THE MIDDLE AGES
David / Donaldson

THE SIXTEENTH CENTURY
Logan / Greenblatt

THE EARLY SEVENTEENTH CENTURY
Lewalski / Adams

THE RESTORATION AND THE EIGHTEENTH CENTURY
Lipking / Monk

THE ROMANTIC PERIOD
Abrams / Stillinger

THE VICTORIAN AGE
Christ / Ford

THE TWENTIETH CENTURY
Stallworthy / Daiches

The Norton Anthology
of English Literature

SEVENTH EDITION
THE MAJOR AUTHORS

The Norton Anthology
of English Literature

SEVENTH EDITION

THE MAJOR AUTHORS

M. H. Abrams, *General Editor*

CLASS OF 1916 PROFESSOR OF ENGLISH EMERITUS,
CORNELL UNIVERSITY

Stephen Greenblatt, *Associate General Editor*

COGAN UNIVERSITY PROFESSOR OF THE HUMANITIES,
HARVARD UNIVERSITY

W · W · NORTON & COMPANY · *New York · London*

Copyright © 2001, 1996, 1987, 1975, 1968, 1962 by W. W. Norton & Company, Inc.
Copyright renewed 1990 by W. W. Norton & Company, Inc.

Since this page cannot legibly accommodate all the copyright notices, pages 2857–59
constitute an extension of the copyright page.

The text of this book is composed in Fairfield Medium
with the display set in Bernhard Modern.
Composition by Binghamton Valley Composition.
Manufacturing by R. R. Donnelley & Sons, Inc.
Book design by Antonina Krass.

Library of Congress Cataloging-in-Publication Data

The Norton anthology of English literature. The major authors / M.H. Abrams, general
editor ; Stephen Greenblatt, associate general editor.—7th ed.
p. cm.
Includes bibliographical references and index.

ISBN 0-393-97619-X—ISBN 0-393-96150-8 (pbk.)

1. English literature. 2. Great Britain—Literary collections. I. Abrams, M. H. (Meyer
Howard), 1912–   II. Greenblatt, Stephen, 1943–

PR1109 .N6 2001
820.8—dc21   00-045229

W. W. Norton & Company, Inc., 500 Fifth Avenue, New York, N.Y. 10110
www.wwnorton.com

W. W. Norton & Company Ltd., 10 Coptic Street, London WC1A 1PU

2 3 4 5 6 7 8 9 0

Contents

The Early Seventeenth Century (1603–1660)   577

The Restoration and the Eighteenth Century
(1660–1785)   855

The Romantic Period (1785–1830)   1313

The Victorian Age (1830–1901)   1859

The Twentieth Century 2271

Preface to the Seventh Edition

The outpouring of English literature overflows all boundaries, including the capacious boundaries of the Major Authors edition of *The Norton Anthology of English Literature*. But these pages manage to contain many of the most remarkable works written in English during centuries of restless creative effort. We have included epic poems and short lyrics; love songs and satires; plays written for performance on the commercial stage and private meditations meant to be perused in silence; prayers, popular ballads, prophecies, ecstatic visions, erotic fantasies, short stories, letters in verse and prose, critical essays, extended prose works of both fiction and nonfiction, and a great deal more. Such works generally form the core of courses that are designed to introduce students to the rich abundance of English literature, with its history not only of gradual development, continuity, and dense internal echoes, but also of radical contingency, sudden change, and startling innovation.

The meaning of the term *literature* has in the course of several centuries shifted from the whole body of writing produced in a particular language to a subset of that writing consisting of works that claim special attention because of their formal beauty and expressive power. But any individual text's claim to attention is subject to constant debate and revision; established texts are jostled both by new arrivals and by previously neglected claimants; and the boundaries between the *literary* and whatever is thought to be *nonliterary* are constantly challenged and redrawn, as are the boundaries between *major* and *minor* authors. Just as there have never been academies in English-speaking countries established to regulate the use of language, so too there have never been firm and settled guidelines for canonizing particular texts. Certain works, however, have achieved and maintained sufficient prominence to serve as widespread models for other writers and as objects of intense and enduring admiration. To present an abundant selection of these works is the purpose of the present volume.

This anthology aims to enable its readers to gauge the achievement of the principal authors it represents by providing generous samplings of their most characteristic and brilliant work. We have tried, wherever possible, not to give a brief glimpse but rather to facilitate a satisfying, sustained engagement with each writer. But we have also included some individual works whose compelling interest merits representation in these pages, even though the scope of this book does not permit a wider survey of the author's writings.

By the designation "major authors," the editors call attention to an unusual power to excite and reward close attention. Our grasp of this power—our notion of where to look for it, how to identify it, and what to do when we find it—does not stand still. There are twenty-one new writers in this Seventh Edition of the Major Authors *Norton Anthology,* eleven of whom are women. To cite a few examples: Aphra Behn's extraordinary seventeenth-century novel of slavery and revolt, *Oroonoko,* is included in its entirety; readers of Romantic poetry now encounter the remarkable Anna Letitia Barbauld, Robert Burns, and Felicia Hemans; and Thomas Carlyle, Elizabeth Gaskell, and Oscar Wilde take their places among the writers of the Victorian age. The innovations are perhaps most visible at the beginning and the end of the anthology, with a celebrated new translation by Seamus Heaney of the Anglo-Saxon epic *Beowulf* and a striking expansion of the selections of modern literature. While the Sixth Edition ended with Dylan Thomas, this edition continues with Philip Larkin, Nadine Gordimer, Derek Walcott, Seamus Heaney, J. M. Coetzee, and Salman Rushdie.

Where do we draw the boundaries? The designation *"English"* provides some obvious limits to the unstable and constantly shifting field of *literature.* But these limits are themselves in constant flux, due in part to the complexity of the territory evoked by the term (as explained in our appendix on "Geographical Nomenclature") and in part to the multinational, multicultural, and hugely expansive character of the language. As Geoffrey Nunberg's informative essay "The Persistence of English," commissioned for this Seventh Edition, makes clear, the variations in the forms of the spoken language that all go by the name of English are so great as to call into question the very notion of a single tongue, and the complex history and diffusion of the language have helped ensure that its literature is enormous. In the momentous process that transformed England into Great Britain and eventually into the center of a huge empire, more and more writers from outside England, beginning with the strong Irish and Scottish presence in the eighteenth century and gradually fanning out into the colonies, were absorbed into and at the same time transformed "English literature."

The term "English Literature" in our title designates two different things. First, it refers to the literary productions of a particular part of the world: the works we include were for the most part written by authors living in the British Isles, that is, in England, Scotland, Wales, and Ireland. Second, it refers to literary works in the English language, a language that has extended far beyond the boundaries of its point of origin. Following the lead of most college courses, we have separated off, for purposes of this anthology, English literature from American literature, but in the selections for the twentieth century we have incorporated a number of texts written in English by authors from other countries. Writers like William Butler Yeats (born in Dublin), Virginia Woolf (born in London), and Dylan Thomas (born in Swansea, Wales) are now being taught, and are here anthologized, alongside such writers as Nadine Gordimer (born in the Transvaal, South Africa), Derek Walcott (born on Saint Lucia in the West Indies), and Salman Rushdie (born in Bombay, India). English literature has ceased to be principally about the identity of a single nation; it is a global phenomenon.

The linguistic mobility and cultural interwining reflected in these texts are not new: the authors assembled in this anthology constitute a linguistic community that has never fit comfortably within any firm geographical or ethnic or national boundaries. It is fitting that among the first works in the volume is an Irish poet's translation of *Beowulf,* a powerful epic written in the Germanic language known as Old English about a singularly restless Scandinavian hero. So too, to glance at a few other authors and writings included here, in the sixteenth century William Tyndale, in exile in the Low Countries and inspired by German religious reformers, translated the New Testament from Greek and thereby changed the course of the English language; in the seventeenth century Aphra Behn deeply touched her readers with a story that moves from Africa, where its hero is born, to South America, where she herself may have briefly resided; and early in the twentieth century Joseph Conrad, born in Ukraine of Polish parents, wrote in eloquent English a celebrated novella whose vision of European empire has been powerfully challenged by such masterful writers as the African-born Nadine Gordimer and J. M. Coetzee.

One of the principal features of *The Norton Anthology of English Literature,* established by its original editors, was a commitment to provide periodic revisions in order to take advantage of newly recovered or better-edited texts, reflect scholarly discoveries and the shifting interests of readers, and keep the anthology in touch with contemporary critical and intellectual concerns. To help us honor this commitment we have, as in past years, profited from a remarkable flow of voluntary corrections and suggestions proposed by students, as well as teachers, who view the anthology with a loyal but critical eye. Moreover, we have again solicited and received detailed information on the works actually assigned, proposals for deletions and additions, and suggestions for improving the editorial matter, from dozens of reviewers from around the world, almost all of them teachers who use the book in their courses. In its evolution, then, this anthology has been the product of an ongoing collaboration among its editors, teachers, and students.

In addition to the new translation of *Beowulf* and to the augmented global approach to twentieth-century literature in English, several other important features of this Seventh Edition merit special mention. As already noted, we have greatly expanded the selection of writing by women in all of the historical periods. The extraordinary, sustained work of scholars in recent years has recovered dozens of significant authors who had been marginalized or neglected by a male-dominated literary tradition and has deepened our understanding of those women writers who had managed, against considerable odds, to claim a place in that tradition. Poets and prose writers whose names were mentioned, if at all, only in specialized literary histories—Marie de France, Mary Herbert, Aemilia Lanyer, Mary Wroth, Katherine Philips, Anne Finch, Frances Burney, Anna Letitia Barbauld, Felicia Hemans, and others—now appear in the company of their male contemporaries. There are in addition two complete long prose works by women: Aphra Behn's *Oroooko* and Virginia Woolf's *A Room of One's Own.*

The novel is, of course, a stumbling block for an anthology. The length of many great novels defies their incorporation in any volume that hopes to include a broad spectrum of literature. At the same time it is difficult to excerpt representative passages from narratives whose power often depends upon amplitude or upon the slow development of character or upon the onrushing urgency of the story. Therefore, better to represent the remarkable achievements of novelists, the publisher makes specially available, in inexpensive and well-edited Norton Anthology Editions, a range of novels, including Jane Austen's *Pride and Prejudice,* Mary Shelley's *Frankenstein,*

Charles Dickens's *Hard Times,* Charlotte Brontë's *Jane Eyre,* and Emily Brontë's *Wuthering Heights.*

Period-by-Period Revisions

The scope of the revisions we have undertaken, the most extensive in the long publishing history of the Major Authors edition of *The Norton Anthology of English Literature,* can be conveyed more fully by a list of some of the principal texts and features that have been added to the present edition.

The Middle Ages. In addition to Seamus Heaney's award-winning translation of *Beowulf,* the selection of Anglo-Saxon poems has also been augmented with *The Dream of the Rood.* We have added an entirely new section, "Legendary Histories of Britain," which provides a key bridge between the Anglo-Saxon period and the time of Chaucer, highlighting an important cluster of texts that trace the origins of Arthurian romance. This section includes legendary histories by Geoffrey of Monmouth, Wace, and Layamon, along with Marie de France's *Lanval* (a Breton lay about King Arthur's court, here in a new verse translation by Alfred David). And we have added selections from the revelations of the visionary anchoress Julian of Norwich.

The Sixteenth Century. A new section on the English Bible brings together contrasting Bible translations; also included is the beautiful marriage ceremony from the Book of Common Prayer. There are newly added letters and the celebrated "Golden Speech" by Queen Elizabeth; Sir Walter Ralegh's darkly eloquent address to Death at the end of his *History of the World;* and several additional sonnets by Sidney and Shakespeare, including "Full many a glorious morning have I seen."

The Early Seventeenth Century. John Donne's Holy Sonnet "O, to vex me, contraries meet in one" joins the already substantial selection of his works; two important parts of her *Salve Deus Rex Judaeorum,* "To the Doubtful Reader" and "Eve's Apology in Defense of Women," are added to the selection of Aemilia Lanyer; Andrew Marvell's haunting mower poems, *The Mower to the Glowworms* and *The Mower's Song,* are now included; and Katherine Philips makes her first appearance in the pages of this anthology.

The Restoration and the Eighteenth Century. Aphra Behn's novel *Oroonoko, or The Royal Slave* is included in full. Some of the issues Behn raises are echoed in a newly included work by Samuel Johnson, "A Brief to Free a Slave," and in chapters from Olaudah Equiano's ground-breaking history of his own enslavement. William Hogarth's remarkably "literary" graphic art is represented by his satiric *Marriage A-la-Mode.* The narrative gifts of Frances Burney, whose long career spans this period and the next, are newly presented by several texts, including her famous, harrowing account of her mastectomy.

The Romantic Period. Five writers have been added: the poets Anna Letitia Barbauld, Robert Burns, and Felicia Dorothea Hemans; and Mary Wollstonecraft, represented by a generous selection of her influential *Vindication,* and Dorothy Wordsworth, whose journal writings and poems are included. The presence of Barbauld, Hemans, Wollstonecraft, and Wordsworth helps to restore women writers, once marginalized in literary histories of the period, to the highly significant place they in fact occupied.

The Victorian Age. The important novelist, short story writer, and biographer Elizabeth Gaskell makes her first appearance in the Major Authors edition of the *Norton Anthology,* along with the celebrated prophet and essayist Thomas Carlyle. Newly added as well are selected works by Oscar Wilde, including his greatest play, *The Importance of Being Earnest.* We have added several poems by Elizabeth Barrett Browning, and we have moved Bernard Shaw's play *Mrs. Warren's Profession* to its chronological place in this section.

The Twentieth Century. The many changes in this section reflect a rethinking of this century's literary history. We now begin with Thomas Hardy and Joseph Conrad, both liminal figures poised between two cultural worlds. The selection from Virginia Woolf includes the whole of her feminist classic, *A Room of One's Own.* To James Joyce's works is added the poignant story *Araby;* Eliot's poems now include *The Hollow Men;* and Samuel Beckett is represented by the complete text of his masterful tragicomedy *Endgame.* Philip Larkin's subtle, ironic voice is heard for the first time in this edition in a selection of his poems. The explosion of brilliant writing in English in "postcolonial" countries around the world is represented by the addition of texts by Nadine Gordimer, Derek Walcott, J. M. Coetzee, and Salman Rushdie. Finally, the inclusion of seven poems by Seamus Heaney provides the occasion to look back again to the beginning of this volume with Heaney's new translation of *Beowulf.* This translation is a reminder that the history of literature is not a straightforward sequence, that the most recent works can double back upon the distant past, and that words set down by men and women who have crumbled into dust can speak to us with astonishing directness.

Editorial Procedures

As in past editions of the Major Authors, the editorial features—period introductions, headnotes, and annotation—are designed to give students the information needed, without imposing an interpretation. In this edition, these editorial features have been thoroughly revised in response to new scholarship. The period introductions and many headnotes have been either entirely or substantially rewritten to be more helpful to students, and all the Selected Bibliographies have been updated.

Several new features reflect the broadened scope of the selections in the anthology. The new introductory essay, "The Persistence of English" by Geoffrey Nunberg, Stanford University and Xerox Palo Alto Research Center, explores the emergence and spread of English and its apparent present-day "triumph" as a world language. It provides an informative and lively point of departure for the study of literatures in English. The endpaper maps have been reconceived and redrawn. Timelines, following each period introduction, help students place their reading in historical and cultural context. So that students can explore literature as a visual medium, the anthology newly offers graphic materials from three periods—Hogarth's *Marriage-A-la-Mode,* engravings by William Blake, and illustrations and paintings by D. G. Rossetti—supplemented with the more than one thousand images available on the Web companion to the *Norton Anthology,* described below.

An appendix, "Poems in Process," reproduces from manuscripts and printed texts the genesis and evolution of a number of poems anthologized here. The much-used section of "Poetic Forms and Literary Terminology" has been revised in this Seventh Edition, along with appendices, newly expanded, on the intricacies of English money, the baronage, and religions. An appendix, "Geographic Nomenclature," has been added to clarify the shifting place-names applied to regions of the British Isles.

Students, no less than scholars, deserve the most accurate texts available; in keeping with this policy, we continue to introduce improved versions of the selections where available. In this edition, for example, in addition to Seamus Heaney's new translation of *Beowulf*, we include Alfred David's new verse translation of Marie de France's *Lanval*. To ease a student's access, we have normalized spelling and capitalization in texts up to and including the Victorian period to follow the conventions of modern English; we leave unaltered, however, texts in which modernizing would change semantic or metrical qualities. In the Twentieth Century, we have restored the original spelling and punctuation to selections retained from the previous edition, in the belief that the authors' choices, when they pose no difficulties for student readers, should be respected.

We continue other editorial procedures that have proved useful in the past. After each work, we cite (when known) the date of composition on the left and the date of first publication on the right; in some instances, the latter is followed by the date of a revised edition for which the author was responsible. We have used square brackets to indicate titles supplied by the editors for the convenience of readers. Whenever a portion of a text has been omitted, we have indicated that omission with three asterisks. If the omitted portion is important for following the plot or argument, we have provided a brief summary within the text or in a footnote. We have extended our longstanding practice of providing marginal glossing of single words and short phrases from medieval and dialect poets (such as Robert Burns) to all the poets in the anthology. Finally, we have adopted a larger and bolder typeface and redesigned the page, so as to make the text more readable and more agreeable to the eye.

Three cardinal innovations, one print and two electronic, greatly increase the anthology's flexibility. The Seventh Edition is available in the traditional one-volume format, in clothbound and paperback versions, and in a new two-volume paperback version comprised of Volume A, covering the Middle Ages through the Restoration and the Eighteenth Century, and Volume B, covering the Romantic Period through the Twentieth Century. By maintaining the same pagination as in the original volume, the two-volume format offers a more portable option for students.

Extending beyond the printed page, the Norton Topics Online Web site (www.wwnorton.com/nael) augments the anthology's already broad representation of the sweep of English literature and greatly enlarges the representation of graphic materials that are relevant to literary studies. For students who wish to extend their exploration of the contexts of this literature, the Web site offers a huge range of related texts, prepared by the anthology editors, and by Myron Tuman, University of Alabama, and Philip Schwyzer, Oxford University. An ongoing venture, the Web site currently offers twenty-one thematic clusters—three per period—of texts and visual images, cross-referenced to the anthology, together with overviews, study explorations, and annotated links to related sites.

The Norton Topics Online Web site enables us to address effectively one of the problems that faces any anthology, however capacious and far-reaching: the need to make available at least some of the vast textual and visual resources that lie just beyond the borders of the selected literary works. The Web makes it possible as well to address another crucial problem: the need to respond to changing interests by adding new works to the printed anthology, without altogether losing the texts that considerations of space force us to drop. The solution, our second electronic innovation, is the Norton Online Archive, an ongoing project that at present includes more than 150 texts dropped from earlier editions of *The Norton Anthology of English Literature*, ranging from the Middle Ages to the early Victorian period (www.wwnorton. com/nael/noa). This archive, which will continue to grow as future editions are revised and altered, provides carefully edited Norton texts, with glosses and notes, that may be downloaded and printed. It will also constitute a valuable record of the ongoing shifts in literary and cultural interest.

Two valuable further features should be mentioned. In response to numerous requests from instructors who use the Audio Companion accompanying the anthology, we are making an expanded version available without charge to students purchasing new copies of *The Norton Anthology of English Literature*, Seventh Edition, The Major Authors. The two compact disks offer readings by the authors of the works represented in the anthology, readings of poems in Old and Middle English and in English dialects, and performances of poems written to be set to music. New to the Audio Companion, Disk 1, are a generous sampling of Seamus Heaney's reading of his translation of *Beowulf*, a selection from *The Battle of Maldon* read by R. D. Fulk, and additional Chaucer selections read by V. A. Kolve. Recordings of the poets Robert Graves, Ted Hughes, Eavan Boland, and Thom Gunn reading their work have been added to Disk 2.

The Course Guide to accompany *The Norton Anthology of English Literature*, by Alfred David (Indiana University), Kelly Hurley (University of Colorado at Boulder), and Philip Schwyzer (Oxford University), has been thoroughly revised and expanded. It contains thematic discussions of selected works in each period, sample reading lists for several kinds of survey and topical courses, study and essay questions, and cross-references to the Web materials and audio recordings that accompany the anthology. A copy of the Guide may be obtained on request from the publisher.

The editors are deeply grateful to the hundreds of teachers worldwide who have helped us to improve the Major Authors edition of *The Norton Anthology of English Literature*. A list of the advisors who prepared in-depth reviews and of the instructors who replied to a detailed questionnaire follows on a separate page, under Acknowledgments. The editors would like to express appreciation for their assistance to Tiffany Beechy (Harvard University), Mitch Cohen (Wissenschaftskolleg zu Berlin), Sandie Byrne (Oxford University), Sarah Cole (Columbia University), Dianne Ferriss (Cornell University), Robert Folkenflik (University of California, Irvine), Robert D. Fulk (Indiana University), Andrew Gurr (The University of Reading), Wendy Hyman (Harvard University), Elissa Linke (Wissenschaftskolleg zu Berlin), Joanna Lipking (Northwestern University), Linda O'Riordan (Wissenschaftskolleg zu Berlin), Ruth Perry (M.I.T.), Leah Price (Harvard University), Ramie Targoff (Yale University), and Douglas Trevor (Harvard University).

The editors give special thanks to Paul Leopold, who drafted the appendix on Geographic Nomenclature and revised the appendix on Religions in England, and to Philip Schwyzer (Oxford University), whose wide-ranging contributions include preparing texts and study materials for the Web site, assisting with the revision of numerous headnotes, and updating appendices on the British baronage and British money. We also thank the many people at Norton who contributed to the Major Authors, Seventh Edition: Julia Reidhead, who served not only as the inhouse supervisor but also as an unfailingly wise and effective collaborator in every aspect of planning and accomplishing this revision; Marian Johnson, developmental editor, who kept the project moving forward with a remarkable blend of focused energy, intelligence, and common sense; Candace Levy, Ann Tappert, Barry Katzen, Lynn Cannon Menges, David Hawkins, and Will Rigby, project and manuscript editors; Julie Tedoff, Web site editor; Diane O'Connor, production manager; Kristin Sheerin and Ann Marcy, permissions managers; Toni Krass, designer; Neil Ryder Hoos, art researcher; and Christa Grenawalt and Brian Baker, editorial assistants. All these friends provided the editors with indispensable help in meeting the challenge of representing justly the unparalleled range and variety of English literature.

M. H. Abrams
Stephen Greenblatt

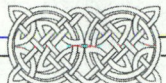

Acknowledgments

Among our many critics, advisors, and friends, the following were of especial help toward the preparation of the Seventh Edition, either by offering advice or by providing critiques of particular periods of the anthology: Jonathon Allison (University of Kentucky), Rebecca Argall (University of Memphis), Christopher Baker (Armstrong Atlantic State University), Mark R. Blackwell (California State University, Chico), Mary Blockley (University of Texas at Austin), James Brown (Charleston State University), Alexander Bruce (Florida Southern College), Yvonne Bruce (The Citadel), Howard Cole (University of Illinois), Natalie B. Cole (Oakland University), Joanne Craig (Bishop's University), R. W. Crump (Louisiana State University), James E. Doan (Nova Southeastern University), Helen V. Emmitt (Virginia Military University), Laura Fasick (Moorhead State University), Suzanne Ferriss (Nova Southeastern University), Julia A. Fesmire (Middle Tennessee State University), Rosemary Fisk (Samford University), Robert Forman (St. John's University, Jamaica), Rosanne Gasse (Brandon University), Ronald W. Harris (Southeastern Louisiana University), Elizabeth Hedrick (University of Texas at Austin), Brooke Hopkins (University of Utah), Susan Jones (Palm Beach Atlantic College), Stewart Justman (University of Montana), Robert G. Laird (Carleton University), Yixiong Liang (Mohawk Valley Community College), David Lindstrom (Colorado State University), Scott Lucas (The Citadel), Paul McCarron (Texas A&M), J. McGinty (Delta College), S. Jaret McKinstry (Charleston College), K. Moore-Jumonville (Taylor University), Patricia Moran (University of California, Davis), Mary A. Papazian (Oakland University), Mary Pharr (Florida Southern College), Jim Read (Allan Hancock College), James A. W. Rembert (The Citadel), William O. Shakespeare (Brigham Young University), Isabel B. Stanley (East Tennessee State University), James W. Stick, Jr. (Des Moines Area Community College), Charlotte Templin (University of Indianapolis), Theresa Mae Thompson (Valdosta State University), Joel Westerholm (Northwestern College, Orange City), Matthew Wikander (University of Toledo), Thomas Willard (University of Arizona), Lloyd Worley (University of North Colorado).

The Persistence of English

Geoffrey Nunberg

Stanford University and Xerox Palo Alto Research Center

THE TRIUMPH OF ENGLISH?

If you measure the success of a language in purely quantitative terms, English is entering the twenty-first century at the moment of its greatest triumph. It has between 400 and 450 million native speakers, perhaps 300 million more who speak it as a second language—well enough, that is, to use it in their daily lives—and somewhere between 500 and 750 million who speak it as a foreign language with various degrees of fluency. The resulting total of between 1.2 billion and 1.5 billion speakers, or roughly a quarter of the world's population, gives English more speakers than any other language (though Chinese has more native speakers). Then, too, English is spoken over a much wider geographical area than any other language and is the predominant lingua franca of most fields of international activity, such as diplomacy, business, travel, science, and technology.

But figures like these can obscure a basic question: what exactly do we mean when we talk about the "English language" in the first place? There is, after all, an enormous range of variation in the forms of speech that go by the name of English in the various parts of the world—or often, even within the speech of a single nation—and it is not obvious why we should think of all of these as belonging to a single language. Indeed, there are some linguists who prefer to talk about "world Englishes," in the plural, with the implication that these varieties may not have much more to unite them than a single name and a common historical origin.

To the general public, these reservations may be hard to understand; people usually assume that languages are natural kinds like botanical species, whose boundaries are matters of scientific fact. But as linguists observe, there is nothing in the forms of English themselves that tells us that it is a single language. It may be that the varieties called "English" have a great deal of vocabulary and structure in common and that English-speakers can usually manage to make themselves understood to one another, more or less (though films produced in one part of the English-speaking world often have to be dubbed or subtitled to make them intelligible to audiences in another). But there are many cases where we find linguistic varieties that are mutually intelligible and grammatically similar, but where speakers nonetheless identify separate languages—for example, Danish and Norwegian, Czech and Slovak, or Dutch and Afrikaans. And on the other hand, there are cases where speakers identify varieties as belonging to a single language even though they are linguistically quite distant from one another: the various "dialects" of Chinese are more different from one another than the Latin offshoots that we identify now as French, Italian, Spanish, and so forth.

Philosophers sometimes compare languages to games, and the analogy is apt here, as well. Trying to determine whether American English and British English or Dutch and Afrikaans are "the same language" is like trying to determine whether baseball and softball are "the same game"—it is not something you can find out just by looking at their rules. It is not surprising, then, that linguists should throw up their hands when someone asks them to determine on linguistic grounds alone whether two varieties belong to a single language. That, they answer, is a political or social determination, not a linguistic one, and they usually go on to cite a well-known quip: "a language is just a dialect with an army and a navy."

There is something to this remark. Since the eighteenth century, it has been widely believed that every nation deserved to have its own language, and declarations of political independence have often been followed by declarations of linguistic independence. Until recently, for example, the collection of similar language varieties that were spoken in most of central Yugoslavia was regarded as a single language, Serbo-Croatian, but once the various regions became independent, their inhabitants began to speak of Croatian, Serbian, and Bosnian as separate languages, even though they are mutually comprehensible and grammatically almost identical.

The English language has avoided this fate (though on occasion it has come closer to breaking up than most people realize). But the unity of a language is never a foregone conclusion. In any speech-community, there are forces always at work to create new differences and varieties: the geographic and social separation of speech-communities, their distinct cultural and practical interests, their contact with other cultures and other languages, and, no less important, a universal fondness for novelty for its own sake, and a desire to speak differently from one's parents or the people in the next town. Left to function on their own, these centrifugal pressures can rapidly lead to the linguistic fragmentation of the speech-community. That is what happened, for example, to the vulgar (that is, "popular") Latin of the late Roman Empire, which devolved into hundreds or thousands of separate dialects (the emergence of the eight or ten standard varieties that we now think of as the Romance languages was a much later development).

Maintaining the unity of a language over an extended time and space, then, requires a more or less conscious determination by its speakers that they have certain communicative interests in common that make it worthwhile to try to curb or modulate the natural tendency to fragmentation and isolation. This determination can be realized in a number of ways. The speakers of a language may decide to use a common spelling system even when dialects become phonetically distinct, to defer to a common set of literary models, to adopt a common format for their dictionaries and grammars, or to make instruction in the standard language a part of the general school curriculum, all of which the English-speaking world has done to some degree. Or in some other places, the nations of the linguistic community may establish academies or other state institutions charged with regulating the use of the language, and even go so far as to publish lists of words that are unacceptable for use in the press or in official publications, as the French have done in recent years. Most important, the continuity of the language rests on speakers' willingness to absorb the linguistic and cultural influences of other parts of the linguistic community.

THE EMERGENCE OF THE ENGLISH LANGUAGE

To recount the history of a language, then, is not simply to trace the development of its various sounds, words, and constructions. Seen from that exclusively linguistic point of view, there would be nothing to distinguish the evolution of Anglo-Saxon into the varieties of modern English from the evolution of Latin into modern French, Italian, and so forth—we would not be able to tell, that is, why English continued to be considered a single language while the Romance languages did not. We also have to follow the play of centrifugal and centripetal forces that kept the language always more or less a unity—the continual process of creation of new dialects and varieties, the countervailing rise of new standards and of mechanisms aimed at maintaining the linguistic center of gravity.

Histories of the English language usually put its origin in the middle of the fifth century, when several Germanic peoples first landed in the place we now call England and began to displace the local inhabitants, the Celts. There is no inherent linguistic reason why we should locate the beginning of the language at this time, rather than with the Norman Conquest of 1066 or in the fourteenth century, say, and in fact the determination that English began with the Anglo-Saxon period was not generally accepted until the nineteenth century. But this point of view has been to a certain extent self-fulfilling, if only because it has led to the addition of Anglo-Saxon works to the canon of English literature, where they remain. Languages are constructions over time as well as over space.

Wherever we place the beginnings of English, though, there was never a time when the language was not diverse. The Germanic peoples who began to arrive in England in the fifth century belonged to a number of distinct tribes, each with its own dialect, and tended to settle in different parts of the country—the Saxons in the southwest, the Angles in the east and north, the Jutes (and perhaps some Franks) in Kent. These differences were the first source of the distinct dialects of the language we now refer to as Anglo-Saxon or Old English. As time went by, the linguistic divisions were reinforced by geography and by the political fragmentation of the country, and later, through contact with the Vikings who had settled the eastern and northern parts of England in the eighth through eleventh centuries.

Throughout this period, though, there were also forces operating to consolidate the language of England. Over the centuries, cultural and political dominance passed from Northumbria in the north to Mercia in the center and then to Wessex in the southwest, where a literary standard emerged in the ninth century, owing in part to the unification of the kingdom and in part to the singular efforts of Alfred the Great (849–899), who encouraged literary production in English and himself translated Latin works into the language. The influence of these standards and the frequent communication between the regions worked to level many of the dialect differences. There is a striking example of the process in the hundreds of everyday words derived from the language of the Scandinavian settlers, which include *dirt, lift, sky, skin, die, birth, weak, seat,* and *want.* All of these spread to general usage from the northern and eastern dialects in which they were first introduced, an indication of how frequent and ordinary were the contacts among the Anglo-Saxons of various parts of the country—and initially, between the Anglo-Saxons and the Scandinavians themselves. (By contrast, the Celtic peoples that the Anglo-Saxons had displaced made relatively few contributions to the language, apart from place-names like *Thames, Avon,* and *Dover.*)

The Anglo-Saxon period came to an abrupt end with the Norman Conquest of 1066. With the introduction of a French-speaking ruling class, the written use of English was greatly reduced for a hundred and fifty years. English did not reappear extensively in written records until the beginning of the thirteenth century, and even then it was only one of the languages of a multilingual community: French was widely used for another two hundred years or so (Parliament was conducted in French until 1362), and Latin was the predominant language of scholarship until the Renaissance. The English language that re-emerged in this period was considerably changed from the language of Alfred's period. Its grammar was simplified, continuing a process already under way before the Conquest, and its vocabulary was enriched by thousands of French loan words. Not surprisingly, given the preeminent role of French among the elite, these included the language of government (*majesty, state, rebel*); of religion (*pastor, ordain, temptation*); of fashion and social life (*button, adorn, dinner*); and of art, literature, and medicine (*painting, chapter, paper, physician*). But the breadth of French influence was not limited to those domains; it also provided simple words like *move, aim, join, solid, chief, clear, air,* and *very.* All of this left the language sufficiently different from Old English to warrant describing it with the name of Middle English, though we should bear in mind that language change is always gradual and that the division of English into neat periods is chiefly a matter of scholarly convenience.

Middle English was as varied a language as Old English was: Chaucer wrote in *Troilus and Criseyde* that "ther is so gret diversite in Englissh" that he was fearful that the text would be misread in other parts of the country. It was only in the fifteenth century or so that anything like a standard language began to emerge, based in the speech of the East Midlands and in particular of London, which reflected the increased centralization of political and economic power in that region. Even then, though, dialect differences remained strong; John Palsgrave complained in 1540 that the speech of university students was tainted by "the rude language used in their native countries [i.e., counties]," which left them unable to express themselves in their "vulgar tongue."

The language itself continued to change as it moved into what scholars describe as the Early Modern English period, which for convenience sake we can date from the year 1500. Around this time, it began to undergo the Great Vowel Shift, as the long vowels engaged in an intricate dance that left them with new phonetic values. (In Chaucer's time, the word *bite* had been pronounced roughly as "beet," *beet* as "bate," *name* as "nahm," and so forth.) The grammar was changing as well; for example, the pronoun *thee* began to disappear, as did the verbal suffix-*eth*, and the modern form of questions began to emerge: in place of "See you that house?" people began to say "Do you see that house?" Most significantly, at least so far as contemporary observers were concerned, the Elizabethans and their successors coined thousands of new words based on Latin and Greek in an effort to make English an adequate replacement for Latin in the writing of philosophy, science, and literature. Many of these words now seem quite ordinary to us—for example, *accommodation*, *frugal*, *obscene*, *premeditated*, and *submerge*, all of which are recorded for the first time in Shakespeare's works. A large proportion of these linguistic experiments, though, never gained a foothold in the language—for example, *illecebrous* for "delicate," *deruncinate* for "to weed," *obtestate* for "call on," or Shakespeare's *disquantity* to mean "diminish." Indeed, some contemporaries ridiculed the pretension and obscurity of these "inkhorn words" in terms that sound very like modern criticisms of bureaucratic and corporate jargon—the rhetorician Thomas Wilson wrote in 1540 of the writers who affected "outlandish English" such that "if some of their mothers were alive, they were not able to tell what they say." But this effect was inevitable: the additions to the standard language that made it a suitable vehicle for art and scholarship could only increase the linguistic distance between the written language used by the educated classes and the spoken language used by other groups.

DICTIONARIES AND RULES

These were essentially growing pains for the standard language, which continued to gain ground in the sixteenth and seventeenth centuries, abetted by a number of developments: the ever-increasing dominance of London and the Southeast, the growth in social and geographic mobility, and in particular the introduction and spread of print, which led both to higher levels of literacy and schooling and to the gradual standardization of English spelling. But even as this process was going on, other developments were both creating new distinctions and investing existing ones with a new importance. For one thing, people were starting to pay more attention to accents based on social class, rather than region, an understandable preoccupation as social mobility increased and speech became a more important indicator of social background. Not surprisingly, the often imperfect efforts of the emerging middle class to speak and dress like their social superiors occasioned some ridicule; Thomas Gainsford wrote in 1616 of the "foppish mockery" of commoners who tried to imitate gentlemen by altering "habit, manner of life, conversation, and even their phrase of speech." Yet even the upper classes were paying more attention to speech as a social indicator than they had in previous ages; as one writer put it, "it is a pitty when a Noble man is better distinguished from a Clowne by his golden laces, than by his good language." (Shakespeare plays on this theme in *I Henry IV* [3.1.250, 257–58] when he has Hotspur tease his wife for swearing too daintily, which makes her sound like "a comfit-maker's wife," rather than "like a lady as thou art," with "a good mouth-filling oath.")

Over the course of the seventeenth and eighteenth centuries, print began to exercise a paradoxical effect on the perception of the language: even as it was serving to codify the standard, it was also making people more aware of variation and more anxious about its consequences. This was largely the result of the growing importance of print, as periodicals, novels, and other new forms became increasingly influential in shaping public opinion, together with the perception that the contributors to the print discourse were drawn from a wider range of backgrounds than in previous periods. As Samuel Johnson wrote: "The present age . . . may be styled, with great propriety, the Age of Authors; for, perhaps, there was never a time when men of all degrees of ability, of every kind of education, of every profession and employment were posting with ardor so general to the press. . . . "

This anxiety about the language was behind the frequent eighteenth-century lamentations that English was "unruled," "barbarous," or, as Johnson put it, "copious without order, and energetick without rule." Some writers looked for a remedy in public institutions modeled on the French Academy. This idea was advocated by John Dryden, Daniel Defoe, Joseph Addison, and most notably by Jonathan Swift, in a 1712 pamphlet called A *Proposal for Correcting, Improving, and Ascertaining* [i.e., "fixing"] *the English Tongue*, which did receive some official attention from the Tory government. But the idea was dropped as a Tory scheme when the Whigs came to power two years later, and by the middle of the eighteenth century, there was wide agreement among all parties that an academy would be an unwarranted intervention in the free conduct of public discourse. Samuel Johnson wrote in the Preface to his *Dictionary* of 1775 that he hoped that "the spirit of English liberty will hinder or destroy" any attempt to set up an academy; and the scientist and radical Joseph Priestly called such an institution "unsuitable to the genius of a *free nation*."

The rejection of the idea of an academy was to be important in the subsequent development of the language. From that time forward, it was clear that the state was not to play a major role in regulating and reforming the language, whether in England or in the other nations of the language community—a characteristic that makes English different from many other languages. (In languages like French and German, for example, spelling reforms can be introduced by official commissions charged with drawing up rules which are then adopted in all textbooks and official publications, a procedure that would be unthinkable in any of the nations of the English-speaking world.) Instead, the task of determining standards was left to private citizens, whose authority rested on their ability to gain general public acceptance.

The eighteenth century saw an enormous growth in the number of grammars and handbooks, which formulated most of the principles of correct English that, for better or worse, are still with us today—the rules for using *who* and *whom*, for example, the injunction against constructions like "very unique," and the curious prejudice against the split infinitive. Even more important was the development of the modern English dictionary. Before 1700, English speakers had to make do with alphabetical lists of "hard-words," a bit like the vocabulary improvement books that are still frequent today; it was only in the early 1700s that scholars began to produce anything like a comprehensive dictionary in the modern sense, a process that culminated in the publication of Samuel Johnson's magisterial *Dictionary* of 1755. It would be hard to argue that these dictionaries did much in fact to reduce variation or to arrest the process of linguistic change (among the words that Johnson objected to, for example, were *belabor, budge, cajole, coax, doff, gambler*, and *job*, all of which have since become part of the standard language). But they did serve to ease the sense of linguistic crisis, by providing a structure for describing the language and points of reference for resolving disputes about grammar and meaning. And while both the understanding of language and the craft of lexicography have made a great deal of progress since Johnson's time, the form of the English-language dictionary is still pretty much as he laid it down. (In this regard, Johnson's *Dictionary* is likely to present a much more familiar appearance to a modern reader than his poetry or periodical essays.)

THE DIFFUSION OF ENGLISH

The Modern English period saw the rise of another sort of variation, as well, as English began to spread over an increasingly larger area. By Shakespeare's time, English was displacing the Celtic languages in Wales, Cornwall, and Scotland, and then in Ireland, where the use of Irish was brutally repressed on the assumption—in retrospect a remarkably obtuse one—that people who were forced to become English in tongue would soon become English in loyalty as well. People in these new parts of the English-speaking world—a term we can begin to use in this period, for English was no longer the language of a single country—naturally used the language in accordance with their own idiom and habits of thought and mixed it with words drawn from the Celtic languages, a number of which eventually entered the speech of the larger linguistic community, for example, *baffle, bun, clan, crag, drab, galore, hubbub, pet, slob, slogan,* and *trousers.*

The development of the language in the New World followed the same process of differentiation. English settlers in North America rapidly developed their own characteristic forms of speech. They retained a number of words that had fallen into disuse in England (*din, clod, trash,* and *fall* for *autumn*) and gave old words new senses (like *corn,* which in England meant simply "grain," or *creek,* originally "an arm of the sea"). They borrowed freely from the other languages they came in contact with. By the time of the American Revolution, the colonists had already taken *chowder, cache, prairie,* and *bureau* from French; *noodle* and *pretzel* from German; *cookie, boss,* and *scow* and *yankee* from the Dutch; and *moose, skunk, chipmunk, succotash, toboggan,* and *tomahawk* from various Indian languages. And they coined new words with abandon. Some of these answered to their specific needs and interests—for example, *squatter, clearing, foothill, watershed, congressional, sidewalk*—but there were thousands of others that had no close connection to the American experience as such, many of which were ultimately adopted by the other varieties of English. *Belittle, influential, reliable, comeback, lengthy, turn down, make good*—all of these were originally American creations; they and other words like them indicate how independently the language was developing in the New World.

This process was repeated wherever English took root—in India, Africa, the Far East, the Caribbean, and Australia and New Zealand; by the late nineteenth century, English bore thousands of souvenirs of its extensive travels. From Africa (sometimes via Dutch) came words like *banana, boorish, palaver, gorilla,* and *guinea;* from the aboriginal languages of Australia came *wombat* and *kangaroo;* from the Caribbean languages came *cannibal, hammock, potato,* and *canoe;* and from the languages of India came *bangle, bun-*

galow, chintz, cot, dinghy, jungle, loot, pariah, pundit, and *thug*. And even lists like these are misleading, since they include only words that worked their way into the general English vocabulary and don't give a sense of the thousands of borrowings and coinages that were used only locally. Nor do they touch on the variation in grammar from one variety to the next. This kind of variation occurs everywhere, but it is particularly marked in regions like the Caribbean and Africa, where the local varieties of English are heavily influenced by English-based creoles—that is, language varieties that use English-based vocabulary with grammars largely derived from African languages. This is the source, for example, of a number of the distinctive syntactic features of the variety used by many inner-city African Americans, like the "invariant *be*" of sentences like *We be living in Chicago*, which signals a state of affairs that holds for an extended period. (Some linguists have suggested that Middle English, in fact, could be thought of as a kind of creolized French.)

The growing importance of these new forms of English, particularly in America, presented a new challenge to the unity of the language. Until the eighteenth century, English was still thought of as essentially a national language. It might be spoken in various other nations and colonies under English control, but it was nonetheless rooted in the speech of England and subject to a single standard. Not surprisingly, Americans came to find this picture uncongenial, and when the United States first declared its independence from Britain, there was a strong sentiment for declaring that "American," too, should be recognized as a separate language. This was the view held by John Adams, Thomas Jefferson, and above all by America's first and greatest lexicographer, Noah Webster, who argued that American culture would naturally come to take a distinct form in the soil of the New World, free from what he described as "the old feudal and hierarchical establishments of England." And if a language was naturally the product and reflection of a national culture, then Americans could scarcely continue to speak "English." As Webster wrote in 1789: "Culture, habits, and language, as well as government should be national. America should have her own distinct from the rest of the world. . . ." It was in the interest of symbolically distinguishing American from English that Webster introduced a variety of spelling changes, such as *honor* and *favor* for *honour* and *favour*, *theater* for *theatre*, *traveled* for *travelled*, and so forth—a procedure that new nations often adopt when they want to make their variety of a language look different from its parent tongue.

In fact Webster's was by no means an outlandish suggestion. Even at the time of American independence, the linguistic differences between America and Britain were as great as those that separate many languages today, and the differences would have become much more salient if Americans had systematically adopted all of the spelling reforms that Webster at one time proposed, such as *wurd, reezon, tung, iz*, and so forth, which would ultimately have left English and American looking superficially no more similar than German and Dutch. Left to develop on their own, English and American might soon have gone their separate ways, perhaps paving the way for the separation of the varieties of English used in other parts of the world.

In the end, of course, the Americans and British decided that neither their linguistic nor their cultural and political differences warranted recognizing distinct languages. Webster himself conceded the point in 1828, when he entitled his magnum opus *An American Dictionary of the English Language*. And by 1862 the English novelist Anthony Trollope could write:

> An American will perhaps consider himself to be as little like an Eng-
> lishman as he is like a Frenchman. But he reads Shakespeare through
> the medium of his own vernacular, and has to undergo the penance of
> a foreign tongue before he can understand Molière. He separates him-
> self from England in politics and perhaps in affection; but he cannot
> separate himself from England in mental culture.

ENGLISH AND ENGLISHNESS

This was a crucial point of transition, which set the English language on a very different course from most of the European languages, where the asso-ciation of language and national culture was being made more strongly than ever before. But the detachment of English from Englishness did not take place overnight. For Trollope and his Victorian contemporaries, the "mental culture" of the English-speaking world was still a creation of England, the embodiment of English social and political values. "The English language," said G. C. Swayne in 1862, "is like the English constitution . . . and perhaps also the English Church, full of inconsistencies and anomalies, yet flourish-ing in defiance of theory." The monumental *Oxford English Dictionary* that the Victorians undertook was conceived in this patriotic spirit. In the words of Archbishop Richard Chevenix Trench, one of the guiding spirits of the OED project:

> We could scarcely have a lesson on the growth of our English tongue,
> we could scarcely follow upon one of its significant words, without
> having unawares a lesson in English history as well, without not merely
> falling upon some curious fact illustrative of our national life, but learn-
> ing also how the great heart which is beating at the centre of that life,
> was being gradually shaped and moulded.

It was this conception of the significance of the language that led, too, to the insistence that the origin of the English language should properly be located in Anglo-Saxon, rather than in the thirteenth or fourteenth centuries, as scholars argued that contemporary English laws and institutions could be traced to a primordial "Anglo-Saxon spirit" in an almost racial line of descent, and that the Anglo-Saxon language was "immediately connected with the original introduction and establishment of their present language and their laws, their liberty, and their religion."

This view of English as the repository of "Anglo-Saxon" political ideals had its appeal in America, as well, particularly in the first decades of the twentieth century, when the crusade to "Americanize" recent immigrants led a number of states to impose severe restrictions on the use of other languages in schools, newspapers, and public meetings, a course that was often justified on the grounds that only speakers of English were in a position to fully appreciate the nuances of democratic thought. As a delegate to a New York State constitutional convention in 1916 put the point: "You have got to learn our language because that is the vehicle of the thought that has been handed down from the men in whose breasts first burned the fire of freedom at the signing of the Magna Carta."

But this view of the language is untenable on both linguistic and historical grounds. It is true that the nations of the English-speaking world have a common political heritage that makes itself known in similar legal systems and an (occasionally shaky) predilection for democratic forms of government. But while there is no doubt that the possession of a common language has helped to reinforce some of these connections, it is not responsible for them. Languages do work to create a common worldview, but not at such a specific level. Words like *democracy* move easily from one language to the next, along with the concepts they name—a good thing for the English-speaking world, since a great many of those ideals of "English democracy," as the writer calls it, owe no small debt to thinkers in Greece, Italy, France, Germany, and a number of other places, and those ideals have been established in many nations that speak languages other than English. (Thirteenth-century England was one of them. We should bear in mind that the Magna Carta that people sometimes like to mention in this context was a Latin document issued by a French-speaking king to French-speaking barons.) For that matter, there are English-speaking nations where democratic institutions have not taken root—nor should we take their continuing health for granted even in the core nations of the English-speaking world.

In the end, the view of English as the repository of Englishness has the effect of marginalizing or disenfranchising large parts of the English-speaking world, particularly those who do not count the political and cultural imposition of Englishness as an unmixed blessing. In most of the places where English has been planted, after all, it has had the British flag flying above it. And for many nations, it has been hard to slough off the sense of English as a colonial language. There is a famous passage in James Joyce's *Portrait of the Artist as a Young Man*, for example, where Stephen Daedelus says of the speech of an English-born dean, "The language in which we are speaking is his not mine," and there are still many people in Ireland and other parts of the English-speaking world who have mixed feelings about the English language: they may use and even love English, but they resent it, too.

Today the view of English as an essentially English creation is impossible to sustain even on purely linguistic grounds; the influences of the rest of the English-speaking world have simply been too great. Already in Trollope's time there were vociferous complaints in England about the growing use of Americanisms, a sign that the linguistic balance of payments between the two communities was tipping westward, and a present-day English writer would have a hard time producing a single paragraph that contained no words that originated in other parts of the linguistic community. Nor, what is more important, could you find a modern British or North American writer whose work was not heavily influenced, directly or indirectly, by the literature of the rest of the linguistic community, particularly after the extraordinary twentieth-century efflorescence of the English-language literatures of other parts of the world. Trying to imagine modern English literature without the contributions of writers like Yeats, Shaw, Joyce, Beckett, Heaney, Walcott, Lessing, Gordimer, Rushdie, Achebe, and Naipaul (to take only some of the writers who are included in this collection) is like trying to imagine an "English" cuisine that made no use of potatoes, tomatoes, corn, noodles, eggplant, olive oil, almonds, bay leaf, curry, or pepper.

THE FEATURES OF "STANDARD ENGLISH"

Where should we look, then, for the common "mental culture" that English-speakers share? This is always a difficult question to answer, partly because the understanding of the language changes from one place and time to the next, and partly because it is hard to say just what sorts of things languages are in the abstract. For all that we may want to think of the English-speaking world as a single community united by a common worldview, it is not a social group comparable to a tribe or people or nation—the sorts of groups that can easily evoke the first-person plural pronoun *we*. (Americans and Australians travel around saying "We gave the world Shakespeare," even though one might think that as paid-up members of the English-speaking community they would be entirely within their rights to do so.)

But we can get some sense of the ties that connect the members of the English-speaking community by starting with the language itself—not just in its forms and rules, but in the centripetal forces spoken of earlier. Forces like these are operating in every language community, it's true, but what gives each language its unique character is the way they are realized, the particular institutions and cultural commonalties which work to smooth differences and create a basis for continued communication—which ensure, in short, that English will continue as a single language, rather than devolve into a collection of dialects that are free to wander wherever they will.

People often refer to this basis for communication as "Standard English," but that term is misleading. There are many linguistic communities that do have a genuine standard variety, a fixed and invariant form of the language that is used for certain kinds of communication. But that notion of the standard would be unsuitable to a language like English, which recognizes no single cultural center and has to allow for a great deal of variation even in the language of published texts. (It is rare to find a single page of an English-language novel or newspaper that does not reveal what nation it was written in.) What English does have, rather, is a collection of standard features—of spelling, of grammar, and of word use—which taken together ensure that certain kinds of communication will be more or less comprehensible in any part of the language community.

The standard features of English are as notable for what they don't contain as for what they do. One characteristic of English, for example, is that it has no standard pronunciation. People pronounce the language according to whatever their regional practice happens to be, and while certain pronunciations may be counted as "good" or "bad" according to local standards, there are no general rules about this, the way there are in French or Italian. (Some New Yorkers may be stigmatized for pronouncing words like *car* and *bard* as 'kah' and 'bahd', but roughly the same *r*-less pronunciation is standard in parts of the American South and in England, South Africa, Australia, and New Zealand.) In this sense, "standard English" exists only as a written language. Of course there is some variation in the rules of written English, as well, such as the American spellings that Webster introduced, but these are relatively minor and tend to date from earlier periods. A particular speech-community can pronounce the words *half* or *car* however it likes, but it can't unilaterally change the way the words are spelled. Indeed, this is one of the unappreciated advantages of the notoriously irregular English spelling system—it is so plainly *un*phonetic that there's no temptation to take it as codifying any particular spoken variety. When you want to define a written standard in a linguistic community that embraces no one standard accent, it's useful to have a spelling system that doesn't tip its hand.

The primacy of the written language is evident in the standard English vocabulary, too, if only indirectly. The fact is that English as such does not give us a complete vocabulary for talking about the world, but only for certain kinds of topics. If you want to talk about vegetables in English, for example, you have to choose among the usages common in one or another region: depending on where you do your shopping, you will talk about *rutabagas*, *scallions*, and *string beans* or *Swedes*, *spring onions*, and *French beans*. That is, you can only talk about vegetables in your capacity as an American, an Englishman, or whatever, not in your capacity as an English-speaker in general. And similarly for fashion (*sweater* vs. *jumper*, *bobby pin* vs. *hair grip*, *vest* vs. *waistcoat*), for car parts (*hood* vs. *bonnet*, *trunk* vs. *boot*), and for food, sport, transport, and furniture, among many other things.

The English-language vocabulary is much more standardized, though, in other areas of the lexicon. We have a large common vocabulary for talking about aspects of our social and moral life—*blatant*, *vanity*, *smug*, *indifferent*, and the like. We have a common repertory of grammatical constructions and "signpost" expressions—for example, adverbs like *arguably*, *literally*, and *of course*—which we use to organize our discourse and tell readers how to interpret it. And there is a large number of common words for talking about the language itself—for example, *slang*, *usage*, *jargon*, *succinct*, and *literate*. (It is striking how many of these words are particular to English. No other language has an exact synonym for *slang*, for example, or a single word that covers the territory that *literate* covers in English, from "able to read and write" to "knowledgeable or educated.")

The common "core vocabulary" of English is not limited to these notions, of course—for example, it includes as well the thousands of technical and scientific terms that are in use throughout the English-speaking world, like *global warming* and *penicillin*, which for obvious reasons are not particularly susceptible to cultural variation. Nor would it be accurate to say that the core vocabulary includes all the words we use to refer to our language or to our social and moral life, many of which have a purely local character. But the existence of a core vocabulary of common English words, as fuzzy as it may prove to be, is an indication of the source of our cultural commonalities. What is notable about words like *blatant*, *arguably*, and *succinct* is that their meanings are defined by reference to our common literature, and in particular to the usage of what the eighteenth-century philosopher George Campbell described as "authors of reputation"—writers whose authority is determined by "the esteem of the public." We would not take the usage of Ezra Pound or Bernard Shaw as authoritative in deciding what words like *sweater* or *rutabaga* mean—they could easily have been wrong about either—but their precedents carry a lot of weight when we come to talking about the meaning of *blatant* and *succinct*. In fact the body of English-language "authors of reputation" *couldn't* be wrong about the meanings of words like these, since it is their usage by these authors that collectively determines what these words mean. And for purposes of defining these words it does not matter where a writer is from. The *American Heritage Dictionary*, for example, uses citations from the Irish writer Samuel Beckett to illustrate the meanings of *exasperate* and *impulsion*, from the African-born Doris Lessing to illustrate the meaning of *efface*, and from the Englishman E. M. Forster to illustrate the meaning of *solitude*; and dictionaries from other communities feel equally free to draw on the whole of English literature to illustrate the meanings of the words of the common vocabulary.

It is this strong connection between our common language and our common literature that gives both the language and the linguistic community their essential unity. Late in the eighteenth century, Samuel Johnson said that Britain had become "a nation of readers," by which he meant not just that people were reading more than ever before, but that participation in the written discourse of English had become in some sense constitutive of the national identity. And while the English-speaking world and its ongoing conversation can no longer be identified with a single nation, that world is still very much a community of readers in this sense. Historically, at least, we use the language in the same way because we read and talk about the same books—not *all* the same books, of course, but a loose and shifting group of works that figure as points of reference for our use of language.

This sense of the core vocabulary based on a common literature is intimately connected to the linguistic culture that English-speakers share—the standards, beliefs, and institutions that keep the various written dialects of the language from flying apart. The English dictionary is a good example. It is true that each part of the linguistic community requires its own dictionaries, given the variation in vocabulary and occasionally in spelling and the rest, but they are all formed on more or less the same model, which is very different from that of the French or the Germans. They all organize their entries in the same way, use the same form of definitions, include the same kind of information, and so on, to the point where we often speak of "*the* dictionary," as if the book were a single, invariant text like "the periodic table." By the same token, the schools in every English-speaking nation generally teach the same principles of good usage, a large number of which date from the grammarians of the eighteenth century. There are a few notable exceptions to this generality (Americans and most other communities outside England abandoned some time ago the effort to keep *shall* and *will* straight and seem to be none the worse off for it), but even in these cases grammarians justify their prescriptions using the same terminology and forms of argument.

THE CONTINUITY OF ENGLISH

To be sure, our collective agreement on standards of language and literature is never more than approximate and is always undergoing redefinition and change. Things could hardly be otherwise, given the varied constitution of the English-speaking community, the changing social background, and the insistence of English-speakers that they must be left to decide these matters on their own, without the intervention of official commissions or academies. It is not surprising that the reference points that we depend on to maintain the continuity of the language should often be controversial, even within a single community, and even less so that different national communities should have different ideas as to who counts as authority or what kinds of texts should be relevant to defining the common core of English words. The most we can ask of our common linguistic heritage is that it give us a general format for adapting the language to new needs and for reinterpreting its significance from one time and place to another.

This is the challenge posed by the triumph of English. Granted, there is no threat to the hegemony of English as a worldwide medium for practical communication. It is a certainty that the nations of the English-speaking community will continue to use the various forms of English to communicate with each other, as well as with the hundreds of millions of people who speak English as a second language (and who in fact outnumber the native speakers of the language by a factor of two or three to one). And with the growth of travel and trade and of media like the Internet, the number of English-speakers is sure to continue to increase.

But none of this guarantees the unity of English as a means of cultural expression. What is striking about the accelerating spread of English over the past two centuries is not so much the number of speakers that the language has acquired, but the remarkable variety of the cultures and communities who use it. The heterogeneity of the linguistic community is evident not just in the emergence of the rich new literatures of Africa, Asia, and the Caribbean, but also in the literatures of what linguists sometimes call the "inner circle" of the English-speaking world—nations like Britain, the United States, Australia, and Canada—where the language is being asked to describe a much wider range of experience than ever before, particularly on behalf of groups who until recently have been largely excluded or marginalized from the collective conversation of the English-speaking world.

Not surprisingly, the speakers of the "new Englishes" use the language with different voices and different rhythms and bring to it different linguistic and cultural backgrounds. The language of a writer like Chinua Achebe reflects the influence not just of Shakespeare and Wordsworth but of proverbs and other forms of discourse drawn from West African oral traditions. Indian writers like R. K. Narayan and Salman Rushdie ground their works not just in the traditional English-language canon but in Sanskrit classics like the epic *Rāmāyana*. The continuing sense that all English-speakers are engaged in a common discourse depends on the linguistic community's being able to accommodate and absorb these new linguistic and literary influences, as it has been able to do in the past.

In all parts of the linguistic community, moreover, there are questions posed by the new media of discourse. Over the past hundred years, the primacy of print has been challenged first by the growth of film, recordings, and the broadcast media, and more recently by the remarkable growth of the Internet, each of which has had its effects on the language. With film and the rest, we have begun to see the emergence of spoken standards that co-exist with the written standard of print, not in the form of a standardized English pronunciation—if anything, pronunciation differences among the communities of the English-speaking world have become more marked over the course of the century—but rather in the use of words, expressions, and rhythms that are particular to speech (there is no better example of this than the universal adoption of the particle *okay*). And the Internet has had the effect of projecting what were previously private forms of written communication, like the personal letter, into something more like models of public discourse, but with a language that is much more informal than the traditional discourse of the novel or newspaper.

It is a mistake to think that any of these new forms of discourse will wholly replace the discourse of print (the Internet, in particular, has shown itself to be an important vehicle for marketing and diffusing print works with much greater efficiency than has ever been possible before). It seems reasonable to assume that a hundred years from now the English-speaking world will still be at heart a community of readers—and of readers of books, among other things. And it is likely, too, that the English language will still be at heart a means of written expression, not just for setting down air schedules and trade statistics, but for doing the kind of cultural work that we have looked for literature to do for us in the past; a medium, that is, for poetry, criticism, history, and fiction. But only time will tell if English will remain a single language—if in the midst of all the diversity, cultural and communicative, people will still be able to discern a single "English literature" and a characteristic English-language frame of mind.

The Norton Anthology
of English Literature

SEVENTH EDITION
THE MAJOR AUTHORS

The Middle Ages
to ca. 1485

43–ca. 420:	Roman invasion and occupation of Britain
ca. 450:	Anglo-Saxon Conquest
597:	St. Augustine arrives in Kent; beginning of Anglo-Saxon conversion to Christianity
871–899:	Reign of King Alfred
1066:	Norman Conquest
1154–1189:	Reign of Henry II
ca. 1200:	Beginnings of Middle English literature
1360–1400:	Geoffrey Chaucer; *Piers Plowman; Sir Gawain and the Green Knight*
1485:	William Caxton's printing of Sir Thomas Malory's *Morte Darthur*, one of the first books printed in England

The Middle Ages designates the time span roughly from the collapse of the Roman Empire to the Renaissance. The adjective "medieval," coined from Latin *medium* (middle) and *aevum* (age), refers to whatever was made, written, or thought during the Middle Ages. The Renaissance was so named by nineteenth-century historians and critics because they associated it with an outburst of creativity attributed to a "rebirth" or revival of Latin and, especially, of Greek learning and literature. The Renaissance was seen as spreading from Italy in the fourteenth and fifteenth centuries to the rest of Europe. The very idea of a "rebirth," however, implies something dormant or lacking in the preceding era. More recently, there has been a tendency to emphasize the continuities between the Middle Ages and the later time now often called the Early Modern period. Medieval authors, of course, did not think of themselves as living in the "middle"; they sometimes expressed the idea that the world was growing old and that theirs was a declining age, close to the end of time. Yet art, literature, and science flourished during the Middle Ages, rooted in the Christian culture that preserved, transmitted, and transformed classical tradition.

Although the Roman Catholic Church provided continuity, the period was one of enormous historical, social, and linguistic change. To emphasize these changes and the events underlying them, we have divided the period into three primary sections: Anglo-Saxon England, Anglo-Norman England, and Middle English Literature in the Fourteenth and Fifteenth Centuries. The Anglo-Saxon invaders, who began their conquest of the southeastern part of Britain around 450, spoke an early form of the language we now call Old English. Old English displays its kinship with other Germanic languages (German or Dutch, for example) much more clearly than does contemporary British and American English, of which Old English is the remote ancestor.

1

As late as the tenth century, part of an Old Saxon poem written on the Continent was transcribed and transliterated into the West Saxon dialect of Old English without presenting problems to its English readers. In form and content Old English literature also has much in common with other Germanic literatures with which it shared a body of heroic as well as Christian stories. The major characters in *Beowulf* are pagan Danes and Geats, and the only connection to England is an obscure allusion to the ancestor of one of the kings of the Angles.

The changes already in progress in the language and culture of Anglo-Saxon England were greatly accelerated by the Norman Conquest of 1066. The ascendancy of a French-speaking ruling class had the effect of adding a vast number of French loan words to the English vocabulary. The conquest resulted in new forms of political organization and administration, architecture, and literary expression. In the twelfth century, through the interest of the Anglo-Normans in British history before the Anglo-Saxon Conquest, not only England but all of Western Europe became fascinated with a legendary hero named Arthur who makes his earliest appearances in Celtic literature. King Arthur and his knights became a staple subject of medieval French, English, and German literature.

Literature in English was performed orally and written throughout the Middle Ages, but the awareness of and pride in a uniquely *English* literature does not actually exist before the late fourteenth century. In 1336 Edward III began a war to enforce his claims to the throne of France; the war continued intermittently for one hundred years until finally the English were driven from all their French territories except for the port of Calais. One result of the war and these losses was a keener sense on the part of England's nobility of their English heritage and identity. Toward the close of the fourteenth century English finally began to displace French as the language for conducting business in Parliament and in the courts of law. Although the high nobility continued to speak French by preference, they were certainly bilingual, whereas some of the earlier Norman kings had known no English at all. It was becoming possible to obtain patronage for literary achievement in English. Chaucer's decision to emulate French and Italian poetry in his own vernacular is an indication of the change taking place in the status of English, and Chaucer's works were greatly to enhance the prestige of English as a vehicle for important literature. He was acclaimed by fifteenth-century poets as the embellisher of the English tongue; later writers called him the English Homer and the father of English poetry. His friend John Gower (1325?–1408) wrote long poems in French and Latin before producing his last major work, the *Confessio Amantis* (The Lover's Confession), which in spite of its Latin title is composed in English. The third and longest of the three primary sections, Middle English Literature in the Fourteenth and Fifteenth Centuries, is thus not only a chronological and linguistic division but implies a new sense of English as a literary medium that could compete with French and Latin in elegance and seriousness.

Texts in Old English and *Sir Gawain and the Green Knight*, which is in a difficult regional dialect of Middle English, are given in translation. Chaucer and other Middle English works may be read in the original, even by the beginner, with the help of marginal glosses and notes. These texts have been spelled in a way that is intended to aid the reader. Analyses of the sounds and grammar of Middle English and of Old and Middle English prosody are discussed on pages 12–18.

ANGLO-SAXON ENGLAND

From the first to the fifth century, England was a province of the Roman Empire and was named Britannia after its Celtic-speaking inhabitants, the Britons. The Britons adapted themselves to Roman civilization, of which the ruins survived to impress the poet of *The Wanderer*, who refers to them as "the old works of giants." The withdrawal of the Roman legions during the fifth century, in a vain attempt to protect Rome itself from the threat of Germanic conquest, left the island vulnerable to seafaring Germanic invaders. These belonged primarily to three related tribes, the Angles, the Saxons, and the Jutes. The name *English* derives from the Angles, and the names of the counties Essex, Sussex, and Wessex refer to the territories occupied by the East, South, and West Saxons.

The Anglo-Saxon occupation was no sudden conquest but extended over decades of fighting against the native Britons. The latter were finally confined to the mountainous region of Wales, where the modern form of their language is spoken alongside English to this day. The Britons had become Christians in the fourth century after the conversion of Emperor Constantine along with most of the rest of the Roman Empire, but for about 150 years after the beginning of the invasion, Christianity was maintained only in the remoter regions where the as yet pagan Anglo-Saxons failed to penetrate. In the year 597, however, a Benedictine monk (afterward St. Augustine of Canterbury) was sent by Pope Gregory as a missionary to King Ethelbert of Kent, the most southerly of the kingdoms into which England was then divided, and about the same time missionaries from Ireland began to preach Christianity in the north. Within 75 years the island was once more predominantly Christian. Before Christianity there had been no books. The impact of Christianity on literacy is evident from the fact that the first extended written specimen of the Old English (Anglo-Saxon) language is a code of laws promulgated by Ethelbert, the first English Christian king.

In the centuries that followed the conversion, England produced many distinguished churchmen. One of the earliest of these was Bede, whose Latin *Ecclesiastical History of the English People*, which tells the story of the conversion and of the English church, was completed in 731; this remains one of our most important sources of knowledge about the period. In the next generation Alcuin (735–804), a man of wide culture, became the friend and adviser of the Frankish emperor Charlemagne, whom he assisted in making the Frankish court a great center of learning; thus by the year 800 English culture had developed so richly that it overflowed its insular boundaries.

In the ninth century the Christian Anglo-Saxons were themselves subjected to new Germanic invasions by the Danes who in their longboats repeatedly ravaged the coast, sacking Bede's monastery among others. The Danes also occupied the northern part of the island, threatening to overrun the rest. They were stopped by Alfred, king of the West Saxons from 871 to 899, who for a time united all the kingdoms of southern England. This most active king was also an enthusiastic patron of literature. He himself translated various works from Latin, the most important of which was Boethius's *Consolation of Philosophy*, a sixth-century Roman work also translated in the fourteenth century by Chaucer. Practically all of Old English poetry is preserved in copies made in the West Saxon dialect after the reign of Alfred.

Old English Poetry

The Anglo-Saxon invaders brought with them a tradition of oral poetry. Because nothing was written down before the conversion to Christianity, we have only circumstantial evidence of what that poetry must have been like. Aside from a few short inscriptions on small artifacts, the earliest records in the English language are in manuscripts produced at monasteries and other religious establishments, beginning in the seventh century. Literacy was mainly restricted to servants of the church, and so it is natural that the bulk of Old English literature deals with religious subjects and is mostly drawn from Latin sources. Manuscripts were costly and time-consuming to produce, because they required the copying of texts word by word onto parchment, a durable material made from the prepared skins of domestic animals (paper would not be used in Europe before the twelfth century). Under these difficult circumstances, few texts were written down that did not pertain directly to the work of the church. Most of Old English poetry is contained in just four manuscripts.

These poems show that the aristocratic heroic and kinship values of Germanic society continued to inspire both clergy and laity in the Christian era. As represented in the relatively small body of Anglo-Saxon heroic poetry that survives, this world shares many characteristics with the heroic world described by Homer. Nations are reckoned as groups of people related by kinship rather than by geographical areas, and kinship is the basis of the heroic code. The tribe is ruled by a chieftain who is called *king*, a word that has "kin" for its root. The *lord* (a word derived from Old English *hlaf*, "loaf," plus *weard*, "protector") surrounds himself with a band of retainers (many of them his blood kindred) who are members of his household. He leads his men in battle and rewards them with the spoils; royal generosity was one of the most important aspects of heroic behavior. In return, the retainers are obligated to fight for their lord to the death, and if he is slain, to avenge him or die in the attempt. Blood vengeance is regarded as a sacred duty, and in poetry, everlasting shame awaits those who fail to observe it.

Even though the heroic world of poetry could be invoked to rally resistance to the Viking invasions, it was already remote from the Christian world of Anglo-Saxon England. Nevertheless, Christian writers like the *Beowulf* poet were fascinated by the distant culture of their pagan ancestors and by the inherent conflict between the heroic code and a religion that teaches that we should "forgive those who trespass against us" and that "all they that take the sword shall perish with the sword." The *Beowulf* poet looks back on that ancient world with admiration for the courage of which it was capable and at the same time with elegiac sympathy for its inevitable doom.

For Anglo-Saxon poetry, it is difficult and probably futile to draw a line between "heroic" and "Christian," for the best poetry crosses that boundary. Much of the Christian poetry is also cast in the heroic mode: although the Anglo-Saxons adapted themselves readily to the ideals of Christianity, they did not do so without adapting Christianity to their own heroic ideal. Thus

Moses and St. Andrew, Christ and God the Father are represented in the style of heroic verse. In the *Dream of the Rood*, the Cross speaks of Christ as "the young hero, . . . strong and stouthearted."

The world of Old English poetry is predominantly harsh. Men are said to be cheerful in the mead hall, but even there they think of struggle in war, of possible triumph but more possible failure. Romantic love—one of the principal topics of later literature—appears hardly at all. Even so, at some of the bleakest moments, the poets powerfully recall the return of spring. The blade of the magic sword with which Beowulf has killed Grendel's mother in her sinister underwater lair begins to melt, "as ice melts / when the Father eases the fetters off the frost / and unravels the water ropes, He who wields power."

Poetic language is created out of a special vocabulary that contains a multiplicity of terms for *lord, warrior, spear, shield*, and so on. Synecdoche and metonymy are common figures of speech as when *keel* is used for "ship" or *iron*, for "sword." A particularly striking effect is achieved by the kenning, a compound of two words in place of another as when *sea* becomes "whale-road" or *body* is called "life-house." The figurative use of language finds playful expression in poetic riddles, of which about one hundred survive. Common (and sometimes uncommon) creatures, objects, or phenomena are described in an enigmatic passage of alliterative verse, and the reader must guess their identity. Sometimes they are personified and ask, "What is my name?"

The overall effect of the language is to formalize and elevate speech. Instead of being straightforward, it moves at a slow and stately pace with steady indirection. A favorite mode of this indirection is irony. A grim irony pervades heroic poetry even at the level of diction where *fighting* is called "battle-play." A favorite device, known by the rhetorical term *litotes*, is ironic understatement. After the monster Grendel has slaughtered the Danes in the great hall Heorot, it stands deserted. The poet observes, "It was easy then to meet with a man / shifting himself to a safer distance."

More than a figure of speech, irony is also a mode of perception in Old English poetry. *Beowulf* is full of ironic balances and contrasts—between the aged Danish king and the youthful Beowulf, and between Beowulf, the high-spirited young warrior at the beginning, and Beowulf, the gray-haired king at the end, facing the dragon and death.

The formal and dignified speech of Old English poetry was always distant from the everyday language of the Anglo-Saxons, and this poetic idiom remained remarkably uniform for the roughly three hundred years before the Norman Conquest. This clinging to old forms—grammatical and orthographic as well as literary—by the Anglo-Saxon church and aristocracy conceals from us the enormous changes that were taking place in the English language and the diversity of its dialects. The dramatic changes between Old and Middle English did not happen overnight or over the course of a single century. The Normans displaced the English ruling class with their own barons and clerics, whose native language was a dialect of Old French that we call Anglo-Norman. Without a ruling literate class to preserve English traditions, the custom of transcribing vernacular texts in an earlier form of the West-Saxon dialect was abandoned, and both language and literature were allowed to develop unchecked in new directions.

ANGLO-NORMAN ENGLAND

The Normans, who took possession of England after the decisive Battle of Hastings (1066), were, like the Anglo-Saxons, descendants of Germanic adventurers who at the beginning of the tenth century had seized a wide part of northern France. Their name is actually a contraction of "Norsemen." A highly adaptable people, they had adopted the French language of the land they had settled in and its Christian religion. Both in Normandy and in Britain they were great builders of castles, with which they enforced their political dominance, and magnificent churches. Norman bishops, who held land and castles like the barons, wielded both political and spiritual authority. The earlier Norman kings of England, however, were often absentee rulers, as much concerned with defending their Continental possessions as with ruling over their English holdings. The English Crown's French territories were enormously increased in 1154 when Henry II, the first of England's Plantagenet kings, ascended the throne. Through his marriage with Eleanor of Aquitaine, the divorced wife of Louis VII of France, Henry had acquired vast provinces in the south of France.

The presence of a French-speaking ruling class in England created exceptional opportunities for linguistic and cultural exchange. Four languages coexisted in the realm of Anglo-Norman England: Latin, as it had been for Bede, remained the international language of learning, used for theology, science, and history. It was not by any means a written language only but a lingua franca by which different nationalities communicated in the church and the newly founded universities. The Norman aristocracy for the most part spoke French, but intermarriage with the native English nobility and the business of daily life between masters and servants encouraged bilingualism. Different branches of the Celtic language group were spoken in Ireland, Wales, Cornwall, and Brittany.

Inevitably there was also literary intercourse among the different languages. The Latin Bible and Latin saints' lives provided subjects for a great deal of Old English as well as Old French poetry and prose. The first medieval drama in the vernacular, *The Play of Adam*, with elaborate stage directions in Latin and realistic dialogue in the Anglo-Norman dialect of French, was probably produced in England during the twelfth century.

The Anglo-Norman aristocracy was especially attracted to Celtic legends and tales that had been circulating orally for centuries. The twelfth-century poets Marie de France and Chrétien de Troyes both claim to have obtained their narratives from Breton storytellers, who were probably bilingual performers of native tales for French audiences. "Breton" may indicate that they came from Brittany, or it may have been a generic term for a Celtic bard. Marie speaks respectfully of the storytellers; Chrétien accuses them of marring their material, which, he boasts, he has retold with an elegant fusion of form and meaning. Marie wrote a series of short romances, which she refers to as "lays" originally told by Bretons. Her versions are the most original and sophisticated examples of the genre that came to be known as the Breton lay, represented here by Marie's *Lanval*. It is very likely that Henry II is the "noble king" to whom she dedicated her lays and that they were written for his court. Chrétien is the principal creator of the romance of chivalry in which knightly adventures are a means of exploring psychological and ethical dilemmas that the knights must solve, in addition to displaying martial prowess in saving ladies from monsters, giants, and wicked knights. Chrétien, like Marie, is thought to have spent time in England at the court of Henry II. Both Marie de France and Chrétien de Troyes were innovators of the genre that has become known as "romance." The word *roman* was initially applied in French to a work written in the French vernacular. Thus the thirteenth-century *Roman de Troie* is a long poem about the Trojan War in French. While this work deals mainly with the siege of Troy, it also includes stories about the love of Troilus for Cressida and of Achilles for the Trojan princess Polyxena. Eventually "romance" acquired the generic associations it has for us as a story about love and adventure. In the late twelfth century, Andreas Capellanus (Andrew the Chaplain) wrote a Latin treatise, the title of which may be translated *The Art of Loving Correctly* [*honeste*]. In one part, Eleanor of Aquitaine, her daughter, the countess Marie de Champagne, and other noble women are cited as a supreme court rendering decisions on difficult questions of love—for example, whether there is greater passion between lovers or between married couples. Whether such "courts of love" were purely imaginary or whether they represent some actual court entertainment, they imply that the literary taste and judgment of women had a significant role in determining the rise of romance in France and Anglo-Norman England.

In Marie's *Lanval* and in Chrétien's romances, the court of King Arthur had already acquired for French audiences a reputation as the most famous center of chivalry. That eminence is owing in large measure to a remarkable book in Latin, *The History of the Kings of Britain*, completed by Geoffrey of Monmouth, ca. 1136–38. Geoffrey claimed to have based his "history" on a book in the British tongue (i.e., Welsh), but no one has ever found such a book. He drew on a few earlier Latin chronicles, but the bulk of his history was probably fabricated from Celtic oral tradition, his familiarity with Roman history and literature, and his own fertile imagination. The climax of the book is the reign of King Arthur, who defeats the Roman armies but is forced to turn back to Britain to counter the treachery of his nephew Mordred. Geoffrey's Latin was rendered into French rhyme by an Anglo-Norman poet called Wace, and Wace's poem was turned by Layamon, an English priest, into a much longer poem that combines English alliterative verse with sporadic rhyme.

Layamon's work is one of many instances where English receives new material directly through French sources, which may be drawn from Celtic or Latin sources. There are two Middle English versions of Marie's *Lanval*, and the English romance called *Yvain and Gawain* is a cruder version of Chrétien's *Le Chevalier au Lion* (The Knight of the Lion). There is a marvelous English lay, *Sir Orfeo*, a version of the Orpheus story in which Orpheus succeeds in rescuing his wife from the other world, for which a French original, if there was one, has never been found. Romance, stripped of its courtly, psychological, and ethical subtleties, had an immense popular appeal for English readers and listeners. Many of these romances are simplified adaptations of more aristocratic French poems and recount in a rollicking and rambling style the adventures of heroes like Guy of Warwick, a poor steward who must prove his knightly worth to win the love of Fair

Phyllis. The ethos of many romances, aristocratic and popular alike, involves a knight proving his worthiness through nobility of character and brave deeds rather than through high birth. In this respect romances reflect the aspirations of a lower order of the nobility to rise in the world, as historically some of these nobles did. William the Marshall, for example, the fourth son of a baron of middle rank, used his talents in war and in tournaments to become tutor to the oldest son of Henry II and Eleanor of Aquitaine. He married a great heiress and became one of the most powerful nobles in England and the subject of a verse biography in French, which often reads like a romance.

MIDDLE ENGLISH LITERATURE IN THE FOURTEENTH AND FIFTEENTH CENTURIES

Throughout the thirteenth and early fourteenth centuries, there are many kinds of evidence that, although French continued to be the principal language of Parliament, law, business, and high culture, English was gaining ground. Several authors of religious and didactic works in English state that they are writing for the benefit of those who do not understand Latin or French. Anthologies are made of miscellaneous works adapted from French for English readers and original pieces in English. Most of the nobility are by now bilingual, and the author of an English romance written early in the fourteenth century declares that he has seen many nobles who cannot speak French. Children of the nobility and the merchant class are now learning French as a second language. By the 1360s the linguistic, political, and cultural climate had been prepared for the flowering of Middle English literature in the writings of Chaucer, Langland, and the *Gawain* poet.

The Fourteenth Century

War and disease were prevalent throughout the Middle Ages but never more devastatingly than during the fourteenth century. In the wars against France, the gains of two spectacular English victories, at Crécy in 1346 and Poitiers in 1356, were gradually frittered away in futile campaigns that ravaged the French countryside without obtaining any clear advantage for the English. In 1348 the first and most virulent epidemic of the bubonic plague—the Black Death—swept Europe, wiping out a quarter to a third of the population. The toll was higher in crowded urban centers. Giovanni Boccaccio's description of the plague in Florence, with which he introduces the *Decameron*, vividly portrays its ravages: "So many corpses would arrive in front of a church every day and at every hour that the amount of holy ground for burials was certainly insufficient for the ancient custom of giving each body its individual place; when all the graves were full, huge trenches were dug in all of the cemeteries of the churches and into them the new arrivals were dumped by the hundreds; and they were packed in there with dirt, one on top of another, like a ship's cargo, until the trench was filled." The resulting scarcity of labor and a sudden expansion of the possibilities for social mobility fostered popular discontent. In 1381 attempts to enforce wage controls and to collect oppressive new taxes provoked a rural uprising in Essex and Kent that dealt a profound shock to the English ruling class. The participants were for the most part tenant farmers, day laborers, apprentices, and rural workers not attached to the big manors. A few of the lower clergy sided with the rebels against their wealthy church superiors; the priest John Ball was among the leaders. The movement was quickly suppressed, but not before sympathizers in London had admitted the rebels through two city gates, which had been barred against them. The insurgents burned down the palace of the hated duke of Lancaster, and they summarily beheaded the archbishop of Canterbury and the treasurer of England, who had taken refuge in the Tower of London. The church had become the target of popular resentment because it was among the greatest of the oppressive landowners and because of the wealth, worldliness, and venality of many of the higher clergy.

These calamities and upheavals nevertheless did not stem the growth of international trade and the influence of the merchant class. In the portrait of Geoffrey Chaucer's merchant, we see the budding of capitalism based on credit and interest. Cities like London ran their own affairs under politically powerful mayors and aldermen. Edward III, chronically in need of money to finance his wars, was obliged to negotiate for revenues with the Commons in the English Parliament, an institution that became a major political force during this period. A large part of the king's revenues depended on taxing the profitable export of English wool to the Continent. The Crown thus became involved in the country's economic affairs, and this involvement led to a need for capable administrators. These were no longer drawn mainly from the church, as in the past, but from a newly educated laity that occupied a rank somewhere between that of the lesser nobility and the upper bourgeoisie. The career of Chaucer, who served Edward III and his successor Richard II in a number of civil posts, is typical of this class—with the exception that Chaucer was also a great poet.

In the fourteenth century, a few poets and intellectuals achieved the status and respect formerly accorded only to the ancients. Marie de France and Chrétien de Troyes had dedicated their works to noble patrons and, in their role as narrators, address themselves as entertainers and sometimes as instructors to court audiences. Dante (1265–1321) made himself the protagonist of *The Divine Comedy*, the sacred poem, as he called it, in which he revealed the secrets of the afterlife. After his death, manuscripts of the work were provided with lengthy commentaries as though it were Scripture, and public readings and lectures were devoted to it. Francesco Petrarch (1304–1374) won an international reputation as a man of letters. He wrote primarily in Latin and contrived to have himself crowned "poet laureate" in emulation of the Roman poets whose works he imitated, but his most famous work is the sonnet sequence he wrote in Italian. Giovanni Boccaccio (1313–1375) was among Petrarch's most ardent admirers and carried on a literary correspondence with him.

Chaucer read these authors along with the ancient Roman poets and drew on them in his own works. Chaucer's *Clerk's Tale* is based on a Latin version Petrarch made from the last tale in Boccaccio's *Decameron*; in his prologue, the Clerk refers to Petrarch as "lauriat poete" whose sweet rhetoric illuminated all Italy with his poetry. Yet in his own time, the English poet Chaucer never attained the kind of laurels that he and others accorded to Petrarch. In his earlier works, Chaucer portrayed himself comically as a diligent reader of old books, as an aspiring apprentice writer, and as an eager spectator on the fringe of a fashionable world of courtiers and poets. In *The House of*

Fame, he relates a dream of being snatched up by a huge golden eagle (the eagle and many other things in this work were inspired by Dante), who transports him to the palace of the goddess of Fame. There he gets to see phantoms, like the shades in Dante's poem, of all the famous authors of antiquity. At the end of his romance *Troilus and Criseyde*, Chaucer asks his "litel book" to kiss the footsteps where the great ancient poets had passed before. Like Dante and Petrarch, Chaucer had an ideal of great poetry and, in his *Troilus* at least, strove to emulate it. But in *The House of Fame* and in his final work, *The Canterbury Tales*, he also views that ideal ironically and distances himself from it. The many surviving documents that record Geoffrey Chaucer's career as a civil servant do not contain a single word to show that he was also a poet. Only in the following centuries would he be canonized as the father of English poetry.

Native traditions held out longest in the west and north, away from London, where Chaucer and his audience were more open to literary fashions from the Continent. Those areas saw a final flowering in the late fourteenth century of the verse form that goes all the way back to Anglo-Saxon England, known as the "Alliterative Revival." An important poem in that tradition is William Langland's dream vision allegory *Piers Plowman*, which assailed corruption in church and state. Admiration for Chaucer's poetry and the controversial nature of Langland's writing assured the survival of their work in many manuscripts. The work of a third major fourteenth-century English poet, who remains anonymous, is known only through a single manuscript, which contains four poems all thought to be by a single author: *Cleanness* and *Patience*, two biblical narratives in alliterative verse; *Pearl*, a moving dream vision in which a grief-stricken father is visited and consoled by his dead child, who has been transformed into a queen in the kingdom of heaven; and *Sir Gawain and the Green Knight*, the finest of all English romances. The plot of *Gawain* involves a folklore motif of a challenge by a supernatural visitor, first found in an Old Irish tale. The poet has made this motif a challenge to King Arthur's court and has framed the tale with allusions at the beginning and end to the legends that link Arthur's reign with the Trojan War and the founding of Rome and of Britain. The poet has a sophisticated awareness of romance as a literary genre and plays a game with both the hero's and the readers' expectations of what is supposed to happen in a romance. One could say that the broader subject of *Sir Gawain and the Green Knight* is "romance" itself, and in this respect the poem resembles Chaucer's *Canterbury Tales* in its author's interest in literary form.

The Fifteenth Century

In 1399 Henry Bolingbroke, the duke of Lancaster, deposed his cousin Richard II, who was murdered in prison. As Henry IV, he successfully defended his crown against several insurrections and passed it on to Henry V, who briefly united the country once more and achieved one last apparently decisive victory over the French at the Battle of Agincourt (1415). The premature death of Henry V, however, left England exposed to the civil wars known as the Wars of the Roses, the red rose being the emblem of the house of Lancaster; the white, of York. These wars did not end until 1485, when Henry Tudor defeated Richard III at Bosworth Field and acceded to the throne as Henry VII.

Social, economic, and literary life continued as they had throughout all of the previous wars. The prosperity of the towns was shown by performances of the mystery plays—a sequence or "cycle" of plays based on the Bible and produced by the city guilds, the organizations representing the various trades and crafts. The cycles of several towns are lost, but those of York, Wakefield, and Chester have been preserved. The play of *Noah's Flood* continued to be performed at Chester until late in the sixteenth century.

While religious works of all kinds continued to be produced, the four-teenth and fifteenth centuries are notable (both in England and on the Con-tinent) for mystical writings in which the authors, many of whom were women, tell of their direct personal experience of God. The anchoress Julian of Norwich spent her life meditating and writing about a series of visions, which she called "showings," that she had received in 1373, when she was thirty years old. Early in the fifteenth century she was still in her cell, attached to a church in Norwich, when she was consulted by Margery Kempe, whom a series of visions had directed to lead a spiritual life. Kempe, a controversial figure, made a pilgrimage to the Holy Land and during the 1430s dictated the first autobiography in English. Both Julian of Norwich and Margery Kempe, in highly individual ways, allow us to see the medieval church and its doctrines from female points of view.

The works of Sir Thomas Malory gave the definitive form in English to the saga of King Arthur and his knights. Malory spent years in prison Englishing a series of Arthurian romances that he translated and abridged chiefly from several enormously long thirteenth-century French prose romances. Malory was a passionate devotee of chivalry, which he personified in his hero Sir Lancelot. In the jealousies and rivalries that finally break up the round table and destroy Arthur's kingdom, Malory saw a distant image of the civil wars of his own time. A manuscript of Malory's works fell into the hands of Wil-liam Caxton (1422?–1491), who had introduced the new art of printing by movable type to England in 1476. Caxton divided Malory's tales into the chapters and books of a single long work, as though it were a chronicle history, and gave it the title *Morte Darthur*, which has stuck to it ever since. Caxton also printed *The Canterbury Tales*, some of Chaucer's earlier works, and Gower's *Confessio Amantis*. Caxton himself translated many of the works he printed for English readers: a history of Troy, a book on chivalry, Aesop's fables, and *The Game and Playe of Chesse*. The new technology extended literacy and made books more easily accessible to new classes of readers. Printing made the production of literature a business and made possible the bitter political and doctrinal disputes that, in the sixteenth century, were waged in print as well as on the field of battle.

MEDIEVAL ENGLISH

The medieval works in this book were composed in different states of our language. Old English, the language that took shape among the Germanic settlers of England, preserved its integrity until the Norman Conquest rad-ically altered English civilization. Middle English, the earliest records of which date from the early twelfth century, was continually changing. Shortly after the introduction of printing at the end of the fifteenth century, it attained the form designated as Early Modern English. Old English is a very heavily inflected language. (That is, the words change form to indicate changes in usage, such as person, number, tense, case, mood, and so on. Most languages have some inflection—for example, the personal pronouns in Modern English have different forms when used as objects—but a "heavily inflected" language is one in which almost all classes of words undergo elaborate patterns of change.) The vocabulary of Old English is almost entirely Germanic. In Middle English, the inflectional system was weakened, and a large number of words were introduced into it from French, so that many of the older native words disappeared. Because of the difficulty of Old English, all selections from it in this book have been given in translation. The present discussion, then, is concerned primarily with the relatively late form of Middle English used by Chaucer and the East Midland dialect in which he wrote.

The chief difficulty with Middle English for the modern reader is caused not by its inflections so much as by its spelling, which may be described as a rough-and-ready phonetic system, and by the fact that it is not a single standardized language, but consists of a number of regional dialects, each with its own peculiarities of sound and its own systems for representing sounds in writing. The Midland dialect—the dialect of London and of Chaucer, which is the ancestor of our own standard speech—differs greatly from the dialect spoken in the west of England (the original dialect of *Piers Plowman*), from that of the northwest (*Sir Gawain* and *the Green Knight*), and from that of the north (*The Second Shepherds' Play*). In this book, the long texts composed in the more difficult dialects have been translated or modernized, and those that—like Chaucer, *Everyman*, the lyrics, and the ballads—appear in the original, have been re-spelled in a way that is designed to aid the reader. The remarks that follow apply chiefly to Chaucer's Midland English, although certain non-Midland dialectal variations are noted if they occur in some of the other selections.

I. The Sounds of Middle English: General Rules

The following general analysis of the sounds of Middle English will enable the reader who has not time for detailed study to read Middle English aloud so as to preserve some of its most essential characteristics, without, however, giving heed to many important details. The next section, "Detailed Analysis," is designed for the reader who wishes to go more deeply into the pronunciation of Middle English.

Middle English differs from Modern English in three principal respects: (1) the pronunciation of the long vowels *a, e, i* (or *y*), *o*, and *u* (spelled *ou, ow*); (2) the fact that Middle English final *e* is often sounded; and (3) the fact that all Middle English consonants are sounded.

1. LONG VOWELS

Middle English vowels are long when they are doubled (*aa, ee, oo*) or when they are terminal (*he, to, holy*); *a, e,* and *o* are long when followed by a single consonant plus a vowel (*name, mete, note*). Middle English vowels are short when they are followed by two consonants.

Long *a* is sounded like the *a* in Modern English "father": *maken, madd*.

Long *e* may be sounded like the *a* in Modern English "name" (ignoring the distinction between the close and open vowel): *be, sweete*.

Long *i* (or *y*) is sounded like the *i* in Modern English "machine": *lif, whit; myn, holy*.

Long *o* may be sounded like the *o* in Modern English "note" (again ignoring the distinction between the close and open vowel): *do, soone*.

Long *u* (spelled *ou, ow*) is sounded like the *oo* in Modern English "goose": *hous, flowr*.

Note that in general Middle English long vowels are pronounced like long vowels in modern European languages other than English. Short vowels and diphthongs, however, may be pronounced as in Modern English.

2. FINAL E

In Middle English syllabic verse, final *e* is sounded like the *a* in "sofa" to provide a needed unstressed syllable: *Another Nonnë with hire haddë she*. But (cf. *hire* in the example) final *e* is suppressed when not needed for the meter. It is commonly silent before words beginning with a vowel or *h*.

3. CONSONANTS

Middle English consonants are pronounced separately in all combinations—*gnat: g-nat; knave: k-nave; write: w-rite; folk: fol-k*. In a simplified system of pronunciation the combination *gh* as in *night* or *thought* may be treated as if it were silent.

II. *The Sounds of Middle English: Detailed Analysis*

1. SIMPLE VOWELS

Sound	Pronunciation	Example
long *a* (spelled *a, aa*)	*a* in "father"	*maken, maad*
short *a*	*o* in "hot"	*cappe*
long *e* close (spelled *e, ee*)	*a* in "name"	*be, sweete*
long *e* open (spelled *e, ee*)	*e* in "there"	*mete, heeth*
short *e*	*e* in "set"	*setten*
final *e*	*a* in "sofa"	*large*
long *i* (spelled *i, y*)	*i* in "machine"	*lif, mym*
short *i*	*i* in "wit"	*wit*
long *o* close (spelled *o, oo*)	*o* in "note"	*do, soone*
long *o* open (spelled *o, oo*)	*oa* in "broad"	*go, goon*
short *o*	*o* in "oft"	*pot*
long *u* when spelled *ou, ow*	*oo* in "goose"	*hous, flowr*
long *u* when spelled *u*	*u* in "pure"	*vertu*
short *u* (spelled *u, o*)	*u* in "full"	*ful, love*

Doubled vowels and terminal vowels are always long, whereas single vowels before two consonants other than *th, ch* are always short. The vowels *a, e,* and *o* are long before a single consonant followed by a vowel: *nāmë, sēkë* (sick), *hōly*. In general, words that have descended into Modern English reflect their original Middle English quantity: *lĭven* (to live), but *līf* (life).

The close and open sounds of long *e* and long *o* may often be identified by the Modern English spellings of the words in which they appear. Original long close *e* is generally represented in Modern English by *ee*: "sweet," "knee," "teeth," "see" have close *e* in Middle English, but so does "be"; original long open *e* is generally represented in Modern English by *ea*: "meat," "heath," "sea," "great," "breath" have open *e* in Middle English. Similarly, original long close *o* is now generally represented by *oo*: "soon," "food," "good," but also "do," "to"; original long open *o* is represented either by *oa* or by *o*: "coat," "boat," "moan," but also "go," "bone," "foe," "home." Notice that original close *o* is now almost always pronounced like the *oo* in "goose," but that original open *o* is almost never so pronounced; thus it is often possible to identify the Middle English vowels through Modern English sounds.

The nonphonetic Middle English spelling of *o* for short *u* has been preserved in a number of Modern English words ("love," "son," "come"), but in others *u* has been restored: "sun" (*sonne*), "run" (*ronne*).

For the treatment of final *e*, see "General Rules," "Final *e*."

2. DIPHTHONGS

Sound	Pronunciation	Example
ai, ay, ei, ay	between *ai* in "aisle" and *ay* in "day"	*saide, day, veine, preye*
au, aw	*ou* in "out"	*chaunge, bawdy*
eu, ew	*ew* in "few"	*newe*
oi, oy	*oy* in "joy"	*joye, point*
ou, ow	*ou* in "thought"	*thought, lowe*

Note that in words with *ou, ow* that in Modern English are sounded with the *ou* of "about," the combination indicates not the diphthong but the simple vowel long *u* (see "Simple Vowels").

3. CONSONANTS

In general, all consonants except *h* were always sounded in Middle English, including consonants that have become silent in Modern English, such as the *g* in *gnaw*, the *k* in *knight*, the *l* in *folk*, and the *w* in *write*. In noninitial *gn*, however, the *g* was silent as in Modern English "sign." Initial *h* was silent in short common English words and in words borrowed from French and may have been almost silent in all words. The combination *gh* as in *night* or *thought* was sounded like the *ch* of German *ich* or *nach*. Note that Middle English *gg* represents both the hard sound of "dagger" and the soft sound of "bridge."

III. *Parts of Speech and Grammar*

1. NOUNS

The plural and possessive of nouns end in *es*, formed by adding *s* or *es* to the singular: *knight, knightes; roote, rootes*; a final consonant is frequently doubled before *es*: *bed, beddes*. A common irregular plural is *yën*, from *yë*, eye.

2. PRONOUNS

The chief differences from Modern English are as follows:

Modern English	Middle English
I	*I, ich (ik* is a northern form)
you (singular)	*thou* (subjective); *thee* (objective)
her	*hir(e), her(e)*
its	*his*
you (plural)	*ye* (subjective); *you* (objective)
their	*hir*
them	*hem*

In formal speech, the second person plural is often used for the singular. The possessive adjectives *my, thy* take *n* before a word beginning with a vowel or *h: thyn yë, myn host.*

3. ADJECTIVES

Adjectives ending in a consonant add final *e* when they stand before the noun they modify and after another modifying word such as *the, this, that,* or nouns or pronouns in the possessive: *a good hors,* but *the (this, my, the kinges) goode hors.* They also generally add *e* when standing before and modifying a plural noun, a noun in the vocative, or any proper noun: *goode men, oh goode man, faire Venus.*

Adjectives are compared by adding *er(e)* for the comparative, *est(e)* for the superlative. Sometimes the stem vowel is shortened or altered in the process: *sweete, swettere, swettest; long, lenger, lengest.*

4. ADVERBS

Adverbs are formed from adjectives by adding *e, ly,* or *liche;* the adjective *fair* thus yields *faire, fairly, fairliche.*

5. VERBS

Middle English verbs, like Modern English verbs, are either "weak" or "strong." Weak verbs form their preterites and past participles with a *t* or *d* suffix and preserve the same stem vowel throughout their systems, although it is sometimes shortened in the preterite and past participle: *love, loved; bend, bent; hear, heard; meet, met.* Strong verbs do not use the *t* or *d* suffix, but vary their stem vowel in the preterite and past participle: *take, took, taken; begin, began, begun; find, found, found.*

The inflectional endings are the same for Middle English strong verbs and weak verbs except in the preterite singular and the imperative singular. In the following paradigms, the weak verbs *loven* (to love) and *heeren* (to hear), and the strong verbs *taken* (to take) and *ginnen* (to begin) serve as models.

	Present Indicative	Preterite Indicative
I	*love, heere*	*loved(e), herde*
	take, ginne	*took, gan*
thou	*lovest, heerest*	*lovedest, herdest*
	takest, ginnest	*tooke, gonne*
he, she, it	*loveth, heereth*	*loved(e), herde*
	taketh, ginneth	*took, gan*
we, ye, they	*love(n) (th), heere(n) (th)*	*loved(e) (en), herde(n)*
	take(n) (th), ginne(n) (th)	*tooke(n), gonne(n)*

The present plural ending *eth* is southern, whereas the *e(n)* ending is Midland and characteristic of Chaucer. In the north, *s* may appear as the ending of all persons of the present. In the weak preterite, when the ending *e* gave a verb three or more syllables, it was frequently dropped. Note that in certain strong verbs like *ginnen* there are two distinct stem vowels in the preterite; even in Chaucer's time, however, one of these had begun to replace the other, and Chaucer occasionally writes *gan* for all persons of the preterite.

	Present Subjunctive	Preterite Subjunctive
Singular	*love, heere*	*lovede, herde*
	take, ginne	*tooke, gonne*
Plural	*love(n), heere(n)*	*lovede(n), herde(n)*
	take(n), ginne(n)	*tooke(n), gonne(n)*

In verbs like *ginnen*, which have two stem vowels in the indicative preterite, it is the vowel of the plural and of the second person singular that is used for the preterite subjunctive.

The imperative singular of most weak verbs is *e: (thou) love*, but of some weak verbs and all strong verbs, the imperative singular is without termination: *(thou) heer, taak, gin*. The imperative plural of all verbs is either *e* or *eth: (ye) love(th), heere(th), take(th), ginne(th)*.

The infinitive of verbs is *e* or *en: love(n), heere(n), take(n), ginne(n)*.

The past participle of weak verbs is the same as the preterite without inflectional ending: *loved, herd*. In strong verbs the ending is either *e* or *en: take(n), gonne(n)*. The prefix *y* often appears on past participles: *yloved, yherd, ytake(n)*.

OLD AND MIDDLE ENGLISH PROSODY

All the poetry of Old English is in the same verse form. The verse unit is the single line, because rhyme was not used to link one line to another, except very occasionally in late Old English. The organizing device of the line is alliteration, the beginning of several words with the same sound ("Foemen fled"). The Old English alliterative line contains, on the average, four principal stresses and is divided into two half-lines of two stresses each by a strong medial caesura, or pause. These two half-lines are linked to each other by the alliteration; at least one of the two stressed words in the first half-line, and often both of them, begin with the same sound as the first stressed word of the second half-line (the second stressed word is generally nonal-literative). The fourth line of *Beowulf* is an example (*sc* has the value of modern *sh*; þ is a runic symbol with the value of modern *th*):

> Oft Scyld Scefing   sceaþena þreatum.

It will be noticed that any vowel alliterates with any other vowel. In addition to the alliteration, the length of the unstressed syllables and their number and pattern is governed by a highly complex set of rules. When sung or intoned—as it was—to the rhythmic strumming of a harp, Old English poetry must have been wonderfully impressive in the dignified, highly formalized way that aptly fits both its subject matter and tone.

The majority of Middle English verse is either in alternately stressed rhyming verse, adapted from French after the conquest, or in alliterative verse that is descended from Old English. The latter preserves the caesura of Old English and in its purest form the same alliterative system, the two stressed words of the first half-line (or at least one of them) alliterating with the first stressed word in the second half-line. But most of the alliterative poets allowed themselves a number of deviations from the norm. All four stressed words may alliterate, as in the first line of *Piers Plowman:*

> In a summer season   when soft was the sun.

Or the line may contain five, six, or even more stressed words, of which all or only the basic minimum may alliterate:

> A *f*air *f*ield *f*ull of   *f*olk *f*ound I therebetween.

There is no rule determining the number of unstressed syllables, and at times some poets seem to ignore alliteration entirely. As in Old English, any vowel may alliterate with any other vowel; furthermore, since initial *h* was silent or lightly pronounced in Middle English, words beginning with *h* are treated as though they began with the following vowel.

There are two general types of stressed verse with rhyme. In the more common, stressed and unstressed syllables alternate regularly as x X x X x X or, with two unstressed syllables intervening as x x X x x X x x X or a combination of the two as x x X x X x x X (of the reverse patterns, only X x X x X x is common in English). There is also a line that can only be defined as containing a predetermined number of stressed syllables but an irregular number and pattern of unstressed syllables. Much Middle English verse has to be read without expectation of regularity; some of this was evidently composed in the irregular meter, but some was probably originally composed according to a strict metrical system that has been obliterated by scribes careless of fine points. One receives the impression that many of the lyrics— as well as the *Second Shepherds' Play*—were at least composed with regular syllabic alternation. In the play *Everyman*, only the number of stresses is generally predetermined but not the number or placement of unstressed syllables.

In pre-Chaucerian verse the number of stresses, whether regularly or irregularly alternated, was most often four, although sometimes the number was three and rose in some poems to seven. Rhyme in Middle English (as in Modern English) may be either between adjacent or alternate lines, or may occur in more complex patterns. Most of the *Canterbury Tales* are in rhymed couplets, the line containing five stresses with regular alternation—technically known as iambic pentameter, the standard English poetic line, perhaps introduced into English by Chaucer. In reading Chaucer and much pre-Chaucerian verse one must remember that the final *e*, which is silent in Modern English, could be pronounced at any time to provide a needed unstressed syllable. Evidence seems to indicate that it was also pronounced at the end of the line, even though it thus produced a line with eleven syllables. Although he was a very regular metricist, Chaucer used various conventional devices that are apt to make the reader stumble until he or she understands them. Final *e* is often not pronounced before a word beginning with a vowel or *h*, and may be suppressed whenever metrically convenient. The same medial and terminal syllables that are slurred in Modern English are apt to be suppressed in Chaucer's English: *Canterb'ry* for *Canterbury*; *ev'r* (perhaps *e'er*) for *evere*. The plural in *es* may either be syllabic or reduced to *s* as in Modern English. Despite these seeming irregularities, Chaucer's verse is not difficult to read if one constantly bears in mind the basic pattern of the iambic pentameter line.

THE MIDDLE AGES

TEXTS	CONTEXTS
	43–ca. 420 Romans conquer Britons; Brittania a province of the Roman Empire
	307–37 Reign of Constantine the Great leads to adoption of Christianity as official religion of the Roman Empire
ca. 405 St. Jerome completes *Vulgate,* Latin translation of the Bible that becomes standard for the Roman Catholic Church	
	432 St. Patrick begins mission to convert Ireland
	ca. 450 Withdrawal of Roman legions; Anglo-Saxon conquest of Britons begins
523 Boethius, *Consolation of Philosophy* (Latin)	
	597 St. Augustine of Canterbury's mission to Kent begins conversion of Anglo-Saxons to Christianity
ca. 658–80 *Cædmon's Hymn,* earliest poem recorded in English	
731 Bede completes *Ecclesiastical History of the English People*	
? ca. 750 *Beowulf* composed	
	ca. 787 First Viking raids on England
	871–99 Reign of King Alfred
ca. 1000 Unique *Beowulf* manuscript written	
	1066 Norman Conquest by William I establishes French-speaking ruling class in England
	1095–1221 Crusades
ca. 1135–38 Geoffrey of Monmouth's Latin *History of the Kings of Britain* gives pseudohistorical status to Arthurian and other legends	
	1152 Future Henry II marries Eleanor of Aquitaine, bringing vast French territories to the English crown
1154 End of *Peterborough Chronicle,* last branch of the *Anglo-Saxon Chronicle*	
? ca. 1165–80 Marie de France, *Lais* in Anglo-Norman French from Breton sources	
ca. 1170–91 Chrétien de Troyes, chivalric romances about knights of the Round Table	**1170** Archbishop Thomas Becket murdered in Canterbury Cathedral
	1182 Birth of St. Francis of Assisi
? ca. 1200 Layamon's *Brut*	
? ca. 1215–25 *Ancrene Riwle*	**1215** Fourth Lateran Council requires annual confession. English barons force King John to seal Magna Carta (the Great Charter) guaranteeing baronial rights

TEXTS	CONTEXTS
ca. 1304–21 Dante Alighieri writing *Divine Comedy*	
	ca. 1337–1453 Hundred Years' War
	1348 Black Death ravages Europe
	1362 English first used in law courts and Parliament
1368 Chaucer, *Book of the Duchess*	
	1372 Chaucer's first journey to Italy
ca. 1375–1400 *Sir Gawain and the Green Knight*	
	1376 Earliest record of performance of drama at York
1377–79 William Langland, *Piers Plowman* (B-Text)	
ca. 1380 John Wycliffe and his followers begin first complete translation of the Bible into English	
	1381 People's uprising briefly takes control of London before being suppressed
ca. 1385–87 Chaucer, *Troilus and Criseyde*	
ca. 1387–89 Chaucer working on *The Canterbury Tales*	
ca. 1390–92 John Gower, *Confessio Amantis*	
	1399 Richard II deposed by his cousin, who succeeds him as Henry IV
	1400 Richard II murdered
	1401 Execution of William Sawtre, first Lollard burned at the stake under new law against heresy
	1415 Henry V defeats French at Agincourt
	1431 English burn Joan of Arc at Rouen
ca. 1432–38 Margery Kempe, *The Book of Margery Kempe*	
ca. 1450–75 Wakefield mystery cycle, *Second Shepherds' Play*	
	1455–85 Wars of the Roses
ca. 1470 Sir Thomas Malory in prison working on *Morte Darthur*	
	1476 William Caxton sets up first printing press in England
1485 Caxton publishes *Morte Darthur,* one of the first books in English to be printed	**1485** The earl of Richmond defeats the Yorkist king, Richard III, at Bosworth Field and succeeds him as Henry VII, founder of the Tudor dynasty
ca. 1510 *Everyman*	
	1575 Last performance of mystery plays at Chester

Anglo-Saxon England

THE DREAM OF THE ROOD

The *Dream of the Rood* (i.e., of the Cross) is the finest of a rather large number of religious poems in Old English. Neither its author nor its date of composition is known. It appears in a late tenth-century manuscript located in Vercelli in northern Italy, a manuscript made up of Old English religious poems and sermons. The poem may antedate its manuscript, because some passages from the Rood's speech were carved, with some variations, in runes on a stone cross at some time after its construction early in the eighth century; this is the famous Ruthwell Cross, which is preserved near Dumfries in southern Scotland. The precise relation of the poem to this cross is, however, uncertain.

The experience of the Rood—its humiliation at the hands of those who changed it from tree to instrument of punishment for criminals, its humility when the young hero Christ mounts it, and its pride as the restored "tree of glory"—has a suggestive relevance to the condition of the sad, lonely, sin-stained Dreamer. His isolation and melancholy is typical of exile figures in Old English poetry. For the Rood, however, glory has replaced torment, and at the end, the Dreamer's description of Christ's triumphant entry into heaven with the souls He has liberated from hell reflects the Dreamer's response to the hope that has been brought to him.

The Dream of the Rood[1]

Listen, I will speak of the best of dreams, of what I dreamed at midnight when men and their voices were at rest. It seemed to me that I saw a most rare tree reach high aloft, wound in light, brightest of beams. All that beacon[2] was covered with gold; gems stood fair where it met the ground, five were above about the crosspiece. Many hosts of angels gazed on it, fair in the form created for them. This was surely no felon's gallows, but holy spirits beheld it there, men upon earth, and all this glorious creation. Wonderful was the triumph-tree, and I stained with sins, wounded with wrongdoings. I saw the tree of glory shine splendidly, adorned with garments, decked with gold: jewels had worthily covered the Lord's tree. Yet through that gold I might perceive ancient agony of wretches, for now it began to bleed on the right side.[3] I was all afflicted with sorrows, I was afraid for that fair sight. I saw that bright beacon change in clothing and color: now it was wet with moisture, drenched with flowing of blood, now adorned with treasure. Yet I, lying

---

1. This prose translation, by E. T. Donaldson, has been based in general on the edition of the poem by John C. Pope, *Seven Old English Poems* (1966).
2. The Old English word *beacen* also means token

or sign and battle standard.
3. The wound Christ received on the Cross was supposed to have been on the right side.

21

there a long while troubled, beheld the Saviour's tree until I heard it give voice: the best of trees began to speak words.

"It was long ago—I remember it still—that I was hewn down at the wood's edge, taken from my stump. Strong foes seized me there, hewed me to the shape they wished to see, commanded me to lift their criminals. Men carried me on their shoulders, then set me on a hill; foes enough fastened me there. Then I saw the Lord of mankind hasten with stout heart, for he would climb upon me. I dared not bow or break against God's word when I saw earth's surface tremble. I might have felled all foes, but I stood fast. Then the young Hero stripped himself—that was God Almighty—strong and stouthearted. He climbed on the high gallows, bold in the sight of many, when he would free mankind. I trembled when the Warrior embraced me, yet I dared not bow to earth, fall to the ground's surface; but I must stand fast. I was raised up, a cross; I lifted up the Mighty King, Lord of the Heavens: I dared not bend. They pierced me with dark nails: the wounds are seen on me, open gashes of hatred. Nor did I dare harm any of them. They mocked us both together. I was all wet with blood, drenched from the side of that Man after he had sent forth his spirit. I had endured many bitter happenings on that hill. I saw the God of Hosts cruelly racked. The shades of night had covered the Ruler's body with their mists, the bright splendor. Shadow came forth, dark beneath the clouds. All creation wept, bewailed the King's fall; Christ was on Cross.

"Yet from afar some came hastening to the Lord.[4] All that I beheld. I was sore afflicted with griefs, yet I bowed to the men's hands, meekly, eagerly. Then they took Almighty God, lifted him up from his heavy torment. The warriors left me standing, covered with blood. I was all wounded with arrows. They laid him down weary of limb, stood at the body's head, looked there upon Heaven's Lord; and he rested there a while, tired after the great struggle. Then warriors began to build him an earth-house in the sight of his slayer,[5] carved it out of bright stone; they set there the Wielder of Triumphs. Then they began to sing him a song of sorrow, desolate in the evening. Then they wished to turn back, weary, from the great Prince; he remained with small company.[6] Yet we[7] stood in our places a good while, weeping. The voice of the warriors departed. The body grew cold, fair house of the spirit. Then some began to fell us to earth—that was a fearful fate! Some buried us in a deep pit. Yet thanes[8] of the Lord, friends, learned of me there. . . . decked me in gold and silver.[9]

"Now you might understand, my beloved man, that I had endured the work of evildoers, grievous sorrows. Now the time has come that men far and wide upon earth honor me—and all this glorious creation—and pray to this beacon. On me God's Son suffered awhile; therefore I tower now glorious under the heavens, and I may heal every one of those who hold me in awe. Of old I became the hardest of torments, most loathed by men, before I opened the right road of life to those who have voices. Behold, the Lord of Glory honored

---

4. According to John 19.38–39, it was Joseph of Arimathea and Nicodemus who received Christ's body from the Cross.
5. I.e., the Cross.
6. I.e., alone (an understatement).
7. I.e., Christ's Cross and those on which the two thieves were crucified.

8. Members of the king's body of warriors.
9. A number of lines describing the finding of the Cross have apparently been lost here. According to the legend, St. Helen, the mother of Constantine the Great, the first Christian emperor, led a Roman expedition that discovered the true Cross in the 4th century.

me over all the trees of the wood, the Ruler of Heaven, just as also he honored his mother Mary, Almighty God for all men's sake, over all woman's kind.

"Now I command you, my beloved man, that you tell men of this vision. Disclose with your words that it is of the tree of glory on which Almighty God suffered for mankind's many sins and the deeds Adam did of old. He tasted death there; yet the Lord arose again to help mankind in his great might. Then he climbed to the heavens. He will come again hither on this earth to seek mankind on Doomsday, the Lord himself, Almighty God, and his angels with him, for then he will judge, he who has power to judge, each one just as in this brief life he has deserved. Nor may any one be unafraid of the word the Ruler will speak. Before his host he will ask where the man is who in the name of the Lord would taste bitter death as he did on the Cross. But then they will be afraid, and will think of little to begin to say to Christ. There need none be afraid who bears on his breast the best of tokens, but through the Cross shall the kingdom be sought by each soul on this earthly journey that thinks to dwell with the Lord."

Then I prayed to the tree, blithe-hearted, confident, there where I was alone with small company. My heart's thoughts were urged on the way hence. I endured many times of longing. Now is there hope of life for me, that I am permitted to seek the tree of triumph, more often than other men honor it well, alone. For it my heart's desire is great, and my hope of protection is directed to the Cross. I do not possess many powerful friends on earth, but they have gone hence from the delights of the world, sought for themselves the King of Glory. They live now in the heavens with the High Father, dwell in glory. And every day I look forward to when the Lord's Cross that I beheld here on earth will fetch me from this short life and bring me then where joy is great, delight in the heavens, where the Lord's folk are seated at the feast, where bliss is eternal. And then may it place me where thenceforth I may dwell in glory, fully enjoy bliss with the saints. May the Lord be my friend, who once here on earth suffered on the gallows-tree for man's sins: he freed us and granted us life, a heavenly home. Hope was renewed, with joys and with bliss, to those who endured fire.[1] The Son was victorious in that foray, mighty and successful. Then he came with his multitude, a host of spirits, into God's kingdom, the Almighty Ruler; and the angels and all the saints who dwelt then in glory rejoiced when their Ruler, Almighty God, came where his home was.

---

1. This and the following sentences refer to the Harrowing (i.e., pillaging) of Hell; after His death on the Cross, Christ descended into Hell, from which He released the souls of certain of the patriarchs and prophets, conducting them triumphantly to Heaven.

BEOWULF

Beowulf, the oldest of the great long poems written in English, may have been composed more than twelve hundred years ago, in the first half of the eighth century, although some scholars would place it as late as the tenth century. As is the case with most Old English poems, the title has been assigned by modern editors, for the manuscripts do not normally give any indication of title or authorship. Linguistic evidence shows that the poem was originally composed in the dialect of what was then Mercia, the Midlands of England today. But in the unique late-tenth-century manuscript preserving the poem, it has been converted into the West-Saxon dialect of the southwest in which most of Old English literature survives. In 1731, before any modern transcript of the text had been made, the manuscript was seriously damaged in a fire that destroyed the building in London that housed the extraordinary collection of medieval English manuscripts made by Sir Robert Bruce Cotton (1571–1631). As a result of the fire and subsequent deterioration, a number of lines and words have been lost from the poem.

It is possible that *Beowulf* may be the lone survivor of a genre of Old English long epics, but it must have been a remarkable and difficult work even in its own day. The poet was reviving the heroic language, style, and pagan world of ancient Germanic oral poetry, a world that was already remote for his contemporaries and that is stranger to the modern reader, in many respects, than the epic world of Homer and Virgil. With the help of *Beowulf* itself, a few shorter heroic poems in Old English, and later poetry and prose in Old Saxon, Old Icelandic, and Middle High German, we can only conjecture what Germanic oral epic must have been like when performed by the Germanic *scop*, or bard. The *Beowulf* poet himself imagines such oral performances by having King Hrothgar's court poet recite a heroic lay at a feast celebrating Beowulf's defeat of Grendel. Many of the words and formulaic expressions in *Beowulf* can be found in other Old English poems, but there are also an extraordinary number of what linguists call *hapax legomena*—that is, words recorded only once in a language. The poet may have found them elsewhere, but the high incidence of such words suggests that he was an original wordsmith in his own right.

Although the poem itself is English in language and origin, it deals not with native Englishmen but with their Germanic forebears, especially with two south Scandinavian tribes, the Danes and the Geats, who lived on the Danish island of Zealand and in southern Sweden. Thus the historical period the poem concerns—insofar as it may be said to refer to history at all—is some centuries before it was written—that is, a time after the initial invasion of England by Germanic tribes in the middle of the fifth century but before the Anglo-Saxon migration was completed. The one datable fact of history mentioned in the poem is a raid on the Franks in which Hygelac, the king of the Geats and Beowulf's lord, was killed, and this raid occurred in the year 520. Yet the poet's elliptical references to quasihistorical and legendary material show that his audience was still familiar with many old stories, the outlines of which we can only infer, sometimes with the help of later analogous tales in other Germanic languages. This knowledge was probably kept alive by other heroic poetry, of which little has been preserved in English, although much may once have existed.

It is now widely believed that *Beowulf* is the work of a single poet who was a Christian and that his poem reflects well-established Christian tradition. The conversion of the Germanic settlers in England had been largely completed during the seventh century. The Danish king Hrothgar's poet sings a song about the Creation (lines 87–98) reminiscent of Cædmon's *Hymn*. The monster Grendel is said to be a descendant of Cain. There are allusions to God's judgment and to fate (*wyrd*) but none to pagan deities. References to the New Testament are notably absent, but Hrothgar and Beowulf often speak of God as though their religion is monotheistic. With sadness the poet relates that, made desperate by Grendel's attacks, the Danes pray for help at heathen shrines—apparently backsliding as the children of Israel and the earliest Anglo-Saxon Christians had sometimes done.

Although Hrothgar and Beowulf are portrayed as morally upright and enlightened pagans, they fully espouse and frequently affirm the values of Germanic heroic poetry. In the poetry depicting this warrior society, the most important of human relationships was that which existed between the warrior—the thane—and his lord, a relationship based less on subordination of one man's will to another's than on mutual trust and respect. When a warrior vowed loyalty to his lord, he became not so much his servant as his voluntary companion, one who would take pride in defending him and fighting in his wars. In return, the lord was expected to take care of his thanes and to reward them richly for their valor; a good king, one like Hrothgar or Beowulf, is referred to by such poetic epithets as "ring-giver" and as the "helmet" and "shield" of his people.

The relationship between kinsmen was also of deep significance to this society. If one of his kinsmen had been slain, a man had a moral obligation either to kill the slayer or to exact the payment of *wergild* (man-price) in compensation. Each rank of society was evaluated at a definite price, which had to be paid to the dead man's kin by the killer if he wished to avoid their vengeance—even if the killing had been an accident. In the absence of any legal code other than custom or any body of law enforcement, it was the duty of the family (often with the lord's support) to execute justice. The payment itself had less significance as wealth than as proof that the kinsmen had done what was right. The failure to take revenge or to exact compensation was considered shameful. Hrothgar's anguish over the murders committed by Grendel is not only for the loss of his men but also for the shame of his inability either to kill Grendel or to exact a "death-price" from the killer. "It is always better / to avenge dear ones than to indulge in mourning" (lines 1384–85), Beowulf says to Hrothgar, who has been thrown back into despair by the revenge-slaying of his old friend Aeschere by Grendel's mother.

Yet the young Beowulf's attempt to comfort the bereaved old king by invoking the code of vengeance may be one of several instances of the poet's ironic treatment of the tragic futility of the never-ending blood feuds. The most graphic example in the poem of that irony is the Finnsburg episode, the lay sung by Hrothgar's hall-poet. The Danish princess Hildeburh, married to the Frisian king Finn—probably to put an end to a feud between those peoples—loses both her brother and her son when a bloody fight breaks out in the hall between a visiting party of Danes and her husband's men. The bodies are cremated together on a huge funeral pyre: "The glutton element flamed and consumed / the dead of both sides. Their great days were gone" (lines 1124–25).

Such feuds, the staple subject of Germanic epic and saga, have only a peripheral place in the poem. Instead, the poem turns on Beowulf's three great fights against preternatural evil, which inhabits the dangerous and demonic space surrounding human society. He undertakes the fight against Grendel to save the Danes from the monster and to exact vengeance for the men Grendel has slain. Another motive is to demonstrate his strength and courage and thereby to enhance his personal glory. Hrothgar's magnificent gifts become the material emblems of that glory. Revenge and glory also motivate Beowulf's slaying of Grendel's mother. He undertakes his last battle against the dragon, however, only because there is no other way to save his own people.

A somber and dignified elegiac mood pervades *Beowulf*. The poem opens and closes with the description of a funeral and is filled with laments for the dead. Our first view of Beowulf is of an ambitious young hero. At the end, he has become an old king, facing the dragon and death. His people mourn him and praise him, as does the poet, for his nobility, generosity, courage, and, what is less common in Germanic heroes, kindness to his people. The poet's elegiac tone may be informed by something more than the duty to "praise a prince whom he holds dear / and cherish his memory when that moment comes / when he has to be convoyed from his bodily home" (lines 3175–77). The entire poem could be viewed as the poet's lament for heroes like Beowulf who went into the darkness without the light of his own Christian faith.

The present verse translation is by the Irish poet Seamus Heaney, who received the Nobel Prize for literature in 1995. Selections from Heaney's own poems appear in this anthology. His *Beowulf* is both a translation of one of the oldest English poems and a personal response to a work that speaks to a modern poet about the violence of our own century and the courage with which some men and women have faced up to it.

TRIBES AND GENEALOGIES

1. The Danes (Bright-, Half-, Ring-, Spear-, North-, East-, South-, West-Danes; Shield-ings, Honor-, Victor-, War-Shieldings; Ing's friends)

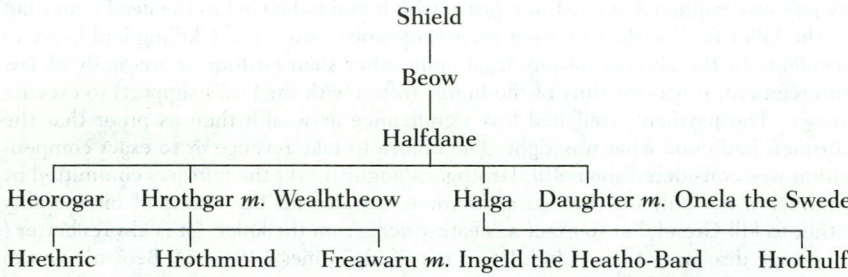

Shield
|
Beow
|
Halfdane

Heorogar   Hrothgar *m.* Wealhtheow   Halga   Daughter *m.* Onela the Swede

Hrethric   Hrothmund   Freawaru *m.* Ingeld the Heatho-Bard   Hrothulf

2. The Geats (Sea-, War-, Weather-Geats)

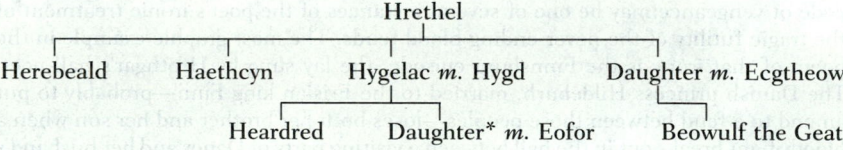

Hrethel

Herebeald   Haethcyn   Hygelac *m.* Hygd   Daughter *m.* Ecgtheow

Heardred   Daughter* *m.* Eofor   Beowulf the Geat

3. The Swedes

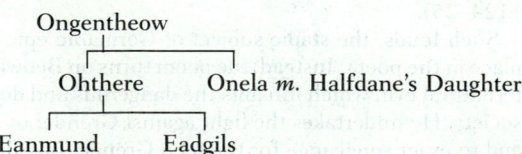

Ongentheow

Ohthere   Onela *m.* Halfdane's Daughter

Eanmund   Eadgils

4. Miscellaneous

A. The Half-Danes (also called Shieldings) involved in the fight at Finnsburg may represent a different tribe from the Danes described above. Their king Hoc had a son, Hnaef, who succeeded him, and a daughter Hildeburh, who married Finn, king of the Jutes.

B. The Jutes or Frisians are represented as enemies of the Danes in the fight at Finnsburg and as allies of the Franks or Hugas at the time Hygelac the Geat made the attack in which he lost his life and from which Beowulf swam home. Also allied with the Franks at this time were the Hetware.

C. The Heatho-Bards (i.e., "Battle-Bards") are represented as inveterate enemies of the Danes. Their king Froda had been killed in an attack on the Danes, and Hrothgar's attempt to make peace with them by marrying his daughter Freawaru to Froda's son Ingeld failed when the latter attacked Heorot. The attack was repulsed, although Heorot was burned.

---

* The daughter of Hygelac who was given to Eofor may have been born to him by a former wife, older than Hygd.

A NOTE ON NAMES

Old English, like Modern German, contained many compound words, most of which have been lost in Modern English. Most of the names in *Beowulf* are compounds. Hrothgar is a combination of words meaning "glory" and "spear"; the name of his older brother, Heorogar, comes from "army" and "spear"; Hrothgar's sons Hrethric and Hrothmund contain the first elements of their father's name combined, respectively, with *ric* (kingdom, empire; Modern German *Reich*) and *mund* (hand, protection). As in the case of the Danish dynasty, family names often alliterate. Masculine names of the warrior class have military associations. The importance of family and the demands of alliteration frequently lead to the designation of characters by formulas identifying them in terms of relationships. Thus Beowulf is referred to as "son of Ecgtheow" or "kinsman of Hygelac" (his uncle and lord).

The Old English spellings of names are mostly preserved in the translation. A few rules of pronunciation are worth keeping in mind. Initial *H* before *r* was sounded, and so Hrothgar's name alliterates with that of his brother Heorogar. The combination *cg* has the value of *dg* in words like "edge." The first element in the name of Beowulf's father "Ecgtheow" is the same word as "edge," and, by the figure of speech called synecdoche (a part of something stands for the whole), *ecg* stands for *sword* and Ecgtheow means "sword-servant."

Beowulf

[PROLOGUE: THE RISE OF THE DANISH NATION]

So. The Spear-Danes[1] in days gone by
and the kings who ruled them had courage and greatness.
We have heard of those princes' heroic campaigns.
  There was Shield Sheafson,[2] scourge of many tribes,
5 a wrecker of mead-benches, rampaging among foes.
This terror of the hall-troops had come far.
A foundling to start with, he would flourish later on
as his powers waxed and his worth was proved.
In the end each clan on the outlying coasts
10 beyond the whale-road had to yield to him
and begin to pay tribute. That was one good king.
  Afterward a boy-child was born to Shield,
a cub in the yard, a comfort sent
by God to that nation. He knew what they had tholed,[3]
15 the long times and troubles they'd come through
without a leader; so the Lord of Life,
the glorious Almighty, made this man renowned.
Shield had fathered a famous son:
Beow's name was known through the north.

---

1. There are different compound names for tribes, often determined by alliteration in Old English poetry. Line 1 reads, "*Hwæt, we Gar-dena in geardagum,*" where alliteration falls on *Gar* (spear) and *gear* (year). Old English hard and soft *g* (spelled *y* in Modern English) alliterate. The compound *geardagum* derives from "year," used in the special sense of "long ago," and "days" and survives in the archaic expression "days of yore."

2. Shield is the name of the founder of the Danish royal line. Sheafson translates *Scefing*, i.e., *sheaf* + the patronymic suffix -*ing*. Because Sheaf was a "foundling" (line 7: *feasceaft funden*, i.e., found destitute) who arrived by sea (lines 45–46), it is likely that as a child Shield brought with him only a sheaf, a symbol of fruitfulness.

3. Suffered, endured.

20 And a young prince must be prudent like that,
giving freely while his father lives
so that afterward in age when fighting starts
steadfast companions will stand by him
and hold the line. Behavior that's admired
25 is the path to power among people everywhere.
　　　Shield was still thriving when his time came
and he crossed over into the Lord's keeping.
His warrior band did what he bade them
when he laid down the law among the Danes:
30 they shouldered him out to the sea's flood,
the chief they revered who had long ruled them.
A ring-whorled prow rode in the harbor,
ice-clad, outbound, a craft for a prince.
They stretched their beloved lord in his boat,
35 laid out by the mast, amidships,
the great ring-giver. Far-fetched treasures
were piled upon him, and precious gear.
I never heard before of a ship so well furbished
with battle-tackle, bladed weapons
40 and coats of mail. The massed treasure
was loaded on top of him: it would travel far
on out into the ocean's sway.
They decked his body no less bountifully
with offerings than those first ones did
45 who cast him away when he was a child
and launched him alone out over the waves.[4]
And they set a gold standard up
high above his head and let him drift
to wind and tide, bewailing him
50 and mourning their loss. No man can tell,
no wise man in hall or weathered veteran
knows for certain who salvaged that load.
　　　Then it fell to Beow to keep the forts.
He was well regarded and ruled the Danes
55 for a long time after his father took leave
of his life on earth. And then his heir,
the great Halfdane,[5] held sway
for as long as he lived, their elder and warlord.
He was four times a father, this fighter prince:
60 one by one they entered the world,
Heorogar, Hrothgar, the good Halga,
and a daughter, I have heard, who was Onela's queen,
a balm in bed to the battle-scarred Swede.
　　　The fortunes of war favored Hrothgar.
65 Friends and kinsmen flocked to his ranks,
young followers, a force that grew
to be a mighty army. So his mind turned

---

4. See n. 2, above. Since Shield was found destitute, "no less bountifully" is litotes or understatement; the ironic reminder that he came with
nothing (line 43) emphasizes the reversal of his

fortunes.
5. Probably named so because, according to one
source, his mother was a Swedish princess.

to hall-building: he handed down orders
for men to work on a great mead-hall
70 meant to be a wonder of the world forever;
it would be his throne-room and there he would dispense
his God-given goods to young and old—
but not the common land or people's lives.[6]
Far and wide through the world, I have heard,
75 orders for work to adorn that wallstead
were sent to many peoples. And soon it stood there
finished and ready, in full view,
the hall of halls. Heorot was the name[7]
he had settled on it, whose utterance was law.
80 Nor did he renege, but doled out rings
and torques at the table. The hall towered,
its gables wide and high and awaiting
a barbarous burning.[8] That doom abided,
but in time it would come: the killer instinct
85 unleashed among in-laws, the blood-lust rampant.[9]

[HEOROT IS ATTACKED]

Then a powerful demon,[1] a prowler through the dark,
nursed a hard grievance. It harrowed him
to hear the din of the loud banquet
every day in the hall, the harp being struck
90 and the clear song of a skilled poet
telling with mastery of man's beginnings,
how the Almighty had made the earth
a gleaming plain girdled with waters;
in His splendor He set the sun and the moon
95 to be earth's lamplight, lanterns for men,
and filled the broad lap of the world
with branches and leaves; and quickened life
in every other thing that moved.
So times were pleasant for the people there
100 until finally one, a fiend out of hell,
began to work his evil in the world.
Grendel was the name of this grim demon
haunting the marches, marauding round the heath
and the desolate fens; he had dwelt for a time
105 in misery among the banished monsters,
Cain's clan, whom the Creator had outlawed
and condemned as outcasts.[2] For the killing of Abel
the Eternal Lord had exacted a price:
Cain got no good from committing that murder
110 because the Almighty made him anathema

6. The king could not dispose of land used by all, such as a common pasture, or of slaves.
7. I.e., "Hart," from antlers fastened to the gables or because the crossed gable-ends resembled a stag's antlers; the hart was also an icon of royalty.
8. An allusion to the future destruction of Heorot by fire, probably in a raid by the Heatho-Bards.
9. As told later (lines 2020–69), Hrothgar plans to marry a daughter to Ingeld, chief of the Heatho-Bards, in hopes of resolving a long-standing feud. See previous note.
1. The poet withholds the name for several lines. He does the same with the name of the hero as well as others.
2. See Genesis 4.9–12.

and out of the curse of his exile there sprang
ogres and elves and evil phantoms
and the giants too who strove with God
time and again until He gave them their reward.

115 So, after nightfall, Grendel set out
for the lofty house, to see how the Ring-Danes
were settling into it after their drink,
and there he came upon them, a company of the best
asleep from their feasting, insensible to pain

120 and human sorrow. Suddenly then
the God-cursed brute was creating havoc:
greedy and grim, he grabbed thirty men
from their resting places and rushed to his lair,
flushed up and inflamed from the raid,

125 blundering back with the butchered corpses.
Then as dawn brightened and the day broke,
Grendel's powers of destruction were plain:
their wassail was over, they wept to heaven
and mourned under morning. Their mighty prince,

130 the storied leader, sat stricken and helpless,
humiliated by the loss of his guard,
bewildered and stunned, staring aghast
at the demon's trail, in deep distress.
He was numb with grief, but got no respite

135 for one night later merciless Grendel
struck again with more gruesome murders.
Malignant by nature, he never showed remorse.
It was easy then to meet with a man
shifting himself to a safer distance

140 to bed in the bothies,[3] for who could be blind
to the evidence of his eyes, the obviousness
of the hall-watcher's hate? Whoever escaped
kept a weather-eye open and moved away.
So Grendel ruled in defiance of right,

145 one against all, until the greatest house
in the world stood empty, a deserted wallstead.
For twelve winters, seasons of woe,
the lord of the Shieldings[4] suffered under
his load of sorrow; and so, before long,

150 the news was known over the whole world.
Sad lays were sung about the beset king,
the vicious raids and ravages of Grendel,
his long and unrelenting feud,
nothing but war; how he would never

155 parley or make peace with any Dane
nor stop his death-dealing nor pay the death-price.[5]
No counselor could ever expect
fair reparation from those rabid hands.

---

3. Huts, outlying buildings. Evidently Grendel wants only to dominate the hall.
4. The descendants of Shield, another name for the Danes.

5. I.e., *wergild* (man-price); monetary compensation for the life of the slain man is the only way, according to Germanic law, to settle a feud peacefully.

All were endangered; young and old
160 were hunted down by that dark death-shadow
who lurked and swooped in the long nights
on the misty moors; nobody knows
where these reavers from hell roam on their errands.
    So Grendel waged his lonely war,
165 inflicting constant cruelties on the people,
atrocious hurt. He took over Heorot,
haunted the glittering hall after dark,
but the throne itself, the treasure-seat,
he was kept from approaching; he was the Lord's outcast.
170   These were hard times, heartbreaking
for the prince of the Shieldings; powerful counselors,
the highest in the land, would lend advice,
plotting how best the bold defenders
might resist and beat off sudden attacks.
175 Sometimes at pagan shrines they vowed
offerings to idols, swore oaths
that the killer of souls[6] might come to their aid
and save the people. That was their way,
their heathenish hope; deep in their hearts
180 they remembered hell. The Almighty Judge
of good deeds and bad, the Lord God,
Head of the Heavens and High King of the World,
was unknown to them. Oh, cursed is he
who in time of trouble has to thrust his soul
185 in the fire's embrace, forfeiting help;
he has nowhere to turn. But blessed is he
who after death can approach the Lord
and find friendship in the Father's embrace.

[THE HERO COMES TO HEOROT]

    So that troubled time continued, woe
190 that never stopped, steady affliction
for Halfdane's son, too hard an ordeal.
There was panic after dark, people endured
raids in the night, riven by the terror.
    When he heard about Grendel, Hygelac's thane
195 was on home ground, over in Geatland.
There was no one else like him alive.
In his day, he was the mightiest man on earth,
highborn and powerful. He ordered a boat
that would ply the waves. He announced his plan:
200 to sail the swan's road and seek out that king,
the famous prince who needed defenders.
Nobody tried to keep him from going,
no elder denied him, dear as he was to them.
Instead, they inspected omens and spurred
205 his ambition to go, whilst he moved about
like the leader he was, enlisting men,

---

6. I.e., the devil. Heathen gods were thought to be devils.

the best he could find; with fourteen others
the warrior boarded the boat as captain,
a canny pilot along coast and currents.
210   Time went by, the boat was on water,
in close under the cliffs.
Men climbed eagerly up the gangplank,
sand churned in surf, warriors loaded
a cargo of weapons, shining war-gear
215   in the vessel's hold, then heaved out,
away with a will in their wood-wreathed ship.
Over the waves, with the wind behind her
and foam at her neck, she flew like a bird
until her curved prow had covered the distance,
220   and on the following day, at the due hour,
those seafarers sighted land,
sunlit cliffs, sheer crags
and looming headlands, the landfall they sought.
It was the end of their voyage and the Geats vaulted
225   over the side, out on to the sand,
and moored their ship. There was a clash of mail
and a thresh of gear. They thanked God
for that easy crossing on a calm sea.
        When the watchman on the wall, the Shieldings' lookout
230   whose job it was to guard the sea-cliffs,
saw shields glittering on the gangplank
and battle-equipment being unloaded
he had to find out who and what
the arrivals were. So he rode to the shore,
235   this horseman of Hrothgar's, and challenged them
in formal terms, flourishing his spear:
"What kind of men are you who arrive
rigged out for combat in your coats of mail,
sailing here over the sea-lanes
240   in your steep-hulled boat? I have been stationed
as lookout on this coast for a long time.
My job is to watch the waves for raiders,
any danger to the Danish shore.
Never before has a force under arms
245   disembarked so openly—not bothering to ask
if the sentries allowed them safe passage
or the clan had consented. Nor have I seen
a mightier man-at-arms on this earth
than the one standing here: unless I am mistaken,
250   he is truly noble. This is no mere
hanger-on in a hero's armor.
So now, before you fare inland
as interlopers, I have to be informed
about who you are and where you hail from.
255   Outsiders from across the water,
I say it again: the sooner you tell
where you come from and why, the better."
        The leader of the troop unlocked his word-hoard;

the distinguished one delivered this answer:

260 "We belong by birth to the Geat people
and owe allegiance to Lord Hygelac.
In his day, my father was a famous man,
a noble warrior-lord named Ecgtheow.
He outlasted many a long winter
265 and went on his way. All over the world
men wise in counsel continue to remember him.
We come in good faith to find your lord
and nation's shield, the son of Halfdane.
Give us the right advice and direction.
270 We have arrived here on a great errand
to the lord of the Danes, and I believe therefore
there should be nothing hidden or withheld between us.
So tell us if what we have heard is true
about this threat, whatever it is,
275 this danger abroad in the dark nights,
this corpse-maker mongering death
in the Shieldings' country. I come to proffer
my wholehearted help and counsel.
I can show the wise Hrothgar a way
280 to defeat his enemy and find respite—
if any respite is to reach him, ever.
I can calm the turmoil and terror in his mind.
Otherwise, he must endure woes
and live with grief for as long as his hall
285 stands at the horizon on its high ground."
　　Undaunted, sitting astride his horse,
the coast-guard answered: "Anyone with gumption
and a sharp mind will take the measure
of two things: what's said and what's done.
290 I believe what you have told me, that you are a troop
loyal to our king. So come ahead
with your arms and your gear, and I will guide you.
What's more, I'll order my own comrades
on their word of honor to watch your boat
295 down there on the strand—keep her safe
in her fresh tar, until the time comes
for her curved prow to preen on the waves
and bear this hero back to Geatland.
May one so valiant and venturesome
300 come unharmed through the clash of battle."
　　So they went on their way. The ship rode the water,
broad-beamed, bound by its hawser
and anchored fast. Boar-shapes[7] flashed
above their cheek-guards, the brightly forged
305 work of goldsmiths, watching over
those stern-faced men. They marched in step,
hurrying on till the timbered hall
rose before them, radiant with gold.

---

7. Carved images of boars were placed on helmets, probably as good luck charms to protect the warriors.

Nobody on earth knew of another
310 building like it. Majesty lodged there,
its light shone over many lands.
So their gallant escort guided them
to that dazzling stronghold and indicated
the shortest way to it; then the noble warrior
315 wheeled on his horse and spoke these words:
"It is time for me to go. May the Almighty
Father keep you and in His kindness
watch over your exploits. I'm away to the sea,
back on alert against enemy raiders."

320 　　It was a paved track, a path that kept them
in marching order. Their mail-shirts glinted,
hard and hand-linked; the high-gloss iron
of their armor rang. So they duly arrived
in their grim war-graith[8] and gear at the hall,
325 and, weary from the sea, stacked wide shields
of the toughest hardwood against the wall,
then collapsed on the benches; battle-dress
and weapons clashed. They collected their spears
in a seafarers' stook, a stand of grayish
330 tapering ash. And the troops themselves
were as good as their weapons.
　　　　　　　　　　Then a proud warrior
questioned the men concerning their origins:
"Where do you come from, carrying these
decorated shields and shirts of mail,
335 these cheek-hinged helmets and javelins?
I am Hrothgar's herald and officer.
I have never seen so impressive or large
an assembly of strangers. Stoutness of heart,
bravery not banishment, must have brought you to Hrothgar."

340 　　The man whose name was known for courage,
the Geat leader, resolute in his helmet,
answered in return: "We are retainers
from Hygelac's band. Beowulf is my name.
If your lord and master, the most renowned
345 son of Halfdane, will hear me out
and graciously allow me to greet him in person,
I am ready and willing to report my errand."

　　Wulfgar replied, a Wendel chief
renowned as a warrior, well known for his wisdom
350 and the temper of his mind: "I will take this message,
in accordance with your wish, to our noble king,
our dear lord, friend of the Danes,
the giver of rings. I will go and ask him
about your coming here, then hurry back
355 with whatever reply it pleases him to give."

　　With that he turned to where Hrothgar sat,
an old man among retainers;

---

8. "Graith": archaic for apparel.

the valiant follower stood foursquare
in front of his king: he knew the courtesies.
360 Wulfgar addressed his dear lord:
"People from Geatland have put ashore.
They have sailed far over the wide sea.
They call the chief in charge of their band
by the name of Beowulf. They beg, my lord,
365 an audience with you, exchange of words
and formal greeting. Most gracious Hrothgar,
do not refuse them, but grant them a reply.
From their arms and appointment, they appear well born
and worthy of respect, especially the one
370 who has led them this far: he is formidable indeed."
    Hrothgar, protector of Shieldings, replied:
"I used to know him when he was a young boy.
His father before him was called Ecgtheow.
Hrethel the Geat⁹ gave Ecgtheow
375 his daughter in marriage. This man is their son,
here to follow up an old friendship.
A crew of seamen who sailed for me once
with a gift-cargo across to Geatland
returned with marvelous tales about him:
380 a thane, they declared, with the strength of thirty
in the grip of each hand. Now Holy God
has, in His goodness, guided him here
to the West-Danes, to defend us from Grendel.
This is my hope; and for his heroism
385 I will recompense him with a rich treasure.
Go immediately, bid him and the Geats
he has in attendance to assemble and enter.
Say, moreover, when you speak to them,
they are welcome to Denmark."
                At the door of the hall,
390 Wulfgar duly delivered the message:
"My lord, the conquering king of the Danes,
bids me announce that he knows your ancestry;
also that he welcomes you here to Heorot
and salutes your arrival from across the sea.
395 You are free now to move forward
to meet Hrothgar in helmets and armor,
but shields must stay here and spears be stacked
until the outcome of the audience is clear."
    The hero arose, surrounded closely
400 by his powerful thanes. A party remained
under orders to keep watch on the arms;
the rest proceeded, led by their prince
under Heorot's roof. And standing on the hearth
in webbed links that the smith had woven,
405 the fine-forged mesh of his gleaming mail-shirt,
resolute in his helmet, Beowulf spoke:

9. Hygelac's father and Beowulf's grandfather.

"Greetings to Hrothgar. I am Hygelac's kinsman,
one of his hall-troop. When I was younger,
I had great triumphs. Then news of Grendel,
410 hard to ignore, reached me at home:
sailors brought stories of the plight you suffer
in this legendary hall, how it lies deserted,
empty and useless once the evening light
hides itself under heaven's dome.
415 So every elder and experienced councilman
among my people supported my resolve
to come here to you, King Hrothgar,
because all knew of my awesome strength.
They had seen me boltered[1] in the blood of enemies
420 when I battled and bound five beasts,
raided a troll-nest and in the night-sea
slaughtered sea-brutes. I have suffered extremes
and avenged the Geats (their enemies brought it
upon themselves; I devastated them).
425 Now I mean to be a match for Grendel,
settle the outcome in single combat.
And so, my request, O king of Bright-Danes,
dear prince of the Shieldings, friend of the people
and their ring of defense, my one request
430 is that you won't refuse me, who have come this far,
the privilege of purifying Heorot,
with my own men to help me, and nobody else.
I have heard moreover that the monster scorns
in his reckless way to use weapons;
435 therefore, to heighten Hygelac's fame
and gladden his heart, I hereby renounce
sword and the shelter of the broad shield,
the heavy war-board: hand-to-hand
is how it will be, a life-and-death
440 fight with the fiend. Whichever one death fells
must deem it a just judgment by God.
If Grendel wins, it will be a gruesome day;
he will glut himself on the Geats in the war-hall,
swoop without fear on that flower of manhood
445 as on others before. Then my face won't be there
to be covered in death: he will carry me away
as he goes to ground, gorged and bloodied;
he will run gloating with my raw corpse
and feed on it alone, in a cruel frenzy
450 fouling his moor-nest. No need then
to lament for long or lay out my body:[2]
if the battle takes me, send back
this breast-webbing that Weland[3] fashioned
and Hrethel gave me, to Lord Hygelac.
455 Fate goes ever as fate must."

---

1. Clotted, sticky.
2. I.e., for burial. Hrothgar will not need to give

Beowulf an expensive funeral.
3. Famed blacksmith in Germanic legend.

Hrothgar, the helmet of Shieldings, spoke:
"Beowulf, my friend, you have traveled here
to favor us with help and to fight for us.
There was a feud one time, begun by your father.
460 With his own hands he had killed Heatholaf
who was a Wulfing; so war was looming
and his people, in fear of it, forced him to leave.
He came away then over rolling waves
to the South-Danes here, the sons of honor.
465 I was then in the first flush of kingship,
establishing my sway over the rich strongholds
of this heroic land. Heorogar,
my older brother and the better man,
also a son of Halfdane's, had died.
470 Finally I healed the feud by paying:
I shipped a treasure-trove to the Wulfings,
and Ecgtheow acknowledged me with oaths of allegiance.
    "It bothers me to have to burden anyone
with all the grief that Grendel has caused
475 and the havoc he has wreaked upon us in Heorot,
our humiliations. My household-guard
are on the wane, fate sweeps them away
into Grendel's clutches—but God can easily
halt these raids and harrowing attacks!
480   "Time and again, when the goblets passed
and seasoned fighters got flushed with beer
they would pledge themselves to protect Heorot
and wait for Grendel with their whetted swords.
But when dawn broke and day crept in
485 over each empty, blood-spattered bench,
the floor of the mead-hall where they had feasted
would be slick with slaughter. And so they died,
faithful retainers, and my following dwindled.
Now take your place at the table, relish
490 the triumph of heroes to your heart's content."

[FEAST AT HEOROT]

    Then a bench was cleared in that banquet hall
so the Geats could have room to be together
and the party sat, proud in their bearing,
strong and stalwart. An attendant stood by
495 with a decorated pitcher, pouring bright
helpings of mead. And the minstrel sang,
filling Heorot with his head-clearing voice,
gladdening that great rally of Geats and Danes.
    From where he crouched at the king's feet,
500 Unferth, a son of Ecglaf's, spoke
contrary words. Beowulf's coming,
his sea-braving, made him sick with envy:
he could not brook or abide the fact
that anyone else alive under heaven
505 might enjoy greater regard than he did:

"Are you the Beowulf who took on Breca
in a swimming match on the open sea,
risking the water just to prove that you could win?
It was sheer vanity made you venture out
510 on the main deep. And no matter who tried,
friend or foe, to deflect the pair of you,
neither would back down: the sea-test obsessed you.
You waded in, embracing water,
taking its measure, mastering currents,
515 riding on the swell. The ocean swayed,
winter went wild in the waves, but you vied
for seven nights; and then he outswam you,
came ashore the stronger contender.
He was cast up safe and sound one morning
520 among the Heatho-Reams, then made his way
to where he belonged in Bronding country,
home again, sure of his ground
in strongroom and bawn.[4] So Breca made good
his boast upon you and was proved right.
525 No matter, therefore, how you may have fared
in every bout and battle until now,
this time you'll be worsted; no one has ever
outlasted an entire night against Grendel."
    Beowulf, Ecgtheow's son, replied:
530 "Well, friend Unferth, you have had your say
about Breca and me. But it was mostly beer
that was doing the talking. The truth is this:
when the going was heavy in those high waves,
I was the strongest swimmer of all.
535 We'd been children together and we grew up
daring ourselves to outdo each other,
boasting and urging each other to risk
our lives on the sea. And so it turned out.
Each of us swam holding a sword,
540 a naked, hard-proofed blade for protection
against the whale-beasts. But Breca could never
move out farther or faster from me
than I could manage to move from him.
Shoulder to shoulder, we struggled on
545 for five nights, until the long flow
and pitch of the waves, the perishing cold,
night falling and winds from the north
drove us apart. The deep boiled up
and its wallowing sent the sea-brutes wild.
550 My armor helped me to hold out;
my hard-ringed chain-mail, hand-forged and linked,
a fine, close-fitting filigree of gold,
kept me safe when some ocean creature
pulled me to the bottom. Pinioned fast

---

4. Fortified outwork of a court or castle. The word was used by English planters in Ulster to describe fortified dwellings they erected on lands confiscated from the Irish [Translator's note].

555   and swathed in its grip, I was granted one
final chance: my sword plunged
and the ordeal was over. Through my own hands,
the fury of battle had finished off the sea-beast.
    "Time and again, foul things attacked me,
560   lurking and stalking, but I lashed out,
gave as good as I got with my sword.
My flesh was not for feasting on,
there would be no monsters gnawing and gloating
over their banquet at the bottom of the sea.
565   Instead, in the morning, mangled and sleeping
the sleep of the sword, they slopped and floated
like the ocean's leavings. From now on
sailors would be safe, the deep-sea raids
were over for good. Light came from the east,
570   bright guarantee of God, and the waves
went quiet; I could see headlands
and buffeted cliffs. Often, for undaunted courage,
fate spares the man it has not already marked.
However it occurred, my sword had killed
575   nine sea-monsters. Such night dangers
and hard ordeals I have never heard of
nor of a man more desolate in surging waves.
But worn out as I was, I survived,
came through with my life. The ocean lifted
580   and laid me ashore, I landed safe
on the coast of Finland.
                        Now I cannot recall
any fight you entered, Unferth,
that bears comparison. I don't boast when I say
that neither you nor Breca were ever much
585   celebrated for swordsmanship
or for facing danger on the field of battle.
You killed your own kith and kin,
so for all your cleverness and quick tongue,
you will suffer damnation in the depths of hell.
590   The fact is, Unferth, if you were truly
as keen or courageous as you claim to be
Grendel would never have got away with
such unchecked atrocity, attacks on your king,
havoc in Heorot and horrors everywhere.
595   But he knows he need never be in dread
of your blade making a mizzle of his blood
or of vengeance arriving ever from this quarter—
from the Victory-Shieldings, the shoulderers of the spear.
He knows he can trample down you Danes
600   to his heart's content, humiliate and murder
without fear of reprisal. But he will find me different.
I will show him how Geats shape to kill
in the heat of battle. Then whoever wants to
may go bravely to mead, when the morning light,
605   scarfed in sun-dazzle, shines forth from the south

and brings another daybreak to the world."
　　Then the gray-haired treasure-giver was glad;
far-famed in battle, the prince of Bright-Danes
and keeper of his people counted on Beowulf,
610　on the warrior's steadfastness and his word.
So the laughter started, the din got louder
and the crowd was happy. Wealhtheow came in,
Hrothgar's queen, observing the courtesies.
Adorned in her gold, she graciously saluted
615　the men in the hall, then handed the cup
first to Hrothgar, their homeland's guardian,
urging him to drink deep and enjoy it
because he was dear to them. And he drank it down
like the warlord he was, with festive cheer.
620　So the Helming woman went on her rounds,
queenly and dignified, decked out in rings,
offering the goblet to all ranks,
treating the household and the assembled troop,
until it was Beowulf's turn to take it from her hand.
625　With measured words she welcomed the Geat
and thanked God for granting her wish
that a deliverer she could believe in would arrive
to ease their afflictions. He accepted the cup,
a daunting man, dangerous in action
630　and eager for it always. He addressed Wealhtheow;
Beowulf, son of Ecgtheow, said:
"I had a fixed purpose when I put to sea.
As I sat in the boat with my band of men,
I meant to perform to the uttermost
635　what your people wanted or perish in the attempt,
in the fiend's clutches. And I shall fulfill that purpose,
prove myself with a proud deed
or meet my death here in the mead-hall."
This formal boast by Beowulf the Geat
640　pleased the lady well and she went to sit
by Hrothgar, regal and arrayed with gold.
　　Then it was like old times in the echoing hall,
proud talk and the people happy,
loud and excited; until soon enough
645　Halfdane's heir had to be away
to his night's rest. He realized
that the demon was going to descend on the hall,
that he had plotted all day, from dawn-light
until darkness gathered again over the world
650　and stealthy night-shapes came stealing forth
under the cloud-murk. The company stood
as the two leaders took leave of each other:
Hrothgar wished Beowulf health and good luck,
named him hall-warden and announced as follows:
655　"Never, since my hand could hold a shield
have I entrusted or given control
of the Danes' hall to anyone but you.

Ward and guard it, for it is the greatest of houses.
Be on your mettle now, keep in mind your fame,
660 beware of the enemy. There's nothing you wish for
that won't be yours if you win through alive."

[THE FIGHT WITH GRENDEL]

Hrothgar departed then with his house-guard.
The lord of the Shieldings, their shelter in war,
left the mead-hall to lie with Wealhtheow,
665 his queen and bedmate. The King of Glory
(as people learned) had posted a lookout
who was a match for Grendel, a guard against monsters,
special protection to the Danish prince.
And the Geat placed complete trust
670 in his strength of limb and the Lord's favor.
He began to remove his iron breast-mail,
took off the helmet and handed his attendant
the patterned sword, a smith's masterpiece,
ordering him to keep the equipment guarded.
675 And before he bedded down, Beowulf,
that prince of goodness, proudly asserted:
"When it comes to fighting, I count myself
as dangerous any day as Grendel.
So it won't be a cutting edge I'll wield
680 to mow him down, easily as I might.
He has no idea of the arts of war,
of shield or sword-play, although he does possess
a wild strength. No weapons, therefore,
for either this night: unarmed he shall face me
685 if face me he dares. And may the Divine Lord
in His wisdom grant the glory of victory
to whichever side He sees fit."
Then down the brave man lay with his bolster
under his head and his whole company
690 of sea-rovers at rest beside him.
None of them expected he would ever see
his homeland again or get back
to his native place and the people who reared him.
They knew too well the way it was before,
695 how often the Danes had fallen prey
to death in the mead-hall. But the Lord was weaving
a victory on His war-loom for the Weather-Geats.
Through the strength of one they all prevailed;
they would crush their enemy and come through
700 in triumph and gladness. The truth is clear:
Almighty God rules over mankind
and always has.
                    Then out of the night
came the shadow-stalker, stealthy and swift.
The hall-guards were slack, asleep at their posts,
705 all except one; it was widely understood
that as long as God disallowed it,

the fiend could not bear them to his shadow-bourne.
One man, however, was in fighting mood,
awake and on edge, spoiling for action.
710   In off the moors, down through the mist-bands
God-cursed Grendel came greedily loping.
The bane of the race of men roamed forth,
hunting for a prey in the high hall.
Under the cloud-murk he moved toward it
715   until it shone above him, a sheer keep
of fortified gold. Nor was that the first time
he had scouted the grounds of Hrothgar's dwelling—
although never in his life, before or since,
did he find harder fortune or hall-defenders.
720   Spurned and joyless, he journeyed on ahead
and arrived at the bawn.[5] The iron-braced door
turned on its hinge when his hands touched it.
Then his rage boiled over, he ripped open
the mouth of the building, maddening for blood,
725   pacing the length of the patterned floor
with his loathsome tread, while a baleful light,
flame more than light, flared from his eyes.
He saw many men in the mansion, sleeping,
a ranked company of kinsmen and warriors
730   quartered together. And his glee was demonic,
picturing the mayhem: before morning
he would rip life from limb and devour them,
feed on their flesh; but his fate that night
was due to change, his days of ravening
had come to an end.
735   Mighty and canny,
Hygelac's kinsman was keenly watching
for the first move the monster would make.
Nor did the creature keep him waiting
but struck suddenly and started in;
740   he grabbed and mauled a man on his bench,
bit into his bone-lappings, bolted down his blood
and gorged on him in lumps, leaving the body
utterly lifeless, eaten up
hand and foot. Venturing closer,
745   his talon was raised to attack Beowulf
where he lay on the bed, he was bearing in
with open claw when the alert hero's
comeback and armlock forestalled him utterly.
The captain of evil discovered himself
750   in a handgrip harder than anything
he had ever encountered in any man
on the face of the earth. Every bone in his body
quailed and recoiled, but he could not escape.
He was desperate to flee to his den and hide
755   with the devil's litter, for in all his days

5. See p. 38, n. 4.

he had never been clamped or cornered like this.
Then Hygelac's trusty retainer recalled
his bedtime speech, sprang to his feet
and got a firm hold. Fingers were bursting,
760 the monster back-tracking, the man overpowering.
The dread of the land was desperate to escape,
to take a roundabout road and flee
to his lair in the fens. The latching power
in his fingers weakened; it was the worst trip
765 the terror-monger had taken to Heorot.
And now the timbers trembled and sang,
a hall-session[6] that harrowed every Dane
inside the stockade: stumbling in fury,
the two contenders crashed through the building.
770 The hall clattered and hammered, but somehow
survived the onslaught and kept standing:
it was handsomely structured, a sturdy frame
braced with the best of blacksmith's work
inside and out. The story goes
775 that as the pair struggled, mead-benches were smashed
and sprung off the floor, gold fittings and all.
Before then, no Shielding elder would believe
there was any power or person upon earth
capable of wrecking their horn-rigged hall
780 unless the burning embrace of a fire
engulf it in flame. Then an extraordinary
wail arose, and bewildering fear
came over the Danes. Everyone felt it
who heard that cry as it echoed off the wall,
785 a God-cursed scream and strain of catastrophe,
the howl of the loser, the lament of the hell-serf
keening his wound. He was overwhelmed,
manacled tight by the man who of all men
was foremost and strongest in the days of this life.
790   But the earl-troop's leader was not inclined
to allow his caller to depart alive:
he did not consider that life of much account
to anyone anywhere. Time and again,
Beowulf's warriors worked to defend
795 their lord's life, laying about them
as best they could, with their ancestral blades.
Stalwart in action, they kept striking out
on every side, seeking to cut
straight to the soul. When they joined the struggle
800 there was something they could not have known at the time,
that no blade on earth, no blacksmith's art
could ever damage their demon opponent.
He had conjured the harm from the cutting edge
of every weapon.[7] But his going away

6. In Hiberno-English the word "session" (*seissiún*
in Irish) can mean a gathering where musicians
and singers perform for their own enjoyment

[Translator's note].
7. Grendel is protected by a charm against metals.

805   out of this world and the days of his life
would be agony to him, and his alien spirit
would travel far into fiends' keeping.
    Then he who had harrowed the hearts of men
with pain and affliction in former times
810   and had given offense also to God
found that his bodily powers failed him.
Hygelac's kinsman kept him helplessly
locked in a handgrip. As long as either lived,
he was hateful to the other. The monster's whole
815   body was in pain; a tremendous wound
appeared on his shoulder. Sinews split
and the bone-lappings burst. Beowulf was granted
the glory of winning; Grendel was driven
under the fen-banks, fatally hurt,
820   to his desolate lair. His days were numbered,
the end of his life was coming over him,
he knew it for certain; and one bloody clash
had fulfilled the dearest wishes of the Danes.
The man who had lately landed among them,
825   proud and sure, had purged the hall,
kept it from harm; he was happy with his nightwork
and the courage he had shown. The Geat captain
had boldly fulfilled his boast to the Danes:
he had healed and relieved a huge distress,
830   unremitting humiliations,
the hard fate they'd been forced to undergo,
no small affliction. Clear proof of this
could be seen in the hand the hero displayed
high up near the roof: the whole of Grendel's
835   shoulder and arm, his awesome grasp.

[CELEBRATION AT HEOROT]

    Then morning came and many a warrior
gathered, as I've heard, around the gift-hall,
clan-chiefs flocking from far and near
down wide-ranging roads, wondering greatly
840   at the monster's footprints. His fatal departure
was regretted by no one who witnessed his trail,
the ignominious marks of his flight
where he'd skulked away, exhausted in spirit
and beaten in battle, bloodying the path,
845   hauling his doom to the demons' mere.[8]
The bloodshot water wallowed and surged,
there were loathsome upthrows and overturnings
of waves and gore and wound-slurry.
With his death upon him, he had dived deep
850   into his marsh-den, drowned out his life
and his heathen soul: hell claimed him there.
    Then away they rode, the old retainers

---

8. A lake or pool, although we learn later that it has an outlet to the sea. Grendel's habitat.

with many a young man following after,
a troop on horseback, in high spirits
855 on their bay steeds. Beowulf's doings
were praised over and over again.
Nowhere, they said, north or south
between the two seas or under the tall sky
on the broad earth was there anyone better
860 to raise a shield or to rule a kingdom.
Yet there was no laying of blame on their lord,
the noble Hrothgar; he was a good king.
    At times the war-band broke into a gallop,
letting their chestnut horses race
865 wherever they found the going good
on those well-known tracks. Meanwhile, a thane
of the king's household, a carrier of tales,
a traditional singer deeply schooled
in the lore of the past, linked a new theme
870 to a strict meter.[9] The man started
to recite with skill, rehearsing Beowulf's
triumphs and feats in well-fashioned lines,
entwining his words.
                    He told what he'd heard
repeated in songs about Sigemund's exploits,[1]
875 all of those many feats and marvels,
the struggles and wanderings of Waels's son,[2]
things unknown to anyone
except to Fitela, feuds and foul doings
confided by uncle to nephew when he felt
880 the urge to speak of them: always they had been
partners in the fight, friends in need.
They killed giants, their conquering swords
had brought them down.
                    After his death
Sigemund's glory   grew and grew
885 *because of his courage   when he killed the dragon,*
the guardian of the hoard.   Under gray stone
he had dared to enter   all by himself
to face the worst   without Fitela.
But it came to pass   that his sword plunged
890 *right through   those radiant scales*
and drove into the wall.   The dragon died of it.
His daring had given him   total possession
of the treasure-hoard,   his to dispose of
however he liked.   He loaded a boat:
895 *Waels's son   weighted her hold*
with dazzling spoils.   The hot dragon melted.
Sigemund's name   was known everywhere.

---

9. I.e., an extemporaneous heroic poem in alliterative verse about Beowulf's deeds.
1. Tales about Sigemund, his nephew Sinfjotli
(Fitela), and his son Sigurth are found in a 13th-
century Old Icelandic collection of legends known
as the *Volsung Saga.* Analogous stories must have
been known to the poet and his audience, though
details differ.
2. Waels is the father of Sigemund.

He was utterly valiant   and venturesome,
a fence round his fighters   and flourished therefore
900 *after King Heremod's*[3]   *prowess declined*
and his campaigns slowed down.   The king was betrayed,
ambushed in Jutland,   overpowered
and done away with.   The waves of his grief
had beaten him down,   made him a burden,
905 *a source of anxiety   to his own nobles:*
that expedition   was often condemned
in those earlier times   by experienced men,
men who relied   on his lordship for redress,
who presumed that the part   of a prince was to thrive
910 *on his father's throne   and defend the nation,*
the Shielding land   where they lived and belonged,
its holdings and strongholds.   Such was Beowulf
in the affection of his friends   and of everyone alive.
But evil entered   into Heremod.

915   Meanwhile, the Danes kept racing their mounts
down sandy lanes. The light of day
broke and kept brightening. Bands of retainers
galloped in excitement to the gabled hall
to see the marvel; and the king himself,
920 guardian of the ring-hoard, goodness in person,
walked in majesty from the women's quarters
with a numerous train, attended by his queen
and her crowd of maidens, across to the mead-hall.
    When Hrothgar arrived at the hall, he spoke,
925 standing on the steps, under the steep eaves,
gazing toward the roofwork and Grendel's talon:
"First and foremost, let the Almighty Father
be thanked for this sight. I suffered a long
harrowing by Grendel. But the Heavenly Shepherd
930 can work His wonders always and everywhere.
Not long since, it seemed I would never
be granted the slightest solace or relief
from any of my burdens: the best of houses
glittered and reeked and ran with blood.
935 This one worry outweighed all others—
a constant distress to counselors entrusted
with defending the people's forts from assault
by monsters and demons. But now a man,
with the Lord's assistance, has accomplished something
940 none of us could manage before now
for all our efforts. Whoever she was
who brought forth this flower of manhood,
if she is still alive, that woman can say
that in her labor the Lord of Ages
945 bestowed a grace on her. So now, Beowulf,
I adopt you in my heart as a dear son.

---

3. Heremod was a bad king, held up by the bard as the opposite of Beowulf, as Sigemund is held up as a heroic prototype of Beowulf.

Nourish and maintain this new connection,
you noblest of men; there'll be nothing you'll want for,
no worldly goods that won't be yours.
950 I have often honored smaller achievements,
recognized warriors not nearly as worthy,
lavished rewards on the less deserving.
But you have made yourself immortal
by your glorious action. May the God of Ages
955 continue to keep and requite you well."
  Beowulf, son of Ecgtheow, spoke:
"We have gone through with a glorious endeavor
and been much favored in this fight we dared
against the unknown. Nevertheless,
960 if you could have seen the monster himself
where he lay beaten, I would have been better pleased.
My plan was to pounce, pin him down
in a tight grip and grapple him to death—
have him panting for life, powerless and clasped
965 in my bare hands, his body in thrall.
But I couldn't stop him from slipping my hold.
The Lord allowed it, my lock on him
wasn't strong enough; he struggled fiercely
and broke and ran. Yet he bought his freedom
970 at a high price, for he left his hand
and arm and shoulder to show he had been here,
a cold comfort for having come among us.
And now he won't be long for this world.
He has done his worst but the wound will end him.
975 He is hasped and hooped and hirpling with pain,
limping and looped in it. Like a man outlawed
for wickedness, he must await
the mighty judgment of God in majesty."
  There was less tampering and big talk then
980 from Unferth the boaster, less of his blather
as the hall-thanes eyed the awful proof
of the hero's prowess, the splayed hand
up under the eaves. Every nail,
claw-scale and spur, every spike
985 and welt on the hand of that heathen brute
was like barbed steel. Everybody said
there was no honed iron hard enough
to pierce him through, no time-proofed blade
that could cut his brutal, blood-caked claw.
990   Then the order was given for all hands
to help to refurbish Heorot immediately:
men and women thronging the wine-hall,
getting it ready. Gold thread shone
in the wall-hangings, woven scenes
995 that attracted and held the eye's attention.
But iron-braced as the inside of it had been,
that bright room lay in ruins now.
The very doors had been dragged from their hinges.

Only the roof remained unscathed
1000 by the time the guilt-fouled fiend turned tail
in despair of his life. But death is not easily
escaped from by anyone:
all of us with souls, earth-dwellers
and children of men, must make our way
1005 to a destination already ordained
where the body, after the banqueting,
sleeps on its deathbed.
          Then the due time arrived
for Halfdane's son to proceed to the hall.
The king himself would sit down to feast.
1010 No group ever gathered in greater numbers
or better order around their ring-giver.
The benches filled with famous men
who fell to with relish; round upon round
of mead was passed; those powerful kinsmen,
1015 Hrothgar and Hrothulf, were in high spirits
in the raftered hall. Inside Heorot
there was nothing but friendship. The Shielding nation
was not yet familiar with feud and betrayal.[4]
    Then Halfdane's son presented Beowulf
1020 with a gold standard as a victory gift,
an embroidered banner; also breast-mail
and a helmet; and a sword carried high,
that was both precious object and token of honor.
So Beowulf drank his drink, at ease;
1025 it was hardly a shame to be showered with such gifts
in front of the hall-troops. There haven't been many
moments, I am sure, when men exchanged
four such treasures at so friendly a sitting.
An embossed ridge, a band lapped with wire
1030 arched over the helmet: head-protection
to keep the keen-ground cutting edge
from damaging it when danger threatened
and the man was battling behind his shield.
Next the king ordered eight horses
1035 with gold bridles to be brought through the yard
into the hall. The harness of one
included a saddle of sumptuous design,
the battle-seat where the son of Halfdane
rode when he wished to join the sword-play:
1040 wherever the killing and carnage were the worst,
he would be to the fore, fighting hard.
Then the Danish prince, descendant of Ing,
handed over both the arms and the horses,
urging Beowulf to use them well.
1045 And so their leader, the lord and guard
of coffer and strongroom, with customary grace

4. Probably an ironic allusion to the future usurpation of the throne from Hrothgar's sons by Hro-
thulf, although no such treachery is recorded of Hrothulf, who is the hero of other Germanic stories.

bestowed upon Beowulf both sets of gifts.
A fair witness can see how well each one behaved.
    The chieftain went on to reward the others:
1050   each man on the bench who had sailed with Beowulf
and risked the voyage received a bounty,
some treasured possession. And compensation,
a price in gold, was settled for the Geat
Grendel had cruelly killed earlier—
1055   as he would have killed more, had not mindful God
and one man's daring prevented that doom.
Past and present, God's will prevails.
Hence, understanding is always best
and a prudent mind. Whoever remains
1060   for long here in this earthly life
will enjoy and endure more than enough.
    They sang then and played to please the hero,
words and music for their warrior prince,
harp tunes and tales of adventure:
1065   there were high times on the hall benches,
and the king's poet performed his part
with the saga of Finn and his sons, unfolding
the tale of the fierce attack in Friesland
where Hnaef, king of the Danes, met death.[5]

1070   *Hildeburh*
            had little cause
    to credit the Jutes:
            son and brother,
    she lost them both
            on the battlefield.
    She, bereft
            and blameless, they
    foredoomed, cut down
            and spear-gored. She,
1075   *the woman in shock,*
            waylaid by grief,
    Hoc's daughter—
            how could she not
    lament her fate
            when morning came
    and the light broke
            on her murdered dears?
    And so farewell
            delight on earth,
1080   *war carried away*

5. The bard's lay is known as the Finnsburg Episode. Its allusive style makes the tale obscure in many details, although some can be filled in from a fragmentary Old English lay, which modern editors have entitled *The Fight at Finnsburg*. Hildeburh, the daughter of the former Danish king Hoc, was married to Finn, king of Friesland, presumably to help end a feud between their peoples. As the episode opens, the feud has already broken out again when a visiting party of Danes, led by Hildeburh's brother Hnaef, who has succeeded their father, is attacked by a tribe called the Jutes. The Jutes are subject to Finn but may be a clan distinct from the Frisians, and Finn does not seem to have instigated the attack. In the ensuing battle, both Hnaef and the son of Hildeburh and Finn are killed, and both sides suffer heavy losses.

Finn's troop of thanes
all but a few.
How then could Finn
hold the line
or fight on
to the end with Hengest,
how save
the rump of his force
from that enemy chief?
1085 So a truce was offered
as follows:[6] first
separate quarters
to be cleared for the Danes,
hall and throne
to be shared with the Frisians.
Then, second:
every day
at the dole-out of gifts
Finn, son of Folcwald,
1090 should honor the Danes,
bestow with an even
hand to Hengest
and Hengest's men
the wrought-gold rings,
bounty to match
the measure he gave
his own Frisians—
to keep morale
in the beer-hall high.
1095 Both sides then
sealed their agreement.
With oaths to Hengest
Finn swore
openly, solemnly,
that the battle survivors
would be guaranteed
honor and status.
No infringement
by word or deed,
1100 no provocation
would be permitted.
Their own ring-giver
after all
was dead and gone,
they were leaderless,
in forced allegiance
to his murderer.
So if any Frisian
stirred up bad blood
1105 with insinuations

6. The truce was offered by Finn to Hengest, who succeeded Hnaef as leader of the Danes.

or taunts about this,
the blade of the sword
                    would arbitrate it.
A funeral pyre
                was then prepared,
effulgent gold
                brought out from the hoard.
The pride and prince
                of the Shieldings lay
1110 awaiting the flame.
                    Everywhere
there were blood-plastered
                        coats of mail.
The pyre was heaped
                with boar-shaped helmets
forged in gold,
                with the gashed corpses
of wellborn Danes—
                many had fallen.
1115 Then Hildeburh
                ordered her own
son's body
                be burnt with Hnaef's,
the flesh on his bones
                        to sputter and blaze
beside his uncle's.
                The woman wailed
and sang keens,
                the warrior went up.[7]
1120 Carcass flame
                swirled and fumed,
they stood round the burial
                        mound and howled
as heads melted,
                crusted gashes
spattered and ran
                bloody matter.
The glutton element
                flamed and consumed
1125 the dead of both sides.
                        Their great days were gone.
Warriors scattered
                to homes and forts
all over Friesland,
                fewer now, feeling
loss of friends.
                Hengest stayed,
lived out that whole
                resentful, blood-sullen

7. The meaning may be, the warrior was placed up on the pyre, or went up in smoke. "Keens": lamentations or dirges for the dead.

1130 winter with Finn,
      homesick and helpless.
  No ring-whorled prow
      could up then
  and away on the sea.
      Wind and water
  raged with storms,
      wave and shingle
  were shackled in ice
      until another year

1135 appeared in the yard
      as it does to this day,
  the seasons constant,
      the wonder of light
  coming over us.
      Then winter was gone,
  earth's lap grew lovely,
      longing woke
  in the cooped-up exile
      for a voyage home—

1140 but more for vengeance,
      some way of bringing
  things to a head:
      his sword arm hankered
  to greet the Jutes.
      So he did not balk
  once Hunlafing
      placed on his lap
  Dazzle-the-Duel,
      the best sword of all,[8]

1145 whose edges Jutes
      knew only too well.
  Thus blood was spilled,
      the gallant Finn
  slain in his home
      after Guthlaf and Oslaf[9]
  back from their voyage
      made old accusation:
  the brutal ambush,
      the fate they had suffered,

1150 all blamed on Finn.
      The wildness in them
  had to brim over.
      The hall ran red
  with blood of enemies.
      Finn was cut down,
  the queen brought away
      and everything

---

8. Hunlafing may be the son of a Danish warrior called Hunlaf. The placing of the sword in Hengest's lap is a symbolic call for revenge.
9. It is not clear whether the Danes have traveled home and then returned to Friesland with reinforcements, or whether the Danish survivors attack once the weather allows them to take ship.

> *the Shieldings could find*
> > *inside Finn's walls—*
1155 *the Frisian king's*
> > *gold collars and gemstones—*
> *swept off to the ship.*
> > *Over sea-lanes then*
> *back to Daneland*
> > *the warrior troop*
> *bore that lady home.*

     The poem was over,
the poet had performed, a pleasant murmur
1160 started on the benches, stewards did the rounds
with wine in splendid jugs, and Wealhtheow came to sit
in her gold crown between two good men,
uncle and nephew, each one of whom
still trusted the other;[1] and the forthright Unferth,
1165 admired by all for his mind and courage
although under a cloud for killing his brothers,
reclined near the king.
     The queen spoke:
"Enjoy this drink, my most generous lord;
raise up your goblet, entertain the Geats
1170 duly and gently, discourse with them,
be open-handed, happy and fond.
Relish their company, but recollect as well
all of the boons that have been bestowed on you.
The bright court of Heorot has been cleansed
1175 and now the word is that you want to adopt
this warrior as a son. So, while you may,
bask in your fortune, and then bequeath
kingdom and nation to your kith and kin,
before your decease. I am certain of Hrothulf.
1180 He is noble and will use the young ones well.
He will not let you down. Should you die before him,
he will treat our children truly and fairly.
He will honor, I am sure, our two sons,
repay them in kind, when he recollects
1185 all the good things we gave him once,
the favor and respect he found in his childhood."
She turned then to the bench where her boys sat,
Hrethric and Hrothmund, with other nobles' sons,
all the youth together; and that good man,
1190 Beowulf the Geat, sat between the brothers.
  The cup was carried to him, kind words
spoken in welcome and a wealth of wrought gold
graciously bestowed: two arm bangles,
a mail-shirt and rings, and the most resplendent
1195 torque of gold I ever heard tell of
anywhere on earth or under heaven.

1. See n. 4, p. 48.

There was no hoard like it since Hama snatched
the Brosings' neck-chain and bore it away
with its gems and settings to his shining fort,
1200   away from Eormenric's wiles and hatred,[2]
and thereby ensured his eternal reward.
Hygelac the Geat, grandson of Swerting,
wore this neck-ring on his last raid;[3]
at bay under his banner, he defended the booty,
1205   treasure he had won. Fate swept him away
because of his proud need to provoke
a feud with the Frisians. He fell beneath his shield,
in the same gem-crusted, kingly gear
he had worn when he crossed the frothing wave-vat.
1210   So the dead king fell into Frankish hands.
They took his breast-mail, also his neck-torque,
and punier warriors plundered the slain
when the carnage ended; Geat corpses
covered the field.
               Applause filled the hall.
1215   Then Wealhtheow pronounced in the presence of the company:
"Take delight in this torque, dear Beowulf,
wear it for luck and wear also this mail
from our people's armory: may you prosper in them!
Be acclaimed for strength, for kindly guidance
1220   to these two boys, and your bounty will be sure.
You have won renown: you are known to all men
far and near, now and forever.
Your sway is wide as the wind's home,
as the sea around cliffs. And so, my prince,
1225   I wish you a lifetime's luck and blessings
to enjoy this treasure. Treat my sons
with tender care, be strong and kind.
Here each comrade is true to the other,
loyal to lord, loving in spirit.
1230   The thanes have one purpose, the people are ready:
having drunk and pledged, the ranks do as I bid."
    She moved then to her place. Men were drinking wine
at that rare feast; how could they know fate,
the grim shape of things to come,
1235   the threat looming over many thanes
as night approached and King Hrothgar prepared
to retire to his quarters? Retainers in great numbers
were posted on guard as so often in the past.
Benches were pushed back, bedding gear and bolsters
1240   spread across the floor, and one man
lay down to his rest, already marked for death.

2. The necklace presented to Beowulf is compared
to one worn by the goddess Freya in Germanic
mythology. In another story it was stolen by Hama
from the Gothic king Eormenric, who is treated as
a tyrant in Germanic legend, but how Eormenric
came to possess it is not known.
3. Later we learn that Beowulf gave the necklace
to Hygd, the queen of his lord Hygelac. Hygelac is
here said to have been wearing it on his last expedition. This is the first of several allusions to Hygelac's death on a raid up the Rhine, the one incident
in the poem that can be connected to a historical
event documented elsewhere.

At their heads they placed their polished timber
battle-shields; and on the bench above them,
each man's kit was kept to hand:
1245   a towering war-helmet, webbed mail-shirt
and great-shafted spear. It was their habit
always and everywhere to be ready for action,
at home or in the camp, in whatever case
and at whatever time the need arose
1250   to rally round their lord. They were a right people.

[ANOTHER ATTACK]

They went to sleep. And one paid dearly
for his night's ease, as had happened to them often,
ever since Grendel occupied the gold-hall,
committing evil until the end came,
1255   death after his crimes. Then it became clear,
obvious to everyone once the fight was over,
that an avenger lurked and was still alive,
grimly biding time. Grendel's mother,
monstrous hell-bride, brooded on her wrongs.
1260   She had been forced down into fearful waters,
the cold depths, after Cain had killed
his father's son, felled his own
brother with a sword. Branded an outlaw,
marked by having murdered, he moved into the wilds,
1265   shunned company and joy. And from Cain there sprang
misbegotten spirits, among them Grendel,
the banished and accursed, due to come to grips
with that watcher in Heorot waiting to do battle.
The monster wrenched and wrestled with him,
1270   but Beowulf was mindful of his mighty strength,
the wondrous gifts God had showered on him:
he relied for help on the Lord of All,
on His care and favor. So he overcame the foe,
brought down the hell-brute. Broken and bowed,
1275   outcast from all sweetness, the enemy of mankind
made for his death-den. But now his mother
had sallied forth on a savage journey,
grief-racked and ravenous, desperate for revenge.
She came to Heorot. There, inside the hall,
1280   Danes lay asleep, earls who would soon endure
a great reversal, once Grendel's mother
attacked and entered. Her onslaught was less
only by as much as an amazon warrior's
strength is less than an armed man's
1285   when the hefted sword, its hammered edge
and gleaming blade slathered in blood,
razes the sturdy boar-ridge off a helmet.
Then in the hall, hard-honed swords
were grabbed from the bench, many a broad shield
1290   lifted and braced; there was little thought of helmets
or woven mail when they woke in terror.

The hell-dam was in panic, desperate to get out,
in mortal terror the moment she was found.
She had pounced and taken one of the retainers
1295 in a tight hold, then headed for the fen.
To Hrothgar, this man was the most beloved
of the friends he trusted between the two seas.
She had done away with a great warrior,
ambushed him at rest.
                    Beowulf was elsewhere.
1300 Earlier, after the award of the treasure,
the Geat had been given another lodging.
    There was uproar in Heorot. She had snatched their trophy,
Grendel's bloodied hand. It was a fresh blow
to the afflicted bawn. The bargain was hard,
1305 both parties having to pay
with the lives of friends. And the old lord,
the gray-haired warrior, was heartsore and weary
when he heard the news: his highest-placed adviser,
his dearest companion, was dead and gone.
1310   Beowulf was quickly brought to the chamber:
the winner of fights, the arch-warrior,
came first-footing in with his fellow troops
to where the king in his wisdom waited,
still wondering whether Almighty God
1315 would ever turn the tide of his misfortunes.
So Beowulf entered with his band in attendance
and the wooden floorboards banged and rang
as he advanced, hurrying to address
the prince of the Ingwins, asking if he'd rested
1320 since the urgent summons had come as a surprise.
    Then Hrothgar, the Shieldings' helmet, spoke:
"Rest? What is rest? Sorrow has returned.
Alas for the Danes! Aeschere is dead.
He was Yrmenlaf's elder brother
1325 and a soul-mate to me, a true mentor,
my right-hand man when the ranks clashed
and our boar-crests had to take a battering
in the line of action. Aeschere was everything
the world admires in a wise man and a friend.
1330 Then this roaming killer came in a fury
and slaughtered him in Heorot. Where she is hiding,
glutting on the corpse and glorying in her escape,
I cannot tell; she has taken up the feud
because of last night, when you killed Grendel,
1335 wrestled and racked him in ruinous combat
since for too long he had terrorized us
with his depredations. He died in battle,
paid with his life; and now this powerful
other one arrives, this force for evil
1340 driven to avenge her kinsman's death.
Or so it seems to thanes in their grief,
in the anguish every thane endures

at the loss of a ring-giver, now that the hand
that bestowed so richly has been stilled in death.
1345   "I have heard it said by my people in hall,
counselors who live in the upland country,
that they have seen two such creatures
prowling the moors, huge marauders
from some other world. One of these things,
1350   as far as anyone ever can discern,
looks like a woman; the other, warped
in the shape of a man, moves beyond the pale
bigger than any man, an unnatural birth
called Grendel by the country people
1355   in former days. They are fatherless creatures,
and their whole ancestry is hidden in a past
of demons and ghosts. They dwell apart
among wolves on the hills, on windswept crags
and treacherous keshes, where cold streams
1360   pour down the mountain and disappear
under mist and moorland.
                                    A few miles from here
a frost-stiffened wood waits and keeps watch
above a mere; the overhanging bank
is a maze of tree-roots mirrored in its surface.
1365   At night there, something uncanny happens:
the water burns. And the mere bottom
has never been sounded by the sons of men.
On its bank, the heather-stepper halts:
the hart in flight from pursuing hounds
1370   will turn to face them with firm-set horns
and die in the wood rather than dive
beneath its surface. That is no good place.
When wind blows up and stormy weather
makes clouds scud and the skies weep,
1375   out of its depths a dirty surge
is pitched toward the heavens. Now help depends
again on you and on you alone.
The gap of danger where the demon waits
is still unknown to you. Seek it if you dare.
1380   I will compensate you for settling the feud
as I did the last time with lavish wealth,
coffers of coiled gold, if you come back."

[BEOWULF FIGHTS GRENDEL'S MOTHER]

Beowulf, son of Ecgtheow, spoke:
"Wise sir, do not grieve. It is always better
1385   to avenge dear ones than to indulge in mourning.
For every one of us, living in this world
means waiting for our end. Let whoever can
win glory before death. When a warrior is gone,
that will be his best and only bulwark.
1390   So arise, my lord, and let us immediately
set forth on the trail of this troll-dam.

I guarantee you: she will not get away,
not to dens under ground nor upland groves
nor the ocean floor. She'll have nowhere to flee to.
1395   Endure your troubles today. Bear up
and be the man I expect you to be."
    With that the old lord sprang to his feet
and praised God for Beowulf's pledge.
Then a bit and halter were brought for his horse
1400   with the plaited mane. The wise king mounted
the royal saddle and rode out in style
with a force of shield-bearers. The forest paths
were marked all over with the monster's tracks,
her trail on the ground wherever she had gone
1405   across the dark moors, dragging away
the body of that thane, Hrothgar's best
counselor and overseer of the country.
So the noble prince proceeded undismayed
up fells and screes, along narrow footpaths
1410   and ways where they were forced into single file,
ledges on cliffs above lairs of water-monsters.
He went in front with a few men,
good judges of the lie of the land,
and suddenly discovered the dismal wood,
1415   mountain trees growing out at an angle
above gray stones: the bloodshot water
surged underneath. It was a sore blow
to all of the Danes, friends of the Shieldings,
a hurt to each and every one
1420   of that noble company when they came upon
Aeschere's head at the foot of the cliff.
    Everybody gazed as the hot gore
kept wallowing up and an urgent war-horn
repeated its notes: the whole party
1425   sat down to watch. The water was infested
with all kinds of reptiles. There were writhing sea-dragons
and monsters slouching on slopes by the cliff,
serpents and wild things such as those that often
surface at dawn to roam the sail-road
1430   and doom the voyage. Down they plunged,
lashing in anger at the loud call
of the battle-bugle. An arrow from the bow
of the Geat chief got one of them
as he surged to the surface: the seasoned shaft
1435   stuck deep in his flank and his freedom in the water
got less and less. It was his last swim.
He was swiftly overwhelmed in the shallows,
prodded by barbed boar-spears,
cornered, beaten, pulled up on the bank,
1440   a strange lake-birth, a loathsome catch
men gazed at in awe.
                Beowulf got ready,
donned his war-gear, indifferent to death;

his mighty, hand-forged, fine-webbed mail
would soon meet with the menace underwater.
1445 It would keep the bone-cage of his body safe:
no enemy's clasp could crush him in it,
no vicious armlock choke his life out.
To guard his head he had a glittering helmet
that was due to be muddied on the mere bottom
1450 and blurred in the upswirl. It was of beaten gold,
princely headgear hooped and hasped
by a weapon-smith who had worked wonders
in days gone by and adorned it with boar-shapes;
since then it had resisted every sword.
1455 And another item lent by Unferth
at that moment of need was of no small importance:
the brehon[4] handed him a hilted weapon,
a rare and ancient sword named Hrunting.
The iron blade with its ill-boding patterns
1460 had been tempered in blood. It had never failed
the hand of anyone who hefted it in battle,
anyone who had fought and faced the worst
in the gap of danger. This was not the first time
it had been called to perform heroic feats.
1465   When he lent that blade to the better swordsman,
Unferth, the strong-built son of Ecglaf,
could hardly have remembered the ranting speech
he had made in his cups. He was not man enough
to face the turmoil of a fight under water
1470 and the risk to his life. So there he lost
fame and repute. It was different for the other
rigged out in his gear, ready to do battle.
   Beowulf, son of Ecgtheow, spoke:
"Wisest of kings, now that I have come
1475 to the point of action, I ask you to recall
what we said earlier: that you, son of Halfdane
and gold-friend to retainers, that you, if I should fall
and suffer death while serving your cause,
would act like a father to me afterward.
1480 If this combat kills me, take care
of my young company, my comrades in arms.
And be sure also, my beloved Hrothgar,
to send Hygelac the treasures I received.
Let the lord of the Geats gaze on that gold,
1485 let Hrethel's son take note of it and see
that I found a ring-giver of rare magnificence
and enjoyed the good of his generosity.
And Unferth is to have what I inherited:
to that far-famed man I bequeath my own
1490 sharp-honed, wave-sheened wonder-blade.
With Hrunting I shall gain glory or die."

4. One of an ancient class of lawyers in Ireland [Translator's note]. The Old English word for Unferth's office, *thyle*, has been interpreted as "orator" and "spokesman."

After these words, the prince of the Weather-Geats
was impatient to be away and plunged suddenly:
without more ado, he dived into the heaving
1495   depths of the lake. It was the best part of a day
before he could see the solid bottom.
    Quickly the one who haunted those waters,
who had scavenged and gone her gluttonous rounds
for a hundred seasons, sensed a human
1500   observing her outlandish lair from above.
So she lunged and clutched and managed to catch him
in her brutal grip; but his body, for all that,
remained unscathed: the mesh of the chain-mail
saved him on the outside. Her savage talons
1505   failed to rip the web of his war-shirt.
Then once she touched bottom, that wolfish swimmer
carried the ring-mailed prince to her court
so that for all his courage he could never use
the weapons he carried; and a bewildering horde
1510   came at him from the depths, droves of sea-beasts
who attacked with tusks and tore at his chain-mail
in a ghastly onslaught. The gallant man
could see he had entered some hellish turn-hole
and yet the water there did not work against him
1515   because the hall-roofing held off
the force of the current; then he saw firelight,
a gleam and flare-up, a glimmer of brightness.
    The hero observed that swamp-thing from hell,
the tarn-hag in all her terrible strength,
1520   then heaved his war-sword and swung his arm:
the decorated blade came down ringing
and singing on her head. But he soon found
his battle-torch extinguished; the shining blade
refused to bite. It spared her and failed
1525   the man in his need. It had gone through many
hand-to-hand fight, had hewed the armor
and helmets of the doomed, but here at last
the fabulous powers of that heirloom failed.
    Hygelac's kinsman kept thinking about
1530   his name and fame: he never lost heart.
Then, in a fury, he flung his sword away.
The keen, inlaid, worm-loop-patterned steel
was hurled to the ground: he would have to rely
on the might of his arm. So must a man do
1535   who intends to gain enduring glory
in a combat. Life doesn't cost him a thought.
Then the prince of War-Geats, warming to this fight
with Grendel's mother, gripped her shoulder
and laid about him in a battle frenzy:
1540   he pitched his killer opponent to the floor
but she rose quickly and retaliated,
grappled him tightly in her grim embrace.
The sure-footed fighter felt daunted,

the strongest of warriors stumbled and fell.
1545 So she pounced upon him and pulled out
a broad, whetted knife: now she would avenge
her only child. But the mesh of chain-mail
on Beowulf's shoulder shielded his life,
turned the edge and tip of the blade.
1550 The son of Ecgtheow would have surely perished
and the Geats lost their warrior under the wide earth
had the strong links and locks of his war-gear
not helped to save him: holy God
decided the victory. It was easy for the Lord,
1555 the Ruler of Heaven, to redress the balance
once Beowulf got back up on his feet.
     Then he saw a blade that boded well,
a sword in her armory, an ancient heirloom
from the days of the giants, an ideal weapon,
1560 one that any warrior would envy,
but so huge and heavy of itself
only Beowulf could wield it in a battle.
So the Shieldings' hero hard-pressed and enraged,
took a firm hold of the hilt and swung
1565 the blade in an arc, a resolute blow
that bit deep into her neck-bone
and severed it entirely, toppling the doomed
house of her flesh; she fell to the floor.
The sword dripped blood, the swordsman was elated.
1570   A light appeared and the place brightened
the way the sky does when heaven's candle
is shining clearly. He inspected the vault:
with sword held high, its hilt raised
to guard and threaten, Hygelac's thane
1575 scouted by the wall in Grendel's wake.
Now the weapon was to prove its worth.
The warrior determined to take revenge
for every gross act Grendel had committed—
and not only for that one occasion
1580 when he'd come to slaughter the sleeping troops,
fifteen of Hrothgar's house-guards
surprised on their benches and ruthlessly devoured,
and as many again carried away,
a brutal plunder. Beowulf in his fury
1585 now settled that score: he saw the monster
in his resting place, war-weary and wrecked,
a lifeless corpse, a casualty
of the battle in Heorot. The body gaped
at the stroke dealt to it after death:
1590 Beowulf cut the corpse's head off.
     Immediately the counselors keeping a lookout
with Hrothgar, watching the lake water,
saw a heave-up and surge of waves
and blood in the backwash. They bowed gray heads,
1595 spoke in their sage, experienced way

about the good warrior, how they never again
expected to see that prince returning
in triumph to their king. It was clear to many
that the wolf of the deep had destroyed him forever.
1600   The ninth hour of the day arrived.
The brave Shieldings abandoned the cliff-top
and the king went home; but sick at heart,
staring at the mere, the strangers held on.
They wished, without hope, to behold their lord,
Beowulf himself.
1605   Meanwhile, the sword
began to wilt into gory icicles
to slather and thaw. It was a wonderful thing,
the way it all melted as ice melts
when the Father eases the fetters off the frost
1610   and unravels the water-ropes, He who wields power
over time and tide: He is the true Lord.
The Geat captain saw treasure in abundance
but carried no spoils from those quarters
except for the head and the inlaid hilt
1615   embossed with jewels; its blade had melted
and the scrollwork on it burned, so scalding was the blood
of the poisonous fiend who had perished there.
Then away he swam, the one who had survived
the fall of his enemies, flailing to the surface.
1620   The wide water, the waves and pools,
were no longer infested once the wandering fiend
let go of her life and this unreliable world.
The seafarers' leader made for land,
resolutely swimming, delighted with his prize,
1625   the mighty load he was lugging to the surface.
His thanes advanced in a troop to meet him,
thanking God and taking great delight
in seeing their prince back safe and sound.
Quickly the hero's helmet and mail-shirt
1630   were loosed and unlaced. The lake settled,
clouds darkened above the bloodshot depths.
With high hearts they headed away
along footpaths and trails through the fields,
roads that they knew, each of them wrestling
1635   with the head they were carrying from the lakeside cliff,
men kingly in their courage and capable
of difficult work. It was a task for four
to hoist Grendel's head on a spear
and bear it under strain to the bright hall.
1640   But soon enough they neared the place,
fourteen Geats in fine fettle,
striding across the outlying ground
in a delighted throng around their leader.
In he came then, the thanes' commander,
1645   the arch-warrior, to address Hrothgar:
his courage was proven, his glory was secure.

Grendel's head was hauled by the hair,
dragged across the floor where the people were drinking,
a horror for both queen and company to behold.
1650 They stared in awe. It was an astonishing sight.

[ANOTHER CELEBRATION AT HEOROT]

Beowulf, son of Ecgtheow, spoke:
"So, son of Halfdane, prince of the Shieldings,
we are glad to bring this booty from the lake.
It is a token of triumph and we tender it to you.
1655 I barely survived the battle under water.
It was hard-fought, a desperate affair
that could have gone badly; if God had not helped me,
the outcome would have been quick and fatal.
Although Hrunting is hard-edged,
1660 I could never bring it to bear in battle.
But the Lord of Men allowed me to behold—
for He often helps the unbefriended—
an ancient sword shining on the wall,
a weapon made for giants, there for the wielding.
1665 Then my moment came in the combat and I struck
the dwellers in that den. Next thing the damascened
sword blade melted; it bloated and it burned
in their rushing blood. I have wrested the hilt
from the enemies' hand, avenged the evil
1670 done to the Danes; it is what was due.
And this I pledge, O prince of the Shieldings:
you can sleep secure with your company of troops
in Heorot Hall. Never need you fear
for a single thane of your sept or nation,
1675 young warriors or old, that laying waste of life
that you and your people endured of yore."
Then the gold hilt was handed over
to the old lord, a relic from long ago
for the venerable ruler. That rare smithwork
1680 was passed on to the prince of the Danes
when those devils perished; once death removed
that murdering, guilt-steeped, God-cursed fiend,
eliminating his unholy life
and his mother's as well, it was willed to that king
1685 who of all the lavish gift-lords of the north
was the best regarded between the two seas.
Hrothgar spoke; he examined the hilt,
that relic of old times. It was engraved all over
and showed how war first came into the world
1690 and the flood destroyed the tribe of giants.
They suffered a terrible severance from the Lord;
the Almighty made the waters rise,
drowned them in the deluge for retribution.
In pure gold inlay on the sword-guards
1695 there were rune-markings correctly incised,
stating and recording for whom the sword

had been first made and ornamented
with its scrollworked hilt. Then everyone hushed
as the son of Halfdane spoke this wisdom:

1700 "A protector of his people, pledged to uphold
truth and justice and to respect tradition,
is entitled to affirm that this man
was born to distinction. Beowulf, my friend,
your fame has gone far and wide,

1705 you are known everywhere. In all things you are even-tempered,
prudent and resolute. So I stand firm by the promise of friendship
we exchanged before. Forever you will be
your people's mainstay and your own warriors'
helping hand.
              Heremod was different,

1710 the way he behaved to Ecgwela's sons.
His rise in the world brought little joy
to the Danish people, only death and destruction.
He vented his rage on men he caroused with,
killed his own comrades, a pariah king

1715 who cut himself off from his own kind,
even though Almighty God had made him
eminent and powerful and marked him from the start
for a happy life. But a change happened,
he grew bloodthirsty, gave no more rings

1720 to honor the Danes. He suffered in the end
for having plagued his people for so long:
his life lost happiness.
              So learn from this
and understand true values. I who tell you
have wintered into wisdom.
              It is a great wonder

1725 how Almighty God in His magnificence
favors our race with rank and scope
and the gift of wisdom; His sway is wide.
Sometimes He allows the mind of a man
of distinguished birth to follow its bent,

1730 grants him fulfillment and felicity on earth
and forts to command in his own country.
He permits him to lord it in many lands
until the man in his unthinkingness
forgets that it will ever end for him.

1735 He indulges his desires; illness and old age
mean nothing to him; his mind is untroubled
by envy or malice or the thought of enemies
with their hate-honed swords. The whole world
conforms to his will, he is kept from the worst

1740 until an element of overweening
enters him and takes hold
while the soul's guard, its sentry, drowses,
grown too distracted. A killer stalks him,
an archer who draws a deadly bow.

1745 And then the man is hit in the heart,

the arrow flies beneath his defenses,
the devious promptings of the demon start.
His old possessions seem paltry to him now.
He covets and resents; dishonors custom
1750 and bestows no gold; and because of good things
that the Heavenly Powers gave him in the past
he ignores the shape of things to come.
Then finally the end arrives
when the body he was lent collapses and falls
1755 prey to its death; ancestral possessions
and the goods he hoarded are inherited by another
who lets them go with a liberal hand.
    "O flower of warriors, beware of that trap.
Choose, dear Beowulf, the better part,
1760 eternal rewards. Do not give way to pride.
For a brief while your strength is in bloom
but it fades quickly; and soon there will follow
illness or the sword to lay you low,
or a sudden fire or surge of water
1765 or jabbing blade or javelin from the air
or repellent age. Your piercing eye
will dim and darken; and death will arrive,
dear warrior, to sweep you away.
    "Just so I ruled the Ring-Danes' country
1770 for fifty years, defended them in wartime
with spear and sword against constant assaults
by many tribes: I came to believe
my enemies had faded from the face of the earth.
Still, what happened was a hard reversal
1775 from bliss to grief. Grendel struck
after lying in wait. He laid waste to the land
and from that moment my mind was in dread
of his depredations. So I praise God
in His heavenly glory that I lived to behold
1780 this head dripping blood and that after such harrowing
I can look upon it in triumph at last.
Take your place, then, with pride and pleasure,
and move to the feast. Tomorrow morning
our treasure will be shared and showered upon you."
1785   The Geat was elated and gladly obeyed
the old man's bidding; he sat on the bench.
And soon all was restored, the same as before.
Happiness came back, the hall was thronged,
and a banquet set forth; black night fell
and covered them in darkness.
1790   Then the company rose
for the old campaigner: the gray-haired prince
was ready for bed. And a need for rest
came over the brave shield-bearing Geat.
He was a weary seafarer, far from home,
1795 so immediately a house-guard guided him out,
one whose office entailed looking after

whatever a thane on the road in those days
might need or require. It was noble courtesy.

[BEOWULF RETURNS HOME]

That great heart rested. The hall towered,
1800 gold-shingled and gabled, and the guest slept in it
until the black raven with raucous glee
announced heaven's joy, and a hurry of brightness
overran the shadows. Warriors rose quickly,
impatient to be off: their own country
1805 was beckoning the nobles; and the bold voyager
longed to be aboard his distant boat.
Then that stalwart fighter ordered Hrunting
to be brought to Unferth, and bade Unferth
take the sword and thanked him for lending it.
1810 He said he had found it a friend in battle
and a powerful help; he put no blame
on the blade's cutting edge. He was a considerate man.
And there the warriors stood in their war-gear,
eager to go, while their honored lord
1815 approached the platform where the other sat.
The undaunted hero addressed Hrothgar.
Beowulf, son of Ecgtheow, spoke:
"Now we who crossed the wide sea
have to inform you that we feel a desire
1820 to return to Hygelac. Here we have been welcomed
and thoroughly entertained. You have treated us well.
If there is any favor on earth I can perform
beyond deeds of arms I have done already,
anything that would merit your affections more,
1825 I shall act, my lord, with alacrity.
If ever I hear from across the ocean
that people on your borders are threatening battle
as attackers have done from time to time,
I shall land with a thousand thanes at my back
1830 to help your cause. Hygelac may be young
to rule a nation, but this much I know
about the king of the Geats: he will come to my aid
and want to support me by word and action
in your hour of need, when honor dictates
1835 that I raise a hedge of spears around you.
Then if Hrethric should think about traveling
as a king's son to the court of the Geats,
he will find many friends. Foreign places
yield more to one who is himself worth meeting."
1840 Hrothgar spoke and answered him:
"The Lord in his wisdom sent you those words
and they came from the heart. I have never heard
so young a man make truer observations.
You are strong in body and mature in mind,
1845 impressive in speech. If it should come to pass
that Hrethel's descendant dies beneath a spear,

if deadly battle or the sword blade or disease
fells the prince who guards your people
and you are still alive, then I firmly believe
1850 the seafaring Geats won't find a man
worthier of acclaim as their king and defender
than you, if only you would undertake
the lordship of your homeland. My liking for you
deepens with time, dear Beowulf.
1855 What you have done is to draw two peoples,
the Geat nation and us neighboring Danes,
into shared peace and a pact of friendship
in spite of hatreds we have harbored in the past.
For as long as I rule this far-flung land
1860 treasures will change hands and each side will treat
the other with gifts; across the gannet's bath,
over the broad sea, whorled prows will bring
presents and tokens. I know your people
are beyond reproach in every respect,
1865 steadfast in the old way with friend or foe."
  Then the earls' defender furnished the hero
with twelve treasures and told him to set out,
sail with those gifts safely home
to the people he loved, but to return promptly.
1870 And so the good and gray-haired Dane,
that highborn king, kissed Beowulf
and embraced his neck, then broke down
in sudden tears. Two forebodings
disturbed him in his wisdom, but one was stronger:
1875 nevermore would they meet each other
face to face. And such was his affection
that he could not help being overcome:
his fondness for the man was so deep-founded,
it warmed his heart and wound the heartstrings
tight in his breast.
1880   The embrace ended
and Beowulf, glorious in his gold regalia,
stepped the green earth. Straining at anchor
and ready for boarding, his boat awaited him.
So they went on their journey, and Hrothgar's generosity
1885 was praised repeatedly. He was a peerless king
until old age sapped his strength and did him
mortal harm, as it has done so many.
  Down to the waves then, dressed in the web
of their chain-mail and war-shirts the young men marched
1890 in high spirits. The coast-guard spied them,
thanes setting forth, the same as before.
His salute this time from the top of the cliff
was far from unmannerly; he galloped to meet them
and as they took ship in their shining gear,
1895 he said how welcome they would be in Geatland.
Then the broad hull was beached on the sand
to be cargoed with treasure, horses and war-gear.

The curved prow motioned; the mast stood high
above Hrothgar's riches in the loaded hold.
1900   The guard who had watched the boat was given
a sword with gold fittings, and in future days
that present would make him a respected man
at his place on the mead-bench.
                              Then the keel plunged
and shook in the sea; and they sailed from Denmark.
1905   Right away the mast was rigged with its sea-shawl;
sail-ropes were tightened, timbers drummed
and stiff winds kept the wave-crosser
skimming ahead; as she heaved forward,
her foamy neck was fleet and buoyant,
1910   a lapped prow loping over currents,
until finally the Geats caught sight of coastline
and familiar cliffs. The keel reared up,
wind lifted it home, it hit on the land.
       The harbor guard came hurrying out
1915   to the rolling water: he had watched the offing
long and hard, on the lookout for those friends.
With the anchor cables, he moored their craft
right where it had beached, in case a backwash
might catch the hull and carry it away.
1920   Then he ordered the prince's treasure-trove
to be carried ashore. It was a short step
from there to where Hrethel's son and heir,
Hygelac the gold-giver, makes his home
on a secure cliff, in the company of retainers.
1925   The building was magnificent, the king majestic,
ensconced in his hall; and although Hygd, his queen,
was young, a few short years at court,
her mind was thoughtful and her manners sure.
Haereth's daughter behaved generously
1930   and stinted nothing when she distributed
bounty to the Geats.
                    Great Queen Modthryth
perpetrated terrible wrongs.[5]
If any retainer ever made bold
to look her in the face, if an eye not her lord's[6]
1935   stared at her directly during daylight,
the outcome was sealed: he was kept bound,
in hand-tightened shackles, racked, tortured
until doom was pronounced—death by the sword,
slash of blade, blood-gush, and death-qualms
1940   in an evil display. Even a queen
outstanding in beauty must not overstep like that.

5. The story of Queen Modthryth's vices is
abruptly introduced as a foil to Queen Hygd's virtues. A transitional passage may have been lost, but
the poet's device is similar to that of using the earlier reference to the wickedness of King Heremod
to contrast with the good qualities of Sigemund
and Beowulf.

6. This could refer to her husband or her father
before her marriage. The story resembles folktales
about a proud princess whose unsuccessful suitors
are all put to death, although the unfortunate victims in this case seem to be guilty only of looking
at her.

A queen should weave peace, not punish the innocent
with loss of life for imagined insults.
But Hemming's kinsman[7] put a halt to her ways
1945 and drinkers round the table had another tale:
she was less of a bane to people's lives,
less cruel-minded, after she was married
to the brave Offa, a bride arrayed
in her gold finery, given away
1950 by a caring father, ferried to her young prince
over dim seas. In days to come
she would grace the throne and grow famous
for her good deeds and conduct of life,
her high devotion to the hero king
1955 who was the best king, it has been said,
between the two seas or anywhere else
on the face of the earth. Offa was honored
far and wide for his generous ways,
his fighting spirit and his farseeing
1960 defense of his homeland; from him there sprang Eomer,
Garmund's grandson, kinsman of Hemming,[8]
his warriors' mainstay and master of the field.

    Heroic Beowulf and his band of men
crossed the wide strand, striding along
1965 the sandy foreshore; the sun shone,
the world's candle warmed them from the south
as they hastened to where, as they had heard,
the young king, Ongentheow's killer
and his people's protector,[9] was dispensing rings
1970 inside his bawn. Beowulf's return
was reported to Hygelac as soon as possible,
news that the captain was now in the enclosure,
his battle-brother back from the fray
alive and well, walking to the hall.
1975 Room was quickly made, on the king's orders,
and the troops filed across the cleared floor.

    After Hygelac had offered greetings
to his loyal thane in a lofty speech,
he and his kinsman, that hale survivor,
1980 sat face to face. Haereth's daughter
moved about with the mead-jug in her hand,
taking care of the company, filling the cups
that warriors held out. Then Hygelac began
to put courteous questions to his old comrade
1985 in the high hall. He hankered to know
every tale the Sea-Geats had to tell:

7. I.e., Offa I, a legendary king of the Angles. We
know nothing about Hemming other than that
Offa was related to him. Offa II (757–96) was king
of Mercia, and although the story is about the second Offa's ancestor on the Continent, this is the
only English connection in the poem and has been
taken as evidence to date its origins to 8th-century
Mercia.

8. I.e., Eomer, Offa's son. See previous note. Garmund was presumably the name of Offa's father.
9. I.e., Hygelac. Ongentheow was king of the
Swedish people called the Shylfings. This is the
first of the references to wars between the Geats
and the Swedes. One of Hygelac's war party named
Eofer was the actual slayer of Ongentheow.

"How did you fare on your foreign voyage,
dear Beowulf, when you abruptly decided
to sail away across the salt water
1990 and fight at Heorot? Did you help Hrothgar
much in the end? Could you ease the prince
of his well-known troubles? Your undertaking
cast my spirits down, I dreaded the outcome
of your expedition and pleaded with you
1995 long and hard to leave the killer be,
let the South-Danes settle their own
blood-feud with Grendel. So God be thanked
I am granted this sight of you, safe and sound."
      Beowulf, son of Ecgtheow, spoke:
2000 "What happened, Lord Hygelac, is hardly a secret
any more among men in this world—
myself and Grendel coming to grips
on the very spot where he visited destruction
on the Victory-Shieldings and violated
2005 life and limb, losses I avenged
so no earthly offspring of Grendel's
need ever boast of that bout before dawn,
no matter how long the last of his evil
family survives.
                        When I first landed
2010 I hastened to the ring-hall and saluted Hrothgar.
Once he discovered why I had come,
the son of Halfdane sent me immediately
to sit with his own sons on the bench.
It was a happy gathering. In my whole life
2015 I have never seen mead enjoyed more
in any hall on earth. Sometimes the queen
herself appeared, peace-pledge between nations,
to hearten the young ones and hand out
a torque to a warrior, then take her place.
2020 Sometimes Hrothgar's daughter distributed
ale to older ranks, in order on the benches:
I heard the company call her Freawaru
as she made her rounds, presenting men
with the gem-studded bowl, young bride-to-be
2025 to the gracious Ingeld,[1] in her gold-trimmed attire.
The friend of the Shieldings favors her betrothal:
the guardian of the kingdom sees good in it
and hopes this woman will heal old wounds
and grievous feuds.
                        But generally the spear
2030 is prompt to retaliate when a prince is killed,
no matter how admirable the bride may be.
      "Think how the Heatho-Bards are bound to feel,
their lord, Ingeld, and his loyal thanes,
when he walks in with that woman to the feast:
2035 Danes are at the table, being entertained,

_____
1. King of the Heatho-Bards; his father, Froda, was killed by the Danes.

honored guests in glittering regalia,
burnished ring-mail that was their hosts' birthright,
looted when the Heatho-Bards could no longer wield
their weapons in the shield-clash, when they went down
2040 with their beloved comrades and forfeited their lives.
Then an old spearman will speak while they are drinking,
having glimpsed some heirloom that brings alive
memories of the massacre; his mood will darken
and heart-stricken, in the stress of his emotion,
2045 he will begin to test a young man's temper
and stir up trouble, starting like this:
'Now, my friend, don't you recognize
your father's sword, his favorite weapon,
the one he wore when he went out in his war-mask
2050 to face the Danes on that final day?
After Withergeld[2] died and his men were doomed,
the Shieldings quickly claimed the field;
and now here's a son of one or other
of those same killers coming through our hall
2055 overbearing us, mouthing boasts,
and rigged in armor that by right is yours.'
And so he keeps on, recalling and accusing,
working things up with bitter words
until one of the lady's retainers lies
2060 spattered in blood, split open
on his father's account.[3] The killer knows
the lie of the land and escapes with his life.
Then on both sides the oath-bound lords
will break the peace, a passionate hate
2065 will build up in Ingeld, and love for his bride
will falter in him as the feud rankles.
I therefore suspect the good faith of the Heatho-Bards,
the truth of their friendship and the trustworthiness
of their alliance with the Danes.
                              But now, my lord,
2070 I shall carry on with my account of Grendel,
the whole story of everything that happened
in the hand-to-hand fight.
                        After heaven's gem
had gone mildly to earth, that maddened spirit,
the terror of those twilights, came to attack us
2075 where we stood guard, still safe inside the hall.
There deadly violence came down on Hondscio
and he fell as fate ordained, the first to perish,
rigged out for the combat. A comrade from our ranks
had come to grief in Grendel's maw:
2080 he ate up the entire body.
There was blood on his teeth, he was bloated and dangerous,
all roused up, yet still unready

---

2. One of the Heatho-Bard leaders.
3. I.e., the young Danish attendant is killed
because his father killed the father of the young

Heatho-Bard who has been egged on by the old
veteran of that campaign.

to leave the hall empty-handed;
renowned for his might, he matched himself against me,
2085   wildly reaching. He had this roomy pouch,
a strange accoutrement, intricately strung
and hung at the ready, a rare patchwork
of devilishly fitted dragon-skins.
I had done him no wrong, yet the raging demon
2090   wanted to cram me and many another
into this bag—but it was not to be
once I got to my feet in a blind fury.
It would take too long to tell how I repaid
the terror of the land for every life he took
2095   and so won credit for you, my king,
and for all your people. And although he got away
to enjoy life's sweetness for a while longer,
his right hand stayed behind him in Heorot,
evidence of his miserable overthrow
2100   as he dived into murk on the mere bottom.
    "I got lavish rewards from the lord of the Danes
for my part in the battle, beaten gold
and much else, once morning came
and we took our places at the banquet table.
2105   There was singing and excitement: an old reciter,
a carrier of stories, recalled the early days.
At times some hero made the timbered harp
tremble with sweetness, or related true
and tragic happenings; at times the king
2110   gave the proper turn to some fantastic tale,
or a battle-scarred veteran, bowed with age,
would begin to remember the martial deeds
of his youth and prime and be overcome
as the past welled up in his wintry heart.
2115   "We were happy there the whole day long
and enjoyed our time until another night
descended upon us. Then suddenly
the vehement mother avenged her son
and wreaked destruction. Death had robbed her,
2120   Geats had slain Grendel, so his ghastly dam
struck back and with bare-faced defiance
laid a man low. Thus life departed
from the sage Aeschere, an elder wise in counsel.
But afterward, on the morning following,
2125   the Danes could not burn the dead body
nor lay the remains of the man they loved
on his funeral pyre. She had fled with the corpse
and taken refuge beneath torrents on the mountain.
It was a hard blow for Hrothgar to bear,
2130   harder than any he had undergone before.
And so the heartsore king beseeched me
in your royal name to take my chances
underwater, to win glory

and prove my worth. He promised me rewards.
2135 Hence, as is well known, I went to my encounter
with the terror-monger at the bottom of the tarn.
For a while it was hand-to-hand between us,
then blood went curling along the currents
and I beheaded Grendel's mother in the hall
2140 with a mighty sword. I barely managed
to escape with my life; my time had not yet come.
But Halfdane's heir, the shelter of those earls,
again endowed me with gifts in abundance.
      "Thus the king acted with due custom.
2145 I was paid and recompensed completely,
given full measure and the freedom to choose
from Hothgar's treasures by Hrothgar himself.
These, King Hygelac, I am happy to present
to you as gifts. It is still upon your grace
2150 that all favor depends. I have few kinsmen
who are close, my king, except for your kind self."
Then he ordered the boar-framed standard to be brought,
the battle-topping helmet, the mail-shirt gray as hoar-frost,
and the precious war-sword; and proceeded with his speech:
2155 "When Hrothgar presented this war-gear to me
he instructed me, my lord, to give you some account
of why it signifies his special favor.
He said it had belonged to his older brother,
King Heorogar, who had long kept it,
2160 but that Heorogar had never bequeathed it
to his son Heoroward, that worthy scion,
loyal as he was. Enjoy it well."
      I heard four horses were handed over next.
Beowulf bestowed four bay steeds
2165 to go with the armor, swift gallopers,
all alike. So ought a kinsman act,
instead of plotting and planning in secret
to bring people to grief, or conspiring to arrange
the death of comrades. The warrior king
2170 was uncle to Beowulf and honored by his nephew:
each was concerned for the other's good.
      I heard he presented Hygd with a gorget,
the priceless torque that the prince's daughter,
Wealhtheow, had given him; and three horses,
2175 supple creatures brilliantly saddled.
The bright necklace would be luminous on Hygd's breast.
      Thus Beowulf bore himself with valor;
he was formidable in battle yet behaved with honor
and took no advantage; never cut down
2180 a comrade who was drunk, kept his temper
and, warrior that he was, watched and controlled
his God-sent strength and his outstanding
natural powers. He had been poorly regarded
for a long time, was taken by the Geats

2185 for less than he was worth:[4] and their lord too
had never much esteemed him in the mead-hall.
They firmly believed that he lacked force,
that the prince was a weakling; but presently
every affront to his deserving was reversed.

2190 The battle-famed king, bulwark of his earls,
ordered a gold-chased heirloom of Hrethel's[5]
to be brought in; it was the best example
of a gem-studded sword in the Geat treasury.
This he laid on Beowulf's lap

2195 and then rewarded him with land as well,
seven thousand hides; and a hall and a throne.
Both owned land by birth in that country,
ancestral grounds; but the greater right
and sway were inherited by the higher born.

[THE DRAGON WAKES]

2200 A lot was to happen in later days
in the fury of battle. Hygelac fell
and the shelter of Heardred's shield proved useless
against the fierce aggression of the Shylfings:[6]
ruthless swordsmen, seasoned campaigners,

2205 they came against him and his conquering nation,
and with cruel force cut him down
so that afterwards
                    the wide kingdom
reverted to Beowulf. He ruled it well
for fifty winters, grew old and wise

2210 as warden of the land
                    until one began
to dominate the dark, a dragon on the prowl
from the steep vaults of a stone-roofed barrow
where he guarded a hoard; there was a hidden passage,
unknown to men, but someone[7] managed

2215 to enter by it and interfere
with the heathen trove. He had handled and removed

4. There is no other mention of Beowulf's unpromising youth. This motif of the "Cinderella hero" and others, such as Grendel's magic pouch, are examples of folklore material, probably circulating orally, that made its way into the poem.
5. Hygelac's father and Beowulf's grandfather.
6. There are several references, some of them lengthy, to the wars between the Geats and the Swedes. Because these are highly allusive and not in chronological order, they are difficult to follow and keep straight. This outline, along with the Genealogies (p. 26), may serve as a guide. *Phase 1*: After the death of the Geat patriarch, King Hrethel (lines 2462–70), Ohthere and Onela, the sons of the Swedish king Ongentheow, invade Geat territory and inflict heavy casualties in a battle at Hreosnahill (lines 2472–78). *Phase 2*: The Geats invade Sweden under Haethcyn, King Hrethel's son who has succeeded him. At the battle of Ravenswood, the Geats capture Ongentheow's queen, but Ongentheow counterattacks, rescues the queen, and kills Haethcyn. Hygelac, Haethcyn's younger brother, arrives with reinforcements; Ongentheow is killed in savage combat with two of Hygelac's men; and the Swedes are routed (lines 2479–89 and 2922–90). *Phase 3*: Eanmund and Eadgils, the sons of Ohthere (presumably dead), are driven into exile by their uncle Onela, who is now king of the Swedes. They are given refuge by Hygelac's son Heardred, who has succeeded his father. Onela invades Geatland and kills Heardred; his retainer Weohstan kills Eanmund; and after the Swedes withdraw, Beowulf becomes king (lines 2204–8, which follow, and 2379–90). *Phase 4*: Eadgils, supported by Beowulf, invades Sweden and kills Onela (lines 2391–96).
7. The following section was damaged by fire. In lines 2215–31 entire words and phrases are missing or indicated by only a few letters. Editorial attempts to reconstruct the text are conjectural and often disagree.

a gem-studded goblet; it gained him nothing,
though with a thief's wiles he had outwitted
the sleeping dragon. That drove him into rage,
2220 as the people of that country would soon discover.
       The intruder who broached the dragon's treasure
and moved him to wrath had never meant to.
It was desperation on the part of a slave
fleeing the heavy hand of some master,
2225 guilt-ridden and on the run,
going to ground. But he soon began
to shake with terror;[8] . . . . . . in shock
the wretch . . . .
. . . . panicked and ran
2230 away with the precious . . . . . .
metalwork. There were many other
heirlooms heaped inside the earth-house,
because long ago, with deliberate care,
somebody now forgotten
2235 had buried the riches of a highborn race
in this ancient cache. Death had come
and taken them all in times gone by
and the only one left to tell their tale,
the last of their line, could look forward to nothing
2240 but the same fate for himself: he foresaw that his joy
in the treasure would be brief.
                              A newly constructed
barrow stood waiting, on a wide headland
close to the waves, its entryway secured.
Into it the keeper of the hoard had carried
2245 all the goods and golden ware
worth preserving. His words were few:
"Now, earth, hold what earls once held
and heroes can no more; it was mined from you first
by honorable men. My own people
2250 have been ruined in war; one by one
they went down to death, looked their last
on sweet life in the hall. I am left with nobody
to bear a sword or to burnish plated goblets,
put a sheen on the cup. The companies have departed.
2255 The hard helmet, hasped with gold,
will be stripped of its hoops; and the helmet-shiner
who should polish the metal of the war-mask sleeps;
the coat of mail that came through all fights,
through shield-collapse and cut of sword,
2260 decays with the warrior. Nor may webbed mail
range far and wide on the warlord's back
beside his mustered troops. No trembling harp,
no tuned timber, no tumbling hawk
swerving through the hall, no swift horse
2265 pawing the courtyard. Pillage and slaughter

---

8. Lines 2227–30 are so damaged that they defy guesswork to reconstruct them.

have emptied the earth of entire peoples."
And so he mourned as he moved about the world,
deserted and alone, lamenting his unhappiness
day and night, until death's flood
brimmed up in his heart.
2270   Then an old harrower of the dark
happened to find the hoard open,
the burning one who hunts out barrows,
the slick-skinned dragon, threatening the night sky
with streamers of fire. People on the farms
2275 are in dread of him. He is driven to hunt out
hoards under ground, to guard heathen gold
through age-long vigils, though to little avail.
For three centuries, this scourge of the people
had stood guard on that stoutly protected
2280 underground treasury, until the intruder
unleashed its fury; he hurried to his lord
with the gold-plated cup and made his plea
to be reinstated. Then the vault was rifled,
the ring-hoard robbed, and the wretched man
2285 had his request granted. His master gazed
on that find from the past for the first time.
    When the dragon awoke, trouble flared again.
He rippled down the rock, writhing with anger
when he saw the footprints of the prowler who had stolen
2290 too close to his dreaming head.
So may a man not marked by fate
easily escape exile and woe
by the grace of God.
                        The hoard-guardian
scorched the ground as he scoured and hunted
2295 for the trespasser who had troubled his sleep.
Hot and savage, he kept circling and circling
the outside of the mound. No man appeared
in that desert waste, but he worked himself up
by imagining battle; then back in he'd go
2300 in search of the cup, only to discover
signs that someone had stumbled upon
the golden treasures. So the guardian of the mound,
the hoard-watcher, waited for the gloaming
with fierce impatience; his pent-up fury
2305 at the loss of the vessel made him long to hit back
and lash out in flames. Then, to his delight,
the day waned and he could wait no longer
behind the wall, but hurtled forth
in a fiery blaze. The first to suffer
2310 were the people on the land, but before long
it was their treasure-giver who would come to grief.
    The dragon began to belch out flames
and burn bright homesteads; there was a hot glow
that scared everyone, for the vile sky-winger
2315 would leave nothing alive in his wake.

Everywhere the havoc he wrought was in evidence.
Far and near, the Geat nation
bore the brunt of his brutal assaults
and virulent hate. Then back to the hoard
2320 he would dart before daybreak, to hide in his den.
He had swinged the land, swathed it in flame,
in fire and burning, and now he felt secure
in the vaults of his barrow; but his trust was unavailing.
    Then Beowulf was given bad news,
2325 the hard truth: his own home,
the best of buildings, had been burned to a cinder,
the throne-room of the Geats. It threw the hero
into deep anguish and darkened his mood:
the wise man thought he must have thwarted
2330 ancient ordinance of the eternal Lord,
broken His commandment. His mind was in turmoil,
unaccustomed anxiety and gloom
confused his brain; the fire-dragon
had razed the coastal region and reduced
2335 forts and earthworks to dust and ashes,
so the war-king planned and plotted his revenge.
The warriors' protector, prince of the hall-troop,
ordered a marvelous all-iron shield
from his smithy works. He well knew
2340 that linden boards would let him down
and timber burn. After many trials,
he was destined to face the end of his days,
in this mortal world, as was the dragon,
for all his long leasehold on the treasure.
2345   Yet the prince of the rings was too proud
to line up with a large army
against the sky-plague. He had scant regard
for the dragon as a threat, no dread at all
of its courage or strength, for he had kept going
2350 often in the past, through perils and ordeals
of every sort, after he had purged
Hrothgar's hall, triumphed in Heorot
and beaten Grendel. He outgrappled the monster
and his evil kin.
                        One of his cruelest
2355 hand-to-hand encounters had happened
when Hygelac, king of the Geats, was killed
in Friesland: the people's friend and lord,
Hrethel's son, slaked a sword blade's
thirst for blood. But Beowulf's prodigious
2360 gifts as a swimmer guaranteed his safety:
he arrived at the shore, shouldering thirty
battle-dresses, the booty he had won.
There was little for the Hetware[9] to be happy about
as they shielded their faces and fighting on the ground

9. A tribe of the Franks allied with the Frisians.

2365 began in earnest. With Beowulf against them,
few could hope to return home.
　　　Across the wide sea, desolate and alone,
the son of Ecgtheow swam back to his people.
There Hygd offered him throne and authority
2370 as lord of the ring-hoard: with Hygelac dead,
she had no belief in her son's ability
to defend their homeland against foreign invaders.
Yet there was no way the weakened nation
could get Beowulf to give in and agree
2375 to be elevated over Heardred as his lord
or to undertake the office of kingship.
But he did provide support for the prince,
honored and minded him until he matured
as the ruler of Geatland.
　　　　　　　　　　　Then over sea-roads
2380 exiles arrived, sons of Ohthere.[1]
They had rebelled against the best of all
the sea-kings in Sweden, the one who held sway
in the Shylfing nation, their renowned prince,
lord of the mead-hall. That marked the end
2385 for Hygelac's son: his hospitality
was mortally rewarded with wounds from a sword.
Heardred lay slaughtered and Onela returned
to the land of Sweden, leaving Beowulf
to ascend the throne, to sit in majesty
2390 and rule over the Geats. He was a good king.
　　　In days to come, he contrived to avenge
the fall of his prince; he befriended Eadgils
when Eadgils was friendless, aiding his cause
with weapons and warriors over the wide sea,
2395 sending him men. The feud was settled
on a comfortless campaign when he killed Onela.
　　　And so the son of Ecgtheow had survived
every extreme, excelling himself
in daring and in danger, until the day arrived
2400 when he had to come face to face with the dragon.
The lord of the Geats took eleven comrades
and went in a rage to reconnoiter.
By then he had discovered the cause of the affliction
being visited on the people. The precious cup
2405 had come to him from the hand of the finder,
the one who had started all this strife
and was now added as a thirteenth to their number.
They press-ganged and compelled this poor creature
to be their guide. Against his will
2410 he led them to the earth-vault he alone knew,
an underground barrow near the sea-billows
and heaving waves, heaped inside
with exquisite metalwork. The one who stood guard

---

1. See p. 74, n. 6, Phases 3 and 4.

was dangerous and watchful, warden of the trove
2415　buried under earth: no easy bargain
would be made in that place by any man.
　　　The veteran king sat down on the cliff-top.
He wished good luck to the Geats who had shared
his hearth and his gold. He was sad at heart,
2420　unsettled yet ready, sensing his death.
His fate hovered near, unknowable but certain:
it would soon claim his coffered soul,
part life from limb. Before long
the prince's spirit would spin free from his body.
2425　　　Beowulf, son of Ecgtheow, spoke:
"Many a skirmish I survived when I was young
and many times of war: I remember them well.
At seven, I was fostered out by my father,
left in the charge of my people's lord.
2430　King Hrethel kept me and took care of me,
was openhanded, behaved like a kinsman.
While I was his ward, he treated me no worse
as a wean[2] about the place than one of his own boys,
Herebeald and Haethcyn, or my own Hygelac.
2435　For the eldest, Herebeald, an unexpected
deathbed was laid out, through a brother's doing,
when Haethcyn bent his horn-tipped bow
and loosed the arrow that destroyed his life.
He shot wide and buried a shaft
2440　in the flesh and blood of his own brother.
That offense was beyond redress, a wrongfooting
of the heart's affections; for who could avenge
the prince's life or pay his death-price?
It was like the misery felt by an old man
2445　who has lived to see his son's body
swing on the gallows. He begins to keen
and weep for his boy, watching the raven
gloat where he hangs: he can be of no help.
The wisdom of age is worthless to him.
2450　Morning after morning, he wakes to remember
that his child is gone; he has no interest
in living on until another heir
is born in the hall, now that his first-born
has entered death's dominion forever.
2455　He gazes sorrowfully at his son's dwelling,
the banquet hall bereft of all delight,
the windswept hearthstone; the horsemen are sleeping,
the warriors under ground; what was is no more.
No tunes from the harp, no cheer raised in the yard.
2460　Alone with his longing, he lies down on his bed
and sings a lament; everything seems too large,
the steadings and the fields.
　　　　　　　　Such was the feeling

---

2. A young child [Northern Ireland; Translator's note].

of loss endured by the lord of the Geats
after Herebeald's death. He was helplessly placed
2465   to set to rights the wrong committed,
could not punish the killer in accordance with the law
of the blood-feud, although he felt no love for him.
Heartsore, wearied, he turned away
from life's joys, chose God's light
2470   and departed, leaving buildings and lands
to his sons, as a man of substance will.
        "Then over the wide sea Swedes and Geats
battled and feuded and fought without quarter.
Hostilities broke out when Hrethel died.[3]
2475   Ongentheow's sons were unrelenting,
refusing to make peace, campaigning violently
from coast to coast, constantly setting up
terrible ambushes around Hreosnahill.
My own kith and kin avenged
2480   these evil events, as everybody knows,
but the price was high: one of them paid
with his life. Haethcyn, lord of the Geats,
met his fate there and fell in the battle.
Then, as I have heard, Hygelac's sword
2485   was raised in the morning against Ongentheow,
his brother's killer. When Eofor cleft
the old Swede's helmet, halved it open,
he fell, death-pale: his feud-calloused hand
could not stave off the fatal stroke.
2490   "The treasures that Hygelac lavished on me
I paid for when I fought, as fortune allowed me,
with my glittering sword. He gave me land
and the security land brings, so he had no call
to go looking for some lesser champion,
2495   some mercenary from among the Gifthas
or the Spear-Danes or the men of Sweden.
I marched ahead of him, always there
at the front of the line; and I shall fight like that
for as long as I live, as long as this sword
2500   shall last, which has stood me in good stead
late and soon, ever since I killed
Dayraven the Frank in front of the two armies.
He brought back no looted breastplate
to the Frisian king but fell in battle,
2505   their standard-bearer, highborn and brave.
No sword blade sent him to his death:
my bare hands stilled his heartbeats
and wrecked the bone-house. Now blade and hand,
sword and sword-stroke, will assay the hoard."

3. See p. 74, n. 6, Phases 1 and 2.

[BEOWULF ATTACKS THE DRAGON]

2510   Beowulf spoke, made a formal boast
for the last time: "I risked my life
often when I was young. Now I am old,
but as king of the people I shall pursue this fight
for the glory of winning, if the evil one will only
2515 abandon his earth-fort and face me in the open."
    Then he addressed each dear companion
one final time, those fighters in their helmets,
resolute and highborn: "I would rather not
use a weapon if I knew another way
2520 to grapple with the dragon and make good my boast
as I did against Grendel in days gone by.
But I shall be meeting molten venom
in the fire he breathes, so I go forth
in mail-shirt and shield. I won't shift a foot
2525 when I meet the cave-guard: what occurs on the wall
between the two of us will turn out as fate,
overseer of men, decides. I am resolved.
I scorn further words against this sky-borne foe.
    "Men-at-arms, remain here on the barrow,
2530 safe in your armor, to see which one of us
is better in the end at bearing wounds
in a deadly fray. This fight is not yours,
nor is it up to any man except me
to measure his strength against the monster
2535 or to prove his worth. I shall win the gold
by my courage, or else mortal combat,
doom of battle, will bear your lord away."
    Then he drew himself up beside his shield.
The fabled warrior in his war-shirt and helmet
2540 trusted in his own strength entirely
and went under the crag. No coward path.
    Hard by the rock-face that hale veteran,
a good man who had gone repeatedly
into combat and danger and come through,
2545 saw a stone arch and a gushing stream
that burst from the barrow, blazing and wafting
a deadly heat. It would be hard to survive
unscathed near the hoard, to hold firm
against the dragon in those flaming depths.
2550 Then he gave a shout. The lord of the Geats
unburdened his breast and broke out
in a storm of anger. Under gray stone
his voice challenged and resounded clearly.
Hate was ignited. The hoard-guard recognized
2555 a human voice, the time was over
for peace and parleying. Pouring forth
in a hot battle-fume, the breath of the monster
burst from the rock. There was a rumble under ground.
Down there in the barrow, Beowulf the warrior

2560   lifted his shield: the outlandish thing
       writhed and convulsed and viciously
       turned on the king, whose keen-edged sword,
       an heirloom inherited by ancient right,
       was already in his hand. Roused to a fury,
2565   each antagonist struck terror in the other.
       Unyielding, the lord of his people loomed
       by his tall shield, sure of his ground,
       while the serpent looped and unleashed itself.
       Swaddled in flames, it came gliding and flexing
2570   and racing toward its fate. Yet his shield defended
       the renowned leader's life and limb
       for a shorter time than he meant it to:
       that final day was the first time
       when Beowulf fought and fate denied him
2575   glory in battle. So the king of the Geats
       raised his hand and struck hard
       at the enameled scales, but scarcely cut through:
       the blade flashed and slashed yet the blow
       was far less powerful than the hard-pressed king
2580   had need of at that moment. The mound-keeper
       went into a spasm and spouted deadly flames:
       when he felt the stroke, battle-fire
       billowed and spewed. Beowulf was foiled
       of a glorious victory. The glittering sword,
2585   infallible before that day,
       failed when he unsheathed it, as it never should have.
       For the son of Ecgtheow, it was no easy thing
       to have to give ground like that and go
       unwillingly to inhabit another home
2590   in a place beyond; so every man must yield
       the leasehold of his days.
                                    Before long
       the fierce contenders clashed again.
       The hoard-guard took heart, inhaled and swelled up
       and got a new wind; he who had once ruled
2595   was furled in fire and had to face the worst.
       No help or backing was to be had then
       from his highborn comrades; that hand-picked troop
       broke ranks and ran for their lives
       to the safety of the wood. But within one heart
2600   sorrow welled up: in a man of worth
       the claims of kinship cannot be denied.
         His name was Wiglaf, a son of Weohstan's,
       a well-regarded Shylfing warrior
       related to Aelfhere.[4] When he saw his lord
2605   tormented by the heat of his scalding helmet,
       he remembered the bountiful gifts bestowed on him,

4. Although Wiglaf is here said to be a Shylfing (i.e., a Swede), in line 2607 we are told his family are Waegmundings, a clan of the Geats, which is also Beowulf's family. It was possible for a family to owe allegiance to more than one nation and to shift sides as a result of feuds. Nothing is known of Aelfhere.

how well he lived among the Waegmundings,
the freehold he inherited from his father[5] before him.
He could not hold back: one hand brandished

2610 the yellow-timbered shield, the other drew his sword—
an ancient blade that was said to have belonged
to Eanmund, the son of Ohthere, the one
Weohstan had slain when he was an exile without friends.
He carried the arms to the victim's kinfolk,

2615 the burnished helmet, the webbed chain-mail
and that relic of the giants. But Onela returned
the weapons to him, rewarded Weohstan
with Eanmund's war-gear. He ignored the blood-feud,
the fact that Eanmund was his brother's son.[6]

2620 Weohstan kept that war-gear for a lifetime,
the sword and the mail-shirt, until it was the son's turn
to follow his father and perform his part.
Then, in old age, at the end of his days
among the Weather-Geats, he bequeathed to Wiglaf
innumerable weapons.

2625 And now the youth
was to enter the line of battle with his lord,
his first time to be tested as a fighter.
His spirit did not break and the ancestral blade
would keep its edge, as the dragon discovered

2630 as soon as they came together in the combat.
Sad at heart, addressing his companions,
Wiglaf spoke wise and fluent words:
"I remember that time when mead was flowing,
how we pledged loyalty to our lord in the hall,

2635 promised our ring-giver we would be worth our price,
make good the gift of the war-gear,
those swords and helmets, as and when
his need required it. He picked us out
from the army deliberately, honored us and judged us

2640 fit for this action, made me these lavish gifts—
and all because he considered us the best
of his arms-bearing thanes. And now, although
he wanted this challenge to be one he'd face
by himself alone—the shepherd of our land,

2645 a man unequaled in the quest for glory
and a name for daring—now the day has come
when this lord we serve needs sound men
to give him their support. Let us go to him,
help our leader through the hot flame

2650 and dread of the fire. As God is my witness,
I would rather my body were robed in the same
burning blaze as my gold-giver's body

5. I.e., Weohstan, who, as explained below, was the slayer of Onela's nephew Eanmund. Possibly, Weohstan joined the Geats under Beowulf after Eanmund's brother, with Beowulf's help, avenged Eanmund's death on Onela and became king of the Shylfings. See p. 74, n. 6, Phase 2.

6. An ironic comment: since Onela wanted to kill Eanmund, he rewarded Weohstan for killing his nephew instead of exacting compensation or revenge.

than go back home bearing arms.
That is unthinkable, unless we have first
2655   slain the foe and defended the life
of the prince of the Weather-Geats. I well know
the things he has done for us deserve better.
Should he alone be left exposed
to fall in battle? We must bond together,
2660   shield and helmet, mail-shirt and sword."
Then he waded the dangerous reek and went
under arms to his lord, saying only:
"Go on, dear Beowulf, do everything
you said you would when you were still young
2665   and vowed you would never let your name and fame
be dimmed while you lived. Your deeds are famous,
so stay resolute, my lord, defend your life now
with the whole of your strength. I shall stand by you."
    After those words, a wildness rose
2670   in the dragon again and drove it to attack,
heaving up fire, hunting for enemies,
the humans it loathed. Flames lapped the shield,
charred it to the boss, and the body armor
on the young warrior was useless to him.
2675   But Wiglaf did well under the wide rim
Beowulf shared with him once his own had shattered
in sparks and ashes.
            Inspired again
by the thought of glory, the war-king threw
his whole strength behind a sword stroke
2680   and connected with the skull. And Naegling snapped.
Beowulf's ancient iron-gray sword
let him down in the fight. It was never his fortune
to be helped in combat by the cutting edge
of weapons made of iron. When he wielded a sword,
2685   no matter how blooded and hard-edged the blade,
his hand was too strong, the stroke he dealt
(I have heard) would ruin it. He could reap no advantage.
    Then the bane of that people, the fire-breathing dragon,
was mad to attack for a third time.
2690   When a chance came, he caught the hero
in a rush of flame and clamped sharp fangs
into his neck. Beowulf's body
ran wet with his life-blood: it came welling out.
    Next thing, they say, the noble son of Weohstan
2695   saw the king in danger at his side
and displayed his inborn bravery and strength.
He left the head alone,[7] but his fighting hand
was burned when he came to his kinsman's aid.
He lunged at the enemy lower down
2700   so that his decorated sword sank into its belly
and the flames grew weaker.

---

7. I.e., he avoided the dragon's flame-breathing head.

Once again the king
gathered his strength and drew a stabbing knife
he carried on his belt, sharpened for battle.
He stuck it deep in the dragon's flank.
2705   Beowulf dealt it a deadly wound.
They had killed the enemy, courage quelled his life;
that pair of kinsmen, partners in nobility,
had destroyed the foe. So every man should act,
be at hand when needed; but now, for the king,
2710   this would be the last of his many labors
and triumphs in the world.
                    Then the wound
dealt by the ground-burner earlier began
to scald and swell; Beowulf discovered
deadly poison suppurating inside him,
2715   surges of nausea, and so, in his wisdom,
the prince realized his state and struggled
toward a seat on the rampart. He steadied his gaze
on those gigantic stones, saw how the earthwork
was braced with arches built over columns.
2720   And now that thane unequaled for goodness
with his own hands washed his lord's wounds,
swabbed the weary prince with water,
bathed him clean, unbuckled his helmet.
   Beowulf spoke: in spite of his wounds,
2725   mortal wounds, he still spoke
for he well knew his days in the world
had been lived out to the end—his allotted time
was drawing to a close, death was very near.
   "Now is the time when I would have wanted
2730   to bestow this armor on my own son,
had it been my fortune to have fathered an heir
and live on in his flesh. For fifty years
I ruled this nation. No king
of any neighboring clan would dare
2735   face me with troops, none had the power
to intimidate me. I took what came,
cared for and stood by things in my keeping,
never fomented quarrels, never
swore to a lie. All this consoles me,
2740   doomed as I am and sickening for death;
because of my right ways, the Ruler of mankind
need never blame me when the breath leaves my body
for murder of kinsmen. Go now quickly,
dearest Wiglaf, under the gray stone
2745   where the dragon is laid out, lost to his treasure;
hurry to feast your eyes on the hoard.
Away you go: I want to examine
that ancient gold, gaze my fill
on those garnered jewels; my going will be easier
2750   for having seen the treasure, a less troubled letting-go
of the life and lordship I have long maintained."

And so, I have heard, the son of Weohstan
quickly obeyed the command of his languishing
war-weary lord; he went in his chain-mail
2755　under the rock-piled roof of the barrow,
exulting in his triumph, and saw beyond the seat
a treasure-trove of astonishing richness,
wall-hangings that were a wonder to behold,
glittering gold spread across the ground,
2760　the old dawn-scorching serpent's den
packed with goblets and vessels from the past,
tarnished and corroding. Rusty helmets
all eaten away. Armbands everywhere,
artfully wrought. How easily treasure
2765　buried in the ground, gold hidden
however skillfully, can escape from any man!
　　And he saw too a standard, entirely of gold,
hanging high over the hoard,
a masterpiece of filigree; it glowed with light
2770　so he could make out the ground at his feet
and inspect the valuables. Of the dragon there was no
remaining sign: the sword had dispatched him.
Then, the story goes, a certain man
plundered the hoard in that immemorial howe,
2775　filled his arms with flagons and plates,
anything he wanted; and took the standard also,
most brilliant of banners.
　　　　　　　　　　　　　　Already the blade
of the old king's sharp killing-sword
had done its worst: the one who had for long
2780　minded the hoard, hovering over gold,
unleashing fire, surging forth
midnight after midnight, had been mown down.
　　Wiglaf went quickly, keen to get back,
excited by the treasure. Anxiety weighed
2785　on his brave heart—he was hoping he would find
the leader of the Geats alive where he had left him
helpless, earlier, on the open ground.
　　So he came to the place, carrying the treasure
and found his lord bleeding profusely,
2790　his life at an end; again he began
to swab his body. The beginnings of an utterance
broke out from the king's breast-cage.
The old lord gazed sadly at the gold.
　　"To the everlasting Lord of all,
2795　to the King of Glory, I give thanks
that I behold this treasure here in front of me,
that I have been allowed to leave my people
so well endowed on the day I die.
Now that I have bartered my last breath
2800　to own this fortune, it is up to you
to look after their needs. I can hold out no longer.
Order my troop to construct a barrow

on a headland on the coast, after my pyre has cooled.
It will loom on the horizon at Hronesness[8]
2805 and be a reminder among my people—
so that in coming times crews under sail
will call it Beowulf's Barrow, as they steer
ships across the wide and shrouded waters."
    Then the king in his great-heartedness unclasped
2810 the collar of gold from his neck and gave it
to the young thane, telling him to use
it and the war-shirt and gilded helmet well.
"You are the last of us, the only one left
of the Waegmundings. Fate swept us away,
2815 sent my whole brave highborn clan
to their final doom. Now I must follow them."
    That was the warrior's last word.
He had no more to confide. The furious heat
of the pyre would assail him. His soul fled from his breast
2820 to its destined place among the steadfast ones.

[BEOWULF'S FUNERAL]

    It was hard then on the young hero,
having to watch the one he held so dear
there on the ground, going through
his death agony. The dragon from underearth,
2825 his nightmarish destroyer, lay destroyed as well,
utterly without life. No longer would his snakefolds
ply themselves to safeguard hidden gold.
Hard-edged blades, hammered out
and keenly filed, had finished him
2830 so that the sky-roamer lay there rigid,
brought low beside the treasure-lodge.
    Never again would he glitter and glide
and show himself off in midnight air,
exulting in his riches: he fell to earth
2835 through the battle-strength in Beowulf's arm.
There were few, indeed, as far as I have heard,
big and brave as they may have been,
few who would have held out if they had had to face
the outpourings of that poison-breather
2840 or gone foraging on the ring-hall floor
and found the deep barrow-dweller
on guard and awake.
                        The treasure had been won,
bought and paid for by Beowulf's death.
Both had reached the end of the road
through the life they had been lent.
2845   Before long
the battle-dodgers abandoned the wood,
the ones who had let down their lord earlier,
the tail-turners, ten of them together.

8. A headland by the sea. The name means "Whalesness."

When he needed them most, they had made off.
2850 Now they were ashamed and came behind shields,
in their battle-outfits, to where the old man lay.
They watched Wiglaf, sitting worn out,
a comrade shoulder to shoulder with his lord,
trying in vain to bring him round with water.
2855 Much as he wanted to, there was no way
he could preserve his lord's life on earth
or alter in the least the Almighty's will.
What God judged right would rule what happened
to every man, as it does to this day.
2860   Then a stern rebuke was bound to come
from the young warrior to the ones who had been cowards.
Wiglaf, son of Weohstan, spoke
disdainfully and in disappointment:
"Anyone ready to admit the truth
2865 will surely realize that the lord of men
who showered you with gifts and gave you the armor
you are standing in—when he would distribute
helmets and mail-shirts to men on the mead-benches,
a prince treating his thanes in hall
2870 to the best he could find, far or near—
was throwing weapons uselessly away.
It would be a sad waste when the war broke out.
Beowulf had little cause to brag
about his armed guard; yet God who ordains
2875 who wins or loses allowed him to strike
with his own blade when bravery was needed.
There was little I could do to protect his life
in the heat of the fray, but I found new strength
welling up when I went to help him.
2880 Then my sword connected and the deadly assaults
of our foe grew weaker, the fire coursed
less strongly from his head. But when the worst happened
too few rallied around the prince.
    "So it is good-bye now to all you know and love
2885 on your home ground, the open-handedness,
the giving of war-swords. Every one of you
with freeholds of land, our whole nation,
will be dispossessed, once princes from beyond
get tidings of how you turned and fled
2890 and disgraced yourselves. A warrior will sooner
die than live a life of shame."
    Then he ordered the outcome of the fight to be reported
to those camped on the ridge, that crowd of retainers
who had sat all morning, sad at heart,
2895 shield-bearers wondering about
the man they loved: would this day be his last
or would he return? He told the truth
and did not balk, the rider who bore
news to the cliff-top. He addressed them all:
2900 "Now the people's pride and love,

the lord of the Geats, is laid on his deathbed,
brought down by the dragon's attack.
Beside him lies the bane of his life,
dead from knife-wounds. There was no way
2905 Beowulf could manage to get the better
of the monster with his sword. Wiglaf sits
at Beowulf's side, the son of Weohstan,
the living warrior watching by the dead,
keeping weary vigil, holding a wake
for the loved and the loathed.
2910   Now war is looming
over our nation, soon it will be known
to Franks and Frisians, far and wide,
that the king is gone. Hostility has been great
among the Franks since Hygelac sailed forth
2915 at the head of a war-fleet into Friesland:
there the Hetware harried and attacked
and overwhelmed him with great odds.
The leader in his war-gear was laid low,
fell among followers: that lord did not favor
2920 his company with spoils. The Merovingian king
has been an enemy to us ever since.
     "Nor do I expect peace or pact-keeping
of any sort from the Swedes. Remember:
at Ravenswood,[9] Ongentheow
2925 slaughtered Haethcyn, Hrethel's son,
when the Geat people in their arrogance
first attacked the fierce Shylfings.
The return blow was quickly struck
by Ohthere's father.[1] Old and terrible,
2930 he felled the sea-king and saved his own
aged wife, the mother of Onela
and of Ohthere, bereft of her gold rings.
Then he kept hard on the heels of the foe
and drove them, leaderless, lucky to get away
2935 in a desperate rout into Ravenswood.
His army surrounded the weary remnant
where they nursed their wounds; all through the night
he howled threats at those huddled survivors,
promised to axe their bodies open
2940 when dawn broke, dangle them from gallows
to feed the birds. But at first light
when their spirits were lowest, relief arrived.
They heard the sound of Hygelac's horn,
his trumpet calling as he came to find them,
2945 the hero in pursuit, at hand with troops.
     "The bloody swathe that Swedes and Geats
cut through each other was everywhere.
No one could miss their murderous feuding.

---

9. The messenger describes in greater detail the
Battle of Ravenswood. See the outline of the Swedish wars on p. 74, n. 6.
1. I.e., Ongentheow.

Then the old man made his move,
2950 pulled back, barred his people in:
Ongentheow withdrew to higher ground.
Hygelac's pride and prowess as a fighter
were known to the earl; he had no confidence
that he could hold out against that horde of seamen,
2955 defend his wife and the ones he loved
from the shock of the attack. He retreated for shelter
behind the earthwall. Then Hygelac swooped
on the Swedes at bay, his banners swarmed
into their refuge, his Geat forces
2960 drove forward to destroy the camp.
There in his gray hairs, Ongentheow
was cornered, ringed around with swords.
And it came to pass that the king's fate
was in Eofor's hands,[2] and in his alone.
2965 Wulf, son of Wonred, went for him in anger,
split him open so that blood came spurting
from under his hair. The old hero
still did not flinch, but parried fast,
hit back with a harder stroke:
2970 the king turned and took him on.
Then Wonred's son, the brave Wulf,
could land no blow against the aged lord.
Ongentheow divided his helmet
so that he buckled and bowed his bloodied head
2975 and dropped to the ground. But his doom held off.
Though he was cut deep, he recovered again.
   "With his brother down, the undaunted Eofor,
Hygelac's thane, hefted his sword
and smashed murderously at the massive helmet
2980 past the lifted shield. And the king collapsed,
the shepherd of people was sheared of life.
Many then hurried to help Wulf,
bandaged and lifted him, now that they were left
masters of the blood-soaked battle-ground.
2985 One warrior stripped the other,
looted Ongenteow's iron mail-coat,
his hard sword-hilt, his helmet too,
and carried the graith[3] to King Hygelac;
he accepted the prize, promised fairly
2990 that reward would come, and kept his word.
For their bravery in action, when they arrived home,
Eofor and Wulf were overloaded
by Hrethel's son, Hygelac the Geat,
with gifts of land and linked rings
2995 that were worth a fortune. They had won glory,
so there was no gainsaying his generosity.

---

2. I.e., he was at Eofor's mercy. Eofor's slaying of
Ongetheow was described in lines 2486–89, where
no mention is made of his brother Wulf's part in
the battle. They are the sons of Wonred. *Eofor*

means boar, and *Wulf* is the Old English spelling
of wolf.
3. Possessions, apparel.

And he gave Eofor his only daughter
to bide at home with him, an honor and a bond.
    "So this bad blood between us and the Swedes,
3000 this vicious feud, I am convinced,
is bound to revive; they will cross our borders
and attack in force when they find out
that Beowulf is dead. In days gone by
when our warriors fell and we were undefended,
3005 he kept our coffers and our kingdom safe.
He worked for the people, but as well as that
he behaved like a hero.
                  We must hurry now
to take a last look at the king
and launch him, lord and lavisher of rings,
3010 on the funeral road. His royal pyre
will melt no small amount of gold:
heaped there in a hoard, it was bought at heavy cost,
and that pile of rings he paid for at the end
with his own life will go up with the flame,
3015 be furled in fire: treasure no follower
will wear in his memory, nor lovely woman
link and attach as a torque around her neck—
but often, repeatedly, in the path of exile
they shall walk bereft, bowed under woe,
3020 now that their leader's laugh is silenced,
high spirits quenched. Many a spear
dawn-cold to the touch will be taken down
and waved on high; the swept harp
won't waken warriors, but the raven winging
3025 darkly over the doomed will have news,
tidings for the eagle of how he hoked and ate,
how the wolf and he made short work of the dead."[4]
    Such was the drift of the dire report
that gallant man delivered. He got little wrong
in what he told and predicted.
3030   The whole troop
rose in tears, then took their way
to the uncanny scene under Earnaness.[5]
There, on the sand, where his soul had left him,
they found him at rest, their ring-giver
3035 from days gone by. The great man
had breathed his last. Beowulf the king
had indeed met with a marvelous death.
    But what they saw first was far stranger:
the serpent on the ground, gruesome and vile,
3040 lying facing him. The fire-dragon
was scaresomely burned, scorched all colors.
From head to tail, his entire length

---

4. The raven, eagle, and wolf—the scavengers
who will feed on the slain—are "the beasts of battle," a common motif in Germanic war poetry.
"Hoked": rooted about [Northern Ireland,
Translator's note].
5. The site of Beowulf's fight with the dragon. The
name means "Eaglesness."

was fifty feet. He had shimmered forth
on the night air once, then winged back
3045 down to his den; but death owned him now,
he would never enter his earth-gallery again.
Beside him stood pitchers and piled-up dishes,
silent flagons, precious swords
eaten through with rust, ranged as they had been
3050 while they waited their thousand winters under ground.
That huge cache, gold inherited
from an ancient race, was under a spell—
which meant no one was ever permitted
to enter the ring-hall unless God Himself,
3055 mankind's Keeper, True King of Triumphs,
allowed some person pleasing to Him—
and in His eyes worthy—to open the hoard.
    What came about brought to nothing
the hopes of the one who had wrongly hidden
3060 riches under the rock-face. First the dragon slew
that man among men, who in turn made fierce amends
and settled the feud. Famous for his deeds
a warrior may be, but it remains a mystery
where his life will end, when he may no longer
3065 dwell in the mead-hall among his own.
So it was with Beowulf, when he faced the cruelty
and cunning of the mound-guard. He himself was ignorant
of how his departure from the world would happen.
The highborn chiefs who had buried the treasure
3070 declared it until doomsday so accursed
that whoever robbed it would be guilty of wrong
and grimly punished for their transgression,
hasped in hell-bonds in heathen shrines.
Yet Beowulf's gaze at the gold treasure
3075 when he first saw it had not been selfish.
    Wiglaf, son of Weohstan, spoke:
"Often when one man follows his own will
many are hurt. This happened to us.
Nothing we advised could ever convince
3080 the prince we loved, our land's guardian,
not to vex the custodian of the gold,
let him lie where he was long accustomed,
lurk there under earth until the end of the world.
He held to his high destiny. The hoard is laid bare,
3085 but at a grave cost; it was too cruel a fate
that forced the king to that encounter.
I have been inside and seen everything
amassed in the vault. I managed to enter
although no great welcome awaited me
3090 under the earthwall. I quickly gathered up
a huge pile of the priceless treasures
handpicked from the hoard and carried them here
where the king could see them. He was still himself,
alive, aware, and in spite of his weakness

3095   he had many requests. He wanted me to greet you
and order the building of a barrow that would crown
the site of his pyre, serve as his memorial,
in a commanding position, since of all men
to have lived and thrived and lorded it on earth
3100   his worth and due as a warrior were the greatest.
Now let us again go quickly
and feast our eyes on that amazing fortune
heaped under the wall. I will show the way
and take you close to those coffers packed with rings
3105   and bars of gold. Let a bier be made
and got ready quickly when we come out
and then let us bring the body of our lord,
the man we loved, to where he will lodge
for a long time in the care of the Almighty."
3110   Then Weohstan's son, stalwart to the end,
had orders given to owners of dwellings,
many people of importance in the land,
to fetch wood from far and wide
for the good man's pyre:
                "Now shall flame consume
3115   our leader in battle, the blaze darken
round him who stood his ground in the steel-hail,
when the arrow-storm shot from bowstrings
pelted the shield-wall. The shaft hit home.
Feather-fledged, it finned the barb in flight."
3120   Next the wise son of Weohstan
called from among the king's thanes
a group of seven: he selected the best
and entered with them, the eighth of their number,
under the God-cursed roof; one raised
3125   a lighted torch and led the way.
No lots were cast for who should loot the hoard
for it was obvious to them that every bit of it
lay unprotected within the vault,
there for the taking. It was no trouble
3130   to hurry to work and haul out
the priceless store. They pitched the dragon
over the cliff-top, let tide's flow
and backwash take the treasure-minder.
Then coiled gold was loaded on a cart
3135   in great abundance, and the gray-haired leader,
the prince on his bier, borne to Hronesness.
    The Geat people built a pyre for Beowulf,
stacked and decked it until it stood foursquare,
hung with helmets, heavy war-shields
3140   and shining armor, just as he had ordered.
Then his warriors laid him in the middle of it,
mourning a lord far-famed and beloved.
On a height they kindled the hugest of all
funeral fires; fumes of woodsmoke
3145   billowed darkly up, the blaze roared

and drowned out their weeping, wind died down
and flames wrought havoc in the hot bone-house,
burning it to the core. They were disconsolate
and wailed aloud for their lord's decease.
3150 A Geat woman too sang out in grief;
with hair bound up, she unburdened herself
of her worst fears, a wild litany
of nightmare and lament: her nation invaded,
enemies on the rampage, bodies in piles,
3155 slavery and abasement. Heaven swallowed the smoke.
  Then the Geat people began to construct
a mound on a headland, high and imposing,
a marker that sailors could see from far away,
and in ten days they had done the work.
3160 It was their hero's memorial; what remained from the fire
they housed inside it, behind a wall
as worthy of him as their workmanship could make it.
And they buried torques in the barrow, and jewels
and a trove of such things as trespassing men
3165 had once dared to drag from the hoard.
They let the ground keep that ancestral treasure,
gold under gravel, gone to earth,
as useless to men now as it ever was.
Then twelve warriors rode around the tomb,
3170 chieftains' sons, champions in battle,
all of them distraught, chanting in dirges,
mourning his loss as a man and a king.
They extolled his heroic nature and exploits
and gave thanks for his greatness; which was the proper thing,
3175 for a man should praise a prince whom he holds dear
and cherish his memory when that moment comes
when he has to be convoyed from his bodily home.
So the Geat people, his hearth-companions,
sorrowed for the lord who had been laid low.
3180 They said that of all the kings upon earth
he was the man most gracious and fair-minded,
kindest to his people and keenest to win fame.

Anglo-Norman England

LEGENDARY HISTORIES OF BRITAIN

During the twelfth century, three authors, who wrote in Latin, Anglo-Norman
French, and Middle English, respectively, created a mostly legendary history of Britain for their Norman overlords (see pp. 6–7). This "history" was set in the remote
past, beginning with a foundation myth—a heroic account of national origins—mod-

eled on Virgil's *Aeneid* and ending with the Anglo-Saxon conquest of the native island-ers, the Britons, in the fifth and sixth centuries. The chief architect of the history is Geoffrey of Monmouth, who was writing his *History of the Kings of Britain* in Latin prose ca. 1136–38. His work was freely translated into French verse by Wace in 1155, and Wace in turn was translated into English alliterative poetry by Layamon.

Geoffrey of Monmouth and Wace wrote their histories of Britain primarily for an audience of noblemen and prelates who were descendants of the Norman conquerors of the Anglo-Saxons. Geoffrey wrote several dedications of his *History*, first to sup-porters of Matilda, the heiress presumptive of Henry I, and, when the Crown went instead to Stephen of Blois, to the new king's allies and to Stephen himself. Layamon tells us that Wace wrote his French version for Eleanor of Aquitaine, queen of Ste-phen's successor, Henry II. The prestige and power of ancient Rome still dominated the historical and political imagination of the feudal aristocracy, and the legendary history of the ancient kings of the Britons, especially of King Arthur, who had defeated Rome itself, served to flatter the self-image and ambitions of the Anglo-Norman bar-ons. Perhaps the destruction of Arthur's kingdom also provided a timely object lesson of the disastrous consequences of civil wars such as those over the English succession in which these lords were engaged.

The selections from Geoffrey of Monmouth and Wace are translated by Alfred David. The Layamon selections are translated by Rosamund Allen.

GEOFFREY OF MONMOUTH

The author of the *History of the Kings of Britain* was a churchman, probably of Welsh or Breton ancestry, who spent much of his life at Oxford. One of his motives in writing the work was undoubtedly to obtain advancement in the church. In the dedications of the *History*, Geoffrey claims that it is merely a translation into Latin of "a very old book in the British language [i.e., Welsh]," which had been loaned to him by his friend Walter, archdeacon of Oxford, but scholars have discounted this story as another one of Geoffrey's many fictions.

Geoffrey began his history with a British foundation myth modeled upon Virgil's *Aeneid*. Out of legends that Rome had been founded by refugees from the fall of Troy, the poet Virgil had created his epic poem the *Aeneid* for Augustus Caesar. Aeneas, carrying his father upon his back, had escaped from the ruins of Troy and, fulfilling prophecies, became the founding father of a new Troy in Italy. The Brit-ons had developed an analogous foundation myth in which a great-grandson of Aeneas called Brutus had led another band of Trojan exiles to establish another Troy, which was named Britain after him. Geoffrey drew upon earlier Latin chron-icles and Welsh oral tradition, but he himself provided his history with a chronol-ogy, a genealogy, a large cast of both historical and legendary characters (among many other stories, he is the first to tell of King Lear and his daughters), and a cyclical sense of the rise and fall of empires. The longest and most original part of the work (over one-fifth of the *History*) is devoted to the birth and reign of King Arthur. In the first part of Arthur's reign, he defeats and drives out the pagan Anglo-Saxon invaders. At the end of his reign the Saxons return at the invitation of the traitor Mordred and, though defeated again by Arthur in his last battle, they ultimately triumph over his successors.

The historicity of Geoffrey's book, although questioned by some of Geoffrey's con-temporary historians, was widely accepted and not fully discredited until the seven-teenth century. In the course of time Arthur was adopted as a national and cultural hero by the English against whose ancestors he had fought, and his court became the international ideal of a splendid chivalric order in the past of which contemporary knighthood was only a faint imitation. Geoffrey of Monmouth himself already declares that in Arthur's time, "Womenfolk became chaste and more virtuous and for their love the knights were ever more daring."

In the following selections, Geoffrey relates the British foundation myth, which he historicizes, amplifies, and fleshes out with details that he regards as classical.

From The History of the Kings of Britain

[THE STORY OF BRUTUS AND DIANA'S PROPHECY]

After the Trojan War, Aeneas with his son Ascanius fled from the destruction of the city and sailed to Italy. Although King Latinus would have received him there with honor, Turnus, the king of the Rutuli, was envious and made war on him. In their rivalry Aeneas prevailed and, having slain Turnus, obtained the kingdom of Italy and Latinus's daughter, Lavinia.

At the end of Aeneas's days, Ascanius was elevated to royal power and founded the city of Alba on the banks of the Tiber. He fathered a son whose name was Silvius. The latter had a secret love affair with a niece of Lavinia's whom he married and got with child. When his father Ascanius learned about this he ordered his wise men to find out the sex of the child that the girl had conceived. When the wise men had made sure of the truth, they said that she would bear a son who would be the death of his father and mother. After travelling through many lands as an exile, he would nevertheless attain to the highest honor. Their prophecies did not turn out to be mistaken. For when her time had come, the woman bore a boy and died in childbirth. The boy was handed over to the midwife and named Brutus. At last, after fifteen years had gone by, the boy went hunting with his father and killed him with a misdirected bowshot. For as the servants were driving some stags into their path, Brutus, believing that he was aiming at them, hit his father below the breast. On account of this death, his relatives, outraged that he should have done such a deed, drove him from Italy.* * *

[The exiled Brutus travels to Greece, where he discovers descendants of Trojan prisoners of war living in slavery. He organizes a successful rebellion against their Greek masters and, like Aeneas before him, leads them on a quest for a new homeland.]

Driven by favorable winds, the Trojans sailed for two days and one night until they made land on an island called Leogetia, which was uninhabited because long ago it had been devastated by pirate raids. So Brutus sent three hundred armed men to explore the island and see whether anything was living on it. They found no one but they killed several kinds of wild animals that they came across in the woods and thickets.

They came to a deserted city where they found a temple of Diana in which a statue of the goddess rendered oracles if someone should consult it. At last they returned to their ships, loaded down with game, and told their comrades about the land and the city. They suggested to their chief that he go to the temple and, after making propitiatory sacrifices, inquire of the goddess what land might afford them a permanent home. When everyone agreed, Brutus with the soothsayer Gero and twelve elders set out for the temple, taking along everything necessary for the sacrifice. When they got there, they bound their brows with headbands and, in preparation of the most ancient rite, they erected three hearths to three gods, namely to Jupiter, Mercury, and Diana. They poured out libations to each one in turn. Before the altar of the goddess, Brutus himself, holding a sacrificial vessel filled with wine and the blood of a white doe in his right hand, raised his face to her statue and broke the silence with these words:[1]

> Mighty goddess of woodlands, terror of the wild boar,
> Thou who art free to traverse the ethereal heavens
> And the mansions of hell, disclose my rights on this earth
> And say what lands it is your wish for us to inhabit,
> What dwelling-place where I shall worship you all my life,
> Where I shall dedicate temples to you with virgin choirs.

After he had spoken this prayer nine times, he walked four times around the altar and poured out the wine he was holding upon the hearth. Then he spread out the hide of the doe before the altar and lay down on it. He tried to doze off and finally fell asleep. It was now the third hour of the night when sweetest slumber overcomes mortals. Then it seemed to him that the goddess was standing before him and speaking to him like this:

> Brutus, where the sun sets beyond the kingdoms of Gaul
> Is an isle in the ocean, closed all around by the sea.
> Once on a time giants lived on that isle in the ocean,
> But now it stands empty and fit to receive your people.
> Seek it out, for it shall be your homeland forever;
> It shall be a second Troy for your descendants.
> There kings shall be born of your seed and to them
> All nations of the round earth shall be subject.

When the vision vanished, Brutus remained in doubt whether what he had seen was only a phantom or whether the actual voice of the goddess had foretold the homeland to which he was to travel. Finally he called his comrades and told them point by point what had happened to him while he slept. Waves of great joy swept over them, and they urged that they return to the ships and, while the wind blew behind them, head with swiftest sail toward the ocean to seek out what the goddess had promised. Without delay they rejoined their comrades and set out on the high seas.

---

1. Brutus's prayer and Diana's prophecy are written as Latin poetry and employ a more formal diction than the prose narrative. The entire episode is meant to show off Geoffrey's classical learning and familiarity with pagan ritual.

WACE

Wace (ca. 1110–ca. 1180) was a Norman cleric, born on the island of Jersey in the English Channel, which was then part of the dukedom of Normandy. Although educated for the church, he seems to have served the laity, perhaps in a secretarial function. All of his extant works, which include saints' lives, *Le Roman de Brut*, and *Le Roman de Rou*, were written in French verse for a lay audience that would have included women like Eleanor of Aquitaine, to whom he dedicated the *Brut*, and Marie de France, who drew on that work in her lays. *Roman* in these titles refers to the fact that they are, respectively, chronicles in French verse about the dynasties of Brutus (first of the kings of Britain) and Rollo (first of the dukes of Normandy).

The *Roman de Brut* is a very free translation in eight-syllable couplets of Geoffrey of Monmouth's Latin prose *History of the Kings of Britain*. Wace has cut some details and added a good deal, including the first mention of the Round Table. He is far more interested than Geoffrey in creating an atmosphere of courtliness—in the way his characters dress, think, speak, and behave. The following selection covers a challenge delivered to Arthur by the Roman emperor Lucius and Arthur's response. This climactic sequence follows an elaborate coronation scene attended by a large gathering of kings and dukes from Britain and overseas who owe allegiance to Arthur and whose lands comprise what might be called the Arthurian Empire. At the feast following his coronation, Arthur's authority is challenged by ambassadors who present an insulting letter from Lucius. Arthur's reply is a masterpiece of feudal rhetoric that would have been admired by Wace's audience.

From Le Roman de Brut

[THE ROMAN CHALLENGE]

Arthur was seated on a dais surrounded by counts and kings when a dozen white-haired, very well-dressed men came into the hall in pairs, one holding the other's hand. Each held an olive branch. They crossed the hall very slowly in an orderly and solemn procession, approached the king and hailed him. They said they had come from Rome as messengers. They unfolded a letter, which one of them gave to Arthur on behalf of the Roman emperor. Listen to what it said:

"Lucius who holds Rome in his domain and is sovereign lord of the Romans, proclaims to King Arthur, his enemy, what he has deserved. I am disdainful in amazement and am amazed with disdain at the inordinate and insane pride with which you have set your sights on Rome. With disdain and amazement I ask myself at whose prompting and from what quarters you have undertaken to pick a quarrel with Rome as long as a single Roman remains alive. You have acted with great recklessness in attacking us who have the right to rule the world and hold supremacy over it. You still don't know, but we shall teach you; you are blind, but we shall make you see what a great thing it is to anger Rome, which has the power to rule over everything. You have presumed beyond your place and crossed the bounds of your authority! Have you any idea who you are and where you come from—you who are taking and holding back the tribute that belongs to us? You are taking our tribute and our lands: why do you hold them, why don't you turn them over, why do you keep them, what right do you have to them? If you keep them any longer, you will be acting most recklessly. And if you are capable of holding them without our forcing you to give them up, you might as well say—an unprecedented miracle!—that the lion flees from the lamb, the wolf from the goat, the greyhound from the hare. But that could never happen, for Nature would not suffer it. Julius Caesar, our ancestor—but maybe you have little respect for him—conquered Britain and imposed a tribute that our people have collected since that time. And we have also been receiving tribute for a long time from the other islands surrounding you. And you have foolishly presumed to take tribute from both of them. Already you were guilty of senseless behavior, but you have committed an even greater insult that touches us still more closely than the losses we have sustained: you killed our vassal Frollo[1] and illegally occupied France. Therefore, since you are not afraid of Rome nor its great power, the Senate summons and orders you—for the summons is an order—to come before it in mid-August, ready, at whatever cost, to make full restitution of what you have taken from them. And thus you will give satisfaction for the wrongs of which we accuse you. But if you delay in any fashion to do what I command you, I will cross the Alps with an army and will deprive you of Britain and France. But I can't imagine that you will await my coming or will defend France against me. I don't think you will dare to face me on this side of the Channel. And even if you stay over there, you will never await my coming. You won't know a place to hide where I won't flush you out. I'll lead you to Rome in chains and hand you over to the Senate."

At these words there was a great uproar, and all were greatly enraged. You could have heard the Britons shouting loudly, calling God as witness and swearing by his name that they were going to punish the messengers. They would have showered them with abuse and insults, but the king rose to his feet and called out to them, "Silence! Silence! Don't lay a hand on these men. They are messengers; they have a master, they are bringing his message; they can say whatever they like. No one shall do them the slightest harm."

When the noise quieted down and the retainers recovered their composure, the king ordered his dukes and counts and his personal advisers to accompany him to a stone tower called the Giant Tower. There he wanted to seek advice on what to reply to the messengers. Side by side the barons and counts were already mounting the stairs, when Cador, the duke of Cornwall, with a smile spoke to the king, who was in front of him, as follows: "I've been afraid," he said, "and have often thought that leisure and peace might spoil the Britons, for leisure is conducive to bad habits and causes many a man to become lazy. Leisure diminishes prowess, leisure promotes lechery, leisure kindles clandestine love affairs. Through prolonged repose and leisure youth gets preoccupied with entertainment and pleasure and backgammon and other games of diversion. By staying put and resting for a long time, we could lose our reputation. Well, we've been asleep, but God has given us a little wake-up call—let us thank him for encouraging the Romans to challenge our country and the others we have conquered. Should the Romans find it in themselves to carry out what they say in that letter, the Britons will still retain their reputation for valor and strength. I never like peace for long, nor shall I love a peace that lasts a long time."

"My lord," said Gawain, "in faith, you're getting upset over nothing. Peace after war is a good thing. The land is better and more beautiful on account of it. It's very good to amuse oneself and to make love. It's for love and for their ladies that knights perform chivalrous deeds."

While bantering in this way, they entered the tower and took their seats. When Arthur saw them sitting down and waiting in silence with full attention, he paused for a moment in thought, then raised his head and spoke:

"Barons," he said, "you who are here, my companions and friends, you have stood by me in good times and bad; you have supported me when I had

---

1. Roman governor of France.

to go to war; you have taken my part whether I won or lost; you have been partners in my loss, and in my gain when I conquered. Thanks to you and your help, I have won many a victory. I have led you through many dangers by land and by sea, in places near and far. I have found you loyal in action and in counsel. I have tested your mettle many times and always found it good. Thanks to you the neighboring countries are subject to me. You have heard the Romans' order, the tenor of the letter, and the overbearingness and arrogance of their demands. They have provoked and threatened us enough, but if God protects us, we shall do away with the Romans. They are rich and have great power, and now we must carefully consider what we can properly and reasonably say and do. Trouble is dealt with better when a strategy has been worked out in advance. If someone sees the arrow in flight, he must get out of the way or shield himself. That is how we must proceed. The Romans want to shoot at us, and we must get ready so that they cannot wound us. They demand tribute from Britain and must have it, so they tell us; they demand the same from the other islands and from France.

"But first I shall reply how matters stand with regard to Britain. They claim that Caesar conquered it; Caesar was a powerful man and carried out his will by force. The Britons could not defend themselves against him, and he exacted tribute from them by force. But might is not right; it is force and superior power. A man does not possess by right what he has taken by force. Therefore, we are allowed to keep by right what they formerly took by force. They have held up to us the damages, losses, humiliations, the sufferings and fears that they inflicted on our ancestors. They boasted that they conquered them and extorted tribute and rents from them. We have all the more right to make them suffer; they have all the more restitution to make to us. We ought to hate those who hated our ancestors and to injure those who injured them. They remind us that they made them suffer, got tribute from them, and demand tribute from us. They want us to suffer the same shame and extortion as our ancestors. They once got tribute from Britain, and so they want to get it from us. By the same reason and with equal cause we can challenge the Romans and dispute our rights. Belinus, who was king of the Britons, and Brennus,[2] duke of the Burgundians, two brothers born in Britain, valiant and wise knights, marched on Rome, laid siege to the city, and took it by assault. They hanged twenty-four hostages in plain sight of their families. When Belinus returned from Rome, he entrusted the city to his brother.

"I won't dwell on Belinus and Brennus but will speak of Constantine. He was British by birth, the son of Helen; he held Rome in his own right. Maximian, king of Britain, conquered France and Germany, crossed the Alps and Lombardy and reigned over Rome. These were my ancestors by direct descent, and each one held Rome in his possession. Now you may hear and understand that we have just as much right to possess Rome as they do to possess Britain. The Romans had our tribute, and my ancestors had theirs.

2. Brennus was not a Briton but a Gaulish chieftain who sacked Rome in the 4th century. Belinus is fictional. Constantine I, who adopted Christianity as the official religion of the Roman Empire, was believed to be British. Maximian (Maximus) was a 5th-century Roman general serving in Britain who abandoned the island when his army proclaimed him emperor and usurped the imperium in civil wars that weakened Rome and left Britain at the mercy of attacks by the Picts, Scots, and Germanic tribes. Geoffrey of Monmouth's earlier accounts of these personages had conflated a tiny amount of fact with a great deal of fiction.

They claim Britain, and I claim Rome. This is the gist of my counsel: that they may have the land and tribute who can take it away from another. As for France and the other lands we have taken from them, they have no right to dispute them since they would not or could not defend them, or perhaps had no right to them because they held them in bondage through force and greed. So let he who can hold all. There is no need to look for any other kind of right. The emperor threatens us. God forbid that he should do us any harm. He says that he will take away our lands and lead me to Rome as a prisoner. He has small regard or fear of me. But, God willing, if he comes to this land, before he leaves again he'll have no stomach to make threats. He defies me, and I defy him: may he possess the lands who is able to take them!"

When King Arthur had spoken what he wanted to his barons, the others spoke in turn while the rest listened. Hoël, king of Brittany, spoke next: "Sire," he said, "in faith, you have spoken many just words; none could have said it better. Send after and mobilize your forces along with us who are here at court. Without delay pass over the sea, pass through Burgundy and France, pass the Alps, conquer Lombardy! Throw the emperor who is defying you into confusion and panic so that he will not have the chance to cause you harm. The Romans have begun a suit that will ruin them. God wants to exalt you: don't hold back and lose any time! Make yourself master of the empire, which is ready to surrender to you of its own will. Remember what is written in the Sibyl's prophecies.[3] Three Britons will be born in Britain who shall conquer Rome by might. Two have already lived and been sovereigns over Rome. The first was Belinus and the second, Constantine. You shall be the third to possess Rome and conquer it by force; in you the Sibyl's prophecy will be fulfilled. Why delay to seize that which God wants to bestow on you? Increase your glory and ours to which we aspire. We may say truly that we are not afraid of blows or wounds or death or hardship or prison so long as we strive for honor. As long as you are in danger, I will lead ten thousand armed knights in your host, and if that should not be enough, I shall mortgage all my lands and give you the gold and silver. I won't keep back a farthing so long as you have need of it!"

3. Reference to the Sibylline books containing prophecies of the Roman Sibyl of Cumae, but these no longer existed and could have been known only by reputation. This prophecy was probably invented by Geoffrey of Monmouth.

LAYAMON

Layamon, an English priest, adapted Wace's *Roman de Brut* into Middle English alliterative verse. His *Brut* (ca. 1190) runs to 16,095 lines, expanding on Wace and adding much new material.

After winning the continental campaign against Lucius, Arthur is forced to return to Britain upon learning that his nephew, Mordred, whom he had left behind as regent, has usurped Arthur's throne and queen. The following selection, a passage added by Layamon, presents Arthur's dream of Mordred's treachery.

Layamon employs a long alliterative line that harks back to Old English poetry, but the two halves of his line are often linked by rhyme as well as by alliteration. Layamon reveals his ties with Germanic literary tradition in other ways. In Arthur's nightmare, the king and Gawain are sitting astride the roof beam of a building like the mead hall Heorot in *Beowulf*—a symbol of the control a king wields over his house and kingdom. On the ground below, Mordred is chopping away at the foundations like the gigantic rodent in Norse mythology that is gnawing away at the roots of Yggdrasil, the great tree, which holds together earth, heaven, and hell.

From Brut

[ARTHUR'S DREAM]

Then came to pass what Merlin spoke of long before,
13965　That the walls of Rome would fall down before Arthur;
This had already happened there in relation to the emperor
Who had fallen in the fighting with fifty thousand men:
That's when Rome with her power was pushed to the ground.
　　And so Arthur really expected to possess all of Rome,
13970　And the most mighty of kings remained there in Burgundy;
　　Now there arrived at this time a bold man on horseback;
News he was bringing for Arthur the king
From Modred, his sister's son: to Arthur he was welcome,
For he thought that he was bringing very pleasant tidings.
13975　Arthur lay there all that long night, talking with the young knight,
Who simply did not like to tell him the truth of what had happened.
The next day, as dawn broke, the household started moving,
And then Arthur got up, and, stretching his arms,
He stood up, and sat down again, as if he felt very sick.
Then a good knight questioned him: "My Lord, how did you get on
13980　　last night?"
Arthur responded (his heart was very heavy):
"Tonight as I was sleeping, where I was lying in my chamber,
There came to me a dream which has made me most depressed:
I dreamed someone had lifted me right on top of some hall
13985　And I was sitting on the hall, astride, as if I was going riding;
All the lands which I possess, all of them I was surveying,
And Gawain sat in front of me, holding in his hands my sword.
Then Modred came marching there with a countless host of men,
Carrying in his hand a massive battle-axe.
13990　He started to hew, with horrible force,
And hacked down all the posts which were holding up the hall.
I saw Guinevere there as well, the woman I love best of all:
The whole roof of that enormous hall with her hands she was
　　pulling down;
The hall started tottering, and I tumbled to the ground,
13995　And broke my right arm, at which Modred said 'Take that!'
Down then fell the hall and Gawain fell as well,
Falling on the ground where both his arms were broken,
So with my left hand I clutched my beloved sword
And struck off Modred's head and it went rolling over the ground,
14000　And I sliced the queen in pieces with my beloved sword,

And after that I dropped her into a dingy pit.
And all my fine subjects set off in flight,
And what in Christendom became of them I had no idea,
Except that I was standing by myself in a vast plain,
14005 And then I started roaming all around across the moors;
There I could see griffins and really gruesome birds.
 "Then a golden lioness came gliding over the downs,
As really lovely a beast as any Our Lord has made.
The lioness ran up to me and put her jaws around my waist,
14010 And off she set, moving away towards the sea,
And I could see the waves, tossing in the sea,
And taking me with her, the lioness plunged into the water.
When we two were in the sea, the waves swept her away from me;
Then a fish came swimming by and ferried me ashore.
14015 Then I was all wet and weary, and I was sick with sorrow.
And upon waking, I started quaking,
And then I started to shudder as if burning up with fire,
And so all night I've been preoccupied with my disturbing dream,
For I know of a certainty this is the end of my felicity,
14020 And all the rest of my life I must suffer grief.
O alas that I do not have here my queen with me, my Guinevere!"
 Then the knight responded: "My Lord, you are mistaken;
Dreams should never be interpreted as harbingers of sorrow!
You are the most mighty prince who has rule in any land,
14025 And the most intelligent of all inhabitants on the earth.
If it should have happened—as may Our Lord not allow it—
That your sister's son, Lord Modred, your own queen might have
     wedded,
And all your royal domains might have annexed in his own name,
Those which you entrusted to him when you intended going to
     Rome,
14030 And if he should have done all this by his treacherous deeds,
Even then you might avenge yourself honorably with arms,
And once again possess your lands and rule over your people,
And destroy your enemies who wish you so much evil,
And slay them, every one alive, so that there is none who survives!"
14035 Then Arthur answered him, most excellent of all kings:
"For as long as is for ever, I have no fear whatever,
That Modred who is my relative, the man I love best,
Would betray all my trust, not for all of my realm,
Nor would Guinevere, my queen, weaken in her allegiance,
14040 She will not begin to, for any man in the world!"
Immediately after these words, the knight gave his answer:
"I am telling you the truth, dear king, for I am merely your
     underling:
Modred has done these things: he has adopted your queen,
And has placed in his own hands your lovely land;
14045 He is king and she is queen; they don't expect your return,
For they don't believe it will be the case that you'll ever come back
     from Rome.
I am your loyal liegeman, and I did see this treason,
And so I have come to you in person to tell you the truth.

Let my head be as pledge of what I have told you,
14050 The truth and no lie, about your beloved queen,
And about Modred, your sister's son, and how he has snatched
　　Britain from you."
　　Then everything went still in King Arthur's hall;
There was great unhappiness for the excellent king,
And because of it the British men were utterly depressed;
14055 Then after a while came the sound of a voice;
All over could be heard the reactions of the British
As they started to discuss in many kinds of expression
How they wished to condemn Modred and the queen
And destroy all the population who had supported Modred.
14060 Most courteous of all Britons, Arthur then called out aloud,
"Sit down quietly, my knights in this assembly,
And then I shall tell you some very strange tales.
Now tomorrow when daylight is sent by our Lord to us,
I wish to be on my way toward entering Britain,
14065 And there I shall kill Modred and burn the queen to death,
And I shall destroy all of them who gave assent to the treason."

MARIE DE FRANCE

Much of twelfth-century French literature was composed in England in the Anglo-Norman dialect (see pp. 6–7). Prominent among the earliest poets writing in the French vernacular, who shaped the genres, themes, and styles of later medieval European poetry, is the author who, in an epilogue to her *Fables,* calls herself Marie de France. That signature tells us only that her given name was Marie and that she was born in France, but circumstantial evidence from her writings shows that she spent much of her life in England. A reference to her in a French poem written in England around 1180 speaks of "dame Marie" who wrote "lais" much loved and praised, read, and heard by counts, barons, and knights and indicates that her poems also appealed to ladies who listened to them gladly and joyfully.

Three works can be safely attributed to Marie, probably written in the following order: the *Lais* [English "lay" refers to a short narrative poem in verse], the *Fables,* and *St. Patrick's Purgatory.* Marie's twelve lays are short romances (they range from 118 to 1,184 lines), each of which deals with a single event or crisis in the affairs of noble lovers. In her prologue, Marie tells us that she had heard these *performed,* and in several of the lays she refers to the Breton language and Breton storytellers—that is, professional minstrels from the French province of Brittany or the Celtic parts of Great Britain. Because no sources of Marie's stories have survived, it is not possible to determine the exact nature of the materials she worked from, but they were probably oral and were presented with the accompaniment of a stringed instrument. Marie's lays provide the basis of the genre that came to be known as the "Breton lay." In the prologue Marie dedicates the work to a "noble king," who is most likely to have been Henry II of England, who reigned from 1154 to 1189.

The portrait of the author that emerges from the combination of these works is of a highly educated noblewoman, proficient in Latin and English as well as her native French, with ideas of her own and a strong commitment to writing. Scholars have proposed several Maries of the period who fit this description to identify the author. A likely candidate is Marie, abbess of Shaftesbury, an illegitimate daughter of Geoffrey of Anjou and thus half-sister of Henry II. Correct or not, such an identification points to the milieu in which Marie moved and to the kind of audience she was addressing.

Many of Marie's lays contain elements of magic and mystery. Medieval readers would recognize that *Lanval* is about a mortal lover and a fairy bride, although the word "fairy" is not used in the tale. In the Middle Ages fairies were not thought of as the small creatures they became in Elizabethan and later literature. Fairies are supernatural, sometimes dangerous, beings who possess magical powers and inhabit another world. Their realm in some respects resembles the human (fairies have kings and queens), and fairies generally keep to themselves and disappear when humans notice them. But the tales are often about crossovers between the human and fairy worlds. Chaucer's *Wife of Bath's Tale* is such a story. In *Lanval* the female fairy world eclipses King Arthur's chivalric court (which Marie had read about in Wace's *Roman de Brut*) in splendor, riches, and generosity.

With Chrétien de Troyes, Marie is among the twelfth-century writers who made love the means of analyzing the individual's relation to his or her society. The only woman writer known to be among the creators of this literature, Marie explores both female and male desire. Her lays portray different kinds of love relationships, both favorably and unfavorably, with both happy and tragic resolutions. They resist reduction to a pattern.

Two Middle English versions of Marie's *Lanval* exist, but we prefer to offer a modern verse translation of the original. Marie wrote in eight-syllable couplets, which was the standard form of French narrative verse, employed also by Wace and Chrétien de Troyes. Here is what the beginning of Marie's prologue to the *Lais* says about her view of a writer's duty and, implicitly, of her own talent:

Ki Deu ad duné escïence	He to whom God has given knowledge
E de parler bon' eloquence	And the gift of speaking eloquently,
Ne s'en deit taisir ne celer,	Must not keep silent nor conceal the gift,
Ainz se deit volunters mustrer.	But he must willingly display it.

Lanval[1]

Another lay to you I'll tell,
Of the adventure that befell
A noble vassal whom they call
In the Breton tongue Lanval.
5   Arthur, the brave and courtly king,
At Carlisle was sojourning
Because the Scots and Picts allied
Were ravaging the countryside;
Of Logres° they had crossed the border   *Arthur's kingdom*
10   Where often they caused great disorder.
He had come there with his host
That spring to hold the Pentecost.

---

1. The translation is by Alfred David and is based on *Marie de France: Lais*, edited by Alfred Ewert (1947).

He lavished ample patronage
On all his noble baronage—
15 That is the knights of the Round Table
(In all the world none are so able).
Lands and wives he gave outright
To all his servants save one knight:
That was Lanval; him he forgot.
20 His men disliked him, too; the lot
Were envious of his handsomeness,
His strength, his courage, his largesse.
There were a few who friendship feigned,
But would by no means have complained
25 Had Lanval met some evil fate.
He was a prince of great estate,
But all his personal property
He gave away for amity,
And he got nothing from the king,
30 Nor would he ask for anything.
Now Lanval is much preoccupied,
Gloomy, seeing the darker side.
My lords, please do not think it rare:
A foreigner is filled with care
35 And sadness in a distant land,
Finding no help at any hand.
    The knight of whom I'm telling you,
In the king's service tried and true,
Mounting upon his steed one day,
40 For pleasure's sake set on his way.
Outside the town he went to ride
Alone into the countryside.
He got off by a running brook,
But there his horse trembled and shook.
45 He unlaced the saddle, set it free,
And let it ramble on the lee.
He folded up his riding gown
To make a pillow and lay down.
Much troubled by his luck's declining,
50 He can't see any silver lining.
There as he lay without a clue,
Two damoiselles hove into view,
The fairest he had ever eyed,
Riding along the riverside.
55 Their clothes were in expensive taste,
Close-fitting tunics, tightly laced,
Made of deep-dyed purple wool.
Their faces were most beautiful.
The elder bore a well-made pair
60 Of basins; of purest gold they were.
My lords, I swear that I'm not lying!
The other held a towel for drying.
The two of them went straightaway
Right to the spot where the knight lay.

65 Lanval, the soul of courtesy,
   Rose to his feet immediately.
   They greeted him first by his name
   And told the reason why they came.
   "Sir Lanval, our damoiselle,
70 Who is so worthy, wise, and *belle*,[2]
   Dispatched us to come after you,
   For she has come here with us, too.
   We shall bring you safely to her:
   See, her pavillion's over there."
75 The knight followed without regard
   For the horse left grazing on the sward.
   The tent to which they bring the knight
   Was fairly pitched, a beauteous sight.
   Not Queen Semiramis of yore,
80 Had she been owner of even more
   Wealth, power, and *savoir*,°   wisdom, know-how
   Nor Octavian, the emperor,
   Could have afforded to pay for
   The right-hand flap of the front door.
85 On top was set an eagle of gold,
   The cost of which cannot be told,
   Nor of the cords and poles which brace
   That structure and hold it in place.
   No earthly king could own this tent
90 For any treasure that he spent.
   Inside the tent the maiden was:
   Not rose nor lily could surpass
   Her beauty when they bloom in May.
   The sumptuous bed on which she lay
95 Was beautiful. The drapes and tassel,
   Sheets and pillows were worth a castle.
   The single gown she wore was sheer
   And made her shapely form appear.
   She'd thrown, in order to keep warm,
100 An ermine stole over her arm,
    White fur with the lining dyed
    Alexandrian purple. But her side,
    Her face, her neck, her bosom
    Showed whiter than the hawthorn blossom.
105 The knight moved toward the bed's head.
    She asked him to sit down and said,
    "Lanval, fair friend, for you I've come,
    For you I've traveled far from home.
    If you are brave and courteous,
110 You'll be more glad and prosperous
    Than ever was emperor or king,
    For I love you over everything."
    Her loveliness transfixed his gaze.

2. Beautiful. Several words and phrases are in French, partly for the sake of rhyme but also as an indication of the great influence that the French language exercised on English. Most of these words can be found in a modern English dictionary.

Love pierced his eyes with its bright rays,
115 Set fire to and scorched his heart.
He gave fair answer on his part.
"Lady," he said, "if this should be
Your wish (and such joy meant for me),
To have me for your paramour,
120 There's no command, you may be sure,
Wise or foolish, what you will,
Which I don't promise to fulfill.
I'll follow only your behest.
For you I'll give up all the rest."
125 When the lady heard him say
That he would love her in this way,
She bestowed on him her heart
And her body, every part.
Now Lanval is on easy street!
130 Whatever his needs are she will meet:
As a gift to him she granted
He should get whatever he wanted—
Money, as fast as he can spend it,
No matter how much, she will send it.
135 The more largesse he gives, the more
Gold and silver in his store.
Now Sir Lanval is harbored well.
To him then spoke the damoiselle:
"_Ami_,"[3] she said, "please understand,
140 I warn and pray you and command:
You must never tell anyone
About the love that you have won.
The consequence I shall declare:
Should people learn of this affair,
145 You shall never again see me,
Nor have my body in your fee."
He promised her that he would do
Whatever thing she told him to.
He lay beside her on the bed:
150 Now is Lanval well bestead.
He stayed with her all afternoon
Until it would be evening soon
And gladly would have stayed all night
Had she consented that he might.
155 But she told him, "Rise up, _Ami_.
You may no longer stay with me.
Get on your way; I shall remain.
But one thing I will tell you plain:
When you would like to talk to me
160 At any rendezvous that's free
Of blame or of unseemliness,
Where one his true love may possess,
I shall attend you at your will

3. Literally "friend," but used as a term of endearment for a lover. The feminine form is _amie_.

All your wishes to fulfill."
165 These words gave him great happiness.
He kissed her, then got up to dress.
The damsels who had brought him there
Gave him expensive clothes to wear.
This world has no such comely squire
170 As Lanval in his new attire.
He was no simpleton or knave.
Water to wash his hands they gave,
Also the towel with which he dried,
And next he was with food supplied.
175 His love ate supper with Lanval,
A thing he did not mind at all.
They served him with great courtesy,
Which he accepted with much glee.
There were many special dishes
180 That the knight found most delicious.
And many times the gallant knight
Kissed his love and held her tight.
After they had cleared the table,
They fetched his horse out of the stable,
185 Harnessed just as it should be.
He had been served luxuriously.
He took his leave, mounted the horse,
And toward town he held his course,
Oftentimes looking to his rear.
190 Lanval was very much in fear
As he went thinking about the maiden,
And his heart with doubts was laden.
What to believe he's all astir;
He thinks he's seen the last of her.
195 Arrived back home, Sir Lanval sees
His men dressed in new liveries.
That night the lavish host he plays,
But no one knows from whence he pays.
In town there is no *chevalier*[4]
200 Who badly needs a place to stay
Whom Lanval doesn't make his guest
And serves him richly of the best.
Lanval gives expensive presents;
Lanval remits the captive's sentence;
205 Lanval puts minstrels in new dress;
Lanval does honors in excess.
There's no stranger nor private friend
On whom Lanval does not spend.
He lives in joy and in delight,
210 Whether it be by day or night.
He sees his lady often, and
Has all the world at his command.
    That same summer, I would say,

4. Knight. Rhymes with -*ay* in French pronunciation.

After the feast of St. John's Day,
215 Thirty knights made an excursion,
For the sake of their diversion,
To a garden beneath the tower
In which the queen had her bower.
Among that party was Gawain
220 And his cousin, the good Yvain.
Sir Gawain spoke, brave and sincere,
Whom everybody held so dear,
"By God, my lords, we've not done right
By our companion, that good knight—
225 Lanval, so free, courtly, and loyal,
Son of a king who's rich and royal—
To leave that nobleman behind."
And straightway they turn back and find
Sir Lanval at his residence
230 And beg that they might take him thence.
    From a window with fine molding
The queen herself leaned out beholding
(Waited on by damsels three)
King Arthur's festive company.
235 She gazed at Lanval and knew him well.
She called out to one damoiselle
And sent her for her maids-in-waiting,
The fairest and most captivating.
With her into the garden then
240 They went to relax with the men.
Thirty she took along and more,
Down the stairs and out the door.
Rejoiced to have the ladies meet them,
The *chevaliers* advance to greet them.
245 Each girl by a knight's hand is led:
Such pleasant talk is not ill-bred.
Lanval goes off alone and turns
Aside from all the rest. He yearns
To hold his love within his arms,
250 To kiss, embrace, and feel her charms.
The joy of others is less pleasant
To him, his own not being present.
When she perceives him stand alone,
The queen straightway to him has gone
255 To sit beside him and reveals
All the passion that she feels:
"Lanval, I've honored you sincerely,
Have cherished you and loved you dearly.
All my love is at your disposal.
260 What do you say to my proposal?
Your mistress I consent to be;
You should receive much joy from me."
"Lady," he said, "hold me excused
Because your love must be refused.
265 I've served the king for many a day;

My faith to him I won't betray.
Never for love, and not for you,
Would I be to my lord untrue."
Made angry by these words, the queen
270 Insultingly expressed her spleen.
"Lanval," she said, "It's evident
That to such pleasures you have no bent.
Often I have heard men aver
That women are not what you prefer.
275 But you have many pretty boys
With whom you like to take your joys.
Faithless coward of low degree,
My lord was badly served when he
Suffered your person to come near.
280 For that he could lose God, I fear."
  Hearing this, Lanval was dismayed;
His answer was not long delayed.
With spite, as he was much upset,
He spoke what soon he would regret.
285 "My lady queen," was his retort,
"I know nothing about that sport.
But I love one, and she loves me;
From every woman I know of, she
Deserves to bear the prize away.
290 And one more thing I wish to say,
So that you may know it plain:
Each serving-maid in her domain,
The poorest girl of the whole crew,
My lady, is worth more than you
295 In beauty of both figure and face,
In good breeding and bounteous grace."
In tears the queen at once repairs
Back to her chamber up the stairs.
Dolorous she is and mortified
300 To be by him thus villified.
She goes to bed where sick she lies,
Vowing never again to rise,
Unless the king grants her redress
For that which caused her such distress.
305 The king had come back from the wood
Cheerful because the day was good.
To the queen's bedroom he attained;
As soon as she saw him, she complained.
Fallen at his feet, she cried, "*Merci!*[5]
310 Lanval has done me infamy."
To be her lover he had affected.
When his advances were rejected,
He had reviled her shamefully
And boasted he had an *amie*
315 So chic, noble, and proud, he said,

5. Exclamation appealing for compassion and favor.

That even her lowliest chambermaid,
The poorest one that might be seen,
Was worthier than she—the queen.
The king grew marvelously wroth,
320 And solemnly he swore an oath:
Unless the knight proved what he'd boasted,
The king would have him hanged or roasted.
Leaving the chamber, the king then
Summoned three of his noblemen.
325 After Lanval they were to go,
Who, feeling enough of grief and woe,
Had returned to his habitation,
Well aware of his situation.
Since he had told of their *amour*,
330 He had lost his love for sure.
In his room alone he languished,
Melancholy and sorely anguished.
He calls his love time and again,
But all his pleadings are in vain.
335 Sighs he utters and complaints,
And from time to time he faints.
A hundred times he cries *merci*
And begs her speak to her *ami*.
He curses both his heart and tongue;
340 A wonder 'tis he lives so long
Without committing suicide.
However much he roared and cried,
Fought with himself and scratched his face,
She would not show him any grace—
345 Even to see her once again.
Alas, how can he bear the pain?
        The king's men have arrived to say
He must to court without delay.
The king had summoned him for this reason:
350 The queen had charged the knight with treason.
Lanval went with them very sadly.
Should he be killed, he'd bear it gladly.
The knight was brought before the king,
Grief-stricken, not saying anything,
355 Like someone in great misery.
The king spoke out indignantly:
"Vassal, you've done lèse-majesté.[6]
You have begun a churlish play,
Me to dishonor and demean
360 And to speak slander of the queen.
It was a foolish boast to call
Your love the noblest one of all,
And her servant—to declare her
Worthier than the queen and fairer.
365   Lanval protested, word for word,

6. Treason against the highest authority.

Any dishonor done to his lord
Respecting the queen's accusation
Of a guilty solicitation.
But of his speech—to give her due—
370   He confessed that it was true.
The mistress he had boasted of
He mourned, for he had lost her love.
Regarding that, he said he'd do
Whatever the court told him to.
375   This put the king in a great fury.
He summoned his knights to act as jury
To tell how to proceed by law
So none might catch him in a flaw.[7]
They obeyed him—the entire lot,
380   Whether they wanted to or not.
They met together to consult
And deemed and judged with this result:
A court day set, Lanval goes free
But must find pledges to guarantee
385   His lord that judgment he'll abide,
Return to court and there be tried
By Arthur's entire baronage,
Not just the palace entourage.[8]
Back to the king the barons bring
390   The judgment of their parleying.
The king demands his sureties,
Thus putting Lanval ill at ease.
A foreigner, he felt chagrin
Since he had neither friend nor kin.
395   Gawain stepped forth and pledged that he
Would stand as Lanval's surety.
And his companions in succession
Each one made the same profession.
The king replied, "He's in your hands
400   At risk to forfeit all your lands
And fiefs, whatever they may be,
Which each of you obtained from me."
The pledges made, the court adjourned,
And Lanval to his place returned.
405   The knights escort him on his way.
They blame and warn him, and they say
To shun excessive melancholy;
And they lay curses on love's folly.
Worried about his mental state,
410   Each day they go investigate
Whether he's taking nourishment
Or to himself is violent.

---

7. The trial of Lanval shows precise knowledge of 12th-century legal procedure concerning the respective rights of the king and his barons. So as not to violate baronial rights, Arthur asks the knights of his household to determine the proper ways to proceed against one of their own.

8. The case is important enough to require judgment by all of Arthur's vassals, not just the immediate household. Hence the delay of the trial.

On the day that had been set,
All King Arthur's barons met.
415 Attending were the king and queen;
Pledges brought Lanval on the scene.
They were all sad on his account—
A hundred of them I could count
Who would have done their best to see
420 Him without trial go scot-free,
For he'd been wrongfully arraigned.
On the charge, the king maintained,
And his response, he must be tried:
And now the barons must decide.
425 To the judgment they go next
Greatly worried and perplexed,
Since the noble foreign guest
In their midst is so hard-pressed.
Some were willing to condemn
430 To oblige their sovereign.
The Duke of Cornwall counselled thus:
"No fault shall be ascribed to us:
Though some may weep and some may play,
Justice must take its lawful way.
435 A vassal by the king denounced,
Whose name—'Lanval'—I heard pronounced,
Has been accused of felony
And charged that mischievously he
To a mistress had pretended
440 And Madame the Queen offended.
By the faith I owe you duly,
In this case, should one speak truly,
The king being the sole adversary,
No defense were necessary,
445 Save for the sake of his lord's name
A man must never speak him shame.
Sir Lanval by his oath must stand,
And the king quitclaim our land,
If the knight can guarantee
450 The coming here of his *amie*.
Should it prove true what he has claimed,
By which the queen felt so defamed,
Of that he'll be judged innocent,
Since he spoke without base intent.
455 But if he cannot prove it so,
In that case we must let him know,
All the king's service he must lose
And banished say his last adieus."
The knight was sent the court's decree
460 And informed by them that he
Must summon his *amie* and send her
To be his witness and defender.
The knight responded that he could not:
To his rescue come she would not.

465 To the judges they made report
That he looked for no support.
The king pressed them to make an ending
And not to keep the queen attending.
    When they came to lay down the law,
470 Two maidens from afar they saw
On two fine steeds, riding apace,
Who were extremely fair of face.
Of purple taffeta a sheath
They wore with nothing underneath.
475 The men took pleasure in the view.
Sir Gawain and three of his crew
Went to Sir Lanval to report
And show the girls coming to court.
Happy, he asked him earnestly
480 If one of them were his *amie*.
He told them that he knew not who
They were, where from, or going to.
The damoiselles rode on withal
Upon their mounts into the hall,
485 And they got off before the dais
There where the king sat at his place.
Their features were of beauty rare;
Their form of speech was debonair:
"King, clear your chambers, if you please,
490 And hang them with silk draperies,
Where my lady may make arrest,
For she wishes to be your guest."
The king gladly gave his consent.
Two of his courtiers he sent
495 To show them to their rooms upstairs.
No more was said of these affairs.
    The king ordered his retinue
To render up their judgment due.
The long procrastination had,
500 He said, made him extremely mad.
"My lord," they answered, "we have acted.
But our attention was distracted
By those ladies we have seen.
But now the court shall reconvene."
505 They reassembled much perturbed,
By too much noise and strife disturbed.
    While they engaged in this debate,
Two damoiselles of high estate—
In silks produced in Phrygia,
510 On mules from Andalusia—
Came riding up the street just then.
This gave great joy to Arthur's men,
Who told each other this must be
The worthy Lanval's remedy.
515 To him there hastened Sir Gawain
With his companions in his train.

"Sir knight," he said, "be of good cheer.
For God's sake speak to us! See here,
Two maidens are approaching us,
520 Most beautiful and decorous;
Surely one must be your *amie*."
Lanval made answer hastily.
He said that he recognized neither.
He didn't know or love them either.
525 Meanwhile the damoiselles had gone
And dismounted before the throne
Where the king was sitting on the dais.
From many there they won great praise
For figure, visage, and complexion.
530 They came much nearer to perfection
Than did the queen, so people said.
The elder was courteous and well-bred.
She spoke her message with much flair:
"King, tell your household to prepare
535 A suite to lodge my lady, who
Is coming here to speak with you."
The king had them conducted where
His men had lodged the previous pair.
As soon as they were from him gone,
540 He told his barons to have done
And give their verdict right away.
There had been far too much delay;
The queen had found it most frustrating
That they so long had kept her waiting.
545   When they were just about to bring
Judgment, a girl was entering
The town, whose beauty, it was clear,
In all the world could have no peer.
She rode upon a milkwhite horse,
550 Which bore her gently down the course.
Its neck and head were shapeliest;
Of all creatures, it was the best.
Splendidly furnished was this mount:
Beneath the heavens, no king or count
555 Could have afforded gear so grand
Unless he sold or pawned his land.
And this is how she was arrayed:
A white linen shift displayed—
There where it was with laces tied—
560 Her slender flanks on either side.
Slim-hipped, her form was *comme il faut*;[9]
Her neck, whiter than branch in snow;
Her eyes were gray; her face was bright;
Her mouth, lovely; nose, set just right;
565 Eyebrows black, forehead fair;
Blonde and curly was her hair.

9. As required, perfectly correct.

Golden wire sheds no such ray
As did her locks against the day.
A mantle was around her drawn,
570   A cloak of deep-dyed purple lawn.
A falcon on her wrist sat still;
A greyhound followed her at will.
In town was neither high nor low,
Old man or child, who did not go
575   And line the streets along the way
To watch as she made her entrée.
And as they stood gazing at her,
Her beauty was no laughing matter.
She rode up to the castle slowly.
580   The judges, seeing her, were wholly
Astonished at that spectacle
And held it for a miracle.
The heart of every single knight
Among them warmed with sheer delight.
585   Those who loved Sir Lanval well
Quickly went to him to tell
About the maiden who perchance,
Please God, brought him deliverance.
"Comrade," they said, "here comes one,
590   Who is neither swart nor dun.
Of all women by land and sea,
She is the fairest that may be.
Lanval heard and raised his eye;
He knew her well and gave a sigh.
595   The blood shot up into his cheeks,
And somewhat hastily he speaks:
"In faith," he said, "that's my *amie*!
Now I don't care if they kill me
If but her mercy is assured,
600   For when I see her, I am cured."
The maid rode through the palace door,
So fair came never there before.
In front of Arthur she got down
With the whole company looking on.
605   Softly she let her mantle fall,
The better to be seen by all.
King Arthur, who was most discreet,
To greet her got up on his feet.
In turn, to honor her the rest
610   Offered their service to the guest.
When they had satisfied their gaze
And greatly sung her beauty's praise,
She made her speech in such a way
As she did not intend to stay:
615   "King, I have loved one of your band—
It's Lanval, there you see him stand.
I would not have the man ill-used—
In your court he has been accused

Of lies he spoke. Take it from me,
620 The queen committed perjury;
He never asked her for her love.
As for the things he boasted of,
If I may be his warranty,
Your barons ought to speak him free."
625 The king agreed he would abide
By what they lawfully decide.
Among them there was no dissent;
Lanval was pronounced innocent.
The damoiselle set off again,
630 Though the king asked her to remain.
Outside there stood a marble rock
With steps to make a mounting block,
From which armed men would get astride
When they from court set out to ride.
635 Lanval climbed up on it before
The damoiselle rode out the door.
Swiftly he sprang the horse to straddle
And sat behind her on the saddle.
To Avalon they came away,
640 Which Breton storytellers say
An island is, most ravishing,
There Lanval has gone, vanishing.
No man has heard more of his fate;
I've nothing further to relate.

FINIS

Middle English Literature in the Fourteenth and Fifteenth Centuries

SIR GAWAIN AND THE GREEN KNIGHT
ca. 1375–1400

The finest Arthurian romance in English survives in only one manuscript, which also contains three religious poems—*Pearl, Patience*, and *Purity*—generally believed to be by the same poet. Nothing is known about the author except what can be inferred from the works. The dialect of the poems locates them in a remote corner of the northwest midlands between Cheshire and Staffordshire, and details of Sir Gawain's journey north show that the author was familiar with the geography of that region. But if author and audience were provincials, *Sir Gawain* and the other poems in the manuscript reveal them to have been highly sophisticated and well acquainted both with the international culture of the high Middle Ages and with ancient native traditions.

Sir Gawain belongs to the so-called Alliterative Revival. After the Norman Conquest, alliterative verse doubtless continued to be recited by oral poets. At the beginning, the *Gawain* poet pretends that this romance is an oral poem and asks the audience to "listen" to a story, which he has "heard." Alliterative verse also continued to appear in Early Middle English texts. Layamon's *Brut* (see pp. 102–04) is the outstanding example. During the late fourteenth century there was a renewed flowering of alliterative poetry, especially in the north and west of Britain, which includes *Piers Plowman* and a splendid poem known as *The Alliterative Morte Darthur*.

The *Gawain* poet's audience evidently valued the kind of alliterative verse that Chaucer's Parson caricatures as "Rum-Ram-Ruf by lettre" (see p. 275, line 43). They would also have understood archaic poetic diction surviving from Old English poetry such as *athel* (noble) and words of Scandinavian origin such as *skete* (quickly) and *skifted* (alternated). They were well acquainted with French Arthurian romances and the latest fashions in clothing, armor, and castle building. In making Sir Gawain, Arthur's sister's son, the preeminent knight of the Round Table, the poet was faithful to an older tradition. The thirteenth-century French romances, which in the next century became the main sources of Sir Thomas Malory, had made Sir Lancelot the best of Arthur's knights and Lancelot's adultery with Queen Guinevere the central event on which the fate of Arthur's kingdom turns. In *Sir Gawain* Lancelot is only one name in a list of Arthur's knights. Arthur is still a youth, and the court is in its springtime. Sir Gawain epitomizes this first blooming of Arthurian chivalry, and the reputation of the court rests upon his shoulders.

Ostensibly, Gawain's head is what is at stake. The main plot belongs to a type folklorists classify as the "Beheading Game," in which a supernatural challenger offers to let his head be cut off in exchange for a return blow. The earliest written occurrence of this motif is in the Middle Irish tale of *Bricriu's Feast*. The *Gawain* poet could have encountered it in several French romances as well as in oral tradition. But the outcome of the game here does not turn only on the champion's courage as it does in

Bricriu's Feast. The *Gawain* poet has devised another series of tests for the hero that link the beheading with his truth, the emblem of which is the pentangle—a five-pointed star—displayed on Gawain's coat of arms and shield. The word *truth* in Middle English means not only what it still means now—a fact, belief, or idea held to be "true"—but what is conveyed by the old-fashioned variant from the same root: *troth*— that is, faith pledged by one's word and owed to a lord, a spouse, or anyone who puts someone else under an obligation. In this respect, Sir Gawain is being measured against a moral and Christian ideal of chivalry. Whether or not he succeeds in that contest is a question carefully left unresolved—perhaps as a challenge for the reader.

The poet has framed Gawain's adventure with references in the first and last stanzas to what are called the "Brutus books," the foundation stories that trace the origins of Rome and Britain back to the destruction of Troy. See, for example, the selection from Geoffrey of Monmouth's *History of the Kings of Britain* (p. 96). A cyclical sense of history as well as of the cycles of the seasons of the year, the generations of human-kind, and of individual lives runs through *Sir Gawain and the Green Knight.*

The poem is written in stanzas that contain a group of alliterative lines (the number of lines in a stanza varies). The line is longer and does not contain a fixed number or pattern of stresses like the classical alliterative measure of Old English poetry. Each stanza closes with five short lines rhyming *a b a b a*. The first of these rhyming lines contains just two (rarely three) syllables and is called the "bob"; the four three-stress lines that follow are called the "wheel." For details on alliterative verse, see "Old and Middle English Prosody" (pp. 16–18). The opening stanza is printed below in Middle English with an interlinear translation. The alliterating sounds, which should be stressed, have been italicized.

Sithen the *sege* and the *assaut* was *sesed* at Troye,
After the siege and the assault was ceased at Troy,

The *borgh brittened* and *brent* to *brondes* and askes,
The city crumbled and burned to brands and ashes,

The *tulk* that the *trammes* of *tresoun* ther wroght
The man who the plots of treason there wrought

Was *tried* for his *tricherie*, the *trewest* on erthe.
Was tried for his treachery, the truest on earth.

Hit was *Ennias* the *athel* and his *highe* kynde,
It was Aeneas the noble and his high race,

That *sithen depreced provinces*, and *patrounes* bicome
Who after subjugated provinces, and lords became

Welneghe of al the *wele* in the *west* iles.
Wellnigh of all the wealth in the west isles.

Fro *riche* Romulus to *Rome ricchis* hym swythe,
Then noble Romulus to Rome proceeds quickly,

With *gret bobbaunce* that *burghe* he *biges* upon fyrst
With great pride that city he builds at first

And *nevenes* hit his aune *nome*, as hit *now* hat;
And names it his own name, as it now is called;

Ticius to Tuskan and *teldes bigynnes,*
Ticius (goes) to Tuscany and houses begins,

Langaberde in *Lumbardie lyftes* up homes,
Longbeard in Lombardy raises up homes,

And *fer* over the French *flod,* Felix Brutus
And far over the English Channel, Felix Brutus

On mony *bonkkes* ful *brode* Bretayn he settes
On many banks very broad Brittain he sets

Wyth wynne,
With joy,

Where *werre* and *wrake* and *wonder*
Where war and revenge and wondrous happenings

Bi sythes has wont therinne,
On occasions have dwelled therein

And oft *bothe blysse* and *blunder*
And often both joy and strife

Ful *skete* has *skyfted* synne.
Very swiftly have alternated since.

Sir Gawain and the Green Knight[1]

Part 1

Since the siege and the assault was ceased at Troy,
The walls breached and burnt down to brands and ashes,
The knight that had knotted the nets of deceit
Was impeached for his perfidy, proven most true,[2]
5 It was high-born Aeneas and his haughty race
That since prevailed over provinces, and proudly reigned
Over well-nigh all the wealth of the West Isles.[3]
Great Romulus[4] to Rome repairs in haste;
With boast and with bravery builds he that city
10 And names it with his own name, that it now bears.
Ticius to Tuscany, and towers raises,
Langobard[5] in Lombardy lays out homes,
And far over the French Sea, Felix Brutus[6]
On many broad hills and high Britain he sets,
15   most fair.

---

1. The Modern English translation is by Marie Borroff (1967), who has reproduced the alliterative meter of the original as well as the "bob" and "wheel," the five-line rhyming group that concludes each of the long irregular stanzas.
2. The treacherous knight is Aeneas, who was a traitor to his city, Troy, according to medieval tradition, but Aeneas was actually tried ("impeached") by the Greeks for his refusal to hand over to them his sister Polyxena.
3. Perhaps Western Europe.
4. The legendary founder of Rome is here given Trojan ancestry, like Aeneas.
5. The reputed founder of Lombardy. "Ticius": not otherwise known.
6. Great-grandson of Aeneas and legendary founder of Britain; not elsewhere given the name Felix (Latin "happy").

Where war and wrack and wonder
By shifts have sojourned there,
And bliss by turns with blunder
In that land's lot had share.

20 And since this Britain was built by this baron great,
Bold boys bred there, in broils delighting,
That did in their day many a deed most dire.
More marvels have happened in this merry land
Than in any other I know, since that olden time,
25 But of those that here built, of British kings,
King Arthur was counted most courteous of all,
Wherefore an adventure I aim to unfold,
That a marvel of might some men think it,
And one unmatched among Arthur's wonders.
30 If you will listen to my lay but a little while,
As I heard it in hall, I shall hasten to tell
anew.
As it was fashioned featly
In tale of derring-do,
35 And linked in measures meetly
By letters tried and true.

This king lay at Camelot[7] at Christmastide;
Many good knights and gay his guests were there,
Arrayed of the Round Table[8] rightful brothers,
40 With feasting and fellowship and carefree mirth.
There true men contended in tournaments many,
Joined there in jousting these gentle knights,
Then came to the court for carol-dancing,
For the feast was in force full fifteen days,
45 With all the meat and the mirth that men could devise,
Such gaiety and glee, glorious to hear,
Brave din by day, dancing by night.
High were their hearts in halls and chambers,
These lords and these ladies, for life was sweet.
50 In peerless pleasures passed they their days,
The most noble knights known under Christ,
And the loveliest ladies that lived on earth ever,
And he the comeliest king, that that court holds,
For all this fair folk in their first age
55 were still.
Happiest of mortal kind,
King noblest famed of will;
You would now go far to find
So hardy a host on hill.

60 While the New Year was new, but yesternight come,
This fair folk at feast two-fold was served,

---

7. Capital of Arthur's kingdom, presumably located in southwest England or southern Wales.
8. According to legend, Merlin made the Round Table after a dispute broke out among Arthur's knights about precedence: it seated one hundred knights. The table described in the poem is not round.

When the king and his company were come in together,
The chanting in chapel achieved and ended.
Clerics and all the court acclaimed the glad season,
65 Cried Noel anew, good news to men;
Then gallants gather gaily, hand-gifts to make,
Called them out clearly, claimed them by hand,
Bickered long and busily about those gifts.
Ladies laughed aloud, though losers they were,
70 And he that won was not angered, as well you will know.[9]
All this mirth they made until meat was served;
When they had washed them worthily, they went to their seats,
The best seated above, as best it beseemed,
Guenevere the goodly queen gay in the midst
75 On a dais well-decked and duly arrayed
With costly silk curtains, a canopy over,
Of Toulouse and Turkestan tapestries rich,
All broidered and bordered with the best gems
Ever brought into Britain, with bright pennies
80   to pay.
                        Fair queen, without a flaw,
                        She glanced with eyes of grey.
                        A seemlier that once he saw,
                        In truth, no man could say.

85 But Arthur would not eat till all were served;
So light was his lordly heart, and a little boyish;
His life he liked lively—the less he cared
To be lying for long, or long to sit,
So busy his young blood, his brain so wild.
90 And also a point of pride pricked him in heart,
For he nobly had willed, he would never eat
On so high a holiday, till he had heard first
Of some fair feat or fray some far-borne tale,
Of some marvel of might, that he might trust,
95 By champions of chivalry achieved in arms,
Or some suppliant came seeking some single knight
To join with him in jousting, in jeopardy each
To lay life for life, and leave it to fortune
To afford him on field fair hap or other.
100 Such is the king's custom, when his court he holds
At each far-famed feast amid his fair host
                        so dear.
                        The stout king stands in state
                        Till a wonder shall appear;
105   He leads, with heart elate,
                        High mirth in the New Year.

So he stands there in state, the stout young king,
Talking before the high table of trifles fair.
There Gawain the good knight by Guenevere sits,
110 With Agravain à la dure main on her other side,

9. The dispensing of New Year's gifts seems to have involved kissing.

Both knights of renown, and nephews of the king.
Bishop Baldwin above begins the table,
And Yvain, son of Urien, ate with him there.
These few with the fair queen were fittingly served;
115   At the side-tables[1] sat many stalwart knights.
Then the first course comes, with clamor of trumpets
That were bravely bedecked with bannerets bright,
With noise of new drums and the noble pipes.
Wild were the warbles that wakened that day
120   In strains that stirred many strong men's hearts.
There dainties were dealt out, dishes rare,
Choice fare to choose, on chargers so many
That scarce was there space to set before the people
The service of silver, with sundry meats,
125   on cloth.
            Each fair guest freely there
            Partakes, and nothing loth;
            Twelve dishes before each pair;
            Good beer and bright wine both.

130   Of the service itself I need say no more,
For well you will know no tittle was wanting.
Another noise and a new was well-nigh at hand,
That the lord might have leave his life to nourish;
For scarce were the sweet strains still in the hall,
135   And the first course come to that company fair,
There hurtles in at the hall-door an unknown rider,
One the greatest on ground in growth of his frame:
From broad neck to buttocks so bulky and thick,
And his loins and his legs so long and so great,
140   Half a giant on earth I hold him to be,
But believe him no less than the largest of men,
And that the seemliest in his stature to see, as he rides,
For in back and in breast though his body was grim,
His waist in its width was worthily small,
145   And formed with every feature in fair accord
                    was he.
            Great wonder grew in hall
            At his hue most strange to see,
            For man and gear and all
150   Were green as green could be.

And in guise all of green, the gear and the man:
A coat cut close, that clung to his sides,
And a mantle to match, made with a lining
Of furs cut and fitted—the fabric was noble,
155   Embellished all with ermine, and his hood beside,
That was loosed from his locks, and laid on his shoulders.
With trim hose and tight, the same tint of green,

---

1. The side tables are on the main floor and run along the walls at a right angle with the high table, which is on a dais.

His great calves were girt, and gold spurs under
He bore on silk bands that embellished his heels,
160 And footgear well-fashioned, for riding most fit.
And all his vesture verily was verdant green;
Both the bosses on his belt and other bright gems
That were richly ranged on his raiment noble
About himself and his saddle, set upon silk,
165 That to tell half the trifles would tax my wits,
The butterflies and birds embroidered thereon
In green of the gayest, with many a gold thread.
The pendants of the breast-band, the princely crupper,
And the bars of the bit were brightly enameled;
170 The stout stirrups were green, that steadied his feet,
And the bows of the saddle and the side-panels both,
That gleamed all and glinted with green gems about.
The steed he bestrides of that same green
     so bright.
175   A green horse great and thick;
    A headstrong steed of might;
    In broidered bridle quick,
    Mount matched man aright.

Gay was this goodly man in guise all of green,
180 And the hair of his head to his horse suited;
Fair flowing tresses enfold his shoulders;
A beard big as a bush on his breast hangs,
That with his heavy hair, that from his head falls,
Was evened all about above both his elbows,
185 That half his arms thereunder were hid in the fashion
Of a king's cap-à-dos,[2] that covers his throat.
The mane of that mighty horse much to it like,
Well curled and becombed, and cunningly knotted
With filaments of fine gold amid the fair green,
190 Here a strand of the hair, here one of gold;
His tail and his foretop twin in their hue,
And bound both with a band of a bright green
That was decked adown the dock with dazzling stones
And tied tight at the top with a triple knot
195 Where many bells well burnished rang bright and clear.
Such a mount in his might, nor man on him riding,
None had seen, I dare swear, with sight in that hall
     so grand.
    As lightning quick and light
200   He looked to all at hand;
    It seemed that no man might
    His deadly dints withstand.

Yet had he no helm, nor hauberk neither,
Nor plate, nor appurtenance appending to arms,

---

2. The word *capados* occurs in this form in Middle English only in *Gawain*, here and in line 572. The translator has interpreted it, as the poet apparently did also, as *cap-à-dos*, i.e., a garment covering its wearer "from head to back," on the model of *cap-à-pie*, "from head to foot," referring to armor.

205 Nor shaft pointed sharp, nor shield for defense,
But in his one hand he had a holly bob
That is goodliest in green when groves are bare,
And an ax in his other, a huge and immense,
A wicked piece of work in words to expound:
210 The head on its haft was an ell long;
The spike of green steel, resplendent with gold;
The blade burnished bright, with a broad edge,
As well shaped to shear as a sharp razor;
Stout was the stave in the strong man's gripe,
215 That was wound all with iron to the weapon's end,
With engravings in green of goodliest work.
A lace lightly about, that led to a knot,
Was looped in by lengths along the fair haft,
And tassels thereto attached in a row,
220 With buttons of bright green, brave to behold.
This horseman hurtles in, and the hall enters;
Riding to the high dais, recked he no danger;
Not a greeting he gave as the guests he o'erlooked,
Nor wasted his words, but "Where is," he said,
225 "The captain of this crowd? Keenly I wish
To see that sire with sight, and to himself say
              my say."
          He swaggered all about
          To scan the host so gay;
230   He halted, as if in doubt
          Who in that hall held sway.

There were stares on all sides as the stranger spoke,
For much did they marvel what it might mean
That a horseman and a horse should have such a hue,
235 Grow green as the grass, and greener, it seemed,
Than green fused on gold more glorious by far.
All the onlookers eyed him, and edged nearer,
And awaited in wonder what he would do,
For many sights had they seen, but such a one never,
240 So that phantom and faerie the folk there deemed it,
Therefore chary of answer was many a champion bold,
And stunned at his strong words stone-still they sat
In a swooning silence in the stately hall.
As all were slipped into sleep, so slackened their speech
245   apace.
          Not all, I think, for dread,
          But some of courteous grace
          Let him who was their head
          Be spokesman in that place.

250 Then Arthur before the high dais that entrance beholds,
And hailed him, as behooved, for he had no fear,
And said "Fellow, in faith you have found fair welcome;
The head of this hostelry Arthur am I;
Leap lightly down, and linger, I pray,

255 And the tale of your intent you shall tell us after."
"Nay, so help me," said the other, "He that on high sits,
To tarry here any time, 'twas not mine errand;
But as the praise of you, prince, is puffed up so high,
And your court and your company are counted the best,
260 Stoutest under steel-gear on steeds to ride,
Worthiest of their works the wide world over,
And peerless to prove in passages of arms,
And courtesy here is carried to its height,
And so at this season I have sought you out.
265 You may be certain by the branch that I bear in hand
That I pass here in peace, and would part friends,
For had I come to this court on combat bent,
I have a hauberk at home, and a helm beside,
A shield and a sharp spear, shining bright,
270 And other weapons to wield, I ween well, to boot,
But as I willed no war, I wore no metal.
But if you be so bold as all men believe,
You will graciously grant the game that I ask
                         by right."
275   Arthur answer gave
                         And said, "Sir courteous knight,
                         If contest bare you crave,
                         You shall not fail to fight."

"Nay, to fight, in good faith, is far from my thought;
280 There are about on these benches but beardless children,
Were I here in full arms on a haughty steed,
For measured against mine, their might is puny.
And so I call in this court for a Christmas game,
For 'tis Yule and New Year, and many young bloods about;
285 If any in this house such hardihood claims,
Be so bold in his blood, his brain so wild,
As stoutly to strike one stroke for another,
I shall give him as my gift this gisarme noble,
This ax, that is heavy enough, to handle as he likes,
290 And I shall bide the first blow, as bare as I sit.
If there be one so wilful my words to assay,
Let him leap hither lightly, lay hold of this weapon;
I quitclaim it forever, keep it as his own,
And I shall stand him a stroke, steady on this floor,
295 So you grant me the guerdon to give him another,
                         sans blame.
                         In a twelvemonth and a day
                         He shall have of me the same;
                         Now be it seen straightway
300   Who dares take up the game."

If he astonished them at first, stiller were then
All that household in hall, the high and the low;
The stranger on his green steed stirred in the saddle,
And roisterously his red eyes he rolled all about,

305 Bent his bristling brows, that were bright green,
    Wagged his beard as he watched who would arise.
    When the court kept its counsel he coughed aloud,
    And cleared his throat coolly, the clearer to speak:
    "What, is this Arthur's house," said that horseman then,
310 "Whose fame is so fair in far realms and wide?
    Where is now your arrogance and your awesome deeds,
    Your valor and your victories and your vaunting words?
    Now are the revel and renown of the Round Table
    Overwhelmed with a word of one man's speech,
315 For all cower and quake, and no cut felt!"
    With this he laughs so loud that the lord grieved;
    The blood for sheer shame shot to his face,
                        and pride.
                With rage his face flushed red,
320   And so did all beside.
                Then the king as bold man bred
                Toward the stranger took a stride.

    And said "Sir, now we see you will say but folly,
    Which whoso has sought, it suits that he find.
325 No guest here is aghast of your great words.
    Give to me your gisarme, in God's own name,
    And the boon you have begged shall straight be granted."
    He leaps to him lightly, lays hold of his weapon;
    The green fellow on foot fiercely alights.
330 Now has Arthur his ax, and the haft grips,
    And sternly stirs it about, on striking bent.
    The stranger before him stood there erect,
    Higher than any in the house by a head and more;
    With stern look as he stood, he stroked his beard,
335 And with undaunted countenance drew down his coat,
    No more moved nor dismayed for his mighty dints
    Than any bold man on bench had brought him a drink
                        of wine.
                Gawain by Guenevere
340   Toward the king doth now incline:
                "I beseech, before all here,
                That this melee may be mine."

    "Would you grant me the grace," said Gawain to the king,
    "To be gone from this bench and stand by you there,
345 If I without discourtesy might quit this board,
    And if my liege lady misliked it not,
    I would come to your counsel before your court noble.
    For I find it not fit, as in faith it is known,
    When such a boon is begged before all these knights,
350 Though you be tempted thereto, to take it on yourself
    While so bold men about upon benches sit,
    That no host under heaven is hardier of will,
    Nor better brothers-in-arms where battle is joined;
    I am the weakest, well I know, and of wit feeblest;

355 And the loss of my life would be least of any;
That I have you for uncle is my only praise;
My body, but for your blood, is barren of worth;
And for that this folly befits not a king,
And 'tis I that have asked it, it ought to be mine,
360 And if my claim be not comely let all this court judge,
                    in sight."
          The court assays the claim,
          And in counsel all unite
          To give Gawain the game
365   And release the king outright.

Then the king called the knight to come to his side,
And he rose up readily, and reached him with speed,
Bows low to his lord, lays hold of the weapon,
And he releases it lightly, and lifts up his hand,
370 And gives him God's blessing, and graciously prays
That his heart and his hand may be hardy both.
"Keep, cousin," said the king, "what you cut with this day,
And if you rule it aright, then readily, I know,
You shall stand the stroke it will strike after."
375 Gawain goes to the guest with gisarme in hand,
And boldly he bides there, abashed not a whit.
Then hails he Sir Gawain, the horseman in green:
"Recount we our contract, ere you come further.
First I ask and adjure you, how you are called
380 That you tell me true, so that trust it I may."
"In good faith," said the good knight, "Gawain am I
Whose buffet befalls you, what'er betide after,
And at this time twelvemonth take you another
With what weapon you will, and with no man else
385   alive."
          The other nods assent:
          "Sir Gawain, as I may thrive,
          I am wondrous well content
          That you this dint shall drive."

390 "Sir Gawain," said the Green Knight, "By God, I rejoice
That your fist shall fetch this favor I seek,
And you have readily rehearsed, and in right terms,
Each clause of my covenant with the king your lord,
Save that you shall assure me, sir, upon oath,
395 That you shall seek me yourself, wheresoever you deem
My lodgings may lie, and look for such wages
As you have offered me here before all this host."
"What is the way there?" said Gawain. "Where do you dwell?
I heard never of your house, by him that made me,
400 Nor I know you not, knight, your name nor your court.
But tell me truly thereof, and teach me your name,
And I shall fare forth to find you, so far as I may,
And this I say in good certain, and swear upon oath."
"That is enough in New Year, you need say no more,"

405   Said the knight in the green to Gawain the noble,
        "If I tell you true, when I have taken your knock,
        And if you handily have hit, you shall hear straightway
        Of my house and my home and my own name;
        Then follow in my footsteps by faithful accord.
410   And if I spend no speech, you shall speed the better:
        You can feast with your friends, nor further trace
                    my tracks.
             Now hold your grim tool steady
             And show us how it hacks."
415   "Gladly, sir; all ready,"
             Says Gawain; he strokes the ax.

        The Green Knight upon ground girds him with care:
        Bows a bit with his head, and bares his flesh:
        His long lovely locks he laid over his crown,
420   Let the naked nape for the need be shown.
        Gawain grips to his ax and gathers it aloft—
        The left foot on the floor before him he set—
        Brought it down deftly upon the bare neck,
        That the shock of the sharp blow shivered the bones
425   And cut the flesh cleanly and clove it in twain,
        That the blade of bright steel bit into the ground.
        The head was hewn off and fell to the floor;
        Many found it at their feet, as forth it rolled;
        The blood gushed from the body, bright on the green,
430   Yet fell not the fellow, nor faltered a whit,
        But stoutly he starts forth upon stiff shanks,
        And as all stood staring he stretched forth his hand,
        Laid hold of his head and heaved it aloft,
        Then goes to the green steed, grasps the bridle,
435   Steps into the stirrup, bestrides his mount,
        And his head by the hair in his hand holds,
        And as steady he sits in the stately saddle
        As he had met with no mishap, nor missing were
                    his head.
440   His bulk about he haled,
             That fearsome body that bled;
             There were many in the court that quailed
             Before all his say was said.

        For the head in his hand he holds right up;
445   Toward the first on the dais directs he the face,
        And it lifted up its lids, and looked with wide eyes,
        And said as much with its mouth as now you may hear:
        "Sir Gawain, forget not to go as agreed,
        And cease not to seek till me, sir, you find,
450   As you promised in the presence of these proud knights.
        To the Green Chapel come, I charge you, to take
        Such a dint as you have dealt—you have well deserved
        That your neck should have a knock on New Year's morn.
        The Knight of the Green Chapel I am well-known to many,

455 Wherefore you cannot fail to find me at last;
Therefore come, or be counted a recreant knight."
With a roisterous rush he flings round the reins,
Hurtles out at the hall-door, his head in his hand,
That the flint-fire flew from the flashing hooves.
460 Which way he went, not one of them knew
Nor whence he was come in the wide world
     so fair.
    The king and Gawain gay
    Make game of the Green Knight there,
465   Yet all who saw it say
    'Twas a wonder past compare.

Though high-born Arthur at heart had wonder,
He let no sign be seen, but said aloud
To the comely queen, with courteous speech,
470 "Dear dame, on this day dismay you no whit;
Such crafts are becoming at Christmastide,
Laughing at interludes, light songs and mirth,
Amid dancing of damsels with doughty knights.
Nevertheless of my meat now let me partake,
475 For I have met with a marvel, I may not deny."
He glanced at Sir Gawain, and gaily he said,
"Now, sir, hang up your ax,[3] that has hewn enough,"
And over the high dais it was hung on the wall
That men in amazement might on it look,
480 And tell in true terms the tale of the wonder.
Then they turned toward the table, these two together,
The good king and Gawain, and made great feast,
With all dainties double, dishes rare,
With all manner of meat and minstrelsy both,
485 Such happiness wholly had they that day
     in hold.
    Now take care, Sir Gawain,
    That your courage wax not cold
    When you must turn again
490   To your enterprise foretold.

Part 2

This adventure had Arthur of handsels[4] first
When young was the year, for he yearned to hear tales;
Though they wanted for words when they went to sup,
Now are fierce deeds to follow, their fists stuffed full.
495 Gawain was glad to begin those games in hall,
But if the end be harsher, hold it no wonder,
For though men are merry in mind after much drink,
A year passes apace, and proves ever new:
First things and final conform but seldom.

---

3. A colloquial expression equivalent to "bury the
hatchet," but here with an appropriate literal sense
also.
4. New Year's presents.

500 And so this Yule to the young year yielded place,
And each season ensued at its set time;
After Christmas there came the cold cheer of Lent,
When with fish and plainer fare our flesh we reprove;
But then the world's weather with winter contends:
505 The keen cold lessens, the low clouds lift;
Fresh falls the rain in fostering showers
On the face of the fields; flowers appear.
The ground and the groves wear gowns of green;
Birds build their nests, and blithely sing
510 That solace of all sorrow with summer comes
ere long.
And blossoms day by day
Bloom rich and rife in throng;
Then every grove so gay
515 Of the greenwood rings with song.

And then the season of summer with the soft winds,
When Zephyr sighs low over seeds and shoots;
Glad is the green plant growing abroad,
When the dew at dawn drops from the leaves,
520 To get a gracious glance from the golden sun.
But harvest with harsher winds follows hard after,
Warns him to ripen well ere winter comes;
Drives forth the dust in the droughty season,
From the face of the fields to fly high in air.
525 Wroth winds in the welkin wrestle with the sun,
The leaves launch from the linden and light on the ground,
And the grass turns to gray, that once grew green.
Then all ripens and rots that rose up at first,
And so the year moves on in yesterdays many,
530 And winter once more, by the world's law,
draws nigh.
At Michaelmas° the moon   *September 29*
Hangs wintry pale in sky;
Sir Gawain girds him soon
535 For travails yet to try.

Till All-Hallows' Day[5] with Arthur he dwells,
And he held a high feast to honor that knight
With great revels and rich, of the Round Table.
Then ladies lovely and lords debonair
540 With sorrow for Sir Gawain were sore at heart;
Yet they covered their care with countenance glad:
Many a mournful man made mirth for his sake.
So after supper soberly he speaks to his uncle
Of the hard hour at hand, and openly says,
545 "Now, liege lord of my life, my leave I take;
The terms of this task too well you know—
To count the cost over concerns me nothing.

5. All Saints' Day, November 1.

But I am bound forth betimes to bear a stroke
From the grim man in green, as God may direct."
550   Then the first and foremost came forth in throng:
Yvain and Eric and others of note,
Sir Dodinal le Sauvage, the Duke of Clarence,
Lionel and Lancelot and Lucan the good,
Sir Bors and Sir Bedivere, big men both,
555   And many manly knights more, with Mador de la Porte.
All this courtly company comes to the king
To counsel their comrade, with care in their hearts;
There was much secret sorrow suffered that day
That one so good as Gawain must go in such wise
560   To bear a bitter blow, and his bright sword
lay by.
He said, "Why should I tarry?"
And smiled with tranquil eye;
"In destinies sad or merry,
565   True men can but try."

He dwelt there all that day, and dressed in the morning;
Asked early for his arms, and all were brought.
First a carpet of rare cost was cast on the floor
Where much goodly gear gleamed golden bright;
570   He takes his place promptly and picks up the steel,
Attired in a tight coat of Turkestan silk
And a kingly cap-à-dos, closed at the throat,
That was lavishly lined with a lustrous fur.
Then they set the steel shoes on his sturdy feet
575   And clad his calves about with comely greaves,
And plate well-polished protected his knees,
Affixed with fastenings of the finest gold.
Fair cuisses enclosed, that were cunningly wrought,
His thick-thewed thighs, with thongs bound fast,
580   And massy chain-mail of many a steel ring
He bore on his body, above the best cloth,
With brace burnished bright upon both his arms,
Good couters and gay, and gloves of plate,
And all the goodly gear to grace him well
585   that tide.
His surcoat blazoned bold;
Sharp spurs to prick with pride;
And a brave silk band to hold
The broadsword at his side.

590   When he had on his arms, his harness was rich,
The least latchet or loop laden with gold;
So armored as he was, he heard a mass,
Honored God humbly at the high altar.
Then he comes to the king and his comrades-in-arms,
595   Takes his leave at last of lords and ladies,
And they clasped and kissed him, commending him to Christ.
By then Gringolet was girt with a great saddle

That was gaily agleam with fine gilt fringe,
New-furbished for the need with nail-heads bright;
600 The bridle and the bars bedecked all with gold;
The breast-plate, the saddlebow, the side-panels both,
The caparison and the crupper accorded in hue,
And all ranged on the red the resplendent studs
That glittered and glowed like the glorious sun.
605 His helm now he holds up and hastily kisses,
Well-closed with iron clinches, and cushioned within;
It was high on his head, with a hasp behind,
And a covering of cloth to encase the visor,
All bound and embroidered with the best gems
610 On broad bands of silk, and bordered with birds,
Parrots and popinjays preening their wings,
Lovebirds and love-knots as lavishly wrought
As many women had worked seven winters thereon,
                              entire.
615   The diadem costlier yet
                       That crowned that comely sire,
                       With diamonds richly set,
                       That flashed as if on fire.

Then they showed forth the shield, that shone all red,
620 With the pentangle[6] portrayed in purest gold.
About his broad neck by the baldric he casts it,
That was meet for the man, and matched him well.
And why the pentangle is proper to that peerless prince
I intend now to tell, though detain me it must.
625 It is a sign by Solomon sagely devised
To be a token of truth, by its title of old,
For it is a figure formed of five points,
And each line is linked and locked with the next
For ever and ever, and hence it is called
630 In all England, as I hear, the endless knot.
And well may he wear it on his worthy arms,
For ever faithful five-fold in five-fold fashion
Was Gawain in good works, as gold unalloyed,
Devoid of all villainy, with virtues adorned
635   in sight.
                       On shield and coat in view
                       He bore that emblem bright,

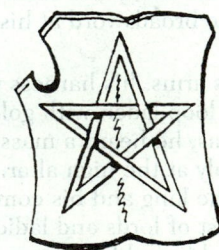

6. A five-pointed star, formed by five lines that are drawn without lifting the pencil from the paper, supposed to have mystical significance; as Solomon's sign (line 625) it was enclosed in a circle.

As to his word most true
And in speech most courteous knight.
640 And first, he was faultless in his five senses,
Nor found ever to fail in his five fingers,
And all his fealty was fixed upon the five wounds
That Christ got on the cross, as the creed tells;
And wherever this man in melee took part,
645 His one thought was of this, past all things else,
That all his force was founded on the five joys[7]
That the high Queen of heaven had in her child.
And therefore, as I find, he fittingly had
On the inner part of his shield her image portrayed,
650 That when his look on it lighted, he never lost heart.
The fifth of the five fives followed by this knight
Were beneficence boundless and brotherly love
And pure mind and manners, that none might impeach,
And compassion most precious—these peerless five
655 Were forged and made fast in him, foremost of men.
Now all these five fives were confirmed in this knight,
And each linked in other, that end there was none,
And fixed to five points, whose force never failed,
Nor assembled all on a side, nor asunder either,
660 Nor anywhere at an end, but whole and entire
However the pattern proceeded or played out its course.
And so on his shining shield shaped was the knot
Royally in red gold against red gules,
That is the peerless pentangle, prized of old
665   in lore.
                Now armed is Gawain gay,
                And bears his lance before,
                And soberly said good day,
                He thought forevermore.

670 He struck his steed with the spurs and sped on his way
So fast that the flint-fire flashed from the stones.
When they saw him set forth they were sore aggrieved,
And all sighed softly, and said to each other,
Fearing for their fellow, "Ill fortune it is
675 That you, man, must be marred, that most are worthy!
His equal on this earth can hardly be found;
To have dealt more discreetly had done less harm,
And have dubbed him a duke, with all due honor.
A great leader of lords he was like to become,
680 And better so to have been than battered to bits,
Beheaded by an elf-man,° for empty pride!   *supernatural being*
Who would credit that a king could be counseled so,
And caught in a cavil in a Christmas game?"
Many were the warm tears they wept from their eyes
685 When goodly Sir Gawain was gone from the court
                    that day.

---

7. Most commonly in Middle English literature, the Annunciation, Nativity, Resurrection, Ascension, and Assumption, although the list varies. These overlap but are not identical with the Five Joyful Mysteries of the Rosary, which were not formally established until the 16th century.

No longer he abode,
But speedily went his way
Over many a wandering road,
690   As I heard my author say.

Now he rides in his array through the realm of Logres,[8]
Sir Gawain, God knows, though it gave him small joy!
All alone must he lodge through many a long night
Where the food that he fancied was far from his plate;
695   He had no mate but his mount, over mountain and plain,
Nor man to say his mind to but almighty God,
Till he had wandered well-nigh into North Wales.
All the islands of Anglesey he holds on his left,
And follows, as he fares, the fords by the coast,
700   Comes over at Holy Head, and enters next
The Wilderness of Wirral[9]—few were within
That had great good will toward God or man.
And earnestly he asked of each mortal he met
If he had ever heard aught of a knight all green,
705   Or of a Green Chapel, on ground thereabouts,
And all said the same, and solemnly swore
They saw no such knight all solely green
                        in hue.
            Over country wild and strange
710   The knight sets off anew;
            Often his course must change
            Ere the Chapel comes in view.

Many a cliff must he climb in country wild;
Far off from all his friends, forlorn must he ride;
715   At each strand or stream where the stalwart passed
'Twere a marvel if he met not some monstrous foe,
And that so fierce and forbidding that fight he must.
So many were the wonders he wandered among
That to tell but the tenth part would tax my wits.
720   Now with serpents he wars, now with savage wolves,
Now with wild men of the woods, that watched from the rocks,
Both with bulls and with bears, and with boars besides,
And giants that came gibbering from the jagged steeps.
Had he not borne himself bravely, and been on God's side,
725   He had met with many mishaps and mortal harms.
And if the wars were unwelcome, the winter was worse,
When the cold clear rains rushed from the clouds
And froze before they could fall to the frosty earth.
Near slain by the sleet he sleeps in his irons
730   More nights than enough, among naked rocks,
Where clattering from the crest the cold stream ran
And hung in hard icicles high overhead.
Thus in peril and pain and predicaments dire

8. One of the names for Arthur's kingdom.
9. Gawain went from Camelot north to the northern coast of Wales, opposite the islands of Anglesey; there he turned east across the Dee to the
forest of Wirral in Cheshire.

He rides across country till Christmas Eve,
735   our knight.
    And at that holy tide
    He prays with all his might
    That Mary may be his guide
    Till a dwelling comes in sight.

740 By a mountain next morning he makes his way
 Into a forest fastness, fearsome and wild;
 High hills on either hand, with hoar woods below,
 Oaks old and huge by the hundred together.
 The hazel and the hawthorn were all intertwined
745 With rough raveled moss, that raggedly hung,
 With many birds unblithe upon bare twigs
 That peeped most piteously for pain of the cold.
 The good knight on Gringolet glides thereunder
 Through many a marsh and mire, a man all alone;
750 He feared for his default, should he fail to see
 The service of that Sire that on that same night
 Was born of a bright maid, to bring us his peace.
 And therefore sighing he said, "I beseech of Thee, Lord,
 And Mary, thou mildest mother so dear,
755 Some harborage where haply I might hear mass
 And Thy matins tomorrow—meekly I ask it,
 And thereto proffer and pray my pater and ave
     and creed."
    He said his prayer with sighs,
760   Lamenting his misdeed;
    He crosses himself, and cries
    On Christ in his great need.

No sooner had Sir Gawain signed himself thrice
 Than he was ware, in the wood, of a wondrous dwelling,
765 Within a moat, on a mound, bright amid boughs
 Of many a tree great of girth that grew by the water—
 A castle as comely as a knight could own,
 On grounds fair and green, in a goodly park
 With a palisade of palings planted about
770 For two miles and more, round many a fair tree.
 The stout knight stared at that stronghold great
 As it shimmered and shone amid shining leaves,
 Then with helmet in hand he offers his thanks
 To Jesus and Saint Julian,[1] that are gentle both,
775 That in courteous accord had inclined to his prayer;
 "Now fair harbor," said he, "I humbly beseech!"
 Then he pricks his proud steed with the plated spurs,
 And by chance he has chosen the chief path
 That brought the bold knight to the bridge's end
780   in haste.
    The bridge hung high in air;

1. Patron saint of hospitality.

The gates were bolted fast;
The walls well-framed to bear
The fury of the blast.

785 The man on his mount remained on the bank
Of the deep double moat that defended the place.
The wall went in the water wondrous deep,
And a long way aloft it loomed overhead.
It was built of stone blocks to the battlements' height,
790 With corbels under cornices in comeliest style;
Watch-towers trusty protected the gate,
With many a lean loophole, to look from within:
A better-made barbican the knight beheld never.
And behind it there hoved a great hall and fair:
795 Turrets rising in tiers, with tines° at their tops,   *spikes*
Spires set beside them, splendidly long,
With finials° well-fashioned, as filigree fine.   *gable ornaments*
Chalk-white chimneys over chambers high
Gleamed in gay array upon gables and roofs;
800 The pinnacles in panoply, pointing in air,
So vied there for his view that verily it seemed
A castle cut of paper for a king's feast.[2]
The good knight on Gringolet thought it great luck
If he could but contrive to come there within
805 To keep the Christmas feast in that castle fair
                              and bright.
                    There answered to his call
                    A porter most polite;
                    From his station on the wall
810   He greets the errant knight.

"Good sir," said Gawain, "Wouldst go to inquire
If your lord would allow me to lodge here a space?"
"Peter!" said the porter, "For my part, I think
So noble a knight will not want for a welcome!"
815 Then he bustles off briskly, and comes back straight,
And many servants beside, to receive him the better.
They let down the drawbridge and duly went forth
And kneeled down on their knees on the naked earth
To welcome this warrior as best they were able.
820 They proffered him passage—the portals stood wide—
And he beckoned them to rise, and rode over the bridge.
Men steadied his saddle as he stepped to the ground,
And there stabled his steed many stalwart folk.
Now come the knights and the noble squires
825 To bring him with bliss into the bright hall.
When his high helm was off, there hied forth a throng
Of attendants to take it, and see to its care;
They bore away his brand° and his blazoned shield;   *sword*
Then graciously he greeted those gallants each one,

2. A common table decoration at feasts.

830 And many a noble drew near, to do the knight honor.
All in his armor into hall he was led,
Where fire on a fair hearth fiercely blazed.
And soon the lord himself descends from his chamber
To meet with good manners the man on his floor.
835 He said, "To this house you are heartily welcome:
What is here is wholly yours, to have in your power
              and sway."
        "Many thanks," said Sir Gawain;
        "May Christ your pains repay!"
840   The two embrace amain
          As men well met that day.

Gawain gazed on the host that greeted him there,
And a lusty fellow he looked, the lord of that place:
A man of massive mold, and of middle age;
845 Broad, bright was his beard, of a beaver's hue,
Strong, steady his stance, upon stalwart shanks,
His face fierce as fire, fair-spoken withal,
And well-suited he seemed in Sir Gawain's sight
To be a master of men in a mighty keep.
850 They pass into a parlor, where promptly the host
Has a servant assigned him to see to his needs,
And there came upon his call many courteous folk
That brought him to a bower where bedding was noble,
With heavy silk hangings hemmed all in gold,
855 Coverlets and counterpanes curiously wrought,
A canopy over the couch, clad all with fur,
Curtains running on cords, caught to gold rings,
Woven rugs on the walls of eastern work,
And the floor, under foot, well-furnished with the same.
860 Amid light talk and laughter they loosed from him then
His war-dress of weight and his worthy clothes.
Robes richly wrought they brought him right soon,
To change there in chamber and choose what he would.
When he had found one he fancied, and flung it about,
865 Well-fashioned for his frame, with flowing skirts,
His face fair and fresh as the flowers of spring,
All the good folk agreed, that gazed on him then,
His limbs arrayed royally in radiant hues,
That so comely a mortal never Christ made
870   as he.
        Whatever his place of birth,
        It seemed he well might be
        Without a peer on earth
        In martial rivalry.

875 A couch before the fire, where fresh coals burned,
They spread for Sir Gawain splendidly now
With quilts quaintly stitched, and cushions beside,
And then a costly cloak they cast on his shoulders
Of bright silk, embroidered on borders and hems,

880 With furs of the finest well-furnished within,
And bound about with ermine, both mantle and hood;
And he sat at that fireside in sumptuous estate
And warmed himself well, and soon he waxed merry.
Then attendants set a table upon trestles broad,
885 And lustrous white linen they laid thereupon,
A saltcellar of silver, spoons of the same.
He washed himself well and went to his place,
Men set his fare before him in fashion most fit.
There were soups of all sorts, seasoned with skill,
890 Double-sized servings, and sundry fish,
Some baked, some breaded, some broiled on the coals,
Some simmered, some in stews, steaming with spice,
And with sauces to sup that suited his taste.
He confesses it a feast with free words and fair;
895 They requite him as kindly with courteous jests,
                              well-sped.
                    "Tonight you fast[3] and pray;
                    Tomorrow we'll see you fed."
                    The knight grows wondrous gay
900   As the wine goes to his head.

Then at times and by turns, as at table he sat,
They questioned him quietly, with queries discreet,
And he courteously confessed that he comes from the court,
And owns him of the brotherhood of high-famed Arthur,
905 The right royal ruler of the Round Table,
And the guest by their fireside is Gawain himself,
Who has happened on their house at that holy feast.
When the name of the knight was made known to the lord,
Then loudly he laughed, so elated he was,
910 And the men in that household made haste with joy
To appear in his presence promptly that day,
That of courage ever-constant, and customs pure,
Is pattern and paragon, and praised without end:
Of all knights on earth most honored is he.
915 Each said solemnly aside to his brother,
"Now displays of deportment shall dazzle our eyes
And the polished pearls of impeccable speech;
The high art of eloquence is ours to pursue
Since the father of fine manners is found in our midst.
920 Great is God's grace, and goodly indeed,
That a guest such as Gawain he guides to us here
When men sit and sing of their Savior's birth
                              in view.
                    With command of manners pure
925   He shall each heart imbue;
                    Who shares his converse, sure,
                    Shall learn love's language true."

---

3. Gawain is said to be "fasting" because the meal, although elaborate, consisted only of fish dishes, appropriate to a fasting day.

When the knight had done dining and duly arose,
The dark was drawing on; the day nigh ended.
930 Chaplains in chapels and churches about
Rang the bells aright, reminding all men
Of the holy evensong of the high feast.
The lord attends alone: his fair lady sits
In a comely closet, secluded from sight.
935 Gawain in gay attire goes thither soon;
The lord catches his coat, and calls him by name,
And has him sit beside him, and says in good faith
No guest on God's earth would he gladlier greet.
For that Gawain thanked him; the two then embraced
940 And sat together soberly the service through.
Then the lady, that longed to look on the knight,
Came forth from her closet with her comely maids.
The fair hues of her flesh, her face and her hair
And her body and her bearing were beyond praise,
945 And excelled the queen herself, as Sir Gawain thought.
He goes forth to greet her with gracious intent;
Another lady led her by the left hand
That was older than she—an ancient, it seemed,
And held in high honor by all men about.
950 But unlike to look upon, those ladies were,
For if the one was fresh, the other was faded:
Bedecked in bright red was the body of one;
Flesh hung in folds on the face of the other;
On one a high headdress, hung all with pearls;
955 Her bright throat and bosom fair to behold,
Fresh as the first snow fallen upon hills;
A wimple the other one wore round her throat;
Her swart chin well swaddled, swathed all in white;
Her forehead enfolded in flounces of silk
960 That framed a fair fillet, of fashion ornate,
And nothing bare beneath save the black brows,
The two eyes and the nose, the naked lips,
And they unsightly to see, and sorrily bleared.
A beldame, by God, she may well be deemed,
965   of pride!
                    She was short and thick of waist,
                    Her buttocks round and wide;
                    More toothsome, to his taste,
                    Was the beauty by her side.

970 When Gawain had gazed on that gay lady,
With leave of her lord, he politely approached;
To the elder in homage he humbly bows;
The lovelier he salutes with a light embrace.
He claims a comely kiss, and courteously he speaks;
975 They welcome him warmly, and straightway he asks
To be received as their servant, if they so desire.
They take him between them; with talking they bring him
Beside a bright fire; bade then that spices

Be freely fetched forth, to refresh them the better,
980 And the good wine therewith, to warm their hearts.
The lord leaps about in light-hearted mood;
Contrives entertainments and timely sports;
Takes his hood from his head and hangs it on a spear,
And offers him openly the honor thereof
985 Who should promote the most mirth at that Christmas feast;
"And I shall try for it, trust me—contend with the best,
Ere I go without my headgear by grace of my friends!"
Thus with light talk and laughter the lord makes merry
To gladden the guest he had greeted in hall
990   that day.
            At the last he called for light
            The company to convey;
            Gawain says goodnight
            And retires to bed straightway.

995 On the morn when each man is mindful in heart
That God's son was sent down to suffer our death,
No household but is blithe for his blessed sake;
So was it there on that day, with many delights.
Both at larger meals and less they were lavishly served
1000 By doughty lads on dais, with delicate fare;
The old ancient lady, highest she sits;
The lord at her left hand leaned, as I hear;
Sir Gawain in the center, beside the gay lady,
Where the food was brought first to that festive board,
1005 And thence throughout the hall, as they held most fit,
To each man was offered in order of rank.
There was meat, there was mirth, there was much joy,
That to tell all the tale would tax my wits,
Though I pained me, perchance, to paint it with care;
1010 But yet I know that our knight and the noble lady
Were accorded so closely in company there,
With the seemly solace of their secret words,
With speeches well-sped, spotless and pure,
That each prince's pastime their pleasures far
1015   outshone.
            Sweet pipes beguile their cares,
            And the trumpet of martial tone;
            Each tends his affairs
            And those two tend their own.

1020 That day and all the next, their disport was noble,
And the third day, I think, pleased them no less;
The joys of St. John's Day° were justly praised,   *December 27*
And were the last of their like for those lords and ladies;
Then guests were to go in the gray morning,
1025 Wherefore they whiled the night away with wine and with mirth,
Moved to the measures of many a blithe carol;
At last, when it was late, took leave of each other,
Each one of those worthies, to wend his way.
Gawain bids goodbye to his goodly host

1030 Who brings him to his chamber, the chimney beside,
And detains him in talk, and tenders his thanks
And holds it an honor to him and his people
That he has harbored in his house at that holy time
And embellished his abode with his inborn grace.
1035 "As long as I may live, my luck is the better
That Gawain was my guest at God's own feast!"
"Noble sir," said the knight, "I cannot but think
All the honor is your own—may heaven requite it!
And your man to command I account myself here
1040 As I am bound and beholden, and shall be, come
                              what may."
                    The lord with all his might
                    Entreats his guest to stay;
                    Brief answer makes the knight:
1045   Next morning he must away.

Then the lord of that land politely inquired
What dire affair had forced him, at that festive time,
So far from the king's court to fare forth alone
Ere the holidays wholly had ended in hall.
1050 "In good faith," said Gawain, "you have guessed the truth:
On a high errand and urgent I hastened away,
For I am summoned by myself to seek for a place—
I would I knew whither, or where it might be!
Far rather would I find it before the New Year
1055 Than own the land of Logres, so help me our Lord!
Wherefore, sir, in friendship this favor I ask,
That you say in sober earnest, if something you know
Of the Green Chapel, on ground far or near,
Or the lone knight that lives there, of like hue of green.
1060 A certain day was set by assent of us both
To meet at that landmark, if I might last,
And from now to the New Year is nothing too long,
And I would greet the Green Knight there, would God but allow,
More gladly, by God's Son, than gain the world's wealth!
1065 And I must set forth to search, as soon as I may;
To be about the business I have but three days
And would as soon sink down dead as desist from my errand."
Then smiling said the lord, "Your search, sir, is done,
For we shall see you to that site by the set time.
1070 Let Gawain grieve no more over the Green Chapel;
You shall be in your own bed, in blissful ease,
All the forenoon, and fare forth the first of the year,
And make the goal by midmorn, to mind your affairs,
                              no fear!
1075   Tarry till the fourth day
                    And ride on the first of the year.
                    We shall set you on your way;
                    It is not two miles from here."

Then Gawain was glad, and gleefully he laughed:
1080 "Now I thank you for this, past all things else!

Now my goal is here at hand! With a glad heart I shall
Both tarry, and undertake any task you devise."
Then the host seized his arm and seated him there;
Let the ladies be brought, to delight them the better,
1085 And in fellowship fair by the fireside they sit;
So gay waxed the good host, so giddy his words,
All waited in wonder what next he would say.
Then he stares on the stout knight, and sternly he speaks:
"You have bound yourself boldly my bidding to do—
1090 Will you stand by that boast, and obey me this once?"
"I shall do so indeed," said the doughty knight;
"While I lie in your lodging, your laws will I follow."
"As you have had," said the host, "many hardships abroad
And little sleep of late, you are lacking, I judge,
1095 Both in nourishment needful and nightly rest;
You shall lie abed late in your lofty chamber
Tomorrow until mass, and meet then to dine
When you will, with my wife, who will sit by your side
And talk with you at table, the better to cheer
1100   our guest.
              A-hunting I will go
              While you lie late and rest."
              The knight, inclining low,
              Assents to each behest.

1105 "And Gawain," said the good host, "agree now to this:
Whatever I win in the woods I will give you at eve,
And all you have earned you must offer to me;
Swear now, sweet friend, to swap as I say,
Whether hands, in the end, be empty or better."
1110 "By God," said Sir Gawain, "I grant it forthwith!
If you find the game good, I shall gladly take part."
"Let the bright wine be brought, and our bargain is done,"
Said the lord of that land—the two laughed together.
Then they drank and they dallied and doffed all constraint,
1115 These lords and these ladies, as late as they chose,
And then with gaiety and gallantries and graceful adieux
They talked in low tones, and tarried at parting.
With compliments comely they kiss at the last;
There were brisk lads about with blazing torches
1120 To see them safe to bed, for soft repose
                    long due.
              Their covenants, yet awhile,
              They repeat, and pledge anew;
              That lord could well beguile
1125   Men's hearts, with mirth in view.

Part 3

Long before daylight they left their beds;
Guests that wished to go gave word to their grooms,
And they set about briskly to bind on saddles,
Tend to their tackle, tie up trunks.

1130 The proud lords appear, appareled to ride,
Leap lightly astride, lay hold of their bridles,
Each one on his way to his worthy house.
The liege lord of the land was not the last
Arrayed there to ride, with retainers many;
1135 He had a bite to eat when he had heard mass;
With horn to the hills he hastens amain.
By the dawn of that day over the dim earth,
Master and men were mounted and ready.
Then they harnessed in couples the keen-scented hounds,
1140 Cast wide the kennel-door and called them forth,
Blew upon their bugles bold blasts three;
The dogs began to bay with a deafening din,
And they quieted them quickly and called them to heel,
A hundred brave huntsmen, as I have heard tell,
1145   together.
              Men at stations meet;
              From the hounds they slip the tether;
              The echoing horns repeat,
              Clear in the merry weather.

1150 At the clamor of the quest, the quarry trembled;
Deer dashed through the dale, dazed with dread;
Hastened to the high ground, only to be
Turned back by the beaters, who boldly shouted.
They harmed not the harts, with their high heads,
1155 Let the bucks go by, with their broad antlers,
For it was counted a crime, in the close season,
If a man of that demesne should molest the male deer.
The hinds were headed up, with "Hey!" and "Ware!"
The does with great din were driven to the valleys.
1160 Then you were ware, as they went, of the whistling of arrows;
At each bend under boughs the bright shafts flew
That tore the tawny hide with their tapered heads.
Ah! they bray and they bleed, on banks they die,
And ever the pack pell-mell comes panting behind;
1165 Hunters with shrill horns hot on their heels—
Like the cracking of cliffs their cries resounded.
What game got away from the gallant archers
Was promptly picked off at the posts below
When they were harried on the heights and herded to the streams:
1170 The watchers were so wary at the waiting-stations,
And the greyhounds so huge, that eagerly snatched,
And finished them off as fast as folk could see
                    with sight.
              The lord, now here, now there,
1175   Spurs forth in sheer delight.
              And drives, with pleasures rare,
              The day to the dark night.

So the lord in the linden-wood leads the hunt
And Gawain the good knight in gay bed lies,
1180 Lingered late alone, till daylight gleamed,

Under coverlet costly, curtained about.
And as he slips into slumber, slyly there comes
A little din at his door, and the latch lifted,
And he holds up his heavy head out of the clothes;
1185   A corner of the curtain he caught back a little
And waited there warily, to see what befell.
Lo! it was the lady, loveliest to behold,
That drew the door behind her deftly and still
And was bound for his bed—abashed was the knight,
1190   And laid his head low again in likeness of sleep;
And she stepped stealthily, and stole to his bed,
Cast aside the curtain and came within,
And set herself softly on the bedside there,
And lingered at her leisure, to look on his waking.
1195   The fair knight lay feigning for a long while,
Conning in his conscience what his case might
Mean or amount to—a marvel he thought it.
But yet he said within himself, "More seemly it were
To try her intent by talking a little."
1200   So he started and stretched, as startled from sleep,
Lifts wide his lids in likeness of wonder,
And signs himself swiftly, as safer to be,
                  with art.
        Sweetly does she speak
1205   And kindling glances dart,
        Blent white and red on cheek
        And laughing lips apart.

"Good morning, Sir Gawain," said that gay lady,
"A slack sleeper you are, to let one slip in!
1210   Now you are taken in a trice—a truce we must make,
Or I shall bind you in your bed, of that be assured."
Thus laughing lightly that lady jested.
"Good morning, good lady," said Gawain the blithe,
"Be it with me as you will; I am well content!
1215   For I surrender myself, and sue for your grace,
And that is best, I believe, and behooves me now."
Thus jested in answer that gentle knight.
"But if, lovely lady, you misliked it not,
And were pleased to permit your prisoner to rise,
1220   I should quit this couch and accoutre me better,
And be clad in more comfort for converse here."
"Nay, not so, sweet sir," said the smiling lady;
"You shall not rise from your bed; I direct you better:
I shall hem and hold you on either hand,
1225   And keep company awhile with my captive knight.
For as certain as I sit here, Sir Gawain you are,
Whom all the world worships, whereso you ride;
Your honor, your courtesy are highest acclaimed
By lords and by ladies, by all living men;
1230   And lo! we are alone here, and left to ourselves:
My lord and his liegemen are long departed,

The household asleep, my handmaids too,
The door drawn, and held by a well-driven bolt,
And since I have in this house him whom all love,
1235 I shall while the time away with mirthful speech
                    at will.
            My body is here at hand,
            Your each wish to fulfill;
            Your servant to command
1240   I am, and shall be still."

"In good faith," said Gawain, "my gain is the greater,
Though I am not he of whom you have heard;
To arrive at such reverence as you recount here
I am one all unworthy, and well do I know it.
1245 By heaven, I would hold me the happiest of men
If by word or by work I once might aspire
To the prize of your praise—'twere a pure joy!"
"In good faith, Sir Gawain," said that gay lady,
"The well-proven prowess that pleases all others,
1250 Did I scant or scout it, 'twere scarce becoming.
But there are ladies, believe me, that had liefer far
Have thee here in their hold, as I have today,
To pass an hour in pastime with pleasant words,
Assuage all their sorrows and solace their hearts,
1255 Than much of the goodly gems and gold they possess.
But laud be to the Lord of the lofty skies,
For here in my hands all hearts' desire
                    doth lie."
            Great welcome got he there
1260   From the lady who sat him by;
            With fitting speech and fair
            The good knight makes reply.

"Madame," said the merry man, "Mary reward you!
For in good faith, I find your beneficence noble.
1265 And the fame of fair deeds runs far and wide,
But the praise you report pertains not to me,
But comes of your courtesy and kindness of heart."
"By the high Queen of heaven" (said she) "I count it not so,
For were I worth all the women in this world alive,
1270 And all wealth and all worship were in my hands,
And I should hunt high and low, a husband to take,
For the nurture I have noted in thee, knight, here,
The comeliness and courtesies and courtly mirth—
And so I had ever heard, and now hold it true—
1275 No other on this earth should have me for wife."
"You are bound to a better man," the bold knight said,
"Yet I prize the praise you have proffered me here,
And soberly your servant, my sovereign I hold you,
And acknowledge me your knight, in the name of Christ."
1280 So they talked of this and that until 'twas nigh noon,
And ever the lady languishing in likeness of love.

With feat words and fair he framed his defense,
For were she never so winsome, the warrior had
The less will to woo, for the wound that his bane
1285   must be.
        He must bear the blinding blow,
        For such is fate's decree:
        The lady asks leave to go;
        He grants it full and free.

1290 Then she gaily said goodbye, and glanced at him, laughing,
And as she stood, she astonished him with a stern speech:
"Now may the Giver of all good words these glad hours repay!
But our guest is not Gawain—forgot is that thought."
"How so?" said the other, and asks in some haste,
1295 For he feared he had been at fault in the forms of his speech.
But she held up her hand, and made answer thus:
"So good a knight as Gawain is given out to be,
And the model of fair demeanor and manners pure,
Had he lain so long at a lady's side,
1300 Would have claimed a kiss, by his courtesy,
Through some touch or trick of phrase at some tale's end."
Said Gawain, "Good lady, I grant it at once!
I shall kiss at your command, as becomes a knight,
And more, lest you mislike, so let be, I pray."
1305 With that she turns toward him, takes him in her arms,
Leans down her lovely head, and lo! he is kissed.
They commend each other to Christ with comely words,
He sees her forth safely, in silence they part,
And then he lies no later in his lofty bed,
1310 But calls to his chamberlain, chooses his clothes,
Goes in those garments gladly to mass,
Then takes his way to table, where attendants wait,
And made merry all day, till the moon rose
                in view
1315   Was never knight beset
        'Twixt worthier ladies two:
        The crone and the coquette;
        Fair pastimes they pursue.

And the lord of the land rides late and long,
1320 Hunting the barren hind over the broad heath.
He had slain such a sum, when the sun sank low,
Of does and other deer, as would dizzy one's wits.
Then they trooped in together in triumph at last,
And the count of the quarry quickly they take.
1325 The lords lent a hand with their liegemen many,
Picked out the plumpest and put them together
And duly dressed the deer, as the deed requires.
Some were assigned the assay of the fat:
Two fingers' width fully they found on the leanest.
1330 Then they slit the slot open and searched out the paunch,
Trimmed it with trencher-knives and tied it up tight.

They flayed the fair hide from the legs and trunk,
Then broke open the belly and laid bare the bowels,
Deftly detaching and drawing them forth.
1335 And next at the neck they neatly parted
The weasand° from the windpipe, and cast away the guts.　　*esophagus*
At the shoulders with sharp blades they showed their skill,
Boning them from beneath, lest the sides be marred;
They breached the broad breast and broke it in twain,
1340 And again at the gullet they begin with their knives,
Cleave down the carcass clear to the breach;
Two tender morsels they take from the throat,
Then round the inner ribs they rid off a layer
And carve out the kidney-fat, close to the spine,
1345 Hewing down to the haunch, that all hung together,
And held it up whole, and hacked it free,
And this they named the numbles,[4] that knew such terms
　　　　　　of art.
　　　　　They divide the crotch in two,
1350　　　　And straightway then they start
　　　　　To cut the backbone through
　　　　　And cleave the trunk apart.

With hard strokes they hewed off the head and the neck,
Then swiftly from the sides they severed the chine,
1355 And the corbie's bone[5] they cast on a branch.
Then they pierced the plump sides, impaled either one
With the hock of the hind foot, and hung it aloft,
To each person his portion most proper and fit.
On a hide of a hind the hounds they fed
1360 With the liver and the lights,° the leathery paunches,　　*lungs*
And bread soaked in blood well blended therewith.
High horns and shrill set hounds a-baying,
Then merrily with their meat they make their way home,
Blowing on their bugles many a brave blast.
1365 Ere dark had descended, that doughty band
Was come within the walls where Gawain waits
　　　　　　at leisure.
　　　　　Bliss and hearth-fire bright
　　　　　Await the master's pleasure;
1370　　　　When the two men met that night,
　　　　　Joy surpassed all measure.

Then the host in the hall his household assembles,
With the dames of high degree and their damsels fair.
In the presence of the people, a party he sends
1375 To convey him his venison in view of the knight.
And in high good-humor he hails him then,
Counts over the kill, the cuts on the tallies,
Holds high the hewn ribs, heavy with fat.
"What think you, sir, of this? Have I thriven well?

4. The other internal organs.　　　　　　5. A bit of gristle assigned to the ravens ("corbies").

1380 Have I won with my woodcraft a worthy prize?"
"In good earnest," said Gawain, "this game is the finest
I have seen in seven years in the season of winter."
"And I give it to you, Gawain," said the goodly host,
"For according to our convenant, you claim it as your own."
1385 "That is so," said Sir Gawain, "the same say I:
What I worthily have won within these fair walls,
Herewith I as willingly award it to you."
He embraces his broad neck with both his arms,
And confers on him a kiss in the comeliest style.
1390 "Have here my profit, it proved no better;
Ungrudging do I grant it, were it greater far."
"Such a gift," said the good host, "I gladly accept—
Yet it might be all the better, would you but say
Where you won this same award, by your wits alone."
1395 "That was no part of the pact; press me no further,
For you have had what behooves; all other claims
                        forbear."
                With jest and compliment
                They conversed, and cast off care;
1400   To the table soon they went;
                Fresh dainties wait them there.

And then by the chimney-side they chat at their ease;
The best wine was brought them, and bounteously served;
And after in their jesting they jointly accord
1405 To do on the second day the deeds of the first:
That the two men should trade, betide as it may,
What each had taken in, at eve when they met.
They seal the pact solemnly in sight of the court;
Their cups were filled afresh to confirm the jest;
1410 Then at last they took their leave, for late was the hour,
Each to his own bed hastening away.
Before the barnyard cock had crowed but thrice
The lord had leapt from his rest, his liegemen as well.
Both of mass and their meal they made short work:
1415 By the dim light of dawn they were deep in the woods
                        away.
                With huntsmen and with horns
                Over plains they pass that day;
                They release, amid the thorns,
1420   Swift hounds that run and bay.

Soon some were on a scent by the side of a marsh;
When the hounds opened cry, the head of the hunt
Rallied them with rough words, raised a great noise.
The hounds that had heard it came hurrying straight
1425 And followed along with their fellows, forty together.
Then such a clamor and cry of coursing hounds
Arose, that the rocks resounded again.
Hunters exhorted them with horn and with voice;
Then all in a body bore off together

1430 Between a mere in the marsh and a menacing crag,
To a rise where the rock stood rugged and steep,
And boulders lay about, that blocked their approach.
Then the company in consort closed on their prey:
They surrounded the rise and the rocks both,
1435 For well they were aware that it waited within,
The beast that the bloodhounds boldly proclaimed.
Then they beat on the bushes and bade him appear,
And he made a murderous rush in the midst of them all;
The best of all boars broke from his cover,
1440 That had ranged long unrivaled, a renegade old,
For of tough-brawned boars he was biggest far,
Most grim when he grunted—then grieved were many,
For three at the first thrust he threw to the earth,
And dashed away at once without more damage.
1445 With "Hi!" "Hi!" and "Hey!" "Hey!" the others followed,
Had horns at their lips, blew high and clear.
Merry was the music of men and of hounds
That were bound after this boar, his bloodthirsty heart
                    to quell.
1450   Often he stands at bay,
                    Then scatters the pack pell-mell;
                    He hurts the hounds, and they
                    Most dolefully yowl and yell.

Men then with mighty bows moved in to shoot,
1455 Aimed at him with their arrows and often hit,
But the points had no power to pierce through his hide,
And the barbs were brushed aside by his bristly brow;
Though the shank of the shaft shivered in pieces,
The head hopped away, wheresoever it struck.
1460 But when their stubborn strokes had stung him at last,
Then, foaming in his frenzy, fiercely he charges,
Hies at them headlong that hindered his flight,
And many feared for their lives, and fell back a little.
But the lord on a lively horse leads the chase;
1465 As a high-mettled huntsman his horn he blows;
He sounds the assembly and sweeps through the brush,
Pursuing this wild swine till the sunlight slanted.
All day with this deed they drive forth the time
While our lone knight so lovesome lies in his bed,
1470 Sir Gawain safe at home, in silken bower
                    so gay.
                    The lady, with guile in heart,
                    Came early where he lay;
                    She was at him with all her art
1475   To turn his mind her way.

She comes to the curtain and coyly peeps in;
Gawain thought it good to greet her at once,
And she richly repays him with her ready words,
Settles softly at his side, and suddenly she laughs,

1480 And with a gracious glance, she begins on him thus:
"Sir, if you be Gawain, it seems a great wonder—
A man so well-meaning, and mannerly disposed,
And cannot act in company as courtesy bids,
And if one takes the trouble to teach him, 'tis all in vain.
1485 That lesson learned lately is lightly forgot,
Though I painted it as plain as my poor wit allowed."
"What lesson, dear lady?" he asked all alarmed;
"I have been much to blame, if your story be true."
"Yet my counsel was of kissing," came her answer then,
1490 "Where favor has been found, freely to claim
As accords with the conduct of courteous knights."
"My dear," said the doughty man, "dismiss that thought;
Such freedom, I fear, might offend you much;
It were rude to request if the right were denied."
1495 "But none can deny you," said the noble dame,
"You are stout enough to constrain with strength, if you choose,
Were any so ungracious as to grudge you aught."
"By heaven," said he, "you have answered well,
But threats never throve among those of my land,
1500 Nor any gift not freely given, good though it be.
I am yours to command, to kiss when you please;
You may lay on as you like, and leave off at will."
                        With this,
                The lady lightly bends
1505   And graciously gives him a kiss;
                The two converse as friends
                Of true love's trials and bliss.

"I should like, by your leave," said the lovely lady,
"If it did not annoy you, to know for what cause
1510 So brisk and so bold a young blood as you,
And acclaimed for all courtesies becoming a knight—
And name what knight you will, they are noblest esteemed
For loyal faith in love, in life as in story;
For to tell the tribulations of these true hearts,
1515 Why, 'tis the very title and text of their deeds,
How bold knights for beauty have braved many a foe,
Suffered heavy sorrows out of secret love,
And then valorously avenged them on villainous churls
And made happy ever after the hearts of their ladies.
1520 And you are the noblest knight known in your time;
No household under heaven but has heard of your fame,
And here by your side I have sat for two days
Yet never has a fair phrase fallen from your lips
Of the language of love, not one little word!
1525 And you, that with sweet vows sway women's hearts,
Should show your winsome ways, and woo a young thing,
And teach by some tokens the craft of true love.
How! are you artless, whom all men praise?
Or do you deem me so dull, or deaf to such words?

1530

Fie! Fie!

In hope of pastimes new

I have come where none can spy;

Instruct me a little, do,

While my husband is not nearby."

1535 "God love you, gracious lady!" said Gawain then;
"It is a pleasure surpassing, and a peerless joy,
That one so worthy as you would willingly come
And take the time and trouble to talk with your knight
And content you with his company—it comforts my heart.
1540 But to take to myself the task of telling of love,
And touch upon its texts, and treat of its themes
To one that, I know well, wields more power
In that art, by a half, than a hundred such
As I am where I live, or am like to become,
1545 It were folly, fair dame, in the first degree!
In all that I am able, my aim is to please,
As in honor behooves me, and am evermore
Your servant heart and soul, so save me our Lord!"
Thus she tested his temper and tried many a time,
1550 Whatever her true intent, to entice him to sin,
But so fair was his defense that no fault appeared,
Nor evil on either hand, but only bliss

they knew.

They linger and laugh awhile;

1555

She kisses the knight so true,

Takes leave in comeliest style

And departs without more ado.

Then he rose from his rest and made ready for mass,
And then a meal was set and served, in sumptuous style;
1560 He dallied at home all day with the dear ladies,
But the lord lingered late at his lusty sport;
Pursued his sorry swine, that swerved as he fled,
And bit asunder the backs of the best of his hounds
When they brought him to bay, till the bowmen appeared
1565 And soon forced him forth, though he fought for dear life,
So sharp were the shafts they shot at him there.
But yet the boldest drew back from his battering head,
Till at last he was so tired he could travel no more,
But in as much haste as he might, he makes his retreat
1570 To a rise on rocky ground, by a rushing stream.
With the bank at his back he scrapes the bare earth,
The froth foams at his jaws, frightful to see.
He whets his white tusks—then weary were all
Those hunters so hardy that hoved round about
1575 Of aiming from afar, but ever they mistrust

his mood.

He had hurt so many by then

That none had hardihood

To be torn by his tusks again,
1580   That was brainsick, and out for blood.

Till the lord came at last on his lofty steed,
Beheld him there at bay before all his folk;
Lightly he leaps down, leaves his courser,
Bares his bright sword, and boldly advances;
1585 Straight into the stream he strides towards his foe.
The wild thing was wary of weapon and man;
His hackles rose high; so hotly he snorts
That many watched with alarm, lest the worst befall.
The boar makes for the man with a mighty bound
1590 So that he and his hunter came headlong together
Where the water ran wildest—the worse for the beast,
For the man, when they first met, marked him with care,
Sights well the slot, slips in the blade,
Shoves it home to the hilt, and the heart shattered,
1595 And he falls in his fury and floats down the water,
                 ill-sped.
           Hounds hasten by the score
           To maul him, hide and head;
           Men drag him in to shore
1600   And dogs pronounce him dead.

With many a brave blast they boast of their prize,
All hallooed in high glee, that had their wind;
The hounds bayed their best, as the bold men bade
That were charged with chief rank in that chase of renown.
1605 Then one wise in woodcraft, and worthily skilled,
Began to dress the boar in becoming style:
He severs the savage head and sets it aloft,
Then rends the body roughly right down the spine;
Takes the bowels from the belly, broils them on coals,
1610 Blends them well with bread to bestow on the hounds.
Then he breaks out the brawn in fair broad flitches,
And the innards to be eaten in order he takes.
The two sides, attached to each other all whole,
He suspended from a spar that was springy and tough;
1615 And so with this swine they set out for home;
The boar's head was borne before the same man
That had stabbed him in the stream with his strong arm,
                 right through.
           He thought it long indeed
1620   Till he had the knight in view;
           At his call, he comes with speed
           To claim his payment due.

The lord laughed aloud, with many a light word,
When he greeted Sir Gawain—with good cheer he speaks.
1625 They fetch the fair dames and the folk of the house;
He brings forth the brawn, and begins the tale
Of the great length and girth, the grim rage as well,

Of the battle of the boar they beset in the wood.
The other man meetly commended his deeds
1630 And praised well the prize of his princely sport,
For the brawn of that boar, the bold knight said,
And the sides of that swine surpassed all others.
Then they handled the huge head; he owns it a wonder,
And eyes it with abhorrence, to heighten his praise.
1635 "Now, Gawain," said the good man, "this game becomes yours
By those fair terms we fixed, as you know full well."
"That is true," returned the knight, "and trust me, fair friend,
All my gains, as agreed, I shall give you forthwith."
He clasps him and kisses him in courteous style,
1640 Then serves him with the same fare a second time.
"Now we are even," said he, "at this evening feast,
And clear is every claim incurred here to date,
           and debt."
        "By Saint Giles!" the host replies,
1645   "You're the best I ever met!
        If your profits are all this size,
        We'll see you wealthy yet!"

Then attendants set tables on trestles about,
And laid them with linen; light shone forth,
1650 Wakened along the walls in waxen torches.
The service was set and the supper brought;
Royal were the revels that rose then in hall
At that feast by the fire, with many fair sports:
Amid the meal and after, melody sweet,
1655 Carol-dances comely and Christmas songs,
With all the mannerly mirth my tongue may describe.
And ever our gallant knight beside the gay lady;
So uncommonly kind and complaisant was she,
With sweet stolen glances, that stirred his stout heart,
1660 That he was at his wits' end, and wondrous vexed;
But he could not rebuff her, for courtesy forbade,
Yet took pains to please her, though the plan might
           go wrong.
        When they to heart's delight
1665   Had reveled there in throng,
        To his chamber he calls the knight,
        And thither they go along.

And there they dallied and drank, and deemed it good sport
To enact their play anew on New Year's Eve,
1670 But Gawain asked again to go on the morrow,
For the time until his tryst was not two days.
The host hindered that, and urged him to stay,
And said, "On my honor, my oath here I take
That you shall get to the Green Chapel to begin your chores
1675 By dawn on New Year's Day, if you so desire.
Wherefore lie at your leisure in your lofty bed,
And I shall hunt hereabouts, and hold to our terms,

And we shall trade winnings when once more we meet,
For I have tested you twice, and true have I found you;
1680 Now think this tomorrow: the third pays for all;
Be we merry while we may, and mindful of joy,
For heaviness of heart can be had for the asking."
This is gravely agreed on and Gawain will stay.
They drink a last draught and with torches depart
1685   to rest.
                    To bed Sir Gawain went:
                    His sleep was of the best;
                    The lord, on his craft intent,
                    Was early up and dressed.

1690 After mass, with his men, a morsel he takes;
Clear and crisp the morning; he calls for his mount;
The folk that were to follow him afield that day
Were high astride their horses before the hall gates.
Wondrous fair were the fields, for the frost was light;
1695 The sun rises red amid radiant clouds,
Sails into the sky, and sends forth his beams.
They let loose the hounds by a leafy wood;
The rocks all around re-echo to their horns;
Soon some have set off in pursuit of the fox,
1700 Cast about with craft for a clearer scent;
A young dog yaps, and is yelled at in turn;
His fellows fall to sniffing, and follow his lead,
Running in a rabble on the right track,
And he scampers all before; they discover him soon,
1705 And when they see him with sight they pursue him the faster,
Railing at him rudely with a wrathful din.
Often he reverses over rough terrain,
Or loops back to listen in the lee of a hedge;
At last, by a little ditch, he leaps over the brush,
1710 Comes into a clearing at a cautious pace,
Then he thought through his wiles to have thrown off the hounds
Till he was ware, as he went, of a waiting-station
Where three athwart his path threatened him at once,
                    all gray.
1715   Quick as a flash he wheels
                    And darts off in dismay;
                    With hard luck at his heels
                    He is off to the wood away.

Then it was heaven on earth to hark to the hounds
1720 When they had come on their quarry, coursing together!
Such harsh cries and howls they hurled at his head
As all the cliffs with a crash had come down at once.
Here he was hailed, when huntsmen met him;
Yonder they yelled at him, yapping and snarling;
1725 There they cried "Thief!" and threatened his life,
And ever the harriers at his heels, that he had no rest.
Often he was menaced when he made for the open,

And often rushed in again, for Reynard was wily;
And so he leads them a merry chase, the lord and his men,
1730 In this manner on the mountains, till midday or near,
While our hero lies at home in wholesome sleep
Within the comely curtains on the cold morning.
But the lady, as love would allow her no rest,
And pursuing ever the purpose that pricked her heart,
1735 Was awake with the dawn, and went to his chamber
In a fair flowing mantle that fell to the earth,
All edged and embellished with ermines fine;
No hood on her head, but heavy with gems
Were her fillet and the fret° that confined her tresses;   ornamental net
1740 Her face and her fair throat freely displayed;
Her bosom all but bare, and her back as well.
She comes in at the chamber-door, and closes it with care,
Throws wide a window—then waits no longer,
But hails him thus airily with her artful words,
1745   with cheer:
          "Ah, man, how can you sleep?
          The morning is so clear!"
          Though dreams have drowned him deep,
          He cannot choose but hear.

1750 Deep in his dreams he darkly mutters
As a man may that mourns, with many grim thoughts
Of that day when destiny shall deal him his doom
When he greets his grim host at the Green Chapel
And must bow to his buffet, bating all strife.
1755 But when he sees her at his side he summons his wits,
Breaks from the black dreams, and blithely answers.
That lovely lady comes laughing sweet,
Sinks down at his side, and salutes him with a kiss.
He accords her fair welcome in courtliest style;
1760 He sees her so glorious, so gaily attired,
So faultless her features, so fair and so bright,
His heart swelled swiftly with surging joys.
They melt into mirth with many a fond smile,
Nor was fair language lacking, to further that hour's
1765   delight.
          Good were their words of greeting;
          Each joyed in other's sight;
          Great peril attends that meeting
          Should Mary forget her knight.

1770 For that high-born beauty so hemmed him about,
Made so plain her meaning, the man must needs
Either take her tendered love or distastefully refuse.
His courtesy concerned him, lest crass he appear,
But more his soul's mischief, should he commit sin
1775 And belie his loyal oath to the lord of that house.
"God forbid!" said the bold knight. "That shall not befall!"
With a little fond laughter he lightly let pass

All the words of special weight that were sped his way;
"I find you much at fault," the fair one said,
1780 "Who can be cold toward a creature so close by your side,
Of all women in this world most wounded in heart,
Unless you have a sweetheart, one you hold dearer,
And allegiance to that lady so loyally knit
That you will never love another, as now I believe.
1785 And, sir, if it be so, then say it, I beg you;
By all your heart holds dear, hide it no longer
                                     with guile."
                        "Lady, by Saint John,"
                        He answers with a smile,
1790   "Lover have I none,
                        Nor will have, yet awhile."

"Those words," said the woman, "are the worst of all,
But I have had my answer, and hard do I find it!
Kiss me now kindly: I can but go hence
1795 To lament my life long like a maid lovelorn."
She inclines her head quickly and kisses the knight,
Then straightens with a sigh, and says as she stands,
"Now, dear, ere I depart, do me this pleasure:
Give me some little gift, your glove or the like,
1800 That I may think on you, man, and mourn the less."
"Now by heavens," said he, "I wish I had here
My most precious possession, to put it in your hands,
For your deeds, beyond doubt, have often deserved
A repayment far passing my power to bestow.
1805 But a love-token, lady, were of little avail;
It is not to your honor to have at this time
A glove as a guerdon from Gawain's hand,
And I am here on an errand in unknown realms
And have no bearers with baggage with becoming gifts,
1810 Which distresses me, madame, for your dear sake.
A man must keep within his compass: account it neither grief
                                     nor slight."
                        "Nay, noblest knight alive,"
                        Said that beauty of body white,
1815   "Though you be loath to give,
                        Yet you shall take, by right."

She reached out a rich ring, wrought all of gold,
With a splendid stone displayed on the band
That flashed before his eyes like a fiery sun;
1820 It was worth a king's wealth, you may well believe.
But he waved it away with these ready words:
"Before God, good lady, I forgo all gifts;
None have I to offer, nor any will I take."
And she urged it on him eagerly, and ever he refused,
1825 And vowed in very earnest, prevail she would not.
And she sad to find it so, and said to him then,
"If my ring is refused for its rich cost—

You would not be my debtor for so dear a thing—
I shall give you my girdle; you gain less thereby."
1830 She released a knot lightly, and loosened a belt
That was caught about her kirtle, the bright cloak beneath,
Of a gay green silk, with gold overwrought,
And the borders all bound with embroidery fine,
And this she presses upon him, and pleads with a smile,
1835 Unworthy though it were, that it would not be scorned.
But the man still maintains that he means to accept
Neither gold nor any gift, till by God's grace
The fate that lay before him was fully achieved.
"And be not offended, fair lady, I beg,
1840 And give over your offer, for ever I must
              decline.
        I am grateful for favor shown
        Past all deserts of mine,
        And ever shall be your own
1845   True servant, rain or shine."

"Now does my present displease you," she promptly inquired,
"Because it seems in your sight so simple a thing?
And belike, as it is little, it is less to praise,
But if the virtue that invests it were verily known,
1850 It would be held, I hope, in higher esteem.
For the man that possesses this piece of silk,
If he bore it on his body, belted about,
There is no hand under heaven that could hew him down,
For he could not be killed by any craft on earth."
1855 Then the man began to muse, and mainly he thought
It was a pearl for his plight, the peril to come
When he gains the Green Chapel to get his reward:
Could he escape unscathed, the scheme were noble!
Then he bore with her words and withstood them no more,
1860 And she repeated her petition and pleaded anew,
And he granted it, and gladly she gave him the belt,
And besought him for her sake to conceal it well,
Lest the noble lord should know—and the knight agrees
That not a soul save themselves shall see it thenceforth
1865   with sight.
        He thanked her with fervent heart,
        As often as ever he might;
        Three times, before they part,
        She has kissed the stalwart knight.

1870 Then the lady took her leave, and left him there,
For more mirth with that man she might not have.
When she was gone, Sir Gawain got from his bed,
Arose and arrayed him in his rich attire;
Tucked away the token the temptress had left,
1875 Laid it reliably where he looked for it after.
And then with good cheer to the chapel he goes,
Approached a priest in private, and prayed to be taught

To lead a better life and lift up his mind,
Lest he be among the lost when he must leave this world.
1880 And shamefaced at shrift he showed his misdeeds
From the largest to the least, and asked the Lord's mercy,
And called on his confessor to cleanse his soul,
And he absolved him of his sins as safe and as clean
As if the dread Day of Doom were to dawn on the morrow.
1885 And then he made merry amid the fine ladies
With deft-footed dances and dalliance light,
As never until now, while the afternoon wore
away.
He delighted all around him,
1890 And all agreed, that day,
They never before had found him
So gracious and so gay.

Now peaceful be his pasture, and love play him fair!
The host is on horseback, hunting afield;
1895 He has finished off this fox that he followed so long:
As he leapt a low hedge to look for the villain
Where he heard all the hounds in hot pursuit,
Reynard comes racing out of a rough thicket,
And all the rabble in a rush, right at his heels.
1900 The man beholds the beast, and bides his time,
And bares his bright sword, and brings it down hard,
And he blenches from the blade, and backward he starts;
A hound hurries up and hinders that move,
And before the horse's feet they fell on him at once
1905 And ripped the rascal's throat with a wrathful din.
The lord soon alighted and lifted him free,
Swiftly snatched him up from the snapping jaws,
Holds him over his head, halloos with a will,
And the dogs bayed the dirge, that had done him to death.
1910 Hunters hastened thither with horns at their lips,
Sounding the assembly till they saw him at last.
When that comely company was come in together,
All that bore bugles blew them at once,
And the others all hallooed, that had no horns.
1915 It was the·merriest medley that ever a man heard,
The racket that they raised for Sir Reynard's soul
that died.
Their hounds they praised and fed,
Fondling their heads with pride,
1920 And they took Reynard the Red
And stripped away his hide.

And then they headed homeward, for evening had come,
Blowing many a blast on their bugles bright.
The lord at long last alights at his house,
1925 Finds fire on the hearth where the fair knight waits,
Sir Gawain the good, that was glad in heart.

With the ladies, that loved him, he lingered at ease;
He wore a rich robe of blue, that reached to the earth
And a surcoat lined softly with sumptuous furs;
1930 A hood of the same hue hung on his shoulders;
With bands of bright ermine embellished were both.
He comes to meet the man amid all the folk,
And greets him good-humoredly, and gaily he says,
"I shall follow forthwith the form of our pledge
1935 That we framed to good effect amid fresh-filled cups."
He clasps him accordingly and kisses him thrice,
As amiably and as earnestly as ever he could.
"By heaven," said the host, "you have had some luck
Since you took up this trade, if the terms were good."
1940 "Never trouble about the terms," he returned at once,
"Since all that I owe here is openly paid."
"Marry!" said the other man, "mine is much less,
For I have hunted all day, and nought have I got
But this foul fox pelt, the fiend take the goods!
1945 Which but poorly repays such precious things
That you have cordially conferred, such kisses three
                      so good."
             "Enough!" said Sir Gawain;
             "I thank you, by the rood!"
1950   And how the fox was slain
             He told him, as they stood.

With minstrelsy and mirth, with all manner of meats,
They made as much merriment as any men might
(Amid laughing of ladies and light hearted girls;
1955 So gay grew Sir Gawain and the goodly host)
Unless they had been besotted, or brainless fools.
The knight joined in jesting with that joyous folk,
Until at last it was late; ere long they must part,
And be off to their beds, as behooved them each one.
1960 Then politely his leave of the lord of the house
Our noble knight takes, and renews his thanks:
"The courtesies countless accorded me here,
Your kindness at this Christmas, may heaven's King repay!
Henceforth, if you will have me, I hold you my liege,
1965 And so, as I have said, I must set forth tomorrow,
If I may take some trusty man to teach, as you promised,
The way to the Green Chapel, that as God allows
I shall see my fate fulfilled on the first of the year."
"In good faith," said the good man, "with a good will
1970 Every promise on my part shall be fully performed."
He assigns him a servant to set him on the path,
To see him safe and sound over the snowy hills,
To follow the fastest way through forest green
                   and grove.
1975   Gawain thanks him again,
             So kind his favors prove,

And of the ladies then
He takes his leave, with love.

Courteously he kissed them, with care in his heart,
1980 And often wished them well, with warmest thanks,
Which they for their part were prompt to repay.
They commend him to Christ with disconsolate sighs;
And then in that hall with the household he parts—
Each man that he met, he remembered to thank
1985 For his deeds of devotion and diligent pains,
And the trouble he had taken to tend to his needs;
And each one as woeful, that watched him depart,
As he had lived with him loyally all his life long.
By lads bearing lights he was led to his chamber
1990 And blithely brought to his bed, to be at his rest.
How soundly he slept, I presume not to say,
For there were matters of moment his thoughts might well
                                        pursue.
        Let him lie and wait;
1995   He has little more to do,
        Then listen, while I relate
        How they kept their rendezvous.

Part 4

Now the New Year draws near, and the night passes,
The day dispels the dark, by the Lord's decree;
2000 But wild weather awoke in the world without:
The clouds in the cold sky cast down their snow
With great gusts from the north, grievous to bear.
Sleet showered aslant upon shivering beasts;
The wind warbled wild as it whipped from aloft,
2005 And drove the drifts deep in the dales below.
Long and well he listens, that lies in his bed;
Though he lifts not his eyelids, little he sleeps;
Each crow of the cock he counts without fail.
Readily from his rest he rose before dawn,
2010 For a lamp had been left him, that lighted his chamber.
He called to his chamberlain, who quickly appeared,
And bade him get him his gear, and gird his good steed,
And he sets about briskly to bring in his arms,
And makes ready his master in manner most fit.
2015 First he clad him in his clothes, to keep out the cold,
And then his other harness, made handsome anew,
His plate-armor of proof, polished with pains,
The rings of his rich mail rid of their rust,
And all was fresh as at first, and for this he gave thanks
2020   indeed.
        With pride he wears each piece,
        New-furbished for his need:
        No gayer from here to Greece;
        He bids them bring his steed.

2025 In his richest raiment he robed himself then:
His crested coat-armor, close-stitched with craft,
With stones of strange virtue on silk velvet set;
All bound with embroidery on borders and seams
And lined warmly and well with furs of the best.
2030 Yet he left not his love-gift, the lady's girdle;
Gawain, for his own good, forgot not that:
When the bright sword was belted and bound on his haunches,
Then twice with that token he twined him about.
Sweetly did he swathe him in that swatch of silk,
2035 That girdle of green so goodly to see,
That against the gay red showed gorgeous bright.
Yet he wore not for its wealth that wondrous girdle,
Nor pride in its pendants, though polished they were,
Though glittering gold gleamed at the tips,
2040 But to keep himself safe when consent he must
To endure a deadly dint, and all defense
                           denied.
                  And now the bold knight came
                  Into the courtyard wide;
2045   That folk of worthy fame
                  He thanks on every side.

Then was Gringolet girt, that was great and huge,
And had sojourned safe and sound, and savored his fare;
He pawed the earth in his pride, that princely steed.
2050 The good knight draws near him and notes well his look,
And says sagely to himself, and soberly swears,
"Here is a household in hall that upholds the right!
The man that maintains it, may happiness be his!
Likewise the dear lady, may love betide her!
2055 If thus they in charity cherish a guest
That are honored here on earth, may they have his reward
That reigns high in heaven—and also you all;
And might I live in this land but a little while,
I should willingly reward you, and well, if I might."
2060 Then he steps into the stirrup and bestrides his mount;
His shield is shown forth; on his shoulder he casts it;
Strikes the side of his steed with his steel spurs,
And he starts across the stones, nor stands any longer
                           to prance.
2065   On horseback was the swain
                  That bore his spear and lance;
                  "May Christ this house maintain
                  And guard it from mischance!"

The bridge was brought down, and the road gates
2070 Unbarred and carried back upon both sides;
He commended him to Christ, and crossed over the planks;
Praised the noble porter, who prayed on his knees
That God save Sir Gawain, and bade him good day,
And went on his way alone with the man

2075   That was to lead him ere long to that luckless place
Where the dolorous dint must be dealt him at last.
Under bare boughs they ride, where steep banks rise,
Over high cliffs they climb, where cold snow clings;
The heavens held aloof, but heavy thereunder
2080   Mist mantled the moors, moved on the slopes.
Each hill had a hat, a huge cape of cloud;
Brooks bubbled and broke over broken rocks,
Flashing in freshets that waterfalls fed.
Roundabout was the road that ran through the wood
2085   Till the sun at that season was soon to rise,

that day.
They were on a hilltop high;
The white snow round them lay;
The man that rode nearby
2090   Now bade his master stay.

"For I have seen you here safe at the set time,
And now you are not far from that notable place
That you have sought for so long with such special pains.
But this I say for certain, since I know you, sir knight,
2095   And have your good at heart, and hold you dear—
Would you heed well my words, it were worth your while—
You are rushing into risks that you reck not of:
There is a villain in yon valley, the veriest on earth,
For he is rugged and rude, and ready with his fists,
2100   And most immense in his mold of mortals alive,
And his body bigger than the best four
That are in Arthur's house, Hector[6] or any.
He gets his grim way at the Green Chapel;
None passes by that place so proud in his arms
2105   That he does not dash him down with his deadly blows,
For he is heartless wholly, and heedless of right,
For be it chaplain or churl that by the Chapel rides,
Monk or mass-priest or any man else,
He would as soon strike him dead as stand on two feet.
2110   Wherefore I say, just as certain as you sit there astride,
You cannot but be killed, if his counsel holds,
For he would trounce you in a trice, had you twenty lives

for sale.
He has lived long in this land
2115   And dealt out deadly bale;
Against his heavy hand
Your power cannot prevail.

"And so, good Sir Gawain, let the grim man be;
Go off by some other road, in God's own name!
2120   Leave by some other land, for the love of Christ,
And I shall get me home again, and give you my word
That I shall swear by God's self and the saints above,
By heaven and by my halidom[7] and other oaths more,

---

6. Either the Trojan hero or one of Arthur's knights.   7. Holiness or, more likely, patron saints.

To conceal this day's deed, nor say to a soul
2125 That ever you fled for fear from any that I knew."
"Many thanks!" said the other man—and demurring he speaks—
"Fair fortune befall you for your friendly words!
And conceal this day's deed I doubt not you would,
But though you never told the tale, if I turned back now,
2130 Forsook this place for fear, and fled, as you say,
I were a caitiff coward; I could not be excused.
But I must to the Chapel to chance my luck
And say to that same man such words as I please,
Befall what may befall through Fortune's will
2135   or whim.
                    Though he be a quarrelsome knave
                    With a cudgel great and grim,
                    The Lord is strong to save:
                    His servants trust in him."

2140 "Marry," said the man, "since you tell me so much,
And I see you are set to seek your own harm,
If you crave a quick death, let me keep you no longer!
Put your helm on your head, your hand on your lance,
And ride the narrow road down yon rocky slope
2145 Till it brings you to the bottom of the broad valley.
Then look a little ahead, on your left hand,
And you will soon see before you that self-same Chapel,
And the man of great might that is master there.
Now goodbye in God's name, Gawain the noble!
2150 For all the world's wealth I would not stay here,
Or go with you in this wood one footstep further!"
He tarried no more to talk, but turned his bridle,
Hit his horse with his heels as hard as he might,
Leaves the knight alone, and off like the wind
2155   goes leaping.
                    "By God," said Gawain then,
                    "I shall not give way to weeping;
                    God's will be done, amen!
                    I commend me to his keeping."

2160 He puts his heels to his horse, and picks up the path;
Goes in beside a grove where the ground is steep,
Rides down the rough slope right to the valley;
And then he looked a little about him—the landscape was wild,
And not a soul to be seen, nor sign of a dwelling,
2165 But high banks on either hand hemmed it about,
With many a ragged rock and rough-hewn crag;
The skies seemed scored by the scowling peaks.
Then he halted his horse, and hoved there a space,
And sought on every side for a sight of the Chapel,
2170 But no such place appeared, which puzzled him sore,
Yet he saw some way off what seemed like a mound,
A hillock high and broad, hard by the water,
Where the stream fell in foam down the face of the steep
And bubbled as if it boiled on its bed below.

2175 The knight urges his horse, and heads for the knoll;
Leaps lightly to earth; loops well the rein
Of his steed to a stout branch, and stations him there.
He strides straight to the mound, and strolls all about,
Much wondering what it was, but no whit the wiser;
2180 It had a hole at one end, and on either side,
And was covered with coarse grass in clumps all without,
And hollow all within, like some old cave,
Or a crevice of an old crag—he could not discern
aright.
2185   "Can this be the Chapel Green?
      Alack!" said the man, "here might
      The devil himself be seen
      Saying matins at black midnight!"

"Now by heaven," said he, "it is bleak hereabouts;
2190 This prayer-house is hideous, half-covered with grass!
Well may the grim man mantled in green
Hold here his orisons, in hell's own style!
Now I feel it is the Fiend, in my five wits,
That has tempted me to this tryst, to take my life;
2195 This is a Chapel of mischance, may the mischief take it!
As accursed a country church as I came upon ever!"
With his helm on his head, his lance in his hand,
He stalks toward the steep wall of that strange house.
Then he heard, on the hill, behind a hard rock,
2200 Beyond the brook, from the bank, a most barbarous din:
Lord! it clattered in the cliff fit to cleave it in two,
As one upon a grindstone ground a great scythe!
Lord! it whirred like a mill-wheel whirling about!
Lord! it echoed loud and long, lamentable to hear!
Then "By heaven," said the bold knight, "that business
2205   up there
Is arranged for my arrival, or else I am much
      misled.
      Let God work! Ah me!
      All hope of help has fled!
2210   Forfeit my life may be
      But noise I do not dread."

Then he listened no longer, but loudly he called,
"Who has power in this place, high parley to hold?
For none greets Sir Gawain, or gives him good day;
2215 If any would a word with him, let him walk forth
And speak now or never, to speed his affairs."
"Abide," said one on the bank above over his head,
"And what I promised you once shall straightway be given."
Yet he stayed not his grindstone, nor stinted its noise,
2220 But worked awhile at his whetting before he would rest,
And then he comes around a crag, from a cave in the rocks,
Hurtling out of hiding with a hateful weapon,
A Danish° ax devised for that day's deed,   *i.e., long-bladed*

With a broad blade and bright, bent in a curve,
2225 Filed to a fine edge—four feet it measured
By the length of the lace that was looped round the haft.
And in form as at first, the fellow all green,
His lordly face and his legs, his locks and his beard,
Save that firm upon two feet forward he strides,
2230 Sets a hand on the ax-head, the haft to the earth;
When he came to the cold stream, and cared not to wade,
He vaults over on his ax, and advances amain
On a broad bank of snow, overbearing and brisk
     of mood.
2235   Little did the knight incline
   When face to face they stood;
   Said the other man, "Friend mine,
   It seems your word holds good!"

"God love you, Sir Gawain!" said the Green Knight then,
2240 "And well met this morning, man, at my place!
And you have followed me faithfully and found me betimes,
And on the business between us we both are agreed:
Twelve months ago today you took what was yours,
And you at this New Year must yield me the same.
2245 And we have met in these mountains, remote from all eyes:
There is none here to halt us or hinder our sport;
Unhasp your high helm, and have here your wages;
Make no more demur than I did myself
When you hacked off my head with one hard blow."
2250 "No, by God," said Sir Gawain, "that granted me life,
I shall grudge not the guerdon, grim though it prove;
Bestow but one stroke, and I shall stand still,
And you may lay on as you like till the last of my part
     be paid."
2255   He proffered, with good grace,
   His bare neck to the blade,
   And feigned a cheerful face:
   He scorned to seem afraid.

Then the grim man in green gathers his strength,
2260 Heaves high the heavy ax to hit him the blow.
With all the force in his frame he fetches it aloft,
With a grimace as grim as he would grind him to bits;
Had the blow he bestowed been as big as he threatened,
A good knight and gallant had gone to his grave.
2265 But Gawain at the great ax glanced up aside,
As down it descended with death-dealing force,
And his shoulders shrank a little from the sharp iron.
Abruptly the brawny man breaks off the stroke,
And then reproved with proud words that prince among knights.
2270 "You are not Gawain the glorious," the green man said,
"That never fell back on field in the face of the foe,
And now you flee for fear, and have felt no harm:
Such news of that knight I never heard yet!

I moved not a muscle when you made to strike,
2275 Nor caviled at the cut in King Arthur's house;
My head fell to my feet, yet steadfast I stood,
And you, all unharmed, are wholly dismayed—
Wherefore the better man I, by all odds,
                                    must be."
2280   Said Gawain, "Strike once more;
            I shall neither flinch nor flee;
            But if my head falls to the floor
            There is no mending me!"

"But go on, man, in God's name, and get to the point!
2285 Deliver me my destiny, and do it out of hand,
For I shall stand to the stroke and stir not an inch
Till your ax has hit home—on my honor I swear it!"
"Have at thee then!" said the other, and heaves it aloft,
And glares down as grimly as he had gone mad.
2290 He made a mighty feint, but marred not his hide;
Withdrew the ax adroitly before it did damage.
Gawain gave no ground, nor glanced up aside,
But stood still as a stone, or else a stout stump
That is held in hard earth by a hundred roots.
2295 Then merrily does he mock him, the man all in green:
"So now you have your nerve again, I needs must strike;
Uphold the high knighthood that Arthur bestowed,
And keep your neck-bone clear, if this cut allows!"
Then was Gawain gripped with rage, and grimly he said,
2300 "Why, thrash away, tyrant, I tire of your threats;
You make such a scene, you must frighten yourself."
Said the green fellow, "In faith, so fiercely you speak
That I shall finish this affair, nor further grace
                                    allow."
2305   He stands prepared to strike
            And scowls with both lip and brow;
            No marvel if the man mislike
            Who can hope no rescue now.

He gathered up the grim ax and guided it well:
2310 Let the barb at the blade's end brush the bare throat;
He hammered down hard, yet harmed him no whit
Save a scratch on one side, that severed the skin;
The end of the hooked edge entered the flesh,
And a little blood lightly leapt to the earth.
2315 And when the man beheld his own blood bright on the snow,
He sprang a spear's length with feet spread wide,
Seized his high helm, and set it on his head,
Shoved before his shoulders the shield at his back,
Bares his trusty blade, and boldly he speaks—
2320 Not since he was a babe born of his mother
Was he once in this world one-half so blithe—
"Have done with your hacking—harry me no more!
I have borne, as behooved, one blow in this place;

If you make another move I shall meet it midway
2325 And promptly, I promise you, pay back each blow
                         with brand.
                 One stroke acquits me here;
                 So did our covenant stand
                 In Arthur's court last year—
2330   Wherefore, sir, hold your hand!"

He lowers the long ax and leans on it there,
Sets his arms on the head, the haft on the earth,
And beholds the bold knight that bides there afoot,
How he faces him fearless, fierce in full arms,
2335 And plies him with proud words—it pleases him well.
Then once again gaily to Gawain he calls,
And in a loud voice and lusty, delivers these words:
"Bold fellow, on this field your anger forbear!
No man has made demands here in manner uncouth,
2340 Nor done, save as duly determined at court.
I owed you a hit and you have it; be happy therewith!
The rest of my rights here I freely resign.
Had I been a bit busier, a buffet, perhaps,
I could have dealt more directly, and done you some harm.
2345 First I flourished with a feint, in frolicsome mood,
And left your hide unhurt—and here I did well
By the fair terms we fixed on the first night;
And fully and faithfully you followed accord:
Gave over all your gains as a good man should.
2350 A second feint, sir, I assigned for the morning
You kissed my comely wife—each kiss you restored.
For both of these there behooved two feigned blows
                         by right.
                 True men pay what they owe;
2355   No danger then in sight.
                 You failed at the third throw,
                 So take my tap, sir knight.

"For that is my belt about you, that same braided girdle,
My wife it was that wore it; I know well the tale,
2360 And the count of your kisses and your conduct too,
And the wooing of my wife—it was all my scheme!
She made trial of a man most faultless by far
Of all that ever walked over the wide earth;
As pearls to white peas, more precious and prized,
2365 So is Gawain, in good faith, to other gay knights.
Yet you lacked, sir, a little in loyalty there,
But the cause was not cunning, nor courtship either,
But that you loved your own life; the less, then, to blame."
The other stout knight in a study stood a long while,
2370 So gripped with grim rage that his great heart shook.
All the blood of his body burned in his face
As he shrank back in shame from the man's sharp speech.
The first words that fell from the fair knight's lips:

"Accursed be a cowardly and covetous heart!
2375 In you is villainy and vice, and virtue laid low!"
Then he grasps the green girdle and lets go the knot,
Hands it over in haste, and hotly he says:
"Behold there my falsehood, ill hap betide it!
Your cut taught me cowardice, care for my life,
2380 And coveting came after, contrary both
To largesse and loyalty belonging to knights.
Now am I faulty and false, that fearful was ever
Of disloyalty and lies, bad luck to them both!
                    and greed.
2385   I confess, knight, in this place,
                Most dire is my misdeed;
                Let me gain back your good grace,
                And thereafter I shall take heed."

Then the other laughed aloud, and lightly he said,
2390 "Such harm as I have had, I hold it quite healed.
You are so fully confessed, your failings made known,
And bear the plain penance of the point of my blade,
I hold you polished as a pearl, as pure and as bright
As you had lived free of fault since first you were born.
2395 And I give you, sir, this girdle that is gold-hemmed
And green as my garments, that, Gawain, you may
Be mindful of this meeting when you mingle in throng
With nobles of renown—and known by this token
How it chanced at the Green Chapel, to chivalrous knights.
2400 And you shall in this New Year come yet again
And we shall finish out our feast in my fair hall,
                    with cheer."
                He urged the knight to stay,
                And said, "With my wife so dear
2405   We shall see you friends this day,
                Whose enmity touched you near."

"Indeed," said the doughty knight, and doffed his high helm,
And held it in his hands as he offered his thanks,
"I have lingered long enough—may good luck be yours,
2410 And he reward you well that all worship bestows!
And commend me to that comely one, your courteous wife,
Both herself and that other, my honoured ladies,
That have trapped their true knight in their trammels so quaint.
But if a dullard should dote, deem it no wonder,
2415 And through the wiles of a woman be wooed into sorrow,
For so was Adam by one, when the world began,
And Solomon by many more, and Samson the mighty—
Delilah was his doom, and David thereafter
Was beguiled by Bathsheba, and bore much distress;
2420 Now these were vexed by their devices—'twere a very joy
Could one but learn to love, and believe them not.
For these were proud princes, most prosperous of old,
Past all lovers lucky, that languished under heaven,

bemused.

2425
And one and all fell prey
To women that they had used;
If I be led astray,
Methinks I may be excused.

"But your girdle, God love you! I gladly shall take
2430 And be pleased to possess, not for the pure gold,
Nor the bright belt itself, nor the beauteous pendants,
Nor for wealth, nor worldly state, nor workmanship fine,
But a sign of excess it shall seem oftentimes
When I ride in renown, and remember with shame
2435 The faults and the frailty of the flesh perverse,
How its tenderness entices the foul taint of sin;
And so when praise and high prowess have pleased my heart,
A look at this love-lace will lower my pride.
But one thing would I learn, if you were not loath,
2440 Since you are lord of yonder land where I have long sojourned
With honor in your house—may you have His reward
That upholds all the heavens, highest on throne!
How runs your right name?—and let the rest go."
"That shall I give you gladly," said the Green Knight then;
2445 "Bercilak de Hautdesert this barony I hold,
Through the might of Morgan le Faye,[8] that lodges at my house,
By subtleties of science and sorcerers' arts,
The mistress of Merlin,[9] she has caught many a man,
For sweet love in secret she shared sometime
2450 With that wizard, that knows well each one of your knights
and you.
Morgan the Goddess, she,
So styled by title true;
None holds so high degree
2455
That her arts cannot subdue.

"She guided me in this guise to your glorious hall,
To assay, if such it were, the surfeit of pride
That is rumored of the retinue of the Round Table.
She put this shape upon me to puzzle your wits,
2460 To afflict the fair queen, and frighten her to death
With awe of that elvish man that eerily spoke
With his head in his hand before the high table.
She was with my wife at home, that old withered lady,
Your own aunt[1] is she, Arthur's half-sister,
2465 The Duchess' daughter of Tintagel, that dear King Uther
Got Arthur on after, that honored is now.
And therefore, good friend, come feast with your aunt;
Make merry in my house; my men hold you dear,

8. Arthur's half-sister, an enchantress who sometimes abetted him, sometimes made trouble for
him.
9. The wise magician who had helped Arthur
become king.

1. Morgan was the daughter of Igraine, duchess
of Tintagel, and her husband the duke; Igraine
conceived Arthur when his father, Uther, lay with
her through one of Merlin's trickeries.

And I wish you as well, sir, with all my heart,
2470   As any man God ever made, for your great good faith."
But the knight said him nay, that he might by no means.
They clasped then and kissed, and commended each other
To the Prince of Paradise, and parted with one
                assent.
2475   Gawain sets out anew;
             Toward the court his course is bent;
             And the knight all green in hue,
             Wheresoever he wished, he went.

Wild ways in the world our worthy knight rides
2480   On Gringolet, that by grace had been granted his life.
He harbored often in houses, and often abroad,
And with many valiant adventures verily he met
That I shall not take time to tell in this story.
The hurt was whole that he had had in his neck,
2485   And the bright green belt on his body he bore,
Oblique, like a baldric, bound at his side,
Below his left shoulder, laced in a knot,
In betokening of the blame he had borne for his fault;
And so to court in due course he comes safe and sound.
2490   Bliss abounded in hall when the high-born heard
That good Gawain was come; glad tidings they thought it.
The king kisses the knight, and the queen as well,
And many a comrade came to clasp him in arms,
And eagerly they asked, and awesomely he told,
2495   Confessed all his cares and discomfitures many,
How it chanced at the Chapel, what cheer made the knight,
The love of the lady, the green lace at last.
The nick on his neck he naked displayed
That he got in his disgrace at the Green Knight's hands,
2500   alone.
             With rage in heart he speaks,
             And grieves with many a groan;
             The blood burns in his cheeks
             For shame at what must be shown.

2505   "Behold, sir," said he, and handles the belt,
"This is the blazon of the blemish that I bear on my neck;
This is the sign of sore loss that I have suffered there
For the cowardice and coveting that I came to there;
This is the badge of false faith that I was found in there,
2510   And I must bear it on my body till I breathe my last.
For one may keep a deed dark, but undo it no whit,
For where a fault is made fast, it is fixed evermore."
The king comforts the knight, and the court all together
Agree with gay laughter and gracious intent
2515   That the lords and the ladies belonging to the Table,
Each brother of that band, a baldric should have,
A belt borne oblique, of a bright green,
To be worn with one accord for that worthy's sake.

So that was taken as a token by the Table Round,
2520 And he honored that had it, evermore after,
As the best book of knighthood bids it be known.
In the old days of Arthur this happening befell;
The books of Brutus' deeds bear witness thereto
Since Brutus, the bold knight, embarked for this land
2525 After the siege ceased at Troy and the city fared
          amiss.
          Many such, ere we were born,
          Have befallen here, ere this.
          May He that was crowned with thorn
2530   Bring all men to His bliss! Amen.

Hony Soyt Qui Mal Pense[2]

2. "Shame be to the man who has evil in his mind." This is the motto of the Order of the Garter, founded ca. 1350: apparently a copyist of the poem associated this order with the one founded to honor Gawain.

GEOFFREY CHAUCER
ca. 1343–1400

Medieval social theory held that society was made up of three "estates": the nobility, composed of a small hereditary aristocracy, whose mission on earth was to rule over and defend the body politic; the church, whose duty was to look after the spiritual welfare of that body; and everyone else, the large mass of commoners who were supposed to do the work that provided for its physical needs. By the late fourteenth century, however, these basic categories were layered into complex, interrelated, and unstable social strata among which birth, wealth, profession, and personal ability all played a part in determining one's status in a world that was rapidly changing economically, politically, and socially. Chaucer's life and his works, especially *The Canterbury Tales*, were profoundly influenced by these forces. A growing and prosperous middle class was beginning to play increasingly important roles in church and state, blurring the traditional class boundaries, and it was into this middle class that Chaucer was born.

Chaucer was the son of a prosperous wine merchant and probably spent his boyhood in the mercantile atmosphere of London's Vintry, where ships docked with wines from France and Spain. Here he would have mixed daily with people of all sorts, heard several languages spoken, become fluent in French, and received schooling in Latin. Instead of apprenticing Chaucer to the family business, however, his father was apparently able to place him, in his early teens, as a page in one of the great aristocratic households of England, that of the countess of Ulster who was married to Prince Lionel, the second son of Edward III. There Chaucer would have acquired the manners and skills required for a career in the service of the ruling class, not only in the role of personal attendant in royal households but in a series of administrative posts.

We can trace Chaucer's official and personal life in a considerable number of surviving historical documents, beginning with a reference, in Elizabeth of Ulster's household accounts, to an outfit he received as a page (1357). He was captured by the French and ransomed in one of Edward III's campaigns during the Hundred Years

War (1359). He was a member of King Edward's personal household (1367) and took part in several diplomatic missions to Spain (1366), France (1368), and Italy (1372). As controller of customs on wool, sheepskins, and leather for the port of London (1374–85), Chaucer audited and kept books on the export taxes, which were one of the Crown's main sources of revenue. During this period he was living in a rent-free apartment over one of the gates in the city wall, probably as a perquisite of the customs job. He served as a justice of the peace and knight of the shire (the title given to members of Parliament) for the county of Kent (1385–86) where he moved after giving up the controllership. As clerk of the king's works (1389–91), Chaucer was responsible for the maintenance of numerous royal residences, parks, and other hold-ings; his duties included supervision of the construction of the nave of Westminster Abbey and of stands and lists for a celebrated tournament staged by Richard II. While the records show Chaucer receiving many grants and annuities in addition to his salary for these services, they also show that at times he was being pressed by creditors and obliged to borrow money.

These activities brought Chaucer into association with the ruling nobility of the kingdom, with Prince Lionel and his younger brother John of Gaunt, duke of Lan-caster, England's most powerful baron during much of Chaucer's lifetime; with their father, King Edward; and with Edward's grandson, who succeeded to the throne as Richard II. Near the end of his life Chaucer addressed a comic *Complaint to His Purse* to Henry IV—John of Gaunt's son, who had usurped the crown from his cousin Richard—as a reminder that the treasury owed Chaucer his annuity. Chaucer's wife, Philippa, served in the households of Edward's queen and of John of Gaunt's second wife, Constance, daughter of the king of Castile. A Thomas Chaucer, who was prob-ably Chaucer's son, was an eminent man in the next generation, and Thomas's daugh-ter Alice was married successively to the earl of Salisbury and the duke of Suffolk. The gap between the commoners and the aristocracy would thus have been bridged by Chaucer's family in the course of three generations.

None of these documents contains any hint that this hardworking civil servant wrote poetry, although poetry would certainly have been among the diversions cul-tivated at English courts in Chaucer's youth. That poetry, however, would have been in French, which still remained the fashionable language and literature of the English aristocracy, whose culture in many ways had more in common with that of the French nobles with whom they warred than with that of their English subjects. Chaucer's earliest models, works by Guillaume de Machaut (1300?–1377) and Jean Froissart (1333?–1400?), the leading French poets of the day, were lyrics and narratives about courtly love, often cast in the form of a dream in which the poet acted as a protagonist or participant in some aristocratic love affair. The poetry of Machaut and Froissart derives from the thirteenth-century *Romance of the Rose*, a long dream allegory in which the dreamer suffers many agonies and trials for the love of a symbolic rosebud. Chaucer's apprentice work may well have been a partial translation of the twenty-one-thousand-line *Romance*. His first important original poem is *The Book of the Duchess*, an elegy in the form of a dream vision commemorating John of Gaunt's first wife, the young duchess of Lancaster, who died in 1368.

The diplomatic mission that sent Chaucer to Italy in 1372 was in all likelihood a milestone in his literary development. Although he may have acquired some knowl-edge of the language and literature from Italian merchants and bankers posted in London, this visit and a subsequent one to Florence (1378) brought him into direct contact with the Italian Renaissance. Probably he acquired manuscripts of works by Dante, Petrarch, and Boccaccio—the last two still alive at the time of Chaucer's visit, although he probably did not meet them. These writers provided him with models of new verse forms, new subject matter, and new modes of representation. *The House of Fame*, still a dream vision, takes the poet on a journey in the talons of a gigantic eagle to the celestial palace of the goddess Fame, a trip that at many points affec-tionately parodies Dante's journey in the *Divine Comedy*. In his dream vision *The

Parliament of Fowls, all the birds meet on St. Valentine's Day to choose their mates; their "parliament" humorously depicts the ways in which different classes in human society think and talk about love. Boccaccio provided sources for two of Chaucer's finest poems—although Chaucer never mentions his name. *The Knight's Tale,* the first of *The Canterbury Tales,* is based on Boccaccio's romance *Il Teseida* (The Story of Theseus). His longest completed poem, *Troilus and Criseyde* (ca. 1385), which tells the story of how Trojan Prince Troilus loved and finally lost Criseyde to the Greek warrior Diomede, is an adaptation of Boccaccio's *Il Filostrato* (The Love-Stricken). Chaucer reworked the latter into one of the greatest love poems in any language. Even if he had never written *The Canterbury Tales, Troilus* would have secured Chaucer a place among the major English poets.

A final dream vision provides the frame for Chaucer's first experiment with a series of tales, the unfinished *Legend of Good Women.* In the dream, Chaucer is accused of heresy and antifeminism by Cupid, the god of love himself, and ordered to do penance by writing a series of "legends," i.e., saints' lives, of Cupid's martyrs, women who were betrayed by false men and died for love. Perhaps a noble patron, possibly Queen Anne, asked the poet to write something to make up for telling about Criseyde's betrayal of Troilus.

Throughout his life Chaucer also wrote moral and religious works, chiefly translations. Besides French, which was a second language for him, and Italian, Chaucer also read Latin. He made a prose translation of the Latin *Consolation of Philosophy,* written by the sixth-century Roman statesman Boethius while in prison awaiting execution for crimes for which he had been unjustly condemned. The *Consolation* became a favorite book for the Middle Ages, providing inspiration and comfort through its lesson that worldly fortune is deceitful and ephemeral and through the platonic doctrine that the body itself is only a prison house for the soul that aspires to eternal things. The influence of Boethius is deeply ingrained in *The Knight's Tale* and *Troilus.* The ballade *Truth* compresses the Boethian and Christian teaching into three stanzas of homely moral advice.

Thus long before Chaucer conceived of *The Canterbury Tales,* his writings were many faceted: they embrace prose and poetry; human and divine love; French, Italian, and Latin sources; secular and religious influences; comedy and philosophy. Moreover, different elements are likely to mix in the same work, often making it difficult to extract from Chaucer simple, direct, and certain meanings.

This Chaucerian complexity owes much to the wide range of Chaucer's learning and his exposure to new literary currents on the Continent but perhaps also to the special social position he occupied as a member of a new class of civil servants. Born into the urban middle class, Chaucer, through his association with the court and service of the Crown, had attained the rank of "esquire," roughly equivalent to what would later be termed a "gentleman." His career brought him into contact with overlapping bourgeois and aristocratic social worlds, without his being securely anchored in either. Although he was born a commoner and continued to associate with commoners in his official life, he did not live as a commoner; and although his training and service at court, his wife's connections, and probably his poetry brought him into contact with the nobility, he must always have been conscious of the fact that he did not really belong to that society of which birth alone could make one a true member. Situated at the intersection of these social worlds, Chaucer had the gift of being able to view with both sympathy and humor the behaviors, beliefs, and pretensions of the diverse people who comprised the levels of society. Chaucer's art of being at once involved in and detached from a given situation is peculiarly his own, but that art would have been appreciated by a small group of friends close to Chaucer's social position—men like Sir Philip de la Vache, to whom Chaucer addressed the humorous envoy to *Truth.* Chaucer belongs to an age when poetry was read aloud. A beautiful frontispiece to a manuscript of *Troilus* pictures the poet's public performance before a magnificently dressed royal audience, and he may well have been invited at times to read his poems at court. But besides addressing a listening audience, to whose allegedly superior taste and sensibility the poet often ironically defers (for example, *The General Prologue*, lines 745–48), Chaucer has in mind discriminating readers whom he might expect to share his sense of humor and his complex attitudes toward the company of "sondry folk" who make the pilgrimage to Canterbury.

The text given here is from E. T. Donaldson's *Chaucer's Poetry: An Anthology for the Modern Reader* (1958, 1975) with some modifications. For *The Canterbury Tales* the Hengwrt Manuscript has provided the textual basis. The spelling has been altered to improve consistency and has been modernized in so far as is possible without distorting the phonological values of the Middle English. A discussion of Middle English pronunciation, grammar, and prosody is included in the introduction to "The Middle Ages" (pp. 11–18).

The Canterbury Tales

Chaucer's original plan for *The Canterbury Tales*—if we assume it to be the same as that which the fictional Host proposes at the end of *The General Prologue*—projected about one hundred twenty stories, two for each pilgrim to tell on the way to Canterbury and two more on the way back. Chaucer actually completed only twenty-two and the beginnings of two others. He did write an ending, for the Host says to the Parson, who tells the last tale, that everyone except him has told "his tale." Indeed, the pilgrims never even get to Canterbury. The work was probably first conceived in 1386, when Chaucer was living in Greenwich, some miles east of London. From his house he might have been able to see the pilgrim road that led toward the shrine of the famous English saint, Thomas à Becket, the archbishop of Canterbury who was murdered in his cathedral in 1170. Medieval pilgrims were notorious tale tellers, and the sight and sound of the bands riding toward Canterbury may well have suggested to Chaucer the idea of using a fictitious pilgrimage as a framing device for a number of stories. Collections of stories linked by such a device were common in the later Middle Ages. Chaucer's contemporary John Gower had used one in his *Confessio Amantis*. The most famous medieval framing tale besides Chaucer's is Boccaccio's *Decameron*, in which ten different narrators each tell a tale a day for ten days. Chaucer could have known the *Decameron*, which contains tales with plots analogous to plots found also in *The Canterbury Tales*, but these stories were widespread, and there is no proof that Chaucer got them from Boccaccio.

Chaucer's artistic exploitation of the device is, in any case, altogether his own. Whereas in Gower a single speaker relates all the stories, and in Boccaccio the ten speakers—three young gentlemen and seven young ladies—all belong to the same sophisticated social elite, Chaucer's pilgrim narrators represent a wide spectrum of ranks and occupations. This device, however, should not be mistaken for "realism." It is highly unlikely that a group like Chaucer's pilgrims would ever have joined together and communicated on such seemingly equal terms. That is part of the fiction, as is the tacit assumption that a group so large could have ridden along listening to one another tell tales in verse. The variety of tellers is matched by the diversity of their tales: tales are assigned to appropriate narrators and juxtaposed to bring out contrasts in genre, style, tone, and values. Thus the Knight's courtly romance about the rivalry of two noble lovers for a lady is followed by the Miller's fabliau of the seduction of an old carpenter's young wife by a student. In several of *The Canterbury Tales* there is a fascinating accord between the narrators and their stories, so that the story takes on rich overtones from what we have learned of its teller in *The General Prologue* and elsewhere, and the character itself grows and is revealed by the story. Chaucer conducts two fictions simultaneously—that of the individual tale and that of the pilgrim to whom he has assigned it. He develops the second fiction not only through *The General Prologue* but also through the "links," the interchanges among pilgrims connecting the stories. These interchanges sometimes lead to quarrels. Thus *The Miller's Tale* offends the Reeve, who takes the figure of the Miller's foolish, cuckolded carpenter as directed personally at himself, and he retaliates with a story satirizing an arrogant miller very much like the pilgrim Miller. The antagonism of the two tellers provides comedy in the links and enhances the comedy of their tales. The links also offer interesting literary commentary on the tales by members of the pilgrim audience, especially the Host, whom the pilgrims have declared "governour" and "juge" of the storytelling. Further dramatic interest is created by the fact that several tales respond to topics taken up by previous tellers. The Wife of Bath's thesis that women should have sovereignty over men in marriage gets a reply from the Clerk, which in turn elicits responses from the Merchant and the Franklin. The tales have their own logic and interest quite apart from the framing fiction; no other medieval framing fiction, however, has such varied and lively interaction between the frame and the individual stories.

The composition of none of the tales can be accurately dated; most of them were written during the last fourteen years of Chaucer's life, although a few were probably written earlier and inserted into *The Canterbury Tales*. The popularity of the poem in late medieval England is attested by the number of surviving manuscripts: more than eighty, none from Chaucer's lifetime. It was also twice printed by William Caxton, who introduced printing to England in 1476, and often reprinted by Caxton's early successors. The manuscripts reflect the unfinished state of the poem—the fact that when he died Chaucer had not made up his mind about a number of details and hence left many inconsistencies. The poem appears in the manuscripts as nine or ten "fragments" or blocks of tales; the order of the poems within each fragment is generally the same, but the order of the fragments themselves varies widely. The fragment containing *The General Prologue;* the Knight's, Miller's, and Reeve's tales; and the Cook's unfinished tale, always comes first, and the fragment consisting of *The Parson's Tale* and *The Retraction* always comes last. But the others, such as that containing the Wife of Bath, the Friar, and the Summoner or that consisting of the Physician and Pardoner or the longest fragment, consisting of six tales concluding with the Nun's Priest's, are by no means stable in relation to one another. The order followed here, that of the Ellesmere manuscript, has been adopted as the most nearly satisfactory.

The General Prologue

Chaucer did not need to make a pilgrimage himself to meet the types of people that his fictitious pilgrimage includes, because most of them had long inhabited literature as well as life: the ideal Knight, who had taken part in all the major expeditions and battles of the crusades during the last half-century; his fashionably dressed son, the Squire, a typical young lover; the lady Prioress, the hunting Monk, and the flattering Friar, who practice the little vanities and larger vices for which such ecclesiastics were conventionally attacked; the prosperous Franklin; the fraudulent Doctor; the lusty and domineering Wife of Bath; the austere Parson; and so on down through the lower orders to that spellbinding preacher and mercenary, the Pardoner, peddling his paper indulgences and phony relics. One meets all these types throughout medieval literature, but particularly in a genre called estates satire, which sets out to expose and pillory typical examples of corruption at all levels of society. A remarkable number of details in *The General Prologue* could have been taken straight out of books as well as drawn from life. Although it has been argued that some of the pilgrims are portraits of actual people, the impression that they are drawn from life is more likely to be a function of Chaucer's art, which is able to endow types with a reality we generally associate only with people we know. The salient features of each pilgrim leap out randomly at the reader, as they might to an observer concerned only with what meets the eye. This imitation of the way our minds actually perceive reality may make us fail to notice the care with which Chaucer has selected his details to give an integrated sketch of the person being described. Most of these details give something more than mere verisimilitude to the description. The pilgrims' facial features, the clothes they wear, the foods they like to eat, the things they say, the work they do are all clues not only to their social rank but to their moral and spiritual condition and, through the accumulation of detail, to the condition of late-medieval society, of which, collectively, they are representative. What uniquely distinguishes Chaucer's prologue from more conventional estates satire, such as the *Prologue* to *Piers Plowman*, is the suppression in all but a few flagrant instances of overt moral judgment. The narrator, in fact, seems to be expressing chiefly admiration and praise at the superlative skills and accomplishments of this particular group, even such dubious ones as the Friar's begging techniques or the Manciple's success in cheating the learned lawyers who employ him. The reader is left free to draw out the ironic implications of details presented with such seeming artlessness, even while falling in with the easygoing mood of "felaweship" that pervades Chaucer's prologue to the pilgrimage.

FROM THE CANTERBURY TALES

The General Prologue

	Whan that April with his° showres soote°	*its / fresh*
	The droughte of March hath perced to the roote,	
	And bathed every veine[1] in swich° licour,°	*such / liquid*
	Of which vertu[2] engendred is the flowr;	
5	Whan Zephyrus eek° with his sweete breeth	*also*
	Inspired[3] hath in every holt° and heeth°	*grove / field*
	The tendre croppes,° and the yonge sonne[4]	*shoots*
	Hath in the Ram his halve cours yronne,	
	And smale fowles° maken melodye	*birds*
10	That sleepen al the night with open yë°—	*eye*
	So priketh hem° Nature in hir corages[5]—	*them*
	Thanne longen folk to goon° on pilgrimages,	*go*
	And palmeres for to seeken straunge strondes	
	To ferne halwes,[6] couthe° in sondry° londes;	*known / various*
15	And specially from every shires ende	
	Of Engelond to Canterbury they wende,	
	The holy blisful martyr[7] for to seeke	
	That hem hath holpen° whan that they were seke.°	*helped / sick*
	Bifel° that in that seson on a day,	*It happened*
20	In Southwerk[8] at the Tabard as I lay,	
	Redy to wenden on my pilgrimage	
	To Canterbury with ful° devout corage,	*very*
	At night was come into that hostelrye	

1. I.e., in plants.
2. By the power of which.
3. Breathed into. "Zephyrus": the west wind.
4. The sun is young because it has run only halfway through its course in Aries, the Ram—the first sign of the zodiac in the solar year.
5. Their hearts.
6. Far-off shrines. "Palmeres": palmers, wide-

ranging pilgrims—especially those who sought out the "straunge strondes" (foreign shores) of the Holy Land.
7. St. Thomas à Becket, murdered in Canterbury Cathedral in 1170.
8. Southwark, site of the Tabard Inn, was then a suburb of London, south of the Thames River.

Wel nine and twenty in a compaignye
25 Of sondry folk, by aventure° yfalle   *chance*
     In felaweshipe, and pilgrimes were they alle
     That toward Canterbury wolden° ride.   *would*
     The chambres and the stables weren wide,
     And wel we weren esed° at the beste.⁹   *accommodated*
30 And shortly,° whan the sonne was to reste,¹   *in brief*
     So hadde I spoken with hem everichoon°   *every one*
     That I was of hir felaweshipe anoon,°   *at once*
     And made forward² erly for to rise,
     To take oure way ther as³ I you devise.°   *describe*
35 But nathelees,° whil I have time and space,⁴   *nevertheless*
     Er° that I ferther in this tale pace,°   *before/proceed*
     Me thinketh it accordant to resoun⁵
     To telle you al the condicioun
     Of eech of hem, so as it seemed me,
40 And whiche they were, and of what degree,°   *social rank*
     And eek° in what array that they were inne: *also*
     And at a knight thanne° wol I first biginne.   *then*
     A Knight ther was, and that a worthy man,
     That fro the time that he first bigan
45 To riden out, he loved chivalrye,
     Trouthe and honour, freedom and curteisye.⁶
     Ful worthy was he in his lordes werre,°   *war*
     And therto hadde he riden, no man ferre,°   *farther*
     As wel in Cristendom as hethenesse,°   *heathen lands*
50 And⁷ evere honoured for his worthinesse.
     At Alisandre⁸ he was whan it was wonne;
     Ful ofte time he hadde the boord bigonne⁹
     Aboven alle nacions in Pruce;
     In Lettou had he reised,° and in Ruce,   *campaigned*
55 No Cristen man so ofte of his degree;
     In Gernade° at the sege eek hadde he be   *Granada*
     Of Algezir, and riden in Belmarye;
     At Lyeis was he, and at Satalye,
     Whan they were wonne; and in the Grete See¹
60 At many a noble arivee° hadde he be.   *military landing*
     At mortal batailes² hadde he been fifteene,
     And foughten for oure faith at Tramissene
     In listes³ thries,° and ay° slain his fo.   *thrice/always*
     This ilke° worthy Knight hadde been also   *same*
65 Sometime with the lord of Palatye⁴

9. In the best possible way.
1. Had set.
2. I.e., (we) made an agreement.
3. Where.
4. I.e., opportunity.
5. It seems to me according to reason.
6. Courtesy. "Trouthe": integrity. "Freedom": generosity of spirit.
7. I.e., and he was.
8. The Knight has taken part in campaigns fought against three groups who threatened Christian Europe during the 14th century: the Muslims in the Near East, from whom Alexandria was seized

after a famous siege; the northern barbarians in Prussia, Lithuania, and Russia; and the Moors in North Africa. The place names in the following lines refer to battlegrounds in these continuing wars.
9. Sat in the seat of honor at military feasts.
1. The Mediterranean.
2. Tournaments fought to the death.
3. Lists, tournament grounds.
4. A Muslim: alliances of convenience were often made during the Crusades between Christians and Muslims.

Again° another hethen in Turkye;   *against*
And everemore he hadde a soverein pris.°   *reputation*
And though that he were worthy, he was wis,[5]
And of his port° as meeke as is a maide.   *demeanor*
70 He nevere yit no vilainye° ne saide   *rudeness*
In al his lif unto no manere wight:[6]
He was a verray,° parfit,° gentil° knight.   *true/perfect/noble*
But for to tellen you of his array,
His hors° were goode, but he was nat gay.[7]   *horses*
75 Of fustian° he wered° a gipoun[8]   *thick cloth/wore*
Al bismotered with his haubergeoun,[9]
For he was late° come from his viage,°   *lately/expedition*
And wente for to doon his pilgrimage.
    With him ther was his sone, a yong Squier,[1]
80 A lovere and a lusty bacheler,
With lokkes crulle° as° they were laid in presse.   *curly/as if*
Of twenty yeer of age he was, I gesse.
Of his stature he was of evene° lengthe,   *moderate*
And wonderly delivere,° and of greet° strengthe.   *agile/great*
85 And he hadde been som time in chivachye[2]
In Flandres, in Artois, and Picardye,
And born him wel as of so litel space,[3]
In hope to stonden in his lady° grace.   *lady's*
    Embrouded° was he as it were a mede,[4]   *embroidered*
90 Al ful of fresshe flowres, white and rede;°   *red*
Singing he was, or floiting,° al the day: *whistling*
He was as fressh as is the month of May.
Short was his gowne, with sleeves longe and wide.
Wel coude he sitte on hors, and faire ride;
95 He coude songes make, and wel endite,°   *compose verse*
Juste[5] and eek° daunce, and wel portraye° and write.   *also/sketch*
So hote° he loved that by nightertale[6]   *hotly*
He slepte namore than dooth a nightingale.
Curteis he was, lowely,° and servisable,   *humble*
100 And carf biforn his fader at the table.[7]
    A Yeman hadde he[8] and servants namo°   *no more*
At that time, for him liste[9] ride so;
And he[1] was clad in cote and hood of greene.
A sheef of pecok arwes,° bright and keene,   *arrows*
105 Under his belt he bar° ful thriftily;°   *bore/properly*
Wel coude he dresse° his takel° yemanly:[2]   *tend to/gear*
His arwes drouped nought with fetheres lowe.

---

5. I.e., he was wise as well as bold.
6. Any sort of person. In Middle English, negatives are multiplied for emphasis, as in these two lines: "nevere," "no," "ne," "no."
7. I.e., gaily dressed.
8. Tunic worn underneath the coat of mail.
9. All rust-stained from his hauberk (coat of mail).
1. The vague term "Squier" (Squire) here seems to be the equivalent of "bacheler" (line 80), a young knight still in the service of an older one.
2. On cavalry expeditions. The places in the next line are sites of skirmishes in the constant warfare between the English and the French.

3. I.e., considering the little time he had been in service.
4. Mead, meadow.
5. Joust, fight in a tournament.
6. At night.
7. It was a squire's duty to carve his lord's meat.
8. I.e., the Knight. The "Yeman" (Yeoman) is an independent commoner who acts as the Knight's military servant.
9. It pleased him to.
1. I.e., the Yeoman.
2. In a workmanlike way.

And in his hand he bar a mighty bowe.
A not-heed° hadde he with a brown visage.   *close-cut head*
110 Of wodecraft wel coude° he al the usage.   *knew*
Upon his arm he bar a gay bracer,[3]
And by his side a swerd° and a bokeler,[4]   *sword*
And on that other side a gay daggere,
Harneised° wel and sharp as point of spere;   *mounted*
115 A Cristophre[5] on his brest of silver sheene;°   *bright*
An horn he bar, the baudrik[6] was of greene.
A forster° was he soothly,° as I gesse.   *forester/truly*
    Ther was also a Nonne, a Prioresse,
That of hir smiling was ful simple and coy.[7]
120 Hir gretteste ooth was but by sainte Loy!°   *Eloi*
And she was cleped° Madame Eglantine.   *named*
Ful wel she soong° the service divine,   *sang*
Entuned° in hir nose ful semely;[8]   *chanted*
And Frenssh she spak ful faire and fetisly,°   *elegantly*
125 After the scole° of Stratford at the Bowe[9]—   *school*
For Frenssh of Paris was to hire unknowe.
At mete° wel ytaught was she withalle:°   *meals/besides*
She leet° no morsel from hir lippes falle,   *let*
Ne wette hir fingres in hir sauce deepe;
130 Wel coude she carye a morsel, and wel keepe°   *take care*
That no drope ne fille° upon hir brest.   *should fall*
In curteisye was set ful muchel hir lest.[1]
Hir over-lippe° wiped she so clene   *upper lip*
That in hir coppe° ther was no ferthing° seene   *cup/bit*
135 Of grece,° whan she dronken hadde hir draughte;   *grease*
Ful semely after hir mete she raughte.°   *reached*
And sikerly° she was of greet disport,[2]   *certainly*
And ful plesant, and amiable of port,°   *mien*
And pained hire to countrefete cheere[3]
140 Of court, and to been statlich° of manere,   *dignified*
And to been holden digne[4] of reverence.
But, for to speken of hir conscience,
She was so charitable and so pitous°   *merciful*
She wolde weepe if that she saw a mous
145 Caught in a trappe, if it were deed° or bledde.   *dead*
Of[5] smale houndes hadde she that she fedde
With rosted flessh, or milk and wastelbreed;°   *fine white bread*
But sore wepte she if oon of hem were deed,
Or if men smoot it with a yerde smerte;[6]
150 And al was conscience and tendre herte.
Ful semely hir wimpel° pinched° was,   *headdress/pleated*
Hir nose tretis,° hir yën° greye as glas,   *well-formed/eyes*

---

3. Wrist guard for archers.
4. Buckler (a small shield).
5. St. Christopher medal.
6. Baldric (a supporting strap).
7. Sincere and shy. The Prioress is the mother superior of her nunnery.
8. In a seemly, proper manner.
9. The French learned in a convent school in

Stratford-at-the-Bow, a suburb of London, was evidently not up to the Parisian standard.
1. I.e., her chief delight lay in good manners.
2. Of great good cheer.
3. And took pains to imitate the behavior.
4. And to be considered worthy.
5. I.e., some.
6. If someone struck it with a rod sharply.

	Hir mouth ful smal, and therto° softe and reed,°	*moreover / red*
	But sikerly° she hadde a fair forheed:	*certainly*
155	It was almost a spanne brood,[7] I trowe,°	*believe*
	For hardily,° she was nat undergrowe.	*assuredly*
	Ful fetis° was hir cloke, as I was war;°	*becoming / aware*
	Of smal° coral aboute hir arm she bar	*dainty*
	A paire of bedes, gauded all with greene,[8]	
160	And theron heeng° a brooch of gold ful sheene,°	*hung / bright*
	On which ther was first writen a crowned A,[9]	
	And after, *Amor vincit omnia*.[1]	
	Another Nonne with hire hadde she	
	That was hir chapelaine,° and preestes three.[2]	*secretary*
165	A Monk ther was, a fair for the maistrye,[3]	
	An outridere[4] that loved venerye,°	*hunting*
	A manly man, to been an abbot able.°	*worthy*
	Ful many a daintee° hors hadde he in stable,	*fine*
	And whan he rood,° men mighte his bridel heere	*rode*
170	Ginglen° in a whistling wind as clere	*jingle*
	And eek° as loude as dooth the chapel belle	*also*
	Ther as this lord was kepere of the celle.[5]	
	The rule of Saint Maure or of Saint Beneit,	
	By cause that it was old and somdeel strait[6]—	
175	This ilke° Monk leet olde thinges pace,°	*same / pass away*
	And heeld° after the newe world the space.°	*held / course*
	He yaf° nought of that text a pulled hen[7]	*gave*
	That saith that hunteres been° nought holy men,	*are*
	Ne that a monk, whan he is recchelees,[8]	
180	Is likned til° a fissh that is waterlees—	*to*
	This is to sayn, a monk out of his cloistre;	
	But thilke° text heeld he nat worth an oystre.	*that same*
	And I saide his opinion was good:	
	What° sholde he studye and make himselven wood°	*why / crazy*
185	Upon a book in cloistre alway to poure,°	*pore*
	Or swinke° with his handes and laboure,	*work*
	As Austin bit?[9] How shal the world be served?	
	Lat Austin have his swink to him reserved!	
	Therefore he was a prikasour° aright.	*hard rider*
190	Grehoundes he hadde as swift as fowl in flight.	
	Of priking° and of hunting for the hare	*riding*
	Was al his lust,° for no cost wolde he spare.	*pleasure*
	I sawgh his sleeves purfiled° at the hand	*fur lined*
	With gris,° and that the fineste of a land;	*gray fur*
195	And for to festne his hood under his chin	
	He hadde of gold wrought a ful curious[1] pin:	

---

7. A handsbreadth wide.
8. Provided with green beads to mark certain prayers. "A paire": string (i.e., a rosary).
9. An *A* with an ornamental crown on it.
1. "Love conquers all."
2. The three get reduced to just one nun's priest.
3. I.e., a superlatively fine one.
4. A monk charged with supervising property distant from the monastery. Monasteries obtained income from large landholdings.

5. Prior of an outlying cell (branch) of the monastery.
6. Somewhat strict. St. Maurus and St. Benedict were authors of monastic rules.
7. He didn't give a plucked hen for that text.
8. Reckless, careless of rule.
9. I.e., as St. Augustine bids. St. Augustine had written that monks should perform manual labor.
1. Of careful workmanship.

A love-knotte in the grettere° ende ther was.   *greater*
His heed was balled,° that shoon as any glas,   *bald*
And eek his face, as he hadde been anoint:
200 He was a lord ful fat and in good point;²
His yën steepe,° and rolling in his heed,   *protruding*
That stemed as a furnais of a leed,³
His bootes souple,° his hors in greet estat°   *supple/condition*
Now certainly he was a fair prelat.⁴
205 He was nat pale as a forpined° gost: *wasted away*
A fat swan loved he best of any rost.
His palfrey° was as brown as is a berye.   *saddle horse*
    A Frere ther was, a wantoune° and a merye,   *jovial*
A limitour,⁵ a ful solempne° man.   *ceremonious*
210 In alle the ordres foure is noon that can°   *knows*
So muche of daliaunce° and fair langage: *sociability*
He hadde maad ful many a mariage
Of yonge wommen at his owene cost;
Unto his ordre he was a noble post.⁶
215 Ful wel biloved and familier was he
With frankelains over al⁷ in his contree,
And with worthy wommen of the town—
For he hadde power of confessioun,
As saide himself, more than a curat,°   *parish priest*
220 For of° his ordre he was licenciat.⁸   *by*
Ful swetely herde he confessioun,
And plesant was his absolucioun.
He was an esy man to yive penaunce
Ther as he wiste to have⁹ a good pitaunce;°   *donation*
225 For unto a poore ordre for to yive
Is signe that a man is wel yshrive,¹
For if he yaf, he dorste make avaunt°   *boast*
He wiste° that a man was repentaunt;   *knew*
For many a man so hard is of his herte
230 He may nat weepe though him sore smerte:²
Therfore, in stede of weeping and prayeres,
Men mote° yive silver to the poore freres.³   *may*
    His tipet° was ay farsed° ful of knives   *hood/stuffed*
And pinnes, for to yiven faire wives;
235 And certainly he hadde a merye note;
Wel coude he singe and playen on a rote;°   *fiddle*
Of yeddinges he bar outrely the pris.⁴
His nekke whit was as the flowr-de-lis;°   *lily*
Therto he strong was as a champioun.

2. In good shape, plump.
3. That glowed like a furnace with a pot in it.
4. Prelate (an important churchman).
5. The "Frere" (Friar) is a member of one of the four religious orders whose members live by begging; as a "limitour" he has been granted by his order exclusive begging rights within a certain limited area.
6. I.e., pillar, a staunch supporter.
7. I.e., with franklins everywhere. Franklins were well-to-do country men.

8. I.e., licensed to hear confessions.
9. Where he knew he would have.
1. Shriven, absolved.
2. Although he is sorely grieved.
3. Before granting absolution, the confessor must be sure the sinner is contrite; moreover, the absolution is contingent on the sinner's performance of an act of satisfaction. In the case of Chaucer's Friar, a liberal contribution served both as proof of contrition and as satisfaction.
4. He absolutely took the prize for ballads.

240　He knew the tavernes wel in every town,
　　　And every hostiler° and tappestere,°　　　　　*innkeeper/barmaid*
　　　Bet° than a lazar or a beggestere.[5]　　　　　*better*
　　　For unto swich a worthy man as he
　　　Accorded nat, as by his facultee,[6]
245　To have with sike° lazars aquaintaunce:　　　　*sick*
　　　It is nat honeste,° it may nought avaunce,°　　*dignified/profit*
　　　For to delen with no swich poraile,[7]
　　　But al with riche, and selleres of vitaile;°　　*foodstuffs*
　　　And over al ther as[8] profit sholde arise,
250　Curteis he was, and lowely of servise.
　　　Ther was no man nowher so vertuous:°　　　　*effective*
　　　He was the beste beggere in his hous.°　　　　*friary*
　　　And yaf a certain ferme for the graunt:[9]
　　　Noon of his bretheren cam ther in his haunt.[1]
255　For though a widwe° hadde nought a sho,°　　*widow/shoe*
　　　So plesant was his *In principio*[2]
　　　Yit wolde he have a ferthing° er he wente;　　*small coin*
　　　His purchas was wel bettre than his rente.[3]
　　　And rage he coude as it were right a whelpe;[4]
260　In love-dayes[5] ther coude he muchel° helpe,　*much*
　　　For ther he was nat lik a cloisterer,
　　　With a thredbare cope, as is a poore scoler,
　　　But he was lik a maister[6] or a pope.
　　　Of double worstede was his semicope,°　　　*short robe*
265　And rounded as a belle out of the presse.°　　*bell mold*
　　　Somwhat he lipsed° for his wantounesse°　　　*lisped/affectation*
　　　To make his Englissh sweete upon his tonge;
　　　And in his harping, whan he hadde songe,°　　*sung*
　　　His yën twinkled in his heed aright
270　As doon the sterres° in the frosty night.　　　*stars*
　　　This worthy limitour was cleped Huberd.
　　　　A Marchant was ther with a forked beerd,
　　　In motelee,[7] and hye on hors he sat,
　　　Upon his heed a Flandrissh° bevere hat,　　　*Flemish*
275　His bootes clasped faire and fetisly.°　　　　*elegantly*
　　　His resons° he spak ful solempnely,　　　　　*opinions*
　　　Souning° alway th' encrees of his winning.°　*implying/profit*
　　　He wolde the see were kept for any thing[8]
　　　Bitwixen Middelburgh and Orewelle.
280　Wel coude he in eschaunge sheeldes[9] selle.

---

5. "Beggestere": female beggar. "Lazar:" leper.
6. It was not suitable because of his position.
7. I.e., poor trash. The oldest order of friars had been founded by St. Francis to administer to the spiritual needs of precisely those classes the Friar avoids.
8. Everywhere.
9. And he paid a certain rent for the privilege of begging.
1. Assigned territory.
2. A friar's usual salutation: "In the beginning [was the Word]" (John 1.1).
3. I.e., the money he got through such activity was more than his proper income.

4. And he could flirt wantonly, as if he were a puppy.
5. Days appointed for the settlement of lawsuits out of court.
6. A man of recognized learning.
7. Motley, a cloth of mixed color.
8. I.e., he wished the sea to be guarded at all costs. The sea route between Middelburgh (in the Netherlands) and Orwell (in Suffolk) was vital to the Merchant's export and import of wool—the basis of England's chief trade at the time.
9. Shields were units of transfer in international credit, which he exchanged at a profit.

This worthy man ful wel his wit bisette:°   *employed*
Ther wiste° no wight° that he was in dette,   *knew / person*
So statly° was he of his governaunce,[1]   *dignified*
With his bargaines,° and with his chevissaunce.°   *bargainings / borrowing*
285 Forsoothe° he was a worthy man withalle;   *in truth*
But, sooth to sayn, I noot° how men him calle.   *don't know*
    A Clerk[2] ther was of Oxenforde also
That unto logik hadde longe ygo.[3]
As lene was his hors as is a rake,
290 And he was nought right fat, I undertake,
But looked holwe,° and therto sobrely.   *hollow*
Ful thredbare was his overeste courtepy,
For he hadde geten him yit no benefice,[4]
Ne was so worldly for to have office.°   *secular employment*
295 For him was levere[5] have at his beddes heed
Twenty bookes, clad in blak or reed,
Of Aristotle and his philosophye,
Than robes riche, or fithele,° or gay sautrye.[6]   *fiddle*
But al be that he was a philosophre[7]
300 Yit hadde he but litel gold in cofre;°   *coffer*
But al that he mighte of his freendes hente,°   *take*
On bookes and on lerning he it spente,
And bisily gan for the soules praye
Of hem that yaf him wherwith to scoleye.°   *study*
305 Of studye took he most cure° and most heede.   *care*
Nought oo° word spak he more than was neede,   *one*
And that was said in forme[8] and reverence,
And short and quik,° and ful of heigh sentence:[9]   *lively*
Souning° in moral vertu was his speeche,   *resounding*
310 And gladly wolde he lerne, and gladly teche.
    A Sergeant of the Lawe, war and wis,[1]
That often hadde been at the Parvis[2]
Ther was also, ful riche of excellence.
Discreet he was, and of greet reverence—
315 He seemed swich, his wordes weren so wise.
Justice he was ful often in assise°   *circuit courts*
By patente[3] and by plein° commissioun.   *full*
For his science° and for his heigh renown   *knowledge*
Of fees and robes hadde he many oon.
320 So greet a purchasour° was nowher noon;   *speculator in land*
Al was fee simple[4] to him in effect—
His purchasing mighte nat been infect.[5]

---

1. The management of his affairs.
2. The Clerk is a student at Oxford; to become a student, he would have had to signify his intention of becoming a cleric, but he was not bound to proceed to a position of responsibility in the church.
3. Who had long since matriculated in philosophy.
4. Ecclesiastical living, such as the income a parish priest receives. "Courtepy": outer cloak.
5. He would rather.
6. Psaltery (a kind of harp).
7. The word may also mean alchemist, someone who tries to turn base metals into gold. The Clerk's

"philosophy" does not pay either way.
8. With decorum.
9. Elevated thought.
1. Wary and wise. The Sergeant is not only a practicing lawyer but one of the high justices of the nation.
2. The Paradise, the porch of St. Paul's Cathedral, a meeting place for lawyers and their clients.
3. Royal warrant.
4. Owned outright without legal impediments.
5. Invalidated on a legal technicality.

Nowher so bisy a man as he ther nas;°   *was not*
And yit he seemed bisier than he was.
325   In termes hadde he caas and doomes⁶ alle
That from the time of King William⁷ were falle.
Therto he coude endite and make a thing,⁸
Ther coude no wight pinchen° at his writing;   *cavil*
And every statut coude° he plein° by rote.⁹   *knew/entire*
330   He rood but hoomly° in a medlee cote,¹   *unpretentiously*
Girt with a ceint° of silk, with barres² smale.   *belt*
Of his array telle I no lenger tale.
A Frankelain³ was in his compaignye:
Whit was his beerd as is the dayesye;°   *daisy*
335   Of his complexion he was sanguin.⁴
Wel loved he by the morwe a sop in win.⁵
To liven in delit° was evere his wone,°   *sensual delight/wont*
For he was Epicurus⁶ owene sone,
That heeld opinion that plein° delit   *full*
340   Was verray° felicitee parfit.°   *true/perfect*
An housholdere and that a greet was he:
Saint Julian⁷ he was in his contree.
His breed, his ale, was always after oon;⁸
A bettre envined° man was nevere noon.   *wine-stocked*
345   Withouten bake mete was nevere his hous,
Of fissh and flessh, and that so plentevous°   *plenteous*
It snewed° in his hous of mete° and drinke,   *snowed/food*
Of alle daintees that men coude thinke.
After° the sondry sesons of the yeer   *according to*
350   So chaunged he his mete° and his soper.°   *dinner/supper*
Ful many a fat partrich hadde he in mewe,°   *cage*
And many a breem,° and many a luce° in stewe.⁹   *carp/pike*
Wo was his cook but if his sauce were
Poinant° and sharp, and redy all his gere.   *spicy*
355   His table dormant in his halle alway
Stood redy covered all the longe day.¹
At sessions ther was he lord and sire.
Ful ofte time he was Knight of the Shire.²
An anlaas° and a gipser° al of silk   *dagger/purse*
360   Heeng at his girdel,³ whit as morne° milk.   *morning*
A shirreve° hadde he been, and countour.⁴   *sheriff*
Was nowhere swich a worthy vavasour.⁵

---

6. Law cases and decisions. "By termes": i.e., by heart.
7. I.e., the Conqueror (reigned 1066–87).
8. Compose and draw up a deed.
9. By heart.
1. A coat of mixed color.
2. Transverse stripes.
3. The "Frankelain" (Franklin) is a prosperous country man, whose lower-class ancestry is no impediment to the importance he has attained in his county.
4. A reference to the fact that the Franklin's temperament, "humor," is dominated by blood as well as to his red face (see p. 188, n. 8).
5. I.e., in the morning he was very fond of a piece of bread soaked in wine.

6. The Greek philosopher whose teaching is popularly believed to make pleasure the chief goal of life.
7. The patron saint of hospitality.
8. Always of the same high quality.
9. Fishpond.
1. Tables were usually dismounted when not in use, but the Franklin kept his mounted and set ("covered"), hence "dormant."
2. County representative in Parliament. "Sessions": i.e., sessions of the justices of the peace.
3. Hung at his belt.
4. Auditor of county finances.
5. Feudal landholder of lowest rank; a provincial gentleman.

An Haberdasshere and a Carpenter,
A Webbe,° a Dyere, and a Tapicer°—   *weaver/tapestry maker*
365   And they were clothed alle in oo liveree[6]
Of a solempne and greet fraternitee.
Ful fresshe and newe hir gere apiked° was;   *trimmed*
Hir knives were chaped° nought with bras,   *mounted*
But al with silver; wrought ful clene and weel
370   Hir girdles and hir pouches everydeel.°   *altogether*
Wel seemed eech of hem a fair burgeis°   *burgher*
To sitten in a yeldehalle° on a dais.   *guildhall*
Everich, for the wisdom that he can,[7]
Was shaply° for to been an alderman.   *suitable*
375   For catel° hadde they ynough and rente,°   *property/income*
And eek hir wives wolde it wel assente—
And elles certain were they to blame:
It is ful fair to been ycleped° "Madame,"   *called*
And goon to vigilies all bifore,[8]
380   And have a mantel royalliche ybore.[9]
     A Cook they hadde with hem for the nones,[1]
To boile the chiknes with the marybones,°   *marrowbones*
And powdre-marchant tart and galingale.[2]
Wel coude he knowe° a draughte of London ale.   *recognize*
385   He coude roste, and seethe,° and broile, and frye, *boil*
Maken mortreux,° and wel bake a pie.   *stews*
But greet harm was it, as it thoughte° me,   *seemed to*
That on his shine a mormal° hadde he,   *ulcer*
For blankmanger,[3] that made he with the beste.
390   A Shipman was ther, woning° fer by weste—°   *dwelling/in the west*
For ought I woot,° he was of Dertemouthe.[4]   *know*
He rood upon a rouncy° as he couthe,[5]   *large nag*
In a gowne of falding° to the knee.   *heavy wool*
A daggere hanging on a laas° hadde he   *strap*
395   Aboute his nekke, under his arm adown.
The hote somer hadde maad his hewe° al brown;   *color*
And certainly he was a good felawe.
Ful many a draughte of win hadde he drawe[6]
Fro Burdeuxward, whil that the chapman sleep:[7]
400   Of nice° conscience took he no keep;°   *fastidious/heed*
If that he faught and hadde the hyer° hand,   *upper*
By water he sente hem hoom to every land.[8]
But of his craft, to rekene wel his tides,
His stremes° and his daungers° him bisides,[9]   *currents/hazards*
405   His herberwe° and his moone, his lodemenage,[1] *anchorage*

---

6. In one livery, i.e., the uniform of their "fraternitee" or guild, a partly religious, partly social organization.
7. Was capable of.
8. I.e., at the head of the procession. "Vigiles":
feasts held on the eve of saints' days.
9. Royally carried.
1. For the occasion.
2. "Powdre-marchant" and "galingale" are flavor-
ing materials.

3. A white stew or mousse.
4. Dartmouth, a port in the southwest of England.
5. As best he could.
6. Drawn, i.e., stolen.
7. Merchant slept. "Fro Burdeuxward": from
Bordeaux; i.e., while carrying wine from Bordeaux
(the wine center of France).
8. He drowned his prisoners.
9. Around him.
1. Pilotage, art of navigation.

There was noon swich from Hulle to Cartage.[2]
Hardy he was and wis to undertake;[3]
With many a tempest hadde his beerd been shake;
He knew alle the havenes° as they were   *harbors*
410 Fro Gotlond to the Cape of Finistere,[4]
And every crike° in Britaine° and in Spaine.   *inlet / Brittany*
His barge ycleped was the Maudelaine.°   *Magdalene*
   With us ther was a Doctour of Physik:°   *medicine*
In al this world ne was ther noon him lik
415 To speken of physik and of surgerye.
For° he was grounded in astronomye,°   *because / astrology*
He kepte° his pacient a ful greet deel[5]   *tended to*
In houres by his magik naturel.[6]
Wel coude he fortunen the ascendent
420 Of his images[7] for his pacient.
He knew the cause of every maladye,
Were it of hoot or cold or moiste or drye,
And where engendred and of what humour:[8]
He was a verray parfit praktisour.[9]
425 The cause yknowe,° and of his° harm the roote,   *known / its*
Anoon he yaf the sike man his boote.°   *remedy*
   Ful redy hadde he his apothecaries
To senden him drogges° and his letuaries,°   *drugs / medicines*
For eech of hem made other for to winne:
430 Hir frendshipe was nought newe to biginne.
Wel knew he the olde Esculapius,[1]
And Deiscorides and eek Rufus,
Olde Ipocras, Hali, and Galien,
Serapion, Razis, and Avicen,
435 Averrois, Damascien, and Constantin,
Bernard, and Gatesden, and Gilbertin.
Of his diete mesurable° was he,   *moderate*
For it was of no superfluitee,
But of greet norissing° and digestible.   *nourishment*
440 His studye was but litel on the Bible.
In sanguin° and in pers° he clad was al,   *blood red / blue*
Lined with taffata and with sendal;°   *silk*
And yit he was but esy of dispence;°   *expenditure*

2. From Hull (in northern England) to Cartagena (in Spain).
3. Shrewd in his undertakings.
4. From Gotland (an island in the Baltic) to Finisterre (the westernmost point in Spain).
5. Closely.
6. Natural—as opposed to black—magic. "In houres": i.e., the astrologically important hours (when conjunctions of the planets might help his recovery).
7. Assign the propitious time, according to the position of stars, for using talismanic images. Such images, representing either the patient himself or points in the zodiac, were thought to be influential on the course of the disease.
8. Diseases were thought to be caused by a disturbance of one or another of the four bodily "humors," each of which, like the four elements, was a compound of two of the elementary qualities

mentioned in line 422: the melancholy humor, seated in the black bile, was cold and dry (like earth); the sanguine, seated in the blood, hot and moist (like air); the choleric, seated in the yellow bile, hot and dry (like fire); the phlegmatic, seated in the phlegm, cold and moist (like water).
9. True perfect practitioner.
1. The Doctor is familiar with the treatises that the Middle Ages attributed to the "great names" of medical history, whom Chaucer names: the purely legendary Greek demigod Aesculapius; the Greeks Dioscorides, Rufus, Hippocrates, Galen, and Serapion; the Persians Hali and Rhazes; the Arabians Avicenna and Averroës; the early Christians John (?) of Damascus and Constantine Afer; the Scotsman Bernard Gordon; the Englishmen John of Gatesden and Gilbert, the former an early contemporary of Chaucer.

He kepte that he wan in pestilence.[2]
445 For° gold in physik is a cordial,[3]   *because*
Therfore he loved gold in special.
    A good Wif was ther of biside Bathe,
But she was somdeel deef,° and that was scathe.°   *a bit deaf/a pity*
Of cloth-making she hadde swich an haunt,°   *skill*
450 She passed° hem of Ypres and of Gaunt.[4]   *surpassed*
In al the parissh wif ne was ther noon
That to the offring[5] bifore hire sholde goon,
And if ther dide, certain so wroth° was she   *angry*
That she was out of alle charitee.
455 Hir coverchiefs° ful fine were of ground°—   *headcovers/texture*
I dorste° swere they weyeden° ten pound   *dare/weighed*
That on a Sonday weren° upon hir heed.   *were*
Hir hosen° weren of fin scarlet reed,°   *leggings/red*
Ful straite yteyd,[6] and shoes ful moiste° and newe. *supple*
460 Bold was hir face and fair and reed of hewe.
She was a worthy womman al hir live:
Housbondes at chirche dore[7] she hadde five,
Withouten° other compaignye in youthe—   *not counting*
But therof needeth nought to speke as nouthe.°   *now*
465 And thries hadde she been at Jerusalem;
She hadde passed many a straunge° streem;   *foreign*
At Rome she hadde been, and at Boloigne,
In Galice at Saint Jame, and at Coloigne:[8]
She coude° muchel of wandring by the waye: *knew*
470 Gat-toothed[9] was she, soothly for to saye.
Upon an amblere[1] esily she sat,
Ywimpled° wel, and on hir heed an hat   *veiled*
As brood as is a bokeler or a targe,[2]
A foot-mantel° aboute hir hipes large,   *riding skirt*
475 And on hir feet a paire of spores° sharpe.   *spurs*
In felaweshipe wel coude she laughe and carpe:° *talk*
Of remedies of love she knew parchaunce,°   *as it happened*
For she coude of that art the olde daunce.[3]
    A good man was ther of religioun,
480 And was a poore Person° of a town,   *parson*
But riche he was of holy thought and werk.
He was also a lerned man, a clerk,
That Cristes gospel trewely° wolde preche;   *faithfully*
His parisshens° devoutly wolde he teche.   *parishioners*
485 Benigne he was, and wonder° diligent,   *wonderfully*
And in adversitee ful pacient,

---

2. He saved the money he made during the plague time.
3. A stimulant. Gold was thought to have some medicinal properties.
4. Ypres and Ghent ("Gaunt") were Flemish cloth-making centers.
5. The offering in church, when the congregation brought its gifts forward.
6. Tightly laced.
7. In medieval times, weddings were performed at the church door.

8. Rome, Boulogne (in France), St. James (of Compostella) in Galicia (Spain), and Cologne (in Germany) were all sites of shrines much visited by pilgrims.
9. Gap-toothed, thought to be a sign of amorousness.
1. Horse with an easy gait.
2. "Bokeler" and "targe": small shields.
3. I.e., she knew all the tricks of that trade.

And swich he was preved° ofte sithes.°   proved / times
Ful loth were him to cursen for his tithes,[4]
But rather wolde he yiven, out of doute,[5]
490   Unto his poore parisshens aboute
Of his offring[6] and eek of his substaunce:°   property
He coude in litel thing have suffisaunce.°   sufficiency
Wid was his parissh, and houses fer asonder,
But he ne lafte° nought for rain ne thonder,   neglected
495   In siknesse nor in meschief,° to visite   misfortune
The ferreste° in his parissh, muche and lite,[7]   farthest
Upon his feet, and in his hand a staf.
This noble ensample° to his sheep he yaf   example
That first he wroughte,[8] and afterward he taughte.
500   Out of the Gospel he tho° wordes caughte,°   those / took
And this figure° he added eek therto: metaphor
That if gold ruste, what shal iren do?
For if a preest be foul, on whom we truste,
No wonder is a lewed° man to ruste.   uneducated
505   And shame it is, if a preest take keep,°   heed
A shiten° shepherde and a clene sheep.   befouled
Wel oughte a preest ensample for to yive
By his clennesse how that his sheep sholde live.
He sette nought his benefice[9] to hire
510   And leet° his sheep encombred in the mire   left
And ran to London, unto Sainte Poules,[1]
To seeken him a chaunterye[2] for soules,
Or with a bretherhede to been withholde,[3]
But dwelte at hoom and kepte wel his folde,
515   So that the wolf ne made it nought miscarye:
He was a shepherde and nought a mercenarye.
And though he holy were and vertuous,
He was to sinful men nought despitous,°   scornful
Ne of his speeche daungerous° ne digne,°   disdainful / haughty
520   But in his teching discreet and benigne,
To drawen folk to hevene by fairnesse
By good ensample—this was his bisinesse.
But it° were any persone obstinat,   if there
What so he were, of heigh or lowe estat,
525   Him wolde he snibben° sharply for the nones:[4]   scold
A bettre preest I trowe° ther nowher noon is.   believe
He waited after[5] no pompe and reverence,
Ne maked him a spiced conscience,[6]
But Cristes lore° and his Apostles twelve   teaching

---

4. He would be most reluctant to invoke excommunication in order to collect his tithes.
5. Without doubt.
6. The offering made by the congregation of his church was at the Parson's disposal.
7. Great and small.
8. I.e., he practiced what he preached.
9. I.e., his parish. A priest might rent his parish to another and take a more profitable position.
1. St. Paul's Cathedral.
2. Chantry, i.e., a foundation that employed

priests for the sole duty of saying masses for the souls of wealthy persons. St. Paul's had many of them.
3. Or to be employed by a brotherhood; i.e., to take a lucrative and fairly easy position as chaplain with a parish guild (see p. 187, 1st n. 6).
4. On the spot, promptly.
5. I.e., expected.
6. Nor did he assume an overfastidious conscience, a holier-than-thou attitude.

530 He taughte, but first he folwed it himselve.
   With him ther was a Plowman, was his brother,
   That hadde ylad° of dong° ful many a fother.[7]   *carried/dung*
   A trewe swinkere° and a good was he,   *worker*
   Living in pees° and parfit charitee.   *peace*
535 God loved he best with al his hoole° herte   *whole*
   At alle times, though him gamed or smerte,[8]
   And thanne his neighebor right as himselve.
   He wolde thresshe, and therto dike° and delve,°   *work hard/dig*
   For Cristes sake, for every poore wight,
540 Withouten hire, if it laye in his might.
   His tithes payed he ful faire and wel,
   Bothe of his propre swink[9] and his catel.°   *property*
   In a tabard° he rood upon a mere.°   *workman's smock/mare*
      Ther was also a Reeve° and a Millere,   *estate manager*
545 A Somnour, and a Pardoner[1] also,
   A Manciple,° and myself—ther were namo.   *steward*
      The Millere was a stout carl° for the nones.   *fellow*
   Ful big he was of brawn° and eek of bones—   *muscle*
   That preved[2] wel, for overal ther he cam
550 At wrastling he wolde have alway the ram.[3]
   He was short-shuldred, brood,° a thikke knarre.[4]   *broad*
   Ther was no dore that he nolde heve of harre,[5]
   Or breke it at a renning° with his heed.°   *running/head*
   His beerd as any sowe or fox was reed,°   *red*
555 And therto brood, as though it were a spade;
   Upon the cop right[6] of his nose he hade
   A werte,° and theron stood a tuft of heres,   *wart*
   Rede as the bristles of a sowes eres;°   *ears*
   His nosethirles° blake were and wide.   *nostrils*
560 A swerd and a bokeler° bar° he by his side.   *shield/bore*
   His mouth as greet was as a greet furnais.°   *furnace*
   He was a janglere° and a Goliardais,[7]   *chatterer*
   And that was most of sinne and harlotries.°   *obscenities*
   Wel coude he stelen corn and tollen thries[8]—
565 And yit he hadde a thombe[9] of gold, pardee.°   *by heaven*
   A whit cote and a blew hood wered° he.   *wore*
   A baggepipe wel coude he blowe and soune,°   *sound*
   And therwithal° he broughte us out of towne.   *therewith*
      A gentil Manciple[1] was ther of a temple,
570 Of which achatours° mighte take exemple   *buyers of food*
   For to been wise in bying of vitaile;°   *victuals*
   For wheither that he paide or took by taile,[2]

---

7. Load.
8. Whether he was pleased or grieved.
9. His own work.
1. "Somnour" (Summoner): server of summonses to the ecclesiastical court. "Pardoner": dispenser of papal pardons (see p. 193, 1st n. 8, and p. 194, n. 5).
2. Proved, i.e., was evident.
3. A ram was frequently offered as the prize in wrestling, a village sport.
4. Sturdy fellow.

5. He would not heave off (its) hinge.
6. Right on the tip.
7. Goliard, teller of ribald stories.
8. Take toll thrice—i.e., deduct from the grain far more than the lawful percentage.
9. Thumb. Ironic allusion to a proverb: "An honest miller has a golden thumb."
1. The Manciple is the business agent of a community of lawyers in London (a "temple").
2. By talley, i.e., on credit.

Algate he waited so in his achat[3]
That he was ay biforn and in good stat.[4]
575   Now is nat that of God a ful fair grace
That swich a lewed° mannes wit shal pace°   *uneducated/surpass*
The wisdom of an heep of lerned men?
Of maistres° hadde he mo than thries ten   *masters*
That weren of lawe expert and curious,°   *cunning*
580 Of whiche ther were a dozeine in that hous
Worthy to been stiwardes of rente° and lond   *income*
Of any lord that is in Engelond,
To make him live by his propre good[5]
In honour dettelees but if he were wood,[6]
585 Or live as scarsly° as him list° desire,   *economically/it pleases*
And able for to helpen al a shire
In any caas° that mighte falle° or happe,   *event/befall*
And yit this Manciple sette hir aller cappe![7]
    The Reeve was a sclendre° colerik[8] man;   *slender*
590 His beerd was shave as neigh° as evere he can;   *close*
His heer was by his eres ful round yshorn;
His top was dokked[9] lik a preest biforn;°   *in front*
Ful longe were his legges and ful lene,
Ylik a staf, ther was no calf yseene.°   *visible*
595 Wel coude he keepe° a gerner° and a binne—   *guard/granary*
Ther was noon auditour coude on him winne.[1]
Wel wiste° he by the droughte and by the rain   *knew*
The yeelding of his seed and of his grain.
His lordes sheep, his neet,° his dayerye,°   *cattle/dairy herd*
600 His swin, his hors, his stoor,° and his pultrye   *stock*
Was hoolly° in this Reeves governinge,   *wholly*
And by his covenant yaf[2] the rekeninge,
Sin° that his lord was twenty-yeer of age.   *since*
There coude no man bringe him in arrerage.[3]
605 Ther nas baillif, hierde, nor other hine,
That he ne knew his sleighte and his covine[4]—
They were adrad° of him as of the deeth.°   *afraid/plague*
His woning° was ful faire upon an heeth;°   *dwelling/meadow*
With greene trees shadwed was his place.
610 He coude bettre than his lord purchace.°   *acquire goods*
Ful riche he was astored° prively.°   *stocked/secretly*
His lord wel coude he plesen subtilly,
To yive and lene° him of his owene good,°   *lend/property*
And have a thank, and yit a cote and hood.
615 In youthe he hadde lerned a good mister:°   *occupation*
He was a wel good wrighte, a carpenter.
This Reeve sat upon a ful good stot°   *stallion*

---

3. Always he was on the watch in his purchasing.
4. Financial condition. "Ay biforn": i.e., ahead of the game.
5. His own money.
6. Out of debt unless he were crazy.
7. This Manciple made fools of them all.
8. Choleric describes a person whose dominant humor is yellow bile (choler)—i.e., a hot-tempered person. The Reeve is the superintendent of a large

farming estate.
9. Cut short; the clergy wore the head partially shaved.
1. I.e., find him in default.
2. And according to his contract he gave.
3. Convict him of being in arrears financially.
4. There was no bailiff (i.e., foreman), shepherd, or other farm laborer whose craftiness and plots he didn't know.

That was a pomely° grey and highte° Scot.   *dapple/was named*
A long surcote° of pers° upon he hade,[5]   *overcoat/blue*
620 And by his side he bar° a rusty blade.   *bore*
Of Northfolk was this Reeve of which I telle,
Biside a town men clepen Baldeswelle.°   *Bawdswell*
Tukked[6] he was as is a frere aboute,
And evere he rood the hindreste of oure route.[7]
625   A Somnour[8] was ther with us in that place
That hadde a fir-reed° cherubinnes[9] face,   *fire-red*
For saucefleem° he was, with yën narwe,   *pimply*
And hoot° he was, and lecherous as a sparwe,°   *hot/sparrow*
With scaled° browes blake and piled[1] beerd: *scabby*
630 Of his visage children were aferd.°   *afraid*
Ther nas quiksilver, litarge, ne brimstoon,
Boras, ceruce, ne oile of tartre noon,[2]
Ne oinement that wolde clense and bite,
That him mighte helpen of his whelkes° white,   *pimples*
635 Nor of the knobbes° sitting on his cheekes.   *lumps*
Wel loved he garlek, oinons, and eek leekes,
And for to drinke strong win reed as blood.
Thanne wolde he speke and crye as he were wood;°   *mad*
And whan that he wel dronken hadde the win,
640 Thanne wolde he speke no word but Latin:
A fewe termes hadde he, two or three,
That he hadde lerned out of som decree;
No wonder is—he herde it al the day,
And eek ye knowe wel how that a jay°   *parrot*
645 Can clepen "Watte"[3] as wel as can the Pope—
But whoso coude in other thing him grope,°   *examine*
Thanne hadde he spent all his philosophye;[4]
Ay *Questio quid juris*[5] wolde he crye.
   He was a gentil harlot° and a kinde;   *rascal*
650 A bettre felawe sholde men nought finde:
He wolde suffre,° for a quart of win,   *permit*
A good felawe to have his concubin
A twelfmonth, and excusen him at the fulle;[6]
Ful prively° a finch eek coude he pulle.[7]   *secretly*
655 And if he foond° owher° a good felawe   *found/anywhere*
He wolde techen him to have noon awe
In swich caas of the Ercedekenes curs,[8]
But if[9] a mannes soule were in his purs,

---

5. He had on.
6. With clothing tucked up like a friar.
7. Hindmost of our group.
8. The "Somnour" (Summoner) is an employee of the ecclesiastical court, whose duty is to bring to court persons whom the archdeacon—the justice of the court—suspects of offenses against canon law. By this time, however, summoners had generally transformed themselves into corrupt detectives who spied out offenders and blackmailed them by threats of summonses.
9. Cherubs, often depicted in art with red faces.
1. Uneven, partly hairless.
2. These are all ointments for diseases affecting the skin, probably diseases of venereal origin.
3. Call out: "Walter"—like modern parrots' "Polly."
4. I.e., learning.
5. "What point of law does this investigation involve?" A phrase frequently used in ecclesiastical courts.
6. Fully. Ecclesiastical courts had jurisdiction over many offenses that today would come under civil law, including sexual offenses.
7. "To pull a finch" (pluck a bird) is to have sexual relations with a woman.
8. Archdeacon's sentence of excommunication.
9. Unless.

For in his purs he sholde ypunisshed be.
660 "Purs is the Ercedekenes helle," saide he.
    But wel I woot he lied right in deede:
Of cursing° oughte eech gilty man him drede,   *excommunication*
For curs wol slee° right as assoiling° savith—   *slay/absolution*
And also war him of a *significavit*.[1]
665   In daunger[2] hadde he at his owene gise°   *disposal*
The yonge girles of the diocise,
And knew hir conseil,° and was al hir reed.[3]   *secrets*
A gerland hadde he set upon his heed
As greet as it were for an ale-stake,[4]
670 A bokeler hadde he maad him of a cake.
    With him ther rood a gentil Pardoner[5]
Of Rouncival, his freend and his compeer,°   *comrade*
That straight was comen fro the Court of Rome.[6]
Ful loude he soong,° "Com hider, love, to me."   *sang*
675 This Somnour bar to him a stif burdoun:[7]
Was nevere trompe° of half so greet a soun.   *trumpet*
    This Pardoner hadde heer as yelow as wex,
But smoothe it heeng° as dooth a strike° of flex;°   *hung/hank/flax*
By ounces[8] heenge his lokkes that he hadde,
680 And therwith he his shuldres overspradde,°   *overspread*
But thinne it lay, by colpons,° oon by oon;   *strands*
But hood for jolitee° wered° he noon,   *nonchalance/wore*
For it was trussed up in his walet:°   *pack*
Him thoughte he rood al of the newe jet.°   *fashion*
685 Dischevelee° save his cappe he rood al bare.   *with hair down*
Swiche glaring yën hadde he as an hare.
A vernicle[9] hadde he sowed upon his cappe,
His walet biforn him in his lappe,
Bretful° of pardon, come from Rome al hoot.°   *brimful/hot*
690 A vois he hadde as smal° as hath a goot;°   *high-pitched/goat*
No beerd hadde he, ne nevere sholde have;
As smoothe it was as it were late yshave:
I trowe° he were a gelding[1] or a mare.   *believe*
But of his craft, fro Berwik into Ware,[2]
695 Ne was ther swich another pardoner;
For in his male° he hadde a pilwe-beer°   *bag/pillowcase*
Which that he saide was Oure Lady veil;
He saide he hadde a gobet° of the sail   *piece*
That Sainte Peter hadde whan that he wente
700 Upon the see, til Jesu Crist him hente.°   *seized*

---

1. And also one should be careful of a *significavit* (the writ that transferred the guilty offender from the ecclesiastical to the civil arm for punishment).
2. Under his domination.
3. Was their chief source of advice.
4. A tavern was signalized by a pole ("ale-stake"), rather like a modern flagpole, projecting from its front wall; on this hung a garland, or "bush."
5. A Pardoner dispensed papal pardon for sins to those who contributed to the charitable institution that he was licensed to represent; this Pardoner purported to be collecting for the hospital of

Roncesvalles ("Rouncival") in Spain, which had a London branch.
6. The papal court.
7. I.e., provided him with a strong bass accompaniment.
8. I.e., thin strands.
9. Portrait of Christ's face as it was said to have been impressed on St. Veronica's handkerchief, i.e., a souvenir reproduction of a famous relic in Rome.
1. A neutered stallion, i.e., a eunuch.
2. I.e., from one end of England to the other.

He hadde a crois° of laton,° ful of stones,   *cross/brassy metal*
And in a glas he hadde pigges bones,
But with thise relikes[3] whan that he foond°   *found*
A poore person° dwelling upon lond,[4]   *parson*
705 Upon° a day he gat° him more moneye   *in/got*
Than that the person gat in monthes twaye;
And thus with feined° flaterye and japes°   *false/tricks*
He made the person and the peple his apes.°   *dupes*
But trewely to tellen at the laste,
710 He was in chirche a noble ecclesiaste;
Wel coude he rede a lesson and a storye,° *liturgical narrative*
But alderbest° he soong an offertorye,[5]   *best of all*
For wel he wiste° whan that song was songe,   *knew*
He moste° preche and wel affile° his tonge *must/sharpen*
715 To winne silver, as he ful wel coude—
Therefore he soong the merierly° and loude. *more merrily*
  Now have I told you soothly in a clause[6]
Th'estaat, th'array, the nombre, and eek the cause
Why that assembled was this compaignye
720 In Southwerk at this gentil hostelrye
That highte the Tabard, faste° by the Belle;[7]   *close*
But now is time to you for to telle
How that we baren us[8] that ilke° night   *same*
Whan we were in that hostelrye alight;
725 And after wol I telle of oure viage,°   *trip*
And al the remenant of oure pilgrimage.
But first I praye you of youre curteisye
That ye n'arette it nought my vilainye[9]
Though that I plainly speke in this matere
730 To telle you hir wordes and hir cheere,°   *behavior*
Ne though I speke hir wordes proprely;°   *accurately*
For this ye knowen also wel as I:
Who so shal telle a tale after a man
He moot° reherce,° as neigh as evere he can, *must/repeat*
735 Everich a word, if it be in his charge,°   *responsibility*
Al speke he[1] nevere so rudeliche and large,°   *broadly*
Or elles he moot telle his tale untrewe,
Or feine° thing, or finde° wordes newe; *make up/devise*
He may nought spare[2] although he were his brother:
740 He moot as wel saye oo word as another.
Crist spak himself ful brode° in Holy Writ,   *broadly*
And wel ye woot no vilainye° is it;   *rudeness*
Eek Plato saith, who so can him rede,
The wordes mote be cosin to the deede.
745 Also I praye you to foryive it me
Al° have I nat set folk in hir degree   *although*
Here in this tale as that they sholde stonde:

3. Relics, i.e., the pigs' bones that the Pardoner represented as saints' bones.
4. Upcountry.
5. Part of the mass sung before the offering of alms.
6. I.e., in a short space.

7. Another tavern in Southwark.
8. Bore ourselves.
9. That you do not attribute it to my boorishness.
1. Although he speak.
2. I.e., spare anyone.

My wit is short, ye may wel understonde.
    Greet cheere made oure Host[3] us everichoon,
750 And to the soper sette he us anoon.°   *at once*
He served us with vitaile° at the beste.   *food*
Strong was the win, and wel to drinke us leste.° *it pleased*
A semely man oure Hoste was withalle
For to been a marchal[4] in an halle;
755 A large man he was, with yën steepe,°   *prominent*
A fairer burgeis° was ther noon in Chepe[5]—   *burgher*
Bold of his speeche, and wis, and wel ytaught,
And of manhood him lakkede right naught.
Eek therto he was right a merye man,
760 And after soper playen he bigan,
And spak of mirthe amonges othere thinges—
Whan that we hadde maad oure rekeninges[6]—
And saide thus, "Now, lordinges, trewely,
Ye been to me right welcome, hertely.°   *heartily*
765 For by my trouthe, if that I shal nat lie,
I sawgh nat this yeer so merye a compaignye
At ones in this herberwe° as is now.   *inn*
Fain° wolde I doon you mirthe, wiste I[7] how. *gladly*
And of a mirthe I am right now bithought,
770 To doon you ese, and it shal coste nought.
    "Ye goon to Canterbury—God you speede;
The blisful martyr quite you youre meede.[8]
And wel I woot as ye goon by the waye
Ye shapen you[9] to talen° and to playe,   *converse*
775 For trewely, confort ne mirthe is noon
To ride by the waye domb as stoon;°   *stone*
And therefore wol I maken you disport
As I saide erst,° and doon you som confort;   *before*
And if you liketh alle, by oon assent,
780 For to stonden at[1] my juggement,
And for to werken as I shall you saye,
Tomorwe whan ye riden by the waye—
Now by my fader° soule that is deed,   *father's*
But° ye be merye I wol yive you myn heed!° *unless/head*
785 Holde up youre handes withouten more speeche."
    Oure counseil was nat longe for to seeche;° *seek*
Us thought it was not worth to make it wis,[2]
And graunted him withouten more avis,° *deliberation*
And bade him saye his voirdit° as him leste.[3] *verdict*
790   "Lordinges," quod he, "now herkneth for the beste;
But taketh it nought, I praye you, in desdain.
This is the point, to speken short and plain,
That eech of you, to shorte° with oure waye   *shorten*
In this viage, shal tellen tales twaye°—   *two*

---

3. The landlord of the Tabard Inn.
4. Marshal, one who was in charge of feasts.
5. Cheapside, business center of London.
6. Had paid our bills.
7. If I knew.
8. Pay you your reward.

9. Intend.
1. Abide by.
2. We didn't think it worthwhile to make an issue of it.
3. It pleased.

795 To Canterburyward, I mene it so,
And hoomward he shal tellen othere two,
Of aventures that whilom° have bifalle;   *once upon a time*
And which of you that bereth him best of alle—
That is to sayn, that telleth in this cas
800 Tales of best sentence° and most solas°—   *meaning/delight*
Shal have a soper at oure aller cost,[4]
Here in this place, sitting by this post,
Whan that we come again fro Canterbury.
And for to make you the more mury°   *merry*
805 I wol myself goodly° with you ride—   *kindly*
Right at myn owene cost—and be youre gide.
And who so wol my juggement withsaye°   *contradict*
Shal paye al that we spende by the waye.
And if ye vouche sauf that it be so,
810 Telle me anoon, withouten wordes mo,°   *more*
And I wol erly shape me[5] therefore."
      This thing was graunted and oure othes swore
With ful glad herte, and prayden[6] him also
That he wolde vouche sauf for to do so,
815 And that he wolde been oure governour,
And of oure tales juge and reportour,°   *accountant*
And sette a soper at a certain pris,°   *price*
And we wol ruled been at his devis,°   *disposal*
In heigh and lowe; and thus by oon assent
820 We been accorded to his juggement.
And therupon the win was fet° anoon;   *fetched*
We dronken and to reste wente eechoon°   *each one*
Withouten any lenger° taryinge.   *longer*
      Amorwe° whan that day bigan to springe   *in the morning*
825 Up roos oure Host and was oure aller cok,[7]
And gadred us togidres in a flok,
And forth we riden, a litel more than pas,°   *walking pace*
Unto the watering of Saint Thomas;[8]
And ther oure Host bigan his hors arreste,°   *halt*
830 And saide, "Lordes, herkneth if you leste:°   *it please*
      Ye woot youre forward° and it you recorde:[9]   *agreement*
If evensong and morwesong° accorde,°   *morning song/agree*
Lat see now who shal telle the firste tale.
As evere mote° I drinken win or ale,   *may*
835 Who so be rebel to my juggement
Shal paye for al that by the way is spent.
Now draweth cut er that we ferrer twinne:[1]
He which that hath the shorteste shal biginne.
      "Sire Knight," quod he, "my maister and my lord,
840 Now draweth cut, for that is myn accord.°   *will*
Cometh neer," quod he, "my lady Prioresse,
And ye, sire Clerk, lat be youre shamefastnesse°—   *modesty*

4. At the cost of us all.
5. Prepare myself.
6. I.e., we prayed.
7. Was rooster for us all.

8. A watering place near Southwark.
9. You recall it.
1. Go farther. "Draweth cut": i.e., draw straws.

Ne studieth nought. Lay hand to, every man!"
       Anoon to drawen every wight bigan,
845 And shortly for to tellen as it was
       Were it by aventure, or sort, or cas,[2]
       The soothe° is this, the cut fil° to the Knight;   truth/fell
       Of which ful blithe and glad was every wight,
       And telle he moste° his tale, as was resoun,   must
850 By forward and by composicioun,[3]
       As ye han herd. What needeth wordes mo?
       And whan this goode man sawgh that it was so,
       As he that wis was and obedient
       To keepe his forward by his free assent,
855 He saide, "Sin° I shal biginne the game,   since
       What, welcome be the cut, in Goddes name!
       Now lat us ride, and herkneth what I saye."
       And with that word we riden forth oure waye,
       And he bigan with right a merye cheere°   countenance
860 His tale anoon, and saide as ye may heere.

---

2. Whether it was luck, fate, or chance.   3. By agreement and compact.

[*The Knight's Tale* is a romance of 2,350 lines, which Chaucer had written before beginning *The Canterbury Tales*—one of several works assumed to be earlier that he inserted into the collection. It is probably the same story, with only minor revisions, that Chaucer referred to in *The Legend of Good Women* as "al the love of Palamon and Arcite." These are the names of the two heroes of *The Knight's Tale*, kinsmen and best friends who are taken prisoner at the siege and destruction of ancient Thebes by Theseus, the ruler of Athens. Gazing out from their prison cell in a tower, they fall in love at first sight and almost at the same moment with Theseus's sister-in-law, Emily, who is taking an early-morning walk in a garden below their window. After a bitter rivalry, they are at last reconciled through a tournament in which Emily is the prize. Arcite wins the tournament but, as he lies dying after being thrown by his horse, he makes a noble speech encouraging Palamon and Emily to marry. The tale is an ambitious combination of classical setting and mythology, romance plot, and themes of fortune and destiny.]

The Miller's Prologue and Tale

The Miller's Tale belongs to a genre known as the "fabliau": a short story in verse that deals satirically, often grossly and fantastically as well as hilariously, with intrigues and deceptions about sex or money (and often both these elements in the same story). These are the tales Chaucer is anticipating in *The General Prologue* when he warns his presumably genteel audience that they must expect some rude speaking (see lines 727–44). An even more pointed apology follows at the end of *The Miller's Prologue*. Fabliau tales exist everywhere in oral literature; as a literary form they flourished in France, especially in the thirteenth century. By having Robin the Miller tell a fabliau to "quit" (to requite or pay back) the Knight's aristocratic romance, Chaucer sets up a dialectic between classes, genres, and styles that he exploits throughout *The Canterbury Tales*.

The Prologue

Whan that the Knight hadde thus his tale ytold,
In al the route° nas° ther yong ne old   *group/was not*
That he ne saide it was a noble storye,
And worthy for to drawen° to memorye,   *recall*
5 And namely° the gentils everichoon.   *especially*
    Oure Hoste lough° and swoor, "So mote I goon,[1]   *laughed*
This gooth aright: unbokeled is the male.°   *pouch*
Lat see now who shal telle another tale.
For trewely the game is wel bigonne.
10 Now telleth ye, sire Monk, if that ye conne,°   *can*
Somwhat to quite° with the Knightes tale."   *repay*
    The Millere, that for dronken[2] was al pale,
So that unnethe° upon his hors he sat,   *with difficulty*
He nolde° avalen° neither hood ne hat,   *would not/take off*
15 Ne abiden no man for his curteisye,
But in Pilates vois[3] he gan to crye,
And swoor, "By armes[4] and by blood and bones,
I can° a noble tale for the nones,   *know*
With which I wol now quite the Knightes tale."
20   Oure Hoste sawgh that he was dronke of ale,
And saide, "Abide, Robin, leve° brother,   *dear*
Som bettre man shal telle us first another.
Abide, and lat us werken thriftily."°   *with propriety*
    "By Goddes soule," quod he, "that wol nat I,
25 For I wol speke or elles go my way."
    Oure Host answerde, "Tel on, a devele way![5]
Thou art a fool; thy wit is overcome."
    "Now herkneth," quod the Millere, "alle and some.[6]
But first I make a protestacioun°   *public affirmation*
30 That I am dronke: I knowe it by my soun.°   *tone of voice*
And therfore if that I misspeke° or saye,   *speak or say wrongly*
Wite it[7] the ale of Southwerk, I you praye;
For I wol telle a legende° and a lif   *saint's life*
Bothe of a carpenter and of his wif,
35 How that a clerk hath set the wrightes cappe."[8]
    The Reeve answerde and saide, "Stint thy clappe![9]
Lat be thy lewed° dronken harlotrye.°   *ignorant/obscenity*
It is a sinne and eek° a greet folye   *also*
To apairen° any man or him defame,   *injure*
40 And eek to bringen wives in swich fame.°   *reputation*
Thou maist ynough of othere thinges sayn."
    This dronken Millere spak ful soone again,
And saide, "Leve° brother Osewold,   *dear*
Who hath no wif, he is no cokewold.°   *cuckold*
45 But I saye nat therfore that thou art oon.

---

1. So might I walk—an oath.
2. I.e., drunkenness.
3. The harsh voice usually associated with the character of Pontius Pilate in the mystery plays.
4. I.e., by God's arms, a blasphemous oath.

5. I.e., in the devil's name.
6. Each and every one.
7. Blame it on.
8 I.e., how a clerk made a fool of a carpenter.
9. Stop your chatter.

Ther ben ful goode wives many oon,°   *a one*
And evere a thousand goode ayains oon badde.
That knowestou wel thyself but if thou madde.°   *rave*
Why artou angry with my tale now?
50   I have a wif, pardee,° as wel as thou,   *by God*
Yit nolde° I, for the oxen in my plough,   *would not*
Take upon me more than ynough°   *enough*
As deemen of myself that I were oon:[1]
I wol bileve wel that I am noon.
55   An housbonde shal nought been inquisitif
Of Goddes privetee,° nor of his wif.   *secrets*
So[2] he may finde Goddes foison° there,   *plenty*
Of the remenant° needeth nought enquere."°   *rest/inquire*
    What sholde I more sayn but this Millere
60   He nolde his wordes for no man forbere,
But tolde his cherles tale in his manere.
M'athinketh° that I shal reherce° it here,   *I regret/repeat*
And therefore every gentil wight I praye,
Deemeth nought, for Goddes love, that I saye
65   Of yvel entente, but for° I moot reherse   *because*
Hir tales alle, be they bet° or werse,   *better*
Or elles falsen° som of my matere.   *falsify*
And therfore, whoso list it nought yheere°   *hear*
Turne over the leef,° and chese° another tale,   *page/choose*
70   For he shal finde ynowe,° grete and smale,   *enough*
Of storial[3] thing that toucheth gentilesse,°   *gentility*
And eek moralitee and holinesse:
Blameth nought me if that ye chese amis.
The Millere is a cherl, ye knowe wel this,
75   So was the Reeve eek, and othere mo,
And harlotrye° they tolden bothe two.   *ribaldry*
Aviseth you,[4] and putte me out of blame:
And eek men shal nought maken ernest of game.

The Tale

    Whilom° ther was dwelling at Oxenforde   *once upon a time*
80   A riche gnof° that gestes heeld to boorde,[5]   *churl*
And of his craft he was a carpenter.
With him ther was dwelling a poore scoler,
Hadde lerned art,[6] but al his fantasye°   *desire*
Was turned for to lere° astrologye,   *learn*
85   And coude a certain of conclusiouns,
To deemen by interrogaciouns,[7]
If that men axed° him in certain houres   *asked*
Whan that men sholde have droughte or elles showres,
Or if men axed him what shal bifalle

---

1. To think that I were one (a cuckold).
2. Provided that.
3. Historical, i.e., true.
4. Take heed.
5. I.e., took in boarders.

6. Who had completed the first stage of university education (the trivium).
7. I.e., and he knew a number of propositions on which to base astrological analyses (which would reveal the matters in the next three lines).

90 Of every thing—I may nat rekene hem alle.
  This clerk was cleped° hende[8] Nicholas.   *called*
 Of derne love he coude, and of solas,[9]
 And therto he was sly and ful privee,°   *secretive*
 And lik a maide meeke for to see.
95 A chambre hadde he in that hostelrye
 Allone, withouten any compaignye,
 Ful fetisly ydight[1] with herbes swoote,°   *sweet*
 And he himself as sweete as is the roote
 Of licoris or any setewale.[2]
100 His *Almageste*[3] and bookes grete and smale,
 His astrelabye, longing for[4] his art,
 His augrim stones,[5] layen faire apart
 On shelves couched° at his beddes heed;   *set*
 His presse° ycovered with a falding reed;[6]   *storage chest*
105 And al above ther lay a gay sautrye,°   *psaltery (harp)*
 On which he made a-nightes melodye
 So swetely that al the chambre roong,°   *rang*
 And *Angelus ad Virginem*[7] he soong,
 And after that he soong the *Kinges Note:*[8]
110 Ful often blessed was his merye throte.
 And thus this sweete clerk his time spente
 After his freendes finding and his rente.[9]
  This carpenter hadde wedded newe° a wif   *lately*
 Which that he loved more than his lif.
115 Of eighteteene yeer she was of age;
 Jalous he was, and heeld hire narwe in cage,
 For she was wilde and yong, and he was old,
 And deemed himself been lik a cokewold.[1]
 He knew nat Caton,[2] for his wit was rude,
120 That bad men sholde wedde his similitude:[3]
 Men sholde wedden after hir estat,[4]
 For youthe and elde° is often at debat.   *age*
 But sith that he was fallen in the snare,
 He moste endure, as other folk, his care.
125 Fair was this yonge wif, and therwithal
 As any wesele° hir body gent and smal.[5]   *weasel*
 A ceint she wered, barred[6] al of silk;
 A barmcloth° as whit as morne° milk   *apron / morning*
 Upon hir lendes,° ful of many a gore;°   *loins / flounce*
130 Whit was hir smok,° and broiden° al bifore *undergarment / embroidered*
 And eek bihinde, on hir coler° aboute,   *collar*

---

8. Courteous, handy, attractive.
9. I.e., he knew about secret love and pleasurable practices.
1. Elegantly furnished.
2. Setwall, a spice.
3. The 2nd-century treatise by Ptolemy, still the standard astronomy textbook.
4. Belonging to. "Astrelabye": astrolabe, an astronomical instrument.
5. Counters used in arithmetic.
6. Red coarse woolen cloth.
7. "The Angel to the Virgin," an Annunciation

hymn.
8. Probably a popular song of the time.
9. In accordance with his friends' provision and his own income.
1. I.e., suspected of himself that he was like a cuckold.
2. Dionysius Cato, the supposed author of a book of maxims used in elementary education.
3. Commanded that one should wed his equal.
4. Men should marry according to their condition.
5. Slender and delicate.
6. A belt she wore, with transverse stripes.

Of° col-blak silk, withinne and eek withoute;   *with*
The tapes° of hir white voluper°   *ribbons/cap*
Were of the same suite of[7] hir coler;
135 Hir filet° brood° of silk and set ful hye;   *headband/broad*
And sikerly° she hadde a likerous° yë;   *certainly/wanton*
Ful smale ypulled[8] were hir browes two,
And tho were bent,° and blake as any slo.°   *arching/sloeberry*
She was ful more blisful on to see
140 Than is the newe perejonette° tree,   *pear*
And softer than the wolle° is of a wether;°   *wool/ram*
And by hir girdel° heeng° a purs of lether,   *belt/hung*
Tasseled with silk and perled with latoun.[9]
In al this world, to seeken up and down,
145 Ther nis no man so wis that coude thenche°   *imagine*
So gay a popelote° or swich° a wenche.   *doll/such*
Ful brighter was the shining of hir hewe
Than in the Towr[1] the noble° yforged newe.   *gold coin*
But of hir song, it was as loud and yerne°   *lively*
150 As any swalwe° sitting on a berne.°   *swallow/barn*
Therto she coude skippe and make game°   *play*
As any kide or calf folwing his dame.°   *mother*
Hir mouth was sweete as bragot or the meeth,[2]
Or hoord of apples laid in hay or heeth.°   *heather*
155 Winsing° she was as is a joly° colt,   *skittish/high-spirited*
Long as a mast, and upright° as a bolt.°   *straight/arrow*
A brooch she bar upon hir lowe coler
As brood as is the boos° of a bokeler;°   *boss/shield*
Hir shoes were laced on hir legges hye.
160 She was a primerole,° a piggesnye,[3]   *primrose*
For any lord to leggen° in his bedde,   *lay*
Or yit for any good yeman to wedde.

Now sire, and eft° sire, so bifel the cas   *again*
That on a day this hende Nicholas
165 Fil° with this yonge wif to rage° and playe,   *happened/flirt*
Whil that hir housbonde was at Oseneye[4]
(As clerkes been ful subtil and ful quainte),°   *clever*
And prively he caughte hire by the queinte,[5]
And saide, "Ywis,° but° if ich° have my wille,   *truly/unless/I*
170 For derne° love of thee, lemman, I spille,"°   *secret/die*
And heeld hire harde by the haunche-bones,°   *thighs*
And saide, "Lemman,° love me al atones,[6]   *sweetheart*
Or I wol dien, also° God me save."   *so*
And she sproong° as a colt dooth in a trave,[7]   *sprang*
175 And with hir heed she wried° faste away;   *twisted*
She saide, "I wol nat kisse thee, by my fay.°   *faith*
Why, lat be," quod she, "lat be, Nicholas!
Or I wol crye 'Out, harrow,° and allas!'   *help*
Do way youre handes, for your curteisye!"

---

7. The same kind as, i.e., black.
8. Delicately plucked.
9. I.e., with brassy spangles on it.
1. The Tower of London, the Mint.
2. "Bragot" and "meeth" are honey drinks.
3. A pig's eye, a name for a common flower.

4. A town near Oxford.
5. Elegant (thing); a euphemism for the female genitals.
6. Right now.
7. Frame for holding a horse to be shod.

180 This Nicholas gan mercy for to crye,
  And spak so faire, and profred him so faste,[8]
  That she hir love him graunted atte laste,
  And swoor hir ooth by Saint Thomas of Kent[9]
  That she wolde been at his comandement,
185 Whan that she may hir leiser[1] wel espye.
  "Myn housbonde is so ful of jalousye
  That but ye waite° wel and been privee   *be on guard*
  I woot right wel I nam but deed,"[2] quod she.
  "Ye moste been ful derne° as in this cas."   *secret*
190 "Nay, therof care thee nought," quod Nicholas.
  "A clerk hadde litherly biset his while,[3]
  But if he coude a carpenter bigile."
  And thus they been accorded and ysworn
  To waite° a time, as I have told biforn.   *watch for*
195 Whan Nicholas hadde doon this everydeel,° *every bit*
  And thakked° hire upon the lendes° weel, *patted/loins*
  He kiste hire sweete, and taketh his sautrye,
  And playeth faste, and maketh melodye.
   Thanne fil° it thus, that to the parissh chirche, *befell*
200 Cristes owene werkes for to wirche,°   *perform*
  This goode wif wente on an haliday:°   *holy day*
  Hir forheed shoon as bright as any day,
  So was it wasshen whan she leet° hir werk. *left*
  Now was ther of that chirche a parissh clerk,[4]
205 The which that was ycleped° Absolon: *called*
  Crul° was his heer, and as the gold it shoon, *curly*
  And strouted° as a fanne[5] large and brode; *spread out*
  Ful straight and evene lay his joly shode.[6]
  His rode° was reed, his yën greye as goos.° *complexion/goose*
210 With Poules window corven[7] on his shoos,
  In hoses° rede he wente fetisly.°   *stockings/elegantly*
  Yclad he was ful smale° and proprely, *finely*
  Al in a kirtel° of a light waget°—   *tunic/blue*
  Ful faire and thikke been the pointes[8] set—
215 And therupon he hadde a gay surplis,° *surplice*
  As whit as is the blosme upon the ris.° *bough*
  A merye child° he was, so God me save. *young man*
  Wel coude he laten blood, and clippe,[9] and shave,
  And maken a chartre of land, or acquitaunce;[1]
220 In twenty manere° coude he trippe and daunce *ways*
  After the scole of Oxenforde tho,°   *then*
  And with his legges casten° to and fro, *prance*
  And playen songes on a smal rubible;° *fiddle*
  Therto he soong somtime a loud quinible,[2]
225 And as wel coude he playe on a giterne:° *guitar*

---

8. I.e., made such vigorous advances.
9. Thomas à Becket.
1. I.e., opportunity.
2. I am no more than dead, I am done for.
3. Poorly employed his time.
4. Assistant to the parish priest, not a cleric or student.
5. Wide-mouthed basket for separating grain from chaff.

6. Parting of the hair.
7. Carved with intricate designs, like the tracery in the windows of St. Paul's.
8. Laces for fastening the tunic and holding up the hose.
9. Let blood and give haircuts. Bleeding was a medical treatment performed by barbers.
1. Legal release. "Chartre": deed.
2. Part requiring a very high voice.

In al the town nas brewhous ne taverne
That he ne visited with his solas,°   *entertainment*
Ther any gailard tappestere[3] was.
But sooth to sayn, he was somdeel squaimous°   *a bit squeamish*
230   Of° farting, and of speeche daungerous.[4]   *about*
    This Absolon, that joly° was and gay,   *pretty, amorous*
Gooth with a cencer° on the haliday,   *incense burner*
Cencing the wives of the parissh faste,
And many a lovely look on hem he caste,
235   And namely° on this carpenteres wif: *especially*
To looke on hire him thoughte a merye lif.
She was so propre° and sweete and likerous,[5]   *neat*
I dar wel sayn, if she hadde been a mous,
And he a cat, he wolde hire hente° anoon.   *pounce on*
240   This parissh clerk, this joly Absolon,
Hath in his herte swich a love-longinge°   *lovesickness*
That of no wif ne took he noon offringe—
For curteisye he saide he wolde noon.
The moone, whan it was night, ful brighte shoon,°   *shone*
245   And Absolon his giterne° hath ytake—   *guitar*
For paramours° he thoughte for to wake—   *love*
And forth he gooth, jolif° and amorous,   *pretty*
Til he cam to the carpenteres hous,
A litel after cokkes hadde ycrowe,
250   And dressed him up by a shot-windowe[6]
That was upon the carpenteres wal.
He singeth in his vois gentil and smal,°   *dainty*
"Now dere lady, if thy wille be,
I praye you that ye wol rewe° on me,"   *have pity*
255   Ful wel accordant to his giterninge.[7]
This carpenter awook and herde him singe,
And spak unto his wif, and saide anoon,
"What, Alison, heerestou nought Absolon
That chaunteth thus under oure bowres° wal?"   *bedroom's*
260   And she answerde hir housbonde therwithal,
"Yis, God woot, John, I heere it everydeel."°   *every bit*
    This passeth forth. What wol ye bet than weel?[8]
Fro day to day this joly Absolon
So woweth° hire that him is wo-bigoon: *woos*
265   He waketh° al the night and al the day;   *stays awake*
He kembed° his lokkes brode[9] and made him gay; *combed*
He woweth hire by menes and brocage,[1]
And swoor he wolde been hir owene page°   *personal servant*
He singeth, brokking° as a nightingale;   *trilling*
270   He sente hire piment,° meeth,° and spiced ale, *spiced wine/mead*
And wafres° piping hoot out of the gleede;°   *pastries/coals*
And for she was of towne,[2] he profred meede°— *money*

---

3. Gay barmaid.
4. Prudish about (vulgar) talk.
5. Wanton, appetizing.
6. Took his position by a hinged window.
7. In harmony with his guitar playing.

8. Better than well.
9. I.e., wide-spreading.
1. By go-betweens and agents.
2. Because she was a town woman.

For som folk wol be wonnen for richesse,
And som for strokes,° and som for gentilesse.   *blows (force)*
275 Somtime to shewe his lightnesse and maistrye,[3]
He playeth Herodes[4] upon a scaffold° hye.   *platform, stage*
But what availeth him as in this cas?
She loveth so this hende Nicholas
That Absolon may blowe the bukkes horn;[5]
280 He ne hadde for his labour but a scorn.
And thus she maketh Absolon hir ape,[6]
And al his ernest turneth til° a jape.°   *to/joke*
Ful sooth is this proverbe, it is no lie;
Men saith right thus: "Alway the nye slye
285 Maketh the ferre leve to be loth."[7]
For though that Absolon be wood° or wroth,   *furious*
By cause that he fer was from hir sighte,
This nye° Nicholas stood in his lighte.   *nearby*
    Now beer° thee wel, thou hende Nicholas,   *bear*
290 For Absolon may waile and singe allas.
    And so bifel it on a Saterday
This carpenter was goon til Oseney,
And hende Nicholas and Alisoun
Accorded been to this conclusioun,
295 That Nicholas shal shapen° hem a wile°   *arrange/trick*
This sely[8] jalous housbonde to bigile,
And if so be this game wente aright,
She sholden sleepen in his arm al night—
For this was his desir and hire° also.   *hers*
300 And right anoon, withouten wordes mo,
This Nicholas no lenger wolde tarye,
But dooth ful softe unto his chambre carye
Bothe mete and drinke for a day or twaye,
And to hir housbonde bad hire for to saye,
305 If that he axed after Nicholas,
She sholde saye she niste° wher he was—   *didn't know*
Of al that day she sawgh him nought with yë:
She trowed° that he was in maladye,   *believed*
For for no cry hir maide coude him calle,
310 He nolde answere for no thing that mighte falle.°   *happen*
    This passeth forth al thilke° Saterday   *this*
That Nicholas stille in his chambre lay,
And eet,° and sleep,° or dide what him leste,[9]   *ate/slept*
Til Sonday that the sonne gooth to reste.
315 This sely carpenter hath greet mervaile
Of Nicholas, or what thing mighte him aile,
And saide, "I am adrad,° by Saint Thomas,   *afraid*
It stondeth nat aright with Nicholas.
God shilde° that he deide sodeinly!   *forbid*

3. Facility and virtuosity.
4. Herod, a role traditionally played as a bully in
the mystery plays.
5. Blow the buck's horn, i.e., go whistle, waste his
time.

6. I.e., thus she makes a monkey out of Absolon.
7. Always the sly man at hand makes the distant
dear one hated.
8. Poor innocent.
9. He wanted.

320 This world is now ful tikel,° sikerly: precarious
    I sawgh today a corps yborn to chirche
    That now a° Monday last I sawgh him wirche.°   on/work
    Go up," quod he unto his knave° anoon,   manservant
    "Clepe° at his dore or knokke with a stoon.°   call/stone
325 Looke how it is and tel me boldely."
        This knave gooth him up ful sturdily,
    And at the chambre dore whil that he stood
    He cride and knokked as that he were wood,°   mad
    "What? How? What do ye, maister Nicholay?
330 How may ye sleepen al the longe day?"
    But al for nought: he herde nat a word.
    An hole he foond ful lowe upon a boord,
    Ther as the cat was wont in for to creepe,
    And at that hole he looked in ful deepe,
335 And atte laste he hadde of him a sighte.
        This Nicholas sat evere caping° uprighte   gaping
    As he hadde kiked° on the newe moone.   gazed
    Adown he gooth and tolde his maister soone
    In what array° he saw this ilke° man.   condition/same
340   This carpenter to blessen him[1] bigan,
    And saide, "Help us, Sainte Frideswide!
    A man woot litel what him shal bitide.
    This man is falle, with his astromye,°   astronomy
    In som woodnesse° or in som agonye.   madness
345 I thoughte ay° wel how that it sholde be: always
    Men sholde nought knowe of Goddes privetee.
    Ye, blessed be alway a lewed° man   ignorant
    That nought but only his bileve° can.°   creed/knows
    So ferde° another clerk with astromye: fared
350 He walked in the feeldes for to prye°   gaze
    Upon the sterres,° what ther sholde bifalle,   stars
    Til he was in a marle-pit[2] yfalle—
    He saw nat that. But yit, by Saint Thomas,
    Me reweth sore[3] for hende Nicholas.
355 He shal be rated of[4] his studying,
    If that I may, by Jesus, hevene king!
    Get me a staf that I may underspore,°   pry up
    Whil that thou, Robin, hevest° up the dore.   heave
    He shal[5] out of his studying, as I gesse."
360 And to the chambre dore he gan him dresse.[6]
    His knave was a strong carl° for the nones,°   fellow/purpose
    And by the haspe he haaf° it up atones: heaved
    Into° the floor the dore fil° anoon.   on/fell
    This Nicholas sat ay as stille as stoon,
365 And evere caped up into the air.
    This carpenter wende° he were in despair,   thought
    And hente° him by the shuldres mightily,   seized
    And shook him harde, and cride spitously,°   vehemently

1. Cross himself.   4. Scolded for.
2. Pit from which a fertilizing clay is dug. 5. I.e., shall come.
3. I sorely pity.   6. Took his stand.

"What, Nicholay, what, how! What! Looke adown!
370   Awaak and thenk on Cristes passioun![7]
I crouche[8] thee from elves and fro wightes."°   *wicked creatures*
Therwith the nightspel saide he anoonrightes[9]
On foure halves° of the hous aboute,   *sides*
And on the thresshfold° on the dore withoute: *threshold*
375   "Jesu Crist and Sainte Benedight,°   *Benedict*
Blesse this hous from every wikked wight!
For nightes nerye the White Pater Noster.[1]
Where wentestou,° thou Sainte Petres soster?°   *did you go/sister*
And at the laste this hende Nicholas
380   Gan for to sike° sore, and saide, "Allas,   *sigh*
Shal al the world be lost eftsoones° now?"   *again*
    This carpenter answerde, "What saistou?
What, thenk on God as we doon, men that swinke."°   *work*
    This Nicholas answerde, "Fecche me drinke,
385   And after wol I speke in privetee
Of certain thing that toucheth me and thee.
I wol telle it noon other man, certain."
    This carpenter gooth down and comth again,
And broughte of mighty° ale a large quart,   *strong*
390   And when that eech of hem hadde dronke his part,
This Nicholas his dore faste shette,°   *shut*
And down the carpenter by him he sette,
And saide, "John, myn hoste lief° and dere,   *beloved*
Thou shalt upon thy trouthe° swere me here   *word of honor*
395   That to no wight thou shalt this conseil° wraye;°   *secret/disclose*
For it is Cristes conseil that I saye,
And if thou telle it man,[2] thou art forlore,°   *lost*
For this vengeance thou shalt have therfore,
That if thou wraye me, thou shalt be wood."[3]
400   "Nay, Crist forbede it, for his holy blood,"
Quod tho this sely° man. "I nam no labbe,°   *innocent/tell-tale*
And though I saye, I nam nat lief to gabbe.[4]
Say what thou wilt, I shal it nevere telle
To child ne wif, by him that harwed helle."[5]
405   "Now John," quod Nicholas, "I wol nought lie.
I have yfounde in myn astrologye,
As I have looked in the moone bright,
That now a Monday next, at quarter night,[6]
Shal falle a rain, and that so wilde and wood,°   *furious*
410   That half so greet was nevere Noees° flood.   *Noah's*
This world," he saide, "in lasse° than an hour   *less*
Shal al be dreint,° so hidous is the showr.   *drowned*
Thus shal mankinde drenche° and lese° hir lif."   *drown/lose*

---

7. I.e., the Crucifixion.
8. Make the sign of the cross on.
9. The night-charm he said right away (to ward off evil spirits).
1. Pater Noster is Latin for "Our Father," the beginning of the Lord's Prayer. The line is obscure, but a conjectural reading would be, "May the White 'Our Father' (or 'Our White Father') [either a prayer or the personification of a protecting power] defend [*nerye*] (us) against nights." The "nightspel" is a jumble of Christian references and pagan superstition.
2. To anyone.
3. Go mad.
4. And though I say it myself, I don't like to gossip.
5. By Him that despoiled hell—i.e., Christ.
6. I.e., shortly before dawn.

This carpenter answerde, "Allas, my wif!
415 And shal she drenche? Allas, myn Alisoun!"
For sorwe of this he fil almost[7] adown,
And saide, "Is there no remedye in this cas?"
    "Why yis, for[8] Gode," quod hende Nicholas,
"If thou wolt werken after lore and reed[9]—
420 Thou maist nought werken after thyn owene heed;°   *head*
For thus saith Salomon that was ful trewe,
'Werk al by conseil and thou shalt nought rewe.'°   *be sorry*
And if thou werken wolt by good conseil,
I undertake, withouten mast or sail,
425 Yit shal I save hire and thee and me.
Hastou nat herd how saved was Noee
Whan that oure Lord hadde warned him biforn
That al the world with water sholde be lorn?"°   *lost*
    "Yis," quod this carpenter, "ful yore° ago."   *long*
430   "Hastou nat herd," quod Nicholas, "also
The sorwe of Noee with his felaweshipe?
Er° that he mighte gete his wif to shipe,   *before*
Him hadde levere,[1] I dar wel undertake,
At thilke time than alle his wetheres[2] blake
435 That she hadde had a ship hirself allone.[3]
And therfore woostou° what is best to doone?   *do you know*
This axeth° haste, and of an hastif° thing   *requires / urgent*
Men may nought preche or maken tarying.
Anoon go gete us faste into this in°   *lodging*
440 A kneeding trough or elles a kimelin°   *brewing tub*
For eech of us, but looke that they be large,°   *wide*
In whiche we mowen swimme as in a barge,[4]
And han therinne vitaile suffisaunt[5]
But for a day—fy° on the remenaunt!   *fie*
445 The water shal aslake° and goon away   *diminish*
Aboute prime[6] upon the nexte day.
But Robin may nat wite° of this, thy knave,   *know*
Ne eek thy maide Gille I may nat save.
Axe nought why, for though thou axe me,
450 I wol nought tellen Goddes privetee.°   *secrets*
Suffiseth thee, but if thy wittes madde,°   *go mad*
To han° as greet a grace as Noee hadde.   *have*
Thy wif shal I wel saven, out of doute.
Go now thy way, and speed thee heraboute.
455 But whan thou hast for hire° and thee and me   *her*
Ygeten us thise kneeding-tubbes three,
Thanne shaltou hangen hem in the roof ful hye,
That no man of oure purveyance° espye.   *preparations*
And whan thou thus hast doon as I have said,
460 And hast oure vitaile faire in hem ylaid,

---

7. Almost fell.
8. I.e., by.
9. Act according to learning and advice.
1. He had rather.
2. Rams. I.e., he'd have given all the black rams
he had.

3. The reluctance of Noah's wife to board the ark
is a traditional comic theme in the mystery plays.
4. In which we can float as in a vessel.
5. Sufficient food.
6. 9 A.M.

And eek an ax to smite the corde atwo,
Whan that the water comth that we may go,
And broke an hole an heigh[7] upon the gable
Unto the gardinward,[8] over the stable,
465 That we may freely passen forth oure way,
Whan that the grete showr is goon away,
Thanne shaltou swimme as merye, I undertake,
As dooth the white doke° after hir drake.   *duck*
Thanne wol I clepe,° 'How, Alison? How, John?   *call*
470 Be merye, for the flood wol passe anoon.'
And thou wolt sayn, 'Hail, maister Nicholay!
Good morwe, I see thee wel, for it is day!'
And thanne shal we be lordes al oure lif
Of al the world, as Noee and his wif.
475 But of oo thing I warne thee ful right:
Be wel avised° on that ilke night   *warned*
That we been entred into shippes boord
That noon of us ne speke nought a word,
Ne clepe, ne crye, but been in his prayere,
480 For it is Goddes owene heeste dere.[9]
Thy wif and thou mote hange fer atwinne,[1]
For that bitwixe you shal be no sinne—
Namore in looking than ther shal in deede.
This ordinance is said: go, God thee speede.
485 Tomorwe at night whan men been alle asleepe,
Into oure kneeding-tubbes wol we creepe,
And sitten there, abiding Goddes grace.
Go now thy way, I have no lenger space°   *time*
To make of this no lenger sermoning.
490 Men sayn thus: 'Send the wise and say no thing.'
Thou art so wis it needeth thee nat teche:
Go save oure lif, and that I thee biseeche."
  This sely carpenter gooth forth his way:
Ful ofte he saide allas and wailaway,
495 And to his wif he tolde his privetee,
And she was war,° and knew it bet° than he, *aware/better*
What al this quainte cast was for to saye.[2]
But nathelees she ferde° as she wolde deye, *acted*
And saide, "Allas, go forth thy way anoon.
500 Help us to scape,° or we been dede eechoon. *escape*
I am thy trewe verray wedded wif:
Go, dere spouse, and help to save oure lif."
  Lo, which a greet thing is affeccioun!° *emotion*
Men may dien of imaginacioun,
505 So deepe° may impression be take.   *deeply*
This sely carpenter biginneth quake;
Him thinketh verrailiche° that he may see *truly*
Noees flood come walwing° as the see   *rolling*

---

7. On high.
8. Toward the garden.
9. Precious commandment.

1. Far apart.
2. What all this clever plan meant.

To drenchen° Alison, his hony dere.   *drown*
510 He weepeth, waileth, maketh sory cheere;
He siketh° with ful many a sory swough,°   *sighs/groan*
And gooth and geteth him a kneeding-trough,
And after a tubbe and a kimelin,
And prively he sente hem to his in,°   *dwelling*
515 And heeng° hem in the roof in privetee;   *hung*
His° owene hand he made laddres three,   *with his*
To climben by the ronges° and the stalkes°   *rungs/uprights*
Unto the tubbes hanging in the balkes,°   *rafters*
And hem vitailed,° bothe trough and tubbe,   *victualed*
520 With breed and cheese and good ale in a jubbe,°   *jug*
Suffising right ynough as for a day.
But er° that he hadde maad al this array,   *before*
He sente his knave, and eek his wenche also,
Upon his neede[3] to London for to go.
525 And on the Monday whan it drow to[4] nighte,
He shette° his dore withouten candel-lighte,   *shut*
And dressed° alle thing as it sholde be,   *arranged*
And shortly up they clomben° alle three.   *climbed*
They seten° stille wel a furlong way.[5]   *sat*
530 "Now, Pater Noster, clum,"[6] saide Nicholay,
And "Clum" quod John, and "Clum" saide Alisoun.
This carpenter saide his devocioun,
And stille he sit° and biddeth° his prayere,   *sits/prays*
Awaiting on the rain, if he it heere.°   *might hear*
535 The dede sleep, for wery bisinesse,
Fil° on this carpenter right as I gesse   *fell*
Aboute corfew time,[7] or litel more.
For travailing of his gost[8] he groneth sore,
And eft° he routeth,° for his heed mislay.[9]   *then/snores*
540 Down of the laddre stalketh Nicholay,
And Alison ful softe adown she spedde:
Withouten wordes mo they goon to bedde
Ther as the carpenter is wont to lie.
Ther was the revel and the melodye,
545 And thus lith° Alison and Nicholas   *lies*
In bisinesse of mirthe and of solas,°   *pleasure*
Til that the belle of Laudes[1] gan to ringe,
And freres° in the chauncel° gonne singe.   *friars/chancel*
This parissh clerk, this amorous Absolon,
550 That is for love alway so wo-bigoon,
Upon the Monday was at Oseneye,
With compaignye him to disporte and playe,
And axed upon caas a cloisterer[2]
Ful prively after John the carpenter;

---

3. On an errand for him.
4. Drew toward.
5. The time it takes to go a furlong (i.e., a few minutes).
6. Hush (?). "Pater Noster": Our Father.
7. Probably about 8 P.M.

8. Affliction of his spirit.
9. Lay in the wrong position.
1. The first church service of the day, before daybreak.
2. Here a member of the religious order of Osney Abbey. "Upon caas": by chance.

555 And he drow him apart out of the chirche,
  And saide, "I noot:[3] I sawgh him here nought wirche°   *work*
  Sith Saterday. I trowe that he be went
  For timber ther oure abbot hath him sent.
  For he is wont for timber for to go,
560 And dwellen atte grange[4] a day or two.
  Or elles he is at his hous, certain.
  Where that he be I can nought soothly sayn."
   This Absolon ful jolif was and light,[5]
  And thoughte, "Now is time to wake al night,
565 For sikerly,° I sawgh him nought stiringe   *certainly*
  Aboute his dore sin day bigan to springe.
  So mote° I thrive, I shal at cokkes crowe   *may*
  Ful prively knokken at his windowe
  That stant° ful lowe upon his bowres° wal.   *stands/bedroom's*
570 To Alison now wol I tellen al
  My love-longing,° for yet I shal nat misse   *lovesickness*
  That at the leeste way[6] I shal hire kisse.
  Som manere confort shal I have, parfay.°   *in faith*
  My mouth hath icched al this longe day:
575 That is a signe of kissing at the leeste.
  Al night me mette[7] eek I was at a feeste.
  Therfore I wol go sleepe an hour or twaye,
  And al the night thanne wol I wake and playe."
   Whan that the firste cok hath crowe, anoon
580 Up rist° this joly lovere Absolon,   *rises*
  And him arrayeth gay at point devis.[8]
  But first he cheweth grain[9] and licoris,
  To smellen sweete, er he hadde kembd° his heer.   *combed*
  Under his tonge a trewe-love[1] he beer,°   *bore*
585 For therby wende° he to be gracious.°   *supposed/pleasing*
  He rometh° to the carpenteres hous,   *strolls*
  And stille he stant° under the shot-windowe—   *stands*
  Unto his brest it raughte,° it was so lowe—   *reached*
  And ofte he cougheth with a semisoun.°   *small sound*
590 "What do ye, hony-comb, sweete Alisoun,
  My faire brid,[2] my sweete cinamome?°   *cinnamon*
  Awaketh, lemman° myn, and speketh to me.   *sweetheart*
  Wel litel thinken ye upon my wo
  That for your love I swete° ther I go.   *sweat*
595 No wonder is though that I swelte° and swete: *melt*
  I moorne as doth a lamb after the tete.°   *teat*
  Ywis, lemman, I have swich love-longinge,
  That lik a turtle° trewe is my moorninge: *dove*
  I may nat ete namore than a maide."
600 "Go fro the windowe, Jakke fool," she saide.
  "As help me God, it wol nat be com-pa-me.°   *come-kiss-me*

---

3. Don't know.
4. The outlying farm belonging to the abbey.
5. Was very amorous and cheerful.
6. I.e., at least.
7. I dreamed.

8. To perfection.
9. Grain of paradise; a spice.
1. Sprig of a cloverlike plant.
2. Bird or bride.

I love another, and elles I were to blame,
Wel bet° than thee, by Jesu, Absolon.   better
Go forth thy way or I wol caste a stoon,
605   And lat me sleepe, a twenty devele way."[3]
"Allas," quod Absolon, "and wailaway,
That trewe love was evere so yvele biset.[4]
Thanne kis me, sin that it may be no bet,
For Jesus love and for the love of me."
610   "Woltou thanne go thy way therwith?" quod she.
"Ye, certes, lemman," quod this Absolon.
"Thanne maak thee redy," quod she. "I come anoon."
And unto Nicholas she saide stille,°   quietly
"Now hust,° and thou shalt laughen al thy fille."   hush
615   This Absolon down sette him on his knees,
And said, "I am a lord at alle degrees,[5]
For after this I hope ther cometh more.
Lemman, thy grace, and sweete brid, thyn ore!"°   mercy
The windowe she undooth, and that in haste.
620   "Have do," quod she, "come of and speed thee faste,
Lest that oure neighebores thee espye."
This Absolon gan wipe his mouth ful drye:
Derk was the night as pich or as the cole,
And at the windowe out she putte hir hole,
625   And Absolon, him fil no bet ne wers,[6]
But with his mouth he kiste hir naked ers,
Ful savourly,° er he were war of this.   with relish
Abak he sterte,° and thoughte it was amis,   started
For wel he wiste a womman hath no beerd.°   beard
630   He felte a thing al rough and longe yherd,°   haired
And saide, "Fy, allas, what have I do?"
"Teehee," quod she, and clapte the windowe to.
And Absolon gooth forth a sory pas.[7]
"A beerd, a beerd!"[8] quod hende Nicholas,
635   "By Goddes corpus,° this gooth faire and weel."   body
This sely Absolon herde everydeel,°   every bit
And on his lippe he gan for anger bite,
And to himself he saide, "I shal thee quite."°   repay
Who rubbeth now, who froteth° now his lippes   wipes
640   With dust, with sond,° with straw, with cloth, with chippes,   sand
But Absolon, that saith ful ofte allas?
"My soule bitake° I unto Satanas,°   commit/Satan
But me were levere[9] than all this town," quod he,
"Of this despit° awroken° for to be.   insult/avenged
645   Allas," quod he, "allas I ne hadde ybleint!"°   turned aside
His hote love was cold and al yqueint,°   quenched
For fro that time that he hadde kist hir ers
Of paramours he sette nought a kers,[1]
For he was heled° of his maladye.   cured

3. In the name of twenty devils.
4. Ill-used.
5. In every way.
6. It befell him neither better nor worse.

7. I.e., walking sadly.
8. A trick (slang), but with a play on line 629.
9. I had rather.
1. He didn't care a piece of cress for woman's love.

650 Ful ofte paramours he gan defye,° *renounce*
And weep° as dooth a child that is ybete. *wept*
A softe paas² he wente over the streete
Until° a smith men clepen daun Gervais,³ *to*
That in his forge smithed plough harneis:° *equipment*
655 He sharpeth shaar and cultour⁴ bisily.
This Absolon knokketh al esily,° *quietly*
And saide, "Undo, Gervais, and that anoon."° *at once*
    "What, who artou?" "It am I, Absolon."
"What, Absolon? What, Cristes sweete tree!° *cross*
660 Why rise ye so rathe?° Ey, benedicite,° *early/bless me*
What aileth you? Som gay girl, God it woot,
Hath brought you thus upon the viritoot.⁵
By Sainte Note, ye woot wel what I mene."
    This Absolon ne roughte nat a bene⁶
665 Of al his play. No word again he yaf:
He hadde more tow on his distaf⁷
Than Gervais knew, and saide, "Freend so dere,
This hote cultour in the chimenee° here, *fireplace*
As lene⁸ it me: I have therwith to doone.
670 I wol bringe it thee again ful soone."
    Gervais answerde, "Certes, were it gold,
Or in a poke nobles alle untold,⁹
Thou sholdest have, as I am trewe smith.
Ey, Cristes fo,¹ what wol ye do therwith?"
675   "Therof," quod Absolon, "be as be may.
I shal wel telle it thee another day."
And caughte the cultour by the colde stele.° *handle*
Ful softe out at the dore he gan to stele,
And wente unto the carpenteres wal:
680 He cougheth first and knokketh therwithal
Upon the windowe, right as he dide er.° *before*
    This Alison answerde, "Who is ther
That knokketh so? I warante² it a thief."
    "Why, nay," quod he, "God woot, my sweete lief,° *dear*
685 I am thyn Absolon, my dereling.° *darling*
Of gold," quod he, "I have thee brought a ring—
My moder yaf it me, so God me save;
Ful fin it is and therto wel ygrave:° *engraved*
This wol I yiven thee if thou me kisse."
690   This Nicholas was risen for to pisse,
And thoughte he wolde amenden³ al the jape:° *joke*
He sholde kisse his ers er that he scape.
And up the windowe dide he hastily,
And out his ers he putteth prively,
695 Over the buttok to the haunche-boon.
    And therwith spak this clerk, this Absolon,

---

2. I.e., quiet walk.
3. Master Gervais.
4. He sharpens plowshare and coulter (the turf cutter on a plow).
5. I.e., on the prowl.
6. Didn't care a bean.

7. I.e., more on his mind.
8. I.e., please lend.
9. Or gold coins all uncounted in a bag.
1. Foe, i.e., Satan.
2. I.e., wager.
3. Improve on.

"Speek, sweete brid, I noot nought wher thou art."
This Nicholas anoon leet flee[4] a fart
As greet as it hadde been a thonder-dent°   *thunderbolt*
700 That with the strook he was almost yblent,°   *blinded*
And he was redy with his iren hoot,°   *hot*
And Nicholas amidde the ers he smoot:°   *smote*
Of° gooth the skin an hande-brede° aboute;   *off/handsbreadth*
The hote cultour brende so his toute°   *buttocks*
705 That for the smert° he wende for to[5] die;   *pain*
As he were wood° for wo he gan to crye,   *crazy*
"Help! Water! Water! Help, for Goddes herte!"
    This carpenter out of his slomber sterte,
And herde oon cryen "Water!" as he were wood,
710 And thoughte, "Allas, now cometh Noweles[6] flood!"
He sette him up[7] withoute wordes mo,
And with his ax he smoot the corde atwo,
And down gooth al: he foond neither to selle
Ne breed ne ale til he cam to the celle,[8]
715 Upon the floor, and ther aswoune° he lay.   *in a faint*
    Up sterte hire[9] Alison and Nicholay,
And criden "Out" and "Harrow" in the streete.
The neighebores, bothe smale and grete,
In ronnen for to gauren° on this man   *gape*
720 That aswoune lay bothe pale and wan,
For with the fal he brosten° hadde his arm;   *broken*
But stonde he moste° unto his owene harm,   *must*
For whan he spak he was anoon bore down[1]
With° hende Nicholas and Alisoun: *by*
725 They tolden every man that he was wood—
He was agast so of Noweles flood,
Thurgh fantasye, that of his vanitee°   *folly*
He hadde ybought him kneeding-tubbes three,
And hadde hem hanged in the roof above,
730 And that he prayed hem, for Goddes love,
To sitten in the roof, *par compaignye*.[2]
    The folk gan laughen at his fantasye.
Into the roof they kiken° and they cape,°   *peer/gape*
And turned al his harm unto a jape,°   *joke*
735 For what so that this carpenter answerde,
It was for nought: no man his reson° herde;   *argument*
With othes grete he was so sworn adown,
That he was holden° wood in al the town,   *considered*
For every clerk anoonright heeld with other:
740 They saide, "The man was wood, my leve brother,"
And every wight gan laughen at this strif.°   *fuss*
Thus swived[3] was the carpenteres wif
For al his keeping° and his jalousye,   *guarding*

4. Let fly.
5. Thought he would.
6. The carpenter is confusing Noah and Noel (Christmas).
7. Got up.
8. He found time to sell neither bread nor ale until

he arrived at the foundation, i.e., he did not take time out.
9. Started.
1. Refuted.
2. For company's sake.
3. The vulgar verb for having sexual intercourse.

And Absolon hath kist hir nether° yë,   *lower*
745 And Nicholas is scalded in the toute:
This tale is doon, and God save al the route!° *company*

The Man of Law's Epilogue

The Reeve has taken *The Miller's Tale* personally and retaliates with a fabliau about a miller whose wife and daughter are seduced by two clerks. Next the Cook begins yet another fabliau, which breaks off after fifty-five lines, thereby closing Fragment I of *The Canterbury Tales*. Chaucer may never have settled on a final order for the tales he completed, but all modern editors, following many manuscripts, agree in putting *The Man of Law's Tale* next. The Man of Law tells a long moralistic tale about the many trials of a heroine called Constance for the virtue she personifies. This tale is finished, but Fragment II shows that *The Canterbury Tales* reaches us as a work in progress, which Chaucer kept revising, creating many problems for its scribes and editors. In the link that introduces him, the Man of Law says he will tell a tale in prose, but the story of Constance turns out to be in a seven-line stanza called rhyme royal. That inconsistency has led to speculation that at one time the Man of Law was assigned a long prose allegory, which Chaucer later reassigned to his own pilgrim persona. In thirty-five manuscripts *The Man of Law's Tale* is followed by an *Epilogue* omitted in twenty-two of the manuscripts that contain more or less complete versions of *The Canterbury Tales*. The often-missing link begins with the Host praising the *Man of Law's Tale* and calling upon the Parson to tell another uplifting tale. The Parson, however, rebukes the Host for swearing. The Host angrily accuses the Parson of being a "Lollard," a derogatory term for followers of the reformist preacher John Wycliffe. This is Chaucer's only overt reference to an important religious and political controversy that anticipates the sixteenth-century English Reformation.

A third speaker, about whose identity the manuscripts disagree (six read "Summoner"; twenty-eight, "Squire"; one, "Shipman"), interrupts with the promise to tell a merry tale. Several modern editions, including the standard one used by scholars, print *The Man of Law's Epilogue* at the end of Fragment II, and begin Fragment III with *The Wife of Bath's Prologue*. Because the third speaker in the former *sounds* like the Wife, an argument has been made that she is the pilgrim who refers to "My joly body" (line 23), who at one time told a fabliau tale in which the narrator speaks of married women in the first person plural ("we," "us," "our"). Chaucer, so the argument goes, later gave that story to the Shipman. If in fact the Wife of Bath did once tell what is now *The Shipman's Tale*, that would be an indication of the exciting new possibilities he discovered in the literary form he had invented.

Oure Host upon his stiropes stood anoon
And saide, "Goode men, herkneth everichoon,
This was a thrifty° tale for the nones,° *proper/occasion*
Sire parissh Preest," quod he, "for Goddes bones,
5 Tel us a tale as was thy forward° yore.° *agreement/earlier*
I see wel that ye lerned men in lore° *teaching*
Can° muche good, by Goddes dignitee." *know*
The Person him answerde, "Benedicite,° *bless me*
What aileth the man so sinfully to swere?"
10 Oure Host answerede, "O Jankin, be ye there?[1]
I smelle a lollere[2] in the wind," quod he.

1. Is that where you're coming from? "Jankin": Johnny; derogatory name for a priest.
2. Contemptuous term for a religious reformer considered radical; a heretic.

"Now, goode men," quod oure Hoste, "herkneth me:
Abideth, for Goddes digne° passioun,   *worthy*
For we shal have a predicacioun.°   *sermon*
15 This lollere here wol prechen us somwhat."
"Nay, by my fader soule, that shal he nat,"
Saide the [Wif of Bathe],³ "here shal he nat preche:
He shal no gospel glosen⁴ here ne teche.
We leven° alle in the grete God," quod [she].   *believe*
20 "He wolde sowen som difficultee
Or sprengen cokkel in oure clene corn.⁵
And therfore, Host, I warne thee biforn,
My joly body shal a tale telle
And I shal clinken you so merye a belle
25 That I shal waken al this compaignye.
But it shal nat been of philosophye,
Ne physlias,⁶ ne termes quainte of lawe:
There is but litel Latin in my mawe."°   *stomach*

The Wife of Bath's Prologue and Tale

In creating the Wife of Bath, Chaucer drew upon a centuries-old tradition of anti-feminist writings that was particularly nurtured by the medieval church. In their conviction that the rational, intellectual, spiritual, and, therefore, higher side of human nature predominated in men, whereas the irrational, material, earthly, and, therefore, lower side of human nature predominated in women, St. Paul and the early Church fathers exalted celibacy and virginity above marriage, although they were also obliged to concede the necessity and sanctity of matrimony. In the fourth century, a monk called Jovinian wrote a tract in which he apparently presented marriage as a positive good rather than as a necessary evil. That tract is known only through St. Jerome's extreme attack upon it. Jerome's diatribe and other antifeminist and anti-matrimonial literature provided Chaucer with a rich body of bookish male "auctoritee" (authority) against which the Wife of Bath asserts her female "experience" and defends her rights and justifies her life as a five-time married woman. In her polemical wars with medieval clerks and her matrimonial wars with her five husbands, the last of whom was once a clerk of Oxenford, the Wife of Bath seems ironically to confirm the accusations of the clerks, but at the same time she succeeds in satirizing the shallowness of the stereotypes of women and marriage in antifeminist writings and in demonstrating how much the largeness and complexity of her own character rise above that stereotype.

The Prologue

Experience, though noon auctoritee
Were in this world, is right ynough for me
To speke of wo that is in mariage:
For lordinges,° sith I twelf yeer was of age—   *gentlemen*
5 Thanked be God that is eterne on live—
Housbondes at chirche dore¹ I have had five

---

3. On the speaker here, see discussion in head-note.
4. Gloss, with the sense of distorting the meaning of scripture.
5. Sow tares (impure doctrine) in our pure wheat.

6. No such word exists. The speaker is coining a professional-sounding term in philosophy, law, or medicine.
1. The actual wedding ceremony was celebrated at the church door, not in the chancel.

(If I so ofte mighte han wedded be),
And alle were worthy men in hir degree.
But me was told, certain, nat longe agoon is,
10 That sith that Crist ne wente nevere but ones°   *once*
To wedding in the Cane[2] of Galilee,
That by the same ensample° taughte he me   *example*
That I ne sholde wedded be but ones.
Herke eek,° lo, which° a sharp word for the nones,[3]   *also/what*
15 Biside a welle, Jesus, God and man,
Spak in repreve° of the Samaritan: *reproof*
"Thou hast yhad five housbondes," quod he,
"And that ilke° man that now hath thee   *same*
Is nat thyn housbonde." Thus saide he certain.
20 What that he mente therby I can nat sayn,
But that I axe° why the fifthe man   *ask*
Was noon housbonde to the Samaritan?[4]
How manye mighte she han in mariage?
Yit herde I nevere tellen in myn age
25 Upon this nombre diffinicioun.°   *definition*
Men may divine° and glosen° up and down,   *guess/interpret*
But wel I woot,° expres,° withouten lie,   *know/expressly*
God bad us for to wexe[5] and multiplye:
That gentil text can I wel understonde.
30   Eek wel I woot° he saide that myn housbonde   *know*
Sholde lete° fader and moder and take to me,[6]   *leave*
But of no nombre mencion made he—
Of bigamye or of octogamye:[7]
Why sholde men thanne speke of it vilainye?
35   Lo, here the wise king daun° Salomon: *master*
I trowe° he hadde wives many oon,[8]   *believe*
As wolde God it leveful° were to me   *permissible*
To be refresshed half so ofte as he.
Which yifte[9] of God hadde he for alle his wives!
40 No man hath swich° that in this world alive is.   *such*
God woot this noble king, as to my wit,°   *knowledge*
The firste night hadde many a merye fit°   *bout*
With eech of hem, so wel was him on live.[1]
Blessed be God that I have wedded five,
45 Of whiche I have piked out the beste,[2]
Bothe of hir nether purs[3] and of hir cheste.°   *money box*
Diverse scoles maken parfit° clerkes,   *perfect*
And diverse practikes[4] in sondry werkes
Maken the werkman parfit sikerly:°   *certainly*
50 Of five housbondes scoleying° am I.   *schooling*

---

2. Cana (see John 2.1).
3. To the purpose.
4. Christ was actually referring to a sixth man who was not married to the Samaritan woman (cf. John 4.6 ff.).
5. I.e., increase (see Genesis 1.28).
6. See Matthew 19.5.
7. I.e., of two or even eight marriages. The Wife of Bath is referring to successive, rather than simultaneous, marriages.
8. Solomon had seven hundred wives and three hundred concubines (1 Kings 11.3).
9. What a gift.
1. I.e., so pleasant a life he had.
2. Whom I have cleaned out of everything worthwhile.
3. Lower purse, i.e., testicles.
4. Practical experiences.

Welcome the sixte whan that evere he shal![5]
For sith I wol nat kepe me chast in al,
Whan my housbonde is fro the world agoon,
Som Cristen man shal wedde me anoon.°   *right away*
55 For thanne th'Apostle[6] saith that I am free
To wedde, a Goddes half, where it liketh me.[7]
He saide that to be wedded is no sinne:
Bet is to be wedded than to brinne.[8]
What rekketh me[9] though folk saye vilainye
60 Of shrewed° Lamech[1] and his bigamye?   *cursed*
I woot wel Abraham was an holy man,
And Jacob eek, as fer as evere I can,°   *know*
And eech of hem hadde wives mo than two,
And many another holy man also.
65   Where can ye saye in any manere age
That hye God defended° mariage   *prohibited*
By expres word? I praye you, telleth me.
Or where comanded he virginitee?
I woot as wel as ye, it is no drede,°   *doubt*
70 Th'Apostle, whan he speketh of maidenhede,°   *virginity*
He saide that precept therof hadde he noon:
Men may conseile a womman to be oon,°   *single*
But conseiling nis° no comandement.   *is not*
He putte it in oure owene juggement.
75 For hadde God comanded maidenhede,
Thanne hadde he dampned° wedding with the deede;[2]   *condemned*
And certes, if there were no seed ysowe,
Virginitee, thanne wherof sholde it growe?
Paul dorste nat comanden at the leeste
80 A thing of which his maister yaf° no heeste.°   *gave/command*
The dart[3] is set up for virginitee:
Cacche whoso may, who renneth° best lat see.   *runs*
But this word is nought take of[4] every wight,°   *person*
But ther as[5] God list° yive it of his might.   *it pleases*
85 I woot wel that th'Apostle was a maide,°   *virgin*
But nathelees, though that he wroot and saide
He wolde that every wight were swich° as he,   *such*
Al nis but conseil to virginitee;
And for to been a wif he yaf me leve
90 Of indulgence; so nis it no repreve°   *disgrace*
To wedde me[6] if that my make° die,   *mate*
Withouten excepcion of bigamye[7]—
Al° were it good no womman for to touche[8]   *although*
(He mente as in his bed or in his couche,

5. I.e., shall come along.
6. St. Paul.
7. I please. "A Goddes half": on God's behalf.
8. "It is better to marry than to burn" (1 Corinthians 7.9). Many of the Wife's citations of St. Paul are from this chapter, often secondhand from St. Jerome's tract *Against Jovinian*.
9. What do I care.
1. The first man whom the Bible mentions as having two wives (Genesis 4.19–24); he is cursed,

however, not for his marriages but for murder.
2. I.e., at the same time.
3. I.e., prize in a race.
4. Understood for, i.e., applicable to.
5. Where.
6. For me to marry.
7. I.e., without there being any legal objection on the score of remarriage.
8. "It is good for a man not to touch a woman" (1 Corinthians 7.1).

95	For peril is bothe fir° and tow° t'assemble—	*fire/flax*
	Ye knowe what this ensample may resemble).⁹	
	This al and som,¹ he heeld virginitee	
	More parfit than wedding in freletee.°	*frailty*
	(Freletee clepe I but if² that he and she	
100	Wolde leden al hir lif in chastitee.)	
	I graunte it wel, I have noon envye	
	Though maidenhede preferre° bigamye:°	*excel/remarriage*
	It liketh hem to be clene in body and gost.°	*spirit*
	Of myn estaat ne wol I make no boost;	
105	For wel ye knowe, a lord in his houshold	
	Ne hath nat every vessel al of gold:	
	Some been of tree,° and doon hir lord servise.	*wood*
	God clepeth° folk to him in sondry wise,	*calls*
	And everich hath of God a propre³ yifte,	
110	Som this, som that, as him liketh shifte.°	*ordain*
	Virginitee is greet perfeccioun,	
	And continence eek with devocioun,	
	But Crist, that of perfeccion is welle,°	*source*
	Bad nat every wight he sholde go selle	
115	Al that he hadde and yive it to the poore,	
	And in swich wise folwe him and his fore:°⁴	*footsteps*
	He spak to hem that wolde live parfitly°—	*perfectly*
	And lordinges, by youre leve, that am nat I.	
	I wol bistowe the flour of al myn age	
120	In th'actes and in fruit of mariage.	
	Telle me also, to what conclusioun°	*end*
	Were membres maad of generacioun	
	And of so parfit wis a wrighte ywrought?⁵	
	Trusteth right wel, they were nat maad for nought.	
125	Glose° whoso wol, and saye bothe up and down	*interpret*
	That they were maked for purgacioun	
	Of urine, and oure bothe thinges smale	
	Was eek° to knowe a femele from a male,	*also*
	And for noon other cause—saye ye no?	
130	Th'experience woot it is nought so.	
	So that the clerkes be nat with me wrothe,	
	I saye this, that they been maad for bothe—	
	That is to sayn, for office° and for ese°	*use/pleasure*
	Of engendrure,° ther we nat God displese.	*procreation*
135	Why sholde men elles in hir bookes sette	
	That man shal yeelde⁶ to his wif hir dette?°	*(marital) debt*
	Now wherwith sholde he make his payement	
	If he ne used his sely° instrument?	*innocent*
	Thanne were they maad upon a creature	
140	To purge urine, and eek for engendrure.	
	But I saye nought that every wight is holde,°	*bound*
	That hath swich harneis° as I to you tolde,	*equipment*

---

9. I.e., what this metaphor may apply to.
1. This is all there is to it.
2. Frailty I call it unless.
3. I.e., his own.

4. Matthew 19.21.
5. And wrought by so perfectly wise a maker.
6. I.e., pay.

To goon and usen hem in engendrure:
Thanne sholde men take of chastitee no cure.°   *heed*
145 Crist was a maide° and shapen as a man,   *virgin*
And many a saint sith that the world bigan,
Yit lived they evere in parfit chastitee.
I nil° envye no virginitee: *will not*
Lat hem be breed° of pured° whete seed,   *bread / refined*
150 And lat us wives hote° barly breed—   *be called*
And yit with barly breed, Mark telle can,
Oure Lord Jesu refresshed many a man.[7]
In swich estaat as God hath cleped us
I wol persevere: I nam nat precious.°   *fastidious*
155 In wifhood wol I use myn instrument
As freely° as my Makere hath it sent.   *generously*
If I be daungerous[8], God yive me sorwe:
Myn housbonde shal it han both eve and morwe,°   *morning*
Whan that him list[9] come forth and paye his dette.
160 An housbonde wol I have, I wol nat lette,[1]
Which shal be bothe my dettour° and my thral,°   *debtor / slave*
And have his tribulacion withal°   *as well*
Upon his flessh whil that I am his wif.
I have the power during al my lif
165 Upon his propre° body, and nat he: *own*
Right thus th'Apostle tolde it unto me,
And bad oure housbondes for to love us weel.
Al this sentence° me liketh everydeel.°   *sense / entirely*

[AN INTERLUDE]

Up sterte° the Pardoner and that anoon: *started*
170 "Now dame," quod he, "by God and by Saint John,
Ye been a noble prechour in this cas.
I was aboute to wedde a wif: allas,
What° sholde I bye° it on my flessh so dere?   *why / purchase*
Yit hadde I levere° wedde no wif toyere."°   *rather / this year*
175 "Abid," quod she, "my tale is nat bigonne.
Nay, thou shalt drinken of another tonne,°   *tun, barrel*
Er° that I go, shal savoure wors than ale.   *before*
And whan that I have told thee forth my tale
Of tribulacion in mariage,
180 Of which I am expert in al myn age—
This is to saye, myself hath been the whippe—
Thanne maistou chese° wheither thou wolt sippe   *choose*
Of thilke° tonne that I shal abroche;°   *this same / open*
Be war of it, er thou too neigh approche,
185 For I shal telle ensamples mo than ten.
'Whoso that nil° be war by othere men,   *will not*
By him shal othere men corrected be.'

---

7. In the descriptions of the miracle of the loaves and fishes, it is actually John, not Mark, who mentions barley bread (6.9).
8. In romance *dangerous* is a term for disdainfulness with which a woman rejects a lover. The Wife means she will not withhold sexual favors, in emulation of God's generosity (line 156).
9. When he wishes to.
1. I will not leave off, desist.

Thise same wordes writeth Ptolomee:
Rede in his *Almageste* and take it there."[2]
190   "Dame, I wolde praye you if youre wil it were,"
Saide this Pardoner, "as ye bigan,
Telle forth youre tale; spareth for no man,
And teche us yonge men of youre practike."°   *mode of operation*
   "Gladly," quod she, "sith it may you like;°   *please*
195 But that I praye to al this compaignye,
If that I speke after my fantasye,[3]
As taketh nat agrief° of that I saye,   *amiss*
For myn entente nis but for to playe."

[THE WIFE CONTINUES]

   Now sire, thanne wol I telle you forth my tale.
200 As evere mote I drinke win or ale,
I shal saye sooth: tho° housbondes that I hadde,   *those*
As three of hem were goode, and two were badde.
The three men were goode, and riche, and olde;
Unnethe° mighte they the statut holde   *scarcely*
205 In which they were bounden unto me—
Ye woot wel what I mene of this, pardee.
As help me God, I laughe whan I thinke
How pitously anight I made hem swinke;°   *work*
And by my fay,° I tolde of it no stoor:[4]   *faith*
210 They hadde me yiven hir land and hir tresor;
Me needed nat do lenger diligence
To winne hir love or doon hem reverence.
They loved me so wel, by God above,
That I ne tolde no daintee of[5] hir love.
215 A wis womman wol bisye hire evere in oon[6]
To gete hire love, ye, ther as she hath noon.
But sith I hadde hem hoolly in myn hand,
And sith that they hadde yiven me al hir land,
What° sholde I take keep° hem for to plese,   *why/care*
220 But it were for my profit and myn ese?
I sette hem so awerke,° by my fay,   *awork*
That many a night they songen° wailaway.   *sang*
The bacon was nat fet° for hem, I trowe,   *brought back*
That some men han in Essexe at Dunmowe.[7]
225 I governed hem so wel after° my lawe   *according to*
That eech of hem ful blisful was and fawe°   *glad*
To bringe me gaye thinges fro the faire;
They were ful glade whan I spak hem faire,
For God it woot, I chidde° hem spitously.°   *chided/cruelly*
230   Now herkneth how I bar me[8] properly:

2. "He who will not be warned by the example of others shall become an example to others." The *Almagest*, an astronomical work by the Greek astronomer and mathematician Ptolemy (2nd century C.E.), contains no such aphorism.
3. If I speak according to my fancy.
4. I set no store by it.
5. Set no value on.
6. Busy herself constantly.
7. At Dunmow, a side of bacon was awarded to the couple who after a year of marriage could claim no quarrels, no regrets, and the desire, if freed, to remarry one another.
8. Bore myself, behaved.

Ye wise wives, that conne understonde,
Thus sholde ye speke and bere him wrong on honde[9]—
For half so boldely can ther no man
Swere and lie as a woman can.
235 I saye nat this by wives that been wise,
But if it be whan they hem misavise.[1]
A wis wif, if that she can hir good,[2]
Shal bere him on hande the cow is wood,[3]
And take witnesse of hir owene maide
240 Of hir assent.[4] But herkneth how I saide:
    "Sire olde cainard,° is this thyn array?[5]   sluggard
Why is my neighebores wif so gay?
She is honoured overal° ther she gooth: wherever
I sitte at hoom; I have no thrifty° cloth.   decent
245 What doostou at my neighebores hous?
Is she so fair? Artou so amorous?
What roune° ye with oure maide, benedicite?[6]   whisper
Sire olde lechour, lat thy japes° be.   tricks, intrigues
And if I have a gossib° or a freend,   confidant
250 Withouten gilt, ye chiden as a feend,
If that I walke or playe unto his hous.
Thou comest hoom as dronken as a mous,
And prechest on thy bench, with yvel preef.[7]
Thou saist to me, it is a greet meschief°   misfortune
255 To wedde a poore womman for costage.[8]
And if that she be riche, of heigh parage,°   descent
Thanne saistou that it is a tormentrye
To suffre hir pride and hir malencolye.°   bad humor
And if that she be fair, thou verray knave,
260 Thou saist that every holour° wol hire have: lecher
She may no while in chastitee abide
That is assailed upon eech a side.
    "Thou saist som folk desiren us for richesse,
Som[9] for oure shap, and som for oure fairnesse,
265 And som for she can outher° singe or daunce,   either
And som for gentilesse and daliaunce,°   flirtatiousness
Som for hir handes and hir armes smale°—   slender
Thus gooth al to the devel by thy tale![1]
Thou saist men may nat keepe[2] a castel wal,
270 It may so longe assailed been overal.°   everywhere
And if that she be foul,° thou saist that she   ugly
Coveiteth° every man that she may see;   desires
For as a spaniel she wol on him lepe,
Til that she finde som man hire to chepe.°   bargain for
275 Ne noon so grey goos gooth ther in the lake,

---

9. Accuse him falsely.
1. Unless it happens that they make a mistake.
2. If she knows what's good for her.
3. Shall persuade him the chough has gone crazy. The chough, a talking bird, was popularly supposed to tell husbands of their wives' infidelity.
4. And call as a witness her maid, who is on her side.

5. I.e., is this how you behave?
6. Bless me.
7. I.e., (may you have) bad luck.
8. Because of the expense.
9. "Som," in this and the following lines, means "one."
1. I.e., according to your story.
2. I.e., keep safe.

As, saistou, wol be withoute make;°   *mate*
And saist it is an hard thing for to weelde°   *possess*
A thing that no man wol, his thankes, heelde.[3]
Thus saistou, lorel,° whan thou goost to bedde,   *wretch*
280 And that no wis man needeth for to wedde,
Ne no man that entendeth° unto hevene—   *aims*
With wilde thonder-dint° and firy levene°   *thunderbolt / lightning*
Mote thy welked nekke be tobroke![4]
Thou saist that dropping° houses and eek smoke   *leaking*
285 And chiding wives maken men to flee
Out of hir owene hous: a, benedicite,
What aileth swich an old man for to chide?
Thou saist we wives wil oure vices hide
Til we be fast,[5] and thanne we wol hem shewe—
290 Wel may that be a proverbe of a shrewe!°   *rascal*
Thou saist that oxen, asses, hors,° and houndes,   *horses*
They been assayed° at diverse stoundes;°   *tried out / times*
Bacins, lavours,° er that men hem bye,°   *washbowls / buy*
Spoones, stooles, and al swich housbondrye,°   *household goods*
295 And so be° pottes, clothes, and array°—   *are / clothing*
But folk of wives maken noon assay
Til they be wedded—olde dotard shrewe!
And thanne, saistou, we wil oure vices shewe.
Thou saist also that it displeseth me
300 But if° that thou wolt praise my beautee,   *unless*
And but thou poure° alway upon my face,   *gaze*
And clepe me 'Faire Dame' in every place,
And but thou make a feeste on thilke day
That I was born, and make me fressh and gay,
305 And but thou do to my norice° honour,   *nurse*
And to my chamberere within my bowr,[6]
And to my fadres folk, and his allies[7]—
Thus saistou, olde barel-ful of lies.
And yit of our apprentice Janekin,
310 For his crispe° heer, shining as gold so fin,   *curly*
And for° he squiereth me bothe up and down,   *because*
Yit hastou caught a fals suspecioun;
I wil° him nat though thou were deed° tomorwe.   *want / dead*
"But tel me this, why hidestou with sorwe[8]
315 The keyes of thy cheste° away fro me?   *money box*
It is my good° as wel as thyn, pardee.   *property*
What, weenestou° make an idiot of oure dame?[9]   *do you think to*
Now by that lord that called is Saint Jame,
Thou shalt nought bothe, though thou were wood,°   *furious*
320 Be maister of my body and of my good:
That oon thou shalt forgo, maugree thine yën.[1]
"What helpeth it of me enquere° and spyen?   *inquire*

3. No man would willingly hold.
4. May thy withered neck be broken!
5. I.e., married.
6. And to my chambermaid within my bedroom.
7. Relatives by marriage.
8. I.e., with sorrow to you.
9. I.e., me, the mistress of the house.
1. Despite your eyes, i.e., despite anything you can do about it.

I trowe thou woldest loke° me in thy cheste.   *lock*
Thou sholdest saye, 'Wif, go wher thee leste.°   *it may please*
325 Taak youre disport.² I nil leve° no tales: *believe*
I knowe you for a trewe wif, dame Alis.'
We love no man that taketh keep or charge³
Wher that we goon: we wol been at oure large.⁴
Of alle men yblessed mote he be
330 The wise astrologen° daun Ptolomee,   *astronomer*
That saith this proverbe in his *Almageste*:
'Of alle men his wisdom is the hyeste
That rekketh° nat who hath the world in honde.'⁵   *cares*
By this proverbe thou shalt understonde,
335 Have thou⁶ ynough, what thar° thee rekke or care   *need*
How merily that othere folkes fare?
For certes, olde dotard, by youre leve,
Ye shal han queinte⁷ right ynough at eve:
He is too greet a nigard that wil werne°   *refuse*
340 A man to lighte a candle at his lanterne;
He shal han nevere the lasse° lighte, pardee.   *less*
Have thou ynough, thee thar nat plaine thee.⁸
    "Thou saist also that if we make us gay
With clothing and with precious array,
345 That it is peril of oure chastitee,
And yit, with sorwe, thou moste enforce thee,⁹
And saye thise wordes in th' Apostles¹ name:
'In habit° maad with chastitee and shame   *clothing*
Ye wommen shal apparaile you,' quod he,
350 'And nat in tressed heer² and gay perree,°   *jewelry*
As perles, ne with gold ne clothes riche.'³
After thy text, ne after thy rubriche,⁴
I wol nat werke as muchel as a gnat.
Thou saidest this, that I was lik a cat:
355 For whoso wolde senge° a cattes skin,   *singe*
Thanne wolde the cat wel dwellen in his in;°   *lodging*
And if the cattes skin be slik° and gay,   *sleek*
She wol nat dwelle in house half a day,
But forth she wol, er any day be dawed,⁵
360 To shewe her skin and goon a-caterwawed.°   *caterwauling*
This is to saye, if I be gay, sire shrewe,
I wol renne° out, my borel° for to shewe.   *run/clothing*
Sir olde fool, what helpeth⁶ thee t'espyen?
Though thou praye Argus with his hundred yën⁷
365 To be my wardecors,° as he can best,   *bodyguard*
In faith, he shal nat keepe° me but me lest:⁸   *guard*

2. Enjoy yourself.
3. Notice or interest.
4. I.e., liberty.
5. Who rules the world.
6. If you have.
7. Elegant, pleasing thing; a euphemism for sexual enjoyment.
8. I.e., you need not complain.
9. Strengthen your position.
1. I.e., St. Paul's.

2. I.e., elaborate hairdo.
3. See 1 Timothy 2.9.
4. Rubric, i.e., direction.
5. Has dawned.
6. What does it help.
7. Argus was a monster whom Juno set to watch over one of Jupiter's mistresses. Mercury put all one hundred of his eyes to sleep and slew him.
8. Unless I please.

Yit coude I make his beerd,[9] so mote I thee.°   *prosper*
"Thou saidest eek that ther been thinges three,
The whiche thinges troublen al this erthe,
370 And that no wight may endure the ferthe.°   *fourth*
O leve° sire shrewe, Jesu shorte° thy lif!   *dear/shorten*
Yit prechestou and saist an hateful wif
Yrekened° is for oon of thise meschaunces.[1]   *is counted*
Been ther nat none othere resemblaunces
375 That ye may likne youre parables to,[2]
But if° a sely° wif be oon of tho?   *unless/innocent*
"Thou liknest eek wommanes love to helle,
To bareine° land ther water may nat dwelle;   *barren*
Thou liknest it also to wilde fir—
380 The more it brenneth,° the more it hath desir   *burns*
To consumen every thing that brent° wol be;   *burned*
Thou saist right° as wormes shende° a tree,   *just/destroy*
Right so a wif destroyeth hir housbonde—
This knowen they that been to wives bonde."°   *bound*
385   Lordinges, right thus, as ye han understonde,
Bar I stifly mine olde housbondes on honde[3]
That thus they saiden in hir dronkenesse—
And al was fals, but that I took witnesse
On Janekin and on my nece also.
390 O Lord, the paine I dide hem and the wo,
Ful giltelees, by Goddes sweete pine!°   *suffering*
For as an hors I coude bite and whine;°   *whinny*
I coude plaine° and° I was in the gilt,   *complain/if*
Or elles often time I hadde been spilt.°   *ruined*
395 Whoso that first to mille comth first grint.°   *grinds*
I plained first: so was oure werre stint.[4]
They were ful glade to excusen hem ful blive°   *quickly*
Of thing of which they nevere agilte hir live.[5]
Of wenches wolde I beren hem on honde,[6]
400 Whan that for sik[7] they mighte unnethe° stonde,   *scarcely*
Yit tikled I his herte for that he
Wende° I hadde had of him so greet cheertee.°   *thought/affection*
I swoor that al my walking out by nighte
Was for to espye wenches that he dighte.[8]
405 Under that colour[9] hadde I many a mirthe.
For al swich wit is yiven us in oure birthe:
Deceite, weeping, spinning God hath yive
To wommen kindely° whil they may live.   *naturally*
And thus of oo thing I avaunte me:[1]
410 At ende I hadde the bet° in eech degree,   *better*
By sleighte or force, or by som manere thing,
As by continuel murmur° or grucching;°   *complaint/grumbling*

9. I.e., deceive him.
1. For the other three misfortunes see Proverbs 30.21–23.
2. Are there no other (appropriate) similitudes to which you might draw analogies?
3. I rigorously accused my old husbands.
4. Our war brought to an end.

5. Of which they were never guilty in their lives.
6. Falsely accuse them.
7. I.e., sickness.
8. Had intercourse with.
9. I.e., pretense.
1. Boast.

Namely° abedde hadden they meschaunce: *especially*
Ther wolde I chide and do hem no plesaunce;[2]
415 I wolde no lenger in the bed abide
If that I felte his arm over my side,
Til he hadde maad his raunson° unto me;   *ransom*
Thanne wolde I suffre him do his nicetee.°   *foolishness (sex)*
And therfore every man this tale I telle:
420 Winne whoso may, for al is for to selle;
With empty hand men may no hawkes lure.
For winning° wolde I al his lust endure,   *profit*
And make me a feined° appetit—   *pretended*
And yit in bacon[3] hadde I nevere delit.
425 That made me that evere I wolde hem chide;
For though the Pope hadde seten° hem biside,   *sat*
I wolde nought spare hem at hir owene boord.°   *table*
For by my trouthe, I quitte° hem word for word.   *repaid*
As help me verray God omnipotent,
430 Though I right now sholde make my testament,
I ne owe hem nat a word that it nis quit.
I broughte it so aboute by my wit
That they moste yive it up as for the beste,
Or elles hadde we nevere been in reste;
435 For though he looked as a wood° leoun,   *furious*
Yit sholde he faile of his conclusioun.°   *object*
    Thanne wolde I saye, "Goodelief, taak keep,[4]
How mekely looketh Wilekin,[5] oure sheep!
Com neer my spouse, lat me ba° thy cheeke—   *kiss*
440 Ye sholden be al pacient and meeke,
And han a sweete-spiced° conscience,   *mild*
Sith ye so preche of Jobes pacience;
Suffreth alway, sin ye so wel can preche;
And but ye do, certain, we shal you teche
445 That it is fair to han a wif in pees.
Oon of us two moste bowen, doutelees,
And sith a man is more resonable
Than womman is, ye mosten been suffrable.°   *patient*
What aileth you to grucche° thus and grone?   *grumble*
450 Is it for ye wolde have my queinte° allone?   *sexual organ*
Why, taak it al—lo, have it everydeel.°   *all of it*
Peter,[6] I shrewe° you but ye° love it weel.   *curse/if you don't*
For if I wolde selle my bele chose,[7]
I coude walke as fressh as is a rose;
455 But I wol keepe it for youre owene tooth.°   *taste*
Ye be to blame. By God, I saye you sooth!"°   *the truth*
Swiche manere° wordes hadde we on honde.   *kind of*
Now wol I speke of my ferthe° housbonde.   *fourth*
    My ferthe housbonde was a revelour°   *reveler*
460 This is to sayn, he hadde a paramour°   *mistress*

2. Give them no pleasure.
3. I.e., old meat.
4. Good friend, take notice.
5. I.e., Willie.

6. By St. Peter.
7. French for "beautiful thing"; a euphemism for sexual organs.

And I was yong and ful of ragerye,°   *passion*
Stibourne° and strong and joly as a pie:° *untamable/magpie*
How coude I daunce to an harpe smale,° *gracefully*
And singe, ywis,° as any nightingale,   *indeed*
465 Whan I hadde dronke a draughte of sweete win.
Metellius, the foule cherl, the swin,
That with a staf birafte° his wif hir lif   *deprived*
For° she drank win, though I hadde been his wif, *because*
Ne sholde nat han daunted° me fro drinke; *frightened*
470 And after win on Venus moste° I thinke, *must*
For also siker° as cold engendreth hail,   *sure*
A likerous° mouth moste han a likerous° tail: *greedy/lecherous*
In womman vinolent° is no defence— *who drinks*
This knowen lechours by experience.
475 But Lord Crist, whan that it remembreth me[8]
Upon my youthe and on my jolitee,
It tikleth me aboute myn herte roote—
Unto this day it dooth myn herte boote° *good*
That I have had my world as in my time.
480 But age, allas, that al wol envenime,° *poison*
Hath me biraft[9] my beautee and my pith°— *vigor*
Lat go, farewel, the devel go therwith!
The flour is goon, ther is namore to telle:
The bren° as I best can now moste I selle; *bran*
485 But yit to be right merye wol I fonde.° *strive*
Now wol I tellen of my ferthe housbonde.
  I saye I hadde in herte greet despit
That he of any other hadde delit,
But he was quit,° by God and by Saint Joce: *paid back*
490 I made him of the same wode a croce[1]—
Nat of my body in no foul manere—
But, certainly, I made folk swich cheere[2]
That in his owene grece I made him frye,
For angre and for verray jalousye.
495 By God, in erthe I was his purgatorye,
For which I hope his soule be in glorye.
For God it woot, he sat ful ofte and soong° *sang*
Whan that his sho ful bitterly him wroong.° *pinched*
Ther was no wight save God and he that wiste° *knew*
500 In many wise how sore I him twiste.
He deide whan I cam fro Jerusalem,
And lith ygrave under the roode-beem,[3]
Al° is his tombe nought so curious[4]   *although*
As was the sepulcre of him Darius,
505 Which that Apelles wroughte subtilly:[5]
It nis but wast to burye him preciously.° *expensively*
Lat him fare wel, God yive his soule reste;

8. When I look back.
9. Has taken away from me.
1. I made him a cross of the same wood. The proverb has much the same sense as the one quoted in
line 493.
2. Pretended to be in love with others.

3. And lies buried under the rood beam (the crucifix beam running between nave and chancel).
4. Carefully wrought.
5. Accordingly to medieval legend, the artist Apelles decorated the tomb of Darius, king of the Persians.

He is now in his grave and in his cheste.°   *coffin*
Now of my fifthe housbonde wol I telle—
510 God lete his soule nevere come in helle—
And yit he was to me the moste shrewe:[6]
That feele I on my ribbes al by rewe,[7]
And evere shal unto myn ending day.
But in oure bed he was so fressh and gay,
515 And therwithal so wel coulde he me glose°   *flatter, coax*
Whan that he wolde han my bele chose,
That though he hadde me bet° on every boon,°   *beaten / bone*
He coude winne again my love anoon.°   *immediately*
I trowe I loved him best for that he
520 Was of his love daungerous[8] to me.
We wommen han, if that I shal nat lie,
In this matere a quainte fantasye:[9]
Waite what[1] thing we may nat lightly° have,   *easily*
Therafter wol we crye al day and crave;
525 Forbede us thing, and that desiren we;
Preesse on us faste, and thanne wol we flee.
With daunger oute we al oure chaffare:[2]
Greet prees° at market maketh dere° ware,   *crowd / expensive*
And too greet chepe is holden at litel pris.[3]
530 This knoweth every womman that is wis.
     My fifthe housbonde—God his soule blesse!—
Which that I took for love and no richesse,
He somtime was a clerk at Oxenforde,
And hadde laft° scole and wente at hoom to boorde   *left*
535 With my gossib,° dwelling in oure town   *confidante*
God have hir soule!—hir name was Alisoun;
She knew myn herte and eek my privetee°   *secrets*
Bet° than oure parissh preest, as mote I thee.° *better / prosper*
To hire biwrayed° I my conseil° al,   *disclosed / secrets*
540 For hadde myn housbonde pissed on a wal,
Or doon a thing that sholde han cost his lif,
To hire,° and to another worthy wif,   *her*
And to my nece which I loved weel,
I wolde han told his conseil everydeel;°   *entirely*
545 And so I dide ful often, God it woot,
That made his face often reed° and hoot°   *red / hot*
For verray shame, and blamed himself for he
Hadde told to me so greet a privetee.
     And so bifel that ones° in a Lente—   *once*
550 So often times I to my gossib wente,
For evere yit I loved to be gay,
And for to walke in March, Averil, and May,
From hous to hous, to heere sondry tales—
That Janekin clerk and my gossib dame Alis
555 And I myself into the feeldes wente.
Myn housbonde was at London al that Lente:

---

6. Worst rascal.
7. In a row.
8. I.e., he played hard to get.
9. Strange fancy.

1. Whatever.
2. (Meeting) with reserve, we spread out our merchandise.
3. Too good a bargain is held at little value.

I hadde the better leiser for to playe,
And for to see, and eek for to be seye°   *seen*
Of lusty folk—what wiste I wher my grace°   *luck*
560 Was shapen° for to be, or in what place?   *destined*
Therfore I made my visitaciouns
To vigilies[4] and to processiouns,
To preching eek, and to thise pilgrimages,
To playes of miracles and to mariages,
565 And wered upon[5] my gaye scarlet gites°—   *gowns*
Thise wormes ne thise motthes ne thise mites,
Upon my peril,[6] frete° hem neveradeel: *ate*
And woostou why? For they were used weel.
     Now wol I tellen forth what happed me.
570 I saye that in the feeldes walked we,
Til trewely we hadde swich daliaunce,°   *flirtation*
This clerk and I, that of my purveyaunce°   *foresight*
I spak to him and saide him how that he,
If I were widwe, sholde wedde me.
575 For certainly, I saye for no bobaunce,°   *boast*
Yit was I nevere withouten purveyaunce
Of mariage n'of othere thinges eek:
I holde a mouses herte nought worth a leek
That hath but oon hole for to sterte° to,   *run*
580 And if that faile thanne is al ydo.[7]
I bar him on hand[8] he hadde enchaunted me
(My dame° taughte me that subtiltee);   *mother*
And eek I saide I mette° of him al night: *dreamed*
He wolde han slain me as I lay upright,°   *on my back*
585 And al my bed was ful of verray blood—
"But yit I hope that ye shul do me good;
For blood bitokeneth° gold, as me was taught."   *signifies*
And al was fals, I dremed of it right naught,
But as I folwed ay my dames° lore°   *mother's / teaching*
590 As wel of that as othere thinges more.
But now sire—lat me see, what shal I sayn?
Aha, by God, I have my tale again.
     Whan that my ferthe housbonde was on beere,°   *funeral bier*
I weep,° algate,° and made sory cheere,   *wept / anyhow*
595 As wives moten,° for it is usage,°   *must / custom*
And with my coverchief covered my visage;
But for I was purveyed° of a make.°   *provided / mate*
I wepte but smale, and that I undertake.°   *guarantee*
     To chirche was myn housbonde born amorwe;[9]
600 With neighebores that for him maden sorwe,
And Janekin oure clerk was oon of tho.
As help me God, whan that I saw him go
After the beere, me thoughte he hadde a paire
Of legges and of feet so clene[1] and faire,
605 That al myn herte I yaf unto his hold.°   *possession*

<hr>

4. Evening service before a religious holiday.   8. I pretended to him.
5. Wore.   9. In the morning.
6. On peril (to my soul), an oath.   1. I.e., neat.
7. I.e., the game is up.

He was, I trowe,° twenty winter old,   *believe*
And I was fourty, if I shal saye sooth—
But yit I hadde alway a coltes tooth:[2]
Gat-toothed[3] was I, and that bicam me weel;
610   I hadde the prente[4] of Sainte Venus seel.°   *seal*
As help me God, I was a lusty oon,
And fair and riche and yong and wel-bigoon,°   *well-situated*
And trewely, as mine housbondes tolde me,
I hadde the beste quoniam[5] mighte be.
615   For certes I am al Venerien
In feeling, and myn herte is Marcien:[6]
Venus me yaf my lust, my likerousnesse,°   *amorousness*
And Mars yaf me my sturdy hardinesse.
Myn ascendent was Taur[7] and Mars therinne—
620   Allas, allas, that evere love was sinne!
I folwed ay° my inclinacioun   *ever*
By vertu of my constellacioun;[8]
That made me I coude nought withdrawe
My chambre of Venus from a good felawe.
625   Yit have I Martes° merk upon my face,   *Mars's*
And also in another privee place.
For God so wis° be my savacioun,°   *surely/salvation*
I loved nevere by no discrecioun,°   *moderation*
But evere folwede myn appetit,
630   Al were he short or long or blak or whit;
I took no keep,° so that he liked° me,   *heed/pleased*
How poore he was, ne eek of what degree.
    What sholde I saye but at the monthes ende
This joly clerk Janekin that was so hende°   *courteous, nice*
635   Hath wedded me with greet solempnitee,°   *splendor*
And to him yaf I al the land and fee°   *property*
That evere was me yiven therbifore—
But afterward repented me ful sore:
He nolde suffre no thing of my list.°   *wish*
640   By God, he smoot° me ones on the list°   *struck/ear*
For that I rente° out of his book a leef,   *tore*
That of the strook° myn ere weex° al deef.   *blow/grew*
Stibourne° I was as is a leonesse,   *stubborn*
And of my tonge a verray jangleresse,°   *chatterbox*
645   And walke I wolde, as I hadde doon biforn,
From hous to hous, although he hadde it[9] sworn;
For which he often times wolde preche,
And me of olde Romain geestes° teche,   *stories*
How he Simplicius Gallus lafte° his wif,   *left*
650   And hire forsook for terme of al his lif,
Nought but for open-heveded he hire sey[1]

2. I.e., youthful appetites.
3. Gap-toothed women were considered to be amorous.
4. Print, i.e., a birthmark.
5. Latin for "because"; another euphemism for a sexual organ.
6. Influenced by Mars. "Venerien": astrologically influenced by Venus.
7. My birth sign was the constellation Taurus, a sign in which Venus is dominant.
8. I.e., horoscope.
9. I.e., the contrary.
1. Just because he saw her bareheaded.

Looking out at his dore upon a day.
Another Romain tolde he me by name
That, for his wif was at a someres° game   *summer's*
655 Withouten his witing,° he forsook hire eke;   *knowledge*
And thanne wolde he upon his Bible seeke
That ilke proverbe of Ecclesiaste[2]
Where he comandeth and forbedeth faste°   *strictly*
Man shal nat suffre his wif go roule° aboute;   *roam*
660 Thanne wolde he saye right thus withouten doute:
"Whoso that buildeth his hous al of salwes,°   *willow sticks*
And priketh° his blinde hors over the falwes,[3] *rides*
And suffreth° his wif to go seeken halwes,°   *allows/shrines*
Is worthy to be hanged on the galwes."°   *gallows*
665 But al for nought—I sette nought an hawe[4]
Of his proverbes n'of his olde sawe;
N' I wolde nat of him corrected be:
I hate him that my vices telleth me,
And so doon mo, God woot, of us than I.
670 This made him with me wood al outrely:°   *entirely*
I nolde nought forbere° him in no cas.   *submit to*
     Now wol I saye you sooth, by Saint Thomas,
Why that I rente° out of his book a leef,   *tore*
For which he smoot me so that I was deef.
675 He hadde a book that gladly night and day
For his disport° he wolde rede alway.   *entertainment*
He cleped it *Valerie*[5] *and Theofraste,*
At which book he lough° alway ful faste;   *laughed*
And eek ther was somtime a clerk at Rome,
680 A cardinal, that highte Saint Jerome,
That made a book[6] again° Jovinian;   *against*
In which book eek ther was Tertulan,
Crysippus, Trotula, and Helouis,[7]
That was abbesse nat fer fro Paris;
685 And eek the Parables of Salomon,
Ovides *Art,*[8] and bookes many oon—
And alle thise were bounden in oo volume.
And every night and day was his custume,
Whan he hadde leiser and vacacioun°   *free time*
690 From other worldly occupacioun,
To reden in this book of wikked wives.
He knew of hem mo legendes and lives
Than been of goode wives in the Bible.
For trusteth wel, it is an impossible°   *impossibility*
695 That any clerk wol speke good of wives,
But if it be of holy saintes lives,

---

2. Ecclesiasticus (25.25).
3. Plowed land.
4. I did not rate at the value of a hawthorn berry.
5. "*Valerie*": i.e., the *Letter of Valerius Concerning Not Marrying,* by Walter Map; "*Theofraste*": Theophrastus's *Book Concerning Marriage.* Medieval manuscripts often contained a number of different works, sometimes, as here, dealing with the same subject.

6. St. Jerome's antifeminist *Against Jovinian.*
7. "Tertulan": i.e., Tertullian, author of treatises on sexual modesty. "Crysippus": mentioned by Jerome as an antifeminist. "Trotula": a female doctor whose presence here is unexplained. "Helouis": i.e., Eloise, whose love affair with the great scholar Abelard was a medieval scandal.
8. Ovid's *Art of Love.* "Parables of Salomon": the biblical Book of Proverbs.

N'of noon other womman nevere the mo—
Who painted the leon, tel me who?[9]
By God, if wommen hadden writen stories,
700 As clerkes han within hir oratories,°   chapels
They wolde han writen of men more wikkednesse
Than al the merk[1] of Adam may redresse.
The children of Mercurye and Venus[2]
Been in hir werking° ful contrarious:°   operation / opposed
705 Mercurye loveth wisdom and science,
And Venus loveth riot° and dispence;°   revelry / spending
And for hir diverse disposicioun
Each falleth in otheres exaltacioun,[3]
And thus, God woot, Mercurye is desolat
710 In Pisces wher Venus is exaltat,[4]
And Venus falleth ther Mercurye is raised:
Therfore no womman of no clerk is praised.
The clerk, whan he is old and may nought do
Of Venus werkes worth his olde sho,°   shoe
715 Thanne sit° he down and writ° in his dotage   sits / writes
That wommen can nat keepe hir mariage.
    But now to purpose why I tolde thee
That I was beten for a book, pardee:
Upon a night Janekin, that was our sire,[5]
720 Redde on his book as he sat by the fire
Of Eva first, that for hir wikkednesse
Was al mankinde brought to wrecchednesse,
For which that Jesu Crist himself was slain
That boughte° us with his herte blood again—   redeemed
725 Lo, heer expres of wommen may ye finde
That womman was the los° of al mankinde.[6]   ruin
    Tho° redde he me how Sampson loste his heres: then
Sleeping his lemman° kitte° it with hir sheres,   lover / cut
Thurgh which treson loste he both his yën.
730 Tho redde he me, if that I shal nat lien,
Of Ercules and of his Dianire,[7]
That caused him to sette himself afire.
    No thing forgat he the sorwe and wo
That Socrates hadde with his wives two—
735 How Xantippa caste pisse upon his heed:
This sely° man sat stille as he were deed;   poor, hapless
He wiped his heed, namore dorste° he sayn   dared
But "Er that thonder stinte,° comth a rain."   stops
    Of Pasipha[8] that was the queene of Crete—
740 For shrewednesse° him thoughte the tale sweete—   malice

9. In one of Aesop's fables, the lion, shown a picture of a man killing a lion, asked who painted the
picture. Had a lion been the artist, of course, the
roles would have been reversed.
1. Mark, sex.
2. I.e., clerks and women, astrologically ruled by
Mercury and Venus, respectively.
3. Because of their contrary positions (as planets),
each one descends (in the belt of the zodiac) as the
other rises, hence one loses its power as the other

becomes dominant.
4. I.e., Mercury is deprived of power in Pisces (the
sign of the Fish), where Venus is most powerful.
5. My husband.
6. The stories of wicked women Chaucer drew
mainly from St. Jerome and Walter Map.
7. Dejanira unwittingly gave Hercules a poisoned
shirt, which hurt him so much that he committed
suicide by fire.
8. Pasiphaë, who had intercourse with a bull.

Fy, speek namore, it is a grisly thing
Of hir horrible lust and hir liking.°   *pleasure*
Of Clytermistra[9] for hir lecherye
That falsly made hir housbonde for to die,
745 He redde it with ful good devocioun.
He tolde me eek for what occasioun
Amphiorax[1] at Thebes loste his lif:
Myn housbonde hadde a legende of his wif
Eriphylem, that for an ouche° of gold   *trinket*
750 Hath prively unto the Greekes told
Wher that hir housbonde hidde him in a place,
For which he hadde at Thebes sory grace.
Of Livia tolde he me and of Lucie:[2]
They bothe made hir housbondes for to die,
755 That oon for love, that other was for hate;
Livia hir housbonde on an even late
Empoisoned hath for that she was his fo;
Lucia likerous° loved hir housbonde so   *lecherous*
That for° he sholde alway upon hire thinke,   *in order that*
760 She yaf him swich a manere love-drinke
That he was deed er it were by the morwe.[3]
And thus algates° housbondes han sorwe.   *in every way*
Thanne tolde he me how oon Latumius
Complained unto his felawe Arrius
765 That in his garden growed swich a tree,
On which he saide how that his wives three
Hanged hemself for herte despitous.[4]
"O leve° brother," quod this Arrius,   *dear*
"Yif me a plante of thilke blessed tree,
770 And in my gardin planted shal it be."
Of latter date of wives hath he red
That some han slain hir housbondes in hir bed
And lete hir lechour dighte[5] hire al the night,
Whan that the cors° lay in the floor upright;°   *corpse/on his back*
775 And some han driven nailes in hir brain
Whil that they sleepe, and thus they han hem slain;
Some han hem yiven poison in hir drinke.
He spak more harm than herte may bithinke,°   *imagine*
And therwithal he knew of mo proverbes
780 Than in this world ther growen gras or herbes:
"Bet° is," quod he, "thyn habitacioun   *better*
Be with a leon or a foul dragoun
Than with a womman using° for to chide."   *accustomed*
"Bet is," quod he, "hye in the roof abide
785 Than with an angry wif down in the hous:
They been so wikked° and contrarious,   *perverse*
They haten that hir housbondes loveth ay."

9. Clytemnestra, who, with her lover, Aegisthus, slew her husband, Agamemnon.
1. Amphiaraus, betrayed by his wife, Eriphyle, and forced to go to the war against Thebes.
2. Livia murdered her husband in behalf of her lover, Sejanus. "Lucie": i.e., Lucilla, who was said to have poisoned her husband, the poet Lucretius, with a potion designed to keep him faithful.
3. He was dead before it was near morning.
4. For malice of heart.
5. Have intercourse with.

He saide, "A womman cast° hir shame away   *casts*

When she cast of° hir smok,"[6] and ferthermo,   *off*

790   "A fair womman, but she be chast also,

Is like a gold ring in a sowes nose."

Who wolde weene,° or who wolde suppose   *think*

The wo that in myn herte was and pine?°   *suffering*

  And whan I sawgh he wolde nevere fine°   *end*

795   To reden on this cursed book al night,

Al sodeinly three leves have I plight°   *snatched*

Out of his book right as he redde, and eke

I with my fist so took[7] him on the cheeke

That in oure fir he fil° bakward adown.   *fell*

800   And up he sterte as dooth a wood° leoun,   *raging*

And with his fist he smoot me on the heed°   *head*

That in the floor I lay as I were deed.°   *dead*

And whan he sawgh how stille that I lay,

He was agast, and wolde have fled his way,

805   Til atte laste out of my swough° I braide:°   *swoon/started*

"O hastou slain me, false thief?" I saide,

"And for my land thus hastou mordred° me?   *murdered*

Er I be deed yit wol I kisse thee."

And neer he cam and kneeled faire adown,

810   And saide, "Dere suster Alisoun,

As help me God, I shal thee nevere smite.

That I have doon, it is thyself to wite.°   *blame*

Foryif it me, and that I thee biseeke."°   *beseech*

And yit eftsoones° I hitte him on the cheeke,   *another time*

815   And saide, "Thief, thus muchel am I wreke.°   *avenged*

Now wol I die: I may no lenger speke."

  But at the laste with muchel care and wo

We fille[8] accorded by us selven two.

He yaf me al the bridel° in myn hand,   *bridle*

820   To han the governance of hous and land,

And of his tonge and his hand also;

And made[9] him brenne° his book anoonright tho.   *burn*

And whan that I hadde geten unto me

By maistrye° al the sovereinetee,°   *skill/dominion*

825   And that he saide, "Myn owene trewe wif,

Do as thee lust° the terme of al thy lif;   *it pleases*

Keep thyn honour, and keep eek myn estat,"

After that day we hadde nevere debat.

God help me so, I was to him as kinde

830   As any wif from Denmark unto Inde,°   *India*

And also trewe, and so was he to me.

I praye to God that sit° in majestee,   *sits*

So blesse his soule for his mercy dere.

Now wol I saye my tale if ye wol heere.

---

6. Undergarment.
7. I.e., hit.

8. I.e., became.
9. I.e., I made.

[ANOTHER INTERRUPTION]

| 835 | The Frere lough° whan he hadde herd all this: | *laughed* |

The Frere lough° whan he hadde herd all this: *laughed*
  "Now dame," quod he, "so have I joye or blis,
  This is a long preamble of a tale."
  And whan the Somnour herde the Frere gale,°   *exclaim*
  "Lo," quod the Somnour, "Goddes armes two,
840 A frere wol entremette him[1] everemo!
  Lo, goode men, a flye and eek a frere
  Wol falle in every dissh and eek matere.
  What spekestou of preambulacioun?
  What, amble or trotte or pisse or go sitte down!
845 Thou lettest° oure disport in this manere."   *hinder*
    "Ye, woltou so, sire Somnour?" quod the Frere.
  "Now by my faith, I shal er that I go
  Telle of a somnour swich a tale or two
  That al the folk shal laughen in this place."
850   "Now elles, Frere, I wol bishrewe° thy face,"   *curse*
  Quod this Somnour, "and I bishrewe me,
  But if I telle tales two or three
  Of freres, er I come to Sidingborne,[2]
  That I shal make thyn herte for to moorne°—   *mourn*
855 For wel I woot thy pacience is goon."
    Oure Hoste cride, "Pees, and that anoon!"
  And saide, "Lat the womman telle hir tale:
  Ye fare as folk that dronken been of ale.
  Do, dame, tel forth youre tale, and that is best."
860   "Al redy, sire," quod she, "right as you lest°—   *it pleases*
  If I have licence of this worthy Frere."
  "Yis, dame," quod he, "tel forth and I wol heere."

The Tale

As was suggested in the headnote to *The Man of Law's Epilogue*, Chaucer may have originally written the fabliau that became *The Shipman's Tale* for the Wife of Bath. If so, then he replaced it with a tale that is not simply appropriate to her character but that develops it even beyond the complexity already revealed in her *Prologue*. The story survives in two other versions in which the hero is Sir Gawain, whose courtesy contrasts sharply with the behavior of the knight in the Wife's tale. As Chaucer has the Wife tell it, the tale expresses her views about the relations of the sexes, her wit and humor, and her fantasies. Like Marie de France's lay *Lanval* (see pp. 105–18), the Wife's tale is about a fairy bride who seeks out and tests a mortal lover.

    In th'olde dayes of the King Arthour,
  Of which that Britouns speken greet honour,
865 Al was this land fulfild of faïrye:[3]
  The elf-queene° with hir joly compaignye   *queen of the fairies*
  Daunced ful ofte in many a greene mede°—   *meadow*
  This was the olde opinion as I rede;

---

1. Intrude himself.
2. Sittingbourne (a town forty miles from London).
3. I.e., filled full of supernatural creatures.

I speke of many hundred yeres ago.
870 But now can no man see none elves mo,
For now the grete charitee and prayeres
Of limitours,[4] and othere holy freres,
That serchen every land and every streem,
As thikke as motes° in the sonne-beem,   *dust particles*
875 Blessing halles, chambres, kichenes, bowres,
Citees, burghes,° castels, hye towres,   *townships*
Thropes, bernes, shipnes,[5] dayeries—
This maketh that ther been no faïries.
For ther as wont to walken was an elf
880 Ther walketh now the limitour himself,
In undermeles° and in morweninges,°   *afternoons/mornings*
And saith his Matins and his holy thinges,
As he gooth in his limitacioun.[6]
Wommen may go saufly° up and down: *safely*
885 In every bussh or under every tree
Ther is noon other incubus[7] but he,
And he ne wol doon hem but[8] dishonour.
   And so bifel it that this King Arthour
Hadde in his hous a lusty bacheler,°   *young knight*
890 That on a day cam riding fro river,[9]
And happed° that, allone as he was born,   *it happened*
He sawgh a maide walking him biforn;
Of which maide anoon, maugree hir heed,[1]
By verray force he rafte° hir maidenheed;   *deprived her of*
895 For which oppression° was swich clamour,   *rape*
And swich pursuite° unto the King Arthour,   *petitioning*
That dampned was this knight for to be deed[2]
By cours of lawe, and sholde han lost his heed—
Paraventure° swich was the statut tho—   *perchance*
900 But that the queene and othere ladies mo
So longe prayeden the king of grace,
Til he his lif him graunted in the place,
And yaf him to the queene, al at hir wille,
To chese° wheither she wolde him save or spille.[3]   *choose*
905 The queene thanked the king with al hir might,
And after this thus spak she to the knight,
Whan that she saw hir time upon a day:
"Thou standest yit," quod she, "in swich array°   *condition*
That of thy lif yit hastou no suretee.°   *guarantee*
910 I graunte thee lif if thou canst tellen me
What thing it is that wommen most desiren:
Be war and keep thy nekke boon° from iren.   *bone*
And if thou canst nat tellen me anoon,°   *right away*
Yit wol I yive thee leve for to goon
915 A twelfmonth and a day to seeche° and lere°   *search/learn*

4. Friars licensed to beg in a certain territory.
5. Thorps (villages), barns, stables.
6. I.e., the friar's assigned area. His "holy thinges" are prayers.
7. An evil spirit that seduces mortal women.
8. "Ne . . . but": only.
9. Hawking, usually carried out on the banks of a stream.
1. Despite her head, i.e., despite anything she could do.
2. This knight was condemned to death.
3. Put to death.

An answere suffisant° in this matere, · · · · · · · · · *satisfactory*
And suretee wol I han er that thou pace,° · · · · · · · *pass*
Thy body for to yeelden in this place."
    Wo was this knight, and sorwefully he siketh.° · · · · *sighs*
920 But what, he may nat doon al as him liketh,
And atte laste he chees° him for to wende, · · · · · · · *chose*
And come again right at the yeres ende,
With swich answere as God wolde him purveye,° · · · · *provide*
And taketh his leve and wendeth forth his waye.
925 He seeketh every hous and every place
Wher as he hopeth for to finde grace,
To lerne what thing wommen love most.
But he ne coude arriven in no coost[4]
Wher as he mighte finde in this matere
930 Two creatures according in fere.[5]
    Some saiden wommen loven best richesse;
Some saide honour, some saide jolinesse;° · · · · · · · *pleasure*
Some riche array, some saiden lust abedde,
And ofte time to be widwe and wedde.
935 Some saide that oure herte is most esed
Whan that we been yflatered and yplesed—
He gooth ful neigh the soothe, I wol nat lie:
A man shal winne us best with flaterye,
And with attendance° and with bisinesse° · · · · · · · *attention/solicitude*
940 Been we ylimed,° bothe more and lesse. · · · · · · · *ensnared*
    And some sayen that we loven best
For to be free, and do right as us lest,° · · · · · · · *it pleases*
And that no man repreve° us of oure vice, · · · · · · · *reprove*
But saye that we be wise and no thing nice.° · · · · · · *foolish*
945 For trewely, ther is noon of us alle,
If any wight wol clawe° us on the galle,° · · · · · · · *rub/sore spot*
That we nil kike° for° he saith us sooth: · · · · · · · *kick/because*
Assaye° and he shal finde it that so dooth. · · · · · · · *try*
For be we nevere so vicious withinne,
950 We wol be holden° wise and clene of sinne. · · · · · · *considered*
    And some sayn that greet delit han we
For to be holden stable and eek secree,[6]
And in oo° purpos stedefastly to dwelle, · · · · · · · *one*
And nat biwraye° thing that men us telle— · · · · · · · *disclose*
955 But that tale is nat worth a rake-stele.° · · · · · · · *rake handle*
Pardee,° we wommen conne no thing hele:° · · · · · · · *by God/conceal*
Witnesse on Mida.° Wol ye heere the tale? · · · · · · · *Midas*
    Ovide, amonges othere thinges smale,
Saide Mida hadde under his longe heres,
960 Growing upon his heed, two asses eres,
The whiche vice° he hidde as he best mighte · · · · · · *defect*
Ful subtilly from every mannes sighte,
That save his wif ther wiste° of it namo. · · · · · · · *knew*
He loved hire most and trusted hire also.

4. I.e., country.
5. Agreeing together.

6. Reliable and also closemouthed.

965 He prayed hire that to no creature
  She sholde tellen of his disfigure.°   *deformity*
   She swoor him nay, for al this world to winne,
  She nolde do that vilainye or sinne
  To make hir housbonde han so foul a name:
970 She nolde nat telle it for hir owene shame.
  But nathelees, hir thoughte that she dyde°   *would die*
  That she so longe sholde a conseil° hide;   *secret*
  Hire thoughte it swal° so sore about hir herte   *swelled*
  That nedely som word hire moste asterte,[7]
975 And sith she dorste nat telle it to no man,
  Down to a mareis° faste° by she ran—   *marsh/close*
  Til she cam there hir herte was afire—
  And as a bitore bombleth[8] in the mire,
  She laide hir mouth unto the water down:
980 "Biwray° me nat, thou water, with thy soun,"° *betray/sound*
  Quod she. "To thee I telle it and namo:°   *to no one else*
  Myn housbonde hath longe asses eres two.
  Now is myn herte al hool,[9] now is it oute.
  I mighte no lenger keep it, out of doute."
985 Here may ye see, though we a time abide,
  Yit oute it moot:° we can no conseil hide.   *must*
  The remenant of the tale if ye wol heere,
  Redeth Ovide, and ther ye may it lere.[1]
   This knight of which my tale is specially,
990 Whan that he sawgh he mighte nat come thereby—
  This is to saye what wommen loven most—
  Within his brest ful sorweful was his gost,°   *spirit*
  But hoom he gooth, he mighte nat sojourne:°   *delay*
  The day was come that hoomward moste° he turne. *must*
995 And in his way it happed him to ride
  In al this care under° a forest side,   *by*
  Wher as he sawgh upon a daunce go
  Of ladies foure and twenty and yit mo;
  Toward the whiche daunce he drow ful yerne,[2]
1000 In hope that som wisdom sholde he lerne.
  But certainly, er he cam fully there,
  Vanisshed was this daunce, he niste° where.   *knew not*
  No creature sawgh he that bar° lif,   *bore*
  Save on the greene he sawgh sitting a wif°—   *woman*
1005 A fouler wight ther may no man devise.°   *imagine*
  Again[3] the knight this olde wif gan rise,
  And saide, "Sire knight, heer forth lith° no way.° *lies/road*
  Telle me what ye seeken, by youre fay.°   *faith*
  Paraventure it may the better be:
1010 Thise olde folk conne° muchel thing," quod she. *know*
   "My leve moder,"° quod this knight, "certain, *mother*
  I nam but deed but if that I can sayn

---

7. Of necessity some word must escape her.
8. Makes a booming noise. "Bittore": bittern, a heron.
9. I.e., sound.

1. Learn. The reeds disclosed the secret by whispering *"aures aselli"* (ass's ears).
2. Drew very quickly.
3. I.e., to meet.

What thing it is that wommen most desire.
Coude ye me wisse,° I wolde wel quite youre hire."[4]   *teach*

1015   "Plight° me thy trouthe here in myn hand," quod she,   *pledge*
"The nexte thing that I requere° thee,   *require of*
Thou shalt it do, if it lie in thy might,
And I wol telle it you er it be night."
    "Have heer my trouthe," quod the knight. "I graunte."

1020   "Thanne," quod she, "I dar me wel avaunte°   *boast*
Thy lif is sauf,° for I wol stande therby.   *safe*
Upon my lif the queene wol saye as I.
Lat see which is the pruddeste° of hem alle   *proudest*
That wereth on[5] a coverchief or a calle°   *headdress*

1025   That dar saye nay of that I shal thee teche.
Lat us go forth withouten lenger speeche."
Tho rouned° she a pistel° in his ere,   *whispered/message*
And bad him to be glad and have no fere.
    Whan they be comen to the court, this knight

1030   Saide he hadde holde his day as he hadde hight,°   *promised*
And redy was his answere, as he saide.
Ful many a noble wif, and many a maide,
And many a widwe—for that they been wise—
The queene hirself sitting as justise,

1035   Assembled been this answere for to heere,
And afterward this knight was bode° appere.   *bidden to*
To every wight comanded was silence,
And that the knight sholde telle in audience°   *open hearing*
What thing that worldly wommen loven best.

1040   This knight ne stood nat stille as dooth a best,°   *beast*
But to his question anoon answerde
With manly vois that al the court it herde.
    "My lige° lady, generally," quod he,   *liege*
"Wommen desire to have sovereinetee°   *dominion*

1045   As wel over hir housbonde as hir love,
And for to been in maistrye him above.
This is youre moste desir though ye me kille.
Dooth as you list:° I am here at youre wille."   *please*
    In al the court ne was ther wif ne maide

1050   Ne widwe that contraried° that he saide,   *contradicted*
But saiden he was worthy han° his lif.   *to have*
    And with that word up sterte° that olde wif,   *started*
Which that the knight sawgh sitting on the greene;
"Mercy," quod she, "my soverein lady queene,

1055   Er that youre court departe, do me right.
I taughte this answere unto the knight,
For which he plighte me his trouthe there
The firste thing I wolde him requere°   *require*
He wolde it do, if it laye in his might.

1060   Bifore the court thanne praye I thee, sire knight,"
Quod she, "that thou me take unto thy wif,
For wel thou woost that I have kept° thy lif.   *saved*

---

4. Repay your trouble.   5. That wears.

If I saye fals, say nay, upon thy fay."
    This knight answerde, "Allas and wailaway,
1065 I woot right wel that swich was my biheeste.°   *promise*
For Goddes love, as chees° a newe requeste: *choose*
Taak al my good and lat my body go."
    "Nay thanne," quod she, "I shrewe° us bothe two.   *curse*
For though that I be foul and old and poore,
1070 I nolde for al the metal ne for ore
That under erthe is grave° or lith° above,   *buried / lies*
But if thy wif I were and eek thy love."
    "My love," quod he. "Nay, my dampnacioun!°   *damnation*
Allas, that any of my nacioun[6]
1075 Sholde evere so foule disparaged° be."   *degraded*
But al for nought, th'ende is this, that he
Constrained was: he needes moste hire wedde,
And taketh his olde wif and gooth to bedde.
    Now wolden some men saye, paraventure,
1080 That for my necligence I do no cure[7]
To tellen you the joye and al th'array
That at the feeste was that ilke day.
To which thing shortly answere I shal:
I saye ther nas no joye ne feeste at al;
1085 Ther nas but hevinesse and muche sorwe.
For prively he wedded hire on morwe,[8]
And al day after hidde him as an owle,
So wo was him, his wif looked so foule.
    Greet was the wo the knight hadde in his thought:
1090 Whan he was with his wif abedde brought,
He walweth° and he turneth to and fro.   *tosses*
His olde wif lay smiling everemo,
And saide, "O dere housbonde, benedicite,°   *bless me*
Fareth° every knight thus with his wif as ye?   *behaves*
1095 Is this the lawe of King Arthures hous?
Is every knight of his thus daungerous?°   *standoffish*
I am youre owene love and youre wif;
I am she which that saved hath youre lif;
And certes yit ne dide I you nevere unright.
1100 Why fare ye thus with me this firste night?
Ye faren like a man hadde lost his wit.
What is my gilt? For Goddes love, telle it,
And it shal been amended if I may."
    "Amended!" quod this knight. "Allas, nay, nay,
1105 It wol nat been amended neveremo.
Thou art so lothly° and so old also,   *hideous*
And therto comen of so lowe a kinde,°   *lineage*
That litel wonder is though I walwe and winde.°   *turn*
So wolde God myn herte wolde breste!"°   *break*
1110 "Is this," quod she, "the cause of youre unreste?"
    "Ye, certainly," quod he. "No wonder is."

---

6. I.e., family.   8. In the morning.
7. I do not take the trouble.

"Now sire," quod she, "I coude amende al this,
If that me liste, er it were dayes three,
So° wel ye mighte bere you[9] unto me.   provided that
1115   "But for ye speken of swich gentilesse°   nobility
As is descended out of old richesse—
That therfore sholden ye be gentilmen—
Swich arrogance is nat worth an hen.
Looke who that is most vertuous alway,
1120   Privee and apert,[1] and most entendeth° ay°   tries / always
To do the gentil deedes that he can,
Taak him for the gretteste° gentilman.   greatest
Crist wol° we claime of him oure gentilesse,   desires that
Nat of oure eldres for hir 'old richesse.'
1125   For though they yive us al hir heritage,
For which we claime to been of heigh parage,°   descent
Yit may they nat biquethe for no thing
To noon of us hir vertuous living,
That made hem gentilmen ycalled be,
1130   And bad[2] us folwen hem in swich degree.
"Wel can the wise poete of Florence,
That highte Dant,[3] speken in this sentence;°   topic
Lo, in swich manere rym is Dantes tale:
'Ful selde° up riseth by his braunches[4] smale   seldom
1135   Prowesse° of man, for God of his prowesse   excellence
Wol that of him we claime oure gentilesse.'
For of oure eldres may we no thing claime
But temporel thing that man may hurte and maime.
Eek every wight woot this as wel as I,
1140   If gentilesse were planted natureelly
Unto a certain linage down the line,
Privee and apert, thanne wolde they nevere fine°   cease
To doon of gentilesse the faire office°—   function
They mighte do no vilainye or vice.
1145   "Taak fir and beer° it in the derkeste hous   bear
Bitwixe this and the Mount of Caucasus,
And lat men shette° the dores and go thenne,°   shut / thence
Yit wol the fir as faire lye° and brenne°   blaze / burn
As twenty thousand men mighte it biholde:
1150   His° office natureel ay wol it holde,   its
Up° peril of my lif, til that it die.   upon
Heer may ye see wel how that genterye°   gentility
Is nat annexed° to possessioun,[5]   related
Sith folk ne doon hir operacioun
1155   Alway, as dooth the fir, lo, in his kinde.°   nature
For God it woot, men may wel often finde
A lordes sone do shame and vilainye;
And he that wol han pris of his gentrye,[6]
For he was boren° of a gentil° hous,   born / noble

9. Behave.   4. I.e., by the branches of a man's family tree.
1. Privately and publicly.   5. I.e., inheritable property.
2. I.e., they bade.   6. Have credit for his noble birth.
3. Dante (see his *Convivio*).

1160 And hadde his eldres noble and vertuous,
And nil himselven do no gentil deedes,
Ne folwen his gentil auncestre that deed° is,   *dead*
He nis nat gentil, be he duc or erl—
For vilaines sinful deedes maken a cherl.
1165 Thy gentilesse[7] nis but renomee°   *renown*
Of thine auncestres for hir heigh bountee,°   *magnanimity*
Which is a straunge° thing for thy persone.   *external*
For gentilesse[8] cometh fro God allone.
Thanne comth oure verray gentilesse of grace:
1170 It was no thing biquethe us with oure place.
Thenketh how noble, as saith Valerius,[9]
Was thilke Tullius Hostilius
That out of poverte° roos to heigh noblesse.   *poverty*
Redeth Senek° and redeth eek Boece:°   *Seneca/Boethius*
1175 Ther shul ye seen expres that no drede° is   *doubt*
That he is gentil that dooth gentil deedes.
And therfore, leve housbonde, I thus conclude:
Al° were it that mine auncestres weren rude,[1]   *although*
Yit may the hye God—and so hope I—
1180 Graunte me grace to liven vertuously.
Thanne am I gentil whan that I biginne
To liven vertuously and waive° sinne.   *avoid*
    "And ther as ye of poverte me repreve,°   *reprove*
The hye God, on whom that we bileve,
1185 In wilful° poverte chees° to live his lif;   *voluntary/chose*
And certes every man, maiden, or wif
May understonde that Jesus, hevene king,
Ne wolde nat chese° a vicious living.   *choose*
Glad poverte is an honeste° thing, certain;   *honorable*
1190 This wol Senek and othere clerkes sayn.
Whoso that halt him paid of[2] his poverte,
I holde him riche al hadde he nat a sherte.°   *shirt*
He that coveiteth[3] is a poore wight,
For he wolde han that is nat in his might;
1195 But he that nought hath, ne coveiteth° have,   *desires to*
Is riche, although we holde him but a knave.
Verray° poverte it singeth proprely.°   *true/appropriately*
Juvenal saith of poverte, 'Merily
The poore man, whan he gooth by the waye,
1200 Biforn the theves he may singe and playe.'
Poverte is hateful good, and as I gesse,
A ful greet bringere out of bisinesse;[4]
A greet amendere eek of sapience°   *wisdom*
To him that taketh it in pacience;
1205 Poverte is thing, although it seeme elenge,°   *wretched*
Possession that no wight wol chalenge;[5]

7. I.e., the gentility you claim.
8. I.e., true gentility.
9. A Roman historian.
1. I.e., low born.

2. Considers himself satisfied with.
3. I.e., suffers desires.
4. I.e., remover of cares.
5. Claim as his property.

Poverte ful often, whan a man is lowe,
Maketh[6] his God and eek himself to knowe;
Poverte a spectacle° is, as thinketh me, *pair of spectacles*
1210 Thurgh which he may his verray° freendes see. *true*
And therfore, sire, sin that I nought you greve,
Of my poverte namore ye me repreve.° *reproach*
 "Now sire, of elde° ye repreve me: *old age*
And certes sire, though noon auctoritee
1215 Were in no book, ye gentils of honour
Sayn that men sholde an old wight doon favour,
And clepe him fader for youre gentilesse—
And auctours[7] shal I finde, as I gesse.
 "Now ther ye saye that I am foul and old:
1220 Thanne drede you nought to been a cokewold,° *cuckold*
For filthe and elde, also mote I thee,[8]
Been grete wardeins° upon chastitee. *guardians*
But nathelees, sin I knowe your delit,
I shal fulfille youre worldly appetit.
1225 "Chees° now," quod she, "oon of thise thinges twaye: *choose*
To han me foul and old til that I deye
And be to you a trewe humble wif,
And nevere you displese in al my lif,
Or elles ye wol han me yong and fair,
1230 And take youre aventure° of the repair[9] *chance*
That shal be to youre hous by cause of me—
Or in some other place, wel may be.
Now chees youreselven wheither° that you liketh." *whichever*
 This knight aviseth him[1] and sore siketh;° *sighs*
1235 But atte laste he saide in this manere:
"My lady and my love, and wif so dere,
I putte me in youre wise governaunce:
Cheseth° youreself which may be most plesaunce° *choose/pleasure*
And most honour to you and me also.
1240 I do no fors the wheither[2] of the two,
For as you liketh it suffiseth° me." *satisfies*
 "Thanne have I gete° of you maistrye," quod she, *got*
"Sin I may chese and governe as me lest?"° *it pleases*
 "Ye, certes, wif," quod he. "I holde it best."
1245 "Kisse me," quod she. "We be no lenger wrothe.
For by my trouthe, I wol be to you bothe—
This is to sayn, ye, bothe fair and good.
I praye to God that I mote sterven wood,[3]
But° I to you be al so good and trewe *unless*
1250 As evere was wif sin that the world was newe.
And but I be tomorn° as fair to seene *tomorrow morning*
As any lady, emperisse, or queene,
That is bitwixe the eest and eek the west,

6. I.e., makes him.   1. Considers.
7. I.e., authorities.   2. I do not care whichever.
8. So may I prosper.   3. Die mad.
9. I.e., visits.

Do with my lif and deeth right as you lest:
1255   Caste up the curtin,[4] looke how that it is."
    And whan the knight sawgh verraily al this,
That she so fair was and so yong therto,
For joye he hente° hire in his armes two;   *took*
His herte bathed in a bath of blisse;
1260   A thousand time arewe° he gan hire kisse,   *in a row*
And she obeyed him in every thing
That mighte do him plesance or liking.°   *pleasure*
And thus they live unto hir lives ende
In parfit° joye. And Jesu Crist us sende   *perfect*
1265   Housbondes meeke, yonge, and fresshe abedde—
And grace t'overbide° hem that we wedde.   *outlive*
And eek I praye Jesu shorte° hir lives   *shorten*
That nought wol be governed by hir wives,
And olde and angry nigardes of dispence°—   *spending*
1270   God sende hem soone a verray° pestilence!   *veritable*

The Pardoner's Prologue and Tale

As with *The Wife of Bath's Prologue* and *Tale, The Pardoner's Prologue* and *Tale* develop in profound and surprising ways the portrait sketched in *The General Prologue*. In his *Prologue* the Pardoner boasts to his fellow pilgrims about his own depravity and the ingenuity with which he abuses his office and extracts money from poor and ignorant people.

The medieval pardoner's job was to collect money for the charitable enterprises, such as hospitals, supported by the church. In return for donations he was licensed by the pope to award token remission of sins that the donor should have repented and confessed. By canon law pardoners were permitted to work only in a prescribed area; within that area they might visit churches during Sunday service, briefly explain their mission, receive contributions, and in the pope's name issue indulgence, which was not considered to be a sale but a gift from the infinite treasury of Christ's mercy made in return for a gift of money. In practice, pardoners ignored the restrictions on their office, made their way into churches at will, preached emotional sermons, and claimed extraordinary power for their pardons.

The Pardoner's Tale is a bombastic sermon against gluttony, gambling, and swearing, which he preaches to the pilgrims to show off his professional skills. The sermon is framed by a narrative that is supposed to function as an *exemplum* (that is, an illustration) of the scriptural text, the one on which the Pardoner, as he tells the pilgrims, always preaches: "*Radix malorum est cupiditas*" (Avarice is the root of evil).

The Introduction

    Oure Hoste gan to swere as he were wood°   *insane*
"Harrow,"° quod he, "by nailes and by blood,[1]   *help*
This was a fals cherl and a fals justise.[2]

---

4. The curtain around the bed.
1. I.e., God's nails and blood.
2. The Host has been affected by the Physicians's sad tale of the Roman maiden Virginia, whose great beauty caused a judge to attempt to obtain

her person by means of a trumped-up lawsuit in which he connived with a "churl" who claimed her as his slave; in order to preserve her chastity, her father killed her.

As shameful deeth as herte may devise
5   Come to thise juges and hir advocats.
Algate° this sely° maide is slain, allas!   *at any rate/innocent*
Allas, too dere boughte she beautee!
Wherfore I saye alday° that men may see   *always*
The yiftes of Fortune and of Nature
10   Been cause of deeth to many a creature.
As bothe yiftes that I speke of now,
Men han ful ofte more for harm than prow.°   *benefit*
   "But trewely, myn owene maister dere,
This is a pitous tale for to heere.
15   But nathelees, passe over, is no fors:³
I praye to God to save thy gentil cors,°   *body*
And eek thine urinals and thy jurdones,⁴
Thyn ipocras and eek thy galiones,⁵
And every boiste° ful of thy letuarye°—   *box/medicine*
20   God blesse hem, and oure lady Sainte Marye.
So mote I theen,⁶ thou art a propre man,
And lik a prelat, by Saint Ronian!⁷
Saide I nat wel? I can nat speke in terme.⁸
But wel I woot, thou doost° myn herte to erme°   *make/grieve*
25   That I almost have caught a cardinacle.⁹
By corpus bones,¹ but if° I have triacle,°   *unless/medicine*
Or elles a draughte of moiste° and corny° ale,   *fresh/malty*
Or but I here anoon° a merye tale,   *at once*
Myn herte is lost for pitee of this maide.
30   "Thou bel ami,² thou Pardoner," he saide,
"Tel us som mirthe or japes° right anoon."   *jokes*
"It shal be doon," quod he, "by Saint Ronion.
But first," quod he, "here at this ale-stake³
I wol bothe drinke and eten of a cake."°   *flat loaf of bread*
35   And right anoon thise gentils gan to crye,
"Nay, lat him telle us of no ribaudye.°   *ribaldry*
Tel us som moral thing that we may lere,°   *learn*
Som wit,⁴ and thanne wol we gladly heere."
   "I graunte, ywis,"° quod he, "but I moot thinke   *certainly*
40   Upon som honeste° thing whil that I drinke."   *decent*

The Prologue

Lordinges—quod he—in chirches whan I preche,
I paine me⁵ to han° an hautein° speeche,   *have/loud*
And ringe it out as round as gooth a belle,
For I can al by rote⁶ that I telle.

---

3. I.e., never mind.
4. Jordans (chamber pots): the Host is somewhat confused in his endeavor to use technical medical terms. "Urinals": vessels for examining urine.
5. A medicine, probably invented on the spot by the Host, named after Galen. "Ipocras": a medicinal drink named after Hippocrates.
6. So might I prosper.
7. St. Ronan or St. Ninian, with a possible play on "runnion" (sexual organ).

8. Speak in technical idiom.
9. Apparently a cardiac condition, confused in the Host's mind with a cardinal.
1. An illiterate oath, mixing "God's bones" with *corpus dei* ("God's body").
2. Fair friend.
3. Sign of a tavern.
4. I.e., something with significance.
5. Take pains.
6. I know all by heart.

45 My theme is alway oon,[7] and evere was:
    Radix malorum est cupiditas.[8]
    First I pronounce whennes° that I come,   *whence*
    And thanne my bulles shewe I alle and some:[9]
    Oure lige lordes seel on my patente,[1]
50 That shewe I first, my body to warente,°   *keep safe*
    That no man be so bold, ne preest ne clerk,
    Me to destourbe of Cristes holy werk.
    And after that thanne telle I forth my tales[2]—
    Bulles of popes and of cardinales,
55 Of patriarkes and bisshopes I shewe,
    And in Latin I speke a wordes fewe,
    To saffron with[3] my predicacioun,°   *preaching*
    And for to stire hem to devocioun.
        Thanne shewe I forth my longe crystal stones,°   *jars*
60 Ycrammed ful of cloutes° and of bones   *rags*
    Relikes been they, as weenen° they eechoon.   *suppose*
    Thanne have I in laton° a shulder-boon   *brass*
    Which that was of an holy Jewes sheep.
    "Goode men," I saye, "take of my wordes keep:°   *notice*
65 If that this boon be wasshe in any welle,
    If cow, or calf, or sheep, or oxe swelle,
    That any worm hath ete or worm ystonge,[4]
    Take water of that welle and wassh his tonge,
    And it is hool[5] anoon. And ferthermoor,
70 Of pokkes° and of scabbe and every soor°   *pox, pustules / sore*
    Shal every sheep be hool that of this welle
    Drinketh a draughte. Take keep eek° that I telle: *also*
    If that the goode man that the beestes oweth°   *owns*
    Wol every wike,° er° that the cok him croweth,   *week / before*
75 Fasting drinken of this welle a draughte—
    As thilke° holy Jew oure eldres taughte—   *that same*
    His beestes and his stoor° shal multiplye.   *stock*
        "And sire, also it heleth jalousye:
    For though a man be falle in jalous rage,
80 Lat maken with this water his potage,°   *soup*
    And nevere shal he more his wif mistriste,°   *mistrust*
    Though he the soothe of hir defaute wiste,[6]
    Al hadde she[7] taken preestes two or three.
        "Here is a mitein° eek that ye may see: *mitten*
85 He that his hand wol putte in this mitein
    He shal have multiplying of his grain,
    Whan he hath sowen, be it whete or otes—
    So that he offre pens or elles grotes.[8]
        "Goode men and wommen, oo thing warne I you:

---

7. I.e., the same. "Theme": biblical text on which
the sermon is based.
8. Avarice is the root of evil (1 Timothy 6.10).
9. Each and every one. "Bulles": papal bulls, official documents.
1. I.e., the pope's or bishop's seal on my papal
license.
2. I go on with my yarn.

3. To add spice to.
4. That has eaten any worm or been bitten by any
snake.
5. I.e., sound.
6. Knew the truth of her infidelity.
7. Even if she had.
8. Pennies, groats, coins.

90   If any wight be in this chirche now
      That hath doon sinne horrible, that he
      Dar nat for shame of it yshriven° be,   *confessed*
      Or any womman, be she yong or old,
      That hath ymaked hir housbonde cokewold,°   *cuckold*
95   Swich° folk shal have no power ne no grace   *such*
      To offren to⁹ my relikes in this place;
      And whoso findeth him out of swich blame,
      He wol come up and offre in Goddes name,
      And I assoile° him by the auctoritee   *absolve*
100   Which that by bulle ygraunted was to me."
          By this gaude° have I wonne, yeer by yeer,   *trick*
      An hundred mark¹ sith° I was pardoner.   *since*
      I stonde lik a clerk in my pulpet,
      And whan the lewed° peple is down yset,   *ignorant*
105   I preche so as ye han herd bifore,
      And telle an hundred false japes° more.   *tricks*
      Thanne paine I me² to strecche forth the nekke,
      And eest and west upon the peple I bekke°   *nod*
      As dooth a douve,° sitting on a berne;°   *dove / barn*
110   Mine handes and my tonge goon so yerne°   *fast*
      That it is joye to see my bisinesse.
      Of avarice and of swich cursednesse°   *sin*
      Is al my preching, for to make hem free°   *generous*
      To yiven hir pens, and namely° unto me,   *especially*
115   For myn entente is nat but for to winne,³
      And no thing for correccion of sinne:
      I rekke° nevere whan that they been beried°   *care / buried*
      Though that hir soules goon a-blakeberied.⁴
      For certes, many a predicacioun°   *sermon*
120   Comth ofte time of yvel entencioun:
      Som for plesance of folk and flaterye,
      To been avaunced° by ypocrisye,   *promoted*
      And som for vaine glorye, and som for hate;
      For whan I dar noon otherways debate,°   *fight*
125   Thanne wol I stinge him⁵ with my tonge smerte°   *sharply*
      In preching, so that he shal nat asterte°   *escape*
      To been defamed falsly, if that he
      Hath trespassed to my bretheren⁶ or to me.
      For though I telle nought his propre name,
130   Men shal wel knowe that it is the same
      By signes and by othere circumstaunces.
      Thus quite° I folk that doon us displesaunces;⁷ *pay back*
      Thus spete° I out my venim under hewe° *spit / false colors*
      Of holinesse, to seeme holy and trewe.
135   But shortly myn entente I wol devise:°   *explain*
      I preche of no thing but for coveitise;°   *covetousness*
      Therfore my theme is yit and evere was

---

9. To make gifts in reverence of.
1. Marks (pecuniary units).
2. I take pains.
3. My intent is only to make money.

4. Go blackberrying, i.e., go to hell.
5. An adversary critical of pardoners.
6. Injured my fellow pardoners.
7. Make trouble for us.

Radix malorum est cupiditas.

Thus can I preche again that same vice
140 Which that I use, and that is avarice.
But though myself be gilty in that sinne,
Yit can I make other folk to twinne°   separate
From avarice, and sore to repente—
But that is nat my principal entente:
145 I preche no thing but for coveitise.
Of this matere it oughte ynough suffise.
Thanne telle I hem ensamples[8] many oon
Of olde stories longe time agoon,
For lewed° peple loven tales olde—   ignorant
150 Swiche° thinges can they wel reporte and holde.[9]   such
What, trowe° ye that whiles I may preche,   believe
And winne gold and silver for° I teche,   because
That I wol live in poverte wilfully?°   voluntarily
Nay, nay, I thoughte° it nevere, trewely,   intended
155 For I wol preche and begge in sondry landes;
I wol nat do no labour with mine handes,
Ne make baskettes and live therby,
By cause I wol nat beggen idelly.[1]
I wol none of the Apostles countrefete:°   imitate
160 I wol have moneye, wolle,° cheese, and whete,   wool
Al were it[2] yiven of the pooreste page,
Or of the pooreste widwe in a village—
Al sholde hir children sterve[3] for famine.
Nay, I wol drinke licour of the vine
165 And have a joly wenche in every town.
But herkneth, lordinges, in conclusioun,
Youre liking° is that I shal telle a tale: pleasure
Now have I dronke a draughte of corny ale,
By God, I hope I shal you telle a thing
170 That shal by reson been at youre liking;
For though myself be a ful vicious man,
A moral tale yit I you telle can,
Which I am wont to preche for to winne.
Now holde youre pees, my tale I wol biginne.

The Tale

175 In Flandres whilom° was a compaignye   once
Of yonge folk that haunteden° folye—   practiced
As riot, hasard, stewes,[4] and tavernes,
Wher as with harpes, lutes, and giternes°   guitars
They daunce and playen at dees° bothe day and night,   dice
180 And ete also and drinke over hir might,[5]
Thurgh which they doon the devel sacrifise

8. Exempla (stories illustrating moral principles).
9. Repeat and remember.
1. I.e., without profit.
2. Even though it were.

3. Even though her children should die.
4. Wild parties, gambling, brothels.
5. Beyond their capacity.

Within that develes temple in cursed wise
By superfluitee° abhominable.   *overindulgence*
Hir othes been so grete and so dampnable
185 That it is grisly for to heere hem swere:
Oure blessed Lordes body they totere[6]—
Hem thoughte that Jewes rente° him nought ynough.   *tore*
And eech of hem at otheres sinne lough.°   *laughed*
And right anoon thanne comen tombesteres,°   *dancing girls*
190 Fetis° and smale,° and yonge frutesteres,[7] *shapely/slender*
Singeres with harpes, bawdes,° wafercres[8]—   *pimps*
Whiche been the verray develes officeres,
To kindle and blowe the fir of lecherye
That is annexed unto glotonye:[9]
195 The Holy Writ take I to my witnesse
That luxure° is in win and dronkenesse.   *lechery*
Lo, how that dronken Lot[1] unkindely°   *unnaturally*
Lay by his doughtres two unwitingly:
So dronke he was he niste° what he wroughte.° *didn't know/did*
200 Herodes, who so wel the stories soughte,[2]
Whan he of win was repleet° at his feeste,   *filled*
Right at his owene table he yaf his heeste°   *command*
To sleen° the Baptist John, ful giltelees.   *slay*
Senek[3] saith a good word doutelees:
205 He saith he can no difference finde
Bitwixe a man that is out of his minde
And a man which that is dronkelewe,°   *drunken*
But that woodnesse, yfallen in a shrewe,[4]
Persevereth lenger than dooth dronkenesse.
210 O glotonye, ful of cursednesse!°   *wickedness*
O cause first of oure confusioun!°   *downfall*
O original of oure dampnacioun,°   *damnation*
Til Crist hadde bought° us with his blood again! *redeemed*
Lo, how dere, shortly for to sayn,
215 Abought° was thilke° cursed vilainye;   *paid for/that same*
Corrupt was al this world for glotonye:
Adam oure fader and his wif also
Fro Paradis to labour and to wo
Were driven for that vice, it is no drede.°   *doubt*
220 For whil that Adam fasted, as I rede,
He was in Paradis; and whan that he
Eet° of the fruit defended° on a tree,   *ate/forbidden*
Anoon he was out cast to wo and paine.
O glotonye, on thee wel oughte us plaine!°   *complain*
225 O, wiste a man[5] how manye maladies
Folwen of excesse and of glotonies,

6. Tear apart (a reference to oaths sworn by parts of His body, such as "God's bones!" or "God's teeth!").
7. Fruit-selling girls.
8. Girl cake vendors.
9. I.e., closely related to gluttony.
1. See Genesis 19.30–36.

2. For the story of Herod and St. John the Baptist, see Mark 6.17–29. "Who so . . . soughte": i.e., whoever looked it up in the Gospel would find.
3. Seneca, the Roman Stoic philosopher.
4. But that madness, occurring in a wicked man.
5. If a man knew.

He wolde been the more mesurable°   *moderate*
Of his diete, sitting at his table.
Allas, the shorte throte, the tendre mouth,
230   Maketh that eest and west and north and south,
In erthe, in air, in water, men to swinke,°   *work*
To gete a gloton daintee mete° and drinke.   *food*
Of this matere, O Paul, wel canstou trete:
"Mete unto wombe,° and wombe eek unto mete,   *belly*
235   Shal God destroyen bothe," as Paulus saith.[6]
Allas, a foul thing is it, by my faith,
To saye this word, and fouler is the deede
Whan man so drinketh of the white and rede[7]
That of his throte he maketh his privee°   *toilet*
240   Thurgh thilke cursed superfluitee.°   *overindulgence*
    The Apostle[8] weeping saith ful pitously,
"Ther walken manye of which you told have I—
I saye it now weeping with pitous vois—
They been enemies of Cristes crois,°   *cross*
245   Of whiche the ende is deeth—wombe is hir god!"[9]
O wombe, O bely, O stinking cod,°   *bag*
Fulfilled° of dong° and of corrupcioun!   *filled full / dung*
At either ende of thee foul is the soun.°   *sound*
How greet labour and cost is thee to finde!°   *provide for*
250   Thise cookes, how they stampe° and straine and grinde, *pound*
And turnen substance into accident[1]
To fulfillen al thy likerous° talent!°   *greedy / appetite*
Out of the harde bones knokke they
The mary,° for they caste nought away   *marrow*
255   That may go thurgh the golet[2] softe and soote.°   *sweetly*
Of spicerye° of leef and bark and roote   *spices*
Shal been his sauce ymaked by delit,
To make him yit a newer appetit.
But certes, he that haunteth swiche delices°   *pleasures*
260   Is deed° whil that he liveth in tho° vices.   *dead / those*
    A lecherous thing is win, and dronkenesse
Is ful of striving° and of wrecchednesse.   *quarreling*
O dronke man, disfigured is thy face!
Sour is thy breeth, foul artou to embrace!
265   And thurgh thy dronke nose seemeth the soun
As though thou saidest ay,° "Sampsoun, Sampsoun." *always*
And yit, God woot,° Sampson drank nevere win.[3] *knows*
Thou fallest as it were a stiked swin;°   *stuck pig*
Thy tonge is lost, and al thyn honeste cure,[4]
270   For dronkenesse is verray sepulture°   *burial*
Of mannes wit° and his discrecioun.   *intelligence*
In whom that drinke hath dominacioun

---

6. See 1 Corinthians 6.13.
7. I.e., white and red wines.
8. I.e., St. Paul.
9. See Philippians 3.18.
1. A philosophic joke, depending on the distinction between inner reality (substance) and outward appearance (accident).
2. Through the gullet.
3. Before Samson's birth an angel told his mother that he would be a Nazarite throughout his life; members of this sect took no strong drink.
4. Care for self-respect.

	He can no conseil° keepe, it is no drede.°	*secrets / doubt*
	Now keepe you fro the white and fro the rede—	
275	And namely° fro the white win of Lepe⁵	*particularly*
	That is to selle in Fisshstreete or in Chepe:⁶	
	The win of Spaine creepeth subtilly	
	In othere wines growing faste° by,	*close*
	Of which ther riseth swich fumositee°	*heady fumes*
280	That whan a man hath dronken draughtes three	
	And weeneth° that he be at hoom in Chepe,	*supposes*
	He is in Spaine, right at the town of Lepe,	
	Nat at The Rochele ne at Burdeux town;⁷	
	And thanne wol he sayn, "Sampsoun, Sampsoun."	
285	But herkneth, lordinges, oo° word I you praye,	*one*
	That alle the soverein actes,⁸ dar I saye,	
	Of victories in the Olde Testament,	
	Thurgh verray God that is omnipotent,	
	Were doon in abstinence and in prayere:	
290	Looketh° the Bible and ther ye may it lere.°	*behold / learn*
	Looke Attila, the grete conquerour,⁹	
	Deide° in his sleep with shame and dishonour,	*died*
	Bleeding at his nose in dronkenesse:	
	A capitain sholde live in sobrenesse.	
295	And overal this, aviseth you¹ right wel	
	What was comanded unto Lamuel²—	
	Nat Samuel, but Lamuel, saye I—	
	Redeth the Bible and finde it expresly,	
	Of win-yiving° to hem that han³ justise:	*wine-serving*
300	Namore of this, for it may wel suffise.	
	And now that I have spoken of glotonye,	
	Now wol I you defende° hasardrye:°	*prohibit / gambling*
	Hasard is verray moder° of lesinges,°	*mother / lies*
	And of deceite and cursed forsweringes,°	*perjuries*
305	Blaspheme of Crist, manslaughtre, and wast° also	*waste*
	Of catel° and of time; and ferthermo,	*property*
	It is repreve° and contrarye of honour	*disgrace*
	For to been holden a commune hasardour,°	*gambler*
	And evere the hyer he is of estat	
310	The more is he holden desolat.⁴	
	If that a prince useth hasardrye,	
	In alle governance and policye	
	He is, as by commune opinioun,	
	Yholde the lasse° in reputacioun.	*less*
315	Stilbon, that was a wis embassadour,	
	Was sent to Corinthe in ful greet honour	
	Fro Lacedomye° to make hir alliaunce,	*Sparta*

5. A town in Spain.
6. Fishstreet and Cheapside in the London market district.
7. The Pardoner is joking about the illegal custom of adulterating fine wines of Bordeaux and La Rochelle with strong Spanish wine.
8. Distinguished deeds.
9. Attila was the leader of the Huns who almost captured Rome in the 5th century.
1. Consider.
2. Lemuel's mother told him that kings should not drink (Proverbs 31.4–5).
3. I.e., administer.
4. I.e. dissolute.

And whan he cam him happede° parchaunce   *it happened*
That alle the gretteste° that were of that lond   *greatest*
320 Playing at the hasard he hem foond,°   *found*
For which as soone as it mighte be
He stal him[5] hoom again to his contree,
And saide, "Ther wol I nat lese° my name,   *lose*
N'I wol nat take on me so greet defame°   *dishonor*
325 You to allye unto none hasardours:
Sendeth othere wise embassadours,
For by my trouthe, me were levere[6] die
Than I you sholde to hasardours allye.
For ye that been so glorious in honours
330 Shal nat allye you with hasardours
As by my wil, ne as by my tretee."°   *treaty*
This wise philosophre, thus saide he.
    Looke eek that to the king Demetrius
The King of Parthes,° as the book[7] saith us,   *Parthians*
335 Sente him a paire of dees° of gold in scorn,   *dice*
For he hadde used hasard therbiforn,
For which he heeld his glorye or his renown
At no value or reputacioun.
Lordes may finden other manere play
340 Honeste° ynough to drive the day away.   *honorable*
    Now wol I speke of othes false and grete
A word or two, as olde bookes trete:
    Greet swering is a thing abhominable,
And fals swering is yit more reprevable.°   *reprehensible*
345 The hye God forbad swering at al—
Witnesse on Mathew.[8] But in special
Of swering saith the holy Jeremie,[9]
"Thou shalt swere sooth thine othes and nat lie,
And swere in doom° and eek in rightwisnesse,°   *equity/righteousness*
350 But idel swering is a cursednesse."°   *wickedness*
    Biholde and see that in the firste Table[1]
Of hye Goddes heestes° honorable   *commandments*
How that the seconde heeste of him is this:
"Take nat my name in idel or amis."
355 Lo, rather° he forbedeth swich swering   *sooner*
Than homicide, or many a cursed thing.
I saye that as by ordre thus it stondeth—
This knoweth that[2] his heestes understondeth
How that the seconde heeste of God is that.
360 And fertherover,° I wol thee telle al plat°   *moreover/plain*
That vengeance shal nat parten° from his hous   *depart*
That of his othes is too outrageous.
"By Goddes precious herte!" and "By his nailes!"°   *fingernails*
And "By the blood of Crist that is in Hailes,[3]

---

5. He stole away.
6. I had rather.
7. The book that relates this and the previous incident is the *Policraticus* of the 12th-century Latin writer John of Salisbury.
8. "But I say unto you, Swear not at all" (Matthew

5.34).
9. Jeremiah 4.2.
1. I.e., the first three of the Ten Commandments.
2. I.e., he that.
3. An abbey in Gloucestershire supposed to possess some of Christ's blood.

365 Sevene is my chaunce,° and thyn is cink and traye!"[4]   *winning number*
"By Goddes armes, if thou falsly playe
This daggere shal thurghout thyn herte go!"
This fruit cometh of the bicche bones[5] two—
Forswering, ire, falsnesse, homicide.
370 Now for the love of Crist that for us dyde,°   *died*
Lete° youre othes bothe grete and smale.   *leave*
But sires, now wol I telle forth my tale.
    Thise riotoures° three of whiche I telle,   *revelers*
Longe erst er prime[6] ronge of any belle,
375 Were set hem in a taverne to drinke,
And as they sat they herde a belle clinke
Biforn a cors° was caried to his grave.   *corpse*
That oon of hem gan callen to his knave:°   *servant*
Go bet,"[7] quod he, "and axe° redily°   *ask/promptly*
380 What cors is this that passeth heer forby,
And looke° that thou reporte his name weel."°   *be sure/well*
    "Sire," quod this boy, "it needeth neveradeel:[8]
It was me told er ye cam heer two houres.
He was, pardee,° an old felawe of youres,   *by God*
385 And sodeinly he was yslain tonight,°   *last night*
Fordronke° as he sat on his bench upright;   *very drunk*
Ther cam a privee° thief men clepeth° Deeth,   *stealthy/call*
That in this contree al the peple sleeth,°   *slays*
And with his spere he smoot his herte atwo,
390 And wente his way withouten wordes mo.
He hath a thousand slain this° pestilence.   *during this*
And maister, er ye come in his presence,
Me thinketh that it were necessarye
For to be war of swich an adversarye;
395 Beeth redy for to meete him everemore:
Thus taughte me my dame.° I saye namore."   *mother*
    "By Sainte Marye," saide this taverner,
"The child saith sooth, for he hath slain this yeer,
Henne° over a mile, within a greet village,   *hence*
400 Bothe man and womman, child and hine[9] and page.
I trowe° his habitacion be there.   *believe*
To been avised° greet wisdom it were   *wary*
Er that he dide a man a dishonour."
    "Ye, Goddes armes," quod this riotour,
405 "Is it swich peril with him for to meete?
I shal him seeke by way and eek by streete,[1]
I make avow to Goddes digne° bones.   *worthy*
Herkneth, felawes, we three been alle ones:°   *of one mind*
Lat eech of us holde up his hand to other
410 And eech of us bicome otheres brother,
And we wol sleen this false traitour Deeth.
He shal be slain, he that so manye sleeth,

---

4. Five and three.
5. I.e., damned dice.
6. Long before 9 A.M.
7. Better, i.e., quick.

8. It isn't a bit necessary.
9. Farm laborer.
1. By highway and byway.

By Goddes dignitee, er it be night."
Togidres han thise three hir trouthes plight[2]
415 To live and dien eech of hem with other,
As though he were his owene ybore° brother.   *born*
And up they sterte,° al dronken in this rage,   *started*
And forth they goon towardes that village
Of which the taverner hadde spoke biforn,
420 And many a grisly ooth thanne han they sworn,
And Cristes blessed body they torente:°   *tore apart*
Deeth shal be deed° if that they may him hente.°   *dead/catch*
  Whan they han goon nat fully half a mile,
Right as they wolde han treden° over a stile,   *stepped*
425 An old man and a poore with hem mette;
This olde man ful mekely hem grette,°   *greeted*
And saide thus, "Now lordes, God you see."[3]
  The pruddeste° of thise riotoures three   *proudest*
Answerde again, "What, carl° with sory grace,   *fellow*
430 Why artou al forwrapped° save thy face?   *muffled up*
Why livestou so longe in so greet age?"
  This olde man gan looke in his visage,
And saide thus, "For° I ne can nat finde   *because*
A man, though that I walked into Inde,°   *India*
435 Neither in citee ne in no village,
That wolde chaunge his youthe for myn age;
And therefore moot° I han myn age stille,   *must*
As longe time as it is Goddes wille.
  "Ne Deeth, allas, ne wol nat have my lif.
440 Thus walke I lik a restelees caitif,°   *wretch*
And on the ground which is my modres° gate   *mother's*
I knokke with my staf bothe erly and late,
And saye, 'Leve° moder, leet me in: *dear*
Lo, how I vanisshe, flessh and blood and skin.
445 Allas, whan shal my bones been at reste?
Moder, with you wolde I chaunge° my cheste[4]   *exchange*
That in my chambre longe time hath be,
Ye, for an haire-clout[5] to wrappe me.'
But yit to me she wol nat do that grace,
450 For which ful pale and welked° is my face.   *withered*
But sires, to you it is no curteisye
To speken to an old man vilainye,°   *rudeness*
But° he trespasse° in word or elles in deede.   *unless/offend*
In Holy Writ ye may yourself wel rede,
455 'Agains[6] an old man, hoor° upon his heed,   *hoar*
Ye shall arise.'[7] Wherfore I yive you reed,°   *advice*
Ne dooth unto an old man noon harm now,
Namore than that ye wolde men dide to you
In age, if that ye so longe abide.[8]
460 And God be with you wher ye go° or ride: *walk*

2. Pledged their words of honor.
3. May God protect you.
4. Chest for one's belongings, used here as the symbol for life—or perhaps a coffin.
5. Haircloth, for a winding sheet.
6. In the presence of.
7. Cf. Leviticus 19.32.
8. I.e., if you live so long.

I moot go thider as I have to go."
   "Nay, olde cherl, by God thou shalt nat so,"
Saide this other hasardour anoon.
"Thou partest nat so lightly,° by Saint John!   *easily*
465 Thou speke° right now of thilke traitour Deeth,   *spoke*
That in this contree alle oure freendes sleeth:
Have here my trouthe, as thou art his espye,°   *spy*
Tel wher he is, or thou shalt it abye,°   *pay for*
By God and by the holy sacrament!
470 For soothly thou art oon of his assent[9]
To sleen us yonge folk, thou false thief."
   "Now sires," quod he, "if that ye be so lief°   *anxious*
To finde Deeth, turne up this crooked way,
For in that grove I lafte° him, by my fay,°   *left/faith*
475 Under a tree, and ther he wol abide:
Nat for youre boost° he wol him no thing hide.   *boast*
See ye that ook?° Right ther ye shal him finde.   *oak*
God save you, that boughte again[1] mankinde,
And you amende." Thus saide this olde man.
480   And everich of thise riotoures ran
Til he cam to that tree, and ther they founde
Of florins° fine of gold ycoined rounde   *coins*
Wel neigh an eighte busshels as hem thoughte—
Ne lenger thanne after Deeth they soughte,
485 But eech of hem so glad was of the sighte,
For that the florins been so faire and brighte,
That down they sette hem by this precious hoord.
The worste of hem he spak the firste word:
   "Bretheren," quod he, "take keep° what that I saye: *heed*
490 My wit is greet though that I bourde° and playe.   *joke*
This tresor hath Fortune unto us yiven
In mirthe and jolitee oure lif to liven,
And lightly° as it cometh so wol we spende.   *easily*
Ey, Goddes precious dignitee, who wende[2]
495 Today that we sholde han so fair a grace?
But mighte this gold be caried fro this place
Hoom to myn hous—or elles unto youres—
For wel ye woot that al this gold is oures—
Thanne were we in heigh felicitee.
500 But trewely, by daye it mighte nat be:
Men wolde sayn that we were theves stronge,°   *flagrant*
And for oure owene tresor doon us honge.[3]
This tresor moste ycaried be by nighte,
As wisely and as slyly as it mighte.
505 Therefore I rede° that cut° amonges us alle   *advise/straws*
Be drawe, and lat see wher the cut wol falle;
And he that hath the cut with herte blithe
Shal renne° to the town, and that ful swithe,°   *run/quickly*
And bringe us breed and win ful prively;

9. I.e., one of his party.   2. Who would have supposed.
1. Redeemed.   3. Have us hanged.

510 And two of us shal keepen° subtilly   *guard*
    This tresor wel, and if he wol nat tarye,
    Whan it is night we wol this tresor carye
    By oon assent wher as us thinketh best."
    That oon of hem the cut broughte in his fest°   *fist*
515 And bad hem drawe and looke wher it wol falle;
    And it fil° on the yongeste of hem alle,   *fell*
    And forth toward the town he wente anoon.
    And also° soone as that he was agoon,°   *as / gone away*
    That oon of hem spak thus unto that other:
520 "Thou knowest wel thou art my sworen brother;
    Thy profit wol I telle thee anoon:
    Thou woost wel that oure felawe is agoon,
    And here is gold, and that ful greet plentee,
    That shall departed° been among us three.   *divided*
525 But nathelees, if I can shape° it so   *arrange*
    That it departed were among us two,
    Hadde I nat doon a freendes turn to thee?"
      That other answerde, "I noot⁴ how that may be:
    He woot that the gold is with us twaye.
530 What shal we doon? What shal we to him saye?"
      "Shal it be conseil?"⁵ saide the firste shrewe.°   *villain*
    "And I shal telle in a wordes fewe
    What we shul doon, and bringe it wel aboute."
      "I graunte," quod that other, "out of doute,
535 That by my trouthe I wol thee nat biwraye."°   *expose*
      "Now," quod the firste, "thou woost wel we be twaye,
    And two of us shal strenger° be than oon: *stronger*
    Looke whan that he is set that right anoon
    Aris as though thou woldest with him playe,
540 And I shal rive° him thurgh the sides twaye,   *pierce*
    Whil that thou strugelest with him as in game,
    And with thy daggere looke thou do the same;
    And thanne shal al this gold departed be,
    My dere freend, bitwixe thee and me.
545 Thanne we may bothe oure lustes° al fulfille,   *desires*
    And playe at dees° right at oure owene wille."   *dice*
    And thus accorded been thise shrewes twaye
    To sleen the thridde, as ye han herd me saye.
      This yongeste, which that wente to the town,
550 Ful ofte in herte he rolleth up and down
    The beautee of thise florins newe and brighte.
    "O Lord," quod he, "if so were that I mighte
    Have al this tresor to myself allone,
    Ther is no man that liveth under the trone°   *throne*
555 Of God that sholde live so merye as I."
    And at the laste the feend oure enemy
    Putte in his thought that he sholde poison beye,°   *buy*
    With which he mighte sleen his felawes twaye—

---

4. Don't know.   5. A secret.

Forwhy° the feend° foond him in swich livinge   *because/devil*
560 That he hadde leve° him to sorwe bringe:[6]   *permission*
For this was outrely° his fulle entente,   *plainly*
To sleen hem bothe, and nevere to repente.
    And forth he gooth—no lenger wolde he tarye—
Into the town unto a pothecarye,°   *apothecary*
565 And prayed him that he him wolde selle
Som poison that he mighte his rattes quelle,°   *kill*
And eek ther was a polcat[7] in his hawe°   *yard*
That, as he saide, his capons hadde yslawe,°   *slain*
And fain he wolde wreke him[8] if he mighte
570 On vermin that destroyed him[9] by nighte.
    The pothecarye answerde, "And thou shalt have
A thing that, also° God my soule save,   *as*
In al this world there is no creature
That ete or dronke hath of this confiture°   *mixture*
575 Nat but the mountance° of a corn° of whete—   *amount/grain*
That he ne shal his lif anoon forlete.°   *lose*
Ye, sterve° he shal, and that in lasse° while   *die/less*
Than thou wolt goon a paas[1] nat but a mile,
The poison is so strong and violent."
580 This cursed man hath in his hand yhent°   *taken*
This poison in a box and sith° he ran   *then*
Into the nexte streete unto a man
And borwed of him large botels three,
And in the two his poison poured he—
585 The thridde he kepte clene for his drinke,
For al the night he shoop him[2] for to swinke°   *work*
In carying of the gold out of that place.
And whan this riotour with sory grace
Hadde filled with win his grete botels three,
590 To his felawes again repaireth he.
    What needeth it to sermone of it more?
For right as they had cast° his deeth bifore,   *plotted*
Right so they han him slain, and that anoon.
And whan that this was doon, thus spak that oon:
595 "Now lat us sitte and drinke and make us merye,
And afterward we wol his body berye."°   *bury*
And with that word it happed him par cas[3]
To take the botel ther the poison was,
And drank, and yaf his felawe drinke also,
600 For which anoon they storven° bothe two.   *died*
    But certes I suppose that Avicen
Wroot nevere in no canon ne in no *fen*[4]
Mo wonder signes[5] of empoisoning
Than hadde thise wrecches two er hir ending:

6. Christian doctrine teaches that the devil may not tempt people except with God's permission.
7. A weasellike animal.
8. He would gladly avenge himself.
9. I.e., were ruining his farming.
1. Take a walk.

2. He was preparing.
3. By chance.
4. The *Canon of Medicine,* by Avicenna, an 11th-century Arabic philosopher, was divided into sections called "fens."
5. More wonderful symptoms.

605 Thus ended been thise homicides two,
And eek the false empoisonere also.
　　O cursed sinne of alle cursednesse!
O traitours homicide, O wikkednesse!
O glotonye, luxure,° and hasardrye!　　　　　　　　　　*lechery*
610 Thou blasphemour of Crist with vilainye
And othes grete of usage° and of pride!　　　　　　　　*habit*
Allas, mankinde, how may it bitide
That to thy Creatour which that thee wroughte,
And with his precious herte blood thee boughte,°　　　*redeemed*
615 Thou art so fals and so unkinde,° allas?　　　　　　　*unnatural*
　　Now goode men, God foryive you youre trespas,
And ware° you fro the sinne of avarice:　　　　　　　　*guard*
Myn holy pardon may you alle warice°—　　　　　　　　*save*
So that ye offre nobles or sterlinges,[6]
620 Or elles silver brooches, spoones, ringes.
Boweth your heed under this holy bulle!
Cometh up, ye wives, offreth of youre wolle!°　　　　　*wool*
Youre name I entre here in my rolle: anoon
Into the blisse of hevene shul ye goon.
625 I you assoile° by myn heigh power—　　　　　　　　　*absolve*
Ye that wol offre—as clene and eek as cleer
As ye were born.—And lo, sires, thus I preche.
And Jesu Crist that is oure soules leeche°　　　　　　　*physician*
So graunte you his pardon to receive,
630 For that is best—I wol you nat deceive.

The Epilogue

　　"But sires, oo word forgat I in my tale:
I have relikes and pardon in my male°　　　　　　　　　*bag*
As faire as any man in Engelond,
Whiche were me yiven by the Popes hond.
635 If any of you wol of devocioun
Offren and han myn absolucioun,
Come forth anoon, and kneeleth here adown,
And mekely receiveth my pardoun,
Or elles taketh pardon as ye wende,°　　　　　　　　　*ride along*
640 Al newe and fressh at every miles ende—
So that ye offre alway newe and newe[7]
Nobles or pens whiche that be goode and trewe.
It is an honour to everich° that is heer　　　　　　　　*everyone*
That ye have a suffisant° pardoner　　　　　　　　　　*competent*
645 T'assoile you in contrees as ye ride,
For aventures° whiche that may bitide:　　　　　　　　　*accidents*
Paraventure ther may falle oon or two
Down of his hors and breke his nekke atwo;
Looke which a suretee° is it to you alle　　　　　　　　*safeguard*
650 That I am in youre felaweshipe yfalle
That may assoile you, bothe more and lasse,[8]

6. "Nobles" and "sterlinges" were valuable coins.　　8. Both high and low (i.e., everybody).
7. Over and over.

Whan that the soule shal fro the body passe.
I rede° that oure Hoste shal biginne,   *advise*
For he is most envoluped° in sinne.   *involved*
655 Com forth, sire Host, and offre first anoon,
And thou shalt kisse the relikes everichoon,°   *each one*
Ye, for a grote: unbokele° anoon thy purs."   *unbuckle*
"Nay, nay," quod he, "thanne have I Cristes curs!
Lat be," quod he, "it shal nat be, so theech!°   *may I prosper*
660 Thou woldest make me kisse thyn olde breech°   *breeches*
And swere it were a relik of a saint,
Though it were with thy fundament° depeint.°   *anus/stained*
But, by the crois which that Sainte Elaine foond,[9]
I wolde I hadde thy coilons° in myn hond,   *testicles*
665 In stede of relikes or of saintuarye.°   *relic-box*
Lat cutte hem of: I wol thee helpe hem carye.
They shal be shrined in an hogges tord."°   *turd*
This Pardoner answerde nat a word:
So wroth he was no word ne wolde he saye.
670 "Now," quod oure Host, "I wol no lenger playe
With thee, ne with noon other angry man."
But right anoon the worthy Knight bigan,
Whan that he sawgh that al the peple lough,°   *laughed*
"Namore of this, for it is right ynough.
675 Sire Pardoner, be glad and merye of cheere,
And ye, sire Host that been to me so dere,
I praye you that ye kisse the Pardoner,
And Pardoner, I praye thee, draw thee neer,
And as we diden lat us laughe and playe."
680 Anoon they kiste and riden forth hir waye.

The Nun's Priest's Tale

In the framing story, *The Nun's Priest's Tale* is linked to a dramatic exchange that
follows *The Monk's Tale*. The latter consists of brief tragedies, the common theme of
which is the fall of famous men and one woman, most of whom are rulers, through
the reversals of Fortune. Like *The Knight's Tale*, this was probably an earlier work of
Chaucer's, one that he never finished. As the Monk's tragedies promise to go on and
on monotonously, the Knight interrupts and politely tells the Monk that his tragedies
are too painful. The Host chimes in to say that the tragedies are "nat worth a bot-
terflye" and asks the Monk to try another subject, but the Monk is offended and
refuses. The Host then turns to the Nun's Priest, that is, the priest who is accompanying the Prioress. The three priests said in *The General Prologue* to have been
traveling with her have apparently been reduced to one.

   The Nun's Priest's Tale is an example of the literary genre known as the "beast
fable," familiar from the fables of Aesop in which animals, behaving like human
beings, point a moral. In the Middle Ages fables often functioned as elementary texts
to teach boys Latin. Marie de France's fables in French are the earliest known vernacular translations. This particular fable derives from an episode in the French

9. I.e., by the cross that St. Helena found. Helena, mother of Constantine the Great, was reputed to have
found the True Cross.

Roman de Renard, a "beast epic," which satirically represents a feudal animal society ruled over by Noble the Lion. Reynard the Fox is a wily trickster hero who is constantly preying upon and outwitting the other animals, although sometimes Reynard himself is outwitted by one of his victims.

In *The Nun's Priest's Tale*, morals proliferate: both the priest-narrator and his hero, Chauntecleer the rooster, spout examples, learned allusions, proverbs, and sententious generalizations, often in highly inflated rhetoric. The simple beast fable is thus inflated into a delightful satire of learning and moralizing and of the pretentious rhetoric by which medieval writers sometimes sought to elevate their works. Among them, we we may include Chaucer himself who in this tale seems to be making affectionate fun of some of his own works like the tragedies which became *The Monk's Tale*.

	A poore widwe somdeel stape° in age	*advanced*
	Was whilom° dwelling in a narwe¹ cotage,	*once upon a time*
	Biside a grove, stonding in a dale:	
	This widwe of which I telle you my tale,	
5	Sin thilke° day that she was last a wif,	*that same*
	In pacience ladde° a ful simple lif.	*led*
	For litel was hir catel° and hir rente,°	*property/income*
	By housbondrye° of swich as God hire sente	*economy*
	She foond° hirself and eek hir doughtren two.	*provided for*
10	Three large sowes hadde she and namo,	
	Three kin,° and eek a sheep that highte° Malle.	*cows/was called*
	Ful sooty was hir bowr° and eek hir halle.	*bedroom*
	In which she eet ful many a sclendre° meel;	*scanty*
	Of poinant° sauce hire needed neveradeel:°	*pungent/not a bit*
15	No daintee morsel passed thurgh hir throte—	
	Hir diete was accordant to hir cote.°	*cottage*
	Repleccioun° ne made hire nevere sik:	*overeating*
	Attempre° diete was al hir physik,°	*moderate/medicine*
	And exercise and hertes suffisaunce.°	*contentment*
20	The goute lette hire nothing for to daunce,²	
	N'apoplexye shente° nat hir heed.°	*hurt/head*
	No win ne drank she, neither whit ne reed:°	*red*
	Hir boord° was served most with whit and blak,³	*table*
	Milk and brown breed, in which she foond no lak;⁴	
25	Seind bacon, and somtime an ey° or twaye,	*egg*
	For she was as it were a manere daye.⁵	
	A yeerd° she hadde, enclosed al withoute	*yard*
	With stikkes, and a drye dich aboute,	
	In which she hadde a cok heet° Chauntecleer:	*named*
30	In al the land of crowing nas° his peer.	*was not*
	His vois was merier than the merye orgon	
	On massedayes that in the chirche goon;⁶	
	Wel sikerer⁷ was his crowing in his logge°	*dwelling*
	Than is a clok or an abbeye orlogge;°	*timepiece*
35	By nature he knew eech ascensioun	

1. I.e., small.
2. The gout didn't hinder her at all from dancing.
3. I.e., milk and bread.
4. Found no fault.
5. I.e., a kind of dairywoman. "Seind": scorched (i.e., broiled).
6. I.e., is played.
7. More reliable.

Of th'equinoxial[8] in thilke town:
For whan degrees fifteene were ascended,
Thanne crew° he that it mighte nat been amended.°   *crowed/improved*
His comb was redder than the fin coral,
40   And batailed° as it were a castel wal;   *battlemented*
His bile° was blak, and as the jeet° it shoon;   *bill/jet*
Like asure[9] were his legges and his toon;°   *toes*
His nailes whitter° than the lilye flowr,   *whiter*
And lik the burned° gold was his colour.   *burnished*
45   This gentil° cok hadde in his governaunce   *noble*
Sevene hennes for to doon al his plesaunce,°   *pleasure*
Whiche were his sustres and his paramours,[1]
And wonder like to him as of colours;
Of whiche the faireste hewed° on hir throte   *colored*
50   Was cleped° faire damoisele Pertelote: *called*
Curteis she was, discreet, and debonaire,°   *meek*
And compaignable,° and bar° hirself so faire,   *companionable/bore*
Sin thilke day that she was seven night old,
That trewely she hath the herte in hold
55   Of Chauntecleer, loken° in every lith.°   *locked/limb*
He loved hire so that wel was him therwith.[2]
But swich a joye was it to heere hem singe,
Whan that the brighte sonne gan to springe,
In sweete accord *My Lief is Faren in Londe*[3]—
60   For thilke time, as I have understonde,
Beestes and briddes couden speke and singe.
    And so bifel that in a daweninge,
As Chauntecleer among his wives alle
Sat on his perche that was in the halle,
65   And next him sat this faire Pertelote,
This Chauntecleer gan gronen in his throte,
As man that in his dreem is drecched° sore.   *troubled*
    And whan that Pertelote thus herde him rore,°   *roar*
She was agast, and saide, "Herte dere,
70   What aileth you to grone in this manere?
Ye been a verray slepere,[4] fy, for shame!"
    And he answerde and saide thus, "Madame,
I praye you that ye take it nat agrief.°   *amiss*
By God, me mette I was in swich meschief[5]
75   Right now, that yit myn herte is sore afright.
Now God," quod he, "my swevene recche aright,[6]
And keepe my body out of foul prisoun!
Me mette° how that I romed up and down   *dreamed*
Within oure yeerd, wher as I sawgh a beest,
80   Was lik an hound and wolde han maad arrest[7]

8. I.e., he knew by instinct each step in the progression of the celestial equator. The celestial
equator was thought to make a 360° rotation
around the earth every twenty-four hours;
therefore, a progression of 15° would be equal to
the passage of an hour (line 37).
9. Blue (lapis lazuli).
1. His sisters and his mistresses.

2. That he was well contented.
3. "My Love Has Gone Away," a popular song of
the time.
4. Sound sleeper.
5. I dreamed that I was in such misfortune.
6. Interpret my dream correctly (i.e., in an auspicious manner).
7. Would have laid hold.

Upon my body, and han had me deed.[8]
His colour was bitwixe yelow and reed,
And tipped was his tail and bothe his eres
With blak, unlik the remenant° of his heres;°   *rest / hairs*
85 His snoute smal, with glowing yën twaye.
Yit of his look for fere almost I deye:°   *die*
This caused me my groning, doutelees."
    "Avoi,"° quod she, "fy on you, hertelees!°   *fie / coward*
Allas," quod she, "for by that God above,
90 Now han ye lost myn herte and al my love!
I can nat love a coward, by my faith.
For certes, what so any womman saith,
We alle desiren, if it mighte be,
To han housbondes hardy, wise, and free,°   *generous*
95 And secree,° and no nigard, ne no fool,   *discreet*
Ne him that is agast of every tool,°   *weapon*
Ne noon avauntour.° By that God above,   *boaster*
How dorste° ye sayn for shame unto youre love   *dare*
That any thing mighte make you aferd?
100 Have ye no mannes herte and han a beerd?°   *beard*
Allas, and conne° ye been agast of swevenes?°   *can / dreams*
No thing, God woot, but vanitee[9] in swevene is!
Swevenes engendren of replexiouns,[1]
And ofte of fume° and of complexiouns,°   *gas / bodily humors*
105 Whan humours been too habundant in a wight.[2]
Certes, this dreem which ye han met° tonight   *dreamed*
Comth of the grete superfluitee
Of youre rede colera,[3] pardee,
Which causeth folk to dreden° in hir dremes   *fear*
110 Of arwes,° and of fir with rede lemes,°   *arrows / flames*
Of rede beestes, that they wol hem bite,
Of contek,° and of whelpes grete and lite[4]—   *strife*
Right° as the humour of malencolye[5]   *just*
Causeth ful many a man in sleep to crye
115 For fere of blake beres° or boles° blake,   *bears / bulls*
Or elles blake develes wol hem take.
Of othere humours coude I tell also
That werken many a man in sleep ful wo,
But I wol passe as lightly° as I can.   *quickly*
120 Lo, Caton,[6] which that was so wis a man,
Saide he nat thus? 'Ne do no fors of[7] dremes.'
Now, sire," quod she, "whan we flee fro the bemes,[8]
For Goddes love, as take som laxatif.
Up° peril of my soule and of my lif,   *upon*
125 I conseile you the beste, I wol nat lie,

---

8. I.e., killed me.
9. I.e., empty illusion.
1. Dreams have their origin in overeating.
2. I.e., when humors (bodily fluids) are too abundant in a person. Pertelote's diagnosis is based on the familiar concept that an excess of one of the bodily humors in a person affected his or her temperament (see p. 188, n. 8).

3. Red bile.
4. And of big and little dogs.
5. I.e., black bile.
6. Dionysius Cato, supposed author of a book of maxims used in elementary education.
7. Pay no attention to.
8. Fly down from the rafters.

That bothe of colere and of malencolye
Ye purge you; and for° ye shal nat tarye,   *in order that*
Though in this town is noon apothecarye,
I shal myself to herbes techen you,
130 That shal been for youre hele° and for youre prow,°   *health/benefit*
And in oure yeerd tho° herbes shal I finde,   *those*
The whiche han of hir propretee by kinde°   *nature*
To purge you binethe and eek above.
Foryet° nat this, for Goddes owene love.   *forget*
135 Ye been ful colerik° of complexioun;   *bilious*
Ware° the sonne in his ascencioun   *beware that*
Ne finde you nat repleet° of humours hote;°   *filled/hot*
And if it do, I dar wel laye° a grote   *bet*
That ye shul have a fevere terciane,[9]
140 Or an agu° that may be youre bane.°   *ague/death*
A day or two ye shul han digestives
Of wormes, er° ye take youre laxatives   *before*
Of lauriol, centaure, and fumetere,[1]
Or elles of ellebor° that groweth there,   *hellebore*
145 Of catapuce, or of gaitres beries,[2]
Of herb-ive° growing in oure yeerd ther merye is[3]—   *herb ivy*
Pekke hem right up as they growe and ete hem in.
Be merye, housbonde, for youre fader° kin!   *father's*
Dredeth no dreem: I can saye you namore."
150 "Madame," quod he, "graunt mercy of youre lore,[4]
But nathelees, as touching daun° Catoun,   *master*
That hath of wisdom swich a greet renown,
Though that he bad no dremes for to drede,
By God, men may in olde bookes rede
155 Of many a man more of auctoritee°   *authority*
Than evere Caton was, so mote I thee,°   *prosper*
That al the revers sayn of his sentence,°   *opinion*
And han wel founden by experience
That dremes been significaciouns
160 As wel of joye as tribulaciouns
That folk enduren in this lif present.
Ther needeth make of this noon argument:
The verray preve[5] sheweth it in deede.
    "Oon of the gretteste auctour[6] that men rede
165 Saith thus, that whilom two felawes wente
On pilgrimage in a ful good entente,
And happed so they comen in a town,
Wher as ther was swich congregacioun
Of peple, and eek so strait of herbergage,[7]
170 That they ne founde as muche as oo cotage
In which they bothe mighte ylogged° be;   *lodged*
Wherfore they mosten° of necessitee   *must*

9. Tertian (recurring every other day).
1. Of laureole, centaury, and fumitory. These, and
the herbs mentioned in the next lines, were all
common medieval medicines used as cathartics.
2. Of caper berry or of gaiter berry.
3. Where it is pleasant.

4. Many thanks for your instruction.
5. Actual experience.
6. I.e., one of the greatest authors (perhaps Cicero
or Valerius Maximus).
7. And also such a shortage of lodging.

As for that night departe° compaignye.   *part*
And eech of hem gooth to his hostelrye,
175   And took his logging as it wolde falle.°   *befall*
That oon of hem was logged in a stalle,
Fer° in a yeerd, with oxen of the plough;   *far away*
That other man was logged wel ynough,
As was his aventure° or his fortune,   *lot*
180   That us governeth alle as in commune.
And so bifel that longe er it were day,
This man mette° in his bed, ther as he lay,   *dreamed*
How that his felawe gan upon him calle,
And saide, 'Allas, for in an oxes stalle
185   This night I shal be mordred° ther I lie!   *murdered*
Now help me, dere brother, or I die!
In alle haste com to me,' he saide.
      "This man out of his sleep for fere abraide,°   *started up*
But whan that he was wakened of his sleep,
190   He turned him and took of this no keep:°   *heed*
Him thoughte his dreem nas but a vanitee.°   *illusion*
Thus twies in his sleeping dremed he,
And atte thridde time yit his felawe
Cam, as him thoughte, and saide, 'I am now slawe:°   *slain*
195   Bihold my bloody woundes deepe and wide.
Aris up erly in the morwe tide,[8]
And atte west gate of the town,' quod he,
'A carte ful of dong° ther shaltou see,   *dung*
In which my body is hid ful prively:
200   Do thilke carte arresten boldely.[9]
My gold caused my mordre, sooth to sayn'
—And tolde him every point how he was slain,
With a ful pitous face, pale of hewe.
And truste wel, his dreem he foond° ful trewe,   *found*
205   For on the morwe° as soone as it was day,   *morning*
To his felawes in° he took the way,   *lodging*
And whan that he cam to this oxes stalle,
After his felawe he bigan to calle.
      "The hostiler° answerde him anoon,   *innkeeper*
210   And saide, 'Sire, youre felawe is agoon:°   *gone away*
As soone as day he wente out of the town.'
      "This man gan fallen in suspecioun,
Remembring on his dremes that he mette;°   *dreamed*
And forth he gooth, no lenger wolde he lette,°   *tarry*
215   Unto the west gate of the town, and foond
A dong carte, wente as it were to donge° lond,   *put manure on*
That was arrayed in that same wise
As ye han herd the dede° man devise;   *dead*
And with an hardy herte he gan to crye,
220   'Vengeance and justice of this felonye!
My felawe mordred is this same night,
And in this carte he lith° gaping upright!°   *lies/on his back*
I crye out on the ministres,' quod he,

8. In the morning.   9. Boldly have this same cart seized.

'That sholde keepe and rulen this citee.
225 Harrow,° allas, here lith my felawe slain!'   *help*
What sholde I more unto this tale sayn?
The peple up sterte° and caste the carte to grounde,   *started*
And in the middel of the dong they founde
The dede man that mordred was al newe.[1]
230   "O blisful God that art so just and trewe,
Lo, how that thou biwrayest° mordre alway!   *disclose*
Mordre wol out, that see we day by day:
Mordre is so wlatsom° and abhominable   *loathsome*
To God that is so just and resonable,
235 That he ne wol nat suffre it heled° be,   *concealed*
Though it abide a yeer or two or three.
Mordre wol out: this my conclusioun.
And right anoon ministres of that town
Han hent° the cartere and so sore him pined,[2]   *seized*
240 And eek the hostiler so sore engined,°   *racked*
That they biknewe° hir wikkednesse anoon,   *confessed*
And were anhanged° by the nekke boon.   *hanged*
Here may men seen that dremes been to drede.[3]
    "And certes, in the same book I rede—
245 Right in the nexte chapitre after this—
I gabbe° nat, so have I joye or blis—   *lie*
Two men that wolde han passed over see
For certain cause into a fer contree,
If that the wind ne hadde been contrarye
250 That made hem in a citee for to tarye,
That stood ful merye upon an haven° side—   *harbor's*
But on a day again° the even-tide   *toward*
The wind gan chaunge, and blewe right as hem leste:[4]
Jolif° and glad they wenten unto reste,   *merry*
255 And casten° hem ful erly for to saile.   *determined*
    "But to that oo man fil° a greet mervaile;   *befell*
That oon of hem, in sleeping as he lay,
Him mette[5] a wonder dreem again the day:
Him thoughte a man stood by his beddes side,
260 And him comanded that he sholde abide,
And saide him thus, 'If thou tomorwe wende,
Thou shalt be dreint:° my tale is at an ende.'   *drowned*
    "He wook and tolde his felawe what he mette,
And prayed him his viage° to lette;°   *voyage/delay*
265 As for that day he prayed him to bide.
    "His felawe that lay by his beddes side
Gan for to laughe, and scorned him ful faste.°   *hard*
'No dreem,' quod he, 'may so myn herte agaste°   *terrify*
That I wol lette for to do my thinges.°   *business*
270 I sette nat a straw by thy dreminges,[6]
For swevenes been but vanitees and japes:[7]
Men dreme alday° of owles or of apes,[8]   *constantly*

1. Recently.
2. Tortured.
3. Worthy of being feared.
4. Just as they wished.

5. He dreamed.
6. I don't care a straw for your dreamings.
7. Dreams are but illusions and frauds.
8. I.e., of absurdities.

And of many a maze° therwithal—   *delusion*
Men dreme of thing that nevere was ne shal.[9]
275   But sith I see that thou wolt here abide,
And thus forsleuthen° wilfully thy tide,°   *waste/time*
God woot, it reweth me;[1] and have good day.'
And thus he took his leve and wente his way.
But er that he hadde half his cours ysailed—
280   Noot I nat why ne what meschaunce it ailed—
But casuelly the shippes botme rente,[2]
And ship and man under the water wente,
In sighte of othere shippes it biside,
That with hem sailed at the same tide.
285   And therfore, faire Pertelote so dere,
By swiche ensamples olde maistou lere°   *learn*
That no man sholde been too recchelees°   *careless*
Of dremes, for I saye thee doutelees
That many a dreem ful sore is for to drede.
290   "Lo, in the lif of Saint Kenelm[3] I rede—
That was Kenulphus sone, the noble king
Of Mercenrike°—how Kenelm mette a thing   *Mercia*
A lite° er he was mordred on a day.   *little*
His mordre in his avision° he sey.°   *dream/saw*
295   His norice° him expounded everydeel°   *nurse/every bit*
His swevene, and bad him for to keepe him[4] weel
For traison, but he nas but seven yeer old,
And therfore litel tale hath he told
Of any dreem,[5] so holy was his herte.
300   By God, I hadde levere than my sherte[6]
That ye hadde rad° his legende as have I.   *read*
"Dame Pertelote, I saye you trewely,
Macrobeus,[7] that writ the *Avisioun*
In Affrike of the worthy Scipioun,
305   Affermeth° dremes, and saith that they been   *confirms*
Warning of thinges that men after seen.
"And ferthermore, I praye you looketh wel
In the Olde Testament of Daniel,
If he heeld° dremes any vanitee.[8]   *considered*
310   "Rede eek of Joseph[9] and ther shul ye see
Wher° dremes be somtime—I saye nat alle—   *whether*
Warning of thinges that shul after falle.
"Looke of Egypte the king daun Pharao,
His bakere and his botelere° also,   *butler*
315   Wher they ne felte noon effect in dremes.[1]
Whoso wol seeke actes of sondry remes°   *realms*
May rede of dremes many a wonder thing.

---

9. I.e., shall be.
1. I'm sorry.
2. I don't know why nor what was the trouble with it—but accidentally the ship's bottom split.
3. Kenelm succeeded his father as king of Mercia at the age of seven, but was slain by his aunt (in 821).
4. Guard himself.
5. Therefore he has set little store by any dream.

6. I.e., I'd give my shirt.
7. Macrobius wrote a famous commentary on Cicero's account in *De Republica* of the dream of Scipio Africanus Minor; the commentary came to be regarded as a standard authority on dream lore.
8. See Daniel 7.
9. See Genesis 37.
1. See Genesis 39–41.

"Lo Cresus, which that was of Lyde° king,   *Lydia*
Mette° he nat that he sat upon a tree,   *dreamed*
320 Which signified he sholde anhanged° be?   *hanged*
"Lo here Andromacha, Ectores° wif,   *Hector's*
That day that Ector sholde lese° his lif,   *lose*
She dremed on the same night biforn
How that the lif of Ector sholde be lorn,°   *lost*
325 If thilke° day he wente into bataile;   *that same*
She warned him, but it mighte nat availe:°   *do any good*
He wente for to fighte nathelees,
But he was slain anoon° of Achilles.   *right away*
But thilke tale is al too long to telle,
330 And eek it is neigh day, I may nat dwelle.
Shortly I saye, as for conclusioun,
That I shal han of this avisioun[2]
Adversitee, and I saye ferthermoor
That I ne telle of[3] laxatives no stoor,
335 For they been venimes,° I woot it weel: *poisons*
I hem defye, I love hem neveradeel.°   *not a bit*
"Now lat us speke of mirthe and stinte° al this.   *stop*
Madame Pertelote, so have I blis,
Of oo thing God hath sente me large grace:
340 For whan I see the beautee of youre face—
Ye been so scarlet reed° aboute youre yën—   *red*
It maketh al my drede for to dien.
For also siker° as *In principio*,[4]   *certain*
Mulier est hominis confusio.[5]
345 Madame, the sentence° of this Latin is,   *meaning*
'Womman is mannes joye and al his blis.'
For whan I feele anight youre softe side—
Al be it that I may nat on you ride,
For that oure perche is maad so narwe, allas—
350 I am so ful of joye and of solas°   *delight*
That I defye bothe swevene and dreem."
And with that word he fleigh° down fro the beem,   *flew*
For it was day, and eek his hennes alle,
And with a "chuk" he gan hem for to calle,
355 For he hadde founde a corn lay in the yeerd.
Real° he was, he was namore aferd:°   *regal/afraid*
He fethered[6] Pertelote twenty time,
And trad hire as ofte er it was prime.[7]
He looketh as it were a grim leoun,
360 And on his toes he rometh up and down:
Him deined[8] nat to sette his foot to grounde.
He chukketh whan he hath a corn yfounde,
And to him rennen° thanne his wives alle.   *run*
Thus royal, as a prince is in his halle,

2. Divinely inspired dream (as opposed to the more ordinary "swevene" or "dreem").
3. Set by.
4. Beginning of the Gospel of St. John that gives the essential premises of Christianity: "In the beginning was the Word."
5. Woman is man's ruination.
6. I.e., embraced.
7. 9 A.M. "Trad": trod, copulated with.
8. He deigned.

365   Leve I this Chauntecleer in his pasture,
    And after wol I telle his aventure.
       Whan that the month in which the world bigan,
    That highte° March, whan God first maked man,   *is called*
    Was compleet, and passed were also,
370   Sin March biran,° thritty days and two,[9]   *passed by*
    Bifel that Chauntecleer in al his pride,
    His sevene wives walking him biside,
    Caste up his yën to the brighte sonne,
    That in the signe of Taurus hadde yronne
375   Twenty degrees and oon and somwhat more,
    And knew by kinde,° and by noon other lore,   *nature*
    That it was prime, and crew with blisful stevene.°   *voice*
    "The sonne," he saide, "is clomben[1] up on hevene
    Fourty degrees and oon and more, ywis.°   *indeed*
380   Madame Pertelote, my worldes blis,
    Herkneth thise blisful briddes° how they singe,   *birds*
    And see the fresshe flowers how they springe:
    Ful is myn herte of revel and solas."
    But sodeinly him fil° a sorweful cas,°   *befell/chance*
385   For evere the latter ende of joye is wo—
    God woot that worldly joye is soone ago,
    And if a rethor° coude faire endite,   *rhetorician*
    He in a cronicle saufly° mighte it write,   *safely*
    As for a soverein notabilitee.[2]
390   Now every wis man lat him herkne me:
    This storye is also° trewe, I undertake,   *as*
    As is the book of *Launcelot de Lake*,[3]
    That wommen holde in ful greet reverence.
    Now wol I turne again to my sentence.°   *main point*
395   A colfox[4] ful of sly iniquitee,
    That in the grove hadde woned° yeres three,   *dwelled*
    By heigh imaginacion forncast,[5]
    The same night thurghout the hegges° brast°   *hedges/burst*
    Into the yeerd ther Chauntecleer the faire
400   Was wont, and eek his wives, to repaire;
    And in a bed of wortes° stille he lay   *cabbages*
    Til it was passed undren° of the day,   *midmorning*
    Waiting his time on Chauntecleer to falle,
    As gladly doon thise homicides alle,
405   That in await liggen to mordre[6] men.
    O false mordrour, lurking in thy den!
    O newe Scariot! Newe Geniloun![7]
    False dissimilour!° O Greek Sinoun,[8]   *dissembler*
    That broughtest Troye al outrely° to sorwe!   *utterly*

---

9. The rhetorical time telling yields the date May 3.
1. Has climbed.
2. Indisputable fact.
3. Romances of the courteous knight Lancelot of the Lake were very popular.
4. Fox with black markings.
5. Predestined by divine planning.

6. That lie in ambush to murder.
7. I.e., Ganelon, who betrayed Roland to the Saracens (in the medieval French epic *The Song of Roland*). "Scariot": Judas Iscariot.
8. Sinon, who persuaded the Trojans to take the Greeks' wooden horse into their city—with, of course, the result that the city was destroyed.

410	O Chauntecleer, accursed be that morwe°	*morning*
	That thou into the yeerd flaugh° fro the bemes!	*flew*
	Thou were ful wel ywarned by thy dremes	
	That thilke day was perilous to thee;	
	But what that God forwoot° moot° needes be,	*foreknows / must*
415	After° the opinion of certain clerkes:	*according to*
	Witnesse on him that any parfit° clerk is	*perfect*
	That in scole is greet altercacioun	
	In this matere, and greet disputisoun,°	*disputation*
	And hath been of an hundred thousand men.	
420	But I ne can nat bulte it to the bren,[9]	
	As can the holy doctour Augustin,	
	Or Boece, or the bisshop Bradwardin[1]—	
	Wheither that Goddes worthy forwiting°	*foreknowledge*
	Straineth me nedely[2] for to doon a thing	
425	("Nedely" clepe I simple necessitee),	
	Or elles if free chois be graunted me	
	To do that same thing or do it naught,	
	Though God forwoot° it er that I was wrought;	*foreknew*
	Or if his witing° straineth neveradeel,	*knowledge*
430	But by necessitee condicionel[3]—	
	I wol nat han to do of swich matere:	
	My tale is of a cok, as ye may heere,	
	That took his conseil of his wif with sorwe,	
	To walken in the yeerd upon that morwe	
435	That he hadde met° the dreem that I you tolde.	*dreamed*
	Wommenes conseils been ful ofte colde,[4]	
	Wommanes conseil broughte us first to wo,	
	And made Adam fro Paradis to go,	
	Ther as he was ful merye and wel at ese.	
440	But for I noot° to whom it mighte displese	*don't know*
	If I conseil of wommen wolde blame,	
	Passe over, for I saide it in my game°—	*sport*
	Rede auctours where they trete of swich matere,	
	And what they sayn of wommen ye may heere—	
445	Thise been the cokkes wordes and nat mine:	
	I can noon harm of no womman divine.°	*guess*
	Faire in the sond° to bathe hire merily	*sand*
	Lith° Pertelote, and alle hir sustres by,	*lies*
	Again° the sonne, and Chauntecleer so free°	*in / noble*
450	Soong° merier than the mermaide in the see—	*sang*
	For Physiologus[5] saith sikerly	
	How that they singen wel and merily.	
	And so bifel that as he caste his yë	
	Among the wortes on a boterflye,°	*butterfly*

9. Sift it to the bran, i.e., get to the bottom of it.
1. St. Augustine, Boethius (6th-century Roman philosopher, whose *Consolation of Philosophy* was translated by Chaucer), and Thomas Bradwardine (archbishop of Canterbury, d. 1349) were all concerned with the interrelationship between people's free will and God's foreknowledge.

2. Constrains me necessarily.
3. Boethius's "conditional necessity" permitted a large measure of free will.
4. I.e., baneful.
5. Supposed author of a bestiary, a book of moralized zoology describing both natural and supernatural animals (including mermaids).

455 He was war of this fox that lay ful lowe.
No thing ne liste him[6] thanne for to crowe,
But cride anoon "Cok cok!" and up he sterte,°   *started*
As man that[7] was affrayed in his herte—
For naturelly a beest desireth flee
460 Fro his contrarye[8] if he may it see,
Though he nevere erst° hadde seen it with his yë.   *before*
This Chauntecleer, whan he gan him espye,
He wolde han fled, but that the fox anoon
Saide, "Gentil sire, allas, wher wol ye goon?
465 Be ye afraid of me that am youre freend?
Now certes, I were worse than a feend
If I to you wolde° harm or vilainye.   *meant*
I am nat come youre conseil° for t'espye,   *secrets*
But trewely the cause of my cominge
470 Was only for to herkne how ye singe:
For trewely, ye han as merye a stevene°   *voice*
As any angel hath that is in hevene.
Therwith ye han in musik more feelinge
Than hadde Boece,[9] or any that can singe.
475 My lord your fader—God his soule blesse!—
And eek youre moder, of hir gentilesse,°   *gentility*
Han in myn hous ybeen, to my grete ese.
And certes sire, ful fain° wolde I you plese.   *gladly*
    "But for men speke of singing, I wol saye,
480 So mote I brouke[1] wel mine yën twaye,
Save ye, I herde nevere man to singe
As dide youre fader in the morweninge.
Certes, it was of herte° al that he soong.°   *heartfelt/sang*
And for to make his vois the more strong,
485 He wolde so paine him[2] that with bothe his yën
He moste winke,[3] so loude wolde he cryen;
And stonden on his tiptoon therwithal,
And strecche forth his nekke long and smal;
And eek he was of swich discrecioun
490 That ther nas no man in no regioun
That him in song or wisdom mighte passe.
I have wel rad° in *Daun Burnel the Asse*[4]   *read*
Among his vers how that ther was a cok,
For a preestes sone yaf him a knok[5]
495 Upon his leg whil he was yong and nice,°   *foolish*
He made him for to lese° his benefice.[6]   *lose*
But certain, ther nis no comparisoun
Bitwixe the wisdom and discrecioun
Of youre fader and of his subtiltee.[7]

---

6. He wished.
7. Like one who.
8. I.e., his natural enemy.
9. Boethius also wrote a treatise on music.
1. So might I enjoy the use of.
2. Take pains.
3. He had to shut his eyes.
4. Master Brunellus, a discontented donkey, was

the hero of a 12th-century satirical poem by Nigel Wireker.
5. Because a priest's son gave him a knock.
6. The offended cock neglected to crow so that his master, now grown to manhood, overslept, missing his ordination and losing his benefice.
7. His (the cock in the story) cleverness.

500	Now singeth, sire, for sainte° charitee!	*holy*
	Lat see, conne° ye youre fader countrefete?"°	*can/imitate*
	This Chauntecleer his winges gan to bete,	
	As man that coude his traison nat espye,	
	So was he ravisshed with his flaterye.	
505	Allas, ye lordes, many a fals flatour°	*flatterer*
	Is in youre court, and many a losengeour°	*deceiver*
	That plesen you wel more, by my faith,	
	Than he that soothfastnesse° unto you saith!	*truth*
	Redeth Ecclesiaste[8] of flaterye.	
510	Beeth war, ye lordes, of hir trecherye.	
	This Chauntecleer stood hye upon his toos,	
	Strecching his nekke, and heeld his yën cloos,	
	And gan to crowe loude for the nones;°	*occasion*
	And daun Russel the fox sterte° up atones,	*jumped*
515	And by the gargat° hente° Chauntecleer,	*throat/seized*
	And on his bak toward the wode him beer,°	*bore*
	For yit ne was ther no man that him sued.°	*followed*
	O destinee that maist nat been eschued!°	*eschewed*
	Allas that Chauntecleer fleigh° fro the bemes!	*flew*
520	Allas his wif ne roughte nat of[9] dremes!	
	And on a Friday fil° al this meschaunce!	*befell*
	O Venus that art goddesse of plesaunce,	
	Sin that thy servant was this Chauntecleer,	
	And in thy service dide al his power—	
525	More for delit than world[1] to multiplye—	
	Why woldestou suffre him on thy day[2] to die?	
	O Gaufred,[3] dere maister soverein,	
	That, whan thy worthy king Richard was slain	
	With shot,[4] complainedest his deeth so sore,	
530	Why ne hadde I now thy sentence and thy lore,[5]	
	The Friday for to chide as diden ye?	
	For on a Friday soothly slain was he.	
	Thanne wolde I shewe you how that I coude plaine°	*lament*
	For Chauntecleres drede and for his paine.	
535	Certes, swich cry ne lamentacioun	
	Was nevere of ladies maad when Ilioun°	*Ilium, Troy*
	Was wonne, and Pyrrus[6] with his straite° swerd,	*drawn*
	Whan he hadde hent° King Priam by the beerd	*seized*
	And slain him, as saith us *Eneidos*,[7]	
540	As maden alle the hennes in the cloos,°	*yard*
	Whan they hadde seen of Chauntecleer the sighte.	
	But sovereinly° Dame Pertelote shrighte°	*supremely/shrieked*
	Ful louder than dide Hasdrubales[8] wif	
	Whan that hir housbonde hadde lost his lif,	

8. The Book of Ecclesiasticus, in the Apocrypha.
9. Didn't care for.
1. I.e., population.
2. Friday is Venus's day.
3. Geoffrey of Vinsauf, a famous medieval rhetorician, who wrote a lament on the death of Richard I in which he scolded Friday, the day on which the king died.

4. I.e., a missile.
5. Thy wisdom and thy learning.
6. Pyrrhus was the Greek who slew Priam, king of Troy.
7. As the *Aeneid* tells us.
8. Hasdrubal was king of Carthage when it was destroyed by the Romans.

545 And that the Romains hadden brend° Cartage;   *burned*
She was so ful of torment and of rage°   *madness*
That wilfully unto the fir she sterte,°   *jumped*
And brende hirselven with a stedefast herte.
O woful hennes, right so criden ye
550 As, whan that Nero brende the citee
Of Rome, criden senatoures wives
For that hir housbondes losten alle hir lives:[9]
Withouten gilt this Nero hath hem slain.
Now wol I turne to my tale again.

555 The sely° widwe and eek hir doughtres two   *innocent*
Herden thise hennes crye and maken wo,
And out at dores sterten° they anoon,   *leapt*
And sien° the fox toward the grove goon,   *saw*
And bar upon his bak the cok away,
560 And criden, "Out, harrow,° and wailaway,   *help*
Ha, ha, the fox," and after him they ran,
And eek with staves many another man;
Ran Colle oure dogge, and Talbot and Gerland,[1]
And Malkin with a distaf in hir hand,
565 Ran cow and calf, and eek the verray hogges,
Sore aferd° for berking of the dogges   *frightened*
And shouting of the men and wommen eke.
They ronne° so hem thoughte hir herte breke;[2]   *ran*
They yelleden as feendes doon in helle;
570 The dokes° criden as men wolde hem quelle;°   *ducks/kill*
The gees for fere flowen° over the trees;   *flew*
Out of the hive cam the swarm of bees;
So hidous was the noise, a, benedicite,°   *bless me*
Certes, he Jakke Straw[3] and his meinee°   *company*
575 Ne made nevere shoutes half so shrille
Whan that they wolden any Fleming kille,
As thilke day was maad upon the fox:
Of bras they broughten bemes° and of box,°   *trumpets/boxwood*
Of horn, of boon,° in whiche they blewe and pouped,°   *bone/tooted*
580 And therwithal they skriked° and they houped°—   *shrieked/whooped*
It seemed as that hevene sholde falle.
Now goode men, I praye you herkneth alle:
Lo, how Fortune turneth° sodeinly   *reverses, overturns*
The hope and pride eek of hir enemy.
585 This cok that lay upon the foxes bak,
In al his drede unto the fox he spak,
And saide, "Sire, if that I were as ye,
Yit sholde I sayn, as wis° God helpe me,   *surely*
'Turneth ayain, ye proude cherles alle!
590 A verray pestilence upon you falle!
Now am I come unto this wodes side,
Maugree your heed,[4] the cok shal here abide.

---

9. According to the legend, Nero not only set fire to Rome (in 64 C.E.) but also put many senators to death.
1. Two other dogs.
2. Would break.

3. One of the leaders of the Uprising of 1381, which was partially directed against the Flemings living in London.
4. Despite your head—i.e., despite anything you can do.

I wol him ete, in faith, and that anoon.' "
　　The fox answerde, "In faith, it shal be doon."
595　And as he spak that word, al sodeinly
　　The cok brak from his mouth deliverly,°　　　　　　*nimbly*
　　And hye upon a tree he fleigh° anoon.　　　　　　　*flew*
　　　　And whan the fox sawgh that he was agoon,
　　"Allas," quod he, "O Chauntecleer, allas!
600　I have to you," quod he, "ydoon trespas,
　　In as muche as I maked you aferd
　　Whan I you hente° and broughte out of the yeerd.　　*seized*
　　But sire, I dide it in no wikke° entente:　　　　　　*wicked*
　　Come down, and I shal telle you what I mente.
605　I shal saye sooth to you, God help me so."
　　　　"Nay thanne," quod he, "I shrewe° us bothe two:　*curse*
　　But first I shrewe myself, bothe blood and bones,
　　If thou bigile me ofter than ones;
　　Thou shalt namore thurgh thy flaterye
610　Do° me to singe and winken with myn yëe.　　　　　*cause*
　　For he that winketh whan he sholde see,
　　Al wilfully, God lat him nevere thee."°　　　　　　*prosper*
　　　　"Nay," quod the fox, "but God yive him meschaunce
　　That is so undiscreet of governaunce°　　　　　　　*self-control*
615　That jangleth° whan he sholde holde his pees."　　*chatters*
　　　　Lo, swich it is for to be reccheless°　　　　　　*careless*
　　And necligent and truste on flaterye.
　　But ye that holden this tale a folye
　　As of a fox, or of a cok and hen,
620　Taketh the moralitee, goode men.
　　For Saint Paul saith that al that writen is
　　To oure doctrine it is ywrit, ywis:[5]
　　Taketh the fruit, and lat the chaf be stille.[6]
　　Now goode God, if that it be thy wille,
625　As saith my lord, so make us alle goode men,
　　And bringe us to his hye blisse. Amen.

Close of *Canterbury Tales*

At the end of *The Canterbury Tales*, Chaucer invokes a common allegorical theme, that life on earth is a pilgrimage. As Chaucer puts it in his moral ballade *Truth*, "Here in noon home . . . / Forth, pilgrim, forth!" In the final fragment, he makes explicit a metaphor that has been implicit all along in the journey to Canterbury. The pilgrims never arrive at the shrine of St. Thomas, but in *The Parson's Tale*, and in its short introduction and in the "Retraction" that follows it, Chaucer seems to be making an end for two pilgrimages that had become one, that of his fiction and that of his life.

In the introduction to the tale we find the twenty-nine pilgrims moving through a nameless little village as the sun sinks to within twenty-nine degrees of the horizon. The atmosphere contains something of both the chill and the urgency of a late autumn afternoon, and we are surprised to find that the pilgrimage is almost over,

5. See Romans 15.4.
6. The "fruit" refers to the kernel of moral or doctrinal meaning; the "chaf," or husk, is the narrative

containing that meaning. The metaphor was commonly applied to scriptural interpretation.

that there is need for haste to make that "good end" that every medieval Christian hoped for. This delicately suggestive passage, rich with allegorical overtones, introduces an extremely long penitential treatise, translated by Chaucer from Latin or French sources. Although often assumed to be an earlier work, it may well have been written by Chaucer to provide the ending for *The Canterbury Tales*.

In the "Retraction" that follows *The Parson's Tale*, Chaucer acknowledges, lists, revokes, and asks forgiveness for his "giltes" (that is, his sins), which consist of having written most of the works on which his reputation as a great poet depends. He thanks Christ and Mary for his religious and moral works. One need not take this as evidence of a spiritual crisis or conversion at the end of his life. The "Retraction" seems to have been written to appear at the end of *The Canterbury Tales*, without censoring any of the tales deemed to be sinful. At the same time, one need not question Chaucer's sincerity. A readiness to deny his own reality before the reality of his God is implicit in many of Chaucer's works, and the placement of the "Retraction" within or just outside the border of the fictional pilgrimage suggests that although Chaucer finally rejected his fictions, he recognized that he and they were inseparable.

From The Parson's Tale

The Introduction

By that[1] the Manciple hadde his tale al ended,
The sonne fro the south line[2] was descended
So lowe, that he has nat to my sighte
Degrees nine and twenty as in highte.
5   Four of the clokke it was, so as I gesse,
For elevene foot, or litel more or lesse,
My shadwe was at thilke time as there,
Of swich feet as° my lengthe parted° were   *as if/divided*
In six feet equal of proporcioun.[3]
10   Therwith the moones exaltacioun[4]—
I mene Libra—always gan ascende,
As we were entring at a thropes° ende.   *village's*
For which oure Host, as he was wont to gie°   *lead*
As in this caas oure joly compaignye,
15   Saide in this wise, "Lordinges everichoon,
Now lakketh us no tales mo than oon:
Fulfild is my sentence° and my decree;   *purpose*
I trowe° that we han herd of ech degree;   *believe*
Almost fulfild is al myn ordinaunce.
20   I praye to God, so yive him right good chaunce
That telleth this tale to us lustily.
Sire preest," quod he, "artou a vicary,°   *vicar*
Or arte a Person? Say sooth, by thy fay.°   *faith*
Be what thou be, ne breek° thou nat oure play,   *break*
25   For every man save thou hath told his tale.
Unbokele and shew us what is in thy male!°   *bag*
For trewely, me thinketh by thy cheere°   *expression*
Thou sholdest knitte up wel a greet matere.
Tel us a fable anoon, for cokkes bones!"[5]

1. By the time that.
2. I.e., the line that runs some 28° to the south of the celestial equator and parallel to it.
3. This detailed analysis merely says that the shad-
ows are lengthening.
4. I.e., the astrological sign in which the moon's influence was dominant.
5. Cock's bones, a euphemism for God's bones.

30   This Person answerde al atones,°   *immediately*
    "Thou getest fable noon ytold for me,
    For Paul, that writeth unto Timothee,
    Repreveth° hem that waiven soothfastnesse,[6]   *reproves*
    And tellen fables and swich wrecchednesse.
35   Why sholde I sowen draf° out of my fest,°   *chaff/fist*
    Whan I may sowen whete if that me lest?[7]
    For which I saye that if you list to heere
    Moralitee and vertuous matere,
    And thanne that ye wol yive me audience,
40   I wol ful fain,° at Cristes reverence,   *gladly*
    Do you plesance leveful° as I can.   *lawful*
    But trusteth wel, I am a southren man:
    I can nat geeste Rum-Ram-Ruf by lettre[8]—
    Ne, God woot, rym holde° I but litel bettre.   *consider*
45   And therfore, if you list—I wol nat glose[9]—
    I wol you telle a merye tale in prose
    To knitte up al this feeste and make an ende.
    And Jesu for his grace wit me sende
    To shewe you the way in this viage°   *journey*
50   Of thilke parfit glorious pilgrimage
    That highte° Jerusalem celestial.   *is called*
    And if ye vouche sauf, anoon I shal
    Biginne upon my tale, for which I praye
    Telle youre avis:° I can no bettre saye.   *opinion*
55   But nathelees, this meditacioun
    I putte it ay under correccioun
    Of clerkes, for I am nat textuel:[1]
    I take but the sentence,° trusteth wel.   *meaning*
    Therefore I make protestacioun°   *public acknowledgment*
60   That I wol stonde to correccioun."
      Upon this word we han assented soone,
    For, as it seemed, it was for to doone[2]
    To enden in som vertuous sentence,°   *doctrine*
    And for to yive him space° and audience;   *time*
65   And bede[3] oure Host he sholde to him saye
    That alle we to telle his tale him praye.
      Oure Hoste hadde the wordes for us alle:
    "Sire preest," quod he, "now faire you bifalle:
    Telleth," quod he, "youre meditacioun.
70   But hasteth you; the sonne wol adown.
    Beeth fructuous,° and that in litel space,°   *fruitful/time*
    And to do wel God sende you his grace.
    Saye what you list, and we wol gladly heere."
    And with that word he saide in this manere.

---

6. Depart from truth (see 1 Timothy 1.4).
7. It pleases me.
8. I.e., I cannot tell stories in the alliterative measure (without rhyme): this form of poetry was not common in southeastern England.
9. I.e., speak in order to please.
1. Literal, faithful to the letter.
2. Necessary to be done.
3. I.e., we bade.

Chaucer's Retraction

Here taketh the makere of this book his leve[4]

Now praye I to hem alle that herkne this litel tretis[5] or rede, that if ther be any thing in it that liketh[6] hem, that therof they thanken oure Lord Jesu Crist, of whom proceedeth al wit[7] and al goodnesse. And if ther be any thing that displese hem, I praye hem also that they arrette it to the defaute of myn unconning,[8] and nat to my wil, that wolde ful fain have said bettre if I hadde had conning. For oure book saith, "Al that is writen is writen for oure doctrine,"[9] and that is myn entente. Wherfore I biseeke[1] you mekely, for the mercy of God, that ye praye for me that Crist have mercy on me and foryive me my giltes, and namely of my translacions and enditinges[2] of worldly vanitees, the whiche I revoke in my retraccions: as is the *Book of Troilus;* the Book also of *Fame;* the *Book of the Five and Twenty Ladies;*[3] the *Book of the Duchesse;* the *Book of Saint Valentines Day of the Parlement of Briddes;* the *Tales of Canterbury,* thilke that sounen into[4] sinne; the *Book of the Leon;*[5] and many another book, if they were in my remembrance, and many a song and many a leccherous lay: that Crist for his grete mercy foryive me the sinne. But of the translacion of Boece[6] *De Consolatione,* and othere bookes of legendes of saintes, and omelies,[7] and moralitee, and devocion, that thanke I oure Lord Jesu Crist and his blisful Moder and alle the saintes of hevene, biseeking hem that they from hennes[8] forth unto my lives ende sende me grace to biwaile my giltes and to studye to the salvacion of my soule, and graunte me grace of verray penitence, confession, and satisfaccion to doon in this present lif, thurgh the benigne grace of him that is king of kinges and preest over alle preestes, that boughte[9] us with the precious blood of his herte, so that I may been oon of hem at the day of doom that shulle be saved. *Qui cum patre et Spiritu Sancto vivis et regnas Deus per omnia saecula.*[1] Amen.

1386–1400

---

4. "Chaucer's Retraction" is the title given to this passage by modern editors. The heading, "*Here . . . leve,*" which does appear in all manuscripts, may be by Chaucer himself or by a scribe.
5. Hear this little treatise, i.e., *The Parson's Tale.*
6. Pleases.
7. Understanding.
8. Ascribe it to the defect of my lack of skill.
9. Romans 15.4.
1. Beseech.

2. Compositions. "Namely": especially.
3. I.e., the *Legend of Good Women.*
4. Those that tend toward.
5. The *Book of the Lion* has not been preserved.
6. Boethius.
7. Homilies.
8. Hence.
9. Redeemed.
1. Who with the Father and the Holy Spirit livest and reignest God forever.

JULIAN OF NORWICH
1342–ca.1416

The "Showings," or "Revelations" as they are also called, were sixteen mystical visions received by the woman known as Julian of Norwich. The name may be one that she adopted when she became an anchoress in a cell attached to the church of St. Julian that still stands in that town on the northeast coast of England. An anchorite (m.) or anchoress (f.) is a religious recluse confined to an enclosure, which he or she has vowed never to leave. At the time of such an enclosing the burial service was performed, signifying that the enclosed person was dead to the world and that the enclosure corresponded to a grave. The point of this confinement was, of course, to pursue more actively the contemplative or spiritual life.

Julian may well have belonged to a religious order at the time that her visions led her to choose the life of an anchoress. We know very little about her except what she tells us in her writings. She is, however, very precise about the date of her visions. They occurred, she tells us, at the age of thirty and a half on May 13, 1373. Four extant wills bequeath sums for Julian's maintenance in her anchorage. The most important document witnessing her life is *The Book of Margery Kempe*. Kempe sought out Julian's advice whether there might be any deception in Kempe's own visions, "for the anchoress," she says, "was expert in such things." Kempe's description of Julian's conversation accords well with the doctrines and personality that emerge from Julian's own book.

A Book of Showings survives in a short and a long version. The longer text, from which the following excerpts are taken, was the product of fifteen and more years of meditation on the meaning of the visions in which much had been obscure to Julian. Apparently the mystical experiences were never repeated, but through constant study and contemplation the showings acquired a greater clarity, richness, and profundity as they continued to be turned over in a mind both gifted with spiritual insight and learned in theology. Her editors document her extensive use of the Bible and her familiarity with medieval religious writings in both English and Latin.

Julian's showings are, in her words, both "ghostly" (that is, spiritual) and "bodily." They embrace powerful visual phenomena such as blood drops running from the crown of thorns and revelations that take place in pure mind. The years of meditation on these showings led her ultimately to a personal, profound, and difficult understanding of the Trinity—the one God in the three persons of the father, the son, and the Holy Spirit—and humanity's participation in that oneness. For Julian, God the father generates the human soul (conceived of as immortal "substance," co-eternal with God); God the son is the mother who bears, nourishes, and redeems (through his own incarnation) sensual human nature; God the Holy Spirit binds deity and humanity in eternal love and grace. Julian expresses such sophisticated theological concepts in language that can be intricate in its logic yet at other times transparently simple. She herself is amazed that God, who is so great and awe inspiring, can be so "homely" (so direct, intimate, and familial) with "a sinful creature." The blood of Christ reminds her of water dripping from the eaves of a house and of the scales of herring. Her concept of Jesus as mother has antecedents in both the Old and New Testaments, in medieval theology, and in the writings of medieval mystics (both men and women).

Julian is an accomplished prose stylist, inheriting a tradition of English religious prose that goes back to the Old English period. Her book is one of many distinguished devotional and mystical works, both English and Continental, composed during the late Middle Ages, such as the *Dialogue* of Catherine of Siena (translated into Middle English as *The Orchard of Syon*) or the anonymous *Cloud of Unknowing*. Julian wrote and rewrote *A Book of Showings* to come to terms with her visions, but, like other visionaries, she felt the visions were not only a personal gift but an obligation. "We are all one," she says, "and I am sure I saw it for the profit of many other."

From A Book of Showings to the Anchoress Julian of Norwich[1]

[THE FIRST REVELATION]

And when I was thirty year old and a half, God sent me a bodily sickness in the which I lay three days and three nights; and on the fourth night I took all my rites of holy church, and went[2] not to have liven till day. And after this I lay two days and two nights; and on the third night I weened[3] oftentimes to have passed, and so weened they that were with me. And yet in this I felt a great loathsomeness[4] to die, but for nothing that was on earth that me liketh to live for, ne[5] for no pain that I was afraid of, for I trusted in God of his mercy. But it was for I would have lived to have loved God better and longer time, that I might by the grace of that living have the more knowing and loving of God in the bliss of heaven. For me thought[6] all that time that I had lived here so little and so short in regard of[7] that endless bliss, I thought: Good Lord, may my living no longer be to thy worship?[8] And I understood by my reason and by the feeling of my pains that I should die; and I assented fully with all the will of my heart to be at God's will.

Thus I endured till day, and by then was my body dead from the middes downward, as to my feeling.[9] Then was I holpen[1] to be set upright, underset[2] with help, for to have the more freedom of my heart to be at God's will, and thinking on God while my life lasted. My curate was sent for to be at my ending, and before he came I had set up my eyen[3] and might not speak. He set the cross before my face and said: "I have brought the image of thy savior; look thereupon and comfort thee therewith." Me thought I was well, for my eyen was set upright into heaven, where I trusted to come by the mercy of God; but nevertheless I assented to set my eyen in the face of the crucifix, if I might, and so I did, for me thought I might longer dure to look even forth than right up.[4] After this my sight began to fail. It waxed as dark about me in the chamber as if it had been night, save in the image of the cross, wherein held a common light; and I wist[5] not how. All that was beside the cross was ugly and fearful to me as[6] it had been much occupied with fiends.

After this the over[7] part of my body began to die so farforth that unneth[8] I had any feeling. My most pain was shortness of breath and failing of life. Then went[9] I verily to have passed. And in this suddenly all my pain was taken from me, and I was as whole, and namely in the over part of my body, as ever I was before. I marvelled of this sudden change, for me thought that it was a privy working of God, and not of kind;[1] and yet by feeling of this ease I trusted never more to have lived, ne the feeling of this ease was no full ease to me, for me thought I had liever[2] have been delivered of this world, for my heart was willfully set thereto.

1. The text is based on that given by Edmund Colledge, O.S.A., and James Walsh, S. J., for the Pontifical Institute of Mediaeval Studies, Toronto (1978), but it has been freely edited and modern spelling has been used where possible.
2. Thought.
3. Supposed.
4. Reluctance.
5. Nor.
6. I thought, [it] thought me.
7. In comparison with.
8. Glory.

9. As it felt to me.
1. Helped.
2. Supported.
3. Eyes.
4. Endure to look straight ahead than straight up.
5. Knew.
6. As if.
7. Upper.
8. To the extent that scarcely.
9. Thought.
1. Nature.
2. Rather.

Then came suddenly to my mind that I should desire the second wound of our Lord's gift and of his grace, that my body might be fulfilled with mind and feeling of his blessed passion, as I had before prayed,[3] for I would that his pains were my pains, with compassion and afterward longing to God. Thus thought me that I might with his grace have the wounds that I had before desired; but in this I desired never no bodily sight ne no manner showing of God, but compassion as me thought that a kind soul might have with our Lord Jesu, that for love would become a deadly[4] man. With him I desired to suffer, living in my deadly body, as God would give me grace.

And in this suddenly I saw the red blood running down from under the garland, hot and freshly, plenteously and lively, right as it was in the time that the garland of thorns was pressed on his blessed head. Right so, both God and man, the same that suffered for me, I conceived truly and mightily that it was himself that shewed it me without any mean.[5]

And in the same showing suddenly the Trinity fulfilled my heart most of joy, and so I understood it shall be in heaven without end to all that shall come there. For the Trinity is God, God is the Trinity. The Trinity is our maker, the Trinity is our keeper, the Trinity is our everlasting lover, the Trinity is endless joy and our bliss, by our Lord Jesu Christ, and in our Lord Jesu Christ. And this was showed in the first sight and in all, for where Jesu appeareth, the blessed Trinity is understand, as to my sight.[6] And I said, "*Benedicite dominus.*"[7] This I said for reverence in my meaning,[8] with a mighty voice, and full greatly was I astoned[9] for wonder and marvel that I had, that he that is so reverend and so dreadful[1] will be so homely[2] with a sinful creature living in this wretched flesh.

* * *

In this same time that I saw this sight of the head bleeding, our good Lord showed a ghostly sight of his homely loving. I saw that he is to us all thing that is good and comfortable to our help. He is our clothing that for love wrappeth us and windeth us, halseth us[3] and all becloses us, hangeth about us for tender love that[4] he may never leave us. And so in this sight I saw that he is all thing that is good, as to my understanding.

And in this he showed a little thing, the quantity of an hazelnut, lying in the palm of my hand, as me seemed, and it was as round as a ball. I looked thereon with the eye of my understanding, and thought: What may this be? And it was answered generally thus: It is all that is made. I marvelled how it might last, for me thought it might suddenly have fallen to nought for[5] littleness. And I was answered in my understanding: It lasteth and ever shall, for God loveth it; and so hath all thing being by the love of God.

* * *

And in all that time that he showed this that I have now said in ghostly sight, I saw the bodily sight lasting of the plenteous bleeding of the head.

---

3. Julian had prayed for three gifts: direct experience of Christ's passion, mortal sickness, and the wounds of true contrition, loving compassion, and a willed desire for God.
4. Mortal.
5. Intermediary.
6. Is understood, as I see it.
7. Blessed be the Lord.

8. Intention.
9. Astonished.
1. Awe-inspiring.
2. Familiar, intimate (the quality of being "at home").
3. Envelops us and embraces us.
4. So that.
5. Because of.

The great drops of blood fell down fro under the garland like pellets, seeming as it had come out of the veins. And in the coming out they were brown red, for the blood was full thick; and in the spreading abroad they were bright red. And when it came at the brows, there they vanished; and not withstanding the bleeding continued till many things were seen and understanded. Nevertheless the fairhead and livelihead continued in the same beauty and liveliness.

The plenteoushead is like to the drops of water that fall of the evesing[6] of an house after a great shower of rain, that fall so thick that no man may number them with no bodily wit.[7] And for the roundness they were like to the scale of herring in the spreading of the forehead.

[JESUS AS MOTHER]

And thus is Jesu our very[8] mother in kind of our first making, and he is our very mother in grace by taking of our kind made. All the fair working and all the sweet kindly offices of dearworthy motherhood is impropered to[9] the second person, for in him we have this goodly will, whole and safe without end, both in kind and in grace, of his own proper goodness.

I understood three manner of beholdings of motherhood in God. The first is ground of our kind making, the second is taking of our kind, and there beginneth the motherhood of grace, the third is motherhood in working.[1] And therein is a forthspreading[2] by the same grace of length and breadth, of high and of deepness without end. And all is one love.

But now me behooveth to say a little more of this forthspreading, as I understood, in the meaning of our Lord: how that we be brought again by the motherhood of mercy and grace into our kindly stead, where that we were in,[3] made by the motherhood of kind love, which kind love never leaveth us.

Our kind mother, our gracious mother (for he would[4] all wholly become our mother in all thing) he took the ground of his work full low[5] and full mildly in the maiden's womb. And that showed he first, where he brought that meek maiden before the eye of my understanding, in the simple stature as she was when she conceived;[6] that is to say our high god, the sovereign wisdom of all, in this low place he arrayed him and dight him[7] all ready in our poor flesh, himself to do the service, he and the office of motherhood in all thing. The mother's service is nearest, readiest, and surest: nearest for it is most of kind, readiest for it is most of love, and sikerest[8] for it is most of truth. This office ne might nor could never none doon to the full but he alone. We wit[9] that all our mothers bear us to pain and to dying. Ah, what is that? But our very Mother Jesu, he alone beareth us to joy and to endless living, blessed moot[1] he be. Thus he sustaineth us within him in love and travail, into the full time that he would suffer the sharpest thorns and griev-

6. Eaves.
7. Intelligence.
8. True.
9. Appropriated to.
1. At work.
2. (Infinite) spreading out, expansion.
3. The natural condition, i.e., the state of grace, that we were in originally.
4. Because he wanted to.

5. I.e., he laid the groundwork for his mission in a very humble place.
6. The appearance of the Virgin in Julian's first vision.
7. Arrayed and dressed himself.
8. Surest.
9. Know.
1. May.

ous pains that ever were or ever shall be, and died at the last. And when he had done, and so borne us to bliss, yet might not all this make aseeth[2] to his marvelous love. And that showed he in these high overpassing words of love: "If I might suffer more I would suffer more."[3] He might no more die, but he would not stint[4] working.

Wherefore him behooveth to find[5] us, for the dearworthy love of motherhood hath made him debtor to us.[6] The mother may give her child sucken her milk, but our precious mother Jesu, he may feed us with himself, and doth full courteously and full tenderly with the blessed sacrament, that is precious food of very life; and with all the sweet sacraments he sustaineth us full mercifully and graciously, and so meant he in these blessed words, where he said: "I it am that holy church preacheth thee and teacheth thee." That is to say: All the health and the life of sacraments, all the virtue and the grace of my word, all the goodness that is ordained in holy church to thee, I it am.

The mother may lay her child tenderly to her breast, but our tender mother Jesu, he may homely lead us into his blessed breast by his sweet open side,[7] and show us therein in party of[8] the godhead and the joys of heaven with ghostly sureness of endless bliss. And that showed he in the tenth revelation, giving the same understanding in this sweet word where he sayeth: "Lo, how I love thee."

* * *

The mother may suffer the child to fall sometime and be diseased[9] in diverse manner of peril come to her child for love. And though our earthly mother may suffer her child to perish, our heavenly mother Jesu may never suffer us that be his children to perish, for he is all mighty, all wisdom, and all love, and so is none but he, blessed mote he be.

But oft times when our falling and our wretchedness is showed to us, we be so sore adread and so greatly ashamed of ourself that unnethes[1] we wit where that we may hold us. But then will not our courteous mother that we flee away, for him were nothing loather;[2] for then he will that we use[3] the condition of a child. For when it is diseased and afeared, it runneth hastily to the mother; and if it may do no more, it crieth on the mother for help with all the might. So will he that we do as the meek child, saying thus: "My kind mother, my gracious mother, my dearworthy mother, have mercy on me. I have made myself foul and unlike to thee, and I may not nor can amend it but with thine help and grace."

And if we feel us not then eased, as soon be we sure that he useth[4] the condition of a wise mother. For if he see that it be for profit to us to mourn and to weep, he suffereth with ruth[5] and pity, into the best time,[6] for love. And he will then that we use the property of a child that ever more kindly trusteth to the love of the mother in weal and in woe. And he will that we

---

2. Bring satisfaction.
3. These and other quotations refer back to Julian's earlier revelations.
4. Stop.
5. Nourish, feed.
6. As any mother is obligated to look after her child.
7. The wound inflicted by a soldier in John 19.34.

8. A part of.
9. Unhappy.
1. Scarcely.
2. Nothing would be more hateful to him.
3. He wants us to experience.
4. Right away we are sure he is practicing.
5. Compassion.
6. Until the right time.

take us mightily to the faith of holy church and find there our dearworthy mother in solace and true understanding with all the blessed common.[7] For one singular person may oftentimes be broken, as it seemeth to the self, but the whole body of holy church was never broken, nor never shall be without end. And therefore a sure thing it is, a good and a gracious, to willen meekly and mightily been fastened and oned to our mother holy church, that is Christ Jesu. For the flood of his mercy that is his dearworthy blood and precious water is plenteous to make us fair and clean. The blessed wounds of our savior be open and enjoy[8] to heal us. The sweet gracious hands of our mother be ready and diligent about us; for he in all this working useth the very office of a kind nurse that hath not else to do but to entend[9] the salvation of her child.

It is his office to save us, it is his worship to do it, and it is his will we know it; for he will we love him sweetly and trust in him meekly and mightily. And this showed he in these gracious words: "I keep thee full surely."

[CONCLUSION]

This book is begun by God's gift and his grace, but it is not yet performed,[1] as to my sight. For charity, pray we all together with God's working, thanking, trusting, enjoying, for thus will our good Lord be prayed, but the understanding that I took in all his own meaning, and in the sweet words where he sayeth full merrily: "I am ground of thy beseeching." For truly I saw and understood in our Lord's meaning that he showed it for he will have it known more than it is. In which knowing he will give us grace to love him and cleave to him, for he beheld his heavenly treasure with so great love on earth that he will give us more light, and solace in heavenly joy, in drawing of our hearts fro sorrow and darkness which we are in.

And fro the time that it was showed, I desired oftentimes to wit[2] in what was our Lord's meaning. And fifteen year after and more, I was answered in ghostly understanding, saying thus: "What, wouldst thou wit thy Lord's meaning in this thing? Wit it well, love was his meaning. Who showeth it thee? Love. What showed he thee? Love. Wherefore showeth he it thee? For love. Hold thee therein, thou shalt wit more in the same. But thou shalt never wit therein other withouten end."

Thus was I learned,[3] that love is our Lord's meaning. And I saw full surely in this and in all, that ere God made us he loved us, which love was never slaked[4] ne never shall. And in this love he hath done all his works, and in this love he hath made all things profitable to us, and in this love our life is everlasting. In our making we had beginning, but the love wherein he made us was in him fro without beginning. In which love we have our beginning, and all this shall we see in God withouten end.

Deo gracias. Explicit liber revelacionum Julyane anacorite Norwyche, cuius anime propicietur deus.[5]

ca. 1390

---

7. Community.
8. Rejoice.
9. Be busy about.
1. Completed.
2. Know.

3. Taught.
4. Abated.
5. Thanks be to God. Here ends the book of revelations of Julian, anchorite of Norwich, on whose soul may God have mercy.

MYSTERY PLAYS

The word *mystery*, as applied to medieval drama, refers to the spiritual mystery of Christ's redemption of humankind, and mystery plays are dramatizations of the Old Testament, which foretells that redemption, and of the New, which recounts it. In England the mysteries were generally composed in cycles containing as many as forty-eight individual plays: a typical cycle would begin with the Creation, continue with the Fall of Man, and proceed through the most significant events of the Old Testament, such as the Flood, to the New Testament, which provided plays on the Nativity, the chief events of Christ's life, the Crucifixion, the Harrowing of Hell (based on sources now deemed apocryphal), and the Last Judgment.

The church had its own drama in Latin, dating back to the tenth century, which developed through the dramatization and elaboration of the liturgy—the regular service—for certain holidays, the Easter morning service in particular. The vernacular drama was once thought to have evolved from the liturgical, passing by stages from the church into the streets of the town. However, even though the vernacular plays at times echo their Latin counterparts and although their authors may have been clerics, the mysteries represent an old and largely independent tradition of vernacular religious drama. As early as the twelfth century a *Play of Adam* in Anglo-Norman French was performed in England, a dramatization of the Fall with highly sophisticated dialogue, characterization, and stagecraft.

During the late fourteenth and the fifteenth centuries the great English mystery cycles, four of which have survived complete, were formed in the towns that, in spite of war and plague, became increasingly prosperous and independent. Most of our knowledge of the plays, apart from the texts themselves, comes through municipal and guild records. Every trade in urban society had its guild, an organization combining the functions of a modern trade union, club, religious society, and political action group. The guilds, which played a major role in the governance of the towns, produced the plays; each guild was responsible for putting on a traditional play during the holidays when the cycles were presented.

The town and guild documents tell us a great deal about the evolution, staging, and all aspects of the production of the cycles. In some of the towns each company had a wagon that served as a stage. The wagon would proceed from one strategic point in the city to another, and the play would be performed a number of times on the same day. The spectators gathered at any one place would never be without a play before them and might see the whole cycle without moving. In other towns, plays were probably acted out in sequence on a platform erected at a single location such as the main city square.

The cycles were performed every year at the time of one of two great early summer festivals—Whitsuntide, the week following the seventh Sunday after Easter, or Corpus Christi, a week later. They served as both religious instruction and entertainment for wide audiences, including unlearned folk like the carpenter in *The Miller's Tale* (lines 405–74), who recalls from them the trouble Noah had getting his wife aboard the ark, but also educated laypeople and clerics, who besides enjoying the sometimes boisterous comedy would find the plays acting out traditional interpretations of Scripture such as the ark as a type, or prefiguration, of the church.

Thus the cycles were public spectacles watched by every layer of society, and they paved the way for the professional theater in the age of Elizabeth I. The rainbow in *Noah's Flood* with its messages of mercy and hope, unites actors and audience in a common faith.

The Chester Play of Noah's Flood

The Chester Play of Noah's Flood The most durable of the four surviving English mystery cycles was that of Chester, which was still occasionally performed when Shakespeare was a boy and was produced for the last time in 1575. The plays, however, remained of great interest to antiquarians and were a source of municipal pride. The five surviving manuscripts are all later than the final performance. Because the cycle had been extensively revised during the sixteenth century, we cannot know what it was like during the medieval period. The text we have is certainly very late. God's lengthy instructions to Noah concerning "clean" and "unclean" beasts reflect a new, probably Protestant, interest in Jewish law, also seen in other plays of the Chester cycle. But the revisers were also concerned to preserve what they felt to be traditional medieval features and, in the case of *Noah's Flood,* to introduce such a feature when it was missing. Thus the entertaining scene in which Noah and his wife quarrel and she gives him a box on the ear is an interpolation based on an old comic tradition that is well attested in the other cycle plays and in Chaucer's *The Miller's Tale.* The Chester play is a typical example of the composite authorship so characteristic of many medieval works, by which a text, passing through many hands and generations, carries with it traces of its past that blend in a rich, although not always smooth mixture. An interesting feature of the play is its stage directions, which show how such business as the animals on the ark was managed. A few additional stage directions are provided in braces.

Noah's Flood[1]

The Waterleaders and Drawers of Dee[2]

CAST OF CHARACTERS

GOD	NOAH'S WIFE
NOAH	SHEM'S WIFE
SHEM	HAM'S WIFE
HAM	JAPHET'S WIFE
JAPHETH	GOSSIPS

And first in some high place—or in the clouds, if it may be—God speaketh to Noah, standing without the ark[3] with all his family.

GOD   I, God, that[4] all this world hath wrought,
    Heaven and earth, and all of nought,
    I see my people in deed and thought
      Are set foully° in sin.   *are mired*
5 My ghost shall not leng in mon,
    That through flesh-liking is my fon,
    But till six score years be comen and gone,
      To look if they will blin.[5]

1. The text is based on that of R. M. Lumiansky and David Mills in *The Chester Mystery Cycle* (1974), but has been freely edited. Spelling has been normalized except in some cases for the sake of rhyme and meter. Stage directions are original except for a few added in braces.
2. The guild responsible for the production of the play, the Waterleaders and Drawers, carted and sold water, a trade appropriate for the producers of Noah's flood.

3. Outside the ark. Evidently the ark is already on stage, although Noah and his family will simulate its building.
4. Who. *That* is used throughout as the relative pronoun.
5. My spirit shall remain with mankind, who through fleshly lust are my foes, only till six score [120] years be come and gone, to see if they will stop [sinning]. I.e., God allows the human race a probationary period to reform (cf. lines 149–50),

Man that I made will I destroy,

10 Beast, worm, and fowl to fly;[6]

For on earth they do me noy,°   *harm*
    The folk that are thereon.

It harmes me so hurtfully,°   *grievously*

The malice that doth now multiply,

15 That sore it grieves me inwardly
    That ever I made mon.

Therefore Noah, my servant free,°   *noble*

That righteous man art as I see,

A ship soon thou shalt make thee

20   Of trees dry and light.

Little chambers therein thou make

And binding slitch also thou take;

Within and without thou ne slake

To annoint it through all thy might.[7]

25 Three hundred cubits it shall be long

And fifty broad to make it strong;

Of height sixty. The meet thou fong;[8]
    Thus measure thou it about.

One window work through thy wit;

30 A cubit of length and breadth make it.

Upon the side a door shall shut,
    For to come in and out.

Eating-places thou make also,

Three roofed chambers on a row,[9]

35 For with water I think to flow°   *drown*
    Man that I can° make.   *did*

Destroyed all the world shall be—

Save thou, thy wife, thy sonnes three,

And their wives also with thee—

40   Shall saved be for thy sake.

NOAH   A, Lord, I thank thee loud and still[1]

That to me art in such will

And spares me and my household to spill.[2]
    As now I soothly° find.   *truly*

45 Thy bidding, Lord, I shall fulfill

Nor never more Thee grieve ne grill,°   *offend*

That such grace has sent me till°   *to me*
    Amonges all mankind.

---

probably a misunderstanding of Genesis 6.3, where God limits the human life span to 120 years. "Mon": man. In the West-Midland dialect, *a* is rounded before a nasal and rhymes with the vowel of *gone* and *on*. Both spellings *mon* and *man* occur in the manuscripts.

6. Animal, reptile, and bird flying.

7. Do not slacken to smear it [to make it water-tight], inside and out, with all your might. "Slitch": mud (for caulking).

8. Take thou the measurement.

9. May refer to three decks, but the text is obscure.

1. Aloud and silent, i.e., at all times.

2. Who are so minded toward me and refrain from destroying me and my household.

Have done, you men and women all,
50 Hie° you, lest this water fall,   *haste*
To work this ship, chamber and hall,
As God hath bidden us do.

SHEM Father, I am already boun:°   *prepared*
An ax I have, by my crown,[3]
55 As sharp as any in all this town,
For to go thereto.

HAM I have a hatchet wonder keen
To bite well, as may be seen;
A better ground,° as I ween,°   *sharpened/think*
60 Is not in all this town.

JAPHETH And I can well make a pin°   *peg*
And with this hammer knock it in.
Go we work but° more din,°   *without/fuss*
And I am ready boun.

65 NOAH'S WIFE And we shall bring timber to,°   *thereto*
For we mun° nothing else do—   *may*
Woman been weak to underfo°   *undertake*
Any great travail.°   *labor*

SHEM'S WIFE Here is a good hackestock;°   *chopping block*
70 On this you may hewe and knock,
Shall none be idle in this flock,
Ne now may no man fail.

HAM'S WIFE And I will go gather slitch,°   *pitch*
The ship for to cleam° and pitch.   *caulk*
75 Annoint° it must be every stitch—   *smeared*
Board, tree,° and pin.   *mast*

JAPHETH'S WIFE And I will gather chippes here
To make a fire for you in fere,°   *together*
And for to dighte° your dinner   *prepare*
80 Against° you come in.   *before*

[*Then they make signs as if they were working with different tools.*]

NOAH Now in the name of God I begin
To make the ship that we shall in,°   *go in*
That we may be ready for to swim°   *float*
At the coming of the flood.
85 These boards I pin here together
To bear us safe from the weather
That we may row both hither and thither
And safe be from this flood.

Of this tree will I make a mast
90 Tied with cables that will last,

---

3. By my head (an oath).

With a sail-yard° for each blast,　　　　　　　　　　*spar*
　　And each thing in their kind.
With topcastle⁴ and bowsprit,
Both cords and ropes I have all meet°　　　　　　*suitable*
95　　To sail forth at the nexte wet;°　　　　　　　　*rain*
　　This ship is at an end.

⟨Wife, in this vessel we shall be kept;
My children and thou, I would in ye leapt.⁵
NOAH'S WIFE　　In faith, Noah, I had as lief thou slept.
100　　For all thy frankish fare,
I will not do after thy rede.⁶
NOAH　　Good wife, do now as I thee bid.
NOAH'S WIFE　　By Christ, not ere I see more need,
　　Though thou stand all day and stare.

105　　NOAH　　Lord, that° women been crabbed ay,°　　*how/always*
And none are meek, I dare well say.
That is well seen by me today
　　In witness of you each one.⁷
Good wife, let be all this bear°　　　　　　　　　*behavior*
110　　That thou makest in this place here,
For all they ween° that thou art master—　　　　*think*
　　And so thou art, by Saint John.⟩

GOD　　Noah, take thou thy meinie,°　　　　　　　*household*
And in the ship hie° that ye be;　　　　　　　　*hasten*
115　　For none so righteous man to me
　　Is now on earth living.
Of clean beasts with thee thou take
Seven and seven ere then thou slake;⁸
He and she, make to make,°　　　　　　　　　　*mate with mate*
120　　Belive in that thou bring.⁹

Of beasts unclean two and two,
Male and female, but mo;°　　　　　　　　　　　*no more*
Of clean fowls seven also
　　The he and she together;
125　　Of fowls unclean, twain and no more,
　　As I of beasts said before,

4. An armed platform at the masthead. "And each thing in their kind": and each kind of thing (required).
5. I would like you to jump aboard. The behavior of Noah's Wife in the next two stanzas and in lines 193–252, both enclosed in angle brackets, is inconsistent with her cooperation and meek words in lines 65–68 and elsewhere. Nor does it make sense that Noah orders her to board the ark before God tells him to take his family inside. Stylistic evidence strongly suggests that these comic exchanges were added, probably in the early 16th century, to bring the Chester play in line with the tradition of the shrewish and recalcitrant Wife of the other mystery cycles.
6. I'd just as soon have you go to bed. In spite of your polite ("Frenchified") manner, I won't follow your direction.
7. As each one of you (i.e., in the audience) witnesses.
8. I.e., seven by seven before you leave off. See Genesis 7.2–4, where God's instructions follow Jewish dietary laws. According to Genesis 6.19–21, Noah is to take only one pair of each.
9. [See] that you bring in quickly.

That shall be saved through my lore,°   *teaching*
   Against° I send this weather.   *before*

Of meats° that may be eaten,   *foods*
130 Into the ship look they be gotten,
For that may be no way forgotten.
   And do this al bedene.°   *at once*
To sustain man and beasts therein.
Ay till the water cease and blin.°   *stop*
135 This world is filled full of sin,
   And that is now well seen.

Seven days been yet coming;°   *are yet to come*
You shall have space° them in to bring.   *time*
After that it is my liking
140   Mankind to annoy.°   *afflict*
Forty days and forty nights
Rain shall fall for their unrights,°   *sins*
And that I have made through mights[1]
   Now think I to destroy.

145 NOAH Lord, at Your bidding I am bain.°   *ready*
Sithen° no other grace will gain,°   *since / avail*
It will I fulfill fain,°   *gladly*
   For gracious I Thee find.
An hundred winters and twenty
150 This ship-making tarried° have I,   *delayed*
If through amendment Thy mercy
   Would fall to mankind.[2]

Have done, ye men and women all;
Hie you lest this water fall,
155 That each beast were in his stall
   And into the ship brought.
Of clean beastes seven shall be,
Of unclean two; thus God bade me.
The flood is nigh, you may well see;
160   Therefore tarry you nought.

[*Then* NOAH *shall go into the ark with all his family, his wife except, and the ark must be boarded[3] round about. And on the boards all the beasts and fowls hereafter rehearsed must be painted, that their words may agree with the pictures.*]

SHEM Sir, here are lions, leopards in;
Horses, mares, oxen, and swine,
Goats, calves, sheep, and kine

---

1. That [which] I have made through [my] power.   mercy (cf. lines 7–8).
2. If through reform mankind would obtain Thy   3. Supplied with boards.

Here sitten thou may see.
165 HAM　Camels, asses, man may find,
　　Buck and doe, hart and hind.
　　All beasts of all manner kind
　　　Here been, as thinketh me.

JAPHETH　Take here cattes, dogges too,
170 　Otters and foxes, fulmarts° also;　　　　　polecats
　　Hares hopping gaily can go
　　　Here have cole° for to eat.　　　　　　cabbage
NOAH'S WIFE　And here are bears, wolves set,
　　Apes, owls, marmoset,
175 　Weasels, squirrels, and ferret;
　　　Here they eat their meat.°　　　　　　food

SHEM'S WIFE　Here are beasts in this house;
　　Here cats maken it crouse;[4]
　　Here a raton,° here a mouse　　　　　　rat
180 　　That standen near together.
HAM'S WIFE　And here are fowles less and more—
　　Herons, cranes, and bittor,°　　　　　　bittern
　　Swanes, peacocks—and them before,
　　　Meat for this weather.

185 JAPHETH'S WIFE　Here are cockes, kites, crowes,
　　Rookes, ravens, many rowes,
　　Duckes, curlews, whoever knowes,
　　　Each one in this kind.
　　And here are doves, digges,° drakes,　　　ducks
190 　Redshanks running through the lakes;
　　And each fowl that leden° makes　　　　　song
　　　In this ship man may find.

⟨NOAH　Wife, come in. Why stands thou there?
　　Thou art ever froward;[5] that dare I swear.
195 　Come, in God's name! Time it were,
　　　For fear lest that we drown!
NOAH'S WIFE　Yea, sir, set up your sail
　　And row forth with evil hail;°　　　　　ill luck
　　For withouten any fail°　　　　　　　　doubt
200 　　I will not out of this town.

　　But° I have my gossips° every one,　　unless/friends
　　One foot further I will not gone.°　　　go
　　They shall not drown, by Saint John,
　　　And° I may save their life.　　　　　　if
205 　They loved me full well, by Christ.
　　But thou wilt let them into thy chist,°　　ark (chest)

4. Have a merry time.　　　　　　　5. Bold, presumptuous.

Else row forth, Noah, when thee list°   *you please*
    And get thee a new wife.

NOAH   Shem, son, lo thy mother is wrow;°   *angry*
210   By God, such another I do not know.
SHEM   Father, I shall fetch her in, I trow,°   *trust*
    Withouten any fail.
    Mother, my father after thee send
    And bids thee into yonder ship wend.°   *go*
215   Look up and see the wind,
        For we been ready to sail.

NOAH'S WIFE   Son, go again to him and say
    I will not come therein today.
NOAH   Come in, Wife, in twenty devils way,[6]
220   Or else stand there without.°   *outside*
HAM   Shall we all fetch her in?
NOAH   Yea, son, in Christ's blessing and mine,
    I would ye hied you betime,
        For of this flood I stand in doubt.[7]

Song

225   THE GOOD GOSSIPS   The flood comes fleeting in full fast,[8]
    On every side that spreadeth full far.
    For fear of drowning I am aghast;
    Good gossip, let us draw near.

    And let us drink ere we depart,
230   For oftentimes we have done so.
    For at one draught thou drink a quart,
    And so will I do ere I go.

NOAH'S WIFE   Here is a pottle of Malmsey[9] good and strong;
    It will rejoice both heart and tongue.
235   Though Noah think us never so long,
    Yet we will drink atyte.°   *at once*

JAPHETH   Mother, we pray you all together—
    For we are here, your own childer°—   *children*
    Come into the ship for fear of the weather,
240   For his love that you bought![1]
NOAH'S WIFE   That will I not for all your call
    But° I have my gossips all.   *unless*
SHEM   I° faith, mother, yet thou shall,   *in*
    Whether thou will or nought.   {*Drags her aboard.*}

6. In the name of twenty devils.
7. I want you to hurry before it's too late because
I'm afraid of the flood.
8. The flood comes flowing in very fast.

9. A sweet wine. "Pottle": two-quart measure.
1. For the love of him who redeemed you (i.e.,
Christ).

245 NOAH   Welcome, wife, into this boat.
   NOAH'S WIFE   {*slaps him*} Have thou that for thy note!°   *trouble*
   NOAH   Aha, Mary,² this is hot!
      It is good for to be still.
      Ah, children, methinks my boat removes.°   *moves off*
250   Our tarrying here me highly grieves.
      Over the land the water spreads;
         God do as He will.⟩

   [*Then they sing and* NOAH *shall speak again.*³]

   NOAH   Ah, great God that art so good,
      That° workes not thy will is wood.°   *whoever / crazy*
255   Now all this world is on a flood.
      As we see well in sight.
      The windows I will shut anon,
      And into my chamber I will gone.
      Till this water, so great one,
260   Is slaked° through Thy might.   *diminished*

   [*Then shall* NOAH *shut the window of the ark, and for a little space within
   the boards he shall be silent; and afterward opening the window and
   looking round about saying:*]

      Now forty days are fully gone.
      Send a raven I will anon,
      If aughtwhere° earth, tree, or stone   *anywhere*
         Be dry in any place.
265   And if this fowl come not again,
      It is a sign, sooth to sayn,°   *truth to say*
      That dry it is on hill or plain,
         And God hath done some grace.

   [*Then he shall send forth a raven, and taking a dove in his hands, let
   him say:*]

      Ah, Lord, wherever this raven be,
270   Somewhere is dry, well I see;
      But yet a dove, by my lewty,°   *faith*
         After I will send.
      Thou wilt turn again to me,
      For of all fowls that may fle°   *fly*
275   Thou art most meek and hend.°   *gentle*

   [*Then he shall send forth the dove; and there shall be another dove in
   the ship, bearing an olive branch in its mouth, which someone shall let*

---

2. [By] Mary (an oath).
3. The manuscripts do not indicate what song

Noah and his family sing. A song might originally
have followed after line 192.

down from the mast into NOAH's *hands with a rope; and then let* NOAH *say:*]

Ah, Lord, blessed be thou ay,
That me hast comfort° thus today.   *comforted*
By this sight I may well say
    This flood begins to cease.
280   My sweet dove to me brought has
A branch of olive from some place,
This betokeneth God has done us some grace,
    And is a sign of peace.

Ah, Lord, honored must Thou be;
285   All earth dries now I see.
But yet till thou command me,
    Hence I will not hie.
All this water is away;
Therefore, as soon as I may,
290   Sacrifice I shall do in fay°   *faith*
    To Thee devoutly.

GOD   Noah, take thy wife anon,
And thy children every one;
Out of the ship thou shalt gone,
295   And they all with thee.
Beasts and all that can fly,
Out anon they shall hie.
On earth to grow and multiply.
    I will that it so be.

300   NOAH   Lord, I thank Thee through Thy might;
Thy bidding shall be done in hight,°   *haste*
And, as fast as I may dight,°   *get ready*
    I will do Thee honor.
And to Thee offer sacrifice
305   Therefore comes in all wise,[4]
For of these beasts that been His,
    Offer I will this store.°   *great number*

[*Then, going out of the ark with his whole family he shall take his animals and birds and offer and sacrifice them.*]

Lord God in majesty,
That such grace has granted me,
310   Where all was lorn,° safe to be,   *lost*
    Therefore now am I boun,°   *ready*
My wife, my children, and my meinie,°   *household*
With sacrifice to honor Thee

---

4. Is, therefore, becoming in every way.

Of beasts, fowls, as Thou mayst see,
315   And full devotioun.

GOD   Noah, to me thou art full able°   *very worthy*
    And thy sacrifice acceptable,
    For I have found thee true and stable,
    On thee now must I min.[5]
320 Wary° earth I will no more   *curse*
    For man's sins that grieve me sore;
    For of youth man full yore
    Has been inclined to sin.[6]

    Ye shall now grow and multiply
325 And earth again to edify.°   *replenish*
    Each beast, and fowl that may fly,
       Shall be feared° of you;   *afraid*
    And fish in sea, all that may flete,°   *swim*
    Shall sustain you, I thee beheet;°   *promise*
330 To eat of them ye ne let
    That clean been you may know.[7]

    Thereas° ye have eaten before   *whereas*
    Trees and roots since ye were bore,°   *born*
    Of clean beasts now, less and more,
335   I give you leave to eat—
    Save blood and flesh both in fere.[8]
    Of wrong dead carrion that is here,
    Eat ye not of that in no manner,
    For that ay ye shall let.[9]

340 Manslaughter also ay ye shall flee,
    For that is not pleasant unto me.
    They that shed blood, he or she,
       Aughtwhere° amongst mankin,°   *anywhere / mankind*
    That blood foully shed shall be
345 And vengeance have, that men shall see.
    Therefore beware now all ye,
       Ye fall not into that sin.

    A forward,° Noah, with thee I make   *covenant*
    And all thy seed for thy sake,
350 Of such vengeance for to slake,[1]
       For now I have my will.
    Here I beheet thee an hest[2]

5. I must now be mindful of you.
6. Because for a very long time man, from his youth, has been inclined to sin.
7. Do not abstain from eating those you know to be clean (Genesis 9.1–3). The eating of meat will henceforth be permissible so long as the dietary laws are observed. "Ye": God speaks not just to Noah but to all the human race.

8. Except for blood and flesh both together (Genesis 9.4).
9. Of wrongly dead carrion (i.e., meat not killed according to dietary law), which is here, of that do not eat at all, for you must always leave that alone.
1. To give over such vengeance (as the flood).
2. Here I make you a promise.

That man, woman, fowl, ne beast,
With water while this world shall last
355   I will no more spill.°   *destroy*

My bow° between you and me   *rainbow*
In the firmament shall be
By very° tokening that you may see   *true*
    That such vengeance shall cease.
360 That man ne woman shall never more
Be wasted by water as hath before;[3]
But for sin that grieveth me sore,
    Therefore this vengeance was.

Where cloudes in the welkin° been,   *sky*
365 That ilke° bow shall be seen,   *same*
In tokening that my wrath and teen°   *anger*
    Shall never thus wroken° be.   *avenged*
The string is turned towards you,
And towards me is bent the bow,[4]
370 That such weather shall never show;[5]
    And this beheet° I thee.   *promise*

My blessing now I give thee here,
To thee, Noah, my servant dear,
For vengeance shall no more appear;
375 And now farewell, my darling dear.

3. Be destroyed by water as has happened.   from the earth at the sky.
4. The rainbow is visualized as a bow aimed away   5. [A sign] that such a flood shall never appear.

SIR THOMAS MALORY
ca. 1405–1471

Morte Darthur (Death of Arthur) is the title that William Caxton, the first English printer, gave to Malory's volume, which Caxton described more accurately in his Preface as "the noble histories of * * * King Arthur and of certain of his knights." The volume begins with the mythical story of Arthur's birth. King Uther Pendragon falls in love with the wife of one of his barons. Merlin's magic transforms Uther into the likeness of her husband, and Arthur is born of this union. The volume ends with the destruction of the Round Table and the deaths of Arthur, Queen Guinevere, and Sir Lancelot, who is Arthur's best knight and the queen's lover. The bulk of the work is taken up with the separate adventures of the knights of the Round Table.

On the evolution of the Arthurian saga, see the headnote to *Legendary Histories of Britain*, p. 94. During the thirteenth century the stories about Arthur and his knights had been turned into a series of enormously long prose romances in French, and it was these, as Caxton informed his readers, "Sir Thomas Malory did take out of certain books of French and reduced into English."

Little was known about the author until the early twentieth century when scholars began to unearth the criminal record of a Sir Thomas Malory of Newbold Revell in Warwickshire. In 1451 he was arrested for the first time to prevent his doing injury—presumably further injury—to a priory in Lincolnshire, and shortly thereafter he was accused of a number of criminal acts. These included escaping from prison after his first arrest, twice breaking into and plundering the Abbey of Coombe, extorting money from various persons, and committing rape. Malory pleaded innocent of all charges. The Wars of the Roses—in which Malory, like the formidable earl of Warwick (the "kingmaker"), whom he seems to have followed, switched sides from Lancaster to York and back again—may account for some of his troubles with the law. After a failed Lancastrian revolt, the Yorkist king, Edward IV, specifically excluded Malory from four amnesties he granted to the Lancastrians.

The identification of this Sir Thomas Malory (there is another candidate with the same name) as the author of the *Morte* was strengthened by the discovery in 1934 of a manuscript that differed from Caxton's text, the only version previously known. The manuscript contained eight separate romances. Caxton, in order to give the impression of a continuous narrative, had welded these together into twenty-one books, subdivided into short chapters with summary chapter headings. Caxton suppressed all but the last of the personal remarks the author had appended to individual tales in the manuscript. At the very end of the book Malory asks "all gentlemen and gentlewomen that readeth this book * * * pray for me while I am alive that God send me good deliverance." The discovery of the manuscript revealed that at the close of the first tale he had written: "this was drawyn by a knight presoner Sir Thomas Malleoré, that God sende him good recover." There is strong circumstantial evidence, therefore, that the book from which the Arthurian legends were passed on to future generations to be adapted in literature, art, and film was written in prison by a man whose violent career might seem at odds with the chivalric ideals he professes.

Such a contradiction—if it really is one—should not be surprising. Nostalgia for an ideal past that never truly existed is typical of much historical romance. Like the slave-owning plantation society of Margaret Mitchell's *Gone with the Wind*, whose southern gentlemen cultivate chivalrous manners and respect for gentlewomen, Malory's Arthurian world is a fiction. In our terms, it cannot even be labeled "historical," although the distinction between romance and history is not one that Malory would have made. Only rarely does he voice skepticism about the historicity of his tale; one such example is his questioning of the myth of Arthur's return. Much of the tragic power of his romance lies in his sense of the irretrievability of past glory in comparison with the sordidness of his own age.

The success of Malory's retelling owes much to his development of a terse and direct prose style, especially the naturalistic dialogue that keeps his narrative close to earth. And both he and many of his characters are masters of understatement who express themselves, in moments of great emotional tension, with a bare minimum of words.

In spite of its professed dedication to service of women, Malory's chivalry is primarily devoted to the fellowship and competitions of aristocratic men. Fighting consists mainly of single combats in tournaments, chance encounters, and battles, which Malory never tires of describing in professional detail. Commoners rarely come into view; when they do, the effect can be chilling—as when pillagers by moonlight plunder the corpses of the knights left on the field of Arthur's last battle. Above all, Malory cherishes an aristocratic male code of honor for which his favorite word is "worship." Men win or lose "worship" through their actions in war and love.

The most "worshipful" of Arthur's knights is Sir Lancelot, the "head of all Christian knights," as he is called in a moving eulogy by his brother, Sir Ector. But Lancelot is compromised by his fatal liaison with Arthur's queen and torn between the incompatible loyalties that bind him as an honorable knight, on the one hand, to his lord Arthur and, on the other, to his lady Guinevere. Malory loves his character Lancelot even to the point of indulging in the fleeting speculation, after Lancelot has been admitted to the queen's chamber, that their activities might have been innocent, "for love that time was not as love is nowadays." But when the jealousy and malice of two wicked knights forces the affair into the open, nothing can avert the breaking up of the fellowship of the Round Table and the death of Arthur himself, which Malory relates with somber magnificence as the passing of a great era.

From Morte Darthur[1]

[THE CONSPIRACY AGAINST LANCELOT AND GUINEVERE]

In May, when every lusty[2] heart flourisheth and burgeoneth, for as the season is lusty to behold and comfortable,[3] so man and woman rejoiceth and gladdeth of summer coming with his fresh flowers, for winter with his rough winds and blasts causeth lusty men and women to cower and to sit fast by the fire—so this season it befell in the month of May a great anger and unhap that stinted not[4] till the flower of chivalry of all the world was destroyed and slain. And all was long upon two unhappy[5] knights which were named Sir Agravain and Sir Mordred that were brethren unto Sir Gawain.[6] For this Sir Agravain and Sir Mordred had ever a privy[7] hate unto the Queen, Dame Guinevere, and to Sir Lancelot, and daily and nightly they ever watched upon Sir Lancelot.

So it misfortuned Sir Gawain and all his brethren were in King Arthur's chamber, and then Sir Agravain said thus openly, and not in no counsel,[8] that many knights might hear: "I marvel that we all be not ashamed both to see and to know how Sir Lancelot lieth daily and nightly by the Queen. And all we know well that it is so, and it is shamefully suffered of us all[9] that we should suffer so noble a king as King Arthur is to be shamed."

Then spoke Sir Gawain and said, "Brother, Sir Agravain, I pray you and charge you, move no such matters no more afore[1] me, for wit you well, I will not be of your counsel."[2]

"So God me help," said Sir Gaheris and Sir Gareth,[3] "we will not be known of your deeds."[4]

"Then will I!" said Sir Mordred.

"I lieve[5] you well," said Sir Gawain, "for ever unto all unhappiness, sir, ye will grant.[6] And I would that ye left all this and make you not so busy, for I know," said Sir Gawain, "what will fall of it."[7]

"Fall whatsoever fall may," said Sir Agravain, "I will disclose it to the King."

"Not by my counsel," said Sir Gawain, "for and[8] there arise war and wrack betwixt[9] Sir Lancelot and us, wit you well, brother, there will many kings and

---

1. The selections given here are from the section that Caxton called book 20, chaps. 1–4, 8–10, and book 21, chaps. 3–7, 10–12, with omissions. In the Winchester manuscript this section is titled "The Most Piteous Tale of the Morte Arthur Saunz Guerdon" (i.e., the death of Arthur without reward or compensation). The text has been based on Winchester, with some readings introduced from the Caxton edition; spelling has been modernized and modern punctuation added.
2. Merry.
3. Pleasant.
4. Misfortune that ceased not.
5. On account of two ill-fated.
6. Gawain and Agravain are sons of King Lot of Orkney and his wife, Arthur's half-sister Morgause.

Mordred is the illegitimate son of Arthur and Morgause.
7. Secret.
8. Secret manner.
9. Put up with by all of us.
1. Before. "Move": propose.
2. On your side. "Wit you well": know well, i.e., give you to understand.
3. Sons of King Lot and Gawain's brothers.
4. A party to your doings.
5. Believe.
6. You will consent to all mischief.
7. Come of it.
8. If.
9. Strife between.

great lords hold with Sir Lancelot. Also, brother, Sir Agravain," said Sir Gawain, "ye must remember how often times Sir Lancelot hath rescued the King and the Queen. And the best of us all had been full cold at the heart-root[1] had not Sir Lancelot been better than we, and that has he proved himself full oft. And as for my part," said Sir Gawain, "I will never be against Sir Lancelot for[2] one day's deed, when he rescued me from King Carados of the Dolorous Tower and slew him and saved my life. Also, brother, Sir Agravain and Sir Mordred, in like wise Sir Lancelot rescued you both and three score and two[3] from Sir Tarquin. And therefore, brother, methinks such noble deeds and kindness should be remembered."

"Do as ye list,"[4] said Sir Agravain, "for I will layne[5] it no longer."

So with these words came in Sir Arthur.

"Now, brother," said Sir Gawain, "stint your noise."[6]

"That will I not," said Sir Agravain and Sir Mordred.

"Well, will ye so?" said Sir Gawain. "Then God speed you, for I will not hear of your tales, neither be of your counsel."

"No more will I," said Sir Gaheris.

"Neither I," said Sir Gareth, "for I shall never say evil by[7] that man that made me knight." And therewithal they three departed making great dole.[8]

"Alas!" said Sir Gawain and Sir Gareth, "now is this realm wholly destroyed and mischieved,[9] and the noble fellowship of the Round Table shall be disparbeled."[1]

So they departed, and then King Arthur asked them what noise they made. "My lord," said Sir Agravain, "I shall tell you, for I may keep[2] it no longer. Here is I and my brother Sir Mordred broke[3] unto my brother Sir Gawain, Sir Gaheris, and to Sir Gareth—for this is all, to make it short—how that we know all that Sir Lancelot holdeth your queen, and hath done long; and we be your sister[4] sons, we may suffer it no longer. And all we woot[5] that ye should be above Sir Lancelot, and ye are the king that made him knight, and therefore we will prove it that he is a traitor to your person."

"If it be so," said the King, "wit[6] you well, he is none other. But I would be loath to begin such a thing but[7] I might have proofs of it, for Sir Lancelot is an hardy knight, and all ye know that he is the best knight among us all. And but if he be taken with the deed,[8] he will fight with him that bringeth up the noise, and I know no knight that is able to match him. Therefore, and[9] it be sooth as ye say, I would that he were taken with the deed."

For, as the French book saith, the King was full loath that such a noise should be upon Sir Lancelot and his queen. For the King had a deeming[1] of it, but he would not hear of it, for Sir Lancelot had done so much for him and for the Queen so many times that, wit you well, the King loved him passingly[2] well.

---

1. Would have been dead.
2. On account of.
3. I.e., sixty-two.
4. You please.
5. Conceal.
6. Stop making scandal.
7. About.
8. Lamentation.
9. Put to shame.
1. Dispersed.

2. Conceal.
3. Revealed.
4. Sister's.
5. Know.
6. Know.
7. Unless.
8. Unless he is caught in the act.
9. If.
1. Suspicion.
2. Exceedingly.

"My lord," said Sir Agravain, "ye shall ride tomorn[3] on hunting, and doubt ye not, Sir Lancelot will not go with you. And so when it draweth toward night, ye may send the Queen word that ye will lie out all that night, and so may ye send for your cooks. And then, upon pain of death, that night we shall take him with the Queen, and we shall bring him unto you, quick[4] or dead."

"I will well,"[5] said the King. "Then I counsel you to take with you sure fellowship."

"Sir," said Sir Agravain, "my brother, Sir Mordred, and I will take with us twelve knights of the Round Table."

"Beware," said King Arthur, "for I warn you, ye shall find him wight."[6]

"Let us deal!"[7] said Sir Agravain and Sir Mordred.

So on the morn King Arthur rode on hunting and sent word to the Queen that he would be out all that night. Then Sir Agravain and Sir Mordred got to them[8] twelve knights and hid themself in a chamber in the castle of Carlisle. And these were their names: Sir Colgrevance, Sir Mador de la Porte, Sir Guingalen, Sir Meliot de Logres, Sir Petipace of Winchelsea, Sir Galeron of Galway, Sir Melion de la Mountain, Sir Ascamore, Sir Gromore Somyr Jour, Sir Curselayne, Sir Florence, and Sir Lovell. So these twelve knights were with Sir Mordred and Sir Agravain, and all they were of Scotland, or else of Sir Gawain's kin, or well-willers[9] to his brother.

So when the night came, Sir Lancelot told Sir Bors[1] how he would go that night and speak with the Queen.

"Sir," said Sir Bors, "ye shall not go this night by my counsel."

"Why?" said Sir Lancelot.

"Sir," said Sir Bors, "I dread me[2] ever of Sir Agravain that waiteth upon[3] you daily to do you shame and us all. And never gave my heart against no going that ever ye went[4] to the queen so much as now, for I mistrust[5] that the King is out this night from the Queen because peradventure he hath lain[6] some watch for you and the Queen. Therefore, I dread me sore of some treason."

"Have ye no dread," said Sir Lancelot, "for I shall go and come again and make no tarrying."

"Sir," said Sir Bors, "that me repents,[7] for I dread me sore that your going this night shall wrath[8] us all."

"Fair nephew," said Sir Lancelot, "I marvel me much why ye say thus, sithen[9] the Queen hath sent for me. And wit you well, I will not be so much a coward, but she shall understand I will[1] see her good grace."

"God speed you well," said Sir Bors, "and send you sound and safe again!"

So Sir Lancelot departed and took his sword under his arm, and so he walked in his mantel,[2] that noble knight, and put himself in great jeopardy.

---

3. Tomorrow.
4. Alive.
5. Readily agree.
6. Strong.
7. Leave it to us.
8. Gathered to themselves.
9. Partisans.
1. Nephew and confidant of Sir Lancelot.
2. I am afraid.
3. Lies in wait.

4. Never misgave my heart against any visit you made.
5. Suspect.
6. Perhaps he has set.
7. I regret.
8. Cause injury to.
9. Since.
1. Wish to.
2. Cloak. Lancelot goes without armor.

And so he passed on till he came to the Queen's chamber, and so lightly he was had[3] into the chamber. And then, as the French book saith, the Queen and Sir Lancelot were together. And whether they were abed or at other manner of disports, me list[4] not thereof make no mention, for love that time[5] was not as love is nowadays.

But thus as they were together there came Sir Agravain and Sir Mordred with twelve knights with them of the Round Table, and they said with great crying and scaring[6] voice: "Thou traitor, Sir Lancelot, now are thou taken!" And thus they cried with a loud voice that all the court might hear it. And these fourteen knights all were armed at all points, as[7] they should fight in a battle.

"Alas!" said Queen Guinevere, "now are we mischieved[8] both!"

"Madam," said Sir Lancelot, "is there here any armor within your chamber that I might cover my body withal? And if there be any, give it me, and I shall soon stint[9] their malice, by the grace of God!"

"Now, truly," said the Queen, "I have none armor neither helm, shield, sword, neither spear, wherefore I dread me sore our long love is come to a mischievous end. For I hear by their noise there be many noble knights, and well I woot they be surely[1] armed, and against them ye may make no resistance. Wherefore ye are likely to be slain, and then shall I be burned! For and[2] ye might escape them," said the Queen, "I would not doubt but that ye would rescue me in what danger that ever I stood in."

"Alas!" said Sir Lancelot, "in all my life thus was I never bestead[3] that I should be thus shamefully slain for lack of mine armor."

But ever in one[4] Sir Agravain and Sir Mordred cried: "Traitor knight, come out of the Queen's chamber! For wit thou well thou art beset so that thou shalt not escape."

"Ah, Jesu mercy!" said Sir Lancelot, "this shameful cry and noise I may not suffer, for better were death at once than thus to endure this pain." Then he took the Queen in his arms and kissed her and said, "Most noblest Christian queen, I beseech you, as ye have been ever my special good lady, and I at all times your poor knight and true unto[5] my power, and as I never failed you in right nor in wrong sithen the first day King Arthur made me knight, that ye will pray for my soul if that I be slain. For well I am assured that Sir Bors, my nephew, and all the remnant of my kin, with Sir Lavain and Sir Urry,[6] that they will not fail you to rescue you from the fire. And therefore, mine own lady, recomfort yourself,[7] whatsoever come of me, that ye go with Sir Bors, my nephew, and Sir Urry and they all will do you all the pleasure that they may, and ye shall live like a queen upon my lands."

"Nay, Sir Lancelot, nay!" said the Queen. "Wit thou well that I will not live long after thy days. But and[8] ye be slain I will take my death as meekly as ever did martyr take his death for Jesu Christ's sake."

"Well, Madam," said Sir Lancelot, "sith it is so that the day is come that

---

3. Quickly he was received.
4. I care. "Disports": pastimes.
5. At that time.
6. Terrifying.
7. Completely, as if.
8. Come to grief.
9. Stop.
1. Securely.
2. If.

3. Beset.
4. In unison.
5. To the utmost of.
6. The brother of Elaine, the Fair Maid of Astolat, and a knight miraculously healed of his wound by Sir Lancelot. "Remnant": rest.
7. Take heart again.
8. If.

our love must depart,[9] wit you well I shall sell my life as dear as I may. And a thousandfold," said Sir Lancelot, "I am more heavier[1] for you than for myself! And now I had liefer[2] than to be lord of all Christendom that I had sure armor upon me, that men might speak of my deeds ere ever I were slain."

"Truly," said the Queen, "and[3] it might please God, I would that they would take me and slay me and suffer[4] you to escape."

"That shall never be," said Sir Lancelot. "God defend me from such a shame! But, Jesu Christ, be Thou my shield and mine armor!" And therewith Sir Lancelot wrapped his mantel about his arm well and surely; and by then they had gotten a great form[5] out of the hall, and therewith they all rushed at the door. "Now, fair lords," said Sir Lancelot, "leave[6] your noise and your rushing, and I shall set open this door, and then may ye do with me what it liketh you."[7]

"Come off,[8] then," said they all, "and do it, for it availeth thee not to strive against us all. And therefore let us into this chamber, and we shall save thy life until thou come to King Arthur."

Then Sir Lancelot unbarred the door, and with his left hand he held it open a little, that but one man might come in at once. And so there came striding a good knight, a much[9] man and a large, and his name was called Sir Colgrevance of Gore. And he with a sword struck at Sir Lancelot mightily. And he put aside[1] the stroke and gave him such a buffet[2] upon the helmet that he fell groveling dead within the chamber door. Then Sir Lancelot with great might drew the knight within[3] the chamber door. And then Sir Lancelot, with help of the Queen and her ladies, he was lightly[4] armed in Colgrevance's armor. And ever stood Sir Agravain and Sir Mordred, crying, "Traitor knight! Come forth out of the Queen's chamber!"

"Sirs, leave[5] your noise," said Sir Lancelot, "for wit you well, Sir Agravain, ye shall not prison me this night. And therefore, and[6] ye do by my counsel, go ye all from this chamber door and make you no such crying and such manner of slander as ye do. For I promise you by my knighthood, and ye will depart and make no more noise, I shall as tomorn appear afore you all and before the King, and then let it be seen which of you all, other else ye all,[7] that will deprove[8] me of treason. And there shall I answer you, as a knight should, that hither I came to the Queen for no manner of mal engine,[9] and that will I prove and make it good upon you with my hands."

"Fie upon thee, traitor," said Sir Agravain and Sir Mordred, "for we will have thee malgré thine head[1] and slay thee, and we list. For we let thee wit we have the choice of[2] King Arthur to save thee other slay thee."

"Ah, sirs," said Sir Lancelot, "is there none other grace with you? Then keep[3] yourself!" And then Sir Lancelot set all open the chamber door and

---

9. Come to an end.
1. More grieved.
2. Rather.
3. If.
4. Allow.
5. Bench.
6. Stop.
7. Pleases you.
8. Go ahead.
9. Big.
1. Fended off.

2. Blow.
3. Inside.
4. Quickly.
5. Stop.
6. If.
7. Or else all of you.
8. Accuse.
9. Evil design.
1. In spite of you.
2. From.
3. Defend.

mightily and knightly he strode in among them. And anon[4] at the first stroke he slew Sir Agravain, and after twelve of his fellows. Within a little while he had laid them down cold to the earth, for there was none of the twelve knights might stand Sir Lancelot one buffet.[5] And also he wounded Sir Mordred, and therewithal he fled with all his might.

And then Sir Lancelot returned again unto the Queen and said, "Madam, now wit you well, all our true love is brought to an end, for now will King Arthur ever be my foe. And therefore, Madam, and it like you[6] that I may have you with me, I shall save you from all manner adventurous[7] dangers."

"Sir, that is not best," said the Queen, "me seemeth, for[8] now ye have done so much harm, it will be best that ye hold you still with this. And if ye see that as tomorn they will put me unto death, then may ye rescue me as ye think best."

"I will well,"[9] said Sir Lancelot, "for have ye no doubt, while I am a man living I shall rescue you." And then he kissed her, and either of them gave other a ring, and so there he left the Queen and went until[1] his lodging.

[WAR BREAKS OUT BETWEEN ARTHUR AND LANCELOT][2]

Then said King Arthur unto Sir Gawain, "Dear nephew, I pray you make ready in your best armor with your brethren, Sir Gaheris and Sir Gareth, to bring my Queen to the fire, there to have her judgment and receive the death."

"Nay, my most noble king," said Sir Gawain, "that will I never do, for wit you well I will never be in that place where so noble a queen as is my lady Dame Guinevere shall take such a shameful end. For wit you well," said Sir Gawain, "my heart will not serve me for to see her die, and it shall never be said that ever I was of your counsel for her death."

"Then," said the King unto Sir Gawain, "suffer[3] your brethren Sir Gaheris and Sir Gareth to be there."

"My lord," said Sir Gawain, "wit you well they will be loath to be there present because of many adventures[4] that is like to fall, but they are young and full unable to say you nay."

Then spake Sir Gaheris and the good knight Sir Gareth unto King Arthur: "Sir, ye may well command us to be there, but wit you well it shall be sore against our will. But and[5] we be there by your straight commandment, ye shall plainly[6] hold us there excused—we will be there in peaceable wise and bear none harness of war upon us."

"In the name of God," said the King, "then make you ready, for she shall have soon[7] her judgment."

"Alas," said Sir Gawain, "that ever I should endure[8] to see this woeful day."

4. Right away.
5. Withstand Sir Lancelot one blow.
6. If it please you.
7. Perilous.
8. Because.
9. Agree.
1. To.
2. Lancelot and Sir Bors mobilize their friends for the rescue of Guinevere. In the morning Mordred reports the events of the night to Arthur who, against Gawain's strong opposition, condemns the queen to be burned, for "the law was such in those days that whatsoever they were, of what estate or degree, if they were found guilty of treason there should be none other remedy but death."
3. Allow.
4. Chance occurrences.
5. If.
6. Openly. "Straight": strict.
7. Right away.
8. Live.

So Sir Gawain turned him and wept heartily, and so he went into his chamber.

And then the Queen was led forth without[9] Carlisle, and anon she was dispoiled into[1] her smock. And then her ghostly father[2] was brought to her to be shriven of her misdeeds.[3] Then was there weeping and wailing and wringing of hands of many lords and ladies, but there were but few in comparison that would bear any armor for to strengthen[4] the death of the Queen.

Then was there one that Sir Lancelot had sent unto that place, which went to espy what time the Queen should go unto her death. And anon as[5] he saw the Queen dispoiled into her smock and shriven, then he gave Sir Lancelot warning. Then was there but spurring and plucking up[6] of horses, and right so they came unto the fire. And who[7] that stood against them, there were they slain—there might none withstand Sir Lancelot. So all that bore arms and withstood them, there were they slain, full many a noble knight. * * * And so in this rushing and hurling, as Sir Lancelot thrang[8] here and there, it misfortuned him[9] to slay Sir Gaheris and Sir Gareth, the noble knight, for they were unarmed and unwares.[1] As the French book saith, Sir Lancelot smote Sir Gaheris and Sir Gareth upon the brain-pans, wherethrough[2] that they were slain in the field, howbeit[3] Sir Lancelot saw them not. And so were they found dead among the thickest of the press.

Then when Sir Lancelot had thus done, and slain and put to flight all that would withstand him, then he rode straight unto Queen Guinevere and made a kirtle[4] and a gown to be cast upon her, and then he made her to be set behind him and prayed her to be of good cheer. Now wit you well the Queen was glad that she was escaped from death, and then she thanked God and Sir Lancelot.

And so he rode his way with the Queen, as the French book saith, unto Joyous Garde,[5] and there he kept her as a noble knight should. And many great lords and many good knights were sent him, and many full noble knights drew unto him. When they heard that King Arthur and Sir Lancelot were at debate,[6] many knights were glad, and many were sorry of their debate.

Now turn we again unto King Arthur, that when it was told him how and in what manner the Queen was taken away from the fire, and when he heard of the death of his noble knights, and in especial Sir Gaheris and Sir Gareth, then he swooned for very pure[7] sorrow. And when he awoke of his swoon, then he said: "Alas, that ever I bore crown upon my head! For now have I lost the fairest fellowship of noble knights that ever held Christian king[8] together. Alas, my good knights be slain and gone away from me. Now within these two days I have lost nigh forty knights and also the noble fellowship of Sir Lancelot and his blood,[9] for now I may nevermore hold them together with my worship.[1] Alas, that ever this war began!"

"Now, fair fellows," said the King, "I charge you that no man tell Sir

---

9. Outside.
1. Undressed down to.
2. Spiritual father, i.e., her priest.
3. For her to be confessed of her sins.
4. Secure.
5. As soon as.
6. Urging forward.
7. Whoever.
8. Pressed. "Hurling": turmoil.
9. He had the misfortune.

1. Unaware.
2. Through which.
3. Although.
4. Petticoat.
5. Lancelot's castle in England.
6. Strife.
7. Sheer.
8. That Christian king ever held.
9. Kin.
1. Glory.

Gawain of the death of his two brethren, for I am sure," said the King, "when he heareth tell that Sir Gareth is dead, he will go nigh out of his mind. Mercy Jesu," said the King, "why slew he Sir Gaheris and Sir Gareth? For I dare say, as for Sir Gareth, he loved Sir Lancelot above all men earthly."[2]

"That is truth," said some knights, "but they were slain in the hurling,[3] as Sir Lancelot thrang in the thickest of the press. And as they were unarmed, he smote them and wist[4] not whom that he smote, and so unhappily[5] they were slain."

"Well," said Arthur, "the death of them will cause the greatest mortal war that ever was, for I am sure that when Sir Gawain knoweth hereof that Sir Gareth is slain, I shall never have rest of him[6] till I have destroyed Sir Lancelot's kin and himself both, other else he to destroy me. And therefore," said the King, "wit you well, my heart was never so heavy as it is now. And much more I am sorrier for my good knights' loss[7] than for the loss of my fair queen; for queens I might have enough, but such a fellowship of good knights shall never be together in no company. And now I dare say," said King Arthur, "there was never Christian king that ever held such a fellowship together. And alas, that ever Sir Lancelot and I should be at debate. Ah, Agravain, Agravain!" said the King, "Jesu forgive it thy soul, for thine evil will that thou and thy brother Sir Mordred haddest unto Sir Lancelot hath caused all this sorrow." And ever among these complaints the King wept and swooned.

Then came there one to Sir Gawain and told him how the Queen was led away with[8] Sir Lancelot, and nigh a four-and-twenty knights slain. "Ah, Jesu, save me my two brethren!" said Sir Gawain. "For full well wist I," said Sir Gawain, "that Sir Lancelot would rescue her, other else he would die in that field. And to say the truth he were not of worship but if he had[9] rescued the Queen, insomuch as she should have been burned for his sake. And as in that," said Sir Gawain, "he hath done but knightly, and as I would have done myself and I had stood in like case. But where are my brethren?" said Sir Gawain. "I marvel that I hear not of them."

Then said that man, "Truly, Sir Gaheris and Sir Gareth be slain."

"Jesu defend!"[1] said Sir Gawain. "For all this world I would not that they were slain, and in especial my good brother Sir Gareth."

"Sir," said the man, "he is slain, and that is great pity."

"Who slew him?" said Sir Gawain.

"Sir Lancelot," said the man, "slew them both."

"That may I not believe," said Sir Gawain, "that ever he slew my good brother Sir Gareth, for I dare say my brother loved him better than me and all his brethren and the King both. Also I dare say, an[2] Sir Lancelot had desired my brother Sir Gareth with him, he would have been with him against the King and us all. And therefore I may never believe that Sir Lancelot slew my brethren."

"Verily, sir," said the man, "it is noised[3] that he slew him."

"Alas," said Sir Gawain, "now is my joy gone." And then he fell down and

---

2. Earthly men.
3. Turmoil.
4. Knew.
5. Unluckily.
6. He will never give me any peace.
7. The loss of my good knights.

8. By.
9. Of honor if he had not.
1. Forbid.
2. If.
3. Reported.

swooned, and long he lay there as he had been dead. And when he arose out of his swoon, he cried out sorrowfully and said, "Alas!" And forthwith he ran unto the King, crying and weeping, and said, "Ah, mine uncle King Arthur! My good brother Sir Gareth is slain, and so is my brother Sir Gaheris, which were two noble knights."

Then the King wept and he both, and so they fell on swooning. And when they were revived, then spake Sir Gawain and said, "Sir, I will go and see my brother Sir Gareth."

"Sir, ye may not see him," said the King, "for I caused him to be interred and Sir Gaheris both, for I well understood that ye would make overmuch sorrow, and the sight of Sir Gareth should have caused your double sorrow."

"Alas, my lord," said Sir Gawain, "how slew he my brother Sir Gareth? Mine own good lord, I pray you tell me."

"Truly," said the King, "I shall tell you as it hath been told me—Sir Lancelot slew him and Sir Gaheris both."

"Alas," said Sir Gawain, "they bore none arms against him, neither of them both."

"I woot not how it was," said the King, "but as it is said, Sir Lancelot slew them in the thickest of the press and knew them not. And therefore let us shape a remedy for to revenge their deaths."

"My king, my lord, and mine uncle," said Sir Gawain, "wit you well, now I shall make you a promise which I shall hold by my knighthood, that from this day forward I shall never fail[4] Sir Lancelot until that one of us have slain the other. And therefore I require you, my lord and king, dress[5] you unto the wars, for wit you well, I will be revenged upon Sir Lancelot; and therefore, as ye will have my service and my love, now haste you thereto and assay[6] your friends. For I promise unto God," said Sir Gawain, "for the death of my brother Sir Gareth I shall seek Sir Lancelot throughout seven kings' realms, but I shall slay him, other else he shall slay me."

"Sir, ye shall not need to seek him so far," said the King, "for as I hear say, Sir Lancelot will abide me and us all within the castle of Joyous Garde. And much people draweth unto him, as I hear say."

"That may I right well believe," said Sir Gawain, "but my lord," he said, "assay your friends and I will assay mine."

"It shall be done," said the King, "and as I suppose I shall be big[7] enough to drive him out of the biggest tower of his castle."

So then the King sent letters and writs throughout all England, both the length and the breadth, for to summon all his knights. And so unto King Arthur drew many knights, dukes, and earls, that he had a great host, and when they were assembled the King informed them how Sir Lancelot had bereft him his Queen. Then the King and all his host made them ready to lay siege about Sir Lancelot where he lay within Joyous Garde.

---

4. Give up the pursuit of.
5. Prepare.

6. Appeal to.
7. Strong.

[THE DEATH OF ARTHUR][8]

So upon Trinity Sunday at night King Arthur dreamed a wonderful dream, and in his dream him seemed that he saw upon a chafflet[9] a chair, and the chair was fast to a wheel, and thereupon sat King Arthur in the richest cloth of gold that might be made. And the King thought there was under him, far from him, an hideous deep black water, and therein was all manner of serpents, and worms, and wild beasts, foul and horrible. And suddenly the King thought that the wheel turned upside down, and he fell among the serpents, and every beast took him by a limb. And then the King cried as he lay in his bed, "Help, help!"

And then knights, squires, and yeomen awaked the King, and then he was so amazed that he wist[1] not where he was. And then so he awaked[2] until it was nigh day, and then he fell on slumbering again, not sleeping nor thoroughly waking. So the King seemed[3] verily that there came Sir Gawain unto him with a number of fair ladies with him. So when King Arthur saw him, he said, "Welcome, my sister's son. I weened ye had been dead. And now I see thee on-live, much am I beholden unto Almighty Jesu. Ah, fair nephew and my sister's son, what been these ladies that hither be come with you?"

"Sir," said Sir Gawain, "all these be ladies for whom I have foughten for when I was man living. And all these are tho[4] that I did battle for in righteous quarrels, and God hath given them that grace, at their great prayer, because I did battle for them for their right, that they should bring me hither unto you. Thus much hath given me leave God, for to warn you of your death. For and ye fight as tomorn[5] with Sir Mordred, as ye both have assigned,[6] doubt ye not ye must be slain, and the most party of your people on both parties. And for the great grace and goodness that Almighty Jesu hath unto you, and for pity of you and many mo other good men there[7] shall be slain, God hath sent me to you of his special grace to give you warning that in no wise ye do battle as tomorn, but that ye take a treatise for a month-day.[8] And proffer you largely,[9] so that tomorn ye put in a delay. For within a month shall come Sir Lancelot with all his noble knights and rescue you worshipfully and slay Sir Mordred and all that ever will hold with him."

Then Sir Gawain and all the ladies vanished. And anon the King called upon his knights, squires, and yeomen, and charged them wightly[1] to fetch his noble lords and wise bishops unto him. And when they were come the King told them of his avision,[2] that Sir Gawain had told him and warned him that, and he fought on the morn, he should be slain. Then the King commanded Sir Lucan the Butler[3] and his brother Sir Bedivere the Bold, with

8. The pope arranges a truce, Guinevere is returned to Arthur, and Lancelot and his kin leave England to become rulers of France. At Gawain's instigation Arthur invades France to resume the war against Lancelot. Word comes to the king that Mordred has seized the kingdom, and Arthur leads his forces back to England. Mordred attacks them upon their landing, and Gawain is mortally wounded and dies, although not before he has repented for having insisted that Arthur fight Lancelot and has written Lancelot to come to the aid of his former lord.
9. Scaffold. "Him seemed": it seemed to him.
1. Knew.
2. Lay awake.

3. It seemed to the king.
4. Those.
5. If you fight tomorrow.
6. Decided.
7. I.e., who there. "Mo": more.
8. For a month from today. "Treatise": treaty, truce.
9. Make generous offers.
1. Quickly.
2. Dream.
3. "Butler" here is probably only a title of high rank, although it was originally used to designate the officer who had charge of wine for the king's table.

two bishops with them, and charged them in any wise to take a treatise for a month-day with Sir Mordred. "And spare not: proffer him lands and goods as much as ye think reasonable."

So then they departed and came to Sir Mordred where he had a grim host of an hundred thousand, and there they entreated[4] Sir Mordred long time. And at the last Sir Mordred was agreed for to have Cornwall and Kent by King Arthur's days,[5] and after that, all England, after the days of King Arthur.

Then were they condescended[6] that King Arthur and Sir Mordred should meet betwixt both their hosts, and everich[7] of them should bring fourteen persons. And so they came with this word unto Arthur. Then said he, "I am glad that this is done," and so he went into the field.

And when King Arthur should depart, he warned all his host that, and they see any sword drawn, "Look ye come on fiercely and slay that traitor Sir Mordred, for I in no wise trust him." In like wise Sir Mordred warned his host that "And ye see any manner of sword drawn, look that ye come on fiercely, and so slay all that ever before you standeth, for in no wise I will not trust for this treatise." And in the same wise said Sir Mordred unto his host, "For I know well my father will be avenged upon me."

And so they met as their pointment[8] was and were agreed and accorded thoroughly. And wine was fetched and they drank together. Right so came an adder out of a little heath-bush, and it stung a knight in the foot. And so when the knight felt him so stung, he looked down and saw the adder. And anon he drew his sword to slay the adder, and thought[9] none other harm. And when the host on both parties saw that sword drawn, then they blew beams,[1] trumpets, and horns, and shouted grimly. And so both hosts dressed them[2] together. And King Arthur took his horse and said, "Alas, this unhappy day!" and so rode to his party, and Sir Mordred in like wise.

And never since was there never seen a more dolefuller battle in no Christian land, for there was but rushing and riding, foining[3] and striking; and many a grim word was there spoken of either to other, and many a deadly stroke. But ever King Arthur rode throughout the battle[4] of Sir Mordred many times and did full nobly, as a noble king should do, and at all times he fainted never. And Sir Mordred did his devoir[5] that day and put himself in great peril.

And thus they fought all the long day, and never stinted[6] till the noble knights were laid to the cold earth. And ever they fought still till it was near night, and by then was there an hundred thousand laid dead upon the down. Then was King Arthur wood-wroth[7] out of measure when he saw his people so slain from him. And so he looked about him and could see no mo[8] of all his host, and good knights left no mo on-live, but two knights: the t'one[9] was Sir Lucan the Butler and [the other] his brother Sir Bedivere. And yet they were full sore wounded.

"Jesu, mercy," said the King, "where are all my noble knights become?[1]

4. Dealt with.
5. During King Arthur's lifetime.
6. Agreed.
7. Each.
8. Arrangement.
9. Meant.
1. A kind of trumpet.
2. Prepared to come.

3. Lunging.
4. Battalion.
5. Knightly duty.
6. Stopped.
7. Mad with rage.
8. Others.
9. That one, i.e., the first.
1. What has become of all my noble knights?

Alas that ever I should see this doleful day! For now," said King Arthur, "I am come to mine end. But would to God," said he, "that I wist[2] now where were that traitor Sir Mordred that has caused all this mischief."

Then King Arthur looked about and was ware where stood Sir Mordred leaning upon his sword among a great heap of dead men.

"Now give me my spear," said King Arthur unto Sir Lucan, "for yonder I have espied the traitor that all this woe hath wrought."

"Sir, let him be," said Sir Lucan, "for he is unhappy.[3] And if ye pass this unhappy day ye shall be right well revenged upon him. And, good lord, remember ye of your night's dream, and what the spirit of Sir Gawain told you tonight, and yet God of his great goodness hath preserved you hitherto. And for God's sake, my lord, leave off by this,[4] for, blessed be God, ye have won the field: for yet we been here three on-live, and with Sir Mordred is not one on-live. And therefore if ye leave off now, this wicked day of destiny is past."

"Now, tide[5] me death, tide me life," said the King, "now I see him yonder alone, he shall never escape mine hands. For at a better avail[6] shall I never have him."

"God speed you well!" said Sir Bedivere.

Then the King got his spear in both his hands and ran toward Sir Mordred, crying and saying, "Traitor, now is thy deathday come!"

And when Sir Mordred saw King Arthur he ran until him with his sword drawn in his hand, and there King Arthur smote Sir Mordred under the shield, with a foin[7] of his spear, throughout the body more than a fathom.[8] And when Sir Mordred felt that he had his death's wound, he thrust himself with the might that he had up to the burr[9] of King Arthur's spear, and right so he smote his father King Arthur with his sword holden in both his hands, upon the side of the head, that the sword pierced the helmet and the tay[1] of the brain. And therewith Sir Mordred dashed down stark dead to the earth.

And noble King Arthur fell in a swough[2] to the earth, and there he swooned oftentimes, and Sir Lucan and Sir Bedivere ofttimes heaved him up. And so, weakly betwixt them, they led him to a little chapel not far from the seaside, and when the King was there, him thought him reasonably eased. Then heard they people cry in the field. "Now go thou, Sir Lucan," said the King, "and do me to wit[3] what betokens that noise in the field."

So Sir Lucan departed, for he was grievously wounded in many places. And so as he yede[4] he saw and harkened by the moonlight how that pillers[5] and robbers were come into the field to pill and to rob many a full noble knight of brooches and bees[6] and of many a good ring and many a rich jewel. And who that were not dead all out there they slew them for their harness[7] and their riches. When Sir Lucan understood this work, he came to the King as soon as he might and told him all what he had heard and seen. "Therefore by my read,"[8] said Sir Lucan, "it is best that we bring you to some town."

---

2. Knew.
3. I.e., unlucky for you.
4. I.e., with this much accomplished.
5. Betide.
6. Advantage.
7. Thrust.
8. I.e., six feet.
9. Hand guard.

1. Edge.
2. Swoon.
3. Let me know.
4. Walked.
5. Plunderers.
6. Bracelets.
7. Armor. "All out": entirely.
8. Advice.

"I would it were so," said the King, "but I may not stand, my head works[9] so. Ah, Sir Lancelot," said King Arthur, "this day have I sore missed thee. And alas that ever I was against thee, for now have I my death, whereof Sir Gawain me warned in my dream."

Then Sir Lucan took up the King the t'one party[1] and Sir Bedivere the other party; and in the lifting up the King swooned and in the lifting Sir Lucan fell in a swoon that part of his guts fell out of his body, and therewith the noble knight's heart burst. And when the King awoke he beheld Sir Lucan how he lay foaming at the mouth and part of his guts lay at his feet.

"Alas," said the King, "this is to me a full heavy[2] sight to see this noble duke so die for my sake, for he would have holpen[3] me that had more need of help than I. Alas that he would not complain him for[4] his heart was so set to help me. Now Jesu have mercy upon his soul."

Then Sir Bedivere wept for the death of his brother.

"Now leave this mourning and weeping, gentle knight," said the King, "for all this will not avail me. For wit thou well, and[5] I might live myself, the death of Sir Lucan would grieve me evermore. But my time passeth on fast," said the King. "Therefore," said King Arthur unto Sir Bedivere, "take thou here Excalibur[6] my good sword and go with it to yonder water's side; and when thou comest there I charge thee throw my sword in that water and come again and tell me what thou sawest there."

"My lord," said Sir Bedivere, "your commandment shall be done, and [I shall] lightly[7] bring you word again."

So Sir Bedivere departed. And by the way he beheld that noble sword, that the pommel and the haft[8] was all precious stones. And then he said to himself, "If I throw this rich sword in the water, thereof shall never come good, but harm and loss." And then Sir Bedivere hid Excalibur under a tree. And so, as soon as he might, he came again unto the King and said he had been at the water and had thrown the sword into the water.

"What saw thou there?" said the King.

"Sir," he said, "I saw nothing but waves and winds."

"That is untruly said of thee," said the King. "And therefore go thou lightly again and do my commandment; as thou art to me lief[9] and dear, spare not, but throw it in."

Then Sir Bedivere returned again and took the sword in his hand. And yet him thought[1] sin and shame to throw away that noble sword. And so eft[2] he hid the sword and returned again and told the King that he had been at the water and done his commandment.

"What sawest thou there?" said the King.

"Sir," he said, "I saw nothing but waters wap and waves wan."[3]

"Ah, traitor unto me and untrue," said King Arthur, "now hast thou betrayed me twice. Who would have weened that thou that has been to me so lief and dear, and thou art named a noble knight, and would betray me for the riches of this sword. But now go again lightly, for thy long tarrying

9. Aches.
1. On one side.
2. Sorrowful.
3. Helped.
4. Because.
5. If.
6. The sword that Arthur had received as a young man from the Lady of the Lake; it is presumably she who catches it when Bedivere finally throws it

into the water.
7. Quickly.
8. Handle. "Pommel": rounded knob on the hilt.
9. Beloved.
1. It seemed to him.
2. Again.
3. The phrase seems to mean "waters wash the shore and waves grow dark."

putteth me in great jeopardy of my life, for I have taken cold. And but if thou do now as I bid thee, if ever I may see thee I shall slay thee mine[4] own hands, for thou wouldest for my rich sword see me dead."

Then Sir Bedivere departed and went to the sword and lightly took it up, and so he went to the water's side; and there he bound the girdle[5] about the hilts, and threw the sword as far into the water as he might. And there came an arm and an hand above the water and took it and clutched it, and shook it thrice and brandished; and then vanished away the hand with the sword into the water. So Sir Bedivere came again to the King and told him what he saw.

"Alas," said the King, "help me hence, for I dread me I have tarried overlong."

Then Sir Bedivere took the King upon his back and so went with him to that water's side. And when they were at the water's side, even fast[6] by the bank hoved[7] a little barge with many fair ladies in it; and among them all was a queen; and all they had black hoods, and all they wept and shrieked when they saw King Arthur.

"Now put me into that barge," said the King; and so he did softly. And there received him three ladies with great mourning, and so they set them[8] down. And in one of their laps King Arthur laid his head, and then the queen said, "Ah, my dear brother, why have ye tarried so long from me? Alas, this wound on your head hath caught overmuch cold." And anon they rowed fromward the land, and Sir Bedivere beheld all tho ladies go froward him.

Then Sir Bedivere cried and said, "Ah, my lord Arthur, what shall become of me, now ye go from me and leave me here alone among mine enemies?"

"Comfort thyself," said the King, "and do as well as thou mayest, for in me is no trust for to trust in. For I must into the vale of Avilion[9] to heal me of my grievous wound. And if thou hear nevermore of me, pray for my soul."

But ever the queen and ladies wept and shrieked that it was pity to hear. And as soon as Sir Bedivere had lost the sight of the barge he wept and wailed and so took the forest, and went[1] all that night. And in the morning he was ware betwixt two holts hoar[2] of a chapel and an hermitage.[3]

* * *

Thus of Arthur I find no more written in books that been authorized,[4] neither more of the very certainty of his death heard I never read,[5] but thus was he led away in a ship wherein were three queens: that one was King Arthur's sister, Queen Morgan la Fée, the t'other[6] was the Queen of North Wales, and the third was the Queen of the Waste Lands. * * *

Now more of the death of King Arthur could I never find but that these ladies brought him to his burials,[7] and such one was buried there that the hermit bore witness that sometime was Bishop of Canterbury.[8] But yet the

---

4. I.e., with mine.
5. Sword belt.
6. Close.
7. Waited.
8. I.e., they sat.
9. A legendary island, sometimes identified with the earthly paradise.
1. Walked. "Took": took to.
2. Ancient copses.
3. In the passage here omitted, Sir Bedivere meets the former bishop of Canterbury, now a hermit, who describes how on the previous night a com-

pany of ladies had brought to the chapel a dead body, asking that it be buried. Sir Bedivere exclaims that the dead man must have been King Arthur and vows to spend the rest of his life there in the chapel as a hermit.
4. That have authority.
5. Tell.
6. The second.
7. Grave.
8. Of whom the hermit, who was formerly bishop of Canterbury, bore witness.

hermit knew not in certain that he was verily the body of King Arthur, for this tale Sir Bedivere, a Knight of the Table Round, made it to be written. Yet some men say in many parts of England that King Arthur is not dead, but had by the will of our Lord Jesu into another place. And men say that he shall come again and he shall win the Holy Cross. Yet I will not say that it shall be so, but rather I will say, Here in this world he changed his life. And many men say that there is written upon his tomb this verse: *Hic iacet Arthurus, rex quondam, rexque futurus.*[9]

[THE DEATHS OF LANCELOT AND GUINEVERE][1]

And thus upon a night there came a vision to Sir Lancelot and charged him, in remission[2] of his sins, to haste him unto Amesbury: "And by then[3] thou come there, thou shalt find Queen Guinevere dead. And therefore take thy fellows with thee, and purvey them of an horse-bier,[4] and fetch thou the corse[5] of her, and bury her by her husband, the noble King Arthur. So this avision[6] came to Lancelot thrice in one night. Then Sir Lancelot rose up ere day and told the hermit.

"It were well done," said the hermit, "that ye made you ready and that ye disobey not the avision."

Then Sir Lancelot took his eight fellows with him, and on foot they yede[7] from Glastonbury to Amesbury, the which is little more than thirty mile, and thither they came within two days, for they were weak and feeble to go. And when Sir Lancelot was come to Amesbury within the nunnery, Queen Guinevere died but half an hour afore. And the ladies told Sir Lancelot that Queen Guinevere told them all ere she passed that Sir Lancelot had been priest near a twelve-month:[8] "and hither he cometh as fast as he may to fetch my corse, and beside my lord King Arthur he shall bury me." Wherefore the Queen said in hearing of them all, "I beseech Almighty God that I may never have power to see Sir Lancelot with my worldly eyes."

"And thus," said all the ladies, "was ever her prayer these two days till she was dead."

Then Sir Lancelot saw her visage, but he wept not greatly, but sighed. And so he did all the observance of the service himself, both the *dirige*[9] and on the morn he sang mass. And there was ordained[1] an horse-bier, and so with an hundred torches ever burning about the corse of the Queen, and ever Sir Lancelot with his eight fellows went about[2] the horse-bier, singing and reading many an holy orison,[3] and frankincense upon the corse incensed.[4]

Thus Sir Lancelot and his eight fellows went on foot from Amesbury unto Glastonbury, and when they were come to the chapel and the hermitage, there she had a *dirige* with great devotion.[5] And on the morn the hermit that

---

9. "Here lies Arthur, who was once king and king will be again."
1. Guinevere enters a convent at Amesbury where Lancelot, returned with his companions to England, visits her, but she commands him never to see her again. Emulating her example, Lancelot joins the bishop of Canterbury and Bedivere in their hermitage where he takes holy orders and is joined in turn by seven of his fellow knights.
2. For the remission.
3. By the time.

4. Provide them with a horse-drawn hearse.
5. Body.
6. Dream.
7. Went.
8. Nearly twelve months.
9. Funeral service.
1. Prepared.
2. Around.
3. Reciting many a prayer.
4. Burned frankincense over the body.
5. Solemnity.

sometime[6] was Bishop of Canterbury sang the mass of requiem with great devotion, and Sir Lancelot was the first that offered, and then als[7] his eight fellows. And then she was wrapped in cered cloth of Rennes, from the top[8] to the toe, in thirtyfold, and after she was put in a web[9] of lead, and then in a coffin of marble.

And when she was put in the earth Sir Lancelot swooned and lay long still, while[1] the hermit came and awaked him, and said, "Ye be to blame, for ye displease God with such manner of sorrow-making."

"Truly," said Sir Lancelot, "I trust I do not displease God, for He knoweth mine intent—for my sorrow was not, nor is not, for any rejoicing of sin, but my sorrow may never have end. For when I remember of her beaulté and of her noblesse[2] that was both with her king and with her,[3] so when I saw his corse and her corse so lie together, truly mine heart would not serve to sustain my careful[4] body. Also when I remember me how by my defaute and mine orgule[5] and my pride that they were both laid full low, that were peerless that ever was living of Christian people, wit you well," said Sir Lancelot, "this remembered, of their kindness and mine unkindness, sank so to mine heart that I might not sustain myself." So the French book maketh mention.

Then Sir Lancelot never after ate but little meat,[6] nor drank, till he was dead, for then he sickened more and more and dried and dwined[7] away. For the Bishop nor none of his fellows might not make him to eat, and little he drank, that he was waxen by a kibbet[8] shorter than he was, that the people could not know him. For evermore, day and night, he prayed, but sometime he slumbered a broken sleep. Ever he was lying groveling on the tomb of King Arthur and Queen Guinevere, and there was no comfort that the Bishop nor Sir Bors, nor none of his fellows could make him—it availed not.

So within six weeks after, Sir Lancelot fell sick and lay in his bed. And then he sent for the Bishop that there was hermit, and all his true fellows. Then Sir Lancelot said with dreary steven,[9] "Sir Bishop, I pray you give to me all my rights that longeth[1] to a Christian man."

"It shall not need you,"[2] said the hermit and all his fellows. "It is but heaviness of your blood. Ye shall be well mended by the grace of God tomorn."

"My fair lords," said Sir Lancelot, "wit you well my careful body will into the earth; I have warning more than now I will say. Therefore give me my rights."

So when he was houseled and annealed[3] and had all that a Christian man ought to have, he prayed the Bishop that his fellows might bear his body to Joyous Garde. (Some men say it was Alnwick, and some men say it was Bamborough.) "Howbeit," said Sir Lancelot, "me repenteth[4] sore, but I made mine avow sometime that in Joyous Garde I would be buried. And because

---

6. Once.
7. Also. "Offered": made his donation.
8. Head. "Cloth of Rennes": A shroud made of fine linen smeared with wax, produced at Rennes.
9. Afterward she was put in a sheet.
1. Until.
2. Her beauty and nobility.
3. That she and her king both had.
4. Sorrowful.

5. My fault and my haughtiness.
6. Food.
7. Wasted.
8. Grown by a cubit.
9. Sad voice.
1. Pertains. "Rights": last sacrament.
2. You shall not need it.
3. Given communion and extreme unction.
4. I am sorry.

of breaking[5] of mine avow, I pray you all, lead me thither." Then there was weeping and wringing of hands among his fellows.

So at a season of the night they all went to their beds, for they all lay in one chamber. And so after midnight, against[6] day, the Bishop that was hermit, as he lay in his bed asleep, he fell upon a great laughter. And therewith all the fellowship awoke and came to the Bishop and asked him what he ailed.[7]

"Ah, Jesu mercy," said the Bishop, "why did ye awake me? I was never in all my life so merry and so well at ease."

"Wherefore?" said Sir Bors.

"Truly," said the Bishop, "here was Sir Lancelot with me, with mo[8] angels than ever I saw men in one day. And I saw the angels heave[9] up Sir Lancelot unto heaven, and the gates of heaven opened against him."

"It is but dretching of swevens,"[1] said Sir Bors, "for I doubt not Sir Lancelot aileth nothing but good."[2]

"It may well be," said the Bishop. "Go ye to his bed and then shall ye prove the sooth."

So when Sir Bors and his fellows came to his bed, they found him stark dead. And he lay as he had smiled, and the sweetest savor[3] about him that ever they felt. Then was there weeping and wringing of hands, and the greatest dole they made that ever made men. And on the morn the Bishop did his mass of Requiem, and after the Bishop and all the nine knights put Sir Lancelot in the same horse-bier that Queen Guinevere was laid in tofore that she was buried. And so the Bishop and they all together went with the body of Sir Lancelot daily, till they came to Joyous Garde. And ever they had an hundred torches burning about him.

And so within fifteen days they came to Joyous Garde. And there they laid his corse in the body of the choir,[4] and sang and read many psalters[5] and prayers over him and about him. And ever his visage was laid open and naked, that all folks might behold him; for such was the custom in tho[6] days that all men of worship should so lie with open visage till that they were buried.

And right thus as they were at their service, there came Sir Ector de Maris that had seven year sought all England, Scotland, and Wales, seeking his brother, Sir Lancelot. And when Sir Ector heard such noise and light in the choir of Joyous Garde, he alight and put his horse from him and came into the choir. And there he saw men sing and weep, and all they knew Sir Ector, but he knew not them. Then went Sir Bors unto Sir Ector and told him how there lay his brother, Sir Lancelot, dead. And then Sir Ector threw his shield, sword, and helm from him, and when he beheld Sir Lancelot's visage, he fell down in a swoon. And when he waked, it were hard any tongue to tell the doleful complaints that he made for his brother.

"Ah, Lancelot!" he said, "thou were head of all Christian knights. And now I dare say," said Sir Ector, "thou Sir Lancelot, there thou liest, that thou were never matched of earthly knight's hand. And thou were the courteoust[7]

---

5. In order not to break.
6. Toward.
7. Ailed him.
8. More.
9. Lift.
1. Illusion of dreams.
2. Has nothing wrong with him.

3. Odor. A sweet scent is a conventional sign in saints' lives of a sanctified death.
4. The center of the chancel, the place of honor.
5. Psalms.
6. Those.
7. Most courteous.

knight that ever bore shield. And thou were the truest friend to thy lover that ever bestrode horse, and thou were the truest lover, of a sinful man,[8] that ever loved woman, and thou were the kindest man that ever struck with sword. And thou were the goodliest person that ever came among press of knights, and thou was the meekest man and the gentlest that ever ate in hall among ladies, and thou were the sternest knight to thy mortal foe that ever put spear in the rest."[9]

Then there was weeping and dolor out of measure.

Thus they kept Sir Lancelot's corse aloft fifteen days, and then they buried it with great devotion. And then at leisure they went all with the Bishop of Canterbury to his hermitage, and there they were together more than a month.

Then Sir Constantine that was Sir Cador's son of Cornwall was chosen king of England, and he was a full noble knight, and worshipfully he ruled this realm. And then this King Constantine sent for the Bishop of Canterbury, for he heard say where he was. And so he was restored unto his bishopric and left that hermitage, and Sir Bedivere was there ever still hermit to his life's end.

Then Sir Bors de Ganis, Sir Ector de Maris, Sir Gahalantine, Sir Galihud, Sir Galihodin, Sir Blamour, Sir Bleoberis, Sir Villiars le Valiant, Sir Clarrus of Clermount, all these knights drew them to their countries. Howbeit[1] King Constantine would have had them with him, but they would not abide in this realm. And there they all lived in their countries as holy men.

And some English books make mention that they went never out of England after the death of Sir Lancelot—but that was but favor of makers.[2] For the French book maketh mention—and is authorized—that Sir Bors, Sir Ector, Sir Blamour, and Sir Bleoberis went into the Holy Land, theras Jesu Christ was quick[3] and dead, and anon as they had stablished their lands;[4] for the book saith so Sir Lancelot commanded them for to do ere ever he passed out of this world. There these four knights did many battles upon the miscreaunts,[5] or Turks, and there they died upon a Good Friday for God's sake.

Here is the end of the whole book of King Arthur and of his noble knights of the Round Table, that when they were whole together there was ever an hundred and forty. And here is the end of *The Death of Arthur*.[6]

I pray you all gentlemen and gentlewomen that readeth this book of Arthur and his knights from the beginning to the ending, pray for me while I am alive that God send me good deliverance. And when I am dead, I pray you all pray for my soul.

For this book was ended the ninth year of the reign of King Edward the Fourth, by Sir Thomas Malory, knight, as Jesu help him for His great might, as he is the servant of Jesu both day and night.

1469–70   1485

---

8. Of any man born in original sin.
9. Support for the butt of the lance.
1. However.
2. The authors' bias.
3. Living. "Theras": where.
4. As soon as they had put their lands in order.

5. Infidels.
6. By the "whole book" Malory refers to the entire work; the *Death of Arthur*, which Caxton made the title of the entire work, refers to the last part of Malory's book.

The Sixteenth Century
1485–1603

At the beginning of the sixteenth century, the English language had almost no prestige abroad, and there were those at home who doubted that it could serve as a suitable medium for serious, elevated, or elegant discourse. Yet by the century's end there were signs of a great increase in what we might call linguistic self-confidence, signs that at least some contemporary observers were aware that something extraordinary had happened to their language. Though in 1600 England still remained somewhat peripheral to the Continent, English had been fashioned into an immensely powerful expressive medium, one whose cadences in the works of Marlowe, Shakespeare, or the translators of the Bible continue after more than four centuries to thrill readers.

How did it come about that by the century's end so many remarkable poems, plays, and prose works were written in English? The answer lies in part in the spectacular creativity of a succession of brilliant writers, the best of whom are represented in these pages. Still, a vital literary culture is the product of a complex process, involving thousands of more modest, half-hidden creative acts sparked by a wide range of motives, some of which we will briefly explore.

THE COURT AND THE CITY

The development of the English language in the sixteenth century is linked at least indirectly to the consolidation and strengthening of the English state. Preoccupied by violent clashes between the thuggish feudal retainers of rival barons, England through most of the fifteenth century had rather limited time and inclination to cultivate rhetorical skills. The social and economic health of the nation had been severely damaged by the so-called Wars of the Roses, a vicious, decades-long struggle for royal power between the noble houses of York and Lancaster. The struggle was resolved with the establishment by Henry VII of the Tudor dynasty that ruled England from 1485 to 1603. The wily Henry was able to counter the multiple and competing power structures characteristic of feudal society and to impose a much stronger central authority and order on the nation. Initiated by the first Tudor sovereign, this consolidation progressed throughout the sixteenth century; by the reign of the last Tudor—Henry's granddaughter, Elizabeth I—though the ruler still needed the consent of Parliament on crucial matters (including the all-important one of raising taxes), the royal court had concentrated in itself much of the nation's power.

The court was a center of culture as well as power: court entertainments such as theater and masque (a sumptuous, elaborately costumed performance of dance, song, and poetry); court fashions in dress and speech; court tastes in painting, music, and poetry—all shaped the taste and the imagination of the country as a whole. Culture and power were not, in any case, easily separable in Tudor England. In a society with no freedom of speech as we understand it and with relatively limited means of mass communication, important public issues were often aired indirectly, through what we might now regard as entertainment, while lyrics that to us seem slight and nonchalant could serve as carefully crafted manifestations of rhetorical agility by aspiring courtiers.

Court culture simultaneously spawned an art of intrigue and one of ostentation. Ambitious men and women sought to call attention to themselves. They did so by the gorgeous, immensely costly clothes they wore—Elizabethan high fashion was among the most extravagantly ornamented in European history—and by the display of their artistic and social skills. The goal was close proximity to the monarch's body (one of the coveted positions in the court of Henry VIII was Groom of the Stool, "close stool" being the Tudor term for toilet). But if proximity held out the promise of wealth and power, it also harbored danger. Festive evenings with the likes of the ruthless Henry VIII were not occasions for relaxation. The court fostered paranoia and an attendant obsession with secrecy, spying, duplicity, and betrayal. Courtiers were highly gifted at crafting and deciphering graceful words with double or triple meanings. Sixteenth-century poets had much to learn from courtiers, the Elizabethan critic George Puttenham observed; indeed many of the best poets in the period, Sir Thomas Wyatt, Sir Philip Sidney, Sir Walter Ralegh, and others, *were* courtiers.

If court culture fostered performances for a small coterie audience, other forces in Tudor England pulled toward a more public sphere. Markets expanded significantly, international trade flourished, and cities throughout the realm experienced a rapid surge in size and importance. London's population in particular soared, from 60,000 in 1520 to 120,000 in 1550 to 375,000 a century later, making it the largest and fastest-growing city not only in England but in all of Europe. Every year in the first half of the seventeenth century about 10,000 people migrated to London from other parts of England—wages in London tended to be around 50 percent higher than in the rest of the country—and it is estimated that one in eight English people lived in London at some point in their lives.

About a decade before Henry VII won his throne, the art of printing from movable metal type, a German invention, had been introduced into England by William Caxton (ca. 1422–1491), who had learned and practiced it in the Low Countries. Though reliable statistics are impossible to come by, literacy seems to have increased during the fifteenth century and still more during the sixteenth, when Protestantism encouraged a direct encounter with the Bible. Printing made books cheaper and more plentiful, providing more opportunity to read and more incentive to learn. The greater availability of books may also have reinforced the trend toward silent reading, a trend that gradually transformed what had been a communal experience into a more intimate encounter with a text.

Yet it would be a mistake to imagine these changes as sudden and dramatic. Manuscripts retained considerable prestige among the elite; throughout the sixteenth and well into the seventeenth centuries court poets in particular were wary of the "stigma of print" that might mark their verse as less exclusive.

RENAISSANCE HUMANISM

During the fifteenth century a few English clerics and government officials had journeyed to Italy and had seen something of the extraordinary cultural and intellectual movement flourishing in the city-states there. That movement, generally known as the Renaissance, involved a rebirth of letters and arts stimulated by the recovery of texts and artifacts from classical antiquity, the development of techniques such as linear perspective, and the creation of powerful new aesthetic norms based on classical models. It also unleashed new ideas and new social, political, and economic forces that gradually displaced the otherworldly and communal values of the Middle Ages. In the brilliant, intensely competitive, and vital world of Leonardo da Vinci and Michelangelo, the submission of the human spirit to penitential discipline gave way to unleashed curiosity, individual self-assertion, and a powerful conviction that man was the measure of all things. "We have made thee neither of heaven nor of earth, neither mortal nor immortal," God tells Adam, in the Florentine Pico della Mirandola's *Oration on the Dignity of Man* (1486), "so that with freedom of choice and with honor, as though the maker and molder of thyself, thou mayest fashion thyself in whatever shape thou shalt prefer." "As though the maker and molder of thyself": this vision of self-fashioning may be glimpsed in the poetry of Petrarch, the sculpture of Donatello, and the statecraft of Lorenzo de' Medici. But in England it was not until Henry VII's reign brought some measure of political stability that the Renaissance could take root, and it was not until the accession of Henry VIII that it began to flower.

This flowering, when it occurred, came not, as in Italy, in the visual arts and architecture. It came rather in the spiritual and intellectual orientation known as humanism. In England and elsewhere, humanism was bound up with struggles over the purposes of education and curriculum reform. Education—predominantly male and conducted by tutors in wealthy families or in grammar schools—was ordered according to the subjects of the medieval *trivium* (grammar, logic, and rhetoric) and *quadrivium* (arithmetic, geometry, astronomy, and music), but humanists helped to shift its focus from training for the church to the general acquisition of "literature," in the sense both of literacy and of cultural knowledge. For some of the more intellectually ambitious humanists, that knowledge extended to ancient Greek, whose enthusiastic adherents began to challenge the entrenched prestige of Latin.

Still, at the core of the curriculum remained the study of Latin, the mastery of which was in effect a prolonged male puberty rite involving pain as well as pleasure. Though some educators counseled mildness, punishment was an established part of the pedagogy of the age, and even gifted students could scarcely have escaped recurrent flogging. The purpose was to train the sons of the nobility and gentry to speak and write good Latin, the language of diplomacy, of the professions, and of all higher learning. Their sisters were always educated at home or in other noble houses. They chiefly learned modern languages, religion, music, and needlework, but they very seldom received the firm grounding in ancient languages and classical literature so central to Renaissance culture.

Humanists committed to classical learning were faced with the question of whether to write their own works in Latin or in English. To many learned men, influenced both by the humanist exaltation of the classical languages and by the characteristic Renaissance desire for eternal fame, the national languages seemed relatively unstable and ephemeral. Intellectuals had long shared a pan-European world of scientific inquiry, so that works by such English scientists as William Gilbert, William Harvey, and Francis Bacon easily joined those by Nicolaus Copernicus, Johannes Kepler, and Andreas Vesalius on the common linguistic ground of Latin. But throughout Europe nationalism and the expansion of the reading public were steadily strengthening the power and allure of the vernacular. The famous schoolmaster Richard Mulcaster (ca. 1530–1611), teacher of the poet Edmund Spenser, captured this emergent sense of national identity in singing the praises of his native tongue: "I love Rome, but London better; I favor Italy, but England more; I honor the Latin, but I worship the English."

THE REFORMATION

There had long been serious ideological and institutional tensions in the religious life of England, but officially at least England in the early sixteenth century had a single religion, Catholicism, whose acknowledged head was the pope in Rome. For its faithful adherents the Catholic church was the central institution in their lives, a universal infallible guide to human existence from cradle to grave and on into the life to come. They were instructed by its teachings, corrected by its discipline, sustained by its sacraments, and comforted by its promises. At Mass, its most sacred ritual, the congregation could witness a miracle, as the priest held aloft the Host and uttered the words that transformed the bread and wine into the body and blood of God incarnate. A vast system of confession, pardons, penance, absolution, indulgences, sacred relics, and ceremonies gave the unmarried male clerical hierarchy great power, at once spiritual and material, over their largely illiterate flock. The Bible, the liturgy, and most of the theological discussions were in Latin, which few lay people could understand; however, religious doctrine and spirituality were mediated to them by the priests, by beautiful church art and music, and by the liturgical ceremonies of daily life—festivals, holy days, baptisms, marriages, exorcisms, and funerals.

Several of the key doctrines and practices of the Catholic church had been challenged in fourteenth-century England by the teachings of John Wycliffe and his followers, known as the Lollards. But the heretical challenge had been ruthlessly suppressed, and the embers of dissent lay largely dormant until they were ignited once again in Germany by Martin Luther, an Augustinian monk and professor of theology at the University of Wittenberg. What began in November 1517 as an academic disputation grew with amazing speed into a bitter, far-reaching, and bloody revolt that forever ruptured the unity of Western Christendom.

When Luther rose up against the ancient church, he did so in the name of private conscience enlightened by a personal reading of the Scriptures. A person of formidable intellectual energy, eloquence, and rhetorical violence, Luther charged that the pope and his hierarchy were the servants of Satan and that the church had degenerated into a corrupt, worldly conspiracy designed to bilk the credulous and subvert secular authority. Salvation depended upon destroying this conspiracy and enabling all of the people to regain direct access to the word of God by means of vernacular translations of the Bible. The common watchwords of the Reformation, as the movement Luther sparked came to be known, were *sola scriptura* and *sola fide*: only the Scriptures (not the church or tradition or the clerical hierarchy) have authority in matters of religion and should determine what an individual must believe and practice; only the faith of the individual (not good works or the scrupulous observance of religious rituals) can effect a Christian's salvation.

These tenets, heretical in the eyes of the Catholic Church, spread and gathered force, especially in Northern Europe, where major leaders like the Swiss pastor Ulrich Zwingli in Zurich and the French theologian John Calvin in Geneva, elaborating various and sometimes conflicting doctrinal principles, organized the populace to overturn the existing church and established new institutional structures. In England, however, the Reformation began less with popular discontent and theological disputation than with dynastic politics and royal greed. Henry VIII, who had received from Pope Leo X the title Defender of the Faith for writing a book against Luther, craved a legitimate son to succeed to the throne, and his queen, Catherine of Aragon, failed to give him one. (Catherine had borne six children, but only a daughter, Mary, survived infancy.) After lengthy negotiations, the pope, under pressure from Catherine's powerful Spanish family, refused to grant the king the divorce he sought in order to marry Anne Boleyn. A series of momentous events followed, as England lurched away from the Church of Rome. In 1531 Henry charged the entire clergy of England with having usurped royal authority in the administration of canon law (the law that governed such matters as divorce). Under extreme pressure, including the threat of mass confiscations and imprisonment, the Convocation of the Clergy begged for pardon and made a donation to the royal coffers of over one hundred thousand pounds.

In 1533 Henry's marriage to Catherine was officially declared null and void and Anne Boleyn was crowned queen. The king was promptly excommunicated by the pope, Clement VII. In the following year, a parliamentary

Act of Succession required an oath from all adult male subjects confirming the new dynastic settlement. Thomas More, the distinguished humanist and former chancellor, and John Fisher, the bishop of Rochester, were among the small number who refused. The Act of Supremacy, passed later in the year, formally declared the king to be "Supreme Head of the Church in England" and again required an oath to this effect. In 1535 and 1536 further acts made it treasonous to refuse the oath of royal supremacy or, as More had tried to do, to remain silent. The first victims were three Carthusian monks who rejected the oath—"How could the king, a layman," said one of them, "be Head of the Church of England?"—and in May 1535 were duly hanged, drawn, and quartered. A few weeks later Fisher and More were convicted and beheaded. Between 1536 and 1539, under the direction of Henry's powerful secretary of state, Thomas Cromwell, England's monasteries were suppressed and their vast wealth seized by the crown.

Royal defiance of the authority of Rome was a key element in the Reformation but did not by itself constitute the establishment of Protestantism in England. On the contrary, in the same year that Fisher and More were martyred for their adherence to Roman Catholicism, twenty-five Protestants, members of a sect known as Anabaptists, were burned for heresy on a single day. Through most of his reign, Henry remained an equal-opportunity persecutor, pitiless to Catholics loyal to Rome and hostile to many of those who espoused Reformation ideas, though these ideas gradually established themselves on English soil.

Even when Henry (in his brief stint as Defender of the Faith) was eager to do so, it proved impossible to eradicate Protestantism, as it would later prove impossible for Protestant monarchs to eradicate Catholicism. In part this persistence in the face of ferocious persecution arose from the willingness of a small core of ardent believers to die for their faith; in part it arose from the ability of even a small number of clandestine printing presses to flood the country with texts that the authorities were unable to suppress. Hence in his role as Defender of the Faith, Henry had driven the great English translator of the Bible, William Tyndale, into exile on the Continent, where he was eventually seized and garroted by Catholic authorities. But Tyndale's eloquent—and distinctly Protestant—translation of the New Testament circulated widely in England, despite repeated attempts by officials to burn every copy. After Henry's break with Rome, Tyndale's version served as the core of the so-called Great Bible, the authorized translation that made the Scriptures available in English to anyone who could read.

Upon Henry's death in 1547, his son, Edward (by his third wife, Jane Seymour), came to the throne, with his maternal uncle, Edward Seymour, the duke of Somerset, as Lord Protector. Both the ten-year-old Edward and his uncle were staunch Protestants, and reformers hastened to transform the English church accordingly. During Edward's brief reign, Thomas Cranmer, the archbishop of Canterbury, formulated the forty-two articles of religion which became the core of Anglican orthodoxy and wrote the first *Book of Common Prayer*, which was officially adopted in 1549 as the basis of English worship services.

The sickly Edward died in 1553, only six years after his accession to the throne, and was succeeded by his half-sister Mary (Henry VIII's daughter by his first wife, Catherine), who immediately took steps to return her kingdom to Roman Catholicism. Though she was unable to get Parliament to agree to return church lands seized under Henry VIII, she restored the Catholic Mass, once again affirmed the authority of the pope, and put down a rebellion that sought to depose her. Seconded by her ardently Catholic husband, Philip II, king of Spain, she initiated a series of religious persecutions that earned her (from her enemies) the name Bloody Mary. Hundreds of Protestants took refuge abroad in cities like Calvin's Geneva; almost three hundred less fortunate Protestants were condemned as heretics and burned at the stake.

Mary died childless in 1558, and her younger half-sister, Elizabeth, became queen. Elizabeth's succession had been by no means assured. For if Protestants regarded Henry VIII's marriage to Catherine as invalid and hence deemed Mary illegitimate, so Catholics regarded his marriage to Anne Boleyn as invalid and hence deemed her daughter, Elizabeth, illegitimate. Henry VIII himself seemed to support both views, since only three years after divorcing Catherine, he beheaded Anne on charges of treason and adultery and urged Parliament to invalidate the marriage. Moreover, though during her sister's reign Elizabeth outwardly complied with the official Catholic religious observance, Mary and her advisers suspected her of Protestant leanings, and the young princess's life was in grave danger. Poised and circumspect, Elizabeth warily evaded the traps that were set for her. When she ascended the throne, her actions were scrutinized for some indication of the country's future course. During her coronation procession, when a girl in an allegorical pageant presented her with a Bible in English translation—banned under Mary's reign—Elizabeth kissed the book, held it up reverently, and laid it to her breast. England had returned to the Reformation.

Many English men and women, of all classes, remained loyal to the old Catholic faith, but English authorities under Elizabeth moved steadily, if cautiously, toward ensuring at least an outward conformity to the official Protestant settlement. Recusants, those who refused to attend regular Sunday services in their parish churches, were heavily fined. Anyone who wished to receive a university degree, to be ordained as a priest in the Church of England, or to be named as an officer of the state had to swear an oath to the royal supremacy. Commissioners were sent throughout the land to confirm that religious services were following the officially approved liturgy and to investigate any reported backsliding into Catholic practice or, alternatively, any attempts to introduce reforms more radical than the queen and her bishops had chosen to embrace, for the Protestant exiles who streamed back were eager not only to undo the damage Mary had done but also to carry the Reformation much further than it had gone. They sought to dismantle the church hierarchy, to purge the calendar of folk customs deemed pagan and the church service of ritual practices deemed superstitious, to dress the clergy in simple garb, and, at the extreme edge, to smash "idolatrous" statues, crucifixes, and altarpieces. Throughout her long reign, however, Elizabeth herself remained cautiously conservative and determined to hold religious zealotry in check.

In the space of a single lifetime, England had gone officially from Roman Catholicism, to Catholicism under the supreme headship of the English king, to a guarded Protestantism, to a more radical Protestantism, to a renewed and aggressive Roman Catholicism, and finally to Protestantism again. Each of these shifts was accompanied by danger, persecution, and death. It was enough to make people wary. Or skeptical. Or extremely agile.

THE ENGLISH AND OTHERNESS

Elizabethan London had a large population of resident aliens, mainly artisans and merchants and their families, from Portugal, Italy, Spain, Germany, and, above all, France and the Netherlands. Many of these people were Protestant refugees, and they were accorded some legal and economic protection by the government. But they were not always welcome to the local populace. Throughout the sixteenth century London was the site of repeated demonstrations and, on occasion, bloody riots against the communities of foreign artisans, who were accused of taking jobs away from Englishmen. There was widespread hostility as well toward the Welsh, the Scots, and above all the Irish, whom the English had for centuries been struggling unsuccessfully to subdue. The kings of England claimed to be rulers of Ireland, but in reality they effectively controlled only a small area known as the Pale, extending north from Dublin. The great majority of the population remained stubbornly Catholic and, despite endlessly reiterated English repression, burning of villages, destruction of crops, seizure of land, and massacres, incorrigibly independent.

Medieval England's Jewish population, the recurrent object of persecution, extortion, and massacre, had been officially expelled by King Edward I in 1290, but Elizabethan England harbored a tiny number of Jews or Jewish converts to Christianity. They were the objects of suspicion and hostility. Elizabethans appear to have been fascinated by Jews and Judaism but quite uncertain whether the terms referred to a people, a foreign nation, a set of strange practices, a living faith, a defunct religion, a villainous conspiracy, or a messianic inheritance. Protestant Reformers brooded deeply on the Hebraic origins of Christianity; government officials ordered the arrest of those "suspected to be Jews"; villagers paid pennies to itinerant fortunetellers who claimed to be descended from Abraham or masters of kabbalistic mysteries; and London playgoers enjoyed the spectacle of the downfall of the wicked Barabas in Christopher Marlowe's *The Jew of Malta* and the forced conversion of Shylock in Shakespeare's *The Merchant of Venice*. Jews were not officially permitted to resettle in England until the middle of the seventeenth century, and even then their legal status was ambiguous.

Sixteenth-century England also had a small African population whose skin color was the subject of pseudoscientific speculation and theological debate. Some Elizabethans believed that Africans' blackness resulted from the climate of the regions where they lived, where, as one traveler put it, they were "so scorched and vexed with the heat of the sun, that in many places they curse it when it riseth." Others held that blackness was a curse inherited from their forefather Cush, the son of Ham (who had, according to Genesis, wickedly exposed the nakedness of his drunken father, Noah). George Best, a proponent of this theory of inherited skin color, reported that "I myself have seen an Ethiopian as black as coal brought into England, who taking a fair English woman to wife, begat a son in all respects as black as the father was, although England were his native country, and an English woman his mother: whereby it seemeth this blackness proceedeth rather of some natural infection of that man."

As the word "infection" suggests, Elizabethans frequently regarded blackness as a physical defect, though the black people who lived in England and Scotland throughout the sixteenth century were also treated as exotic curiosities. At his marriage to Anne of Denmark, James VI of Scotland (the son of Mary, Queen of Scots; as James I of England, he succeeded Elizabeth in 1603) entertained his bride and her family by commanding four naked black youths to dance before him in the snow. (The youths died of exposure shortly afterward.) In 1594, in the festivities celebrating the baptism of James's son, a "Black-Moor" entered pulling an elaborately decorated chariot that was, in the original plan, supposed to be pulled by a lion. In England there was a black trumpeter in the courts of Henry VII and Henry VIII, while Elizabeth had at least two black servants, one an entertainer, the other a page. Africans became increasingly popular as servants in aristocratic and gentle households in the last decades of the sixteenth century.

Some of these Africans were almost certainly slaves, though the legal status of slavery in England was ambiguous. In Cartwright's Case (1569), the court ruled "that England was too Pure an Air for Slaves to breathe in," but there is evidence that black slaves were owned in Elizabethan and Jacobean England. Moreover, by the mid-sixteenth century the English had become involved in the profitable trade that carried African slaves to the New World. In 1562 John Hawkins embarked on his first slaving voyage, transporting some three hundred Africans from the Guinea coast to Hispaniola, where they were sold for ten thousand pounds. Elizabeth is reported to have said of this venture that it was "detestable, and would call down the Vengeance of Heaven upon the Undertakers." Nevertheless, she invested in Hawkins's subsequent voyages and loaned him ships.

Elizabeth also invested in other enterprises that combined aggressive nationalism and the pursuit of profit. In 1493 the pope had divided the New World between the Spanish and the Portuguese by drawing a line from pole to pole (hence Brazil speaks Portuguese today and the rest of Latin America speaks Spanish): the English were not in the picture. But by the end of Edward VI's reign the Company of Merchant Adventurers was founded, and Englishmen began to explore Asia and North America. Some of these adventurers turned to piracy, preying on Spanish ships that were returning laden with wealth extracted from their New World possessions. (The pope had ruled that the Indians were human beings—and hence could be converted to Christianity—but the ruling did nothing to prevent their enslavement and brutal exploitation.) English acts of piracy soon became a private undeclared war, with the queen and her courtiers covertly investing in the raids but accepting no responsibility for them. The greatest of many astounding exploits was the voyage of Francis Drake (1577–80): he sailed through the Strait of Magellan, pillaged Spanish towns on the Pacific, reached as far north as San Francisco, crossed to the Philippines, and returned around the Cape of Good Hope; he came back with a million pounds in treasure, and his investors earned a dividend of 5,000 percent. Queen Elizabeth knighted him on the deck of his ship, *The Golden Hind*.

A FEMALE MONARCH IN A MALE WORLD

In the last year of Mary's reign, the Scottish Calvinist minister John Knox thundered against what he called "the monstrous regiment of women." After the Protestant Elizabeth came to the throne the following year, Knox and his religious brethren were less inclined to denounce all female rulers, but in England, as elsewhere in Europe, there remained a widespread conviction that women were unsuited to wield power over men. Many men seem to have regarded the capacity for rational thought as exclusively male; women, they assumed, were led only by their passions. While gentlemen mastered the arts of rhetoric and warfare, gentlewomen were expected to display the virtues of silence and good housekeeping. Among upper-class males, the will to dominate others was acceptable and indeed admired; the same will in women was condemned as a grotesque and dangerous aberration.

Apologists for the queen countered these prejudices by appealing to historical precedent and legal theory. History offered inspiring examples of just female rulers, notably Deborah, the biblical prophetess who had judged Israel. In the legal sphere, crown lawyers advanced the theory of "the king's two bodies." As England's crowned head, Elizabeth's person was mystically divided between her mortal "body natural" and the immortal "body politic." While the queen's natural body was inevitably subject to the failings of human flesh, the body politic was timeless and perfect. In political terms, therefore, Elizabeth's sex was a matter of no consequence, a thing indifferent.

Elizabeth, who had received a fine humanist education and an extended, dangerous lesson in the art of survival, made it immediately clear that she intended to rule in more than name only. Like many Renaissance monarchs, Elizabeth was drawn to the idea of royal absolutism, the theory that ultimate power was quite properly concentrated in her person and indeed that God had appointed her to be His deputy in the kingdom. In reality, Elizabeth's power was not absolute. The government had a network of spies, informers and *agents provocateurs*, but it lacked a standing army, a national police force, an efficient system of communication, and an extensive bureaucracy. Above all, the queen had limited financial resources and needed to turn periodically to an independent and often recalcitrant Parliament, which by long tradition had the sole right to levy taxes and to grant subsidies. Members of the House of Commons were elected from their boroughs, not appointed by the monarch, and though the queen had considerable influence over their decisions, she could by no means dictate policy. Under these constraints, Elizabeth ruled through a combination of adroit political maneuvering and imperious command, all the while enhancing her authority in the eyes of both court and country by means of an extraordinary cult of love.

"We all loved her," Elizabeth's godson Sir John Harington wrote, with just a touch of irony, a few years after the queen's death, "for she said she loved us." Ambassadors, courtiers, and parliamentarians all submitted to Elizabeth's cult of love, in which the queen's gender was transformed from a potential liability into a significant asset. Those who approached her generally did so on their knees and were expected to address her with the most extravagant compliments; she in turn spoke, when it suited her to do so, in a comparable language of love. The court moved in an atmosphere of romance, with music, dancing, plays, and the elaborate, fancy-dress entertainments called masques. The queen adorned herself in dazzling clothes and rich jewels. When she went on one of her summer "progresses," ceremonial journeys through her land, she looked like an exotic, sacred image in a religious cult of love, and her noble hosts virtually bankrupted themselves to lavish upon her the costliest pleasures. England's leading artists, such as the poet Spenser and the painter Nicholas Hilliard, enlisted themselves in the celebration of Elizabeth's mystery, likening her to the goddesses of mythology and the heroines of the Bible: Diana, Astraea, Cynthia, Deborah.

There was a sober, even grim aspect to these poetical fantasies: Elizabeth was brilliant at playing one dangerous faction off against another, now turning her gracious smiles on one favorite, now honoring his hated rival, now suddenly looking elsewhere and raising an obscure upstart to royal favor. And when she was disobeyed or when she felt that her prerogatives had been challenged, she was capable of an anger that, as Harington put it, "left no doubtings whose daughter she was." Thus when Sir Walter Ralegh, one of the queen's glittering favorites, married without her knowledge or consent, he found himself promptly imprisoned in the Tower of London. Or when the Protestant polemicist John Stubbs ventured to publish a pamphlet stridently denouncing the queen's proposed marriage to the French Catholic duke of Anjou, Stubbs and his publisher were arrested and had their right hands chopped off. (After receiving the blow, the now prudent Stubbs lifted his hat with his remaining hand and cried, "God save the Queen!")

The queen's marriage negotiations were a particularly fraught issue. When she came to the throne at twenty-five, speculation about a suitable match, already widespread, intensified and remained for decades at a fever pitch, for the stakes were high. If Elizabeth died childless, the Tudor line would come to an end. The nearest heir was her cousin Mary, Queen of Scots, a Catholic whose claim was supported by France and by the papacy and whose penchant for sexual and political intrigue confirmed the worst fears of English Protestants. The obvious way to avert the nightmare was for Elizabeth to marry and produce an heir, and the pressure upon her to do so was intense.

More than the royal succession hinged on the question of the queen's marriage; Elizabeth's perceived eligibility was a vital factor in the complex machinations of international diplomacy. A dynastic marriage between the queen of England and a foreign ruler would forge an alliance sufficient to alter the balance of power in Europe. The English court hosted a steady stream of ambassadors from kings and princelings eager to win the hand of the royal maiden, and Elizabeth, who prided herself on speaking fluent French and Italian (and on reading Latin and Greek), played her romantic part with exemplary skill, sighing and spinning the negotiations out for months and even years. Most probably, she never meant to marry any of her numerous foreign (and domestic) suitors. Such a decisive act would have meant the end of her independence, as well as the end of the marriage game by which she played one power off against another. One day she would seem to be on the verge of accepting a proposal; the next, she would vow never to forsake her virginity. "She is a princess," the French ambassador remarked, "who can act any part she pleases."

THE KINGDOM IN DANGER

Beset by Catholic and Protestant extremists, Elizabeth contrived to forge a moderate compromise that enabled her realm to avert the massacres and civil wars that poisoned France and other countries on the Continent. But menace was never far off, and there were continual fears of conspiracy, rebellion, and assassination. Many of the fears swirled around Mary, Queen of Scots, who had been driven from her own kingdom in 1567 and had taken refuge in England. Her presence, under a kind of house arrest, was the source of intense anxiety and helped generate continual rumors of plots, some of them real enough, others imaginary, still others fabricated by the secret agents of the government's intelligence service under the direction of Sir Francis Walsingham.

The queen's life seemed to be in great danger after Pope Gregory XIII's proclamation in 1580 that the assassination of the great heretic Elizabeth (who had been excommunicated a decade before) would not constitute a mortal sin. The immediate effect of the proclamation was to make life more difficult for English Catholics, most of whom were loyal to the queen but who fell under grave suspicion. Suspicion was intensified by the clandestine presence of English Jesuits, trained at seminaries abroad and smuggled back into England to serve the Roman Catholic cause. When, after several botched conspiracies had been disclosed, Elizabeth's spymaster Walsingham unearthed another assassination plot in the correspondence between the Queen of Scots and the Catholic Anthony Babington, the wretched Mary's fate was sealed. After vacillating, a very reluctant Elizabeth signed the death warrant, and her cousin was beheaded.

The long-anticipated military confrontation with Catholic Spain was now unavoidable. Elizabeth learned that Philip II, her former brother-in-law and one-time suitor, was preparing to send an enormous fleet against her island realm. The Armada was to sail to the Netherlands, where a Spanish army would be waiting to embark and invade England. Barring its way was England's small fleet of well-armed and highly maneuverable fighting vessels, backed up by ships from the merchant navy. The Invincible Armada reached English waters in July 1588, only to be routed in one of the most famous and decisive naval battles in European history. Then, in what many viewed as an Act of God on behalf of Protestant England, the Spanish fleet was dispersed and all but destroyed by violent storms.

As England braced itself to withstand the invasion that never came, Elizabeth appeared in person to review a detachment of soldiers assembled at Tilbury. Dressed in a white gown and a silver breastplate, she declared that though some among her councillors had urged her not to appear before a large crowd of armed men, she would never fail to trust the loyalty of her faithful and loving subjects. Nor did she fear the Spanish armies. "I know I have the body but of a weak and feeble woman," Elizabeth declared, "but I have the heart and stomach [i.e., valor] of a king, and of a king of England too." In this celebrated speech, Elizabeth displayed many of her most memorable qualities: her self-consciously theatrical command of grand public occasion, her subtle blending of magniloquent rhetoric and the language of love, her strategic appropriation of traditionally masculine qualities, and her great personal courage. "We princes," she once remarked, "are set on stages in the sight and view of all the world."

WRITERS, PRINTERS, AND PATRONS

The career of professional writer in sixteenth-century England was almost impossible: there was no such thing as author's copyright, no royalties paid to an author according to the sales of his book, and virtually no notion that anyone could make a decent living through the creation of works of literature. Writers sold their manuscripts to the printer or bookseller outright, for what now seem like ridiculously low prices. Freedom of the press did not exist. Writers and printers were supposed to abide by stringent government regulations. The political, judicial, and ecclesiastical authorities that enforced these regulations could mete out severe punishments for breaches of censorship and other infractions: fines, interrogation, imprisonment; even branding, mutilation, and execution. Not surprisingly, therefore, literary texts sometimes bear traces of self-censorship and often deploy strategies of indirection designed to evade official scrutiny. It was potentially dangerous to put pen to paper and so unprofitable that it is a wonder that any serious original writing was published at all.

Fortunately, the system of state censorship was inefficient, and many men and women of the sixteenth century had a passionate determination to make themselves heard. The *Short-Title Catalogue* of the Bibliographical Society, which lists works published in English between 1475 and 1640, includes more than 26,000 items, and that is an incomplete list. To these we must add the many manuscripts in which poems and other literary texts were circulated, especially those by authors of higher rank, and the commonplace books in which people jotted down poems and prose passages they considered worth keeping.

Elizabethan writers of exalted social standing, like the earl of Surrey or Sir Philip Sidney, thought of themselves as courtiers, statesmen, and landowners; poetry was for them an indispensable social grace and a deeply pleasurable, exalted form of play. Writers of lower rank sought careers as civil servants, secretaries, tutors, and clerics; they might take up more or less permanent residence in a noble household, or, more casually, offer their literary work to actual or prospective patrons, in the hope of protection, career advancement, or financial reward. Remuneration for writing prose or poetry came mostly in the form of gifts from wealthy patrons, who sought to enhance their status and gratify their vanity through the achievements and lavish praises of their clients. Some Elizabethan patrons, though, were well-educated humanists motivated by aesthetic interests, and with them, patronage extended beyond financial support to the creation of lively literary and intellectual circles.

In addition to the court and the great families as dispensers of patronage, the city of London and the two universities also had a substantial impact on the period's literature. London was the center of the book trade, the nursery of a fledgling middle-class reading public, and, most important, the home of the public theaters. Before Elizabeth's time, the universities were mainly devoted to educating the clergy, and that remained an important part of their function. But in the second half of the century, the sons of the gentry and the aristocracy were going in increasing numbers to the universities and the Inns of Court (law schools), not in order to take religious orders or to practice law but to prepare for public service or the management of their estates. Other, less affluent students, such as Marlowe and Spenser, attended Oxford and Cambridge on scholarship. A group of graduates, including Thomas Nashe, enlivened the literary scene in London in the 1590s, but the precarious lives of these so-called "university wits" testify to the difficulties they encountered in their quixotic attempt to survive by their writing skill. The diary of Philip Henslowe, a leading theatrical manager, has entry after entry showing university graduates in prison or in debt or at best eking out a miserable existence patching plays.

Women had no access to grammar schools, the universities, or the Inns of Court and, when not altogether illiterate, received for the most part only a rudimentary education. While Protestantism, with its emphasis on reading Scripture, certainly helped to improve female literacy in the sixteenth century, girls were rarely encouraged to pursue their studies. Indeed, while girls were increasingly taught to read, they were not necessarily taught to write, for the latter skill in women was considered to be at the very least useless, at the worst dangerous. When the prominent humanist Sir Thomas Smith thinks of how he should describe his country's social order, he declares that "we do reject women, as those whom nature hath made to keep home and to nourish their family and children, and not to meddle with matters abroad, nor to bear office in a city or commonwealth." Then, with a kind of nervous glance over his shoulder, he makes an exception of those few in whom "the blood is respected, not the age nor the sex": for example, the queen. Every piece of writing by a woman from this period is a triumph over nearly impossible odds.

TUDOR STYLE: ORNAMENT, PLAINNESS, AND WONDER

Renaissance literature is the product of a rhetorical culture, a culture steeped in the arts of persuasion and trained to process complex verbal signals. (The contemporary equivalent would be the ease with which we deal with complex visual signals, effortlessly processing such devices as fade-out, montage, crosscutting, and morphing.) In 1512, Erasmus published a work called *De copia* that taught its readers how to cultivate "copiousness," verbal richness, in discourse. The work obligingly provides, as a sample, a list of 144 different ways of saying "Thank you for your letter."

In Renaissance England, certain syntactic forms of patterns of words known as "figures" (also called "schemes") were shaped and repeated in order to confer beauty or heighten expressive power. Figures were usually known by their Greek and Latin names, though in an Elizabethan rhetorical manual, *The Arte of English Poesie*, George Puttenham made a valiant if short-lived attempt to give them English equivalents, such as "Hyperbole, or the Overreacher," "Ironia, or the Dry Mock," and "Ploce, or the Doubler." Those who received a grammar-school education throughout Europe at almost any point between the Roman Empire and the eighteenth century probably knew by heart the names of up to one hundred such figures, just as they knew by heart their multiplication tables. According to one scholar's count, William Shakespeare knew and made use of about two hundred.

As certain grotesquely inflated Renaissance texts attest, lessons from *De copia* and similar rhetorical guides could encourage prolixity and verbal self-display. Elizabethans had a taste for elaborate ornament in language as in clothing, jewelry, and furniture, and, if we are to appreciate their accomplishments, it helps to set aside the modern preference, particularly in prose, for unadorned simplicity and directness. When, in one of the age's most fashionable works of prose fiction, John Lyly wishes to explain that the vices of his young hero, Euphues, are tarnishing his virtues, he offers a small flood of synonymous images: "The freshest colors soonest fade, the teenest [i.e., keenest] razor soonest turneth his edge, the finest cloth is soonest eaten with moths." The euphistic multiplication of figures was soon ridiculed by Shakespeare and others, but its pleasure is deeply rooted in rhetorical culture, and most of the greatest Renaissance writers used to it extraordinary effect. Consider, for example, the succession of images in Shakespeare's sonnet 73:

> That time of year thou mayst in me behold
> When yellow leaves, or none, or few, do hang
> Upon those boughs which shake against the cold,
> Bare ruined choirs, where late the sweet birds sang.
> In me thou seest the twilight of such day
> As after sunset fadeth in the west;
> Which by and by black night doth take away,
> Death's second self that seals up all in rest.
> In me thou seest the glowing of such fire
> That on the ashes of his youth doth lie,
> As the deathbed whereon it must expire,
> Consumed with that which it was nourished by.
> This thou perceiv'st, which makes thy love more strong,
> To love that well, which thou must leave ere long.

What seems merely repetitious in Lyly here becomes a subtle, poignant amplification of the perception of decay, through the succession of images from winter (or late fall) to twilight to the last glow of a dying fire. Each of these images is in turn sensitively explored, so that, for example, the season is figured by bare boughs that shiver, as if they were human, and then these anthropomorphized tree branches in turn are figured as the ruined choirs of a church where services were once sung. No sooner is the image of singers in a church choir evoked than these singers are instantaneously transmuted back into the songbirds who, in an earlier season, had sat upon the boughs, while these sweet birds in turn conjure up the poet's own vanished youth. And this nostalgic gaze extends, at least glancingly, to the chancels of the Catholic abbeys reduced to ruins by Protestant iconoclasm and the dissolution of the monasteries. All of this within the first four lines: here and elsewhere Shakespeare, along with other poets of his time, contrives to freight the small compass and tight formal constraints of the sonnet—fourteen lines of iambic pentameter in three principal rhyming patterns—with remarkable emotional intensity, psychological nuance, and imagistic complexity. The effect is what Christopher Marlowe called "infinite riches in a little room."

Elizabethans were certainly capable of admiring plainness of speech, and such poets as Thomas Nashe and, in the early seventeenth century, Ben Jonson wrote restrained, aphoristic, moralizing lyrics in a plain style whose power depends precisely on the avoidance of richly figurative verbal pyrotechnics. This power is readily apparent in the wintry spareness of Nashe's *A Litany in Time of Plague*, with its grim refrain:

> Wit with his wantonness
> Tasteth death's bitterness;
> Hell's executioner
> Hath no ears for to hear
> What vain art can reply.
> I am sick, I must die.
> Lord, have mercy on us!

Here the linguistic playfulness beloved by Elizabethan culture is scorned as an ineffectual "vain art" to which the executioner, death, is utterly indifferent.

But here and in other plain-style poetry, the somber, lapidary effect depends on a tacit recognition of the allure of the suppleness, grace, and sweet harmony that the dominant literary artists of the period so assiduously cultivated. Many sixteenth-century poems were written to be set to music, but even those that were not often aspire in their metrical and syllabic virtuosity to the complex pleasures of madrigals or to the sweet fluency of airs. In poetry and music, as in gardens, architecture and dance, Elizabethans had a taste for elaborate, intricate, but perfectly regular designs. They admired form, valued the artist's manifest control of the medium, and took pleasure in the highly patterned surfaces of things. Suspicion of surfaces, impatience with order, the desire to rip away the mask in order to discover a hidden core of experiential truth: these responses to art, highly characteristic of later periods, are far less in evidence in Renaissance aesthetics than is a delight in pattern.

Such an emphasis on conspicuous pattern might seem to encourage an art as stiff as the starched ruffs that ladies and gentlemen wore around their necks, but the period's fascination with order was conjoined with a profound interest in persuasively conveying the movements of the mind and heart. Syntax in the sixteenth century was looser, more flexible than our own and punctuation less systematic. If the effect is sometimes confusing, it also enabled writers confidently to follow the twists and turns of thought or perception. Such confidence emanates from Sir Walter Ralegh's deeply melancholy, deeply ironic apostrophe to Death at the close of *The History of the World*, written when he was a prisoner in the Tower:

> O eloquent, just, and mighty Death! Whom none could advise, thou hast persuaded; what none hath dared, thou hast done; and whom all the world hath flattered, thou only hast cast out of the world and despised; thou hast drawn together all the far-stretched greatness, all the pride, cruelty, and ambition of man, and covered it all over with these two narrow words: *Hic jacet!* [Here lies]

Death is triumphant here, but so is Ralegh's eloquent, just, and mighty language.

The power of *wonder* that animates much Elizabethan prose—as if the world were being seen clearly and distinctly for the first time—characterizes much of the period's poetry as well. In his *Defense of Poesy*, the most important work of literary criticism in sixteenth-century England, Sidney claims that this power is also a moral power. All other arts, he argues, are subjected to fallen, imperfect nature, but the poet alone is free to range "within the zodiac of his own wit" and create a second nature, superior to the one we are condemned to inhabit: "Her world is brazen, the poets only deliver a golden." The poet's golden world in this account is not an escapist fantasy; it is a model to be emulated in actual life, an ideal to be brought into reality as completely as possible. It is difficult to say, of course, how seriously this project of realization was taken—though the circumstances of Sidney's own death suggest that he may have been attempting to enact on the battlefield an ideal image of Protestant chivalry. A didactic role for poetry is, in any case, urged not by Sidney alone but by most Elizabethan poets. Human sinfulness has corrupted life, robbing it of the sweet wholesomeness that it had once possessed in Eden, but poetry can mark the way back to a more virtuous and fulfilled existence. And not only mark the way: poetry, Sidney and others argue, has a unique persuasive force that shatters inertia and impels readers toward the good they glimpse in its ravishing lines.

This force, attributed to the energy and vividness of figurative language, made poetry a fitting instrument not only for such high-minded enterprises as moral exhortation, prayer, and praise, and for such uplifting narratives as the legends of religious and national heroes, but also for such verbal actions as cursing, lamenting, flattering, and seducing. The almost inexhaustible range of motives was given some order by literary conventions that functioned as shared cultural codes, enabling poets to elicit particular responses from readers and to relate their words to other times, other languages, and other cultures. We can glimpse a few of the ways in which these literary codes worked by looking briefly at the two that are, for modern readers, the least familiar: pastoral and heroic.

The conventions of the pastoral mode present a world inhabited by shepherds and shepherdesses who are chiefly concerned to tend their flocks, fall in love, and engage in friendly singing contests. The mode celebrated leisure, humility, and contentment, exalting the simple country life over the city and its business, the military camp and its violence, the court and its burdens of rule. Pastoral motifs could be deployed in different genres. Pastoral songs commonly expressed the joys of the shepherd's life or disappointment in love. Pastoral dialogues between shepherds might conceal serious, satiric comment on abuses in the great world under the guise of homely, local concerns. There were pastoral funeral elegies, pastoral dramas, pastoral romances (prose fiction), and even pastoral episodes within epics. Probably the most famous pastoral poem of the period is Marlowe's *The Passionate Shepherd to His Love*, an erotic invitation whose promise of gold buckles, coral clasps, and amber studs serves to remind us that, however much it sings of naïve innocence, the mode is ineradicably sophisticated and urban.

With its rustic characters, simple concerns, and modest scope, the pastoral mode was regarded as situated at the opposite extreme from heroic, with its values of honor, martial courage, loyalty, leadership, and endurance and its glorification of a nation or people. The chief genre here was the epic, typically a long, exalted poem in the high style, based on a heroic story from the nation's distant past and imitating Homer and Virgil in structure and motifs. Renaissance poets throughout Europe undertook to honor their nations and their vernacular languages by writing this most prestigious kind of poetry. In sixteenth-century England the major success in heroic poetry is Spenser's *Faerie Queene*, properly speaking, a romantic epic in that it draws more heavily on the romance conventions employed by the great Italian poets Ariosto and Tasso—tangled, episodic plots, exotic adventures and marvels, and a fundamental concern with love as well as war—than on the classical epics. To these basic elements Spenser also conjoins medieval allegory, pastoral, satire, mythological narrative, comedy, philosophical meditation, and many other literary conventions in a strange, wonderful blend. The spectacular mixing of genres in Spenser's poem is only an extreme instance of a general Elizabethan indifference to the generic purity admired by writers, principally on the Continent, who adhered to Aristotle's *Poetics*. Where such neoclassicists attempted to observe rigid stylistic boundaries, English poets tended to approach the different genres in the spirit of Sidney's inclusivism: "if severed they be good, the conjunction cannot be hurtful."

THE ELIZABETHAN THEATER

If Sidney welcomed the experimental intertwining of genres in both poetry and prose—and his own *Arcadia*, a prose romance incorporating both pastoral and heroic elements, confirms that he did—there was one place where he found it absurd: the theater. He condemned the conjunction of high and low characters in "mongrel" tragicomedies that mingled "kings and clowns." Moreover, in the spirit of neoclassical advocacy of the "dramatic unities," Sidney disliked the ease with which the action on the bare stage ("where you shall have Asia of the one side, and Afric of the other") violated the laws of time and space. "Now you shall have three ladies walk to gather flowers," he writes in *The Defense of Poesy*, "and then we must believe the stage to be a garden. By and by we hear news of shipwreck in the same place: and then we are to blame if we accept it not for a rock." The irony is that this mocking account, written probably in 1579, anticipates by a few years the stupendous achievements of Marlowe and Shakespeare, whose plays joyously break every rule that Sidney thought it essential to observe.

A permanent, freestanding public theater in England dates only from Shakespeare's own lifetime. A London playhouse, the Red Lion, is first mentioned in 1567, and James Burbage's playhouse, The Theater, was built in 1576. But it is quite misleading to identify English drama exclusively with the new, specially constructed playhouses, for in fact there was a rich and vital theatrical tradition in England stretching back for centuries. Several towns in late medieval England were the sites of annual festivals that mounted elaborate cycles of plays depicting the great biblical stories, from the creation of the world to Christ's Passion and its miraculous aftermath.

But early English theater was not restricted to these civic and religious festivals. Performers acted in town halls and the halls of guilds and aristocratic mansions, on scaffolds erected in town squares and marketplaces, on pageant wagons in the streets, and in innyards. By the fifteenth century, and probably earlier, there were organized companies of players traveling under noble patronage. Such companies earned a precarious living providing amusement, while enhancing the prestige of the patron whose livery they wore and whose protection they enjoyed. (Otherwise, by statutes enjoining productive labor, actors without another, ordinary trade could have been classified as vagabonds and whipped or branded.) This practice explains why the professional acting companies of Shakespeare's time, including Shakespeare's own, attached themselves to a nobleman and were technically his servants (the Lord Chamberlain's Men, the Lord Admiral's Men, etc.), even though virtually all their time was devoted to entertaining the public from whom most of their income derived.

Before the construction of the public theaters, the playing companies often performed short plays called "interludes" that were, in effect, staged dialogues on religious, moral, and political themes. The structure of such plays reflects the training in argumentation that students received in Tudor schools and, in particular, the sustained practice in examining both sides of a difficult question. Some of Shakespeare's amazing ability to look at critical issues from multiple perspectives may be traced back to this practice and the dramatic interludes it helped to inspire.

Another major form of theater that flourished in England in the fifteenth century and continued on into the sixteenth was the morality play. Like the mysteries, moralities addressed questions of the ultimate fate of the soul. They did so, however, not by rehearsing scriptural stories but by dramatizing allegories of spiritual struggle. Typically, a person named Human or Mankind or Youth is faced with a choice between a pious life in the company of such associates as Mercy, Discretion, and Good Deeds and a dissolute life among riotous companions like Lust or Mischief.

If such plays sound more than a bit like sermons, it is because they were. The church was a profoundly different institution from the theater, but its professionals shared some of the same rhetorical skills. It would be grossly misleading to regard churchgoing and playgoing as comparable entertainments, but clerical attacks on the theater sometimes make it sound as if ministers thought themselves to be in direct competition with professional players. The players, for their part, were generally too discreet to present themselves in a similar light, yet they almost certainly understood their craft as relating to sermons with an uneasy blend of emulation and rivalry.

Play-acting, whether of tragedies, comedies, or any of the other Elizabethan forms, took its place alongside other forms of public expression and entertainment as well. Perhaps the most important, from the perspective of the theater, were music and dance, since these were directly and repeatedly incorporated into plays. Moreover, virtually all plays in the period, including Shakespeare's, apparently ended with a dance. Brushing off the theatrical gore and changing their expressions from woe to pleasure, the actors in plays like *Doctor Faustus* and *King Lear* would presumably have received the audience's applause and then bid for a second round by performing a stately pavane or a lively jig.

Plays, music, and dancing were by no means the only shows in town. There were jousts, tournaments, royal entries, religious processions, pageants in honor of newly installed civic officials or ambassadors arriving from abroad;

wedding masques, court masques, and costumed entertainments known as Disguisings or Mummings; juggling acts, fortune tellers, exhibitions of swordsmanship, mountebanks, folk healers, storytellers, magic shows; bear-baiting, bullbaiting, cockfighting, and other blood sports; folk festivals such as Maying, the Feast of Fools, Carnival, and Whitsun Ales. For several years, Elizabethan Londoners were delighted by a trained animal—Banks's Horse—that could, it was thought, do arithmetic and answer questions. And there was always the grim but compelling spectacle of public shaming, mutilation, and execution.

Most English towns had stocks and whipping posts. Drunks, fraudulent merchants, adulterers, and quarrelers could be placed in carts or mounted backward on asses and paraded through the streets for crowds to jeer and throw refuse at. Women accused of being scolds could be publicly muzzled by an iron device called a brank or tied to a "cucking stool" and dunked in the river. Convicted criminals could have their ears cut off, their noses slit, their foreheads branded. Public beheadings and hangings were common. In the worst cases, felons were sentenced to be "hanged by the neck, and being alive cut down, and your privy members to be cut off, and your bowels to be taken out of your belly and there burned, you being alive." In the dismem-berment with which Marlowe's Doctor Faustus ends, the audience was wit-nessing the theatrical equivalent of the execution of criminals and traitors that they could have also watched in the flesh, as it were, nearby.

Doctor Faustus was performed by the Lord Admiral's Men at the Rose Theater, one of four major public playhouses that by the mid-1590s were feverishly competing for crowds of spectators. These playhouses (including Shakespeare's famous Globe Theater, which opened in 1599) each accom-modated some two thousand spectators and generally followed the same design: they were oval in shape, with an unroofed yard in the center where stood the groundlings (apprentices, servants, and others of the lower classes) and three rising tiers around the yard for men and women able to pay a higher price for places to sit and a roof over their heads. A large platform stage jutted out into the yard, surrounded on three sides by spectators (see the conjectural drawing of an Elizabethan playhouse, in the appendices to this volume). These financially risky ventures relied on admission charges—it was an innovation of this period to have money advanced in the expectation of pleasure rather than offered to servants as a reward—and counted on habitual playgoing fueled by a steady supply of new plays. The public play-houses were all located outside the limits of the city of London and, accord-ingly, beyond the jurisdiction of city authorities generally hostile to dramatic spectacles. Eventually, indoor theaters, artificially lighted and patronized by a more select audience, were also built, secured under conditions that would allow them some protection from those who wished to shut them down.

Why should what we now regard as one of the undisputed glories of the age have aroused so much hostility? One answer, curiously enough, is traffic: plays drew large audiences, and residents objected to the crowds, the noise, and the crush of carriages. Other, more serious concerns were public health and crime. It was thought that many diseases, including the dreaded bubonic plague, were spread by noxious odors, and the packed playhouses were obvi-ous breeding grounds for infection. (Patrons often tried to protect themselves by sniffing nosegays or stuffing cloves in their nostrils.) The large crowds drew pickpockets, cutpurses, and other scoundrels. On one memorable afternoon a pickpocket was caught in the act and tied for the duration of the play to one of the posts that held up the canopy above the stage. The theater was, moreover, a well-known haunt of prostitutes, and, it was alleged, a place where innocent maids were seduced and respectable matrons corrupted. It was darkly rumored that "chambers and secret places" adjoined the theater galleries, and, in any case, taverns, disreputable inns, and whorehouses were close at hand.

There were other charges as well. Plays were performed in the afternoon and therefore drew people, especially the young, away from their work. They were schools of idleness, luring apprentices from their trades, law students from their studies, housewives from their kitchens, and potentially pious souls from the sober meditations to which they might otherwise devote themselves. Moralists warned that the theaters were nests of sedition, and religious polemicists, especially Puritans, obsessively focusing on the use of boy actors to play the female parts, charged that theatrical transvestism excited illicit sexual desires, both heterosexual and homosexual.

But the playing companies had powerful allies, including Queen Elizabeth herself, and continuing popular support. One theater historian has estimated that between the late 1560s and 1642, when the playhouses were shut down by the English Civil War, well over fifty million visits were paid to the London theater, an astonishing figure for a city that had, by our standards, a very modest population. Plays were performed without the scene breaks and intermissions to which we are accustomed; there was no scenery and few props, but costumes were usually costly and elaborate. The players formed what would now be called repertory companies—that is, they filled the roles of each play from members of their own group, not employing outsiders. They performed a number of different plays on consecutive days, and the principal actors were shareholders in the profits of the company. Boys were apprenticed to actors just as they had been apprenticed to master craftsmen in the guilds; they took the women's parts in plays until their voices changed. The plays might be bought for the company from hack writers, or, as in Shakespeare's company, the group might include an actor-playwright who could supply it with some (though by no means all) of its plays. The script remained the property of the company, but a popular play was eagerly sought by the printers, and the companies, which generally tried to keep their plays from appearing in print, sometimes had trouble guarding their rights. The editors of the first collected edition of Shakespeare, the First Folio (1623), complain about the prior publication of "divers stolen and surreptitious copies" of his plays, "maimed and deformed by the frauds and stealths of injurious imposters."

SURPRISED BY TIME

All of the ways we cut up time into units are inevitably distortions. The dividing line between centuries was not, as far as we can tell, a highly significant one for people in the Renaissance, and many of the most important literary careers cross into the seventeenth century without a self-conscious moment of reflection. But virtually everyone must have been aware that the long reign of England's Queen Elizabeth was nearing its end, and this impending closure occasioned considerable anxiety. Childless, the last of her line, Elizabeth had steadfastly refused to name a successor. She continued to make brilliant speeches, to receive the extravagant compliments of her flatterers, and to exercise her authority—in 1601, she had her favorite, the headstrong earl of Essex, executed for attempting to raise an insurrection. But, as her seventieth birthday approached, she was clearly, as Ralegh put it, "a lady surprised by time." She suffered from bouts of ill health and melancholy; her godson, Sir John Harington, was dismayed to see her pacing through the rooms of her palace, striking at the tapestries with a sword. Her more astute advisers—among them Lord Burghley's son, Sir Robert Cecil, who had succeeded his father as her principal counselor—secretly entered into correspondence with the likeliest claimant to the throne, James VI of Scotland. Though the English queen had executed his Catholic mother, Mary, Queen of Scots, the Protestant James had continued to exchange polite letters with Elizabeth. It was at least plausible, as officially claimed, that in her dying breath, on March 24, 1603, Elizabeth designated James as her successor. A jittery nation that had feared a possible civil war lit bonfires to welcome its new king. But in a very few years, the English began to express nostalgia for the rule of "Good Queen Bess" and to look back on her reign as a magnificent high point in the history and culture of their nation.

THE SIXTEENTH CENTURY

TEXTS	CONTEXTS
	1485 Accession of Henry VII inaugurates Tudor dynasty
	1499 Desiderius Erasmus first visits England; meets Thomas More
ca. 1504 Amerigo Vespucci, *New World* and *Four Voyages*	**ca. 1504** Leonardo paints Mona Lisa
	1508–12 Michelangelo paints Sistine Chapel ceiling
	1509 Death of Henry VII; accession of Henry VIII
1511 Erasmus, *Praise of Folly*	
	1513 James IV of Scotland killed at Battle of Flodden; succeeded by James V
1516 More, *Utopia*. Ludovico Ariosto, *Orlando furioso*	
ca. 1517 John Skelton, *The Tunning of Elinour Rumming*	**1517** Martin Luther's Ninety-Five Theses; beginning of the Reformation in Germany
	1519 Cortés invades Mexico. Magellen begins his voyage around the world
1520s–30s Thomas Wyatt's poems circulating in manuscript	**1521** Pope Leo X names Henry VIII "Defender of the Faith"
1525 William Tyndale's English translation of the New Testament	
1528 Baldessare Castiglione, *The Courtier*	
	1529–32 More is Lord Chancellor
1532 Nicolò Machiavelli, *The Prince* (written 1513)	**1532–34** Henry VIII divorces Catherine of Aragon to marry Anne Boleyn; Elizabeth I born; Henry declares himself head of the English church
	1535 More beheaded
1537 John Calvin, *The Institution of Christian Religion*	**1537** Establishment of Calvin's theocracy at Geneva
	1542 Roman Inquisition. James IV of Scotland dies; succeeded by daughter Mary
1543 Copernicus, *On the Revolution of the Spheres*	
1547 *Book of Homilies*	**1547** Death of Henry VIII; accession of Protestant Edward VI
1549 *Book of Common Prayer*	**1553** Death of Edward VI; accession of Catholic Queen Mary, daughter of Catherine of Aragon
	1555–56 Archbishop Cranmer and former bishops Latimer and Ridley burned at the stake
1557 Tottel's *Songs and Sonnets* (printed poems by Wyatt, Surrey, and others)	
	1558 Mary dies; succeeded by Protestant Elizabeth I

TEXTS	CONTEXTS
1563 John Foxe, *Acts and Monuments*	
1565 Thomas Norton and Thomas Sackville, *Gorboduc*, first English blank-verse tragedy (acted in 1561)	
1567 Arthur Golding, translation of Ovid's *Metamorphoses*	**1567** Mary, Queen of Scots, abdicates; succeeded by her son James VI; Mary imprisoned in England
	1570 Elizabeth I excommunicated by Pope Pius V
	1576 James Burbage's playhouse, The Theater, built in London
	1576–77 Frobisher's voyage to North America
	1577–80 Drake's circumnavigation
1578 John Lyly, *Euphues*	
1579 Edmund Spenser, *Shepheardes Calender*	
1580 Montaigne, *Essays*	
	1583 Irish rebellion crushed
	1584–87 Sir Walter Ralegh's earliest attempts to colonize Virginia
	1586–87 Mary, Queen of Scots, tried for treason and executed
ca. 1587–90 Marlowe's *Tamburlaine* acted. Shakespeare begins career as actor and playwright	
1588 Thomas Hariot, *A Brief and True Report of Virginia*	**1588** Failed invasion of the Spanish Armada
1589 Richard Hakluyt, *The Principal Navigations . . . of the English Nation*	
1590 Sir Philip Sidney, *Arcadia* (posthumously published); Spenser, *The Faerie Queene*, Books 1–3	
1591 Sidney, *Astrophil and Stella*	
ca. 1592 John Donne's earliest poems circulating in manuscript	
1595 Sidney, *The Defense of Poesy*	**1595** Ralegh's voyage to Guiana
1596 Spenser, *The Faerie Queene*, Books 4–6 (with Books 1–3)	
1598 Ben Jonson, *Every Man in His Humor*	**1599** Globe Theater opens
	1603 Elizabeth I dies; succeeded by James VI of Scotland (as James I), inaugurating the Stuart dynasty

SIR THOMAS WYATT THE ELDER
1503–1542

Thomas Wyatt made his career in the shifting, dangerous currents of Renaissance courts, and court culture, with its power struggles, sexual intrigues, and sophisticated tastes, shaped his remarkable achievements as a poet. The son of a gentleman who early linked his fortunes to the Tudor dynasty, Wyatt was educated at St. John's College, Cambridge, and then entered the service of Henry VIII, becoming clerk of the king's jewels, a member of diplomatic missions to France and the Low Countries, and, in 1537–39, ambassador to the court of the Emperor Charles V in Spain. The years he spent abroad as a diplomat had a significant impact upon his writing, most obvious in his translations. Diplomacy, with its veiled threats, subtle indirection, and cynical role-playing, may have had a more indirect impact as well, reinforcing the lessons in self-display and self-concealment that Wyatt would have received at the English court.

Life in the orbit of the ruthless, unpredictable Henry VIII was competitive and risky. When, in the late 1530s, Wyatt wrote to his son of the "thousand dangers and hazards, enmities, hatreds, prisonments, despites, and indignations" he had faced, he was not exaggerating. He probably came closest to the executioner's axe when in 1536 he was imprisoned in the Tower of London along with several others accused of having adulterous affairs with the queen, Anne Boleyn. As his poem *Who list his wealth and ease retain* implies, Wyatt may have watched from his cell the execution of the queen and her alleged lovers, but he himself was spared, as he was spared a few years later, when he was again imprisoned in the Tower on charges of high treason brought by his enemies at court. His death, at the age of thirty-nine, came from a fever.

It is not surprising, given his career, that many of Wyatt's poems express an intense longing for "steadfastness" and an escape from the corruption, anxiety, and duplicity of the court. But of course the eloquent celebration of simplicity and truthfulness can itself be a cunning strategy. Wyatt was a master of the game of poetic self-display. Again and again he represents himself as a plain-speaking and steadfast man, betrayed by the "doubleness" of a fickle mistress or the instability of fortune. At this distance it is impossible to know how much this account corresponds to reality, but we can admire, as Wyatt's contemporaries did, the rhetorical deftness of the performance.

In a move with momentous consequences for English poetry, Wyatt introduced into English the sonnet, a fourteen-line poem in pentameter with a complex, inter-twining rhyme scheme. For the most part, he took his subject matter from Petrarch's sonnets, but his rhyme schemes came from other Italian models. The most common rhyme scheme in Wyatt's sonnets is *abba abba cddc ee*; the more typical Italian structure—an octave (the first eight lines) followed, after a turn in the sense, by a sestet (the last six lines)—was already beginning to change into the characteristic "English" structure for the sonnet, three quatrains and a couplet.

In his translations of Petrarchan sonnets, such as *Whoso list to hunt*, Wyatt tends to turn the idealizing of the woman into disillusionment and complaint. For the lover in Petrarch's poems, love is a transcendent experience; for the lover in Wyatt's poems, it is obsessive and embittering. The tone of bitterness carries over to many poems less closely linked to Italian and French models, poems with short stanzas and refrains in the manner of the native English "ballet" (pronounced to rhyme with *mallet*) or dance-song. Some of the ballets, to be sure, strike a note of jaunty independence, often tinged with misogyny, but melancholy complaint is rarely very distant. Perhaps the poem that most brilliantly captures Wyatt's blend of passion, anger, cynicism, longing, and pain is *They flee from me*.

Wyatt never published a collection of his own poems, and very little of his verse appeared in print during his lifetime. In 1557 (fifteen years after his death), the printer Richard Tottel included 97 poems attributed to Wyatt among the 271 poems in his miscellany, *Songs and Sonnets*. Wyatt was not primarily concerned with regularity of accent and smoothness of rhythm. By the time Tottel's collection was published, Wyatt's deliberately rough, vigorous, and expressive metrical practice was felt to be crude, and Tottel (or someone in his printing house) smoothed out the versification. We print Wyatt's poems in the versions found in the Egerton Manuscript (E. MS.), a manuscript that contains poems in Wyatt's own hand and corrections in his hand of scribal copies of his poems, and in the Arundel Manuscript (A. MS.).

The long love that in my thought doth harbor[1]

The long love that in my thought doth harbor,
And in mine heart doth keep his residence,
Into my face presseth with bold pretense
And therein campeth, spreading his banner.[2]
She that me learneth to love and suffer   5
And will that my trust and lust's negligence[3]
Be reined by reason, shame,° and reverence,   *modesty*
With his hardiness taketh displeasure.
Wherewithal unto the heart's forest he fleeth,
Leaving his enterprise with pain and cry,   10
And there him hideth, and not appeareth.
What may I do, when my master feareth,
But in the field with him to live and die?
For good is the life ending faithfully.

                                          E. MS.

Whoso list to hunt[1]

Whoso list° to hunt, I know where is an hind,°   *cares / female deer*
But as for me, alas, I may no more.
The vain travail hath wearied me so sore,
I am of them that farthest cometh behind.
Yet may I, by no means, my wearied mind   5
Draw from the deer, but as she fleeth afore,
Fainting I follow. I leave off, therefore,
Since in a net I seek to hold the wind.
Who list her hunt, I put him out of doubt,

1. Wyatt's version of poem 140 of Petrarch's *Rime sparse* (Scattered Rhymes); his younger friend, the earl of Surrey, also translated it (p. 344).
2. I.e., the speaker's blush. The first four lines of this sonnet introduce the "conceit" (or elaborately sustained metaphor) of Love as a warrior who, "with bold pretense" (i.e., making bold claim), flaunts his presence by means of the "banner." Elaborate metaphors of this kind are common in Petrarchan (and Elizabethan) love poetry, and often, as in this instance, an entire sonnet will turn

on a single conceit.
3. I.e., my open and careless revelation of my love. "Learneth": teaches.
1. An adaptation of Petrarch's *Rima* 190, perhaps influenced by commentators on Petrarch, who said that *Noli me tangere quia Caesaris sum* ("Touch me not, for I am Caesar's") was inscribed on the collars of Caesar's hinds, which were then set free and were presumably safe from hunters. Wyatt's sonnet is usually supposed to refer to Anne Boleyn, in whom Henry VIII became interested in 1526.

10 As well as I, may spend his time in vain.
And graven with diamonds in letters plain
There is written, her fair neck round about,
"*Noli me tangere,* for Caesar's I am,
And wild for to hold, though I seem tame."

E. MS.

They flee from me

They flee from me, that sometime did me seek
With naked foot stalking° in my chamber.   *walking softly*
I have seen them gentle, tame, and meek
That now are wild and do not remember
5 That sometime they put themself in danger
To take bread at my hand; and now they range,
Busily seeking with a continual change.

Thanked be fortune it hath been otherwise
Twenty times better; but once in special,
10 In thin array, after a pleasant guise,
When her loose gown from her shoulders did fall,
And she me caught in her arms long and small,°   *slender*
Therewithal sweetly did me kiss
And softly said, "Dear heart, how like you this?"

15 It was no dream, I lay broad waking.
But all is turned, thorough my gentleness,
Into a strange fashion of forsaking;
And I have leave to go, of her goodness,
And she also to use newfangleness.°   *fickleness*
20 But since that I so kindely[1] am served,
I fain would know what she hath deserved.

E. MS.

My lute, awake!

My lute, awake! Perform the last
Labor that thou and I shall waste,
And end that I have now begun;
For when this song is sung and past,
5 My lute, be still, for I have done.

As to be heard where ear is none,
As lead to grave in marble stone,[1]

---

1. Naturally, but with an ironic suggestion of the modern meaning of "kindly." In Wyatt's spelling, the word should presumably be pronounced as three syllables.

1. I.e., when sound may be heard with no ear to hear it or when soft lead is able to carve ("grave") hard marble.

My song may pierce her heart as soon.
Should we then sigh or sing or moan?
10 No, no, my lute, for I have done.

The rocks do not so cruelly
Repulse the waves continually
As she my suit and affectiön.
So that I am past remedy,
15 Whereby my lute and I have done.

Proud of the spoil that thou hast got
Of simple hearts, thorough love's shot,
By whom, unkind, thou hast them won,
Think not he hath his bow forgot,
20 Although my lute and I have done.

Vengeance shall fall on thy disdain
That makest but game on earnest pain.
Think not alone under the sun
Unquit° to cause thy lovers plain,° *unrevenged / to complain*
25 Although my lute and I have done.

Perchance thee lie withered and old
The winter nights that are so cold,
Plaining in vain unto the moon.
Thy wishes then dare not be told.
30 Care then who list,° for I have done. *likes*

And then may chance thee to repent
The time that thou hast lost and spent
To cause thy lovers sigh and swoon.
Then shalt thou know beauty but lent,
35 And wish and want as I have done.

Now cease, my lute. This is the last
Labor that thou and I shall waste,
And ended is that we begun.
Now is this song both sung and past;
40 My lute, be still, for I have done.

            E. MS.

Stand whoso list[1]

Stand whoso list° upon the slipper° top *cares to / slippery*
Of court's estates,° and let me here rejoice *high positions*
And use me quiet without let or stop,[2]
Unknown in court, that hath such brackish joys.
5 In hidden place so let my days forth pass
That when my years be done withouten noise,

---

1. A translation of Seneca, *Thyestes*, lines 391–
403.

2. Comport myself quietly without hindrance or
impediment from others.

I may die aged after the common trace.°   *way*
For him death grippeth right hard by the crop°   *throat*
That is much known of other, and of himself, alas,
10   Doth die unknown, dazed, with dreadful° face.   *fearful*

A. MS.

HENRY HOWARD, EARL OF SURREY
1517–1547

The axe that beheaded Surrey at the age of thirty had been hanging over his head for much of his life. In the court of Henry VIII, it was dangerous to be a potential claimant to the throne, and Surrey was descended from kings on both sides of his family. He was brought up at Windsor Castle as the close companion of Henry VIII's illegitimate son, the duke of Richmond, who married Surrey's sister. As the eldest son of the duke of Norfolk, the chief bulwark of the old Catholic aristocracy against the rising tide of "new men" and the reformed religion, Surrey was the heir not only to the Howard family's great wealth but also to their immense pride, their sense at once of noble privilege and of obligation. Like his father and grandfather, he was a brave and able soldier, serving in Henry VIII's French wars as "Lieutenant General of the King on Sea and Land." He was also repeatedly imprisoned for rash behavior, on one occasion for striking a courtier, on another for wandering through the streets of London breaking the windows of sleeping townspeople. In 1541 Surrey used his family connections—his first cousin, Catherine Howard, was queen—to secure the release from the Tower of his close friend, the poet Thomas Wyatt, who had been accused of treason. But a year later, Catherine Howard was executed for adultery. Power returned to the rival family of the former queen Jane Seymour, who had died in childbirth giving a son and heir to the aging Henry VIII. Surrey's situation was already precarious, and his vocal opposition to the Seymours, with their strong Protestant leanings, sealed his fate. Convicted of treason, he had the grim distinction of being Henry's last victim.

Poets and critics of the later sixteenth century, fascinated by Surrey's noble rank and his tragic fate, routinely praised him as one of the very greatest English poets. The full title of Tottel's influential miscellany, published in 1557 (ten years after Surrey's death), is *Songs and Sonnets written by the Right Honorable Lord Henry Howard Late Earl of Surrey and Other*. The principal "other" here is his older friend Wyatt, with whose poetry Surrey's is closely linked. Poets who circulated their verse in manuscript in a courtly milieu, both shared a passion for French and Italian poetry, especially for Petrarch's sonnets. Surrey established a form for these that was used by Shakespeare and that has become known as the English sonnet: three quatrains and a couplet, all in iambic pentameter and rhyming *abab cdcd efef gg*. Even more significant, he was the first English poet to publish in blank verse—unrhymed iambic pentameter—a verse form so popular in the succeeding centuries that it has come to seem almost indigenous to the language. The work in which he used his "strange meter," as the publisher called it, was a translation of part of Virgil's *Aeneid*. (Book 4 was published in 1554 and Book 2 in 1557.) Whether in blank verse or in rhyming forms, Surrey managed with exceptional skill the rhythmic fluency of the five-stress line, initiating the ease and grace that distinguish so many Elizabethan lyrics.

Love, that doth reign and live within my thought[1]

Love, that doth reign and live within my thought,
And built his seat within my captive breast,
Clad in the arms wherein with me he fought,
Oft in my face he doth his banner rest.
5 But she that taught me love and suffer pain,
My doubtful hope and eke° my hot desire   *also*
With shamefast° look to shadow and refrain,   *modest*
Her smiling grace converteth straight to ire.
And coward Love, then, to the heart apace
10 Taketh his flight, where he doth lurk and plain,°   *complain*
His purpose lost, and dare not show his face.
For my lord's guilt thus faultless bide I pain,
Yet from my lord shall not my foot remove:
Sweet is the death that taketh end by love.

1557

1. Cf. Surrey's version of Petrarch's *Rima* 140 with Wyatt's adaptation of the same original (p. 340).

THE ENGLISH BIBLE

Protestantism required direct lay access to the Bible, which meant in practice the widespread availability of vernacular translations. The Roman Catholic Church had not always and everywhere opposed such translations, but it generally preferred that the populace encounter the Scriptures through the interpretations of the priests, trained to read the Latin translation known as the Vulgate. In times of great conflict this preference for clerical mediation hardened into outright prohibition of vernacular translation and into persecution and book burning.

Zealous Protestants set out, in the teeth of fierce opposition, to put the Bible into the hands of the laity. A remarkable translation of the New Testament, by an English Lutheran named William Tyndale, was printed on the Continent and smuggled into England in 1525; Tyndale's translation of the Pentateuch, the first five books of the Hebrew Bible, followed in 1530. Many copies of these translations were seized and destroyed, as was the translator himself, but the printing press made it extremely difficult for authorities to eradicate books for which there was a passionate demand. The English Bible was a force that could not be suppressed, and it became, in its various forms, the single most important book of the sixteenth century.

Tyndale's translation was completed by an associate, Miles Coverdale, whose rendering of the Psalms proved to be particularly influential. Their joint labor was the basis for the Great Bible (1539), the first authorized version of the Bible in English, a copy of which was ordered to be placed in every church in the kingdom. With the accession of Edward VI, many editions of the Bible followed, but the process was sharply reversed when Mary came to the throne in 1553. Along with people condemned as heretics, English Bibles were burned in great bonfires.

Marian persecution was indirectly responsible for what would become the most scholarly Protestant English Bible, the translation known as the Geneva Bible, prepared, with extensive, learned, and often fiercely polemical marginal notes, by English exiles in Calvin's Geneva and widely diffused in England after Elizabeth came to the throne. In addition, Elizabethan church authorities ordered a careful revision of the Great Bible, and this version, known as the Bishops' Bible, was the one read in the churches. The success of the Geneva Bible in particular prompted those Elizabethan Catholics who now in turn found themselves in exile to bring out a vernacular translation of their own, the Douay-Rheims version, in order to counter the Protestant readings and glosses.

After Elizabeth's death in 1603, King James I and his bishops ordered that a revised translation of the entire Bible be undertaken by a group of forty-seven scholars. The result was the Authorized Version, more popularly known as the King James Bible.

In the passage selected here, 1 Corinthians 13, Tyndale's use of the word "love," echoed by the Geneva Bible, is set against the Catholic "charity." The latter term would gesture toward the religious doctrine of "works," against the Protestant insistence on salvation by faith alone. It is a sign of the conservative, moderate Protestantism of the King James version that it too opts for "charity."

From Tyndale's Translation

Though I spake with the tongues of men and angels, and yet had no love, I were even as sounding brass: or as a tinkling cymbal. And though I could prophesy, and understood all secrets, and all knowledge: yea, if I had all faith, so that I could move mountains out of their places, and yet had no love, I were nothing. And though I bestowed all my goods to feed the poor, and though I gave my body even that I burned, and yet had no love, it profiteth me nothing.

Love suffereth long, and is courteous. Love envieth not. Love doth not frowardly,[1] swelleth not, dealeth not dishonestly, seeketh not her own, is not provoked to anger, thinketh not evil, rejoiceth not in iniquity: but rejoiceth in the truth, suffereth all things, believeth all things, hopeth all things, endureth in all things. Though that prophesying fail, other[2] tongues shall cease, or knowledge vanish away, yet love falleth never away.

For our knowledge is unperfect and our prophesying is unperfect. But when that which is perfect is come, then that which is unperfect shall be done away. When I was a child, I spake as a child, I understood as a child, I imagined as a child. But as soon as I was a man, I put away childishness. Now we see in a glass,[3] even in a dark speaking: but then shall we see face to face. Now I know unperfectly: but then shall I know even as I am known. Now abideth faith, hope, and love, even these three: but the chief of these is love.

1525, 1535

From The Geneva Bible[1]

Though I speak with the tongues of men and Angels, and have not love, I am as sounding brass, or a tinkling cymbal. [2]And though I had the gift of

---

1. Perversely, evilly.
2. Or.
3. Mirror. "Dark": obscure, unclear. This metaphor of indirect and imperfect sight seems to

derive from Plato's Allegory of the Cave (*Republic* 7).

1. The Geneva Bible is the earliest English version printed with verse divisions.

prophecy, and knew all secrets and all knowledge, yea, if I had all faith, so that I could remove mountains, and had not love, I were nothing. [3]And though I feed the poor with all my goods, and though I give my body, that I be burned, and have not love, it profiteth me nothing. [4]Love suffereth long: it is bountiful: love envieth not: love doth not boast itself: it is not puffed up: [5]It disdaineth not: it seeketh not her own things: it is not provoked to anger: it thinketh not evil: [6]It rejoiceth not in iniquity, but rejoiceth in the truth: [7]It suffereth all things: it believeth all things: it hopeth all things: it endureth all things. [8]Love doth never fall away, though that prophesyings be abolished, or the tongues cease, or knowledge vanish away. [9]For we know in part, and we prophesy in part. [10]But when that which is perfect is come, then that which is in part shall be abolished. [11]When I was a child, I spake as a child, I understood as a child, I thought as a child: but when I became a man, I put away childish things. [12]For now we see through a glass darkly:[2] but then shall we see face to face. Now I know in part: but then shall I know even as I am known. [13]And now abideth faith, hope, and love, even these three: but the chiefest of these is love.

1560, 1602

From The Douay-Rheims Version

If I speak with the tongues of men and of Angels, and have not charity, I am become as sounding brass, or a tinkling cymbal. [2]And if I should have prophecy, and knew all mysteries, and all knowledge, and if I should have all faith so that I could remove mountains, and have not charity, I am nothing. [3]And if I should distribute all my goods to be meat[1] for the poor, and if I should deliver my body so that I burn, and have not charity, it doth profit me nothing.

[4]Charity is patient, is benign: charity envieth not, dealeth not perversely: is not puffed up, [5]is not ambitious, seeketh not her own, is not provoked to anger, thinketh not evil: [6]rejoiceth not upon iniquity, but rejoiceth with the truth: [7]suffereth all things, believeth all things, hopeth all things, beareth all things. [8]Charity never falleth away: whether prophecies shall be made void, or tongues shall cease, or knowledge shall be destroyed. [9]For in part we know, and in part we prophesy. [10]But when that shall come that is perfect, that shall be made void that is in part. [11]When I was a little one, I spake as a little one, I understood as a little one, I thought as a little one. But when I was made a man, I did away the things that belonged to a little one. [12]We see now by a glass in a dark sort: but then face to face. Now I know in part: but then I shall know as also I am known. [13]And now there remain faith, hope, charity, these three, but the greater of these is charity.

1582

2. By means of a mirror, obscurely.   1. Food (in general).

From The Authorized (King James) Version

Though I speak with the tongues of men and of angels, and have not charity, I am become as sounding brass, or a tinkling cymbal. [2]And though I have the gift of prophecy, and understand all mysteries, and all knowledge; and though I have all faith, so that I could remove mountains, and have no charity, I am nothing. [3]And though I bestow all my goods to feed the poor, and though I give my body to be burned, and have not charity, it profiteth me nothing. [4]Charity suffereth long, and is kind; charity envieth not; charity vaunteth not itself, is not puffed up, [5]doth not behave itself unseemly, seeketh not her own, is not easily provoked, thinketh no evil; [6]rejoiceth not in iniquity, but rejoiceth in the truth; [7]beareth all things, believeth all things, hopeth all things, endureth all things. [8]Charity never faileth: but whether there be prophecies, they shall fail; whether there be tongues, they shall cease; whether there be knowledge, it shall vanish away. [9]For we know in part, and we prophesy in part. [10]But when that which is perfect is come, then that which is in part shall be done away. [11]When I was a child, I spake as a child, I understood as a child, I thought as a child: but when I became a man, I put away childish things. [12]For now we see through a glass, darkly; but then face to face: now I know in part; but then shall I know even as also I am known. And now abideth faith, hope, charity, these three; but the greatest of these is charity.

1611

BOOK OF COMMON PRAYER

The Protestant attack on Catholic rituals and the demand for worship in the vernacular led during the reign of Edward VI to the preparation of an English liturgical book, authorized to be the official and only text for public worship in England. Initiated by the Act of Uniformity in 1549, the work's principal architect was Thomas Cranmer (1489–1556). Cranmer, the archbishop of Canterbury, was at first careful to translate and shape the old Latin liturgy into a moderate, occasionally ambiguous compromise between Catholic and Protestant positions. His thorough revision in 1552 put the *Book of Common Prayer* much more decisively into the Protestant camp. Banned by the Catholic Mary Tudor, during whose reign Cranmer was executed, the *Book of Common Prayer* was restored, with small revisions, by Elizabeth, and has remained the basis of Anglican worship ever since. Cranmer was, among his other accomplishments, a brilliant prose stylist, and the cadences of the *Book of Common Prayer* have had a profound influence on the English language. The selection, part of the marriage service, is from the version used during the reign of Elizabeth.

From The Book of Common Prayer and Administration of the Sacraments and Other Rites and Ceremonies in the Church of England

From *The Form of Solemnization of Matrimony*

* * * At the day appointed for solemnization of matrimony, the persons to be married shall come into the body of the church with their friends and neighbors. And there the priest shall thus say:

Dearly beloved friends, we are gathered together here in the sight of God, and in the face of his congregation, to join together this man and this woman in holy matrimony, which is an honorable estate,[1] instituted of God in paradise, in the time of man's innocency, signifying unto us the mystical union that is betwixt Christ and his church: which holy estate Christ adorned and beautified with his presence and first miracle that he wrought in Cana of Galilee,[2] and is commended of Saint Paul to be honorable among all men,[3] and therefore is not to be enterprised[4] nor taken in hand unadvisedly, lightly, or wantonly, to satisfy men's carnal lusts and appetites, like brute beasts that have no understanding; but reverently, discreetly, advisedly, soberly, and in the fear of God, duly considering the causes for the which matrimony was ordained. One was, the procreation of children, to be brought up in the fear and nurture of the Lord, and praise of God. Secondly, it was ordained for a remedy against sin, and to avoid fornication, that such persons as have not the gift of continency might marry, and keep themselves undefiled members of Christ's body.[5] Thirdly, for the mutual society, help, and comfort that the one ought to have of the other, both in prosperity and adversity: into the which holy estate these two persons present come now to be joined. Therefore if any man can show any just cause why they may not lawfully be joined together, let him now speak, or else hereafter forever hold his peace.

And also speaking to the persons that shall be married, he shall say:

I require and charge you (as you will answer at the dreadful day of judgment, when the secrets of all hearts shall be disclosed) that if either of you do know any impediment why ye may not be lawfully joined together in matrimony, that ye confess it. For be ye well assured, that so many as be coupled together otherwise than God's word doth allow are not joined together by God, neither is their matrimony lawful.

At which day of marriage, if any man do allege and declare any impediment why they may not be coupled together in matrimony by God's law or the laws of this realm; and will be bound, and sufficient sureties with him, to the parties, or else put in a caution,[6] to the full value of such charges as the persons to be married doth sustain, to prove his allegation: then the solemnization must be deferred unto such time as the truth be tried. If no impediment be alleged, then shall the curate[7] say unto the man,

1. State, condition.
2. He changed water into wine (John 2.1–11).
3. "Marriage is honorable in all, and the bed undefiled: but whoremongers and adulterers God will judge" (Hebrews 13.4).

4. Undertaken.
5. The church.
6. Surety.
7. A clergyman who has charge of a parish.

N.[8] Wilt thou have this woman to thy wedded wife, to live together after God's ordinance in the holy estate of matrimony? Wilt thou love her, comfort her, honor and keep her, in sickness and in health? And forsaking all other, keep thee only to her, so long as you both shall live?

The man shall answer,

I will.

Then shall the priest say to the woman,

N. Wilt thou have this man to thy wedded husband, to live together after God's ordinance in the holy estate of matrimony? Wilt thou obey him and serve him, love, honor, and keep him, in sickness and in health, and forsaking all other, keep thee only unto him, so long as you both shall live?

The woman shall answer,

I will.

Then shall the minister say,

Who giveth this woman to be married unto this man?

And the minister receiving the woman at her father or friend's hands, shall cause the man to take the woman by the right hand, and so either to give their troth[9] to other. The man first saying:

I N. take thee N. to my wedded wife, to have and to hold from this day forward, for better, for worse, for richer, for poorer, in sickness and in health, to love and to cherish, till death us depart,[1] according to God's holy ordinance: and thereto I plight thee my troth.

Then shall they loose their hands, and the woman taking again the man by the right hand shall say:

I N. take thee N. to my wedded husband, to have and to hold from this day forward, for better, for worse, for richer, for poorer, in sickness and in health, to love, cherish, and to obey, till death us depart, according to God's holy ordinance: and thereto I give thee my troth.

Then shall they again loose their hands, and the man shall give unto the woman a ring, laying the same upon the book with the accustomed duty[2] to the priest and clerk. And the priest taking the ring, shall deliver it unto the man, to put it upon the fourth finger of the woman's left hand. And the man taught by the priest shall say:

With this ring I thee wed: with my body I thee worship: and with all my worldly goods I thee endow. In the name of the Father, and of the Son, and of the Holy Ghost. Amen.

Then the man leaving the ring upon the fourth finger of the woman's left hand, the minister shall say:

O eternal God, creator and preserver of all mankind, giver of all spiritual grace, the author of everlasting life: send thy blessing upon these thy servants, this man and this woman, whom we bless in thy name; that as Isaac

---

8. Name—i.e., the minister inserts the man's given name here.
9. Truth—i.e., pledge.

1. Part.
2. Payment. "Book": Bible.

and Rebecca lived faithfully together,[3] so these persons may surely perform and keep the vow and covenant betwixt them made, whereof this ring given and received is a token and pledge, and may ever remain in perfect love and peace together, and live according unto thy laws: through Jesus Christ our Lord. Amen.

Then shall the priest join their right hands together, and say:

Those whom God hath joined together, let no man put asunder.

Then shall the minister speak unto the people:

Forasmuch as N. and N. have consented together in holy wedlock, and have witnessed the same before God and this company, and thereto have given and pledged their troth, either to other, and have declared the same by giving and receiving of a ring, and by joining of hands: I pronounce that they be man and wife together. In the name of the Father, and of the Son, and of the Holy Ghost. Amen.

And the minister shall add this blessing:

God the Father, God the Son, God the Holy Ghost, bless, preserve, and keep you: the Lord mercifully with his favor look upon you, and so fill you with all spiritual benediction and grace that you may so live together in this life that in the world to come you may have life everlasting. Amen.

1559

3. In Genesis 24–27.

QUEEN ELIZABETH
1533–1603

Elizabeth I, queen of England from 1558 to 1603, set her mark indelibly on the age that has come to bear her name. Endowed with intelligence, courage, cunning, and a talent for self-display, she managed to survive and flourish in a world that would have easily crushed a weaker person. Her birth was a disappointment to her father, Henry VIII, who had hoped for a male heir to the throne, and her prospects were further dimmed when her mother, Anne Boleyn, was executed three years later on charges of adultery and treason. At six years old, observers noted, Elizabeth had as much gravity as if she had been forty.

Under distinguished tutors, including the Protestant humanist Roger Ascham, the young princess received a rigorous education, with training in classical and modern languages, history, rhetoric, theology, and moral philosophy. Her religious orientation was Protestant, which put her in great danger during the reign of her Catholic older half-sister, Mary. Imprisoned in the Tower, interrogated and constantly spied upon, Elizabeth steadfastly professed innocence, loyalty, and a pious abhorrence of heresy. Upon Mary's death, she ascended the throne and quickly made clear that the official religion of the land would be Protestantism.

Elizabeth also made it clear that she would not be a figurehead. She gathered around her an able group of advisers, but she held firmly to the reins of power, playing one faction against another, conducting diplomatic affairs in her fluent French and Latin, and negotiating with an often contentious Parliament. Under great pressure to marry, she entered into protracted courtships with princely suitors, including the French duke of Anjou, but she ultimately refused all offers and declared repeatedly that she was wedded to her country.

In the face of deep skepticism about the ability of any woman to rule, Elizabeth strategically blended imperiousness with an elaborate cult of love. Her courtiers and advisers, on their knees, approached the queen, glittering in jewels and gorgeous gowns, and addressed her in extravagant terms that conjoined romantic passion and religious veneration. Artists and poets celebrated her in mythological dress—as Diana, the chaste goddess of the moon; Astraea, the goddess of justice; Gloriana, the queen of the fairies. Though she could suddenly veer whenever she chose toward bluntness and anger, Elizabeth herself often contrived to transform the language of politics into the language of love. "We all loved her," her godson John Harington wrote with a touch of irony, "for she said she loved us."

Throughout her life Elizabeth took pride in her command of languages and her felicity of expression. Her own writing includes carefully crafted letters and speeches on several state occasions; verse translations of selections from the Psalms, Petrarch, Seneca, and Horace; prose translations from Boethius, Plutarch, and the French Protestant Queen Margaret of Navarre; and a few original poems. The original poems known to be hers deal with actual events in her life. They are chiefly in octosyllabics or poulter's measure (rhyming couplets in which the first line has twelve and the second line fourteen syllables) and are rough-hewn, vigorous, and moralistic.

The doubt of future foes[1]

The doubt° of future foes exiles my present joy,   *fear*
And wit° me warns to shun such snares as threaten mine   *intelligence*
   annoy.[2]
For falsehood now doth flow, and subjects' faith doth ebb,[3]
Which would not be, if reason ruled or wisdom weaved the web.
5 But clouds of toys untried do cloak aspiring minds,
Which turn to rain of late repent, by course of changèd winds.[4]
The top of hope supposed, the root of ruth° will be,   *sorrow*
And fruitless all their graffèd guiles, as shortly ye shall see.[5]
The dazzled eyes with pride, which great ambition blinds,
10 Shall be unsealed by worthy wights° whose foresight falsehood   *men*
   finds.
The daughter of debate,[6] that eke° discord doth sow   *also*
Shall reap no gain where former rule[7] hath taught still° peace to   *stable*
   grow.
No foreign banished wight shall anchor in this port;

1. The poem concerns Elizabeth's Roman Catholic cousin Mary Stuart, queen of Scotland, who in 1567 sought refuge in England from her rebellious subjects. Mary was the focus of several Catholic conspiracies to place her on the English throne in place of Elizabeth.
2. I.e., threaten to harm ("annoy") me.
3. I.e., the tide of faith (loyalty) is ebbing, yielding to the rising tide of falsehood.
4. Clouds of tricks ("toys") not yet tested and detected ("untried") hide the "aspiring minds" of

ambitious foes, but those clouds will turn at last into rains of repentance.
5. The deceptions ("guiles") grafted ("graffèd") into them will not bear fruit.
6. Mary Stuart also was sometimes called "Mother of Debate," because she was constantly the focus of conspiracies and plots.
7. "Former rule": either the reign of Henry VIII or that of Edward VI, which established the Reformation in England.

Our realm it brooks no stranger's force, let them elsewhere resort.
15   Our rusty sword with rest,[8] shall first his edge employ
To poll their tops[9] that seek such change and gape for future joy.

ca. 1568   1589

On Monsieur's Departure[1]

I grieve and dare not show my discontent,
I love and yet am forced to seem to hate,
I do, yet dare not say I ever meant,
I seem stark mute but inwardly do prate.°   *chatter*
5   I am and not, I freeze and yet am burned,
Since from myself another self I turned.

My care is like my shadow in the sun,
Follows me flying, flies when I pursue it,
Stands and lies by me, doth what I have done.[2]
10   His too familiar care[3] doth make me rue° it.   *regret*
No means I find to rid him from my breast,
Till by the end of things it be suppressed.

Some gentler passion slide into my mind,
For I am soft and made of melting snow;
15   Or be more cruel, love, and so be kind.
Let me or° float or sink, be high or low.   *either*
Or let me live with some more sweet content,
Or die and so forget what love ere meant.

ca. 1582   1823

Letters

To Sir Amyas Paulet[1]

[ca. September 1586]

Amyas, my most faithful and careful servant, God reward thee treblefold in the double for thy most troublesome charge[2] so well discharged. If you knew, my Amyas, how kindly, besides most dutifully, my grateful heart accepts and prizes your spotless endeavors and faultless actions, your wise orders and safe regard, performed in so dangerous and crafty a charge, it would ease your travails and rejoice your heart, in which I charge you place

---

8. Sword rusty from disuse.
9. Strike off their heads.
1. The heading, present in two manuscripts, identifies the occasion of this poem as the breaking off of marriage negotiations between Queen Elizabeth and the French duke of Anjou in 1582. A third manuscript implies instead an association with Elizabeth's favorite, the earl of Essex, who led an abortive rebellion and was executed for treason in 1601.
2. Does everything I do.

3. I.e., my own care (i.e., sorrow) that he caused.
1. Paulet was the keeper of Mary, Queen of Scots, who had been imprisoned in England since 1567. In 1586 a number of her supporters, led by Anthony Babington, plotted to murder Elizabeth and place Mary on the throne. The plot was discovered, and the plotters were executed in September. Mary, who had been complicit with them, was placed under stricter confinement.
2. Duty, responsibility.

this most just thought, that I cannot balance in any weight of my judgment the value that I prize you at, and suppose no treasures to countervail such a faith. If I reward not such deserts, let me lack when I have most need of you, if I acknowledge not such merit, *non omnibus dictum*.[3]

Let your wicked murderess know how, with hearty sorrow, her vile deserts compel these orders; and bid her from me, ask God forgiveness for her treacherous dealings towards the savior of her life many a year, to the intolerable peril of my own, and yet, not contented with so many forgivenesses, must fault again so horribly, far passing woman's thought, much less a princess; instead of excusing whereof, not one can sorrow, it being so plainly confessed by the authors[4] of my guiltless death. Let repentance take place, and let not the fiend possess her, so as her better part may not be lost, for which I pray with hands lifted up to Him that may both save and spill.[5]

With my most loving adieu and prayer for thy long life, your most assured and loving sovereign, as thereby by good deserts induced.

1854

To Henry III, king of France[1]

January 1587

Sir, my Good Brother,

The old ground, on which I have often based my letters, appears to me so changed at present, that I am compelled to alter the style, and instead of returning thanks, to use complaints. My God! How could you be so unreasonable as to reproach the injured party, and to compass the death of an innocent one by allowing her to become the prey of a murderess? But, without reference to my rank, which is nowise inferior to your own, nor to my friendship to you, most sincere, for I have wellnigh forfeited all reputation among the princes of my own religion,[2] by neglecting them in order to prevent disturbances in your dominions; exposed to dangers such as scarcely any prince ever was before; expecting, at least, some ostensible reasons and offers for security against the daily danger, for the epilogue of this whole negotiation: you are, in spite of all this, so blinded by the words of those who I pray may not ruin you, that instead of a thousand thanks, which I had merited for such singular services, Monsieur de Bellievre has addressed language to my ears, which, in truth, I know not well how to interpret. For that you should be angry at my saving my own life seems to me the threat of an enemy, which, I assure you, will never put me in fear, but is the shortest way to make me dispatch the cause of so much mischief. Let me, I pray you, understand in what sense I am to take these words; for I will not live an hour to endure that any prince whatsoever should boast that he had humbled me

3. In context, the phrase (which means "not said to [or by] all") is obscure. Perhaps Elizabeth's meaning is "if indeed I do not proclaim such merit to all."
4. I.e., the conspirators.
5. Destroy.
1. Translated from the original French by Agnes Strickland. In the aftermath of the conspiracy to set her on the throne, Mary was tried, convicted, and sentenced to death. On January 6, 1587, Mon-

sieur de Bellievre, a special ambassador from the king of France, Henry III (to whose predecessor, Henry II, Mary had briefly enjoyed a dynastic marriage, ended by the young king's death in 1560), pleaded Mary's cause before Elizabeth. The threats included in his remarks prompted her to write this strong letter to his master. On February 8 Mary was beheaded.
2. I.e., other Protestant monarchs.

into drinking such a cup as that. Monsieur de Bellievre has, indeed, somewhat softened his language, by adding that you in nowise wish any danger to accrue to me, and still less to cause me any. I therefore write you these few words, and if it please you to act accordingly, you shall never find a truer friend; but if otherwise, I neither am in so low a place, nor govern realms so inconsiderable, that I should in right and honor yield to any living prince who would injure me; and I doubt not, by the grace of God, to make my cause good for my own security.

I beseech you to think rather of the means of maintaining than of diminishing my friendship. Your realm, my good brother, cannot abide many enemies. Give not the rein, in God's name, to wild horses, lest they should shake you from your saddle. I say this to you out of a true and upright heart, and implore the Creator to grant you long and happy life.

Elizabeth

1854

Speech to the Troops at Tilbury[1]

My loving people: We have been persuaded by some that are careful of[2] our safety, to take heed how we commit ourselves to armed multitudes, for fear of treachery. But I assure you I do not desire to live to distrust my faithful and loving people. Let tyrants fear! I have always so behaved myself that, under God, I have placed my chief strength and safeguard in the loyal hearts and goodwill of my subjects; and therefore I am come amongst you, as you see, at this time, not for my recreation and disport, but being resolved, in the midst of the heat of the battle, to live or die amongst you all; to lay down for my God, and for my kingdom, and for my people, my honor and my blood, even in the dust. I know I have the body but of a weak and feeble woman; but I have the heart and stomach of a king, and of a king of England too,[3] and think foul scorn that Parma[4] or Spain, or any prince of Europe, should dare to invade the borders of my realm; to which, rather than any dishonor should grow by me, I myself will take up arms, I myself will be your general, judge, and rewarder of every one of your virtues in the field. I know already, for your forwardness you have deserved rewards and crowns;[5] and we do assure you on the word of a prince, they shall be duly paid you. In the meantime, my lieutenant-general[6] shall be in my stead, than whom never prince commanded a more noble or worthy subject; not doubting but by your obedience to my general, by your concord in the camp, and your valor in the

---

1. Delivered by Elizabeth to the land forces assembled at Tilbury (Essex) to repel the anticipated invasion of the Spanish Armada, a fleet of warships sent by Philip II. The Armada was defeated at sea and never reached England, a miraculous deliverance and sign of God's special favor to Elizabeth and to England, in the general view.
2. Anxious about.
3. An allusion to the concept of the king's (or queen's) two bodies, the one natural and mortal,

the other an ideal and enduring political construct. "Stomach": valor.
4. Alexander Farnese, duke of Parma, allied with (the king of) Spain and expected to join with him in the invasion of England.
5. An English monetary unit.
6. Robert Dudley, earl of Leicester, led her armies; he was the queen's favorite courtier and at one time rumored to be her lover and a prospective husband.

field, we shall shortly have a famous victory over those enemies of my God, of my kingdoms, and of my people.

1588   1752

The "Golden Speech"[1]

Mr. Speaker: We have heard your declaration and perceive your care of our state,[2] by falling into the consideration of a grateful acknowledgment of such benefits as you have received; and that your coming is to present thanks unto us, which I accept with no less joy than your loves can have desire to offer such a present.

I do assure you that there is no prince that loveth his subjects better, or whose love can countervail our love. There is no jewel, be it of never so rich a price, which I prefer before this jewel, I mean your love, for I do more esteem it than any treasure or riches: for that we know how to prize, but love and thanks I count inestimable. And though God has raised me high, yet this I count the glory of my crown, that I have reigned with your loves. This makes me that I do not so much rejoice that God hath made me to be a queen as to be a queen over so thankful a people. Therefore I have cause to wish nothing more than to content the subject, and that is a duty which I owe. Neither do I desire to live longer days than that I may see your prosperity, and that is my only desire. And as I am that person that still, yet under God, hath delivered you, so I trust, by the almighty power of God, that I still shall be His instrument to preserve you from envy, peril, dishonor, shame, tyranny, and oppression, partly by means of your intended helps, which we take very acceptably, because it manifests the largeness of your loves and loyalties unto your sovereign.

Of myself I must say this: I never was any greedy, scraping grasper, nor a strait fast-holding prince, nor yet a waster; my heart was never set on worldly goods, but only for my subjects' good. What you do bestow on me I will not hoard up, but receive it to bestow on you again. Yea, mine own properties I count yours, to be expended for your good. Therefore render unto them, I beseech you, Mr. Speaker, such thanks as you imagine my heart yieldeth, but my tongue cannot express.

1. Elizabeth's speech to her last Parliament, 1601. The designation "Golden Speech" stems from the headnote to a version of it printed near the end of the Puritan interregnum (1659?): "This speech ought to be set in letters of gold, that as well the majesty, prudence, and virtue of this royal queen might in general most exquisitely appear, as also that her religious love and tender respect which she particularly and constantly did bear to her Parliament in unfeigned sincerity might (to the shame and perpetual disgrace and infamy of some of her successors) be nobly and truly vindicated." The royal prerogatives included the right to grant or sell "letters patent," which gave the recipient monopoly control of some branch of commerce. (Sir Walter Ralegh, for example, was given the exclusive right, for a period of thirty years, to license all taverns.) Discontent with the monopolies—which had resulted in higher prices for a wide range of commodities, including such basic ones as salt and starch—came to a head in the Parliament of 1601. Under parliamentary pressure (and in return for a subsidy granted to her treasury), Elizabeth agreed to revoke some of the most obnoxious patents and to allow the courts to rule freely on charges brought against the holders of others. She invited members of Parliament who wished to offer thanks for this largess to come to her in a body, and on November 30 received about 150 of them at Whitehall palace. After effusive remarks by the speaker of the House of Commons (John Croke), the queen responded more or less as recorded here. (Elizabeth revised the speech for publication; and none of the surviving versions of it—which differ considerably—was printed earlier than about 1628.)

2. Rank, position.

Mr. Speaker, I would wish you and the rest to stand up, for I shall yet trouble you with longer speech.[3]

Mr. Speaker, you give me thanks, but I doubt me I have more cause to thank you all than you me: and I charge you to thank them of the House of Commons from me, for had I not received a knowledge from you, I might have fallen into the lap of an error only for lack of true information.

Since I was queen, yet never did I put my pen to any grant but that upon pretext and semblance made unto me that it was both good and beneficial to the subjects in general, though a private profit to some of my ancient servants who had deserved well. But the contrary being found by experience, I am exceedingly beholding to such subjects as would move the same at first. And I am not so simple to suppose but that there be some of the Lower House[4] whom these grievances never touched, and for them I think they speak out of zeal to their countries[5] and not out of spleen or malevolent affection, as being parties grieved. And I take it exceeding grateful from them, because it gives us to know that no respects or interests had moved them other than the minds[6] they bear to suffer no diminution of our honor and our subjects' love unto us. The zeal of which affection, tending to ease my people and knit their hearts unto me, I embrace with a princely care.

Far above all earthly treasure I esteem my people's love, more than which I desire not to merit. That my grants should be grievous to my people and oppressions to be privileged under color of our patents, our kingly dignity shall not suffer[7] it. Yea, when I heard it, I could give no rest to my thoughts until I had reformed it.[8] Shall they think to escape unpunished that have thus oppressed you and have been respectless of their duty and regardless of our honor? No, Mr. Speaker, I assure you, were it more for conscience' sake than for any glory or increase of love that I desire these errors, troubles, vexations, and oppressions done by these varlets and lewd[9] persons, not worthy the name of subjects, should not escape without condign punishment. But I perceive they dealt with me like physicians who, ministering a drug, make it more acceptable by giving it a good aromatical savor, or, when they give pills, do gild them all over.

I have ever used to set the last judgment day before mine eyes and so to rule as I shall be judged to answer before a higher Judge. To Whose judgment seat I do appeal that never thought was cherished in my heart that tended not to my people's good. And if my kingly bounty have been abused and my grants turned to the hurt of my people, contrary to my will and meaning, or if any in authority under me have neglected or perverted what I have committed to them, I hope God will not lay their culps[1] and offenses to my charge. And though there were danger in repealing our grants, yet what danger would not I rather incur for your own good, than I would suffer them still to continue?

I know the title of a king is a glorious title, but assure yourself that the shining glory of princely authority hath not so dazzled the eyes of our understanding but that we well know and remember that we also are to yield an account of our actions before the Great Judge. To be a king and wear a crown

---

3. Up to this point, the assemblage had evidently been kneeling.
4. The House of Commons.
5. Their constituents.
6. Intentions.
7. Allow. "Color": pretext.

8. In fact, Elizabeth was extremely slow to respond to the grievances, which had, for example, previously been raised in the Parliament of 1597.
9. Base.
1. Sins.

is more glorious to them that see it than it is pleasure to them that bear it. For myself, I was never so much enticed with the glorious name of a king or royal authority of a queen as delighted that God hath made me this instrument to maintain His truth and glory, and to defend this kingdom, as I said, from peril, dishonor, tyranny, and oppression.

There will never queen sit in my seat with more zeal to my country or care to my subjects, and that will sooner with willingness yield and venture her life for your good and safety than myself. And though you have had and may have many princes more mighty and wise sitting in this seat, yet you never had or shall have any that will be more careful and loving.

Should I ascribe anything to myself and my sexly weakness, I were not worthy to live then, and of all most unworthy of the mercies I have had from God, Who hath ever yet given me a heart which never yet feared foreign or home enemies. I speak it to give God the praise as a testimony before you, and not to attribute anything unto myself. For I, O Lord, what am I, whom practices and perils past should not fear?[2] O what can I do? That I should speak for any glory, God forbid!

This, Mr. Speaker, I pray you deliver unto the House, to whom heartily recommend me. And so I commit you all to your best fortunes and further counsels. And I pray you, Mr. Comptroller, Mr. Secretary,[3] and you of my council, that before these gentlemen depart into their countries,[4] you bring them all to kiss my hand.

1601   ca. 1628

---

2. Frighten. "Practices": treacherous schemes.
3. William Knollys, earl of Banbury, and Robert

Cecil, earl of Salisbury.
4. Districts.

EDMUND SPENSER
1552–1599

Edmund Spenser set out, consciously and deliberately, to become the great English poet of his age. In a culture in which most accomplished poetry was written by those who were, or at least professed to be, principally interested in something else— advancement at court, diplomacy, statecraft, or the church—Spenser's ambition was altogether remarkable, and it is still more remarkable that he succeeded in reaching his goal. Unlike such poets as Wyatt, Surrey, and Sidney, born to privilege and social distinction, Spenser was born to parents of modest means and station, in London, probably in 1552. He nonetheless received an impressive education, first at the Merchant Taylors' School, under its demanding humanist headmaster, Richard Mulcaster, then at Pembroke College, Cambridge, where he was enrolled as a "sizar" or poor (meaning impoverished) scholar. In the Puritan environment of Cambridge, where the popular preacher Thomas Cartwright was beginning to make the authorities uneasy, Spenser started as a poet by translating some poems for a volume of anti-Catholic propaganda. He also began his friendship with Gabriel Harvey, an eccentric Cambridge don, humanist, and pamphleteer. Their correspondence shows that both men were passionately interested in theories of poetry and in experiments in quantitative versification in English.

After receiving the B.A. degree in 1573 and the M.A. in 1576, Spenser served as personal secretary and aide to several prominent men, including Dr. John Young, bishop of Rochester; and the earl of Leicester, the queen's principal favorite. During his employment in Leicester's household he came to know Sir Philip Sidney and his friend Sir Edward Dyer, courtiers who sought to promote a new English poetry. Spenser's contribution to the movement was *The Shepheardes Calender*, published in 1579 and dedicated to Sidney.

In *The Shepheardes Calender* Spenser used a deliberately archaic language, partly in homage to Chaucer, whose work he praised as a "well of English undefiled," and partly to achieve a rustic effect, in keeping with the feigned simplicity of pastoral poetry's shepherd singers. Sidney did not approve; in his *Defense of Poesy* he wrote, "*The Shepheardes Calender* hath much poetry in his eclogues, indeed worthy the reading, if I be not deceived. (That same framing of his style to an old rustic language I dare not allow, since neither Theocritus in Greek, Virgil in Latin, nor Sannazaro in Italian did affect it.)" Another classical purist, Ben Jonson, growled that Spenser "writ no language," and, in the eighteenth century, Samuel Johnson described the language of *The Shepheardes Calender* as "studied barbarity." Johnson's characterization is, in a way, quite accurate, for Spenser was attempting to conjure up a native English style to which he could wed the classical mode of the pastoral. Moreover, since pastoral was traditionally viewed as the prelude in a great national poet's career to more ambitious undertakings, Spenser was also in effect announcing his extravagant ambition.

There are thirteen different meters in *The Shepheardes Calender*. Some of these Spenser invented, some he adapted, but most of them were novel; only three or four were at all common in 1579. Spenser was a prolific experimenter who went on to make further innovations in his later poems: the special rhyme scheme of the Spenserian sonnet; the remarkably beautiful adaptation of the Italian *canzone* forms for the *Epithalamion* and *Prothalamion*; and the nine-line stanza of *The Faerie Queene*, with its hexameter (six-stress) line at the end, are the best known. Spenser is sometimes called the "poet's poet" because so many later English poets learned the art of versification from him. In the nineteenth century alone his influence may be seen in Shelley's *Revolt of Islam*, Byron's *Childe Harold's Pilgrimage*, Keats's *Eve of St. Agnes*, and Tennyson's *The Lotus-Eaters*.

The year after the publication of *The Shepheardes Calender*, Spenser went to Ireland as secretary and aide to Lord Grey of Wilton, lord deputy of Ireland. Although he tried continually to obtain appointments in England and to secure the patronage of the queen, he spent the rest of his career in Ireland, holding various minor government posts and hence participating actively in the English struggle against those who resisted their colonial authority. The grim realities of that struggle—massacre, the burning of miserable hovels and of crops with the deliberate intention of starving the inhabitants, the forced relocation of whole communities, the manipulation of treason charges so as to facilitate the seizure of lands, the endless repetition of acts of military "justice" calculated to intimidate and break the spirit—may be glimpsed in distorted and on occasion direct form throughout Spenser's writings, along with dreamlike depictions of the beauty of the Irish landscape. Those writings probably include *A View of the Present State of Ireland*, an anonymously published apology for the repressive English regime.

Spenser was rewarded for his efforts in Ireland with a castle and 3,028 acres of expropriated land at Kilcolman in the province of Munster. There he was visited by another colonist and poet, the powerful and well-connected Sir Walter Ralegh, to whom Spenser showed the great chivalric epic on which he was at work. With Ralegh's influential backing, Spenser traveled to England and published, in 1590, the first three books of *The Faerie Queene*, which made a strong bid for the queen's favor and patronage. He was rewarded with a handsome pension of fifty pounds a year for life, though the queen's principal councilor, Lord Burghley, is said to have complained that it was a lot for a song. Soon after, Spenser published a volume of poems called *Complaints*; a pastoral called *Colin Clouts Come Home Againe* (1595), commenting on the courtiers and ladies at the center of English court life at the time of his 1590 visit; his sonnet cycle, *Amoretti*; and two wedding poems, *Epithalamion* and *Prothalamion*. The six-book *Faerie Queene* was published in 1596, with some revisions in the first part and a changed ending to Book 3 to provide a bridge to the added books; the two so-called Mutability cantos and two stanzas of a third—perhaps part of an intended seventh book—appeared posthumously in the edition of 1609.

In 1598 there was an uprising in Munster, and rebels burned down the house in which Spenser lived. The poet fled with his wife; their newborn baby is said to have died in the flames. Spenser was sent to England with messages from the besieged English garrison. He died in Westminster on January 13, 1599, and was buried near his beloved Chaucer in what is now called the Poets' Corner of Westminster Abbey.

Spenser cannot be put into neatly labeled categories. His work is steeped in Renaissance Neoplatonism but is also earthy and practical. He is a lover and celebrator of physical beauty yet also a profound analyst of good and evil in all their perplexing shapes and complexities. In his early days he was strongly influenced by Puritanism, remained a thoroughgoing Protestant all his life, and portrayed the Roman Catholic church as a demonic villain in *The Faerie Queene*; yet his understanding of faith and of sin owes much to Catholic thinkers. He is a poet of sensuous images yet also something of an iconoclast, deeply suspicious of the power of images (material and verbal) to turn into idols. He is an idealist, drawn to courtesy, gentleness, and exquisite moral refinement, yet also a celebrant of English nationalism, empire, and martial power. He is in some ways a backward-looking poet who paid homage to Chaucer, used archaic language, and compared his own age unfavorably with the feudal past. Yet as a British epic poet and poet-prophet, he points forward to the poetry of the Romantics and especially Milton—who himself paid homage to the "sage and serious" Spenser as "a better teacher than Scotus or Aquinas."

Because it was a deliberate choice on Spenser's part that his language should seem antique, his poetry is always printed in the original spelling and punctuation; a few of the most confusing punctuation marks have, however, been altered in the present text. Spenser also spells words variably in such a way as to suggest rhymes to the eye or to suggest etymologies (often incorrect ones). This inconsistency in his spelling is typical of his time; in the sixteenth century people varied even the spelling of their own names.

The Faerie Queene

In a letter to Sir Walter Ralegh, appended to the first, 1590, edition of *The Faerie Queene*, Spenser describes his exuberant, multifaceted poem as an allegory—an extended metaphor or "dark conceit"—and invites us to interpret the characters and adventures in the several books in terms of the particular virtues and vices they enact or come to embody. Thus the Redcrosse Knight in Book 1 is the knight of Holiness (and also St. George, the patron saint of England); Sir Guyon in Book 2 is the knight of Temperance; the female knight Britomart in Book 3 is the knight of Chastity (chastity here meaning chaste love leading to marriage). The heroes of Books 4, 5, and 6 represent Friendship, Justice, and Courtesy. The poem's general end, Spenser writes, is "to fashion a gentleman or noble person in vertuous and gentle discipline," and the individual moral qualities, taken together, constitute the ideal human being.

However, Spenser's allegory is not as simple as the letter to Ralegh might suggest, and the fashioning of identity proves to be anything but straightforward. Far from being the static embodiments of abstract moral precepts, the knights have a surprisingly complex, altogether human relation to their allegorical identities, identities into which they grow only through painful trial and error in the course of their adventures. These adventures repeatedly take the form of mortal combat with sworn enemies—hence the Redcrosse Knight of Holiness smites the "Saracen" (that is, Muslim) Sansfoy (literally, "without faith")—but the enemies are revealed more often than not to be weirdly dissociated aspects of the knights themselves: when he encounters Sansfoy, Redcrosse has just been faithless to his lady Una, and his most dangerous enemy ultimately proves to be his own despair. Accordingly, the meaning of the various characters, episodes, and places is richly complex, revealed to us (and to the characters themselves) only by degrees.

The complexity is heightened by the inclusion, in addition to the moral allegory, of an historical allegory to which Spenser calls attention, in the letter to Ralegh, by observing that both the Faerie Queene and Britomart are personifications of Queen Elizabeth. Throughout the poem there is a dense network of allusions to events, issues, and particular persons in England and Ireland—for example, the queen, her rival Mary, Queen of Scots, the Spanish Armada, the English Reformation, the controversies over religious images, and the bitter colonial struggles against Irish rebellion. Some of Spenser's characters are identified by conventional symbols and attributes that would have been obvious to every reader of his time. For example, such a reader would know immediately that a woman who wears a miter and scarlet clothes and who dwells near the river Tiber represents (in one sense at least) the Roman Catholic Church, which had often been identified by Protestant preachers with the Whore of Babylon in the Book of Revelation. Marginal notes jotted in early copies of The Faerie Queene suggest, however, that there was no consensus among Spenser's contemporaries about the precise historical referents of others of the poem's myriad figures. (Sir Walter Ralegh's wife Bess, for example, seems to have identified many of the virtuous female characters as allegorical representations of herself.) Spenser's poem may be enjoyed as a fascinating story with multiple meanings, a story that works on several levels at once and continually eludes the full and definitive allegorical explanation it constantly promises to deliver.

The poem is also an epic. The organization of each book into twelve cantos imitates the twelve books of Virgil's great Latin epic, the Aeneid, and, like Virgil, Spenser is deeply concerned with the dangerous struggles and painful renunciations required to achieve the highest values of human civilization. The heroic deeds of Spenser's brave knights are the achievements of individual aristocratic men and women, not the triumphs of armies or communities united in serving a common purpose, not even the triumph of the virtually invisible royal court of Gloriana, the Faerie Queene. Yet, taken together, the disjointed adventures of these solitary warriors constitute in Spenser's fervent vision the glory of Britain, the collective memory of its heroic past and the promise of a still more glorious future. And if the Faerie Queene herself is consigned to the margins of the poem that bears her name, she nonetheless is the symbolic embodiment of a shared national destiny, a destiny that reaches beyond mere political success to participate in the ultimate, millennial triumph of good over evil.

If The Faerie Queene is thus an epic celebration of Queen Elizabeth, the Protestant faith, and the English nation, it is also a chivalric romance, full of jousting knights and damsels in distress, dragons, witches, enchanted trees, wicked magicians, giants, dark caves, shining castles, and "paynims" (with French names). A clear, pleasant stream may be dangerous to drink from because to do so produces loss of strength. A pious hermit may prove to be a cunningly disguised villain. Houses, castles, and gardens are often places of education and challenge or of especially dense allegorical significance, as if they possess special, half-hidden keys to the meaning of the books in which they appear. As a romance, Spenser's poem is designed to produce wonder, to enthrall its readers with sprawling plots, marvelous adventures, heroic characters, ravishing descriptions, and esoteric mysteries.

The Faerie Queene constantly intertwines diverse literary and pictorial traditions. Entire episodes are adapted from two great Italian romantic epics, Orlando furioso (Orlando Mad, 1516), by Ariosto, and Gerusalemme liberata (Jerusalem Delivered, 1575), by Tasso. Ariosto and Tasso in turn were closely following Homer, Virgil, and Ovid, as well as other ancient poets. (For a Renaissance poet, borrowing from and reworking older materials was thought praiseworthy.) Places such as Lucifera's castle, individual attributes such as Una's lamb, and certain stock characters, with their names, physiognomies, and costumes, came to Spenser from the classics and the Bible, from theologians, from folk tales and medieval pageants, from tapestries, paintings, and collections of emblems.

The whole of The Faerie Queene is written in a remarkable nine-line stanza of closely interlocking rhymes (ababbcbcc), the first eight lines with five stresses each (iambic pentameter) and the final line with six stresses (iambic hexameter or alexandrine). The stanza gives the work a certain formal regularity, but the various books are composed on quite different structural principles. Book 1 is almost entirely self-contained; it has been called a miniature epic in itself, centering on the adventures of one principal hero, Redcrosse, who at length achieves the quest he undertakes at Una's behest: killing the dragon who has imprisoned her parents and thereby winning her as his bride. The spiritual allegory is similarly self-contained; it presents the Christian struggling heroically against many evils and temptations—doctrinal error, hypocrisy, the Seven Deadly Sins, and despair—to some of which he succumbs before finally emerging triumphant. It shows him separated from the one true faith and, aided by many interventions of divine grace, at length reunited with it once more. Then it treats his purgation from sin, his education in the House of Holiness, and his final salvation.

To some degree a lack of closure characterizes all of The Faerie Queene, including the more self-contained of the six finished books, and it is fitting that there survives the fragment of another book, the cantos of Mutability, in which Spenser broods on the tension in nature between systematic order and ceaseless change. The poem as a whole is built around principles that pull tautly against one another: a commitment to a life of constant struggle and a profound longing for rest; a celebration of human heroism and a perception of ineradicable human sinfulness; a vision of evil as a terrifyingly potent force and a vision of evil as mere emptiness and filth; a faith in the supreme value of visionary art and a recurrent suspicion that art is dangerously allied to graven images and deception. That Spenser's knights never quite reach the havens they seek may reflect irresolvable tensions to which we owe much of the power and beauty of this great, unfinished work.

From THE FAERIE QUEENE

From The First Booke of The Faerie Queene

Contayning
The Legende of the
Knight of the Red Crosse,
or
Of Holinesse

Canto 1

The Patron of true Holinesse,
Foule Errour doth defeate:
Hypocrisie him to entrappe,
Doth to his home entreate.

1

	A Gentle Knight was pricking° on the plaine,	*spurring*
	Ycladd in mightie armes and silver shielde,	
	Wherein old dints of deepe wounds did remaine,	
	The cruell markes of many a bloudy fielde;	
5	Yet armes till that time did he never wield:[1]	
	His angry steede did chide his foming bitt,	
	As much disdayning to the curbe to yield:	
	Full jolly° knight he seemd, and faire did sitt,	*gallant*
	As one for knightly giusts° and fierce encounters fitt.	*tourneys, jousts*

2

10	But on his brest a bloudie Crosse he bore,	
	The deare remembrance of his dying Lord,	
	For whose sweete sake that glorious badge he wore,	
	And dead as living ever him adored:	
	Upon his shield the like was also scored,	
15	For soveraine[2] hope, which in his helpe he had:	
	Right faithfull true[3] he was in deede and word,	
	But of his cheere[4] did seeme too solemne sad;°	*grave*
	Yet nothing did he dread, but ever was ydrad.°	*dreaded, feared*

3

20	Upon a great adventure he was bond,	
	That greatest Gloriana to him gave,	
	That greatest Glorious Queene of Faerie Lond,	
	To winne him worship,° and her grace to have,	*honor*
	Which of all earthly things he most did crave;	

---

1. Redcrosse wears the armor of the Christian man, as Spenser explained in the letter to Ralegh. It bears the dents of every Christian's fight against evil.
2. Having greatest power (often applied to medical remedies).
3. An echo of Revelation 19.11: "And I saw heaven opened; and behold a white horse; and he that sat upon him was called Faithful and True."
4. Facial expression, mood.

And ever as he rode, his hart did earne°   *yearn*
25 To prove his puissance in battell brave
Upon his foe, and his new force to learne;
Upon his foe, a Dragon horrible and stearne.

4

A lovely Ladie rode him faire beside,
Upon a lowly Asse more white then snow,
30 Yet she much whiter, but the same did hide
Under a vele, that wimpled° was full low, *lying in folds*
And over all a blacke stole she did throw,
As one that inly mournd: so was she sad,
And heavie sat upon her palfrey slow:
35 Seemèd in heart some hidden care she had,
And by her in a line a milke white lambe she lad.

5

So pure an innocent, as that same lambe,
She was in life and every vertuous lore,
And by descent from Royall lynage came
40 Of ancient Kings and Queenes, that had of yore
Their scepters stretcht from East to Westerne shore,
And all the world in their subjection held;
Till that infernall feend with foule uprore
Forwasted° all their land, and them expeld: *laid waste*
45 Whom to avenge, she had this Knight from far compeld.° *summoned*

6

Behind her farre away a Dwarfe did lag,
That lasie seemd in being ever last,
Or wearied with bearing of her bag
Of needments at his backe. Thus as they past,
50 The day with cloudes was suddeine overcast,
And angry Jove an hideous storme of raine
Did poure into his Lemans⁵ lap so fast,
That every wight° to shrowd° it did constrain, *creature / cover*
And this faire couple eke° to shroud themselves were fain.° *also / eager*

7

55 Enforst to seeke some covert nigh at hand,
A shadie grove not far away they spide,
That promist ayde the tempest to withstand:
Whose loftie trees yclad with sommers pride,
Did spred so broad, that heavens light did hide,
60 Not perceable° with power of any starre: *penetrable*
And all within were pathes and alleies wide,
With footing worne, and leading inward farre:
Faire harbour that them seemes; so in they entred arre.

5. His lover's, i.e., the earth's.

8

And foorth they passe, with pleasure forward led,
65   Joying to heare the birdes sweete harmony,
    Which therein shrouded from the tempest dred,°   *fearful*
    Seemd in their song to scorne the cruell sky.
    Much can° they prayse the trees, so straight and hy,   *did*
    The sayling Pine, the Cedar proud and tall,
70   The vine-prop Elme, the Poplar never dry,
    The builder Oake, sole king of forrests all,
The Aspine good for staves, the Cypresse funerall.

9

The Laurell, meed° of mightie Conquerours   *reward*
    And Poets sage, the Firre that weepeth still,[6]
75   The Willow worne of forlorne Paramours,
    The Eugh° obedient to the benders will,   *yew*
    The Birch for shaftes, the Sallow° for the mill,   *willow*
    The Mirrhe sweete bleeding in the bitter wound,
    The warlike Beech, the Ash for nothing ill,
80   The fruitfull Olive, and the Platane° round,   *plane-tree*
The carver Holme,[7] the Maple seeldom inward sound.

10

Led with delight, they thus beguile the way,
    Untill the blustring storme is overblowne;
    When weening° to returne, whence they did stray,   *thinking*
85   They cannot finde that path, which first was showne,
    But wander too and fro in wayes unknowne,
    Furthest from end then, when they neerest weene,
    That makes them doubt, their wits be not their owne:
    So many pathes, so many turnings seene,
90 That which of them to take, in diverse doubt they been.

11

At last resolving forward still to fare,
    Till that some end they finde or° in or out,   *either*
    That path they take, that beaten seemed most bare,
    And like to lead the labyrinth about°   *out of*
95   Which when by tract they hunted had throughout,
    At length it brought them to a hollow cave,
    Amid the thickest woods. The Champion stout
    Eftsoones° dismounted from his courser brave,   *forthwith*
And to the Dwarfe a while his needlesse spere[8] he gave.

12

100 "Be well aware,"° quoth then that Ladie milde,   *watchful*
    "Least suddaine mischiefe° ye too rash provoke: *misfortune*

---

6. I.e., exudes resin continuously. Spenser in these stanzas imitates Chaucer's catalog of trees in the *Parliament of Fowls*; the convention goes back to Ovid.

7. Holly or holm-oak, both suitable for carving.

8. "Needlesse" because the spear is used only on horseback. "By tract" (line 95): by following the track.

The danger hid, the place unknowne and wilde,
Breedes dreadfull doubts: Oft fire is without smoke,
And perill without show: therefore your stroke
105   Sir knight with-hold, till further triall made."
"Ah Ladie," said he, "shame were to revoke°   draw back
The forward footing for° an hidden shade: because of
Vertue gives her selfe light, through darkenesse for to wade."

13

"Yea but," quoth she, "the perill of this place
110   I better wot then° you, though now too late   know than
To wish you backe returne with foule disgrace,
Yet wisedome warnes, whilest foot is in the gate,
To stay the stepe, ere forcèd to retrate.
This is the wandring wood, this Errours den,
115   A monster vile, whom God and man does hate:
Therefore I read° beware." "Fly fly," quoth then   advise
The fearefull Dwarfe: "this is no place for living men."

14

But full of fire and greedy hardiment,°   boldness
The youthfull knight could not for ought° be staide,   anything
120   But forth unto the darksome hole he went,
And lookèd in: his glistring° armor made   shining
A litle glooming light, much like a shade,
By which he saw the ugly monster plaine,
Halfe like a serpent horribly displaide,[9]
125   But th' other halfe did womans shape retaine,
Most lothsom, filthie, foule, and full of vile disdaine.°   loathsomeness

15

And as she lay upon the durtie ground,
Her huge long taile her den all overspred,
Yet was in knots and many boughtes° upwound,   coils
130   Pointed with mortall sting. Of her there bred
A thousand yong ones, which she dayly fed,
Sucking upon her poisonous dugs, eachone
Of sundry shapes, yet all ill favorèd:
Soone as that uncouth° light upon them shone,   unfamiliar
135   Into her mouth they crept, and suddain all were gone.

16

Their dam upstart, out of her den effraide,°   alarmed
And rushèd forth, hurling her hideous taile
About her cursèd head, whose folds displaid°   extended
Were stretcht now forth at length without entraile.°   coiling
140   She lookt about, and seeing one in mayle
Armèd to point,° sought backe to turne againe;   i.e., completely
For light she hated as the deadly bale,°   injury

9. That Errour is half serpent reminds us of the primal error in Eden, which the serpent instigated. The description echoes both classical and biblical monsters (cf. Revelation 9.7–10).

Ay wont° in desert darknesse to remain,   *ever accustomed*
Where plaine none might her see, nor she see any plaine.

17

145 Which when the valiant Elfe[1] perceived, he lept
  As Lyon fierce upon the flying pray,
  And with his trenchand° blade her boldly kept *cutting*
  From turning backe, and forcèd her to stay:
  Therewith enraged she loudly gan to bray,
150 And turning fierce, her speckled taile advaunst,
  Threatning her angry sting, him to dismay:° *defeat*
  Who nought aghast, his mightie hand enhaunst:° *lifted up*
The stroke down from her head unto her shoulder glaunst.

18

Much daunted with that dint,° her sence was dazd, *blow*
155 Yet kindling rage, her selfe she gathered round,
  And all attonce her beastly body raizd
  With doubled forces high above the ground:
  Tho° wrapping up her wrethèd sterne arownd, *then*
  Lept fierce upon his shield, and her huge traine° *tail*
160 All suddenly about his body wound,
  That hand or foot to stirre he strove in vaine:
God helpe the man so wrapt in Errours endlesse traine.

19

His Lady sad to see his sore constraint,° *fettered state*
  Cride out, "Now now Sir knight, shew what ye bee,
165 Add faith unto your force, and be not faint:
  Strangle her, else she sure will strangle thee."
  That when he heard, in great perplexitie,[2]
  His gall did grate for griefe° and high disdaine, *wrath*
  And knitting all his force got one hand free,
170 Wherewith he grypt her gorge° with so great paine, *throat*
That soone to loose her wicked bands did her constraine.

20

Therewith she spewd out of her filthy maw
  A floud of poyson horrible and blacke,
  Full of great lumpes of flesh and gobbets raw,
175 Which stunck so vildly, that it forst him slacke
  His grasping hold, and from her turne him backe:
  Her vomit full of bookes and papers was,[3]
  With loathly frogs and toades, which eyes did lacke,
  And creeping sought way in the weedy gras:
180 Her filthy parbreake° all the place defilèd has.[4] *vomit*

---

1. I.e., knight of Faerie Land.
2. In both the usual sense and the sense of "entangled condition."
3. Alluding (at one level) to books and pamphlets of Catholic propaganda, notably attacks on Queen Elizabeth.
4. Revelation 16.13: "And I saw three unclean spirits like frogs come out of the mouth of the dragon, and out of the mouth of the beast, and out of the mouth of the false prophet."

21

As when old father Nilus gins to swell
   With timely° pride above the Aegyptian vale,   *in season*
   His fattie° waves do fertile slime outwell,   *rich*
   And overflow each plaine and lowly dale:
185   But when his later spring gins to avale,°   *subside*
   Huge heapes of mudd he leaves, wherein there breed
   Ten thousand kindes of creatures, partly male
   And partly female of his fruitfull seed;
Such ugly monstrous shapes elswhere may no man reed.°   *see*

22

190 The same so sore annoyèd has the knight,
   That welnigh chokèd with the deadly stinke,
   His forces faile, ne can no longer fight.
   Whose corage when the feend perceived to shrinke,
   She pourèd forth out of her hellish sinke
195   Her fruitfull cursèd spawne of serpents small,
   Deformèd monsters, fowle, and blacke as inke,
   Which swarming all about his legs did crall,
And him encombred sore, but could not hurt at all.

23

As gentle Shepheard in sweete even-tide,
200   When ruddy Phoebus gins to welke° in west,   *sink*
   High on an hill, his flocke to vewen wide,
   Markes° which do byte their hasty supper best;   *observes*
   A cloud of combrous° gnattes do him molest,   *encumbering*
   All striving to infixe their feeble stings,
205   That from their noyance he no where can rest,
   But with his clownish° hands their tender wings   *rustic*
He brusheth oft, and oft doth mar their murmurings.

24

Thus ill bestedd,° and fearful more of shame,   *situated*
   Then of the certaine perill he stood in,
210   Halfe furious unto his foe he came,
   Resolved in minde all suddenly to win,
   Or soone to lose, before he once would lin;°   *cease*
   And strooke at her with more then manly force,
   That from her body full of filthie sin
215   He raft° her hatefull head without remorse;   *cut away*
A streame of cole black bloud forth gushèd from her corse.

25

Her scattred brood, soone as their Parent deare
   They saw so rudely° falling to the ground,   *with great force*
   Groning full deadly, all with troublous feare,
220   Gathred themselves about her body round,
   Weening° their wonted entrance to have found   *thinking*
At her wide mouth: but being there withstood

They flockèd all about her bleeding wound,
And suckèd up their dying mothers blood,
225 Making her death their life, and eke° her hurt their good.   *also*

26

That detestable sight him much amazde,°   *stunned*
To see th' unkindly Impes° of heaven accurst,   *unnatural offspring*
Devoure their dam; on whom while so he gazd,
Having all satisfide their bloudy thirst,
230 Their bellies swolne he saw with fulnesse burst,
And bowels gushing forth: well worthy end
Of such as drunke her life, the which them nurst;
Now needeth him no lenger labour spend,
His foes have slaine themselves, with whom he should contend.

27

235 His Ladie seeing all, that chaunst, from farre
Approcht in hast to greet° his victorie,   *congratulate*
And said, "Faire knight, borne under happy starre,
Who see your vanquisht foes before you lye;
Well worthy be you of that Armorie,°   *armor*
240 Wherein ye have great glory wonne this day,
And prooved your strength on a strong enimie,
Your first adventure: many such I pray,
And henceforth ever wish, that like succeed it may."

28

Then mounted he upon his Steede againe,
245 And with the Lady backward sought to wend;°   *go*
That path he kept, which beaten was most plaine,
Ne ever would to any by-way bend,
But still did follow one unto the end,
The which at last out of the wood them brought.
250 So forward on his way (with God to frend)°   *with God as friend*
He passèd forth, and new adventure sought;
Long way he travelèd, before he heard of ought.

29

At length they chaunst to meet upon the way
An aged Sire, in long blacke weedes yclad,[5]
255 His feete all bare, his beard all hoarie gray,
And by his belt his booke he hanging had;
Sober he seemde, and very sagely sad,°   *grave*
And to the ground his eyes were lowly bent,
Simple in shew, and voyde of malice bad,
260 And all the way he prayèd, as he went,
And often knockt his brest, as one that did repent.

30

He faire the knight saluted, louting° low,   *bowing*
Who faire him quited,° as that courteous was: *answered*

5. Dressed in long black garments.

And after askèd him, if he did know
265   Of straunge adventures, which abroad did pas.
"Ah my deare Sonne," quoth he, "how should, alas,
Silly° old man, that lives in hidden cell,   *simple*
Bidding his beades° all day for his trespas,   *saying his prayers*
Tydings of warre and worldly trouble tell?
270 With holy father sits not with such things to mell.[6]

31

"But if of daunger which hereby doth dwell,
And homebred evill ye desire to heare,
Of a straunge man I can you tidings tell,
That wasteth all this countrey farre and neare."
275   "Of such," said he, "I chiefly do inquere,
And shall you well reward to shew the place,
In which that wicked wight his dayes doth weare.°   *spend*
For to all knighthood it is foule disgrace,
That such a cursed creature lives so long a space."

32

280 "Far hence," quoth he, "in wastfull° wildernesse   *desolate*
His dwelling is, by which no living wight
May ever passe, but thorough great distresse."
"Now," sayd the Lady, "draweth toward night,
And well I wote, that of your later° fight   *recent*
285   Ye all forwearied be: for what so strong,
But wanting rest will also want of might?
The Sunne that measures heaven all day long,
At night doth baite° his steedes the Ocean waves emong.   *feed, refresh*

33

"Then with the Sunne take Sir, your timely rest,
290 And with new day new worke at once begin:
Untroubled night they say gives counsell best."
"Right well Sir knight ye have advisèd bin,"
Quoth then that agèd man; "the way to win
Is wisely to advise:° now day is spent;   *take thought*
295   Therefore with me ye may take up your In°   *lodging*
For this same night." The knight was well content.
So with that godly father to his home they went.

34

A little lowly Hermitage it was,
Downe in a dale, hard by a forests side,
300 Far from resort of people, that did pas
In travell to and froe: a little wyde°   *apart*
There was an holy Chappell edifyde,°   *built*
Wherein the Hermite dewly wont° to say   *was accustomed*
His holy things° each morne and eventyde: *prayers*
305   Thereby a Christall streame did gently play,
Which from a sacred fountaine wellèd forth alway.

6. I.e., it is not fitting for a holy hermit to meddle ("mell") with such things.

35

Arrivèd there, the little house they fill,
    Ne looke for entertainement, where none was:
    Rest is their feast, and all things at their will;
310   The noblest mind the best contentment has.
    With faire discourse the evening so they pas:
    For that old man of pleasing wordes had store,
    And well could file° his tongue as smooth as glas;   *polish*
    He told of Saintes and Popes, and evermore
315 He strowd an *Ave-Mary*[7] after and before.

36

The drouping Night thus creepeth on them fast,
    And the sad humour;° loading their eye liddes,   *heavy moisture*
    As messenger of Morpheus° on them cast   *god of dreams*
    Sweet slombring deaw, the which to sleepe them biddes.
320   Unto their lodgings then his guestes he riddes:°   *leads*
    Where when all drownd in deadly sleepe;° he findes,   *sleep like death*
    He to his study goes, and there amiddes
    His Magick bookes and artes of sundry kindes,
He seekes out mighty charmes, to trouble sleepy mindes.

37

325 Then choosing out few wordes most horrible
    (Let none them read), thereof did verses frame,
    With which and other spelles like terrible,
    He bade awake blacke Plutoes griesly Dame,[8]
    And cursèd heaven, and spake reprochfull shame
330   Of highest God, the Lord of life and light;
    A bold bad man, that dared to call by name
    Great Gorgon,[9] Prince of darknesse and dead night,
At which Cocytus quakes, and Styx is put to flight.

38

And forth he cald out of deepe darknesse dred
335   Legions of Sprights, the which like little flyes;[1]
    Fluttring about his ever damnèd hed,
    A-waite whereto their service he applyes,
    To aide his friends, or fray° his enimies: *frighten*
    Of those he chose out two, the falsest twoo,
340   And fittest for to forge true-seeming lyes;
    The one of them he gave a message too,
The other by him selfe staide other worke to doo.

39

He making speedy way through spersèd° ayre,   *dispersed*
    And through the world of waters wide and deepe,
345   To Morpheus house doth hastily repaire.

---

7. "Hail Mary"—that is, a Catholic prayer.
8. Proserpine, as patron of witchcraft.
9. Demogorgon, in some myths the progenitor of all the gods, so powerful that the mention of his name causes hell's rivers (Styx and Cocytus) to tremble.
1. The simile associates him with Beelzebub (Lord of Flies).

Amid the bowels of the earth full steepe,
And low, where dawning day doth never peepe,
His dwelling is; there Tethys° his wet bed   *the wife of Ocean*
Doth ever wash, and Cynthia[2] still° doth steepe   *continually*
350   In silver deaw his ever-drouping hed,
Whiles sad° Night over him her mantle black doth spred.   *sober*

40

Whose double gates he findeth lockèd fast,
The one faire framed of burnisht Yvory,
The other all with silver overcast;
355   And wakefull dogges before them farre do lye,
Watching to banish Care their enimy,
Who oft is wont° to trouble gentle Sleepe.   *accustomed to*
By them the Sprite doth passe in quietly,
And unto Morpheus comes, whom drownèd deepe
360   In drowsie fit he findes: of nothing he takes keepe.°   *notice*

41

And more, to lulle him in his slumber soft,
A trickling streame from high rocke tumbling downe
And ever-drizling raine upon the loft,
Mixt with a murmuring winde, much like the sowne°   *sound*
365   Of swarming Bees, did cast him in a swowne:°   *swoon*
No other noyse, nor peoples troublous cryes,
As still° are wont t'annoy the wallèd towne,   *always*
Might there be heard: but carelesse° Quiet lyes,   *free from care*
Wrapt in eternall silence farre from enemyes.[3]

42

370   The messenger approching to him spake,
But his wast° wordes returnd to him in vaine: *wasted*
So sound he slept, that nought mought° him awake.   *might*
Then rudely he him thrust, and pusht with paine,°   *effort*
Whereat he gan to stretch: but he againe
375   Shooke him so hard, that forcèd him to speake.
As one then in a dreame, whose dryer braine[4]
Is tost with troubled sights and fancies° weake,   *fantasies*
He mumbled soft, but would not all his silence breake.

43

The Sprite then gan more boldly him to wake,
380   And threatned unto him the dreaded name
Of Hecate:° whereat he gan to quake,   *queen of Hades*
And lifting up his lumpish head, with blame
Halfe angry askèd him, for what° he came.   *why*
"Hither," quoth he, "me Archimago[5] sent,
385   He that the stubborne Sprites can wisely tame,

2. Diana, the goddess of the moon.
3. Spenser is imitating descriptions of the house of Morpheus in Chaucer and Ovid.
4. According to the old physiology, elderly people and other light sleepers had too little moisture in the brain.
5. The name can be construed as meaning both "archmagician" and "architect of images."

He bids thee to him send for his intent
A fit false dreame, that can delude the sleepers sent."°   *senses*

44

The God obayde, and calling forth straight way
A diverse° dreame out of his prison darke,   *distracting*
390   Delivered it to him, and downe did lay
His heavie head, devoide of carefull carke,°   *anxious concerns*
Whose sences all were straight benumbd and starke.
He backe returning by the Yvorie dore,[6]
Remounted up as light as chearefull Larke,
395   And on his litle winges the dreame he bore
In hast unto his Lord, where he him left afore.

45

Who all this while with charmes and hidden artes,
Had made a Lady of that other Spright,
And framed of liquid ayre her tender partes
400   So lively,° and so like in all mens sight,   *lifelike*
That weaker° sence it could have ravisht quight: *too weak*
The maker selfe for all his wondrous witt,
Was nigh beguilèd with so goodly sight:
Her all in white he clad, and over it
405   Cast a blacke stole, most like to seeme for Una[7] fit.°   *fitting*

46

Now when that ydle dreame was to him brought
Unto that Elfin knight he bad him fly,
Where he slept soundly void of evill thought
And with false shewes abuse his fantasy,°   *imagination*
410   In sort as° he him schoolèd privily: *in the way that*
And that new creature borne without her dew°   *unnaturally*
Full of the makers guile, with usage sly
He taught to imitate that Lady trew,
Whose semblance she did carrie under feignèd hew.°   *form*

47

415   Thus well instructed, to their worke they hast
And comming where the knight in slomber lay
The one upon his hardy head him plast,°   *placed*
And made him dreame of loves and lustfull play
That nigh his manly hart did melt away,
420   Bathèd in wanton blis and wicked joy:
Then seemèd him his Lady by him lay,
And to him playnd,° how that false wingèd boy;°   *complained / Cupid*
Her chast hart had subdewd, to learne Dame pleasures toy.°   *lustful play*

---

6. According to Homer (*Odyssey* 19.562–67) and Virgil (*Aeneid* 6.893–96), false dreams come through Sleep's ivory gate, true dreams through his gate of horn.

7. Her name means "one, unity." Elizabethan readers would know the Latin phrase *Una Vera Fides* ("one true faith") and also the proverb "Truth is one."

48

And she her selfe of beautie soveraigne Queene
425   Faire Venus seemde unto his bed to bring
 Her, whom he waking evermore did weene°   *think*
 To be the chastest flowre, that ay° did spring   *ever*
 On earthly braunch, the daughter of a king,
 Now a loose Leman° to vile service bound: *paramour*
430   And eke° the Graces seemèd all to sing,   *also*
 Hymen iô Hymen, dauncing all around,
Whilst freshest Flora her with Yvie girlond crownd.[8]

49

In this great passion of unwonted° lust,   *unaccustomed*
 Or wonted feare of doing ought amis,
435   He started up, as seeming to mistrust°   *suspect*
 Some secret ill, or hidden foe of his:
 Lo there before his face his Lady is,
 Under blake stole hyding her bayted hooke,
 And as halfe blushing offred him to kis,
440   With gentle blandishment and lovely° looke,   *loving*
Most like that virgin true, which for her knight him took.

50

All cleane dismayd to see so uncouth° sight,   *unseemly*
 And halfe enragèd at her shamelesse guise,
 He thought have slaine her in his fierce despight:°   *indignation*
445   But hasty heat tempring with sufferance wise,
 He stayde his hand, and gan himselfe advise
 To prove his sense, and tempt° her faignèd truth.   *test*
 Wringing her hands in wemens pitteous wise,
 Tho can° she weepe, to stirre up gentle ruth,°   *then did / pity*
450   Both for her noble bloud, and for her tender youth.

51

And said, "Ah Sir, my liege Lord and my love,
 Shall I accuse the hidden cruell fate,
 And mightie causes wrought in heaven above,
 Or the blind God, that doth me thus amate,°   *dismay*
455   For° hopèd love to winne me certaine hate?   *instead of*
 Yet thus perforce° he bids me do, or die.   *forcibly*
 Die is my dew:[9] yet rew° my wretched state   *pity*
 You, whom my hard avenging destinie
Hath made judge of my life or death indifferently.

52

460   "Your owne deare sake forst me at first to leave
 My Fathers kingdome," There she stopt with teares;

---

8. The three graces of classical mythology were personifications of grace and beauty; here they sing a call to the pleasures of the marriage bed (Hymen was god of marriage). In the March eclogue of *The Shepheardes Calender,* E. K. glossed Flora as "the Goddesse of flowres, but indede (as saith Tacitus) a famous harlot."

9. I.e., I deserve to die.

Her swollen hart her speach seemd to bereave,
And then againe begun, "My weaker yeares
Captived to fortune and frayle worldly feares,
465   Fly to your faith for succour and sure ayde:
Let me not dye in languor° and long teares.   sorrow
"Why Dame," quoth he, "what hath ye thus dismayd?
What frayes° ye, that were wont to comfort me affrayd?"   frightens

53

"Love of your selfe," she said, "and deare° constraint   dire
470   Lets me not sleepe, but wast the wearie night
In secret anguish and unpittied plaint,
Whiles you in carelesse sleepe are drownèd quight."
Her doubtfull words made that redoubted[1] knight
Suspect her truth: yet since no untruth he knew,
475   Her fawning love with foule disdainefull spight
He would not shend,° but said, "Deare dame I rew,   reject
That for my sake unknowne such griefe unto you grew.

54

"Assure your selfe, it fell not all to ground;
For all so deare as life is to my hart,
480   I deeme your love, and hold me to you bound;
Ne let vaine feares procure your needlesse smart,°   pain
Where cause is none, but to your rest depart."
Not all content, yet seemd she to appease°   cease
Her mournefull plaintes, beguilèd° of her art,   foiled
485   And fed with words, that could not chuse but please,
So slyding softly forth, she turnd° as to her ease.   returned

55

Long after lay he musing at her mood,
Much grieved to thinke that gentle Dame so light,°   frivolous
For whose defence he was to shed his blood.
490   At last dull wearinesse of former fight
Having yrockt a sleepe his irkesome spright,°   weary mind
That troublous dreame gan freshly tosse his braine,
With bowres and beds, and Ladies deare delight:
But when he saw his labour all was vaine,
495   With that misformèd spright[2] he backe returnd againe.

1. Dreaded, also doubting again. "Doubtfull": 2. I.e., with the spirit impersonating Una.
fearful, also questionable.

From *Canto 2*

[REDCROSSE WINS "FIDESSA"]

The guilefull great Enchaunter parts
The Redcrosse Knight from Truth:
Into whose stead faire falshood steps,
And workes him wofull ruth.

1

By this the Northerne wagoner had set
    His seven fold teame behind the stedfast starre,[3]
    That was in Ocean waves yet never wet,
    But firme is fixt, and sendeth light from farre
5   To all, that in the wide deepe wandring arre:
    And chearefull Chaunticlere with his note shrill
    Had warnèd once, that Phoebus fiery carre[4]
    In hast was climbing up the Easterne hill,
Full envious that night so long his roome did fill.

2

10 When those accursèd messengers of hell,
    That feigning dreame, and that faire-forgèd Spright
    Came to their wicked maister, and gan tell
    Their bootelesse° paines, and ill succeeding night: *useless*
    Who all in rage to see his skilfull might
15 Deluded so, gan threaten hellish paine
    And sad Proserpines wrath, them to affright.
But when he saw his threatning was but vaine,
He cast about, and searcht his balefull° bookes againe.   *deadly*

3

Eftsoones° he tooke that miscreated faire,   *forthwith*
20 And that false other Spright, on whom he spred
    A seeming body of the subtile° aire,   *rarefied*
    Like a young Squire, in loves and lusty-hed
    His wanton dayes that ever loosely led,
    Without regard of armes and dreaded fight:
25 Those two he tooke, and in a secret bed,
    Covered with darknesse and misdeeming° night,   *misleading*
Them both together laid, to joy in vaine delight.

4

Forthwith he runnes with feignèd faithfull hast
    Unto his guest, who after troublous sights
30 And dreames, gan now to take more sound repast,°   *rest*
    Whom suddenly he wakes with fearefull frights,
    As one aghast with feends or damnèd sprights,
    And to him cals, "Rise rise unhappy Swaine,

3. I.e., by this time the Big Dipper had set behind the North Star.

4. The chariot of the sun. "Chaunticlere": Chanticleer is the generic name for a rooster.

That here wex° old in sleepe, whiles wicked wights   grow
35   Have knit themselves in Venus shamefull chaine;
Come see, where your false Lady doth her honour staine."

5

All in amaze he suddenly up start
With sword in hand, and with the old man went;
Who soone him brought into a secret part,
40   Where that false couple were full closely ment°   mingled
In wanton lust and lewd embracèment:
Which when he saw, he burnt with gealous fire,
The eye of reason was with rage yblent,°   blinded
And would have slaine them in his furious ire,
45 But hardly° was restreinèd of° that aged sire.   with difficulty / by

6

Returning to his bed in torment great,
And bitter anguish of his guiltie sight,
He could not rest, but did his stout heart eat,
And wast his inward gall with deepe despight,°   malice
50   Yrkesome° of life, and too long lingring night.   tired
At last faire Hesperus⁵ in highest skie
Had spent his lampe, and brought forth dawning light,
Then up he rose, and clad him hastily;
The Dwarfe him brought his steed: so both away do fly.

7

55 Now when the rosy-fingred Morning faire,
Weary of aged Tithones⁶ saffron bed,
Had spred her purple robe through deawy aire,
And the high hils Titan° discoverèd,°   the sun / revealed
The royall virgin shooke off drowsy-hed,
60   And rising forth out of her baser° bowre,   too lowly
Lookt for her knight, who far away was fled,
And for her Dwarfe, that wont to wait each houre:
Then gan she waile and weepe, to see that woefull stowre.°   affliction

8

And after him she rode with so much speede
65   As her slow beast could make; but all in vaine:
For him so far had borne his light-foot steede,
Prickèd with wrath and fiery fierce disdaine,°   indignation
That him to follow was but fruitlesse paine;
Yet she her weary limbes would never rest,
70   But every hill and dale, each wood and plaine
Did search, sore grievèd in her gentle brest,
He so ungently left her, whom she lovèd best.

5. The morning star.
6. Tithonus is the husband of Aurora, goddess of the dawn.

9

But subtill° Archimago, when his guests   *cunning*
    He saw divided into double parts,
75   And Una wandring in woods and forrests,
    Th' end of his drift,° he praisd his divelish arts   *plot*
    That had such might over true meaning harts;
    Yet rests not so, but other meanes doth make,
    How he may worke unto her further smarts:
80   For her he hated as the hissing snake,
And in her many troubles did most pleasure take.

10

He then devisde himselfe how to disguise;
    For by his mightie science° he could take   *knowledge*
    As many formes and shapes in seeming wise,°   *in appearance*
85   As ever Proteus[7] to himselfe could make:
    Sometime a fowle, sometime a fish in lake,
    Now like a foxe, now like a dragon fell,°   *fierce*
    That of himselfe he oft for feare would quake,
    And oft would flie away. O who can tell
90   The hidden power of herbes, and might of Magicke spell?

11

But now seemde best, the person to put on
    Of that good knight, his late beguilèd guest:
    In mighty armes he was yclad anon,
    And silver shield: upon his coward brest
95   A bloudy crosse, and on his craven crest
    A bounch of haires discolourd diversly:°   *variously colored*
    Full jolly° knight he seemde, and well addrest,°   *gallant / armed*
    And when he sate upon his courser free,
Saint George himself ye would have deemèd him to be.

12

100   But he the knight, whose semblaunt° he did beare,   *likeness*
    The true Saint George was wandred far away,
    Still flying from° his thoughts and gealous feare;   *because of*
    Will was his guide,[8] and griefe led him astray.
    At last him chaunst to meete upon the way
105   A faithlesse Sarazin° all armed to point,   *Saracen*
    In whose great shield was writ with letters gay
    Sans foy:[9] full large of limbe and every joint
He was, and carèd not for God or man a point.°   *at all*

13

He had a faire companion of his way,
110   A goodly Lady clad in scarlot red,

---

7. A sea god who could change his shape at will
(*Odyssey* 4.398–424).
8. Will should itself be under the guidance of rea-

son or truth.
9. Literally, without faith, faithless.

Purfled° with gold and pearle of rich assay,[1]   *decorated*
And like a Persian mitre on her hed
She wore, with crownes and owches° garnishèd, *brooches*
The which her lavish lovers to her gave;[2]
115 Her wanton° palfrey all was overspred   *unruly*
With tinsell trappings, woven like a wave,
Whose bridle rung with golden bels and bosses brave.° *handsome studs*

14

With faire disport° and courting dalliaunce   *diversion*
She intertainde her lover all the way:
120 But when she saw the knight his speare advaunce,
She soone left off her mirth and wanton play,
And bad her knight addresse him to the fray:
His foe was nigh at hand. He prickt with pride
And hope to winne his Ladies heart that day,
125 Forth spurrèd fast: adowne his coursers side
The red bloud trickling staind the way, as he did ride.

15

The knight of the Redcrosse when him he spide,
Spurring so hote with rage dispiteous,°   *cruel*
Gan fairely couch° his speare, and towards ride: *lower*
130 Soone meete they both, both fell and furious,
That daunted with their forces hideous,
Their steeds do stagger, and amazèd stand,
And eke° themselves too rudely rigorous,° *also / violent*
Astonied° with the stroke of their owne hand, *stunned*
135 Do backe rebut,° and each to other yeeldeth land. *recoil*

16

As when two rams stird with ambitious pride,
Fight for the rule of the rich fleecèd flocke,
Their hornèd fronts so fierce on either side
Do meete, that with the terrour of the shocke
140 Astonied both, stand sencelesse as a blocke,
Forgetfull of the hanging° victory: *in the balance*
So stood these twaine, unmovèd as a rocke,
Both staring fierce, and holding idely
The broken reliques of their former cruelty.

17

145 The Sarazin sore daunted with the buffe
Snatcheth his sword, and fiercely to him flies;
Who well it wards, and quyteth° cuff with cuff: *requites*
Each others equall puissaunce envies,

---

1. Proven valuable by analysis.
2. The lady's garb associates her with the Whore of Babylon (Revelation 17.3–4): "And I saw a woman sit upon a scarlet colored beast, full of names of blasphemy, having seven heads and ten horns. And the woman was arrayed in purple and scarlet color, and decked with gold and precious stones and pearls, having a golden cup in her hand full of abominations and filthiness of her fornication."

And through their iron sides with cruell spies°   *looks*
150 Does seeke to perce: repining courage yields
  No foote to foe. The flashing fier flies
  As from a forge out of their burning shields,
And streames of purple bloud new dies the verdant fields.

18

"Curse on that Crosse," quoth then the Sarazin,
155 "That keepes thy body from the bitter fit;°   *death pangs*
  Dead long ygoe I wote° thou haddest bin,   *thought*
  Had not that charme from thee forwarnèd° it: *prevented*
  But yet I warne thee now assurèd° sitt,   *securely*
  And hide thy head." Therewith upon his crest
160 With rigour° so outrageous he smitt,   *violence*
  That a large share it hewd out of the rest,
And glauncing downe his shield, from blame him fairely blest.[3]

19

Who thereat wondrous wroth, the sleeping spark
  Of native vertue° gan eftsoones revive,   *strength*
165 And at his haughtie helmet making mark,
  So hugely° stroke, that it the steele did rive, *mightily*
  And cleft his head. He tumbling downe alive,
  With bloudy mouth his mother earth did kis
  Greeting his grave: his grudging° ghost did strive *complaining*
170 With the fraile flesh; at last it flitted is,
Whither the soules do fly of men, that live amis.

20

The Lady when she saw her champion fall,
  Like the old ruines of a broken towre,
  Staid not to waile his woefull funerall,°   *death*
175 But from him fled away with all her powre;
  Who after her as hastily gan scowre,°   *scurry*
  Bidding the Dwarfe with him to bring away
  The Sarazins shield, signe of the conqueroure.
  Her soone he overtooke, and bad to stay,
180 For present cause was none of dread her to dismay.

21

She turning backe with ruefull countenaunce,
  Cride, "Mercy mercy Sir vouchsafe to show
  On silly° Dame, subject to hard mischaunce, *helpless*
  And to your mighty will." Her humblesse low
185 In so ritch weedes° and seeming glorious show, *clothes*
  Did much emmove his stout heroicke heart,
  And said, "Deare dame, your suddein overthrow
  Much rueth° me; but now put feare apart,   *grieves*
And tell, both who ye be, and who that tooke your part."

3. Preserved him from harm.

22

190 Melting in teares, then gan she thus lament;
    "The wretched woman, whom unhappy howre
    Hath now made thrall° to your commandèment,   *slave*
    Before that angry heavens list to lowre,°   *frown*
    And fortune false betraide me to your powre
195   Was (O what now availeth that I was!)
    Borne the sole daughter of an Emperour,
    He that the wide West under his rule has,
    And high hath set his throne, where Tiberis doth pas.[4]

23

    "He in the first flowre of my freshest age,
200   Betrothèd me unto the onely haire°   *heir*
    Of a most mighty king, most rich and sage;
    Was never Prince so faithfull and so faire,
    Was never Prince so meeke and debonaire;°   *gracious*
    But ere my hopèd day of spousall shone,
205   My dearest Lord fell from high honours staire,
    Into the hands of his accursèd fone,°   *foes*
    And cruelly was slaine, that shall I ever mone.[5]

24

    "His blessed body spoild of lively breath,
    Was afterward, I know not how, convaid°   *carried away*
210   And fro me hid: of whose most innocent death
    When tidings came to me unhappy maid,
    O how great sorrow my sad soule assaid.°   *afflicted*
    Then forth I went his woefull corse to find,
    And many yeares throughout the world I straid,
215   A virgin widow, whose deepe wounded mind
    With love, long time did languish as the striken hind.°   *deer*

25

    "At last it chauncèd this proud Sarazin
    To meete me wandring, who perforce° me led   *by violence*
    With him away, but yet could never win
220   The fort, that Ladies hold in soveraigne dread.
    There lies he now with foule dishonour dead,
    Who whiles he livde, was callèd proud Sans foy,
    The eldest of three brethren, all three bred
    Of one bad sire, whose youngest is Sans joy,
225 And twixt them both was borne the bloudy bold Sans loy.[6]

26

    "In this sad plight, friendlesse, unfortunate,
    Now miserable I Fidessa° dwell,   *Faith*

---

4. The Tiber River runs through Rome. The lady is hence associated with the Catholic church. Her father, she says, is ruler of the west—but Una's father had the rule of both east *and* west (1.1.41); historically, the true church once embraced east and west.
5. The lady claims to have been betrothed to Christ, bridegroom of the church.
6. Literally, without law. *Sans joy* means "without joy, darkness of spirit."

Craving of you in pitty of my state,
To do none° ill, if please ye not do well."   *no*
230   He in great passion all this while did dwell,°   *continue*
More busying his quicke eyes, her face to view,
Then his dull eares, to heare what she did tell;
And said, "Faire Lady hart of flint would rew
The undeservèd woes and sorrowes, which ye shew.

27

235   "Henceforth in safe assuraunce may ye rest,
Having both found a new friend you to aid,
And lost an old foe, that did you molest:
Better new friend than an old foe is° said."   *it is*
With chaunge of cheare the seeming simple maid
240   Let fall her eyen, as shamefast° to the earth,   *as if modestly*
And yeelding soft, in that she nought gain-said,
So forth they rode, he feining° seemely merth,   *simulating*
And she coy lookes: so dainty they say maketh derth.[7]

Summary   In the second half of the canto, Redcrosse and his new companion seek relief from the blazing sun in the shade of two trees. Plucking a bough from one of them to make a garland for the lady, he is astonished to hear a groaning voice from within the tree. The voice is that of a knight named Fradubio (Brother Doubt), who explains that he and his beloved have been metamorphosed into trees by a wicked witch named Duessa. Unbeknownst to him, Redcrosse is in the company of this witch.

Canto 3 *Summary*   In search of the knight who has abandoned her, Una encounters a lion who licks her hands and accompanies her in her wanderings. They take refuge for the night in the cottage of a superstitious old woman and her daughter. During the night the daughter's lover, a robber of churches, returns to the cottage with booty for her and is torn to pieces by the lion. Seeking revenge, the old woman encounters Archimago and tells him where to find Una. The magician presents himself to Una disguised as Redcrosse, but his plan backfires when he is attacked by the Saracen Sans loy (brother of the slain Sans foy). Sans loy then kills the faithful lion and abducts Una, leaving Archimago lying wounded.

From *Canto 4*

[THE HOUSE OF PRIDE]

To sinfull house of Pride, Duessa
guides the faithfull knight,
Where brothers death to wreak° Sansjoy   *avenge*
doth chalenge him to fight.

1

Young knight, what ever that dost armes professe,
And through long labours huntest after fame,
Beware of fraud, beware of ficklenesse,
In choice, and change of thy deare lovèd Dame,

7. Proverbial: what's dear is rare; here, coyness creates unsatisfied desire.

5   Least thou of her beleeve too lightly blame,
    And rash misweening° doe thy hart remove: *misjudgment*
    For unto knight there is no greater shame,
    Then lightnesse and inconstancie in love;
    That doth this Redcrosse knights ensample° plainly prove.   *example*

2

10   Who after that he had faire Una lorne,°   *forsaken*
    Through light misdeeming° of her loialtie,   *misjudging*
    And false Duessa in her sted had borne,°   *taken as companion*
    Called Fidess', and so supposd to bee;
    Long with her traveild, till at last they see
15   A goodly building, bravely garnishèd,°   *adorned*
    The house of mightie Prince it seemd to bee:
    And towards it a broad high way[8] that led,
All bare through peoples feet, which thither traveilèd.

3

Great troupes of people traveild thitherward
20   Both day and night, of each degree and place,°   *rank*
    But few returnèd, having scapèd hard,°   *with difficulty*
    With balefull° beggerie, or foule disgrace,   *wretched*
    Which ever after in most wretched case,
    Like loathsome lazars,° by the hedges lay.   *lepers*
25   Thither Duessa bad him bend his pace:°   *direct his steps*
    For she is wearie of the toilesome way,
    And also nigh consumèd is the lingring day.

4

A stately Pallace built of squarèd bricke,
    Which cunningly was without morter laid,
30   Whose wals were high, but nothing strong, nor thick,
    And golden foile° all over them displaid,   *thin layer of gold*
    That purest skye with brightnesse they dismaid:°   *outdid*
    High lifted up were many loftie towres,
    And goodly galleries farre over laid,°   *placed above*
35   Full of faire windowes, and delightfull bowres;
And on the top a Diall told the timely howres.[9]

5

It was a goodly heape° for to behould,   *building*
    And spake the praises of the workmans wit;°   *skill*
    But full great pittie, that so faire a mould°   *structure*
40   Did on so weake foundation ever sit:
    For on a sandie hill,[1] that still did flit,°   *shift*
    And fall away, it mounted was full hie,
    That every breath of heaven shakèd it:

---

8. "Broad is the way that leadeth to destruction" (Matthew 7.13).
9. A sundial measured the hours of the day.
1. Matthew 7.26–27: "A foolish man . . . built his house upon the sand: And the rain descended, and the floods came, and the winds blew, and beat upon that house; and it fell; and great was the fall of it."

And all the hinder parts, that few could spie,
45   Were ruinous and old, but painted cunningly.

6

Arrivèd there they passèd in forth right;
    For still to all the gates stood open wide,
    Yet charge of them was to a Porter hight°   *committed*
    Cald Malvenù,[2] who entrance none denide:
50   Thence to the hall, which was on every side,
    With rich array and costly arras dight:[3]
    Infinite sorts of people did abide
    There waiting long, to win the wishèd sight
Of her, that was the Lady of that Pallace bright.

7

55   By them they passe, all gazing on them round,
    And to the Presence[4] mount; whose glorious vew
    Their frayle amazèd senses did confound:
    In living Princes court none ever knew
    Such endlesse richesse, and so sumptuous shew;
60   Ne Persia selfe, the nourse of pompous pride
    Like ever saw. And there a noble crew
    Of Lordes and Ladies stood on every side,
Which with their presence faire, the place much beautifide.

8

High above all a cloth of State° was spred,   *canopy*
65   And a rich throne, as bright as sunny day,
    On which there sate most brave embellishèd°   *handsomely clad*
    With royall robes and gorgeous array,
    A mayden Queene, that shone as Titans° ray,   *the sun's*
    In glistring gold, and peerelesse pretious stone:
70   Yet her bright blazing beautie did assay°   *attempt*
    To dim the brightnesse of her glorious throne,
As envying her selfe, that too exceeding shone.

9

Exceeding shone, like Phoebus fairest childe,
    That did presume his fathers firie wayne,°   *chariot*
75   And flaming mouthes of steedes unwonted° wilde   *unusually*
    Through highest heaven with weaker° hand to rayne; *too weak*
    Proud of such glory and advancement vaine,
    While flashing beames do daze his feeble eyen,
    He leaves the welkin° way most beaten plaine,   *heavenly*
80   And rapt° with whirling wheeles, inflames the skyen, *carried away*
With fire not made to burne, but fairely for to shyne.[5]

---

2. The name means unwelcome. In courtly love allegories, the porter is often called Bienvenu or Bel-accueil ("welcome").
3. Decorated with costly wall hangings.

4. Presence chamber, where a sovereign receives guests.
5. Phaëton tried to drive the chariot of Phoebus, his father, but set the skies on fire and fell.

10

So proud she shynèd in her Princely state,
   Looking to heaven; for earth she did disdayne,
   And sitting high; for lowly° she did hate: *lowliness*
85   Lo underneath her scornefull feete, was layne
   A dreadfull Dragon with an hideous trayne,°   *tail*
   And in her hand she held a mirrhour bright,[6]
   Wherein her face she often vewèd fayne,°   *with pleasure*
   And in her selfe-loved semblance tooke delight;
90 For she was wondrous faire, as any living wight.

11

Of griesly° Pluto she the daughter was,   *horrid*
   And sad Proserpina the Queene of hell;
   Yet did she thinke her pearelesse worth to pas° *surpass*
   That parentage, with pride so did she swell,
95 And thundring Jove, that high in heaven doth dwell,
   And wield° the world, she claymèd for her syre, *govern*
   Or if that any else did Jove excell:
   For to the highest she did still aspyre,
Or if ought° higher were then that, did it desyre. *anything*

12

100 And proud Lucifera men did her call,
   That made her selfe a Queene, and crownd to be,
   Yet rightfull kingdome she had none at all,
   Ne heritage of native soveraintie,
   But did usurpe with wrong and tyrannie
105 Upon the scepter, which she now did hold:
   Ne ruld her Realmes with lawes, but pollicie,° *political cunning*
   And strong advizement of six wisards old,
That with their counsels bad her kingdome did uphold.

13

Soone as the Elfin knight in presence came,
110 And false Duessa seeming Lady faire,
   A gentle Husher,° Vanitie by name   *usher*
   Made rowme, and passage for them did prepaire:
   So goodly° brought them to the lowest staire *graciously*
   Of her high throne, where they on humble knee
115 Making obeyssance,° did the cause declare, *submission*
   Why they were come, her royall state to see,
To prove° the wide report of her great Majestee. *verify*

14

With loftie eyes, halfe loth to looke so low,
   She thankèd them in her disdainefull wise,° *manner*
120 Ne other grace vouchsafèd them to show

---

6. Pride and figures associated with her in Renaissance literature and art often hold a mirror, emblematic of self-love.

Of Princesse worthy, scarse them bad arise.
Her Lordes and Ladies all this while devise°   *make ready*
Themselves to setten forth to straungers sight:
Some frounce° their curlèd haire in courtly guise,   *frizzle*
125 Some prancke° their ruffes, and others trimly dight° *pleat / arrange*
Their gay attire: each others greater pride does spight.[7]

15

Goodly they all that knight do entertaine,
  Right glad with him to have increast their crew:
  But to Duess' each one himselfe did paine
130 All kindnesse and faire courtesie to shew;
  For in that court whylome° her well they knew: *formerly*
  Yet the stout Faerie mongst the middest° crowd   *thickest*
  Thought all their glorie vaine in knightly vew,
  And that great Princesse too exceeding prowd,
135 That to strange° knight no better countenance° allowd. *stranger / favor*

16

Suddein upriseth from her stately place
  The royall Dame, and for her coche doth call:
  All hurtlen° forth and she with Princely pace,   *rush*
  As faire Aurora in her purple pall,[8]
140 Out of the East the dawning day doth call:
  So forth she comes: her brightnesse brode° doth blaze;   *abroad*
  The heapes of people thronging in the hall,
  Do ride° each other, upon her to gaze: *climb up*
Her glorious glitterand° light doth all mens eyes amaze.   *glittering*

17

145 So forth she comes, and to her coche does clyme,
  Adornèd all with gold, and girlonds gay,
  That seemd as fresh as Flora in her prime,
  And strove to match, in royall rich array,
  Great Junos golden chaire,° the which they say   *chariot*
150 The Gods stand gazing on, when she does ride
  To Joves high house through heavens bras-pavèd way
  Drawne of faire Pecocks, that excell in pride,
And full of Argus eyes their tailes dispredden wide.[9]

18

But this was drawne of six unequall beasts,
155 On which her six sage Counsellours did ryde,
  Taught to obay their bestiall beheasts,
  With like conditions to their kinds applyde:[1]

7. Each begrudges the others' greater pride.
8. Goddess of dawn, in her crimson robe ("purple pall").
9. Peacocks, with their tails outspread ("dispredden wide"), are a symbol of pride. The hundred-eyed monster Argus was set by Juno to watch Io, Jupiter's love. When Mercury killed Argus, his eyes were put in the peacock's tail feathers.
1. Because riders and their mounts are alike bestial, the same conditions pertain (are "applyde") to both natures ("kinds"). This procession of the Seven Deadly Sins—of which Pride is queen—had a long tradition in medieval art and literature (see also Marlowe, *Dr. Faustus* 5.280–330, pp. 475–76).

Of which the first, that all the rest did guyde,
Was sluggish Idlenesse the nourse of sin;
160   Upon a slouthfull Asse he chose to ryde,
Arayd in habit blacke, and amis thin,[2]
Like to an holy Monck, the service to begin.

19

  And in his hand his Portesse° still he bare,   *breviary*
That much was worne, but therein little red,
165   For of devotion he had little care,
Still drownd in sleepe, and most of his dayes ded;
Scarse could he once uphold his heavie hed,
To looken, whether it were night or day:
May seeme the wayne° was very evill led,   *chariot*
170   When such an one had guiding of the way,
That knew not, whether right he went, or else astray.

20

From worldly cares himselfe he did esloyne,°   *withdraw*
And greatly shunnèd manly exercise,
From every worke he chalengèd essoyne,°   *claimed exemption*
175   For contemplation sake: yet otherwise,
His life he led in lawlesse riotise;°   *riotous conduct*
By which he grew to grievous malady;
For in his lustlesse° limbs through evill guise°   *feeble / living*
A shaking fever raignd continually:
180   Such one was Idlenesse, first of this company.

21

And by his side rode loathsome Gluttony,
Deformèd creature, on a filthie swyne,
His belly was up-blowne with luxury.°   *indulgence*
And eke with fatnesse swollen were his eyne,
185   And like a Crane his necke was long and fyne,[3]
With which he swallowd up excessive feast,
For want whereof poore people oft did pyne;°   *starve*
And all the way, most like a brutish beast,
He spuèd up his gorge,[4] that° all did him deteast.   *so that*

22

190   In greene vine leaves he was right fitly clad;
For other clothes he could not weare for heat,
And on his head an yvie girland had,[5]
From under which fast trickled downe the sweat:
Still as he rode, he somewhat° still did eat,   *something*

---

2. Idleness wears the gown ("habit") and hood or amice ("amis") of a monk. Traditionally, Idleness led the procession of the deadly sins.
3. The crane is a common symbol of gluttony because its long and thin ("fyne") neck allows extended pleasure in swallowing.
4. Vomited up what he had swallowed.
5. He resembles the drunken satyr Silenus, foster father of Bacchus, god of wine; ivy is sacred to Bacchus.

195	And in his hand did beare a bouzing° can,	*drinking*
	Of which he supt so oft, that on his seat	
	His dronken corse° he scarse upholden can,	*body*
	In shape and life more like a monster, then° a man.	*than*

23

	Unfit he was for any worldly thing,	
200	And eke unhable once° to stirre or go,°	*at all / walk*
	Not meet° to be of counsell to a king,	*fit*
	Whose mind in meat and drinke was drownèd so,	
	That from his friend he seldome knew his fo:	
	Full of diseases was his carcas blew,	
205	And a dry dropsie through his flesh did flow:	
	Which by misdiet daily greater grew:	
	Such one was Gluttony, the second of that crew.	

24

	And next° to him rode lustfull Lechery,	*just after*
	Upon a bearded Goat,[6] whose rugged haire,	
210	And whally° eyes (the signe of gelosy,°)	*glaring / jealousy*
	Was like the person selfe, whom he did beare:	
	Who rough, and blacke, and filthy did appeare,	
	Unseemely man to please faire Ladies eye;	
	Yet he of Ladies oft was lovèd deare,	
215	When fairer faces were bid standen by:°	*away*
	O who does know the bent of womens fantasy?	

25

	In a greene gowne he clothèd was full faire,	
	Which underneath did hide his filthinesse,	
	And in his hand a burning hart he bare,	
220	Full of vaine follies, and new fangleness:°	*fickleness*
	For he was false, and fraught with ficklenesse,	
	And learnèd had to love with secret lookes,	
	And well could daunce, and sing with ruefulnesse,°	*pathos*
	And fortunes tell, and read in loving bookes,[7]	
225	And thousand other wayes, to bait his fleshly hookes.	

26

	Inconstant man, that lovèd all he saw,	
	And lusted after all, that he did love,	
	Ne would his looser life be tide to law,	
	But joyd weake wemens hearts to tempt and prove°	*try*
230	If from their loyall loves he might them move;	
	Which lewdnesse fild him with reprochfull paine	
	Of that fowle evill, which all men reprove,	
	That rots the marrow, and consumes the braine:°	*i.e., syphilis*
	Such one was Lecherie, the third of all this traine.	

6. Traditional symbol of Lust.
7. Either manuals on the art of love (e.g., Ovid's *Ars Amatoria*) or erotic books.

27

235 And greedy Avarice by him did ride,
      Upon a Camell loaden all with gold;[8]
      Two iron coffers hong on either side,
      With precious mettall full, as they might hold,
      And in his lap an heape of coine he told;°   *counted*
240   For of his wicked pelfe° his God he made,   *money*
      And unto hell him selfe for money sold;
      Accursèd usurie was all his trade,
  And right and wrong ylike in equall ballaunce waide.[9]

28

  His life was nigh unto deaths doore yplast,
245   And thread-bare cote, and cobled shoes he ware,
      Ne scarse good morsell all his life did tast,
      But both from backe and belly still did spare,
      To fill his bags, and richesse to compare;°   *acquire*
      Yet chylde ne kinsman living had he none
250   To leave them to; but thorough daily care
      To get, and nightly feare to lose his owne,
  He led a wretched life unto him selfe unknowne.

29

  Most wretched wight, whom nothing might suffise,
      Whose greedy lust did lacke in greatest store,°   *plenty*
255   Whose need had end, but no end covetise,
      Whose wealth was want, whose plenty made him pore,
      Who had enough, yet wishèd ever more;
      A vile disease, and eke in foote and hand
      A grievous gout tormented him full sore,
260   That well he could not touch, not go,° nor stand: *walk*
  Such one was Avarice, the fourth of this faire band.

30

  And next to him malicious Envie rode,
      Upon a ravenous wolfe, and still° did chaw   *continually*
      Betweene his cankred° teeth a venemous tode,   *infected*
265   That all the poison ran about his chaw;°   *jaw*
      But inwardly he chawèd his owne maw°   *entrails*
      At neighbours wealth, that made him ever sad;
      For death it was, when any good he saw,
      And wept, that cause of weeping none he had,
270 But when he heard of harme, he wexèd wondrous glad.

31

  All in a kirtle of discolourd say[1]
      He clothèd was, ypainted full of eyes;

---

8. The camel as a symbol of avarice is based on Matthew 19.24: "It is easier for a camel to go through the eye of a needle, than for a rich man to enter into the kingdom of God."

9. I.e., he made no distinction between right and wrong.

1. Jacket of many-colored wool.

And in his bosome secretly there lay
An hatefull Snake,[2] the which his taile uptyes
275   In many folds, and mortall sting implyes.°   *enfolds*
Still as he rode, he gnasht his teeth, to see
Those heapes of gold with griple Covetyse,°   *grasping Avarice*
And grudgèd at the great felicitie
Of proud Lucifera, and his owne companie.

32

280   He hated all good workes and vertuous deeds,
And him no lesse, that any like did use,°   *perform*
And who with gracious bread the hungry feeds,
His almes for want of faith he doth accuse;[3]
So every good to bad he doth abuse:°   *twist*
285   And eke° the verse of famous Poets witt   *also*
He does backebite, and spightfull poison spues
From leprous mouth on all, that ever writt:
Such one vile Envie was, that fifte in row did sitt.

33

And him beside rides fierce revenging Wrath,
290   Upon a Lion, loth for to be led;
And in his hand a burning brond° he hath,   *sword*
The which he brandisheth about his hed;
His eyes did hurle forth sparkles fiery red,
And starèd sterne on all, that him beheld,
295   As ashes pale of hew and seeming ded;
And on his dagger still his hand he held,
Trembling through hasty rage, when choler° in him sweld.   *anger*

34

His ruffin° raiment all was staind with blood,   *disorderly*
Which he had spilt, and all to rags yrent,°   *torn*
300   Through unadvisèd rashnesse woxen wood,[4]
For of his hands he had no governement,°   *control*
Ne cared for bloud in his avengement:
But when the furious fit was overpast,
His cruell facts° he often would repent;   *actions*
305   Yet wilfull man he never would forecast,
How many mischieves should ensue his heedlesse hast.[5]

35

Full many mischiefes follow cruell Wrath;
Abhorrèd bloudshed, and tumultuous strife,
Unmanly murder, and unthrifty scath,[6]
310   Bitter despight,° with rancours rusty knife,   *malice*
And fretting griefe the enemy of life;

2. Traditional attribute of Envy.
3. Envy perversely discounts others' good works by attributing them to a selfish motive: the desire to compensate (in God's eyes) for lack of faith.
4. Grown insane.
5. I.e., he never would foresee ("forecast") the calamities his "heedless haste" caused.
6. I.e., inhuman murder and destructive harm.

All these, and many evils moe° haunt ire,°   more / anger
   The swelling Splene,[7] and Frenzy raging rife,
   The shaking Palsey, and Saint Fraunces fire:[8]
315 Such one was Wrath, the last of this ungoldly tire.°   train

36

And after all, upon the wagon beame
   Rode Sathan, with a smarting whip in hand,
   With which he forward lasht the laesie teme,
   So oft as Slowth° still in the mire did stand.   Idleness
320 Huge routs° of people did about them band,   crowds
   Showting for joy, and still before their way
   A foggy mist had covered all the land;
   And underneath their feet, all scattered lay
Dead sculs and bones of men, whose life had gone astray.

Summary   In the remainder of the canto, the third Saracen brother, Sans joy, arrives at the House of Pride and demands to do battle with Redcrosse. Lucifera intervenes and orders them to meet in a formal combat on the following day. Duessa visits Sans joy in the night, warning him of the power of Redcrosse's invulnerable armor, and promising him her secret aid.

Canto 5 Summary   Just as Redcrosse is about to slay Sans joy in combat, the Saracen vanishes in a magical cloud created by Duessa. To heal the wounded Sans joy, the witch enlists the help of Night, the queen of darkness who is grandmother of the three Saracen brothers. Together they take Sans joy down to Hades, the classical underworld. There he will be healed by the legendary physician Aesculapius, who has the power to raise the dead and is himself immortal, but doomed to live forever in Hades. Meanwhile, Redcrosse's companion the dwarf discovers Lucifera's dungeon, where the bodies of the proud are cast in heaps. With the dwarf, Redcrosse flees in the night, stumbling over piled-up corpses as he makes his escape, and Duessa returns to find him gone.

Canto 6 Summary   Sans loy intends to rape Una, but is frightened away by a band of fauns and satyrs (mythological creatures who are men above the waist and goats below). They take Una and proceed to worship her as a goddess, in spite of her attempts to teach them true religion. She is discovered among them by Satyrane, a wild but virtuous knight born of a human mother and a satyr father. Together they escape her idolators. They then meet with a pilgrim who informs them that Redcrosse has been slain by Sans loy. Satyrane seeks out the Saracen and they do battle. Una flees in terror and is pursued by the pilgrim, who is revealed as Archimago in disguise.

Cantos 7 and 8 Summary   Still disguised as Fidessa, Duessa pursues and finds Redcrosse. He drinks from a fountain which robs him of strength. The enfeebled knight is discovered lying with Duessa by the giant Orgoglio (Pride), who easily conquers Redcrosse and casts him into his dungeon. The giant pampers Duessa, attiring her as the Whore of Babylon in Revelation (a figure associated by Protestants with the papacy), and mounting her on a seven-headed beast. Meanwhile, the dwarf finds Una and reveals to her what has happened. Una sets out in search of Redcrosse and meets with Prince Arthur—the future king of Britain whose story runs through all the books of *The Faerie Queene*. She tells Arthur her story, explaining that Redcrosse

---

7. Organ associated with anger in Renaissance physiology.

8. St. Anthony's fire, erysipelas, or the flaming itch; appropriate to Wrath.

has been assigned by the Faerie Queene to rescue her parents, the king and queen of Eden, from a dragon. Arthur promises to rescue Redcrosse. In an epic fight, he defeats and kills Orgoglio, after stunning the giant and the beast with the divine brightness of his shield. Arthur seizes the keys to Orgoglio's dungeon from the giant's ancient foster-father, Ignaro (Ignorance), and liberates the starving Redcrosse. They strip Duessa, who is revealed as a filthy, bestial hag. She hides herself in the wilderness.

From *Canto 9*

His loves and lignage° Arthur tells:	*lineage*
The knights knit friendly bands:°	*bonds*
Sir Trevisan flies from Despayre,	
Whom Redcrosse knight withstands.	

Summary   In the first part of the canto, Arthur tells Redcrosse and Una of his past life. Taken from his mother at birth, Arthur is ignorant of his lineage, but has been told by the magician Merlin that he is heir to a king. After being visited by the Faerie Queene in a dream, in which she lay beside him on the grass, he has fallen in love with her. The knights then exchange vows of friendship and gifts. Arthur gives Redcrosse a precious liquid which heals wounds, while Redcrosse gives him the New Testament. Arthur then rides off in search of the Faerie Queene. Una looks with concern at Redcrosse, who remains weak and weary from his recent ordeal.

[REDCROSSE MEETS DESPAIRE]

21

	So as they traveild, lo they gan espy	
	An armèd knight towards them gallop fast,	
	That seemèd from some fearèd foe to fly,	
	Or other griesly thing, that him agast.°	*terrified*
185	Still as he fled, his eye was backward cast,	
	As if his feare still followed him behind;	
	Als flew his steed, as he his bands had brast,°	*broken*
	And with his wingèd heeles did tread the wind,	
	As he had beene a fole of Pegasus his kind.[9]	

22

190	Nigh as he drew, they might perceive his head	
	To be unarmd, and curld uncombèd heares	
	Upstaring° stiffe, dismayd with uncouth° dread;	*bristling / unknown*
	Nor drop of bloud in all his face appeares	
	Nor life in limbe: and to increase his feares,	
195	In fowle reproch° of knighthoods faire degree,°	*disgrace / condition*
	About his neck an hempen rope he weares,	
	That with his glistring armes does ill agree;	
	But he of rope or armes has now no memoree.	

23

	The Redcrosse knight toward him crossèd fast,	
200	To weet, what mister° wight was so dismayd:	*kind of*

9. I.e., as if he had been a foal of a horse like Pegasus (a flying horse).

There him he finds all sencelesse and aghast,
That of him selfe he seemd to be afrayd;
Whom hardly he from flying forward stayd,
Till he these wordes to him deliver might;
205 "Sir knight, aread° who hath ye thus arayd,   declare
And eke from whom make ye this hasty flight:
For never knight I saw in such misseeming° plight."   unseemly

24

He answerd nought at all, but adding new
Feare to his first amazment, staring wide
210 With stony eyes, and hartlesse hollow hew,[1]
Astonisht stood, as one that had aspide
Infernall furies, with their chaines untide.
Him yet againe, and yet againe bespake
The gentle knight; who nought to him replide,
215 But trembling every joynt did inly quake,
And foltring tongue at last these words seemd forth to shake.

25

"For Gods deare love, Sir knight, do me not stay;
For loe he comes, he comes fast after mee."
Eft° looking backe would faine have runne away;   again
220 But he him forst to stay, and tellen free
The secret cause of his perplexitie:°   distress
Yet nathemore° by his bold hartie speach,   not at all
Could his bloud-frosen hart emboldned bee,
But through his boldnesse rather feare did reach,
225 Yet forst, at last he made through silence suddein breach.

26

"And am I now in safetie sure," quoth he,
"From him, that would have forcèd me to dye?
And is the point of death now turnd fro mee,
That I may tell this haplesse history?"
230 "Feare nought:" quoth he, "no daunger now is nye."
"Then shall I you recount a ruefull cace,"°   event
Said he, "the which with this unlucky eye
I late beheld, and had not greater grace
Me reft° from it, had bene partaker of the place.[2]   carried

27

235 "I lately chaunst (Would I had never chaunst)
With a faire knight to keepen companee,
Sir Terwin[3] hight,° that well himselfe advaunst   named
In all affaires, and was both bold and free,
But not so happie as mote happie bee:
240 He loved, as was his lot, a Ladie gent,°   gentle

---

1. I.e., with blanched, bloodless countenance.
2. I.e., shared the same fate.
3. His name may connote weariness or fatigue ("terwyn").

That him againe° loved in the least degree: *in return*
For she was proud, and of too high intent,°   *mind*
And joyd to see her lover languish and lament.

28

"From whom returning sad and comfortlesse,°   *desolate*
245   As on the way together we did fare,
We met that villen (God from him me blesse°)   *defend*
That cursèd wight, from whom I scapt whyleare,°   *a while before*
A man of hell, that cals himselfe Despaire;[4]
Who first us greets, and after faire areedes°   *tells*
250   Of tydings strange, and of adventures rare:
So creeping close, as Snake in hidden weedes,
Inquireth of our states, and of our knightly deedes.

29

"Which when he knew, and felt our feeble harts
Embost° with bale,° and bitter byting griefe,   *exhausted/sorrow*
255   Which love had launchèd° with his deadly darts,   *pierced*
With wounding words and termes of foule repriefe°   *insult*
He pluckt from us all hope of due reliefe,
That earst us held in love of lingring life;
Then hopelesse hartlesse, gan the cunning thiefe
260   Perswade us die, to stint° all further strife: *end*
To me he lent this rope, to him a rustie knife.

30

"With which sad instrument of hastie death,
That wofull lover, loathing lenger° light,   *longer*
A wide way made to let forth living breath.
265   But I more fearefull, or more luckie wight,
Dismayd with that deformèd dismall sight,
Fled fast away, halfe dead with dying feare:°   *fear of death*
Ne yet assur'd of life by you, Sir knight,
Whose like infirmitie like chaunce may beare:
270   But God you never let his charmèd speeches heare."[5]

31

"How may a man," said he, "with idle speach
Be wonne, to spoyle° the Castle of his health?"   *destroy*
"I wote," quoth he, "whom triall° late did teach,   *experience*
That like would not[6] for all this worldes wealth:
275   His subtill tongue, like dropping honny, mealt'th°   *melts*
Into the hart, and searcheth every vaine,
That ere one be aware, by secret stealth
His powre is reft, and weaknesse doth remaine.
O never Sir desire to try° his guilefull traine."°   *test/treachery*

4. Despair is the ultimate Christian sin, denying
the possibility of Divine mercy and grace.
5. I.e., may God never let you hear his mesmer-
izing ("charmed") speeches.
6. I.e., would not do the like again.

32

280 "Certes,"° said he, "hence shall I never rest,   *surely*
    Till I that treachours art have heard and tride;
    And you Sir knight, whose name mote° I request,   *might*
    Of grace° do me unto his cabin° guide."   *favor/cave*
    "I that hight° Trevisan," quoth he, "will ride   *am called*
285   Against my liking backe, to doe you grace:°   *a favor*
    But nor for gold nor glee⁷ will I abide
    By you, when ye arrive in that same place;
  For lever° had I die, then° see his deadly face."   *rather/than*

33

    Ere long they come, where that same wicked wight
290   His dwelling has, low in an hollow cave,
    Farre underneath a craggie clift ypight,°   *placed*
    Darke, dolefull, drearie, like a greedie grave,
    That still for carrion carcases doth crave:
    On top whereof aye dwelt the ghastly Owle,⁸
295   Shrieking his balefull note, which ever drave
    Farre from that haunt all other chearefull fowle;
  And all about it wandring ghostes did waile and howle.

34

    And all about old stockes° and stubs of trees,   *stumps*
    Whereon nor fruit, nor leafe was ever seene,
300   Did hang upon the ragged rocky knees;°   *crags*
    On which had many wretches hangèd beene,
    Whose carcases were scattered on the greene,
    And throwne about the cliffs. Arrivèd there,
    That bare-head knight for dread and dolefull teene,°   *grief*
305   Would faine° have fled, ne durst approachen neare,   *gladly*
  But th' other forst him stay, and comforted in feare.

35

    That darkesome cave they enter, where they find
    That cursèd man, low sitting on the ground,
    Musing full sadly in his sullein° mind;   *morose*
310   His griesie° lockes, long growen, and unbound,   *gray*
    Disordred hong about his shoulders round,
    And hid his face; through which his hollow eyne
    Lookt deadly dull, and starèd as astound;
    His raw-bone cheekes through penurie and pine,°   *starvation*
315 Were shronke into his jawes, as° he did never dine.   *as if*

36

    His garment nought but many ragged clouts,°   *rags*
    With thornes together pind and patchèd was,
    The which his naked sides he wrapt abouts;
    And him beside there lay upon the gras

---

7. Song; i.e., anything you can say to me.   8. Traditionally a messenger of death.

320   A drearie° corse, whose life away did pas,   *bloody*
       All wallowd in his owne yet luke-warme blood,
       That from his wound yet wellèd fresh alas;
       In which a rustie° knife fast fixèd stood,   *bloodstained*
       And made an open passage for the gushing flood.

37

325   Which piteous spectacle, approving° trew   *confirming*
       The wofull tale that Trevisan had told,
       When as the gentle Redcrosse knight did vew,
       With firie zeale he burnt in courage bold,
       Him to avenge, before his bloud were cold,
330   And to the villein said, "Thou agèd damnèd wight,
       The author of this fact,° we here behold,   *deed*
       What justice can but judge against thee right,
       With thine owne bloud to price° his bloud, here shed in sight?"   *pay for*

38

       "What franticke fit," quoth he,° "hath thus distraught   *i.e., Despaire*
335   Thee, foolish man, so rash a doome° to give?   *judgment*
       What justice ever other judgement taught,
       But he should die, who merites not to live?
       None else to death this man despayring drive,°   *drove*
       But his owne guiltie mind deserving death.
340   Is then unjust to each his due to give?
       Or let him die, that loatheth living breath?
       Or let him die at ease, that liveth here uneath?°   *in unease*

39

       "Who travels by the wearie wandring way,
       To come unto his wishèd home in haste,
345   And meetes a flood, that doth his passage stay,
       Is not great grace to helpe him over past,
       Or free his feet, that in the myre sticke fast?
       Most envious man, that grieves at neighbours good,
       And fond,° that joyest in the woe thou hast,   *foolish*
350   Why wilt not let him passe, that long hath stood
       Upon the banke, yet wilt thy selfe not passe the flood?

40

       "He there does now enjoy eternall rest
       And happie ease, which thou doest want and crave,
       And further from it daily wanderest:
355   What if some litle paine the passage have,
       That makes fraile flesh to feare the bitter wave?
       Is not short paine well borne, that brings long ease,
       And layes the soule to sleepe in quiet grave?
       Sleepe after toyle, port after stormie seas,
360   Ease after warre, death after life does greatly please."[9]

9. Despaire's arguments on behalf of suicide as against a painful life are derived, like those of Hamlet in his third soliloquy (*Hamlet* 3.1.58–90), principally from Seneca, Marcus Aurelius, other ancient Stoics, and Old Testament statements on divine justice.

41

The knight much wondred at his suddeine wit,°   *quick intelligence*
      And said, "The terme of life is limited,
      Ne may a man prolong, nor shorten it;
      The souldier may not move from watchfull sted,[1]
365   Nor leave his stand, untill his Captaine bed."°   *commands*
      "Who life did limit by almightie doome,"
      Quoth he,° "knowes best the termes establishèd;   *Despaire*
      And he, that points the Centonell his roome,°   *station*
Doth license him depart at sound of morning droome.[2]

42

370   "Is not his deed, what ever thing is donne,
      In heaven and earth? did not he all create
      To die againe? all ends that was begonne.
      Their times in his eternall booke of fate
      Are written sure, and have their certaine° date.   *fixed*
375   Who then can strive with strong necessitie,
      That holds the world in his still chaunging state,
      Or shunne the death ordaynd by destinie?
When houre of death is come, let none aske whence, nor why.

43

      "The lenger° life, I wote° the greater sin,   *longer / know*
380   The greater sin, the greater punishment:
      All those great battels, which thou boasts to win,
      Through strife, and bloud-shed, and avengement,
      Now praysd, hereafter deare° thou shalt repent: *bitterly*
385   For life must life, and bloud must bloud repay.[3]
      Is not enough thy evill life forespent?
      For he, that once hath missèd the right way,
The further he doth goe, the further he doth stray.

44

      "Then do no further goe, no further stray,
      But here lie downe, and to thy rest betake,
390   Th' ill to prevent, that life ensewen may.[4]
      For what hath life, that may it lovèd make,
      And gives not rather cause it to forsake?
      Feare, sicknesse, age, losse, labour, sorrow, strife,
      Paine, hunger, cold, that makes the hart to quake;
395   And ever fickle fortune rageth rife,
All which, and thousands mo° do make a loathsome life.   *more*

45

      "Thou wretched man, of death hast greatest need,
      If in true ballance thou wilt weigh thy state:

---

1. The sentry post assigned him.
2. Drum, with a pun on *doom.*
3. An echo of Genesis 9.6: "Whoso sheddeth

man's blood, by man shall his blood be shed."
4. I.e., to prevent the evil that will ensue in the rest of your life.

For never knight, that darèd warlike deede,
400   More lucklesse disaventures° did amate:°   *mishaps/daunt*
Witnesse the dongeon deepe, wherein of late
Thy life shut up, for death so oft did call;
And though good lucke prolongèd hath thy date,°   *span of life*
Yet death then, would the like mishaps forestall,
405 Into the which hereafter thou maiest happen fall.°   *happen to fall*

46

"Why then doest thou, O man of sin, desire
To draw thy dayes forth to their last degree?
Is not the measure of thy sinfull hire°   *service to sin*
High heapèd up with huge iniquitie,
410 Against the day of wrath,° to burden thee?   *Judgment Day*
Is not enough that to this Ladie milde
Thou falsèd° hast thy faith with perjurie,   *betrayed*
And sold thy selfe to serve Duessa vilde,°   *vile*
With whom in all abuse thou hast thy selfe defilde?

47

415 "Is not he just, that all this doth behold
From highest heaven, and beares an equall° eye?   *impartial*
Shall he thy sins up in his knowledge fold,
And guiltie be of thine impietie?
Is not his law, Let every sinner die:[5]
420 Die shall all flesh? what then must needs be donne,
Is it not better to doe willinglie,
Then linger, till the glasse° be all out ronne?   *hourglass*
Death is the end of woes: die soone, O faeries sonne."

48

The knight was much enmovèd with his speach,
425 That as a swords point through his hart did perse,
And in his conscience made a secret breach,
Well knowing true all, that he did reherse°   *recount*
And to his fresh remembrance did reverse°   *bring back*
The ugly vew of his deformèd crimes,
430 That all his manly powres it did disperse,
As he were charmèd with inchaunted rimes,
That oftentimes he quakt, and fainted oftentimes.

49

In which amazement, when the Miscreant°   *misbeliever*
Perceivèd him to waver weake and fraile,
435 Whiles trembling horror did his conscience dant,°   *daunt*
And hellish anguish° did his soule assaile,   *i.e., fear of hell*
To drive him to despaire, and quite to quaile,°   *be dismayed*
He shewed him painted in a table° plaine,   *picture*

---

5. Despaire cites only half of the Scripture verse: "The wages of sin is death; but the gift of God is eternal life through Jesus Christ our Lord" (Romans 6.23).

The damnèd ghosts, that doe in torments waile,
440 And thousand feends that doe them endlesse paine
With fire and brimstone, which for ever shall remaine.

50

The sight whereof so throughly him dismaid,
That nought but death before his eyes he saw,
And ever burning wrath before him laid,
445 By righteous sentence of th' Almighties law:
Then gan the villein him to overcraw,°   *exult over*
And brought unto him swords, ropes, poison, fire,
And all that might him to perdition draw;
And bad him choose, what death he would desire:
450 For death was due to him, that had provokt Gods ire.

51

But when as none of them he saw him take,
He to him raught° a dagger sharpe and keene,   *reached*
And gave it him in hand: his hand did quake,
And tremble like a leafe of Aspin greene,
455 And troubled bloud through his pale face was seene
To come, and goe with tydings from the hart,
As it a running messenger had beene.
At last resolved to worke his finall smart,
He lifted up his hand, that backe againe did start.

52

460 Which when as Una saw, through every vaine
The crudled° cold ran to her well of life,°   *congealing/heart*
As in a swowne: but soone relived° againe,   *revived*
Out of his hand she snatcht the cursèd knife,
And threw it to the ground, enragèd rife,°   *deeply*
465 And to him said, "Fie, fie, faint harted knight,
What meanest thou by this reprochfull° strife?   *deserving reproach*
Is this the battell, which thou vauntst to fight
With the fire-mouthèd Dragon, horrible and bright?

53

"Come, come away, fraile, feeble, fleshly wight,
470 Ne let vaine words bewitch thy manly hart,
Ne divelish thoughts dismay thy constant spright.
In heavenly mercies hast thou not a part?
Why shouldst thou then despeire, that chosen[6] art?
Where justice growes, there grows eke° greater grace,   *also*
475 The which doth quench the brond of hellish smart,
And that accurst hand-writing[7] doth deface.°   *blot out*
Arise, Sir knight arise, and leave this cursèd place."

---

6. Cf. 2 Thessalonians 2.13: "God hath from the beginning chosen you to salvation through sanctification of the Spirit and belief of the truth."
7. An echo of Colossians 2.14: "Blotting out the handwriting of ordinances [i.e., the Old Testament Law] that was against us, which was contrary to us, and took it out of the way, nailing it to his cross."

54

So up he rose, and thence amounted° streight.　　　*mounted his horse*
Which when the carle° beheld, and saw his guest　　　*churl*
480　Would safe depart, for° all his subtill sleight,　　　*in spite of*
He chose an halter from among the rest,
And with it hung himselfe, unbid° unblest.　　　*unprayed for*
But death he could not worke himselfe thereby;
For thousand times he so himselfe had drest,°　　　*made ready*
485　Yet nathelesse it could not doe° him die,　　　*make*
Till he should die his last, that is eternally.

From *Canto 10*

Her faithfull knight faire Una brings
to house of Holinesse,
Where he is taught repentance, and
the way to heavenly blesse.°　　　*bliss*

Summary　In the first part of the canto, Una brings Redcrosse to the House of Holinesse to be healed in body and spirit. The house is kept by Dame Caelia (Heavenly) with her three daughters Fidelia (Faith), Speranza (Hope), and Charissa (Charity, or Love). Redcrosse is welcomed and given counsel by Fidelia and Speranza, but remains wracked by guilt and suicidal impulses. He is entrusted to the doctor Patience and undergoes a painful cure with Penance, Remorse, and Repentance. He next comes to Charissa, who instructs him in love and good deeds and places him in the hands of a godly matron, Mercie. She leads him along a narrow and thorny path to a holy Hospitall (hostel), kept by seven Bead-men (men of prayer), where Redcrosse learns to frame his life in righteousness. Redcrosse and Mercie then continue on their way.

46

Thence forward by that painfull way they pas,
Forth to an hill, that was both steepe and hy;
On top whereof a sacred chappell was,
And eke a litle Hermitage thereby,
410　Wherein an agèd holy man did lye,°　　　*live*
That day and night said his devotion,
Ne other worldly busines did apply;[8]
His name was heavenly Contemplation;
Of God and goodnesse was his meditation.

47

415　Great grace that old man to him given had;
For God he often saw from heavens hight,
All° were his earthly eyen both blunt° and bad,　　　*although / dim*
And through great age had lost their kindly° sight,　　　*natural*
Yet wondrous quick and persant° was his spright,°　　　*piercing / spirit*
420　As Eagles eye, that can behold the Sunne:
That hill they scale with all their powre and might,
That his frayle thighes nigh wearie and fordonne°　　　*exhausted*
Gan faile, but by her helpe the top at last he wonne.

---

8. I.e., he did not attend to any worldly activities.

48

There they do finde that godly agèd Sire,
425   With snowy lockes adowne his shoulders shed,
As hoarie frost with spangles doth attire
The mossy braunches of an Oke halfe ded.
Each bone might through his body well be red,°   *seen*
And every sinew seene through° his long fast: *because of*
430   For nought he cared his carcas long unfed;
His mind was full of spirituall repast,
And pyned° his flesh, to keepe his body low° and chast.   *starved/thin*

49

Who when these two approching he aspide,
At their first presence grew agrievèd sore,⁹
435   That forst him lay his heavenly thoughts aside;
And had he not that Dame respected more,°   *greatly*
Whom highly he did reverence and adore,
He would not once have movèd for the knight.
They him saluted standing far afore;°   *away*
440   Who well them greeting, humbly did requight,°   *respond*
And askèd, to what end they clomb° that tedious height.   *had climbed*

50

"What end," quoth she, "should cause us take such paine,
But that same end, which every living wight
Should make his marke,° high heaven to attaine?   *goal*
445   Is not from hence the way, that leadeth right
To that most glorious house, that glistreth bright
With burning starres, and everliving fire,
Whereof the keyes are to thy hand behight°   *entrusted*
By wise Fidelia? she doth thee require,
450   To shew it to this knight, according° his desire."   *granting*

51

"Thrise happy man," said then the father grave,
"Whose staggering steps thy° steady hand doth lead,   *i.e., Mercy's*
And shewes the way, his sinfull soule to save.
Who better can the way to heaven aread°   *direct*
455   Then thou thy selfe, that was both borne and bred
In heavenly throne, where thousand Angels shine?
Thou doest the prayers of the righteous sead°   *seed*
Present before the majestie divine,
And his avenging wrath to clemencie incline.

52

460   "Yet since thou bidst, thy pleasure shalbe donne.
Then come thou man of earth,¹ and see the way,
That never yet was seene of Faeries sonne,
That never leads the traveiler astray,

---

9. I.e., he was at first sorely grieved at their arrival.
1. An allusion to humankind's formation from the

dust of the earth (Genesis 2.7) and also to the
knight's name (see below, stanza 66 and note 2).

But after labours long, and sad delay,
465 Brings them to joyous rest and endlesse blis.
But first thou must a season fast and pray,
Till from her bands the spright assoilèd° is,   *spirit released*
And have her strength recured° from fraile infirmitis."   *recovered*

53

That done, he leads him to the highest Mount;
470 Such one, as that same mighty man of God,
That bloud-red billowes like a wallèd front
On either side disparted° with his rod,   *parted asunder*
Till that his army dry-foot through them yod,°   *went*
Dwelt fortie dayes upon; where writ in stone
475 With bloudy letters by the hand of God,
The bitter doome of death and balefull mone²
He did receive, whiles flashing fire about him shone.

54

Or like that sacred hill, whose head full hie,
Adornd with fruitfull Olives all arownd,
480 Is, as it were for endlesse memory
Of that deare Lord, who oft thereon was fownd,
For ever with a flowring girlond crownd:
Or like that pleasaunt Mount, that is for ay
Through famous Poets verse each where° renownd,   *everywhere*
485 On which the thrise three learned Ladies play
Their heavenly notes, and make full many a lovely lay.³

55

From thence, far off he unto him did shew
A litle path, that was both steepe and long,
Which to a goodly Citie led his vew;
490 Whose wals and towres were builded high and strong
Of perle and precious stone, that earthly tong
Cannot describe, nor wit of man can tell;
Too high a ditty° for my simple song;   *subject*
The Citie of the great king hight it well,
495 Wherein eternall peace and happinesse doth dwell.

56

As he thereon stood gazing, he might see
The blessed Angels to and fro descend
From highest heaven, in gladsome companee,
And with great joy into that Citie wend,
500 As commonly° as friend does with his frend.⁴   *familiarly*
Whereat he wondred much, and gan enquere,

---

2. I.e., the Ten Commandments ("bloudy letters") carried with them the judgment ("doome") of death and pain (causing sorrowful moans—"balefull mone").
3. Song. The mountain is successively compared with Mount Sinai, where Moses, after parting the "bloud-red billowes" of the Red Sea, received the tablets of the Ten Commandments; to the Mount of Olives, associated with Christ; and to Mount Parnassus, where the Nine Muses of art and poetry dwelt.
4. Cf. Jacob's ladder, which "reached to heaven; and behold the angels of God ascending and descending on it" (Genesis 28.12).

What stately building durst so high extend
Her loftie towres unto the starry sphere,
And what unknowen nation there empeopled were.

57

505   "Faire knight," quoth he, "Hierusalem that is,
      The new Hierusalem, that God has built
      For those to dwell in, that are chosen his,
      His chosen people purged from sinfull guilt,
      With pretious bloud, which cruelly was spilt
510   On cursèd tree, of that unspotted lam,[5]
      That for the sinnes of all the world was kilt:
      Now are they Saints all in that Citie sam,°   together
      More deare unto their God, then younglings to their dam."[6]

58

      "Till now," said then the knight, "I weenèd well,
515   That great Cleopolis,[7] where I have beene,
      In which that fairest Faerie Queene doth dwell,
      The fairest Citie was, that might be seene;
      And that bright towre all built of christall cleene,°   clear
      Panthea,[8] seemd the brightest thing, that was:
520   But now by proofe all otherwise I weene;
      For this great Citie that[9] does far surpas,
      And this bright Angels towre quite dims that towre of glas."

59

      "Most trew," then said the holy agèd man;
      "Yet is Cleopolis for earthly frame,°   structure
525   The fairest peece,° that eye beholden can: masterpiece
      And well beseemes° all knights of noble name,   becomes
      That covet in th' immortall booke of fame
      To be eternizèd, that same to haunt,°   frequent
      And doen their service to that soveraigne Dame,
530   That glorie does to them for guerdon° graunt: reward
      For she is heavenly borne, and heaven may justly vaunt.°   claim

60

      "And thou faire ymp,° sprong out from English race,   youth
      How ever now accompted° Elfins sonne,   accounted
      Well worthy doest thy service for her grace,°   favor
535   To aide a virgin desolate foredonne.°   undone
      But when thou famous victorie hast wonne,
      And high emongst all knights hast hong thy shield,
      Thenceforth the suit° of earthly conquest shonne,   pursuit

---

5. Lamb; a reference to Christ (the lamb of God),
whose death on the cross ("cursèd tree") purged
the guilt of sin from those "chosen his."
6. The New Jerusalem is described in Revelation
21–22; "the nations of them which are saved shall
walk in the light of it" (21.24).
7. London, Camelot—the earthly counterpart of

the Heavenly Kingdom.
8. Reminiscent of the temple of glass in Chaucer's
House of Fame; perhaps intended to allude to Richmond Palace or Westminster Abbey.
9. I.e., The New Jerusalem far surpasses Cleopolis
("that").

And wash thy hands from guilt of bloudy field:
540 For bloud can nought but sin, and wars but sorrowes yield.

61

"Then seeke this path, that I to thee presage,°   *show prophetically*
Which after all to heaven shall thee send;
Then peaceably thy painefull° pilgrimage   *laborious*
To yonder same Hierusalem do bend,
545 Where is for thee ordaind a blessèd end:
For thou emongst those Saints, whom thou doest see,
Shalt be a Saint, and thine owne nations frend
And Patrone: thou Saint George shalt callèd bee,
Saint George of mery England, the signe of victoree."[1]

62

550 "Unworthy wretch," quoth he, "of so great grace,
How dare I thinke such glory to attaine?"
"These that have it attaind, were in like cace,"
Quoth he, "as wretched, and lived in like paine."
"But deeds of armes must I at last be faine,°   *content (to leave)*
555 And Ladies love to leave so dearely bought?"
"What need of armes, where peace doth ay remaine,"
Said he, "and battailes none are to be fought?
As for loose loves are° vaine, and vanish into nought."   *i.e., they are*

63

"O let me not," quoth he, "then turne againe
560 Backe to the world, whose joyes so fruitlesse are;
But let me here for aye in peace remaine,
Or streight way on that last long voyage fare,
That nothing may my present hope empare."°   *impair*
"That may not be," said he, "ne maist thou yit
565 Forgo that royall maides bequeathèd care,°   *charge*
Who did her cause into thy hand commit,
Till from her cursèd foe thou have her freely quit."°   *released*

64

"Then shall I soone," quoth he, "so God me grace,
Abet° that virgins cause disconsolate,   *maintain*
570 And shortly backe returne unto this place
To walke this way in Pilgrims poore estate.
But now aread,° old father, why of late   *declare*
Didst thou behight° me borne of English blood,   *call*
Whom all a Faeries sonne doen nominate?"°   *name*
575 "That word shall I," said he, "avouchen° good,   *prove*
Sith° to thee is unknowne the cradle of thy brood.   *since*

---

1. Spenser's conception of St. George, patron saint of England, draws on the *Legenda Aurea* (*The Golden Legend*—a medieval manual of ecclesias- tical lore, translated into English by William Caxton in 1487) and on pictures, tapestries, pageants, and folklore.

65

"For well I wote,° thou springst from ancient race   *know*
   Of Saxon kings, that have with mightie hand
   And many bloudie battailes fought in place°   *there*
580 High reard their royall throne in Britane land,
   And vanquisht them, unable to withstand:
   From thence a Faerie thee unweeting reft,°   *secretly stole*
   There as thou slepst in tender swadling band,
   And her base Elfin brood there for thee left.
585 Such men do Chaungelings call, so chaungd by Faeries theft.

66

"Thence she thee brought into this Faerie lond,
   And in an heapèd furrow did thee hyde,
   Where thee a Ploughman all unweeting° fond,   *unknowing*
   As he his toylesome teme° that way did guyde,   *team of oxen*
590 And brought thee up in ploughmans state to byde,
   Whereof Georgos he thee gave to name;[2]
   Till prickt° with courage, and thy forces pryde,   *spurred*
   To Faery court thou cam'st to seeke for fame,
   And prove thy puissaunt armes, as seemes thee best
     became."°   *as best suited you*

67

595 "O holy Sire," quoth he, "how shall I quight°   *repay*
   The many favours I with thee have found,
   That hast my name and nation red aright,
   And taught the way that does to heaven bound?"°   *go*
   This said, adowne he lookèd to the ground,
600 To have returnd, but dazèd° were his eyne,   *dazzled*
   Through passing° brightnesse, which did quite confound   *surpassing*
   His feeble sence, and too exceeding shyne.
   So darke are earthly things compard to things divine.

68

At last whenas himselfe he gan to find,°   *recover*
605 To Una back he cast him to retire;
   Who him awaited still with pensive° mind.   *anxious*
   Great thankes and goodly meed° to that good syre,   *gift*
   He thence departing gave for his paines hyre.°   *reward*
   So came to Una, who him joyd to see,
610 And after litle rest, gan him desire,
   Of her adventure mindfull for to bee.
   So leave they take of Caelia, and her daughters three.

---

2. I.e., as a name. *Georgos* is Greek for "farmer" (cf. Virgil's *Georgics*, on farming).

Canto 11

The knight with that old Dragon fights
two dayes incessantly:
The third him overthrowes, and gayns
most glorious victory.

1

High time now gan it wex° for Una faire,   *grow*
  To thinke of those her captive Parents deare,
  And their forwasted kingdome to repaire:³
  Whereto whenas they now approachèd neare,
5 With hartie° words her knight she gan to cheare,   *bold*
  And in her modest manner thus bespake;
  "Deare knight, as deare, as ever knight was deare,
  That all these sorrowes suffer for my sake,
High heaven behold the tedious toyle, ye for me take.

2

10 "Now are we come unto my native soyle,
  And to the place, where all our perils dwell;
  Here haunts that feend, and does his dayly spoyle,
  Therefore henceforth be at your keeping well,°   *be well on your guard*
  And ever ready for your foeman fell.
15 The sparke of noble courage now awake,
  And strive your excellent selfe to excell;
  That shall ye evermore renowmèd make,
Above all knights on earth, that batteill undertake."

3

And pointing forth, "lo yonder is," said she,
20 "The brasen towre in which my parents deare
  For dread of that huge feend emprisond be,
  Whom I from far see on the walles appeare,
  Whose sight my feeble soule doth greatly cheare:
  And on the top of all I do espye
25 The watchman wayting tydings glad to heare,
  That O my parents might I happily
Unto you bring, to ease you of your misery."

4

With that they heard a roaring hideous sound,
  That all the ayre with terrour fillèd wide,
30 And seemd uneath° to shake the stedfast ground.   *almost*
  Eftsoones that dreadfull Dragon they espide,
  Where stretcht he lay upon the sunny side
  Of a great hill, himselfe like a great hill.
  But all so soone, as he from far descride

---

3. I.e., to restore their kingdom, laid waste (by the dragon).

35   Those glistring armes, that heaven with light did fill,
        He rousd himselfe full blith,° and hastned them untill.°   *joyfully / toward*

                              5
        Then bad the knight his Lady yede° aloofe,   *go*
          And to an hill her selfe withdraw aside,
          From whence she might behold that battailles proof°   *outcome*
40   And eke° be safe from daunger far descryde: *also*
          She him obayd, and turnd a little wyde.°   *aside*
          Now O thou sacred Muse, most learnèd Dame,
          Faire ympe° of Phoebus, and his aged bride,[4]   *child*
          The Nourse of time, and everlasting fame,
45   That warlike hands ennoblest with immortall name;

                              6
        O gently come into my feeble brest,
          Come gently, but not with that mighty rage,
          Wherewith the martiall troupes thou doest infest,°   *arouse*
          And harts of great Heroës doest enrage,
50   That nought their kindled courage may aswage,
          Soone as thy dreadfull trompe° begins to sownd;   *trumpet*
          The God of warre with his fiers equipage
          Thou doest awake, sleepe never he so sownd,°   *sound*
        And scarèd nations doest with horrour sterne astown.°   *appall*

                              7
55   Faire Goddesse lay that furious fit° aside,   *strain*
          Till I of warres and bloudy Mars do sing[5]
          And Briton fields with Sarazin bloud bedyde,
          Twixt that great faery Queene and Paynim king,
          That with their horrour heaven and earth did ring,
60   A worke of labour long, and endlesse prayse:
          But now a while let downe that haughtie string,
          And to my tunes thy second tenor rayse,[6]
        That I this man of God his godly armes may blaze.°   *proclaim*

                              8
        By this the dreadfull Beast drew nigh to hand,
65   Halfe flying, and halfe footing° in his hast,   *walking*
          That with his largenesse measurèd much land,
          And made wide shadow under his huge wast;°   *girth*
          As mountaine doth the valley overcast.
          Approching nigh, he rearèd high afore
70   His body monstrous, horrible, and vast,
          Which to increase his wondrous greatnesse more,
        Was swolne with wrath, and poyson, and with bloudy gore.

4. I.e., Mnemosyne (memory), mother of the
Muses.
5. Perhaps a reference to a projected but unwritten book of *The Faerie Queene*.

6. The "haughtie" (high-pitched) mode would be
appropriate to a large-scale epic war; the "second
tenor" (lower in pitch) to this present battle.

9

And over, all with brasen scales was armd,
  Like plated coate of steele, so couchèd neare,°   *placed so closely*
75 That nought mote perce,[7] ne might his corse° be harmd   *body*
  With dint of sword, nor push of pointed speare;
  Which as an Eagle, seeing pray appeare,
  His aery Plumes doth rouze,° full rudely dight,°   *shake / ruggedly arrayed*
  So shakèd he, that horrour was to heare,
80 For as the clashing of an Armour bright,
Such noyse his rouzèd scales did send unto the knight.

10

His flaggy° wings when forth he did display,   *drooping*
  Were like two sayles, in which the hollow wynd
  Is gathered full, and worketh speedy way:
85 And eke the pennes,° that did his pineons bynd,   *quills*
  Were like mayne-yards, with flying canvas lynd,
  With which whenas him list the ayre to beat,
  And there by force unwonted° passage find,   *unaccustomed*
  The cloudes before him fled for terrour great,
90 And all the heavens stood still amazèd with his threat.

11

His huge long tayle wound up in hundred foldes,
  Does overspred his long bras-scaly backe,
  Whose wreathèd boughts° when ever he unfoldes,   *coils*
  And thicke entangled knots adown does slacke,
95 Bespotted as with shields° of red and blacke,   *scales*
  It sweepeth all the land behind him farre,
  And of three furlongs does but litle lacke;
  And at the point two stings in-fixèd arre,
Both deadly sharpe, that sharpest steele exceeden farre.

12

100 But stings and sharpest steele did far exceed°   *i.e., were far exceeded by*
  The sharpnesse of his cruell rending clawes;
  Dead was it sure, as sure as death in deed,°   *in its effect*
  What ever thing does touch his ravenous pawes,
  Or what within his reach he ever drawes.
105 But his most hideous head my toung to tell
  Does tremble: for his deepe devouring jawes
  Wide gapèd, like the griesly° mouth of hell,   *horrid*
Through which into his darke abisse all ravin° fell.   *prey, booty*

13

And that° more wondrous was, in either jaw   *what*
110 Threeranckes of yron teeth enraungèd were,
  In which yet trickling bloud and gobbets raw° *chunks of undigested food*

7. Nothing might pierce.

Of late° devourèd bodies did appeare,   *recently*
That sight thereof bred cold congealèd feare:
Which to increase, and all at once to kill,
115   A cloud of smoothering smoke and sulphur seare°   *burning*
Out of his stinking gorge° forth steemèd still,   *maw*
That all the ayre about with smoke and stench did fill.

14

His blazing eyes, like two bright shining shields,
Did burne with wrath, and sparkled living fyre;
120   As two broad Beacons, set in open fields,
Send forth their flames farre off to every shyre,°   *shire*
And warning give, that enemies conspyre,
With fire and sword the region to invade;
So flamed his eyne° with rage and rancorous yre:°   *eyes/ire*
125   But farre within, as in a hollow glade,
Those glaring lampes were set, that made a dreadfull shade.

15

So dreadfully he towards him did pas,
Forelifting up aloft his speckled brest,
And often bounding on the brusèd gras,
130   As for great joyance of his newcome guest.
Eftsoones he gan advance his haughtie crest,
As chauffèd° Bore his bristles doth upreare,   *angry*
And shoke his scales to battell readie drest;°   *prepared*
That made the Redcrosse knight nigh quake for feare,
135   As bidding bold defiance to his foeman neare.

16

The knight gan fairely couch° his steadie speare,   *rest, aim*
And fiercely ran at him with rigorous° might: *violent*
The pointed steele arriving rudely° theare,   *roughly*
His harder hide would neither perce, nor bight,
140   But glauncing by forth passèd forward right;
Yet sore amovèd with so puissant push,
The wrathfull beast about him turnèd light,°   *quickly*
And him so rudely passing by, did brush
With his long tayle, that horse and man to ground did rush.

17

145   Both horse and man up lightly rose againe,
And fresh encounter towards him addrest:
But th' idle stroke yet backe recoyld in vaine,
And found no place his° deadly point to rest.   *its*
Exceeding rage enflamed the furious beast,
150   To be avengèd of so great despight;°   *outrage*
For never felt his imperceable brest
So wondrous force, from hand of living wight;
Yet had he provèd° the powre of many a puissant knight.   *tested*

18

Then with his waving wings displayèd wyde,
155   Himselfe up high he lifted from the ground,
    And with strong flight did forcibly divide
    The yielding aire, which nigh too feeble found
    Her flitting° partes, and element unsound,°   *moving / weak*
    To beare so great a weight: he cutting way
160   With his broad sayles, about him soarèd round:
    At last low stouping with unweldie sway,°   *ponderous force*
Snatcht up both horse and man, to beare them quite away.

19

Long he them bore above the subject plaine,°   *i.e., the ground below*
    So farre as Ewghen° bow a shaft may send,   *yewen, of yew*
165   Till struggling strong did him at last constraine,
    To let them downe before his flightès end:
    As hagard° hauke presuming to contend   *untamed*
    With hardie fowle, above his hable might,°   *able power*
    His wearie pounces° all in vaine doth spend,   *claws*
170   To trusse° the pray too heavie for his flight;   *seize*
Which comming downe to ground, does free it selfe by fight.

20

He so disseizèd of his gryping grosse,[8]
    The knight his thrilant° speare againe assayd   *piercing*
    In his bras-plated body to embosse,°   *plunge*
175   And three mens strength unto the stroke he layd;
    Wherewith the stiffe beame quakèd, as affrayd,
    And glauncing from his scaly necke, did glyde
    Close under his left wing, then broad displayd.
    The percing steele there wrought a wound full wyde,
180   That with the uncouth° smart the Monster lowdly cryde.   *unfamiliar*

21

He cryde, as raging seas are wont to rore,
    When wintry storme his wrathfull wreck does threat,
    The rolling billowes beat the ragged shore,
    As they the earth would shoulder from her seat,
185   And greedie gulfe° does gape, as he would eat   *i.e., the sea*
    His neighbour element° in his revenge: *earth*
    Then gin the blustring brethren° boldly threat,   *the winds*
    To move the world from off his stedfast henge,°   *axis*
And boystrous battell make, each other to avenge.

22

190   The steely head stucke fast still in his flesh,
    Till with his cruell clawes he snatcht the wood,
    And quite a sunder broke. Forth flowèd fresh

---

8. Freed from his formidable grip.

A gushing river of blacke goarie° blood,   clotted
That drownèd all the land, whereon he stood;
195   The stream thereof would drive a water-mill.
Trebly augmented was his furious mood
With bitter sense of his deepe rooted ill,°   injury
That flames of fire he threw forth from his large nosethrill.

23

His hideous tayle then hurlèd he about,
200   And therewith all enwrapt the nimble thyes°   thighs
Of his froth-fomy steed, whose courage stout
Striving to loose the knot, that fast him tyes,
Himselfe in streighter° bandes too rash implyes,⁹   tighter
That to the ground he is perforce constraynd
205   To throw his rider: who can° quickly ryse   did
From off the earth, with durty bloud distaynd,°   defiled
For that reprochfull fall right fowly he disdaynd.

24

And fiercely tooke his trenchand° blade in hand,   sharp
With which he stroke so furious and so fell,
210   That nothing seemd the puissance could withstand:
Upon his crest the hardned yron fell,
But his more hardned crest was armd so well,
That deeper dint therein it would not make;¹
Yet so extremely did the buffe° him quell,°   blow/dismay
215   That from thenceforth he shund the like to take,
But when he saw them come, he did them still forsake.°   avoid

25

The knight was wrath to see his stroke beguyld,°   foiled
And smote againe with more outrageous might;
But backe againe the sparckling steele recoyld,
220   And left not any marke, where it did light;
As if in Adamant rocke it had bene pight.°   struck against
The beast impatient of his smarting wound,
And of so fierce and forcible despight,°   powerful injury
Thought with his wings to stye° above the ground;   mount
225   But his late wounded wing unserviceable found.

26

Then full of griefe and anguish vehement,
He lowdly brayd, that like was never heard,
And from his wide devouring oven sent
A flake° of fire, that flashing in his beard,   flash
230   Him all amazd, and almost made affeard;
The scorching flame sore swingèd° all his face,   singed
And through his armour all his bodie seard,

---

9. I.e., too quickly entangles.   1. I.e., it could not make a deep gash there.

That he could not endure so cruell cace,°   *plight*
But thought his armes to leave, and helmet to unlace.

27

235   Not that great Champion of the antique world,
      Whom famous Poetes verse so much doth vaunt,
      And hath for twelve huge labours high extold,
      So many furies and sharpe fits did haunt,
      When him the poysoned garment did enchaunt
240   With Centaures bloud, and bloudie verses charmed,
      As did this knight twelve thousand dolours° daunt,   *pains*
      Whom fyrie steele now burnt, that earst° him armed,   *formerly*
That erst him goodly armed, now most of all him harmed.[2]

28

     Faint, wearie, sore, emboylèd, grievèd, brent°   *burned*
245   With heat, toyle, wounds, armes, smart, and inward fire
      That never man such mischiefes° did torment;   *misfortunes*
      Death better were, death did he oft desire,
      But death will never come, when needes require.
      Whom so dismayd when that his foe beheld,
250   He cast to suffer him no more respire,°   *live*
      But gan his sturdie sterne° about to weld,°   *tail/lash*
And him so strongly stroke, that to the ground him feld.

29

     It fortunèd (as faire it then befell)
      Behind his backe unweeting,° where he stood,   *unnoticed*
255   Of auncient time there was a springing well,
      From which fast trickled forth a silver flood,
      Full of great vertues, and for med'cine good.
      Whylome,° before that cursèd Dragon got   *formerly*
      That happie land, and all with innocent blood
260   Defyld those sacred waves, it rightly hot°   *was called*
The Well of Life,[3] ne yet his vertues° had forgot.   *powers*

30

     For unto life the dead it could restore,
      And guilt of sinfull crimes cleane wash away,
      Those that with sicknesse were infected sore,
265   It could recure, and agèd long decay
      Renew, as one were borne that very day.
      Both Silo this, and Jordan did excell,
      And th' English Bath, and eke the german Spau,

2. Redcrosse's fire baptism is compared with the burning shirt of Nessus, which killed Hercules, "that great Champion of the antique world" (line 235). His "twelve huge labours" are paralleled to the knight's "twelve thousand dolours."
3. An allusion to Revelation 22.1–2: "And he showed me a pure river of water of life, clear as crystal, proceeding out of the throne of God, and of the Lamb. In the midst of the street of it, and on either side of the river, was the tree of life which bare twelve manner of fruits and yielded her fruit every month: and the leaves of the tree were for the healing of the nations."

Ne can Cephise, nor Hebrus match this well:
270 Into the same the knight backe overthrowen, fell.[4]

31

Now gan the golden Phoebus for to steepe
His fierie face in billowes of the west,
And his faint steedes watred in Ocean deepe,
Whiles from their journall° labours they did rest,   *daily*
275 When that infernall Monster, having kest°   *cast*
His wearie foe into that living well,
Can° high advaunce his broad discoloured brest,   *did*
Above his wonted pitch,° with countenance fell,°   *height / sinister*
And clapt his yron wings, as victor he did dwell.°   *remain*

32

280 Which when his pensive Ladie saw from farre,
Great woe and sorrow did her soule assay,°   *assail*
As weening that the sad end of the warre,
And gan to highest God entirely° pray,   *earnestly*
That fearèd chaunce° from her to turne away;   *fate*
285 With folded hands and knees full lowly bent
All night she watcht, ne once adowne would lay
Her daintie limbs in her sad dreriment,°   *dismal condition*
But praying still did wake, and waking did lament.

33

The morrow next gan early to appeare,
290 That° Titan° rose to runne his daily race;   *when / the sun god*
But early ere the morrow next gan reare
Out of the sea faire Titans deawy face,
Up rose the gentle virgin from her place,
And lookèd all about, if she might spy
295 Her lovèd knight to move his manly pace:
For she had great doubt of his safety,
Since late she saw him fall before his enemy.

34

At last she saw, where he upstarted brave
Out of the well, wherein he drenchèd lay;
300 As Eagle fresh out of the Ocean wave,
Where he hath left his plumes all hoary gray,
And deckt himselfe with feathers youthly gay,
Like Eyas° hauke up mounts unto the skies,   *young*
His newly budded pineons to assay,
305 And marveiles at himselfe, still as he flies:
So new this new-borne knight to battell new did rise.[5]

---

4. The Well of Life, with its powers of renewal, is successively compared with waters of the Bible, of England and Europe, and of classical antiquity. In Siloam ("Silo") a blind man was cured by Christ (John 9.7); the crossing of the river Jordan saved the Jews (Deuteronomy 27.2–9), and Christ was baptized therein (Matthew 3.16). "Bath" and "Spau" (Spa) were famed for their medicinal waters. "Cephise" and "Hebrus" in Greece were noted for purifying and healing powers.
5. Legend had it that the eagle could renew its youth by bathing in a spring.

35

Whom when the damnèd feend so fresh did spy,
  No wonder if he wondred at the sight,
  And doubted, whether his late enemy
310 It were, or other new supplièd knight.
  He, now to prove his late renewèd might,
  High brandishing his bright deaw-burning blade,
  Upon his crested scalpe so sore did smite,
  That to the scull a yawning wound it made:
315 The deadly dint° his dullèd senses all dismaid.   *blow*

36

I wote° not, whether the revenging steele   *know*
  Were hardnèd with that holy water dew,
  Wherein he fell, or sharper edge did feele,
  Or his baptizèd hands now greater° grew;   *stronger*
320 Or other secret vertue° did ensew;   *power*
  Else never could the force of fleshly arme,
  Ne molten mettall in his bloud embrew:°   *plunge*
  For till that stownd° could never wight him harme,   *moment*
  By subtilty, nor slight,° nor might, nor mighty charme.   *trickery*

37

325 The cruell wound enragèd him so sore,
  That loud he yellèd for exceeding paine;
  As hundred ramping Lyons seemed to rore,
  Whom ravenous hunger did thereto constraine:
  Then gan he tosse aloft his stretchèd traine,°   *tail*
330 And therewith scourge the buxome° aire so sore,   *yielding*
  That to his force to yeelden it was faine;°   *obliged*
  Ne ought his sturdie strokes might stand afore,[6]
  That high trees overthrew, and rocks in peeces tore.

38

The same advauncing high above his head,
335 With sharpe intended° sting so rude° him smot,   *extended/roughly*
  That to the earth him drove, as stricken dead,
  Ne living wight would have him life behot:[7]
  The mortall sting his angry needle shot
  Quite through his shield, and in his shoulder seasd,
340 Where fast it stucke, ne would there out be got:
  The griefe° thereof him wondrous sore diseasd,°   *pain/afflicted*
  Ne might his ranckling paine with patience be appeasd.

39

But yet more mindfull of his honour deare,
  Then of the grievous smart, which him did wring,°   *torment*
345 From loathèd soile he can° him lightly reare,   *did*

6. I.e., neither could anything ("ought") stand before his violent ("sturdie") strokes.

7. Promised. I.e., no one would have thought he could survive the blow.

And strove to loose the farre infixèd sting:
Which when in vaine he tryde with struggeling,
Inflamed with wrath, his raging blade he heft,°   *heaved*
And strooke so strongly, that the knotty string
350   Of his huge taile he quite a sunder cleft,
Five joynts thereof he hewd, and but the stump him left.

40

Hart cannot thinke, what outrage,° and what cryes,   *violent clamor*
With foule enfouldred[8] smoake and flashing fire,
The hell-bred beast threw forth unto the skyes,
355   That all was coverèd with darknesse dire:
Then fraught° with rancour, and engorgèd° ire,   *filled / swollen*
He cast at once him to avenge for all,
And gathering up himselfe out of the mire,
With his uneven wings did fiercely fall
360   Upon his sunne-bright shield, and gript it fast withall.

41

Much was the man encombred with his hold,
In feare to lose his weapon in his paw,
Ne wist yet, how his talents° to unfold;   *talons*
Nor harder was from Cerberus[9] greedie jaw
365   To plucke a bone, then° from his cruell claw   *than*
To reave° by strength the gripèd gage° away: *seize / prize*
Thrise he assayd it from his foot to draw,
And thrise in vaine to draw it did assay,
It booted nought to thinke, to robbe him of his pray.

42

370   Tho° when he saw no power might prevaile,   *then*
His trustie sword he cald to his last aid,
Wherewith he fiercely did his foe assaile,
And double blowes about him stoutly laid,
That glauncing fire out of the yron plaid;
375   As sparckles from the Andvile° use to fly,   *anvil*
When heavie hammers on the wedge are swaid;°   *struck*
Therewith at last he forst him to unty°   *loosen*
One of his grasping feete, him to defend thereby.

43

The other foot, fast fixèd on his shield,
380   Whenas no strength, nor stroks mote° him constraine   *might*
To loose, ne yet the warlike pledge to yield,
He smot thereat with all his might and maine,
That nought so wondrous puissance might sustaine;
Upon the joynt the lucky steele did light,
385   And made such way, that hewd it quite in twaine;
The paw yet missèd not his minisht° might,   *lessened*
But hong still on the shield, as it at first was pight.°   *placed*

---

8. Black as a thundercloud.   9. The dog that guards the mouth of hell.

44

For griefe thereof, and divelish despight,
 From his infernall fournace forth he threw
390 Huge flames, that dimmèd all the heavens light,
 Enrold in duskish smoke and brimstone blew;
 As burning Aetna from his boyling stew°   *cauldron*
 Doth belch out flames, and rockes in peeces broke,
 And ragged ribs of mountaines molten new
395 Enwrapt in coleblacke clouds and filthy smoke,
That all the land with stench, and heaven with horror choke.

45

The heate whereof, and harmefull pestilence
 So sore him noyd,° that forst him to retire   *troubled*
 A little backward for his best defence,
400 To save his bodie from the scorching fire,
 Which he from hellish entrailes did expire.°   *breathe out*
 It chaunst (eternall God that chaunce did guide)
 As he recoylèd backward, in the mire
 His nigh forwearied feeble feet did slide,
405 And downe he fell, with dread of shame sore terrifide.

46

There grew a goodly tree him faire beside,
 Loaden with fruit and apples rosie red,
 As they in pure vermilion had beene dide,
 Whereof great vertues over all were red:° *everywhere were told*
410 For happie life to all, which thereon fed,
 And life eke everlasting did befall:
 Great God it planted in that blessed sted°   *place*
 With his almightie hand, and did it call
The Tree of Life, the crime of our first fathers fall.[1]

47

415 In all the world like was not to be found,
 Save in that soile, where all good things did grow,
 And freely sprong out of the fruitfull ground,
 As incorrupted Nature did them sow,
 Till that dread Dragon all did overthrow.
420 Another like faire tree eke grew thereby,
 Whereof who so did eat, eftsoones did know
 Both good and ill: O mornefull memory:
That tree through one mans fault hath doen us all to dy.° *i.e., killed us*

48

From that first tree forth flowd, as from a well,
425 A trickling streame of Balme, most soveraine° *powerful for cures*

---

1. Genesis 2.9 describes the Tree of Life and also the Tree of Knowledge of Good and Evil, both of which God planted in the Garden of Eden. The "crime of our first fathers fall" is that Adam, in eating of the second and being banished from Eden, separated himself—and (according to Christian doctrine) us—from the first. The Tree of Life appears again in the New Jerusalem (Revelation 22.2).

And daintie deare,° which on the ground still fell,   *precious*
And overflowèd all the fertill plaine,
As it had deawèd bene with timely° raine: *seasonable*
Life and long health that gratious° ointment gave,   *full of grace*
430   And deadly woundes could heale, and reare° againe   *raise*
The senselesse corse appointed° for the grave.   *made ready*
Into that same he fell: which did from death him save.[2]

49

For nigh thereto the ever damnèd beast
Durst not approch, for he was deadly made,°   *i.e., a child of death*
435   And all that life preservèd, did detest:
Yet he it oft adventured° to invade.   *attempted*
By this the drouping day-light gan to fade,
And yeeld his roome to sad succeeding night,
Who with her sable mantle gan to shade
440   The face of earth, and wayes of living wight,
And high her burning torch set up in heaven bright.

50

When gentle Una saw the second fall
Of her deare knight, who wearie of long fight,
And faint through losse of bloud, moved not at all,
445   But lay as in a dreame of deepe delight,
Besmeard with pretious Balme, whose vertuous might
Did heale his wounds, and scorching heat alay,[3]
Againe she stricken was with sore affright,
And for his safetie gan devoutly pray;
450 And watch the noyous° night, and wait for joyous day.   *noxious*

51

The joyous day gan early to appeare,
And faire Aurora from the deawy bed
Of aged Tithone gan her selfe to reare,[4]
With rosie cheekes, for shame as blushing red;
455   Her golden lockes for haste were loosely shed
About her eares, when Una her did marke
Clymbe to her charet, all with flowers spred,
From heaven high to chase the chearelesse darke;
With merry note her loud salutes the mounting larke.

52

460   Then freshly up arose the doughtie knight,
All healèd of his hurts and woundès wide,
And did himselfe to battell readie dight;°   *prepare*
Whose early foe awaiting him beside

---

2. The healing balm flowing from the Tree of Life is understood to be Christ's blood, shed to redeem humankind from eternal damnation.
3. Cf. Revelation 2.7, 11: "To him that overcometh will I give to eat of the tree of life" and "He that overcometh shall not be hurt of the second death."
4. Aurora is goddess of the dawn, Tithonus her husband ("aged" because he was granted everlasting life without everlasting youth).

To have devourd, so soone as day he spyde,
465   When now he saw himselfe so freshly reare,
As if late fight had nought him damnifyde,°   *injured*
He woxe° dismayd, and gan his fate to feare;   *grew*
Nathlesse° with wonted rage he him advaunced neare.   *nevertheless*

53

And in his first encounter, gaping wide,
470   He thought attonce him to have swallowed quight,
And rusht upon him with outragious pride;
Who him r'encountring fierce, as hauke in flight,
Perforce rebutted° backe. The weapon bright   *drove*
Taking advantage of his open jaw,
475   Ran through his mouth with so importune° might,   *violent*
That deepe emperst his darksome hollow maw,
And back retyrd,[5] his life bloud forth with all did draw.

54

So downe he fell, and forth his life did breath,
That vanisht into smoke and cloudès swift;
480   So downe he fell, that th' earth him underneath
Did grone, as feeble so great load to lift;
So downe he fell, as an huge rockie clift,
Whose false° foundation waves have washt away,   *insecure*
With dreadfull poyse° is from the mayneland rift,° *falling weight / split*
485   And rolling downe, great Neptune doth dismay;
So downe he fell, and like an heapèd mountaine lay.

55

The knight himselfe even trembled at his fall,
So huge and horrible a masse it seemed;
And his deare Ladie, that beheld it all,
490   Durst not approch for dread, which she misdeemed,°   *misjudged*
But yet at last, when as the direfull feend
She saw not stirre, off-shaking vaine affright,
She nigher drew, and saw that joyous end:
Then God she praysd, and thankt her faithfull knight,
495 That had atchiev'd so great a conquest by his might.

Canto 12 *Summary*   The king and queen of Eden emerge from the castle with all their followers and gaze in wonder at the dead dragon. A great banquet is held in the castle, and Redcrosse and Una are betrothed, though Redcrosse must still fulfill his pledge to serve the Faerie Queene in war for six more years. A messenger arrives bearing a letter from Fidessa (Duessa), in which she charges Redcrosse with breach of promise and seeks to prevent his marriage to Una. Redcrosse explains to the king how he was led astray by Duessa's wicked arts. The messenger is revealed by Una as Archimago and thrown into a dungeon. The king then performs the wedding ceremony. They live in happiness for some time, until Redcrosse must return to the Faerie Queene, leaving Una to mourn.

5. I.e., on being drawn back.

From The Second Booke of The Faerie Queene

Contayning
The Legend of Sir Guyon,
or
Of Temperaunce

Summary   Book 2 deals with Temperance, a virtue encompassing moderation, balance, and self-discipline. Sir Guyon, the Knight of Temperance, is accompanied for most of his journey by the faithful Palmer, who represents reason. His quest is to capture the lustful enchantress Acrasia, who seduces men and turns them into beasts. On his journey, Guyon must face and overcome a series of challenges involving different kinds of passion and desire: wrath, lust, mirth, ambition, and greed. In the seventh canto he enters the underworld realm of Mammon, god of wealth, and survives three days there without succumbing to any of a host of temptations. This experience leaves him exhausted spiritually and physically. After a sojourn with Prince Arthur in the House of Alma, an allegorical representation of the properly disciplined human body ruled by the rational soul, Guyon and the Palmer resume their quest. Together they travel by boat to Acrasia's Bower of Bliss, passing by a host of dangers and temptations on the way.

From *Canto 12*

[THE BOWER OF BLISS]¹

42

370 Thence passing forth, they shortly do arrive,
Whereas the Bowre of Blisse was situate;
A place pickt out by choice of best alive,°   *the best living artisans*
That natures worke by art can imitate:
In which what ever in this worldly state
375 Is sweet, and pleasing unto living sense,
Or that may dayntiest fantasie aggrate,°   *please, satisfy*
Was pourèd forth with plentifull dispence,°   *liberality*
And made there to abound with lavish affluence.

43

Goodly it was enclosèd round about,
380 Aswell their entred guests to keepe within,
As those unruly beasts to hold without;
Yet was the fence thereof but weake and thin;
Nought feard their force, that fortilage° to win,   *fortress*
But wisedomes powre, and temperaunces might,
385 By which the mightiest things efforcèd bin:°   *are compelled*
And eke° the gate was wrought of substaunce light,   *also*
Rather for pleasure, then° for battery or fight.   *than*

44

Yt framèd was of precious yvory,
That seemd a worke of admirable wit;°   *marvelous skill*

---

1. The Bower of Bliss, perhaps the most famous of Spenser's symbolic places, has been variously interpreted. Some critics emphasize its aspects of sterility and artifice; others, its seductive and threatening eroticism and idolatry akin to that associated with the New World and Ireland.

390   And therein all the famous history
        Of Jason and Medaea was ywrit;
        Her mighty charmes, her furious loving fit,
        His goodly conquest of the golden fleece,
        His falsèd° faith, and love too lightly flit,°   *violated/altering*
395   The wondred° Argo, which in venturous peece[2]   *admired*
First through the Euxine seas bore all the flowr of Greece.[3]

45

      Ye might have seene the frothy billowes fry°   *foam*
        Under the ship, as thorough them she went,
        That seemd the waves were into yvory,
400   Or yvory into the waves were sent;
        And other where the snowy substaunce sprent°   *sprinkled*
        With vermell,° like the boyes bloud[4] therein shed,   *vermilion*
        A piteous spectacle did represent,
        And otherwhiles° with gold besprinkelèd;   *elsewhere*
405   Yt seemd th' enchaunted flame, which did Creüsa wed.[5]

46

All this, and more might in that goodly gate
        Be red; that ever open stood to all,
        Which thither came: but in the Porch there sate
        A comely personage of stature tall,
410   And semblaunce° pleasing, more then naturall,   *appearance*
        That travellers to him seemd to entize;
        His looser° garment to the ground did fall,   *too loose*
        And flew about his heeles in wanton wize,
Not fit for speedy pace, or manly exercize.

47

415   They in that place him Genius° did call: *presiding spirit*
        Not that celestiall powre,[6] to whom the care
        Of life, and generatiön of all
        That lives, pertaines in charge particulare,
        Who wondrous things concerning our welfare,
420   And strange phantomes doth let us oft forsee,
        And oft of secret ill bids us beware:
That is our Selfe, whom though we do not see,
Yet each doth in him selfe it well perceive to bee.

48

Therefore a God him sage Antiquity
425   Did wisely make, and good Agdistes call:
        But this same was to that quite contrary,

---

2. I.e., adventurous vessel.
3. Jason, in his ship the *Argo*, sought the Golden Fleece of the king of Colchis; the witch Medea, the king's daughter, fell in love with him and used "her mighty charmes" to help him obtain it.
4. Refers to Absyrtus, Medea's younger brother, whose body she cut into pieces and scattered to delay her father's pursuit.

5. Jason later deserted Medea for Creüsa. In revenge, Medea gave the girl a dress that burst into flame when she put it on; the flame consumed and thus "wed" her.
6. I.e., not Agdistes (see next stanza), the god of generation. The true Agdistes appears in the Garden of Adonis canto (3.6, stanzas 31–33).

The foe of life, that good envyes° to all,   grudges
That secretly doth us procure° to fall,   cause
Through guilefull semblaunts,° which he makes us see.   illusions
430   He of this Gardin had the governall,°   management
And Pleasures porter was devizd° to bee,   appointed
Holding a staffe in hand for more formalitee.

49

With diverse flowres he daintily was deckt,
And strowèd round about, and by his side
435   A mighty Mazer bowle[7] of wine was set,
As if it had to him bene sacrifide;°   consecrated
Wherewith all new-come guests he gratifide:
So did he eke Sir Guyon passing by:
But he his idle curtesie defide,
440   And overthrew his bowle disdainfully;
And broke his staffe, with which he charmèd semblants sly.[8]

50

Thus being entred, they behold around
A large and spacious plaine, on every side
Strowed with pleasauns,° whose faire grassy ground   gardens
445   Mantled with greene, and goodly beautifide
With all the ornaments of Floraes° pride,   goddess of flowers
Wherewith her mother Art, as halfe in scorne
Of niggard Nature, like a pompous bride
Did decke her, and too lavishly adorne,
450   When forth from virgin bowre she comes in th' early morne.

51

Thereto the Heavens alwayes Joviall,[9]
Lookt on them lovely,° still in stedfast state,   lovingly
Ne° suffred storme nor frost on them to fall,   nor
Their tender buds or leaves to violate,
455   Nor scorching heat, nor cold intemperate
T' afflict the creatures, which therein did dwell,
But the milde aire with season moderate
Gently attempred, and disposd so well,
That still it breathèd forth sweet spirit° and holesome smell.   breath

52

460   More sweet and holesome, then the pleasaunt hill
Of Rhodope, on which the Nimphe, that bore
A gyaunt babe, her selfe for griefe did kill;
Or the Thessalian Tempe, where of yore
Faire Daphne Phoebus hart with love did gore;
465   Or Ida, where the Gods lov'd to repaire,°   resort

7. A drinking cup of maple.
8. Raised deceitful apparitions. The rod and bowl are traditional emblems of enchantment (cf.
Duessa's cup, 1.8, stanza 14).
9. Serene and beneficent, as influenced by the planet Jupiter.

When ever they their heavenly bowres forlore;°   *deserted*
Or sweet Parnasse, the haunt of Muses faire;[1]
Or Eden selfe, if ought with Eden mote compaire.

53

Much wondred Guyon at the faire aspect
470   Of that sweet place, yet suffred no delight
To sincke into his sence, nor mind affect,
But passèd forth, and lookt still forward right,°   *straight ahead*
Bridling his will, and maistering his might:
Till that he came unto another gate;
475   No gate, but like one, being goodly dight°   *arrayed*
With boughes and braunches, which did broad dilate°   *spread out*
Their clasping armes, in wanton wreathings intricate.

54

So fashionèd a Porch with rare device,°   *design*
Archt over head with an embracing vine,
480   Whose bounches hanging downe, seemed to entice
All passers by, to tast their lushious wine,
And did themselves into their hands incline,
As freely offering to be gatherèd:
Some deepe empurpled as the Hyacint,[2]
485   Some as the Rubine,° laughing sweetly red,   *ruby*
Some like faire Emeraudes, not yet well ripenèd.

55

And them amongst, some were of burnisht gold,
So made by art, to beautifie the rest,
Which did themselves emongst the leaves enfold,
490   As lurking from the vew of covetous guest,
That the weake bowes,° with so rich load opprest,   *boughs*
Did bowe adowne, as over-burdenèd.
Under that Porch a comely dame did rest,
Clad in faire weedes,° but fowle disderèd,   *garments*
495 And garments loose, that seemd unmeet for womanhed.°   *womanhood*

56

In her left hand a Cup of gold she held,
And with her right the riper° fruit did reach,   *overripe*
Whose sappy liquor, that with fulnesse sweld,
Into her cup she scruzd,° with daintie breach°   *squeezed/crushing*
500   Of her fine fingers, without fowle empeach,°   *injury*
That so faire wine-presse made the wine more sweet:
Thereof she usd to give to drinke to each,

---

1. The nymph Rhodope, who had a "gyaunt babe," Athos, by Neptune, was turned into a mountain. Daphne, another nymph, charmed Apollo so that he pursued her until she prayed for aid and was turned into a laurel tree. Mount Ida was the scene of the rape of Ganymede by Jupiter, the judgment of Paris, and the gods' vantage point for viewing the Trojan War. Mount Parnassus is the home of the Muses.
2. The hyacinth or jacinth, a sapphire-colored stone.

Whom passing by she happenèd to meet:
It was her guise,° all Straungers goodly so to greet.   *custom*

57

505 So she to Guyon offred it to tast;
Who taking it out of her tender hond,
The cup to ground did violently cast,
That all in peeces it was broken fond,°   *found*
And with the liquor stainèd all the lond:°   *land*
510 Whereat Excesse exceedingly was wroth,
Yet no'te° the same amend, ne yet withstond,   *knew not how to*
But suffered him to passe, all° were she loth;   *although*
Who nought regarding her displeasure forward goth.

58

There the most daintie Paradise on ground,
515 It selfe doth offer to his sober eye,
In which all pleasures plenteously abound,
And none does others happinesse envye:
The painted° flowres, the trees upshooting hye,   *brightly colored*
The dales for shade, the hilles for breathing space,
520 The trembling groves, the Christall° running by;   *clear stream*
And that, which all faire workes doth most aggrace,°   *add grace to*
The art, which all that wrought, appearèd in no place.

59

One would have thought (so cunningly, the rude,
And scornèd parts were mingled with the fine)
525 That nature had for wantonesse ensude°   *imitated*
Art, and that Art at nature did repine;°   *complain*
So striving each th' other to undermine,
Each did the others worke more beautifie;
So diff'ring both in willes, agreed in fine:°   *in the end*
530 So all agreed through sweete diversitie,
This Gardin to adorne with all varietie.

60

And in the midst of all, a fountaine stood,
Of richest substaunce, that on earth might bee,
So pure and shiny, that the silver flood
535 Through every channell running one might see;
Most goodly it with curious imageree
Was over-wrought, and shapes of naked boyes,
Of which some seemd with lively jollitee,
To fly about, playing their wanton toyes,°   *sports*
540 Whilest others did them selves embay° in liquid joyes.   *bathe*

61

And over all, of purest gold was spred,
A trayle of yvie in his native hew:
For the rich mettall was so colourèd,

That wight, who did not well avis'd° it vew,   *carefully*
545 Would surely deeme it to be yvie trew:
Low his lascivious armes adown did creepe,
That themselves dipping in the silver dew,
Their fleecy flowres they tenderly did steepe,
Which° drops of Christall seemd for wantones°   *on which/wantonness*
    to weepe.

62

550 Infinit streames continually did well
Out of this fountaine, sweet and faire to see,
The which into an ample laver° fell,   *basin*
And shortly grew to so great quantitie,
That like a little lake it seemd to bee;
555 Whose depth exceeded not three cubits[3] hight,
That through the waves one might the bottom see,
All pav'd beneath with Jaspar shining bright,
That seemd the fountaine in that sea did sayle upright.

63

And all the margent° round about was set,   *border*
560 With shady Laurell trees, thence to defend°   *ward off*
The sunny beames, which on the billowes bet,°   *beat*
And those which therein bathèd, mote offend.°   *harm*
As Guyon hapned by the same to wend,
Two naked Damzelles he therein espyde,
565 Which therein bathing, seemèd to contend,
And wrestle wantonly, ne car'd to hyde,
Their dainty parts from vew of any, which them eyde.

64

Sometimes the one would lift the other quight
Above the waters, and then downe againe
570 Her plong,° as over maisterèd by might,   *plunge*
Where both awhile would coverèd remaine,
And each the other from to rise° restraine;   *rising*
The whiles their snowy limbes, as through a vele,
So through the Christall waves appearèd plaine:
575 Then suddeinly both would themselves unhele,°   *uncover*
And th' amarous sweet spoiles to greedy eyes revele.

65

As that faire Starre, the messenger of morne,[4]
His deawy face out of the sea doth reare:
Or as the Cyprian goddess,[5] newly borne
580 Of th' Oceans fruitfull froth,° did first appeare: *foam*
Such seemèd they, and so their yellow heare

---

3. A cubit is about twenty inches (thus the depth is less than five feet).
4. "His" in the next line implies that the reference is not to Venus but to Phosphorus (or Heophorus),

the minor male divinity sometimes identified with the morning star.
5. Venus, one of whose principal shrines was on the island of Cyprus.

Christalline humour° droppèd downe apace.   clear water
Whom such when Guyon saw, he drew him neare,
And somewhat gan relent his earnest pace,
585   His stubborne brest gan secret pleasaunce to embrace.

66

The wanton Maidens him espying, stood
     Gazing a while at his unwonted guise;°   manner
     Then th' one her selfe low duckèd in the flood,
     Abasht, that her a straunger did avise:°   see
590   But th' other rather higher did arise,
     And her two lilly paps aloft displayd,
     And all, that might his melting hart entise
     To her delights, she unto him bewrayed:°   revealed
The rest hid underneath, him more desirous made.

67

595   With that, the other likewise up arose,
     And her faire lockes, which formerly were bownd
     Up in one knot, she low adowne did lose:°   loosen
     Which flowing long and thick, her cloth'd arownd,
     And th' yvorie in golden mantle gownd:
600   So that faire spectacle from him was reft,°   taken
     Yet that, which reft it, no lesse faire was fownd:
     So hid in lockes and waves from lookers theft,
Nought but her lovely face she for his looking left.

68

Withall she laughèd, and she blusht withall,
605   That blushing to her laughter gave more grace,
     And laughter to her blushing, as did fall:
     Now when they spide the knight to slacke his pace,
     Them to behold, and in his sparkling face
     The secret signes of kindled lust appeare,
610   Their wanton meriments they did encreace,
     And to him beckned, to approch more neare,
And shewd him many sights, that courage cold could reare.[6]

69

On which when gazing him the Palmer saw,
     He much rebukt those wandring eyes of his,
615   And counseld well, him forward thence did draw.
     Now are they come nigh to the Bowre of blis
     Of her fond favorites so named amis:
     When thus the Palmer; "Now Sir, well avise;°   take care
     For here the end of all our travell is:
620   Here wonnes° Acrasia, whom we must surprise,   dwells
Else she will slip away, and all our drift° despise."   plan, effort

6. That could arouse sexual desire ("courage") when cold.

70

Eftsoones they heard a most melodious sound,
 Of all that mote delight a daintie eare,
 Such as attonce might not on living ground,
625 Save in this Paradise, be heard elswhere:
 Right hard it was, for wight, which did it heare,
 To read,° what manner musicke that mote bee: *discern*
 For all that pleasing is to living eare,
 Was there consorted in one harmonee,
630 Birdes, voyces, instruments, windes, waters, all agree.

71

The joyous birdes shrouded in chearefull shade,
 Their notes unto the voyce attempred° sweet;   *attuned*
 Th' Angelicall soft trembling voyces made
 To th' instruments divine respondence meet:°   *fitting*
635 The silver sounding instruments did meet°   *join*
 With the base murmure of the waters fall:
 The waters fall with difference discreet,°   *distinct variations*
 Now soft, now loud, unto the wind did call:
 The gentle warbling wind low answerèd to all.

72

640 There, whence that Musick seemèd heard to bee,
 Was the faire Witch her selfe[7] now solacing,
 With a new Lover, whom through sorceree
 And witchcraft, she from farre did thither bring:
 There she had him now layd a slombering,
645 In secret shade, after long wanton joyes:
 Whilst round about them pleasauntly did sing
 Many faire Ladies, and lascivious boyes,
 That ever mixt their song with light licentious toyes.°   *amorous play*

73

And all that while, right over him she hong,
650 With her false° eyes fast fixèd in his sight,   *deceitful*
 As seeking medicine, whence she was stong,
 Or greedily depasturing° delight: *feeding on*
 And oft inclining downe with kisses light,
 For feare of waking him, his lips bedewd,
655 And through his humid eyes did sucke his spright,
 Quite molten into lust and pleasure lewd;
 Wherewith she sighèd soft, as if his case she rewd.°   *pitied*

74

The whiles some one did chaunt this lovely lay:[8]
 "Ah see, who so faire thing doest faine° to see,   *delight*

7. Acrasia—whose name means both "excess" and "impotence"—bears many resemblances to Circe (in *Odyssey* 10 as well as the more witchlike and seductive figure in Ovid's *Metamorphoses* 14) and also to the enchantresses of Italian romance who derive from Circe: Acratia in Trissino's *L'Italia liberata* and Armida in Tasso's *Gerusalemme liberata*. Much of the description in this scene is imitated from Armida's garden.

8. The song ("lay") of stanzas 74 and 75 imitates that in *Gerusalemme liberata* 16.14–15; this is a classic statement of the *carpe florem* theme—pick the flower of youth before it fades.

660 In springing flowre the image of thy day;
Ah see the Virgin Rose, how sweetly shee
Doth first peepe forth with bashfull modestee,
That fairer seemes, the lesse ye see her may;
Lo see soone after, how more bold and free
665 Her barèd bosome she doth broad display;
Loe see soone after, how she fades, and falles away.

75

"So passeth, in the passing of a day,
Of mortall life the leafe, the bud, the flowre,
Ne more doth flourish after first decay,
670 That earst° was sought to decke both bed and bowre,   *formerly*
Of many a Ladie, and many a Paramowre: *lover*
Gather therefore the Rose, whilest yet is prime,°   *(its) springtime*
For soone comes age, that will her pride deflowre:
Gather the Rose of love, whilest yet is time,
675 Whilest loving thou mayst lovèd be with equal crime."

76

He ceast, and then gan all the quire of birdes
Their diverse notes t' attune unto his lay,
As in approvance of his pleasing words.
The constant paire⁹ heard all, that he did say,
680 Yet swarvèd not, but kept their forward way,
Through many covert groves, and thickets close,
In which they creeping did at last display°   *discover*
That wanton Ladie, with her lover lose,°   *loose, wanton*
Whose sleepie head she in her lap did soft dispose.

77

685 Upon a bed of Roses she was layd,
As faint through heat, or dight to° pleasant sin,   *ready for*
And was arayd, or rather disarayd,
All in a vele of silke and silver thin,
That hid no whit her alablaster skin,
690 But rather shewd more white, if more might bee:
More subtile web Arachne° cannot spin,   *the spider*
Nor the fine nets, which oft we woven see
Of scorchèd deaw, do not in th' aire more lightly flee.°   *float*

78

Her snowy brest was bare to readie spoyle
695 Of hungry eies, which n'ote° therewith be fild,   *could not*
And yet through languor of her late sweet toyle,
Few drops, more cleare then Nectar, forth distild,
That like pure Orient perles¹ adowne it trild,°   *trickled*
And her faire eyes sweet smyling in delight,
700 Moystened their fierie beames, with which she thrild°   *pierced*

9. I.e., Guyon and the Palmer.   1. Lustrous pearls of the East.

Fraile harts, yet quenchèd° not; like starry light   *killed*
Which sparckling on the silent waves, does seeme more bright.

79

The young man sleeping by her, seemd to bee
  Some goodly swayne of honorable place,°   *rank*
705 That certès it great pittie was to see
  Him his nobilitie so foule deface;°   *disgrace*
  A sweet regard,° and amiable grace,   *demeanor*
  Mixèd with manly sternnesse did appeare
  Yet sleeping, in his well proportioned face,
710 And on his tender lips the downy heare
Did now but freshly spring, and silken blossomes beare.

80

His warlike armes, the idle instruments
  Of sleeping praise,° were hong upon a tree,   *worthiness*
  And his brave shield, full of old moniments,°   *marks of honor*
715 Was fowly ra'st,° that none the signes might see;   *erased*
  Ne for them, ne for honour carèd hee,
  Ne ought, that did to his advauncement tend,
  But in lewd loves, and wastfull luxuree,°   *licentiousness*
  His dayes, his goods, his bodie he did spend:
720 O horrible enchantment, that him so did blend.°   *blind*

81

The noble Elfe,[2] and carefull Palmer drew
  So nigh them, minding nought, but lustfull game,
  That suddein forth they on them rusht, and threw
  A subtile net, which onely for the same
725 The skilfull Palmer formally° did frame.   *expressly*
  So held them under fast, the whiles the rest
  Fled all away from feare of fowler shame.
  The faire Enchauntresse, so unwares opprest,°   *surprised*
Tryde all her arts, and all her sleights, thence out to wrest.

82

730 And eke° her lover strove: but all in vaine;   *also*
  For that same net so cunningly was wound,
  That neither guile, nor force might it distraine.°   *tear*
  They tooke them both, and both them strongly bound
  In captive bandes,° which there they readie found: *bonds*
735 But her in chaines of adamant[3] he tyde;
  For nothing else might keepe her safe and sound;
  But Verdant[4] (so he hight°) he soone untyde,   *was called*
And counsell sage in steed° thereof to him applyde.   *instead*

---

2. Knight of Faerie Land, here, Guyon.
3. Steel or some other extremely hard substance.

4. His name, meaning "green," points to aspects of his nature.

83

But all those pleasant bowres and Pallace brave,°   *splendid*
740 Guyon broke downe, with rigour pittilesse;
 Ne ought their goodly workmanship might save
 Them from the tempest of his wrathfulnesse,
 But that their blisse he turn'd to balefulnesse:° *distress*
 Their groves he feld, their gardins did deface,
745 Their arbers spoyle, their Cabinets° suppresse,   *bowers*
 Their banket° houses burne, their buildings race,° *banquet / raze*
And of the fairest late, now made the fowlest place.

84

Then led they her away, and eke that knight
 They with them led, both sorrowfull and sad:
750 The way they came, the same retourn'd they right,
 Till they arrivèd, where they lately had
 Charm'd those wild-beasts, that rag'd with furie mad.
 Which now awaking, fierce at them gan fly,
 As in their mistresse reskew, whom they lad;°   *led*
755 But them the Palmer soone did pacify.
Then Guyon askt, what meant those beastes, which there did ly.

85

Said he, "These seeming beasts are men indeed,
 Whom this Enchauntresse hath transformèd thus,
 Whylome° her lovers, which her lusts did feed,   *formerly*
760 Now turnèd into figures hideous,
 According to their mindes like monstruous."[5]
 "Sad end," quoth he, "of life intemperate,
 And mournefull meed° of joyes delicious: *reward*
 But Palmer, if it mote thee so aggrate,°   *please*
765 Let them returnèd be unto their former state."

86

Streight way he with his vertuous° staffe them strooke, *powerful*
 And streight of beasts they comely men became;
 Yet being men they did unmanly looke,
 And starèd ghastly, some for inward shame,
770 And some for wrath, to see their captive Dame:
 But one above the rest in speciall,
 That had an hog beene late, hight° Grille[6] by name, *called*
 Repinèd greatly, and did him miscall,°   *revile*
That had from hoggish forme him brought to naturall.

87

775 Said Guyon, "See the mind of beastly man,
 That hath so soone forgot the excellence
 Of his creation, when he life began,

---

5. Even as their own minds were similarly monstrous. Circe changed Odysseus's companions into animals, but Odysseus had a charm to release them.

6. According to one of Plutarch's dialogues, a man named Gryllus ("fierce," "cruel"), having been changed into a hog by Circe, refused to be restored to human form by Odysseus.

That now he chooseth, with vile difference,°   *preference*
To be a beast, and lacke intelligence."
780   To whom the Palmer thus, "The donghill kind
Delights in filth and foule incontinence:
Let Grill be Grill, and have his hoggish mind,
But let us hence depart, whilest wether serves and wind."

1590, 1596

Amoretti and Epithalamion

In the early 1590s the widowed Spenser wooed and won Elizabeth Boyle, who became his wife in 1594. The next year he published a small volume that included the sonnet sequence *Amoretti* ("little loves" or "little cupids") and the *Epithalamion*. Several of the sonnets explicitly address an "Elizabeth," and the volume's subtitle, "Written not long since," suggest that these poems, taken together, are a portrait of Spenser's recent courtship and marriage. It was unusual to write sonnets about a happy and successful love; traditionally, the sonneteer's love was for someone painfully inaccessible. Spenser rehearses some of the conventional motifs of frustration and longing, but his cycle of polished, eloquent poems leads toward joyous possession. Thus, for example, in sonnet 67 ("Lyke as a huntman after weary chace"), he transforms a Petrarchan lament into a vision of unexpected fulfillment.

Spenser's great celebration of this fulfillment is the *Epithalamion*. A learned poet, he was acutely conscious that he was writing within a tradition: an epithalamion is a wedding song whose Greek name conveys that it was sung on the threshold of the bridal chamber. The genre, which goes back at least as far as Sappho (ca. 612 B.C.E.), was widely practiced by the Latin poets, particularly Catullus, and imitated in the Renaissance. Its elements typically include an invocation of the Muses, followed by a celebratory description of the procession of the bride, the religious rites, the singing and dancing at the wedding party, the preparations for the wedding night, and the sexual consummation of the marriage.

In long, flowing stanzas, Spenser follows these conventions closely, adapting them with exquisite delicacy to his small-town Irish setting and native folklore. But his first stanza announces a major innovation: "So I unto myselfe alone will sing." Traditionally, the poet of an epithalamion was an admiring observer, a kind of master of ceremonies; by combining the roles of poet and bridegroom, Spenser transforms a genial social performance into a passionate lyric utterance. Equally remarkable innovations are the complex stanza form, for which no direct model has been discovered, and the still more complex overall structure. That structure is a triumph of symbolic patterning; the more scholars have studied it, the more elaborate the order they have uncovered. For example, the poem has exactly 365 long lines (composed of five or more metrical feet) matching the number of days in the year. There are twenty-four stanzas, counting the closing "envoy," matching the hours of one full day. Of these stanzas, the first sixteen describe the course of the day, in which the woods echo the various sounds; the last eight describe the night, a time of silence in which the woods no longer echo. (At the summer solstice [cf. line 266 and note 2] in the latitude of Ireland, night falls after sixteen hours of daylight.)

This subtle and rich poetic structure conjures up not only a single day of celebration but also, beyond this particular event, an orderly, harmonious universe, with a hidden pattern of coherence and regularity. If the *Epithalamion* goes to remarkable lengths to affirm this pattern, it is perhaps because it also registers so insistently all that threatens the enduring happiness of wedded love and indeed of human life itself. The greatest threat is the force over which the poem exercises its greatest power: time.

From Amoretti

Sonnet 1

Happy ye leaves[1] when as those lilly hands,
   Which hold my life in their dead doing° might,   *killing*
   Shall handle you and hold in loves soft bands,°   *bonds*
   Lyke captives trembling at the victors sight.
5 And happy lines, on which with starry light,
   Those lamping° eyes will deigne sometimes to look   *flashing*
   And reade the sorrowes of my dying spright,°   *spirit*
   Written with teares in harts close° bleeding book.   *secret*
   And happy rymes bath'd in the sacred brooke
10   Of Helicon[2] whence she derivèd is,
   When ye behold that Angels blessèd looke,
   My soules long lackèd foode, my heavens blis.
Leaves, lines, and rymes, seeke her to please alone,
   Whom if ye please, I care for other none.

Sonnet 34[3]

Lyke as a ship that through the Ocean wyde,
   By conduct of some star doth make her way,
   Whenas a storme hath dimd her trusty guyde,
   Out of her course doth wander far astray:
5 So I whose star, that wont° with her bright ray   *was accustomed*
   Me to direct, with cloudes is overcast,
   Doe wander now in darknesse and dismay,
   Through hidden perils round about me plast.°   *placed*
   Yet hope I well, that when this storme is past
10   My Helice[4] the lodestar of my lyfe
   Will shine again, and looke on me at last,
   With lovely light to cleare my cloudy grief.
Till then I wander carefull° comfortlesse,   *full of cares*
   In secret sorow and sad pensivenesse.

Sonnet 54

Of this worlds Theatre in which we stay,
   My love like the Spectator ydly sits
   Beholding me that all the pageants° play,   *roles*
   Disguysing diversly my troubled wits.
5 Sometimes I joy when glad occasion fits,
   And mask in myrth lyke to a Comedy:
   Soone after when my joy to sorrow flits,
   I waile and make my woes a Tragedy.
Yet she beholding me with constant eye,

---

1. I.e., of the book: pages.
2. The "sacred brooke" is Hippocrene, which flows from Mount Helicon, the mountain sacred

to the Muses.
3. An adaptation of Petrarch's *Rima* 189.
4. The Big Dipper or North Star.

10   Delights not in my merth nor rues my smart:°   *pities my hurt*
        But when I laugh she mocks, and when I cry
        She laughes and hardens evermore her hart.
    What then can move her? if nor merth nor mone,°   *moan*
        She is no woman, but a sencelesse stone.

Sonnet 64[5]

Comming to kisse her lyps (such grace I found)
    Me seemd I smelt a gardin of sweet flowres
    That dainty odours from them threw around,
    For damzels fit to decke their lovers bowres.
5 Her lips did smell lyke unto Gillyflowers,°   *carnations*
    Her ruddy cheeks lyke unto Roses red;
    Her snowy browes lyke budded Bellamoures,[6]
    Her lovely eyes like Pincks but newly spred,
Her goodly bosome lyke a Strawberry bed,
10   Her neck lyke to a bounch of Cullambynes;
    Her brest lyke lillyes, ere theyr leaves be shed,
    Her nipples lyke yong blossomd Jessemynes.°   *jasmines*
Such fragrant flowres doe give most odorous smell,
    But her sweet odour did them all excell.

Sonnet 67[7]

Lyke as a huntsman after weary chace,
    Seeing the game from him escapt away,
    Sits downe to rest him in some shady place,
    With panting hounds beguilèd of their pray:
5 So after long pursuit and vaine assay,°   *attempt*
    When I all weary had the chace forsooke,
    The gentle deare returnd the selfe-same way,
    Thinking to quench her thirst at the next° brooke.   *nearby*
There she beholding me with mylder looke,
10   Sought not to fly, but fearelesse still did bide:
    Till I in hand her yet halfe trembling tooke,
    And with her owne goodwill hir fyrmely tyde.
Strange thing me seemd to see a beast so wyld,
    So goodly wonne with her owne will beguyld.°   *entangled*

Sonnet 75

One day I wrote her name upon the strand,°   *beach*
    But came the waves and washèd it away:

5. Much of the imagery of this sonnet is imitated from the Song of Solomon 4.10–16.
6. Unidentified flower, evidently white.

7. An imitation of Petrarch's *Rima* 190 but with a very different ending. Cf. Wyatt's *Whoso list to hunt*, p. 340.

Agayne I wrote it with a second hand,
But came the tyde, and made my paynes his pray.°   *prey*
5 "Vayne man," sayd she, "that doest in vaine assay,°   *attempt*
A mortall thing so to immortalize,
For I my selfe shall lyke to this decay,
And eek° my name bee wypèd out lykewize."   *also*
"Not so," quod° I, "let baser things devize°   *quoth/contrive*
10 To dy in dust, but you shall live by fame:
My verse your vertues rare shall eternize,
And in the heavens wryte your glorious name.
Where whenas death shall all the world subdew,
Our love shall live, and later life renew."

Sonnet 79

Men call you fayre, and you doe credit° it,   *believe*
For that your selfe ye dayly such doe see:
But the trew fayre,° that is the gentle wit,   *beauty*
And vertuous mind, is much more praysd of me.
5 For all the rest, how ever fayre it be,
Shall turne to nought and loose that glorious hew:°   *form*
But onely that is permanent and free
From frayle corruption, that doth flesh ensew.°   *outlast*
That is true beautie: that doth argue you
10 To be divine and borne of heavenly seed:
Deriv'd from that fayre Spirit,° from whom al true   *i.e., God*
And perfect beauty did at first proceed.
He onely fayre, and what he fayre hath made:
All other fayre, lyke flowres, untymely fade.

        1595

Epithalamion

Ye learnèd sisters which have oftentimes
Beene to me ayding, others to adorne:[1]
Whom ye thought worthy of your gracefull rymes,
That even the greatest did not greatly scorne
5 To heare theyr names sung in your simple layes,
But joyèd in theyr prayse.
And when ye list° your owne mishaps to mourne,   *chose*
Which death, or love, or fortunes wreck did rayse,
Your string could soone to sadder tenor° turne,   *mood*
10 And teach the woods and waters to lament
Your dolefull dreriment.°   *sorrow*
Now lay those sorrowfull complaints aside,
And having all your heads with girland crownd,
Helpe me mine owne loves prayses to resound,
15 Ne let the same of° any be envide: *by*

---

1. To write poems in praise of others. The "learned sisters" are the Muses.

So Orpheus did for his owne bride,[2]
So I unto my selfe alone will sing,
The woods shall to me answer and my Eccho ring.

20 Early before the worlds light giving lampe,
His golden beame upon the hils doth spred,
Having disperst the nights unchearefull dampe,
Doe ye awake, and with fresh lustyhed°   *vigor*
Go to the bowre° of my belovèd love,   *bedchamber*
My truest turtle dove,
25 Bid her awake; for Hymen[3] is awake,
And long since ready forth his maske to move,
With his bright Tead[4] that flames with many a flake,°   *spark*
And many a bachelor to waite on him,
In theyr fresh garments trim.
30 Bid her awake therefore and soone her dight,°   *dress*
For lo the wishèd day is come at last,
That shall for al the paynes and sorrowes past,
Pay to her usury° of long delight: *interest*
And whylest she doth her dight,
35 Doe ye to her of joy and solace sing,
That all the woods may answer and your Eccho ring.

Bring with you all the Nymphes that you can
        heare°   *that can hear you*
Both of the rivers and the forrests greene:
And of the sea that neighbours to her neare,
40 Al with gay girlands goodly wel beseene.°   *beautified*
And let them also with them bring in hand,
Another gay girland
For my fayre love of lillyes and of roses,
Bound truelove wize° with a blew silke riband.   *i.e., in a love knot*
45 And let them make great store of bridale poses,°   *posies*
And let them eeke° bring store of other flowers   *also*
To deck the bridale bowers.
And let the ground whereas her foot shall tread,
For feare the stones her tender foot should wrong
50 Be strewed with fragrant flowers all along,
And diapred lyke the discolored mead.[5]
Which done, doe at her chamber dore awayt,
For she will waken strayt,°   *straightway*
The whiles doe ye this song unto her sing,
55 The woods shall to you answer and your Eccho ring.

Ye Nymphes of Mulla[6] which with careful heed,
The silver scaly trouts doe tend full well,
And greedy pikes which use therein to feed,

---

2. Orpheus, archetype of the poet in classical antiquity, was famous for his love for his wife, Eurydice.
3. The god of marriage, who leads a "maske" or procession at weddings.

4. A ceremonial torch, associated with marriages since classical times.
5. Ornamented like the many-colored meadow.
6. The vale of Mulla, near Spenser's home in Ireland.

(Those trouts and pikes all others doo excell)
60 And ye likewise, which keepe the rushy lake,
Where none doo fishes take,
Bynd up the locks the which hang scatterd light,
And in his waters which your mirror make,
Behold your faces as the christall bright,
65 That when you come whereas° my love doth lie,   *where*
No blemish she may spie.
And eke° ye lightfoot mayds which keepe the deere,   *also*
That on the hoary mountayne use to towre,[7]
And the wylde wolves which seeke them to devoure,
70 With your steele darts doo chace from comming neer
Be also present heere,
To helpe to decke her and to help to sing,
That all the woods may answer and your Eccho ring.

Wake, now my love, awake; for it is time,
75 The Rosy Morne long since left Tithones bed,[8]
All ready to her silver coche° to clyme,   *coach*
And Phoebus gins to shew his glorious hed.
Hark how the cheerefull birds do chaunt theyr laies° *songs*
And carroll of loves praise.
80 The merry Larke hir mattins° sings aloft,   *morning prayers*
The thrush replyes, the Mavis descant playes,
The Ouzell shrills, the Ruddock warbles soft,[9]
So goodly all agree with sweet consent,
To this dayes merriment.
85 Ah my deere love why doe ye sleepe thus long,
When meeter° were that ye should now awake, *more fitting*
T' awayt the comming of your joyous make,°   *mate*
And hearken to the birds lovelearnèd song,
The deawy leaves among.
90 For they of joy and pleasance to you sing,
That all the woods them answer and theyr Eccho ring.

My love is now awake out of her dreame,
And her fayre eyes like stars that dimmèd were
With darksome cloud, now shew theyr goodly beams
95 More bright then Hesperus° his head doth rere. *evening star*
Come now ye damzels, daughters of delight,
Helpe quickly her to dight,°   *adorn*
But first come ye fayre houres which were begot
In Joves sweet paradice, of Day and Night,
100 Which doe the seasons of the yeare allot,

7. A falconry term meaning to occupy heights. "The deere": all wild animals, kept by the forest nymphs.
8. See Song of Solomon 2.10–13: "Rise up, my love, my fair one, and come away. For, lo, the winter is past, the rain is over and gone; the flowers appear on the earth; the time of the singing of birds is come." In classical myth, Tithonus is the aged husband of Aurora, the dawn.
9. "Descant": a melody or counterpoint written above a musical theme—a soprano obbligato. The "Mavis" is the song thrush; the "Ouzell," the blackbird (which sings in England); and the "Ruddock," the European robin. The birds' concert is a convention of medieval love poetry.

And al that ever in this world is fayre
Doe make and still° repayre.   *continuously*
And ye three handmayds of the Cyprian Queene,[1]
The which doe still adorne her beauties pride,
105   Helpe to addorne my beautifullest bride:
And as ye her array, still throw betweene°   *at intervals*
Some graces to be seene,
And as ye use° to Venus, to her sing,   *are accustomed*
The whiles the woods shal answer and your Eccho ring.

110   Now is my love all ready forth to come,
Let all the virgins therefore well awayt,
And ye fresh boyes that tend upon her groome
Prepare your selves; for he is comming strayt.°   *straightway*
Set all your things in seemely good aray°   *order*
115   Fit for so joyfull day,
The joyfulst day that ever sunne did see.
Faire Sun, shew forth thy favourable ray,
And let thy lifull° heat not fervent be   *life-giving*
For feare of burning her sunshyny face,
120   Her beauty to disgrace.
O fayrest Phoebus, father of the Muse,[2]
If ever I did honour thee aright,
Or sing the thing, that mote° thy mind delight,   *might*
Doe not thy servants simple boone° refuse,   *request*
125   But let this day let this one day be myne,
Let all the rest be thine.
Then I thy soverayne prayses loud wil sing,
That all the woods shal answer and theyr Eccho ring.

Harke how the Minstrels gin° to shrill aloud   *begin*
130   Their merry Musick that resounds from far,
The pipe, the tabor,° and the trembling Croud,[3]   *small drum*
That well agree withouten breach or jar.°   *discord*
But most of all the Damzels doe delite,
When they their tymbrels° smyte,   *tambourines*
135   And thereunto doe daunce and carrol sweet,
That all the sences they doe ravish quite,
The whyles the boyes run up and downe the street,
Crying aloud with strong confusèd noyce,
As if it were one voyce.
140   *Hymen iô Hymen, Hymen*[4] they do shout,
That even to the heavens theyr shouting shrill
Doth reach, and all the firmament doth fill,
To which the people standing all about,
As in approvance doe thereto applaud

---

1. The Graces attending on Venus ("Cyprian Queene"), representing brightness, joy, and bloom.
2. Phoebus (Apollo), god of the sun, was also god of music and poetry, but he was not normally regarded as the father of the Nine Muses (Zeus was).
3. Primitive fiddle. Spenser here designates Irish, not classical, instruments and music for the classical masque or ballet.
4. The name of the god of marriage, used as a conventional exclamation at weddings.

145 And loud advaunce her laud,°   *praise*
   And evermore they *Hymen Hymen* sing,
   That all the woods them answer and theyr Eccho ring.

   Loe where she comes along with portly° pace   *stately*
   Lyke Phoebe from her chamber of the East,
150 Arysing forth to run her mighty race,[5]
   Clad all in white, that seemes° a virgin best.   *beseems, suits*
   So well it her beseems that ye would weene°   *think*
   Some angell she had beene.
   Her long loose yellow locks lyke golden wyre,
155 Sprinckled with perle, and perling° flowres a tweene, *winding*
   Doe lyke a golden mantle her attyre,
   And being crownèd with a girland greene,
   Seeme lyke some mayden Queene.
   Her modest eyes abashèd to behold
160 So many gazers, as on her do stare,
   Upon the lowly ground affixèd are.
   Ne dare lift up her countenance too bold,
   But blush to heare her prayses sung so loud,
   So farre from being proud.
165 Nathlesse doe ye still loud her prayses sing.
   That all the woods may answer and your Eccho ring.

   Tell me ye merchants daughters did ye see
   So fayre a creature in your towne before,
   So sweet, so lovely, and so mild as she,
170 Adornd with beautyes grace and vertues store,
   Her goodly eyes lyke Saphyres shining bright,
   Her forehead yvory white,
   Her cheekes lyke apples which the sun hath rudded,° *made red*
   Her lips lyke cherryes charming men to byte,
175 Her brest like to a bowle of creame uncrudded,° *uncurdled*
   Her paps lyke lyllies budded,
   Her snowie necke lyke to a marble towre,
   And all her body like a pallace fayre,
   Ascending uppe with many a stately stayre,
180 To honors seat and chastities sweet bowre.[6]
   Why stand ye still ye virgins in amaze,
   Upon her so to gaze,
   Whiles ye forget your former lay to sing,
   To which the woods did answer and your Eccho ring.

185 But if ye saw that which no eyes can see,
   The inward beauty of her lively spright,°   *living spirit, soul*
   Garnisht with heavenly guifts of high degree,
   Much more then would ye wonder at that sight,

---

5. Phoebe is the moon, a virgin like the bride; the reference to her anticipates the night.
6. The head, where the higher faculties are. The catalog of qualities is a convention in love poetry (cf. Song of Solomon 4–8).

And stand astonisht lyke to those which red°   *saw*
190 Medusaes mazeful hed.[7]
There dwels sweet love and constant chastity,
Unspotted fayth and comely womanhood,
Regard of honour and mild modesty,
There vertue raynes as Queene in royal throne,
195 And giveth lawes alone.
The which the base° affections doe obay,   *lower*
And yeeld theyr services unto her will,
Ne thought of thing uncomely ever may
Thereto approch to tempt her mind to ill.
200 Had ye once seene these her celestial threasures,
And unrevealèd pleasures,
Then would ye wonder and her prayses sing,
That all the woods should answer and your Eccho ring.

Open the temple gates unto my love,
205 Open them wide that she may enter in,[8]
And all the postes adorne as doth behove,[9]
And all the pillours deck with girlands trim,
For to recyve this Saynt with honour dew,
That commeth in to you.
210 With trembling steps and humble reverence,
She commeth in, before th' almighties vew,
Of her ye virgins learne obedience,
When so ye come into those holy places,
To humble your proud faces:
215 Bring her up to th' high altar, that she may
The sacred ceremonies there partake,
The which do endless matrimony make,
And let the roring Organs loudly play
The praises of the Lord in lively notes,
220 The whiles with hollow throates
The Choristers the joyous Antheme sing,
That all the woods may answere and theyr Eccho ring.

Behold whiles she before the altar stands
Hearing the holy priest that to her speakes
225 And blesseth her with his two happy hands,
How the red roses flush up in her cheekes,
And the pure snow with goodly vermill° stayne,   *vermilion*
Like crimsin dyde in grayne,°   *fast color*
That even th' Angels which continually,
230 About the sacred Altare doe remaine,
Forget their service and about her fly,
Ofte peeping in her face that seemes more fayre,
The more they on it stare.

---

7. Medusa, one of the Gorgons, had serpents instead of hair (hence a "mazeful hed"): the effect on beholders was to turn them to stone.
8. Cf. Psalm 24.7: "Lift up your heads, O ye gates; and be ye lift up, ye everlasting doors; and the King of glory shall come in."
9. As is proper. The doorposts were trimmed for weddings in classical times, and the custom was often referred to in classical and later love poetry.

But her sad° eyes still fastened on the ground,   *serious*
235 Are governèd with goodly modesty,
That suffers not one looke to glaunce awry,
Which may let in a little thought unsownd.
Why blush ye love to give to me your hand,
The pledge of all our band?°   *bond, tie*
240 Sing ye sweet Angels, Alleluya sing,
That all the woods may answere and your Eccho ring.

Now al is done; bring home the bride againe,
Bring home the triumph of our victory,
Bring home with you the glory of her gaine,[1]
245 With joyance bring her and with jollity.
Never had man more joyfull day then this,
Whom heaven would heape with blis.
Make feast therefore now all this live long day,
This day for ever to me holy is,
250 Poure out the wine without restraint or stay,
Poure not by cups, but by the belly full,
Poure out to all that wull,°   *want it*
And sprinkle all the postes and wals with wine,
That they may sweat, and drunken be withall.
255 Crowne ye God Bacchus° with a coronall,°   *god of wine/garland*
And Hymen also crowne with wreathes of vine,
And let the Graces daunce unto the rest;
For they can doo it best:
The whiles the maydens doe theyr carroll sing,
260 To which the woods shall answer and theyr Eccho ring.

Ring ye the bels, ye young men of the towne,
And leave your wonted° labors for this day: *usual*
This day is holy; doe ye write it downe,
That ye for ever it remember may.
265 This day the sunne is in his chiefest hight,
With Barnaby the bright,[2]
From whence declining daily by degrees,
He somewhat loseth of his heat and light,
When once the Crab[3] behind his back he sees.
270 But for this time it ill ordainèd was,
To chose the longest day in all the yeare,
And shortest night, when longest fitter weare:
Yet never day so long, but late° would passe.   *at last*
Ring ye the bels, to make it weare away,
275 And bonefiers° make all day,   *bonfires*
And daunce about them, and about them sing:
That all the woods may answer, and your Eccho ring.

Ah when will this long weary day have end,
And lende me leave to come unto my love?

1. I.e., the glory of gaining her.
2. St. Barnabas's Day, at the time of the summer solstice.

3. The constellation Cancer between Gemini and Leo. The sun, passing through the zodiac, leaves the Crab behind toward the end of July.

280   How slowly do the houres theyr numbers spend?
How slowly does sad Time his feathers move?
Hast thee O fayrest Planet to thy home
Within the Westerne fome:
Thy tyred steedes long since have need of rest.[4]
285   Long though it be, at last I see it gloome,
And the bright evening star° with golden creast°   *Hesperus / crest*
Appeare out of the East.
Fayre childe of beauty, glorious lampe of love
That all the host of heaven in rankes doost lead,
290   And guydest lovers through the nightès dread,
How chearefully thou lookest from above,
And seemst to laugh atweene thy twinkling light
As joying in the sight
Of these glad many which for joy doe sing,
295   That all the woods them answer and theyr Eccho ring.

Now ceasse ye damsels your delights forepast;
Enough is it, that all the day was youres:
Now day is doen, and night is nighing fast:
Now bring the Bryde into the brydall boures.
300   Now night is come, now soone her disaray,
And in her bed her lay;
Lay her in lillies and in violets,
And silken courteins over her display,°   *spread*
And odourd° sheetes, and Arras° coverlets.   *perfumed / tapestry*
305   Behold how goodly my faire love does ly
In proud humility;
Like unto Maia,[5] when as Jove her tooke,
In Tempe,[6] lying on the flowry gras,
Twixt sleepe and wake, after she weary was,
310   With bathing in the Acidalian brooke.[7]
Now it is night, ye damsels may be gon,
And leave my love alone,
And leave likewise your former lay to sing:
The woods no more shall answere, nor your Eccho ring.

315   Now welcome night, thou night so long expected,
That long daies labour doest at last defray,°   *pay for*
And all my cares, which cruell love collected,
Hast sumd in one, and cancellèd for aye:
Spread thy broad wing over my love and me,
320   That no man may us see,
And in thy sable mantle us enwrap,
From feare of perrill and foule horror free.
Let no false treason seeke us to entrap,
Nor any dread disquiet once annoy

4. The sun's chariot completes its daily course in the western sea.
5. The eldest and most beautiful of the seven daughters of Atlas. (They were stellified as the Pleiades.) Jove fathered Mercury on her.
6. The Vale of Tempe in Thessaly (not, however, traditionally the site of Jove's encounter with Maia).
7. The Acidalian brook is associated with Venus.

325 The safety of our joy:
But let the night be calme and quietsome,
Without tempestuous storms or sad afray:°   *fear*
Lyke as when Jove with fayre Alcmena[8] lay,
When he begot the great Tirynthian groome:
330 Or lyke as when he with thy selfe[9] did lie,
And begot Majesty.
And let the mayds and yongmen cease to sing:
Ne let the woods them answer, nor theyr Eccho ring.

Let no lamenting cryes, nor dolefull teares,
335 Be heard all night within nor yet without:
Ne let false whispers, breeding hidden feares,
Breake gentle sleepe with misconceivèd dout.°   *fear*
Let no deluding dreames, nor dreadful sights
Make sudden sad affrights;
340 Ne let housefyres, nor lightnings helpelesse harmes,
Ne let the Pouke,[1] nor other evill sprights,
Ne let mischivous witches with theyr charmes,
Ne let hob Goblins, names whose sence we see not,
Fray° us with things that be not.   *terrify*
345 Let not the shriech Oule, nor the Storke be heard:
Nor the night Raven that still° deadly yels,[2]   *continuously*
Nor damnèd ghosts cald up with mighty spels,
Nor griesly° vultures make us once affeard: *horrid*
Ne let th' unpleasant Quyre of Frogs still croking
350 Make us to wish theyr choking.
Let none of these theyr drery accents sing;
Ne let the woods them answer, nor theyr Eccho ring.

But let stil Silence trew night watches keepe,
That sacred peace may in assurance rayne,
355 And tymely Sleep, when it is tyme to sleepe,
May poure his limbs forth on your pleasant playne,
The whiles an hundred little wingèd loves,°   *cupids (or amoretti)*
Like divers fethered doves,
Shall fly and flutter round about your bed,
360 And in the secret darke, that none reproves,
Their prety stealthes shal worke, and snares shal spread
To filch away sweet snatches of delight,
Conceald through covert night.
Ye sonnes of Venus, play your sports at will,
365 For greedy pleasure, carelesse of your toyes,°   *amorous dallying*
Thinks more upon her paradise of joyes,
Then° what ye do, albe it good or ill.   *than*
All night therefore attend your merry play,
For it will soone be day:

---

8. The mother of Hercules ("the great Tirynthian groome"). Jove made that first night last as long as three.
9. Night. This is Spenser's own myth.
1. Puck, Robin Goodfellow—here more powerful

and evil than Shakespeare made him.
2. The owl and the night raven were birds of ill omen; the stork, in Chaucer's *Parliament of Fowls*, is called an avenger of adultery.

370 Now none doth hinder you, that say or sing,
Ne will the woods now answer, nor your Eccho ring.

Who is the same, which at my window peepes?
Or whose is that faire face, that shines so bright,
Is it not Cinthia,[3] she that never sleepes,
375 But walkes about high heaven al the night?
O fayrest goddesse, do thou not envy
My love with me to spy:
For thou likewise didst love, though now unthought,°   *not thought of*
And for a fleece of woll,° which privily,   *wool*
380 The Latmian shephard[4] once unto thee brought,
His pleasures with thee wrought,
Therefore to us be favorable now;
And sith° of wemens labours thou hast charge,[5]   *since*
And generation goodly dost enlarge,
385 Encline thy will t' effect our wishfull vow,
And the chast wombe informe° with timely seed,   *give life to*
That may our comfort breed:
Till which we cease our hopefull hap° to sing,   *fortune we hope for*
Ne let the woods us answer, nor our Eccho ring.

390 And thou great Juno, which with awful might
The lawes of wedlock still dost patronize,
And the religion° of the faith first plight   *sanctity*
With sacred rites hast taught to solemnize:
And eeke° for comfort often callèd art   *also*
395 Of women in their smart,°   *labor*
Eternally bind thou this lovely band,°   *bond*
And all thy blessings unto us impart.
And thou glad Genius,[6] in whose gentle hand,
The bridale bowre and geniall bed remaine,
400 Without blemish or staine,
And the sweet pleasures of theyr loves delight
With secret ayde doest succour and supply,
Till they bring forth the fruitfull progeny,
Send us the timely fruit of this same night.
405 And thou fayre Hebe,[7] and thou Hymen free,
Grant that it may so be.
Til which we cease your further prayse to sing,
Ne any woods shall answer, nor your Eccho ring.

And ye high heavens, the temple of the gods,
410 In which a thousand torches flaming bright
Doe burne, that to us wretched earthly clods,
In dreadful darknesse lend desirèd light;
And all ye powers which in the same remayne,
More than we men can fayne,°   *imagine*

---

3. Cynthia (or Diana) is goddess of the moon.
4. Endymion, beloved by the moon. The "fleece of woll," however, comes from another story—that of Pan's enticement of the moon.

5. Diana is, as Lucina, patroness of births. The "labours" are, of course, those of childbirth.
6. Patron of sex, pregnancy, and reproduction.
7. Patron of youth and freedom.

415 Poure out your blessing on us plentiously,
And happy influence upon us raine,
That we may raise a large posterity,
Which from the earth, which they may long possesse,
With lasting happinesse,
420 Up to your haughty pallaces may mount,
And for the guerdon° of theyr glorious merit   reward
May heavenly tabernacles there inherit,
Of blessèd Saints for to increase the count.
So let us rest, sweet love, in hope of this,
425 And cease till then our tymely joyes to sing,
The woods no more us answer, nor our Eccho ring.

Song made in lieu of many ornaments,
With which my love should duly have bene dect,°   adorned
Which cutting off through hasty accidents,
430 Ye would not stay your dew time to expect,°   await
But promist both to recompens,
Be unto her a goodly ornament,
And for short time an endlesse moniment.[8]

1595

8. The envoy is traditionally apologetic in tone: the poem is offered as a substitute for wedding presents ("ornaments") that did not arrive in time for the wedding. But this elaborate poem is itself a "goodly ornament," for it stands as a timeless monument of art to the passing day that it celebrates.

SIR WALTER RALEGH
1552–1618

The brilliant and versatile Sir Walter Ralegh was a soldier, courtier, philosopher, explorer and colonist, student of science, historian, and poet. Born to West Country gentry of modest means, Ralegh amassed great wealth thanks to his position at court, leading him to be denounced by some as an upstart and hated by others as a rapacious monopolist. He fought ruthlessly in Ireland and Cádiz, directed the colonization of Virginia, introduced the potato to Ireland and tobacco to Europe, brought Spenser from Ireland to the English court, conducted scientific experiments, led expeditions to Guiana in an unsuccessful effort to find gold, and wrote several reports urging England to challenge Spanish dominance in the New World. He was known for his violent temper, his dramatic sense of life, his extravagant dress, his skepticism in religious matters, his bitter hatred of Spain, and his great favor with Queen Elizabeth, interrupted in 1592 when he seduced, and then married, one of her ladies-in-waiting. His long poem to the queen, *The Ocean to Cynthia,* remains in fragments of manuscript, one of more than five hundred lines. His best-known shorter poems include the reply to Marlowe's *Passionate Shepherd* and *The Lie,* an attack on social classes and institutions which itself provoked many replies. His active resistance to printing his poems—in one case he forced a printer to recall a volume and paste a slip of paper over his initials—makes it very difficult to put the copies that circulated in manuscript in any reliable chronological order.

King James suspected Ralegh of opposing his succession and threw him into the Tower of London in 1603 on trumped-up charges of treason; there he remained for the rest of his life save for an ill-fated last voyage to Guiana in 1617, which again failed to discover gold. In prison he wrote his long, unfinished *History of the World*, which begins with the Creation, emphasizes the providential punishment of evil princes, and projects a treatment of English history—although not of recent events because, he declared, he who follows truth too closely at the heels might get kicked in the teeth. The work was to have been dedicated to Henry, prince of Wales, Ralegh's most powerful friend and supporter, who declared, "Only my father would keep such a bird in a cage." But Henry died in 1612, and Ralegh broke off his narrative at 168 B.C.E. Six years later James, bowing to Spanish pressure, had Ralegh executed on the old treason charge.

The Nymph's Reply to the Shepherd

If all the world and love were young,
And truth in every shepherd's tongue,
These pretty pleasures might me move
To live with thee and be thy love.

5   Time drives the flocks from field to fold
When rivers rage and rocks grow cold,
And Philomel° becometh dumb;   *the nightingale*
The rest complains of cares to come.

The flowers do fade, and wanton fields
10 To wayward winter reckoning yields;
A honey tongue, a heart of gall,
Is fancy's spring, but sorrow's fall.

Thy gowns, thy shoes, thy beds of roses,
Thy cap, thy kirtle,° and thy posies   *skirt, outer petticoat*
15 Soon break, soon wither, soon forgotten—
In folly ripe, in reason rotten.

Thy belt of straw and ivy buds,
Thy coral clasps and amber studs,
All these in me no means can move
20 To come to thee and be thy love.

But could youth last and love still breed,
Had joys no date° nor age no need,   *ending*
Then these delights my mind might move
To live with thee and be thy love.

1600

From The History of the World

[CONCLUSION: ON DEATH]

It is * * * Death alone that can suddenly make man to know himself. He tells the proud and insolent that they are but abjects,[1] and humbles them at the instant; makes them cry, complain, and repent, yea, even to hate their forepassed happiness. He takes the account of the rich, and proves him a beggar, a naked beggar, which hath interest in nothing but in the gravel that fills his mouth. He holds a glass before the eyes of the most beautiful, and makes them see therein their deformity and rottenness, and they acknowledge it.

O eloquent, just, and mighty Death! Whom none could advise, thou hast persuaded; what none hath dared, thou hast done; and whom all the world hath flattered, thou only hast cast out of the world and despised; thou hast drawn together all the far-stretched greatness, all the pride, cruelty, and ambition of man, and covered it all over with these two narrow words: *Hic jacet!*[2] * * *

1614

1. Castoffs.
2. Latin for "Here lies," often carved on tombstones.

SIR PHILIP SIDNEY
1554–1586

Knight, soldier, poet, friend, and patron, Sidney seemed to the Elizabethans to embody all the traits of character and personality they admired. When he was killed in battle in the Low Countries at the age of thirty-two, fighting for the Protestant cause against the hated Spanish, all England mourned. Stories, possibly apocryphal, began immediately to circulate about his gallantry on the battlefield—grievously wounded, he gave his water to a dying footsoldier with the words "Thy necessity is yet greater than mine"—and about his astonishing self-composure as he himself lay dying: suffering from his putrifying, gangrenous wound, Sidney composed a song and had it sung by his deathbed. When his corpse was brought back to England for burial, the spectacular funeral procession, one of the most elaborate ever staged, almost bankrupted his father-in-law, Francis Walsingham, the wealthy head of Queen Elizabeth's secret service.

Philip Sidney's father was Sir Henry Sidney, thrice lord deputy (governor) of Ireland, and his mother was a sister of Robert Dudley, earl of Leicester, the most spectacular and powerful of all the queen's favorites. He attended Oxford but left without taking a degree and completed his education by extended travels on the Continent. There he met many of the most important people of the time, from kings and queens to philosophers, theologians, and poets. In France he witnessed the Massacre of St. Bartholomew's Day, which began in Paris on August 24, 1572, and raged through France for more than a month, as Catholic mobs incited by Queen Catherine de Medici slaughtered perhaps 50,000 Huguenots (French Protestants). This experience undoubtedly strengthened Sidney's ardent Protestantism, which had been inculcated by his family background and education. In an intense correspondence with his mentor, the Burgundian humanist Hubert Languet, he brooded on how he could help to save Europe from what he viewed as the Roman Catholic menace.

When he returned to England Sidney found the direct path to heroic action blocked by the caution and hard-nosed realism of Queen Elizabeth and her principal advisers. Though she sent him on some diplomatic missions, the queen clearly regarded the zealous young man with considerable skepticism. As a prominent, well-connected courtier with literary interests, Sidney actively encouraged authors such as Edward Dyer, Fulke Greville, and, most important, the young Edmund Spenser. But he clearly longed to be something more than an influential patron of letters. In 1580 his Protestant convictions led him publicly to oppose Queen Elizabeth's projected marriage to the Catholic duke of Anjou. The queen, who hated interference with her diplomatic maneuvers, angrily dismissed Sidney from the court.

He retired to Wilton, the estate of his beloved and learned sister, Mary Herbert, countess of Pembroke, and there he wrote a long, elaborate epic romance in prose called *Arcadia*. Two other influential works by Sidney have had still more lasting importance. One of these was a major piece of critical prose that was published after his death under two titles, *The Defense of Poesy* and *An Apology for Poetry*. In this long essay Sidney eloquently defends poetry (his term for all imaginative literature) against its attackers and, in the process, greatly exalts the role of the poet, the freedom of the imagination, and the moral value of fiction.

Perhaps Sidney's finest literary achievement is *Astrophil and Stella* ("Starlover and Star"), the first of the major Elizabethan sonnet cycles. The 108 sonnets and eleven songs rely heavily, as do virtually all sonnets in the period, on the conventions established by the great fourteenth-century Italian poet Petrarch and his many Italian, French, and Spanish imitators. These conventions bequeathed a loose framework of plot, marking the stages of a love relationship from its starting point in the lover's attraction to the lady's beauty, through various trials, sufferings, conflicts, and occasional encouragements, to a conclusion in which nothing is resolved. The poet undertook to produce an anatomy of love, displaying its shifting and often contradictory states: hope and despair, tenderness and bitterness, exultation and modesty, bodily desire and spiritual transcendence. Petrarch had deployed a series of ingenious metaphors to describe these states, but by Sidney's time the metaphors—love as a freezing fire, the beloved's glance as an arrow striking the lover's heart, and so forth—had through endless repetition become familiar and predictable.

In an elaborate game of literary masks, psychological risk-taking, and open secrets, Sidney manages to infuse these conventions with an extraordinary vigor and freshness. The sequence of poems, with its dazzling display of technical virtuosity, provides tantalizing glimpses of identifiable characters and, still more, a sustained and remarkably intimate portrait of the poet's inner life. Sidney was hardly indifferent to his privacy: "I assure you before God," he had written once in an angry letter to his father's private secretary, "that if ever I know you do so much as read any letter I write to my father, without his commandment or my consent, I will thrust my dagger into you. And trust to it, for I speak it in earnest." Yet in *Astrophil and Stella* he seems to hold up a mirror to every nuance of his emotional being. The sense of the poet's daring self-exposure, his hinting at intimate psychological and social secrets, has provoked much biographical speculation centered on Sidney's ambiguous relationship with Penelope Devereux, the original of Stella. A marriage between the two had been proposed in 1576 and was talked about for some years, but in 1581 she married Lord Robert Rich, and two years later Sidney also married. (At their high social rank, marriages were negotiated in the interests of the powerful families involved, not of the individuals.) Some of the sonnets contain sly puns on the name *Rich*, and it seems likely that there are autobiographical elements in the shadowy narrative sketched by the work. But the principal focus of the sonnets is not a narrative of events or an unfolding relationship. Rather, *Astrophil and Stella* explores the lover's state of mind and soul, the contradictory impulses, intense desires, and frustrations that haunt him.

In 1585 Sidney tried to join Sir Francis Drake's West Indian expedition but was prevented by the queen; instead, she appointed him governor of Flushing in the Netherlands, where as a volunteer and knight-errant he engaged in several vicious skirmishes in the war against Spain. At Zutphen on September 13, 1586, leading a charge against great odds, Sidney was wounded in the thigh, shortly after he had thrown away his thigh armor in an ill-fated chivalric gesture. He died after lingering for twenty-six days.

Sidney called poetry his "unelected vocation," and, in keeping with the norms of his class, he did not publish any of his major literary works himself. His ambition, continually thwarted, was to be a man of action whose deeds would affect his country's destiny. Yet he was the author of the most ambitious work of prose fiction, the most important piece of literary criticism, and the most influential sonnet cycle of the Elizabethan age.

From Astrophil and Stella

1[1]

> Loving in truth, and fain° in verse my love to show,   *desirous*
> That the dear She might take some pleasure of my pain,
> Pleasure might cause her read, reading might make her know,
> Knowledge might pity win, and pity grace obtain,
> 5   I sought fit words to paint the blackest face of woe,
> Studying inventions fine, her wits to entertain,
> Oft turning others' leaves, to see if thence would flow
> Some fresh and fruitful showers upon my sunburned brain.
> But words came halting forth, wanting Invention's stay;°   *prop*
> 10 Invention, Nature's child, fled step-dame Study's blows,
> And others' feet still seemed but strangers in my way.
> Thus great with child to speak, and helpless in my throes,
> Biting my trewand° pen, beating myself for spite,   *truant*
> "Fool," said my Muse to me, "look in thy heart and write."

2

> Not at first sight, nor with a dribbèd[2] shot
> Love gave the wound, which while I breathe will bleed,
> But known worth did in mine[3] of time proceed,
> Till by degrees it had full conquest got.
> 5   I saw and liked, I liked but lovèd not,
> I loved, but straight did not what *Love* decreed;
> At length to Love's decrees, I, forced, agreed,
> Yet with repining at so partial° lot.   *unfair*
> Now even that footstep of lost liberty
> 10 Is gone, and now like slave-borne Muscovite,[4]

---

1. One of six sonnets in the sequence written in hexameters.
2. Ineffectual or at random.
3. Tunnel dug to undermine a besieged fortress.

4. Inhabitant of Muscovy, an important Russian principality ruled from Moscow; 16th-century travel books describe Muscovites as contented slaves.

I call it praise to suffer tyranny;
And now employ the remnant of my wit,°   *intelligence*
  To make myself believe that all is well,
  While with a feeling skill I paint my hell.

6

Some lovers speak, when they their muses entertain,
Of hopes begot by fear, of wot° not what desires,   *know*
Of force of heavenly beams infusing hellish pain,
Of living deaths, dear wounds, fair storms, and freezing fires;[5]
5   Some one his song in Jove, and Jove's strange tales attires,
Broidered with bulls and swans, powdered with golden rain;[6]
Another humbler wit to shepherd's pipe retires,
Yet hiding royal blood full oft in rural vein.[7]
  To some a sweetest plaint a sweetest style affords,[8]
10   While tears pour out his ink, and sighs breathe out his words,
His paper pale despair, and pain his pen doth move.
  I can speak what I feel, and feel as much as they,
  But think that all the map of my state I display,
When trembling voice brings forth that I do Stella love.

20

Fly, fly, my friends, I have my death-wound, fly;
See there that boy, that murth'ring° boy, I say,   *murdering*
Who, like a thief, hid in dark bush doth lie
Till bloody bullet get him wrongful prey.
5   So tyran° he no fitter place could spy,   *tyrant*
Nor so fair level° in so secret stay,°   *aim/stopping place*
As that sweet black° which veils the heav'nly eye;   *pupil*
There himself with his shot he close° doth lay.   *secretly*
  Poor passenger,° pass now thereby I did,   *passerby*
10   And stay'd, pleas'd with the prospect of the place,
While that black hue from me the bad guest hid;
But straight I saw motions of lightning grace,
  And then descried the glist'ring° of his dart;   *glittering*
  But ere I could fly thence, it pierc'd my heart.

28

You that with allegory's curious frame
  Of others' children changelings use to make,
  With me those pains, for God's sake, do not take;
  I list not° dig so deep for brazen fame.   *I don't care to*
5   When I say Stella, I do mean the same
  Princess of beauty for whose only sake

---

5. Conventional Petrarchan oxymorons.
6. I.e., embroidered with mythological figures. Jove courted Europa in the shape of a bull; Leda, as a swan; and Danaë, as a golden shower.
7. Pastoral allegory. By convention, a pastoral

poet pipes his songs on an oaten or reed pipe.
8. Overuse of the word *sweet* in love complaints, with allusion to the very musical *dolce stil nuovo* (sweet new style) associated with Dante and his Italian contemporaries.

The reins of love I love, though never slake,°   *slack*
And joy therein, though nations count it shame.
   I beg no subject to use eloquence,[9]
10 Nor in hid ways do guide philosophy;
Look at my hands for no such quintessence,[1]
   But know that I in pure simplicity
     Breathe out the flames which burn within my heart,
     Love only reading unto me this art.

31

With how sad steps, O Moon, thou climb'st the skies,
   How silently, and with how wan a face!
   What, may it be that even in heavenly place
That busy archer° his sharp arrows tries?   *Cupid*
5 Sure, if that long-with-love-acquainted eyes
   Can judge of love, thou feel'st a lover's case;
   I read it in thy looks: thy languished grace,
To me that feel the like, thy state descries.
     Then even of fellowship, O Moon, tell me,
10 Is constant love deemed there but want of wit?
Are beauties there as proud as here they be?
Do they above love to be loved, and yet
     Those lovers scorn whom that love doth possess?
     Do they call virtue there ungratefulness?[2]

52

A strife is grown between Virtue and Love,
   While each pretends° that Stella must be his: *claims*
   Her eyes, her lips, her all, saith Love, do this,
Since they do wear his badge,[3] most firmly prove.
5 But Virtue thus that title doth disprove:
   That Stella (O dear name) that Stella is
   That virtuous soul, sure heir of heavenly bliss;
Not this fair outside, which our hearts doth move.
     And therefore, though her beauty and her grace
10 Be Love's indeed, in Stella's self he may
By no pretence claim any manner° place.   *kind of*
     Well, Love, since this demur° our suit[4] doth stay,°   *objection / stop*
     Let Virtue have that Stella's self; yet thus,
     That Virtue but° that body grant to us.   *only*

71

Who will in fairest book of Nature know
   How Virtue may best lodged in beauty be,

---

9. I.e., I don't ask for a topic simply as an excuse to display my rhetorical skills.
1. The mysterious "fifth element" of matter (supplementary to earth, air, fire, and water), which alchemists labored to extract.
2. I.e., is the lady's ingratitude considered virtue

in heaven (as here)? Also, is the lover's virtue (fidelity) considered distasteful in heaven (as here)?
3. Device or livery worn to identify someone's (here, Cupid's) servants.
4. "Courtship," in addition to the legal meaning.

Let him but learn of Love to read in thee,
Stella, those fair lines, which true goodness show.
5   There shall he find all vices' overthrow,
        Not by rude force, but sweetest sovereignty
        Of reason, from whose light those night-birds[5] fly;
That inward sun in thine eyes shineth so.
And not content to be Perfection's heir
10   Thyself, dost strive all minds that way to move, *perceive*
Who mark° in thee what is in thee most fair.[6]
So while thy beauty draws the heart to love,
        As fast° thy Virtue bends that love to good; *at the same rate*
        "But, ah," Desire still cries, "give me some food."

72

Desire, though thou my old companion art,
        And oft so clings to my pure Love that I
        One from the other scarcely can descry,° *distinguish*
While each doth blow the fire of my heart,
5   Now from thy fellowship I needs must part:
        Venus is taught with Dian's wings to fly;[7]
        I must no more in thy sweet passions lie;
Virtue's gold now must head my Cupid's dart.
        Service and honor, wonder with delight,
10   Fear to offend, will worthy to appear,[8]
Care shining in mine eyes, faith in my sprite:° *spirit*
These things are left me by my only dear;
        But thou, Desire, because thou wouldst have all,
        Now banished art. But yet alas how shall?

74

I never drank of Aganippe well,
        Nor ever did in shade of Tempe[9] sit;
        And Muses scorn with vulgar brains to dwell;
Poor layman I, for sacred rites unfit.
5   Some do I hear of Poets' fury° tell, *inspiration*
But God wot,° wot not what they mean by it; *knows*
And this I swear by blackest brook of hell,[1]
I am no pick-purse of another's wit.
        How falls it then that with so smooth an ease
10   My thoughts I speak, and what I speak doth flow
In verse, and that my verse best wits doth please?
        Guess we the cause. "What, is it thus?" Fie no.
        "Or so?" Much less. "How then?" Sure thus it is:
        My lips are sweet, inspired with Stella's kiss.[2]

5. The owl, for example, was an emblem of various vices.
6. I.e., her virtue, which is fairer even than her beauty.
7. Diana, goddess of the moon and patron of chastity; Venus, goddess of beauty and love, mother of Cupid.
8. The phrase can mean either "the wish to appear worthy" or "desire that is worthy to appear [i.e., not shameful]."
9. Valley beside Mount Olympus, sacred to Apollo, the god of song. "Aganippe": fountain at the foot of Mount Helicon in Greece, sacred to the Muses.
1. The most binding of all oaths were those sworn by the river Styx.
2. A kiss he stole from Stella when he caught her napping (Song 2).

108[3]

When Sorrow (using mine own fire's might)
   Melts down his lead into my boiling breast,
   Through that dark furnace to my heart oppressed
There shines a joy from thee, my only light;
5 But soon as thought of thee breeds my delight,
   And my young soul flutters to thee, his nest,
   Most rude Despair, my daily unbidden guest,
Clips straight° my wings, straight wraps me in his night,   *immediately*
   And makes me then bow down my head and say,
10 "Ah, what doth Phoebus'° gold that wretch avail,   *god of the sun*
Whom iron doors do keep from use of day?"
So strangely (alas) thy works in me prevail,
   That in my woes for thee thou art my joy,
   And in my joys for thee my only annoy.

1582?   1591, 1598

Leave me, O Love[1]

Leave me, O Love which reachest but to dust,
And thou my mind aspire to higher things;
Grow rich in that which never taketh rust:
Whatever fades but fading pleasure brings.

5 Draw in thy beams, and humble all thy might
To that sweet yoke where lasting freedoms be;
Which breaks the clouds and opens forth the light,
That doth both shine and give us sight to see.

O take fast hold; let that light be thy guide
10 In this small course which birth draws out to death,
And think how evil becometh him to slide,
Who seeketh heav'n, and comes of heav'nly breath.[2]
   Then farewell world, thy uttermost I see;
   Eternal Love, maintain thy life in me.

ca. 1581   1598

---

3. In many sonnet sequences, as here, the final sonnet brings no resolution.
1. This poem is from *Certain Sonnets*, a miscellany of thirty-two poems (not all of them sonnets

in the modern sense) apparently written before *Astrophil and Stella*.
2. I.e., it ill becomes one who has a soul and seeks heaven to "slide" to earthly things.

MARY (SIDNEY) HERBERT, COUNTESS OF PEMBROKE
1562–1621

When her brother, the celebrated courtier and author Philip Sidney, died in 1586, Mary Sidney, the countess of Pembroke, became the custodian not only of his writings but also of his last name. Though her marriage in 1577 to Henry Herbert, the second earl of Pembroke, represented a great social advance for her family—her offspring would no longer be members of the gentry but rather would be among the nation's tiny number of landed aristocrats—yet throughout her life the countess of Pembroke held onto her identity as a Sidney.

She had good reason to do so. The Sidneys were celebrated for their generous support of poets, clergy, alchemists, naturalists, scientists, and musicians. The Pembroke country estate, Wilton, quickly became a gathering place for thinkers who enjoyed the countess's patronage and shared her staunch Protestant convictions and her literary interests. Books, pamphlets, and scores of poems were dedicated in the 1590s and thereafter to her, as well as to her brother Robert (his country house, Penshurst, is praised in a well-known poem by Ben Jonson). Nicholas Breton and Samuel Daniel in particular benefited from her support, as did her niece, goddaughter, and frequent companion, Mary Wroth.

In one of the dedicatory poems to *Salve Deus Rex Judaeorum*, Aemilia Lanyer praises Mary Sidney not only for her generosity toward poets but also for those "works that are more deep and more profound." These include her translation of Robert Garnier's neoclassical French tragedy *Antonius* and a prose translation of the religious tract *A Discourse of Life and Death* by the French Protestant Philippe de Mornay. Her translation of Petrarch's *Triumph of Death* was the first in English to maintain the original *terza rima* (a particularly challenging rhyme scheme for an English versifier). Although translation was considered an especially appropriate genre for women to work in, it is a mistake to assume that Mary Sidney's efforts as a poet are merely derivative: Elizabethans understood that translation offered the opportunity not only for the display of linguistic and technical skills but also for the indirect expression of personal and political concerns. Mary Sidney also expressed these concerns directly: among her original poems was a powerful elegy for her brother Philip and a short pastoral entertainment for Queen Elizabeth.

Mary Sidney was best known for having prepared a composite edition of Philip Sidney's *Arcadia* and for contributing the larger number (107) of the series of 150 poetic translations of the psalms begun by her brother. Her very free renderings recreate the psalms as English poems, using an amazing variety of stanzaic and metrical patterns and some strikingly effective images. This widely circulated and influential volume was an important bridge between the many metrical paraphrases of psalms in this period and the works of the great religious lyric poets of the seventeenth century, especially George Herbert. Donne's poem *Upon the Translation of the Psalms by Sir Philip Sidney and the Countess of Pembroke His Sister* testifies to that importance: "They tell us *why*, and teach us *how* to sing."

To the Angel Spirit of the Most Excellent Sir Philip Sidney[1]

> To thee, pure sprite,° to thee alone's addressed   *spirit*
>   This coupled work, by double int'rest thine:

1. This is the dedicatory poem to the translation of the Psalms begun by Philip Sidney and completed, after his death, by Mary.

First raised by thy blessed hand, and what is mine
Inspired by thee, thy secret power impressed.°   *i.e., investing her*
5   So dared my Muse with thine itself combine,
As mortal stuff with that which is divine.
Thy light'ning beams give luster to the rest,

That heaven's king may deign his own transformed
In substance no, but superficial tire°   *attire*
10   By thee put on; to praise, not to aspire
To those high tones, so in themselves adorned,
Which angels sing in their celestial choir,
And all of tongues with soul and voice admire
These sacred hymns thy kingly prophet[2] formed.

15   Oh, had that soul which honor brought to rest
Too soon not left, and reft° the world of all   *deprived*
What man could show, which we perfection call,
This half-maimed piece had sorted° with the best.   *consorted, equaled*
Deep wounds enlarged, long festered in their gall,
20   Fresh bleeding smart;° not eye- but heart-tears fall.   *pain, grief*
Ah memory, what needs this new arrest?°   *delay*

Yet here behold (oh, wert thou to behold!)
This° finished now, thy matchless Muse begun,   *the translation*
The rest but pieced, as left by thee undone.
25   Pardon (oh, blessed soul) presumption too too bold,
If love and zeal such error ill become,[3]
'Tis zealous love, love which hath never done,
Nor can enough in world of words unfold.

And sith° it hath no further scope to go,   *since*
30   Nor other purpose but to honor thee,
Thee in thy works, where all the Graces[4] be,
As little streams with all their all do flow
To their great sea, due tribute's grateful fee;
So press my thoughts, my burdened thoughts, in me,
35   To pay the debt of infinites I owe

To thy great worth. Exceeding Nature's store,°   *abundance*
Wonder of men, sole° born perfection's kind,   *alone*
Phoenix[5] thou wert. So rare thy fairest mind,
Heav'nly adorned, Earth justly might adore,
40   Where truthful praise in highest glory shined,
For there alone° was praise to truth confined;   *i.e., in heaven*
And where but there to live forevermore?

2. The Old Testament King David, supposed author of the Psalms. Herbert says that in translating the Psalms her brother intended not to rival the originals—which angels sing and which all those learned in ancient languages ("all of tongues") admire—but simply to praise God.
3. I.e., if it's unbecoming for (her) love and zeal to have presumed to complete the translation.
4. The three Graces of classical mythology, goddesses who presided over all social pleasures and polite accomplishments.
5. The phoenix was a mythical Arabian bird, only one of which existed at any one time. Often associated with Christ, it symbolizes unique perfection.

Oh! When to this accompt,° this cast-up° sum,   *account/totaled*
   This reckoning made, this audit of my woe,
45   I call my thoughts, whence so strange passions flow,
How works my heart, my senses stricken dumb?
   That would thee[6] more than ever heart could show,
   And all too short:° who knew thee best doth know   *inadequate*
There lives no wit° that may thy praise become.°   *mind/express*

50   Truth I invoke (who scorn elsewhere to move,
   Or here in aught my blood should partialize),[7]
   Truth, sacred Truth, thee sole to solemnize.
Those precious rights well known best minds approve;
   And who but doth, hath wisdom's open eyes,
55   Not owly blind the fairest light still flies,
Confirm no less?[8] At least 'tis sealed above,°   *acknowledged in heaven*

Where thou art fixed among thy fellow lights:
   My day put out, my life in darkness cast,
   Thy angel's soul with highest angels placed
60   There blessèd sings enjoying heav'n-delights,
   Thy maker's praise, as far from earthly taste
   As here thy works so worthily embraced
By all of worth, where never envy bites.

As goodly buildings to some glorious end
65   Cut off by Fate, before the Graces had
   Each wond'rous part in all their beauties clad,
Yet so much done, as art could not amend;[9]
   So thy rare works to which no wit can add,
   In all men's eyes, which are not blindly mad,
70   Beyond compare, above all praise extend.

Immortal monuments of thy fair fame,
   Though not complete, nor in the reach of thought,
   How on that passing peacetime would have wrought,
Had Heav'n so spared the life of life to frame
75   The rest?[1] But ah, such loss! Hath this world aught
   Can equal it? Or which like grievance brought?
Yet there will live thy ever-praisèd name.

To which these dearest off'rings of my heart,
   Dissolved to ink, while pen's impressions move
80   The bleeding veins of never-dying love,
I render here: these wounding lines of smart,
   Sad characters indeed of simple love,
   Not art nor skill, which abler wits do prove,°   *experience*
Of my full soul receive the meanest part.[2]

---

6. I.e., my thoughts would (if they could) praise you.
7. I scorn demonstrating partiality to my kinsman.
8. I.e., those who have the open eyes of wisdom— are not blind like an owl always fleeing the fairest light—will confirm what I've said about Sidney's worth.
9. I.e., the part that was completed could not be improved upon; the same is true of Sidney's unfinished literary works.
1. If heaven had spared your life so that you could have completed your representation of human life.
2. The least part—all that she, with her limitations as a writer, is able to express. Professions of a writer's inadequacy are conventional.

85　Receive these hymns,° these obsequies° receive:　　*the psalms/funeral rites*
　　　If any mark of thy sweet sprite appear,
　　　Well are they born; no title else shall bear.
　　I can no more. Dear soul, I take my leave;
　　　Sorrow still strives, would mount thy highest sphere,
90　　Presuming so just cause might meet thee there.[3]
　　Oh happy change, could so I take my leave!

ca. 1595　　　　　　　　　　　　　　　　　　　　　　　　　1623

Psalm 52

　　　Tyrant, why swell'st thou thus,
　　　　　Of mischief vaunting?
　　　Since help from God to us
　　　　　Is never wanting.

5　　Lewd lies thy tongue contrives,
　　　　　Loud lies it soundeth;
　　　Sharper than sharpest knives
　　　　　With lies it woundeth.

　　　Falsehood thy wit° approves,　　　　　　　　　　*mind*
10　　　All truth rejected:
　　　Thy will all vices loves,
　　　　　Virtue neglected.

　　　Not words from cursèd thee,
　　　　　But gulfs° are pourèd;　　　　　*abysses, yawning chasms*
15　　Gulfs wherein daily be
　　　　　Good men devourèd.

　　　Think'st thou to bear it° so?　　　　*bear it off, triumph*
　　　　　God shall displace thee;
　　　God shall thee overthrow,
20　　　Crush thee, deface thee.

　　　The just shall fearing see
　　　　　These fearful chances,
　　　And laughing shoot at thee
　　　　　With scornful glances.

25　　Lo, lo, the wretched wight,
　　　　　Who, God disdaining,
　　　His mischief made his might,
　　　　　His guard his gaining.°　　　　　　　　　　*riches*

　　　I as an olive tree
30　　　Still green shall flourish:

3. My sorrow would mount to heaven to meet you, presuming that the justness of my cause would allow me (however personally unworthy) entrance there.

God's house the soil shall be
 My roots to nourish.
My trust on his true love
 Truly attending,
35 Shall never thence remove,
 Never see ending.

Thee will I honor still,
 Lord, for this justice;
There fix my hopes I will
40 Where thy saints' trust is.

Thy saints trust in thy name,
 Therein they joy them:
Protected by the same,
 Nought° can annoy° them.   *nothing / harm*

ca. 1595   1823

MICHAEL DRAYTON
1563–1631

Michael Drayton was born about a year before Shakespeare and in the same county, Warwickshire. He had a long career as poet, extending from the early 1590s until well into the seventeenth century. He collaborated on plays, wrote scriptural paraphrases, pastorals, odes, poetic epistles, verse legends, and a historical epic called *The Barons' Wars*. His self-styled masterpiece is *Poly-Olbion*, a thirty-thousand-line historical-geographical poem celebrating all the counties of England and Wales. He made a significant contribution as well to the period's vogue for sonnets, publishing a sequence called *Idea's Mirror* (1594) that, following substantial revision, he republished as *Idea*. It was in fact Drayton's standard practice to revise and add to his poems in each new edition, so that one can trace his response to shifting fashions, his rethinking of his antiquarian fascinations, and his development from an Elizabethan to a seventeenth-century poet.

From Idea

61

Since there's no help, come, let us kiss and part;
Nay, I have done, you get no more of me,
And I am glad, yea glad with all my heart
That thus so cleanly I myself can free.
5 Shake hands forever, cancel all our vows,
And when we meet at any time again,
Be it not seen in either of our brows

That we one jot of former love retain.
Now at the last gasp of love's latest breath,
10 When, his pulse failing, passion speechless lies,
When faith is kneeling by his bed of death,
And innocence is closing up his eyes;
Now if thou wouldst, when all have given him over,
From death to life thou mightst him yet recover.

1619

CHRISTOPHER MARLOWE
1564–1593

The son of a Canterbury shoemaker, Christopher Marlowe was born two months
before William Shakespeare. In 1580 he went to Corpus Christi College, Cambridge,
on a scholarship that was ordinarily awarded to students preparing for the ministry.
He held the scholarship for the maximum time, six years, but did not take holy orders.
Instead, he began to write plays. When he applied for his Master of Arts degree in
1587, the university was about to deny it to him on the ground that he intended to
go abroad to Rheims, the center of Catholic intrigue and propaganda against Elizabeth, and remain there. But the Privy Council intervened and requested that because
Marlowe had done the queen "good service"—evidently as some kind of secret
agent—he be granted his degree at the next commencement. "It is not Her Majesty's
pleasure," the government officials added, "that anyone employed as he had been in
matters touching the benefit of his country should be defamed by those that are
ignorant in the affairs he went about." Although much sensational information about
Marlowe has been discovered in modern times, we are still largely "ignorant in the
affairs he went about." The likeliest possibility is that he served as a spy or *agent
provocateur* against English Catholics who were conspiring to overthrow the Protestant regime.

   Before he left Cambridge, Marlowe had certainly written his tremendously successful play *Tamburlaine* and perhaps also, in collaboration with his younger Cambridge contemporary, Thomas Nashe, the tragedy of *Dido, Queen of Carthage.*
Tamburlaine dramatizes the exploits of a fourteenth-century Mongol warrior who rose
from humble origins to conquer a huge territory that extended from the Black Sea to
Delhi. In some sixteenth-century chronicles, Tamburlaine is represented as God's
scourge, the instrument of divine wrath. In Marlowe's play there are few if any
glimpses of a transcendent design. His hero is the vehicle for the expression of boundless energy and ambition, the impulse to strive ceaselessly for absolute power. When
one of his victims accuses him of bloody cruelty, Tamburlaine answers that strife,
restlessness, and unfettered ambition are embedded in the laws of nature and in basic
human psychology:

> Nature that framed us of four elements
> Warring within our breasts for regiment,
> Doth teach us all to have aspiring minds;
> Our souls, whose faculties can comprehend
> The wondrous architecture of the world

And measure every wandering planet's course,
Still climbing after knowledge infinite,
And always moving as the restless spheres,
Wills us to wear ourselves and never rest
Until we reach the ripest fruit of all,
That perfect bliss and sole felicity,
The sweet fruition of an earthly crown.

The English theater audience had never before heard such resonant, immensely energetic blank verse. The great period of Elizabethan drama was launched by what Marlowe called his "high astounding terms."

From the time of his first theatrical success, when he was twenty-three, Marlowe had only six years to live. They were not calm years. In 1589 he was involved in a brawl with one William Bradley, in which the poet Thomas Watson intervened and killed Bradley. Both poets were jailed, but Watson got off on a plea of self-defense, and Marlowe was released. In 1591 Marlowe was living in London with the playwright Thomas Kyd, who later, under torture, gave information to the Privy Council accusing him of atheism and treason. On May 30, 1593, at an inn in the London suburb of Deptford, Marlowe was killed by a dagger thrust, purportedly in an argument over the bill. Modern scholars have discovered that the murderer and the others present in the room at the inn had connections to the world of spies, double agents, and swindlers to which Marlowe himself was in some way linked. Those who were arrested in connection with the murder were briefly held and then quietly released.

In the turbulent years before his death at the age of twenty-nine, Marlowe composed five more plays: a sequel to *Tamburlaine*; *The Massacre at Paris*; two major tragedies, *The Jew of Malta* and *Doctor Faustus*; and a chronicle history play about the tragic fate of a homosexual king, *Edward II*.

The Passionate Shepherd to His Love[1]

Come live with me and be my love,
And we will all the pleasures prove°   test, experience
That valleys, groves, hills, and fields,
Woods, or steepy mountain yields.

5   And we will sit upon the rocks,
Seeing the shepherds feed their flocks,
By shallow rivers to whose falls
Melodious birds sing madrigals.

And I will make thee beds of roses
10   And a thousand fragrant posies,
A cap of flowers, and a kirtle°   skirt
Embroidered all with leaves of myrtle;

A gown made of the finest wool
Which from our pretty lambs we pull;
15   Fair linèd slippers for the cold,
With buckles of the purest gold;

---

1. This pastoral lyric of invitation is one of the most famous of Elizabethan songs, and a few lines from it are sung in Shakespeare's *Merry Wives of* *Windsor*. Many poets have written replies to it, the best known of which is by Sir Walter Ralegh (p. 443).

A belt of straw and ivy buds,
With coral clasps and amber studs:
And if these pleasures may thee move,
20   Come live with me, and be my love.

The shepherd swains shall dance and sing
For thy delight each May morning:
If these delights thy mind may move,
Then live with me and be my love.

1599, 1600

Doctor Faustus

Marlowe's major dramas, *Tamburlaine, The Jew of Malta,* and *Doctor Faustus,* all portray heroes who passionately seek power—the power of rule, the power of money, and the power of knowledge, respectively. Each of the heroes is an overreacher, striving to get beyond the conventional boundaries established to contain the human will.

Unlike Tamburlaine, whose aim and goal is "the sweet fruition of an earthly crown," and Barabas, the Jew of Malta, who lusts for "infinite riches in a little room," Faustus seeks the power and voluptuous pleasure that come from forbidden knowledge. To get this power Faustus must make—or chooses to make—a bargain with Lucifer. This is an old folklore motif, but it would have been taken seriously in a time when belief in the reality of devils was almost universal. The story's power over its original audience is vividly suggested by the numerous accounts of uncanny events at performances of the play: strange noises in the theater or extra devils who suddenly appeared among the actors on stage, causing panic.

In the opening soliloquy, Marlowe's Faustus bids farewell to each of his studies—logic, medicine, law, and divinity—as something he has used up. He turns instead to black magic, but the devil exacts a fearful price in exchange: the eternal damnation of Faustus's soul. This fate would also have been taken literally by an Elizabethan audience. Faustus aspires to be more than a man: "A sound magician is a mighty god," he declares. His fall is caused by the same pride and ambition that caused the fall of the angels in heaven and of humankind in the Garden of Eden. But it is characteristic of Marlowe that he makes those aspirations nonetheless magnificent.

The immediate source of the play is a German narrative called, in its English translation, *The History of the Damnable Life and Deserved Death of Doctor John Faustus.* That source supplies Marlowe's drama with the scenes of horseplay and low practical joking that contrast so markedly with the passages of huge ambition. It is quite possible that these comic scenes are the work of a collaborator; but no other Elizabethan could have written the first scene (with its brilliant representation of the insatiable aspiring mind of the hero), the ecstatic address to Helen of Troy, or the searing scene of Faustus's last hour. And though compared with these celebrated passages, the comic scenes often seem crude, they too contribute to the overarching vision of Faustus's fate: the half-trivial, half-daring exploits, the alternating states of bliss and despair, the questions that are not answered and the answers that bring no real satisfaction, the heroic wanderings that lead nowhere.

Marlowe's play exists in two very different forms: the A text (1604) and the much longer B text (1616), which, according to theatrical records, contains yet more scenes by other hands and which has also been revised to conform to the severe censorship statutes of 1606. We use Roma Gill's edition, based on the A text.

The Tragical History
of Doctor Faustus

DRAMATIS PERSONAE[1]

CHORUS
DR. JOHN FAUSTUS
WAGNER, *his servant, a student*
VALDES
CORNELIUS } *his friends, magicians*
THREE SCHOLARS
GOOD ANGEL
EVIL ANGEL
MEPHASTOPHILIS
LUCIFER
BELZEBUB
OLD MAN
CLOWN
ROBIN
RAFE } *ostlers at an inn*
VINTNER
HORSE-COURSER
THE POPE
THE CARDINAL OF LORRAINE
CHARLES V, EMPEROR OF GERMANY
A KNIGHT *at the* EMPEROR'S *court*
DUKE OF VANHOLT
DUCHESS OF VANHOLT

Spirits presenting
THE SEVEN DEADLY SINS
   PRIDE
   COVETOUSNESS
   WRATH
   ENVY
   GLUTTONY
   SLOTH
   LECHERY
ALEXANDER THE GREAT *and his* PARAMOUR
HELEN OF TROY

ATTENDANTS, FRIARS, *and* DEVILS

Prologue

[*Enter* CHORUS.][2]
CHORUS   Not marching now in fields of Thrasimene,
   Where Mars[3] did mate° the Carthaginians,   *join with*
   Nor sporting in the dalliance of love,

---

1. There is no list of characters in the A text. The one here is an editorial construction.
2. A single actor who recited a prologue to an act or a whole play, and occasionally delivered an epi-

logue.
3. God of war. The battle of Lake Trasimene (217 B.C.E.) was one of the Carthaginian leader Hannibal's great victories.

In courts of kings where state° is overturned,   *political power*

5   Nor in the pomp of proud audacious deeds,
Intends our Muse to vaunt his heavenly verse:
Only this (Gentlemen) we must perform,
The form of Faustus' fortunes good or bad.
To patient judgments we appeal our plaud,°   *applause*
10   And speak for Faustus in his infancy:
Now is he born, his parents base of stock,
In Germany, within a town called Rhodes;
Of riper years to Wittenberg[4] he went,
Whereas° his kinsmen chiefly brought him up.   *where*
15   So soon he profits in divinity,
The fruitfull plot of scholarism graced,
That shortly he was graced with doctor's name,[5]
Excelling all, whose sweet delight disputes[6]
In heavenly matters of theology.
20   Till, swollen with cunning,° of a self-conceit,   *knowledge*
His waxen wings did mount above his reach,
And melting heavens conspired his overthrow.[7]
For falling to a devilish exercise,
And glutted more with learning's golden gifts,
25   He surfeits upon cursed necromancy:°   *black magic*
Nothing so sweet as magic is to him,
Which he prefers before his chiefest bliss.[8]
And this the man[9] that in his study sits.   [*Exit.*]

SCENE 1

[*Enter* FAUSTUS *in his study.*]
FAUSTUS   Settle thy studies, Faustus, and begin
To sound the depth of that thou wilt profess:
Having commenced, be a divine in show,[1]
Yet level° at the end of every art,   *aim*
5   And live and die in Aristotle's works.
Sweet *Analytics,* 'tis thou hast ravished me:
Bene disserere est finis logices.[2]
Is, to dispute well, logic's chiefest end?
Affords this art no greater miracle?
10   Then read no more, thou hast attained the end;
A greater subject fitteth Faustus' wit.°   *intellect*
Bid *on kai me on* farewell; Galen[3] come:
Seeing, *ubi desinit philosophus, ibi incipit medicus.*[4]
Be a physician, Faustus, heap up gold,

4. The famous university where Martin Luther studied, as did Shakespeare's Hamlet and Horatio. "Rhodes": Roda, or Stadtroda, in Germany.
5. The lines play on two senses of *graced*: he so (1) adorned the place ("plot") of scholarship—i.e., the university—that shortly he was (2) honored with a doctor's degree.
6. Referring to formal disputations, academic exercises that took the place of examinations.
7. In Greek myth, Icarus flew too near the sun on wings of feathers and wax made by his father, Daedalus; the wax melted, and he fell into the sea and drowned.
8. The salvation of his soul.

9. Apparently a cue for the Chorus to draw aside the curtain to the enclosed space at the rear of the stage.
1. In external appearance. "Commenced": graduated, i.e., received the doctor's degree.
2. To carry on a disputation well is the end or purpose of logic. "*Analytics*": the title of two treatises on logic by Aristotle.
3. The ancient authority on medicine (2nd century C.E.). The Greek means, "Being and not being," i.e., philosophy.
4. Where the philosopher leaves off the physician begins.

15 And be eternized for some wondrous cure.
    Summum bonum medicinae sanitas:[5]
    The end of physic° is our body's health.   medicine
    Why Faustus, hast thou not attained that end?
    Is not thy common talk found aphorisms?[6]
20 Are not thy bills° hung up as monuments,   prescriptions
    Whereby whole cities have escaped the plague,
    And thousand desperate maladies been eased?
    Yet art thou still but Faustus, and a man.
    Couldst thou make men to live eternally,
25 Or, being dead, raise them to life again,
    Then this profession were to be esteemed.
    Physic farewell! Where is Justinian?[7]
    Si una eademque res legatur duobus,
    Alter rem alter valorem rei, etc.[8]
30 A pretty case of paltry legacies:
    Exhereditare filium non potest pater nisi . . .[9]
    Such is the subject of the Institute,
    And universal body of the law:
    This study fits a mercenary drudge
35 Who aims at nothing but external trash!
    Too servile and illiberal for me.
    When all is done, divinity is best:
    Jerome's Bible,[1] Faustus, view it well:
    Stipendium peccati mors est: ha! *Stipendium, etc.*[2]
40 The reward of sin is death? That's hard.
    Si pecasse negamus, fallimur, et nulla est in nobis veritas.[3]
    If we say that we have no sin,
    We deceive ourselves, and there's no truth in us.
    Why then belike we must sin,
45 And so consequently die.
    Ay, we must die an everlasting death.
    What doctrine call you this? *Che sarà, sarà:*[4]
    What will be, shall be! Divinity, adieu!
    These metaphysics° of magicians,   basic principles
50 And necromantic books are heavenly!
    Lines, circles, schemes, letters, and characters!
    Ay, these are those that Faustus most desires.
    O what a world of profit and delight,
    Of power, of honor, of omnipotence
55 Is promised to the studious artisan![5]
    All things that move between the quiet° poles   unmoving
    Shall be at my command: emperors and kings
    Are but obeyed in their several provinces,
    Nor can they raise the wind, or rend the clouds;
60 But his dominion that exceeds in this
    Stretcheth as far as doth the mind of man:

5. The Latin is translated in the line below.
6. I.e., generally accepted wisdom.
7. Roman emperor and authority on law (483–565 C.E.), author of the *Institutes.*
8. If something is bequeathed to two persons, one shall have the thing itself, the other something of equal value.
9. A father cannot disinherit his son unless . . .

1. The Latin translation, or "Vulgate," of St. Jerome (ca. 340–420 C.E.).
2. Romans 6.23, translated in the line below.
3. 1 John 1.8, translated in the next two lines.
4. Translated in the first half of the next line.
5. A master of the occult arts, such as necromancy.

A sound magician is a mighty god.
Here Faustus, try thy brains to gain a deity.
                [*Enter* WAGNER.]
Wagner, commend me to my dearest friends,
65   The German Valdes, and Cornelius,
Request them earnestly to visit me.
WAGNER   I will sir.   [*Exit.*]
FAUSTUS   Their conference will be a greater help to me
Than all my labors, plod I ne'er so fast.
                [*Enter the* GOOD ANGEL *and the* EVIL ANGEL.]
70   GOOD ANGEL   O Faustus, lay that damnèd book aside,
And gaze not on it, lest it tempt thy soul,
And heap God's heavy wrath upon thy head:
Read, read the Scriptures; that is blasphemy.
EVIL ANGEL   Go forward, Faustus, in that famous art,
75   Wherein all nature's treasury is contained:
Be thou on earth as Jove[6] is in the sky,
Lord and commander of these elements.   [*Exeunt.*]
FAUSTUS   How am I glutted with conceit° of this!   *filled with the idea*
Shall I make spirits fetch me what I please,
80   Resolve me of all ambiguities,
Perform what desperate enterprise I will?
I'll have them fly to India[7] for gold,
Ransack the ocean for orient pearl,
And search all corners of the new-found world
85   For pleasant fruits and princely delicates.
I'll have them read me strange philosophy,
And tell the secrets of all foreign kings;
I'll have them wall all Germany with brass,
And make swift Rhine circle fair Wittenberg;[8]
90   I'll have them fill the public schools[9] with silk,
Wherewith the students shall be bravely° clad.   *splendidly*
I'll levy soldiers with the coin they bring,
And chase the Prince of Parma[1] from our land,
And reign sole king of all our provinces.
95   Yea, stranger engines for the brunt of war
Than was the fiery keel at Antwerp's bridge,[2]
I'll make my servile spirits to invent.
Come German Valdes and Cornelius,
And make me blest with your sage conference.
                [*Enter* VALDES *and* CORNELIUS.]
100   Valdes, sweet Valdes, and Cornelius,
Know that your words have won me at the last
To practise magic and concealed arts;
Yet not your words only, but mine own fantasy,
That will receive no object[3] for my head,

6. God, a common substitution in Elizabethan drama.
7. "India" could refer to the West Indies, America, or Ophir (in the east).
8. Wittenberg is in fact on the Elbe River.
9. The university lecture rooms.
1. The duke of Parma was the Spanish governor-

general of the Low Countries, 1579–92.
2. A reference to the burning ship sent by the Netherlanders in 1585 against the barrier on the river Scheldt that Parma had built as a part of the blockade of Antwerp.
3. That will pay no attention to physical reality.

105 But ruminates on necromantic skill.
Philosophy is odious and obscure,
Both law and physic are for petty wits;
Divinity is basest of the three,
Unpleasant, harsh, contemptible, and vile.
110 'Tis magic, magic that hath ravished me.
Then, gentle friends, aid me in this attempt,
And I, that have with concise syllogisms
Graveled° the pastors of the German church,   *confounded*
And made the flowering pride of Wittenberg
115 Swarm to my problems,[4] as the infernal spirits
On sweet Musaeus when he came to hell,
Will be as cunning as Agrippa was,
Whose shadows made all Europe honor him.[5]
VALDES   Faustus, these books, thy wit, and our experience
120 Shall make all nations to canonize us.
As Indian Moors[6] obey their Spanish lords,
So shall the spirits of every element
Be always serviceable to us three.
Like lions shall they guard us when we please,
125 Like Almaine rutters° with their horsemen's staves,   *German horsemen*
Or Lapland giants trotting by our sides;
Sometimes like women, or unwedded maids,
Shadowing° more beauty in their airy brows   *harboring*
Than in the white breasts of the Queen of Love.
130 From Venice shall they drag huge argosies,
And from America the golden fleece
That yearly stuffs old Philip's° treasury,   *Philip II, king of Spain*
If learnèd Faustus will be resolute.
FAUSTUS   Valdes, as resolute am I in this
135 As thou to live, therefore object it not.[7]
CORNELIUS   The miracles that magic will perform
Will make thee vow to study nothing else.
He that is grounded in astrology,
Enriched with tongues,° well seen° in minerals,   *languages/expert*
140 Hath all the principles magic doth require:
Then doubt not, Faustus, but to be renowned
And more frequented for this mystery°   *craft*
Than heretofore the Delphian oracle.[8]
The spirits tell me they can dry the sea,
145 And fetch the treasure of all foreign wrecks,
Ay, all the wealth that our forefathers hid
Within the massy° entrails of the earth.   *massive*
Then tell me, Faustus, what shall we three want?
FAUSTUS   Nothing, Cornelius. O this cheers my soul!
150 Come, show me some demonstrations magical,
That I may conjure in some lusty° grove,   *flourishing, beautiful*

4. Lectures in logic and mathematics.
5. Musaeus was a mythical singer, son of Orpheus; it was, however, Orpheus who charmed the denizens of hell with his music. Cornelius Agrippa, German author of *The Vanity and Uncertainty of Arts and Sciences* (1530), was popularly supposed to have had the power of calling up the "shadows" or shades of the dead.
6. Dark-skinned native Americans.
7. Do not make it a condition.
8. The oracle of Apollo at Delphi in Greece.

And have these joys in full possessiön.
VALDES   Then haste thee to some solitary grove,
And bear wise Bacon's and Abanus'[9] works,
155   The Hebrew Psalter, and New Testament;
And whatsoever else is requisite
We will inform thee ere our conference cease.
CORNELIUS   Valdes, first let him know the words of art,
And then, all other ceremonies learned,
160   Faustus may try his cunning by himself.
VALDES   First, I'll instruct thee in the rudiments,
And then wilt thou be perfecter than I.
FAUSTUS   Then come and dine with me, and after meat
We'll canvass every quiddity° thereof: *essential feature*
165   For ere I sleep, I'll try what I can do.
This night I'll conjure,° though I die therefore.   *call up spirits*
[*Exeunt.*]

SCENE 2

[*Enter two* SCHOLARS.]
1 SCHOLAR   I wonder what's become of Faustus, that was wont to
make our schools ring with *sic probo*.[1]
2 SCHOLAR   That shall we know; for see, here comes his boy.[2]
[*Enter* WAGNER.]
SCHOLAR   How now sirra, where's thy master?
5   WAGNER   God in heaven knows.
2 SCHOLAR   Why, dost not thou know?
WAGNER   Yes I know, but that follows not.
1 SCHOLAR   Go to sirra, leave your jesting, and tell us where he is.
WAGNER   That follows not necessary by force of argument, that you,
10   being licentiates,[3] should stand upon't; therefore acknowledge your
error, and be attentive.
2 SCHOLAR   Why, didst thou not say thou knew'st?
WAGNER   Have you any witness on't?
1 SCHOLAR   Yes sirra, I heard you.
15   WAGNER   Ask my fellow if I be a thief.
2 SCHOLAR   Well, you will not tell us.
WAGNER   Yes sir, I will tell you; yet if you were not dunces you would
never ask me such a question. For is not he *corpus naturale*? And
is not that *mobile*?[4] Then wherefore should you ask me such a ques-
20   tion? But that I am by nature phlegmatic,[5] slow to wrath, and prone
to lechery—to love I would say—it were not for you to come within
forty foot of the place of execution,[6] although I do not doubt to see
you both hanged the next sessions. Thus having triumphed over
you, I will set my countenance like a precisian,[7] and begin to speak
25   thus: Truly my dear brethren, my master is within at dinner with
Valdes and Cornelius, as this wine, if it could speak, it would inform

9. Roger Bacon, the medieval friar and scientist popularly thought to be a magician, and Pietro d'Abano, 13th-century alchemist.
1. Thus I prove; a phrase in scholastic disputation.
2. Poor student acting as servant to earn his living.
3. Graduate students.
  Corpus naturale et mobile ("matter natural and vable") was a scholastic definition of the subject

matter of physics. Wagner is here parodying the language of learning at the university.
5. Dominated by the phlegm, one of the four humors of medieval medicine and psychology.
6. The dining room.
7. Puritan. The rest of his speech is in the style of the Puritans.

your worships. And so the Lord bless you, preserve you, and keep
you, my dear brethren, my dear brethren. [*Exit.*]

1 SCHOLAR   Nay then, I fear he is fallen into that damned art, for
30   which they two are infamous through the world.

2 SCHOLAR   Were he a stranger, and not allied to me, yet should I
grieve for him. But come, let us go and inform the Rector,[8] and see
if he by his grave counsel can reclaim him.

1 SCHOLAR   Ay, but I fear me nothing can reclaim him.

35   2 SCHOLAR   Yet let us try what we can do. [*Exeunt.*]

SCENE 3

[*Enter* FAUSTUS *to conjure.*]

FAUSTUS   Now that the gloomy shadow of the earth,
Longing to view Orion's drizzling look,[9]
Leaps from th'antarctic world unto the sky,
And dims the welkin° with her pitchy breath,   sky
5   Faustus, begin thine incantations,
And try if devils will obey thy hest,
Seeing thou hast prayed and sacrificed to them.
Within this circle[1] is Jehovah's name,
Forward and backward anagrammatized;
10   Th'abbreviated names of holy saints,
Figures of every adjunct to the heavens,
And characters of signs and erring stars,[2]
By which the spirits are enforced to rise.
Then fear not Faustus, but be resolute,
15   And try the uttermost magic can perform.
Sint mihi dei Acherontis propitii! Valeat numen triplex Jehovae!
Ignei, aerii, aquatici, terreni spiritus salvete! Orientis princeps, Bel-
zebub inferni ardentis monarcha, et Demogorgon, propitiamus vos ut
appareat et surgat Mephastophilis. Quid tu moraris? Per Jehovam,
20   *Gehennam, et consecratam aquam quam nunc spargo, signumque*
crucis quod nunc facio, et per vota nostra, ipse nunc surgat nobis
dicatus Mephastophilis.[3]

        [*Enter a* DEVIL.]
I charge thee to return and change thy shape,
Thou art too ugly to attend on me;
25   Go and return an old Franciscan friar,
That holy shape becomes a devil best. [*Exit* DEVIL.]
I see there's virtue° in my heavenly words!   power
Who would not be proficient in this art?
How pliant is this Mephastophilis,
30   Full of obedience and humility,
Such is the force of magic and my spells.

---

8. The head of a German university.
9. The constellation Orion appears at the beginning of winter. The phrase is a reminiscence of Virgil.
1. The magic circle drawn on the ground, within which the magician would be safe from the spirits he conjured.
2. The moving planets. "Adjunct": heavenly body, thought to be joined to the solid firmament of the sky. "Characters of signs": signs of the zodiac and the planets.

3. May the gods of the lower regions favor me! Farewell to the Trinity! Hail, spirits of fire, air, water, and earth! Prince of the East, Belzebub, monarch of burning hell, and Demogorgon, we pray to you that Mephastophilis may appear and rise. What are you waiting for? By Jehovah, Gehenna, and the holy water that I now sprinkle, and the sign of the cross that I now make, and by our vows, may Mephastophilis himself now rise to serve us.

Now Faustus, thou art conjurer laureate
That canst command great Mephastophilis.
Quin redis, Mephastophilis, fratris imagine![4]
[*Enter* MEPHASTOPHILIS.]

35 MEPHASTOPHILIS   Now Faustus, what would'st thou have me do?
FAUSTUS   I charge thee wait upon me whilst I live,
To do whatever Faustus shall command,
Be it to make the moon drop from her sphere,
Or the ocean to overwhelm the world.
40 MEPHASTOPHILIS   I am a servant to great Lucifer,
And may not follow thee without his leave;
No more than he commands must we perform.
FAUSTUS   Did not he charge thee to appear to me?
MEPHASTOPHILIS   No, I came now hither of mine own accord.
45 FAUSTUS   Did not my conjuring speeches raise thee? Speak!
MEPHASTOPHILIS   That was the cause, but yet *per accidens*,[5]
For when we hear one rack[6] the name of God,
Abjure the Scriptures, and his savior Christ,
We fly in hope to get his glorious soul;
50 Nor will we come unless he use such means
Whereby he is in danger to be damned:
Therefore the shortest cut for conjuring
Is stoutly to abjure the Trinity,
And pray devoutly to the prince of hell.
55 FAUSTUS   So Faustus hath already done, and holds this principle:
There is no chief but only Belzebub,
To whom Faustus doth dedicate himself.
This word damnation terrifies not him,
For he confounds hell in Elysium:
60 His ghost be with the old philosophers.[7]
But leaving these vain trifles of men's souls,
Tell me, what is that Lucifer thy lord?
MEPHASTOPHILIS   Arch-regent and commander of all spirits.
FAUSTUS   Was not that Lucifer an angel once?
65 MEPHASTOPHILIS   Yes Faustus, and most dearly loved of God.
FAUSTUS   How comes it then that he is prince of devils?
MEPHASTOPHILIS   O, by aspiring pride and insolence,
For which God threw him from the face of heaven.
FAUSTUS   And what are you that live with Lucifer?
70 MEPHASTOPHILIS   Unhappy spirits that fell with Lucifer,
Conspired against our God with Lucifer,
And are forever damned with Lucifer.
FAUSTUS   Where are you damned?
MEPHASTOPHILIS   In hell.
75 FAUSTUS   How comes it then that thou art out of hell?
MEPHASTOPHILIS   Why this is hell, nor am I out of it.
Think'st thou that I, who saw the face of God,
And tasted the eternal joys of heaven,
Am not tormented with ten thousand hells

---

4. Return, Mephastophilis, in the shape of a friar.
5. The immediate, not ultimate, cause.
6. Torture (by anagrammatizing).

7. Faustus considers hell to be the Elysium of the classical philosophers, not the Christian hell of torment.

80   In being deprived of everlasting bliss?[8]
     O Faustus, leave these frivolous demands,
     Which strike a terror to my fainting soul.
    FAUSTUS   What, is great Mephastophilis so passionate
     For being deprivèd of the joys of heaven?
85   Learn thou of Faustus manly fortitude,
     And scorn those joys thou never shalt possess.
     Go bear these tidings to great Lucifer,
     Seeing Faustus hath incurred eternal death
     By desperate thoughts against Jove's deity:
90   Say, he surrenders up to him his soul
     So he will spare him four and twenty years,
     Letting him live in all voluptuousness,
     Having thee ever to attend on me,
     To give me whatsoever I shall ask,
95   To tell me whatsoever I demand,
     To slay mine enemies, and aid my friends,
     And always be obedient to my will.
     Go, and return to mighty Lucifer,
     And meet me in my study at midnight
100   And then resolve me of thy master's mind.[9]
    MEPHASTOPHILIS   I will, Faustus.   [*Exit.*]
    FAUSTUS   Had I as many souls as there be stars,
     I'd give them all for Mephastophilis.
     By him I'll be great emperor of the world,
105   And make a bridge through the moving air
     To pass the ocean with a band of men;
     I'll join the hills that bind the Afric shore,
     And make that land continent to Spain,
     And both contributory to my crown.
110   The emperor[1] shall not live but by my leave,
     Nor any potentate of Germany.
     Now that I have obtained what I desire,
     I'll live in speculation° of this art   *contemplation*
     Till Mephastophilis return again.   [*Exit.*]

SCENE 4

[*Enter* WAGNER *and the* CLOWN.[2]]

    WAGNER   Sirra boy, come hither.
    CLOWN   How, boy? Zounds, boy! I hope you have seen many boys
     with such pickadevants as I have. Boy, quotha![3]
    WAGNER   Tell me sirra, hast thou any comings in?[4]
5   CLOWN   Ay, and goings out too; you may see else.[5]
    WAGNER   Alas poor slave, see how poverty jesteth in his nakedness!
     The villain is bare, and out of service,[6] and so hungry that I know

---

8. This is the punishment of loss of God's presence, which is supposed to be the greatest torment of hell.
9. I.e., give me his decision.
1. The Holy Roman Emperor.
2. Not a court jester (as in some of Shakespeare's plays) but an older stock character, a rustic buffoon.

3. Says he. The point of the clown's retort is that he is a man and wears a beard. "Zounds": an oath, meaning "God's wounds." "Pickadevants": small, pointed beards.
4. Income, but the clown then puns on the literal meaning.
5. I.e., if you don't believe me.
6. Out of a job.

he would give his soul to the devil for a shoulder of mutton, though it were blood raw.

10 CLOWN   How, my soul to the devil for a shoulder of mutton though 'twere blood raw? Not so good friend; by'rlady,[7] I had need have it well roasted, and good sauce to it, if I pay so dear.

WAGNER   Well, wilt thou serve me, and I'll make thee go like *qui mihi discipulus*?[8]

15 CLOWN   How, in verse?

WAGNER   No sirra; in beaten silk and stavesacre.[9]

CLOWN   How, how, knavesacre?[1] Ay I thought that was all the land his father left him! Do ye hear, I would be sorry to rob you of your living.

20 WAGNER   Sirra, I say in stavesacre.

CLOWN   Oho, oho, stavesacre! Why then belike, if I were your man, I should be full of vermin.

WAGNER   So thou shalt, whether thou be'st with me or no. But sirra, leave your jesting, and bind your self presently unto me for seven

25   years, or I'll turn all the lice about thee into familiars,[2] and they shall tear thee in pieces.

CLOWN   Do you hear, sir? You may save that labor: they are too familiar with me already—zounds, they are as bold with my flesh as if they had paid for my meat and drink.

30 WAGNER   Well, do you hear, sirra? Hold, take these guilders.[3]

CLOWN   Gridirons; what be they?

WAGNER   Why, French crowns.[4]

CLOWN   'Mass, but for the name of French crowns a man were as good have as many English counters![5] And what should I do with

35   these?

WAGNER   Why, now, sirra, thou art at an hour's warning whensoever or wheresoever the devil shall fetch thee.

CLOWN   No, no, here take your gridirons again.

WAGNER   Truly I'll none of them.

40 CLOWN   Truly but you shall.

WAGNER   Bear witness I gave them him.

CLOWN   Bear witness I give them you again.

WAGNER   Well, I will cause two devils presently to fetch thee away. Baliol[6] and Belcher!

45 CLOWN   Let your Baliol and your Belcher come here, and I'll knock[7] them, they were never so knocked since they were devils! Say I should kill one of them, what would folks say? Do ye see yonder tall fellow in the round slop?[8] He has killed the devil! So I should be called "Killdevil" all the parish over.

[*Enter two* DEVILS, *and the* CLOWN *runs up and down crying.*]

50 WAGNER   Baliol and Belcher, spirits, away!   [*Exeunt* DEVILS.]

CLOWN   What, are they gone? A vengeance on them! They have vile long nails. There was a he devil and a she devil. I'll tell you how

7. An oath: "by Our Lady."

8. You who are my pupil (the opening phrase of a poem on how students should behave, from Lily's *Latin Grammar*, ca. 1509). Wagner means "like a proper servant of a learned man."

9. A kind of delphinium used for killing vermin.

1. Wordplay, here and below.

2. Familiar spirits, demons.

3. Coins.

4. French crowns, legal tender in England at this period, were easily counterfeited.

5. Worthless tokens.

6. Probably a corruption of Belial.

7. Beat.

8. Baggy pants. "Tall": fine.

you shall know them: all he devils has horns, and all she devils has clefts and cloven feet.

55 WAGNER   Well sirra, follow me.

CLOWN   But do you hear? If I should serve you, would you teach me to raise up Banios and Belcheos?

WAGNER   I will teach thee to turn thyself to anything, to a dog, or a cat, or a mouse, or a rat, or anything.

60 CLOWN   How! A Christian fellow to a dog, or a cat, a mouse, or a rat? No, no sir, if you turn me into anything, let it be in the likeness of a little pretty frisking flea, that I may be here, and there, and everywhere. O I'll tickle the pretty wenches' plackets! I'll be amongst them, i'faith.[9]

65 WAGNER   Well sirra, come.

CLOWN   But, do you hear, Wagner . . . ?

WAGNER   How? Baliol and Belcher!

CLOWN   O Lord I pray, sir, let Banio and Belcher go sleep.

WAGNER   Villain, call me Master Wagner; and let thy left eye be dia-
70 metarily fixed upon my right heel, with *quasi vestigias nostras insis-
tere.*[1]   [*Exit.*]

CLOWN   God forgive me, he speaks Dutch fustian![2] Well, I'll follow him, I'll serve him; that's flat.   [*Exit.*]

SCENE 5

[*Enter* FAUSTUS *in his study.*]

FAUSTUS   Now Faustus, must thou needs be damned,
And canst thou not be saved.
What boots° it then to think of God or heaven?   avails
Away with such vain fancies, and despair,
5 Despair in God, and trust in Belzebub.
Now go not backward: no, Faustus, be resolute;
Why waverest thou? O, something soundeth in mine ears:
"Abjure this magic, turn to God again."
Ay, and Faustus will turn to God again.
10 To God? He loves thee not:
The god thou servest is thine own appetite
Wherein is fixed the love of Belzebub.
To him I'll build an altar and a church,
And offer lukewarm blood of newborn babes.

[*Enter* GOOD ANGEL *and* EVIL.]

15 GOOD ANGEL   Sweet Faustus, leave that execrable art.

FAUSTUS   Contrition, prayer, repentance: what of them?

GOOD ANGEL   O they are means to bring thee unto heaven.

EVIL ANGEL   Rather illusions, fruits of lunacy,
That makes men foolish that do trust them most.

20 GOOD ANGEL   Sweet Faustus, think of heaven, and heavenly things.

EVIL ANGEL   No Faustus, think of honor and of wealth.

[*Exeunt.*]

FAUSTUS   Of wealth!
Why, the signory of Emden[3] shall be mine,

9. In faith. "Plackets": slits in garments—but with an obvious sexual allusion.
1. A pedantic way of saying "Follow my footsteps."

"Diametarily": diametrically.
2. Gibberish.
3. A wealthy German trade center.

When Mephastophilis shall stand by me.
25   What god can hurt thee, Faustus? Thou art safe,
   Cast no more doubts. Come, Mephastophilis,
   And bring glad tidings from great Lucifer.
   Is't not midnight? Come, Mephastophilis:
   Veni, veni, Mephastophile![4]
        [*Enter* MEPHASTOPHILIS.]
30   Now tell, what says Lucifer thy lord?
   MEPHASTOPHILIS   That I shall wait on Faustus whilst he lives,
   So he will buy my service with his soul.
   FAUSTUS   Already Faustus hath hazarded that for thee.
   MEPHASTOPHILIS   But Faustus, thou must bequeath it solemnly,
35   And write a deed of gift with thine own blood,
   For that security craves great Lucifer.
   If thou deny it, I will back to hell.
   FAUSTUS   Stay, Mephastophilis, and tell me,
   What good will my soul do thy lord?
40   MEPHASTOPHILIS   Enlarge his kingdom.
   FAUSTUS   Is that the reason he tempts us thus?
   MEPHASTOPHILIS   *Solamen miseris socios habuisse doloris.*[5]
   FAUSTUS   Have you any pain that tortures others?
   MEPHASTOPHILIS   As great as have the human souls of men.
45   But tell me Faustus, shall I have thy soul?
   And I will be thy slave and wait on thee,
   And give thee more than thou hast wit to ask.
   FAUSTUS   Ay Mephastophilis, I give it thee.
   MEPHASTOPHILIS   Then stab thine arm courageously,
50   And bind thy soul, that at some certain day
   Great Lucifer may claim it as his own,
   And then be thou as great as Lucifer.
   FAUSTUS   Lo Mephastophilis, for love of thee,
   I cut my arm, and with my proper° blood   own
55   Assure my soul to be great Lucifer's,
   Chief lord and regent of perpetual night.
   View here the blood that trickles from mine arm,
   And let it be propitious for my wish.
   MEPHASTOPHILIS   But Faustus, thou must write it
60   In manner of a deed of gift.
   FAUSTUS   Ay, so I will; but, Mephastophilis,
   My blood congeals and I can write no more.
   MEPHASTOPHILIS   I'll fetch thee fire to dissolve it straight.   [*Exit.*]
   FAUSTUS   What might the staying of my blood portend?
65   Is it unwilling I should write this bill?°   contract
   Why streams it not, that I may write afresh:
   "Faustus gives to thee his soul"? Ah, there it stayed!
   Why should'st thou not? Is not thy soul thine own?
   Then write again: "Faustus gives to thee his soul."
        [*Enter* MEPHASTOPHILIS *with a chafer° of coals.*]   *a portable grate*
70   MEPHASTOPHILIS   Here's fire, come Faustus, set it on.
   FAUSTUS   So, now the blood begins to clear again.

4. Come, come, Mephastophilis!   5. Misery loves company.

Now will I make an end immediately.
MEPHASTOPHILIS   Oh what will not I do to obtain his soul!
FAUSTUS   *Consummatum est,*[6] this bill is ended,
75   And Faustus hath bequeathed his soul to Lucifer.
But what is this inscription on mine arm?
Homo fuge.° Whither should I fly?   O man, fly
If unto God, he'll throw me down to hell;
My senses are deceived, here's nothing writ;
80   I see it plain, here in this place is writ,
Homo fuge! Yet shall not Faustus fly.
MEPHASTOPHILIS   I'll fetch him somewhat to delight his mind.   [*Exit.*]
        [*Enter with* DEVILS, *giving crowns and rich apparel to* FAUS-
        TUS, *and dance, and then depart.*]
FAUSTUS   Speak, Mephastophilis, what means this show?
MEPHASTOPHILIS   Nothing, Faustus, but to delight thy mind withal,
85   And to show thee what magic can perform.
FAUSTUS   But may I raise up spirits when I please?
MEPHASTOPHILIS   Ay, Faustus, and do greater things than these.
FAUSTUS   Then there's enough for a thousand souls!
Here, Mephastophilis, receive this scroll,
90   A deed of gift of body and of soul:
But yet conditionally, that thou perform
All articles prescribed between us both.
MEPHASTOPHILIS   Faustus, I swear by hell and Lucifer
To effect all promises between us made.
95   FAUSTUS   Then hear me read them. On these conditions following:
First, that Faustus may be a spirit[7] *in form and substance.*
Secondly, that Mephastophilis shall be his servant, and at his com-
mand.
Thirdly, that Mephastophilis shall do for him, and bring him whatso-
100   *ever.*
Fourthly, that he shall be in his chamber or house invisible.
Lastly, that he shall appear to the said John Faustus at all times, in
what form or shape soever he please.
I, John Faustus of Wittenberg, doctor, by these presents,[8] *do give both*
105   *body and soul to Lucifer, Prince of the East, and his minister Mephas-*
tophilis; and furthermore grant unto them that, four and twenty years
being expired, the articles above-written inviolate, full power to fetch
or carry the said John Faustus, body and soul, flesh, blood, or goods,
into their habitation wheresoever.
110   *By me John Faustus.*
MEPHASTOPHILIS   Speak, Faustus: do you deliver this as your deed?
FAUSTUS   Ay, take it; and the devil give thee good on't.
MEPHASTOPHILIS   Now, Faustus, ask what thou wilt.
FAUSTUS   First will I question with thee about hell:
115   Tell me, where is the place that men call hell?
MEPHASTOPHILIS   Under the heavens.
FAUSTUS   Ay, but whereabouts?
MEPHASTOPHILIS   Within the bowels of these elements,
Where we are tortured and remain for ever.

---

6. It is finished; a blasphemy, because these are
the words of Christ on the Cross (John 19.30).

7. I.e., have the supernatural powers of a spirit.
8. Legal articles.

120   Hell hath no limits, nor is circumscribed
       In one self place; for where we are is hell,
       And where hell is, there must we ever be.
       And to conclude, when all the world dissolves,
       And every creature shall be purified,
125   All places shall be hell that is not heaven.
       FAUSTUS   Come, I think hell's a fable.
       MEPHASTOPHILIS   Ay, think so still, till experience change thy
          mind.
       FAUSTUS   Why? think'st thou then that Faustus shall be damned?
130   MEPHASTOPHILIS   Ay, of necessity, for here's the scroll
          Wherein thou hast given thy soul to Lucifer.
       FAUSTUS   Ay, and body too; but what of that?
          Think'st thou that Faustus is so fond° to imagine   foolish
          That after this life there is any pain?
135   Tush, these are trifles and mere old wives' tales.
       MEPHASTOPHILIS   But Faustus, I am an instance to prove the con-
          trary;
          For I am damned, and am now in hell.
       FAUSTUS   How, now in hell? Nay, and this be hell, I'll willingly be
          damned here! What? walking, disputing, etc. . . . . But leaving off
140   this, let me have a wife, the fairest maid in Germany, for I am
          wanton and lascivious, and cannot live without a wife.
       MEPHASTOPHILIS   How, a wife? I prithee Faustus, talk not of a wife.⁹
       FAUSTUS   Nay sweet Mephastophilis, fetch me one, for I will have
          one.
145   MEPHASTOPHILIS   Well, thou wilt have one; sit there till I come.
          I'll fetch thee a wife in the devil's name.   [Exit.]
          [Enter with a DEVIL dressed like a woman, with fireworks.]
       MEPHASTOPHILIS   Tell, Faustus, how dost thou like thy wife?
       FAUSTUS   A plague on her for a hot whore!
       MEPHASTOPHILIS   Tut, Faustus, marriage is but a ceremonial toy;
150   If thou lovest me, think no more of it.
          I'll cull thee out the fairest courtesans
          And bring them every morning to thy bed:
          She whom thine eye shall like, thy heart shall have,
          Be she as chaste as was Penelope,
155   As wise as Saba,¹ or as beautiful
          As was bright Lucifer before his fall.
          Hold, take this book, peruse it thoroughly:
          The iterating° of these lines brings gold;   repeating
          The framing° of this circle on the ground   drawing
160   Brings whirlwinds, tempests, thunder and lightning.
          Pronounce this thrice devoutly to thyself,
          And men in armor shall appear to thee,
          Ready to execute what thou desirest.
       FAUSTUS   Thanks, Mephastophilis, yet fain would I have a book
165   wherein I might behold all spells and incantations, that I might raise
          up spirits when I please.
       MEPHASTOPHILIS   Here they are in this book.   [There turn to them.]

9. Mephastophilis cannot produce a wife for
Faustus because marriage is a sacrament.

1. The queen of Sheba. "Penelope": the wife of
Ulysses, famed for chastity and fidelity.

FAUSTUS   Now would I have a book where I might see all characters
and planets of the heavens, that I might know their motions and
170   dispositions.
MEPHASTOPHILIS   Here they are too.   [*Turn to them.*]
FAUSTUS   Nay, let me have one book more, and then I have done,
wherein I might see all plants, herbs, and trees that grow upon the
earth.
175   MEPHASTOPHILIS   Here they be.
FAUSTUS   O thou art deceived!
MEPHASTOPHILIS   Tut, I warrant thee.   [*Turn to them.*]
FAUSTUS   When I behold the heavens, then I repent,
And curse thee, wicked Mephastophilis,
180   Because thou hast deprived me of those joys.
MEPHASTOPHILIS   Why Faustus,
Think'st thou that heaven is such a glorious thing?
I tell thee 'tis not half so fair as thou,
Or any man that breathes on earth.
185   FAUSTUS   How prov'st thou that?
MEPHASTOPHILIS   It was made for man, therefore is man more excel-
lent.
FAUSTUS   If it were made for man, 'twas made for me:
I will renounce this magic, and repent.
      [*Enter* GOOD ANGEL *and* EVIL ANGEL.]
190   GOOD ANGEL   Faustus, repent, yet° God will pity thee.   *still*
EVIL ANGEL   Thou art a spirit,° God cannot pity thee.   *evil spirit, devil*
FAUSTUS   Who buzzeth in mine ears I am a spirit?
Be I a devil, yet God may pity me.
Ay, God will pity me if I repent.
195   EVIL ANGEL   Ay, but Faustus never shall repent.   [*Exeunt.*]
FAUSTUS   My heart's so hardened[2] I cannot repent!
Scarce can I name salvation, faith, or heaven,
But fearful echoes thunders in mine ears,
"Faustus, thou are damned"; then swords and knives,
200   Poison, guns, halters,° and envenomed steel   *ropes for hanging*
Are laid before me to dispatch myself:
And long ere this I should have slain myself,
Had not sweet pleasure conquered deep despair.
Have I not made blind Homer sing to me
205   Of Alexander's[3] love, and Oenon's death?
And hath not he that built the walls of Thebes
With ravishing sound of his melodious harp,[4]
Made music with my Mephastophilis?
Why should I die then, or basely despair?
210   I am resolved! Faustus shall ne'er repent.
Come, Mephastophilis, let us dispute again,
And argue of divine astrology.
Tell me, are there many heavens above the moon?

---

2. Hardness of heart is the desperate spiritual
state of the reprobate who will suffer eternal damnation.
3. Alexander is another name for Paris, the lover
of Oenone; later he deserted her and abducted
Helen, causing the Trojan War. Oenone refused to

heal the wounds Paris received in battle, and when
he died of them, she killed herself in remorse.
4. The legendary musician Amphion, whose harp
caused stones, of themselves, to form the walls of
Thebes.

Are all celestial bodies but one globe,
215 As is the substance of this centric earth?[5]
MEPHASTOPHILIS   As are the elements, such are the spheres,
Mutually folded in each other's orb.
And, Faustus, all jointly move upon one axletree
Whose termine° is termed the world's wide pole,   *end*
220 Nor are the names of Saturn, Mars, or Jupiter
Feigned, but are erring stars.[6]
FAUSTUS   But tell me, have they all one motion, both *situ et tempore*?[7]
MEPHASTOPHILIS   All jointly move from east to west in four-and-
twenty hours upon the poles of the world, but differ in their motion
225 upon the poles of the zodiac.[8]
FAUSTUS   Tush, these slender trifles Wagner can decide!
Hath Mephastophilis no greater skill?
Who knows not the double motion of the planets?
The first is finished in a natural day, the second thus: as Saturn in
230 thirty years; Jupiter in twelve; Mars in four; the Sun, Venus, and
Mercury in a year; the Moon in twenty-eight days. Tush, these are
freshmen's suppositions. But tell me, hath every sphere a dominion
or *intelligentia*?[9]
MEPHASTOPHILIS   Ay.
235 FAUSTUS   How many heavens or spheres are there?
MEPHASTOPHILIS   Nine: the seven planets, the firmament, and the
empyreal heaven.[1]
FAUSTUS   Well, resolve me then in this question: why have we not
conjunctions, oppositions,[2] aspects, eclipses, all at one time, but in
240 some years we have more, in some less?
MEPHASTOPHILIS   *Per inaequalem motum respectu totius.*[3]
FAUSTUS   Well, I am answered. Tell me who made the world?
MEPHASTOPHILIS   I will not.
FAUSTUS   Sweet Mephastophilis, tell me.
245 MEPHASTOPHILIS   Move° me not, for I will not tell thee.   *anger*
FAUSTUS   Villain, have I not bound thee to tell me anything?
MEPHASTOPHILIS   Ay, that is not against our kingdom; but this is.
Think thou on hell, Faustus, for thou art damned.
FAUSTUS   Think, Faustus, upon God, that made the world.
250 MEPHASTOPHILIS   Remember this.   [*Exit.*]
FAUSTUS   Ay, go accursèd spirit, to ugly hell,
'Tis thou hast damned distressèd Faustus' soul:
Is't not too late?
        [*Enter* GOOD ANGEL *and* EVIL.]
EVIL ANGEL   Too late.
255 GOOD ANGEL   Never too late, if Faustus will repent.
EVIL ANGEL   If thou repent, devils shall tear thee in pieces.

---

5. Faustus asks whether all the apparently different heavenly bodies form really "one globe" like the
earth. Mephastophilis answers that like the elements, which are separate but combined, the heavenly bodies are separate but their spheres are
enfolded and they move on one axletree.
6. It is appropriate to give individual names to Saturn, Mars, Jupiter, and the other planets—which
are called wandering, or "erring" stars. The fixed
stars were in the eighth sphere (the firmament, or
crystalline sphere).
7. In position and time.

8. The common axletree on which all the spheres
revolve.
9. An angel, or intelligence, thought to be the
source of motion in each sphere.
1. The ninth sphere was the immovable empyrean.
2. "Conjunctions": the apparent joinings of two
planets. "Oppositions": when two planets are most
remote.
3. Because of their unequal velocities within the
system.

GOOD ANGEL   Repent, and they shall never raze° thy skin.   tear
    [*Exeunt.*]
FAUSTUS   Ah Christ my Savior! seek to save
Distressèd Faustus' soul!
    [*Enter* LUCIFER, BELZEBUB, *and* MEPHASTOPHILIS.]
260 LUCIFER   Christ cannot save thy soul, for he is just.
There's none but I have interest in the same.
FAUSTUS   O who art thou that look'st so terrible?
LUCIFER   I am Lucifer, and this is my companion prince in hell.
FAUSTUS   O Faustus, they are come to fetch away thy soul!
265 LUCIFER   We come to tell thee thou dost injure us.
Thou talk'st of Christ, contrary to thy promise.
Thou should'st not think of God; think of the devil,
And his dam[4] too.
FAUSTUS   Nor will I henceforth: pardon me in this,
270 And Faustus vows never to look to heaven,
Never to name God, or to pray to him,
To burn his Scriptures, slay his ministers,
And make my spirits pull his churches down.
LUCIFER   Do so, and we will highly gratify thee. Faustus, we are
275 come from hell to show thee some pastime; sit down, and thou shalt
see all the Seven Deadly Sins[5] appear in their proper shapes.
FAUSTUS   That sight will be as pleasing unto me as Paradise was to
Adam, the first day of his creation.
LUCIFER   Talk not of Paradise, nor creation, but mark this show; talk
280 of the devil and nothing else. Come away.
    [*Enter the* SEVEN DEADLY SINS.]
Now Faustus, examine them of their several names and dispositions.
FAUSTUS   What art thou, the first?
PRIDE   I am Pride: I disdain to have any parents. I am like to Ovid's
285 flea,[6] I can creep into every corner of a wench: sometimes like a
periwig, I sit upon her brow; or like a fan of feathers, I kiss her lips.
Indeed I do—what do I not! But fie, what a scent is here? I'll not
speak another word, except the ground were perfumed and covered
with cloth of arras.[7]
290 FAUSTUS   What art thou, the second?
COVETOUSNESS   I am Covetousness, begotten of an old churl in an
old leathern bag; and might I have my wish, I would desire that this
house, and all the people in it, were turned to gold, that I might
lock you up in my good chest. O my sweet gold!
295 FAUSTUS   What art thou, the third?
WRATH   I am Wrath. I had neither father nor mother: I leaped out
of a lion's mouth when I was scarce half an hour old, and ever since
I have run up and down the world, with this case of rapiers, wounding myself when I had nobody to fight withal. I was born in hell—
300 and look to it, for some of you shall be my father.
FAUSTUS   What art thou, the fourth?

---

4. Mother. "The devil and his dam" was a common
colloquial expression.
5. Pride, avarice, lust, anger, gluttony, envy, and
sloth, called deadly because they lead to spirtual
death. All other sins are said to grow out of them
(cf. the procession of the Seven Deadly Sins in

Spenser's *The Faerie Queene* 1.4, stanzas 16–36,
pp. 385–90).
6. A salacious medieval poem *Carmen de Pulice*
(Song of the Flea) was attributed to Ovid.
7. Arras in Flanders exported fine cloth used for
tapestry hangings. "Except": unless.

ENVY   I am Envy, begotten of a chimney-sweeper and an oyster-wife.
I cannot read, and therefore wish all books were burnt; I am lean
with seeing others eat—O that there would come a famine through
305   all the world, that all might die, and I live alone; then thou should'st
see how fat I would be! But must thou sit and I stand? Come down,
with a vengeance!

FAUSTUS   Away, envious rascal! What art thou, the fifth?

GLUTTONY   Who, I sir? I am Gluttony. My parents are all dead, and
310   the devil a penny they have left me but a bare pension, and that is
thirty meals a day and ten bevers[8]—a small trifle to suffice nature.
O, I come of a royal parentage: my grandfather was a gammon[9] of
bacon, my grandmother a hogshead of claret wine; my godfathers
were these: Peter Pickled-Herring, and Martin Martlemas-Beef.[1] O,
315   but my godmother! She was a jolly gentlewoman, and well-beloved
in every good town and city; her name was Mistress Margery March-
Beer.[2] Now, Faustus, thou hast heard all my progeny;[3] wilt thou bid
me to supper?

FAUSTUS   No, I'll see thee hanged; thou wilt eat up all my victuals.

320 GLUTTONY   Then the devil choke thee!

FAUSTUS   Choke thyself, Glutton. What art thou, the sixth?

SLOTH   I am Sloth; I was begotten on a sunny bank, where I have
lain ever since—and you have done me great injury to bring me
from thence. Let me be carried thither again by Gluttony and Lech-
325   ery. I'll not speak another word for a king's ransom.

FAUSTUS   What are you, Mistress Minx, the seventh and last?

LECHERY   Who, I sir? I am one that loves an inch of raw mutton
better than an ell of fried stockfish;[4] and the first letter of my name
begins with Lechery.

330 LUCIFER   Away! To hell, to hell!   [*Exeunt the* SINS.]
Now Faustus, how dost thou like this?

FAUSTUS   O this feeds my soul!

LUCIFER   Tut, Faustus, in hell is all manner of delight.

FAUSTUS   O might I see hell, and return again, how happy were I
335   then!

LUCIFER   Thou shalt; I will send for thee at midnight. In meantime,
take this book, peruse it thoroughly, and thou shalt turn thyself into
what shape thou wilt.

FAUSTUS   Great thanks, mighty Lucifer; this will I keep as chary[5] as
340   my life.

LUCIFER   Farewell, Faustus; and think on the devil.

FAUSTUS   Farewell, great Lucifer; come, Mephastophilis.
                                                 [*Exeunt* OMNES.]

SCENE 6

[*Enter* ROBIN *the ostler*[6] *with a book in his hand.*]

ROBIN   O this is admirable! here I ha' stolen one of Doctor Faustus'
conjuring books, and i'faith I mean to search some circles[7] for my

---

8. Snacks.
9. The lower side of pork, including the leg.
1. Meat, salted to preserve it during the winter,
was prepared around Martinmas (November 11).
2. A rich ale, made in March.
3. Ancestry, lineage.

4. Dried cod. "Mutton": frequently a bawdy term
in Elizabethan English; here, the penis. "Ell": forty-
five inches.
5. Carefully.
6. Hostler, stablehand.
7. Magicians' circles, but with a sexual innuendo.

own use: now will I make all the maidens in our parish dance at my pleasure stark naked before me, and so by that means I shall see
5 more than ere I felt or saw yet.

[*Enter* RAFE *calling* ROBIN.]

RAFE   Robin, prithee come away, there's a gentleman tarries to have his horse, and he would have his things rubbed and made clean. He keeps such a chafing[8] with my mistress about it, and she has sent me to look thee out. Prithee, come away.
10 ROBIN   Keep out, keep out; or else you are blown up, you are dismembered, Rafe. Keep out, for I am about a roaring[9] piece of work.
RAFE   Come, what dost thou with that same book? Thou canst not read!
ROBIN   Yes, my master and mistress shall find that I can read—he
15 for his forehead,[1] she for her private study. She's born to bear with me,[2] or else my art fails.
RAFE   Why Robin, what book is that?
ROBIN   What book? Why the most intolerable[3] book for conjuring that ere was invented by any brimstone devil.
20 RAFE   Canst thou conjure with it?
ROBIN   I can do all these things easily with it: first, I can make thee drunk with 'ipocrase[4] at any tavern in Europe for nothing, that's one of my conjuring works.
RAFE   Our master parson says that's nothing.
25 ROBIN   True, Rafe! And more, Rafe, if thou hast any mind to Nan Spit, our kitchen maid, then turn her and wind her to thy own use, as often as thou wilt, and at midnight.
RAFE   O brave Robin! Shall I have Nan Spit, and to mine own use? On that condition I'll feed thy devil with horsebread as long as he
30 lives, of free cost.[5]
ROBIN   No more, sweet Rafe; let's go and make clean our boots which lie foul upon our hands, and then to our conjuring in the devil's name.   [*Exeunt.*]

CHORUS 2

[*Enter* WAGNER *solus.*]

WAGNER   Learned Faustus,
To know the secrets of astronomy
Graven in the book of Jove's high firmament,
Did mount himself to scale Olympus'[6] top.
5 Being seated in a chariot burning bright,
Drawn by the strength of yokèd dragons' necks.
He now is gone to prove cosmography,[7]
And, as I guess, will first arrive at Rome
To see the pope, and manner of his court,
10 And take some part of holy Peter's feast,[8]
That to this day is highly solemnized.   [*Exit* WAGNER.]

8. Scolding.
9. Dangerous.
1. That is, Robin intends to give his master horns—cuckold him.
2. I.e., bear his weight, or bear him a child.
3. Irresistible.
4. Robin's pronunciation of *hippocras*, a spiced wine.
5. Free of charge. "Horsebread": fodder.
6. The home of the gods in Greek mythology.
7. To test the accuracy of maps.
8. St. Peter's feast is June 29.

SCENE 7

[*Enter* FAUSTUS *and* MEPHASTOPHILIS.]
FAUSTUS   Having now, my good Mephastophilis,
    Passed with delight the stately town of Trier,[9]
    Environed round with airy mountain tops,
    With walls of flint, and deep entrenchèd lakes,°   *moats*
5   Not to be won by any conquering prince;
    From Paris next, coasting° the realm of France,   *traversing*
    We saw the river Main fall into Rhine,
    Whose banks are set with groves of fruitful vines;
    Then up to Naples, rich Campania,
10   With buildings fair and gorgeous to the eye,
    The streets straight forth, and paved with finest brick,
    Quarters the town in four equivalents;
    There saw we learned Maro's[1] golden tomb,
    The way° he cut, an English mile in length,   *tunnel*
15   Thorough a rock of stone in one night's space.
    From thence to Venice, Padua, and the rest,
    In midst of which a sumptuous temple° stands   *St. Mark's in Venice*
    That threats the stars with her aspiring top.
    Thus hitherto hath Faustus spent his time.
20   But tell me now, what resting place is this?
    Hast thou, as erst° I did command,   *earlier*
    Conducted me within the walls of Rome?
MEPHASTOPHILIS   Faustus, I have; and because we will not be unpro-
    vided, I have taken up his holiness' privy chamber for our use.
25 FAUSTUS   I hope his holiness will bid us welcome.
MEPHASTOPHILIS   Tut, 'tis no matter, man, we'll be bold with his
    good cheer.
    And now, my Faustus, that thou may'st perceive
    What Rome containeth to delight thee with,
30   Know that this city stands upon seven hills
    That underprop the groundwork of the same;
    Just through the midst runs flowing Tiber's stream,
    With winding banks, that cut it in two parts;
    Over the which four stately bridges lean,
35   That makes safe passage to each part of Rome.
    Upon the bridge called Ponte Angelo
    Erected is a castle passing strong,[2]
    Within whose walls such store of ordinance are
    And double cannons, framed of carvèd brass,
40   As match the days within one complete year—
    Besides the gates and high pyramides°   *obelisks*
    Which Julius Caesar brought from Africa.
FAUSTUS   Now by the kingdoms of infernal rule,
    Of Styx, Acheron, and the fiery lake
45   Of ever-burning Phlegethon,[3] I swear
    That I do long to see the monuments
    And situation of bright-splendent Rome.

9. Treves (in Prussia).
1. Virgil's. In medieval legend the Roman poet Virgil was considered a magician whose powers produced a tunnel on the promontory of Posilippo at Naples, near his tomb.
2. Actually the castle is on the bank, not the bridge. "Passing": surpassingly.
3. Classical names for rivers of the underworld.

Come therefore, let's away.

MEPHASTOPHILIS   Nay, Faustus, stay. I know you'd fain see the pope,
50   And take some part of holy Peter's feast,
Where thou shalt see a troup of bald-pate friars,
Whose *summum bonum*[4] is in belly-cheer.

FAUSTUS   Well, I am content to compass[5] then some sport,
And by their folly make us merriment.
55   Then charm me that I may be invisible, to do what I please unseen
of any whilst I stay in Rome.

MEPHASTOPHILIS [*casts a spell on him*].   So Faustus, now do what
thou wilt, thou shalt not be discerned.

[*Sound a sennet;*[6] *enter the* POPE *and the* CARDINAL OF LOR-
RAINE *to the banquet, with* FRIARS *attending.*]

POPE   My lord of Lorraine, will't please you draw near.
60   FAUSTUS   Fall to; and the devil choke you and[7] you spare.

POPE   How now, who's that which spake? Friars, look about.

1 FRIAR   Here's nobody, if it like[8] your holiness.

POPE   My lord, here is a dainty dish was sent to me from the bishop
of Milan.
65   FAUSTUS   I thank you, sir.   [*Snatch it.*]

POPE   How now, who's that which snatched the meat from me? Will
no man look? My lord, this dish was sent me from the cardinal of
Florence.

FAUSTUS   You say true? I'll have't.   [*Snatch it.*]
70   POPE   What, again! My lord, I'll drink to your grace.

FAUSTUS   I'll pledge your grace.   [*Snatch the cup.*]

LORRAINE   My lord, it may be some ghost newly crept out of purgatory come to beg a pardon of your holiness.

POPE   It may be so; friars; prepare a dirge[9] to lay the fury of this ghost.
75   Once again my lord, fall to.   [*The* POPE *crosseth himself.*]

FAUSTUS   What, are you crossing of your self? Well, use that trick no
more, I would advise you.

[*Cross again.*]

FAUSTUS   Well, there's the second time; aware the third! I give you
fair warning.

[*Cross again, and* FAUSTUS *hits him a box of the ear, and they
all run away.*]
80   FAUSTUS   Come on, Mephastophilis, what shall we do?

MEPHASTOPHILIS   Nay, I know not; we shall be cursed with bell,
book, and candle.[1]

FAUSTUS   How! Bell, book, and candle; candle, book, and bell,
Forward and backward, to curse Faustus to hell.
85   Anon you shall hear a hog grunt, a calf bleat, and an ass bray,
Because it is St. Peter's holy day.

[*Enter all the* FRIARS *to sing the Dirge.*]

1 FRIAR   Come brethren, let's about our business with good devotion.

[*Sing this.*]

---

4. The greatest good; often refers to God.
5. Take part in.
6. A set of notes on the trumpet or cornet.
7. If. "Fall to": get on with it.
8. Please.

9. A requiem mass. But what actually follows is a
litany of curses. "Pledge": toast.
1. The traditional paraphernalia for cursing and
excommunication.

Cursed be he that stole away his holiness' meat from the table.
90   Maledicat Dominus.[2]
Cursed be he that struck his holiness a blow on the face.
    Maledicat Dominus.
Cursed be he that took Friar Sandelo a blow on the pate.
    Maledicat Dominus.
95   Cursed be he that disturbeth our holy dirge.
    Maledicat Dominus.
Cursed be he that took away his holiness' wine.
    Maledicat dominus.
        Et omnes sancti.[3] Amen.
    [Beat the FRIARS, and fling fireworks among them, and so Exeunt.]

SCENE 8

[Enter ROBIN and RAFE with a silver goblet.]

ROBIN   Come, Rafe, did not I tell thee we were forever made by this
    Doctor Faustus' book? Ecce signum![4] Here's a simple purchase for
    horsekeepers: our horses shall eat no hay as long as this lasts.
    [Enter the VINTNER.]
RAFE   But Robin, here comes the vintner.
5 ROBIN   Hush, I'll gull him supernaturally! Drawer,[5] I hope all is paid;
    God be with you. Come, Rafe.
VINTNER   Soft, sir, a word with you. I must yet have a goblet paid
    from you ere you go.
ROBIN   I, a goblet, Rafe? I, a goblet? I scorn you: and you are but a
10   &c.[6] . . . I, a goblet? Search me.
VINTNER   I mean so, sir, with your favor.   [Searches ROBIN.]
ROBIN   How say you now?
VINTNER   I must say somewhat to your fellow; you, sir!
RAFE   Me, sir? Me, sir? Search your fill. Now sir, you may be ashamed
15   to burden honest men with a matter of truth.
VINTNER [searches RAFE]   Well, t'one of you hath this goblet about
    you.
ROBIN   You lie, drawer; 'tis afore me. Sirra you, I'll teach ye to
    impeach honest men: [to RAFE] stand by. [to the VINTNER] I'll scour
20   you for a goblet—stand aside, you were best—I charge you in the
    name of Belzebub—look to the goblet, Rafe!
VINTNER   What mean you, sirra?
ROBIN   I'll tell you what I mean: [he reads] Sanctobulorum Periphras-
    ticon—nay, I'll tickle you, vintner—look to the goblet, Rafe—Poly-
25   pragmos Belseborams framanto pacostiphos tostis Mephastophilis,
    &c. . . .[7]
        [Enter MEPHASTOPHILIS: sets squibs[8] at their backs: they run
        about.]
VINTNER   O nomine Domine![9] What mean'st thou, Robin? Thou hast
    no goblet.
RAFE   Peccatum peccatorum![1] Here's thy goblet, good vintner.

---

2. May the Lord curse him.
3. And all the saints (also curse him).
4. Behold the proof.
5. Wine-drawer. "Gull": trick.
6. The actor might ad lib abuse at this point.
7. Dog-Latin, as Robin attempts to conjure from Faustus's book.

8. Firecrackers. Evidently Mephastophilis is on stage only long enough to set off the firecrackers and is not seen by Robin, Rafe, or the Vintner. He then reenters at line 32.
9. In the name of the Lord; the Latin invocations are used in swearing.
1. Sin of sins!

30 ROBIN   *Misericordia pro nobis*![2] What shall I do? Good devil, forgive
        me now, and I'll never rob thy library more.
        [*Enter to them* MEPHASTOPHILIS.]
    MEPHASTOPHILIS   Vanish, villains, th'one like an ape, another like a
        bear, the third an ass, for doing this enterprise.   [*Exit* VINTNER.]
        Monarch of hell, under whose black survey
35   Great potentates do kneel with awful fear;
        Upon whose altars thousand souls do lie;
        How am I vexèd with these villains' charms!
        From Constantinople am I hither come,
        Only for pleasure of these damnèd slaves.
40 ROBIN   How, from Constantinople? You have had a great journey!
        Will you take sixpence in your purse to pay for your supper, and be
        gone?
    MEPHASTOPHILIS   Well, villains, for your presumption, I transform
        thee into an ape, and thee into a dog; and so begone!   [*Exit.*]
45 ROBIN   How, into an ape? That's brave: I'll have fine sport with the
        boys; I'll get nuts and apples enow.[3]
    RAFE   And I must be a dog.
    ROBIN   I'faith, thy head will never be out of the potage[4] pot.
                                         [*Exeunt.*]

CHORUS 3

[*Enter* CHORUS.[5]]
CHORUS   When Faustus had with pleasure ta'en the view
        Of rarest things, and royal courts of kings,
        He stayed his course, and so returnèd home;
        Where such as bare his absence but with grief—
5   I mean his friends and nearest companions—
        Did gratulate his safety with kind words.
        And in their conference of what befell,
        Touching his journey through the world and air,
        They put forth questions of astrology,
10   Which Faustus answered with such learnèd skill,
        As they admired and wondered at his wit.
        Now is his fame spread forth in every land:
        Amongst the rest the emperor is one,
        Carolus the Fifth,[6] at whose palace now
15   Faustus is feasted 'mongst his noblemen.
        What there he did in trial of his art
        I leave untold: your eyes shall see performed.   [*Exit.*]

SCENE 9

[*Enter* EMPEROR, FAUSTUS, *and a* KNIGHT, *with Attendants.*]
EMPEROR   Master Doctor Faustus, I have heard strange report of thy
        knowledge in the black art, how that none in my empire, nor in the
        whole world, can compare with thee for the rare effects of magic.
        They say thou hast a familiar spirit, by whom thou canst accomplish
5   what thou list! This therefore is my request: that thou let me see

---

2. Have mercy on us!
3. Enough. "Brave": splendid.
4. Porridge.

5. I.e., Wagner.
6. The Holy Roman Emperor Charles V (reigned
1519–1556).

some proof of thy skill, that mine eyes may be witnesses to confirm
what mine ears have heard reported. And here I swear to thee, by
the honor of mine imperial crown, that whatever thou dost, thou
shalt be in no ways prejudiced or endamaged.

10 KNIGHT [*aside*] I'faith, he looks much like a conjuror.

FAUSTUS My gracious sovereign, though I must confess myself far
inferior to the report men have published, and nothing answerable
to the honor of your imperial majesty, yet for that love and duty
binds me thereunto, I am content to do whatsoever your majesty

15 shall command me.

EMPEROR Then Doctor Faustus, mark what I shall say. As I was
sometime solitary set within my closet,[7] sundry thoughts arose
about the honor of mine ancestors—how they had won by prowess
such exploits, got such riches, subdued so many kingdoms, as we

20 that do succeed, or they that shall hereafter possess our throne,
shall (I fear me) never attain to that degree of high renown and
great authority. Amongst which kings is Alexander the Great,[8] chief
spectacle of the world's pre-eminence:
The bright shining of whose glorious acts

25 Lightens the world with his reflecting beams;
As when I hear but motion° made of him,   *mention*
It grieves my soul I never saw the man.
If therefore thou, by cunning of thine art,
Canst raise this man from hollow vaults below,

30 Where lies entombed this famous conqueror,
And bring with him his beauteous paramour,[9]
Both in their right shapes, gesture, and attire
They used to wear during their time of life,
Thou shalt both satisfy my just desire,

35 And give me cause to praise thee whilst I live.

FAUSTUS My gracious lord, I am ready to accomplish your request,
so far forth as by art and power of my spirit I am able to perform.

KNIGHT [*aside*] I'faith, that's just nothing at all.

FAUSTUS But, if it like your grace, it is not in my ability to present

40 before your eyes the true substantial bodies of those two deceased
princes, which long since are consumed to dust.

KNIGHT [*aside*] Ay, marry,[1] master doctor, now there's a sign of grace
in you, when you will confess the truth.

FAUSTUS But such spirits as can lively resemble Alexander and his

45 paramour shall appear before your grace, in that manner that they
best lived in, in their most flourishing estate: which I doubt not
shall sufficiently content your imperial majesty.

EMPEROR Go to, master doctor, let me see them presently.[2]

KNIGHT Do you hear, master doctor? You bring Alexander and his

50 paramour before the emperor!

FAUSTUS How then, sir?

KNIGHT I'faith, that's as true as Diana turned me to a stag.

FAUSTUS No sir; but when Actaeon died, he left the horns[3] for you!
Mephastophilis, begone!   [*Exit* MEPHASTOPHILIS.]

---

7. Private chamber.
8. The emperor traces his ancestry to the great
world conqueror (356–323 B.C.E.).
9. Probably Roxana, Alexander's wife.
1. To be sure.
2. Immediately.

3. Horns were traditionally a sign of the cuckolded
husband (cf. Scene 6, lines 14–15). "Actaeon": the
hunter of classical legend who happened to see the
goddess Diana bathing. For punishment he was
changed into a stag; he was then chased and killed
by his own hounds.

55   KNIGHT   Nay, and[4] you go to conjuring I'll be gone. [*Exit* KNIGHT.]
     FAUSTUS   I'll meet with you anon for interrupting me so. Here they
     are, my gracious lord.
              [*Enter* MEPHASTOPHILIS *with* ALEXANDER *and his* PARAMOUR.]
     EMPEROR   Master doctor, I heard this lady, while she lived, had a
     wart or mole in her neck; how shall I know whether it be so or no?
60   FAUSTUS   Your highness may boldly go and see.
              [*The* EMPEROR *examines the lady's neck.*]
     EMPEROR   Sure, these are no spirits, but the true substantial bodies
     of those two deceased princes.
              [*Exit* ALEXANDER (*and his* PARAMOUR).]
     FAUSTUS   Will't please your highness now to send for the knight that
     was so pleasant with me here of late?
65   EMPEROR   One of you call him forth.
              [*Enter the* KNIGHT *with a pair of horns on his head.*]
     EMPEROR   How now, sir knight? Why, I had thought thou hadst
     been a bachelor, but now I see thou hast a wife that not only gives
     thee horns but makes thee wear them! Feel on thy head.
     KNIGHT   Thou damnèd wretch and execrable dog,
70   Bred in the concave of some monstrous rock,
     How dar'st thou thus abuse a gentleman?
     Villain, I say, undo what thou hast done.
     FAUSTUS   O not so fast, sir, there's no haste but good. Are you
     remembered[5] how you crossed me in my conference with the
75   emperor? I think I have met with[6] you for it.
     EMPEROR   Good master doctor, at my entreaty release him; he hath
     done penance sufficient.
     FAUSTUS   My gracious lord, not so much for the injury he offered me
     here in your presence as to delight you with some mirth, hath Faus-
80   tus worthily requited this injurious knight; which being all I desire,
     I am content to release him of his horns. And, sir knight, hereafter
     speak well of scholars: Mephastophilis, transform him straight.[7]
     Now, my good lord, having done my duty, I humbly take my leave.
     EMPEROR   Farewell, master doctor; yet ere you go, expect from me a
85   bounteous reward.
              [*Exit* EMPEROR (*and his* ATTENDANTS).]
     FAUSTUS   Now, Mephastophilis, the restless course
     That time doth run with calm and silent foot,
     Shortening my days and thread of vital life,
     Calls for the payment of my latest years;
90   Therefore, sweet Mephastophilis, let us make haste to Wittenberg.
     MEPHASTOPHILIS   What, will you go on horseback or on foot?
     FAUSTUS   Nay, till I am past this fair and pleasant green, I'll walk on
     foot.

SCENE 10

              [*Enter a* HORSE-COURSER.[8]]
     HORSE-COURSER   I have been all this day seeking one Master Fus-
     tian: 'mass,[9] see where he is! God save you, master doctor.

---

4. If.
5. Have you forgotten. "No haste but good": a
proverb: no point hurrying, unless it's to good
effect.
6. Been revenged upon.

7. Immediately.
8. Horse trader, traditionally a sharp bargainer or
cheat.
9. By the Mass. "Fustian": the horse-courser's
mispronunciation of Faustus's name.

FAUSTUS   What, horse-courser: you are well met.

HORSE-COURSER   Do you hear, sir; I have brought you forty dollars[1]
5   for your horse.

FAUSTUS   I cannot sell him so: if thou lik'st him for fifty, take him.

HORSE-COURSER   Alas sir, I have no more. I pray you speak for me.

MEPHASTOPHILIS   I pray you let him have him; he is an honest fellow,
and he has a great charge[2]—neither wife nor child.

10 FAUSTUS   Well, come, give me your money; my boy will deliver him
to you. But I must tell you one thing before you have him: ride him
not into the water at any hand.

HORSE-COURSER   Why sir, will he not drink of all waters?

FAUSTUS   O yes, he will drink of all waters, but ride him not into the
15   water. Ride him over hedge or ditch, or where thou wilt, but not
into the water.

HORSE-COURSER   Well sir. Now am I made man forever: I'll not leave
my horse for forty! If he had but the quality of hey ding ding, hey
ding ding,[3] I'd make a brave living on him! He has a buttock as slick
20   as an eel. Well, God b'y,[4] sir; your boy will deliver him me. But hark
ye sir, if my horse be sick, or ill at ease, if I bring his water[5] to you,
you'll tell me what it is?

              [*Exit* HORSE-COURSER.]

FAUSTUS   Away, you villain! What, dost think I am a horse-doctor?
What art thou, Faustus, but a man condemned to die?
25   Thy fatal time doth draw to final end.
Despair doth drive distrust unto my thoughts:
Confound these passions with a quiet sleep.
Tush, Christ did call the thief upon the cross;[6]
Then rest thee, Faustus, quiet in conceit.°   *in mind*

              [*Sleep in his chair.*]

      [*Enter* HORSE-COURSER *all wet, crying.*]

30 HORSE-COURSER   Alas, alas, Doctor Fustian, quoth 'a: 'mass, Doctor
Lopus[7] was never such a doctor! H'as given me a purgation, h'as
purged me of forty dollars! I shall never see them more. But yet,
like an ass as I was, I would not be ruled by him; for he bade me I
should ride him into no water. Now I, thinking my horse had had
35   some rare quality that he would not have had me known of, I, like
a vent'rous youth, rid him into the deep pond at the town's end. I
was no sooner in the middle of the pond, but my horse vanished
away, and I sat upon a bottle[8] of hay, never so near drowning in my
life! But I'll seek out my doctor, and have my forty dollars again, or
40   I'll make it the dearest[9] horse. O, yonder is his snipper-snapper! Do
you hear, you hey-pass,[1] where's your master?

MEPHASTOPHILIS   Why, sir, what would you? You cannot speak with
him.

HORSE-COURSER   But I will speak with him.

45 MEPHASTOPHILIS   Why, he's fast asleep; come some other time.

---

1. Common German coins.
2. Burden.
3. I.e., he wishes his horse were a stallion, not a gelding, so he could put him to stud.
4. Good-bye (contracted from "God be with you").
5. Urine.
6. In Luke 23.39–43 one of the two thieves crucified with Jesus is promised paradise.

7. In February 1594 Roderigo Lopez, the queen's personal physician, was executed for plotting to poison her. Obviously Marlowe, who died in 1593, did not write the line.
8. Bundle.
9. Most expensive.
1. A conjurer's phrase. "Snipper-snapper": insignificant youth, whipper-snapper.

HORSE-COURSER   I'll speak with him now, or I'll break his glass-
windows[2] about his ears.
MEPHASTOPHILIS   I tell thee, he has not slept this eight nights.
HORSE-COURSER   And he have not slept this eight weeks I'll speak
50   with him.
MEPHASTOPHILIS   See where he is, fast asleep.
HORSE-COURSER   Ay, this is he; God save ye master doctor, master
doctor, master Doctor Fustian, forty dollars, forty dollars for a bottle
of hay.
55   MEPHASTOPHILIS   Why, thou seest he hears thee not.
HORSE-COURSER   So ho ho; so ho ho.[3] [halloo in his ear] No, will you
not wake? I'll make you wake ere I go. [pull him by the leg, and pull
it away] Alas, I am undone! What shall I do?
FAUSTUS   O my leg, my leg! Help, Mephastophilis! Call the officers!
60   My leg, my leg!
MEPHASTOPHILIS   Come villain, to the constable.
HORSE-COURSER   O Lord, sir! Let me go, and I'll give you forty dollars
more.
MEPHASTOPHILIS   Where be they?
65   HORSE-COURSER   I have none about me: come to my ostry[4] and I'll
give them you.
MEPHASTOPHILIS   Begone quickly!
[HORSE-COURSER runs away.]
FAUSTUS   What, is he gone? Farewell he: Faustus has his leg again,
and the horse-courser—I take it—a bottle of hay for his labor! Well,
70   this trick shall cost him forty dollars more.
[Enter WAGNER.]
How now, Wagner, what's the news with thee?
WAGNER   Sir, the Duke of Vanholt doth earnestly entreat your company.
FAUSTUS   The Duke of Vanholt! An honorable gentleman, to whom
75   I must be no niggard of my cunning. Come, Mephastophilis, let's
away to him.   [Exeunt.]

SCENE 11

[FAUSTUS and MEPHASTOPHILIS return to the stage. Enter to
them the DUKE and the DUCHESS; the DUKE speaks.]
DUKE   Believe me, master doctor, this merriment hath much pleased
me.
FAUSTUS   My gracious Lord, I am glad it contents you so well: but it
may be, madam, you take no delight in this; I have heard that great-
5   bellied women do long for some dainties or other—what is it,
madam? Tell me, and you shall have it.
DUCHESS   Thanks, good master doctor; and for I see your courteous
intent to pleasure me, I will not hide from you the thing my heart
desires. And were it now summer, as it is January and the dead of
10   winter, I would desire no better meat than a dish of ripe grapes.
FAUSTUS   Alas madam, that's nothing! Mephastophilis, begone! [Exit
MEPHASTOPHILIS.] Were it a greater thing than this, so it would

2. Spectacles.   4. Hostelry, inn.
3. The huntsman's cry, when he sights the quarry.

content you, you should have it. [*Enter* MEPHASTOPHILIS *with the grapes.*] Here they be, madam; will't please you taste on them?

15   DUKE   Believe me, master doctor, this makes me wonder above the rest: that being in the dead time of winter, and in the month of January, how you should come by these grapes?

      FAUSTUS   If it like your grace, the year is divided into two circles over the whole world, that when it is here winter with us, in the contrary
20   circle it is summer with them, as in India, Saba,[5] and farther countries in the east; and by means of a swift spirit that I have, I had them brought hither, as ye see. How do you like them, madam; be they good?

      DUCHESS   Believe me, master doctor, they be the best grapes that ere
25   I tasted in my life before.

      FAUSTUS   I am glad they content you so, madam.

      DUKE   Come madam, let us in, where you must well reward this learned man for the great kindness he hath showed to you.

      DUCHESS   And so I will, my lord; and whilst I live, rest beholding for
30   this courtesy.

      FAUSTUS   I humbly thank your grace.

      DUKE   Come, master doctor, follow us, and receive your reward.

                                             [*Exeunt.*]

CHORUS 4

[*Enter* WAGNER *solus.*]

WAGNER   I think my master means to die shortly,
      For he hath given to me all his goods!
      And yet methinks, if that death were near,
      He would not banquet, and carouse, and swill
5   Amongst the students, as even now he doth,
      Who are at supper with such belly-cheer
      As Wagner ne'er beheld in all his life.
      See where they come: belike the feast is ended.

                                               [*Exit.*]

SCENE 12

[*Enter* FAUSTUS (*and* MEPHASTOPHILIS), *with two or three* SCHOLARS.]

1 SCHOLAR   Master Doctor Faustus, since our conference about fair ladies, which was the beautifulest in all the world, we have determined with ourselves that Helen of Greece was the admirablest lady that ever lived. Therefore, master doctor, if you will do us that favor
5   as to let us see that peerless dame of Greece, whom all the world admires for majesty, we should think ourselves much beholding unto you.

      FAUSTUS   Gentlemen, for that I know your friendship is unfeigned,
      And Faustus' custom is not to deny
10   The just requests of those that wish him well,
      You shall behold that peerless dame of Greece,
      No otherways for pomp and majesty
      Than when Sir Paris crossed the seas with her

5. Sheba, Yemen.

And brought the spoils to rich Dardania.°   *Troy*

15   Be silent then, for danger is in words.
          [*Music sounds, and* HELEN *passeth over the stage.*]
    2 SCHOLAR   Too simple is my wit to tell her praise,
      Whom all the world admires for majesty.
    3 SCHOLAR   No marvel though the angry Greeks pursued
      With ten years' war the rape of such a queen,
20   Whose heavenly beauty passeth all compare.
    1 SCHOLAR   Since we have seen the pride of Nature's works
      And only paragon of excellence,
      Let us depart; and for this glorious deed
      Happy and blest be Faustus evermore.
25 FAUSTUS   Gentlemen farewell; the same I wish to you.
                           [*Exeunt* SCHOLARS.]
         [*Enter an* OLD MAN.]
    OLD MAN   Ah Doctor Faustus, that I might prevail
      To guide thy steps unto the way of life,
      By which sweet path thou may'st attain the goal
      That shall conduct thee to celestial rest.
30   Break heart, drop blood, and mingle it with tears,
      Tears falling from repentant heaviness
      Of thy most vile and loathsome filthiness,
      The stench whereof corrupts the inward soul
      With such flagitious° crimes of heinous sins,   *villainous*
35   As no commiseration may expel
      But mercy, Faustus, of thy savior sweet,
      Whose blood alone must wash away thy guilt.
    FAUSTUS   Where art thou, Faustus? Wretch, what hast thou done!
      Damned art thou, Faustus, damned; despair and die!
40   Hell calls for right, and with a roaring voice
      Says, "Faustus, come: thine hour is come!"
          [MEPHASTOPHILIS *gives him a dagger.*]
      And Faustus will come to do thee right.
    OLD MAN   Ah stay, good Faustus, stay thy desperate steps!
      I see an angel hovers o'er thy head
45   And with a vial full of precious grace
      Offers to pour the same into thy soul!
      Then call for mercy, and avoid despair.
    FAUSTUS   Ah my sweet friend, I feel thy words
      To comfort my distressed soul;
50   Leave me awhile to ponder on my sins.
    OLD MAN   I go, sweet Faustus; but with heavy cheer,°   *i.e., heavy heart*
      Fearing the ruin of thy hopeless soul.   [*Exit.*]
    FAUSTUS   Accursèd Faustus, where is mercy now?
      I do repent, and yet I do despair:
55   Hell strives with grace for conquest in my breast!
      What shall I do to shun the snares of death?
    MEPHASTOPHILIS   Thou traitor, Faustus: I arrest thy soul
      For disobedience to my sovereign lord.
      Revolt,[6] or I'll in piecemeal tear thy flesh.
60 FAUSTUS   Sweet Mephastophilis, entreat thy lord
      To pardon my unjust presumptiön;

6. Turn back (to your allegiance to Lucifer).

And with my blood again I will confirm
My former vow I made to Lucifer.
MEPHASTOPHILIS   Do it then quickly, with unfeignèd heart,
65   Lest greater danger do attend thy drift.°   *intent*
FAUSTUS   Torment, sweet friend, that base and crooked age
That durst dissuade me from thy Lucifer,
With greatest torments that our hell affords.
MEPHASTOPHILIS   His faith is great, I cannot touch his soul,
70   But what I may afflict his body with
I will attempt—which is but little worth.
FAUSTUS   One thing, good servant, let me crave of thee,
To glut the longing of my heart's desire:
That I might have unto my paramour
75   That heavenly Helen which I saw of late,
Whose sweet embracings may extinguish clean
These thoughts that do dissuade me from my vow:
And keep mine oath I made to Lucifer.
MEPHASTOPHILIS   Faustus, this, or what else thou shalt desire,
80   Shall be performed in twinkling of an eye.
            [*Enter* HELEN.]
FAUSTUS   Was this the face that launched a thousand ships,
And burnt the topless[7] towers of Ilium?°   *Troy*
Sweet Helen, make me immortal with a kiss:
Her lips sucks forth my soul, see where it flies!
85   Come Helen, come, give me my soul again.
Here will I dwell, for heaven be in these lips,
And all is dross that is not Helena!
            [*Enter* OLD MAN.]
I will be Paris, and for love of thee,
Instead of Troy shall Wittenberg be sacked;
90   And I will combat with weak Menelaus,°   *Helen's husband*
And wear thy colors on my plumèd crest:
Yea, I will wound Achilles in the heel,[8]
And then return to Helen for a kiss.
O thou art fairer than the evening air,
95   Clad in the beauty of a thousand stars,
Brighter art thou than flaming Jupiter
When he appeared to hapless Semele;[9]
More lovely than the monarch of the sky
In wanton Arethusa's azured arms;[1]
100   And none but thou shalt be my paramour.
            [*Exeunt* (FAUSTUS *and* HELEN).]
OLD MAN   Accursèd Faustus, miserable man,
That from thy soul exclud'st the grace of heaven
And fliest the throne of His tribunal seat!
            [*Enter the* DEVILS.]
Satan begins to sift me with his pride,[2]

---

7. So high they seemed to have no tops.
8. Achilles could only be wounded in his heel—
where he was shot by Paris.
9. A Theban girl, loved by Jupiter and destroyed
by the fire of his lightning when he appeared to her
in his full splendor.

1. Arethusa was the nymph of a fountain, as well
as the fountain itself; she excited the passion of
the river god Alpheus, who was by some accounts
related to the sun.
2. To test me with his strength.

105   As in this furnace God shall try my faith.
       My faith, vile hell, shall triumph over thee!
       Ambitious fiends, see how the heavens smiles
       At your repulse, and laughs your state° to scorn.   *royal power*
       Hence hell, for hence I fly unto my God.   [*Exeunt.*]

SCENE 13

[*Enter* FAUSTUS *with the* SCHOLARS.]

FAUSTUS   Ah, gentlemen!

1 SCHOLAR   What ails Faustus?

FAUSTUS   Ah, my sweet chamber-fellow, had I lived with thee, then had I lived still; but now I die eternally. Look, comes he not, comes
5   he not?

2 SCHOLAR   What means Faustus?

3 SCHOLAR   Belike he is grown into some sickness by being over-solitary.

1 SCHOLAR   If it be so, we'll have physicians to cure him; 'tis but a
10   surfeit:[3] never fear, man.

FAUSTUS   A surfeit of deadly sin, that hath damned both body and soul.

2 SCHOLAR   Yet Faustus, look up to heaven; remember God's mercies are infinite.

15 FAUSTUS   But Faustus' offense can ne'er be pardoned! The serpent that tempted Eve may be saved, but not Faustus. Ah gentlemen, hear me with patience, and tremble not at my speeches, though my heart pants and quivers to remember that I have been a student here these thirty years—O would I had never seen Wittenberg,
20   never read book—and what wonders I have done, all Wittenberg can witness—yea, all the world; for which Faustus hath lost both Germany and the world—yea, heaven itself—heaven, the seat of God, the throne of the blessed, the kingdom of joy; and must remain in hell forever—hell, ah, hell forever! Sweet friends, what shall
25   become of Faustus, being in hell forever?

3 SCHOLAR   Yet Faustus, call on God.

FAUSTUS   On God, whom Faustus hath abjured? On God, whom Faustus hath blasphemed? Ah my God—I would weep, but the devil draws in my tears! gush forth blood, instead of tears—yea, life and
30   soul! O, he stays my tongue! I would lift up my hands, but see, they hold them, they hold them!

ALL   Who, Faustus?

FAUSTUS   Lucifer and Mephastophilis! Ah gentlemen, I gave them my soul for my cunning.

35 ALL   God forbid!

FAUSTUS   God forbade it indeed, but Faustus hath done it: for the vain pleasure of four-and-twenty years hath Faustus lost eternal joy and felicity. I writ them a bill with mine own blood, the date is expired, the time will come, and he will fetch me.

40 1 SCHOLAR   Why did not Faustus tell us of this before, that divines might have prayed for thee?

FAUSTUS   Oft have I thought to have done so, but the devil threatened to tear me in pieces if I named God, to fetch both body and

---

3. Indigestion caused by overeating.

soul, if I once gave ear to divinity; and now 'tis too late. Gentlemen
45 away, lest you perish with me!

2 SCHOLAR   O what shall we do to save Faustus?

3 SCHOLAR   God will strengthen me. I will stay with Faustus.

1 SCHOLAR   Tempt not God, sweet friend, but let us into the next
room, and there pray for him.

50 FAUSTUS   Ay, pray for me, pray for me; and what noise soever ye hear,
come not unto me, for nothing can rescue me.

2 SCHOLAR   Pray thou, and we will pray, that God may have mercy
upon thee.

FAUSTUS   Gentlemen, farewell. If I live till morning, I'll visit you; if
55 not, Faustus is gone to hell.

ALL   Faustus, farewell.   [*Exeunt* SCHOLARS.]
       [*The clock strikes eleven.*]

FAUSTUS   Ah Faustus,
Now hast thou but one bare hour to live,
And then thou must be damned perpetually.
60 Stand still, you ever-moving spheres of heaven,
That time may cease, and midnight never come.
Fair Nature's eye, rise, rise again, and make
Perpetual day, or let this hour be but
A year, a month, a week, a natural day,
65 That Faustus may repent and save his soul.
O lente, lente currite noctis equi![4]
The stars move still, time runs, the clock will strike,
The devil will come, and Faustus must be damned.
O I'll leap up to my God! Who pulls me down?
70 See, see where Christ's blood streams in the firmament!
One drop would save my soul, half a drop: ah my Christ—
Ah, rend not my heart for naming of my Christ;
Yet will I call on him—O spare me, Lucifer!
Where is it now? 'Tis gone: and see where God
75 Stretcheth out his arm, and bends his ireful brows!
Mountains and hills, come, come and fall on me,
And hide me from the heavy wrath of God.
No, no?
Then will I headlong run into the earth:
80 Earth, gape! O no, it will not harbor me.
You stars that reigned at my nativity,
Whose influence hath allotted death and hell,
Now draw up Faustus like a foggy mist
Into the entrails of yon laboring cloud,
85 That when you vomit forth into the air
My limbs may issue from your smoky mouths,
So that my soul may but ascend to heaven.[5]
       [*The watch strikes.*]
Ah, half the hour is past: 'twill all be past anon.
O God, if thou wilt not have mercy on my soul,
90 Yet for Christ's sake, whose blood hath ransomed me,
Impose some end to my incessant pain:

---

4. Slowly, slowly run, O horses of the night; adapted from a line in Ovid's *Amores*.
5. Faustus wants to be drawn up into a cloud, which would compact his body into a thunderstone so that his soul, thus purified, might ascend to heaven.

Let Faustus live in hell a thousand years,
A hundred thousand, and at last be saved.
O no end is limited to damnèd souls!
95 Why wert thou not a creature wanting soul?
Or why is this immortal that thou hast?
Ah, Pythagoras' *metempsychosis*[6]—were that true,
This soul should fly from me, and I be changed
Unto some brutish beast:
100 All beasts are happy, for when they die,
Their souls are soon dissolved in elements;
But mine must live still° to be plagued in hell.   *always*
Cursed be the parents that engendered me:
No, Faustus, curse thy self, curse Lucifer,
105 That hath deprived thee of the joys of heaven.
        [*The clock striketh twelve.*]
O it strikes, it strikes! Now body, turn to air,
Or Lucifer will bear thee quick° to hell.   *alive*
        [*Thunder and lightning.*]
O soul, be changed into little water drops,
And fall into the ocean, ne'er be found.
110 My God, my God, look not so fierce on me!
        [*Enter* DEVILS.]
Adders and serpents, let me breathe awhile!
Ugly hell gape not! Come not, Lucifer!
I'll burn my books—ah, Mephastophilis!
        [*Exeunt with him.*]

Epilogue

[*Enter* CHORUS.]
Cut is the branch that might have grown full straight,
And burnèd is Apollo's laurel bough,[7]
That sometime grew within this learnèd man.
Faustus is gone! Regard his hellish fall,
5   Whose fiendful fortune° may exhort the wise   *devilish fate*
Only to wonder at[8] unlawful things:
Whose deepness doth entice such forward wits
To practice more than heavenly power permits.   [*Exit.*]

Terminat hora diem, terminat author opus.[9]

1604, 1616

---

6. Pythagoras's doctrine of the transmigration of souls.
7. The laurel crown of Apollo symbolizes (among other things) learning and wisdom.

8. Be content simply to observe with awe.
9. The hour ends the day, the author ends his work; this motto was probably added by the printer.

WILLIAM SHAKESPEARE
1564–1616

William Shakespeare was born in the small market town of Stratford-on-Avon in April (probably April 23) 1564. His father, a successful glovemaker, landowner, money-lender, and dealer in agricultural commodities, was elected to several important posts in local government but later suffered financial and social reverses, possibly as a result of adherence to the Catholic faith. Shakespeare almost certainly attended the free Stratford grammar school, where he could have acquired a reasonably impressive education, including a respectable knowledge of Latin, but he did not proceed to Oxford or Cambridge. There are legends about Shakespeare's youth but no docu-mented facts. The first record we have of his life after his christening is that of his marriage in 1582, at age eighteen, to Anne Hathaway, eight years his senior. A daugh-ter, Susanna, was born six months later, in 1583, and twins, Hamnet and Judith, in 1585. We possess no information about his activities for the next seven years, but by 1592 he was in London as an actor and apparently already well known as a playwright, for a rival dramatist, Robert Greene, refers to him resentfully in *A Groatsworth of Wit* as "an upstart crow, beautified with our feathers."

At this time, there were several companies of professional actors in London and in the provinces. What connection Shakespeare had with one or more of them before 1592 is conjectural, but we do know of his long and fruitful connection with the most successful troupe, the Lord Chamberlain's Men, who later, when James I came to the throne, became the King's Men. Shakespeare not only acted with this company but eventually became a leading shareholder and the principal playwright. Then as now, making a living in the professional theater was not easy: competition among the repertoire companies was stiff, civic officials and religious moralists regarded play-acting as a sinful, time-wasting nuisance and tried to ban it altogether, government officials exercised censorship over the contents of the plays, and periodic outbreaks of bubonic plague led to temporary closing of the London theaters. But Shakespeare's company, which included some of the most famous actors of the day, nonetheless thrived and in 1599 began to perform in the Globe, a fine, open-air theater that the company built for itself on the south bank of the Thames. The company also per-formed frequently at court and, after 1608, at Blackfriars, an indoor London theater. Already by 1597 Shakespeare had so prospered that he was able to purchase New Place, a handsome house in Stratford; he could now call himself a gentleman, as his father had (probably with the financial assistance of his successful playwright son) been granted a coat of arms the previous year.

Shakespeare himself evidently had no interest in preserving for posterity the sum of his writings, let alone in clarifying the chronology of his works or in specifying which plays he wrote alone and which with collaborators. He wrote plays for perfor-mance by his company, and his scripts existed in his own handwritten manuscripts or in scribal copies, in playhouse prompt books, and probably in pirated texts based on shorthand reports of a performance or on reconstructions from memory by an actor or spectator. None of these manuscript versions has survived. Eighteen of his plays were published during his lifetime in the small-format, inexpensive books called quartos; to these were added eighteen other plays, never before printed, in the large, expensive folio volume of *Mr. William Shakespeares Comedies, Histories, & Tragedies* (1623), published seven years after his death. This First Folio, edited by two of his friends and fellow actors, John Heminges and Henry Condell, is organized by genre and makes no attempt to establish a chronology. We do not know how long a time would normally have elapsed between the writing of a play and its first per-formance, nor, with a very few exceptions, do we know with any certainty the month or even the year of the first performance of Shakespeare's plays. But scholars have gradually assembled a considerable archive of evidence, both external and internal, for dating the composition of the plays.

Shakespeare began his career, probably in the early 1590s, by writing both comedies and history plays. The earliest of these histories, generally based on the accounts of English kings written by Raphael Holinshed and other sixteenth-century chroniclers, seem theatrically vital but crude, as does an early attempt at tragedy, *Titus Andronicus*. But Shakespeare very quickly moved on to create, in *Richard III* (ca. 1592), a brilliantly conceived central character and to display a dazzling command of histrionic rhetoric and an overarching moral vision of English history. In the later 1590s he wrote a sequence of profoundly searching and ambitious history plays—*Richard II*, the first and second parts of *Henry IV*, and *Henry V*—which together explore the death throes of feudal England and the birth of the modern nation-state ruled by a charismatic monarch.

Shakespeare's first comedies show even fewer signs of an apprenticeship. *The Comedy of Errors*, one of his early efforts in this genre, already displays a rare command of the resources of comedy—mistaken identity, madcap confusion, and the threat of disaster, giving way in the end to reconciliation, recovery, and love. Successful as are these early histories and comedies, and indicative of an extraordinary theatrical talent, Shakespeare's achievement only a few years later would still have been all but impossible to foresee. Starting with *A Midsummer Night's Dream* (ca. 1595), he wrote an unprecedented succession of romantic comedies—*The Merchant of Venice, The Merry Wives of Windsor, Much Ado About Nothing, As You Like It*, and *Twelfth Night* (ca. 1601)—whose poetic richness and emotional complexity remain unmatched.

In the same year that Shakespeare wrote *Twelfth Night*, often regarded as the greatest of his comedies, he also probably wrote *Hamlet*, initiating an outpouring of great tragic dramas: *Othello, King Lear, Macbeth, Antony and Cleopatra*, and *Coriolanus*. These plays, written from 1601 to 1607, seem to mark a major shift in sensibility, an existential and metaphysical darkening that many readers think must have originated in a deep personal anguish, perhaps caused by the death of his father, John, in 1601.

Whatever the truth of these speculations—and we have no direct testimony either to support or to undermine them—there appears to have occurred in the same period a shift as well in Shakespeare's comic sensibility. The comedies written between 1601 and 1604, *Troilus and Cressida, All's Well That Ends Well*, and *Measure for Measure*, are sufficiently different from the earlier comedies—more biting in tone, more uneasy with comic conventions, more ruthlessly questioning of the values of the characters and the resolutions of the plots—to have led some modern scholars to classify them as "problem plays" or "dark comedies." Another group of plays, among the last that Shakespeare wrote, similarly constitutes a distinct category not recognized by the editors of the First Folio. *Pericles, Cymbeline, The Winter's Tale*, and *The Tempest*, written between 1608 and 1611, when Shakespeare had developed a remarkably fluid, dreamlike sense of plot and a poetic style that could veer, apparently effortlessly, from the tortured to the ineffably sweet, are now commonly known as the "romances." These plays share an interest in the moral and emotional life less of the adolescents who dominate the earlier comedies than of their parents. The "romances" are deeply concerned with patterns of loss and recovery, suffering and redemption, despair and renewal. They have seemed to many critics to constitute a self-conscious conclusion to a career that opened with histories and comedies and passed through the dark and tormented tragedies. Shakespeare evidently wrote the last of his plays in Stratford, where he retired about 1610. He died in 1616, shortly after the marriage festivities for his daughter Judith. His best epitaph is a famous line from a poem that his friend and rival Ben Jonson wrote in the First Folio: "He was not of an age, but for all time!"

Sonnets

In Elizabethan England aristocratic patronage, with the money, protection and prestige it alone could provide, was probably a professional writer's most important asset. This patronage, or at least Shakespeare's quest for it, is most visible in his dedication in 1593 and 1594 of his narrative poems, *Venus and Adonis* and *The Rape of Lucrece*, to the young nobleman Henry Wriothesley, earl of Southampton. What return the poet got for his exquisite offerings is unknown. We do know that among wits and gallants the narrative poems won Shakespeare a fine reputation as an immensely stylish and accomplished poet. This reputation was enhanced as well by manuscript circulation of his sonnets, which were mentioned admiringly in print more than ten years before they were published in 1609 (apparently without his personal supervision and perhaps without his consent).

Shakespeare's sonnets are quite unlike the other sonnet sequences of his day, notably in his almost unprecedented choice of a beautiful young man (rather than a lady) as the principal object of praise, love, and idealizing devotion and in his portrait of a dark, sensuous, and sexually promiscuous mistress (rather than the usual chaste and aloof blond beauty). Nor are the moods confined to what the Renaissance thought were those of the despairing Petrarchan lover: they include delight, pride, melancholy, shame, disgust, and fear. Shakespeare's sequence suggests a story, although the details are vague, and there is even doubt whether the sonnets as published are in an order established by the poet himself. Certain motifs are evident: an introductory series (1 to 17) celebrates the beauty of a young man and urges him to marry and beget children who will bear his image. The subsequent long sequence (18 to 126), passionately focused on the same beloved young man, develops as a dominant motif the transience and destructive power of time, countered only by the force of love and the permanence of poetry. The remaining sonnets focus chiefly on the so-called Dark Lady as an alluring but degrading object of desire. Some sonnets (like 144) intimate a love triangle involving the speaker, the male friend, and the woman; others take note of a rival poet (sometimes identified as George Chapman or Christopher Marlowe). The biographical background of the sonnets has inspired a mountain of speculation, but very little of it has any factual support.

Though there are many variations, Shakespeare's most frequent rhyme scheme in the sonnets is *abab cdcd efef gg*. This so-called Shakespearean pattern often (though not always) calls attention to three distinct quatrains (each of which may develop a separate metaphor), followed by a closing couplet that may either confirm or pull sharply against what has gone before. Startling shifts in direction may occur in lines other than the closing ones; consider, for example, the twists and turns in the opening lines of sonnet 138: "When my love swears that she is made of truth, / I do believe her, though I know she lies." Shakespeare's sonnets as a whole are strikingly intense, conveying a sense of high psychological and moral stakes. They are also remarkably dense, written with a daunting energy, concentration, and compression. Often the main idea of the poem may be grasped quickly, but the precise movement of thought and feeling, the links among the shifting images, the syntax, tone, and rhetorical structure prove immensely challenging. These are poems that famously reward rereading.

SONNETS

*To the Only Begetter of
These Ensuing Sonnets
Mr. W. H. All Happiness
and That Eternity
Promised
By
Our Ever-Living Poet
Wisheth
the Well-Wishing
Adventurer in
Setting Forth
T. T.*[1]

3

Look in thy glass° and tell the face thou viewest   *mirror*
Now is the time that face should form another,
Whose fresh repair if now thou not renewest,
Thou dost beguile the world, unbless some mother.
5   For where is she so fair whose uneared° womb   *unplowed*
Disdains the tillage of thy husbandry?
Or who is he so fond° will be the tomb   *foolish*
Of his self-love, to stop posterity?
Thou art thy mother's glass, and she in thee
10   Calls back the lovely April of her prime;
So thou through windows of thine age shalt see,
Despite of wrinkles, this thy golden time.
     But if thou live rememb'red not to be,
     Die single, and thine image dies with thee.

12

When I do count the clock that tells the time
And see the brave° day sunk in hideous night,   *splendid*
When I behold the violet past prime
And sable curls all silvered o'er with white,
5   When lofty trees I see barren of leaves,
Which erst° from heat did canopy the herd   *formerly*
And summer's green all girded up in sheaves
Borne on the bier with white and bristly beard:

---

1. This odd dedication bears the initials of the publisher, Thomas Thorpe. The W. H. addressed here may or may not be the male friend addressed in sonnets 1 to 126. Leading candidates for that role are Henry Wriothesley, earl of Southampton, the dedicatee of *Venus and Adonis* (1593) and *The Rape of Lucrece* (1594), and William Herbert, earl of Pembroke, a dedicatee of the First Folio. But there is no hard evidence to support these or other suggested identifications of the male friend or of the so-called Dark Lady; these sonnet personages may or may not have had real-life counterparts.

Since all the sonnets save two were first published in 1609, we do not repeat the date after each one. Numbers 138 and 144 were first published in 1599, in a verse miscellany called *The Passionate Pilgrim*.

Then of thy beauty do I question make°   *speculate*
10   That thou among the wastes of time must go,
Since sweets and beauties do themselves forsake,
And die as fast as they see others grow,
     And nothing 'gainst Time's scythe can make defense
     Save breed, to brave[2] him when he takes thee hence.

15

When I consider every thing that grows
Holds° in perfection but a little moment;   *remains*
That this huge stage presenteth naught but shows
Whereon the stars in secret influence comment;[3]
5   When I perceive that men as plants increase,
Cheerèd and checked[4] even by the selfsame sky,
Vaunt[5] in their youthful sap, at height decrease,
And wear their brave state out of memory;[6]
Then the conceit° of this inconstant stay   *conception*
10   Sets you most rich in youth before my sight,
Where wasteful Time debateth[7] with Decay
To change your day of youth to sullied° night,   *soiled, blackened*
And all in war with Time for love of you,
     As he takes from you, I ingraft[8] you new.

18

Shall I compare thee to a summer's day?
Thou art more lovely and more temperate:
Rough winds do shake the darling buds of May,
And summer's lease hath all too short a date;
5   Sometime too hot the eye of heaven shines,
And often is his gold complexion dimmed;
And every fair from fair sometime declines,
By chance or nature's changing course untrimmed.[9]
But thy eternal summer shall not fade,
10   Nor lose possession of that fair thou ow'st;°   *ownest*
Nor shall death brag thou wander'st in his shade,
When in eternal lines to time thou grow'st:°   *are grafted*
     So long as men can breathe or eyes can see,
     So long lives this, and this gives life to thee.[1]

2. Defy. "Breed": offspring.
3. The stars secretly affect human actions.
"Shows": (1) appearances, (2) performances.
4. Encouraged and reproached or stopped.
5. Exult, display themselves.
6. Wear their showy splendor out and are forgotten.
7. (1)Fights, (2) joins forces.

8. Renew by grafting, implant beauty again (by my verse).
9. Stripped of gay apparel.
1. The boast of immortality for one's verse was a convention going back to the classics. It may be thought to imply not egotism on the part of the poet but faith in the permanence of poetry.

19

Devouring Time, blunt thou the lion's paws,
And make the earth devour her own sweet brood;
Pluck the keen teeth from the fierce tiger's jaws,
And burn the long-lived phoenix in her blood;[2]
5   Make glad and sorry seasons as thou fleet'st,
And do whate'er thou wilt, swift-footed Time,
To the wide world and all her fading sweets,
But I forbid thee one most heinous crime:
O carve not with thy hours my love's fair brow,
10   Nor draw no lines there with thine antique[3] pen;
Him in thy course untainted[4] do allow,
For beauty's pattern to succeeding men.
     Yet do thy worst, old Time: despite thy wrong,
     My love shall in my verse ever live young.

20

A woman's face with Nature's own hand painted[5]
Hast thou, the master mistress of my passion;[6]
A woman's gentle heart but not acquainted
With shifting change as is false women's fashion;
5   An eye more bright than theirs, less false in rolling,°   *roving*
Gilding the object whereupon it gazeth;
A man in hue all hues[7] in his controlling,
Which steals men's eyes and women's souls amazeth.
And for a woman wert thou first created,
10   Till Nature as she wrought thee fell a-doting,[8]
And by addition me of thee defeated,
By adding one thing to my purpose nothing.
     But since she pricked[9] thee out for women's pleasure,
     Mine be thy love, and thy love's use their treasure.[1]

absurd

29

When, in disgrace° with Fortune and men's eyes,   *disfavor*
I all alone beweep my outcast state,
And trouble deaf heaven with my bootless° cries,   *futile*
And look upon myself and curse my fate,
5   Wishing me like to one more rich in hope,
Featured like him, like him with friends possessed,[2]
Desiring this man's art° and that man's scope,°   *skill / ability*

2. In full vigor of life (a hunting term). The phoenix was a mythical bird that lived five hundred years, then died in flames to rise again from its ashes.
3. (1) Old, (2) fantastic.
4. (1) Undefiled, (2) untouched by a weapon (a term from jousting).
5. I.e., not made up with cosmetics.
6. (1) Strong feeling, (2) poem.
7. "Hue" probably means appearance or form. In the first edition, "hues" is spelled "*Hews*," which some have taken as indicating a pun on a proper name. It has also been suggested that "man in" is a copyist's or compositor's misreading of "maiden."
8. (1) Crazy, (2) infatuated.
9. Marked, with obvious sexual pun.
1. (1) Sexual enjoyment, (2) interest (as in usury).
2. I.e., I wish I had one man's looks, another man's friends.

With what I most enjoy contented least;
Yet in these thoughts myself almost despising,
10 Haply I think on thee, and then my state[3]
(Like to the lark at break of day arising
From sullen earth) sings hymns at heaven's gate;
   For thy sweet love remembered such wealth brings
   That then I scorn to change my state with kings.

30

When to the sessions[4] of sweet silent thought
I summon up remembrance of things past,
I sigh the lack of many a thing I sought,
And with old woes new wail° my dear time's waste: *bewail anew*
5 Then can I drown an eye (unused to flow)
For precious friends hid in death's dateless° night,   *endless*
And weep afresh love's long since canceled woe,
And moan th' expense° of many a vanished sight: *loss*
Then can I grieve at grievances foregone,°   *former*
10 And heavily from woe to woe tell° o'er   *count*
The sad account of fore-bemoanèd moan,
Which I new pay as if not paid before.
   But if the while I think on thee, dear friend,
   All losses are restored and sorrows end.

33

Full many a glorious morning have I seen
Flatter the mountain tops with sovereign eye,°   *sunlight*
Kissing with golden face the meadows green,
Gilding pale streams with heavenly alchemy;
5 Anon° permit the basest° clouds to ride   *(but) soon / darkest*
With ugly rack° on his celestial face,   *cloudy mask*
And from the forlorn world his visage hide,
Stealing unseen to west with this disgrace.
Even so my sun one early morn did shine
10 With all triumphant splendor on my brow;
But out, alack,° he was but one hour mine;   *alas*
The region° cloud hath masked him from me now.   *high*
   Yet him for this my love no whit disdaineth:
   Suns of the world may stain° when heaven's sun staineth.   *darken*

35

No more be grieved at that which thou hast done:
Roses have thorns, and silver fountains mud.

---

3. Condition, state of mind; but in line 14 there is
a pun on *state* meaning chair of state, throne.

4. Sittings of court. "Summon up" (next line) continues the metaphor.

Clouds and eclipses stain° both moon and sun, · · · · *dim*
And loathsome canker° lives in sweetest bud. · · · *rose worm*
5 All men make faults, and even I in this,
Authorizing thy trespass with compare,
Myself corrupting, salving thy amiss,° · · · · *palliating your offense*
Excusing thy sins more than thy sins are;
For to thy sensual fault I bring in sense°— · · · *reason*
10 Thy adverse party is thy advocate—
And 'gainst myself a lawful plea commence.
Such civil war is in my love and hate,
      That I an accessary needs must be
      To that sweet thief which sourly robs from me.

55

Not marble, nor the gilded monuments
Of princes, shall outlive this powerful rhyme;
But you shall shine more bright in these contents
Than unswept stone, besmeared with sluttish time.[5]
5 When wasteful war shall statues overturn,
And broils root out the work of masonry,
Nor Mars his° sword nor war's quick fire shall burn · · · *neither Mars's*
The living record of your memory.
'Gainst death and all-oblivious enmity[6]
10 Shall you pace forth; your praise shall still find room
Even in the eyes of all posterity
That wear this world out to the ending doom.° · · · *Judgment Day*
      So, till the judgment that yourself arise,[7]
      You live in this, and dwell in lovers' eyes.

60

Like as the waves make towards the pebbled shore,
So do our minutes hasten to their end;
Each changing place with that which goes before,
In sequent toil all forwards do contend.[8]
5 Nativity, once in the main° of light, · · · · *broad expanse*
Crawls to maturity, wherewith being crowned,
Crooked eclipses 'gainst his glory fight,
And Time that gave doth now his gift confound.
Time doth transfix the flourish set on youth
10 And delves the parallels[9] in beauty's brow,
Feeds on the rarities of nature's truth,
And nothing stands but for his scythe to mow.

5. I.e., than in a stone tomb or effigy that time wears away and covers with dust.
6. The enmity of oblivion, of being forgotten.
7. Until you rise from the dead on Judgment Day.
8. Toiling and following each other, the waves struggle to press forward.
9. Digs the parallel furrows (wrinkles). "Transfix the flourish": remove the embellishment. To "flourish" is also to blossom.

And yet to times in hope° my verse shall stand,   *future times*
Praising thy worth, despite his cruel hand.

65

Since[1] brass, nor stone, nor earth, nor boundless sea,
But sad mortality o'ersways their power,
How with this rage° shall beauty hold a plea,   *destructive power*
Whose action is no stronger than a flower?
5 O how shall summer's honey breath hold out
Against the wrackful° siege of batt'ring days,   *destructive*
When rocks impregnable are not so stout,
Nor gates of steel so strong, but Time decays?
O fearful meditation! where, alack,
10 Shall Time's best jewel from Time's chest[2] lie hid?
Or what strong hand can hold his swift foot back?
Or who his spoil° of beauty can forbid?   *ravaging*
    O none, unless this miracle have might,
    That in black ink my love may still shine bright.

71

No longer mourn for me when I am dead
Than you shall hear the surly sullen bell[3]
Give warning to the world that I am fled
From this vile world, with vilest worms to dwell:
5 Nay, if you read this line, remember not
The hand that writ it; for I love you so,
That I in your sweet thoughts would be forgot,
If thinking on me then should make you woe.
Oh, if, I say, you look upon this verse
10 When I perhaps compounded am with clay,
Do not so much as my poor name rehearse,
But let your love even with my life decay;
    Lest the wise world should look into your moan,
    And mock you with me after I am gone.

73

That time of year thou mayst in me behold
When yellow leaves, or none, or few, do hang
Upon those boughs which shake against the cold,
Bare ruined choirs,[4] where late the sweet birds sang.
5 In me thou seest the twilight of such day

1. I.e., because there is neither.
2. I.e., from being coffered up by Time.
3. The bell was tolled to announce the death of a member of the parish—one stroke for each year of

his or her life.
4. The part of a church where divine service was sung.

As after sunset fadeth in the west;
Which by and by black night doth take away,
Death's second self that seals up all in rest.
In me thou seest the glowing of such fire
10 That on the ashes of his youth doth lie,
As the deathbed whereon it must expire,
Consumed with that which it was nourished by.[5]
  This thou perceiv'st, which makes thy love more strong,
  To love that well, which thou must leave ere long.

74

But be contented; when that fell[6] arrest
Without all bail shall carry me away,
My life hath in this line some interest,[7]
Which for memorial still° with thee shall stay.   *always*
5 When thou reviewest this, thou dost review
The very part was° consecrate to thee.   *i.e., which was*
The earth can have but earth, which is his due;
My spirit is thine, the better part of me.
So then thou hast but lost the dregs of life,
10 The prey of worms, my body being dead,
The coward conquest of a wretch's knife,[8]
Too base of thee to be rememberèd.
  The worth of that is that which it contains,[9]
  And that is this, and this with thee remains.

87

Farewell: thou art too dear[1] for my possessing,
And like enough thou know'st thy estimate.°   *value*
The charter° of thy worth gives thee releasing;   *deed, contract for property*
My bonds in thee are all determinate.°   *expired*
5 For how do I hold thee but by thy granting,
And for that riches where is my deserving?
The cause of this fair gift in me is wanting,
And so my patent° back again is swerving.   *title*
Thy self thou gav'st, thy own worth then not knowing,
10 Or me, to whom thou gav'st it, else mistaking;
So thy great gift, upon misprision° growing,   *mistake, oversight*
Comes home again, on better judgment making.
  Thus have I had thee as a dream doth flatter,
  In sleep a king, but waking no such matter.

---

5. Choked by the ashes of that which once nourished its flame.
6. Cruel. Hamlet says, "this fell sergeant / Death
is strict in his arrest" (5.2.278–79).
7. Share, participation. "In this line": i.e., poetry.

8. Death's weapon (like Time's scythe).
9. I.e., the only value of the body is that it contains
the spirit.
1. (1) Expensive, (2) beloved.

94

They that have power to hurt and will do none,
That do not do the thing they most do show,°   *seem to do*
Who, moving others, are themselves as stone,
Unmovèd, cold, and to temptation slow;
5   They rightly do inherit heaven's graces
And husband nature's riches from expense;[2]
They are the lords and owners of their faces,
Others but stewards of their excellence.
The summer's flower is to the summer sweet,
10   Though to itself it only live and die,
But if that flower with base infection meet,
The basest weed outbraves° his dignity: *surpasses*
     For sweetest things turn sourest by their deeds;
     Lilies that fester smell far worse than weeds.[3]

97

How like a winter hath my absence been
From thee, the pleasure of the fleeting year!
What freezings have I felt, what dark days seen!
What old December's bareness everywhere!
5   And yet this time removed[4] was summer's time,
The teeming autumn, big with rich increase,
Bearing the wanton burthen of the prime,[5]
Like widowed wombs after their lords' decease;
Yet this abundant issue seemed to me
10   But hope of orphans and unfathered fruit;
For summer and his pleasures wait on thee,
And, thou away, the very birds are mute;
     Or, if they sing, 'tis with so dull a cheer°   *disposition*
     That leaves look pale, dreading the winter's near.

106

When in the chronicle of wasted° time   *past*
I see descriptions of the fairest wights,°   *persons*
And beauty making beautiful old rhyme
In praise of ladies dead and lovely knights,
5   Then, in the blazon[6] of sweet beauty's best,
Of hand, of foot, of lip, of eye, of brow,
I see their antique pen would have expressed

---

2. I.e., they do not squander nature's gifts.
3. This line also appears in *Edward III* (2.1.451), an apocryphal Shakespearean play licensed December 1, 1595.
4. I.e., when I was absent.

5. Spring, which has engendered the lavish crop ("wanton burthen") that autumn is now left to bear.
6. Catalog of excellencies.

Even such a beauty as you master now.
So all their praises are but prophecies
10 Of this our time, all you prefiguring;
And, for they looked but with divining eyes,[7]
They had not skill enough your worth to sing:
    For we, which now behold these present days,
    Have eyes to wonder, but lack tongues to praise.

107

Not mine own fears, nor the prophetic soul
Of the wide world dreaming on things to come,[8]
Can yet the lease of my true love control,
Supposed as forfeit to a confinèd doom.[9]
5 The mortal moon hath her eclipse endured,
And the sad augurs mock their own presage;[1]
Incertainties now crown themselves assured,
And peace[2] proclaims olives of endless age.
Now with the drops of this most balmy time
10 My love looks fresh, and death to me subscribes,°   *submits*
Since, spite of him, I'll live in this poor rhyme,
While he insults o'er dull and speechless tribes:
    And thou in this shalt find thy monument,
    When tyrants' crests and tombs of brass are spent.°   *wasted away*

116

Let me not to the marriage of true minds
Admit impediments;[3] love is not love
Which alters when it alteration finds,
Or bends with the remover to remove:
5 O, no, it is an ever-fixèd mark,[4]
That looks on tempests and is never shaken;
It is the star to every wand'ring bark,
Whose worth's unknown, although his highth[5] be taken.
Love's not Time's fool,° though rosy lips and cheeks   *plaything, victim*
10 Within his[6] bending sickle's compass come;
Love alters not with his brief hours and weeks,
But bears it out even to the edge of doom.°   *brink of Judgment Day*

7. Because ("for") they were able only ("but") to foresee prophetically.
8. This sonnet refers to contemporary events and the prophecies, common in Elizabethan almanacs, of disaster.
9. I.e., can yet put an end to my love, which I thought doomed to early forfeiture.
1. The "mortal moon" is Queen Elizabeth; her "eclipse" is probably her climacteric year, her sixty-third (thought meaningful because the product of two "significant" numbers, 7 and 9), which ended in September 1596. The sober astrologers ("sad augurs") now ridicule their own predictions ("pres-age") of catastrophe, because they turned out to be false.
2. Probably the agreement between Henry IV of France and Elizabeth.
3. From the marriage service: "If any of you know cause or just impediment why these persons should not be joined together . . ."
4. Seamark (cf. *landmark*).
5. The star's value is incalculable, although its "highth" (altitude) may be known and used for practical purposes.
6. Time's (as also in line 11).

If this be error and upon me proved,
I never writ, nor no man ever loved.

129

Th' expense of spirit in a waste of shame
Is lust in action;[7] and till action, lust
Is perjured, murd'rous, bloody, full of blame,
Savage, extreme, rude,° cruel, not to trust;   *brutal*
5   Enjoyed no sooner but despisèd straight:
Past reason hunted; and no sooner had,
Past reason hated, as a swallowed bait,
On purpose laid to make the taker mad:
Mad in pursuit, and in possession so;
10 Had, having, and in quest to have, extreme;
A bliss in proof[8] and proved, a very° woe;   *true*
Before, a joy proposed; behind, a dream.
    All this the world well knows; yet none knows well
    To shun the heaven that leads men to this hell.

130

My mistress' eyes are nothing like the sun;[9]
Coral is far more red than her lips' red;
If snow be white, why then her breasts are dun;
If hairs be wires, black wires grow on her head.
5   I have seen roses damasked,° red and white,   *variegated*
But no such roses see I in her cheeks;
And in some perfumes is there more delight
Than in the breath that from my mistress reeks.[1]
I love to hear her speak, yet well I know
10 That music hath a far more pleasing sound;
I grant I never saw a goddess go;°   *walk*
My mistress, when she walks, treads on the ground.
    And yet, by heaven, I think my love as rare°   *admirable, extraordinary*
    As any she belied° with false compare.   *misrepresented*

135

Whoever hath her wish, thou hast thy *Will*,[2]
And *Will* to boot, and *Will* in overplus;

---

7. The word order here is inverted and slightly
obscures the meaning. Lust, when put into action,
expends "spirit" (life, vitality; also semen) in a
"waste" (desert; also with a pun on *waist*) of shame.
8. A bliss during the experience.
9. An anti-Petrarchan sonnet. All of the details
commonly attributed by other Elizabethan sonneteers to their ladies are here denied to the poet's

mistress.
1. Not with our pejorative sense, but simply "emanates."
2. (1) Wishes, (2) carnal desire, (3) the male and
female sexual organs, (4) a lover—Shakespeare?—
named Will. This is one of three, possibly four,
sonnets punning on the word.

More than enough am I that vex thee still,°   *always*
To thy sweet will making addition thus.
5   Wilt thou, whose will is large and spacious,
Not once vouchsafe° to hide my will in thine?   *consent*
Shall will in others seem right gracious,
And in° my will no fair acceptance shine?   *in the case of*
The sea, all water, yet receives rain still,
10   And in abundance addeth to his store,°   *plenty*
So thou being rich in *Will* add to thy *Will*
One will of mine to make thy large *Will* more.
        Let no unkind, no fair beseechers kill;[3]
        Think all but one, and me in that one *Will*.

138

When my love swears that she is made of truth,
I do believe her, though I know she lies,[4]
That she might think me some untutored youth,
Unlearnèd in the world's false subtleties.
5   Thus vainly thinking that she thinks me young,
Although she knows my days are past the best,[5]
Simply° I credit her false-speaking tongue: *like a simpleton*
On both sides thus is simple truth suppressed.
But wherefore says she not she is unjust?°   *unfaithful*
10   And wherefore say not I that I am old?
Oh, love's best habit[6] is in seeming trust,
And age in love loves not to have years told.°   *counted*
        Therefore I lie with her and she with me,
        And in our faults by lies we flattered be.

144

Two loves I have of comfort and despair,[7]
Which like two spirits do suggest me still:°   *tempt me constantly*
The better angel is a man right fair,
The worser spirit a woman colored ill.°   *dark*
5   To win me soon to hell, my female evil
Tempteth my better angel from my side,
And would corrupt my saint to be a devil,
Wooing his purity with her foul pride.[8]
And whether that my angel be turned fiend
10   Suspect I may, yet not directly tell;
But being both from me, both to each[9] friend,
I guess one angel in another's hell.[1]

3. I.e., do not kill with unkindness any of your
wooers.
4. With the obvious sexual pun (as also in lines
13–14). "Made of truth": (1) is utterly honest, (2)
is faithful.
5. Shakespeare was thirty-five or younger when he
wrote this sonnet (it first appeared in *The Passion-*

ate Pilgrim, 1599).
6. Appearance, deportment.
7. I have two beloveds, one bringing me comfort
and the other despair.
8. (1) Vanity, (2) sexuality.
9. Each other. "From": away from.
1. A double entendre.

Yet this shall I ne'er know, but live in doubt,
Till my bad angel fire my good one out.[2]

146

Poor soul, the center of my sinful earth,
Lord of[3] these rebel powers that thee array,[4]
Why dost thou pine within and suffer dearth,
Painting thy outward walls so costly gay?
5   Why so large cost, having so short a lease,
Dost thou upon thy fading mansion spend?
Shall worms, inheritors of this excess,
Eat up thy charge?[5] Is this thy body's end?
Then, soul, live thou upon thy servant's loss,
10   And let that pine to aggravate thy store;[6]
Buy terms divine in selling hours of dross;[7]
Within be fed, without be rich no more.
    So shalt thou feed on death, that feeds on men,
    And death once dead, there's no more dying then.

147

My love is as a fever, longing still°   *continually*
For that which longer nurseth[8] the disease,
Feeding on that which doth preserve the ill,°   *maintain the illness*
Th' uncertain sickly appetite[9] to please.
5   My reason, the physician to my love,
Angry that his prescriptions are not kept,
Hath left me, and I desperate now approve
Desire is death, which physic did except.[1]
Past cure I am, now reason is past care,[2]
10   And frantic mad with evermore unrest;
My thoughts and my discourse as madmen's are,
At random from the truth, vainly expressed;[3]
    For I have sworn thee fair, and thought thee bright,
    Who art as black as hell, as dark as night.

1 Henry IV

With a succession of plays written in the 1590s, Shakespeare helped to invent and perfect a theatrical genre known as the history play, a staging of momentous events and crucial figures from England's past. Depicting on the public

---

2. I.e., until she infects him with venereal disease.
3. An emendation. The 1609 edition repeats the last three words of line 1. Other suggestions are "Thrall to," "Starved by," "Pressed by," and leaving the repetition but dropping "that thee" in line 2.
4. Dress out, often used in a military sense.
5. What you have spent so much on.
6. Let "that" (i.e., the body) deteriorate to increase ("aggravate") the soul's riches ("thy store").

7. Refuse, rubbish. "Terms": long periods.
8. (1) Nourishes, (2) takes care of.
9. (1) Desire for food, (2) lust.
1. I.e., I learn by experience that desire, which rejected reason's medicine, is death.
2. I.e., medical care (of me). The line is a version of the proverb "past cure, past care."
3. Wide of the mark and senselessly uttered.

stage contemporary figures such as Queen Elizabeth or her glittering courtiers would not have been at all prudent: both the Elizabethan theater and the printing press were censored, and it was dangerous to represent or to reflect in public on those in power. As Sir Walter Ralegh remarked, explaining why he was writing a history of the ancient past, he who follows truth too close on the heels is likely to have his teeth kicked out. But Shakespeare contrived to reflect with remarkable candor on his own society and on the underlying forces that shaped the nation's destiny. He did so by powerfully chronicling a series of violent struggles in the fourteenth and fifteenth centuries that, as he depicts them, constituted the birth pangs of the modern world.

Henry IV, Part One is part of what is often termed Shakespeare's Second Tetralogy (that is, the sequence of four plays comprising *Richard II*, the two parts of *Henry IV*, and *Henry V*). But each of these was clearly intended to be enjoyed independently of the others. First printed in 1598, *1 Henry IV* had been performed on the stage and at court before publication, and from that time to this it has remained one of Shakespeare's most popular plays.

In *Richard II*, the tough, efficient Bullingbrook overthrows his weak, irresponsible young cousin, King Richard II. Vain, surrounded by flatterers, and deluded by poetic dreams of his own grandeur, Richard had precipitated the events that led to his downfall by unjustly exiling Bullingbrook and then seizing his inheritance. At the close of the play, Bullingbrook, now on the throne as King Henry IV, has the imprisoned Richard II murdered. By this act—ridding himself, as he puts it, of his "buried fear"—he hopes to stabilize and secure his rule and the rule after him of his son and heir Prince Hal.

But the buried fear proves to be a persistent nightmare. Deposing a legitimate king, one who had been duly anointed by the church and thereby invested with enormous symbolic significance, is an act whose long-term consequences are difficult to control. Several characters express the anxious sense that there is a curse now hanging over the land, a curse that will bring what the bishop of Carlisle grimly predicts: "Disorder, horror, fear, and mutiny" (*Richard II* 4.1.137). And, even without metaphysical dread, there are ample grounds for concern, since a variety of political and social forces are threatening to tear the kingdom apart. The usurper Bullingbrook's struggle to maintain his power in the face of a succession of civil wars and rebellions lies at the heart of the two parts of *Henry IV*. Bound up with this struggle is the transformation of his son, Prince Hal, from a dissolute wastrel to a staunch prop of the regime and a worthy successor to monarchical authority. In *Henry V*, Hal, having succeeded to his father's throne, secures this transformation, becoming in the process an English national hero. Leading his brave, heavily outnumbered troops, he conquers France at the Battle of Agincourt.

Shakespeare drew his historical material from prose chronicle histories, specifically Raphael Holinshed's *Chronicle of England, Scotland, and Ireland*, as well as from Samuel Daniel's historical poem, *The Civil Wars*, and an earlier anonymously authored play about Henry V, *The Famous Victories of Henry V*. These sources gave him the main outlines of his plot: the beleaguered Henry IV is threatened by a rebellion among his nobles, especially the powerful Percy family that had earlier helped him topple Richard II. This family, whose stronghold lay in Northumberland, in the north of England, is joined by other dangerous forces situated on the Celtic-speaking peripheries of the kingdom: the Scots, led by the redoutable Earl of Douglas, and the Welsh, led by the charismatic, volatile magician Owen Glendower. These menacing powers had been kept at bay by Henry IV's allies, but the erstwhile allies have now become the king's most dangerous enemies: the gallant, impetuous Henry Percy or Hotspur, who has naturally followed his father, the earl of Northumberland, and his uncle, the earl of Worcester, into rebellion, and Edmund Mortimer, who had a strong claim to succeed Richard II to the throne and who has now married Glendower's daughter.

From his sources Shakespeare also derived a portrait of Prince Hal as a prodigal son, a wild youth cavorting with a disorderly crew of drunks, thieves, and whores. The chief among these dissipated friends was a fat knight whom Shakespeare originally called Sir John Oldcastle. The choice of name turned out to be an unfortunate one. The historical Oldcastle had at one time fought for Henry IV but was charged with rebellion and executed; Protestants in the sixteenth century said that he was a martyr who had actually been killed for his religious beliefs, many of which anticipated the tenets of the Reformation. Oldcastle's powerful descendants vehemently objected to the identification of their illustrious ancestor with the corrupt, wheezing, hilarious scoundrel on stage, and Shakespeare was forced to come up with another name. Under the altered name—Sir John Falstaff—the character has come to be widely regarded as Shakespeare's greatest comic creation.

Shakespeare, who never felt tied to a strict observance of historical accuracy, made many changes in his source materials, most notably, perhaps, reconceiving the character of Hotspur. In the *Chronicle*, he is older than Hal's father, but Shakespeare makes him Hal's foil, coeval, and rival—a charismatic and brave warrior, as Hal finally proves to be, but also (unlike Hal) fiery and impatient, scornful of the soft, civilized arts of music and poetry, and single-mindedly driven by ambition for honor and fame. In reworking his sources Shakespeare highlights psychological conflicts: Hal's need to define himself in relation to two very different fathers—the tense, care-worn Henry IV and his witty, disreputable surrogate father, Falstaff—and against his glittering, siblinglike rival, Hotspur.

1 Henry IV is centrally concerned with political power: its sources, uses, theatrical manifestations, ambiguities, psychological costs, and subversions. Recent criticism has focused attention on several key questions: how far does this play (and the tetralogy) serve to reinforce the "Tudor myth" of providential kingship? And to what extent does it undermine that myth of divinely-sanctioned legitimacy by exposing the basis of kingship as Machiavellian force and fraud? How far does Prince Hal's transformation make him the embodiment of an ideal monarch who fulfills his filial and regal responsibilities? And to what extent is that idealization undercut by Hal's self-proclaimed hypocrisy and play-acting (and in *2 Henry IV* by his cold-hearted repudiation of Falstaff)? The scheme of Hal's moral redemption is carefully laid out in his soliloquy at the close of the first tavern scene: "By how much better than my word I am," he declares, "By so much shall I falsify men's hopes" (1.2.165–66). To falsify men's hopes is to exceed their expectations, but it is also to disappoint their expectations, to deceive men, to turn hopes into fictions, to betray.

At issue are not only the contradictory desires and expectations centered on Hal—the competing hopes of his royal father and his tavern cronies—but also the fantasies continually aroused by the play of innate grace, limitless playfulness, absolute friendship, generosity, and trust. Those fantasies are symbolized by certain echoing, talismanic phrases ("when thou art king?"), and they are bound up with the overall vividness, intensity, and richness of the theatrical practice itself: the play's multiplicity of brilliant characters, its intensely differentiated settings, its dazzling verbal wit, its mingling of high comedy, farce, epic heroism, and tragedy. *1 Henry IV* awakens a dream of superabundance, which is given its irresistible embodiment in Falstaff.

In structure, the play moves back and forth between court (whether that of the king or of the rebels) and tavern, and it sets the affairs of state in counterpoint to the affairs of bawds, thieves, and drunkards. The fulcrum in this precarious balance is Falstaff, for generations of readers and critics the play's most fascinating figure. A number of literary antecedents lie behind Shakespeare's character: the braggart soldier of Roman comedy, the stock character called the Vice in medieval morality plays, the carnival Lord of Misrule, the figure of Gluttony from the pageant of the Seven Deadly Sins, the picaresque rogue or highwayman, and the sanctimonious hypocrite from popular satires on Elizabethan puritanism. What is most striking about Falstaff perhaps is his sheer comic excess: he is liar, glutton, knave, coward, thief, lecher, drunkard, wit, philosopher, skilled rhetorician, cynic, master parodist, confidence man, parasite, and friend. Shakespeare continued to mine his inexhaustible exuberance in *2 Henry IV* and also (reportedly by Queen Elizabeth's express command) in a comedy of middle-class life, *The Merry Wives of Windsor*.

The First Part of King Henry the Fourth

DRAMATIS PERSONAE

KING HENRY THE FOURTH
HENRY, *Prince of Wales* } *Sons to the* KING
PRINCE JOHN OF LANCASTER }
EARL OF WESTMORELAND
SIR WALTER BLUNT
THOMAS PERCY, *Earl of Worcester*
HENRY PERCY, *Earl of Northumberland*
HENRY PERCY, *surnamed* HOTSPUR, *his son*
EDMUND MORTIMER, *Earl of March*
RICHARD SCROOP, *Archbishop of York*
ARCHIBALD, *Earl of Douglas*
OWEN GLENDOWER
SIR RICHARD VERNON
SIR MICHAEL, *a friend to the* ARCHBISHOP OF YORK
SIR JOHN FALSTAFF
POINS }
GADSHILL } *Companions of* FALSTAFF
PETO }
BARDOLPH }
LADY PERCY, *wife to* HOTSPUR, *and sister to* MORTIMER
LADY MORTIMER, *daughter to* GLENDOWER, *and wife to* MORTIMER
MISTRESS QUICKLY, *hostess of a tavern in Eastcheap*
LORDS, OFFICERS, SHERIFF, VINTNER, CHAMBERLAIN, DRAWERS, *two* CARRIERS, TRAVELERS, *and* ATTENDANTS

England and Wales

Act 1

SCENE 1

[*Enter the* KING, PRINCE JOHN OF LANCASTER, THE EARL OF WEST-MORELAND, SIR WALTER BLUNT, *with others.*]

KING   So shaken as we are, so wan with care,
    Find we a time for frighted peace to pant,[1]
    And breathe short-winded accents of new broils[2]
    To be commenced in stronds° afar remote.   *strands, regions*
5   No more the thirsty entrance[3] of this soil
    Shall daub her lips with her own children's blood;
    No more shall trenching war channel her fields,

1. I.e., let us allow peace to catch her breath.   3. Parched mouth.
2. I.e., news of new wars.

Nor bruise her flow'rets with the armèd hoofs
Of hostile paces.[4] Those opposèd eyes,
10   Which, like the meteors of a troubled heaven,
All of one nature, of one substance bred,
Did lately meet in the intestine shock[5]
And furious close° of civil butchery,   *encounter*
Shall now, in mutual well-beseeming ranks,
15   March all one way and be no more opposed
Against acquaintance, kindred, and allies.
The edge of war, like an ill-sheathèd knife,
No more shall cut his master. Therefore, friends,
As far as to the sepulchre of Christ,—
20   Whose soldier now, under whose blessed cross
We are impressèd° and engaged to fight,   *enlisted*
Forthwith a power[6] of English shall we levy,
Whose arms were molded in their mother's womb
To chase these pagans in those holy fields
25   Over whose acres walked those blessed feet
Which fourteen hundred years ago were nailed
For our advantage on the bitter cross.
But this our purpose now is twelve month old,
And bootless° 'tis to tell you we will go.   *useless*
30   Therefore we meet not now.[7] Then let me hear
Of you, my gentle cousin° Westmoreland,   *kinsman*
What yesternight our Council did decree
In forwarding this dear expedience.[8]
WESTMORELAND   My liege, this haste was hot in questiòn,
35   And many limits of the charge[9] set down
But yesternight, when all athwart[1] there came
A post° from Wales loaden with heavy news,   *messenger*
Whose worst was that the noble Mortimer,
Leading the men of Herefordshire to fight
40   Against the irregular° and wild Glendower,   *guerrilla*
Was by the rude hands of that Welshman taken,
A thousand of his people butcherèd,
Upon whose dead corpse° there was such misuse,   *corpses*
Such beastly shameless transformatiòn,
45   By those Welshwomen done as may not be
Without much shame retold or spoken of.
KING   It seems then that the tidings of this broil
Brake off our business for the Holy Land.
WESTMORELAND   This matched with other did, my gracious lord,
50   For more uneven and unwelcome news
Came from the north, and thus it did import:
On Holyrood Day[2] the gallant Hotspur there,

4. The tread of war horses.
5. Internal violence, civil war.
6. Army. He is planning a crusade, in expiation of his guilt for the death of Richard II.
7. I.e., that is not the reason for our present meeting.

8. Important, urgent matter.
9. Assignment of military responsibilities. "Hot in question": actively discussed.
1. Interrupting, crossing our purpose.
2. Holy Cross Day (September 14).

Young Harry Percy, and brave Archibald,
That ever-valiant and approvèd Scot,
At Holmedon met,
Where they did spend a sad and bloody hour,
As by discharge of their artillery,
And shape of likelihood,[3] the news was told;
For he that brought them[4] in the very heat
And pride° of their contention did take horse,   *height*
Uncertain of the issue any way.
KING   Here is a dear, a true industrious friend,
Sir Walter Blunt, new lighted from his horse,
Stained with the variation of each soil
Betwixt that Holmedon and this seat of ours;
And he hath brought us smooth and welcome news.
The Earl of Douglas is discomfited;
Ten thousand bold Scots, two and twenty knights
Balked° in their own blood did Sir Walter see   *heaped*
On Holmedon's plains. Of prisoners Hotspur took
Mordake Earl of Fife, and eldest son
To beaten Douglas, and the Earl of Athol,
Of Murray, Angus, and Menteith;
And is not this an honorable spoil,
A gallant prize? Ha, cousin, is it not?
WESTMORELAND   In faith,
It is a conquest for a prince to boast of.
KING   Yea, there thou mak'st me sad and mak'st me sin
In envy that my Lord Northumberland
Should be the father to so blest a son,
A son who is the theme of honor's tongue,
Amongst a grove the very straightest plant,
Who is sweet Fortune's minion° and her pride;   *favorite*
Whilst I, by looking on the praise of him,
See riot and dishonor stain the brow
Of my young Harry. O that it could be proved
That some night-tripping fairy had exchanged
In cradle-clothes our children where they lay,
And called mine Percy, his Plantagenet![5]
Then would I have his Harry, and he mine.
But let him from my thoughts. What think you, coz,
Of this young Percy's pride? The prisoners
Which he in this adventure hath surprised
To his own use he keeps, and sends me word
I shall have none but Mordake Earl of Fife.
WESTMORELAND   This is his uncle's teaching, this is Worcester,
Malevolent to you in all aspects,[6]
Which makes him prune himself,[7] and bristle up

55
60
65
70
75
80
85
90
95

3. Probable inference.
4. I.e., the news (usually a plural in Shakespeare).
5. The family name of the English royal family.
6. Hostile in every way. The figure is from astrology.
7. Plume himself. "Bristle up" and "crest" continue the image, which is that of a fighting cock.

The crest of youth against your dignity.
100 KING   But I have sent for him to answer this;
   And for this cause awhile we must neglect
   Our holy purpose to Jerusalem.
   Cousin, on Wednesday next our council we
   Will hold at Windsor, so inform the lords;
105 But come yourself with speed to us again,
   For more is to be said and to be done
   Than out of anger can be utterèd.
WESTMORELAND   I will, my liege.   [Exeunt.]

SCENE 2

[Enter HENRY, PRINCE OF WALES, and SIR JOHN FALSTAFF.]

FALSTAFF   Now Hal, what time of day is it, lad?
PRINCE   Thou art so fat-witted with drinking of old sack,[8] and unbuttoning
   thee after supper, and sleeping upon benches after noon, that thou hast
   forgotten to demand that truly which thou wouldst truly know. What a
5   devil hast thou to do with the time of the day? Unless hours were cups
   of sack, and minutes capons, and clocks the tongues of bawds, and dials
   the signs of leaping-houses,[9] and the blessed sun himself a fair hot wench
   in flame-colored taffeta, I see no reason why thou shouldst be so superfluous to demand the time of the day.
10 FALSTAFF   Indeed you come near me now, Hal, for we that take purses go
   by the moon and the seven stars, and not by Phoebus,[1] he, "that wandering knight so fair." And I prithee, sweet wag, when thou art king, as,
   God save thy grace—majesty I should say, for grace[2] thou wilt have
   none—
15 PRINCE   What, none?
FALSTAFF   No, by my troth, not so much as will serve to be prologue to an
   egg and butter.
PRINCE   Well, how then? come, roundly, roundly.[3]
FALSTAFF   Marry then, sweet wag, when thou art king, let not us that are
20   squires of the night's body be called thieves of the day's beauty;[4] let us
   be Diana's foresters, gentlemen of the shade, minions of the moon; and
   let men say we be men of good government, being governed as the sea
   is, by our noble and chaste mistress the moon, under whose countenance
   we steal.
25 PRINCE   Thou sayest well, and it holds well too, for the fortune of us that
   are the moon's men doth ebb and flow like the sea, being governed as
   the sea is by the moon. As for proof now: a purse of gold most resolutely
   snatched on Monday night and most dissolutely spent on Tuesday morning, got with swearing "Lay by" and spent with crying "Bring in," now in

8. Dry Spanish wine.
9. Whorehouses.
1. The sun. Falstaff then quotes from a popular ballad.
2. A triple pun: (1) "your Grace," the correct manner of addressing a prince or duke; (2) the divine influence that produces sanctity; and (3) a short

prayer before a meal—hence Falstaff's allusion to "egg and butter," a common hasty breakfast.
3. Plainly.
4. Two puns: (1) a "squire of the body" was an attendant on a knight and (2) "body" would be pronounced bawdy. "Beauty" also puns with booty, which thieves take. Diana is the moon goddess.

30 as low an ebb as the foot of the ladder and by and by in as high a flow
as the ridge of the gallows.[5]

FALSTAFF   By the Lord thou sayest true, lad. And is not my hostess of the
tavern a most sweet wench?

PRINCE   As the honey of Hybla, my old lad of the castle.[6] And is not a buff
35 jerkin a most sweet robe of durance?[7]

FALSTAFF   How now, how now, mad wag! what, in thy quips and thy quid-
dities?[8] what a plague have I to do with a buff jerkin?

PRINCE   Why, what a pox[9] have I to do with my hostess of the tavern?

FALSTAFF   Well, thou hast called her to a reckoning[1] many a time and oft.

40 PRINCE   Did I ever call for thee to pay thy part?

FALSTAFF   No, I'll give thee thy due, thou hast paid all there.

PRINCE   Yea, and elsewhere, so far as my coin would stretch, and where
it would not I have used my credit.

FALSTAFF   Yea, and so used it that were it not here apparent that thou art
45 heir apparent[2]—but I prithee, sweet wag, shall there be gallows standing
in England when thou art king? and resolution thus fobbed as it is with
the rusty curb of old father antic[3] the law? Do not thou, when thou art
king, hang a thief.

PRINCE   No, thou shalt.

50 FALSTAFF   Shall I? O rare! By the Lord, I'll be a brave judge.

PRINCE   Thou judgest false already; I mean thou shalt have the hanging
of the thieves and so become a rare hangman.

FALSTAFF   Well, Hal, well; and in some sort it jumps with my humor[4] as
well as waiting in the court, I can tell you.

55 PRINCE   For obtaining of suits?[5]

FALSTAFF   Yea, for obtaining of suits, whereof the hangman hath no lean
wardrobe. 'Sblood, I am as melancholy as a gib cat or a lugged[6] bear.

PRINCE   Or an old lion, or a lover's lute.

FALSTAFF   Yea, or the drone of a Lincolnshire bagpipe.

60 PRINCE   What sayest thou to a hare, or the melancholy of Moorditch?[7]

FALSTAFF   Thou hast the most unsavory similes and art indeed the most
comparative,[8] rascalliest, sweet young prince. But Hal, I prithee, trouble
me no more with vanity. I would to God thou and I knew where a commodity of good names were to be bought. An old lord of the council rated[9]
65 me the other day in the street about you, sir, but I marked him not; and
yet he talked very wisely, but I regarded him not; and yet he talked wisely,
and in the street too.

5. The "foot of the ladder" is at the bottom of the
gallows (robbery was a hanging offense); the
"ridge" is the crosspiece at the top. "Lay by": hand
over (a robber's command to the victim). "Bring
in": a customer's command for more drink at a tavern.
6. A reference to Falstaff's original name, Oldcastle. Hybla is a town in Sicily, famous for honey.
7. A pun: (1) lasting quality, (2) imprisonment.
"Buff jerkin": the leather jacket worn by a sheriff's
sergeant.
8. Quibbles.
9. Common oath, alluding to venereal disease.
1. The bill; also (here) sexual intercourse.
2. "Here" and "heir" would pun in Elizabethan

pronunciation.
3. A clown. "Resolution": bravery. "Fobbed":
cheated.
4. I.e., agrees with my disposition.
5. Special favors, but "clothing" in the next line.
The hangman was given the clothes of his victims.
6. Baited (in the bearbaiting pits a bear was
attacked by dogs as a public amusement).
" 'Sblood": God's blood, a common oath. "Gib cat":
tomcat.
7. A foul-smelling ditch on the outskirts of London. The "hare" was traditionally associated with
melancholy.
8. Given to (insulting) comparisons.
9. Scolded, berated.

PRINCE Thou didst well, for wisdom cries out in the streets and no man
regards it.[1]

70 FALSTAFF O, thou hast damnable iteration[2] and art indeed able to corrupt
a saint. Thou hast done much harm upon me, Hal, God forgive thee for
it! Before I knew thee, Hal, I knew nothing, and now am I, if a man
should speak truly, little better than one of the wicked. I must give over
this life, and I will give it over; by the Lord, an[3] I do not, I am a villain;

75 I'll be damned for never a king's son in Christendom.

PRINCE Where shall we take a purse tomorrow, Jack?

FALSTAFF Zounds, where thou wilt, lad; I'll make one; an I do not, call
me villain and baffle[4] me.

PRINCE I see a good amendment of life in thee—from praying to purse-

80 taking.

FALSTAFF Why, Hal, 'tis my vocation,[5] Hal; 'tis no sin for a man to labor
in his vocation.

[*Enter* POINS.]

Poins! Now shall we know if Gadshill[6] have set a match. O, if men were
to be saved by merit, what hole in hell were hot enough for him? This is

85 the most omnipotent villain that ever cried "stand" to a true man.

PRINCE Good morrow, Ned.

POINS Good morrow, sweet Hal. What says Monsieur Remorse? what says
Sir John Sack and Sugar? Jack! how agrees the devil and thee about thy
soul, that thou soldest him on Good Friday last for a cup of Madeira and

90 a cold capon's leg?

PRINCE Sir John stands to his word; the devil shall have his bargain, for
he was never yet a breaker of proverbs; he will give the devil his due.

POINS Then art thou damned for keeping thy word with the devil.

PRINCE Else he had been damned for cozening[7] the devil.

95 POINS But my lads, my lads, tomorrow morning by four o'clock, early at
Gadshill, there are pilgrims going to Canterbury with rich offerings, and
traders riding to London with fat purses. I have vizards for you all, you
have horses for yourselves; Gads hill lies[8] tonight in Rochester; I have
bespoke supper tomorrow night in Eastcheap;[9] we may do it as secure

100 as sleep. If you will go, I will stuff your purses full of crowns; if you will
not, tarry at home and be hanged.

FALSTAFF Hear ye, Yedward[1] if I tarry at home and go not, I'll hang you
for going.

POINS You will, chops?[2]

105 FALSTAFF Hal, wilt thou make one?

PRINCE Who, I rob? I a thief? not I, by my faith.

---

1. Prince Hal is quoting Proverbs 1.20 and 24.
2. Repetition, especially of sacred texts.
3. If.
4. A knight in the days of chivalry was "baffled" or
disgraced by having his shield hung upside down,
signaling his loss of rank. "Zounds": a common
oath, a contraction of "by God's wounds" (i.e.,
Jesus' wounds on the Cross).
5. Falstaff is here making fun of the Puritan doctrine of "calling" or vocation, based on the parable
of the talents (Matthew 25.25ff.).
6. Both a man and a place: the place is a hill

twenty-seven miles from London on the road to
Rochester; it was notorious for robberies. The
man, so called from the place, is the thieves' "setter," who arranges when and where the robbery
will occur.
7. Cheating.
8. Lodges. "Vizards": masks.
9. A thoroughfare in London, site of Mistress
Quickly's tavern.
1. Dialect for Edward.
2. Fat face.

FALSTAFF   There's neither honesty, manhood, nor good fellow ship in thee, nor thou camest not of the blood royal, if thou darest not stand for[3] ten shillings.

PRINCE   Well then, once in my days I'll be a madcap.

FALSTAFF   Why, that's well said.

PRINCE   Well, come what will, I'll tarry at home.

FALSTAFF   By the Lord, I'll be a traitor then, when thou art king.

PRINCE   I care not.

POINS   Sir John, I prithee leave the prince and me alone; I will lay him down such reasons for this adventure that he shall go.

FALSTAFF   Well, God give thee the spirit of persuasion and him the ears of profiting, that what thou speakest may move and what he hears may be believed, that the true prince may (for recreation sake) prove a false thief; for the poor abuses of the time want countenance.[4] Farewell; you shall find me in Eastcheap.

PRINCE   Farewell, thou latter spring, farewell, Allhallown summer![5]

[⟨Exit FALSTAFF.⟩][6]

POINS   Now, my good sweet honey lord, ride with us tomorrow; I have a jest to execute that I cannot manage alone. Falstaff, Bardolph, Peto, and Gadshill shall rob those men that we have already waylaid;[7] yourself and I will not be there, and when they have the booty, if you and I do not rob them, cut this head off from my shoulders.

PRINCE   How shall we part with them in setting forth?

POINS   Why, we will set forth before or after them, and appoint them a place of meeting, wherein it is at our pleasure to fail, and then will they adventure upon the exploit themselves, which they shall have no sooner achieved but we'll set upon them.

PRINCE   Yea, but 'tis like that they will know us by our horses, by our habits,[8] and by every other appointment to be ourselves.

POINS   Tut, our horses they shall not see—I'll tie them in the wood; our vizards we will change after we leave them: and, sirrah, I have cases of buckram for the nonce,[9] to immask our noted outward garments.

PRINCE   Yea, but I doubt they will be too hard[1] for us.

POINS   Well, for two of them, I know them to be as true-bred cowards as ever turned back; and for the third, if he fight longer than he sees reason, I'll forswear arms. The virtue of this jest will be the incomprehensible lies that this same fat rogue will tell us when we meet at supper: how thirty at least he fought with; what wards,[2] what blows, what extremities he endured; and in the reproof[3] of this lies the jest.

---

3. A pun: "stand for" means both "represent" and "fight for." "Royal" is also a pun: the coin called *royal* was worth ten shillings.
4. A satirical reference to the common complaint that the nobility did not properly give "countenance" to (i.e., encourage) good causes and to the Puritan habit of attacking the "abuses of the time." This entire speech parodies the language of the Puritans.
5. I.e., Indian summer; All Hallows' Day (All Saints' Day) is November 1. The two epithets are intended to suggest how unseasonable it is for Falstaff, an old man, to be engaged in youthful, hood-

lum exploits.
6. This stage direction, like some others in the play, does not appear in the earliest editions; it was added by a later editor. All such interpolated directions are indicated in our text by the special double brackets used here.
7. Set an ambush for.
8. Clothes.
9. I.e., outer clothes (of a coarse, stiff cloth) for the occasion.
1. I.e., too many. "Doubt": suspect.
2. Defensive postures.
3. Disproof.

145 PRINCE   Well, I'll go with thee. Provide us all things necessary and meet
me tomorrow night⁴ in Eastcheap; there I'll sup. Farewell.

POINS   Farewell, my lord.   [*Exit* POINS.]

PRINCE   I know you all, and will awhile uphold
The unyoked humor° of your idleness;   *undisciplined whim*
150 Yet herein will I imitate the sun,
Who doth permit the base contagious° clouds   *pestilence-breeding*
To smother up his beauty from the world,
That, when he please again to be himself,
Being wanted, he may be more wondered at
155 By breaking through the foul and ugly mists
Of vapors that did seem to strangle him.
If all the year were playing holidays,
To sport would be as tedious as to work;
But when they seldom come, they wished-for come,
160 And nothing pleaseth but rare accidents.
So, when this loose behavior I throw off
And pay the debt I never promisèd,
By how much better than my word I am,
By so much shall I falsify men's hopes,
165 And like bright metal on a sullen ground,°   *dull background*
My reformation, glitt'ring o'er my fault,
Shall show more goodly and attract more eyes
Than that which hath no foil° to set it off.   *contrast*
I'll so offend to make offense a skill,
170 Redeeming time⁵ when men think least I will.   [*Exit.*]

SCENE 3

[*Enter the* KING, NORTHUMBERLAND, WORCESTER, HOTSPUR,
SIR WALTER BLUNT, *with others.*]

KING   My blood hath been too cold and temperate,
Unapt to stir at these indignities,
And you have found me,⁶ for accordingly
You tread upon my patience; but be sure
5 I will from henceforth rather be myself,
Mighty and to be feared, than my condition,°   *disposition*
Which hath been smooth as oil, soft as young down,
And therefore lost that title of respect
Which the proud soul ne'er pays but to the proud.

10 WORCESTER   Our house, my sovereign liege, little deserves
The scourge of greatness to be used on it,
And that same greatness too which our own hands
Have holp° to make so portly.°   *helped/stately*

NORTHUMBERLAND   My lord—

4. Either the text should read "tonight" (before the
robbery) or else Shakespeare intends to show
Prince Hal's mind intent, not on the robbery, but
on its aftermath. The soliloquy of the Prince that
follows has provoked much critical discussion.

5. Making good use of time, following the advice
given to Christians in a non-Christian world (see
Ephesians 5.16). "Skill": piece of good policy.
6. Discovered this to be true.

15 KING   Worcester, get thee gone, for I do see
      Danger and disobedience in thine eye;
      O, sir, your presence is too bold and peremptory,
      And majesty might never yet endure
      The moody frontier of a servant brow.[7]
20   You have good leave to leave us; when we need
      Your use and counsel we shall send for you.   [*Exit* WORCESTER.]
      You were about to speak.   [⟨*to* NORTHUMBERLAND⟩]
  NORTHUMBERLAND.   Yea, my good lord.
      Those prisoners in your highness' name demanded,
      Which Harry Percy here at Holmedon took,
25   Were, as he says, not with such strength denied
      As is delivered to your majesty.
      Either envy° therefore or misprisiòn°   *malice / mistake*
      Is guilty of this fault, and not my son.
  HOTSPUR   My liege, I did deny no prisoners.
30   But I remember, when the fight was done,
      When I was dry with rage and extreme toil,
      Breathless and faint, leaning upon my sword,
      Came there a certain lord, neat and trimly dressed,
      Fresh as a bridegroom, and his chin new reaped
35   Showed like a stubble-land at harvest-home.
      He was perfumèd like a milliner,[8]
      And 'twixt his finger and his thumb he held
      A pouncet box,° which ever and anon   *perfume box*
      He gave his nose and took 't away again;
40   Who therewith angry, when it next came there,
      Took it in snuff;[9] and still he smiled and talked,
      And as the soldiers bore dead bodies by,
      He called them untaught knaves, unmannerly,
      To bring a slovenly° unhandsome corse°   *disgusting / corpse*
45   Betwixt the wind and his nobility.
      With many holiday and lady terms[1]
      He questioned me; amongst the rest, demanded
      My prisoners in your majesty's behalf.
      I then, all smarting with my wounds being cold,
50   To be so pestered with a popinjay,°   *parrot*
      Out of my grief and my impatience
      Answered neglectingly I know not what,
      He should, or he should not—for he made me mad
      To see him shine so brisk and smell so sweet
55   And talk so like a waiting-gentlewoman
      Of guns and drums and wounds, God save the mark!
      And telling me the sovereign'st° thing on earth   *most curative*
      Was parmaceti[2] for an inward bruise,

---

7. I.e., a servant's brow showing defiance, like a
fortification ("frontier").
8. Not a maker of hats, but a dealer in perfumes,
women's gloves, etc.

9. I.e., was annoyed at it, with a pun on *snuffing
it up.*
1. Affected and effeminate language.
2. Spermaceti, whale oil used as an ointment.

And that it was great pity, so it was,
60 This villanous saltpeter[3] should be digged
Out of the bowels of the harmless earth,
Which many a good tall° fellow had destroyed   *brave*
So cowardly, and but for these vile guns
He would himself have been a soldier.
65 This bald° unjointed chat of his, my lord,   *trivial*
I answered indirectly as I said,
And I beseech you, let not his report
Come current[4] for an accusation
Betwixt my love and your high majesty.
70 BLUNT   The circumstance considered, good my lord,
Whate'er Lord Harry Percy then had said
To such a person and in such a place,
At such a time, with all the rest retold,
May reasonably die and never rise
75 To do him wrong or any way impeach
What then he said, so he unsay it now.
KING   Why, yet° he doth deny his prisoners,   *still*
But° with proviso and exceptiòn,   *except*
That we at our own charge shall ransom straight°   *immediately*
80 His brother-in-law, the foolish Mortimer,
Who, on my soul, hath willfully betrayed
The lives of those that he did lead to fight
Against that great magician, damned Glendower,
Whose daughter, as we hear, the Earl of March
85 Hath lately married. Shall our coffers then
Be emptied to redeem a traitor home?
Shall we buy treason? and indent with fears,[5]
When they have lost and forfeited themselves?
No, on the barren mountains let him starve;
90 For I shall never hold that man my friend
Whose tongue shall ask me for one penny cost
To ransom home revolted Mortimer.
HOTSPUR   Revolted Mortimer!
He never did fall off, my sovereign liege,
95 But by the chance of war. To prove that true
Needs no more but one tongue for all those wounds,
Those mouthèd wounds which valiantly he took
When on the gentle Severn's[6] sedgy bank
In single opposition, hand to hand,
100 He did confound° the best part of an hour   *spend*
In changing hardiment[7] with great Glendower;
Three times they breathed° and three times   *paused for breath*
did they drink

---

3. Used in gunpowder.
4. Be considered valid.
5. Enter into a contract with cowards.
6. A river on the England-Wales border. Wounds are often likened to mouths in Shakespeare. The

image may derive from their appearance and from the idea that they could speak as witnesses to what caused them (cf. *Julius Caesar* 3.2.229–231 and *Richard III* 1.2.55–56).
7. Testing prowess and exchanging blows.

Upon agreement of swift Severn's flood,
Who then, affrighted with their bloody looks,
105 Ran fearfully among the trembling reeds,
And hid his crisp[8] head in the hollow bank
Bloodstainèd with these valiant combatants.
Never did bare and rotten policy°   *craftiness, conspiracy*
Color° her working with such deadly wounds,   *disguise*
110 Nor never could the noble Mortimer
Receive so many, and all willingly;
Then let not him be slandered with revolt.
KING   Thou dost belie him, Percy, thou dost belie him;
He never did encounter with Glendower.
115 I tell thee,
He durst as well have met the devil alone
As Owen Glendower for an enemy.
Art thou not ashamed? But, sirrah,[9] henceforth
Let me not hear you speak of° Mortimer;   *mention*
120 Send me your prisoners with the speediest means,
Or you shall hear in such a kind from me
As will displease you. My Lord Northumberland,
We license your departure with your son.
Send us your prisoners, or you will hear of it.
       [*Exeunt* KING, 〈BLUNT, *and train*〉].
125 HOTSPUR   An if the devil come and roar for them
I will not send them; I will after straight
And tell him so, for I will ease my heart
Albeit I make a hazard of my head.
NORTHUMBERLAND   What, drunk with choler?° stay and   *anger*
       pause awhile.
Here comes your uncle.
       [*Enter* WORCESTER.]
130 HOTSPUR   Speak of Mortimer!
Zounds, I will speak of him, and let my soul
Want mercy if I do not join with him;
Yea, on his part° I'll empty all these veins,   *behalf*
And shed my dear blood drop by drop in the dust,
135 But I will lift the downtrod Mortimer
As high in the air as this unthankful king,
As this ingrate° and cankered° Bullingbrook.   *ungrateful / malignant*
NORTHUMBERLAND   Brother, the king hath made your nephew mad.
WORCESTER   Who struck this heat up after I was gone?
140 HOTSPUR   He will, forsooth, have all my prisoners;
And when I urged the ransom once again
Of my wife's brother, then his cheek looked pale,
And on my face he turned an eye of death,
Trembling even at the name of Mortimer.
145 WORCESTER   I cannot blame him; was not he proclaimed

8. I.e., curly (because of the waves).
9. A form of "sir," but used familiarly, and sometimes, as here, with a tone of contempt.

By Richard, that dead is, the next of blood?
NORTHUMBERLAND   He was—I heard the proclamatìon;
    And then it was when the unhappy king
    (Whose wrongs in us God pardon!¹) did set forth
150 Upon his Irish expeditiòn;
    From whence he intercepted did return
    To be deposed and shortly murderèd.
WORCESTER   And for whose death we in the world's wide mouth
    Live scandalized and foully spoken of.
155 HOTSPUR   But soft, I pray you; did King Richard then
    Proclaim my brother² Edmund Mortimer
    Heir to the crown?
NORTHUMBERLAND   He did; myself did hear it.
HOTSPUR   Nay, then I cannot blame his cousin king
    That wished him on the barren mountains starve.
160 But shall it be that you, that set the crown
    Upon the head of this forgetful man
    And for his sake wear the detested blot
    Of murderous subornation³—shall it be
    That you a world of curses undergo,
165 Being the agents, or base second means,°   tools, helpers
    The cords, the ladder, or the hangman rather?
    O pardon me that I descend so low
    To show the line and the predicament
    Wherein you range⁴ under this subtle king!
170 Shall it for shame be spoken in these days,
    Or fill up chronicles in time to come,
    That men of your nobility and power
    Did gage° them both in an unjust behalf,°   pledge / cause
    As both of you—God pardon it!—have done,
175 To put down Richard, that sweet lovely rose,
    And plant this thorn, this canker,⁵ Bullingbrook?
    And shall it in more shame be further spoken,
    That you are fooled, discarded, and shook off
    By him for whom these shames ye underwent?
180 No; yet time serves wherein you may redeem
    Your banished honors and restore yourselves
    Into the good thoughts of the world again,
    Revenge the jeering and disdained° contempt   disdainful
    Of this proud king, who studies day and night
185 To answer all the debt he owes to you
    Even with the bloody payment of your deaths:
    Therefore, I say—
WORCESTER   Peace, cousin, say no more;
    And now I will unclasp a secret book,
    And to your quick-conceiving discontents
190 I'll read you matter deep and dangerous,
    As full of peril and adventurous spirit

---

1. I.e., God pardon in us the wrongs we did to him.
2. Brother-in-law.
3. I.e., the stain of aiding and abetting murder.

4. I.e., to show the position and the category (or class) in which you are placed.
5. A wild rose, also a diseased spot in a nose.

As to o'er-walk a current roaring loud
On the unsteadfast footing of a spear.[6]
HOTSPUR   If he fall in, good night, or sink or swim.
195 Send danger from the east unto the west,
So° honor cross it from the north to south,   *provided that*
And let them grapple. O, the blood more stirs
To rouse a lion than to start[7] a hare!
NORTHUMBERLAND   Imagination of some great exploit
200 Drives him beyond the bounds of patience.
HOTSPUR   By heaven, methinks it were an easy leap
To pluck bright honor from the pale-faced moon,
Or dive into the bottom of the deep,
Where fathom line could never touch the ground,
205 And pluck up drownèd honor by the locks,
So he that doth redeem her thence might wear
Without corrival° all her dignities;   *rival*
But out upon this half-faced fellowship![8]
WORCESTER   He apprehends a world of figures[9] here,
210 But not the form of what he should attend.
Good cousin, give me audience for a while.
HOTSPUR   I cry you mercy.[1]
WORCESTER   Those same noble Scots
That are your prisoners—
HOTSPUR   I'll keep them all;
By God, he shall not have a Scot of them;
215 No, if a Scot would save his soul he shall not.
I'll keep them, by his hand.
WORCESTER   You start away
And lend no ear unto my purposes.
Those prisoners you shall keep.
HOTSPUR   Nay, I will; that's flat.
He said he would not ransom Mortimer,
220 Forbade my tongue to speak of Mortimer,
But I will find him when he lies asleep,
And in his ear I'll holla "Mortimer!"
Nay,
I'll have a starling shall be taught to speak[2]
225 Nothing but "Mortimer," and give it him
To keep his anger still in motion.
WORCESTER   Hear you, cousin, a word.
HOTSPUR   All studies here I solemnly defy,
Save how to gall° and pinch this Bullingbrook,   *irritate*
230 And that same sword-and-buckler[3] Prince of Wales,
But that I think his father loves him not
And would be glad he met with some mischance,
I would have him poisoned with a pot of ale.[4]

6. A spear laid down as a footbridge.
7. Arouse, in hunting.
8. Miserable sharing (of honor) with someone else.
9. Rhetorical figures of speech.
1. Beg your pardon.

2. Starlings used to be taught to speak, as parrots are now.
3. Weapons used by the lowest class of soldiers and servants. Gentlemen used rapiers.
4. The drink of the lower classes.

WORCESTER   Farewell, kinsman; I'll talk to you
235   When you are better tempered to attend.
NORTHUMBERLAND   Why, what a wasp-stung and impatient fool
      Art thou to break into this woman's mood,
      Tying thine ear to no tongue but thine own!
HOTSPUR   Why, look you, I am whipped and scourged with rods,
240   Nettled and stung with pismires,° when I hear   *ants*
      Of this vile politician Bullingbrook.
      In Richard's time—what do you call the place?—
      A plague upon it, it is in Gloucestershire—
      'Twas where the madcap duke his uncle kept,°   *lived*
245   His uncle York, where I first bow'd my knee
      Unto this king of smiles, this Bullingbrook
      'Sblood!—
      When you and he came back from Ravenspurgh.
NORTHUMBERLAND   At Berkeley castle.
250 HOTSPUR   You say true.
      Why, what a candy deal of courtesy
      This fawning greyhound[5] then did proffer me!
      "Look when his infant fortune came to age,"
      And "gentle Harry Percy," and "kind cousin";
255   O, the devil take such cozeners![6] God forgive me!
      Good uncle, tell your tale; I have done.
WORCESTER   Nay, if you have not, to it again;
      We will stay your leisure.
HOTSPUR   I have done, i' faith.
WORCESTER   Then once more to your Scottish prisoners.
260   Deliver them up without their ransom straight,
      And make the Douglas' son your only mean
      For powers in Scotland, which, for divers reasons
      Which I shall send you written, be assured
      Will easily be granted. You, my lord, [⟨*to* NORTHUMBERLAND⟩]
265   Your son in Scotland being thus employed,
      Shall secretly into the bosom creep
      Of that same noble prelate well beloved,
      The archbishop.
HOTSPUR   Of York, is it not?
270 WORCESTER   True; who bears hard
      His brother's death at Bristol, the Lord Scroop.
      I speak not this in estimation,°   *by conjecture*
      As what I think might be, but what I know
      Is ruminated, plotted, and set down,
275   And only stays but to behold the face
      Of that occasion that shall bring it on.
HOTSPUR   I smell it; upon my life, it will do well.
NORTHUMBERLAND   Before the game is afoot, thou still let'st slip.[7]

---

5. A complex image that occurs in Shakespeare several times (cf. *Hamlet* 3.2.50–52 and *Antony and Cleopatra* 4.12.20–23). The idea of fawning or flattery called up to Shakespeare's mind the image of a dog begging for sweetmeats ("candy").

6. Cheaters, with, of course, a pun on *cousin*.
7. An image from hunting. The meaning is "You always ('still') release the dogs before we are ready to pursue the game."

HOTSPUR   Why, it cannot choose but be a noble plot;
280   And then the power of Scotland and of York
      To join with Mortimer, ha?
WORCESTER   And so they shall.
HOTSPUR   In faith, it is exceedingly well aimed.
WORCESTER   And 'tis no little reason bids us speed,
285   For, bear ourselves as even as we can,
      The king will always think him in our debt,
      And think we think ourselves unsatisfied,
      Till he hath found a time to pay us home;
      And see already how he doth begin
290   To make us strangers to his looks of love.
HOTSPUR   He does, he does; we'll be revenged on him.
WORCESTER   Cousin, farewell. No further go in this
      Than I by letters shall direct your course.
      When time is ripe, which will be suddenly,
295   I'll steal to Glendower and Lord Mortimer,
      Where you and Douglas and our powers at once,
      As I will fashion it, shall happily meet,
      To bear our fortunes in our own strong arms,
      Which now we hold at much uncertainty.
300   NORTHUMBERLAND   Farewell, good brother; we shall thrive, I trust.
HOTSPUR   Uncle, adieu; O, let the hours be short
      Till fields and blows and groans applaud our sport!   [*Exeunt.*]

Act 2

SCENE 1

[*Enter a* CARRIER *with a lantern in his hand.*]

FIRST CARRIER   Heigh-ho! an it be not four by the day, I'll be hanged;
      Charles' wain[9] is over the new chimney, and yet our horse not packed.
      What, ostler!
OSTLER [*within*]   Anon, anon.
5   FIRST CARRIER   I prithee, Tom, beat Cut's saddle,[1] put a few flocks in the
      point;[2] poor jade, is wrung in the withers out of all cess.[3]
      [*Enter another* CARRIER.]
SECOND CARRIER   Peas and beans are as dank here as a dog, and that is
      the next way to give poor jades the bots;[4] this house is turned upside
      down since Robin Ostler died.
10   FIRST CARRIER   Poor fellow, never joyed since the price of oats rose; it was
      the death of him.
SECOND CARRIER   I think this be the most villainous house in all London
      road for fleas; I am stung like a tench.[5]
FIRST CARRIER   Like a tench! by the mass, there is ne'er a king christen[6]
15   could be better bit than I have been since the first cock.

8. Raising an army.
9. The constellation of the Great Bear, or Big Dipper.
1. A saddle was beaten to make it soft. "Cut" is a name for a horse with a docked tail.
2. Pieces of wool under the point of the saddle.

3. I.e., is sore excessively in the shoulders.
4. I.e., that is the easiest way to give poor nags worms in the stomach.
5. A fish covered with red spots, like fleabites.
6. Christian king.

SECOND CARRIER   Why, they will allow us ne'er a jordan, and then we leak
in your chimney, and your chamber-lye breeds fleas like a loach.[7]

FIRST CARRIER   What, ostler! come away and be hanged, come away!

SECOND CARRIER   I have a gammon of bacon and two razes[8] of ginger, to
20   be delivered as far as Charing Cross.

FIRST CARRIER   God's body! the turkeys in my pannier[9] are quite starved.
What, ostler! A plague on thee, hast thou never an eye in thy head? canst
not hear? An 'twere not as good deed as drink to break the pate on thee,
I am a very villain. Come and be hanged! hast no faith in thee?

   [Enter GADSHILL.]

25   GADSHILL   Good morrow, carriers. What's o'clock?

FIRST CARRIER   I think it be two o'clock.

GADSHILL   I prithee lend me thy lantern to see my gelding in the stable.

FIRST CARRIER   Nay, by God, soft; I know a trick worth two of that, i' faith.

GADSHILL   I pray thee lend me thine.

30   SECOND CARRIER   Aye, when? canst tell?[1] Lend me thy lantern, quoth he?
marry, I'll see thee hanged first.

GADSHILL   Sirrah carrier, what time do you mean to come to London?

SECOND CARRIER   Time enough to go to bed with a candle, I warrant thee.
Come, neighbor Mugs, we'll call up the gentlemen; they will along with
35   company, for they have great charge.[2]

   [Exeunt ⟨CARRIERS⟩.]

GADSHILL   What ho! chamberlain!

   [Enter CHAMBERLAIN.]

CHAMBERLAIN   At hand, quoth pickpurse.

GADSHILL   That's even as fair as At hand, quoth the chamberlain, for thou
variest no more from picking of purses than giving direction doth from
40   laboring; thou layest the plot how.[3]

CHAMBERLAIN   Good morrow, Master Gadshill. It holds current[4] that I
told you yesternight; there's a franklin in the weald of Kent[5] hath brought
three hundred marks with him in gold—I heard him tell it to one of his
company last night at supper—a kind of auditor, one that hath abun-
45   dance of charge[6] too, God knows what. They are up already and call for
eggs and butter; they will away presently.[7]

GADSHILL   Sirrah, if they meet not with Saint Nicholas' clerks,[8] I'll give
thee this neck.

CHAMBERLAIN   No, I'll none of it; I pray thee, keep that for the hangman,
50   for I know thou worshipest Saint Nicholas as truly as a man of falsehood
may.

GADSHILL   What talkest thou to me of the hangman? if I hang, I'll make
a fat pair of gallows; for if I hang, old Sir John hangs with me, and thou
knowest he is no starveling. Tut! there are other Trojans[9] that thou

---

7. A fish that breeds prolifically. "Jordan": chamber pot. "Chamber-lye": urine.
8. Roots. "Gammon": haunch.
9. Basket.
1. A colloquial expression of contemptuous
refusal.
2. Valuable cargo.
3. A pun: "giving direction" means supervising, as
contrasted with "laboring," but it was also the
name for informing thieves about the journeys of

prospective victims (laying "the plot how").
4. Remains true.
5. A section of that county, formerly wooded.
"Franklin": a freeholder, just below a gentleman in
rank.
6. Considerable property. "Auditor": revenue officer.
7. At once.
8. Highwaymen.
9. Roisterers, good fellows.

55 dream'st not of, the which for sport sake are content to do the profession
some grace, that would, if matters should be looked into, for their own
credit sake make all whole. I am joined with no foot land-rakers, no long-
staff sixpenny strikers,[1] none of these mad mustachio purple-hued maltworms, but with nobility and tranquility, burgomasters and great oneyers,
60 such as can hold in,[2] such as will strike sooner than speak, and speak
sooner than drink, and drink sooner than pray; and yet, zounds, I lie, for
they pray continually to their saint, the commonwealth, or rather, not
pray to her but prey on her, for they ride up and down on her and make
her their boots.[3]
65 CHAMBERLAIN   What, the commonwealth their boots? will she hold out
water in foul way?[4]
GADSHILL   She will, she will; justice hath liquored her.[5] We steal as in a
castle, cocksure; we have the receipt of fern seed,[6] we walk invisible.
CHAMBERLAIN   Nay, by my faith, I think you are more beholding to the
70 night than to fern seed for your walking invisible.
GADSHILL   Give me thy hand; thou shalt have a share in our purchase,[7] as
I am a true man.
CHAMBERLAIN   Nay, rather let me have it, as you are a false thief.
GADSHILL   Go to; *homo* is a common name to all men. Bid the ostler bring
75 my gelding out of the stable. Farewell, you muddy[8] knave.[*Exeunt.*]

SCENE 2

[*Enter* PRINCE *and* POINS.]

POINS   Come shelter, shelter; I have removed Falstaff's horse, and he frets
like a gummed velvet.
PRINCE   Stand close.[9]
[*Enter* FALSTAFF.]
FALSTAFF   Poins! Poins, and be hanged! Poins!
5 PRINCE   Peace, ye fat-kidneyed rascal! what a brawling dost thou keep!
FALSTAFF   Where's Poins, Hal?
PRINCE   He is walked up to the top of the hill; I'll go seek him.
[(*He pretends to go, but hides onstage with* POINS.)]
FALSTAFF   I am accursed to rob in that thief's company; the rascal hath
removed my horse, and tied him I know not where. If I travel but four
10 foot by the squier[1] further afoot, I shall break my wind. Well, I doubt
not but to die a fair death for all this, if I 'scape hanging for killing that
rogue. I have forsworn his company hourly any time this two and twenty
years, and yet I am bewitched with the rogue's company. If the rascal
have not given me medicines to make me love him, I'll be hanged; it
15 could not be else; I have drunk medicines. Poins! Hal! a plague upon
you both! Bardolph! Peto! I'll starve ere I'll rob a foot further. An 'twere

1. Small-time thieves. "Land-rakers": footpads.
2. Keep secret. "Purple-hued maltworms": flushed, swaggering barflies. "Oneyers": dignitaries.
3. Booty.
4. Keep one dry in muddy roads, i.e., give protection.
5. I.e., those who control the laws have greased (or bribed) her.

6. I.e., we have the recipe for fern seed (supposed to make one invisible).
7. Takings.
8. Muddleheaded.
9. Hide. "Gummed velvet": cheap velvet was treated with gum to make the pile stiff; as a result it soon fretted or wore away.
1. Ruler, yardstick.

not as good a deed as drink to turn true man and to leave these rogues, I am the veriest varlet that ever chewed with a tooth. Eight yards of uneven ground is threescore and ten miles afoot with me, and the stony-hearted villains know it well enough; a plague upon it when thieves cannot be true one to another! [*They whistle.*] Whew! A plague upon you all! Give me my horse, you rogues; give me my horse, and be hanged!

PRINCE   Peace, ye fat-guts! lie down; lay thine ear close to the ground and list if thou canst hear the tread of travelers.

FALSTAFF   Have you any levers to lift me up again, being down? 'Sblood, I'll not bear my own flesh so far afoot again for all the coin in thy father's exchequer. What a plague mean ye to colt me thus?

PRINCE   Thou liest; thou art not colted, thou art uncolted.[2]

FALSTAFF   I prithee, good Prince, Hal, help me to my horse, good king's son.

PRINCE   Out, ye rogue! shall I be your ostler?

FALSTAFF   Go hang thyself in thine own heir-apparent garters![3] If I be ta'en, I'll peach for this. An I have not ballads made on you all and sung to filthy tunes, let a cup of sack be my poison; when a jest is so forward, and afoot too! I hate it.

    [*Enter* GADSHILL.]

GADSHILL   Stand.

FALSTAFF   So I do, against my will.

POINS [*coming forward with* BARDOLPH *and* PETO]   O, 'tis our setter; I know his voice. Bardolph, what news?

BARDOLPH   Case[4] ye, case ye, on with your vizards; there's money of the king's coming down the hill; 'tis going to the king's exchequer.

FALSTAFF   You lie, you rogue; 'tis going to the king's tavern.

GADSHILL   There's enough to make us all.

FALSTAFF   To be hanged.

PRINCE   Sirs, you four shall front them in the narrow lane; Ned Poins and I will walk lower; if they 'scape from your encounter, then they light on us.

PETO   How many be there of them?

GADSHILL   Some eight or ten.

FALSTAFF   Zounds, will they not rob us?

PRINCE   What, a coward, Sir John Paunch?

FALSTAFF   Indeed, I am not John of Gaunt, your grandfather, but yet no coward, Hal.

PRINCE   Well, we leave that to the proof.

POINS   Sirrah Jack, thy horse stands behind the hedge; when thou need'st him, there thou shalt find him. Farewell, and stand fast.

FALSTAFF   Now cannot I strike him, if I should be hanged.

PRINCE [⟨*aside to* POINS⟩]   Ned, where are our disguises?

POINS [⟨*aside*⟩]   Here, hard by; stand close.

    [⟨*Exeunt* PRINCE *and* POINS.⟩]

---

2. You have had your horse stolen. "To colt": trick.
3. As heir apparent to the throne, Hal would be a

knight of the Order of the Garter.
4. Mask.

60 FALSTAFF Now, my masters, happy man be his dole,[5] say I; every man to
his business.

[*Enter the* TRAVELERS.]

FIRST TRAVELER Come, neighbor, the boy shall lead our horses down the
hill; we'll walk afoot awhile, and ease our legs.

THIEVES Stand!

65 TRAVELERS Jesus bless us!

FALSTAFF Strike; down with them; cut the villains' throats. Ah, whoreson
caterpillars,[6] bacon-fed knaves, they hate us youth! Down with them,
fleece them.

TRAVELERS O, we are undone, both we and ours forever!

70 FALSTAFF Hang ye, gorbellied knaves, are ye undone? No, ye fat chuffs,[7]
I would your store were here! On, bacons, on! What, ye knaves, young
men must live! You are grand jurors, are ye? we'll jure ye, faith.

[*Here they rob them and bind them. Exeunt.*]

[*Enter the* PRINCE *and* POINS *in buckram.*]

PRINCE The thieves have bound the true men. Now could thou and I rob
the thieves and go merrily to London; it would be argument[8] for a week,

75 laughter for a month, and a good jest forever.

POINS Stand close; I hear them coming.

[*Enter the* THIEVES *again.*]

FALSTAFF Come, my masters, let us share, and then to horse before day.
An the Prince and Poins be not two arrant cowards, there's no equity
stirring;[9] there's no more valor in that Poins than in a wild duck.

80 PRINCE Your money!

POINS Villains!

[*As they are sharing, the* PRINCE *and* POINS *set upon them; they all run
away; and* FALSTAFF, *after a blow or two, runs away too, leaving the booty
behind them.*]

PRINCE Got with much ease. Now merrily to horse;
The thieves are all scattered and possessed with fear
So strongly that they dare not meet each other;

85 Each takes his fellow for an officer.
Away, good Ned. Falstaff sweats to death,
And lards the lean earth as he walks along;
Were't not for laughing, I should pity him.

POINS How the fat rogue roared! [*Exeunt.*]

SCENE 3

[*Enter* HOTSPUR, *alone, reading a letter.*]

HOTSPUR "But for mine own part, my lord, I could be well contented to
be there, in respect of the love I bear your house." He could be contented;
why is he not, then? In respect of the love he bears our house, he shows
in this, he loves his own barn better than he loves our house. Let me see

5 some more. "The purpose you undertake is dangerous." Why, that's cer-

---

5. I.e., good luck!
6. "Caterpillars of the commonwealth" was a common phrase, referring to rogues. Falstaff here
applies ridiculously inappropriate terms to the
travelers and to himself (e.g., "youth").
7. Misers. "Gorbellied": fat.
8. Subject of stories.
9. There's no justice.

tain. 'Tis dangerous to take a cold, to sleep, to drink; but I tell you, my lord fool, out of this nettle, danger, we pluck this flower, safety.[1] "The purpose you undertake is dangerous, the friends you have named uncertain, the time itself unsorted,[2] and your whole plot too light for the counterpoise of so great an opposition." Say you so, say you so? I say unto you again, you are a shallow cowardly hind,[3] and you lie. What a lackbrain is this! By the Lord, our plot is a good plot as ever was laid, our friends true and constant; a good plot, good friends, and full of expectation; an excellent plot, very good friends. What a frosty-spirited rogue is this! Why, my lord of York[4] commends the plot and the general course of the action. Zounds, an I were now by this rascal I could brain him with his lady's fan. Is there not my father, my uncle, and myself? Lord Edmund Mortimer, my lord of York, and Owen Glendower? is there not besides the Douglas? have I not all their letters to meet me in arms by the ninth of the next month, and are they not some of them set forward already? What a pagan rascal is this, an infidel! Ha! you shall see now in very sincerity of fear and cold heart, will he to the king and lay open all our proceedings. O, I could divide myself and go to buffets,[5] for moving[6] such a dish of skim milk with so honorable an action! Hang him! let him tell the king. We are prepared; I will set forward tonight.

    [*Enter his* LADY.]

How now, Kate! I must leave you within these two hours.

LADY   O, my good lord, why are you thus alone?
For what offense have I this fortnight been
A banished woman from my Harry's bed?
Tell me, sweet lord, what is 't that takes from thee
Thy stomach,° pleasure, and thy golden sleep?   *appetite*
Why dost thou bend thine eyes upon the earth,
And start so often when thou sit'st alone?
Why hast thou lost the fresh blood in thy cheeks,
And given my treasures and my rights of thee
To thick-eyed musing and cursed melancholy?
In thy faint slumbers I by thee have watched
And heard thee murmur tales of iron wars,
Speak terms of manage° to thy bounding steed,   *horsemanship*
Cry "Courage! to the field!" And thou hast talked
Of sallies and retires, of trenches, tents,
Of palisadoes, frontiers, parapets,
Of basilisks, of cannon, culverin,[7]
Of prisoners' ransom and of soldiers slain,
And all the currents of a heady fight.
Thy spirit within thee hath been so at war
And thus hath so bestirred thee in thy sleep
That beads of sweat have stood upon thy brow
Like bubbles in a late-disturbèd stream,

---

1. The nettle if touched tenderly will sting; if grasped firmly, will not.
2. Unsuitable.
3. Peasant.
4. The archbishop of York.

5. Split myself in two and let the parts fight each other.
6. Urging.
7. Three kinds of artillery (named here in decreasing order of weight).

50 And in thy face strange motions have appeared
Such as we see when men restrain their breath
On some great sudden hest.° O, what portents are these?   *command*
Some heavy business hath my lord in hand
And I must know it, else he loves me not.
HOTSPUR What, ho!
                    [⟨*Enter* SERVANT.⟩]
55   Is Gilliams with the packet gone?
SERVANT He is, my lord, an hour ago.
HOTSPUR Hath Butler brought those horses from the sheriff?
SERVANT One horse, my lord, he brought even now.
HOTSPUR What horse? a roan, a crop-ear, is it not?
SERVANT It is, my lord.
60 HOTSPUR   That roan shall be my throne.
Well, I will back° him straight; O Esperance![8]   *mount*
Bid Butler lead him forth into the park.   [⟨*Exit* SERVANT.⟩]
LADY But hear you, my lord.
HOTSPUR What say'st thou, my lady?
65 LADY What is it carries you away?
HOTSPUR Why, my horse, my love, my horse.
LADY Out, you mad-headed ape!
A weasel hath not such a deal of spleen[9]
As you are tossed with. In faith
70 I'll know your business, Harry, that I will.
I fear my brother Mortimer doth stir
About his title, and hath sent for you
To line° his enterprise; but if you go[1]—   *support*
HOTSPUR So far afoot, I shall be weary, love.
75 LADY Come, come, you paraquito,° answer me   *parrot*
Directly unto this question that I ask.
In faith, I'll break thy little finger, Harry,
An if thou wilt not tell me all things true.
HOTSPUR Away,
80 Away, you trifler! Love! I love thee not,
I care not for thee, Kate; this is no world
To play with mammets° and to tilt with lips;   *dolls*
We must have bloody noses and cracked crowns,[2]
And pass them current too. God's me, my horse!
85 What say'st thou, Kate? what wouldst thou have with me?
LADY Do you not love me? do you not, indeed?
Well, do not then, for since you love me not
I will not love myself. Do you not love me?
Nay, tell me if you speak in jest or no.
90 HOTSPUR Come, wilt thou see me ride?
And when I am o' horseback, I will swear

---

8. The battle cry of the Percies: "Hope!"
9. The spleen was supposed to be the source of sudden and violent emotions. The weasel was considered a very impetuous animal.
1. Besides its ordinary sense, which Lady Percy

uses, "go" also meant "walk," the sense in which Hotspur takes it.
2. Broken heads, with a pun on *crowns* as coins and with allusion to the overthrow of kings.

I love thee infinitely. But hark you, Kate,
I must not have you henceforth question me
Whither I go, nor reason whereabout;
95 Whither I must, I must; and, to conclude,
This evening must I leave you, gentle Kate.
I know you wise, but yet no farther wise
Than Harry Percy's wife; constant you are,
But yet a woman, and for secrecy
100 No lady closer; for I well believe
Thou wilt not utter what thou dost not know,
And so far will I trust thee, gentle Kate.
LADY   How! so far?
HOTSPUR   Not an inch further. But hark you, Kate,
105 Whither I go, thither shall you go too;
Today will I set forth, tomorrow you.
Will this content you, Kate?
LADY   It must of force.³   [*Exeunt.*]

SCENE 4

[*Enter the* PRINCE *and* POINS.]

PRINCE   Ned, prithee come out of that fat⁴ room, and lend me thy hand
to laugh a little.
POINS   Where hast been, Hal?
PRINCE   With three or four loggerheads⁵ amongst three or four-score hogs-
5 heads. I have sounded the very bass string of humility. Sirrah, I am sworn
brother to a leash of drawers,⁶ and can call them all by their christen
names, as Tom, Dick, and Francis. They take it already upon their salvation, that though I be but Prince of Wales, yet I am the king of courtesy, and tell me flatly I am no proud Jack, like Falstaff, but a Corinthian,⁷
10 a lad of mettle, a good boy—by the Lord, so they call me—and when I
am king of England I shall command all the good lads in Eastcheap.
They call drinking deep, dyeing scarlet, and when you breathe in your
watering⁸ they cry "hem!" and bid you play it off. To conclude, I am so
good a proficient in one quarter of an hour that I can drink with any
15 tinker in his own language during my life. I tell thee, Ned, thou hast lost
much honor, that thou wert not with me in this action. But, sweet Ned—
to sweeten which name of Ned, I give thee this penny worth of sugar,
clapped even now into my hand by an underskinker,⁹ one that never
spake other English in his life than "Eight shillings and sixpence," and
20 "You are welcome," with this shrill addition, "Anon, anon, sir! Score a
pint of bastard in the Half-Moon,"¹ or so. But, Ned, to drive away the
time till Falstaff come, I prithee do thou stand in some by-room, while
I question my puny drawer to what end he gave me the sugar, and do

---

3. Of necessity.
4. Vat. This establishes that the scene is a tavern.
5. Blockheads.
6. Group of tapsters, waiters.
7. Good fellow.
8. Drink.

9. Assistant waiter.
1. I.e., charge a pint of "bastard" (a sweet Spanish
wine) to a customer in the room called "Half-
Moon." "Anon": immediately (the reply of a servant
when called, equivalent to "Coming!").

thou never leave calling "Francis," that his tale to me may be nothing
25 but "Anon." Step aside, and I'll show thee a precedent.[2]

POINS   Francis!

PRINCE   Thou art perfect.

POINS   Francis!   [⟨*Exit* POINS.⟩]
        [*Enter* DRAWER.]

FRANCIS   Anon, anon, sir. Look down into the Pomgarnet,[3] Ralph.

30 PRINCE   Come hither, Francis.

FRANCIS   My lord?

PRINCE   How long hast thou to serve,[4] Francis?

FRANCIS   Forsooth, five years, and as much as to—

POINS [*within*]   Francis!

35 FRANCIS   Anon, anon, sir.

PRINCE   Five year! by 'r Lady, a long lease for the clinking of pewter. But,
        Francis, darest thou be so valiant as to play the coward with thy indenture
        and show it a fair pair of heels and run from it?

FRANCIS   O Lord, sir, I'll be sworn upon all the books[5] in England, I could
40   find in my heart—

POINS [*within*]   Francis!

FRANCIS   Anon, sir.

PRINCE   How old art thou, Francis?

FRANCIS   Let me see—about Michaelmas[6] next I shall be—

45 POINS [*within*]   Francis!

FRANCIS   Anon, sir. Pray stay a little, my lord.

PRINCE   Nay, but hark you, Francis: for the sugar thou gavest me, 'twas a
        pennyworth, was't not?

FRANCIS   O Lord, I would it had been two!

50 PRINCE   I will give thee for it a thousand pound; ask me when thou wilt,
        and thou shalt have it.

POINS [*within*]   Francis!

FRANCIS   Anon, anon.

PRINCE   Anon, Francis? No, Francis, but tomorrow, Francis; or Francis,
55   o' Thursday, or indeed, Francis, when thou wilt. But, Francis!

FRANCIS   My lord?

PRINCE   Wilt thou rob this leathern-jerkin, crystal-button, not-pated,
        agate-ring, puke-stocking, caddis-garter,[7] smooth-tongue, Spanish-
        pouch—

60 FRANCIS   O Lord, sir, who do you mean?

PRINCE   Why, then, your brown bastard is your only drink, for
        look you, Francis, your white canvas doublet will sully. In Barbary, sir,
        it cannot come to so much.[8]

FRANCIS   What, sir?

65 POINS [*within*]   Francis!

PRINCE   Away, you rogue, dost thou not hear them call?

---

2. Example.
3. Pomegranate (another room in the tavern).
4. I.e., to finish out his apprenticeship, usually a
seven-year period under an "indenture" or agreement.
5. I.e., Bibles.
6. September 29.

7. Worsted tape garter. "Leathern-jerken":
leather-jacketed. "Not-pated": with short hair.
"Puke": dark gray.
8. Deliberate nonsense to confuse Francis and
one of the first instances of double-talk in English
literature.

[*Here they both call him; the drawer stands amazed, not knowing which way to go.*]

[*Enter* VINTNER.]

VINTNER   What, stand'st thou still, and hear'st such a calling? Look to the guests within. [*Exit* FRANCIS.] My lord, old Sir John with half-a-dozen more are at the door; shall I let them in?

70   PRINCE   Let them alone awhile, and then open the door. [*Exit* VINTNER.] Poins!

[*Enter* POINS.]

POINS   Anon, anon, sir.

PRINCE   Sirrah, Falstaff and the rest of the thieves are at the door; shall we be merry?

75   POINS   As merry as crickets, my lad. But hark ye, what cunning match have you made with this jest of the drawer? come, what's the issue?

PRINCE   I am now of all humors[9] that have showed themselves humors since the old days of goodman Adam to the pupil[1] age of this present twelve o'clock at midnight.

[⟨*Enter* FRANCIS.⟩]

80   What's o'clock, Francis?

FRANCIS   Anon, anon, sir.   [⟨*Exit.*⟩]

PRINCE   That ever this fellow should have fewer words than a parrot, and yet the son of a woman! His industry is upstairs and downstairs, his eloquence the parcel[2] of a reckoning. I am not yet of Percy's mind, the
85   Hotspur of the north, he that kills me some six or seven dozen of Scots at a breakfast, washes his hands, and says to his wife "Fie upon this quiet life! I want work." "O my sweet Harry," says she, "how many hast thou killed today?" "Give my roan horse a drench," says he, and answers "Some fourteen," an hour after, "a trifle, a trifle." I prithee, call in Falstaff; I'll
90   play Percy, and that damned brawn shall play Dame Mortimer his wife. "Rivo!"[3] says the drunkard. Call in ribs, call in tallow.

[*Enter* FALSTAFF, ⟨GADSHILL, BARDOLPH, *and* PETO, FRANCIS *following with wine*⟩.]

POINS   Welcome, Jack; where hast thou been?

FALSTAFF   A plague of all cowards, I say, and a vengeance too, marry and amen! Give me a cup of sack, boy. Ere I lead this life long, I'll sew nether
95   stocks[4] and mend them and foot them too. A plague of all cowards! Give me a cup of sack, rogue. Is there no virtue extant?   [*He drinks.*]

PRINCE   Didst thou ever see Titan[5] kiss a dish of butter, pitiful-hearted butter that melted at the sweet tale of the sun's? If thou didst, then behold that compound.

100   FALSTAFF   You rogue, here's lime in this sack too;[6] there is nothing but roguery to be found in villainous man, yet a coward is worse than a cup of sack with lime in it. A villainous coward! Go thy ways, old Jack, die when thou wilt; if manhood, good manhood, be not forgot upon the face of the earth, then am I a shotten herring.[7] There lives not three good
105   men unhanged in England, and one of them is fat and grows old. God

9. Temperaments, dispositions, i.e., as a result of teasing the servant, I am now in the mood for anything.
1. Youthful.
2. Item.

3. Drink up!
4. Stockings.
5. The sun.
6. Lime was used to make wine sparkle.
7. A herring that has cast its spawn and is lean.

help the while; a bad world, I say. I would I were a weaver; I could sing psalms[8] or anything. A plague of all cowards, I say still.

PRINCE   How now, woolsack, what mutter you?

FALSTAFF   A king's son! If I do not beat thee out of thy kingdom with a dagger of lath,[9] and drive all thy subjects afore thee like a flock of wild geese, I'll never wear hair on my face more. You Prince of Wales!

PRINCE   Why, you whoreson round man, what's the matter?

FALSTAFF   Are not you a coward? answer me to that; and Poins there?

POINS   Zounds, ye fat paunch, an ye call me coward, by the Lord I'll stab thee.

FALSTAFF   I call thee coward! I'll see thee damned ere I call thee coward; but I would give a thousand pound I could run as fast as thou canst. You are straight enough in the shoulders, you care not who sees your back; call you that backing of your friends? A plague upon such backing! give me them that will face me. Give me a cup of sack; I am a rogue if I drunk today.

PRINCE   O villain! thy lips are scarce wiped since thou drunk'st last.

FALSTAFF   All's one for that. [*He drinks.*] A plague of all cowards, still say I.

PRINCE   What's the matter?

FALSTAFF   What's the matter! there be four of us here have ta'en a thousand pound this day morning.

PRINCE   Where is it, Jack? where is it?

FALSTAFF   Where is it? taken from us it is—a hundred upon poor four of us.

PRINCE   What, a hundred, man?

FALSTAFF   I am a rogue if I were not at half-sword[1] with a dozen of them two hours together. I have 'scaped by miracle. I am eight times thrust through the doublet, four through the hose,[2] my buckler cut through and through, my sword hacked like a handsaw—*ecce signum!*[3] I never dealt better since I was a man; all would not do. A plague of all cowards! Let them speak; if they speak more or less than truth, they are villains and the sons of darkness.

PRINCE   Speak, sirs; how was it?

GADSHILL   We four set upon some dozen—

FALSTAFF   Sixteen at least, my lord.

GADSHILL   And bound them.

PETO   No, no, they were not bound.

FALSTAFF   You rogue, they were bound, every man of them, or I am a Jew else, an Ebrew Jew.

GADSHILL   As we were sharing, some six or seven fresh men set upon us—

FALSTAFF   And unbound the rest, and then come in the other.

PRINCE   What, fought you with them all?

FALSTAFF   All! I know not what you call all, but if I fought not with fifty of them, I am a bunch of radish; if there were not two or three and fifty upon poor old Jack, then am I no two-legged creature.

PRINCE   Pray God you have not murdered some of them.

8. Protestant weavers from Flanders were notorious for singing psalms.
9. A stick used by Vice in the old morality plays.

1. At half a sword's length.
2. Breeches.
3. Here's the proof!

FALSTAFF   Nay, that's past praying for; I have peppered two of them. Two
I am sure I have paid, two rogues in buckram suits. I tell thee what, Hal,
155   if I tell thee a lie, spit in my face, call me horse. Thou knowest my old
ward; here I lay,[4] and thus I bore my point. Four rogues in buckram let
drive at me—

PRINCE   What, four? thou saidst but two even now.

FALSTAFF   Four, Hal; I told thee four.

160   POINS   Aye, aye, he said four.

FALSTAFF   These four came all a-front, and mainly[5] thrust at me. I made
me no more ado but took all their seven points in my target,[6] thus.

PRINCE   Seven? why, there were but four even now.

FALSTAFF   In buckram?

165   POINS   Aye, four, in buckram suits.

FALSTAFF   Seven, by these hilts, or I am a villain else.

PRINCE   Prithee, let him alone; we shall have more anon.

FALSTAFF   Dost thou hear me, Hal?

PRINCE   Aye, and mark thee too, Jack.

170   FALSTAFF   Do so, for it is worth the listening to. These nine in buckram
that I told thee of—

PRINCE   So, two more already.

FALSTAFF   Their points being broken—

POINS   Down fell their hose.[7]

175   FALSTAFF   Began to give me ground; but I followed me close, came in foot
and hand, and with a thought[8] seven of the eleven I paid.

PRINCE   O monstrous! eleven buckram men grown out of two!

FALSTAFF   But, as the devil would have it, three misbegotten knaves in
Kendal green[9] came at my back and let drive at me, for it was so dark,
180   Hal, that thou couldst not see thy hand.

PRINCE   These lies are like their father that begets them—gross as a mountain, open, palpable. Why, thou clay-brained guts, thou knotty-pated
fool, thou whoreson, obscene, greasy tallow-catch[1]—

FALSTAFF   What, art thou mad? art thou mad? is not the truth the truth?

185   PRINCE   Why, how couldst thou know these men in Kendal green, when
it was so dark thou couldst not see thy hand? come, tell us your reason.
What sayest thou to this?

POINS   Come, your reason, Jack, your reason.

FALSTAFF   What, upon compulsion? Zounds, an I were at the strappado,
190   or all the racks[2] in the world, I would not tell you on compulsion. Give
you a reason on compulsion! if reasons[3] were as plentiful as blackberries,
I would give no man a reason upon compulsion, I.

PRINCE   I'll be no longer guilty of this sin; this sanguine coward, this bed-
presser, this horseback-breaker, this huge hill of flesh—

195   FALSTAFF   'Sblood, you starveling, you eelskin, you dried neat's tongue,
you bull's pizzle, you stockfish![4] O for breath to utter what is like thee!

---

4. This was my stance. "Ward": defense.
5. Strongly.
6. Shield.
7. Poins puns on the other meaning of *points*: the
laces used to tie a man's hose to his doublet.
8. As quick as thought.
9. A coarse cloth.

1. Piece of tallow from which chandlers made
candles
2. "Strappado" and "racks" are methods of torture.
3. A pun on the word *raisin*, which was spelled and
pronounced like *reason* in Elizabethan England.
4. I.e., you ox tongue, you bull's penis, you dried
cod!

you tailor's yard, you sheath, you bow case, you vile standing-tuck[5]—

PRINCE   Well, breathe awhile, and then to it again; and when thou hast
tired thyself in base comparisons, hear me speak but this.

200   POINS   Mark, Jack.

PRINCE   We two saw you four set on four and bound them, and were
masters of their wealth. Mark now, how a plain tale shall put you down.
Then did we two set on you four; and, with a word, outfaced you from
your prize, and have it, yea, and can show it you here in the house; and,

205   Falstaff, you carried your guts away as nimbly, with as quick dexterity,
and roared for mercy and still run and roared, as ever I heard bullcalf.
What a slave art thou, to hack thy sword as thou hast done, and then say
it was in fight! What trick, what device, what starting-hole,[6] canst thou
now find out to hide thee from this open and apparent shame?

210   POINS   Come, let's hear, Jack; what trick hast thou now?

FALSTAFF   By the Lord, I knew ye as well as he that made ye. Why, hear
you, my masters: was it for me to kill the heir apparent? should I turn
upon the true prince? why, thou knowest I am as valiant as Hercules;
but beware instinct; the lion will not touch the true prince.[7] Instinct is

215   a great matter; I was now a coward on instinct. I shall think the better
of myself and thee during my life; I for a valiant lion, and thou for a true
prince. But, by the Lord, lads, I am glad you have the money. Hostess,
clap to the doors; watch[8] tonight, pray tomorrow. Gallants, lads, boys,
hearts of gold, all the titles of good fellowship come to you! What, shall

220   we be merry? shall we have a play extempore?

PRINCE   Content; and the argument[9] shall be thy running away.

FALSTAFF   Ah, no more of that, Hal, an thou lovest me!

[*Enter* HOSTESS.]

HOSTESS   O Jesu, my lord the prince!

PRINCE   How now, my lady the hostess! what sayest thou to me?

225   HOSTESS   Marry, my lord, there is a nobleman of the court at door would
speak with you; he says he comes from your father.

PRINCE   Give him as much as will make him a royal[1] man, and send him
back again to my mother.

FALSTAFF   What manner of man is he?

230   HOSTESS   An old man.

FALSTAFF   What doth gravity out of his bed at midnight? Shall I give him
his answer?

PRINCE   Prithee, do, Jack.

FALSTAFF   Faith, and I'll send him packing.   [*Exit.*]

235   PRINCE   Now, sirs. By 'r Lady, you fought fair; so did you, Peto; so did
you, Bardolph; you are lions too, you ran away upon instinct, you will
not touch the true prince; no, fie!

BARDOLPH   Faith, I ran when I saw others run.

PRINCE   Faith, tell me now in earnest, how came Falstaff's sword so

240   hacked?

---

5. Stiff rapier.
6. Evasion.
7. In many medieval romances the lion, as king of
beasts, shows respect for royalty.

8. Stay up.
9. Plot or story.
1. A "royal" was half of a pound sterling, a "noble"
was a third.

PETO Why, he hacked it with his dagger, and said he would swear truth out of England but he would make you believe it was done in fight, and persuaded us to do the like.

BARDOLPH Yea, and to tickle our noses with speargrass to make them bleed, and then to beslubber our garments with it and swear it was the blood of true men. I did that I did not this seven year before, I blushed to hear his monstrous devices.

PRINCE O villain, thou stolest a cup of sack eighteen years ago, and wert taken with the manner,[2] and ever since thou hast blushed extempore. Thou hadst fire and sword on thy side, and yet thou ran'st away; what instinct hadst thou for it?

BARDOLPH My lord, do you see these meteors? do you behold these exhalations?[3]

PRINCE I do.

BARDOLPH What think you they portend?

PRINCE Hot livers and cold purses.[4]

BARDOLPH Choler, my lord, if rightly taken.

PRINCE No, if rightly taken, halter.[5]

[Enter FALSTAFF.]

Here comes lean Jack, here comes bare-bone. How now, my sweet creature of bombast,[6] how long is 't ago, Jack, since thou sawest thine own knee?

FALSTAFF My own knee! when I was about thy years, Hal, I was not an eagle's talon in the waist; I could have crept into any alderman's thumb ring. A plague of sighing and grief—it blows a man up like a bladder. There's villainous news abroad; here was Sir John Bracy from your father; you must to the court in the morning. That same mad fellow of the north, Percy, and he of Wales, that gave Amamon the bastinado[7] and made Lucifer cuckold and swore the devil his true liegeman upon the cross of a Welsh hook[8]—what a plague call you him?

POINS O, Glendower.

FALSTAFF Owen, Owen, the same; and his son-in-law Mortimer, and old Northumberland, and that sprightly Scot of Scots, Douglas, that runs o' horseback up a hill perpendicular—

PRINCE He that rides at high speed and with his pistol kills a sparrow flying.

FALSTAFF You have hit it.

PRINCE So did he never the sparrow.

FALSTAFF Well, that rascal hath good mettle in him; he will not run.

PRINCE Why, what a rascal art thou then, to praise him so for running!

FALSTAFF O' horseback, ye cuckoo; but afoot he will not budge a foot.

PRINCE Yes, Jack, upon instinct.

FALSTAFF I grant ye, upon instinct. Well, he is there too, and one Mordake, and a thousand blue-caps[9] more. Worcester is stolen away tonight; thy father's beard is turned white with the news; you may buy land now

---

2. In the act.
3. "Fire" and the allusions to "meteors" and "exhalations" (shooting stars) refer to Bardolph's red nose.
4. I.e., drunkenness and poverty.
5. Hangman's noose, with a pun on *collar*.

"Choler": fiery complexion, indicating a choleric (angry) temperament.
6. Padding, stuffing.
7. A beating, cudgeling. "Amamon": a devil.
8. A long spear with a hook on it.
9. Scots.

285   as cheap as stinking mackerel.

PRINCE   Why then, it is like, if there come a hot June, and this civil buf-
feting hold, we shall buy maidenheads as they buy hobnails, by the hundreds.

FALSTAFF   By the mass, lad, thou sayest true; it is like we shall have good
290   trading that way. But tell me, Hal, art not thou horrible afeard? thou
being heir apparent, could the world pick thee out three such enemies
again as that fiend Douglas, that spirit Percy, and that devil Glendower?
Art thou not horribly afraid? doth not thy blood thrill at it?

PRINCE   Not a whit, i' faith; I lack some of thy instinct.

295 FALSTAFF   Well, thou wilt be horribly chid tomorrow when thou comest
to thy father; if thou love me, practice an answer.

PRINCE   Do thou stand for[1] my father and examine me upon the particulars of my life.

FALSTAFF   Shall I? Content. This chair shall be my state,[2] this dagger my
300   scepter, and this cushion my crown.

PRINCE   Thy state is taken for a joint-stool,[3] thy golden scepter for a leaden
dagger, and thy precious rich crown for a pitiful bald crown!

FALSTAFF   Well, an the fire of grace be not quite out of thee, now shalt
thou be moved. Give me a cup of sack to make my eyes look red, that it
305   may be thought I have wept, for I must speak in passion, and I will do it
in King Cambyses'[4] vein.

PRINCE   Well, here is my leg.[5]

FALSTAFF   And here is my speech. Stand aside, nobility.

HOSTESS   O Jesu, this is excellent sport, i' faith!

310 FALSTAFF   Weep not, sweet queen, for trickling tears are vain.

HOSTESS   O, the father, how he holds his countenance!

FALSTAFF   For God's sake, lords, convey my tristful queen,
For tears do stop the floodgates of her eyes.[6]

HOSTESS   O Jesu, he doth it as like one of these harlotry players as ever I
315   see!

FALSTAFF   Peace, good pint pot, peace, good ticklebrain. Harry, I do not
only marvel where thou spendest thy time, but also how thou art accompanied, for though the camomile,[7] the more it is trodden on the faster it
grows, so youth, the more it is wasted the sooner it wears. That thou art
320   my son, I have partly thy mother's word, partly my own opinion, but
chiefly a villainous trick of thine eye and a foolish hanging of thy nether
lip that doth warrant[8] me. If then thou be son to me, here lies the point;
why, being son to me, art thou so pointed at? Shall the blessed sun of
heaven prove a micher[9] and eat blackberries? a question not to be asked.
325   Shall the son of England prove a thief and take purses? a question to be
asked. There is a thing, Harry, which thou hast often heard of and it is
known to many in our land by the name of pitch. This pitch, as ancient
writers do report, doth defile; so doth the company thou keepest: for,

1. Represent.
2. Throne.
3. An ordinary stool, made by a joiner (cabinet-maker).
4. Like the bombastic hero of the old play *Cambyses*.
5. I.e., he bows, makes an obeisance.
6. Falstaff's blank verse lines parody the old-fashioned tragedies of the 1570s and 1580s.
7. An aromatic herb. The style in this speech is a parody of Euphuism, the ornate, elaborate, balanced style made popular by Lyly's *Euphues*.
8. Assure.
9. Truant.

Harry, now I do not speak to thee in drink but in tears, not in pleasure
but in passion, not in words only, but in woes also: and yet there is a
virtuous man whom I have often noted in thy company, but I know not
his name.

PRINCE What manner of man, an it like[1] your majesty?

FALSTAFF A goodly portly man, i' faith, and a corpulent; of a cheerful look,
a pleasing eye and a most noble carriage, and, as I think, his age some
fifty, or, by 'r Lady, inclining to threescore; and now I remember me, his
name is Falstaff. If that man should be lewdly given, he deceiveth me,
for, Harry, I see virtue in his looks. If then the tree may be known by the
fruit, as the fruit by the tree, then, peremptorily I speak it, there is virtue
in that Falstaff; him keep with, the rest banish. And tell me now, thou
naughty varlet, tell me, where hast thou been this month?

PRINCE Dost thou speak like a king? Do thou stand for me, and I'll play
my father.

FALSTAFF Depose me? if thou dost it half so gravely, so majestically, both
in word and matter, hang me up by the heels for a rabbit-sucker[2] or a
poulter's hare.

PRINCE Well, here I am set.[3]

FALSTAFF And here I stand; judge, my masters.

PRINCE Now, Harry, whence come you?

FALSTAFF My noble lord, from Eastcheap.

PRINCE The complaints I hear of thee are grievous.

FALSTAFF 'Sblood, my lord, they are false: nay, I'll tickle ye for a young
prince, i' faith.

PRINCE Swearest thou, ungracious boy? Henceforth ne'er look on me.
Thou art violently carried away from grace; there is a devil haunts thee
in the likeness of an old fat man; a tun[4] of man is thy companion. Why
dost thou converse with that trunk of humors, that bolting-hutch of
beastliness, that swollen parcel of dropsies, that huge bombard[5] of sack,
that stuffed cloak-bag of guts, that roasted Manningtree ox with the pudding in his belly, that reverend vice,[6] that gray iniquity, that father ruffian, that vanity in years? Wherein is he good, but to taste sack and drink
it? wherein neat and cleanly, but to carve a capon and eat it? wherein
cunning, but in craft? wherein crafty, but in villainy? wherein villainous,
but in all things? wherein worthy, but in nothing?

FALSTAFF I would your grace would take me with you; whom means your
grace?

PRINCE That villainous abominable misleader of youth, Falstaff, that old
white-bearded Satan.

FALSTAFF My lord, the man I know.

PRINCE I know thou dost.

FALSTAFF But to say I know more harm in him than in myself were to say
more than I know. That he is old the more the pity, his white hairs do
witness it; but that he is, saving your reverence, a whoremaster, that I

---

1. If it please.
2. Suckling rabbit.
3. Seated.
4. Large barrel.
5. Leather wine vessel. "Bolting-hutch": trough.

6. The Vice was a comic character in the old
morality plays. Falstaff is in some respects a
descendant of this type character. "Manningtree":
a town in Essex, noted for barbecues. "Pudding":
sausage.

utterly deny. If sack and sugar be a fault, God help the wicked! if to be
375 old and merry be a sin, then many an old host that I know is damned; if
to be fat be to be hated, then Pharaoh's lean kine[7] are to be loved. No,
my good lord, banish Peto, banish Bardolph, banish Poins, but for sweet
Jack Falstaff, kind Jack Falstaff, true Jack Falstaff, valiant Jack Falstaff,
and therefore more valiant, being as he is old Jack Falstaff, banish not
380 him thy Harry's company, banish not him thy Harry's company; banish
plump Jack, and banish all the world.
PRINCE   I do, I will.   [⟨A knocking heard.⟩]
                                                      [⟨Exeunt HOSTESS and BARDOLPH.⟩]
            [Enter BARDOLPH, running.]
BARDOLPH   O, my lord, my lord, the sheriff with a most monstrous watch
    is at the door.
385 FALSTAFF   Out, ye rogue! Play out the play; I have much to say in the
    behalf of that Falstaff.
            [Enter the HOSTESS.]
HOSTESS   O Jesu, my lord, my lord!
FALSTAFF   Heigh, heigh! the devil rides upon a fiddlestick;[8] what's the mat-
    ter?
390 HOSTESS   The sheriff and all the watch are at the door; they are come to
    search the house. Shall I let them in?
FALSTAFF   Dost thou hear, Hal? never call a true piece of gold a counter-
    feit; thou art essentially mad, without seeming so.[9]
PRINCE   And thou a natural coward, without instinct.
395 FALSTAFF   I deny your major;[1] if you will deny the sheriff, so; if not, let
    him enter. If I become not a cart as well as another man, a plague on
    my bringing up! I hope I shall as soon be strangled with a halter as
    another.[2]
PRINCE   Go hide thee behind the arras; the rest walk up above.[3] Now my
400 masters, for a true face and good conscience.
FALSTAFF   Both which I have had; but their date is out,[4] and therefore I'll
    hide me.
PRINCE   Call in the sheriff.
                                          [Exeunt ⟨all except the PRINCE and POINS⟩.]
            [Enter SHERIFF and the CARRIER.]
    Now, master sheriff, what is your will with me?
405 SHERIFF   First pardon me, my lord. A hue and cry
    Hath followed certain men unto this house.
PRINCE   What men?
SHERIFF   One of them is well known, my gracious lord,
    A gross fat man.
CARRIER   As fat as butter.
410 PRINCE   The man, I do assure you, is not here,

---

7. In the dream Joseph interpreted (Genesis
41.19–21).
8. I.e., there's a commotion.
9. I.e., don't give a true man (me, Falstaff) away
as a thief. He goes on to accuse the prince, in his
reversal of values in the play scene, of being out of
his mind, though he appears rational.
1. Your major premise (that I, Falstaff, am a cow-

ard).
2. I.e., I hope my fat neck will not make the process of strangling on the gallows longer for me than
for the rest of you. The "cart" is the wagon on
which criminals were taken to be hanged.
3. On the balcony. "Arras": the hangings or draperies that covered the walls.
4. Lease has expired.

For I myself at this time have employed him,
And, sheriff, I will engage my word to thee
That I will by tomorrow dinnertime
Send him to answer thee or any man
415 For anything he shall be charged withal;
And so let me entreat you leave the house.
SHERIFF   I will, my lord. There are two gentlemen
Have in this robbery lost three hundred marks.
PRINCE   It may be so; if he have robbed these men
420 He shall be answerable; and so farewell.
SHERIFF   Good night, my noble lord.
PRINCE   I think it is good morrow, is it not?
SHERIFF   Indeed, my lord, I think it be two o'clock.
    [*Exeunt* ⟨SHERIFF *and* CARRIER.⟩]
PRINCE   This oily rascal is known as well as Paul's.[5] Go call him forth.
425 POINS   Falstaff!—Fast asleep behind the arras, and snorting like a horse.
PRINCE   Hark, how hard he fetches breath. Search his pockets. [*He searcheth his pockets, and findeth certain papers.*] What hast thou found?
POINS   Nothing but papers, my lord.
PRINCE   Let's see what they be: read them.
430 POINS [*reads*]   "Item, a capon.   .   .   .   .   .   2s. 2d.
                Item, sauce.   .   .   .   .   .   .   4d.
                Item, sack, two gallons.   .   .   5s. 8d.
                Item, anchovies and sack   .   2s. 6d.
                after supper.   .   .   .   .   .   .
                Item, bread.   .   .   .   .   .   ob."[6]
435 PRINCE   O monstrous! but one halfpennyworth of bread to this intolerable deal of sack! What there is else, keep close; we'll read it at more advantage; there let him sleep till day. I'll to the court in the morning. We must all to the wars, and thy place shall be honorable. I'll procure this fat rogue a charge of foot,[7] and I know his death will be a march of
440 twelvescore. The money shall be paid back again with advantage. Be with me betimes[8] in the morning, and so good morrow, Poins.
POINS   Good morrow, good my lord.   [*Exeunt.*]

Act 3

SCENE 1

[*Enter* HOTSPUR, WORCESTER, LORD MORTIMER, *and* OWEN GLENDOWER.]

MORTIMER   These promises are fair, the parties sure,
      And our induction° full of prosperous hope.   *initial step*
HOTSPUR   Lord Mortimer, and cousin Glendower,
      Will you sit down?
5   And uncle Worcester; a plague upon it,
      I have forgot the map.
GLENDOWER   No, here it is.

5. St. Paul's Cathedral.
6. Oble, a halfpenny.
7. Company of infantry.
8. Early. "Twelvescore": i.e., 240 yards.

Sit, cousin Percy, sit, good cousin Hotspur,
For by that name as oft as Lancaster[9]
Doth speak of you, his cheek looks pale and with
10 A rising sigh he wisheth you in heaven.
HOTSPUR   And you in hell as often as he hears Owen Glendower spoke of.
GLENDOWER   I cannot blame him; at my nativity
The front° of heaven was full of fiery shapes,   *forehead*
Of burning cressets,° and at my birth   *lamps*
15 The frame and huge foundation of the earth
Shaked like a coward.
HOTSPUR   Why, so it would have done at the same season if your mother's
cat had but kittened, though yourself had never been born.
GLENDOWER   I say the earth did shake when I was born.
20 HOTSPUR   And I say the earth was not of my mind,
If you suppose as fearing you it shook.
GLENDOWER   The heavens were all on fire, the earth did tremble.
HOTSPUR   O then the earth shook to see the heavens on fire,
And not in fear of your nativity.
25 Diseasèd nature oftentimes breaks forth
In strange eruptions; oft the teeming earth
Is with a kind of colic pinched and vexed
By the imprisoning of unruly wind
Within her womb, which for enlargement striving
30 Shakes the old beldam° earth and topples down   *old woman*
Steeples and moss-grown towers. At your birth
Our grandam earth, having this distemperature,°   *ailment*
In passion shook.
GLENDOWER   Cousin, of many men
I do not bear these crossings. Give me leave
35 To tell you once again that at my birth
The front of heaven was full of fiery shapes,
The goats ran from the mountains, and the herds
Were strangely clamorous to the frighted fields.
These signs have marked me extraordinary,
40 And all the courses of my life do show
I am not in the roll of common men.
Where is he living, clipped in with[1] the sea
That chides the banks of England, Scotland, Wales,
Which calls me pil or hath read to me?
45 And bring him out that is but woman's son
Can trace me in the tedious ways of art[2]
And hold me pace in deep experiments.
HOTSPUR   I think there's no man speaks better Welsh. I'll to dinner.
MORTIMER   Peace, cousin Percy; you will make him mad.
50 GLENDOWER   I can call spirits from the vasty deep.
HOTSPUR   Why, so can I, or so can any man;
But will they come when you do call for them?

9. I.e., King Henry IV. To call him by his lesser
title is insulting.

1. Within the limits of.
2. Follow me in practicing difficult magic.

GLENDOWER   Why, I can teach you, cousin, to command
    The devil.
55   HOTSPUR   And I can teach thee, coz, to shame the devil
    By telling truth; tell truth and shame the devil.[3]
    If thou have power to raise him, bring him hither,
    And I'll be sworn I have power to shame him hence.
    O, while you live, tell truth and shame the devil!
60   MORTIMER   Come, come, no more of this unprofitable chat.
    GLENDOWER   Three times hath Henry Bullingbrook made head
    Against my power, thrice from the banks of Wye
    And sandy-bottomed Severn have I sent him
    Bootless[4] home and weather-beaten back.
65   HOTSPUR   Home without boots, and in foul weather too!
    How 'scapes he agues,° in the devil's name?   *fevers and chills*
    GLENDOWER   Come, here is the map; shall we divide our right
    According to our threefold order ta'en?[5]
    MORTIMER   The archdeacon hath divided it
70   Into three limits very equally:
    England, from Trent and Severn hitherto,
    By south and east is to my part assigned;
    All westward, Wales beyond the Severn shore,
    And all the fertile land within that bound,
75   To Owen Glendower; and, dear coz, to you
    The remnant northward lying off from Trent.
    And our indentures tripartite are drawn,
    Which being sealèd interchangeably,
    A business that this night may execute,
80   Tomorrow, cousin Percy, you and I
    And my good Lord of Worcester will set forth
    To meet your father and the Scottish power,
    As is appointed us, at Shrewsbury.
    My father[6] Glendower is not ready yet,
85   Nor shall we need his help these fourteen days.
    Within that space you may have drawn together
    Your tenants, friends, and neighboring gentlemen.
    GLENDOWER   A shorter time shall send me to you, lords,
    And in my conduct shall your ladies come,
90   From whom you ow must steal and take no leave,
    For there will be a world of water shed
    Upon the parting of your wives and you.
    HOTSPUR   Methinks my moiety,° north from Burton here,   *share*
    In quantity equals not one of yours;
95   See how this river comes me cranking° in,   *curving*
    And cuts me from the best of all my land
    A huge half-moon, a monstrous cantle° out.   *corner*
    I'll have the current in this place dammed up;
    And here the smug° and silver Trent shall run   *smooth*

---

3. A proverb.
4. Unsuccessful; but Hotspur takes it in the other
sense.

5. Divide our property according to the arrangement for division into three parts.
6. Father-in-law.

100

In a new channel, fair and evenly;
It shall not wind with such a deep indent
To rob me of so rich a bottom° here.   *valley*

GLENDOWER   Not wind? it shall, it must; you see it doth.

MORTIMER   Yea, but

105

Mark how he bears his course, and runs me up
With like advantage on the other side;
Gelding the opposèd continent[7] as much
As on the other side it takes from you.

WORCESTER   Yea, but a little charge will trench him here

110

And on this north side win this cape of land,
And then he runs straight and even.

HOTSPUR   I'll have it so; a little charge will do it.

GLENDOWER   I'll not have it altered.

HOTSPUR   Will not you?

GLENDOWER   No, nor you shall not.

HOTSPUR   Who shall say me nay?

115

GLENDOWER   Why, that will I.

HOTSPUR   Let me not understand you then; speak it in Welsh.

GLENDOWER   I can speak English, lord, as well as you,
For I was trained up in the English court,
Where, being but young, I framèd to the harp

120

Many an English ditty lovely well
And gave the tongue a helpful ornament,
A virtue that was never seen in you.

HOTSPUR   Marry,
And I am glad of it with all my heart;

125

I had rather be a kitten and cry mew
Than one of these same meter ballad-mongers;
I had rather hear a brazen canstick turned,[8]
Or a dry wheel grate on the axletree,
And that would set my teeth nothing on edge,

130

Nothing so much as mincing° poetry;   *affected*
'Tis like the forced gait of a shuffling° nag.   *hobbled*

GLENDOWER   Come, you shall have Trent turned.

HOTSPUR   I do not care; I'll give thrice so much land
To any well-deserving friend;

135

But in the way of bargain, mark ye me,
I'll cavil° on the ninth part of a hair.   *quibble*
Are the indentures drawn? shall we be gone?

GLENDOWER   The moon shines fair; you may be away by night.
I'll haste the writer, and withal

140

Break with° your wives of your departure hence.   *inform*
I am afraid my daughter will run mad,
So much she doteth on her Mortimer.   [*Exit.*]

MORTIMER   Fie, cousin Percy, how you cross my father!

HOTSPUR   I cannot choose; sometime he angers me

---

7. I.e., cutting off from the opposite side.   8. A brass candlestick turned on a lathe.

145 With telling me of the moldwarp⁹ and the ant,
Of the dreamer Merlin and his prophecies,
And of a dragon and a finless fish,
A clip-winged griffin and a molten raven,
A couching lion and a ramping¹ cat,
150 And such a deal of skimble-skamble stuff
As puts me from my faith. I tell you what;
He held me last night at least nine hours
In reckoning up the several devils' names
That were his lackeys. I cried "hum" and "well, go to,"
155 But marked him not a word. O, he is as tedious
As a tired horse, a railing° wife,   nagging
Worse than a smoky house. I had rather live
With cheese and garlic in a windmill,² far,
Than feed on cates° and have him talk to me   delicacies
160 In any summer house in Christendom.
MORTIMER   In faith, he is a worthy gentleman,
Exceedingly well read, and profited
In strange concealments,³ valiant as a lion
And wondrous affable and as bountiful
165 As mines of India. Shall I tell you, cousin?
He holds your temper° in a high respect   character
And curbs himself even of his natural scope
When you come 'cross his humor; faith, he does.
I warrant you that man is not alive
170 Might so have tempted him as you have done
Without the taste of danger and reproof;
But do not use it oft, let me entreat you.
WORCESTER   In faith, my lord, you are too willful-blame,
And since your coming hither have done enough
175 To put him quite beside his patience.
You must needs learn, lord, to amend this fault.
Though sometimes it show greatness, courage, blood°—   breeding
And that's the dearest grace it renders you—
Yet oftentimes it doth present harsh rage,
180 Defect of manners, want of government,°   self-control
Pride, haughtiness, opinion,° and disdain;   arrogance
The least of which haunting a nobleman
Loseth men's hearts and leaves behind a stain
Upon the beauty of all parts besides,
185 Beguiling them of commendation.
HOTSPUR   Well, I am schooled; good manners be your speed!
Here come our wives, and let us take our leave.
                [Enter GLENDOWER with the ladies.]

---

9. Mole. According to the chronicler Holinshed there were prophecies in which Henry IV was referred to as "a moldwarp, cursed of God." Merlin was the famous prophet of King Arthur's court; many later prophecies were attributed to him.
1. "Couching" and "ramping" are Hotspur's ver-

sions of the heraldic terms "couchant" (lying down) and "rampant" (erect, on hind feet).
2. Cheese and garlic would be smelly, and the living quarters in a mill would be noisy.
3. Experienced in secret mysteries.

MORTIMER   This is the deadly spite that angers me;
My wife can speak no English, I no Welsh.
190 GLENDOWER   My daughter weeps; she will not part with you,
She'll be a soldier too, she'll to the wars.
MORTIMER   Good father, tell her that she and my aunt Percy
Shall follow in your conduct speedily.
    [GLENDOWER *speaks to her in Welsh, and she answers him in the same.*]
GLENDOWER   She is desperate here; a peevish self-willed harlotry,[4] one
195 that no persuasion can do good upon.
    [*The lady speaks in Welsh.*]
MORTIMER   I understand thy looks; that pretty Welsh
Which thou pour'st down from these swelling heavens[5]
I am too perfect in; and, but for shame,
In such a parley should I answer thee.[6]
    [*The lady speaks again in Welsh.*]
200 I understand thy kisses and thou mine,
And that's a feeling disputation,
But I will never be a truant, love,
Till I have learned thy language, for thy tongue
Makes Welsh as sweet as ditties highly penned,
205 Sung by a fair queen in a summer's bower,
With ravishing division,° to her lute.   *musical variation*
GLENDOWER   Nay, if you melt, then will she run mad.
    [*The lady speaks again in Welsh.*]
MORTIMER   O, I am ignorance itself in this!
GLENDOWER   She bids you on the wanton rushes[7] lay you down
210 And rest your gentle head upon her lap,
And she will sing the song that pleaseth you
And on your eyelids crown the god of sleep,
Charming your blood with pleasing heaviness,°   *drowsiness*
Making such difference 'twixt wake and sleep
215 As is the difference betwixt day and night
The hour before the heavenly-harnessed team[8]
Begins his golden progress in the east.
MORTIMER   With all my heart I'll sit and hear her sing;
By that time will our book,[9] think, be drawn.
220 GLENDOWER   Do so:
And those musicians that shall play to you
Hang in the air a thousand leagues from hence,
And straight they shall be here; sit, and attend.
HOTSPUR   Come, Kate, thou art perfect in lying down; come, quick,
225 quick, that I may lay my head in thy lap.
LADY PERCY   Go, ye giddy goose.
    [*The music plays.*]
HOTSPUR   Now I perceive the devil understands Welsh,
And 'tis no marvel, he is so humorous.[1]

4. Wench; used affectionately, not seriously.
5. I.e., tears from her eyes.
6. Cry likewise.
7. The dry reeds used as a floor covering in Elizabethan England.
8. The horses of the sun.
9. The indenture.
1. Capricious, governed by humors.

By 'r Lady, he is a good musician.

230 LADY PERCY   Then should you be nothing but musical, for you are altogether governed by humors. Lie still, ye thief, and hear the lady sing
in Welsh.

HOTSPUR   I had rather hear Lady, my brach,[2] howl in Irish.

LADY PERCY   Wouldst thou have thy head broken?

235 HOTSPUR   No.

LADY PERCY   Then be still.

HOTSPUR   Neither; 'tis a woman's fault.[3]

LADY PERCY   Now God help thee.

HOTSPUR   To the Welsh lady's bed.

240 LADY PERCY   What's that?

HOTSPUR   Peace! she sings.

    [Here the lady sings a Welsh song.]

HOTSPUR   Come, Kate, I'll have your song too.

LADY PERCY   Not mine, in good sooth.°   *truth*

HOTSPUR   Not yours, in good sooth! Heart! you swear like a comfitmaker's[4]

245   wife. "Not you, in good sooth," and "as true as I live," and "as God shall
mend me," and "as sure as day,"
And givest such sarcenet° surety for thy oaths   *thin silk*
As if thou never walk'st further than Finsbury.[5]
Swear me, Kate, like a lady as thou art,

250 A good mouth-filling oath, and leave "in sooth,"
And such protest of pepper-gingerbread,
To velvet-guards and Sunday citizens.[6]
Come, sing.

LADY PERCY   I will not sing.

255 HOTSPUR   'Tis the next way to turn tailor, or be redbreast teacher.[7] An the
indentures be drawn, I'll away within these two hours; and so, come in
when ye will.   *[Exit.]*

GLENDOWER   Come, come, Lord Mortimer, you are as slow
As hot Lord Percy is on fire to go.

260 By this our book is drawn; we will but seal,
And then to horse immediately.

MORTIMER   With all my heart.   *[Exeunt.]*

SCENE 2

[Enter the KING, PRINCE OF WALES, *and others.]*

KING   Lords, give us leave; the Prince of Wales and I
Must have some private conference; but be near at hand,
For we shall presently have need of you.   *[Exeunt* LORDS.]
I know not whether God will have it so

---

2. My bitch hound, Lady.
3. Hotspur sarcastically reverses the usual saying about women and talkativeness.
4. Confectioner's.
5. A recreation ground outside London, frequented by citizens and their wives on Sundays, but not by ladies of Lady Percy's class.
6. City folk out for a stroll on Sunday. "Pepper-

gingerbread": i.e., such tame oaths, as crumbly and unsubstantial as gingerbread. "Velvet-guards": respectable people of the middle class, who wore velvet stripes on their clothes.
7. I.e., it is the easiest way to become a tailor (supposedly tailors sang at their work) or a person who teaches birds to sing. Hotspur is equally scornful of music and of people who work for a living.

5   For some displeasing service I have done,
     That, in his secret doom, out of my blood[8]
     He'll breed revengement and a scourge for me;
     But thou dost in thy passages° of life   actions
     Make me believe that thou art only marked
10   For the hot vengeance and the rod of heaven
     To punish my mistreadings.° Tell me else,   misdeeds
     Could such inordinate and low desires,
     Such poor, such bare, such lewd,° such mean attempts,   low
     Such barren pleasures, rude society
15   As thou art matched withal and grafted to
     Accompany the greatness of thy blood
     And hold their level with thy princely heart?
PRINCE   So please your majesty, I would I could
     Quit[9] all offenses with as clear excuse
20   As well as I am doubtless° I can purge   sure
     Myself of many I am charged withal;
     Yet such extenuation let me beg,
     As, in reproof of many tales devised
     (Which oft the ear of greatness needs must hear)
25   By smiling pickthanks° and base newsmongers,°   flatterers / tattletales
     I may, for some things true, wherein my youth
     Hath faulty wandered and irregular,
     Find pardon on my true submission.
KING   God pardon thee; yet let me wonder, Harry,
30   At thy affections, which doth hold a wing
     Quite from the flight of all thy ancestors.
     Thy place in council thou hast rudely lost,
     Which by thy younger brother is supplied,
     And art almost an alien to the hearts
35   Of all the court and princes of my blood.
     The hope and expectation of thy time[1]
     Is ruined, and the soul of every man
     Prophetically do forethink thy fall.
     Had I so lavish of my presence been,
40   So common-hackneyed[2] in the eyes of men,
     So stale and cheap to vulgar company,
     Opinion,[3] that did help me to the crown,
     Had still kept loyal to possession
     And left me in reputeless banishment,
45   A fellow of no mark nor likelihood.
     By being seldom seen, I could not stir
     But like a comet I was wondered at,
     That men would tell their children "This is he";
     Others would say "Where, which is Bullingbrook?"
50   And then I stole all courtesy from heaven,

8. Unknown judgment, through my son.   2. Cheapened, vulgarized.
9. Acquit myself of.   3. Popularity, public opinion.
1. Lifetime.

And dressed myself in such humility.
That I did pluck allegiance from men's hearts,
Loud shouts and salutations from their mouths,
Even in the presence of the crownèd king.
55 Thus did I keep my person fresh and new,
My presence like a robe pontifical,
Ne'er seen but wondered at; and so my state,[4]
Seldom but sumptuous, showed like a feast
And wan° by rareness such solemnity.[5]   won
60 The skipping king, he ambled up and down
With shallow jesters and rash° bavin[6] wits,   quick
Soon kindled and soon burnt, carded his state,[7]
Mingled his royalty with cap'ring fools,
Had his great name profanèd with their scorns
65 And gave his countenance° against his name[8]   authority
To laugh at gibing boys and stand the push
Of every beardless vain comparative,[9]
Grew a companion to the common streets,
Enfeoffed himself to popularity,[1]
70 That, being daily swallowed by men's eyes,
They surfeited with honey and began
To loathe the taste of sweetness, whereof a little
More than a little is by much too much.
So when he had occasion to be seen
75 He was but as the cuckoo is in June,[2]
Heard, not regarded, seen, but with such eyes
As, sick and blunted with community,°   commonness
Afford no extraordinary gaze
Such as is bent on sunlike majesty
80 When it shines seldom in admiring eyes,
But rather drowsed and hung their eyelids down,
Slept in his face[3] and rendered such aspèct°   looks
As cloudy° men use to their adversaries,   sullen
Being with his presence glutted, gorged, and full.
85 And in that very line, Harry, standest thou,
For thou hast lost thy princely privilege
With vile participation.[4] Not an eye
But is a-weary of thy common sight,
Save mine, which hath desired to see thee more,
90 Which now doth that I would not have it do,
Make blind itself with foolish tenderness.
PRINCE   I shall hereafter, my thrice gracious lord,

---

4. Public ceremonial appearances.
5. "Such solemnity": i.e., the greatest possible majestic effect.
6. Brushwood; the image is explained in the next line.
7. Degraded his royal dignity; "card" also means "to adulterate wine."
8. Reputation.

9. Tolerate the impertinent witticisms of every beardless youth.
1. Made himself the common property of the public.
2. The cuckoo is noticed in April, when its song is first heard; by June it is commonplace.
3. I.e., yawned in his face.
4. Association with vile companions.

Be more myself.

KING   For all the world
As thou art to this hour was Richard then
95   When I from France set foot at Ravenspurgh,
And even as I was then is Percy now.
Now, by my scepter and my soul to boot,
He hath more worthy interest to the state
Than thou the shadow of succession;[5]
100   For of no right, nor color[6] like to right,
He doth fill fields with harness° in the realm,   *armor*
Turns head against the lion's armèd jaws,[7]
And, being no more in debt to years than thou,
Leads ancient lords and reverend bishops on
105   To bloody battles and to bruising arms.
What never-dying honor hath he got
Against renownèd Douglas! whose high deeds,
Whose hot incursions° and great name in arms   *raids*
Holds from all soldiers chief majority°   *superiority*
110   And military title capital[8]
Through all the kingdoms that acknowledge Christ.
Thrice hath this Hotspur, Mars in swaddling clothes,
This infant warrior, in his enterprises
Discomfited great Douglas, ta'en him once,
115   Enlargèd° him and made a friend of him,   *freed*
To fill the mouth of deep defiance up[9]
And shake the peace and safety of our throne.
And what say you to this? Percy, Northumberland,
The Archbishop's grace of York, Douglas, Mortimer,
120   Capitulate[1] against us and are up.
But wherefore do I tell these news to thee?
Why, Harry, do I tell thee of my foes,
Which art my nearest and dearest enemy?
Thou that art like enough through vassal fear,
125   Base inclinatiòn and the start of spleen,[2]
To fight against me under Percy's pay,
To dog his heels and curtsy at his frowns,
To show how much thou art degenerate.

PRINCE   Do not think so; you shall not find it so;
130   And God forgive them that so much have swayed
Your majesty's good thoughts away from me.
I will redeem all this on Percy's head
And in the closing of some glorious day
Be bold to tell you that I am your son,
135   When I will wear a garment all of blood

---

5. I.e., Hotspur's claim to the throne is more solid, because of his achievements, than is Hal's, which rests only on shadowy rights of succession by birth.
6. False pretense.
7. I.e., takes military action against the king's army.
8. Has the greatest reputation among soldiers.
9. I.e., to swell the chorus of defiance.
1. Raise a head, revolt.
2. Unreasoning impulse.

And stain my favors° in a bloody mask, *features*
Which, washed away, shall scour my shame with it;
And that shall be the day, whene'er it lights,
That this same child of honor and renown,
140 This gallant Hotspur, this all-praisèd knight,
And your unthought-of Harry chance to meet.
For every honor sitting on his helm—
Would they were multitudes, and on my head
My shames redoubled!—for the time will come
145 That I shall make this northern youth exchange
His glorious deeds for my indignities.
Percy is but my factor,° good my lord, *agent*
To engross up° glorious deeds on my behalf, *collect, acquire*
And I will call him to so strict account,
150 That he shall render every glory up,
Yea, even the slightest worship° of his time, *honor*
Or I will tear the reckoning from his heart.
This in the name of God I promise here,
The which if He be pleased I shall perform,
155 I do beseech your majesty, may salve
The long-grown wounds of my intemperance;
If not, the end of life cancels all bands,° *bonds, debts*
And I will die a hundred thousand deaths
Ere break the smallest parcel of this vow.
160 KING   A hundred thousand rebels die in this;
Thou shalt have charge and sovereign trust herein.
            [*Enter* BLUNT.]
How now, good Blunt? thy looks are full of speed.
BLUNT   So hath the business that I come to speak of.
Lord Mortimer of Scotland hath sent word
165 That Douglas and the English rebels met
The eleventh of this month at Shrewsbury;
A mighty and a fearful head° they are, *power*
If promises be kept on every hand,
As ever offered foul play in a state.
170 KING   The Earl of Westmoreland set forth today,
With him my son, Lord John of Lancaster,
For this advertisement° is five days old. *news*
On Wednesday next, Harry, you shall set forward;
On Thursday we ourselves will march. Our meeting
175 Is Bridgenorth and, Harry, you shall march
Through Gloucestershire, by which account,° *method*
Our business valued,³ some twelve days hence
Our general forces at Bridgenorth shall meet.
Our hands are full of business: let's away;
180 Advantage feeds him fat while men delay.⁴ [*Exeunt.*]

---

3. According to estimates.
4. I.e., the rebels' "advantage" (opportunity) grows as the king's men delay.

SCENE 3

[*Enter* FALSTAFF *and* BARDOLPH.]

FALSTAFF   Bardolph, am I not fall'n away vilely⁵ since this last action? do
I not bate? do I not dwindle? Why, my skin hangs about me like an old
lady's loose gown; I am withered like an old applejohn. Well, I'll repent,
and that suddenly, while I am in some liking;⁶ I shall be out of heart
shortly, and then I shall have no strength to repent. An I have not forgotten what the inside of a church is made of, I am a peppercorn, a
brewer's horse. The inside of a church! Company, villainous company,
hath been the spoil of me.

BARDOLPH   Sir John, you are so fretful you cannot live long.

FALSTAFF   Why, there is it; come sing me a bawdy song, make me merry.
I was as virtuously given as a gentleman need to be: virtuous enough:
swore little; diced not above seven times a week; went to a bawdyhouse
not above once in a quarter—of an hour; paid money that I borrowed
three or four times; lived well and in good compass; and now I live out
of all order, out of all compass.

BARDOLPH   Why, you are so fat, Sir John, that you must needs be out of
all compass, out of all reasonable compass, Sir John.

FALSTAFF   Do thou amend thy face, and I'll amend my life; thou art our
admiral,⁷ thou bearest the lantern in the poop, but 'tis in the nose of
thee; thou art the Knight of the Burning Lamp.

BARDOLPH   Why, Sir John, my face does you no harm.

FALSTAFF   No, I'll be sworn; I make as good use of it as many a man doth
of a death's-head or a *memento mori*.⁸ I never see thy face but I think
upon hell-fire and Dives⁹ that lived in purple, for there he is in his robes,
burning, burning. If thou wert any way given to virtue, I would swear by
thy face; my oath should be "By this fire, that's God's angel"; but thou
art altogether given over, and wert indeed, but for the light in thy face,
the son of utter darkness. When thou ran'st up Gadshill in the night to
catch my horse, if I did not think thou hadst been an *ignis fatuus* or a
ball of wildfire,¹ there's no purchase in money. O, thou art a perpetual
triumph, an everlasting bonfire light!² Thou hast saved me a thousand
marks in links³ and torches, walking with thee in the night betwixt tavern
and tavern, but the sack that thou hast drunk me would have bought me
lights as good cheap at the dearest chandler's in Europe. I have maintained that salamander⁴ of yours with fire any time this two and thirty
years, God reward me for it.

BARDOLPH   'Sblood, I would my face were in your belly!

FALSTAFF   God-a-mercy! so should I be sure to be heartburnt.

[*Enter* HOSTESS.]

---

5. Lose weight. "Last action": i.e., the Gadshill
robbery.
6. In good condition, in the mood. "Applejohn":
an apple with a wrinkled skin.
7. Flagship.
8. I.e., a skull or some other reminder of death.
9. The rich man who would not give food to Lazarus and was punished in hell for it (Luke 16.19–

31).
1. A firework used for military purposes. "*Ignis
fatuus*": will-o'-the-wisp.
2. Illumination at a public festival.
3. Small torches carried at night.
4. Lizards that supposedly lived in fire and ate it.
"Chandler's": candlemaker's.

How now, Dame Partlet[5] the hen! have you inquired yet who picked my
40 pocket?

HOSTESS   Why, Sir John, what do you think, Sir John? do you think I keep
thieves in my house? I have searched, I have inquired, so has my husband, man by man, boy by boy, servant by servant; the tithe[6] of a hair
was never lost in my house before.

45 FALSTAFF   Ye lie, hostess; Bardolph was shaved and lost many a hair, and
I'll be sworn my pocket was picked. Go to, you are a woman, go.

HOSTESS   Who, I? no, I defy thee; God's light, I was never called so in
mine own house before.

FALSTAFF   Go to, I know you well enough.

50 HOSTESS   No, Sir John; you do not know me, Sir John. I know you, Sir
John; you owe me money, Sir John, and now you pick a quarrel to beguile
me of it; I bought you a dozen of shirts to your back.

FALSTAFF   Dowlas, filthy dowlas; I have given them away to bakers' wives,
and they have made bolters[7] of them.

55 HOSTESS   Now, as I am a true woman, holland of eight shillings an ell.[8]
You owe money here besides, Sir John, for your diet and by-drinkings,[9]
and money lent you, four and twenty pound.

FALSTAFF   He had his part of it; let him pay.

HOSTESS   He? alas, he is poor; he hath nothing.

60 FALSTAFF   How! poor? look upon his face; what call you rich? let them
coin his nose, let them coin his cheeks; I'll not pay a denier. What, will
you make a younker[1] of me? shall I not take mine ease in mine inn but
I shall have my pocket picked? I have lost a seal ring of my grandfather's
worth forty mark.[2]

65 HOSTESS   O Jesu, I have heard the prince tell him I know not how oft that
that ring was copper.

FALSTAFF   How! the prince is a Jack, a sneak-up;[3] 'sblood, an he were here,
I would cudgel him like a dog if he would say so.

[Enter the PRINCE ⟨and POINS⟩, marching, and FALSTAFF meets them
playing upon his truncheon like a fife.]

How now, lad, is the wind in that door, i' faith? must we all march?

70 BARDOLPH   Yea, two and two, Newgate fashion.[4]

HOSTESS   My lord, I pray you hear me.

PRINCE   What say'st thou, Mistress Quickly? How doth thy husband? I
love him well; he is an honest man.

HOSTESS   Good my lord, hear me.

75 FALSTAFF   Prithee let her alone, and list to me.

PRINCE   What say'st thou, Jack?

FALSTAFF   The other night I fell asleep here behind the arras and had my
pocket picked; this house is turned bawdyhouse, they pick pockets.

PRINCE   What didst thou lose, Jack?

80 FALSTAFF   Wilt thou believe me, Hal? three or four bonds of forty pound
apiece, and a seal ring of my grandfather's.

5. A nickname from the hen in Chaucer's *The
Nun's Priest's Tale;* in Shakespeare's time a conventional name for a scolding woman.
6. Tenth part.
7. Sieves for flour. "Dowlas": a coarse cloth.
8. Forty-five inches. "Holland": fine linen.

9. Drinks between meals.
1. Youngster, novice. "Denier": French penny,
worth a tenth of an English penny.
2. A mark was worth two-thirds of a pound.
3. A sneak. "Jack": rascal.
4. Chained together, like prisoners at Newgate.

PRINCE   A trifle, some eightpenny matter.

HOSTESS   So I told him, my lord, and I said I heard your grace say so; and,
my lord, he speaks most vilely of you, like a foul-mouthed man as he is,
85   and said he would cudgel you.

PRINCE   What, he did not?

HOSTESS   There's neither faith, truth, nor womanhood in me else.

FALSTAFF   There's no more faith in thee than in a stewed prune, nor no
more truth in thee than in a drawn[5] fox, and for womanhood Maid Mar-
90   ian may be the deputy's wife of the ward[6] to thee. Go, you thing, go.

HOSTESS   Say, what thing, what thing?

FALSTAFF   What thing! why, a thing to thank God on.

HOSTESS   I am no thing to thank God on, I would thou shouldst know it;
I am an honest man's wife, and, setting thy knighthood aside,[7] thou art
95   a knave to call me so.

FALSTAFF   Setting thy womanhood aside, thou art a beast to say otherwise.

HOSTESS   Say, what beast, thou knave, thou?

FALSTAFF   What beast? why, an otter.

PRINCE   An otter, Sir John, why an otter?

100   FALSTAFF   Why, she's neither fish nor flesh, a man knows not where to
have her.[8]

HOSTESS   Thou art an unjust man in saying so; thou or any man knows
where to have me, thou knave, thou!

PRINCE   Thou sayest true, hostess, and he slanders thee most grossly.

105   HOSTESS   So he doth you, my lord, and said this other day you ought[9] him
a thousand pound.

PRINCE   Sirrah, do I owe you a thousand pound?

FALSTAFF   A thousand pound, Hal! A million. Thy love is worth a million;
thou owest me thy love.

110   HOSTESS   Nay, my lord, he called you Jack, and said he would
cudgel you.

FALSTAFF   Did I, Bardolph?

BARDOLPH   Indeed, Sir John, you said so.

FALSTAFF   Yea, if he said my ring was copper.

115   PRINCE   I say 'tis copper; darest thou be as good as thy word now?

FALSTAFF   Why, Hal, thou knowest, as thou art but man, I dare; but as
thou art prince, I fear thee as I fear the roaring of the lion's whelp.

PRINCE   And why not as the lion?

FALSTAFF   The king himself is to be feared as the lion; dost thou think I'll
120   fear thee as I fear thy father? Nay, an I do, I pray God my girdle[1] break.

PRINCE   O, if it should, how would thy guts fall about thy knees! But,
sirrah, there's no room for faith, truth, nor honesty in this bosom of thine;
it is all filled up with guts and midriff. Charge an honest woman with
picking thy pocket! Why, thou whoreson, impudent, embossed rascal[2] if

---

5. Hunted. Stewed prunes were commonly served
in bawdyhouses, as a supposed protection against
venereal disease.
6. "Maid Marian" was a female character of low
morals in the popular Robin Hood plays; a "deputy's wife of the ward" would be a respectable
woman.
7. I.e., ignoring, or intending no disrespect to, the

rank of knighthood. Falstaff intentionally misun-
derstands the phrase.
8. I.e., how to understand her. But the Hostess's
retort is, unconsciously, equivalent to saying that
she is completely promiscuous.
9. Owed.
1. Belt.
2. Swollen rascal.

125 there were anything in thy pocket but tavern-reckonings, memorandums
of bawdyhouses, and one poor pennyworth of sugar candy to make thee
long-winded, if thy pocket were enriched with any other injuries[3] but
these, I am a villain. And yet you will stand to it, you will not pocket up
wrong; art thou not ashamed?

130 FALSTAFF   Dost thou hear, Hal? thou knowest in the state of innocency
Adam fell, and what should poor Jack Falstaff do in the days of villainy?
Thou seest I have more flesh than another man, and therefore more
frailty.[4] You confess then, you picked my pocket?

PRINCE   It appears so by the story.

135 FALSTAFF   Hostess, I forgive thee; go make ready breakfast, love thy husband, look to thy servants, cherish thy guests; thou shalt find me tractable to any honest reason; thou seest I am pacified still.[5] Nay, prithee
begone. [Exit HOSTESS.] Now, Hal, to the news at court; for the robbery,
lad, how is that answered?

140 PRINCE   O, my sweet beef, I must still be good angel to thee; the money
is paid back again.

FALSTAFF   O, I do not like that paying back; 'tis a double labor.

PRINCE   I am good friends with my father and may do anything.

FALSTAFF   Rob me the exchequer the first thing thou doest, and do it with
145 unwashed hands[6] too.

BARDOLPH   Do, my lord.

PRINCE   I have procured thee, Jack, a charge of foot.

FALSTAFF   I would it had been of horse.[7] Where shall I find one that can
steal well? O for a fine thief, of the age of two and twenty or thereabouts!
150 I am heinously unprovided. Well, God be thanked for these rebels, they
offend none but the virtuous; I laud them, I praise them.

PRINCE   Bardolph!

BARDOLPH   My lord?

PRINCE   Go bear this letter to Lord John of Lancaster, to my brother John;
155 this to my Lord of Westmoreland. [Exit BARDOLPH.] Go, Poins, to horse,
to horse; for thou and I have thirty miles to ride yet ere dinnertime. [Exit
POINS.] Jack, meet me tomorrow in the Temple Hall at two o'clock in
the afternoon.
There shalt thou know thy charge, and there receive
160 Money and order for their furniture.[8]
The land is burning, Percy stands on high,
And either we or they must lower lie.   [⟨Exit.⟩]

FALSTAFF   Rare words, brave world! Hostess, my breakfast, come.
O, I could wish this tavern were my drum![9]   [Exit.]

Act 4

SCENE 1

[Enter HOTSPUR, WORCESTER, and DOUGLAS.]

HOTSPUR   Well said, my noble Scot. If speaking truth
In this fine age were not thought flattery,

---

3. Things, the loss of which you claim as injuries.
4. "The flesh is frail is proverbial" (cf. Matthew 26.41), meaning the flesh is weak.
5. Always easily pacified.
6. I.e., hastily.

7. Cavalry. "A charge of foot": command of a company of foot soldiers.
8. Furnishings, equipment.
9. Headquarters.

Such attribution° should the Douglas have   praise
As not a soldier of this season's stamp
5   Should go so general current[1] through the world.
By God, I cannot flatter; I do defy
The tongues of soothers,° but a braver[2] place   flatterers
In my heart's love hath no man than yourself;
Nay, task me to my word,[3] approve° me, lord.   prove, test
10   DOUGLAS   Thou art the king of honor;
No man so potent breathes upon the ground
But I will beard him.[4]
HOTSPUR   Do so, and 'tis well.
     [Enter a MESSENGER with letters.]
What letters hast thou there?—I can but thank you.
MESSENGER   These letters come from your father.
15   HOTSPUR   Letters from him! why comes he not himself?
MESSENGER   He cannot come, my lord; he is grievous sick.
HOTSPUR   Zounds! how has he the leisure to be sick
In such a justling° time? Who leads his power?   turbulent
Under whose government come they along?
20   MESSENGER   His letters bears his mind, not I, my lord.
WORCESTER   I prithee tell me, doth he keep his bed?
MESSENGER   He did, my lord, four days ere I set forth,
And at the time of my departure thence
He was much feared by his physicíans.
25   WORCESTER   I would the state of time[5] had first been whole
Ere he by sickness had been visited;
His health was never better worth than now.
HOTSPUR   Sick now! droop now! this sickness doth infect
The very lifeblood of our enterprise;
30   'Tis catching hither, even to our camp.
He writes me here that inward sickness—
And that his friends by deputation could not
So soon be drawn,[6] nor did he think it meet
To lay so dangerous and dear a trust
35   On any soul removed[7] but on his own.
Yet doth he give us bold advertisement
That with our small conjunction[8] we should on
To see how fortune is disposed to us;
For, as he writes, there is no quailing now,
40   Because the king is certainly possessed°   informed
Of all our purposes. What say you to it?
WORCESTER   Your father's sickness is a maim to us.
HOTSPUR   A perilous gash, a very limb lopped off;
And yet in faith it is not; his present want[9]
45   Seems more than we shall find it. Were it good
To set the exact wealth of all our states

---

1. I.e., that not a soldier of this age's coinage
should achieve such currency.
2. More distinguished.
3. Compare my actions with my speech.
4. I.e., I will take on anybody, however powerful.

5. Public affairs. "Feared by": feared for by.
6. Could not quickly be organized under a deputy.
7. Other person.
8. Unified forces.
9. Our present awareness of his absence.

All at one cast, to set so rich a main
On the nice hazard[1] of one doubtful hour?
It were not good, for therein should we read
50 The very bottom and the soul of hope,[2]
The very list,° the very utmost bound   limit
Of all our fortunes.
DOUGLAS   Faith, and so we should,
Where now remains a sweet reversiòn.[3]
We may boldly spend upon the hope of what
55 Is to come in;
A comfort of retirement[4] lives in this.
HOTSPUR   A rendezvous, a home to fly unto,
If that the devil and mischance look big
Upon the maidenhead of our affairs.[5]
60 WORCESTER   But yet I would your father had been here.
The quality and hair° of our attempt   character
Brooks° no division; it will be thought   allows
By some that know not why he is away
That wisdom, loyalty, and mere dislike
65 Of our proceedings kept the earl from hence.
And think how such an apprehensiòn
May turn the tide of fearful factiòn°   conspiracy
And breed a kind of question in our cause,
For well you know we of the off'ring° side   challenging
70 Must keep aloof from strict arbitrement,°   investigation
And stop all sight-holes, every loop° from whence   loophole
The eye of reason may pry in upon us.
This absence of your father's draws a curtain,
That shows the ignorant a kind of fear
Before not dreamt of.
75 HOTSPUR   You strain too far.
I rather of his absence make this use:
It lends a luster and more great opinion,
A larger dare to our great enterprise,
Than if the earl were here, for men must think,
80 If we without his help can make a head
To push against a kingdom, with his help
We shall o'erturn it topsy-turvy down.
Yet all goes well, yet all our joints are whole.
DOUGLAS   As heart can think; there is not such a word
85 Spoke of in Scotland as this term of fear.
              [Enter SIR RICHARD VERNON.]
HOTSPUR   My cousin Vernon, welcome, by my soul!
VERNON   Pray God my news be worth a welcome, lord.
The Earl of Westmoreland, seven thousand strong,
Is marching hitherwards; with him Prince John.
HOTSPUR   No harm; what more?

---

1. Risky chance. "Main": stake, in betting.
2. Foundation and essence of our expectations.
3. A fund to be inherited in the future.

4. Sustaining place to fall back on.
5. I.e., threaten the beginning of our affairs.

90 VERNON   And further I have learned
   The king himself in person is set forth,
   Or hitherwards intended speedily,
   With strong and mighty preparatiòn.
   HOTSPUR   He shall be welcome too. Where is his son,
95 The nimble-footed madcap Prince of Wales,
   And his comrades that daft° the world aside   push
   And bid it pass?
   VERNON   All furnished, all in arms,
   All plumed like estridges° that with the wind   ostriches
   Bated, like eagles having lately bathed,[6]
100 Glittering in golden coats like images,
    As full of spirit as the month of May,
    And gorgeous as the sun at midsummer,
    Wanton as youthful goats, wild as young bulls.
    I saw young Harry, with his beaver° on,   helmet
105 His cushes[7] on his thighs, gallantly armed,
    Rise from the ground like feathered Mercury,
    And vaulted with such ease into his seat,
    As if an angel dropped down from the clouds,
    To turn and wind° a fiery Pegasus[8]   direct
110 And witch the world with noble horsemanship.
    HOTSPUR   No more, no more. Worse than the sun in March
    This praise doth nourish agues.[9] Let them come;
    They come like sacrifices in their trim,
    And to the fire-eyed maid of smoky war[1]
115 All hot and bleeding will we offer them;
    The mailèd Mars shall on his altar sit
    Up to the ears in blood. I am on fire
    To hear this rich reprisal° is so nigh   prize
    And yet not ours. Come, let me taste my horse,
120 Who is to bear me like a thunderbolt
    Against the bosom of the Prince of Wales;
    Harry to Harry shall, hot horse to horse,
    Meet and ne'er part till one drop down a corse.
    O that Glendower were come!
    VERNON   There is more news;
125 I learned in Worcester, as I rode along,
    He cannot draw his power[2] this fourteen days.
    DOUGLAS   That's the worst tidings that I hear of yet.
    WORCESTER   Aye, by my faith, that bears a frosty sound.
    HOTSPUR   What may the king's whole battle° reach unto?   army
    VERNON   To thirty thousand.
130 HOTSPUR   Forty let it be;
    My father and Glendower being both away,

---

6. Eagles were supposed to renew their youth by
bathing in the ocean. "Bated": fluttering their
wings.
7. Cuisses, armor for the thighs.
8. A winged horse.

9. Fevers. Malaria was thought to be caused by
vapors from the marshes, drawn up by the sun in
spring.
1. Bellona, goddess of war.
2. Assemble his forces.

The powers of us may serve so great a day.
Come, let us take a muster speedily;
Doomsday is near; die all, die merrily.
135 DOUGLAS   Talk not of dying; I am out of fear
Of death or death's hand for this one-half year.   [*Exeunt.*]

SCENE 2

[*Enter* FALSTAFF *and* BARDOLPH.]

FALSTAFF   Bardolph, get thee before to Coventry; fill me a bottle of sack,
our soldiers shall march through. We'll to Sutton Co'fil'³ tonight.
BARDOLPH   Will you give me money, captain?
FALSTAFF   Lay out, lay out.
5 BARDOLPH   This bottle makes an angel.⁴
FALSTAFF   An if it do, take it for thy labor; and if it make twenty, take them
all; I'll answer the coinage. Bid my lieutenant Peto meet me at town's
end.
BARDOLPH   I will, captain; farewell.   [*Exit.*]
10 FALSTAFF   If I be not ashamed of my soldiers, I am a soused gurnet. I have
misused the king's press⁵ damnably. I have got in exchange of a hundred
and fifty soldiers three hundred and odd pounds. I press me none but
good householders, yeomen's sons, inquire me out contracted bachelors,
such as had been asked twice on the banns,⁶ such a commodity of warm
15 slaves as had as lieve hear the devil as a drum, such as fear the report of
a caliver⁷ worse than a struck fowl or a hurt wild duck. I pressed me
none but such toasts-and-butter⁸ with hearts in their bellies no bigger
than pins' heads, and they have bought out their services, and now my
whole charge consists of ancients,⁹ corporals, lieutenants, gentlemen of
20 companies, slaves as ragged as Lazarus in the painted cloth where the
glutton's dogs licked his sores, and such as indeed were never soldiers,
but discarded unjust serving-men, younger sons to younger brothers,
revolted tapsters and ostlers trade-fall'n,¹ the cankers² of a calm world
and a long peace, ten times more dishonorable ragged than an old-fac'd
25 ancient,³ and such have I to fill up the rooms of them that have bought
out their services, that you would think that I had a hundred and fifty
tattered prodigals lately come from swine-keeping, from eating draff⁴ and
husks. A mad fellow met me on the way and told me I had unloaded all
the gibbets and pressed the dead bodies. No eye hath seen such scare-
30 crows. I'll not march through Coventry with them, that's flat; nay, and
the villains march wide betwixt the legs, as if they had gyves⁵ on, for
indeed I had the most of them out of prison. There's but a shirt and a
half in all my company, and the half shirt is two napkins tacked together

---

3. Sutton Coldfield, about twenty-five miles from Coventry.
4. Ten shillings' worth.
5. The draft or impressment of soldiers into service. "Soused gurnet": pickled anchovy.
6. Notice of approaching marriage, announced three times publicly in church before the marriage could take place.
7. Musket. "Commodity": collection. "Warm":

well-to-do.
8. Sissies.
9. Ensigns.
1. Hostlers out of work.
2. Canker worms.
3. Frayed flag.
4. Garbage. The prodigal son, in the Bible, fed on husks before returning to the paternal board.
5. Leg-irons.

and thrown over the shoulders like a herald's coat without sleeves, and
35 the shirt, to say the truth, stolen from my host at Saint Alban's, or the
red-nose innkeeper of Daventry. But that's all one; they'll find linen
enough on every hedge.[6]

[*Enter the* PRINCE *and the* LORD OF WESTMORELAND.]

PRINCE   How now, blown Jack! how now, quilt![7]

FALSTAFF   What, Hal, how now, mad wag! what a devil dost thou in War-
40 wickshire? My good Lord of Westmoreland, I cry you mercy; I thought
your honor had already been at Shrewsbury.

WESTMORELAND   Faith, Sir John, 'tis more than time that I were there,
and you too; but my powers are there already. The king, I can tell you,
looks for us all; we must away all night.

45 FALSTAFF   Tut, never fear me; I am as vigilant as a cat to steal cream.

PRINCE   I think, to steal cream indeed, for thy theft hath already made
thee butter. But tell me, Jack, whose fellows are these that come after?

FALSTAFF   Mine, Hal, mine.

PRINCE   I did never see such pitiful rascals.

50 FALSTAFF   Tut, tut, good enough to toss,[8] food for powder, food for powder; they'll fill a pit as well as better; tush, man, mortal men, mortal men.

WESTMORELAND   Aye, but, Sir John, methinks they are exceeding poor and
bare, too beggarly.

FALSTAFF   Faith, for their poverty I know not where they had that, and for
55 their bareness I am sure they never learned that of me.

PRINCE   No, I'll be sworn, unless you call three fingers[9] on the ribs bare.
But, sirrah, make haste; Percy is already in the field.

FALSTAFF   What, is the king encamped?

WESTMORELAND   He is, Sir John; I fear we shall stay too long.

60 FALSTAFF   Well,
To the latter end of a fray and the beginning of a feast
Fits a dull fighter and a keen guest.   [*Exeunt.*]

SCENE 3

[*Enter* HOTSPUR, WORCESTER, DOUGLAS, *and* VERNON.]

HOTSPUR   We'll fight with him tonight.

WORCESTER   It may not be.

DOUGLAS   You give him then advantage.

VERNON   Not a whit.

HOTSPUR   Why say you so? looks he not for supply?

VERNON   So do we.

HOTSPUR   His is certain, ours is doubtful.

5 WORCESTER   Good cousin, be advised; stir not tonight.

VERNON   Do not, my lord.

DOUGLAS   You do not counsel well;
You speak it out of fear and cold heart.

VERNON   Do me no slander, Douglas; by my life,

---

6. Laundry was customarily hung on hedges to
dry.
7. Padded material, a substitute for armor.

8. I.e., on a pike, or long spear.
9. Layers of fat. A finger was three-quarters of an
inch.

And I dare well maintain it with my life,
10   If well-respected honor[1] bid me on,
I hold as little counsel with weak fear
As you, my lord, or any Scot that this day lives.
Let it be seen tomorrow in the battle
Which of us fears.
DOUGLAS   Yea, or tonight.
VERNON   Content.
15   HOTSPUR   Tonight, say I.
VERNON   Come, come, it may not be. I wonder much,
Being men of such great leading as you are,
That you foresee not what impediments
Drag back our expedition;[2] certain horse
20   Of my cousin Vernon's are not yet come up,
Your uncle Worcester's horse came but today,
And now their pride and mettle is asleep,
Their courage with hard labor tame and dull,
That not a horse is half the half of himself.
25   HOTSPUR   So are the horses of the enemy
In general, journey-bated[3] and brought low;
The better part of ours are full of rest.
WORCESTER   The number of the king exceedeth ours;
For God's sake, cousin, stay till all come in.
[*The trumpet sounds a parley. Enter* SIR WALTER BLUNT.]
30   BLUNT   I come with gracious offers from the king,
If you vouchsafe me hearing and respect.
HOTSPUR   Welcome, Sir Walter Blunt; and would to God
You were of our determinàtion!
Some of us love you well, and even those some
35   Envy your great deservings and good name
Because you are not of our quality,[4]
But stand against us like an enemy.
BLUNT   And God defend° but still° I should stand so,   *forbid / always*
So long as out of limit and true rule
40   You stand against anointed majesty.
But to my charge. The king hath sent to know
The nature of your griefs, and whereupon
You conjure from the breast of civil peace
Such bold hostility, teaching his duteous land
45   Audacious cruelty. If that the king
Have any way your good deserts forgot,
Which he confesseth to be manifold,
He bids you name your griefs, and with all speed
You shall have your desires with interest
50   And pardon absolute for yourself and these
Herein misled by your suggestiòn.°   *temptation*
HOTSPUR   The king is kind, and well we know the king

---

1. Well-considered (not rash, like Hotspur's).
2. Retard our speed.
3. Tired from travel.
4. Fellowship, party.

Knows at what time to promise, when to pay.
My father and my uncle and myself
55 Did give him that same royalty he wears;
And when he was not six and twenty strong,
Sick in the world's regard, wretched and low,
A poor unminded outlaw sneaking home,
My father gave him welcome to the shore;
60 And when he heard him swear and vow to God
He came but to be Duke of Lancaster,
To sue his livery⁵ and beg his peace,
With tears of innocency and terms of zeal,
My father, in kind heart and pity moved,
65 Swore him assistance and performed it too.
Now when the lords and barons of the realm
Perceived Northumberland did lean to him,
The more and less came in with cap and knee,⁶
Met him in boroughs, cities, villages,
70 Attended him on bridges, stood in lanes,
Laid gifts before him, proffered him their oaths,
Gave him their heirs as pages, followed him
Even at the heels in golden multitudes.
He presently, as greatness knows itself,
75 Steps me a little higher than his vow,
Made to my father while his blood was poor
Upon the naked shore at Ravenspurgh,
And now, forsooth, takes on him to reform
Some certain edicts and some strait° decrees   *strict*
80 That lie too heavy on the commonwealth,
Cries out upon abuses, seems to weep
Over his country's wrongs, and by this face,°   *pretense*
This seeming brow of justice, did he win
The hearts of all that he did angle for;
85 Proceeded further, cut me off the heads
Of all the favorites that the absent king
In deputation left behind him here,
When he was personal⁷ in the Irish war.
BLUNT Tut, I came not to hear this.
HOTSPUR   Then to the point.
90 In short time after he deposed the king,
Soon after that deprived him of his life,
And in the neck of that tasked⁸ the whole state;
To make that worse, suffered his kinsman March
(Who is, if every owner were well placed,
95 Indeed his king) to be engaged⁹ in Wales,
There without ransom to lie forfeited;
Disgraced¹ me in my happy victories,

---

5. I.e., claim title to his late father's lands (held by King Richard II).
6. Cap in hand and on bended knee; i.e., offering homage.
7. Actively participating in person.
8. I.e., immediately after that, (he) taxed.
9. Pawned as a hostage.
1. I.e., did not favor.

    Sought to entrap me by intelligence,°   *spying*
    Rated[2] mine uncle from the council board,
100   In rage dismissed my father from the court,
    Broke oath on oath, committed wrong on wrong,
    And in conclusion drove us to seek out
    This head of safety,[3] and withal to pry
    Into his title, the which we find
105   Too indirect for long continuance.
BLUNT   Shall I return this answer to the king?
HOTSPUR   Not so, Sir Walter; we'll withdraw awhile.
    Go to the king, and let there be impawned°   *pledged*
    Some surety° for a safe return again,   *guarantee*
110   And in the morning early shall mine uncle
    Bring him our purposes; and so farewell.
BLUNT   I would you would accept of grace and love.
HOTSPUR   And may be so we shall.
BLUNT   Pray God you do.   *[Exeunt.]*

SCENE 4

[*Enter the* ARCHBISHOP OF YORK *and* SIR MICHAEL.]
ARCHBISHOP   Hie, good Sir Michael; bear this sealèd brief°   *letter*
    With wingèd haste to the lord marshal,
    This to my cousin Scroop, and all the rest
    To whom they are directed. If you knew
5   How much they do import you would make haste.
SIR MICHAEL   My good lord,
    I guess their tenor.
ARCHBISHOP   Like enough you do.
    Tomorrow, good Sir Michael, is a day
    Wherein the fortune of ten thousand men
10   Must bide the touch;[4] for, sir, at Shrewsbury,
    As I am truly given to understand,
    The king with mighty and quick-raisèd power
    Meets with Lord Harry; and I fear, Sir Michael,
    What with the sickness of Northumberland,
15   Whose power was in the first proportiòn,[5]
    And what with Owen Glendower's absence thence,
    Who with them was a rated[6] sinew too
    And comes not in, o'er-ruled by prophecies—
    I fear the power of Percy is too weak
20   To wage an instant trial with the king.
SIR MICHAEL   Why, my good lord, you need not fear;
    There is Douglas and Lord Mortimer.
ARCHBISHOP   No, Mortimer is not there.
SIR MICHAEL   But there is Mordake, Vernon, Lord Harry Percy,
25   And there is my Lord of Worcester and a head

---

2. Angrily dismissed.
3. Army for our safety.
4. Stand the test.

5. The largest part.
6. Highly regarded.

Of gallant warriors, noble gentlemen.

ARCHBISHOP   And so there is; but yet the king hath drawn
The special head[7] of all the land together:
The Prince of Wales, Lord John of Lancaster,
30 The noble Westmoreland, and warlike Blunt,
And many more corrivals° and dear° men   *associates / noble*
O estimation and command in arms.

SIR MICHAEL   Doubt not, my lord, they shall be well opposed.

ARCHBISHOP   I hope no less, yet needful 'tis to fear,
35 And to prevent° the worst, Sir Michael, speed;   *forestall*
For if Lord Percy thrive not, ere the king
Dismiss his power, he means to visit° us,   *attack*
For he hath heard of our confederacy,
And 'tis but wisdom to make strong against him;
40 Therefore make haste. I must go write again
To other friends; and so farewell, Sir Michael.   [*Exeunt.*]

Act 5

SCENE 1

[*Enter the* KING, PRINCE OF WALES, PRINCE JOHN OF LANCASTER, SIR
WALTER BLUNT, *and* FALSTAFF.]

KING   How bloodily the sun begins to peer
Above yon busky° hill! The day looks pale   *wooded*
At his distemp'rature.[8]

PRINCE   The southern wind
Doth play the trumpet to his purposes,[9]
5 And by his hollow whistling in the leaves
Foretells a tempest and a blustering day.

KING   Then with the losers let it sympathize,
For nothing can seem foul to those that win.
    [*The trumpet sounds. Enter* WORCESTER ⟨*and* VERNON⟩.]
How now, my lord of Worcester! 'Tis not well
10 That you and I should meet upon such terms
As now we meet. You have deceived our trust
And made us doff our easy robes of peace,
To crush° our old limbs in ungentle steel;   *enfold, cramp*
This is not well, my lord, this is not well.
15 What say you to it? will you again unknit
This churlish knot of all-abhorrèd war
And move in that obedient orb[1] again
Where you did give a fair and natural light,
And be no more an exhaled meteor,[2]
20 A prodigy of fear and a portent
Of broachèd mischief to the unborn times?[3]

---

7. Principal army.
8. I.e., the sun's illness or malevolence.
9. I.e., the sun's intentions; the southern wind supports them.
1. Regular orbit, as of a planet.
2. Meteors were thought to be made of gas

exhaled by a planet and were commonly associated with civil commotion.
3. I.e., of harm or disaster opened up ("broached") to plague the future. "Mischief" conveyed a tronger meaning to Shakespeare than it does to us.

WORCESTER   Hear me, my liege:
 For mine own part I could be well content
 To entertain the lag end of my life
25 With quiet hours, for I do protest
 I have not sought the day of this dislike.
KING   You have not sought it! how comes it then?
FALSTAFF   Rebellion lay in his way, and he found it.
PRINCE   Peace, chewet,[4] peace!
30   WORCESTER   It pleased your majesty to turn your looks
 Of favor from myself and all our house,
 And yet I must remember° you, my lord,   *remind*
 We were the first and dearest of your friends.
 For you my staff of office did I break
35 In Richard's time, and posted day and night
 To meet you on the way and kiss your hand
 When yet you were in place and in account
 Nothing so strong and fortunate as I.
 It was myself, my brother, and his son
40 That brought you home and boldly did outdare
 The dangers of the time. You swore to us,
 And you did swear that oath at Doncaster,
 That you did nothing purpose 'gainst the state
 Nor claim no further than your new-fall'n[5] right,
45 The seat of Gaunt, dukedom of Lancaster.
 To this we swore our aid. But in short space
 It rained down fortune showering on your head
 And such a flood of greatness fell on you,
 What with our help, what with the absent king,
50 What with the injuries of a wanton time,
 The seeming sufferances° that you had borne, *sufferings*
 And the contrarious winds that held the king
 So long in his unlucky Irish wars
 That all in England did repute him dead;
55 And from this swarm of fair advantages
 You took occasion to be quickly wooed
 To gripe the general sway[6] into your hand,
 Forgot your oath to us at Doncaster,
 And being fed by us you used us so
60 As that ungentle gull[7] the cuckoo's bird
 Useth the sparrow, did oppress our nest,
 Grew by our feeding to so great a bulk
 That even our love durst not come near your sight
 For fear of swallowing;[8] but with nimble wing
65 We were enforced for safety sake to fly
 Out of your sight and raise this present head,
 Whereby we stand opposèd by such means

4. Chattering bird.
5. Recently inherited.
6. Seize power over the whole state.

7. Rude nestling; the cuckoo hatches its young in other birds' nests.
8. Being swallowed.

As you yourself have forged against yourself
By unkind usage, dangerous countenance,[9]
70　　And violation of all faith and troth
Sworn to us in your younger enterprise.
KING　These things indeed you have articulate,[1]
Proclaimed at market crosses, read in churches,
To face° the garment of rebellion　　　　　　　　　　　　　　*decorate*
75　　With some fine color that may please the eye
Of fickle changelings and poor discontents,
Which gape and rub the elbow at the news
Of hurlyburly innovation;
And never yet did insurrection want
80　　Such water colors to impaint his cause,
Nor moody beggars starving for a time
Of pellmell havoc and confusion.
PRINCE　In both our armies there is many a soul
Shall pay full dearly for this encounter,
85　　If once they join in trial. Tell your nephew
The Prince of Wales doth join with all the world
In praise of Henry Percy; by my hopes,
This present enterprise set off his head,[2]
I do not think a braver gentleman,
90　　More active-valiant or more valiant-young,
More daring or more bold, is now alive
To grace this latter age with noble deeds.
For my part, I may speak it to my shame,
I have a truant been to chivalry—
95　　And so I hear he doth account me too—
Yet this before my father's majesty:
I am content that he shall take the odds
Of his great name and estimation,
And will, to save the blood on either side,
100　　Try fortune with him in a single fight.
KING　And, Prince of Wales, so dare we venture thee,
Albeit considerations infinite
Do make° against it. No, good Worcester, no,　　　　　　　　*weigh*
We love our people well; even those we love
105　　That are misled upon your cousin's part;
And, will they take the offer of our grace,
Both he and they and you, yea, every man
Shall be my friend again and I'll be his.
So tell your cousin, and bring me word
110　　What he will do; but if he will not yield,
Rebuke and dread correction wait on° us　　　　　　　　　　*accompany*
And they shall do their office. So, be gone;
We will not now be troubled with reply.

9. Threatening looks.　　　　　　　　　　　　2. Deducted from his account.
1. Drawn up in detail.

We offer fair; take it advisedly.
    [*Exit* WORCESTER ⟨*and* VERNON.⟩]

115 PRINCE   It will not be accepted, on my life;
    The Douglas and the Hotspur both together
    Are confident against the world in arms.

KING   Hence, therefore, every leader to his charge,
    For on their answer will we set on them,
120   And God befriend us, as our cause is just!
    [*Exeunt all but the* PRINCE *and* FALSTAFF.]

FALSTAFF   Hal, if thou see me down in the battle and bestride me, so; 'tis
a point of friendship.

PRINCE   Nothing but a colossus can do thee that friendship. Say thy
prayers, and farewell.

125 FALSTAFF   I would 'twere bedtime, Hal, and all well.

PRINCE   Why, thou owest God a death.   [⟨*Exit.*⟩]

FALSTAFF   'Tis not due yet; I would be loath to pay him before his day.
What need I be so forward with him that calls not on me? Well, 'tis no
matter; honor pricks me on. Yea, but how if honor prick me off when I
130 come on? How then? can honor set to a leg? No. Or an arm? No. Or
take away the grief[3] of a wound? No. Honor hath no skill in surgery,
then? No. What is honor? A word. What is in that word honor? what is
that honor? Air. A trim reckoning![4] Who hath it? He that died o'Wednesday. Doth he feel it? No. Doth he hear it? No. 'Tis insensible,[5] then? Yea,
135 to the dead. But will it not live with the living? No. Why? Detraction will
not suffer it. Therefore I'll none of it; Honor is a mere scutcheon.[6] And
so ends my catechism.   [*Exit.*]

SCENE 2

[*Enter* WORCESTER *and* SIR RICHARD VERNON.]

WORCESTER   O no, my nephew must not know, Sir Richard,
    The liberal and kind offer of the king.

VERNON   'Twere best he did.

WORCESTER   Then are we all undone.
    It is not possible, it cannot be,
5   The king should keep his word in loving us;
    He will suspect us still and find a time
    To punish this offense in other faults.
    Suspicion all our lives shall be stuck full of eyes,
    For treason is but trusted like the fox
10   Who, ne'er so tame, so cherished and locked up,
    Will have a wild trick of his ancestors;
    Look how we can, or sad or merrily,
    Interpretation will misquote° our looks,   *misinterpret*
    And we shall feed like oxen at a stall,
15   The better cherished, still the nearer death.
    My nephew's trespass may be well forgot;

---

3. Pain.
4. A fine totaling of the bill.

5. Not capable of being felt.
6. A coat of arms, often put on a tombstone.

It hath the excuse of youth and heat of blood
And an adopted name of privilege,[7]
A harebrained Hotspur, governed by a spleen.[8]
20 All his offenses live upon my head
And on his father's; we did train° him on,   *entice*
And, his corruption being ta'en from us,[9]
We, as the spring of all, shall pay for all.
Therefore, good cousin, let not Harry know
25 In any case the offer of the king.
VERNON   Deliver what you will; I'll say 'tis so.
Here comes your cousin.
        [*Enter* HOTSPUR ⟨*and* DOUGLAS⟩.]
HOTSPUR   My uncle is returned;
Deliver up my Lord of Westmoreland.
30 Uncle, what news?
WORCESTER   The king will bid you battle presently.°   *immediately*
DOUGLAS   Defy him by the Lord of Westmoreland.
HOTSPUR   Lord Douglas, go you and tell him so.
DOUGLAS   Marry, and shall, and very willingly.   [*Exit.*]
35 WORCESTER   There is no seeming mercy in the king.
HOTSPUR   Did you beg any? God forbid!
WORCESTER   I told him gently of our grievances,
Of his oath-breaking, which he mended thus,
By now forswearing[1] that he is forsworn;
40 He calls us rebels, traitors, and will scourge
With haughty arms this hateful name in us.
        [*Enter* DOUGLAS.]
DOUGLAS   Arm, gentlemen, to arms! for I have thrown
A brave defiance in King Henry's teeth,
And Westmoreland, that was engaged,[2] did hear it,
45 Which cannot choose but bring him quickly on.
WORCESTER   The Prince of Wales stepped forth before the king,
And, nephew, challenged you to single fight.
HOTSPUR   O, would the quarrel lay upon our heads,
And that no man might draw short breath today
50 But I and Harry Monmouth! Tell me, tell me,
How showed his tasking?° seemed it in contempt?   *challenge*
VERNON   No, by my soul; I never in my life
Did hear a challenge urged more modestly,
Unless a brother should a brother dare
55 To gentle exercise and proof of arms.
He gave you all the duties[3] of a man,
Trimmed up your praises with a princely tongue,
Spoke your deservings like a chronicle,
Making you ever better than his praise
60 By still dispraising praise valued° with you;   *compared*

___

7. A nickname that gives him privileges.
8. Impetuous temperament.
9. Being attributed to.

1. Swearing falsely.
2. Held as a hostage.
3. Good qualities.

And, which became him like a prince indeed,
He made a blushing cital[4] of himself,
And chid his truant youth with such a grace
As if he mastered there a double spirit
65   Of teaching and of learning instantly.
There did he pause; but let me tell the world,
If he outlive the envy° of this day,   malice
England did never owe° so sweet a hope,   own
So much miscònstrued in his wantonness.°   frivolity
70   HOTSPUR   Cousin, I think thou art enamoured
On his follies; never did I hear
Of any prince so wild a liberty.[5]
But be he as he will, yet once ere night
I will embrace him with a soldier's arm,
75   That he shall shrink under my courtesy.
Arm, arm with speed; and, fellows, soldiers, friends,
Better consider what you have to do
Than I, that have not well the gift of tongue,
Can lift your blood up with persuasiòn.
          [Enter a MESSENGER.]
80   MESSENGER   My lord, here are letters for you.
HOTSPUR   I cannot read them now.
O gentlemen, the time of life is short!
To spend that shortness basely were too long,
If life did ride upon a dial's point,
85   Still° ending at the arrival of an hour;[6]   always
And if we live, we live to tread on kings,
If die, brave death when princes die with us!
Now, for our consciences, the arms are fair,
When the intent of bearing them is just.
          [Enter another MESSENGER.]
90   MESSENGER   My lord, prepare; the king comes on apace.
HOTSPUR   I thank him that he cuts me from my tale,
For I profess not talking; only this—
Let each man do his best; and here draw I
A sword whose temper I intend to stain
95   With the best blood that I can meet withal
In the adventure of this perilous day.
Now, Esperance! Percy![7] and set on.
Sound all the lofty instruments of war,
And by that music let us all embrace;
100 For, heaven to earth,[8] some of us never shall
A second time do such a courtesy.
          [The trumpets sound. They embrace and exeunt.]

4. Mention, recital.
5. Reckless dissipation.
6. Hotspur's meaning is that a base life would be too long even if it lasted only one hour. "Dial's

point": hands of a clock.
7. Hope, Percy! (the family motto).
8. I.e., the odds are heaven to earth that.

SCENE 3

[*The* KING *enters with his power. Alarum*[9] *to the battle.*
Then enter DOUGLAS *and* SIR WALTER BLUNT.]

BLUNT What is thy name, that in the battle thus
  Thou crossest me? what honor dost thou seek
  Upon my head?

DOUGLAS   Know then, my name is Douglas,
  And I do haunt thee in the battle thus
5 Because some tell me that thou art a king.[1]

BLUNT   They tell thee true.

DOUGLAS   The Lord of Stafford dear° today hath bought   *expensively*
  Thy likeness, for instead of thee, King Harry,
  This sword hath ended him; so shall it thee,
10 Unless thou yield thee as my prisoner.

BLUNT   I was not born a yielder, thou proud Scot,
  And thou shalt find a king that will revenge
  Lord Stafford's death.   [*They fight.* DOUGLAS *kills* BLUNT.]
      [*Enter* HOTSPUR.]

HOTSPUR   O Douglas, hadst thou fought at Holmedon thus,
15 I never had triumphed upon a Scot.

DOUGLAS   All's done, all's won; here breathless lies the king.

HOTSPUR   Where?

DOUGLAS   Here.

HOTSPUR   This, Douglas? No, I know this face full well;
20 A gallant knight he was, his name was Blunt;
  Semblably furnished like the king himself.

DOUGLAS   Ah fool, go with thy soul whither it goes!
  A borrowed title hast thou bought too dear;
  Why didst thou tell me that thou wert a king?

25 HOTSPUR   The king hath many marching in his coats.

DOUGLAS   Now, by my sword, I will kill all his coats;
  I'll murder all his wardrobe, piece by piece,
  Until I meet the king.

HOTSPUR   Up and away!
  Our soldiers stand full fairly for the day.   [*Exeunt.*]
      [*Alarum. Enter* FALSTAFF *alone.*]

30 FALSTAFF   Though I could 'scape shot-free[2] at London, I fear the shot here;
  here's no scoring but upon the pate. Soft, who are you? Sir Walter Blunt;
  there's honor for you, here's no vanity! I am as hot as molten lead, and
  as heavy too; God keep lead out of me! I need no more weight than mine
  own bowels. I have led my ragamuffins where they are peppered; there's
35 not three of my hundred and fifty left alive, and they are for the town's
  end, to beg during life. But who comes here?
      [*Enter the* PRINCE.]

PRINCE   What, stand'st thou idle here? lend me thy sword;
  Many a nobleman lies stark and stiff

---

9. Trumpet signal.
1. Blunt and others are dressed to look like the king.

2. Scot-free, without paying the bill at a tavern. "Scoring" continues the pun; it means (1) marking up a charge, (2) cutting with a sword.

Under the hoofs of vaunting enemies,
40 Whose deaths are yet unrevenged; I prithee, lend me thy sword.
FALSTAFF   O Hal, I prithee give me leave to breathe awhile. Turk Gregory[3]
never did such deeds in arms as I have done this day. I have paid Percy,
I have made him sure.
PRINCE   He is indeed, and living to kill thee. I prithee, lend me thy sword.
45 FALSTAFF   Nay, before God, Hal, if Percy be alive, thou get'st not my
sword; but take my pistol if thou wilt.
PRINCE   Give it me; what, is it in the case?
FALSTAFF   Aye, Hal; 'tis hot, 'tis hot; there's that will sack a city.
[*The* PRINCE *draws it out, and finds it to be a bottle of sack.*]
PRINCE   What, is it a time to jest and dally now?
[*He throws the bottle at him. Exit.*]
50 FALSTAFF   Well, if Percy be alive, I'll pierce him. If he do come in my way,
so; if he do not, if I come in his willingly, let him make a carbonado[4] of
me. I like not such grinning honor as Sir Walter hath; give me life, which
if I can save, so; if not, honor comes unlooked for, and there's an end.
[*Exit.*]

SCENE 4

[*Alarum. Excursions.*[5] *Enter the* KING, *the* PRINCE, PRINCE JOHN OF
LANCASTER, *and* EARL OF WESTMORELAND.]
KING   I prithee,
Harry, withdraw thyself; thou bleed'st too much.
Lord John of Lancaster, go you with him.
LANCASTER   Not I, my lord, unless I did bleed too.
5 PRINCE   I beseech your majesty, make up,°   advance
Lest your retirement do amaze° your friends.   dismay
KING   I will do so.
My Lord of Westmoreland, lead him to his tent.
WESTMORELAND   Come, my lord, I'll lead you to your tent.
10 PRINCE   Lead me, my lord? I do not need your help,
And God forbid a shallow scratch should drive
The Prince of Wales from such a field as this,
Where stained nobility lies trodden on,
And rebels' arms triumph in massacres!
15 LANCASTER   We breathe too long; come, cousin Westmoreland,
Our duty this way lies; for God's sake, come.
[⟨*Exeunt* PRINCE JOHN *and* WESTMORELAND.⟩]
PRINCE   By God, thou hast deceived me, Lancaster;
I did not think thee lord of such a spirit.
Before, I loved thee as a brother, John,
20 But now I do respect thee as my soul.
KING   I saw him hold Lord Percy at the point
With lustier maintenance than I did look for
Of such an ungrown warrior.
PRINCE   O, this boy

3. Falstaff combines Pope Gregory VII, of whom   4. A cubed steak.
fantastic stories were told, with "Turk" (the Turks   5. Brief appearances and exits of soldiers fighting.
were noted for ferocity).

Lends mettle to us all!   [*Exit.*]
          [*Enter* DOUGLAS.]

25   DOUGLAS   Another king! they grow like Hydra's heads.[6]
          I am the Douglas, fatal to all those
          That wear those colors on them; what art thou,
          That counterfeit'st the person of a king?
     KING   The king himself, who, Douglas, grieves at heart
30   So many of his shadows° thou hast met   *likenesses*
          And not the very king. I have two boys
          Seek Percy and thyself about the field,
          But seeing thou fall'st on me so luckily
          I will assay thee; so defend thyself.
35   DOUGLAS   I fear thou art another counterfeit,
          And yet, in faith, thou bearest thee like a king;
          But mine I am sure thou art, whoe'er thou be.
          And thus I win thee.
          [*They fight; the* KING *being in danger, enter* PRINCE OF WALES.]
     PRINCE   Hold up thy head, vile Scot, or thou art like
40   Never to hold it up again! the spirits
          Of valiant Shirley, Stafford, Blunt, are in my arms;
          It is the Prince of Wales that threatens thee,
          Who never promiseth but he means to pay.
          [*They fight;* DOUGLAS *flieth.*]
          Cheerly, my lord; how fares your grace?
45   Sir Nicholas Gawsey hath for succor sent,
          And so hath Clifton; I'll to Clifton straight.
     KING   Stay, and breathe awhile.
          Thou hast redeemed thy lost opinion,°   *reputation*
          And showed thou makest some tender of[7] my life
50   His fair rescue thou hast brought to me.
     PRINCE   O God, they did me too much injury
          That ever said I hearkened for your death.
          If it were so, I might have let alone
          The insulting hand of Douglas over you,
55   Which would have been as speedy in your end
          As all the poisonous potions in the world
          And saved the treacherous labor of your son.
     KING   Make up to Clifton; I'll to Sir Nicholas Gawsey.   [*Exit.*]
          [*Enter* HOTSPUR.]
     HOTSPUR   If I mistake not, thou art Harry Monmouth.
60   PRINCE   Thou speak'st as if I would deny my name.
     HOTSPUR   My name is Harry Percy.
     PRINCE   Why then I see
          A very valiant rebel of the name.
          I am the Prince of Wales, and think not, Percy,
          To share with me in glory any more:
65   Two stars keep not their motion in one sphere,°   *orbit*

6. The heads of this fabulous monster grew back   7. I.e., you have some concern for.
as fast as they could be cut off.

Nor can one England brook° a double reign   *endure*
Of Harry Percy and the Prince of Wales.
HOTSPUR   Nor shall it, Harry, for the hour is come
To end the one of us; and would to God
70   Thy name in arms were now as great as mine!
PRINCE   I'll make it greater ere I part from thee,
And all the budding honors on thy crest
I'll crop to make a garland for my head.
HOTSPUR   I can no longer brook thy vanities.   *[They fight.]*
      [Enter FALSTAFF.]
75 FALSTAFF   Well said, Hal, to it, Hal! Nay, you shall find no boy's play here,
I can tell you.
      [Enter DOUGLAS; *he fighteth with* FALSTAFF, *who falls down as if he were
      dead.* ⟨*Exit* DOUGLAS.⟩ *The* PRINCE *killeth* PERCY.]
HOTSPUR   O Harry, thou hast robbed me of my youth!
I better brook the loss of brittle life
Than those proud titles thou hast won of me;
80   They wound my thoughts worse than thy sword my flesh;
But thought's the slave of life, and life time's fool,
And time, that takes survey of all the world,
Must have a stop. O, I could prophesy,
But that the earthy and cold hand of death
85   Lies on my tongue; no, Percy, thou art dust,
And food for—   *[⟨Dies.⟩]*
PRINCE   For worms, brave Percy; fare thee well, great heart!
Ill-weaved ambition, how much art thou shrunk!
When that this body did contain a spirit
90   A kingdom for it was too small a bound,
But now two paces of the vilest earth
Is room enough; this earth that bears thee dead
Bears not alive so stout° a gentleman.   *valiant*
If thou wert sensible of courtesy,
95   I should not make so dear° a show of zeal;   *open*
But let my favors hide thy mangled face[8]
And, even in thy behalf, I'll thank myself
For doing these fair rites of tenderness.
Adieu, and take thy praise with thee to heaven;
100   Thy ignominy sleep with thee in the grave,
But not remembered in thy epitaph!
      [He spieth FALSTAFF *on the ground.]*
What, old acquaintance, could not all this flesh
Keep in a little life? Poor Jack, farewell;
I could have better spared a better man.
105   O, I should have a heavy miss of thee,
If I were much in love with vanity!°   *frivolity*
Death hath not struck so fat a deer today,
Though many dearer,° in this bloody fray.   *nobler*
Emboweled° will I see thee by and by;   *embalmed*
110   Till then in blood by noble Percy lie.   *[Exit.]*

8. Prince Hal here covers Hotspur's face with a scarf.

FALSTAFF [*rising up*]   Emboweled! if thou embowel me today, I'll give you
leave to powder[9] me and eat me tomorrow. 'Sblood, 'twas time to counterfeit, or that hot termagant Scot had paid me scot and lot[1] too. Counterfeit? I lie, I am no counterfeit; to die is to be a counterfeit, for he is but
115 the counterfeit of a man who hath not the life of a man; but to counterfeit
dying when a man thereby liveth is to be no counterfeit, but the true and
perfect image of life indeed. The better part[2] of valor is discretion, in the
which better part I have saved my life. Zounds, I am afraid of this gunpowder Percy, though he be dead; how if he should counterfeit too and
120 rise? By my faith, I am afraid he would prove the better counterfeit.
Therefore I'll make him sure; yea, and I'll swear I killed him. Why may
not he rise as well as I? Nothing confutes me but eyes, and nobody sees
me. Therefore, sirrah [*stabbing him*], with a new wound in your thigh,
come you along with me.

> [*He takes up* HOTSPUR *on his back.*]
> [*Enter the* PRINCE *and* JOHN OF LANCASTER.]

125 PRINCE   Come, brother John, full bravely hast thou fleshed°   *initiated*
Thy maiden sword.
LANCASTER   But soft, whom have we here?
Did you not tell me this fat man was dead?
PRINCE   I did; I saw him dead,
Breathless and bleeding on the ground. Art thou alive?
130 Or is it fantasy° that plays upon our eyesight?   *illusion*
I prithee speak; we will not trust our eyes
Without our ears; thou art not what thou seem'st.
FALSTAFF   No, that's certain, I am not a double man; but if I be not Jack
Falstaff, then am I a Jack.[3] There is Percy [*throwing the body down*]; if
135 your father will do me any honor, so; if not, let him kill the next Percy
himself. I look to be either earl or duke, I can assure you.
PRINCE   Why, Percy I killed myself and saw thee dead.
FALSTAFF   Didst thou? Lord, Lord, how this world is given to lying! I grant
you I was down and out of breath, and so was he; but we rose both at
140 an instant and fought a long hour by Shrewsbury clock. If I may be
believed, so; if not, let them that should reward valor bear the sin upon
their own heads. I'll take it upon my death, I gave him this wound in the
thigh; if the man were alive and would deny it, zounds, I would make
him eat a piece of my sword.
145 LANCASTER   This is the strangest tale that ever I heard.
PRINCE   This is the strangest fellow, brother John.
Come, bring your luggage nobly on your back;
For my part, if a lie may do thee grace,
I'll gild it with the happiest terms I have.
> [*A retreat is sounded.*]
150 The trumpet sounds retreat;[4] the day is ours.
Come, brother, let us to the highest[5] of the field,
To see what friends are living, who are dead.

---

9. Pickle.
1. Completely. "Termagant": violent.
2. Quality, not "portion."
3. I.e., a worthless fellow.

4. The signal to stop pursuit of the defeated
enemy.
5. Highest part.

[*Exeunt* ⟨PRINCE OF WALES *and* LANCASTER⟩.]

FALSTAFF   I'll follow, as they say, for reward. He that rewards me, God
reward him! If I do grow great, I'll grow less, for I'll purge[6] and leave
155   sack, and live cleanly as a nobleman should do.   [*Exit.*]

SCENE 5

[*The trumpets sound. Enter the* KING, PRINCE OF WALES, PRINCE JOHN
OF LANCASTER, EARL OF WESTMORELAND, *with* WORCESTER *and* VER-
NON *prisoners.*]

KING   Thus ever did rebellion find rebuke.
     Ill-spirited Worcester, did not we send grace,
     Pardon, and terms of love to all of you?
     And wouldst thou turn our offers contrary,
5   Misuse the tenor of thy kinsman's trust?
     Three knights upon our party slain today,
     A noble earl and many a creature else
     Had been alive this hour,
     If like a Christian thou hadst truly borne
10   Betwixt our armies true intelligence.
WORCESTER   What I have done my safety urged me to,
     And I embrace this fortune patiently,
     Since not to be avoided it falls on me.
KING   Bear Worcester to the death and Vernon too;
15   Other offenders we will pause upon.
                    [*Exeunt* WORCESTER *and* VERNON ⟨*guarded*⟩.]
     How goes the field?
PRINCE   The noble Scot, Lord Douglas, when he saw
     The fortune of the day quite turned from him,
     The noble Percy slain, and all his men
20   Upon the foot of fear,[7] fled with the rest,
     And falling from a hill he was so bruised
     That the pursuers took him. At my tent
     The Douglas is, and I beseech your grace
     I may dispose of him.
KING   With all my heart.
25   PRINCE   Then, brother John of Lancaster, to you
     This honorable bounty shall belong;
     Go to the Douglas and deliver him
     Up to his pleasure, ransomless and free;
     His valor shown upon our crests today
30   Hath taught us how to cherish such high deeds
     Even in the bosom of our adversaries.
LANCASTER   I thank your grace for this high courtesy,
     Which I shall give away immediately.
KING   Then this remains, that we divide our power.
35   You, son John and my cousin Westmoreland,
     Towards York shall bend you with your dearest° speed   greatest

---

6. Take laxatives, also repent. "Grow great": i.e.,   7. Fleeing in panic.
become either earl or duke.

To meet Northumberland and the prelate Scroop,
Who, as we hear, are busily in arms;
Myself and you, son Harry, will towards Wales
40 To fight with Glendower and the Earl of March.
Rebellion in this land shall lose his sway,
Meeting the check[8] of such another day;
And since this business so fair is done,
Let us not leave till all our own be won.   [*Exeunt.*]

1598

8. (1) Hindrance, (2) rebuke.

THOMAS NASHE
1567–1601

Thomas Nashe, a Cambridge graduate, was a versatile writer of controversial pamphlets, satires, plays, a novel, and lyric verse. He was one of the so-called University Wits who in the late 1580s came to London and wrote for the stage and the press. They lived short and precarious lives: Nashe was about thirty-three when he died; his friend Christopher Marlowe died at twenty-nine; George Peele, at thirty; and Robert Greene, at thirty-two. Nashe's polemical enemy was an older man, Gabriel Harvey, Spenser's friend; Nashe exchanged a series of vituperative and slanderous pamphlets with Harvey in which Nashe's talent for invective and mockery was exploited to the fullest. In June 1599 the ecclesiastical authorities ordered that "all Nashe's books and Doctor Harvey's books be taken wheresoever they may be found and that none of their books be ever printed hereafter."

Nashe wrote a festive comedy, *Summer's Last Will and Testament*; an attack on women called *The Anatomy of Absurdity*; an attack on social abuses of every kind titled *Pierce Penniless, His Supplication to the Devil*; and a strident comparison between the sins of the Jews that led to the destruction of Jerusalem and the current morals and manners of London, called *Christ's Tears Over Jerusalem*. His picaresque narrative, *The Unfortunate Traveler or the Life of Jack Wilton*, recounts the adventures of the young hero all over Europe, including fictive encounters with Erasmus and the poet Surrey, the massacre of the Protestant radicals in Germany, and harrowing, melodramatic exploits in seductive, corrupt, and plague-ridden Italy. Nashe's outlook, like that of many satirists, was conservative; he attacked innovation and praised the purported stability and order of the past. But there is something wild and extreme in his vision of the world, and his prose style, which sometimes sounds like modern experimental fiction, is headlong, impatient, colloquial, and vivid.

A Litany in Time of Plague[1]

Adieu, farewell, earth's bliss,
This world uncertain is;

1. This lyric is from *A Pleasant Comedy Called Summer's Last Will and Testament,* acted before the archbishop of Canterbury in his palace at Croydon in 1592 and published in 1600.

Fond° are life's lustful joys,   *foolish*
Death proves them all but toys,°   *trifles*
5   None from his darts can fly;
I am sick, I must die.
    Lord, have mercy on us!

Rich men, trust not in wealth,
Gold cannot buy you health;
10 Physic himself must fade,
All things to end are made.
The plague full swift goes by;
I am sick, I must die.
    Lord, have mercy on us!

15 Beauty is but a flower
Which wrinkles will devour;
Brightness falls from the air,
Queens have died young and fair,
Dust hath closèd Helen's eye.
20 I am sick, I must die.
    Lord, have mercy on us!

Strength stoops unto the grave,
Worms feed on Hector brave;
Swords may not fight with fate,
25 Earth still holds ope her gate.
"Come, come!" the bells do cry.
I am sick, I must die.
    Lord, have mercy on us!

Wit with his wantonness
30 Tasteth death's bitterness;
Hell's executioner
Hath no ears for to hear
What vain art can reply.
I am sick, I must die.
35   Lord, have mercy on us!

Haste, therefore, each degree,
To welcome destiny;
Heaven is our heritage,
Earth but a player's stage;
40 Mount we unto the sky.
I am sick, I must die.
    Lord, have mercy on us!

1592   1600

The Early Seventeenth Century
1603–1660

1603: Death of Elizabeth I; accession of James I, first Stuart king of England
1605: The Gunpowder Plot, a failed effort by Catholic extremists to blow up Parliament and the king
1620: Arrival of the Pilgrims in the New World aboard the *Mayflower*
1625: Death of James I; accession of Charles I
1642: Outbreak of civil war: theaters closed
1649: Execution of Charles I; beginning of Commonwealth and Protectorate, known inclusively as the Interregnum (1649–60)
1660: End of the Protectorate; Restoration of Charles II

When Queen Elizabeth died on March 24, 1603, after more than four decades on the throne, her kinsman James VI of Scotland succeeded her as James I of England without the disruptions or attempted *coups* that had been feared. The nation breathed a sigh of relief and expected a new beginning. The change from an aged queen without progeny to a thirty-six-year-old king, with an attractive queen, Anne of Denmark, and children who could assure the succession, was cause for celebration. But there was also cause for unease, as the nation saw itself exchanging an English Deborah, whom God had favored with a miraculous victory over the Spanish Armada and who had declared herself married to her people, for an aloof Scotsman with a foreign entourage that might displace English place-seekers. The atmosphere and anxieties at the change of regimes are suggested by an entry in the diary of Lady Anne Clifford, then thirteen years old:

> About 10 o'clock King *James* was proclaimed in *Cheapside* by all the Council with great joy and triumph. I went to see and hear. This peaceable coming-in of the King was unexpected of all sorts of people. . . . At this time we used to go very much to *Whitehall*, and walked much in the garden which was frequented by lords and ladies, my Mother [Margaret Clifford, countess of Cumberland] being all full of hopes, every man expecting mountains and finding molehills. . . . We all went to *Tibbalds* [Theobalds] to see the King who used my Mother and aunt very graciously, but we all saw a great change between the fashion of the Court as it is now and of that in the Queen's time, for we were all lousy by sitting in the chamber of Sir *Thomas Erskine*. . . . About this time my Aunt *Warwick* went to meet the Queen [enroute from Scotland]. . . . Then my Mother and I went on our journey to overtake her, and killed three horses that day with extremity of heat. . . .

> Upon the 25th of July the King and Queen were crowned at *Westminster*, my Father and Mother both attended in their robes, my Aunt of *Bath* and my Uncle *Russell*, which solemn sight my Mother would not let me see because the plague was hot in *London*.

Because of the plague, public celebrations of the coronation were postponed until the following year, when the king made an elaborate progress through the City of London. He passed through ceremonial arches and viewed pageants that represented him in terms suited to his patriarchal and absolutist royal style: a Roman Augustus, a wise Solomon, a Sun King, and the ruler of a newly constituted Britain with England and Scotland linked. The progress was designed to testify to an ideal relationship between a ruler and his people, but it revealed tensions and misunderstandings on both sides. Unlike Elizabeth, James thoroughly disliked exposing himself at such close quarters to the tumultuous crowds. His plans for a full union between his two kingdoms found little favor with the English people. The relationships between the monarch and his people and between England and Scotland would be sources of deep and recurrent conflict throughout his reign, and long afterward.

Traditional literary and historical periods are arbitrary, and their association with monarchs' reigns even more so. Broad political and cultural movements—the Reformation, exploration and colonization, the rising bourgeois class in the cities, the printing press and the expansion of literacy, conflicts over gender roles, changes in perceptions of the self and of authorship—have a much longer time-frame. They span the centuries (roughly 1500–1700) that scholars refer to as the Renaissance when they mean to emphasize breaks with medieval culture and the Early Modern Period when they mean to emphasize seeds of the modern world. Nor do authors' lives and careers neatly conform to the conventional periods. Shakespeare wrote his great tragedies and romances in James I's reign; Donne wrote his elegies, satires, and some love poems in the last decade of Queen Elizabeth's. Milton completed *Paradise Lost* and wrote two other major poems in the 1660s. Yet recognizing the years 1603–60 as a period brings into focus important political, intellectual, cultural, and stylistic currents that bear directly upon literary production. It also permits attention to changes in worldview that helped shape the cultural and literary scene: Galileo's astronomy, Bacon's empiricism, justifications for revolution, and the seismic shift in consciousness that, in 1649, allowed for the formal trial, conviction, and execution of an anointed king.

STATE AND CHURCH, 1603–40

Soon after James I's ascension, the Elizabethan settlement in church and state began to unravel. By great astuteness, by appointing brilliant ministers, and by playing complex roles as female monarch and Petrarchan lady, eliciting both obedience and love, Elizabeth had managed to maintain control over her Parliaments, retain the loyalty and devotion of most of her subjects, and win respect abroad. The Stuart kings, James I and his son Charles I, were unable to do this, engaging in constant confrontations with their Parliaments and subjects over taxes, religion, unpopular ministers, and parliamentary rights. Elizabeth did not try to define precisely how power is divided in what was usually described as a "mixed" government of Monarch, Lords, and Commons. James, while yet in Scotland, published two arguments for royal absolutism, *The True Law of Free Monarchies* (1597) and *Basilikon Doran* (1598). These works, both reissued in 1603, proclaim the divine right of kings as God's deputies and as fathers of their people and explain that monarchs are "free" in that they are accountable only to God. A series of analogies is seen to structure a patriarchal social order: as God is absolute ruler of the universe, so is the king of his people and the father of his family. James also claimed a role as shaper of culture in other published works, among them original poems, a translation of the psalms, a treatise on witchcraft, and a vigorous polemic against tobacco.

By contrast with Elizabeth's, James's court was disorderly and indecorous, marked by hard drinking and late-night feasting, a craze for hunting, and great extravagance. While Elizabeth had created eight new peers, James created sixty, selling peerages and noble titles as a means of raising funds. The court was in a constant state of financial crisis. As early as 1605, the king lamented that "it is a horror to me to think of the height of my place, the greatness of my debts, and the smallness of my means." Unlike Elizabeth, James had to maintain separate households for his queen and for the heir apparent, Prince Henry. The three courts had markedly different styles. The queen's household had places for female as well as male courtiers and separate channels for patronage, the most important being the queen's favorite, Lucy Russell, countess of Bedford, who was a major patron of Donne and Jonson. Prince Henry also patronized authors and scholars (among them Sir Walter Ralegh, who was writing, in prison, his *History of the World*, and George Chapman, who was translating Homer). His household became a focus for militant Protestants who were seeking more reform at home and more vigorous support of Protestantism abroad.

James himself relied increasingly on favorites who became channels for patronage in all spheres: first Robert Car, earl of Somerset, then George Villiers, duke of Buckingham. The attachment James formed for these favorites was highly romantic. "God so love me," the king wrote to Buckingham, "as I only desire to live in the world for your sake, and that I would rather live banished in any part of the earth with you than live a sorrowful widow's life without you." Such sentiments, not surprisingly, gave rise to widespread rumors of homosexual activities at court. The rumors are certainly plausible, though the surviving evidence of same-sex relationships in Early Modern England is extremely difficult to interpret. Sodomy was a crime punishable by death, but prosecutions were extremely rare. English law simply declined to recognize the possibility of lesbian acts. From Shakespeare's sonnets to James's letters, we find avowals of love and desire between men which may sometimes be formal expressions of affection based on classical models, or, alternatively, expressions of passionate physical and spiritual love. The interpretive difficulty is compounded by the absence in the period of any clear reference to homosexual "identity," though there are many references to same-sex acts and feelings. What is clear is that male friendships at the court of James and elsewhere were suffused with an eroticism, at once delightful and threatening, that subsequent periods policed more anxiously.

Religious tensions mounted during James's reign. The divisive energies of the Reformation had been tamed under Elizabeth by the establishment of a national church that accommodated, more or less comfortably, the great majority of her subjects, whether mostly Catholic or mostly Protestant in their religious views. During the first decade of James's reign, this accommodation held. The discovery and thwarting of the "Gunpowder Plot" in 1605, in which Guy Fawkes and a band of Roman Catholic conspirators plotted to blow up the Houses of Parliament and seize control of the government, unified English Protestants in a wave of anti-Catholic sentiment and support for the monarch. James, it seemed, had been preserved by a divine miracle even as Elizabeth had been by the defeat of the Armada. Also, the king's sponsorship of the so-called King James Bible (the Authorized Version, 1611) was a powerful force for Protestant unity.

Religion was such a vital cement for maintaining social and political order that, for almost everybody, genuine separation of church and state was unthinkable. Yet Christians thought it absolutely vital for their salvation or damnation to make right decisions about controversial theological issues: what to believe about predestination? how to conduct public worship? how to read, understand, and explicate scripture? what private devotions and meditations to use? what church was established by Christ? how to know if one is saved? So it is not surprising that Roman Catholics and various kinds of Puritans resisted the Established Church and that the Established Church tried to repress that opposition.

There were still many open or covert Roman Catholics who paid stiff fines for recusancy (failing to take the sacrament in the Established Church). They were also barred from taking degrees in the universities or holding public office or practicing at the bar, since to do so required an oath recognizing the monarch's supremacy over the church. Catholic priests, if captured, might be executed as traitors in the usual grisly fashion of hanging, drawing, disemboweling, and quartering. Yet there were Catholics in high places. Some ancient noble houses held to the old religion. And when Queen Anne refused to take the sacrament at her coronation there was intense speculation that she was a covert Catholic, speculation that continued (without being actually proved) throughout the reign.

From the other side, Puritans, as they were disparagingly called, pressed for more reformation in doctrine, ritual, and especially in church government, so as to bring the English church into closer conformity with the Presbyterian Church organization in Geneva, as established by the Protestants reformer John Calvin. Theology as such was not the issue, since much of the clergy accepted some version of Calvinism, as did King James. However, within that consensus Puritans tended to hold more extreme views about predestination (God's consignment of individuals to salvation or damnation—election and reprobation—without reference to their own acts or merit) and about the total depravity of humankind after the Fall. Many Puritans sought to remain within the Established Church but wanted to eliminate what they saw as the "popish" elements in the liturgy of *The Book of Common Prayer* and the "idolatrous" religious images in churches, e.g., religious statues, stained-glass windows, and an ornate high altar. They emphasized preaching and reading the Bible, not sacraments, as the core of religious practice; they sought moral and social reform through laws governing recreation, sabbath-keeping, drunkenness, and public order; and they emphasized the individual's direct responsibility for his or her own faith and for fulfilling his or her vocation or calling in the world, counting success as a possible indicator of election to salvation. The largest Puritan denomination, the Presbyterians, held that the Bible mandated church government by Presbyters (ministers), Lay Elders, and Synods (regional and national convocations) and agitated to substitute that organization for the Established Church hierarchy of archbishops, bishops, and priests. Some separatist Puritans (Congregationalists, Brownists, Anabaptists) wanted no national church, only individual gathered churches of the elect; some of them went to Holland or New England to escape repression.

Prince Henry's sudden death in 1612 dashed the hopes of Puritans and other reformist Protestants, prompting an outpouring of funeral elegies and laments reminiscent of the response to Sir Philip Sidney's early death in 1586. Prince Charles became heir apparent, and Henry's role as a potential leader of international Protestantism was partly filled by Frederick, Elector Palatine, who married James's daughter Elizabeth in 1613. Reformist Protestants urged James to take an active military role in the Thirty-Years' War (1618–48), which erupted over Frederick's claims to Bohemia and raged all over Europe, pitting Protestant against Roman Catholic nations. But James sought, unsuccessfully, to play peacemaker in that conflict. In 1623 he set plans in motion to marry Prince Charles to the Catholic Infanta of Spain, but when those plans collapsed over religious issues the nation was overjoyed. When Charles married the French princess Henrietta Maria instead there was little objection: though Catholic, she was at least not Spanish. The English antipathy to Catholic Spain reached back to Mary Tudor's reign (with her Spanish husband, Phillip II) and it intensified to white heat with the threat of invasion by the Spanish Armada (1588).

The ascent of Charles I to the throne in 1625 brought a palpable change in monarchical style. Unlike his father, Charles was not a theorist of royal absolutism and the divine right of kings, but he acted on those principles with consistency and inflexibility. By temperament James was given to compromise, whereas Charles held out for his royal prerogatives. He dissolved Parliament three times and in 1629 began nearly a decade of "personal rule" without Parliament, raising money through special taxes that were widely denounced as illegal and governing through a much-hated cabinet council: Buckingham, the earl of Strafford, and Archbishop Laud. Religious conflicts also intensified. Queen Henrietta Maria brought with her from France to England an entourage of Roman Catholic priests and followers and promoted the conversion to Catholicism of several English noblewomen in her court. The appointment in 1633 of William Laud as archbishop of Canterbury, the ecclesiastical head of the English Church, proved to be a watershed event. Throughout the 1630s Laud promoted the rapid growth of a high Anglican faction within the church, conforming its ceremony, ritual, and doctrine more closely to Roman Catholicism. The altar rather than the pulpit again dominated the church, making the eucharist the primary element in worship, rather than preaching. Ministers of Puritan tendency were dispossessed of their livings, and the full liturgy of *The Book of Common Prayer* was required in every parish. In theology Laud threw down the gauntlet to much of the nation by imposing an Arminian rather than a Calvinist interpretation on the

Thirty-Nine Articles of the Church of England—a doctrine of Free Will, that is, rather than Predestination.

Through both reigns, but especially that of Charles, resistance to Stuart absolutism came from several quarters. The Commons in Parliament insisted on their own rights and powers and demanded reforms in return for voting subsidies. As the peerage grew more impoverished, due in part to changes in agriculture but also to the expense of maintaining their status in the lavish courts, many peers of ancient lineage grew increasingly disaffected. Some Puritans and reform-minded clergy found ways to urge their causes in the pulpit and the press. Also, the wealthy bourgeois in the cities gained considerable power as sources of needed funds: they often supplied loans to the Crown and also funded exploration and colonization in the New World and elsewhere through such corporations as the East and West India Companies.

As the 1630s drew to a close, Archbishop Laud and Charles attempted to impose *The Book of Common Prayer* and episcopal organization upon Presbyterian Scotland. When the Scots resisted, Charles took this as a direct challenge to his authority, being persuaded that to dismantle ecclesiastical hierarchy threatened hierarchy everywhere and ultimately the Crown: "No Bishop, No King." Charles's military action against Scotland (The First and Second Bishops' Wars in 1639–40) was funded by extra-legal taxes, but met with abject failure. Exacerbating the situation, Laud laid down new canons for the English church, requiring full conformity in liturgy and preaching and an oath from all clergy opposing any change in the church government then in place. Riots in the London streets and Scots occupation of several northern English cities forced Charles to call the so-called "Long Parliament," which would soon be managing a revolution.

LITERATURE AND CULTURE, 1603–40

The earlier seventeenth century brought old and new ideas about the nature of things into sharp opposition. An inherited body of concepts and images was still available to be used by Donne, Burton, and others, even as they were being questioned or displaced: the Ptolemaic universe with its nine concentric spheres whose movements produce music, its circling sun and fixed earth, and its assumption of perfection above the moon and corruption beneath; the four elements—fire, air, water, earth—that comprise the matter of all things; and the four humors of the body—choler, blood, phlegm, and melancholy—that determine temperament and in great imbalance make for disease, mental and physical. Jacobeans thought of themselves as especially prone to melancholy: Shakespeare's Hamlet and Jacques in *As You Like It* are melancholics, and Robert Burton wrote a massive and thoroughly delightful treatise on the malady, which he thought universal, *The Anatomy of Melancholy* (1621). Milton's title figure in *Il Penseroso* is a benign exemplar of that temperament, which was commonly associated with scholars. Key concepts of this inherited system were order and analogy, often rendered in striking literary images. Donne was especially fond of the macrocosm/microcosm parallel according to which the human being is seen as "a little world" or recapitulation of the world itself; and almost everyone believed in some version of the "chain" of being that links and orders all species hierarchically.

But this system, with its *a priori* assumptions and reliance upon ancient authority, was challenged by Francis Bacon's new emphasis on scientific method, as well as by actual experiments such as Gabriel Harvey's discovery of the circulation of the blood and Galileo's telescope, which supplied evidence confirming the Copernican astronomy. Galileo dislodged the earth from its former fixed and stable position at the center of the cosmos and, in defiance of all ordinary observation, sent it whirling about the sun; he also found evidence of change and corruption in the heavens and advanced mind-boggling speculations about life on other planets and infinite universes. Donne, like other writers of his age, responded to the new ideas, giving voice to the anxieties they produced in his *Anatomy of the World*:

> And new philosophy calls all in doubt,
> The element of fire is quite put out;
> The sun is lost, and the earth, and no man's wit
> Can well direct him where to look for it.

Milton, however, embraced the new science, referring with pride to a visit during his European tour to "the famous Galileo, grown old, a prisoner to the Inquisition for thinking in astronomy otherwise than the Franciscan and Dominican licensers thought." In *Paradise Lost* he made complex poetic use of the astronomical controversy.

In both reigns, the court was an important site of literary activity. Births, marriages, and funerals in the royal family prompted celebratory or elegiac verse, as did other royal occasions. Queen Anne played a major role in giving distinctive form and prominence to the court masque, traditionally presented at Christmastide and most often on Twelfth Night (January 6). The spectacular and extravagant masques devised by Inigo Jones, written by Ben Jonson, and danced by royal and noble personages portray King James as source of all power and splendor in the kingdom. Masques customarily end with the masquers unmasking and dancing with other courtiers, symbolizing the fusion of the ideal world and the Stuart court. But masques produced and danced by Queen Anne and her ladies also served to assert their own interests and power and to enact some resistance to the king's control.

Beyond the court, some noblemen retained their status as powerful local patrons with many clients, including poets and playwrights. Especially prominent were the interrelated families of the Sidneys at Penshurst and the Herberts at Wilton. Ben Jonson's country-house poem *To Penshurst* celebrates the Sidney estate as an alternative ideal to the court, hospitable alike to poets and kings; his collection of poems *The Forest* also includes several other poems associated with the Sidney family. Aemilia Lanyer's country-house poem of about the same date, *The Description of Cooke-Ham*, celebrates the estate occupied by Margaret Clifford, countess of Cumberland, and her daughter Anne (author of the *Diary* quoted above), crediting her residence there with nurturing her poetry. Jonson's book of *Epigrams* and Lanyer's dedicatory poems construct imagined communities of worthy personages and patrons honored by and honoring the poet. Coteries of friends also promoted and circulated literary works. Donne addressed several verse letters and some of his *Songs and Sonnets* to male friends in the law courts and at court; later he became part of a coterie formed around his patron, Lucy Russell, countess of Bedford, with whom he sometimes exchanged poems.

The church also promoted writing of several kinds: treatises of devotion, meditation, and instruction; controversial tracts (like Donne's *Pseudo-Martyr* against the Roman Catholics); cases of conscience that work out difficult moral issues in complex situations; and especially sermons. This is an age in which everyone heard sermons at least once and often twice on Sunday, as well as on all days of special religious or national celebration. Sermons were at least an hour long and often much longer. Congregants, especially children, were urged to outline them, repeat them later, and meditate on them. The essence of a sermon, Protestants agreed, is the careful exposition of Scripture, and its purpose is to instruct and move. Gifted Church of England preachers like Donne called on all the resources of artful rhetoric and elegant style to enthrall their congregations. They probed the words and phrases of a Scripture text by wordplay, allusions, conceits, and quotations from the learned languages. By contrast, many Puritans sought a logical, undecorated style that would display God's word in its own splendor, unadorned by human wit.

The City of London was also an important site for literary creation. City officials commissioned Lord Mayors' pageants and other civic entertainments. Also, the numerous booksellers contracted for and published books of domestic advice, devotional treatises, "how-to-do-it" manuals, and tracts of political and religious controversy. The theaters continued to flourish in the Liberties just outside the City, and therefore not under London's jurisdiction; this was the only sphere in which authors could support themselves by writing. Shakespeare was at the height of his powers: *King Lear, Othello, Macbeth, Twelfth Night, The Tempest*, and several others were staged during the early years of James's reign. So were Ben Jonson's major comedies—*Volpone, The Alchemist*, and *Epicoene*—as well as *Bartholomew Fair*, Jonson's contribution to City Comedy. That new kind, practiced by Thomas Middleton, Thomas Heywood, and others, drew satirical and comic matter from the life of London. The most important new playwright was John Webster, whose dark tragedies *The Duchess of Malfi* and *The White Devil* combined gothic horror with poetry of stunning beauty.

This era saw important changes in poetic fashion. Several prominent Elizabethan genres were no longer much in evidence: long allegorical or mythological narratives, sonnet sequences, and pastoral poems. Nor were such stylistic features as nature imagery, florid ornament, and sonorous lyricism. The norm was coming to be short, very concentrated poems in a colloquial and often witty "plain style." The major poets of these years, Donne, Jonson, and George Herbert, led this shift, as well as the rise to prominence of other genres: love elegy and satire after the classical models of Ovid and Horace, epigram, verse epistle, dramatic monologue, meditative religious lyric, and country-house poem. These three poets represent three distinct modes of authorship, but have in common a pronounced anxiety about the nature of literary production and the relation of the author to society. All three exercised an important influence on poets of the next generation.

John Donne, whose imprudent marriage cost him a much-desired career in the court bureaucracy but who later became a famous preacher and dean of St. Paul's Cathedral, cast himself in the older mold of gentleman amateur, circulating his poems in manuscript to friends and coterie circles, and largely avoiding print publication (his poems were published posthumously in

1633). In both their style and their content, Donne's poems were designed to be read by a select few rather than the public at large. His best poems explore the private worlds of love and religion, often developing passionate dialectical arguments that set them in anxious opposition to the public world. His style is characterized by learned terms and images, speechlike and often unmelodic verses, and strikingly dramatic language that often evokes a scene in progress. It is also characterized by witty play with paradoxes, ironies and the conjunction of opposites, as in the so-called "metaphysical conceit"—a surprising metaphor that (as Samuel Johnson later observed) links together images from very different ranges of experience. Donne took particular delight in challenging his sophisticated readers by interchanging the vocabularies of sexual and religious love both in his love poems and in his religious poems. Donne has sometimes been regarded as the founder of a "metaphysical school" of poetry, but that classification is not very useful. We find some echoes of Donne's style in some later poets such as Thomas Carew, who praised Donne as "Monarch of wit," John Cleveland, Abraham Cowley, and Andrew Marvell. But neither they nor the other poets sometimes linked with Donne (Herbert, Vaughan, Crashaw, Traherne) can be usefully classified as members of a "school," since none of them is very like Donne, nor are they like one another.

Ben Jonson staked his claim as a new kind of professional author when he published his court masques, his plays for the public theater, and two collections of poems in an elegant folio titled *Works* in the same year (1616) that King James published his treatises and poems under the same title. Jonson's finest poems celebrate the social world of friendship and community and embody the classical values of simplicity, restraint, economy, decorum, good workmanship, and art. Important principles of his poetics can be gleaned from his comments on poets and poetry to his friend, William Drummond of Hawthornden, and from his volume of extracts from classical sources: that nature first and then art makes the poet; that the poet's formation demands wit, judgment, and the proper imitation of models; and that the ideal poetic style is strong and plain (not abstruse like Donne's): "Pure and neat language I love, yet plain and customary." A ruling principle for Jonson is decorum—the proper fit of style to subject. Another is that the best art conceals art. In contrast to Donne, Jonson cast himself as the father of a brood of poetic sons—known as the Tribe or Sons of Ben—and met regularly with some of them in the Apollo Room of the Devil Tavern in London. Robert Herrick and many of the poets known as Cavaliers for their attachment to the court—Carew, Lovelace, Suckling—either acknowledged the relationship or gave some evidence of it.

George Herbert, pastor to a small country parish, was a very different kind of author from Donne, who wrote to please his friends and patrons, or Jonson, who wrote to instruct the court and country. Herbert destroyed his secular verse in English and turned his volume of religious verse over to a friend on his deathbed, desiring him to print it if he thought it would be useful "to some dejected poor soul" and otherwise to burn it. The 177 lyrics contained in that volume, *The Temple* (1633), display a complex religious sensibility and great artistic subtlety in an amazing variety of kinds, stanzaic forms, and rhythmic patterns. In several of these poems, Herbert agonized about the paradoxical necessity, and at the same time impossibility, of a

Christian poet giving fit and sincere praise to God. He also questioned whether literary art is appropriate to divine praises and if so, what kind of art? Several poems renounce old poetic styles and ornaments for a new, plain, devotional, and biblical mode, exploring the question posed in *Jordan I*, "Is there in truth no beauty?" Herbert was the major influence on the next generation of religious lyric poets and was explicitly recognized as such by Henry Vaughan and Richard Crashaw.

The Jacobean era (so-called from King James I) also saw the emergence of what would become a major new prose genre, the familiar essay. Francis Bacon brought it to England in a form very different from the intimate, tentative, conversational essay developed some decades earlier in France by Montaigne. Bacon's fifty-eight short sketches have, by contrast, a pithy, sententious style and a tone of cool objectivity, as if presenting society's accumulated practical wisdom on such topics as *Marriage and the Single Life, Truth, Simulation and Dissimulation, Ambition, Followers and Friends*, and *Suitors*. Bacon's other works are analyses of the state of knowledge in England and proposals for placing it on a scientific basis of induction and experimentation. His fictional utopia *The New Atlantis* imagines a society based on the Baconian dream of scientific learning and research.

These years mark the entry of Englishwomen, in some numbers, into authorship and publication. Their works rewrite discourses that repress or diminish women—patriarchy, gender hierarchy, the apostle Paul's teachings on marriage—and shape several genres to women's concerns. Most of these women were from the nobility or gentry and all were educated above the norm for women in the period. Some wrote private diaries and autobiographies that remained in manuscript, published mothers' manuals, or polemics defending women's worthiness against attacks. Aemilia Lanyer is the first Englishwoman to publish a substantial volume of original poems (1611), containing poetic dedications, a long poem on Christ's passion, and a country-house poem, all defending women's interests and worth. Elizabeth Cary, Lady Falkland, is the first Englishwoman to publish a tragedy, *Mariam* (1613), a Senecan closet drama that probes the situation of a queen-wife subjected to domestic and political tyranny. Lady Mary Wroth, niece of Sir Philip Sidney and the countess of Pembroke, wrote three works that are firsts for an Englishwoman. Her Petrarchan sonnet sequence *Pamphilia to Amphilanthus* (1621) gives voice and subjectivity to the woman lover-poet. It was published with her long prose romance *Urania* (1621), which presents a range of women's responses to life and love as well as many spheres for women's exercise of agency and power—as rulers, counselors, scholars, storytellers, poets, and seers. Her unpublished pastoral tragicomedy *Love's Victory* depicts a nonhierarchical pastoral world whose ideality depends on female friendships and female control.

When Charles and Henrietta Maria came to the throne in 1625, the changed court style in this Caroline era directly affected the arts and literature. As the Puritan Lucy Hutchinson recalled, "The fools and bawds, mimics and catamites of the former court grew out of fashion," to be replaced by a new sophistication and refinement and a courtly code idealizing female beauty, heterosexual love, and harmony. Charles and his queen were art collectors on a large scale and patrons of such painters as Rubens and Van Dyke; the latter portrayed Charles in magnificent, heroic poses, mounted on a splendid white stallion. A fashionable artistic and literary cult of platonic love mythologized the two monarchs as the ideal Platonic hermaphrodite, their union joining together heroic virtue and divine beauty or love. In this milieu several courtier-poets—Carew, Suckling, Waller—wrote playful, sophisticated, sometimes delicate and sometimes licentious love lyrics on *carpe diem* themes: seize the day, time passes swiftly, make love now.

During the 1630s, the culture wars intensified between the Caroline court and the Laudian church on the one hand and the reformist Protestant and Puritan opposition on the other. In 1633 Charles reissued James I's *Book of Sports*, prescribing the continuation of traditional holiday festivities and Sunday sports in every parish in an effort to extend the cultural control of the court throughout the country. Puritans denounced both court festivities and country sports on religious grounds: they regarded masques, maypoles, and morris dances as palpable occasions of sin and the Sunday sports as profanations of the Sabbath. Also, many saw connections between the sophisticated pastoralism, Neoplatonism, and representations of ritual in the court masques and the Queen's Roman Catholicism. William Prynne had staked out the most extreme Puritan position, publishing in November 1632 a passionate tirade of over one thousand pages against stage-plays, masques, masque dancing, maypoles, and rural festivals, country sports on the Sabbath, Laudian ritual, stained-glass windows, and much more. He associated the court arts—"effeminate mixed dancing, lascivious pictures, wanton fashions, face painting . . . amorous pastorals, lascivious effeminate music"— with licentiousness, effeminacy, and seduction to popery. Worse, his reference to "Women actors, notorious whores" was thought to refer to the queen and her ladies, then rehearsing a pastoral play at court. For this cultural critique Prynne was stripped of his academic degrees, ejected from the legal profession, set in the pillory at Westminster and Cheapside, had his books burned and his ears cut off, and was sentenced to life imprisonment. The severity of the punishment indicates the perceived danger of his book, which one judge claimed would "effect disobedience to the state, and a general dislike unto all governments."

Milton's early poems display astonishing artistic virtuosity rooted in literary and generic traditions, but they also respond to the tensions of these years. Milton repudiated courtly and Laudian aesthetics and also Prynne's wholesale prohibitions, developing reformed versions of pastoral, masque, and hymn. His lovely hymn *On the Morning of Christ's Nativity* (1629) contains a long section on the casting out of idols at Christ's birth which resonates with contemporary Puritan resistance to Laudian "idolatry." And his magnificent pastoral funeral elegy *Lycidas* contains a vehement denunciation of the establishment clergy as "Blind Mouths"—both ignorant and greedy— who deprive their flocks of spiritual nourishment.

THE REVOLUTIONARY ERA, 1640–60

Now almost four hundred years after the execution of Charles I, the English Revolution is still not quite over. Its aftershocks can be felt in the politically heated debate over its causes, which continues to this day. On the one hand, many historians see the revolution as the consequence, at least in part, of long-term changes in the English society and economy. They point to the conflict between new (capitalist) and old (feudal) modes of production in agriculture, industry, and trade and to the rising power and ambition of the gentry, the urban bourgeoisie, and those known as the "middling sort" of people in town and country. The frustrated demands of these classes for a greater measure of economic, political, and religious freedom led to rising social tensions and eventually civil war and revolution. This view, championed by Marxists among others, has been opposed by a revisionist school which emphasizes short-term and avoidable causes of the war. These historians point to a number of unlucky chance events, personal psychological factors, and poor decisions made by a small group of individuals. The political overtones of this clash of historians are unmistakeable. The debate over whether this was Europe's first bourgeois revolution or merely the consequence (as one scholar has argued) of Charles I's attempts to compensate for a sense of masculine inadequacy is ultimately a debate about the nature of history. As such it is not only about the events of the past, but about the shape of the future.

Whatever causes contributed to the outbreak of hostilities, there is no doubt that the twenty-year revolutionary period left the English economy far more open to the development of capitalist production. It also saw the development of concepts central to bourgeois liberal thought and soon to influence John Locke and the theorists of the American and French revolutions: religious toleration, separation of church and state, social contract, popular sovereignty, representative government, and republicanism. These concepts developed out of years of prolonged and bitter dispute centering around three fundamental questions: What kind of church government is laid down in Scripture and should therefore be settled in England? What should be the relation between church and state? What is the ultimate source of political power? The theories that evolved in response to these questions contain the seeds of much that is familiar in modern thought, mixed with much that seems forbiddingly alien. It is vital to bear in mind that the participants in these debates were not working their way (vaguely and haphazardly) toward modern liberalism, but responding (clearly and powerfully) to the most fundamental problems of their day. The debate was especially bitter and the need to find the right answers particularly intense for the many Millenarians among them, who believed that their day was very near to being the last day of all.

When the so-called "Long Parliament" convened in 1640, it had no intention of mounting a revolution and executing a king, but it was intent on securing and expanding its rights in the face of the king's perceived absolutist tendencies. Parliament set about to abolish extra-legal taxes and courts; to bring to trial and at length execute the king's hated ministers, Strafford and Laud; to rein in the bishops' power; to provide for triennial parliaments; and to remain in session until they themselves agreed to disband. As Parliament debated such matters, legitimate and underground presses poured forth a flood of treatises denouncing or supporting the bishops, *The Book of Common Prayer*, and the competing ecclesiastical models, creating a lively public forum for political discussion. That forum was also shaped by the little weekly newsbooks—the ancestors of our newpapers—which reported events at home and abroad from different political perspectives: royalist, parliamentarian, republican, army. Some of these so-called "Mercuries" were official government publications; some were licensed and quasi-official; some were fly-by-night affairs that lasted a few weeks, disappeared when the censors came after them, and then reappeared under different names.

Puritans were united in passionate opposition to the bishops, associating them with popery, tyranny over conscience, evil counsel to the king, and pompous excesses in lifestyle. Many, including Milton, demanded that they be cast out of the church, "root and branch." Puritan pamphlets sounded watchwords that were to be constantly repeated over the next two decades. One such was the call for "Godly Preachers." Another was "Holy Community," which some found embodied in the nation as a whole, some in a national church, and some in gathered churches of elect "saints." Another was "Covenant," registering the Puritan sense of being in a covenantal relation with God, whether as individuals, families, church members, or nation. Still another was the reference to England as a "New Israel," a new chosen people called to reform church and state, perhaps in preparation for Christ's Millennial Kingdom—the thousand-year reign of Christ with the saints which was to follow the Last Judgment.

In late 1641 events began to move quickly, though not inevitably, toward war. As the rift widened between Parliament and the king, and mobs of London apprentices kept up the pressure, horrific news came of an uprising in Ireland, with perhaps thirty thousand English and Scottish Protestants massacred by the enraged Catholic populace which they had dispossessed, persecuted for religion, and reduced to poverty. Parliament refused to fund the king for an invasion of Ireland, fearing he would instead invade England with an Irish army. When Charles sought to arrest five members of Parliament for treason, Londoners rose in arms against him. Negotiations for compromise broke down over the issues that would derail them at every future stage: control of the army and episcopacy. On July 12, 1642, Parliament voted to raise an army, and on August 22 the king stood before a force of some two thousand horse and foot at Nottingham, unfurled his royal standard, and summoned his liegemen to his aid. Civil war had officially begun with its agonizing divisions, not only between but within regions of the country, cities, towns, rural communities, social classes, Parliament, the army, and even families.

Parliament and the Presbyterian clergy who managed the First Civil War (1642–46) had limited aims: to secure the rights of Parliament, to limit the king's control over the army and the church, and to settle some version of Presbyterianism as the national established church. They had no desire to depose the king, and indeed both Scots and English swore in their *Solemn League and Covenant* to uphold the king's person and authority even as they also swore to advance reformation, the rights of Parliament, and the peoples' liberties. They justified taking arms against the king by the Calvinist theory of contract, according to which political power was transferred by the people to "Magistrates" generally, so that "subordinate magistrates" (Parliament) could mount resistance to a king when, like Charles, he endangered religion and his subjects' liberties. The king set up court and an alternative parliament in Oxford, to which many in the House of Lords and some in the Commons resorted. As the Puritan armies moved through the country, fighting at Edgehill, Marston Moor, Naseby, and elsewhere, they also undertook an iconoclastic crusade to stamp out idolatry, often destroying religious images and stained-glass windows and lopping the heads off of statues, as an earlier generation of radical Protestants had done at the time of the English Reformation. The effects of these ravages can still be seen in English cathedrals and churches.

The Toleration Controversy that erupted in 1643 exposed deep divisions among Puritans. Presbyterians insisted that it was the Christian magistrates' duty to settle a national Presbyterian Church and enforce conformity to it, repressing all dissent. But some secular-minded Parliamentarians thought that broad toleration was the key to civic harmony, while Congegationalists, Independents, and Baptists in the gathered churches and in the army vehemently opposed any national church and pressed for toleration. Most, however, stopped well short of the argument in *The Bloody Tenant* (1644) by the Baptist Roger Williams, recently returned from New England, that Christ has mandated complete separation of church and state and toleration of all religions, even Roman Catholics, Jews, and Muslims. As the revolution wore on, other sects sprang up, also seeking toleration: Seekers, Finders, Antinomians, the Family of Love, Fifth Monarchists, Quakers, Muggletonians, Ranters, and more. The orthodox were aghast, attempting unsuccessfully to stem the tide with laws against blasphemy and for censorship and with treatises like Thomas Edward's massive catalogue of dangerous sects and heresies, *Gangreana* (1646). Milton joined the toleration controversy with *Areopagitica* (1644), arguing vigorously against press censorship and for a very broad though not complete religious toleration.

The defeat of the royalist army in 1646 led to difficult, protracted negotiations and a brief Second Civil War in 1648, in which the king was again beaten, and at length brought to trial. That dramatic spectacle began on January 20 in the crowded Great Hall at Westminster, where Charles heard himself accused of "High Treason and other High Crimes," specifically that he had broken his coronation oath, sought "unlimited and tyrannical power," attempted to overthrow the peoples' liberties and their foundation in successive Parliaments, and "traitorously and maliciously" made war against the Parliament and people. Every day Charles wore his hat in defiance of the court's authority and refused to answer the charges, insisting that a divinely anointed king could not be judged by any earthly power. On January 27 he was sentenced to be beheaded as a "Tyrant, Traitor, Murderer, and public Enemy," with fifty-nine commissioners signing the death warrant. On January 30, on a black-draped scaffold stage erected, ironically enough, outside the Banquetting Room at Whitehall where Charles had danced so many masque roles, he now acted his last role with dignity and courage. Andrew Marvell described the execution scene memorably in *An Horatian Ode*.

The Rump Parliament, the part of the House of Commons that was allowed to remain after the army expelled royalist and Presbyterian members (Pride's Purge), immediately established a new government "in way of a republic, without King or House of Lords" and with a Council of State as executive. Some classically educated supporters of the revolution saw themselves as reviving the forms of Athenian democracy and the Roman republic. As Hobbes later remarked, these men had absorbed the works of Demosthenes, Cicero, Livy, and others in which "popular government was extolled by the glorious name of liberty, and monarchy disgraced by the name of tyranny," and so "fell in love with their forms of government." But whatever their ideals, those in power in the infant republic (1649–54) found they could not afford to be doctrinaire or hold new elections while the state was threatened on all sides. The Scots and Irish immediately proclaimed the exiled prince—in France with his mother, Henrietta Maria—as Charles II and gathered armies to invade England; invasion was also threatened from Europe. Royalist newsletters and Presbyterian pulpits exploded in fury, pronouncing it sacrilege to execute a king anointed by God. The government party, including Milton, had to argue somewhat uncomfortably that popular sovereignty for the present could only extend to the "well affected" and that the good men raised up by God to serve the cause of liberty—the Rump and the army—could act for the whole people.

But the new establishment was not threatened by royalists alone. The Rump and the army were at odds with one another, divided within themselves, and attacked by a chorus of voices demanding far more radical religious and political reform. Millenarians and Fifth Monarchists called for political power to be given to regenerate "Saints," in preparation for the last days and the thousand-year reign of Christ. Quakers were seen to defy state and church authority by refusing to take oaths or remove their hats and by denouncing ministers in their own pulpits—practices that often landed them in prison. The rank and file of the army contained many so-called Levellers, who held that "all power is originally and essentially in the whole body of the people" and insisted that voting rights should not be limited to men of property. Still more threatening in principle if not in fact were the "True Levellers" or Diggers, a few poor men who set out on April 1, 1649, to cultivate waste lands in Surrey as a symbolic claim to rights in the common lands and, in theory, to all property; their leader, Gerrard Winstanley, wrote eloquent manifestos urging their Christian communist program. Most alarming of all, out of all proportion to their scant numbers, were the Ranters, who believed that because God dwelt in them none of their acts could be sinful; some acted on that belief by running naked in the streets, or by open sexual license, or by blaspheming and swearing (hence their name).

The threat of invasion was dispelled by Oliver Cromwell's victories in Ireland and Scotland. The war in Ireland was especially bloody as Cromwell's army slaughtered the native Irish without quarter in a frenzy of religious hatred. The republic gained international prestige by winning notable sea victories in the Anglo-Dutch War (1652–54), which erupted over trade rivalries and supremacy in the English Channel. But, given continued popular disaffection, the republic's leaders still could not find a way to call new elections, and relations between the Rump and army grew worse. In 1653 Cromwell expelled the Rump and convened a new legislature dominated by radical sectaries and Millenarians. This so-called "Barebones" Parliament, nicknamed for a prominent member, Praisegod Barebone, self-destructed in less than six months, and at the end of the year Cromwell was sworn in as Protector for life under England's first written constitution. The transition was comparatively smooth, save for outraged republicans opposed to any "single person," Fifth Monarchists who thought Cromwell had usurped the place of "King Jesus" soon to appear, and royalists who continued to act in the interests of Charles II. Many property owners adhered to Cromwell as the only hope for stability and settlement, while others, including Milton, did so because religious liberty was more secure with him than with the Rump or the other parliaments. Quakers and Ranters continued to receive harsh treatment, though Cromwell intervened sometimes to rescue Quakers from prison. He also began a program to readmit Jews to England, partly in the interests of trade but also to open the way for their conversion, supposedly a precursor of the last days as prophesied in the New Testament Book of Revelation.

Cromwell succumbed to a virulent influenza epidemic and died on September 3, 1658. Had he lived longer he might have restored monarchy to England by having himself crowned; his last constitution contained several monarchical features. In early 1660, in conditions of mounting chaos, General George Monk marched from Scotland to London proclaiming his firm support for the republic, but he soon called elections for a new "full and free" parliament that everyone knew would restore the king. As Monk played out his hand and negotiated secretly with Charles, royalist and Presbyterian preachers ridiculed and denounced the republic in pulpit and press. A few republicans and radicals made last-ditch efforts to stave off the inevitable: the last polemic plea for the Good Old Cause was probably Milton's *Ready and Easy Way to Establish a Free Commonwealth*, published in late April 1660. On May 8, 1660, Charles II was officially proclaimed king; he landed at Dover on May 25 and made a triumphal entry into London four days later.

Over the next few years some regicides were executed and others were imprisoned, the court and the Anglican church were restored to full glory, and Puritan dissenters were harshly repressed. But royal absolutism was not restored. Parliament was now a force to be reckoned with; and the merchant classes, filled with dissenters, had powerful economic leverage. Less than three decades after Charles II returned, his brother, the Roman Catholic King James II, who had succeeded because Charles had no legitimate progeny, was frightened into fleeing the country in the so-called "Glorious Revolution" of 1688. The throne was transferred to the Dutch Protestant William of Orange and his wife, Mary, a daughter of James II. The English revolution was apparently dismantled in 1660, but its long-term effects profoundly changed English institutions and English society.

LITERATURE AND CULTURE, 1640–60

One of Parliament's first acts after hostilities began in 1642 was to abolish public sports and stage plays as unsuited to the calamitous times, "being spectacles of pleasure, too commonly expressing lascivious mirth and levity." The last play produced was Richard Brome's *A Jovial Crew: Or, The Merry Beggars*. During the next fifteen years, London theaters were dismantled and destroyed: the Globe, Blackfriars, the Phoenix, the Fortune, and the beargardens. Dramatic literature continued to be published—some Caroline plays in the 1640s and Brome's play in 1652. Also, both royalists and antiroyalists wrote play-pamphlets about real-life dramas, such as *The Famous Tragedie of King Charles I. Basely Butchered* (1649). Despite the prohibitions, some plays were put on stage in England. Beaumont and Fletcher's *Wit without Money* was performed in February 1648 at the Red Bull Theater. Under the Protectorate, some erstwhile royalist playwrights used the new fashion for opera to develop "reformed" dramas. William Davenant's *First Day's Entertainment at Rutland House* (1656) and James Shirley's *Cupid and Death* were presented in quasi-private circumstances, but Davenant's *Cruelty of the Spaniards in Peru* (1658) was performed in the more public venue of the Cockpit Theater. This and other Davenant plays of the late 1650s dramatize crusades against the Turks and the Spaniards, emphasizing colonial and imperial myths.

During the revolutionary era many royalist authors found support in hard times from circles of friends. Also, with the disruption of their usual patronage networks, many decided to publish their verse. During the 1640s the bookseller Herbert Moseley collected and published volumes of poems by the Cavalier poets Thomas Carew, Sir John Denham, Edmund Waller, Sir John Suckling, James Shirley, Richard Lovelace, and Robert Herrick. Some of these poets fought for their king; others were imprisoned or fled abroad with the queen or went into "internal exile" at home. Their poems, some dating from the 1630s, celebrate royalist culture and the courtly ideal of the good life: wine, good food, good friends, good verses, hospitality, and loyalty to the king. One characteristic genre for them is the elegant love lyric, often with a *carpe diem* theme; other common themes are friendship and retirement. Stylistically, their verses are characterized by urbanity, smoothness, and (especially with Herrick) diligent attention to classical models. Several poems in Herrick's delightful collection of short lyrics, *Hesperides* (1648), celebrate those rural, quasi-pagan harvest festivals and May-day rituals so much criticized by Puritans. Others underscore the volume's dominant theme: "time's trans-shifting," the transience of all life, beauty, and poetry. Waller and Denham helped set the fashion for melodic rhymed stanzas and iambic pentameter couplets, which were to become normative verse patterns after the Restoration. The poems of Suckling and Lovelace construct a quintessential Cavalier persona with the qualities usually associated with those supporters of the king and queen. He talks amusingly, bawdily, charmingly, and sometimes sadly about the joys and tribulations of love, the conflicts of love and honor, loyalty to friends, and the trials of the times. He presents himself as an amateur, writing verse in the midst of a life devoted to more important matters: war, love, the king's service, and the endurance of loss.

During the 1650s, royalists wrote lyric poems in places removed from the hostile centers of parliamentary power. Henry Vaughan in Wales wrote religious verse expressing his intense longing for past biblical eras of innocence and for the perfection of heaven or the millennium, and representing himself in the present as a solitary wanderer seeking out the vestiges of God in nature. Also in Wales, Katherine Philips wrote and circulated in manuscript poems that celebrate female friends in the Platonic terms normally reserved for male friendships. Their publication after the Restoration brought Philips some celebrity as "The Matchless Orinda." Richard Crashaw, an exile in Paris and Rome and a convert to Roman Catholicism, is England's only major baroque poet. His poems treat typical baroque topics—weeping Magdalens, infant Saviors, rosy cherubs, tender Virgins, tormented martyrs, ecstatic saints—in the lush, sensuous language that, according to Counter-Reformation aesthetics, could reveal the spiritual by stimulating the senses. Margaret Cavendish, duchess of Newcastle, also in exile with the queen in Paris, published two collections of lyrics when she returned to England in

1653; a number of these poems are about her own role as poet. After the Restoration she published several dramas and her remarkable utopian romance, *The Blazing World* (1668), which imagines a world governed by an empress with absolute power to rule as she will and learn what she wishes. Cavendish claims for herself as author a comparable absolutism in creating fictional worlds.

The most important English philosopher and political theorist of the earlier seventeenth century, Thomas Hobbes, was also an exile in Paris, as long-time tutor and secretary in the Cavendish family. While there he developed his materialist philosophy and psychology, his critique of language, and, in *Leviathan* (1651), his unflinching analysis and defense of absolute and indivisible sovereignty based on social contract. As his argument validates whatever government is in power and can preserve peace and security—whether Stuart kings, the republic, or Cromwell—he was distrusted by royalists and republicans alike. Claims of royal legitimacy and assertions of the rights and liberties of the people are alike irrelevant in Hobbes's political theory.

Several prose works by royalists have become classics of their respective prose genres. They seem to have little or nothing to do with the contemporary scene but in fact they carry a political charge. In his *Life of Donne*, Izaak Walton went some distance toward producing a scholarly biography: he drew on his personal knowledge of Donne in his later years, collected facts and sometimes dubious anecdotes from those who knew him, and read his letters and personal papers. But Walton's overall design presents Donne as a latter-day St. Augustine—rakish in youth, saintly in his later life as dean of St. Paul's. Published as a preface to a collection of Donne's sermons in 1640, when religious tensions were growing and war loomed on the horizon, Walton's work makes Donne a modern "saint" of Anglicanism. Later, Walton wrote an enormously popular treatise on fishing, *The Complete Angler* (1653), presenting it as a dialogue between Walton's warm-hearted persona, Piscator the angler, and a hunter, Venator, a figure for busy, warlike Puritans. Sir Thomas Browne published *Religio Medici* (A Doctor's Religion) in 1642/43, offering it as a portrait of his mind. Browne presents himself as a genial, speculative doctor who contains in himself many paradoxes and idiosyncratic views but willingly submits his judgment to the Church of England, who loves ritual and ceremony, who finds nothing human foreign to him, and who can sympathize with and worship with all Christians, even Roman Catholics. The subtext presents him as a model of Anglican inclusiveness and charity, a sharp contrast to reforming Puritans bent on ridding the church of its errors. Browne's other works published in this period display his Baconian, antiquarian, and mystical sides. The omnipresent prose genre of the revolutionary era was the polemic tract. Tracts large and small addressed all aspects of all the religious, social, and political controversies. Many voices are memorable for their rhetorical and literary power amid that hubbub: the Leveller John Lilburne, the Digger Gerrard Winstanley, the tolerationist Roger Williams, the prophet Anna Trapnall, and Milton.

It is no surprise that the revolutionary era gave new impetus to women's writing. The overturning of boundaries and the circumstances of war that placed women in novel and sometimes dangerous situations gave them unusual events to chronicle and prompted self-discovery. Autobiographies of three royalist women, Lady Anne Halkett, Lady Anne Fanshaw, and Margaret Cavendish, duchess of Newcastle, all published after the Restoration, report their emotions, their love relationships, and their sometimes daring activities during those trying days. On the revolutionary side, Lucy Hutchinson's *Memoir* of her husband, Colonel John Hutchinson, treats his life with her and his significant role in the war and in government within a narrative that is also a republican history of those times; it was first published in 1806, along with an autobiographical fragment dealing with her early life. She left in manuscript several poems on personal and political themes. Leveller women joined the polemic fray, offering petitions and manifestos in support of their imprisoned husbands and their cause. Quaker women came into their own as preachers and sometimes writers of tracts, authorized by Quaker belief that all persons should testify to what the Inner Light of the Spirit communicates to them. Among the Quaker Margaret Fell's several treatises is one justifying women speaking in church. Female prophets came forth in some numbers during the revolution, their claims to divine inspiration gaining currency from the widespread belief that the Spirit was moving in unexpected ways. The published prophecies of Lady Eleanor Davies, Mary Cary, and Anna Trapnell often carried a strong political critique of Charles or Cromwell. Trapnell dictated her ecstatic visions to scribes, but she also wrote a lively autobiographical report of her adventures and persecution during a missionary journey in the west of England.

If the royalist side claimed most of the poets and the writers of literary prose during this period, the revolution could claim the best of them: Marvell and Milton. During several regimes, Andrew Marvell maintained his independent vision and his firm commitment to religious toleration. He wrote most of his supremely artful lyrics and political poems while at Nunappleton in 1650–52, tutoring the daughter of the retired parliamentary general Sir Thomas Fairfax; in 1657 he joined his friend Milton in the office of Cromwell's Latin Secretariat. All of his poems play wittily with genre and literary convention. His love poems span the spectrum from *carpe diem* invitations to love to neoplatonic affirmations of the absolute split between soul and body, to near-postmodern perceptions that what attracts love is only an unstable set of shifting images. His pastorals, spoken as dramatic monologues by such unusual figures as Damon the Mower, disrupt pastoral norms of contentment and harmony between humans and nature. Several of his political poems are praises of Cromwell, but the finest of them, *An Horatian Ode upon Cromwell's Return from Ireland,* also invites sympathy for the executed king. It recognizes Cromwell as a providential force and celebrates his Irish victory, but also indicates the potential danger in his military successes and meteoric rise to power as a kind of Caesar. Marvell's very long poem celebrating his patron's estate, *Upon Appleton House,* attains something like epic scope, as it locates the static, mythic features traditionally celebrated in country-house poems within the course of providential history in Israel and England, a history that includes the chaotic events of the English revolution.

Milton's commitment to the revolution was unwavering, early to late, despite his disillusion when it failed to realize his fundamental ideals: religious toleration for all Protestants and the free circulation of ideas without prior censorship. He argued for those ideals in the most impressive and enduring polemic of the age, his eloquent, brilliantly imagistic *Areopagitica*

(1644). First as self-appointed advisor to the state, then as its official defender, he addressed the other great issues under debate and argued for his own positions: removal of the bishops "root and branch"; the necessity of divorce for incompatibility so as to relieve widespread human unhappiness; justifications for tyrannicide and republican government based on natural law and popular sovereignty; the right of those who love liberty to act, if necessary, for the whole people; denial to magistrates of any power over religion; church disestablishment; the manifest evils of kingship; and the divine preference for republican government. He was a Puritan, but both his theological heterodoxies and his poetic vision mark him as a distinctly unusual one.

During the twenty years in which he wrote polemics in support of these causes, Milton also wrote several sonnets, revising that small kind to accommodate large public and private topics: a threatened attack by the royalist army on London; praise of and advice to Cromwell about the church; agonizing questions posed by his blindness; and the massacre of the proto-Protestant Waldensians by Roman Catholic forces in the Piedmont. In 1645 he published his collected poems in a double volume, English and Latin, offering it as a counterstatement to the royalist volumes of the 1640s. He wrote some part of *Paradise Lost* in the 1650s and completed it after the Restoration, encompassing in it all he had thought, read, and experienced of tyranny, political rhetoric, evil, deception, love, the need for human companionship, the woes and the good of human life. This stunning, cosmic, blank-verse epic assimilates and critiques the epic tradition and Milton's entire intellectual and literary heritage, classical and Christian. Yet it has at its center not martial heroes but a domestic pair, whose challenge is to discover how to live the good human life day by day, in Eden and later in the fallen world, amid intense emotional pressures and the seductions of evil.

Seventeenth-century poetry and prose retains its hold on readers because so much of it is so very good, fusing (as T. S. Eliot recognized) intellectual strength, emotional passion, and linguistic artfulness. We have in Donne and Marvell love poetry at once cerebral, witty, and passionate; in Donne and Herbert religious poetry at once deeply felt and highly artful; in Jonson tough-minded analyses of what is worthy of praise and blame in the social order; in Herrick some of the most exquisite short lyrics in the English language; in Crashaw the most extravagantly baroque as well as, arguably, the most musical poet in our literature. We watch English prose become a highly flexible instrument, suited to informal essays, scientific or political treatises, religious meditation, biography and autobiography, and vigorous polemic. We observe a number of literary forms evolve for the analysis or dramatization or representation of the self: dramatic monologues portraying the self or several imagined selves in various love situations; religious meditations on the state of the soul; meditations on personal experiences like illness; intellectual or spiritual autobiographies; sermons in which the preacher takes himself as example. Finally, we have in Milton an epic poet who assumed the role of inspired prophet, envisioning a world produced by God but shaped by human choice and imagination.

THE EARLY SEVENTEENTH CENTURY

TEXTS	CONTEXTS
1603 James I, *Basilikon Doran* reissued	1603 Death of Elizabeth I; accession of James I. Plague
1604 William Shakespeare, *Othello*	
1605 Shakespeare, *King Lear*. Ben Jonson, *The Masque of Blackness*. Francis Bacon, *The Advancement of Learning*	1605 Gunpowder Plot, failed effort by Roman Catholic extremists to blow up Parliament
1606 Jonson, *Volpone*. Shakespeare, *MacBeth*	
	1607 Founding of Jamestown colony in Virginia
1609 Shakespeare, *Sonnets*	1609 Galileo's telescope
1611 "King James" Bible (Authorized Version). Shakespeare, *The Tempest*. John Donne, *The First Anniversary*. Aemilia Lanyer, *Salve Deus Rex Judaeorum*	
1612 Donne, *The Second Anniversary*	1612 Death of Prince Henry
1613 Elizabeth Cary, *The Tragedy of Mariam*	
1614 John Webster, *The Duchess of Malfi*	
1616 Jonson, *Works*. James I, *Works*	1616 Death of Shakespeare
	1618 Beginning of the Thirty Years War
	1619 First African slaves in North America exchanged by Dutch frigate for food and supplies at Jamestown
1620 Bacon, *Novum Organum*	1620 Pilgrims land at Plymouth
1621 Mary Wroth, *The Countess of Montgomery's Urania*. Robert Burton, *Anatomy of Melancholy*	1621 Donne appointed dean of St. Paul's Cathedral
1623 Shakespeare, First Folio	
	1625 Death of James I; accession of Charles I; Charles I marries Henrietta Maria
	1629 Charles I dissolves Parliament
1633 Donne, *Poems*. George Herbert, *The Temple*	1633 Galileo forced by the Inquisition to recant the Copernican theory
1637 John Milton, *Lycidas*	
1640 Thomas Carew, *Poems*	1640 Long Parliament called (1640–53). Archbishop Laud impeached
1642 Thomas Browne, *Religio Medici*. Milton, *Reason of Church Government*	1642 First Civil War begins (1642–46). Parliament closes the theaters
1643 Milton, *Doctrine and Discipline of Divorce*	1643 Accession of Louis XIV of France
1644 Milton, *Areopagitica*	
1645 Milton, *Poems*. Edmund Waller, *Poems*	1645 Archbishop Laud executed. Royalists defeated at Naseby

TEXTS	CONTEXTS
1648 Robert Herrick, *Hesperides*	**1648** Second Civil War. Pride's Purge of Parliament
1649 Milton, *Eikonoklastes*	**1649** Trial and execution of Charles I. Republic declared. Milton becomes Latin Secretary (1649–59)
1650 Henry Vaughan, *Silex Scintillans* (Part II, 1655)	
1651 Thomas Hobbes, *Leviathan*. Andrew Marvell, *Upon Appleton House* (unpublished)	
	1652 Dutch War (1652–53)
	1653 Cromwell made Lord Protector
	1658 Death of Cromwell; his son Richard made Protector
1660 Milton, *Ready and Easy Way to Establish a Free Commonwealth*	**1660** Restoration of Charles II to throne. Royal Society founded
	1662 Charles II marries Catherine of Braganza
	1665 The Great Plague
1666 Margaret Cavendish, *The Blazing World*	**1666** The Great Fire
1667 Milton, *Paradise Lost* (in ten books). Katherine Philips, *Collected Poems*. John Dryden, *Annus Mirabilis*	
1671 Milton, *Paradise Regained* and *Samson Agonistes*	
1674 Milton, *Paradise Lost* (in twelve books)	**1674** Death of Milton
1681 Marvell, *Poems*, published posthumously	

JOHN DONNE
1572–1631

Lovers' eyeballs threaded on a string. A god who assaults the human heart with a battering ram. A teardrop that encompasses and drowns the world. John Donne's poems abound with startling images, some of them exalting and others grotesque. With his strange and playful intelligence, expressed in puns, paradoxes, and the elaborately sustained metaphors known as "conceits," Donne has enthralled and sometimes enraged readers from his day to our own. The tired clichés of love poetry—cheeks like roses, hearts pierced by the arrows of love—emerge reinvigorated and radically transformed by his hand, demanding from the reader an unprecedented level of mental alertness and engagement. Donne prided himself on his wit and displayed it not only in his conceits but in his grasp of learned and obscure discourses ranging from theology to alchemy, from cosmology to law. Yet for all their ostentatious intellectuality, Donne's poems never give the impression of being academic exercises put into verse. Rather, they are intense dramatic monologues in which the speaker's ideas and feelings seem to shift and evolve from one line to the next. Donne's prosody is equally dramatic, mirroring in its variable and jagged rhythms the effect of speech (and eliciting from his classically minded contemporary Ben Jonson the gruff observation that "Donne, for not keeping of accent deserved hanging").

Donne began life as an outsider, and in some respects remained one until death. He was born in London in 1572 into a devout Roman Catholic household. The family was prosperous, but, as the poet later remarked, none had suffered more heavily for its loyalty to the Catholic Church: "I have been ever kept awake in a meditation of martyrdom." Donne was distantly related to the great Catholic humanist and martyr Sir Thomas More. Closer to home, a Jesuit uncle was executed by the brutal method of hanging, drawing, quartering, and disemboweling, and his own brother Henry, arrested for harboring a priest, died in prison of the plague. As a Catholic in Protestant England, growing up in decades when anti-Roman feeling reached new heights, Donne could not expect any kind of public career, nor even to receive a university degree (he left Oxford without one and studied law for a time at the Inns of Court). What he could reasonably expect instead was prejudice, official harrassment, and crippling financial penalties. He chose not to live under such conditions. At some point in the 1590s, having returned to London after travels abroad, and having devoted some years to studying theological issues, Donne converted to the English Church.

The poems that belong with certainty to this period of his life—the five Satires and most of the Elegies—reveal a man both fascinated by and keenly critical of English society. Four of the satires treat commonplace Elizabethan topics—foppish and obsequious courtiers, bad poets, corrupt lawyers and a corrupt court—but are unique both in their visceral revulsion and in their intellectual excitement. Donne uses striking images of pestilence, itchy lust, vomit, excrement, and pox to create a unique satiric world, busy, vibrant, and corrupt, in which his dramatic speakers have only to step outside the door to be innundated by all the fools and knaves in Christendom. By contrast, the third satire treats the quest for true religion—the question that preoccupied him above all others in these years—in terms that are serious, passionately witty, and deeply felt. Donne argues that honest doubting search is better than the facile acceptance of any religious tradition, epitomizing that point brilliantly in the image of Truth on a high and craggy hill, very difficult to climb. What is certain is that society's values are of no help whatsoever to the individual seeker—none will escape the final judgment by pleading that "A Harry, or a Martin taught [them] this." In the love Elegies Donne seems intent on making up for his social powerlessness through witty representations of mastery in the bedroom and of adventurous travel.

In *Elegy 16* he imagines his speaker embarking on a journey "O'er the white Alps" and with mingled tenderness and condescension argues down a naive mistress's proposal to accompany him. And in *Elegy 19,* his fondling of a naked lover becomes in a famous conceit the equivalent of exploration in America. Donne's interest in satire and elegy—classical Roman genres which he helped introduce to English verse—is itself significant. He wrote in English, but he reached out to other traditions.

If Donne's conversion to the Church of England promised him security, social acceptance, and the possibility of a public career, that promise was soon to be cruelly withdrawn. In 1596–97 he participated in the earl of Essex's military expeditions against Catholic Spain in Cádiz and the Azores (the experience prompted two remarkable descriptive poems of life at sea, *The Storm* and *The Calm*) and upon his return became secretary to Sir Thomas Egerton, Lord Keeper of the Great Seal. This should have been the beginning of a successful public career. But his secret marriage in 1601 to Egerton's seventeen-year-old niece Ann More enraged Donne's employer and the bride's wealthy father; Donne was briefly imprisoned and dismissed from service. The poet was reduced to a retired country life beset by financial insecurity and a rapidly increasing family; Ann bore twelve children (not counting miscarriages) by the time she died at age thirty-three. At one point, Donne wrote despairingly that while the death of a child would mean one less mouth to feed, he could not afford the burial expenses. In this bleak period, he wrote but dared not publish a paradoxical defense of suicide (*Biathanatos*).

As his family grew, Donne made every effort to reinstate himself in the favor of the great. To win the approval of James I, he penned *Pseudo-Martyr* (1610), defending the king's insistence that Catholics take the Oath of Allegiance. This set an irrevocable public stamp on his renunciation of Catholicism, and Donne followed up with a witty satire on the Jesuits, *Ignatius his Conclave* (1611). In the same period he was producing a steady stream of occasional poems for friends and patrons such as Somerset (the king's favorite), the countess of Bedford, and Magdalen Herbert, and for small coteries of courtiers and ladies. Like most gentlemen of his era, Donne saw poetry as a polite accomplishment rather than as a trade or vocation, and in consequence he circulated his poems in manuscript but left most of them uncollected and unpublished. In 1611 and 1612, however, he published the first and second *Anniversaries* on the death of the daughter of his patron, Sir Robert Drury.

For some years King James had urged an ecclesiastical career on Donne, denying him any other means of advancement. In 1615 Donne finally consented, overcoming his sense of unworthiness and the pull of other ambitions. He was ordained in the Church of England and entered upon a distinguished career as court preacher, reader in divinity at Lincoln's Inn, and dean of St. Paul's. Donne's metaphorical style, bold erudition, and dramatic wit established him as a great preacher in an age that appreciated learned sermons powerfully delivered. Some 160 of his sermons survive, preached to monarchs and courtiers, lawyers and London magistrates, city merchants and trading companies. As a distinguished clergyman in the Church of England, Donne had traveled an immense distance from the religion of his childhood and the adventurous life of his twenties. Yet in his sermons and late poems we find the same brilliant and idiosyncratic mind at work, refashioning his profane conceits to serve a new and higher purpose. In *Expostulation 19* he praises God as the greatest of literary stylists: "a figurative, a metaphorical God," imagining God as a conceit-maker like himself. In poems, meditations, and sermons, Donne came increasingly to be engaged in anxious contemplation of his own mortality. In *A Hymn to God my God in my Sickness,* Donne imagines himself spread out on his deathbed like a map showing the route to the next world. Only a few days before his death he preached *Death's Duel,* a terrifying analysis of all life as a decline toward death and dissolution which contemporaries termed his own funeral sermon. On his deathbed, according to his contemporary biographer Izaak Walton, Donne had a portrait made of himself in his shroud and meditated on it daily. Meditations upon skulls as emblems of mortality were common in the period, but nothing is more characteristic of Donne than to find a way to meditate on his own skull.

Given the shape of Donne's career, it is no surprise that his poems and prose works display an astonishing variety of attitudes, viewpoints, and feelings on the great subjects of love and religion. Yet this variety cannot be fully explained in biographical terms. The poet's own attempt to distinguish between Jack Donne, the young rake, and Dr. Donne, the grave and religious dean of St. Paul's, is (perhaps intentionally) misleading. We do not know the time and circumstances for most of Donne's verses, but it is clear that many of his finest religious poems predate his ordination, and it is possible that he continued to add to the love poems known as his *Songs and Sonnets* after he entered the Church. Theological language abounds in his love poetry, and daringly erotic images occur in his religious verse.

Although they were not widely known in his lifetime, Donne's *Songs and Sonnets* have been the cornerstone of his reputation almost since their publication in 1633. The title associates them with the popular miscellanies of love poems and sonnet sequences in the Petrarchan tradition, but they directly challenge the popular Petrarchan sonnet sequences of the 1590s. The collection contains only one formal sonnet, the "Songs" are not notably lyrical, and Donne draws upon and transforms a whole range of literary traditions concerned with love. Like Petrarch, Donne can present himself as the despairing lover of an unattainable lady (*The Funeral*); like Ovid he can be lighthearted, witty, cynical, and frankly lustful (*The Flea, The Indifferent*); like the Neoplatonists, he espouses a theory of transcendant love, but he breaks from them with his insistence in many poems on the union of physical and spiritual love. What binds these poems together and grants them enduring power is their compelling immediacy. The speaker is always in the throes of intense emotion, and that emotion is not static but constantly shifting and evolving with the turns of the poet's thought. Donne seems supremely present in these poems, standing behind their various speakers. Where Petrarchan poets exhaustively catalogue their beloved's physical features (though in highly conventional terms), Donne's speakers tell us little or nothing about the loved woman, or about the male friends imagined as audience for many poems. Donne's repeated insistence that the private world of lovers is superior to the wider public world, or that it somehow contains all of that world, or obliterates it, is understandable in light of the many disappointments of his career. Yet this was also a poet who threw himself headlong into life, love, and sexuality, and later into the very visible public role of court and city preacher.

Donne was long grouped with Herbert, Vaughan, Crashaw, Marvell, Traherne, and Cowley under the heading of "Metaphysical Poets." The expression was first employed by critics like Samuel Johnson and William Hazlitt, who found the intricate conceits and self-conscious learning of these poets incompatible with poetic beauty and sincerity. Early in the twentieth century, T. S. Eliot sought to restore their reputation, attributing to them a unity of thought and feeling which had since their time been lost. Today the term "Metaphysicals" seems more an obstacle than an aid to understanding these very different poets. There was certainly no formal "school" of metaphysical poetry, and the characteristics ascribed to it by later critics pertain chiefly to Donne. Like Ben Jonson, John Donne had a large influence on the succeeding generation, but he remains a singularity.

FROM SONGS AND SONNETS[1]

The Flea[2]

Mark but this flea, and mark in this,
How little that which thou deniest me is;
Me it sucked first, and now sucks thee,
And in this flea our two bloods mingled be;
5   Thou know'st that this cannot be said
A sin, or shame, or loss of maidenhead,
    Yet this enjoys before it woo,
      And pampered swells with one blood made of two,[3]
    And this, alas, is more than we would do.

10   Oh stay, three lives in one flea spare,
Where we almost, nay more than married are.
This flea is you and I, and this
Our marriage bed and marriage temple is;
Though parents grudge, and you, we are met,
15   And cloistered[4] in these living walls of jet.°   *black*
    Though use° make you apt to kill[5] me,   *habit*
      Let not to that, self-murder added be,
    And sacrilege, three sins in killing three.

  Cruel and sudden, hast thou since
20   Purpled thy nail in blood of innocence?
Wherein could this flea guilty be,
Except in that drop which it sucked from thee?
Yet thou triumph'st, and say'st that thou
Find'st not thy self nor me the weaker now;
25   'Tis true; then learn how false fears be:
    Just so much honor, when thou yield'st to me,
    Will waste, as this flea's death took life from thee.

                                    1633

The Good-Morrow

I wonder, by my troth, what thou and I
Did, till we loved? Were we not weaned till then,
But sucked on country pleasures, childishly?

1. Donne's love poems were written over nearly two decades, beginning around 1595; they were not published in Donne's lifetime but circulated widely in manuscript. The title *Songs and Sonnets* was supplied in the second edition (1635), which grouped the poems by kind, but neither this arrangement nor the more haphazard organization of the first edition (1633) is Donne's own. In Donne's time the term sonnet often meant simply "love lyric," and in fact there is only one formal sonnet in this collection. For the poems we present we follow the 1635 edition, beginning with the extremely popular poem *The Flea*.
2. This insect afforded a popular erotic theme for poets all over Europe, deriving from a pseudo-Ovidian medieval poem in which a lover envies the flea for the liberties it takes with his mistress's body.
3. The swelling suggests pregnancy.
4. As in a convent or monastery.
5. "Kill" carries an allusion to sexual intercourse.

Or snorted° we in the seven sleepers' den?[1] *snored*
5 'Twas so; but° this, all pleasures fancies be. *except for*
If ever any beauty I did see,
Which I desired, and got, 'twas but a dream of thee.

And now good morrow to our waking souls,
Which watch not one another out of fear;
10 For love all love of other sights controls,
And makes one little room an everywhere.
Let sea-discoverers to new worlds have gone,
Let maps to others, worlds on worlds have shown:
Let us possess one world;[2] each hath one, and is one.

15 My face in thine eye, thine in mine appears,
And true plain hearts do in the faces rest;
Where can we find two better hemispheres,
Without sharp North, without declining West?
Whatever dies was not mixed equally;[3]
20 If our two loves be one, or thou and I
Love so alike that none do slacken, none can die.

1633

Song

Go and catch a falling star,
    Get with child a mandrake root,[1]
Tell me where all past years are,
    Or who cleft the Devil's foot,
5 Teach me to hear mermaids° singing, *sirens*
Or to keep off envy's stinging,
        And find
        What wind
Serves to advance an honest mind.

do these impossible things—try

10 If thou beest born to strange sights,
    Things invisible to see,
Ride ten thousand days and nights,
    Till age snow white hairs on thee,
Thou, when thou return'st, wilt tell me *but you can't...*
15 All strange wonders that befell thee,
        And swear
        No where
Lives a woman true, and fair.

1. Cave in Ephesus where, according to legend, seven Christian youths hid from pagan persecutors and slept for 187 years.
2. "Our world" in many manuscripts.
3. Scholastic philosophy taught that when the elements were imperfectly ("not equally") mixed, matter was mutable and mortal; conversely, when the elements were perfectly mixed, matter was immutable and hence immortal.

1. The mandrake root, or mandragora, is forked like the lower part of the human body. It was thought to shriek when pulled from the ground and to kill all humans who heard it; it was also (paradoxically) thought to help women conceive.

If thou find'st one, let me know,
20   Such a pilgrimage were sweet;
Yet do not, I would not go,
   Though at next door we might meet;
Though she were true when you met her,
And last till you write your letter,
25   Yet she
   Will be
False, ere I come, to two, or three.

1633

[handwritten marginal note: Hyperbole comic exaggeration not 7, but the stereotype.]

The Undertaking

I have done one braver thing
   Than all the Worthies[1] did,
And yet a braver thence doth spring,
   Which is, to keep that hid.

5 It were but madness now t' impart
   The skill of specular stone,[2]
When he which can have learned the art
   To cut it, can find none.

So, if I now should utter this,
10   Others (because no more
Such stuff to work upon, there is)
   Would love but as before.

But he who loveliness within
   Hath found, all outward loathes,
15 For he who color loves, and skin,
   Loves but their oldest clothes.

If, as I have, you also do
   Virtue attired in woman see,
And dare love that, and say so too,
20   And forget the He and She;

And if this love, though placèd so,
   From profane men you hide,
Which will no faith on this bestow,
   Or, if they do, deride;

25 Then you have done a braver thing
   Than all the Worthies did;

1. According to medieval legend, the Nine Worthies, or supreme heroes of history, included three Jews (Joshua, David, Judas Maccabeus), three pagans (Hector, Alexander, Julius Caesar), and three Christians (Arthur, Charlemagne, Godfrey of Bouillon).
2. A transparent or translucent material, reputed to have been used in antiquity for windows, but no longer known. Great skill was needed to cut it.

And a braver thence will spring,
Which is, to keep that hid.

1633

The Sun Rising[1]

Busy old fool, unruly sun,
  Why dost thou thus
Through windows and through curtains call on us?
Must to thy motions lovers' seasons run?
5   Saucy pedantic wretch, go chide
        Late schoolboys and sour prentices,
    Go tell court huntsmen that the King will ride,[2]
    Call country ants to harvest offices;[3]
Love, all alike, no season knows nor clime,
10 Nor hours, days, months, which are the rags of time.

    Thy beams, so reverend and strong
      Why shouldst thou think?
I could eclipse and cloud them with a wink,
But that I would not lose her sight so long;
15   If her eyes have not blinded thine,
        Look, and tomorrow late, tell me,
    Whether both th' Indias of spice and mine[4]
    Be where thou leftst them, or lie here with me.
Ask for those kings whom thou saw'st yesterday,
20 And thou shalt hear, All here in one bed lay.

    She is all states,° and all princes I,   nations
      Nothing else is.
Princes do but play us; compared to this,
All honor's mimic, all wealth alchemy.
25   Thou, sun, art half as happy as we,
        In that the world's contracted thus;
    Thine age asks ease, and since thy duties be
    To warm the world, that's done in warming us.
Shine here to us, and thou art everywhere;
30 This bed thy center is,[5] these walls thy sphere.

1633

The Indifferent[1]

I can love both fair and brown,[2]
Her whom abundance melts, and her whom want betrays,

1. Some lines of this poem recall Ovid, *Amores*
1.13.
2. King James was very fond of hunting.
3. Autumn chores. "Country ants": farm drudges.
4. The India of "spice" is East India; that of "mine"
(gold) is the West Indies.

5. According to the old Ptolemaic astronomy, the
earth was the center of the sun's orbit, and the
sun's motion was contained within its sphere.
1. Some lines of this poem recall Ovid, *Amores*
2.4.
2. Both blond and brunet.

Her who loves loneness best, and her who masks and plays,
Her whom the country formed, and whom the town,
5   Her who believes, and her who tries,°   *tests*
Her who still weeps with spongy eyes,
And her who is dry cork, and never cries;
I can love her, and her, and you, and you,
I can love any, so she be not true.

10   Will no other vice content you?
Will it not serve your turn to do as did your mothers?
Or have you all old vices spent, and now would find out others?
Or doth a fear that men are true torment you?
O we are not, be not you so;
15   Let me, and do you, twenty know.
Rob me, but bind me not, and let me go.
Must I, who came to travail thorough³ you,
Grow your fixed subject, because you are true?

Venus heard me sigh this song,
20   And by love's sweetest part, variety, she swore,
She heard not this till now; and that it should be so no more.
She went, examined, and returned ere long,
And said, Alas, some two or three
Poor heretics in love there be,
25   Which think to 'stablish dangerous constancy.
But I have told them, Since you will be true,
You shall be true to them who are false to you.

                                1633

The Canonization¹

For God's sake hold your tongue, and let me love,
   Or chide my palsy, or my gout,
My five gray hairs, or ruined fortune, flout,
   With wealth your state, your mind with arts improve,
5   Take you a course, get you a place,²
      Observe His Honor, or His Grace,³
Or the King's real, or his stampèd face⁴
     Contemplate; what you will, approve,°   *try, test*
     So you will let me love.

10   Alas, alas, who's injured by my love?
   What merchant's ships have my sighs drowned?
Who says my tears have overflowed his ground?
   When did my colds a forward° spring remove?⁵   *early*
   When did the heats which my veins fill

---

3. Through. "Travail": grief, but also journey, travel.
1. The poem plays off against the Roman Catholic process of determining that certain persons are saints, proper objects of veneration and prayer.
2. An appointment, at court or elsewhere. "Take you a course": follow some career.
3. Pay court to some lord or bishop.
4. On coins; "real" (royal) refers also to a particular Spanish coin.
5. Petrarchan lovers traditionally sigh, weep, and are frozen by their mistresses' neglect.

15   Add one man to the plaguy bill?[6]
    Soldiers find wars, and lawyers find out still
        Litigious men, which quarrels move,
        Though she and I do love.

    Call us what you will, we are made such by love;
20   Call her one, me another fly,
    We're tapers too, and at our own cost die,[7]
        And we in us find the eagle and the dove.[8]
        The phoenix riddle hath more wit
        By us: we two being one, are it.
25 So, to one neutral thing both sexes fit.
        We die and rise the same, and prove
        Mysterious by this love.

    We can die by it, if not live by love,
        And if unfit for tombs and hearse
30 Our legend be, it will be fit for verse;
        And if no piece of chronicle we prove,
        We'll build in sonnets pretty rooms;[9]
    As well a well-wrought urn becomes°   *befits*
The greatest ashes, as half-acre tombs,
35   And by these hymns,[1] all shall approve°   *confirm*
    Us canonized for love:

    And thus invoke us: You whom reverend love
        Made one another's hermitage;
    You, to whom love was peace, that now is rage,
40   Who did the whole world's soul contract,[2] and drove
        Into the glasses of your eyes
        (So made such mirrors, and such spies,°   *spyglasses, telescopes*
    That they did all to you epitomize)
        Countries, towns, courts:[3] Beg from above
45   A pattern of your love!

                                                            1633

---

6. Deaths from the plague, which raged in summer, were recorded by parish in weekly bills.
7. Flies were emblems of transience and lustfulness; tapers (candles) attract flies to their death and also consume themselves. "Die" in the punning terminology of the period means to experience orgasm, and there was a superstition that intercourse shortens life.
8. The eagle signifies strength and vision; the dove, meekness and mercy. The phoenix was a mythic Arabian bird, only one of which existed at any one time. After living five hundred years, it was consumed by fire, then rose triumphantly from its ashes a new bird. Thus it was a symbol of immor-

tality and sometimes associated with Christ. "Eagle" and "dove" are also alchemical terms for processes leading to the rise of "phoenix," a stage in the transmutation of metals to gold.
9. "Rooms" (punning on the Italian meaning of "stanza") will contain their exploits, as prose chronicle histories contain great deeds done in the world.
1. The lover's own poems.
2. An alternative meaning is "extract."
3. "Countries, towns, courts" are objects of the verb "drove." The notion is that eyes both see and reflect the outside world, and so can contain all of it.

Air and Angels

Twice or thrice had I loved thee,
Before I knew thy face or name;
So in a voice, so in a shapeless flame,
Angels affect us oft, and worshipped be;
5   Still° when, to where thou wert, I came,   *always*
Some lovely glorious nothing[1] I did see.
    But since my soul, whose child love is,
Takes limbs of flesh, and else could nothing do,[2]
    More subtle° than the parent is   *rarified*
10 Love must not be, but take a body too;
    And therefore what thou wert, and who,
       I bid love ask, and now
That it assume thy body I allow,
And fix itself in thy lip, eye, and brow.
15 Whilst thus to ballast love I thought,
    And so more steadily to have gone,
With wares which would sink° admiration,   *overwhelm*
I saw I had love's pinnace° overfraught;°   *small boat/overballasted*
    Every thy hair for love to work upon
20 Is much too much, some fitter must be sought;
    For, nor in nothing, nor in things
Extreme and scatt'ring° bright, can love inhere. *diffused, dazzling*
    Then as an angel, face and wings
Of air, not pure as it, yet pure doth wear,
25   So thy love may be my love's sphere;[3]
       Just such disparity
As is 'twixt air and angels' purity,
'Twixt women's love and men's will ever be.[4]

                         1633

Break of Day[1]

'Tis true, 'tis day; what though it be?
O wilt thou therefore rise from me?
Why should we rise because 'tis light?
Did we lie down because 'twas night?
5 Love, which in spite of darkness brought us hither,
Should in despite of light keep us together.
Light hath no tongue, but is all eye;
If it could speak as well as spy,
This were the worst that it could say,

---

1. Spiritual beauty, the true object of love in Neoplatonic philosophy.
2. My soul could not function unless it were in a
body.
3. Each sphere was thought to be governed by an
angel (an intelligence).
4. It was commonly believed that angels, when
they appeared to humans, assumed a body of air

which, though pure, was less so than the angel's
spiritual essence.
1. An aubade, or song of the lovers' parting at
dawn, this poem is unusual for Donne in having a
female speaker. The poem was given a musical setting and published in 1622, in William Corkine's
Second Book of Ayers.

10   That being well, I fain would stay,
      And that I loved my heart and honor so
      That I would not from him, that had them, go.

      Must business thee from hence remove?
      O, that's the worst disease of love.
15   The poor, the foul, the false, love can
      Admit, but not the busied man.
      He which hath business, and makes love, doth do
      Such wrong, as when a married man doth woo.

1622, 1633

A Valediction:[1] Of Weeping

        Let me pour forth
My tears before thy face whilst I stay here,
For thy face coins them, and thy stamp° they bear,   *image*
And by this mintage they are something worth,
5   For thus they be
        Pregnant of thee;
Fruits of much grief they are, emblems° of more—   *symbols*
When a tear falls, that Thou falls which it bore,
So thou and I are nothing then, when on a diverse° shore.   *different*

10   On a round ball
A workman that hath copies by can lay
An Europe, Afric, and an Asia,
And quickly make that, which was nothing, all;[2]
        So doth each tear
15   Which thee doth wear,[3]
A globe, yea world, by that impression grow,
Till thy tears mixed with mine do overflow
This world; by waters sent from thee, my heaven dissolvèd so.

        O more than moon,
20   Draw not up seas to drown me in thy sphere;[4]
Weep me not dead in thine arms, but forbear
To teach the sea what it may do too soon.
        Let not the wind
        Example find
25   To do me more harm than it purposeth;
Since thou and I sigh one another's breath,
Whoe'er sighs most is cruelest, and hastes the other's death.

1633

1. A farewell poem, one of four so titled in the *Songs and Sonnets*. Another is *A Valediction: Forbidding Mourning*, p. 611.
2. I.e., on a blank globe one can place maps of the continents and so convert a cypher ("nothing") into the whole world ("all").
3. Bears your image.
4. A star or planet with more power of attraction than the moon might not only affect tides but draw the very seas unto itself.

Love's Alchemy

Some that have deeper digged love's mine than I,
Say where his centric° happiness doth lie: central
   I have loved, and got, and told,
But should I love, get, tell, till I were old,
5 I should not find that hidden mystery;
     O, 'tis imposture all:
And as no chemic° yet the elixir[1] got,   alchemist
   But glorifies his pregnant pot[2]
   If by the way to him befall
10 Some odoriferous thing, or medicinal;
   So lovers dream a rich and long delight,
   But get a winter-seeming summer's night.[3]

Our ease, our thrift, our honor, and our day,
Shall we for this vain bubble's shadow pay?
15   Ends love in this, that my man°   servant
Can be as happy as I can, if he can
Endure the short scorn of a bridegroom's play?
   That loving wretch that swears
'Tis not the bodies marry, but the minds,
20   Which he in her angelic finds,
   Would swear as justly that he hears,
In that day's rude hoarse minstrelsy, the spheres.[4]
   Hope not for mind in women; at their best
Sweetness and wit, they are but mummy, possessed.[5]

1633

The Apparition

When by thy scorn, O murderess, I am dead,
And that thou thinkst thee free
From all solicitation from me,
Then shall my ghost come to thy bed,
5 And thee, feigned vestal,[1] in worse arms shall see;
Then thy sick taper will begin to wink,°   flicker
And he whose thou art then, being tired before,
Will, if thou stir, or pinch to wake him, think
     Thou call'st for more,

1. A magic medicine sought by alchemists and reputed to heal all ills.
2. A fertile (and womb-shaped) retort, calling up the common analogy between producing the elixir of life and human generation.
3. A night cold as in winter and short as in summer.
4. The perfect harmony of the planets, moving in concentric crystalline spheres, is contrasted with the boistrous serenade of pots, pans, and trumpets,

performed on the wedding night.
5. The syntax of the last two lines is unclear, and they are punctuated differently in various copies. The 1633 edition reads: "at their best, / Sweetnesse, and wit they'are, but, *mummy*, possesst." Many modern editors punctuate as we do here. "Mummy" suggests a corpselike body, without mind or spirit.
1. Virgins consecrated to the Roman goddess Vesta.

10 And in false sleep will from thee shrink,
And then, poor aspen wretch,[2] neglected thou
Bathed in a cold quicksilver sweat[3] wilt lie
    A verier° ghost than I;   *truer*
What I will say, I will not tell thee now,
15 Lest that preserve thee; and since my love is spent,
I had rather thou shouldst painfully repent,
Than by my threatenings rest still innocent.

                                                1633

A Valediction: Forbidding Mourning[1]

As virtuous men pass mildly away,
    And whisper to their souls to go,
Whilst some of their sad friends do say
    The breath goes now, and some say, No;

5 So let us melt, and make no noise,
    No tear-floods, nor sigh-tempests move;
'Twere profanation° of our joys   *desecration*
    To tell the laity our love.

Moving of th' earth brings harms and fears,
10   Men reckon what it did and meant;
But trepidation of the spheres,
    Though greater far, is innocent.[2]

Dull sublunary[3] lovers' love
    (Whose soul is sense) cannot admit
15 Absence, because it doth remove
    Those things which elemented° it.   *composed*

But we, by a love so much refined
    That our selves know not what it is,
Inter-assurèd of the mind,
20   Care less, eyes, lips, and hands to miss.

Our two souls therefore, which are one,
    Though I must go, endure not yet
A breach, but an expansion,
    Like gold to airy thinness beat.

2. Aspen leaves flutter in the slightest breeze.
3. Sweating in terror; quicksilver (mercury) was a stock prescription for venereal disease, and sweating was part of the cure.
1. For "valediction" see p. 609, n. 1. Izaak Walton speculated that this poem was addressed to Donne's wife on the occasion of his trip to the Continent in 1611, but there is no proof of that. Donne was, however, apprehensive about that trip; Walton also heard that, while abroad, Donne had a startling vision of his wife holding a dead baby at about the time she gave birth to a stillborn child.
2. Earthquakes cause damage and were thought to be portentous. Trepidation (in the Ptolemaic cosmology, an oscillation of the ninth or crystalline sphere imparted to all the inner spheres), though a much more violent motion than an earthquake, is neither destructive nor sinister.
3. Beneath the moon, therefore earthly, sensual, and subject to change.

25 If they be two, they are two so
        As stiff twin compasses⁴ are two;
    Thy soul, the fixed foot, makes no show
        To move, but doth, if th' other do.

    And though it in the center sit,
30   Yet when the other far doth roam,
    It leans and hearkens after it,
        And grows erect, as that comes home.

    Such wilt thou be to me, who must,
        Like th' other foot, obliquely run;
35 Thy firmness makes my circle just,
        And makes me end where I begun.

                                                    1633

The Ecstasy¹

    Where, like a pillow on a bed,
        A pregnant bank swelled up to rest
    The violet's reclining head,
        Sat we two, one another's best.

5   Our hands were firmly cemented
        With a fast balm° which thence did spring,   *perspiration*
    Our eye-beams² twisted, and did thread
        Our eyes upon one double string;

    So to intergraft our hands, as yet
10   Was all our means to make us one,
    And pictures in our eyes to get°   *beget*
        Was all our propagation.³

    As 'twixt two equal armies Fate
        Suspends uncertain victory,
15 Our souls (which to advance their state
        Were gone out) hung 'twixt her and me;

    And whilst our souls negotiate there,
        We like sepulchral statues lay;
    All day the same our postures were,
20   And we said nothing all the day.

    If any, so by love refined
        That he soul's language understood,

4. The two legs of a geometer's or draughtsman's compass. This simile is the most famous example of the "metaphysical conceit" (see "Figurative language," in the "Literary Terminology" appendix to this volume).
1. From *ekstasis* (Greek), a movement of the soul outside of the body.
2. Invisible shafts of light, thought of as going out of the eyes and thereby enabling one to see things.
3. Reflections of each in the other's eyes, often called "making babies."

And by good love were grown all mind,
   Within convenient distance stood,

25 He (though he know not which soul spake,
   Because both meant, both spake the same)
Might thence a new concoction[4] take,
   And part far purer than he came.

This ecstasy doth unperplex,
30   We said, and tell us what we love;
We see by this it was not sex;
   We see we saw not what did move;°   *motivate us*

But as all several° souls contain   *separate*
   Mixture of things, they know not what,
35 Love these mixed souls doth mix again,
   And makes both one, each this and that.

A single violet transplant,
   The strength, the color, and the size
(All which before was poor and scant)
40   Redoubles still, and multiplies.

When love with one another so
   Interinanimates two souls,
That abler soul, which thence doth flow,
   Defects of loneliness controls.

45 We then, who are this new soul, know
   Of what we are composed and made,
For th' atomies° of which we grow   *components*
   Are souls, whom no change can invade.

But O alas, so long, so far
50   Our bodies why do we forbear?
They are ours, though they are not we; we are
   The intelligences, they the sphere.[5]

We owe them thanks because they thus
   Did us to us at first convey,
55 Yielded their forces, sense, to us,
   Nor are dross to us, but allay.[6]

On man heaven's influence works not so
   But that it first imprints the air:[7]
So soul into the soul may flow,
60   Though it to body first repair.°   *go*

---

4. In the alchemical sense of sublimation or purification.
5. In Ptolemaic astronomy, each planet, set in a transparent "sphere" that revolved and so carried it around the earth, was inhabited by a controlling angelic "intelligence."
6. "Dross" is an impurity that weakens metal; "allay" (alloy) strengthens it.
7. Astrological influences were thought to work on people through the medium of the surrounding air.

As our blood labors to beget
    Spirits[8] as like souls as it can,
Because such fingers need° to knit   *are needed*
    That subtle knot which makes us man,

65   So must pure lovers' souls descend
        T' affections, and to faculties
Which sense may reach and apprehend;
    Else a great prince in prison lies.

To our bodies turn we then, that so
70   Weak men on love revealed may look;
Love's mysteries[9] in souls do grow,
    But yet the body is his book.

And if some lover, such as we,
    Have heard this dialogue of one,[1]
75   Let him still mark° us; he shall see   *observe*
    Small change when we are to bodies gone.

1633

The Funeral

Whoever comes to shroud me, do not harm
    Nor question much
That subtle wreath of hair which crowns my arm;
The mystery, the sign you must not touch,
5   For 'tis my outward soul,
Viceroy to that, which then to heaven being gone,
    Will leave this to control,
And keep these limbs, her[1] provinces, from dissolution.

For if the sinewy thread[2] my brain lets fall
10   Through every part
Can tie those parts and make me one of all,
These hairs which upward grew, and strength and art
    Have from a better brain,
Can better do it; except° she meant that I   *unless*
15   By this should know my pain,
As prisoners then are manacled, when they're condemned to die.

Whate'er she meant by it, bury it with me,
    For since I am
Love's martyr, it might breed idolatry,

---

8. Subtle substances thought to be produced by the blood to serve as intermediaries between body and soul.
9. The implied comparison is with God's mysteries, which are revealed and may be read in the book of Nature and the book of Scripture.

1. "Dialogue of one" because "both meant, both spake the same" (line 26).
1. The soul's, but also the mistress's (cf. "she," line 14).
2. The nervous system.

20 If into others' hands these relics³ came:
    As 'twas humility
To afford to it all that a soul can do,
    So 'tis some bravery,
That since you would save⁴ none of me, I bury some of you.

1633

The Relic

When my grave is broke up again
Some second guest to entertain
    (For graves have learned that woman-head°   *female trait*
    To be to more than one a bed),¹
5   And he that digs it spies
A bracelet of bright hair about the bone,
     Will he not let us alone,
And think that there a loving couple lies,
Who thought that this device might be some way
10 To make their souls, at the last busy day,°   *Judgment Day*
Meet at this grave, and make a little stay?

    If this fall in a time, or land,
    Where mis-devotion² doth command,
     Then he that digs us up will bring
15   Us to the Bishop and the King,
To make us relics; then
Thou shalt be a Mary Magdalen, and I
     A something else thereby;
All women shall adore us, and some men;
20 And since at such times, miracles are sought,
I would have that age by this paper taught
What miracles we harmless lovers wrought.

    First, we loved well and faithfully,
    Yet knew not what we loved, nor why,
25   Difference of sex no more we knew,
     Than our guardian angels do;
     Coming and going, we
Perchance might kiss, but not between those meals;³
     Our hands ne'er touched the seals°   *sexual organs*
30 Which nature, injured by late law, sets free:⁴
These miracles we did: but now, alas,

3. Body parts or other objects belonging to a saint, venerated by Roman Catholics.
4. All the early printed texts read "have" (which carries sexual connotations), while many manuscripts read "save."
1. Graves were often used to inter successive corpses, the bones of previous occupants being deposited in charnel houses.
2. False devotion, superstition, i.e., Roman Catholicism.
3. The kiss of salutation and parting.
4. Human law forbids the free love permitted by nature. "Late": recent (comparatively speaking).

All measure and all language I should pass,
Should I tell what a miracle she was.

1633

Elegy[1] 16. On His Mistress

By our first strange and fatal interview,
By all desires which thereof did ensue,
By our long starving hopes, by that remorse°   pity
Which my words' masculine persuasive force
5 Begot in thee, and by the memory
Of hurts which spies and rivals threatened me,
I calmly beg; but by thy father's wrath,
By all pains which want and divorcement hath,
I conjure thee; and all the oaths which I
10 And thou have sworn to seal joint constancy
Here I unswear and overswear them thus:
Thou shalt not love by ways so dangerous.
Temper, oh fair love, love's impetuous rage;
Be my true mistress still, not my feigned page.[2]
15 I'll go, and, by thy kind leave, leave behind
Thee, only worthy to nurse in my mind
Thirst to come back. Oh, if thou die before,
My soul from other lands to thee shall soar.
Thy (else almighty) beauty cannot move
20 Rage from the seas, nor thy love teach them love,
Nor tame wild Boreas' harshness.[3] Thou hast read
How roughly he in pieces shiverèd
Fair Orithea, whom he swore he loved.
Fall ill or good, 'tis madness to have proved°   sought out
25 Dangers unurged; feed on this flattery,
That absent lovers one in th' other be.
Dissemble nothing, not a boy, nor change
Thy body's habit,° nor mind's; be not strange   clothing
To thyself only; all will spy in thy face
30 A blushing womanly discovering grace.
Richly clothed apes are called apes, and as soon
Eclipsed as bright we call the moon the moon.
Men of France, changeable chameleons,
Spitals° of diseases, shops of fashions,   hospitals
35 Love's fuellers[4] and the rightest company

1. In Latin poetry, an elegy is not necessarily a funeral lament but simply a discursive or reflective poem written in "elegiacs" (unrhymed couplets of alternating dactylic hexameters and pentameters). The subject matter primarily associated with this meter was sex, the most famous collection of elegies being Ovid's *Amores*. Several of Donne's elegies—almost all written in the 1590s—take Ovid as their principal model and resemble him in ingenious wit and in frank and unapologetic erot-icism. *Elegy 16* is highly dramatic.
2. The speaker's mistress wanted to accompany him abroad, disguised as a page boy. Such escapades occasionally took place in real life; in 1605, Elizabeth Southwell, disguised as a page, went abroad with Sir Robert Dudley.
3. God of the north wind; Ovid in *Metamorphoses* 6 describes the wild force with which Boreas abducted Orithea.
4. Providers of aphrodisiacs.

Of players which upon the world's stage be,
Will quickly know thee, and know[5] thee; and alas!
Th' indifferent° Italian, as we pass   *bisexual*
His warm land, well content to think thee page,
40 Will hunt thee with such lust and hideous rage
As Lot's fair guests were vexed.[6] But none of these
Nor spongy, hydroptic[7] Dutch shall thee displease
If thou stay here. O stay here, for, for thee,
England is only a worthy gallery
45 To walk in expectation, till from thence
Our greatest king call thee to his presence.[8]
When I am gone, dream me some happiness,
Nor let thy looks our long-hid love confess;
Nor praise nor dispraise me, bless nor curse
50 Openly love's force, nor in bed fright thy nurse
With midnight's startings, crying out "Oh, oh!
Nurse, oh my love is slain, I saw him go
O'er the white Alps alone; I saw him, I,
Assailed, fight, taken, stabbed, bleed, fall, and die."
55 Augur me better chance, except dread Jove
Think it enough for me t' have had thy love.

                                                    1635

Elegy 19. To His Mistress Going to Bed[1]

Come, Madam, come, all rest my powers defy,
Until I labor, I in labor lie.[2]
The foe oft-times, having the foe in sight,
Is tired with standing though he never fight.
5 Off with that girdle,° like heaven's zone° glistering,   *belt/zodiac*
But a far fairer world encompassing.
Unpin that spangled breastplate[3] which you wear
That th' eyes of busy fools may be stopped there.
Unlace yourself, for that harmonious chime — clock/watch
10 Tells me from you that now it is bed-time.
Off with that happy busk,° which I envy,   *bodice*
That still can be and still can stand so nigh.
Your gown going off, such beauteous state reveals
As when from flowery meads th' hill's shadow steals.
15 Off with that wiry coronet and show
The hairy diadem which on you doth grow;
Now off with those shoes, and then safely tread

---

5. "Know" in the sexual sense. "Alas" may pun on "a lass."
6. The inhabitants of Sodom brought destruction on themselves when they tried to rape two angels who visited Lot in the guise of young men (Genesis 19.1–11).
7. Dropsical, thus insatiably thirsty.
8. Throne rooms commonly had antechambers (galleries) where visitors waited until the monarch was ready to see them.
1. This poem reworks the central situation of Ovid's *Amores* 1.5 in much more dramatic terms.
2. Labor in the dual sense of "get to work (sexually)" and "distress."
3. The stomacher, an ornamental, often jeweled, covering for the chest, worn under the lacing of the bodice.

give me
permission

In this love's hallowed temple, this soft bed.
In such white robes, heaven's angels used to be
20 Received by men; thou, angel, bring'st with thee
A heaven like Mahomet's paradise;[4] and though
Ill spirits walk in white, we easily know
By this these angels from an evil sprite,
Those set our hairs, but these our flesh upright.

hands
are
licenced

25 License my roving hands, and let them go
Before, behind, between, above, below.
O my America! my new-found-land,
My kingdom, safeliest when with one man manned,
My mine of precious stones, my empery,°   empire
30 How blest am I in this discovering thee!
To enter in these bonds is to be free;
There where my hand is set, my seal shall be.[5]
    Full nakedness! All joys are due to thee.
As souls unbodied, bodies unclothed must be,
35 To taste whole joys. Gems which you women use
Are like Atalanta's balls,[6] cast in men's views,
That when a fool's eye lighteth on a gem,
His earthly soul may covet theirs, not them.
Like pictures, or like books' gay coverings, made
40 For laymen, are all women thus arrayed;
Themselves are mystic books, which only we
(Whom their imputed grace will dignify)
Must see revealed.[7] Then since that I may know,
As liberally as to a midwife show
45 Thyself: cast all, yea, this white linen hence,
Here is no penance, much less innocence.[8]
    To teach thee, I am naked first; why then
What need'st thou have more covering than a man?

1669

Satire 3

In satire the author holds a subject up to ridicule or to scorn. Like his elegies, Donne's five verse satires were written in his twenties and are in the forefront of an effort in the 1590s (by Donne, Ben Jonson, Joseph Hall, and John Marston) to naturalize those classical forms in England. While elements of satire figure in many different kinds of literature, the great models for formal verse satire were the Roman poets Horace and Juvenal, the former for an urbanely witty style, the latter for an indignant or angry manner. While Donne's other satires call on these models, his

---

4. A place of sensual pleasure, thought to be populated by seductive houris for the delectation of the faithful.
5. The jokes mingle law with sex: where he has signed a document (placed his hand) he will now place his seal; and in the bonds of her arms he will find freedom.
6. Atalanta, running a race against her suitor Hippomenes, was beaten when he dropped golden balls (apples) for her to pick up. Donne reverses the story.

7. By granting favors to their lovers, women impute to them grace that they don't deserve, as God (in Calvinist doctrine) imputes grace to undeserving sinners. Laymen can only look at the covers of mystic books (women) but "we" elect can read them.
8. Some manuscripts read: "There is no penance due to innocence." White garments would be appropriate either for the innocent virgin or for the sinner doing formal penance.

third satire more nearly resembles a third Roman satirist, Persius, known for an abstruse style and moralizing manner. This work is a strenuous discussion of an acute theological problem, for the age and for Donne himself: How may one discover the true Christian church among so many claimants to that role? At the time Donne wrote this, he was in the process of leaving the Roman Catholic Church of his heritage for the Church of England.

Satire 3

  Kind pity chokes my spleen;[1] brave scorn forbids
  Those tears to issue which swell my eyelids;
  I must not laugh, nor weep° sins, and be wise: *lament*
  Can railing then cure these worn maladies?
5 Is not our mistress, fair Religion,
  As worthy of all our souls' devotion
  As virtue was to the first blinded age?[2]
  Are not heaven's joys as valiant to assuage
  Lusts, as earth's honor was to them?° Alas,   *pagans*
10 As we do them in means, shall they surpass
  Us in the end, and shall thy father's spirit
  Meet blind philosophers in heaven, whose merit
  Of strict life may be imputed faith,[3] and hear
  Thee, whom he taught so easy ways and near
15 To follow, damned? O, if thou dar'st, fear this;
  This fear great courage and high valor is.
  Dar'st thou aid mutinous Dutch,[4] and dar'st thou lay
  Thee in ships, wooden sepulchers, a prey
  To leaders' rage, to storms, to shot, to dearth?° *famine*
20 Dar'st thou dive seas and dungeons° of the earth? *mines, caves*
  Hast thou courageous fire to thaw the ice
  Of frozen North discoveries?[5] and thrice
  Colder than salamanders, like divine
  Children in the oven,[6] fires of Spain, and the line,
25 Whose countries limbecks to our bodies be,
  Canst thou for gain bear?[7] And must every he
  Which cries not "Goddess!" to thy mistress, draw,° *fight a duel*
  Or eat thy poisonous words? Courage of straw!
  O desperate coward, wilt thou seem bold, and
30 To thy foes and his° (who made thee to stand *God's*
  Sentinel in his world's garrison) thus yield,
  And for forbidden wars leave th' appointed field?[8]

1. The seat of bile, hence scorn and ridicule.
2. The age of paganism, blind to Christianity but capable of natural morality ("virtue").
3. Donne's formulation wittily turns on its head the key concept of reformed Protestant theology—that salvation is to be achieved only by imputing Christ's merits to Christians through faith—by suggesting that virtuous pagans might be saved by imputing faith to them on the basis of their moral life.
4. English volunteers took frequent part with the Dutch in their wars against Spain. Donne himself had sailed in two raiding expeditions against the Spanish.
5. Many explorers tried to find a northwest passage to the Pacific.
6. In the biblical story (Daniel 3), Shadrach, Meshack, and Abednego were rescued from a fiery furnace. The salamander (a lizardlike creature) was thought to be so cold-blooded that it could live in fire.
7. The object of "bear" is "fires of Spain, and the line"—inquisitorial and equatorial heats, which roast people as chemists heat materials in "limbecks" (alembics, or vessels for distilling).
8. Of moral struggle.

Know thy foes: The foul Devil (whom thou
Strivest to please) for hate, not love, would allow
35 Thee fain his whole realm to be quit;° and as   *to satisfy you*
The world's all parts wither away and pass,[9]
So the world's self, thy other loved foe, is
In her decrepit wane, and thou, loving this,
Dost love a withered and worn strumpet; last,
40 Flesh (itself's death) and joys which flesh can taste
Thou lovest; and thy fair goodly soul, which doth
Give this flesh power to taste joy, thou dost loathe.
Seek true religion. O, where? Mirreus,[1]
Thinking her unhoused here, and fled from us,
45 Seeks her at Rome; there, because he doth know
That she was there a thousand years ago.
He loves her rags so, as we here obey
The statecloth[2] where the Prince sat yesterday.
Crantz to such brave loves will not be enthralled,
50 But loves her only, who at Geneva is called
Religion—plain, simple, sullen, young,
Contemptuous, yet unhandsome; as among
Lecherous humors,° there is one that judges   *temperaments*
No wenches wholesome but coarse country drudges.
55 Graius stays still at home here, and because
Some preachers, vile ambitious bawds, and laws
Still new, like fashions, bid him think that she
Which dwells with us is only perfect, he
Embraceth her whom his godfathers will
60 Tender to him, being tender, as wards still
Take such wives as their guardians offer, or
Pay values.[3] Careless Phrygius doth abhor
All, because all cannot be good, as one
Knowing some women whores, dares marry none.
65 Graccus loves all as one, and thinks that so
As women do in divers countries go
In divers habits, yet are still one kind,
So doth, so is religion; and this blind-
ness too much light breeds;[4] but unmoved thou
70 Of force° must one, and forced but one allow;   *necessity*
And the right; ask thy father which is she,
Let him ask his; though truth and falsehood be
Near twins, yet truth a little elder is;
Be busy to seek her, believe me this,
75 He's not of none, nor worst, that seeks the best.[5]
To adore, or scorn an image, or protest,
May all be bad; doubt wisely; in strange way

9. The common belief that the world was growing
old and becoming decrepit.
1. The satiric types in this passage represent different creeds: "Mirreus" is a Roman Catholic;
"Crantz" an austere Calvinist Presbyterian of
Geneva; "Graius" a Church of England Erastian
who believes in any religion sponsored by the state;
"Phrygius" a skeptic; and "Graccus" a complete rel-
ativist.

2. The royal canopy, a symbol of kingly power.
3. If minors in care of a guardian (in wardship)
rejected the wives offered ("tendered") to them
they had to pay fines ("values").
4. I.e., being blind to the differences between
religions, Graccus has too much light to see where
truth might lie.
5. The person who seeks the best church is neither an unbeliever nor the worst sort of believer.

To stand inquiring right, is not to stray;
To sleep, or run wrong, is. On a huge hill,
80 Cragged and steep, Truth stands, and he that will
Reach her, about must, and about must go,
And what the hill's suddenness resists, win so;
Yet strive so, that before age, death's twilight,
Thy soul rest, for none can work in that night.[6]
85 To will° implies delay, therefore now do.   intend a future act
Hard deeds, the body's pains; hard knowledge too
The mind's endeavors reach,° and mysteries   achieve
Are like the sun, dazzling, yet plain to all eyes.
Keep the truth which thou hast found; men do not stand
90 In so ill case here, that God hath with his hand
Signed kings' blank charters to kill whom they hate,
Nor are they vicars, but hangmen to fate.[7]
Fool and wretch, wilt thou let thy soul be tied
To man's laws, by which she shall not be tried
95 At the last day? O, will it then boot° thee   profit
To say a Philip, or a Gregory,
A Harry, or a Martin taught thee this?[8]
Is not this excuse for mere° contraries   complete
Equally strong? Cannot both sides say so?
100 That thou mayest rightly obey power, her bounds know;
Those passed, her nature and name is changed; to be
Then humble to her is idolatry.
As streams are, power is; those blest flowers that dwell
At the rough stream's calm head, thrive and prove well,
105 But having left their roots, and themselves given
To the stream's tyrannous rage, alas, are driven
Through mills, and rocks, and woods, and at last, almost
Consumed in going, in the sea are lost:
So perish souls, which more choose men's unjust
110 Power from God claimed, than God himself to trust.

1633

From Holy Sonnets[1]

1

Thou hast made me, and shall thy work decay?
Repair me now, for now mine end doth haste;
I run to death, and death meets me as fast,
And all my pleasures are like yesterday.

6. Echoes John 9.4, "the night cometh, when no
man can work."
7. Kings are not God's vicars on earth, with license
("blank charters") to persecute or kill whomever
they wish on grounds of religion.
8. "Philip" is Philip II of Spain, "Gregory" is Pope
Gregory XIII or XIV, "Harry" is England's Henry
VIII, and "Martin" is Martin Luther.
1. Donne wrote a variety of religious poems
(called "Divine Poems"), including a group of nine-

teen *Holy Sonnets* that reflect his interest in Jesuit
and especially Protestant meditative procedures.
He probably began writing them about 1609, a
decade or so after leaving the Catholic church. Our
selections follow the traditional numbering established in Sir Herbert Grierson's influential edition,
since for most of these sonnets we cannot tell
when they were written or in what order they were
intended to appear.

5   I dare not move my dim eyes any way,
     Despair behind, and death before doth cast
     Such terror, and my feeble flesh doth waste
     By sin in it, which it towards hell doth weigh.°   *incline, weigh down*
     Only thou art above, and when towards thee
10   By thy leave I can look, I rise again;
     But our old subtle foe so tempteth me
     That not one hour myself I can sustain.
     Thy grace may wing° me to prevent° his art,   *give wings to / forestall*
     And thou like adamant° draw mine iron heart.   *magnetic lodestone*

1635

5

     I am a little world[2] made cunningly
     Of elements, and an angelic sprite;°   *spirit, soul*
     But black sin hath betrayed to endless night
     My world's both parts, and O, both parts must die.
5   You which beyond that heaven which was most high
     Have found new spheres, and of new lands can write,[3]
     Pour new seas in mine eyes, that so I might
     Drown my world with my weeping earnestly,
     Or wash it if it must be drowned no more.[4]
10   But O, it must be burnt! Alas, the fire
     Of lust and envy have burnt it heretofore,
     And made it fouler; let their flames retire,
     And burn me, O Lord, with a fiery zeal
     Of thee and thy house, which doth in eating heal.[5]

1635

7

     At the round earth's imagined corners,[6] blow
     Your trumpets, angels; and arise, arise
     From death, you numberless infinities
     Of souls, and to your scattered bodies go:
5   All whom the flood did, and fire[7] shall, o'erthrow,
     All whom war, dearth,° age, agues,° tyrannies,   *famine / fevers*
     Despair, law, chance hath slain, and you whose eyes
     Shall behold God, and never taste death's woe.[8]
     But let them sleep, Lord, and me mourn a space;
10   For, if above all these, my sins abound,
     'Tis late to ask abundance of thy grace
     When we are there. Here on this lowly ground,

2. The traditional idea of the human being as microcosm (a "little world"), containing in miniature all the features of the macrocosm or great world.
3. Astronomers, especially Galileo.
4. God promised Noah (Genesis 9.11) never to flood the earth again.
5. See Psalm 69.9: "For the zeal of thine house hath eaten me up." These lines refer to three kinds of flame—those of the Last Judgment, those of lust and envy, and those of zeal, which alone save.
6. Cf. Revelations 7.1: "I saw four angels standing on the four corners of the earth."
7. Noah's flood, and the universal conflagration at the end of the world (Revelation 6.11).
8. Those who will be alive at the Second Coming (cf. Luke 9.27).

Teach me how to repent; for that's as good
As if thou hadst sealed my pardon with thy blood.

1633

9

If poisonous minerals, and if that tree[9]
Whose fruit threw death on else-immortal us,
If lecherous goats, if serpents envious[1]
Cannot be damned, alas! why should I be?
5 Why should intent or reason, born in me,
Make sins, else equal, in me more heinous?
And, mercy being easy and glorious
To God, in his stern wrath why threatens he?
But who am I that dare dispute with thee
10 O God? Oh, of thine only worthy blood
And my tears, make a heavenly Lethean[2] flood,
And drown in it my sin's black memory.
That thou remember them some claim as debt;
I think it mercy if thou wilt forget.[3]

1633

10

Death, be not proud, though some have callèd thee
Mighty and dreadful, for thou art not so;
For those whom thou think'st thou dost overthrow
Die not, poor Death, nor yet canst thou kill me.
5 From rest and sleep, which but thy pictures be,
Much pleasure; then from thee much more must flow,
And soonest our best men with thee do go,
Rest of their bones, and soul's delivery.[4]
Thou art slave to fate, chance, kings, and desperate men,
10 And dost with poison, war, and sickness dwell,
And poppy° or charms can make us sleep as well   *opium*
And better than thy stroke; why swell'st° thou then?   *puff with pride*
One short sleep past, we wake eternally
And death shall be no more; Death, thou shalt die.[5]

1633

13

What if this present were the world's last night?
Mark in my heart, O soul, where thou dost dwell,

---

9. The Tree of Knowledge of Good and Evil, whose fruit was forbidden to Adam and Eve in Eden.
1. Traits commonly associated with these creatures.
2. In classical mythology, the waters of the river Lethe in the underworld caused total forgetful-

ness.
3. Cf. Jeremiah 31.34: "I will forgive their iniquity, and I will remember their sins no more."
4. I.e., to find rest for their bones and freedom ("delivery") for their souls.
5. Cf. 1 Corinthians 15.26: "The last enemy that shall be destroyed is death."

The picture of Christ crucified, and tell
Whether that countenance can thee affright.
5 Tears in his eyes quench the amazing light,
Blood fills his frowns, which from his pierced head fell;
And can that tongue adjudge thee unto hell
Which prayed forgiveness for his foes' fierce spite?
No, no; but as in my idolatry
10 I said to all my profane° mistresses,   *earthly*
Beauty of pity, foulness only is
A sign of rigor:[6] so I say to thee,
To wicked spirits are horrid shapes assigned,
This beauteous form assures a piteous mind.

                                                          1633

14

Batter my heart, three-personed God; for you
As yet but knock, breathe, shine, and seek to mend;
That I may rise and stand, o'erthrow me, and bend
Your force to break, blow, burn, and make me new.
5 I, like an usurped town, to another due,
Labor to admit you, but O, to no end;
Reason, your viceroy[7] in me, me should defend,
But is captived, and proves weak or untrue.
Yet dearly I love you, and would be loved fain,°   *gladly*
10 But am betrothed[8] unto your enemy.
Divorce me, untie or break that knot again;
Take me to you, imprison me, for I,
Except° you enthrall me, never shall be free,   *unless*
Nor ever chaste, except you ravish[9] me.

                                                          1633

18

Show me, dear Christ, thy spouse[1] so bright and clear.
What! is it she which on the other shore
Goes richly painted? or which, robbed and tore,
Laments and mourns in Germany and here?[2]
5 Sleeps she a thousand, then peeps up one year?
Is she self-truth, and errs? now new, now outwore?
Doth she, and did she, and shall she evermore
On one, on seven, or on no hill appear?[3]

---

6. In Neoplatonic theory, beautiful features are the sign of a compassionate mind, while ugliness signifies the contrary.
7. The governor in your stead.
8. Humanity's relationship with God has been described in terms of marriage and adultery from the time of the Hebrew prophets.
9. Rape, also overwhelm with wonder. "Enthrall": enslave, also enchant.
1. The church is commonly called the bride of Christ. Cf. Revelation 19.7–8: "The marriage of the Lamb is come, and his wife hath made herself ready. / And to her was granted that she should be arrayed in fine linen, clean and white."
2. I.e., neither the painted woman (the Church of Rome) nor the ravished virgin (the Lutheran and Calvinist churches in Germany and England) seem very like a bride.
3. The church on one hill is probably Solomon's temple on Mount Moriah; that on seven hills is the Church of Rome; that on no hill is the Presbyterian church of Geneva.

Dwells she with us, or like adventuring knights
10 First travel we to seek, and then make love?
Betray, kind husband, thy spouse to our sights,
And let mine amorous soul court thy mild dove,
Who is most true and pleasing to thee then
When she is embraced and open to most men.[4]

1899

19

Oh, to vex me, contraries meet in one:
Inconstancy unnaturally hath begot
A constant habit; that when I would not
I change in vows, and in devotion.
5 As humorous is my contrition
As my profane love, and as soon forgot:
As riddlingly distempered, cold and hot,[5]
As praying, as mute, as infinite, as none.
I durst not view heaven yesterday; and today
10 In prayers, and flattering speeches I court God:
Tomorrow I quake with true fear of his rod.
So my devout fits come and go away
Like a fantastic ague:[6] save that here
Those are my best days, when I shake with fear.

1899

Hymn to God My God, in My Sickness[1]

Since I am coming to that holy room
    Where, with thy choir of saints for evermore,
I shall be made thy music; as I come
    I tune the instrument here at the door,
5   And what I must do then, think[2] now before.

Whilst my physicians by their love are grown
    Cosmographers, and I their map, who lie
Flat on this bed, that by them may be shown
    That this is my southwest discovery[3]
10   Per fretum febris,[4] by these straits to die,

4. The final lines wittily rework, with startling sexual associations, Song of Solomon 5.2: "Open to me, my sister, my love, my dove, my undefiled." That biblical book was often interpreted as the song of love between Christ and the church.
5. Arising from the unbalanced humors, changeable.
6. A fever, attended with paroxysms of hot and cold and trembling fits. "Fantastic": capricious, extravagant.
1. Though Izaak Walton, Donne's pious biographer, assigns this poem to the last days of his life, it was probably written in December 1623.
2. This and the previous poem are less hymns (songs of praise) than meditations preparing (tuning the instrument) for such hymns.
3. South is the region of heat, west the region of sunset and death.
4. Through the straits of fever, with a pun on straits as sufferings, rigors, and a geographical reference to the Strait of Magellan.

I joy, that in these straits, I see my West;
  For, though their currents yield return to none,
What shall my West hurt me? As West and East
  In all flat maps (and I am one) are one,[5]
15   So death doth touch the resurrection.

Is the Pacific Sea my home? Or are
  The Eastern riches?° Is Jerusalem?   *Cathay, China*
Anyan,[6] and Magellan, and Gibraltar,
  All straits, and none but straits, are ways to them,
20   Whether where Japhet dwelt, or Cham, or Shem.[7]

We think that Paradise and Calvary,
  Christ's cross and Adam's tree, stood in one place;
Look, Lord and find both Adams[8] met in me;
  As the first Adam's sweat surrounds my face,
25   May the last Adam's blood my soul embrace.

So, in his purple wrapped,[9] receive me, Lord;
  By these his thorns give me his other crown;
And, as to others' souls I preached thy word,
  Be this my text, my sermon to mine own:
30   Therefore that he may raise the Lord throws down.

                          1635

A Hymn to God the Father[1]

Wilt thou forgive that sin where I begun,
  Which is my sin, though it were done before?[2]
Wilt thou forgive that sin through which I run,
  And do run still, though still I do deplore?
5   When thou hast done,[3] thou hast not done,
      For I have more.

Wilt thou forgive that sin by which I have won
  Others to sin? and made my sin their door?
Wilt thou forgive that sin which I did shun
10   A year or two, but wallowed in a score?
      When thou hast done, thou hast not done,
      For I have more.

5. If a flat map is pasted on a round globe, west and east meet.

6. Anian, a strait on the west coast of America, shown on early maps as separating America from Asia.

7. The three sons of Noah by whom the world was repopulated after the Flood (Genesis 10). The descendants of Japhet were thought to inhabit Europe; those of Cham (Ham), Africa; and those of Shem, Asia.

8. Adam and Christ. Legend had it that Christ's cross was erected on the spot, or at least in the region, where the tree forbidden to Adam in Eden had stood.

9. In his blood, also in his kingly robes.

1. This hymn was used as a congregational hymn. Walton tells us that Donne wrote it during his illness of 1623, had it set to music, and was delighted to hear it performed (as it frequently was) by the choir of St. Paul's Cathedral.

2. I.e., he inherits the original sin of Adam and Eve.

3. In the refrains, Donne puns on his own name and may pun on his wife's maiden name, Ann More.

I have a sin of fear, that when I have spun
My last thread, I shall perish on the shore;
15   Swear by thy self, that at my death thy Son
Shall shine as he shines now and heretofore;
And, having done that, thou hast done,
I fear[4] no more.

1633

From Devotions upon Emergent Occasions[1]

Meditation 17

Nunc lento sonitu dicunt, morieris.
Now this bell tolling softly for another, says to me, Thou must die.

Perchance he for whom this bell[2] tolls may be so ill as that he knows not it tolls for him; and perchance I may think myself so much better than I am, as that they who are about me and see my state may have caused it to toll for me, and I know not that. The church is catholic, universal, so are all her actions; all that she does belongs to all. When she baptizes a child, that action concerns me; for that child is thereby connected to that head which is my head too, and ingrafted into that body[3] whereof I am a member. And when she buries a man, that action concerns me: all mankind is of one author and is one volume; when one man dies, one chapter is not torn out of the book, but translated[4] into a better language; and every chapter must be so translated. God employs several translators; some pieces are translated by age, some by sickness, some by war, some by justice; but God's hand is in every translation, and his hand shall bind up all our scattered leaves again for that library where every book shall lie open to one another. As therefore the bell that rings to a sermon calls not upon the preacher only, but upon the congregation to come, so this bell calls us all; but how much more me, who am brought so near the door by this sickness. There was a contention as far as a suit[5] (in which piety and dignity, religion and estimation,[6] were mingled) which of the religious orders should ring to prayers first in the morning; and it was determined that they should ring first that rose earliest. If we understand aright the dignity of this bell that tolls for our evening prayer, we would be glad to make it ours by rising early, in that application, that it might be ours as well as his whose indeed it is. The bell doth toll for him that thinks it doth; and though it intermit again, yet from that minute that that occasion wrought upon him, he is united to God. Who casts not up his eye to the sun when it rises? but who takes off his eye from a comet when that breaks out?

4. Some manuscripts read "have."
1. Donne's *Devotions* were composed in the aftermath of his serious illness in the winter of 1623, though Donne characteristically writes as if the events of the illness were happening as he describes them. The *Devotions* recount in twenty-three sections the stages ("emergent occasions") of the illness and recovery: the term associates the exercise with a popular kind of Protestant meditation on the occasions that daily life presents to us. Each section contains a "meditation upon our

human condition," an "expostulation and debatement with God," and a prayer to God. The book was published almost immediately, offering its meditation on an intensely personal experience as exemplary for others.
2. The "passing bell" for the dying.
3. The church.
4. Punning on the literal sense, "carried across."
5. Controversy that went as far as a lawsuit.
6. Self-esteem.

Who bends not his ear to any bell which upon any occasion rings? but who can remove it from that bell which is passing a piece of himself out of this world? No man is an island, entire of itself; every man is a piece of the continent, a part of the main.[7] If a clod be washed away by the sea, Europe is the less, as well as if a promontory were, as well as if a manor of thy friend's or of thine own were. Any man's death diminishes me, because I am involved in mankind; and therefore never send to know for whom the bell tolls; it tolls for thee.[8] Neither can we call this a begging of misery or a borrowing of misery, as though we were not miserable enough of ourselves but must fetch in more from the next house, in taking upon us the misery of our neighbors. Truly it were an excusable covetousness if we did; for affliction is a treasure, and scarce any man hath enough of it. No man hath affliction enough that is not matured and ripened by it, and made fit for God by that affliction. If a man carry treasure in bullion, or in a wedge of gold, and have none coined into current moneys, his treasure will not defray[9] him as he travels. Tribulation is treasure in the nature of it, but it is not current money in the use of it, except we get nearer and nearer our home, heaven, by it. Another man may be sick too, and sick to death, and this affliction may lie in his bowels as gold in a mine and be of no use to him; but this bell that tells me of his affliction digs out and applies that gold to me, if by this consideration of another's danger I take mine own into contemplation and so secure myself by making my recourse to my God, who is our only security.

1623   1624

7. Mainland.   novel *For Whom the Bell Tolls.*
8. This phrase gave Hemingway the title for his   9. Meet his expenses.

AEMILIA LANYER
1569–1645

Aemilia Lanyer was the first Englishwoman to publish a substantial volume of original poems and the first to make an overt bid for patronage, as previously only a male poet of the era might. She was daughter to an Italian-Jewish family of court musicians (the Bassanos), and for some years the mistress of Queen Elizabeth's Lord Chamberlain, Henry Cary, Lord Hunsdon, forty-five years her senior and a notable patron of the arts, including Shakespeare's company. Apparently to cover a pregnancy by him that resulted in a son named Henry, she married into another family of gentlemen musicians attached to the courts of Elizabeth I and James I. Educated in the aristocratic household of the countess of Kent and supported in style by Hunsdon, her fortunes declined after her marriage to Alfonso Lanyer, and her efforts to find some niche at the Jacobean court came to nothing. The gossipy notebooks of the astrologer Simon Forman record some of these facts from information Lanyer provided when consulting him about her fortunes. She evidently resided for some time in the bookish and cultivated household of Margaret Clifford, countess of Cumberland, and Margaret's young daughter Anne Clifford, receiving there some encouragement in learning, piety, and poetry, as well as, perhaps, some support in the unusual venture of offering her poems for publication.

Lanyer's single volume of poems, *Salve Deus Rex Judaeorum* (1611), has a decided feminist thrust. A series of dedicatory poems to former and would-be patronesses praises them as a community of contemporary good women. The title poem, a baroque meditation on Christ's Passion which at times invites some comparison with Donne and Crashaw, contrasts the good women who are part of the Passion story with the weak and evil men portrayed there and also incorporates a defense of Eve and all women. That defense and Lanyer's prose epistle "To the Virtuous Reader" are spirited contributions to the so-called *querelle des femmes*, a massive body of writings both serious and satiric that extends over several centuries and argues the issue of women's worthiness or fault-iness in several genres and languages: some examples include Chaucer's *Wife of Bath's Prologue and Tale*, John Knox's denunciation of Mary Queen of Scots, and Shake-speare's *Taming of the Shrew*. The final poem in Lanyer's volume, *The Description of Cooke-ham*, celebrates in elegiac mode the crown estate occasionally occupied by the countess of Cumberland, portraying it as an Edenic paradise of women, now lost. This poem may or may not have been written before Ben Jonson's *To Penshurst*—commonly thought to have inaugurated the "country-house" genre in English literature—but Lan-yer's poem can claim priority in publication. These two poems offer an instructive com-parison, constructing male and female conceptions of an idealized social order that respond in very different ways to contemporary gender ideology.

From Salve Deus Rex Judaeorum[1]

To the Doubtful Reader[2]

Gentle Reader, if thou desire to be resolved, why I give this title, *Salve Deus Rex Judaeorum*, know for certain, that it was delivered unto me in sleep many years before I had any intent to write in this manner, and was quite out of my memory, until I had written the Passion of Christ, when imme-diately it came into my remembrance, what I had dreamed long before. And thinking it a significant token[3] that I was appointed to perform this work, I gave the very same words I received in sleep as the fittest title I could devise for this book.

Eve's Apology in Defense of Women[4]

Now Pontius Pilate is to judge the cause°   *case*
Of faultless Jesus, who before him stands,
Who neither hath offended prince, nor laws,
Although he now be brought in woeful bands.
5   O noble governor, make thou yet a pause,
Do not in innocent blood inbrue° thy hands;   *stain*
     But hear the words of thy most worthy wife,[5]
     Who sends to thee, to beg her Savior's life.

---

1. "Hail God, King of the Jews," a variant of the inscription affixed to Christ's cross.
2. Lanyer placed this explanation at the end of her volume, not the beginning, as a further authorizing gesture. Invoking the familiar genre of the dream vision, she lays claim to some kind of poetic, and even divine, inspiration. "Doubtful": doubting.
3. Sign.
4. Lanyer supplies the title for this subsection of the *Salve Deus* on her title page. Eve is not, how-ever, the speaker; rather, the narrator presents

Eve's "Apology" (defense of her actions), which is also a defense of all women. She does so by means of an apostrophe (impassioned address) to Pilate, the Roman official who authorized the crucifixion of Jesus. Lanyer makes Pilate and Adam represen-tatives of the male gender, whereas Eve and Pilate's wife represent womankind.
5. Pilate's wife wrote her husband a letter urging Pilate to spare Jesus, about whom she had a warn-ing dream (Matthew 27.19).

Let barb'rous cruelty far depart from thee,
10   And in true justice take affliction's part;
Open thine eyes, that thou the truth may'st see.
Do not the thing that goes against thy heart,
Condemn not him that must thy Savior be;
But view his holy life, his good desert.
15   Let not us women glory in men's fall.[6]
    Who had power given to overrule us all.

Till now your indiscretion sets us free.
And makes our former fault much less appear;
Our mother Eve, who tasted of the tree,
20   Giving to Adam what she held most dear,
Was simply good, and had no power to see;[7]
The after-coming harm did not appear:
    The subtle serpent that our sex betrayed
    Before our fall so sure a plot had laid.

25   That undiscerning ignorance perceived
No guile or craft that was by him intended;
For had she known of what we were bereaved,[8]
To his request she had not condescended.
But she, poor soul, by cunning was deceived;
30   No hurt therein her harmless heart intended:
    For she alleged° God's word, which he° denies,   *asserted / serpent*
    That they should die, but even as gods be wise.

But surely Adam cannot be excused;
Her fault though great, yet he was most to blame;
35   What weakness offered, strength might have refused,
Being lord of all, the greater was his shame.
Although the serpent's craft had her abused,
God's holy word ought all his actions frame,°   *determine*
    For he was lord and king of all the earth,
40   Before poor Eve had either life or breath,

Who being framed° by God's eternal hand   *fashioned*
The perfectest man that ever breathed on earth;
And from God's mouth received that strait° command,   *strict*
The breach whereof he knew was present death;
45   Yea, having power to rule both sea and land,
Yet with one apple won to lose that breath[9]
    Which God had breathed in his beauteous face,
    Bringing us all in danger and disgrace.

---

6. The fall of Adam, and the prospective fall of Pilate.
7. In Eden, Eve ate the forbidden fruit first, at the serpent's bidding. Genesis commentary usually emphasized Eve's full knowledge that God had forbidden them on pain of death and banishment from Eden to eat the fruit of the Tree of Knowledge of Good and Evil; her action was usually ascribed to intemperance, pride, and ambition.

8. Deprived, specifically of eternal life. In Genesis 3, Eve was enticed by the serpent to eat the forbidden fruit; she in turn enticed her husband. God expelled them from Eden, condemning Adam to hard labor, Eve to pain in childbirth and subjection to her husband, and both to suffering and death.
9. The breath of life, which would have been eternal.

And then to lay the fault on Patience' back,
50 That we (poor women) must endure it all.
We know right well he did discretion lack,
Being not persuaded thereunto at all.
If Eve did err, it was for knowledge sake;
The fruit being fair persuaded him to fall:
55   No subtle serpent's falsehood did betray him;
        If he would eat it, who had power to stay° him?   *prevent*

Not Eve, whose fault was only too much love,
Which made her give this present to her dear,
That what she tasted he likewise might prove,°   *experience*
60 Whereby his knowledge might become more clear;
He never sought her weakness to reprove
With those sharp words which he of God did hear;
        Yet men will boast of knowledge, which he took
        From Eve's fair hand, as from a learned book.

65 If any evil did in her remain,
Being made of him,[1] he was the ground of all.
If one of many worlds[2] could lay a stain
Upon our sex, and work so great a fall
To wretched man by Satan's subtle train,[3]
70 What will so foul a fault amongst you all?
        Her weakness did the serpent's words obey,
        But you in malice God's dear Son betray,

Whom, if unjustly you condemn to die,
Her sin was small to what you do commit;
75 All mortal sins[4] that do for vengeance cry
Are not to be compared unto it.
If many worlds would altogether try
By all their sins the wrath of God to get,
        This sin of yours surmounts them all as far
80   As doth the sun another little star.[5]

Then let us have our liberty again,
And challenge° to yourselves no sovereignty.   *claim*
You came not in the world without our pain,
Make that a bar against your cruelty;
85 Your fault being greater, why should you disdain
Our being your equals, free from tyranny?
        If one weak woman simply did offend,
        This sin of yours hath no excuse nor end,

To which, poor souls, we never gave consent.
90 Witness, thy wife, O Pilate, speaks for all,

1. Genesis 2.21–22 reports God's creation of Eve from Adam's rib.
2. May allude to the commonplace that man is a little world, applying it here to woman.
3. Tradition identifies Satan with the serpent, although that identification is not made in Genesis.
4. Sins punishable by damnation.
5. In the Ptolemaic system, the sun was larger than the other planets and the fixed stars.

Who did but dream, and yet a message sent
That thou shouldest have nothing to do at all
With that just man[6] which, if thy heart relent,
Why wilt thou be a reprobate° with Saul[7]   *damned*
95   To seek the death of him that is so good,
For thy soul's health to shed his dearest blood?

1611

The Description of Cooke-ham[1]

Farewell (sweet *Cooke-ham*) where I first obtained
Grace[2] from that grace where perfect grace remained;
And where the muses gave their full consent,
I should have power the virtuous to content;
5   Where princely palace[3] willed me to indite,
The sacred story of the soul's delight.
Farewell (sweet place) where virtue then did rest,
And all delights did harbor in her breast;
Never shall my sad eyes again behold
10   Those pleasures which my thoughts did then unfold.
Yet you (great Lady) Mistress of that place,
From whose desires did spring this work of grace;
Vouchsafe to think upon those pleasures past,
As fleeting worldly joys that could not last,
15   Or, as dim shadows of celestial pleasures,
Which are desired above all earthly treasures.
Oh how (methought) against° you thither came,   *in preparation for*
Each part did seem some new delight to frame!
The house received all ornaments to grace it,
20   And would endure no foulness to deface it.
And walks put on their summer liveries,[4]
And all things else did hold like similes:[5]
The trees with leaves, with fruits, with flowers clad,
Embraced each other, seeming to be glad,
25   Turning themselves to beauteous Canopies,
To shade the bright sun from your brighter eyes;
The crystal streams with silver spangles graced,
While by the glorious sun they were embraced;

6. Christ.
7. King of Israel who sought the death of God's annointed prophet-king, David. The parallel is with Pilate, who sought Christ's death.
1. The poem was written in honor of Margaret Clifford, countess of Cumberland, and celebrates a royal estate leased to her brother, at which the countess occasionally resided. The poem should be compared with Jonson's *To Penshurst*. Lanyer's poem is based on a familiar classical topic, the "Farewell to a Place," which had its most famous development in Virgil's *Eclogue* 1. Lanyer makes extensive use of the common pastoral motif of nature's active sympathy with and response to human emotion—which later came to be called

the "pathetic fallacy."
2. Here, both God's grace and the favor of Her Grace, the Countess of Cumberland. Lanyer attributes both her religious conversion and her vocation as poet to a period of residence at Cookeham in the countess's household. We do not know how long or under what circumstances Lanyer resided there.
3. Apparently a reference to the countess as her patron, commissioning her Passion poem.
4. Distinctive garments worn by persons in the service of great families, to indicate whose servants they were.
5. Behaved in similar fashion.

The little birds in chirping notes did sing,
30 To entertain both you and that sweet spring.
And *Philomela*[6] with her sundry lays,
Both you and that delightful place did praise.
Oh how me thought each plant, each flower, each tree
Set forth their beauties then to welcome thee!
35 The very hills right humbly did descend,
When you to tread on them did intend.
And as you set your feet, they still did rise,
Glad that they could receive so rich a prize.
The gentle winds did take delight to be
40 Among those woods that were so graced by thee,
And in sad murmur uttered pleasing sound,
That pleasure in that place might more abound.
The swelling banks delivered all their pride
When such a *Phoenix*[7] once they had espied.
45 Each arbor, bank, each seat, each stately tree,
Thought themselves honored in supporting thee.
The pretty birds would oft come to attend thee,
Yet fly away for fear they should offend thee;
The little creatures in the burrough by
50 Would come abroad to sport them in your eye,
Yet fearful of the bow in your fair hand,
Would run away when you did make a stand.
Now let me come unto that stately tree,
Wherein such goodly prospects you did see;
55 That oak that did in height his fellows pass,
As much as lofty trees, low growing grass,
Much like a comely cedar straight and tall,
Whose beauteous stature far exceeded all.
How often did you visit this fair tree,
60 Which seeming joyful in receiving thee,
Would like a palm tree spread his arms abroad,
Desirous that you there should make abode;
Whose fair green leaves much like a comely veil,
Defended° *Phoebus* when he would assail;   *defended against, resisted*
65 Whose pleasing boughs did yield a cool fresh air,
Joying° his happiness when you were there.   *enjoying*
Where being seated, you might plainly see
Hills, vales, and woods, as if on bended knee
They had appeared, your honor to salute,
70 Or to prefer some strange unlooked-for suit;[8]
All interlaced with brooks and crystal springs,
A prospect fit to please the eyes of kings.
And thirteen shires appeared all in your sight,

---

6. In myth, Philomela was raped by her brother-in-law Tereus, who also tore out her tongue; the gods transformed her into a nightingale. Here the bird's song is joyous but later mournful (line 189), associating her own woes with those of Cookeham at the women's departure.
7. Mythical bird that lived alone of its kind for five

hundred years, then was consumed in flame and reborn from its own ashes; metaphorically, a person of rare excellence. "All their pride": fish (cf. *To Penshurst*, lines 31–36).
8. To urge some unexpected petition, as to a monarch.

Europe could not afford much more delight.
75   What was there then but gave you all content,
While you the time in meditation spent
Of their Creator's power, which there you saw,
In all his creatures held a perfect law;
And in their beauties did you plain descry°   *perceive*
80   His beauty, wisdom, grace, love, majesty.
In these sweet woods how often did you walk,
With Christ and his Apostles there to talk;
Placing his holy Writ in some fair tree
To meditate what you therein did see.
85   With *Moses* you did mount his holy hill
To know his pleasure, and perform his will.[9]
With lowly *David* you did often sing
His holy hymns to Heaven's eternal King.[1]
And in sweet music did your soul delight
90   To sound his praises, morning, noon, and night.
With blessed *Joseph* you did often feed
Your pined brethren, when they stood in need.[2]
And that sweet Lady sprung from *Clifford's* race,
Of noble *Bedford's* blood, fair stem of grace,[3]
95   To honorable *Dorset* now espoused,[4]
In whose fair breast true virtue then was housed,
Oh what delight did my weak spirits find
In those pure parts of her well framéd mind.
And yet it grieves me that I cannot be
100   Near unto her, whose virtues did agree
With those fair ornaments of outward beauty,
Which did enforce from all both love and duty.
Unconstant Fortune, thou art most to blame,
Who casts us down into so low a frame
105   Where our great friends we cannot daily see,
So great a difference is there in degree.[5]
Many are placed in those orbs of state,
Parters[6] in honor, so ordained by Fate,
Nearer in show, yet farther off in love,
110   In which, the lowest always are above.[7]
But whither am I carried in conceit,
My wit too weak to conster° of the great.   *construe*
Why not? although we are but born of earth,
We may behold the heavens, despising death;
115   And loving heaven that is so far above,

---

9. You sought out and followed God's law, like
Moses, who received the Ten Commandments on
Mount Sinai.
1. You often sang David's psalms.
2. Like Joseph, who fed the starving Israelites in
Egypt, you fed the hungry.
3. Main line of the family tree. Anne Clifford, only
surviving child of the seaman-adventurer George
Clifford, third earl of Cumberland, and the countess, a Russell (of "Bedford's blood"). She was
tutored by Samuel Daniel and her *Diary* offers

interesting insights into this period.
4. Anne Clifford was married to Richard Sackville,
third earl of Dorset, on February 25, 1609; the reference helps date Lanyer's poem.
5. These lines and lines 117–25 probably exaggerate Lanyer's former familiarity with Anne Clifford.
6. Separators, i.e., the various honorific ranks
"orbs of state" act to separate person from person.
7. An egalitarian sentiment playing on the Christian notion that in spiritual things—love and charity—the poor and lowly surpass the great ones.

May in the end vouchsafe us entire love.[8]
Therefore sweet memory do thou retain
Those pleasures past, which will not turn again:
Remember beauteous *Dorset's* former sports,[9]
120 So far from being touched by ill reports,
Wherein myself did always bear a part,
While reverend love presented my true heart.
Those recreations let me bear in mind,
Which her sweet youth and noble thoughts did find,
125 Whereof deprived, I evermore must grieve,
Hating blind Fortune, careless to relieve.
And you sweet Cooke-ham, whom these ladies leave,
I now must tell the grief you did conceive
At their departure, when they went away,
130 How everything retained a sad dismay.
Nay long before, when once an inkling came,
Methought each thing did unto sorrow frame:
The trees that were so glorious in our view,
Forsook both flowers and fruit, when once they knew
135 Of your depart, their very leaves did wither,
Changing their colors as they grew together.
But when they saw this had no power to stay you,
They often wept, though, speechless, could not pray you,
Letting their tears in your fair bosoms fall,
140 As if they said, Why will ye leave us all?
This being vain, they cast their leaves away
Hoping that pity would have made you stay:
Their frozen tops, like age's hoary hairs,
Shows their disasters, languishing in fears.
145 A swarthy riveled rind° all over spread,   bark
Their dying bodies half alive, half dead.
But your occasions[1] called you so away
That nothing there had power to make you stay.
Yet did I see a noble grateful mind
150 Requiting each according to their kind,
Forgetting not to turn and take your leave
Of these sad creatures, powerless to receive
Your favor, when with grief you did depart,
Placing their former pleasures in your heart,
155 Giving great charge to noble memory
There to preserve their love continually.
But specially the love of that fair tree,
That first and last you did vouchsafe to see,
In which it pleased you oft to take the air
160 With noble *Dorset*, then a virgin fair,
Where many a learned book was read and scanned,
To this fair tree, taking me by the hand,
You did repeat the pleasures which had passed,

8. I.e., we (lowly) may also love God and enjoy
God's love, and hence are equal to anyone.
9. As was common, Anne Clifford is here referred
to by her husband's title.

1. After her husband's death (1605) Margaret
Clifford chiefly resided in her dower properties in
the north; Anne Clifford was married in 1609.

Seeming to grieve they could no longer last.
165   And with a chaste, yet loving kiss took leave,
Of which sweet kiss I did it soon bereave,°   *take from it*
Scorning a senseless creature should possess
So rare a favor, so great happiness.
No other kiss it could receive from me,
170   For fear to give back what it took of thee,
So I ungrateful creature did deceive it
Of that which you in love vouchsafed to leave it.
And though it oft had given me much content,
Yet this great wrong I never could repent;
175   But of the happiest made it most forlorn,
To show that nothing's free from Fortune's scorne,
While all the rest with this most beauteous tree
Made their sad comfort sorrow's harmony.
The flowers that on the banks and walks did grow,
180   Crept in the ground, the grass did weep for woe.
The winds and waters seemed to chide together
Because you went away they knew not whither;
And those sweet brooks that ran so fair and clear,
With grief and trouble wrinkled did appear.
185   Those pretty birds that wonted were to sing,
Now neither sing, nor chirp, nor use their wing,
But with their tender feet on some bare spray,
Warble forth sorrow, and their own dismay.
Fair *Philomela* leaves her mournful ditty,
190   Drowned in deep sleep, yet can procure no pity.
Each arbor, bank, each seat, each stately tree
Looks bare and desolate now for want of thee,
Turning green tresses into frosty gray,
While in cold grief they wither all away.
195   The sun grew weak, his beams no comfort gave,
While all green things did make the earth their grave.
Each brier, each bramble, when you went away
Caught fast your clothes, thinking to make you stay;
Delightful Echo wonted° to reply   *was accustomed*
200   To our last words, did now for sorrow die;
The house cast off each garment that might grace it,
Putting on dust and cobwebs to deface it.
All desolation then there did appear,
When you were going whom they held so dear.
205   This last farewell to *Cooke-ham* here I give,
When I am dead thy name in this may live,
Wherein I have performed her noble hest°   *commission*
Whose virtues lodge in my unworthy breast,
And ever shall, so long as life remains,
210   Tying my life to her by those rich chains.[2]

1611

___

2. Her virtues.

BEN JONSON
1572–1637

In 1616 Ben Jonson published his *Works*, earning howls of derision and incredulity from many who were astounded to see mere plays and poems collected under the same title the king gave to his political treatises. Many of Jonson's contemporaries shied away from publication, either because, like Donne, they wrote for small coterie audiences, or because, like Shakespeare, they wrote for theater companies which preferred not to let go of the scripts. Jonson knew and admired both Donne and Shakespeare, and more than any Jacobean belonged to both of their very different worlds, but in publishing his *Works* he broke with them and laid claim to an altogether higher literary status. He had risen from very humble beginnings to become England's unofficial poet laureate, with a pension from the king and honorary degrees from both universities. If he was not the first professional author in England, he was the first to invest that role with dignity and respectability. His published *Works*, over which he labored with painstaking and pedantic care, are designed to testify to an extraordinary feat of self-transformation.

Jonson's early life was tough and turbulent. The posthumous son of a London clergyman, he was educated at Westminster school under the great antiquarian scholar William Camden. There he developed his love of classical learning, but lacking the resources to continue his education, Jonson was forced to turn to his stepfather's trade of bricklaying, a life he "could not endure." He escaped by joining the English forces in Flanders, where, as he later boasted, he killed a man in single combat before the eyes of two armies. Back in London, his attempt to make a living as an actor and playwright almost ended in early disaster. He was imprisoned in 1597 for collaborating with Thomas Nashe on the scandalous play *The Isle of Dogs* (now lost), and shortly after his release he killed one of his fellow actors in a duel. Jonson escaped the gallows by pleading benefit of clergy (a medieval privilege allowing felons who could read Latin to be tried by a more lenient ecclesiastical court). His learning had saved his life, but he emerged from captivity branded on the thumb, and with another mark against him as well. Under the influence of a priest imprisoned with him, he had converted to Catholicism (around the time that John Donne was abandoning that faith). Jonson was now more than ever a marginal figure, distrusted by the society that he satirized brilliantly in his early plays.

Jonson's fortunes improved with the accession of James I, though not at once. In 1603 he was called before the Privy Council to answer charges of "popery and treason" found in his play *Sejanus*. Little more than a year later he was in jail again for his part in the play *Eastward Ho*, which openly mocked the king's Scots accent and propensity for selling knighthoods. But Jonson was now on the way to establishing himself at the new court. In 1605 he received the commission to organize the Twelfth Night entertainment; *The Masque of Blackness* was the first of twenty-four masques he would produce for the court, most of them in collaboration with the architect and scene designer Inigo Jones. In the same years that he was writing the masques he produced his greatest works for the public theater. His first successful play, *Every Man in His Humor* (1598), had inaugurated the so-called "comedy of humors," in which the ruling eccentricities or passions of the characters (thought to be caused by physiological imbalance) are exposed to ridicule. He capitalized on this success with the comedies *Volpone* (1606), *The Alchemist* (1610), and *Bartholomew Fair* (1614). Jonson preserved the detached, satiric perspective of an outsider, but he was rising in society and making accommodations where necessary. In 1605, when suspicion fell upon him as a Catholic following the exposure of the Gunpowder Plot, he showed his loyalty by agreeing to serve as a spy for the Privy Council. Five years later he would return to the Church of England.

Although he rose to a position of eminent respectability, Jonson seems to have been possessed all his life by an uncontrollably quarrelsome spirit. Indeed, much of his best work emerged out of fierce tensions with his collaborators and contemporaries. At the turn of the century he became embroiled in the so-called "War of the Theaters," in which he satirized and was satirized by his fellow playwrights John Marston and Thomas Dekker. Later, his long collaborative partnership with Inigo Jones was marked by ever more bitter rivalry over the relative importance of words and scenery in the making of masques. Jonson also poured scorn and invective on the public theater audiences who failed, in his view, to appreciate the classical unities he brought to his plots. The failure of his play *The New Inn* elicited his *Ode to Himself* (1629), a disgusted farewell to the "loathed stage." Yet even after a stroke in 1629 left him partially paralyzed and confined to his home, Jonson continued to write for the stage, and was at work on a new play when he died in 1637.

In spite of his antagonistic nature, Jonson had a great capacity for friendship. His friends included Shakespeare, Donne, Francis Bacon, and John Selden, and in later years he gathered about himself a group of admiring younger men known as the "Sons of Ben," whose numbers included Herrick, Carew, and Suckling. He was a fascinating and inexhaustible conversationalist, as recorded by his friend William Drummond of Hawthornden, who carefully noted down Jonson's off-the-cuff opinions on a wide variety of subjects, ranging from his fellow poets to his sexual predilections. Jonson also moved easily among the great of the land, though in poems like *Celebration of Charis* he shows himself cutting a ridiculous figure in the fashionable world. His patrons included Lady Mary Wroth and Sir Walter Ralegh and members of the Sidney and Herbert families. In *To Penshurst*, a celebration of Robert Sidney's country estate, Jonson offers an ideal image of a social order in which a virtuous patriarchal governor offers ready hospitality to guests of all stations, from poets to kings.

To Penshurst, together with Aemilia Lanyer's *Description of Cooke-ham*, inaugurated the small genre of the "country-house poem" in England. Jonson tried his hand, usually with success, at a wide range of poetic genres, including epitaph and epigram, love and funeral elegy, verse satire and verse letter, song and ode. More often than not he looked back to classical precedents. From the Roman poets Horace and Martial he derived not only generic models but an ideal vision of the artist and society against which he measured himself and the court he served. In many poems he adopted the persona of "bluff Ben," a witty, keenly perceptive, and scrupulously honest judge of men and women. The classical values Jonson most admired are enumerated in his longest epigram, *Inviting a Friend to Supper*, which describes a dinner party characterized by moderation, civility, graciousness, and pleasure that delights without enslaving—all contrasting sharply with the excess and licentiousness that marked the banquets and entertainments of imperial Rome and Stuart England. Yet the poet who produced this image of perfect moderation was notorious in his life as a drinker and a glutton with, as he puts it in *My Picture Left in Scotland*, a "mountain belly." Jonson was a man of immense appetites, which found expression in his art as well as in his life. His best works seethe with an almost uncontrollable imaginative energy and lust for abundance. Even his profound classical learning manifests this impulse. The notes and references to learned authorities which spill across the margins of his *Works* can be seen as the literary equivalent of food and drink piled high on the poet's table. Years of hardship had taught Jonson to seek his feasts in his imagination, and he could make the most mundane object the basis for flights of high fancy. As he told Drummond, he once "consumed a whole night in lying looking to his great toe, about which he had seen Tartars and Turks, Romans and Carthaginians fight in his imagination." In Drummond's view, Jonson was "oppressed with fantasy." Perhaps it was so—but Jonson's capacity for fantasy also produced a wide variety of plays, masques, and poems, in styles ranging from witty comedy to delicate lyricism.

FROM EPIGRAMS[1]

To My Book

It will be looked for, book, when some but see
    Thy title, *Epigrams,* and named of me,
Thou should'st be bold, licentious, full of gall,
    Wormwood° and sulphur, sharp and toothed[2] withal,   *bitter-tasting plant*
5 Become a petulant thing, hurl ink and wit
    As madmen stones, not caring whom they hit.
Deceive their malice who could wish it so,
    And by thy wiser temper let men know
Thou art not covetous of least self-fame
10 Made from the hazard of another's shame[3]—
Much less with lewd, profane, and beastly phrase
    To catch the world's loose laughter or vain gaze.
He that departs° with his own honesty   *parts*
    For vulgar praise, doth it too dearly buy.

1616

On My First Daughter[1]

Here lies, to each her parents' ruth,°   *grief*
    Mary, the daughter of their youth;
Yet all heaven's gifts being heaven's due,
    It makes the father less to rue.
5 At six months' end she parted hence
    With safety of her innocence;
Whose soul heaven's queen, whose name she bears,
    In comfort of her mother's tears,
Hath placed amongst her virgin-train:
10 Where, while that severed doth remain,
This grave partakes the fleshly birth;°   *the body*
    Which cover lightly, gentle earth![2]

1616

---

1. Epigrams are commonly thought of as brief, witty, incisive poems of personal invective, often with a surprise turn at the end. But when Jonson included in his collected *Works* of 1616 a separate section headed "Epigrams (Book 1)," he was using the word in a more liberal sense. His "epigrams" included (besides some sharp and satiric verses) several poems of compliment and courtesy, some memorial epitaphs, and a verse letter, *Inviting a Friend to Supper. To My Book* and the next several poems come from this section. The "Book 1" of Jonson's title implied a "Book 2"; there are a number of epigramlike verses scattered through his later poetry, but Jonson never assembled them under any such title.
2. The distinction between toothed (biting) and toothless (general) satires—originally made by Joseph Hall (1574–1656), who claimed to be the first English satirist—was a commonplace.
3. Here, as often elsewhere, Jonson echoes the greatest Roman epigrammatist, Martial.
1. Probably written in the late 1590s, in Jonson's Roman Catholic period (ca. 1598–1610).
2. A common sentiment in Latin epitaphs.

To John Donne

Donne, the delight of Phoebus° and each Muse,   *god of poetry*
Who, to thy one, all other brains refuse;[1]
Whose every work, of thy most early wit,
Came forth example and remains so yet;
5   Longer a-knowing than most wits do live,
And which no affection praise enough can give.
To it[2] thy language, letters, arts, best life,
Which might with half mankind maintain a strife.
All which I meant to praise, and yet I would,
10   But leave, because I cannot as I should.

                               1616

On Giles and Joan

Who says that Giles and Joan at discord be?
   Th' observing neighbors no such mood can see.
Indeed, poor Giles repents he married ever,
   But that his Joan doth too. And Giles would never
5   By his free will be in Joan's company;
   No more would Joan he should. Giles riseth early,
And having got him out of doors is glad;
   The like is Joan. But turning home is sad,
And so is Joan. Ofttimes, when Giles doth find
10   Harsh sights at home, Giles wisheth he were blind:
All this doth Joan. Or that his long-yearned[1] life
   Were quite outspun. The like wish hath his wife.
The children that he keeps Giles swears are none
   Of his begetting; and so swears his Joan.
15   In all affections she concurreth still.
   If now, with man and wife, to will and nill°   *not will*
The self-same things a note of concord be,
   I know no couple better can agree.

                               1616

On My First Son

Farewell, thou child of my right hand,[1] and joy;
My sin was too much hope of thee, loved boy:
Seven years thou wert lent to me, and I thee pay,
Exacted by thy fate, on the just day.
5   O could I lose all father now! For why
Will man lament the state he should envy,

---

1. I.e., the muses shower their favors exclusively on you.
2. In addition to your wit.
1. Spun from long skeins of yarn.

1. A literal translation of the Hebrew name "Benjamin," which implies the meaning "dexterous" or "fortunate." The boy was born in 1596 and died on his birthday in 1603.

To have so soon 'scaped world's and flesh's rage,
And, if no other misery, yet age?
Rest in soft peace, and asked, say, "Here doth lie
10   Ben Jonson his best piece of poetry."[2]
For whose sake henceforth all his vows be such
As what he loves may never like too much.[3]

1616

To Lucy, Countess of Bedford, with Mr. Donne's Satires[1]

Lucy, you brightness[2] of our sphere, who are
Life of the Muses' day, their morning star!
If works, not th' authors, their own grace should look,°   *have regard to*
Whose poems would not wish to be your book?
5   But these, desired by you, the maker's ends
Crown with their own. Rare poems ask rare friends.
Yet satires, since the most of mankind be
Their unavoided° subject, fewest see: *inevitable*
For none e'er took that pleasure in sin's sense,
10   But, when they heard it taxed, took more offense.
They then that, living where the matter is bred,[3]
Dare for these poems yet both ask and read
And like them too, must needfully, though few,
Be of the best: and 'mongst those, best are you;
15   Lucy, you brightness of our sphere, who are
The Muses' evening, as their morning star.[4]

1616

Inviting a Friend to Supper

Tonight, grave sir, both my poor house and I
Do equally desire your company:
Not that we think us worthy such a guest,
But that your worth will dignify our feast
5   With those that come; whose grace may make that seem
Something, which else could hope for no esteem.
It is the fair acceptance, Sir, creates
The entertainment perfect: not the cates.°   *food*
Yet shall you have, to rectify your palate,
10   An olive, capers, or some better salad
Ushering the mutton; with a short-legged hen,

2. Poet and father are both makers, Jonson's favorite term for the poet.
3. The obscure grammar of the last lines allows for various readings; "like" may carry the sense of "please."
1. With this poem, Jonson offered a manuscript collection of Donne's satires (see p. 618), such as commonly passed from hand to hand in court circles.
2. Lucy's name derives from the Latin *lux*, meaning light.
3. I.e., at court.
4. The planet Venus is called Lucifer (light-bearing) when it appears before sunrise, Hesperus when it appears after sunset.

If we can get her, full of eggs, and then
Lemons and wine for sauce; to these, a coney°   rabbit
Is not to be despaired of for our money;
15   And though fowl now be scarce, yet there are clerks,°   scholars
The sky not falling, think we may have larks.
I'll tell you of more, and lie, so you will come:
Of partridge, pheasant, woodcock, of which some
May yet be there; and godwit if we can,
20   Knot, rail, and ruff, too.[1] Howsoe'er, my man°   servant
Shall read a piece of Virgil, Tacitus,
Livy, or of some better book to us,
Of which we'll speak our minds amidst our meat;
And I'll profess° no verses to repeat: promise
25   To this,° if aught appear which I not know of,   add to this
That will the pastry, not my paper, show of.[2]
Digestive cheese and fruit there sure will be;
But that which most doth take my muse and me
Is a pure cup of rich Canary wine,
30   Which is the Mermaid's now, but shall be mine;
Of which, had Horace or Anacreon[3] tasted,
Their lives, as do their lines, till now had lasted.
Tobacco, Nectar, or the Thespian spring[4]
Are all but Luther's beer to this I sing.
35   Of this we will sup free but moderately,
And we will have no Pooly or Parrot[5] by;
Nor shall our cups make any guilty men,
But at our parting we will be as when
We innocently met. No simple word
40   That shall be uttered at our mirthful board
Shall make us sad next morning, or affright
The liberty that we'll enjoy tonight.

                                                            1616

Epitaph on S. P., a Child of Queen Elizabeth's Chapel[1]

Weep with me, all you that read
This little story;
And know for whom a tear you shed,
Death's self is sorry.
5   'Twas a child that so did thrive
In grace and feature,
As Heaven and Nature seemed to strive
Which owned the creature.
Years he numbered scarce thirteen

1. All these are edible birds.
2. I.e., papers may appear, but they will be under pies (to keep them from sticking to the pan), not for declamation.
3. Horace and Anacreon (one in Latin, the other in Greek) wrote many poems in praise of wine. The Mermaid tavern was a favorite haunt of the poets; sweet wine from the Canary Islands was popular in England.
4. One of two springs on Mount Helicon, both reputed to be sources of poetic inspiration. Com-

pared to Canary, all these other intoxicants are no better than inferior German beer.
5. Pooly and Parrot were government spies, though their conjunction also suggests a talkative bird, Poll Parrot. While a Roman Catholic and even after, Jonson had reason to be wary of undercover agents.
1. Salomon Pavy, a boy actor in the troupe known as the Children of Queen Elizabeth's Chapel, who had appeared in several of Jonson's plays; he died in 1602.

10   When Fates turned cruel,
     Yet three filled zodiacs had he been
       The stage's jewel;[2]
     And did act (what now we moan)
       Old men so duly,°   *aptly*
15   As, sooth, the Parcae° thought him one,   *Fates*
       He played so truly.
     So, by error, to his fate
       They all consented;
     But, viewing him since (alas, too late),
20   They have repented,
     And have sought (to give new birth)
       In baths[3] to steep him;
     But, being so much too good for earth,
       Heaven vows to keep him.

                                1616

FROM THE FOREST[1]

To Penshurst[2]

Thou art not, Penshurst, built to envious show,
   Of touch[3] or marble; nor canst boast a row
Of polished pillars, or a roof of gold;
   Thou hast no lantern° whereof tales are told,   *cupola*
5 Or stair, or courts; but stand'st an ancient pile,
   And, these grudged at,[4] art reverenced the while.
Thou joy'st in better marks, of soil, of air,
   Of wood, of water; therein thou art fair.
Thou hast thy walks for health, as well as sport;
10   Thy mount, to which the dryads° do resort,   *wood nymphs*
Where Pan and Bacchus their high feasts have made,
   Beneath the broad beech and the chestnut shade;
That taller tree, which of a nut was set
   At his great birth where all the Muses met.[5]
15 There in the writhèd bark are cut the names
   Of many a sylvan,° taken with his flames;   *countryman*
And thence the ruddy satyrs[6] oft provoke
   The lighter fauns to reach thy Lady's Oak.[7]
Thy copse° too, named of Gamage,[8] thou hast there,   *little woods*

---

2. He had been on the stage for three seasons.
3. Perhaps such magic baths as that of Medea, which restored Jason's father to his first youth (Ovid, *Metamorphoses* 7).
1. In the 1616 *Works*, Jonson grouped some of his nonepigrammatic poems under the heading *The Forest*, a translation of the term *Sylvae*, meaning a poetic miscellany. *To Penshurst* and the two following poems are from that group.
2. Penshurst, in Kent, was the estate of Robert Sidney, Viscount Lisle (later, earl of Leicester), a younger brother of the poet Sir Philip Sidney (see p. 444). Along with Lanyer's *The Description of Cooke-ham* (p. 632), this poem inaugurated the small genre of English "country-house" poems.
3. Touchstone, a fine black (and expensive) variety of basalt.
4. More pretentious houses attract envy.
5. Sir Philip Sidney was born at Penshurst.
6. Satyrs and fauns were woodland spirits. Satyrs, with the body of a man and the legs (and horns) of a goat, were symbols of lechery. "Provokes": challenges to a race.
7. Named after a lady of the house who went into labor under its branches.
8. Lady Barbara (Gamage) Sidney, wife of Sir Robert.

20   That never fails to serve thee seasoned deer
        When thou wouldst feast or exercise thy friends.
          The lower land, that to the river bends,
        Thy sheep, thy bullocks, kine,° and calves do feed;   *cattle*
          The middle grounds thy mares and horses breed.
25   Each bank doth yield thee conies;° and the tops,°   *rabbits/high ground*
          Fertile of wood, Ashore and Sidney's copse,
        To crown thy open table, doth provide
          The purpled pheasant with the speckled side;
        The painted partridge lies in every field,
30   And for thy mess is willing to be killed.
        And if the high-swollen Medway[9] fail thy dish,
          Thou hast thy ponds, that pay thee tribute fish:
        Fat agèd carps that run into thy net,
          And pikes, now weary their own kind to eat,
35   As loath the second draught or cast to stay,
          Officiously° at first themselves betray;   *dutifully*
        Bright eels that emulate them, and leap on land
          Before the fisher, or into his hand.
        Then hath thy orchard fruit, thy garden flowers,
40   Fresh as the air, and new as are the hours.
        The early cherry, with the later plum,
          Fig, grape, and quince, each in his time doth come;
        The blushing apricot and woolly peach
          Hang on thy walls, that every child may reach.
45   And though thy walls be of the country stone,
          They're reared with no man's ruin, no man's groan;
        There's none that dwell about them wish them down;
          But all come in, the farmer and the clown,°   *peasant*
        And no one empty-handed, to salute
50   Thy lord and lady, though they have no suit.°   *request to make*
        Some bring a capon, some a rural cake,
          Some nuts, some apples; some that think they make
         The better cheeses bring them, or else send
          By their ripe daughters, whom they would commend
55   This way to husbands, and whose baskets bear
          An emblem of themselves in plum or pear.
        But what can this (more than express their love)
          Add to thy free provisions, far above
         The need of such? whose liberal board doth flow
60   With all that hospitality doth know;
        Where comes no guest but is allowed to eat,
          Without his fear, and of thy lord's own meat;
         Where the same beer and bread, and selfsame wine,
          That is his lordship's shall be also mine,
65   And I not fain to sit (as some this day
          At great men's tables), and yet dine away.[1]
        Here no man tells° my cups; nor, standing by,   *counts*
          A waiter doth my gluttony envy,

9. The local river.
1. Different courses might be served to different   guests, depending on their social status. The lord
     would have the best food.

But gives me what I call, and lets me eat;
70   He knows below° he shall find plenty of meat.   *in the servants' quarters*
Thy tables hoard not up for the next day;
    Nor, when I take my lodging, need I pray
For fire, or lights, or livery; all is there,
    As if thou then wert mine, or I reigned here:
75 There's nothing I can wish, for which I stay.°   *wait*
    That found King James when, hunting late this way
With his brave son, the Prince,[2] they saw thy fires
    Shine bright on every hearth, as the desires
Of thy Penates° had been set on flame   *Roman household gods*
80   To entertain them; or the country came
With all their zeal to warm their welcome here.
    What (great I will not say, but) sudden cheer
Didst thou then make 'em! and what praise was heaped
    On thy good lady then, who therein reaped
85 The just reward of her high housewifery;
    To have her linen, plate, and all things nigh,
When she was far; and not a room but dressed
    As if it had expected such a guest!
These, Penshurst, are thy praise, and yet not all.
90   Thy lady's noble, fruitful, chaste withal.
His children thy great lord may call his own,
    A fortune in this age but rarely known.
They are, and have been, taught religion; thence
    Their gentler spirits have sucked innocence.
95 Each morn and even they are taught to pray,
    With the whole household, and may, every day,
Read in their virtuous parents' noble parts
    The mysteries of manners, arms, and arts.
Now, Penshurst, they that will proportion° thee   *compare*
100   With other edifices, when they see
Those proud, ambitious heaps, and nothing else,
    May say, their lords have built, but thy lord dwells.

1616

Song: To Celia[1]

    Drink to me only with thine eyes,
        And I will pledge with mine;
    Or leave a kiss but in the cup,
        And I'll not look for wine.
5   The thirst that from the soul doth rise
        Doth ask a drink divine:
    But might I of Jove's nectar sup,
        I would not change for thine.

2. Prince Henry, the heir apparent, who died in November 1612.
1. These famous lines are a patchwork of five separate prose passages by Philostratus, a Greek sophist (3rd century C.E.). The music that has made it a barroom favorite is by an anonymous 18th-century composer.

I sent thee late a rosy wreath,
10   Not so much honoring thee,
As giving it a hope that there
    It could not withered be.
But thou thereon didst only breathe,
    And sent'st it back to me;
15 Since when it grows and smells, I swear,
    Not of itself, but thee.

1616

To Heaven

Good and great God, can I not think of thee
    But it must straight my melancholy be?
Is it interpreted in me disease
    That, laden with my sins, I seek for ease?
5 Oh, be thou witness, that the reins[1] dost know
    And hearts of all, if I be sad for show,
And judge me after, if I dare pretend
    To aught but grace, or aim at other end.
As thou art all, so be thou all to me,
10 First, midst, and last, converted° one and three,   *interchanging*
My faith, my hope, my love; and in this state,
    My judge, my witness, and my advocate.
Where have I been this while exiled from thee,
    And whither rapt,° now thou but stoop'st to me?   *carried off*
15 Dwell, dwell here still: Oh, being everywhere,
    How can I doubt to find thee ever here?
I know my state, both full of shame and scorn,
    Conceived in sin and unto labor born,
Standing with fear, and must with horror fall,
20 And destined unto judgment after all.
I feel my griefs too, and there scarce is ground
    Upon my flesh to inflict another wound.
Yet dare I not complain or wish for death
    With holy Paul,[2] lest it be thought the breath
25 Of discontent; or that these prayers be
    For weariness of life, not love of thee.

1616

My Picture Left in Scotland[1]

I now think Love is rather deaf than blind,
    For else it could not be

---

1. Literally, kidneys, but also the seat of the affections, with a glance at Psalm 7.9: "the righteous God trieth the hearts and reins."
2. "Who shall deliver me from the body of this death?" (Roman 7.24).

1. After his walking tour of Scotland in 1618–19, Jonson sent a manuscript version of this poem to William Drummond, with whom he had stayed. The woman of the poem may or may not be a real person.

              That she
      Whom I adore so much should so slight me
5   And cast my love behind;
      I'm sure my language to her was as sweet,
                  And every close° did meet   *cadence*
              In sentence° of as subtle feet,   *wise sayings*
                  As hath the youngest he
10   That sits in shadow of Apollo's tree.[2]

      O, but my conscious fears
              That fly my thoughts between,
              Tell me that she hath seen
              My hundreds of gray hairs,
15   Told seven and forty years,
      Read so much waist[3] as she cannot embrace
      My mountain belly and my rocky face;
      And all these through her eyes have stopped her ears.

1619   1640–41

              Queen and Huntress[1]

          Queen and huntress, chaste and fair,
          Now the sun is laid to sleep,
          Seated in thy silver chair,
          State in wonted manner keep;
5   Hesperus entreats thy light,
          Goddess excellently bright.

          Earth, let not thy envious shade
          Dare itself to interpose;[2]
          Cynthia's shining orb was made
10   Heaven to clear, when day did close.
          Bless us then with wishèd sight,
          Goddess excellently bright.

          Lay thy bow of pearl apart,
          And thy crystal-shining quiver;
15   Give unto the flying hart
          Space to breathe, how short soever.
          Thou that mak'st a day of night,
          Goddess excellently bright.

                                              1600

---

2. The god of poetry.
3. With a pun on waste.
1. Also from *Cynthia's Revels* (4.3), this song is sung by Hesperus, the evening star, to Cynthia or

Diana, goddess of chastity and the moon—with whom Queen Elizabeth was constantly compared.
2. Eclipses were thought to portend evil.

Though I Am Young[1]

Though I am young and cannot tell
    Either what Death or Love is well,
Yet I have heard they both bear darts,
    And both do aim at human hearts.
5   And then again, I have been told
    Love wounds with heat, as Death with cold;
So that I fear they do but bring
    Extremes to touch, and mean one thing.

As in a ruin we it call
10   One thing to be blown up or fall;
Or to our end like way may have
    By a flash of lightning or a wave;
So Love's inflamèd shaft or brand
    May kill as soon as Death's cold hand;
15   Except[2] Love's fires the virtue have
    To fright the frost out of the grave.

1640–41

Still to Be Neat[1]

Still to be neat, still to be dressed
As° you were going to a feast,   *as though*
Still to be powdered, still perfumed;
Lady, it is to be presumed,
5   Though art's hid causes are not found,
All is not sweet, all is not sound.

Give me a look, give me a face
That makes simplicity a grace;
Robes loosely flowing, hair as free—
10   Such sweet neglect more taketh me
Than all the adulteries of art.
They strike mine eyes, but not my heart.

1609

To the Memory of My Beloved, The Author, Mr. William Shakespeare, and What He Hath Left Us[1]

To draw no envy, Shakespeare, on thy name,
    Am I thus ample° to thy book and fame,   *copious*

---

1. This song is sung in *The Sad Shepherd*, by Karolin; the pastoral simplicity of his character is caught in the naive monosyllables of the poem.
2. Unless.

1. Sung in the play *Epicoene*, this song concerns the art of makeup, but also art more generally.
1. This poem was prefixed to the first Folio of Shakespeare's plays (1623).

While I confess thy writings to be such
    As neither man nor muse can praise too much.
5 'Tis true, and all men's suffrage.° But these ways   *consent*
    Were not the paths I meant unto thy praise;
For silliest° ignorance on these may light,   *simplest*
    Which, when it sounds at best, but echoes right;
Or blind affection, which doth ne'er advance
10   The truth, but gropes, and urgeth all by chance;
Or crafty malice might pretend this praise,
    And think to ruin where it seemed to raise.
These are as° some infamous bawd or whore   *as though*
    Should praise a matron. What could hurt her more?
15 But thou art proof against them, and, indeed,
    Above th' ill fortune of them, or the need.
I therefore will begin. Soul of the age!
    The applause! delight! the wonder of our stage!
My Shakespeare, rise; I will not lodge thee by
20   Chaucer or Spenser, or bid Beaumont lie
A little further to make thee a room:[2]
    Thou art a monument without a tomb,
And art alive still while thy book doth live,
    And we have wits to read and praise to give.
25 That I not mix thee so, my brain excuses,
    I mean with great, but disproportioned° Muses;   *not comparable*
For, if I thought my judgment were of years,
    I should commit thee surely with thy peers,
And tell how far thou didst our Lyly outshine,
30   Or sporting Kyd, or Marlowe's mighty line.[3]
And though thou hadst small Latin and less Greek,[4]
    From thence to honor thee I would not seek°   *lack*
For names, but call forth thund'ring Aeschylus,
    Euripides, and Sophocles to us,
35 Pacuvius, Accius, him of Cordova dead,[5]
    To life again, to hear thy buskin° tread   *symbol of tragedy*
And shake a stage; or, when thy socks° were on,   *symbol of comedy*
    Leave thee alone for the comparison
Of all that insolent Greece or haughty Rome
40   Sent forth, or since did from their ashes come.
Triumph, my Britain; thou hast one to show
    To whom all scenes° of Europe homage owe.   *stages*
He was not of an age, but for all time!
    And all the Muses still were in their prime
45 When like Apollo he came forth to warm
    Our ears, or like a Mercury to charm.
Nature herself was proud of his designs,

---

2. Chaucer, Spenser, and Francis Beaumont were buried in Westminster Abbey; Shakespeare, in Stratford.
3. John Lily, Thomas Kyd, and Christopher Marlowe were Elizabethan dramatists contemporary or nearly contemporary with Shakespeare.
4. Shakespeare's Latin was pretty good, but Jonson is judging by the standard of his own remarkable scholarship.
5. Marcus Pacuvius, Lucius Accius (2nd century B.C.E.) and "him of Cordova," Seneca the Younger (Ist century C.E.), were Latin tragedians. Seneca's tragedies had a large influence on Elizabethan revenge tragedy.

And joyed to wear the dressing of his lines,
Which were so richly spun, and woven so fit,
50 As, since, she will vouchsafe no other wit:
The merry Greek, tart Aristophanes,
Neat Terence, witty Plautus[6] now not please,
But antiquated and deserted lie,
As they were not of Nature's family.
55 Yet must I not give Nature all; thy Art,
My gentle Shakespeare, must enjoy a part.
For though the poet's matter° Nature be,   subject matter
His Art doth give the fashion;° and that he   form, style
Who casts° to write a living line must sweat   undertakes
60 (Such as thine are) and strike the second heat
Upon the Muses' anvil; turn the same,
And himself with it, that he thinks to frame,
Or for the laurel he may gain a scorn;
For a good poet's made as well as born.
65 And such wert thou! Look how the father's face
Lives in his issue; even so the race
Of Shakespeare's mind and manners brightly shines
In his well-turnèd and true-filèd lines,
In each of which he seems to shake a lance,[7]
70 As brandished at the eyes of ignorance.
Sweet swan of Avon, what a sight it were
To see thee in our waters yet appear,
And make those flights upon the banks of Thames
That so did take Eliza and our James![8]
75 But stay; I see thee in the hemisphere
Advanced and made a constellation there![9]
Shine forth, thou star of poets, and with rage
Or influence[1] chide or cheer the drooping stage,
Which, since thy flight from hence, hath mourned like night,
80 And despairs day, but for thy volume's light.

1623

6. Aristophanes, an ancient Greek satirist and writer of comedy; Terence and Plautus (2nd and 3rd centuries B.C.E.), Roman writers of comedy.
7. Pun on Shake-speare.
8. Queen Elizabeth and King James.

9. Heroes and demigods were typically exalted after death to a place among the stars.
1. "Rage" and "influence" describe the supposed effects of the planets on earthly affairs. "Rage" also implies poetic inspiration.

MARY WROTH
1587–1651?

Lady Mary Wroth was the most prolific, self-conscious, and impressive female author of the Jacobean era. Her published work (1621) include two firsts for an English-woman: a 558-page romance, *The Countess of Montgomery's Urania*, which includes more than fifty poems; and appended to it a Petrarchan lyric sequence that had circulated some years in manuscript, 103 sonnets and elegant songs titled *Pamphilia to Amphilanthus*. Wroth left unpublished a very long but unfinished continuation of the *Urania* and a pastoral drama, *Love's Victory*, also a first for an Englishwoman. Her achievement was fostered by her strong sense of identity as a Sidney, heir to the literary talent and cultural role of her famous uncle Sir Philip Sidney, her famous aunt Mary Sidney Herbert, countess of Pembroke, who may have served as mentor to her, and her father Robert Sidney, Viscount Lisle, author of a recently discovered sonnet sequence. But she used that heritage transgressively to replace heroes with heroines in genres employed by the male Sidney authors—notably Philip Sidney's *Astrophil and Stella* and *The Countess of Pembroke's Arcadia*—transforming their gender politics and exploring the poetics and situation of women writers.

As Robert Sidney's eldest daughter, she lived and was educated at Penshurst, the Sidney country house celebrated by Ben Jonson, and was often at her aunt's "little college" at Wilton. She danced at court in *The Masque of Blackness* and perhaps in other masques; she was married (incompatibly) at age seventeen to Sir Robert Wroth of Durrance and Loughton Manor, whose office it was to facilitate the king's hunting; and she was patron to several poets, including Jonson. He celebrated her in two epigrams and in a verse letter honoring her husband, dedicated his great comedy *The Alchemist* to her, and claimed in his only sonnet (p. 1408) that the artistry and erotic power of her sonnets had made him "a better lover, and much better poet." After her husband's death she carried on a long-standing love affair with her married first cousin, William Herbert, earl of Pembroke, himself a poet, a powerful courtier, and a patron of the theater and of literature. That relationship produced two children and occasioned some scandal.

The significant names in the title of Wroth's Petrarchan sequence, *Pamphilia* ("all-loving") *to Amphilanthus* ("lover of two"), are from characters in her romance who at times shadow Wroth and her lover Pembroke. Though it was passé by Wroth's time, the Petrarchan lyric sequence had long served as the major genre for analyzing a male lover's desire, passions, frustrations, and fantasies (and sometimes his career anxieties), so it was the obvious beginning point for a woman poet undertaking the construction of subjectivity in a female lover-speaker. Wroth does not, however, simply reverse roles: Pamphilia addresses very few sonnets to Amphilanthus and seldom assumes the Petrarchan lover's position of abject servitude to a cruel beloved; instead, she proclaims subjection to Cupid, usually identified with the force of her own desire. This radical revision identifies female desire as the source and center of the love relationship and celebrates the woman lover-poet's movement from the bondage of chaotic passion to the freedom of self-chosen constancy.

Wroth's romance, *Urania*, breaks the romance convention of a plot centered on courtship, portraying instead married heroines and their love relationships, both inside and outside of marriage. It is in part an idealizing fantasy in which all the principal characters are queens, kings, and emperors, with the power and comparative freedom such positions allow. However the landscape is not Arcadia or Fairyland but war-torn Europe and Asia, and the romance fantasy, with Spenserian symbolic places and knights fighting evil tyrants and monsters, only partially overlays a rigidly patriarchal Jacobean world rife with rape, incest, arranged or forced marriages, jealous husbands, tortured women, and endangered children. Those conditions, affecting all women from shepherdesses to queens, are rendered in large part through the numerous stories interpolated in romance fashion within the principal plots. The male heroes are courageous fighters and attractive lovers, but all are flawed by inconstancy. The higher heroism involves attainment or preservation of personal integrity and agency in love amid intense social and psychological pressures and constraints, and it belongs to a few women, chief among them Pamphilia, the good queen and heroine of constancy; Urania, the wise counselor who wins through to self-knowledge and makes wise choices in love; and Veralinda, who marries her true lover after great trials. A major means of self-definition and agency for almost all Wroth's female characters is storytelling and making poems. Women compose twice as many of the poems as men do, and Pamphilia (Wroth's surrogate) is singled out as a poet by vocation by the number and recognized excellence of her poems.

The *Urania* was widely assumed by contemporaries to be a *roman á clef*, alluding not only to Sidney-Pembroke-Wroth affairs but also at times to notable scandals and personages of the Jacobean court. A public outcry from one such target, Lord Edward Denny, elicited from Wroth a spirited and satiric response; she also made an offer to the king's minister Buckingham to withdraw the work from circulation. There is, however, no evidence that she actually did so, though the uproar may have discouraged her from publishing part II of the romance and her pastoral drama.

From The Countess of Montgomery's Urania[1]

From *The First Book*

When the spring began to appear like the welcome messenger of summer, one sweet (and in that more sweet) morning, after Aurora[2] had called all careful eyes to attend the day, forth came the fair shepherdess Urania[3] (fair indeed; yet that far too mean a title for her, who for beauty deserved the highest style[4] could be given by best-knowing judgments). Into the mead[5] she came, where usually she drove her flocks to feed, whose leaping and wantonness showed they were proud of such a guide: but she, whose sad thoughts led her to another manner of spending her time, made her soon leave them, and follow her late-begun custom; which was (while they delighted themselves) to sit under some shade, bewailing her misfortune; while they fed, to feed upon her own sorrow and tears, which at this time she began again to summon, sitting down under the shade of a well-spread beech; the ground (then blest) and the tree, with full and fine-leaved branches, growing proud to bear and shadow such perfections. But she regarding nothing, in comparison of her woe, thus proceeded in her grief: "Alas Urania," said she (the true servant to misfortune), "of any misery that can befall woman, is not this the most and greatest which thou art fallen into? Can there be any near the unhappiness of being ignorant, and that in the highest kind, not being certain of mine own estate or birth? Why was I not still continued in the belief I was, as I appear, a shepherdess, and daughter to a shepherd? My ambition then went no higher than this estate, now flies it to a knowledge; then was I contented, now perplexed. O ignorance, can thy dullness yet procure so sharp a pain? and that such a thought as makes me now aspire unto knowledge? How did I joy in this poor life, being quiet? blest in the love of those I took for parents, but now by them I know the contrary, and by that knowledge, now to know myself. Miserable Urania,

1. Wroth's title echoes *The Countess of Pembroke's Arcadia*, the romance written by her uncle, Sir Philip Sidney. The countess of Montgomery was Susan (Vere) Herbert, Wroth's close friend and the sister-in-law of her lover, William Herbert. The opening of *Urania* is meant to be compared to (and contrasted with) the opening of the *Arcadia*, in which two shepherds lament the absence of their beloved, the mysterious shepherdess Urania.
2. The Greek goddess of the dawn.
3. The name has multiple associations: the Muse of Astronomy, the Muse of Christian Poetry, a sur-

name for Aphrodite (Venus) designating Heavenly Beauty. It was also an honorific commonly bestowed on Wroth's aunt, Mary Sidney, countess of Pembroke. In Wroth's romance, Urania is a foundling adopted by shepherds but actually the daughter of the king of Naples: after losing one lover and gaining another, she marries, becomes a matriarch, and is throughout (as in this episode) a counselor of others.
4. Title.
5. Meadow.

worse art thou now than these thy lambs; for they know their dams, while thou dost live unknown of any." By this were others come into that mead with their flocks: but she, esteeming her sorrowing thoughts her best and choicest company, left that place, taking a little path which brought her to the further side of the plain, to the foot of the rocks, speaking as she went these lines, her eyes fixed upon the ground, her very soul turned into mourning.

> Unseen, unknown, I here alone complain
>   To rocks, to hills, to meadows, and to springs,
> Which can no help return to ease my pain,
>   But back my sorrows the sad Echo[6] brings.
> 5 Thus still increasing are my woes to me,
>   Doubly resounded by that moanful voice,
> Which seems to second me in misery,
>   And answer gives like friend of mine own choice.
> Thus only she doth my companion prove,
> 10   The others silently do offer ease.
> But those that grieve, a grieving note do love;
>   Pleasures to dying eyes bring but disease:
> And such am I, who daily ending live,
> Wailing a state which can no comfort give.

In this passion she went on, till she came to the foot of a great rock, she thinking of nothing less than ease, sought how she might ascend it; hoping there to pass away her time more peaceably with loneliness, though not to find least respite from her sorrow, which so dearly she did value, as by no means she would impart it to any. The way was hard, though by some windings making the ascent pleasing. Having attained the top, she saw under some hollow trees the entry into the rock: she fearing nothing but the continuance of her ignorance, went in; where she found a pretty room, as if that stony place had yet in pity, given leave for such perfections to come into the heart as chiefest, and most beloved place, because most loving. The place was not unlike the ancient (or the descriptions of ancient) Hermitages, instead of hangings, covered and lined with ivy, disdaining aught else should come there, that being in such perfection. This richness in Nature's plenty made her stay to behold it, and almost grudge the pleasant fulness of content that place might have, if sensible, while she must know to taste of torments. As she was thus in passion mixed with pain, throwing her eyes as wildly as timorous lovers do for fear of discovery, she perceived a little light, and such a one, as a chink doth oft discover to our sights. She curious to see what this was, with her delicate hands put the natural ornament aside, discerning a little door, which she putting from her, passed through it into another room, like the first in all proportion; but in the midst there was a square stone, like to a pretty table, and on it a wax-candle burning; and by that a paper,[7] which had suffered itself patiently to receive the discovering of

---

6. In classical mythology Echo was a wood nymph who pined away in unrequited love for the handsome Narcissus until only her voice remained (Ovid, *Metamorphoses* 3).
7. The episode alludes to an episode in Sidney's

Old Arcadia (181) in which one of the heroines, Cleophila, enters a darkened cave illuminated by a single candle and finds a poem on top of a stone table.

so much of it, as presented this sonnet (as it seemed newly written) to her sight.

> Here all alone in silence might I mourn:
>> But how can silence be where sorrows flow?
> Sighs with complaints have poorer pains out-worne;
>> But broken hearts can only true grief show.
> 5 Drops of my dearest blood shall let Love know
>> Such tears for her I shed, yet still do burn,
> As no spring can quench least part of my woe,
>> Till this live earth, again to earth doe turne.
> Hateful all thought of comfort is to me,
> 10 Despised day, let me still night possess;
> Let me all torments feel in their excesse,
>> And but this light allow my state to see.
> Which still doth waste, and wasting as this light,
> Are my sad days unto eternal night.

"Alas Urania!" sighed she. "How well do these words, this place, and all agree with thy fortune? Sure poor soul thou wert here appointed to spend they days, and these rooms ordained to keep thy tortures in; none being assuredly so matchlessly unfortunate."

Turning from the table, she discerned in the room a bed of boughs, and on it a man lying, deprived of outward sense, as she thought, and of life, as she at first did fear, which struck her into a great amazement: yet having a brave spirit, though shadowed under a mean habit,[8] she stepped unto him, whom she found not dead, but laid upon his back, his head a little to her wards, his arms folded on his breast, hair long, and beard disordered, manifesting all care;[9] but care itself had left him: curiousness thus far afforded him, as to be perfectly discerned the most exact piece of misery; apparel he had suitable to the habitation, which was a long gray[1] robe. This grieveful spectacle did much amaze the sweet and tender-hearted Shepherdess; especially, when she perceived (as she might by the help of the candle) the tears which distilled from his eyes; who seeming the image of death, yet had this sign of worldly sorrow, the drops falling in that abundance, as if there were a kind strife among them, to rid their Master first of that burdenous[2] carriage; or else meaning to make a flood, and so drown their woeful patient in his own sorrow, who yet lay still, but then fetching a deep groan from the profoundest part of his soul, he said:

"Miserable Perissus,[3] canst thou thus live, knowing she that gave thee life is gone? Gone, O me! and with her all my joy departed. Wilt thou (unblessed creature) lie here complaining for her death, and know she died for thee? Let truth and shame make thee do something worthy of such a love, ending thy days like thyself, and one fit to be her servant. But that I must not do: then thus remain and foster storms, still to torment thy wretched soul withall, since all are little, and too too little for such a loss. O dear Limena,[4] loving Limena, worthy Limena, and more rare, constant Limena: perfections deli-

---

8. Garment.
9. Trouble.
1. Gray is typically associated with mourning and despair.

2. Burdensome.
3. Perissus: Lost one.
4. Limena: Woman of home or threshold.

cately feigned to be in women were verified in thee, was such worthiness framed only to be wondered at by the best, but given as a prey to base and unworthy jealousy? When were all worthy parts joined in one, but in thee (my best Limena)? Yet all these grown subject to a creature ignorant of all but ill; like unto a Fool, who in a dark Cave, that hath but one way to get out, having a candle, but not the understanding what good it doth him, puts it out: this ignorant wretch not being able to comprehend thy virtues, did so by thee in thy murder, putting out the world's light, and men's admiration: Limena, Limena, O my Limena."

With that he fell from complaining into such a passion, as weeping and crying were never in so woeful a perfection, as now in him; which brought as deserved a compassion from the excellent Shepherdess, who already had her heart so tempered with grief, as that it was apt to take any impression that it would come to seal withall. Yet taking a brave courage to her, she stepped unto him, kneeling down by his side, and gently pulling him by the arm, she thus spoke.

"Sir," said she, "having heard some part of your sorrows, they have not only made me truly pity you, but wonder at you; since if you have lost so great a treasure, you should not lie thus leaving her and your love unrevenged, suffering her murderers to live, while you lie here complaining; and if such perfections be dead in her, why make you not the Phoenix[5] of your deeds live again, as to new life raised out of the revenge you should take on them? Then were her end satisfied, and you deservedly accounted worthy of her favor, if she were so worthy as you say."

"If she were, O God," cried out Perissus, "what devilish spirit art thou, that thus dost come to torture me? But now I see you are a woman; and therefore not much to be marked, and less resisted: but if you know charity, I pray now practice it, and leave me who am afflicted sufficiently without your company; or if you will stay, discourse not to me."

"Neither of these will I do," said she.

"If you be then," said he, "some fury of purpose sent to vex me, use your force to the uttermost in martyring me; for never was there a fitter subject, then the heart of poor Perissus is."

"I am no fury," replied the divine Urania, "nor hither come to trouble you, but by accident lighted on this place; my cruel hap being such, as only the like can give me content, while the solitariness of this like cave might give me quiet, though not ease. Seeking for such a one, I happened hither; and this is the true cause of my being here, though now I would use it to a better end if I might: Wherefore favor me with the knowledge of your grief; which heard, it may be I shall give you some counsel, and comfort in your sorrow."

"Cursed may I be," cried he, "if ever I take comfort, having such cause of mourning: but because you are, or seem to be afflicted, I will not refuse to satisfy your demand, but tell you the saddest story that ever was rehearsed by dying man to living woman, and such a one, as I fear will fasten too much sadness in you; yet should I deny it, I were to blame, being so well known to these senseless places; as were they sensible of sorrow, they would condole,

5. Mythical bird which could rise with new life after being consumed in flame.

or else amazed at such cruelty stand dumb as they do, to find that man should be so inhuman."

* * *

SONG[6]

Love what art thou? A vain thought
In our minds by fant'sy wrought.
Idle smiles did thee beget,
While fond wishes made the net
5   Which so many fools have caught.

Love what art thou? Light and fair,
Fresh as morning, clear as th' air.
But too soon thy evening change
Makes thy worth with coldness range;
10   Still thy joy is mixt with care.

Love what art thou? A sweet flower
Once full blown,° dead in an hour.   *in full bloom*
Dust in wind as staid remains
As thy pleasure or our gains,
15   If thy humor° change, to lour.   *whim*

Love what art thou? Childish, vain,
Firm as bubbles made by rain,
Wantonness thy greatest pride.
These foul faults thy virtues hide—
20   But babes can no staidness gain.

Love what art thou? Causeless cursed,
Yet alas these not the worst:
Much more of thee may be said.
But thy law I once obeyed,
25   Therefore say no more at first.

1621

From Pamphilia to Amphilanthus[1]

1

When night's black mantle could most darkness prove,
And sleep, death's image, did my senses hire

---

6. This song, one of a group of eclogues that marks the conclusion of book 1 of the *Urania*, is sung to a shepherdess by a shepherd, "being, as it seemed, fallen out with Love."
1. Pamphilia ("All-loving") is the protagonist of *Urania*. Her unfaithful beloved's name means "Lover of Two." These characters are first cousins, like Mary Wroth and William Herbert; their names adumbrate the main theme of both the romance and the appended sonnet sequence, constancy in

the face of unfaithfulness.
Pamphilia to Amphilanthus is broken into several separately numbered series (the first of which includes forty-eight sonnets, with songs inserted after every sixth sonnet except the last). In Josephine A. Roberts's edition of Wroth's poetry, the poems are numbered consecutively throughout the work; we have adopted this convenient renumbering.

From knowledge of myself, then thoughts did move
Swifter than those most swiftness need require.
5 In sleep, a chariot drawn by winged desire
I saw, where sat bright Venus, Queen of Love,
And at her feet, her son,[2] still adding fire
To burning hearts, which she did hold above.
But one heart flaming more than all the rest
10 The goddess held, and put it to my breast.
"Dear son, now shut,"[3] said she: "thus must we win."
He her obeyed, and martyred my poor heart.
I, waking, hoped as dreams it would depart:
Yet since, O me, a lover I have been.

16

Am I thus conquered? Have I lost the powers
That to withstand, which joys to ruin me?[4]
Must I be still while it my strength devours,
And captive leads me prisoner, bound, unfree?
5 Love first shall leave men's fant'sies to them free,[5]
Desire shall quench Love's flames, spring hate sweet showers,
Love shall loose all his darts, have sight, and see
His shame, and wishings hinder happy hours.
Why should we not Love's purblind° charms resist?   *completely blind*
10 Must we be servile, doing what he list?°   *what pleases him*
No, seek some host to harbor thee: I fly
Thy babish tricks, and freedom do profess.
But O my hurt makes my lost heart confess
I love, and must: So farewell liberty.

40

False hope which feeds but to destroy, and spill[6]
What it first breeds; unnatural to the birth
Of thine own womb; conceiving but to kill,
And plenty gives to make the greater dearth,[7]
5 So tyrants do who falsely ruling earth
Outwardly grace them,[8] and with profits fill,
Advance those who appointed are to death,
To make their greater fall to please their will.
Thus shadow° they their wicked vile intent,   *conceal*
10 Coloring evil with a show of good
While in fair shows their malice so is spent;[9]
Hope kills the heart, and tyrants shed the blood.
For hope deluding brings us to the pride
Of our desires the farther down to slide.

2. Cupid.
3. I.e., shut the burning heart into Pamphilia's breast.
4. I.e., have I lost the power to withstand love ("That"), which takes pleasure in ruining me?
5. I.e., this and the other impossibilities that follow will occur before I surrender to love.
6. Kill. The image is of miscarriage or infanticide.
7. I.e., gives abundance only to make scarcity more painful afterward.
8. I.e., those whom they mean to destroy (see the next line).
9. Expended, employed. "Shows": appearances.

68

My pain, still smothered in my grievèd breast,
   Seeks for some ease, yet cannot passage find
   To be discharged of this unwelcome guest:
   When most I strive, most fast his burdens bind,
5   Like to a ship on Goodwin's¹ cast by wind,
   The more she strives, more deep in sand is pressed,
   Till she be lost; so am I, in this kind,°   *manner*
   Sunk, and devoured, and swallowed by unrest,
Lost, shipwracked, spoiled, debarred of smallest hope,
10   Nothing of pleasure left; save thoughts have scope,
   Which wander may. Go then, my thoughts, and cry
Hope's perished, Love tempest-beaten, Joy lost:
   Killing Despair hath all these blessings crossed.
   Yet Faith still cries, Love will not falsify.

74

SONG

Love a child is ever crying,
   Please him, and he straight is flying;
   Give him, he the more is craving,
   Never satisfied with having.

5   His desires have no measure,
   Endless folly is his treasure;
   What he promiseth he breaketh:
   Trust not one word that he speaketh.

He vows nothing but false matter,
10   And to cozen you he'll flatter.
   Let him gain the hand,° he'll leave you,   *the upper hand*
   And still glory to deceive you.

He will triumph in your wailing,
   And yet cause be of your failing:
15   These his virtues are, and slighter
   Are his gifts, his favors lighter.

Feathers are as firm in staying,
   Wolves no fiercer in their preying.
   As a child then leave him crying,
20   Nor seek him, so given to flying.

---

1. Goodwin Sands, a line of shoals at the entrance to the Strait of Dover.

From *A Crown of Sonnets Dedicated to Love*[2]

77

In this strange labyrinth how shall I turn?
   Ways° are on all sides, while the way I miss: *paths*
   If to the right hand, there in love I burn;
   Let me go forward, therein danger is;
5 If to the left, suspicion hinders bliss,
   Let me° turn back, Shame cries I ought return,   *if I*
   Nor faint though crosses[3] with my fortunes kiss;
   Stand still is harder, although sure to mourn.[4]
Then let me take the right- or left-hand way;
10   Go forward, or stand still, or back retire;
   I must these doubts endure without allay°   *abatement*
   Or help, but travail find for my best hire.[5]
Yet that which most my troubled sense doth move
Is to leave all, and take the thread of love.[6]

1621

2. The "crown" is a difficult poetic form (originally Italian and usually known by its Italian name, *corona*) in which the last line of each poem serves as the first line of the next, until a circle is completed by the last line of the final poem, which is the same as the first line of the first one. The number of poems varies from seven to (as in Wroth's *corona*) fourteen.

   In contrast to the errant-child Cupid of the preceding part of the sequence, Love in this series is a mature and just monarch, whose true service

ennobles lovers. The crown is in part a recantation of the harsh judgment of love earlier in the sequence. But Pamphilia relapses into melancholy afterward.
3. Troubles, adversity. "Faint": lose heart.
4. I.e., certain to make me mourn.
5. I.e., I find travail (with a pun on "travel," the spelling in the 1621 edition) is my only reward.
6. Ariadne gave Theseus a thread to follow so as to find his way out of the Labyrinth, after killing the Minotaur at its center.

GEORGE HERBERT
1593–1633

Unlike the learned and witty style of the work of his friend John Donne, Herbert's style in his single volume of religious poetry, *The Temple*, is deceptively simple, marked by ease and grace. But it is also marked by self-irony, a remarkable intellectual and emotional range, and a highly conscious artistry that is evident in the poems' tight construction, exact diction, perfect control of tone, and great variety of stanzaic forms and rhythmic patterns. As well, these poems reflect Herbert's struggle to define his relationship to God through biblical metaphors that are also invested with the tensions and anxieties those relationships held in his own society: king and subject, lord and courtier, master and servant, father and child, bridegroom and bride, friend to friend of inferior status. None of Herbert's secular English poems survives, so his reputation rests on this single volume, published posthumously. *The Temple* contains a long prefatory poem, *The Church-Porch*, and a long concluding poem, *Church Militant*, which together enclose a collection of 177 short lyrics entitled *The Church*, among which are sonnets, songs, hymns, laments, meditative poems, dialogue poems, acrostic poems, emblematic poems, and more. Herbert's own description of the collection is apt: "a picture of the many spiritual conflicts that have passed between God and my soul." Izaak Walton reports that Herbert gave the manuscript to his friend

Nicholas Farrar, head of a quasi-monastic community at Little Gidding, with instructions to publish it if he thought it would "turn to the advantage of any dejected poor soul" and otherwise to burn it. Fortunately, Farrar chose to publish, and *The Temple* became the major influence on the religious lyric poets of the Caroline age: Henry Vaughan, Richard Crashaw, Thomas Traherne, and even Edward Taylor, the American colonial poet.

The fifth son of an eminent Welsh family, Herbert's upbringing and that of his nine siblings was carefully monitored by his mother, Magdalen Herbert, patron and friend of Donne and several other scholars and poets. Herbert was educated at Westminster School and at Trinity College, Cambridge, where he subsequently held a fellowship and wrote Latin poetry: elegies on the death of Prince Henry (1612), witty epigrams, poems on Christ's passion and death, and poems defending the rites of the English Church. In 1620 he was appointed "public orator," the official spokesman and correspondent for the university; this was a step toward a career at court or in public service, as was his election as Member of Parliament from Montgomery in 1624. But that route was closed off by the death of influential patrons and the change of monarchs. Like Donne, Herbert hesitated for some years before being ordained, but in 1630 he took up pastoral duties in the small country parish at Bemerton in Wiltshire. Whereas Donne preached to monarchs and statesmen, Herbert ministered to a few cottagers and none of his sermons survive. His small book on the duties of his new life, *A Priest to the Temple; or, The Country Parson*, testifies to the earnestness and joy (but also to the aristocratic uneasiness) with which he embraced that role. In chronic bad health he lived only three more years—performing pastoral duties assiduously, writing and revising his poems, playing music, and listening to organ and choir at nearby Salisbury cathedral.

Herbert locates himself in the church through many poems that treat church liturgy, architecture, and art—e.g., *Church Monuments* and *The Windows*—but his primary emphasis is always on the soul's inner architecture. Unlike Donne's poems, Herbert's poems do not voice anxious fears about his salvation or about his desperate sins and helplessness; his anxieties center rather on his relationship with Christ, most often represented as that of friend with friend. Many poems register the speaker's distress over the vacillations and regressions in this relationship, over his lack of "fruition" in God's service, and over the instability in his own nature, purposes, and temperament. In several dialogic poems the speaker's difficulties and anxieties are alleviated or resolved by the voice of a divine friend heard within or recalled through a scripture text (as in *The Collar*). In poem after poem he resists but has to come to terms with the fact that his relationship with Christ is always radically unequal, that Christ must both initiate it and make possible his own response. He struggles constantly with the paradox that, as the works of a Christian poet, his poems ought to give fit and sincere praise to God but that they cannot possibly do so—an issue explored in *The Altar*, the two *Jordan* poems, *Easter*, *The Forerunners*, and many more.

His recourse is to develop a biblical poetics that renounces conventional poetic styles—"fiction and false hair"—so as to depend on God's "art" wrought in his own soul and displayed in the language, metaphors, and symbolism of the Bible. He makes scant use of Donnean learned imagery drawn from such areas as cosmology or medicine or Scholastic philosophy, but his allusions carry profound significances. A biblical metaphor provides the unifying motif for the volume: the New Testament temple in the human heart (1 Corinthians 3.16). Another recurring biblical metaphor represents the Christian as plant or tree or flower in God's garden, needing pruning, rain, and nurture. Many poems are related to religious emblems: shaped poems like *The Altar* that present image and picture at once, or others like *Life* that might stand as commentaries on an emblem, here, a posy. Other poems allude to typological symbolism, which reads persons and events in the Old Testament as types or foreshadowings of Christ, the fulfillment or antitype; often, as in *The Bunch of Grapes*, Herbert locates both type and antitype in the speaker's soul.

FROM *THE TEMPLE*[1]

The Altar[2]

A broken A L T A R , Lord, thy servant rears,
Made of a heart, and cemented with tears:
    Whose parts are as thy hand did frame;
    No workman's tool hath touched the same.[3]
5   A H E A R T alone
                        Is   such   a   stone,
                        As   nothing   but
                        Thy power doth cut.
                        Wherefore each part
10   Of my hard heart
                        Meets in this frame,
                        To praise thy Name:
    That, if I chance to hold my peace,
    These stones to praise thee may not cease.[4]
15 Oh let thy blessed S A C R I F I C E be mine,
    And   sanctify   this   A L T A R   to   be   thine.

Redemption[1]

Having been tenant long to a rich lord,
    Not thriving, I resolvèd to be bold,
And make a suit unto him, to afford
    A new small-rented lease, and cancel th' old.[2]

5   In heaven at his manor I him sought:
    They told me there that he was lately gone
About some land which he had dearly bought
    Long since on earth, to take possession.

    I straight returned, and knowing his great birth,
10   Sought him accordingly in great resorts—
    In cities, theaters, gardens, parks, and courts:
    At length I heard a ragged noise and mirth

1. The title of Herbert's volume sets his poems in relation to David's Psalms for the Temple at Jerusalem; his are new covenant "psalms" for the New Testament temple in the heart. All of the following poems come from this volume, published in 1633.
2. A variety of emblem poem. Emblems customarily have three parts: a picture, a motto, and a poem. This kind collapses picture and poem into one, presenting the emblem image by its very shape. Shaped poems have been used by the occasional author from Hellenistic times to Dylan Thomas.
3. A reference to Exodus 20.25, in which the Lord enjoins Moses to build an altar of uncut stones,

not touched by any tool, and also to Psalm 51.7: "A broken and the contrite heart, O God, thou wilt not despise."
4. A reference to Luke 19.40: "I tell you that, if these should hold their peace, the stones would immediately cry out." Herbert's poems obtain much of their resonance from the biblical echoes they incorporate.
1. Literally, "buying back." In this beautifully concise sonnet Herbert figures God as a landlord, himself as a discontented tenant.
2. I.e., to ask him for a new lease, with a smaller rent; the figure points to the New Testament supplanting the Old.

Of thieves and murderers; there I him espied,
Who straight, "Your suit is granted," said, and died.

Easter Wings[1]

Lord, who createdst man in wealth and store,°   *abundance*
Though foolishly he lost the same,
Decaying more and more
Till he became
5   Most poor:
With thee
O let me rise
As larks, harmoniously,
And sing this day thy victories:
10   Then shall the fall further the flight in me.[2]

My tender age in sorrow did begin:
And still with sicknesses and shame
Thou didst so punish sin,
That I became
15   Most thin.
With thee
Let me combine,
And feel this day thy victory;
For, if I imp[3] my wing on thine,
20   Affliction shall advance the flight in me.

Jordan (1)[1]

Who says that fictions only and false hair
Become a verse? Is there in truth no beauty?
Is all good structure in a winding stair?
May no lines pass, except they do their duty°   *pay reverence to*
5   Not to a true, but painted chair?[2]

Is it no verse, except enchanted groves
And sudden arbors shadow coarse-spun lines?[3]
Must purling° streams refresh a lover's loves?   *rippling*
Must all be veiled,[4] while he that reads, divines,
10   Catching the sense at two removes?

1. Another emblem poem whose shape presents the emblem picture; the lines, increasing and decreasing, imitate flight, and also the spiritual experience of falling and rising. Early editions printed the poem with the lines running vertically, making the wing shape more apparent.
2. The idea of the "Fortunate Fall," which brought humankind so great a redeemer.
3. In falconry, to insert feathers in a bird's wing.
1. The river Jordan, which the Israelites crossed to enter the promised land, was also taken as a symbol for baptism.
2. It was the custom for men to bow before a throne, whether it was occupied or not (see Donne, *Satire* 3, lines 47–48, p. 618), but to require bowing before a throne in a painting would be ridiculous.
3. "Sudden," i.e., that appear unexpectedly (an artificial effect much sought after in landscape gardening). "Shadow": shade.
4. As in allegory.

Shepherds[5] are honest people: let them sing;
　　Riddle who list,° for me, and pull for prime:[6]　　　　*wishes*
I envy no man's nightingale or spring;
Nor let them punish me with loss of rhyme,
15　　Who plainly say, *My God, My King.*[7]

The Collar[1]

I struck the board[2] and cried, "No more;
　　　　I will abroad!
What? shall I ever sigh and pine?
My lines and life are free, free as the road,
5　　Loose as the wind, as large as store.
　　　　Shall I be still in suit?[3]
Have I no harvest but a thorn
To let me blood, and not restore
What I have lost with cordial° fruit?　　　　*restorative to the heart*
10　　　　Sure there was wine
　　Before my sighs did dry it; there was corn
　　Before my tears did drown it.
Is the year only lost to me?
　　　　Have I no bays[4] to crown it,
15　No flowers, no garlands gay? all blasted?
　　　　All wasted?
Not so, my heart; but there is fruit,
　　　　And thou hast hands.
Recover all thy sigh-blown age
20　On double pleasures: leave thy cold dispute
Of what is fit and not. Forsake thy cage,
　　　　Thy rope of sands,
Which petty thoughts have made, and made to thee
Good cable,[5] to enforce and draw,
25　　　　And be thy law,
While thou didst wink and wouldst not see.
　　　　Away! take heed;
　　　　I will abroad.
Call in thy death's-head[6] there; tie up thy fears.
30　　　　He that forbears
　　To suit and serve his need,
　　　　Deserves his load."
But as I raved and grew more fierce and wild
　　　　At every word,

5. Conventional pastoral poets.
6. To draw a lucky card in the game of primero. "For me": as far as I am concerned.
7. Echoes Psalm 145.1: "my God, O king."
1. The emblematic title at first suggests a clerical collar that has become a slave's collar; also, punningly, it comes to suggest the speaker's choler (anger) and, perhaps, the caller that he at last hears.
2. Table, with perhaps an allusion to the communion table.
3. In attendance, waiting on someone for a favor.
4. The poet's laurel wreath, symbol of recognized accomplishment.
5. Christian restrictions on behavior, which the "petty thoughts" of the docile believer have made into strong bonds.
6. Skull, emblem of human mortality, and often used as an object for meditation.

35 Methoughts I heard one calling, *Child!*[7]
    And I replied, *My Lord.*

The Pulley[1]

When God at first made man,
Having a glass of blessings standing by,
"Let us," said he, "pour on him all we can:
Let the world's riches, which dispersèd lie,
5   Contract into a span."

So strength first made a way;
Then beauty flowed, then wisdom, honor, pleasure.
When almost all was out, God made a stay,
Perceiving that, alone of all his treasure,
10   Rest in the bottom lay.[2]

"For if I should," said he,
"Bestow this jewel also on my creature,
He would adore my gifts instead of me,
And rest in Nature, not the God of Nature;
15   So both should losers be.

"Yet let him keep the rest,
But keep them with repining restlessness:
Let him be rich and weary, that at least,
If goodness lead him not, yet weariness
20   May toss him to my breast."

The Flower

How fresh, O Lord, how sweet and clean
Are thy returns! even as the flowers in spring,
To which, besides their own demesne,°   *domain, demeanor*
The late-past frosts tributes of pleasure bring.
5   Grief melts away
           Like snow in May,
As if there were no such cold thing.

Who would have thought my shriveled heart
Could have recovered greenness? It was gone
10   Quite underground; as flowers depart
To see their mother-root, when they have blown,°   *bloomed*
           Where they together

---

7. The call "Child" reminds the speaker of Paul's words (Romans 8.14–17) that Christians are not in "bondage again to fear" but are children of God, "and if children, then heirs."
1. The poem inverts the legend of Pandora's box, which released all manner of evils when opened, but left Hope trapped inside.
2. "Rest" has two senses: "remainder" and "repose."

All the hard weather,
Dead to the world, keep house unknown.

15 These are thy wonders, Lord of power,
Killing and quickening, bringing down to hell
And up to heaven in an hour,
Making a chiming of a passing-bell.[1]
We say amiss
20 This or that is:
Thy word is all, if we could spell.

O that I once past changing were,
Fast in thy Paradise, where no flower can wither!
Many a spring I shoot up fair,
25 Offering° at heaven, growing and groaning thither;   aiming
Nor doth my flower
Want a spring shower,[2]
My sins and I joining together.

But while I grow in a straight line,
30 Still upwards bent, as if heaven were mine own,
Thy anger comes, and I decline:
What frost to that? what pole is not the zone
Where all things burn,
When thou dost turn,
35 And the least frown of thine is shown?[3]

And now in age I bud again,
After so many deaths I live and write;
I once more smell the dew and rain,
And relish versing. O my only light,
40 It cannot be
That I am he
On whom thy tempests fell all night.

These are thy wonders, Lord of love,
To make us see we are but flowers that glide;°   slip silently away
45 Which when we once can find and prove,[4]
Thou hast a garden for us where to bide;
Who would be more,
Swelling through store,
Forfeit their Paradise by their pride.

Love (3)

Love bade me welcome: yet my soul drew back,
Guilty of dust and sin.

1. The "passing-bell," intended to mark the death
of a parishioner, is tolled in a monotone; a chiming
bell offers pleasant variety.
2. Tears of contrition.

3. I.e., compared with God's wrath, what polar
chill would not seem like the heat of the equator?
4. Experience.

But quick-eyed Love, observing me grow slack°   *hesitant*
    From my first entrance in,
5 Drew nearer to me, sweetly questioning
    If I lacked anything.[1]

"A guest," I answered, "worthy to be here":
    Love said, "You shall be he."
"I, the unkind, ungrateful? Ah, my dear,
10   I cannot look on thee."
Love took my hand, and smiling did reply,
    "Who made the eyes but I?"

"Truth, Lord; but I have marred them; let my shame
    Go where it doth deserve."
15 "And know you not," says Love, "who bore the blame?"
    "My dear, then I will serve."
"You must sit down," says Love, "and taste my meat."
    So I did sit and eat.[2]

---

1. The first question of shopkeepers and tavern waiters to an entering customer would be "What d'ye lack?" (i.e., want).
2. In addition to the sacrament of Communion, the reference is especially to the final communion in heaven, when the Lord "shall gird himself, and make them to sit down to meat, and will come forth and serve them" (Luke 12.37).

ROBERT HERRICK
1591–1674

Robert Herrick is the most devoted of the Sons of Ben, though his epigrams and lyrics (like Jonson's) also show the direct influence of classical poets: Horace, Anacreon, Catullus, Tibullus, Ovid, and Martial. Born in London the son of a goldsmith and apprenticed for some years in that craft, Herrick took B.A. and M.A. degrees at Cambridge and consorted in the early 1620s with Jonson and his "tribe," meeting regularly at the Apollo Room. After his ordination in 1623, he apparently served as chaplain to various noblemen and in that role joined Buckingham's failed military expedition to rescue French Protestants at Rhé in 1627. In 1630 he was installed as vicar of Dean Prior in Devonshire but found much to dislike about rural life in the West Country. Expelled as a royalist in 1647, he apparently lived in and about London until the Restoration, when he was reinstated at Dean Prior and lived there until his death.

His single volume of poems, *Hesperides* (1648), with its appended book of religious poems, *Noble Numbers*, contains over four hundred short poems which, at first glance, seem mostly playful and charming, remarkable for their exquisite and unerring artistry and perfect decorum. Many are love poems on the *Carpe Diem* theme—seize the day, time is fleeting, make love now; a famous example is the elegant song *To the Virgins, to Make Much of Time*. But Herrick's range is much wider than is sometimes recognized: he moves from the pastoral to the cynical, from an almost rococo elegance to coarse, even vulgar, epigrams, and from the didactic to the dramatic. Also, he derives mythic energy and power from certain recurring motifs. One is metamorphosis, "times trans-shifting," the transience of all natural things. Another is celebration—festivals and feasts—evoking the social, ritualistic, and even anthropological signficances and energies contained in rural harvest festivals (*The Hock-Cart*) or the May Day rituals described in what is perhaps his finest poem, *Corinna's Going A-Maying*. Yet another is the classical but also perennial ideal of the "good life," defined in his terms as "cleanly wantonness." For Herrick this involves love devoid of high passion (the several mistresses he addresses seem interchangeable and not very real); the pleasures of food, drink, and song; delight in the beauty of surfaces (as in *Upon Julia's Clothes*); and finally, the creation of poetry as some ballast against the ravages of time.

These poems, published just months before the execution of Charles I, seem almost oblivious to the catastrophes of the war and the political turmoil. But they are not. Poems celebrating rural feasts and festivals, ceremonial social occasions, and the rituals of good fellowship reinforce the old conservative values of social stability, tradition, and order threatened by the Puritan revolution. Several poems that draw upon the Celtic mythology of fairy folk make their feasts, temples, worship, and ceremonies stand in for the forbidden ceremonies of the Laudian church and a life governed by ritual. Still other poems, like *The Hock-Cart* and *Corinna's Going A-Maying*, celebrate the kind of rural festivals that were at the center of the culture wars between royalists and Puritans. Both James I and Charles I urged such activities in their *Book of Sports* as a means of reinforcing hierarchical relations and traditional institutions in the countryside and deflecting discontent, while Puritans vigorously opposed these activities on those accounts and as occasions for drunkenness and licentiousness.

The Vine

I dreamed this mortal part of mine
Was metamorphosed to a vine,
Which, crawling one and every way,
Enthralled my dainty Lucia.[1]
5   Methought, her long small legs and thighs
I with my tendrils did surprise;
Her belly, buttocks, and her waist
By my soft nervelets were embraced.
About her head I writhing hung,
10   And with rich clusters (hid among
The leaves) her temples I behung,
So that my Lucia seemed to me
Young Bacchus ravished by his tree.°   *the grapevine*
My curls about her neck did crawl,
15   And arms and hands they did enthrall,
So that she could not freely stir
(All parts there made one prisoner).
But when I crept with leaves to hide
Those parts which maids keep unespied,
20   Such fleeting pleasures there I took
That with the fancy I awoke,

---

1. For the sake of both rhyme and meter, the name of this lady is given three syllables here; in line 12 it has only two.

And found (ah me!) this flesh of mine
More like a stock than like a vine.

Delight in Disorder[1]

A sweet disorder in the dress
Kindles in clothes a wantonness.
A lawn° about the shoulders thrown   *fine linen scarf*
Into a fine distractiòn;
5   An erring° lace, which here and there   *wandering*
Enthralls the crimson stomacher;[2]
A cuff neglectful, and thereby
Ribbons to flow confusedly;
A winning wave, deserving note,
10   In the tempestuous petticoat;
A careless shoestring, in whose tie
I see a wild civility:
Do more bewitch me than when art
Is too precise[3] in every part.

Corinna's Going A-Maying

Get up! get up for shame! the blooming morn
Upon her wings presents the god unshorn.[1]
    See how Aurora throws her fair
    Fresh-quilted colors through the air:[2]
5   Get up, sweet slug-a-bed, and see
    The dew bespangling herb and tree.
Each flower has wept and bowed toward the east
Above an hour since, yet you not dressed;
    Nay, not so much as out of bed?
10   When all the birds have matins° said,   *morning prayer*
    And sung their thankful hymns, 'tis sin,
    Nay, profanation° to keep in,   *impiety*
Whenas a thousand virgins on this day
Spring, sooner than the lark, to fetch in May.[3]

15   Rise, and put on your foliage, and be seen
    To come forth, like the springtime, fresh and green,
        And sweet as Flora.[4] Take no care
        For jewels for your gown or hair;
        Fear not; the leaves will strew

1. One of several poems in this period in which
women's dress is a means by which to explore the
relation of nature and art. See Jonson's *Still to Be
Neat*, p. 648.
2. An ornamental covering of the chest, worn
under the laces of the bodice.
3. "Precise" and "precision" were terms used satirically about Puritans. Herrick, in praising feminine
disarray, is at one level praising the "sprezzatura"

or careless grace of Cavalier art.
1. Apollo, the sun god; sunbeams are seen as his
flowing locks.
2. Aurora is goddess of the dawn.
3. On May Day morning, it was the custom to
gather whitethorn blossoms and trim the house
with them.
4. Flora, Italian goddess of flowers, had her festival in the spring.

20   Gems in abundance upon you;
        Besides, the childhood of the day has kept,
        Against° you come, some orient pearls[5] unwept;   *until*
            Come and receive them while the light
            Hangs on the dew-locks of the night,
25   And Titan° on the eastern hill   *the sun*
        Retires himself, or else stands still
    Till you come forth. Wash, dress, be brief in praying:
    Few beads[6] are best when once we go a-Maying.

        Come, my Corinna, come; and, coming, mark
30   How each field turns° a street, each street a park   *turns into*
            Made green and trimmed with trees; see how
            Devotion gives each house a bough
            Or branch: each porch, each door ere this,
            An ark, a tabernacle is,[7]
35   Made up of whitethorn neatly interwove,
        As if here were those cooler shades of love.
            Can such delights be in the street
            And open fields, and we not see 't?
            Come, we'll abroad; and let's obey
40   The proclamation[8] made for May,
    And sin no more, as we have done, by staying;
    But, my Corinna, come, let's go a-Maying.

        There's not a budding boy or girl this day
    But is got up and gone to bring in May;
45   A deal of youth, ere this, is come
            Back, and with whitethorn laden, home.
            Some have dispatched their cakes and cream
            Before that we have left to dream;
    And some have wept, and wooed, and plighted troth,
50   And chose their priest, ere we can cast off sloth.
            Many a green-gown[9] has been given,
            Many a kiss, both odd and even;[1]
            Many a glance, too, has been sent
            From out the eye, love's firmament;
55   Many a jest told of the keys betraying
        This night, and locks picked; yet we're not a-Maying.

        Come, let us go while we are in our prime,
        And take the harmless folly of the time.
            We shall grow old apace, and die
60   Before we know our liberty.
            Our life is short, and our days run
            As fast away as does the sun;

5. Pearls from the orient were especially lustrous, like drops of dew.
6. Rosary beads of the "old" Catholic religion, but more generally, a casual term for prayers.
7. The doorways, ornamented with whitethorn, are like the Hebrew Ark of the Covenant, or the sanctuary that housed it (Leviticus 23.40–42: "Ye shall take you on the first day the boughs of goodly trees . . .").
8. Probably a reference to Charles I's "Declaration to his subjects concerning lawful sports."
9. Got by rolling in the grass.
1. Kisses are odd and even in kissing games.

And, as a vapor or a drop of rain,
Once lost, can ne'er be found again,
65   So when or you or I are made
A fable, song, or fleeting shade,
All love, all liking, all delight
Lies drowned with us in endless night.[2]
Then while time serves, and we are but decaying,
70   Come, my Corinna, come, let's go a-Maying.

To the Virgins, to Make Much of Time

Gather ye rosebuds while ye may,
    Old time is still a-flying;[1]
And this same flower that smiles today,
    Tomorrow will be dying.

5   The glorious lamp of heaven, the sun,
    The higher he's a-getting,
The sooner will his race be run,[2]
    And nearer he's to setting.

That age is best which is the first,
10   When youth and blood are warmer;
But being spent, the worse, and worst
    Times still succeed the former.

Then be not coy, but use your time,
    And while ye may, go marry;
15   For having lost but once your prime,
    You may forever tarry.

Upon Julia's Clothes

Whenas in silks my Julia goes,
Then, then, methinks, how sweetly flows
That liquefaction of her clothes.

Next, when I cast mine eyes and see
5   That brave[1] vibration each way free,
Oh, how that glittering taketh me!

---

2. Some echoes of the apocryphal book Wisdom of Solomon 2.1–8: "For the ungodly said . . . the breath of our nostrils is as smoke, and a little spark . . . and our life shall pass away as the trace of a cloud. . . . Come on therefore . . . Let us crown ourselves with rose buds before they be withered." This *carpe diem* sentiment is a frequent theme in classical love poetry.

1. Translates the Latin *tempus fugit*.
2. In classical myth, the sun was taken to be the chariot of Phoebus Apollo, which he drove across the heavens daily.
1. Splendid, glorious.

RICHARD LOVELACE
1618–1657

Usually linked with Suckling as a quintessential Cavalier, Richard Lovelace was described by a contemporary as "the most amiable and beautiful person that ever eye beheld." Born into a wealthy Kentish family, he was educated at Oxford, and, like Suckling, fought for his king in Scotland (in both expeditions, 1639 and 1640). But he was not a libertine and his poems, in contrast with Suckling's, often exalt women, love, and honor. Also, he shared with his king a serious interest in art, especially the paintings of Rubens, Van Dyke, and Lely. He was imprisoned for a few months in 1642 for supporting the "Kentish Petition" that urged restoration of the king to his ancient rights; in *To Althea, from Prison,* he finds freedom from external bondage in the Cavalier ideals of women, wine, and royalism. During 1643–46 he fought in Holland and France and in the king's armies in England, and was wounded abroad. In a general roundup of known royalists in 1648 he was imprisoned for ten months, and while there prepared his poems for publication under the title *Lucasta* (1649). Besides witty and charming love songs, that volume includes the plaintive ballad about the conflict between love and honor, *To Lucasta, Going to the Wars,* and also a poem that presents the Cavalier ideal at its most attractive: *The Grasshopper.* That emblematic summer creature is taken to symbolize the loss of the king and the carefree Cavalier life in the Puritan "winter," but Lovelace finds in the fellowship of Cavalier friends a nobler version of the good life and a truer kingship. After 1649 he endured a decade of penury, largely dependent on the largess of his friend and fellow royalist, Charles Cotton. His remaining poems appeared in 1659 as *Lucasta: Postume Poems.*

From Lucasta

To Lucasta, Going to the Wars

Tell me not, sweet, I am unkind,
    That from the nunnery
Of thy chaste breast and quiet mind
    To war and arms I fly.

5 True, a new mistress now I chase,
    The first foe in the field;
And with a stronger faith embrace
    A sword, a horse, a shield.

Yet this inconstancy is such
10   As you too shall adore;
I could not love thee, dear, so much,
    Loved I not honor more.

1649

To Althea, from Prison

When Love with unconfinèd wings
    Hovers within my gates,

And my divine Althea brings
    To whisper at the grates;
5 When I lie tangled in her hair
    And fettered to her eye,
The gods[1] that wanton° in the air   *play*
    Know no such liberty.

When flowing cups run swiftly round,
10   With no allaying Thames,[2]
Our careless heads with roses bound,
    Our hearts with loyal flames;
When thirsty grief in wine we steep,
    When healths and draughts go free,
15 Fishes that tipple in the deep
    Know no such liberty.

When, like committed linnets,[3] I
    With shriller throat shall sing
The sweetness, mercy, majesty,
20   And glories of my king;
When I shall voice aloud how good
    He is, how great should be,
Enlargèd winds, that curl the flood,
    Know no such liberty.

25 Stone walls do not a prison make,
    Nor iron bars a cage;
Minds innocent and quiet take
    That for an hermitage.
If I have freedom in my love,
30   And in my soul am free,
Angels alone, that soar above,
    Enjoy such liberty.

                            1649

1. Some versions read "birds" instead of "gods."   in the wine.
2. No mixture of water (as from the River Thames)   3. Caged finches.

KATHERINE PHILIPS
1632–1664

The best-known woman poet of her own and the next generation, Katherine Philips was honored as "The Matchless Orinda," the classical name she chose for herself in her poetic addresses to a coterie of chiefly female friends, especially Mary Aubrey (M. A.) and Anne Owen (Lucasia). Sometimes reminiscent of Donne's love lyrics and sometimes of the ancient Greek Sappho's erotic lyrics to women, these poems develop an exalted ideal of female friendship as a Platonic union of souls. Born to a well-to-do Presbyterian family and educated at Mrs. Salmon's Presbyterian school, Philips was taken to Wales when her mother remarried. In 1648 at age seventeen she was married to James Philips, thirty-eight years her senior and a prominent Presbyterian magistrate and Member of Parliament. They lived together twelve years, chiefly in the small Welsh town of Cardigan, and had two children: Hector, whose death a few days after birth prompted one of her most moving poems, and Katherine, who lived to adulthood. A royalist despite her Puritan family connections, Philips forged connections with other displaced royalists. Her poems circulated in manuscript and elicited high praise from Vaughan in *Olor Iscanus*. They include elegies, epitaphs, poems at parting, and friendship poems to women and men, but also poetry on political themes: a denunciation of the regicide, *Upon the Double Murder of King Charles,* and panegyrics on the restored Stuarts. At the Restoration, James Philips barely escaped execution as a regicide, had his estates confiscated, and lost his seat in parliament, but Katherine became a favorite at Court, promoted by her friend Sir Charles Cotterell ("Poliarchus"), who was master of ceremonies. In Ireland attempting (unsuccessfully) to redeem an investment, she translated Corneille's *Pompey* and her friend the earl of Orrery produced and printed it in Dublin in 1663. The first edition of her poems, apparently pirated, appeared in 1664, the same year she died of smallpox. Her friend Cotterell brought out an authorized edition in 1667.

A Married State[1]

A married state affords but little ease
The best of husbands are so hard to please.
This in wives' careful° faces you may spell   *full of cares*
Though they dissemble their misfortunes well.
5   A virgin state is crowned with much content;[2]
It's always happy as it's innocent.
No blustering husbands to create your fears;
No pangs of childbirth to extort your tears;
No children's cries for to offend your ears;
10 Few worldly crosses to distract your prayers:
Thus are you freed from all the cares that do
Attend on matrimony and a husband too.
Therefore Madam, be advised by me
Turn, turn apostate to love's levity,
15 Suppress wild nature if she dare rebel.
There's no such thing as leading apes in hell.[3]

ca. 1646   Ms; 1988

1. In a manuscript (Orielton MSS Box 24 at the National Library of Wales) this poem appears with another by Philips, addressed to Anne Barlow (whom she probably met in 1646); this one is probably also for Barlow. Both are signed by her maiden name, C. Fowler, so were evidently written before her marriage in 1648.
2. Praise of the single life is a common topic in women's poetry.
3. Proverbially, the fate of spinsters.

Upon the Double Murder of King Charles

In Answer to a Libelous Rhyme made by V. P.[1]

I think not on the state, nor am concerned
Which way soever that great helm[2] is turned,
But as that son whose father's danger nigh
Did force his native dumbness, and untie
His fettered organs: so here is a cause
That will excuse the breach of nature's laws.[3]
Silence were now a sin: nay passion now
Wise men themselves for merit would allow.[4]
What noble eye could see (and careless pass)
The dying lion kicked by every ass?
Hath Charles so broke God's laws, he must not have
A quiet crown, nor yet a quiet grave?
Tombs have been sanctuaries; thieves lie here
Secure from all their penalty and fear.
Great Charles his double misery was this,
Unfaithful friends, ignoble enemies;
Had any heathen been this prince's foe,
He would have wept to see him injured so.
His title was his crime, they'd reason good
To quarrel at the right they had withstood.
He broke God's laws, and therefore he must die,
And what shall then become of thee and I?
Slander must follow treason; but yet stay,
Take not our reason with our king away.
Though you have seized upon all our defense,
Yet do not sequester° our common sense.   *confiscate*
But I admire not at this new supply:
No bounds will hold those who at scepters fly.
Christ will be King, but I ne'er understood,
His subjects built his kingdom up with blood
(Except their own) or that he would dispense
With his commands, though for his own defense.
Oh! to what height of horror are they come
Who dare pull down a crown, tear up a tomb![5]

5
10
15
20
25
30

1649?   1664

---

1. The itinerant Welsh preacher Vavasour Powell was a Fifth Monarchist and an ardent republican who justified the regicide on the ground that Christ's second coming was imminent, when he would rule with his saints, putting down all earthly kings. His poem, which Philips is answering, has not survived, but the likelihood is that both were written shortly after Charles I's execution (January 30, 1649).

2. Steering wheel for the "ships" of state.
3. Breaking the supposed law of nature that excludes women from speaking about public affairs.
4. Wise men, especially Stoic philosophers, normally counsel the firm control or elimination of passions.
5. Their slanders tear up Charles's tomb after his death.

Friendship's Mystery, To My Dearest *Lucasia*[1]

1

Come, my *Lucasia*, since we see
   That Miracles Men's faith do move,
By wonder and by prodigy
   To the dull angry world let's prove
5   There's a Religion in our Love.

2

For though we were designed t' agree,
   That Fate no liberty destroys,
But our Election is as free
   As Angels, who with greedy choice
10   Are yet determined to their joys[2]

3

Our hearts are doubled by the loss,
   Here Mixture is Addition grown;
We both diffuse,° and both engross:°   *spread out / collect*
   And we whose minds are so much one,
15   Never, yet ever are alone.

4

We court our own Captivity
   Than Thrones more great and innocent:
'Twere banishment to set free,
   Since we wear fetters whose intent
20   Not bondage is, but Ornament.

5

Divided joys are tedious found,
   And griefs united easier grow:
We are selves but by rebound,
   And all our Titles shuffled so,
25   Both Princes, and both Subjects too.[3]

6

Our Hearts are mutual Victims laid,
   While they (such power in Friendship lies)
Are Altars, Priests, and Off'rings made:
   And each Heart which thus kindly° dies,   *benevolently, naturally*
30   Grows deathless by the Sacrifice.

1655, 1664

1. This poem was first printed, with a musical setting by the royalist musician and composer Henry Lawes, as "Mutual Affection betweene *Orinda* and *Lucasia*" in Lawes's *The Second Book of Ayres* (1655); our text is from *Poems by the most deservedly admired Mrs. Katherine Philips, the matchless Orinda* (1667). Lucasia is Philips's name for her friend Anne Owen.
2. Angels, though created with free will, were thought to have become fixed in goodness when they turned toward God in the first moments after their creation.
3. Compare Donne, *The Sun Rising*, lines 21–22: "She is all states, and all princes, I" (p. 605).

To Mrs. M. A.[1] at Parting

I have examined and do find,
    Of all that favor me
There's none I grieve to leave behind
    But only only thee.
5 To part with thee I needs must die,
Could parting separate thee and I.

But neither chance nor compliment
    Did element our love:
'Twas sacred sympathy was lent
10   Us from the choir above.
(That friendship fortune did create,
Still fears a wound from time or fate.)

Our changed and mingled souls are grown
    To such acquaintance now,
15 That if each would resume their own,
    Alas! we know not how.
We have each other so engrossed
That each is in the union lost.[2]

And thus we can no absence know,
20   Nor shall we be confined;
Our active souls will daily go
    To learn each other's mind.
Nay, should we never meet to sense,
Our souls would hold intelligence.°   *would still commune*

Inspirèd with a flame divine,
25   I scorn to court a stay;[3]
For from that noble soul of thine
    I ne'er can be away.
But I shall weep when thou dost grieve;
30 Nor can I die whilst thou dost live.

By my own temper I shall guess
    At thy felicity,
And only like my happiness
    Because it pleaseth thee.
35 Our hearts at any time will tell
If thou or I be sick or well.

1. M. A. was Mary Aubrey, the first and, until she married, the dearest member of Philips's "Society of Friendship." Orinda's valedictory poem to her—which Keats admired enough to copy it out in full in an early letter—recalls some of Donne's lyrics, especially *A Valediction: Forbidding Mourning* (p. 611).
2. These lines play upon the Neoplatonic idea of friendship and spiritual love—two souls become one.
3. Postponement (of their parting).

All honor, sure, I must pretend,°   *aspire to*
   All that is good or great:
She that would be Rosania's⁴ friend
40   Must be at least complete.
If I have any bravery,
   'Tis cause I have so much of thee.

Thy leiger° soul in me shall lie,   *ambassadorial*
   And all thy thoughts reveal;
45   Then back again with mine shall fly,
   And thence to me shall steal.
Thus still to one another tend:
   Such is the sacred name of friend.

Thus our twin souls in one shall grow,
50   And teach the world new love,
Redeem the age and sex, and show
   A flame fate dares not move:
And courting death to be our friend,
Our lives, together too, shall end.

55   A dew shall dwell upon our tomb
   Of such a quality
That fighting armies, thither come,
   Shall reconcilèd be.
We'll ask no epitaph, but say:
60   ORINDA and ROSANIA.

1664

On the Death of My First and Dearest Child, Hector Philips[1]

Twice forty months in wedlock[2] I did stay,
   Then had my vows crowned with a lovely boy.
And yet in forty days[3] he dropped away;
   O swift vicissitude of human joy!

5   I did but see him, and he disappeared,
   I did but touch the rosebud, and it fell;
A sorrow unforeseen and scarcely feared,
   So ill can mortals their afflictions spell.°   *discern*

And now, sweet babe, what can my trembling heart
10   Suggest to right my doleful fate or thee?

---

4. The poetic name Philips gave to Mary Aubrey.
1. In a manuscript the subtitle reads, "born the 23d of April, and died the 2d of May 1655. Set by Mr. Lawes." There is however no extant musical setting.
2. Philips was married in August 1648.
3. The subtitle indicates that he lived barely ten days; the change here is clearly for the parallelism.

Tears are my muse, and sorrow all my art,
  So piercing groans must be thy elegy.

Thus whilst no eye is witness of my moan,
  I grieve thy loss (Ah, boy too dear to live!),
15 And let the unconcernèd world alone,
  Who neither will, nor can, refreshment give.

An off'ring too for thy sad tomb I have,
  Too just a tribute to thy early hearse.
Receive these gasping numbers to thy grave,
20   The last of thy unhappy mother's verse.[4]

1655   1667

---

4. This was not in fact Philips's last poem, but the sentiment is both true to human feeling and common
in elegy. She had one other child, a year later—a daughter, Katherine, who survived her.

ANDREW MARVELL
1621–1678

Andrew Marvell's finest poems are second to none in this or any other period. He
wrote less than Donne, Jonson, and Herbert did, but his range is in some ways greater,
as he claimed both the private worlds of love and religion and the public worlds of
political and satirical poetry and prose. His overriding concern with art, his elegant,
well-crafted, limpid style, and the cool balance and reserve of some poems align him
with Ben Jonson, but his paradoxes and complexities of tone, his use of dramatic
monologue, and his witty, dialectical arguments associate him with Donne. Above all,
he is a supremely original poet, so complex and elusive that it is often hard to know
what he really thought about the subjects he treats. Many of his poems were published
posthumously in 1681, some thirty years after they were written, by a woman who
claimed to be his widow but was probably his housekeeper. So their date and order
of composition is often in doubt, as is his authorship of some anonymous works.

  The son of a Church of England clergyman, Marvell grew up in Yorkshire, attended
Trinity College, Cambridge (perhaps deriving the persistant strain of Neoplatonism
in his poetry from the academics known as the Cambridge Platonists), ran off to
London, and converted to Roman Catholicism until his father put an end to both
ventures. He returned to Cambridge, took his degree in 1639, and stayed on as a
scholar until his father's death in 1641. During the years of the Civil Wars (1642–
47), he traveled in France, Italy, Holland and Spain; much later he said of the Puritan
"Good Old Cause" that it was "too good to have been fought for." While his earliest
poems associate him with royalists, those after 1649 celebrate the Commonwealth
and Cromwell, sometimes with ambivalence but recognizing divine providence in the
political changes. From 1650 to 1652 he lived at Nunappleton as tutor to the twelve-
year-old daughter of Thomas Fairfax, who had given over his command of the Parliamentary army to Cromwell because he was unwilling to invade Scotland. In these
years of retirement and ease, Marvell probably wrote most of his love lyrics and pastorals as well as *Upon Appleton House*. Subsequently he was tutor to Cromwell's ward,
William Dutton, and traveled with him on the Continent; in 1657 he joined the blind

Milton, at Milton's request, in the post of Latin secretary to Cromwell's Council of State. Marvell accepted the Restoration but maintained his own independent vision and his abiding belief in religious toleration, a mixed state, and constitutional government. He helped his friend Milton avoid execution for his revolutionary polemics and helped negotiate Milton's release from a brief imprisonment. Elected a Member of Parliament in 1659 from his hometown, Hull in Yorkshire, he held that post until 1678, focusing his attention on the needs of his district; on two occasions he went on diplomatic missions—to Holland and Russia. His (necessarily anonymous) anti-royalist polemics of these years include his best-known prose work, *The Rehearsal Transprosed* (1672–73), which defends Puritan dissenters and denounces censorship with verve and wit, and several verse satires that ridicule Charles II and his ministers. He also wrote a brilliant poem of criticism and interpretation on Milton's *Paradise Lost* that was prefixed to the second edition (1674).

Many of Marvell's poems explore the human condition in terms of fundamental dichotomies that resist resolution. In religious or philosophical poems like *The Coronet* or *The Dialogue Between the Soul and Body*, the conflict is between nature and grace, or body and soul, or poetic creation and sacrifice. In love poems such as *The Definition of Love* or *To His Coy Mistress* it is often between flesh and spirit, or physical sex and platonic love, or idealizing courtship and the ravages of time. In pastorals like the Mower poems and *The Garden* the opposition is between nature and art, or the fallen and Edenic state, or violent passion and contentment. Marvell's most subtle and complex political poem, *An Horatian Ode upon Cromwell's Return from Ireland*, sets stable traditional order and ancient right against providential revolutionary change, and the goods and costs of retirement and peace against those of action and war. *Upon Appleton House* also opposes the attractions of various kinds of retirement to the duties of action and reformation.

Marvell's stylistic experiments and transformations of genres produce striking aesthetic effects. Many of his dramatic monologues are voiced by named, naive personas—the Mower, the Nymph complaining—who stand at some remove from the author. One of his most remarkable figures—the phrase "Like a green thought in a green shade" from *The Garden*—derives its power from the unanalyzable suggestiveness the entire poem invests in the term "green." *To His Coy Mistress,* perhaps the best known of the century's *carpe diem* poems, is voiced by a witty and urbane speaker in balanced and artful couplets, but its rapid shifts from the world of fantasy to the charnal house of reality raise questions as to whether this is a clever seduction poem or a probing of existential angst, and whether Marvell intends to endorse or critique this speaker's view of passion and sex.

To His Coy Mistress[1]

> Had we but world enough, and time,
> This coyness, lady, were no crime.
> We would sit down, and think which way
> To walk, and pass our long love's day.
> 5   Thou by the Indian Ganges' side

---

1. One of the most famous *carpe diem* (seize the day) poems of the period, it develops the motifs of time and space, introduced in line 1.

Shouldst rubies find; I by the tide
Of Humber would complain.[2] I would
Love you ten years before the Flood,
And you should, if you please, refuse
10 Till the conversion of the Jews.[3]
My vegetable love should grow
Vaster than empires, and more slow;
An hundred years should go to praise
Thine eyes, and on thy forehead gaze;
15 Two hundred to adore each breast,
But thirty thousand to the rest:
An age at least to every part,
And the last age should show your heart.
For, lady, you deserve this state,°   *dignity*
20 Nor would I love at lower rate.
    But at my back I always hear
Time's wingèd chariot hurrying near;
And yonder all before us lie
Deserts of vast eternity.
25 Thy beauty shall no more be found,
Nor, in thy marble vault, shall sound
My echoing song; then worms shall try
That long-preserved virginity,
And your quaint[4] honor turn to dust,
30 And into ashes all my lust:
The grave's a fine and private place,
But none, I think, do there embrace.
    Now therefore, while the youthful hue
Sits on thy skin like morning dew,[5]
35 And while thy willing soul transpires
At every pore with instant fires,[6]
Now let us sport us while we may,
And now, like amorous birds of prey,
Rather at once our time devour
40 Than languish in his slow-chapped[7] power.
Let us roll all our strength and all
Our sweetness up into one ball,
And tear our pleasures with rough strife
Thorough° the iron gates of life:[8]   *` through*
45 Thus, though we cannot make our sun
Stand still, yet we will make him run.[9]

2. The exotic river Ganges is on one side of the world, the Humber river flows past Marvell's city, Hull, on the opposite side. Complaints are poems of plaintive, unavailing love.
3. Popular belief had it that the Jews were to be converted just before the Last Judgment. The exaggerated offers in this stanza play off against conventional hyperbolic declarations of love in Petrarchan poetry.
4. "Quaint" puns on "out of date" and *queynte*, a term for the female genitals.

5. The text reads "glew," which could be correct, but "dew" is a common emendation.
6. Urgent, sudden enthusiasm. "Transpires": breathes forth.
7. Slowly devouring jaws.
8. One manuscript reads "grates," a somewhat different figure for the sexual act proposed.
9. The sun stood still for Joshua (Joshua 10.12) in his war against Gibeon; see the very different resolution in Donne's *The Sun Rising* (p. 605).

The Definition of Love

My Love is of a birth as rare
As 'tis, for object, strange and high;
It was begotten by Despair
Upon Impossibility.

5 Magnanimous Despair alone
Could show me so divine a thing,
Where feeble Hope could ne'er have flown
But vainly flapped its tinsel wing.

And yet I quickly might arrive
10 Where my extended soul is fixed;[1]
But Fate does iron wedges drive,
And always crowds itself betwixt.

For Fate with jealous eye does see
Two perfect loves, nor lets them close;°   unite
15 Their union would her ruin be,
And her tyrannic power depose.[2]

And therefore her decrees of steel
Us as the distant poles have placed
(Though Love's whole world on us doth wheel),[3]
20 Not by themselves to be embraced,

Unless the giddy heaven fall,
And earth some new convulsion tear,
And, us to join, the world should all
Be cramped into a planisphere.[4]

25 As lines, so loves oblique may well
Themselves in every angle greet;[5]
But ours, so truly parallel,
Though infinite, can never meet.

Therefore the love which us doth bind,
30 But Fate so enviously debars,
Is the conjunction of the mind,
And opposition of the stars.[6]

---

1. The soul has extended itself from the speaker's body and fixed itself to his lover.
2. Two perfections, united, would not be subject to change and thereby to Fate.
3. Rotates as on its axis.
4. A two-dimensional map of the world; Marvell images a round globe collapsed into a flat pancake shape, top to bottom, which would bring the two poles together.
5. Oblique lines can touch in angles, as might "oblique" lovers that (in one meaning of the term) "deviate from right conduct or thought."
6. Conjunction is the coming together of two heavenly bodies in the same sign of the zodiac; "opposition" places them at diametrical opposites.

The Mower to the Glowworms

Ye living lamps, by whose dear light
The nightingale does sit so late,
And studying all the summer night
Her matchless songs does meditate,

5 Ye country comets, that portend
No war nor prince's funeral,
Shining unto no higher end
Than to presage the grass's fall;

Ye glowworms, whose officious° flame   *zealous, attentive*
10 To wand'ring mowers shows the way,
That in the night have lost their aim,
And after foolish fires° do stray;   *will-o-the-wisps*

Your courteous fires in vain you waste,
Since Juliana here is come,
15 For she my mind hath so displaced
That I shall never find my home.

The Mower's Song

My mind was once the true survey
Of all these meadows fresh and gay,
And in the greenness of the grass
Did see its hopes[1] as in a glass;°   *mirror*
5 When Juliana came, and she,
What I do to the grass, does to my thoughts and me.[2]

But these, while I with sorrow pine,
Grew more luxuriant still and fine,
That not one blade of grass you spied
10 But had a flower on either side;
When Juliana came, and she,
What I do to the grass, does to my thoughts and me.

Unthankful meadows, could you so
A fellowship so true forego,
15 And in your gaudy May-games[3] meet,
While I lay trodden under feet?
When Juliana came, and she,
What I do to the grass, does to my thoughts and me.

But what you in compassion ought
20 Shall now by my revenge be wrought,
And flowers, and grass, and I, and all,

---

1. Green is the color of hope.
2. The alexandrine (12-syllable line) used here is
the only example of a refrain in Marvell.

3. Festivals and merrymaking marked the first of
May.

Will in one common ruin fall;
For Juliana comes, and she,
What I do to the grass, does to my thoughts and me.

25   And thus ye meadows, which have been
Companions of my thoughts more green,
Shall now the heraldry become
With which I shall adorn my tomb;
For Juliana comes, and she,
30   What I do to the grass, does to my thoughts and me.

The Garden

How vainly men themselves amaze°   bewilder
To win the palm, the oak, or bays,[1]
And their uncessant labors see
Crowned from some single herb or tree,
5   Whose short and narrow-vergèd° shade   edged
Does prudently their toils upbraid;
While all flowers and all trees do close°   unite, agree
To weave the garlands of repose!

Fair Quiet, have I found thee here,
10   And Innocence, thy sister dear?
Mistaken long, I sought you then
In busy companies of men.
Your sacred plants, if here below,°   on earth
Only among the plants will grow;
15   Society is all but rude,
To° this delicious solitude.   compared to

No white nor red[2] was ever seen
So amorous as this lovely green.
Fond lovers, cruel as their flame,
20   Cut in these trees their mistress' name:
Little, alas, they know or heed
How far these beauties hers exceed!
Fair trees, wheresoe'er your barks I wound,
No name shall but your own be found.[3]

25   When we have run our passion's heat,
Love hither makes his best retreat.
The gods, that mortal beauty chase,
Still in a tree did end their race:
Apollo hunted Daphne so,
30   Only that she might laurel grow;
And Pan did after Syrinx speed,
Not as a nymph, but for a reed.[4]

1. Honors, respectively, for military, civic, and poetic achievement.
2. Colors traditionally associated with female beauty.
3. Marvell proposes to carve in the bark of trees, not *Sylvia* or *Laura*, but *Beech* and *Oak*.

4. Apollo, the god of poetry, chased Daphne until she turned into a laurel (the emblematic reward of poets); Pan pursued Syrinx until she became a reed, out of which he made panpipes. The gods' motives were, of course, sexual, not horticultural.

What wondrous life in this I lead!
Ripe apples drop about my head;
35 The luscious clusters of the vine
Upon my mouth do crush their wine;
The nectarine and curious° peach   *exquisite*
Into my hands themselves do reach;
Stumbling on melons[5] as I pass,
40 Insnared with flowers, I fall on grass.

Meanwhile the mind, from pleasure less,[6]
Withdraws into its happiness;
The mind, that ocean where each kind
Does straight° its own resemblance find;[7]   *immediately*
45 Yet it creates, transcending these,
Far other worlds and other seas,
Annihilating all that's made
To a green thought in a green shade.

Here at the fountain's sliding foot,
50 Or at some fruit tree's mossy root,
Casting the body's vest° aside,   *garment*
My soul into the boughs does glide:
There like a bird it sits and sings,
Then whets° and combs its silver wings,   *preen*
55 And, till prepared for longer flight,
Waves in its plumes the various light.[8]

Such was that happy garden-state,
While man there walked without a mate:
After a place so pure and sweet,
60 What other help could yet be meet![9]
But 'twas beyond a mortal's share
To wander solitary there:
Two paradises 'twere in one
To live in paradise alone.

65 How well the skillful gardener drew
Of flowers and herbs this dial new,[1]
Where from above the milder sun
Does through a fragrant zodiac run;

5. "Melons," with etymological roots in the Greek word for *apple*, may recall the apple over which all humankind stumbled.
6. "Less" may modify either "pleasure" or "mind."
7. As the ocean supposedly contained a counterpart of every creature on land, so the ocean of the mind holds the innate ideas of all things (in Neo-

platonic philosophy).
8. The multicolored light of this world, contrasted with the white radiance of eternity.
9. Genesis 2.18 recounts the Lord's decision to make a "help meet" for Adam, Eve.
1. The garden itself is laid out as a sundial.

And as it works, th' industrious bee
70 Computes its time[2] as well as we!
How could such sweet and wholesome hours
Be reckoned but with herbs and flowers?

2. With a pun on thyme.

MARGARET CAVENDISH
1623–1673

Margaret (Lucas) Cavendish, duchess of Newcastle, wrote and published numerous works during the Interregnum and Restoration era, in a great variety of genres: poetry (*Poems and Fancies*, 1653), essays (*Philosophical Fancies*, 1653, *The World's Olio*, 1655), short fiction (*Nature's Pictures*, 1656), autobiography (*A True Relation of My Birth, Breeding, and Life*, 1656), utopian romance (*The Blazing World*, 1666), scientific essays chiefly critical of the new science, letters, a biography of her husband (*The Life of . . . William Cavendish*, 1667), and some eighteen plays, of which one, *The Forced Marriage*, was produced in 1670. Most were published in lavish editions, at the Newcastles' own expense, and at the time they elicited more derision than praise: for a woman, especially an aristocratic woman, to publish works dealing so intimately with her desires, opinions, personal circumstances, and aspirations to fame and authorship was seen by many as disgraceful. Samuel Pepys concluded, after reading her life of her husband the duke, that she was "a mad, conceited, ridiculous woman, and he an ass to suffer [her] to write what she writes to him and of him." Her fantastic dress and sometimes idiosyncratic social behavior abetted that characterization: she took pride in "singularity" and even insisted on paying a visit to the all-male Royal Society. But the philosopher Thomas Hobbes thought well of her, and her rediscoverers in recent decades have been impressed by her works and her self-construction as a female author.

Her autobiography analyzes her responses to the circumstances of her life: born into a wealthy royalist family that encouraged her disposition to read and write; accepted as maid of honor by Queen Henrietta Maria, whom she followed into exile in Paris; married there (1645) to the widowed William Cavendish, thirty years her senior, who was one of Charles I's generals and later duke of Newcastle; exiled with him for fifteen years on the Continent, where (his estates having been sequestered) they ran up exorbitant debts; and restored to status and fortune after the Restoration. The duke, who was himself something of a poet, playwright, and philosopher, encouraged, supported, and promoted Margaret's literary endeavors—for which she was profoundly grateful. In polemical prefaces to her several works, she develops a fragmentary poetics, trenchantly defends her right to publish and to participate in contemporary intellectual exchange, defends women's rational powers, and decries their educational disadvantages and exclusion from the public domain.

The Blazing World Part romance, part utopia, and part science fiction, *The Blazing World* is also an idealized version of Cavendish's own ideas and fantasies in that it portrays the effortless rise of a woman to absolute power. It begins in the vein of romance: a young woman is abducted and miraculously saved as a tempest carries the abductors' boat to the North Pole and on to another universe, the Blazing World, whose emperor promptly marries her and turns over the entire government of the realm to her. It takes on a utopian character, as the new Empress learns from the fantastically diverse inhabitants about their numerous scientific experiments and about the royalist politics and religious uniformity of the place. She then brings Margaret Cavendish to be her scribe and returns with Margaret (in the state of disembodied spirits and platonic friends) to visit and learn about Margaret's world and Margaret's husband, the duke; she also puts down a rebellion at home and subjects other nations to her beneficent rule. Cavendish's preface makes a bold claim for authorial self-sufficiency, equating her creation and rule over her textual world with the conquering and ruling of empires by Caesar and Alexander. She undertakes to emphasize the satisfactions of authorship, but in doing so she also underscores the social and political restrictions on women that have confined her sphere of action to an imagined world.

The Description of a New World, Called The Blazing World[1]

To the Reader

* * * This is the reason, why I added this piece of fancy to my philosophical observations, and joined them as two worlds at the ends of their poles; both for my own sake, to divert my studious thoughts, which I employed in the contemplation thereof, and to delight the reader with variety, which is always pleasing. But lest my fancy should stray too much, I chose such a fiction as would be agreeable to the subject treated of in the former parts; it is a description of a *new world,* not such as *Lucian's* or the *French*-man's world in the moon;[2] but a world of my own creating, which I call the *Blazing World*: the first part whereof is *romancical,* the second philosophical, and the third is merely *fancy,* or (as I may call it) *fantastical,* which if it add any satisfaction to you, I shall account my self a happy *creatoress*; if not, I must be content to live a melancholy life in my own world; I cannot call it a poor world, if poverty be only want of gold, silver, and jewels; for there is more gold in it than all the chemists ever did, and (as I verily believe) will ever be able to make. As for the rocks of diamonds, I wish with all my soul they might be shared amongst my noble female friends, and upon that condition, I would willingly quit my part; and of the gold I should only desire so much as might suffice to repair my noble lord and husband's losses:[3] for I am not covetous, but as ambitious as ever any of my sex was, is, or can be; which makes, that though I cannot be *Henry* the Fifth, or *Charles* the Second, yet I endeavor to be *Margaret* the First; and although I have neither power, time nor occasion to conquer the world as *Alexander* and *Caesar* did; yet rather than not to be mistress of one, since Fortune and the Fates would give me none, I

---

1. *The Blazing World* was published in 1666 and 1668, together with Newcastle's *Observations upon Experimental Philosophy,* a critique of the new science emphasizing the limitations of experiment founded on human perception, and such machines as the microscope and telescope.
2. Cyrano de Bergerac (1620–1655), author of *Histoire comique conenant les états et empires de la lune* (1657). The Greek satirist Lucian of Samo-

sata (125–200? C.E.) wrote dialogues about an imaginary voyage, translated in 1634.
3. Cavendish's husband, William, was formally banished from England and his estates confiscated in 1649; they were all restored after the Restoration. During his banishment Margaret estimated that he suffered financial losses of around £940,000.

have made a world of my own: for which no body, I hope, will blame me, since it is in every one's power to do the like.

---

* * * No sooner was the Lady brought before the Emperor, but he conceived her to be some goddess, and offered to worship her; which she refused, telling him, (for by that time she had pretty well learned their language) that although she came out of another world, yet was she but a mortal; at which the Emperor rejoicing, made her his wife, and gave her an absolute power to rule and govern all that world as she pleased. But her subjects, who could hardly be persuaded to believe her mortal, tendered her all the veneration and worship due to a deity . . .

Their priests and governors were princes of the imperial blood, and made eunuchs for that purpose; and as for the ordinary sort of men in that part of the world where the Emperor resided, they were of several complexions; not white, black, tawny, olive or ash-coloured; but some appeared of an azure, some of a deep purple, some of a grass-green, some of a scarlet, some of an orange color, etc. Which colors and complexions, whether they were made by the bare reflection of light, without the assistance of small particles, or by the help of well-ranged and ordered atoms; or by a continual agitation of little globules; or by some pressing and reacting motion, I am not able to determine. The rest of the inhabitants of that world, were men of several different sorts, shapes, figures, dispositions, and humors, as I have already made mention heretofore; some were bear-men, some worm-men, some fish- or mear-men,[4] otherwise called sirens; some bird-men, some fly-men, some ant-men, some geese-men, some spider-men, some lice-men, some fox-men, some ape-men, some jackdaw-men, some magpie-men, some parrot-men, some satyrs, some giants, and many more, which I cannot all remember; and of these several sorts of men, each followed such a profession as was most proper for the nature of their species, which the Empress encouraged them in, especially those that had applied themselves to the study of several arts and sciences; for they were as ingenious and witty in the invention of profitable and useful arts, as we are in our world, nay, more; and to that end she erected schools, and founded several societies. The bear-men were to be her experimental philosophers, the bird-men her astronomers, the fly-, worm- and fish-men her natural philosophers, the ape-men her chemists, the satyrs her Galenic physicians, the fox-men her politicians, the spider- and lice-men her mathematicians, the jackdaw-, magpie- and parrot-men her orators and logicians, the giants her architects, etc. But before all things, she having got a sovereign power from the Emperor over all the world, desired to be informed both of the manner of their religion and government, and to that end she called the priests and statesmen, to give her an account of either. Of the statesmen she enquired, first, why they had so few laws? To which they answered, that many laws made many divisions, which most commonly did breed factions, and at last break out into open wars. Next, she asked, why they preferred the monarchical form of government before any other? They answered, that as it was natural for one body to have but one head, so it was also natural for a politic body to have but one governor; and that a

---

4. Mermen, the male counterparts of mermaids.

commonwealth, which had many governors was like a monster with many heads: besides, said they, a monarchy is a divine form of government, and agrees most with our religion; for as there is but one God, whom we all unanimously worship and adore with one faith, so we are resolved to have but one Emperor, to whom we all submit with one obedience.

Then the Empress seeing that the several sorts of her subjects had each their churches apart, asked the priests whether they were of several religions? They answered her Majesty, that there was no more but one religion in all that world, nor no diversity of opinions in that same religion; for though there were several sorts of men, yet had they all but one opinion concerning the worship and adoration of God. The Empress asked them, whether they were Jews, Turks, or Christians? We do not know, said they, what religions those are; but we do all unanimously acknowledge, worship and adore the only, omnipotent, and eternal God, with all reverence, submission, and duty. Again, the Empress enquired, whether they had several forms of worship? They answered, no: for our devotion and worship consists only in prayers, which we frame according to our several necessities, in petitions, humiliations, thanksgiving, etc. Truly, replied the Empress, I thought you had been either Jews, or Turks, because I never perceived any women in your congregations; but what is the reason, you bar them from your religious assemblies? It is not fit, said they, that men and women should be promiscuously together in time of religious worship; for their company hinders devotion, and makes many, instead of praying to God, direct their devotion to their mistresses. But, asked the Empress, have they no congregation of their own, to perform the duties of divine worship, as well as men? No, answered they: but they stay at home, and say their prayers by themselves in their closets.[5] Then the Empress desired to know the reason why the priests and governors of their world were made eunuchs? They answered, to keep them from marriage; for women and children most commonly make disturbance both in church and state. But, said she, women and children have no employment in church or state. 'Tis true, answered they; but although they are not admitted to public employments, yet are they so prevalent[6] with their husbands and parents, that many times by their importunate persuasions, they cause as much, nay, more mischief secretly, than if they had the management of public affairs.

* * * * *

[THE EMPRESS BRINGS THE DUCHESS OF NEWCASTLE TO THE BLAZING WORLD]

After some time, when the spirits had refreshed themselves in their own vehicles, they sent one of their nimblest spirits, to ask the Empress, whether she would have a scribe. * * * Then the spirit asked her, whether she would have the soul of a living or a dead man? Why, said the Empress, can the soul quit a living body, and wander or travel abroad? Yes, answered he, for according to Plato's doctrine, there is a conversation of souls, and the souls of lovers live in the bodies of their beloved. Then I will have, answered she, the soul of some ancient famous writer, either of Aristotle, Pythagoras, Plato, Epicurus,[7] or the like. The spirit said, that those famous men were very learned,

---

5. Private chambers.
6. I.e., they prevail so much.
7. Classical philosophers and founders, respec-

tively, of schools of philosophy: the Peripatetics, the Pythagoreans, the Academics, the Epicureans.

subtle, and ingenious writers, but they were so wedded to their own opinions, that they would never have the patience to be scribes. Then, said she, I'll have the soul of one of the most famous modern writers, as either of Galileo, Gassendus, Descartes, Helmont, Hobbes, H. More, etc.[8] The spirit answered, that they were fine ingenious writers, but yet so self-conceited, that they would scorn to be scribes to a woman. But, said he, there's a lady, the Duchess of Newcastle, which although she is not one of the most learned, eloquent, witty and ingenious, yet is she a plain and rational writer, for the principle of her writings, is sense and reason, and she will without question, be ready to do you all the service she can. This lady then, said the Empress, will I choose for my scribe, neither will the Emperor have reason to be jealous, she being one of my own sex. In truth, said the spirit, husbands have reason to be jealous of platonic lovers, for they are very dangerous, as being not only very intimate and close, but subtle and insinuating. You say well, replied the Empress; wherefore I pray send me the Duchess of New-castle's soul; which the spirit did; and after she came to wait on the Empress, at her first arrival the Empress embraced and saluted her with a spiritual kiss.

* * *

[THE DUCHESS WANTS A WORLD TO RULE]

Well, said the Duchess, setting aside this dispute, my ambition is, that I would fain be as you are, that is, an Empress of a world, and I shall never be at quiet until I be one. I love you so well, replied the Empress, that I wish with all my soul, you had the fruition of your ambitious desire, and I shall not fail to give you my best advice how to accomplish it; the best informers are the immaterial spirits, and they'll soon tell you, whether it be possible to obtain your wish. But, said the Duchess, I have little acquaintance with them, for I never knew any before the time you sent for me. They know you, replied the Empress; for they told me of you, and were the means and instru-ment of your coming hither: wherefore I'll confer with them, and enquire whether there be not another world, whereof you may be Empress as well as I am of this? No sooner had the Empress said this, but some immaterial spirits came to visit her, of whom she enquired, whether there were but there worlds in all, to wit, the Blazing World where she was in, the world which she came from, and the world where the Duchess lived? The spirits answered, that there were more numerous worlds than the stars which appeared in these three mentioned worlds. Then the Empress asked, whether it was not possible, that her dearest friend the Duchess of Newcastle, might be Empress of one of them?[9] Although there be numerous, nay, infinite worlds, answered the spirits, yet none is without government. But is none of these worlds so weak, said she, that it may be surprised or conquered? The spirits answered, that Lucian's world of lights, had been for some time in a snuff, but of late years one Helmont had got it, who since he was Emperor

---

8. Galileo Galilei (1564–1642), Italian astrono-mer and defender of the Copernican system; Pierre Gassendi (1592–1655), proponent of a mechanis-tic theory of matter; René Descartes (1596–1650), French mathematician and philosopher who had a major influence on the new science; Jan Baptista Van Helmont (1577–1644), Flemish chemist; Thomas Hobbes, English mechanistic philosopher

and political scientist, author of *Leviathan*; Henry More (1614–1687), one of the antimaterialist Cambridge Platonists.
9. Speculation about multiple inhabited worlds was an occasional topic in texts on the new astron-omy. Milton's Raphael introduces the idea to Adam (*Paradise Lost* 8.148–52).

of it, had so strengthened the immortal parts thereof with mortal out-works, as it was for the present impregnable. Said the Empress, if there be such an infinite number of worlds, I am sure, not only my friend, the Duchess, but any other might obtain one. Yes, answered the spirits, if those worlds were uninhabited; but they are as populous as this, your Majesty governs. Why, said the Empress, it is not impossible to conquer a world. No, answered the spirits, but, for the most part, conquerors seldom enjoy their conquest, for they being more feared than loved, most commonly come to an untimely end. If you will but direct me, said the Duchess to the spirits, which world is easiest to be conquered, her Majesty will assist me with means, and I will trust to fate and fortune; for I had rather die in the adventure of noble achievements, than live in obscure and sluggish security; since by the one, I may live in a glorious fame, and by the other I am buried in oblivion. The spirits answered, that the lives of fame were like other lives; for some lasted long, and some died soon. 'Tis true, said the Duchess; but yet the shortest-lived fame lasts longer than the longest life of man. But, replied the spirits, if occasion does not serve you, you must content yourself to live without such achievements that may gain you a fame: but we wonder, proceeded the spirits, that you desire to be Empress of a terrestrial world, whenas you can create yourself a celestial world if you please. What, said the Empress, can any mortal be a creator? Yes, answered the spirits; for every human creature can create an immaterial world fully inhabited by immaterial creatures, and populous of immaterial subjects, such as we are, and all this within the compass of the head or skull; nay, not only so, but he may create a world of what fashion and government he will, and give the creatures thereof such motions, figures, forms, colors, perceptions, etc. as he pleases, and make whirlpools, lights, pressures and reactions, etc. as he thinks best; nay, he may make a world full of veins, muscles, and nerves, and all these to move by one jolt or stroke: also he may alter that world as often as he pleases, or change it from a natural world, to an artificial; he may make a world of ideas, a world of atoms, a world of lights, or whatsoever his fancy leads him to. And since it is in your power to create such a world, what need you to venture life, reputation and tranquility, to conquer a gross material world? . . . You have converted me, said the Duchess to the spirits, from my ambitious desire; wherefore I'll take your advice, reject and despise all the worlds without me, and create a world of my own.

* * *

The Epilogue to the Reader

By this poetical description, you may perceive, that my ambition is not only to be Empress, but Authoress of a whole world; and that the worlds I have made, both the Blazing and the other Philosophical World, mentioned in the first part of this description, are framed and composed of the most pure, that is, the rational parts of matter, which are the parts of my mind; which creation was more easily and suddenly effected, than the conquests of the two famous monarchs of the world, Alexander and Caesar:[1] neither have I made such disturbances, and caused so many dissolutions of particulars, otherwise named deaths, as they did; for I have destroyed but some

---

1. Alexander the Great and Julius Caesar were both famed as conquerors of much of the world known to them.

few men in a little boat, which died through the extremity of cold, and that by the hand of Justice, which was necessitated to punish their crime of stealing away a young and beauteous lady.[2] And in the formation of those worlds, I take more delight and glory, than ever Alexander or Caesar did in conquering this terrestrial world; and though I have made my Blazing World, a peaceable world, allowing it but one religion, one language, and one government; yet could I make another world, as full of factions, divisions, and wars, as this is of peace and tranquility; and the rational figures of my mind might express as much courage to fight, as Hector and Achilles[3] had; and be as wise as Nestor, as eloquent as Ulysses, and as beautiful as Helen. But I esteeming peace before war, wit before policy, honesty before beauty; instead of the figures of Alexander, Caesar, Hector, Achilles, Nestor, Ulysses, Helen, etc. chose rather the figure of honest Margaret Newcastle, which now I would not change for all this terrestrial world; and if any should like the world I have made, and be willing to be my subjects, they may imagine themselves such, and they are such, I mean, in their minds, fancies or imaginations; but if they cannot endure to be subjects, they may create worlds of their own, and govern themselves as they please: but yet let them have a care, not to prove unjust usurpers, and to rob me of mine; for concerning the Philosophical World, I am Empress of it myself; and as for the Blazing World, it having an Empress already, who rules it with great wisdom and conduct, which Empress is my dear Platonic friend; I shall never prove so unjust, treacherous and unworthy to her, as to disturb her government, much less to depose her from her imperial throne, for the sake of any other; but rather choose to create another world for another friend.

1666, 1668

2. A reference to the romancelike incident with which *The Blazing World* begins, the abduction of a young woman by a party of adventurers, whose boat was blown in a tempest to the North Pole, where they perished (except for the woman, who entered into the Blazing World).

3. The principal heroes of Homer's *Iliad*, Hector the Trojan and Achilles the Greek. "Nestor": wise advisor to the Greeks. "Ulysses": hero of Homer's *Odyssey*. "Helen": her beauty caused the Trojan War, as it prompted the Trojan Paris to steal her away from her Greek husband, Menelaus.

JOHN MILTON
1608–1674

When he was thirty, John Milton proclaimed himself the future author of a great English epic. He promised a poem devoted to the glory of the nation, centering around the deeds of King Arthur or some other ancient hero. When Milton finally published his epic thirty years later, readers found instead a poem set in Heaven, Hell, and the garden of Eden, in which traditional heroism is denigrated and England not once mentioned. What lay between the youthful promise and the eventual fulfillment was a career marked by private tragedy and public controversy. Milton tells us much about both these experiences in his works, which combine an intense self-scrutiny and concern with authorship with urgent intervention in the great questions of his time. It is scarcely possible to treat Milton's career separately from the history of England in his lifetime, not only because he was an active participant in public affairs but also because he himself refused to distinguish between his private life and affairs of church and state. When he signed himself, as he often did, "John Milton, Englishman," he did not simply mean *an* Englishman. As England's self-appointed prophetic bard, Milton saw himself as spokesman for the nation as a whole, even when he found himself in a minority of one. Milton was a man who devoted his life to public causes, but whose understanding of those causes often arose out of the most personal concerns.

The young Milton self-consciously set out to follow the steps of the ideal poetic career—beginning with pastoral and ending with epic—modeled on that of the Roman poet Virgil. In this approach to his vocation, he stood at the opposite end of the spectrum from such Cavalier contemporaries as Suckling and Lovelace, who turned to verse with an air of studied carelessness. Milton began by writing occasional poems in Latin and several English poems in the pastoral mode: lyrics, the masque *Comus* (1634), and the pastoral elegy *Lycidas* (1683). These are extraordinary works in their own right, which crown and transform their respective genres, but Milton also undertook them as preparation for the greater genres of tragedy and epic. He was embarking on a road previously traveled by Edmund Spenser, whom he called "a better teacher than Scotus or Aquinas." Milton resembles Spenser in certain ways, above all in his constant use of myth and archetype, alluding to and juxtaposing biblical and classical stories. But Milton's learning was greater than Spenser's. As part of his preparation for a poetic career, he undertook a six-year program of self-directed reading in ancient and modern theology, philosophy, history, science, politics, and literature. His command of languages included Latin, Greek, Hebrew and its dialects, Italian, French, Spanish, and Dutch. The sum of the western literary and intellectual heritage impinged on his writing as immediately and directly as the circumstances of his own life, but he continually reconceived the ideas, literary forms, and values of this heritage to make them relevant to himself and his age.

For Milton to devote six years of his adult life to an obscure course of private study required extraordinary confidence in the service he hoped to perform for God and country. It also, of course, required money, which was provided by his father, who was a successful scrivener—a combination of solicitor, investment advisor, and money lender. Although Milton enjoyed the company of some aristocrats and was profoundly grateful that his father spared him from the grubby business of making money, he belonged to the London bourgeoisie. His father's business dealings and loans at interest paid for private tutors in his youth, for his education at St. Paul's, one of the finest schools in the land, for his seven years at Cambridge and the six years of reading that followed, and for his "grand tour" of France, Italy, and Switzerland at the age of thirty. Yet Milton's connection with the class that stood to benefit most directly from Europe's first bourgeois revolution does not account for his passionate political views. His brother, Christopher, fought on the royalist side. For the Milton brothers, as for most of their contemporaries, the civil wars did not appear as a confrontation of class interests, but as a conflict between radically differing theories of government and, above all, religion.

From the outbreak of the conflict until his death, Milton was allied with the Puritan cause. Yet his religious opinions developed throughout his life, from relative orthodoxy in his youth to ever more heretical positions in his later years. Milton went up to Cambridge in 1625 with every intention of taking orders in the Church of England. In the hindsight of 1642, he blamed the lack of reformation and the corruption in the English Church under Archbishop Laud for forcing him to abandon that goal, proclaiming himself "church-outed by the Prelates." Milton's change of direction must also have been linked to the fastidious contempt he expressed for the ignorant and clownish clergymen-in-making who were his fellow students at Cambridge: "They thought themselves gallant men, and I thought them fools." Those fellow students dubbed Milton "The Lady of Christ's College." Above all, Milton came to believe that he was destined to serve his language, his country, and his God as a poet. In his first major English poem, the hymn *On the Morning of Christ's Nativity* (written at the age of twenty-one), Milton had already begun to construct himself as a prophetic bard. His sense of poetic mission grew over the next decade, accompanied by growing disillusion with the Church of England. Both are present in *Lycidas* (1638), written to lament the untimely death of his Cambridge contemporary Edward King. The figure of King recedes in the poem next to Milton's anxious contemplation of poetry as a vocation and his furious diatribe against the corrupt Anglican clergy who leave their charges prey to the "grim wolf" of Catholicism. Yet while he was in Italy on the Grand Tour (1638–39), Milton delighted in exchanging verses and learned compliments with various Catholic intellectuals and men of letters, some of whom became friends. Milton could always maintain friendships and family relationships across ideological divides.

Upon his return to England, Milton opened a school and was soon involved in Presbyterian efforts to depose the bishops and reform Church liturgy, writing five "Antiprelatical" tracts denouncing and satirizing bishops. These were the first in a remarkable series of political interventions which occupied Milton for the next twenty years, until the disaster (for him) of the Restoration. He wrote successively on church government, divorce, education, freedom of the press, regicide, and republicanism. He also served as Latin Secretary to the Commonwealth Government (1649–53) and to Oliver Cromwell's Protectorate (1654–58), writing the official letters—mostly in Latin—to foreign governments and heads of state. Yet Milton was the very opposite of a faceless spokesman for a party line. From the beginning to the end of his polemical career, his publications show an extraordinary courage and independence of thought. In his tracts advocating divorce on the grounds of incompatibility and with the right to remarry, he adopted and vigorously defended a position almost unheard of at the time, one which required a boldly antiliteral reading of the gospels. In *Areopagitica*, he put forward an impassioned defense of a free press against a Parliament determined to restore effective censorship. And just as he was among the first to attack the power of the bishops, so he was virtually the last defender of the "Good Old Cause" of the Revolution; the second edition of his *Ready and Easy Way to Establish a Free Commonwealth* appeared in late April 1660, scarcely two weeks before the Restoration.

Several of these treatises were also prompted by personal concerns or crises. In his polemical tract *The Reason of Church Government Urged Against Prelaty*, Milton devoted several pages to a discussion of his poetic vocation and the great works he might produce in the future. His writings on divorce, which can hardly have seemed the most pressing of issues in the strife-torn years 1643–45, were motivated by his personal experience of a disastrous marriage. Aged thirty-three, inexperienced with women, and idealistic about marriage as in essence a union of minds and spirits, he had wedded a young woman of seventeen, Mary Powell, who returned to her royalist family just a few months after the marriage. Milton responded by turning his private grief into a matter of public controversy. The fact that his tracts on divorce could not be licensed and were roundly denounced in Parliament, from pulpits, and in print prompted him in turn to write *Areopagitica*, his famous defense of a free press and the free commerce in ideas. Yet he saw all these personal issues—a reformed poetry, the domestic liberty to be achieved through needful divorce, and a free press—as vital to the creation of a reformed English culture.

In the years that followed, Milton suffered a series of agonizing tragedies. Mary Powell returned to him in 1645, but died in childbirth in 1652, leaving four children; the only son, John, died a few months later. In the same year, Milton became totally blind. Whatever the medical causes, Milton himself attributed his blindness to late nights of reading in his youth and his exertions in writing defenses of the execution of Charles I and the new republic. Milton married again in 1656, apparently happily, but his new wife, Katherine Woodcock, was dead two years later, along with their infant daughter. Katherine is probably the subject of his sonnet *Methought I Saw My Late Espousèd Saint*, a moving dream-vision poignant with the sense of loss—both of sight and of love. Milton had little time for poetry in these years, but his few sonnets revolutionized the genre, overlaying the Petrarchan metrical structure with an urgent rhetorical voice and using the small sonnet form, hitherto confined mainly to matters of love, for new and grand subjects: praise of Cromwell mixed with admonition and political advice; a prophetic denunciation calling down God's vengeance for Protestants massacred in Piedmont; an emotion-filled account of his continuing struggle to come to terms with his blindness as part of God's providence.

Milton's courageous defense of the Revolution down to the last possible moment could have spelled disaster for him upon the return of Charles II. For several months after that event, he was in hiding, his life in danger, but friends, especially the poet Andrew Marvell, managed his pardon and later his release from a brief imprisonment. He lived out his last years in reduced circumstances, plagued by ever more serious attacks of gout but grateful for the domestic comforts provided by his third wife, Elizabeth Minshull, whom he married in 1663 and who survived him. In such conditions, dismayed by the defeat of his political and religious cause, totally blind and often ill, threatened by the horrific plague of 1665 and the great fire of 1666, and entirely dependent on amanuenses and friends to transcribe his dictation, he completed the great epic poem that undertakes to "justify the ways of God to men." *Paradise Lost* radically reconceives the epic genre and epic heroism, choosing as protagonists a domestic couple rather than martial heroes, and degrading the military glory celebrated in epic tradition in favor of the "better fortitude / Of patience and heroic martyrdom." Michael's prophecy to Adam makes clear that the course of human history is tragic, that the world will remain "to good malignant, to bad men benign" until the Second Coming of Christ. Yet it also makes clear that throughout history God will raise up prophets and heroes to resist wicked tyrants and corrupt societies.

In his final years, Milton continued to pursue subjects that had interested him from his youth, publishing works on grammar and logic chiefly written during his days as schoolmaster, a *History of Britain* (1670) from earliest times to the Norman Conquest, and a treatise urging toleration for Puritan dissenters (1673). He also continued work on his *Christian Doctrine*, a Latin treatise which reveals how far Milton had moved from the orthodoxies of his day. The work denies the Trinity (making Christ and the Holy Spirit much inferior to God the Father), insists upon free will (against Calvinist predestination), and privileges the inspiration of the Spirit over the Scriptures and the Ten Commandments. Such radical and heterodox positions could not be made public in his lifetime, certainly not in the repressive conditions of the Restoration, and Milton's *Christian Doctrine* was lost to view for over 150 years.

In 1671 Milton published two poems which resonate with echoes of the harsh repression and the moral and political challenges Puritan dissenters faced after the Restoration. *Paradise Regained*, a brief epic in four books, treats Jesus' Temptation in the Wilderness as a hard intellectual struggle through which the hero comes to understand himself and his mission and defeats Satan by renouncing the whole panoply of false or faulty versions of the good life and of his kingdom. *Samson Agonistes*, a classical tragedy, is the more harrowing for the resemblances between its tragic hero and its author. The deeply flawed, pain-wracked, blind, and defeated Samson struggles, in dialogues with his visitors, to gain self-knowledge, discovering at last a desperate way to triumph over his captors and offer his people a chance to regain their freedom. In these last poems, Milton sought to educate his readers in moral and political wisdom and virtue. Only through such inner transformation, Milton now firmly believed, would men and women come to value—and so perhaps reclaim—the intellectual, religious, and political freedom he so vigorously promoted in his prose and poetry.

On Shakespeare[1]

What needs my Shakespeare for his honored bones
The labor of an age in pilèd stones,
Or that his hallowed relics should be hid
Under a star-ypointing[2] pyramid?
5   Dear son of memory,[3] great heir of fame,
What° need'st thou such weak witness of thy name?   *why*
Thou in our wonder and astonishment
Hast built thyself a livelong° monument.   *enduring*
For whilst to th' shame of slow-endeavoring art
10   Thy easy numbers flow, and that each heart
Hath from the leaves of thy unvalued° book   *invaluable*
Those Delphic[4] lines with deep impression took,
Then thou, our fancy of itself bereaving,
Dost make us marble with too much conceiving;[5]
15   And so sepùlchered in such pomp dost lie,
That kings for such a tomb would wish to die.

1630   1632

L'Allegro[1]

Hence loathèd Melancholy,[2]
   Of Cerberus[3] and blackest midnight born,
In Stygian[4] cave forlorn
   'Mongst horrid shapes, and shrieks, and sights unholy,
5   Find out some uncouth° cell,   *desolate*
   Where brooding Darkness spreads his jealous wings,
And the night-raven sings;
   There under ebon shades and low-browed rocks,
As ragged as thy locks,
10   In dark Cimmerian[5] desert ever dwell.
But come thou goddess fair and free,
In heaven yclept Euphrosyne,[6]

1. This tribute, Milton's first published poem, appeared in the Second Folio of Shakespeare's plays (1632).
2. A Spenserian archaism.
3. As "son of memory" Shakespeare is a brother of the Muses, who are the daughters of Mnemosyne (Memory).
4. Apollo, god of poetry, had his oracle at Delphi.
5. Shakespeare's mesmerized readers are themselves his (marble) monument.
1. The companion poems *L'Allegro* and *Il Penseroso* are both written in tetrameter couplets, but Milton's virtuosity produces entirely different tempos and sound qualities in the two poems. The Italian titles name, respectively, the cheerful, mirthful man and the melancholy, contemplative man. The poems are carefully balanced and their different values celebrated, though *Penseroso's* greater length and final coda may intimate that life's superiority. Mirth, the presiding deity of *Allegro*, is described in terms that evoke Botticelli's presen-

tation of the Grace Euphrosone (youthful mirth) and her sisters in his *Primavera*.
2. The black Melancholy recognized and here exorcized by Mirth's man is a disease leading to madness; *Il Penseroso* celebrates melancholy as the temperament of the scholarly, contemplative man, represented in Durer's famous engraving *Melancholy*. Robert Burton's *Anatomy of Melancholy* treats the entire range of possibilities.
3. The three-headed hellhound of classical mythology.
4. Near the river Styx, in the underworld.
5. Homer's Cimmereans (*Odyssey* 11.13–19) live on the outer edge of the world, in perpetual darkness.
6. The three Graces—Euphrosyne (four syllables) figuring Youthful Mirth, Aglaia, Brilliance, and Thalia, Bloom—were commonly taken to be offspring of Venus (Love and Beauty) and Bacchus (god of wine). Milton proceeds, however, to devise another, more innocent parentage for Euphrosyne

And by men, heart-easing Mirth,
Whom lovely Venus at a birth
15   With two sister Graces more
To ivy-crownèd Bacchus bore;
Or whether (as some sager sing)
The frolic wind that breathes the spring,
Zephyr with Aurora playing,
20   As he met her once a-Maying,
There on beds of violets blue,
And fresh-blown° roses washed in dew,   newly opened
Filled her with thee a daughter fair,
So buxom,° blithe, and debonair.   lively
25   Haste thee nymph, and bring with thee
Jest and youthful Jollity,
Quips° and Cranks,° and wanton Wiles,   witty sayings/jokes
Nods, and Becks,° and wreathèd Smiles,   beckonings
Such as hang on Hebe's[7] cheek,
30   And love to live in dimple sleek;
Sport that wrinkled Care derides,
And Laughter holding both his sides.
Come, and trip it° as ye go   dance
On the light fantastic toe,
35   And in thy right hand lead with thee
The mountain nymph, sweet Liberty;
And if I give thee honor due,
Mirth, admit me of thy crew
To live with her and live with thee
40   In unreprovèd° pleasures free;   irreproachable
To hear the lark begin his flight,
And, singing, startle the dull night,
From his watch-tower in the skies,
Till the dappled dawn doth rise;
45   Then to come in spite of° sorrow,   in defiance of
And at my window bid good morrow,
Through the sweetbriar or the vine,
Or the twisted eglantine.
While the cock with lively din
50   Scatters the rear of darkness thin,
And to the stack or the barn door,
Stoutly struts his dames before;
Oft listening how the hounds and horn
Cheerly rouse the slumbering morn,
55   From the side of some hoar hill,
Through the high wood echoing shrill.
Sometime walking not unseen
By hedgerow elms, on hillocks green,
Right against the eastern gate,
60   Where the great sun begins his state,[8]
Robed in flames and amber light,

(ascribing it to "some sager," lines 17–24): Zephyr,
the West Wind, and Aurora, goddess of the Dawn.
7. Goddess of youth and cupbearer to the gods.
8. Stately procession, as by a monarch.

The clouds in thousand liveries dight;°   *dressed*
While the plowman near at hand
Whistles o'er the furrowed land,
65   And the milkmaid singeth blithe,
And the mower whets his scythe,
And every shepherd tells his tale
Under the hawthorn in the dale.
Straight mine eye hath caught new pleasures
70   Whilst the landscape round it measures,
Russet lawns and fallows° gray,   *plowed land*
Where the nibbling flocks do stray,
Mountains on whose barren breast
The laboring clouds do often rest;
75   Meadows trim with daisies pied,°   *multicolored*
Shallow brooks, and rivers wide.
Towers and battlements it sees
Bosomed high in tufted trees,
Where perhaps some beauty lies,
80   The cynosure[9] of neighboring eyes.
Hard by, a cottage chimney smokes
From betwixt two agèd oaks,
Where Corydon and Thyrsis met
Are at their savory dinner set
85   Of herbs and other country messes,
Which the neat-handed° Phyllis dresses;   *dexterous*
And then in haste her bower she leaves,
With Thestylis[1] to bind the sheaves;
Or if the earlier season lead
90   To the tanned° haycock in the mead.   *sun-dried*
Sometimes with secure° delight   *careless*
The upland hamlets will invite,
When the merry bells ring round
And the jocund rebecks[2] sound
95   To many a youth and many a maid,
Dancing in the checkered shade;
And young and old come forth to play
On a sunshine holiday,
Till the livelong daylight fail;
100   Then to the spicy nut-brown ale,
With stories told of many a feat,
How fairy Mab the junkets[3] eat;
She was pinched and pulled, she said,
And he, by friar's lantern led,
105   Tells how the drudging goblin[4] sweat
To earn his cream-bowl duly set,
When in one night, ere glimpse of morn,

9. Literally, the bright polestar, by which mariners steer; here, a splendid object, much gazed at.
1. Milton uses traditional names from classical pastoral—"Corydon," "Thyrsis," "Phyllis," "Thestylis"—for his rustic English shepherds.
2. A small three-stringed fiddle. "Jocund": merry, sprightly.

3. Sweetmeats, especially with cream. Queen Mab is the fairy queen, consort of Oberon. "She" and "he" in the next two lines are country folk telling of their experiences with fairies.
4. Robin Goodfellow, alias Puck, Pook, or Hobgoblin. "Friar's lantern": will-o'-the-wisp.

His shadowy flail hath threshed the corn
That ten day-laborers could not end;
110 Then lies him down the lubber fiend,[5]
And stretched out all the chimney's° length,   *fireplace's*
Basks at the fire his hairy strength;
And crop-full out of doors he flings
Ere the first cock his matin rings.
115 Thus done the tales, to bed they creep,
By whispering winds soon lulled asleep.
Towered cities please us then,
And the busy hum of men,
Where throngs of knights and barons bold
120 In weeds of peace high triumphs[6] hold,
With store of ladies, whose bright eyes
Rain influence,[7] and judge the prize
Of wit or arms, while both contend
To win her grace, whom all commend.
125 There let Hymen[8] oft appear
In saffron robe, with taper clear,
And pomp and feast and revelry,
With masque and antique° pageantry;   *ancient, also antic*
Such sights as youthful poets dream
130 On summer eves by haunted stream.
Then to the well-trod stage anon,
If Jonson's learned sock be on,
Or sweetest Shakespeare, fancy's child,
Warble his native wood-notes wild.[9]
135 And ever against eating cares;[1]
Lap me in soft Lydian airs,[2]
Married to immortal verse
Such as the meeting soul may pierce
In notes with many a winding bout°   *circuit*
140 Of linkèd sweetness long drawn out,
With wanton heed and giddy cunning,
The melting voice through mazes running,
Untwisting all the chains that tie
The hidden soul of harmony;
145 That Orpheus' self may heave his head
From golden slumber on a bed
Of heaped Elysian flowers, and hear
Such strains as would have won the ear
Of Pluto, to have quite set free
150 His half-regained Eurydice.[3]

5. Robin traditionally did all manner of drudging work for people, to be rewarded with a bowl of cream.
6. Pageants. "Weeds of peace": courtly raiment.
7. The ladies' eyes are stars and so have astrological influence over the men.
8. Roman god of marriage. An orange-yellow (saffron) robe and a torch are his attributes.
9. It was conventional to contrast Jonson as a "learned" poet and Shakespeare as a "natural" one, but L'Allegro's views and choices of literature also

suits with his nature. "Sock": the comedian's low-heeled slipper, contrasted with the tragedian's buskin, a high-heeled boot.
1. "Eating cares" (Horace, *Odes* 2.11.18) is one of many classical echoes in the poem.
2. Plato considered "Lydian airs" to be enervating, soft, and sensual; he preferred the solemn Doric mode. Some others thought Lydian airs relaxing and delightful.
3. Orpheus's music so moved Pluto that he agreed to release his dead wife Eurydice (four syllables,

These delights if thou canst give,
Mirth, with thee I mean to live.[4]

ca. 1631   1645

Il Penseroso[1]

Hence vain deluding Joys,[2]
    The brood of Folly without father bred,
How little you bestead,°   *avail*
    Or fill the fixèd mind with all your toys°   *trifles*
5   Dwell in some idle brain,
    And fancies fond° with gaudy shapes possess,   *foolish*
As thick and numberless
    As the gay motes that people the sunbeams,
Or likest hovering dreams,
10   The fickle pensioners of Morpheus'[3] train.
But hail thou Goddess sage and holy,
Hail, divinest Melancholy,
Whose saintly visage is too bright
To hit° the sense of human sight,   *suit*
15 And therefore to our weaker view
O'erlaid with black, staid Wisdom's hue;[4]
Black, but such as in esteem,
Prince Memnon's sister[5] might beseem,
Or that starred Ethiope queen[6] that strove
20 To set her beauty's praise above
The sea nymphs, and their powers offended.
Yet thou art higher far descended;
Thee bright-haired Vesta long of yore
To solitary Saturn bore;[7]
25 His daughter she (in Saturn's reign
Such mixture was not held a stain).
Oft in glimmering bowers and glades
He met her, and in secret shades
Of woody Ida's inmost grove,
30 While yet there was no fear of Jove.
Come pensive nun, devout and pure,

accent on the second) from the underworld, but
he violated the condition set—that he not look
back at her—and so lost her again. Milton often
uses Orpheus as a figure for the poet.
4. The final lines echo Marlowe's *The Passionate
Shepherd to His Love* (p. 457): "If these delights
thy mind may move, / Then live with me, and be
my love."
1. Melancholy's man celebrates a melancholy that
does not produce madness but the scholarly temperament, ruled by Saturn. See note 2 to *L'Allegro*.
2. For Melancholy's man, Mirth is not the innocent joys of *L'Allegro*, but "vain deluding Joys."
3. Morpheus is the god of sleep. "Pensioners": followers.
4. The melancholy humor, caused by black bile,
was thought to make the face dark or saturnine—

from the ancient god, Saturn, allegorized in Neoplatonic philosophy as "the collective angelic
mind."
5. Memnon, in *Odyssey* 11, was a handsome Ethiopian prince; his sister Himera's beauty was mentioned by later commentators. Cf. Song of
Solomon 1.5, "I am black but comely."
6. Cassiopeia was turned into a constellation
("starred") for bragging that she was more beautiful than the sea nymphs.
7. Vesta, daughter of Saturn, was goddess of the
household and a virgin, as were her priestesses.
Milton invented the story of her sexual congress
with Saturn on Mount Ida, resulting in Melancholy's birth. Saturn ruled the gods and the world
during the Golden Age, which ended when he was
murdered by his son Jove.

Sober, steadfast, and demure,
All in a robe of darkest grain,°   color
Flowing with majestic train,
35   And sable stole⁸ of cypress lawn
Over thy decent° shoulders drawn.   comely, modestly covered
Come, but keep thy wonted state,
With even step and musing gait,
And looks commercing with the skies,
40   Thy rapt soul sitting in thine eyes:
There held in holy passion still,
Forget thyself to marble,⁹ till
With a sad° leaden downward cast°   grave, dignified / glance
Thou fix them on the earth as fast.
45   And join with thee calm Peace and Quiet,
Spare Fast, that oft with gods doth diet,
And hears the Muses in a ring
Aye° round about Jove's altar sing.   continually
And add to these retired Leisure,
50   That in trim gardens takes his pleasure;
But first, and chiefest, with thee bring
Him that yon soars on golden wing,
Guiding the fiery-wheelèd throne,
The cherub Contemplatiòn;¹
55   And the mute Silence hist° along,   summon
'Less Philomel² will deign a song,
In her sweetest, saddest plight,
Smoothing the rugged brow of night,
While Cynthia³ checks her dragon yoke
60   Gently o'er th' accustomed oak;
Sweet bird that shunn'st the noise of folly,
Most musical, most melancholy!
Thee chantress oft the woods among
I woo to hear thy evensong;⁴
65   And missing thee, I walk unseen
On the dry smooth-shaven green,
To behold the wandering moon,
Riding near her highest noon,
Like one that had been led astray
70   Through the heaven's wide pathless way;
And oft as if her head she bowed,
Stooping through a fleecy cloud.
Oft on a plat° of rising ground,   plot, open field
I hear the far-off curfew sound
75   Over some wide-watered shore,
Swinging slow with sullen° roar;   deep, mournful

8. A delicate black cloth.
9. Still as a statue.
1. The special function of cherubim is contemplation of God; Milton alludes also (line 53) to their identification with the wheels of the mystical chariot/throne of God described by Ezekiel (Ezekiel 10).
2. The nightingale (the bird into which Philomela was transformed after her rape by her brother-in-

law Tereus) traditionally sings a mournful song.
3. Goddess of the moon, also associated with Hecate, goddess of the underworld, who drives a pair of sleepless dragons.
4. The evening liturgy traditionally sung by cloistered monks and nuns ("chantress" evokes such a singer); L'Allegro's cock, by contrast, calls hearers to the morning liturgy, matins (line 114).

Or if the air will not permit,
Some still removèd place will fit,
Where glowing embers through the room
80 Teach light to counterfeit a gloom,
Far from all resort of mirth,
Save the cricket on the hearth,
Or the bellman's[5] drowsy charm,
To bless the doors from nightly harm;
85 Or let my lamp at midnight hour
Be seen in some high lonely tower,
Where I may oft outwatch the Bear,[6]
With thrice-great Hermes,[7] or unsphere
The spirit of Plato to unfold
90 What worlds or what vast regions hold
The immortal mind that hath forsook
Her mansion in this fleshly nook;
And of those demons[8] that are found
In fire, air, flood, or under ground,
95 Whose power hath a true consent°   agreement
With planet, or with element.
Sometime let gorgeous Tragedy
In sceptered pall[9] come sweeping by,
Presenting Thebes, or Pelops' line,
100 Or the tale of Troy divine,[1]
Or what (though rare) of later age
Ennobled hath the buskined[2] stage.
But, O sad virgin, that thy power
Might raise Musaeus[3] from his bower,
105 Or bid the soul of Orpheus[4] sing
Such notes as, warbled to the string,
Drew iron tears down Pluto's cheek,
And made Hell grant what Love did seek.
Or call up him[5] that left half told
110 The story of Cambuscan bold,
Of Camball and of Algarsife,
And who had Canacee to wife,
That owned the virtuous° ring and glass,   having magical powers
And of the wondrous horse of brass,
115 On which the Tartar king did ride;
And if aught else great bards beside
In sage and solemn tunes have sung,

5. Night watchman who rang a bell to mark the hours.
6. The Great Bear constellation never sets in northern skies.
7. Various esoteric books (actually written in the 3rd and 4th centuries) were attributed to an ancient Egyptian, Hermes Trismegistus ("thrice great"). Neoplatonists made him the father of all knowledge; later he became a patron of magicians and alchemists. To "unsphere" Plato is to bring him magically back to earth from whatever sphere he now inhabits—in practical terms, by reading his books.
8. Demons, halfway between gods and men, pre-side over the four elements.
9. Royal robe, worn by tragic actors.
1. Tragedies about Thebes include Sophocles' Oedipus cycle, those about the line of Pelops, Aeschylus's Oresteia, and those about Troy, Euripedes' Trojan Women.
2. The buskin (high boot) of tragedy, contrasted with the sock of comedy (L'Allegro, line 132).
3. Mythical poet-priest of the pre-Homeric age, supposedly a son or pupil of Orpheus.
4. For the story of Orpheus, see L'Allegro, line 145, and note.
5. Chaucer, whose Squire's Tale is unfinished.

Of tourneys and of trophies hung,
Of forests and enchantments drear,
120 Where more is meant than meets the ear.[6]
Thus, Night, oft see me in thy pale career,
Till civil-suited Morn[7] appear,
Not tricked and frounced as she was wont
With the Attic boy to hunt,
125 But kerchiefed in a comely cloud,
While rocking winds are piping loud,
Or ushered with a shower still,°   *gentle*
When the gust hath blown his fill,
Ending on the rustling leaves,
130 With minute drops from off the eaves.
And when the sun begins to fling
His flaring beams, me, Goddess, bring
To archèd walks of twilight groves,
And shadows brown that Sylvan[8] loves
135 Of pine or monumental oak,
Where the rude ax with heavèd stroke
Was never heard the nymphs to daunt,
Or fright them from their hallowed haunt.
There in close covert° by some brook,   *hidden place*
140 Where no profaner eye may look,
Hide me from day's garish eye,
While the bee with honeyed thigh,
That at her flowery work doth sing,
And the waters murmuring
145 With such consort° as they keep,   *musical harmony*
Entice the dewy-feathered sleep;
And let some strange mysterious dream
Wave at his wings in airy stream
Of lively portraiture displayed
150 Softly on my eyelids laid.
And as I wake, sweet music breathe
Above, about, or underneath,
Sent by some spirit to mortals good,
Or th' unseen genius° of the wood.   *guardian deity*
155 But let my due feet never fail
To walk the studious cloister's pale,°   *enclosure*
And love the high embowèd roof,
With antic pillars massy proof,[9]
And storied windows richly dight,[1]
160 Casting a dim religious light.
There let the pealing organ blow
To the full-voiced choir below,
In service high and anthems clear,
As may with sweetness, through mine ear,

---

6. A capsule definition of allegory.
7. The now soberly dressed Aurora, goddess of the dawn, once fell in love with Cephalus ("the Attic boy") and hunted with him. "Tricked and frounced": adorned and with frizzled hair.
8. Roman god of woodlands.
9. Massive and strong. "Antic": covered with quaint or grotesque carvings, also antique.
1. Dressed. "Storied windows": stained-glass windows depicting biblical stories.

165 Dissolve me into ecstasies,
And bring all heaven before mine eyes.
And may at last my weary age
Find out the peaceful hermitage,
The hairy gown and mossy cell,
170 Where I may sit and rightly spell°   *study*
Of every star that heaven doth shew,
And every herb that sips the dew,
Till old experience do attain
To something like prophetic strain.
175 These pleasures, Melancholy, give,[2]
And I with thee will choose to live.

ca. 1631   1645

Lycidas

Milton wrote this pastoral elegy for a volume of Latin, Greek, and English poems, *Justa Eduourdo King Naufrago* (1638), commemorating the death by shipwreck of his college classmate Edward King, three years younger than himself. King was not a close friend, but Milton's deepest emotions, anxieties, and fears are engaged here because, as poet and minister, King could serve him as a kind of alter ego. Still engaged in preparing himself, at the age of twenty-nine, for his projected poetic career, Milton was forced to recognize the uncertainty of all human endeavors. King's death posed the problem of mortality in its most agonizing form: the death of the young, the unfulfilled, the good, seems to deny all meaning to life, to demonstrate the uselessness of exceptional talent, lofty ambition, and noble ideals of service to God.

While the poem expresses Milton's anxieties, it also serves as an announcement of his grand ambitions. Like Edmund Spenser, Milton saw mastery of pastoral mode as the first step in a great poetic career. In *Lycidas* that mastery is complete. In the tradition which Milton received from classical and Renaissance predecessors, including Theocritus, Virgil, Petrarch, and Spenser, the pastoral landscape was invested with profound significances that had little indeed to do with the hard life of agricultural labor. The carefree shepherds who engage in singing contests, watch contentedly over their grazing sheep, fall in love, and write poetry offer an image or human life in harmony with nature and the seasonal processes of fruition and mellowing before the winter of death. The classical image of the shepherd as poet is mingled with the Christian understanding of the shepherd as pastor (Christ is the Good Shepherd), and sometimes as the prophet called to his mission from the fields, like David or Isaiah. Milton calls on all these associations, along with other motifs specific to pastoral funeral elegy: the recollection of past friendship, a questioning of destiny for cutting short this life, a procession of mourners (often mythological figures), and a "flower passage" in which nature pays tribute to the dead shepherd.

Lycidas uses but continually tests and challenges the assumptions and conventions of pastoral elegy, making for profound tensions and clashes of tone. The pastoral "oaten flute" is interrupted by divine pronouncements and bitter invective; nature seems rife with examples of meaningless waste and early death; the "blind Fury" often cuts off the poet's "thin-spun life" before he can win fame; good pastors die young while corrupt "Blind Mouths" remain; and Nature cannot even pay her tribute of

---

2. Compare this version of the echo from Marlowe's *Passionate Shepherd* with that with which *L'Allegro* ends.

flowers to Lycidas's funeral bier since he welters in the deep, his bones hurled to the "bottom of the monstrous world." In response to these fierce challenges come pronouncements by Apollo and St. Peter, and images of protection and resurrection in nature and myth, culminating in a new vision of pastoral: in heaven Lycidas enjoys a perfected pastoral existence, and in the coda, the consoled shepherd arises and carries his song to "pastures new." Milton's questioning thus leads to a final reassertion of confidence in his calling as national poet. Moreover, in the headnote added in the 1645 volume of his *Poems*, he lays claim to prophetic authority, for the Anglican clergy he denounced as corrupt in 1638 had mostly been expelled from their livings by Puritan reformers in 1645.

Lycidas

IN THIS MONODY[1] THE AUTHOR BEWAILS A LEARNED FRIEND,
UNFORTUNATELY DROWNED IN HIS PASSAGE FROM CHESTER ON THE
IRISH SEAS, 1637. AND BY OCCASION FORETELLS THE RUIN OF OUR
CORRUPTED CLERGY, THEN IN THEIR HEIGHT.

    Yet once more, O ye laurels, and once more
Ye myrtles brown, with ivy never sere,[2]
I come to pluck your berries harsh and crude,°   *unripe*
And with forced fingers rude,°   *unskilled*
5   Shatter your leaves before the mellowing year.
Bitter constraint, and sad occasion dear,°   *heartfelt, also dire*
Compels me to disturb your season due;
For Lycidas is dead, dead ere his prime,[3]
Young Lycidas, and hath not left his peer.
10 Who would not sing for Lycidas? He knew
Himself to sing, and build the lofty rhyme.[4]
He must not float upon his watery bier
Unwept, and welter° to the parching wind,   *be tossed about*
Without the meed° of some melodious tear.°   *reward/elegy*
15   Begin then, sisters of the sacred well[5]
That from beneath the seat of Jove doth spring,
Begin, and somewhat loudly sweep the string.
Hence with denial vain, and coy excuse;
So may some gentle Muse[6]
20 With lucky words favor my destined urn,
And as he passes turn,
And bid fair peace be to my sable shroud.
For we were nursed upon the selfsame hill,
Fed the same flock, by fountain, shade, and rill.
25   Together both, ere the high lawns° appeared   *upland pastures*
Under the opening eyelids of the morn,

1. A dirge sung by a single voice, though this one incorporates several other voices. This Miltonic headnote was added in the edition of 1645; it identifies Milton as a prophet in the passage denouncing the clergy in this 1638 poem (lines 112–31) and invites the reader to remember Milton's 1641–42 polemics against the English bishops and church government (now dismantled).
2. "Laurels," associated with Apollo and poetry; "myrtle," associated with Venus and love; "ivy,"

associated with Bacchus and frenzy (also learning). All three are evergreens ("never sere") linked to poetic inspiration.
3. King was twenty-five.
4. King had written several poems of compliment in the patronage mode, chiefly on members of the royal family.
5. The nine (sister) Muses called (probably) from the fountain Aganippe, near Mount Helicon.
6. Here, some kindly poet.

We drove afield, and both together heard
What time the grayfly winds her sultry horn,[7]
Battening our flocks with the fresh dews of night,
30   Oft till the star that rose at evening bright
Toward heaven's descent had sloped his westering wheel.[8]
Meanwhile the rural ditties were not mute,
Tempered to th' oaten flute,[9]
Rough satyrs danced, and fauns with cloven heel
35   From the glad sound would not be absent long,
And old Damoetas[1] loved to hear our song.

But O the heavy change, now thou art gone,
Now thou art gone, and never must return!
Thee, shepherd, thee the woods and desert caves,
40   With wild thyme and the gadding° vine o'ergrown,   *wandering*
And all their echoes mourn.
The willows and the hazel copses green
Shall now no more be seen,
Fanning their joyous leaves to thy soft lays.
45   As killing as the canker° to the rose,   *cankerworm*
Or taint-worm[2] to the weanling herds that graze,
Or frost to flowers that their gay wardrobe wear
When first the white-thorn blows;[3]
Such, Lycidas, thy loss to shepherd's ear.

50   Where were ye, nymphs,[4] when the remorseless deep
Closed o'er the head of your loved Lycidas?
For neither were ye playing on the steep
Where your old bards, the famous Druids,[5] lie,
Nor on the shaggy top of Mona high,
55   Nor yet where Deva spreads her wizard stream:[6]
Ay me! I fondly dream—
Had ye been there—for what could that have done?
What could the Muse[7] herself that Orpheus bore,
The Muse herself, for her enchanting[8] son
60   Whom universal Nature did lament,
When by the rout[9] that made the hideous roar
His gory visage down the stream was sent,
Down the swift Hebrus to the Lesbian shore?
Alas! What boots° it with incessant care   *profits*
65   To tend the homely slighted shepherd's trade,
And strictly meditate the thankless Muse?[1]

---

7. I.e., heard the grayfly when she buzzes. "Battening" (next line): feeding.
8. Hesperus, the evening star.
9. Panpipes, played traditionally by shepherds in pastoral.
1. A type name from pastoral poetry, possibly referring to some particular tutor at Cambridge. "Satyrs": goat-legged woodland creatures, Pan's boisterous attendants.
2. Internal parasite fatal to newly weaned lambs.
3. Hawthorne in bloom.
4. Nature deities.
5. Priestly poet-kings of Celtic Britain, who worshiped the forces of nature. They are buried on the mountain ("steep") Kerig-y-Druidion in Wales.
6. Deva, the river Dee in Cheshire, was magic

("wizard") because its shifting stream foretold prosperity or dearth for the land. "Mona" is the island of Anglesey. All these places are in the West Country, near where King drowned.
7. Calliope, Muse of epic poetry, was the mother of Orpheus.
8. Implies both song and magic; the root word survives in "incantation."
9. Orpheus's song was drowned out by the screams of a mob ("rout") of Thracian women, the Bacchantes, who then were able to tear him to pieces and throw his gory head into the river Hebrus, which carried it—still singing—to the island of Lesbos, bringing that island the gift of poetry.
1. I.e., study to write poetry (a Virgilian phrase).

Were it not better done as others use,
To sport with Amaryllis in the shade,
Or with the tangles of Neaera's hair?[2]
70   Fame is the spur that the clear spirit doth raise
(That last infirmity of noble mind)
To scorn delights, and live laborious days;
But the fair guerdon° when we hope to find,   *reward*
And think to burst out into sudden blaze,
75   Comes the blind Fury[3] with th' abhorrèd shears,
And slits the thin-spun life. "But not the praise,"
Phoebus replied, and touched my trembling ears;[4]
"Fame is no plant that grows on mortal soil,
Nor in the glistering foil[5]
80   Set off to th' world, nor in broad rumor lies,
But lives and spreads aloft by those pure eyes,
And perfect witness of all-judging Jove;
As he pronounces lastly on each deed,
Of so much fame in heaven expect thy meed."°   *reward*
85   O fountain Arethuse, and thou honored flood,
Smooth-sliding Mincius, crowned with vocal reeds,
That strain I heard was of a higher mood.[6]
But now my oat° proceeds,   *pastoral flute*
And listens to the herald of the sea[7]
90   That came in Neptune's plea.
He asked the waves, and asked the felon° winds,   *savage*
"What hard mishap hath doomed this gentle swain?"
And questioned every gust of rugged° wings   *stormy*
That blows from off each beakèd promontory;
95   They knew not of his story,
And sage Hippotades[8] their answer brings,
That not a blast was from his dungeon strayed;
The air was calm, and on the level brine,
Sleek Panope[9] with all her sisters played.
100   It was that fatal and perfidious bark,
Built in th' eclipse,[1] and rigged with curses dark,
That sunk so low that sacred head of thine.
     Next Camus,[2] reverend sire, went footing slow,
His mantle hairy, and his bonnet sedge,°   *formed of reeds*
105   Inwrought with figures dim, and on the edge
Like to that sanguine flower inscribed with woe.[3]
"Ah! who hath reft," quoth he, "my dearest pledge?"

---

2. "Amaryllis" and "Neaera" (*Nee-eye-ra*), conventional names for pretty shepherdesses wooed in song by pastoral shepherds.
3. Atropos, one of the three Fates, whose scissors cuts the thread of human life after her sisters spin and measure it. Milton makes her a savage, and blind, Fury.
4. Phoebus Apollo, god of poetic inspiration. In *Eclogue* 6.3–4 he plucked Virgil's ears, warning him against impatient ambition.
5. Flashy, glittering metal foil, set under a gem to enhance its brilliance.
6. Arethusa was a fountain in Sicily associated with Greek pastoral poetry (Theocritus), Mincius

a river in Lombardy associated with Latin pastoral (Virgil); Milton invokes them as a return to the pastoral after the "higher mood" of Apollo's speech.
7. Triton, who comes gathering evidence about the accident for Neptune's court.
8. Aeolus, god of winds.
9. The chief Nereid or sea nymph.
1. Eclipses were taken as evil omens.
2. God of the river Cam, representing Cambridge University.
3. Like the *AI AI* cry of grief supposedly found on the hyacinth, a "sanguine flower" sprung from the blood of the youth Hyacinthus, beloved of Apollo and accidentally killed by him.

Last came and last did go
The pilot of the Galilean lake;[4]
110 Two massy keys he bore of metals twain
(The golden opes, the iron shuts amain).°   *forever*
He shook his mitered locks, and stern bespake:
"How well could I have spared for° thee, young swain,   *in place of*
Enow° of such as for their bellies' sake   *enough (plural)*
115 Creep and intrude and climb into the fold![5]
Of other care they little reckoning make,
Than how to scramble at the shearers' feast,[6]
And shove away the worthy bidden guest.
Blind mouths![7] that scarce themselves know how to hold
120 A sheep-hook, or have learned aught else the least
That to the faithful herdsman's art belongs!
What recks it them? What need they? They are sped;[8]
And when they list,° their lean° and flashy songs   *choose / meager*
Grate on their scrannel° pipes of wretched straw.   *harsh, thin*
125 The hungry sheep look up, and are not fed,
But swoln with wind, and the rank mist they draw,°   *inhale*
Rot inwardly,[9] and foul contagion spread,
Besides what the grim wolf with privy paw[1]
Daily devours apace, and nothing said.
130 But that two-handed engine at the door[2]
Stands ready to smite once, and smite no more."
      Return, Alpheus,[3] the dread voice is past,
That shrunk thy streams; return, Sicilian muse,
And call the vales, and bid them hither cast
135 Their bells and flowerets of a thousand hues.[4]
Ye valleys low where the mild whispers use,°   *frequent*
Of shades and wanton winds, and gushing brooks,
On whose fresh lap the swart star sparely looks,[5]
Throw hither all your quaint enameled eyes,[6]
140 That on the green turf suck the honeyed showers,
And purple all the ground with vernal flowers.

4. St. Peter, originally a fisherman on the sea of
Galilee, was Christ's chief apostle; his keys open
and shut the gates of heaven. He wears a bishop's
miter (line 112): Milton in his antiprelatical tracts
allows for a special role for apostles but denies any
distinction in office between bishops and ministers
in the later church.
5. Cf. John 10.1: "He that entereth not by the door
into the sheepfold, but climbeth up some other
way, the same is a thief and a robber."
6. Festive suppers for the sheepshearers (hence,
the material rewards of their ministry). "Worthy
bidden guest": cf. Matthew 22.8, the parable of the
marriage feast, "they which were bidden were not
worthy."
7. This audacious metaphor collapses them into
these reprehensible qualities, blindness, as
opposed to the oversight the term *episcopus*
(bishop) signifies; gluttony, as opposed to the feeding of flocks proper to pastors. "Sheep-hook" (line
120): the bishop's staff is in the form of a shepherd's crook.
8. Provided for. "What recks it them?": what do
they care?

9. Sheep-rot is used as an allegory of church corruption by both Petrarch and Dante.
1. I.e., Roman Catholicism, whose agents operated in secret ("privy"). Conversions in the court
of the Roman Catholic queen Henrietta Maria
were notorious.
2. A celebrated crux, variously explained as the
two houses of Parliament, St. Peter's keys, the two-
edged sword of the gospel, a sword wielded by two
hands, and by other guesses; what is clear is the
denunciation of impending, apocalyptic vengeance. In Matthew 24.33 the Last Judgment is
said to be "even at the doors."
3. A river in Arcadia, fabled to pass unmixed
through the sea before mixing its waters with the
"fountain Arethuse" in Sicily, again reviving the
pastoral mode after the fierce denunciation of
Peter (see lines 85–87).
4. A catalogue of flowers was a common pastoral
topic. "Bells": bell-shaped flowers.
5. The Dog Star, Sirius, associated with the heats
of late summer.
6. Flowers curiously patterned and adorned with
many colors.

Bring the rathe° primrose that forsaken dies,   *early*
The tufted crow-toe, and pale jessamine,[7]
The white pink, and the pansy freaked° with jet,   *flecked*
145 The glowing violet,
The musk-rose, and the well-attired woodbine,
With cowslips wan° that hang the pensive head,   *pale*
And every flower that sad embroidery wears:
Bid amaranthus[8] all his beauty shed,
150 And daffadillies fill their cups with tears,
To strew the laureate hearse° where Lycid lies.   *laurel-decked bier*
For so to interpose a little ease,
Let our frail thoughts dally with false surmise.[9]
Ay me! whilst thee the shores and sounding seas
155 Wash far away, where'er thy bones are hurled,
Whether beyond the stormy Hebrides,[1]
Where thou perhaps under the whelming° tide   *roaring, overwhelming*
Visit'st the bottom of the monstrous world;
Or whether thou, to our moist vows denied,
160 Sleep'st by the fable of Bellerus old,[2]
Where the great vision of the guarded mount
Looks toward Namancos and Bayona's hold;[3]
Look homeward angel now, and melt with ruth:°   *pity*
And, O ye dolphins,[4] waft the hapless youth.
165   Weep no more, woeful shepherds, weep no more,
For Lycidas your sorrow is not dead,
Sunk though he be beneath the wat'ry floor;
So sinks the day-star° in the ocean bed,   *the sun*
And yet anon repairs his drooping head,
170 And tricks° his beams, and with new-spangled ore   *adorns, trims*
Flames in the forehead of the morning sky:
So Lycidas sunk low, but mounted high,
Through the dear might of him[5] that walked the waves,
Where, other groves and other streams along,[6]
175 With nectar pure his oozy° locks he laves,   *moist*
And hears the unexpressive nuptial song,[7]
In the blest kingdoms meek of joy and love.
There entertain him all the saints above,
In solemn troops and sweet societies
180 That sing, and singing in their glory move,
And wipe the tears forever from his eyes.

---

7. White jasmine. "Tufted crow-toe": hyacinth or
buttercup, growing in clusters. "Woodbine" (line
146): honeysuckle.
8. In Greek, "unfading," a legendary flower of
immortality, one that never fades.
9. False, because Lycidas's body is not here to
receive floral and poetic tributes.
1. Islands off the coast of Scotland, the northern
terminus of the Irish Sea.
2. A fabulous giant invented by Milton as the origin of the Latin name for Land's End in Cornwall,
Bellerium. "Monstrous world" (line 158): filled
with monsters, also, immense.
3. St. Michael's Mount in Cornwall, where the
archangel was said to have appeared to fishermen

in 495, and from which he is envisioned as looking
over the Atlantic toward a region and fortress (Bayona's hold) in northern Spain, thereby guarding
Protestant England against the continuing Roman
Catholic threat.
4. Dolphins brought the Greek poet Arion safely
ashore, for love of his verse, and also performed
other sea rescues.
5. Christ, who rescued Peter when he tried and
failed to do so (Matthew 14.25–31).
6. See Revelation 22.1–2, on the "pure river of
water of life," and the "tree of life, which bare
twelve manner of fruits."
7. Inexpressible hymn of joy sung "at the marriage
supper of the Lamb" (Revelation 19).

Now, Lycidas, the shepherds weep no more;
Henceforth thou art the genius[8] of the shore,
In thy large recompense, and shalt be good
185   To all that wander in that perilous flood.
    Thus sang the uncouth swain[9] to th' oaks and rills,
While the still morn went out with sandals gray;
He touched the tender stops of various quills,[1]
With eager thought warbling his Doric[2] lay:
190   And now the sun had stretched out all the hills,
And now was dropped into the western bay;
At last he rose, and twitched his mantle blue:[3]
Tomorrow to fresh woods, and pastures new.

November 1637   1638

Areopagitica   In this most literary of his tracts, Milton sets forth a trenchant defense of intellectual liberty that has had a powerful influence on the evolving liberal conception of the freedom of speech, press, and thought. His target is the Press Ordinance of June 14, 1643, Parliament's attempt to crack down on the flood of pamphlets (including Milton's own controversial treatises on divorce) that poured forth both from legal and from underground presses as the Civil War raged. Like Tudor and Stuart censorship laws, Parliament's ordinance demanded that works be registered with the Stationers and licensed by the censors before publication, and that both author and publisher be identified, on pain of fines and imprisonment for both. Milton vigorously protests the prepublication licensing of books, arguing that such measures have only been used by, and are only fit for, degenerate cultures. In the regenerate English nation, now "rousing herself like a strong man after sleep," men and women must be allowed to develop in virtue by participating in the clash and conflict of ideas. Truth will always overcome falsehood in reasoned debate. Thus, in opposition to the Presbyterians then in power, Milton defends widespread religious toleration, though with restrictions on Roman Catholicism, which, like most of his Protestant contemporaries, he viewed as a political threat and a tyranny binding individual conscience to the Pope.

    The title associates the tract with the speech of the Greek orator Isocrates to the Areopagus, the Council of the Wise in Athens. Learned readers would have recognized the irony of this; while Isocrates instructed the council to reform Athens by careful supervision of the private lives of citizens, Milton argues that only liberty and removal of censorship can advance reformation. This association explains the oratorical tone of the tract, which was, in fact, subtitled "A Speech." Milton's style is elevated, eloquent, dense with poetic figures, and ranges in tone from satire and ridicule to urgent pleading and florid praise. His arguments and principles are often couched in striking images and phrases. One example is his passionate testimony to the potency and inestimable value of books: "As good almost kill a man as kill a good book . . ." Most memorable is his ringing credo that echoes down the centuries to protest every new tyranny: "Give me the liberty to know, to utter, and to argue freely according to conscience, above all liberties."

---

8. Local guardian spirit.
9. Another voice now seems to take over from the previously heard voice of the "uncouth swain" (unknown, unskilled shepherd).
1. The oaten stalks of panpipes.

2. Rustic, the dialect of Theocritus and other famous Greek pastoral poets.
3. The color of hope. "Twitched": pulled up around his shoulders.

From Areopagitica

I deny not, but that it is of greatest concernment in the Church and Commonwealth, to have a vigilant eye how Books demean[1] themselves as well as men; and thereafter to confine, imprison, and do sharpest justice on them as malefactors:[2] For Books are not absolutely dead things, but do contain a potency of life in them to be as active as that soul was whose progeny they are; nay they do preserve as in a vial the purest efficacy and extraction of that living intellect that bred them. I know they are as lively, and as vigorously productive, as those fabulous Dragon's teeth; and being sown up and down, may chance to spring up armed men.[3] And yet on the other hand unless wariness be used, as good almost kill a Man as kill a good Book; who kills a Man kills a reasonable creature, God's Image; but he who destroys a good Book, kills reason it self, kills the Image of God, as it were in the eye. Many a man lives a burden to the Earth; but a good Book is the precious life-blood of a master spirit, embalmed and treasured up on purpose to a life beyond life. 'Tis true, no age can restore a life, whereof perhaps there is no great loss; and revolutions of ages do not oft recover the loss of a rejected truth, for the want of which whole Nations fare the worse. We should be wary therefore what persecution we raise against the living labors of public men, how we spill that seasoned life of man preserved and stored up in Books; since we see a kind of massacre, whereof the execution ends not in the slaying of an elemental life, but strikes at that ethereal and fifth essence,[4] the breath of reason it self, slays an immortality rather then a life. But lest I should be condemned of introducing licence, while I oppose Licensing, I refuse not the pains to be so much Historical, as will serve to show what hath been done by ancient and famous Commonwealths, against this disorder, till the very time that this project of licensing crept out of the *Inquisition*,[5] was catched up by our Prelates, and hath caught some of our Presbyters.[6] * * *

* * *Good and evil we know in the field of this world grow up together almost inseparably; and the knowledge of good is so involved and interwoven with the knowledge of evil, and in so many cunning resemblances hardly to be discerned, that those confused seeds which were imposed on Psyche as an incessant labor to cull out and sort asunder[7] were not more intermixed. It was from out the rind of one apple tasted, that the knowledge of good and evil, as two twins cleaving together, leaped forth into the world. And perhaps this is that doom which Adam fell into of knowing good and evil, that is to say of knowing good by evil.

---

1. Behave.
2. Milton allows that books may be called to account after publication, if they are proved to contain libels or other manifest crimes (he leaves this quite vague).
3. After Cadmus killed a dragon on his way to founding Thebes, on a god's advice he sowed the dragon's teeth, which sprang up as an army, the belligerent forefathers of Sparta.
4. Quintessence, a pure, mystical substance above the four elements (fire, air, water, earth).
5. The Roman Catholic institution for suppressing heresy, especially strong in Spain.

6. The Presbyterians, powerful in the Parliament, were striving to establish theirs as the national church and suppress others; Milton, who began by supporting them in *The Reason of Church Government* and his other antiprelatical tracts (1641–42), now rejects them, in large part because they seek to supplant one repressive church with another.
7. Angry at her son Cupid's love for Psyche, Venus set the girl many trials, among them to sort out a vast mound of mixed seeds, but the ants took pity on her and did the work.

As therefore the state of man now is, what wisdom can there be to choose, what continence to forbear, without the knowledge of evil? He that can apprehend and consider vice with all her baits and seeming pleasures, and yet abstain, and yet distinguish, and yet prefer that which is truly better, he is the true wayfaring[8] Christian. I cannot praise a fugitive and cloistered virtue, unexercised and unbreathed,[9] that never sallies out and sees her adversary, but slinks out of the race where that immortal garland is to be run for, not without dust and heat. Assuredly we bring not innocence into the world, we bring impurity much rather; that which purifies us is trial, and trial is by what is contrary. That virtue therefore which is but a youngling in the contemplation of evil, and knows not the utmost that vice promises to her followers, and rejects it, is but a blank virtue, not a pure; her whiteness is but an excremental[1] whiteness; which was the reason why our sage and serious poet Spenser (whom I dare be known to think a better teacher than Scotus or Aquinas[2]), describing true temperance under the person of Guyon, brings him in with his palmer through the cave of Mammon and the bower of earthly bliss, that he might see and know, and yet abstain.

Since therefore the knowledge and survey of vice is in this world so necessary to the constituting of human virtue, and the scanning of error to the confirmation of truth, how can we more safely, and with less danger, scout into the regions of sin and falsity than by reading all manner of tractates and hearing all manner of reason? And this is the benefit which may be had of books promiscuously read.

But of the harm that may result hence, three kinds are usually reckoned. First is feared the infection that may spread; but then all human learning and controversy in religious points must remove out of the world, yea, the Bible itself; for that ofttimes relates blasphemy not nicely,[3] it describes the carnal sense of wicked men not unelegantly, it brings in holiest men passionately murmuring against providence through all the arguments of Epicurus;[4] in other great disputes it answers dubiously and darkly to the common reader.[5]

* * *

To sequester out of the world into Atlantic and Utopian politics,[6] which never can be drawn into use, will not mend our condition, but to ordain wisely as in this world of evil, in the midst whereof God hath placed us unavoidably. . . . Impunity and remissness, for certain, are the bane of a

8. The printed text reads "wayfaring," calling up the image of the Christian pilgrim; several presentation copies correct it (by hand) to "warfaring," calling up the image of the Christian warrior. Both suit the passage.
9. Not forced by exertion to breathe hard. "Immortal garland" (next line): the prize for the winner of a race, as figure for the "crown of life" promised to those who endure temptation (James 1.12).
1. Exterior only.
2. Duns Scotus and Thomas Aquinas, major Scholastic theologians. Guyon, the hero of Book II of the *Faerie Queene*, passes through the Cave of Mammon (symbolic of all worldly goods and honors) without his Palmer-guide, but that figure does accompany him through the Bower of

Bliss.
3. Daintily.
4. Greek philosopher (342–270 B.C.E.) who taught that happiness is the greatest good, and that virtue should be practiced because it brings happiness; some of his followers equated happiness with sensual enjoyment. Milton may be thinking of the biblical book of Ecclesiastes.
5. Milton goes on to argue that a fool can find material for folly in the best books, and a wise person material for wisdom in the worst. Also, one cannot remove evil by censoring books without also censoring ballads, fiddlers, clothing, conversation, and all social life.
6. Milton alludes to Thomas More's *Utopia* and Francis Bacon's *New Atlantis*.

commonwealth; but here the great art lies, to discern in what the law is to bid restraint and punishment, and in what things persuasion only is to work. If every action which is good or evil in man at ripe years were to be under pittance[7] and prescription and compulsion, what were virtue but a name, what praise could be then due to well-doing, what gramercy[8] to be sober, just, or continent?

Many there be that complain of divine providence for suffering Adam to transgress; foolish tongues! when God gave him reason, he gave him freedom to choose, for reason is but choosing; he had been else a mere artificial Adam, such an Adam as he is in the motions.[9] We ourselves esteem not of that obedience, or love, or gift, which is of force: God therefore left him free, set before him a provoking object, ever almost in his eyes; herein consisted his merit, herein the right of his reward, the praise of his abstinence.[1] Wherefore did he create passions within us, pleasures round about us, but that these rightly tempered are the very ingredients of virtue? They are not skillful considerers of human things, who imagine to remove sin by removing the matter of sin; for, besides that it is a huge heap increasing under the very act of diminishing, though some part of it may for a time be withdrawn from some persons, it cannot from all, in such a universal thing as books are; and when this is done, yet the sin remains entire. Though ye take from a covetous man all his treasure, he has yet one jewel left: ye cannot bereave him of his covetousness. Banish all objects of lust, shut up all youth into the severest discipline that can be exercised in any hermitage, ye cannot make them chaste that came not thither so: such great care and wisdom is required to the right managing of this point.

Suppose we could expel sin by this means; look how much we thus expel of sin, so much we expel of virtue: for the matter of them both is the same; remove that, and ye remove them both alike. This justifies the high providence of God, who, though he commands us temperance, justice, continence, yet pours out before us, even to a profuseness, all desirable things, and gives us minds that can wander beyond all limit and satiety. Why should we then affect a rigor contrary to the manner of God and of nature, by abridging or scanting those means, which books freely permitted are, both to the trial of virtue and the exercise of truth? It would be better done to learn that the law must needs be frivolous which goes to restrain things uncertainly and yet equally working to good and to evil. And were I the chooser, a dram of well-doing should be preferred before many times as much the forcible hindrance of evil-doing. For God sure esteems the growth and completing of one virtuous person more than the restraint of ten vicious.

*   *   *

What advantage is it to be a man over it is to be a boy at school, if we have only scaped the ferula[2] to come under the fescue of an Imprimatur; if serious and elaborate writings, as if they were no more than the theme of a grammar-

---

7. Rationing.
8. Reward, thanks.
9. Puppet shows.
1. Compare Milton's representation of Adam and Eve in Eden in *Paradise Lost*.

2. "Ferula": a schoolmaster's rod; "fescue": a pointer. Milton's keen sense of the affront to scholars and scholarship, and to himself, is evident in this passage.

lad under his pedagogue, must not be uttered without the cursory eyes of a temporizing and extemporizing licenser?[3] He who is not trusted with his own actions, his drift not being known to be evil, and standing to the hazard of law and penalty, has no great argument to think himself reputed, in the commonwealth wherein he was born, for other than a fool or a foreigner.

When a man writes to the world, he summons up all his reason and deliberation to assist him; he searches, meditates, is industrious, and likely consults and confers with his judicious friends, after all which done he takes himself to be informed in what he writes, as well as any that writ before him. If in this the most consummate act of his fidelity and ripeness, no years, no industry, no former proof of his abilities can bring him to that state of maturity as not to be still mistrusted and suspected (unless he carry all his considerate diligence, all his midnight watchings, and expense of Palladian[4] oil, to the hasty view of an unleisured licenser, perhaps much his younger, perhaps far his inferior in judgment, perhaps one who never knew the labor of bookwriting), and if he be not repulsed, or slighted, must appear in print like a puny[5] with his guardian, and his censor's hand on the back of his title to be his bail and surety that he is no idiot, or seducer; it cannot be but a dishonor and derogation to the author, to the book, to the privilege and dignity of learning. * * *

And how can a man teach with authority, which is the life of teaching, how can he be a doctor in his book as he ought to be, or else had better be silent, whenas all he teaches, all he delivers, is but under the tuition, under the correction of his patriarchal[6] licenser to blot or alter what precisely accords not with the hide-bound humor which he calls his judgment? When every acute reader upon the first sight of a pedantic license, will be ready with these like words to ding the book a quoit's[7] distance from him: "I hate a pupil teacher, I endure not an instructor that comes to me under the wardship of an overseeing fist. I know nothing of the licenser, but that I have his own hand here for his arrogance; who shall warrant me his judgment?"

"The State, sir," replies the stationer, but has a quick return: "The State shall be my governors, but not my critics; they may be mistaken in the choice of a licenser, as easily as this licenser may be mistaken in an author."

* * *

Well knows he who uses to consider, that our faith and knowledge thrives by exercise, as well as our limbs and complexion.[8] Truth is compared in Scripture to a streaming fountain;[9] if her waters flow not in a perpetual progression, they sicken into a muddy pool of conformity and tradition. A man may be a heretic in the truth; and if he believe things only because his pastor says so, or the Assembly[1] so determines, without knowing other reason, though his belief be true, yet the very truth he holds becomes his heresy.

* * *

3. He temporizes in following the times, and acts by whim (extemporizes).
4. Pertaining to Pallas Athena, goddess of wisdom.
5. A minor, hence, young, unseasoned.
6. Taking on the role of a father; also, standing in for ecclesiastical patriarchs or prelates (like Archbishop Laud).

7. A flat disc of stone or metal, thrown as an exercise of strength or skill.
8. Constitution, the proper mingling of qualities in the body.
9. In Psalm 85.11.
1. The Westminster Assembly, convened by Parliament in 1643 to reorganize the English church along Presbyterian lines.

Truth indeed came once into the world with her Divine Master, and was a perfect shape most glorious to look on: but when he ascended, and his apostles after him were laid asleep, then straight arose a wicked race of deceivers, who, as that story goes of the Egyptian Typhon with his conspirators, how they dealt with the good Osiris,[2] took the virgin Truth, hewed her lovely form into a thousand pieces, and scattered them to the four winds. From that time ever since, the sad friends of Truth, such as durst appear, imitating the careful search that Isis made for the mangled body of Osiris, went up and down gathering up limb by limb, still as they could find them. We have not yet found them all, Lords and Commons, nor ever shall do, till her Master's second coming; he shall bring together every joint and member, and shall mold them into an immortal feature of loveliness and perfection. Suffer not these licensing prohibitions to stand at every place of opportunity, forbidding and disturbing them that continue seeking, that continue to do our obsequies[3] to the torn body of our martyred saint.

We boast our light; but if we look not wisely on the sun itself, it smites us into darkness. Who can discern those planets that are oft combust,[4] and those stars of brightest magnitude that rise and set with the sun, until the opposite motion of their orbs bring them to such a place in the firmament where they may be seen evening or morning? The light which we have gained was given us, not to be ever staring on, but by it to discover onward things more remote from our knowledge. It is not the unfrocking of a priest, the unmitering of a bishop, and the removing him from off the Presbyterian shoulders, that will make us a happy nation. No, if other things as great in the church, and in the rule of life both economical and political, be not looked into and reformed, we have looked so long upon the blaze that Zwinglius and Calvin[5] hath beaconed up to us, that we are stark blind.

There be who perpetually complain of schisms and sects, and make it such a calamity that any man dissents from their maxims. 'Tis their own pride and ignorance which causes the disturbing, who neither will hear with meekness, nor can convince; yet all must be suppressed which is not found in their syntagma.[6] They are the troublers, they are the dividers of unity, who neglect and permit not others to unite those disseevered pieces which are yet wanting to the body of Truth. To be still searching what we know not by what we know, still closing up truth to truth as we find it (for all her body is homogeneal and proportional), this is the golden rule in theology as well as in arithmetic, and makes up the best harmony in a church; not the forced and outward union of cold and neutral and inwardly divided minds.

Lords and Commons of England, consider what nation it is whereof ye are, and whereof ye are the governors: a nation not slow and dull, but of a quick, ingenious, and piercing spirit, acute to invent, subtle and sinewy to discourse, not beneath the reach of any point the highest that human capacity can soar to. Therefore the studies of learning in her deepest sciences have been so ancient and so eminent among us, that writers of good antiquity and

---

2. Plutarch tells, in *Isis and Osiris*, of Typhon's scattering the fragments of his brother Osiris and of Isis's efforts to recover them.
3. Funeral or commemorative rites.
4. Burned up; in astrology, so close to the sun as

not to be visible.
5. Zwingli and Calvin, famous Protestant reformers, were mainstays of the Presbyterian cause. "Economical": domestic.
6. Compilations of beliefs, creeds.

ablest judgment have been persuaded that even the school of Pythagoras and the Persian wisdom took beginning from the old philosophy of this island.[7] And that wise and civil Roman, Julius Agricola, who governed once here for Caesar, preferred the natural wits of Britain before the labored studies of the French. Nor is it for nothing that the grave and frugal Transylvanian sends out yearly from as far as the mountainous borders of Russia, and beyond the Hercynian wilderness, not their youth, but their staid men, to learn our language and our theologic arts.[8]

Yet that which is above all this, the favor and the love of heaven we have great argument to think in a peculiar manner propitious and propending[9] towards us. Why else was this nation chosen before any other, that out of her, as out of Zion,[1] should be proclaimed and sounded forth the first tidings and trumpet of Reformation to all Europe? And had it not been the obstinate perverseness of our prelates against the divine and admirable spirit of Wycliffe to suppress him as a schismatic and innovator, perhaps neither the Bohemian Huss and Jerome,[2] no, nor the name of Luther or of Calvin, had been ever known: the glory of reforming all our neighbors had been completely ours. But now, as our obdurate clergy have with violence demeaned the matter, we are become hitherto the latest and the backwardest scholars of whom[3] God offered to have made us the teachers.

Now once again by all concurrence of signs, and by the general instinct of holy and devout men, as they daily and solemnly express their thoughts, God is decreeing to begin some new and great period in his church, even to the reforming of Reformation itself; what does he then but reveal himself to his servants, and as his manner is, first to his Englishmen? I say, as his manner is, first to us, though we mark not the method of his counsels, and are unworthy. Behold now this vast city: a city of refuge,[4] the mansion house of liberty, encompassed and surrounded with his protection; the shop of war hath not there more anvils and hammers waking, to fashion out the plates[5] and instruments of armed justice in defense of beleaguered truth, than there be pens and heads there, sitting by their studious lamps, musing, searching, revolving new notions and ideas wherewith to present, as with their homage and their fealty, the approaching Reformation: others as fast reading, trying all things, assenting to the force of reason and convincement.

What could a man require more from a nation so pliant and so prone to seek after knowledge? What wants there to such a towardly[6] and pregnant soil, but wise and faithful laborers, to make a knowing people, a nation of prophets,[7] of sages, and of worthies? We reckon more than five months yet

7. Some speculation existed as to whether the Pythagorean notion of the transmigration of souls might trace back to the Druids, but the notion was mostly denied.
8. The "civil" (cultured, civilized) Agricola's opinion of the British intellect (referred to next) is found in Tacitus's *Life of Agricola*. Transylvania (now Romania) was an independent Protestant country whose citizens sometimes came to England to study. "Hercynian wilderness": Roman name for a forested and mountainous region of Germany.
9. Inclining, favorable. "Argument": reason.
1. Mount Zion, in Jerusalem, the site of the Temple.

2. John Wycliffe was a 14th-century English reformer and translator of the Bible, whose books were forbidden by Pope Alexander V in 1409. John Huss spread Wycliffe's doctrines on the Continent; he was burned at the stake in 1415, as was (the next year) his follower Jerome of Prague.
3. Of those whom. "Demeaned": conducted, degraded.
4. Numbers 35 instructs the Jews to establish "cities of refuge" where those accused of crimes are protected from "revengers of blood."
5. Plate mail, for armor.
6. Favorable.
7. In Numbers 11.29 Moses reproaches Joshua, who complained of the presence of other prophets:

to harvest; there need not be five weeks; had we but eyes to lift up, the fields are white already.[8] Where there is much desire to learn, there of necessity will be much arguing, much writing, many opinions; for opinion in good men is but knowledge in the making. Under these fantastic terrors of sect and schism we wrong the earnest and zealous thirst after knowledge and understanding which God hath stirred up in this city.

What some lament of, we rather should rejoice at, should rather praise this pious forwardness among men, to reassume the ill-deputed care of their religion into their own hands again. A little generous prudence, a little forbearance of one another, and some grain of charity might win all these diligences to join, and unite into one general and brotherly search after truth; could we but forego this prelatical tradition of crowding free consciences and Christian liberties into canons and precepts of men. I doubt not, if some great and worthy stranger should come among us, wise to discern the mold and temper of a people, and how to govern it, observing the high hopes and aims, the diligent alacrity of our extended thoughts and reasonings in the pursuance of truth and freedom, but that he would cry out as Pyrrhus did, admiring the Roman docility and courage: "If such were my Epirots, I would not despair the greatest design that could be attempted, to make a church or kingdom happy."[9] Yet these are the men cried out against for schismatics and sectaries;[1] as if, while the temple of the Lord was building, some cutting, some squaring the marble, others hewing the cedars, there should be a sort of irrational men, who could not consider there must be many schisms and many dissections[2] made in the quarry and in the timber, ere the house of God can be built. And when every stone is laid artfully together, it cannot be united into a continuity, it can but be contiguous in this world; neither can every piece of the building be of one form; nay rather the perfection consists in this, that out of many moderate varieties and brotherly dissimilitudes that are not vastly disproportional, arises the goodly and the graceful symmetry that commends the whole pile and structure. Let us therefore be more considerate builders, more wise in spiritual architecture, when great reformation is expected. For now the time seems come, wherein Moses the great prophet may sit in heaven rejoicing to see that memorable and glorious wish of his fulfilled, when not only our seventy elders, but all the Lord's people, are become prophets.[3]

* * *

Methinks I see in my mind a noble and puissant nation rousing herself like a strong man after sleep, and shaking her invincible locks:[4] methinks I see her as an eagle mewing[5] her mighty youth, and kindling her undazzled

---

"Enviest thou for my sake? Would God that all the Lord's people were prophets."

8. Milton is paraphrasing Christ's words to his disciples (John 4.35): "Lift up your eyes, and look on the fields: for they are white already to harvest."

9. Though King Pyrrhus of Epirus beat the Roman armies at Heraclea in 280 B.C.E., he was much impressed by their discipline.

1. "Schismatics": those who cut up or divide the church; "sectaries": members of Protestant communions outside the national church.

2. Milton is playing on the literal meaning of

"schism," cutting up or dividing.

3. Again alluding to Numbers 11.29, Milton equates the English assembly of clergy to set doctrine and church order (the Westminster Assembly) with the Jewish Sanhedrin of seventy elders.

4. The allusion is to Samson, whose uncut hair made him invincible, when he frustrated the first three attempts of Delilah and the Philistines to subdue him in sleep (Judges 16.6–14).

5. Molting, when the eagle sheds it feathers and thereby renews its coat; eagles were thought to be able to look directly at the sun.

eyes at the full midday beam; purging and unscaling her long-abused sight at the fountain itself of heavenly radiance; while the whole noise of timorous and flocking birds, with those also that love the twilight, flutter about, amazed at what she means, and in their envious gabble would prognosticate[6] a year of sects and schisms.

What should ye do then, should ye suppress all this flowery crop of knowledge and new light sprung up and yet springing daily in this city? Should ye set an oligarchy of twenty engrossers[7] over it, to bring a famine upon our minds again, when we shall know nothing but what is measured to us by their bushel? Believe it, Lords and Commons, they who counsel ye to such a suppressing do as good as bid ye suppress yourselves; and I will soon show how.[8]

* * *

And now the time in special is by privilege to write and speak what may help to the further discussing of matters in agitation. The temple of Janus with his two controversial faces might now not unsignificantly be set open.[9] And though all the winds of doctrine were let loose to play upon the earth, so Truth be in the field, we do injuriously by licensing and prohibiting to misdoubt her strength. Let her and Falsehood grapple; who ever knew Truth put to the worse in a free and open encounter? Her[1] confuting is the best and surest suppressing. He who hears what praying there is for light and clearer knowledge to be sent down among us would think of other matters to be constituted beyond the discipline of Geneva framed and fabricked already to our hands.[2]

Yet when the new light which we beg for shines in upon us, there be who envy and oppose if it come not first in at their casements. What a collusion is this, whenas we are exhorted by the wise man to use diligence, to seek for wisdom as for hidden treasures early and late,[3] that another order shall enjoin us to know nothing but by statute. When a man hath been laboring the hardest labor in the deep mines of knowledge, hath furnished out his findings in all their equipage, drawn forth his reasons as it were a battle[4] ranged, scattered and defeated all objections in his way, calls out his adversary into the plain, offers him the advantage of wind and sun if he please, only that he may try the matter by dint of argument; for his opponents then to skulk, to lay ambushments, to keep a narrow bridge of licensing where the challenger should pass, though it be valor enough in soldiership, is but weakness and cowardice in the wars of Truth.

For who knows not that Truth is strong, next to the Almighty? She needs no policies nor stratagems nor licensings to make her victorious—those are

---

6. Predict.
7. Engrossers, much hated in the English countryside, bought up great quantities of grain and held it for times of famine, selling it at high prices; Milton equates them with the twenty authorized printers, the stationers.
8. Milton argues that Parliament, by its own liberalizing reforms to date, has created the vigorous and inquiring minds it now seeks to suppress.
9. Janus, as god of beginnings and endings, had two faces looking in opposite directions; a door

dedicated to him in Rome was kept open in time of war, closed in time of peace.
1. I.e., Falsehood's.
2. Milton was already disenchanted with Genevan "Discipline" (Presbyterian church government) and within a year or so would be writing, "New Presbyter is but Old Priest, writ large." "Fabricked": fabricated.
3. Solomon's advice in Proverbs 8.11.
4. Line of battle. Wind and sun (below) were significant advantages in a fight with swords.

the shifts and the defenses that error uses against her power. Give her but room, and do not bind her when she sleeps, for then she speaks not true, as the old Proteus[5] did, who spake oracles only when he was caught and bound, but then rather she turns herself into all shapes except her own, and perhaps tunes her voice according to the time, as Micaiah did before Ahab,[6] until she be adjured into her own likeness.

Yet it is not impossible that she may have more shapes than one. What else is all that rank of things indifferent, wherein Truth may be on this side or on the other without being unlike herself? What but a vain shadow else is the abolition of those ordinances, that handwriting nailed to the cross?[7] what great purchase is this Christian liberty which Paul so often boasts of? His doctrine is that he who eats or eats not, regards a day or regards it not, may do either to the Lord.[8] How many other things might be tolerated in peace and left to conscience, had we but charity, and were it not the chief stronghold of our hypocrisy to be ever judging one another? I fear yet this iron yoke of outward conformity hath left a slavish print upon our necks; the ghost of a linen decency[9] yet haunts us. We stumble and are impatient at the least dividing of one visible congregation from another, though it be not in fundamentals; and through our forwardness to suppress and our backwardness to recover any enthralled piece of truth out of the grip of custom, we care not[1] to keep truth separated from truth, which is the fiercest rent and disunion of all. We do not see that while we still affect by all means a rigid and external formality, we may as soon fall again into a gross conforming stupidity, a stark and dead congealment of "wood and hay and stubble," forced and frozen together, which is more to the sudden degenerating of a church than many sub-dichotomies of petty schisms.

Not that I can think well of every light separation, or that all in a church is to be expected "gold and silver and precious stones."[2] It is not possible for man to sever the wheat from the tares, the good fish from the other fry; that must be the angels' ministry at the end of mortal things.[3] Yet if all cannot be of one mind—as who looks they should be?—this doubtless is more wholesome, more prudent, and more Christian, that many be tolerated rather than all compelled. I mean not tolerated popery and open superstition, which, as it extirpates all religions and civil supremacies, so itself should be extirpate, provided first that all charitable and compassionate means be used to win and regain the weak and the misled; that also which is impious or evil absolutely, either against faith or manners,[4] no law can possibly permit that intends not to unlaw itself; but those neighboring differences or rather indifferences are what I speak of, whether in some point of doctrine or of discipline, which though they

5. The sea god who could change shape at will, to avoid capture (*Odyssey* 4).

6. Micaiah, a prophet of God, tried for a time to disguise an unpleasant prophecy from King Ahab but then spoke truth when adjured to do so (1 Kings 22.10–28).

7. The locution, from Colossians 2.14, implies that the crucifixion canceled all the rules and penalties of the Mosaic law. Paul's doctrine of Christian liberty is expressed in Galatians 5 and elsewhere.

8. In the Lord's service.

9. The scraps of white linen around the necks and wrists of gentlemen (and white bands around the necks of clergymen) are made emblems of formal piety.

1. Scruple not.

2. The contrast between "wood, hay, stubble" and "gold, silver, precious stones" is from 1 Corinthians 3.12.

3. In Matthew 13.24–30, 36–43, Christ in a parable tells his disciples to let the wheat and tares (weeds) grow up together till harvest time.

4. Morals.

may be many yet need not interrupt "the unity of spirit," if we could but find among us the "bond of peace."[5]

In the meanwhile, if anyone would write and bring his helpful hand to the slow-moving reformation which we labor under, if truth have spoken to him before others, or but seemed at least to speak, who hath so bejesuited[6] us that we should trouble that man with asking license to do so worthy a deed? And not consider this, that if it come to prohibiting, there is not aught more likely to be prohibited than truth itself; whose first appearance to our eyes bleared and dimmed with prejudice and custom is more unsightly and unplausible than many errors, even as the person is of many a great man slight and contemptible to see to. And what do they tell us vainly of new opinions, when this very opinion of theirs, that none must be heard but whom they like, is the worst and newest opinion of all others, and is the chief cause why sects and schisms do so much abound, and true knowledge is kept at distance from us; besides yet a greater danger which is in it. For when God shakes a kingdom[7] with strong and healthful commotions to a general reforming, it is not untrue that many sectaries and false teachers are then busiest in seducing; but yet more true it is that God then raises to his own work men of rare abilities and more than common industry, not only to look back and revise what hath been taught heretofore, but to gain further and go on some new enlightened steps in the discovery of truth.

✳   ✳   ✳

1644

Sonnets

Between 1630 and 1658 Milton wrote twenty-four sonnets. Five in Italian constitute a mini-Petrarchan sequence on a perhaps imaginary Italian lady. The rest, in English, are individual poems on a wide variety of topics and occasions though not on the usual sonnet topics (love, as in the sequences of Sidney, Spenser, and Shakespeare, or religious devotion, as in that of Donne). Milton writes sometimes about personal crises (his blindness, the death of his wife), sometimes about political issues or personages (Cromwell, the persecuting Parliament), sometimes about friends and friendship (Cyriack Skinner, Lady Margaret Ley), sometimes about historical events (a threatened royalist attack on London, the massacre of Protestants in Piedmont); and his tone ranges from Jonsonian urbanity to prophetic denunciation. The form of the sonnets is Petrarchan (see "Poetic Forms and Literary Terminology," in the appendices to this volume), but in the later sonnets especially (e.g., the Blindness and Piedmont sonnets) the sense runs on from line to line, overriding the expected end-stopped lines and the octave/sestet shift. There is some precedent for this in the Italian sonneteer Giovanni Della Casa, but not for the powerful tension Milton creates as meaning and emotion strive within and against the metrical form of the Petrarchan sonnet. Milton's new ways with the sonnet had a profound and acknowledged influence on the Romantic poets, especially Wordsworth and Shelley.

5. The quoted phrases are from Ephesians 4.3.
6. Imposed on us Jesuit ideas (of censorship).
7. Milton alludes to Haggai 2.7: "I will shake all nations, and the desire of all nations shall come, and I will fill this house with glory, saith the Lord of hosts."

Sonnets

How Soon Hath Time

How soon hath Time, the subtle thief of youth,
   Stol'n on his wing my three and twentieth year!
   My hasting days fly on with full career,
   But my late spring no bud or blossom shew'th.
5 Perhaps my semblance might deceive[1] the truth,
   That I to manhood am arrived so near,
   And inward ripeness doth much less appear,
   That some more timely-happy spirits endu'th.°   *endows*
   Yet be it less or more, or soon or slow,
10 It shall be still in strictest measure even[2]
   To that same lot, however mean or high,
Toward which Time leads me, and the will of Heaven;
   All is, if I have grace to use it so,
   As ever in my great Taskmaster's eye.[3]

1632?   1645

When I Consider How My Light Is Spent[1]

When I consider how my light is spent,°   *extinguished*
   Ere half my days,[2] in this dark world and wide,
   And that one talent which is death to hide[3]
   Lodged with me useless, though my soul more bent
5 To serve therewith my Maker, and present
   My true account, lest he returning chide;
   "Doth God exact day-labor, light denied?"[4]
   I fondly° ask; but Patience to prevent°   *foolishly / forestall*
   That murmur, soon replies, "God doth not need
10 Either man's work or his own gifts; who best
   Bear his mild yoke, they serve him best. His state°   *splendor*
   Is kingly.[5] Thousands at his bidding speed
   And post o'er land and ocean without rest:
   They also serve who only stand and wait."

1652?   1673

---

1. Misrepresent. "Semblance": appearance.
2. Equal, adequate. "It": Milton's inner growth. "Even / To that same lot": conformed to the appointed destiny.
3. The final lines allow for various readings. "Taskmaster" identifies God with the parable (Matthew 20.1–16) in which a vineyard keeper takes on workers throughout the day, paying the same wages to those hired at the first and at the eleventh hour.
1. Apparently written soon after Milton lost his sight entirely in 1652.
2. Milton was forty-three in 1652; he is obviously not thinking of the biblical lifespan of seventy, but perhaps of that of his father, who died at eighty-four.
3. In the parable of the talents (Matthew 25.14–

30), a crucial text for Puritans, the servants who put their master's money ("talents") to earn interest for him were praised while the servant who buried the single talent he was given was deprived of it and cast into outer darkness. Milton puns on "literary talent." "Useless" (line 4) carries a pun on usury, the return expected by the Master.
4. Milton also alludes here to the parable of the vineyard keeper (see *How Soon Hath Time*, n. 3). Also to John 9.4, spoken by Jesus before curing a blind man: "I must work the works of him that sent me, while it is day: the night cometh, when no man can work."
5. The changed metaphor for God—from master who needs to profit from his workers to King—allows the inference that those who "stand and wait" may be placed nearest the throne.

On the Late Massacre in Piedmont[1]

Avenge,[2] O Lord, thy slaughtered saints, whose bones
Lie scattered on the Alpine mountains cold;
Even them who kept thy truth so pure of old
When all our fathers worshiped stocks and stones,[3]
5   Forget not: in thy book[4] record their groans
Who were thy sheep and in their ancient fold
Slain by the bloody Piemontese that rolled
Mother with infant down the rocks. Their moans
The vales redoubled to the hills, and they
10   To heaven. Their martyred blood and ashes sow
O'er all th' Italian fields, where still doth sway
The triple tyrant:[5] that from these may grow
A hundredfold, who having learnt thy way
Early may fly the Babylonian woe.[6]

1655   1673

Methought I Saw My Late Espousèd Saint[1]

Methought I saw my late espousèd saint
Brought to me like Alcestis[2] from the grave,
Whom Jove's great son to her glad husband gave,
Rescued from death by force though pale and faint.
5   Mine, as whom[3] washed from spot of childbed taint,
Purification in the old law did save,[4]
And such, as yet once more I trust to have
Full sight of her in heaven without restraint,
Came vested all in white, pure as her mind.
10   Her face was veiled, yet to my fancied sight[5]

1. The Waldensians (or Vaudois) were a proto-Protestant sect dating to the 12th century, who lived in the valleys of northern Italy (the Piedmont) and southern France; Protestants considered them a remnant retaining Apostolic purity, free of Catholic superstitions and graven images ("stocks and stones"). The treaty that had allowed them freedom of worship was bypassed in 1655 when the armies of the Catholic duke of Savoy conducted a massacre, razing villages, committing unspeakable atrocities, and hurling women and children from the mountaintops. Protestant Europe was outraged, and in his capacity as Cromwell's Latin secretary Milton translated and wrote several letters about the episode. The sonnet incorporates details from such letters and the contemporary newsbooks. Here Milton transforms the sonnet into a prophetic denunciation.
2. Cf. Revelation 6.9–10: "The souls of them that were slain for the word of God . . . cried with a loud voice, saying 'How long, O Lord, holy and true, dost thou not judge and avenge our blood?'"
3. Pagan gods of wood and stone, but with allusion to Roman Catholic "idols."
4. Cf. Revelation 20.12: "The dead were judged out of those things which were written in the books, according to their works." "Sheep": echoes Romans 8.36: "We are accounted as sheep for the slaughter."

5. The pope, wearing his tiara with three crowns. The passage alludes to Tertullian's maxim that "the blood of the martyrs is the seed of the church"; also to the parable of the sower (Matthew 13.3), some of whose seed brought forth fruit "an hundredfold"; and also to Cadmus, who sowed dragon's teeth that sprang forth armed men.
6. Protestants often identified the Roman Church with the whore of Babylon (Revelation 17–18).
1. There is some critical debate as to whether this poem refers to Milton's first wife, Mary Powell, who died in May 1652 three days after giving birth to her third daughter, or his second wife, Katherine Woodcock, who died in February 1658, after giving birth (in October 1657) to a daughter. The text can support either, but the latter seems more likely. The sonnet is couched as a dream vision.
2. In Euripedes' Alcestis, Alcestis, wife of Admetus, is rescued from the underworld by Hercules ("Jove's great son") and restored, veiled, to Admetus; he is overjoyed when he lifts the veil, but she must remain silent until she is ritually cleansed.
3. As one whom.
4. The Mosaic Law (Leviticus 12.4–8) prescribed periods for the purification of women after childbirth (eighty days for a daughter).
5. She is veiled like Alcestes and Milton's sight of her is only "fancied"; he never saw the face of his second wife, Katherine.

> Love, sweetness, goodness, in her person shined
> So clear, as in no face with more delight.
> But O, as to embrace me she inclined,
> I waked, she fled, and day brought back my night.

1658   1673

Paradise Lost   The setting of Milton's great epic encompasses Heaven, Hell, primordial Chaos, and the planet Earth. It features battles among immortal spirits, voyages through space, and lakes of fire. Yet its protagonists are a married couple living in a garden, and its climax consists in the eating of a piece of fruit. *Paradise Lost* is ultimately about the human condition, the Fall that caused "all our woe," and the promise and means of restoration. It is also about knowing and choosing, about free will. In the opening passages of Books 1, 3, 7, and 9, Milton highlights the choices and difficulties he faced in creating his poem. His central characters—Satan, Beelzebub, Abdiel, Adam, and Eve—are confronted with hard choices under the pressure of powerful desires and sometimes devious temptations. Milton's readers, too, are continually challenged to choose and to reconsider their most basic assumptions about freedom, heroism, work, pleasure, language, nature, and love. The great themes of *Paradise Lost* are intimately linked to the political questions at stake in the English Revolution and Restoration, but the connection is by no means simple or straightforward. This is a poem in which Satan leads a revolution against an absolute monarch and in which questions of tyranny, servitude, and liberty are debated in a Parliament in Hell. Milton's readers are hereby challenged to rethink these topics and, like Abdiel debating with Satan in Books 5 and 6, to make crucial distinctions.

In Milton's time, the conventions of epic poetry comprised a familiar recipe. The action should begin *in medias res* (in the middle of things), following the poet's statement of his theme and invocation of his Muse. The reader could expect grand battles and love affairs, supernatural intervention, a descent into the underworld, catalogs of warriors, and epic similes. Milton had absorbed the epic tradition in its entirety, and his poem abounds with echoes of Homer and Virgil, the fifteenth-century Italians Tasso and Ariosto, and the English Spenser. But in *Paradise Lost* he at once heightens epic conventions and values and utterly transforms them. This is the epic to end all epics. Milton gives us the first and greatest of all wars (between God and Satan) and the first and greatest of love affairs (between Adam and Eve). His theme is the destiny of the entire human race, caught up in the temptation and Fall of our first "grand parents."

Milton challenges his readers in *Paradise Lost*, at once fulfilling and defying all of our expectations. Nothing in the epic tradition or in biblical interpretation can prepare us for the Satan who hurtles into view in Book 1, with his awesome energy and defiance, incredible fortitude, and, above all, magnificent rhetoric. For some readers, including Blake and Shelley, Satan has been the true hero of the poem. But Milton is engaged in a radical re-evaluation of epic values, and Satan's version of heroism must be contrasted with those of the loyal Abdiel and the Son of God. Moreover, the poem's truly epic action takes place not on the battlefield but in the moral and domestic arena. Milton's Adam and Eve are not conventional epic heroes, but neither are they the conventional Adam and Eve. Their state of innocence is not childlike, tranquil, and free of sexual desire. Instead, the first couple enjoy sex, experience tension and passion, make mistakes of judgment, and grow in knowledge. Their task is to prune what is unruly in their own natures as they prune the vegetation in their garden, for both have the capacity to grow wild. Their relationship exhibits gender hierarchy, but Milton's early readers may have been surprised by the fullness and complexity of Eve's character and the centrality of her role, not only in the Fall but in the promised restoration.

We expect in epics a grand style, and Milton's style engulfs us from the outset with its energy and power, as those rushing, enjambed, blank-verse lines propel us along with only a few pauses for line endings or grammar (there is only one full-stop in the first twenty-six lines). The elevated diction and complex syntax, the sonorities and patternings, make a magnificent music. But that music is an entire orchestra of tones, including the high political rhetoric of Satan in Books 1 and 2, the evocative sensuousness of the descriptions of Eden, the delicacy of Eve's love lyric to Adam in Book 4, the relatively plain speech of God in Book 3, and the speech rhythms of Adam and Eve's marital quarrel in Book 9. This majestic achievement depends on the poet's rejection of heroic couplets, the norm for epic and tragedy in the Restoration, vigorously defended by Dryden, but denounced by Milton in his note on "The Verse." The choice of verse form was, like so many other things in Milton's life, in part a question of politics. Milton's terms associate the "troublesome and modern bondage of rhyming" with Restoration monarchy and repression of dissidents and present his use of unrhymed blank verse as a recovery of "ancient liberty."

FROM PARADISE LOST

SECOND EDITION (1674)[1]

The Verse

The measure is English heroic verse without rhyme, as that of Homer in Greek and of Virgil in Latin; rhyme being no necessary adjunct or true ornament of poem or good verse, in longer works especially, but the invention of a barbarous age, to set off wretched matter[2] and lame meter; graced indeed since by the use of some famous modern poets,[3] carried away by custom, but much to their own vexation, hindrance, and constraint to express many things otherwise, and for the most part worse than else they would have expressed them. Not without cause therefore some both Italian[4] and Spanish poets of prime note have rejected rhyme both in longer and shorter works, as have also long since our best English tragedies, as a thing of itself, to all judicious ears, trivial and of no true musical delight; which consists only in apt numbers,[5] fit quantity of syllables, and the sense variously drawn out from one verse into another, not in the jingling sound of like endings, a fault avoided by the learned ancients both in poetry and all good oratory. This neglect then of rhyme so little is to be taken for a defect, though it may seem so perhaps to vulgar readers, that it rather is to be esteemed an example set,

1. The first edition (1667) presented *Paradise Lost* in ten books; the second (1674) recast it into twelve books after the Virgilian model, splitting the original Books 7 and 10.
2. Perhaps the bawdy content of the Latin songs composed by Goliardic poets of the Middle Ages;

they learned rhyme from medieval hymns.
3. Notably, Dryden. See his *Essay of Dramatic Poesy*, p. 913.
4. Trissino and Tasso.
5. Appropriate rhythm.

the first in English, of ancient liberty recovered to heroic poem from the troublesome and modern bondage of rhyming.

Book 1

The Argument[1]

This first book proposes, first in brief, the whole subject, man's disobedience, and the loss thereupon of Paradise wherein he was placed: then touches the prime cause of his fall, the Serpent, or rather Satan in the Serpent; who revolting from God, and drawing to his side many legions of angels, was by the command of God driven out of Heaven with all his crew into the great deep. Which action passed over, the poem hastes into the midst of things,[2] presenting Satan with his angels now fallen into Hell, described here, not in the center[3] (for Heaven and Earth may be supposed as yet not made, certainly not yet accursed) but in a place of utter darkness, fitliest called Chaos: here Satan with his angels lying on the burning lake, thunderstruck and astonished, after a certain space recovers, as from confusion, calls up him who next in order and dignity lay by him; they confer of their miserable fall. Satan awakens all his legions, who lay till then in the same manner confounded; they rise, their numbers, array of battle, their chief leaders named, according to the idols known afterwards in Canaan and the countries adjoining. To these Satan directs his speech, comforts them with hope yet of regaining Heaven, but tells them lastly of a new world and new kind of creature to be created, according to an ancient prophecy or report in Heaven; for that angels were long before this visible creation, was the opinion of many ancient Fathers.[4] To find out the truth of this prophecy, and what to determine[5] thereon he refers to a full council. What his associates thence attempt. Pandemonium the palace of Satan rises, suddenly built out of the deep: the infernal peers there sit in council.

Of man's first disobedience, and the fruit[1]
Of that forbidden tree, whose mortal° taste   *deadly*
Brought death into the world, and all our woe,
With loss of Eden, till one greater Man[2]
5 Restore us, and regain the blissful seat,
Sing Heav'nly Muse,[3] that on the secret top
Of Oreb, or of Sinai, didst inspire
That shepherd, who first taught the chosen seed,
In the beginning how the heav'ns and earth
10 Rose out of Chaos: or if Sion hill[4]

1. *Paradise Lost* appeared originally without any sort of prose aid to the reader, but the printer asked Milton for some "Arguments," or summary explanations of the action in the various books, and these were prefixed to later issues of the poem. We reprint the "Argument" for the first book.
2. According to Horace, the epic poet should begin, "*in medias res.*"
3. I.e., of the earth.
4. Church Fathers, the Christian writers of the first centuries.
5. I.e., what action to take.
1. Eve's apple, and all the consequences of eating

it. This first Proem (lines 1–26) combines the epic statement of theme and invocation.
2. Christ, the second Adam.
3. In Greek mythology, Urania, Muse of astronomy; here, however, by the references to Oreb and Sinai, identified with the Muse who inspired Moses ("that shepherd") to write Genesis and the other four books of the Pentateuch for the instruction of the Jews ("the chosen seed").
4. Mount Zion: the site of Solomon's Temple. "Siloa's Brook": a spring near the Temple where Christ cured a blind man.

Delight thee more, and Siloa's brook that flowed
Fast by the oracle of God; I thence
Invoke thy aid to my advent'rous song,
That with no middle flight intends to soar
15 Above th' Aonian mount,[5] while it pursues
Things unattempted yet in prose or rhyme.[6]
And chiefly thou O Spirit,[7] that dost prefer
Before all temples th' upright heart and pure,
Instruct me, for thou know'st; thou from the first
20 Wast present, and with mighty wings outspread
Dove-like sat'st brooding[8] on the vast abyss
And mad'st it pregnant: what in me is dark
Illumine, what is low raise and support;
That to the height of this great argument°   subject, theme
25 I may assert Eternal Providence,
And justify° the ways of God to men.   show the justice of
      Say first, for Heav'n hides nothing from thy view
Nor the deep tract of Hell, say first what cause[9]
Moved our grand parents in that happy state,
30 Favored of Heav'n so highly, to fall off
From their Creator, and transgress his will
For° one restraint, lords of the world besides?°   because of / otherwise
Who first seduced them to that foul revolt?
Th' infernal Serpent; he it was, whose guile
35 Stirred up with envy and revenge, deceived
The mother of mankind, what time° his pride   when
Had cast him out from Heav'n, with all his host
Of rebel angels, by whose aid aspiring
To set himself in glory above his peers,°   equals
40 He trusted to have equaled the Most High,
If he opposed; and with ambitious aim
Against the throne and monarchy of God
Raised impious war in Heav'n and battle proud
With vain attempt. Him the Almighty Power
45 Hurled headlong flaming from th' ethereal sky
With hideous ruin and combustion down
To bottomless perdition, there to dwell
In adamantine[1] chains and penal fire,
Who durst defy th' Omnipotent to arms.
50 Nine times the space[2] that measures day and night
To mortal men, he with his horrid crew
Lay vanquished, rolling in the fiery gulf
Confounded though immortal: but his doom
Reserved him to more wrath; for now the thought
55 Both of lost happiness and lasting pain

5. Helicon, home of the classical Muses. Milton will attempt to surpass Homer and Virgil.
6. Paradoxically, Milton vaunts his originality in a translated line from Ariosto's *Orlando Furioso* 1.2. The allusion also challenges the romantic epic in Ariosto's tradition.
7. An impulse or voice or power of God.
8. A composite of phrases and ideas from Genesis 1.2 ("And the earth was without form, and void, and darkness was upon the face of the deep. And

the Spirit of God moved upon the face of the waters"). Only a small number of Milton's many allusions to the Bible (in many versions) can be indicated in the notes. Milton's brooding dove image comes from the Latin (Tremellius) Bible version, "incubabat."
9. An opening question like this is an epic convention.
1. A mythical substance of great hardness.
2. Extent of time, linear distances.

Torments him; round he throws his baleful° eyes   *malignant*
That witnessed huge affliction and dismay
Mixed with obdúrate pride and steadfast hate:
At once as far as angels ken° he views   *range of sight*
60   The dismal situation waste and wild,
A dungeon horrible, on all sides round
As one great furnace flamed, yet from those flames
No light,[3] but rather darkness visible
Served only to discover sights of woe,
65   Regions of sorrow, doleful shades, where peace
And rest can never dwell, hope never comes
That comes to all;[4] but torture without end
Still urges,° and a fiery deluge, fed   *always provokes*
With ever-burning sulphur unconsumed:
70   Such place Eternal Justice had prepared
For those rebellious, here their prison ordained
In utter darkness, and their portion set
As far removed from God and light of Heav'n
As from the center thrice to th' utmost pole.[5]
75   O how unlike the place from whence they fell!
There the companions of his fall, o'erwhelmed
With floods and whirlwinds of tempestuous fire,
He soon discerns, and welt'ring° by his side   *rolling in the waves*
One next himself in power, and next in crime,
80   Long after known in Palestine, and named
Beëlzebub.[6] To whom th' Arch-Enemy,
And thence in Heav'n called Satan,[7] with bold words
Breaking the horrid silence thus began.
     "If thou beest he; but O how fall'n![8] how changed
85   From him, who in the happy realms of light
Clothed with transcendent brightness didst outshine
Myriads though bright: if he whom mutual league,
United thoughts and counsels, equal hope
And hazard in the glorious enterprise,
90   Joined with me once, now misery hath joined
In equal ruin: into what pit thou seest
From what height fall'n, so much the stronger proved
He with his thunder:° and till then who knew   *thunderbolt*
The force of those dire arms? Yet not for those,
95   Nor what the potent victor in his rage
Can else inflict, do I repent or change,
Though changed in outward luster, that fixed mind

3. Omitting the verb conveys abruptly the paradox, fire without light.
4. The phrase alludes to Dante ("All hope abandon, ye who enter here").
5. Milton makes use of various images of the cosmos in *Paradise Lost*: (1) The earth is the center of the (Ptolemaic) cosmos of ten concentric spheres; (2) The earth and the whole cosmos are an appendage hanging from Heaven by a golden chain; (3) The cosmos seems Copernican from the angels' perspective (see Book 8). Here, the fall from Heaven to Hell is described as thrice as far as the distance from the center (earth) to the outermost

sphere.
6. A Phoenician deity, or Baal (the name means "Lord of Flies"). He is called the prince of devils in Matthew 12.24. As with the other fallen angels, his angelic name has been obliterated, and he is now called by the name he will bear as a pagan deity. That literary strategy evokes all the evil associations attaching to those names in human history.
7. In Hebrew the name means "adversary."
8. Alludes to Isaiah 14.12: "How art thou fallen from heaven, O Lucifer, Son of the morning."

And high disdain, from sense of injured merit,
That with the mightiest raised me to contend,
100 And to the fierce contention brought along
Innumerable force of Spirits armed
That durst dislike his reign, and me preferring,
His utmost power with adverse power opposed
In dubious° battle on the plains of Heav'n,   *of uncertain outcome*
105 And shook his throne. What though the field be lost?
All is not lost; the unconquerable will,
And study° of revenge, immortal hate,   *intense consideration*
And courage never to submit or yield:
And what is else not to be overcome?[9]
110 That glory never shall his wrath or might
Extort from me. To bow and sue for grace
With suppliant knee, and deify his power
Who from the terror of this arm so late
Doubted° his empire, that were low indeed,   *feared for*
115 That were an ignominy and shame beneath
This downfall; since by fate the strength of gods[1]
And this empyreal substance cannot fail,°   *cease to exist*
Since through experience of this great event
In arms not worse, in foresight much advanced,
120 We may with more successful hope resolve
To wage by force or guile eternal war
Irreconcilable, to our grand foe,
Who now triúmphs, and in th' excess of joy
Sole reigning holds the tyranny of Heav'n."
125   So spake th' apostate angel, though in pain,
Vaunting aloud, but racked with deep despair:
And him thus answered soon his bold compeer.°   *comrade, equal*
  "O Prince, O Chief of many thronéd Powers,
That led th' embattled Seraphim[2] to war
130 Under thy conduct, and in dreadful deeds
Fearless, endangered Heav'ns perpetual King;
And put to proof his high supremacy,
Whether upheld by strength, or chance, or fate;
Too well I see and rue the dire event,°   *outcome*
135 That with sad overthrow and foul defeat
Hath lost us Heav'n, and all this mighty host
In horrible destruction laid thus low,
As far as gods and heav'nly essences
Can perish: for the mind and spirit remains
140 Invincible, and vigor soon returns,
Though all our glory extinct, and happy state
Here swallowed up in endless misery.
But what if he our conqueror (whom I now
Of force° believe almighty, since no less   *necessarily*

9. I.e., what else does it mean not to be overcome?
1. A term commonly used in the poem for angels. But to Satan and his followers it means more, as Satan claims the position of a god, subject to fate but nothing else. Their substance is "empyreal" (of the empyrean).

2. According to tradition, there were nine orders of angels, arranged hierarchically—seraphim, cherubim, thrones, dominions, virtues, powers, principalities, archangels, and angels. The poem makes use of some of these titles, but does not keep this hierarchy.

145   Than such could have o'erpow'red such force as ours)
      Have left us this our spirit and strength entire
      Strongly to suffer and support our pains,
      That we may so suffice° his vengeful ire,   *satisfy*
      Or do him mightier service as his thralls
150   By right of war, whate'er his business be
      Here in the heart of Hell to work in fire,
      Or do his errands in the gloomy deep;
      What can it then avail though yet we feel
      Strength undiminished, or eternal being
155   To undergo eternal punishment?"
      Whereto with speedy words th' Arch-Fiend replied.
         "Fall'n Cherub, to be weak is miserable
      Doing or suffering: but of this be sure,
      To do aught good never will be our task,
160   But ever to do ill our sole delight,
      As being the contrary to his high will
      Whom we resist. If then his providence
      Out of our evil seek to bring forth good,
      Our labor must be to pervert that end,
165   And out of good still to find means of evil;
      Which ofttimes may succeed, so as perhaps
      Shall grieve him, if I fail° not, and disturb   *err*
      His inmost counsels from their destined aim.
      But see the angry victor hath recalled
170   His ministers of vengeance and pursuit
      Back to the gates of Heav'n: the sulphurous hail
      Shot after us in storm, o'erblown hath laid°   *calmed*
      The fiery surge, that from the precipice
      Of Heav'n received us falling, and the thunder,
175   Winged with red lightning and impetuous rage,
      Perhaps hath spent his shafts, and ceases now
      To bellow through the vast and boundless deep.
      Let us not slip° th' occasion, whether scorn,   *let slip*
      Or satiate fury yield it from our foe.
180   Seest thou yon dreary plain, forlorn and wild,
      The seat of desolation, void of light,
      Save what the glimmering of these livid° flames   *bluish*
      Casts pale and dreadful? Thither let us tend
      From off the tossing of these fiery waves,
185   There rest, if any rest can harbor there,
      And reassembling our afflicted powers,°   *armies*
      Consult how we may henceforth most offend°   *harm, vex*
      Our enemy, our own loss how repair,
      How overcome this dire calamity,
190   What reinforcement we may gain from hope,
      If not what resolution from despair."[3]
         Thus Satan talking to his nearest mate
      With head uplift above the wave, and eyes
      That sparkling blazed, his other parts besides

---

3. Five of the last nine lines of Satan's speech rhyme.

195 Prone on the flood, extended long and large
　　Lay floating many a rood,[4] in bulk as huge
　　As whom° the fables name of monstrous size,　　　　*as those whom*
　　Titanian, or Earth-born, that warred on Jove,
　　Briareos or Typhon,[5] whom the den
200 By ancient Tarsus held, or that sea-beast
　　Leviathan,[6] which God of all his works
　　Created hugest that swim th' ocean stream:
　　Him haply slumb'ring on the Norway foam
　　The pilot of some small night-foundered° skiff,　　*overcome by night*
205 Deeming some island, oft, as seamen tell,[7]
　　With fixèd anchor in his scaly rind
　　Moors by his side under the lee,° while night　　*out of the wind*
　　Invests° the sea, and wishèd morn delays:　　　　*covers*
　　So stretched out huge in length the Arch-Fiend lay
210 Chained on the burning lake, nor ever thence
　　Had ris'n or heaved his head, but that the will
　　And high permission of all-ruling Heaven
　　Left him at large to his own dark designs,
　　That with reiterated crimes he might
215 Heap on himself damnation, while he sought
　　Evil to others, and enraged might see
　　How all his malice served but to bring forth
　　Infinite goodness, grace and mercy shown
　　On man by him seduced, but on himself
220 Treble confusion, wrath and vengeance poured.
　　Forthwith upright he rears from off the pool
　　His mighty stature; on each hand the flames
　　Driv'n backward slope their pointing spires,° and rolled　　*points of flames*
　　In billows, leave i' th' midst a horrid° vale.　　　*dreadful, bristling*
225 Then with expanded wings he steers his flight
　　Aloft, incumbent on° the dusky air　　　　　　　*resting on*
　　That felt unusual weight, till on dry land
　　He lights,° if it were land that ever burned　　　　*alights*
　　With solid, as the lake with liquid fire,
230 And such appeared in hue; as when the force
　　Of subterranean wind transports a hill
　　Torn from Pelorus, or the shattered side
　　Of thund'ring Etna,[8] whose combustible
　　And fueled entrails thence conceiving fire,
235 Sublimed° with mineral fury, aid the winds,　　　*vaporized*
　　And leave a singèd bottom all involved°　　　　*enveloped*
　　With stench and smoke: such resting found the sole
　　Of unblest feet. Him followed his next mate,

4. An old unit of measure, between six and eight yards.
5. Both the Titans, led by Briareos (said to have had a hundred hands), and the earth-born Giants, represented by Typhon (who lived in Cilicea near Tarsus and was said to have had a hundred heads), fought with Jove. They were punished by being thrown into the underworld. Christian mythographers found in these stories an analogy to Satan's revolt and punishment.

6. The whale, often identified with the great sea-monster and enemy of the Lord in Isaiah 17.1 and the crocodilelike dragon of Job 41. Both were also identified with Satan.
7. The story of the deceived sailor and the illusory island was a commonplace, but the reference to Norway suggests a 16th-century version by Olaus Magnus, a Swedish historian.
8. Pelorus and Etna are volcanic mountains in Sicily.

Both glorying to have scaped the Stygian° flood   *Styxlike, hellish*
240 As gods, and by their own recovered strength,
Not by the sufferance° of supernal power.   *permission*
    "Is this the region, this the soil, the clime,"
Said then the lost Archangel, "this the seat°   *estate*
That we must change for Heav'n, this mournful gloom
245 For that celestial light? Be it so, since he
Who now is sovran can dispose and bid
What shall be right: farthest from him is best
Whom reason hath equaled, force hath made supreme
Above his equals. Farewell happy fields
250 Where joy for ever dwells: Hail horrors, hail
Infernal world, and thou profoundest Hell
Receive thy new possessor: one who brings
A mind not to be changed by place or time.
The mind is its own place, and in itself
255 Can make a Heav'n of Hell, a Hell of Heav'n.⁹
What matter where, if I be still the same,
And what I should be, all but less than° he   *barely less than*
Whom thunder hath made greater? Here at least
We shall be free; th' Almighty hath not built
260 Here for his envy,¹ will not drive us hence:
Here we may reign secure, and in my choice
To reign is worth ambition though in Hell:
Better to reign in Hell, than serve in Heav'n.²
But wherefore let we then our faithful friends,
265 Th' associates and copartners of our loss
Lie thus astonished° on th' oblivious pool,³   *stunned*
And call them not to share with us their part
In this unhappy mansion, or once more
With rallied arms to try what may be yet
270 Regained in Heav'n, or what more lost in Hell?"
    So Satan spake, and him Beëlzebub
Thus answered. "Leader of those armies bright,
Which but th' Omnipotent none could have foiled,
If once they hear that voice, their liveliest pledge
275 Of hope in fears and dangers, heard so oft
In worst extremes, and on the perilous edge°   *front lines*
Of battle when it raged, in all assaults
Their surest signal, they will soon resume
New courage and revive, though now they lie
280 Groveling and prostrate on yon lake of fire,
As we erewhile, astounded and amazed,
No wonder, fall'n such a pernicious highth."
    He scarce had ceased when the superior Fiend
Was moving toward the shore; his ponderous shield
285 Ethereal temper,⁴ massy, large and round,

---

9. Compare Satan's soliloquy, 4.33–113.
1. I.e., because he desires this place.
2. An ironic echo of *Odyssey* 11.489–91, where the shade of Achilles tells Odysseus that it is better to be a farmhand on earth than king among the

dead.
3. The epithet "oblivious" is transferred from the fallen angels to the pool in which they have fallen.
4. I.e., tempered in celestial fire.

Behind him cast; the broad circumference
Hung on his shoulders like the moon, whose orb
Through optic glass the Tuscan artists views[5]
At evening from the top of Fesole,
290   Or in Valdarno, to descry new lands,
Rivers or mountains in her spotty globe.
His spear, to equal which the tallest pine
Hewn on Norwegian hills, to be the mast
Of some great ammiral,° were but a wand,   *admiral's ship*
295   He walked with to support uneasy steps
Over the burning marl,° not like those steps   *soil*
On heaven's azure; and the torrid clime
Smote on him sore besides, vaulted with fire;
Nathless° he so endured, till on the beach   *nevertheless*
300   Of that inflamed° sea, he stood and called   *flaming*
His legions, angel forms, who lay entranced
Thick as autumnal leaves that strow the brooks
In Vallombrosa,[6] where th' Etrurian shades
High overarched embow'r;° or scattered sedge°   *form bowers/seaweed*
305   Afloat, when with fierce winds Orion[7] armed
Hath vexed the Red Sea coast, whose waves o'erthrew
Busiris[8] and his Memphian chivalry,
While with perfidious hatred they pursued
The sojourners of Goshen, who beheld
310   From the safe shore their floating carcasses
And broken chariot wheels; so thick bestrown
Abject and lost lay these, covering the flood,
Under amazement of their hideous change.
He called so loud, that all the hollow deep
315   Of Hell resounded. "Princes, Potentates,
Warriors, the flow'r of heav'n, once yours, now lost,
If such astonishment as this can seize
Eternal Spirits: or have ye chos'n this place
After the toil of battle to repose
320   Your wearied virtue,° for the ease you find   *strength, valor*
To slumber here, as in the vales of Heav'n?
Or in this abject posture have ye sworn
To adore the conqueror? who now beholds
Cherub and Seraph rolling in the flood
325   With scattered arms and ensigns,° till anon   *battle flags*
His swift pursuers from Heav'n gates discern
Th' advantage, and descending tread us down
Thus drooping, or with linkèd thunderbolts
Transfix us to the bottom of this gulf.
330   Awake, arise, or be for ever fall'n."

5. Galileo, who looked through a telescope ("optic glass") from the hill town of Fesole outside Florence, in the valley of the Arno river ("Valdarno," val d'Arno). In 1610 he published a book describing the mountains on the moon.
6. The name means "shady valley," a region high in the Apennines, about twenty miles from Florence, in Tuscany ("Etruria"). Similes comparing the numberless dead to falling leaves are frequent in epic (e.g., *Aeneid* 6.309–10).
7. Orion is a constellation whose rising near sunset in late summer and autumn was associated with storms in the Red Sea.
8. Mythical Egyptian pharaoh, whom Milton associates with the pharaoh of Exodus 14 who pursued the Israelites ("sojourners of Goshen") into the Red Sea, which God parted for them. His "chivalry" are horsemen from Memphis.

They heard, and were abashed, and up they sprung
Upon the wing, as when men wont to watch
On duty, sleeping found by whom they dread,
Rouse and bestir themselves ere well awake.
335 Nor did they not perceive[9] the evil plight
In which they were, or the fierce pains not feel;
Yet to their general's voice they soon obeyed
Innumerable. As when the potent rod
Of Amram's son[1] in Egypt's evil day
340 Waved round the coast, up called a pitchy cloud
Of locusts, warping° on the eastern wind,   *floating*
That o'er the realm of impious Pharaoh hung
Like night, and darkened all the land of Nile:
So numberless were those bad angels seen
345 Hovering on wing under the cope° of Hell   *roof*
'Twixt upper, nether, and surrounding fires;
Till, as a signal giv'n, th' uplifted spear
Of their great Sultan[2] waving to direct
Their course, in even balance down they light
350 On the firm brimstone, and fill all the plain;
A multitude, like which the populous North
Poured never from her frozen loins, to pass
Rhene or the Danaw, when her barbarous sons
Came like a deluge on the South, and spread
355 Beneath Gibraltar to the Libyan sands.[3]
Forthwith from every squadron and each band
The heads and leaders thither haste where stood
Their great commander; godlike shapes and forms
Excelling human, princely dignities,
360 And powers that erst in Heaven sat on thrones;
Though of their names in heav'nly records now
Be no memorial, blotted out and razed°   *erased*
By their rebellion, from the Books of Life.
Nor had they yet among the sons of Eve
365 Got them new names, till wand'ring o'er the earth,
Through God's high sufferance for the trial of man,
By falsities and lies the greatest part
Of mankind they corrupted to forsake
God their Creator, and th' invisible
370 Glory of him that made them, to transform
Oft to the image of a brute, adorned
With gay religions° full of pomp and gold,   *showy rites*
And devils to adore for deities:
Then were they known to men by various names,
375 And various idols through the heathen world.
      Say, Muse, their names then known, who first, who last,[4]
Roused from the slumber on that fiery couch,

---

9. The double negatives make a positive: they did
perceive both plight and pain.
1. Moses, who drew down a plague of locusts on
Egypt (Exodus 10.12–15).
2. A first use of this description of Satan as an
Oriental despot.

3. The barbarian invasions of Rome began with
crossings of the Rhine ("Rhene") and Danube
("Danaw") rivers and spread across Spain, via Gibraltar, to North Africa.
4. The catalog of gods here is an epic convention;
Homer catalogs ships; Virgil, warriors.

At their great emperor's call, as next in worth
Came singly° where he stood on the bare strand,   *one at a time*
380 While the promiscuous° crowd stood yet aloof.   *mixed*
    The chief were those who from the pit of Hell
Roaming to seek their prey on earth, durst fix
Their seats long after next the seat of God,[5]
Their altars by his altar, gods adored
385 Among the nations round, and durst abide
Jehovah thund'ring out of Zion, throned
Between the Cherubim;[6] yea, often placed
Within his sanctuary itself their shrines,
Abomination; and with cursèd things
390 His holy rites, and solemn feasts profaned,
And with their darkness durst affront his light.
First Moloch,[7] horrid king besmeared with blood
Of human sacrifice, and parents' tears,
Though for the noise of drums and timbrels° loud   *tambourines*
395 Their children's cries unheard, that passed through fire
To his grim idol. Him the Ammonite[8]
Worshiped in Rabba and her wat'ry plain,
In Argob and in Basan, to the stream
Of Utmost Arnon. Nor content with such
400 Audacious neighborhood, the wisest heart
Of Solomon he led by fraud to build
His temple right against the temple of God
On that opprobrious hill, and made his grove
The pleasant valley of Hinnom, Tophet thence
405 And black Gehenna called, the type of Hell.[9]
Next Chemos,[1] th' obscene dread of Moab's sons,
From Aroer to Nebo, and the wild
Of southmost Abarim; in Hesebon
And Horanaim, Seon's realm, beyond
410 The flow'ry dale of Sibma clad with vines,
And Elealè to th' Asphaltic Pool.[2]
Peor[3] his other name, when he enticed
Israel in Sittim on their march from Nile
To do him wanton rites, which cost them woe.
415 Yet thence his lustful orgies he enlarged
Even to that hill of scandal,[4] by the grove
Of Moloch homicide, lust hard by hate;

---

5. The first group of devils come from the Middle East, close neighbors of Jehovah "throned" in his sanctuary in Jerusalem.
6. Golden cherubim adorned opposite ends of the gold cover on the Ark of the Covenant.
7. Moloch was a sun god, sometimes represented as a roaring bull or with a calf's head, within whose brazen image living children were supposedly burned as sacrifices.
8. The Ammonites lived east of the Jordan. "Rabba" is modern Amman, in Jordan; "Argob," "Basan," "utmost Arnon" are lands east of the Dead Sea.
9. The rites of Moloch on "that opprobrious hill" (the Mount of Olives), just opposite the Jewish temple, and in the valley of Hinnom so polluted those places that they were turned into the refuse dump of Jerusalem. Under the name "Tophet" and "Gehenna," Hinnom became a type of Hell.
1. Chemos or Chemosh, associated with Moloch in 1 Kings 11.7, was the god of the Moabites, whose lands (many drawn from Isaiah 15–16) are mentioned in the following lines.
2. The Dead Sea.
3. The story of Peor seducing the Israelites in Sittim is told in Numbers 15.
4. The Mount of Olives where Solomon built temples for Chemos and Moloch (1 Kings 11.7); epithets were commonly attached to the names of gods, as here, Moloch "homicide." Josiah (next line) destroyed pagan idols in Jerusalem and other cities (2 Chronicles 34).

Till good Josiah drove them thence to Hell.
With these came they, who from the bord'ring flood
420 Of old Euphrates to the brook that parts
Egypt from Syrian ground,[5] had general names
Of Baalim and Ashtaroth, those male,
These feminine.[6] For Spirits when they please
Can either sex assume, or both; so soft
425 And uncompounded is their essence pure,
Not tied or manacled with joint or limb,
Nor founded on the brittle strength of bones,
Like cumbrous flesh; but in what shape they choose
Dilated or condensed, bright or obscure,
430 Can execute their airy purposes,
And works of love or enmity fulfill.
For those the race of Israel oft forsook
Their Living Strength, and unfrequented left
His righteous altar, bowing lowly down
435 To bestial gods; for which their heads as low
Bowed down in battle, sunk before the spear
Of despicable foes. With these in troop
Came Astoreth, whom the Phoenicians called
Astartè, queen of Heav'n, with crescent horns;
440 To whose bright image nightly by the moon
Sidonian virgins[7] paid their vows and songs,
In Sion also not unsung, where stood
Her temple on th' offensive mountain,[8] built
By that uxorious king, whose heart though large,
445 Beguiled by fair idolatresses, fell
To idols foul. Thammuz[9] came next behind,
Whose annual wound in Lebanon allured
The Syrian damsels to lament his fate
In amorous ditties all a summer's day,
450 While smooth Adonis[1] from his native work
Ran purple to the sea, supposed with blood
Of Thammuz yearly wounded: the love-tale
Infected Sion's daughters with like heat,
Whose wanton passions in the sacred porch
455 Ezekiel[2] saw, when by the vision led
His eye surveyed the dark idolatries
Of alienated Judah. Next came one
Who mourned in earnest, when the captive ark
Maimed his brute image, head and hands lopped off
460 In his own temple, on the grunsel edge,[3]

---

5. Palestine lies between the Euphrates and "the brook of Besor" (1 Samuel 30.10).
6. Plural forms, masculine and feminine, respectively, denoting aspects of the sun god Baal and the moon goddess Astarte.
7. Sidon and Tyre were the chief cities of Phoenicia.
8. The Mount of Olives again. "That uxorious king" (next line) is Solomon, who "loved many strange women" (2 Kings 11.1–8).
9. A Syrian god, supposedly killed by a boar in

Lebanon; his Greek form was Adonis, beloved of Aphrodite and god of the solar year. Annual festivals mourned his death and celebrated his revival as signifying the death and rebirth of vegetation.
1. Here, the Lebanese river named for the deity because every spring it turned blood-red from sedimentary mud.
2. The prophet complained that Jewish women were worshipping Thammuz (Ezekiel 8.14).
3. When the Philistines stole the ark of God, they placed it in the temple of their sea god, Dagon, but

Where he fell flat, and shamed his worshipers:
Dagon his name, sea monster, upward man
And downward fish: yet had his temple high
Reared in Azotus, dreaded through the coast
465 Of Palestine, in Gath and Ascalon[4]
And Accaron and Gaza's frontier bounds.
Him followed Rimmon,[5] whose delightful seat
Was fair Damascus, on the fertile banks
Of Abbana and Pharphar, lucid streams.
470 He also against the house of God was bold:
A leper once he lost and gained a king,[6]
Ahaz his sottish conqueror, whom he drew
God's altar to disparage and displace
For one of Syrian mode, whereon to burn
475 His odious off'rings, and adore the gods
Whom he had vanquished. After these appeared
A crew who under names of old renown,
Osiris, Isis, Orus[7] and their train
With monstrous shapes and sorceries abused
480 Fanatic Egypt and her priests, to seek
Their wand'ring gods disguised in brutish forms
Rather than human. Nor did Israel scape
Th' infection when their borrowed gold composed
The calf in Oreb:[8] and the rebel king
485 Doubled that sin in Bethel and in Dan,
Lik'ning his Maker to the grazèd ox,[9]
Jehovah, who in one night when he passed
From Egypt marching, equaled° with one stroke   levelled
Both her first-born and all her bleating gods.[1]
490 Belial came last,[2] than whom a spirit more lewd
Fell not from Heaven, or more gross to love
Vice for itself: to him no temple stood
Or altar smoked; yet who more oft than he
In temples and at altars, when the priest
495 Turns atheist, as did Eli's sons,[3] who filled
With lust and violence the house of God.
In courts and palaces he also reigns
And in luxurious cities, where the noise
Of riot ascends above their loftiest tow'rs,

---

in the morning the mutilated statue of Dagon was found on the threshhold ("grunsel edge") (1 Samuel 5.1–5).
4. The five chief cities of the Philistines, sites of Dagon's worship.
5. A Phoenician god whose temple was in Damascus.
6. A Syrian general, Naaman, was cured of leprosy and converted from worship of Rimmon by the waters of the Jordan (2 Kings 5), while King Ahaz, an Israelite monarch who conquered Damascus, was converted there to Rimmon's worship.
7. The second group of devils include the Egyptian gods driven from Heaven by the revolt of the giants (Ovid, *Metamorphoses* 5) and forced to wander in "monstrous" (next line) animal disguises.
8. In the wilderness of Egypt, while Moses was

receiving the Law, Aaron made a golden calf, thought to be an idol of the Egyptian god Apis and made of ornaments brought out of Egypt (Exodus 32).
9. Jereboam, "the rebel king" who led the ten tribes of Israel in revolt against Solomon's son, Reheboam; he doubled Aaron's sin by making two golden calves (1 Kings 12–30).
1. Jehovah smote the firstborn of all Egyptian families as well as their gods (Exodus 12.12).
2. Belial was never worshiped as a god; his name means "wickedness," but its use in phrases like "sons of Belial" encouraged personification.
3. Priests who were termed "sons of Belial" because they seized for themselves offerings made to God and lay with prostitutes (1 Samuel 2.12–22).

500 And injury and outrage: and when night
Darkens the streets, then wander forth the sons
Of Belial, flown° with insolence and wine.[4]   *flushed*
Witness the streets of Sodom, and that night
In Gibeah,[5] when the hospitable door
505 Exposed a matron to avoid worse rape.
      These were the prime in order and in might;
The rest were long to tell, though far renowned,
Th' Ionian gods, of Javan's issue held
Gods, yet confessed later than Heav'n and Earth
510 Their boasted parents;[6] Titan Heav'n's first-born
With his enormous brood, and birthright seized
By younger Saturn, he from mightier Jove,
His own and Rhea's son, like measure found;
So Jove usurping reigned:[7] these first in Crete
515 And Ida known, thence on the snowy top
Of cold Olympus ruled the middle air
Their highest heav'n; or on the Delphian cliff,
Or in Dodona, and through all the bounds
Of Doric land;[8] or who with Saturn old
520 Fled over Adria to th' Hesperian fields,
And o'er the Celtic roamed the utmost isles.[9]
      All these and more came flocking; but with looks
Downcast and damp,° yet such wherein appeared   *depressed, dazed*
Obscure some glimpse of joy, to have found their chief
525 Not in despair, to have found themselves not lost
In loss itself; which on his count'nance cast
Like doubtful hue:[1] but he his wonted pride
Soon recollecting, with high words, that bore
Semblance of worth, not substance, gently raised
530 Their fainting courage, and dispelled their fears.
Then straight commands that at the warlike sound
Of trumpets loud and clarions be upreared
His mighty standard; that proud honor claimed
Azazel[2] as his right, a Cherub tall:
535 Who forthwith from the glittering staff unfurled
Th' imperial ensign, which full high advanced
Shone like a meteor streaming to the wind
With gems and golden luster rich emblazed,
Seraphic arms and trophies:[3] all the while

---

4. This passage, with its present-tense verbs, invites application to current examples—like Cavaliers at court and Restoration London.
5. Lot begged the Sodomites to rape his daughter rather than his (male) angel guests (Genesis 19); in Gibeah a Levite avoided worse (homosexual) rape by surrendering his concubine to riotous "sons of Belial" (Judges 19.21–30).
6. The Ionian Greeks ("Javan's issue," i.e., of the line of Javan, grandson of Noah) regarded the Titans as gods; their supposed parents were Heaven (Uranus) and Earth (Gaea).
7. The Titan Chronos, or Saturn, deposed his elder brother, married his sister Rhea, and ruled until he was deposed by his son, Zeus (Jove), who

had been reared in secret on Mount Ida in Crete.
8. Zeus and the other Olympian gods had their seat on Mount Olympus, in "middle air"; they were worshiped in Delphi, Dodona, and throughout Greece ("Doric lands").
9. Saturn, after his downfall, fled over "Adria" (the Adriatic Sea) to "the Hesperian fields" (Italy), crossed the "Celtic" fields of France, and thence to Britain, the "utmost isles."
1. Satan's face reflected the same mixed emotions.
2. Traditionally, one of the four standard-bearers in Satan's army. "Clarions" (line 532): small, shrill trumpets.
3. Their flags bear the heraldic arms of the various orders of angels and memorials of their battles.

540 Sonorous metal° blowing martial sounds: *trumpets*
At which the universal host upsent
A shout that tore Hell's concave,° and beyond   *vault*
Frighted the reign of Chaos and old Night.[4]
All in a moment through the gloom were seen
545 Ten thousand banners rise into the air
With orient° colors waving: with them rose   *lustrous*
A forest huge of spears: and thronging helms
Appeared, and serried° shields in thick array   *pushed close together*
Of depth immeasurable: anon they move
550 In perfect phalanx to the Dorian[5] mood
Of flutes and soft recorders; such as raised
To highth of noblest temper heroes old
Arming to battle, and instead of rage
Deliberate valor breathed, firm and unmoved
555 With dread of death to flight or foul retreat,
Nor wanting power to mitigate and swage°   *assuage*
With solemn touches, troubled thoughts, and chase
Anguish and doubt and fear and sorrow and pain
From mortal or immortal minds. Thus they
560 Breathing united force with fixèd thought
Moved on in silence to soft pipes that charmed
Their painful steps o'er the burnt soil; and now
Advanced in view they stand, a horrid° front   *bristling with spears*
Of dreadful length and dazzling arms, in guise
565 Of warriors old with ordered spear and shield,
Awaiting what command their mighty chief
Had to impose. He through the armèd files
Darts his experienced eye, and soon traverse°   *across*
The whole battalion views, their order due,
570 Their visages and stature as of gods,
Their number last he sums. And now his heart
Distends with pride, and hard'ning in his strength
Glories: for never since created man[6]
Met such embodied force, as named° with these   *composed*
575 Could merit more than that small infantry[7]
Warred on by cranes: though all the giant brood
Of Phlegra with th' heroic race were joined
That fought at Thebes and Ilium,[8] on each side
Mixed with auxiliar° gods; and what resounds   *allied*
580 In fable or romance of Uther's son
Begirt with British and Armoric knights;
And all who since, baptized or infidel
Jousted in Aspramont or Montalban,
Damasco, or Marocco, or Trebisond,

4. In *Paradise Lost* 2.894–909, 959–70 Chaos and Night rule the region of unformed matter between Heaven and earth.
5. Severe, martial music used by the Spartans marching to battle. "Phalanx": battle formation.
6. I.e., since the creation of man.
7. Pygmies (little people, with a pun on *infants*) had periodic fights with the cranes, in Pliny's account. Compared with Satan's forces, all other armies are puny.
8. In Greek mythology, the Giants fought the gods at Phlegra in Macedonia; in Roman myth, it was at Phlegra in Italy. Satan's forces surpass them, even if joined with the Seven who fought against Thebes and the whole Greek host that besieged Troy ("Illium").

585 Or whom Biserta sent from Afric shore
When Charlemain with all his peerage fell
By Fontarabbia.[9] Thus far these beyond
Compare of mortal prowess, yet observed°   *obeyed*
Their dread commander: he above the rest
590 In shape and gesture proudly eminent
Stood like a tow'r; his form had yet not lost
All her[1] original brightness, nor appeared
Less than Archangel ruined, and th' excess
Of glory obscured: as when the sun new-ris'n
595 Looks through the horizontal° misty air   *on the horizon*
Shorn of his beams, or from behind the moon
In dim eclipse° disastrous twilight sheds   *ill-starred*
On half the nations, and with fear of change
Perplexes monarchs. Darkened so, yet shone
600 Above them all th' Archangel: but his face
Deep scars of thunder had intrenched,° and care   *furrowed*
Sat on his faded cheek, but under brows
Of dauntless courage, and considerate° pride   *conscious, deliberate*
Waiting revenge: cruel his eye, but cast
605 Signs of remorse and passion° to behold   *compassion, pain*
The fellows of his crime, the followers rather
(Far other once beheld in bliss) condemned
For ever now to have their lot in pain,
Millions of Spirits for his fault amerced°   *deprived*
610 Of Heav'n, and from eternal splendors flung
For his revolt, yet faithful how they stood,
Their glory withered: as when Heaven's fire
Hath scathed the forest oaks, or mountain pines,
With singèd top their stately growth though bare
615 Stands on the blasted heath. He now prepared
To speak; whereat their doubled ranks they bend
From wing to wing, and half enclose him round
With all his peers: attention held them mute.
Thrice he essayed, and thrice, in spite of scorn,
620 Tears such as angels weep burst forth: at last
Words interwove with sighs found out their way.
   "O myriads of immortal Spirits, O Powers
Matchless, but with th' Almighty, and that strife
Was not inglorious, though th' event° was dire,   *outcome*
625 As this place testifies, and this dire change
Hateful to utter: but what power of mind
Foreseeing or presaging, from the depth
Of knowledge past or present, could have feared,
How such united force of gods, how such
630 As stood like these, could ever know repulse?
For who can yet believe, though after loss,

---

9. Satan's forces also surpass the "British or Armoric" (from Brittany) knights who fought with King Arthur ("Uther's son"), and all the romance knights who fought at the famous named sites in the following lines. Roncevalles, near Fontarabba, was the place where Charlemagne's "peerage," including his best knight, Roland, were defeated in battle (though not Charlemagne himself).
1. "Forma" in Latin is feminine.

That all these puissant° legions, whose exile   *potent, powerful*
Hath emptied Heav'n, shall fail to reascend
Self-raised, and repossess their native seat?
635 For me, be witness all the host of Heav'n,
If counsels different,° or danger shunned   *contradictory*
By me, have lost our hopes. But he who reigns
Monarch in Heav'n, till then as one secure
Sat on his throne, upheld by old repute,
640 Consent or custom, and his regal state
Put forth at full, but still his strength concealed,
Which tempted our attempt,[2] and wrought our fall.
Henceforth his might we know, and know our own
So as not either to provoke, or dread
645 New war, provoked; our better part remains
To work in close design, by fraud or guile
What force effected not: that he no less
At length from us may find, who overcomes
By force, hath overcome but half his foe.
650 Space may produce new worlds; whereof so rife°   *common*
There went a fame° in Heav'n that he ere long   *rumor*
Intended to create, and therein plant
A generation, whom his choice regard
Should favor equal to the sons of Heaven:
655 Thither, if but to pry, shall be perhaps
Our first eruption,° thither or elsewhere: *breaking out*
For this infernal pit shall never hold
Celestial Spirits in bondage, not th' abyss
Long under darkness cover. But these thoughts
660 Full counsel must mature: peace is despaired,
For who can think submission? War then, war
Open or understood° must be resolved."   *covert*
     He spake: and to confirm his words, out flew
Millions of flaming swords, drawn from the thighs
665 Of mighty Cherubim; the sudden blaze
Far round illumined Hell: highly they raged
Against the Highest, and fierce with graspèd arms
Clashed on their sounding shields the din of war,[3]
Hurling defiance toward the vault of Heav'n.
670   There stood a hill not far whose grisly top
Belched fire and rolling smoke; the rest entire
Shone with a glossy scurf,° undoubted sign   *crust*
That in his womb was hid metallic ore,
The work of sulphur.[4] Thither winged with speed
675 A numerous brígade hastened. As when bands
Of pioneers° with spade and pickax armed   *military engineers*
Forerun the royal camp, to trench a field,
Or cast a rampart. Mammon[5] led them on,

2. Satan is an inveterate punster.
3. Like Roman legionaires, the fallen angels applaud by beating swords on shields.
4. Sulfur and mercury were considered the basic substances of all metals.

5. Mammon, an abstract word for riches, came to be personified and associated with the god of wealth, Plutus, and so with Pluto, god of the underworld. Cf. Matthew 6.24: "Ye cannot serve God and Mammon."

Mammon, the least erected Spirit that fell
680 From Heav'n, for ev'n in Heav'n his looks and thoughts
Were always downward bent, admiring more
The riches of Heav'n's pavement, trodden gold,
Than aught divine or holy else enjoyed
In vision beatific: by him first
685 Men also, and by his suggestion taught,
Ransacked the center, and with impious hands
Rifled the bowels of their mother earth
For treasures better hid. Soon had his crew
Opened into the hill a spacious wound
690 And digged out ribs of gold. Let none admire°   *wonder*
That riches grow in Hell; that soil may best
Deserve the precious bane.° And here let those   *poison*
Who boast in mortal things, and wond'ring tell
Of Babel, and the works of Memphian kings,[6]
695 Learn how their greatest monuments of fame,
And strength and art are easily outdone
By Spirits reprobate, and in an hour
What in an age they with incessant toil
And hands innumerable scarce perform.
700 Nigh on the plain in many cells prepared,
That underneath had veins of liquid fire
Sluiced from the lake, a second multitude
With wondrous art founded° the massy ore,   *melted*
Severing° each kind, and scummed the bullion dross:° *separating/boiling dregs*
705 A third as soon had formed within the ground
A various mold, and from the boiling cells
By strange conveyance filled each hollow nook,
As in an organ from one blast of wind
To many a row of pipes the soundboard breathes.
710 Anon out of the earth a fabric huge
Rose like an exhalation, with the sound
Of dulcet symphonies and voices sweet,[7]
Built like a temple, where pilasters° round   *columns set in a wall*
Were set, and Doric pillars[8] overlaid
715 With golden architrave; nor did there want
Cornice or frieze, with bossy° sculptures grav'n;   *embossed*
The roof was fretted° gold. Not Babylon,   *richly ornamented*
Nor great Alcairo such magnificence
Equaled in all their glories, to enshrine
720 Belus or Serapis[9] their gods, or seat
Their kings, when Egypt with Assyria strove
In wealth and luxury. Th' ascending pile
Stood fixed° her stately height, and straight° the doors *complete/at once*
Opening their brazen folds discover wide
725 Within, her ample spaces, o'er the smooth
And level pavement: from the archèd roof

---

6. The Tower of Babel and the pyramids of Egypt.
7. After melting the gold with fire from the lake and pouring it into molds, the devils cause their building to rise as by magic, to the sounds of marvelous music.
8. Doric pillars are severe and plain. The devils'

palace combines classical architectural features with elaborate ornamentation, suggesting, perhaps, St. Peter's in Rome.
9. At Babylon in Assyria there were temples to "Belus" or Baal; at Alcairo (modern Cairo, ancient Memphis) in Egypt they were to Osiris ("Serapis").

Pendent by subtle magic many a row
Of starry lamps and blazing cressets[1] fed
With naphtha and asphaltus yielded light
730 As from a sky. The hasty multitude
Admiring entered, and the work some praise
And some the architect: his hand was known
In Heav'n by many a towered structure high,
Where sceptered angels held their residence,
735 And sat as princes, whom the Súpreme King
Exalted to such power, and gave to rule,
Each in his hierarchy, the orders bright.
Nor was his name unheard or unadored
In ancient Greece and in Ausonian land
740 Men called him Mulciber[2] and how he fell
From Heav'n, they fabled, thrown by angry Jove
Sheer o'er the crystal battlements: from morn
To noon he fell, from noon to dewy eve,
A summer's day; and with the setting sun
745 Dropped from the zenith like a falling star,
On Lemnos th' Aégean isle: thus they relate,
Erring; for he with this rebellious rout
Fell long before; nor aught availed him now
To have built in Heav'n high tow'rs; nor did he scape
750 By all his engines, but was headlong sent
With his industrious crew to build in Hell.
    Meanwhile the wingèd heralds by command
Of sovran power, with awful ceremony
And trumpet's sound throughout the host proclaim
755 A solemn council forthwith to be held
At Pandemonium,[3] the high capitol
Of Satan and his peers:° their summons called   *nobles*
From every band and squarèd regiment
By place° or choice° the worthiest; they anon   *rank/election*
760 With hundreds and with thousands trooping came
Attended: all access was thronged, the gates
And porches wide, but chief the spacious hall
(Though like a covered field, where champions bold
Wont ride in armed, and at the Soldan's° chair   *sultan's*
765 Defied the best of paynim° chivalry   *pagan*
To mortal combat or career with lance)
Thick swarmed, both on the ground and in the air,
Brushed with the hiss of rustling wings. As bees
In springtime, when the sun with Taurus[4] rides,
770 Pour forth their populous youth about the hive
In clusters; they among fresh dews and flowers
Fly to and fro, or on the smoothèd plank,
The suburb of their straw-built citadel,
New rubbed with balm, expatiate and confer[5]

---

1. Basketlike lamps, hung from the ceiling.
2. Hephaestus, or Vulcan, was sometimes known in "Ausonian land" (Italy) as "Mulciber." The story of Jove's tossing him out of heaven is told in book 1 of the *Iliad*.
3. "Pandemonium" (a Miltonic coinage) means

literally "All-Demons," an inversion of Pantheon, "All Gods."
4. The sun is in the zodiacal sign of Taurus from about April 19 to May 20.
5. Spread out and discuss. Bee similes were common in epic from Homer on; also, the bees' (roy-

775 Their state affairs. So thick the aery crowd
Swarmed and were straitened; till the signal giv'n,
Behold a wonder! They but now who seemed
In bigness to surpass Earth's giant sons
Now less than smallest dwarfs, in narrow room
780 Throng numberless, like that Pygmean race
Beyond the Indian mount,[6] or fairy elves,
Whose midnight revels, by a forest side
Or fountain some belated peasant sees,
Or dreams he sees, while overhead the moon
785 Sits arbitress,° and nearer to the earth   witness
Wheels her pale course: they on their mirth and dance
Intent, with jocund° music charm his ear;[7]   merry
At once with joy and fear his heart rebounds.
Thus incorporeal Spirits to smallest forms
790 Reduced their shapes immense, and were at large,
Though without number still amidst the hall
Of that infernal court. But far within
And in their own dimensions like themselves
The great Seraphic Lords and Cherubim
795 In close recess and secret conclave sat,
A thousand demi-gods on golden seats,
Frequent and full.[8] After short silence then
And summons read, the great consult[9] began.

Book 2

High on a throne of royal state, which far
Outshone the wealth of Ormus and of Ind,[1]
Or where the gorgeous East with richest hand
Show'rs on her kings barbaric pearl and gold,
5 Satan exalted sat, by merit raised
To that bad eminence; and from despair
Thus high uplifted beyond hope, aspires
Beyond thus high, insatiate to pursue
Vain war with Heav'n, and by success° untaught   the outcome
10 His proud imaginations° thus displayed.   schemes
    "Powers and Dominions,[2] deities of Heaven,
For since no deep within her gulf can hold
Immortal vigor, though oppressed and fall'n,
I give not Heav'n for lost. From this descent
15 Celestial Virtues rising, will appear
More glorious and more dread than from no fall,
And trust themselves to fear no second fate.
Me though just right, and the fixed laws of Heav'n
Did first create your leader, next, free choice,

---

alist) society was often cited in political argument.
The simile prepares for the sudden contraction of
the devils, who can shrink or dilate at will.
6. The pygmies were supposed to live beyond the
Himalayas.
7. The belated peasant's.

8. Crowded together, and in full complement.
9. Consultation, often secret and seditious.
1. India. "Ormus": an island in the Persian Gulf,
modern Hormuz, famous for pearls.
2. Angelic orders.

20   With what besides, in counsel or in fight,
     Hath been achieved of merit, yet this loss
     Thus far at least recovered, hath much more
     Established in a safe unenvied throne
     Yielded with full consent. The happier state
25   In Heaven, which follows dignity, might draw
     Envy from each inferior; but who here
     Will envy whom the highest place exposes
     Foremost to stand against the Thunderer's aim
     Your bulwark, and condemns to greatest share
30   Of endless pain? Where there is then no good
     For which to strive, no strife can grow up there
     From faction; for none sure will claim in Hell
     Precédence, none, whose portion is so small
     Of present pain, that with ambitious mind
35   Will covet more. With this advantage then
     To union, and firm faith, and firm accord,
     More than can be in Heav'n, we now return
     To claim our just inheritance of old,
     Surer to prosper than prosperity
40   Could have assured us;[3] and by what best way,
     Whether of open war or covert guile,[4]
     We now debate; who can advise, may speak."
       He ceas'd, and next him Moloch, sceptered king
     Stood up, the strongest and the fiercest Spirit
45   That fought in Heav'n; now fiercer by despair:
     His trust was with th' Eternal to be deemed
     Equal in strength, and rather than be less
     Cared not to be at all; with that care lost
     Went all his fear: of God, or Hell, or worse
50   He recked° not, and these words thereafter spake.   *cared*
       "My sentence° is for open war: of wiles,   *judgment*
     More unexpert,° I boast not: them let those   *less experienced*
     Contrive who need, or when they need, not now.
     For while they sit contriving, shall the rest,
55   Millions that stand in arms, and longing wait
     The signal to ascend, sit lingering here
     Heav'n's fugitives, and for their dwelling-place
     Accept this dark opprobrious den of shame,
     The prison of his tyranny who reigns
60   By our delay? No, let us rather choose
     Armed with Hell flames and fury all at once
     O'er Heav'n's high tow'rs to force resistless way,
     Turning our tortures into horrid° arms   *bristling, horrifying*
     Against the Torturer; when to meet the noise
65   Of his almighty engine° he shall hear   *the thunderbolt*
     Infernal thunder, and for lightning see
     Black fire and horror shot with equal rage
     Among his angels; and his throne itself

---

3. Note the play on "sure—prosper—prosperity—
assure," a favorite device of Milton's.
4. A typical epic convention (in Homer, Virgil,

Tasso, and elsewhere) involved councils debating
war or peace, with spokesmen on each side. Satan
offers only the option of war, open or covert.

Mixed with Tartarean[5] sulfur, and strange fire,
70 His own invented torments. But perhaps
The way seems difficult and steep to scale
With upright wing against a higher foe.
Let such bethink them, if the sleepy drench°   *large draught*
Of that forgetful° lake benumb not still,   *causing oblivion*
75 That in our proper° motion we ascend   *natural*
Up to our native seat: descent and fall
To us is adverse. Who but felt of late
When the fierce foe hung on our broken rear
Insulting,[6] and pursued us through the deep,
80 With what compulsion and laborious flight
We sunk thus low? Th' ascent is easy then;
Th' event° is feared; should we again provoke   *outcome*
Our stronger, some worse way his wrath may find
To our destruction: if there be in Hell
85 Fear to be worse destroyed: what can be worse
Than to dwell here, driven out from bliss, condemned
In this abhorrèd deep to utter woe;
Where pain of unextinguishable fire
Must exercise° us without hope of end   *vex, afflict*
90 The vassals[7] of his anger, when the scourge
Inexorably, and the torturing hour
Calls us to penance? More destroyed than thus
We should be quite abolished and expire.
What fear we then? What° doubt we to incense   *why*
95 His utmost ire? which to the high enraged,
Will either quite consume us, and reduce
To nothing this essential,° happier far   *essence*
Than miserable to have eternal being:
Or if our substance be indeed divine,
100 And cannot cease to be, we are at worst
On this side nothing;[8] and by proof we feel
Our power sufficient to disturb his Heav'n,
And with perpetual inroads to alarm,
Though inaccessible, his fatal[9] throne:
105 Which if not victory is yet revenge."

     He ended frowning, and his look, denounced°   *portended*
Desperate revenge, and battle dangerous
To less than gods. On th' other side up rose
Belial, in act more graceful and humane;°   *civil, polite*
110 A fairer person lost not Heav'n; he seemed
For dignity composed and high exploit:
But all was false and hollow; though his tongue
Dropped manna, and could make the worse appear
The better reason,[1] to perplex and dash°   *confuse*

5. Tartarus is a classical name for hell.
6. With the Latin sense of stamping on; also, triumphantly scorning.
7. Servants, but perhaps also, vessels.
8. I.e., we cannot be worse off than we are now, and still live.
9. Established by Fate; also, deadly.

1. The Sophists, mercenary teachers of rhetoric in ancient Greece, were denounced by Plato for making "the worse appear / The better reason." "His tongue / Dropped manna": his honeyed words seemed like the manna supplied to the Israelites in the desert.

115 Maturest counsels: for his thoughts were low;
To vice industrious, but to nobler deeds
Timorous and slothful: yet he pleased the ear,
And with persuasive accent thus began.
      "I should be much for open war, O Peers,
120 As not behind in hate; if what was urged
Main reason to persuade immediate war,
Did not dissuade me most, and seem to cast
Ominous conjecture on the whole success:
When he who most excells in fact° of arms,   *feat*
125 In what he counsels and in what excels
Mistrustful, grounds his courage on despair
And utter dissolution, as the scope
Of all his aim, after some dire revenge.
First, what revenge? The tow'rs of Heav'n are filled
130 With arméd watch, that render all access
Impregnable; oft on the bordering deep
Encamp their legions, or with óbscure wing
Scout far and wide into the realm of Night,
Scorning surprise. Or could we break our way
135 By force, and at our heels all Hell should rise
With blackest insurrection, to confound
Heav'n's purest light, yet our great enemy
All incorruptible would on his throne
Sit unpolluted, and th' ethereal mold[2]
140 Incapable of stain would soon expel
Her mischief, and purge off the baser fire
Victorious. Thus repulsed, our final hope
Is flat despair: we must exasperate
Th' almighty victor to spend all his rage,
145 And that must end us, that must be our cure,
To be no more; sad cure; for who would lose,
Though full of pain, this intellectual being,
Those thoughts that wander through eternity,
To perish rather, swallowed up and lost
150 In the wide womb of uncreated night,
Devoid of sense and motion? And who knows,
Let this be good, whether our angry foe
Can give it, or will ever? How he can
Is doubtful; that he never will is sure.
155 Will he, so wise, let loose at once his ire,
Belike° through impotence, or unaware,   *perhaps*
To give his enemies their wish, and end
Them in his anger, whom his anger saves
To punish endless? 'Wherefore cease we then?'
160 Say they who counsel war, 'We are decreed,
Reserved and destined to eternal woe;
Whatever doing, what can we suffer more,
What can we suffer worse?' Is this then worst,
Thus sitting, thus consulting, thus in arms?

2. Heavenly substance, derived from "ether," the fifth and purest element, thought to be incorruptible.

165 What when we fled amain,° pursued and strook°   *headlong/struck*
    With Heav'n's afflicting thunder, and besought
    The deep to shelter us? This Hell then seemed
    A refuge from those wounds. Or when we lay
    Chained on the burning lake? That sure was worse.
170 What if the breath that kindled those grim fires
    Awaked should blow them into sevenfold rage
    And plunge us in the flames? Or from above
    Should intermitted° vengeance arm again   *suspended*
    His red right hand to plague us? What if all
175 Her° stores were opened, and this firmament   *Hell's*
    Of Hell should spout her cataracts° of fire,   *cascades*
    Impendent³ horrors, threat'ning hideous fall
    One day upon our heads; while we perhaps
    Designing or exhorting glorious war,
180 Caught in a fiery tempest shall be hurled
    Each on his rock transfixed, the sport and prey
    Of racking whirlwinds, or for ever sunk
    Under yon boiling ocean, wrapped in chains;
    There to converse with everlasting groans,
185 Unrespited, unpitied, unreprieved,
    Ages of hopeless end; this would be worse.
    War therefore, open or concealed, alike
    My voice dissuades; for what can force or guile⁴
    With him, or who deceive his mind, whose eye
190 Views all things at one view? He from Heav'n's high
    All these our motions° vain, sees and derides;   *proposals*
    Not more almighty to resist our might
    Than wise to frustrate all our plots and wiles.
    Shall we then live thus vile, the race of Heav'n
195 Thus trampled, thus expelled to suffer here
    Chains and these torments? Better these than worse
    By my advice; since fate inevitable
    Subdues us, and omnipotent decree,
    The victor's will. To suffer, as to do,
200 Our strength is equal, nor the law unjust
    That so ordains: this was at first resolved,
    If we were wise, against so great a foe
    Contending, and so doubtful what might fall.
    I laugh, when those who at the spear are bold
205 And vent'rous, if that fail them, shrink and fear
    What yet they know must follow, to endure
    Exile, or ignominy, or bonds, or pain,
    The sentence of their conqueror: This is now
    Our doom; which if we can sustain and bear,
210 Our Súpreme Foe in time may much remit
    His anger, and perhaps thus far removed
    Not mind us not offending, satisfied
    With what is punished; whence these raging fires

3. In the Latin sense, hanging down, threatening.
4. The verb "accomplish" or "achieve" is understood.

Will slacken, if his breath stir not their flames.
215 Our purer essence then will overcome
Their noxious vapor, or inured° not feel,   *accustomed*
Or changed at length, and to the place conformed
In temper and in nature, will receive
Familiar the fierce heat, and void of pain;
220 This horror will grow mild, this darkness light,
Besides what hope the never-ending flight
Of future days may bring, what chance, what change
Worth waiting, since our present lot appears
For happy though but ill, for ill not worst,[5]
225 If we procure not to ourselves more woe."
      Thus Belial, with words clothed in reason's garb,
Counseled ignoble ease and peaceful sloth,
Not peace: and after him thus Mammon spake.
      "Either to disenthrone the King of Heav'n
230 We war, if war be best, or to regain
Our own right lost: him to unthrone we then
May hope when everlasting fate shall yield
To fickle chance, and Chaos judge the strife:
The former vain to hope argues° as vain   *proves*
235 The latter: for what place can be for us
Within Heav'n's bound, unless Heav'n's Lord supreme
We overpower? Suppose he should relent
And publish grace to all, on promise made
Of new subjection; with what eyes could we
240 Stand in his presence humble, and receive
Strict laws imposed, to celebrate his throne
With warbled hymns, and to his Godhead sing
Forced hallelujahs; while he lordly sits
Our envied Sovran, and his altar breathes
245 Ambrosial° odors and ambrosial flowers,   *fragrant, immortal*
Our servile offerings. This must be our task
In Heav'n, this our delight; how wearisome
Eternity so spent in worship paid
To whom we hate. Let us not then pursue
250 By force impossible, by leave obtained
Unácceptable, though in Heav'n, our state
Of splendid vassalage,° but rather seek   *servitude*
Our own good from ourselves, and from our own
Live to ourselves, though in this vast recess,
255 Free, and to none accountable, preferring
Hard liberty before the easy yoke
Of servile pomp. Our greatness will appear
Then most conspicuous, when great things of small,
Useful of hurtful, prosperous of adverse
260 We can create, and in what place soe'er
Thrive under evil, and work ease out of pain
Through labor and endurance. This deep world

---

5. I.e., from the point of view of happiness, the devils are in ill state; from the point of view of evil, they could be worse.

Of darkness do we dread? How oft amidst
Thick clouds and dark doth Heav'n's all-ruling Sire
265 Choose to reside, his glory unobscured,
And with the majesty of darkness round
Covers his throne; from whence deep thunders roar
Must'ring their rage, and Heav'n resembles Hell?
As he our darkness, cannot we his light
270 Imitate when we please? This desert soil
Wants° not her hidden luster, gems and gold;   lacks
Nor want we skill or art, from whence to raise
Magnificence; and what can Heav'n show more?
Our torments also may in length of time
275 Become our elements, these piercing fires
As soft as now severe, our temper° changed   constitution
Into their temper; which must needs remove
The sensible of pain.⁶ All things invite
To peaceful counsels, and the settled state
280 Of order, how in safety best we may
Compose° our present evils, with regard   come to terms with
Of what we are and where, dismissing quite
All thoughts of war: ye have what I advise."
     He scarce had finished, when such murmur filled
285 Th' assembly, as when hollow rocks retain
The sound of blust'ring winds, which all night long
Had roused the sea, now with hoarse cadence lull
Seafaring men o'erwatched,° whose bark by chance   worn out from watching
Or pinnace° anchors in a craggy bay   boat
290 After the tempest: such applause was heard
As Mammon ended, and his sentence pleased,
Advising peace: for such another field°   battlefield
They dreaded worse than Hell: so much the fear
Of thunder and the sword of Michaël⁷
295 Wrought still within them; and no less desire
To found this nether empire, which might rise
By policy,° and long process of time,   statecraft
In emulation opposite to Heav'n.
Which then Beëlzebub perceived, than whom,
300 Satan except, none higher sat, with grave
Aspect he rose, and in his rising seemed
A pillar of state; deep on his front° engraven   brow
Deliberation sat and public care;
And princely counsel in his face yet shone,
305 Majestic though in ruin: sage he stood
With Atlantean⁸ shoulders fit to bear
The weight of mightiest monarchies; his look
Drew audience and attention still as night
Or summer's noontide air, while thus he spake.
310   "Thrones and imperial Powers, offspring of Heav'n
Ethereal Virtues; or these titles⁹ now
Must we renounce, and changing style be called

---

6. Pain felt by the senses.
7. The warrior angel, chief of the angelic armies.
8. Worthy of Atlas, the Titan who as a punishment

for rebellion was condemned to hold up the heavens on his shoulders.
9. The official titles of angelic orders.

Princes of Hell? for so the popular vote
Inclines, here to continue, and build up here

315 A growing empire. Doubtless! while we dream,
And know not that the King of Heav'n hath doomed
This place our dungeon, not our safe retreat
Beyond his potent arm, to live exempt
From Heav'n's high jurisdiction, in new league

320 Banded against his throne, but to remain
In strictest bondage, though thus far removed,
Under th' inevitable curb, reserved
His captive multitude: for he, be sure,
In height or depth, still first and last will reign

325 Sole King, and of his kingdom lose no part
By our revolt, but over Hell extend
His empire, and with iron scepter rule
Us here, as with his golden those in Heav'n.
What° sit we then projecting peace and war?   *why*

330 War hath determined us,[1] and foiled with loss
Irreparable; terms of peace yet none
Vouchsafed or sought; for what peace will be giv'n
To us enslaved, but custody severe,
And stripes, and arbitrary punishment

335 Inflicted? And what peace can we return,
But, to our power,[2] hostility and hate,
Untamed reluctance,° and revenge though slow,   *resistance*
Yet ever plotting how the conqueror least
May reap his conquest, and may least rejoice

340 In doing what we most in suffering feel?
Nor will occasion want,° nor shall we need   *be lacking*
With dangerous expedition to invade
Heav'n, whose high walls fear no assault or siege,
Or ambush from the deep. What if we find

345 Some easier enterprise? There is a place
(If ancient and prophetic fame° in Heav'n   *rumor*
Err not) another world, the happy seat
Of some new race called Man, about this time
To be created like to us, though less

350 In power and excellence, but favored more
Of him who rules above; so was his will
Pronounced among the gods, and by an oath,
That shook Heav'n's whole circumference, confirmed.
Thither let us bend all our thoughts, to learn

355 What creatures there inhabit, of what mold,
Or substance, how endued,° and what their power,   *endowed*
And where their weakness, how attempted° best,   *attacked, tempted*
By force or subtlety. Though Heav'n be shut,
And Heav'n's high arbitrator sit secure

360 In his own strength, this place may lie exposed,
The utmost border of his kingdom, left
To their defense who hold it:[3] here perhaps

---

1. I.e., war has decided the question for us, but
also limited us.

2. I.e., to the best of our power.
3. To be defended by the occupants.

Some advantageous act may be achieved
By sudden onset, either with Hell fire
365 To waste° his whole creation, or possess   *lay waste*
All as our own, and drive as we were driven,
The puny habitants, or if not drive,
Seduce them to our party, that their God
May prove their foe, and with repenting hand
370 Abolish his own works.[4] This would surpass
Common revenge, and interrupt his joy
In our confusion, and our joy upraise
In his disturbance; when his darling sons
Hurled headlong to partake with us, shall curse
375 Their frail original,° and faded bliss,   *originator, parent*
Faded so soon. Advise° if this be worth   *consider*
Attempting, or to sit in darkness here
Hatching vain empires." Thus Beëlzebub
Pleaded his devilish counsel, first devised
380 By Satan, and in part proposed: for whence,
But from the author of all ill could spring
So deep a malice, to confound° the race   *ruin*
Of mankind in one root,[5] and earth with Hell
To mingle and involve, done all to spite
385 The great Creator? But their spite still serves
His glory to augment. The bold design
Pleased highly those infernal States,° and joy   *nobles*
Sparkled in all their eyes; with full assent
They vote: whereat his speech he thus renews.
390   "Well have ye judged, well ended long debate,
Synod of gods, and like to what ye are,
Great things resolved, which from the lowest deep
Will once more lift us up, in spite of fate,
Nearer our ancient seat; perhaps in view
395 Of those bright confines, whence with neighboring arms
And opportune excursion we may chance
Re-enter Heav'n; or else in some mild zone
Dwell not unvisited of Heav'n's fair light
Secure, and at the bright'ning orient beam
400 Purge off this gloom; the soft delicious air,
To heal the scar of these corrosive fires
Shall breathe her balm. But first whom shall we send
In search of this new world, whom shall we find
Sufficient? Who shall tempt° with wand'ring feet   *attempt, venture*
405 The dark unbottomed infinite abyss
And through the palpable obscure[6] find out
His uncouth° way, or spread his aery flight   *unknown*
Upborne with indefatigable wings
Over the vast abrupt,[7] ere he arrive

---

4. Cf. Genesis 6.7: "And the Lord said, I will destroy man [and all other creatures]; for it repenteth me that I have made them."
5. Adam, the first man, is the "root" of the human race.

6. Darkness so thick it can be felt (cf. Exodus 10.21).
7. Chaos, a striking example of sound imitating sense.

410 The happy isle? what strength, what art can then
Suffice, or what evasion bear him safe
Through the strict senteries° and stations thick   *sentries*
Of angels watching round? Here he had need
All circumspection, and we now no less
415 Choice° in our suffrage; for on whom we send,   *discrimination*
The weight of all and our last hope relies."
        This said, he sat; and expectation held
His look suspense,[8] awaiting who appeared
To second, or oppose, or undertake
420 The perilous attempt: but all sat mute,
Pondering the danger with deep thoughts; and each
In other's count'nance read his own dismay
Astonished. None among the choice and prime
Of those Heav'n-warring champions could be found
425 So hardy as to proffer or accept
Alone the dreadful voyage; till at last
Satan, whom now transcendent glory raised
Above his fellows, with monarchal pride
Conscious of highest worth, unmoved thus spake.
430   "O progeny of Heav'n, empyreal Thrones,
With reason hath deep silence and demur°   *hesitation*
Seized us, though undismayed: long is the way
And hard, that out of Hell leads up to light;
Our prison strong, this huge convex of fire,
435 Outrageous to devour, immures us round
Ninefold,[9] and gates of burning adamant
Barred over us prohibit all egress.
These passed, if any pass, the void profound
Of unessential Night receives him next
440 Wide gaping, and with utter loss of being
Threatens him, plunged in that abortive gulf.[1]
If thence he scape into whatever world,
Or unknown region, what remains him less°   *awaits him except*
Than unknown dangers and as hard escape?
445 But I should ill become this throne, O Peers,
And this imperial sovranty, adorned
With splendor, armed with power, if aught proposed
And judged of public moment,° in the shape   *importance*
Of difficulty or danger could deter
450 Me from attempting. Wherefore do I assume
These royalties, and not refuse to reign,
Refusing° to accept as great a share   *if I refuse*
Of hazard as of honor, due alike
To him who reigns, and so much to him due
455 Of hazard more, as he above the rest
High honored sits? Go therefore mighty Powers,
Terror of Heav'n, though fall'n; intend° at home,   *consider*
While here shall be our home, what best may ease

8. I.e., everyone sat waiting in suspense.
9. Hell's fiery walls and gate have nine thicknesses
(see lines 645ff.).

1. Chaos is a womb in which all potential forms
fragment (see lines 900ff.) "Unessential" (line
439): i.e., having no real essence.

The present misery, and render Hell
460 More tolerable; if there be cure or charm
To respite or deceive, or slack the pain
Of this ill mansion: intermit no watch
Against a wakeful foe, while I abroad
Through all the coasts of dark destruction seek
465 Deliverance for us all: this enterprise
None shall partake with me." Thus saying rose
The monarch, and prevented° all reply,   *forestalled*
Prudent, lest from his resolution raised°   *roused*
Others among the chief might offer now
470 (Certain to be refused) what erst they feared;
And so refused might in opinion stand
His rivals, winning cheap the high repute
Which he through hazard huge must earn. But they
Dreaded not more th' adventure than his voice
475 Forbidding; and at once with him they rose;
Their rising all at once was as the sound
Of thunder heard remote. Towards him they bend
With awful° reverence prone; and as a god   *full of awe*
Extol him equal to the Highest in Heav'n:
480 Nor failed they to express how much they praised,
That for the general safety he despised
His own: for neither do the Spirits damned
Lose all their virtue; lest bad men should boast
Their specious° deeds on earth, which glory excites,   *pretending to worth*
485 Or close° ambition varnished o'er with zeal.   *secret*
     Thus they their doubtful consultations dark
Ended rejoicing in their matchless chief:
As when from mountain tops the dusky clouds
Ascending, while the north wind sleeps, o'erspread
490 Heav'n's cheerful face, the louring element°   *threatening sky*
Scowls o'er the darkened landscape snow, or show'r;
If chance the radiant sun with farewell sweet
Extend his evening beam, the fields revive,
The birds their notes renew, and bleating herds
495 Attest their joy, that hill and valley rings.
O shame to men! Devil with devil damned
Firm concord holds, men only disagree
Of creatures rational, though under hope
Of heavenly grace: and God proclaiming peace,
500 Yet live in hatred, enmity, and strife
Among themselves, and levy cruel wars,
Wasting the earth, each other to destroy:
As if (which might induce us to accord)
Man had not hellish foes enow° besides,   *enough*
505 That day and night for his destruction wait.
     The Stygian council thus dissolved; and forth
In order came the grand infernal peers:
Midst came their mighty paramount,° and seemed   *supreme ruler*
Alone th' antagonist of Heav'n, nor less
510 Than Hell's dread emperor with pomp supreme,

And god-like imitated state; him round
A globe° of fiery Seraphim enclosed   *band, circle*
With bright emblazonry and horrent[2] arms.
Then of their session ended they bid cry
515　With trumpet's regal sound the great result:
Toward the four winds four speedy Cherubim
Put to their mouths the sounding alchemy[3]
By herald's voice explained; the hollow abyss
Heard far and wide, and all the host of hell
520　With deaf'ning shout, returned them loud acclaim.
Thence more at ease their minds and somewhat raised
By false presumptuous hope, the rangèd° powers   *arrayed in ranks*
Disband, and wand'ring, each his several way
Pursues, as inclination or sad choice
525　Leads him perplexed, where he may likeliest find
Truce to his restless thoughts, and entertain°   *while away*
The irksome hours, till his great chief return.
Part on the plain, or in the air sublime°   *aloft*
Upon the wing, or in swift race contend,
530　As at th' Olympian games or Pythian fields;[4]
Part curb their fiery steeds, or shun the goal[5]
With rapid wheels, or fronted° brígades form.   *confronting*
As when to warn proud cities war appears
Waged in the troubled sky, and armies rush
535　To battle in the clouds,[6] before each van°   *vanguard*
Prick° forth the aery knights, and couch their spears   *spur*
Till thickest legions close; with feats of arms
From either end of Heav'n the welkin° burns.   *sky*
Others with vast Typhoean[7] rage more fell
540　Rend up both rocks and hills, and ride the air
In Whirlwind; Hell scarce holds the wild uproar.
As when Alcides from Oechalia crowned
With conquest, felt th' envenomed robe, and tore
Through pain up by the roots Thessalian pines,
545　And Lichas from the top of Oeta threw
Into th' Euboic sea.[8] Others more mild,
Retreated in a silent valley, sing
With notes angelical to many a harp
Their own heroic deeds and hapless fall
550　By doom of battle; and complain that fate
Free virtue should enthrall to force or chance.
Their song was partial,° but the harmony   *prejudiced*
(What could it less when Spirits immortal sing?)
Suspended° Hell, and took with ravishment   *held in suspense*
555　The thronging audience. In discourse more sweet

2. Bristling. "Emblazonry": decorated shields.
3. Trumpets (made of the goldlike alloy, brass).
4. The Olympic games were held at Olympia, the Pythian games at Delphi. Games celebrating a (usually dead) hero are an epic convention.
5. To drive a chariot as close as possible around a column without hitting it.
6. The appearance of warfare in the skies, reported before several notable battles, portends

trouble on earth.
7. Like that of Typhon, the hundred-headed Titan (see 1.199).
8. Wearing a poisoned robe given him in a deception, Hercules in his dying agonies threw his beloved companion Lichas, along with a good part of Mount Oeta, into the sea of Euboea, near Thermopylae.

(For eloquence the soul, song charms the sense)
Others apart sat on a hill retired,
In thoughts more elevate, and reasoned high
Of providence, foreknowledge, will, and fate,
560   Fixed fate, free will, foreknowledge absolute,
And found no end, in wand'ring mazes lost.
Of good and evil much they argued then,
Of happiness and final misery,
Passion and apathy,[9] and glory and shame,
565   Vain wisdom all, and false philosophy:
Yet with a pleasing sorcery could charm
Pain for a while or anguish, and excite
Fallacious hope, or arm th' obdurèd° breast   *hardened*
With stubborn patience as with triple steel.
570   Another part in squadrons and gross° bands,   *solid, dense*
On bold adventure to discover wide
That dismal world, if any clime perhaps
Might yield them easier habitation, bend
Four ways their flying march, along the banks
575   Of four infernal rivers that disgorge
Into the burning lake their baleful streams:[1]
Abhorrèd Styx the flood of deadly hate,
Sad Acheron of sorrow, black and deep;
Cocytus, named of lamentation loud
580   Heard on the rueful stream; fierce Phlegethon
Whose waves of torrent fire inflame with rage.
Far off from these a slow and silent stream,
Lethe the river of oblivion rolls
Her wat'ry labyrinth, whereof who drinks,
585   Forthwith his former state and being forgets,
Forgets both joy and grief, pleasure and pain.
Beyond this flood a frozen continent
Lies dark and wild, beat with perpetual storms
Of whirlwind and dire hail, which on firm land
590   Thaws not, but gathers heap,[2] and ruin seems
Of ancient pile; all else deep snow and ice,
A gulf profound as that Serbonian bog[3]
Betwixt Damiata and Mount Casius old,
Where armies whole have sunk: the parching air
595   Burns frore,° and cold performs th' effect of fire.   *frozen*
Thither by harpy-footed[4] Furies haled,
At certain revolutions° all the damned   *recurring times*
Are brought: and feel by turns the bitter change
Of fierce extremes, extremes by change more fierce,
600   From beds of raging fire to starve° in ice   *make numb*

---

9. The Stoic goal of freedom from passion.
1. These four rivers are traditional in hellish geography. Milton distinguishes them by the original meanings of their Greek names: Styx means "hateful," Acheron "woeful," etc. Lethe is "far off" and quite different from the others, oblivion being a desired state in Hell.

2. In a heap, resembling the ruin of an old building ("ancient pile").
3. Lake Serbonis, once famous for its quicksands, lies near the city of Damiata, just east of the Nile.
4. Taloned. In Greek mythology the harpies (monsters with women's faces) carried off individuals to the Furies, who avenged crimes.

Their soft ethereal warmth, and there to pine
Immovable, infixed, and frozen round,
Periods of time; thence hurried back to fire.
They ferry over this Lethean sound
605 Both to and fro, their sorrow to augment,
And wish and struggle, as they pass, to reach
The tempting stream, with one small drop to lose
In sweet forgetfulness all pain and woe,
All in one moment, and so near the brink;
610 But fate withstands, and to oppose th' attempt
Medusa[5] with Gorgonian terror guards
The ford, and of itself the water flies
All taste of living wight, as once it fled
The lip of Tantalus.[6] Thus roving on
615 In cónfused march forlorn, th' advent'rous bands
With shudd'ring horror pale, and eyes aghast
Viewed first their lamentable lot, and found
No rest: through many a dark and dreary vale
They passed, and many a region dolorous,
620 O'er many a frozen, many a fiery alp,°   *volcano*
Rocks, caves, lakes, fens, bogs, dens, and shades of death,
A universe of death, which God by curse
Created evil, for evil only good,
Where all life dies, death lives, and nature breeds,
625 Perverse, all monstrous, all prodigious things,
Abominable, inutterable, and worse
Than fables yet have feigned, or fear conceived,
Gorgons and Hydras, and Chimeras[7] dire.
    Meanwhile the Adversary of God and man,
630 Satan, with thoughts inflamed of highest design,
Puts on swift wings,° and towards the gates of hell   *flies swiftly*
Explores his solitary flight; sometimes
He scours the right-hand coast, sometimes the left,
Now shaves with level wing the deep, then soars
635 Up to the fiery concave° tow'ring high.   *vault*
As when far off at sea a fleet descried
Hangs on the clouds, by equinoctial winds°   *from the equator*
Close sailing from Bengala,° or the isles   *Bengal*
Of Ternate and Tidore,[8] whence merchants bring
640 Their spicy drugs: they on the trading flood
Through the wide Ethiopian to the Cape
Ply stemming nightly toward the pole:[9] so seemed
Far off the flying Fiend. At last appear
Hell bounds high reaching to the horrid roof,
645 And thrice threefold the gates; three folds were brass,

5. One of the three Gorgons, women with snaky hair, scaly bodies, and boar's tusks, the sight of whose faces changed men to stone.
6. Tantalus, afflicted with a raging thirst, stood in the middle of a lake, the water of which always receded when he tried to drink (hence, "tantalize").
7. The Hydra was a serpent whose multiple heads

grew back when severed; the Chimera was a fire-breathing creature, part lion, part dragon, part goat.
8. Two of the Molucca or "Spice" Islands, modern Indonesia.
9. The South Pole. "Ethiopian": the Indian Ocean. "The Cape" is the Cape of Good Hope.

Three iron, three of adamantine rock,
Impenetrable, impaled with circling fire,
Yet unconsumed. Before the gates there sat
On either side a formidable shape;[1]

650   The one seemed woman to the waist, and fair,
But ended foul in many a scaly fold
Voluminous and vast, a serpent armed
With mortal sting: about her middle round
A cry° of hell-hounds never ceasing barked   *pack*

655   With wide Cerberean[2] mouths full loud, and rung
A hideous peal: yet, when they list, would creep,
If aught disturbed their noise, into her womb,
And kennel there, yet there still barked and howled,
Within unseen. Far less abhorred than these

660   Vexed Scylla[3] bathing in the sea that parts
Calabria from the hoarse Trinacrian shore:
Nor uglier follow the night-hag,[4] when called
In secret, riding through the air she comes
Lured with the smell of infant blood, to dance

665   With Lapland witches, while the laboring° moon   *troubled*
Eclipses at their charms.° The other shape,   *magic*
If shape it might be called that shape had none
Distinguishable in member, joint, or limb,
Or substance might be called that shadow seemed,

670   For each seemed either; black it stood as night,
Fierce as ten Furies, terrible as hell,
And shook a dreadful dart; what seemed his head
The likeness of a kingly crown had on.
Satan was now at hand, and from his seat

675   The monster moving onward came as fast
With horrid strides. Hell trembled as he strode.
Th' undaunted Fiend what this might be admired,°   *wondered*
Admired, not feared; God and his Son except,
Created thing naught valued he nor shunned;

680   And with disdainful look thus first began.
     "Whence and what art thou, execrable shape,
That dar'st, though grim and terrible, advance
Thy miscreated front° athwart my way   *misshapen face*
To yonder gates? Through them I mean to pass,

685   That be assured, without leave asked of thee:
Retire, or taste° thy folly, and learn by proof,   *experience*
Hell-born, not to contend with Spirits of Heav'n."
     To whom the goblin full of wrath replied:
"Art thou that traitor angel, art thou he,

690   Who first broke peace in Heav'n and faith, till then

---

1. The allegorical figures of Sin and Death are founded on James 1.15: "Then when lust hath conceived, it bringeth forth sin: and sin, when it is finished, bringeth forth death." But the incestuous relations of Sin and Death are Milton's own invention. Physically, Sin is modeled on Virgil's or Ovid's Scylla, with some touches adopted from Spenser's Error. Death is a traditional figure, vague and vast.
2. Like Cerberus, the multiheaded hound of Hell.

3. Circe, out of jealousy, threw poison into the water where Scylla bathed, in the straits between Calabria and Sicily ("Trinacria"); the poison caused Scylla to develop a ring of barking, snapping dogs around her waist.
4. Hecate (three syllables), goddess of sorcery. She attends orgies of witches in Lapland (famous for witchcraft), drawn by the blood of babies sacrificed for the occasion.

Unbroken, and in proud rebellious arms
Drew after him the third part of Heav'n's sons
Conjured° against the Highest, for which both thou   *sworn together*
And they outcast from God, are here condemned
695 To waste eternal days in woe and pain?
And reckon'st thou thyself with Spirits of Heav'n,
Hell-doomed, and breath'st defiance here and scorn,
Where I reign king, and to enrage thee more,
Thy king and lord? Back to thy punishment,
700 False fugitive, and to thy speed add wings,
Lest with a whip of scorpions I pursue
Thy ling'ring, or with one stroke of this dart
Strange horror seize thee, and pangs unfelt before."
      So spake the grisly terror, and in shape,
705 So speaking and so threat'ning, grew tenfold
More dreadful and deform: on th' other side
Incensed with indignation Satan stood
Unterrified, and like a comet burned
That fires the length of Ophiuchus[5] huge
710 In th' arctic sky, and from his horrid° hair   *bristling*
Shakes pestilence and war. Each at the head
Leveled his deadly aim; their fatal hands
No second stroke intend, and such a frown
Each cast at th' other, as when, two black clouds
715 With Heav'n's artillery fraught,[6] come rattling on
Over the Caspian,[7] then stand front to front
Hov'ring a space, till winds the signal blow
To join their dark encounter in mid-air:
So frowned the mighty combatants, that Hell
720 Grew darker at their frown, so matched they stood;
For never but once more was either like
To meet so great a foe.[8] And now great deeds
Had been achieved, whereof all Hell had rung,
Had not the snaky sorceress that sat
725 Fast by Hell gate, and kept the fatal key,
Ris'n, and with hideous outcry rushed between.
      "O father, what intends thy hand," she cried,
"Against thy only son?[9] What fury O son,
Possesses thee to bend that mortal dart
730 Against thy father's head? And know'st for whom;
For him who sits above and laughs the while
At thee ordained his drudge, to execute
Whate'er his wrath, which he calls justice, bids,
His wrath which one day will destroy ye both."
735 She spake, and at her words the hellish pest
Forbore, then these to her Satan returned.
      "So strange thy outcry, and thy words so strange
Thou interposest, that my sudden hand

---

5. A vast northern constellation, "The Serpent Bearer."
6. Loaded with thunderbolts.
7. The Caspian is a particularly stormy area.

8. I.e., the Son of God.
9. Sin, Death, and Satan, in their various interrelations, parody obscenely the relations between God and the Son, Adam and Eve.

Prevented° spares to tell thee yet by deeds   *forestalled*
740   What it intends; till first I know of thee,
What thing thou art, thus double-formed, and why
In this infernal vale first met thou call'st
Me father, and that phantasm call'st my son?
I know thee not, nor ever saw till now
745   Sight more detestable than him and thee."
      T' whom thus the portress of Hell gate replied:
"Hast thou forgot me then, and do I seem
Now in thine eye so foul, once deemed so fair
In Heav'n, when at th' assembly, and in sight
750   Of all the Seraphim with thee combined
In bold conspiracy against Heav'n's King,
All on a sudden miserable pain
Surprised thee, dim thine eyes, and dizzy swum
In darkness, while thy head flames thick and fast
755   Threw forth, till on the left side op'ning wide,
Likest to thee in shape and count'nance bright,
Then shining heav'nly fair, a goddess armed
Out of thy head I sprung:[1] amazement seized
All th' host of Heav'n; back they recoiled afraid
760   At first, and called me Sin, and for a sign
Portentous held me; but familiar grown,
I pleased, and with attractive graces won
The most averse, thee chiefly, who full oft
Thyself in me thy perfect image viewing
765   Becam'st enamored, and such joy thou took'st
With me in secret, that my womb conceived
A growing burden. Meanwhile war arose,
And fields were fought in Heav'n; wherein remained
(For what could else) to our almighty foe
770   Clear victory, to our part loss and rout
Through all the empyrean: down they fell
Driv'n headlong from the pitch° of Heaven, down   *summit*
Into this deep, and in the general fall
I also; at which time this powerful key
775   Into my hand was giv'n, with charge to keep
These gates for ever shut, which none can pass
Without my op'ning. Pensive here I sat
Alone, but long I sat not, till my womb
Pregnant by thee, and now excessive grown
780   Prodigious motion felt and rueful throes.
At last this odious offspring whom thou seest
Thine own begotten, breaking violent way
Tore through my entrails, that with fear and pain
Distorted, all my nether shape thus grew
785   Transformed: but he my inbred enemy
Forth issued, brandishing his fatal dart
Made to destroy: I fled, and cried out 'Death';
Hell trembled at the hideous name, and sighed

---

1. As Athena sprang full-grown from the head of Zeus.

From all her caves, and back resounded 'Death.'
790 I fled, but he pursued (though more, it seems,
Inflamed with lust than rage) and swifter far,
Me overtook his mother all dismayed,
And in embraces forcible and foul
Engend'ring with me, of that rape begot
795 These yelling monsters that with ceaseless cry
Surround me, as thou saw'st, hourly conceived
And hourly born, with sorrow infinite
To me, for when they list,° into the womb   _wish_
That bred them they return, and howl and gnaw
800 My bowels, their repast; then bursting forth
Afresh with conscious terrors vex me round,
That rest or intermission none I find.
Before mine eyes in opposition sits
Grim Death my son and foe, who sets them on,
805 And me his parent would full soon devour
For want of other prey, but that he knows
His end with mine involved; and knows that I
Should prove a bitter morsel, and his bane,
Whenever that shall be; so fate pronounced.
810 But thou O father, I forewarn thee, shun
His deadly arrow; neither vainly hope
To be invulnerable in those bright arms,
Though tempered heav'nly, for that mortal dint,°   _blow_
Save he who reigns above, none can resist."
815 She finished, and the subtle Fiend his lore° _lesson_
Soon learned, now milder, and thus answered smooth.
"Dear daughter, since thou claim'st me for thy sire,
And my fair son here show'st me, the dear pledge
Of dalliance had with thee in Heav'n, and joys
820 Then sweet, now sad to mention, through dire change
Befall'n us unforeseen, unthought of, know
I come no enemy, but to set free
From out this dark and dismal house of pain,
Both him and thee, and all the heav'nly host
825 Of Spirits that in our just pretenses° armed   _claims_
Fell with us from on high: from them I go
This uncouth errand sole,[2] and one for all
Myself expose, with lonely steps to tread
Th' unfounded° deep, and through the void immense _bottomless_
830 To search with wand'ring quest a place foretold
Should be, and, by concurring signs, ere now
Created vast and round, a place of bliss
In the purlieus° of Heav'n, and therein placed _outskirts_
A race of upstart creatures, to supply
835 Perhaps our vacant room, though more removed,
Lest Heav'n surcharged° with potent multitude _overcrowded_
Might hap to move new broils:° be this or aught _controversies_
Than this more secret now designed, I haste

2. Unknown journey—a parody of Christ's errand on earth (3.236–65).

To know, and this once known, shall soon return,
840 And bring ye to the place where thou and Death
Shall dwell at ease, and up and down unseen
Wing silently the buxom° air, embalmed°   *yielding / made fragrant*
With odors; there ye shall be fed and filled
Immeasurably, all things shall be your prey."
845 He ceased, for both seemed highly pleased, and Death
Grinned horrible a ghastly smile, to hear
His famine° should be filled, and blessed his maw   *ravenous hunger*
Destined to that good hour: no less rejoiced
His mother bad, and thus bespake her sire.
850   "The key of this infernal pit by due,
And by command of Heav'n's all-powerful King
I keep, by him forbidden to unlock
These adamantine gates; against all force
Death ready stands to interpose his dart,
855 Fearless to be o'ermatched by living might.
But what owe I to his commands above
Who hates me, and hath hither thrust me down
Into this gloom of Tartarus profound,
To sit in hateful office here confined,
860 Inhabitant of Heav'n, and heav'nly-born,
Here in perpetual agony and pain,
With terrors and with clamors compassed round
Of mine own brood, that on my bowels feed?
Thou art my father, thou my author, thou
865 My being gav'st me; whom should I obey
But thee, whom follow? Thou wilt bring me soon
To that new world of light and bliss, among
The gods who live at ease, where I shall reign
At thy right hand voluptuous,[3] as beseems
870 Thy daughter and thy darling, without end."
        Thus saying, from her side the fatal key,
Sad instrument of all our woe, she took;
And towards the gate rolling her bestial train,[4]
Forthwith the huge portcullis high up drew,
875 Which but herself not all the Stygian powers°   *armies of Hell*
Could once have moved; then in the key-hole turns
Th' intricate wards, and every bolt and bar
Of massy iron or solid rock with ease
Unfastens: on a sudden open fly
880 With impetuous recoil and jarring sound
Th' infernal doors, and on their hinges grate
Harsh thunder, that the lowest bottom shook
Of Erebus.° She opened, but to shut   *Hell*
Excelled° her power; the gates wide open stood,   *exceeded*
885 That with extended wings a bannered host
Under spread ensigns° marching might pass through   *flags, standards*
With horse and chariots ranked in loose array;

---

3. As the Son sits at God's right hand, Sin will at   *Paradise Lost* 3.250–80.
Satan's, a blasphemous parody of the Creed and of   4. I.e. accompanied by her yelping offspring.

So wide they stood, and like a furnace mouth
Cast forth redounding° smoke and ruddy flame.   *billowing*
890 Before their eyes in sudden view appear
The secrets of the hoary deep, a dark
Illimitable° ocean without bound,   *without limit*
Without dimension, where length, breadth, and height,
And time and place are lost; where eldest Night
895 And Chaos, ancestors of Nature, hold
Eternal anarchy, amidst the noise
Of endless wars, and by confusion stand.
For Hot, Cold, Moist, and Dry, four champions fierce
Strive here for mastery, and to battle bring
900 Their embryon atoms;[5] they around the flag
Of each his faction, in their several clans,
Light-armed or heavy, sharp, smooth, swift or slow,
Swarm populous, unnumbered as the sands
Of Barca or Cyrene's torrid soil,[6]
905 Levied to side with warring winds, and poise[7]
Their lighter wings. To whom these most adhere,
He rules a moment; Chaos[8] umpire sits,
And by decision more embroils the fray
By which he reigns: next him high arbiter
910 Chance governs all. Into this wild abyss,
The womb of Nature and perhaps her grave,
Of neither sea, nor shore, nor air, nor fire,
But all these in their pregnant causes° mixed   *seeds*
Confus'dly, and which thus must ever fight,
915 Unless th' Almighty Maker them ordain
His dark materials to create more worlds,
Into this wild abyss the wary Fiend
Stood on the brink of Hell and looked a while,
Pondering his voyage; for no narrow frith°   *channel, firth*
920 He had to cross. Nor was his ear less pealed°   *dinned*
With noises loud and ruinous (to compare
Great things with small) than when Bellona[9] storms,
With all her battering engines bent to raze
Some capital city; or less than if this frame°   *structure*
925 Of Heav'n were falling, and these elements
In mutiny had from her axle torn
The steadfast earth. At last his sail-broad vans°   *wings*
He spreads for flight, and in the surging smoke
Uplifted spurns the ground, thence many a league
930 As in a cloudy chair ascending rides
Audacious, but that seat soon failing, meets
A vast vacuity: all unawares
Flutt'ring his pennons[1] vain plumb down he drops

---

5. These subatomic qualities combine together in nature to form the four elements, fire, earth, water, and air, but they struggle endlessly in Chaos, where the atoms of these elements remain undeveloped (in "embryo").
6. Cities built on the shifting sands of North Africa.

7. Give weight to. "Levied": both enlisted and raised up.
8. Chaos is both the place where confusion reigns and personified confusion itself.
9. Goddess of war.
1. Useless wings ("pinions").

Ten thousand fathom deep, and to this hour
935 Down had been falling, had not by ill chance
The strong rebuff° of some tumultuous cloud   counterblast
Instinct° with fire and niter° hurried him   filled/saltpeter
As many miles aloft: that fury stayed,
Quenched in a boggy Syrtis,[2] neither sea,
940 Nor good dry land: night foundered on he fares,
Treading the crude consistence, half on foot,
Half flying; behoves° him now both oar and sail.   befits
As when a gryphon through the wilderness
With wingèd course o'er hill or moory° dale,   marshy
945 Pursues the Arimaspian, who by stealth
Had from his wakeful custody purloined
The guarded gold:[3] so eagerly the Fiend
O'er bog or steep, through strait, rough, dense, or rare,
With head, hands, wings, or feet pursues his way,
950 And swims or sinks, or wades, or creeps, or flies:
At length a universal hubbub wild
Of stunning sounds and voices all confused
Borne through the hollow dark assaults his ear
With loudest vehemence: thither he plies,
955 Undaunted to meet there whatever Power
Or Spirit of the nethermost abyss
Might in that noise reside, of whom to ask
Which way the nearest coast of darkness lies
Bordering on light; when straight behold the throne
960 Of Chaos, and his dark pavilion spread
Wide on the wasteful deep; with him enthroned
Sat sable-vested Night, eldest of things,
The consort of his reign; and by them stood
Orcus and Ades,[4] and the dreaded name
965 Of Demogorgon,[5] Rumor next and Chance,
And Tumult and Confusion all embroiled,
And Discord with a thousand various mouths.
    T' whom Satan turning boldly, thus. "Ye Powers
And Spirits of this nethermost abyss,
970 Chaos and ancient Night, I come no spy,
With purpose to explore or to disturb
The secrets of your realm, but by constraint
Wand'ring this darksome desert, as my way
Lies through your spacious empire up to light,
975 Alone, and without guide, half lost, I seek
What readiest path leads where your gloomy bounds
Confine with° Heav'n; or if some other place   border on
From your dominion won, th' Ethereal King
Possesses lately, thither to arrive
980 I travel this profound;° direct my course;   deep pit
Directed, no mean recompense it brings

2. Quicksand in North African gulfs, famous for
their shifting sandbars.
3. Gryphons, fabulous creatures, half-eagle, half-
lion, hoarded gold which was stolen from them by
the one-eyed Arimaspians.
4. Latin and Greek names of Pluto, god of Hell.
5. A mysterious deity associated with Fate; Milton
elsewhere identifies him with Chaos.

To your behoof,° if I that region lost,   *on your behalf*
All usurpation thence expelled, reduce
To her original darkness and your sway
985 (Which is my present journey)[6] and once more
Erect the standard there of ancient Night;
Yours be th' advantage all, mine the revenge."
    Thus Satan; and him thus the anarch[7] old
With falt'ring speech and visage incomposed°   *disordered*
990 Answered. "I know thee, stranger, who thou art,
That mighty leading angel, who of late
Made head against Heav'n's King, though overthrown.
I saw and heard, for such a numerous host
Fled not in silence through the frighted deep
995 With ruin upon ruin, rout on rout,
Confusion worse confounded; and Heav'n gates
Poured out by millions her victorious bands
Pursuing. I upon my frontiers here
Keep residence; if all I can will serve,
1000 That little which is left so to defend,
Encroached on still° through our intestine broils°   *constantly/civil wars*
Weak'ning the scepter of old Night: first Hell
Your dungeon stretching far and wide beneath;
Now lately heaven and earth,[8] another world
1005 Hung o'er my realm, linked in a golden chain
To that side Heav'n from whence your legions fell:
If that way be your walk, you have not far;
So much the nearer danger; go and speed;
Havoc and spoil and ruin are my gain."
1010   He ceased; and Satan stayed not to reply,
But glad that now his sea should find a shore,
With fresh alacrity and force renewed
Springs upward like a pyramid of fire
Into the wild expanse, and through the shock
1015 Of fighting elements, on all sides round
Environed wins his way; harder beset
And more endangered, than when Argo passed
Through Bosporus betwixt the justling rocks:[9]
Or when Ulysses on the larboard shunned
1020 Charybdis, and by th' other whirlpool steered.[1]
So he with difficulty and labor hard
Moved on, with difficulty and labor he;
But he once passed, soon after when man fell,
Strange alteration! Sin and Death amain°   *at full speed*
1025 Following his track, such was the will of Heav'n,
Paved after him a broad and beaten way
Over the dark abyss, whose boiling gulf

---

6. The purpose of my present journey.
7. Chaos is not monarch of his realm but, appropriately, "anarch," nonruler.
8. The cosmos, with its own "heaven" (not the empyrean, the Heaven of God and the angels).
9. Jason and his fifty Argonauts, sailing through the Bosporus to the Black Sea in pursuit of the

Golden Fleece, had to pass through the Symplegades, or clashing rocks.
1. Homer's Ulysses, sailing where Italy almost touches Sicily, had to pass between Charybdis, a whirlpool, and Scylla, a monster who devoured six of his men (not another whirlpool, as used here).

Tamely endured a bridge of wondrous length
From Hell continued reaching th' utmost orb[2]
1030　Of this frail world; by which the Spirits perverse
With easy intercourse pass to and fro
To tempt or punish mortals, except whom
God and good angels guard by special grace.
But now at last the sacred influence
1035　Of light appears, and from the walls of Heav'n
Shoots far into the bosom of dim Night
A glimmering dawn; here Nature first begins
Her farthest verge,° and Chaos to retire　　　　　　　*threshold*
As from her outmost works a broken foe
1040　With tumult less and with less hostile din,
That° Satan with less toil, and now with ease　　　　　*so that*
Wafts on the calmer wave by dubious light
And like a weather-beaten vessel holds°　　　　　　　*makes for*
Gladly the port, though shrouds and tackle torn;
1045　Or in the emptier waste, resembling air
Weighs° his spread wings, at leisure to behold　　　　*balances*
Far off th' empyreal Heav'n, extended wide
In circuit, undetermined square or round,
With opal tow'rs and battlements adorned
1050　Of living sapphire, once his native seat;
And fast by hanging in a golden chain
This pendent world,° in bigness as a star　　　　　　*universe*
Of smallest magnitude close by the moon.
Thither full fraught with mischievous revenge,
1055　Accursed, and in a cursèd hour, he hies.

From Book 3

[THE INVOCATION, THE COUNCIL IN HEAVEN, AND THE CONCLUSION OF SATAN'S JOURNEY]

Hail holy Light, offspring of Heav'n first-born,
Or of th' Eternal coeternal beam
May I express thee unblamed?[1] Since God is light,
And never but in unapproachèd light
5　Dwelt from eternity, dwelt then in thee,
Bright effluence of bright essence increate.°　　　　*uncreated, eternal*
Or hear'st thou rather[2] pure ethereal stream,
Whose fountain who shall tell? Before the sun,
Before the heavens thou wert, and at the voice
10　Of God, as with a mantle didst invest°　　　　　　*cover*
The rising world of waters dark and deep,
Won from the void and formless infinite.
Thee I revisit now with bolder wing,

2. The bridge ends on the outermost sphere of the ten concentric spheres making up the universe.
1. This second Proem or invocation (3.1–55) is a hymn to Light, addressed either as the first crea-

ture of God or as coeternal with God, with allusion to 1 John 1.5, "God is Light, and in him is no darkness at all."
2. I.e., would you rather be called (a Latinism).

Escaped the Stygian pool, though long detained
15 In that obscure sojourn, while in my flight
Through utter and through middle darkness[3] borne
With other notes than to th' Orphéan lyre[4]
I sung of Chaos and eternal Night,
Taught by the Heav'nly Muse[5] to venture down
20 The dark descent, and up to reascend,
Though hard and rare: thee I revisit safe,
And feel thy sovran vital lamp; but thou
Revisit'st not these eyes, that roll in vain
To find thy piercing ray, and find no dawn;
25 So thick a drop serene hath quenched their orbs,
Or dim suffusion[6] veiled. Yet not the more
Cease I to wander where the Muses haunt
Clear spring, or shady grove, or sunny hill,
Smit with the love of sacred song; but chief
30 Thee Sion[7] and the flow'ry brooks beneath
That wash thy hallowed feet, and warbling flow,
Nightly I visit: nor sometimes forget°   *always remember*
Those other two equaled with me in fate,[8]
So were I equaled with them in renown,
35 Blind Thamyris and blind Maeonides,
And Tiresias and Phineus prophets old,[9]
Then feed on thoughts, that voluntary move
Harmonious numbers;° as the wakeful bird°   *verses / nightingale*
Sings darkling,° and in shadiest covert hid   *in the dark*
40 Tunes her nocturnal note. Thus with the year
Seasons return, but not to me returns
Day, or the sweet approach of ev'n or morn,
Or sight of vernal bloom, or summer's rose,
Or flocks, or herds, or human face divine;
45 But cloud instead, and ever-during dark
Surrounds me, from the cheerful ways of men
Cut off, and for the book of knowledge° fair   *Book of Nature*
Presented with a universal blank
Of nature's works to me expunged and razed,°   *erased*
50 And wisdom at one entrance quite shut out.
So much the rather thou celestial Light
Shine inward, and the mind through all her powers
Irradiate, there plant eyes, all mist from thence
Purge and disperse, that I may see and tell
55 Of things invisible to mortal sight.
    Now had the Almighty Father from above,
From the pure empyrean where he sits
High throned above all height, bent down his eye,

---

3. Hell is "utter" (i.e., outer) darkness; Chaos is
middle darkness.
4. One of the so-called Orphic Hymns is *To Night*,
and Orpheus himself visited the underworld. But
Milton's song, Christian and epic, is of a different
kind.
5. Urania (though not named until 7.1).
6. Cataract—*suffusio nigra*. "Drop serene": *gutta
serena*, the medical term for Milton's kind of blind-

ness.
7. The mountain of scriptural inspiration, with its
brooks Siloa and Kidron.
8. I.e., blind like me.
9. Thamyris was a blind Thracian poet, who lived
before Homer; "Maeonides" is an epithet of
Homer; Tiresias was the blind prophet of Thebes;
Phineus was a blind king and seer (*Aeneid* 3).

His own works and their works at once to view:
60 Above him all the sanctities° of Heaven   *angels*
Stood thick as stars, and from his sight received
Beatitude past utterance; on his right
The radiant image of his glory sat,
His only Son; on earth he first beheld
65 Our two first parents, yet the only two
Of mankind, in the happy garden placed,
Reaping immortal fruits of joy and love,
Uninterrupted joy, unrivaled love
In blissful solitude; he then surveyed
70 Hell and the gulf between, and Satan there
Coasting the wall of Heav'n on this side Night
In the dun° air sublime,° and ready now   *dusky/above*
To stoop with wearied wings, and willing feet
On the bare outside of this world,° that seemed   *universe*
75 Firm land embosomed without firmament,°   *atmosphere*
Uncertain which, in ocean or in air.
Him God beholding from his prospect high,
Wherein past, present, future he beholds,
Thus to his only Son foreseeing spake.
80   "Only begotten Son, seest thou what rage
Transports our Adversary, whom no bounds
Prescribed, no bars of Hell, nor all the chains
Heaped on him there, nor yet the main° abyss   *vast*
Wide interrupt[1] can hold; so bent he seems
85 On desperate revenge, that shall redound
Upon his own rebellious head. And now
Through all restraint broke loose he wings his way
Not far off Heav'n, in the precincts of light,
Directly towards the new-created world,
90 And man there placed, with purpose to essay
If him by force he can destroy, or worse,
By some false guile pervert; and shall pervert;
For man will hearken to his glozing° lies,   *flattering*
And easily transgress the sole command,
95 Sole pledge of his obedience: so will fall
He and his faithless progeny: whose fault?
Whose but his own? Ingrate, he had of me
All he could have; I made him just and right,
Sufficient to have stood, though free to fall.
100 Such I created all th' ethereal Powers
And Spirits, both them who stood and them who failed;
Freely they stood who stood, and fell who fell.
Not free, what proof could they have giv'n sincere
Of true allegiance, constant faith or love,
105 Where only what they needs must do, appeared,
Not what they would? What praise could they receive?
What pleasure I from such obedience paid,

---

1. Forming a wide breach between Heaven and Hell.

When will and reason (reason also is choice)
Useless and vain, of freedom both despoiled,
110 Made passive both, had served necessity,
Not me. They therefore as to right belonged,
So were created, nor can justly accuse
Their Maker, or their making, or their fate,
As if predestination overruled
115 Their will, disposed by absolute decree
Or high foreknowledge; they themselves decreed
Their own revolt, not I: if I foreknew,
Foreknowledge had no influence on their fault,
Which had no less proved certain unforeknown.[2]
120 So without least impulse or shadow of fate,
Or aught by me immutably foreseen,
They trespass, authors to themselves in all
Both what they judge and what they choose; for so
I formed them free, and free they must remain,
125 Till they enthrall themselves: I else must change
Their nature, and revoke the high decree
Unchangeable, eternal, which ordained
Their freedom, they themselves ordained their fall.
The first sort[3] by their own suggestion fell,
130 Self-tempted, self-depraved: man falls deceived
By the other first: man therefore shall find grace,
The other none: in mercy and justice both,
Through Heav'n and earth, so shall my glory excel,
But mercy first and last shall brightest shine."
135   Thus while God spake, ambrosial fragrance filled
All Heav'n, and in the blessèd Spirits elect°   *unfallen*
Sense of new joy ineffable diffused:
Beyond compare the Son of God was seen
Most glorious, in him all his Father shone
140 Substantially expressed, and in his face
Divine compassion visibly appeared,
Love without end, and without measure grace,
Which uttering thus he to his Father spake.
"O Father, gracious was that word which closed
145 Thy sovran sentence, that man should find grace;
For which both Heav'n and earth shall high extol
Thy praises, with th' innumerable sound
Of hymns and sacred songs, wherewith thy throne
Encompassed shall resound thee ever blessed.
150 For should man finally be lost, should man
Thy creature late so loved, thy youngest son
Fall circumvented thus by fraud, though joined
With his own folly? That be from thee far,
That far be from thee, Father, who art judge
155 Of all things made, and judgest only right.[4]

2. I.e., if I had not foreknown it.
3. Satan and his crew.
4. The Son echoes (or rather foreshadows) Abra-

ham pleading with the Lord to spare Sodom: "That
be far from thee to do after this manner, to slay
the righteous with the wicked . . . that be far from

Or shall the Adversary[5] thus obtain
His end, and frustrate thine, shall he fulfill
His malice, and thy goodness bring to naught,
Or proud return though to his heavier doom,
160 Yet with revenge accomplished, and to Hell
Draw after him the whole race of mankind,
By him corrupted? Or wilt thou thyself
Abolish thy creation, and unmake,
For him, what for thy glory thou hast made?
165 So should thy goodness and thy greatness both
Be questioned and blasphemed° without defense."   *reviled*
   To whom the great Creator thus replied.
"O Son, in whom my soul hath chief delight,
Son of my bosom, Son who art alone
170 My Word, my wisdom, and effectual might,[6]
All hast thou spoken as my thoughts are, all
As my eternal purpose hath decreed:
Man shall not quite be lost, but saved who will,
Yet not of will in him, but grace in me
175 Freely vouchsafed; once more I will renew
His lapsèd powers, though forfeit and enthralled
By sin to foul exorbitant desires;
Upheld by me, yet once more he shall stand
On even ground against his mortal foe,
180 By me upheld, that he may know how frail
His fall'n condition is, and to me owe
All his deliv'rance, and to none but me.
Some I have chosen of peculiar grace
Elect above the rest;[7] so is my will:
185 The rest shall hear me call, and oft be warned°   *warned about*
Their sinful state, and to appease betimes
Th' incensèd Deity, while offered grace
Invites; for I will clear their senses dark,
What may suffice, and soften stony hearts
190 To pray, repent, and bring obedience due.
To prayer, repentance, and obedience due,
Though but endeavored with sincere intent,
Mine ear shall not be slow, mine eye not shut.
And I will place within them as a guide
195 My umpire conscience, whom if they will hear,
Light after light well used they shall attain,[8]
And to the end persisting, safe arrive.
This my long sufferance and my day of grace
They who neglect and scorn, shall never taste;
200 But hard be hardened, blind be blinded more,

---

thee. Shall not the Judge of all the earth do right?"
(Genesis 18.25).
5. *Satan* in Hebrew means "adversary."
6. God's speech is rhythmic and sometimes
rhymed.
7. In this speech, Milton's God rejects the Calvinist doctrine that he had from the beginning predestined the damnation or salvation of each

individual soul; he claims rather that grace sufficient for salvation is offered to all, enabling everyone, if they choose to do so, to believe and
persevere. He does, however, assert his right to give
special grace to some.
8. By using the light of conscience well they will
gain more light.

That they may stumble on, and deeper fall;
And none but such from mercy I exclude.
But yet all is not done; man disobeying,
Disloyal breaks his fealty, and sins
205   Against the high supremacy of Heav'n,
Affecting° Godhead, and so losing all,   aspiring to
To expiate his treason hath naught left,
But to destruction sacred and devote,°   consecrated
He with his whole posterity must die,
210   Die he or justice must; unless for him
Some other able, and as willing, pay
The rigid satisfaction, death for death.
Say heav'nly Powers, where shall we find such love,
Which of ye will be mortal to redeem
215   Man's mortal crime,⁹ and just th' unjust to save,
Dwells in all heaven charity so dear?"
        He asked, but all the heav'nly choir stood mute,¹
And silence was in Heav'n; on man's behalf
Patron or intercessor none appeared,
220   Much less that durst upon his own head draw
The deadly forfeiture, and ransom set.
And now without redemption all mankind
Must have been lost, adjudged to death and Hell
By doom severe, had not the Son of God,
225   In whom the fullness dwells of love divine,
His dearest mediation° thus renewed.   intercession
        "Father, thy word is passed, man shall find grace;
And shall grace not find means, that finds her way,
The speediest of thy wingèd messengers,
230   To visit all thy creatures, and to all
Comes unprevented,° unimplored, unsought,   unanticipated
Happy for man, so coming; he her aid
Can never seek, once dead in sins and lost;
Atonement for himself or offering meet,
235   Indebted and undone, hath none to bring:
Behold me then, me for him, life for life
I offer, on me let thine anger fall;
Account me man; I for his sake will leave
Thy bosom, and this glory next to thee
240   Freely put off, and for him lastly die
Well pleased, on me let Death wreck all his rage;
Under his gloomy power I shall not long
Lie vanquished; thou hast giv'n me to possess
Life in myself forever, by thee I live,
245   Though now to Death I yield, and am his due
All that of me can die, yet that debt paid,
Thou wilt not leave me in the loathsome grave
His prey, nor suffer my unspotted soul
Forever with corruption there to dwell;

---

9. "Mortal" means "human" in line 214, but   1. Compare the devils in the Great Consult,
"deadly" in line 215.   2.420–26.

250 But I shall rise victorious, and subdue
My vanquisher, spoiled of his vaunted spoil;
Death his death's wound shall then receive, and stoop
Inglorious, of his mortal sting disarmed.
I through the ample air in triumph high
255 Shall lead Hell captive maugre° Hell, and show   *in spite of*
The powers of darkness bound.[2] Thou at the sight
Pleased, out of Heaven shalt look down and smile,
While by thee raised I ruin[3] all my foes,
Death last, and with his carcass glut the grave:
260 Then with the multitude of my redeemed
Shall enter Heaven long absent, and return,
Father, to see thy face, wherein no cloud
Of anger shall remain, but peace assured,
And reconcilement; wrath shall be no more
265 Thenceforth, but in thy presence joy entire."
    His words here ended, but his meek aspéct
Silent yet spake, and breathed immortal love
To mortal men, above which only shone
Filial obedience: as a sacrifice
270 Glad to be offered, he attends the will
Of his great Father. Admiration° seized   *wonder*
All Heav'n, what this might mean, and wither tend
Wond'ring; but soon th' Almighty thus replied:
    "O thou in Heav'n and earth the only peace
275 Found out for mankind under wrath, O thou
My sole complacence!° well thou know'st how dear   *pleasure, delight*
To me are all my works, nor man the least
Though last created, that for him I spare
Thee from my bosom and right hand, to save,
280 By losing thee a while, the whole race lost.
Thou therefore whom[4] thou only canst redeem,
Their nature also to thy nature join;
And be thy self man among men on earth,
Made flesh, when time shall be, of virgin seed,
285 By wondrous birth: be thou in Adam's room
The head of all mankind, though Adam's son.[5]
As in him perish all men, so in thee
As from a second root shall be restored,
As many as are restored, without thee none.
290 His crime makes guilty all his sons; thy merit
Imputed shall absolve them who renounce
Their own both righteous and unrighteous deeds,[6]
And live in thee transplanted, and from thee
Receive new life. So man, as is most just,

---

2. The Son's triumph is represented in a series of paradoxes—a vanquisher vanquished, a spoiler spoiled, Death dead, Hell captured in all Hell's despite.
3. In the Latin sense, throw down.
4. The antecedent of "whom" is, loosely construed, the "their nature" that follows it.
5. The Son of God, who long antedates the creation of Adam and who is actually the first created

being (3.383), is later incarnated in Jesus Christ; he is called Second Adam and "Son of Man" by reason of his descent from the first man, Adam. Cf. 1 Corinthians 15.22: "For as in Adam all die, even so in Christ shall all be made alive."
6. The merit of Christ attributed vicariously ("imputed") to human beings frees from original sin those who renounce their own deeds, good and bad, and hope to be saved by faith.

295 Shall satisfy for man, be judged and die,
     And dying rise, and rising with him raise
     His brethren, ransomed with his own dear life.
     So heav'nly love shall outdo hellish hate,
     Giving to death, and dying to redeem,
300 So dearly to redeem what hellish hate
     So easily destroyed, and still destroys
     In those who, when they may, accept not grace.
     Nor shalt thou by descending to assume
     Man's nature, lessen or degrade thine own.
305 Because thou hast, though throned in highest bliss
     Equal to God, and equally enjoying
     God-like fruition,° quitted all to save   state
     A world from utter loss, and hast been found
     By merit more than birthright Son of God,[7]
310 Found worthiest to be so by being good,
     Far more than great or high; because in thee
     Love hath abounded more than glory abounds.
     Therefore thy humiliation shall exalt
     With thee thy manhood also to this throne;
315 Here shalt thou sit incarnate, here shalt reign
     Both God and man, Son both of God and man,
     Anointed[8] universal King; all power
     I give thee, reign forever, and assume
     Thy merits; under thee as Head Supreme
320 Thrones, Princedoms, Powers, Dominions[9] I reduce:
     All knees to thee shall bow, of them that bide
     In Heaven, or earth, or under earth in Hell;
     When thou attended gloriously from Heav'n
     Shalt in the sky appear, and from thee send
325 The summoning Archangels to proclaim
     Thy dread tribunal: forthwith from all winds°   directions
     The living, and forthwith the cited° dead   summoned
     Of all past ages to the general doom
     Shall hasten, such a peal shall rouse their sleep.
330 Then all thy saints assembled, thou shalt judge
     Bad men and angels, they arraigned° shall sink   accursed
     Beneath thy sentence; Hell, her numbers full,
     Thenceforth shall be forever shut. Meanwhile
     The world shall burn, and from her ashes spring
335 New Heav'n and earth, wherein the just shall dwell,[1]
     And after all their tribulations long
     See golden days, fruitful of golden deeds,
     With joy and love triumphing, and fair truth.
     Then thou thy regal scepter shalt lay by,
340 For regal scepter then no more shall need,°   be needed
     God shall be all in all. But all ye gods,°   angels

7. A heterodox doctrine, that Christ was Son of God by merit. Compare with Satan (2.5).
8. "The Anointed" in Hebrew means messiah.
9. Orders of angels.
1. Milton's description of the Last Judgment draws on several biblical texts, including Matthew 24.30–31, and 25.31–32; the account of the burning and re-creation of Heaven and earth is from 2 Peter 3.12–13.

Adore him, who to compass all this dies,
Adore the Son, and honor him as me."
　　No sooner had th' Almighty ceased, but all
345　The multitude of angels with a shout
Loud as from numbers without number, sweet
As from blest voices, uttering joy, Heav'n rung[2]
With jubilee, and loud hosannas filled
Th' eternal regions: lowly reverent
350　Towards either throne[3] they bow, and to the ground
With solemn adoration down they cast
Their crowns inwove with amarant[4] and gold,
Immortal amarant, a flow'r which once
In Paradise, fast by the Tree of Life
355　Began to bloom, but soon for man's offense
To Heav'n removed where first it grew, there grows,
And flow'rs aloft shading the Fount of Life,
And where the river of bliss through midst of Heav'n
Rolls o'er Elysian[5] flow'rs her amber° stream;　　　*pure*
360　With these that never fade the Spirits elect
Bind their resplendent locks inwreathed with beams,
Now in loose garlands thick thrown off, the bright
Pavement that like a sea of jasper shone
Impurpled with celestial roses smiled.
365　Then crowned again their golden harps they took,
Harps ever tuned, that glittering by their side
Like quivers hung, and with preamble sweet
Of charming symphony they introduce
Their sacred song, and waken raptures high;
370　No voice exempt,° no voice but well could join　　　*excluded*
Melodious part, such concord is in Heav'n.
　　Thee Father first they sung omnipotent,
Immutable, immortal, infinite,
Eternal King; thee Author of all being,
375　Fountain of light, thyself invisible
Amidst the glorious brightness where thou sitt'st
Throned inaccessible, but when thou shad'st
The full blaze of thy beams, and through a cloud
Drawn round about thee like a radiant shrine,[6]
380　Dark with excessive bright thy skirts appear,
Yet dazzle Heav'n, that brightest Seraphim
Approach not, but with both wings veil their eyes.
Thee next they sang of all creation first,[7]
Begotten Son, Divine Similitude,
385　In whose conspicuous count'nance, without cloud
Made visible, th' Almighty Father shines,
Whom else no creature can behold;[8] on thee

---

2. "Multitude" (line 345) is the subject of the sentence, "rung" the verb, and "Heav'n" the object.
3. Thrones of God and the Son.
4. In Greek, "unfading," a legendary immortal flower.
5. Milton draws freely, for his Christian Heaven, on descriptions of the classical paradisal place, the

Elysian Fields.
6. Note the turn from theological debate to images that evoke a more mystical aspect of God.
7. The Son is not eternal, as in Trinitarian doctrine, but rather, God's first creation.
8. If it were not for the Son who is God's image, no creature could see God.

Impressed th' effulgence of his glory abides,
Transfused on thee his ample spirit rests.
390 He Heav'n of heavens and all the Powers therein
By thee created, and by thee threw down
Th' aspiring Dominations.[9] Thou that day
Thy Father's dreadful thunder didst not spare,
Nor stop thy flaming chariot wheels, that shook
395 Heav'n's everlasting frame, while o'er the necks
Thou drov'st of warring angels disarrayed.
Back from pursuit thy Powers° with loud acclaim   *angels*
Thee only extolled, Son of thy Father's might,
To execute fierce vengeance on his foes,
400 Not so on man; him through their malice fall'n,
Father of mercy and grace, thou didst not doom
So strictly, but much more to pity incline:
No sooner did thy dear and only Son
Perceive thee purposed not to doom° frail man   *judge*
405 So strictly, but much more to pity inclined,
He to appease thy wrath, and end the strife
Of mercy and justice in thy face discerned,
Regardless of the bliss wherein he sat
Second to thee, offered himself to die
410 For man's offense. O unexampled love,
Love nowhere to be found to be found less than divine!
Hail Son of God, Saviour of men, thy name
Shall be the copious matter of my[1] song
Henceforth, and never shall my harp thy praise
415 Forget, nor from thy Father's praise disjoin.
      Thus they in Heav'n, above the starry sphere,
Their happy hours in joy and hymning spent.
Meanwhile upon the firm opacous° globe   *opaque*
Of this round world, whose first convex divides
420 The luminous inferior orbs, enclosed
From Chaos and th' inroad of Darkness old,
Satan alighted walks:[2] a globe far off
It seemed, now seems a boundless continent
Dark, waste, and wild, under the frown of Night
425 Starless exposed, and ever-threatening storms
Of Chaos blust'ring round, inclement sky;
Save on that side which from the wall of Heav'n
Though distant far some small reflection gains
Of glimmering air less vexed with tempest loud:
430 Here walked the Fiend at large in spacious field.
As when a vulture on Imaus bred,
Whose snowy ridge the roving Tartar bounds,[3]
Dislodging from a region scarce of prey
To gorge the flesh of lambs or yeanling° kids   *newborn*

9. The rebel angels.
1. Either Milton here quotes the angels singing as a single chorus, or he associates himself with their song, or both.
2. Satan is on the outermost of the ten concentric spheres that make up the cosmos.
3. Imaus, a ridge of mountains beyond the modern Himalayas, runs north through Asia from modern Afghanistan to the Arctic Circle.

435   On hills where flocks are fed, flies toward the springs
       Of Ganges or Hydaspes, Indian streams;[4]
       But in his way lights on the barren plains
       Of Sericana, where Chineses drive
       With sails and wind their cany wagons light:
440   So on this windy sea of land, the Fiend
       Walked up and down alone bent on his prey,
       Alone, for other creature in this place
       Living or lifeless to be found was none,
       None yet, but store hereafter from the earth
445   Up hither like aërial vapors flew
       Of all things transitory and vain, when sin
       With vanity had filled the works of men:
       Both all things vain, and all who in vain things
       Built their fond hopes of glory or lasting fame,
450   Or happiness in this or th' other life;
       All who have their reward on earth, the fruits
       Of painful superstition and blind zeal,
       Naught seeking but the praise of men, here find
       Fit retribution, empty as their deeds;
455   All th' unaccomplished° works of nature's hand,   *imperfect*
       Abortive, monstrous, or unkindly° mixed,   *unnatural*
       Dissolved on earth, fleet° hither, and in vain,   *float*
       Till final dissolution, wander here,
       Not in the neighboring moon, as some[5] have dreamed;
460   Those argent° fields more likely habitants,   *silver*
       Translated saints,[6] or middle Spirits hold
       Betwixt th' angelical and human kind:
       Hither of ill-joined sons and daughters born
       First from the ancient world those giants came
465   With many a vain exploit, though then renowned:[7]
       The builders next of Babel on the plain
       Of Sennaär,[8] and still with vain design
       New Babels, had they wherewithal, would build:
       Others came single; he who to be deemed
470   A god, leaped fondly° into Etna flames,   *foolishly*
       Empedocles, and he who to enjoy
       Plato's Elysium, leaped into the sea,
       Cleombrotus, and many more too long,[9]
       Embryos and idiots, eremites° and friars   *hermits*
475   White, black, and gray, with all their trumpery.[1]
       Here pilgrims roam, that strayed so far to seek
       In Golgotha[2] him dead, who lives in Heav'n;

---

4. Both the Ganges and Hydaspes (a tributary of the Indus) rise from the mountains of northern India. Sericana (line 438) is a region in Northwest China.
5. Milton's Paradise of Fools (named in line 496) was inspired by Ariosto's Limbo of Vanity in *Orlando Furioso* (book 34, lines 73ff.); Milton's region is reserved for deluded victims of misplaced devotion, chiefly Roman Catholics.
6. Holy men like Enoch and Elijah, transported to Heaven while yet alive.
7. Giants, born of unnatural marriages between the "sons of God" and the daughters of men (Genesis 6.4), are creatures unkindly mixed.
8. Shinar, the plain of Babel (Genesis 11.2–9); the Tower of Babel is an emblem of human pride and folly.
9. I.e., it would take too long to name them. Both Empedocles and Cleombrotus foolishly carried piety to the point of suicide.
1. The white friars are Carmelites; the black, Dominicans; and the gray, Franciscans. "Trumpery": religious paraphernalia.
2. Place where Christ was crucified.

And they who to be sure of paradise
Dying put on the weeds° of Dominic,   *garments*
480 Or in Franciscan think to pass disguised;[3]
They pass the planets seven, and pass the fixed,
And that crystálline sphere whose balance weighs
The trepidation talked, and that first moved;[4]
And now Saint Peter at Heav'n's wicket seems
485 To wait them with his keys, and now at foot
Of Heav'n's ascent they lift their feet, when lo
A violent crosswind from either coast
Blows them transverse ten thousand leagues awry
Into the devious° air. Then might ye see   *erratic*
490 Cowls, hoods and habits[5] with their wearers tossed
And fluttered into rags; then relics, beads,
Indulgences, dispenses, pardons, bulls,
The sport of winds: all these upwhirled aloft
Fly o'er the backside° of the world far off   *rump*
495 Into a limbo large and broad, since called
The Paradise of Fools, to few unknown
Long after, now unpeopled, and untrod;
All this dark globe the Fiend found as he passed,
And long he wandered, till at last a gleam
500 Of dawning light turned thitherward in haste
His traveled° steps; far distant he descries   *travel-weary*
Ascending by degrees° magnificent   *steps*
Up to the wall of heaven a structure high,
At top whereof, but far more rich appeared
505 The work as of a kingly palace gate
With frontispiece° of diamond and gold   *pediment*
Embellished; thick with sparkling orient° gems   *lustrous*
The portal shone, inimitable on earth,
By model, or by shading pencil drawn.
510 The stairs were such as whereon Jacob saw
Angels ascending and descending, bands
Of guardians bright, when he from Esau fled
To Padan-Aram in the field of Luz,
Dreaming by night under the open sky,
515 And waking cried, "This is the gate of Heav'n."[6]
Each stair mysteriously was meant, nor stood
There always, but drawn up to Heav'n sometimes
Viewless,° and underneath a bright sea flowed   *invisible*
Of jasper, or of liquid pearl, whereon
520 Who after came from earth, sailing arrived,
Wafted by angels, or flew o'er the lake
Rapt in a chariot drawn by fiery steeds.[7]
The stairs were then let down, whether to dare

3. Some try to trick God into granting them salvation by wearing on their deathbeds the garb of various religious orders.

4. Milton follows their souls through the spheres of the moon and sun, the five then-known planets, the fixed stars, and the sphere responsible for the "trepidation" (a periodic corrective shudder of the cosmos), up to the *primum mobile* or prime mover. The next step seems to be the empyreal Heaven.

5. The dress of religious orders, together with (next lines) rosary beads, saints' relics, various kinds of pardon for sins, and papal decrees ("bulls").

6. The story of Jacob's vision is summarized from Genesis 28.1–19; the stairs of the ladder allegorically ("mysteriously") represent stages of spiritual growth.

7. Elijah was wafted to heaven in a chariot.

The Fiend by easy ascent, or aggravate
525 His sad exclusion from the doors of bliss.
Direct against which opened from beneath,
Just o'er the blissful seat of Paradise,
A passage down to th' earth, a passage wide,[8]
Wider by far than that of aftertimes
530 Over Mount Zion, and, though that were large,
Over the Promised Land to God so dear,
By which, to visit oft those happy tribes,
On high behests his angels to and fro
Passed frequent, and his eye with choice° regard   discriminating
535 From Paneas the fount of Jordan's flood
To Beërsaba, where the Holy Land
Borders on Egypt and the Arabian shore;[9]
So wide the op'ning seemed, where bounds were set
To darkness, such as bound the ocean wave.
540 Satan from hence now on the lower stair
That scaled by steps of gold to Heaven gate
Looks down with wonder at the sudden view
Of all this world at once. As when a scout
Through dark and desert ways with peril gone
545 All night; at last by break of cheerful dawn
Obtains° the brow of some high-climbing hill,   gains
Which to his eye discovers unaware
The goodly prospect of some foreign land
First seen, or some renowned metropolis
550 With glistering spires and pinnacles adorned,
Which now the rising sun gilds with his beams.
Such wonder seized, though after Heaven seen,
The Spirit malign, but much more envy seized
At sight of all this world beheld so fair.
555 Round he surveys, and well might, where he stood
So high above the circling canopy
Of night's extended shade; from eastern point
Of Libra to the fleecy star that bears
Andromeda far off Atlantic seas[1]
560 Beyond th' horizon; then from pole to pole
He views in breadth, and without longer pause
Down right into the world's first region throws
His flight precipitant, and winds with ease
Through the pure marble° air his oblique way   sparkling
565 Amongst innumerable stars, that shone
Stars distant, but nigh hand seemed other worlds,
Or other worlds they seemed, or happy isles,
Like those Hesperian gardens famed of old,
Fortunate fields, and groves and flow'ry vales,[2]
570 Thrice happy isles, but who dwelt happy there

8. A passage through the crystalline spheres, otherwise impenetrable.
9. From Paneas (or Dan) in northern Palestine to Beersaba, or Beersheba, near the Egyptian border—the entire land of Israel.
1. In the zodiac, Libra is diametrically opposite Aries, or the Ram ("the fleecy star"), which seems to carry the constellation Andromeda on its back.
2. The gardens of the Hesperides and the "fortunate isles" of Greek mythology, classical versions of paradise, lay far out in the Atlantic.

He stayed not to inquire: above them all
The golden sun in splendor likest Heaven
Allured his eye: thither his course he bends
Through the calm firmament; but up or down
575 By center, or eccentric, hard to tell,
Or longitude,[3] where the great luminary
Aloof the vulgar constellations thick,
That from his lordly eye keep distance due,
Dispenses light from far; they as they move
580 Their starry dance in numbers that compute
Days, months, and years, towards his all-cheering lamp
Turn swift their various motions, or are turned
By his magnetic beam, that gently warms
The universe, and to each inward part
585 With gentle penetration, though unseen,
Shoots invisible virtue° even to the deep: influence, strength
So wondrously was set his station bright.

Summary   Landing on the bright orb of the sun, Satan disguises himself as a
youthful cherub and approaches the solar guardian, the archangel Uriel. Pretending
interest in the new great works of God, he gets directions to Earth and Adam's bower,
then spirals down and on Mount Niphates (in modern Iran), overlooking the site of
Paradise.

From Book 4

[SATAN'S ENTRY INTO PARADISE; ADAM AND EVE IN THEIR BOWER]

O for that warning voice, which he who saw
Th' Apocalypse, heard cry in heaven aloud,
Then when the Dragon, put to second rout,
Came furious down to be revenged on men,
5 "Woe to the inhabitants on earth!"[1] that now,
While time was, our first parents had been warned
The coming of their secret foe, and scaped
Haply° so scaped his mortal° snare; for now   happily / deadly
Satan, now first inflamed with rage, came down,
10 The tempter ere° th' accuser of mankind,   before being
To wreck° on innocent frail man his loss   avenge, wreak
Of that first battle, and his flight to Hell:
Yet not rejoicing in his speed, though bold,
Far off and fearless, nor with cause to boast,
15 Begins his dire attempt, which nigh the birth
Now rolling, boils in his tumultuous breast,
And like a devilish engine back recoils

---

3. Milton leaves open whether the sun or the earth
is at the center of the cosmos.
1. John of Patmos, in Revelation 12.3–12, hears

such a cry during a second war in Heaven, between
the Dragon and the angels.

Upon himself; horror and doubt distract
His troubled thoughts, and from the bottom stir
20   The Hell within him, for within him Hell
He brings, and round about him, nor from Hell
One step no more than from himself can fly
By change of place: now conscience wakes despair
That slumbered, wakes the bitter memory
25   Of what he was, what is, and what must be
Worse; of worse deeds worse sufferings must ensue.
Sometimes towards Eden which now in his view
Lay pleasant, his grieved look he fixes sad,
Sometimes towards Heav'n and the full-blazing sun,
30   Which now sat high in his meridian tow'r:[2]
Then much revolving,° thus in sighs began.   *pondering*
    "O thou that with surpassing glory crowned,[3]
Look'st from thy sole dominion like the god
Of this new world: at whose sight all the stars
35   Hide their diminished heads; to thee I call,
But with no friendly voice, and add thy name
O sun, to tell thee how I hate thy beams
That bring to my remembrance from what state
I fell, how glorious once above thy sphere;
40   Till pride and worse ambition threw me down
Warring in Heav'n against Heav'n's matchless King:
Ah wherefore! he deserved no such return
From me, whom he created what I was
In that bright eminence, and with his good
45   Upbraided none,[4] nor was his service hard.
What could be less than to afford him praise,
The easiest recompense, and pay him thanks,
How due! yet all his good proved ill in me,
And wrought but malice; lifted up so high
50   I 'sdained° subjection, and thought one step higher   *disdained*
Would set me highest, and in a moment quit°   *pay*
The debt immense of endless gratitude,
So burthensome still° paying, still to owe;   *always*
Forgetful what from him I still received,
55   And understood not that a grateful mind
By owing owes not, but still pays, at once
Indebted and discharged; what burden then?
O had his powerful destiny ordained
Me some inferior angel, I had stood
60   Then happy; no unbounded hope had raised
Ambition. Yet why not? some other Power°   *angel*
As great might have aspired, and me though mean
Drawn to his part; but other Powers as great
Fell not, but stand unshaken, from within

---

2. Midday, the height of noon.
3. Milton's nephew, Edward Phillips, said that this soliloquy was written "several years before the poem was begun," and was intended to begin a

drama on the topic, *Adam Unparadised.*
4. Demanded no return for his benefits (James 1.5).

65 Or from without, to all temptations armed.
Hadst thou[5] the same free will and power to stand?
Thou hadst: whom hast thou then or what to accuse,
But Heav'n's free love dealt equally to all?
Be then his love accursed, since love or hate,
70 To me alike, it deals eternal woe.
Nay cursed be thou; since against his thy will
Chose freely what it now so justly rues.
Me miserable![6] which way shall I fly
Infinite wrath, and infinite despair?
75 Which way I fly is Hell; myself am Hell;[7]
And in the lowest deep a lower deep
Still threat'ning to devour me opens wide,
To which the Hell I suffer seems a Heav'n.
O then at last relent! is there no place
80 Left for repentance, none for pardon left?
None left but by submission; and that word
Disdain forbids me, and my dread of shame
Among the Spirits beneath, whom I seduced
With other promises and other vaunts
85 Than to submit, boasting I could subdue
Th' Omnipotent. Ay me, they little know
How dearly I abide° that boast so vain,   *pay the penalty for*
Under what torments inwardly I groan:
While they adore me on the throne of hell,
90 With diadem and scepter high advanced
The lower still I fall, only supreme
In misery; such joy ambition finds.
But say I could repent and could obtain
By act of grace[8] my former state; how soon
95 Would hight recall high thoughts, how soon unsay
What feigned submission swore: ease would recant
Vows made in pain, as violent° and void.   *forced*
For never can true reconcilement grow
Where wounds of deadly hate have pierced so deep:
100 Which would but lead me to a worse relapse,
And heavier fall: so should I purchase dear
Short intermission bought with double smart.
This knows my punisher; therefore as far
From granting he, as I from begging peace:
105 All hope excluded thus, behold instead
Of us outcast, exiled, his new delight,
Mankind created, and for him this world.
So farewell hope, and with hope farewell fear,
Farewell remorse: all good to me is lost;
110 Evil be thou my good; by thee at least
Divided empire with Heav'n's King I hold

---

5. Compare Satan's address to himself here with Adam's soliloquy in parallel circumstances (10.758ff.).
6. A Latinism, *me miserum!*

7. Compare Satan's earlier claim that "the mind is its own place" (1.254).
8. The technical term for a formal pardon.

By thee, and more than half perhaps will reign;
As man ere long, and this new world shall know."
    Thus while he spake, each passion dimmed his face
115 Thrice changed with pale,° ire, envy and despair,   *pallor*
Which marred his borrowed visage, and betrayed
Him counterfeit, if any eye beheld.
For heav'nly minds from such distempers foul
Are ever clear. Whereof he soon aware,
120 Each perturbation smoothed with outward calm,
Artificer of fraud; and was the first
That practiced falsehood under saintly show,
Deep malice to conceal, couched° with revenge: *hidden*
Yet not enough had practiced to deceive
125 Uriel once warned; whose eye pursued him down
The way he went, and on th' Assyrian mount°   *Niphates*
Saw him disfigured, more than could befall
Spirit of happy sort: his gestures fierce
He marked and mad demeanor, then alone,
130 As he supposed, all unobserved, unseen.
    So on he fares, and to the border comes
Of Eden, where delicious Paradise,[9]
Now nearer, crowns with her enclosure green,
As with a rural mound the champaign head°   *open summit*
135 Of a steep wilderness, whose hairy sides
With thicket overgrown, grotesque[1] and wild,
Access denied; and overhead up grew
Insuperable highth of loftiest shade,
Cedar, and pine, and fir, and branching palm,
140 A sylvan scene, and as the ranks ascend
Shade above shade, a woody theater[2]
Of stateliest view. Yet higher than their tops
The verdurous wall of Paradise up sprung:
Which to our general sire gave prospect large
145 Into his nether empire neighboring round.
And higher than that wall a circling row
Of goodliest trees loaden with fairest fruit,
Blossoms and fruits at once of golden hue
Appeared, with gay enameled° colors mixed: *bright*
150 On which the sun more glad impressed his beams
Than in fair evening cloud, or humid bow,°   *rainbow*
When God hath show'red the earth; so lovely seemed
That landscape: and of pure now purer air[3]
Meets his approach, and to the heart inspires°   *infuses*
155 Vernal delight and joy, able to drive°   *drive out*
All sadness but despair: now gentle gales
Fanning their odoriferous° wings dispense   *fragrance-bearing*
Native perfumes, and whisper whence they stole
Those balmy spoils. As when to them who sail

---

9. Paradise is a delightful ("delicious") garden on top of a steep hill situated in the east of the land of Eden.
1. Characterized by interwoven, tangled vines and branches.
2. As if in a Greek amphitheater, the trees are set row on row.
3. The air becomes still purer.

160 Beyond the Cape of Hope,° and now are past   *Cape of Good Hope*
Mozambic, off at sea northeast winds blow
Sabean odors from the spicy shore
Of Araby the Blest,[4] with such delay
Well pleased they slack their course, and many a league
165 Cheered with the grateful° smell old Ocean smiles.   *pleasing*
So entertained those odorous sweets the Fiend
Who came their bane, though with them better pleased
Than Asmodeus with the fishy fume,
That drove him, though enamored, from the spouse
170 Of Tobit's son,[5] and with a vengeance sent
From Media post to Egypt, there fast bound.
    Now to th'ascent of that steep savage° hill   *wooded, wild*
Satan had journeyed on, pensive and slow;
But further way found none, so thick entwined,
175 As one continued brake,° the undergrowth   *thicket*
Of shrubs and tangling bushes had perplexed
All path of man or beast that passed that way:
One gate there only was, and that looked east
On th' other side: which when th' arch-felon saw
180 Due entrance he disdained, and in contempt,
At one slight bound high overleaped all bound
Of hill or highest wall, and sheer within
Lights on his feet. As when a prowling wolf,
Whom hunger drives to seek new haunt for prey,
185 Watching where shepherds pen their flocks at eve
In hurdled cotes° amid the field secure,   *pens of woven reeds*
Leaps o'er the fence with ease into the fold:
Or as a thief bent to unhoard the cash
Of some rich burgher, whose substantial doors,
190 Cross-barred and bolted fast, fear no assault,
In at the window climbs, or o'er the tiles;
So clomb° this first grand thief into God's fold: *climbed*
So since into his church lewd hirelings[6] climb.
Thence up he flew, and on the Tree of Life,
195 The middle tree and highest there that grew,
Sat like a cormorant;[7] yet not true life
Thereby regained, but sat devising death
To them who lived; nor on the virtue° thought   *power*
Of that life-giving plant, but only used
200 For prospect,° what well used had been the pledge   *as a lookout*
Of immortality. So little knows
Any, but God alone, to value right
The good before him, but perverts best things
To worst abuse, or to their meanest use.
205   Beneath him with new wonder now he views

4. *Arabia Felix* (modern Yemen). "Sabean": the biblical Sheba.
5. The Apocryphal book of Tobit tells of Tobias, Tobit's son, who married Sara and avoided the fate of her previous seven husbands (killed on their wedding night by the demon Asmodeus) by following the instructions of the angel Raphael and mak-

ing a fishy smell to drive him off; Asmodeus then fled to Egypt where Raphael bound him.
6. Base men interested only in money; Milton would have clergymen not paid by the state, to ensure their purity of motive.
7. A sea bird, noted for gluttony.

To all delight of human sense exposed
In narrow room nature's whole wealth, yea more,
A heav'n on earth: for blissful Paradise
Of God the garden was, by him in the east
210 Of Eden planted; Eden stretched her line
From Auran eastward to the royal tow'rs
Of great Seleucia, built by Grecian kings,
Or where the sons of Eden long before
Dwelt in Telassar:[8] in this pleasant soil
215 His far more pleasant garden God ordained;
Out of the fertile ground he caused to grow
All trees of noblest kind for sight, smell, taste;
And all amid them stood the Tree of Life,
High eminent, blooming ambrosial° fruit   divinely fragrant
220 Of vegetable gold; and next to life
Our death the Tree of Knowledge grew fast by,
Knowledge of good bought dear by knowing ill.
Southward through Eden[9] went a river large,
Nor changed his course, but through the shaggy hill
225 Passed underneath engulfed, for God had thrown
That mountain as his garden mold° high raised   rich earth
Upon the rapid current, which through veins
Of porous earth with kindly° thirst up drawn,   natural
Rose a fresh fountain, and with many a rill
230 Watered the garden; thence united fell
Down the steep glade, and met the nether flood,
Which from his darksome passage now appears,
And now divided into four main streams,
Runs diverse, wand'ring many a famous realm
235 And country whereof here needs no account,
But rather to tell how, if art could tell,
How from that sapphire fount the crispèd° brooks,   wavy, rippling
Rolling on orient pearl and sands of gold,
With mazy error[1] under pendent shades
240 Ran nectar, visiting each plant, and fed
Flow'rs worthy of Paradise which not nice° art   fastidious
In beds and curious knots, but nature boon°   bounteous
Poured forth profuse on hill and dale and plain,
Both where the morning sun first warmly smote
245 The open field, and where the unpierced shade
Embrowned° the noontide bow'rs. Thus was this place,   darkened
A happy rural seat of various view,[2]
Groves whose rich trees wept odorous gums and balm,
Others whose fruit burnished with golden rind
250 Hung amiable,° Hesperian fables true,[3]   lovely

8. "Auran" is the province of Hauran on the eastern border of Israel. "Selucia," a powerful city on
the Tigris, near modern Baghdad, was founded by
one of Alexander's generals ("built by Grecian
kings"). "Telassar" is another Near Eastern kingdom.
9. The Tigris (identified at 9.71) flowed under the

hill.
1. From Latin *errare*, wandering.
2. Like a country estate, with a variety of prospects.
3. These were real golden apples, by contrast to
those feigned golden apples of the Hesperides,
fabled paradisal islands in the Western Ocean.

If true, here only, and of delicious taste:
Betwixt them lawns, or level downs, and flocks
Grazing the tender herb, were interposed,
Or palmy hillock, or the flow'ry lap
255   Of some irriguous° valley spread her store,   *well-watered*
Flow'rs of all hue, and without thorn the rose:
Another side, umbrageous° grots and caves   *shady*
Of cool recess, o'er which the mantling° vine   *enveloping*
Lays forth her purple grape, and gently creeps
260   Luxuriant; meanwhile murmuring waters fall
Down the slope hills, dispersed, or in a lake,
That to the fringèd bank with myrtle crowned,
Her crystal mirror holds, unite their streams.
The birds their choir apply; airs,[4] vernal airs,
265   Breathing the smell of field and grove, attune
The trembling leaves, while universal Pan[5]
Knit° with the Graces and the Hours in dance   *clasping hands*
Led on th' eternal spring. Not that fair field
Of Enna, where Proserpine gathering flow'rs
270   Herself a fairer flow'r by gloomy Dis
Was gathered, which cost Ceres all that pain
To seek her through the world; nor that sweet grove
Of Daphne by Orontes, and th' inspired
Castalian spring,[6] might with this Paradise
275   Of Eden strive; nor that Nyseian isle
Girt with the river Triton, where old Cham,
Whom Gentiles Ammon call and Libyan Jove,
Hid Amalthea and her florid° son   *wine-flushed*
Young Bacchus from his stepdame Rhea's eye;[7]
280   Nor where Abassin kings their issue guard,
Mount Amara,[8] though this by some supposed
True Paradise under the Ethiop line°   *equator*
By Nilus'° head, enclosed with shining rock,   *Nile's*
A whole day's journey high, but wide remote
285   From this Assyrian garden,° where the Fiend   *Eden*
Saw undelighted all delight, all kind
Of living creatures new to sight and strange:
   Two of far nobler shape erect and tall,
God-like erect, with native honor clad
290   In naked majesty seemed lords of all,
And worthy seemed, for in their looks divine
The image of their glorious Maker shone,
Truth, wisdom, sanctitude severe and pure,

---

4. Both breezes and melodies. "Their choir apply": practice their songs.
5. The god of all nature—"pan" in Greek means "all."
6. Milton compares Paradise with famous beauty spots of antiquity. Enna in Sicily was a lovely meadow from which "Proserpine" was kidnapped by "gloomy Dis" (i.e., Pluto); her mother Ceres sought her throughout the world. The grove of Daphne, near Antioch and the Orontes River in the

Near East, had a spring called "Castalia" after the Muses' fountain near Parnassus.
7. The isle of Nysa in the river Triton in Tunisia was where Ammon (an Egyptian god, identified with Cham or Ham, the son of Noah) hid Bacchus, his child by Amalthea (who later became the god of wine), away from the eyes of his wife Rhea.
8. Atop Mount Amara, the "Abassin" (Abyssinian) king had a splendid palace in a paradisal garden.

Severe but in true filial freedom placed;
295 Whence true authority in men;[9] though both
Not equal, as their sex not equal seemed;
For contemplation he and valor formed,
For softness she and sweet attractive grace,
He for God only, she for God in him:[1]
300 His fair large front° and eye sublime declared   *forehead*
Absolute rule; and hyacinthine[2] locks
Round from his parted forelock manly hung
Clust'ring, but not beneath his shoulders broad:
She as a veil down to the slender waist
305 Her unadorned golden tresses wore
Disheveled, but in wanton ringlets waved
As the vine curls her tendrils,[3] which implied
Subjection, but required with gentle sway,°   *persuasion*
And by her yielded, by him best received,
310 Yielded with coy° submission, modest pride,   *shyly reserved*
And sweet reluctant amorous delay.
Nor those mysterious parts were then concealed,
Then was not guilty shame, dishonest° shame   *unchaste*
Of nature's works, honor dishonorable,
315 Sin-bred, how have ye troubled all mankind
With shows instead, mere shows of seeming pure,
And banished from man's life his happiest life,
Simplicity and spotless innocence.
So passed they naked on, nor shunned the sight
320 Of God or angel, for they thought no ill:
So hand in hand they passed, the loveliest pair
That ever since in love's embraces met,
Adam the goodliest man of men since born
His sons, the fairest of her daughters Eve.
325 Under a tuft of shade that on a green
Stood whispering soft, by a fresh fountain side
They sat them down, and after no more toil
Of their sweet gard'ning labor than sufficed
To recommend cool Zephyr,[4] and made ease
330 More easy, wholesome thirst and appetite
More grateful, to their supper fruits they fell,
Nectarine° fruits which the compliant boughs   *sweet as nectar*
Yielded them, sidelong as they sat recline
On the soft downy bank damasked with flow'rs:
335 The savory pulp they chew, and in the rind
Still as they thirsted scoop the brimming stream;
Nor gentle purpose,° nor endearing smiles   *conversation*
Wanted,° nor youthful dalliance as beseems   *lacked*
Fair couple, linked in happy nuptial league,
340 Alone as they. About them frisking played

9. This phrase underscores Milton's idea that true freedom involves obedience to natural superiors (i.e., God).
1. The phrase has as its context 1 Corinthians 11.3: "The head of every man is Christ; and the head of the woman is the man."

2. A classical metaphor for hair curled in the form of hyacinth petals, and perhaps also implying dark or flowing.
3. Eve's hair is curly, abundant, not subjected to rigid control, like the vegetation in Paradise.
4. I.e., to make a cool breeze welcome.

All beasts of th' earth, since wild, and of all chase°   *a game preserve*
In wood or wilderness, forest or den;
Sporting the lion ramped,° and in his paw   *stood on hind legs*
Dandled the kid; bears, tigers, ounces,° pards°   *lynxes/leopards*
345 Gamboled before them; th' unwieldy elephant
To make them mirth used all his might, and wreathed
His lithe proboscis;° close the serpent sly   *trunk*
Insinuating,° wove with Gordian twine   *writhing, twisting*
His braided train,⁵ and of his fatal guile
350 Gave proof unheeded; others on the grass
Couched, and now filled with pasture gazing sat,
Or bedward ruminating:° for the sun   *chewing the cud*
Declined was hasting now with prone° career   *sinking*
To th' Ocean Isles,° and in th' ascending scale   *the Azores*
355 Of Heav'n the stars that usher evening rose:
When Satan still in gaze, as first he stood,
Scarce thus at length failed speech recovered sad.
    "O Hell! what do mine eyes with grief behold,
Into our room of bliss thus high advanced
360 Creatures of other mold, earth-born perhaps,
Not Spirits, yet to heav'nly Spirits bright
Little inferior; whom my thoughts pursue
With wonder, and could love, so lively shines
In them divine resemblance, and such grace
365 The hand that formed them on their shape hath poured.
Ah gentle pair, ye little think how nigh
Your change approaches, when all these delights
Will vanish and deliver ye to woe,
More woe, the more your taste is now of joy;
370 Happy, but for so happy° ill secured   *such happiness*
Long to continue, and this high seat your heav'n
Ill fenced for heav'n to keep out such a foe
As now is entered; yet no purposed foe
To you whom I could pity thus forlorn
375 Though I unpitied: league with you I seek,
And mutual amity so strait,° so close,   *intimate*
That I with you must dwell, or you with me
Henceforth; my dwelling haply may not please
Like this fair Paradise, your sense, yet such
380 Accept your Maker's work; he gave it me,
Which I as freely give; Hell shall unfold,
To entertain you two, her widest gates,
And send forth all her kings; there will be room,
Not like these narrow limits, to receive
385 Your numerous offspring; if no better place,
Thank him who puts me loath to this revenge
On you who wrong me not for° him who wronged.   *in place of*
And should I at your harmless innocence
Melt, as I do, yet public reason just,

---

5. Checkered body. "Gordian twine": cords as convoluted as the Gordian knot which Alexander the Great had to cut with his sword.

390 Honor and empire with revenge enlarged
By conquering this new world, compels me now
To do what else though damned I should abhor."[6]
    So spake the Fiend, and with necessity,
The tyrant's plea, excused his devilish deeds.
395 Then from his lofty stand on that high tree
Down he alights among the sportful herd
Of those four-footed kinds, himself now one,
Now other, as their shape served best his end
Nearer to view his prey, and unespied
400 To mark what of their state he more might learn
By word or action marked: about them round
A lion now he stalks with fiery glare,
Then as a tiger, who by chance hath spied
In some purlieu° two gentle fawns at play,   *outskirts of a forest*
405 Straight couches close, then rising changes oft
His couchant watch, as one who chose his ground
Whence rushing he might surest seize them both
Gripped in each paw: when Adam first of men
To first of women Eve thus moving speech
410 Turned him all ear to hear new utterance flow:
    "Sole partner and sole° part of all these joys,   *chief*
Dearer thyself than all; needs must the Power
That made us, and for us this ample world
Be infinitely good, and of his good
415 As liberal and free as infinite,
That raised us from the dust and placed us here
In all this happiness, who at his hand
Have nothing merited, nor can perform
Aught whereof he hath need, he who requires
420 From us no other service than to keep
This one, this easy charge, of all the trees
In Paradise that bear delicious fruit
So various, not to taste that only Tree
Of Knowledge, planted by the Tree of Life,
425 So near grows death to life, whate'er death is,
Some dreadful thing no doubt; for well thou know'st
God hath pronounced it death to taste that Tree,
The only sign of our obedience left
Among so many signs of power and rule
430 Conferred upon us, and dominion giv'n
Over all other creatures that possess
Earth, air, and sea. Then let us not think hard
One easy prohibition, who enjoy
Free leave so large to all things else, and choice
435 Unlimited of manifold delights:
But let us ever praise him, and extol
His bounty, following our delightful task
To prune these growing plants, and tend these flow'rs,
Which were it toilsome, yet with thee were sweet."

---

6. Satan's excuse—reason of state, public interest, empire, etc.—is called "the tyrant's plea" in line 394.

440 　　　To whom thus Eve replied. "O thou for whom
　　　And from whom I was formed flesh of thy flesh,
　　　And without whom am to no end, my guide
　　　And head, what thou hast said is just and right.
　　　For we to him indeed all praises owe,
445 　　　And daily thanks, I chiefly who enjoy
　　　So far the happier lot, enjoying thee
　　　Preeminent by so much odds,° while thou　　　　　　　*advantage*
　　　Like consort to thyself canst nowhere find.
　　　That day I oft remember, when from sleep
450 　　　I first awaked, and found myself reposed°　　　　　　　*resting*
　　　Under a shade on flowers, much wond'ring where
　　　And what I was, whence thither brought, and how.
　　　Not distant far from thence a murmuring sound
　　　Of waters issued from a cave and spread
455 　　　Into a liquid plain, then stood unmoved
　　　Pure as th' expanse of Heav'n; I thither went
　　　With unexperienced thought, and laid me down
　　　On the green bank, to look into the clear
　　　Smooth lake, that to me seemed another sky.
460 　　　As I bent down to look, just opposite,
　　　A shape within the wat'ry gleam appeared
　　　Bending to look on me, I started back,
　　　It started back, but pleased I soon returned,
　　　Pleased it returned as soon with answering looks
465 　　　Of sympathy and love; there I had fixed
　　　Mine eyes till now, and pined with vain° desire,[7]　　　　*futile*
　　　Had not a voice thus warned me, 'What thou seest,
　　　What there thou seest fair creature is thyself,
　　　With thee it came and goes: but follow me,
470 　　　And I will bring thee where no shadow stays°　　　　　*hinders*
　　　Thy coming, and thy soft embraces, he
　　　Whose image thou art, him thou shalt enjoy
　　　Inseparably thine, to him shalt bear
　　　Multitudes like thyself, and thence be called
475 　　　Mother of human race': what could I do,
　　　But follow straight° invisibly thus led?　　　　　　　　*at once*
　　　Till I espied thee, fair indeed and tall,
　　　Under a platan,° yet methought less fair,　　　　　　　*plane tree*
　　　Less winning soft, less amiably mild,
480 　　　Than that smooth wat'ry image; back I turned,
　　　Thou following cried'st aloud, 'Return fair Eve,
　　　Whom fli'st thou? Whom thou fli'st, of him thou art,
　　　His flesh, his bone; to give thee being I lent
　　　Out of my side to thee, nearest my heart
485 　　　Substantial life, to have thee by my side
　　　Henceforth an individual° solace dear;　　　　　*inseparable, distinct*
　　　Part of my soul I seek thee, and thee claim
　　　My other half': with that thy gentle hand

7. Eve's experience reprises (but with significant differences) the story of Narcissus, who fell in love with his own reflection and was transformed into a flower.

Seized mine, I yielded, and from that time see
490 How beauty is excelled by manly grace
And wisdom, which alone is truly fair."
     So spake our general mother, and with eyes
Of conjugal attraction unreproved,
And meek surrender, half embracing leaned
495 On our first father, half her swelling breast
Naked met his under the flowing gold
Of her loose tresses hid: he in delight
Both of her beauty and submissive charms
Smiled with superior love, as Jupiter
500 On Juno smiles, when he impregns° the clouds   *impregnates*
That shed May flowers; and pressed her matron lip
With kisses pure: aside the Devil turned
For envy, yet with jealous leer malign
Eyed them askance, and to himself thus plained.°   *complained*
505   "Sight hateful, sight tormenting! thus these two
Imparadised in one another's arms
The happier Eden, shall enjoy their fill
Of bliss on bliss, while I to Hell am thrust,
Where neither joy nor love, but fierce desire,
510 Among our other torments not the least,
Still° unfulfilled with pain of longing pines;   *always*
Yet let me not forget what I have gained
From their own mouths; all is not theirs it seems:
One fatal tree there stands of Knowledge called,
515 Forbidden them to taste: Knowledge forbidden?
Suspicious, reasonless. Why should their Lord
Envy° them that? Can it be sin to know,   *begrudge*
Can it be death? And do they only stand
By ignorance, is that their happy state,
520 The proof of their obedience and their faith?
O fair foundation laid whereon to build
Their ruin! Hence I will excite their minds
With more desire to know, and to reject
Envious commands, invented with design
525 To keep them low whom knowledge might exalt
Equal with gods; aspiring to be such,
They taste and die: what likelier can ensue?
But first with narrow search I must walk round
This garden, and no corner leave unspied;
530 A chance, but chance[8] may lead where I may meet
Some wand'ring Spirit of Heav'n, by fountain side,
Or in thick shade retired, from him to draw
What further would be learnt. Live while ye may,
Yet happy pair; enjoy, till I return,
535 Short pleasures, for long woes are to succeed."
     So saying, his proud step he scornful turned,
But with sly circumspection, and began
Through wood, through waste, o'er hill, o'er dale his roam.°   *act of wandering*

8. An opportunity, even if only by luck.

Meanwhile in utmost longitude, where Heav'n
540 With earth and ocean meets, the setting sun
Slowly descended, and with right aspéct
Against the eastern gate of Paradise
Leveled his evening rays.⁹ it was a rock
Of alabaster,¹ piled up to the clouds,
545 Conspicuous far, winding with one ascent
Accessible from earth, one entrance high;
The rest was craggy cliff, that overhung
Still as it rose, impossible to climb.
Betwixt these rocky pillars Gabriel² sat
550 Chief of th' angelic guards, awaiting night;
About him exercised heroic games
Th' unarmèd youth of Heav'n, but nigh at hand
Celestial armory, shields, helms, and spears
Hung high with diamond flaming, and with gold.
555 Thither came Uriel, gliding through the even
On a sunbeam, swift as a shooting star
In autumn thwarts° the night, when vapors fired   *passes across*
Impress the air, and shows the mariner
From what point of his compass to beware
560 Impetuous winds:³ he thus began in haste.
    "Gabriel, to thee thy course by lot hath giv'n
Charge and strict watch that to this happy place
No evil thing approach or enter in;
This day at hight of noon came to my sphere
565 A Spirit, zealous, as he seemed, to know
More of th' Almighty's works, and chiefly man
God's latest image: I described° his way   *descried, observed*
Bent all on speed, and marked his airy gait;°   *path*
But in the mount that lies from Eden north,
570 Where he first lighted, soon discerned his looks
Alien from Heav'n, with passions foul obscured:
Mine eye pursued him still, but under shade°   *trees*
Lost sight of him; one of the banished crew
I fear, hath ventured from the deep, to raise
575 New troubles; him thy care must be to find."
    To whom the wingèd warrior thus returned:
"Uriel, no wonder if thy perfect sight,
Amid the sun's bright circle where thou sitt'st,
See far and wide. In at this gate none pass
580 The vigilance here placed, but such as come
Well known from Heav'n; and since meridian hour°   *noon*
No creature thence: if Spirit of other sort,
So minded, have o'erleaped these earthy bounds
On purpose, hard thou know'st it to exclude
585 Spiritual substance with corporeal bar.
But if within the circuit of these walks,

---

9. Setting in the west, the sun struck the eastern gate from the inside, at a 90-degree angle.
1. White, translucent marble veined with colors.
2. In Hebrew, "Strength of God." A tradition (cf.

Enoch 20.7) gave Gabriel charge of Paradise.
3. Shooting stars were thought to indicate by the direction of their fall the source of oncoming storms. "Vapors fired": heat lightning.

In whatsoever shape he lurk, of whom
Thou tell'st, by morrow dawning I shall know."
　　So promised he, and Uriel to his charge
590　Returned on that bright beam, whose point now raised
Bore him slope downward to the sun now fall'n
Beneath th' Azorès; whether the prime orb,
Incredible how swift, had thither rolled
Diurnal,° or this less volúble° earth　　　　　　　　　　*daily / swift-turning*
595　By shorter flight to th' east,[4] had left him there
Arraying with reflected purple and gold
The clouds that on his western throne attend.
Now came still evening on, and twilight gray
Had in her sober livery all things clad;
600　Silence accompanied, for beast and bird,
They to their grassy couch, these to their nests
Were slunk, all but the wakeful nightingale;
She all night long her amorous descant° sung;　　　　　　　　*melody*
Silence was pleased: now glowed the firmament
605　With living sapphires: Hesperus[5] that led
The starry host, rode brightest, till the moon
Rising in clouded majesty, at length
Apparent° queen unveiled her peerless light,　　　　　　　*clearly seen*
And o'er the dark her silver mantle threw.
610　　　When Adam thus to Eve: "Fair consort, th' hour
Of night, and all things now retired to rest
Mind us of like repose, since God hath set
Labor and rest, as day and night to men
Successive, and the timely dew of sleep
615　Now falling with soft slumbrous weight inclines
Our eyelids; other creatures all day long
Rove idle unemployed, and less need rest;
Man hath his daily work of body or mind
Appointed, which declares his dignity,
620　And the regard of Heav'n on all his ways;
While other animals unactive range,
And of their doings God takes no account.
Tomorrow ere fresh morning streak the east
With first approach of light, we must be ris'n,
625　And at our pleasant labor, to reform
Yon flow'ry arbors, yonder alleys green,
Our walk at noon, with branches overgrown,
That mock our scant manuring,° and require　　　　　　　*cultivating*
More hands than ours to lop their wanton growth:
630　Those blossoms also, and those dropping gums,
That lie bestrown unsightly and unsmooth,
Ask riddance,° if we mean to tread with ease;　　　　　*need to be cleared*
Meanwhile, as nature wills, night bids us rest."
　　To whom thus Eve with perfect beauty adorned.
635　"My author and disposer, what thou bidd'st

___

4. Here and elsewhere Milton leaves open the
question of whether the sun moves around the
earth, or vice versa.
5. The evening star, Venus.

Unargued I obey; so God ordains,
God is thy law, thou mine: to know no more
Is woman's happiest knowledge and her praise.
With thee conversing I forget all time.
640 All seasons° and their change, all please alike.   *times of day*
Sweet[6] is the breath of morn, her rising sweet,
With charm[7] of earliest birds; pleasant the sun
When first on this delightful land he spreads
His orient beams, on herb, tree, fruit, and flow'r,
645 Glist'ring with dew; fragrant the fertile earth
After soft showers; and sweet the coming on
Of grateful evening mild, then silent night
With this her solemn bird° and this fair moon,   *the nightingale*
And these the gems of heav'n, her starry train:
650 But neither breath of morn when she ascends
With charm of earliest birds, nor rising sun
On this delightful land, nor herb, fruit, flow'r,
Glist'ring with dew, nor fragrance after showers,
Nor grateful evening mild, nor silent night
655 With this her solemn bird, nor walk by moon,
Or glittering starlight without thee is sweet.
But wherefore all night long shine these, for whom
This glorious sight, when sleep hath shut all eyes?"
      To whom our general ancestor replied.
660 "Daughter of God and man, accomplished Eve,[8]
Those have their course to finish, round the earth,
By morrow evening, and from land to land
In order, though to nations yet unborn,
Minist'ring light prepared, they set and rise;
665 Lest total darkness should by night regain
Her old possession, and extinguish life
In nature and all things, which these soft° fires   *agreeable*
Not only enlighten, but with kindly° heat   *natural, benevolent*
Of various influence foment and warm,
670 Temper or nourish, or in part shed down
Their stellar virtue on all kinds that grow
On earth, made hereby apter to receive
Perfection from the sun's more potent ray.[9]
These then, though unbeheld in deep of night,
675 Shine not in vain, nor think, though men were none,
That Heav'n would want spectators, God want praise;
Millions of spiritual creatures walk the earth
Unseen, both when we wake, and when we sleep:
All these with ceaseless praise his works behold
680 Both day and night: how often from the steep
Of echoing hill or thicket have we heard
Celestial voices to the midnight air,

---

6. With this embedded lyric, Eve displays her literary talents as author of an elegant love song, son-
netlike and replete with striking rhetorical figures
of circularity and repetition.
7. Blended singing of many birds.

8. Having many talents and achievements; perfect, complete.
9. The stars were thought to have their own occult
influence, and also to moderate that of the sun.

Sole, or responsive each to other's note
Singing their great Creator: oft in bands
685   While they keep watch, or nightly rounding walk,
With heav'nly touch of instrumental sounds
In full harmonic number joined, their songs
Divide[1] the night, and lift our thoughts to Heaven."
     Thus talking hand in hand alone they passed
690   On to their blissful bower; it was a place
Chos'n by the sovran Planter, when he framed°   *fashioned*
All things to man's delightful use; the roof
Of thickest covert was inwoven shade
Laurel and myrtle, and what higher grew
695   Of firm and fragrant leaf; on either side
Acanthus, and each odorous bushy shrub
Fenced up the verdant wall; each beauteous flow'r,
Iris all hues, roses, and jessamine°   *jasmine*
Reared high their flourished° heads between, and wrought   *flowering*
700   Mosaic; underfoot the violet,
Crocus, and hyacinth with rich inlay
Broidered the ground, more colored than with stone
Of costliest emblem:° other creature here   *inlaid work*
Beast, bird, insect, or worm durst enter none,
705   Such was their awe of man. In shadier bower
More sacred and sequestered,° though but feigned,   *secluded*
Pan or Silvanus never slept, nor nymph,
Nor Faunus[2] haunted. Here in close recess
With flowers, garlands, and sweet-smelling herbs
710   Espousèd Eve decked first her nuptial bed,
And heav'nly choirs the hymenean° sung,   *wedding song*
What day the genial[3] angel to our sire
Brought her in naked beauty more adorned,
More lovely than Pandora, whom the gods
715   Endowed with all their gifts, and O too like
In sad event,° when to the unwiser son   *outcome*
Of Japhet brought by Hermes, she ensnared
Mankind with her fair looks, to be avenged
On him who had stole Jove's authentic fire.[4]
720   Thus at their shady lodge arrived, both stood,
Both turned, and under open sky adored
The God that made both sky, air, earth and Heav'n
Which they beheld, the moon's resplendent globe
And starry pole:° "Thou also mad'st the night,   *sky*
725   Maker Omnipotent, and thou the day,
Which we in our appointed work employed
Have finished happy in our mutual help

---

1. Mark the watches of the night; also, perform musical "divisions," elaborate melodic passages.
2. Forest and field divinities of classical mythology.
3. Presiding over marriage and generation.
4. Pandora (the name means "all gifts") was an artificial woman, molded of clay, bestowed by the gods on Epimetheus, brother of Prometheus (who angered Jove by stealing fire from heaven). She brought a box that foolish Epimetheus opened, releasing all the ills of the human race, leaving only hope inside. The brothers were sons of Iapetos, whom Milton identifies with Japhet, Noah's third son. The Eve-Pandora parallel was often noted.

And mutual love, the crown of all our bliss
Ordained by thee, and this delicious place
730 For us too large, where thy abundance wants
Partakers, and uncropped falls to the ground.
But thou hast promised from us two a race
To fill the earth, who shall with us extol
Thy goodness infinite, both when we wake,
735 And when we seek, as now, thy gift of sleep."
   This said unanimous, and other rites
Observing none, but adoration pure
Which God likes best,[5] into their inmost bow'r
Handed° they went; and eased° the putting off   *hand in hand / spared*
740 These troublesome disguises which we wear,
Straight side by side were laid, nor turned I ween°   *surmise*
Adam from his fair spouse, nor Eve the rites
Mysterious[6] of connubial love refused:
Whatever hypocrites austerely talk
745 Of purity and place and innocence,
Defaming as impure what God declares
Pure, and commands to some, leaves free to all.
Our Maker bids increase,[7] who bids abstain
But our destroyer, foe to God and man?
750 Hail wedded Love, mysterious law, true source
Of human offspring, sole propriety°   *private property*
In Paradise of all things common else.
By thee adulterous lust was driv'n from men
Among the bestial herds to range, by thee
755 Founded in reason, loyal, just, and pure,
Relations dear, and all the charities°   *loves*
Of father, son, and brother first were known.
Far be it, that I should write thee sin or blame,
Or think thee unbefitting holiest place,
760 Perpetual fountain of domestic sweets,
Whose bed is undefiled and chaste pronounced,
Present, or past, as saints and patriarchs used.[8]
Here Love his golden shafts employs, here lights
His constant lamp, and waves his purple wings,
765 Reigns here and revels;[9] not in the bought smile
Of harlots, loveless, joyless, unendeared,
Casual fruition, nor in court amours,
Mixed dance, or wanton masque, or midnight ball,
Or serenade, which the starved° lover sings   *perished with cold*
770 To his proud fair, best quitted with disdain.
These lulled by nightingales embracing slept,
And on their naked limbs the flow'ry roof

---

5. Like many Puritans, Milton objected to set
forms of prayer, so Adam and Eve pray spontaneously (therefore sincerely), but also, paradoxically,
together. Their prayer develops variations on
Psalm 104.20–24.
6. Awe-inspiring. St. Paul (Ephesians 5.32) calls
the union of man and woman a "mystery" parallel-

ing that of Christ and the Church.
7. Genesis 1.28.
8. Throughout history ("present or past"), Old and
New Testament worthies have "used" matrimony
as a noble estate.
9. The "golden shafts" (arrows) of Cupid produce
true love, his lead-tipped arrows, hate.

Show'red roses, which the morn repaired.° Sleep on,   *replaced*
Blest pair; and O yet happiest if ye seek
775   No happier state, and know to know no more.[1]

Summary   Fulfilling his promise to Uriel, Gabriel divides his night watch into
search parties, assigning Ithuriel and Zephon to guard closely the bower of Adam and
Eve. They find Satan in the bower, whispering in the ear of the sleeping Eve,
and bring him before Gabriel. A battle impends, but is averted by a heavenly signal,
and Satan flees out of Paradise.

From Book 5

[EVE'S DREAM: TROUBLE IN PARADISE]

Now Morn her rosy steps in th' eastern clime
Advancing, sowed the earth with orient pearl,°   *sparkling dew*
When Adam waked, so customed, for his sleep
Was aery light, from pure digestion bred,
5   And temperate vapors bland,° which th' only sound   *gentle, balmy*
Of leaves and fuming rills, Aurora's fan,[1]
Lightly dispersed, and the shrill matin° song   *morning*
Of birds on every bough; so much the more
His wonder was to find unawakened Eve
10   With tresses discomposed, and glowing cheek,
As through unquiet rest: he on his side
Leaning half-raised, with looks of cordial° love   *heartfelt*
Hung over her enamored, and beheld
Beauty, which whether waking or asleep
15   Shot forth peculiar° graces; then with voice   *its own*
Mild, as when Zephyrus on Flora[2] breathes,
Her hand soft touching, whispered thus: "Awake
My fairest, my espoused, my lastest found,
Heav'n's last best gift, my ever new delight,
20   Awake, the morning shines, and the fresh field
Calls us, we lose the prime, to mark how spring
Our tended plants, how blows° the citron grove,   *blooms*
What drops the myrrh, and what the balmy reed,°   *balsam*
How nature paints her colors, how the bee
25   Sits on the bloom extracting liquid sweet."[3]
   Such whispering waked her, but with startled eye
On Adam, whom embracing, thus she spake:
   "O sole in whom my thoughts find all repose,

1. Know enough to be content with what you
know.
1. Rustling leaves stirred by Aurora, goddess of the
dawn.
2. Zephyrus is god of the gentle west wind, Flora
goddess of flowers.
3. Adam sings a morning love song (*aubade*) to

Eve, which works variations on Song of Solomon
2.10–12: "Rise up, my love, my fair one, and come
away. . . . The flowers appear on the earth; the
time of the singing of birds is come." Compare
Satan's serenade (5.38–47), a parody of Adam's
aubade and the Song of Solomon. "Prime" (line
21): first hour of the day.

My glory, my perfection, glad I see
30 Thy face, and morn returned, for I this night,
Such night till this I never passed, have dreamed,
If dreamed, not as I oft am wont, of thee,
Works of day past, or morrow's next design,
But of offense and trouble, which my mind
35 Knew never till this irksome night. Methought
Close at mine ear one called me forth to walk
With gentle voice, I thought it thine; it said,
'Why sleep'st thou Eve? now is the pleasant time,
The cool, the silent, save where silence yields
40 To the night-warbling bird, that now awake
Tunes sweetest his love-labored song; now reigns
Full-orbed the moon, and with more pleasing light
Shadowy sets off the face of things, in vain,
If none regard; heav'n wakes with all his eyes,°   stars
45 Whom to behold but thee, nature's desire,
In whose sight all things joy, with ravishment
Attracted by thy beauty still° to gaze.'   continually
I rose as at thy call, but found thee not;
To find thee I directed then my walk;
50 And on, me thought, alone I passed through ways
That brought me on a sudden to the tree
Of interdicted knowledge: fair it seemed,
Much fairer to my fancy than by day:
And as I wond'ring looked, beside it stood
55 One shaped and winged like one of those from Heav'n
By us oft seen; his dewy locks distilled
Ambrosia;° on that tree he also gazed;   heavenly fragrance
And 'O fair plant,' said he, 'with fruit surcharged,
Deigns none to ease thy load and taste thy sweet,
60 Nor god,° nor man; is knowledge so despised?   angel
Or envy, or what reserve forbids to taste?[4]
Forbid who will, none shall from me withhold
Longer thy offered good, why else set here?'
This said he paused not, but with vent'rous arm
65 He plucked, he tasted; me damp horror chilled
At such bold words vouched with° a deed so bold: backed by
But he thus overjoyed, 'O fruit divine,
Sweet of thyself, but much more sweet thus cropped,
Forbidden here, it seems, as only fit
70 For gods, yet able to make gods of men:
And why not gods of men, since good, the more
Communicated, more abundant grows,
The author not impaired,° but honored more?   injured, diminished
Here, happy creature, fair angelic Eve,
75 Partake thou also; happy though thou art,
Happier thou may'st be, worthier canst not be:
Taste this, and be henceforth among the gods
Thyself a goddess, not to earth confined,

4. I.e., does envy or some other barrier ("reserve") forbid your being tasted?

But sometimes in the air, as we, sometimes
80 Ascend to Heav'n, by merit thine, and see
What life the gods live there, and such live thou.'
So saying, he drew nigh, and to me held,
Even to my mouth of that same fruit held part
Which he had plucked; the pleasant savory smell
85 So quickened appetite, that I, me thought,
Could not but taste. Forthwith up to the clouds
With him I flew, and underneath beheld
The earth outstretched immense, a prospect wide
And various: wond'ring at my flight and change
90 To this high exaltation: suddenly
My guide was gone, and I, methought, sunk down,
And fell asleep; but O how glad I waked
To find this but a dream!" Thus Eve her night
Related, and thus Adam answered sad.°   gravely, soberly
95   "Best image of myself and dearer half,
The trouble of thy thoughts this night in sleep
Affects me equally; nor can I like
This uncouth° dream, of evil sprung I fear;   strange, unpleasant
Yet evil whence? in thee can harbor none,
100 Created pure. But know that in the soul
Are many lesser faculties[5] that serve
Reason as chief; among these fancy next
Her office holds; of all external things,
Which the five watchful senses represent,
105 She forms imaginations,° aery shapes,   images
Which reason joining or disjoining, frames
All what we affirm or what deny, and call
Our knowledge or opinion; then retires
Into her private cell when nature rests.
110 Oft in her absence mimic fancy wakes
To imitate her; but misjoining shapes,
Wild work produces oft, and most in dreams,
Ill matching words and deeds long past or late.
Some such resemblances methinks I find
115 Of our last evening's talk in this thy dream,[6]
But with addition strange; yet be not sad.
Evil into the mind of god[7] or man
May come and go, so unapproved,[8] and leave
No spot or blame behind: which gives me hope
120 That what in sleep thou didst abhor to dream,
Waking thou never wilt consent to do.
Be not disheartened then, nor cloud those looks
That wont to be more cheerful and serene
Than when fair morning first smiles on the world,
125 And let us to our fresh employments rise

5. Adam's explanation of the dream (lines 100–113) summarizes the orthodox faculty psychology and dream theory of Milton's time—one among many kinds of knowledge with which unfallen man was endowed.

6. Adam recalls his own words in 4.411–39.

7. Probably "angel" as elsewhere, but perhaps God, whose omniscience must encompass knowledge of evil as well as good.

8. If not approved of, or not acted on (put to the proof).

Among the groves, the fountains, and the flow'rs
That open now their choicest bosomed smells
Reserved from night, and kept for thee in store."
    So cheered he his fair spouse, and she was cheered,
130 But silently a gentle tear let fall
From either eye, and wiped them with her hair;
Two other precious drops that ready stood,
Each in their crystal sluice, he ere they fell
Kissed as the gracious signs of sweet remorse
135 And pious° awe, that feared to have offended.   dutiful

Summary   Before going to work at their rural tasks, Adam and Eve recite their spontaneous morning prayers. God, seeing and pitying their unprotected innocence, dispatches Raphael to warn them of approaching dangers. The affable archangel enters the bower just about noontime and is promptly invited to join the midday meal, an invitation that he gladly accepts.

[A VISIT WITH THE ANGEL. THE SCALE OF NATURE]

    * * * So to the sylvan lodge
They came, that like Pomona's⁹ arbor smiled
With flow'rets decked° and fragrant smells; but Eve   covered
380 Undecked, save with herself more lovely fair
Than wood-nymph, or the fairest goddess feigned
Of three that in Mount Ida naked strove,¹
Stood to entertain her guest from Heav'n; no veil
She needed, virtue-proof,° no thought infirm   armored in virtue
385 Altered her cheek. On whom the Angel "Hail"
Bestowed, the holy salutation used
Long after to blest Mary, second Eve.²
    "Hail mother of mankind, whose fruitful womb
Shall fill the world more numerous with thy sons
390 Than with these various fruits the trees of God
Have heaped this table." Raised of grassy turf
Their table was, and mossy seats had round,
And on her ample square from side to side
All autumn piled, though spring and autumn here
395 Danced hand in hand. A while discourse they hold;
No fear lest dinner cool; when thus began
Our author:° "Heav'nly stranger, please to taste   forefather
These bounties which our Nourisher, from whom
All perfect good unmeasured out, descends,
400 To us for food and for delight hath caused

9. The Roman goddess of fruit trees.
1. On Mount Ida, Venus, Juno, and Minerva "strove" naked for the title of the most beautiful; Paris awarded the prize (the apple of discord) to Venus, which led to the rape of Helen and the Tro-

jan War.
2. Cf. the angel's words to Mary announcing that she would bear a son, Jesus (Luke 1.28): "Hail, thou that art highly favored, the Lord is with thee: blessed art thou among women."

The earth to yield; unsavory food perhaps
To spiritual natures; only this I know,
That one Celestial Father gives to all."
        To whom the angel: "Therefore what he gives
405 (Whose praise be ever sung) to man in part
Spiritual, may of° purest Spirits be found   by
No ingrateful food: and food alike those pure
Intelligential substances require³
As doth your rational; and both contain
410 Within them every lower faculty
Of sense, whereby they hear, see, smell, touch, taste,
Tasting concoct, digest, assimilate,⁴
And corporeal to incorporeal turn.
For know, whatever was created, needs
415 To be sustained and fed; of elements
The grosser feeds the purer, earth the sea,
Earth and the sea feed air, the air those fires
Ethereal, and as lowest first the moon;
Whence in her visage round those spots, unpurged
420 Vapors not yet into her substance turned.⁵
Nor doth the moon no nourishment exhale
From her moist continent to higher orbs.⁶
The sun that light imparts to all, receives
From all his alimental° recompense   nourishing
425 In humid exhalations, and at even
Sups with the ocean:⁷ though in Heav'n the trees
Of life ambrosial fruitage bear, and vines
Yield nectar,⁸ though from off the boughs each morn
We brush mellifluous° dews, and find the ground   honey-flowing
430 Covered with pearly grain; yet God hath here
Varied his bounty so with new delights,
As may compare with Heaven; and to taste
Think not I shall be nice."° So down they sat,   fastidious, finicky
And to their viands fell, nor seemingly°   in show
435 The angel, nor in mist, the common gloss°   explanation
Of theologians, but with keen dispatch
Of real hunger, and concoctive° heat   digestive
To transubstantiate;⁹ what redounds, transpires
Through Spirits with ease; nor wonder, if by fire
440 Of sooty coal the empiric° alchemist   experimental

3. Milton's angels ("intelligential substances") require real food, even as "rational" men do (see below, lines 430–38). As a monist (believer that all creation is of one matter), Milton denied the more common (dualistic) idea that angels are pure spirit, holding instead that they are of a very highly refined material substance.
4. Three stages in digestion.
5. Here Raphael describes lunar spots as still-undigested vapors (in keeping with his exposition of the universal need of nourishment); in 1.287–91 he referred to moonspots in Galileo's terms, as landscape features.
6. A double negative: the moon does exhale such nourishment to other planets.

7. Milton explains evaporation as the sun dining off moisture exhaled from the oceans.
8. Ambrosia is the food and nectar the drink of the classical gods; Milton adds "pearly grain" (line 430), like the manna showered on the Israelites in the desert (Exodus 16.14).
9. In common theological use, transubstantiation is the Roman Catholic doctrine that the bread and wine of the eucharist become the body and blood of Christ. Milton vigorously denied that doctrine, but he describes the angels' transforming of earthly food into their more highly refined spiritual substance as a true transubstantiation. The excess ("what redounds") is exhaled ("transpires") through angelic pores.

Can turn, or holds it possible to turn
Metals of drossiest ore to perfect gold
As from the mine. Meanwhile at table Eve
Ministered naked, and their flowing cups
445 With pleasant liquors crowned.° O innocence   *filled to the brim*
Deserving Paradise! if ever, then,
Then had the Sons of God excuse t' have been
Enamored at that sight,[1] but in those hearts
Love unlibidinous° reigned, nor jealousy   *without lust*
450 Was understood, the injured lover's hell.
    Thus when with meats and drinks they had sufficed,
Not burdened nature, sudden mind arose
In Adam, not to let th' occasion pass
Given him by this great conference to know
455 Of things above his world, and of their being
Who dwell in Heav'n, whose excellence he saw
Transcend his own so far, whose radiant forms
Divine effulgence,° whose high power so far   *shining forth*
Exceeded human, and his wary speech
460 Thus to th' empyreal minister he framed:
    "Inhabitant with God, now know I well
Thy favor, in this honor done to man,
Under whose lowly roof thou hast vouchsafed
To enter and these earthly fruits to taste,
465 Food not of angels, yet accepted so,
As that more willingly thou couldst not seem
At Heav'n's high feasts t' have fed: yet what compare?"
    To whom the wingèd Hierarch replied:
"O Adam, one Almighty is, from whom
470 All things proceed, and up to him return,
If not depraved from good, created all
Such to perfection, one first matter all,[2]
Endued with various forms, various degrees
Of substance, and in things that live, of life;
475 But more refined, more spiritous, and pure,
As nearer to him placed or nearer tending
Each in their several active spheres assigned,
Till body up to spirit work, in bounds
Proportioned to each kind.[3] So from the root
480 Springs lighter the green stalk, from thence the leaves
More airy, last the bright consummate flow'r
Spirits odórous breathes:[4] flow'rs and their fruit

1. Genesis 6.2 tells of the marriage of the daughters of men with the sons of God, usually identified as sons of Seth, but a patristic tradition (alluded to here) identifies them as angels.
2. Milton held that the universe was created out of Chaos, not out of nothing: the primal matter of Chaos had its origin in God, who subsequently created all things from that matter (see 7.168–73, 210–42). This materialist "monism" denies sharp distinctions between angels and men, spirit and matter: all beings are of one substance, of varying degrees of refinement and life.
3. Milton's version of the chain of being qualifies

natural hierarchy by allowing for movement up or down; beings may become increasingly "spiritual" or increasingly gross (as the rebel angels do), depending on their moral choices—"nearer tending."
4. The plant figure—root, stalk, leaves, flowers, and fruit—provides an illustration of the dynamism of being in the universe and further explains why Raphael can eat the fruit. Such food is then transformed (next lines) into various orders of "spirits"—"vital," "animal," and "intellectual" (fluids in the blood that sustain life, sensation, motion, and finally intellect and its functions, "fancy,"

Man's nourishment, by gradual scale sublimed°   *purified*
To vital spirits aspire, to animal,
485 To intellectual, give both life and sense,
Fancy° and understanding, whence the soul   *imagination*
Reason receives, and reason is her being,
Discursive, or intuitive;⁵   *discourse*
Is oftest yours, the latter most is ours,
490 Differing but in degree, of kind the same.
Wonder not then, what God for you saw good
If I refuse not, but convert, as you,
To proper° substance; time may come when men   *our own*
With angels may participate, and find
495 No inconvenient diet, nor too light fare:
And from these corporal nutriments perhaps
Your bodies may at last turn all to spirit,
Improved by tract° of time, and winged ascend   *passage*
Ethereal as we, or may at choice
500 Here or in heav'nly paradises dwell;
If ye be found obedient, and retain
Unalterably firm his love entire
Whose progeny you are. Meanwhile enjoy
Your fill what happiness this happy state
505 Can comprehend, incapable° of more."   *unable to contain*
    To whom the patriarch of mankind replied:
"O favorable Spirit, propitious guest,
Well hast thou taught the way that might direct
Our knowledge, and the scale of nature set
510 From center to circumference, whereon
In contemplation of created things
By steps we may ascend to God. * * *

Summary   After this mingled explanation and warning, Raphael, by way of emphasizing the danger that threatens Adam and Eve, enters upon the story of Satan's revolt and fall. Satan, pretending that God's exaltation of the Son was an offense to angelic dignity, persuaded the angels under his command—a third of the heavenly host—to go off and set up a camp in the north of Heaven. When he revealed his rebellious purpose, however, one of these angels refused to embrace it. The seraph Abdiel, though scorned by Satan and all his legions, denounced the rebellion and returned, heroically alone, to the ranks of God's followers.

Book 6 Summary   Continuing the story of the war in Heaven, Raphael describes the assembling of the armies and a first skirmish in which Satan is both

---

"understanding," and "reason"), indicating that the soul is also material.
5. Traditionally, on the dualist assumption that angels are pure spirit and humans a combination of matter and spirit, angelic intuition (immediate

apprehension of truth) was absolutely distinguished from human "discourse" of reason (arguing from premises to conclusions). Milton, denying that assumption, makes the distinction only relative, a matter of "degree" (line 490).

insulted and wounded by Abdiel. After the first day's battle, the evil angels retire discomfited; but overnight Satan invents cannon, with which, on the second day, the good angels are put to some disorder. In the fury of the fight, however, they pull up mountains by the roots and bury the cannon beneath them; thus the issue remains inconclusive. On the third day, God withdraws all His armies and sends the Son alone into battle; the Son drives His enemies irresistibly over the wall of Heaven, and after falling nine days through Chaos they are swallowed up in Hell.

From Book 7

[THE INVOCATION]

Descend from Heav'n Urania,[1] by that name
If rightly thou art called, whose voice divine
Following, above th' Olympian hill I soar,
Above the flight of Pegasean wing.[2]
5   The meaning, not the name I call: for thou
Nor of the muses nine, nor on the top
Of old Olympus dwell'st, but heav'nly born
Before the hills appeared, or fountain flowed,
Thou with eternal Wisdom[3] didst converse,°   associate
10 Wisdom thy sister, and with her didst play
In presence of th' Almighty Father, pleased
With thy celestial song. Up led by thee
Into the Heav'n of Heav'ns I have presumed,
An earthly guest, and drawn empyreal air,
15 Thy temp'ring;° with like safety guided down   made suitable by thee
Return me to my native element:
Lest from this flying steed unreined (as once
Bellerophon,[4] though from a lower clime)°   region
Dismounted, on th' Aleian field I fall
20 Erroneous° there to wander and forlorn.   straying
Half yet remains unsung, but narrower bound
Within the visible diurnal sphere;[5]
Standing on earth, not rapt° above the pole,   transported, enraptured
More safe I sing with mortal voice, unchanged
25 To hoarse or mute, though fall'n on evil days,
On evil days though fall'n on evil tongues;
In darkness, and with dangers compassed round,[6]

1. Urania, the Greek Muse of Astronomy, had been made into the Muse of Christian Poetry by DuBartas and other religious poets. Milton, however, constructs another derivation for her (line 5ff.). Milton begins Book 7 with a third Proem (lines 1–39).
2. Pegasus, the flying horse of inspired poetry, suggests (in connection with Bellerophon, line 18) Milton's sense of perilous audacity in writing this poem.
3. In Proverbs 8.24–31 Wisdom tells of her activities before the Creation: "Then I was by him [God], as one brought up with him; and I was daily his delight, rejoicing always before him." Milton describes "eternal Wisdom" as a "daughter" of God (personification of his wisdom), and devises a myth

in which the Muse of Divine Poetry ("celestial song," line 12) is Wisdom's "sister"—also, thereby, originating from God.
4. Bellerophon incurred the gods' anger when he tried to fly to heaven upon Pegasus; Zeus sent an insect to sting the horse, and Bellerophon fell down to the "Aleian field" (plain of error), where he wandered alone and blind until his death.
5. The universe, which appears to rotate daily.
6. After the Restoration of Charles II (May 1660) and until the passage of the Act of Oblivion (August 1660), Milton was in danger of death and dismemberment (like Orpheus, lines 34–35); several of his republican colleagues were hanged, drawn, and quartered for their part in the revolution and regicide.

And solitude; yet not alone, while thou
Visit'st my slumbers nightly, or when morn
30 Purples the east: still govern thou my song,
Urania, and fit audience find, though few.
But drive far off the barbarous dissonance
Of Bacchus and his revelers,[7] the race
Of that wild rout that tore the Thracian bard
35 In Rhodope, where woods and rocks had ears
To rapture, till the savage clamor drowned
Both harp and voice; nor could the Muse[8] defend
Her son. So fail not thou, who thee implores:
For thou art heav'nly, she an empty dream.

Summary   At Adam's request, Raphael continues his narration and describes
how God, to replace the fallen angels, created the world, its creatures, and finally
man, in the course of six days; the story of the creation concludes, on the seventh
day, with a chorus of thanksgiving by the angels.

From Book 8

Summary   Adam, to prolong his visit with Raphael, asks why so many and such
splendid stars seem to be at the service of the earth, which appears smaller and less
noble than they. At this point Eve discreetly takes her leave. Replying to Adam's
question, Raphael proposes various astronomical possibilities, but gives no conclusive
answer, advising Adam to concern himself with matters closer to home. The angel,
on the other hand, is much interested to hear the story, which Adam proposes to tell,
of his own creation.

[ADAM DESCRIBES HIS OWN CREATION AND THAT OF EVE; HAVING
REPEATED HIS WARNING, THE ANGEL DEPARTS]

So spake the godlike Power, and thus our sire:
250 "For man to tell how human life began
Is hard; for who himself beginning knew?[1]
Desire with thee still longer to converse
Induced me. As new-waked from soundest sleep
Soft on the flow'ry herb I found me laid
255 In balmy sweat, which with his beams the sun
Soon dried, and on the reeking° moisture fed.   *steaming*
Straight toward heav'n my wond'ring eyes I turned,
And gazed a while the ample sky, till raised
By quick instinctive motion up I sprung

7. The music of the "Thracian Bard" Orpheus,
type of the poet, charmed even "woods and rocks,"
but his song was drowned out by the Bacchantes,
a "wild rout" of screaming women who murdered
and dismembered him and threw his body parts
into the Hebrus River, which rises in the "Rhodope" mountains. Milton fears that a similar "bar-

barous dissonance" unleashed by the Restoration
will drown out his voice and threaten his life.
8. Orpheus's mother is Calliope, Muse of Epic
Poetry.
1. Compare Satan's inability to remember his origins (5.859–63) from which he infers self-creation,
whereas Adam infers a Maker (278).

260 As thitherward endeavoring, and upright
    Stood on my feet; about me round I saw
    Hill, dale, and shady woods, and sunny plains,
    And liquid lapse° of murmuring streams; by these,   *flow*
    Creatures that lived, and moved, and walked, or flew,
265 Birds on the branches warbling; all things smiled,
    With fragrance and with joy my heart o'erflowed.
    Myself I then perused, and limb by limb
    Surveyed, and sometimes went,° and sometimes ran   *walked*
    With supple joints, as lively vigor led:
270 But who I was, or where, or from what cause,
    Knew not; to speak I tried, and forthwith spake,
    My tongue obeyed and readily could name
    Whate'er I saw.² 'Thou sun,' said I, 'fair light,
    And thou enlightened earth, so fresh and gay,
275 Ye hills and dales, ye rivers, woods, and plains,
    And ye that live and move, fair creatures, tell,
    Tell, if ye saw, how came I thus, how here?
    Not of myself; by some great Maker then,
    In goodness and in power preeminent;
280 Tell me, how may I know him, how adore,
    From whom I have that thus I move and live,
    And feel that I am happier than I know.'
    While thus I called, and strayed I knew not whither,
    From where I first drew air, and first beheld
285 This happy light, when answer none returned,
    On a green shady bank profuse of flow'rs
    Pensive I sat me down; there gentle sleep
    First found me, and with soft oppression seized
    My drowsèd sense, untroubled, though I thought
290 I then was passing to my former state
    Insensible, and forthwith to dissolve:
    When suddenly stood at my head a dream,
    Whose inward apparition gently moved
    My fancy to believe I yet had being,
295 And lived: one came, methought, of shape divine,
    And said, 'Thy mansion° wants° thee, Adam, rise,   *habitation/lacks*
    First man, of men innumerable ordained
    First father, called by thee I come thy guide
    To the garden of bliss, thy seat° prepared.'   *residence*
300 So saying, by the hand he took me raised,
    And over fields and waters, as in air
    Smooth sliding without step, last led me up
    A woody mountain whose high top was plain,
    A circuit wide, enclosed, with goodliest trees
305 Planted, with walks, and bowers, that what I saw
    Of earth before scarce pleasant seemed. Each tree
    Load'n with fairest fruit, that hung to the eye
    Tempting, stirred in me sudden appetite
    To pluck and eat; whereat I waked, and found

---

2. Adam's ability to name the creatures was said to signify his intuitive understanding of their natures.

310 Before mine eyes all real, as the dream
Had lively° shadowed: here had new begun   *vividly*
My wand'ring, had not he who was my guide
Up hither, from among the trees appeared,
Presence Divine. Rejoicing, but with awe
315 In adoration at his feet I fell
Submiss:° he reared me, and 'Whom thou sought'st I am,'   *submissive*
Said mildly, 'Author of all this thou seest
Above, or round about thee or beneath.
This paradise I give thee, count it thine
320 To till and keep,° and of the fruit to eat: *care for*
Of every tree that in the garden grows
Eat freely with glad heart; fear here no dearth:
But of the tree whose operation° brings   *action*
Knowledge of good and ill, which I have set
325 The pledge of thy obedience and thy faith,
Amid the garden by the Tree of Life,
Remember what I warn thee, shun to taste,
And shun the bitter consequence: for know,
The day thou eat'st thereof, my sole command
330 Transgressed, inevitably thou shalt die;
From that day mortal, and this happy state
Shalt lose, expelled from hence into a world
Of woe and sorrow.'³ Sternly he pronounced
The rigid interdiction,° which resounds   *prohibition*
335 Yet dreadful in mine ear, though in my choice
Not to incur; but soon his clear aspéct
Returned and gracious purpose° thus renewed: *speech*
'Not only these fair bounds, but all the earth
To thee and to thy race I give; as lords
340 Possess it, and all things that therein live,
Or live in sea, or air, beast, fish, and fowl.
In sign whereof each bird and beast behold
After their kinds; I bring them to receive
From thee their names, and pay thee fealty
345 With low subjection; understand the same
Of fish within their wat'ry residence,
Not hither summoned, since they cannot change
Their element to draw the thinner air.'
As thus he spake, each bird and beast behold
350 Approaching two and two, these° cow'ring low   *the beasts*
With blandishment,° each bird stooped on his wing.   *flattering gesture*
I named them, as they passed, and understood
Their nature, with such knowledge God endued
My sudden apprehension:⁴ but in these
355 I found not what methought I wanted still;
And to the heav'nly Vision thus presumed:
    " 'O by what name, for thou above all these,

---

3. Compare God's commands to Adam (Genesis
1.28–39, 2.16–17) with Milton's elaboration here.
4. Adam had already begun naming the sun and
features of the earth (lines 72–73), but here he
names (and thereby shows he understands) all living creatures.

Above mankind, or aught than mankind higher,
Surpassest far my naming,[5] how may I
360 Adore thee, Author of this universe,
And all this good to man, for whose well-being
So amply, and with hands so liberal
Thou hast provided all things: but with me
I see not who partakes. In solitude
365 What happiness, who can enjoy alone,
Or all enjoying, what contentment find?'
Thus I presumptuous; and the Vision bright,
As with a smile more brightened, thus replied:
    " 'What call'st thou solitude? Is not the earth
370 With various living creatures, and the air
Replenished,° and all these at thy command   *fully stocked*
To come and play before thee? Know'st thou not
Their language and their ways? They also know,°   *have understanding*
And reason not contemptibly; with these
375 Find pastime, and bear rule; thy realm is large.'
So spake the Universal Lord, and seemed
So ordering. I with leave of speech implored,
And humble deprecation thus replied:
    " 'Let not my words offend thee, Heav'nly Power,
380 My Maker, be propitious while I speak.
Hast thou not made me here thy substitute,
And these inferior far beneath me set?
Among unequals what society
Can sort,° what harmony or true delight?   *agree*
385 Which must be mutual, in proportion due
Giv'n and received; but in disparity
The one intense, the other still remiss[6]
Cannot well suit with either, but soon prove
Tedious alike. Of fellowship I speak
390 Such as I seek, fit to participate°   *partake of*
All rational delight, wherein the brute
Cannot be human consort; they rejoice
Each with their kind, lion with lioness;
So fitly them in pairs thou hast combined;
395 Much less can bird with beast, or fish with fowl
So well converse,° nor with the ox the ape;   *associate*
Worse then can man with beast, and least of all.'
    "Whereto th' Almighty answered, not displeased:
'A nice° and subtle happiness I see   *fastidious*
400 Thou to thyself proposest, in the choice
Of thy associates, Adam, and wilt taste
No pleasure, though in pleasure, solitary.
What think'st thou then of me, and this my state?
Seem I to thee sufficiently possessed

---

5. Adam reasons, as the Scholastics did, from the creatures to the fact of a Creator, but he cannot name (and so indicates that he cannot understand) God, except as God reveals himself.

6. As with poorly matched musical instruments, Adam's string is too taut ("intense") and the animals' is too slack ("remiss") to be in harmony ("suit").

405　Of happiness, or not? who am alone
　　From all eternity, for none I know
　　Second to me or like, equal much less.
　　How have I then with whom to hold converse
　　Save with the creatures which I made, and those
410　To me inferior, infinite descents
　　Beneath what other creatures are to thee?'
　　　"He ceased, I lowly answered: 'To attain
　　The height and depth of thy eternal ways
　　All human thoughts come short, Supreme of things;
415　Thou in thyself art perfect, and in thee
　　Is no deficience found; not so is man,
　　But in degree, the cause of his desire
　　By conversation with his like to help,
　　Or solace his defects.[7] No need that thou
420　Shouldst propagate, already infinite;
　　And through all numbers absolute, though One;[8]
　　But man by number is to manifest
　　His single imperfection, and beget
　　Like of his like, his image multiplied,
425　In unity defective, which requires
　　Collateral° love, and dearest amity.　　　　　　　　　　*mutual*
　　Thou in thy secrecy° although alone,　　　　　　　　　*seclusion*
　　Best with thyself accompanied, seek'st not
　　Social communication, yet so pleased,
430　Canst raise thy creature to what height thou wilt
　　Of union or communion, deified;
　　I by conversing cannot these erect
　　From prone, nor in their ways complacence° find.'　　*satisfaction*
　　Thus I emboldened spake, and freedom used
435　Permissive,° and acceptance found, which gained　　*permitted*
　　This answer from the gracious Voice Divine:
　　　"'Thus far to try thee, Adam, I was pleased,
　　And find thee knowing not of beasts alone,
　　Which thou hast rightly named, but of thyself,
440　Expressing well the spirit within thee free,
　　My image, not imparted to the brute,
　　Whose fellowship therefore unmeet for thee
　　Good reason was thou freely shouldst dislike,
　　And be so minded still. I, ere thou spak'st,
445　Knew it not good for man to be alone,
　　And no such company as then thou saw'st
　　Intended thee, for trial only brought,
　　To see how thou couldst judge of fit and meet:
　　What next I bring shall please thee, be assured,
450　Thy likeness, thy fit help, thy other self,
　　Thy wish, exactly to thy heart's desire.'[9]

7. God is absolutely perfect, man only relatively so
("in degree"), and thereby needs companionship
with a fit mate to assuage ("solace") the "defects"
arising from solitariness.
8. God, though One, contains all numbers, but
man has to remedy the "imperfection" of being single (line 423) by procreating and thereby multiplying his single and thereby "defective" image (line
425).
9. Compare the account in Genesis 2.18 with Milton's elaboration.

"He ended, or I heard no more, for now
My earthly by his heav'nly overpowered,
Which it had long stood under,° strained to the height   *been exposed to*
455 In that celestial colloquy sublime,
As with an object that excels° the sense,   *exceeds*
Dazzled and spent, sunk down, and sought repair
Of sleep, which instantly fell on me, called
By nature as in aid, and closed mine eyes.
460 Mine eyes he closed, but open left the cell
Of fancy° my internal sight, by which   *imagination*
Abstract° as in a trance methought I saw,   *withdrawn*
Though sleeping, where I lay, and saw the shape
Still glorious before whom awake I stood;
465 Who stooping opened my left side, and took
From thence a rib, with cordial° spirits warm,   *from the heart*
And life-blood streaming fresh; wide was the wound,
But suddenly with flesh filled up and healed:
The rib he formed and fashioned with his hands;
470 Under his forming hands a creature grew,[1]
Manlike, but different sex, so lovely fair
That what seemed fair in all the world seemed now
Mean, or in her summed up, in her contained
And in her looks, which from that time infused
475 Sweetness into my heart, unfelt before,
And into all things from her air° inspired   *mien, look*
The spirit of love and amorous delight.
She disappeared, and left me dark, I waked
To find her, or for ever to deplore
480 Her loss, and other pleasures all abjure:
When out of hope, behold her, not far off,
Such as I saw her in my dream, adorned
With what all earth or heaven could bestow
To make her amiable:° on she came,   *lovely*
485 Led by her heav'nly Maker, though unseen,[2]
And guided by his voice, nor uninformed
Of nuptial sanctity and marriage rites:
Grace was in all her steps, Heav'n in her eye,
In every gesture dignity and love.
490 I overjoyed could not forbear aloud:
    " 'This turn hath made amends; thou hast fulfilled
Thy words, Creator bounteous and benign,
Giver of all things fair, but fairest this
Of all thy gifts, nor enviest.° I now see   *give reluctantly*
495 Bone of my bone, flesh of my flesh, my self
Before me; woman is her name, of man
Extracted; for this cause he shall forgo
Father and mother, and to his wife adhere;
And they shall be one flesh, one heart, one soul.'[3]
500   "She heard me thus, and though divinely brought,

1. Compare the *Creation of Eve* by the Italian
painter Paolo Veronese (1528–1588).
2. Compare Eve's version of these events (4.440–

91).
3. Compare the account in Genesis 2.23–24.

Yet innocence and virgin modesty,
Her virtue and the conscience°   *consciousness*
That would be wooed, and not unsought be won,
Not obvious,° not obtrusive,° but retired,   *bold/forward*
505 The more desirable, or to say all,
Nature herself, though pure of sinful thought,
Wrought in her so that, seeing me, she turned;
I followed her, she what was honor knew,
And with obsequious° majesty approved   *compliant*
510 My pleaded reason. To the nuptial bow'r
I led her blushing like the morn: all heav'n,
And happy constellations on that hour
Shed their selectest influence; the earth
Gave sign of gratulation,° and each hill;   *rejoicing, congratulation*
515 Joyous the birds; fresh gales and gentle airs[4]
Whispered it to the woods, and from their wings
Flung rose, flung odors from the spicy shrub,
Disporting,° till the amorous bird of night°   *frolicking/nightingale*
Sung spousal, and bid haste the evening star°   *Venus*
520 On his hill top, to light the bridal lamp.
      Thus I have told thee all my state, and brought
My story to the sum of earthly bliss
Which I enjoy, and must confess to find
In all things else delight indeed, but such
525 As used or not, works in the mind no change,
Nor vehement desire, these delicacies
I mean of taste, sight, smell, herbs, fruits, and flow'rs,
Walks, and the melody of birds; but here
Far otherwise, transported° I behold,   *enraptured*
530 Transported touch; here passion first I felt,
Commotion° strange, in all enjoyments else   *mental agitation*
Superior and unmoved, here only weak
Against the charm of beauty's powerful glance.
Or° nature failed in me, and left some part   *either*
535 Not proof enough such object to sustain,°   *withstand*
Or from my side subducting,° took perhaps   *subtracting*
More than enough; at least on her bestowed
Too much of ornament, in outward show
Elaborate, of inward less exact.
540 For well I understand in the prime end
Of nature her th' inferior, in the mind
And inward faculties, which most excel,
In outward also her resembling less
His image who made both, and less expressing
545 The character of that dominion giv'n
O'er other creatures; yet when I approach
Her loveliness, so absolute° she seems   *perfect, independent*
And in herself complete, so well to know
Her own, that what she wills to do or say,
550 Seems wisest, virtuousest, discreetest, best;
All higher knowledge in her presence falls

4. Both breezes and melodies. "Gales": winds.

Degraded, wisdom in discourse with her
Loses discount'nanced,° and like folly shows;   *disconcerted, abashed*
Authority and reason on her wait,
555   As one intended first, not after made
Occasionally;° and to consúmmate all,   *incidentally*
Greatness of mind and nobleness their seat
Build in her loveliest, and create an awe
About her, as a guard angelic placed."
560   To whom the angel with contracted brow:
        "Accuse not nature, she hath done her part;
Do thou but thine, and be not diffident°   *mistrustful*
Of wisdom, she deserts thee not, if thou
Dismiss not her, when most thou need'st her nigh,
565   By áttributing overmuch to things
Less excellent, as thou thyself perceiv'st.
For what admir'st thou, what transports thee so,
An outside? Fair no doubt, and worthy well
Thy cherishing, thy honoring, and thy love,
570   Not thy subjection: weigh with her thyself;
Then value: ofttimes nothing profits more
Than self-esteem, grounded on just and right
Well managed; of that skill the more thou know'st,
The more she will acknowledge thee her head,[5]
575   And to realities yield all her shows:
Made so adorn for thy delight the more,
So awful,° that with honor thou may'st love   *awe-inspiring*
Thy mate, who sees when thou art seen least wise.
But if the sense of touch whereby mankind
580   Is propagated seem such dear delight
Beyond all other, think the same vouchsafed
To cattle and each beast; which would not be
To them made common and divulged,° if aught   *imparted generally*
Therein enjoyed were worthy to subdue
585   The soul of man, or passion in him move.
What higher in her society thou find'st
Attractive, human, rational, love still;
In loving thou dost well, in passion not,
Wherein true love consists not; love refines
590   The thoughts, and heart enlarges, hath his seat
In reason, and is judicious, is the scale[6]
By which to heav'nly love thou may'st ascend,
Not sunk in carnal pleasure, for which cause
Among the beasts no mate for thee was found."
595   To whom thus half abashed Adam replied.
"Neither her outside formed so fair, nor aught
In procreation common to all kinds
(Though higher of the genial[7] bed by far,
And with mysterious reverence I deem)

---

5. See 1 Corinthians 11.31: "The head of every man is Christ; and the head of the woman is the man; and the head of Christ is God."
6. The ladder of love, a Neoplatonic concept for the movement from sensual love to higher forms, and ultimately to love of God.

7. Both nuptial and generative. Adam takes respectful issue with the apparent denigration of human sex in Raphael's account of the Neoplatonic ladder, which prompts his question about angelic sex (lines 615–17).

600 So much delights me, as those graceful acts,
Those thousand decencies° that daily flow   *fitting acts*
From all her words and actions, mixed with love
And sweet compliance, which declare unfeigned
Union of mind, or in us both one soul;
605 Harmony to behold in wedded pair
More grateful than harmonious sound to the ear.
Yet these subject not; I to thee disclose
What inward thence I feel, not therefore foiled,°   *overcome*
Who meet with various objects, from the sense
610 Variously representing;⁸ yet still free
Approve the best, and follow what I approve.
To love thou blam'st me not, for love thou say'st
Leads up to Heav'n, is both the way and guide;
Bear with me then, if lawful what I ask;
615 Love not the heav'nly Spirits, and how their love
Express they, by looks only, or do they mix
Irradiance, virtual or immediate° touch?"   *actual*
    To whom the angel with a smile that glowed
Celestial rosy red, love's proper hue,⁹
620 Answered. "Let it suffice thee that thou know'st
Us happy, and without love no happiness.
Whatever pure thou in the body enjoy'st
(And pure thou wert created) we enjoy
In eminence,° and obstacle find none   *surprisingly*
625 Of membrane, joint, or limb, exclusive bars:
Easier than air with air, if Spirits embrace,
Total they mix, union of pure with pure
Desiring; nor restrained conveyance need
As flesh to mix with flesh, or soul with soul.
630 But I can now no more; the parting sun
Beyond the earth's green cape¹ and verdant isles
Hesperian sets, my signal to depart.
Be strong, live happy, and love, but first of all
Him whom to love is to obey, and keep
635 His great command; take heed lest passion sway
Thy judgment to do aught, which else free will
Would not admit;° thine and of all thy sons   *permit*
The weal or woe in thee is placed; beware.
I in thy persevering shall rejoice,
640 And all the blest: stand fast; to stand or fall
Free in thine own arbitrament° it lies.   *determination*
Perfect within, no outward aid require;°   *depend on*
And all temptation to transgress repel."
    So saying, he arose; whom Adam thus
645 Followed with benediction. "Since to part,
Go heavenly guest, ethereal messenger,

---

8. I.e., various objects, variously represented to me by my senses.
9. This is not likely to be an embarrassed blush: red is the color traditionally associated with Seraphim who burn with ardor. Raphael's smile also

glows with friendship for Adam and appreciation of his perceptive inference about angelic love.
1. Cape Verde near Dakar and the islands off that coast are the westernmost ("Hesperian") points of Africa.

Sent from whose sovran goodness I adore.
Gentle to me and affable hath been
Thy condescension, and shall be honored ever
650 With grateful memory: thou to mankind
Be good and friendly still, and oft return."
    So parted they, the angel up to Heav'n
From the thick shade, and Adam to his bow'r.

Book 9

No more of talk where God or angel guest
With man, as with his friend, familiar used
To sit indulgent, and with him partake
Rural repast, permitting him the while
5 Venial° discourse unblamed: I now must change   *pardonable*
Those notes to tragic; foul distrust, and breach
Disloyal on the part of man, revolt,
And disobedience: on the part of Heav'n
Now alienated, distance and distaste,°   *aversion*
10 Anger and just rebuke, and judgment giv'n,
That brought into this world a world of woe,
Sin and her shadow Death, and misery
Death's harbinger: sad task, yet argument
Not less but more heroic than the wrath
15 Of stern Achilles on his foe pursued
Thrice fugitive about Troy wall; or rage
Of Turnus for Lavinia disespoused,
Or Neptune's ire or Juno's, that so long
Perplexed the Greek and Cytherea's son;[1]
20 If answerable° style I can obtain   *fitting*
Of my celestial patroness, who deigns
Her nightly visitation unimplored,[2]
And dictates to me slumb'ring, or inspires
Easy my unpremeditated verse:
25 Since first this subject for heroic song
Pleased me long choosing, and beginning late;
Not sedulous° by nature to indite   *eager*
Wars, hitherto the only argument°   *subject*
Heroic deemed, chief mastery to dissect
30 With long and tedious havoc fabled knights
In battles feigned; the better fortitude
Of patience and heroic martyrdom
Unsung; or to describe races and games,
Or tilting furniture,[3] emblazoned shields,

---

1. In this fourth proem (lines 1–47), after signaling his change from pastoral to tragic mode (lines
1–6), Milton emphasizes tragic elements in several
classical epics: Achilles pursuing Hector three
times around Troy wall before killing him (*Iliad*
22); Turnus fighting Aeneas over the loss of his
betrothed Lavinia and killed by him; Odysseus
("the Greek") and Aeneas ("Cytherea's son," i.e.,
Venus's son) tormented ("perplexed") by Neptune

(Poseidon) and Juno, respectively.
2. Milton does not here invoke the Muse but testifies to her customary nightly visits. Milton's
nephew reports that he often awoke in the morning
with lines of poetry fully formed in his head, ready
to dictate them to an amanuensis.
3. Equipment for jousting; "impresses quaint":
cunningly designed heraldic devices on shields;
"caparisons": ornamental trappings or armor for

35 Impresses quaint, caparisons and steeds;
    Bases and tinsel trappings, gorgeous knights
    At joust and tournament; then marshaled feast
    Served up in hall with sewers,° and seneschals;°   *waiters/stewards*
    The skill of artifice° or office mean,   *mechanic art*
40 Not that which justly gives heroic name
    To person or to poem. Me of these
    Nor skilled nor studious, higher argument
    Remains,[4] sufficient of itself to raise
    That name, unless an age too late, or cold
45 Climate, or years damp my intended wing
    Depressed, and much they may, if all be mine,
    Not hers who brings it nightly to my ear.
        The sun was sunk, and after him the star
    Of Hesperus,[5] whose office is to bring
50 Twilight upon the earth, short arbiter
    'Twixt day and night, and now from end to end
    Night's hemisphere had veiled the horizon round:
    When Satan who late fled[6] before the threats
    Of Gabriel out of Eden, now improved°   *increased*
55 In meditated fraud and malice, bent
    On man's destruction, maugre what might hap
    Of heavier on himself,[7] fearless returned.
    By night he fled, and at midnight returned
    From compassing the earth, cautious of day,
60 Since Uriel regent of the sun descried
    His entrance, and forewarned the Cherubim
    That kept their watch; thence full of anguish driv'n,
    The space of seven continued nights he rode
    With darkness, thrice the equinoctial line°   *equator*
65 He circled, four times crossed the car of Night
    From pole to pole, traversing each colure;[8]
    On the eighth returned, and on the coast averse°   *turned away*
    From entrance on Cherubic watch, by stealth
    Found unsuspected way. There was a place,
70 Now not, though sin, not time, first wrought the change,
    Where Tigris at the foot of Paradise
    Into a gulf shot under ground, till part
    Rose up a fountain by the Tree of Life;
    In with the river sunk, and with it rose
75 Satan involved in rising mist, then sought
    Where to lie hid. Sea he had searched and land
    From Eden over Pontus,[9] and the pool

---

horses; "bases": cloth coverings for horses. After
rejecting the classical epic subjects, Milton here
rejects the familiar topics of romance.
4. For a heroic poem. He proceeds to recap worries he has voiced before: that the times might not
be receptive to such poems ("age too late"), that
the "cold/Climate" of England or his own
advanced age might "damp" (benumb, dampen) his
"intended wing/Depressed" (poetic flights held
down, kept from soaring).
5. Venus, the Evening Star.
6. At the end of Book 4.
7. I.e., despite ("maugre") what might result in

heavier punishments for himself.
8. The colures are two great circles that intersect
at right angles at the poles. By circling the globe
from east to west at the equator and then over the
north and south poles, Satan can remain in darkness, keeping the earth between himself and the
sun. "Car of Night" (line 65): the earth's shadow,
imagined as the chariot of the goddess Night.
9. The Black Sea. Satan's journey (lines 77–82)
takes him from there to the Sea of Azov in Russia
("Maeotis"), beyond the river "Ob" in Siberia,
which flows into the Arctic Ocean, then south to
Antarctica; thence west from "Orontes" (a river in

Maeotis, up beyond the river Ob;
Downward as far Antarctic; and in length
80 West from Orontes to the ocean barred
At Darien, thence to the land where flows
Ganges and Indus: thus the orb he roamed
With narrow search; and with inspection deep
Considered every creature, which of all
85 Most opportune might serve his wiles, and found
The serpent subtlest beast of all the field.[1]
Him after long debate, irresolute°   *undecided*
Of° thoughts revolved, his final sentence° chose   *among / decision*
Fit vessel, fittest imp° of fraud, in whom   *offshoot*
90 To enter, and his dark suggestions hide
From sharpest sight: for in the wily snake,
Whatever sleights° none would suspicious mark,   *artifices*
As from his wit and native subtlety
Proceeding, which in other beasts observed
95 Doubt° might beget of diabolic pow'r   *suspicion*
Active within beyond the sense of brute.
Thus he resolved, but first from inward grief
His bursting passion into plaints thus poured:
        "O earth, how like to Heav'n, if not preferred
100 More justly, seat worthier of gods, as built
With second thoughts, reforming what was old!
For what God after better worse would build?
Terrestrial heav'n, danced round by other heav'ns
That shine, yet bear their bright officious° lamps,   *dutiful*
105 Light above light, for thee alone, as seems,[2]
In thee concent'ring all their precious beams
Of sacred influence: as God in Heav'n
Is center, yet extends to all, so thou
Centring receiv'st from all those orbs; in thee,
110 Not in themselves, all their known virtue appears
Productive in herb, plant, and nobler birth
Of creatures animate with gradual life
Of growth, sense, reason,[3] all summed up in man.
With what delight could I have walked thee round,
115 If I could joy in aught, sweet interchange
Of hill and valley, rivers, woods and plains,
Now land, now sea, and shores with forest crowned,
Rocks, dens, and caves; but I in none of these
Find place or refuge; and the more I see
120 Pleasures about me, so much more I feel
Torment within me, as from the hateful siege°   *conflict*
Of contraries; all good to me becomes
Bane,° and in Heav'n much worse would be my state.   *poison*
But neither here seek I, no nor in Heav'n
125 To dwell, unless by mastering Heav'n's Supreme;

Syria) across the Atlantic to "Darien" (the Isthmus
of Panama), then across the Pacific and Asia to
India where the "Ganges" and "Indus" rivers flow.
1. The serpent is so described in Genesis 3.1.
2. Like Adam (8.15ff.) and Eve (4.657) but not

Raphael (8.114–78), Satan assumes a Ptolemaic
universe centered on the earth and humankind.
3. Graduated in steps ("gradual," line 113) from
vegetable to animal to rational forms (souls); cf.
5.469–90.

Nor hope to be myself less miserable
By what I seek, but others to make such
As I, though thereby worse to me redound:
For only in destroying I find ease
130 To my relentless thoughts; and him[4] destroyed,
Or won to what may work his utter loss,
For whom all this was made, all this will soon
Follow, as to him linked in weal or woe:
In woe then; that destruction wide may range:
135 To me shall be the glory sole among
The infernal Powers, in one day to have marred
What he Almighty styled, six nights and days
Continued making, and who knows how long
Before had been contriving, though perhaps
140 Not longer than since I in one night freed
From servitude inglorious well-nigh half
Th' angelic name, and thinner left the throng
Of his adorers. He to be avenged,
And to repair his numbers thus impaired,
145 Whether such virtue° spent of old now failed   power
More angels to create, if they at least
Are his created, or to spite us more,
Determined to advance into our room
A creature formed of earth, and him endow,
150 Exalted from so base original,°   origin
With heav'nly spoils, our spoils: what he decreed
He effected; man he made, and for him built
Magnificent this world, and earth his seat,
Him lord pronounced, and, O indignity!
155 Subjected to his service angel wings,
And flaming ministers to watch and tend
Their earthy charge: of these the vigilance
I dread, and to elude, thus wrapped in mist
Of midnight vapor glide obscure, and pry
160 In every bush and brake, where hap° may find   luck
The serpent sleeping, in whose mazy folds
To hide me, and the dark intent I bring.
O foul descent![5] that I who erst contended
With gods to sit the highest, am now constrained
165 Into a beast, and mixed with bestial slime,
This essence to incarnate and imbrute,
That to the height of deity aspired;
But what will not ambition and revenge
Descend to? Who aspires must down as low
170 As high he soared, obnoxious° first or last   exposed
To basest things. Revenge, at first though sweet,
Bitter ere long back on itself recoils;
Let it; I reck° not, so it light well aimed,   care
Since higher I fall short, on him who next

---

4. Adam. "This" (line 132): the universe.
5. Satan "imbruting" himself in a snake parodies,

grotesquely, the Son's incarnation in human form,
as Christ.

175 Provokes my envy, this new favorite
Of Heav'n, this man of clay, son of despite,
Whom us the more to spite his Maker raised
From dust: spite then with spite is best repaid."
So saying, through each thicket dank or dry,
180 Like a black mist low creeping, he held on
His midnight search, where soonest he might find
The serpent: him fast sleeping soon he found
In labyrinth of many a round self-rolled,
His head the midst, well stored with subtle wiles:
185 Not yet in horrid shade or dismal den,
Nor nocent° yet, but on the grassy herb   harmful, guilty
Fearless unfeared he slept: in at his mouth
The Devil entered, and his brutal° sense,   animal
In heart or head, possessing soon inspired
190 With act intelligential: but his sleep
Disturbed not, waiting close° th' approach of morn.   hidden
Now whenas sacred light began to dawn
In Eden on the humid flow'rs, that breathed
Their morning incense, when all things that breathe,
195 From th' earth's great altar send up silent praise
To the Creator, and his nostrils fill
With grateful° smell, forth came the human pair   pleasing
And joined their vocal worship to the choir
Of creatures wanting° voice; that done, partake   lacking
200 The season, prime° for sweetest scents and airs: best
Then cómmune how that day they best may ply
Their growing work; for much their work outgrew
The hands' dispatch of two gard'ning so wide.
And Eve first to her husband thus began:
205 "Adam, well may we labor still° to dress   continually
This garden, still to tend plant, herb and flow'r,
Our pleasant task enjoined, but till more hands
Aid us, the work under our labor grows,
Luxurious° by restraint; what we by day   luxuriant
210 Lop overgrown, or prune, or prop, or bind,
One night or two with wanton growth derides,
Tending to wild. Thou therefore now advise
Or hear what to my mind first thoughts present,
Let us divide our labors, thou where choice
215 Leads thee, or where most needs, whether to wind
The woodbine round this arbor, or direct
The clasping ivy where to climb, while I
In yonder spring° of roses intermixed   growth
With myrtle, find what to redress° till noon: set upright
220 For while so near each other thus all day
Our task we choose, what wonder if so near
Looks intervene and smiles, or object new
Casual discourse draw on, which intermits
Our day's work brought to little, though begun
225 Early, and th' hour of supper comes unearned."
To whom mild answer Adam thus returned:

"Sole Eve, associate sole,[6] to me beyond
Compare above all living creatures dear,
Well hast thou motioned,° well thy thoughts employed   *proposed*
230 How we might best fulfill the work which here
God hath assigned us, nor of me shalt pass
Unpraised: for nothing lovelier can be found
In woman, than to study household good,
And good works in her husband to promote.[7]
235 Yet not so strictly hath our Lord imposed
Labor, as to debar us when we need
Refreshment, whether food, or talk between,
Food of the mind, or this sweet intercourse
Of looks and smiles, for smiles from reason flow,
240 To brute denied, and are of love the food,
Love not the lowest end of human life.
For not to irksome toil, but to delight
He made us, and delight to reason joined.
These paths and bowers doubt not but our joint hands
245 Will keep from wilderness with ease, as wide
As we need walk, till younger hands ere long
Assist us: but if much convérse perhaps
Thee satiate, to short absence I could yield.
For solitude sometimes is best society,
250 And short retirement urges sweet return.
But other doubt possesses me, lest harm
Befall thee severed from me; for thou know'st
What hath been warned us, what malicious foe
Envying our happiness, and of his own
255 Despairing, seeks to work us woe and shame
By sly assault; and somewhere nigh at hand
Watches, no doubt, with greedy hope to find
His wish and best advantage, us asunder,
Hopeless to circumvent us joined, where each
260 To other speedy aid might lend at need;
Whether his first design be to withdraw
Our fealty from God, or to disturb
Conjugal love, than which perhaps no bliss
Enjoyed by us excites his envy more;
265 Or° this, or worse, leave not the faithful side   *whether*
That gave thee being, still shades thee and protects.
The wife, where danger or dishonor lurks,
Safest and seemliest by her husband stays,
Who guards her, or with her the worst endures."
270   To whom the virgin[8] majesty of Eve,
As one who loves, and some unkindness meets,
With sweet austere composure thus replied.
    "Offspring of Heav'n and earth, and all earth's lord,
That such an enemy we have, who seeks

---

6. Adam puns on "sole" as "unrivaled" and "only" (cf. 4.411).
7. Adam's compliments owe something to the praises of a good wife in Proverbs 31.

8. The term here means unspotted or peerless; Milton has insisted at the end of Books 4 and 8 that Adam and Eve have sex.

275 Our ruin, both by thee informed I learn,
     And from the parting angel overheard
     As in a shady nook I stood behind,
     Just then returned at shut of evening flow'rs.[9]
     But that thou shouldst my firmness therefore doubt
280 To God or thee, because we have a foe
     May tempt it, I expected not to hear.
     His violence thou fear'st not, being such,
     As we, not capable of death or pain,
     Can either not receive, or can repel.
285 His fraud is then thy fear, which plain infers
     Thy equal fear that my firm faith and love
     Can by his fraud be shaken or seduced;
     Thoughts, which how found they harbor in thy breast,
     Adam, misthought of° her to thee so dear?"   *misapplied to*
290   To whom with healing words Adam replied.
     "Daughter of God and man, immortal Eve,
     For such thou art, from sin and blame entire:°   *untouched*
     Not diffident° of thee do I dissuade   *distrustful*
     Thy absence from my sight, but to avoid
295 Th' attempt itself, intended by our foe.
     For he who tempts, though in vain, at least asperses°   *bespatters*
     The tempted with dishonor foul, supposed
     Not incorruptible of faith, not proof
     Against temptation: thou thyself with scorn
300 And anger wouldst resent the offered wrong,
     Though ineffectual found; misdeem not then,
     If such affront I labor to avert
     From thee alone, which on us both at once
     The enemy, though bold, will hardly dare,
305 Or daring, first on me th' assault shall light.
     Nor thou his malice and false guile contemn;
     Subtle he needs must be, who could seduce
     Angels, nor think superfluous others' aid.
     I from the influence of thy looks receive
310 Access° in every virtue, in thy sight   *increase*
     More wise, more watchful, stronger, if need were
     Of outward strength; while shame, thou looking on,
     Shame to be overcome or overreached°   *outwitted*
     Would utmost vigor raise, and raised unite.
315 Why shouldst not thou like sense within thee feel
     When I am present, and thy trial choose
     With me, best witness of thy virtue tried."
        So spake domestic Adam in his care
     And matrimonial love; but Eve, who thought
320 Less° attribúted to her faith sincere,   *too little*
     Thus her reply with accent sweet renewed.
        "If this be our condition, thus to dwell

9. Somewhat confusing, since Eve heard the full story of the war in Heaven and Raphael's earlier warnings; Raphael's parting words (8.630–43), overheard by Eve, do not mention Satan but warn Adam to resist his passion for Eve. He does, however, reiterate the charge to obey the "great command" and repel temptation.

In narrow circuit straitened° by a foe,　　　　　　*confined*
Subtle or violent, we not endued
325　Single with like defense, wherever met,
How are we happy, still° in fear of harm?　　　　　*always*
But harm precedes not sin: only our foe
Tempting affronts us with his foul esteem
Of our integrity: his foul esteem
330　Sticks no dishonor on our front,° but turns　　　　*forehead*
Foul on himself; then wherefore shunned or feared
By us? who rather double honor gain
From his surmise proved false, find peace within,
Favor from Heav'n, our witness from th' event.°　　*outcome*
335　And what is faith, love, virtue unassayed
Alone, without exterior help sustained?[1]
Let us not then suspect our happy state
Left so imperfect by the Maker wise,
As not secure to single° or combined.　　　　　　*one alone*
340　Frail is our happiness, if this be so,
And Eden were no Eden thus exposed."
　　　To whom thus Adam fervently replied.
"O woman, best are all things as the will
Of God ordained them, his creating hand
345　Nothing imperfect or deficient left
Of all that he created, much less man,
Or aught that might his happy state secure,
Secure from outward force; within himself
The danger lies, yet lies within his power:
350　Against his will he can receive no harm.
But God left free the will, for what obeys
Reason, is free, and reason he made right,[2]
But bid her well beware, and still erect,°　　　　　*alert*
Lest by some fair appearing good surprised
355　She dictate false, and misinform the will
To do what God expressly hath forbid.
Not then mistrust, but tender love enjoins,
That I should mind° thee oft, and mind thou me.　*remind, pay heed to*
Firm we subsist,° yet possible to swerve,　　　　　*stand, exist*
360　Since reason not impossibly may meet
Some specious° object by the foe suborned,　　　　*deceptively attractive*
And fall into deception unaware,
Not keeping strictest watch, as she was warned.
Seek not temptation then, which to avoid
365　Were better, and most likely if from me
Thou sever not: trial will come unsought.
Wouldst thou approve° thy constancy, approve　　*prove*
First thy obedience; th' other who can know,
Not seeing thee attempted, who attest?
370　But if thou think, trial unsought may find
Us both securer° than thus warned thou seem'st,　*overconfident*

---

1. Compare and contrast *Areopagitica*, p. 710.
2. Right reason, a classical concept accommo-

dated to Christian thought, is the God-given power
to apprehend truth and moral law.

Go; for thy stay, not free, absents thee more;
Go in thy native innocence, rely
On what thou hast of virtue, summon all,
375 For God towards thee hath done his part, do thine."
      So spake the patriarch of mankind, but Eve
Persisted, yet submiss, though last, replied:
"With thy permission then, and thus forewarned
Chiefly by what thy own last reasoning words
380 Touched only, that our trial, when least sought,
May find us both perhaps far less prepared,
The willinger I go, nor much expect
A foe so proud will first the weaker seek;
So bent, the more shall shame him his repulse."
385 Thus saying, from her husband's hand her hand
Soft she withdrew, and like a wood-nymph light[3]
Oread or Dryad, or of Delia's train,
Betook her to the groves, but Delia's self
In gait surpassed and goddess-like deport,°   *bearing*
390 Though not as she with bow and quiver armed,
But with such gardening tools as art yet rude,
Guiltless of fire[4] had formed, or angels brought.
To Pales, or Pomona, thus adorned,
Likest she seemed[5] Pomona when she fled
395 Vertumnus, or to Ceres in her prime,
Yet virgin of Proserpina from Jove.
Her long with ardent look his eye pursued
Delighted, but desiring more her stay.
Oft he to her his charge of quick return
400 Repeated, she to him as oft engaged
To be returned by noon amid the bow'r,
And all things in best order to invite
Noontide repast, or afternoon's repose.
O much deceived, much failing,° hapless° Eve,   *erring/unlucky*
405 Of thy presumed return! event perverse!
Thou never from that hour in Paradise
Found'st either sweet repast, or sound repose;
Such ambush hid among sweet flow'rs and shades
Waited with hellish rancor imminent
410 To intercept thy way, or send thee back
Despoiled of innocence, of faith, of bliss.
For now, and since first break of dawn the Fiend,
Mere serpent in appearance, forth was come,
And on his quest, where likeliest he might find
415 The only two of mankind, but in them
The whole included race, his purposed prey.

---

3. Light-footed, with overtones of "fickle" or "frivolous." "Oread": a mountain nymph. "Dryad": a wood nymph. "Delia": Diana, born on the isle of Delos, hunted with a "train" of nymphs.
4. Having no experience of fire, not needed in Paradise. Milton may be alluding to the guilt of Prometheus, who stole fire from heaven.
5. These goddesses, like Eve, are associated with agriculture (lines 393–96)—Pales, with flocks and pastures; Pomona, with fruit trees, Ceres with harvests—and the latter two foreshadow Eve's situation. Pomona was chased by the wood god "Vertumnus" in many guises before surrendering to him; Ceres was impregnated by Jove with Proserpina—later carried off to Hades by Pluto.

In bow'r and field he sought, where any tuft
Of grove or garden-plot more pleasant lay,
Their tendance or plantation[6] for delight,
420　By fountain or by shady rivulet
He sought them both, but wished his hap° might find　　　　luck
Eve separate; he wished, but not with hope
Of what so seldom chanced, when to his wish,
Beyond his hope, Eve separate he spies,
425　Veiled in a cloud of fragrance, where she stood,
Half spied, so thick the roses bushing round
About her glowed, oft stooping to support
Each flow'r of slender stalk, whose head though gay
Carnation, purple, azure, or specked with gold,
430　Hung drooping unsustained, them she upstays
Gently with myrtle band, mindless° the while,　　　　heedless
Herself, though fairest unsupported flow'r
From her best prop so far, and storm so nigh.[7]
Nearer he drew, and many a walk traversed
435　Of stateliest covert, cedar, pine, or palm,
Then voluble° and bold, now hid, now seen　　　　undulating
Among thick-woven arborets° and flow'rs　　　　small trees
Embordered on each bank, the hand° of Eve:　　　　handiwork
Spot more delicious than those gardens feigned
440　Or of revived Adonis, or renowned
Alcinous, host of old Laertes' son,
Or that, not mystic, where the sapient king
Held dalliance with his fair Egyptian spouse.[8]
Much he the place admired, the person more.
445　As one who long in populous city pent,
Where houses thick and sewers annoy° the air,　　　　make noisome, befoul
Forth issuing on a summer's morn to breathe
Among the pleasant villages and farms
Adjoined, from each thing met conceives delight,
450　The smell of grain, or tedded grass, or kine,[9]
Or dairy, each rural sight, each rural sound;
If chance with nymph-like step fair virgin pass,
What pleasing seemed, for° her now pleases more,　　　　because of
She most, and in her look sums all delight.
455　Such pleasure took the Serpent to behold
This flow'ry plat,° the sweet recess° of Eve　　　　plot / retreat
Thus early, thus alone; her heav'nly form
Angelic, but more soft, and feminine,
Her graceful innocence, her every air°　　　　manner
460　Of gesture or least action overawed
His malice, and with rapine sweet[1] bereaved
His fierceness of the fierce intent it brought:

6. I.e., which they had cultivated or planted for
their pleasure.
7. The conceit of the flower-gatherer who is herself gathered evokes the story of Proserpina, to
whom it was applied in 4.269–71.
8. The gardens of Adonis were beauty spots
named for the lovely youth loved by Venus, killed
by a boar, and subsequently revived; Odysseus
("Laertes' son") was entertained by "Alcinous" in

his beautiful gardens; Solomon ("the sapient king")
entertained his "fair Egyptian spouse," the Queen
of Sheba, in a real garden (not "mystic," or
"feigned," as the others were).
9. Cattle. "Tedded": spread out to dry, like hay.
1. From Latin "rapere," to seize, the root of both
"rape" and "rapture," underscoring the paradox of
the ravisher (temporarily) ravished.

That space the Evil One abstracted° stood   *withdrawn*
From his own evil, and for the time remained
465   Stupidly good,° of enmity disarmed,   *good because stupefied*
Of guile, of hate, of envy, of revenge;
But the hot hell that always in him burns,
Though in mid-heav'n, soon ended his delight,
And tortures him now more, the more he sees
470   Of pleasure not for him ordained: then soon
Fierce hate he recollects, and all his thoughts
Of mischief gratulating,° thus excites: *greeting*
    "Thoughts, whither have ye led me, with what sweet
Compulsion thus transported to forget
475   What hither brought us, hate, not love, nor hope
Of Paradise for Hell, hope here to taste
Of pleasure, but all pleasure to destroy,
Save what is in destroying, other joy
To me is lost. Then let me not let pass
480   Occasion which now smiles, behold alone
The woman, opportune° to all attempts,   *open*
Her husband, for I view far round, not nigh,
Whose higher intellectual more I shun,
And strength, of courage haughty,° and of limb   *exalted*
485   Heroic built, though of terrestrial° mold,   *earthly*
Foe not informidable, exempt from wound,
I not; so much hath Hell debased, and pain
Enfeebled me, to what I was in Heav'n.
She fair, divinely fair, fit love for gods,
490   Not terrible,° though terror be in love   *terrifying*
And beauty, not° approached by stronger hate,   *unless*
Hate stronger, under show of love well feigned,
The way which to her ruin now I tend."
    So spake the Enemy of mankind, enclosed
495   In serpent, inmate bad, and toward Eve
Addressed his way, not with indented° wave,   *zigzag*
Prone on the ground, as since, but on his rear,
Circular base of rising folds, that tow'red
Fold above fold a surging maze, his head
500   Crested aloft, and carbuncle° his eyes;   *deep red*
With burnished neck of verdant gold, erect
Amidst his circling spires,° that on the grass   *coils*
Floated redundant:° pleasing was his shape,   *in swelling waves*
And lovely, never since of serpent kind
505   Lovelier, not those that in Illyria changed
Hermione and Cadmus, or the god
In Epidaurus;[2] nor to which transformed
Ammonian Jove, or Capitoline was seen,
He with Olympias, this with her who bore
510   Scipio, the height of Rome.[3] With tract° oblique   *course*

2. The legendary founder of Thebes, "Cadmus," and his wife Harmonia (Milton's "Hermione") were changed to serpents when they went to "Illyria" in old age; Aesculapius, god of healing, sometimes came forth as a serpent fron his temple in "Epidaurus."

3. Jupiter Ammon ("Ammonian Jove") made love to "Olympias" in the form of a snake, and sired Alexander the Great; the Jupiter worshipped in Rome ("Capitoline") also in serpent form, sired Scipio Africanus, the savior and great leader ("height") of Rome.

At first, as one who sought accéss, but feared
To interrupt, sidelong he works his way.
As when a ship by skilful steersman wrought
Nigh river's mouth or foreland, where the wind
515   Veers oft, as oft so steers, and shifts her sail;
So varied he, and of his tortuous train
Curled many a wanton° wreath in sight of Eve,   luxuriant, sportive
To lure her eye; she busied heard the sound
Of rustling leaves, but minded not, as used
520   To such disport before her through the field,
From every beast, more duteous at her call,
Than at Circean⁴ call the herd disguised.
He bolder now, uncalled before her stood;
But as in gaze admiring: oft he bowed
525   His turret crest, and sleek enameled° neck,   multicolored
Fawning, and licked the ground whereon she trod.
His gentle dumb expression turned at length
The eye of Eve to mark his play; he glad
Of her attention gained, with serpent tongue
530   Organic, or impulse of vocal air,⁵
His fraudulent temptation thus began.
      "Wonder not, sovran mistress, if perhaps
Thou canst, who art sole wonder, much less arm
Thy looks, the heav'n of mildness, with disdain,
535   Displeased that I approach thee thus, and gaze
Insatiate, I thus single, nor have feared
Thy awful brow, more awful thus retired.
Fairest resemblance of thy Maker fair,
Thee all things living gaze on, all things thine
540   By gift, and thy celestial beauty adore
With ravishment beheld, there best beheld
Where universally admired; but here
In this enclosure wild, these beasts among,
Beholders rude, and shallow to discern
545   Half what in thee is fair, one man except,
Who sees thee? (and what is one?) who shouldst be seen
A goddess among gods, adored and served
By angels numberless, thy daily train."⁶
      So glozed° the Tempter, and his proem° tuned;   flattered/prelude
550   Into the heart of Eve his words made way,
Though at the voice much marveling; at length
Not unamazed she thus in answer spake.
"What may this mean? Language of man pronounced
By tongue of brute, and human sense expressed?
555   The first at least of these I thought denied
To beasts, whom God on their creation-day
Created mute to all articulate sound;
The latter I demur,° for in their looks   hesitate about
Much reason, and in their actions oft appears.

---

4. Circe, in the *Odyssey*, transformed men to
beasts and was attended by an obedient herd.
5. Satan either used the actual tongue of the ser-

pent or impressed the air with his own voice.
6. Satan's entire speech is couched in the extravagant praises of the Petrarchan love convention.

560 Thee, serpent, subtlest beast of all the field
I knew, but not with human voice endued;°   *endowed*
Redouble then this miracle, and say,
How cam'st thou speakable° of mute, and how   *able to speak*
To me so friendly grown above the rest
565 Of brutal kind, that daily are in sight?
Say, for such wonder claims attention due."
    To whom the guileful Tempter thus replied:
"Empress of this fair world, resplendent Eve,
Easy to me it is to tell thee all
570 What thou command'st, and right thou shouldst be obeyed:
I was at first as other beasts that graze
The trodden herb, of abject thoughts and low,
As was my food, nor aught but food discerned
Or sex, and apprehended nothing high:
575 Till on a day roving the field, I chanced
A goodly tree far distant to behold
Loaden with fruit of fairest colors mixed,
Ruddy and gold: I nearer drew to gaze;
When from the boughs a savory odor blown,
580 Grateful to appetite, more pleased my sense
Than smell of sweetest fennel, or the teats
Of ewe or goat dropping with milk at ev'n,[7]
Unsucked of lamb or kid, that tend their play.
To satisfy the sharp desire I had
585 Of tasting those fair apples, I resolved
Not to defer;° hunger and thirst at once,   *delay*
Powerful persuaders, quickened at the scent
Of that alluring fruit, urged me so keen.
About the mossy trunk I wound me soon,
590 For high from ground the branches would require
Thy utmost reach or Adam's: round the tree
All other beasts that saw, with like desire
Longing and envying stood, but could not reach.
Amid the tree now got, where plenty hung
595 Tempting so nigh, to pluck and eat my fill
I spared° not, for such pleasure till that hour   *refrained*
At feed or fountain never had I found.
Sated at length, ere long I might perceive
Strange alteration in me, to degree
600 Of reason in my inward powers,[8] and speech
Wanted° not long, though to this shape retained.   *lacked*
Thenceforth to speculations high or deep
I turned my thoughts, and with capacious mind
Considered all things visible in Heav'n,
605 Or earth, or middle,° all things fair and good;   *regions between*

---

7. According to Pliny, serpents ate fennel to aid in shedding their skins and to sharpen their eyesight; folklore had it that they drank the milk of sheep and goats.

8. There is no precedent in Genesis or the inter-

pretative tradition for Satan's powerfully persuasive argument by analogy based on the snake's supposed experience of attaining to reason and speech by eating the forbidden fruit.

But all that fair and good in thy divine
Semblance, and in thy beauty's heav'nly ray
United I beheld; no fair° to thine   *beauty*
Equivalent or second, which compelled
610 Me thus, though importune° perhaps, to come   *inopportunely*
And gaze, and worship thee of right declared
Sovran of creatures, universal dame."⁹
    So talked the spirited¹ sly snake; and Eve
Yet more amazed unwary thus replied:
615   "Serpent, thy overpraising leaves in doubt
The virtue° of that fruit, in thee first proved: *power*
But say, where grows the tree, from hence how far?
For many are the trees of God that grow
In Paradise, and various, yet unknown
620 To us, in such abundance lies our choice,
As leaves a greater store of fruit untouched,
Still hanging incorruptible, till men
Grow up to their provision,² and more hands
Help to disburden nature of her birth."
625   To whom the wily adder, blithe and glad:
"Empress, the way is ready, and not long,
Beyond a row of myrtles, on a flat,
Fast by a fountain, one small thicket past
Of blowing myrrh and balm;³ if thou accept
630 My conduct,° I can bring thee thither soon."   *guidance*
    "Lead then," said Eve. He leading swiftly rolled
In tangles, and made intricate seem straight,
To mischief swift. Hope elevates, and joy
Brightens his crest, as when a wand'ring fire,°   *will-o'-the-wisp*
635 Compact° of unctuous° vapor, which the night   *composed/oily*
Condenses, and the cold environs round,
Kindled through agitation to a flame,
Which oft, they say, some evil spirit attends,
Hovering and blazing with delusive light,
640 Misleads th' amazed° night-wanderer from his way   *bewildered*
To bogs and mires, and oft through pond or pool,
There swallowed up and lost, from succor far.
So glistered the dire snake, and into fraud
Led Eve our credulous mother, to the tree
645 Of prohibition, root of all our woe;
Which when she saw, thus to her guide she spake:
    "Serpent, we might have spared our coming hither,
Fruitless to me, though fruit be here to excess,
The credit of whose virtue° rest with thee,   *power*
650 Wondrous indeed, if cause of such effects.
But of this tree we may not taste nor touch;
God so commanded, and left that command

---

9. Satan continues his Petrarchan language of courtship.
1. Both inspired by and possessed by an evil spirit, Satan.

2. I.e., until the numbers of the human race are such as to consume the food God has provided.
3. Blooming trees that exude the aromatic gums, myrrh and balm (balsam).

Sole daughter of his voice;[4] the rest, we live
Law to ourselves, our reason is our law."

655   To whom the Tempter guilefully replied:
"Indeed? hath God then said that of the fruit
Of all these garden trees ye shall not eat,
Yet lords declared of all in earth or air?"

    To whom thus Eve yet sinless: "Of the fruit
660 Of each tree in the garden we may eat,
But of the fruit of this fair tree amidst
The garden, God hath said, 'Ye shall not eat
Thereof, nor shall ye touch it, lest ye die.' "[5]

    She scarce had said, though brief, when now more bold
665 The Tempter, but with show of zeal and love
To man, and indignation at his wrong,
New part puts on, and as to passion moved,
Fluctuates disturbed, yet comely, and in act
Raised,[6] as of some great matter to begin.

670 As when of old some orator renowned
In Athens or free Rome, where eloquence
Flourished, since mute, to some great cause addressed,
Stood in himself collected, while each part,
Motion, each act won audience ere the tongue,°   *before speaking*
675 Sometimes in high began, as no delay
Of preface brooking[7] through his zeal of right.
So standing, moving, or to high upgrown
The Tempter all impassioned thus began:

    "O sacred, wise, and wisdom-giving plant,
680 Mother of science,° now I feel thy power   *knowledge*
Within me clear, not only to discern
Things in their causes, but to trace the ways
Of highest agents, deemed however wise.
Queen of this universe, do not believe
685 Those rigid threats of death; ye shall not die:
How should ye? By the fruit? It gives you life
To knowledge.[8] By the Threat'ner? Look on me,
Me who have touched and tasted, yet both live,
And life more perfect have attained than fate
690 Meant me, by vent'ring higher than my lot.
Shall that be shut to man, which to the beast
Is open? Or will God incense his ire
For such a petty trespass, and not praise
Rather your dauntless virtue,° whom the pain   *courage*
695 Of death denounced,° whatever thing death be,   *threatened*
Deterred not from achieving what might lead
To happier life, knowledge of good and evil;

4. God's only direct commandment (in Hebrew, *Bath Kol*, "daughter of a voice" from heaven). Otherwise, they follow the moral law of nature, known to them perfectly by their unfallen reason, "our reason is our law."
5. Eve's formulation indicates her "sufficient" understanding of the prohibition and the conditions of life in Eden.
6. Drawn up to full dignity. Satan as the snake

takes on the role of a Greek or Roman orator defending liberty (lines 671–72), a Demosthenes or a Cicero.
7. Bursting into the middle of his speech without a preface, and "upgrown" to the impassioned high style ("high") at once (lines 675–78).
8. I.e., life as well as knowledge, and a better life enhanced by knowledge, which Satan in the snake presents as a "magical" property of the tree.

Of good, how just?⁹ Of evil, if what is evil
Be real, why not known, since easier shunned?
700 God therefore cannot hurt ye, and be just;
Not just, not God;¹ not feared then, nor obeyed:
Your fear itself of death removes the fear.
Why then was this forbid? Why but to awe,
Why but to keep ye low and ignorant,
705 His worshipers; he knows that in the day
Ye eat thereof, your eyes that seem so clear,
Yet are but dim, shall perfectly be then
Opened and cleared, and ye shall be as gods,
Knowing both good and evil as they know.
710 That ye should be as gods, since I as man,
Internal man, is but proportion meet,
I of brute human, ye of human gods.²
So ye shall die perhaps, by putting off
Human, to put on gods, death to be wished,
715 Though threatened, which no worse than this can bring.
And what are gods that man may not become
As they, participating° godlike food?   *partaking of*
The gods³ are first, and that advantage use
On our belief, that all from them proceeds;
720 I question it, for this fair earth I see,
Warmed by the sun, producing every kind,
Them nothing: if they all° things, who enclosed   *produce all*
Knowledge of good and evil in this tree,
That whoso eats thereof, forthwith attains
725 Wisdom without their leave? And wherein lies
Th' offense, that man should thus attain to know?
What can your knowledge hurt him, or this tree
Impart against his will if all be his?
Or is it envy, and can envy dwell
730 In heav'nly breasts? These, these and many more
Causes import° your need of this fair fruit.   *prove*
Goddess humane,⁴ reach then, and freely taste."
     He ended, and his words replete with guile
Into her heart too easy entrance won:
735 Fixed on the fruit she gazed, which to behold
Might tempt alone, and in her ears the sound
Yet rung of his persuasive words, impregned°   *impregnated*
With reason, to her seeming, and with truth;
Meanwhile the hour of noon drew on, and waked
740 An eager appetite, raised by the smell
So savory of that fruit, which with desire,
Inclinable now grown to touch or taste,
Solicited her longing eye;⁵ yet first
Pausing a while, thus to herself she mused:

9. I.e., how can it be just to forbid the knowledge
of good?
1. Satan's sophism invites atheism: if God forbids
knowledge of good and evil he is not just, therefore
not God, therefore his threat of death need not be
feared.

2. Satan invites the aspiration to divinity, based on
analogy to the supposed experience of the snake.
3. Hereafter, Satan speaks of "gods," not God.
4. Both "human" and "gracious" or "kindly."
5. All Eve's senses—sight, hearing, smell, taste,
and touch—are solicited by the fruit.

745   "Great are thy virtues,° doubtless, best of fruits,   *powers*
        Though kept from man, and worthy to be admired,
        Whose taste, too long forborne, at first assay°   *try*
        Gave elocution to the mute, and taught
        The tongue not made for speech to speak thy praise:
750   Thy praise he also who forbids thy use,
        Conceals not from us, naming thee the Tree
        Of Knowledge, knowledge both of good and evil;
        Forbids us then to taste, but his forbidding
        Commends thee more, while it infers° the good   *implies*
755   By thee communicated, and our want:°   *lack*
        For good unknown, sure is not had, or had
        And yet unknown, is as not had at all.
        In plain° then, what forbids he but to know,   *in plain words*
        Forbids us good, forbids us to be wise?
760   Such prohibitions bind not. But if death
        Bind us with after-bands,° what profits then   *later bonds*
        Our inward freedom? In the day we eat
        Of this fair fruit, our doom is, we shall die.
        How dies the serpent? He hath eat'n and lives,
765   And knows, and speaks, and reasons, and discerns,
        Irrational till then. For us alone
        Was death invented? Or to us denied
        This intellectual food, for beasts reserved?
        For beasts it seems: yet that one beast which first
770   Hath tasted, envies° not, but brings with joy   *begrudges*
        The good befall'n him, author unsuspect,[6]
        Friendly to man, far from deceit or guile.
        What fear I then, rather what know to fear
        Under this ignorance of good and evil,
775   Of God or death, of law or penalty?
        Here grows the cure of all, this fruit divine,
        Fair to the eye, inviting to the taste,
        Of virtue° to make wise: what hinders then   *power*
        To reach, and feed at once both body and mind?"
780   So saying, her rash hand in evil hour
        Forth reaching to the fruit, she plucked, she eat.[7]
        Earth felt the wound, and nature from her seat
        Sighing through all her works gave signs of woe,
        That all was lost. Back to the thicket slunk
785   The guilty serpent, and well might, for Eve
        Intent now wholly on her taste, naught else
        Regarded, such delight till then, as seemed,
        In fruit she never tasted, whether true
        Or fancied so, through expectation high
790   Of knowledge, nor was Godhead from her thought.
        Greedily she engorged without restraint,
        And knew not eating death:[8] satiate at length,
        And heightened as with wine, jocund° and boon,°   *merry/jolly*

---

6. An authority or informant beyond suspicion.
7. Ate: an accepted past tense, pronounced *et*.
8. I.e., she is eating death and doesn't know it, or

experience it yet, but also, punning, death is eating
her too.

Thus to herself she pleasingly began:
795   "O sovran, virtuous, precious of all trees
In Paradise, of operation blest
To sapience, hitherto obscured, infamed,[9]
And thy fair fruit let hang, as to no end
Created; but henceforth my early care,
800 Not without song, each morning, and due praise
Shall tend thee, and the fertile burden ease
Of thy full branches offered free to all;
Till dieted by thee I grow mature
In knowledge, as the gods who all things know;
805 Though others envy what they cannot give;
For had the gift been theirs,[1] it had not here
Thus grown. Experience, next to thee I owe,
Best guide; not following thee, I had remained
In ignorance, thou open'st wisdom's way,
810 And giv'st accéss, though secret° she retire.   *hidden*
And I perhaps am secret° Heav'n is high,   *unseen*
High and remote to see from thence distinct
Each thing on earth; and other care perhaps
May have diverted from continual watch
815 Our great Forbidder, safe with all his spies
About him. But to Adam in what sort°   *guise*
Shall I appear? shall I to him make known
As yet my change, and give him to partake
Full happiness with me, or rather not,
820 But keep the odds° of knowledge in my power   *advantage*
Without copartner? so to add what wants°   *lacks*
In female sex, the more to draw his love,
And render me more equal, and perhaps,
A thing not undesirable, sometime
825 Superior; for inferior who is free?[2]
This may be well: but what if God have seen,
And death ensue? Then I shall be no more,
And Adam wedded to another Eve,
Shall live with her enjoying, I extinct;
830 A death to think. Confirmed then I resolve,
Adam shall share with me in bliss or woe:
So dear I love him, that with him all deaths
I could endure, without him live no life."
    So saying, from the tree her step she turned,
835 But first low reverence done, as to the power
That dwelt within,[3] whose presence had infused
Into the plant sciential° sap, derived   *knowledge-producing*
From nectar, drink of gods. Adam the while
Waiting desirous her return, had wove
840 Of choicest flow'rs a garland to adorn
Her tresses, and her rural labors crown,
As reapers oft are wont their harvest queen.

9. Slandered. "Sapience": both knowledge and tasting (Latin, *sapere*).
1. Like Satan, Eve now conflates gods and God,

ascribing envy but also lack of power to "them."
2. Cf. Satan, 1.248–63, 5.790–97.
3. Eve ends with idolatry, worship of the tree.

Great joy he promised to his thoughts, and new
Solace in her return, so long delayed;
845   Yet oft his heart, divine of° something ill,   *foreboding*
Misgave him; he the falt'ring measure° felt;   *heartbeat*
And forth to meet her went, the way she took
That morn when first they parted; by the Tree
Of Knowledge he must pass; there he her met,
850   Scarce from the tree returning; in her hand
A bough of fairest fruit that downy smiled,
New gathered, and ambrosial smell diffused.
To him she hasted, in her face excuse
Came prologue,[4] and apology to prompt,
855   Which with bland° words at will she thus addressed.   *mild, coaxing*
    "Hast thou not wondered, Adam, at my stay?
Thee I have missed, and thought it long, deprived
Thy presence, agony of love till now
Not felt, nor shall be twice, for never more
860   Mean I to try, what rash untried I sought,
The pain of absence from thy sight. But strange
Hath been the cause, and wonderful to hear:
This tree is not as we are told, a tree
Of danger tasted,° nor to evil unknown   *if tasted*
865   Op'ning the way, but of divine effect
To open eyes, and make them gods who taste;
And hath been tasted such: the serpent wise,
Or° not restrained as we, or not obeying,   *either*
Hath eaten of the fruit, and is become,
870   Not dead, as we are threatened, but thenceforth
Endued with human voice and human sense,
Reasoning to admiration,° and with me   *cause wonder*
Persuasively° hath so prevailed, that I   *by persuasion*
Have also tasted, and have also found
875   Th' effects to correspond, opener mine eyes,
Dim erst,° dilated spirits, ampler heart,   *before*
And growing up to godhead; which for thee
Chiefly I sought, without thee can despise.
For bliss, as thou hast part, to me is bliss,
880   Tedious, unshared with thee, and odious soon.
Thou therefore also taste, that equal lot
May join us, equal joy, as equal love;
Lest thou not tasting, different degree°   *rank*
Disjoin us, and I then too late renounce
885   Deity for thee, when fate will not permit."[5]
    Thus Eve with count'nance blithe her story told;
But in her cheek distemper[6] flushing glowed.
On th' other side, Adam, soon as he heard
The fatal trespass done by Eve, amazed,°   *stunned*
890   Astonied° stood and blank, while horror chill   *petrified*
Ran through his veins, and all his joints relaxed;

---

4. I.e., excuse came like the prologue in a play, and apology (justification, self-defense) served as prompter.

5. Compare Eve in soliloquy, lines 817–31.

6. I.e., disorder arising from disturbance of the balance of humors in the body, intoxication.

From his slack hand the garland wreathed for Eve
Down dropped, and all the faded roses shed:
Speechless he stood and pale, till thus at length
895 First to himself he inward silence broke:
"O fairest of creation, last and best
Of all God's works, creature in whom excelled
Whatever can to sight or thought be formed,
Holy, divine, good, amiable, or sweet!
900 How art thou lost, how on a sudden lost,
Defaced, deflow'red, and now to death devote?°   *doomed*
Rather how hast thou yielded to transgress
The strict forbiddance, how to violate
The sacred° fruit forbidd'n! some cursèd fraud   *consecrated*
905 Of enemy hath beguiled thee, yet unknown,
And me with thee hath ruined, for with thee
Certain my resolution is to die;
How can I live without thee, how forgo
Thy sweet converse and love so dearly joined,
910 To live again in these wild woods forlorn?
Should God create another Eve, and I
Another rib afford, yet loss of thee
Would never from my heart; no no, I feel
The link of nature draw me: flesh of flesh,
915 Bone of my bone thou art,[7] and from thy state
Mine never shall be parted, bliss or woe."
       So having said, as one from sad dismay
Recomforted, and after thoughts disturbed
Submitting to what seemed remédiless,
920 Thus in calm mood his words to Eve he turned:
       "Bold deed thou hast presumed, advent'rous Eve,
And peril great provoked, who thus hast dared
Had it been only coveting to eye
That sacred fruit, sacred° to abstinence,   *set apart*
925 Much more to taste it under ban to touch.
But past who can recall, or done undo?
Not God omnipotent, nor fate; yet so
Perhaps thou shalt not die, perhaps the fact°   *deed*
Is not so heinous now, foretasted fruit,
930 Profaned first by the serpent, by him first
Made common and unhallowed ere our taste;
Nor yet on him found deadly, he yet lives,
Lives, as thou saidst, and gains to live as man
Higher degree of life, inducement strong
935 To us, as likely tasting to attain
Proportional ascent, which cannot be
But to be gods, or angels demi-gods.
Nor can I think that God, Creator wise,
Though threat'ning, will in earnest so destroy
940 Us his prime creatures, dignified so high,
Set over all his works, which in our fall,

---

7. Adam echoes Genesis 2.23–24.

For us created, needs with us must fail,
Dependent made; so God shall uncreate,
Be frustrate, do, undo, and labor lose,
945 Not well conceived of God, who though his power
Creation could repeat, yet would be loath
Us to abolish, lest the Adversary°   Satan
Triumph and say; 'Fickle their state whom God
Most favors, who can please him long? Me first
950 He ruined, now mankind; whom will he next?'
Matter of scorn, not to be given the Foe.
However I with thee have fixed my lot,
Certain° to undergo like doom; if death   resolved
Consort° with thee, death is to me as life;   associate
955 So forcible within my heart I feel
The bond of nature draw me to my own,
My own in thee, for what thou art is mine;
Our state cannot be severed, we are one,
One flesh; to lose thee were to lose myself."
960   So Adam, and thus Eve to him replied:
"O glorious trial of exceeding[8] love,
Illustrious evidence, example high!
Engaging me to emulate, but short
Of thy perfection, how shall I attain,
965 Adam, from whose dear side I boast me sprung,
And gladly of our union hear thee speak,
One heart, one soul in both; whereof good proof
This day affords, declaring thee resolved,
Rather than death or aught° than death more dread   anything other
970 Shall separate us, linked in love so dear,
To undergo with me one guilt, one crime,
If any be, of tasting this fair fruit,
Whose virtue,° for of good still good proceeds,   power
Direct, or by occasion° hath presented   indirectly
975 This happy trial of thy love, which else
So eminently never had been known.
Were it° I thought death menaced would ensue°   if / result from
This my attempt, I would sustain alone
The worst, and not persuade thee, rather die
980 Deserted, than oblige° thee with a fact°   bind / deed
Pernicious to thy peace, chiefly assured
Remarkably so late of thy so true,
So faithful love unequaled;[9] but I feel
Far otherwise th' event,° not death, but life   result
985 Augmented, opened eyes, new hopes, new joys,
Taste so divine, that what of sweet before
Hath touched my sense, flat seems to this, and harsh.
On my experience, Adam, freely taste,
And fear of death deliver to the winds."
990   So saying, she embraced him, and for joy

---

8. The word, which Eve intends as praise, carries   9. I.e., since I have so recently been assured of
the implication of "excessive."   your unparalleled love.

Tenderly wept, much won that he his love
Had so ennobled, as of choice to incur
Divine displeasure for her sake, or death.
In recompense (for such compliance bad
995 Such recompense best merits) from the bough
She gave him of that fair enticing fruit
With liberal hand: he scrupled not to eat
Against his better knowledge, not deceived,[1]
But fondly° overcome with female charm.   foolishly
1000 Earth trembled from her entrails, as again
In pangs, and nature gave a second groan;
Sky loured, and muttering thunder, some sad drops
Wept at completing of the mortal sin
Original;[2] while Adam took no thought,
1005 Eating his fill, nor Eve to iterate°   repeat
Her former trespass feared, the more to soothe
Him with her loved society, that now
As with new wine intoxicated both
They swim in mirth, and fancy that they feel
1010 Divinity within them breeding wings
Wherewith to scorn the earth: but that false fruit
Far other operation first displayed,
Carnal desire inflaming, he on Eve
Began to cast lascivious eyes, she him
1015 As wantonly repaid; in lust they burn:
Till Adam thus 'gan Eve to dalliance move:
        "Eve, now I see thou art exact of taste,
And elegant, of sapience[3] no small part,
Since to each meaning savor we apply,
1020 And palate call judicious; I the praise
Yield thee, so well this day thou hast purveyed.°   provided
Much pleasure we have lost, while we abstained
From this delightful fruit, nor known till now
True relish, tasting; if such pleasure be
1025 In things to us forbidden, it might be wished,
For this one tree had been forbidden ten.
But come, so well refreshed, now let us play,
As meet° is, after such delicious fare;   appropriate
For never did thy beauty since the day
1030 I saw thee first and wedded thee, adorned
With all perfections, so inflame my sense
With ardor to enjoy thee, fairer now
Than ever, bounty of this virtuous tree."
        So said he, and forbore not glance or toy°   caress
1035 Of amorous intent, well understood
Of° Eve, whose eye darted contagious fire.   by
Her hand he seized, and to a shady bank,

---

1. Cf. 1 Timothy 2.14: "And Adam was not deceived, but the woman being deceived was in the transgression."
2. The theological doctrine that all Adam's descendants are stained by Adam's sin, and are thereby subject to physical death and (unless saved by grace) to damnation.
3. Adam commends Eve for her fine ("exact") and discriminating ("elegant") taste, as a part of "sapience," which means both "taste" and "wisdom."

Thick overhead with verdant roof embow'red
He led her nothing loath; flow'rs were the couch,
1040   Pansies, and violets, and asphodel,
And hyacinth, earth's freshest softest lap.
There they their fill of love and love's disport
Took largely, of their mutual guilt the seal,
The solace of their sin, till dewy sleep
1045   Oppressed them, wearied with their amorous play.
Soon as the force of that fallacious fruit,
That with exhilarating vapor bland°   *pleasing*
About their spirits had played, and inmost powers
Made err, was now exhaled, and grosser sleep
1050   Bred of unkindly° fumes,° with conscious dreams   *unnatural / vapors*
Encumbered,° now had left them, up they rose   *oppressed*
As from unrest, and each the other viewing,
Soon found their eyes how opened, and their minds
How darkened; innocence, that as a veil
1055   Had shadowed them from knowing ill, was gone,
Just confidence, and native righteousness,
And honor from about them, naked left
To guilty shame: he° covered, but his robe   *shame*
Uncovered more. So rose the Danite strong
1060   Hercúlean Samson from the harlot-lap
Of Philistéan Dálilah, and waked
Shorn of his strength,[4] they destitute and bare
Of all their virtue: silent, and in face
Confounded long they sat, as strucken mute,
1065   Till Adam, though not less than Eve abashed,
At length gave utterance to these words constrained:°   *forced*
    "O Eve, in evil[5] hour thou didst give ear
To that false worm, of whomsoever taught
To counterfeit man's voice, true in our fall,
1070   False in our promised rising; since our eyes
Opened we find indeed, and find we know
Both good and evil, good lost and evil got,[6]
Bad fruit of knowledge, if this be to know,
Which leaves us naked thus, of honor void,
1075   Of innocence, of faith, of purity,
Our wonted° ornaments now soiled and stained,   *former*
And in our faces evident the signs
Of foul concupiscence;[7] whence evil store;
Even shame, the last of evils; of the first
1080   Be sure then. How shall I behold the face
Henceforth of God or angel, erst with joy
And rapture so oft beheld? Those heav'nly shapes

---

4. Samson, of the tribe of Dan, told the "harlot"
Philistine Delilah that the secret of his strength
(like that of Hercules) lay in his hair; she sheared
it off while he slept, and when he awoke he was
easily captured and blinded by his enemies.
5. Adam's bitter pun—Eve, evil—repudiates the
actual etymology of Eve, "life," which Adam will
later reaffirm (11.159–61).

6. Milton, like most commentators, derives the
tree's name from the event (4.222, 11.84–89).
7. The theological term for the unruly human passions and desires seen as one effect of the Fall, a
sign of abundance ("store") of evils. If "shame" is
the "last" evil, the "first" is probably the guiltiness
that produces it, according to Milton's *Christian
Doctrine* (1.12).

Will dazzle now this earthly, with their blaze
Insufferably bright. O might I here
1085 In solitude live savage, in some glade
Obscured, where highest woods impenetrable
To star or sunlight, spread their umbrage° broad,   shadow, foliage
And brown as evening: cover me ye pines,
Ye cedars, with innumerable boughs
1090 Hide me, where I may never see them more.
But let us now, as in bad plight, devise
What best may for the present serve to hide
The parts of each from other, that seem most
To shame obnoxious,° and unseemliest seen,   exposed
1095 Some tree whose broad smooth leaves together sewed,
And girded on our loins, may cover round
Those middle parts, that this newcomer, shame,
There sit not, and reproach us as unclean."
     So counseled he, and both together went
1100 Into the thickest wood, there soon they chose
The fig tree,[8] not that kind for fruit renowned,
But such as at this day to Indians known
In Malabar or Deccan spreads her arms
Branching so broad and long, that in the ground
1105 The bended twigs take root, and daughters grow
About the mother tree, a pillared shade
High overarched, and echoing walks between;
There oft the Indian herdsman shunning heat
Shelters in cool, and tends his pasturing herds
1110 At loopholes cut through thickest shade: those leaves
They gathered, broad as Amazonian targe,°   shields
And with what skill they had, together sewed,
To gird their waist, vain covering if to hide
Their guilt and dreaded shame. O how unlike
1115 To that first naked glory. Such of late
Columbus found th' American so girt
With feathered cincture,° naked else and wild,   belt
Among the trees on isles and woody shores.
Thus fenced, and as they thought, their shame in part
1120 Covered, but not at rest or ease of mind,
They sat them down to weep, nor only tears
Rained at their eyes, but high winds worse within
Began to rise, high passions, anger, hate,
Mistrust, suspicion, discord, and shook sore
1125 Their inward state of mind, calm region once
And full of peace, now tossed and turbulent:
For understanding ruled not, and the will
Heard not her lore, both in subjection now
To sensual appetite, who from beneath
1130 Usurping over sovran reason claimed

---

8. The banyan, or Indian fig, has small leaves, but the account Milton draws on from Gerard's *Herbal* (1597) contains the details of lines 1104–11; "Malabar" and "Deccan" are in southern India.

Superior sway: from thus distempered breast,[9]
Adam, estranged° in look and altered style,   *unlike himself*
Speech intermitted thus to Eve renewed:
   "Would thou hadst hearkened to my words, and stayed
1135 With me, as I besought thee, when that strange
Desire of wand'ring this unhappy morn,
I know not whence possessed thee; we had then
Remained still happy, not as now, despoiled
Of all our good, shamed, naked, miserable.
1140 Let none henceforth seek needless cause to approve°   *prove*
The faith they owe; when earnestly they seek
Such proof, conclude, they then begin to fail."
   To whom soon moved with touch of blame thus Eve:
"What words have passed thy lips, Adam severe,
1145 Imput'st thou that to my default, or will
Of wand'ring, as thou call'st it, which who knows
But might as ill have happened thou being by,
Or to thyself perhaps: hadst thou been there,
Or here th' attempt, thou couldst not have discerned
1150 Fraud in the serpent, speaking as he spake;
No ground of enmity between us known,
Why he should mean me ill, or seek to harm.
Was I to have never parted from thy side?
As good have grown there still a lifeless rib.
1155 Being as I am, why didst not thou the head
Command me absolutely not to go,
Going into such danger as thou saidst?
Too facile° then thou didst not much gainsay,   *easy, mild*
Nay didst permit, approve, and fair dismiss.
1160 Hadst thou been firm and fixed in thy dissent,
Neither had I transgressed, nor thou with me."
   To whom then first incensed Adam replied.
"Is this the love, is this the recompense
Of mine to thee, ingrateful Eve, expressed°   *demonstrated*
1165 Immutable when thou wert lost, not I,
Who might have lived and joyed immortal bliss,
Yet willingly chose rather death with thee:
And am I now upbraided, as the cause
Of thy transgressing? not enough severe,
1170 It seems, in thy restraint: what could I more?
I warned thee, I admonished thee, foretold
The danger, and the lurking enemy
That lay in wait; beyond this had been force,
And force upon free will hath here no place.
1175 But confidence then bore thee on, secure°   *self-assured*
Either to meet no danger, or to find
Matter of glorious trial; and perhaps
I also erred in overmuch admiring
What seemed in thee so perfect, that I thought

9. The immediate psychological effects of the Fall are evident in the subjection of reason to the lower faculties of sensual appetite.

1180 No evil durst attempt thee, but I rue
That error now, which is become my crime,
And thou th' accuser. Thus it shall befall
Him who to worth in women overtrusting
Lets her will rule; restraint she will not brook,° *accept*
1185 And left to herself, if evil thence ensue,
She first his weak indulgence will accuse."
 Thus they in mutual accusation spent
The fruitless hours, but neither self-condemning,
And of their vain contést appeared no end.

From Book 10

Summary When it is known in Heaven that man has fallen, God sends his Son to pass judgment on the sinners. Having found them in the garden, he hears their confession and passes instant sentence, cursing the serpent, condemning Eve to the pains of childbirth and Adam to those of daily toil; but in mercy, he clothes the human couple both outwardly with skins of beasts and inwardly with his righteousness. Meanwhile Sin and Death, sitting by Hell-gate, feel new strength, and pass across Chaos, leaving a great bridge behind them. On their way they meet with their parent, Satan, learn of his success on Earth, and press eagerly forward in hopes of destroying humankind altogether. Satan, on the other hand, continues his flight back toward Hell, where he is to report to his constituents.

[CONSEQUENCES OF THE FALL]

 * * *   Th' other way Satan went down
415 The causey° to Hell gate; on either side *causeway*
Disparted Chaos over-built exclaimed,
And with rebounding surge the bars assailed,
That scorned his indignation.[1] Through the gate,
Wide open and unguarded, Satan passed,
420 And all about found desolate; for those[2]
Appointed to sit there, had left their charge,
Flown to the upper world; the rest were all
Far to the inland retired, about the walls
Of Pandemonium, city and proud seat
425 Of Lucifer, so by allusion° called, *metaphor*
Of that bright star[3] to Satan paragoned.
There kept their watch the legions, while the grand[4]
In council sat, solicitous° what chance *anxious*
Might intercept their emperor sent, so he
430 Departing gave command, and they observed.
As when the Tartar[5] from his Russian foe

---

1. Chaos is the instinctive enemy of all order, so hostile to the bridge built over it.
2. Sin and Death.
3. Satan before his fall was Lucifer, the Light-bringer, and the Morning Star is named Lucifer because it is compared ("paragoned") to him.
4. The "grand infernal peers" who govern (cf. 2.507).
5. The simile compares the fallen angels, with-drawn from other regions of Hell to guard their

metropolis, to Tartars retiring before attacking Russians and Persians before the attacking Turks (lines 431–39). "Astracan": a region west of the Caspian Sea inhabited by Russia and defended against Turks and Tartars; "Aladule": the region of Armenia, from which the last Persian ruler, called "Anadule," a "Bactrian Sophi" (Persian Shah), was forced to retreat from the Turks, to Tabriz ("Tauris") and Kazvin ("Casbeen").

By Astracan over the snowy plains
Retires, or Bactrian Sophi from the horns
Of Turkish crescent, leaves all waste beyond
435 The realm of Aladule, in his retreat
To Tauris or Casbeen: so these the late
Heav'n-banished host, left desert utmost Hell
Many a dark league, reduced° in careful watch   *drawn together*
Round their metropolis, and now expecting
440 Each hour their great adventurer from the search
Of foreign worlds: he through the midst unmarked,°   *unnoticed*
In show plebeian angel militant
Of lowest order,° passed; and from the door   *private*
Of that Plutonian[6] hall, invisible
445 Ascended his high throne, which under state°   *canopy*
Of richest texture spread, at th' upper end
Was placed in regal luster. Down a while
He sat, and round about him saw unseen:
At last as from a cloud his fulgent head
450 And shape star-bright appeared, or brighter, clad
With what permissive° glory since his fall   *permitted*
Was left him, or false glitter: all amazed
At that so sudden blaze the Stygian[7] throng
Bent their aspéct, and whom they wished beheld,
455 Their mighty chief returned: loud was th' acclaim:
Forth rushed in haste the great consulting peers,
Raised from their dark divan,[8] and with like joy
Congratulant approached him, who with hand
Silence, and with these words attention won:
460   "Thrones, Dominations, Princedoms, Virtues, Powers,
For in possession such, not only of right,
I call ye[9] and declare ye now, returned
Successful beyond hope, to lead ye forth
Triumphant out of this infernal pit
465 Abominable, accurst, the house of woe,
And dungeon of our tyrant: now possess,
As lords, a spacious world, to our native heaven
Little inferior, by my adventure hard
With peril great achieved. Long were to tell
470 What I have done, what suffered, with what pain
Voyaged th' unreal,° vast, unbounded deep   *unformed*
Of horrible confusion, over which
By Sin and Death a broad way now is paved
To expedite your glorious march; but I
475 Toiled out my uncouth° passage, forced to ride   *strange*
Th' untractable abyss, plunged in the womb
Of unoriginal[1] Night and Chaos wild,
That jealous of their secrets fiercely opposed

6. Pertaining to Pluto, ruler of the classical underworld.
7. Of the river Styx in Hades, the river of hate.
8. The Turkish Council of State (continuing the

comparisons with oriental despotism).
9. I.e., you now have these titles not only by right
but by possession (from the conquest on earth).
1. Having no origin, uncreated.

My journey strange, with clamorous uproar
480 Protesting[2] Fate supreme; thence how I found
The new-created world, which fame in Heav'n
Long had foretold, a fabric wonderful
Of absolute perfection, therein man
Placed in a paradise, by our exile
485 Made happy: him by fraud I have seduced
From his Creator, and the more to increase
Your wonder, with an apple. He thereat
Offended, worth your laughter, hath giv'n up
Both his beloved man and all his world,
490 To Sin and Death a prey, and so to us,
Without our hazard, labor, or alarm,
To range in, and to dwell, and over man
To rule, as over all he should have ruled.
True is, me also he hath judged, or rather
495 Me not, but the brute serpent in whose shape
Man I deceived; that which to me belongs,
Is enmity, which he will put between
Me and mankind; I am to bruise his heel;
His seed, when is not set, shall bruise my head:
500 A world who would not purchase with a bruise,
Or much more grievous pain? Ye have th' account
Of my performance: what remains, ye gods,
But up and enter now into full bliss."[3]
      So having said, a while he stood, expecting
505 Their universal shout and high applause.
To fill his ear, when contrary he hears
On all sides, from innumerable tongues
A dismal universal hiss, the sound
Of public scorn; he wondered, but not long
510 Had leisure, wond'ring at himself now more;
His visage drawn he felt to sharp and spare,
His arms clung to his ribs, his legs entwining
Each other, till supplanted° down he fell   *tripped up*
A monstrous serpent on his belly prone,
515 Reluctant,° but in vain, a greater power   *struggling*
Now ruled him, punished in the shape he sinned,
According to his doom: he would have spoke,
But hiss for hiss returned with forkèd tongue
To forkèd tongue, for now were all transformed
520 Alike, to serpents[4] all as accessories
To his bold riot:° dreadful was the din   *revolt*
Of hissing through the hall, thick swarming now
With complicated° monsters, head and tail,   *tangled*
Scorpion[5] and asp, and amphisbaena dire,

---

2. Protesting both to, and against, Fate.
3. Ironically, the final word of Satan's proud, triumphal speech rhymes with and so prepares for the "hiss" that will soon greet him, as his would-be triumph is turned by God to abject humiliation.
4. The scene recalls Dante's vivid description of the thieves metamorphosed to snakes in *Inferno* 24–25.

5. The "Scorpion" has a venomous sting at the tip of the tail; "asp" is a small Egyptian viper; "amphisbaena" supposedly had a head at each end; "Cerastes" is an asp with horny projections over each eye; "hydrus" and "ellops" were mythical water snakes; "dipsas" was a mythical snake whose bite caused raging thirst.

525　Cerastes horned, hydrus, and ellops drear,
　　　And dipsas (not so thick swarmed once the soil
　　　Bedropped with blood of Gorgon,[6] or the isle
　　　Ophiusa) but still greatest he the midst,
　　　Now dragon grown, larger than whom the sun
530　Engendered in the Pythian vale on slime,
　　　Huge Python,[7] and his power no less he seemed
　　　Above the rest still to retain; they all
　　　Him followed issuing forth to th' open field,
　　　Where all yet left of that revolted rout
535　Heav'n-fall'n, in station stood or just array,[8]
　　　Sublime° with expectation when to see　　　　　　　　*raised up*
　　　In triumph issuing forth their glorious chief;
　　　They saw, but other sight instead, a crowd
　　　Of ugly serpents; horror on them fell,
540　And horrid sympathy; for what they saw,
　　　They felt themselves now changing; down their arms,
　　　Down fell both spear and shield, down they as fast,
　　　And the dire hiss renewed, and the dire form
　　　Catched by contagion, like in punishment,
545　As in their crime. Thus was th' applause they meant,
　　　Turned to exploding hiss, triumph to shame
　　　Cast on themselves from their own mouths. There stood
　　　A grove hard by, sprung up with this their change,
　　　His will who reigns above, to aggravate
550　Their penance,° laden with fair fruit, like that　　　　*punishment*
　　　Which grew in Paradise, the bait of Eve
　　　Used by the Tempter: on that prospect strange
　　　Their earnest eyes they fixed, imagining
　　　For one forbidden tree a multitude
555　Now ris'n, to work them further woe or shame;
　　　Yet parched with scalding thirst and hunger fierce,
　　　Though to delude them sent, could not abstain,
　　　But on they rolled in heaps, and up the trees
　　　Climbing, sat thicker than the snaky locks
560　That curled Megaera:[9] greedily they plucked
　　　The fruitage fair to sight, like that which grew
　　　Near that bituminous lake where Sodom flamed;[1]
　　　This more delusive, not the touch, but taste
　　　Deceived; they fondly° thinking to allay　　　　　　*foolishly*
565　Their appetite with gust,° instead of fruit　　　　　　*relish*
　　　Chewed bitter ashes, which th' offended taste
　　　With spattering noise rejected: oft they assayed,°　　*attempted*
　　　Hunger and thirst constraining, drugged as oft,
　　　With hatefulest disrelish writhed their jaws
570　With soot and cinders filled; so oft they fell

6. Drops of blood from the Gorgon Medusa's severed head turned into snakes; "Ophiusa" in Greek means "isle of snakes."
7. A gigantic serpent engendered from the slime left by Deucalion's flood; Apollo slew him and appropriated the "Pythian" vale and shrine at Delphi.
8. I.e., at their posts or on parade.
9. One of three Furies with snaky hair.
1. Sodom apples reputedly grew on the spot where the accursed city once stood, now the Dead Sea ("that bituminous lake"); the apples look good, but dissolve into ashes when eaten.

Into the same illusion, not as man
Whom they triumphed once lapsed.[2] Thus were they plagued
And worn with famine, long and ceaseless hiss,
Till their lost shape, permitted, they resumed,[3]
575 Yearly enjoined, some say, to undergo
This annual humbling certain numbered days,
To dash their pride, and joy for man seduced.
However some tradition they dispersed
Among the heathen of their purchase° got,   plunder
580 And fabled how the serpent, whom they called
Ophion with Eurynome,[4] the wide-
Encroaching Eve perhaps, had first the rule
Of high Olympus, thence by Saturn driv'n
And Ops, ere yet Dictaean Jove was born.

Summary Sin and Death proceed without further interruption to Earth, and
enter into possession of it. God sees their arrival and declines to interfere, but prophesies that their triumph will be only temporary; in due course they will be forced back
to Hell again, and forever. Meanwhile, the angels are ordered to twist the Earth on
its axis, disorder the planets so their influence will in future be bad as well as good,
and rearrange the cosmos generally. In consequence, the temperate climate of Paradise at once gives way to extremes of heat and cold, and furious winds begin to blow
across the ruined planet.

[ADAM, EVE, AND THE FIRST STEPS TO REDEMPTION]

* * * Thus began
Outrage from lifeless things; but Discord first
Daughter of Sin, among th' irrational,
Death introduced through fierce antipathy:[5]
710 Beast now with beast gan war, and fowl with fowl,
And fish with fish; to graze the herb° all leaving,   grass
Devour'd each other; nor stood much in awe
Of man, but fled him, or with count'nance grim
Glared on him passing: these were from without
715 The growing miseries, which Adam saw
Already in part, though hid in gloomiest shade,
To sorrow abandoned, but worse felt within,
And in a troubled sea of passion tossed,
Thus to disburden sought with sad complaint:
720   "O miserable of happy![6] Is this the end

2. Unlike man who fell once, they try to eat the
dissolving apples over and over again.
3. God permitted them to regain their "lost form"
as fallen angels; but they are undergoing a slower,
natural metamorphosis into grosser substance by
their continuing commitment to and choice of evil.
4. The Titan "Ophion" (whose name means
"snake") and his wife "Eurynome" ("the wide-
reacher") ruled Olympus until driven away by "Saturn" and his wife "Ops," who were in turn

overthrown by "Jove," who lived on the mountain
"Dicte." Milton suggests that these may represent
versions of the story transmitted by the fallen
angels to the pagans (lines 578–84).
5. "Discord" (personified as daughter of Sin)
introduced Death among the animals ("the irrational") by stirring up "antipathy" among them.
6. Adam's complaint begins with the classical formula for a tragic fall or *peripeteia*, the change from
happiness to misery.

Of this new glorious world, and me so late
The glory of that glory, who now become
Accurst of blessèd, hide me from the face
Of God, whom to behold was then my height
725 Of happiness: yet well, if here would end
The misery, I deserved it, and would bear
My own deservings; but this will not serve;
All that I eat or drink, or shall beget,
Is propagated[7] curse. O voice once heard
730 Delightfully, 'Increase and multiply,'
Now death to hear! For what can I increase
Or multiply, but curses on my head?
Who of all ages to succeed, but feeling
The evil on him brought by me, will curse
735 My head: 'Ill fare our ancestor impure,
For this we may thank Adam'; but his thanks
Shall be the execration; so besides
Mine own that bide upon[8] me, all from me
Shall with a fierce reflux on me redound,
740 On me as on their natural center light
Heavy, though in their place. O fleeting joys
Of Paradise, dear bought with lasting woes!
Did I request thee, Maker, from my clay
To mold me man, did I solicit thee
745 From darkness to promote me, or here place
In this delicious garden? As my will
Concurred not to my being, it were but right
And equal° to reduce me to my dust,   *just*
Desirous to resign, and render back
750 All I received, unable to perform
Thy terms too hard, by which I was to hold
The good I sought not. To the loss of that,
Sufficient penalty, why hast thou added
The sense of endless woes? Inexplicable
755 Thy justice seems; yet to say truth, too late
I thus contest; then should have been refused
Those terms whatever, when they were proposed:
Thou[9] didst accept them; wilt thou enjoy the good,
Then cavil the conditions? And though God
760 Made thee without thy leave, what if thy son
Prove disobedient, and reproved, retort,
'Wherefore didst thou beget me? I sought it not:'
Wouldst thou admit for his contempt of thee
That proud excuse? Yet him not thy election,°   *choice*
765 But natural necessity begot.

---

7. Handed down from one generation to the next.
8. I.e., Adam's "own" curse will remain ("bide") with him, and the curse ("execration") of "all" who descend from him will "redound" on him as to their natural "center"; objects so placed ("in their place," line 741) were thought to be weightless ("light") but these curses will be "heavy."
9. Adam turns from addressing God to address himself.

God made thee of choice his own, and of his own
To serve him, thy reward was of his grace,
Thy punishment then justly is at his will.
Be it so, for I submit, his doom is fair,
770 That dust I am, and shall to dust return:
O welcome hour whenever! Why delays
His hand to execute what his decree
Fixed on this day? Why do I overlive,
Why am I mocked with death, and lengthened out
775 To deathless pain? How gladly would I meet
Mortality my sentence, and be earth
Insensible, how glad would lay me down
As in my mother's lap! There I should rest
And sleep secure; his dreadful voice no more
780 Would thunder in my ears, no fear of worse
To me and to my offspring would torment me
With cruel expectation. Yet one doubt
Pursues me still, lest all I° cannot die,   *all of me*
Lest that pure breath of life, the spirit of man
785 Which God inspired, cannot together perish
With this corporeal clod; then in the grave,
Or in some other dismal place, who knows
But I shall die a living death? O thought
Horrid, if true! Yet why? It was but breath
790 Of life that sinned; what dies but what had life
And sin? The body properly hath neither.
All of me then shall die:[1] let this appease
The doubt, since human reach no further knows.
For though the Lord of all be infinite,
795 Is his wrath also? Be it, man is not so,
But mortal doomed. How can he exercise
Wrath without end on man whom death must end?
Can he make deathless death? That were to make
Strange contradiction, which to God himself
800 Impossible is held, as argument
Of weakness, not of power. Will he draw out,
For anger's sake, finite to infinite
In punished man, to satisfy his rigor
Satisfied never; that were to extend
805 His sentence beyond dust and nature's law,
By which all causes else according still
To the reception of their matter act,
Not to th' extent of their own sphere.[2] But say
That death be not one stroke, as I supposed,
810 Bereaving° sense, but endless misery   *taking away*

---

1. After debating the matter, Adam concludes that
the soul dies with the body; Milton in his *Christian
Doctrine* worked out this "mortalist" doctrine, with
its corollary, that both soul and body rise at the
Last Judgment.

2. Adam convinces himself that "finite" matter
(line 802) cannot suffer "infinite" punishment by
an axiom of traditional philosophy, that by
"nature's law" (line 805) the actions of agents are
limited by the nature of the object they act upon.

From this day onward, which I feel begun
Both in me, and without° me, and so last   *outside of*
To perpetuity; ay me, that fear
Comes thund'ring back with dreadful revolution°   *recurrence*
815   On my defenseless head; both Death and I
Am found eternal, and incorporate° both,   *made one body*
Nor I on my part single, in me all
Posterity stands cursed: fair patrimony
That I must leave ye, sons; O were I able
820   To waste it all myself, and leave ye none!
So disinherited how would ye bless
Me now your curse! Ah, why should all mankind
For one man's fault thus guiltless be condemned,
If guiltless? But from me what can proceed,
825   But all corrupt, both mind and will depraved,
Not to do° only, but to will the same   *act*
With me? How can they then acquitted stand
In sight of God? Him after all disputes
Forced I absolve: all my evasions vain
830   And reasonings, though through mazes, lead me still
But to my own conviction: first and last
On me, me only, as the source and spring
Of all corruption, all the blame lights due;
So might the wrath.[3] Fond° wish! Couldst thou support   *foolish*
835   That burden heavier than the earth to bear,
Than all the world much heavier, though divided
With that bad woman? Thus what thou desir'st,
And what thou fear'st, alike destroys all hope
Of refuge, and concludes thee miserable
840   Beyond all past example and future,
To Satan only like both crime and doom.
O conscience, into what abyss of fears
And horrors hast thou driv'n me; out of which
I find no way, from deep to deeper plunged!"
845   Thus Adam to himself lamented loud
Through the still night, not now, as ere man fell,
Wholesome and cool, and mild, but with black air
Accompanied, with damps° and dreadful gloom,   *noxious vapors*
Which to his evil conscience represented
850   All things with double terror: on the ground
Outstretched he lay, on the cold ground, and oft
Cursed his creation, Death as oft accused
Of tardy execution, since denounced°   *pronounced*
The day of his offense: "Why comes not Death,"
855   Said he, "with one thrice-accéptáble stroke
To end me? Shall Truth fail to keep her word,
Justice divine not hasten to be just?
But Death comes not at call, Justice divine

---

3. Cf. the Son's offer to accept all humankind's guilt (3.236), and Eve's similar offer (10.935–36).

Mends not her slowest pace for prayers or cries.
860 O woods, O fountains, hillocks, dales and bow'rs,
With other echo late I taught your shades
To answer, and resound far other song."[4]
Whom thus afflicted when sad Eve beheld,
Desolate where she sat, approaching nigh,
865 Soft words to his fierce passion she assayed;
But her with stern regard he thus repelled:
　　"Out of my sight, thou serpent,[5] that name best
Befits thee with him leagued, thyself as false
And hateful; nothing wants,° but that thy shape,   *is lacking*
870 Like his, and color serpentine may show
Thy inward fraud, to warn all creatures from thee
Henceforth; lest that too heav'nly form, pretended[6]
To hellish falsehood, snare them. But° for thee   *except*
I had persisted happy, had not thy pride
875 And wand'ring vanity, when least was safe,
Rejected my forewarning, and disdained
Not to be trusted, longing to be seen
Though by the Devil himself, him overweening°   *overconfident*
To overreach, but with the serpent meeting
880 Fooled and beguiled, by him thou, I by thee,
To trust thee from my side, imagined wise,
Constant, mature, proof against all assaults,
And understood not all was but a show
Rather than solid virtue, all but a rib
885 Crooked by nature, bent, as now appears,
More to the part siníster° from me drawn,   *the left side*
Well if thrown out, as supernumerary[7]
To my just number found. O why did God,
Creator wise, that peopled highest heav'n
890 With Spirits masculine,[8] create at last
This novelty on earth, this fair defect
Of nature,[9] and not fill the world at once
With men as angels without feminine,
Or find some other way to generate
895 Mankind? This mischief had not then befall'n,
And more that shall befall, innumerable
Disturbances on earth through female snares,
And strait conjunction[1] with this sex: for either
He never shall find out fit mate, but such
900 As some misfortune brings him, or mistake,
Or whom he wishes most shall seldom gain

---

4. Cf. their morning hymn (5.153–208).
5. Adam's bitter, misogynistic outcry begins with reference to the patristic notion that the name Eve, aspirated, means "serpent."
6. Held in front of, as a cover or mask.
7. It was supposed that Adam had thirteen ribs on the left side, so he could spare one for the creation of Eve and still retain the proper ("just") number,

twelve.
8. The Miltonic Bard indicated that angels can assume at will "either sex . . . or both" (1.424).
9. Aristotle had claimed that the female is a defective male.
1. Close, hard-pressing, binding union: Adam goes on to project the problems of future marriages.

Through her perverseness, but shall see her gained
By a far worse, or if she love, withheld
By parents, or his happiest choice too late
905 Shall meet, already linked and wedlock-bound
To a fell° adversary, his hate or shame: *bitter*
Which infinite calamity shall cause
To human life, and household peace confound."
    He added not, and from her turned, but Eve
910 Not so repulsed, with tears that ceased not flowing,
And tresses all disordered, at his feet
Fell humble, and embracing them, besought
His peace, and thus proceeded in her plaint:
    "Forsake me not thus, Adam, witness Heav'n
915 What love sincere, and reverence in my heart
I bear thee, and unweeting° have offended,   *unintentionally*
Unhappily deceived; thy suppliant
I beg, and clasp thy knees;² bereave me not,
Whereon I live, thy gentle looks, thy aid,
920 Thy counsel in this uttermost distress,
My only strength and stay: forlorn of thee,
Whither shall I betake me, where subsist?
While yet we live, scarce one short hour perhaps,
Between us two let there be peace, both joining,
925 As joined in injuries, one enmity
Against a foe by doom express° assigned us,   *explicit judgment*
That cruel serpent: on me exercise not
Thy hatred for this misery befall'n,
On me already lost, me than thyself
930 More miserable; both have sinned, but thou
Against God only, I against God and thee,
And to the place of judgment will return,
There with my cries importune Heaven, that all
The sentence from thy head removed may light
935 On me, sole cause to thee of all this woe,
Me me only just object of his ire."³
    She ended weeping, and her lowly plight,°   *posture*
Immovable till peace obtained from fault
Acknowledged and deplored, in Adam wrought
940 Commiseration; soon his heart relented
Towards her, his life so late and sole delight,
Now at his feet submissive in distress,
Creature so fair his reconcilement seeking,
His counsel whom she had displeased, his aid;
945 As one disarmed, his anger all he lost,
And thus with peaceful words upraised her soon:
    "Unwary, and too desirous, as before,
So now of what thou know'st not, who desir'st

---

2. Eve assumes the posture of the classical suppliant, clasping the knees of the one she begs from.

3. Eve also echoes the Son's offer (3.236). Cf.
Adam's cry (10.832).

The punishment all on thyself; alas!
950 Bear thine own first, ill able to sustain
His full wrath whose thou feel'st as yet least part,[4]
And my displeasure bear'st so ill. If prayers
Could alter high decrees, I to that place
Would speed before thee, and be louder heard,
955 That on my head all might be visited,
Thy frailty and infirmer sex forgiv'n,
To me committed and by me exposed.
But rise, let us no more contend, nor blame
Each other, blamed enough elsewhere, but strive
960 In offices of love, how we may light'n
Each other's burden in our share of woe;
Since this day's death denounced, if aught I see,
Will prove no sudden, but a slow-paced evil,
A long day's dying to augment our pain,
965 And to our seed (O hapless seed!) derived."°   passed on
     To whom thus Eve, recovering heart, replied:
"Adam, by sad experiment I know
How little weight my words with thee can find,
Found so erroneous, thence by just event°   consequence
970 Found so unfortunate; nevertheless,
Restored by thee, vile as I am, to place
Of new acceptance, hopeful to regain
Thy love, the sole contentment of my heart
Living or dying, from thee I will not hide
975 What thoughts in my unquiet breast are ris'n,
Tending to some relief of our extremes,
Or end, though sharp and sad, yet tolerable,
As in our evils, and of easier choice.
If care of our descent perplex us most,[5]
980 Which must be born to certain woe, devoured
By Death at last, and miserable it is
To be to others cause of misery,
Our own begotten, and of our loins to bring
Into this cursèd world a woeful race,
985 That after wretched life must be at last
Food for so foul a monster, in thy power
It lies, yet ere conception to prevent
The race unblest, to being yet unbegot.
Childless thou art, childless remain; so Death
990 Shall be deceived° his glut, and with us two   cheated of
Be forced to satisfy his rav'nous maw.
But if thou judge it hard and difficult,
Conversing, looking, loving, to abstain
From love's due rites, nuptial embraces sweet,

---

4. I.e., you could hardly bear God's "full wrath"
since you are so distraught when you feel only the
smallest part of it, and you can "ill" bear my dis-

pleasure (line 952).
5. I.e., if concern for our descendants most torment ("perplex") us.

995   And with desire to languish without hope,
        Before the present object[6] languishing
        With like desire, which would be misery
        And torment less than none of what we dread,
        Then both ourselves and seed at once to free
1000   From what we fear for both, let us make short,°   *lose no time*
        Let us seek Death, or he not found, supply
        With our own hands his office on ourselves;
        Why stand we longer shivering under fears,
        That show no end but death, and have the power,
1005   Of many ways to die the shortest choosing,
        Destruction with destruction to destroy."
            She ended here, or vehement despair
        Broke off the rest; so much of death her thoughts
        Had entertained, as dyed her cheeks with pale.
1010   But Adam with such counsel nothing swayed,
        To better hopes his more attentive mind
        Laboring had raised, and thus to Eve replied.
            "Eve thy contempt of life and pleasure seems
        To argue in thee something more sublime
1015   And excellent than what thy mind contemns;°   *despises*
        But self-destruction therefore sought, refutes
        That excellence thought in thee, and implies,
        Not thy contempt, but anguish and regret
        For loss of life and pleasure overloved.
1020   Or if thou covet death, as utmost end
        Of misery, so thinking to evade
        The penalty pronounced, doubt not but God
        Hath wiselier armed his vengeful ire than so
        To be forestalled; much more I fear lest death
1025   So snatched will not exempt us from the pain
        We are by doom to pay: rather such acts
        Of contumacy° will provoke the Highest   *contempt*
        To make death in us live. Then let us seek
        Some safer resolution, which methinks
1030   I have in view, calling to mind with heed
        Part of our sentence, that thy seed shall bruise
        The serpent's head; piteous amends, unless
        Be meant, whom I conjecture, our grand foe
        Satan, who in the serpent hath contrived
1035   Against us this deceit: to crush his head
        Would be revenge indeed; which will be lost
        By death brought on ourselves, or childless days
        Resolved, as thou proposest; so our foe
        Shall scape his punishment ordained, and we
1040   Instead shall double ours upon our heads.
        No more be mentioned then of violence

6. I.e., Eve herself, who then projects her own frustrated desire if they were to forgo sex.

Against ourselves, and wilful barrenness,
That cuts us off from hope, and savors only
Rancor and pride, impatience and despite,
1045 Reluctance° against God and his just yoke   *resistance*
Laid on our necks. Remember with what mild
And gracious temper he both heard and judged
Without wrath or reviling; we expected
Immediate dissolution, which we thought
1050 Was meant by death that day, when lo, to thee
Pains only in child-bearing were foretold,
And bringing forth, soon recompensed with joy,
Fruit of thy womb:[7] on me the curse aslope
Glanced on the ground,[8] with labor I must earn
1055 My bread; what harm? Idleness had been worse;
My labor will sustain me; and lest cold
Or heat should injure us, his timely care
Hath unbesought provided, and his hands
Clothed us unworthy, pitying while he judged;
1060 How much more, if we pray him, will his ear
Be open, and his heart to pity incline,
And teach us further by what means to shun
Th' inclement seasons, rain, ice, hail and snow,
Which now the sky with various face begins
1065 To show us in this mountain, while the winds
Blow moist and keen, shattering° the graceful locks   *scattering*
Of these fair spreading trees; which bids us seek
Some better shroud,° some better warmth to cherish   *shelter*
Our limbs benumbed, ere this diurnal star°   *the sun*
1070 Leave cold the night, how we his gathered beams
Reflected, may with matter sere foment,
Or by collision of two bodies grind
The air attrite to fire,[9] as late the clouds
Justling or pushed with winds rude in their shock
1075 Tine° the slant° flame driv'n down   *ignite / slanting*
Kindles the gummy bark of fir or pine,
And sends a comfortable heat from far,
Which might supply° the sun: such fire to use,   *take the place of*
And what may else be remedy or cure
1080 To evils which our own misdeeds have wrought,
He will instruct us praying, and of grace
Beseeching him, so as we need not fear
To pass commodiously this life, sustained
By him with many comforts, till we end
1085 In dust, our final rest and native home.
What better can we do, than to the place

---

7. Adam's unconscious echo of Elizabeth's address to Mary, mother of Jesus (Luke 1.41–42), "Blessed is the fruit of thy womb," lays the ground for their fuller understanding of the promise about the "seed" of the woman.
8. I.e., the curse, like a spear that almost missed its target, glanced aside and hit the ground.
9. Adam projects the invention of fire: they might, by striking two bodies together, rub ("attrite") the air into fire by friction; or else (line 1070) focus reflected sunbeams (through some equivalent of glass) on dry ("sere") matter.

Repairing where he judged us, prostrate fall
Before him reverent, and there confess
Humbly our faults, and pardon beg, with tears
1090 Watering the ground, and with our sighs the air
Frequenting,° sent from hearts contrite, in sign   *filling*
Of sorrow unfeigned, and humiliation meek.
Undoubtedly he will relent and turn
From his displeasure; in whose look serene,
1095 When angry most he seemed and most severe,
What else but favor, grace, and mercy shone?"
     So spake our father penitent, nor Eve
Felt less remorse: they forthwith to the place
Repairing where he judged them prostrate fell
1100 Before him reverent, and both confessed
Humbly their faults, and pardon begged, with tears
Watering the ground, and with their sighs the air
Frequenting, sent from hearts contrite, in sign
Of sorrow unfeigned, and humiliation meek.[1]

Book 11 *Summary*   The prayers of Adam and Eve prove acceptable to God.
But while humankind may now hope for ultimate redemption, humans may no longer
dwell in Paradise; and Michael, the warrior archangel, is dispatched to explain the
sentence, offer some hope for the future, and dismiss Adam and Eve from the happy
garden. Adam is at first overcome with grief; but the angel encourages him, and while
Eve is put in a trance, Adam is raised to the peak of a high hill and shown in a vision
the future of the human race as far as the flood of Noah.

From Book 12

Summary   Continuing his instruction of Adam, Michael relates the history of
the world from the time of Noah through the coming of Christ, whose ascent into
Heaven and triumph over Death after the Crucifixion he describes.

[THE DEPARTURE FROM EDEN]

     So spake th' Archangel Michaël, then paused,
As at the world's great period;° and our sire   *consummation*
Replete with joy and wonder thus replied:
     "O goodness infinite, goodness immense!
470 That all this good of evil shall produce,
And evil turn to good; more wonderful
Than that which by creation first brought forth
Light out of darkness! Full of doubt I stand,
Whether I should repent me now of sin
475 By me done and occasioned, or rejoice
Much more, that much more good thereof shall spring,
To God more glory, more good will to men

---

1. The final six lines repeat, almost word for word, lines 1086–92, with only six lines separating them; this provides strong closure, as the poet describes Adam's proposed gesture of repentance carried out in every detail.

From God, and over wrath grace shall abound.[1]
But say, if our Deliverer up to Heav'n
480 Must reascend, what will betide the few
His faithful, left among th' unfaithful herd,
The enemies of truth; who then shall guide
His people, who defend? Will they not deal
Worse with his followers than with him they dealt?"
485   "Be sure they will," said th' angel; "but from Heav'n
He to his own a Comforter will send,[2]
The promise of the Father, who shall dwell
His Spirit within them, and the law of faith
Working through love, upon their hearts shall write,
490 To guide them in all truth, and also arm
With spiritual armor, able to resist
Satan's assaults, and quench his fiery darts,[3]
What° man can do against them, not afraid,   *as much as*
Though to the death, against such cruelties
495 With inward consolations recompensed,
And oft supported so as shall amaze
Their proudest persecutors: for the Spirit
Poured first on his apostles, whom he sends
To evangelize the nations, then on all
500 Baptized, shall them with wondrous gifts endue°   *endow*
To speak all tongues, and do all miracles,
As did their Lord before them. Thus they win
Great numbers of each nation to receive
With joy the tidings brought from Heav'n: at length
505 Their ministry performed, and race well run,
Their doctrine and their story written left,[4]
They die; but in their room, as they forewarn,
Wolves shall succeed for teachers, grievous wolves,
Who all the sacred mysteries of Heav'n
510 To their own vile advantages shall turn
Of lucre and ambition, and the truth
With superstitions and traditions taint,[5]
Left only in those written records pure,
Though not but by the Spirit understood.
515 Then shall they seek to avail themselves of names,°   *honors*
Places° and titles, and with these to join   *offices*
Secular power, though feigning still to act

1. These lines do not formulate the medieval idea of the *felix culpa*—that the Fall was fortunate in bringing humans greater happiness than they would otherwise have enjoyed—only that the Fall has provided God an occasion to bring still greater good out of evil. The poem makes clear that Adam and Eve would have grown in perfection and advanced to Heaven had they not sinned.
2. The Holy Spirit, who for Milton is much subordinate to both Father and Son.
3. Cf. Ephesians 6.11–16: "Put on the whole armor of God, that ye may be able to stand against the wiles of the devil. . . . Above all, taking the shield of faith, wherewith ye shall be able to quench all the fiery darts of the wicked." The subsequent history (lines 493–505) is that of the early Christian church in apostolic times.
4. I.e., in the Gospels and Epistles.
5. The history summarized in lines 510–40 is of the corruption of the Christian church by superstitions, traditions, and persecutions of conscience in patristic times under the popes and the Christian emperors, but also extending to the Last Day. The terms point especially to what Milton saw as the revival of "popish" superstitions in the English Church of the Restoration, and to the fierce persecution of Dissenters.

By spiritual, to themselves appropriating
The Spirit of God, promised alike and giv'n
520 To all believers;[6] and from that pretense,
Spiritual laws by carnal° power shall force   *fleshly, worldly*
On every conscience; laws which none shall find
Left them enrolled, or what the Spirit within
Shall on the heart engrave.[7] What will they then
525 But force the Spirit of Grace itself, and bind
His consort Liberty; what, but unbuild
His living temples,[8] built by faith to stand,
Their own faith not another's: for on earth
Who against faith and conscience can be heard
530 Infallible?[9] Yet many will presume:
Whence heavy persecution shall arise
On all who in the worship persevere
Of Spirit and Truth; the rest, far greater part,
Will deem in outward rites and specious forms
535 Religion satisfied; Truth shall retire
Bestuck with sland'rous darts, and works of faith
Rarely be found: so shall the world go on,
To good malignant, to bad men benign,
Under her own weight groaning, till the day
540 Appear of respiration° to the just,   *respite*
And vengeance to the wicked, at return
Of him so lately promised to thy aid,
The Woman's Seed,[1] obscurely then foretold,
Now ampler known thy Saviour and thy Lord,
545 Last in the clouds from Heav'n to be revealed
In glory of the Father, to dissolve
Satan with his perverted world, then raise
From the conflagrant mass,° purged and refined,   *the burning world*
New heav'ns, new earth, ages of endless date
550 Founded in righteousness and peace of love,
To bring forth fruits joy and eternal bliss."
    He ended; and thus Adam last replied:
"How soon hath thy prediction, seer blest,
Measured this transient world, the race of time,
555 Till time stand fixed: beyond is all abyss,
Eternity, whose end no eye can reach.
Greatly instructed I shall hence depart,
Greatly in peace of thought, and have my fill
Of knowledge, what° this vessel can contain;   *as much as*

6. These lines affirm the Protestant principle of every Christian's right to interpret Scripture according to the "inner light" of the Spirit, and denounce (as Milton consistently did in his tracts) the use of civil ("carnal") power to enforce orthodoxy.
7. I.e., there is nothing in Scripture or in the Spirit's inner teaching that sanctions persecution for conscience.
8. Cf. 1 Corinthians 3.16: "Know ye not that ye are the temple of God?" "His consort Liberty": Mil-

ton typically insists that Christ's gospel and the Spirit of God teach liberty, religious and civil, alluding as here to 2 Corinthians 3.17: "Where the Spirit of the Lord is, there is Liberty."
9. An attack on papal claims to infallibility, asserted though not yet proclaimed as doctrine.
1. Michael's story ends with the full explication of the promised "Woman's Seed" as Christ, and with the renewal of all things after the Last Judgment (lines 545–51).

560 Beyond which was my folly to aspire.
Henceforth I learn, that to obey is best,
And love with fear the only God, to walk
As in his presence, ever to observe
His providence, and on him sole depend,
565 Merciful over all his works, with good
Still overcoming evil, and by small
Accomplishing great things, by things deemed weak
Subverting worldly strong, and worldly wise
By simply meek; that suffering for truth's sake
570 Is fortitude to highest victory,
And to the faithful death the gate of life;
Taught this by his example whom I now
Acknowledge my Redeemer ever blest."
    To whom thus also th' angel last replied:
575 "This having learnt, thou hast attained the sum
Of wisdom; hope no higher, though all the stars
Thou knew'st by name,[2] and all th' ethereal powers,
All secrets of the deep, all nature's works,
Or works of God in heav'n, air, earth, or sea,
580 And all the riches of this world enjoy'dst,
And all the rule, one empire; only add
Deeds to thy knowledge answerable,° add faith,   *corresponding*
Add virtue, patience, temperance, add love,
By name to come called charity, the soul
585 Of all the rest: then wilt thou not be loath
To leave this Paradise, but shalt possess
A paradise within thee, happier far.
Let us descend now therefore from this top
Of speculation;° for the hour precise   *hill of speculation*
590 Exacts° our parting hence; and see the guards,   *requires*
By me encamped on yonder hill, expect
Their motion,° at whose front a flaming sword,   *await their orders*
In signal of remove, waves fiercely round;
We may no longer stay: go, waken Eve;
595 Her also I with gentle dreams have calmed
Portending good, and all her spirits composed
To meek submission: thou at season fit
Let her with thee partake what thou hast heard,
Chiefly what may concern her faith to know,
600 The great deliverance by her seed to come
(For by the Woman's Seed) on all mankind.
That ye may live, which will be many days,
Both in one faith unanimous though sad,
With cause for evils past, yet much more cheered
605 With meditation on the happy end."
    He ended, and they both descend the hill;
Descended, Adam to the bow'r where Eve

---

2. Michael glances back at Raphael's warning in Book 8 that Adam should concern himself first with matters pertaining to his own life and world, rather than speculating overmuch about the cosmos.

Lay sleeping ran before, but found her waked;
And thus with words not sad she him received:
610   "Whence thou return'st, and whither went'st, I know;
For God is also in sleep, and dreams advise,[3]
Which he hath sent propitious, some great good
Presaging, since with sorrow and heart's distress
Wearied I fell asleep: but now lead on;
615 In me is no delay; with thee to go,
Is to stay here; without thee here to stay,
Is to go hence unwilling; thou to me
Art all things under heav'n,[4] all places thou,
Who for my wilful crime art banished hence.
620 This further consolation yet secure
I carry hence; though all by me is lost,
Such favor I unworthy am vouchsafed,
By me the Promised Seed shall all restore."
   So spake our mother Eve, and Adam heard
625 Well pleased, but answered not; for now too nigh
Th' Archangel stood, and from the other hill
To their fixed station, all in bright array
The Cherubim descended; on the ground
Gliding metéorous,° as evening mist   *like a meteor*
630 Ris'n from a river o'er the marish° glides,   *marsh*
And gathers ground fast at the laborer's heel
Homeward returning. High in front advanced,
The brandished sword of God before them blazed
Fierce as a comet; which with torrid heat,
635 And vapor° as the Libyan air adust,°   *smoke / parched*
Began to parch that temperate clime; whereat
In either hand the hast'ning angel caught
Our ling'ring parents, and to th' eastern gate
Led them direct, and down the cliff as fast
640 To the subjected° plain; then disappeared.   *low-lying*
They looking back, all th' eastern side beheld
Of Paradise, so late their happy seat,°   *estate*
Waved over by that flaming brand,° the gate   *sword*
With dreadful faces thronged and fiery arms:
645 Some natural tears they dropped, but wiped them soon;
The world was all before them, where to choose
Their place of rest, and Providence their guide:
They hand in hand with wand'ring steps and slow,
Through Eden took their solitary way.[5]

1674

---

3. The lines suggest that Eve's dream has provided her a parallel (if lesser) prophecy to Adam's visions and instruction. Cf. Numbers 12.6: "If there be a prophet among you, I the Lord will make myself known unto him in a vision, and will speak to him in a dream."
4. Eve has the last word in the poem, a love-song recalling her lovely prelapsarian lyric (4.641ff.).

Her language also recalls Ruth's promise to accompany her mother-in-law, Naomi (Ruth 1.16). In her last lines (621–23) she rather surprisingly characterizes herself as the central epic protagonist of Milton's poem.
5. The paradox, "hand in hand" / "solitary," is especially resonant.

The Restoration and the Eighteenth Century 1660–1785

1660:	Charles II restored to the English throne
1688–89:	The Glorious Revolution: deposition of James II and accession of William of Orange
1700:	Death of John Dryden
1707:	Act of Union unites Scotland and England, which thus become "Great Britain"
1714:	Rule by House of Hanover begins with accession of George I
1744–45:	Deaths of Alexander Pope and Jonathan Swift
1784:	Death of Samuel Johnson

The Restoration and the eighteenth century were times of enormous growth and change in England—or Great Britain, as the nation came to be called after 1707, when the Act of Union joined Scotland to England and Wales. Britain became a world power, an empire on which the sun never set. But it also changed internally. England had always been an agricultural nation; most people were farmers who spent their lives in the neighborhoods where they were born. Gradually their horizons expanded. As the population doubled, to more than ten million, the balance of power shifted toward cities, while trades and industries multiplied and standards of living rose. Moreover, Great Britain became a literate nation, a nation of readers. Almost everyone read the new periodicals and novels that reflected the lives of ordinary women and men, and writers learned to cater to the public. Common interests linked the British Isles; among famous authors, Jonathan Swift, Edmund Burke, Richard Sheridan, and Oliver Goldsmith came from Ireland, and James Thomson, David Hume, and James Boswell came from Scotland. Britons also ventured abroad. In a series of wars against France from 1689 to 1763, colonies were annexed around the world, from Canada in the west to India in the east, and an aggressive market economy—including a lucrative slave trade—brought in unprecedented wealth. At the same time, such developments strained the old ways of life. The gulf widened between rich and poor; individual interests and rights took the place of hierarchical values; and new class conflicts turned people against one another. Regret for what had been lost—the communities and beliefs that gave each person a place to belong to—competed with an eagerness for what had been gained—new ideas and pleasures, new chances to rise. The struggle between these opposing visions affects every phase of eighteenth-century life.

RELIGION AND POLITICS

The Restoration of 1660—the return of Charles Stuart to England—brought hope to a nation divided against itself, exhausted by twenty years of civil wars. Almost all of Charles's subjects welcomed him home, for after the abdication of Richard Cromwell in 1659 the country had seemed at the brink of chaos, and Britons were eager to believe that their king would bring order and law and a spirit of mildness back into the national life. But no political settlement could be stable until religious issues had been resolved. The restoration of the monarchy meant that the established church would also be restored, and though Charles was willing to pardon or ignore many former enemies (such as Milton), the bishops and Anglican clergy were less tolerant of dissent. When Parliament reimposed the Book of Common Prayer in 1662, and then in 1664 barred Nonconformists from religious meetings outside the established church, thousands of clergymen resigned their livings, and the jails were filled with preachers like John Bunyan who refused to be silenced. In 1673 the Test Act required all holders of civil and military offices to take the sacrament in an Anglican Church and to deny belief in transubstantiation. Thus Protestant Dissenters and Roman Catholics were largely excluded from public life; for instance, Alexander Pope, a Catholic, could not attend a university, own land, or vote. The scorn of Anglicans for Nonconformist zeal or "enthusiasm" (a belief in private revelation) bursts out in Samuel Butler's popular *Hudibras* (1663), a caricature of Presbyterians and Independents. And English Catholics were widely regarded as potential traitors who had probably set the great fire that destroyed much of London in 1666.

Yet the triumph of the established church did not resolve the constitutional issues that had divided Charles I and Parliament. Charles II had promised to govern through Parliament, but slyly tried to consolidate royal power. Steering away from crises, he hid his Catholic sympathies and avoided a test of strength with Parliament—except on one occasion. In 1678 the report of the Popish Plot, in which Catholics would rise and murder their Protestant foes, terrified London; and though the charge turned out to be a fraud, the House of Commons exploited the fear by trying to force Charles to exclude his Catholic brother, James, duke of York, from succession to the throne. The turmoil of this period is captured brilliantly by Dryden's *Absalom and Achitophel* (1681). Finally, Charles defeated the Exclusion Bill by dissolving Parliament. But the crisis resulted in a basic division of the country between two new political parties. The party that supported the king came to be called Tories; the king's opponents, Whigs. By the end of the century the two parties had developed opposing attitudes on most important issues. The Tories, who drew their strength from the landed gentry and country clergy, represented conservative values; they strongly supported the Crown and the Anglican Church as the pillars of social and political stability. Convinced that only those with local ties and deep roots in the land could rule responsibly, they were hostile to the rising influence of the new moneyed interests. The Whigs were more progressive and diverse: many powerful nobles, jealous of the powers of the Crown; the merchants and financiers of London; a number of bishops and low-church clergymen; and the Dissenters. What held them together were policies of toleration and support of commerce.

Neither party could live with James II. After he came to the throne in 1685, he claimed the right to make his own laws, suspended the Test Act, and began to fill the army and government with fellow Catholics. Matters came to a head in 1688, when the birth of a son confronted the nation with the prospect of a Catholic dynasty. Secret negotiations paved the way for the Dutchman William of Orange, a champion of Protestantism and the husband of James's Protestant daughter Mary. William landed with a small army in southwestern England and marched toward London. As he advanced, the king's allies faded away, and James fled to a permanent exile in France. The house of Stuart would be heard from again. For more than half a century some loyal Jacobites (from the Latin *Jacobus*, "James"), especially in Scotland, supported James, his son ("the Old Pretender"), and his grandson ("the Young Pretender" or "Bonnie Prince Charlie") as the legitimate rulers of Britain. Moreover, a good many writers, from Aphra Behn and Dryden (and arguably Pope and Johnson) to Robert Burns, privately sympathized with Jacobitism. But after the failure of one last rising in 1745, the cause would dwindle gradually into a wistful sentiment. In retrospect, the coming of William and Mary in 1688—the Glorious, or Bloodless, Revolution—had calmed the fierce divisions within the nation and prepared the way for a unified Great Britain.

A lasting settlement followed. In 1689 a Bill of Rights revoked James's actions; it limited the powers of the Crown, reaffirmed the supremacy of Parliament, and guaranteed some individual rights. The same year the Toleration Act relaxed the strain of religious conflict by granting a limited freedom of worship to Dissenters (although not to Catholics or Jews) so long as they swore allegiance to the Crown. This proved to be a workable compromise; and with the passage of the Act of Settlement in 1701, putting Sophia, electress of Hanover, and her descendants in line for the throne (as the granddaughter of James I, she was the closest Protestant relative of Princess Anne, James II's younger daughter, whose sole surviving child died in that year), the difficult problems that had so long divided England seemed resolved. The principles established in 1689 endured unaltered in essentials until the Reform Bill of 1832.

During Anne's reign (1702–14), new political tensions embittered the nation. England and its allies defeated France and Spain in the War of the Spanish Succession (1702–13)—a Whig war, supported by Whig lords and London merchants, who grew rich on war profits and gained by weakening the power of France and Spain. The spoils included new colonies and the *asiento,* a contract to supply slaves to the Spanish Empire. The hero of the war, Captain-General John Churchill, duke of Marlborough, won the famous victory of Blenheim; was showered with honors and wealth; and with his duchess, dominated the queen until 1710. But the Whigs and Marlborough pushed their luck too hard. When the Whigs tried to reward the Dissenters for their loyalty by removing the Test, Anne fought back to defend the established church. She dismissed her Whig ministers and the Marlboroughs and called in Robert Harley and the brilliant young Henry St. John to form a Tory ministry. These ministers were popular with writers; they employed

Defoe and Swift and commissioned Matthew Prior to negotiate the Peace of Utrecht (1713). But to Swift's despair—he later burlesqued events at court in *Gulliver's Travels*—a bitter rivalry broke out between Harley (then earl of Oxford) and St. John (then Viscount Bolingbroke). Though Bolingbroke succeeded in ousting Oxford, the death of Anne in 1714 reversed his fortunes. George I (Sophia's son) became the first Hanoverian king, and the vindictive Whigs returned to power. Harley was imprisoned in the Tower of London until 1717; and Bolingbroke, charged with being a Jacobite traitor, fled to France. Pardoned in 1723, he came back to England and directed the opposition to Robert Walpole, while playing the gentleman-philosopher-farmer and helping Pope to plan *An Essay on Man*. Government was now securely in the hands of the Whigs.

The three Georges who occupied the throne during the rest of the century presided over a nation that grew increasingly prosperous through war, trade, colonization, consumer capitalism, and the beginnings of industrialism. George I (reigned 1714–27) and George II (reigned 1727–60) were German at heart; they spoke broken English and took little interest in England's affairs. Hence ministers became more important and more independent of the Crown than they had ever been before. Through royal indifference and the ambition and skill of Walpole, the first "prime minister," the modern system of ministerial government began to develop. Walpole rose to power as a result of the "South Sea bubble" (1720), a stock market crash; and his ability to restore confidence and keep the country running smoothly—as well as to juggle money—would mark his long ascendancy (1721–42). He was a master of the patronage system, installing his dependents in government offices and controlling the House of Commons by buying off its members. But he did not buy off the wits, and they were offended. Gay's *Beggar's Opera* (1728) and Fielding's *Jonathan Wild* (1743) draw interesting parallels between great criminals and great politicians, and Pope's *Dunciad* uses Walpole as an emblem of the corruption and commercialization of the whole social fabric. Yet Pope himself had made a fortune by marketing his poems as cleverly as he wrote them. Increasingly, authors, like politicians, rose in the world by giving the public what it wanted. Walpole was unwilling to go to war (and fell because he managed it badly); but the next major English statesman, William Pitt the Elder, appealed to the patriotism of common people and called for the expansion of British power and commerce overseas. The defeat of the French in the Seven Years' War (1756–63), especially in North America, was largely his doing.

The long reign of George III (1760–1820) was dominated by two great concerns: the emergence of Britain as a colonial power and the cry for a new social order based on liberty and radical reform. In 1763 the Peace of Paris consolidated British rule over Canada and India, and not even the later loss of the American colonies could stem the rise of the empire. Great Britain was no longer an isolated island but a nation with interests and responsibilities around the world. At home, however, there was discontent. The wealth brought to England by industrialism and foreign trade had not spread to the working classes. It seemed to many that the bonds of custom that once held people together had broken, and now money alone was respected. Protestants turned against Catholics; in 1780 the Gordon Riots put London temporarily under mob rule. The king was popular with his subjects and tried to take government into his own hands, rising above all parties, but his efforts often backfired—as when the American colonists mistook him for a tyrant. From 1788 to the end of his life, moreover, an inherited disease (porphyria) periodically unhinged his mind, as in a memorable scene described by Frances Burney. Meanwhile, reformers such as John Wilkes and Richard Price called for a new political democracy. Fear of their radicalism would contribute to the British reaction against the French Revolution. In the last decades of the century, British authors would be torn between two opposing attitudes: loyalty to the old traditions of subordination, mutual obligations, and local self-sufficiency; and yearning for a new dispensation founded on principles of liberty, the rule of reason, and human rights.

THE CONTEXT OF IDEAS

The political turbulence of the seventeenth century subsided only gradually during the period after the Restoration (1660–1700), and literature also registered a conflict of values. John Milton's major poems, a culmination of Renaissance art, appeared at the same time that John Dryden was leading the way to a new age of elegance. Bunyan's *Pilgrim's Progress* expressed the Nonconformist conscience at the same time that the earl of Rochester expressed the creed of a libertine and rake. In the theater, witty, bawdy comedies—written and acted by women as well as men—reflected the style of a fun-loving, dissolute court. Charles set a mixed example for the nation. A lover of pleasure and women, he was always ready to sacrifice principles to live in comfort. But he also took a genuine interest in new ideas and supported the arts and sciences. French and Italian musicians, as well as painters from the Low Countries, migrated to England; and playhouses—closed by the Puritans since 1642—sprang back to life. In 1660 Charles authorized two new companies of actors: the King's Players and the Duke's. Two years later he chartered the Royal Society of London for the Improving of Natural Knowledge, thus giving official approval to the scientific revolution that was reshaping views of the world. Early in the century, Francis Bacon had called for an advancement of learning based on direct observations of nature; and two wonderful inventions, the microscope and telescope, had begun to reveal that nature is more extravagant—teeming with tiny creatures and boundless galaxies—than anyone had ever imagined. Now experiments came into vogue, in thought and morals as well as science and art. The sense that new worlds were being discovered could be unnerving, but it was also exciting.

Skepticism and freethinking flourished during the late seventeenth century. The civil wars had turned the world upside down; if a king could be executed, what authority was safe? Even after the Restoration, the question remained. One answer had been offered by Thomas Hobbes, whose *Leviathan* (1651) had argued that only an absolute government could check the "perpetual and restless desire of power" in all human beings, a competition that would lead to the "war of every man against every man" unless the final power were vested in some sovereign. Hobbes's emphasis on the predatory passions that drive both human nature and society was detested by the church and attacked on all sides. Yet his ideas influenced many young people, especially the libertines who devoted their lives to a quest for pleasure and power. His pessimistic view of human nature also provoked, by way of reaction, an optimistic insistence on the natural goodness of humanity, which would become an article of faith for many in the eighteenth century. Another influential point of view was philosophic skepticism. Originating in ancient Greece, skepticism revived in the all-questioning essays of the Frenchman Michel de Montaigne (1533–1592). The skeptic argued that all knowledge derives from our senses but that, because our senses do not report the world accurately, reliable knowledge is impossible to achieve. The safest course is to remember that most beliefs rest on opinion and not to hunger for some ultimate, inaccessible truth. Butler, Dryden, and Rochester were among those who followed this doctrine. But though skeptics might doubt the results of human reasoning, they were not precluded from religious beliefs. As Dryden asserted after converting to Catholicism, to accept the mysteries of Christianity one needs faith alone.

The new science also encouraged a challenge to traditional wisdom and learning. The ancients (and the fathers of the church) had not known about the solar system, the circulation of the blood, the existence of microscopic organisms, or the law of gravity. In this respect the moderns were much wiser. But the school curriculum still began with years of Latin and Greek. Humanistic education had long relied on standard ancient texts, which were supposed to teach the student everything necessary for understanding life. Hence a battle of books broke out in the late seventeenth century between the champions of ancient and of modern learning; Swift, Pope, and other British writers fought for the ancients. Nevertheless, modern habits of thought began to dominate intellectual life as scientists discovered new worlds in outer space or under the microscope, other thinkers began to speculate that our world is plural (or multicultural) and that its most basic institutions—systems of government, marriage, the church, the distribution of wealth—could always be organized in some different way. Schemes for reforming society preoccupied many writers. Both Mary Astell and Daniel Defoe, for instance, proposed model schools for the education of women.

As views of nature changed, so did philosophy and religion. What we call "science" today was then grouped under "natural history" (the collection and description of facts of nature), "natural philosophy" (the study of the causes of what happens in nature), and "natural religion" (the study of nature as a book written by God). And the discovery of laws of nature, such as Boyle's law (the pressure and volume of a gas are inversely proportional) or Newton's laws of optics and celestial mechanics, seemed evidence of a universal order in creation. Theologically, the elegant simplicity of that order supported the idea of a divine intelligence whose presence might be deduced from his works, as a watch implies a watchmaker. For Deists like Bolingbroke, religion did not depend on mystery or superstition, but only on reason, which taught the goodness and wisdom of natural law and its creator. Many orthodox Christians shuddered at the vision of a vast, impersonal machine of nature. Instead they rested their faith on the revelation of Scripture, the scheme of salvation in which Christ died to redeem our sins. Newton himself spent much of his life exploring mysteries of Scripture. Yet many others, like Pope in *An Essay on Man*, insisted that they saw no contradiction between the books of nature and Relevation.

Philosophers also claimed to be following nature. The main line of British philosophy—which runs from Bacon and Hobbes through John Locke, George Berkeley, and David Hume—can be characterized broadly as empiricism, the doctrine that regards all knowledge as derived from experience. However much they disagree with one another, eighteenth-century philosophers typically shun metaphysics—the search for essential or ultimate principles of reality, transcending the physical—in favor of more practical concerns: how do we know what we know, and how can we best put that knowledge to use? Reasoning from what they know most immediately, their own minds and perceptions, they draw conclusions about the natural basis of the ways that human beings behave, especially in morals and politics. British philosophers like to appeal to common sense. Accepting the limits of human intelligence and power, they settle for the possible. Thus Locke, the philosopher who most influenced others, expresses the temper of his times in the *Essay Concerning Human Understanding* (1690):

> If by this inquiry into the nature of the understanding, I can discover the powers thereof; how far they reach; to what things they are in any degree proportionate; and where they fail us, I suppose it may be of use, to prevail with the busy mind of man to be more cautious in meddling with things exceeding its comprehension; to stop when it is at the utmost extent of its tether; and to sit down in a quiet ignorance of those things which, upon examination, are found to be beyond the reach of our capacities. . . . Our business here is not to know all things, but those which concern our conduct.

These words might be taken as the creed of eighteenth-century England. Such a position is Swift's, when he inveighs against metaphysics, abstract logical deductions, and theoretical science. It is similar to Pope's warning against human presumption in *An Essay on Man*. It prompts Johnson to talk of "the business of living" and to restrain the flights of unbridled imagination. And it helps account for the Anglican clergy's dislike of emotion and "enthusiasm" in religion, and for their emphasis on good works, rather than faith, as the way to salvation. Locke's empiricism pervaded eighteenth-century British thought on politics, education, and morals as well as philosophy; Johnson's great *Dictionary* (1755) uses more than fifteen hundred illustrations from his writings.

During the early eighteenth century, the most heated challenges to authority tended to cool. The Act of Settlement and the Act of Union, reducing some tensions within the nation, seemed paralleled by a growing consensus in manners and ideas. Addison and Steele are the masters of that consensus. Attracting a national audience, the *Tatler* (1709–11) and the *Spectator* (1711–12; 1714) both produced and reflected an urbane social ideal, an intellectual life in which all sorts of people could mingle, as in the streets and parks of a thriving city like London. Here a large middle-class public learned to think and behave politely. Through most of the century, as prosperity grew, the rifts in the nation seemed patched. In the provinces as well as in London, in Scotland as well as in England, a standard of good manners came to be shared.

An optimistic view of the ties that bind people together extended to human nature. Rejecting Hobbes, and minimizing original sin, some eighteenth-century thinkers asserted that human beings are naturally good and find their highest happiness by being good to others. In midcentury a new word, *sen-*

timental, suddenly came into fashion. Those who trusted humanity looked for virtue in instinctive and social impulses rather than in a code of conduct sanctioned by divine law. The cult of sensibility fostered a philanthropy that led to social reforms seldom envisioned in earlier times—to the improvement of jails, the relief of imprisoned debtors, the establishment of foundling hospitals and homes for penitent prostitutes, and ultimately the abolition of the slave trade. And it also loosed a ready flow of feeling and tears, sympathetic responses to the joys and sorrows of fellow human beings. The doctrine of natural goodness, popularized by Rousseau, suggested that civilization corrupts us and that if we lived in a state of nature, like "noble savages," we might retain a childlike innocence and virtue. Such notions encouraged an interest in primitive societies and in poets who were reputed to draw their inspiration directly from nature, like the thresher Stephen Duck, the milkmaid Ann Yearsley, and the plowman Robert Burns. William Wordsworth's fascination with children and simple, rural people grows out of the eighteenth-century wish to believe in natural goodness and genius.

As the wave of sentimentalism mounted, it was balanced by a rise of religious feeling. The evangelical revival known as Methodism began in the 1730s, led by three Oxford graduates: John Wesley (1703–1791), his brother Charles (1707–1788), and George Whitefield (1714–1770). The Methodists took their gospel to the common people, warning that all were sinners and damned, unless they accepted "amazing grace," salvation through faith. Nor did the insistence of Methodists on faith over works as the way to salvation prevent them or their Anglican allies from fighting for social reforms. The campaign to abolish slavery and the slave trade was driven largely by a passion to save souls.

Both sentimentalism and evangelicalism placed a new importance on individuals—their private encounters with one another or with a personal god. The older hierarchical system had tended to subordinate individuals to their social rank or station. In the eighteenth century that fixed system began to break down, and people's sense of themselves began to change. The difference between the self as it appears to us in introspection and the identity that others fasten on us—for instance, between the person a woman feels herself to be and the generic "woman" whose role she is supposed to fill— becomes a major interest of eighteenth-century writing. Anne Finch, Lady Mary Wortley Montagu, and Burney all grapple, in their own ways, with the problem of how to stay true to their own core of feelings in spite of social expectations. Similarly, a new kind of fiction, the novel, devotes unprecedented attention to what particular characters are thinking and feeling. In such a world, an institution like marriage begins to be defined as a means to self-fulfillment and personal happiness rather than as a family alliance. By the end of the century many issues of politics and the law revolve around rights, not traditions. The modern individual had been invented; no product of the age is more enduring.

LITERARY PRINCIPLES

The literature of the period between 1660 and 1785 divides conveniently into three lesser periods of about forty years each. The first, extending to the death of Dryden in 1700, is characterized by an effort to bring a new refinement to English literature according to sound critical principles of what is fitting and right; the second, ending with the deaths of Pope in 1744 and Swift in 1745, extends that effort to a wider circle of readers, with special satirical attention to what is unfitting and wrong; the third, concluding with the death of Johnson in 1784 and the publication of Cowper's *The Task* in 1785, confronts the old principles with revolutionary ideas that would come to the fore in the Romantic movement of the late eighteenth and early nineteenth centuries.

Apparently, a sudden change of taste took place about 1660. The change had been long prepared, however, by a trend in European culture, especially in seventeenth-century France: the desire for an elegant simplicity. Reacting against the difficulty and occasional extravagance of late Renaissance literature, writers and critics called for a new restraint, clarity, regularity, and good sense. Donne's "metaphysics" and Milton's bold storming of heaven, for instance, seemed overdone to some Restoration readers. Hence Dryden and Andrew Marvell both were tempted to revise *Paradise Lost*, smoothing away its sublime but arduous idiosyncrasies. The "easy, natural" wit that such writers prefer, surprising but seldom shocking, may well reflect a yearning for peace and order after the violent extremism of the civil wars. Postwar writing aims to be disarming, to counsel a middle way among opposing parties.

This movement produced in France an impressive body of classical literature that distinguished the age of Louis XIV. In England it produced a literature often termed "Augustan," after the writers—Virgil, Horace, and Ovid—who flourished during the reign of Augustus Caesar, the first Roman emperor. In 1660 there was hope that Charles would be a better Augustus, bringing England the civilized virtues of an Augustan age. The King and his followers brought back from exile an admiration of French literature, as well as French fashions, and the theoretical "correctness" of such writers as Pierre Corneille, René Rapin, and Nicolas Boileau came into vogue. The effort to formulate rules of good writing appealed to Dryden and later to Pope. Even Shakespeare had sometimes been careless; and although writers could not expect to surpass his genius, they might hope to avoid his faults. But "neoclassical" English literature aimed to be not only classical but *new*. When Dryden and Pope make use of Greek or Latin or French poets, they convert them to English traditions of variety, freewheeling fancy, and humor. Chaucer, Spenser, Shakespeare, Jonson, and Milton (as well as Homer, Virgil, Horace, Longinus, and Corneille) helped form the literary consciousness of the new age.

If Charles had never lived abroad, English literature would probably still have turned toward an ideal of elegant simplicity. Jonson's poems and criticism had brought the classicizing tendencies of the English Renaissance to a focus. His closed heroic couplets set an example for Edmund Waller and Sir John Denham, whom Dryden considered the principal "refiners" of English metrics. By 1625 one "son of Ben," Sir John Beaumont, anticipated the critical standards of Dryden and Pope, in couplets very much like theirs:

> Pure phrase, fit epithets, a sober care
> Of metaphors, descriptions clear, yet rare,

Similitudes contracted, smooth and round,
Not vexed by learning, but with Nature crowned:
Strong figures drawn from deep inventions, springs,
Consisting less in words, and more in things:
A language not affecting ancient times,
Nor Latin shreds, by which the pedant climbs.
(*To His Late Majesty, Concerning the True Form of
English Poetry*)

Such standards, alien to the verse of Donne, Richard Crashaw, or Milton, suggest that a native classicism, serene and graceful, existed side by side with metaphysical poetry. The emphasis on the correct ("pure"), the appropriate ("fit"), restraint and discipline ("sober care"), clarity, the fresh and surprising ("rare"), nature, strength, freedom from pedantry indicates exactly the direction English poets were to follow after the Restoration.

Above all, the new simplicity of style aimed to give pleasure to readers— to write about passions that everyone could recognize in language that everyone could understand. According to Dryden, Donne's amorous verse mistakenly "perplexes the minds of the fair sex with nice speculations of philosophy, when he should engage their hearts, and entertain them with the softnesses of love." Dryden's poems would not make that mistake; like subsequent English critics, he values poetry according to its power to move an audience. Readers, in turn, were supposed to cooperate with authors through the exercise of their own imaginations, creating pictures in the mind.

What poets most tried to see and represent was *Nature*—a word of many meanings. The Augustans focused especially on one meaning: Nature as the universal and permanent elements in human experience. External nature— the landscape—attracted attention throughout the eighteenth century as a source of pleasure and an object of inquiry. But as Finch muses on the landscape, in *A Nocturnal Reverie,* it is her own soul she discovers. Pope's injunction to the critic, "First follow Nature," has primarily *human* nature in view. Nature consists of the enduring, general truths that have been, are, and will be true for everyone in all times, everywhere. Hence the business of the poet, according to Johnson's *Rasselas,* is not "to number the streaks of the tulip" but "to examine, not the individual, but the species; to remark general properties and large appearances . . . to exhibit in his portraits of nature such prominent and striking features as recall the original to every mind." The general need not exclude the particular. In *The Vanity of Human Wishes,* Johnson describes the sorrows of an old woman: "Now kindred Merit fills the sable Bier, / Now lacerated Friendship claims a tear." Here "kindred Merit" refers particularly to a worthy relative who has died, and "lacerated Friendship" refers to a friend who has been wasted by violence or disease. Yet Merit and Friendship are also personifications, and the lines imply that the woman may be mourning the passing of goodness like her own or a broken friendship; values and sympathies can die as well as people. This play on words is not a pun. Rather, it indicates a state of mind in which life assumes the form of a perpetual allegory and some abiding truth shines through each circumstance and moment as it passes. The particular is already the general, in good eighteenth-century verse.

To study Nature was also to study the ancients. Nature and Homer, according to Pope, were the same; and both Pope and his readers applied

Horace's satires on Rome to their own world, because Horace had expressed the perennial forms of life. Moreover, modern writers could learn from the ancients how to practice their craft. If a poem is an object to be made, the *poet* (a word derived from the Greek for "maker") must make the object to proper specifications. Thus poets were taught to plan their works in one of the classical "kinds" or genres—epic, tragedy, comedy, pastoral, satire, or ode—to choose a language appropriate to that genre, and to select the right style and tone and rhetorical figures. The rules of art, as Pope had said, "are Nature methodized." At the same time, however, writers needed *wit*: quickness of mind, inventiveness, a knack for conceiving images and metaphors and for perceiving resemblances between things apparently unlike. Shakespeare had surpassed the ancients themselves in wit, and no one could deny that Pope was witty. Hence a major project of the age was to combine good method with wit, or judgment with fancy. Nature intended them to be one, and the role of judgment was not to suppress passion, energy, and originality but to make them more effective through discipline: "The wingèd courser, like a generous horse, / Shows most true mettle when you check his course."

The test of a poet's true mettle is language. When Wordsworth, in the preface to *Lyrical Ballads* (1800), declared that he wrote "in a selection of the language really used by men," he went on to attack eighteenth-century poets for their use of an artificial and stock "poetic diction." Many poets did employ a special language. When used mechanically it could become a mannerism. But Thomas Gray contrives subtle, expressive effects from artificial diction and syntax, as in the ironic inflation of *Ode on the Death of a Favorite Cat* or a famous stanza from *Elegy Written in a Country Churchyard*:

> The boast of heraldry, the pomp of power,
>> And all that beauty, all that wealth e'er gave,
> Awaits alike the inevitable hour.
>> The paths of glory lead but to the grave.

It is easy to misread the first sentence. What is the subject of *awaits*? The answer must be *hour* (the only available singular noun), which lurks at the end of the sentence, ready to spring a trap not only on the reader but on all those aristocratic, powerful, beautiful, wealthy people who forget that their hour will come. Moreover, the intricacy of that sentence sets off the simplicity of the next, which says the same thing with deadly directness. The artful mix in the *Elegy* of a special poetic language—a language that nobody speaks—with sentiments that everybody feels helps account for the poem's enduring popularity.

Versification also tests a poet's skill. The heroic couplet was brought to such perfection by Pope, Johnson thought, that "to attempt any further improvement of versification will be dangerous." Pope's couplets, in rhymed iambic pentameter, typically present a complete statement, closed by a punctuation mark. Within the binary system of these two lines, as in a digital computer, a world of distinctions can be compressed. The second line of the couplet might closely parallel the first in structure and meaning, for instance, or the two lines might antithetically play against each other. Similarly, because normally the length of a pentameter line requires a slight pause called a "caesura" ("Know then thyself, presume not God to scan"), one part of the line can be made parallel with or antithetical to the other or even to one part of the following line. Sir John Denham's *Cooper's Hill* (1642) includes a passage, quoted and parodied for many years, that illustrates these effects. The poem addresses the Thames and builds up a witty comparison between the flow of a river and the flow of verse (italics are added to highlight the terms compared):

	O could I flow like thee,	and make thy stream
Parallelism:	*My great example,*	as it is *my theme!*
Double balance:	Though *deep,* yet *clear,*	though *gentle,* yet not *dull,*
Double balance:	*Strong* without *rage,*	without *o'erflowing, full.*

Once Dryden and Pope had bound such passages more tightly together with alliteration and assonance, the typical metrical-rhetorical wit of the new age had been perfected. For most of the eighteenth century its only metrical rival was blank verse: iambic pentameter that does not rhyme and is not closed in couplets. Milton's blank verse in *Paradise Lost* provided one model, and the dramatic blank verse of Shakespeare and Dryden provided another. This more expansive form appealed to poets who cared less for wit than for stories and thoughts with plenty of room to develop.

Yet not all poets chose to compete with Pope's wit or Milton's heroic striving. Ordinary people also wrote and read verse, and many of them neither knew nor regarded the classics. Only a minority of men, and very few women, had the chance to study Latin and Greek, but that did not keep a good many from playing with verse as a pastime or writing about their own lives. Hence the eighteenth century is the first age to reflect the modern tension between "high" and "low" art. While the heroic couplet was being perfected, doggerel also thrived, and Milton's blank verse was sometimes reduced to describing a drunk or an oyster. Burlesque and broad humor characterize the common run of eighteenth-century verse. As the audience for poetry became more diversified, so did the subject matter. No readership was too small to address; Isaac Watts, and later Anna Laetitia Barbauld and William Blake, wrote songs for children. The rise of unconventional forms and topics of verse subverted an older poetic ideal: the Olympian art that only a handful of the elect could possibly master. The eighteenth century brought poetry down to earth. In the future, art that claimed to be high would have to find ways to distinguish itself from the low.

RESTORATION LITERATURE, 1660–1700

Dryden brought England a *modern* literature between 1660 and 1700. He combined a cosmopolitan outlook on the latest European trends with some of the richness and variety he admired in Chaucer and Shakespeare. In most of the important contemporary forms—occasional verse, comedy, tragedy, heroic play, ode, satire, translation, and critical essay—both his example and his precepts influenced others. As a critic, he spread the word that English literature, particularly his own, could vie with the best of the past. As a translator, he made such classics as Ovid and Virgil available to a wide public; for the first time, a large number of women and men without a formal education could feel included in the literary world.

The effort to reach a new audience is clearly marked by Restoration prose.

The styles of Donne's sermons, of Milton's pamphlets, or of Browne's treatises now seemed too elaborate and rhetorical for simple communication. In polite literature, exemplified by Cowley, Dryden, and Sir William Temple, the ideal of good prose came to be a style with the ease and poise of well-bred urbane conversation. This is a social prose for a sociable age. Later, it became the mainstay of essayists like Addison and Steele, of eighteenth-century novelists, and of the host of brilliant eighteenth-century letter writers, including Montagu, Horace Walpole, Gray, Cowper, and Burney, who still give readers the sense of being their intimate friends.

Yet despite its broad appeal to the public, Restoration literature kept its ties to an aristocratic heroic ideal. The "fierce wars and faithful loves" of epic poems were expected to offer patterns of virtue for noble emulation. These ideals lived on in popular French prose romances, in Behn's *Oroonoko*, and in heroic plays like those written by Dryden, which push to extremes the conflict between love and honor in the hearts of impossibly valiant heroes and impossibly high-minded and attractive heroines.

But comedy was the real distinction of Restoration drama. The best plays of Sir George Etherege (*The Man of Mode*, 1676), William Wycherley (*The Country Wife*, 1675), Aphra Behn (*The Rover*, 1677), William Congreve (*Love for Love*, 1695; *The Way of the World*, 1700), and later George Farquhar (*The Beaux' Stratagem*, 1707) can still hold the stage today. These "comedies of manners" pick social behavior apart, exposing the nasty struggles for power among the upper classes, who use wit, manners and sex as weapons.

During the 1690s "Societies for the Reformation of Manners" began to attack the blasphemy and obscenity they detected on stage, and they sometimes brought offenders to trial. The clergyman Jeremy Collier spoke for the moral outrage of the pious middle classes. The wits retreated. The temper of comedy softened; at the end of the century, the heroes and heroines were often good-natured and decent. Ladies could safely attend the theater, where several of the leading playwrights were women, such as Mary Pix, Susanna Centlivre, and Catharine Trotter. When Dryden died in 1700, a more respectable society was coming into being. One of the tasks that, early in the next century, Steele and Addison undertook in the *Tatler* and *Spectator* and Pope in *An Essay on Criticism* was to rehabilitate "wit" by making it the servant of social and moral decorum.

Decorum was also enforced by the clubs where literary people gathered. The coffeehouses of London served as informal meeting places; first founded in 1652, they numbered in the hundreds by the turn of the century. Collectively they functioned as a new kind of national forum, a public sphere. There men could smoke, drink chocolate or coffee, read newspapers, write and receive letters, gossip, do business, argue, and observe the oddities of character for which the English were famous. Eventually clubs like Addison's imaginary Spectator Club came to preside over literary life. Their members helped determine the tone of literature, the reputations of writers, the success or failure of plays, and the character of the *Spectator* itself. At first women were excluded. Around 1750, however, some intellectual women (known as bluestockings because they wore homely worsted hose instead of black silk) established clubs of their own under the leadership of Elizabeth Montagu, and gradually men joined them for literary conversation.

EIGHTEENTH-CENTURY LITERATURE, 1700–45

Early in the century a new and brilliant group of writers took the stage: Swift, with *A Tale of a Tub* (1704–10); Addison, with *The Campaign* (1705), a poetic celebration of the battle of Blenheim; Prior, with *Poems on Several Occasions* (1707); Steele, with the *Tatler* (1709); and the youthful Pope, in the same year, with his *Pastorals*. These writers consolidate and popularize the social graces of the previous age. Determined to preserve good sense and civilized values, they turn their wit against fanaticism and innovation. Hence this is a great age of satire. Deeply conservative but also playful, the finest works often cast a strange light on modern times by viewing them through the screen of classical myths and classical forms. Thus Pope exposes the frivolity of fashionable London, in *The Rape of the Lock,* through the incongruity of verse that casts the idle rich as epic heroes. Such incongruities are not entirely negative. They also provide a fresh perspective on things that had once seemed too low for poetry to notice them—for instance, in *The Rape of the Lock,* a girl putting on her makeup. In this way a parallel with classical literature can show not only how far the modern world has fallen but also how much has stayed the same in the lives of ordinary, unheroic people.

At the same time, a new sort of reading matter began to appeal to an audience eager to be entertained. The reading public expanded dramatically during the eighteenth century, and its recruits included upper-class women and the prosperous men and women of the growing middle class. The popular press churned out a succession of newspapers; periodical essays in the manner of the *Tatler;* miscellaneous collections of verse and prose; and finally, in 1731, the first magazine, the *Gentleman's Magazine,* followed not only by imitations but also by successful literary journals like the *Monthly Review* (1749) and the *Critical Review* (1756). Each audience attracted some periodical tailored to it, as with the *Female Tatler* (1709) and Eliza Haywood's *Female Spectator* (1744–46). The new journalism satisfied a hunger for information about politics, science, philosophy, and literature as well as for scandal and gossip. As the number of readers grew, so did the demand for writers. Grub Street, where many poor London writers lived, became a synonym for hacks and scandal mongers. To Pope and Swift, these drudges represented a serious threat to the dignity of authorship and humanistic learning. But it was the public, not a few wealthy patrons, that eighteenth-century writers had to please. Johnson began his career as an employee of the *Gentleman's Magazine,* then took the job of putting together a dictionary, and only gradually emerged as a major author. Nor could the novel have come into being without the new customers for print, who wanted to read about people whose lives were like their own.

As the readership changed, so did kinds of literature. Lyric poetry, one of the glories of the late sixteenth and early seventeenth centuries, became in the Restoration a minor, graceful mode, often used to flatter a patron or mistress. Between 1700 and 1740, however, the forms of poetry shifted. The sonnet now seemed an archaic, courtly form; lyrics went out of fashion, replaced by descriptive and didactic verse, along with such popular genres as the ballad, the hymn, the burlesque. A similar shift in taste occurred in the drama. The moral reform of the 1690s, together with an increasingly optimistic view of human nature, made Restoration rakes seem libels on humanity. The old comedy of manners was replaced by a new kind, later called "sentimental" not only because goodness triumphs over vice but also because it deals in high moral sentiments rather than witty dialogue and because the embarrassments of its heroines and heroes move the audience not to laughter but to tears. Some plays resisted the tide. Gay's cynical *Beggar's Opera* (1728) was a tremendous success, and later in the century the comedies of Goldsmith and Sheridan proved that sentiment is not necessarily an enemy to wit and laughter. Yet larger and larger audiences responded more to spectacles and special effects than to sophisticated writing. Although the *stage* prospered during the eighteenth century, and the star system produced idolized actors and actresses (such as David Garrick and Sarah Siddons), the authors of *drama* tended to fade to the background.

The rising tide of popular taste also provoked a reaction. Pope and Swift and other satirists turned their weapons against what they perceived as the coarsening and corruption of public life and the arts. Early in his career, Pope (like Dryden before him) had set out to make the texts and principles of classical literature available to everyone who could read English. His translations of Homer brought the epic tradition home to Britain, earning him enormous profits. But eventually he came to fear that the barbarians were winning. Politics contributed to this despair; both Pope and Swift were Tory satirists in an age of Whig domination. Tories stood fast against the social and economic changes that were transforming Britain from an island kingdom into a world power and from an agrarian into a mercantile society. A new nexus of cash and credit seemed to be driving out the civic humanism that put the nation ahead of private interests. Moral revulsion—especially against the wheeling and dealing perfected by Walpole—fueled the satirists' rage. In his last great work, *The Dunciad,* Pope imagines the tragic victory of Chaos and Night over Order and Art. Swift emphasizes that the world is going mad. The abandonment of practical reality to crackbrained theories of science, religious fanaticism, and romantic illusions leaves no recourse— except a saving remnant of laughter.

A wholly different sort of poetry accompanied the age of satire. Since the seventeenth century, no poems had been more popular than those about the pleasures of retirement, which invited the reader to dream about a safe retreat in the country or to meditate, like Finch, on scenery and the soul. But after 1726, when Thomson published *Winter,* the first of his cycle on the seasons, the poetry of natural description came into its own. Tourists as well as poets roamed the countryside, frequently quoting verse as they gazed at some evocative scene. Wordsworth's love of external nature draws on eighteenth-century sources; *Tintern Abbey* is very much a poem of the century in which it was written. During the course of the century, Britons learned to enjoy not only the tamed and gentrified nature of landscape gardens and fields but also a thrilling pleasure or fear in the presence of "the sublime" in nature: rushing waters, wild prospects, and mountains shrouded in mist. Whether enthusiasts went to the landscape in search of God or merely of heightened sensations, they came back feeling that they had been touched by something beyond the life they knew, by something that could hardly be expressed. Pope had written of "a grace beyond the reach of art, / Which, without passing through the judgment, gains / The heart, and all its end at once attains"; but many of his successors identified that appeal to feeling—and avoidance of judgment—with poetry itself. The presence of the sublime in nature, as well as in the emotions of writers and readers, would be a staple of literature for decades to come.

THE EMERGENCE OF NEW LITERARY THEMES AND MODES, 1740–85

When Matthew Arnold called the eighteenth century an "age of prose," he meant to belittle its poetry, but he also stated a significant fact: great prose does dominate the age. Until the 1740s, poetry tended to set the standards of literature. But the growth of new kinds of prose took the initiative away from verse. Novelists became better known than poets; no writers of mid-century were more admired or popular than Samuel Richardson and Henry Fielding. And intellectual prose also flourished, with the achievements of Johnson in the essay and literary criticism; of Boswell in biography; of Hume in philosophy; of Burke in politics; of Edward Gibbon in history; of Sir Joshua Reynolds in aesthetics; of Gilbert White in natural history; and of Adam Smith in economics. Each of these authors is a master stylist, whose effort to express himself clearly and fully demands an art as carefully wrought as poetry. An unprecedented effort to formulate the first principles of philosophy, history, psychology, and art required a new style of persuasion.

Johnson helped codify that language, not only with his writings but with the first great English *Dictionary* (1755). This work established him as a national man of letters; eventually the period would be known as "the Age of Johnson." But his dominance was based on an ideal of service to others. The *Dictionary* illustrates its definitions with more than 114,000 quotations from the best English writers, thus building a bridge from past to present usage; and Johnson's essays, poems, and criticism also reflect his desire to preserve the lessons of the past. Yet he looks to the future as well, trying both to reach and to mold a nation of readers. If Johnson speaks for his age, one reason is his faith in common sense and the common reader. "By the common sense of readers uncorrupted with literary prejudices," he wrote in the last of his *Lives of the Poets* (1781), "must be finally decided all claim to poetical honors." A similar respect for the good judgment of ordinary people, and for standards of taste and behavior that anyone can share, marks many writers of the age. Both Burke, the great conservative statesman and author, and Thomas Paine, his radical adversary, proclaim themselves apostles of common sense. Moreover, the poets whom everyone read relied on verse that could do justice to the feelings of simple people. Gray's *Elegy*, Goldsmith's *The Deserted Village*, Crabbe's *The Village*, and the lyrics of Burns all strive to make poetry from and for the lives of common men and women.

Nevertheless, an age of great prose can burden its poets. The generation of talented young poets who emerged about the time of Pope's death, a group that includes Gray, William Collins, Mark Akenside, and the brothers Joseph and Thomas Warton, seems afraid that the spirit of poetry might be dying, driven out by the spirit of prose, by uninspiring truth, by the end of superstitions that had once peopled the land with poetic fairies and demons. In an age barren of magic, they ask, where has poetry gone? That question haunts many poems, suffusing them with melancholy. The prototype of the mid-eighteenth-century poet was Milton's *Il Penseroso*, a night-loving solitary who broods on the "far-off curfew" or the plangent organ in the twilight of a Gothic church. Such a figure has little in common with poets like Dryden and Pope, social beings who live in a crowded world and seldom confess their private feelings in public. The melancholy poet withdraws into himself and yearns to be living in some other time and place.

Poets who muse in silence are never far from thoughts of death, and a morbid fascination with suicide and the grave preoccupies many midcentury poets. Pope's *Essay on Man* had taken a sunny view of providence; Edward Young's *The Complaint: or Night Thoughts on Life, Death, and Immortality* (1742–46), an immensely long poem in blank verse, is darkened by Christian fear of the life to come. But the "graveyard school" pays less attention to religion than to images of decay. Surrounded by medieval ruins and tombs, the spirits of graveyard poets tremble and sink. The revival of Gothic architectural styles, most famously in Horace Walpole's tiny pseudo-Gothic castle, Strawberry Hill, influenced literary styles as well. Walpole's *Castle of Otranto* (1765), a dreamlike tale of terror set in a simulacrum of Strawberry Hill, created a mode of fiction that retains its popularity to the present day. In a typical Gothic romance, amid the glooms and secret passages of some remote castle, the laws of nightmare replace the laws of probability. Forbidden themes—incest, murder, necrophilia, atheism, and the torments of sexual desire—are allowed free play; repressed anxieties and terrors rise to the surface of the narrative. In serious novels of social purpose, like William Godwin's *Caleb Williams* (1794) and Mary Wollstonecraft's *Maria, or The Wrongs of Woman* (1798); and Mary Shelley, the daughter of Wollstonecraft and Godwin, eventually composed a romantic nightmare, *Frankenstein* (1818), that continues to haunt our dreams.

When poets looked for a renewal of poetry, however, they sought it not so much in the Gothic as in their own imaginations and feelings. In his *Ode to Fancy* (1746), Joseph Warton associated "fancy" with visions in the wilderness and spontaneous passions; the true poet was no longer defined as a craftsman or maker but as a seer or nature's priest. "The public has seen all that art can do," William Shenstone wrote in 1761, welcoming James Macpherson's *Ossian*, "and they want the more striking efforts of wild, original, enthusiastic genius." Macpherson filled the bill. His primitive, sentimental epics, supposedly translated from an ancient Gaelic warrior-bard, won the hearts of readers around the world; Napoleon and Thomas Jefferson, for instance, both thought that Ossian was greater than Homer. At the same time, many of the best poets of the period identified with the recluse or the outcast. Collins, Smart, and Cowper all were isolated from society by fits of madness, and only a handful of readers noticed the extraordinary work of Smart or later of William Blake.

Meanwhile, a different sort of poetry flourished: humorous, personal, and down to earth. As the reading public expanded, so did the number of people who tried their hand at verse; and they wrote about whatever interested them. Women and men described the details of their lives in homely images and graphic language. Such poets were not afraid to deal with beggars and barbers and chimney sweeps, or to sing the joys of village sports or the bustle of washing day. For much of the public, poetry offered the pleasures of self-expression and companionship. Cowper, the most popular poet of the later part of the century, won his readers with a modest, intimate kind of verse, seldom departing far from the accents of friendly conversation. Women especially prized his poems, and poets like Anna Seward and Charlotte Smith helped revive the lyric. Amid revolutions in society and thought, poets were asked to teach their readers how to respond—above all, how to feel. The next generation would try to answer that call.

THE BEGINNING OF THE NOVEL

The modern novel came into its own in the 1740s. Prose fiction had existed, to be sure, since ancient times; the Greeks and Romans wrote stories about the tribulations of love, and narrative traditions lie behind the Bible and most other sacred writings. Other early types of prose fiction include Sir Philip Sidney's courtly *Arcadia* and Lady Mary Wroth's *Urania*; the earthy tales of Thomas Nashe and Thomas Deloney; the long French romances of the seventeenth century, blending chivalric adventure and courtly love; and in a world apart, Bunyan's vivid allegories of the spiritual quests and battles of wayfaring Christians. Nor were clear distinctions drawn between history and fiction; Behn's *Oroonoko* is both. In the early eighteenth century, writers often mixed facts with their fiction, as when they whipped up scandalous versions of current events or reported some famous criminal's "true story." The master of this genre was Daniel Defoe. A middle-class writer, he did not seek upper-class readers (though *Robinson Crusoe*, 1719, appealed to all classes). Instead he aimed at shopkeepers, apprentices, and servants, a readership avid for racy stories, usually laced with moral indignation. Defoe shows his readers a world that they know, where unheroic people try to cope with practical problems, like finding a trustworthy spouse or simply staying alive. Nor was he alone in writing about and for women. For the first time in British history, a critical mass of female readers and writers carried weight with publishers. Jane Barker and Mary Davys, along with many others, brought women's work and daily lives as well as love affairs to fiction. Such stories were not only amusing but also served as models of conduct; they influenced the stories that real people told about themselves.

Samuel Richardson conceived the idea of *Pamela, or Virtue Rewarded* (1740) while compiling a little book of model letters. The letters grew into a story about a captivating young servant who resists her master's base designs on her virtue until he gives up and marries her. The combination of a high moral tone with sexual titillation and a minute analysis of the heroine's emotions and state of mind proved irresistible to readers. Richardson caught the attention of all literate Europe and once and for all established the novel as we know it: a serious form that can also be a popular success. He topped that success with *Clarissa* (1747–48). In the conflict between the libertine Lovelace, an attractive and diabolical aristocrat, and the angelic Clarissa, a middle-class paragon who struggles to stay pure, Richardson caught the ideals and tensions of a society whose values were in flux. No earlier author had involved readers so much in the feelings and motives of characters, examined minute by minute—this is the longest novel in English—until they seem more real than people we meet every day.

Like Richardson, Henry Fielding had a gift for writing dramatic scenes; in the 1730s he had been the best comic playwright in England. But Fielding looked down on Richardson's pious middle-class values. *Joseph Andrews* (1742) begins by turning *Pamela* farcically upside-down, as Joseph (Pamela's brother) defends his chastity from the lewd advances of Lady Booby. Fielding's true model, however, is Cervantes' great *Don Quixote* (1605–15), from which he took an ironic, antiromantic style, a plot of wandering around the countryside, and an idealistic central character (Parson Adams) who keeps mistaking appearances for reality. The ambition of writing what Fielding called "a comic epic-poem in prose" went still further in *The History of Tom Jones, A Foundling* (1749). Crowded with incidents and comments on the state of England, the novel contrasts a good-natured, generous, wayward hero (who needs to learn prudence) with cold-hearted people who use moral codes and the law for their own selfish interests. This emphasis on instinctive virtue and vice, instead of Richardson's devotion to good principles, put off respectable readers like Johnson and Burney. But Coleridge thought that *Tom Jones* (along with *Oedipus Rex* and Jonson's *Alchemist*) was one of "the three most perfect plots ever planned."

Remarkable experiments in fiction run through the later part of the century, anticipating many of the forms that novelists still use today. Tobias Smollett's picaresque *Roderick Random* (1748) and *Humphry Clinker* (1771) delight in coarse practical jokes, the freaks and strong odors of life. But the most *novel* novelist of the age was Laurence Sterne, a humorous, sentimental clergyman who loves to play tricks on his readers. *The Life and Opinions of Tristram Shandy* (1760–67) abandons clock time for psychological time, whimsically follows chance associations, interrupts its own stories, violates the conventions of print by putting chapters 18 and 19 after chapter 25, sneaks in double entendres, and seems ready to go on forever. And yet these games get us inside the characters' minds, as if the world were as capricious as our thoughts. Sterne's self-conscious art implies that people's private obsessions shape their lives—or help create reality itself. Present-day novelists still play the games he invented.

At the same time, the focus on eccentric or individual points of view, along with the popularity of fiction—Gothic or sentimental—that indulged in extreme states of feeling, freed many writers to question the norms of behavior. Identifying with characters in novels, readers might find themselves. That seems to have been especially true for women. By the end of the century most of the leading British novelists were women—Burney, Ann Radcliffe, and later Maria Edgeworth—and the novel was often considered a feminine preserve. For that reason, perhaps, it lost some prestige. When two young women spend their time reading novels together, in *Northanger Abbey,* the young Jane Austen defends them against some critic (presumably male) who might accuse them of frivolity: " 'It is only a novel!' . . . only some work in which the greatest powers of the mind are displayed, in which the most thorough knowledge of human nature, the happiest delineation of its varieties, the liveliest effusions of wit and humour, are conveyed to the world in the best chosen language." Novels, she argues, not only give pleasure to women but foster their education. Yet men were already beginning to take back the novel. Although today no English novelist of manners seems greater than Austen, early in the nineteenth century it was Walter Scott whose novels everyone read; and the historical novel, filled with scenes of men at work and war, largely superseded more intimate forms. That broader canvas would mark out the future of fiction.

CONTINUITY AND REVOLUTION

The history of eighteenth-century literature was first composed by the Romantics, who wrote it to serve their own interests. Prizing originality, they naturally preferred to stress how different they were from writers of the previous age. Later historians have tended to follow their lead, competing to prove that everything changed in 1776, or 1789, or 1798. This revolutionary view of history accounts for what happened to the word *revolution*. The older meaning referred to a movement around a point, a recurrence or cycle, as in the revolutions of the planets; the newer meaning signified a violent break with the past, an overthrow of the existing order, as in the Big Bang or the French Revolution. Romantic rhetoric made heavy use of such dramatic upheavals. Yet every history devoted to truth must take account of both sorts of revolution, of continuities as well as changes. The ideals that many Romantics made their own—the passion for liberty and equality, the founding of justice on individual rights, the distrust of institutions, the love of nature, the reverence for imagination, and even the embrace of change—were grown from seeds that had been planted long before. Nor did Augustan literature abruptly vanish on that day in 1798 when Wordsworth and Coleridge anonymously published a small and unsuccessful volume of poems called *Lyrical Ballads*. Even when they rebel against the work of Pope and Johnson and Gray, Romantic writers incorporate much of their language and values.

What Restoration and eighteenth-century literature passed on to the future, in fact, was chiefly a set of unresolved problems. The age of Enlightenment was also, in England, an age that insisted on holding fast to older beliefs and customs; the age of population explosion was also an age of individualism; the age that developed the slave trade was also the age that gave rise to the abolitionist movement; the age that codified rigid standards of conduct for women was also an age when many women took the chance to read and write and think for themselves; the age of reason was also the age when sensibility flourished; the last classical age was also the first modern age. These contradictions are far from abstract; writers were forced to choose their own directions. When young James Boswell looked for a mentor whose biography he might write, he considered not only Samuel Johnson but also David Hume, whose skeptical views of morality, truth, and religion were everything Johnson abhorred. The two writers seem to inhabit different worlds, yet Boswell traveled freely between them. That was exciting and also instructive. "Without Contraries is no progression," according to one citizen of Johnson's London, William Blake, who also thought that "Opposition is true Friendship." Good conversation was a lively eighteenth-century art, and sharp disagreements did not keep people from talking. The conversations the period started have not ended yet.

THE RESTORATION AND THE EIGHTEENTH CENTURY

TEXTS	CONTEXTS
1660 Samuel Pepys begins his diary.	1660 Charles II restored to the throne. Reopening of the theaters
1662 Samuel Butler, *Hudibras,* part 1	1662 Act of Uniformity requires all clergy to obey the Church of England. Chartering of the Royal Society
	1666 Fire destroys the City of London
1667 John Milton, *Paradise Lost*	
1668 John Dryden, *Essay of Dramatic Poesy*	1668 Dryden becomes Poet Laureate
	1673 Test Act requires all officeholders to swear allegiance to Anglicanism
1678 John Bunyan, *Pilgrim's Progress,* part 1	1678 The "Popish Plot" inflames anti-Catholic feeling
1681 Dryden, *Absalom and Achitophel*	1681 Charles II dissolves Parliament
	1685 Death of Charles II. James II, his Catholic brother, takes the throne
1687 Sir Isaac Newton, *Principia Mathematica*	
1688 Aphra Behn, *Oroonoko*	1688–89 The Glorious Revolution; James II exiled and succeeded by his Protestant daughter, Mary, and her husband, William of Orange
1690 John Locke, *An Essay Concerning Human Understanding*	
1700 William Congreve, *The Way of the World.* Mary Astell, *Some Reflections upon Marriage*	
	1702 Death of William III; succession of Anne (Protestant daughter of James II)
1704 Jonathan Swift, *A Tale of a Tub.* Newton, *Opticks*	
	1707 Act of Union with Scotland
	1710 Tories take power
1711 Alexander Pope, *An Essay on Criticism.* Joseph Addison and Sir Richard Steele, *The Spectator* (1711–12, 1714)	
	1714 Death of Queen Anne; George I (great-grandson of James I) becomes the first Hanoverian king; Tory government replaced by Whigs
1716 Lady Mary Wortley Montagu writes her letters from Turkey (1716–18)	
1717 Pope, *The Rape of the Lock*	
1719 Daniel Defoe, *Robinson Crusoe*	
	1720 South Sea Bubble collapses
	1721 Robert Walpole comes to power

TEXTS	CONTEXTS
1726　Swift, *Gulliver's Travels*	
	1727　George I dies; George II succeeds
1728　John Gay, *The Beggar's Opera*	
1733　Pope, *An Essay on Man*	
	1737　Licensing Act censors the stage
1740　Samuel Richardson, *Pamela*	
1742　Henry Fielding, *Joseph Andrews*	1742　Walpole resigns
1743　Pope, *The Dunciad* (final version). William Hogarth, *Marriage A-la-Mode*	
1746　William Collins's *Odes*	1746　Charles Edward Stuart's defeat at Culloden ends the last Jacobite rebellion
1747　Richardson, *Clarissa*	
	1748　Treaty of Aix-la-Chapelle
1749　Fielding, *Tom Jones*	
1751　Thomas Gray, *Elegy Written in a Country Churchyard*	1751　Robert Clive seizes Arcot, the prelude to English control of India
1755　Samuel Johnson, *Dictionary*	
	1756　Beginning of Seven Years War
1759　Johnson, *Rasselas*. Voltaire, *Candide*	1759　James Wolfe's capture of Quebec assures British control of Canada
1760　Laurence Sterne, *Tristram Shandy* (1760–67)	1760　George III succeeds to the throne
1765　Johnson's edition of Shakespeare	
	1768　Captain James Cook voyages to Australia and New Zealand
1770　Oliver Goldsmith, *The Deserted Village*	
	1775　American Revolution (1775–83). James Watt produces steam engines
1776　Adam Smith, *The Wealth of Nations*	
1778　Frances Burney, *Evelina*	
1779　Johnson, *Lives of the Poets* (1779–81)	
	1780　Gordon Riots in London
1783　George Crabbe, *The Village*	1783　William Pitt becomes Prime Minister
1785　William Cowper, *The Task*	

JOHN DRYDEN
1631–1700

Although John Dryden's parents seem to have sided with Parliament against the king, there is no evidence that the poet grew up in a strict Puritan family. His father, a country gentleman of moderate fortune, gave his son a gentleman's education at Westminster School, under the renowned Dr. Richard Busby, who used the rod as a pedagogical aid in imparting a sound knowledge of the learned languages and literatures to his charges (among others John Locke and Matthew Prior). From Westminster, Dryden went to Trinity College, Cambridge, where he took his A.B. in 1654. His first important poem, *Heroic Stanzas* (1659), was written to commemorate the death of Cromwell. The next year, however, in *Astraea Redux,* Dryden joined his countrymen in celebrating the return of Charles II to his throne. During the rest of his life Dryden was to remain entirely loyal to Charles and to his successor, James II.

Dryden is the commanding literary figure of the last four decades of the seventeenth century. Every important aspect of the life of his times—political, religious, philosophical, artistic—finds expression somewhere in his writings. Dryden is the least personal of poets. He is not at all the solitary, subjective poet listening to the murmur of his own voice and preoccupied with his own feelings, but rather a citizen of the world commenting publicly on matters of public concern.

From the beginning to the end of his literary career, Dryden's nondramatic poems are most typically occasional poems, which celebrate particular events of a public character—a coronation, a military victory, a death, or a political crisis. Such poems are social and ceremonial, written not for the self but for the nation. Between 1664 and 1681, however, Dryden was mainly a playwright. The newly chartered theaters needed a modern repertory, and he set out to supply the need. In the style of the time, he produced rhymed heroic plays, in which incredibly noble heroes and heroines face incredibly difficult choices between love and honor; comedies, in which male and female rakes engage in intrigue and bright repartee; and later, libretti for the newly introduced dramatic form, the opera. His one great tragedy, *All for Love* (1677), in blank verse, adapts Shakespeare's *Antony and Cleopatra* to the unities of time, place, and action. As his *An Essay of Dramatic Poesy* (1668) shows, Dryden had studied the works of the great playwrights of Greece and Rome, of the English Renaissance, and of contemporary France, seeking sound theoretical principles on which to construct the new drama that the age demanded. Because he took literature seriously and enjoyed discussing it, he became, almost casually, what Samuel Johnson called him: "the father of English criticism." His abilities as both poet and dramatist brought him to the attention of the king, who in 1668 made him poet laureate. Two years later the post of historiographer royal was added to the laureateship at a combined stipend of £200, enough money to live on.

Between 1678 and 1681, when he was nearing fifty, Dryden discovered his great gift for writing formal verse satire. A quarrel with the playwright Thomas Shadwell prompted the mock-heroic episode *Mac Flecknoe,* probably written in 1678 or 1679 but not published until 1682. Out of the stresses occasioned by the Popish Plot (1678) and its political aftermath came his major political satires, *Absalom and Achitophel* (1681), and *The Medal* (1682), his final attack on the villain of *Absalom and Achitophel,* the earl of Shaftesbury. Twenty years' experience as poet and playwright had prepared him technically for the triumph of *Absalom and Achitophel.* He had mastered the heroic couplet, having fashioned it into an instrument suitable in his hands for every sort of discourse from the thrust and parry of quick logical argument, to lyric feeling, rapid narrative, or forensic declamation. Thanks to this long discipline, he was able in one stride to rival the masters of verse satire: Horace, Juvenal, Persius, in ancient Rome, and Boileau, his French contemporary.

The consideration of religious and political questions that the events of 1678–81 forced on Dryden brought a new seriousness to his mind and works. In 1682 he published *Religio Laici,* a poem in which he examined the grounds of his religious faith and defended the middle way of the Anglican Church against the rationalism of Deism on the one hand and the authoritarianism of Rome on the other. But he had moved closer to Rome than he perhaps realized when he wrote the poem. Charles II died in 1685 and was succeeded by his Catholic brother, James II. Within a year Dryden and his two sons were converted to Catholicism. Though his enemies accused him of opportunism, he proved his sincerity by his steadfast loyalty to the Roman Church after James abdicated and the Protestant William and Mary came in; as a result he was to lose his offices and their much-needed stipends. From his new position as a Roman Catholic, Dryden wrote in 1687 *The Hind and the Panther,* in which a milk-white Hind (the Roman Church) and a spotted Panther (the Anglican Church) eloquently debate theology. The Hind has the better of the argument, but Dryden already knew that James's policies were failing, and with them the Catholic cause in England.

Dryden was now nearing sixty, with a family to support on a much-diminished income. To earn a living, he resumed writing plays and turned to translations. In 1693 appeared his versions of Juvenal and Persius, with the long dedicatory epistle on satire; and in 1697, his greatest achievement in this mode, the works of Virgil. At the very end, two months before his death, came the *Fables Ancient and Modern,* prefaced by one of the finest of his critical essays and made up of translations from Ovid, Boccaccio, and Chaucer.

What was the nature of Dryden's achievement? First and foremost, he brought the pleasures of literature to the ever-increasing reading public of Britain. As a critic and translator, he made many classics available to men and women who lacked a classical education. His canons of taste and theoretical principles would set the standard for the next generation. As a writer of prose, he helped establish a popular new style, shaped to the cadences of good conversation. Johnson praised its apparent artlessness: "every word seems to drop by chance, though it falls into its proper place. Nothing is cold or languid; the whole is airy, animated, and vigorous . . . though all is easy, nothing is feeble; though all seems careless, there is nothing harsh." Although Dryden's plays went out of fashion, his poems did not. His satire inspired the most brilliant verse satirist of the next century, Alexander Pope, and the energy and variety of his metrics launched the long-standing vogue of heroic couplets. Augustan style is at its best in his poems: lively, dignified, precise, and always musical—a flexible instrument of public speech. "By him we were taught *sapere et fari,* to think naturally and express forcibly," Johnson concluded. "What was said of Rome, adorned by Augustus, may be applied by an easy metaphor to English poetry embellished by Dryden, *lateritiam invenit, marmoream reliquit,* he found it brick, and he left it marble."

Song from *Marriage à la Mode*

I

Why should a foolish marriage vow,
    Which long ago was made,
Oblige us to each other now,
    When passion is decayed?
5 We loved, and we loved, as long as we could,
    Till our love was loved out in us both;
But our marriage is dead when the pleasure is fled:
    'Twas pleasure first made it an oath.

2

If I have pleasures for a friend,
10   And farther love in store,
What wrong has he whose joys did end,
     And who could give no more?
'Tis a madness that he should be jealous of me,
     Or that I should bar him of another:
15   For all we can gain is to give ourselves pain,
     When neither can hinder the other.

ca. 1672   1673

Absalom and Achitophel

In 1678 a dangerous crisis, both religious and political, threatened to undo the Restoration settlement and to precipitate England once again into civil war. The Popish Plot and its aftermath not only whipped up extreme anti-Catholic passions, but led between 1679 and 1681 to a bitter political struggle between Charles II (whose adherents came to be called Tories) and the earl of Shaftesbury (whose followers were termed Whigs). The issues were nothing less than the prerogatives of the crown and the possible exclusion of the king's Catholic brother, James, duke of York, from his position as heir-presumptive to the throne. Charles's cool courage and brilliant, if unscrupulous, political genius saved the throne for his brother and gave at least temporary peace to his people.

Charles was a Catholic at heart—he received the last rites of that church on his deathbed—and was eager to do what he could do discreetly for the relief of his Catholic subjects, who suffered severe civil and religious disabilities imposed by their numerically superior Protestant compatriots. James openly professed the Catholic religion, an awkward fact politically, for he was next in line of succession because Charles had no legitimate children. The household of the duke, as well as that of Charles's neglected queen, Catherine of Braganza, inevitably became the center of Catholic life and intrigue at court and consequently of Protestant prejudice and suspicion.

No one understood, however, that the situation was explosive until 1678, when Titus Oates (a renegade Catholic convert of infamous character) offered sworn testimony of the existence of a Jesuit plot to assassinate the king, burn London, massacre Protestants, and reestablish the Roman Church.

The country might have kept its head and come to realize (what no historian has doubted) that Oates and his confederates were perjured rascals, as Charles himself quickly perceived. But panic was created by the discovery of the body of a prominent London justice of the peace, Sir Edmund Berry Godfrey, who a few days before had received for safekeeping a copy of Oates's testimony. The murder, immediately ascribed to the Catholics, has never been solved. Fear and indignation reached a hysterical pitch when the seizure of the papers of the duke of York's secretary revealed that he had been in correspondence with the confessor of Louis XIV regarding the reestablishment of the Roman Church in England. Before the terror subsided many innocent men were executed on the increasingly bold and always false evidence of Oates and his accomplices.

The earl of Shaftesbury, the duke of Buckingham, and others quickly took advantage of the situation. With the support of the Commons and the City of London, they moved to exclude the duke of York from the succession. Between 1679 and 1681 Charles and Shaftesbury were engaged in a mighty struggle. The Whigs found a candidate of their own in the king's favorite illegitimate son, the handsome and engaging duke of Monmouth, whom they advanced as a proper successor to his father. They urged Charles to legitimize him, and when he refused, they whispered that there was proof that the king had secretly married Monmouth's mother. The young man allowed himself to be used against his father. He was sent on a triumphant progress through western England, where he was enthusiastically received. Twice an Exclusion Bill nearly passed both houses. But by early 1681 Charles had secured his own position by secretly accepting from Louis XIV a three-year subsidy that made him independent of Parliament, which had tried to force his hand by refusing to vote him funds. He summoned Parliament to meet at Oxford in the spring of 1681, and a few moments after the Commons had passed the Exclusion Bill, in a bold stroke he abruptly dissolved Parliament, which never met again during his reign. Already, as Charles was aware, a reaction had set in against the violence of the Whigs. In midsummer, when he felt it safe to move against his enemies, Shaftesbury was sent to the Tower of London, charged with high treason. In November, the grand jury, packed with Whigs, threw out the indictment, and the earl was free, but his power was broken, and he lived only two more years.

Shortly before the grand jury acted, Dryden published anonymously the first part of *Absalom and Achitophel*, apparently hoping to influence their verdict. The issues in question were grave; the chief actors, the most important men in the realm. Dryden, therefore, could not use burlesque and caricature as had Butler, or the mock heroic as he himself had done in *Mac Flecknoe*. Only a heroic style and manner were appropriate to his weighty material, and the poem is most original in its blending of the heroic and the satiric. Dryden's task called for all his tact and literary skill; he had to mention, but to gloss over, the king's faults: his indolence and love of pleasure; his neglect of his wife, and his devotion to his mistresses—conduct that had left him with many children, but no heir except his Catholic brother. He had to deal gently with Monmouth, whom Charles still loved. And he had to present, or appear to present, the king's case objectively.

The remarkable parallels between the rebellion of Absalom against his father King David (2 Samuel 13–18) had already been remarked in sermons, satires, and pamphlets. Dryden took the hint and gave contemporary events a due distance and additional dignity by approaching them indirectly through their biblical analogues. The poem is famous for its brilliant portraits of the king's enemies and friends, but equally admirable are the temptation scene (which, like other passages, is indebted to *Paradise Lost*) and the remarkably astute analysis of the Popish Plot itself.

A second part of *Absalom and Achitophel* appeared in 1682. Most of it is the work of Nahum Tate, but lines 310–509, which include the devastating portraits of Doeg and Og (two Whig poets, Elkanah Settle and Thomas Shadwell), are certainly by Dryden.

Absalom and Achitophel: A Poem

In pious times, ere priestcraft did begin,
Before polygamy was made a sin;
When man on many multiplied his kind,
Ere one to one was cursedly confined;
5   When nature prompted and no law denied
Promiscuous use of concubine and bride;
Then Israel's monarch after Heaven's own heart,[1]
His vigorous warmth did variously impart

---

1. David ("a man after [God's] own heart," according to 1 Samuel 13.14) represents Charles II.

To wives and slaves; and, wide as his command,
10   Scattered his Maker's image through the land.
Michal,[2] of royal blood, the crown did wear,
A soil ungrateful to the tiller's care:
Not so the rest; for several mothers bore
To godlike David several sons before.
15   But since like slaves his bed they did ascend,
No true succession could their seed attend.
Of all this numerous progeny was none
So beautiful, so brave, as Absalom:[3]
Whether, inspired by some diviner lust,
20   His father got him with a greater gust,°   *relish, pleasure*
Or that his conscious destiny made way,
By manly beauty, to imperial sway.
Early in foreign fields he won renown,
With kings and states allied to Israel's crown:[4]
25   In peace the thoughts of war he could remove,
And seemed as he were only born for love.
Whate'er he did, was done with so much ease,
In him alone 'twas natural to please;
His motions all accompanied with grace;
30   And paradise was opened in his face.
With secret joy indulgent David viewed
His youthful image in his son renewed:
To all his wishes nothing he denied;
And made the charming Annabel[5] his bride.
35   What faults he had (for who from faults is free?)
His father could not, or he would not see.
Some warm excesses which the law forbore,
Were construed youth that purged by boiling o'er:
And Amnon's murther,[6] by a specious name,
40   Was called a just revenge for injured fame.
Thus praised and loved the noble youth remained,
While David, undisturbed, in Sion° reigned.   *London*
But life can never be sincerely° blest;   *wholly*
Heaven punishes the bad, and proves° the best.   *tests*
45   The Jews,° a headstrong, moody, murmuring race, *English*
As ever tried the extent and stretch of grace;
God's pampered people, whom, debauched with ease,
No king could govern, nor no God could please
(Gods they had tried of every shape and size
50   That god-smiths could produce, or priests devise);[7]
These Adam-wits, too fortunately free,
Began to dream they wanted liberty;[8]

2. One of David's wives, who represents the childless queen, Catherine of Braganza.
3. James Scott, duke of Monmouth (1649–1685).
4. Monmouth had won repute as a soldier fighting for France against Holland and for Holland against France.
5. Anne Scott, duchess of Buccleuch (pronounced *Bue-cloo*), a beauty and a great heiress.
6. Absalom killed his half-brother Amnon, who had raped Absalom's sister Tamar (2 Samuel

13.28–29). The parallel with Monmouth is vague. He is known to have committed acts of violence in his youth, but certainly not fratricide.
7. Dryden recalls the political and religious controversies that, since the Reformation, had divided England and finally caused civil wars.
8. Adam rebelled because he felt that he lacked ("wanted") liberty, because he was forbidden to eat the fruit of one tree.

And when no rule, no precedent was found,
Of men by laws less circumscribed and bound,
55 They led their wild desires to woods and caves,
And thought that all but savages were slaves.
They who, when Saul was dead, without a blow,
Made foolish Ishbosheth[9] the crown forgo;
Who banished David did from Hebron[1] bring,
60 And with a general shout proclaimed him king:
Those very Jews, who, at their very best,
Their humor° more than loyalty expressed,   *caprice*
Now wondered why so long they had obeyed
An idol monarch, which their hands had made;
65 Thought they might ruin him they could create,
Or melt him to that golden calf,[2] a state.°   *republic*
But these were random bolts;° no formed design   *shots*
Nor interest made the factious crowd to join:
The sober part of Israel, free from stain,
70 Well knew the value of a peaceful reign;
And, looking backward with a wise affright,
Saw seams of wounds, dishonest° to the sight: *disgraceful*
In contemplation of whose ugly scars
They cursed the memory of civil wars.
75 The moderate sort of men, thus qualified,°   *assuaged*
Inclined the balance to the better side;
And David's mildness managed it so well,
The bad found no occasion to rebel.
But when to sin our biased[3] nature leans,
80 The careful Devil is still at hand with means;
And providently pimps for ill desires:
The Good Old Cause[4] revived, a plot requires.
Plots, true or false, are necessary things,
To raise up commonwealths and ruin kings.
85   The inhabitants of old Jerusalem
Were Jebusites;[5] the town so called from them;
And theirs the native right.
But when the chosen people° grew more strong,   *Protestants*
The rightful cause at length became the wrong;
90 And every loss the men of Jebus bore,
They still were thought God's enemies the more.
Thus worn and weakened, well or ill content,
Submit they must to David's government:
Impoverished and deprived of all command,
95 Their taxes doubled as they lost their land;
And, what was harder yet to flesh and blood,
Their gods disgraced, and burnt like common wood.[6]

---

9. Saul's son; he stands for Richard Cromwell, who succeeded his father as lord protector. "Saul": Oliver Cromwell.
1. Where David reigned over Judah after the death of Saul and before he became king of Israel (2 Samuel 1–5). Charles had been crowned in Scotland in 1651.
2. The image worshiped by the children of Israel during the period that Moses spent on Mount

Sinai, receiving the law from God.
3. Inclined (cf. *Mac Flecknoe*, line 189 and n. 5, p. 908).
4. The Commonwealth. Dryden stigmatizes the Whigs by associating them with subversion.
5. Roman Catholics. The original name of Jerusalem (here, London) was Jebus.
6. Such oppressive laws against Roman Catholics date from the time of Elizabeth I.

This set the heathen priesthood[7] in a flame;
For priests of all religions are the same:
100 Of whatsoe'er descent their godhead be,
Stock, stone, or other homely pedigree,
In his defense his servants are as bold,
As if he had been born of beaten gold.
The Jewish rabbins,[8] though their enemies,
105 In this conclude them honest men and wise:
For 'twas their duty, all the learned think,
To espouse his cause, by whom they eat and drink.
From hence began that Plot, the nation's curse,
Bad in itself, but represented worse;
110 Raised in extremes, and in extremes decried;
With oaths affirmed, with dying vows denied;
Not weighed or winnowed by the multitude;
But swallowed in the mass, unchewed and crude.
Some truth there was, but dashed° and brewed with lies,   *adulterated*
115 To please the fools, and puzzle all the wise.
Succeeding times did equal folly call,
Believing nothing, or believing all.
The Egyptian rites the Jebusites embraced,
Where gods were recommended by their taste.[9]
120 Such savory deities must needs be good,
As served at once for worship and for food.
By force they could not introduce these gods,
For ten to one in former days was odds;
So fraud was used (the sacrificer's trade):
125 Fools are more hard to conquer than persuade.
Their busy teachers mingled with the Jews,
And raked for converts even the court and stews:°   *brothels*
Which Hebrew priests the more unkindly took,
Because the fleece accompanies the flock.[1]
130 Some thought they God's anointed° meant to slay   *the king*
By guns, invented since full many a day:
Our author swears it not; but who can know
How far the Devil and Jebusites may go?
This Plot, which failed for want of common sense,
135 Had yet a deep and dangerous consequence:
For, as when raging fevers boil the blood,
The standing lake soon floats into a flood,
And every hostile humor, which before
Slept quiet in its channels, bubbles o'er;
140 So several factions from this first ferment
Work up to foam, and threat the government.
Some by their friends, more by themselves thought wise,
Opposed the power to which they could not rise.
Some had in courts been great, and thrown from thence,

---

7. Roman Catholic clergy.
8. Anglican clergy.
9. Here Dryden sneers at the doctrine of transubstantiation. "Egyptian": French, therefore Catholic.

1. Dryden charges that the Anglican clergy ("Hebrew priests") resented proselytizing by Catholics chiefly because they stood to lose their tithes ("fleece").

145　Like fiends were hardened in impenitence;
　　　Some, by their monarch's fatal mercy, grown
　　　From pardoned rebels kinsmen to the throne,
　　　Were raised in power and public office high;
　　　Strong bands, if bands ungrateful men could tie.
150　　　Of these the false Achitophel[2] was first;
　　　A name to all succeeding ages cursed:
　　　For close designs, and crooked counsels fit;
　　　Sagacious, bold, and turbulent of wit;°　　　　　　unruly imagination
　　　Restless, unfixed in principles and place;
155　In power unpleased, impatient of disgrace:
　　　A fiery soul, which, working out its way, ⎫
　　　Fretted the pygmy body to decay, ⎬
　　　And o'er-informed the tenement of clay.[3] ⎭
　　　A daring pilot in extremity;
160　Pleased with the danger, when the waves went high,
　　　He sought the storms; but, for a calm unfit,
　　　Would steer too nigh the sands, to boast his wit.
　　　Great wits are sure to madness near allied,[4]
　　　And thin partitions do their bounds divide;
165　Else why should he, with wealth and honor blest,
　　　Refuse his age the needful hours of rest?
　　　Punish a body which he could not please;
　　　Bankrupt of life, yet prodigal of ease?
　　　And all to leave what with his toil he won,
170　To that unfeathered two-legged thing,[5] a son;
　　　Got, while his soul did huddled° notions try;　　　confused, hurried
　　　And born a shapeless lump, like anarchy.
　　　In friendship false, implacable in hate,
　　　Resolved to ruin or to rule the state.
175　To compass this the triple bond[6] he broke, ⎫
　　　The pillars of the public safety shook, ⎬
　　　And fitted Israel for a foreign yoke; ⎭
　　　Then seized with fear, yet still affecting fame,
　　　Usurped a patriot's all-atoning name.
180　So easy still it proves in factious times,
　　　With public zeal to cancel private crimes.
　　　How safe is treason, and how sacred ill,
　　　Where none can sin against the people's will!
　　　Where crowds can wink, and no offense be known,
185　Since in another's guilt they find their own!
　　　Yet fame deserved, no enemy can grudge;

2. Anthony Ashley Cooper, first earl of Shaftesbury (1621–1683). He had served in the parliamentary army and been a member of Cromwell's council of state. He later helped bring back Charles and, in 1670, was made a member of the notorious Cabal Ministry, which formed an alliance with Louis XIV in which England betrayed her ally, Holland, and joined France in war against that country. In 1672 he became lord chancellor, but with the dissolution of the cabal in 1673, he was removed from office. Lines 146–49 apply perfectly to him.

3. The soul is thought of as the animating principle, the force that puts the body in motion. Shaftesbury's body seemed too small to house his fiery, energetic soul.
4. "Great wits": men of genius. That genius and madness are akin is a very old idea.
5. Cf. Plato's definition of a human: "a featherless biped."
6. The triple alliance of England, Sweden, and Holland against France, 1668. Shaftesbury helped to bring about the war against Holland in 1672.

The statesman we abhor, but praise the judge.
In Israel's courts ne'er sat an Abbethdin[7]
With more discerning eyes, or hands more clean;
190 Unbribed, unsought, the wretched to redress;
Swift of dispatch, and easy of access.
Oh, had he been content to serve the crown,
With virtues only proper to the gown;
Or had the rankness of the soil been freed
195 From cockle, that oppressed the noble seed;
David for him his tuneful harp had strung,
And Heaven had wanted one immortal song.[8]
But wild Ambition loves to slide, not stand,
And Fortune's ice prefers to Virtue's land.
200 Achitophel, grown weary to possess
A lawful fame, and lazy happiness,
Disdained the golden fruit to gather free,
And lent the crowd his arm to shake the tree.
Now, manifest of° crimes contrived long since,   *detected in*
205 He stood at bold defiance with his prince;
Held up the buckler of the people's cause
Against the crown, and skulked behind the laws.
The wished occasion of the Plot he takes;
Some circumstances finds, but more he makes.
210 By buzzing emissaries fills the ears
Of listening crowds with jealousies° and fears   *suspicions*
Of arbitrary counsels brought to light,
And proves the king himself a Jebusite.
Weak arguments! which yet he knew full well
215 Were strong with people easy to rebel.
For, governed by the moon, the giddy Jews
Tread the same track when she the prime renews;
And once in twenty years, their scribes record,[9]
By natural instinct they change their lord.
220 Achitophel still wants a chief, and none
Was found so fit as warlike Absalom:
Not that he wished his greatness to create
(For politicians neither love nor hate),
But, for he knew his title not allowed,
225 Would keep him still depending on the crowd,
That kingly power, thus ebbing out, might be
Drawn to the dregs of a democracy.[1]
Him he attempts with studied arts to please,
And sheds his venom in such words as these:
230   "Auspicious prince, at whose nativity

7. The chief of the seventy elders who composed the Jewish supreme court. The allusion is to Shaftesbury's serving as lord chancellor from 1672 to 1673. Dryden's praise of Shaftesbury's integrity in this office, by suggesting a balanced judgment, makes his condemnation of the statesman more effective than it might otherwise have been.
8. I.e., David would have had occasion to write one fewer song of praise to heaven. The reference may be to 2 Samuel 22 or to Psalm 4.

9. The moon "renews her prime" when its several phases recur on the same day of the solar calendar—i.e., complete a cycle—as happens approximately every twenty years. The crisis between Charles I and Parliament began to grow acute about 1640; Charles II returned in 1660; it is now 1680 and a full cycle has been completed.
1. To Dryden, "democracy" meant popular government. The "dregs of a democracy" would be mob rule.

Some royal planet[2] ruled the southern sky;
Thy longing country's darling and desire;
Their cloudy pillar and their guardian fire:
Their second Moses, whose extended wand
235   Divides the seas, and shows the promised land;[3]
Whose dawning day in every distant age
Has exercised the sacred prophet's rage:
The people's prayer, the glad diviners' theme,
The young men's vision, and the old men's dream![4]
240   Thee, savior, thee, the nation's vows[5] confess,
And, never satisfied with seeing, bless:
Swift unbespoken pomps thy steps proclaim,
And stammering babes are taught to lisp thy name.
How long wilt thou the general joy detain,
245   Starve and defraud the people of thy reign?
Content ingloriously to pass thy days
Like one of Virtue's fools that feeds on praise;
Till thy fresh glories, which now shine so bright,
Grow stale and tarnish with our daily sight.
250   Believe me, royal youth, thy fruit must be
Or gathered ripe, or rot upon the tree.
Heaven has to all allotted, soon or late,
Some lucky revolution of their fate;
Whose motions if we watch and guide with skill
255   (For human good depends on human will),
Our Fortune rolls as from a smooth descent,
And from the first impression takes the bent;
But, if unseized, she glides away like wind,
And leaves repenting Folly far behind.
260   Now, now she meets you with a glorious prize,
And spreads her locks before her as she flies.[6]
Had thus old David, from whose loins you spring,
Not dared, when Fortune called him, to be king,
At Gath[7] an exile he might still remain,
265   And heaven's anointing[8] oil had been in vain.
Let his successful youth your hopes engage;
But shun the example of declining age;
Behold him setting in his western skies,
The shadows lengthening as the vapors rise.
270   He is not now, as when on Jordan's sand[9]
The joyful people thronged to see him land,
Covering the beach, and blackening all the strand;

2. A planet whose influence destines him to kingship.
3. After their exodus from Egypt under the leadership of Moses, whose "extended wand" separated
the waters of the Red Sea so that they crossed over
on dry land, the Israelites were led in their forty-
year wandering in the wilderness by a pillar of
cloud by day and a pillar of fire by night (Exodus
13–14).
4. Cf. Joel 2.28.
5. Solemn promises of fidelity.
6. Achitophel gives to Fortune the traditional

attributes of the allegorical personification of
Opportunity: bald except for a forelock, she can be
seized only as she approaches.
7. Brussels, where Charles spent his last years in
exile. David took refuge from Saul in Gath (1 Samuel 27.4).
8. After God rejected Saul, he sent Samuel to
anoint the boy David, as a token that he should
finally come to the throne (1 Samuel 16.1–13).
9. The seashore at Dover, where Charles landed
(May 25, 1660).

But, like the Prince of Angels, from his height
Comes tumbling downward with diminished light;[1]
275 Betrayed by one poor plot to public scorn
(Our only blessing since his cursed return),
Those heaps of people which one sheaf did bind,
Blown off and scattered by a puff of wind.
What strength can he to your designs oppose,
280 Naked of friends, and round beset with foes?
If Pharaoh's[2] doubtful succor he should use,
A foreign aid would more incense the Jews:
Proud Egypt would dissembled friendship bring;
Foment the war, but not support the king:
285 Nor would the royal party e'er unite
With Pharaoh's arms to assist the Jebusite;
Or if they should, their interest soon would break,
And with such odious aid make David weak.
All sorts of men by my successful arts,
290 Abhorring kings, estrange their altered hearts
From David's rule: and 'tis the general cry,
'Religion, commonwealth, and liberty.'[3]
If you, as champion of the public good,
Add to their arms a chief of royal blood,
295 What may not Israel hope, and what applause
Might such a general gain by such a cause?
Not barren praise alone, that gaudy flower
Fair only to the sight, but solid power;
And nobler is a limited command,
300 Given by the love of all your native land,
Than a successive title,[4] long and dark,
Drawn from the moldy rolls of Noah's ark."
       What cannot praise effect in mighty minds,
When flattery soothes, and when ambition blinds!
305 Desire of power, on earth a vicious weed,
Yet, sprung from high, is of celestial seed:
In God 'tis glory; and when men aspire,
'Tis but a spark too much of heavenly fire.
The ambitious youth, too covetous of fame,
310 Too full of angels' metal[5] in his frame,
Unwarily was led from virtue's ways,
Made drunk with honor, and debauched with praise.
Half loath, and half consenting to the ill
(For loyal blood within him struggled still),
315 He thus replied: "And what pretense have I
To take up arms for public liberty?
My father governs with unquestioned right;
The faith's defender, and mankind's delight,
Good, gracious, just, observant of the laws:

1. Cf. the fall of Satan in *Paradise Lost* 1.50–124, which dims the brightness of the archangel. The choice of the undignified word *tumbling* is deliberate.
2. Louis XIV of France.
3. Cf. line 82 and n. 4.

4. A title to the crown based on succession.
5. An alternative spelling of *mettle* (i.e., spirit). But a pun on "metal" is intended, as is obvious from the pun "angel" (a purely intellectual being and a coin). Ambition caused the revolt of the angels in heaven.

320 And heaven by wonders has espoused his cause.
Whom has he wronged in all his peaceful reign?
Who sues for justice to his throne in vain?
What millions has he pardoned of his foes,
Whom just revenge did to his wrath expose?
325 Mild, easy, humble, studious of our good,
Inclined to mercy, and averse from blood;
If mildness ill with stubborn Israel suit,
His crime is God's beloved attribute.
What could he gain, his people to betray,
330 Or change his right for arbitrary sway?
Let haughty Pharaoh curse with such a reign
His fruitful Nile, and yoke a servile train.
If David's rule Jerusalem displease,
The Dog Star⁶ heats their brains to this disease.
335 Why then should I, encouraging the bad,
Turn rebel and run popularly mad?
Were he a tyrant, who, by lawless might
Oppressed the Jews, and raised the Jebusite,
Well might I mourn; but nature's holy bands
340 Would curb my spirits and restrain my hands:
The people might assert° their liberty,   *claim*
But what was right in them were crime in me.
His favor leaves me nothing to require,
Prevents my wishes, and outruns desire.
345 What more can I expect while David lives?
All but his kingly diadem he gives:
And that"—But there he paused; then sighing, said—
"Is justly destined for a worthier head.
For when my father from his toils shall rest
350 And late augment the number of the blest,
His lawful issue shall the throne ascend,
Or the collateral line,⁷ where that shall end.
His brother, though oppressed with vulgar spite,
Yet dauntless, and secure of native right,
355 Of every royal virtue stands possessed;
Still dear to all the bravest and the best.
His courage foes, his friends his truth proclaim;
His loyalty the king, the world his fame.
His mercy even the offending crowd will find,
360 For sure he comes of a forgiving kind.⁸
Why should I then repine at heaven's decree,
Which gives me no pretense to royalty?
Yet O that fate, propitiously inclined,
Had raised my birth, or had debased my mind;
365 To my large soul not all her treasure lent,
And then betrayed it to a mean descent!
I find, I find my mounting spirits bold,

6. Sirius, which in midsummer rises and sets with the sun and is thus associated with the maddening heat of the "dog days."
7. In the event of Charles's dying without legiti-

mate issue, the throne would constitutionally pass to his brother, James, or his descendants, the "collateral line."
8. Race, in the sense of family.

And David's part disdains my mother's mold.
Why am I scanted by a niggard birth?[9]
370　My soul disclaims the kindred of her earth;
And, made for empire, whispers me within,
'Desire of greatness is a godlike sin.'"
　　Him staggering so when hell's dire agent found,[1]
While fainting Virtue scarce maintained her ground,
375　He pours fresh forces in, and thus replies:
　　"The eternal god, supremely good and wise,
Imparts not these prodigious gifts in vain:
What wonders are reserved to bless your reign!
Against your will, your arguments have shown,
380　Such virtue's only given to guide a throne.
Not that your father's mildness I contemn,
But manly force becomes the diadem.
'Tis true he grants the people all they crave;
And more, perhaps, than subjects ought to have:
385　For lavish grants suppose a monarch tame,
And more his goodness than his wit° proclaim.　　　*intelligence*
But when should people strive their bonds to break,
If not when kings are negligent or weak?
Let him give on till he can give no more,
390　The thrifty Sanhedrin[2] shall keep him poor;
And every shekel which he can receive,
Shall cost a limb of his prerogative.[3]
To ply him with new plots shall be my care;
Or plunge him deep in some expensive war;
395　Which when his treasure can no more supply,
He must, with the remains of kingship, buy.
His faithful friends our jealousies and fears
Call Jebusites, and Pharaoh's pensioners;
Whom when our fury from his aid has torn,
400　He shall be naked left to public scorn.
The next successor, whom I fear and hate,
My arts have made obnoxious to the state;
Turned all his virtues to his overthrow,
And gained our elders[4] to pronounce a foe.
405　His right, for sums of necessary gold,
Shall first be pawned, and afterward be sold;
Till time shall ever-wanting David draw,
To pass your doubtful title into law:
If not, the people have a right supreme
410　To make their kings; for kings are made for them.
All empire is no more than power in trust,
Which, when resumed, can be no longer just.
Succession, for the general good designed,

9. I.e., why am I limited by a sordid birth?
1. Observe the Miltonic inversion, which helps maintain the epic tone.
2. The highest judicial counsel of the Jews, here, Parliament.
3. The Whigs hoped to limit the special privileges of the Crown (the royal "prerogative") by refusing

to vote money to Charles. He circumvented them by living on French subsidies and refusing to summon Parliament.
4. The chief magistrates and rulers of the Jews. Shaftesbury had won over ("gained") country gentlemen and nobles to his hostile view of James.

In its own wrong a nation cannot bind;
415 If altering that the people can relieve,
Better one suffer than a nation grieve.
The Jews well know their power: ere Saul they chose,[5]
God was their king, and God they durst depose.
Urge now your piety,[6] your filial name,
420 A father's right and fear of future fame;
The public good, that universal call,
To which even heaven submitted, answers all.
Nor let his love enchant your generous mind;
'Tis Nature's trick to propagate her kind.
425 Our fond begetters, who would never die,
Love but themselves in their posterity.
Or let his kindness by the effects be tried,
Or let him lay his vain pretense aside.
God said he loved your father; could he bring
430 A better proof than to anoint him king?
It surely showed he loved the shepherd well,
Who gave so fair a flock as Israel.
Would David have you thought his darling son?
What means he then, to alienate[7] the crown?
435 The name of godly he may blush to bear:
'Tis after God's own heart[8] to cheat his heir.
He to his brother gives supreme command;
To you a legacy of barren land,[9]
Perhaps the old harp, on which he thrums his lays,
440 Or some dull Hebrew ballad in your praise.
Then the next heir, a prince severe and wise,
Already looks on you with jealous eyes;
Sees through the thin disguises of your arts,
And marks your progress in the people's hearts.
445 Though now his mighty soul its grief contains,
He meditates revenge who least complains;
And, like a lion, slumbering in the way,
Or sleep dissembling, while he waits his prey,
His fearless foes within his distance draws,
450 Constrains his roaring, and contracts his paws;
Till at the last, his time for fury found,
He shoots with sudden vengeance from the ground;
The prostrate vulgar° passes o'er and spares,   common people
But with a lordly rage his hunters tears.
455 Your case no tame expedients will afford:
Resolve on death, or conquest by the sword,
Which for no less a stake than life you draw;
And self-defense is nature's eldest law.
Leave the warm people no considering time;

5. Before Saul, the first king of Israel, came to the throne, the Jews were governed by judges. Similarly Oliver Cromwell ("Saul") as lord protector took over the reins of government, after he had dissolved the Rump Parliament in 1653.
6. Dutifulness to a parent.

7. In law, to convey the title to property to another person.
8. An irony (cf. line 7 and n. 1).
9. James was given the title of generalissimo in 1678. In 1679 Monmouth was banished and withdrew to Holland.

460   For then rebellion may be thought a crime.
      Prevail yourself of what occasion gives,
      But try your title while your father lives;
      And that your arms may have a fair pretense,°   *pretext*
      Proclaim you take them in the king's defense;
465   Whose sacred life each minute would expose
      To plots, from seeming friends, and secret foes.
      And who can sound the depth of David's soul?
      Perhaps his fear his kindness may control.
      He fears his brother, though he loves his son,
470   For plighted vows too late to be undone.
      If so, by force he wishes to be gained,
      Like women's lechery, to seem constrained.°   *forced*
      Doubt not; but when he most affects the frown,
      Commit a pleasing rape upon the crown.
475   Secure his person to secure your cause:
      They who possess the prince, possess the laws."
         He said, and this advice above the rest
      With Absalom's mild nature suited best:
      Unblamed of life (ambition set aside),
480   Not stained with cruelty, nor puffed with pride,
      How happy had he been, if destiny
      Had higher placed his birth, or not so high!
      His kingly virtues might have claimed a throne,
      And blest all other countries but his own.
485   But charming greatness since so few refuse,
      'Tis juster to lament him than accuse.
      Strong were his hopes a rival to remove,
      With blandishments to gain the public love;
      To head the faction while their zeal was hot,
490   And popularly prosecute the Plot.
      To further this, Achitophel unites
      The malcontents of all the Israelites;
      Whose differing parties he could wisely join,
      For several ends, to serve the same design:
495   The best (and of the princes some were such),
      Who thought the power of monarchy too much;
      Mistaken men, and patriots in their hearts;
      Not wicked, but seduced by impious arts.
      By these the springs of property were bent,
500   And wound so high, they cracked the government.
      The next for interest sought to embroil the state,
      To sell their duty at a dearer rate;
      And make their Jewish markets of the throne,
      Pretending public good, to serve their own.
505   Others thought kings an useless heavy load,
      Who cost too much, and did too little good.
      These were for laying honest David by,
      On principles of pure good husbandry.°   *economy*
      With them joined all the haranguers of the throng,
510   That thought to get preferment by the tongue.

Who follow next, a double danger bring,
Not only hating David, but the king:
The Solymaean rout,[1] well-versed of old
In godly faction, and in treason bold;
515 Cowering and quaking at a conqueror's sword,
But lofty to a lawful prince restored;
Saw with disdain an ethnic[2] plot begun,
And scorned by Jebusites to be outdone.
Hot Levites[3] headed these; who, pulled before
520 From the ark, which in the Judges' days they bore,
Resumed their cant, and with a zealous cry
Pursued their old beloved theocracy:
Where Sanhedrin and priest enslaved the nation,
And justified their spoils by inspiration:[4]
525 For who so fit for reign as Aaron's race,[5]
If once dominion they could found in grace?
These led the pack; though not of surest scent,
Yet deepest-mouthed[6] against the government.
A numerous host of dreaming saints succeed,
530 Of the true old enthusiastic breed:[7]
'Gainst form and order they their power employ,
Nothing to build, and all things to destroy.
But far more numerous was the herd of such,
Who think too little, and who talk too much.
535 These out of mere instinct, they knew not why,
Adored their fathers' God and property;
And, by the same blind benefit of fate,
The Devil and the Jebusite did hate:
Born to be saved, even in their own despite,
540 Because they could not help believing right.
Such were the tools; but a whole Hydra more
Remains, of sprouting heads too long to score.
Some of their chiefs were princes of the land:
In the first rank of these did Zimri[8] stand;
545 A man so various, that he seemed to be

1. I.e., London rabble. Solyma was a name for
Jerusalem.
2. Gentile; here, Roman Catholic.
3. I.e., Presbyterian clergymen. The tribe of Levi,
assigned to duties in the tabernacle, carried the ark
of the covenant during the forty-year sojourn in the
wilderness (Numbers 4). Under the Commonwealth ("in the Judges' days") Presbyterianism
became the state religion, and its clergy, therefore,
"bore the ark." The Act of Uniformity (1662)
forced the Presbyterian clergy out of their livings:
in short, before the Popish Plot, they had been
"pulled from the ark." They are represented here
as joining the Whigs in the hope of restoring the
commonwealth, "their old beloved theocracy."
4. Observe in these lines the cluster of disparaging
words: "cant," "zealous," "inspiration." Dryden
shared Samuel Butler's contempt for the irration-
ality of Dissenters.
5. Priests had to be descendants of Aaron (Exodus
28.1, Numbers 18.7).
6. Loudest. The phrase is applied to hunting dogs.

"Pack" and "scent" sustain the image.
7. "Dreaming saints": a term used by certain Dissenters for those elected to salvation. The extreme
fanaticism of the "saints" and their claims to inspiration are characterized as a form of religious madness ("enthusiastic").
8. George Villiers, second duke of Buckingham
(1628–1687), wealthy, brilliant, dissolute, and
unstable. He had been an influential member of
the cabal, but after 1673 had joined Shaftesbury
in opposition to the court party. This is the least
political of the satirical portraits in the poem.
Buckingham had been the chief author of The
Rehearsal (1671), the play that satirized the heroic
play and ridiculed Dryden in the character of Mr.
Bayes. Politics gave Dryden an opportunity to
retaliate. He comments on this portrait in his A
Discourse Concerning the Original and Progress of
Satire. Dryden had two biblical Zimris in mind: the
Zimri destroyed for his lustfulness and blasphemy
(Numbers 25) and the conspirator and regicide of
1 Kings 16.8–20 and 2 Kings 9.31.

Not one, but all mankind's epitome:
Stiff in opinions, always in the wrong;
Was everything by starts, and nothing long;
But, in the course of one revolving moon,
550 Was chymist,° fiddler, statesman, and buffoon: *chemist*
Then all for women, painting, rhyming, drinking,
Besides ten thousand freaks that died in thinking.
Blest madman, who could every hour employ,
With something new to wish, or to enjoy!
555 Railing° and praising were his usual themes;   *reviling, abusing*
And both (to show his judgment) in extremes:
So over-violent, or over-civil,
That every man, with him, was God or Devil.
In squandering wealth was his peculiar art:
560 Nothing went unrewarded but desert.
Beggared by fools, whom still° he found° too late,   *constantly/found out*
He had his jest, and they had his estate.
He laughed himself from court; then sought relief
By forming parties, but could ne'er be chief;
565 For, spite of him, the weight of business fell
On Absalom and wise Achitophel:
Thus, wicked but in will, of means bereft,
He left not faction, but of that was left.
    Titles and names 'twere tedious to rehearse
570 Of lords, below the dignity of verse.
Wits, warriors, Commonwealth's men, were the best;
Kind husbands, and mere nobles, all the rest.
And therefore, in the name of dullness, be
The well-hung Balaam and cold Caleb, free;
575 And canting Nadab let oblivion damn,
Who made new porridge for the paschal lamb.[9]
Let friendship's holy band some names assure;
Some their own worth, and some let scorn secure.
Nor shall the rascal rabble here have place,
580 Whom kings no titles gave, and God no grace:
Not bull-faced Jonas,[1] who could statutes draw
To mean rebellion, and make treason law.
But he, though bad, is followed by a worse,
The wretch who heaven's anointed dared to curse:
585 Shimei,[2] whose youth did early promise bring
Of zeal to God and hatred to his king,
Did wisely from expensive sins refrain,

9. The lamb slain during Passover; here, Christ. The identities of Balaam, Caleb, and Nadab have not been certainly established, although various Whig nobles have been suggested. For Balaam see Numbers 22–24; for Caleb, Numbers 13–14; and for Nadab, Leviticus 10.1–2. "Well-hung": fluent of speech or sexually potent or both. "Cold" would contrast with the second meaning of well-hung. "Canting" points to a Nonconformist, as does "new porridge," for Dissenters referred to the Book of Common Prayer contemptuously as "porridge," a hodgepodge, unsubstantial stuff.

1. Sir William Jones, attorney general, had been largely responsible for the passage of the first Exclusion Bill by the House of Commons. He prosecuted the accused in the Popish Plot.
2. Shimei cursed and stoned David when he fled into the wilderness during Absalom's revolt (2 Samuel 16.5–14). His name is used here for one of the two sheriffs of London: Slingsby Bethel, a Whig, former republican, and virulent enemy of Charles. He packed juries with Whigs and so secured the acquittal of enemies of the court, among them Shaftesbury himself.

And never broke the Sabbath, but for gain;
Nor ever was he known an oath to vent,
590 Or curse, unless against the government.
Thus heaping wealth, by the most ready way
Among the Jews, which was to cheat and pray,
The city, to reward his pious hate
Against his master, chose him magistrate.
595 His hand a vare° of justice did uphold;   staff
His neck was loaded with a chain of gold.
During his office, treason was no crime;
The sons of Belial[3] had a glorious time;
For Shimei, though not prodigal of pelf,
600 Yet loved his wicked neighbor as himself.
When two or three were gathered to declaim ⎤
Against the monarch of Jerusalem,   ⎬
Shimei was always in the midst of them;   ⎦
And if they cursed the king when he was by,
605 Would rather curse than break good company.
If any durst his factious friends accuse,
He packed a jury of dissenting Jews;
Whose fellow-feeling in the godly cause
Would free the suffering saint from human laws.
610 For laws are only made to punish those
Who serve the king, and to protect his foes.
If any leisure time he had from power
(Because 'tis sin to misemploy an hour),
His business was, by writing, to persuade
615 That kings were useless, and a clog to trade;
And, that his noble style he might refine,
No Rechabite[4] more shunned the fumes of wine.
Chaste were his cellars, and his shrieval board[5]
The grossness of a city feast abhorred:
620 His cooks, with long disuse, their trade forgot;
Cool was his kitchen, though his brains were hot,
Such frugal virtue malice may accuse,
But sure 'twas necessary to the Jews:
For towns once burnt[6] such magistrates require
625 As dare not tempt God's providence by fire.
With spiritual food he fed his servants well,
But free from flesh that made the Jews rebel;
And Moses' laws he held in more account,
For forty days of fasting in the mount.[7]
630 To speak the rest, who better are forgot,
Would tire a well-breathed witness of the Plot.
Yet, Corah,[8] thou shalt from oblivion pass:

3. Sons of wickedness (cf. Milton, *Paradise Lost* 1.490–505). Dryden probably intended a pun on Balliol, the Oxford college in which leading Whigs stayed during the brief and fateful meeting of Parliament at Oxford in 1681.
4. An austere Jewish sect that drank no wine (Jeremiah 35.2–19).
5. Sheriff's dinner table.

6. London burned in 1666.
7. Mount Sinai, where, during a fast of forty days, Moses received the law (Exodus 34.28).
8. Or Korah, a rebellious Levite, swallowed up by the earth because of his crimes (Numbers 16). Corah is Titus Oates, the self-appointed, perjured, and "well-breathed" (long-winded) witness of the plot.

Erect thyself, thou monumental brass,
High as the serpent of thy metal made,[9]
635 While nations stand secure beneath thy shade.
What though his birth were base, yet comets rise
From earthy vapors, ere they shine in skies.
Prodigious actions may as well be done
By weaver's issue,[1] as by prince's son.
640 This arch-attestor for the public good
By that one deed ennobles all his blood.
Who ever asked the witnesses' high race
Whose oath with martyrdom did Stephen[2] grace?
Ours was a Levite, and as times went then,
645 His tribe were God Almighty's gentlemen.
Sunk were his eyes, his voice was harsh and loud,
Sure signs he neither choleric[3] was nor proud:
His long chin proved his wit; his saintlike grace
A church vermilion, and a Moses' face.[4]
650 His memory, miraculously great,
Could plots, exceeding man's belief, repeat;
Which therefore cannot be accounted lies,
For human wit could never such devise.
Some future truths are mingled in his book;
655 But where the witness failed, the prophet spoke:
Some things like visionary flights appear;
The spirit caught him up, the Lord knows where,
And gave him his rabbinical degree,
Unknown to foreign university.[5]
660 His judgment yet his memory did excel;
Which pieced his wondrous evidence so well,
And suited to the temper of the times,
Then groaning under Jebusitic crimes.
Let Israel's foes suspect his heavenly call,
665 And rashly judge his writ apocryphal;[6]
Our laws for such affronts have forfeits made:
He takes his life, who takes away his trade.
Were I myself in witness Corah's place,
The wretch who did me such a dire disgrace
670 Should whet my memory, though once forgot,
To make him an appendix of my plot.
His zeal to heaven made him his prince despise,
And load his person with indignities;
But zeal peculiar privilege affords,
675 Indulging latitude to deeds and words;
And Corah might for Agag's murder[7] call,

---

9. Moses erected a brazen serpent to heal the Jews bitten by fiery serpents (Numbers 21.4–9). "Brass" also means impudence or shamelessness.
1. Oates's father, a clergyman, belonged to an obscure family of ribbon weavers.
2. The first Christian martyr, accused by false witnesses (Acts 6–7).
3. Prone to anger.
4. Moses' face shone when he came down from Mount Sinai with the tables of the law (Exodus

34.29–30). Oates's face suggests high living, not spiritual illumination.
5. Oates falsely claimed to be a doctor of divinity in the University of Salamanca.
6. Not inspired and hence excluded from Holy Writ.
7. Agag is probably one of the five Catholic peers executed for the Popish Plot in 1680, most likely Lord Stafford, against whom Oates fabricated testimony; he is almost certainly not, as is usually sug-

In terms as coarse as Samuel used to Saul.
What others in his evidence did join
(The best that could be had for love or coin),
680 In Corah's own predicament will fall;
For *witness* is a common name to all.
　　Surrounded thus with friends of every sort,
Deluded Absalom forsakes the court:
Impatient of high hopes, urged with renown,
685 And fired with near possession of a crown.
The admiring crowd are dazzled with surprise,
And on his goodly person feed their eyes:
His joy concealed, he sets himself to show,
On each side bowing popularly[8] low;
690 His looks, his gestures, and his words he frames,
And with familiar ease repeats their names.
Thus formed by nature, furnished out with arts,
He glides unfelt into their secret hearts.
Then, with a kind compassionating look,
695 And sighs, bespeaking pity ere he spoke,
Few words he said; but easy those and fit,
More slow than Hybla-drops,[9] and far more sweet.
　　"I mourn, my countrymen, your lost estate;
Though far unable to prevent your fate:
700 Behold a banished man, for your dear cause
Exposed a prey to arbitrary laws!
Yet oh! that I alone could be undone,
Cut off from empire, and no more a son!
Now all your liberties a spoil are made; ⎫
705 Egypt° and Tyrus° intercept your trade, ⎬ France/Holland
And Jebusites your sacred rites invade. ⎭
My father, whom with reverence yet I name,
Charmed into ease, is careless of his fame;
And, bribed with petty sums of foreign gold,
710 Is grown in Bathsheba's[1] embraces old;
Exalts his enemies, his friends destroys;
And all his power against himself employs.
He gives, and let him give, my right away;
But why should he his own, and yours betray?
715 He only, he can make the nation bleed,
And he alone from my revenge is freed.
Take then my tears (with that he wiped his eyes),
'Tis all the aid my present power supplies:
No court-informer can these arms accuse;
720 These arms may sons against their fathers use:
And 'tis my wish, the next successor's reign
May make no other Israelite complain."
　　　　Youth, beauty, graceful action seldom fail;

---

gested, Sir Edmund Berry Godfrey (see headnote, p. 879). "Agag's murder" and Samuel's coarse terms to Saul are in 1 Samuel 15.
8. "So as to please the crowd" (Johnson's *Dictionary*).
9. The famous honey of Hybla in Sicily.
1. With whom David committed adultery (2 Samuel 11); here, Charles II's French mistress, Louise de Keroualle, duchess of Portsmouth.

But common interest always will prevail;
725 And pity never ceases to be shown
To him who makes the people's wrongs his own.
The crowd (that still believe their kings oppress)
With lifted hands their young Messiah bless:
Who now begins his progress to ordain
730 With chariots, horsemen, and a numerous train;
From east to west his glories he displays,[2]
And, like the sun, the promised land surveys.
Fame runs before him as the morning star,
And shouts of joy salute him from afar:
735 Each house receives him as a guardian god,
And consecrates the place of his abode:
But hospitable treats did most commend
Wise Issachar,[3] his wealthy western friend.
This moving court, that caught the people's eyes,
740 And seemed but pomp, did other ends disguise:
Achitophel had formed it, with intent
To sound the depths, and fathom, where it went,
The people's hearts; distinguish friends from foes,
And try their strength, before they came to blows.
745 Yet all was colored with a smooth pretense
Of specious love, and duty to their prince.
Religion, and redress of grievances,
Two names that always cheat and always please,
Are often urged; and good King David's life
750 Endangered by a brother and a wife.[4]
Thus, in a pageant show, a plot is made,
And peace itself is war in masquerade.
O foolish Israel! never warned by ill,
Still the same bait, and circumvented still!
755 Did ever men forsake their present ease,
In midst of health imagine a disease;
Take pains contingent mischiefs to foresee,
Make heirs for monarchs, and for God decree?
What shall we think![5] Can people give away
760 Both for themselves and sons, their native sway?
Then they are left defenseless to the sword
Of each unbounded, arbitrary lord:
And laws are vain, by which we right enjoy,
If kings unquestioned can those laws destroy.
765 Yet if the crowd be judge of fit and just,
And kings are only officers in trust,
Then this resuming covenant was declared
When kings were made, or is forever barred.
If those who gave the scepter could not tie

---

2. In 1680 Monmouth made a progress through the west of England, seeking popular support for his cause.

3. Thomas Thynne of Longleat. He entertained Monmouth on his journey in the west. "Wise" is, of course, ironic.

4. Titus Oates had sworn that both James, duke of York, and the queen were involved in a similar plot to poison Charles II.

5. In the passage that follows, Dryden states his political philosophy. He bases the royal authority on a covenant entered into by the governor and the governed.

770 By their own deed their own posterity,
How then could Adam bind his future race?
How could his forfeit on mankind take place?
Or how could heavenly justice damn us all,
Who ne'er consented to our father's fall?
775 Then kings are slaves to those whom they command,
And tenants to their people's pleasure stand.
Add, that the power for property allowed
Is mischievously seated in the crowd;
For who can be secure of private right,
780 If sovereign sway may be dissolved by might?
Nor is the people's judgment always true:
The most may err as grossly as the few;
And faultless kings run down, by common cry,
For vice, oppression, and for tyranny.
785 What standard is there in a fickle rout,
Which, flowing to the mark,° runs faster out?   °highwater mark
Nor only crowds, but Sanhedrins may be
Infected with this public lunacy,[6]
And share the madness of rebellious times,
790 To murder monarchs for imagined crimes.[7]
If they may give and take whene'er they please,
Not kings alone (the Godhead's images),
But government itself at length must fall
To nature's state, where all have right to all.
795 Yet, grant our lords the people kings can make,
What prudent men a settled throne would shake?
For whatsoe'er their sufferings were before,
That change they covet makes them suffer more.
All other errors but disturb a state,
800 But innovation is the blow of fate.
If ancient fabrics nod, and threat to fall,
To patch the flaws, and buttress up the wall,
Thus far 'tis duty; but here fix the mark;
For all beyond it is to touch our ark.[8]
805 To change foundations, cast the frame anew,
Is work for rebels, who base ends pursue,
At once divine and human laws control,
And mend the parts by ruin of the whole.
The tampering world is subject to this curse,
810 To physic their disease into a worse.
  Now what relief can righteous David bring?
How fatal 'tis to be too good a king!
Friends he has few, so high the madness grows:
Who dare be such, must be the people's foes:
815 Yet some there were, even in the worst of days;
Some let me name, and naming is to praise.
  In this short file Barzillai[9] first appears;

---

6. The fickle crowd flows and ebbs like the tide, which is pulled back and forth by the moon (hence "lunacy," after the Latin *luna*, or "moon").
7. An allusion to the execution of Charles I.
8. Uzzah was struck dead because he sacrilegiously touched the Ark of the Covenant (2 Samuel 6.6–7).
9. James Butler, duke of Ormond (1610–1688). He was famous for his loyalty to the Stuart cause. He fought for Charles I in Ireland, and when that cause was hopeless, he joined Charles II in his exile abroad. He spent a large fortune on behalf of the

Barzillai, crowned with honor and with years:
Long since, the rising rebels he withstood
820 In regions waste, beyond the Jordan's flood:
Unfortunately brave to buoy the State;
But sinking underneath his master's fate:
In exile with his godlike prince he mourned;
For him he suffered, and with him returned.
825 The court he practiced, not the courtier's art:
Large was his wealth, but larger was his heart:
Which well the noblest objects knew to choose,
The fighting warrior, and recording Muse.
His bed could once a fruitful issue boast;
830 Now more than half a father's name is lost.
His eldest hope,[1] with every grace adorned,
By me (so Heaven will have it) always mourned,
And always honored, snatched in manhood's prime
By unequal fates, and Providence's crime:
835 Yet not before the goal of honor won,
All parts fulfilled of subject and of son;
Swift was the race, but short the time to run.
O narrow circle, but of power divine,
Scanted in space, but perfect in thy line!
840 By sea, by land, thy matchless worth was known,
Arms thy delight, and war was all thy own:
Thy force, infused, the fainting Tyrians° propped;   *the Dutch*
And haughty Pharaoh found his fortune stopped.
Oh ancient honor! Oh unconquered hand,
845 Whom foes unpunished never could withstand!
But Israel was unworthy of thy name:
Short is the date of all immoderate fame.
It looks as Heaven our ruin had designed,
And durst not trust thy fortune and thy mind.
850 Now, free from earth, thy disencumbered soul
Mounts up, and leaves behind the clouds and starry pole:
From thence thy kindred legions mayst thou bring,
To aid the guardian angel of thy king.
Here stop my Muse, here cease thy painful flight;
855 No pinions can pursue immortal height:
Tell good Barzillai thou canst sing no more,
And tell thy soul she should have fled before:
Or fled she with his life, and left this verse
To hang on her departed patron's hearse?
860 Now take thy steepy flight from heaven, and see
If thou canst find on earth another *he*:
Another *he* would be too hard to find;
See then whom thou canst see not far behind.
Zadoc the priest, whom, shunning power and place,
865 His lowly mind advanced to David's grace:
With him the Sagan of Jerusalem,
Of hospitable soul, and noble stem;

---

king and continued to serve him loyally after the
Restoration.
1. Ormond's son, Thomas, earl of Ossory (1634–

1680), a famous soldier and like his father devoted
to Charles II.

Him of the western dome, whose weighty sense
Flows in fit words and heavenly eloquence.
870 The prophets' sons,² by such example led,
To learning and to loyalty were bred:
For colleges on bounteous kinds depend,
And never rebel was to arts a friend.
To these succeed the pillars of the laws,
875 Who best could plead, and best can judge a cause.
Next them a train of loyal peers ascend;
Sharp-judging Adriel, the Muses' friend,
Himself a Muse—in Sanhedrin's debate
True to his prince, but not a slave of state:
880 Whom David's love with honors did adorn,
That from his disobedient son were torn.
Jotham of piercing wit, and pregnant thought,
Indued by nature, and by learning taught
To move assemblies, who but only tried
885 The worse a while, then chose the better side;
Nor chose alone, but turned the balance too;
So much the weight of one brave man can do.
Hushai,³ the friend of David in distress,
In public storms, of manly steadfastness:
890 By foreign treaties he informed his youth,
And joined experience to his native truth.
His frugal care supplied the wanting throne,
Frugal for that, but bounteous of his own:
'Tis easy conduct when exchequers flow,
895 But hard the task to manage well the low;
For sovereign power is too depressed or high,
When kings are forced to sell, or crowds to buy.
Indulge one labor more, my weary Muse,
For Amiel:⁴ who can Amiel's praise refuse?
900 Of ancient race by birth, but nobler yet
In his own worth, and without title great:
The Sanhedrin long time as chief he ruled,
Their reason guided, and their passion cooled:
So dexterous was he in the crown's defense,
905 So formed to speak a loyal nation's sense,
That, as their band was Israel's tribes in small,
So fit was he to represent them all.
Now rasher charioteers the seat ascend,
Whose loose careers his steady skill commend:
910 They like the unequal ruler of the day,
Misguide the seasons, and mistake the way;
While he withdrawn at their mad labor smiles,
And safe enjoys the sabbath of his toils.

---

2. The boys of Westminster School, which Dryden had attended. "Zadoc": William Sancroft, archbishop of Canterbury. "Sagan": Henry Compton, bishop of London. "Him of the western dome": John Dolben, dean of Westminster.

3. Laurence Hyde, earl of Rochester. "Adriel": John Sheffield, earl of Mulgrave. "Jotham": George Savile, marquis of Halifax.
4. Edward Seymour, speaker of the House of Commons.

These were the chief, a small but faithful band ⎤
915 Of worthies, in the breach who dared to stand, ⎬
And tempt the united fury of the land. ⎦
With grief they viewed such powerful engines bent,
To batter down the lawful government:
A numerous faction, with pretended frights,
920 In Sanhedrins to plume the regal rights;
The true successor from the court removed:[5]
The Plot, by hireling witnesses, improved.
These ills they saw, and, as their duty bound,
They showed the king the danger of the wound:
925 That no concessions from the throne would please,
But lenitives[6] fomented the disease;
That Absalom, ambitious of the crown,
Was made the lure to draw the people down;
That false Achitophel's pernicious hate
930 Had turned the Plot to ruin Church and State:
The council violent, the rabble worse;
That Shimei taught Jerusalem to curse.
⠀⠀With all these loads of injuries oppressed,
And long revolving, in his careful breast,
935 The event of things, at last, his patience tired,
Thus from his royal throne, by Heaven inspired,
The godlike David spoke: with awful fear
His train their Maker in their master hear.
⠀⠀"Thus long have I, by native mercy swayed,
940 My wrongs dissembled, my revenge delayed:
So willing to forgive the offending age,
So much the father did the king assuage.
But now so far my clemency they slight,
The offenders question my forgiving right.
945 That one was made for many, they contend;
But 'tis to rule; for that's a monarch's end.
They call my tenderness of blood, my fear;
Though manly tempers can the longest bear.
Yet, since they will divert my native course,
950 'Tis time to show I am not good by force.
Those heaped affronts that haughty subjects bring,
Are burdens for a camel, not a king:
Kings are the public pillars of the State,
Born to sustain and prop the nation's weight:
955 If my young Samson will pretend a call
To shake the column, let him share the fall:[7]
But, oh, that yet he would repent and live!
How easy 'tis for parents to forgive!
With how few tears a pardon might be won
960 From nature, pleading for a darling son!
Poor pitied youth, by my paternal care
Raised up to all the height his frame could bear:

5. The duke of York had been banished from England.

6. Any medicine that relieves pain.

7. Judges 16.

Had God ordained his fate for empire born,
He would have given his soul another turn:
965 Gulled° with a patriot's name, whose modern sense   *deceived*
Is one that would by law supplant his prince:
The people's brave, the politician's tool;
Never was patriot yet, but was a fool.
Whence comes it that religion and the laws
970 Should more be Absalom's than David's cause?
His old instructor, ere he lost his place,
Was never thought indued with so much grace.[8]
Good heavens, how faction can a patriot paint!
My rebel ever proves my people's saint:
975 Would *they* impose an heir upon the throne?
Let Sanhedrins be taught to give their own.
A king's at least a part of government,
And mine as requisite as their consent;
Without my leave a future king to choose,
980 Infers a right the present to depose:
True, they petition me to approve their choice;
But Esau's hands suit ill with Jacob's voice.[9]
My pious subjects for my safety pray,
Which to secure, they take my power away.
985 From plots and treasons Heaven preserve my years,
But save me most from my petitioners.
Unsatiate as the barren womb or grave;
God cannot grant so much as they can crave.
What then is left but with a jealous eye
990 To guard the small remains of royalty?
The law shall still direct my peaceful sway,
And the same law teach rebels to obey:
Votes shall no more established power control—
Such votes as make a part exceed the whole:
995 No groundless clamors shall my friends remove,
Nor crowds have power to punish ere they prove:
For gods and godlike kings, their care express,
Still to defend their servants in distress.
O that my power to saving were confined:
1000 Why am I forced, like Heaven, against my mind, ⎫
To make examples of another kind?   ⎬
Must I at length the sword of justice draw?   ⎭
O curst effects of necessary law!
How ill my fear they by my mercy scan!
1005 Beware the fury of a patient man.
Law they require, let Law then show her face;
They could not be content to look on Grace,
Her hinder parts, but with a daring eye
To tempt the terror of her front and die.[1]
1010 By their own arts, 'tis righteously decreed,
Those dire artificers of death shall bleed.

---

8. The earl of Shaftesbury.
9. Genesis 27.22.

1. Moses was not allowed to see the countenance
of Jehovah (Exodus 33.20–23).

Against themselves their witnesses will swear,
Till viper-like their mother Plot they tear:
And suck for nutriment that bloody gore,
1015 Which was their principle of life before.
Their Belial with their Belzebub² will fight;
Thus on my foes, my foes shall do me right:
Nor doubt the event; for factious crowds engage,
In their first onset, all their brutal rage.
1020 Then let 'em take an unresisted course,
Retire and traverse, and delude their force:
But when they stand all breathless, urge the fight,
And rise upon 'em with redoubled might:
For lawful power is still superior found,
1025 When long driven back, at length it stands the ground."
    He said. The Almighty, nodding, gave consent;
And peals of thunder shook the firmament.
Henceforth a series of new time began,
The mighty years in long procession ran:
1030 Once more the godlike David was restored,
And willing nations knew their lawful lord.

1681

Mac Flecknoe

The target of this superb satire, which is cast in the form of a mock-heroic episode, is Thomas Shadwell (1640–1692), the playwright, with whom Dryden had been on good terms for a number of years, certainly as late as March 1678. Shadwell considered himself the successor of Ben Jonson and the champion of the type of comedy that Jonson had written, the "comedy of humors," in which each character is presented under the domination of a single psychological trait or eccentricity, his humor. His plays are not without merit, but they are often clumsy and prolix and certainly much inferior to Jonson's. For many years he had conducted a public argument with Dryden on the merits of Jonson's comedies, which he thought Dryden undervalued. Exactly what moved Dryden to attack him is a matter of conjecture: he may simply have grown progressively bored and irritated by Shadwell and his tedious argument. The poem seems to have been written in late 1678 or 1679 and to have circulated only in manuscript until it was printed in 1682 in a pirated edition by an obscure publisher. By that time, the two playwrights were alienated by politics as well as by literary quarrels. Shadwell was a violent Whig and the reputed author of a sharp attack on Dryden as the Tory author of *Absalom and Achitophel* and *The Medal*. It was probably for this reason that the printer added the subtitle referring to Shadwell's Whiggism in the phrase "true-blue-Protestant poet." Political passions were running high, and sales would be helped if the poem seemed to refer to the events of the day.

Whereas Butler had debased and degraded his victims by using burlesque, caricature, and the grotesque, Dryden exposed Shadwell to ridicule by using the devices of mock epic, which treats the low, mean, or absurd in the grand language, lofty style, and solemn tone of epic poetry. The obvious disparity between subject and style makes the satiric point. In 1678, a prolific, untalented writer, Richard Flecknoe, died. Dryden conceived the idea of presenting Shadwell (the self-proclaimed heir of Ben Jonson, the laureate) as the son and successor of Flecknoe—hence *Mac* (i.e., son of)

2. A god of the Philistines. "Belial": the incarnation of all evil.

Flecknoe—from whom he inherits the throne of dullness. Flecknoe in the triple role of king, priest, and poet hails his successor, pronounces a panegyric on his perfect fitness for the throne, anoints and crowns him, foretells his glorious reign, and as he sinks (leaden dullness cannot soar), leaves his mantle to fall symbolically on Shadwell's shoulders. The poem abounds in literary allusions—to Roman legend and history and to the *Aeneid*, to Cowley's fragmentary epic *The Davideis*, to *Paradise Lost*, and to Shadwell's own plays. Biblical allusions add an unexpected dimension of incongruous dignity to the low scene. The coronation takes place in the City, to the plaudits of the citizens, who are fit to admire only what is dull. In 217 lines, Dryden created an image of Shadwell that has fixed his reputation to this day.

Mac Flecknoe

Or a Satire upon the True-Blue-Protestant Poet, T. S.

All human things are subject to decay,
And when fate summons, monarchs must obey.
This Flecknoe found, who, like Augustus,[1] young
Was called to empire, and had governed long;
5   In prose and verse, was owned, without dispute,
Through all the realms of Nonsense, absolute.
This aged prince, now flourishing in peace,
And blest with issue of a large increase,
Worn out with business, did at length debate
10   To settle the succession of the state;
And, pondering which of all his sons was fit
To reign, and wage immortal war with wit,
Cried: " 'Tis resolved; for nature pleads that he
Should only rule, who most resembles me.
15   Sh——[2] alone my perfect image bears,
Mature in dullness from his tender years:
Sh—— alone, of all my sons, is he
Who stands confirmed in full stupidity.
The rest to some faint meaning make pretense,
20   But Sh—— never deviates into sense.
Some beams of wit on other souls may fall,
Strike through, and make a lucid interval;
But Sh——'s genuine night admits no ray,
His rising fogs prevail upon the day.
25   Besides, his goodly fabric[3] fills the eye,
And seems designed for thoughtless majesty:
Thoughtless as monarch oaks that shade the plain,
And, spread in solemn state, supinely reign.
Heywood and Shirley were but types of thee,[4]
30   Thou last great prophet of tautology.[5]

1. In 31 B.C.E. Octavian became the first Roman emperor at the age of thirty-two. He assumed the title Augustus in 27 B.C.E.
2. Thomas Shadwell. The initial and second letter of the name followed by a dash give the appearance, but only the appearance, of protecting Dryden's victim by concealing his name. A common device in the satire of the period.
3. His body. Shadwell was a corpulent man.

4. Thomas Heywood (ca. 1570–1641) and James Shirley (1596–1666), playwrights popular before the closing of the theaters in 1642 but now out of fashion. They are introduced here as "types" (i.e., prefigurings) of Shadwell, in the sense that Solomon was regarded as an Old Testament prefiguring of Christ, the "last [final] great prophet."
5. Unnecessary repetition of meaning in different words.

Even I, a dunce of more renown than they,
Was sent before but to prepare thy way;
And, coarsely clad in Norwich drugget,[6] came
To teach the nations in thy greater name.[7]

35 My warbling lute, the lute I whilom° strung,   *formerly*
When to King John of Portugal[8] I sung,
Was but the prelude to that glorious day,
When thou on silver Thames didst cut thy way,
With well-timed oars before the royal barge,

40 Swelled with the pride of thy celestial charge;
And big with hymn, commander of a host,
The like was ne'er in Epsom blankets tossed.[9]
Methinks I see the new Arion[1] sail,
The lute still trembling underneath thy nail.

45 At thy well-sharpened thumb from shore to shore
The treble squeaks for fear, the basses roar;
Echoes from Pissing Alley Sh—— call,
And Sh—— they resound from Aston Hall.
About thy boat the little fishes throng,

50 As at the morning toast° that floats along.   *sewage*
Sometimes, as prince of thy harmonious band,
Thou wield'st thy papers in thy threshing hand,
St. André's[2] feet ne'er kept more equal time,
Not ev'n the feet of thy own *Psyche's* rhyme;

55 Though they in number as in sense excel:
So just, so like tautology, they fell,
That, pale with envy, Singleton[3] forswore ⎫
The lute and sword, which he in triumph bore, ⎬
And vowed he ne'er would act Villerius[4] more." ⎭

60 Here stopped the good old sire, and wept for joy
In silent raptures of the hopeful boy.
All arguments, but most his plays, persuade,
That for anointed dullness[5] he was made.

Close to the walls which fair Augusta° bind   *London*
65 (The fair Augusta much to fears inclined),[6]
An ancient fabric,° raised to inform the sight,   *building*
There stood of yore, and Barbican it hight:
A watchtower once; but now, so fate ordains,
Of all the pile an empty name remains.

70 From its old ruins brothel houses rise,

---

6. A coarse woolen cloth. Flecknoe was a Catholic priest.
7. The parallel between Flecknoe, as forerunner of Shadwell, and John the Baptist, as forerunner of Jesus, is made plain in lines 32–34 by the use of details and even words taken from Matthew 3.3–4 and John 1.23.
8. Flecknoe boasted of the patronage of the Portuguese king.
9. A reference to Shadwell's comedy *Epsom Wells* and to the farcical scene in his *Virtuoso*, in which Sir Samuel Hearty is tossed in a blanket.
1. A legendary Greek poet. Returning home by sea, he was robbed and thrown overboard by the sailors, but was saved by a dolphin that had been charmed by his music.
2. A French dancer who designed the choreography of Shadwell's opera *Psyche* (1675). Dryden's sneer at the mechanical metrics of the songs in *Psyche* is justified.
3. John Singleton (d. 1686), a musician at the Theatre Royal.
4. A character in Sir William Davenant's *Siege of Rhodes* (1656), the first English opera.
5. The anticipated phrase is "anointed *majesty*." English kings are anointed with oil at their coronations.
6. This line alludes to the fears excited by the Popish Plot (cf. *Absalom and Achitophel*, p. 880).

Scenes of lewd loves, and of polluted joys,
Where their vast courts the mother-strumpets keep,
And, undisturbed by watch, in silence sleep.
Near these a Nursery[7] erects its head,
75 Where queens are formed, and future heroes bred;
Where unfledged actors learn to laugh and cry,
Where infant punks° their tender voices try,   *prostitutes*
And little Maximins[8] the gods defy.
Great Fletcher never treads in buskins here,
80 Nor greater Jonson dares in socks[9] appear;
But gentle Simkin[1] just reception finds
Amidst this monument of vanished minds:
Pure clinches° the suburbian Muse affords,   *puns*
And Panton[2] waging harmless war with words.
85 Here Flecknoe, as a place to fame well known,
Ambitiously design'd his Sh——'s throne;
For ancient Dekker[3] prophesied long since,
That in this pile would reign a mighty prince,
Born for a scourge of wit, and flail of sense;
90 To whom true dullness should some *Psyches* owe,
But worlds of *Misers* from his pen should flow;
Humorists and *Hypocrites*[4] it should produce,
Whole Raymond families, and tribes of Bruce.
    Now Empress Fame had published the renown
95 Of Sh——'s coronation through the town.
Roused by report of Fame, the nations meet,
From near Bunhill, and distant Watling Street.[5]
No Persian carpets spread the imperial way,
But scattered limbs of mangled poets lay;
100 From dusty shops neglected authors come,
Martyrs of pies, and relics of the bum.[6]
Much Heywood, Shirley, Ogilby[7] there lay,
But loads of Sh—— almost choked the way.
Bilked stationers for yeomen stood prepared,
105 And Herringman was captain of the guard.[8]
The hoary prince in majesty appeared,
High on a throne of his own labors reared.
At his right hand our young Ascanius sate,
Rome's other hope, and pillar of the state.
110 His brows thick fogs, instead of glories, grace,

---

7. The name of a training school for young actors.
8. Maximin is the cruel emperor in Dryden's *Tyrannic Love* (1669), notorious for his bombast.
9. "Buskins" and "socks" were the symbols of tragedy and comedy. John Fletcher (1579–1625), the playwright and collaborator with Francis Beaumont (ca. 1584–1616).
1. A popular character in low farces.
2. Said to have been a celebrated punster.
3. Thomas Dekker (ca. 1572–1632), the playwright, whom Jonson had satirized in *The Poetaster.*
4. Three of Shadwell's plays; *The Hypocrite*, a failure, was not published. "Raymond" and "Bruce" (line 93) are characters in *The Humorists* and *The Virtuoso*, respectively.

5. Because Bunhill is about a quarter of a mile and Watling Street little more than half a mile from the site of the Nursery, where the coronation is held, Shadwell's fame is narrowly circumscribed. Moreover, his subjects live in the heart of the City, regarded by men of wit and fashion as the abode of bad taste and middle-class vulgarity.
6. Unsold books eventually went to bakers' shops and privies.
7. John Ogilby, a translator of Homer and Virgil, ridiculed by both Dryden and Pope as a bad poet.
8. "Bilked stationers": cheated publishers, acting as "yeomen" of the guard, led by Henry Herringman, who until 1679 was the publisher of both Shadwell and Dryden.

And lambent dullness played around his face.[9]
As Hannibal did to the altars come,
Sworn by his sire a mortal foe to Rome,[1]
So Sh—— swore, nor should his vow be vain,
115 That he till death true dullness would maintain;
And, in his father's right, and realm's defense,
Ne'er to have peace with wit, nor truce with sense.
The king himself the sacred unction[2] made,
As king by office, and as priest by trade.
120 In his siníster° hand, instead of ball,   *left*
He placed a mighty mug of potent ale;
Love's Kingdom to his right he did convey,
At once his scepter, and his rule of sway;
Whose righteous lore the prince had practiced young,
125 And from whose loins recorded *Psyche* sprung.
His temples, last, with poppies were o'erspread,
That nodding seemed to consecrate his head.[3]
Just at that point of time, if fame not lie,
On his left hand twelve reverend owls did fly.[4]
130 So Romulus, 'tis sung, by Tiber's brook,
Presage of sway from twice six vultures took.
The admiring throng loud acclamations make,
And omens of his future empire take.
The sire then shook the honors[5] of his head,
135 And from his brows damps of oblivion shed
Full on the filial dullness: long he stood, ⎫
Repelling from his breast the raging god;   ⎬
At length burst out in this prophetic mood: ⎭
   "Heavens bless my son, from Ireland let him reign
140 To far Barbadoes on the western main;[6]
Of his dominion may no end be known,
And greater than his father's be his throne;
Beyond *Love's Kingdom* let him stretch his pen!"
He paused, and all the people cried, "Amen."
145 Then thus continued he: "My son, advance
Still in new impudence, new ignorance.
Success let others teach, learn thou from me
Pangs without birth, and fruitless industry.
Let *Virtuosos* in five years be writ;
150 Yet not one thought accuse thy toil of wit.
Let gentle George[7] in triumph tread the stage,

9. "Ascanius": or Īulus, son of Aeneas. Virgil referred to him as *"spes altera Romae"* ("Rome's other hope," *Aeneid* 12.168). As Troy fell, he was marked as favored by the gods when a flickering ("lambent") flame played round his head (*Aeneid* 2.680–84).
1. Hannibal, who almost conquered Rome in 216 B.C.E., during the second Punic War, took this oath at the age of nine (Livy 21.1).
2. The sacramental oil, used in the coronation.
3. During the coronation a British monarch holds two symbols of the throne: a globe ("ball") representing the world in the left hand and a scepter in the right. Shadwell's symbols of monarchy are a

mug of ale; Flecknoe's dreary play *Love's Kingdom*; and a crown of poppies, which suggest heaviness, dullness, and drowsiness. The poppies also refer obliquely to Shadwell's addiction to opium.
4. Birds of night, appropriate substitutes for the twelve vultures whose flight confirmed to Romulus the destined site of Rome, of which he was founder and king.
5. Ornaments, hence locks.
6. Shadwell's empire is vast but empty.
7. Sir George Etherege (ca. 1635–1691), a writer of brilliant comedies. In the next couplet Dryden names characters from his plays.

Make Dorimant betray, and Loveit rage;
Let Cully, Cockwood, Fopling, charm the pit,
And in their folly show the writer's wit.
155 Yet still thy fools shall stand in thy defense,
And justify their author's want of sense.
Let 'em be all by thy own model made
Of dullness, and desire no foreign aid;
That they to future ages may be known,
160 Not copies drawn, but issue of thy own.
Nay, let thy men of wit too be the same,
All full of thee, and differing but in name.
But let no alien S—dl—y[8] interpose,
To lard with wit[9] thy hungry *Epsom* prose.
165 And when false flowers of rhetoric thou wouldst cull,
Trust nature, do not labor to be dull;
But write thy best, and top; and, in each line,
Sir Formal's[1] oratory will be thine:
Sir Formal, though unsought, attends thy quill,
170 And does thy northern dedications[2] fill.
Nor let false friends seduce thy mind to fame,
By arrogating Jonson's hostile name.
Let father Flecknoe fire thy mind with praise,
And uncle Ogilby thy envy raise.
175 Thou art my blood, where Jonson has no part:
What share have we in nature, or in art?
Where did his wit on learning fix a brand,
And rail at arts he did not understand?
Where made he love in Prince Nicander's vein,[3]
180 Or swept the dust in *Psyche's* humble strain?
Where sold he bargains, 'whip-stitch,[4] kiss my arse,'
Promised a play and dwindled to a farce?[5]
When did his Muse from Fletcher scenes purloin,
As thou whole Eth'rege dost transfuse to thine?
185 But so transfused, as oil on water's flow,
His always floats above, thine sinks below.
This is thy province, this thy wondrous way,
New humors to invent for each new play:
This is that boasted bias[6] of thy mind,
190 By which one way, to dullness, 'tis inclined;
Which makes thy writings lean on one side still,
And, in all changes, that way bends thy will.
Nor let thy mountain-belly make pretense
Of likeness; thine's a tympany[7] of sense.

---

8. Sir Charles Sedley (1638–1701), wit, rake, poet, and playwright. Dryden hints that he contributed more than the prologue to Shadwell's *Epsom Wells*.

9. This phrase recalls a sentence in Burton's *Anatomy of Melancholy*: "They lard their lean books with the fat of others' works."

1. Sir Formal Trifle, the ridiculous and vapid orator in *The Virtuoso*.

2. Shadwell frequently dedicated his works to the duke of Newcastle and members of his family.

3. In *Psyche*.

4. A nonsense word frequently used by Sir Samuel Hearty in *The Virtuoso*. To "sell bargains" is to answer an innocent question with a coarse or indecent phrase, as in this line.

5. Low comedy that depends largely on situation rather than wit, consistently condemned by Dryden and other serious playwrights.

6. In bowling, the spin given to the bowl that causes it to swerve. Dryden closely parodies a passage in Shadwell's epilogue to *The Humorists*.

7. A swelling in some part of the body caused by wind.

195 A tun° of man in thy large bulk is writ,   *large cask*
But sure thou'rt but a kilderkin° of wit.   *small cask*
Like mine, thy gentle numbers feebly creep;
Thy tragic Muse gives smiles, thy comic sleep.
With whate'er gall thou sett'st thyself to write,
200 Thy inoffensive satires never bite.
In thy felonious heart though venom lies,
It does but touch thy Irish pen,[8] and dies.
Thy genius calls thee not to purchase fame
In keen iambics,° but mild anagram.   *sharp satire*
205 Leave writing plays, and choose for thy command
Some peaceful province in acrostic land.
There thou may'st wings display and altars raise,
And torture one poor word ten thousand ways.[9]
Or, if thou wouldst thy different talent suit,
210 Set thy own songs, and sing them to thy lute."
  He said: but his last words were scarcely heard⎫
For Bruce and Longville had a trap prepared, ⎬
And down they sent the yet declaiming bard.[1] ⎭
Sinking he left his drugget robe behind,
215 Borne upwards by a subterranean wind.
The mantle fell to the young prophet's part,[2]
With double portion of his father's art.

ca. 1679   1682

To the Memory of Mr. Oldham[1]

Farewell, too little, and too lately known,
Whom I began to think and call my own:
For sure our souls were near allied, and thine
Cast in the same poetic mold with mine.
5 One common note on either lyre did strike,
And knaves and fools[2] we both abhorred alike.
To the same goal did both our studies drive;
The last set out the soonest did arrive.
Thus Nisus fell upon the slippery place,
10 While his young friend[3] performed and won the race.
O early ripe! to thy abundant store
What could advancing age have added more?
It might (what nature never gives the young)
Have taught the numbers° of thy native tongue. *metrics, verse*

8. Dryden accuses Flecknoe and his "son" of being Irish. Ireland suggested only poverty, superstition, and barbarity to 17th-century Londoners.
9. "Wings" and "altars" refer to poems in the shape of these objects as in George Herbert's *Easter Wings* (p. 662) and *The Altar* (p. 661). "Anagram": the transposition of letters in a word so as to make a new one. "Acrostic": a poem in which the first letter of each line, read downward, makes up the name of the person or thing that is the subject of the poem. Dryden is citing instances of triviality and overingenuity in literature.
1. In *The Virtuoso*, Bruce and Longville play this trick on Sir Formal Trifle while he makes a speech.

2. When the prophet Elijah was carried to heaven in a chariot of fire borne on a whirlwind, his mantle fell on his successor, the younger prophet Elisha (2 Kings 2.8–14). Flecknoe, prophet of dullness, naturally cannot ascend, but must sink.
1. John Oldham (1653–1683), the young poet whose *Satires upon the Jesuits* (1681) won Dryden's admiration. This elegy was published in Oldham's *Remains in Verse and Prose* (1684).
2. The objects of satire.
3. Nisus, on the point of winning a footrace, slipped in a pool of blood. His "young friend" was Euryalus (Virgil's *Aeneid* 5.315–39).

15 But satire needs not those, and wit will shine
Through the harsh cadence of a rugged line.[4]
A noble error, and but seldom made,
When poets are by too much force betrayed.
Thy generous fruits, though gathered ere their prime, ⎫
20 Still showed a quickness;[5] and maturing time   ⎬
But mellows what we write to the dull sweets of rhyme. ⎭
Once more, hail and farewell;[6] farewell, thou young,
But ah too short, Marcellus[7] of our tongue;
Thy brows with ivy, and with laurels bound;[8]
25 But fate and gloomy night encompass thee around.

1684

A Song for St. Cecilia's Day[1]

I

From harmony, from heavenly harmony
   This universal frame began:
     When Nature underneath a heap
      Of jarring atoms lay,
5   And could not heave her head,
The tuneful voice was heard from high:
    "Arise, ye more than dead."
Then cold, and hot, and moist, and dry,[2]
   In order to their stations leap,
10   And Music's power obey.
From harmony, from heavenly harmony
   This universal frame began:
    From harmony to harmony
Through all the compass of the notes it ran,
15 The diapason[3] closing full in man.

---

4. Dryden repeats the Renaissance idea that the satirist should avoid smoothness and affect rough meters ("harsh cadence").
5. Sharpness of flavor.
6. Dryden echoes the famous words that conclude Catullus's elegy to his brother: "*Atque in perpetuum, frater, ave atque vale*" ("And forever, brother, hail and farewell!").
7. The nephew of Augustus, adopted by him as his successor. After winning military fame as a youth, he died at the age of twenty. Virgil celebrated him in the *Aeneid* 6.854–86. The last line of Dryden's poem is a reminiscence of *Aeneid* 6.866.
8. The poet's wreath (cf. Milton's *Lycidas*, lines 1–2, p. 703).
1. St. Cecilia, a Roman lady, was an early Christian martyr. She has long been regarded as the patroness of music and the supposed inventor of the organ. Celebrations of her festival day (November 22) in England were usually devoted to music and the praise of music, and from about 1683 to 1703 the Musical Society in London annually commemorated it with a religious service and a public concert. This concert always included an ode written and set to music for the occasion, of which the two by Dryden (*A Song for St. Cecilia's Day*, 1687, and *Alexander's Feast*, 1697) are the most distinguished. G. B. Draghi, an Italian brought to England by Charles II, set this ode to music; but Handel's fine score, composed in 1739, has completely obscured the original setting. This is an irregular ode in the manner of Cowley. In stanzas 3–6, Dryden boldly attempted to suggest in the sounds of his words the characteristic tones of the instruments mentioned.
2. "Nature": created nature, ordered by the Divine Wisdom out of chaos, which Dryden, adopting the physics of the Greek philosopher Epicurus, describes as composed of the warring and discordant ("jarring") atoms of the four elements: earth, fire, water, and air ("cold," "hot," "moist," and "dry").
3. The entire compass of tones in the scale. Dryden is thinking of the Chain of Being, the ordered creation from inanimate nature up to humans, God's latest and final work. The just gradations of notes in a scale are analogous to the equally just gradations in the ascending scale of created beings. Both are the result of harmony.

2

What passion cannot Music raise and quell![4]
    When Jubal struck the corded shell,[5]
    His listening brethren stood around,
    And, wondering, on their faces fell
20   To worship that celestial sound.
Less than a god they thought there could not dwell
        Within the hollow of that shell
        That spoke so sweetly and so well.
What passion cannot Music raise and quell!

3

25 The trumpet's loud clangor
        Excites us to arms,
    With shrill notes of anger,
        And mortal alarms.
    The double double double beat
30   Of the thundering drum
    Cries: "Hark! the foes come;
    Charge, charge, 'tis too late to retreat."

4

    The soft complaining flute
    In dying notes discovers
35 The woes of hopeless lovers,
Whose dirge is whispered by the warbling lute.

5

    Sharp violins[6] proclaim
Their jealous pangs, and desperation,
Fury, frantic indignation,
40 Depth of pains, and height of passion,
    For the fair, disdainful dame.

6

    But O! what art can teach,
    What human voice can reach,
    The sacred organ's praise?
45   Notes inspiring holy love,
    Notes that wing their heavenly ways
    To mend the choirs above.

7

Orpheus[7] could lead the savage race;
And trees unrooted left their place,

4. The power of music to describe, evoke, or subdue emotion ("passion") is a frequent theme in
17th-century literature. In stanzas 2–6, the poet
considers music as awakening religious awe, warlike courage, sorrow for unrequited love, jealousy
and fury, and the impulse to worship God.
5. According to Genesis 4.21, Jubal was the inventor of the lyre and the pipe. Dryden imagines
Jubal's lyre to have been made of a tortoise shell

("corded shell").
6. A reference to the bright tone of the modern
violin, introduced into England at the Restoration.
The tone of the old-fashioned viol is much duller.
7. Legendary poet, son of one of the Muses, who
played so wonderfully on the lyre that wild beasts
("the savage race") grew tame and followed him,
as did even rocks and trees.

50   Sequacious of° the lyre;   *following*
            But bright Cecilia raised the wonder higher:
            When to her organ vocal breath was given,
            An angel heard, and straight appeared,[8]
            Mistaking earth for heaven.

                         GRAND CHORUS

55   *As from the power of sacred lays*
                The spheres began to move,
            And sung the great Creator's praise[9]
                To all the blest above;
            So, when the last and dreadful hour
60   *This crumbling pageant[1] shall devour,*
            The trumpet shall be heard on high, ⎫
            The dead shall live, the living die, ⎬
            And Music shall untune the sky.[2]   ⎭

                                                                            1687

Epigram on Milton[1]

            Three poets,[2] in three distant ages born,
            Greece, Italy, and England did adorn.
            The first in loftiness of thought surpassed,
            The next in majesty, in both the last:
5   The force of Nature could no farther go;
            To make a third, she joined the former two.

                                                                            1688

CRITICISM

Because Dryden liked to talk about literature, he became a critic, indeed the first comprehensive critic in England. The Elizabethans, largely impelled by the example of Italian humanists, had produced an interesting but unsystematic body of critical writings. Dryden could look back to such pioneer works as George Puttenham's *Art of English Poesy* (1589), Sir Philip Sidney's *Defense of Poesy* (1595), Samuel Daniel's *Defense of Rhyme* (ca. 1603), and Ben Jonson's *Timber, or Discoveries* (1641). These and later writings Dryden knew, as he knew the ancients and the important contemporary French critics, notably Pierre Corneille, Fr. René Rapin, and Nicolas Boileau. Taken as a whole, his critical prefaces and dedications, which appeared between 1664 and 1700, are the work of a man of independent mind who has made his own synthesis of critical canons from wide reading, a great deal of thinking, and the constant prac-

---

8. According to the legend, it was Cecilia's piety, not her music, that brought an angel to visit her.
9. As it was harmony that ordered the universe, so it was angelic song ("sacred lays") that put the celestial bodies ("spheres") in motion. The harmonious chord that results from the traditional "music of the spheres" is a hymn of "praise" sung by created nature to its "Creator."
1. The universe: the stage on which the drama of human salvation has been acted out.

2. The "last trump" of 1 Corinthians 15.52, which will announce the Resurrection and the Last Judgment. Dryden develops his theme of harmony as order in such a way as to give full emphasis of the splendid paradox ("Music shall *untune*") in the final line of the ode.
1. Engraved beneath the portrait of Milton in Jacob Tonson's edition of *Paradise Lost* (1688).
2. I.e., Homer, Virgil, and Milton.

tice of the art of writing. As a critic he is no one's disciple, and he has the saving grace of being always willing to change his mind.

All but a very few of Dryden's critical works (most notably *An Essay of Dramatic Poesy*) grew out of the works to which they served as prefaces: comedies, heroic plays, tragedies, translations, and poems of various sorts. Each work posed problems that Dryden was eager to discuss with his readers, and the topics that he treated proved to be important in the development of the new literature of which he was the principal apologist. He dealt with the processes of literary creation, the poet's relation to tradition, the forms of modern drama, the craft of poetry, and above all the genius of earlier poets: Shakespeare, Jonson, Chaucer, Juvenal, Horace, Homer, and Virgil. For nearly forty years this voice was heard in the land; and when it was finally silenced, a set of critical standards had come into existence and a new age had been given its direction.

From An Essay of Dramatic Poesy[1]

[SHAKESPEARE AND BEN JONSON COMPARED]

"To begin, then, with Shakespeare. He was the man who of all modern, and perhaps ancient poets, had the largest and most comprehensive soul. All the images of Nature were still present to him, and he drew them, not laboriously, but luckily; when he describes anything, you more than see it, you feel it too. Those who accuse him to have wanted learning, give him the greater commendation: he was naturally learned; he needed not the spectacles of books to read Nature; he looked inwards, and found her there. I cannot say he is everywhere alike; were he so, I should do him injury to compare him with the greatest of mankind. He is many times flat, insipid; his comic wit degenerating into clenches, his serious swelling into bombast. But he is always great when some great occasion is presented to him; no man can say he ever had a fit subject for his wit and did not then raise himself as high above the rest of poets,

Quantum lenta solent inter viburna cupressi[2]

The consideration of this made Mr. Hales[3] of Eton say that there was no subject of which any poet ever writ, but he would produce it much better treated of in Shakespeare; and however others are now generally preferred

---

1. With the reopening of the theaters in 1660, older plays were revived, but despite their power and charm, they seemed old-fashioned. Although new playwrights, ambitious to create a modern English drama, soon appeared, they were uncertain of their direction. What, if anything, useful could they learn from the dramatic practice of the ancients? Should they ignore the English dramatists of the late 16th and early 17th centuries? Should they make their example the vigorous contemporary drama of France? Dryden addresses himself to these and other problems in this essay, his first extended piece of criticism. Its purpose, he tells us, was "chiefly to vindicate the honor of our English writers from the censure of those who unjustly prefer the French before them." Its method is skeptical: Dryden presents several points of view, but imposes none. The form is a dialogue among friends, like the *Tusculan Disputations* or the *Brutus* of Cicero. Crites praises the drama of

the ancients; Eugenius protests against their authority and argues for the idea of progress in the arts; Lisideius urges the excellence of French plays; and Neander, speaking in the climactic position, defends the native tradition and the greatness of Shakespeare, Fletcher, and Jonson. The dialogue takes place on June 3, 1665, in a boat on the Thames. The four friends are rowed downstream to listen to the cannonading of the English and Dutch fleets, engaged in battle off the Suffolk coast. As the gunfire recedes they are assured of victory and order their boatman to return to London, and naturally enough they fall to discussing the number of bad poems that the victory will evoke.

2. As do cypresses among the bending shrubs (Latin; Virgil's *Eclogues* 1.25).

3. The learned John Hales (1584–1656), provost of Eton. He is reputed to have said this to Jonson himself.

before him, yet the age wherein he lived, which had contemporaries with him Fletcher and Jonson, never equaled them to him in their esteem: and in the last king's[4] court, when Ben's reputation was at highest, Sir John Suckling,[5] and with him the greater part of the courtiers, set our Shakespeare far above him. . . .

"As for Jonson, to whose character I am now arrived, if we look upon him while he was himself (for his last plays were but his dotages), I think him the most learned and judicious writer which any theater ever had. He was a most severe judge of himself, as well as others. One cannot say he wanted wit, but rather that he was frugal of it. In his works you find little to retrench[6] or alter. Wit, and language, and humor also in some measure, we had before him; but something of art[7] was wanting to the drama till he came. He managed his strength to more advantage than any who preceded him. You seldom find him making love in any of his scenes or endeavoring to move the passions; his genius was too sullen and saturnine[8] to do it gracefully, especially when he knew he came after those who had performed both to such an height. Humor was his proper sphere:[9] and in that he delighted most to represent mechanic people.[1] He was deeply conversant in the ancients, both Greek and Latin, and he borrowed boldly from them: there is scarce a poet or historian among the Roman authors of those times whom he has not translated in *Sejanus* and *Catiline*.[2] But he has done his robberies so openly, that one may see he fears not to be taxed by any law. He invades authors like a monarch; and what would be theft in other poets is only victory in him. With the spoils of these writers he so represents old Rome to us, in its rites, ceremonies, and customs, that if one of their poets had written either of his tragedies, we had seen less of it than in him. If there was any fault in his language, 'twas that he weaved it too closely and laboriously, in his serious plays:[3] perhaps, too, he did a little too much Romanize our tongue, leaving the words which he translated almost as much Latin as he found them: wherein, though he learnedly followed the idiom of their language, he did not enough comply with the idiom of ours. If I would compare him with Shakespeare, I must acknowledge him the more correct poet, but Shakespeare the greater wit.[4] Shakespeare was the Homer, or father of our dramatic poets; Jonson was the Virgil, the pattern of elaborate writing; I admire him, but I love Shakespeare. To conclude of him; as he has given us the most correct plays, so in the precepts which he has laid down in his *Discoveries*, we have as many and profitable rules for perfecting the stage, as any wherewith the French can furnish us."

1668

---

4. Charles I.
5. Courtier, poet, playwright, much admired in Dryden's time for his wit and the easy naturalness of his style.
6. Delete.
7. Craftsmanship.
8. Heavy.
9. In Jonson's comedies the characters are seen under the domination of some psychological trait,

ruling passion, or affectation—i.e., some "humor"—that makes them unique and ridiculous.
1. I.e., artisans.
2. Jonson's two Roman plays, dated 1605 and 1611, respectively.
3. This is the reading of the first edition. Curiously enough, in the second edition Dryden altered the phrase to "in his comedies especially."
4. Genius.

From A Discourse Concerning the Original and Progress of Satire[1]

[THE ART OF SATIRE]

* * * How easy is it to call rogue and villain, and that wittily! But how hard to make a man appear a fool, a blockhead, or a knave without using any of those opprobrious terms! To spare the grossness of the names, and to do the thing yet more severely, is to draw a full face, and to make the nose and cheeks stand out, and yet not to employ any depth of shadowing.[2] This is the mystery of that noble trade, which yet no master can teach to his apprentice; he may give the rules, but the scholar is never the nearer in his practice. Neither is it true that this fineness of raillery[3] is offensive. A witty man is tickled while he is hurt in this manner, and a fool feels it not. The occasion of an offense may possibly be given, but he cannot take it. If it be granted that in effect this way does more mischief; that a man is secretly wounded, and though he be not sensible himself, yet the malicious world will find it out for him; yet there is still a vast difference betwixt the slovenly butchering of a man, and the fineness of a stroke that separates the head from the body, and leaves it standing in its place. A man may be capable, as Jack Ketch's[4] wife said of his servant, of a plain piece of work, a bare hanging; but to make a malefactor die sweetly was only belonging to her husband. I wish I could apply it to myself, if the reader would be kind enough to think it belongs to me. The character of Zimri in my *Absalom*[5] is, in my opinion, worth the whole poem: it is not bloody, but it is ridiculous enough; and he, for whom it was intended, was too witty to resent it as an injury. If I had railed,[6] I might have suffered for it justly; but I managed my own work more happily, perhaps more dexterously. I avoided the mention of great crimes, and applied myself to the representing of blindsides, and little extravagancies; to which, the wittier a man is, he is generally the more obnoxious.[7] It succeeded as I wished; the jest went round, and he was laughed at in his turn who began the frolic. * * *

1693

---

1. This passage is an excerpt from the long and rambling preface that served as the dedication of a translation of the satires of the Roman satirists Juvenal and Persius to Charles Sackville, sixth earl of Dorset. The translations were made by Dryden and other writers, among them William Congreve. Dryden traces the origin and development of verse satire in Rome and in a very fine passage contrasts Horace and Juvenal as satiric poets. It is plain that he prefers the "tragic" satire of Juvenal to the urbane and laughing satire of Horace. But in the passage printed here, he praises his own satiric character of Zimri (the duke of Buckingham) in *Absalom and Achitophel* for the very reason that it

is modeled on Horatian "raillery," not Juvenalian invective.
2. Early English miniaturists prided themselves on the art of giving roundness to the full face without painting in shadows.
3. Satirical mirth, good-natured satire.
4. A notorious public executioner of Dryden's time (d. 1686). His name later became a generic term for all members of his profession.
5. *Absalom and Achitophel*, lines 544–68 (p. 892).
6. Reviled, abused. Observe that the verb differed in meaning from its noun, defined above.
7. Liable.

APHRA BEHN
1640?–1689

"A woman wit has often graced the stage," Dryden wrote in 1681. Soon after actresses first appeared in English public theaters, there was an even more striking debut by a woman writer who boldly signed her plays and talked back to her critics. In a dozen years, Aphra Behn turned out at least that many plays, discovering fresh dramatic possibilities in casts that included women with warm bodies and clever heads. She also drew attention as a warm and witty poet of love. When writing for the stage became less profitable, she turned to the emerging field of prose fiction, composing a pioneering epistolary novel, *Love Letters Between a Nobleman and His Sister,* and diverse short tales—not to mention a raft of translations from the French, pindarics to her beloved Stuart rulers, compilations, prologues, complimentary verses, all the piecework and puffery that were the stock in trade of the Restoration town wit. She worked in haste and with flair for nearly two decades and more than held her own as a professional writer. In the end, no author of her time—except Dryden himself—proved more versatile, more alive to new currents of thought, or more inventive in recasting fashionable forms.

Much of Behn's life remains a mystery. Although her books have been accompanied—and often all but buried—by volumes of rumor, hard facts are elusive. She was almost certainly from East Kent; she may well have been named Johnson. But she herself seems to have left no record of her date and place of birth, her family name and upbringing, or the identity of the shadowy Mr. Behn whom she reportedly married. Her many references to nuns and convents, as well as praise for prominent Catholic lords (*Oroonoko* is dedicated to one), have prompted speculation that she may have been raised as a Catholic and educated in a convent abroad. Without doubt, she drew on a range of worldly experience that would be closed to women in the more genteel ages to come. The circumstantial detail of *Oroonoko* supports her claim that she was in the new sugar colony of Surinam early in 1664. Perhaps she exaggerated her social position to enhance her tale, but many particulars—from dialect words and the location of plantations to methods of selling and torturing slaves—can be authenticated. During the trade war that broke out in 1665—which left her "vast and charming world" a Dutch prize—Behn traveled to the Low Countries on a spying mission for King Charles II. The king could be lax about payment, however, and Behn had to petition desperately to escape debtor's prison. In 1670 she brought out her first plays, "forced to write for bread," she confessed, "and not ashamed to own it."

In London, Behn flourished in the cosmopolitan world of the playhouse and the court. Dryden and other wits encouraged her; she mixed with actresses and managers and playwrights and exchanged verses with a lively literary set that she called her "cabal." Surviving letters record a passionate, troubled attachment to a lawyer named John Hoyle, a bisexual with libertine views. She kept up with the most advanced thinking and joined public debates with pointed satire against the Whigs. But the festivity of the Restoration world was fading out in bitter party acrimony. In 1682 Behn was placed under arrest for "abusive reflections" on the king's illegitimate son, the Whig duke of Monmouth (Dryden's Absalom). Her Royalist opinions and the immodesty of her public role made her a target; gleeful lampoons declared that she was aging and ill and once again poor. She responded by bringing out her works at a still faster rate, composing *Oroonoko,* her dedication claims, "in a few hours . . . for I never rested my pen a moment for thought." In some last works she recorded her hope that her writings would live: "I value fame as much as if I had been born a hero." When she died she was buried in Westminster Abbey.

"All women together ought to let flowers fall upon the grave of Aphra Behn," Virginia Woolf wrote, "for it was she who earned them the right to speak their minds."

Behn herself spoke her mind. She scorned hypocrisy and calculation in her society and commented freely on religion, science, and philosophy. Moreover, she spoke as a woman. Denied the classical education of most male authors, she dismissed "musty rules" and lessons and relished the immediate human appeal of popular forms. Her first play, *The Forced Marriage,* exposes the bondage of matches arranged for money and status, and many later works invoke the powerful natural force of love, whose energy breaks through conventions. In a range of genres, from simple pastoral songs to complex plots of intrigue, she candidly explores the sexual feelings of women, their schooling in disguise, their need to "love upon the honest square" (for this her work was later denounced as coarse and impure). *Oroonoko* represents another departure for Behn and prose fiction. It achieves something new both in its narrative form and in extending some of her favorite themes to an original subject: the destiny of a black male hero on a world historical stage.

Oroonoko cannot be classified as fact or fiction, realism or romance. In the still unshaped field of prose narrative—where a "history" could mean any story, true or false—Behn combined the attractions of three older forms. First, she presents the work as a memoir, a personal account of what she has heard and seen. According to a friend, Behn had told this tale over and over; perhaps that explains the conversational ease with which she turns back and forth, interpreting faraway scenes for her readers at home. Second, *Oroonoko* is a travel narrative in three parts. It turns west to a new world often extolled as a paradise, then east to Africa and the amorous intrigues of a corrupt old-world court (popular reading fare), then finally west again with its hero across the infamous "Middle Passage"—over which millions of slaves would be transported during the next century—to the conflicts of a raw colonial world. Exotic scenes fascinate Behn, but she wants even more to talk to people and learn about their ways of life. As in imaginary voyages, from Sir Thomas More's *Utopia* to *Gulliver's Travels* and *Rasselas,* encounters with foreign cultures sharply challenge Europeans to reexamine themselves. Behn's primitive Indians and noble Africans live by a code of virtue, by principles of fidelity and honor, that "civilized" Christians often ignore or betray. Oroonoko embodies this code. Above all, the book is his biography. Courageous, high-minded, and great hearted, he rivals the heroes of classical epics and Plutarch's *Lives* and is equally worthy of fame. Nor does he lack gentler virtues. Like the heroes of seventeenth-century heroic dramas and romances, he shines in the company of women and proves his nobility by his passionate and constant love for Imoinda, his ideal counterpart. Yet finally a contradiction dooms Oroonoko: he is at once prince and chattel, a "royal slave."

Behn handles her forms dynamically, drawing out their inner discords and tensions. In the biography, Oroonoko's deepest values are turned against him. His trust in friendship and scrupulous truth to his word expose him to the treachery of Europeans who calculate human worth on a yardstick of profit. A hero cannot survive in such a world. His self-respect demands action, even when he can find no clear path through the tangle of assurances and lies. Moreover, the colony too seems tangled in contradictions. Behn's travel narrative reveals a broken paradise where, in the absence of secure authority, the settlers descend into a series of unstable alliances, improvised power relations, and escalating suspicions. Here every term—friend and foe, tenderness and brutality, savagery and civilization—can suddenly turn into its opposite. And the author also seems caught between worlds. The cultivated Englishwoman who narrates and acts in this memoir thinks highly of her hero's code of honor and shares his contempt for the riffraff who plague him. Yet her own role is ambiguous: she lacks the power to save Oroonoko and might even be viewed as implicated in his downfall. Only as a writer can she take control, preserving the hero in her work.

The story of Oroonoko did not end with Behn. Compassion for the royal slave and outrage at his fate were enlisted in the long battle against the slave trade. Reprinted, translated, serialized, dramatized, and much imitated, *Oroonoko* helped teach a mass audience to feel for all victims of the brutal commerce in human beings. A hundred years later, the popular writer Hannah More testified to the widening influence of the story: "No individual griefs my bosom melt, / For millions feel what Oroonoko felt." Women especially identified with the experience of personal injustice and everyday indignity—the pain of being treated as something less than fully human. Perhaps it is appropriate that the writer who made the suffering of the royal slave famous had known the pride and lowliness of being "a female pen."

Oroonoko, or The Royal Slave[1]

I do not pretend, in giving you the history of this royal slave, to entertain my reader with the adventures of a feigned hero, whose life and fortunes fancy may manage at the poet's pleasure; nor in relating the truth, design to adorn it with any accidents but such as arrived in earnest to him. And it shall come simply into the world, recommended by its own proper merits and natural intrigues, there being enough of reality to support it, and to render it diverting, without the addition of invention.

I was myself an eyewitness to a great part of what you will find here set down, and what I could not be witness of, I received from the mouth of the chief actor in this history, the hero himself, who gave us the whole transactions of his youth; and though I shall omit for brevity's sake a thousand little accidents of his life, which, however pleasant to us, where history was scarce and adventures very rare, yet might prove tedious and heavy to my reader, in a world where he finds diversions for every minute, new and strange. But we who were perfectly charmed with the character of this great man were curious to gather every circumstance of his life.

The scene of the last part of his adventures lies in a colony in America called Surinam,[2] in the West Indies.

But before I give you the story of this gallant slave, 'tis fit I tell you the manner of bringing them to these new colonies, for those they make use of there are not natives of the place; for those we live with in perfect amity, without daring to command 'em, but on the contrary caress 'em with all the brotherly and friendly affection in the world, trading with 'em for their fish, venison, buffaloes,[3] skins, and little rarities; as marmosets, a sort of monkey as big as a rat or weasel but of a marvelous and delicate shape, and has face and hands like a human creature, and *cousheries*,[4] a little beast in the form and fashion of a lion, as big as a kitten, but so exactly made in all parts like that noble beast, that it is it in miniature. Then for little parakeetoes, great parrots, macaws, and a thousand other birds and beasts of wonderful and surprising forms, shapes, and colors. For skins of prodigious snakes, of which there are some threescore yards in length, as is the skin of one that may be seen at his Majesty's antiquaries'; where are also some rare flies[5] of amazing forms and colors, presented to 'em by myself, some as big as my fist, some less, and all of various excellencies, such as art cannot imitate. Then we

---

1. The text, prepared by Joanna Lipking, is based on the 1688 edition, the sole edition published during Behn's lifetime. The critical edition of G. C. Duchovnay (diss., Indiana, 1971), which collates the four 17th-century editions, has been consulted.
2. A British sugar colony on the South American coast east of Venezuela; later Dutch Guiana.
3. Wild oxen of various species.
4. A name appearing in local descriptions, but the animal is not clearly identified; probably the lion-headed marmoset or perhaps the *cujara* (Portuguese), a rodent known as the rice rat.
5. Butterflies.

trade for feathers, which they order into all shapes, make themselves little short habits of 'em, and glorious wreaths for their heads, necks, arms and legs, whose tinctures are unconceivable. I had a set of these presented to me, and I gave 'em to the King's theater, and it was the dress of the Indian Queen,[6] infinitely admired by persons of quality, and were unimitable. Besides these, a thousand little knacks and rarities in nature, and some of art, as their baskets, weapons, aprons, et cetera. We dealt with 'em with beads of all colors, knives, axes, pins and needles, which they used only as tools to drill holes with in their ears, noses, and lips, where they hang a great many little things, as long beads, bits of tin, brass, or silver beat thin, and any shining trinket. The beads they weave into aprons about a quarter of an ell long, and of the same breadth,[7] working them very prettily in flowers of several colors of beads; which apron they wear just before 'em, as Adam and Eve did the fig leaves, the men wearing a long stripe of linen which they deal with us for. They thread these beads also on long cotton threads and make girdles to tie their aprons to, which come twenty times or more about the waist, and then cross, like a shoulder belt, both ways, and round their necks, arms, and legs. This adornment, with their long black hair, and the face painted in little specks or flowers here and there, makes 'em a wonderful figure to behold.

Some of the beauties which indeed are finely shaped, as almost all are, and who have pretty features, are very charming and novel; for they have all that is called beauty, except the color, which is a reddish yellow; or after a new oiling, which they often use to themselves, they are of the color of a new brick, but smooth, soft, and sleek. They are extreme[8] modest and bashful, very shy and nice of being touched. And though they are all thus naked, if one lives forever among 'em there is not to be seen an indecent action or glance; and being continually used to see one another so unadorned, so like our first parents before the Fall, it seems as if they had no wishes; there being nothing to heighten curiosity, but all you can see you see at once, and every moment see, and where there is no novelty there can be no curiosity. Not but I have seen a handsome young Indian dying for love of a very beautiful young Indian maid; but all his courtship was to fold his arms, pursue her with his eyes, and sighs were all his language; while she, as if no such lover were present, or rather, as if she desired none such, carefully guarded her eyes from beholding him, and never approached him but she looked down with all the blushing modesty I have seen in the most severe and cautious of our world. And these people represented to me an absolute idea of the first state of innocence, before man knew how to sin. And 'tis most evident and plain that simple Nature is the most harmless, inoffensive, and virtuous mistress. 'Tis she alone, if she were permitted, that better instructs the world than all the inventions of man. Religion would here but destroy that tranquillity they possess by ignorance, and laws would but teach 'em to know offense, of which now they have no notion. They once made mourning and fasting for the death of the English governor, who had given his hand to come on such a day to 'em and neither came nor sent, believing when once

---

6. The title character in the 1664 heroic play by Sir Robert Howard and John Dryden, which was noted for its lavish production. There are contemporary records of "speckled plumes" and feather headdresses.
7. About a foot square.
8. Extremely.

a man's word was passed, nothing but death could or should prevent his keeping it. And when they saw he was not dead, they asked him what name they had for a man who promised a thing he did not do. The governor told them, such a man was a liar, which was a word of infamy to a gentleman. Then one of 'em replied, "Governor, you are a liar, and guilty of that infamy." They have a native justice which knows no fraud, and they understand no vice or cunning, but when they are taught by the white men. They have plurality of wives, which, when they grow old, they serve those that succeed 'em, who are young, but with a servitude easy and respected; and unless they take slaves in war, they have no other attendants.

Those on that continent where I was had no king, but the oldest war captain was obeyed with great resignation. A war captain is a man who has led them on to battle with conduct[9] and success, of whom I shall have occasion to speak more hereafter, and of some other of their customs and manners, as they fall in my way.

With these people, as I said, we live in perfect tranquillity and good understanding, as it behooves us to do, they knowing all the places where to seek the best food of the country and the means of getting it, and for very small and unvaluable trifles, supply us with what 'tis impossible for us to get; for they do not only in the wood and over the savannas, in hunting, supply the parts of hounds, by swiftly scouring through those almost impassable places, and by the mere activity of their feet run down the nimblest deer and other eatable beasts; but in the water one would think they were gods of the rivers, or fellow citizens of the deep, so rare an art they have in swimming, diving, and almost living in water, by which they command the less swift inhabitants of the floods. And then for shooting, what they cannot take, or reach with their hands, they do with arrows, and have so admirable an aim that they will split almost a hair; and at any distance that an arrow can reach, they will shoot down oranges and other fruit, and only touch the stalk with the dart's point, that they may not hurt the fruit. So that they being, on all occasions, very useful to us, we find it absolutely necessary to caress 'em as friends, and not to treat 'em as slaves; nor dare we do other, their numbers so far surpassing ours in that continent.

Those then whom we make use of to work in our plantations of sugar are Negroes, black slaves altogether, which are transported thither in this manner. Those who want slaves make a bargain with a master or captain of a ship and contract to pay him so much apiece, a matter of twenty pound a head for as many as he agrees for, and to pay for 'em when they shall be delivered on such a plantation. So that when there arrives a ship laden with slaves, they who have so contracted go aboard and receive their number by lot; and perhaps in one lot that may be for ten, there may happen to be three or four men, the rest women and children. Or be there more or less of either sex, you are obliged to be contented with your lot.

Coramantien,[1] a country of blacks so called, was one of those places in which they found the most advantageous trading for these slaves, and thither

---

9. Capacity to lead.

1. Not a country but a British-held fort and slave market on the Gold Coast of Africa, in modern-day Ghana. As the slave trade expanded, the slaves and workers shipped out from the region (who came to be called Cormantines) impressed many European observers by their beauty and bearing, their fierceness in war, and their extreme dignity under captivity or torture.

most of our great traders in that merchandise trafficked; for that nation is very warlike and brave, and having a continual campaign, being always in hostility with one neighboring prince or other, they had the fortune to take a great many captives; for all they took in battle were sold as slaves, at least those common men who could not ransom themselves. Of these slaves so taken, the general only has all the profit; and of these generals, our captains and masters of ships buy all their freights.

The King of Coramantien was himself a man of a hundred and odd years old, and had no son, though he had many beautiful black wives; for most certainly there are beauties that can charm of that color. In his younger years he had had many gallant men to his sons, thirteen of which died in battle, conquering when they fell; and he had only left him for his successor one grandchild, son to one of these dead victors, who, as soon as he could bear a bow in his hand and a quiver at his back, was sent into the field, to be trained up by one of the oldest generals to war; where, from his natural inclination to arms and the occasions given him, with the good conduct of the old general, he became, at the age of seventeen, one of the most expert captains and bravest soldiers that ever saw the field of Mars. So that he was adored as the wonder of all that world, and the darling of the soldiers. Besides, he was adorned with a native beauty so transcending all those of his gloomy race that he struck an awe and reverence even in those that knew not his quality; as he did in me, who beheld him with surprise and wonder, when afterwards he arrived in our world.

He had scarce arrived at his seventeenth year, when fighting by his side, the general was killed with an arrow in his eye, which the Prince Oroonoko (for so was this gallant Moor[2] called) very narrowly avoided; nor had he, if the general, who saw the arrow shot, and perceiving it aimed at the Prince, had not bowed his head between, on purpose to receive it in his own body rather than it should touch that of the Prince, and so saved him.

'Twas then, afflicted as Oroonoko was, that he was proclaimed general in the old man's place; and then it was, at the finishing of that war, which had continued for two years, that the Prince came to court, where he had hardly been a month together from the time of his fifth year to that of seventeen; and 'twas amazing to imagine where it was he learned so much humanity; or to give his accomplishments a juster name, where 'twas he got that real greatness of soul, those refined notions of true honor, that absolute generosity, and that softness that was capable of the highest passions of love and gallantry, whose objects were almost continually fighting men, or those mangled or dead; who heard no sounds but those of war and groans. Some part of it we may attribute to the care of a Frenchman of wit and learning, who, finding it turn to very good account to be a sort of royal tutor to this young black, and perceiving him very ready, apt, and quick of apprehension, took a great pleasure to teach him morals, language, and science, and was for it extremely beloved and valued by him. Another reason was, he loved, when he came from war, to see all the English gentlemen that traded thither, and did not only learn their language but that of the Spaniards also, with whom he traded afterwards for slaves.

I have often seen and conversed with this great man, and been a witness

2. Loosely used for any black-skinned person.

to many of his mighty actions, and do assure my reader the most illustrious courts could not have produced a braver man, both for greatness of courage and mind, a judgment more solid, a wit more quick, and a conversation more sweet and diverting. He knew almost as much as if he had read much. He had heard of and admired the Romans; he had heard of the late civil wars in England, and the deplorable death of our great monarch,[3] and would discourse of it with all the sense and abhorrence of the injustice imaginable. He had an extreme good and graceful mien, and all the civility of a well-bred great man. He had nothing of barbarity in his nature, but in all points addressed himself as if his education had been in some European court.

This great and just character of Oroonoko gave me an extreme curiosity to see him, especially when I knew he spoke French and English, and that I could talk with him. But though I had heard so much of him, I was as greatly surprised when I saw him as if I had heard nothing of him, so beyond all report I found him. He came into the room and addressed himself to me, and some other women, with the best grace in the world. He was pretty tall, but of a shape the most exact that can be fancied. The most famous statuary[4] could not form the figure of a man more admirably turned from head to foot. His face was not of that brown, rusty black which most of that nation are, but a perfect ebony or polished jet. His eyes were the most awful that could be seen, and very piercing, the white of 'em being like snow, as were his teeth. His nose was rising and Roman, instead of African and flat; his mouth the finest shaped that could be seen, far from those great turned lips which are so natural to the rest of the Negroes. The whole proportion and air of his face was so noble and exactly formed that, bating[5] his color, there could be nothing in nature more beautiful, agreeable, and handsome. There was no one grace wanting that bears the standard of true beauty. His hair came down to his shoulders by the aids of art; which was by pulling it out with a quill and keeping it combed, of which he took particular care. Nor did the perfections of his mind come short of those of his person, for his discourse was admirable upon almost any subject; and whoever had heard him speak would have been convinced of their errors, that all fine wit is confined to the white men, especially to those of Christendom, and would have confessed that Oroonoko was as capable even of reigning well, and of governing as wisely, had as great a soul, as politic[6] maxims, and was as sensible of power, as any prince civilized in the most refined schools of humanity and learning, or the most illustrious courts.

This prince, such as I have described him, whose soul and body were so admirably adorned, was (while yet he was in the court of his grandfather), as I said, as capable of love as 'twas possible for a brave and gallant man to be; and in saying that, I have named the highest degree of love, for sure, great souls are most capable of that passion.

I have already said, the old general was killed by the shot of an arrow, by

---

3. Charles I, beheaded in 1649 during the civil wars between Royalists and Parliamentarians. In 1688, this remark and others would have signaled Behn's ardent support of James II, the last of the Stuart kings, who would be forced into exile within the year.
4. Sculptor.
5. Except for. The singling out of Africans with European looks or moral values is by no means unique to Behn; for example, Edward Long's 1774 *History of Jamaica* reports of the Cormantines that "their features are very different from the rest of the African Negroes, being smaller, and more of the European turn."
6. Shrewd, sagacious.

the side of this prince, in battle, and that Oroonoko was made general. This old dead hero had one only daughter left of his race, a beauty that, to describe her truly, one need say only she was female to the noble male, the beautiful black Venus to our young Mars, as charming in her person as he, and of delicate virtues. I have seen an hundred white men sighing after her, and making a thousand vows at her feet, all vain and unsuccessful. And she was, indeed, too great for any but a prince of her own nation to adore.

Oroonoko coming from the wars (which were now ended), after he had made his court to his grandfather, he thought in honor he ought to make a visit to Imoinda, the daughter of his foster-father, the dead general; and to make some excuses to her, because his preservation was the occasion of her father's death; and to present her with those slaves that had been taken in this last battle, as the trophies of her father's victories. When he came, attended by all the young soldiers of any merit, he was infinitely surprised at the beauty of this fair queen of night, whose face and person was so exceeding all he had ever beheld; that lovely modesty with which she received him; that softness in her look, and sighs, upon the melancholy occasion of this honor that was done by so great a man as Oroonoko, and a prince of whom she had heard such admirable things: the awfulness[7] wherewith she received him, and the sweetness of her words and behavior while he stayed, gained a perfect conquest over his fierce heart, and made him feel the victor could be subdued. So that having made his first compliments, and presented her a hundred and fifty slaves in fetters, he told her with his eyes that he was not insensible of her charms; while Imoinda, who wished for nothing more than so glorious a conquest, was pleased to believe she understood that silent language of newborn love, and from that moment put on all her additions to beauty.

The Prince returned to court with quite another humor than before; and though he did not speak much of the fair Imoinda, he had the pleasure to hear all his followers speak of nothing but the charms of that maid, insomuch that, even in the presence of the old king, they were extolling her and heightening, if possible, the beauties they had found in her. So that nothing else was talked of, no other sound was heard in every corner where there were whisperers, but "Imoinda! Imoinda!"

'Twill be imagined Oroonoko stayed not long before he made his second visit, nor, considering his quality, not much longer before he told her he adored her. I have often heard him say that he admired[8] by what strange inspiration he came to talk things so soft and so passionate, who never knew love, nor was used to the conversation[9] of women; but (to use his own words) he said, most happily some new and till then unknown power instructed his heart and tongue in the language of love, and at the same time, in favor of him, inspired Imoinda with a sense of his passion. She was touched with what he said, and returned it all in such answers as went to his very heart, with a pleasure unknown before. Nor did he use those obligations[1] ill that love had done him, but turned all his happy moments to the best advantage; and as he knew no vice, his flame aimed at nothing but honor, if such a distinction may be made in love; and especially in that country, where men

7. Reverence.
8. Marveled.
9. Company.
1. Benefits.

take to themselves as many as they can maintain, and where the only crime and sin with woman is to turn her off, to abandon her to want, shame, and misery. Such ill morals are only practiced in Christian countries, where they prefer the bare name of religion, and, without virtue or morality, think that's sufficient. But Oroonoko was none of those professors, but as he had right notions of honor, so he made her such propositions as were not only and barely such; but contrary to the custom of his country, he made her vows she should be the only woman he would possess while he lived; that no age or wrinkles should incline him to change, for her soul would be always fine and always young, and he should have an eternal idea in his mind of the charms she now bore, and should look into his heart for that idea when he could find it no longer in her face.

After a thousand assurances of his lasting flame, and her eternal empire over him, she condescended to receive him for her husband, or rather, received him as the greatest honor the gods could do her.

There is a certain ceremony in these cases to be observed, which I forgot to ask him how performed; but 'twas concluded on both sides that, in obedience to him, the grandfather was to be first made acquainted with the design, for they pay a most absolute resignation to the monarch, especially when he is a parent also.

On the other side, the old king, who had many wives and many concubines, wanted not court flatterers to insinuate in his heart a thousand tender thoughts for this young beauty, and who represented her to his fancy as the most charming he had ever possessed in all the long race of his numerous years. At this character his old heart, like an extinguished brand, most apt to take fire, felt new sparks of love and began to kindle; and now grown to his second childhood, longed with impatience to behold this gay thing, with whom, alas! he could but innocently play. But how he should be confirmed she was this wonder, before he used his power to call her to court (where maidens never came, unless for the King's private use), he was next to consider; and while he was so doing, he had intelligence brought him that Imoinda was most certainly mistress to the Prince Oroonoko. This gave him some chagrin; however, it gave him also an opportunity, one day when the Prince was a-hunting, to wait on a man of quality, as his slave and attendant, who should go and make a present to Imoinda as from the Prince; he should then, unknown, see this fair maid, and have an opportunity to hear what message she would return the Prince for his present, and from thence gather the state of her heart and degree of her inclination. This was put in execution, and the old monarch saw, and burned. He found her all he had heard, and would not delay his happiness, but found he should have some obstacle to overcome her heart; for she expressed her sense of the present the Prince had sent her in terms so sweet, so soft and pretty, with an air of love and joy that could not be dissembled, insomuch that 'twas past doubt whether she loved Oroonoko entirely. This gave the old king some affliction, but he salved it with this, that the obedience the people pay their king was not at all inferior to what they paid their gods; and what love would not oblige Imoinda to do, duty would compel her to.

He was therefore no sooner got to his apartment but he sent the royal veil to Imoinda, that is, the ceremony of invitation: he sends the lady he has a mind to honor with his bed a veil, with which she is covered, and secured for the King's use; and 'tis death to disobey, besides held a most impious disobedience.

'Tis not to be imagined the surprise and grief that seized this lovely maid at this news and sight. However, as delays in these cases are dangerous and pleading worse than treason, trembling, and almost fainting, she was obliged to suffer herself to be covered and led away.

They brought her thus to court; and the King, who had caused a very rich bath to be prepared, was led into it, where he sat under a canopy, in state, to receive this longed-for virgin; whom he having commanded should be brought to him, they (after disrobing her) led her to the bath, and making fast the doors, left her to descend. The King, without more courtship, bade her throw off her mantle and come to his arms. But Imoinda, all in tears, threw herself on the marble, on the brink of the bath, and besought him to hear her. She told him, as she was a maid, how proud of the divine glory she should have been, of having it in her power to oblige her king; but as by the laws he could not, and from his royal goodness would not, take from any man his wedded wife, so she believed she should be the occasion of making him commit a great sin, if she did not reveal her state and condition, and tell him she was another's, and could not be so happy to be his.

The King, enraged at this delay, hastily demanded the name of the bold man that had married a woman of her degree without his consent. Imoinda, seeing his eyes fierce and his hands tremble (whether with age or anger, I know not, but she fancied the last), almost repented she had said so much, for now she feared the storm would fall on the Prince. She therefore said a thousand things to appease the raging of his flame, and to prepare him to hear who it was with calmness; but before she spoke, he imagined who she meant, but would not seem to do so, but commanded her to lay aside her mantle and suffer herself to receive his caresses; or by his gods, he swore that happy man whom she was going to name should die, though it were even Oroonoko himself. "Therefore," said he, "deny this marriage, and swear thyself a maid." "That," replied Imoinda, "by all our powers I do, for I am not yet known to my husband." " 'Tis enough," said the King; " 'tis enough to satisfy both my conscience and my heart." And rising from his seat, he went and led her into the bath, it being in vain for her to resist.

In this time the Prince, who was returned from hunting, went to visit his Imoinda, but found her gone; and not only so, but heard she had received the royal veil. This raised him to a storm, and in his madness they had much ado to save him from laying violent hands on himself. Force first prevailed, and then reason. They urged all to him that might oppose his rage, but nothing weighed so greatly with him as the King's old age, uncapable of injuring him with Imoinda. He would give way to that hope, because it pleased him most, and flattered best his heart. Yet this served not altogether to make him cease his different passions, which sometimes raged within him, and sometimes softened into showers. 'Twas not enough to appease him, to tell him his grandfather was old and could not that way injure him, while he retained that awful duty which the young men are used there to pay to their grave relations. He could not be convinced he had no cause to sigh and mourn for the loss of a mistress he could not with all his strength and courage retrieve. And he would often cry, "O my friends! Were she in walled cities or confined from me in fortifications of the greatest strength, did enchantments or monsters detain her from me, I would venture through any hazard to free her. But here, in the arms of a feeble old man, my youth, my violent love, my trade in arms, and all my vast desire of glory avail me nothing. Imoinda is as irrecoverably lost to me as if she were snatched by the cold arms of Death. Oh! she is never to be retrieved. If I would wait tedious years, till fate should bow the old king to his grave, even that would not leave me Imoinda free; but still that custom that makes it so vile a crime for a son to marry his father's wives or mistresses would hinder my happiness, unless I would either ignobly set an ill precedent to my successors, or abandon my country and fly with her to some unknown world, who never heard our story."

But it was objected to him that his case was not the same; for Imoinda being his lawful wife, by solemn contract, 'twas he was the injured man and might if he so pleased take Imoinda back, the breach of the law being on his grandfather's side; and that if he could circumvent him and redeem her from the Otan, which is the palace of the King's women, a sort of seraglio, it was both just and lawful for him so to do.

This reasoning had some force upon him, and he should have been entirely comforted, but for the thought that she was possessed by his grandfather. However, he loved so well that he was resolved to believe what most favored his hope, and to endeavor to learn from Imoinda's own mouth what only she could satisfy him in, whether she was robbed of that blessing which was only due to his faith and love. But as it was very hard to get a sight of the women (for no men ever entered into the Otan but when the King went to entertain himself with some one of his wives or mistresses, and 'twas death at any other time for any other to go in), so he knew not how to contrive to get a sight of her.

While Oroonoko felt all the agonies of love, and suffered under a torment the most painful in the world, the old king was not exempted from his share of affliction. He was troubled for having been forced by an irresistible passion to rob his son[2] of a treasure he knew could not but be extremely dear to him, since she was the most beautiful that ever had been seen, and had besides all the sweetness and innocence of youth and modesty, with a charm of wit surpassing all. He found that, however she was forced to expose her lovely person to his withered arms, she could only sigh and weep there, and think of Oroonoko; and oftentimes could not forbear speaking of him, though her life were, by custom, forfeited by owning her passion. But she spoke not of a lover only, but of a prince dear to him to whom she spoke, and of the praises of a man who, till now, filled the old man's soul with joy at every recital of his bravery, or even his name. And 'twas this dotage on our young hero that gave Imoinda a thousand privileges to speak of him without offending, and this condescension in the old king that made her take the satisfaction of speaking of him so very often.

Besides, he many times inquired how the Prince bore himself; and those of whom he asked, being entirely slaves to the merits and virtues of the Prince, still answered what they thought conduced best to his service; which was to make the old king fancy that the Prince had no more interest in Imoinda, and had resigned her willingly to the pleasure of the King; that he diverted himself with his mathematicians, his fortifications, his officers, and his hunting.

2. I.e., grandson.

This pleased the old lover, who failed not to report these things again to Imoinda, that she might, by the example of her young lover, withdraw her heart, and rest better contented in his arms. But however she was forced to receive this unwelcome news, in all appearance with unconcern and content, her heart was bursting within, and she was only happy when she could get alone, to vent her griefs and moans with sighs and tears.

What reports of the Prince's conduct were made to the King, he thought good to justify as far as possibly he could by his actions, and when he appeared in the presence of the King, he showed a face not at all betraying his heart. So that in a little time, the old man being entirely convinced that he was no longer a lover of Imoinda, he carried him with him in his train to the Otan, often to banquet with his mistress. But as soon as he entered, one day, into the apartment of Imoinda with the King, at the first glance from her eyes, notwithstanding all his determined resolution, he was ready to sink in the place where he stood, and had certainly done so but for the support of Aboan, a young man who was next to him; which, with his change of countenance, had betrayed him, had the King chanced to look that way. And I have observed, 'tis a very great error, in those who laugh when one says a Negro can change color, for I have seen 'em as frequently blush, and look pale, and that as visibly as ever I saw in the most beautiful white. And 'tis certain that both these changes were evident, this day, in both these lovers. And Imoinda, who saw with some joy the change in the Prince's face, and found it in her own, strove to divert the King from beholding either by a forced caress, with which she met him, which was a new wound in the heart of the poor dying Prince. But as soon as the King was busied in looking on some fine thing of Imoinda's making, she had time to tell the Prince with her angry but love-darting eyes that she resented his coldness, and bemoaned her own miserable captivity. Nor were his eyes silent, but answered hers again, as much as eyes could do, instructed by the most tender and most passionate heart that ever loved. And they spoke so well and so effectually, as Imoinda no longer doubted but she was the only delight and the darling of that soul she found pleading in 'em its right of love, which none was more willing to resign than she. And 'twas this powerful language alone that in an instant conveyed all the thoughts of their souls to each other, that[3] they both found there wanted but opportunity to make them both entirely happy. But when he saw another door opened by Onahal, a former old wife of the King's who now had charge of Imoinda, and saw the prospect of a bed of state made ready with sweets and flowers for the dalliance of the King, who immediately led the trembling victim from his sight into that prepared repose, what rage, what wild frenzies seized his heart! which forcing to keep within bounds, and to suffer without noise, it became the more insupportable, and rent his soul with ten thousand pains. He was forced to retire to vent his groans, where he fell down on a carpet and lay struggling a long time, and only breathing now and then, "—O Imoinda!"

When Onahal had finished her necessary affair within, shutting the door, she came forth to wait till the King called; and hearing someone sighing in the other room, she passed on, and found the Prince in that deplorable condition, which she thought needed her aid. She gave him cordials, but all in vain, till finding the nature of his disease by his sighs and naming Imoinda.

3. So that.

She told him, he had not so much cause as he imagined to afflict himself, for if he knew the King so well as she did, he would not lose a moment in jealousy, and that she was confident that Imoinda bore, at this minute, part in his affliction. Aboan was of the same opinion, and both together persuaded him to reassume his courage; and all sitting down on the carpet, the Prince said so many obliging things to Onahal that he half persuaded her to be of his party. And she promised him she would thus far comply with his just desires, that she would let Imoinda know how faithful he was, what he suffered, and what he said.

This discourse lasted till the King called, which gave Oroonoko a certain satisfaction, and with the hope Onahal had made him conceive, he assumed a look as gay as 'twas possible a man in his circumstances could do; and presently after, he was called in with the rest who waited without. The King commanded music to be brought, and several of his young wives and mistresses came all together by his command to dance before him; where Imoinda performed her part with an air and grace so passing all the rest as her beauty was above 'em, and received the present ordained as a prize. The Prince was every moment more charmed with the new beauties and graces he beheld in this fair one. And while he gazed, and she danced, Onahal was retired to a window with Aboan.

This Onahal, as I said, was one of the cast[4] mistresses of the old king; and 'twas these (now past their beauty) that were made guardians or governants[5] to the new and the young ones, and whose business it was to teach them all those wanton arts of love with which they prevailed and charmed heretofore in their turn; and who now treated the triumphing happy ones with all the severity, as to liberty and freedom, that was possible, in revenge of those honors they rob them of; envying them those satisfactions, those gallantries and presents, that were once made to themselves, while youth and beauty lasted, and which they now saw pass regardless by, and paid only to the bloomings. And certainly nothing is more afflicting to a decayed beauty than to behold in itself declining charms that were once adored, and to find those caresses paid to new beauties to which once she laid a claim; to hear 'em whisper as she passes by, "That once was a delicate woman." These abandoned ladies therefore endeavor to revenge all the despites[6] and decays of time on these flourishing happy ones. And 'twas this severity that gave Oroonoko a thousand fears he should never prevail with Onahal to see Imoinda. But, as I said, she was now retired to a window with Aboan.

This young man was not only one of the best quality,[7] but a man extremely well made and beautiful; and coming often to attend the King to the Otan, he had subdued the heart of the antiquated Onahal, which had not forgot how pleasant it was to be in love. And though she had some decays in her face, she had none in her sense and wit; she was there agreeable still, even to Aboan's youth, so that he took pleasure in entertaining her with discourses of love. He knew also that to make his court to these she-favorites was the way to be great, these being the persons that do all affairs and business at court. He had also observed that she had given him glances more tender and inviting than she had done to others of his quality. And now, when he saw

---

4. Cast-off.
5. Female teachers or chaperones.

6. Insults.
7. Rank.

that her favor could so absolutely oblige the Prince, he failed not to sigh in her ear and to look with eyes all soft upon her, and give her hope that she had made some impressions on his heart. He found her pleased at this, and making a thousand advances to him; but the ceremony ending and the King departing broke up the company for that day, and his conversation.

Aboan failed not that night to tell the Prince of his success, and how advantageous the service of Onahal might be to his amour with Imoinda. The Prince was overjoyed with this good news and besought him, if it were possible, to caress her so as to engage her entirely, which he could not fail to do, if he complied with her desires. "For then," said the Prince, "her life lying at your mercy, she must grant you the request you make in my behalf." Aboan understood him, and assured him he would make love so effectually that he would defy the most expert mistress of the art to find out whether he dissembled it or had it really. And 'twas with impatience they waited the next opportunity of going to the Otan.

The wars came on, the time of taking the field approached, and 'twas impossible for the Prince to delay his going at the head of his army to encounter the enemy. So that every day seemed a tedious year till he saw his Imoinda, for he believed he could not live if he were forced away without being so happy. 'Twas with impatience, therefore, that he expected the next visit the King would make, and according to his wish, it was not long.

The parley of the eyes of these two lovers had not passed so secretly but an old jealous lover could spy it; or rather, he wanted not flatterers who told him they observed it. So that the Prince was hastened to the camp, and this was the last visit he found he should make to the Otan; he therefore urged Aboan to make the best of this last effort, and to explain himself so to Onahal that she, deferring her enjoyment of her young lover no longer, might make way for the Prince to speak to Imoinda.

The whole affair being agreed on between the Prince and Aboan, they attended the King, as the custom was, to the Otan, where, while the whole company was taken up in beholding the dancing and antic postures the women-royal made to divert the King, Onahal singled out Aboan, whom she found most pliable to her wish. When she had him where she believed she could not be heard, she sighed to him, and softly cried, "Ah, Aboan! When will you be sensible of my passion? I confess it with my mouth, because I would not give my eyes the lie; and you have but too much already perceived they have confessed my flame. Nor would I have you believe that because I am the abandoned mistress of a king, I esteem myself altogether divested of charms. No, Aboan; I have still a rest[8] of beauty enough engaging, and have learned to please too well not to be desirable. I can have lovers still, but will have none but Aboan." "Madam," replied the half-feigning youth, "you have already, by my eyes, found you can still conquer, and I believe 'tis in pity of me you condescend to this kind confession. But, Madam, words are used to be so small a part of our country courtship, that 'tis rare one can get so happy an opportunity as to tell one's heart, and those few minutes we have are forced to be snatched for more certain proofs of love than speaking and sighing; and such I languish for."

He spoke this with such a tone that she hoped it true, and could not

8. Remnant.

forbear believing it; and being wholly transported with joy, for having subdued the finest of all the King's subjects to her desires, she took from her
ears two large pearls and commanded him to wear 'em in his. He would have
refused 'em, crying, "Madam, these are not the proofs of your love that I
expect; 'tis opportunity, 'tis a lone hour only, that can make me happy." But
forcing the pearls into his hand, she whispered softly to him, "Oh! Do not
fear a woman's invention, when love sets her a-thinking." And pressing his
hand, she cried, "This night you shall be happy. Come to the gate of the
orange groves behind the Otan, and I will be ready, about midnight, to
receive you." 'Twas thus agreed, and she left him, that no notice might be
taken of their speaking together.

The ladies were still dancing, and the King, laid on a carpet, with a great
deal of pleasure was beholding them, especially Imoinda, who that day
appeared more lovely than ever, being enlivened with the good tidings Onahal had brought her of the constant passion the Prince had for her. The
Prince was laid on another carpet at the other end of the room, with his eyes
fixed on the object of his soul; and as she turned or moved, so did they, and
she alone gave his eyes and soul their motions. Nor did Imoinda employ her
eyes to any other use than in beholding with infinite pleasure the joy she
produced in those of the Prince. But while she was more regarding him than
the steps she took, she chanced to fall, and so near him as that, leaping with
extreme force from the carpet, he caught her in his arms as she fell; and
'twas visible to the whole presence[9] the joy wherewith he received her. He
clasped her close to his bosom, and quite forgot that reverence that was due
to the mistress of a king, and that punishment that is the reward of a boldness
of this nature; and had not the presence of mind of Imoinda (fonder of his
safety than her own) befriended him, in making her spring from his arms
and fall into her dance again, he had at that instant met his death; for the
old king, jealous to the last degree, rose up in rage, broke all the diversion,
and led Imoinda to her apartment, and sent out word to the Prince to go
immediately to the camp, and that if he were found another night in court
he should suffer the death ordained for disobedient offenders.

You may imagine how welcome this news was to Oroonoko, whose unseasonable transport and caress of Imoinda was blamed by all men that loved
him; and now he perceived his fault, yet cried that for such another moment,
he would be content to die.

All the Otan was in disorder about this accident; and Onahal was particularly concerned, because on the Prince's stay depended her happiness, for
she could no longer expect that of Aboan. So that ere they departed, they
contrived it so that the Prince and he should come both that night to the
grove of the Otan, which was all of oranges and citrons, and that there they
should wait her orders.

They parted thus, with grief enough, till night, leaving the King in possession of the lovely maid. But nothing could appease the jealousy of the old
lover. He would not be imposed on, but would have it that Imoinda made a
false step on purpose to fall into Oroonoko's bosom, and that all things
looked like a design on both sides; and 'twas in vain she protested her innocence. He was old and obstinate, and left her more than half assured that
his fear was true.

---

9. Company.

The King going to his apartment sent to know where the Prince was, and if he intended to obey his command. The messenger returned and told him, he found the Prince pensive and altogether unpreparing for the campaign, that he lay negligently on the ground, and answered very little. This confirmed the jealousy of the King, and he commanded that they should very narrowly and privately watch his motions, and that he should not stir from his apartment but one spy or other should be employed to watch him. So that the hour approaching wherein he was to go to the citron grove, and taking only Aboan along with him, he leaves his apartment, and was watched to the very gate of the Otan, where he was seen to enter, and where they left him, to carry back the tidings to the King.

Oroonoko and Aboan were no sooner entered but Onahal led the Prince to the apartment of Imoinda, who, not knowing anything of her happiness, was laid in bed. But Onahal only left him in her chamber, to make the best of his opportunity, and took her dear Aboan to her own, where he showed the heighth of complaisance for his prince, when, to give him an opportunity, he suffered himself to be caressed in bed by Onahal.

The Prince softly wakened Imoinda, who was not a little surprised with joy to find him there; and yet she trembled with a thousand fears. I believe he omitted saying nothing to this young maid that might persuade her to suffer him to seize his own, and take the rights of love; and I believe she was not long resisting those arms where she so longed to be; and having opportunity, night and silence, youth, love and desire, he soon prevailed, and ravished in a moment what his old grandfather had been endeavoring for so many months.

'Tis not to be imagined the satisfaction of these two young lovers; nor the vows she made him that she remained a spotless maid till that night, and that what she did with his grandfather had robbed him of no part of her virgin honor, the gods in mercy and justice having reserved that for her plighted lord, to whom of right it belonged. And 'tis impossible to express the transports he suffered, while he listened to a discourse so charming from her loved lips, and clasped that body in his arms for whom he had so long languished; and nothing now afflicted him but his sudden departure from her; for he told her the necessity and his commands, but should depart satisfied in this, that since the old king had hitherto not been able to deprive him of those enjoyments which only belonged to him, he believed for the future he would be less able to injure him; so that abating the scandal of the veil, which was no otherwise so than that she was wife to another, he believed her safe, even in the arms of the King, and innocent; yet would he have ventured at the conquest of the world, and have given it all, to have had her avoided that honor of receiving the royal veil. 'Twas thus, between a thousand caresses, that both bemoaned the hard fate of youth and beauty, so liable to that cruel promotion. 'Twas a glory that could well have been spared here, though desired and aimed at by all the young females of that kingdom.

But while they were thus fondly employed, forgetting how time ran on, and that the dawn must conduct him far away from his only happiness, they heard a great noise in the Otan, and unusual voices of men; at which the Prince, starting from the arms of the frighted Imoinda, ran to a little battle-ax he used to wear by his side, and having not so much leisure as to put on his habit, he opposed himself against some who were already opening the door; which they did with so much violence that Oroonoko was not able to defend it, but was forced to cry out with a commanding voice, "Whoever ye are that have the boldness to attempt to approach this apartment thus rudely, know that I, the Prince Oroonoko, will revenge it with the certain death of him that first enters. Therefore stand back, and know, this place is sacred to love and me this night; tomorrow 'tis the King's."

This he spoke with a voice so resolved and assured that they soon retired from the door, but cried, " 'Tis by the King's command we are come; and being satisfied by thy voice, O Prince, as much as if we had entered, we can report to the King the truth of all his fears, and leave thee to provide for thy own safety, as thou art advised by thy friends."

At these words they departed, and left the Prince to take a short and sad leave of his Imoinda, who, trusting in the strength of her charms, believed she should appease the fury of a jealous king by saying she was surprised, and that it was by force of arms he got into her apartment. All her concern now was for his life, and therefore she hastened him to the camp, and with much ado prevailed on him to go. Nor was it she alone that prevailed; Aboan and Onahal both pleaded, and both assured him of a lie that should be well enough contrived to secure Imoinda. So that at last, with a heart sad as death, dying eyes, and sighing soul, Oroonoko departed and took his way to the camp.

It was not long after the King in person came to the Otan, where, beholding Imoinda with rage in his eyes, he upbraided her wickedness and perfidy, and threatening her royal lover, she fell on her face at his feet, bedewing the floor with her tears and imploring his pardon for a fault which she had not with her will committed, as Onahal, who was also prostrate with her, could testify; that unknown to her, he had broke into her apartment, and ravished her. She spoke this much against her conscience, but to save her own life 'twas absolutely necessary she should feign this falsity. She knew it could not injure the Prince, he being fled to an army that would stand by him against any injuries that should assault him. However, this last thought of Imoinda's being ravished changed the measures of his revenge; and whereas before he designed to be himself her executioner, he now resolved she should not die. But as it is the greatest crime in nature amongst 'em to touch a woman after having been possessed by a son, a father, or a brother, so now he looked on Imoinda as a polluted thing, wholly unfit for his embrace; nor would he resign her to his grandson, because she had received the royal veil. He therefore removes her from the Otan, with Onahal; whom he put into safe hands, with order they should be both sold off as slaves to another country, either Christian or heathen; 'twas no matter where.

This cruel sentence, worse than death, they implored might be reversed; but their prayers were vain, and it was put in execution accordingly, and that with so much secrecy that none, either without or within the Otan, knew anything of their absence or their destiny.

The old king, nevertheless, executed this with a great deal of reluctancy; but he believed he had made a very great conquest over himself, when he had once resolved, and had performed what he resolved. He believed now that his love had been unjust, and that he could not expect the gods, or Captain of the Clouds (as they call the unknown power), should suffer a better consequence from so ill a cause. He now begins to hold Oroonoko excused, and to say he had reason for what he did. And now everybody could assure the King how passionately Imoinda was beloved by the Prince; even those confessed it now, who said the contrary before his flame was abated. So that the King being old, and not able to defend himself in war, and having no sons of all his race remaining alive but only this, to maintain him on his throne; and looking on this as a man disobliged, first by the rape of his mistress, or rather wife; and now by depriving of him wholly of her, he feared, might make him desperate and do some cruel thing, either to himself or his old grandfather, the offender: he began to repent him extremely of the contempt he had, in his rage, put on Imoinda. Besides, he considered he ought in honor to have killed her for this offense, if it had been one. He ought to have had so much value and consideration for a maid of her quality as to have nobly put her to death, and not to have sold her like a common slave, the greatest revenge and the most disgraceful of any; and to which they a thousand times prefer death, and implore it, as Imoinda did, but could not obtain that honor. Seeing therefore it was certain that Oroonoko would highly resent this affront, he thought good to make some excuse for his rashness to him; and to that end he sent a messenger to the camp, with orders to treat with him about the matter, to gain his pardon, and to endeavor to mitigate his grief; but that by no means he should tell him she was sold, but secretly put to death, for he knew he should never obtain his pardon for the other.

When the messenger came, he found the Prince upon the point of engaging with the enemy; but as soon as he heard of the arrival of the messenger, he commanded him to his tent, where he embraced him and received him with joy; which was soon abated by the downcast looks of the messenger, who was instantly demanded the cause by Oroonoko, who, impatient of delay, asked a thousand questions in a breath, and all concerning Imoinda. But there needed little return, for he could almost answer himself of all he demanded, from his sighs and eyes. At last, the messenger casting himself at the Prince's feet, and kissing them with all the submission of a man that had something to implore which he dreaded to utter, he besought him to hear with calmness what he had to deliver to him, and to call up all his noble and heroic courage to encounter with his words, and defend himself against the ungrateful[1] things he must relate. Oroonoko replied, with a deep sigh and a languishing voice, "I am armed against their worst efforts—; for I know they will tell me, Imoinda is no more—and after that, you may spare the rest." Then, commanding him to rise, he laid himself on a carpet, under a rich pavilion, and remained a good while silent, and was hardly heard to sigh. When he was come a little to himself, the messenger asked him leave to deliver that part of his embassy which the Prince had not yet divined. And the Prince cried, "I permit thee—." Then he told him the affliction the old king was in, for the rashness he had committed in his cruelty to Imoinda; and how he deigned to ask pardon for his offense, and to implore the Prince would not suffer that loss to touch his heart too sensibly, which now all the gods could not restore him, but might recompense him in glory, which he begged he would pursue; and that Death, that common revenger of all injuries, would soon even the account between him and a feeble old man.

Oroonoko bade him return his duty to his lord and master, and to assure

1. Offensive.

him, there was no account of revenge to be adjusted between them; if there were, 'twas he was the aggressor, and that Death would be just and, maugre[2] his age, would see him righted; and he was contented to leave his share of glory to youths more fortunate and worthy of that favor from the gods. That henceforth he would never lift a weapon or draw a bow, but abandon the small remains of his life to sighs and tears, and the continual thoughts of what his lord and grandfather had thought good to send out of the world, with all that youth, that innocence, and beauty.

After having spoken this, whatever his greatest officers and men of the best rank could do, they could not raise him from the carpet, or persuade him to action and resolutions of life; but commanding all to retire, he shut himself into his pavilion all that day, while the enemy was ready to engage; and wondering at the delay, the whole body of the chief of the army then addressed themselves to him, and to whom they had much ado to get admittance. They fell on their faces at the foot of his carpet, where they lay and besought him with earnest prayers and tears to lead 'em forth to battle, and not let the enemy take advantages of them; and implored him to have regard to his glory, and to the world, that depended on his courage and conduct. But he made no other reply to all their supplications but this, that he had now no more business for glory; and for the world, it was a trifle not worth his care. "Go," continued he, sighing, "and divide it amongst you; and reap with joy what you so vainly prize, and leave me to my more welcome destiny."

They then demanded what they should do, and whom he would constitute in his room, that the confusion of ambitious youth and power might not ruin their order and make them a prey to the enemy. He replied, he would not give himself the trouble—; but wished 'em to choose the bravest man amongst 'em, let his quality or birth be what it would. "For, O my friends!" said he, "it is not titles make men brave or good, or birth that bestows courage and generosity, or makes the owner happy. Believe this, when you behold Oroonoko, the most wretched and abandoned by fortune of all the creation of the gods." So turning himself about, he would make no more reply to all they could urge or implore.

The army, beholding their officers return unsuccessful, with sad faces and ominous looks that presaged no good luck, suffered a thousand fears to take possession of their hearts, and the enemy to come even upon 'em, before they would provide for their safety by any defense; and though they were assured by some, who had a mind to animate 'em, that they should be immediately headed by the Prince, and that in the meantime Aboan had orders to command as general, yet they were so dismayed for want of that great example of bravery that they could make but a very feeble resistance; and at last downright fled before the enemy, who pursued 'em to the very tents, killing 'em. Nor could all Aboan's courage, which that day gained him immortal glory, shame 'em into a manly defense of themselves. The guards that were left behind about the Prince's tent, seeing the soldiers flee before the enemy and scatter themselves all over the plain, in great disorder, made such outcries as roused the Prince from his amorous slumber, in which he had remained buried for two days without permitting any sustenance to approach him. But in spite of all his resolutions, he had not the constancy of grief to

2. In spite of. Oroonoko is saying that he will die first.

that degree, as to make him insensible of the danger of his army; and in that instant he leaped from his couch and cried, "—Come, if we must die, let us meet Death the noblest way; and 'twill be more like Oroonoko to encounter him at an army's head, opposing the torrent of a conquering foe, than lazily on a couch to wait his lingering pleasure, and die every moment by a thousand wrecking[3] thoughts; or be tamely taken by an enemy, and led a whining, lovesick slave to adorn the triumphs of Jamoan, that young victor, who already is entered beyond the limits I had prescribed him."

While he was speaking, he suffered his people to dress him for the field, and sallying out of his pavilion, with more life and vigor in his countenance than ever he showed, he appeared like some divine power descended to save his country from destruction; and his people had purposely put on him all things that might make him shine with most splendor, to strike a reverend awe into the beholders. He flew into the thickest of those that were pursuing his men, and being animated with despair, he fought as if he came on purpose to die, and did such things as will not be believed that human strength could perform, and such as soon inspired all the rest with new courage and new order. And now it was that they began to fight indeed, and so as if they would not be outdone even by their adored hero; who, turning the tide of the victory, changing absolutely the fate of the day, gained an entire conquest; and Oroonoko having the good fortune to single out Jamoan, he took him prisoner with his own hand, having wounded him almost to death.

This Jamoan afterwards became very dear to him, being a man very gallant and of excellent graces and fine parts; so that he never put him amongst the rank of captives, as they used to do, without distinction, for the common sale or market; but kept him in his own court, where he retained nothing of the prisoner but the name, and returned no more into his own country, so great an affection he took for Oroonoko; and by a thousand tales and adventures of love and gallantry flattered[4] his disease of melancholy and languishment, which I have often heard him say had certainly killed him, but for the conversation of this prince and Aboan, and the French governor he had from his childhood, of whom I have spoken before, and who was a man of admirable wit, great ingenuity and learning, all which he had infused into his young pupil. This Frenchman was banished out of his own country for some heretical notions he held, and though he was a man of very little religion, he had admirable morals and a brave soul.

After the total defeat of Jamoan's army, which all fled, or were left dead upon the place, they spent some time in the camp, Oroonoko choosing rather to remain a while there in his tents than enter into a palace or live in a court where he had so lately suffered so great a loss. The officers, therefore, who saw and knew his cause of discontent, invented all sorts of diversions and sports to entertain their prince; so that what with those amusements abroad and others at home, that is, within their tents, with the persuasions, arguments, and care of his friends and servants that he more peculiarly prized, he wore off in time a great part of that chagrin and torture of despair which the first efforts of Imoinda's death had given him. Insomuch as having received a thousand kind embassies from the King, and invitations to return to court, he obeyed, though with no little reluctancy; and when he did so,

3. Racking.
4. Soothed.

there was a visible change in him, and for a long time he was much more melancholy than before. But time lessens all extremes, and reduces 'em to mediums and unconcern; but no motives or beauties, though all endeavored it, could engage him in any sort of amour, though he had all the invitations to it, both from his own youth and others' ambitions and designs.

Oroonoko was no sooner returned from this last conquest, and received at court with all the joy and magnificence that could be expressed to a young victor, who was not only returned triumphant but beloved like a deity, when there arrived in the port an English ship.

This person[5] had often before been in these countries and was very well known to Oroonoko, with whom he had trafficked for slaves, and had used to do the same with his predecessors.

This commander was a man of a finer sort of address and conversation, better bred and more engaging than most of that sort of men are, so that he seemed rather never to have been bred out of a court than almost all his life at sea. This captain therefore was always better received at court than most of the traders to those countries were; and especially by Oroonoko, who was more civilized, according to the European mode, than any other had been, and took more delight in the white nations, and above all men of parts and wit. To this captain he sold abundance of his slaves, and for the favor and esteem he had for him, made him many presents, and obliged him to stay at court as long as possibly he could. Which the captain seemed to take as a very great honor done him, entertaining the Prince every day with globes and maps, and mathematical discourses and instruments; eating, drinking, hunting, and living with him with so much familiarity that it was not to be doubted but he had gained very greatly upon the heart of this gallant young man. And the captain, in return of all these mighty favors, besought the Prince to honor his vessel with his presence, some day or other, to dinner, before he should set sail; which he condescended to accept, and appointed his day. The captain, on his part, failed not to have all things in a readiness, in the most magnificent order he could possibly. And the day being come, the captain in his boat, richly adorned with carpets and velvet cushions, rowed to the shore to receive the Prince, with another longboat where was placed all his music and trumpets, with which Oroonoko was extremely delighted; who met him on the shore attended by his French governor, Jamoan, Aboan, and about a hundred of the noblest of the youths of the court. And after they had first carried the Prince on board, the boats fetched the rest off; where they found a very splendid treat, with all sorts of fine wines, and were as well entertained as 'twas possible in such a place to be.

The Prince, having drunk hard of punch and several sorts of wine, as did all the rest (for great care was taken they should want nothing of that part of the entertainment), was very merry, and in great admiration of the ship, for he had never been in one before; so that he was curious of beholding every place where he decently might descend. The rest, no less curious, who were not quite overcome with drinking, rambled at their pleasure fore and aft, as their fancies guided 'em. So that the captain, who had well laid his design before, gave the word, and seized on all his guests; they clapping great irons suddenly on the Prince, when he was leaped down in the hold to view

5. The ship's captain.

that part of the vessel, and locking him fast down, secured him. The same treachery was used to all the rest; and all in one instant, in several places of the ship, were lashed fast in irons, and betrayed to slavery. That great design over, they set all hands to work to hoise[6] sail; and with as treacherous and fair a wind, they made from the shore with this innocent and glorious prize, who thought of nothing less than such an entertainment.

Some have commended this act as brave in the captain; but I will spare my sense of it, and leave it to my reader to judge as he pleases.

It may be easily guessed in what manner the Prince resented this indignity, who may be best resembled to a lion taken in a toil; so he raged, so he struggled for liberty, but all in vain; and they had so wisely managed his fetters that he could not use a hand in his defense, to quit himself of a life that would by no means endure slavery, nor could he move from the place where he was tied to any solid part of the ship, against which he might have beat his head, and have finished his disgrace that way. So that being deprived of all other means, he resolved to perish for want of food. And pleased at last with that thought, and toiled and tired by rage and indignation, he laid himself down, and sullenly resolved upon dying, and refused all things that were brought him.

This did not a little vex the captain, and the more so because he found almost all of 'em of the same humor; so that the loss of so many brave slaves, so tall and goodly to behold, would have been very considerable. He therefore ordered one to go from him (for he would not be seen himself) to Oroonoko, and to assure him he was afflicted for having rashly done so unhospitable a deed, and which could not be now remedied, since they were far from shore; but since he resented it in so high a nature, he assured him he would revoke his resolution, and set both him and his friends ashore on the next land they should touch at; and of this the messenger gave him his oath, provided he would resolve to live. And Oroonoko, whose honor was such as he never had violated a word in his life himself, much less a solemn asseveration, believed in an instant what this man said, but replied, he expected for a confirmation of this to have his shameful fetters dismissed. This demand was carried to the captain, who returned him answer that the offense had been so great which he had put upon the Prince that he durst not trust him with liberty while he remained in the ship, for fear lest by a valor natural to him, and a revenge that would animate that valor, he might commit some outrage fatal to himself and the King his master, to whom his vessel did belong. To this Oroonoko replied, he would engage his honor to behave himself in all friendly order and manner, and obey the command of the captain, as he was lord of the King's vessel and general of those men under his command.

This was delivered to the still doubting captain, who could not resolve to trust a heathen, he said, upon his parole,[7] a man that had no sense or notion of the God that he worshipped. Oroonoko then replied, he was very sorry to hear that the captain pretended to the knowledge and worship of any gods who had taught him no better principles than not to credit as he would be credited; but they told him the difference of their faith occasioned that distrust. For the captain had protested to him upon the word of a Christian, and sworn in the name of a great god, which if he should violate, he would

---

6. Hoist.

7. Word of honor.

expect eternal torment in the world to come. "Is that all the obligation he has to be just to his oath?" replied Oroonoko. "Let him know I swear by my honor; which to violate, would not only render me contemptible and despised by all brave and honest men, and so give myself perpetual pain, but it would be eternally offending and diseasing all mankind, harming, betraying, circumventing and outraging all men; but punishments hereafter are suffered by one's self, and the world takes no cognizances whether this god have revenged 'em or not, 'tis done so secretly and deferred so long. While the man of no honor suffers every moment the scorn and contempt of the honester world, and dies every day ignominiously in his fame, which is more valuable than life. I speak not this to move belief, but to show you how you mistake, when you imagine that he who will violate his honor will keep his word with his gods." So turning from him with a disdainful smile, he refused to answer him, when he urged him to know what answer he should carry back to his captain; so that he departed without saying any more.

The captain pondering and consulting what to do, it was concluded that nothing but Oroonoko's liberty would encourage any of the rest to eat, except the Frenchman, whom the captain could not pretend to keep prisoner, but only told him he was secured because he might act something in favor of the Prince, but that he should be freed as soon as they came to land. So that they concluded it wholly necessary to free the Prince from his irons, that he might show himself to the rest; that they might have an eye upon him, and that they could not fear a single man.

This being resolved, to make the obligation the greater, the captain himself went to Oroonoko; where after many compliments, and assurances of what he had already promised, he receiving from the Prince his parole and his hand for his good behavior, dismissed his irons and brought him to his own cabin; where after having treated and reposed him a while, for he had neither eat[8] nor slept in four days before, he besought him to visit those obstinate people in chains, who refused all manner of sustenance, and entreated him to oblige 'em to eat, and assure 'em of their liberty the first opportunity.

Oroonoko, who was too generous not to give credit to his words, showed himself to his people, who were transported with excess of joy at the sight of their darling prince, falling at his feet and kissing and embracing 'em, believing, as some divine oracle, all he assured 'em. But he besought 'em to bear their chains with that bravery that became those whom he had seen act so nobly in arms; and that they could not give him greater proofs of their love and friendship, since 'twas all the security the captain (his friend) could have, against the revenge, he said, they might possibly justly take for the injuries sustained by him. And they all with one accord assured him, they could not suffer enough, when it was for his repose and safety.

After this they no longer refused to eat, but took what was brought 'em, and were pleased with their captivity, since by it they hoped to redeem the Prince, who, all the rest of the voyage, was treated with all the respect due to his birth, though nothing could divert his melancholy; and he would often sigh for Imoinda, and think this a punishment due to his misfortune, in having left that noble maid behind him that fatal night, in the Otan, when he fled to the camp.

---

8. The past form of *eat*.

Possessed with a thousand thoughts of past joys with this fair young person, and a thousand griefs for her eternal loss, he endured a tedious voyage, and at last arrived at the mouth of the river of Surinam, a colony belonging to the King of England, and where they were to deliver some part of their slaves. There the merchants and gentlemen of the country going on board to demand those lots of slaves they had already agreed on, and, amongst those, the overseers of those plantations where I then chanced to be, the captain, who had given the word, ordered his men to bring up those noble slaves in fetters whom I have spoken of; and having put 'em some in one and some in other lots, with women and children (which they call pickaninnies), they sold 'em off as slaves to several merchants and gentlemen; not putting any two in one lot, because they would separate 'em far from each other, not daring to trust 'em together, lest rage and courage should put 'em upon contriving some great action, to the ruin of the colony.

Oroonoko was first seized on, and sold to our overseer, who had the first lot, with seventeen more of all sorts and sizes, but not one of quality with him. When he saw this, he found what they meant, for, as I said, he understood English pretty well; and being wholly unarmed and defenseless, so as it was in vain to make any resistance, he only beheld the captain with a look all fierce and disdainful, upbraiding him with eyes that forced blushes on his guilty cheeks; he only cried, in passing over the side of the ship, "Farewell, sir. 'Tis worth my suffering, to gain so true a knowledge both of you and of your gods by whom you swear." And desiring those that held him to forbear their pains, and telling 'em he would make no resistance, he cried, "Come, my fellow slaves; let us descend, and see if we can meet with more honor and honesty in the next world we shall touch upon." So he nimbly leaped into the boat, and showing no more concern, suffered himself to be rowed up the river with his seventeen companions.

The gentleman that bought him was a young Cornish gentleman whose name was Trefry, a man of great wit and fine learning, and was carried into those parts by the Lord——, Governor,[9] to manage all his affairs. He reflecting on the last words of Oroonoko to the captain, and beholding the richness of his vest,[1] no sooner came into the boat but he fixed his eyes on him; and finding something so extraordinary in his face, his shape and mien, a greatness of look and haughtiness in his air, and finding he spoke English, had a great mind to be inquiring into his quality and fortune; which, though Oroonoko endeavored to hide, by only confessing he was above the rank of common slaves, Trefry soon found he was yet something greater than he confessed, and from that moment began to conceive so vast an esteem for him that he ever after loved him as his dearest brother, and showed him all the civilities due to so great a man.

Trefry was a very good mathematician and a linguist, could speak French and Spanish; and in the three days they remained in the boat (for so long were they going from the ship to the plantation) he entertained Oroonoko so agreeably with his art and discourse, that he was no less pleased with Trefry than he was with the Prince; and he thought himself at least fortunate in this, that since he was a slave, as long as he would suffer himself to remain

9. Lord Willoughby of Parham, coproprietor of Surinam by royal grant. John Treffry was his plan-

tation overseer.
1. An outer garment or robe.

so, he had a man of so excellent wit and parts for a master. So that before they had finished their voyage up the river, he made no scruple of declaring to Trefry all his fortunes, and most part of what I have here related, and put himself wholly into the hands of his new friend, whom he found resenting all the injuries were done him, and was charmed with all the greatness of his actions; which were recited with that modesty and delicate sense as wholly vanquished him, and subdued him to his interest. And he promised him on his word and honor, he would find the means to reconduct him to his own country again, assuring him, he had a perfect abhorrence of so dishonorable an action, and that he would sooner have died than have been the author of such a perfidy. He found the Prince was very much concerned to know what became of his friends, and how they took their slavery; and Trefry promised to take care about the inquiring after their condition, and that he should have an account of 'em.

Though, as Oroonoko afterwards said, he had little reason to credit the words of a *backearary*,[2] yet he knew not why, but he saw a kind of sincerity and awful truth in the face of Trefry; he saw an honesty in his eyes, and he found him wise and witty enough to understand honor; for it was one of his maxims, a man of wit could not be a knave or villain.

In their passage up the river they put in at several houses for refreshment, and ever when they landed, numbers of people would flock to behold this man; not but their eyes were daily entertained with the sight of slaves, but the fame of Oroonoko was gone before him, and all people were in admiration of his beauty. Besides, he had a rich habit on, in which he was taken, so different from the rest, and which the captain could not strip him of, because he was forced to surprise his person in the minute he sold him. When he found his habit made him liable, as he thought, to be gazed at the more, he begged Trefry to give him something more befitting a slave, which he did, and took off his robes. Nevertheless, he shone through all; and his osenbrigs (a sort of brown holland[3] suit he had on) could not conceal the graces of his looks and mien, and he had no less admirers than when he had his dazzling habit on. The royal youth appeared in spite of the slave, and people could not help treating him after a different manner, without designing it. As soon as they approached him, they venerated and esteemed him; his eyes insensibly commanded respect, and his behavior insinuated it into every soul. So that there was nothing talked of but this young and gallant slave, even by those who yet knew not that he was a prince.

I ought to tell you that the Christians never buy any slaves but they give 'em some name of their own, their native ones being likely very barbarous and hard to pronounce; so that Mr. Trefry gave Oroonoko that of Caesar, which name will live in that country as long as that (scarce more) glorious one of the great Roman; for 'tis most evident, he wanted[4] no part of the personal courage of that Caesar, and acted things as memorable, had they been done in some part of the world replenished with people and historians that might have given him his due. But his misfortune was to fall in an obscure world, that afforded only a female pen to celebrate his fame; though

2. White person or master; a variant of *backra*, from an Ibo word transported with the slaves to Surinam and the Caribbean.

3. Coarse cotton or linen, sometimes called osnaburg, after a German cloth-manufacturing town.
4. Lacked.

I doubt not but it had lived from others' endeavors, if the Dutch, who imme-diately after his time took that country,[5] had not killed, banished, and dis-persed all those that were capable of giving the world this great man's life, much better than I have done. And Mr. Trefry, who designed it, died before he began it, and bemoaned himself for not having undertook it in time.

For the future, therefore, I must call Oroonoko Caesar, since by that name only he was known in our western world, and by that name he was received on shore at Parham House, where he was destined a slave. But if the King himself (God bless him) had come ashore, there could not have been greater expectations by all the whole plantation, and those neighboring ones, than was on ours at that time; and he was received more like a governor than a slave. Notwithstanding, as the custom was, they assigned him his portion of land, his house, and his business, up in the plantation. But as it was more for form than any design to put him to his task, he endured no more of the slave but the name, and remained some days in the house, receiving all visits that were made him, without stirring towards that part of the plantation where the Negroes were.

At last he would needs go view his land, his house, and the business assigned him. But he no sooner came to the houses of the slaves, which are like a little town by itself, the Negroes all having left work, but they all came forth to behold him, and found he was that prince who had, at several times, sold most of 'em to these parts; and from a veneration they pay to great men, especially if they know 'em, and from the surprise and awe they had at the sight of him, they all cast themselves at his feet, crying out in their language, "Live, O King! Long live, O King!" and kissing his feet, paid him even divine homage.

Several English gentleman were with him; and what Mr. Trefry had told 'em was here confirmed, of which he himself before had no other witness than Caesar himself. But he was infinitely glad to find his grandeur con-firmed by the adoration of all the slaves.

Caesar, troubled with their over-joy and over-ceremony, besought 'em to rise and to receive him as their fellow slave, assuring them he was no better. At which they set up with one accord a most terrible and hideous mourning and condoling, which he and the English had much ado to appease; but at last they prevailed with 'em, and they prepared all their barbarous music, and everyone killed and dressed something of his own stock (for every family has their land apart, on which, at their leisure times, they breed all eatable things), and clubbing it together,[6] made a most magnificent supper, inviting their *Grandee Captain*, their prince, to honor it with his presence; which he did, and several English with him; where they all waited on him, some play-ing, others dancing before him all the time, according to the manners of their several nations, and with unwearied industry endeavoring to please and delight him.

While they sat at meat Mr. Trefry told Caesar that most of these young slaves were undone in love with a fine she-slave, whom they had had about six months on their land. The Prince, who never heard the name of love

---

5. In 1667 the Dutch attacked and conquered Surinam, and England ceded it by treaty in exchange for New York.
6. Contributing jointly.

without a sigh, nor any mention of it without the curiosity of examining further into that tale, which of all discourses was most agreeable to him, asked how they came to be so unhappy as to be all undone for one fair slave. Trefry, who was naturally amorous and loved to talk of love as well as anybody, proceeded to tell him, they had the most charming black that ever was beheld on their plantation, about fifteen or sixteen years old, as he guessed; that for his part, he had done nothing but sigh for her ever since she came, and that all the white beauties he had seen never charmed him so absolutely as this fine creature had done; and that no man, of any nation, ever beheld her that did not fall in love with her; and that she had all the slaves perpetually at her feet, and the whole country resounded with the fame of Clemene, "for so," said he, "we have christened her. But she denies us all with such a noble disdain, that 'tis a miracle to see that she, who can give such eternal desires, should herself be all ice and all unconcern. She is adorned with the most graceful modesty that ever beautified youth; the softest sigher—that, if she were capable of love, one would swear she languished for some absent happy man; and so retired, as if she feared a rape even from the god of day,[7] or that the breezes would steal kisses from her delicate mouth. Her task of work some sighing lover every day makes it his petition to perform for her, which she accepts blushing and with reluctancy, for fear he will ask her a look for a recompense, which he dares not presume to hope, so great an awe she strikes into the hearts of her admirers." "I do not wonder," replied the Prince, "that Clemene should refuse slaves, being as you say so beautiful, but wonder how she escapes those who can entertain her as you can do; or why, being your slave, you do not oblige her to yield." "I confess," said Trefry, "when I have, against her will, entertained her with love so long as to be transported with my passion, even above decency, I have been ready to make use of those advantages of strength and force nature has given me. But oh! she disarms me with that modesty and weeping, so tender and so moving that I retire, and thank my stars she overcame me." The company laughed at his civility to a slave, and Caesar only applauded the nobleness of his passion and nature, since that slave might be noble or, what was better, have true notions of honor and virtue in her. Thus passed they this night, after having received from the slaves all imaginable respect and obedience.

The next day Trefry asked Caesar to walk, when the heat was allayed, and designedly carried him by the cottage of the fair slave, and told him she whom he spoke of last night lived there retired. "But," says he, "I would not wish you to approach, for I am sure you will be in love as soon as you behold her." Caesar assured him he was proof against all the charms of that sex, and that if he imagined his heart could be so perfidious to love again, after Imoinda, he believed he should tear it from his bosom. They had no sooner spoke, but a little shock dog[8] that Clemene had presented her, which she took great delight in, ran out; and she, not knowing anybody was there, ran to get it in again, and bolted out on those who were just speaking of her. When seeing them, she would have run in again, but Trefry caught her by the hand and cried, "Clemene, however you fly a lover, you ought to pay some respect to this stranger" (pointing to Caesar). But she, as if she had

7. The sun.
8. A long-haired dog or poodle, especially associated with women of fashion.

resolved never to raise her eyes to the face of a man again, bent 'em the more to the earth when he spoke, and gave the Prince the leisure to look the more at her. There needed no long gazing or consideration to examine who this fair creature was; he soon saw Imoinda all over her; in a minute he saw her face, her shape, her air, her modesty, and all that called forth his soul with joy at his eyes, and left his body destitute of almost life; it stood without motion, and for a minute knew not that it had a being; and I believe he had never come to himself, so oppressed he was with over-joy, if he had not met with this allay, that he perceived Imoinda fall dead in the hands of Trefry. This awakened him, and he ran to her aid and caught her in his arms, where by degrees she came to herself; and 'tis needless to tell with what transports, what ecstasies of joy, they both a while beheld each other, without speaking; then snatched each other to their arms; then gaze again, as if they still doubted whether they possessed the blessing they grasped; but when they recovered their speech, 'tis not to be imagined what tender things they expressed to each other, wondering what strange fate had brought 'em again together. They soon informed each other of their fortunes, and equally bewailed their fate; but at the same time they mutually protested that even fetters and slavery were soft and easy, and would be supported with joy and pleasure, while they could be so happy to possess each other and to be able to make good their vows. Caesar swore he disdained the empire of the world while he could behold his Imoinda; and she despised grandeur and pomp, those vanities of her sex, when she could gaze on Oroonoko. He adored the very cottage where she resided, and said that little inch of the world would give him more happiness than all the universe could do; and she vowed it was a palace, while adorned with the presence of Oroonoko.

Trefry was infinitely pleased with this novel,[9] and found this Clemene was the fair mistress of whom Caesar had before spoke; and was not a little satisfied that heaven was so kind to the Prince as to sweeten his misfortunes by so lucky an accident; and leaving the lovers to themselves, was impatient to come down to Parham House (which was on the same plantation) to give me an account of what had happened. I was as impatient to make these lovers a visit, having already made a friendship with Caesar, and from his own mouth learned what I have related; which was confirmed by his Frenchman, who was set on shore to seek his fortunes, and of whom they could not make a slave, because a Christian, and he came daily to Parham Hill to see and pay his respects to his pupil prince. So that concerning and interesting myself in all that related to Caesar, whom I had assured of liberty as soon as the Governor arrived, I hasted presently to the place where the lovers were, and was infinitely glad to find this beautiful young slave (who had already gained all our esteems, for her modesty and her extraordinary prettiness) to be the same I had heard Caesar speak so much of. One may imagine then we paid her a treble respect; and though, from her being carved in fine flowers and birds all over her body, we took her to be of quality before, yet when we knew Clemene was Imoinda, we could not enough admire her.

I had forgot to tell you that those who are nobly born of that country are so delicately cut and rased[1] all over the forepart of the trunk of their bodies, that it looks as if it were japanned, the works being raised like high point round the edges of the flowers. Some are only carved with a little flower or bird at the sides of the temples, as was Caesar; and those who are so carved over the body resemble our ancient Picts,[2] that are figured in the chronicles, but these carvings are more delicate.

From that happy day Caesar took Clemene for his wife, to the general joy of all people; and there was as much magnificence as the country would afford at the celebration of this wedding: and in a very short time after she conceived with child, which made Caesar even adore her, knowing he was the last of his great race. This new accident made him more impatient of liberty, and he was every day treating with Trefry for his and Clemene's liberty, and offered either gold or a vast quantity of slaves, which should be paid before they let him go, provided he could have any security that he should go when his ransom was paid. They fed him from day to day with promises, and delayed him till the Lord Governor should come; so that he began to suspect them of falsehood, and that they would delay him till the time of his wife's delivery and make a slave of that too, for all the breed is theirs to whom the parents belong. This thought made him very uneasy, and his sullenness gave them some jealousies[3] of him; so that I was obliged, by some persons who feared a mutiny (which is very fatal sometimes in those colonies, that abound so with slaves that they exceed the whites in vast numbers), to discourse with Caesar, and to give him all the satisfaction I possibly could; they knew he and Clemene were scarce an hour in a day from my lodgings, that they eat with me, and that I obliged 'em in all things I was capable of. I entertained him with the lives of the Romans, and great men, which charmed him to my company, and her with teaching her all the pretty works[4] that I was mistress of, and telling her stories of nuns, and endeavoring to bring her to the knowledge of the true God. But of all discourses Caesar liked that the worst, and would never be reconciled to our notions of the Trinity, of which he ever made a jest; it was a riddle, he said, would turn his brain to conceive, and one could not make him understand what faith was. However, these conversations failed not altogether so well to divert him that he liked the company of us women much above the men, for he could not drink, and he is but an ill companion in that country that cannot. So that obliging him to love us very well, we had all the liberty of speech with him, especially myself, whom he called his Great Mistress; and indeed my word would go a great way with him. For these reasons, I had opportunity to take notice to him that he was not well pleased of late as he used to be, was more retired and thoughtful; and told him I took it ill he should suspect we would break our words with him, and not permit both him and Clemene to return to his own kingdom, which was not so long a way but when he was once on his voyage he would quickly arrive there. He made me some answers that showed a doubt in him, which made me ask him what advantage it would be to doubt. It would but give us a fear of him, and possibly compel us to treat him so as I should be very loath to behold; that is, it might occasion his confinement. Perhaps this was not so luckily spoke of me, for I perceived he resented that word, which I strove to soften again in vain. However, he

2. A North British people appearing in histories of England and Scotland.

3. Suspicions.

4. Decorative needlework or other handiwork.

assured me that whatsoever resolutions he should take, he would act nothing upon the white people; and as for myself and those upon that plantation where he was, he would sooner forfeit his eternal liberty, and life itself, than lift his hand against his greatest enemy on that place. He besought me to suffer no fears upon his account, for he could do nothing that honor should not dictate; but he accused himself for having suffered slavery so long; yet he charged that weakness on Love alone, who was capable of making him neglect even glory itself, and for which now he reproaches himself every moment of the day. Much more to this effect he spoke, with an air impatient enough to make me know he would not be long in bondage; and though he suffered only the name of a slave, and had nothing of the toil and labor of one, yet that was sufficient to render him uneasy; and he had been too long idle, who used to be always in action and in arms. He had a spirit all rough and fierce, and that could not be tamed to lazy rest; and though all endeavors were used to exercise himself in such actions and sports as this world afforded, as running, wrestling, pitching the bar,[5] hunting and fishing, chasing and killing tigers[6] of a monstrous size, which this continent affords in abundance, and wonderful snakes, such as Alexander is reported to have encountered at the river of Amazons,[7] and which Caesar took great delight to overcome, yet these were not actions great enough for his large soul, which was still panting after more renowned action.

Before I parted that day with him, I got, with much ado, a promise from him to rest yet a little longer with patience, and wait the coming of the Lord Governor, who was every day expected on our shore; he assured me he would, and this promise he desired me to know was given perfectly in complaisance to me, in whom he had an entire confidence.

After this, I neither thought it convenient to trust him much out of our view, nor did the country, who feared him; but with one accord it was advised to treat him fairly, and oblige him to remain within such a compass, and that he should be permitted as seldom as could be to go up to the plantations of the Negroes or, if he did, to be accompanied by some that should be rather in appearance attendants than spies. This care was for some time taken, and Caesar looked upon it as a mark of extraordinary respect, and was glad his discontent had obliged 'em to be more observant to him. He received new assurance from the overseer, which was confirmed to him by the opinion of all the gentlemen of the country, who made their court to him. During this time that we had his company more frequently than hitherto we had had, it may not be unpleasant to relate to you the diversions we entertained him with, or rather he us.

My stay was to be short in that country, because my father died at sea, and never arrived to possess the honor was designed him (which was lieutenant general of six and thirty islands, besides the continent[8] of Surinam) nor the advantages he hoped to reap by them; so that though we were obliged to continue on our voyage, we did not intend to stay upon the place. Though, in a word, I must say thus much of it, that certainly had his late Majesty, of

---

5. A game in which players compete in throwing a heavy bar or rod.

6. Wild cats, including the South American jaguar and cougar.

7. Alexander the Great is supposed to have encountered both snakes and Amazons in a campaign against India.

8. "Land not disjoined by the sea from other lands" (Johnson's *Dictionary*).

sacred memory, but seen and known what a vast and charming world he had been master of in that continent, he would never have parted so easily with it to the Dutch. 'Tis a continent whose vast extent was never yet known, and may contain more noble earth than all the universe besides, for, they say, it reaches from east to west, one way as far as China and another to Peru. It affords all things both for beauty and use; 'tis there eternal spring, always the very months of April, May, and June; the shades are perpetual, the trees bearing at once all degrees of leaves and fruit, from blooming buds to ripe autumn: groves of oranges, lemons, citrons, figs, nutmegs, and noble aromatics, continually bearing their fragrancies. The trees appearing all like nosegays adorned with flowers of different kinds; some are all white, some purple, some scarlet, some blue, some yellow; bearing, at the same time, ripe fruit and blooming young, or producing every day new. The very wood of all these trees has an intrinsic value above common timber, for they are, when cut, of different colors, glorious to behold, and bear a price considerable, to inlay withal. Besides this they yield rich balm and gums, so that we make our candles of such an aromatic substance as does not only give a sufficient light, but, as they burn, they cast their perfumes all about. Cedar is the common firing, and all the houses are built with it. The very meat we eat, when set on the table, if it be native, I mean of the country, perfumes the whole room; especially a little beast called an armadilly, a thing which I can liken to nothing so well as a rhinoceros; 'tis all in white armor, so jointed that it moves as well in it as if it had nothing on; this beast is about the bigness of a pig of six weeks old. But it were endless to give an account of all the diverse wonderful and strange things that country affords, and which we took a very great delight to go in search of, though those adventures are oftentimes fatal and at least dangerous. But while we had Caesar in our company on these designs we feared no harm, nor suffered any.

As soon as I came into the country, the best house in it was presented me, called St. John's Hill. It stood on a vast rock of white marble, at the foot of which the river ran a vast depth down, and not to be descended on that side; the little waves still dashing and washing the foot of this rock made the softest murmurs and purlings in the world; and the opposite bank was adorned with such vast quantities of different flowers eternally blowing,[9] and every day and hour new, fenced behind 'em with lofty trees of a thousand rare forms and colors, that the prospect was the most ravishing that fancy can create.[1] On the edge of this white rock, towards the river, was a walk or grove of orange and lemon trees, about half the length of the Mall[2] here, whose flowery and fruit-bearing branches met at the top and hindered the sun, whose rays are very fierce there, from entering a beam into the grove; and the cool air that came from the river made it not only fit to entertain people in, at all the hottest hours of the day, but refreshed the sweet blossoms and made it always sweet and charming; and sure the whole globe of the world cannot show so delightful a place as this grove was. Not all the gardens of boasted Italy can produce a shade to outvie this, which nature had joined with art to render so exceeding fine; and 'tis a marvel to see how such vast

---

9. Blooming.
1. The original editions read "the most raving that sands can create," altered to "ravishing" in the third edition, which also corrects the next sentence, "fruity bear branches."
2. Fashionable walk in St. James's Park in London.

trees, as big as English oaks, could take footing on so solid a rock and in so little earth as covered that rock; but all things by nature there are rare, delightful, and wonderful. But to our sports.

Sometimes we would go surprising,[3] and in search of young tigers in their dens, watching when the old ones went forth to forage for prey; and oftentimes we have been in great danger and have fled apace for our lives when surprised by the dams. But once, above all other times, we went on this design, and Caesar was with us, who had no sooner stolen a young tiger from her nest but, going off, we encountered the dam, bearing a buttock of a cow which he[4] had torn off with his mighty paw, and going with it towards his den. We had only four women, Caesar, and an English gentleman, brother to Harry Martin, the great Oliverian;[5] we found there was no escaping this enraged and ravenous beast. However, we women fled as fast as we could from it; but our heels had not saved our lives if Caesar had not laid down his cub, when he found the tiger quit her prey to make the more speed towards him, and taking Mr. Martin's sword, desired him to stand aside, or follow the ladies. He obeyed him, and Caesar met this monstrous beast of might, size, and vast limbs, who came with open jaws upon him; and fixing his awful stern eyes full upon those of the beast, and putting himself into a very steady and good aiming posture of defense, ran his sword quite through his breast down to his very heart, home to the hilt of the sword. The dying beast stretched forth her paw, and going to grasp his thigh, surprised with death in that very moment, did him no other harm than fixing her long nails in his flesh very deep, feebly wounded him, but could not grasp the flesh to tear off any. When he had done this, he hallooed to us to return, which, after some assurance of his victory, we did, and found him lugging out the sword from the bosom of the tiger, who was laid in her blood on the ground; he took up the cub, and with an unconcern that had nothing of the joy or gladness of a victory, he came and laid the whelp at my feet. We all extremely wondered at his daring, and at the bigness of the beast, which was about the heighth of a heifer but of mighty, great, and strong limbs.

Another time, being in the woods, he killed a tiger which had long infested that part, and borne away abundance of sheep and oxen, and other things that were for the support of those to whom they belonged; abundance of people assailed this beast, some affirming they had shot her with several bullets quite through the body at several times, and some swearing they shot her through the very heart, and they believed she was a devil rather than a mortal thing. Caesar had often said he had a mind to encounter this monster, and spoke with several gentlemen who had attempted her, one crying, "I shot her with so many poisoned arrows," another with his gun in this part of her, and another in that; so that he, remarking all these places where she was shot, fancied still he should overcome her by giving her another sort of a wound than any had yet done; and one day said (at the table), "What trophies and garlands, ladies, will you make me, if I bring you home the heart of this ravenous beast that eats up all your lambs and pigs?" We all promised he should be rewarded at all our hands. So taking a bow, which he choosed out

---

3. A military term for making sudden raids.
4. The jarring mixture of pronouns in the two accounts of the tigers (wild cats) may suggest a reluctance to use a feminine pronoun in moments of extreme violence. The first account was left uncorrected in all four 17th-century editions.
5. Supporter of Oliver Cromwell.

of a great many, he went up in the wood, with two gentlemen, where he imagined this devourer to be; they had not passed very far in it but they heard her voice, growling and grumbling, as if she were pleased with something she was doing. When they came in view, they found her muzzling in the belly of a new ravished sheep, which she had torn open; and seeing herself approached, she took fast hold of her prey with her forepaws and set a very fierce raging look on Caesar, without offering to approach him, for fear at the same time of losing what she had in possession. So that Caesar remained a good while, only taking aim, and getting an opportunity to shoot her where he designed; 'twas some time before he could accomplish it, and to wound her and not kill her would but have enraged her more, and endangered him. He had a quiver of arrows at his side, so that if one failed he could be supplied; at last, retiring a little, he gave her opportunity to eat, for he found she was ravenous, and fell to as soon as she saw him retire, being more eager of her prey than of doing new mischiefs. When he going softly to one side of her, and hiding his person behind certain herbage that grew high and thick, he took so good aim that, as he intended, he shot her just into the eye, and the arrow was sent with so good a will and so sure a hand that it stuck in her brain, and made her caper and become mad for a moment or two; but being seconded by another arrow, he fell dead upon the prey. Caesar cut him open with a knife, to see where those wounds were that had been reported to him, and why he did not die of 'em. But I shall now relate a thing that possibly will find no credit among men, because 'tis a notion commonly received with us, that nothing can receive a wound in the heart and live; but when the heart of this courageous animal was taken out, there were seven bullets of lead in it, and the wounds seamed up with great scars, and she lived with the bullets a great while, for it was long since they were shot. This heart the conqueror brought up to us, and 'twas a very great curiosity, which all the country came to see, and which gave Caesar occasion of many fine discourses, of accidents in war and strange escapes.

At other times he would go a-fishing; and discoursing on that diversion, he found we had in that country a very strange fish, called a numb eel[6] (an eel of which I have eaten), that while it is alive, it has a quality so cold, that those who are angling, though with a line of never so great a length with a rod at the end of it, it shall, in the same minute the bait is touched by this eel, seize him or her that holds the rod with benumbedness, that shall deprive 'em of sense for a while; and some have fallen into the water, and others dropped as dead on the banks of the rivers where they stood, as soon as this fish touches the bait. Caesar used to laugh at this, and believed it impossible a man could lose his force at the touch of a fish, and could not understand that philosophy,[7] that a cold quality should be of that nature. However, he had a great curiosity to try whether it would have the same effect on him it had on others, and often tried, but in vain. At last the sought for fish came to the bait, as he stood angling on the bank; and instead of throwing away the rod or giving it a sudden twitch out of the water, whereby he might have caught both the eel and have dismissed the rod, before it could have too much power over him, for experiment sake he grasped it but the harder, and fainting fell into the river; and being still possessed of the rod, the tide carried

6. Electric eel.
7. "Hypothesis or system upon which natural effects are explained" (Johnson's *Dictionary*).

him, senseless as he was, a great way, till an Indian boat took him up, and perceived when they touched him a numbness seize them, and by that knew the rod was in his hand; which with a paddle (that is, a short oar) they struck away, and snatched it into the boat, eel and all. If Caesar were almost dead with the effect of this fish, he was more so with that of the water, where he had remained the space of going a league, and they found they had much ado to bring him back to life. But at last they did, and brought him home, where he was in a few hours well recovered and refreshed, and not a little ashamed to find he should be overcome by an eel, and that all the people who heard his defiance would laugh at him. But we cheered him up; and he being convinced, we had the eel at supper, which was a quarter of an ell about and most delicate meat, and was of the more value, since it cost so dear as almost the life of so gallant a man.

About this time we were in many mortal fears about some disputes the English had with the Indians, so that we could scarce trust ourselves, without great numbers, to go to any Indian towns or place where they abode, for fear they should fall upon us, as they did immediately after my coming away; and that it was in the possession of the Dutch, who used 'em not so civilly as the English, so that they cut in pieces all they could take, getting into houses and hanging up the mother and all her children about her, and cut a footman I left behind me all in joints, and nailed him to trees.

This feud began while I was there, so that I lost half the satisfaction I proposed, in not seeing and visiting the Indian towns. But one day, bemoaning of our misfortunes upon this account, Caesar told us we need not fear, for if we had a mind to go, he would undertake to be our guard. Some would, but most would not venture; about eighteen of us resolved and took barge, and after eight days arrived near an Indian town. But approaching it, the hearts of some of our company failed, and they would not venture on shore; so we polled who would and who would not. For my part, I said if Caesar would, I would go; he resolved; so did my brother and my woman, a maid of good courage. Now none of us speaking the language of the people, and imagining we should have a half diversion in gazing only and not knowing what they said, we took a fisherman that lived at the mouth of the river, who had been a long inhabitant there, and obliged him to go with us. But because he was known to the Indians, as trading among 'em, and being by long living there become a perfect Indian in color, we, who resolved to surprise 'em by making 'em see something they never had seen (that is, white people), resolved only myself, my brother and woman should go; so Caesar, the fisherman, and the rest, hiding behind some thick reeds and flowers that grew on the banks, let us pass on towards the town, which was on the bank of the river all along. A little distant from the houses, or huts, we saw some dancing, others busied in fetching and carrying of water from the river. They had no sooner spied us but they set up a loud cry, that frighted us at first; we thought it had been for those that should kill us, but it seems it was of wonder and amazement. They were all naked, and we were dressed so as is most commode[8] for the hot countries, very glittering and rich, so that we appeared extremely fine; my own hair was cut short, and I had a taffety cap with black feathers on my head; my brother was in a stuff[9] suit, with silver loops and buttons and abundance of green ribbon. This was all infinitely surprising to

8. Suitable.   9. Woven fabric, worsted.

them, and because we saw them stand still till we approached 'em, we took heart and advanced, came up to 'em, and offered 'em our hands; which they took, and looked on us round about, calling still for more company; who came swarming out, all wondering and crying out *"Tepeeme,"* taking their hair up in their hands and spreading it wide to those they called out to, as if they would say (as indeed it signified) "Numberless wonders," or not to be recounted, no more than to number the hair of their heads. By degrees they grew more bold, and from gazing upon us round, they touched us, laying their hands upon all the features of our faces, feeling our breasts and arms, taking up one petticoat, then wondering to see another; admiring our shoes and stockings, but more our garters, which we gave 'em, and they tied about their legs, being laced with silver lace at the ends, for they much esteem any shining things. In fine, we suffered 'em to survey us as they pleased, and we thought they would never have done admiring us. When Caesar and the rest saw we were received with such wonder, they came up to us; and finding the Indian trader whom they knew (for 'tis by these fishermen, called Indian traders, we hold a commerce with 'em, for they love not to go far from home, and we never go to them), when they saw him therefore they set up a new joy, and cried, in their language, "Oh! here's our *tiguamy,* and we shall now know whether those things can speak." So advancing to him, some of 'em gave him their hands and cried, *"Amora tiguamy,"* which is as much as, "How do you?" or "Welcome, friend," and all with one din began to gabble to him, and asked if we had sense and wit; if we could talk of affairs of life and war, as they could do; if we could hunt, swim, and do a thousand things they use. He answered 'em, we could. Then they invited us into their houses, and dressed venison and buffalo for us; and going out, gathered a leaf of a tree called a *sarumbo* leaf, of six yards long, and spread it on the ground for a tablecloth; and cutting another in pieces instead of plates, setting us on little bow Indian stools, which they cut out of one entire piece of wood and paint in a sort of japan work. They serve everyone their mess on these pieces of leaves, and it was very good, but too high seasoned with pepper. When we had eat, my brother and I took out our flutes and played to 'em, which gave 'em new wonder; and I soon perceived, by an admiration that is natural to these people, and by the extreme ignorance and simplicity of 'em, it were not difficult to establish any unknown or extravagant religion among them, and to impose any notions or fictions upon 'em. For seeing a kinsman of mine set some paper afire with a burning glass, a trick they had never before seen, they were like to have adored him for a god, and begged he would give them the characters or figures of his name, that they might oppose it against winds and storms; which he did, and they held it up in those seasons, and fancied it had a charm to conquer them, and kept it like a holy relic. They are very superstitious, and called him the great *Peeie,* that is, prophet. They showed us their Indian *Peeie,* a youth of about sixteen years old, as handsome as nature could make a man. They consecrate a beautiful youth from his infancy, and all arts are used to complete him in the finest manner, both in beauty and shape. He is bred to all the little arts and cunning they are capable of, to all the legerdemain tricks and sleight of hand, whereby he imposes upon the rabble, and is both a doctor in physic and divinity; and by these tricks makes the sick believe he sometimes eases their pains, by drawing from the afflicted part little serpents, or odd flies, or worms, or any strange thing; and though they have besides undoubted good remedies for almost all their diseases, they cure the patient more by fancy than by medicines, and make themselves feared, loved, and reverenced. This young *Peeie* had a very young wife, who seeing my brother kiss her, came running and kissed me; after this they kissed one another, and made it a very great jest, it being so novel; and new admiration and laughing went round the multitude, that they never will forget that ceremony, never before used or known. Caesar had a mind to see and talk with their war captains, and we were conducted to one of their houses, where we beheld several of the great captains, who had been at council. But so frightful a vision it was to see 'em no fancy can create; no such dreams can represent so dreadful a spectacle. For my part I took 'em for hobgoblins or fiends rather than men; but however their shapes appeared, their souls were very humane and noble; but some wanted their noses, some their lips, some both noses and lips, some their ears, and others cut through each cheek with long slashes, through which their teeth appeared; they had other several formidable wounds and scars, or rather dismemberings. They had *comitias* or little aprons before 'em, and girdles of cotton, with their knives naked, stuck in it; a bow at their backs and a quiver of arrows on their thighs; and most had feathers on their heads of diverse colors. They cried "*Amora tiguamy*" to us at our entrance, and were pleased we said as much to 'em; they seated us, and gave us drink of the best sort, and wondered, as much as the others had done before, to see us. Caesar was marveling as much at their faces, wondering how they should all be so wounded in war; he was impatient to know how they all came by those frightful marks of rage or malice, rather than wounds got in noble battle. They told us, by our interpreter, that when any war was waging, two men chosen out by some old captain whose fighting was past, and who could only teach the theory of war, these two men were to stand in competition for the generalship, or great war captain; and being brought before the old judges, now past labor, they are asked what they dare do to show they are worthy to lead an army. When he who is first asked, making no reply, cuts off his nose, and throws it contemptibly[1] on the ground; and the other does something to himself that he thinks surpasses him, and perhaps deprives himself of lips and an eye; so they slash on till one gives out, and many have died in this debate. And 'tis by a passive valor they show and prove their activity, a sort of courage too brutal to be applauded by our black hero; nevertheless he expressed his esteem of 'em.

In this voyage Caesar begot so good an understanding between the Indians and the English that there were no more fears or heart-burnings during our stay, but we had a perfect, open, and free trade with 'em. Many things remarkable and worthy reciting we met with in this short voyage, because Caesar made it his business to search out and provide for our entertainment, especially to please his dearly adored Imoinda, who was a sharer in all our adventures; we being resolved to make her chains as easy as we could, and to compliment the Prince in that manner that most obliged him.

As we were coming up again, we met with some Indians of strange aspects; that is, of a larger size and other sort of features than those of our country. Our Indian slaves that rowed us asked 'em some questions, but they could

---

1. With contempt.

not understand us; but showed us a long cotton string with several knots on it, and told us, they had been coming from the mountains so many moons as there were knots. They were habited in skins of a strange beast, and brought along with 'em bags of gold dust, which, as well as they could give us to understand, came streaming in little small channels down the high mountains when the rains fell; and offered to be the convoy to any body or persons that would go to the mountains. We carried these men up to Parham, where they were kept till the Lord Governor came. And because all the country was mad to be going on this golden adventure, the Governor by his letters commanded (for they sent some of the gold to him) that a guard should be set at the mouth of the river of Amazons[2] (a river so called, almost as broad as the river of Thames) and prohibited all people from going up that river, it conducting to those mountains of gold. But we going off for England before the project was further prosecuted, and the Governor being drowned in a hurricane, either the design died, or the Dutch have the advantage of it. And 'tis to be bemoaned what his Majesty lost by losing that part of America.

Though this digression is a little from my story, however since it contains some proofs of the curiosity and daring of this great man, I was content to omit nothing of his character.

It was thus for some time we diverted him; but now Imoinda began to show she was with child, and did nothing but sigh and weep for the captivity of her lord, herself, and the infant yet unborn, and believed if it were so hard to gain the liberty of two, 'twould be more difficult to get that for three. Her griefs were so many darts in the great heart of Caesar; and taking his opportunity one Sunday when all the whites were overtaken in drink, as there were abundance of several trades and slaves for four years[3] that inhabited among the Negro houses, and Sunday was their day of debauch (otherwise they were a sort of spies upon Caesar), he went pretending out of goodness to 'em to feast amongst 'em; and sent all his music, and ordered a great treat for the whole gang, about three hundred Negroes; and about a hundred and fifty were able to bear arms, such as they had, which were sufficient to do execution[4] with spirits accordingly. For the English had none but rusty swords that no strength could draw from a scabbard, except the people of particular quality, who took care to oil 'em and keep 'em in good order. The guns also, unless here and there one, or those newly carried from England, would do no good or harm; for 'tis the nature of that country to rust and eat up iron, or any metals but gold and silver. And they are very unexpert at the bow, which the Negroes and Indians are perfect masters of.

Caesar, having singled out these men from the women and children, made an harangue to 'em of the miseries and ignominies of slavery, counting up all their toils and sufferings, under such loads, burdens, and drudgeries as were fitter for beasts than men, senseless brutes than human souls. He told 'em, it was not for days, months, or years, but for eternity; there was no end to be of their misfortunes. They suffered not like men, who might find a glory and fortitude in oppression, but like dogs that loved the whip and bell,[5] and fawned the more they were beaten. That they had lost the divine quality of

2. The mouth of the Amazon, in Brazil, is far distant from Surinam.
3. Tradesmen, and whites who for crimes or debt were indentured for a fixed period.

4. Harm, slaughter.
5. Proverbial for something that distracts from comfort or pleasure, from the protective charm on chariots of triumphing generals in ancient Rome.

men and were become insensible asses, fit only to bear; nay, worse: an ass, or dog, or horse, having done his duty, could lie down in retreat and rise to work again, and while he did his duty endured no stripes; but men, villainous, senseless men such as they, toiled on all the tedious week till Black Friday;[6] and then, whether they worked or not, whether they were faulty or meriting, they promiscuously, the innocent with the guilty, suffered the infamous whip, the sordid stripes, from their fellow slaves, till their blood trickled from all parts of their body, blood whose every drop ought to be revenged with a life of some of those tyrants that impose it. "And why," said he, "my dear friends and fellow sufferers, should we be slaves to an unknown people? Have they vanquished us nobly in fight? Have they won us in honorable battle? And are we by the chance of war become their slaves? This would not anger a noble heart, this would not animate a soldier's soul; no, but we are bought and sold like apes or monkeys, to be the sport of women, fools, and cowards, and the support of rogues, runagades,[7] that have abandoned their own countries for rapine, murders, thefts, and villainies. Do you not hear every day how they upbraid each other with infamy of life, below the wildest savages; and shall we render obedience to such a degenerate race, who have no one human virtue left to distinguish 'em from the vilest creatures? Will you, I say, suffer the lash from such hands?" They all replied, with one accord, "No, no, no; Caesar has spoke like a great captain, like a great king."

After this he would have proceeded, but was interrupted by a tall Negro of some more quality than the rest; his name was Tuscan; who bowing at the feet of Caesar, cried, "My lord, we have listened with joy and attention to what you have said, and, were we only men, would follow so great a leader through the world. But oh! consider, we are husbands and parents too, and have things more dear to us than life, our wives and children, unfit for travel in these unpassable woods, mountains, and bogs; we have not only difficult lands to overcome, but rivers to wade, and monsters to encounter, ravenous beasts of prey—." To this, Caesar replied that honor was the first principle in nature that was to be obeyed; but as no man would pretend to that, without all the acts of virtue, compassion, charity, love, justice, and reason, he found it not inconsistent with that to take an equal care of their wives and children as they would of themselves; and that he did not design, when he led them to freedom and glorious liberty, that they should leave that better part of themselves to perish by the hand of the tyrant's whip. But if there were a woman among them so degenerate from love and virtue to choose slavery before the pursuit of her husband, and with the hazard of her life to share with him in his fortunes, that such a one ought to be abandoned, and left as a prey to the common enemy.

To which they all agreed—and bowed. After this, he spoke of the impassable woods and rivers, and convinced 'em, the more danger, the more glory. He told them that he had heard of one Hannibal, a great captain, had cut his way through mountains of solid rocks;[8] and should a few shrubs oppose them, which they could fire before 'em? No, 'twas a trifling excuse to men resolved to die or overcome. As for bogs, they are with a little labor filled and

---

6. Here a day of customary beating; more widely, a Friday bringing some notable disaster, from students' slang for examination day.

7. Renegades or fugitives.

8. The Carthaginian general and his troops literally hacked their way down the Alps into Italy to attack Rome.

hardened; and the rivers could be no obstacle, since they swam by nature, at least by custom, from their first hour of their birth. That when the children were weary they must carry them by turns, and the woods and their own industry would afford them food. To this they all assented with joy.

Tuscan then demanded what he would do. He said, they would travel towards the sea, plant a new colony, and defend it by their valor; and when they could find a ship, either driven by stress of weather or guided by Providence that way, they would seize it and make it a prize, till it had transported them to their own countries; at least, they should be made free in his kingdom, and be esteemed as his fellow sufferers, and men that had the courage and the bravery to attempt, at least, for liberty; and if they died in the attempt it would be more brave than to live in perpetual slavery.

They bowed and kissed his feet at this resolution, and with one accord vowed to follow him to death. And that night was appointed to begin their march; they made it known to their wives, and directed them to tie their hamaca[9] about their shoulder and under their arm like a scarf, and to lead their children that could go, and carry those that could not. The wives, who pay an entire obedience to their husbands, obeyed, and stayed for 'em where they were appointed. The men stayed but to furnish themselves with what defensive arms they could get; and all met at the rendezvous, where Caesar made a new encouraging speech to 'em, and led 'em out.

But as they could not march far that night, on Monday early, when the overseers went to call 'em all together to go to work, they were extremely surprised to find not one upon the place, but all fled with what baggage they had. You may imagine this news was not only suddenly spread all over the plantation, but soon reached the neighboring ones; and we had by noon about six hundred men they call the militia of the county, that came to assist us in the pursuit of the fugitives. But never did one see so comical an army march forth to war. The men of any fashion would not concern themselves, though it were almost the common cause; for such revoltings are very ill examples, and have very fatal consequences oftentimes in many colonies. But they had a respect for Caesar, and all hands were against the Parhamites, as they called those of Parham plantation, because they did not, in the first place, love the Lord Governor, and secondly they would have it that Caesar was ill used, and baffled with;[1] and 'tis not impossible but some of the best in the country was of his counsel in this flight, and depriving us of all the slaves; so that they of the better sort would not meddle in the matter. The deputy governor,[2] of whom I have had no great occasion to speak, and who was the most fawning fair-tongued fellow in the world and one that pretended the most friendship to Caesar, was now the only violent man against him; and though he had nothing, and so need fear nothing, yet talked and looked bigger than any man. He was a fellow whose character is not fit to be mentioned with the worst of the slaves. This fellow would lead his army forth to meet Caesar, or rather to pursue him; most of their arms were of those sort of cruel whips they call cat with nine tails; some had rusty useless guns for show, others old basket hilts[3] whose blades had never seen the light in this age, and others had long staffs and clubs. Mr. Trefry went along, rather

---

9. Hammock.
1. Cheated.
2. William Byam. There are recorded complaints

against him for high-handedness and from him about insubordination by settlers and slaves.
3. Swords with protective hilt guards.

to be a mediator than a conqueror in such a battle; for he foresaw and knew, if by fighting they put the Negroes into despair, they were a sort of sullen fellows that would drown or kill themselves before they would yield; and he advised that fair means was best. But Byam was one that abounded in his own wit and would take his own measures.

It was not hard to find these fugitives; for as they fled they were forced to fire and cut the woods before 'em, so that night or day they pursued 'em by the light they made and by the path they had cleared. But as soon as Caesar found he was pursued, he put himself in a posture of defense, placing all the women and children in the rear, and himself with Tuscan by his side, or next to him, all promising to die or conquer. Encouraged thus, they never stood to parley, but fell on pell-mell upon the English, and killed some and wounded a good many, they having recourse to their whips as the best of their weapons. And as they observed no order, they perplexed the enemy so sorely with lashing 'em in the eyes; and the women and children seeing their husbands so treated, being of fearful cowardly dispositions, and hearing the English cry out, "Yield and live, yield and be pardoned," they all run in amongst their husbands and fathers, and hung about 'em, crying out, "Yield, yield; and leave Caesar to their revenge"; that by degrees the slaves abandoned Caesar, and left him only Tuscan and his heroic Imoinda; who, grown big as she was, did nevertheless press near her lord, having a bow and a quiver full of poisoned arrows, which she managed with such dexterity that she wounded several, and shot the governor into the shoulder; of which wound he had like to have died, but that an Indian woman, his mistress, sucked the wound and cleansed it from the venom. But however, he stirred not from the place till he had parleyed with Caesar, who he found was resolved to die fighting, and would not be taken; no more would Tuscan, or Imoinda. But he, more thirsting after revenge of another sort than that of depriving him of life, now made use of all his art of talking and dissembling, and besought Caesar to yield himself upon terms which he himself should propose, and should be sacredly assented to and kept by him. He told him, it was not that he any longer feared him, or could believe the force of two men, and a young heroine, could overcome all them, with all the slaves now on their side also; but it was the vast esteem he had for his person, the desire he had to serve so gallant a man, and to hinder himself from the reproach hereafter of having been the occasion of the death of a prince whose valor and magnanimity deserved the empire of the world. He protested to him, he looked upon this action as gallant and brave, however tending to the prejudice of his lord and master, who would by it have lost so considerable a number of slaves; that this flight of his should be looked on as a heat of youth, and rashness of a too forward courage, and an unconsidered impatience of liberty, and no more; and that he labored in vain to accomplish that which they would effectually perform as soon as any ship arrived that would touch on his coast. "So that if you will be pleased," continued he, "to surrender yourself, all imaginable respect shall be paid you; and yourself, your wife, and child, if it be here born, shall depart free out of our land."

But Caesar would hear of no composition;[4] though Byam urged, if he pursued and went on in his design, he would inevitably perish, either by

4. Settlement.

great snakes, wild beasts, or hunger; and he ought to have regard to his wife, whose condition required ease, and not the fatigues of tedious travel, where she could not be secured from being devoured. But Caesar told him, there was no faith in the white men or the gods they adored, who instructed 'em in principles so false that honest men could not live amongst 'em; though no people professed so much, none performed so little; that he knew what he had to do when he dealt with men of honor, but with them a man ought to be eternally on his guard, and never to eat and drink with Christians without his weapon of defense in his hand; and for his own security, never to credit one word they spoke. As for the rashness and inconsiderateness of his action, he would confess the governor is in the right; and that he was ashamed of what he had done, in endeavoring to make those free who were by nature slaves, poor wretched rogues, fit to be used as Christians' tools; dogs, treacherous and cowardly, fit for such masters; and they wanted only but to be whipped into the knowledge of the Christian gods to be the vilest of all creeping things, to learn to worship such deities as had not power to make 'em just, brave, or honest. In fine, after a thousand things of this nature, not fit here to be recited, he told Byam he had rather die than live upon the same earth with such dogs. But Trefry and Byam pleaded and protested together so much that Trefry, believing the governor to mean what he said, and speaking very cordially himself, generously put himself into Caesar's hands, and took him aside and persuaded him, even with tears, to live, by surrendering himself, and to name his conditions. Caesar was overcome by his wit and reasons, and in consideration of Imoinda; and demanding what he desired, and that it should be ratified by their hands in writing, because he had perceived that was the common way of contract between man and man, amongst the whites. All this was performed, and Tuscan's pardon was put in, and they surrender to the governor, who walked peaceably down into the plantation with 'em, after giving order to bury their dead. Caesar was very much toiled with the bustle of the day, for he had fought like a fury; and what mischief was done he and Tuscan performed alone, and gave their enemies a fatal proof that they durst do anything and feared no mortal force.

But they were no sooner arrived at the place where all the slaves receive their punishments of whipping, but they laid hands on Caesar and Tuscan, faint with heat and toil; and surprising them, bound them to two several stakes, and whipped them in a most deplorable and inhuman manner, rending the very flesh from their bones; especially Caesar, who was not perceived to make any moan or to alter his face, only to roll his eyes on the faithless governor, and those he believed guilty, with fierceness and indignation; and to complete his rage, he saw every one of those slaves, who but a few days before adored him as something more than mortal, now had a whip to give him some lashes, while he strove not to break his fetters; though if he had, it were impossible. But he pronounced a woe and revenge from his eyes, that darted fire that 'twas at once both awful and terrible to behold.

When they thought they were sufficiently revenged on him, they untied him, almost fainting with loss of blood from a thousand wounds all over his body, from which they had rent his clothes, and led him bleeding and naked as he was, and loaded him all over with irons; and then rubbed his wounds, to complete their cruelty, with Indian pepper, which had like to have made him raving mad; and in this condition made him so fast to the ground that he could not stir, if his pains and wounds would have given him leave. They spared Imoinda, and did not let her see this barbarity committed towards her lord, but carried her down to Parham and shut her up; which was not in kindness to her, but for fear she should die with the sight, or miscarry, and then they should lose a young slave and perhaps the mother.

You must know, that when the news was brought on Monday morning that Caesar had betaken himself to the woods and carried with him all the Negroes, we were possessed with extreme fear, which no persuasions could dissipate, that he would secure himself till night, and then that he would come down and cut all our throats. This apprehension made all the females of us fly down the river, to be secured; and while we were away they acted this cruelty. For I suppose I had authority and interest enough there, had I suspected any such thing, to have prevented it; but we had not gone many leagues but the news overtook us that Caesar was taken and whipped like a common slave. We met on the river with Colonel Martin, a man of great gallantry, wit, and goodness, and whom I have celebrated in a character of my new comedy[5] by his own name, in memory of so brave a man. He was wise and eloquent and, from the fineness of his parts, bore a great sway over the hearts of all the colony. He was a friend to Caesar, and resented this false dealing with him very much. We carried him back to Parham, thinking to have made an accommodation; when we came, the first news we heard was that the governor was dead of a wound Imoinda had given him; but it was not so well. But it seems he would have the pleasure of beholding the revenge he took on Caesar, and before the cruel ceremony was finished, he dropped down; and then they perceived the wound he had on his shoulder was by a venomed arrow, which, as I said, his Indian mistress healed by sucking the wound.

We were no sooner arrived but we went up to the plantation to see Caesar, whom we found in a very miserable and unexpressible condition; and I have a thousand times admired how he lived, in so much tormenting pain. We said all things to him that trouble, pity, and good nature could suggest, protesting our innocency of the fact and our abhorrence of such cruelties; making a thousand professions of services to him and begging as many pardons for the offenders, till we said so much that he believed we had no hand in his ill treatment; but told us he could never pardon Byam; as for Trefry, he confessed he saw his grief and sorrow for his suffering, which he could not hinder, but was like to have been beaten down by the very slaves for speaking in his defense. But for Byam, who was their leader, their head—and should, by his justice and honor, have been an example to 'em—for him, he wished to live, to take a dire revenge of him, and said, "It had been well for him if he had sacrificed me, instead of giving me the contemptible[6] whip." He refused to talk much, but begging us to give him our hands, he took 'em, and protested never to lift up his to do us any harm. He had a great respect for Colonel Martin, and always took his counsel like that of a parent, and assured him he would obey him in anything but his revenge on Byam. "Therefore," said he, "for his own safety, let him speedily dispatch me; for if I could

---

5. *The Younger Brother, or The Amorous Jilt*, not produced until 1696 despite this piece of promo-tion.

6. Showing contempt.

dispatch myself I would not, till that justice were done to my injured person, and the contempt of a soldier. No, I would not kill myself, even after a whipping, but will be content to live with that infamy, and be pointed at by every grinning slave, till I have completed my revenge; and then you shall see that Oroonoko scorns to live with the indignity that was put on Caesar." All we could do could get no more words from him; and we took care to have him put immediately into a healing bath to rid him of his pepper, and ordered a chirurgeon[7] to anoint him with healing balm, which he suffered; and in some time he began to be able to walk and eat. We failed not to visit him every day, and to that end had him brought to an apartment at Parham.

The governor was no sooner recovered, and had heard of the menaces of Caesar, but he called his council; who (not to disgrace them, or burlesque the government there) consisted of such notorious villains as Newgate[8] never transported; and possibly originally were such who understood neither the laws of God or man, and had no sort of principles to make 'em worthy the name of men; but at the very council table would contradict and fight with one another, and swear so bloodily that 'twas terrible to hear and see 'em. (Some of 'em were afterwards hanged when the Dutch took possession of the place, others sent off in chains.) But calling these special rulers of the nation together, and requiring their counsel in this weighty affair, they all concluded that (Damn 'em) it might be their own cases; and that Caesar ought to be made an example to all the Negroes, to fright 'em from daring to threaten their betters, their lords and masters; and at this rate no man was safe from his own slaves; and concluded, *nemine contradicente*,[9] that Caesar should be hanged.

Trefry then thought it time to use his authority, and told Byam his command did not extend to his lord's plantation, and that Parham was as much exempt from the law as Whitehall;[1] and that they ought no more to touch the servants of the Lord——(who there represented the King's person) than they could those about the King himself; and that Parham was a sanctuary; and though his lord were absent in person, his power was still in being there, which he had entrusted with him as far as the dominions of his particular plantations reached, and all that belonged to it; the rest of the country, as Byam was lieutenant to his lord, he might exercise his tyranny upon. Trefry had others as powerful, or more, that interested themselves in Caesar's life, and absolutely said he should be defended. So turning the governor and his wise council out of doors (for they sat at Parham House), they set a guard upon our landing place, and would admit none but those we called friends to us and Caesar.

The governor having remained wounded at Parham till his recovery was completed, Caesar did not know but he was still there; and indeed, for the most part his time was spent there, for he was one that loved to live at other people's expense; and if he were a day absent, he was ten present there, and used to play and walk and hunt and fish with Caesar. So that Caesar did not at all doubt, if he once recovered strength, but he should find an opportunity of being revenged on him. Though after such a revenge, he could not hope to live, for if he escaped the fury of the English mobile,[2] who perhaps would

---

7. Surgeon.
8. The major London prison, from which criminals were transported to the colonies.
9. No one disagreeing (Latin).

1. The king's palace in London. Treffry stands as Lord Willoughby's deputy on his private land, Byam in the colony at large.
2. Common people or mob.

have been glad of the occasion to have killed him, he was resolved not to survive his whipping; yet he had, some tender hours, a repenting softness, which he called his fits of coward, wherein he struggled with Love for the victory of his heart, which took part with his charming Imoinda there; but for the most part his time was passed in melancholy thought and black designs. He considered, if he should do this deed and die, either in the attempt or after it, he left his lovely Imoinda a prey, or at best a slave, to the enraged multitude; his great heart could not endure that thought. "Perhaps," said he, "she may be first ravished by every brute, exposed first to their nasty lusts and then a shameful death." No; he could not live a moment under that apprehension, too insupportable to be borne. These were his thoughts and his silent arguments with his heart, as he told us afterwards; so that now resolving not only to kill Byam but all those he thought had enraged him, pleasing his great heart with the fancied slaughter he should make over the whole face of the plantation, he first resolved on a deed, that (however horrid it at first appeared to us all), when we had heard his reasons, we thought it brave and just. Being able to walk and, as he believed, fit for the execution of his great design, he begged Trefry to trust him into the air, believing a walk would do him good, which was granted him; and taking Imoinda with him, as he used to do in his more happy and calmer days, he led her up into a wood, where, after (with a thousand sighs, and long gazing silently on her face, while tears gushed, in spite of him, from his eyes) he told her his design first of killing her, and then his enemies, and next himself, and the impossibility of escaping, and therefore he told her the necessity of dying, he found the heroic wife faster pleading for death than he was to propose it, when she found his fixed resolution, and on her knees besought him not to leave her a prey to his enemies. He (grieved to death) yet pleased at her noble resolution, took her up, and embracing her with all the passion and languishment of a dying lover, drew his knife to kill this treasure of his soul, this pleasure of his eyes; while tears trickled down his cheeks, hers were smiling with joy she should die by so noble a hand, and be sent in her own country (for that's their notion of the next world) by him she so tenderly loved and so truly adored in this; for wives have a respect for their husbands equal to what any other people pay a deity, and when a man finds any occasion to quit his wife, if he love her, she dies by his hand; if not, he sells her, or suffers some other to kill her. It being thus, you may believe the deed was soon resolved on; and 'tis not to be doubted but the parting, the eternal leave-taking of two such lovers, so greatly born, so sensible,[3] so beautiful, so young, and so fond, must be very moving, as the relation of it was to me afterwards.

All that love could say in such cases being ended, and all the intermitting irresolutions being adjusted, the lovely, young, and adored victim lays herself down before the sacrificer; while he, with a hand resolved and a heart breaking within, gave the fatal stroke; first cutting her throat, and then severing her yet smiling face from that delicate body, pregnant as it was with fruits of tenderest love. As soon as he had done, he laid the body decently on leaves and flowers, of which he made a bed, and concealed it under the same coverlid of nature; only her face he left yet bare to look on. But when he found she was dead and past all retrieve, never more to bless him with her eyes and soft language, his grief swelled up to rage; he tore, he raved, he

3. Sensitive.

roared, like some monster of the wood, calling on the loved name of Imoinda. A thousand times he turned the fatal knife that did the deed toward his own heart, with a resolution to go immediately after her; but dire revenge, which now was a thousand times more fierce in his soul than before, prevents him; and he would cry out, "No; since I have sacrificed Imoinda to my revenge, shall I lose that glory which I have purchased so dear as at the price of the fairest, dearest, softest creature that ever nature made? No, no!" Then, at her name, grief would get the ascendant of rage, and he would lie down by her side and water her face with showers of tears, which never were wont to fall from those eyes. And however bent he was on his intended slaughter, he had not power to stir from the sight of this dear object, now more beloved and more adored than ever.

He remained in this deploring condition for two days, and never rose from the ground where he had made his sad sacrifice. At last, rousing from her side, and accusing himself with living too long now Imoinda was dead, and that the deaths of those barbarous enemies were deferred too long, he resolved now to finish the great work; but offering to rise, he found his strength so decayed that he reeled to and fro, like boughs assailed by contrary winds; so that he was forced to lie down again, and try to summons all his courage to his aid. He found his brains turned round, and his eyes were dizzy, and objects appeared not the same to him they were wont to do; his breath was short, and all his limbs surprised with a faintness he had never felt before. He had not eat in two days, which was one occasion of this feebleness, but excess of grief was the greatest; yet still he hoped he should recover vigor to act his design, and lay expecting it yet six days longer, still mourning over the dead idol of his heart, and striving every day to rise, but could not.

In all this time you may believe we were in no little affliction for Caesar and his wife; some were of opinion he was escaped never to return; others thought some accident had happened to him. But however, we failed not to send out an hundred people several ways to search for him; a party of about forty went that way he took, among whom was Tuscan, who was perfectly reconciled to Byam. They had not gone very far into the wood but they smelt an unusual smell, as of a dead body; for stinks must be very noisome that can be distinguished among such a quantity of natural sweets as every inch of that land produces. So that they concluded they should find him dead, or somebody that was so. They passed on towards it, as loathsome as it was, and made such a rustling among the leaves that lie thick on the ground, by continual falling, that Caesar heard he was approached; and though he had during the space of these eight days endeavored to rise, but found he wanted strength, yet looking up and seeing his pursuers, he rose and reeled to a neighboring tree, against which he fixed his back; and being within a dozen yards of those that advanced and saw him, he called out to them and bid them approach no nearer, if they would be safe. So that they stood still, and hardly believing their eyes, that would persuade them that it was Caesar that spoke to 'em, so much was he altered, they asked him what he had done with his wife, for they smelt a stink that almost struck them dead. He, pointing to the dead body, sighing, cried, "Behold her there." They put off the flowers that covered her with their sticks, and found she was killed, and cried out, "Oh, monster! that hast murdered thy wife." Then asking him why he did so cruel a deed, he replied, he had no leisure to answer impertinent questions. "You may go back," continued he, "and tell the faithless governor he may thank fortune that I am breathing my last, and that my arm is too feeble to obey my heart in what it had designed him." But his tongue faltering, and trembling, he could scarce end what he was saying. The English, taking advantage by his weakness, cried, "Let us take him alive by all means." He heard 'em; and as if he had revived from a fainting, or a dream, he cried out, "No, gentlemen, you are deceived; you will find no more Caesars to be whipped, no more find a faith in me. Feeble as you think me, I have strength yet left to secure me from a second indignity." They swore all anew, and he only shook his head and beheld them with scorn. Then they cried out, "Who will venture on this single man? Will nobody?" They stood all silent while Caesar replied, "Fatal will be the attempt to the first adventurer, let him assure himself," and at that word, held up his knife in a menacing posture. "Look ye, ye faithless crew," said he, " 'tis not life I seek, nor am I afraid of dying," and at that word cut a piece of flesh from his own throat, and threw it at 'em; "yet still I would live if I could, till I had perfected my revenge. But oh! it cannot be; I feel life gliding from my eyes and heart, and if I make not haste, I shall yet fall a victim to the shameful whip." At that, he ripped up his own belly, and took his bowels and pulled 'em out, with what strength he could; while some, on their knees imploring, besought him to hold his hand. But when they saw him tottering, they cried out, "Will none venture on him?" A bold English cried, "Yes, if he were the devil" (taking courage when he saw him almost dead); and swearing a horrid oath for his farewell to the world, he rushed on him; Caesar, with his armed hand, met him so fairly as stuck him to the heart, and he fell dead at his feet. Tuscan, seeing that, cried out, "I love thee, O Caesar, and therefore will not let thee die, if possible." And running to him, took him in his arms; but at the same time warding a blow that Caesar made at his bosom, he received it quite through his arm; and Caesar having not the strength to pluck the knife forth, though he attempted it, Tuscan neither pulled it out himself nor suffered it to be pulled out, but came down with it sticking in his arm; and the reason he gave for it was, because the air should not get into the wound. They put their hands across, and carried Caesar between six of 'em, fainted as he was, and they thought dead, or just dying; and they brought him to Parham, and laid him on a couch, and had the chirurgeon immediately to him, who dressed his wounds and sewed up his belly, and used means to bring him to life, which they effected. We ran all to see him, and if before we thought him so beautiful a sight, he was now so altered that his face was like a death's head blacked over, nothing but teeth and eyeholes. For some days we suffered nobody to speak to him, but caused cordials to be poured down his throat, which sustained his life; and in six or seven days he recovered his senses. For you must know that wounds are almost to a miracle cured in the Indies, unless wounds in the legs, which rarely ever cure.

When he was well enough to speak, we talked to him, and asked him some questions about his wife, and the reasons why he killed her; and he then told us what I have related of that resolution, and of his parting; and he besought us we would let him die, and was extremely afflicted to think it was possible he might live; he assured us if we did not dispatch him, he would prove very fatal to a great many. We said all we could to make him live, and gave him new assurances; but he begged we would not think so poorly of him, or of his love to Imoinda, to imagine we could flatter him to life again; but the chirurgeon assured him he could not live, and therefore he need not fear. We were all (but Caesar) afflicted at this news; and the sight was gashly;[4] his discourse was sad, and the earthly smell about him so strong that I was persuaded to leave the place for some time (being myself but sickly, and very apt to fall into fits of dangerous illness upon any extraordinary melancholy). The servants and Trefry and the chirurgeons promised all to take what possible care they could of the life of Caesar, and I, taking boat, went with other company to Colonel Martin's, about three days' journey down the river; but I was no sooner gone, but the governor taking Trefry about some pretended earnest business a day's journey up the river, having communicated his design to one Banister, a wild Irishman and one of the council, a fellow of absolute barbarity, and fit to execute any villainy, but was rich: he came up to Parham, and forcibly took Caesar, and had him carried to the same post where he was whipped; and causing him to be tied to it, and a great fire made before him, he told him he should die like a dog, as he was. Caesar replied, this was the first piece of bravery that ever Banister did, and he never spoke sense till he pronounced that word; and if he would keep it, he would declare, in the other world, that he was the only man of all the whites that ever he heard speak truth. And turning to the men that bound him, he said, "My friends, am I to die, or to be whipped?" And they cried, "Whipped! No, you shall not escape so well." And then he replied, smiling, "A blessing on thee," and assured them they need not tie him, for he would stand fixed like a rock, and endure death so as should encourage them to die. "But if you whip me," said he, "be sure you tie me fast."

He had learned to take tobacco; and when he was assured he should die, he desired they would give him a pipe in his mouth, ready lighted, which they did; and the executioner came, and first cut off his members,[5] and threw them into the fire; after that, with an ill-favored knife, they cut his ears, and his nose, and burned them; he still smoked on, as if nothing had touched him. Then they hacked off one of his arms, and still he bore up, and held his pipe; but at the cutting off the other arm, his head sunk, and his pipe dropped, and he gave up the ghost, without a groan or a reproach. My mother and sister were by him all the while, but not suffered to save him, so rude and wild were the rabble, and so inhuman were the justices, who stood by to see the execution, who after paid dearly enough for their insolence. They cut Caesar in quarters, and sent them to several of the chief plantations. One quarter was sent to Colonel Martin, who refused it, and swore he had rather see the quarters of Banister and the governor himself than those of Caesar on his plantations, and that he could govern his Negroes without terrifying and grieving them with frightful spectacles of a mangled king.

Thus died this great man, worthy of a better fate, and a more sublime wit than mine to write his praise; yet, I hope, the reputation of my pen is considerable enough to make his glorious name to survive to all ages, with that of the brave, the beautiful, and the constant Imoinda.

1688

---

4. Ghastly. 5. Genitals.

ANNE FINCH,
COUNTESS OF WINCHILSEA
1661–1720

Born into an ancient country family, Anne Kingsmill became a maid of honor at the court of Charles II. There she met Colonel Heneage Finch; in 1684 they married. During the short reign of James II they prospered at court, but at the king's fall in 1688 they were forced to retire, eventually settling on a beautiful family estate at Eastwell, in Kent, near the south coast of England. Here Colonel Finch became, in 1712, earl of Winchilsea, and here Lady Winchilsea wrote most of her poems, influenced, she said, by "the solitude and security of the country," and by "objects naturally inspiring soft and poetical imaginations." Her *Miscellany Poems on Several Occasions, Written by a Lady* were published in 1713. One poem, *The Spleen*, a description of the mysterious melancholic illness from which she and many other fashionable people suffered, achieved some fame; Pope seems to refer to it when he invokes the goddess Spleen in *The Rape of the Lock*. But Winchilsea's larger reputation began only a century later, when Wordsworth praised her for keeping her eye on external nature and for a style "often admirable, chaste, tender, and vigorous."

The Introduction[1]

Did I my lines intend for public view,
How many censures would their faults pursue!
Some would, because such words they do affect,
Cry they're insipid, empty, uncorrect.
5 And many have attained, dull and untaught,
The name of wit, only by finding fault.[2]
True judges might condemn their want of wit;
And all might say, they're by a woman writ.
Alas! a woman that attempts the pen,
10 Such an intruder on the rights of men,
Such a presumptuous creature is esteemed,
The fault can by no virtue be redeemed.
They tell us we mistake our sex and way;
Good breeding, fashion, dancing, dressing, play
15 Are the accomplishments we should desire;
To write, or read, or think, or to enquire,
Would cloud our beauty, and exhaust our time,
And interrupt the conquests of our prime;
Whilst the dull manage of a servile house
20 Is held by some our utmost art and use.
    Sure 'twas not ever thus, nor are we told
Fables,[3] of women that excelled of old;
To whom, by the diffusive hand of heaven,
Some share of wit and poetry was given.
25 On that glad day on which the Ark[4] returned,

1. This preface to Winchilsea's work was never published during her lifetime, for reasons explained in the poem itself.
2. Pronounced *fawt*.

3. Idle stories or lies.
4. The Ark of the Covenant, restored to Jerusalem by David (1 Chronicles 15).

The holy pledge for which the land had mourned,
The joyful tribes attend it on the way,
The Levites do the sacred charge convey,
Whilst various instruments before it play;
30 Here holy virgins in the concert join,[5]
The louder notes to soften and refine,
And with alternate verse[6] complete the hymn divine.
    Lo! the young poet,° after God's own heart,   *David*
By Him inspired and taught the Muses' art,
35 Returned from conquest a bright chorus meets,
That sing his slain ten thousand in the streets.[7]
In such loud numbers[8] they his acts declare,
Proclaim the wonders of his early war,
That Saul upon the vast applause does frown,
40 And feels its mighty thunder shake the crown.
What can the threatened judgment now prolong?[9]
Half of the kingdom is already gone;
The fairest half, whose influence guides the rest,
Have David's empire o'er their hearts confessed.
45   A woman here leads fainting Israel on,
She fights, she wins, she triumphs with a song,[1]
Devout, majestic, for the subject fit,
And far above her arms, exalts her wit,
Then to the peaceful, shady palm withdraws,
50 And rules the rescued nation with her laws.
    How are we fallen! fallen by mistaken rules,
And education's, more than nature's fools;
Debarred from all improvements of the mind,
And to be dull, expected and designed;°   *intended*
55 And if some one would soar above the rest,
With warmer fancy and ambition pressed,
So strong the opposing faction still appears,
The hopes to thrive can ne'er outweigh the fears.
Be cautioned, then, my Muse, and still retired;
60 Nor be despised, aiming to be admired;
Conscious of wants, still with contracted wing,
To some few friends and to thy sorrows sing.
For groves of laurel thou wert never meant;
Be dark enough thy shades, and be thou there content.

1689?   1903

A Nocturnal Reverie

In such a night,[1] when every louder wind
Is to its distant cavern safe confined;

5. Pronounced *jine*.
6. A series of couplets. The choir of virgins, not mentioned in Chronicles, is imagined by Winchilsea as chanting every other line, responsively, as in some of the Psalms.
7. 1 Samuel 18.6–7.
8. Measures of music and verse.
9. What can now stave off the threatened judg-

ment? Saul's doom ("judgment") had been prophesied: God would replace him with a better king.
1. The prophet and judge Deborah sang to praise the Lord for the victory she herself had brought about (Judges 4–5).
1. This phrase, repeated twice below, echoes the same repeated phrase in the night piece that opens act 5 of *The Merchant of Venice*.

And only gentle Zephyr fans his wings,
And lonely Philomel,° still waking, sings;   *nightingale*
5   Or from some tree, famed for the owl's delight,
She, hollowing clear, directs the wanderer right:
In such a night, when passing clouds give place,
Or thinly veil the heavens' mysterious face;
When in some river, overhung with green,
10 The waving moon and trembling leaves are seen;
When freshened grass now bears itself upright,
And makes cool banks to pleasing rest invite,
Whence springs the woodbind, and the bramble-rose,
And where the sleepy cowslip sheltered grows;
15 Whilst now a paler hue the foxglove takes,
Yet checkers still with red the dusky brakes:
When scattered glow-worms, but in twilight fine,
Show trivial beauties watch their hour to shine;
Whilst Salisbury² stands the test of every light,
20 In perfect charms, and perfect virtue bright:
When odors, which declined repelling day,
Through temperate air uninterrupted stray;
When darkened groves their softest shadows wear,
And falling waters we distinctly hear;
25 When through the gloom more venerable shows
Some ancient fabric,° awful in repose,   *edifice*
While sunburnt hills their swarthy looks conceal,
And swelling haycocks thicken up the vale:
When the loosed horse now, as his pasture leads,
30 Comes slowly grazing through the adjoining meads,
Whose stealing pace, and lengthened shade we fear,
Till torn-up forage in his teeth we hear:
When nibbling sheep at large pursue their food,
And unmolested kine rechew the cud;
35 When curlews cry beneath the village walls,
And to her straggling brood the partridge calls;
Their shortlived jubilee the creatures keep,
Which but endures, whilst tyrant man does sleep;
When a sedate content the spirit feels,
40 And no fierce light disturbs, whilst it reveals;
But silent musings urge the mind to seek
Something, too high for syllables to speak;
Till the free soul to a composedness charmed,
Finding the elements of rage disarmed,
45 O'er all below a solemn quiet grown,
Joys in the inferior world,³ and thinks it like her own:
In such a night let me abroad remain,
Till morning breaks, and all's confused again;
Our cares, our toils, our clamors are renewed,
50 Or pleasures, seldom reached, again pursued.

1713

2. Probably Lady Salisbury, the daughter of a
friend. The sense is that this lady differs from others more trivial, who like glowworms look fine only
one hour a day.
3. The world of nature (compared to the world of
the soul).

JONATHAN SWIFT
1667–1745

Jonathan Swift—a posthumous child—was born of English parents in Dublin. Through the generosity of an uncle he was educated at Kilkenny School and Trinity College, Dublin, but before he could fix on a career, the troubles that followed upon James II's abdication and subsequent invasion of Ireland drove Swift along with other Anglo-Irish to England. Between 1689 and 1699 he was more or less continuously a member of the household of his kinsman Sir William Temple, an urbane, civilized man, a retired diplomat, and a friend of King William. During these years Swift read widely, rather reluctantly decided on the church as a career and so took orders, and discovered his astonishing gifts as a satirist. About 1696–97 he wrote his powerful satires on corruptions in religion and learning, *A Tale of a Tub* and *The Battle of the Books*, which were published in 1704 and reached their final form only in the fifth edition of 1710. These were the years in which he slowly came to maturity. When, at the age of thirty-two, he returned to Ireland as chaplain to the lord justice, the earl of Berkeley, he had a clear sense of his genius.

For the rest of his life, Swift devoted his talents to politics and religion—not clearly separated at the time—and most of his works in prose were written to further a specific cause. As a clergyman, a spirited controversialist, and a devoted supporter of the Anglican Church he was hostile to all who seemed to threaten it—Deists, free-thinkers, Roman Catholics, Nonconformists, or merely Whig politicians. In 1710 he abandoned the Whigs, because he opposed their indifference to the welfare of the Anglican Church in Ireland and their desire to repeal the Test Act, which required all holders of offices of state to take the Sacrament according to the Anglican rites, thus excluding Roman Catholics and Dissenters. Welcomed by the Tories, he became the most brilliant political journalist of the day, serving the government of Oxford and Bolingbroke as editor of the party organ, the *Examiner*, and as author of its most powerful articles, as well as writing longer pamphlets in support of important policies, such as that favoring the Peace of Utrecht (1713). He was greatly valued by the two ministers, who admitted him to social intimacy, although never to their counsels. The reward of his services was not the English bishopric that he had a right to expect, but the deanship of St. Patrick's Cathedral in Dublin, which came to him in 1713, a year before the death of Queen Anne and the fall of the Tories put an end to all his hopes of preferment in England.

In Ireland, where he lived unwillingly, he became not only an efficient ecclesiastical administrator but also, in 1724, the leader of Irish resistance to English oppression. Under the pseudonym "M. B. Drapier," he published the famous series of public letters that aroused the country to refuse to accept £100,000 in new copper coins (minted in England by William Wood, who had obtained his patent through court corruption), which, it was feared, would further debase the coinage of the already poverty-stricken kingdom. Although his authorship of the letters was known to all Dublin, no one could be found to earn the £300 offered by the government for information as to the identity of the drapier. Swift is still venerated in Ireland as a national hero. He earned the right to refer to himself in the epitaph that he wrote for his tomb as a vigorous defender of liberty.

His last years were less happy. Swift had suffered most of his adult life from what we now recognize as Ménière's disease, which affects the inner ear, causing dizziness, nausea, and deafness. After 1739, when he was seventy-two years old, his infirmities cut him off from his duties as dean, and from then on his social life dwindled. In 1742 guardians were appointed to administer his affairs, and his last three years were spent in gloom and lethargy. But this dark ending should not put his earlier life, so full of energy and humor, into a shadow. The writer of the satires was a man in full control of great intellectual powers.

For all his involvement in public affairs, Swift seems to stand apart from his con-temporaries—a striking figure among the statesmen of the time, a writer who towered above others by reason of his imagination, mordant wit, and emotional intensity. He has been called a misanthrope, a hater of humanity, and *Gulliver's Travels* has been considered an expression of savage misanthropy. It is true that Swift proclaimed him-self a misanthrope in a letter to Pope, declaring that though he loved individuals, he hated "that animal called man" in general, and offering a new definition of the species as not *animal rationale* ("a rational animal") but as merely *animal rationis capax* ("an animal *capable* of reason"). This, he declared, is the "great foundation" on which his "misanthropy" was erected. Swift was stating not his hatred of his fellow creatures but his antagonism to the current optimistic view that human nature is essentially good. To the "philanthropic" flattery that sentimentalism and Deistic rationalism were paying to human nature, Swift opposed a more ancient and plausible view: that human nature is deeply and permanently flawed and that we can do nothing with or for the human race until we recognize its moral and intellectual limitations. In his epitaph he spoke of the "fierce indignation" that had torn his heart, an indignation that found superb expression in his greatest satires. It was provoked by the constant spectacle of creatures capable of reason, and therefore of reasonable conduct, stead-fastly refusing to live up to their capabilities.

Swift is a master of prose. He defined a good style as "proper words in proper places," a more complex and difficult saying than at first appears. Clear, simple, concrete diction, uncomplicated syntax, economy and conciseness of language mark all his writings. His is a style that shuns ornaments and singularity of all kinds, a style that grows more tense and controlled the more fierce the indignation that it is called on to express. The virtues of his prose are those of his poetry, which shocks us with its hard look at the facts of life and the body. It is unpoetic poetry, devoid of, indeed as often as not mocking at, inspiration, romantic love, cosmetic beauty, easily assumed literary attitudes, and conventional poetic language. Like the prose, it is predominantly satiric in purpose, but not without its moments of comedy and light-heartedness, though written most often not so much to divert as to reform the reader.

A Description of a City Shower

    Careful observers may foretell the hour
    (By sure prognostics) when to dread a shower:
    While rain depends,[1] the pensive cat gives o'er
    Her frolics, and pursues her tail no more.
5   Returning home at night, you'll find the sink°   *sewer*
    Strike your offended sense with double stink.
    If you be wise, then go not far to dine;
    You'll spend in coach hire more than save in wine.
    A coming shower your shooting corns presage,
10 Old aches throb, your hollow tooth will rage.
    Sauntering in coffeehouse is Dulman seen;
    He damns the climate and complains of spleen.[2]
       Meanwhile the South, rising with dabbled wings,
    A sable cloud athwart the welkin flings,
15 That swilled more liquor than it could contain,
    And, like a drunkard, gives it up again.

1. Impends, is imminent. An example of elevated diction used frequently throughout the poem to gain a mock dignity, comically inappropriate to the homely and realistic subject.
2. It was commonly believed at this time that the Englishman's tendency to melancholy ("the spleen") was attributable to the rainy climate. "Dulman": a type name (from "dull man"), like Congreve's "Petulant" or "Witwoud."

Brisk Susan whips her linen from the rope,
While the first drizzling shower is borne aslope:
Such is that sprinkling which some careless quean°   wench, slut
20   Flirts on you from her mop, but not so clean:
You fly, invoke the gods; then turning, stop
To rail; she singing, still whirls on her mop.
Not yet the dust had shunned the unequal strife,
But, aided by the wind, fought still for life,
25   And wafted with its foe by violent gust,
'Twas doubtful which was rain and which was dust.
Ah! where must needy poet seek for aid,
When dust and rain at once his coat invade?
Sole coat, where dust cemented by the rain
30   Erects the nap, and leaves a mingled stain.
      Now in contiguous drops the flood comes down,
Threatening with deluge this devoted town.
To shops in crowds the daggled° females fly,   mud-spattered
Pretend to cheapen° goods, but nothing buy.   bargain for
35   The Templar spruce, while every spout's abroach,³
Stays till 'tis fair, yet seems to call a coach.
The tucked-up sempstress walks with hasty strides,
While streams run down her oiled umbrella's sides.
Here various kinds, by various fortunes led,
40   Commence acquaintance underneath a shed.
Triumphant Tories and desponding Whigs
Forget their feuds,⁴ and join to save their wigs.
Boxed in a chair° the beau impatient sits,   sedan chair
While spouts run clattering o'er the roof by fits,
45   And ever and anon with frightful din
The leather sounds;⁵ he trembles from within.
So when Troy chairmen bore the wooden steed,
Pregnant with Greeks impatient to be freed
(Those bully Greeks, who, as the moderns do,
50   Instead of paying chairmen, run them through),⁶
Laocoön struck the outside with his spear,
And each imprisoned hero quaked for fear.⁷
      Now from all parts the swelling kennels⁸ flow,
And bear their trophies with them as they go:
55   Filth of all hues and odors seem to tell
What street they sailed from, by their sight and smell.
They, as each torrent drives with rapid force,
From Smithfield or St. Pulchre's shape their course,
And in huge confluence joined at Snow Hill ridge,
60   Fall from the conduit prone to Holborn Bridge.⁹

3. Pouring out water. "The Templar": a young
man engaged in studying law. In the literature of
the period the Templar is usually depicted as
neglecting his professional studies for the sake of
dissipation and the pursuit of literature.
4. The Whig ministry had just fallen and the
Tories, led by Harley and St. John, were forming
the government with which Swift was to be closely
associated until the death of the queen in 1714.
5. The roof of the sedan chair was made of leather.

6. Run them through with their swords. The bully,
always prone to violence, was a familiar figure in
London streets and places of amusement.
7. *Aeneid* 2.40–53.
8. The open gutters in the middle of the street.
9. An accurate description of the drainage system
of this part of London—the eastern edge of Holborn and West Smithfield, which lie outside the
old walls west and east of Newgate. The great cattle and sheep markets were in Smithfield. The

Sweepings from butchers' stalls, dung, guts, and blood,
Drowned puppies, stinking sprats,° all drenched in mud,   } *small herrings*
Dead cats, and turnip tops, come tumbling down the flood.[1]

1710

Gulliver's Travels

Gulliver's Travels is Swift's most enduring satire. Although full of allusions to recent and current events, it still rings true today, for its objects are human failings and the defective political, economic, and social institutions that they call into being. Swift adopts an ancient satirical device: the imaginary voyage. Lemuel Gulliver, the narrator, is a ship's surgeon, a moderately well educated man, kindly, resourceful, cheerful, inquiring, patriotic, truthful, and rather unimaginative—in short, a reasonably decent example of humanity, with whom a reader can readily identify. He undertakes four voyages, all of which end disastrously among "several remote nations of the world." In the first, Gulliver is shipwrecked in the empire of Lilliput, where he finds himself a giant among a diminutive people, charmed by their miniature city and amused by their toylike prettiness. But in the end they prove to be treacherous, malicious, ambitious, vengeful, and cruel. As we read we grow disenchanted with the inhabitants of this fanciful kingdom, and then gradually we begin to recognize our likeness to them, especially in the disproportion between our natural pettiness and our boundless and destructive passions. In the second voyage, Gulliver is abandoned by his shipmates in Brobdingnag, a land of giants, creatures ten times as large as Europeans. Though he fears that such monsters must be brutes, the reverse proves to be the case. Brobdingnag is something of a utopia, governed by a humane and enlightened prince who is the embodiment of moral and political wisdom. In the long interview in which Gulliver pridefully enlarges on the glories of England and its political institutions, the king reduces him to resentful silence by asking questions that reveal the difference between what England is and what it ought to be. In Brobdingnag, Gulliver finds himself a Lilliputian, his pride humbled by his helpless state and his human vanity diminished by the realization that his body must have seemed as disgusting to the Lilliputians as do the bodies of the Brobdingnagians to him.

In the third voyage, to Laputa, Swift is chiefly concerned with attacking extremes of theoretical and speculative reasoning, whether in science, politics, or economics. Much of this voyage is an allegory of political life under the administration of the Whig minister, Sir Robert Walpole. The final voyage sets Gulliver between a race of horses, Houyhnhnms (prounced *Hwín-ims*), who live entirely by reason except for a few well-controlled and muted social affections, and their slaves, the Yahoos, whose bodies are obscene caricatures of the human body and who have no glimmer of reason but are mere creatures of appetite and passion.

When *Gulliver's Travels* first appeared, everyone read it—children for the story and politicians for the satire of current affairs—and ever since it has retained a hold on readers of every kind. Almost unique in world literature, it is simple enough for children, complex enough to carry adults beyond their depth. Swift's art works on many levels. First of all, there is the sheer playfulness of the narrative. Through Gulliver's eyes, we gaze on marvel after marvel: a tiny girl who threads an invisible needle with invisible silk or a white mare who threads a needle between pastern and hoof. The

---

church of St. Sepulchre ("St. Pulchre's") stood opposite Newgate Prison. Holborn Conduit was at the foot of Snow Hill. It drained into Fleet Ditch, an evil-smelling open sewer, at Holborn Bridge.

1. In Falkner's edition of Swift's *Works* (Dublin, 1735) a note almost certainly suggested by Swift points to the concluding triplet, with its resonant final alexandrine, as a burlesque of a mannerism of Dryden and other Restoration poets and claims that Swift's ridicule banished the triplet from contemporary poetry.

travels, like a fairy story, transport us to imaginary worlds that function with a perfect, fantastic logic different from our own; Swift exercises our sense of vision. But beyond that, he exercises our perceptions of meaning. In *Gulliver's Travels,* things are seldom what they seem; irony, probing or corrosive, underlies almost every word. In the last chapter, Gulliver insists that the example of the Houyhnhnms has made him incapable of telling a lie—but the oath he swears is quoted from Sinon, whose lies to the Trojans persuaded them to accept the Trojan *horse.* Swift trains us to read alertly, to look beneath the surface. Yet on its deepest level, the book does not offer final meanings, but a question: What is a human being? Voyaging through imaginary worlds, we try to find ourselves. Are we prideful insects or lords of creation? brutes or reasonable beings? In the last voyage, Swift pushes such questions, and Gulliver himself, almost beyond endurance; hating his own humanity, Gulliver forgets who he is. For the reader, however, the outcome cannot be so clear. Swift does not set out to satisfy our minds but to vex and unsettle them. And he leaves us at the moment when the mixed face of humanity—the pettiness of the Lilliputians, the savagery of the Yahoos, the innocence of Gulliver himself—begins to look strangely familiar, like our own faces in a mirror.

Swift's full title for this work was *Travels into Several Remote Nations of the World. In Four Parts. By Lemuel Gulliver, First a Surgeon, and then a Captain of several Ships.* In the first edition (1726), either the bookseller or Swift's friends Charles Ford, Pope, and others, who were concerned in getting the book anonymously into print, altered and omitted so much of the original manuscript (because of its dangerous political implications) that Swift was seriously annoyed. When, in 1735, the Dublin bookseller George Faulkner brought out an edition of Swift's works, the dean seems to have taken pains, surreptitiously, to see that a more authentic version of the work was published. This text is the basis of modern editions.

From Gulliver's Travels

A Letter from Captain Gulliver to His Cousin Sympson[1]

I hope you will be ready to own publicly, whenever you shall be called to it, that by your great and frequent urgency you prevailed on me to publish a very loose and uncorrect account of my travels; with direction to hire some young gentlemen of either University to put them in order, and correct the style, as my Cousin Dampier[2] did by my advice, in his book called *A Voyage round the World.* But I do not remember I gave you power to consent that anything should be omitted, and much less that anything should be inserted: therefore, as to the latter, I do here renounce everything of that kind; particularly a paragraph about her Majesty the late Queen Anne, of most pious and glorious memory; although I did reverence and esteem her more than any of human species. But you, or your interpolator, ought to have considered that as it was not my inclination, so was it not decent to praise any animal of our composition before my master Houyhnhnm; and besides, the fact was altogether false; for to my knowledge, being in England during some part of her Majesty's reign, she did govern by a chief Minister; nay, even by two successively; the first whereof was the Lord of Godolphin, and the sec-

---

1. In this letter, first published in 1735, Swift complains, among other matters, of the alterations in his original text made by the publisher, Benjamin Motte, in the interest of what he considered political discretion.

2. William Dampier (1652–1715), the explorer, whose account of his circumnavigation of the globe Swift had read.

ond the Lord of Oxford; so that you have made me *say the thing that was not.*
Likewise, in the account of the Academy of Projectors, and several passages
of my discourse to my master Houyhnhnm, you have either omitted some
material circumstances, or minced or changed them in such a manner, that
I do hardly know mine own work. When I formerly hinted to you something
of this in a letter, you were pleased to answer that you were afraid of giving
offense; that people in power were very watchful over the press; and apt not
only to interpret, but to punish everything which looked like an *innuendo*
(as I think you called it). But pray, how could that which I spoke so many
years ago, and at above five thousand leagues distance, in another reign, be
applied to any of the Yahoos, who now are said to govern the herd; especially,
at a time when I little thought on or feared the unhappiness of living under
them. Have not I the most reason to complain, when I see these very Yahoos
carried by Houyhnhnms in a vehicle, as if these were brutes, and those the
rational creatures? And, indeed, to avoid so monstrous and detestable a sight
was one principal motive of my retirement hither.[3]

Thus much I thought proper to tell you in relation to yourself, and to the
trust I reposed in you.

I do in the next place complain of my own great want of judgment, in being
prevailed upon by the intreaties and false reasonings of you and some others,
very much against mine own opinion, to suffer my travels to be published.
Pray bring to your mind how often I desired you to consider, when you
insisted on the motive of public good, that the Yahoos were a species of
animals utterly incapable of amendment by precepts or examples; and so it
hath proved; for instead of seeing a full stop put to all abuses and corruptions,
at least in this little island, as I had reason to expect, behold, after above six
months warning, I cannot learn that my book hath produced one single effect
according to mine intentions; I desired you would let me know by a letter,
when party and faction were extinguished; judges learned and upright; plead-
ers honest and modest, with some tincture of common sense; and Smithfield[4]
blazing with pyramids of law books; the young nobility's education entirely
changed; the physicians banished; the female Yahoos abounding in virtue,
honor, truth, and good sense; courts and levees of great ministers thoroughly
weeded and swept; wit, merit, and learning rewarded; all disgracers of the
press in prose and verse, condemned to eat nothing but their own cotton,[5]
and quench their thirst with their own ink. These, and a thousand other
reformations, I firmly counted upon by your encouragement; as indeed they
were plainly deducible from the precepts delivered in my book. And, it must
be owned that seven months were a sufficient time to correct every vice and
folly to which Yahoos are subject; if their natures had been capable of the
least disposition to virtue or wisdom; yet so far have you been from answering
mine expectation in any of your letters, that on the contrary, you are loading
our carrier every week with libels, and keys, and reflections, and memoirs,
and second parts; wherein I see myself accused of reflecting upon great
statesfolk; of degrading human nature (for so they have still the confidence
to style it) and of abusing the female sex. I find likewise, that the writers of
those bundles are not agreed among themselves; for some of them will not

3. To Nottinghamshire.
4. A part of London containing many bookshops.

5. Presumably their paper.

allow me to be author of mine own travels; and others make me author of books to which I am wholly a stranger.

I find likewise that your printer hath been so careless as to confound the times, and mistake the dates of my several voyages and returns; neither assigning the true year, or the true month, or day of the month; and I hear the original manuscript is all destroyed, since the publication of my book. Neither have I any copy left; however, I have sent you some corrections, which you may insert, if ever there should be a second edition; and yet I cannot stand to them, but shall leave that matter to my judicious and candid readers, to adjust it as they please.

I hear some of our sea Yahoos find fault with my sea language, as not proper in many parts, nor now in use. I cannot help it. In my first voyages, while I was young, I was instructed by the oldest mariners, and learned to speak as they did. But I have since found that the sea Yahoos are apt, like the land ones, to become new fangled in their words; which the latter change every year; insomuch, as I remember upon each return to mine own country, their old dialect was so altered, that I could hardly understand the new. And I observe, when any Yahoo comes from London out of curiosity to visit me at mine own house, we neither of us are able to deliver our conceptions in a manner intelligible to the other.[6]

If the censure of Yahoos could any way affect me, I should have great reason to complain that some of them are so bold as to think my book of travels a mere fiction out of mine own brain; and have gone so far as to drop hints that the Houyhnhnms, and Yahoos have no more existence than the inhabitants of Utopia.

Indeed I must confess that as to the people of Lilliput, Brobdingrag (for so the word should have been spelled, and not erroneously Brobdingnag) and Laputa, I have never yet heard of any Yahoo so presumptuous as to dispute their being, or the facts I have related concerning them; because the truth immediately strikes every reader with conviction. And, is there less probability in my account of the Houyhnhnms or Yahoos, when it is manifest as to the latter, there are so many thousands even in this city, who only differ from their brother brutes in Houyhnhnmland, because they use a sort of a jabber, and do not go naked. I wrote for their amendment, and not their approbation. The united praise of the whole race would be of less consequence to me, than the neighing of those two degenerate Houyhnhnms I keep in my stable; because, from these, degenerate as they are, I still improve in some virtues, without any mixture of vice.

Do these miserable animals presume to think that I am so far degenerated as to defend my veracity; Yahoo as I am, it is well known through all Houyhnhnmland, that by the instructions and example of my illustrious master, I was able in the compass of two years (although I confess with the utmost difficulty) to remove that infernal habit of lying, shuffling, deceiving, and equivocating, so deeply rooted in the very souls of all my species; especially the Europeans.

I have other complaints to make upon this vexatious occasion; but I forbear troubling myself or you any further. I must freely confess that since my last

6. Swift was the inveterate enemy of slang.

return, some corruptions of my Yahoo nature have revived in me by conversing with a few of your species, and particularly those of mine own family, by an unavoidable necessity; else I should never have attempted so absurd a project as that of reforming the Yahoo race in this kingdom; but I have now done with all such visionary schemes for ever.

1727?   1735

The Publisher to the Reader

The author of these travels, Mr. Lemuel Gulliver, is my ancient and intimate friend; there is likewise some relation between us by the mother's side. About three years ago Mr. Gulliver, growing weary of the concourse of curious people coming to him at his house in Redriff,[7] made a small purchase of land, with a convenient house, near Newark, in Nottinghamshire, his native country; where he now lives retired, yet in good esteem among his neighbors.

Although Mr. Gulliver were born in Nottinghamshire, where his father dwelt, yet I have heard him say his family came from Oxfordshire; to confirm which, I have observed in the churchyard at Banbury, in that county, several tombs and monuments of the Gullivers.

Before he quitted Redriff, he left the custody of the following papers in my hands, with the liberty to dispose of them as I should think fit. I have carefully perused them three times; the style is very plain and simple; and the only fault I find is that the author, after the manner of travelers, is a little too circumstantial. There is an air of truth apparent through the whole; and indeed the author was so distinguished for his veracity, that it became a sort of proverb among his neighbors at Redriff, when anyone affirmed a thing, to say, it was as true as if Mr. Gulliver had spoke it.

By the advice of several worthy persons, to whom, with the author's permission, I communicated these papers, I now venture to send them into the world; hoping they may be, at least for some time, a better entertainment to our young noblemen, than the common scribbles of politics and party.

This volume would have been at least twice as large, if I had not made bold to strike out innumerable passages relating to the winds and tides, as well as to the variations and bearings in the several voyages; together with the minute descriptions of the management of the ship in storms, in the style of sailors; likewise the account of the longitudes and latitudes, wherein I have reason to apprehend that Mr. Gulliver may be a little dissatisfied; but I was resolved to fit the work as much as possible to the general capacity of readers. However, if my own ignorance in sea affairs shall have led me to commit some mistakes, I alone am answerable for them; and if any traveler hath a curiosity to see the whole work at large, as it came from the hand of the author, I will be ready to gratify him.

As for any further particulars relating to the author, the reader will receive satisfaction from the first pages of the book.

RICHARD SYMPSON

7. Rotherhithe, a district in southern London, below Tower Bridge, then frequented by sailors.

Part 1. A Voyage to Lilliput

CHAPTER 1. *The author gives some account of himself and family; his first inducements to travel. He is shipwrecked, and swims for his life; gets safe on shore in the country of Lilliput; is made a prisoner, and carried up the country.*

My father had a small estate in Nottinghamshire; I was the third of five sons. He sent me to Emanuel College in Cambridge, at fourteen years old, where I resided three years, and applied myself close to my studies: but the charge of maintaining me (although I had a very scanty allowance) being too great for a narrow fortune, I was bound apprentice to Mr. James Bates, an eminent surgeon in London, with whom I continued four years; and my father now and then sending me small sums of money, I laid them out in learning navigation, and other parts of the mathematics, useful to those who intend to travel, as I always believed it would be some time or other my fortune to do. When I left Mr. Bates, I went down to my father; where, by the assistance of him and my uncle John, and some other relations, I got forty pounds, and a promise of thirty pounds a year to maintain me at Leyden: there I studied physic[8] two years and seven months, knowing it would be useful in long voyages.

Soon after my return from Leyden, I was recommended by my good master Mr. Bates, to be surgeon to the *Swallow,* Captain Abraham Pannell commander; with whom I continued three years and a half, making a voyage or two into the Levant[9] and some other parts. When I came back, I resolved to settle in London, to which Mr. Bates, my master, encouraged me; and by him I was recommended to several patients. I took part of a small house in the Old Jury; and being advised to alter my condition, I married Mrs.[1] Mary Burton, second daughter to Mr. Edmond Burton, hosier, in Newgate Street, with whom I received four hundred pounds for a portion.

But, my good master Bates dying in two years after, and I having few friends, my business began to fail; for my conscience would not suffer me to imitate the bad practice of too many among my brethren. Having therefore consulted with my wife, and some of my acquaintance, I determined to go again to sea. I was surgeon successively in two ships, and made several voyages, for six years, to the East and West Indies; by which I got some addition to my fortune. My hours of leisure I spent in reading the best authors, ancient and modern, being always provided with a good number of books; and when I was ashore, in observing the manners and dispositions of the people, as well as learning their language; wherein I had a great facility by the strength of my memory.

The last of these voyages not proving very fortunate, I grew weary of the sea, and intended to stay at home with my wife and family. I removed from the Old Jury to Fetter Lane, and from thence to Wapping, hoping to get business among the sailors; but it would not turn to account. After three years' expectation that things would mend, I accepted an advantageous offer

8. The University of Leyden, in Holland, was a center for the study of "physic" (medicine).
9. The eastern Mediterranean.

1. "Mrs." (pronounced "Mistress") designated any woman, married or unmarried. "Old Jury": a street (once "Old Jewry") in the City of London.

from Captain William Prichard, master of the *Antelope*, who was making a voyage to the South Sea. We set sail from Bristol, May 4th, 1699, and our voyage at first was very prosperous.

It would not be proper, for some reasons, to trouble the reader with the particulars of our adventures in those seas: let it suffice to inform him, that in our passage from thence to the East Indies we were driven by a violent storm to the northwest of Van Diemen's Land.[2] By an observation, we found ourselves in the latitude of 30 degrees 2 minutes south. Twelve of our crew were dead by immoderate labor, and ill food, the rest were in a very weak condition. On the fifth of November, which was the beginning of summer in those parts, the weather being very hazy, the seamen spied a rock, within half a cable's length of the ship; but the wind was so strong, that we were driven directly upon it, and immediately split. Six of the crew, of whom I was one, having let down the boat into the sea, made a shift to get clear of the ship, and the rock. We rowed by my computation about three leagues, till we were able to work no longer, being already spent with labor while we were in the ship. We therefore trusted ourselves to the mercy of the waves; and in about half an hour the boat was overset by a sudden flurry from the north. What became of my companions in the boat, as well as of those who escaped on the rock, or were left in the vessel, I cannot tell; but conclude they were all lost. For my own part, I swam as fortune directed me, and was pushed forward by wind and tide. I often let my legs drop, and could feel no bottom; but when I was almost gone, and able to struggle no longer, I found myself within my depth; and by this time the storm was much abated. The declivity was so small, that I walked near a mile before I got to the shore, which I conjectured was about eight o'clock in the evening. I then advanced forward near half a mile, but could not discover any sign of houses or inhabitants; at least I was in so weak a condition, that I did not observe them. I was extremely tired, and with that, and the heat of the weather, and about half a pint of brandy that I drank as I left the ship, I found myself much inclined to sleep. I lay down on the grass, which was very short and soft, where I slept sounder than ever I remember to have done in my life, and as I reckoned, above nine hours; for when I awaked, it was just daylight. I attempted to rise, but was not able to stir: for as I happened to lie on my back, I found my arms and legs were strongly fastened on each side to the ground; and my hair, which was long and thick, tied down in the same manner. I likewise felt several slender ligatures across my body, from my armpits to my thighs. I could only look upwards; the sun began to grow hot, and the light offended my eyes. I heard a confused noise about me, but in the posture I lay, could see nothing except the sky. In a little time I felt something alive moving on my left leg, which advancing gently forward over my breast, came almost up to my chin; when bending my eyes downwards as much as I could, I perceived it to be a human creature not six inches high,[3] with a bow and arrow in his hands, and a quiver at his back. In the meantime, I felt at least forty more of the same kind (as I conjectured) following the first. I was in the utmost astonishment, and roared so loud, that they all ran back in a

---

2. Tasmania.
3. Lilliput is scaled, fairly consistently, at one-twelfth of Gulliver's world.

fright; and some of them, as I was afterwards told, were hurt with the falls they got by leaping from my sides upon the ground. However, they soon returned; and one of them, who ventured so far as to get a full sight of my face, lifting up his hands and eyes by way of admiration,[4] cried out in a shrill, but distinct voice, *Hekinah Degul*: the others repeated the same words several times, but I then knew not what they meant. I lay all this while, as the reader may believe, in great uneasiness; at length, struggling to get loose, I had the fortune to break the strings, and wrench out the pegs that fastened my left arm to the ground; for, by lifting it up to my face, I discovered the methods they had taken to bind me; and, at the same time, with a violent pull, which gave me excessive pain, I a little loosened the strings that tied down my hair on the left side; so that I was just able to turn my head about two inches. But the creatures ran off a second time, before I could seize them; whereupon there was a great shout in a very shrill accent; and after it ceased, I heard one of them cry aloud, *Tolgo phonac*; when in an instant I felt above an hundred arrows discharged on my left hand, which pricked me like so many needles; and besides they shot another flight into the air, as we do bombs in Europe, whereof many, I suppose, fell on my body (though I felt them not) and some on my face, which I immediately covered with my left hand. When this shower of arrows was over, I fell a groaning with grief and pain; and then striving again to get loose, they discharged another volley larger than the first, and some of them attempted with spears to stick me in the sides; but, by good luck, I had on me a buff jerkin,[5] which they could not pierce. I thought it the most prudent method to lie still; and my design was to continue so till night, when, my left hand being already loose, I could easily free myself: and as for the inhabitants, I had reason to believe I might be a match for the greatest armies they could bring against me, if they were all of the same size with him that I saw. But fortune disposed otherwise of me. When the people observed I was quiet, they discharged no more arrows: but by the noise increasing, I knew their numbers were greater; and about four yards from me, over-against my right ear, I heard a knocking for above an hour, like people at work; when turning my head that way, as well as the pegs and strings would permit me, I saw a stage erected about a foot and a half from the ground, capable of holding four of the inhabitatnts, with two or three ladders to mount it: from whence one of them, who seemed to be a person of quality, made me a long speech, whereof I understood not one syllable. But I should have mentioned, that before the principal person began his oration, he cried out three times, *Langro Dehul san*: (these words and the former were afterwards repeated and explained to me). Whereupon immediately about fifty of the inhabitants came, and cut the strings that fastened the left side of my head, which gave me the liberty of turning it to the right, and of observing the person and gesture of him who was to speak. He appeared to be of a middle age, and taller than any of the other three who attended him; whereof one was a page who held up his train, and seemed to be somewhat longer than my middle finger; the other two stood one on each side to support him. He acted every part of an orator, and I could observe many periods[6] of threatenings, and others of promises, pity and kind-

---

4. Wonderment.
5. Leather jacket.

6. In rhetoric, complete, well-constructed sentences.

ness. I answered in a few words, but in the most submissive manner, lifting up my left hand and both my eyes to the sun, as calling him for a witness; and being almost famished with hunger, having not eaten a morsel for some hours before I left the ship, I found the demands of nature so strong upon me, that I could not forbear showing my impatience (perhaps against the strict rules of decency) by putting my finger frequently on my mouth, to signify that I wanted food. The Hurgo (for so they call a great lord, as I afterwards learned) understood me very well. He descended from the stage, and commanded that several ladders should be applied to my sides, on which above an hundred of the inhabitants mounted, and walked towards my mouth, laden with baskets full of meat, which had been provided and sent thither by the King's orders upon the first intelligence he received of me. I observed there was the flesh of several animals, but could not distinguish them by the taste. There were shoulders, legs, and loins shaped like those of mutton, and very well dressed, but smaller than the wings of a lark. I eat them by two or three at a mouthful, and took three loaves at a time, about the bigness of musket bullets. They supplied me as fast as they could, showing a thousand marks of wonder and astonishment at my bulk and appetite. I then made another sign that I wanted drink. They found by my eating that a small quantity would not suffice me; and being a most ingenious people, they slung up with great dexterity one of their largest hogsheads; then rolled it towards my hand, and beat out the top; I drank it off at a draught, which I might well do, for it hardly held half a pint, and tasted like a small wine of Burgundy, but much more delicious. They brought me a second hogshead, which I drank in the same manner, and made signs for more, but they had none to give me. When I had performed these wonders, they shouted for joy, and danced upon my breast, repeating several times as they did at first, *Hekinah Degul.* They made me a sign that I should throw down the two hogsheads, but first warned the people below to stand out of the way, crying aloud, *Borach Mivola,* and when they saw the vessels in the air, there was an universal shout of *Hekinah Degul.* I confess I was often tempted, while they were passing backwards and forwards on my body, to seize forty or fifty of the first that came in my reach, and dash them against the ground. But the remembrance of what I had felt, which probably might not be the worst they could do; and the promise of honor I made them, for so I interpreted my submissive behavior, soon drove out those imaginations. Besides, I now considered myself as bound by the laws of hospitality to a people who had treated me with so much expense and magnificence. However, in my thoughts I could not sufficiently wonder at the intrepidity of these diminutive mortals, who durst venture to mount and walk on my body, while one of my hands was at liberty, without trembling at the very sight of so prodigious a creature as I must appear to them. After some time, when they observed that I made no more demands for meat, there appeared before me a person of high rank from his Imperial Majesty. His Excellency, having mounted on the small of my right leg, advanced forwards up to my face, with about a dozen of his retinue. And producing his credentials under the Signet Royal, which he applied[7] close to my eyes, spoke about ten minutes, without any signs of anger, but with a kind of determinate resolution; often pointing forwards,

7. Brought.

which, as I afterwards found, was towards the capital city, about half a mile distant, whither it was agreed by his Majesty in council that I must be conveyed. I answered in a few words, but to no purpose, and made a sign with my hand that was loose, putting it to the other (but over his Excellency's head, for fear of hurting him or his train) and then to my own head and body, to signify that I desired my liberty. It appeared that he understood me well enough; for he shook his head by way of disapprobation, and held his hand in a posture to show that I must be carried as a prisoner. However, he made other signs to let me understand that I should have meat and drink enough, and very good treatment. Whereupon I once more thought of attempting to break my bonds; but again, when I felt the smart of their arrows upon my face and hands, which were all in blisters, and many of the darts still sticking in them; and observing likewise that the number of my enemies increased; I gave tokens to let them know that they might do with me what they pleased. Upon this the *Hurgo* and his train withdrew, with much civility and cheerful countenances. Soon after I heard a general shout, with frequent repetitions of the words, *Peplom Selan,* and I felt great numbers of the people on my left side relaxing the cords to such a degree, that I was able to turn upon my right, and to ease myself with making water; which I very plentifully did, to the great astonishment of the people, who conjecturing by my motions what I was going to do, immediately opened to the right and left on that side, to avoid the torrent which fell with such noise and violence from me. But before this, they had daubed my face and both my hands with a sort of ointment very pleasant to the smell, which in a few minutes removed all the smart of their arrows. These circumstances, added to the refreshment I had received by their victuals and drink, which were very nourishing, disposed me to sleep. I slept about eight hours, as I was afterwards assured; and it was no wonder; for the physicians, by the Emperor's order, had mingled a sleeping potion in the hogsheads of wine.

It seems that upon the first moment I was discovered sleeping on the ground after my landing, the Emperor had early notice of it by an express; and determined in council that I should be tied in the manner I have related (which was done in the night while I slept), that plenty of meat and drink should be sent me, and a machine prepared to carry me to the capital city.

This resolution perhaps may appear very bold and dangerous, and I am confident would not be imitated by any prince in Europe on the like occasion; however, in my opinion it was extremely prudent as well as generous. For supposing these people had endeavored to kill me with their spears and arrows while I was asleep; I should certainly have awaked with the first sense of smart, which might so far have roused my rage and strength, as to enable me to break the strings wherewith I was tied; after which, as they were not able to make resistance, so they could expect no mercy.

These people are most excellent mathematicians, and arrived to a great perfection in mechanics by the countenance and encouragement of the Emperor, who is a renowned patron of learning. This prince hath several machines fixed on wheels, for the carriage of trees and other great weights. He often builds his largest men of war, whereof some are nine foot long, in the woods where the timber grows, and has them carried on these engines[8]

8. Contrivances.

three or four hundred yards to the sea. Five hundred carpenters and engineers were immediately set at work to prepare the greatest engine they had. It was a frame of wood raised three inches from the ground, about seven foot long and four wide, moving upon twenty-two wheels. The shout I heard was upon the arrival of this engine, which it seems set out in four hours after my landing. It was brought parallel to me as I lay. But the principal difficulty was to raise and place me in this vehicle. Eighty poles, each of one foot high, were erected for this purpose, and very strong cords of the bigness of packthread were fastened by hooks to many bandages, which the workmen had girt round my neck, my hands, my body, and my legs. Nine hundred of the strongest men were employed to draw up these cords by many pulleys fastened on the poles; and thus, in less than three hours, I was raised and slung into the engine, and there tied fast. All this I was told, for while the whole operation was performing, I lay in a profound sleep, by the force of that soporiferous[9] medicine infused into my liquor. Fifteen hundred of the Emperor's largest horses, each about four inches and a half high, were employed to draw me towards the metropolis, which, as I said, was half a mile distant.

About four hours after we began our journey, I awaked by a very ridiculous accident; for, the carriage being stopped a while to adjust something that was out of order, two or three of the young natives had the curiosity to see how I looked when I was asleep; they climbed up into the engine, and advancing very softly to my face, one of them, an officer in the guards, put the sharp end of his half-pike a good way up into my left nostril, which tickled my nose like a straw, and made me sneeze violently: whereupon they stole off unperceived, and it was three weeks before I knew the cause of my awaking so suddenly. We made a long march the remaining part of the day, and rested at night with five hundred guards on each side of me half with torches, and half with bows and arrows, ready to shoot me if I should offer to stir. The next morning at sunrise we continued our march, and arrived within two hundred yards of the city gates about noon. The Emperor and all his court came out to meet us, but his great officers would by no means suffer his Majesty to endanger his person by mounting on my body.

At the place where the carriage stopped, there stood an ancient temple, esteemed to be the largest in the whole kingdom, which having been polluted some years before by an unnatural murder,[1] was, according to the zeal of those people, looked on as profane, and therefore had been applied to common use, and all the ornaments and furniture carried away. In this edifice it was determined I should lodge. The great gate fronting to the north was about four foot high, and almost two foot wide, through which I could easily creep. On each side of the gate was a small window not above six inches from the ground: into that on the left side, the King's smiths conveyed fourscore and eleven chains, like those that hang to a lady's watch in Europe, and almost as large, which were locked to my left leg with six and thirty padlocks. Over against this temple, on the other side of the great highway, at twenty foot distance, there was a turret at least five foot high. Here the Emperor ascended with many principal lords of his court, to have an oppor-

9. Inducing unnatural sleep.
1. Presumably a reference to the execution of Charles I, who was sentenced in Westminster Hall.

tunity of viewing me, as I was told, for I could not see them. It was reckoned that above an hundred thousand inhabitants came out of the town upon the same errand; and in spite of my guards, I believe there could not be fewer than ten thousand, at several times, who mounted upon my body by the help of ladders. But a proclamation was soon issued to forbid it upon pain of death. When the workmen found it was impossible for me to break loose, they cut all the strings that bound me; whereupon I rose up with as melancholy a disposition as ever I had in my life. But the noise and astonishment of the people at seeing me rise and walk are not to be expressed. The chains that held my left leg were about two yards long, and gave me not only the liberty of walking backwards and forwards in a semicircle; but, being fixed within four inches of the gate, allowed me to creep in, and lie at my full length in the temple.

CHAPTER 2. *The Emperor of Lilliput, attended by several of the nobility, comes to see the author in his confinement. The Emperor's person and habit described. Learned men appointed to teach the author their language. He gains favor by his mild disposition. His pockets are searched, and his sword and pistols taken from him.*

When I found myself on my feet, I looked about me, and must confess I never beheld a more entertaining prospect. The country round appeared like a continued garden, and the inclosed fields, which were generally forty foot psquare, resembled so many beds of flowers. These fields were intermingled with woods of half a stang,[2] and the tallest trees, as I could judge, appeared to be seven foot high. I viewed the town on my left hand, which looked like the painted scene of a city in a theater.

I had been for some hours extremely pressed by the necessities of nature; which was no wonder, it being almost two days since I had last disburthened myself. I was under great difficulties between urgency and shame. The best expedient I could think on, was to creep into my house, which I accordingly did; and shutting the gate after me, I went as far as the length of my chain would suffer; and discharged my body of that uneasy load. But this was the only time I was ever guilty of so uncleanly an action; for which I cannot but hope the candid reader will give some allowance, after he hath maturely and impartially considered my case, and the distress I was in. From this time my constant practice was, as soon as I rose, to perform that business in open air, at the full extent of my chain, and due care was taken every morning before company came, that the offensive matter should be carried off in wheelbarrows by two servants appointed for that purpose. I would not have dwelt so long upon a circumstance, that perhaps at first sight may appear not very momentous, if I had not thought it necessary to justify my character in point of cleanliness to the world; which I am told some of my maligners have been pleased, upon this and other occasions, to call in question.

When this adventure was at an end, I came back out of my house, having occasion for fresh air. The Emperor was already descended from the tower, and advancing on horseback towards me, which had like to have cost him dear; for the beast, although very well trained, yet wholly unused to such a

2. A quarter of an acre.

sight, which appeared as if a mountain moved before him, reared up on his hinder feet: but that prince, who is an excellent horseman, kept his seat, until his attendants ran in, and held the bridle, while his Majesty had time to dismount. When he alighted, he surveyed me round with great admiration, but kept beyond the length of my chains. He ordered his cooks and butlers, who were already prepared, to give me victuals and drink, which they pushed forward in a sort of vehicles upon wheels until I could reach them. I took these vehicles, and soon emptied them all; twenty of them were filled with meat, and ten with liquor; each of the former afforded me two or three good mouthfuls, and I emptied the liquor of ten vessels, which was contained in earthen vials, into one vehicle, drinking it off at a draught; and so I did with the rest. The Empress, and young princes of the blood, of both sexes, attended by many ladies, sat at some distance in their chairs; but upon the accident that happened to the Emperor's horse, they alighted, and came near his person; which I am now going to describe. He is taller, by almost the breadth of my nail, than any of his court, which alone is enough to strike an awe into the beholders. His features are strong and masculine, with an Austrian lip, and arched nose, his complexion olive, his countenance[3] erect, his body and limbs well proportioned, all his motions graceful, and his deportment majestic. He was then past his prime, being twenty-eight years and three quarters old, of which he had reigned about seven, in great felicity, and generally victorious. For the better convenience of beholding him, I lay on my side, so that my face was parallel to his, and he stood but three yards off: however, I have had him since many times in my hand, and therefore cannot be deceived in the description. His dress was very plain and simple, the fashion of it between the Asiatic and the European; but he had on his head a light helmet of gold, adorned with jewels, and a plume on the crest. He held his sword drawn in his hand, to defend himself, if I should happen to break loose; it was almost three inches long, the hilt and scabbard were gold enriched with diamonds. His voice was shrill, but very clear and articulate, and I could distinctly hear it when I stood up. The ladies and courtiers were all most magnificently clad, so that the spot they stood upon seemed to resemble a petticoat spread on the ground, embroidered with figures of gold and silver. His Imperial Majesty spoke often to me, and I returned answers, but neither of us could understand a syllable. There were several of his priests and lawyers present (as I conjectured by their habits) who were commanded to address themselves to me, and I spoke to them in as many languages as I had the least smattering of, which were High and Low Dutch, Latin, French, Spanish, Italian, and Lingua Franca;[4] but all to no purpose. After about two hours the court retired, and I was left with a strong guard, to prevent the impertinence, and probably the malice of the rabble, who were very impatient to crowd about me as near as they durst; and some of them had the impudence to shoot their arrows at me as I sat on the ground by the door of my house, whereof one very narrowly missed my left eye. But the colonel ordered six of the ringleaders to be seized, and thought no punishment so proper as to deliver them bound into my hands, which some of his soldiers accordingly did, pushing them forwards with the butt-ends of their

---

3. Bearing, appearance. Swift may be satirically idealizing George I, whom most of the British thought gross.

4. A jargon, based on Italian, used by traders in the Mediterranean. "High and Low Dutch": German and Dutch.

pikes into my reach; I took them all in my right hand, put five of them into my coat-pocket; and as to the sixth, I made a countenance as if I would eat him alive. The poor man squalled terribly, and the colonel and his officer were in much pain, especially when they saw me take out my penknife: but I soon put them out of fear; for, looking mildly, and immediately cutting the strings he was bound with, I set him gently on the ground, and away he ran. I treated the rest in the same manner, taking them one by one out of my pocket, and I observed both the soldiers and people were highly obliged at this mark of my clemency, which was represented very much to my advantage at court.

Towards night I got with some difficulty into my house, where I lay on the ground, and continued to do so about a fortnight; during which time the Emperor gave orders to have a bed prepared for me. Six hundred beds of the common measure were brought in carriages, and worked up in my house; an hundred and fifty of their beds sewn together made up the breadth and length, and these were four double, which however kept me but very indifferently from the hardness of the floor, that was of smooth stone. By the same computation they provided me with sheets, blankets, and coverlets, tolerable enough for one who had been so long enured to hardships as I.

As the news of my arrival spread through the kingdom, it brought prodigious numbers of rich, idle, and curious people to see me; so that the villages were almost emptied, and great neglect of tillage and household affairs must have ensued, if his Imperial Majesty had not provided by several proclamations and orders of state against this inconveniency. He directed that those who had already beheld me should return home, and not presume to come within fifty yards of my house without license from court; whereby the secretaries of state got considerable fees.

In the mean time, the Emperor held frequent councils to debate what course should be taken with me; and I was afterwards assured by a particular friend, a person of great quality, who was as much in the secret as any, that the court was under many difficulties concerning me. They apprehended[5] my breaking loose, that my diet would be very expensive, and might cause a famine. Sometimes they determined to starve me, or at least to shoot me in the face and hands with poisoned arrows, which would soon dispatch me: but again they considered, that the stench of so large a carcass might produce a plague in the metropolis, and probably spread through the whole kingdom. In the midst of these consultations, several officers of the army went to the door of the great council chamber; and two of them being admitted, gave an account of my behavior to the six criminals above-mentioned; which made so favorable an impression in the breast of his Majesty, and the whole board, in my behalf, that an imperial commission was issued out, obliging all the villages nine hundred yards round the city to deliver in every morning six beeves, forty sheep, and other victuals for my sustenance; together with a proportionable quantity of bread and wine, and other liquors: for the due payment of which his Majesty gave assignments[6] upon his treasury. For this prince lives chiefly upon his own demesnes; seldom except upon great occasions raising any subsidies upon his subjects, who are bound to attend him in his wars at their own expense. An establishment was also made of six

---

5. Anticipated with fear.   6. Formal mandates of revenue.

hundred persons to be my domestics, who had board-wages allowed for their maintenance, and tents built for them very conveniently on each side of my door. It was likewise ordered, that three hundred tailors should make me a suit of clothes after the fashion of the country: that six of his Majesty's greatest scholars should be employed to instruct me in their language: and, lastly, that the Emperor's horses, and those of the nobility, and troops of guards, should be exercised in my sight, to accustom themselves to me. All these orders were duly put in execution; and in about three weeks I made a great progress in learning their language; during which time the Emperor frequently honored me with his visits, and was pleased to assist my masters in teaching me. We began already to converse together in some sort; and the first words I learned, were to express my desire that he would please to give me my liberty; which I every day repeated on my knees.[7] His answer, as I could apprehend, was, that this must be a work of time, not to be thought on without the advice of his council; and that first I must *Lumos kelmin pesso desmar lon emposo;* that is, swear a peace with him and his kingdom. However, that I should be used with all kindness; and he advised me to acquire by my patience and discreet behavior, the good opinion of himself and his subjects. He desired I would not take it ill, if he gave orders to certain proper officers to search me; for probably I might carry about me several weapons, which must needs be dangerous things, if they answered the bulk of so prodigious a person.[8] I said, his Majesty should be satisfied, for I was ready to strip myself, and turn up my pockets before him. This I delivered part in words, and part in signs. He replied, that by the laws of the kingdom, I must be searched by two of his officers; that he knew this could not be done without my consent and assistance; that he had so good an opinion of my generosity and justice, as to trust their persons in my hands; that whatever they took from me should be returned when I left the country, or paid for at the rate which I would set upon them. I took up the two officers in my hands, put them first into my coat-pockets, and then into every other pocket about me, except my two fobs, and another secret pocket which I had no mind should be searched, wherein I had some little necessaries of no consequence to any but myself. In one of my fobs there was a silver watch, and in the other a small quantity of gold in a purse. These gentlemen, having pen, ink, and paper about them, made an exact inventory of everything they saw; and when they had done, desired I would set them down, that they might deliver it to the Emperor. This inventory I afterwards translated into English, and is word for word as follows.

Imprimis, In the right coat-pocket of the Great Man-Mountain (for so I interpret the words *Quinbus Flestrin*) after the strictest search, we found only one great piece of coarse cloth, large enough to be a foot-cloth for your Majesty's chief room of state. In the left pocket, we saw a huge silver chest, with a cover of the same metal, which we the searchers were not able to lift. We desired it should be opened; and one of us, stepping into it, found himself up to the mid leg in a sort of dust, some

---

7. Gulliver's plea for liberty and the threat of starvation or rebellion he represents to his captors suggest the situation of Ireland with respect to England.

8. When the Whigs came into power in 1715, the leading Tories, who included Swift's friends Oxford and Bolingbroke (Robert Harley and Henry St. John) as well as Swift himself, were investigated by a committee of secrecy.

part whereof flying up to our faces, set us both a sneezing for several times together. In his right waistcoat-pocket, we found a prodigious bundle of white thin substances, folded one over another, about the bigness of three men, tied with a strong cable, and marked with black figures; which we humbly conceive to be writings; every letter almost half as large as the palm of our hands. In the left there was a sort of engine, from the back of which were extended twenty long poles, resembling the palisados[9] before your Majesty's court; wherewith we conjecture the Man-Mountain combs his head; for we did not always trouble him with questions, because we found it a great difficulty to make him understand us. In the large pocket on the right side of his middle cover (so I translate the word *ranfu-lo*, by which they meant my breeches) we saw a hollow pillar of iron, about the length of a man, fastened to a strong piece of timber, larger than the pillar; and upon one side of the pillar were huge pieces of iron sticking out, cut into strange figures; which we know not what to make of. In the left pocket, another engine of the same kind. In the smaller pocket on the right side, were several round flat pieces of white and red metal, of different bulk; some of the white, which seemed to be silver, were so large and heavy, that my comrade and I could hardly lift them. In the left pocket were two black pillars irregularly shaped: we could not, without difficulty, reach the top of them as we stood at the bottom of his pocket. One of them was covered, and seemed all of a piece; but at the upper end of the other, there appeared a white round substance, about twice the bigness of our heads. Within each of these was inclosed a prodigious plate of steel; which, by our orders, we obliged him to show us, because we apprehended they might be dangerous engines. He took them out of their cases, and told us, that in his own country his practice was to shave his beard with one of these, and to cut his meat with the other. There were two pockets which we could not enter: these he called his fobs; they were two large slits cut into the top of his middle cover, but squeezed close by the pressure of his belly. Out of the right fob hung a great silver chain, with a wonderful kind of engine at the bottom. We directed him to draw out whatever was at the end of the chain, which appeared to be a globe, half silver, and half of some transparent metal: for on the transparent side we saw certain strange figures circularly drawn, and thought we could touch them, until we found our fingers stopped with that lucid substance. He put this engine to our ears, which made an incessant noise like that of a watermill. And we conjecture it is either some unknown animal, or the god that he worships: but we are more inclined to the latter opinion, because he assured us (if we understood him right, for he expressed himself very imperfectly), that he seldom did any thing without consulting it. He called it his oracle, and said it pointed out the time for every action of his life. From the left fob he took out a net almost large enough for a fisherman, but contrived to open and shut like a purse, and served him for the same use: we found therein several massy pieces of yellow metal, which if they be of real gold, must be of immense value.

Having thus, in obedience to your Majesty's commands, diligently searched all his pockets, we observed a girdle[1] about his waist made of

9. Fences of stakes.   1. Belt.

the hide of some prodigious animal; from which, on the left side, hung a sword of the length of five men; and on the right, a bag or pouch divided into cells; each cell capable of holding three of your Majesty's subjects. In one of these cells were several globes or balls of a most ponderous metal, about the bigness of our heads, and required a strong hand to lift them: the other cell contained a heap of certain black grains, but of no great bulk or weight, for we could hold above fifty of them in the palms of our hands.

This is an exact inventory of what we found about the body of the Man-Mountain; who used us with great civility, and due respect to your Majesty's commission. Signed and sealed on the fourth day of the eighty-ninth moon of your Majesty's auspicious reign.

CLEFREN FRELOCK, MARSI FRELOCK.

When this inventory was read over to the Emperor, he directed me to deliver up the several particulars. He first called for my scimitar, which I took out, scabbard and all. In the meantime he ordered three thousand of his choicest troops (who then attended him) to surround me at a distance, with their bows and arrows just ready to discharge: but I did not observe it; for my eyes were wholly fixed upon his Majesty. He then desired me to draw my scimitar, which, although it had got some rust by the sea water, was in most parts exceeding bright. I did so, and immediately all the troops gave a shout between terror and surprise; for the sun shone clear, and the reflection dazzled their eyes, as I waved the scimitar to and fro in my hand. His Majesty, who is a most magnanimous[2] prince, was less daunted than I could expect; he ordered me to return it into the scabbard, and cast it on the ground as gently as I could, about six foot from the end of my chain. The next thing he demanded was one of the hollow iron pillars, by which he meant my pocket-pistols. I drew it out, and at his desire, as well as I could, expressed to him the use of it, and charging it only with powder, which by the closeness of my pouch happened to escape wetting in the sea (an inconvenience that all prudent mariners take special care to provide against), I first cautioned the Emperor not to be afraid; and then I let it off in the air. The astonishment here was much greater than at the sight of my scimitar. Hundreds fell down as if they had been struck dead; and even the Emperor, although he stood his ground, could not recover himself in some time. I delivered up both my pistols in the same manner as I had done my scimitar, and then my pouch of powder and bullets; begging him that the former might be kept from fire; for it would kindle with the smallest spark, and blow up his imperial palace into the air. I likewise delivered up my watch, which the Emperor was very curious to see; and commanded two of his tallest yeomen of the guards to bear it on a pole upon their shoulders, as draymen in England do a barrel of ale. He was amazed at the continual noise it made, and the motion of the minute-hand, which he could easily discern; for their sight is much more acute than ours: he asked the opinions of his learned men about him, which were various and remote, as the reader may well imagine without my repeating; although indeed I could not very perfectly understand them. I then gave up my silver and copper money, my purse with nine large pieces of gold, and

---

2. Courageous, great-spirited. Magnanimity, the relation (direct or inverse) between the size of the body and the soul, is a central concern of the first two parts of the *Travels*.

some smaller ones; my knife and razor, my comb and silver snuffbox, my handkerchief and journal book. My scimitar, pistols, and pouch, were conveyed in carriages to his Majesty's stores; but the rest of my goods were returned me.

I had, as I before observed, one private pocket which escaped their search, wherein there was a pair of spectacles (which I sometimes use for the weakness of my eyes), a pocket perspective,[3] and several other little conveniences; which, being of no consequence to the Emperor, I did not think myself bound in honor to discover, and I apprehended they might be lost or spoiled if I ventured them out of my possession.

CHAPTER 3. *The author diverts the Emperor and his nobility of both sexes in a very uncommon manner. The diversions of the court of Lilliput described. The author hath his liberty granted him upon certain conditions.*

My gentleness and good behavior had gained so far on the Emperor and his court, and indeed upon the army and people in general, that I began to conceive hopes of getting my liberty in a short time. I took all possible methods to cultivate this favorable disposition. The natives came by degrees to be less apprehensive of any danger from me. I would sometimes lie down, and let five or six of them dance on my hand. And at last the boys and girls would venture to come and play at hide-and-seek in my hair. I had now made a good progress in understanding and speaking their language. The Emperor had a mind one day to entertain me with several of the country shows; wherein they exceed all nations I have known, both for dexterity and magnificence. I was diverted with none so much as that of the rope-dancers, performed upon a slender white thread, extended about two foot, and twelve inches from the ground. Upon which I shall desire liberty, with the reader's patience, to enlarge a little.

This diversion is only practiced by those persons who are candidates for great employments, and high favor, at court. They are trained in this art from their youth, and are not always of noble birth, or liberal education. When a great office is vacant either by death or disgrace (which often happens) five or six of those candidates petition the Emperor to entertain his Majesty and the court with a dance on the rope; and whoever jumps the highest without falling, succeeds in the office. Very often the chief ministers themselves are commanded to show their skill, and to convince the Emperor that they have not lost their faculty. Flimnap,[4] the Treasurer, is allowed to cut a caper on the strait rope, at least an inch higher than any other lord in the whole empire. I have seen him do the summerset several times together upon a trencher[5] fixed on the rope, which is no thicker than a common packthread in England. My friend Reldresal, Principal Secretary for Private Affairs, is, in my opinion, if I am not partial, the second after the Treasurer; the rest of the great officers are much upon a par.

These diversions are often attended with fatal accidents, whereof great numbers are on record. I myself have seen two or three candidates break a limb. But the danger is much greater when the ministers themselves are

3. Telescope.
4. Sir Robert Walpole, the Whig head of the government, was notorious in Swift's circle for his
political acrobatics.
5. Plate. "Summerset": somersault.

commanded to show their dexterity; for, by contending to excel themselves and their fellows, they strain so far, that there is hardly one of them who hath not received a fall; and some of them two or three. I was assured, that a year or two before my arrival, Flimnap would have infallibly broke his neck, if one of the King's cushions,[6] that accidentally lay on the ground, had not weakened the force of his fall.

There is likewise another diversion, which is only shown before the Emperor and Empress, and first minister, upon particular occasions. The Emperor lays on a table three fine silken threads of six inches long. One is blue, the other red, and the third green.[7] These threads are proposed as prizes for those persons whom the Emperor hath a mind to distinguish by a peculiar mark of his favor. The ceremony is performed in his Majesty's great chamber of state; where the candidates are to undergo a trial of dexterity very different from the former, and such as I have not observed the least resemblance of in any other country of the old or the new world. The Emperor holds a stick in his hands, both ends parallel to the horizon, while the candidates, advancing one by one, sometimes leap over the stick, sometimes creep under it backwards and forwards several times, according as the stick is advanced or depressed. Sometimes the Emperor holds one end of the stick, and his first minister the other; sometimes the minister has it entirely to himself. Whoever performs his part with most agility, and holds out the longest in *leaping* and *creeping*, is rewarded with the blue-colored silk; the red is given to the next, and the green to the third, which they all wear girt twice round about the middle; and you see few great persons about this court who are not adorned with one of these girdles.

The horses of the army, and those of the royal stables, having been daily led before me, were no longer shy, but would come up to my very feet, without starting. The riders would leap them over my hand as I held it on the ground; and one of the Emperor's huntsmen, upon a large courser, took[8] my foot, shoe and all; which was indeed a prodigious leap. I had the good fortune to divert the Emperor one day after a very extraordinary manner. I desired he would order several sticks of two foot high, and the thickness of an ordinary cane, to be brought me; whereupon his Majesty commanded the master of his woods to give directions accordingly; and the next morning six woodmen arrived with as many carriages, drawn by eight horses to each. I took nine of these sticks, and fixing them firmly in the ground in a quadrangular figure, two foot and a half square, I took four other sticks, and tied them parallel at each corner, about two foot from the ground; then I fastened my handkerchief to the nine sticks that stood erect, and extended it on all sides till it was as tight as the top of a drum; and the four parallel sticks, rising about five inches higher than the handkerchief, served as ledges on each side. When I had finished my work, I desired the Emperor to let a troop of his best horse, twenty-four in number, come and exercise upon this plain. His Majesty approved of the proposal, and I took them up one by one in my hands, ready mounted and armed, with the proper officers to exercise them. As soon as they got into order, they divided into two parties, performed mock skirmishes, discharged blunt arrows, drew their swords, fled and pursued,

6. A mistress of George I was supposed to have helped restore Walpole to office in 1721.
7. The Orders of the Garter, the Bath, and the

Thistle, conferred for services to the king.
8. Jumped over.

attacked and retired; and in short discovered the best military discipline I ever beheld. The parallel sticks secured them and their horses from falling over the stage; and the Emperor was so much delighted, that he ordered this entertainment to be repeated several days; and once was pleased to be lifted up, and give the word of command; and, with great difficulty, persuaded even the Empress herself to let me hold her in her close chair[9] within two yards of the stage, from whence she was able to take a full view of the whole performance. It was my good fortune that no ill accident happened in these entertainments, only once a fiery horse that belonged to one of the captains pawing with his hoof struck a hole in my handkerchief, and his foot slipping, he overthrew his rider and himself; but I immediately relieved them both; for covering the hole with one hand, I set down the troop with the other, in the same manner as I took them up. The horse that fell was strained in the left shoulder, but the rider got no hurt, and I repaired my handkerchief as well as I could; however, I would not trust to the strength of it any more in such dangerous enterprises.

About two or three days before I was set at liberty, as I was entertaining the court with these kinds of feats, there arrived an express to inform his Majesty that some of his subjects, riding near the place where I was first taken up, had seen a great black substance lying on the ground, very oddly shaped, extending its edges round as wide as his Majesty's bedchamber, and rising up in the middle as high as a man; that it was no living creature, as they at first apprehended, for it lay on the grass without motion, and some of them had walked round it several times; that by mounting upon each other's shoulders, they had got to the top, which was flat and even; and stamping upon it they found it was hollow within; that they humbly conceived it might be something belonging to the Man-Mountain, and if his Majesty pleased, they would undertake to bring it with only five horses. I presently[1] knew what they meant; and was glad at heart to receive this intelligence. It seems upon my first reaching the shore after our shipwreck, I was in such confusion, that before I came to the place where I went to sleep, my hat, which I had fastened with a string to my head while I was rowing, and had stuck on all the time I was swimming, fell off after I came to land; the string, as I conjecture, breaking by some accident which I never observed, but thought my hat had been lost at sea. I intreated his Imperial Majesty to give orders it might be brought to me as soon as possible, describing to him the use and the nature of it: and the next day the wagoners arrived with it, but not in a very good condition; they had bored two holes in the brim, within an inch and half of the edge, and fastened two hooks in the holes; these hooks were tied by a long cord to the harness, and thus my hat was dragged along for above half an English mile: but the ground in that country being extremely smooth and level, it received less damage than I expected.

Two days after this adventure, the Emperor, having ordered that part of his army which quarters in and about his metropolis to be in a readiness, took a fancy of diverting himself in a very singular manner. He desired I would stand like a colossus, with my legs as far asunder as I conveniently could. He then commanded his general (who was an old experienced leader,

---

9. An enclosed or sedan chair.   1. Immediately.

and a great patron of mine) to draw up the troops in close order, and march them under me; the foot[2] by twenty-four in a breast, and the horse by sixteen, with drums beating, colors flying, and pikes advanced. This body consisted of three thousand foot, and a thousand horse. His Majesty gave orders, upon pain of death, that every soldier in his march should observe the strictest decency with regard to my person; which, however, could not prevent some of the younger officers from turning up their eyes as they passed under me. And, to confess the truth, my breeches were at that time in so ill a condition, that they afforded some opportunities for laughter and admiration.

I had sent so many memorials and petitions for my liberty, that his Majesty at length mentioned the matter first in the cabinet, and then in a full council; where it was opposed by none, except Skyresh Bolgolam,[3] who was pleased, without any provocation, to be my mortal enemy. But it was carried against him by the whole board, and confirmed by the Emperor. That minister was *Galbet,* or Admiral of the Realm; very much in his master's confidence, and a person well versed in affairs, but of a morose and sour complexion.[4] However, he was at length persuaded to comply; but prevailed that the articles and conditions upon which I should be set free, and to which I must swear, should be drawn up by himself. These articles were brought to me by Skyresh Bolgolam in person, attended by two under-secretaries, and several persons of distinction. After they were read, I was demanded to swear to the performance of them; first in the manner of my own country, and afterwards in the method prescribed by their laws; which was to hold my right foot in my left hand, to place the middle finger of my right hand on the crown of my head, and my thumb on the tip of my right ear. But because the reader may perhaps be curious to have some idea of the style and manner of expression peculiar to that people, as well as to know the articles upon which I recovered my liberty, I have made a translation of the whole instrument,[5] word for word, as near as I was able; which I here offer to the public.

GOLBASTO MOMAREN EVLAME GURDILO SHEFIN MULLY ULLY GUE, most mighty Emperor of Lilliput, delight and terror of the universe, whose dominions extend five thousand blustrugs (about twelve miles in circumference) to the extremities of the globe; Monarch of all Monarchs; taller than the sons of men; whose feet press down to the center, and whose head strikes against the sun; at whose nod the princes of the earth shake their knees; pleasant as the spring, comfortable as the summer, fruitful as autumn, dreadful as winter. His most sublime Majesty proposeth to the Man-Mountain, lately arrived at our celestial dominions, the following articles, which by a solemn oath he shall be obliged to perform.

First, The Man-Mountain shall not depart from our dominions, without our license under our great seal.

Secondly, He shall not presume to come into our metropolis, without our express order; at which time the inhabitants shall have two hours warning, to keep within their doors.

Thirdly, The said Man-Mountain shall confine his walks to our prin-

---

2. Foot soldiers or infantry.
3. The earl of Nottingham, an enemy of Swift.
4. Disposition.
5. A formal legal document.

cipal high roads; and not offer to walk or lie down in a meadow, or field of corn.

Fourthly, As he walks the said roads, he shall take the utmost care not to trample upon the bodies of any of our loving subjects, their horses, or carriages, nor take any of our said subjects into his hands, without their own consent.

Fifthly, If an express require extraordinary dispatch, the Man-Mountain shall be obliged to carry in his pocket the messenger and horse, a six days' journey once in every moon, and return the said messenger back (if so required) safe to our Imperial Presence.

Sixthly, He shall be our ally against our enemies in the island of Blefuscu, and do his utmost to destroy their fleet, which is now preparing to invade us.

Seventhly, That the said Man-Mountain shall, at his times of leisure, be aiding and assisting to our workmen, in helping to raise certain great stones, towards covering the wall of the principal park, and other our royal buildings.

Eighthly, That the said Man-Mountain shall, in two moons' time, deliver in an exact survey of the circumference of our dominions by a computation of his own paces round the coast.

Lastly, That upon his solemn oath to observe all the above articles, the said Man-Mountain shall have a daily allowance of meat and drink sufficient for the support of 1,728 of our subjects; with free access to our Royal Person, and other marks of our favor. Given at our palace at Belfaborac the twelfth day of the ninety-first moon of our reign.

I swore and subscribed to these articles with great cheerfulness and content, although some of them were not so honorable as I could have wished; which proceeded wholly from the malice of Skyresh Bolgolam the High Admiral: whereupon my chains were immediately unlocked, and I was at full liberty: the Emperor himself in person did me the honor to be by at the whole ceremony. I made my acknowledgements by prostrating myself at his Majesty's feet: but he commanded me to rise; and after many gracious expressions, which, to avoid the censure of vanity, I shall not repeat, he added, that he hoped I should prove a useful servant, and well deserve all the favors he had already conferred upon me, or might do for the future.

The reader may please to observe, that in the last article for the recovery of my liberty, the Emperor stipulates to allow me a quantity of meat and drink, sufficient for the support of 1,728 Lilliputians. Some time after, asking a friend at court how they came to fix on that determinate number, he told me, that his Majesty's mathematicians, having taken the height of my body by the help of a quadrant, and finding it to exceed theirs in the proportion of twelve to one, they concluded from the similarity of their bodies, that mine must contain at least 1,728 of theirs, and consequently would require as much food as was necessary to support that number of Lilliputians. By which, the reader may conceive an idea of the ingenuity of that people, as well as the prudent and exact economy of so great a prince.

CHAPTER 4. *Mildendo, the metropolis of Lilliput, described, together with the Emperor's palace. A conversation between the author and a principal secretary, concerning the affairs of that empire; the author's offers to serve the Emperor in his wars.*

The first request I made after I had obtained my liberty, was, that I might have license to see Mildendo, the metropolis; which the Emperor easily granted me, but with a special charge to do no hurt, either to the inhabitants, or their houses. The people had notice by proclamation of my design to visit the town. The wall which encompassed it is two foot and an half high, and at least eleven inches broad, so that a coach and horses may be driven very safely round it; and it is flanked with strong towers at ten foot distance. I stepped over the great western gate, and passed very gently, and sideling[6] through the two principal streets, only in my short waistcoat, for fear of damaging the roofs and eaves of the houses with the skirts of my coat. I walked with the utmost circumspection, to avoid treading on any stragglers, who might remain in the streets, although the orders were very strict, that all people should keep in their houses, at their own peril. The garret windows and tops of houses were so crowded with spectators, that I thought in all my travels I had not seen a more populous place. The city is an exact square, each side of the wall being five hundred foot long. The two great streets, which run cross and divide it into four quarters, are five foot wide. The lanes and alleys, which I could not enter, but only viewed them as I passed, are from twelve to eighteen inches. The town is capable of holding five hundred thousand souls. The houses are from three to five stories. The shops and markets well provided.

The Emperor's palace is in the center of the city, where the two great streets meet. It is enclosed by a wall of two foot high, and twenty foot distant from the buildings. I had his Majesty's permission to step over this wall; and the space being so wide between that and the palace, I could easily view it on every side. The outward court is a square of forty foot, and includes two other courts: in the inmost are the royal apartments, which I was very desirous to see, but found it extremely difficult; for the great gates, from one square into another, were but eighteen inches high, and seven inches wide. Now the buildings of the outer court were at least five foot high; and it was impossible for me to stride over them, without infinite damage to the pile, although the walls were strongly built of hewn stone, and four inches thick. At the same time the Emperor had a great desire that I should see the magnificence of his palace; but this I was not able to do till three days after, which I spent in cutting down with my knife some of the largest trees in the royal park, about an hundred yards distance from the city. Of these trees I made two stools, each about three foot high, and strong enough to bear my weight. The people having received notice a second time, I went again through the city to the palace, with my two stools in my hands. When I came to the side of the outer court, I stood upon one stool, and took the other in my hand: this I lifted over the roof, and gently set it down on the space between the first and second court, which was eight foot wide. I then stepped over the buildings very conveniently from one stool to the other, and drew up the first after me with a hooked stick. By this contrivance I got into the inmost court; and lying down upon my side, I applied my face to the windows

6. Sideways.

of the middle stories, which were left open on purpose, and discovered the most splendid apartments that can be imagined. There I saw the Empress, and the young princes in their several lodgings, with their chief attendants about them. Her Imperial Majesty was pleased to smile very graciously upon me and gave me out of the window her hand to kiss.

But I shall not anticipate the reader with farther descriptions of this kind, because I reserve them for a greater work, which is now almost ready for the press; containing a general description of this empire, from its first erection, through a long series of princes, with a particular account of their wars and politics, laws, learning, and religion; their plants and animals, their peculiar manners and customs, with other matters very curious and useful; my chief design at present being only to relate such events and transactions as happened to the public, or to myself, during a residence of about nine months in that empire.

One morning, about a fortnight after I had obtained my liberty, Reldresal, Principal Secretary (as they style him) of Private Affairs, came to my house, attended only by one servant. He ordered his coach to wait at a distance, and desired I would give him an hour's audience; which I readily consented to, on account of his quality, and personal merits, as well as of the many good offices he had done me during my solicitations at court. I offered to lie down, that he might the more conveniently reach my ear; but he chose rather to let me hold him in my hand during our conversation. He began with compliments on my liberty, said he might pretend to some merit in it; but, however, added, that if it had not been for the present situation of things at court, perhaps I might not have obtained it so soon. For, said he, as flourishing a condition as we appear to be in to foreigners, we labor under two mighty evils; a violent faction at home, and the danger of an invasion by a most potent enemy from abroad. As to the first, you are to understand, that for above seventy moons past, there have been two struggling parties in the empire, under the names of *Tramecksan*, and *Slamecksan*,[7] from the high and low heels on their shoes, by which they distinguish themselves.

It is alleged indeed, that the high heels are most agreeable to our ancient constitution: but however this be, his Majesty hath determined to make use of only low heels in the administration of the government and all offices in the gift of the crown; as you cannot but observe; and particularly, that his Majesty's imperial heels are lower at least by a *drurr* than any of his court; (*drurr* is a measure about the fourteenth part of an inch). The animosities between these two parties run so high, that they will neither eat nor drink, nor talk with each other. We compute the *Tramecksan*, or High-Heels, to exceed us in number; but the power is wholly on our side. We apprehend his Imperial Highness, the heir to the crown, to have some tendency towards the High-Heels; at least we can plainly discover one of his heels higher than the other, which gives him a hobble in his gait.[8] Now, in the midst of these intestine disquiets, we are threatened with an invasion from the island of Blefuscu,[9] which is the other great empire of the universe, almost as large and powerful as this of his Majesty. For as to what we have heard you affirm, that there are other kingdoms and states in the world, inhabited by human

---

7. Tory (High Church) and Whig (Low Church).
8. The Prince of Wales (later George II) had friends in both parties.
9. France.

creatures as large as yourself, our philosophers are in much doubt; and would rather conjecture that you dropped from the moon, or one of the stars; because it is certain, that an hundred mortals of your bulk would, in a short time, destroy all the fruits and cattle of his Majesty's dominions. Besides, our histories of six thousand moons make no mention of any other regions, than the two great empires of Lilliput and Blefuscu. Which two mighty powers have, as I was going to tell you, been engaged in a most obstinate war for six and thirty moons past. It began upon the following occasion. It is allowed on all hands, that the primitive way of breaking eggs before we eat them, was upon the larger end: but his present Majesty's grandfather, while he was a boy, going to eat an egg, and breaking it according to the ancient practice, happened to cut one of his fingers. Whereupon the Emperor his father published an edict, commanding all his subjects, upon great penalties, to break the smaller end of their eggs. The people so highly resented this law, that our histories tell us there have been six rebellions raised on that account; wherein one emperor lost his life, and another his crown.[1] These civil commotions were constantly fomented by the monarchs of Blefuscu; and when they were quelled, the exiles always fled for refuge to that empire. It is computed, that eleven thousand persons have, at several times, suffered death, rather than submit to break their eggs at the smaller end. Many hundred large volumes have been published upon this controversy: but the books of the Big-Endians have been long forbidden, and the whole party rendered incapable by law of holding employments.[2] During the course of these troubles, the emperors of Blefuscu did frequently expostulate by their ambassadors, accusing us of making a schism in religion, by offending against a fundamental doctrine of our great prophet Lustrog, in the fifty-fourth chapter of the *Brundecral* (which is their Alcoran[3]). This, however, is thought to be a mere strain upon the text: for the words are these; *That all true believers shall break their eggs at the convenient end:* and which is the convenient end, seems, in my humble opinion, to be left to every man's conscience, or at least in the power of the chief magistrate[4] to determine. Now the Big-Endian exiles have found so much credit in the Emperor of Blefuscu's court, and so much private assistance and encouragement from their party here at home, that a bloody war hath been carried on between the two empires for six and thirty moons with various success;[5] during which time we have lost forty capital ships, and a much greater number of smaller vessels, together with thirty thousand of our best seamen and soldiers; and the damage received by the enemy is reckoned to be somewhat greater than ours. However, they have now equipped a numerous fleet, and are just preparing to make a descent upon us; and his Imperial Majesty, placing great confidence in your valor and strength, hath commanded me to lay this account of his affairs before you.

I desired the Secretary to present my humble duty to the Emperor, and to let him know, that I thought it would not become me, who was a foreigner,

1. Swift's satirical allegory of the strife between Catholics (Big-Endians) and Protestants (Little-Endians) touches on Henry VIII (who "broke" with the Pope), Charles I (who lost his life), and James II (who lost his crown).

2. The Test Act (1673) prevented Catholics and Nonconformists from holding office unless they accepted the Anglican Sacrament.

3. Koran.

4. Ruler, sovereign. Swift himself accepted the right of the king to determine religious observances.

5. Reminiscent of the War of the Spanish Succession (1701–13).

to interfere with parties; but I was ready, with the hazard of my life, to defend his person and state against all invaders.

CHAPTER 5. *The author by an extraordinary stratagem prevents an invasion. A high title of honor is conferred upon him. Ambassadors arrive from the Emperor of Blefuscu, and sue for peace. The Empress's apartment on fire by an accident; the author instrumental in saving the rest of the palace.*

The empire of Blefuscu is an island situated to the north north-east side of Lilliput, from whence it is parted only by a channel of eight hundred yards wide. I had not yet seen it, and upon this notice of an intended invasion, I avoided appearing on that side of the coast, for fear of being discovered by some of the enemy's ships, who had received no intelligence of me; all intercourse between the two empires having been strictly forbidden during the war, upon pain of death; and an embargo laid by our Emperor upon all vessels whatsoever. I communicated to his Majesty a project I had formed of seizing the enemy's whole fleet; which, as our scouts assured us, lay at anchor in the harbor ready to sail with the first fair wind. I consulted the most experienced seamen upon the depth of the channel, which they had often plumbed; who told me, that in the middle at high water it was seventy *glumgluffs* deep, which is about six foot of European measure; and the rest of it fifty *glumgluffs* at most. I walked to the northeast coast over against Blefuscu; where, lying down behind a hillock, I took out my small pocket perspective glass, and viewed the enemy's fleet at anchor, consisting of about fifty men of war, and a great number of transports: I then came back to my house, and gave order (for which I had a warrant) for a great quantity of the strongest cable and bars of iron. The cable was about as thick as packthread and the bars of the length and size of a knitting-needle. I trebled the cable to make it stronger, and for the same reason I twisted three of the iron bars together, bending the extremities into a hook. Having thus fixed fifty hooks to as many cables, I went back to the northeast coast, and putting off my coat, shoes, and stockings, walked into the sea in my leathern jerkin, about half an hour before high water. I waded with what haste I could, and swam in the middle about thirty yards until I felt the ground; I arrived at the fleet in less than half an hour. The enemy was so frighted when they saw me, that they leaped out of their ships, and swam to shore, where there could not be fewer than thirty thousand souls. I then took my tackling, and fastening a hook to the hole at the prow of each, I tied all the cords together at the end. While I was thus employed, the enemy discharged several thousand arrows, many of which stuck in my hands and face; and besides the excessive smart, gave me much disturbance in my work. My greatest apprehension was for my eyes, which I should have infallibly lost, if I had not suddenly thought of an expedient. I kept, among other little necessaries, a pair of spectacles in a private pocket, which, as I observed before, had escaped the Emperor's searchers. These I took out, and fastened as strongly as I could upon my nose; and thus armed went on boldly with my work in spite of the enemy's arrows; many of which struck against the glasses of my spectacles, but without any other effect, further than a little to discompose them. I had now fastened all the hooks, and taking the knot in my hand, began to pull; but not a ship would stir, for they were all too fast by their anchors, so that the boldest part of my enterprise remained. I therefore let go the cord, and leaving the hooks fixed to the ships, I resolutely cut with my knife the cables that fastened the anchors, receiving about two hundred shots in my face and hands; then I took up the knotted end of the cables to which my hooks were tied; and with great ease drew fifty of the enemy's largest men-of-war after me.

The Blefuscudians, who had not the least imagination of what I intended, were at first confounded with astonishment. They had seen me cut the cables, and thought my design was only to let the ships run adrift, or fall foul on each other: but when they perceived the whole fleet moving in order, and saw me pulling at the end, they set up such a scream of grief and despair, that it is almost impossible to describe or conceive. When I had got out of danger, I stopped a while to pick out the arrows that stuck in my hands and face, and rubbed on some of the same ointment that was given me at my first arrival, as I have formerly mentioned. I then took off my spectacles, and waiting about an hour until the tide was a little fallen, I waded through the middle with my cargo, and arrived safe at the royal port of Lilliput.

The Emperor and his whole court stood on the shore, expecting the issue of this great adventure. They saw the ships move forward in a large half-moon, but could not discern me, who was up to my breast in water. When I advanced to the middle of the channel, they were yet more in pain, because I was under water to my neck. The Emperor concluded me to be drowned, and that the enemy's fleet was approaching in a hostile manner: but he was soon eased of his fears, for the channel growing shallower every step I made, I came in a short time within hearing; and holding up the end of the cable by which the fleet was fastened, I cried in a loud voice, Long live the most puissant Emperor of Lilliput! This great prince received me at my landing with all possible encomiums, and created me a *Nardac* upon the spot, which is the highest title of honor among them.

His Majesty desired I would take some other opportunity of bringing all the rest of his enemy's ships into his ports. And so unmeasurable is the ambition of princes, that he seemed to think of nothing less than reducing the whole empire of Blefuscu into a province, and governing it by a viceroy; of destroying the Big-Endian exiles, and compelling that people to break the smaller end of their eggs, by which he would remain sole monarch of the whole world. But I endeavored to divert him from this design, by many arguments drawn from the topics of policy as well as justice: and I plainly protested, that I would never be an instrument of bringing a free and brave people into slavery. And when the matter was debated in council, the wisest part of the ministry were of my opinion.

This open bold declaration of mine was so opposite to the schemes and politics of his Imperial Majesty, that he could never forgive me; he mentioned it in a very artful manner at council, where I was told that some of the wisest appeared, at least by their silence, to be of my opinion; but others, who were my secret enemies, could not forbear some expressions, which by a side-wind[6] reflected on me. And from this time began an intrigue between his Majesty and a junta of ministers maliciously bent against me, which broke out in less than two months, and had like to have ended in my utter destruc-

6. Indirectly.

tion. Of so little weight are the greatest services to princes, when put into the balance with a refusal to gratify their passions.[7]

About three weeks after this exploit, there arrived a solemn embassy from Blefuscu, with humble offers of a peace; which was soon concluded upon conditions very advantageous to our Emperor; wherewith I shall not trouble the reader. There were six ambassadors, with a train of about five hundred persons; and their entry was very magnificent, suitable to the grandeur of their master, and the importance of their business. When their treaty was finished, wherein I did them several good offices by the credit I now had, or at least appeared to have at court, their Excellencies, who were privately told how much I had been their friend, made me a visit in form. They began with many compliments upon my valor and generosity; invited me to that kingdom in the Emperor their master's name; and desired me to show them some proofs of my prodigious strength, of which they had heard so many wonders; wherein I readily obliged them, but shall not interrupt the reader with the particulars.

When I had for some time entertained their Excellencies to their infinite satisfaction and surprise, I desired they would do me the honor to present my most humble respects to the Emperor their master, the renown of whose virtues had so justly filled the whole world with admiration, and whose royal person I resolved to attend before I returned to my own country. Accordingly, the next time I had the honor to see our Emperor, I desired his general license to wait on the Blefuscudian monarch, which he was pleased to grant me, as I could plainly perceive, in a very cold manner; but could not guess the reason, till I had a whisper from a certain person, that Flimnap and Bolgolam had represented my intercourse with those ambassadors as a mark of disaffection, from which I am sure my heart was wholly free. And this was the first time I began to conceive some imperfect idea of courts and ministers.

It is to be observed, that these ambassadors spoke to me by an interpreter; the languages of both empires differing as much from each other as any two in Europe, and each nation priding itself upon the antiquity, beauty, and energy of their own tongues, with an avowed contempt for that of their neighbor; yet our Emperor, standing upon the advantage he had got by the seizure of their fleet, obliged them to deliver their credentials, and make their speech, in the Lilliputian tongue. And it must be confessed, that from the great intercourse of trade and commerce between both realms, from the continual reception of exiles, which is mutual among them, and from the custom in each empire to send their young nobility and richer gentry to the other, in order to polish themselves, by seeing the world, and understanding men and manners, there are few persons of distinction, or merchants, or seamen, who dwell in the maritime parts, but what can hold conversation in both tongues; as I found some weeks after, when I went to pay my respects to the Emperor of Blefuscu, which in the midst of great misfortunes, through the malice of my enemies, proved a very happy adventure to me, as I shall relate in its proper place.

The reader may remember, that when I signed those articles upon which I recovered my liberty, there were some which I disliked upon account of

7. After a series of British naval victories, the Treaty of Utrecht (1713) had ended the war with France, but the Tory ministers who engineered the peace were subsequently accused of having sold out to the enemy.

their being too servile, neither could any thing but an extreme necessity have forced me to submit. But being now a *Nardac,* of the highest rank in that empire, such offices[8] were looked upon as below my dignity, and the Emperor (to do him justice) never once mentioned them to me. However, it was not long before I had an opportunity of doing his Majesty, at least as I then thought, a most signal service. I was alarmed at midnight with the cries of many hundred people at my door; by which being suddenly awaked, I was in some kind of terror. I heard the word *burglum* repeated incessantly; several of the Emperor's court, making their way through the crowd, intreated me to come immediately to the palace, where her Imperial Majesty's apartment was on fire, by the carelessness of a maid of honor, who fell asleep while she was reading a romance. I got up in an instant; and orders being given to clear the way before me, and it being likewise a moonshine night, I made a shift to get to the palace without trampling on any of the people. I found they had already applied ladders to the walls of the apartment, and were well provided with buckets, but the water was at some distance. These buckets were about the size of a large thimble, and the poor people supplied me with them as fast as they could; but the flame was so violent, that they did little good. I might easily have stifled it with my coat, which I unfortunately left behind me for haste, and came away only in my leathern jerkin. The case seemed wholly desperate and deplorable; and this magnificent palace would have infallibly been burnt down to the ground, if, by a presence of mind, unusual to me, I had not suddenly thought of an expedient. I had the evening before drank plentifully of a most delicious wine, called *glimigrim* (the Blefuscudians call it *flunec,* but ours is esteemed the better sort), which is very diuretic. By the luckiest chance in the world, I had not discharged myself of any part of it. The heat I had contracted by coming very near the flames, and by my laboring to quench them, made the wine begin to operate by urine; which I voided in such a quantity, and applied so well to the proper places, that in three minutes the fire was wholly extinguished; and the rest of that noble pile, which had cost so many ages in erecting, preserved from destruction.

It was now daylight, and I returned to my house, without waiting to congratulate with the Emperor; because, although I had done a very eminent piece of service, yet I could not tell how his Majesty might resent the manner by which I had performed it: for, by the fundamental laws of the realm, it is capital[9] in any person, of what quality soever, to make water within the precincts of the palace. But I was a little comforted by a message from his Majesty, that he would give orders to the Grand Justiciary for passing my pardon in form; which, however, I could not obtain. And I was privately assured, that the Empress, conceiving the greatest abhorrence of what I had done,[1] removed to the most distant side of the court, firmly resolved that those buildings should never be repaired for her use; and, in the presence of her chief confidents, could not forbear vowing revenge.

CHAPTER 6. *Of the inhabitants of Lilliput; their learning, laws, and customs, the manner of educating their children. The author's way of living in that country. His vindication of a great lady.*

---

8. Duties.
9. Punishable by death.
1. Queen Anne, whom Swift called "a royal

prude," strongly objected to the coarseness of *A Tale of a Tub.*

Although I intend to leave the description of this empire to a particular treatise, yet in the mean time I am content to gratify the curious reader with some general ideas. As the common size of the natives is somewhat under six inches, so there is an exact proportion in all other animals, as well as plants and trees: for instance, the tallest horses and oxen are between four and five inches in height, the sheep an inch and a half, more or less; their geese about the bigness of a sparrow; and so the several gradations downwards, till you come to the smallest, which, to my sight, were almost invisible; but nature hath adapted the eyes of the Lilliputians to all objects proper for their view: they see with great exactness, but at no great distance. And to show the sharpness of their sight towards objects that are near, I have been much pleased with observing a cook pulling[2] a lark, which was not so large as a common fly; and a young girl threading an invisible needle with invisible silk. Their tallest trees are about seven foot high; I mean some of those in the great royal park, the tops whereof I could but just reach with my fist clinched. The other vegetables[3] are in the same proportion; but this I leave to the reader's imagination.

I shall say but little at present of their learning, which for many ages hath flourished in all its branches among them: but their manner of writing is very peculiar; being neither from the left to the right, like the Europeans; nor from the right to the left, like the Arabians; nor from up to down, like the Chinese; nor from down to up, like the Cascagians;[4] but aslant from one corner of the paper to the other, like ladies in England.

They bury their dead with their heads directly downwards; because they hold an opinion that in eleven thousand moons they are all to rise again; in which period, the earth (which they conceive to be flat) will turn upside down, and by this means they shall, at their resurrection, be found ready standing on their feet. The learned among them confess the absurdity of this doctrine; but the practice still continues, in compliance to the vulgar.

There are some laws and customs in this empire very peculiar; and if they were not so directly contrary to those of my own dear country, I should be tempted to say a little in their justification. It is only to be wished, that they were as well executed. The first I shall mention relateth to informers. All crimes against the state are punished here with the utmost severity; but if the person accused make his innocence plainly to appear upon his trial, the accuser is immediately put to an ignominious death; and out of his goods or lands, the innocent person is quadruply recompensed for the loss of his time, for the danger he underwent, for the hardship of his imprisonment, and for all the charges he hath been at in making his defense. Or, if that fund be deficient, it is largely[5] supplied by the crown. The Emperor doth also confer on him some public mark of his favor; and proclamation is made of his innocence through the whole city.

They look upon fraud as a greater crime than theft, and therefore seldom fail to punish it with death; for they allege, that care and vigilance, with a very common understanding, may preserve a man's goods from thieves; but honesty hath no fence against superior cunning: and since it is necessary that there should be a perpetual intercourse of buying and selling, and deal-

2. Plucking.
3. Plants.

4. Swift's invention.
5. Fully.

ing upon credit, where fraud is permitted or connived at, or hath no law to punish it, the honest dealer is always undone, and the knave gets the advantage. I remember when I was once interceding with the King for a criminal who had wronged his master of a great sum of money, which he had received by order, and ran away with; and happening to tell his Majesty, by way of extenuation, that it was only a breach of trust, the Emperor thought it monstrous in me to offer, as a defense, the greatest aggravation of the crime: and truly, I had little to say in return, farther than the common answer, that different nations had different customs; for, I confess, I was heartily ashamed.

Although we usually call reward and punishment the two hinges upon which all government turns, yet I could never observe this maxim to be put in practice by any nation, except that of Lilliput. Whoever can there bring sufficient proof that he hath strictly observed the laws of his country for seventy-three moons, hath a claim to certain privileges, according to his quality[6] and condition of life, with a proportionable sum of money out of a fund appropriated for that use: he likewise acquires the title of *Snilpall*, or *Legal*, which is added to his name, but doth not descend to his posterity. And these people thought it a prodigious defect of policy among us, when I told them that our laws were enforced only by penalties, without any mention of reward. It is upon this account that the image of Justice, in their courts of judicature, is formed with six eyes, two before, as many behind, and on each side one, to signify circumspection; with a bag of gold open in her right hand, and a sword sheathed in her left, to show she is more disposed to reward than to punish.

In choosing persons for all employments, they have more regard to good morals than to great abilities; for, since government is necessary to mankind, they believe that the common size of human understandings is fitted to some station or other; and that Providence never intended to make the management of public affairs a mystery, to be comprehended only by a few persons of sublime genius, of which there seldom are three born in an age: but they suppose truth, justice, temperance, and the like, to be in every man's power; the practice of which virtues, assisted by experience and a good intention, would qualify any man for the service of his country, except where a course of study is required. But they thought the want of moral virtues was so far from being supplied by superior endowments of the mind, that employments could never be put into such dangerous hands as those of persons so qualified; and at least, that the mistakes committed by ignorance in a virtuous disposition would never be of such fatal consequence to the public weal, as the practices of a man whose inclinations led him to be corrupt, and had great abilities to manage, to multiply, and defend his corruptions.

In like manner, the disbelief of a divine Providence renders a man uncapable of holding any public station; for since kings avow themselves to be the deputies of Providence, the Lilliputians think nothing can be more absurd than for a prince to employ such men as disown the authority under which he acteth.

In relating these and the following laws, I would only be understood to mean the original institutions, and not the most scandalous corruptions into

6. Social position.

which these people are fallen by the degenerate nature of man. For as to that infamous practice of acquiring great employments by dancing on the ropes, or badges of favor and distinction by leaping over sticks, and creeping under them, the reader is to observe, that they were first introduced by the grandfather of the Emperor now reigning; and grew to the present height by the gradual increase of party and faction.

Ingratitude is among them a capital crime, as we read it to have been in some other countries; for they reason thus, that whoever makes ill returns to his benefactor, must needs be a common enemy to the rest of mankind, from whom he hath received no obligation; and therefore such a man is not fit to live.

Their notions relating to the duties of parents and children differ extremely from ours. For, since the conjunction of male and female is founded upon the great law of nature, in order to propagate and continue the species, the Lilliputians will needs have it, that men and women are joined together like other animals, by the motives of concupiscence; and that their tenderness towards their young proceedeth from the like natural principle: for which reason they will never allow, that a child is under any obligation to his father for begetting him, or to his mother for bringing him into the world; which, considering the miseries of human life, was neither a benefit in itself, nor intended so by his parents, whose thoughts in their love-encounters were otherwise employed. Upon these, and the like reasonings, their opinion is, that parents are the last of all others to be trusted with the education of their own children: and therefore they have in every town public nurseries, where all parents, except cottagers[7] and laborers, are obliged to send their infants of both sexes to be reared and educated when they come to the age of twenty moons; at which time they are supposed to have some rudiments of docility. These schools are of several kinds, suited to different qualities, and to both sexes. They have certain professors[8] well skilled in preparing children for such a condition of life as befits the rank of their parents, and their own capacities as well as inclinations. I shall first say something of the male nurseries, and then of the female.

The nurseries for males of noble or eminent birth are provided with grave and learned professors, and their several deputies. The clothes and food of the children are plain and simple. They are bred up in the principles of honor, justice, courage, modesty, clemency, religion, and love of their country; they are always employed in some business, except in the times of eating and sleeping, which are very short, and two hours for diversions, consisting of bodily exercises. They are dressed by men until four years of age, and then are obliged to dress themselves, although their quality be ever so great; and the women attendants, who are aged proportionably to ours at fifty, perform only the most menial offices. They are never suffered to converse with servants, but go together in small or greater numbers to take their diversions, and always in the presence of a professor, or one of his deputies; whereby they avoid those early bad impressions of folly and vice to which our children are subject. Their parents are suffered to see them only twice a year; the visit is not to last above an hour; they are allowed to kiss the child at meeting and parting; but a professor, who always standeth by on those occasions, will not

7. Agricultural workers, peasants.   8. Professional teachers.

suffer them to whisper, or use any fondling expressions, or bring any presents of toys, sweetmeats, and the like.

The pension from each family for the education and entertainment[9] of a child, upon failure of due payment, is levied by the Emperor's officers.

The nurseries for children of ordinary gentlemen, merchants, traders, and handicrafts, are managed proportionably after the same manner; only those designed for trades are put out apprentices at seven years old; whereas those of persons of quality continue in their exercises until fifteen, which answers to one and twenty with us: but the confinement is gradually lessened for the last three years.

In the female nurseries, the young girls of quality are educated much like the males, only they are dressed by orderly servants of their own sex, but always in the presence of a professor or deputy, until they come to dress themselves, which is at five years old. And if it be found that these nurses ever presume to entertain the girls with frightful or foolish stories, or the common follies practiced by chambermaids among us, they are publicly whipped thrice about the city, imprisoned for a year, and banished for life to the most desolate parts of the country. Thus the young ladies there are as much ashamed of being cowards and fools as the men; and despise all personal ornaments beyond decency and cleanliness: neither did I perceive any difference in their education, made by their difference of sex, only that the exercises of the females were not altogether so robust; and that some rules were given them relating to domestic life, and a smaller compass of learning was enjoined them: for their maxim is, that among people of quality, a wife should be always a reasonable and agreeable companion, because she cannot always be young. When the girls are twelve years old, which among them is the marriageable age, their parents or guardians take them home, with great expressions of gratitude to the professors, and seldom without tears of the young lady and her companions.

In the nurseries of females of the meaner sort, the children are instructed in all kinds of works proper for their sex, and their several degrees:[1] those intended for apprentices are dismissed at seven years old, the rest are kept to eleven.

The meaner families who have children at these nurseries are obliged, besides their annual pension, which is as low as possible, to return to the steward of the nursery a small monthly share of their gettings, to be a portion for the child; and therefore all parents are limited in their expenses by the law. For the Lilliputians think nothing can be more unjust, than that people, in subservience to their own appetites, should bring children into the world, and leave the burthen of supporting them on the public. As to persons of quality, they give security to appropriate a certain sum for each child, suitable to their condition; and these funds are always managed with good husbandry, and the most exact justice.

The cottagers and laborers keep their children at home, their business being only to till and cultivate the earth; and therefore their education is of little consequence to the public; but the old and diseased among them are supported by hospitals: for begging is a trade unknown in this empire.

And here it may perhaps divert the curious reader, to give some account

9. Sustenance.   1. Various social ranks.

of my domestic,[2] and my manner of living in this country, during a residence of nine months and thirteen days. Having a head mechanically turned, and being likewise forced by necessity, I had made for myself a table and chair convenient enough, out of the largest trees in the royal park. Two hundred sempstresses were employed to make me shirts, and linen for my bed and table, all of the strongest and coarsest kind they could get; which, however, they were forced to quilt together in several folds; for the thickest was some degrees finer than lawn. Their linen is usually three inches wide, and three foot make a piece. The sempstresses took my measure as I lay on the ground, one standing at my neck, and another at my mid-leg, with a strong cord extended, that each held by the end, while the third measured the length of the cord with a rule of an inch long. Then they measured my right thumb, and desired no more; for by a mathematical computation, that twice round the thumb is one round the wrist, and so on to the neck and the waist; and by the help of my old shirt, which I displayed on the ground before them for a pattern, they fitted me exactly. Three hundred tailors were employed in the same manner to make me clothes; but they had another contrivance for taking my measure. I kneeled down, and they raised a ladder from the ground to my neck; upon this ladder one of them mounted, and let fall a plumb-line from my collar to the floor, which just answered the length of my coat; but my waist and arms I measured myself. When my clothes were finished, which was done in my house (for the largest of theirs would not have been able to hold them), they looked like the patchwork made by the ladies in England, only that mine were all of a color.

I had three hundred cooks to dress my victuals, in little convenient huts built about my house, where they and their families lived, and prepared me two dishes apiece. I took up twenty waiters in my hand, and placed them on the table; an hundred more attended below on the ground, some with dishes of meat, and some with barrels of wine, and other liquors, slung on their shoulders; all which the waiters above drew up as I wanted, in a very ingenious manner, by certain cords, as we draw the bucket up a well in Europe. A dish of their meat was a good mouthful, and a barrel of their liquor a reasonable draught. Their mutton yields to ours, but their beef is excellent. I have had a sirloin so large, that I have been forced to make three bites of it; but this is rare. My servants were astonished to see me eat it bones and all, as in our country we do the leg of a lark. Their geese and turkeys I usually eat at a mouthful, and I must confess they far exceed ours. Of their smaller fowl I could take up twenty or thirty at the end of my knife.

One day his Imperial Majesty, being informed of my way of living, desired that himself and his royal consort, with the young princes of the blood of both sexes, might have the happiness (as he was pleased to call it) of dining with me. They came accordingly, and I placed them upon chairs of state on my table, just over against me, with their guards about them. Flimnap the Lord High Treasurer attended there likewise, with his white staff; and I observed he often looked on me with a sour countenance, which I would not seem to regard, but eat more than usual, in honor to my dear country, as well as to fill the court with admiration. I have some private reasons to believe, that this visit from his Majesty gave Flimnap an opportunity of doing

2. Household.

me ill offices to his master. That minister had always been my secret enemy, although he outwardly caressed me more than was usual to the moroseness of his nature. He represented to the Emperor the low condition of his treasury; that he was forced to take up money at great discount; that exchequer bills[3] would not circulate under nine per cent below par; that I had cost his Majesty above a million and a half of *sprugs* (their greatest gold coin, about the bigness of a spangle); and upon the whole, that it would be advisable in the Emperor to take the first fair occasion of dismissing me.

I am here obliged to vindicate the reputation of an excellent lady, who was an innocent sufferer upon my account. The Treasurer took a fancy to be jealous of his wife, from the malice of some evil tongues, who informed him that her Grace had taken a violent affection for my person; and the court-scandal ran for some time that she once came privately to my lodging. This I solemnly declare to be a most infamous falsehood, without any grounds, farther than that her Grace was pleased to treat me with all innocent marks of freedom and friendship. I own she came often to my house, but always publicly, nor ever without three more in the coach, who were usually her sister and young daughter, and some particular acquaintance; but this was common to many other ladies of the court. And I still appeal to my servants round, whether they at any time saw a coach at my door without knowing what persons were in it. On those occasions, when a servant had given me notice, my custom was to go immediately to the door; and, after paying my respects, to take up the coach and two horses very carefully in my hands (for if there were six horses, the postillion always unharnessed four) and place them on a table, where I had fixed a moveable rim quite round, of five inches high, to prevent accidents. And I have often had four coaches and horses at once on my table full of company, while I sat in my chair leaning my face towards them; and when I was engaged with one set, the coachmen would gently drive the others round my table. I have passed many an afternoon very agreeably in these conversations. But I defy the Treasurer, or his two informers (I will name them, and let them make their best of it) Clustril and Drunlo, to prove that any person ever came to me *incognito*, except the Secretary Reldresal, who was sent by express command of his Imperial Majesty, as I have before related. I should not have dwelt so long upon this particular, if it had not been a point wherein the reputation of a great lady is so nearly concerned, to say nothing of my own; although I had the honor to be a *Nardac*, which the Treasurer himself is not; for all the world knows he is only a *Clumglum*, a title inferior by one degree, as that of a marquis is to a duke in England; yet I allow he preceded me in right of his post. These false informations, which I afterwards came to the knowledge of, by an accident not proper to mention, made the Treasurer show his lady for some time an ill countenance, and me a worse; for although he was at last undeceived and reconciled to her, yet I lost all credit with him; and found my interest decline very fast with the Emperor himself, who was indeed too much governed by that favorite.

---

3. Government bills of credit. Walpole was noted as a canny financier.

CHAPTER 7. *The author, being informed of a design to accuse him of high treason, makes his escape to Blefuscu. His reception there.*

Before I proceed to give an account of my leaving this kingdom, it may be proper to inform the reader of a private intrigue which had been for two months forming against me.

I had been hitherto all my life a stranger to courts, for which I was unqualified by the meanness of my condition. I had indeed heard and read enough of the dispositions of great princes and ministers; but never expected to have found such terrible effects of them in so remote a country, governed, as I thought, by very different maxims from those in Europe.

When I was just preparing to pay my attendance on the Emperor of Blefuscu, a considerable person at court (to whom I had been very serviceable at a time when he lay under the highest displeasure of his Imperial Majesty) came to my house very privately at night in a close chair, and without sending his name, desired admittance. The chairmen were dismissed; I put the chair, with his Lordship in it, into my coat-pocket; and giving orders to a trusty servant to say I was indisposed and gone to sleep, I fastened the door of my house, placed the chair on the table, according to my usual custom, and sat down by it. After the common salutations were over, observing his Lordship's countenance full of concern, and enquiring into the reason, he desired I would hear him with patience, in a matter that highly concerned my honor and my life. His speech was to the following effect, for I took notes of it as soon as he left me.

You are to know, said he, that several committees of council have been lately called in the most private manner on your account: and it is but two days since his Majesty came to a full resolution.

You are very sensible that Skyresh Bolgolam (*Galbet,* or High Admiral) hath been your mortal enemy almost ever since your arrival. His original reasons I know not; but his hatred is much increased since your great success against Blefuscu, by which his glory, as Admiral, is obscured. This lord, in conjunction with Flimnap the High Treasurer, whose enmity against you is notorious on account of his lady, Limtoc the General, Lalcon the Chamberlain, and Balmuff the Grand Justiciary, have prepared articles of impeachment against you, for treason, and other capital crimes.[4]

This preface made me so impatient, being conscious of my own merits and innocence, that I was going to interrupt; when he entreated me to be silent, and thus proceeded.

Out of gratitude for the favors you have done me, I procured information of the whole proceedings, and a copy of the articles, wherein I venture my head for your service.

Articles of Impeachment against Quinbus Flestrin (*the* Man-Mountain).

ARTICLE 1

Whereas, by a statute made in the reign of his Imperial Majesty Calin Deffar Plune, it is enacted, that whoever shall make water within the

---

4. After the Whigs had investigated Oxford and Bolingbroke, both were impeached for high treason, on charges of being sympathetic to the Jacobites and the French.

precincts of the royal palace shall be liable to the pains and penalties of high treason: notwithstanding, the said Quinbus Flestrin, in open breach of the said law, under color of extinguishing the fire kindled in the apartment of his Majesty's most dear imperial consort, did maliciously, traitorously, and devilishly, by discharge of his urine, put out the said fire kindled in the said apartment, lying and being within the precincts of the said royal palace; against the statute in that case provided, etc., against the duty, etc.

ARTICLE 2

That the said Quinbus Flestrin, having brought the imperial fleet of Blefuscu into the royal port, and being afterwards commanded by his Imperial Majesty to seize all the other ships of the said empire of Blefuscu, and reduce that empire to a province, to be governed by a viceroy from hence; and to destroy and put to death not only all the Big-Endian exiles, but likewise all the people of that empire who would not immediately forsake the Big-Endian heresy: he, the said Flestrin, like a false traitor against his most auspicious, serene, Imperial Majesty, did petition to be excused from the said service, upon pretense of unwillingness to force the consciences, or destroy the liberties and lives of an innocent people.

ARTICLE 3

That, whereas certain ambassadors arrived from the court of Blefuscu to sue for peace in his Majesty's court: he the said Flestrin did, like a false traitor, aid, abet, comfort, and divert the said ambassadors; although he knew them to be servants to a prince who was lately an open enemy to his Imperial Majesty, and in open war against his said Majesty.

ARTICLE 4

That the said Quinbus Flestrin, contrary to the duty of a faithful subject, is now preparing to make a voyage to the court and empire of Blefuscu, for which he hath received only verbal license from his Imperial Majesty; and under color of the said license, doth falsely and traitorously intend to take the said voyage, and thereby to aid, comfort, and abet the Emperor of Blefuscu, so late an enemy, and in open war with his Imperial Majesty aforesaid.

There are some other articles, but these are the most important, of which I have read you an abstract.

In the several debates upon this impeachment, it must be confessed that his Majesty gave many marks of his great *lenity*; often urging the services you had done him, and endeavoring to extenuate your crimes. The Treasurer and Admiral insisted that you should be put to the most painful and ignominious death, by setting fire on your house at night; and the General was to attend with twenty thousand men armed with poisoned arrows, to shoot you on the face and hands. Some of your servants were to have private orders to strew a poisonous juice on your shirts and sheets, which would soon make you tear your own flesh, and die in the utmost torture. The General came into the same opinion; so that for a long time there was a majority against you. But his Majesty resolving, if possible, to spare your life, at last brought off[5] the Chamberlain.

Upon this incident, Reldresal, Principal Secretary for Private Affairs, who always approved[6] himself your true friend, was commanded by the Emperor to deliver his opinion, which he accordingly did; and therein justified the good thoughts you have of him. He allowed your crimes to be great; but that still there was room for mercy, the most commendable virtue in a prince, and for which his Majesty was so justly celebrated. He said, the friendship between you and him was so well known to the world, that perhaps the most honorable board might think him partial: however, in obedience to the command he had received, he would freely offer his sentiments. That if his Majesty, in consideration of your services, and pursuant to his own merciful disposition, would please to spare your life, and only give order to put out both your eyes, he humbly conceived, that by this expedient justice might in some measure be satisfied, and all the world would applaud the *lenity* of the Emperor, as well as the fair and generous proceedings of those who have the honor to be his counselors. That the loss of your eyes would be no impediment to your bodily strength, by which you might still be useful to his Majesty. That blindness is an addition to courage, by concealing dangers from us; that the fear you had for your eyes was the greatest difficulty in bringing over the enemy's fleet; and it would be sufficient for you to see by the eyes of the ministers, since the greatest princes do no more.

This proposal was received with the utmost disapprobation by the whole board. Bolgolam, the Admiral, could not preserve his temper; but rising up in fury, said, he wondered how the Secretary durst presume to give his opinion for preserving the life of a traitor: that the services you had performed were, by all true reasons of state, the great aggravation of your crimes; that you, who were able to extinguish the fire by discharge of urine in her Majesty's apartment (which he mentioned with horror), might, at another time, raise an inundation by the same means, to drown the whole palace; and the same strength which enabled you to bring over the enemy's fleet might serve, upon the first discontent, to carry it back: that he had good reasons to think you were a Big-Endian in your heart; and as treason begins in the heart before it appears in overt acts, so he accused you as a traitor on that account, and therefore insisted you should be put to death.

The Treasurer was of the same opinion; he showed to what straits his Majesty's revenue was reduced by the charge of maintaining you, which would soon grow insupportable: that the Secretary's expedient of putting out your eyes was so far from being a remedy against this evil, that it would probably increase it; as it is manifest from the common practice of blinding some kind of fowl, after which they fed the faster, and grew sooner fat: that his sacred Majesty, and the council, who are your judges, were in their own consciences fully convinced of your guilt; which was a sufficient argument to condemn you to death, without the formal proofs required by the strict letter of the law.

But his Imperial Majesty, fully determined against capital punishment,

5. Won over.   6. Proved.

was graciously pleased to say, that since the council thought the loss of your eyes too easy a censure, some other may be inflicted hereafter. And your friend the Secretary humbly desiring to be heard again, in answer to what the Treasurer had objected concerning the great charge his Majesty was at in maintaining you, said, that his Excellency, who had the sole disposal of the Emperor's revenue, might easily provide against this evil, by gradually lessening your establishment; by which, for want of sufficient food, you would grow weak and faint, and lose your appetite, and consequently decay and consume in a few months; neither would the stench of your carcass be then so dangerous, when it should become more than half diminished; and immediately upon your death, five or six thousand of his Majesty's subjects might, in two or three days, cut your flesh from your bones, take it away by cart-loads, and bury it in distant parts to prevent infection; leaving the skeleton as a monument of admiration to posterity.

Thus by the great friendship of the Secretary, the whole affair was compromised. It was strictly enjoined, that the project of starving you by degrees should be kept a secret; but the sentence of putting out your eyes was entered on the books; none dissenting except Bolgolam the Admiral, who being a creature of the Empress, was perpetually instigated by her Majesty to insist upon your death; she having borne perpetual malice against you, on account of that infamous and illegal method you took to extinguish the fire in her apartment.

In three days your friend the Secretary will be directed to come to your house, and read before you the articles of impeachment; and then to signify the great lenity and favor of his Majesty and council; whereby you are only condemned to the loss of your eyes, which his Majesty doth not question you will gratefully and humbly submit to; and twenty of his Majesty's surgeons will attend, in order to see the operation well performed, by discharging very sharp-pointed arrows into the balls of your eyes, as you lie on the ground.

I leave to your prudence what measures you will take; and to avoid suspicion, I must immediately return in as private a manner as I came.

His Lordship did so, and I remained alone, under many doubts and perplexities of mind.

It was a custom introduced by this prince and his ministry (very different, as I have been assured, from the practices of former times), that after the court had decreed any cruel execution, either to gratify the monarch's resentment, or the malice of a favorite, the Emperor always made a speech to his whole council, expressing his great lenity and tenderness, as qualities known and confessed by all the world. This speech was immediately published through the kingdom; nor did any thing terrify the people so much as those encomiums on his Majesty's mercy; because it was observed, that the more these praises were enlarged and insisted on, the more inhuman was the punishment, and the sufferer more innocent. Yet as to myself, I must confess, having never been designed for a courtier, either by my birth or education, I was so ill a judge of things, that I could not discover the lenity and favor of this sentence, but conceived it (perhaps erroneously) rather to be rigorous than gentle. I sometimes thought of standing my trial; for although I could not deny the facts alleged in the several articles, yet I hoped they would admit of some extenuations. But having in my life perused many state trials, which I ever observed to terminate as the judges thought fit to direct, I durst not rely on so dangerous a decision, in so critical a juncture, and against such powerful enemies. Once I was strongly bent upon resistance: for while I had liberty, the whole strength of that empire could hardly subdue me, and I might easily with stones pelt the metropolis to pieces; but I soon rejected that project with horror, by remembering the oath I had made to the Emperor, the favors I received from him, and the high title of *Nardac* he conferred upon me. Neither had I so soon learned the gratitude of courtiers, to persuade myself that his Majesty's present severities acquitted me of all past obligations.

At last I fixed upon a resolution, for which it is probable I may incur some censure, and not unjustly; for I confess I owe the preserving my eyes, and consequently my liberty, to my own great rashness and want of experience: because if I had then known the nature of princes and ministers, which I have since observed in many other courts, and their methods of treating criminals less obnoxious than myself, I should with great alacrity and readiness have submitted to so *easy* a punishment. But hurried on by the precipitancy of youth, and having his Imperial Majesty's license to pay my attendance upon the Emperor of Blefuscu, I took this opportunity, before the three days were elapsed, to send a letter to my friend the Secretary, signifying my resolution of setting out that morning for Blefuscu,[7] pursuant to the leave I had got; and without waiting for an answer, I went to that side of the island where our fleet lay. I seized a large man of war, tied a cable to the prow, and lifting up the anchors, I stripped myself, put my clothes (together with my coverlet, which I carried under my arm) into the vessel; and drawing it after me, between wading and swimming, arrived at the royal port of Blefuscu, where the people had long expected me. They lent me two guides to direct me to the capital city, which is of the same name; I held them in my hands until I came within two hundred yards of the gate; and desired them to signify my arrival to one of the secretaries, and let him know, I there waited his Majesty's commands. I had an answer in about an hour, that his Majesty, attended by the royal family, and great officers of the court, was coming out to receive me. I advanced a hundred yards; the Emperor, and his train, alighted from their horses, the Empress and ladies from their coaches; and I did not perceive they were in any fright or concern. I lay on the ground to kiss his Majesty's and the Empress's hand. I told his Majesty that I was come according to my promise, and with the license of the Emperor my master, to have the honor of seeing so mighty a monarch, and to offer him any service in my power, consistent with my duty to my own prince; not mentioning a word of my disgrace, because I had hitherto no regular information of it, and might suppose myself wholly ignorant of any such design; neither could I reasonably conceive that the Emperor would discover the secret while I was out of his power: wherein, however, it soon appeared I was deceived.

I shall not trouble the reader with the particular account of my reception at this court, which was suitable to the generosity of so great a prince; nor of the difficulties I was in for want of a house and bed, being forced to lie on the ground, wrapped up in my coverlet.

7. Before his trial for treason could be held, Bolingbroke had escaped to France.

CHAPTER 8. *The author, by a lucky accident, finds means to leave Blefuscu; and, after some difficulties, returns safe to his native country.*

Three days after my arrival, walking out of curiosity to the northeast coast of the island, I observed, about half a league off, in the sea, somewhat that looked like a boat overturned. I pulled off my shoes and stockings, and wading two or three hundred yards, I found the object to approach nearer by force of the tide; and then plainly saw it to be a real boat, which I supposed might, by some tempest, have been driven from a ship. Whereupon I returned immediately towards the city, and desired his Imperial Majesty to lend me twenty of the tallest vessels he had left after the loss of his fleet, and three thousand seamen under the command of his Vice Admiral. This fleet sailed round, while I went back the shortest way to the coast where I first discovered the boat; I found the tide had driven it still nearer; the seamen were all provided with cordage, which I had beforehand twisted to a sufficient strength. When the ships came up, I stripped myself, and waded till I came within an hundred yards of the boat; after which I was forced to swim till I got up to it. The seamen threw me the end of the cord, which I fastened to a hole in the fore-part of the boat, and the other end to a man of war: but I found all my labor to little purpose; for being out of my depth, I was not able to work. In this necessity, I was forced to swim behind, and push the boat forwards as often as I could, with one of my hands; and the tide favoring me, I advanced so far, that I could just hold up my chin and feel the ground. I rested two or three minutes, and then gave the boat another shove, and so on till the sea was no higher than my armpits. And now the most laborious part being over, I took out my other cables which were stowed in one of the ships, and fastening them first to the boat, and then to nine of the vessels which attended me, the wind being favorable, the seamen towed, and I shoved till we arrived within forty yards of the shore; and waiting till the tide was out, I got dry to the boat, and by the assistance of two thousand men, with ropes and engines, I made a shift to turn it on its bottom, and found it was but little damaged.

I shall not trouble the reader with the difficulties I was under by the help of certain paddles, which cost me ten days making, to get my boat to the royal port of Blefuscu; where a mighty concourse of people appeared upon my arrival, full of wonder at the sight of so prodigious a vessel. I told the Emperor that my good fortune had thrown this boat in my way, to carry me to some place from whence I might return into my native country; and begged his Majesty's orders for getting materials to fit it up, together with license to depart; which, after some kind expostulations, he was pleased to grant.

I did very much wonder, in all this time, not to have heard of any express relating to me from our Emperor to the court of Blefuscu. But I was afterwards given privately to understand, that his Imperial Majesty, never imagining I had the least notice of his designs, believed I was only gone to Blefuscu in performance of my promise, according to the license he had given me, which was well known at our court; and would return in a few days when that ceremony was ended. But he was at last in pain at my long absence; and, after consulting with the Treasurer, and the rest of that cabal, a person of quality was dispatched with the copy of the articles against me. This envoy had instructions to represent to the monarch of Blefuscu the great lenity of his master, who was content to punish me no further than with the loss of my eyes; that I had fled from justice, and if I did not return in two hours, I should be deprived of my title of *Nardac,* and declared a traitor. The envoy further added, that in order to maintain the peace and amity between both empires, his master expected, that his brother of Blefuscu would give orders to have me sent back to Lilliput, bound hand and foot, to be punished as a traitor.

The Emperor of Blefuscu, having taken three days to consult, returned an answer consisting of many civilities and excuses. He said, that as for sending me bound, his brother knew it was impossible; that although I had deprived him of his fleet, yet he owed great obligations to me for many good offices I had done him in making the peace. That however, both their Majesties would soon be made easy; for I had found a prodigious vessel on the shore, able to carry me on the sea, which he had given order to fit up with my own assistance and direction; and he hoped in a few weeks both empires would be freed from so insupportable an incumbrance.

With this answer the envoy returned to Lilliput, and the monarch of Blefuscu related to me all that had passed, offering me at the same time (but under the strictest confidence) his gracious protection, if I would continue in his service; wherein although I believed him sincere, yet I resolved never more to put any confidence in princes or ministers, where I could possibly avoid it; and therefore, with all due acknowledgements for his favorable intentions, I humbly begged to be excused. I told him, that since fortune, whether good or evil, had thrown a vessel in my way, I was resolved to venture myself in the ocean, rather than be an occasion of difference between two such mighty monarchs. Neither did I find the Emperor at all displeased; and I discovered by a certain accident, that he was very glad of my resolution, and so were most of his ministers.

These considerations moved me to hasten my departure somewhat sooner than I intended; to which the court, impatient to have me gone, very readily contributed. Five hundred workmen were employed to make two sails to my boat, according to my directions, by quilting thirteen fold of their strongest linen together. I was at the pains of making ropes and cables, by twisting ten, twenty or thirty of the thickest and strongest of theirs. A great stone that I happened to find, after a long search by the seashore, served me for an anchor. I had the tallow of three hundred cows for greasing my boat, and other uses. I was at incredible pains in cutting down some of the largest timber trees for oars and masts, wherein I was, however, much assisted by his Majesty's ship-carpenters, who helped me in smoothing them, after I had done the rough work.

In about a month, when all was prepared, I sent to receive his Majesty's commands, and to take my leave. The Emperor and royal family came out of the palace; I lay down on my face to kiss his hand, which he very graciously gave me: so did the Empress, and young princes of the blood. His Majesty presented me with fifty purses of two hundred *sprugs* apiece, together with his picture at full length, which I put immediately into one of my gloves, to keep it from being hurt. The ceremonies at my departure were too many to trouble the reader with at this time.

I stored the boat with the carcasses of an hundred oxen, and three hundred sheep, with bread and drink proportionable, and as much meat ready dressed as four hundred cooks could provide. I took with me six cows and two bulls alive, with as many ewes and rams, intending to carry them into my own country, and propagate the breed. And to feed them on board, I had a good bundle of hay, and a bag of corn.[8] I would gladly have taken a dozen of the natives; but this was a thing the Emperor would by no means permit; and besides a diligent search into my pockets, his Majesty engaged my honor not to carry away any of his subjects, although with their own consent and desire.

Having thus prepared all things as well as I was able, I set sail on the twenty-fourth day of September, 1701, at six in the morning; and when I had gone about four leagues to the northward, the wind being at southeast, at six in the evening, I descried a small island about half a league to the northwest. I advanced forward, and cast anchor on the lee-side of the island, which seemed to be uninhabited. I then took some refreshment, and went to my rest. I slept well, and as I conjecture at least six hours; for I found the day broke in two hours after I awaked. It was a clear night; I eat my breakfast before the sun was up; and heaving anchor, the wind being favorable, I steered the same course that I had done the day before, wherein I was directed by my pocket compass. My intention was to reach, if possible, one of those islands which I had reason to believe lay to the northeast of Van Diemen's Land. I discovered nothing all that day; but upon the next, about three in the afternoon, when I had by my computation made twenty-four leagues from Blefuscu, I descried a sail steering to the southeast; my course was due east. I hailed her, but could get no answer; yet I found I gained upon her, for the wind slackened. I made all the sail I could, and in half an hour she spied me, then hung out her ancient,[9] and discharged a gun. It is not easy to express the joy I was in upon the unexpected hope of once more seeing my beloved country, and the dear pledges[1] I had left in it. The ship slackened her sails, and I came up with her between five and six in the evening, September 26; but my heart leapt within me to see her English colors. I put my cows and sheep into my coat-pockets and got on board with all my little cargo of provisions. The vessel was an English merchantman, returning from Japan by the North and South Seas;[2] the captain, Mr. John Biddel of Deptford, a very civil man, and an excellent sailor. We were now in the latitude of 30 degrees south; there were about fifty men in the ship; and here I met an old comrade of mine, one Peter Williams, who gave me a good character to the captain. This gentleman treated me with kindness, and desired I would let him know what place I came from last, and whither I was bound; which I did in few words; but he thought I was raving, and that the dangers I underwent had disturbed my head; whereupon I took my black cattle and sheep out of my pocket, which, after great astonishment, clearly convinced him of my veracity. I then showed him the gold given me by the Emperor of Blefuscu, together with his Majesty's picture at full length, and some other rarities of that country. I gave him two purses of two hundred *sprugs* each, and promised, when we arrived in England, to make him a present of a cow and a sheep big with young.

I shall not trouble the reader with a particular account of this voyage; which was very prosperous for the most part. We arrived in the Downs[3] on

---

8. Wheat, not maize.
9. Flag.
1. Hostages (i.e., his family).

2. North and South Pacific.
3. A rendezvous for ships off the southeast coast of England.

the 13th of April, 1702. I had only one misfortune, that the rats on board carried away one of my sheep; I found her bones in a hole, picked clean from the flesh. The rest of my cattle I got safe on shore, and set them a grazing in a bowling-green at Greenwich, where the fineness of the grass made them feed very heartily, though I had always feared the contrary; neither could I possibly have preserved them in so long a voyage, if the captain had not allowed me some of his best biscuit, which rubbed to powder, and mingled with water, was their constant food. The short time I continued in England, I made a considerable profit by showing my cattle to many persons of quality, and others: and before I began my second voyage, I sold them for six hundred pounds. Since my last return, I find the breed is considerably increased, especially the sheep; which I hope will prove much to the advantage of the woolen manufacture, by the fineness of the fleeces.

I stayed but two months with my wife and family; for my insatiable desire of seeing foreign countries would suffer me to continue no longer. I left fifteen hundred pounds with my wife, and fixed her in a good house at Redriff. My remaining stock I carried with me, part in money, and part in goods, in hopes to improve my fortunes. My eldest uncle, John, had left me an estate in land, near Epping, of about thirty pounds a year; and I had a long lease of the Black Bull in Fetter Lane, which yielded me as much more: so that I was not in any danger of leaving my family upon the parish.[4] My son Johnny, named so after his uncle, was at the grammar school, and a towardly[5] child. My daughter Betty (who is now well married, and has children) was then at her needlework. I took leave of my wife, and boy and girl, with tears on both sides; and went on board the *Adventure*, a merchant-ship of three hundred tons, bound for Surat, Captain John Nicholas of Liverpool, Commander. But my account of this voyage must be referred to the second part of my *Travels*.

Part 2. A Voyage to Brobdingnag

CHAPTER 1. *A great storm described. The longboat sent to fetch water; the Author goes with it to discover the country. He is left on shore, is seized by one of the natives, and carried to a farmer's house. His reception there, with several accidents that happened there. A description of the inhabitants.*

Having been condemned by nature and fortune to an active and restless life, in ten months after my return I again left my native country, and took shipping in the Downs on the 20th day of June, 1702, in the *Adventure*, Captain John Nicholas, a Cornish man, Commander, bound for Surat.[6] We had a very prosperous gale till we arrived at the Cape of Good Hope, where we landed for fresh water, but discovering a leak we unshipped our goods and wintered there; for the Captain falling sick of an ague, we could not leave the Cape till the end of March. We then set sail, and had a good voyage

4. On welfare (living on charity given by the parish).
5. Promising.
6. In India. The geography of the voyage (described next) is simple: The *Adventure*, after sailing up the east coast of Africa to about five degrees south of the equator (the "Line"), is blown

past India into the Malay Archipelago, north of the islands of Buru and Ceram. The storm then drives the ship northward and eastward, away from the coast of Siberia ("Great Tartary") into the northeast Pacific, at that time unexplored. Brobdingnag lies somewhere in the vicinity of Alaska.

till we passed the Straits of Madagascar; but having got northward of that island, and to about five degrees south latitude, the winds, which in those seas are observed to blow a constant equal gale between the north and west from the beginning of December to the beginning of May, on the 19th of April began to blow with much greater violence and more westerly than usual, continuing so far twenty days together, during which time we were driven a little to the east of the Molucca Islands and about three degrees northward of the Line, as our Captain found by an observation he took the 2nd of May, at which time the wind ceased, and it was a perfect calm, whereat I was not a little rejoiced. But he, being a man well experienced in the navigation of those seas, bid us all prepare against a storm, which accordingly happened the day following: for a southern wind, called the southern monsoon, began to set in.

Finding it was likely to overblow,[7] we took in our spritsail, and stood by to hand the foresail; but making foul weather, we looked the guns were all fast, and handed the mizzen. The ship lay very broad off, so we thought it better spooning before the sea, than trying or hulling. We reefed the foresail and set him, we hauled aft the foresheet; the helm was hard aweather. The ship wore bravely. We belayed the fore-downhaul; but the sail was split, and we hauled down the yard and got the sail into the ship, and unbound all the things clear of it. It was a very fierce storm; the sea broke strange and dangerous. We hauled off upon the lanyard of the whipstaff, and helped the man at helm. We would not get down our topmast, but let all stand, because she scudded before the sea very well, and we knew that the topmast being aloft, the ship was the wholesomer, and made better way through the sea, seeing we had searoom. When the storm was over, we set foresail and mainsail, and brought the ship to. Then we set the mizzen, main topsail and the fore topsail. Our course was east-northeast, the wind was at southwest. We got the starboard tacks aboard, we cast off our weather braces and lifts; we set in the lee braces, and hauled forward by the weather bowlings, and hauled them tight, and belayed them, and hauled over the mizzen tack to windward, and kept her full and by as near as she would lie.

During this storm, which was followed by a strong wind west-southwest, we were carried by my computation about five hundred leagues to the east, so that the oldest sailor on board could not tell in what part of the world we were. Our provisions held out well, our ship was staunch, and our crew all in good health; but we lay in the utmost distress for water. We thought it best to hold on the same course rather than turn more northerly, which might have brought us to the northwest parts of Great Tartary, and into the frozen sea.

On the 16th day of June, 1703, a boy on the topmast discovered land. On the 17th we came in full view of a great island or continent (for we knew not whether) on the south side whereof was a small neck of land jutting out into the sea, and a creek[8] too shallow to hold a ship of above one hundred tons. We cast anchor within a league of this creek, and our Captain sent a dozen of his men well armed in the longboat, with vessels for water if any could be found. I desired his leave to go with them that I might see the

7. This paragraph is taken almost literally from Samuel Sturmy's *Mariner's Magazine* (1669). Swift is ridiculing the use of technical terms by writers of popular voyages.
8. A small bay or cove, affording anchorage.

country and make what discoveries I could. When we came to land we saw no river or spring, nor any sign of inhabitants. Our men therefore wandered on the shore to find out some fresh water near the sea, and I walked alone about a mile on the other side, where I observed the country all barren and rocky. I now began to be weary, and seeing nothing to entertain my curiosity, I returned gently down towards the creek; and the sea being full in my view, I saw our men already got into the boat, and rowing for life to the ship. I was going to hollow after them, although it had been to little purpose, when I observed a huge creature walking after them in the sea as fast as he could; he waded not much deeper than his knees and took prodigious strides, but our men had the start of him half a league, and the sea thereabouts being full of sharp-pointed rocks, the monster was not able to overtake the boat. This I was afterwards told, for I durst not stay to see the issue of that adventure, but ran as fast as I could the way I first went, and then climbed up a steep hill, which gave me some prospect of the country. I found it fully cultivated; but that which first surprised me was the length of the grass, which, in those grounds that seemed to be kept for hay, was about twenty foot high.[9]

I fell into a highroad, for so I took it to be, although it served to the inhabitants only as a footpath through a field of barley. Here I walked on for some time, but could see little on either side, it being now near harvest, and the corn[1] rising at least forty foot. I was an hour walking to the end of this field, which was fenced in with a hedge of at least one hundred and twenty foot high, and the trees so lofty that I could make no computation of their altitude. There was a stile to pass from this field into the next: it had four steps, and a stone to cross over when you came to the utmost. It was impossible for me to climb this stile, because every step was six foot high, and the upper stone above twenty. I was endeavoring to find some gap in the hedge when I discovered one of the inhabitants in the next field advancing towards the stile, of the same size with him whom I saw in the sea pursuing our boat. He appeared as tall as an ordinary spire-steeple, and took about ten yards at every stride, as near as I could guess. I was struck with the utmost fear and astonishment, and ran to hide myself in the corn, from whence I saw him at the top of the stile, looking back into the next field on the right hand; and heard him call in a voice many degrees louder than a speaking trumpet; but the noise was so high in the air that at first I certainly thought it was thunder. Whereupon seven monsters like himself came towards him with reaping hooks in their hands, each hook about the largeness of six scythes. These people were not so well clad as the first, whose servants or laborers they seemed to be. For, upon some words he spoke, they went to reap the corn in the field where I lay. I kept from them at as great a distance as I could, but was forced to move with extreme difficulty, for the stalks of the corn were sometimes not above a foot distant, so that I could hardly squeeze my body betwixt them. However, I made a shift to go forward till I came to a part of the field where the corn had been laid by the rain and wind; here it was impossible for me to advance a step, for the stalks were so interwoven that I could not creep through, and the beards of the fallen ears so strong

9. Swift's intention, not always carried out accurately, is that everything in Brobdingnag should be, in relation to our familiar world, on a scale of ten to one.
1. Wheat.

and pointed that they pierced through my clothes into my flesh. At the same time I heard the reapers not above an hundred yards behind me. Being quite dispirited with toil, and wholly overcome by grief and despair, I lay down between two ridges and heartily wished I might there end my days. I bemoaned my desolate widow and fatherless children; I lamented my own folly and willfulness in attempting a second voyage against the advice of all my friends and relations. In this terrible agitation of mind, I could not forbear thinking of Lilliput, whose inhabitants looked upon me as the greatest prodigy that ever appeared in the world; where I was able to draw an imperial fleet in my hand, and perform those other actions which will be recorded forever in the chronicles of that empire, while posterity shall hardly believe them, although attested by millions. I reflected what a mortification it must prove to me to appear as inconsiderable in this nation as one single Lilliputian would be among us. But this I conceived was to be the least of my misfortunes; for as human creatures are observed to be more savage and cruel in proportion to their bulk, what could I expect but to be a morsel in the mouth of the first among these enormous barbarians who should happen to seize me? Undoubtedly philosophers are in the right when they tell us that nothing is great or little otherwise than by comparison. It might have pleased fortune to let the Lilliputians find some nation where the people were as diminutive with respect to them as they were to me. And who knows but that even this prodigious race of mortals might be equally overmatched in some distant part of the world, whereof we have yet no discovery?

Scared and confounded as I was, I could not forbear going on with these reflections; when one of the reapers approaching within ten yards of the ridge where I lay, made me apprehend that with the next step I should be squashed to death under his foot, or cut in two with his reaping hook. And therefore when he was again about to move, I screamed as loud as fear could make me. Whereupon the huge creature trod short, and looking round about under him for some time, at last espied me as I lay on the ground. He considered a while with the caution of one who endeavors to lay hold on a small dangerous animal in such a manner that it shall not be able either to scratch or to bite him, as I myself have sometimes done with a weasel in England. At length he ventured to take me up behind by the middle between his forefinger and thumb, and brought me within three yards of his eyes, that he might behold my shape more perfectly. I guessed his meaning, and my good fortune gave me so much presence of mind that I resolved not to struggle in the least as he held me in the air about sixty foot from the ground, although he grievously pinched my sides, for fear I should slip through his fingers. All I ventured was to raise mine eyes towards the sun, and place my hands together in a supplicating posture, and to speak some words in an humble melancholy tone, suitable to the condition I then was in. For I apprehended every moment that he would dash me against the ground, as we usually do any little hateful animal which we have a mind to destroy. But my good star would have it that he appeared pleased with my voice and gestures, and began to look upon me as a curiosity, much wondering to hear me pronounce articulate words, although he could not understand them. In the meantime I was not able to forbear groaning and shedding tears and turning my head towards my sides, letting him know, as well as I could, how cruelly I was hurt by the pressure of his thumb and finger. He seemed to apprehend my meaning; for, lifting up the lappet[2] of his coat, he put me gently into it, and immediately ran along with me to his master, who was a substantial farmer, and the same person I had first seen in the field.

The farmer having (as I supposed by their talk) received such an account of me as his servant could give him, took a piece of a small straw about the size of a walking staff, and therewith lifted up the lappets of my coat, which it seems he thought to be some kind of covering that nature had given me. He blew my hairs aside to take a better view of my face. He called his hinds[3] about him, and asked them (as I afterwards learned) whether they had ever seen in the fields any little creature that resembled me. He then placed me softly on the ground upon all four; but I got immediately up, and walked slowly backwards and forwards, to let those people see I had no intent to run away. They all sat down in a circle about me, the better to observe my motions. I pulled off my hat, and made a low bow towards the farmer; I fell on my knees, and lifted up my hands and eyes, and spoke several words as loud as I could; I took a purse of gold out of my pocket, and humbly presented it to him. He received it on the palm of his hand, then applied it close to his eye to see what it was, and afterwards turned it several times with the point of a pin (which he took out of his sleeve), but could make nothing of it. Whereupon I made a sign that he should place his hand on the ground; I then took the purse, and opening it, poured all the gold into his palm. There were six Spanish pieces of four pistoles each, beside twenty or thirty smaller coins. I saw him wet the tip of his little finger upon his tongue, and take up one of my largest pieces, and then another; but he seemed to be wholly ignorant what they were. He made me a sign to put them again into my purse, and the purse again into my pocket, which after offering to him several times, I thought it best to do.

The farmer by this time was convinced I must be a rational creature. He spoke often to me, but the sound of his voice pierced my ears like that of a water mill, yet his words were articulate enough. I answered as loud as I could in several languages, and he often laid his ear within two yards of me, but all in vain, for we were wholly unintelligible to each other. He then sent his servants to their work, and taking his handkerchief out of his pocket, he doubled and spread it on his hand, which he placed flat on the ground with the palm upwards, making me a sign to step into it, as I could easily do, for it was not above a foot in thickness. I thought it my part to obey, and for fear of falling, laid myself at full length upon the handkerchief, with the remainder of which he lapped me up to the head for further security, and in this manner carried me home to his house. There he called his wife, and showed me to her; but she screamed and ran back as women in England do at the sight of a toad or a spider. However, when she had a while seen my behavior, and how well I observed the signs her husband made, she was soon reconciled, and by degrees grew extremely tender of me.

It was about twelve at noon, and a servant brought in dinner. It was only one substantial dish of meat (fit for the plain condition of an husbandman) in a dish of about four-and-twenty foot diameter. The company were the farmer and his wife, three children, and an old grandmother. When they were sat down, the farmer placed me at some distance from him on the table,

---

2. Flap or fold. 3. Farm servants.

which was thirty foot high from the floor. I was in a terrible fright, and kept as far as I could from the edge, for fear of falling. The wife minced a bit of meat, then crumbled some bread on a trencher, and placed it before me. I made her a low bow, took out my knife and fork, and fell to eat; which gave them exceeding delight. The mistress sent her maid for a small dram cup, which held about two gallons, and filled it with drink; I took up the vessel with much difficulty in both hands, and in a most respectful manner drank to her ladyship's health, expressing the words as loud as I could in English; which made the company laugh so heartily that I was almost deafened with the noise. This liquor tasted like a small cider,[4] and was not unpleasant. Then the master made me a sign to come to his trencher side; but as I walked on the table, being in great surprise all the time, as the indulgent reader will easily conceive and excuse, I happened to stumble against a crust, and fell flat on my face, but received no hurt. I got up immediately, and observing the good people to be in much concern, I took my hat (which I held under my arm out of good manners) and waving it over my head, made three huzzas to show I had got no mischief by my fall. But advancing forwards toward my master (as I shall henceforth call him), his youngest son who sat next him, an arch boy of about ten years old, took me up by the legs, and held me so high in the air that I trembled every limb; but his father snatched me from him, and at the same time gave him such a box on the left ear as would have felled an European troop of horse to the earth, ordering him to be taken from the table. But being afraid the boy might owe me a spite, and well remembering how mischievous all children among us naturally are to sparrows, rabbits, young kittens, and puppy dogs, I fell on my knees, and pointing to the boy, made my master to understand, as well as I could, that I desired his son might be pardoned. The father complied, and the lad took his seat again; whereupon I went to him and kissed his hand, which my master took, and made him stroke me gently with it.

In the midst of dinner, my mistress's favorite cat leaped into her lap. I heard a noise behind me like that of a dozen stocking weavers at work; and turning my head, I found it proceeded from the purring of this animal, who seemed to be three times larger than an ox, as I computed by the view of her head and one of her paws, while her mistress was feeding and stroking her. The fierceness of this creature's countenance altogether discomposed me, although I stood at the farther end of the table, about fifty foot off, and although my mistress held her fast for fear she might give a spring and seize me in her talons. But it happened there was no danger, for the cat took not the least notice of me when my master placed me within three yards of her. And as I have been always told, and found true by experience in my travels, that flying or discovering[5] fear before a fierce animal is a certain way to make it pursue or attack you, so I resolved in this dangerous juncture to show no manner of concern. I walked with intrepidity five or six times before the very head of the cat, and came within half a yard of her; whereupon she drew herself back, as if she were more afraid of me. I had less apprehension concerning the dogs, whereof three or four came into the room, as it is usual in farmers' houses; one of which was a mastiff, equal in bulk to four elephants, and a greyhound, somewhat taller than the mastiff, but not so large.

4. I.e., weak cider.   5. Revealing.

When dinner was almost done, the nurse came in with a child of a year old in her arms, who immediately spied me, and began a squall that you might have heard from London Bridge to Chelsea, after the usual oratory of infants, to get me for a plaything. The mother out of pure indulgence took me up, and put me towards the child, who presently seized me by the middle, and got my head in his mouth, where I roared so loud that the urchin was frighted and let me drop; and I should infallibly have broke my neck if the mother had not held her apron under me. The nurse to quiet her babe made use of a rattle, which was a kind of hollow vessel filled with great stones, and fastened by a cable to the child's waist: but all in vain, so that she was forced to apply the last remedy by giving it suck. I must confess no object ever disgusted me so much as the sight of her monstrous breast, which I cannot tell what to compare with so as to give the curious reader an idea of its bulk, shape, and color. It stood prominent six foot, and could not be less than sixteen in circumference. The nipple was about half the bigness of my head, and the hue both of that and the dug so varified with spots, pimples, and freckles that nothing could appear more nauseous: for I had a near sight of her, she sitting down the more conveniently to give suck, and I standing on the table. This made me reflect upon the fair skins of our English ladies, who appear so beautiful to us, only because they are of our own size, and their defects not to be seen but through a magnifying glass, where we find by experiment that the smoothest and whitest skins look rough and coarse and ill colored.

I remember when I was at Lilliput, the complexion of those diminutive people appeared to me the fairest in the world; and talking upon this subject with a person of learning there, who was an intimate friend of mine, he said that my face appeared much fairer and smoother when he looked on me from the ground than it did upon a nearer view when I took him up in my hand and brought him close, which he confessed was at first a very shocking sight. He said he could discover great holes in my skin; that the stumps of my beard were ten times stronger than the bristles of a boar, and my complexion made up of several colors altogether disagreeable: although I must beg leave to say for myself that I am as fair as most of my sex and country and very little sunburnt by all my travels. On the other side, discoursing of the ladies in that Emperor's court, he used to tell me one had freckles, another too wide a mouth, a third too large a nose; nothing of which I was able to distinguish. I confess this reflection was obvious enough; which however I could not forbear, lest the reader might think those vast creatures were actually deformed: for I must do them justice to say they are a comely race of people; and particularly the features of my master's countenance, although he were but a farmer, when I beheld him from the height of sixty foot, appeared very well proportioned.

When dinner was done, my master went out to his laborers; and as I could discover by his voice and gesture, gave his wife a strict charge to take care of me. I was very much tired and disposed to sleep, which my mistress perceiving, she put me on her own bed, and covered me with a clean white handkerchief, but larger and coarser than the mainsail of a man-of-war.

I slept about two hours, and dreamed I was at home with my wife and children, which aggravated my sorrows when I awaked and found myself alone in a vast room, between two and three hundred foot wide, and above two hundred high, lying in a bed twenty yards wide. My mistress was gone about her household affairs, and had locked me in. The bed was eight yards from the floor. Some natural necessities required me to get down; I durst not presume to call, and if I had, it would have been in vain with such a voice as mine at so great a distance from the room where I lay to the kitchen where the family kept. While I was under these circumstances, two rats crept up the curtains, and ran smelling backwards and forwards on the bed. One of them came up almost to my face; whereupon I rose in a fright, and drew out my hanger[6] to defend myself. These horrible animals had the boldness to attack me on both sides, and one of them held his forefeet at my collar; but I had the good fortune to rip up his belly before he could do me any mischief. He fell down at my feet; and the other seeing the fate of his comrade, made his escape, but not without one good wound on the back, which I gave him as he fled, and made the blood run trickling from him. After this exploit I walked gently to and fro on the bed, to recover my breath and loss of spirits. These creatures were of the size of a large mastiff, but infinitely more nimble and fierce; so that if I had taken off my belt before I went to sleep, I must have infallibly been torn to pieces and devoured. I measured the tail of the dead rat, and found it to be two yards long, wanting an inch; but it went against my stomach to drag the carcass off the bed, where it lay still bleeding; I observed it had yet some life, but with a strong slash cross the neck, I thoroughly dispatched it.

Soon after, my mistress came into the room, who seeing me all bloody, ran and took me up in her hand. I pointed to the dead rat, smiling and making other signs to show I was not hurt, whereat she was extremely rejoiced, calling the maid to take up the dead rat with a pair of tongs, and throw it out of the window. Then she set me on a table, where I showed her my hanger all bloody, and wiping it on the lappet of my coat, returned it to the scabbard. I was pressed to do more than one thing, which another could not do for me, and therefore endeavored to make my mistress understand that I desired to be set down on the floor; which after she had done, my bashfulness would not suffer me to express myself farther than by pointing to the door, and bowing several times. The good woman with much difficulty at last perceived what I would be at, and taking me up again in her hand, walked into the garden, where she set me down. I went on one side about two hundred yards; and beckoning to her not to look or to follow me, I hid myself between two leaves of sorrel, and there discharged the necessities of nature.

I hope the gentle reader will excuse me for dwelling on these and the like particulars, which however insignificant they may appear to groveling vulgar minds, yet will certainly help a philosopher[7] to enlarge his thoughts and imagination, and apply them to the benefit of public as well as private life, which was my sole design in presenting this and other accounts of my travels to the world; wherein I have been chiefly studious of truth, without affecting any ornaments of learning or of style. But the whole scene of this voyage made so strong an impression on my mind, and is so deeply fixed in my memory, that in committing it to paper I did not omit one material circumstance; however, upon a strict review, I blotted out several passages of less

---

6. A short, broad sword.
7. "Vulgar": commonplace, uncultivated, in contrast to the scientist ("philosopher"); an irony.

moment which were in my first copy, for fear of being censured as tedious and trifling, whereof travelers are often, perhaps not without justice, accused.

CHAPTER 2. *A description of the farmer's daughter. The Author carried to a market town, and then to the metropolis. The particulars of his journey.*

My mistress had a daughter of nine years old, a child of towardly parts for her age, very dexterous at her needle, and skillful in dressing her baby.[8] Her mother and she contrived to fit up the baby's cradle for me against night: the cradle was put into a small drawer of a cabinet, and the drawer placed upon a hanging shelf for fear of the rats. This was my bed all the time I stayed with those people, although made more convenient by degrees as I began to learn their language, and make my wants known. This young girl was so handy, that after I had once or twice pulled off my clothes before her, she was able to dress and undress me, although I never gave her that trouble when she would let me do either myself. She made me seven shirts, and some other linen of as fine cloth as could be got, which indeed was coarser than sackcloth, and these she constantly washed for me with her own hands. She was likewise my schoolmistress to teach me the language: when I pointed to anything, she told me the name of it in her own tongue, so that in a few days I was able to call for whatever I had a mind to. She was very good-natured, and not above forty foot high, being little for her age. She gave me the name of *Grildrig,* which the family took up, and afterwards the whole kingdom. The word imports what the Latins call *nanunculus,* the Italian *homunceletino,*[9] and the English *mannikin.* To her I chiefly owe my preservation in that country: we never parted while I was there; I called her my *Glumdalclitch,* or little nurse: and I should be guilty of great ingratitude if I omitted this honorable mention of her care and affection towards me, which I heartily wish it lay in my power to requite as she deserves, instead of being the innocent but unhappy instrument of her disgrace, as I have too much reason to fear.

It now began to be known and talked of in the neighborhood that my master had found a strange animal in the field, about the bigness of a *splack-nuck,* but exactly shaped in every part like a human creature, which it likewise imitated in all its actions: seemed to speak in a little language of its own, had already learned several words of theirs, went erect upon two legs, was tame and gentle, would come when it was called, do whatever it was bid, had the finest limbs in the world, and a complexion fairer than a nobleman's daughter of three years old. Another farmer who lived hard by, and was a particular friend of my master, came on a visit on purpose to inquire into the truth of this story. I was immediately produced, and placed upon a table, where I walked as I was commanded, drew my hanger, put it up again, made my reverence to my master's guest, asked him in his own language how he did, and told him he was welcome, just as my little nurse had instructed me. This man, who was old and dimsighted, put on his spectacles to behold me better, at which I could not forbear laughing very heartily, for

---

8. Doll. "Towardly parts": promising abilities.
9. The Latin and Italian words are Swift's own

coinages, as, of course, are the various words from the Brobdingnagian language.

his eyes appeared like the full moon shining into a chamber at two windows. Our people, who discovered the cause of my mirth, bore me company in laughing, at which the old fellow was fool enough to be angry and out of countenance. He had the character of a great miser, and to my misfortune he well deserved it by the cursed advice he gave my master to show me as a sight upon a market day in the next town, which was half an hour's riding, about two and twenty miles from our house. I guessed there was some mischief contriving when I observed my master and his friend whispering long together, sometimes pointing at me; and my fears made me fancy that I overheard and understood some of their words. But the next morning Glumdalclitch, my little nurse, told me the whole matter, which she had cunningly picked out from her mother. The poor girl laid me on her bosom, and fell a weeping with shame and grief. She apprehended some mischief would happen to me from rude vulgar folks, who might squeeze me to death, or break one of my limbs by taking me in their hands. She had also observed how modest I was in my nature, how nicely I regarded my honor, and what an indignity I should conceive it to be exposed for money as a public spectacle to the meanest of the people. She said her papa and mamma had promised that Grildrig should be hers; but now she found they meant to serve her as they did last year, when they pretended to give her a lamb, and yet, as soon as it was fat, sold it to a butcher. For my own part, I may truly affirm that I was less concerned than my nurse. I had a strong hope, which never left me, that I should one day recover my liberty; and as to the ignominy of being carried about for a monster, I considered myself to be a perfect stranger in the country, and that such a misfortune could never be charged upon me as a reproach, if ever I should return to England; since the King of Great Britain himself, in my condition, must have undergone the same distress.

My master, pursuant to the advice of his friend, carried me in a box the next market day to the neighboring town, and took along with him his little daughter, my nurse, upon a pillion[1] behind him. The box was close on every side, with a little door for me to go in and out, and a few gimlet holes to let in air. The girl had been so careful to put the quilt of her baby's bed into it, for me to lie down on. However, I was terribly shaken and discomposed in this journey, although it were but of half an hour. For the horse went about forty foot at every step, and trotted so high that the agitation was equal to the rising and falling of a ship in a great storm, but much more frequent. Our journey was somewhat further than from London to St. Albans. My master alighted at an inn which he used to frequent; and after consulting a while with the innkeeper, and making some necessary preparations, he hired the *Grultrud,* or crier, to give notice through the town of a strange creature to be seen at the Sign of the Green Eagle, not so big as a *splacknuck* (an animal in that country very finely shaped, about six foot long), and in every part of the body resembling an human creature; could speak several words and perform an hundred diverting tricks.

I was placed upon a table in the largest room of the inn, which might be near three hundred foot square. My little nurse stood on a low stool close to the table, to take care of me, and direct what I should do. My master, to avoid a crowd, would suffer only thirty people at a time to see me. I walked

---

1. A pad attached to the hinder part of a saddle, on which a second person, usually a woman, could ride.

about on the table as the girl commanded; she asked me questions as far as she knew my understanding of the language reached, and I answered them as loud as I could. I turned about several times to the company, paid my humble respects, said they were welcome, and used some other speeches I had been taught. I took up a thimble filled with liquor, which Glumdalclitch had given me for a cup, and drank their health. I drew out my hanger, and flourished with it after the manner of fencers in England. My nurse gave me part of a straw, which I exercised as pike, having learned the art in my youth. I was that day shown to twelve sets of company, and as often forced to go over again with the same fopperies, till I was half dead with weariness and vexation. For those who had seen me made such wonderful reports that the people were ready to break down the doors to come in. My master for his own interest would not suffer anyone to touch me except my nurse; and, to prevent danger, benches were set round the table at such a distance as put me out of everybody's reach. However, an unlucky schoolboy aimed a hazel-nut directly at my head, which very narrowly missed me; otherwise, it came with so much violence that it would have infallibly knocked out my brains, for it was almost as large as a small pumpion:[2] but I had the satisfaction to see the young rogue well beaten, and turned out of the room.

My master gave public notice that he would show me again the next market day, and in the meantime he prepared a more convenient vehicle for me, which he had reason enough to do; for I was so tired with my first journey, and with entertaining company for eight hours together, that I could hardly stand upon my legs or speak a word. It was at least three days before I recovered my strength; and that I might have no rest at home, all the neighboring gentlemen from an hundred miles round, hearing of my fame, came to see me at my master's own house. There could not be fewer than thirty persons with their wives and children (for the country is very populous); and my master demanded the rate of a full room whenever he showed me at home, although it were only to a single family. So that for some time I had but little ease every day of the week (except Wednesday, which is their Sabbath) although I were not carried to the town.

My master finding how profitable I was like to be, resolved to carry me to the most considerable cities of the kingdom. Having therefore provided himself with all things necessary for a long journey, and settled his affairs at home, he took leave of his wife; and upon the 17th of August, 1703, about two months after my arrival, we set out for the metropolis, situated near the middle of that empire, and about three thousand miles distance from our house. My master made his daughter Glumdalclitch ride behind him. She carried me on her lap in a box tied about her waist. The girl had lined it on all sides with the softest cloth she could get, well quilted underneath, furnished it with her baby's bed, provided me with linen and other necessaries, and made everything as convenient as she could. We had no other company but a boy of the house, who rode after us with the luggage.

My master's design was to show me in all the towns by the way, and to step out of the road for fifty or an hundred miles to any village or person of quality's house where he might expect custom. We made easy journeys of not above seven or eight score miles a day: for Glumdalclitch, on purpose to

2. Pumpkin.

spare me, complained she was tired with the trotting of the horse. She often took me out of my box at my own desire, to give me air and show me the country, but always held me fast by leading strings. We passed over five or six rivers many degrees broader and deeper than the Nile or the Ganges; and there was hardly a rivulet so small as the Thames at London Bridge. We were ten weeks in our journey, and I was shown in eighteen large towns, besides many large villages and private families.

On the 26th day of October, we arrived at the metropolis, called in their language *Lorbrulgrud*, or Pride of the Universe. My master took a lodging in the principal street of the city, not far from the royal palace, and put out bills in the usual form, containing an exact description of my person and parts. He hired a large room between three and four hundred foot wide. He provided a table sixty foot in diameter, upon which I was to act my part, and palisadoed it round three foot from the edge, and as many high, to prevent my falling over. I was shown ten times a day to the wonder and satisfaction of all people. I could now speak the language tolerably well, and perfectly understood every word that was spoken to me. Besides, I had learned their alphabet, and could make a shift to explain a sentence here and there; for Glumdalclitch had been my instructor while we were at home, and at leisure hours during our journey. She carried a little book in her pocket, not much larger than a Sanson's *Atlas*;[3] it was a common treatise for the use of young girls, giving a short account of their religion: out of this she taught me my letters, and interpreted the words.

CHAPTER 3. *The Author sent for to Court. The Queen buys him of his master, the farmer, and presents him to the King. He disputes with his Majesty's great scholars. An apartment at Court provided for the Author. He is in high favor with the Queen. He stands up for the honor of his own country. His quarrels with the Queen's dwarf.*

The frequent labors I underwent every day made in a few weeks a very considerable change in my health: the more my master got by me, the more unsatiable he grew. I had quite lost my stomach, and was almost reduced to a skeleton. The farmer observed it, and concluding I soon must die, resolved to make as good a hand of me as he could. While he was thus reasoning and resolving with himself, a *Slardral*, or Gentleman Usher, came from Court, commanding my master to carry me immediately thither for the diversion of the Queen and her ladies. Some of the latter had already been to see me and reported strange things of my beauty, behavior, and good sense. Her Majesty and those who attended her were beyond measure delighted with my demeanor. I fell on my knees and begged the honor of kissing her Imperial foot; but this gracious princess held out her little finger towards me (after I was set on a table), which I embraced in both my arms, and put the tip of it, with the utmost respect, to my lip. She made me some general questions about my country and my travels, which I answered as distinctly and in as few words as I could. She asked whether I would be content to live at Court. I bowed down to the board of the table, and humbly answered that I was my master's slave, but if I were at my own disposal, I should be proud to devote

___
3. I.e., over two feet long and about two feet wide.

my life to her Majesty's service. She then asked my master whether he were willing to sell me at a good price. He, who apprehended I could not live a month, was ready enough to part with me, and demanded a thousand pieces of gold, which were ordered him on the spot, each piece being about the bigness of eight hundred moidores;[4] but, allowing for the proportion of all things between that country and Europe, and the high price of gold among them, was hardly so great a sum as a thousand guineas would be in England. I then said to the Queen, since I was now her Majesty's most humble creature and vassal, I must beg the favor that Glumdalclitch, who had always tended me with so much care and kindness, and understood to do it so well, might be admitted into her service, and continue to be my nurse and instructor. Her Majesty agreed to my petition, and easily got the farmer's consent, who was glad enough to have his daughter preferred at Court; and the poor girl herself was not able to hide her joy. My late master withdrew, bidding me farewell, and saying he had left me in a good service; to which I replied not a word, only making him a slight bow.

The Queen observed my coldness, and when the farmer was gone out of the apartment, asked me the reason. I made bold to tell her Majesty that I owed no other obligation to my late master than his not dashing out the brains of a poor harmless creature found by chance in his field; which obligation was amply recompensed by the gain he had made in showing me through half the kingdom, and the price he had now sold me for. That the life I had since led was laborious enough to kill an animal of ten times my strength. That my health was much impaired by the continual drudgery of entertaining the rabble every hour of the day; and that if my master had not thought my life in danger, her Majesty perhaps would not have got so cheap a bargain. But as I was out of all fear of being ill treated under the protection of so great and good an Empress, the Ornament of Nature, the Darling of the World, the Delight of her Subjects, the Phoenix of the Creation; so I hoped my late master's apprehensions would appear to be groundless, for I already found my spirits to revive by the influence of her most august presence.

This was the sum of my speech, delivered with great improprieties and hesitation; the latter part was altogether framed in the style peculiar to that people, whereof I learned some phrases from Glumdalclitch, while she was carrying me to Court.

The Queen, giving great allowance for my defectiveness in speaking, was however surprised at so much wit and good sense in so diminutive an animal. She took me in her own hand, and carried me to the King, who was then retired to his cabinet.[5] His Majesty, a prince of much gravity, and austere countenance, not well observing my shape at first view, asked the Queen after a cold manner how long it was since she grew fond of a *splacknuck*; for such it seems he took me to be, as I lay upon my breast in her Majesty's right hand. But this princess, who hath an infinite deal of wit and humor, set me gently on my feet upon the scrutore,[6] and commanded me to give his Majesty an account of myself, which I did in a very few words; and Glumdalclitch, who attended at the cabinet door, and could not endure I should be out of

---

4. Portuguese coins.
5. Private apartment.

6. Writing desk.

her sight, being admitted, confirmed all that had passed from my arrival at her father's house.

The King, although he be as learned a person as any in his dominions, had been educated in the study of philosophy and particularly mathematics; yet when he observed my shape exactly, and saw me walk erect, before I began to speak, conceived I might be a piece of clockwork (which is in that country arrived to a very great perfection) contrived by some ingenious artist. But when he heard my voice, and found what I delivered to be regular and rational, he could not conceal his astonishment. He was by no means satisfied with the relation I gave him of the manner I came into his kingdom, but thought it a story concerted between Glumdalclitch and her father, who had taught me a set of words to make me sell at a higher price. Upon this imagination he put several other questions to me, and still received rational answers, no otherwise defective than by a foreign accent, and an imperfect knowledge in the language, with some rustic phrases which I had learned at the farmer's house, and did not suit the polite style of a court.

His Majesty sent for three great scholars who were then in their weekly waiting (according to the custom in that country). These gentlemen, after they had a while examined my shape with much nicety, were of different opinions concerning me. They all agreed that I could not be produced according to the regular laws of nature, because I was not framed with a capacity of preserving my life, either by swiftness, or climbing of trees, or digging holes in the earth. They observed by my teeth, which they viewed with great exactness, that I was a carnivorous animal; yet most quadrupeds being an overmatch for me, and field mice, with some others, too nimble, they could not imagine how I should be able to support myself, unless I fed upon snails and other insects; which they offered, by many learned arguments, to evince that I could not possibly do. One of them seemed to think that I might be an embryo, or abortive birth. But this opinion was rejected by the other two, who observed my limbs to be perfect and finished, and that I had lived several years, as it was manifested from my beard, the stumps whereof they plainly discovered through a magnifying glass. They would not allow me to be a dwarf, because my littleness was beyond all degrees of comparison; for the Queen's favorite dwarf, the smallest ever known in that kingdom, was nearly thirty foot high. After much debate, they concluded unanimously that I was only *relplum scalcath*, which is interpreted literally, *lusus naturae*; a determination exactly agreeable to the modern philosophy of Europe, whose professors, disdaining the old evasion of *occult causes*, whereby the followers of Aristotle endeavor in vain to disguise their ignorance, have invented this wonderful solution of all difficulties, to the unspeakable advancement of human knowledge.[7]

After this decisive conclusion, I entreated to be heard a word or two. I applied myself to the King, and assured his Majesty that I came from a country which abounded with several millions of both sexes, and of my own stature, where the animals, trees, and houses were all in proportion, and where by consequence I might be as able to defend myself, and to find sus-

---

7. Swift had contempt for both the medieval Schoolmen, who discussed "occult causes," the unknown causes of observable effects, and modern scientists, who, he believed, often concealed their ignorance by using equally meaningless terms. "*Lusus naturae*": one of nature's sports, or roughly, freaks.

tenance, as any of his Majesty's subjects could do here; which I took for a full answer to those gentlemen's arguments. To this they only replied with a smile of contempt, saying that the farmer had instructed me very well in my lesson. The King, who had a much better understanding, dismissing his learned men, sent for the farmer, who by good fortune was not yet gone out of town; having therefore first examined him privately, and then confronted him with me and the young girl, his Majesty began to think that what we told him might possibly be true. He desired the Queen to order that a particular care should be taken of me, and was of opinion that Glumdalclitch should still continue in her office of tending me, because he observed we had a great affection for each other. A convenient apartment was provided for her at Court; she had a sort of governess appointed to take care of her education, a maid to dress her, and two other servants for menial offices; but the care of me was wholly appropriated to herself. The Queen commanded her own cabinetmaker to contrive a box that might serve me for a bedchamber, after the model that Glumdalclitch and I should agree upon. This man was a most ingenious artist, and according to my directions, in three weeks finished for me a wooden chamber of sixteen foot square and twelve high, with sash windows, a door, and two closets, like a London bedchamber. The board that made the ceiling was to be lifted up and down by two hinges, to put in a bed ready furnished by her Majesty's upholsterer, which Glumdalclitch took out every day to air, made it with her own hands, and letting it down at night, locked up the roof over me. A nice[8] workman, who was famous for little curiosities, undertook to make me two chairs, with backs and frames, of a substance not unlike ivory, and two tables, with a cabinet to put my things in. The room was quilted on all sides, as well as the floor and the ceiling, to prevent any accident from the carelessness of those who carried me, and to break the force of a jolt when I went in a coach. I desired a lock for my door to prevent rats and mice from coming in: the smith, after several attempts, made the smallest that ever was seen among them, for I have known a larger at the gate of a gentleman's house in England. I made a shift[9] to keep the key in a pocket of my own, fearing Glumdalclitch might lose it. The Queen likewise ordered the thinnest silks that could be gotten, to make me clothes, not much thicker than an English blanket, very cumbersome till I was accustomed to them. They were after the fashion of the kingdom, partly resembling the Persian, and partly the Chinese, and are a very grave, decent habit.

The Queen became so fond of my company that she could not dine without me. I had a table placed upon the same at which her Majesty ate, just at her left elbow, and a chair to sit on. Glumdalclitch stood upon a stool on the floor, near my table, to assist and take care of me. I had an entire set of silver dishes and plates, and other necessaries, which, in proportion to those of the Queen, were not much bigger than what I have seen of the same kind in a London toyshop,[1] for the furniture of a baby-house: these my little nurse kept in her pocket in a silver box and gave me at meals as I wanted them, always cleaning them herself. No person dined with the Queen but the two Princesses Royal, the elder sixteen years old, and the younger at that time thirteen and a month. Her Majesty used to put a bit of meat upon one of my

8. Exact.
9. Contrived.

1. A shop for selling knickknacks.

dishes, out of which I carved for myself; and her diversion was to see me eat in miniature. For the Queen (who had indeed but a weak stomach) took up at one mouthful as much as a dozen English farmers could eat at a meal, which to me was for some time a very nauseous sight. She would craunch the wing of a lark, bones and all, between her teeth, although it were nine times as large as that of a full-grown turkey; and put a bit of bread into her mouth as big as two twelve-penny loaves. She drank out of a golden cup, above a hogshead at a draught. Her knives were twice as long as a scythe set straight upon the handle. The spoons, forks, and other instruments were all in the same proportion. I remember when Glumdalclitch carried me out of curiosity to see some of the tables at Court, where ten or a dozen of these enormous knives and forks were lifted up together, I thought I had never till then beheld so terrible a sight.

It is the custom that every Wednesday (which, as I have before observed, was their Sabbath) the King and Queen, with the royal issue of both sexes, dine together in the apartment of his Majesty, to whom I was now become a favorite; and at these times my little chair and table were placed at his left hand, before one of the salt-cellars. This prince took a pleasure in conversing with me, inquiring into the manners, religion, laws, government, and learning of Europe; wherein I gave him the best account I was able. His apprehension was so clear, and his judgment so exact, that he made very wise reflections and observations upon all I said. But I confess that after I had been a little too copious in talking of my own beloved country, of our trade and wars by sea and land, of our schisms in religion and parties in the state, the prejudices of his education prevailed so far that he could not forbear taking me up in his right hand, and stroking me gently with the other, after an hearty fit of laughing, asked me whether I were a Whig or a Tory. Then turning to his first minister, who waited behind him with a white staff, near as tall as the mainmast of the *Royal Sovereign*,[2] he observed how contemptible a thing was human grandeur, which could be mimicked by such diminutive insects as I: "and yet," said he, "I dare engage, these creatures have their titles and distinctions of honor; they contrive little nests and burrows, that they call houses and cities; they make a figure in dress and equipage; they love, they fight, they dispute, they cheat, they betray." And thus he continued on, while my color came and went several times with indignation to hear our noble country, the mistress of arts and arms, the scourge of France, the arbitress of Europe, the seat of virtue, piety, honor, and truth, the pride and envy of the world, so contemptuously treated.

But as I was not in a condition to resent injuries, so, upon mature thoughts, I began to doubt whether I were injured or no. For, after having been accustomed several months to the sight and converse of this people, and observed every object upon which I cast my eyes to be of proportionable magnitude, the horror I had first conceived from their bulk and aspect was so far worn off that if I had then beheld a company of English lords and ladies in their finery and birthday clothes,[3] acting their several parts in the most courtly manner of strutting and bowing and prating, to say the truth, I should have been strongly tempted to laugh as much at them as this King and his grandees did at me. Neither indeed could I forbear smiling at myself

---

2. One of the largest ships in the Royal Navy. At the English court the lord treasurer bore a white staff as the symbol of his office.

3. Courtiers dressed with special splendor on the monarch's birthday.

when the Queen used to place me upon her hand towards a looking glass, by which both our persons appeared before me in full view together; and there could be nothing more ridiculous than the comparison; so that I really began to imagine myself dwindled many degrees below my usual size.

Nothing angered and mortified me so much as the Queen's dwarf, who being of the lowest stature that was ever in that country (for I verily think he was not full thirty foot high) became so insolent at seeing a creature so much beneath him that he would always affect to swagger and look big as he passed by me in the Queen's antechamber, while I was standing on some table talking with the lords or ladies of the court; and he seldom failed of a smart word or two upon my littleness, against which I could only revenge myself by calling him brother, challenging him to wrestle, and such repartees as are usual in the mouths of Court pages. One day at dinner this malicious little cub was so nettled with something I had said to him that, raising himself upon the frame of Her Majesty's chair, he took me up by the middle, as I was sitting down, not thinking any harm, and let me drop into a large silver bowl of cream, and then ran away as fast as he could. I fell over head and ears, and if I had not been a good swimmer, it might have gone very hard with me; for Glumdalclitch in that instant happened to be at the other end of the room, and the Queen was in such a fright that she wanted presence of mind to assist me. But my little nurse ran to my relief, and took me out, after I had swallowed above a quart of cream. I was put to bed; however, I received no other damage than the loss of a suit of clothes, which was utterly spoiled. The dwarf was soundly whipped, and as further punishment, forced to drink up the bowl of cream into which he had thrown me; neither was he ever restored to favor: for soon after the Queen bestowed him to a lady of high quality, so that I saw him no more, to my very great satisfaction; for I could not tell to what extremity such a malicious urchin might have carried his resentment.

He had before served me a scurvy trick, which set the Queen a laughing, although at the same time she were heartily vexed, and would have immediately cashiered him, if I had not been so generous as to intercede. Her Majesty had taken a marrow bone upon her plate, and after knocking out the marrow, placed the bone again in the dish, erect as it stood before; the dwarf watching his opportunity, while Glumdalclitch was gone to the sideboard, mounted upon the stool she stood on to take care of me at meals, took me up in both hands, and squeezing my legs together, wedged them into the marrow bone above my waist, where I stuck for some time, and made a very ridiculous figure. I believe it was near a minute before anyone knew what was become of me, for I thought it below me to cry out. But, as princes seldom get their meat hot, my legs were not scalded, only my stockings and breeches in a sad condition. The dwarf at my entreaty had no other punishment than a sound whipping.

I was frequently rallied by the Queen upon account of my fearfulness, and she used to ask me whether the people of my country were as great cowards as myself. The occasion was this. The kingdom is much pestered with flies in summer, and these odious insects, each of them as big as a Dunstable lark, hardly gave me any rest while I sat at dinner, with their continual humming and buzzing about my ears. They would sometimes alight upon my victuals, and leave their loathsome excrement or spawn behind, which to me was very visible, although not to the natives of that country, whose large optics were not so acute as mine in viewing smaller objects. Sometimes they would fix upon my nose or forehead, where they stung me to the quick, smelling very offensively; and I could easily trace that viscous matter, which our naturalists tell us enables those creatures to walk with their feet upwards upon a ceiling. I had much ado to defend myself against these detestable animals, and could not forbear starting when they came on my face. It was the common practice of the dwarf to catch a number of these insects in his hand, as schoolboys do among us, and let them out suddenly under my nose, on purpose to frighten me, and divert the Queen. My remedy was to cut them in pieces with my knife as they flew in the air, wherein my dexterity was much admired.

I remember one morning when Glumdalclitch had set me in my box upon a window, as she usually did in fair days to give me air (for I durst not venture to let the box be hung on a nail out of the window, as we do with cages in England), after I had lifted up one of my sashes, and sat down at my table to eat a piece of sweet cake for my breakfast, above twenty wasps, allured by the smell, came flying into the room, humming louder than the drones of as many bagpipes. Some of them seized my cake, and carried it piecemeal away; others flew about my head and face, confounding me with the noise, and putting me in the utmost terror of their stings. However, I had the courage to rise and draw my hanger, and attack them in the air. I dispatched four of them, but the rest got away, and I presently shut my window. These insects were as large as partridges; I took out their stings, found them an inch and a half long, and as sharp as needles. I carefully preserved them all, and having since shown them with some other curiosities in several parts of Europe, upon my return to England I gave three of them to Gresham College,[4] and kept the fourth for myself.

CHAPTER 4. *The country described. A proposal for correcting modern maps. The King's palace, and some account of the metropolis. The Author's way of traveling. The chief temple described.*

I now intend to give the reader a short description of this country, as far as I had traveled in it, which was not above two thousand miles round Lorbrulgrud the metropolis. For the Queen, whom I always attended, never went further when she accompanied the King in his progresses, and there stayed till his Majesty returned from viewing his frontiers. The whole extent of this prince's dominions reacheth about six thousand miles in length, and from three to five in breadth. From whence I cannot but conclude that our geographers of Europe are in a great error by supposing nothing but sea between Japan and California: for it was ever my opinion that there must be a balance of earth to counterpoise the great continent of Tartary; and therefore they ought to correct their maps and charts by joining this vast tract of land to the northwest parts of America, wherein I shall be ready to lend them my assistance.

The kingdom is a peninsula, terminated to the northeast by a ridge of mountains thirty miles high, which are altogether impassable by reason of the volcanoes upon the tops. Neither do the most learned know what sort of mortals inhabit beyond those mountains, or whether they be inhabited at all.

---

4. The Royal Society, in its earliest years, met in Gresham College.

On the three other sides it is bounded by the ocean. There is not one seaport in the whole kingdom; and those parts of the coasts into which the rivers issue are so full of pointed rocks, and the sea generally so rough, that there is no venturing with the smallest of their boats; so that these people are wholly excluded from any commerce with the rest of the world. But the large rivers are full of vessels, and abound with excellent fish, for they seldom get any from the sea, because the sea fish are of the same size with those in Europe, and consequently not worth catching; whereby it is manifest that nature, in the production of plants and animals of so extraordinary a bulk, is wholly confined to this continent, of which I leave the reasons to be determined by philosophers. However, now and then they take a whale that happens to be dashed against the rocks, which the common people feed on heartily. These whales I have known so large that a man could hardly carry one upon his shoulders; and sometimes for curiosity they are brought in hampers to Lorbrulgrud: I saw one of them in a dish at the King's table, which passed for a rarity, but I did not observe he was fond of it; for I think indeed the bigness disgusted him, although I have seen one somewhat larger in Greenland.

The country is well inhabited, for it contains fifty-one cities, near an hundred walled towns, and a great number of villages. To satisfy my curious reader, it may be sufficient to describe Lorbrulgrud. This city stands upon almost two equal parts on each side the river that passes through. It contains above eight thousand houses, and about six hundred thousand inhabitants. It is in length three *glonglungs* (which make about fifty-four English miles) and two and a half in breadth, as I measured it myself in the royal map made by the King's order, which was laid on the ground on purpose for me, and extended an hundred feet; I paced the diameter and circumference several times barefoot, and computing by the scale, measured it pretty exactly.

The King's palace is no regular edifice, but an heap of buildings about seven miles round: the chief rooms are generally two hundred and forty foot high, and broad and long in proportion. A coach was allowed to Glumdalclitch and me, wherein her governess frequently took her out to see the town, or go among the shops; and I was always of the party, carried in my box, although the girl at my own desire would often take me out, and hold me in her hand, that I might more conveniently view the houses and the people as we passed along the streets. I reckoned our coach to be about a square of Westminster Hall,[5] but not altogether so high; however, I cannot be very exact. One day the governess ordered our coachman to stop at several shops, where the beggars, watching their opportunity, crowded to the sides of the coach, and gave me the most horrible spectacles that ever an English eye beheld. There was a woman with a cancer in her breast, swelled to a monstrous size, full of holes, in two or three of which I could have easily crept, and covered my whole body. There was a fellow with a wen in his neck, larger than five woolpacks, and another with a couple of wooden legs, each about twenty foot high. But the most hateful sight of all was the lice crawling on their clothes. I could see distinctly the limbs of these vermin with my naked eye, much better than those of an European louse through a microscope,

---

5. The ancient hall, now incorporated into the Houses of Parliament, where the law courts then sat. Swift presumably means the square of its breadth (just under sixty-eight feet).

and their snouts with which they rooted like swine. They were the first I had ever beheld; and I should have been curious enough to dissect one of them if I had proper instruments (which I unluckily left behind me in the ship), although indeed the sight was so nauseous that it perfectly turned my stomach.

Besides the large box in which I was usually carried, the Queen ordered a smaller one to be made for me, of about twelve foot square and ten high, for the convenience of traveling, because the other was somewhat too large for Glumdalclitch's lap, and cumbersome in the coach; it was made by the same artist, whom I directed in the whole contrivance. This traveling closet was an exact square with a window in the middle of three of the squares, and each window was latticed with iron wire on the outside, to prevent accidents in long journeys. On the fourth side, which had no windows, two strong staples were fixed, through which the person that carried me, when I had a mind to be on horseback, put in a leathern belt, and buckled it about his waist. This was always the office of some grave trusty servant in whom I could confide, whether I attended the King and Queen in their progresses, or were disposed to see the gardens, or pay a visit to some great lady or minister of state in the court, when Glumdalclitch happened to be out of order: for I soon began to be known and esteemed among the greatest officers, I suppose more upon account of their Majesties' favor than any merit of my own. In journeys, when I was weary of the coach, a servant on horseback would buckle my box, and place it on a cushion before him; and there I had a full prospect of the country on three sides from my three windows. I had in this closet a field bed and a hammock hung from the ceiling, two chairs and a table, neatly screwed to the floor to prevent being tossed about by the agitation of the horse or the coach. And having been long used to sea voyages, those motions, although sometimes very violent, did not much discompose me.

When I had a mind to see the town, it was always in my traveling closet, which Glumdalclitch held in her lap in a kind of open sedan, after the fashion of the country, borne by four men, and attended by two others in the Queen's livery. The people, who had often heard of me, were very curious to crowd about the sedan; and the girl was complaisant enough to make the bearers stop, and to take me in her hand that I might be more conveniently seen.

I was very desirous to see the chief temple, and particularly the tower belonging to it, which is reckoned the highest in the kingdom. Accordingly one day my nurse carried me thither, but I may truly say I came back disappointed; for the height is not above three thousand foot, reckoning from the ground to the highest pinnacle top; which, allowing for the difference between the size of those people and us in Europe, is no great matter for admiration, nor at all equal in proportion (if I rightly remember) to Salisbury steeple.[6] But, not to detract from a nation to which during my life I shall acknowledge myself extremely obliged, it must be allowed that whatever this famous tower wants in height is amply made up in beauty and strength. For the walls are near an hundred foot thick, built of hewn stone, whereof each is about forty foot square, and adorned on all sides with statues of gods and emperors cut in marble larger than the life, placed in their several niches. I

6. One of the most beautiful Gothic steeples in England is that of Salisbury Cathedral, 404 feet high.

measured a little finger which had fallen down from one of these statues, and lay unperceived among some rubbish, and found it exactly four foot and an inch in length. Glumdalclitch wrapped it up in a handkerchief, and carried it home in her pocket to keep among other trinkets, of which the girl was very fond, as children at her age usually are.

The King's kitchen is indeed a noble building, vaulted at top, and about six hundred foot high. The great oven is not so wide by ten paces as the cupola at St. Paul's:[7] for I measured the latter on purpose after my return. But if I should describe the kitchen grate, the prodigious pots and kettles, the joints of meat turning on the spits, with many other particulars, perhaps I should be hardly believed; at least a severe critic would be apt to think I enlarged a little, as travelers are often suspected to do. To avoid which censure, I fear I have run too much into the other extreme, and that if this treatise should happen to be translated into the language of Brobdingnag (which is the general name of that kingdom) and transmitted thither, the King and his people would have reason to complain that I had done them an injury by a false and diminutive representation.

His Majesty seldom keeps above six hundred horses in his stables: they are generally from fifty-four to sixty foot high. But when he goes abroad on solemn days, he is attended for state by a militia guard of five hundred horse, which indeed I thought was the most splendid sight that could be ever beheld, till I saw part of his army in battalia,[8] whereof I shall find another occasion to speak.

CHAPTER 5. *Several adventures that happened to the Author. The execution of a criminal. The Author shows his skill in navigation.*

I should have lived happy enough in that country if my littleness had not exposed me to several ridiculous and troublesome accidents, some of which I shall venture to relate. Glumdalclitch often carried me into the gardens of the court in my smaller box, and would sometimes take me out of it and hold me in her hand, or set me down to walk. I remember, before the dwarf left the Queen, he followed us one day into those gardens; and my nurse having set me down, he and I being close together near some dwarf apple trees, I must needs show my wit by a silly allusion between him and the trees, which happens to hold in their language as it doth in ours. Whereupon, the malicious rogue watching his opportunity, when I was walking under one of them, shook it directly over my head, by which a dozen apples, each of them near as large as a Bristol barrel, came tumbling about my ears; one of them hit me on the back as I chanced to stoop, and knocked me down flat on my face, but I received no other hurt; and the dwarf was pardoned at my desire, because I had given the provocation.

Another day Glumdalclitch left me on a smooth grassplot to divert myself while she walked at some distance with her governess. In the meantime there suddenly fell such a violent shower of hail that I was immediately by the force of it struck to the ground: and when I was down, the hailstones gave me such cruel bangs all over the body as if I had been pelted with tennis balls;[9] however I made a shift to creep on all four, and shelter myself by lying

---

7. The cupola of St. Paul's Cathedral in London is 108 feet in diameter.
8. Battle array.

9. Eighteenth-century tennis balls, unlike the modern, were very hard.

on my face on the lee side of a border of lemon thyme, but so bruised from head to foot that I could not go abroad in ten days. Neither is this at all to be wondered at, because nature in that country observing the same proportion through all her operations, a hailstone is near eighteen hundred times as large as one in Europe; which I can assert upon experience, having been so curious to weigh and measure them.

But a more dangerous accident happened to me in the same garden when my little nurse, believing she had put me in a secure place, which I often entreated her to do that I might enjoy my own thoughts, and having left my box at home to avoid the trouble of carrying it, went to another part of the garden with her governess and some ladies of her acquaintance. While she was absent and out of hearing, a small white spaniel belonging to one of the chief gardeners, having got by accident into the garden, happened to range near the place where I lay. The dog following the scent, came directly up, and taking me in his mouth, ran straight to his master, wagging his tail, and set me gently on the ground. By good fortune he had been so well taught that I was carried between his teeth without the least hurt, or even tearing my clothes. But the poor gardener, who knew me well, and had a great kindness for me, was in a terrible fright. He gently took me up in both his hands, and asked me how I did; but I was so amazed and out of breath that I could not speak a word. In a few minutes I came to myself, and he carried me safe to my little nurse, who by this time had returned to the place where she left me, and was in cruel agonies when I did not appear nor answer when she called; she severely reprimanded the gardener on account of his dog. But the thing was hushed up and never known at court; for the girl was afraid of the Queen's anger; and truly, as to myself, I thought it would not be for my reputation that such a story should go about.

This accident absolutely determined Glumdalclitch never to trust me abroad for the future out of her sight. I had been long afraid of this resolution, and therefore concealed from her some little unlucky adventures that happened in those times when I was left by myself. Once a kite hovering over the garden made a stoop[1] at me, and if I had not resolutely drawn my hanger, and run under a thick espalier, he would have certainly carried me away in his talons. Another time walking to the top of a fresh molehill, I fell to my neck in the hole through which that animal had cast up the earth, and coined some lie, not worth remembering, to excuse myself for spoiling my clothes. I likewise broke my right shin against the shell of a snail, which I happened to stumble over, as I was walking alone, and thinking on poor England.

I cannot tell whether I were more pleased or mortified to observe in those solitary walks that the smaller birds did not appear to be at all afraid of me; but would hop about within a yard distance, looking for worms and other food with as much indifference and security as if no creature at all were near them. I remember a thrush had the confidence to snatch out of my hand with his bill a piece of cake that Glumdalclitch had just given me for my breakfast. When I attempted to catch any of these birds, they would boldly turn against me, endeavoring to pick my fingers, which I durst not venture within their reach; and then they would hop back unconcerned to hunt for worms or snails, as they did before. But one day I took a thick cudgel, and

1. Swoop. "Kite": a bird of prey.

threw it with all my strength so luckily at a linnet that I knocked him down, and seizing him by the neck with both my hands, ran with him in triumph to my nurse. However, the bird, who had only been stunned, recovering himself, gave me so many boxes with his wings on both sides of my head and body, though I held him at arm's length, and was out of the reach of his claws, that I was twenty times thinking to let him go. But I was soon relieved by one of our servants, who wrung off the bird's neck, and I had him next day for dinner, by the Queen's command. This linnet, as near as I can remember, seemed to be somewhat larger than an English swan.

The Maids of Honor often invited Glumdalclitch to their apartments, and desired she would bring me along with her, on purpose to have the pleasure of seeing and touching me. They would often strip me naked from top to toe and lay me at full length in their bosoms; wherewith I was much disgusted, because, to say the truth, a very offensive smell came from their skins, which I do not mention or intend to the disadvantage of those excellent ladies, for whom I have all manner of respect; but I conceive that my sense was more acute in proportion to my littleness, and that those illustrious persons were no more disagreeable to their lovers, or to each other, than people of the same quality are with us in England. And, after all, I found their natural smell was much more supportable than when they used perfumes, under which I immediately swooned away. I cannot forget that an intimate friend of mine in Lilliput took the freedom in a warm day, when I had used a good deal of exercise, to complain of a strong smell about me, although I am as little faulty that way as most of my sex: but I suppose his faculty of smelling was as nice with regard to me as mine was to that of this people. Upon this point, I cannot forbear doing justice to the Queen, my mistress, and Glumdalclitch, my nurse, whose persons were as sweet as those of any lady in England.

That which gave me most uneasiness among these Maids of Honor, when my nurse carried me to visit them, was to see them use me without any manner of ceremony, like a creature who had no sort of consequence. For they would strip themselves to the skin and put on their smocks in my presence, while I was placed on their toilet[2] directly before their naked bodies; which, I am sure, to me was very far from being a tempting sight, or from giving me any other emotions than those of horror and disgust. Their skins appeared so coarse and uneven, so variously colored, when I saw them near, with a mole here and there as broad as a trencher, and hairs hanging from it thicker than pack-threads, to say nothing further concerning the rest of their persons. Neither did they at all scruple, while I was by, to discharge what they had drunk, to the quantity of at least two hogsheads, in a vessel that held above three tuns. The handsomest among these Maids of Honor, a pleasant frolicsome girl of sixteen, would sometimes set me astride upon one of her nipples, with many other tricks, wherein the reader will excuse me for not being over particular. But I was so much displeased that I entreated Glumdalclitch to contrive some excuse for not seeing that young lady any more.

One day a young gentleman, who was nephew to my nurse's governess, came and pressed them both to see an execution. It was of a man who had

---

2. Toilet table.

murdered one of that gentleman's intimate acquaintance. Glumdalclitch was prevailed on to be of the company, very much against her inclination, for she was naturally tender-hearted: and as for myself, although I abhorred such kind of spectacles, yet my curiosity tempted me to see something that I thought must be extraordinary. The malefactor was fixed in a chair upon a scaffold erected for the purpose, and his head cut off at a blow with a sword of about forty foot long. The veins and arteries spouted up such a prodigious quantity of blood, and so high in the air, that the great *jet d'eau* at Versailles was not equal for the time it lasted; and the head, when it fell on the scaffold floor, gave such a bounce,[3] as made me start, although I were at least half an English mile distant.

The Queen, who often used to hear me talk of my sea voyages, and took all occasions to divert me when I was melancholy, asked me whether I understood how to handle a sail or an oar, and whether a little exercise of rowing might not be convenient for my health. I answered that I understood both very well. For although my proper employment had been to be surgeon or doctor to the ship, yet often, upon a pinch, I was forced to work like a common mariner. But I could not see how this could be done in their country, where the smallest wherry was equal to a first-rate man-of-war among us, and such a boat as I could manage would never live in any of their rivers. Her Majesty said, if I would contrive a boat, her own joiner should make it, and she would provide a place for me to sail in. The fellow was an ingenious workman and, by my instructions, in ten days finished a pleasure boat with all its tackling, able conveniently to hold eight Europeans. When it was finished, the Queen was so delighted that she ran with it in her lap to the King, who ordered it to be put in a cistern full of water, with me in it, by way of trial; where I could not manage my two sculls, or little oars, for want of room. But the Queen had before contrived another project. She ordered the joiner to make a wooden trough of three hundred foot long, fifty broad, and eight deep; which being well pitched to prevent leaking, was placed on the floor along the wall in an outer room of the palace. It had a cock near the bottom to let out the water when it began to grow stale, and two servants could easily fill it in half an hour. Here I often used to row for my own diversion, as well as that of the Queen and her ladies, who thought themselves well entertained with my skill and agility. Sometimes I would put up my sail, and then my business was only to steer, while the ladies gave me a gale with their fans; and when they were weary, some of the pages would blow my sail forward with their breath, while I showed my art by steering starboard or larboard as I pleased. When I had done, Glumdalclitch always carried my boat into her closet, and hung it on a nail to dry.

In this exercise I once met an accident which had like to have cost me my life. For one of the pages having put my boat into the trough, the governess who attended Glumdalclitch very officiously[4] lifted me up to place me in the boat; but I happened to slip through her fingers, and should have infallibly fallen down forty foot upon the floor, if by the luckiest chance in the world I had not been stopped by a corking-pin that stuck in the good gentlewoman's stomacher;[5] the head of the pin passed between my shirt and the waistband

---

3. A sudden noise. "*Jet d'eau* at Versailles": this fountain rose over forty feet in the air.
4. Kindly, dutifully.

5. An ornamental covering for the front and upper part of the body. "Corking-pin": a pin of the largest size.

of my breeches, and thus I was held by the middle in the air until Glumdalclitch ran to my relief.

Another time, one of the servants, whose office it was to fill my trough every third day with fresh water, was so careless to let a huge frog (not perceiving it) slip out of his pail. The frog lay concealed till I was put into my boat, but then seeing a resting place, climbed up, and made it lean so much on one side that I was forced to balance it with all my weight on the other, to prevent overturning. When the frog was got in, it hopped at once half the length of the boat, and then over my head, backwards and forwards, daubing my face and clothes with its odious slime. The largeness of its features made it appear the most deformed animal that can be conceived. However, I desired Glumdalclitch to let me deal with it alone. I banged it a good while with one of my sculls, and at last forced it to leap out of the boat.

But the greatest danger I ever underwent in that kingdom was from a monkey, who belonged to one of the clerks of the kitchen. Glumdalclitch had locked me up in her closet, while she went somewhere upon business or a visit. The weather being very warm, the closet window was left open, as well as the windows in the door of my bigger box, in which I usually lived, because of its largeness and conveniency. As I sat quietly meditating at my table, I heard something bounce in at the closet window, and skip about from one side to the other, whereat, although I was much alarmed, yet I ventured to look out, but stirred not from my seat; and then I saw this frolicsome animal, frisking and leaping up and down, till at last he came to my box, which he seemed to view with great pleasure and curiosity, peeping in at the door and every window. I retreated to the farther corner of my room, or box, but the monkey looking in at every side, put me into such a fright that I wanted presence of mind to conceal myself under the bed, as I might easily have done. After some time spent in peeping, grinning, and chattering, he at last espied me, and reaching one of his paws in at the door, as a cat does when she plays with a mouse, although I often shifted place to avoid him, he at length seized the lappet of my coat (which, being made of that country cloth, was very thick and strong) and dragged me out. He took me up in his right forefoot, and held me as a nurse does a child she is going to suckle, just as I have seen the same sort of creature do with a kitten in Europe: and when I offered to struggle, he squeezed me so hard that I thought it more prudent to submit. I have good reason to believe that he took me for a young one of his own species, by his often stroking my face very gently with his other paw. In these diversions he was interrupted by a noise at the closet door, as if somebody were opening it, whereupon he suddenly leaped up to the window at which he had come in, and thence upon the leads and gutters, walking upon three legs, and holding me in the fourth, till he clambered up to a roof that was next to ours. I heard Glumdalclitch give a shriek at the moment he was carrying me out. The poor girl was almost distracted: that quarter of the palace was all in an uproar; the servants ran for ladders; the monkey was seen by hundreds in the court, sitting upon the ridge of a building, holding me like a baby in one of his forepaws and feeding me with the other, by cramming into my mouth some victuals he had squeezed out of the bag on one side of his chaps, and patting me when I would not eat; whereat many of the rabble below could not forebear laughing; neither do I think they justly ought to be blamed, for without question the sight was ridiculous enough to everybody but myself. Some of the people threw up stones, hoping to drive the monkey down; but this was strictly forbidden, or else very probably my brains had been dashed out.

The ladders were now applied, and mounted by several men; which the monkey observing, and finding himself almost encompassed, not being able to make speed enough with his three legs, let me drop on a ridge tile, and made his escape. Here I sat for some time three hundred yards from the ground, expecting every moment to be blown down by the wind, or to fall by my own giddiness, and come tumbling over and over from the ridge to the eaves. But an honest lad, one of my nurse's footmen, climbed up, and putting me into his breeches pocket, brought me down safe.

I was almost choked with the filthy stuff the monkey had crammed down my throat; but my dear little nurse picked it out of my mouth with a small needle, and then I fell a vomiting, which gave me great relief. Yet I was so weak and bruised in the sides with the squeezes given me by this odious animal that I was forced to keep my bed a fortnight. The King, Queen, and all the Court sent every day to inquire after my health, and her Majesty made me several visits during my sickness. The monkey was killed, and an order made that no such animal should be kept about the palace.

When I attended the King after my recovery, to return him thanks for his favors, he was pleased to rally me a good deal upon this adventure. He asked me what my thoughts and speculations were while I lay in the monkey's paw, how I liked the victuals he gave me, his manner of feeding, and whether the fresh air on the roof had sharpened my stomach. He desired to know what I would have done upon such an occasion in my own country. I told his Majesty that in Europe we had no monkeys, except such as were brought for curiosities from other places, and so small that I could deal with a dozen of them together, if they presumed to attack me. And as for that monstrous animal with whom I was so lately engaged (it was indeed as large as an elephant), if my fears had suffered me to think so far as to make use of my hanger (looking fiercely and clapping my hand upon the hilt as I spoke) when he poked his paw into my chamber, perhaps I should have given him such a wound as would have made him glad to withdraw it with more haste than he put it in. This I delivered in a firm tone, like a person who was jealous lest his courage should be called in question. However, my speech produced nothing else besides a loud laughter, which all the respect due to his Majesty from those about him could not make them contain. This made me reflect how vain an attempt it is for a man to endeavor doing himself honor among those who are out of all degree of equality or comparison with him. And yet I have seen the moral of my own behavior very frequent in England since my return, where a little contemptible varlet, without the least title to birth, person, wit, or common sense, shall presume to look with importance, and put himself upon a foot with the greatest persons of the kingdom.

I was every day furnishing the court with some ridiculous story; and Glumdalclitch, although she loved me to excess, yet was arch enough to inform the Queen whenever I committed any folly that she thought would be diverting to her Majesty. The girl, who had been out of order, was carried by her governess to take the air about an hour's distance, or thirty miles from town. They alighted out of the coach near a small footpath in a field, and Glumdalclitch setting down my traveling box, I went out of it to walk. There was a cow dung in the patch, and I must needs try my activity by attempting to leap over it. I took a run, but unfortunately jumped short, and found myself just in the middle up to my knees. I waded through with some difficulty, and one of the footmen wiped me as clean as he could with his handkerchief; for I was filthily bemired, and my nurse confined me to my box till we returned home, where the Queen was soon informed of what had passed and the footmen spread it about the Court, so that all the mirth, for some days, was at my expense.

CHAPTER 6. *Several contrivances of the Author to please the King and Queen. He shows his skill in music. The King inquires into the state of Europe, which the Author relates to him. The King's observations thereon.*

I used to attend the King's levee once or twice a week, and had often seen him under the barber's hand, which indeed was at first very terrible to behold. For the razor was almost twice as long as an ordinary scythe. His Majesty, according to the custom of the country, was only shaved twice a week. I once prevailed on the barber to give me some of the suds or lather, out of which I picked forty or fifty of the strongest stumps of hair. I then took a piece of fine wood, and cut it like the back of a comb, making several holes in it at equal distance with as small a needle as I could get from Glumdalclitch. I fixed in the stumps so artificially,[6] scraping and sloping them with my knife towards the points, that I made a very tolerable comb; which was a seasonable supply, my own being so much broken in the teeth that it was almost useless; neither did I know any artist in that country so nice and exact as would undertake to make me another.

And this puts me in mind of an amusement wherein I spent many of my leisure hours. I desired the Queen's woman to save for me the combings of her Majesty's hair, whereof in time I got a good quantity; and consulting with my friend the cabinetmaker, who had received general orders to do little jobs for me, I directed him to make two chair frames, no larger than those I had in my box, and then to bore little holes with a fine awl round those parts where I designed the backs and seats; through these holes I wove the strongest hairs I could pick out, just after the manner of cane chairs in England. When they were finished, I made a present of them to her Majesty, who kept them in her cabinet, and used to show them for curiosities, as indeed they were the wonder of every one that beheld them. The Queen would have made me sit upon one of these chairs, but I absolutely refused to obey her, protesting I would rather die a thousand deaths than place a dishonorable part of my body on those precious hairs that once adorned her Majesty's head. Of these hairs (as I had always a mechanical genius) I likewise made a neat little purse above five foot long, with her Majesty's name deciphered in gold letters, which I gave to Glumdalclitch by the Queen's consent. To say the truth, it was more for show than use, being not of strength to bear the weight of the larger coins; and therefore she kept nothing in it but some little toys[7] that girls are fond of.

The King, who delighted in music, had frequent consorts[8] at court, to

6. Skillfully.
7. Trifles.
8. Concerts.

which I was sometimes carried, and set in my box on a table to hear them; but the noise was so great that I could hardly distinguish the tunes. I am confident that all the drums and trumpets of a royal army, beating and sounding together just at your ears, could not equal it. My practice was to have my box removed from the places where the performers sat, as far as I could, then to shut the doors and windows of it, and draw the window curtains, after which I found their music not disagreeable.

I had learned in my youth to play a little upon the spinet. Glumdalclitch kept one in her chamber, and a master attended twice a week to teach her: I call it a spinet, because it somewhat resembled that instrument, and was played upon in the same manner. A fancy came into my head that I would entertain the King and Queen with an English tune upon this instrument. But this appeared extremely difficult: for the spinet was near sixty foot long, each key being almost a foot wide; so that, with my arms extended, I could not reach to above five keys, and to press them down required a good smart stroke with my fist, which would be too great a labor and to no purpose. The method I contrived was this: I prepared two round sticks about the bigness of common cudgels; they were thicker at one end than the other, and I covered the thicker ends with a piece of a mouse's skin, that by rapping on them I might neither damage the tops of the keys, nor interrupt the sound. Before the spinet a bench was placed, about four foot below the keys, and I was put upon the bench. I ran sideling upon it that way and this, as fast as I could, banging the proper keys with my two sticks; and made a shift to play a jig, to the great satisfaction of both their Majesties: but it was the most violent exercise I ever underwent, and yet I could not strike above sixteen keys, nor, consequently, play the bass and treble together, as other artists do; which was a great disadvantage to my performance.

The King, who, as I before observed, was a prince of excellent understanding, would frequently order that I should be brought in my box and set upon the table in his closet. He would then command me to bring one of my chairs out of the box, and sit down within three yards distance upon the top of the cabinet, which brought me almost to a level with his face. In this manner I had several conversations with him. I one day took the freedom to tell his Majesty that the contempt he discovered towards Europe, and the rest of the world, did not seem answerable to those excellent qualities of mind that he was master of. That reason did not extend itself with the bulk of the body: on the contrary, we observed in our country that the tallest persons were usually least provided with it. That among other animals, bees and ants had the reputation of more industry, art, and sagacity than many of the larger kinds; and that, as inconsiderable as he took me to be, I hoped I might live to do his Majesty some signal service. The King heard me with attention, and began to conceive a much better opinion of me than he had before. He desired I would give him as exact an account of the government of England as I possibly could; because, as fond as princes commonly are of their own customs (for so he conjectured of other monarchs, by my former discourses), he should be glad to hear of anything that might deserve imitation.

Imagine with thyself, courteous reader, how often I then wished for the tongue of Demosthenes or Cicero, that might have enabled me to celebrate the praise of my own dear native country in a style equal to its merits and felicity.

I began my discourse by informing his Majesty that our dominions consisted of two islands, which composed three mighty kingdoms under one sovereign, beside our plantations in America. I dwelt long upon the fertility of our soil, and the temperature[9] of our climate. I then spoke at large upon the constitution of an English Parliament, partly made up of an illustrious body called the House of Peers, persons of the noblest blood, and of the most ancient and ample patrimonies. I described that extraordinary care always taken of their education in arts and arms, to qualify them for being counselors born to the king and kingdom; to have a share in the legislature, to be members of the highest Court of Judicature, from whence there could be no appeal; and to be champions always ready for the defense of their prince and country, by their valor, conduct, and fidelity. That these were the ornament and bulwark of the kingdom, worthy followers of their most renowned ancestors, whose honor had been the reward of their virtue, from which their posterity were never once known to degenerate. To these were joined several holy persons, as part of that assembly, under the title of Bishops, whose peculiar business it is to take care of religion, and of those who instruct the people therein. These were searched and sought out through the whole nation, by the prince and his wisest counselors, among such of the priesthood as were most deservedly distinguished by the sanctity of their lives and the depth of their erudition, who were indeed the spiritual fathers of the clergy and the people.

That the other part of the Parliament consisted of an assembly called the House of Commons, who were all principal gentlemen, freely picked and culled out by the people themselves, for their great abilities and love of their country, to represent the wisdom of the whole nation. And these two bodies make up the most august assembly in Europe, to whom, in conjunction with the prince, the whole legislature is committed.

I then descended to the Courts of Justice, over which the Judges, those venerable sages and interpreters of the law, presided, for determining the disputed rights and properties of men, as well as for the punishment of vice, and protection of innocence. I mentioned the prudent management of our treasury, the valor and achievements of our forces by sea and land. I computed the number of our people, by reckoning how many millions there might be of each religious sect, or political party among us. I did not omit even our sports and pastimes, or any other particular which I thought might redound to the honor of my country. And I finished all with a brief historical account of affairs and events in England for about an hundred years past.

This conversation was not ended under five audiences, each of several hours, and the King heard the whole with great attention, frequently taking notes of what I spoke, as well as memorandums of several questions he intended to ask me.

When I had put an end to these long discourses, his Majesty in a sixth audience consulting his notes, proposed many doubts, queries, and objections, upon every article. He asked what methods were used to cultivate the minds and bodies of our young nobility, and in what kind of business they commonly spent the first and teachable part of their lives. What course was

9. Temperateness.

taken to supply that assembly when any noble family became extinct. What qualifications were necessary in those who were to be created new lords. Whether the humor[1] of the prince, a sum of money to a Court lady or a prime minister, or a design of strengthening a party opposite to the public interest, ever happened to be motives in those advancements. What share of knowledge these lords had in the laws of their country, and how they came by it, so as to enable them to decide the properties of their fellow subjects in the last resort. Whether they were always so free from avarice, partialities, or want that a bribe or some other sinister view could have no place among them. Whether those holy lords I spoke of were constantly promoted to that rank upon account of their knowledge in religious matters, and the sanctity of their lives; had never been compliers with the times while they were common priests, or slavish prostitute chaplains to some nobleman, whose opinions they continued servilely to follow after they were admitted into that assembly.

He then desired to know what arts were practiced in electing those whom I called Commoners. Whether a stranger with a strong purse might not influence the vulgar voters to choose him before their own landlord or the most considerable gentleman in the neighborhood. How it came to pass that people were so violently bent upon getting into this assembly, which I allowed to be a great trouble and expense, often to the ruin of their families, without any salary or pension: because this appeared such an exalted strain of virtue and public spirit that his Majesty seemed to doubt it might possibly not be always sincere; and he desired to know whether such zealous gentlemen could have any views of refunding themselves for the charges and trouble they were at, by sacrificing the public good to the designs of a weak and vicious prince in conjunction with a corrupted ministry. He multiplied his questions, and sifted me thoroughly upon every part of this head, proposing numberless inquiries and objections, which I think it not prudent or convenient to repeat.

Upon what I said in relation to our Courts of Justice, his Majesty desired to be satisfied in several points: and this I was the better able to do, having been formerly almost ruined by a long suit in chancery, which was decreed for me with costs. He asked what time was usually spent in determining between right and wrong, and what degree of expense. Whether advocates and orators had liberty to plead in causes manifestly known to be unjust, vexatious, or oppressive. Whether party in religion or politics were observed to be of any weight in the scale of justice. Whether those pleading orators were persons educated in the general knowledge of equity, or only in provincial, national, and other local customs. Whether they or their judges had any part in penning those laws which they assumed the liberty of interpreting and glossing upon at their pleasure. Whether they had ever at different times pleaded for and against the same cause, and cited precedents to prove contrary opinions. Whether they were a rich or a poor corporation. Whether they received any pecuniary reward for pleading or delivering their opinions. And particularly whether they were ever admitted as members in the lower senate.

1. Whim.

He fell next upon the management of our treasury, and said he thought my memory had failed me, because I computed our taxes at about five or six millions a year, and when I came to mention the issues,[2] he found they sometimes amounted to more than double, for the notes he had taken were very particular in this point; because he hoped, as he told me, that the knowledge of our conduct might be useful to him, and he could not be deceived in his calculations. But if what I told him were true, he was still at a loss how a kingdom could run out of its estate like a private person. He asked me, who were our creditors? and where we should find money to pay them? He wondered to hear me talk of such chargeable and extensive wars; that certainly we must be a quarrelsome people, or live among very bad neighbors, and that our generals must needs be richer than our kings.[3] He asked what business we had out of our own islands, unless upon the score of trade or treaty or to defend the coasts with our fleet. Above all, he was amazed to hear me talk of a mercenary standing army[4] in the midst of peace, and among a free people. He said if we were governed by our own consent in the persons of our representatives, he could not imagine of whom we were afraid, or against whom we were to fight; and would hear my opinion whether a private man's house might not better be defended by himself, his children, and family, than by half a dozen rascals picked up at a venture[5] in the streets for small wages, who might get an hundred times more by cutting their throats.

He laughed at my odd kind of arithmetic (as he was pleased to call it) in reckoning the numbers of our people by a computation drawn from the several sects among us in religion and politics. He said he knew no reason why those who entertain opinions prejudicial to the public should be obliged to change, or should not be obliged to conceal them. And as it was tyranny in any government to require the first, so it was weakness not to enforce the second: for a man may be allowed to keep poisons in his closet, but not to vend them about for cordials.[6]

He observed that among the diversions of our nobility and gentry I had mentioned gaming. He desired to know at what age this entertainment was usually taken up, and when it was laid down; how much of their time it employed; whether it ever went so high as to affect their fortunes; whether mean, vicious people, by their dexterity in that art, might not arrive at great riches, and sometimes keep our very nobles in dependence, as well as habituate them to vile companions, wholly take them from the improvement of their minds, and force them, by the losses they received, to learn and practice that infamous dexterity upon others.

He was perfectly astonished with the historical account I gave him of our affairs during the last century, protesting it was only an heap of conspiracies, rebellions, murders, massacres, revolutions, banishments, the very worst effects that avarice, faction, hypocrisy, perfidiousness, cruelty, rage, madness, hatred, envy, lust, malice, or ambition could produce.

His Majesty in another audience was at the pains to recapitulate the sum of all I had spoken; compared the questions he made with the answers I had

2. Expenditures.
3. An allusion to the enormous fortune gained by the duke of Marlborough, formerly captain-general of the army, whom Swift detested.
4. Since the declaration of the Bill of Rights (1689), a standing army without authorization by Parliament had been illegal. Swift and the Tories in general were vigilant in their opposition to such an army.
5. By chance.
6. Medicines to stimulate the heart, or, equally commonly, liqueurs.

given; then taking me into his hands, and stroking me gently, delivered himself in these words, which I shall never forget, nor the manner he spoke them in. "My little friend Grildrig, you have made a most admirable panegyric upon your country. You have clearly proved that ignorance, idleness, and vice are the proper ingredients for qualifying a legislator. That laws are best explained, interpreted, and applied by those whose interests and abilities lie in perverting, confounding, and eluding them. I observe among you some lines of an institution which in its original might have been tolerable; but these half erased, and the rest wholly blurred and blotted by corruptions. It doth not appear from all you have said how any one virtue is required towards the procurement of any one station among you; much less that men are ennobled on account of their virtue, that priests are advanced for their piety or learning, soldiers for their conduct or valor, judges for their integrity, senators for the love of their country, or counselors for their wisdom. As for yourself," continued the King, "who have spent the greatest part of your life in traveling, I am well disposed to hope you may hitherto have escaped many vices of your country. But by what I have gathered from your own relation, and the answers I have with much pains wringed and extorted from you, I cannot but conclude the bulk of your natives to be the most pernicious race of little odious vermin that nature ever suffered to crawl upon the surface of the earth."

CHAPTER 7. *The Author's love of his country. He makes a proposal of much advantage to the King; which is rejected. The King's great ignorance in politics. The learning of that country very imperfect and confined. Their laws, and military affairs, and parties in the State.*

Nothing but an extreme love of truth could have hindered me from concealing this part of my story. It was in vain to discover my resentments, which were always turned into ridicule: and I was forced to rest with patience while my noble and most beloved country was so injuriously treated. I am heartily sorry as any of my readers can possibly be that such an occasion was given, but this prince happened to be so curious and inquisitive upon every particular that it could not consist either with gratitude or good manners to refuse giving him what satisfaction I was able. Yet thus much I may be allowed to say in my own vindication: that I artfully eluded many of his questions, and gave to every point a more favorable turn by many degrees than the strictness of truth would allow. For I have always borne that laudable partiality to my own country, which Dionysius Halicarnassensis[7] with so much justice recommends to an historian. I would hide the frailties and deformities of my political mother, and place her virtues and beauties in the most advantageous light. This was my sincere endeavor in those many discourses I had with that mighty monarch, although it unfortunately failed of success.

But great allowances should be given to a King who lives wholly secluded from the rest of the world, and must therefore be altogether unacquainted with the manners and customs that most prevail in other nations: the want of which knowledge will ever produce many *prejudices*, and a certain *nar-*

---

7. A Greek rhetorician and historian, who flourished ca. 25 B.C.E. His history of Rome was written to reconcile the Greeks to their Roman masters.

rowness of thinking, from which we and the politer countries of Europe are wholly exempted. And it would be hard indeed if so remote a prince's notions of virtue and vice were to be offered as a standard for all mankind.

To confirm what I have now said, and further to show the miserable effects of a *confined education,* I shall here insert a passage which will hardly obtain belief. In hopes to ingratiate myself farther into his Majesty's favor, I told him of an invention discovered between three and four hundred years ago, to make a certain powder, into an heap of which the smallest spark of fire falling would kindle the whole in a moment, although it were as big as a mountain, and make it all fly up in the air together, with a noise and agitation greater than thunder. That a proper quantity of this powder rammed into an hollow tube of brass or iron, according to its bigness, would drive a ball of iron or lead with such violence and speed as nothing was able to sustain its force. That the largest balls thus discharged would not only destroy whole ranks of an army at once, but batter the strongest walls to the ground; sink down ships with a thousand men in each, to the bottom of the sea; and, when linked together by a chain, would cut through masts and rigging; divide hundreds of bodies in the middle, and lay all waste before them. That we often put this powder into large hollow balls of iron, and discharged them by an engine into some city we were besieging; which would rip up the pavements, tear the houses to pieces, burst and throw splinters on every side, dashing out the brains of all who came near. That I knew the ingredients very well, which were cheap and common; I understood the manner of compounding them, and could direct his workmen how to make those tubes of a size proportionable to all other things in his Majesty's kingdom, and the largest need not be above two hundred foot long; twenty or thirty of which tubes, charged with the proper quantity of powder and balls, would batter down the walls of the strongest town in his dominions in a few hours; or destroy the whole metropolis, if ever it should pretend to dispute his absolute commands. This I humbly offered to his Majesty as a small tribute of acknowledgement in return of so many marks that I had received of his royal favor and protection.

The King was struck with horror at the description I had given of those terrible engines and the proposal I had made. He was amazed how so impotent and groveling an insect as I (these were his expressions) could entertain such inhuman ideas, and in so familiar a manner as to appear wholly unmoved at all the scenes of blood and desolation which I had painted as the common effects of those destructive machines; whereof he said some evil genius, enemy to mankind, must have been the first contriver. As for himself, he protested that although few things delighted him so much as new discoveries in art or in nature, yet he would rather lose half his kingdom than be privy to such a secret, which he commanded me, as I valued my life, never to mention any more.

A strange effect of *narrow principles* and *short views!* that a prince possessed of every quality which procures veneration, love, and esteem; of strong parts, great wisdom, and profound learning; endued with admirable talents for government, and almost adored by his subjects; should from a *nice, unnecessary scruple,* whereof in Europe we can have no conception, let slip an opportunity put into his hands that would have made him absolute master of the lives, the liberties, and the fortunes of his people. Neither do I say this with the least intention to detract from the many virtues of that excellent King, whose character I am sensible will on this account be very much lessened in the opinion of an English reader: but I take this defect among them to have risen from their ignorance; they not having hitherto reduced politics into a science, as the more acute wits of Europe have done. For I remember very well, in a discourse one day with the King, when I happened to say there were several thousand books among us written upon the art of government, it gave him (directly contrary to my intention) a very mean opinion of our understandings. He professed both to abominate and despise all *mystery, refinement,* and *intrigue,* either in a prince or a minister. He could not tell what I meant by *secrets of state,* where an enemy or some rival nation were not in the case. He confined the knowledge of governing within very *narrow bounds:* to common sense and reason, to justice and lenity, to the speedy determination of civil and criminal causes, with some other obvious topics which are not worth considering. And he gave it for his opinion that whoever could make two ears of corn or two blades of grass to grow upon a spot of ground where only one grew before would deserve better of mankind and do more essential service to his country than the whole race of politicians[8] put together.

The learning of this people is very defective, consisting only in morality, history, poetry, and mathematics; wherein they must be allowed to excel. But the last of these is wholly applied to what may be useful in life, to the improvement of agriculture and all mechanical arts; so that among us it would be little esteemed. And as to ideas, entities, abstractions, and transcendentals,[9] I could never drive the least conception into their heads.

No law of that country must exceed in words the number of letters in their alphabet, which consists only in two and twenty. But indeed few of them extend even to that length. They are expressed in the most plain and simple terms, wherein those people are not mercurial enough to discover above one interpretation. And to write a comment upon any law is a capital crime. As to the decision of civil causes, or proceedings against criminals, their precedents are so few that they have little reason to boast of any extraordinary skill in either.

They have had the art of printing as well as the Chinese, time out of mind. But their libraries are not very large; for that of the King's, which is reckoned the biggest, doth not amount to above a thousand volumes, placed in a gallery of twelve hundred foot long, from whence I had liberty to borrow what books I pleased. The Queen's joiner had contrived in one of the Glumdalclitch's rooms a kind of wooden machine five and twenty foot high, formed like a standing ladder; the steps were each fifty foot long. It was indeed a movable pair of stairs, the lowest end placed at ten foot distance from the wall of the chamber. The book I had a mind to read was put up leaning against the wall. I first mounted to the upper step of the ladder, and turning my face towards the book began at the top of the page, and so walking to the right and left about eight or ten paces according to the length of the lines, till I had gotten a little below the level of mine eyes, and then descending gradually till I came to the bottom: after which I mounted again, and began the other page

8. By *politicians,* Swift means something like our modern political scientists or theorists.

9. In Swift's time, *transcendental* was practically synonymous with *metaphysical.*

in the same manner, and so turned over the leaf, which I could easily do with both my hands, for it was as thick and stiff as a pasteboard, and in the largest folios not above eighteen or twenty foot long.

Their style is clear, masculine, and smooth, but not florid; for they avoid nothing more than multiplying unnecessary words or using various expressions. I have perused many of their books, especially those in history and morality. Among the rest, I was much diverted with a little old treatise, which always lay in Glumdalclitch's bedchamber, and belonged to her governess, a grave elderly gentlewoman, who dealt in writings of morality and devotion. The book treats of the weakness of human kind, and is in little esteem, except among the women and the vulgar. However, I was curious to see what an author of that country could say upon such a subject. This writer went through all the usual topics of European moralists: showing how diminutive, contemptible, and helpless an animal was man in his own nature; how unable to defend himself from the inclemencies of the air, or the fury of wild beasts; how much he was excelled by one creature in strength, by another in speed, by a third in foresight, by a fourth in industry. He added that nature was degenerated in these latter declining ages of the world, and could now produce only small abortive births in comparison of those in ancient times. He said it was very reasonable to think, not only that the species of men were originally much larger, but also that there must have been giants in former ages; which, as it is asserted by history and tradition, so it hath been confirmed by huge bones and skulls casually dug up in several parts of the kingdom, far exceeding the common dwindled race of man in our days. He argued that the very laws of nature absolutely required we should have been made in the beginning of a size more large and robust, not so liable to destruction from every little accident of a tile falling from a house, or a stone cast from the hand of a boy, or of being drowned in a little brook. From this way of reasoning, the author drew several moral applications useful in the conduct of life, but needless here to repeat. For my own part, I could not avoid reflecting how universally this talent was spread, of drawing lectures in morality, or indeed rather matter of discontent and repining, from the quarrels we raise with nature. And I believe, upon a strict inquiry, those quarrels might be shown as ill grounded among us as they are among that people.

As to their military affairs, they boast that the King's army consists of an hundred and seventy-six thousand foot and thirty-two thousand horse: if that may be called an army which is made up of tradesmen in the several cities, and farmers in the country, whose commanders are only the nobility and gentry, without pay or reward. They are indeed perfect enough in their exercises, and under very good discipline, wherein I saw no great merit; for how should it be otherwise, where every farmer is under the command of his own landlord, and every citizen under that of the principal men in his own city, chosen after the manner of Venice by ballot?

I have often seen the militia of Lorbrulgrud drawn out to exercise in a great field near the city, of twenty miles square. They were in all not above twenty-five thousand foot, and six thousand horse; but it was impossible for me to compute their number, considering the space of ground they took up. A cavalier mounted on a large steed might be about an hundred foot high. I have seen this whole body of horse, upon a word of command, draw their swords at once, and brandish them in the air. Imagination can figure nothing so grand, so surprising, and so astonishing. It looked as if ten thousand flashes of lightning were darting at the same time from every quarter of the sky.

I was curious to know how this prince, to whose dominions there is no access from any other country, came to think of armies, or to teach his people the practice of military discipline. But I was soon informed, both by conversation and reading their histories. For in the course of many ages they have been troubled with the same disease to which the whole race of mankind is subject: the nobility often contending for power, the people for liberty, and the King for absolute dominion. All which, however happily tempered by the laws of the kingdom, have been sometimes violated by each of the three parties, and have more than once occasioned civil wars, the last whereof was happily put an end to by this prince's grandfather in a general composition;[1] and the militia, then settled with common consent, hath been ever since kept in the strictest duty.

CHAPTER 8. *The King and Queen make a progress to the frontiers. The Author attends them. The manner in which he leaves the country very particularly related. He returns to England.*

I had always a strong impulse that I should some time recover my liberty, though it were impossible to conjecture by what means, or to form any project with the least hope of succeeding. The ship in which I sailed was the first ever known to be driven within sight of that coast; and the King had given strict orders that if at any time another appeared, it should be taken ashore, and with all its crew and passengers brought in a tumbrel[2] to Lorbrulgrud. He was strongly bent to get me a woman of my own size, by whom I might propagate the breed: but I think I should rather have died than undergone the disgrace of leaving a posterity to be kept in cages like tame canary birds, and perhaps in time sold about the kingdom to persons of quality for curiosities. I was indeed treated with much kindness: I was the favorite of a great King and Queen, and the delight of the whole Court, but it was upon such a foot as ill became the dignity of human kind. I could never forget those domestic pledges I had left behind me. I wanted to be among people with whom I could converse upon even terms, and walk about the streets and fields without fear of being trod to death like a frog or a young puppy. But my deliverance came sooner than I expected, and in a manner not very common; the whole story and circumstances of which I shall faithfully relate.

I had now been two years in this country; and about the beginning of the third, Glumdalclitch and I attended the King and Queen in progress to the south coast of the kingdom. I was carried as usual in my traveling box, which, as I have already described, was a very convenient closet of twelve foot wide. I had ordered a hammock to be fixed by silken ropes from the four corners at the top, to break the jolts when a servant carried me before him on horseback, as I sometimes desired; and would often sleep in my hammock while we were upon the road. On the roof of my closet, set not directly over

---

1. A political settlement based on general agreement of all parties.　2. A farm wagon.

the middle of the hammock, I ordered the joiner to cut out a hole of a foot square to give me air in hot weather as I slept, which hole I shut at pleasure with a board that drew backwards and forwards through a groove.

When we came to our journey's end, the King thought proper to pass a few days at a palace he hath near Flanflasnic, a city within eighteen English miles of the seaside. Glumdalclitch and I were much fatigued; I had gotten a small cold, but the poor girl was so ill as to be confined to her chamber. I longed to see the ocean, which must be the only scene of my escape, if ever it should happen. I pretended to be worse than I really was, and desired leave to take the fresh air of the sea with a page whom I was very fond of, and who had sometimes been trusted with me. I shall never forget with what unwillingness Glumdalclitch consented, nor the strict charge she gave the page to be careful of me, bursting at the same time into a flood of tears, as if she had some foreboding of what was to happen. The boy took me out in my box about half an hour's walk from the palace, towards the rocks on the seashore. I ordered him to set me down, and lifting up one of my sashes, cast many a wistful melancholy look towards the sea. I found myself not very well, and told the page that I had a mind to take a nap in my hammock, which I hoped would do me good. I got in, and the boy shut the window close down, to keep out the cold. I soon fell asleep: and all I can conjecture is that while I slept, the page, thinking no danger could happen, went among the rocks to look for birds' eggs; having before observed him from my window searching about, and picking up one or two in the clefts. Be that as it will, I found myself suddenly awaked with a violent pull upon the ring which was fastened at the top of my box for the conveniency of carriage. I felt my box raised very high in the air, and then borne forward with prodigious speed. The first jolt had like to have shaken me out of my hammock, but afterwards the motion was easy enough. I called out several times as loud as I could raise my voice, but all to no purpose. I looked towards my windows, and could see nothing but the clouds and sky. I heard a noise just over my head like the clapping of wings, and then began to perceive the woeful condition I was in; that some eagle had got the ring of my box in his beak, with an intent to let it fall on a rock, like a tortoise in a shell, and then pick out my body and devour it. For the sagacity and smell of this bird enable him to discover his quarry at a great distance, although better concealed than I could be within a two-inch board.

In a little time I observed the noise and flutter of wings to increase very fast, and my box was tossed up and down like a signpost in a windy day. I heard several bangs or buffets, as I thought, given to the eagle (for such I am certain it must have been that held the ring of my box in his beak), and then all on a sudden felt myself falling perpendicularly down for above a minute, but with such incredible swiftness that I almost lost my breath. My fall was topped by a terrible squash, that sounded louder to mine ears than the cataract of Niagara; after which I was quite in the dark for another minute, and then my box began to rise so high that I could see light from the tops of my windows. I now perceived that I was fallen into the sea. My box, by the weight of my body, the goods that were in, and the broad plates of iron fixed for strength at the four corners of the top and bottom, floated above five foot deep in water. I did then and do now suppose that the eagle which flew away with my box was pursued by two or three others, and forced to let me drop while he was defending himself against the rest, who hoped to share in the prey. The plates of iron fastened at the bottom of the box (for those were the strongest) preserved the balance while it fell, and hindered it from being broken on the surface of the water. Every joint of it was well grooved, and the door did not move on hinges, but up and down like a sash; which kept my closet so tight that very little water came in. I got with much difficulty out of my hammock, having first ventured to draw back the slip-board on the roof already mentioned, contrived on purpose to let in air, for want of which I found myself almost stifled.

How often did I then wish myself with my dear Glumdalclitch, from whom one single hour had so far divided me! And I may say with truth that in the midst of my own misfortune, I could not forbear lamenting my poor nurse, the grief she would suffer for my loss, the displeasure of the Queen, and the ruin of her fortune. Perhaps many travelers have not been under greater difficulties and distress than I was at this juncture, expecting every moment to see my box dashed in pieces, or at least overset by the first violent blast or a rising wave. A breach in one single pane of glass would have been imme-diate death, nor could anything have preserved the windows but the strong lattice wires placed on the outside against accidents in traveling. I saw the water ooze in at several crannies, although the leaks were not considerable, and I endeavored to stop them as well as I could. I was not able to lift up the roof of my closet, which otherwise I certainly should have done, and sat on the top of it, where I might at least preserve myself from being shut up, as I may call it, in the hold. Or, if I escaped these dangers for a day or two, what could I expect but a miserable death of cold and hunger! I was four hours under these circumstances, expecting and indeed wishing every moment to be my last.

I have already told the reader that there were two strong staples fixed upon that side of my box which had no window and into which the servant, who used to carry me on horseback, would put a leathern belt, and buckle it about his waist. Being in this disconsolate state, I heard, or at least thought I heard, some kind of grating noise on that side of my box where the staples were fixed; and soon after I began to fancy that the box was pulled or towed along in the sea; for I now and then felt a sort of tugging, which made the waves rise near the tops of my windows, leaving me almost in the dark. This gave me some faint hopes of relief, although I was not able to imagine how it could be brought about. I ventured to unscrew one of my chairs, which were always fastened to the floor; and having made a hard shift to screw it down again directly under the slipping-board that I had lately opened, I mounted on the chair, and putting my mouth as near as I could to the hole, I called for help in a loud voice, and in all the languages I understood. I then fastened my handkerchief to a stick I usually carried, and thrusting it up the hole, waved it several times in the air, that if any boat or ship were near, the seamen might conjecture some unhappy mortal to be shut up in the box.

I found no effect from all I could do, but plainly perceived my closet to be moved along; and in the space of an hour or better, that side of the box where the staples were, and had no window, struck against something that was hard. I apprehended it to be a rock, and found myself tossed more than ever. I plainly heard a noise upon the cover of my closet, like that of a cable, and the grating of it as it passed through the ring. I then found myself hoisted up by degrees at least three foot higher than I was before. Whereupon I again thrust up my stick and handkerchief, calling for help till I was almost hoarse. In return to which, I heard a great shout repeated three times, giving me such transports of joy as are not to be conceived but by those who feel them. I now heard a trampling over my head, and somebody calling through the hole with a loud voice in the English tongue: "If there be anybody below, let them speak." I answered, I was an Englishman, drawn by ill fortune into the greatest calamity that ever any creature underwent, and begged, by all that was moving, to be delivered out of the dungeon I was in. The voice replied, I was safe, for my box was fastened to their ship; and the carpenter should immediately come and saw an hole in the cover, large enough to pull me out. I answered, that was needless and would take up too much time, for there was no more to be done but let one of the crew put his finger into the ring, and take the box out of the sea into the ship, and so into the captain's cabin. Some of them, upon hearing me talk so wildly, thought I was mad; others laughed; for indeed it never came into my head that I was now got among people of my own stature and strength. The carpenter came, and in a few minutes sawed a passage about four foot square; then let down a small ladder, upon which I mounted, and from thence was taken into the ship in a very weak condition.

The sailors were all in amazement, and asked me a thousand questions, which I had no inclination to answer. I was equally confounded at the sight of so many pygmies, for such I took them to be, after having so long accustomed my eyes to the monstrous objects I had left. But the Captain, Mr. Thomas Wilcocks, an honest, worthy Shropshire man, observing I was ready to faint, took me into his cabin, gave me a cordial to comfort me, and made me turn in upon his own bed, advising me to take a little rest, of which I had great need. Before I went to sleep I gave him to understand that I had some valuable furniture in my box, too good to be lost, a fine hammock, an handsome field bed, two chairs, a table, and a cabinet; that my closet was hung on all sides, or rather quilted with silk and cotton; that if he would let one of the crew bring my closet into his cabin, I would open it before him and show him my goods. The Captain, hearing me utter these absurdities, concluded I was raving; however (I suppose to pacify me), he promised to give order as I desired, and going upon deck, sent some of his men down into my closet, from whence (as I afterwards found) they drew up all my goods and stripped off the quilting; but the chairs, cabinet, and bedstead, being screwed to the floor, were much damaged by the ignorance of the seamen, who tore them up by force. Then they knocked off some of the boards for the use of the ship; and when they had got all they had a mind for, let the hulk drop into the sea, which, by reason of many breaches made in the bottom and sides, sunk to rights.[3] And indeed I was glad not to have been a spectator of the havoc they made, because I am confident it would have sensibly touched me, by bringing former passages into my mind, which I had rather forget.

I slept some hours, but perpetually disturbed with dreams of the place I had left, and the dangers I had escaped. However, upon waking, I found myself much recovered. It was now about eight o'clock at night, and the Captain ordered supper immediately, thinking I had already fasted too long.

3. At once; altogether.

He entertained me with great kindness, observing me not to look wildly, or talk inconsistently; and when we were left alone, desired I would give him a relation of my travels, and by what accident I came to be set adrift in that monstrous wooden chest. He said that about twelve o'clock at noon, as he was looking through his glass, he spied it at a distance, and thought it was a sail, which he had a mind to make,[4] being not much out of his course, in hopes of buying some biscuit, his own beginning to fall short. That, upon coming nearer, and finding his error, he sent out his longboat to discover what I was; that his men came back in a fright, swearing they had seen a swimming house. That he laughed at their folly, and went himself in the boat, ordering his men to take a strong cable along with them. That the weather being calm, he rowed round me several times, observed my windows, and the wire lattices that defended them. That he discovered two staples upon one side, which was all of boards, without any passage for light. He then commanded his men to row up to that side, and fastening a cable to one of the staples, ordered his men to tow my chest (as he called it) towards the ship. When it was there, he gave directions to fasten another cable to the ring fixed in the cover, and to raise up my chest with pulleys, which all the sailors were not able to do above two or three foot. He said they saw my stick and handkerchief thrust out of the hole, and concluded that some unhappy man must be shut up in the cavity. I asked whether he or the crew had seen any prodigious birds in the air about the time he first discovered me. To which he answered that, discoursing this matter with the sailors while I was asleep, one of them said he had observed three eagles flying towards the north, but remarked nothing of their being larger than the usual size (which I suppose must be imputed to the great height they were at), and he could not guess the reason of my question. I then asked the Captain how far he reckoned we might be from land; he said, by the best computation he could make, we were at least an hundred leagues. I assured him that he must be mistaken by almost half; for I had not left the country from whence I came above two hours before I dropped into the sea. Whereupon he began again to think that my brain was disturbed, of which he gave me a hint, and advised me to go to bed in a cabin he had provided. I assured him I was well refreshed with his good entertainment and company, and as much in my senses as ever I was in my life. He then grew serious and desired to ask me freely whether I were not troubled in mind by the consciousness of some enormous crime, for which I was punished at the command of some prince, by exposing me in that chest, as great criminals in other countries have been forced to sea in a leaky vessel without provisions; for although he should be sorry to have taken so ill[5] a man into his ship, yet he would engage his word to set me safe on shore in the first port where we arrived. He added that his suspicions were much increased by some very absurd speeches I had delivered at first to the sailors, and afterwards to himself, in relation to my closet or chest, as well as by my odd looks and behavior while I was at supper.

I begged his patience to hear me tell my story, which I faithfully did from the last time I left England to the moment he first discovered me. And as truth always forceth its way into rational minds, so this honest, worthy gentleman, who had some tincture of learning, and very good sense, was imme-

4. Overtake.   5. Evil.

diately convinced of my candor and veracity. But further to confirm all I had said, I entreated him to give order that my cabinet should be brought, of which I kept the key in my pocket (for he had already informed me how the seamen disposed of my closet). I opened it in his presence and showed him the small collection of rarities I made in the country from whence I had been so strangely delivered. There was the comb I had contrived out of the stumps of the King's beard, and another of the same materials, but fixed into a paring of her Majesty's thumbnail, which served for the back. There was a collection of needles and pins from a foot to half a yard long; four wasp-stings, like joiners' tacks; some combings of the Queen's hair; a gold ring which one day she made me a present of in a most obliging manner, taking it from her little finger, and throwing it over my head like a collar. I desired the Captain would please to accept this ring in return for his civilities, which he absolutely refused. I showed him a corn that I had cut off with my own hand from a Maid of Honor's toe; it was about the bigness of a Kentish pippin, and grown so hard that, when I returned to England, I got it hollowed into a cup and set in silver. Lastly, I desired him to see the breeches I had then on, which were made of a mouse's skin.

I could force nothing on him but a footman's tooth, which I observed him to examine with great curiosity, and found he had a fancy for it. He received it with abundance of thanks, more than such a trifle could deserve. It was drawn by an unskillful surgeon in a mistake from one of Glumdalclitch's men, who was afflicted with the toothache; but it was as sound as any in his head. I got it cleaned, and put it into my cabinet. It was about a foot long, and four inches in diameter.

The Captain was very well satisfied with this plain relation I had given him, and said he hoped when we returned to England I would oblige the world by putting it in paper and making it public. My answer was that I thought we were already overstocked with books of travels; that nothing could now pass which was not extraordinary; wherein I doubted some authors less consulted truth than their own vanity or interest, or the diversion of ignorant readers. That my story could contain little besides common events, without those ornamental descriptions of strange plants, trees, birds, and other animals, or the barbarous customs and idolatry of savage people, with which most writers abound. However, I thanked him for his good opinion, and promised to take the matter into my thoughts.

He said he wondered at one thing very much, which was to hear me speak so loud, asking me whether the King or Queen of that country were thick of hearing. I told him it was what I had been used to for above two years past, and that I admired[6] as much at the voices of him and his men, who seemed to me only to whisper, and yet I could hear them well enough. But, when I spoke in that country, it was like a man talking in the street to another looking out from the top of a steeple, unless when I was placed on a table, or held in any person's hand. I told him I had likewise observed another thing: that when I first got into the ship, and the sailors stood all about me, I thought they were the most little contemptible creatures I had ever beheld. For indeed while I was in that prince's country, I could never endure to look in a glass after my eyes had been accustomed to such prodigious objects, because the comparison gave me so despicable a conceit[7] of myself. The

6. Wondered.　　　　　　　　　　7. Notion.

Captain said that while we were at supper he observed me to look at everything with a sort of wonder, and that I often seemed hardly able to contain my laughter; which he knew not well how to take, but imputed it to some disorder in my brain. I answered, it was very true; and I wondered how I could forbear, when I saw his dishes of the size of a silver threepence, a leg of pork hardly a mouthful, a cup not so big as a nutshell; and so I went on, describing the rest of his household stuff and provisions after the same manner. For, although the Queen had ordered a little equipage of all things necessary for me while I was in her service, yet my ideas were wholly taken up with what I saw on every side of me, and I winked at my own littleness, as people do at their own faults. The Captain understood my raillery very well, and merrily replied with the old English proverb, that he doubted[8] my eyes were bigger than my belly, for he did not observe my stomach so good, although I had fasted all day; and continuing in his mirth, protested he would have gladly given an hundred pounds to have seen my closet in the eagle's bill, and afterwards in its fall from so great an height into the sea; which would certainly have been a most astonishing object, worthy to have the description of it transmitted to future ages: and the comparison of Phaeton[9] was so obvious, that he could not forbear applying it, although I did not much admire the conceit.

The Captain having been at Tonquin,[1] was in his return to England driven northeastward to the latitude of 44 degrees, and of longitude 143. But meeting a trade wind two days after I came on board him, we sailed southward a long time, and coasting New Holland[2] kept our course west-southwest, and then south-southwest till we doubled the Cape of Good Hope. Our voyage was very prosperous, but I shall not trouble the reader with a journal of it. The Captain called in at one or two ports, and sent in his longboat for provisions and fresh water; but I never went out of the ship till we came into the Downs, which was on the third day of June, 1706, about nine months after my escape. I offered to leave my goods in security for payment of my freight; but the Captain protested he would not receive one farthing. We took kind leave of each other, and I made him promise he would come to see me at my house in Redriff. I hired a horse and guide for five shillings, which I borrowed of the Captain.

As I was on the road, observing the littleness of the houses, the trees, the cattle, and the people, I began to think myself in Lilliput. I was afraid of trampling on every traveler I met, and often called aloud to have them stand out of the way, so that I had like to have gotten one or two broken heads for my impertinence.

When I came to my own house, for which I was forced to inquire, one of the servants opening the door, I bent down to go in (like a goose under a gate) for fear of striking my head. My wife ran out to embrace me, but I stooped lower than her knees, thinking she could otherwise never be able to reach my mouth. My daughter kneeled to ask my blessing, but I could not see her till she arose, having been so long used to stand with my head and eyes erect to above sixty foot; and then I went to take her up with one hand by the waist. I looked down upon the servants and one or two friends who

---

8. Feared.
9. Son of Helios, the sun god, whose unsuccessful attempt to drive his father's chariot led to his death, when he lost control and was hurled by Zeus

from the sky, falling into the river Eridanus, where he drowned.
1. Tonkin, now in Vietnam.
2. Australia.

were in the house, as if they had been pygmies and I a giant. I told my wife she had been too thrifty; for I found she had starved herself and her daughter to nothing. In short, I behaved myself so unaccountably that they were all of the Captain's opinion when he first saw me, and concluded I had lost my wits. This I mention as an instance of the great power of habit and prejudice.

In a little time I and my family and friends came to a right understanding; but my wife protested I should never go to sea any more, although my evil destiny so ordered that she had not power to hinder me; as the reader may know hereafter. In the meantime I here conclude the second part of my unfortunate voyages.

From Part 3. A Voyage to Laputa, Balnibarbi, Glubbdubdrib, Luggnagg, and Japan

* * *

[THE FLYING ISLAND OF LAPUTA][3]

CHAPTER 2. *The humors and dispositions of the Laputans described. An account of their learning. Of the King and his court. The author's reception there. The inhabitants subject to fears and disquietudes. An account of the women.*

At my alighting I was surrounded by a crowd of people, but those who stood nearest seemed to be of better quality. They beheld me with all the marks and circumstances of wonder; neither indeed was I much in their debt, having never till then seen a race of mortals so singular in their shapes, habits, and countenances. Their heads were all reclined to the right, or the left; one of their eyes turned inward, and the other directly up to the zenith. Their outward garments were adorned with the figures of suns, moons, and stars, interwoven with those of fiddles, flutes, harps, trumpets, guitars, harpsichords, and many more instruments of music, unknown to us in Europe.[4] I observed here and there many in the habits of servants, with a blown bladder fastened like a flail to the end of a short stick, which they carried in their hands. In each bladder was a small quantity of dried pease or little pebbles (as I was afterwards informed). With these bladders they now and then flapped the mouths and ears of those who stood near them, of which practice I could not then conceive the meaning. It seems, the minds of these people are so taken up with intense speculations, that they neither can speak, or attend to the discourses of others, without being roused by some external taction[5] upon the organs of speech and hearing; for which reason those persons who are able to afford it always keep a flapper (the original is *climenole*) in their family, as one of their domestics; nor ever walk abroad or make visits without him. And the business of this officer is, when two or more persons are in company, gently to strike with his bladder the mouth of him who is to speak, and the right ear of him or them to whom the speaker

---

3. In the first chapter of part 3 Gulliver starts on his third voyage, but is captured by pirates and set adrift. Just as he is about to despair, a vast flying island appears in the sky, and the inhabitants draw him up with pulleys.

4. The Laputans represent contemporary specu-

lation, deplored by Swift, about abstract theories of science, mathematics, and music. Both the Royal Society and Sir Isaac Newton took an interest in the mathematical basis of music.

5. Touch.

addresseth himself. This flapper is likewise employed diligently to attend his master in his walks, and upon occasion to give him a soft flap on his eyes, because he is always so wrapped up in cogitation, that he is in manifest danger of falling down every precipice, and bouncing his head against every post; and in the streets, of jostling others, or being jostled himself into the kennel.[6]

It was necessary to give the reader this information, without which he would be at the same loss with me, to understand the proceedings of these people, as they conducted me up the stairs to the top of the island, and from thence to the royal palace. While we were ascending, they forgot several times what they were about, and left me to myself, till their memories were again roused by their flappers; for they appeared altogether unmoved by the sight of my foreign habit and countenance, and by the shouts of the vulgar, whose thoughts and minds were more disengaged.

At last we entered the palace, and proceeded into the chamber of presence; where I saw the King seated on his throne, attended on each side by persons of prime quality. Before the throne was a large table filled with globes and spheres, and mathematical instruments of all kinds. His Majesty took not the least notice of us, although our entrance was not without sufficient noise, by the concourse of all persons belonging to the court. But he was then deep in a problem, and we attended at least an hour before he could solve it. There stood by him on each side a young page, with flaps in their hands, and when they saw he was at leisure, one of them gently struck his mouth, and the other his right ear; at which he started like one awaked on the sudden, and looking towards me, and the company I was in, recollected the occasion of our coming, whereof he had been informed before. He spoke some words, whereupon immediately a young man with a flap came up to my side, and flapped me gently on the right ear; but I made signs as well as I could, that I had no occasion for such an instrument; which as I afterwards found gave his Majesty and the whole court a very mean opinion of my understanding. The King, as far as I could conjecture, asked me several questions, and I addressed myself to him in all the languages I had. When it was found that I could neither understand nor be understood, I was conducted by his order to an apartment in his palace (this prince being distinguished above all his predecessors for his hospitality to strangers),[7] where two servants were appointed to attend me. My dinner was brought, and four persons of quality, whom I remembered to have seen very near the King's person, did me the honor to dine with me. We had two courses, of three dishes each. In the first course there was a shoulder of mutton, cut into an equilateral triangle; a piece of beef into a rhomboid; and a pudding into a cycloid. The second course was two ducks, trussed up into the form of fiddles; sausages and pudding resembling flutes and hautboys,[8] and a breast of veal in the shape of a harp. The servants cut our bread into cones, cylinders, parallelograms, and several other mathematical figures.

While we were at dinner, I made bold to ask the names of several things in their language, and those noble persons, by the assistance of their flappers, delighted to give me answers, hoping to raise my admiration of their great

6. Gutter.
7. George I, a patron of music and science, had filled his court with Hanoverians when he came to England in 1714.
8. Oboes.

abilities, if I could be brought to converse with them. I was soon able to call for bread and drink, or whatever else I wanted.

After dinner my company withdrew, and a person was sent to me by the King's order, attended by a flapper. He brought with him pen, ink, and paper, and three or four books; giving me to understand by signs, that he was sent to teach me the language. We sat together four hours, in which time I wrote down a great number of words in columns, with the translations over against them. I likewise made a shift to learn several short sentences. For my tutor would order one of my servants to fetch something, to turn about, to make a bow, to sit, or stand, or walk, and the like. Then I took down the sentence in writing. He showed me also in one of his books the figures of the sun, moon, and stars, the zodiac, the tropics and polar circles, together with the denominations of many figures of planes and solids. He gave me the names and descriptions of all the musical instruments, and the general terms of art in playing on each of them. After he had left me, I placed all my words with their interpretations in alphabetical order. And thus in a few days, by the help of a very faithful memory, I got some insight into their language.

The word, which I interpret the *Flying* or *Floating Island,* is in the original *Laputa;* whereof I could never learn the true etymology. *Lap* in the old obsolete language signifieth *high,* and *untuh* a *governor;* from which they say by corruption was derived *Laputa,* from *Lapuntuh.* But I do not approve of this derivation, which seems to be a little strained. I ventured to offer to the learned among them a conjecture of my own, that *Laputa* was *quasi Lap outed; Lap* signifying properly the dancing of the sunbeams in the sea, and *outed* a wing, which however I shall not obtrude, but submit to the judicious reader.[9]

Those to whom the King had entrusted me, observing how ill I was clad, ordered a tailor to come next morning, and take my measure for a suit of clothes. This operator did his office after a different manner from those of his trade in Europe. He first took my altitude by a quadrant, and then, with rule and compasses, described the dimensions and outlines of my whole body; all which he entered upon paper, and in six days brought my clothes very ill made, and quite out of shape, by happening to mistake a figure in the calculation. But my comfort was, that I observed such accidents very frequent, and little regarded.

During my confinement for want of clothes, and by an indisposition that held me some days longer, I much enlarged my dictionary; and when I went next to court, was able to understand many things the King spoke, and to return him some kind of answers. His Majesty had given orders that the island should move northeast and by east, to the vertical point over Lagado, the metropolis of the whole kingdom, below upon the firm earth. It was about ninety leagues distant, and our voyage lasted four days and a half. I was not in the least sensible of the progressive motion made in the air by the island. On the second morning, about eleven o'clock, the King himself in person, attended by his nobility, courtiers, and officers, having prepared all their musical instruments, played on them for three hours without intermission, so that I was quite stunned with the noise; neither could I possibly guess the meaning, till my tutor informed me. He said, that the people of their island

9. Gulliver overlooks a likelier etymology: Spanish *la puta,* "the whore."

had their ears adapted to hear the music of the spheres, which always played at certain periods; and the court was now prepared to bear their part in whatever instrument they most excelled.

In our journey towards Lagado, the capital city, his Majesty ordered that the island should stop over certain towns and villages, from whence he might receive the petitions of his subjects. And to this purpose, several packthreads were let down with small weights at the bottom. On these packthreads the people strung their petitions, which mounted up directly like the scraps of paper fastened by schoolboys at the end of the string that holds their kite.[1] Sometimes we received wine and victuals from below, which were drawn up by pulleys.

The knowledge I had in mathematics gave me great assistance in acquiring their phraseology, which depended much upon that science and music; and in the latter I was not unskilled. Their ideas are perpetually conversant in lines and figures. If they would, for example, praise the beauty of a woman, or any other animal, they describe it by rhombs, circles, parallelograms, ellipses, and other geometrical terms; or else by words of art drawn from music, needless here to repeat. I observed in the King's kitchen all sorts of mathematical and musical instruments, after the figures of which they cut up the joints that were served to his Majesty's table.

Their houses are very ill built, the walls bevil, without one right angle in any apartment; and this defect ariseth from the contempt they bear for practical geometry; which they despise as vulgar and mechanic, those instructions they give being too refined for the intellectuals of their workmen; which occasions perpetual mistakes. And although they are dextrous enough upon a piece of paper, in the management of the rule, the pencil, and the divider, yet in the common actions and behavior of life I have not seen a more clumsy, awkward, and unhandy people, nor so slow and perplexed in their conceptions upon all other subjects, except those of mathematics and music. They are very bad reasoners, and vehemently given to opposition, unless when they happen to be of the right opinion, which is seldom their case. Imagination, fancy, and invention, they are wholly strangers to, nor have any words in their language by which those ideas can be expressed; the whole compass of their thoughts and mind being shut up within the two forementioned sciences.

Most of them, and especially those who deal in the astronomical part, have great faith in judicial astrology, although they are ashamed to own it publicly. But what I chiefly admired,[2] and thought altogether unaccountable, was the strong disposition I observed in them towards news and politics; perpetually enquiring into public affairs, giving their judgments in matters of state; and passionately disputing every inch of a party opinion. I have indeed observed the same disposition among most of the mathematicians I have known in Europe; although I could never discover the least analogy between the two sciences; unless those people suppose, that because the smallest circle hath as many degrees as the largest, therefore the regulation and management of the world require no more abilities than the handling and turning of a globe. But I rather take this quality to spring from a very

1. Petitioners, that is, might as well go fly a kite. Throughout this section Swift satirizes the "distance" of George I (who spent much of his time in Hanover) from his British subjects.
2. Wondered at.

common infirmity of human nature, inclining us to be more curious and conceited in matters where we have least concern, and for which we are least adapted either by study or nature.

These people are under continual disquietudes, never enjoying a minute's peace of mind; and their disturbances proceed from causes which very little affect the rest of mortals. Their apprehensions arise from several changes they dread in the celestial bodies. For instance; that the earth, by the continual approaches of the sun towards it, must in course of time be absorbed or swallowed up. That the face of the sun will by degrees be encrusted with its own effluvia,[3] and give no more light to the world. That the earth very narrowly escaped a brush from the tail of the last comet, which would have infallibly reduced it to ashes; and that the next, which they have calculated for one and thirty years hence, will probably destroy us.[4] For, if in its perihelion it should approach within a certain degree of the sun (as by their calculations they have reason to dread), it will conceive a degree of heat ten thousand times more intense than that of red-hot glowing iron; and in its absence from the sun, carry a blazing tail ten hundred thousand and fourteen miles long; through which if the earth should pass at the distance of one hundred thousand miles from the nucleus, or main body of the comet, it must in its passage be set on fire, and reduced to ashes. That the sun daily spending its rays without any nutriment to supply them, will at last be wholly consumed and annihilated; which must be attended with the destruction of this earth, and of all the planets that receive their light from it.

They are so perpetually alarmed with the apprehensions of these and the like impending dangers, that they can neither sleep quietly in their beds, nor have any relish for the common pleasures or amusements of life. When they meet an acquaintance in the morning, the first question is about the sun's health, how he looked at his setting and rising, and what hopes they have to avoid the stroke of the approaching comet. This conversation they are apt to run into with the same temper that boys discover in delighting to hear terrible stories of sprites and hobgoblins, which they greedily listen to, and dare not go to bed for fear.

The women of the island have abundance of vivacity; they contemn their husbands, and are exceedingly fond of strangers, whereof there is always a considerable number from the continent below, attending at court, either upon affairs of the several towns and corporations, or their own particular occasions; but are much despised, because they want the same endowments. Among these the ladies choose their gallants: but the vexation is, that they act with too much ease and security; for the husband is always so rapt in speculation, that the mistress and lover may proceed to the greatest familiarities before his face, if he be but provided with paper and implements, and without his flapper at his side.

The wives and daughters lament their confinement to the island, although I think it the most delicious spot of ground in the world; and although they live here in the greatest plenty and magnificence, and are allowed to do whatever they please, they long to see the world, and take the diversions of the metropolis, which they are not allowed to do without a particular license from the King; and this is not easy to be obtained, because the people of

---

3. Sunspots.
4. Halley's comet, some astronomers had feared, might strike the earth on its next appearance

(1758). All the disasters that disquiet the Laputans had occurred to English scientists as possible implications of Newtonian theory.

quality have found by frequent experience, how hard it is to persuade their women to return from below. I was told that a great court lady, who had several children, is married to the prime minister, the richest subject in the kingdom, a very graceful person, extremely fond of her, and lives in the finest palace of the island, went down to Lagado, on the pretense of health, there hid herself for several months, till the King sent a warrant to search for her, and she was found in an obscure eating-house all in rags, having pawned her clothes to maintain an old deformed footman, who beat her every day, and in whose company she was taken much against her will. And although her husband received her with all possible kindness, and without the least reproach, she soon after contrived to steal down again with all her jewels, to the same gallant, and hath not been heard of since.

This may perhaps pass with the reader rather for an European or English story, than for one of a country so remote. But he may please to consider, that the caprices of womankind are not limited by any climate or nation; and that they are much more uniform than can be easily imagined.

In about a month's time I had made a tolerable proficiency in their language, and was able to answer most of the King's questions, when I had the honor to attend him. His Majesty discovered not the least curiosity to enquire into the laws, government, history, religion, or manners of the countries where I had been; but confined his questions to the state of mathematics, and received the account I gave him with great contempt and indifference, though often roused by his flapper on each side.[5]

*   *   *

[THE ACADEMY OF LAGADO][6]
FROM CHAPTER 5.

The first professor I saw was in a very large room, with forty pupils about him. After salutation, observing me to look earnestly upon a frame, which took up the greatest part of both the length and breadth of the room, he said, perhaps I might wonder to see him employed in a project for improving speculative knowledge by practical and mechanical operations. But the world would soon be sensible[7] of its usefulness, and he flattered himself that a more noble, exalted thought never sprang in any other man's head. Everyone knew how laborious the usual method is of attaining to arts and sciences; whereas by his contrivance the most ignorant person at a reasonable charge, and with a little bodily labor, may write books in philosophy, poetry, politics, law, mathematics, and theology, without the least assistance from genius or study. He then led me to the frame, about the sides whereof all his pupils stood in ranks. It was twenty foot square, placed in the middle of the room. The superficies[8] was composed of several bits of wood, about the bigness of a die, but some larger than others. They were all linked together by slender wires. These bits of wood were covered on every square with papers pasted

5. In the omitted chapters, Gulliver visits countries that show the consequences of modern learning. After an account of the Flying Island, whose power of motion (derived from a giant magnet or lodestone) allows it to dominate the regions below, he descends to Balnibarbi, a once fertile land now ruined by the fanciful projects of impractical scientists. In the Grand Academy of Lagado he meets many professors who are contriving such perverse "improvements" as making clothes from cobwebs or breeding naked sheep. Then he visits the part of the academy devoted to speculative learning.

6. The Grand Academy of Lagado satirizes the Royal Society of London, an organization founded in 1662 to encourage the pursuit of scientific knowledge. Some of the projects described by Swift resemble the experiments or speculations of British scientists at the time.

7. Aware.

8. Surface.

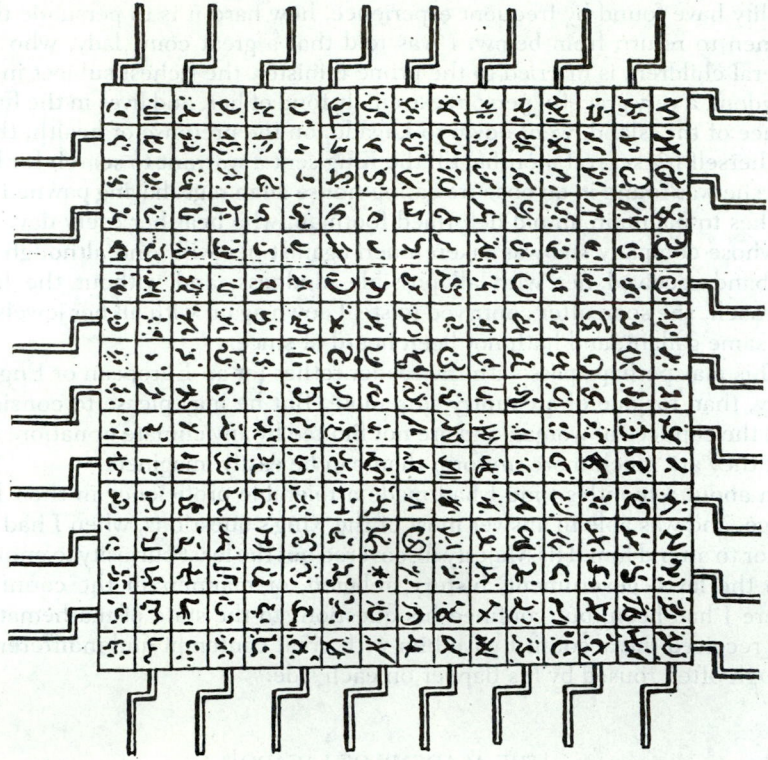

on them; and on these papers were written all the words of their language in their several moods, tenses, and declensions, but without any order. The professor then desired me to observe, for he was going to set his engine at work. The pupils at his command took each of them hold of an iron handle, whereof there were forty fixed round the edges of the frame; and giving them a sudden turn, the whole disposition[9] of the words was entirely changed. He then commanded six and thirty of the lads to read the several lines softly as they appeared upon the frame; and where they found three or four words together that might make part of a sentence, they dictated to the four remaining boys who were scribes. This work was repeated three or four times, and at every turn the engine was so contrived that the words shifted into new places, as the square bits of wood moved upside down.

Six hours a day the young students were employed in this labor; and the professor showed me several volumes in large folio already collected, of broken sentences, which he intended to piece together, and out of those rich materials to give the world a complete body of all arts and sciences; which however might be still improved, and much expedited, if the public would raise a fund for making and employing five hundred such frames in Lagado, and oblige the managers to contribute in common their several[1] collections.

9. Arrangement.   1. Separate.

He assured me, that this invention had employed all his thoughts from his youth, that he had emptied the whole vocabulary into his frame, and made the strictest computation of the general proportion there is in books between the numbers of particles, nouns, and verbs, and other parts of speech.

I made my humblest acknowledgments to this illustrious person for his great communicativeness, and promised if ever I had the good fortune to return to my native country, that I would do him justice, as the sole inventor of this wonderful machine; the form and contrivance of which I desired leave to delineate upon paper as in the figure here annexed. I told him, although it were the custom of our learned in Europe to steal inventions from each other, who had thereby at least this advantage, that it became a controversy which was the right owner, yet I would take such caution, that he should have the honor entire without a rival.

We next went to the school of languages, where three professors sat in consultation upon improving that of their own country.[2]

The first project was to shorten discourse by cutting polysyllables into one, and leaving out verbs and participles, because in reality all things imaginable are but nouns.

The other was a scheme for entirely abolishing all words whatsoever; and this was urged as a great advantage in point of health as well as brevity. For it is plain, that every word we speak is in some degree a diminution of our lungs by corrosion, and consequently contributes to the shortening of our lives. An expedient was therefore offered, that since words are only names for *things*, it would be more convenient for all men to carry about them such *things* as were necessary to express the particular business they are to discourse on. And this invention would certainly have taken place, to the great ease as well as health of the subject, if the women in conjunction with the vulgar and illiterate had not threatened to raise a rebellion, unless they might be allowed the liberty to speak with their tongues, after the manner of their forefathers. Such constant irreconcilable enemies to science[3] are the common people. However, many of the most learned and wise adhere to the new scheme of expressing themselves by *things,* which hath only this inconvenience attending it, that if a man's business be very great, and of various kinds, he must be obliged in proportion to carry a greater bundle of *things* upon his back, unless he can afford one or two strong servants to attend him. I have often beheld two of those sages almost sinking under the weight of their packs, like pedlars among us, who when they met in the streets would lay down their loads, open their sacks, and hold conversation for an hour together, then put up their implements, help each other to resume their burdens, and take their leave.

But for short conversations a man may carry implements in his pockets and under his arms, enough to supply him, and in his house he cannot be at a loss; therefore the room where company meet who practice this art is full of all *things* ready at hand, requisite to furnish matter for this kind of artificial converse.[4]

Another great advantage proposed by this invention was that it would serve

2. Many contemporary scientists had proposed a philosophical language that would eliminate the treacherous disparity between words and things and thus allow accurate scientific discourse.

3. Knowledge.

4. The Royal Society had sponsored a collection intended to contain one specimen of every thing in the world.

as an universal language to be understood in all civilized nations, whose goods and utensils are generally of the same kind, or nearly resembling, so that their uses might easily be comprehended. And thus, ambassadors would be qualified to treat with foreign princes or ministers of state to whose tongues they were utter strangers.

I was at the mathematical school, where the master taught his pupils after a method scarce imaginable to us in Europe. The proposition and demonstration were fairly written on a thin wafer, with ink composed of a cephalic tincture.[5] This the student was to swallow upon a fasting stomach, and for three days following eat nothing but bread and water. As the wafer digested, the tincture mounted to his brain, bearing the proposition along with it. But the success hath not hitherto been answerable, partly by some error in the *quantum* or composition, and partly by the perverseness of lads, to whom this bolus[6] is so nauseous that they generally steal aside, and discharge it upwards before it can operate; neither have they been yet persuaded to use so long an abstinence as the prescription requires.[7]

* * *

[THE STRULDBRUGGS]

CHAPTER 10. *The Luggnaggians commended. A particular description of the struldbruggs, with many conversations between the author and some eminent persons upon that subject.*

The Luggnaggians are a polite[8] and generous people, and although they are not without some share of that pride which is peculiar to all eastern countries, yet they show themselves courteous to strangers, especially such who are countenanced by the court. I had many acquaintance among persons of the best fashion, and being always attended by my interpreter, the conversation we had was not disagreeable.

One day in much good company, I was asked by a person of quality, whether I had seen any of their *struldbruggs* or *immortals*. I said I had not; and desired he would explain to me what he meant by such an appellation, applied to a mortal creature. He told me, that sometimes, although very rarely, a child happened to be born in a family with a red circular spot in the forehead, directly over the left eyebrow, which was an infallible mark that it should never die. The spot, as he described it, was about the compass of a silver threepence, but in the course of time grew larger, and changed its color; for at twelve years old it became green, so continued till five and twenty, then turned to a deep blue; at five and forty it grew coal black, and as large as an English shilling; but never admitted any farther alteration. He said these births were so rare, that he did not believe there could be above eleven hundred *struldbruggs* of both sexes in the whole kingdom, of which he computed about fifty in the metropolis, and among the rest a young girl born about three years ago. That these productions were not peculiar to any family, but a mere effect of chance; and the children of the *struldbruggs* themselves were equally mortal with the rest of the people.

---

5. A solution or dye directed toward the head.
6. A large pill. "*Quantum*": amount.
7. In the omitted chapters Gulliver hears projects for improving politics and offers some of his own. He sails to Glubbdubdrib, the Island of Sorcerers,

where he talks with the spirits of the dead; he learns that history is a pack of lies and that humanity has degenerated since ancient times. He is then received by the king of Luggnagg.
8. Refined, cultivated.

I freely own myself to have been struck with inexpressible delight upon hearing this account: and the person who gave it me happening to understand the Balnibarbian language, which I spoke very well, I could not forbear breaking out into expressions perhaps a little too extravagant. I cried out as in a rapture: Happy nation, where every child hath at least a chance for being immortal! Happy people who enjoy so many living examples of ancient virtue, and have masters ready to instruct them in the wisdom of all former ages! But happiest beyond all comparison are those excellent *struldbruggs*, who being born exempt from that universal calamity of human nature, have their minds free and disengaged, without the weight and depression of spirits caused by the continual apprehension of death. I discovered my admiration that I had not observed any of these illustrious persons at court; the black spot on the forehead being so remarkable a distinction, that I could not have easily overlooked it; and it was impossible that his Majesty, a most judicious prince, should not provide himself with a good number of such wise and able counselors. Yet perhaps the virtue of those reverend sages was too strict for the corrupt and libertine manners of a court. And we often find by experience that young men are too opinionative[9] and volatile to be guided by the sober dictates of their seniors. However, since the King was pleased to allow me access to his royal person, I was resolved upon the very first occasion to deliver my opinion to him on this matter freely, and at large by the help of my interpreter; and whether he would please to take my advice or no, yet in one thing I was determined, that his Majesty having frequently offered me an establishment in this country, I would with great thankfulness accept the favor, and pass my life here in the conversation of those superior beings the *struldbruggs*, if they would please to admit me.

The gentleman to whom I addressed my discourse, because (as I have already observed) he spoke the language of Balnibarbi, said to me with a sort of a smile, which usually ariseth from pity to the ignorant, that he was glad of any occasion to keep me among them, and desired my permission to explain to the company what I had spoke. He did so; and they talked together for some time in their own language, whereof I understood not a syllable, neither could I observe by their countenances what impression my discourse had made on them. After a short silence the same person told me, that his friends and mine (so he thought fit to express himself) were very much pleased with the judicious remarks I had made on the great happiness and advantages of immortal life; and they were desirous to know in a particular manner, what scheme of living I should have formed to myself, if it had fallen to my lot to have been born a *struldbrugg*.

I answered, it was easy to be eloquent on so copious and delightful a subject, especially to me who have been often apt to amuse myself with visions of what I should do if I were a king, a general, or a great lord; and upon this very case I had frequently run over the whole system how I should employ myself, and pass the time if I were sure to live forever.

That, if it had been my good fortune to come into the world a *struldbrugg*, as soon as I could discover my own happiness by understanding the difference between life and death, I would first resolve by all arts and methods whatsoever to procure myself riches: in the pursuit of which, by thrift and management, I might reasonably expect in about two hundred years to be

9. Speculative, impractical.

the wealthiest man in the kingdom. In the second place, I would from my earliest youth apply myself to the study of arts and sciences, by which I should arrive in time to excel all others in learning. Lastly, I would carefully record every action and event of consequence that happened in the public, impartially draw the characters of the several successions of princes, and great ministers of state; with my own observations on every point. I would exactly set down the several changes in customs, languages, fashions of dress, diet and diversions. By all which acquirements, I should be a living treasury of knowledge and wisdom, and certainly become the oracle of the nation.

I would never marry after threescore, but live in an hospitable manner, yet still on the saving side. I would entertain myself in forming and directing the minds of hopeful young men, by convincing them from my own remembrance, experience and observation, fortified by numerous examples, of the usefulness of virtue in public and private life. But my choice and constant companions should be a set of my own immortal brotherhood, among whom I would elect a dozen from the most ancient down to my own contemporaries. Where any of these wanted fortunes, I would provide them with convenient lodges round my own estate, and have some of them always at my table, only mingling a few of the most valuable among you mortals, whom length of time would harden me to lose with little or no reluctance, and treat your posterity after the same manner; just as a man diverts himself with the annual succession of pinks and tulips in his garden, without regretting the loss of those which withered the preceding year.

These *struldbruggs* and I would mutually communicate our observations and memorials[1] through the course of time; remark the several gradations by which corruption steals into the world, and oppose it in every step, by giving perpetual warning and instruction to mankind; which, added to the strong influence of our own example, would probably prevent that continual degeneracy of human nature, so justly complained of in all ages.

Add to all this, the pleasure of seeing the various revolutions of states and empires; the changes in the lower and upper world;[2] ancient cities in ruins; and obscure villages become the seats of kings. Famous rivers lessening into shallow brooks; the ocean leaving one coast dry, and overwhelming another; the discovery of many countries yet unknown. Barbarity overrunning the politest nations, and the most barbarous becoming civilized. I should then see the discovery of the longitude, the perpetual motion, the universal medicine,[3] and many other great inventions brought to the utmost perfection.

What wonderful discoveries should we make in astronomy, by outliving and confirming our own predictions, by observing the progress and returns of comets, with the changes of motion in the sun, moon and stars.

I enlarged upon many other topics, which the natural desire of endless life and sublunary happiness could easily furnish me with. When I had ended, and the sum of my discourse had been interpreted as before to the rest of the company, there was a good deal of talk among them in the language of the country, not without some laughter at my expense. At last the same gentleman who had been my interpreter said, he was desired by the rest to

---

1. Memories.
2. Earth and heaven; figuratively, common people and the ruling class. "Revolutions": cycles.
3. The *elixir vitae*, an alchemical formula to pre-

serve life forever, was considered by Swift an impossible dream, like a method for calculating longitude at sea, or a perpetual motion machine.

set me right in a few mistakes, which I had fallen into through the common imbecility[4] of human nature, and upon that allowance was less answerable for them. That this breed of *struldbruggs* was peculiar to their country, for there were no such people either in Balnibarbi or Japan, where he had the honor to be ambassador from his Majesty, and found the natives in both those kingdoms very hard to believe that the fact was possible; and it appeared from my astonishment when he first mentioned the matter to me, that I received it as a thing wholly new, and scarcely to be credited. That in the two kingdoms above mentioned, where during his residence he had conversed very much, he observed long life to be the universal desire and wish of mankind. That whoever had one foot in the grave was sure to hold back the other as strongly as he could. That the oldest had still hopes of living one day longer, and looked on death as the greatest evil, from which nature always prompted him to retreat; only in this island of Luggnagg the appetite for living was not so eager, from the continual example of the *struldbruggs* before their eyes.

That the system of living contrived by me was unreasonable and unjust, because it supposed a perpetuity of youth, health, and vigor, which no man could be so foolish to hope, however extravagant he might be in his wishes. That the question therefore was not whether a man would choose to be always in the prime of youth, attended with prosperity and health; but how he would pass a perpetual life under all the usual disadvantages which old age brings along with it. For although few men will avow their desires of being immortal upon such hard conditions, yet in the two kingdoms before mentioned of Balnibarbi and Japan, he observed that every man desired to put off death for some time longer, let it approach ever so late; and he rarely heard of any man who died willingly, except he were incited by the extremity of grief or torture. And he appealed to me whether in those countries I had traveled, as well as my own, I had not observed the same general disposition.

After this preface he gave me a particular account of the *struldbruggs* among them. He said they commonly acted like mortals, till about thirty years old, after which by degrees they grew melancholy and dejected, increasing in both till they came to fourscore. This he learned from their own confession; for otherwise there not being above two or three of that species born in an age, they were too few to form a general observation by. When they came to fourscore years, which is reckoned the extremity of living in this country, they had not only all the follies and infirmities of other old men, but many more which arose from the dreadful prospect of never dying. They were not only opinionative, peevish, covetous, morose, vain, talkative; but uncapable of friendship, and dead to all natural affection, which never descended below their grandchildren. Envy and impotent desires are their prevailing passions. But those objects against which their envy seems principally directed, are the vices of the younger sort, and the deaths of the old. By reflecting on the former, they find themselves cut off from all possibility of pleasure; and whenever they see a funeral, they lament and repine that others are gone to an harbor of rest, to which they themselves never can hope to arrive. They have no remembrance of anything but what they learned and observed in their youth and middle age, and even that is very imperfect.

4. Weakness.

And for the truth or particulars of any fact, it is safer to depend on common traditions than upon their best recollections. The least miserable among them appear to be those who turn to dotage, and entirely lose their memories; these meet with more pity and assistance, because they want[5] many bad qualities which abound in others.

If a *struldbrugg* happen to marry one of his own kind, the marriage is dissolved of course by the courtesy of the kingdom, as soon as the younger of the two comes to be fourscore. For the law thinks it a reasonable indulgence, that those who are condemned without any fault of their own to a perpetual continuance in the world, should not have their misery doubled by the load of a wife.

As soon as they have completed the term of eighty years, they are looked on as dead in law; their heirs immediately succeed to their estates, only a small pittance is reserved for their support; and the poor ones are maintained at the public charge. After that period they are held incapable of any employment of trust or profit; they cannot purchase land, or take leases, neither are they allowed to be witnesses in any cause, either civil or criminal, not even for the decision of meers[6] and bounds.

At ninety they lose their teeth and hair; they have at that age no distinction of taste, but eat and drink whatever they can get, without relish or appetite. The diseases they were subject to still continue without increasing or diminishing. In talking they forget the common appellation of things, and the names of persons, even of those who are their nearest friends and relations. For the same reason they never can amuse themselves with reading, because their memory will not serve to carry them from the beginning of a sentence to the end, and by this defect they are deprived of the only entertainment whereof they might otherwise be capable.

The language of this country being always upon the flux, the *struldbruggs* of one age do not understand those of another; neither are they able after two hundred years to hold any conversation (farther than by a few general words) with their neighbors the mortals; and thus they lie under the disadvantage of living like foreigners in their own country.

This was the account given me of the *struldbruggs*, as near as I can remember. I afterwards saw five or six of different ages, the youngest not above two hundred years old, who were brought to me at several times by some of my friends; but although they were told that I was a great traveler, and had seen all the world, they had not the least curiosity to ask me a question; only desired I would give them *slumskudask,* or a token of remembrance; which is a modest way of begging, to avoid the law that strictly forbids it, because they are provided for by the public, although indeed with a very scanty allowance.

They are despised and hated by all sorts of people; when one of them is born, it is reckoned ominous, and their birth is recorded very particularly; so that you may know their age by consulting the registry, which however hath not been kept above a thousand years past, or at least hath been destroyed by time or public disturbances. But the usual way of computing how old they are, is by asking them what kings or great persons they can remember, and then consulting history; for infallibly the last prince in their mind did not begin his reign after they were fourscore years old.

---

5. Lack.   6. Boundaries.

They were the most mortifying sight I ever beheld; and the women more horrible than the men. Besides the usual deformities in extreme old age, they acquired an additional ghastliness in proportion to their number of years, which is not to be described; and among half a dozen I soon distinguished which was the oldest, although there were not above a century or two between them.

The reader will easily believe, that from what I had heard and seen, my keen appetite for perpetuity of life was much abated. I grew heartily ashamed of the pleasing visions I had formed; and thought no tyrant could invent a death into which I would not run with pleasure from such a life. The King heard of all that had passed between me and my friends upon this occasion, and rallied[7] me very pleasantly; wishing I would send a couple of *struldbruggs* to my own country, to arm our people against the fear of death; but this it seems is forbidden by the fundamental laws of the kingdom; or else I should have been well content with the trouble and expense of transporting them.

I could not but agree, that the laws of this kingdom relating to the *struldbruggs,* were founded upon the strongest reasons, and such as any other country would be under the necessity of enacting in the like circumstances. Otherwise, as avarice is the necessary consequent of old age, those immortals would in time become proprietors of the whole nation, and engross[8] the civil power; which, for want of abilities to manage, must end in the ruin of the public.[9]

* * *

Part 4. A Voyage to the Country of the Houyhnhnms[1]

CHAPTER 1. *The Author sets out as Captain of a ship. His men conspire against him, confine him a long time to his cabin, set him on shore in an unknown land. He travels up into the country. The Yahoos, a strange sort of animal, described. The Author meets two Houyhnhnms.*

I continued at home with my wife and children about five months in a very happy condition, if I could have learned the lesson of knowing when I was well. I left my poor wife big with child, and accepted an advantageous offer made me to be Captain of the *Adventure,* a stout merchantman of 350 tons; for I understood navigation well, and being grown weary of a surgeon's employment at sea, which however I could exercise upon occasion, I took a skillful young man of that calling, one Robert Purefoy, into my ship. We set sail from Portsmouth upon the 7th day of September, 1710; on the 14th we met with Captain Pocock of Bristol, at Tenariff,[2] who was going to the Bay of Campeachy[3] to cut logwood. On the 16th he was parted from us by a storm; I heard since my return that his ship foundered and none escaped, but one cabin boy. He was an honest man and a good sailor, but a little too positive in his own opinions, which was the cause of his destruction, as it hath been of several others. For if he had followed my advice, he might at this time have been safe at home with his family as well as myself.

---

7. Ridiculed.
8. Absorb, monopolize.
9. In the omitted chapter, Gulliver sails to Japan, where a Dutch ship provides him passage back to Europe.

1. Pronounced *hwin-ims*. The word suggests the neigh characteristic of a horse.
2. Teneriffe, one of the Canary Islands.
3. Campeche, in the Gulf of Mexico.

I had several men died in my ship of calentures,[4] so that I was forced to get recruits out of Barbadoes and the Leeward Islands, where I touched by the direction of the merchants who employed me; which I had soon too much cause to repent, for I found afterwards that most of them had been buccaneers. I had fifty hands on board; and my orders were that I should trade with the Indians in the South Sea, and make what discoveries I could. These rogues whom I had picked up debauched my other men, and they all formed a conspiracy to seize the ship and secure me; which they did one morning, rushing into my cabin, and binding me hand and foot, threatening to throw me overboard, if I offered to stir. I told them I was their prisoner, and would submit. This they made me swear to do, and then unbound me, only fastening one of my legs with a chain near my bed, and placed a sentry at my door with his piece charged, who was commanded to shoot me dead if I attempted my liberty. They sent me down victuals and drink, and took the government of the ship to themselves. Their design was to turn pirates and plunder the Spaniards, which they could not do, till they got more men. But first they resolved to sell the goods in the ship, and then go to Madagascar for recruits, several among them having died since my confinement. They sailed many weeks, and traded with the Indians; but I knew not what course they took, being kept close prisoner in my cabin, and expecting nothing less than to be murdered, as they often threatened me.

Upon the 9th day of May, 1711, one James Welch came down to my cabin; and said he had orders from the Captain to set me ashore. I expostulated with him, but in vain; neither would he so much as tell me who their new Captain was. They forced me into the longboat, letting me put on my best suit of clothes, which were as good as new, and a small bundle of linen, but no arms except my hanger; and they were so civil as not to search my pockets, into which I conveyed what money I had, with some other little necessaries. They rowed about a league, and then set me down on a strand. I desired them to tell me what country it was; they all swore, they knew no more than myself, but said that the Captain (as they called him) was resolved, after they had sold the lading, to get rid of me in the first place where they discovered land. They pushed off immediately, advising me to make haste, for fear of being overtaken by the tide, and bade me farewell.

In this desolate condition I advanced forward, and soon got upon firm ground, where I sat down on a bank to rest myself, and consider what I had best to do. When I was a little refreshed, I went up into the country, resolving to deliver myself to the first savages I should meet, and purchase my life from them by some bracelets, glass rings, and other toys, which sailors usually provide themselves with in those voyages, and whereof I had some about me. The land was divided by long rows of trees, not regularly planted, but naturally growing; there was great plenty of grass, and several fields of oats. I walked very circumspectly for fear of being surprised, or suddenly shot with an arrow from behind, or on either side. I fell into a beaten road, where I saw many tracks of human feet, and some of cows, but most of horses. At last I beheld several animals in a field, and one or two of the same kind sitting in trees. Their shape was very singular, and deformed, which a little

---

4. "A distemper peculiar to sailors, in hot climates; wherein they imagine the sea to be green fields, and will throw themselves into it, if not restrained" (Johnson's *Dictionary*).

discomposed me, so that I lay down behind a thicket to observe them better. Some of them coming forward near the place where I lay, gave me an opportunity of distinctly marking their form. Their heads and breasts were covered with a thick hair, some frizzled and others lank; they had beards like goats, and a long ridge of hair down their backs, and the fore parts of their legs and feet; but the rest of their bodies were bare, so that I might see their skins, which were of a brown buff color. They had no tails, nor any hair at all on their buttocks, except about the anus; which, I presume Nature had placed there to defend them as they sat on the ground; for this posture they used, as well as lying down, and often stood on their hind feet. They climbed high trees, as nimbly as a squirrel, for they had strong extended claws before and behind, terminating in sharp points, and hooked. They would often spring, and bound, and leap with prodigious agility. The females were not so large as the males; they had long lank hair on their heads, and only a sort of down on the rest of their bodies, except about the anus, and pudenda. Their dugs hung between their forefeet, and often reached almost to the ground as they walked. The hair of both sexes was of several colors, brown, red, black, and yellow. Upon the whole, I never beheld in all my travels so disagreeable an animal, or one against which I naturally conceived so strong an antipathy. So that thinking I had seen enough, full of contempt and aversion, I got up and pursued the beaten road, hoping it might direct me to the cabin of some Indian. I had not gone far when I met one of these creatures full in my way, and coming up directly to me. The ugly monster, when he saw me, distorted several ways every feature of his visage, and stared as at an object he had never seen before; then approaching nearer, lifted up his forepaw, whether out of curiosity or mischief, I could not tell; but I drew my hanger, and gave him a good blow with the flat side of it; for I durst not strike him with the edge, fearing the inhabitants might be provoked against me, if they should come to know that I had killed or maimed any of their cattle. When the beast felt the smart, he drew back, and roared so loud, that a herd of at least forty came flocking about me from the near field, howling and making odious faces; but I ran to the body of a tree, and leaning my back against it, kept them off, by waving my hanger. Several of this cursed brood getting hold of the branches behind, leaped up into the tree, from whence they began to discharge their excrements on my head; however, I escaped pretty well, by sticking close to the stem of the tree, but was almost stifled with the filth, which fell about me on every side.

In the midst of this distress, I observed them all to run away on a sudden as fast as they could; at which I ventured to leave the tree, and pursue the road, wondering what it was that could put them into this fright. But looking on my left hand, I saw a horse walking softly in the field; which my persecutors having sooner discovered, was the cause of their flight. The horse started a little when he came near me, but soon recovering himself, looked full in my face with manifest tokens of wonder; he viewed my hands and feet, walking round me several times. I would have pursued my journey, but he placed himself directly in the way, yet looking with a very mild aspect, never offering the least violence. We stood gazing at each other for some time; at last I took the boldness, to reach my hand towards his neck, with a design to stroke it; using the common style and whistle of jockies when they are going to handle a strange horse. But this animal, seeming to receive my civilities with disdain, shook his head, and bent his brows, softly raising up his left forefoot to remove my hand. Then he neighed three or four times, but in so different a cadence, that I almost began to think he was speaking to himself in some language of his own.

While he and I were thus employed, another horse came up; who applying himself to the first in a very formal manner, they gently struck each other's right hoof before, neighing several times by turns, and varying the sound, which seemed to be almost articulate. They went some paces off, as if it were to confer together, walking side by side, backward and forward, like persons deliberating upon some affair of weight; but often turning their eyes towards me, as it were to watch that I might not escape. I was amazed to see such actions and behavior in brute beasts; and concluded with myself that if the inhabitants of this country were endued with a proportionable degree of reason, they must needs be the wisest people upon earth. This thought gave me so much comfort, that I resolved to go forward until I could discover some house or village, or meet with any of the natives, leaving the two horses to discourse together as they pleased. But the first, who was a dapple grey, observing me to steal off, neighed after me in so expressive a tone that I fancied myself to understand what he meant; whereupon I turned back, and came near him, to expect his farther commands; but concealing my fear as much as I could; for I began to be in some pain, how this adventure might terminate; and the reader will easily believe I did not much like my present situation.

The two horses came up close to me, looking with great earnestness upon my face and hands. The grey steed rubbed my hat all round with his right fore hoof, and discomposed it so much that I was forced to adjust it better, by taking it off, and settling it again; whereat both he and his companion (who was a brown bay) appeared to be much surprised; the latter felt the lappet of my coat, and finding it to hang loose about me, they both looked with new signs of wonder. He stroked my right hand, seeming to admire the softness, and color; but he squeezed it so hard between his hoof and his pastern, that I was forced to roar; after which they both touched me with all possible tenderness. They were under great perplexity about my shoes and stockings, which they felt very often, neighing to each other, and using various gestures, not unlike those of a philosopher, when he would attempt to solve some new and difficult phenomenon.

Upon the whole, the behavior of these animals was so orderly and rational, so acute and judicious, that I at last concluded, they must needs be magicians, who had thus metamorphosed themselves upon some design; and seeing a stranger in the way, were resolved to divert themselves with him; or perhaps were really amazed at the sight of a man so very different in habit, feature, and complexion from those who might probably live in so remote a climate. Upon the strength of this reasoning, I ventured to address them in the following manner: "Gentlemen, if you be conjurers, as I have good cause to believe, you can understand any language; therefore I make bold to let your worships know that I am a poor distressed Englishman, driven by his misfortunes upon your coast; and I entreat one of you, to let me ride upon his back, as if he were a real horse, to some house or village, where I can be relieved. In return of which favor, I will make you a present of this knife and bracelet" (taking them out of my pocket). The two creatures stood silent while I spoke, seeming to listen with great attention; and when I had ended, they neighed frequently towards each other, as if they were engaged in serious conversation. I plainly observed, that their language expressed the passions very well, and the words might with little pains be resolved into an alphabet more easily than the Chinese.

I could frequently distinguish the word *Yahoo*,[5] which was repeated by each of them several times; and although it were impossible for me to conjecture what it meant, yet while the two horses were busy in conversation, I endeavored to practice this word upon my tongue; and as soon as they were silent, I boldly pronounced "Yahoo" in a loud voice, imitating, at the same time, as near as I could, the neighing of a horse; at which they were both visibly surprised, and the grey repeated the same word twice, as if he meant to teach me the right accent, wherein I spoke after him as well as I could, and found myself perceivably to improve every time, although very far from any degree of perfection. Then the bay tried me with a second word, much harder to be pronounced; but reducing it to the English orthography, may be spelt thus, *Houyhnhnm*. I did not succeed in this so well as the former, but after two or three farther trials, I had better fortune; and they both appeared amazed at my capacity.

After some farther discourse, which I then conjectured might relate to me, the two friends took their leaves, with the same compliment of striking each other's hoof; and the grey made me signs that I should walk before him; wherein I thought it prudent to comply, till I could find a better director. When I offered to slacken my pace, he would cry, "Hhuun, Hhuun"; I guessed his meaning, and gave him to understand, as well as I could that I was weary, and not able to walk faster; upon which, he would stand a while to let me rest.

CHAPTER 2. *The Author conducted by a Houyhnhnm to his house. The house described. The Author's reception. The food of the Houyhnhnms. The Author in distress for want of meat is at last relieved. His manner of feeding in that country.*

Having traveled about three miles, we came to a long kind of building, made of timber, stuck in the ground, and wattled across; the roof was low, and covered with straw. I now began to be a little comforted, and took out some toys, which travelers usually carry for presents to the savage Indians of America and other parts, in hopes the people of the house would be thereby encouraged to receive me kindly. The horse made me a sign to go in first; it was a large room with a smooth clay floor, and a rack and manger extending the whole length on one side. There were three nags, and two mares, not eating, but some of them sitting down upon their hams, which I very much wondered at; but wondered more to see the rest employed in domestic business. The last seemed but ordinary cattle; however this confirmed my first opinion, that a people who could so far civilize brute animals must needs excel in wisdom all the nations of the world. The grey came in just after, and thereby prevented any ill treatment, which the others might

5. Perhaps compounded from two expressions of disgust, *yah* and *ugh* (or *hoo*), common in the 18th century.

have given me. He neighed to them several times in a style of authority, and received answers.

Beyond this room there were three others, reaching the length of the house, to which you passed through three doors, opposite to each other, in the manner of a vista; we went through the second room towards the third; here the grey walked in first, beckoning me to attend.[6] I waited in the second room, and got ready my presents, for the master and mistress of the house; they were two knives, three bracelets of false pearl, a small looking glass and a bead necklace. The horse neighed three or four times, and I waited to hear some answers in a human voice, but I heard no other returns than in the same dialect, only one or two a little shriller than his. I began to think that this house must belong to some person of great note among them, because there appeared so much ceremony before I could gain admittance. But, that a man of quality should be served all by horses, was beyond my comprehension. I feared my brain was disturbed by my sufferings and misfortunes; I roused myself, and looked about me in the room where I was left alone; this was furnished as the first, only after a more elegant manner. I rubbed my eyes often, but the same objects still occurred. I pinched my arms and sides, to awaken myself, hoping I might be in a dream. I then absolutely concluded that all these appearances could be nothing else but necromancy and magic. But I had no time to pursue these reflections; for the grey horse came to the door, and made me a sign to follow him into the third room; where I saw a very comely mare, together with a colt and foal, sitting on their haunches, upon mats of straw, not unartfully made, and perfectly neat and clean.

The mare soon after my entrance, rose from her mat, and coming up close, after having nicely observed my hands and face, gave me a most contemptuous look; then turning to the horse, I heard the word Yahoo often repeated betwixt them; the meaning of which word I could not then comprehend, although it were the first I had learned to pronounce; but I was soon better informed, to my everlasting mortification: for the horse beckoning to me with his head, and repeating the word, "Hhuun, Hhuun," as he did upon the road, which I understood was to attend him, led me out into a kind of court, where was another building at some distance from the house. Here we entered, and I saw three of those detestable creatures, which I first met after my landing, feeding upon roots, and the flesh of some animals, which I afterwards found to be that of asses and dogs, and now and then a cow dead by accident or disease. They were all tied by the neck with strong withes, fastened to a beam; they held their food between the claws of their forefeet, and tore it with their teeth.

The master horse ordered a sorrel nag, one of his servants, to untie the largest of these animals, and take him into a yard. The beast and I were brought close together; and our countenances diligently compared, both by master and servant, who thereupon repeated several times the word "Yahoo." My horror and astonishment are not to be described, when I observed, in this abominable animal, a perfect human figure; the face of it indeed was flat and broad, the nose depressed, the lips large, and the mouth wide; but these differences are common to all savage nations, where the lineaments of the countenance are distorted by the natives suffering their infants to lie

6. To wait. "Vista": a long, open corridor.

groveling on the earth, or by carrying them on their backs, nuzzling with their face against the mother's shoulders. The forefeet of the Yahoo differed from my hands in nothing else but the length of the nails, the coarseness and brownness of the palms, and the hairiness on the backs. There was the same resemblance between our feet, with the same differences, which I knew very well, although the horses did not, because of my shoes and stockings; the same in every part of our bodies, except as to hairiness and color, which I have already described.

The great difficulty that seemed to stick with the two horses was to see the rest of my body so very different from that of a Yahoo, for which I was obliged to my clothes, whereof they had no conception; the sorrel nag offered me a root, which he held (after their manner, as we shall describe in its proper place) between his hoof and pastern; I took it in my hand, and having smelled it, returned it to him again as civilly as I could. He brought out of the Yahoo's kennel a piece of ass's flesh, but it smelled so offensively that I turned from it with loathing; he then threw it to the Yahoo, by whom it was greedily devoured. He afterwards showed me a wisp of hay, and a fetlock full of oats; but I shook my head, to signify that neither of these were food for me. And indeed, I now apprehended that I must absolutely starve, if I did not get to some of my own species; for as to those filthy Yahoos, although there were few greater lovers of mankind, at that time, than myself, yet I confess I never saw any sensitive being so detestable on all accounts; and the more I came near them, the more hateful they grew, while I stayed in that country. This the master horse observed by my behavior, and therefore sent the Yahoo back to his kennel. He then put his forehoof to his mouth, at which I was much surprised, although he did it with ease, and with a motion that appeared perfectly natural; and made other signs to know what I would eat; but I could not return him such an answer as he was able to apprehend; and if he had understood me, I did not see how it was possible to contrive any way for finding myself nourishment. While we were thus engaged, I observed a cow passing by; whereupon I pointed to her, and expressed a desire to let me go and milk her. This had its effect; for he led me back into the house, and ordered a mare-servant to open a room, where a good store of milk lay in earthen and wooden vessels, after a very orderly and cleanly manner. She gave me a large bowl full, of which I drank very heartily, and found myself well refreshed.

About noon I saw coming towards the house a kind of vehicle, drawn like a sledge by four Yahoos. There was in it an old steed, who seemed to be of quality; he alighted with his hind feet forward, having by accident got a hurt in his left forefoot. He came to dine with our horse, who received him with great civility. They dined in the best room, and had oats boiled in milk for the second course, which the old horse eat warm, but the rest cold. Their mangers were placed circular in the middle of the room, and divided into several partitions, round which they sat on their haunches upon bosses of straw. In the middle was a large rack with angles answering to every partition of the manger. So that each horse and mare eat their own hay, and their own mash of oats and milk, with much decency and regularity. The behavior of the young colt and foal appeared very modest; and that of the master and mistress extremely cheerful and complaisant to their guest. The grey ordered me to stand by him; and much discourse passed between him and his friend concerning me, as I found by the stranger's often looking on me, and the frequent repetition of the word Yahoo.

I happened to wear my gloves; which the master grey observing, seemed perplexed; discovering signs of wonder what I had done to my forefeet; he put his hoof three or four times to them, as if he would signify, that I should reduce them to their former shape, which I presently did, pulling off both my gloves, and putting them into my pocket. This occasioned farther talk, and I saw the company was pleased with my behavior, whereof I soon found the good effects. I was ordered to speak the few words I understood; and while they were at dinner, the master taught me the names for oats, milk, fire, water, and some others which I could readily pronounce after him, having from my youth a great facility in learning languages.

When dinner was done, the master horse took me aside, and by signs and words made me understand the concern he was in that I had nothing to eat. Oats in their tongue are called *hlunnh*. This word I pronounced two or three times; for although I had refused them at first, yet upon second thoughts, I considered that I could contrive to make a kind of bread, which might be sufficient with milk to keep me alive, till I could make my escape to some other country, and to creatures of my own species. The horse immediately ordered a white mare-servant of his family to bring me a good quantity of oats in a sort of wooden tray. These I heated before the fire as well as I could, and rubbed them till the husks came off, which I made a shift to winnow from the grain; I ground and beat them between two stones, then took water, and made them into a paste or cake, which I toasted at the fire, and eat warm with milk. It was at first a very insipid diet, although common enough in many parts of Europe, but grew tolerable by time; and having been often reduced to hard fare in my life, this was not the first experiment I had made how easily nature is satisfied. And I cannot but observe that I never had one hour's sickness, while I staid in this island. It is true, I sometimes made a shift to catch a rabbit, or bird, by springes[7] made of Yahoos' hairs; and I often gathered wholesome herbs, which I boiled, or eat as salads with my bread; and now and then, for a rarity, I made a little butter, and drank the whey. I was at first at a great loss for salt; but custom soon reconciled the want of it; and I am confident that the frequent use of salt among us is an effect of luxury, and was first introduced only as a provocative to drink; except where it is necessary for preserving of flesh in long voyages, or in places remote from great markets. For we observe no animal to be fond of it but man;[8] and as to myself, when I left this country, it was a great while before I could endure the taste of it in anything that I eat.

This is enough to say upon the subject of my diet, wherewith other travelers fill their books, as if the readers were personally concerned whether we fare well or ill. However, it was necessary to mention this matter, lest the world should think it impossible that I could find sustenance for three years in such a country, and among such inhabitants.

When it grew towards evening, the master horse ordered a place for me to lodge in; it was but six yards from the house, and separated from the stable of the Yahoos. Here I got some straw, and covering myself with my own

---

7. Snares.
8. Gulliver is, of course, in error; many animals require salt.

clothes, slept very sound. But I was in a short time better accommodated, as the reader shall know hereafter, when I come to treat more particularly about my way of living.

CHAPTER 3. *The Author studious to learn the language, the Houyhnhnm his master assists in teaching him. The language described. Several Houyhnhnms of quality come out of curiosity to see the Author. He gives his master a short account of his voyage.*

My principal endeavor was to learn the language, which my master (for so I shall henceforth call him) and his children, and every servant of his house were desirous to teach me. For they looked upon it as a prodigy, that a brute animal should discover such marks of a rational creature. I pointed to everything, and enquired the name of it, which I wrote down in my journal book when I was alone, and corrected my bad accent, by desiring those of the family to pronounce it often. In this employment, a sorrel nag, one of the under servants, was very ready to assist me.

In speaking, they pronounce through the nose and throat, and their language approaches nearest to the High Dutch or German, of any I know in Europe; but is much more graceful and significant. The Emperor Charles V made almost the same observation, when he said, that if he were to speak to his horse, it should be in High Dutch.[9]

The curiosity and impatience of my master were so great, that he spent many hours of his leisure to instruct me. He was convinced (as he afterwards told me) that I must be a Yahoo, but my teachableness, civility, and cleanliness astonished him; which were qualities altogether so opposite to those animals. He was most perplexed about my clothes, reasoning sometimes with himself whether they were a part of my body; for I never pulled them off till the family were asleep, and got them on before they waked in the morning. My master was eager to learn from whence I came; how I acquired those appearances of reason, which I discovered in all my actions; and to know my story from my own mouth, which he hoped he should soon do by the great proficiency I made in learning and pronouncing their words and sentences. To help my memory, I formed all I learned into the English alphabet, and writ the words down with the translations. This last, after some time, I ventured to do in my master's presence. It cost me much trouble to explain to him what I was doing; for the inhabitants have not the least idea of books or literature.

In about ten weeks time I was able to understand most of his questions; and in three months could give him some tolerable answers. He was extremely curious to know from what part of the country I came, and how I was taught to imitate a rational creature; because the Yahoos (whom he saw I exactly resembled in my head, hands, and face, that were only visible) with some appearance of cunning, and the strongest disposition to mischief, were observed to be the most unteachable of all brutes. I answered that I came over the sea, from a far place, with many others of my own kind, in a great hollow vessel made of the bodies of trees; that my companions forced me to

---

9. The emperor is supposed to have said that he would speak to his God in Spanish, to his mistress in Italian, and to his horse in German.

land on this coast, and then left me to shift for myself. It was with some difficulty, and by the help of many signs, that I brought him to understand me. He replied that I must needs be mistaken, or that I *said the thing which was not*. (For they have no word in their language to express lying or falsehood.) He knew it was impossible that there could be a country beyond the sea, or that a parcel of brutes could move a wooden vessel whither they pleased upon water. He was sure no Houyhnhnm alive could make such a vessel, or would trust Yahoos to manage it.

The word Houyhnhnm, in their tongue, signifies a Horse; and in its etymology, the Perfection of Nature. I told my master that I was at a loss for expression, but would improve as fast as I could; and hoped in a short time I should be able to tell him wonders. He was pleased to direct his own mare, his colt, and foal, and the servants of the family to take all opportunities of instructing me; and every day for two or three hours, he was at the same pains himself. Several horses and mares of quality in the neighborhood came often to our house, upon the report spread of a wonderful Yahoo, that could speak like a Houyhnhnm, and seemed in his words and actions to discover some glimmerings of reason. These delighted to converse with me; they put many questions, and received such answers as I was able to return. By all which advantages, I made so great a progress, that in five months from my arrival, I understood whatever was spoke, and could express myself tolerably well.

The Houyhnhnms who came to visit my master, out of a design of seeing and talking with me, could hardly believe me to be a right Yahoo, because my body had a different covering from others of my kind. They were astonished to observe me without the usual hair or skin, except on my head, face, and hands; but I discovered that secret to my master, upon an accident, which happened about a fortnight before.

I have already told the reader, that every night when the family were gone to bed, it was my custom to strip and cover myself with my clothes; it happened one morning early, that my master sent for me, by the sorrel nag, who was his valet; when he came, I was fast asleep, my clothes fallen off on one side, and my shirt above my waist. I awaked at the noise he made, and observed him to deliver his message in some disorder; after which he went to my master, and in a great fright gave him a very confused account of what he had seen. This I presently discovered; for going as soon as I was dressed, to pay my attendance upon his honor, he asked me the meaning of what his servant had reported; that I was not the same thing when I slept as I appeared to be at other times; that his valet assured him, some part of me was white, some yellow, at least not so white, and some brown.

I had hitherto concealed the secret of my dress, in order to distinguish myself as much as possible, from that cursed race of Yahoos; but now I found it in vain to do so any longer. Besides, I considered that my clothes and shoes would soon wear out, which already were in a declining condition, and must be supplied by some contrivance from the hides of Yahoos, or other brutes; whereby the whole secret would be known. I therefore told my master, that in the country from whence I came, those of my kind always covered their bodies with the hairs of certain animals prepared by art, as well for decency, as to avoid inclemencies of air both hot and cold; of which, as to my own person I would give him immediate conviction, if he pleased to command me; only desiring his excuse, if I did not expose those parts that Nature taught us to conceal. He said, my discourse was all very strange, but especially the last part; for he could not understand why Nature should teach us to conceal what Nature had given. That neither himself nor family were ashamed of any parts of their bodies; but however I might do as I pleased. Whereupon, I first unbuttoned my coat, and pulled it off. I did the same with my waistcoat; I drew off my shoes, stockings, and breeches. I let my shirt down to my waist, and drew up the bottom, fastening it like a girdle about my middle to hide my nakedness.

My master observed the whole performance with great signs of curiosity and admiration. He took up all my clothes in his pastern, one piece after another, and examined them diligently; he then stroked my body very gently, and looked round me several times; after which he said, it was plain I must be a perfect Yahoo; but that I differed very much from the rest of my species, in the whiteness and smoothness of my skin, my want of hair in several parts of my body, the shape and shortness of my claws behind and before, and my affectation of walking continually on my two hinder feet. He desired to see no more; and gave me leave to put on my clothes again, for I was shuddering with cold.

I expressed my uneasiness at his giving me so often the appellation of Yahoo, an odious animal, for which I had so utter an hatred and contempt. I begged he would forbear applying that word to me, and take the same order in his family, and among his friends whom he suffered to see me. I requested likewise, that the secret of my having a false covering to my body might be known to none but himself, at least as long as my present clothing should last; for as to what the sorrel nag his valet had observed, his honor might command him to conceal it.

All this my master very graciously consented to; and thus the secret was kept till my clothes began to wear out, which I was forced to supply by several contrivances, that shall hereafter be mentioned. In the meantime, he desired I would go on with my utmost diligence to learn their language, because he was more astonished at my capacity for speech and reason, than at the figure of my body, whether it were covered or no; adding that he waited with some impatience to hear the wonders which I promised to tell him.

From thenceforward he doubled the pains he had been at to instruct me; he brought me into all company, and made them treat me with civility, because, as he told them privately, this would put me into good humor, and make me more diverting.

Every day when I waited on him, beside the trouble he was at in teaching, he would ask me several questions concerning myself, which I answered as well as I could; and by those means he had already received some general ideas, although very imperfect. It would be tedious to relate the several steps, by which I advanced to a more regular conversation, but the first account I gave of myself in any order and length was to this purpose:

That, I came from a very far country, as I already had attempted to tell him, with about fifty more of my own species; that we traveled upon the seas, in a great hollow vessel made of wood, and larger than his honor's house. I described the ship to him in the best terms I could; and explained by the help of my handkerchief displayed, how it was driven forward by the wind. That, upon a quarrel among us, I was set on shore on this coast, where I walked forward without knowing whither, till he delivered me from the persecution of those execrable Yahoos. He asked me who made the ship, and how it was possible that the Houyhnhnms of my country would leave it to the management of brutes? My answer was that I durst proceed no farther in my relation, unless he would give me his word and honor that he would not be offended; and then I would tell him the wonders I had so often promised. He agreed; and I went on by assuring him, that the ship was made by creatures like myself, who in all the countries I had traveled, as well as in my own, were the only governing, rational animals; and that upon my arrival hither, I was as much astonished to see the Houyhnhnms act like rational beings, as he or his friends could be in finding some marks of reason in a creature he was pleased to call a Yahoo; to which I owned my resemblance in every part, but could not account for their degenerate and brutal nature. I said farther, that if good fortune ever restored me to my native country, to relate my travels hither, as I resolved to do, everybody would believe that I *said the thing which was not,* that I invented the story out of my own head; and with all possible respect to himself, his family, and friends, and under his promise of not being offended, our countrymen would hardly think it probable, that a Houyhnhnm should be the presiding creature of a nation, and a Yahoo the brute.

CHAPTER 4. *The Houyhnhnms' notion of truth and falsehood. The Author's discourse disapproved by his master. The Author gives a more particular account of himself, and the accidents of his voyage.*

My master heard me with great appearances of uneasiness in his countenance; because *doubting* or *not believing* are so little known in this country, that the inhabitants cannot tell how to behave themselves under such circumstances. And I remember in frequent discourses with my master concerning the nature of manhood, in other parts of the world, having occasion to talk of *lying* and *false representation,* it was with much difficulty that he comprehended what I meant; although he had otherwise a most acute judgment. For he argued thus: that the use of speech was to make us understand one another, and to receive information of facts; now if anyone *said the thing which was not,* these ends were defeated; because I cannot properly be said to understand him; and I am so far from receiving information, that he leaves me worse than in ignorance; for I am led to believe a thing *black* when it is *white,* and *short* when it is *long.* And these were all the notions he had concerning the faculty of *lying,* so perfectly well understood, and so universally practiced among human creatures.

To return from this digression; when I asserted that the Yahoos were the only governing animals in my country, which my master said was altogether past his conception, he desired to know, whether we had Houyhnhnms among us, and what was their employment. I told him we had great numbers; that in summer they grazed in the fields, and in winter were kept in houses, with hay and oats, where Yahoo servants were employed to rub their skins smooth, comb their manes, pick their feet, serve them with food, and make their beds. "I understand you well," said my master; "it is now very plain from all you have spoken, that whatever share of reason the Yahoos pretend to, the Houyhnhnms are your masters; I heartily wish our Yahoos would be so tractable." I begged his honor would please to excuse me from proceeding any farther, because I was very certain that the account he expected from me would be highly displeasing. But he insisted in commanding me to let him know the best and the worst; I told him he should be obeyed. I owned that the Houyhnhnms among us, whom we called Horses, were the most generous[1] and comely animal we had; that they excelled in strength and swiftness; and when they belonged to persons of quality, employed in traveling, racing, and drawing chariots, they were treated with much kindness and care, till they fell into diseases, or became foundered in the feet; but then they were sold, and used to all kind of drudgery till they died; after which their skins were stripped and sold for what they were worth, and their bodies left to be devoured by dogs and birds of prey. But the common race of horses had not so good fortune, being kept by farmers and carriers, and other mean people, who put them to greater labor, and feed them worse. I described as well as I could, our way of riding; the shape and use of a bridle, a saddle, a spur, and a whip; of harness and wheels. I added, that we fastened plates of a certain hard substance called iron at the bottom of their feet, to preserve their hoofs from being broken by the stony ways on which we often traveled.

My master, after some expressions of great indignation, wondered how we dared to venture upon a Houyhnhnm's back; for he was sure, that the weakest servant in his house would be able to shake off the strongest Yahoo; or by lying down, and rolling upon his back, squeeze the brute to death. I answered that our horses were trained up from three or four years old to the several uses we intended them for; that if any of them proved intolerably vicious, they were employed for carriages; that they were severely beaten while they were young for any mischievous tricks; that the males, designed for the common use of riding or draught, were generally castrated about two years after their birth, to take down their spirits, and make them more tame and gentle; that they were indeed sensible of rewards and punishments; but his honor would please to consider that they had not the least tincture of reason any more than the Yahoos in this country.

It put me to the pains of many circumlocutions to give my master a right idea of what I spoke; for their language doth not abound in variety of words, because their wants and passions are fewer than among us. But it is impossible to express his noble resentment at our savage treatment of the Houyhnhnm race; particularly after I had explained the manner and use of castrating horses among us, to hinder them from propagating their kind, and to render them more servile. He said, if it were possible there could be any country where Yahoos alone were endued with reason, they certainly must be the governing animal, because reason will in time always prevail against brutal strength. But, considering the frame of our bodies, and especially of mine, he thought no creature of equal bulk was so ill-contrived for employing that reason in the common offices of life; whereupon he desired to know whether those among whom I lived resembled me or the Yahoos of his country. I assured him that I was as well shaped as most of my age; but the younger and the females were much more soft and tender, and the skins of the latter generally as white as milk. He said I differed indeed from other Yahoos, being

1. Noble.

much more cleanly, and not altogether so deformed; but in point of real advantage, he thought I differed for the worse. That my nails were of no use either to my fore or hinder feet; as to my forefeet, he could not properly call them by that name, for he never observed me to walk upon them; that they were too soft to bear the ground; that I generally went with them uncovered, neither was the covering I sometimes wore on them of the same shape, or so strong as that on my feet behind. That I could not walk with any security; for if either of my hinder feet slipped, I must inevitably fall. He then began to find fault with other parts of my body; the flatness of my face, the prominence of my nose, my eyes placed directly in front, so that I could not look on either side without turning my head; that I was not able to feed myself without lifting one of my forefeet to my mouth; and therefore nature had placed those joints to answer that necessity. He knew not what could be the use of those several clefts and divisions in my feet behind; that these were too soft to bear the hardness and sharpness of stones without a covering made from the skin of some other brute; that my whole body wanted a fence against heat and cold, which I was forced to put on and off every day with tediousness and trouble. And lastly, that he observed every animal in his country naturally to abhor the Yahoos, whom the weaker avoided, and the stronger drove from them. So that supposing us to have the gift of reason, he could not see how it were possible to cure that natural antipathy which every creature discovered against us; nor consequently, how we could tame and render them serviceable. However, he would (as he said) debate the matter no farther, because he was more desirous to know my own story, the country where I was born, and the several actions and events of my life before I came hither.

I assured him how extremely desirous I was that he should be satisfied in every point; but I doubted much whether it would be possible for me to explain myself on several subjects whereof his honor could have no conception, because I saw nothing in his country to which I could resemble them. That however, I would do my best, and strive to express myself by similitudes, humbly desiring his assistance when I wanted proper words; which he was pleased to promise me.

I said, my birth was of honest parents, in an island called England, which was remote from this country, as many days journey as the strongest of his honor's servants could travel in the annual course of the sun. That I was bred a surgeon, whose trade it is to cure wounds and hurts in the body, got by accident or violence. That my country was governed by a female man, whom we called a queen. That I left it to get riches, whereby I might maintain myself and family when I should return. That in my last voyage, I was Commander of the ship and had about fifty Yahoos under me, many of which died at sea, and I was forced to supply them by others picked out from several nations. That our ship was twice in danger of being sunk; the first time by a great storm, and the second, by striking against a rock. Here my master interposed, by asking me, how I could persuade strangers out of different countries to venture with me, after the losses I had sustained, and the hazards I had run. I said, they were fellows of desperate fortunes, forced to fly from the places of their birth, on account of their poverty or their crimes. Some were undone by lawsuits; others spent all they had in drinking, whoring, and gaming; others fled for treason; many for murder, theft, poisoning, robbery, perjury, forgery, coining false money; for committing rapes or sodomy; for flying from their colors, or deserting to the enemy; and most of them had broken prison. None of these durst return to their native countries for fear of being hanged, or of starving in a jail; and therefore were under a necessity of seeking a livelihood in other places.

During this discourse, my master was pleased often to interrupt me. I had made use of many circumlocutions in describing to him the nature of the several crimes, for which most of our crew had been forced to fly their country. This labor took up several days conversation before he was able to comprehend me. He was wholly at a loss to know what could be the use or necessity of practicing those vices. To clear up which I endeavored to give him some ideas of the desire of power and riches; of the terrible effects of lust, intemperance, malice, and envy. All this I was forced to define and describe by putting of cases, and making suppositions. After which, like one whose imagination was struck with something never seen or heard of before, he would lift up his eyes with amazement and indignation. Power, government, war, law, punishment, and a thousand other things had no terms, wherein that language could express them; which made the difficulty almost insuperable to give my master any conception of what I meant; but being of an excellent understanding, much improved by contemplation and converse, he at last arrived at a competent knowledge of what human nature in our parts of the world is capable to perform; and desired I would give him some particular account of that land, which we call Europe, especially, of my own country.

CHAPTER 5. *The Author, at his master's commands, informs him of the state of England. The causes of war among the princes of Europe. The Author begins to explain the English Constitution.*

The reader may please to observe that the following extract of many conversations I had with my master contains a summary of the most material points, which were discoursed at several times for above two years; his honor often desiring fuller satisfaction as I farther improved in the Houyhnhnm tongue. I laid before him, as well as I could, the whole state of Europe; I discoursed of trade and manufactures, of arts and sciences; and the answers I gave to all the questions he made, as they arose upon several subjects, were a fund of conversation not to be exhausted. But I shall here only set down the substance of what passed between us concerning my own country, reducing it into order as well as I can, without any regard to time or other circumstances, while I strictly adhere to truth. My only concern is that I shall hardly be able to do justice to my master's arguments and expressions; which must needs suffer by my want of capacity, as well as by a translation into our barbarous English.

In obedience therefore to his honor's commands, I related to him the Revolution under the Prince of Orange; the long war with France entered into by the said Prince, and renewed by his successor the present queen; wherein the greatest powers of Christendom were engaged, and which still continued. I computed at his request, that about a million of Yahoos might have been killed in the whole progress of it; and perhaps a hundred or more cities taken, and five times as many ships burned or sunk.[2]

2. Gulliver relates recent English history: the Glorious Revolution (1688–89) and the War of Spanish Succession (1703–13). He greatly exaggerates the casualties in the war.

He asked me what were the usual causes or motives that made one country to go to war with another. I answered, they were innumerable; but I should only mention a few of the chief. Sometimes the ambition of princes, who never think they have land or people enough to govern; sometimes the corruption of ministers, who engage their master in a war in order to stifle or divert the clamor of the subjects against their evil administration. Difference in opinions hath cost many millions of lives; for instance, whether flesh be bread, or bread be flesh; whether the juice of a certain berry be blood or wine; whether whistling be a vice or a virtue; whether it be better to kiss a post, or throw it into the fire; what is the best color for a coat, whether black, white, red, or grey; and whether it should be long or short, narrow or wide, dirty or clean;[3] with many more. Neither are any wars so furious and bloody, or of so long continuance, as those occasioned by difference in opinion, especially if it be in things indifferent.[4]

Sometimes the quarrel between two princes is to decide which of them shall dispossess a third of his dominions, where neither of them pretend to any right. Sometimes one prince quarreleth with another, for fear the other should quarrel with him. Sometimes a war is entered upon, because the enemy is too strong, and sometimes because he is too weak. Sometimes our neighbors want the things which we have, or have the things which we want; and we both fight, till they take ours or give us theirs. It is a very justifiable cause of war to invade a country after the people have been wasted by famine, destroyed by pestilence, or embroiled by factions amongst themselves. It is justifiable to enter into a war against our nearest ally, when one of his towns lies convenient for us, or a territory of land, that would render our dominions round and compact. If a prince send forces into a nation, where the people are poor and ignorant, he may lawfully put half of them to death, and make slaves of the rest, in order to civilize and reduce them from their barbarous way of living. It is a very kingly, honorable, and frequent practice, when one prince desires the assistance of another to secure him against an invasion, that the assistant, when he hath driven out the invader, should seize on the dominions himself, and kill, imprison, or banish the prince he came to relieve. Alliance by blood or marriage is a sufficient cause of war between princes; and the nearer the kindred is, the greater is their disposition to quarrel. Poor nations are hungry, and rich nations are proud; and pride and hunger will ever be at variance. For these reasons, the trade of a soldier is held the most honorable of all others: because a soldier is a Yahoo hired to kill in cold blood as many of his own species, who have never offended him, as possibly he can.

There is likewise a kind of beggarly princes in Europe, not able to make war by themselves, who hire out their troops to richer nations for so much a day to each man; of which they keep three fourths to themselves, and it is the best part of their maintenance; such are those in many northern parts of Europe.[5]

"What you have told me," said my master, "upon the subject of war, doth indeed discover most admirably the effects of that reason you pretend to. However, it is happy that the shame is greater than the danger; and that

3. Gulliver refers to the religious controversies of the Reformation and Counter-Reformation: the doctrine of transubstantiation, the use of music in church services, the veneration of the crucifix, and the wearing of priestly vestments.
4. Of little consequence.
5. A satiric glance at George I, who, as elector of Hanover, had dealt in this trade.

Nature hath left you utterly uncapable of doing much mischief; for your mouths lying flat with your faces, you can hardly bite each other to any purpose, unless by consent. Then, as to the claws upon your feet before and behind, they are so short and tender, that one of our Yahoos would drive a dozen of yours before him. And therefore in recounting the numbers of those who have been killed in battle, I cannot but think that you have *said the thing which is not*."

I could not forbear shaking my head and smiling a little at his ignorance. And, being no stranger to the art of war, I gave him a description of cannons, culverins, muskets, carabines, pistols, bullets, powder, swords, bayonets, battles, sieges, retreats, attacks, undermines, countermines, bombardments, sea fights; ships sunk with a thousand men; twenty thousand killed on each side; dying groans, limbs flying in the air; smoke, noise, confusion, trampling to death under horses' feet; flight, pursuit, victory; fields strewed with carcasses left for food to dogs, and wolves, and birds of prey; plundering, stripping, ravishing, burning, and destroying. And, to set forth the valor of my own dear countrymen, I assured him that I had seen them blow up a hundred enemies at once in a siege, and as many in a ship; and beheld the dead bodies drop down in pieces from the clouds, to the great diversion of all the spectators.

I was going on to more particulars, when my master commanded me silence. He said, whoever understood the nature of Yahoos might easily believe it possible for so vile an animal, to be capable of every action I had named, if their strength and cunning equaled their malice. But, as my discourse had increased his abhorrence of the whole species, so he found it gave him a disturbance in his mind, to which he was wholly a stranger before. He thought his ears being used to such abominable words, might by degrees admit them with less detestation. That, although he hated the Yahoos of this country, yet he no more blamed them for their odious qualities, than he did a *gnnayh* (a bird of prey) for its cruelty, or a sharp stone for cutting his hoof. But, when a creature pretending to reason could be capable of such enormities, he dreaded lest the corruption of that faculty might be worse than brutality itself. He seemed therefore confident, that instead of reason, we were only possessed of some quality fitted to increase our natural vices; as the reflection from a troubled stream returns the image of an ill-shapen body, not only larger, but more distorted.

He added that he had heard too much upon the subject of war, both in this and some former discourses. There was another point which a little perplexed him at present. I had said that some of our crew left their country on account of being ruined by law: that I had already explained the meaning of the word; but he was at a loss how it should come to pass, that the law which was intended for every man's preservation, should be any man's ruin. Therefore he desired to be farther satisfied what I meant by law, and the dispensers thereof, according to the present practice in my own country; because he thought Nature and Reason were sufficient guides for a reasonable animal, as we pretended to be, in showing us what we ought to do, and what to avoid.

I assured his honor that law was a science wherein I had not much conversed, further than by employing advocates, in vain, upon some injustices that had been done me. However, I would give him all the satisfaction I was able.

I said there was a society of men among us, bred up from their youth in the art of proving by words multiplied for the purpose, that white is black, and black is white, according as they are paid. To this society all the rest of the people are slaves.

"For example. If my neighbor hath a mind to my cow, he hires a lawyer to prove that he ought to have my cow from me. I must then hire another to defend my right; it being against all rules of law that any man should be allowed to speak for himself. Now in this case, I who am the true owner lie under two great disadvantages. First, my lawyer being practiced almost from his cradle in defending falsehood is quite out of his element when he would be an advocate for justice, which as an office unnatural, he always attempts with great awkwardness, if not with ill-will. The second disadvantage is that my lawyer must proceed with great caution, or else he will be reprimanded by the judges, and abhorred by his brethren, as one who would lessen the practice of the law. And therefore I have but two methods to preserve my cow. The first is to gain over my adversary's lawyer with a double fee; who will then betray his client, by insinuating that he hath justice on his side. The second way is for my lawyer to make my cause appear as unjust as he can; by allowing the cow to belong to my adversary; and this if it be skillfully done, will certainly bespeak the favor of the bench.

"Now, your honor is to know that these judges are persons appointed to decide all controversies of property, as well as for the trial of criminals; and picked out from the most dextrous lawyers who are grown old or lazy; and having been biased all their lives against truth and equity, lie under such a fatal necessity of favoring fraud, perjury, and oppression, that I have known some of them to have refused a large bribe from the side where justice lay, rather than injure the faculty,[6] by doing anything unbecoming their nature or their office.

"It is a maxim among these lawyers, that whatever hath been done before may legally be done again; and therefore they take special care to record all the decisions formerly made against common justice and the general reason of mankind. These, under the name of *precedents,* they produce as authorities to justify the most iniquitous opinions; and the judges never fail of directing accordingly.

"In pleading, they studiously avoid entering into the merits of the cause; but are loud, violent, and tedious in dwelling upon all circumstances which are not to the purpose. For instance, in the case already mentioned, they never desire to know what claim or title my adversary hath to my cow; but whether the said cow were red or black; her horns long or short; whether the field I graze her in be round or square; whether she were milked at home or abroad; what diseases she is subject to, and the like. After which they consult precedents, adjourn the cause, from time to time, and in ten, twenty, or thirty years come to an issue.

"It is likewise to be observed, that this society hath a peculiar cant and jargon of their own, that no other mortal can understand, and wherein all their laws are written, which they take special care to multiply; whereby they have wholly confounded the very essence of truth and falsehood, of right and wrong; so that it will take thirty years to decide whether the field, left me by my ancestors for six generations, belong to me, or to a stranger three hundred miles off.

6. Profession.

"In the trial of persons accused for crimes against the state, the method is much more short and commendable: the judge first sends to sound the disposition of those in power; after which he can easily hang or save the criminal, strictly preserving all the forms of law."

Here my master interposing said it was a pity that creatures endowed with such prodigious abilities of mind as these lawyers, by the description I gave of them, must certainly be, were not rather encouraged to be instructors of others in wisdom and knowledge. In answer to which, I assured his honor that in all points out of their own trade, they were usually the most ignorant and stupid generation among us, the most despicable in common conversation, avowed enemies to all knowledge and learning; and equally disposed to pervert the general reason of mankind, in every other subject of discourse as in that of their own profession.

CHAPTER 6. *A continuation of the state of England, under Queen Anne. The character of a first minister in the courts of Europe.*

My master was yet wholly at a loss to understand what motives could incite this race of lawyers to perplex, disquiet, and weary themselves by engaging in a confederacy of injustice, merely for the sake of injuring their fellow animals; neither could he comprehend what I meant in saying they did it for hire. Whereupon I was at much pains to describe to him the use of money, the materials it was made of, and the value of the metals; that when a Yahoo had got a great store of this precious substance, he was able to purchase whatever he had a mind to; the finest clothing, the noblest houses, great tracts of land, the most costly meats and drinks; and have his choice of the most beautiful females. Therefore since money alone was able to perform all these feats, our Yahoos thought they could never have enough of it to spend or to save, as they found themselves inclined from their natural bent either to profusion or avarice. That the rich man enjoyed the fruit of the poor man's labor, and the latter were a thousand to one in proportion to the former. That the bulk of our people was forced to live miserably, by laboring every day for small wages to make a few live plentifully. I enlarged myself much on these and many other particulars to the same purpose, but his honor was still to seek,[7] for he went upon a supposition that all animals had a title to their share in the productions of the earth; and especially those who presided over the rest. Therefore he desired I would let him know what these costly meats were, and how any of us happened to want[8] them. Whereupon I enumerated as many sorts as came into my head, with the various methods of dressing them, which could not be done without sending vessels by sea to every part of the world, as well for liquors to drink, as for sauces, and innumerable other conveniencies. I assured him, that this whole globe of earth must be at least three times gone round, before one of our better female Yahoos could get her breakfast, or a cup to put it in. He said, "That must needs be a miserable country which cannot furnish food for its own inhabitants." But what he chiefly wondered at, was how such vast tracts of ground as I described, should be wholly without fresh water, and the people put to the necessity of sending over the sea for drink. I replied that England (the dear place of my nativity) was computed to produce three times the quantity

7. Still did not understand. 8. Lack.

of food, more than its inhabitants are able to consume, as well as liquors extracted from grain, or pressed out of the fruit of certain trees, which made excellent drink; and the same proportion in every other convenience of life. But, in order to feed the luxury and intemperance of the males, and the vanity of the females, we sent away the greatest part of our necessary things to other countries, from whence in return we brought the materials of diseases, folly, and vice, to spend among ourselves. Hence it follows of necessity, that vast numbers of our people are compelled to seek their livelihood by begging, robbing, stealing, cheating, pimping, forswearing, flattering, suborning, forging, gaming, lying, fawning, hectoring, voting, scribbling, star gazing, poisoning, whoring, canting, libeling, freethinking, and the like occupations; every one of which terms, I was at much pains to make him understand.

That, wine was not imported among us from foreign countries, to supply the want of water or other drinks, but because it was a sort of liquid which made us merry, by putting us out of our senses; diverted all melancholy thoughts, begat wild extravagant imaginations in the brain, raised our hopes, and banished our fears; suspended every office of reason for a time, and deprived us of the use of our limbs, until we fell into a profound sleep; although it must be confessed, that we always awaked sick and dispirited; and that the use of this liquor filled us with diseases, which made our lives uncomfortable and short.

But beside all this, the bulk of our people supported themselves by furnishing the necessities or conveniencies of life to the rich, and to each other. For instance, when I am at home and dressed as I ought to be, I carry on my body the workmanship of an hundred tradesmen; the building and furniture of my house employ as many more; and five times the number to adorn my wife.

I was going on to tell him of another sort of people, who get their livelihood by attending the sick; having upon some occasions informed his honor that many of my crew had died of diseases. But here it was with the utmost difficulty that I brought him to apprehend what I meant. He could easily conceive that a Houyhnhnm grew weak and heavy a few days before his death; or by some accident might hurt a limb. But that nature, who worketh all things to perfection, should suffer any pains to breed in our bodies, he thought impossible; and desired to know the reason of so unaccountable an evil. I told him, we fed on a thousand things which operated contrary to each other; that we eat when we were not hungry, and drank without the provocation of thirst; that we sat whole nights drinking strong liquors without eating a bit, which disposed us to sloth, inflamed our bodies, and precipitated or prevented digestion. That, prostitute female Yahoos acquired a certain malady, which bred rottenness in the bones of those who fell into their embraces; that this and many other diseases were propagated from father to son; so that great numbers come into the world with complicated maladies upon them; that it would be endless to give him a catalogue of all diseases incident to human bodies; for they could not be fewer than five or six hundred, spread over every limb, and joint; in short, every part, external and intestine, having diseases appropriated to each. To remedy which, there was a sort of people bred up among us, in the profession or pretense of curing the sick. And because I had some skill in the faculty, I would in gratitude to his honor let him know the whole mystery and method by which they proceed.

Their fundamental is that all diseases arise from repletion; from whence they conclude, that a great evacuation of the body is necessary, either through the natural passage, or upwards at the mouth. Their next business is, from herbs, minerals, gums, oils, shells, salts, juices, seaweed, excrements, barks of trees, serpents, toads, frogs, spiders, dead men's flesh and bones, birds, beasts and fishes, to form a composition for smell and taste the most abominable, nauseous, and detestable, that they can possibly contrive, which the stomach immediately rejects with loathing, and this they call a vomit. Or else from the same storehouse, with some other poisonous additions, they command us to take in at the orifice above or below (just as the physician then happens to be disposed) a medicine equally annoying and disgustful to the bowels; which relaxing the belly, drives down all before it; and this they call a purge, or a clyster. For nature (as the physicians allege) having intended the superior anterior orifice only for the intromission of solids and liquids, and the inferior posterior for ejection, these artists ingeniously considering that in all diseases nature is forced out of her seat; therefore to replace her in it, the body must be treated in a manner directly contrary, by interchanging the use of each orifice; forcing solids and liquids in at the anus, and making evacuations at the mouth.

But, besides real diseases, we are subject to many that are only imaginary, for which the physicians have invented imaginary cures; these have their several names, and so have the drugs that are proper for them; and with these our female Yahoos are always infested.

One great excellency in this tribe is their skill at prognostics, wherein they seldom fail; their predictions in real diseases, when they rise to any degree of malignity, generally portending death, which is always in their power, when recovery is not, and therefore, upon any unexpected signs of amendment, after they have pronounced their sentence, rather than be accused as false prophets, they know how to approve[9] their sagacity to the world by a seasonable dose.

They are likewise of special use to husbands and wives, who are grown weary of their mates; to eldest sons, to great ministers of state, and often to princes.

I had formerly upon occasion discoursed with my master upon the nature of government in general, and particularly of our own excellent constitution, deservedly the wonder and envy of the whole world. But having here accidently mentioned a minister of state, he commanded me some time after to inform him what species of Yahoo I particularly meant by that appellation.

I told him that a first or chief minister of state, whom I intended to describe, was a creature wholly exempt from joy and grief, love and hatred, pity and anger; at least makes use of no other passions but a violent desire of wealth, power, and titles; that he applies his words to all uses, except to the indication of his mind; that he never tells a truth, but with an intent that you should take it for a lie; nor a lie, but with a design that you should take it for a truth; that those he speaks worst of behind their backs are in the surest way to preferment; and whenever he begins to praise you to others or

9. Prove.

to yourself, you are from that day forlorn. The worst mark you can receive is a promise, especially when it is confirmed with an oath; after which every wise man retires, and gives over all hopes.

There are three methods by which a man may rise to be chief minister: the first is by knowing how with prudence to dispose of a wife, a daughter, or a sister; the second, by betraying or undermining his predecessor; and the third is by a furious zeal in public assemblies against the corruptions of the court. But a wise prince would rather choose to employ those who practice the last of these methods; because such zealots prove always the most obsequious and subservient to the will and passions of their master. That, these ministers having all employments at their disposal, preserve themselves in power by bribing the majority of a senate or great council; and at last by an expedient called an Act of Indemnity[1] (whereof I described the nature to him) they secure themselves from after reckonings, and retire from the public, laden with the spoils of the nation.

The palace of a chief minister is a seminary to breed up others in his own trade; the pages, lackies, and porter, by imitating their master, become ministers of state in their several districts, and learn to excel in the three principal ingredients, of insolence, lying, and bribery. Accordingly, they have a subaltern court paid to them by persons of the best rank; and sometimes by the force of dexterity and impudence, arrive through several gradations to be successors to their lord.

He is usually governed by a decayed wench, or favorite footman, who are the tunnels through which all graces are conveyed, and may properly be called, in the last resort, the governors of the kingdom.

One day, my master, having heard me mention the nobility of my country, was pleased to make me a compliment which I could not pretend to deserve: that, he was sure, I must have been born of some noble family, because I far exceeded in shape, color, and cleanliness, all the Yahoos of his nation, although I seemed to fail in strength, and agility, which must be imputed to my different way of living from those other brutes; and besides, I was not only endowed with the faculty of speech, but likewise with some rudiments of reason, to a degree, that with all his acquaintance I passed for a prodigy.

He made me observe, that among the Houyhnhnms, the white, the sorrel, and the iron grey were not so exactly shaped as the bay, the dapple grey, and the black; nor born with equal talents of mind, or a capacity to improve them; and therefore continued always in the condition of servants, without ever aspiring to match out of their own race, which in that country would be reckoned monstrous and unnatural.

I made his honor my most humble acknowledgments for the good opinion he was pleased to conceive of me; but assured him at the same time, that my birth was of the lower sort, having been born of plain, honest parents, who were just able to give me a tolerable education; that, nobility among us was altogether a different thing from the idea he had of it; that, our young noblemen are bred from their childhood in idleness and luxury; that, as soon as years will permit, they consume their vigor, and contract odious diseases among lewd females; and when their fortunes are almost ruined, they marry

---

1. An act passed at each session of Parliament to protect ministers of state who in good faith might have acted illegally.

some woman of mean birth, disagreeable person, and unsound constitution, merely for the sake of money, whom they hate and despise. That, the productions of such marriages are generally scrofulous, rickety or deformed children; by which means the family seldom continues above three generations, unless the wife take care to provide a healthy father among her neighbors, or domestics, in order to improve and continue the breed. That a weak diseased body, a meager countenance, and sallow complexion are the true marks of noble blood; and a healthy robust appearance is so disgraceful in a man of quality, that the world concludes his real father to have been a groom or a coachman. The imperfections of his mind run parallel with those of his body; being a composition of spleen, dullness, ignorance, caprice, sensuality, and pride.

Without the consent of this illustrious body, no law can be enacted, repealed, or altered, and these nobles have likewise the decision of all our possessions without appeal.

CHAPTER 7. *The Author's great love of his native country. His master's observations upon the constitution and administration of England, as described by the Author, with parallel cases and comparisons. His master's observations upon human nature.*

The reader may be disposed to wonder how I could prevail on myself to give so free a representation of my own species, among a race of mortals who were already too apt to conceive the vilest opinion of humankind, from that entire congruity betwixt me and their Yahoos. But I must freely confess that the many virtues of those excellent quadrupeds placed in opposite view to human corruptions had so far opened my eyes, and enlarged my understanding, that I began to view the actions and passions of man in a very different light; and to think the honor of my own kind not worth managing;[2] which, besides, it was impossible for me to do before a person of so acute a judgment as my master, who daily convinced me of a thousand faults in myself, whereof I had not the least perception before, and which with us would never be numbered even among human infirmities. I had likewise learned from his example an utter detestation of all falsehood or disguise; and truth appeared so amiable to me, that I determined upon sacrificing everything to it.

Let me deal so candidly with the reader as to confess that there was yet a much stronger motive for the freedom I took in my representation of things. I had not been a year in this country, before I contracted such a love and veneration for the inhabitants, that I entered on a firm resolution never to return to humankind, but to pass the rest of my life among these admirable Houyhnhnms in the contemplation and practice of every virtue; where I could have no example or incitement to vice. But it was decreed by fortune, my perpetual enemy, that so great a felicity should not fall to my share. However, it is now some comfort to reflect that in what I said of my countrymen, I extenuated their faults as much as I durst before so strict an examiner; and upon every article, gave as favorable a turn as the matter would bear. For, indeed, who is there alive that will not be swayed by his bias and partiality to the place of his birth?

2. Taking care of.

I have related the substance of several conversations I had with my master, during the greatest part of the time I had the honor to be in his service; but have indeed for brevity sake omitted much more than is here set down.

When I had answered all his questions, and his curiosity seemed to be fully satisfied; he sent for me one morning early, and commanding me to sit down at some distance (an honor which he had never before conferred upon me), he said he had been very seriously considering my whole story, as far as it related both to myself and my country; that, he looked upon us as a sort of animals to whose share, by what accident he could not conjecture, some small pittance of reason had fallen, whereof we made no other use than by its assistance to aggravate our natural corruptions, and to acquire new ones which nature had not given us. That we disarmed ourselves of the few abilities she had bestowed; had been very successful in multiplying our original wants, and seemed to spend our whole lives in vain endeavors to supply them by our own inventions. That, as to myself, it was manifest I had neither the strength or agility of a common Yahoo; that I walked infirmly on my hinder feet; had found out a contrivance to make my claws of no use or defense, and to remove the hair from my chin, which was intended as a shelter from the sun and the weather. Lastly, that I could neither run with speed, nor climb trees like my brethren (as he called them) the Yahoos in this country.

That our institutions of government and law were plainly owing to our gross defects in reason, and by consequence, in virtue; because reason alone is sufficient to govern a rational creature; which was therefore a character we had no pretense to challenge, even from the account I had given of my own people; although he manifestly perceived, that in order to favor them, I had concealed many particulars, and often *said the thing which was not*.

He was the more confirmed in this opinion, because he observed that I agreed in every feature of my body with other Yahoos, except where it was to my real disadvantage in point of strength, speed, and activity, the shortness of my claws, and some other particulars where Nature had no part; so, from the representation I had given him of our lives, our manners, and our actions, he found as near a resemblance in the disposition of our minds. He said the Yahoos were known to hate one another more than they did any different species of animals; and the reason usually assigned was the odiousness of their own shapes, which all could see in the rest, but not in themselves. He had therefore begun to think it not unwise in us to cover our bodies, and by that invention, conceal many of our deformities from each other, which would else be hardly supportable. But he now found he had been mistaken; and that the dissensions of those brutes in his country were owing to the same cause with ours, as I had described them. For, if (said he) you throw among five Yahoos as much food as would be sufficient for fifty, they will instead of eating peaceably, fall together by the ears, each single one impatient to have all to itself; and therefore a servant was usually employed to stand by while they were feeding abroad, and those kept at home were tied at a distance from each other. That, if a cow died of age or accident, before a Houyhnhnm could secure it for his own Yahoos, those in the neighborhood would come in herds to seize it, and then would ensue such a battle as I had described, with terrible wounds made by their claws on both sides, although they seldom were able to kill one another, for want of such convenient instruments of death as we had invented. At other times the like battles have been fought between the Yahoos of several neighborhoods without any visible cause; those of one district watching all opportunities to surprise the next before they are prepared. But if they find their project hath miscarried, they return home, and for want of enemies, engage in what I call a civil war among themselves.

That, in some fields of his country, there are certain shining stones of several colors, whereof the Yahoos are violently fond; and when part of these stones are fixed in the earth, as it sometimes happeneth, they will dig with their claws for whole days to get them out, and carry them away, and hide them by heaps in their kennels; but still looking round with great caution, for fear their comrades should find out their treasure. My master said he could never discover the reason of this unnatural appetite, or how these stones could be of any use to a Yahoo; but now he believed it might proceed from the same principle of avarice, which I had ascribed to mankind. That he had once, by way of experiment, privately removed a heap of these stones from the place where one of his Yahoos had buried it, whereupon, the sordid animal missing his treasure, by his loud lamenting brought the whole herd to the place, there miserably howled, then fell to biting and tearing the rest; began to pine away, would neither eat nor sleep, nor work, till he ordered a servant privately to convey the stones into the same hole, and hide them as before; which when his Yahoo had found, he presently recovered his spirits and good humor; but took care to remove them to a better hiding place; and hath ever since been a very serviceable brute.

My master farther assured me, which I also observed myself, that in the fields where these shining stones abound, the fiercest and most frequent battles are fought, occasioned by perpetual inroads of the neighboring Yahoos.

He said it was common when two Yahoos discovered such a stone in a field, and were contending which of them should be the proprietor, a third would take the advantage, and carry it away from them both; which my master would needs contend to have some resemblance with our suits at law; wherein I thought it for our credit not to undeceive him; since the decision he mentioned was much more equitable than many decrees among us; because the plaintiff and defendant there lost nothing beside the stone they contended for; whereas our courts of equity would never have dismissed the cause while either of them had anything left.

My master continuing his discourse said there was nothing that rendered the Yahoos more odious, than their undistinguished appetite to devour everything that came in their way, whether herbs, roots, berries, corrupted flesh of animals, or all mingled together; and it was peculiar in their temper, that they were fonder of what they could get by rapine or stealth at a greater distance, than much better food provided for them at home. If their prey held out, they would eat till they were ready to burst, after which nature had pointed out to them a certain root that gave them a general evacuation.

There was also another kind of root very juicy, but something rare and difficult to be found, which the Yahoos sought for with much eagerness, and would suck it with great delight; it produced the same effects that wine hath upon us. It would make them sometimes hug, and sometimes tear one another; they would howl and grin, and chatter, and reel, and tumble, and then fall asleep in the mud.

I did indeed observe that the Yahoos were the only animals in this country subject to any diseases; which however, were much fewer than horses have among us, and contracted not by any ill treatment they meet with, but by the nastiness and greediness of that sordid brute. Neither has their language any more than a general appellation for those maladies; which is borrowed from the name of the beast, and called *Hnea Yahoo*, or the Yahoo's Evil; and the cure prescribed is a mixture of their own dung and urine, forcibly put down the Yahoo's throat. This I have since often known to have been taken with success, and do here freely recommend it to my countrymen, for the public good, as an admirable specific against all diseases produced by repletion.

As to learning, government, arts, manufactures, and the like, my master confessed he could find little or no resemblance between the Yahoos of that country and those in ours. For he only meant to observe what parity there was in our natures. He had heard indeed some curious Houyhnhnms observe that in most herds there was a sort of ruling Yahoo (as among us there is generally some leading or principal stag in a park) who was always more deformed in body, and mischievous in disposition, than any of the rest. That this leader had usually a favorite as like himself as he could get, whose employment was to lick his master's feet and posteriors, and drive the female Yahoos to his kennel; for which he was now and then rewarded with a piece of ass's flesh. This favorite is hated by the whole herd; and therefore to protect himself, keeps always near the person of his leader. He usually continues in office till a worse can be found; but the very moment he is discarded, his successor, at the head of all the Yahoos in that district, young and old, male and female, come in a body, and discharge their excrements upon him from head to foot. But how far this might be applicable to our courts and favorites, and ministers of state, my master said I could best determine.

I durst make no return to this malicious insinuation, which debased human understanding below the sagacity of a common hound, who hath judgment enough to distinguish and follow the cry of the ablest dog in the pack, without being ever mistaken.

My master told me there were some qualities remarkable in the Yahoos, which he had not observed me to mention, or at least very slightly, in the accounts I had given him of humankind. He said, those animals, like other brutes, had their females in common; but in this they differed, that the she-Yahoo would admit the male while she was pregnant; and that the hes would quarrel and fight with the females as fiercely as with each other. Both which practices were such degrees of infamous brutality, that no other sensitive creature ever arrived at.

Another thing he wondered at in the Yahoos was their strange disposition to nastiness and dirt; whereas there appears to be a natural love of cleanliness in all other animals. As to the two former accusations, I was glad to let them pass without any reply, because I had not a word to offer upon them in defense of my species, which otherwise I certainly had done from my own inclinations. But I could have easily vindicated humankind from the imputation of singularity upon the last article, if there had been any swine in that country (as unluckily for me there were not) which although it may be a sweeter quadruped than a Yahoo, cannot I humbly conceive in justice pretend to more cleanliness; and so his honor himself must have owned, if he had seen their filthy way of feeding, and their custom of wallowing and sleeping in the mud.

My master likewise mentioned another quality, which his servants had discovered in several Yahoos, and to him was wholly unaccountable. He said, a fancy would sometimes take a Yahoo, to retire into a corner, to lie down and howl, and groan, and spurn away all that came near him, although he were young and fat, and wanted neither food nor water; nor did the servants imagine what could possibly ail him. And the only remedy they found was to set him to hard work, after which he would infallibly come to himself. To this I was silent out of partiality to my own kind; yet here I could plainly discover the true seeds of spleen,[3] which only seizeth on the lazy, the luxurious, and the rich; who, if they were forced to undergo the same regimen, I would undertake for the cure.

His Honor had farther observed, that a female Yahoo would often stand behind a bank or a bush, to gaze on the young males passing by, and then appear, and hide, using many antic gestures and grimaces; at which time it was observed, that she had a most offensive smell; and when any of the males advanced, would slowly retire, looking back, and with a counterfeit show of fear, run off into some convenient place where she knew the male would follow her.

At other times, if a female stranger came among them, three or four of her own sex would get about her, and stare and chatter, and grin, and smell her all over; and then turn off with gestures that seemed to express contempt and disdain.

Perhaps my master might refine a little in these speculations, which he had drawn from what he observed himself, or had been told by others; however, I could not reflect without some amazement, and much sorrow, that the rudiments of lewdness, coquetry, censure, and scandal, should have place by instinct in womankind.

I expected every moment that my master would accuse the Yahoos of those unnatural appetites in both sexes, so common among us. But Nature it seems hath not been so expert a schoolmistress; and these politer pleasures are entirely the productions of art and reason, on our side of the globe.

CHAPTER 8. *The Author relateth several particulars of the Yahoos. The great virtues of the Houyhnhnms. The education and exercises of their youth. Their general assembly.*

As I ought to have understood human nature much better than I supposed it possible for my master to do, so it was easy to apply the character he gave of the Yahoos to myself and my countrymen; and I believed I could yet make farther discoveries from my own observation. I therefore often begged his honor to let me go among the herds of Yahoos in the neighborhood; to which he always very graciously consented, being perfectly convinced that the hatred I bore those brutes would never suffer me to be corrupted by them; and his honor ordered one of his servants, a strong sorrel nag, very honest and good-natured, to be my guard; without whose protection I durst not

3. Hypochondria.

undertake such adventures. For I have already told the reader how much I was pestered by those odious animals upon my first arrival. I afterwards failed very narrowly three or four times of falling into their clutches, when I happened to stray at any distance without my hanger. And I have reason to believe, they had some imagination that I was of their own species, which I often assisted myself, by stripping up my sleeves, and shewing my naked arms and breast in their sight, when my protector was with me; at which times they would approach as near as they durst, and imitate my actions after the manner of monkeys, but ever with great signs of hatred; as a tame jackdaw with cap and stockings is always persecuted by the wild ones, when he happens to be got among them.

They are prodigiously nimble from their infancy; however, I once caught a young male of three years old, and endeavored by all marks of tenderness to make it quiet; but the little imp fell a squalling, scratching, and biting with such violence, that I was forced to let it go; and it was high time, for a whole troop of old ones came about us at the noise; but finding the cub was safe (for away it ran) and my sorrel nag being by, they durst not venture near us. I observed the young animal's flesh to smell very rank, and the stink was somewhat between a weasel and a fox, but much more disagreeable. I forgot another circumstance (and perhaps I might have the reader's pardon, if it were wholly omitted) that while I held the odious vermin in my hands, it voided its filthy excrements of a yellow liquid substance, all over my clothes; but by good fortune there was a small brook hard by, where I washed myself as clean as I could; although I durst not come into my master's presence until I were sufficiently aired.

By what I could discover, the Yahoos appear to be the most unteachable of all animals, their capacities never reaching higher than to draw or carry burdens. Yet I am of opinion, this defect ariseth chiefly from a perverse, restive disposition. For they are cunning, malicious, treacherous and revengeful. They are strong and hardy, but of a cowardly spirit, and by consequence insolent, abject, and cruel. It is observed that the red-haired of both sexes are more libidinous and mischievous than the rest, whom yet they much exceed in strength and activity.

The Houyhnhnms keep the Yahoos for present use in huts not far from the house; but the rest are sent abroad to certain fields, where they dig up roots, eat several kinds of herbs, and search about for carrion, or sometimes catch weasels and *luhimuhs* (a sort of wild rat) which they greedily devour. Nature hath taught them to dig deep holes with their nails on the side of a rising ground, wherein they lie by themselves; only the kennels of the females are larger, sufficient to hold two or three cubs.

They swim from their infancy like frogs, and are able to continue long under water, where they often take fish, which the females carry home to their young. And upon this occasion, I hope the reader will pardon my relating an odd adventure.

Being one day abroad with my protector the sorrel nag, and the weather exceeding hot, I entreated him to let me bathe in a river that was near. He consented, and I immediately stripped myself stark naked, and went down softly into the stream. It happened that a young female Yahoo standing behind a bank, saw the whole proceeding; and inflamed by desire, as the nag and I conjectured, came running with all speed, and leaped into the water within five yards of the place where I bathed. I was never in my life so terribly frighted; the nag was grazing at some distance, not suspecting any harm. She embraced me after a most fulsome manner; I roared as loud as I could, and the nag came galloping towards me, whereupon she quitted her grasp, with the utmost reluctancy, and leaped upon the opposite bank, where she stood gazing and howling all the time I was putting on my clothes.

This was matter of diversion to my master and his family, as well as of mortification to myself. For now I could no longer deny that I was a real Yahoo, in every limb and feature, since the females had a natural propensity to me as one of their own species; neither was the hair of this brute of a red color (which might have been some excuse for an appetite a little irregular) but black as a sloe, and her countenance did not make an appearance altogether so hideous as the rest of the kind; for I think, she could not be above eleven years old.

Having already lived three years in this country, the reader I suppose will expect that I should, like other travelers, give him some account of the manners and customs of its inhabitants, which it was indeed my principal study to learn.

As these noble Houyhnhnms are endowed by Nature with a general disposition to all virtues, and have no conceptions or ideas of what is evil in a rational creature; so their grand maxim is to cultivate reason, and to be wholly governed by it. Neither is reason among them a point problematical as with us, where men can argue with plausibility on both sides of a question; but strikes you with immediate conviction; as it must needs do where it is not mingled, obscured, or discolored by passion and interest. I remember it was with extreme difficulty that I could bring my master to understand the meaning of the word "opinion," or how a point could be disputable; because reason taught us to affirm or deny only where we are certain; and beyond our knowledge we cannot do either. So that controversies, wranglings, disputes, and positiveness in false or dubious propositions are evils unknown among the Houyhnhnms. In the like manner when I used to explain to him our several systems of natural philosophy,[4] he would laugh that a creature pretending to reason should value itself upon the knowledge of other people's conjectures, and in things, where that knowledge, if it were certain, could be of no use. Wherein he agreed entirely with the sentiments of Socrates, as Plato delivers them, which I mention as the highest honor I can do that prince of philosophers. I have often since reflected what destruction such a doctrine would make in the libraries of Europe; and how many paths to fame would be then shut up in the learned world.

Friendship and benevolence are the two principal virtues among the Houyhnhnms; and these not confined to particular objects, but universal to the whole race. For a stranger from the remotest part is equally treated with the nearest neighbor, and wherever he goes, looks upon himself as at home. They preserve decency and civility in the highest degrees, but are altogether ignorant of ceremony. They have no fondness for their colts or foals; but the care they take in educating them proceedeth entirely from the dictates of reason. And I observed my master to show the same affection to his neighbor's issue that he had for his own. They will have it that Nature teaches

4. Science.

them to love the whole species, and it is reason only that maketh a distinction of persons, where there is a superior degree of virtue.

When the matron Houyhnhnms have produced one of each sex, they no longer accompany with their consorts, except they lose one of their issue by some casualty, which very seldom happens; but in such a case they meet again; or when the like accident befalls a person whose wife is past bearing, some other couple bestows on him one of their own colts, and then go together a second time, until the mother be pregnant. This caution is necessary to prevent the country from being overburdened with numbers. But the race of inferior Houyhnhnms bred up to be servants is not so strictly limited upon this article; these are allowed to produce three of each sex, to be domestics in the noble families.

In their marriages they are exactly careful to choose such colors as will not make any disagreeable mixture in the breed. Strength is chiefly valued in the male, and comeliness in the female; not upon the account of love, but to preserve the race from degenerating; for, where a female happens to excel in strength, a consort is chosen with regard to comeliness. Courtship, love, presents, jointures, settlements, have no place in their thoughts, or terms whereby to express them in their language. The young couple meet and are joined, merely because it is the determination of their parents and friends; it is what they see done every day; and they look upon it as one of the necessary actions in a reasonable being. But the violation of marriage, or any other unchastity, was never heard of; and the married pair pass their lives with the same friendship and mutual benevolence that they bear to all others of the same species who come in their way, without jealousy, fondness, quarreling, or discontent.

In educating the youth of both sexes, their method is admirable, and highly deserveth our imitation. These are not suffered to taste a grain of oats, except upon certain days, till eighteen years old; nor milk, but very rarely; and in summer they graze two hours in the morning, and as many in the evening, which their parents likewise observe; but the servants are not allowed above half that time; and a great part of the grass is brought home, which they eat at the most convenient hours when they can be best spared from work.

Temperance, industry, exercise, and cleanliness are the lessons equally enjoined to the young ones of both sexes; and my master thought it monstrous in us to give the females a different kind of education from the males, except in some articles of domestic management; whereby, as he truly observed, one half of our natives were good for nothing but bringing children into the world; and to trust the care of their children to such useless animals, he said was yet a greater instance of brutality.

But the Houyhnhnms train up their youth to strength, speed, and hardiness, by exercising them in running races up and down steep hills, or over hard stony grounds; and when they are all in a sweat, they are ordered to leap over head and ears into a pond or a river. Four times a year the youth of certain districts meet to show their proficiency in running, and leaping, and other feats of strength or agility; where the victor is rewarded with a song made in his or her praise. On this festival the servants drive a herd of Yahoos into the field, laden with hay, and oats, and milk for a repast to the Houyhnhnms; after which these brutes are immediately driven back again, for fear of being noisome to the assembly.

Every fourth year, at the vernal equinox, there is a representative council of the whole nation, which meets in a plain about twenty miles from our house, and continueth about five or six days. Here they inquire into the state and condition of the several districts; whether they abound or be deficient in hay or oats, or cows or Yahoos? And wherever there is any want (which is but seldom) it is immediately supplied by unanimous consent and contribution. Here likewise the regulation of children is settled: as for instance, if a Houyhnhnm hath two males, he changeth one of them with another who hath two females, and when a child hath been lost by any casualty, where the mother is past breeding, it is determined what family in the district shall breed another to supply the loss.

CHAPTER 9. *A grand debate at the general assembly of the Houyhnhnms, and how it was determined. The learning of the Houyhnhnms. Their buildings. Their manner of burials. The defectiveness of their language.*

One of these grand assemblies was held in my time, about three months before my departure, whither my master went as the representative of our district. In this council was resumed their old debate, and indeed, the only debate that ever happened in their country; whereof my master after his return gave me a very particular account.

The question to be debated was whether the Yahoos should be exterminated from the face of the earth. One of the members for the affirmative offered several arguments of great strength and weight, alleging that, as the Yahoos were the most filthy, noisome, and deformed animal which nature ever produced, so they were the most restive and indocible,[5] mischievous, and malicious; they would privately suck the teats of the Houyhnhnms' cows; kill and devour their cats, trample down their oats and grass, if they were not continually watched; and commit a thousand other extravagancies. He took notice of a general tradition, that Yahoos had not been always in their country, but that many ages ago, two of these brutes appeared together upon a mountain; whether produced by the heat of the sun upon corrupted mud and slime, or from the ooze and froth of the sea, was never known. That these Yahoos engendered, and their brood in a short time grew so numerous as to overrun and infest the whole nation. That the Houyhnhnms to get rid of this evil, made a general hunting, and at last enclosed the whole herd; and destroying the older, every Houyhnhnm kept two young ones in a kennel, and brought them to such a degree of tameness as an animal so savage by nature can be capable of acquiring, using them for draught and carriage. That there seemed to be much truth in this tradition, and that those creatures could not be *ylnhniamshy* (or aborigines of the land) because of the violent hatred the Houyhnhnms as well as all other animals bore them; which although their evil disposition sufficiently deserved, could never have arrived at so high a degree, if they had been aborigines, or else they would have long since been rooted out. That the inhabitants taking a fancy to use the service of the Yahoos, had very imprudently neglected to cultivate the breed of asses, which were a comely animal, easily kept, more tame and orderly, without any offensive smell, strong enough for labor, although they yield to the other

5. Unteachable.

in agility of body; and if their braying be no agreeable sound, it is far preferable to the horrible howlings of the Yahoos.

Several others declared their sentiments to the same purpose, when my master proposed an expedient to the assembly, whereof he had indeed borrowed the hint from me. He approved of the tradition, mentioned by the honorable member, who spoke before; and affirmed, that the two Yahoos said to be first seen among them, had been driven thither over the sea; that coming to land, and being forsaken by their companions, they retired to the mountains, and degenerating by degrees, became in process of time much more savage than those of their own species in the country from whence these two originals came. The reason of his assertion was that he had now in his possession a certain wonderful Yahoo (meaning myself) which most of them had heard of, and many of them had seen. He then related to them how he first found me; that my body was all covered with an artificial composure of the skins and hairs of other animals; that I spoke in a language of my own, and had thoroughly learned theirs; that I had related to him the accidents which brought me thither; that when he saw me without my covering, I was an exact Yahoo in every part, only of a whiter color, less hairy and with shorter claws. He added how I had endeavored to persuade him that in my own and other countries the Yahoos acted as the governing, rational animal, and held the Houyhnhnms in servitude; that he observed in me all the qualities of a Yahoo, only a little more civilized by some tincture of reason, which however was in a degree as far inferior to the Houyhnhnm race as the Yahoos of their country were to me; that among other things, I mentioned a custom we had of castrating Houyhnhnms when they were young, in order to render them tame; that the operation was easy and safe; that it was no shame to learn wisdom from brutes, as industry is taught by the ant, and building by the swallow (for so I translate the world *lyhannh*, although it be a much larger fowl). That this invention might be practiced upon the younger Yahoos here, which, besides rendering them tractable and fitter for use, would in an age put an end to the whole species without destroying life. That in the meantime the Houyhnhnms should be exhorted to cultivate the breed of asses, which, as they are in all respects more valuable brutes, so they have this advantage, to be fit for service at five years old, which the other are not till twelve.

This was all my master thought fit to tell me at that time, of what passed in the grand council. But he was pleased to conceal one particular, which related personally to myself, whereof I soon felt the unhappy effect, as the reader will know in its proper place, and from whence I date all the succeeding misfortunes of my life.

The Houyhnhnms have no letters, and consequently, their knowledge is all traditional. But there happening few events of any moment among a people so well united, naturally disposed to every virtue, wholly governed by reason, and cut off from all commerce with other nations, the historical part is easily preserved without burdening their memories. I have already observed that they are subject to no diseases, and therefore can have no need of physicians. However, they have excellent medicines composed of herbs, to cure accidental bruises and cuts in the pastern or frog of the foot by sharp stones, as well as other maims and hurts in the several parts of the body.

They calculate the year by the revolution of the sun and the moon, but use no subdivisions into weeks. They are well enough acquainted with the motions of those two luminaries, and understand the nature of eclipses; and this is the utmost progress of their astronomy.

In poetry they must be allowed to excel all other mortals; wherein the justness of their similes, and the minuteness, as well as exactness of their descriptions, are indeed inimitable. Their verses abound very much in both of these, and usually contain either some exalted notions of friendship and benevolence, or the praises of those who were victors in races and other bodily exercises. Their buildings, although very rude and simple, are not inconvenient, but well contrived to defend them from all injuries of cold and heat. They have a kind of tree, which at forty years old loosens in the root, and falls with the first storm; it grows very straight, and being pointed like stakes with a sharp stone (for the Houyhnhnms know not the use of iron), they stick them erect in the ground about ten inches asunder, and then weave in oat straw, or sometimes wattles, betwixt them. The roof is made after the same manner, and so are the doors.

The Houyhnhnms use the hollow part between the pastern and the hoof of their forefeet as we do our hands, and this with greater dexterity than I could at first imagine. I have seen a white mare of our family thread a needle (which I lent her on purpose) with that joint. They milk their cows, reap their oats, and do all the work which requires hands in the same manner. They have a kind of hard flints, which by grinding against other stones they form into instruments that serve instead of wedges, axes, and hammers. With tools made of these flints, they likewise cut their hay, and reap their oats, which there groweth naturally in several fields. The Yahoos draw home the sheaves in carriages, and the servants tread them in certain covered huts, to get out the grain, which is kept in stores. They make a rude kind of earthen and wooden vessels, and bake the former in the sun.

If they can avoid casualties, they die only of old age, and are buried in the obscurest places that can be found, their friends and relations expressing neither joy nor grief at their departure; nor does the dying person discover the least regret that he is leaving the world, any more than if he were upon returning home from a visit to one of his neighbors; I remember my master having once made an appointment with a friend and his family to come to his house upon some affair of importance; on the day fixed, the mistress and her two children came very late; she made two excuses, first for her husband, who, as she said, happened that very morning to *lhnuwnh*. The word is strongly expressive in their language, but not easily rendered into English; it signifies, *to retire to his first Mother*. Her excuse for not coming sooner was that her husband dying late in the morning, she was a good while consulting her servants about a convenient place where his body should be laid; and I observed she behaved herself at our house, as cheerfully as the rest. She died about three months after.

They live generally to seventy or seventy-five years, very seldom to four-score; some weeks before their death they feel a gradual decay, but without pain. During this time they are much visited by their friends, because they cannot go abroad with their usual ease and satisfaction. However, about ten days before their death, which they seldom fail in computing, they return the visits that have been made by those who are nearest in the neighborhood, being carried in a convenient sledge drawn by Yahoos; which vehicle they use, not only upon this occasion, but when they grow old, upon long journeys, or when they are lamed by any accident. And therefore when the dying Houyhnhnms return those visits, they take a solemn leave of their friends, as if they were going to some remote part of the country, where they designed to pass the rest of their lives.

I know not whether it may be worth observing, that the Houyhnhnms have no word in their language to express anything that is evil, except what they borrow from the deformities or ill qualities of the Yahoos. Thus they denote the folly of a servant, an omission of a child, a stone that cuts their feet, a continuance of foul or unseasonable weather, and the like, by adding to each the epithet of Yahoo. For instance, *hhnm Yahoo, whnaholm Yahoo, ynlhmndwihlma Yahoo,* and an ill-contrived house, *ynholmhnmrohlnw Yahoo.*

I could with great pleasure enlarge farther upon the manners and virtues of this excellent people; but intending in a short time to publish a volume by itself expressly upon that subject, I refer the reader thither. And in the meantime, proceed to relate my own sad catastrophe.

CHAPTER 10. *The Author's economy, and happy life among the Houyhnhnms. His great improvement in virtue, by conversing with them. Their conversations. The Author hath notice given him by his master that he must depart from the country. He falls into a swoon for grief, but submits. He contrives and finishes a canoe, by the help of a fellow servant, and puts to sea at a venture.*

I had settled my little economy to my own heart's content. My master had ordered a room to be made for me after their manner, about six yards from the house; the sides and floors of which I plastered with clay, and covered with rush mats of my own contriving; I had beaten hemp, which there grows wild, and made of it a sort of ticking; this I filled with the feathers of several birds I had taken with springes made of Yahoos' hairs, and were excellent food. I had worked two chairs with my knife, the sorrel nag helping me in the grosser and more laborious part. When my clothes were worn to rags, I made myself others with the skins of rabbits, and of a certain beautiful animal about the same size, called *nnuhnoh,* the skin of which is covered with a fine down. Of these I likewise made very tolerable stockings. I soled my shoes with wood which I cut from a tree, and fitted to the upper leather, and when this was worn out, I supplied it with the skins of Yahoos, dried in the sun. I often got honey out of hollow trees, which I mingled with water, or eat it with my bread. No man could more verify the truth of these two maxims, that *Nature is very easily satisfied;* and, that *Necessity is the mother of invention.* I enjoyed perfect health of body, and tranquility of mind; I did not feel the treachery or inconstancy of a friend, nor the inquiries of a secret or open enemy. I had no occasion of bribing, flattering, or pimping to procure the favor of any great man, or of his minion. I wanted no fence against fraud or oppression; here was neither physician to destroy my body, nor lawyer to ruin my fortune; no informer to watch my words and actions, or forge accusations against me for hire; here were no gibers, censurers, backbiters, pickpockets, highwaymen, housebreakers, attorneys, bawds, buffoons, gamesters, politicians, wits, splenetics, tedious talkers, controvertists, ravishers, murderers, robbers, virtuosos;[6] no leaders or followers of party and faction;

6. Savants; those who pursue special interests in the arts or sciences.

no encouragers to vice, by seducement or examples; no dungeons, axes, gibbets, whipping posts, or pillories; no cheating shopkeepers or mechanics; no
pride, vanity or affectation; no fops, bullies, drunkards, strolling whores, or
poxes; no ranting, lewd, expensive wives; no stupid, proud pedants; no importunate, overbearing, quarrelsome, noisy, roaring, empty, conceited, swearing
companions; no scoundrels raised from the dust upon the merit of their vices;
or nobility thrown into it on account of their virtues; no lords, fiddlers,
judges, or dancing masters.

I had the favor of being admitted to several Houyhnhnms, who came to
visit or dine with my master; where his honor graciously suffered me to wait
in the room, and listen to their discourse. Both he and his company would
often descend to ask me questions, and receive my answers. I had also sometimes the honor of attending my master in his visits to others. I never presumed to speak, except in answer to a question; and then I did it with inward
regret, because it was a loss of so much time for improving myself; but I was
infinitely delighted with the station of an humble auditor in such conversations, where nothing passed but what was useful, expressed in the fewest
and most significant words; where (as I have already said) the greatest
decency was observed, without the least degree of ceremony; where no person spoke without being pleased himself, and pleasing his companions;
where there was no interruption, tediousness, heat, or difference of sentiments. They have a notion, that when people are met together, a short silence
doth much improve conversation; this I found to be true; for during those
little intermissions of talk, new ideas would arise in their minds, which very
much enlivened the discourse. Their subjects are generally on friendship and
benevolence; on order and economy; sometimes upon the visible operations
of nature, or ancient traditions; upon the bounds and limits of virtue; upon
the unerring rules of reason; or upon some determinations, to be taken at
the next great assembly; and often upon the various excellencies of poetry. I
may add, without vanity, that my presence often gave them sufficient matter
for discourse, because it afforded my master an occasion of letting his friends
into the history of me and my country, upon which they were all pleased to
descant in a manner not very advantageous to human kind; and for that
reason I shall not repeat what they said; only I may be allowed to observe
that his honor, to my great admiration, appeared to understand the nature
of Yahoos much better than myself. He went through all our vices and follies,
and discovered many which I had never mentioned to him; by only supposing
what qualities a Yahoo of their country, with a small proportion of reason,
might be capable of exerting; and concluded, with too much probability, how
vile as well as miserable such a creature must be.

I freely confess, that all the little knowledge I have of any value was
acquired by the lectures I received from my master, and from hearing the
discourses of him and his friends; to which I should be prouder to listen,
than to dictate to the greatest and wisest assembly in Europe. I admired the
strength, comeliness, and speed of the inhabitants; and such a constellation
of virtues in such amiable persons produced in me the highest veneration.
At first, indeed, I did not feel that natural awe which the Yahoos and all other
animals bear towards them; but it grew upon me by degrees, much sooner
than I imagined, and was mingled with a respectful love and gratitude, that
they would condescend to distinguish me from the rest of my species.

When I thought of my family, my friends, my countrymen, or human race in general, I considered them as they really were, Yahoos in shape and disposition, perhaps a little more civilized, and qualified with the gift of speech; but making no other use of reason than to improve and multiply those vices, whereof their brethren in this country had only the share that nature allotted them. When I happened to behold the reflection of my own form in a lake or fountain, I turned away my face in horror and detestation of myself, and could better endure the sight of a common Yahoo than of my own person. By conversing with the Houyhnhnms, and looking upon them with delight, I fell to imitate their gait and gesture, which is now grown into a habit; and my friends often tell me in a blunt way, that I trot like a horse; which, however, I take for a great compliment. Neither shall I disown, that in speaking I am apt to fall into the voice and manner of the Houyhnhnms, and hear myself ridiculed on that account without the least mortification.

In the midst of this happiness, when I looked upon myself to be fully settled for life, my master sent for me one morning a little earlier than his usual hour. I observed by his countenance that he was in some perplexity, and at a loss how to begin what he had to speak. After a short silence, he told me, he did not know how I would take what he was going to say; that, in the last general assembly, when the affair of the Yahoos was entered upon, the representatives had taken offense at his keeping a Yahoo (meaning myself) in his family more like a Houyhnhnm than a brute animal. That he was known frequently to converse with me, as if he could receive some advantage of pleasure in my company; that such a practice was not agreeable to reason or nature, or a thing ever heard of before among them. The assembly did therefore exhort him, either to employ me like the rest of my species, or command me to swim back to the place from whence I came. That the first of these expedients was utterly rejected by all the Houyhnhnms who had ever seen me at his house or their own; for, they alleged, that because I had some rudiments of reason, added to the natural pravity[7] of those animals, it was to be feared, I might be able to seduce them into the woody and mountainous parts of the country, and bring them in troops by night to destroy the Houyhnhnms' cattle, as being naturally of the ravenous kind, and averse from labor.

My master added that he was daily pressed by the Houyhnhnms of the neighborhood to have the assembly's exhortation executed, which he could not put off much longer. He doubted[8] it would be impossible for me to swim to another country; and therefore wished I would contrive some sort of vehicle resembling those I had described to him, that might carry me on the sea; in which work I should have the assistance of his own servants, as well as those of his neighbors. He concluded that for his own part he could have been content to keep me in his service as long as I lived; because he found I had cured myself of some bad habits and dispositions, by endeavoring, as far as my inferior nature was capable, to imitate the Houyhnhnms.

I should here observe to the reader, that a decree of the general assembly in this country is expressed by the word *hnhloayn*, which signifies an exhortation, as near as I can render it; for they have no conception how a rational creature can be compelled, but only advised, or exhorted; because no person can disobey reason without giving up his claim to be a rational creature.

7. Corruption.   8. Feared.

I was struck with the utmost grief and despair at my master's discourse; and being unable to support the agonies I was under, I fell into a swoon at his feet; when I came to myself, he told me that he concluded I had been dead (for these people are subject to no such imbecilities of nature). I answered, in a faint voice, that death would have been too great an happiness; that although I could not blame the assembly's exhortation, or the urgency of his friends; yet in my weak and corrupt judgment, I thought it might consist with reason to have been less rigorous. That I could not swim a league, and probably the nearest land to theirs might be distant above an hundred; that many materials, necessary for making a small vessel to carry me off, were wholly wanting in this country, which, however, I would attempt in obedience and gratitude to his honor, although I concluded the thing to be impossible, and therefore looked on myself as already devoted[9] to destruction. That the certain prospect of an unnatural death was the least of my evils; for, supposing I should escape with life by some strange adventure, how could I think with temper[1] of passing my days among Yahoos, and relapsing into my old corruptions, for want of examples to lead and keep me within the paths of virtue. That I knew too well upon what solid reasons all the determinations of the wise Houyhnhnms were founded, not to be shaken by arguments of mine, a miserable Yahoo; and therefore after presenting him with my humble thanks for the offer of his servants' assistance in making a vessel, and desiring a reasonable time for so difficult a work, I told him I would endeavor to preserve a wretched being; and, if ever I returned to England, was not without hopes of being useful to my own species by celebrating the praises of the renowned Houyhnhnms, and proposing their virtues to the imitation of mankind.

My master in a few words made me a very gracious reply, allowed me the space of two months to finish my boat, and ordered the sorrel nag, my fellow servant (for so at this distance I may presume to call him), to follow my instructions, because I told my master that his help would be sufficient, and I knew he had a tenderness for me.

In his company my first business was to go to that part of the coast where my rebellious crew had ordered me to be set on shore. I got upon a height, and looking on every side into the sea, fancied I saw a small island towards the northeast; I took out my pocket glass, and could then clearly distinguish it about five leagues off, as I computed; but it appeared to the sorrel nag to be only a blue cloud; for, as he had no conception of any country besides his own, so he could not be as expert in distinguishing remote objects at sea, as we who so much converse in that element.

After I had discovered this island, I considered no farther; but resolved, it should, if possible, be the first place of my banishment, leaving the consequence to fortune.

I returned home, and consulting with the sorrel nag, we went into a copse at some distance, where I with my knive, and he with a sharp flint fastened very artificially,[2] after their manner, to a wooden handle, cut down several oak wattles about the thickness of a walking staff, and some larger pieces. But I shall not trouble the reader with a particular description of my own mechanics; let it suffice to say, that in six weeks time, with the help of the

9. Doomed.   2. Artfully.
1. Equanimity.

sorrel nag, who performed the parts that required most labor, I finished a sort of Indian canoe; but much larger, covering it with the skins of Yahoos, well stitched together, with hempen threads of my own making. My sail was likewise composed of the skins of the same animal; but I made use of the youngest I could get, the older being too tough and thick; and I likewise provided myself with four paddles. I laid in a stock of boiled flesh, of rabbits and fowls; and took with me two vessels, one filled with milk, and the other with water.

I tried my canoe in a large pond near my master's house, and then corrected in it what was amiss, stopping all the chinks with Yahoo's tallow, till I found it staunch, and able to bear me and my freight. And when it was as complete as I could possibly make it, I had it drawn on a carriage very gently by Yahoos, to the seaside, under the conduct of the sorrel nag and another servant.

When all was ready, and the day came for my departure, I took leave of my master and lady, and the whole family, my eyes flowing with tears and my heart quite sunk with grief. But his honor, out of curiosity, and perhaps (if I may speak it without vanity) partly out of kindness, was determined to see me in my canoe; and got several of his neighboring friends to accompany him. I was forced to wait above an hour for the tide, and then observing the wind very fortunately bearing towards the island to which I intended to steer my course, I took a second leave of my master; but as I was going to prostrate myself to kiss his hoof, he did me the honor to raise it gently to my mouth. I am not ignorant how much I have been censured for mentioning this last particular. Detractors are pleased to think it improbable that so illustrious a person should descend to give so great a mark of distinction to a creature so inferior as I. Neither have I forgot how apt some travelers are to boast of extraordinary favors they have received. But, if these censurers were better acquainted with the noble and courteous disposition of the Houyhnhnms, they would soon change their opinion. I paid my respects to the rest of the Houyhnhnms in his honor's company; then getting into my canoe, I pushed off from shore.

CHAPTER 11. *The Author's dangerous voyage. He arrives at New Holland, hoping to settle there. Is wounded with an arrow by one of the natives. Is seized and carried by force into a Portuguese ship. The great civilities of the Captain. The Author arrives at England.*

I began this desperate voyage on February 15, 1714/5,[3] at 9 o'clock in the morning. The wind was very favorable; however, I made use at first only of my paddles; but considering I should soon be weary, and that the wind might probably chop about, I ventured to set up my little sail, and thus, with the help of the tide, I went at the rate of a league and a half an hour, as near as I could guess. My master and his friends continued on the shore, till I was almost out of sight; and I often heard the sorrel nag (who always loved me) crying out, *"Hnuy illa nyha maiah Yahoo"* ("Take care of thyself, gentle Yahoo").

My design was, if possible, to discover some small island uninhabited, yet

---

3. I.e., 1715, by modern dating. The year began on March 25.

sufficient by my labor to furnish me with necessaries of life, which I would have thought a greater happiness than to be first minister in the politest court of Europe, so horrible was the idea I conceived of returning to live in the society and under the government of Yahoos. For in such a solitude as I desired, I could at least enjoy my own thoughts, and reflect with delight on the virtues of those inimitable Houyhnhnms, without any opportunity of degenerating into the vices and corruptions of my own species.

The reader may remember what I related when my crew conspired against me, and confined me to my cabin, how I continued there several weeks, without knowing what course we took; and when I was put ashore in the longboat, how the sailors told me with oaths, whether true or false, that they knew not in what part of the world we were. However, I did then believe us to be about 10 degrees southward of the Cape of Good Hope, or about 45 degrees southern latitude, as I gathered from some general words I overheard among them, being I supposed to the southeast in their intended voyage to Madagascar. And although this were but little better than conjecture, yet I resolved to steer my course eastward, hoping to reach the southwest coast of New Holland, and perhaps some such island as I desired, lying westward of it. The wind was full west, and by six in the evening I computed I had gone eastward at least eighteen leagues; when I spied a very small island about half a league off, which I soon reached. It was nothing but a rock with one creek, naturally arched by the force of tempests. Here I put in my canoe, and climbing a part of the rock, I could plainly discover land to the east, extending from south to north. I lay all night in my canoe; and repeating my voyage early in the morning, I arrived in seven hours to the southeast point of New Holland. This confirmed me in the opinion I have long entertained, that the maps and charts place this country at least three degrees more to the east than it really is; which thought I communicated many years ago to my worthy friend Mr. Herman Moll,[4] and gave him my reasons for it, although he hath rather chosen to follow other authors.

I saw no inhabitants in the place where I landed; and being unarmed, I was afraid of venturing far into the country. I found some shellfish on the shore, and eat them raw, not daring to kindle a fire, for fear of being discovered by the natives. I continued three days feeding on oysters and limpets, to save my own provisions; and I fortunately found a brook of excellent water, which gave me great relief.

On the fourth day, venturing out early a little too far, I saw twenty or thirty natives upon a height, not above five hundred yards from me. They were stark naked, men, women, and children round a fire, as I could discover by the smoke. One of them spied me, and gave notice to the rest; five of them advanced towards me, leaving the women and children at the fire. I made what haste I could to the shore, and getting into my canoe, shoved off; the savages observing me retreat, ran after me; and before I could get far enough into the sea, discharged an arrow, which wounded me deeply on the inside of my left knee. (I shall carry the mark to my grave.) I apprehended the arrow might be poisoned; and paddling out of the reach of their darts (being a calm day) I made a shift to suck the wound, and dress it as well as I could.

I was at a loss what to do, for I durst not return to the same landing place,

4. A famous contemporary map maker.

but stood to the north, and was forced to paddle; for the wind, although very gentle, was against me, blowing northwest. As I was looking about for a secure landing place, I saw a sail to the north northeast, which appearing every minute more visible, I was in some doubt whether I should wait for them or no; but at last my detestation of the Yahoo race prevailed; and turning my canoe, I sailed and paddled together to the south, and got into the same creek from whence I set out in the morning, choosing rather to trust myself among these barbarians than live with European Yahoos. I drew up my canoe as close as I could to the shore, and hid myself behind a stone by the little brook, which, as I have already said, was excellent water.

The ship came within half a league of this creek, and sent out her longboat with vessels to take in fresh water (for the place it seems was very well known), but I did not observe it until the boat was almost on shore; and it was too late to seek another hiding place. The seamen at their landing observed my canoe, and rummaging it all over, easily conjectured that the owner could not be far off. Four of them well armed searched every cranny and lurking hole, till at last they found me flat on my face behind the stone. They gazed a while in admiration at my strange uncouth dress; my coat made of skins, my wooden-soled shoes, and my furred stockings; from whence, however, they concluded I was not a native of the place, who all go naked. One of the seamen in Portuguese bid me rise, and asked who I was. I understood that language very well, and getting upon my feet, said I was a poor Yahoo, banished from the Houyhnhnms, and desired they would please to let me depart. They admired to hear me answer them in their own tongue, and saw by my complexion I must be an European; but were at a loss to know what I meant by Yahoos and Houyhnhnms, and at the same time fell a laughing at my strange tone in speaking, which resembled the neighing of a horse. I trembled all the while betwixt fear and hatred; I again desired leave to depart, and was gently moving to my canoe; but they laid hold on me, desiring to know what country I was of? whence I came? with many other questions. I told them I was born in England, from whence I came about five years ago, and then their country and ours was at peace. I therefore hoped they would not treat me as an enemy, since I meant them no harm, but was a poor Yahoo, seeking some desolate place where to pass the remainder of his unfortunate life.

When they began to talk, I thought I never heard or saw any thing so unnatural; for it appeared to me as monstrous as if a dog or a cow should speak in England, or a Yahoo in Houyhnhnmland. The honest Portuguese were equally amazed at my strange dress, and the odd manner of delivering my words, which however they understood very well. They spoke to me with great humanity, and said they were sure their Captain would carry me *gratis* to Lisbon, from whence I might return to my own country; that two of the seamen would go back to the ship, to inform the Captain of what they had seen, and receive his orders; in the meantime, unless I would give my solemn oath not to fly, they would secure me by force. I thought it best to comply with their proposal. They were very curious to know my story, but I gave them very little satisfaction; and they all conjectured, that my misfortunes had impaired my reason. In two hours the boat, which went laden with vessels of water, returned with the Captain's commands to fetch me on board. I fell on my knees to preserve my liberty; but all was in vain, and the men having tied me with cords, heaved me into the boat, from whence I was taken into the ship, and from thence into the Captain's cabin.

His name was Pedro de Mendez; he was a very courteous and generous person; he entreated me to give some account of myself, and desired to know what I would eat or drink; said I should be used as well as himself, and spoke so many obliging things, that I wondered to find such civilities from a Yahoo. However, I remained silent and sullen; I was ready to faint at the very smell of him and his men. At last I desired something to eat out of my own canoe; but he ordered me a chicken and some excellent wine, and then directed that I should be put to bed in a very clean cabin. I would not undress myself, but lay on the bedclothes; and in half an hour stole out, when I thought the crew was at dinner; and getting to the side of the ship, was going to leap into the sea, and swim for my life, rather than continue among Yahoos. But one of the seamen prevented me, and having informed the Captain, I was chained to my cabin.

After dinner Don Pedro came to me, and desired to know my reason for so desperate an attempt; assured me he only meant to do me all the service he was able; and spoke so very movingly, that at last I descended to treat him like an animal which had some little portion of reason. I gave him a very short relation of my voyage; of the conspiracy against me by my own men; of the country where they set me on shore, and of my five years residence there. All which he looked upon as if it were a dream or a vision; whereat I took great offense; for I had quite forgot the faculty of lying, so peculiar to Yahoos in all countries where they preside, and consequently the disposition of suspecting truth in others of their own species. I asked him whether it were the custom of his country to *say the thing that was not?* I assured him I had almost forgot what he meant by falsehood; and if I had lived a thousand years in Houyhnhnmland, I should never have heard a lie from the meanest servant. That I was altogether indifferent whether he believed me or no; but however, in return for his favors, I would give so much allowance to the corruption of his nature, as to answer any objection he would please to make; and he might easily discover the truth.

The Captain, a wise man, after many endeavors to catch me tripping in some part of my story, at last began to have a better opinion of my veracity. But he added that since I professed so inviolable an attachment to truth, I must give him my word of honor to bear him company in this voyage without attempting anything against my life; or else he would continue me a prisoner till we arrived at Lisbon. I gave him the promise he required; but at the same time protested that I would suffer the greatest hardships rather than return to live among Yahoos.

Our voyage passed without any considerable accident. In gratitude to the Captain I sometimes sat with him at his earnest request, and strove to conceal my antipathy against humankind, although it often broke out; which he suffered to pass without observation. But the greatest part of the day, I confined myself to my cabin, to avoid seeing any of the crew. The Captain had often entreated me to strip myself of my savage dress, and offered to lend me the best suit of clothes he had. This I would not be prevailed on to accept, abhorring to cover myself with anything that had been on the back of a

Yahoo. I only desired he would lend me two clean shirts, which having been washed since he wore them, I believed would not so much defile me. These I changed every second day, and washed them myself.

We arrived at Lisbon, Nov. 5, 1715. At our landing, the Captain forced me to cover myself with his cloak, to prevent the rabble from crowding about me. I was conveyed to his own house; and at my earnest request, he led me up to the highest room backwards.[5] I conjured him to conceal from all persons what I had told him of the Houyhnhnms; because the least hint of such a story would not only draw numbers of people to see me, but probably put me in danger of being imprisoned, or burned by the Inquisition. The Captain persuaded me to accept a suit of clothes newly made; but I would not suffer the tailor to take my measure; however, Don Pedro being almost of my size, they fitted me well enough. He accoutered me with other necessaries, all new, which I aired for twenty-four hours before I would use them.

The Captain had no wife, nor above three servants, none of which were suffered to attend at meals; and his whole deportment was so obliging, added to very good human understanding, that I really began to tolerate his company. He gained so far upon me, that I ventured to look out of the back window. By degrees I was brought into another room, from whence I peeped into the street, but drew my head back in a fright. In a week's time he seduced me down to the door. I found my terror gradually lessened, but my hatred and contempt seemed to increase. I was at last bold enough to walk the street in his company, but kept my nose well stopped with rue, or sometimes with tobacco.

In ten days, Don Pedro, to whom I had given some account of my domestic affairs, put it upon me as a point of honor and conscience that I ought to return to my native country, and live at home with my wife and children. He told me there was an English ship in the port just ready to sail, and he would furnish me with all things necessary. It would be tedious to repeat his arguments, and my contradictions. He said it was altogether impossible to find such a solitary island as I had desired to live in; but I might command in my own house, and pass my time in a manner as recluse as I pleased.

I complied at last, finding I could not do better. I left Lisbon the 24th day of November, in an English merchantman, but who was the Master I never inquired. Don Pedro accompanied me to the ship, and lent me twenty pounds. He took kind leave of me, and embraced me at parting; which I bore as well as I could. During this last voyage I had no commerce with the Master, or any of his men; but pretending I was sick kept close in my cabin. On the fifth of December, 1715, we cast anchor in the Downs about nine in the morning, and at three in the afternoon I got safe to my house at Redriff.

My wife and family received me with great surprise and joy, because they concluded me certainly dead; but I must freely confess, the sight of them filled me only with hatred, disgust, and contempt; and the more, by reflecting on the near alliance I had to them. For although since my unfortunate exile from the Houyhnhnm country, I had compelled myself to tolerate the sight of Yahoos, and to converse with Don Pedro de Mendez; yet my memory and imaginations were perpetually filled with the virtues and ideas of those

5. At the rear.

exalted Houyhnhnms. And when I began to consider that by copulating with one of the Yahoo species, I had become a parent of more, it struck me with the utmost shame, confusion, and horror.

As soon as I entered the house, my wife took me in her arms, and kissed me; at which, having not been used to the touch of that odious animal for so many years, I fell in a swoon for almost an hour. At the time I am writing, it is five years since my last return to England. During the first year I could not endure my wife or children in my presence, the very smell of them was intolerable; much less could I suffer them to eat in the same room. To this hour they dare not presume to touch my bread, or drink out of the same cup; neither was I ever able to let one of them take me by the hand. The first money I laid out was to buy two young stone-horses,[6] which I keep in a good stable, and next to them the groom is my greatest favorite; for I feel my spirits revived by the smell he contracts in the stable. My horses understand me tolerably well; I converse with them at least four hours every day. They are strangers to bridle or saddle; they live in great amity with me, and friendship to each other.

CHAPTER 12. *The Author's veracity. His design in publishing this work. His censure of those travelers who swerve from the truth. The Author clears himself from any sinister ends in writing. His native country commended. The right of the crown to those countries described by the Author is justified. The difficulty of conquering them. The Author takes his last leave of the reader; proposeth his manner of living for the future; gives good advice, and concludeth.*

Thus gentle reader, I have given thee a faithful history of my travels for sixteen years, and above seven months; wherein I have not been so studious of ornament as of truth. I could perhaps like others have astonished thee with strange improbable tales; but I rather chose to relate plain matter of fact in the simplest manner and style; because my principal design was to inform, and not to amuse thee.

It is easy for us who travel into remote countries, which are seldom visited by Englishmen or other Europeans, to form descriptions of wonderful animals both at sea and land. Whereas a traveler's chief aim should be to make men wiser and better, and to improve their minds by the bad as well as good example of what they deliver concerning foreign places.

I could heartily wish a law were enacted, that every traveler, before he were permitted to publish his voyages, should be obliged to make oath before the Lord High Chancellor that all he intended to print was absolutely true to the best of his knowledge; for then the world would no longer be deceived as it usually is, while some writers, to make their works pass the better upon the public, impose the grossest falsities on the unwary reader. I have perused several books of travels with great delight in my younger days; but, having since gone over most parts of the globe, and been able to contradict many fabulous accounts from my own observation, it hath given me a great disgust against this part of reading, and some indignation to see the credulity of mankind so impudently abused. Therefore, since my acquaintance were pleased to think my poor endeavors might not be unacceptable to my coun-

6. Stallions.

try, I imposed on myself as a maxim, never to be swerved from, that I would *strictly adhere to truth;* neither indeed can I be ever under the least temptation to vary from it, while I retain in my mind the lectures and example of my noble master, and the other illustrious Houyhnhnms, of whom I had so long the honor to be an humble hearer.

> ——*Nec si miserum Fortuna Sinonem*
> *Finxit, vanum etiam, mendacemque improba finget.*[7]

I know very well how little reputation is to be got by writings which require neither genius nor learning, nor indeed any other talent, except a good memory, or an exact *Journal.* I know likewise, that writers of travels, like dictionary-makers, are sunk into oblivion by the weight and bulk of those who come last, and therefore lie uppermost. And it is highly probable that such travelers who shall hereafter visit the countries described in this work of mine, may be detecting my errors (if there be any) and adding many new discoveries of their own, jostle me out of vogue, and stand in my place, making the world forget that ever I was an author. This indeed would be too great a mortification if I wrote for fame; but, as my sole intention was the PUBLIC GOOD, I cannot be altogether disappointed. For, who can read the virtues I have mentioned in the glorious Houyhnhnms, without being ashamed of his own vices, when he considers himself as the reasoning, governing animal of his country? I shall say nothing of those remote nations where Yahoos preside; amongst which the least corrupted are the Brobdingnagians, whose wise maxims in morality and government it would be our happiness to observe. But I forbear descanting further, and rather leave the judicious reader to his own remarks and applications.

I am not a little pleased that this work of mine can possibly meet with no censurers; for what objections can be made against a writer who relates only plain facts that happened in such distant countries, where we have not the least interest with respect either to trade or negotiations? I have carefully avoided every fault with which common writers of travels are often too justly charged. Besides, I meddle not the least with any party, but write without passion, prejudice, or ill-will against any man or number of men whatsoever. I write for the noblest end, to inform and instruct mankind, over whom I may, without breach of modesty, pretend to some superiority, from the advantages I received by conversing so long among the most accomplished Houyhnhnms. I write without any view towards profit or praise. I never suffer a word to pass that may look like a reflection, or possibly give the least offense even to those who are most ready to take it. So that, I hope, I may with justice pronounce myself an Author perfectly blameless; against whom the tribes of answerers, considerers, observers, reflectors, detecters, remarkers will never be able to find matter for exercising their talents.

I confess it was whispered to me that I was bound in duty as a subject of England, to have given in a memorial[8] to a secretary of state, at my first coming over; because, whatever lands are discovered by a subject, belong to the Crown. But I doubt whether our conquests in the countries I treat of would be as easy as those of Ferdinando Cortez over the naked Americans.

---

7. Nor if Fortune had molded Sinon for misery, will she also in spite mold him as false and lying (Latin; Virgil's *Aeneid* 2.79–80).

8. Statement of facts for government use.

The Lilliputians, I think, are hardly worth the charge of a fleet and army to reduce them; and I question whether it might be prudent or safe to attempt the Brobdingnagians; or, whether an English army would be much at their ease with the Flying Island over their heads. The Houyhnhnms, indeed, appear not to be so well prepared for war, a science to which they are perfect strangers, and especially against missive weapons. However, supposing myself to be a minister of state, I could never give my advice for invading them. Their prudence, unanimity, unacquaintedness with fear, and their love of their country would amply supply all defects in the military art. Imagine twenty thousand of them breaking into the midst of an European army, confounding the ranks, overturning the carriages, battering the warriors' faces into mummy, by terrible yerks[9] from their hinder hoofs: for they would well deserve the character given to Augustus, *Recalcitrat undique tutus*.[1] But instead of proposals for conquering that magnanimous nation, I rather wish they were in a capacity or disposition to send a sufficient number of their inhabitants for civilizing Europe; by teaching us the first principles of Honor, Justice, Truth, Temperance, public Spirit, Fortitude, Chastity, Friendship, Benevolence, and Fidelity. The names of all which virtues are still retained among us in most languages, and are to be met with in modern as well as ancient authors, which I am able to assert from my own small reading.

But I had another reason which made me less forward to enlarge his majesty's dominions by my discoveries: to say the truth, I had conceived a few scruples with relation to the distributive justice of princes upon those occasions. For instance, a crew of pirates are driven by a storm they know not whither; at length a boy discovers land from the topmast; they go on shore to rob and plunder; they see an harmless people, are entertained with kindness, they give the country a new name, they take formal possession of it for the king, they set up a rotten plank or a stone for a memorial, they murder two or three dozen of the natives, bring away a couple more by force for a sample, return home, and get their pardon. Here commences a new dominion acquired with a title by Divine Right. Ships are sent with the first opportunity; the natives driven out or destroyed, their princes tortured to discover their gold; a free license given to all acts of inhumanity and lust; the earth reeking with the blood of its inhabitants: and this execrable crew of butchers employed in so pious an expedition is a *modern colony* sent to convert and civilize an idolatrous and barbarous people.

But this description, I confess, doth by no means affect the British nation, who may be an example to the whole world for their wisdom, care, and justice in planting colonies; their liberal endowments for the advancement of religion and learning; their choice of devout and able pastors to propagate Christianity; their caution in stocking their provinces with people of sober lives and conversations from this the Mother Kingdom; their strict regard to the distribution of justice, in supplying the civil administration through all their colonies with officers of the greatest abilities, utter strangers to corruption: and to crown all, by sending the most vigilant and virtuous governors, who have no other views than the happiness of the people over whom they preside, and the honor of the king their master.

9. Kicks. "Mummy": pulp.
1. He kicks backward, at every point on his guard (Latin; Horace's *Satires* 2.1.20).

But, as those countries which I have described do not appear to have any desire of being conquered, and enslaved, murdered, or driven out by colonies, nor abound either in gold, silver, sugar, or tobacco, I did humbly conceive they were by no means proper objects of our zeal, our valor, or our interest. However, if those whom it may concern, think fit to be of another opinion, I am ready to depose, when I shall be lawfully called, that no European did ever visit these countries before me. I mean, if the inhabitants ought to be believed.

But, as to the formality of taking possession in my sovereign's name, it never came once into my thoughts; and if it had, yet as my affairs then stood, I should perhaps in point of prudence and self-preservation have put it off to a better opportunity.

Having thus answered the only objection that can be raised against me as a traveler, I here take a final leave of my courteous readers, and return to enjoy my own speculations in my little garden at Redriff; to apply those excellent lessons of virtue which I learned among the Houyhnhnms; to instruct the Yahoos of my own family as far as I shall find them docible animals; to behold my figure often in a glass, and thus if possible habituate myself by time to tolerate the sight of a human creature; to lament the brutality of Houyhnhnms in my own country, but always treat their persons with respect, for the sake of my noble master, his family, his friends, and the whole Houyhnhnm race, whom these of ours have the honor to resemble in all their lineaments, however their intellectuals came to degenerate.

I began last week to permit my wife to sit at dinner with me, at the farthest end of a long table; and to answer (but with the utmost brevity) the few questions I ask her. Yet the smell of a Yahoo continuing very offensive, I always keep my nose well stopped with rue, lavender, or tobacco leaves. And although it be hard for a man late in life to remove old habits, I am not altogether out of hopes in some time to suffer a neighbor Yahoo in my company, without the apprehensions I am yet under of his teeth or his claws.

My reconcilement to the Yahoo kind in general might not be so difficult, if they would be content with those vices and follies only which nature hath entitled them to. I am not in the least provoked at the sight of a lawyer, a pickpocket, a colonel, a fool, a lord, a gamester, a politician, a whoremonger, a physician, an evidence,[2] a suborner, an attorney, a traitor, or the like: this is all according to the due course of things. But when I behold a lump of deformity, and diseases both in body and mind, smitten with *pride,* it immediately breaks all the measures of my patience; neither shall I be ever able to comprehend how such an animal and such a vice could tally together. The wise and virtuous Houyhnhnms, who abound in all excellencies that can adorn a rational creature, have no name for this vice in their language, which hath no terms to express anything that is evil, except those whereby they describe the detestable qualities of their Yahoos, among which they were not able to distinguish this of pride, for want of thoroughly understanding human nature, as it showeth itself in other countries, where that animal presides. But I, who had more experience, could plainly observe some rudiments of it among the wild Yahoos.

But the Houyhnhnms, who live under the government of reason, are no

2. Witness.

more proud of the good qualities they possess, than I should be for not wanting a leg or an arm, which no man in his wits would boast of, although he must be miserable without them. I dwell the longer upon this subject from the desire I have to make the society of an English Yahoo by any means not insupportable; and therefore I here entreat those who have any tincture of this absurd vice, that they will not presume to appear in my sight.

1726, 1735

A Modest Proposal[1]

FOR PREVENTING THE CHILDREN OF POOR PEOPLE IN IRELAND FROM BEING A BURDEN TO THEIR PARENTS OR COUNTRY, AND FOR MAKING THEM BENEFICIAL TO THE PUBLIC

It is a melancholy object to those who walk through this great town[2] or travel in the country, when they see the streets, the roads, and cabin doors, crowded with beggars of the female sex, followed by three, four, or six children, all in rags and importuning every passenger for an alms. These mothers, instead of being able to work for their honest livelihood, are forced to employ all their time in strolling to beg sustenance for their helpless infants, who, as they grow up, either turn thieves for want of work, or leave their dear native country to fight for the Pretender in Spain, or sell themselves to the Barbadoes.[3]

I think it is agreed by all parties that this prodigious number of children in the arms, or on the backs, or at the heels of their mothers, and frequently of their fathers, is in the present deplorable state of the kingdom a very great additional grievance; and therefore whoever could find out a fair, cheap, and easy method of making these children sound, useful members of the commonwealth would deserve so well of the public as to have his statue set up for a preserver of the nation.

But my intention is very far from being confined to provide only for the children of professed beggars; it is of a much greater extent, and shall take in the whole number of infants at a certain age who are born of parents in effect as little able to support them as those who demand our charity in the streets.

1. *A Modest Proposal* is an example of Swift's favorite satiric devices used with superb effect. Irony (from the deceptive adjective *modest* in the title to the very last sentence) pervades the piece. A rigorous logic deduces ghastly arguments from a premise so quietly assumed that readers assent before they are aware of what that assent implies. Parody, at which Swift is adept, allows him to glance sardonically at the by then familiar figure of the benevolent humanitarian (forerunner of the modern sociologist, social worker, and economic planner) concerned to correct a social evil by means of a theoretically conceived plan. The proposer, as naive as he is apparently logical and kindly, ignores and therefore emphasizes for the reader the enormity of his plan. The whole is an elaboration of a rather trite metaphor: "The English are devouring the Irish." But there is noth-

ing trite about the pamphlet, which expresses in Swift's most controlled style his pity for the oppressed, ignorant, populous, and hungry Catholic peasants of Ireland and his anger at the rapacious English absentee landlords, who were bleeding the country white with the silent approbation of Parliament, ministers, and the crown.
2. Dublin.
3. James Francis Edward Stuart (1688–1766), the son of James II, was claimant ("Pretender") to the throne of England from which the Glorious Revolution had barred his succession. Catholic Ireland was loyal to him, and Irishmen joined him in his exile on the Continent. Because of the poverty in Ireland, many Irishmen emigrated to the West Indies and other British colonies in America; they paid their passage by binding themselves to work for a stated period for one of the planters.

As to my own part, having turned my thoughts for many years upon this important subject, and maturely weighed the several schemes of other projectors,[4] I have always found them grossly mistaken in their computation. It is true, a child just dropped from its dam may be supported by her milk for a solar year, with little other nourishment; at most not above the value of two shillings, which the mother may certainly get, or the value in scraps, by her lawful occupation of begging; and it is exactly at one year old that I propose to provide for them in such a manner as instead of being a charge upon their parents or the parish, or wanting food and raiment for the rest of their lives, they shall on the contrary contribute to the feeding, and partly to the clothing, of many thousands.

There is likewise another great advantage in my scheme, that it will prevent those voluntary abortions, and that horrid practice of women murdering their bastard children, alas, too frequent among us, sacrificing the poor innocent babes, I doubt, more to avoid the expense than the shame, which would move tears and pity in the most savage and inhuman breast.

The number of souls in this kingdom[5] being usually reckoned one million and a half, of these I calculate there may be about two hundred thousand couple whose wives are breeders; from which number I subtract thirty thousand couples who are able to maintain their own children, although I apprehend there cannot be so many under the present distresses of the kingdom; but this being granted, there will remain an hundred and seventy thousand breeders. I again subtract fifty thousand for those women who miscarry, or whose children die by accident or disease within the year. There only remain an hundred and twenty thousand children of poor parents annually born. The question therefore is, how this number shall be reared and provided for, which, as I have already said, under the present situation of affairs, is utterly impossible by all the methods hitherto proposed. For we can neither employ them in handicraft or agriculture; we neither build houses (I mean in the country) nor cultivate land. They can very seldom pick up a livelihood by stealing till they arrive at six years old, except where they are of towardly parts;[6] although I confess they learn the rudiments much earlier, during which time they can however be looked upon only as probationers, as I have been informed by a principal gentleman in the county of Cavan, who protested to me that he never knew above one or two instances under the ages of six, even in a part of the kingdom so renowned for the quickest proficiency in that art.

I am assured by our merchants that a boy or a girl before twelve years old is no salable commodity; and even when they come to this age they will not yield above three pounds, or three pounds and half a crown at most on the Exchange; which cannot turn to account either to the parents or the kingdom, the charge of nutriment and rags having been at least four times that value.

I shall now therefore humbly propose my own thoughts, which I hope will not be liable to the least objection.

I have been assured by a very knowing American of my acquaintance in London, that a young healthy child well nursed is at a year old a most deli-

4. Devisers of schemes.
5. Ireland.
6. Promising abilities.

cious, nourishing, and wholesome food, whether stewed, roasted, baked, or boiled; and I make no doubt that it will equally serve in a fricassee or a ragout.[7]

I do therefore humbly offer it to public consideration that of the hundred and twenty thousand children, already computed, twenty thousand may be reserved for breed, whereof only one fourth part to be males, which is more than we allow to sheep, black cattle, or swine; and my reason is that these children are seldom the fruits of marriage, a circumstance not much regarded by our savages, therefore one male will be sufficient to serve four females. That the remaining hundred thousand may at a year old be offered in sale to the persons of quality and fortune through the kingdom, always advising the mother to let them suck plentifully in the last month, so as to render them plump and fat for a good table. A child will make two dishes at an entertainment for friends; and when the family dines alone, the fore or hind quarter will make a reasonable dish, and seasoned with a little pepper or salt will be very good boiled on the fourth day, especially in winter.

I have reckoned upon a medium that a child just born will weigh twelve pounds, and in a solar year if tolerably nursed increaseth to twenty-eight pounds.

I grant this food will be somewhat dear, and therefore very proper for landlords, who, as they have already devoured most of the parents, seem to have the best title to the children.

Infant's flesh will be in season throughout the year, but more plentiful in March, and a little before and after. For we are told by a grave author, an eminent French physician,[8] that fish being a prolific diet, there are more children born in Roman Catholic countries about nine months after Lent than at any other season; therefore, reckoning a year after Lent, the markets will be more glutted than usual, because the number of popish infants is at least three to one in this kingdom; and therefore it will have one other collateral advantage, by lessening the number of Papists among us.

I have already computed the charge of nursing a beggar's child (in which list I reckon all cottagers, laborers, and four fifths of the farmers) to be about two shillings per annum, rags included; and I believe no gentleman would repine to give ten shillings for the carcass of a good fat child, which, as I have said, will make four dishes of excellent nutritive meat, when he hath only some particular friend or his own family to dine with him. Thus the squire will learn to be a good landlord, and grow popular among the tenants; the mother will have eight shillings net profit, and be fit for the work till she produces another child.

Those who are more thrifty (as I must confess the times require) may flay the carcass; the skin of which artificially[9] dressed will make admirable gloves for ladies, and summer boots for fine gentlemen.

As to our city of Dublin, shambles[1] may be appointed for this purpose in the most convenient parts of it, and butchers we may be assured will not be wanting; although I rather recommend buying the children alive, and dressing them hot from the knife as we do roasting pigs.

A very worthy person, a true lover of his country, and whose virtues I highly

7. A highly seasoned meat stew.
8. François Rabelais (ca. 1494–1553), a humorist and satirist, by no means grave.
9. Skillfully.
1. Slaughterhouses.

esteem, was lately pleased in discoursing on this matter to offer a refinement upon my scheme. He said that many gentlemen of this kingdom, having of late destroyed their deer, he conceived that the want of venison might be well supplied by the bodies of young lads and maidens, not exceeding fourteen years of age nor under twelve, so great a number of both sexes in every county being now ready to starve for want of work and service; and these to be disposed of by their parents, if alive, or otherwise by their nearest relations. But with due deference to so excellent a friend and so deserving a patriot, I cannot be altogether in his sentiments; for as to the males, my American acquaintance assured me from frequent experience that their flesh was generally tough and lean, like that of our schoolboys, by continual exercise, and their taste disagreeable; and to fatten them would not answer the charge. Then as to the females, it would, I think with humble submission, be a loss to the public, because they soon would become breeders themselves; and besides, it is not improbable that some scrupulous people might be apt to censure such a practice (although indeed very unjustly) as a little bordering upon cruelty; which I confess, hath always been with me the strongest objection against any project, how well soever intended.

But in order to justify my friend, he confessed that this expedient was put into his head by the famous Psalmanazar,[2] a native of the island Formosa, who came from thence to London above twenty years ago, and in conversation told my friend that in his country when any young person happened to be put to death, the executioner sold the carcass to persons of quality as a prime dainty; and that in his time the body of a plump girl of fifteen, who was crucified for an attempt to poison the emperor, was sold to his Imperial Majesty's prime minister of state, and other great mandarins of the court, in joints from the gibbet, at four hundred crowns. Neither indeed can I deny that if the same use were made of several plump young girls in this town, who without one single groat to their fortunes cannot stir abroad without a chair, and appear at the playhouse and assemblies in foreign fineries which they never will pay for, the kingdom would not be the worse.

Some persons of a desponding spirit are in great concern about that vast number of poor people who are aged, diseased, or maimed, and I have been desired to employ my thoughts what course may be taken to ease the nation of so grievous an encumbrance. But I am not in the least pain upon that matter, because it is very well known that they are every day dying and rotting by cold and famine, and filth and vermin, as fast as can be reasonably expected. And as to the younger laborers, they are now in almost as hopeful a condition. They cannot get work, and consequently pine away for want of nourishment to a degree that if at any time they are accidentally hired to common labor, they have not strength to perform it; and thus the country and themselves are happily delivered from the evils to come.

I have too long digressed, and therefore shall return to my subject. I think the advantages by the proposal which I have made are obvious and many, as well as of the highest importance.

For first, as I have already observed, it would greatly lessen the number of Papists, with whom we are yearly overrun, being the principal breeders of the nation as well as our most dangerous enemies; and who stay at home on

2. George Psalmanazar (ca. 1679–1763), a famous impostor. A Frenchman, he imposed himself on English bishops, noblemen, and scientists as a Formosan. He wrote an entirely fictitious account of Formosa, in which he described human sacrifices and cannibalism.

purpose to deliver the kingdom to the Pretender, hoping to take their advantage by the absence of so many good Protestants, who have chosen rather to leave their country than stay at home and pay tithes against their conscience to an Episcopal curate.

Secondly, the poorer tenants will have something valuable of their own, which by law may be made liable to distress,[3] and help to pay their landlord's rent, their corn and cattle being already seized and money a thing unknown.

Thirdly, whereas the maintenance of an hundred thousand children, from two years old and upwards, cannot be computed at less than ten shillings a piece per annum, the nation's stock will be thereby increased fifty thousand pounds per annum, besides the profit of a new dish introduced to the tables of all gentlemen of fortune in the kingdom who have any refinement in taste. And the money will circulate among ourselves, the goods being entirely of our own growth and manufacture.

Fourthly, the constant breeders, besides the gain of eight shillings sterling per annum by the sale of their children, will be rid of the charge of maintaining them after the first year.

Fifthly, this food would likewise bring great custom to taverns, where the vintners will certainly be so prudent as to procure the best receipts for dressing it to perfection, and consequently have their houses frequented by all the fine gentlemen, who justly value themselves upon their knowledge in good eating; and a skillful cook, who understands how to oblige his guests, will contrive to make it as expensive as they please.

Sixthly, this would be a great inducement to marriage, which all wise nations have either encouraged by rewards or enforced by laws and penalties. It would increase the care and tenderness of mothers toward their children, when they were sure of a settlement for life to the poor babes, provided in some sort by the public, to their annual profit instead of expense. We should see an honest emulation among the married women, which of them could bring the fattest child to the market. Men would become as fond of their wives during the time of their pregnancy as they are now of their mares in foal, their cows in calf, or sows when they are ready to farrow; nor offer to beat or kick them (as is too frequent a practice) for fear of a miscarriage.

Many other advantages might be enumerated. For instance, the addition of some thousand carcasses in our exportation of barreled beef, the propagation of swine's flesh, and improvement in the art of making good bacon, so much wanted among us by the great destruction of pigs, too frequent at our tables, which are no way comparable in taste or magnificence to a well-grown, fat, yearling child, which roasted whole will make a considerable figure at a lord mayor's feast or any other public entertainment. But this and many others I omit, being studious of brevity.

Supposing that one thousand families in this city would be constant customers for infants' flesh, besides others who might have it at merry meetings, particularly weddings and christenings, I compute that Dublin would take off annually about twenty thousand carcasses, and the rest of the kingdom (where probably they will be sold somewhat cheaper) the remaining eighty thousand.

I can think of no one objection that will probably be raised against this

---

3. Distraint, i.e., the seizing, through legal action, of property for the payment of debts and other obligations.

proposal, unless it should be urged that the number of people will be thereby much lessened in the kingdom. This I freely own, and it was indeed one principal design in offering it to the world. I desire the reader will observe, that I calculate my remedy for this one individual kingdom of Ireland and for no other that ever was, is, or I think ever can be upon earth. Therefore let no man talk to me of other expedients: of taxing our absentees at five shillings a pound: of using neither clothes nor household furniture except what is of our own growth and manufacture: of utterly rejecting the materials and instruments that promote foreign luxury: of curing the expensiveness of pride, vanity, idleness, and gaming in our women: of introducing a vein of parsimony, prudence, and temperance: of learning to love our country, in the want of which we differ even from Laplanders and the inhabitants of Topinamboo:[4] of quitting our animosities and factions, nor acting any longer like the Jews, who were murdering one another at the very moment their city was taken:[5] of being a little cautious not to sell our country and conscience for nothing: of teaching landlords to have at least one degree of mercy toward their tenants: lastly, of putting a spirit of honesty, industry, and skill into our shopkeepers; who, if a resolution could now be taken to buy only our native goods, would immediately unite to cheat and exact upon us in the price, the measure, and the goodness, nor could ever yet be brought to make one fair proposal of just dealing, though often and earnestly invited to it.[6]

Therefore I repeat, let no man talk to me of these and the like expedients, till he hath at least some glimpse of hope that there will ever be some hearty and sincere attempt to put them in practice.

But as to myself, having been wearied out for many years with offering vain, idle, visionary thoughts, and at length utterly despairing of success, I fortunately fell upon this proposal, which, as it is wholly new, so it hath something solid and real, of no expense and little trouble, full in our own power, and whereby we can incur no danger in disobliging England. For this kind of commodity will not bear exportation, the flesh being of too tender a consistence to admit a long continuance in salt, although perhaps I could name a country which would be glad to eat up our whole nation without it.[7]

After all, I am not so violently bent upon my own opinion as to reject any offer proposed by wise men, which shall be found equally innocent, cheap, easy, and effectual. But before something of that kind shall be advanced in contradiction to my scheme, and offering a better, I desire the author or authors will be pleased maturely to consider two points. First, as things now stand, how they will be able to find food and raiment for an hundred thousand useless mouths and backs. And secondly, there being a round million of creatures in human figure throughout this kingdom, whose sole subsistence put into a common stock would leave them in debt two millions of pounds sterling, adding those who are beggars by profession to the bulk of farmers, cottagers, and laborers, with their wives and children who are beggars in effect; I desire those politicians who dislike my overture, and may perhaps be so bold to attempt an answer, that they will first ask the parents

4. I.e., even Laplanders love their frozen, infertile country and the savage tribes of Brazil love their jungle more than the Anglo-Irish love Ireland.
5. During the siege of Jerusalem by the Roman emperor Titus, who captured and destroyed the city in 70 C.E., bloody fights broke out between

factions of fanatics.
6. Swift himself had made all these proposals in various pamphlets. In editions printed during his lifetime the various proposals were italicized to indicate that Swift is no longer being ironic.
7. I.e., England.

of these mortals whether they would not at this day think it a great happiness to have been sold for food at a year old in the manner I prescribe, and thereby have avoided such a perpetual sense of misfortunes as they have since gone through by the oppression of landlords, the impossibility of paying rent without money or trade, the want of common sustenance, with neither house nor clothes to cover them from the inclemencies of the weather, and the most inevitable prospect of entailing the like or greater miseries upon their breed forever.

I profess, in the sincerity of my heart, that I have not the least personal interest in endeavoring to promote this necessary work, having no other motive than the public good of my country, by advancing our trade, providing for infants, relieving the poor, and giving some pleasure to the rich. I have no children by which I can propose to get a single penny; the youngest being nine years old, and my wife past childbearing.

1729

ALEXANDER POPE
1688–1744

Alexander Pope is the only important writer of his generation who was solely a man of letters. Because he could not, as a Roman Catholic, attend a university, vote, or hold public office, he was excluded from the sort of patronage that was bestowed by statesmen on many writers during the reign of Anne. This disadvantage he turned into a positive good, for the translation of Homer's *Iliad* and *Odyssey,* which he undertook for profit as well as for fame, gave him ample means to live the life of an independent suburban gentleman. After 1718 he lived hospitably in his villa by the Thames at Twickenham (then pronounced *Twit'nam*), entertaining his friends and converting his five acres of land into a diminutive landscape garden. Almost exactly a century earlier, William Shakespeare had earned enough to retire to a country estate at Stratford—but he had been an actor-manager as well as a playwright; Pope was the first English writer to demonstrate that literature alone could be a gainful profession.

Ill health plagued Pope almost from birth. Crippled early by tuberculosis of the bone, he never grew taller than four and a half feet. In later life he suffered from violent headaches and required constant attention from servants. But Pope did not allow his infirmities to hold him back; he was always a master at making the best of what he had. Around 1700 his father, a well-to-do, retired London merchant, moved to a small property at Binfield in Windsor Forest. There, in rural surroundings, young Pope completed his education by reading whatever he pleased, "like a boy gathering flowers in the woods and fields just as they fall in his way"; and there, encouraged by his father, he began to write verse. He was already an accomplished poet in his teens; no English poet has ever been more precocious.

Pope's first striking success as a poet was *An Essay on Criticism* (1711), which brought him Joseph Addison's approval and an intemperate personal attack from the critic John Dennis, who was angered by a casual reference to himself in the poem. *The Rape of the Lock,* both in its original shorter version of 1712 and in its more elaborate version of 1714, proved the author a master not only of metrics and of language but also of witty, urbane satire. In *An Essay on Criticism,* Pope had excelled all his predecessors in writing a didactic poem after the example of Horace; in the *Rape,* he had written the most brilliant mock epic in the language. But there was another vein in Pope's youthful poetry, a tender concern with natural beauty and love. The *Pastorals* (1709), his first publication, and *Windsor Forest* (1713; much of it was written earlier) abound in visual imagery and descriptive passages of ideally ordered nature; they remind us that Pope was an amateur painter. The *Elegy to the Memory of an Unfortunate Lady* and *Eloisa to Abelard,* published in the collected poems of 1717, dwell on the pangs of unhappy lovers (Pope himself never married). And even the long task of translating Homer; the "dull duty" of editing Shakespeare; and in middle age, his preoccupation with ethical and satirical poetry did not make less fine his keen sense of beauty in nature and art.

Pope's early poetry brought him to the attention of the leading wits of the town, with whom he began to associate in the masculine world of coffeehouse and tavern. Most of them were Whigs. But after the fall of the Whigs in 1710 and the formation of the Tory government under Robert Harley (later earl of Oxford) and Henry St. John (later Viscount Bolingbroke) party loyalties bred bitterness among the wits as among the politicians. By 1712, Pope had made the acquaintance of another group of writers, all Tories, who were soon his intimate friends: Jonathan Swift, by then the close associate of Harley and St. John and the principal propagandist for their policies; Dr. John Arbuthnot, physician to the queen, a learned scientist, a wit, and a man of humanity and integrity; John Gay, the poet, who in 1728 was to create *The Beggar's Opera,* the greatest theatrical success of the century; and the poet Thomas Parnell. Through them he became the friend and admirer of Oxford and later the intimate of Bolingbroke. In 1714 this group formed a club for satirizing all sorts of false learning. The friends proposed to write jointly the biography of a learned fool whom they named Martinus Scriblerus (Martin the Scribbler), whose life and opinions would be a running commentary on educated nonsense. Some amusing episodes were later rewritten and published as the *Memoirs of Martinus Scriblerus* (1741). The real importance of the club, however, is that it fostered a satiric temper that would be expressed in such mature works of the friends as *Gulliver's Travels, The Beggar's Opera,* and *The Dunciad.*

"The life of a wit is a warfare on earth," said Pope, generalizing from his own experience. Throughout his career, enemies jealous of his success derided his crippled body as well as his writings. But he was a fighter who struck back, always giving better than he got. Pope's literary warfare began in 1713, when he announced his intention of translating the *Iliad* and sought subscribers to a deluxe edition of the work. Subscribers came in droves, but the Whig writers who surrounded Addison at Button's Coffee House did all they could to discredit the venture. The eventual success of the first published installment of his *Iliad* in 1715 did not obliterate Pope's resentment against Addison and his "little senate"; and he took his revenge in the damaging portrait of Addison (under the name of Atticus), which was later included in the *Epistle to Dr. Arbuthnot* (1735), lines 193–214. The not unjustified attacks on Pope's edition of Shakespeare (1725) by the learned Shakespeare scholar Lewis Theobald (Pope always spelled and pronounced the name "Tibbald" in his satires), led to Theobald's appearance as king of the dunces in *The Dunciad* (1728). In this impressive poem Pope stigmatized his literary enemies as agents of all that he disliked and feared in the tendencies of his time—the vulgarization of taste and the arts consequent on the rapid growth of the reading public and the development of journalism, magazines, and other popular and cheap publications, which spread scandal, sensationalism, and political partisanship—in short the new commercial spirit of the nation that was corrupting not only the arts but, as Pope saw it, the national life itself.

In the 1730s Pope moved on to philosophical, ethical, and political subjects in *An Essay on Man,* the *Epistles to Several Persons,* and the *Imitations of Horace.* The reigns of George I and George II appeared to him, as to Swift and other Tories, a period of rapid moral, political, and cultural deterioration. The agents of decay fed on the rise of moneyed (as opposed to landed) wealth, which accounted for the political corruption encouraged by Sir Robert Walpole and the court party, and the corruption of all aspects of the national life by a vulgar class of *nouveaux riches*. Pope assumed the role of the champion of traditional values: of right reason, humanistic learning, sound art, good taste, and public virtue. It was fortunate that most of his enemies happened to illustrate various degrees of unreason, pedantry, bad art, vulgar taste, and at best, indifferent morals. In such an age, Pope implies, it is impossible for such a man like him—honest, truthful, blunt—not to write satire.

Pope was a master of style. From first to last, his verse is notable for its rhythmic variety, despite the apparently rigid metrical unit—the heroic couplet—in which he wrote; for the precision of meaning and the harmony (or expressive disharmony) of his language; and for the union of maximum conciseness with maximum complexity. Variety and harmony can be observed in even so short a passage as lines 71–76 of the pastoral *Summer* (1709), lines so lyrical that, in *Semele,* Handel set them to music. In the passage quoted below (as also in the following quotation), only those rhetorical stresses that distort the normal iambic flow of the verse have been marked; internal pauses within the line are indicated by single and double bars, alliteration and assonance by italics.

> Óh déign to visit our *f*orsaken *seats*,
>
> The mossy *f*ountains ‖ and the *green retreats!*
>
> Where'er yóu wálk ‖ cóol *g*áles shall *f*an the *glade,*
>
> Trées whére yóu sít ‖ shall cro*w*d into a sha*de:*
>
> Where'er yóu tŕead ‖ the bl*u*shing *f*lowers shall rise,
>
> And all thíngs *f*lóurish where yóu túrn your eyes.

Pope has attained metrical variety by the free substitution of trochees and spondees for the normal iambs; he has achieved rhythmic variety by arranging phrases and clauses (units of syntax and logic) of different lengths within single lines and couplets, so that the passage moves with the sinuous fluency of thought and feeling; and he not only has chosen musical combinations of words but has also subtly modulated the harmony of the passage by unobtrusive patterns of alliteration and assonance.

Contrast with this pastoral passage lines 16–25 of the *Epilogue to the Satires, Dialogue* 2 (1738), in which Pope is not making music but imitating actual conversation so realistically that the metrical pattern and the integrity of the couplet and individual line seem to be destroyed (although in fact they remain in place). In a dialogue with a friend who warns him that his satire is too personal, indeed mere libel, the poet-satirist replies:

> Yé státesmen, | priests of one religion all!
>
> Yé trádesmen vile ‖ in army, court, or hall!
>
> Yé réverend atheists. ‖ F. Scandal! | name them, | Who?
>
> P. Why that's the thing you bid me not to do.
>
> Whó stárved a sister, ‖ who foreswore a debt,
>
> Í néver named; ‖ the town's inquiring yet.
>
> The poisoning dame—| F. Yóu méan—| P. I don't—| F. Yóu dó.

P. Sée, nów Í kéep the secret, ‖ and nót yóu!

The bribing statesman—| F. Hóld, ‖ tóo hígh you go.

P. The bribed elector—‖ F. There you stoop tóo lów.

In such a passage the language and rhythms of poetry merge with the language and rhythms of impassioned living speech.

A fine example of Pope's ability to derive the maximum of meaning from the most economic use of language and image is the description of the manor house in which lives old Cotta, the miser (*Epistle to Lord Bathurst*, lines 187–96):

> Like some lone Chartreuse stands the good old Hall,
> Silence without, and fasts within the wall;
> No raftered roofs with dance and tabor sound,
> No noontide bell invites the country round;
> Tenants with sighs the smokeless towers survey,
> And turn the unwilling steeds another way;
> Benighted wanderers, the forest o'er,
> Curse the saved candle and unopening door;
> While the gaunt mastiff growling at the gate,
> Affrights the beggar whom he longs to eat.

The first couplet of this passage associates the "Hall," symbol of English rural hospitality, with the Grande Chartreuse, the monastery in the French Alps, which, although a place of "silence" and "fasts" for the monks, afforded food and shelter to all travelers. Then the dismal details of Cotta's miserly dwelling provide a stark contrast, and the meaning of the scene is concentrated in the grotesque image of the last couplet: the half-starved watchdog and the frightened beggar confronting each other in mutual hunger.

But another sort of variety derives from Pope's respect for the idea that the different kinds of literature have their different and appropriate styles. Thus *An Essay on Criticism*, an informal discussion of literary theory, is written, like Horace's *Art of Poetry* (a similarly didactic poem), in a plain style, the easy language of well-bred talk. *The Rape of the Lock*, "a heroi-comical poem" (that is, a comic poem that treats trivial material in an epic style), employs the lofty heroic language that John Dryden had perfected in his translation of Virgil and introduces amusing parodies of passages in *Paradise Lost*; parodies later raised to truly Miltonic sublimity and complexity by the conclusion of *The Dunciad*. *Eloisa to Abelard* renders the brooding, passionate voice of its heroine in a declamatory language, given to sudden outbursts and shifts of tone, that recalls the stage. The grave epistles that make up *An Essay on Man*, a philosophical discussion of such majestic themes as the Creator and His creation, the universe, human nature, society, and happiness, are written in a stately forensic language and tone and constantly employ the traditional rhetorical figures. The *Imitations of Horace*, and above all, the *Epistle to Dr. Arbuthnot*, his finest poem "in the Horatian way," reveal Pope's final mastery of the plain style of Horace's epistles and satires and support his image of himself as the heir of the Roman poet. In short, no other poet of the century can equal Pope in the range of his materials, the diversity of his poetic styles, and the wizardry of his technique.

An Essay on Criticism

There is no pleasanter introduction to the canons of taste in the English Augustan age than Pope's *An Essay on Criticism*. As Addison said in his review in *Spectator* 253, it assembles the "most known and most received observations on the subject of literature and criticism." Pope was attempting to do for his time what Horace, in his *Art of Poetry,* and what Nicolas Boileau (French poet of the age of Louis XIV), in his *L'Art Poétique,* had done for theirs. Horace is Pope's model not only for principles of criticism but also for style, especially in the simple, conversational language and the tone of well-bred ease.

In framing his critical creed, Pope did not try for novelty: he wished merely to give to generally accepted doctrines pleasing and memorable expression and make them useful to modern poets. Here one meets the key words of neoclassical criticism: *wit, Nature, ancients, rules,* and *genius. Wit* in the poem is a word of many meanings—a clever remark or the person who makes it, a conceit, liveliness of mind, inventiveness, fancy, genius, a genius, and poetry itself, among others. *Nature* is an equally ambiguous word, meaning not "things out there" or "the outdoors" but most important that which is representative, universal, permanent in human experience as opposed to the idiosyncratic, the individual, the temporary. In line 21, *Nature* comes close to meaning "intuitive knowledge." In line 52, it means that half-personified power manifested in the cosmic order, which in its modes of working is a model for art. The reverence felt by most Augustans for the great writers of ancient Greece and Rome raised the question how far the authority of these *ancients* extended. Were their works to be received as models to be conscientiously imitated? Were the *rules* received from them or deducible from their works to be accepted as prescriptive laws or merely convenient guides? Was individual *genius* to be bound by what has been conventionally held to be *Nature,* by the authority of the *ancients,* and by the legalistic pedantry of *rules?* Or could it go its own way?

In part 1 of the *Essay,* Pope constructs a harmonious system in which he effects a compromise among all these conflicting forces—a compromise that is typically eighteenth century in spirit. Part 2 analyzes the causes of faulty criticism. Part 3 characterizes the good critic and praises the great critics of the past.

From An Essay on Criticism

Part 1

'Tis hard to say, if greater want of skill
Appear in writing or in judging ill;
But of the two less dangerous is the offense
To tire our patience than mislead our sense.
5 Some few in that, but numbers err in this,
Ten censure° wrong for one who writes amiss;   *judge*
A fool might once himself alone expose,
Now one in verse makes many more in prose.
   'Tis with our judgments as our watches, none
10 Go just alike, yet each believes his own.
In poets as true genius is but rare,
True taste as seldom is the critic's share;
Both must alike from Heaven derive their light,
These born to judge, as well as those to write.
15 Let such teach others who themselves excel,
And censure freely who have written well.
Authors are partial to their wit, 'tis true,
But are not critics to their judgment too?
   Yet if we look more closely, we shall find
20 Most have the seeds of judgment in their mind:
Nature affords at least a glimmering light;
The lines, though touched but faintly, are drawn right.

But as the slightest sketch, if justly traced, ⎫
Is by ill coloring but the more disgraced, ⎬
25 So by false learning is good sense defaced: ⎭
Some are bewildered in the maze of schools,
And some made coxcombs[1] Nature meant but fools.
In search of wit these lose their common sense,
And then turn critics in their own defense:
30 Each burns alike, who can, or cannot write,
Or with a rival's or an eunuch's spite.
All fools have still an itching to deride,
And fain would be upon the laughing side.
If Maevius[2] scribble in Apollo's spite,
35 There are who judge still worse than he can write.
 Some have at first for wits, then poets passed,
Turned critics next, and proved plain fools at last.
Some neither can for wits nor critics pass,
As heavy mules are neither horse nor ass.
40 Those half-learn'd witlings, numerous in our isle,
As half-formed insects on the banks of Nile;[3]
Unfinished things, one knows not what to call,
Their generation's so equivocal:
To tell° them would a hundred tongues require,   *reckon, count*
45 Or one vain wit's, that might a hundred tire.
 But you who seek to give and merit fame,
And justly bear a critic's noble name,
Be sure yourself and your own reach to know,
How far your genius, taste, and learning go;
50 Launch not beyond your depth, but be discreet,
And mark that point where sense and dullness meet.
 Nature to all things fixed the limits fit,
And wisely curbed proud man's pretending wit.
As on the land while here the ocean gains,
55 In other parts it leaves wide sandy plains;
Thus in the soul while memory prevails,
The solid power of understanding fails;
Where beams of warm imagination play,
The memory's soft figures melt away.
60 One science[4] only will one genius fit,
So vast is art, so narrow human wit.
Not only bounded to peculiar arts,
But oft in those confined to single parts.
Like kings we lose the conquests gained before,
65 By vain ambition still to make them more;
Each might his several province well command,
Would all but stoop to what they understand.
 First follow Nature, and your judgment frame
By her just standard, which is still the same;
70 Unerring Nature, still divinely bright,
One clear, unchanged, and universal light,

---

1. Superficial pretenders to learning.
2. A silly poet alluded to contemptuously by Virgil in *Eclogue* 3 and by Horace in *Epode* 10.
3. The ancients believed that many forms of life were spontaneously generated in the fertile mud of the Nile.
4. Branch of learning.

Life, force, and beauty must to all impart,
At once the source, and end, and test of art.
Art from that fund each just supply provides,
75 Works without show, and without pomp presides.
In some fair body thus the informing soul
With spirits feeds, with vigor fills the whole,
Each motion guides, and every nerve sustains;
Itself unseen, but in the effects remains.
80 Some, to whom Heaven in wit has been profuse,
Want as much more to turn it to its use;
For wit and judgment often are at strife,
Though meant each other's aid, like man and wife.
'Tis more to guide than spur the Muse's steed,
85 Restrain his fury than provoke his speed;
The wingèd courser,[5] like a generous° horse,   *spirited, highly bred*
Shows most true mettle when you check his course.
   Those rules of old discovered, not devised,
Are Nature still, but Nature methodized;
90 Nature, like liberty, is but restrained
By the same laws which first herself ordained.
   Hear how learn'd Greece her useful rules indites,
When to repress and when indulge our flights:
High on Parnassus' top her sons she showed,
95 And pointed out those arduous paths they trod;
Held from afar, aloft, the immortal prize,
And urged the rest by equal steps to rise.
Just precepts thus from great examples given,
She drew from them what they derived from Heaven.
100 The generous critic fanned the poet's fire,
And taught the world with reason to admire.
Then criticism the Muse's handmaid proved,
To dress her charms, and make her more beloved:
But following wits from that intention strayed,
105 Who could not win the mistress, wooed the maid;
Against the poets their own arms they turned,
Sure to hate most the men from whom they learned.
So modern 'pothecaries, taught the art
By doctors's bills° to play the doctor's part,   *prescriptions*
110 Bold in the practice of mistaken rules,
Prescribe, apply, and call their masters fools.
Some on the leaves of ancient authors prey,
Nor time nor moths e'er spoiled so much as they.
Some dryly plain, without invention's aid,
115 Write dull receipts[6] how poems may be made.
These leave the sense their learning to display,
And those explain the meaning quite away.
   You then whose judgment the right course would steer,
Know well each ancient's proper character;
120 His fable,[7] subject, scope° in every page;   *aim, purpose*

5. Pegasus, associated with the Muses and poetic inspiration.
6. Formulas for preparing a dish; recipes. Pope himself wrote an amusing burlesque, *Receipt to*

Make an Epic Poem, first published in the *Guardian* 78 (1713).
7. Plot or story of a play or poem.

Religion, country, genius of his age:
Without all these at once before your eyes,
Cavil you may, but never criticize.
Be Homer's works your study and delight,
125 Read them by day, and meditate by night;
Thence form your judgment, thence your maxims bring,
And trace the Muses upward to their spring.
Still with itself compared, his text peruse;
And let your comment be the Mantuan Muse.
130   When first young Maro[8] in his boundless mind
A work to outlast immortal Rome designed,
Perhaps he seemed above the critic's law,
And but from Nature's fountains scorned to draw;
But when to examine every part he came,
135 Nature and Homer were, he found, the same.
Convinced, amazed, he checks the bold design, ⎫
And rules as strict his labored work confine ⎬
As if the Stagirite[9] o'erlooked each line. ⎭
Learn hence for ancient rules a just esteem;
140 To copy Nature is to copy them.
    Some beauties yet no precepts can declare,
For there's a happiness as well as care.[1]
Music resembles poetry, in each ⎫
Are nameless graces which no methods teach, ⎬
145 And which a master hand alone can reach. ⎭
If, where the rules not far enough extend
(Since rules were made but to promote their end)
Some lucky license answers to the full
The intent proposed, that license is a rule.
150 Thus Pegasus, a nearer way to take,
May boldly deviate from the common track.
Great wits sometimes may gloriously offend,
And rise to faults true critics dare not mend;
From vulgar bounds with brave disorder part,
155 And snatch a grace beyond the reach of art,
Which, without passing through the judgment, gains
The heart, and all its end at once attains.
In prospects thus, some objects please our eyes, ⎫
Which out of Nature's common order rise, ⎬
160 The shapeless rock, or hanging precipice. ⎭
But though the ancients thus their rules invade
(As kings dispense with laws themselves have made)
Moderns, beware! or if you must offend
Against the precept, ne'er transgress its end;
165 Let it be seldom, and compelled by need;
And have at least their precedent to plead.

8. Virgil. He was born in a village adjacent to Mantua in Italy, hence "Mantuan Muse." His epic, the *Aeneid*, was modeled on Homer's *Iliad* and *Odyssey* and was considered to be a refinement on the Greek poems. Thus it could be thought of as a commentary ("comment") on Homer's poems.
9. Aristotle, native of Stagira, from whose *Poetics* later critics formulated strict rules for writing tragedy and the epic.
1. I.e., no rules ("precepts") can explain ("declare") some beautiful effects in a work of art that can be the result only of inspiration or good luck ("happiness"), not of painstaking labor ("care").

The critic else proceeds without remorse,
Seizes your fame, and puts his laws in force.
   I know there are, to whose presumptuous thoughts
170 Those freer beauties, even in them, seem faults.[2]
Some figures monstrous and misshaped appear,
Considered singly, or beheld too near,
Which, but proportioned to their light or place,
Due distance reconciles to form and grace.
175 A prudent chief not always must display
His powers in equal ranks and fair array,
But with the occasion and the place comply,
Conceal his force, nay seem sometimes to fly.
Those oft are stratagems which errors seem,
180 Nor is it Homer nods, but we that dream.
   Still green with bays each ancient altar stands
Above the reach of sacrilegious hands,
Secure from flames, from envy's fiercer rage,
Destructive war, and all-involving age.
185 See, from each clime the learn'd their incense bring!
Here in all tongues consenting° paeans ring!   *agreeing, concurring*
In praise so just let every voice be joined,[3]
And fill the general chorus of mankind.
Hail, bards triumphant! born in happier days,
190 Immortal heirs of universal praise!
Whose honors with increase of ages grow,
As streams roll down, enlarging as they flow;
Nations unborn your mighty names shall sound,
And worlds applaud that must not yet be found!
195 Oh, may some spark of your celestial fire,
The last, the meanest of your sons inspire
(That on weak wings, from far, pursues your flights,
Glows while he reads, but trembles as he writes)
To teach vain wits a science little known,
200 To admire superior sense, and doubt their own!

Part 2

   Of all the causes which conspire to blind
Man's erring judgment, and misguide the mind,
What the weak head with strongest bias rules,
Is pride, the never-failing vice of fools.
205 Whatever Nature has in worth denied,
She gives in large recruits° of needful pride;   *supplies*
For as in bodies, thus in souls, we find
What wants in blood and spirits, swelled with wind:
Pride, where wit fails, steps in to our defense,
210 And fills up all the mighty void of sense.
If once right reason drives that cloud away,
Truth breaks upon us with resistless day.
Trust not yourself: but your defects to know,

2. Pronounced *fawts*.   3. Pronounced *jined*.

Make use of every friend—and every foe.
215   A little learning is a dangerous thing;
Drink deep, or taste not the Pierian spring.[4]
There shallow draughts intoxicate the brain,
And drinking largely sobers us again.
Fired at first sight with what the Muse imparts,
220 In fearless youth we tempt° the heights of arts,   *attempt*
While from the bounded level of our mind
Short views we take, nor see the lengths behind;
But more advanced, behold with strange surprise
New distant scenes of endless science rise!
225 So pleased at first the towering Alps we try,
Mount o'er the vales, and seem to tread the sky,
The eternal snows appear already past,
And the first clouds and mountains seem the last;
But, those attained, we tremble to survey
230 The growing labors of the lengthened way,
The increasing prospect tires our wandering eyes,
Hills peep o'er hills, and Alps on Alps arise!
    A perfect judge will read each work of wit
With the same spirit that its author writ:
235 Survey the whole, nor seek slight faults to find
Where Nature moves, and rapture warms the mind;
Nor lose, for that malignant dull delight,
The generous pleasure to be charmed with wit.
But in such lays as neither ebb nor flow,
240 Correctly cold, and regularly low,
That, shunning faults, one quiet tenor keep,
We cannot blame indeed—but we may sleep.
In wit, as nature, what affects our hearts
Is not the exactness of peculiar parts;
245 'Tis not a lip, or eye, we beauty call,
But the joint force and full result of all.
Thus when we view some well-proportioned dome[5]
(The world's just wonder, and even thine, O Rome!),
No single parts unequally surprise,
250 All comes united to the admiring eyes:
No monstrous height, or breadth, or length appear;
The whole at once is bold and regular.
    Whoever thinks a faultless piece to see,
Thinks what ne'er was, nor is, nor e'er shall be.
255 In every work regard the writer's end,
Since none can compass more than they intend;
And if the means be just, the conduct true,
Applause, in spite of trivial faults, is due.
As men of breeding, sometimes men of wit,
260 To avoid great errors must the less commit,
Neglect the rules each verbal critic lays,
For not to know some trifles is a praise.

---

4. The spring in Pieria on Mount Olympus, sacred
to the Muses.

5. The dome of St. Peter's, designed by Michelangelo.

Most critics, fond of some subservient art,
Still make the whole depend upon a part:
265 They talk of principles, but notions prize,
And all to one loved folly sacrifice.
    Once on a time La Mancha's knight,[6] they say,
A certain bard encountering on the way,
Discoursed in terms as just, with looks as sage,
270 As e'er could Dennis,[7] of the Grecian stage;
Concluding all were desperate sots and fools
Who durst depart from Aristotle's rules.
Our author, happy in a judge so nice,
Produced his play, and begged the knight's advice;
275 Made him observe the subject and the plot,
The manners, passions, unities; what not?
All which exact to rule were brought about,
Were but a combat in the lists left out.
"What! leave the combat out?" exclaims the knight.
280 "Yes, or we must renounce the Stagirite."
"Not so, by Heaven!" he answers in a rage,
"Knights, squires, and steeds must enter on the stage."
"So vast a throng the stage can ne'er contain."
"Then build a new, or act it in a plain."
285   Thus critics of less judgment than caprice,
Curious,° not knowing, not exact, but nice,°   *laborious/fussy*
Form short ideas, and offend in arts
(As most in manners), by a love to parts.
    Some to conceit[8] alone their taste confine,
290 And glittering thoughts struck out at every line;
Pleased with a work where nothing's just or fit,
One glaring chaos and wild heap of wit.
Poets, like painters, thus unskilled to trace
The naked nature and the living grace,
295 With gold and jewels cover every part,
And hide with ornaments their want of art.
True wit is Nature to advantage dressed,
What oft was thought, but ne'er so well expressed;
Something whose truth convinced at sight we find,
300 That gives us back the image of our mind.
As shades more sweetly recommend the light,
So modest plainness sets off sprightly wit;
For works may have more wit than does them good,
As bodies perish through excess of blood.
305   Others for language all their care express,
And value books, as women men, for dress.
Their praise is still—the style is excellent;
The sense they humbly take upon contènt.°   *mere acquiescence*
Words are like leaves; and where they most abound,

---

6. Don Quixote. The story comes not from Cervantes's novel, but from a spurious sequel to it by Don Alonzo Fernandez de Avellaneda.
7. John Dennis (1657–1734), although one of the leading critics of the time, was frequently ridiculed by the wits for his irascibility and pomposity. Pope apparently did not know Dennis personally, but his jibe at him in part 3 of this poem made him a bitter enemy.
8. Pointed wit, ingenuity and extravagance, or affectation in the use of figures, especially similes and metaphors.

310 Much fruit of sense beneath is rarely found.
False eloquence, like the prismatic glass,
Its gaudy colors spreads on every place;[9]
The face of Nature we no more survey,
All glares alike, without distinction gay.
315 But true expression, like the unchanging sun, ⎫
Clears and improves whate'er it shines upon; ⎬
It gilds all objects, but it alters none. ⎭
Expression is the dress of thought, and still
Appears more decent as more suitable.
320 A vile conceit in pompous words expressed
Is like a clown° in regal purple dressed: °rustic, boor
For different styles with different subjects sort,
As several garbs with country, town, and court.
Some by old words to fame have made pretense,
325 Ancients in phrase, mere moderns in their sense.
Such labored nothings, in so strange a style,
Amaze the unlearn'd, and make the learned smile;
Unlucky as Fungoso[1] in the play, ⎫
These sparks with awkward vanity display ⎬
330 What the fine gentleman wore yesterday; ⎭
And but so mimic ancient wits at best,
As apes our grandsires in their doublets dressed.
In words as fashions the same rule will hold,
Alike fantastic if too new or old:
335 Be not the first by whom the new are tried,
Nor yet the last to lay the old aside.
    But most by numbers° judge a poet's song,   °versification
And smooth or rough with them is right or wrong.
In the bright Muse though thousand charms conspire,
340 Her voice is all these tuneful fools admire,
Who haunt Parnassus but to please their ear,
Not mend their minds; as some to church repair, ⎬
Not for the doctrine, but the music there.
These equal syllables alone require,
345 Though oft the ear the open vowels tire,[2]
While expletives[3] their feeble aid do join,
And ten low words oft creep in one dull line:
While they ring round the same unvaried chimes,
With sure returns of still expected rhymes;
350 Where'er you find "the cooling western breeze,"
In the next line, it "whispers through the trees";
If crystal streams "with pleasing murmurs creep,"
The reader's threatened (not in vain) with "sleep";
Then, at the last and only couplet fraught
355 With some unmeaning thing they call a thought,
A needless Alexandrine[4] ends the song

---

9. A very up-to-date scientific reference. Newton's *Optics*, which dealt with the prism and the spectrum, had been published in 1704, although his theories had been known earlier.
1. A character in Ben Jonson's comedy *Every Man out of His Humor* (1599).
2. In lines 345–57 Pope cleverly contrives to make

his own metrics or diction illustrate the faults that he is exposing.
3. Words used merely to achieve the necessary number of feet in a line of verse.
4. A line of verse containing six iambic feet; it is illustrated in the next line.

That, like a wounded snake, drags its slow length along.
Leave such to tune their own dull rhymes, and know
What's roundly smooth or languishingly slow;
360 And praise the easy vigor of a line
Where Denham's strength and Waller's sweetness join.[5]
True ease in writing comes from art, not chance,
As those move easiest who have learned to dance.
'Tis not enough no harshness gives offense,
365 The sound must seem an echo to the sense.
Soft is the strain when Zephyr gently blows,
And the smooth stream in smoother numbers flows;
But when loud surges lash the sounding shore,
The hoarse, rough verse should like the torrent roar.
370 When Ajax strives some rock's vast weight to throw,
The line too labors, and the words move slow;
Not so when swift Camilla scours the plain,
Flies o'er the unbending corn, and skims along the main.
Hear how Timotheus'[6] varied lays surprise,
375 And bid alternate passions fall and rise!
While at each change the son of Libyan Jove°   Alexander the Great
Now burns with glory, and then melts with love;
Now his fierce eyes with sparkling fury glow,
Now sighs steal out, and tears begin to flow:
380 Persians and Greeks like turns of nature[7] found
And the world's victor stood subdued by sound!
The power of music all our hearts allow,
And what Timotheus was, is Dryden now.
        Avoid extremes; and shun the fault of such
385 Who still are pleased too little or too much.
At every trifle scorn to take offense:
That always shows great pride, or little sense.
Those heads, as stomachs, are not sure the best,
Which nauseate all, and nothing can digest.
390 Yet let not each gay turn thy rapture move;
For fools admire,° but men of sense approve:[8]   wonder
As things seem large which we through mists descry,
Dullness is ever apt to magnify.
        Some foreign writers, some our own despise;
395 The ancients only, or the moderns prize.
Thus wit, like faith, by each man is applied
To one small sect, and all are damned beside.
Meanly they seek the blessing to confine,
And force that sun but on a part to shine,
400 Which not alone the southern wit sublimes,°   raises up, purifies
But ripens spirits in cold northern climes;
Which from the first has shone on ages past,
Enlights the present, and shall warm the last;
Though each may feel increases and decays,

5. Dryden, whom Pope echoes here, considered Sir John Denham (1615–1669) and Edmund Waller (1606–1687) to have been the principal shapers of the closed pentameter couplet. He had distinguished the "strength" of the one and the "sweetness" of the other.

6. The musician in Dryden's *Alexander's Feast.* Pope retells the story of that poem in the following lines.
7. Alternations of feelings.
8. Judge favorably only after due deliberation.

405　And see now clearer and now darker days.
　　　Regard not then if wit be old or new,
　　　But blame the false and value still the true.
　　　　　Some ne'er advance a judgment of their own,
　　　But catch the spreading notion of the town;
410　They reason and conclude by precedent,
　　　And own stale nonsense which they ne'er invent.
　　　Some judge of authors' names, not works, and then
　　　Nor praise nor blame the writings, but the men.
　　　Of all this servile herd the worst is he
415　That in proud dullness joins with quality,[9]
　　　A constant critic at the great man's board,
　　　To fetch and carry nonsense for my lord.
　　　What woeful stuff this madrigal would be
　　　In some starved hackney sonneteer° or me!　　　　　　　*hireling poet*
420　But let a lord once own the happy lines,
　　　How the wit brightens! how the style refines!
　　　Before his sacred name flies every fault,
　　　And each exalted stanza teems with thought!
　　　　　The vulgar thus through imitation err;
425　As oft the learn'd by being singular;
　　　So much they scorn the crowd, that if the throng
　　　By chance go right, they purposely go wrong.
　　　So schismatics[1] the plain believers quit,
　　　And are but damned for having too much wit.
430　Some praise at morning what they blame at night,
　　　But always think the last opinion right.
　　　A Muse by these is like a mistress used,
　　　This hour she's idolized, the next abused;
　　　While their weak heads like towns unfortified,
435　'Twixt sense and nonsense daily change their side.
　　　Ask them the cause; they're wiser still, they say;
　　　And still tomorrow's wiser than today.
　　　We think our fathers fools, so wise we grow;
　　　Our wiser sons, no doubt, will think us so.
440　Once school divines[2] this zealous isle o'erspread;
　　　Who knew most sentences[3] was deepest read.
　　　Faith, Gospel, all seemed made to be disputed,
　　　And none had sense enough to be confuted.
　　　Scotists and Thomists now in peace remain
445　Amidst their kindred cobwebs in Duck Lane.[4]
　　　If faith itself has different dresses worn,
　　　What wonder modes in wit should take their turn?
　　　Oft, leaving what is natural and fit,
　　　The current folly proves the ready wit;
450　And authors think their reputation safe,
　　　Which lives as long as fools are pleased to laugh.

9. People of high rank.
1. Those who have divided the church on points of theology. Pope stressed the first syllable, the pronunciation approved by Johnson in his *Dictionary*.
2. The medieval theologians, such as the followers of Duns Scotus and St. Thomas Aquinas, mentioned below.
3. Allusion to Peter Lombard's *Book of Sentences*, a book esteemed by Scholastic philosophers.
4. Street where publishers' remainders and secondhand books were sold.

Some valuing those of their own side or mind,
Still make themselves the measure of mankind:
Fondly° we think we honor merit then,   *foolishly*
455 When we but praise ourselves in other men.
Parties in wit attend on those of state,
And public faction doubles private hate.
Pride, Malice, Folly against Dryden rose,
In various shapes of parsons, critics, beaux;
460 But sense survived, when merry jests were past;
For rising merit will buoy up at last.
Might he return and bless once more our eyes,
New Blackmores and new Milbourns must arise.[5]
Nay, should great Homer lift his awful head,
465 Zoilus[6] again would start up from the dead.
Envy will merit, as its shade, pursue,
But like a shadow, proves the substance true;
For envied wit, like Sol eclipsed, makes known
The opposing body's grossness, not its own.
470 When first that sun too powerful beams displays,
It draws up vapors which obscure its rays;
But even those clouds at last adorn its way,
Reflect new glories, and augment the day.
     Be thou the first true merit to befriend;
475 His praise is lost who stays till all commend.
Short is the date, alas! of modern rhymes,
And 'tis but just to let them live betimes.
No longer now that golden age appears,
When patriarch wits survived a thousand years:
480 Now length of fame (our second life) is lost,
And bare threescore is all even that can boast;
Our sons their fathers' failing language see,
And such as Chaucer is, shall Dryden be.[7]
So when the faithful pencil has designed
485 Some bright idea of the master's mind,
Where a new world leaps out at his command,
And ready Nature waits upon his hand;
When the ripe colors soften and unite,
And sweetly melt into just shade and light;
490 When mellowing years their full perfection give,
And each bold figure just begins to live,
The treacherous colors the fair art betray,
And all the bright creation fades away!
     Unhappy wit, like most mistaken things,
495 Atones not for that envy which it brings.
In youth alone its empty praise we boast,
But soon the short-lived vanity is lost;
Like some fair flower the early spring supplies,

5. Sir Richard Blackmore, physician and poet, had attacked Dryden for the immorality of his plays; Rev. Luke Milbourn had attacked his translation of Virgil.
6. A Greek critic of the 4th century B.C.E., who wrote a book of carping criticism of Homer.

7. The radical changes that took place in the English language between the death of Chaucer in 1400 and the death of Dryden in 1700 suggested that in another three hundred years Dryden would be unintelligible. Latin seemed the only means of attaining enduring fame.

That gaily blooms, but even in blooming dies.
500 What is this wit, which must our cares employ?
The owner's wife, that other men enjoy;
Then most our trouble still when most admired,
And still the more we give, the more required;
Whose fame with pains we guard, but lose with ease,
505 Sure some to vex, but never all to please;
'Tis what the vicious fear, the virtuous shun,
By fools 'tis hated, and by knaves undone!
　　If wit so much from ignorance undergo,
Ah, let not learning too commence its foe!
510 Of old those met rewards who could excel,
And such were praised who but endeavored well;
Though triumphs were to generals only due,
Crowns were reserved to grace the soldiers too.[8]
Now they who reach Parnassus' lofty crown
515 Employ their pains to spurn some others down;
And while self-love each jealous writer rules,
Contending wits become the sport of fools;
But still the worst with most regret commend,
For each ill author is as bad a friend.
520 To what base ends, and by what abject ways,
Are mortals urged through sacred[9] lust of praise!
Ah, ne'er so dire a thirst of glory boast,
Nor in the critic let the man be lost!
Good nature and good sense must ever join;
525 To err is human, to forgive divine . . .

1709   1711

The Rape of the Lock

The Rape of the Lock is based on an actual episode that provoked a quarrel between two prominent Catholic families. Pope's friend John Caryll, to whom the poem is addressed (line 3), suggested that Pope write it, in the hope that a little laughter might serve to soothe ruffled tempers. Lord Petre had cut off a lock of hair from the head of the lovely Arabella Fermor (often spelled "Farmer" and doubtless so pronounced), much to the indignation of the lady and her relatives. In its original version of two cantos and 334 lines, published in 1712, *The Rape of the Lock* was a great success. In 1713 a new version was undertaken against the advice of Addison, who considered the poem perfect as it was first written. Pope greatly expanded the earlier version, adding the delightful "machinery" (i.e., the supernatural agents in epic action) of the Sylphs, Belinda's toilet, the card game, and the visit to the Cave of Spleen in canto 4. In 1717, with the addition of Clarissa's speech on good humor, the poem assumed its final form.

With delicate fancy and playful wit, Pope elaborated the trivial episode that occasioned the poem into the semblance of an epic in miniature, the most nearly perfect heroicomical poem in English. The verse abounds in parodies and echoes of the *Iliad*, the *Aeneid*, and *Paradise Lost*, thus constantly forcing the reader to compare small things with great. The familiar devices of epic are observed, but the incidents or

8. To celebrate Roman victories, valiant soldiers
were decorated with a variety of crowns.

9. Accursed. The phrase imitates Virgil's *auri sacra famis*, "accursed hunger for gold" (*Aeneid* 3.57).

characters are beautifully proportioned to the scale of mock epic. The *Rape* tells of war, but it is the drawing-room war between the sexes; it has its heroes and heroines, but they are beaux and belles; it has its supernatural characters ("machinery"), but they are Sylphs (borrowed, as Pope tells us in his engaging dedicatory letter, from Rosicrucian lore)—creatures of the air, the souls of dead coquettes, with tasks appropriate to their nature—or the Gnome Umbriel, once a prude on earth; it has its epic game, played on the "velvet plain" of the card table, its feasting heroes, who sip coffee and gossip, and its battle, fought with the clichés of compliment and conceits, with frowns and angry glances, with snuff and bodkin; it has the traditional epic journey to the underworld—here the Cave of Spleen, emblematic of the ill nature of female hypochondriacs. And Pope creates a world in which these actions take place, a world that is dense with beautiful objects: brocades, ivory and tortoiseshell, cosmetics and diamonds, lacquered furniture, silver teapot, delicate chinaware. It is a world that is constantly in motion and that sparkles and glitters with light, whether the light of the sun or of Belinda's eyes or that light into which the "fluid" bodies of the Sylphs seem to dissolve as they flutter in shrouds and around the mast of Belinda's ship. Though Pope laughs at this world and its creatures—and remembers that a grimmer, darker world surrounds it (3.19–24 and 5.145–48)—he makes us very much aware of its beauty and charm.

The epigraph may be translated, "I was unwilling, Belinda, to ravish your locks; but I rejoice to have conceded this to your prayers" (Martial's *Epigrams* 12.84.1–2). Pope substituted his heroine for Martial's Polytimus. The epigraph is intended to suggest that the poem was published at Miss Fermor's request.

The Rape of the Lock

An Heroi-Comical Poem

Nolueram, Belinda, tuos violare capillos;
sed juvat hoc precibus me tribuisse tuis.
—MARTIAL

TO MRS. ARABELLA FERMOR

MADAM,
It will be in vain to deny that I have some regard for this piece, since I dedicate it to you. Yet you may bear me witness, it was intended only to divert a few young ladies, who have good sense and good humor enough to laugh not only at their sex's little unguarded follies, but at their own. But as it was communicated with the air of a secret, it soon found its way into the world. An imperfect copy having been offered to a bookseller, you had the good nature for my sake to consent to the publication of one more correct; this I was forced to, before I had executed half my design, for the machinery was entirely wanting to complete it.

The machinery, Madam, is a term invented by the critics, to signify that part which the deities, angels, or demons are made to act in a poem; for the ancient poets are in one respect like many modern ladies: let an action be never so trivial in itself, they always make it appear of the utmost importance. These machines I determined to raise on a very new and odd foundation, the Rosicrucian[1] doctrine of spirits.

---

1. A system of arcane philosophy introduced into England from Germany in the 17th century.

I know how disagreeable it is to make use of hard words before a lady; but 'tis so much the concern of a poet to have his works understood, and particularly by your sex, that you must give me leave to explain two or three difficult terms.

The Rosicrucians are a people I must bring you acquainted with. The best account I know of them is in a French book called Le Comte de Gabalis,[2] which both in its title and size is so like a novel, that many of the fair sex have read it for one by mistake. According to these gentlemen, the four elements are inhabited by spirits, which they call Sylphs, Gnomes, Nymphs, and Salamanders. The Gnomes or Demons of earth delight in mischief; but the Sylphs, whose habitation is in the air, are the best-conditioned creatures imaginable. For they say, any mortals may enjoy the most intimate familiarities with these gentle spirits, upon a condition very easy to all true adepts, an inviolate preservation of chastity.

As to the following cantos, all the passages of them are as fabulous as the vision at the beginning, or the transformation at the end (except the loss of your hair, which I always mention with reverence). The human persons are as fictitious as the airy ones; and the character of Belinda, as it is now managed, resembles you in nothing but in beauty.

If this poem had as many graces as there are in your person, or in your mind, yet I could never hope it should pass through the world half so uncensured as you have done. But let its fortune be what it will, mine is happy enough, to have given me this occasion of assuring you that I am, with the truest esteem,

MADAM,

Your most obedient, humble servant,

A. POPE

Canto 1

What dire offense from amorous causes springs,
What mighty contests rise from trivial things,
I sing—This verse to Caryll, Muse! is due:
This, even Belinda may vouchsafe to view:
5   Slight is the subject, but not so the praise,
If she inspire, and he approve my lays.
   Say what strange motive, Goddess! could compel
A well-bred lord to assault a gentle belle?
Oh, say what stranger cause, yet unexplored,
10   Could make a gentle belle reject a lord?
In tasks so bold can little men engage,
And in soft bosoms dwells such mighty rage?
   Sol through white curtains shot a timorous ray,
And oped those eyes that must eclipse the day.
15   Now lapdogs give themselves the rousing shake,
And sleepless lovers, just at twelve, awake:
Thrice rung the bell, the slipper knocked the ground,
And the pressed watch[3] returned a silver sound.

---

2. By the Abbé de Montfaucon de Villars, published in 1670.
3. A watch that chimes the hour and the quarter hour when the stem is pressed down. "Knocked the ground": summons to a maid.

Belinda still her downy pillow pressed,
20   Her guardian Sylph prolonged the balmy rest.
'Twas he had summoned to her silent bed
The morning dream that hovered o'er her head.
A youth more glittering than a birthnight beau[4]
(That even in slumber caused her cheek to glow)
25   Seemed to her ear his winning lips to lay,
And thus in whispers said, or seemed to say:
      "Fairest of mortals, thou distinguished care
Of thousand bright inhabitants of air!
If e'er one vision touched thy infant thought,
30   Of all the nurse and all the priest have taught,
Of airy elves by moonlight shadows seen,
The silver token, and the circled green,[5]
Or virgins visited by angel powers,
With golden crowns and wreaths of heavenly flowers,
35   Hear and believe! thy own importance know,
Nor bound thy narrow views to things below.
Some secret truths, from learned pride concealed,
To maids alone and children are revealed:
What though no credit doubting wits may give?
40   The fair and innocent shall still believe.
Know, then, unnumbered spirits round thee fly,
The light militia of the lower sky:
These, though unseen, are ever on the wing,
Hang o'er the box, and hover round the Ring.[6]
45   Think what an equipage thou hast in air,
And view with scorn two pages and a chair.°   *sedan chair*
As now your own, our beings were of old,
And once enclosed in woman's beauteous mold;
Thence, by a soft transition, we repair
50   From earthly vehicles to these of air.
Think not, when woman's transient breath is fled,
That all her vanities at once are dead:
Succeeding vanities she still regards,
And though she plays no more, o'erlooks the cards.
55   Her joy in gilded chariots, when alive,
And love of ombre,[7] after death survive.
For when the Fair in all their pride expire,
To their first elements[8] their souls retire:
The sprites of fiery termagants in flame
60   Mount up, and take a Salamander's[9] name.
Soft yielding minds to water glide away,
And sip, with Nymphs, their elemental tea.[1]

4. Courtiers wore especially fine clothes on the sovereign's birthday.
5. Rings of bright green grass, which are common in England even in winter, were held to be due to the round dances of fairies. According to popular belief fairies skim off the cream from jugs of milk left standing overnight and leave a coin ("silver token") in payment.
6. The "box" in the theater and the fashionable circular drive ("Ring") in Hyde Park.
7. The popular card game (see n. 8, p. 1143).

8. The four elements out of which all things were believed to have been made were fire, water, earth, and air. One or another of these elements was supposed to be predominant in both the physical and the psychological makeup of each human being. In this context they are spoken of as "humors."
9. A lizardlike animal, in antiquity believed to live in fire. Each element was inhabited by a spirit, as the following lines explain.
1. Pronounced *tay*.

The graver prude sinks downward to a Gnome,
In search of mischief still on earth to roam.
65 The light coquettes in Sylphs aloft repair,
And sport and flutter in the fields of air.
   "Know further yet; whoever fair and chaste
Rejects mankind, is by some Sylph embraced:
For spirits, freed from mortal laws, with ease
70 Assume what sexes and what shapes they please.[2]
What guards the purity of melting maids,
In courtly balls, and midnight masquerades,
Safe from the treacherous friend, the daring spark,
The glance by day, the whisper in the dark,
75 When kind occasion prompts their warm desires,
When music softens, and when dancing fires?
'Tis but their Sylph, the wise Celestials know,
Though Honor is the word with men below.
   "Some nymphs there are, too conscious of their face,
80 For life predestined to the Gnomes' embrace.
These swell their prospects and exalt their pride,
When offers are disdained, and love denied:
Then gay ideas° crowd the vacant brain,   *showy images*
While peers, and dukes, and all their sweeping train,
85 And garters, stars, and coronets[3] appear,
And in soft sounds, 'your Grace'° salutes their ear.   *a duchess*
'Tis these that early taint the female soul,
Instruct the eyes of young coquettes to roll,
Teach infant cheeks a bidden blush to know,
90 And little hearts to flutter at a beau.
   "Oft, when the world imagine women stray,
The Sylphs through mystic mazes guide their way,
Through all the giddy circle they pursue,
And old impertinence° expel by new.   *trifle*
95 What tender maid but must a victim fall
To one man's treat, but for another's ball?
When Florio speaks, what virgin could withstand,
If gentle Damon did not squeeze her hand?
With varying vanities, from every part,
100 They shift the moving toyshop[4] of their heart;
Where wigs with wigs, with sword-knots sword-knots strive,
Beaux banish beaux, and coaches coaches drive.
This erring mortals levity may call;
Oh, blind to truth! the Sylphs contrive it all.
105   "Of these am I, who thy protection claim,
A watchful sprite, and Ariel is my name.
Late, as I ranged the crystal wilds of air,
In the clear mirror of thy ruling star
I saw, alas! some dread event impend,
110 Ere to the main this morning sun descend,
But Heaven reveals not what, or how, or where:

---

2. Cf. *Paradise Lost* 1.427–31; this is one of many
allusions to that poem in the *Rape*.

3. Emblems of nobility.
4. A shop stocked with baubles and trifles.

Warned by the Sylph, O pious maid, beware!
This to disclose is all thy guardian can:
Beware of all, but most beware of Man!"
115   He said; when Shock,[5] who thought she slept too long,
Leaped up, and waked his mistress with his tongue.
'Twas then, Belinda, if report say true,
Thy eyes first opened on a billet-doux;
Wounds, charms, and ardors were no sooner read,
120 But all the vision vanished from thy head.
    And now, unveiled, the toilet stands displayed,
Each silver vase in mystic order laid.
First, robed in white, the nymph intent adores,
With head uncovered, the cosmetic powers.
125 A heavenly image in the glass appears;
To that she bends, to that her eyes she rears.
The inferior priestess, at her altar's side,
Trembling begins the sacred rites of Pride.
Unnumbered treasures ope at once, and here
130 The various offerings of the world appear;
From each she nicely culls with curious toil,
And decks the goddess with the glittering spoil.
This casket India's glowing gems unlocks,
And all Arabia breathes from yonder box.
135 The tortoise here and elephant unite,
Transformed to combs, the speckled and the white.
Here files of pins extend their shining rows,
Puffs, powders, patches, Bibles,[6] billet-doux.
Now awful Beauty puts on all its arms;
140 The fair each moment rises in her charms,
Repairs her smiles, awakens every grace,
And calls forth all the wonders of her face;
Sees by degrees a purer blush arise,
And keener lightnings quicken in her eyes.
145 The busy Sylphs surround their darling care,
These set the head, and those divide the hair,
Some fold the sleeve, whilst others plait the gown;
And Betty's[7] praised for labors not her own.

Canto 2

    Not with more glories, in the ethereal plain,
The sun first rises o'er the purpled Main,
Than, issuing forth, the rival of his beams
Launched on the bosom of the silver Thames.
5 Fair nymphs and well-dressed youths around her shone,
But every eye was fixed on her alone.
On her white breast a sparkling cross she wore,
Which Jews might kiss, and infidels adore.
Her lively looks a sprightly mind disclose,

---

5. A long-haired poodle, Belinda's lapdog.
6. It has been suggested that Pope intended here not "Bibles," but "bibelots" (trinkets), but this interpretation has not gained wide acceptance.
7. Belinda's maid, the "inferior priestess" mentioned in line 127.

10   Quick as her eyes, and as unfixed as those:
     Favors to none, to all she smiles extends;
     Oft she rejects, but never once offends.
     Bright as the sun, her eyes the gazers strike,
     And, like the sun, they shine on all alike.
15   Yet graceful ease, and sweetness void of pride,
     Might hide her faults, if belles had faults to hide:
     If to her share some female errors fall,
     Look on her face, and you'll forget 'em all.
       This nymph, to the destruction of mankind,
20   Nourished two locks which graceful hung behind
     In equal curls, and well conspired to deck
     With shining ringlets her smooth ivory neck.
     Love in these labyrinths his slaves detains,
     And mighty hearts are held in slender chains.
25   With hairy springes[8] we the birds betray,
     Slight lines of hair surprise the finny prey,
     Fair tresses man's imperial race ensnare,
     And beauty draws us with a single hair.
       The adventurous Baron the bright locks admired,
30   He saw, he wished, and to the prize aspired.
     Resolved to win, he meditates the way,
     By force to ravish, or by fraud betray;
     For when success a lover's toil attends,
     Few ask if fraud or force attained his ends.
35   For this, ere Phoebus rose, he had implored
     Propitious Heaven, and every power adored,
     But chiefly Love—to Love an altar built,
     Of twelve vast French romances, neatly gilt.
     There lay three garters, half a pair of gloves,
40   And all the trophies of his former loves.
     With tender billet-doux he lights the pyre,
     And breathes three amorous sighs to raise the fire.
     Then prostrate falls, and begs with ardent eyes
     Soon to obtain, and long possess the prize:
45   The powers gave ear, and granted half his prayer,
     The rest the winds dispersed in empty air.
       But now secure the painted vessel glides,
     The sunbeams trembling on the floating tides,
     While melting music steals upon the sky,
50   And softened sounds along the waters die.
     Smooth flow the waves, the zephyrs gently play,
     Belinda smiled, and all the world was gay.
     All but the Sylph—with careful thoughts oppressed,
     The impending woe sat heavy on his breast.
55   He summons straight his denizens of air;
     The lucid squadrons round the sails repair:
     Soft o'er the shrouds aërial whispers breathe
     That seemed but zephyrs to the train beneath.
     Some to the sun their insect-wings unfold,

---

8. Snares; pronounced *sprin-jez.*

60　Waft on the breeze, or sink in clouds of gold.
　　Transparent forms too fine for mortal sight,
　　Their fluid bodies half dissolved in light,
　　Loose to the wind their airy garments flew,
　　Thin glittering textures of the filmy dew,
65　Dipped in the richest tincture of the skies,
　　Where light disports in ever-mingling dyes,
　　While every beam new transient colors flings,
　　Colors that change whene'er they wave their wings.
　　Amid the circle, on the gilded mast,
70　Superior by the head was Ariel placed;
　　His purple⁹ pinions opening to the sun,
　　He raised his azure wand, and thus begun:
　　　"Ye Sylphs and Sylphids, to your chief give ear!
　　Fays, Fairies, Genïi, Elves, and Daemons, hear!
75　Ye know the spheres and various tasks assigned
　　By laws eternal to the aërial kind.
　　Some in the fields of purest ether play,
　　And bask and whiten in the blaze of day.
　　Some guide the course of wandering orbs on high,
80　Or roll the planets through the boundless sky.
　　Some less refined, beneath the moon's pale light
　　Pursue the stars that shoot athwart the night,
　　Or suck the mists in grosser air below,
　　Or dip their pinions in the painted bow,
85　Or brew fierce tempests on the wintry main,
　　Or o'er the glebe° distill the kindly rain.　　　　*cultivated field*
　　Others on earth o'er human race preside,
　　Watch all their ways, and all their actions guide:
　　Of these the chief the care of nations own,
90　And guard with arms divine the British Throne.
　　　"Our humbler province is to tend the Fair,
　　Not a less pleasing, though less glorious care:
　　To save the powder from too rude a gale,
　　Nor let the imprisoned essences exhale;
95　To draw fresh colors from the vernal flowers;
　　To steal from rainbows e'er they drop in showers
　　A brighter wash;° to curl their waving hairs,　　　*cosmetic lotion*
　　Assist their blushes, and inspire their airs,
　　Nay oft, in dreams invention we bestow,
100　To change a flounce, or add a furbelow.
　　　"This day black omens threat the brightest fair,
　　That e'er deserved a watchful spirit's care;
　　Some dire disaster, or by force or slight,
　　But what, or where, the Fates have wrapped in night:
105　Whether the nymph shall break Diana's¹ law,
　　Or some frail china jar receive a flaw,
　　Or stain her honor, or her new brocade,
　　Forget her prayers, or miss a masquerade,

---

9. In 18th-century poetic diction the word might mean bloodred, purple, or simply (as is likely here) brightly colored. The word derives from Virgil's *Eclogue* 9.40, *purpureum*. An example of the Latinate nature of some poetic diction of the period.
1. Diana was the goddess of chastity.

Or lose her heart, or necklace, at a ball;
110 Or whether Heaven has doomed that Shock must fall.
Haste, then, ye spirits! to your charge repair:
The fluttering fan be Zephyretta's care;
The drops[2] to thee, Brillante, we consign;
And, Momentilla, let the watch be thine;
115 Do thou, Crispissa,[3] tend her favorite Lock;
Ariel himself shall be the guard of Shock.
     "To fifty chosen Sylphs, of special note,
We trust the important charge, the petticoat;
Oft have we known that sevenfold fence to fail,
120 Though stiff with hoops, and armed with ribs of whale.
Form a strong line about the silver bound,
And guard the wide circumference around.
     "Whatever spirit, careless of his charge,
His post neglects, or leaves the fair at large,
125 Shall feel sharp vengeance soon o'ertake his sins,
Be stopped in vials, or transfixed with pins,
Or plunged in lakes of bitter washes lie,
Or wedged whole ages in a bodkin's[4] eye;
Gums and pomatums shall his flight restrain,
130 While clogged he beats his silken wings in vain,
Or alum styptics with contracting power
Shrink his thin essence like a riveled[5] flower:
Or, as Ixion[6] fixed, the wretch shall feel
The giddy motion of the whirling mill,
135 In fumes of burning chocolate shall glow,
And tremble at the sea that froths below!"
     He spoke; the spirits from the sails descend;
Some, orb in orb, around the nymph extend;
Some thread the mazy ringlets of her hair;
140 Some hang upon the pendants of her ear:
With beating hearts the dire event they wait,
Anxious, and trembling for the birth of Fate.

Canto 3

     Close by those meads, forever crowned with flowers,
Where Thames with pride surveys his rising towers,
There stands a structure of majestic frame,
Which from the neighboring Hampton[7] takes its name.
5 Here Britain's statesmen oft the fall foredoom
Of foreign tyrants and of nymphs at home;
Here thou, great Anna! whom three realms obey,
Dost sometimes counsel take—and sometimes tea.
     Hither the heroes and the nymphs resort,

---

2. Diamond earrings. Observe the appropriateness of the names of the Sylphs to their assigned functions.
3. From Latin *crispere*, "to curl."
4. A blunt needle with a large eye, used for drawing ribbon through eyelets in the edging of women's garments.

5. To "rivel" is to "contract into wrinkles and corrugations" (Johnson's *Dictionary*).
6. In the Greek myth, he was punished in the underworld by being bound on an everturning wheel.
7. Hampton Court, the royal palace, about fifteen miles up the Thames from London.

10 To taste awhile the pleasures of a court;
 In various talk the instructive hours they passed,
 Who gave the ball, or paid the visit last;
 One speaks the glory of the British Queen,
 And one describes a charming Indian screen;
15 A third interprets motions, looks, and eyes;
 At every word a reputation dies.
 Snuff, or the fan, supply each pause of chat,
 With singing, laughing, ogling, and all that.
  Meanwhile, declining from the noon of day,
20 The sun obliquely shoots his burning ray;
 The hungry judges soon the sentence sign,
 And wretches hang that jurymen may dine;
 The merchant from the Exchange returns in peace,
 And the long labors of the toilet cease.
25 Belinda now, whom thirst of fame invites,
 Burns to encounter two adventurous knights,
 At ombre[8] singly to decide their doom,
 And swells her breast with conquests yet to come.
 Straight the three bands prepare in arms to join,
30 Each band the number of the sacred nine.
 Soon as she spreads her hand, the aërial guard
 Descend, and sit on each important card:
 First Ariel perched upon a Matadore,
 Then each according to the rank they bore;
35 For Sylphs, yet mindful of their ancient race,
 Are, as when women, wondrous fond of place.
  Behold, four Kings in majesty revered,
 With hoary whiskers and a forky beard;
 And four fair Queens whose hands sustain a flower,
40 The expressive emblem of their softer power;
 Four Knaves in garbs succinct,° a trusty band,   *girded up*
 Caps on their heads, and halberts in their hand;
 And parti-colored troops, a shining train,
 Draw forth to combat on the velvet plain.
45 The skillful nymph reviews her force with care;
 "Let Spades be trumps!" she said, and trumps they were.
  Now move to war her sable Matadores,
 In show like leaders of the swarthy Moors.
 Spadillio first, unconquerable lord!
50 Led off two captive trumps, and swept the board.
 As many more Manillio forced to yield,
 And marched a victor from the verdant field.
 Him Basto followed, but his fate more hard
 Gained but one trump and one plebeian card.

8. The game of ombre that Belinda plays against the baron and another young man is too complicated for complete explication here. Pope has carefully arranged the cards so that Belinda wins. The baron's hand is strong enough to be a threat, but the third player's is of little account. The hand is played exactly according to the rules of ombre, and Pope's description of the cards is equally accurate. Each player holds nine cards (line 30). The "Mata-dores" (line 33), when spades are trump, are "Spadillio" (line 49), the ace of spades; "Manillio" (line 51), the two of spades; and "Basto" (line 53), the ace of clubs. Belinda holds all three of these. (For a more complete description of ombre, see *The Rape of the Lock and Other Poems*, ed. Geoffrey Tillotson, in the Twickenham Edition of Pope's poems, vol. 2, Appendix C.)

55 With his broad saber next, a chief in years,
The hoary Majesty of Spades appears,
Puts forth one manly leg, to sight revealed,
The rest his many-colored robe concealed.
The rebel Knave, who dares his prince engage,
60 Proves the just victim of his royal rage.
Even mighty Pam,[9] that kings and queens o'erthrew
And mowed down armies in the fights of loo,
Sad chance of war! now destitute of aid,
Falls undistinguished by the victor Spade.

65   Thus far both armies to Belinda yield;
Now to the Baron fate inclines the field.
His warlike amazon her host invades,
The imperial consort of the crown of Spades.
The Club's black tyrant first her victim died,
70 Spite of his haughty mien and barbarous pride.
What boots the regal circle on his head,
His giant limbs, in state unwieldy spread?
That long behind he trails his pompous robe,
And of all monarchs only grasps the globe?

75   The Baron now his Diamonds pours apace;
The embroidered King who shows but half his face,
And his refulgent Queen, with powers combined,
Of broken troops an easy conquest find.
Clubs, Diamonds, Hearts, in wild disorder seen,
80 With throngs promiscuous strew the level green.
Thus when dispersed a routed army runs,
Of Asia's troops, and Afric's sable sons,
With like confusion different nations fly,
Of various habit, and of various dye,
85 The pierced battalions disunited fall
In heaps on heaps; one fate o'erwhelms them all.

The Knave of Diamonds tries his wily arts,
And wins (oh, shameful chance!) the Queen of Hearts.
At this, the blood the virgin's cheek forsook,
90 A livid paleness spreads o'er all her look;
She sees, and trembles at the approaching ill,
Just in the jaws of ruin, and Codille.[1]
And now (as oft in some distempered state)
On one nice trick depends the general fate.

95 An Ace of Hearts steps forth: the King unseen
Lurked in her hand, and mourned his captive Queen.
He springs to vengeance with an eager pace,
And falls like thunder on the prostrate Ace.
The nymph exulting fills with shouts the sky,
100 The walls, the woods, and long canals reply.

O thoughtless mortals! ever blind to fate,
Too soon dejected, and too soon elate:
Sudden these honors shall be snatched away,
And cursed forever this victorious day.

---

9. The knave of clubs, the highest trump in the game of loo.

1. The term applied to losing a hand at cards.

105   For lo! the board with cups and spoons is crowned,
        The berries crackle, and the mill turns round;[2]
        On shining altars of Japan[3] they raise
        The silver lamp; the fiery spirits blaze:
        From silver spouts the grateful liquors glide,
110   While China's earth receives the smoking tide.
        At once they gratify their scent and taste,
        And frequent cups prolong the rich repast.
        Straight hover round the fair her airy band;
        Some, as she sipped, the fuming liquor fanned,
115   Some o'er her lap their careful plumes displayed,
        Trembling, and conscious of the rich brocade.
        Coffee (which makes the politician wise,
        And see through all things with his half-shut eyes)
        Sent up in vapors to the Baron's brain
120   New stratagems, the radiant Lock to gain.
        Ah, cease, rash youth! desist ere 'tis too late,
        Fear the just Gods, and think of Scylla's[4] fate!
        Changed to a bird, and sent to flit in air,
        She dearly pays for Nisus' injured hair!
125   But when to mischief mortals bend their will,
        How soon they find fit instruments of ill!
        Just then, Clarissa drew with tempting grace
        A two-edged weapon from her shining case:
        So ladies in romance assist their knight,
130   Present the spear, and arm him for the fight.
        He takes the gift with reverence, and extends
        The little engine on his fingers' ends;
        This just behind Belinda's neck he spread,
        As o'er the fragrant steams she bends her head.
135   Swift to the Lock a thousand sprites repair,
        A thousand wings, by turns, blow back the hair,
        And thrice they twitched the diamond in her ear,
        Thrice she looked back, and thrice the foe drew near.
        Just in that instant, anxious Ariel sought
140   The close recesses of the virgin's thought;
        As on the nosegay in her breast reclined,
        He watched the ideas rising in her mind,
        Sudden he viewed, in spite of all her art,
        An earthly lover lurking at her heart.
145   Amazed, confused, he found his power expired,
        Resigned to fate, and with a sigh retired.
        The Peer now spreads the glittering forfex° wide,   *scissors*
        To enclose the Lock; now joins it, to divide.
        Even then, before the fatal engine closed,
150   A wretched Sylph too fondly interposed;
        Fate urged the shears, and cut the Sylph in twain

2. I.e., coffee is roasted and ground.
3. I.e., small, lacquered tables. "Altars" suggests the ritualistic character of coffee drinking in Belinda's world.
4. Scylla, daughter of Nisus, was turned into a sea bird because, for the sake of her love for Minos of Crete, who was besieging her father's city of Megara, she cut from her father's head the purple lock on which his safety depended. She is not the Scylla of "Scylla and Charybdis."

(But airy substance soon unites again):
The meeting points the sacred hair dissever
From the fair head, forever and forever!
155   Then flashed the living lightning from her eyes,
And screams of horror rend the affrighted skies.
Not louder shrieks to pitying heaven are cast,
When husbands, or when lapdogs breathe their last;
Or when rich china vessels fallen from high,
160 In glittering dust and painted fragments lie!
"Let wreaths of triumph now my temples twine,"
The victor cried, "the glorious prize is mine!
While fish in streams, or birds delight in air,
Or in a coach and six the British fair,
165 As long as *Atalantis*[5] shall be read,
Or the small pillow grace a lady's bed,
While visits shall be paid on solemn days,
When numerous wax-lights in bright order blaze,
While nymphs take treats, or assignations give,
170 So long my honor, name, and praise shall live!
   "What time would spare, from steel receives its date,
And monuments, like men, submit to fate!
Steel could the labor of the Gods destroy,
And strike to dust the imperial towers of Troy;
175 Steel could the works of mortal pride confound,
And hew triumphal arches to the ground.
What wonder then, fair nymph! thy hairs should feel,
The conquering force of unresisted steel?"

Canto 4

   But anxious cares the pensive nymph oppressed,
And secret passions labored in her breast.
Not youthful kings in battle seized alive,
Not scornful virgins who their charms survive,
5 Not ardent lovers robbed of all their bliss,
Not ancient ladies when refused a kiss,
Not tyrants fierce that unrepenting die,
Not Cynthia when her manteau's° pinned awry,   *wrap*
E'er felt such rage, resentment, and despair,
10 As thou, sad virgin! for thy ravished hair.
   For, that sad moment, when the Sylphs withdrew
And Ariel weeping from Belinda flew,
Umbriel,[6] a dusky, melancholy sprite
As ever sullied the fair face of light,
15 Down to the central earth, his proper scene,
Repaired to search the gloomy Cave of Spleen.°   *Ill Humor*
   Swift on his sooty pinions flits the Gnome,
And in a vapor reached the dismal dome.
No cheerful breeze this sullen region knows,

---

5. Delariviere Manley's *New Atalantis* (1709) was notorious for its thinly concealed allusions to con-

temporary scandals.
6. The name suggests shade and darkness.

20 The dreaded east is all the wind that blows.
Here in a grotto, sheltered close from air,
And screened in shades from day's detested glare,
She sighs forever on her pensive bed,
Pain at her side, and Megrim° at her head.   *headache*
25 Two handmaids wait the throne: alike in place
But differing far in figure and in face.
Here stood Ill-Nature like an ancient maid,
Her wrinkled form in black and white arrayed;
With store of prayers for mornings, nights, and noons,
30 Her hand is filled; her bosom with lampoons.
There Affectation, with a sickly mien,
Shows in her cheek the roses of eighteen,
Practiced to lisp, and hang the head aside,
Faints into airs, and languishes with pride,
35 On the rich quilt sinks with becoming woe,
Wrapped in a gown, for sickness and for show.
The fair ones feel such maladies as these,
When each new nightdress gives a new disease.
A constant vapor[7] o'er the palace flies,
40 Strange phantoms rising as the mists arise;
Dreadful as hermit's dreams in haunted shades,
Or bright as visions of expiring maids.
Now glaring fiends, and snakes on rolling spires,°   *coils*
Pale specters, gaping tombs, and purple fires;
45 Now lakes of liquid gold, Elysian scenes,
And crystal domes, and angels in machines.[8]
Unnumbered throngs on every side are seen
Of bodies changed to various forms by Spleen.
Here living teapots stand, one arm held out,
50 One bent; the handle this, and that the spout:
A pipkin° there, like Homer's tripod,[9] walks;   *earthen pot*
Here sighs a jar, and there a goose pie talks;
Men prove with child, as powerful fancy works,
And maids, turned bottles, call aloud for corks.
55 Safe passed the Gnome through this fantastic band,
A branch of healing spleenwort[1] in his hand.
Then thus addressed the Power: "Hail, wayward Queen!
Who rule the sex to fifty from fifteen:
Parent of vapors and of female wit,
60 Who give the hysteric or poetic fit,
On various tempers act by various ways,
Make some take physic, others scribble plays;
Who cause the proud their visits to delay,
And send the godly in a pet to pray.
65 A nymph there is that all your power disdains,
And thousands more in equal mirth maintains.

7. Emblematic of "the vapors," a fashionable hypochondria, melancholy, or peevishness.
8. Mechanical devices used in the theaters for spectacular effects. The catalog of hallucinations draws on the sensational stage effects popular with contemporary audiences.

9. In *Iliad* 18.373–77, Vulcan furnishes the gods with self-propelling "tripods" (three-legged stools).
1. An herb, efficacious against the spleen. Pope alludes to the golden bough that Aeneas and the Cumaean sibyl carry with them for protection into the underworld in *Aeneid* 6.

But oh! if e'er thy Gnome could spoil a grace,
Or raise a pimple on a beauteous face,
Like citron-waters[2] matrons' cheeks inflame,
70 Or change complexions at a losing game;
If e'er with airy horns[3] I planted heads,
Or rumpled petticoats, or tumbled beds,
Or caused suspicion when no soul was rude,
Or discomposed the headdress of a prude,
75 Or e'er to costive lapdog gave disease,
Which not the tears of brightest eyes could ease,
Hear me, and touch Belinda with chagrin:°   ill humor
That single act gives half the world the spleen."
    The Goddess with a discontented air
80 Seems to reject him though she grants his prayer.
A wondrous bag with both her hands she binds,
Like that where once Ulysses held the winds;[4]
There she collects the force of female lungs,
Sighs, sobs, and passions, and the war of tongues.
85 A vial next she fills with fainting fears,
Soft sorrows, melting griefs, and flowing tears.
The Gnome rejoicing bears her gifts away,
Spreads his black wings, and slowly mounts to day.
    Sunk in Thalestris'[5] arms the nymph he found,
90 Her eyes dejected and her hair unbound.
Full o'er their heads the swelling bag he rent,
And all the Furies issued at the vent.
Belinda burns with more than mortal ire,
And fierce Thalestris fans the rising fire.
95 "O wretched maid!" she spread her hands, and cried
(While Hampton's echoes, "Wretched maid!" replied),
"Was it for this you took such constant care
The bodkin, comb, and essence to prepare?
For this your locks in paper durance bound,
100 For this with torturing irons wreathed around?
For this with fillets strained your tender head,
And bravely bore the double loads of lead?[6]
Gods! shall the ravisher display your hair,
While the fops envy, and the ladies stare!
105 Honor forbid! at whose unrivaled shrine
Ease, pleasure, virtue, all, our sex resign.
Methinks already I your tears survey,
Already hear the horrid things they say,
Already see you a degraded toast,
110 And all your honor in a whisper lost!
How shall I, then, your helpless fame defend?

2. Brandy flavored with orange or lemon peel.
3. The symbol of the cuckold, the man whose wife has been unfaithful to him; here "airy," because they exist only in the jealous suspicions of the husband, the victim of the mischievous Umbriel.
4. Aeolus (later conceived of as god of the winds) gave Ulysses a bag containing all the winds adverse to his voyage home. When his ship was in sight of

Ithaca, his companions opened the bag and the storms that ensued drove Ulysses far away (*Odyssey* 10.19ff.).
5. The name is borrowed from a queen of the Amazons, hence a fierce and warlike woman.
6. The frame on which the elaborate coiffures of the day were arranged.

'Twill then be infamy to seem your friend!
And shall this prize, the inestimable prize,
Exposed through crystal to the gazing eyes,
115 And heightened by the diamond's circling rays,
On that rapacious hand forever blaze?
Sooner shall grass in Hyde Park Circus grow,
And wits take lodgings in the sound of Bow;[7]
Sooner let earth, air, sea, to chaos fall,
120 Men, monkeys, lapdogs, parrots, perish all!"
     She said; then raging to Sir Plume repairs,
And bids her beau demand the precious hairs
(Sir Plume of amber snuffbox justly vain,
And the nice conduct of a clouded cane).
125 With earnest eyes, and round unthinking face,
He first the snuffbox opened, then the case,
And thus broke out—"My Lord, why, what the devil!
Z——ds! damn the lock! 'fore Gad, you must be civil!
Plague on 't! 'tis past a jest—nay prithee, pox!
130 Give her the hair"—he spoke, and rapped his box.
     "It grieves me much," replied the Peer again,
"Who speaks so well should ever speak in vain.
But by this Lock, this sacred Lock I swear
(Which never more shall join its parted hair;
135 Which never more its honors shall renew,
Clipped from the lovely head where late it grew),
That while my nostrils draw the vital air,
This hand, which won it, shall forever wear."
He spoke, and speaking, in proud triumph spread
140 The long-contended honors[8] of her head.
     But Umbriel, hateful Gnome, forbears not so;
He breaks the vial whence the sorrows flow.
Then see! the nymph in beauteous grief appears,
Her eyes half languishing, half drowned in tears;
145 On her heaved bosom hung her drooping head,
Which with a sigh she raised, and thus she said:
     "Forever cursed be this detested day,
Which snatched my best, my favorite curl away!
Happy! ah, ten times happy had I been,
150 If Hampton Court these eyes had never seen!
Yet am not I the first mistaken maid,
By love of courts to numerous ills betrayed.
Oh, had I rather unadmired remained
In some lone isle, or distant northern land;
155 Where the gilt chariot never marks the way,
Where none learn ombre, none e'er taste bohea![9]
There kept my charms concealed from mortal eye,
Like roses that in deserts bloom and die.
What moved my mind with youthful lords to roam?
160 Oh, had I stayed, and said my prayers at home!

---

7. A person born within sound of the bells of St. Mary-le-Bow in Cheapside is said to be a cockney. No fashionable wit would have so vulgar an address.
8. Ornaments, hence locks; a Latinism.
9. A costly sort of tea.

'Twas this the morning omens seemed to tell;
Thrice from my trembling hand the patch box[1] fell;
The tottering china shook without a wind,
Nay, Poll sat mute, and Shock was most unkind!
165   A Sylph too warned me of the threats of fate,
In mystic visions, now believed too late!
See the poor remnants of these slighted hairs!
My hands shall rend what e'en thy rapine spares.
These in two sable ringlets taught to break,
170   Once gave new beauties to the snowy neck.
The sister lock now sits uncouth, alone,
And in its fellow's fate foresees its own;
Uncurled it hangs, the fatal shears demands,
And tempts once more thy sacrilegious hands.
175   Oh, hadst thou, cruel! been content to seize
Hairs less in sight, or any hairs but these!"

Canto 5

She said: the pitying audience melt in tears.
But Fate and Jove had stopped the Baron's ears.
In vain Thalestris with reproach assails,
For who can move when fair Belinda fails?
5   Not half so fixed the Trojan[2] could remain,
While Anna begged and Dido raged in vain.
Then grave Clarissa graceful waved her fan;
Silence ensued, and thus the nymph began:
"Say, why are beauties praised and honored most,
10   The wise man's passion, and the vain man's toast?
Why decked with all that land and sea afford,
Why angels called, and angel-like adored?
Why round our coaches crowd the white-gloved beaux,
Why bows the side box from its inmost rows?
15   How vain are all these glories, all our pains,
Unless good sense preserve what beauty gains;
That men may say when we the front box grace,
'Behold the first in virtue as in face!'
Oh! if to dance all night, and dress all day,
20   Charmed the smallpox, or chased old age away,
Who would not scorn what housewife's cares produce,
Or who would learn one earthly thing of use?
To patch, nay ogle, might become a saint,
Nor could it sure be such a sin to paint.
25   But since, alas! frail beauty must decay,
Curled or uncurled, since locks will turn to gray;
Since painted, or not painted, all shall fade,
And she who scorns a man must die a maid;
What then remains but well our power to use,

---

1. To hold the ornamental patches of court plaster
worn on the face by both sexes.
2. Aeneas, who forsook Dido at the bidding of the
gods, despite her reproaches and the supplications
of her sister Anna. Virgil compares him to a steadfast oak that withstands a storm (*Aeneid* 4.437–
43).

30 And keep good humor still whate'er we lose?
And trust me, dear, good humor can prevail
When airs, and flights, and screams, and scolding fail.
Beauties in vain their pretty eyes may roll;
Charms strike the sight, but merit wins the soul."[3]
35   So spoke the dame, but no applause ensued;
Belinda frowned, Thalestris called her prude.
"To arms, to arms!" the fierce virago cries,
And swift as lightning to the combat flies.
All side in parties, and begin the attack;
40 Fans clap, silks rustle, and tough whalebones crack;
Heroes' and heroines' shouts confusedly rise,
And bass and treble voices strike the skies.
No common weapons in their hands are found,
Like Gods they fight, nor dread a mortal wound.
45   So when bold Homer makes the Gods engage,
And heavenly breasts with human passions rage;
'Gainst Pallas, Mars; Latona, Hermes arms;
And all Olympus rings with loud alarms:
Jove's thunder roars, heaven trembles all around,
50 Blue Neptune storms, the bellowing deeps resound:
Earth shakes her nodding towers, the ground gives way,
And the pale ghosts start at the flash of day!
   Triumphant Umbriel on a sconce's[4] height
Clapped his glad wings, and sat to view the fight:
55 Propped on the bodkin spears, the sprites survey
The growing combat, or assist the fray.
   While through the press enraged Thalestris flies,
And scatters death around from both her eyes,
A beau and witling perished in the throng,
60 One died in metaphor, and one in song.
"O cruel nymph! a living death I bear,"
Cried Dapperwit, and sunk beside his chair.
A mournful glance Sir Fopling upwards cast,
"Those eyes are made so killing"—was his last.
65 Thus on Maeander's flowery margin lies
The expiring swan, and as he sings he dies.
   When bold Sir Plume had drawn Clarissa down,
Chloe stepped in, and killed him with a frown;
She smiled to see the doughty hero slain,
70 But, at her smile, the beau revived again.
   Now Jove suspends his golden scales in air,
Weighs the men's wits against the lady's hair;
The doubtful beam long nods from side to side;
At length the wits mount up, the hairs subside.
75   See, fierce Belinda on the Baron flies,
With more than usual lightning in her eyes;
Nor feared the chief the unequal fight to try,
Who sought no more than on his foe to die.

3. The speech is a close parody of Pope's own translation of the speech of Sarpedon to Glaucus, first published in 1709 and slightly revised in his version of the *Iliad* (12.371–96).
4. Candlestick fastened on the wall.

But this bold lord with manly strength endued,
80 She with one finger and a thumb subdued:
Just where the breath of life his nostrils drew,
A charge of snuff the wily virgin threw;
The Gnomes direct, to every atom just,
The pungent grains of titillating dust.
85 Sudden, with starting tears each eye o'erflows,
And the high dome re-echoes to his nose.
    "Now meet thy fate," incensed Belinda cried,
And drew a deadly bodkin[5] from her side.
(The same, his ancient personage to deck,
90 Her great-great-grandsire wore about his neck,
In three seal rings; which after, melted down,
Formed a vast buckle for his widow's gown:
Her infant grandame's whistle next it grew,
The bells she jingled, and the whistle blew;
95 Then in a bodkin graced her mother's hairs,
Which long she wore, and now Belinda wears.)
    "Boast not my fall," he cried, "insulting foe!
Thou by some other shalt be laid as low.
Nor think to die dejects my lofty mind:
100 All that I dread is leaving you behind!
Rather than so, ah, let me still survive,
And burn in Cupid's flames—but burn alive."
    "Restore the Lock!" she cries; and all around
"Restore the Lock!" the vaulted roofs rebound.
105 Not fierce Othello in so loud a strain
Roared for the handkerchief that caused his pain.[6]
But see how oft ambitious aims are crossed,
And chiefs contend till all the prize is lost!
The lock, obtained with guilt, and kept with pain,
110 In every place is sought, but sought in vain:
With such a prize no mortal must be blessed,
So Heaven decrees! with Heaven who can contest?
    Some thought it mounted to the lunar sphere,
Since all things lost on earth are treasured there.
115 There heroes' wits are kept in ponderous vases,
And beaux' in snuffboxes and tweezer cases.
There broken vows and deathbed alms are found,
And lovers' hearts with ends of riband bound,
The courtier's promises, and sick man's prayers,
120 The smiles of harlots, and the tears of heirs,
Cages for gnats, and chains to yoke a flea,
Dried butterflies, and tomes of casuistry.
    But trust the Muse—she saw it upward rise,
Though marked by none but quick, poetic eyes
125 (So Rome's great founder to the heavens withdrew,[7]
To Proculus alone confessed in view);

---

5. Here, an ornamental hairpin shaped like a dagger.
6. *Othello* 3.4.
7. Romulus, the "founder" and first king of Rome,
was snatched to heaven in a storm cloud while reviewing his army in the Campus Martius (Livy 1.16).

A sudden star, it shot through liquid air,
And drew behind a radiant trail of hair.
Not Berenice's locks first rose so bright,[8]
130   The heavens bespangling with disheveled light.
The Sylphs behold it kindling as it flies,
And pleased pursue its progress through the skies.
      This the beau monde shall from the Mall[9] survey,
And hail with music its propitious ray.
135   This the blest lover shall for Venus take,
And send up vows from Rosamonda's Lake.[1]
This Partridge[2] soon shall view in cloudless skies,
When next he looks through Galileo's eyes;°   telescope
And hence the egregious wizard shall foredoom
140   The fate of Louis, and the fall of Rome.
      Then cease, bright nymph! to mourn thy ravished hair,
Which adds new glory to the shining sphere!
Not all the tresses that fair head can boast
Shall draw such envy as the Lock you lost.
145   For, after all the murders of your eye,
When, after millions slain, yourself shall die:
When those fair suns shall set, as set they must,
And all those tresses shall be laid in dust,
This Lock the Muse shall consecrate to fame,
150   And 'midst the stars inscribe Belinda's name.

1712   1714

An Essay on Man

Pope's philosophical poem, *An Essay on Man*, is a fragment of an ambitious but never completed scheme for what the poet referred to as his "ethic work," which was to have been a large survey of human nature, society, and morals. The work is dedicated to Henry St. John (pronounced *Sín-jun*), Viscount Bolingbroke (1678–1751), the brilliant, though erratic, secretary of state in the Tory ministry of 1710–14, whom Pope had come to know through Jonathan Swift. After the accession of George I he fled to France, attainted of treason, but was pardoned and allowed to return in 1723. He settled near Pope at Dawley farm and a close friendship developed between the two men. In their conversations Bolingbroke, who fancied himself a philosopher, helped Pope formulate the optimistic system that is expounded in this poem. Yet it is clear that the poem would have been pretty much what it is had the two men never met, for it expresses doctrines widely circulated and generally accepted at the time by enlightened minds throughout Europe. The *Essay* gives memorable expression to ideas about the nature of the universe and our place in it, ideas on which eighteenth-century optimism rested.

Pope's purpose is to "vindicate the ways of God to man," a phrase that consciously echoes *Paradise Lost* 1.26. Like John Milton, Pope faces the problem of the existence of evil in a world presumed to be the creation of a good God. *Paradise Lost* is biblical

---

8. Berenice, the wife of Ptolemy III, dedicated a lock of her hair to the gods to ensure her husband's safe return from war. It was turned into a constellation.
9. A walk laid out by Charles II in St. James's Park (London), a resort for strollers of all sorts.

1. In St. James's Park; associated with unhappy lovers.
2. John Partridge, an astrologer whose annually published predictions had been amusingly satirized by Swift and other wits in 1708.

in content, Christian in doctrine; *An Essay on Man* avoids all specifically Christian doctrines, not because Pope disbelieved them, but because "man," the subject of the poem, includes millions who never heard of Christianity, and Pope is concerned with the universal. Milton tells a mythological story. Pope writes in abstract terms.

The *Essay* is divided into four epistles. In the first Pope asserts the essential order and goodness of the universe and the rightness of our place in it. The other epistles deal with how we may emulate in our nature and in society the cosmic harmony revealed in the first epistle. The second seeks to show how we may attain a psychological harmony that can become the basis of a virtuous life through the cooperation of self-love and the passions (both necessary to our complete humanity) with reason, the controller and director. The third is concerned with the individual in society, which, it teaches, was created through the cooperation of self-love (the egoistic drives that motivate us) and social love (our dependence on others, our inborn benevolence). The fourth is concerned with happiness, which lies within the reach of all, for it is dependent on virtue, which becomes possible when—though only when—self-love is transmuted into love of others and love of God. Such, in brief summary, are Pope's main ideas, expressed in many phrases so memorable that they have detached themselves from the poem and become part of daily speech.

From An Essay on Man

TO HENRY ST. JOHN, LORD BOLINGBROKE

Epistle 1. Of the Nature and State of Man,
With Respect to the Universe

Awake, my St. John! leave all meaner things
To low ambition, and the pride of kings.
Let us (since life can little more supply
Than just to look about us and to die)
5 Expatiate free° o'er all this scene of man;   *range freely*
A mighty maze! but not without a plan;
A wild, where weeds and flowers promiscuous shoot,
Or garden, tempting with forbidden fruit.
Together let us beat this ample field,
10 Try what the open, what the covert yield;
The latent tracts, the giddy heights, explore
Of all who blindly creep, or sightless soar;
Eye Nature's walks, shoot folly as it flies,
And catch the manners living as they rise;
15 Laugh where we must, be candid° where we can;   *kindly*
But vindicate the ways of God to man.

1. Say first, of God above, or man below,
What can we reason, but from what we know?
Of man, what see we but his station here,
20 From which to reason, or to which refer?
Through worlds unnumbered though the God be known,
'Tis ours to trace him only in our own.
He, who through vast immensity can pierce,
See worlds on worlds compose one universe,
25 Observe how system into system runs,
What other planets circle other suns,

What varied being peoples every star,
May tell why Heaven has made us as we are.
But of this frame the bearings, and the ties,
30   The strong connections, nice dependencies,
Gradations just, has thy pervading soul
Looked through? or can a part contain the whole?
    Is the great chain, that draws all to agree,
And drawn supports, upheld by God, or thee?[1]

35   2. Presumptuous man! the reason wouldst thou find,
Why formed so weak, so little, and so blind?
First, if thou canst, the harder reason guess,
Why formed no weaker, blinder, and no less!
Ask of thy mother earth, why oaks are made
40   Taller or stronger than the weeds they shade?
Or ask of yonder argent fields above,
Why Jove's satellites[2] are less than Jove?
    Of systems possible, if 'tis confessed
That Wisdom Infinite must form the best,
45   Where all must full or not coherent be,
And all that rises, rise in due degree;
Then, in the scale of reasoning life, 'tis plain,
There must be, somewhere, such a rank as man:
And all the question (wrangle e'er so long)
50   Is only this, if God has placed him wrong?
    Respecting man, whatever wrong we call,
May, must be right, as relative to all.
In human works, though labored on with pain,
A thousand movements scarce one purpose gain;
55   In God's, one single can its end produce;
Yet serves to second too some other use.
So man, who here seems principal alone,
Perhaps acts second to some sphere unknown,
Touches some wheel, or verges to some goal;
60   'Tis but a part we see, and not a whole.
    When the proud steed shall know why man restrains
His fiery course, or drives him o'er the plains;
When the dull ox, why now he breaks the clod,
Is now a victim, and now Egypt's god:
65   Then shall man's pride and dullness comprehend
His actions', passions', being's use and end;
Why doing, suffering, checked, impelled; and why
This hour a slave, the next a deity.
    Then say not man's imperfect, Heaven in fault;
70   Say rather, man's as perfect as he ought;
His knowledge measured to his state and place,
His time a moment, and a point his space.
If to be perfect in a certain sphere,[3]
What matter, soon or late, or here or there?

---

1. For the chain of being, see Addison's *The Spectator* 519 and lines 207–58.
2. In his *Dictionary,* Johnson notes and condemns

Pope's giving this word four syllables, as in Latin.
3. I.e., in one's "state and place."

75   The blest today is as completely so,
      As who began a thousand years ago.

      3. Heaven from all creatures hides the book of Fate,
      All but the page prescribed, their present state:
      From brutes what men, from men what spirits know:
80   Or who could suffer being here below?
      The lamb thy riot dooms to bleed today,
      Had he thy reason, would he skip and play?
      Pleased to the last, he crops the flowery food,
      And licks the hand just raised to shed his blood.
85   O blindness to the future! kindly given,
      That each may fill the circle marked by Heaven:
      Who sees with equal eye, as God of all,
      A hero perish, or a sparrow fall,
      Atoms or systems° into ruin hurled,   *solar systems*
90   And now a bubble burst, and now a world.
          Hope humbly then; with trembling pinions soar;
      Wait the great teacher Death, and God adore!
      What future bliss, he gives not thee to know,
      But gives that hope to be thy blessing now.
95   Hope springs eternal in the human breast:
      Man never is, but always to be blest:
      The soul, uneasy and confined from home,
      Rests and expatiates in a life to come.
          Lo! the poor Indian, whose untutored mind
100   Sees God in clouds, or hears him in the wind;
      His soul proud Science never taught to stray
      Far as the solar walk, or milky way;
      Yet simple Nature to his hope has given,
      Behind the cloud-topped hill, an humbler heaven;
105   Some safer world in depth of woods embraced,
      Some happier island in the watery waste,
      Where slaves once more their native land behold,
      No fiends torment, no Christians thirst for gold!
      To be, contents his natural desire,
110   He asks no angel's wing, no seraph's fire;
      But thinks, admitted to that equal sky,
      His faithful dog shall bear him company.

          4. Go, wiser thou! and, in thy scale of sense,
      Weigh thy opinion against Providence;
115   Call imperfection what thou fancy'st such,
      Say, here he gives too little, there too much;
      Destroy all creatures for thy sport or gust,[4]
      Yet cry, if man's unhappy, God's unjust;
      If man alone engross not Heaven's high care,
120   Alone made perfect here, immortal there:
      Snatch from his hand the balance and the rod,
      Rejudge his justice, be the God of God!

4. "Sense of tasting" (Johnson's *Dictionary*).

In pride, in reasoning pride, our error lies;
All quit their sphere, and rush into the skies.
125 Pride still is aiming at the blest abodes,
Men would be angels, angels would be gods.
Aspiring to be gods, if angels fell,
Aspiring to be angels, men rebel:
And who but wishes to invert the laws
130 Of order, sins against the Eternal Cause.

    5. Ask for what end the heavenly bodies shine,
Earth for whose use? Pride answers, " 'Tis for mine:
For me kind Nature wakes her genial power,
Suckles each herb, and spreads out every flower;
135 Annual for me, the grape, the rose renew
The juice nectareous, and the balmy dew;
For me, the mine a thousand treasures brings;
For me, health gushes from a thousand springs;
Seas roll to waft me, suns to light me rise;
140 My footstool earth, my canopy the skies."
    But errs not Nature from this gracious end,
From burning suns when livid deaths descend,
When earthquakes swallow, or when tempests sweep
Towns to one grave, whole nations to the deep?
145 "No," 'tis replied, "the first Almighty Cause
Acts not by partial, but by general laws;
The exceptions few; some change since all began,
And what created perfect?"—Why then man?
If the great end be human happiness,
150 Then Nature deviates; and can man do less?
As much that end a constant course requires
Of showers and sunshine, as of man's desires;
As much eternal springs and cloudless skies,
As men forever temperate, calm, and wise.
155 If plagues or earthquakes break not Heaven's design,
Why then a Borgia, or a Catiline?[5]
Who knows but he whose hand the lightning forms,
Who heaves old ocean, and who wings the storms,
Pours fierce ambition in a Caesar's mind,
160 Or turns young Ammon[6] loose to scourge mankind?
From pride, from pride, our very reasoning springs;
Account for moral, as for natural things:
Why charge we Heaven in those, in these acquit?
In both, to reason right is to submit.
165   Better for us, perhaps, it might appear,
Were there all harmony, all virtue here;
That never air or ocean felt the wind;
That never passion discomposed the mind:

5. The Renaissance Italian family of the Borgias was notorious for its crimes: ruthless lust for power, cruelty, rapaciousness, treachery, and murder (especially by poisoning). Cesare Borgia (1476–1507), son of Pope Alexander VI, is here referred to. Lucius Sergius Catiline (ca. 108–62 B.C.E.), an ambitious, greedy, and cruel conspirator against the Roman state, was denounced in Cicero's famous orations before the senate and in the Forum.
6. Alexander the Great.

But ALL subsists by elemental strife;
170 And passions are the elements of life.
The general ORDER, since the whole began,
Is kept in Nature, and is kept in man.

    6. What would this man? Now upward will he soar,
And little less than angel, would be more;
175 Now looking downwards, just as grieved appears
To want the strength of bulls, the fur of bears.
Made for his use all creatures if he call,
Say what their use, had he the powers of all?
Nature to these, without profusion, kind,
180 The proper organs, proper powers assigned;
Each seeming want compènsated of course,
Here with degrees of swiftness, there of force;
All in exact proportion to the state;
Nothing to add, and nothing to abate.
185 Each beast, each insect, happy in its own;
Is Heaven unkind to man, and man alone?
Shall he alone, whom rational we call,
Be pleased with nothing, if not blessed with all?
    The bliss of man (could pride that blessing find)
190 Is not to act or think beyond mankind;
No powers of body or of soul to share,
But what his nature and his state can bear.
Why has not man a microscopic eye?
For this plain reason, man is not a fly.
195 Say what the use, were finer optics given,
To inspect a mite, not comprehend the heaven?
Or touch, if tremblingly alive all o'er,
To smart and agonize at every pore?
Or quick effluvia⁷ darting through the brain,
200 Die of a rose in aromatic pain?
If nature thundered in his opening ears,
And stunned him with the music of the spheres,
How would he wish that Heaven had left him still
The whispering zephyr, and the purling rill?
205 Who finds not Providence all good and wise,
Alike in what it gives, and what denies?

    7. Far as creation's ample range extends,
The scale of sensual,° mental powers ascends: *sensory*
Mark how it mounts, to man's imperial race,
210 From the green myriads in the peopled grass:
What modes of sight betwixt each wide extreme,
The mole's dim curtain, and the lynx's beam:⁸
Of smell, the headlong lioness between,

---

7. According to the philosophy of Epicurus (adopted by Robert Boyle, the chemist, and other 17th-century scientists), the senses are stirred to perception by being bombarded through the pores by steady streams of "effluvia," incredibly thin and tiny—but material—images of the objects that surround us.

8. One of several early theories of vision held that the eye casts a beam of light that makes objects visible.

And hound sagacious[9] on the tainted green:
215 Of hearing, from the life that fills the flood,
To that which warbles through the vernal wood:
The spider's touch, how exquisitely fine!
Feels at each thread, and lives along the line:
In the nice° bee, what sense so subtly true   *exact, accurate*
220 From poisonous herbs extracts the healing dew:
How instinct varies in the groveling swine,
Compared, half-reasoning elephant, with thine!
'Twixt that, and reason, what a nice barrier,[1]
Forever separate, yet forever near!
225 Remembrance and reflection how allied;
What thin partitions sense from thought divide:
And middle natures, how they long to join,
Yet never pass the insuperable line!
Without this just gradation, could they be
230 Subjected, these to those, or all to thee?
The powers of all subdued by thee alone,
Is not thy reason all these powers in one?

    8. See, through this air, this ocean, and this earth,
All matter quick, and bursting into birth.
235 Above, how high progressive life may go!
Around, how wide! how deep extend below!
Vast Chain of Being! which from God began,
Natures ethereal, human, angel, man,
Beast, bird, fish, insect, what no eye can see,
240 No glass can reach! from Infinite to thee,
From thee to nothing.—On superior powers
Were we to press, inferior might on ours:
Or in the full creation leave a void,
Where, one step broken, the great scale's destroyed:
245 From Nature's chain whatever link you strike,
Tenth or ten thousandth, breaks the chain alike.
    And, if each system in gradation roll
Alike essential to the amazing whole,
The least confusion but in one, not all
250 That system only, but the whole must fall.
Let earth unbalanced from her orbit fly,
Planets and suns run lawless through the sky,
Let ruling angels from their spheres be hurled,
Being on being wrecked, and world on world,
255 Heaven's whole foundations to their center nod,
And Nature tremble to the throne of God:
All this dread ORDER break—for whom? for thee?
Vile worm!—oh, madness, pride, impiety!

    9. What if the foot, ordained the dust to tread,
260 Or hand, to toil, aspired to be the head?

---

9. Quick of scent.   1. Pronounced *ba-réer*.

What if the head, the eye, or ear repined
To serve mere engines to the ruling Mind?[2]
Just as absurd, to mourn the tasks or pains,
The great directing MIND of ALL ordains.
265   All are but parts of one stupendous whole,
Whose body Nature is, and God the soul;
That, changed through all, and yet in all the same,
Great in the earth, as in the ethereal frame,
Warms in the sun, refreshes in the breeze,
270   Glows in the stars, and blossoms in the trees,
Lives through all life, extends through all extent,
Spreads undivided, operates unspent,
Breathes in our soul, informs our mortal part,
As full, as perfect, in a hair as heart;
275   As full, as perfect, in vile man that mourns,
As the rapt seraph that adores and burns;
To him no high, no low, no great, no small;
He fills, he bounds, connects, and equals all.

        10. Cease then, nor ORDER imperfection name:
280   Our proper bliss depends on what we blame.
Know thy own point: this kind, this due degree
Of blindness, weakness, Heaven bestows on thee.
Submit—In this, or any other sphere,
Secure to be as blest as thou canst bear:
285   Safe in the hand of one disposing Power,
Or in the natal, or the mortal hour.
All Nature is but art, unknown to thee;
All chance, direction, which thou canst not see;
All discord, harmony not understood;
290   All partial evil, universal good:
And, spite of pride, in erring reason's spite,
One truth is clear: Whatever IS, is RIGHT.

        From *Epistle 2. Of the Nature and State of Man
        With Respect to Himself, as an Individual*

        1. Know then thyself, presume not God to scan;
The proper study of mankind is Man.
Placed on this isthmus of a middle state,
A being darkly wise, and rudely great:
5   With too much knowledge for the skeptic side,
With too much weakness for the Stoic's pride,
He hangs between; in doubt to act, or rest,
In doubt to deem himself a god, or beast;
In doubt his mind or body to prefer,
10   Born but to die, and reasoning but to err;
Alike in ignorance, his reason such,
Whether he thinks too little, or too much:

2. Cf. 1 Corinthians 12.14–26.

Chaos of thought and passion, all confused;
Still by himself abused, or disabused;
15   Created half to rise, and half to fall;
Great lord of all things, yet a prey to all;
Sole judge of truth, in endless error hurled:
The glory, jest, and riddle of the world!

*   *   *   1733

Epistle 2. To a Lady   *Epistle 2. To a Lady* is one of four poems that Pope grouped together under the title *Epistles to Several Persons* but that have usually been known by the less appropriate title *Moral Essays*. They were conceived as parts of Pope's ambitious "ethic work," of which only the first part, *An Essay on Man*, was completed. *Epistle* 1 treats the characters of men and *Epistle* 2, the characters of women. The other two epistles are concerned with the use of riches, a subject that engaged Pope's attention during the 1730s, because he distrusted the influence on private morals and public life of the rapidly growing wealth of England under the first Hanoverians.

    Epistle 2 combines two literary forms: the satire on women, and the verse letter to a particular person—here Martha Blount (1690–1763), Pope's closest female friend, whose remark in line 2 sets the theme of the poem. The first section (to line 198) sketches a portrait gallery of ladies that illustrates their inconsistency and volatility. As an amateur painter, Pope is fascinated by the problem of catching such contrary types: the affected, the soft-natured, the cunning, the whimsical, the witty, and the silly. The next part of the poem (lines 199–248) develops Pope's favorite theory of the ruling passion—the idea that each person is driven by a single irresistible desire—and argues that women are limited to two passions: love of pleasure and love of power. The final part (line 249 to the end) describes an ideal woman, good-natured, sensible, and well balanced, who is identified with Blount herself.

    Like every satire on women, *Epistle* 2 is shaped by stereotypes: women are fickle, frail, and subordinate to men. Yet much of the poem undermines those prejudices by showing the real difficulties of women's lives. "By man's oppression cursed," they waste their talents on trivial pursuits and "die of nothing but a rage to live." The poem shares that restlessness. If women are full of contradictions, so are Pope's couplets, torn between sympathy and satiric bite. The poet finds himself strangely attracted to what he disapproves, and many female readers, then and now, have felt the same way about the poem.

Epistle 2. To a Lady

Of the Characters of Women

Nothing so true as what you once let fall,
"Most women have no characters at all."
Matter too soft a lasting mark to bear,
And best distinguished by black, brown, or fair.
5   How many pictures[1] of one nymph we view,

---

1. Ladies of the 17th and 18th centuries were often painted in the costumes and attitudes of fanciful, mythological, or historical characters.

All how unlike each other, all how true!
Arcadia's countess, here, in ermined pride,
Is, there, Pastora by a fountain side.
Here Fannia, leering on her own good man,
10   And there, a naked Leda with a swan.[2]
Let then the fair one beautifully cry,
In Magdalen's loose hair and lifted eye,
Or dressed in smiles of sweet Cecilia shine,[3]
With simpering angels, palms, and harps divine;
15   Whether the charmer sinner it, or saint it,
If folly grow romantic,° I must paint it.   *extravagant*
    Come then, the colors and the ground[4] prepare!
Dip in the rainbow, trick° her off in air;   *sketch*
Choose a firm cloud, before it fall, and in it
20   Catch, ere she change, the Cynthia[5] of this minute.
    Rufa, whose eye quick-glancing o'er the park,
Attracts each light gay meteor of a spark,°   *beau*
Agrees as ill with Rufa studying Locke,
As Sappho's diamonds with her dirty smock,
25   Or Sappho at her toilet's greasy task,[6]
With Sappho fragrant at an evening masque:
So morning insects that in muck begun,
Shine, buzz, and flyblow[7] in the setting sun.
    How soft is Silia! fearful to offend,
30   The frail one's advocate, the weak one's friend:
To her, Calista proved her conduct nice,
And good Simplicius asks of her advice.
Sudden, she storms! she raves! You tip the wink,
But spare your censure; Silia does not drink.
35   All eyes may see from what the change arose,
All eyes may see—a pimple on her nose.
    Papillia,[8] wedded to her amorous spark,
Sighs for the shades—"How charming is a park!"
A park is purchased, but the fair he sees
40   All bathed in tears—"Oh, odious, odious trees!"
    Ladies, like variegated tulips, show;
'Tis to their changes half their charms we owe;
Their happy spots the nice admirer take,
Fine by defect, and delicately weak.
45   'Twas thus Calypso[9] once each heart alarmed,
Awed without virtue, without beauty charmed;
Her tongue bewitched as oddly as her eyes,
Less wit than mimic, more a wit than wise;
Strange graces still, and stranger flights she had,
50   Was just not ugly, and was just not mad;

2. Leda was seduced by Zeus, who approached her in the form of a swan.
3. St. Mary Magdalen and St. Cecilia were often painted in the manner described.
4. The first coatings of paint on the canvas before the figures in the picture are sketched in.
5. One of the names of Diana, goddess of the moon, a notoriously changeable heavenly body.
6. Lady Mary Wortley Montagu, although beau-tiful as a young woman, became notorious for her slatternly appearance and personal uncleanliness. Both Sappho and Montagu were poets.
7. Deposit their eggs.
8. The name comes from Latin for "butterfly."
9. The name is borrowed from the fascinating god-dess who detained Odysseus on her island for seven years after the fall of Troy, thus preventing his return to his kingdom, Ithaca.

Yet ne'er so sure your passion to create,
As when she touched the brink of all we hate.
    Narcissa's[1] nature, tolerably mild,
To make a wash,° would hardly stew a child;   *cosmetic lotion*
55 Has even been proved to grant a lover's prayer,
And paid a tradesman once to make him stare,
Gave alms at Easter, in a Christian trim,
And made a widow happy, for a whim.
Why then declare good nature is her scorn,
60 When 'tis by that alone she can be borne?
Why pique all mortals, yet affect a name?
A fool to pleasure, yet a slave to fame:
Now deep in Taylor and the *Book of Martyrs*,[2]
Now drinking citron with his Grace and Chartres.[3]
65 Now conscience chills her, and now passion burns;
And atheism and religion take their turns;
A very heathen in the carnal part,
Yet still a sad, good Christian at her heart.
    See Sin in state, majestically drunk;
70 Proud as a peeress, prouder as a punk;°   *harlot*
Chaste to her husband, frank° to all beside,   *licentious*
A teeming mistress, but a barren bride.
What then? let blood and body bear the fault,
Her head's untouched, that noble seat of thought:
75 Such this day's doctrine—in another fit
She sins with poets through pure love of wit.
What has not fired her bosom or her brain?
Caesar and Tallboy, Charles[4] and Charlemagne.
As Helluo,[5] late dictator of the feast,
80 The nose of hautgout,[6] and the tip of taste,
Criticked your wine, and analyzed your meat,
Yet on plain pudding deigned at home to eat;
So Philomedé,[7] lecturing all mankind
On the soft passion, and the taste refined,
85 The address, the delicacy—stoops at once,
And makes her hearty meal upon a dunce.
    Flavia's a wit, has too much sense to pray;
To toast our wants and wishes, is her way;
Nor asks of God, but of her stars, to give
90 The mighty blessing, "while we live, to live."

---

1. Type of extreme self-love. Narcissus, a beautiful youth, fell in love with his own image when he saw it reflected in a fountain.
2. John Foxe's *Acts and Monuments*, usually referred to as Foxe's *Book of Martyrs*, was a household book in most Protestant families in the 17th and 18th centuries. A record of the Protestants who perished for their faith under the persecution of Mary Tudor (1553–58), it was instrumental in keeping anti-Catholic sentiments alive. Jeremy Taylor, 17th-century Anglican divine, whose *Holy Living and Holy Dying* was often reprinted in the 18th century.
3. Francis Chartres was a debauchee often mentioned by Pope. "His Grace" is usually said to be the duke of Wharton, an old enemy of Swift's and a notorious libertine. "Citron": citron water, brandy flavored with lemon or orange peels.
4. "Charles," as F. W. Bateson points out, was a generic name for a footman in the period. "Tallboy": a crude young man in Richard Brome's comedy *The Jovial Crew* (1641) or the opera adapted from the play (1731).
5. Glutton (Latin).
6. "Anything with a strong relish or strong scent, as overkept venison" (Johnson's *Dictionary*).
7. The name is Pope's adaptation of a Greek epithet meaning "laughter-loving," frequently applied to Aphrodite, the goddess of love.

Then all for death, that opiate of the soul!
Lucretia's dagger, Rosamonda's bowl.[8]
Say, what can cause such impotence of mind?
A spark too fickle, or a spouse too kind.
95   Wise wretch! with pleasures too refined to please,
With too much spirit to be e'er at ease,
With too much quickness ever to be taught,
With too much thinking to have common thought:
You purchase pain with all that joy can give,
100   And die of nothing but a rage to live.
    Turn then from wits; and look on Simo's mate,
No ass so meek, no ass so obstinate:
Or her, that owns her faults, but never mends,
Because she's honest, and the best of friends:
105   Or her, whose life the Church and scandal share,
Forever in a passion, or a prayer:
Or her, who laughs at hell, but (like her Grace)
Cries, "Ah! how charming, if there's no such place!"
Or who in sweet vicissitude appears
110   Of mirth and opium, ratafie[9] and tears,
The daily anodyne, and nightly draught,
To kill those foes to fair ones, time and thought.
Woman and fool are two hard things to hit,
For true no-meaning puzzles more than wit.
115   But what are these to great Atossa's[1] mind?
Scarce once herself, by turns all womankind!
Who, with herself, or others, from her birth
Finds all her life one warfare upon earth:
Shines in exposing knaves, and painting fools,
120   Yet is whate'er she hates and ridicules.
No thought advances, but her eddy brain
Whisks it about, and down it goes again.
Full sixty years the world has been her trade,
The wisest fool much time has ever made.
125   From loveless youth to unrespected age,
No passion gratified except her rage.
So much the fury still outran the wit,
The pleasure missed her, and the scandal hit.
Who breaks with her, provokes revenge from hell,
130   But he's a bolder man who dares be well:[2]
Her every turn with violence pursued,
Nor more a storm her hate than gratitude:
To that each passion turns, or soon or late;
Love, if it makes her yield, must make her hate:
135   Superiors? death! and equals? what a curse!
But an inferior not dependent? worse.
Offend her, and she knows not to forgive;

---

8. According to tradition, the "fair Rosamonda," mistress of Henry II, was forced by Queen Eleanor to drink poison. Lucretia, violated by Tarquin, committed suicide.
9. "A fine liquor, prepared from the kernels of apricots and spirits" (Johnson's *Dictionary*).

1. Atossa, daughter of Cyrus, emperor of Persia (d. 529 B.C.E.). If the duchess of Buckinghamshire is alluded to, the name is appropriate, for she was the natural daughter of James II.
2. Be in her favor.

Oblige her, and she'll hate you while you live:
But die, and she'll adore you—Then the bust
140 And temple rise—then fall again to dust.
Last night, her lord was all that's good and great;
A knave this morning, and his will a cheat.
Strange! by the means defeated of the ends,
By spirit robbed of power, by warmth of friends,
145 By wealth of followers! without one distress
Sick of herself through very selfishness!
Atossa, cursed with every granted prayer,
Childless with all her children, wants an heir.
To heirs unknown descends the unguarded store,
150 Or wanders, Heaven-directed, to the poor.
    Pictures like these, dear Madam, to design,
Asks no firm hand, and no unerring line;
Some wandering touches, some reflected light,
Some flying stroke alone can hit 'em right:
155 For how should equal colors do the knack?[3]
Chameleons who can paint in white and black?
    "Yet Chloe sure was formed without a spot—"
Nature in her then erred not, but forgot.
"With every pleasing, every prudent part,
160 Say, what can Chloe want?"—She wants a heart.
She speaks, behaves, and acts just as she ought;
But never, never, reached one generous thought.
Virtue she finds too painful an endeavor,
Content to dwell in decencies forever.
165 So very reasonable, so unmoved,
As never yet to love, or to be loved.
She, while her lover pants upon her breast,
Can mark[4] the figures on an Indian chest;
And when she sees her friend in deep despair,
170 Observes how much a chintz exceeds mohair.
Forbid it Heaven, a favor or a debt
She e'er should cancel—but she may forget.
Safe is your secret still in Chloe's ear;
But none of Chloe's shall you ever hear.
175 Of all her dears she never slandered one,
But cares not if a thousand are undone.
Would Chloe know if you're alive or dead?
She bids her footman put it in her head.
Chloe is prudent—Would you too be wise?
180 Then never break your heart when Chloe dies.
    One certain portrait may (I grant) be seen,
Which Heaven has varnished out, and made a *Queen*:[5]
The same forever! and described by all
With truth and goodness, as with crown and ball.
185 Poets heap virtues, painters gems at will,
And show their zeal, and hide their want of skill.

---

3. Do the trick.
4. Pay attention to.

5. Pope refers as usual to Queen Caroline with
disapprobation.

'Tis well—but, artists! who can paint or write,
To draw the naked is your true delight.
That robe of quality so struts and swells,
190 None see what parts of Nature it conceals:
The exactest traits of body or of mind,
We owe to models of an humble kind.
If Queensberry[6] to strip there's no compelling,
'Tis from a handmaid we must take a Helen.
195 From peer or bishop 'tis no easy thing
To draw the man who loves his God, or king:
Alas! I copy (or my draft would fail)
From honest Mah'met or plain Parson Hale.[7]
    But grant, in public men sometimes are shown,
200 A woman's seen in private life alone:
Our bolder talents in full light displayed;
Your virtues open fairest in the shade.
Bred to disguise, in public 'tis you hide;
There, none distinguish 'twixt your shame or pride,
205 Weakness or delicacy; all so nice,
That each may seem a virtue, or a vice.
    In men, we various ruling passions find;
In women, two almost divide the kind;
Those, only fixed, they first or last obey,
210 The love of pleasure, and the love of sway.
That, Nature gives; and where the lesson taught
Is but to please, can pleasure seem a fault?
Experience, this; by man's oppression cursed,
They seek the second not to lose the first.
215   Men, some to business, some to pleasure take;
But every woman is at heart a rake;
Men, some to quiet, some to public strife;
But every lady would be queen for life.
    Yet mark the fate of a whole sex of queens!
220 Power all their end, but beauty all the means:
In youth they conquer, with so wild a rage,
As leaves them scarce a subject in their age:
For foreign glory, foreign joy, they roam;
No thought of peace or happiness at home.
225 But wisdom's triumph is well-timed retreat,
As hard a science to the fair as great!
Beauties, like tyrants, old and friendless grown,
Yet hate repose, and dread to be alone,
Worn out in public, weary every eye,
230 Nor leave one sigh behind them when they die.
    Pleasures the sex, as children birds, pursue,
Still out of reach, yet never out of view,
Sure, if they catch, to spoil the toy at most,
To covet flying, and regret when lost:
235 At last, to follies youth could scarce defend,

---

6. The duchess of Queensberry, whom Pope valued because of her kindness to his friend John Gay, had been a famous beauty.

7. Dr. Stephen Hales, an Anglican clergyman and friend of Pope. Mahomet was a Turkish servant of George I.

It grows their age's prudence to pretend;
Ashamed to own they gave delight before,
Reduced to feign it, when they give no more:
As hags hold sabbaths, less for joy than spite,
240 So these their merry, miserable night;[8]
Still round and round the ghosts of beauty glide,
And haunt the places where their honor died.
　　See how the world its veterans rewards!
A youth of frolics, an old age of cards;
245 Fair to no purpose, artful to no end,
Young without lovers, old without a friend;
A fop their passion, but their prize a sot;
Alive, ridiculous, and dead, forgot!
　　Ah friend! to dazzle let the vain design;
250 To raise the thought, and touch the heart be thine!
That charm shall grow, while what fatigues the Ring[9]
Flaunts and goes down, an unregarded thing:
So when the sun's broad beam has tired the sight,
All mild ascends the moon's more sober light,
255 Serene in virgin modesty she shines,
And unobserved the glaring orb declines.
　　Oh! blest with temper, whose unclouded ray
Can make tomorrow cheerful as today;
She, who can love a sister's charms, or hear
260 Sighs for a daughter with unwounded ear;
She, who ne'er answers till a husband cools,
Or, if she rules him, never shows she rules;
Charms by accepting, by submitting sways,
Yet has her humor most, when she obeys;
265 Lets fops or fortune fly which way they will;
Disdains all loss of tickets° or Codille;[1]　　　　　*lottery tickets*
Spleen, vapors, or smallpox, above them all,
And mistress of herself, though China[2] fall.
　　And yet, believe me, good as well as ill,
270 Woman's at best a contradiction still.
Heaven, when it strives to polish all it can
Its last best work, but forms a softer man;
Picks from each sex, to make the favorite blest,
Your love of pleasure, our desire of rest:
275 Blends, in exception to all general rules,
Your taste of follies, with our scorn of fools:
Reserve with frankness, art with truth allied,
Courage with softness, modesty with pride;
Fixed principles, with fancy ever new;
280 Shakes all together, and produces—you.
　　Be this a woman's fame: with this unblest,
Toasts live a scorn, and queens may die a jest.
This Phoebus promised (I forget the year)

---

8. I.e., evenings on which ladies entertained guests. "Sabbaths": obscene rites popularly supposed to be held by witches ("hags").
9. The fashionable drive in Hyde Park.

1. The loss of a hand at the card games of ombre or quadrille.
2. Pope refers punningly to the chinaware that fashionable women collected enthusiastically.

When those blue eyes first opened on the sphere;
285 Ascendant Phoebus watched that hour with care,
Averted half your parents' simple prayer;
And gave you beauty, but denied the pelf
That buys your sex a tyrant o'er itself.
The generous god, who wit and gold refines,
290 And ripens spirits as he ripens mines,[3]
Kept dross for duchesses, the world shall know it,
To you gave sense, good humor, and a poet.

1735, 1744

Epistle to Dr. Arbuthnot

Dr. John Arbuthnot (1667–1735), to whom Pope addressed his best-known verse epistle, was distinguished both as a physician and as a man of wit. He had been one of the liveliest members of the Martinus Scriblerus Club, helping his friends create the character and shape the career of the learned pedant whose memoirs the club had undertaken to write.

Pope had long been meditating such a poem, which was to be both an attack on his detractors and a defense of his own character and career. In his usual way, he had jotted down hints, lines, couplets, and fragments over a period of two decades, but the poem might never have been completed had it not been for two events: Arbuthnot, from his deathbed, wrote to urge Pope to continue his abhorrence of vice and to express it in his writings and, during 1733, Pope was the victim of two bitter attacks by "persons of rank and fortune," as the *Advertisement* has it. The *Verses Addressed to the Imitator of Horace* was the work of Lady Mary Wortley Montagu, helped by her friend Lord Hervey (pronounced *Harvey*), a close friend and confidant of Queen Caroline. *An Epistle to a Doctor of Divinity from a Nobleman at Hampton Court* was the work of Lord Hervey alone. Montagu, it must be admitted, had provocation enough, especially in Pope's recent reference to her in *The First Satire of the Second Book of Horace*, lines 83–84, but Hervey had little to complain of beyond occasional covert references to him as "Lord Fanny." At any rate, the two scurrilous attacks goaded Pope into action, and the poem was completed by the end of the summer of 1734.

The epistle is a masterpiece of poetic rhetoric. The very fact that it is addressed to Arbuthnot, a man generally known to be honest and kind, seems to guarantee the integrity of the *I* of the poem and to diminish the moral stature of his enemies. This acquisition of virtue through association, an effective stroke, is supported by every device of persuasive rhetoric—reasonable argument and emotional appeals, subtly suggestive imagery, and superbly controlled shifts in tone and style—which help sway the reader's judgment to the side of the speaker. The poem opens in the flat language of commonplace prose discourse, tinged with a wry humor and a tone of exasperation: "Shut, shut the door, good John! (fatigued, I said)" and as it progresses it rises or falls in language and style according to the emotions that the speaker expresses—anger, contempt, amusement, sarcasm, mock self-pity, indignation, hatred, affection, gratitude, and tenderness—to return at the end to the homely tone of the opening.

It is not clear that Pope intended the poem to be thought of as a dialogue, as it has usually been printed since Warburton's edition of 1751. The original edition, while suggesting interruptions in the flow of the monologue, kept entirely to the form of a

---

3. Phoebus Apollo, as god of poetry "ripens wit"; as god of the sun, he "ripens mines," for respectable scientific theory held that the sun's rays mature precious metals in the earth.

letter. The introduction of the friend, who speaks from time to time, converts the
original letter into a dramatic dialogue.

Epistle to Dr. Arbuthnot

Advertisement

TO THE FIRST PUBLICATION OF THIS *Epistle*

This paper is a sort of bill of complaint, begun many years since, and drawn
up by snatches, as the several occasions offered. I had no thoughts of publishing it, till it pleased some persons of rank and fortune (the authors of
Verses to the Imitator of Horace, and of an *Epistle to a Doctor of Divinity from
a Nobleman at Hampton Court*) to attack, in a very extraordinary manner,
not only my writings (of which, being public, the public is judge) but my
person, morals, and family, whereof, to those who know me not, a truer
information may be requisite. Being divided between the necessity to say
something of myself, and my own laziness to undertake so awkward a task,
I thought it the shortest way to put the last hand to this epistle. If it have
anything pleasing, it will be that by which I am most desirous to please, the
truth and the sentiment; and if anything offensive, it will be only to those I
am least sorry to offend, the vicious or the ungenerous.

Many will know their own pictures in it, there being not a circumstance
but what is true; but I have, for the most part, spared their names, and they
may escape being laughed at, if they please.

I would have some of them know, it was owing to the request of the learned
and candid friend to whom it is inscribed, that I make not as free use of
theirs as they have done of mine. However, I shall have this advantage, and
honor, on my side, that whereas, by their proceeding, any abuse may be
directed at any man, no injury can possibly be done by mine, since a nameless
character can never be found out, but by its truth and likeness. P.

P. Shut, shut the door, good John![1] (fatigued, I said),
Tie up the knocker, say I'm sick, I'm dead.
The Dog Star[2] rages! nay 'tis past a doubt
All Bedlam,[3] or Parnassus, is let out:
5 Fire in each eye, and papers in each hand,
They rave, recite, and madden round the land.
   What walls can guard me, or what shades can hide?
They pierce my thickets, through my grot[4] they glide,
By land, by water, they renew the charge,
10 They stop the chariot, and they board the barge.
No place is sacred, not the church is free;
Even Sunday shines no Sabbath day to me:
Then from the Mint[5] walks forth the man of rhyme,

1. John Serle, Pope's gardener.
2. Sirius, associated with the period of greatest
heat (and hence of madness) because it sets with
the sun in late summer. August, in ancient Rome,
was the season for reciting poetry.
3. Bethlehem Hospital for the insane, in London.
4. The subterranean passage under the road that

separated his house at Twickenham from his garden became, in Pope's hands, a romantic grotto
ornamented with shells and mirrors.
5. A place in Southwark where debtors were free
from arrest (they could not be arrested anywhere
on Sundays).

Happy! to catch me just at dinner time.

15   Is there a parson, much bemused in beer,
A maudlin poetess, a rhyming peer,
A clerk foredoomed his father's soul to cross,
Who pens a stanza when he should engross?[6]
Is there who, locked from ink and paper,[7] scrawls
20 With desperate charcoal round his darkened walls?
All fly to Twit'nam,[8] and in humble strain
Apply to me to keep them mad or vain.
Arthur,[9] whose giddy son neglects the laws,
Imputes to me and my damned works the cause:
25 Poor Cornus[1] sees his frantic wife elope,
And curses wit, and poetry, and Pope.
    Friend to my life (which did not you prolong,
The world had wanted many an idle song)
What drop or nostrum° can this plague remove?   *medicine*
30 Or which must end me, a fool's wrath or love?
A dire dilemma! either way I'm sped,[2]
If foes, they write, if friends, they read me dead.
Seized and tied down to judge, how wretched I!
Who can't be silent, and who will not lie.
35 To laugh were want of goodness and of grace,
And to be grave exceeds all power of face.
I sit with sad civility, I read
With honest anguish and an aching head,
And drop at last, but in unwilling ears,
40 This saving counsel, "Keep your piece nine years."[3]
    "Nine years!" cries he, who high in Drury Lane,[4]
Lulled by soft zephyrs through the broken pane,
Rhymes ere he wakes, and prints before term[5] ends,
Obliged by hunger and request of friends:
45 "The piece, you think, is incorrect? why, take it,
I'm all submission, what you'd have it, make it."
    Three things another's modest wishes bound,
My friendship, and a prologue, and ten pound.
    Pitholeon[6] sends to me: "You know his Grace,
50 I want a patron; ask him for a place."
Pitholeon libeled me—"but here's a letter
Informs you, sir, 'twas when he knew no better.
Dare you refuse him? Curll[7] invites to dine,

---

6. Write out legal documents.
7. Is there some madman who, locked up without ink or paper . . . ?
8. I.e., Twickenham, Pope's villa on the bank of the Thames, a few miles above Hampton Court.
9. Arthur Moore, whose son, James Moore Smythe, dabbled in literature. Moore Smythe had earned Pope's enmity by using in one of his plays some unpublished lines from Pope's *Epistle 2. To a Lady* in spite of Pope's objections.
1. Latin for "horn," the traditional emblem of the cuckold.
2. "Destroyed; killed" (Johnson's *Dictionary*).
3. The advice of Horace in *Art of Poetry* (line 388).
4. I.e., living in a garret in Drury Lane, site of one

of the theaters and the haunt of the profligate.
5. One of the four annual periods in which the law courts are in session and with which the publishing season coincided.
6. "A foolish poet of Rhodes, who pretended much to Greek" [Pope's note]. He is Leonard Welsted, who translated Longinus and had attacked and slandered Pope (see line 375).
7. Edmund Curll, shrewd and disreputable bookseller, published pirated works, works falsely ascribed to reputable writers, scandalous biographies, and other ephemera. Pope had often attacked him and had assigned to him a low role in *The Dunciad*.

He'll write a *Journal,* or he'll turn divine."[8]
55 Bless me! a packet.—" 'Tis a stranger sues,
A virgin tragedy, an orphan Muse."
If I dislike it, "Furies, death, and rage!"
If I approve, "Commend it to the stage."
There (thank my stars) my whole commission ends,
60 The players and I are, luckily, no friends.
Fired that the house reject him, " 'Sdeath, I'll print it,
And shame the fools—Your interest, sir, with Lintot!"[9]
Lintot, dull rogue, will think your price too much.
"Not, sir, if you revise it, and retouch."
65 All my demurs but double his attacks;
At last he whispers, "Do; and we go snacks."°   *shares*
Glad of a quarrel, straight I clap the door,
"Sir, let me see your works and you no more."
  'Tis sung, when Midas' ears began to spring
70 (Midas, a sacred person and a king),
His very minister who spied them first,
(Some say his queen) was forced to speak, or burst.[1]
And is not mine, my friend, a sorer case,
When every coxcomb perks them in my face?
75   A. Good friend, forbear! you deal in dangerous things.
I'd never name queens, ministers, or kings;
Keep close to ears, and those let asses prick;
'Tis nothing——P. Nothing? if they bite and kick?
Out with it, *Dunciad!* let the secret pass,
80 That secret to each fool, that he's an ass:
The truth once told (and wherefore should we lie?)
The queen of Midas slept, and so may I.
  You think this cruel? take it for a rule,
No creature smarts so little as a fool.
85 Let peals of laughter, Codrus! round thee break,
Thou unconcerned canst hear the mighty crack.
Pit, box, and gallery in convulsions hurled,
Thou stand'st unshook amidst a bursting world.
Who shames a scribbler? break one cobweb through,
90 He spins the slight, self-pleasing thread anew:
Destroy his fib or sophistry, in vain;
The creature's at his dirty work again,
Throned in the center of his thin designs,
Proud of a vast extent of flimsy lines.
95 Whom have I hurt? has poet yet or peer
Lost the arched eyebrow or Parnassian sneer?
And has not Colley[2] still his lord and whore?
His butchers Henley? his freemasons Moore?

8. I.e., he will attack Pope in the *London Journal* or write a treatise on theology, as Welsted in fact did.
9. Bernard Lintot, publisher of Pope's Homer and other early works.
1. Midas, king of ancient Lydia, had the bad taste to prefer the flute-playing of Pan to that of Apollo, whereupon the god endowed him with ass's ears. It was his barber (not his wife or his minister) who discovered the secret and whispered it into a hole in the earth. The reference to "queen" and "minister" makes it plain that Pope is alluding to George II, Queen Caroline, and Walpole.
2. Colley Cibber, the laureate. John Henley, known as "Orator" Henley, an independent preacher of marked eccentricity, was popular among the lower orders, especially for his elocution.

Does not one table Bavius still admit?
100   Still to one bishop Philips³ seem a wit?
Still Sappho⁴——A. Hold! for god's sake—you'll offend.
No names—be calm—learn prudence of a friend.
I too could write, and I am twice as tall;
But foes like these!——P. One flatterer's worse than all.
105   Of all mad creatures, if the learn'd are right,
It is the slaver kills, and not the bite.
A fool quite angry is quite innocent:
Alas! 'tis ten times worse when they repent.

One dedicates in high heroic prose,
110   And ridicules beyond a hundred foes;
One from all Grub Street⁵ will my fame defend,
And, more abusive, calls himself my friend.
This prints my letters,⁶ that expects a bribe,
And others roar aloud, "Subscribe, subscribe!"⁷
115   There are, who to my person pay their court:
I cough like Horace, and, though lean, am short;
Ammon's great son° one shoulder had too high,   *Alexander the Great*
Such Ovid's nose,⁸ and "Sir! you have an eye—"
Go on, obliging creatures, make me see
120   All that disgraced my betters met in me.
Say for my comfort, languishing in bed,
"Just so immortal Maro° held his head":   *Virgil*
And when I die, be sure you let me know
Great Homer died three thousand years ago.

125   Why did I write? what sin to me unknown
Dipped me in ink, my parents', or my own?
As yet a child, nor yet a fool to fame,
I lisped in numbers, for the numbers came.
I left no calling for this idle trade,
130   No duty broke, no father disobeyed.
The Muse but served to ease some friend, not wife,
To help me through this long disease, my life,
To second, Arbuthnot! thy art and care,
And teach the being you preserved, to bear.°   *endure*

135   A. But why then publish? P. Granville the polite,
And knowing Walsh, would tell me I could write;
Well-natured Garth inflamed with early praise,
And Congreve loved, and Swift endured my lays;
The courtly Talbot, Somers, Sheffield, read;
140   Even mitered Rochester would nod the head,

3. The "bishop" is Hugh Boulter, bishop of Armagh; he had employed as his secretary Ambrose Philips (1674–1749), whose insipid simplicity of manner in poetry earned him the nickname of "Namby-Pamby." Bavius, the bad poet alluded to in Virgil's *Eclogue* 3.
4. Lady Mary Wortley Montagu.
5. A term denoting the whole society of literary, political, and journalistic hack writers.
6. In 1726 Curll had surreptitiously acquired and

published without permission some of Pope's letters to Henry Cromwell.
7. To ensure the financial success of a work, the public was often asked to "subscribe" to it by taking a certain number of copies before printing was undertaken. Pope's Homer was published in this manner.
8. Ovid's family name, Naso, suggests the Latin word *nasus* ("nose"), hence the pun.

And St. John's self (great Dryden's friends before)
With open arms received one poet more.[9]
Happy my studies, when by these approved!
Happier their author, when by these beloved!
145 From these the world will judge of men and books,
Not from the Burnets, Oldmixons, and Cookes.[1]
   Soft were my numbers; who could take offense
While pure description held the place of sense?
Like gentle Fanny's[2] was my flowery theme,
150 A painted mistress, or a purling stream.
Yet then did Gildon draw his venal quill;[3]
I wished the man a dinner, and sat still.
Yet then did Dennis[4] rave in furious fret;
I never answered, I was not in debt.
155 If want provoked, or madness made them print,
I waged no war with Bedlam or the Mint.
   Did some more sober critic come abroad?
If wrong, I smiled; if right, I kissed the rod.
Pains, reading, study are their just pretense,
160 And all they want is spirit, taste, and sense.
Commas and points they set exactly right,
And 'twere a sin to rob them of their mite.
Yet ne'er one sprig of laurel graced these ribalds,
From slashing Bentley down to piddling Tibbalds.[5]
165 Each wight who reads not, and but scans and spells,
Each word-catcher that lives on syllables,
Even such small critics some regard may claim,
Preserved in Milton's or in Shakespeare's name.
Pretty! in amber to observe the forms
170 Of hairs, or straws, or dirt, or grubs, or worms!
The things, we know, are neither rich nor rare,
But wonder how the devil they got there.
   Were others angry? I excused them too;
Well might they rage; I gave them but their due.
175 A man's true merit 'tis not hard to find;
But each man's secret standard in his mind,
That casting weight[6] pride adds to emptiness,
This, who can gratify? for who can guess?
The bard[7] whom pilfered pastorals renown,

9. The purpose of this list is to establish Pope as
the successor of Dryden and thus to place him far
above his Grub Street persecutors. George Granville, Lord Lansdowne, poet and statesman; William Walsh, poet and critic; Sir Samuel Garth,
physician and mock-epic poet; William Congreve,
the playwright; the statesmen Charles Talbot, duke
of Shrewsbury; Lord Sommers; John Sheffield,
duke of Buckinghamshire; and Francis Atterbury,
bishop of Rochester, had all been associated with
Dryden in his later years and had all encouraged
the young Pope.
1. Thomas Burnet, John Oldmixon, and Thomas
Cooke: Pope identifies them in a note as "authors
of secret and scandalous history."
2. John, Lord Hervey, whom Pope satirizes in the
character of Sporus (lines 305–33).
3. Charles Gildon, minor critic and scribbler,
who, Pope believed, early attacked him at the insti-

gation of Addison; hence "venal quill."
4. John Dennis (see *An Essay on Criticism*, n. 7,
p. 1129).
5. Lewis Theobald (1688–1744), whose minute
learning in Elizabethan literature had enabled him
to expose Pope's defects as an editor of Shakespeare in 1726. Pope made him king of the Dunces
in *The Dunciad* of 1728. Richard Bentley (1662–
1742), the eminent classical scholar, seemed to
both Pope and Swift the perfect type of the pedant:
he is called "slashing" because, in his edition of
Paradise Lost (1732), he had set in square brackets
all passages that he disliked on the grounds they
had been slipped into the poem without the blind
poet's knowledge.
6. The weight that turns the scale; here, the
"deciding factor."
7. Ambrose Philips, Pope's rival in pastoral poetry
in 1709, when their pastorals were published in

180　Who turns a Persian tale for half a crown,
　　Just writes to make his barrenness appear,
　　And strains from hard-bound brains eight lines a year:
　　He, who still wanting, though he lives on theft,
　　Steals much, spends little, yet has nothing left;
185　And he who now to sense, now nonsense leaning,
　　Means not, but blunders round about a meaning:
　　And he whose fustian's so sublimely bad,
　　It is not poetry, but prose run mad:
　　All these, my modest satire bade translate,
190　And owned that nine such poets made a Tate.[8]
　　How did they fume, and stamp, and roar, and chafe!
　　And swear, not Addison himself was safe.

　　　　Peace to all such! but were there one whose fires
　　True Genius kindles, and fair Fame inspires;
195　Blessed with each talent and each art to please,
　　And born to write, converse, and live with ease:
　　Should such a man, too fond to rule alone,
　　Bear, like the Turk, no brother near the throne;
　　View him with scornful, yet with jealous eyes,
200　And hate for arts that caused himself to rise;
　　Damn with faint praise, assent with civil leer,
　　And without sneering, teach the rest to sneer;
　　Willing to wound, and yet afraid to strike,
　　Just hint a fault, and hesitate dislike;
205　Alike reserved to blame or to commend,
　　A timorous foe, and a suspicious friend;
　　Dreading even fools; by flatterers besieged,
　　And so obliging that he ne'er obliged;
　　Like Cato, give his little senate[9] laws,
210　And sit attentive to his own applause;
　　While wits and Templars° every sentence raise,　　　　*law students*
　　And wonder with a foolish face of praise—
　　Who but must laugh, if such a man there be?
　　Who would not weep, if Atticus[1] were he?
215　　　What though my name stood rubric[2] on the walls
　　Or plastered posts, with claps,° in capitals?　　　　*posters*
　　Or smoking forth, a hundred hawkers' load,
　　On wings of winds came flying all abroad?
　　I sought no homage from the race that write;
220　I kept, like Asian monarchs, from their sight:
　　Poems I heeded (now berhymed so long)
　　No more than thou, great George! a birthday song.

Tonson's 6th *Miscellany*. Philips had also translated some Persian tales (cf. line 100).
8. Nahum Tate, poet laureate from 1692 to 1715.
His popular rewriting of Shakespeare's *King Lear*
provided a happy ending; he wrote most of part 2
of *Absalom and Achitophel*. The line refers to the
old adage that it takes nine tailors to make one
man.
9. Addison's tragedy *Cato* had been a sensational
success in 1713. Pope had written the prologue, in
which occurs the line, "While Cato gives his little

senate laws." The satirical reference here is to
Addison in the role of arbiter of taste among his
friends and admirers, mostly Whigs, at Button's
Coffee House. It was these people who had worked
against the success of Pope's Homer.
1. Pope's satiric pseudonym for Addison; Atticus
(109–32 B.C.E.) was a wealthy man of letters and
a friend of Cicero, known as a wise and disinterested man.
2. In red letters.

I ne'er with wits or witlings passed my days
To spread about the itch of verse and praise;
225 Nor like a puppy daggled through the town
To fetch and carry sing-song up and down;
Nor at rehearsals sweat, and mouthed, and cried,
With handkerchief and orange at my side;
But sick of fops, and poetry, and prate,
230 To Bufo left the whole Castalian[3] state.
    Proud as Apollo on his forkèd hill,[4]
Sat full-blown Bufo, puffed by every quill;
Fed with soft dedication all day long,
Horace and he went hand in hand in song.
235 His library (where busts of poets dead
And a true Pindar stood without a head)
Received of wits an undistinguished race,
Who first his judgment asked, and then a place:
Much they extolled his pictures, much his seat,[5]
240 And flattered every day, and some days eat:
Till grown more frugal in his riper days,
He paid some bards with port, and some with praise;
To some a dry rehearsal was assigned,
And others (harder still) he paid in kind.
245 Dryden alone (what wonder?) came not nigh;
Dryden alone escaped this judging eye:
But still the great have kindness in reserve;
He helped to bury whom he helped to starve.
    May some choice patron bless each gray goose quill!
250 May every Bavius have his Bufo still!
So when a statesman wants a day's defense,
Or envy holds a whole week's war with sense,
Or simple pride for flattery makes demands,
May dunce by dunce be whistled off my hands!
255 Blessed be the great! for those they take away,
And those they left me—for they left me Gay;[6]
Left me to see neglected genius bloom,
Neglected die, and tell it on his tomb;
Of all thy blameless life the sole return
260 My verse, and Queensberry weeping o'er thy urn!
Oh, let me live my own, and die so too!
("To live and die is all I have to do")[7]
Maintain a poet's dignity and ease,
And see what friends, and read what books I please;
265 Above a patron, though I condescend
Sometimes to call a minister my friend.
I was not born for courts or great affairs;

---

3. The Castalian spring on Mount Parnassus was sacred to Apollo and the Muses. "Bufo": a type of tasteless patron of the arts. (*Bufo* means "toad" in Latin.)
4. Mount Parnassus had two peaks, one sacred to Apollo, one to Bacchus.
5. Estate. Pronounced *sate* and rhymed in next line with "eat" (*ate*).
6. John Gay (1685–1732), author of *The Beggar's Opera* and other delightful works, dear friend of Swift and Pope. His failure to obtain patronage from the court intensified Pope's hostility to the Whig administration and the queen. Gay spent the last years of his life under the protection of the duke and duchess of Queensberry.
7. A quotation from John Denham's poem *Of Prudence*.

I pay my debts, believe, and say my prayers,
Can sleep without a poem in my head,
270 Nor know if Dennis be alive or dead.
    Why am I asked what next shall see the light?
Heavens! was I born for nothing but to write?
Has life no joys for me? or (to be grave)
Have I no friend to serve, no soul to save?
275 "I found him close with Swift"—"Indeed? no doubt"
Cries prating Balbus, "something will come out."
'Tis all in vain, deny it as I will.
"No, such a genius never can lie still,"
And then for mine obligingly mistakes
280 The first lampoon Sir Will or Bubo[8] makes.
Poor guiltless I! and can I choose but smile,
When every coxcomb knows me by my style?
    Cursed be the verse, how well soe'er it flow,
That tends to make one worthy man my foe,
285 Give virtue scandal, innocence a fear,
Or from the soft-eyed virgin steal a tear!
But he who hurts a harmless neighbor's peace,
Insults fallen worth, or beauty in distress,
Who loves a lie, lame slander helps about,
290 Who writes a libel, or who copies out:
That fop whose pride affects a patron's name,
Yet absent, wounds an author's honest fame;
Who can your merit selfishly approve,
And show the sense of it without the love;
295 Who has the vanity to call you friend,
Yet wants the honor, injured, to defend;
Who tells whate'er you think, whate'er you say,
And, if he lie not, must at least betray:
Who to the dean and silver bell can swear,
300 And sees at Cannons what was never there:[9]
Who reads but with a lust to misapply,
Make satire a lampoon, and fiction, lie:
A lash like mine no honest man shall dread,
But all such babbling blockheads in his stead.
305   Let Sporus[1] tremble—— A. What? that thing of silk,
Sporus, that mere white curd of ass's milk?[2]
Satire or sense, alas! can Sporus feel?
Who breaks a butterfly upon a wheel?
    P. Yet let me flap this bug with gilded wings,
310 This painted child of dirt, that stinks and stings;
Whose buzz the witty and the fair annoys,
Yet wit ne'er tastes, and beauty ne'er enjoys;

---

8. Sir William Yonge, Whig politician and poet-aster. George Bubb ("Bubo") Dodington, a Whig patron of letters.
9. Pope's enemies had accused him of satirizing Cannons, the ostentatious estate of the duke of Chandos, in his description of Timon's villa in the *Epistle to Burlington*. This Pope quite justly denied. The bell of Timon's chapel was of silver, and there preached a dean who "never mentions

Hell to ears polite."
1. John, Lord Hervey, effeminate courtier and confidant of Queen Caroline (see the headnote to *Epistle to Dr. Arbuthnot*, p. 1168). The original Sporus was a boy, whom the emperor Nero publicly married (see Suetonius's life of Nero in *The Twelve Caesars*).
2. Drunk by invalids.

So well-bred spaniels civilly delight
In mumbling of the game they dare not bite.
315 Eternal smiles his emptiness betray,
As shallow streams run dimpling all the way.
Whether in florid impotence he speaks,
And, as the prompter breathes, the puppet squeaks;
Or at the ear of Eve,[3] familiar toad,
320 Half froth, half venom, spits himself abroad,
In puns, or politics, or tales, or lies,
Or spite, or smut, or rhymes, or blasphemies.
His wit all seesaw between *that* and *this*,
Now high, now low, now master up, now miss,
325 And he himself one vile antithesis.
Amphibious thing! that acting either part,
The trifling head or the corrupted heart,
Fop at the toilet, flatterer at the board,
Now trips a lady, and now struts a lord.
330 Eve's tempter thus the rabbins[4] have expressed,
A cherub's face, a reptile all the rest;
Beauty that shocks you, parts that none will trust,
Wit that can creep, and pride that licks the dust.
    Not fortune's worshiper, nor fashion's fool,
335 Not lucre's madman, nor ambition's tool,
Not proud, nor servile, be one poet's praise,
That if he pleased, he pleased by manly ways:
That flattery, even to kings, he held a shame,
And thought a lie in verse or prose the same:
340 That not in fancy's maze he wandered long,
But stooped[5] to truth, and moralized his song:
That not for fame, but virtue's better end,
He stood the furious foe, the timid friend,
The damning critic, half approving wit,
345 The coxcomb hit, or fearing to be hit;
Laughed at the loss of friends he never had,
The dull, the proud, the wicked, and the mad;
The distant threats of vengeance on his head,
The blow unfelt, the tear he never shed;
350 The tale revived, the lie so oft o'erthrown,
The imputed trash, and dullness not his own;
The morals blackened when the writings 'scape,
The libeled person, and the pictured shape;[6]
Abuse on all he loved, or loved him, spread,
355 A friend in exile, or a father dead;
The whisper, that to greatness still too near,
Perhaps yet vibrates on his Sovereign's ear—
Welcome for thee, fair virtue! all the past:
For thee, fair virtue! welcome even the last!
360   A. But why insult the poor, affront the great?

3. The queen; the allusion is to *Paradise Lost*
(4.799–809).
4. Scholars of and authorities on Jewish law and
doctrine.

5. The falcon is said to "stoop" to its prey when it
swoops down and seizes it in flight.
6. Pope's deformity was frequently ridiculed and
occasionally caricatured.

P. A knave's a knave to me in every state:
Alike my scorn, if he succeed or fail,
Sporus at court, or Japhet[7] in a jail,
A hireling scribbler, or a hireling peer,
365 Knight of the post[8] corrupt, or of the shire,
If on a pillory, or near a throne,
He gain his prince's ear, or lose his own.
   Yet soft by nature, more a dupe than wit,
Sappho° can tell you how this man was bit:°   *Montagu / deceived*
370 This dreaded satirist Dennis will confess
Foe to his pride, but friend to his distress:[9]
So humble, he has knocked at Tibbald's door,
Has drunk with Cibber, nay, has rhymed for Moore.
Full ten years slandered, did he once reply?
375 Three thousand suns went down on Welsted's lie.
To please a mistress one aspersed his life;
He lashed him not, but let her be his wife.
Let Budgell charge low Grub Street on his quill,
And write whate'er he pleased, except his will;[1]
380 Let the two Curlls of town and court,[2] abuse
His father, mother, body, soul, and muse.
Yet why? that father held it for a rule,
It was a sin to call our neighbor fool;
That harmless mother thought no wife a whore:
385 Hear this, and spare his family, James Moore!
Unspotted names, and memorable long,
If there be force in virtue, or in song.
   Of gentle blood (part shed in honor's cause,
While yet in Britain honor had applause)
390 Each parent sprung——A. What fortune, pray?——P. Their own,
And better got than Bestia's[3] from the throne.
Born to no pride, inheriting no strife,
Nor marrying discord in a noble wife,
Stranger to civil and religious rage,
395 The good man walked innoxious through his age.
No courts he saw, no suits would ever try,
Nor dared an oath,[4] nor hazarded a lie.
Unlearn'd, he knew no schoolman's subtle art,
No language but the language of the heart.
400 By nature honest, by experience wise,
Healthy by temperance, and by exercise;
His life, though long, to sickness passed unknown,
His death was instant, and without a groan.
Oh, grant me thus to live, and thus to die!

7. Japhet Crook, a notorious forger.
8. One who lives by selling false evidence.
9. Pope wrote the prologue to Cibber's *Provoked Husband* (1728) when that play was performed for Dennis's benefit, shortly before the old critic died.
1. Eustace Budgell attacked the *Grub Street Journal* for publishing what he took to be a squib by Pope charging him with having forged the will of Dr. Matthew Tindal.
2. I.e., the publisher and Lord Hervey.

3. Probably the duke of Marlborough, whose vast fortune was made through the favor of Queen Anne. The actual Bestia was a corrupt Roman consul.
4. As a Catholic, Pope's father refused to take the Oaths of Allegiance and Supremacy and the oath against the pope. He thus rendered himself vulnerable to the many repressive anti-Catholic laws then in force.

405   Who sprung from kings shall know less joy than I.
     O friend! may each domestic bliss be thine!
    Be no unpleasing melancholy mine:
    Me, let the tender office long engage,
    To rock the cradle of reposing age,
410   With lenient arts extend a mother's breath,
    Make languor smile, and smooth the bed of death,
    Explore the thought, explain the asking eye,
    And keep a while one parent from the sky![5]
    On cares like these if length of days attend,
415   May Heaven, to bless those days, preserve my friend,
    Preserve him social, cheerful, and serene,
    And just as rich as when he served a Queen![6]
     A. Whether that blessing be denied or given,
    Thus far was right—the rest belongs to Heaven.

                                        1735

The Dunciad: Book the Fourth

The fourth book of *The Dunciad*, Pope's last major work, was originally intended as a continuation of *An Essay on Man*. To Jonathan Swift, the spiritual ancestor of the poem, Pope confided in 1736 that he was at work on a series of epistles on the uses of human reason and learning, to conclude with "a satire against the misapplication of all these, exemplified by pictures, characters, and examples." But the epistles never appeared; instead, the satire grew until it took their place. As Pope surveyed England in his last years, the complex literary and social order that had sustained him seemed to be crumbling. It was a time for desperate measures, for satire. And the means of retribution was at hand, in the structure of Pope's own *Dunciad*, the long work that had already impaled so many enemies.

The first *Dunciad*, published in three books in 1728, is a mock-epic reply to Pope's critics and other petty authors. Its hero and victim, Lewis Theobald, had attacked Pope's edition of Shakespeare (1725); other victims had offended Pope either by personal abuse or simply by ineptitude. Inspired by Dryden's *Mac Flecknoe*, *The Dunciad* celebrates the triumph of the hordes of Grub Street. Indeed, so many obscure hacks were mentioned that a *Dunciad Variorum* (1729) was soon required, in which mock-scholarly notes identify the victims, "since it is only in this monument that they must expect to survive." But a modern reader need not catch every reference to enjoy the dazzling wit of the poem, or the sheer sense of fun with which Pope remakes the London literary world into a tiny insane fairground of his own.

The New Dunciad (1742), however, plays a far more serious game: here Pope takes aim at the rot of the whole social fabric. The satire goes deep, and works at many levels, which for convenience may be divided into four. (1) Politics: From 1721 to 1742 England had been ruled by the Whig supremacy of Robert Walpole, first minister. To Pope and his circle, the immensely powerful Walpole (no friend of poets) seemed a crass and greedy vulgarian, like his monarch George II. It is no accident, in the kingdom of *The Dunciad*, that Dulness personified sits on a throne. (2) Society: Just as the action of the *Aeneid* had been the removal of the empire of Troy to Latium, the action of *The Dunciad*, according to Pope, is "the removal of the empire of Dul-

---

5. Pope was a tender and devoted son. His mother had died in 1733, and the earliest version of these lines dates from 1731, when the poet was nursing her through a serious illness.

6. Pope alludes to the fact that Arbuthnot, a man of strict probity, left the queen's service no wealthier than when he entered it.

ness from the City of London to the polite world, Westminster"; that is, the abdication of civility in favor of commerce and financial interests. In modern England, authors write for money, and ministers govern for profit; conspicuous consumption (especially the consumption of paper by scribblers) has replaced the old values of the yeoman and the aristocrat. In 1743, Pope revised the original *Dunciad,* substituting the actor and poet laureate Colley Cibber for Theobald as the hero and incorporating *The New Dunciad* as the fourth book (the version printed here). Dulness, he implies, has achieved her final triumph; Cibber is laureate in England. (3) Education: The word *dunce* is derived from the Scholastic philosopher John Duns Scotus (ca. 1265–1308), whose name had come to stand for silly and useless subtlety, logical hairsplitting. Pope, as an heir of the Renaissance, believes that the central subject of education must always be its relevance for human behavior: "The proper study of mankind is Man," and moral philosophy, the relation of individuals to each other and to the world, should be the teacher's first and last concern. By contrast, Dunces waste their time on grammar (words alone) or the "science" of the collector (things alone); they never comprehend that word and thing, like spirit and matter, are essentially dead unless they join. (4) Religion: At its deepest level, the subject of *The Dunciad* is the undoing of God's creation. Many passages from the fourth book echo *Paradise Lost,* and one of Pope's starting places seems to be Satan's threat to return the world to its original darkness, chaos, and ancient night (*Paradise Lost* 2.968–87). *The Dunciad* ends in a great apocalypse, with a yawn that signals the death of *Logos;* as words have become meaningless, so has the whole creation, which the Lord called forth with words. Here Pope invokes, with terrifying intensity, the old idea that God was the first poet, whose poem was the world, and suggests that the sickness of the word has infected all nature. But there is one consolation: out of non-art itself, out of matter without spirit and substance without essence, the poet creates his own final artistic triumph, and makes a poem.

From The Dunciad

From *Book the Fourth*

Yet, yet a moment, one dim ray of light
Indulge, dread Chaos, and eternal Night!
Of darkness visible[1] so much be lent,
As half to show, half veil the deep intent.
5 Ye Powers![2] whose mysteries restored I sing,
To whom Time bears me on his rapid wing,
Suspend a while your force inertly strong,
Then take at once the poet and the song.
   Now flamed the Dog-star's[3] unpropitious ray,
10 Smote every brain, and withered every bay,[4]
Sick was the sun, the owl forsook his bower,
The moon-struck prophet felt the madding hour:
Then rose the seed[5] of Chaos, and of Night,
To blot out Order, and extinguish Light,
15 Of dull and venal a new world to mold,
And bring Saturnian days of lead and gold.[6]

1. Cf. *Paradise Lost* 1.63.
2. Chaos and Night, invoked in place of the Muse, because "the restoration of their empire is the action of the poem" [Pope's note].
3. Sirius, associated with the heat of summer and the madness of poets (see *Epistle to Dr. Arbuthnot,* line 3, p. 1169).
4. The laurel, whose garlands are bestowed on poets.
5. The Goddess Dulness.
6. Saturn ruled during the golden age; the new age of "gold" will be reestablished by the dull and venal.

She mounts the throne: her head a cloud concealed,
In broad effulgence all below revealed,
('Tis thus aspiring Dulness ever shines)
20   Soft on her lap her Laureate son[7] reclines.
    Beneath her foot-stool, Science groans in chains,
And Wit dreads exile, penalties and pains.
There foamed rebellious Logic, gagged and bound,
There, stripped, fair Rhetoric languished on the ground;
25   His blunted arms by Sophistry are born,
And shameless Billingsgate[8] her robes adorn.
Morality, by her false guardians drawn,
Chicane in furs, and Casuistry in lawn,[9]
Gasps, as they straighten at each end the cord,
30   And dies, when Dulness gives her Page[1] the word.

*   *   *

[THE EDUCATOR]

135   Now crowds on crowds around the Goddess press,
Each eager to present the first address.[2]
Dunce scorning dunce beholds the next advance,
But fop shows fop superior complaisance.
When lo! a specter[3] rose, whose index-hand
140   Held forth the virtue of the dreadful wand;
His beavered brow a birchen garland wears,[4]
Dropping with infant's blood, and mother's tears.
O'er every vein a shuddering horror runs;
Eton and Winton shake through all their sons.
145   All flesh is humbled, Westminster's bold race[5]
Shrink, and confess the Genius[6] of the place:
The pale boy-Senator yet tingling stands,
And holds his breeches close with both his hands.
    Then thus. "Since Man from beast by words is known,
150   Words are Man's province, words we teach alone.
When reason doubtful, like the Samian letter,[7]
Points him two ways, the narrower is the better.
Placed at the door of learning, youth to guide,
We never suffer it to stand too wide.
155   To ask, to guess, to know, as they commence,
As fancy opens the quick springs of sense,
We ply the memory, we load the brain,
Bind rebel wit, and double chain on chain,
Confine the thought, to exercise the breath;[8]

7. Colley Cibber, the poet laureate.
8. Fishmarket slang, which now covers the noble science of rhetoric.
9. Chicanery (legal trickery) wears the ermine robe of a judge; casuistry wears the linen sleeves of a bishop.
1. Sir Francis Page, a notorious hanging judge; or court page, used to strangle criminals in Turkey; or page of writing on which a dull author "kills" moral sentiments.
2. The goddess, newly enthroned, is receiving petitions and congratulations.
3. The ghost of Dr. Busby, stern headmaster of Westminster School.

4. He wears a hat (beaver) and a garland of birch twigs, used for flogging. "Wand": cane used for beating.
5. Alumni of Westminster School, with a play on the justices and members of Parliament who meet at Westminster Hall.
6. I.e., admit that Dr. Busby is the presiding deity (Genius).
7. The letter Y, which Pythagoras (a native of Samos) used as an emblem of the different roads of virtue and vice.
8. Students are taught only to recite the classic poets by heart.

160 And keep them in the pale of words till death.
Whate'er the talents, or howe'er designed,
We hang one jingling padlock on the mind:
A poet the first day, he dips his quill;
And what the last? a very poet still.
165 Pity! the charm works only in our wall,
Lost, lost too soon in yonder House or Hall."⁹

* * *

[THE TRIUMPH OF DULNESS]

Then blessing all,¹ "Go children of my care!
580 To practice now from theory repair.
All my commands are easy, short, and full:
My sons! be proud, be selfish, and be dull.
Guard my prerogative, assert my throne:
This nod confirms each privilege your own.
585 The cap and switch be sacred to his Grace;²
With staff and pumps³ the Marquis lead the race;
From stage to stage the licensed⁴ Earl may run,
Paired with his fellow-charioteer the sun;
The learned baron butterflies design,
590 Or draw to silk Arachne's subtle line;°   spiderweb
The Judge to dance his brother Sergeant⁵ call;
The Senator at cricket urge the ball;
The Bishop stow (pontific luxury!)
An hundred souls of turkeys in a pie;⁶
595 The sturdy squire to Gallic masters° stoop,   French chefs
And drown his lands and manors in a soup.
Others import yet nobler arts from France,
Teach kings to fiddle, and make senates dance.
Perhaps more high some daring son may soar,⁷
600 Proud to my list to add one monarch more;
And nobly conscious, Princes are but things
Born for First Ministers, as slaves for kings,
Tyrant supreme! shall three estates command,
And MAKE ONE MIGHTY DUNCIAD OF THE LAND!"
605 More she had spoke, but yawned—All Nature nods:
What mortal can resist the yawn of Gods?
Churches and chapels instantly it reached;
(St. James's first, for leaden Gilbert⁸ preached)
Then catched the schools; the Hall scarce kept awake;
610 The Convocation gaped,⁹ but could not speak:
Lost was the Nation's Sense,° nor could be found,   Parliament

9. The House of Commons and Westminster Hall, where law cases were heard. The eloquence learned by rote disappears on occasions for public speaking.
1. Having conferred her titles, Dulness bids each of the rulers of England to indulge in the triviality closest to his heart.
2. His Grace, a duke who loves horse racing, is to use the cap and switch of a jockey.
3. Footmen, who wore pumps (low-cut shoes for running), were matched in races.
4. The license required by the owner of a stage-

coach; also privileged or licentious.
5. A lawyer or legislative officer. Formal ceremonies at the Inns of Court are said to have resembled a country dance, "a call of sergeants."
6. According to Pope, a hundred turkeys had been "not unfrequently deposited in one Pye in the Bishopric of Durham."
7. A bold, direct attack on Walpole.
8. Dr. John Gilbert, dean of Exeter.
9. The Convocation, an assembly of clergy consulting on ecclesiastical affairs, had been adjourned since 1717.

While the long solemn unison went round:
Wide, and more wide, it spread o'er all the realm;
Even Palinurus[1] nodded at the helm:
615   The vapor mild o'er each committee crept;
Unfinished treaties in each office slept;
And chiefless armies dozed out the campaign;
And navies yawned for orders on the main.
     O Muse! relate (for you can tell alone,
620   Wits have short memories, and dunces none)
Relate, who first, who last resigned to rest;
Whose heads she partly, whose completely blessed;
What charms could faction, what ambition lull,
The venal quiet, and entrance the dull;
625   'Till drowned was sense, and shame, and right, and wrong—
O sing, and hush the nations with thy song!
. . . .
In vain, in vain,—the all-composing Hour
Resistless falls: The Muse obeys the Power.
She comes! she comes![2] the sable throne behold
630   Of Night primeval, and of Chaos old!
Before her, Fancy's gilded clouds decay,
And all its varying rainbows die away.
Wit shoots in vain its momentary fires,
The meteor drops, and in a flash expires.
635   As one by one, at dread Medea's strain,
The sickening stars fade off the ethereal plain;[3]
As Argus' eyes by Hermes' wand oppressed,
Closed one by one to everlasting rest;[4]
Thus at her felt approach, and secret might,
640   Art after Art goes out, and all is Night.
See skulking Truth to her old cavern fled,[5]
Mountains of casuistry heaped o'er her head!
Philosophy, that leaned on Heaven before,
Shrinks to her second cause,[6] and is no more.
645   Physic[7] of Metaphysic begs defense,
And Metaphysic calls for aid on Sense!
See Mystery[8] to Mathematics fly!
In vain! they gaze, turn giddy, rave, and die.
Religion blushing veils her sacred fires,
650   And unawares Morality expires.
Nor public flame, nor private, dares to shine;
Nor human spark is left, nor glimpse divine!
Lo! thy dread Empire, Chaos! is restored;
Light dies before thy uncreating word:[9]

---

1. The pilot of Aeneas's ship; here Walpole.
2. Having triumphed in the contemporary world of affairs, Dulness (like her antitype Christ) has a Second Coming, a prophetic vision in which she extinguishes the light of the arts and sciences.
3. In Seneca's *Medea,* the stars obey the curse of Medea, a magician and avenger.
4. Argus, Hera's hundred-eyed watchman, was charmed to sleep and slain by Hermes.
5. Alluding to the saying of Democritus, that Truth lay at the bottom of a deep well [Pope's note].

6. Science (philosophy) no longer accepts God as the first cause or final explanation of how all things came to be; instead, it accepts only the second or material cause and tries to account for all things by physical principles alone.
7. Natural science in general.
8. A religious truth known only through divine revelation.
9. Cf. God's first creating words in Genesis, "Let there be light."

655   Thy hand, great Anarch! lets the curtain fall;
     And Universal Darkness buries All.

1743

LADY MARY WORTLEY MONTAGU
1689–1762

In her early teens Lady Mary Pierrepont did something that well-bred young women were not supposed to do: she secretly taught herself Latin. The act reveals many traits that would characterize her as a mature woman: curiosity, love of learning, intelligence, ambition, and independence of mind. The eldest daughter of a wealthy Whig peer, she grew up amid a glittering London circle that included Addison, Steele, Congreve, and later Pope and Gay. But she was not content to live the life of a dutiful aristocratic daughter. Unlike most women in her time, she married for love, and when her husband, Edward Wortley Montagu, was appointed ambassador to Constantinople in 1716, she took the opportunity of traveling through Europe, studying the language and customs of Turkey, and even visiting harems; her "Turkish Letters," published in 1763, would establish her as one of the great letter writers in English. She also pioneered in introducing smallpox inoculation to England. Returning home in 1718, she spent unhappy years that included bitter political quarrels with Pope (who satirized her as "Sappho" in *Epistle 2. To a Lady*) and the gradual failure of her marriage. Then she fell in love with a young Italian author, Francesco Algarotti. In 1739 she traveled to Italy hoping to see him; but the passion that had kindled in their letters was quenched when he failed to join her. She spent the rest of her life abroad, and died soon after returning to London in 1762. Montagu is remembered chiefly for her letters, but was also admired in her own time as a poet. Her verse, though often casual, reveals the strong mind of a woman who is not willing to accept the stereotypes imposed on her by men and who insists on preserving her freedom of choice. Her sexual candor and punishing wit demand respect; and the poems, like Montagu herself, are never dull.

The Lover: A Ballad

    At length, by so much importunity pressed,
    Take, (Molly),[1] at once, the inside of my breast;
    This stupid indifference so often you blame
    Is not owing to nature, to fear, or to shame;
5   I am not as cold as a Virgin in lead,[2]
    Nor is Sunday's sermon so strong in my head;
    I know but too well how time flies along,
    That we live but few years and yet fewer are young.

---

1. Molly Skerrett, a friend of Lady Mary, was the mistress of Sir Robert Walpole. The ideal "lover" of the title, however, is not to be identified with any particular person.

2. I.e., an image of the Virgin Mary, either as a leaden statue or as a stained-glass window framed in lead.

But I hate to be cheated, and never will buy
10   Long years of repentance for moments of joy.
Oh was there a man (but where shall I find
Good sense and good nature so equally joined?)
Would value his pleasure, contribute to mine,
Not meanly would boast, nor lewdly design,°   *plot*
15   Not over severe, yet not stupidly vain,
For I would have the power though not give the pain;

No pedant yet learnèd, not rakehelly gay
Or laughing because he has nothing to say,
To all my whole sex obliging and free,
20   Yet never be fond of any but me;
In public preserve the decorums are just,
And show in his eyes he is true to his trust,
Then rarely approach, and respectfully bow,
Yet not fulsomely pert, nor yet foppishly low.

25   But when the long hours of public are past
And we meet with champagne and a chicken at last,
May every fond pleasure that hour endear,
Be banished afar both discretion and fear,
Forgetting or scorning the airs of the crowd
30   He may cease to be formal, and I to be proud,
Till lost in the joy we confess that we live,
And he may be rude, and yet I may forgive.

And that my delight may be solidly fixed,
Let the friend and the lover be handsomely mixed,
35   In whose tender bosom my soul might confide,
Whose kindness can sooth me, whose counsel could guide.
From such a dear lover as here I describe
No danger should fright me, no millions should bribe;
But till this astonishing creature I know,
40   As I long have lived chaste, I will keep myself so.

I never will share with the wanton coquette,
Or be caught by a vain affectation of wit.
The toasters and songsters may try all their art
But never shall enter the pass of my heart.
45   I loathe the lewd rake, the dressed fopling despise;
Before such pursuers the nice° virgin flies;   *fastidious*
And as Ovid has sweetly in parables told
We harden like trees, and like rivers are cold.[3]

1747

---

3. In Ovid's *Metamorphoses*, Daphne, to escape Apollo, was turned into a laurel, and Arethusa, escaping
Alpheus, became a fountain.

Epistle from Mrs. Yonge to Her Husband[1]

Think not this paper comes with vain pretense
To move your pity, or to mourn th' offense.
Too well I know that hard obdurate heart;
No softening mercy there will take my part,
5   Nor can a woman's arguments prevail,
When even your patron's wise example fails.[2]
But this last privilege I still retain;
Th' oppressed and injured always may complain.
    Too, too severely laws of honor bind
10   The weak submissive sex of womankind.
If sighs have gained or force compelled our hand,
Deceived by art, or urged by stern command,
Whatever motive binds the fatal tie,
The judging world expects our constancy.
15   Just heaven! (for sure in heaven does justice reign,
Though tricks below that sacred name profane)
To you appealing I submit my cause,
Nor fear a judgment from impartial laws.
All bargains but conditional[3] are made;
20   The purchase void, the creditor unpaid;
Defrauded servants are from service free;
A wounded slave regains his liberty.
For wives ill used no remedy remains,
To daily racks condemned, and to eternal chains.
25   From whence is this unjust distinction grown?
Are we not formed with passions like your own?
Nature with equal fire our souls endued,
Our minds as haughty, and as warm our blood;
O'er the wide world your pleasures you pursue,
30   The change is justified by something new;
But we must sigh in silence—and be true.
Our sex's weakness you expose and blame
(Of every prattling fop the common theme),
Yet from this weakness you suppose is due
35   Sublimer virtue than your Cato[4] knew.
Had heaven designed us trials so severe,

---

1. In 1724 the notorious libertine William Yonge, separated from his wife, Mary, discovered that she (like him) had committed adultery. He sued her lover, Colonel Norton, for damages and collected £1,500. Later that year, according to the law of the time, he petitioned the Houses of Parliament for a divorce. The case was tried in public, Mrs. Yonge's love letters were read aloud, and two men testified that they had found her and Norton "together in naked bed." Yonge was granted the divorce, his wife's dowry, and the greater part of her fortune.
    Although the *Epistle* is obviously based on this sensational affair, it is also a work of imagination. Like Pope's *Eloisa to Abelard*—to which the author himself called Montagu's attention—it takes the form of a heroic epistle, the passionate outcry of an abandoned woman. The poet, entering into the feelings of Mary Yonge, justifies her conduct with

reasons both of the heart and of the head. The objects of her attack include the institution of marriage, which binds wives in "eternal chains"; the double standard of morality, which requires chastity from women but not men; the hypocrisy of society, which condemns the very behavior it secretly lusts after; and the craven greed and cruelty of the husband himself. But 18th-century women seldom dared to speak like this in public, and the *Epistle* was not published until the 1970s.
2. Sir Robert Walpole, William Yonge's friend at court, was rumored to tolerate his own wife's infidelities.
3. Only conditionally.
4. The asceticism and self-discipline of the Roman statesman Cato had been emphasized in Addison's famous tragedy *Cato* (1713).

It would have formed our tempers then to bear.
  And I have borne (oh what have I not borne!)
The pang of jealousy, the insults of scorn.
40 Wearied at length, I from your sight remove,
And place my future hopes in secret love.
In the gay bloom of glowing youth retired,
I quit the woman's joy to be admired,
With that small pension your hard heart allows,
45 Renounce your fortune, and release your vows.
To custom (though unjust) so much is due;
I hide my frailty from the public view.
My conscience clear, yet sensible of shame,
My life I hazard, to preserve my fame.
50 And I prefer this low inglorious state ⎫
To vile dependence on the thing I hate— ⎬
But you pursue me to this last retreat. ⎭
Dragged into light, my tender crime is shown
And every circumstance of fondness known.
55 Beneath the shelter of the law you stand,
And urge my ruin with a cruel hand,
While to my fault thus rigidly severe,
Tamely submissive to the man you fear.[5]
    This wretched outcast, this abandoned wife,
60 Has yet this joy to sweeten shameful life:
By your mean conduct, infamously loose,
You are at once my accuser and excuse.
Let me be damned by the censorious prude
(Stupidly dull, or spiritually lewd),
65 My hapless case will surely pity find
From every just and reasonable mind.
When to the final sentence I submit,
The lips condemn me, but their souls acquit.
    No more my husband, to your pleasures go,
70 The sweets of your recovered freedom know.
Go: court the brittle friendship of the great,
Smile at his board,° or at his levee[6] wait;   *dining table*
And when dismissed, to madam's toilet[7] fly,
More than her chambermaids, or glasses,° lie,   *mirrors*
75 Tell her how young she looks, how heavenly fair,
Admire the lilies and the roses there.
Your high ambition may be gratified,
Some cousin of her own be made your bride,
And you the father of a glorious race
80 Endowed with Ch——l's strength and Low——r's face.[8]

1724   1972

5. I.e., Walpole. Montagu suggests that the whole political establishment of England takes sides against Mary Yonge.
6. Morning reception of visitors.
7. It was fashionable for women like Lady Walpole to receive visitors during the last stages of dressing (their "toilet").
8. General Churchill was rumored to have had an affair with Lady Walpole; Antony Lowther was a notorious gallant. The author implies that William Yonge's next wife may be as untrue as his first. Mary Yonge remarried immediately after her divorce; five years later Yonge himself (whose divorce had made him rich) married the daughter of a baron.

WILLIAM HOGARTH
1697–1764

William Hogarth was a Londoner born and bred; the life of the city, both high and low, fills all his work. His early life was hard. When his father, a writer and teacher, failed in business, the family was confined to the area of the Fleet, the debtor's prison. Hogarth never forgot "the cruel treatment" of his father by booksellers, and he resolved to make his living without relying on dealers; he would always be aggressively independent. Apprenticed as an engraver, he trained himself to sketch scenes quickly or catch them in memory. He also learned to paint, studying with the Serjeant Painter to the King, Sir James Thornhill, whose daughter he married (late in life Hogarth himself would become Serjeant Painter). Gradually he won a reputation for portraits and conversation pieces—group portraits in which members of a family or assembly interact in a social situation. But his popular fame was forged by sets of pictures that told a story: *A Harlot's Progress* (1731–32), *A Rake's Progress* (1734–35), and *Marriage A-la-Mode* (1743–45). First Hogarth painted these Modern Moral Subjects (as he called them), then prints were made and sold in large editions. He also found new ways to market and protect his work; a copyright bill to ban cheap imitations of prints was known as "Hogarth's Act." Despite this success, however, his ambition to redefine British standards of art led to frustration. The high regard and high prices for continental old masters were too well entrenched to be undermined. Hogarth did not get prestigious commissions, and his *Analysis of Beauty* (1753), an effort to fix "the fluctuating ideas of taste" by appealing to practical observations, not academic rules, was poorly received. Political and aesthetic controversies embittered his final years.

Writers have always loved Hogarth's satiric art, and many have claimed him as one of their own. Swift, Fielding, and Sterne associated their work with his; Horace Walpole considered him more "a writer of comedy with a pencil" than a painter; Charles Lamb compared him to Shakespeare; and William Hazlitt included him among the great English comic writers. This emphasis may slight Hogarth's importance in the history of art. His attempts to found a British school that looked at life and nature directly, not through a haze of ideas or reverence for the past, and to give pleasure to common people, not only to critics and connoisseurs, opened the eyes of many artists to come. But Hogarth is also a great storyteller, someone to *read*. Like novels and plays, his pictures have plots and morals; they ask us not only to look but also to think. Yet looking and thinking are always intertwined. The mind delights in riddles, according to Hogarth; and as he revised his work he stuffed in more and more clues, like a mystery writer. A feast of interpretation draws the reader in. So many expressive details crowd the pictures, so many keys to character and meaning, that viewers often become obsessed with figuring them out. Even inanimate objects can speak; playwrights rely on words, as Walpole pointed out, but "it was reserved to Hogarth to write a scene of furniture."

The furniture is particularly eloquent in *Marriage A-la-Mode*; note, for example, the fallen chairs in Plates 2 and 6. Hogarth took special pains with this series. The audience at which he aimed, as well as the subject matter, belonged to high society; and the art too is highly refined. A sinuous line weaves through each picture, leading the reader on, and each piece of bric-a-brac carries a message of lavish excess. Yet the story itself is brutally straightforward. A disastrous forced marriage stands at the center: a rich but miserly merchant buys the worthless son of an aristocrat for his restless daughter, and with nothing in common the couple destroy one another. The crisis of values that Hogarth depicts was bringing about radical changes in English life. In the tension between a fading aristocracy, both morally and financially bankrupt, and an upwardly mobile middle class, greedy for power but culturally insecure, the marriage reflects a society that has lost all sense of right and wrong. The artist plays no favorites. The aristocratic Squanderfields are not only vain, effete, and dissipated but also lacking in taste; the wan mythological paintings on their walls are just the sort of pretentious, overpriced art that Hogarth hates. But the vulgar Dutch art on the merchant's walls (in Plate 6) seems even worse, and his daughter falls for every extravagant, spurious fashion (in Plate 4). Nor do the parasites who live off these easy marks offer any hope. Lawyer and doctor, bawd and servant pave the road to ruin. Hogarth's satire warns against the spreading corruption of modern times, when self-interest eats into marriage and old values die. Look hard, he tells the public. These objects make up the world we live in. We might become these people.

Marriage A-la-Mode

Plate 1. *The Marriage Contract.* Lord Squanderfield points to the family tree, going back to William the Conquerer, that his son will bring to the marriage. Coronets are blazed all over the room, from the top of the canopy at the upper left to the side of the prostrate dog on the lower right. The earl, though hobbled by gout, is proud. But he has run out of money: construction has stopped on the Palladian mansion seen through the window. Sitting across from him, a squinting merchant grasps the marriage settlement. Some of the coins and banknotes he has placed on the table have been taken up by a scrawny usurer, who hands the earl a mortgage in return. At the right the betrothed sit back to back, uncaring as the dogs chained to each other below. The vacuous viscount pinches snuff and gazes at himself in a mirror, which ominously reflects the image of lawyer Silvertongue, who sharpens his pen as he bends unctuously over the bride-to-be. Pouting, she twirls her wedding ring in a handkerchief. Disasters from mythology cover the walls. A bombastic portrait of the earl as Jupiter, astride a cannon, dominates the room; and in a candle sconce on the right Medusa glowers over the scene.

Plate 2. *After the Marriage*.   By now the couple are used to ignoring each other. The morning after a spree, the rumpled, exhausted viscount slouches in a chair. His broken sword has dropped on the carpet, and a lapdog sniffs at a woman's cap in his pocket—souvenirs of the night. Lolling and stretching in an unladylike pose, his wife too is half asleep. She has spent the night home but not alone. *Hoyle on Whist* lies before her, cards are scattered on the floor, and the overturned chair, book of music, and violin cases suggest that some player may have departed in haste. A steward carries away a sheaf of bills—only one paid—and the household ledger; a Methodist (*Regeneration* is in his pocket), he petitions heaven to look down on these heathens. Oriental idols decorate the mantel over the fireplace, surmounted by a broken-nosed Roman bust that frowns like the steward and a painting of Cupid playing the bagpipes. On the left, amid the shrubbery of a rococo clock, a cat leers over fish and a Buddha smiles. In the next room, a dozing servant fails to notice that a candle has set fire to a chair. Next to a row of saints, a curtain does not quite cover a bawdy painting from which a naked foot peeps.

Plate 3. *The Scene with the Quack.*   The husband has come to this chamber of medical horrors in search of a cure. The pillbox he holds toward the quack has not done its job, and he raises his cane as if with a playful threat. Evidently the little girl who stands between his legs is infected. She dabs a sore on her lip, and her ageless face may hint that she is not as young and pure as she looks. Her cap resembles the cap in Plate 2; she is the husband's mistress. Perhaps the beauty spot on his neck also covers a sore. The bowlegged Monsieur de la Pillule comfortably wipes his glasses; he has seen all this before. Between the two men an angry woman, fortified by a massive hoop skirt, opens a knife. She may be the wife of the quack, defending her man, or else a bawd who resents the charge that her girls are damaged goods. Medical oddities and monstrosities clutter the room, along with portents of death. The viscount's cane points to a cabinet where a wigged head looks at a skeleton that seems to be groping a cadaver; the tripod above evokes a gallows tree. At the far left, in front of a laboratory door, are two of the doctor's inventions: machines for setting bones and uncorking bottles. Their similarity to instruments of torture hints at how useful the doctor's assistance will be.

Plate 4. *The Countess's Levee.*   In her bedchamber at rising (*levée*; French), the countess receives some guests and puts on a show. Her husband is now earl (note the coronets), and they have a child (note the rattle on her chair). While a hairdresser curls her locks, she hangs on the words of Silvertongue, who makes himself at home (note his portrait on the upper right wall). Tonight they will be going to a masquerade ball, like the one on the screen he gestures toward; his left hand holds the tickets. At the far right a puffy, bedizened castrato sings, accompanied by a flute. His audience includes a self-absorbed dandy in curl-papers; a man who appreciatively smirks and opens his hand, from which a fan dangles; a snoring husband, holding his riding-crop like a baton; and his enraptured wife, who leans forward as if about to swoon. Unobserved by the others, a black servant, bearing a cup of chocolate, smiles in amazement at these precious airs. At the lower left another black servant, a boy in a turban, grins at gewgaws purchased at an auction. His finger points both to Actaeon's horns, the sign of a cuckold, and to the couple as they arrange their tryst. Wall paintings illustrate unnatural sex: Lot's seduction by his daughters, Jupiter embracing Io, and the rape of Ganymede.

Plate 5. *The Death of the Earl.* The melodramatic tableau at the center, as the earl totters toward death and the countess kneels to beg forgiveness, imitates paintings of Christ descending from the cross while Mary Magdalen mourns. But the surroundings are sordid. At a house of ill repute, the Turk's Head Bagnio, the countess and Silvertongue have been surprised in bed. The earl has broken in (key and socket on the floor) and drawn his sword, and the lawyer has run him through. As the horrified owner and constable enter, under a watchman's lantern, the killer, still in his nightshirt, flees through a window. A fire, outside the picture on the lower right, casts lurid light on the victim; the shadow of the tongs encircles the murder weapon. Costumed as a nun and friar, the lovers have come from a masquerade, and their discarded masks and clothes show they were in haste. Pills (presumably mercury, prescribed for venereal disease) have spilled from an overturned table on the right, beside an advertisement for the bagnio, a corset, and a bundle of firewood. The portrait of a streetwalker, a squirrel perched on her hand, leers over the countess; on the wall behind the earl an uplifted blade is about to sever a child, in the Judgment of Solomon. At the top left St. Luke, the patron of artists, inscribes these transgressions.

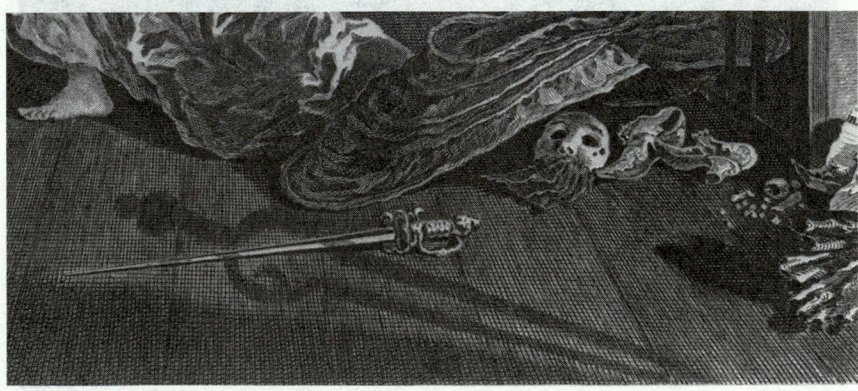

Plate 6. *The Death of the Countess.* "Counseller Silvertongues Last Dying Speech," a paper on the floor announces, and a bottle of laudanum has dropped beside it. News of her lover's execution has driven the countess to poison herself. Slumped in a chair, she is already dead; on the far right a doctor steals away. Her father calmly slides the ring from her finger. This is his house; a window with cobwebs and broken panes opens on London Bridge, in the heart of the City. No luxury here. The furnishings are sparse, the floor is bare, and the dining table holds only one egg and a few leftovers, including a pathetic boar's head from which a starving hound is tearing scraps. The art is equally cheap: a pissing boy, a jumbled still life, a pipe set alight by the glowing nose of a drunk. At the center, beneath a coatrack, a stout apothecary (stomach pump and julep in his pocket) points toward the empty bottle in reproof and pokes the servant who brought it—an idiot wearing a coat many sizes too large, the merchant's hand-me-down. The service staff is completed by a withered old woman who holds out the countess's little child for one last hug and kiss. But the mark on the child's cheek and the brace on its leg imply that disease has passed to the next generation. This noble family will have no heir.

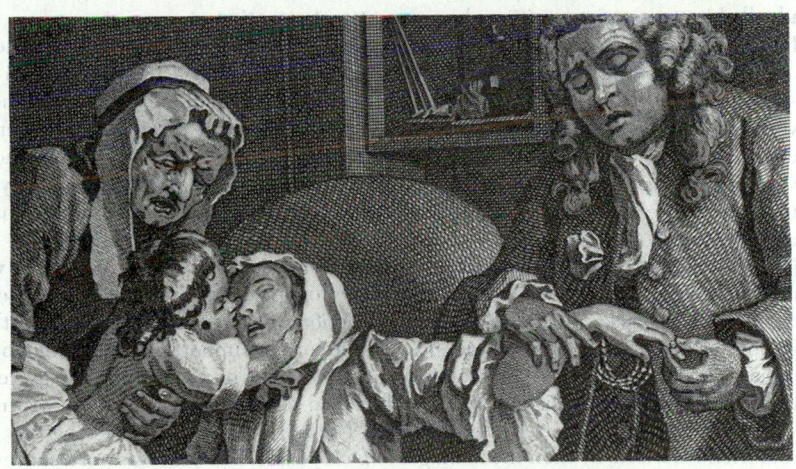

SAMUEL JOHNSON
1709–1784

Samuel Johnson was famous as a talker in his own time, and his conversation (preserved by James Boswell and others) has been famous ever since. But his wisdom survives above all in his writings: a few superb poems; the grave *Rambler* essays, which established his reputation as a stylist and a moralist; the lessons about life in *Rasselas* and the *Lives of the Poets;* and literary criticism that ranks among the best in English. The virtues of the talk and the writings are the same. They come hot from a mind well stored with knowledge, searingly honest, humane, and quick to seize the unexpected but appropriate image of truth. Johnson's wit is timeless, for it deals with the great facts of human experience, with hope and happiness and loss and duty and the fear of death. Whatever topic he addresses, whatever the form in which he writes, he holds to one commanding purpose: to see life as it is.

Two examples must suffice here. When Anna Williams wondered why a man should make a beast of himself through drunkenness, Johnson answered that "he who makes a beast of himself gets rid of the pain of being a man." In this reply Williams's tired metaphor is so charged with an awareness of the dark aspects of human life that it comes almost unbearably alive. Such moments characterize Johnson's writings as well. For instance, in reviewing the book of a fatuous would-be philosopher who blandly explained away the pains of poverty by declaring that a kindly providence compensates the poor by making them more hopeful, more healthy, more easily pleased, and less sensitive than the rich, Johnson retorted: "The poor indeed are insensible of many little vexations which sometimes embitter the possessions and pollute the enjoyments of the rich. They are not pained by casual incivility, or mortified by the mutilation of a compliment; but this happiness is like that of a malefactor who ceases to feel the cords that bind him when the pincers are tearing his flesh."

Johnson had himself known the pains of poverty. During his boyhood and youth, his father's financial circumstances steadily worsened, so that he was forced to leave Oxford before he had taken a degree. An early marriage to a well-to-do widow, Elizabeth ("Tetty") Porter, more than twenty years older than he, enabled him to open a school. But the school failed, and he moved to London to make his way as a writer. The years between 1737, when he first arrived there with his pupil David Garrick (later to become the leading actor of his generation), and 1755, when the publication of the *Dictionary* established his reputation, were often difficult. He supported himself at first as best he could by doing hack work for the *Gentleman's Magazine,* but gradually his own original writings began to attract attention.

In 1747 Johnson published the *Plan* of his *Dictionary,* and he spent the the next seven years compiling it—although he had expected to finish it in three. When in 1748 Dr. Adams, a friend from Oxford days, questioned his ability to carry out such a work alone so fast and reminded him that the *Dictionary* of the French Academy had needed forty academicians working for forty years, Johnson replied with humorous jingoism: "Sir, thus it is. This is the proportion. Let me see; forty times forty is sixteen hundred. As three to sixteen hundred, so is the proportion of an Englishman to a Frenchman."

Johnson's achievement in compiling the *Dictionary* seems even greater when we realize that he was writing some of his best essays and poems during the same period. Although the booksellers who published the *Dictionary* paid him what was then the large sum of £1,575, it was not enough to enable him to support his household, buy materials, and pay the wages of the six assistants whom he employed year by year until the task was accomplished. He therefore had to earn more money by writing. In 1749, his early tragedy *Irene* (pronounced *I-re-nĕ*) was produced at long last by his old friend Garrick, by then the manager of Drury Lane. The play was not a success, although Johnson made some profit from it. In the same year appeared his finest poem, *The Vanity of Human Wishes*. With the *Rambler* (1750–52) and the *Idler* (1758–60), two series of periodical essays, Johnson found a devoted audience, but his pleasure was tempered by the death of his wife in 1752. He never remarried.

Boswell said of the *Rambler* essays that "in no writings whatever can be found more bark and steel [i.e., quinine and iron] for the mind." Moral strength and health; the importance of applying reason to experience; the test of virtue by what we do, not what we say or "feel"; faith in God: these are the centers to which Johnson's moral writings always return. What Johnson uniquely offers us is the quality of his understanding of the human condition, based on wide reading but always ultimately referred to his own passionate and often anguished experience. Such understanding had to be fought for again and again.

Johnson is thought of as the great generalizer, but what gives his generalizations strength is that they are rooted in the particulars of his self-knowledge. He had constantly to fight against what he called "filling the mind" with illusions to avoid the call of duty, his own black melancholy, and the realities of life. His theme of themes is expressed in the title *The Vanity of Human Wishes*: the dangerous but all-pervasive power of wishful thinking, the feverish intrusion of desires and hopes that distort reality and lead to false expectations. Almost all of Johnson's major writings—verse satire, moral essay, or the prose fable *Rasselas* (1759)—express this theme. In *Rasselas* it is called "the hunger of imagination, which preys upon life," picturing things as one would like them to be, not as they are. The travelers who are the fable's protagonists pursue some formula for happiness; they reflect our naive hope, against the lessons of experience, that one choice of life will make us happy forever.

During this time of great activity, Johnson developed his characteristic style: the rotund periods, proceeding through balanced or parallel words; phrases or clauses moving to carefully controlled rhythms, in language that is characteristically general, often Latinate, and frequently polysyllabic. It is a style at the opposite extreme from Jonathan Swift's simplicity or Joseph Addison's neatness. In Johnson's writings this style never becomes obscure or turgid, for even a very complex sentence reveals—as it should—the structure of the thought, and the learned words are always precisely used. While reading early scientists to collect words for the *Dictionary*, he developed a new vocabulary: for example, *obtund, exuberate, fugacity,* and *frigorific*. But he used many of these strange words in conversation as well as in his writings, often with a peculiarly Johnsonian felicity, describing the operations of the mind with a scientific precision.

After Johnson received his pension in 1762, he no longer had to write for a living, and because he held that "no man but a blockhead" ever wrote for any other reason, he produced as little as he decently could during the last twenty years of his life. His edition of Shakespeare, long delayed, was published in 1765, with a fine preface and fascinating notes. His last important work is the *Lives of the Poets*, which came out in two parts in 1779 and 1781. These biographical and critical prefaces were commissioned by a group of booksellers who had joined together to publish a large collection of the English poets and who wished to give their venture the prestige that Johnson would lend it. The poets to be included (except for four insisted on by Johnson) were selected by the booksellers according to current fashions. Therefore the collection begins with Abraham Cowley and John Milton and ends with Thomas Gray, and it omits such standard poets as Geoffrey Chaucer, Edmund Spenser, Sir Philip Sidney, John Donne, and Andrew Marvell.

In the *Lives of the Poets* and in the earlier *Life of Richard Savage* (1744), Johnson did much to advance the art of biography in England. Biography had long been associated with panegyrics or scandalous memoirs; and therefore Johnson's insistence on truth, even about the subject's defects, and on concrete, often minute, details was a new departure, disliked by many readers. "The biographical part of literature is what I love most," Johnson said, for he found every biography useful in revealing the human nature that all of us share. His insistence on truth in biography (and knowing that Boswell intended to write his life, he insisted that he should write it truthfully) was owing to his conviction that only a truthful work can be trusted to help us with the business of living.

The ideal poet, according to Johnson, has a genius for making the things we see every day seem new. The same might be said of Johnson himself as a critic. He is our great champion, in criticism, of common sense and the common reader. Without denying the right of the poet to flights of imagination, he also insists that poems must make sense, please readers, and help us not only understand the world but cope with it. Johnson holds poems to the truth, as he sees it: the principles of nature, logic, religion, and morality. Not even Shakespeare can be excused when "he sacrifices virtue to convenience" and "seems to write without any moral purpose." Yet Johnson is no worshiper of authority or mere "correctness." As a critic he is always the empiricist, testing theory by practice. His determination to judge literature by its truth to life, not by abstract rules, is perfectly illustrated by his treatment of the doctrine of the three unities in the *Preface* to Shakespeare. Johnson is never afraid to state the obvious, whether the lack of human interest in *Paradise Lost* or Shakespeare's temptation by puns. But at its best, as in the praise of Milton or Shakespeare, his criticism engages some of the deepest questions about literature: why it endures, and how it helps us endure.

The Vanity of Human Wishes This poem is an imitation of Juvenal's *Satire 10*. Although it closely follows the order and the ideas of the Latin poem, it remains a very personal work, for Johnson has used the Roman Stoic's satire as a means of expressing his own sense of the tragic and comic in human life. He has tried to reproduce in English verse the qualities he thought especially Juvenalian: stateliness, pointed sentences, and declamatory grandeur. The poem is difficult because of the extreme compactness of the style: every line is forced to convey the greatest possible amount of meaning. Johnson's poetic theory demanded that the poet should deal in the general rather than mere particulars, but he certainly did not intend that the general should fade into the abstract: observe, for example, how he makes abstract nouns concrete, active, and dramatic by using them as subjects of active and dramatic verbs: "Hate *dogs* their flight, and Insult *mocks* their end" (line 78). But the difficulty of the poem is also related to its theme, the difficulty of seeing anything clearly on this earth. In a world of blindness and illusion, human beings must struggle to find a point of view that will not deceive them, and a happiness that can last.

The Vanity of Human Wishes

In Imitation of the Tenth Satire of Juvenal

> Let Observation, with extensive view,
> Survey mankind, from China to Peru;
> Remark each anxious toil, each eager strife,
> And watch the busy scenes of crowded life;
> 5 Then say how hope and fear, desire and hate
> O'erspread with snares the clouded maze of fate,
> Where wavering man, betrayed by venturous pride
> To tread the dreary paths without a guide,
> As treacherous phantoms in the mist delude,

10 Shuns fancied ills, or chases airy good;
    How rarely Reason guides the stubborn choice,
    Rules the bold hand, or prompts the suppliant voice;
    How nations sink, by darling schemes oppressed,
    When Vengeance listens to the fool's request.
15 Fate wings with every wish the afflictive dart,
    Each gift of nature, and each grace of art;
    With fatal heat impetuous courage glows,
    With fatal sweetness elocution flows,
    Impeachment stops the speaker's powerful breath,
20 And restless fire precipitates on death.
        But scarce observed, the knowing and the bold
    Fall in the general massacre of gold;
    Wide-wasting pest! that rages unconfined,
    And crowds with crimes the records of mankind;
25 For gold his sword the hireling ruffian draws,
    For gold the hireling judge distorts the laws;
    Wealth heaped on wealth, nor truth nor safety buys,
    The dangers gather as the treasures rise.
        Let History tell where rival kings command,
30 And dubious title shakes the madded land,
    When statutes glean the refuse of the sword,
    How much more safe the vassal than the lord;
    Low skulks the hind° beneath the rage of power,   peasant
    And leaves the wealthy traitor[1] in the Tower,
35 Untouched his cottage, and his slumbers sound,
    Though Confiscation's vultures hover round.
        The needy traveler, serene and gay,
    Walks the wild heath, and sings his toil away.
    Does envy seize thee? crush the upbraiding joy,
40 Increase his riches and his peace destroy;
    New fears in dire vicissitude invade,
    The rustling brake° alarms, and quivering shade,   thicket
    Nor light nor darkness bring his pain relief,
    One shows the plunder, and one hides the thief.
45   Yet still one general cry the skies assails,
    And gain and grandeur load the tainted gales;
    Few know the toiling statesman's fear or care,
    The insidious rival and the gaping heir.
        Once more, Democritus,[2] arise on earth,
50 With cheerful wisdom and instructive mirth,
    See motley life in modern trappings dressed,
    And feed with varied fools the eternal jest:
    Thou who couldst laugh where Want enchained Caprice,
    Toil crushed Conceit, and man was of a piece;
55 Where Wealth unloved without a mourner died;
    And scarce a sycophant was fed by Pride;
    Where ne'er was known the form of mock debate,
    Or seen a new-made mayor's unwieldy state;

---

1. Johnson first wrote "bonny traitor," recalling the Jacobite uprising of 1745 and the execution of four of its Scot leaders.

2. A Greek philosopher of the late 5th century B.C.E., remembered as the "laughing philosopher" because men's follies only moved him to mirth.

Where change of favorites made no change of laws,
60   And senates heard before they judged a cause;
How wouldst thou shake at Britain's modish tribe,
Dart the quick taunt, and edge the piercing gibe?
Attentive truth and nature to descry,
And pierce each scene with philosophic eye.
65   To thee were solemn toys or empty show
The robes of pleasure and the veils of woe:
All aid the farce, and all thy mirth maintain,
Whose joys are causeless, or whose griefs are vain.
     Such was the scorn that filled the sage's mind,
70   Renewed at every glance on human kind;
How just that scorn ere yet thy voice declare,
Search every state, and canvass every prayer.
     Unnumbered suppliants crowd Preferment's gate,
Athirst for wealth, and burning to be great;
75   Delusive Fortune hears the incessant call,
They mount, they shine, evaporate, and fall.
On every stage the foes of peace attend,
Hate dogs their flight, and Insult mocks their end.
Love ends with hope, the sinking statesman's door
80   Pours in the morning worshiper no more;[3]
For growing names the weekly scribbler lies,
To growing wealth the dedicator flies;
From every room descends the painted face,
That hung the bright palladium[4] of the place;
85   And smoked in kitchens, or in auctions sold,
To better features yields the frame of gold;
For now no more we trace in every line
Heroic worth, benevolence divine:
The form distorted justifies the fall,
90   And Detestation rids the indignant wall.
     But will not Britain hear the last appeal,
Sign her foes' doom, or guard her favorites' zeal?
Through Freedom's sons no more remonstrance rings,
Degrading nobles and controlling kings;
95   Our supple tribes repress their patriot throats,
And ask no questions but the price of votes;
With weekly libels and septennial ale,[5]
Their wish is full to riot and to rail.
     In full-blown dignity, see Wolsey[6] stand,
100 Law in his voice, and fortune in his hand:
To him the church, the realm, their powers consign,
Through him the rays of regal bounty shine;
Turned by his nod the stream of honor flows,

3. Statesmen gave interviews and received friends and petitioners at levees, or morning receptions.
4. An image of Pallas Athena, which fell from heaven and was preserved at Troy. Not until it was stolen by Diomedes could the city fall to the Greeks.
5. Ministers and even the king freely bought support by bribing Members of Parliament, who in turn won elections by buying votes. "Weekly libels": politically motivated lampoons published in the weekly newspapers. "Septennial ale": the ale given away by candidates at parliamentary elections, held at least every seven years.
6. Thomas Cardinal Wolsey (ca. 1475–1530), lord chancellor and favorite of Henry VIII. Shakespeare dramatized his fall in *Henry VIII*.

His smile alone security bestows:
105 Still to new heights his restless wishes tower,
Claim leads to claim, and power advances power;
Till conquest unresisted ceased to please,
And rights submitted, left him none to seize.
At length his sovereign frowns—the train of state
110 Mark the keen glance, and watch the sign to hate.
Where'er he turns, he meets a stranger's eye,
His suppliants scorn him, and his followers fly;
At once is lost the pride of awful state,
The golden canopy, the glittering plate,
115 The regal palace, the luxurious board,
The liveried army, and the menial lord.
With age, with cares, with maladies oppressed,
He seeks the refuge of monastic rest.
Grief aids disease, remembered folly stings,
120 And his last sighs reproach the faith of kings.
        Speak thou, whose thoughts at humble peace repine,
Shall Wolsey's wealth, with Wolsey's end be thine?
Or liv'st thou now, with safer pride content,
The wisest justice on the banks of Trent?
125 For why did Wolsey, near the steeps of fate,
On weak foundations raise the enormous weight?
Why but to sink beneath misfortune's blow,
With louder ruin to the gulfs below?
        What gave great Villiers[7] to the assassin's knife,
130 And fixed disease on Harley's closing life?
What murdered Wentworth, and what exiled Hyde,
By kings protected, and to kings allied?
What but their wish indulged in courts to shine,
And power too great to keep or to resign?
135 When first the college rolls receive his name,
The young enthusiast quits his ease for fame;
Through all his veins the fever of renown
Burns from the strong contagion of the gown:
O'er Bodley's dome his future labors spread,
140 And Bacon's[8] mansion trembles o'er his head.
Are these thy views? proceed, illustrious youth,
And Virtue guard thee to the throne of Truth!
Yet should thy soul indulge the generous heat,
Till captive Science yields her last retreat;
145 Should Reason guide thee with her brightest ray,
And pour on misty Doubt resistless day;
Should no false kindness lure to loose delight,
Nor praise relax, nor difficulty fright;

7. George Villiers, first duke of Buckingham, favorite of James I and Charles I, was assassinated in 1628. Mentioned in the following lines: Robert Harley, earl of Oxford, chancellor of the exchequer and later lord treasurer under Queen Anne (1710–14), impeached and imprisoned by the Whigs in 1715. Thomas Wentworth, earl of Strafford, intimate and adviser of Charles I, impeached by the Long Parliament and executed in 1641. Edward Hyde, earl of Clarendon ("to kings allied" because his daughter married James, duke of York), lord chancellor under Charles II (impeached in 1667, he fled to the Continent).
8. Roger Bacon (ca. 1214–1294), scientist and philosopher, taught at Oxford, where his study, according to tradition, would collapse when a man greater than he should appear at Oxford. "Bodley's dome": the Bodleian Library, Oxford.

Should tempting Novelty thy cell refrain,
150　And Sloth effuse her opiate fumes in vain;
Should Beauty blunt on fops her fatal dart,
Nor claim the triumph of a lettered heart;
Should no disease thy torpid veins invade,
Nor Melancholy's phantoms haunt thy shade;
155　Yet hope not life from grief or danger free,
Nor think the doom of man reversed for thee:
Deign on the passing world to turn thine eyes,
And pause a while from letters, to be wise;
There mark what ills the scholar's life assail,
160　Toil, envy, want, the patron,[9] and the jail.
See nations slowly wise, and meanly just,
To buried merit raise the tardy bust.
If dreams yet flatter, once again attend,
Hear Lydiat's life, and Galileo's[1] end.
165　　Nor deem, when Learning her last prize bestows,
The glittering eminence exempt from foes;
See when the vulgar 'scapes, despised or awed,
Rebellion's vengeful talons seize on Laud.[2]
From meaner minds, though smaller fines content,
170　The plundered palace or sequestered rent;[3]
Marked out by dangerous parts he meets the shock,
And fatal Learning leads him to the block:
Around his tomb let Art and Genius weep,
But hear his death, ye blockheads, hear and sleep.
175　　The festal blazes, the triumphal show,
The ravished standard, and the captive foe,
The senate's thanks, the gazette's pompous tale,
With force resistless o'er the brave prevail.
Such bribes the rapid Greek° o'er Asia whirled,　　*Alexander the Great*
180　For such the steady Romans shook the world;
For such in distant lands the Britons shine,
And stain with blood the Danube or the Rhine;
This power has praise that virtue scarce can warm,
Till fame supplies the universal charm.
185　Yet Reason frowns on War's unequal game,
Where wasted nations raise a single name,
And mortgaged states their grandsires' wreaths regret
From age to age in everlasting debt;
Wreaths which at last the dear-bought right convey
190　To rust on medals, or on stones decay.
　　On what foundation stands the warrior's pride?
How just his hopes, let Swedish Charles[4] decide;

---

9. In the first edition, "garret." For the reason of the change see Boswell's *Life of Johnson* (p. 1278).
1. Galileo (1564–1642), famous astronomer, was imprisoned as a heretic by the Inquisition in 1633; he died blind. Thomas Lydiat (1572–1646), Oxford scholar, died impoverished because of his Royalist sympathies.
2. Appointed archbishop of Canterbury by

Charles I, William Laud followed rigorously High Church policies and was executed by order of the Long Parliament in 1645.
3. During the Commonwealth, the estates of many Royalists were pillaged and their incomes confiscated ("sequestered") by the state.
4. Charles XII of Sweden (1682–1718). Defeated by the Russians at Pultowa (1709), he escaped to

A frame of adamant, a soul of fire,
No dangers fright him, and no labors tire;
195 O'er love, o'er fear, extends his wide domain,
Unconquered lord of pleasure and of pain;
No joys to him pacific scepters yield,
War sounds the trump, he rushes to the field;
Behold surrounding kings their powers combine,
200 And one capitulate, and one resign;[5]
Peace courts his hand, but spreads her charms in vain;
"Think nothing gained," he cries, "till naught remain,
On Moscow's walls till Gothic standards fly,
And all be mine beneath the polar sky."
205 The march begins in military state,
And nations on his eye suspended wait;
Stern Famine guards the solitary coast,
And Winter barricades the realms of Frost;
He comes, nor want nor cold his course delay—
210 Hide, blushing Glory, hide Pultowa's day:
The vanquished hero leaves his broken bands,
And shows his miseries in distant lands;
Condemned a needy supplicant to wait,
While ladies interpose, and slaves debate.
215 But did not Chance at length her error mend?
Did no subverted empire mark his end?
Did rival monarchs give the fatal wound?
Or hostile millions press him to the ground?
His fall was destined to a barren strand,
220 A petty fortress, and a dubious hand;
He left the name at which the world grew pale,
To point a moral, or adorn a tale.
    All times their scenes of pompous woes afford,
From Persia's tyrant to Bavaria's lord.[6]
225 In gay hostility, and barbarous pride,
With half mankind embattled at his side,
Great Xerxes comes to seize the certain prey,
And starves exhausted regions in his way;
Attendant Flattery counts his myriads o'er,
230 Till counted myriads soothe his pride no more;
Fresh praise is tried till madness fires his mind,
The waves he lashes, and enchains the wind;
New powers are claimed, new powers are still bestowed,
Till rude resistance lops the spreading god;
235 The daring Greeks deride the martial show,
And heap their valleys with the gaudy foe;
The insulted sea with humbler thoughts he gains,

Turkey and tried to form an alliance against Russia with the sultan. Returning to Sweden, he attacked Norway and was killed in the attack on Fredriks-hald.
5. Frederick IV of Denmark capitulated to Charles in 1700. Augustus II of Poland resigned his throne to Charles in 1704.

6. The Elector Charles Albert caused the War of the Austrian Succession (1740–48) when he contested the crown of the empire with Maria Theresa ("Fair Austria" in line 245). "Persia's tyrant": Xerxes invaded Greece and was totally defeated in the sea battle off Salamis, 480 B.C.E.

A single skiff to speed his flight remains;
The encumbered oar scarce leaves the dreaded coast
240 Through purple billows and a floating host.
    The bold Bavarian, in a luckless hour,
Tries the dread summits of Caesarean power,
With unexpected legions bursts away,
And sees defenseless realms receive his sway;
245 Short sway! fair Austria spreads her mournful charms,
The queen, the beauty, sets the world in arms;
From hill to hill the beacon's rousing blaze
Spreads wide the hope of plunder and of praise;
The fierce Croatian, and the wild Hussar,[7]
250 With all the sons of ravage crowd the war;
The baffled prince in honor's flattering bloom
Of hasty greatness finds the fatal doom;
His foes' derision, and his subjects' blame,
And steals to death from anguish and from shame.
255   Enlarge my life with multitude of days!
In health, in sickness, thus the suppliant prays;
Hides from himself his state, and shuns to know,
That life protracted is protracted woe.
Time hovers o'er, impatient to destroy,
260 And shuts up all the passages of joy;
In vain their gifts the bounteous seasons pour,
The fruit autumnal, and the vernal flower;
With listless eyes the dotard views the store,
He views, and wonders that they please no more;
265 Now pall the tasteless meats, and joyless wines,
And Luxury with sighs her slave resigns.
Approach, ye minstrels, try the soothing strain,
Diffuse the tuneful lenitives[8] of pain:
No sounds, alas! would touch the impervious ear,
270 Though dancing mountains witnessed Orpheus[9] near;
Nor lute nor lyre his feeble powers attend,
Nor sweeter music of a virtuous friend,
But everlasting dictates crowd his tongue,
Perversely grave, or positively wrong.
275 The still returning tale, and lingering jest,
Perplex the fawning niece and pampered guest,
While growing hopes scarce awe the gathering sneer,
And scarce a legacy can bribe to hear;
The watchful guests still hint the last offense,
280 The daughter's petulance, the son's expense,
Improve his heady rage with treacherous skill,
And mold his passions till they make his will.
    Unnumbered maladies his joints invade,
Lay siege to life and press the dire blockade;
285 But unextinguished avarice still remains,
And dreaded losses aggravate his pains;

---

7. Hungarian light cavalry.
8. Medicines that relieve pain.

9. A legendary poet who played on the lyre so
beautifully that wild beasts were spellbound.

He turns, with anxious heart and crippled hands,
His bonds of debt, and mortgages of lands;
Or views his coffers with suspicious eyes,
290   Unlocks his gold, and counts it till he dies.
    But grant, the virtues of a temperate prime
Bless with an age exempt from scorn or crime;
An age that melts with unperceived decay,
And glides in modest innocence away;
295   Whose peaceful day Benevolence endears,
Whose night congratulating Conscience cheers;
The general favorite as the general friend:
Such age there is, and who shall wish its end?
    Yet even on this her load Misfortune flings,
300   To press the weary minutes' flagging wings;
New sorrow rises as the day returns,
A sister sickens, or a daughter mourns.
Now kindred Merit fills the sable bier,
Now lacerated Friendship claims a tear;
305   Year chases year, decay pursues decay,
Still drops some joy from withering life away;
New forms arise, and different views engage,
Superfluous lags the veteran[1] on the stage,
Till pitying Nature signs the last release,
310   And bids afflicted Worth retire to peace.
    But few there are whom hours like these await,
Who set unclouded in the gulfs of Fate.
From Lydia's monarch[2] should the search descend,
By Solon cautioned to regard his end,
315   In life's last scene what prodigies surprise,
Fears of the brave, and follies of the wise!
From Marlborough's eyes the streams of dotage flow,
And Swift[3] expires a driveler and a show.
    The teeming mother, anxious for her race,
320   Begs for each birth the fortune of a face:
Yet Vane could tell what ills from beauty spring;
And Sedley[4] cursed the form that pleased a king.
Ye nymphs of rosy lips and radiant eyes,
Whom Pleasure keeps too busy to be wise,
325   Whom Joys with soft varieties invite,
By day the frolic, and the dance by night;
Who frown with vanity, who smile with art,
And ask the latest fashion of the heart;
What care, what rules your heedless charms shall save,
330   Each nymph your rival, and each youth your slave?
Against your fame with Fondness Hate combines,
The rival batters, and the lover mines.

---

1. A veteran of life, not of war.
2. Croesus, the wealthy and fortunate king, was warned by Solon not to count himself happy until he ceased to live. He lost his crown to Cyrus the Great of Persia.
3. Jonathan Swift, who passed the last four years of his life in utter senility. John Churchill, duke of Marlborough, England's brilliant general during most of the War of the Spanish Succession (1702–13).
4. Catherine Sedley, mistress of James II. Anne Vane, mistress of Frederick, prince of Wales (son of George II).

With distant voice neglected Virtue calls,
Less heard and less, the faint remonstrance falls;
335 Tired with contempt, she quits the slippery reign,
And Pride and Prudence take her seat in vain.
In crowd at once, where none the pass defend,
The harmless freedom, and the private friend.
The guardians yield, by force superior plied:
340 To Interest, Prudence; and to Flattery, Pride.
Now Beauty falls betrayed, despised, distressed,
And hissing Infamy proclaims the rest.
   Where then shall Hope and Fear their objects find?
Must dull Suspense corrupt the stagnant mind?
345 Must helpless man, in ignorance sedate,
Roll darkling down the torrent of his fate?
Must no dislike alarm, no wishes rise,
No cries invoke the mercies of the skies?
Inquirer, cease; petitions yet remain,
350 Which Heaven may hear, nor deem religion vain.
Still raise for good the supplicating voice,
But leave to Heaven the measure and the choice.
Safe in his power, whose eyes discern afar
The secret ambush of a specious prayer.
355 Implore his aid, in his decisions rest,
Secure, whate'er he gives, he gives the best.
Yet when the sense of sacred presence fires,
And strong devotion to the skies aspires,
Pour forth thy fervors for a healthful mind,
360 Obedient passions, and a will resigned;
For love, which scarce collective man can fill;[5]
For patience sovereign o'er transmuted ill;
For faith, that panting for a happier seat,
Counts death kind Nature's signal of retreat:
365 These goods for man the laws of Heaven ordain,
These goods he grants, who grants the power to gain;
With these celestial Wisdom calms the mind,
And makes the happiness she does not find.

1749

On the Death of Dr. Robert Levet[1]

Condemned to Hope's delusive mine,
  As on we toil from day to day,
By sudden blasts, or slow decline,
  Our social comforts drop away.

5 Well tried through many a varying year,
  See Levet to the grave descend;

---

5. Which humankind as a whole can hardly over-
task.
1. An unlicensed physician, who lived in Johnson's house for many years and who died in 1782.

His practice was among the very poor. Boswell
wrote: "He was of a strange grotesque appearance,
stiff and formal in his manner, and seldom said a
word while any company was present."

Officious,[2] innocent, sincere,
 Of every friendless name the friend.

Yet still he fills Affection's eye,
10 Obscurely wise, and coarsely kind;
Nor, lettered Arrogance, deny
 Thy praise to merit unrefined.

When fainting Nature called for aid,
 And hovering Death prepared the blow,
15 His vigorous remedy displayed
 The power of art without the show.

In Misery's darkest caverns known,
 His useful care was ever nigh,
Where hopeless Anguish poured his groan,
20 And lonely Want retired to die.

No summons mocked by chill delay,
 No petty gain disdained by pride,
The modest wants of every day
 The toil of every day supplied.

25 His virtues walked their narrow round,
 Nor made a pause, nor left a void;
And sure the Eternal Master found
 The single talent well employed.[3]

The busy day, the peaceful night,
30 Unfelt, uncounted, glided by;
His frame was firm, his powers were bright,
 Though now his eightieth year was nigh.

Then with no throbbing fiery pain,
 No cold gradations of decay,
35 Death broke at once the vital chain,
 And freed his soul the nearest way.

1783

Rasselas

Johnson wrote *Rasselas* in January 1759, during the evenings of one week, a remarkable instance of his ability to write rapidly and brilliantly under the pressure of necessity. His mother lay dying in Lichfield. Her son, famous for his *Dictionary,* was nonetheless oppressed by poverty and in great need of ready money with which to make her last days comfortable, pay her funeral expenses, and settle

2. "Kind, doing good offices" (Johnson's *Dictionary*).
3. In the parable of the talents (Matthew 25.14–

30), Jesus suggests that salvation will be granted to those who make good use of their abilities, however small.

her small debts. He was paid £100 for the first edition of *Rasselas,* but not in time to attend her deathbed or her funeral.

Rasselas is a philosophical fable cast in the popular form of an Oriental tale, a type of fiction that owed its popularity to the vogue of the *Arabian Nights,* first translated into English in the early eighteenth century. Because the work is a fable, we should not approach it as a novel: psychologically credible characters and a series of intricately involved actions that lead to a necessary resolution and conclusion are not to be found in *Rasselas.* Instead we are meant to reflect on the ideas and to savor the melancholy resonance and intelligence of the stately prose that expresses them. Johnson arranges the incidents of the fable to test a variety of possible solutions to a problem: What choice of life will bring us happiness? (*The Choice of Life* was his working title for the book.) Many ways of life are examined in turn, and each is found wanting. Johnson does not pretend to have solved the problem. Rather, he locates the sources of discontent in a basic principle of human nature: the "hunger of imagination which preys incessantly upon life" (chapter 32) and which lures us to "listen with credulity to the whispers of fancy and pursue with eagerness the phantoms of hope" (chapter 1). The tale is a gentle satire on one of the perennial topics of satirists: the folly of all of us who stubbornly cling to our illusions despite the evidence of experience. *Rasselas* is not all darkness and gloom, for Johnson's theme invites comic as well as tragic treatment, and some of the episodes evoke that laughter of the mind that is the effect of high comedy. In its main theme, however—the folly of cherishing the dream of ever attaining unalloyed happiness in a world that can never wholly satisfy our desires—and in many of the sayings of its characters, especially of the sage Imlac, *Rasselas* expresses some of Johnson's own deepest convictions.

From The History of Rasselas, Prince of Abyssinia

Chapter 1. Description of a Palace in a Valley

Ye who listen with credulity to the whispers of fancy, and pursue with eagerness the phantoms of hope; who expect that age will perform the promises of youth, and that the deficiencies of the present day will be supplied by the morrow—attend to the history of Rasselas, prince of Abyssinia.

Rasselas was the fourth son of the mighty emperor in whose dominions the Father of Waters[1] begins his course; whose bounty pours down the streams of plenty, and scatters over half the world the harvests of Egypt.

According to the custom which has descended from age to age among the monarchs of the torrid zone, Rasselas was confined in a private palace, with the other sons and daughters of Abyssinian royalty, till the order of succession should call him to the throne.

The place which the wisdom or policy of antiquity had destined for the residence of the Abyssinian princes was a spacious valley[2] in the kingdom of Amhara, surrounded on every side by mountains, of which the summits overhang the middle part. The only passage by which it could be entered was a cavern that passed under a rock, of which it has long been disputed whether it was the work of nature or of human industry. The outlet of the cavern was concealed by a thick wood, and the mouth which opened into the valley was

---

1. The Nile.
2. Johnson had read of the Happy Valley in the Portuguese Jesuit Father Lobo's book on Abyssinia, which he translated in 1735. The description in this and the immediately following paragraphs illustrates Johnson's preference for the "general" over the "particular" (see chap. 10). It owes something to the description of the Garden in *Paradise Lost* 4, and Coleridge's *Kubla Khan* owes something to it.

closed with gates of iron, forged by the artificers of ancient days, so massy that no man could, without the help of engines, open or shut them.

From the mountains on every side rivulets descended that filled all the valley with verdure and fertility, and formed a lake in the middle, inhabited by fish of every species, and frequented by every fowl whom nature has taught to dip the wing in water. This lake discharged its superfluities by a stream, which entered a dark cleft of the mountain on the northern side, and fell with dreadful noise from precipice to precipice till it was heard no more.

The sides of the mountains were covered with trees, the banks of the brooks were diversified with flowers; every blast shook spices from the rocks, and every month dropped fruits upon the ground. All animals that bite the grass, or browse the shrub, whether wild or tame, wandered in this extensive circuit, secured from beasts of prey by the mountains which confined them. On one part were flocks and herds feeding in the pastures, on another all the beasts of chase frisking in the lawns; the sprightly kid was bounding on the rocks, the subtle monkey frolicking in the trees, and the solemn elephant reposing in the shade. All the diversities of the world were brought together, the blessings of nature were collected, and its evils extracted and excluded.

The valley, wide and fruitful, supplied its inhabitants with the necessaries of life, and all delights and superfluities were added at the annual visit which the emperor paid his children, when the iron gate was opened to the sound of music, and during eight days everyone that resided in the valley was required to propose whatever might contribute to make seclusion pleasant, to fill up the vacancies of attention, and lessen the tediousness of time. Every desire was immediately granted. All the artificers of pleasure were called to gladden the festivity; the musicians exerted the power of harmony, and the dancers showed their activity before the princes, in hope that they should pass their lives in this blissful captivity, to which those only were admitted whose performance was thought able to add novelty to luxury. Such was the appearance of security and delight which this retirement afforded, that they to whom it was new always desired that it might be perpetual; and as those on whom the iron gate had once closed were never suffered to return, the effect of longer experience could not be known. Thus every year produced new schemes of delight and new competitors for imprisonment.

The palace stood on an eminence, raised about thirty paces above the surface of the lake. It was divided into many squares or courts, built with greater or less magnificence according to the rank of those for whom they were designed. The roofs were turned into arches of massy stone, joined with a cement that grew harder by time, and the building stood from century to century, deriding the solstitial rains and equinoctial hurricanes, without need of reparation.

This house, which was so large as to be fully known to none but some ancient officers, who successively inherited the secrets of the place, was built as if suspicion herself had dictated the plan. To every room there was an open and secret passage; every square had a communication with the rest, either from the upper stories by private galleries, or by subterranean passages from the lower apartments. Many of the columns had unsuspected cavities, in which a long race of monarchs had reposited their treasures. They then closed up the opening with marble, which was never to be removed but in the utmost exigencies of the kingdom, and recorded their accumulations in a book, which was itself concealed in a tower, not entered but by the emperor, attended by the prince who stood next in succession.

Chapter 2. The Discontent of Rasselas in the Happy Valley

Here the sons and daughters of Abyssinia lived only to know the soft vicissitudes of pleasure and repose, attended by all that were skillful to delight, and gratified with whatever the senses can enjoy. They wandered in gardens of fragrance, and slept in the fortresses of security. Every art was practiced to make them pleased with their own condition. The sages who instructed them told them of nothing but the miseries of public life, and described all beyond the mountains as regions of calamity, where discord was always raging, and where man preyed upon man.

To heighten their opinion of their own felicity, they were daily entertained with songs, the subject of which was the *happy valley*. Their appetites were excited by frequent enumerations of different enjoyments, and revelry and merriment was the business of every hour, from the dawn of morning to the close of even.

These methods were generally successful; few of the princes had ever wished to enlarge their bounds, but passed their lives in full conviction that they had all within their reach that art or nature could bestow, and pitied those whom fate had excluded from this seat of tranquility, as the sport of chance and the slaves of misery.

Thus they rose in the morning and lay down at night, pleased with each other and with themselves; all but Rasselas, who, in the twenty-sixth year of his age, began to withdraw himself from their pastimes and assemblies, and to delight in solitary walks and silent meditation. He often sat before tables covered with luxury, and forgot to taste the dainties that were placed before him; he rose abruptly in the midst of the song, and hastily retired beyond the sound of music. His attendants observed the change, and endeavored to renew his love of pleasure. He neglected their officiousness, repulsed their invitations, and spent day after day on the banks of rivulets sheltered with trees, where he sometimes listened to the birds in the branches, sometimes observed the fish playing in the stream, and anon cast his eyes upon the pastures and mountains filled with animals, of which some were biting the herbage, and some sleeping among the bushes.

This singularity of his humor made him much observed. One of the sages, in whose conversation he had formerly delighted, followed him secretly, in hope of discovering the cause of his disquiet. Rasselas, who knew not that anyone was near him, having for some time fixed his eyes upon the goats that were browsing among the rocks, began to compare their condition with his own.

"What," said he, "makes the difference between man and all the rest of the animal creation? Every beast that strays beside me has the same corporal necessities with myself; he is hungry, and crops the grass, he is thirsty, and drinks the stream, his thirst and hunger are appeased, he is satisfied, and sleeps; he rises again, and he is hungry, he is again fed, and is at rest. I am hungry and thirsty like him, but when thirst and hunger cease, I am not at rest; I am, like him, pained with want, but am not, like him, satisfied with fullness. The intermediate hours are tedious and gloomy; I long again to be hungry that I may again quicken my attention. The birds peck the berries or the corn, and fly away to the groves, where they sit in seeming happiness on the branches, and waste their lives in tuning one unvaried series of sounds. I likewise can call the lutanist and the singer, but the sounds that pleased me yesterday weary me today, and will grow yet more wearisome tomorrow. I can discover within me no power of perception which is not glutted with its proper pleasure, yet I do not feel myself delighted. Man has surely some latent sense for which this place affords no gratification, or he has some desires distinct from sense, which must be satisfied before he can be happy."

After this he lifted up his head, and seeing the moon rising, walked towards the palace. As he passed through the fields, and saw the animals around him, "Ye," said he, "are happy, and need not envy me that walk thus among you, burthened with myself; nor do I, ye gentle beings, envy your felicity, for it is not the felicity of man. I have many distresses from which ye are free; I fear pain when I do not feel it; I sometimes shrink at evils recollected, and sometimes start at evils anticipated. Surely the equity of Providence has balanced peculiar sufferings with peculiar enjoyments."

With observations like these the prince amused himself as he returned, uttering them with a plaintive voice, yet with a look that discovered him to feel some complacence in his own perspicacity, and to receive some solace of the miseries of life from consciousness of the delicacy with which he felt, and the eloquence with which he bewailed them. He mingled cheerfully in the diversions of the evening, and all rejoiced to find that his heart was lightened.

Chapter 3. The Wants of Him That Wants Nothing

On the next day his old instructor, imagining that he had now made himself acquainted with his disease of mind, was in the hope of curing it by counsel, and officiously sought an opportunity of conference, which the prince, having long considered him as one whose intellects were exhausted, was not very willing to afford. "Why," said he, "does this man thus intrude upon me; shall I be never suffered to forget those lectures which pleased only while they were new, and to become new again must be forgotten?" He then walked into the wood, and composed himself to his usual meditations; when, before his thoughts had taken any settled form, he perceived his pursuer at his side, and was at first prompted by his impatience to go hastily away; but, being unwilling to offend a man whom he had once reverenced and still loved, he invited him to sit down with him on the bank.

The old man, thus encouraged, began to lament the change which had been lately observed in the prince, and to inquire why he so often retired from the pleasures of the palace, to loneliness and silence. "I fly from pleasure," said the prince, "because pleasure has ceased to please; I am lonely because I am miserable, and am unwilling to cloud with my presence the happiness of others." "You, sir," said the sage, "are the first who has complained of misery in the *happy valley*. I hope to convince you that your complaints have no real cause. You are here in full possession of all that the emperor of Abyssinia can bestow; here is neither labor to be endured nor danger to be dreaded, yet here is all that labor or danger can procure or purchase. Look round and tell me which of your wants is without supply; if you want nothing, how are you unhappy?"

"That I want nothing," said the prince, "or that I know not what I want, is the cause of my complaint; if I had any known want, I should have a certain wish; that wish would excite endeavor, and I should not then repine to see the sun move so slowly towards the western mountain, or lament when the day breaks, and sleep will no longer hide me from myself. When I see the kids and the lambs chasing one another, I fancy that I should be happy if I had something to pursue. But, possessing all that I can want, I find one day and one hour exactly like another, except that the latter is still more tedious than the former. Let your experience inform me how the day may now seem as short as in my childhood, while nature was yet fresh and every moment showed me what I never had observed before. I have already enjoyed too much; give me something to desire."

The old man was surprised at this new species of affliction and knew not what to reply, yet was unwilling to be silent. "Sir," said he, "if you had seen the miseries of the world you would know how to value your present state." "Now," said the prince, "you have given me something to desire. I shall long to see the miseries of the world, since the sight of them is necessary to happiness."[3]

* * *

Chapter 6. A Dissertation on the Art of Flying

Among the artists that had been allured into the happy valley, to labor for the accommodation and pleasure of its inhabitants, was a man eminent for his knowledge of the mechanic powers, who had contrived many engines[4] both of use and recreation. By a wheel, which the stream turned, he forced the water into a tower, whence it was distributed to all the apartments of the palace. He erected a pavillion in the garden, around which he kept the air always cool by artificial showers. One of the groves, appropriated to the ladies, was ventilated by fans, to which the rivulet that run through it gave a constant motion; and instruments of soft music were placed at proper distances, of which some played by the impulse of the wind, and some by the power of the stream.

This artist was sometimes visited by Rasselas, who was pleased with every kind of knowledge, imagining that the time would come when all his acquisitions should be of use to him in the open world. He came one day to amuse himself in his usual manner, and found the master busy in building a sailing chariot: he saw that the design was practicable upon a level surface, and with expressions of great esteem solicited its completion. The workman was pleased to find himself so much regarded by the prince, and resolved to gain yet higher honors. "Sir," said he, "you have seen but a small part of what the mechanic sciences can perform. I have been long of opinion, that, instead of the tardy conveyance of ships and chariots, man might use the swifter migration of wings; that the fields of air are open to knowledge, and that only ignorance and idleness need crawl upon the ground."

This hint rekindled the prince's desire of passing the mountains; having seen what the mechanist had already performed, he was willing to fancy that he could do more; yet resolved to inquire further before he suffered hope to afflict him by disappointment. "I am afraid," said he to the artist, "that your

---

3. In chapters 4 and 5, Rasselas dreams about escaping the valley.

4. Machines. "Mechanic powers": the forces that cause things to move.

imagination prevails over your skill, and that you now tell me rather what you wish than what you know. Every animal has his element assigned him; the birds have the air, and man and beasts the earth." "So," replied the mechanist, "fishes have the water, in which yet beasts can swim by nature, and men by art. He that can swim needs not despair to fly: to swim is to fly in a grosser fluid, and to fly is to swim in a subtler. We are only to proportion our power of resistance to the different density of the matter through which we are to pass. You will be necessarily upborn by the air, if you can renew any impulse upon it, faster than the air can recede from the pressure."

"But the exercise of swimming," said the prince, "is very laborious; the strongest limbs are soon wearied; I am afraid the act of flying will be yet more violent, and wings will be of no great use, unless we can fly further than we can swim."

"The labor of rising from the ground," said the artist "will be great, as we see it in the heavier domestic fowls; but, as we mount higher, the earth's attraction, and the body's gravity, will be gradually diminished, till we shall arrive at a region where the man will float in the air without any tendency to fall: no care will then be necessary, but to move forwards, which the gentlest impulse will effect. You, Sir, whose curiosity is so extensive, will easily conceive with what pleasure a philosopher, furnished with wings, and hovering in the sky, would see the earth, and all its inhabitants, rolling beneath him, and presenting to him successively, by its diurnal motion, all the countries within the same parallel. How must it amuse the pendent spectator to see the moving scene of land and ocean, cities and deserts! To survey with equal security the marts of trade, and the fields of battle; mountains infested by barbarians, and fruitful regions gladdened by plenty, and lulled by peace! How easily shall we then trace the Nile through all his passage; pass over to distant regions, and examine the face of nature from one extremity of the earth to the other!"

"All this," said the prince, "is much to be desired, but I am afraid that no man will be able to breathe in these regions of speculation and tranquility. I have been told, that respiration is difficult upon lofty mountains, yet from these precipices, though so high as to produce great tenuity of the air, it is very easy to fall: therefore I suspect, that from any height, where life can be supported, there may be danger of too quick descent."

"Nothing," replied the artist, "will ever be attempted, if all possible objections must be first overcome. If you will favor my project I will try the first flight at my own hazard. I have considered the structure of all volant[5] animals, and find the folding continuity of the bat's wings most easily accommodated to the human form. Upon this model I shall begin my task tomorrow, and in a year expect to tower into the air beyond the malice or pursuit of man. But I will work only on this condition, that the art shall not be divulged, and that you shall not require me to make wings for any but ourselves."

"Why," said Rasselas, "should you envy others so great an advantage? All skill ought to be exerted for universal good; every man has owed much to others, and ought to repay the kindness that he has received."

"If men were all virtuous," returned the artist, "I should with great alacrity

5. Able to fly.

teach them all to fly. But what would be the security of the good, if the bad could at pleasure invade them from the sky? Against an army sailing through the clouds neither walls, nor mountains, nor seas, could afford any security. A flight of northern savages might hover in the wind, and light at once with irresistible violence upon the capital of a fruitful region that was rolling under them. Even this valley, the retreat of princes, the abode of happiness, might be violated by the sudden descent of some of the naked nations that swarm on the coast of the southern sea."

The prince promised secrecy, and waited for the performance, not wholly hopeless of success. He visited the work from time to time, observed its progress, and remarked many ingenious contrivances to facilitate motion, and unite levity with strength. The artist was every day more certain that he should leave vultures and eagles behind him, and the contagion of his confidence seized upon the prince.

In a year the wings were finished, and, on a morning appointed, the maker appeared furnished for flight on a little promontory: he waved his pinions a while to gather air, then leaped from his stand, and in an instant dropped into the lake. His wings, which were of no use in the air, sustained him in the water, and the prince drew him to land, half dead with terror and vexation.[6]

* * *

Chapter 10. Imlac's History Continued. A Dissertation upon Poetry

"Wherever I went, I found that poetry was considered as the highest learning, and regarded with a veneration somewhat approaching to that which man would pay to the angelic nature. And yet it fills me with wonder that, in almost all countries, the most ancient poets are considered as the best: whether it be that every other kind of knowledge is an acquisition gradually attained, and poetry is a gift conferred at once; or that the first poetry of every nation surprised them as a novelty, and retained the credit by consent which it received by accident at first; or whether, as the province of poetry is to describe nature and passion, which are always the same, the first writers took possession of the most striking objects for description and the most probable occurrences for fiction, and left nothing to those that followed them, but transcription of the same events, and new combinations of the same images—whatever be the reason, it is commonly observed that the early writers are in possession of nature, and their followers of art; that the first excel in strength and invention, and the latter in elegance and refinement.

"I was desirous to add my name to this illustrious fraternity. I read all the poets of Persia and Arabia, and was able to repeat by memory the volumes that are suspended in the mosque of Mecca. But I soon found that no man was ever great by imitation. My desire of excellence impelled me to transfer my attention to nature and to life. Nature was to be my subject, and men to be my auditors: I could never describe what I had not seen; I could not hope to move those with delight or terror, whose interests and opinions I did not understand.

---

6. In chapters 7–9, Rasselas comes to know Imlac, a scholar and poet who knows the great world outside the valley and who tells the story of his life.

"Being now resolved to be a poet, I saw everything with a new purpose; my sphere of attention was suddenly magnified; no kind of knowledge was to be overlooked. I ranged mountains and deserts for images and resemblances, and pictured upon my mind every tree of the forest and flower of the valley. I observed with equal care the crags of the rock and the pinnacles of the palace. Sometimes I wandered along the mazes of the rivulet, and sometimes watched the changes of the summer clouds. To a poet nothing can be useless. Whatever is beautiful, and whatever is dreadful, must be familiar to his imagination; he must be conversant with all that is awfully vast or elegantly little. The plants of the garden, the animals of the wood, the minerals of the earth, and meteors of the sky, must all concur to store his mind with inexhaustible variety: for every idea[7] is useful for the enforcement or decoration of moral or religious truth; and he who knows most will have most power of diversifying his scenes, and of gratifying his reader with remote allusions and unexpected instruction.

"All the appearances of nature I was therefore careful to study, and every country which I have surveyed has contributed something to my poetical powers."

"In so wide a survey," said the prince, "you must surely have left much unobserved. I have lived till now within the circuit of these mountains, and yet cannot walk abroad without the sight of something which I have never beheld before, or never heeded."

"The business of a poet," said Imlac, "is to examine, not the individual, but the species; to remark general properties and large appearances; he does not number the streaks of the tulip, or describe the different shades in the verdure of the forest. He is to exhibit in his portraits of nature such prominent and striking features as recall the original to every mind, and must neglect the minuter discriminations, which one may have remarked and another have neglected, for those characteristics which are alike obvious to vigilance and carelessness.

"But the knowledge of nature is only half the task of a poet; he must be acquainted likewise with all the modes of life. His character requires that he estimate the happiness and misery of every condition; observe the power of all the passions in all their combinations, and trace the changes of the human mind, as they are modified by various institutions and accidental influences of climate or custom, from the sprightliness of infancy to the despondence of decrepitude. He must divest himself of the prejudices of his age or country; he must consider right and wrong in their abstracted and invariable state; he must disregard present laws and opinions, and rise to general and transcendental[8] truths, which will always be the same. He must, therefore, content himself with the slow progress of his name, contemn the applause of his own time, and commit his claims to the justice of posterity. He must write as the interpreter of nature and the legislator of mankind, and consider himself as presiding over the thoughts and manners of future generations, as a being superior to time and place.

"His labor is not yet at an end; he must know many languages and many sciences; and, that his style may be worthy of his thoughts, must by incessant

7. Mental image.
8. "General; pervading many particulars" (Johnson's *Dictionary*).

practice familiarize to himself every delicacy of speech and grace of harmony."

Chapter 11. Imlac's Narrative Continued. A Hint on Pilgrimage

Imlac now felt the enthusiastic fit, and was proceeding to aggrandize his own profession, when the prince cried out: "Enough! thou hast convinced me that no human being can ever be a poet. Proceed with thy narration."

"To be a poet," said Imlac, "is indeed very difficult." "So difficult," returned the prince, "that I will at present hear no more of his labors. Tell me whither you went when you had seen Persia."

"From Persia," said the poet, "I traveled through Syria, and for three years resided in Palestine, where I conversed with great numbers of the northern and western nations of Europe, the nations which are now in possession of all power and all knowledge, whose armies are irresistible, and whose fleets command the remotest parts of the globe. When I compared these men with the natives of our own kingdom, and those that surround us, they appeared almost another order of beings. In their countries it is difficult to wish for anything that may not be obtained; a thousand arts, of which we never heard, are continually laboring for their convenience and pleasure; and whatever their own climate has denied them is supplied by their commerce."

"By what means," said the prince, "are the Europeans thus powerful, or why, since they can so easily visit Asia and Africa for trade or conquest, cannot the Asiatics and Africans invade their coasts, plant colonies in their ports, and give laws to their natural princes? The same wind that carries them back would bring us thither."

"They are more powerful, sir, than we," answered Imlac, "because they are wiser; knowledge will always predominate over ignorance, as man governs the other animals. But why their knowledge is more than ours, I know not what reason can be given, but the unsearchable will of the Supreme Being."

"When," said the prince with a sigh, "shall I be able to visit Palestine, and mingle with this mighty confluence of nations? Till that happy moment shall arrive, let me fill up the time with such representations as thou canst give me. I am not ignorant of the motive that assembles such numbers in that place, and cannot but consider it as the center of wisdom and piety, to which the best and wisest men of every land must be continually resorting."

"There are some nations," said Imlac, "that send few visitants to Palestine; for many numerous and learned sects in Europe concur to censure pilgrimage as superstitious, or deride it as ridiculous."

"You know," said the prince, "how little my life has made me acquainted with diversity of opinions. It will be too long to hear the arguments on both sides; you, that have considered them, tell me the result."

"Pilgrimage," said Imlac, "like many other acts of piety, may be reasonable or superstitious, according to the principles upon which it is performed. Long journeys in search of truth are not commanded. Truth, such as is necessary to the regulation of life, is always found where it is honestly sought. Change of place is no natural cause of the increase of piety, for it inevitably produces dissipation of mind. Yet, since men go every day to view the fields where great actions have been performed, and return with stronger impressions of the event, curiosity of the same kind may naturally dispose us to view that country whence our religion had its beginning; and I believe no man surveys those awful scenes without some confirmation of holy resolutions. That the Supreme Being may be more easily propitiated in one place than in another is the dream of idle superstition, but that some places may operate upon our own minds in an uncommon manner is an opinion which hourly experience will justify. He who supposes that his vices may be more successfully combated in Palestine, will, perhaps, find himself mistaken, yet he may go thither without folly; he who thinks they will be more freely pardoned, dishonors at once his reason and religion."

"These," said the prince, "are European distinctions. I will consider them another time. What have you found to be the effect of knowledge? Are those nations happier than we?"

"There is so much infelicity," said the poet, "in the world that scarce any man has leisure from his own distresses to estimate the comparative happiness of others. Knowledge is certainly one of the means of pleasure, as is confessed by the natural desire which every mind feels of increasing its ideas. Ignorance is mere privation, by which nothing can be produced; it is a vacuity in which the soul sits motionless and torpid for want of attraction; and, without knowing why, we always rejoice when we learn, and grieve when we forget. I am therefore inclined to conclude that if nothing counteracts the natural consequence of learning, we grow more happy as our minds take a wider range.

"In enumerating the particular comforts of life, we shall find many advantages on the side of the Europeans. They cure wounds and diseases with which we languish and perish. We suffer inclemencies of weather which they can obviate. They have engines for the despatch of many laborious works, which we must perform by manual industry. There is such communication between distant places that one friend can hardly be said to be absent from another. Their policy removes all public inconveniences; they have roads cut through their mountains, and bridges laid upon their rivers. And, if we descend to the privacies of life, their habitations are more commodious, and their possessions are more secure."

"They are surely happy," said the prince, "who have all these conveniencies, of which I envy none so much as the facility with which separated friends interchange their thoughts."

"The Europeans," answered Imlac, "are less unhappy than we, but they are not happy. Human life is everywhere a state in which much is to be endured, and little to be enjoyed."[9]

* * *

Chapter 15. The Prince and Princess Leave the Valley, and See Many Wonders

The prince and princess had jewels sufficient to make them rich whenever they came into a place of commerce, which, by Imlac's direction, they hid in their clothes, and, on the night of the next full moon, all left the valley. The princess was followed only by a single favorite, who did not know whither she was going.

9. In chapters 12–14, Rasselas and Imac, assisted by Nekayah, Rasselas's sister, succeed in making a tunnel through the mountain.

They clambered through the cavity, and began to go down on the other side. The princess and her maid turned their eyes towards every part, and, seeing nothing to bound their prospect, considered themselves as in danger of being lost in a dreary vacuity. They stopped and trembled. "I am almost afraid," said the princess, "to begin a journey of which I cannot perceive an end, and to venture into this immense plain where I may be approached on every side by men whom I never saw." The prince felt nearly the same emotions, though he thought it more manly to conceal them.

Imlac smiled at their terrors, and encouraged them to proceed; but the princess continued irresolute till she had been imperceptibly drawn forward too far to return.

In the morning they found some shepherds in the field, who set milk and fruits before them. The princess wondered that she did not see a palace ready for her reception, and a table spread with delicacies; but, being faint and hungry, she drank the milk and ate the fruits, and thought them of a higher flavor than the products of the valley.

They traveled forward by easy journeys, being all unaccustomed to toil or difficulty, and knowing, that though they might be missed, they could not be pursued. In a few days they came into a more populous region, where Imlac was diverted with the admiration which his companions expressed at the diversity of manners, stations and employments.

Their dress was such as might not bring upon them the suspicion of having any thing to conceal, yet the prince, wherever he came, expected to be obeyed, and the princess was frighted, because those that came into her presence did not prostrate themselves before her. Imlac was forced to observe them with great vigilance, lest they should betray their rank by their unusual behavior, and detained them several weeks in the first village to accustom them to the sight of common mortals.

By degrees the royal wanderers were taught to understand that they had for a time laid aside their dignity, and were to expect only such regard as liberality and courtesy could procure. And Imlac, having, by many admonitions, prepared them to endure the tumults of a port, and the ruggedness of the commercial race, brought them down to the seacoast.

The prince and his sister, to whom every thing was new, were gratified equally at all places, and therefore remained for some months at the port without any inclination to pass further. Imlac was content with their stay, because he did not think it safe to expose them, unpracticed in the world, to the hazards of a foreign country.

At last he began to fear lest they should be discovered, and proposed to fix a day for their departure. They had no pretensions to judge for themselves, and referred the whole scheme to his direction. He therefore took passage in a ship to Suez; and, when the time came, with great difficulty prevailed on the princess to enter the vessel. They had a quick and prosperous voyage, and from Suez traveled by land to Cairo.

Chapter 16. They Enter Cairo, and Find Every Man Happy

As they approached the city, which filled the strangers with astonishment, "This," said Imlac to the prince, "is the place where travelers and merchants assemble from all the corners of the earth. You will here find men of every character and every occupation. Commerce is here honorable. I will act as a merchant, and you shall live as strangers, who have no other end of travel than curiosity. It will soon be observed that we are rich; our reputation will procure us access to all whom we shall desire to know; you will see all the conditions of humanity, and enable yourself at leisure to make your *choice of life*."

They now entered the town, stunned by the noise, and offended by the crowds. Instruction had not yet so prevailed over habit, but that they wondered to see themselves pass undistinguished along the street, and met by the lowest of the people without reverence or notice. The princess could not at first bear the thought of being leveled with the vulgar,[1] and for some days continued in her chamber, where she was served by her favorite, Pekuah, as in the palace of the valley.

Imlac, who understood traffic,[2] sold part of the jewels the next day, and hired a house, which he adorned with such magnificence that he was immediately considered as a merchant of great wealth. His politeness attracted many acquaintance, and his generosity made him courted by many dependents. His table was crowded by men of every nation, who all admired his knowledge, and solicited his favor. His companions, not being able to mix in the conversation, could make no discovery of their ignorance or surprise, and were gradually initiated in the world as they gained knowledge of the language.

The prince had, by frequent lectures, been taught the use and nature of money; but the ladies could not for a long time comprehend what the merchants did with small pieces of gold and silver, or why things of so little use should be received as equivalent to the necessaries of life.

They studied the language two years, while Imlac was preparing to set before them the various ranks and conditions of mankind. He grew acquainted with all who had anything uncommon in their fortune or conduct. He frequented the voluptuous and the frugal, the idle and the busy, the merchants and the men of learning.

The prince being now able to converse with fluency, and having learned the caution necessary to be observed in his intercourse with strangers, began to accompany Imlac to places of resort, and to enter into all assemblies, that he might make his *choice of life*.

For some time he thought choice needless, because all appeared to him equally happy. Wherever he went he met gaiety and kindness, and heard the song of joy or the laugh of carelessness. He began to believe that the world overflowed with universal plenty, and that nothing was withheld either from want or merit; that every hand showered liberality, and every heart melted with benevolence: "And who then," says he, "will be suffered to be wretched?"

Imlac permitted the pleasing delusion, and was unwilling to crush the hope of inexperience, till one day, having sat awhile silent, "I know not," said the prince, "what can be the reason that I am more unhappy than any of our friends. I see them perpetually and unalterably cheerful, but feel my own mind restless and uneasy. I am unsatisfied with those pleasures which I seem most to court; I live in the crowds of jollity, not so much to enjoy company as to shun myself, and am only loud and merry to conceal my sadness."

"Every man," said Imlac, "may, by examining his own mind, guess what

1. Ordinary people.   2. Commerce.

passes in the minds of others; when you feel that your own gaiety is counterfeit, it may justly lead you to suspect that of your companions not to be sincere. Envy is commonly reciprocal. We are long before we are convinced that happiness is never to be found, and each believes it possessed by others, to keep alive the hope of obtaining it for himself. In the assembly where you passed the last night, there appeared such sprightliness of air, and volatility of fancy, as might have suited beings of an higher order, formed to inhabit serener regions, inaccessible to care or sorrow; yet, believe me, prince, there was not one who did not dread the moment when solitude should deliver him to the tyranny of reflection."

"This," said the prince, "may be true of others, since it is true of me; yet, whatever be the general infelicity of man, one condition is more happy than another, and wisdom surely directs us to take the least evil in the *choice of life.*"

"The causes of good and evil," answered Imlac, "are so various and uncertain, so often entangled with each other, so diversified by various relations, and so much subject to accidents which cannot be foreseen, that he who would fix his condition upon incontestable reasons of preference must live and die inquiring and deliberating."

"But, surely," said Rasselas, "the wise men, to whom we listen with reverence and wonder, chose that mode of life for themselves which they thought most likely to make them happy."

"Very few," said the poet, "live by choice. Every man is placed in his present condition by causes which acted without his foresight, and with which he did not always willingly cooperate; and therefore you will rarely meet one who does not think the lot of his neighbor better than his own."

"I am pleased to think," said the prince, "that my birth has given me at least one advantage over others, by enabling me to determine for myself. I have here the world before me. I will review it at leisure; surely happiness is somewhere to be found."

Chapter 17. The Prince Associates with Young Men of Spirit and Gaiety

Rasselas rose next day, and resolved to begin his experiments upon life. "Youth," cried he, "is the time of gladness: I will join myself to the young men, whose only business is to gratify their desires, and whose time is all spent in a succession of enjoyments."

To such societies he was readily admitted, but a few days brought him back weary and disgusted. Their mirth was without images,[3] their laughter without motive; their pleasures were gross and sensual, in which the mind had no part; their conduct was at once wild and mean; they laughed at order and at law, but the frown of power dejected, and the eye of wisdom abashed them.

The prince soon concluded, that he should never be happy in a course of life of which he was ashamed. He thought it unsuitable to a reasonable being to act without a plan, and to be sad or cheerful only by chance. "Happiness," said he, "must be something solid and permanent, without fear and without uncertainty."

But his young companions had gained so much of his regard by their

3. Ideas.

frankness and courtesy, that he could not leave them without warning and remonstrance. "My friends," said he, "I have seriously considered our manners and our prospects, and find that we have mistaken our own interest. The first years of man must make provision for the last. He that never thinks never can be wise. Perpetual levity must end in ignorance; and intemperance, though it may fire the spirits for an hour, will make life short or miserable. Let us consider that youth is of no long duration, and that in maturer age, when the enchantments of fancy shall cease, and phantoms of delight dance no more about us, we shall have no comforts but the esteem of wise men, and the means of doing good. Let us, therefore, stop, while to stop is in our power: let us live as men who are sometime to grow old, and to whom it will be the most dreadful of all evils not to count their past years but by follies, and to be reminded of their former luxuriance of health only by the maladies which riot has produced."

They stared a while in silence one upon another, and, at last, drove him away by a general chorus of continued laughter.

The consciousness that his sentiments were just, and his intentions kind, was scarcely sufficient to support him against the horror of derision. But he recovered his tranquillity, and pursued his search.

Chapter 18. *The Prince Finds a Wise and Happy Man*

As he was one day walking in the street, he saw a spacious building which all were, by the open doors, invited to enter: he followed the stream of people, and found it a hall or school of declamation, in which professors read lectures to their auditory. He fixed his eye upon a sage raised above the rest, who discoursed with great energy on the government of the passions. His look was venerable, his action graceful, his pronunciation clear, and his diction elegant. He showed with great strength of sentiment and variety of illustration that human nature is degraded and debased, when the lower faculties predominate over the higher; that when fancy, the parent of passion, usurps the dominion of the mind, nothing ensues but the natural effect of unlawful government, perturbation, and confusion; that she betrays the fortresses of the intellect to rebels, and excites her children to sedition against reason, their lawful sovereign. He compared reason to the sun, of which the light is constant, uniform and lasting; and fancy to a meteor, of bright but transitory luster, irregular in its motion, and delusive in its direction.

He then communicated the various precepts given from time to time for the conquest of passion, and displayed the happiness of those who had obtained the important victory, after which man is no longer the slave of fear, nor the fool of hope; is no more emaciated by envy, inflamed by anger, emasculated by tenderness, or depressed by grief; but walks on calmly through the tumults or the privacies of life, as the sun pursues alike his course through the calm or the stormy sky.

He enumerated many examples of heroes immovable by pain or pleasure, who looked with indifference on those modes or accidents to which the vulgar give the names of good and evil. He exhorted his hearers to lay aside their prejudices, and arm themselves against the shafts of malice or misfortune, by invulnerable patience; concluding that this state only was happiness, and that this happiness was in everyone's power.

Rasselas listened to him with the veneration due to the instructions of a superior being, and, waiting for him at the door, humbly implored the liberty of visiting so great a master of true wisdom. The lecturer hesitated a moment, when Rasselas put a purse of gold into his hand, which he received with a mixture of joy and wonder.

"I have found," said the prince at his return to Imlac, "a man who can teach all that is necessary to be known; who, from the unshaken throne of rational fortitude, looks down on the scenes of life changing beneath him. He speaks, and attention watches his lips. He reasons, and conviction closes his periods. This man shall be my future guide; I will learn his doctrines, and imitate his life."

"Be not too hasty," said Imlac, "to trust or to admire the teachers of morality: they discourse like angels, but they live like men."

Rasselas, who could not conceive how any man could reason so forcibly without feeling the cogency of his own arguments, paid his visit in a few days, and was denied admission. He had now learned the power of money, and made his way by a piece of gold to the inner apartment, where he found the philosopher in a room half darkened, with his eyes misty and his face pale. "Sir," said he, "you are come at a time when all human friendship is useless; what I suffer cannot be remedied, what I have lost cannot be supplied. My daughter, my only daughter, from whose tenderness I expected all the comforts of my age, died last night of a fever. My views, my purposes, my hopes are at an end; I am now a lonely being, disunited from society."

"Sir," said the prince, "mortality is an event by which a wise man can never be surprised; we know that death is always near, and it should therefore always be expected." "Young man," answered the philosopher, "you speak like one that has never felt the pangs of separation." "Have you then forgot the precepts," said Rasselas, "which you so powerfully enforced? Has wisdom no strength to arm the heart against calamity? Consider that external things are naturally variable, but truth and reason are always the same." "What comfort," said the mourner, "can truth and reason afford me? Of what effect are they now, but to tell me that my daughter will not be restored?"

The prince, whose humanity would not suffer him to insult misery with reproof, went away, convinced of the emptiness of rhetorical sound, and the inefficacy of polished periods and studied sentences.[4]

Chapter 19. A Glimpse of Pastoral Life

He was still eager upon the same inquiry; and having heard of a hermit that lived near the lowest cataract of the Nile, and filled the whole country with the fame of his sanctity, resolved to visit his retreat, and inquire whether that felicity which public life could not afford was to be found in solitude; and whether a man whose age and virtue made him venerable could teach any peculiar art of shunning evils, or enduring them.

Imlac and the princess agreed to accompany him, and, after the necessary preparations, they began their journey. Their way lay through fields, where shepherds tended their flocks and the lambs were playing upon the pasture. "This," said the poet, "is the life which has been often celebrated for its innocence and quiet; let us pass the heat of the day among the shepherds'

4. Maxims or moral axioms. "Periods": complete sentences.

tents, and know whether all our searches are not to terminate in pastoral simplicity."

The proposal pleased them, and they induced the shepherds, by small presents and familiar questions, to tell their opinion of their own state. They were so rude and ignorant, so little able to compare the good with the evil of the occupation, and so indistinct in their narratives and descriptions, that very little could be learned from them. But it was evident that their hearts were cankered with discontent; that they considered themselves as condemned to labor for the luxury of the rich, and looked up with stupid malevolence toward those that were placed above them.

The princess pronounced with vehemence that she would never suffer these envious savages to be her companions, and that she should not soon be desirous of seeing any more specimens of rustic happiness; but could not believe that all the accounts of primeval pleasures were fabulous, and was yet in doubt whether life had anything that could be justly preferred to the placid gratifications of fields and woods. She hoped that the time would come, when, with a few virtuous and elegant companions, she could gather flowers planted by her own hand, fondle the lambs of her own ewe, and listen, without care, among brooks and breezes, to one of her maidens reading in the shade.

Chapter 20. *The Danger of Prosperity*

On the next day they continued their journey, till the heat compelled them to look round for shelter. At a small distance they saw a thick wood, which they no sooner entered than they perceived that they were approaching the habitations of men. The shrubs were diligently cut away to open walks where the shades were darkest; the boughs of opposite trees were artificially interwoven; seats of flowery turf were raised in vacant spaces, and a rivulet, that wantoned along the side of a winding path, had its banks sometimes opened into small basins, and its stream sometimes obstructed by little mounds of stone heaped together to increase its murmurs.

They passed slowly through the wood, delighted with such unexpected accommodations, and entertained each other with conjecturing what, or who, he could be, that, in those rude and unfrequented regions, had leisure and art for such harmless luxury.

As they advanced, they heard the sound of music, and saw youths and virgins dancing in the grove; and, going still further, beheld a stately palace built upon a hill surrounded with woods. The laws of eastern hospitality allowed them to enter, and the master welcomed them like a man liberal and wealthy.

He was skilful enough in appearances soon to discern that they were no common guests, and spread his table with magnificence. The eloquence of Imlac caught his attention, and the lofty courtesy of the princess excited his respect. When they offered to depart he entreated their stay, and was the next day still more unwilling to dismiss them than before. They were easily persuaded to stop, and civility grew up in time to freedom and confidence.

The prince now saw all the domestics cheerful, and all the face of nature smiling round the place, and could not forbear to hope that he should find here what he was seeking; but when he was congratulating the master upon his possessions, he answered with a sigh, "My condition has indeed the appearance of happiness, but appearances are delusive. My prosperity puts my life in danger; the Bassa of Egypt is my enemy, incensed only by my wealth and popularity. I have been hitherto protected against him by the princes of the country; but, as the favor of the great is uncertain, I know not how soon my defenders may be persuaded to share the plunder with the Bassa. I have sent my treasures into a distant country, and, upon the first alarm, am prepared to follow them. Then will my enemies riot in my mansion, and enjoy the gardens which I have planted."

They all joined in lamenting his danger, and deprecating his exile; and the princess was so much disturbed with the tumult of grief and indignation, that she retired to her apartment. They continued with their kind inviter a few days longer, and then went forward to find the hermit.

Chapter 21. The Happiness of Solitude. The Hermit's History

They came on the third day, by the direction of the peasants, to the hermit's cell: it was a cavern in the side of a mountain, over-shadowed with palm-trees; at such a distance from the cataract, that nothing more was heard than a gentle uniform murmur, such as composed the mind to pensive meditation, especially when it was assisted by the wind whistling among the branches. The first rude essay of nature had been so much improved by human labor, that the cave contained several apartments, appropriated to different uses, and often afforded lodging to travelers, whom darkness or tempests happened to overtake.

The hermit sat on a bench at the door, to enjoy the coolness of the evening. On one side lay a book with pens and papers, on the other mechanical instruments of various kinds. As they approached him unregarded, the princess observed that he had not the countenance of a man that had found, or could teach, the way to happiness.

They saluted him with great respect, which he repaid like a man not unaccustomed to the forms of courts. "My children," said he, "if you have lost your way, you shall be willingly supplied with such conveniencies for the night as this cavern will afford. I have all that nature requires, and you will not expect delicacies in a hermit's cell."

They thanked him, and, entering, were pleased with the neatness and regularity of the place. The hermit set flesh and wine before them, though he fed only upon fruits and water. His discourse was cheerful without levity, and pious without enthusiasm.[5] He soon gained the esteem of his guests, and the princess repented of her hasty censure.

At last Imlac began thus: "I do not now wonder that your reputation is so far extended; we have heard at Cairo of your wisdom, and came hither to implore your direction for this young man and maiden in the *choice of life*."

"To him that lives well," answered the hermit, "every form of life is good; nor can I give any other rule for choice, than to remove from all apparent evil."

---

5. "A vain belief of private revelation; a vain confidence of divine favor or communication" (Johnson's *Dictionary*).

"He will remove most certainly from evil," said the prince, "who shall devote himself to that solitude which you have recommended by your example."

"I have indeed lived fifteen years in solitude," said the hermit, "but have no desire that my example should gain any imitators. In my youth I professed arms, and was raised by degrees to the highest military rank. I have traversed wide countries at the head of my troops, and seen many battles and sieges. At last, being disgusted by the preferment of a younger officer, and feeling that my vigor was beginning to decay, I resolved to close my life in peace, having found the world full of snares, discord, and misery. I had once escaped from the pursuit of the enemy by the shelter of this cavern, and therefore chose it for my final residence. I employed artificers to form it into chambers, and stored it with all that I was likely to want.

"For some time after my retreat, I rejoiced like a tempest-beaten sailor at his entrance into the harbor, being delighted with the sudden change of the noise and hurry of war, to stillness and repose. When the pleasure of novelty went away, I employed my hours in examining the plants which grow in the valley, and the minerals which I collected from the rocks. But that inquiry is now grown tasteless and irksome. I have been for some time unsettled and distracted: my mind is disturbed with a thousand perplexities of doubt, and vanities of imagination, which hourly prevail upon me, because I have no opportunities of relaxation or diversion. I am sometimes ashamed to think that I could not secure myself from vice, but by retiring from the exercise of virtue, and begin to suspect that I was rather impelled by resentment, than led by devotion, into solitude. My fancy riots in scenes of folly, and I lament that I have lost so much, and have gained so little. In solitude, if I escape the example of bad men, I want likewise the counsel and conversation of the good. I have been long comparing the evils with the advantages of society, and resolve to return into the world tomorrow. The life of a solitary man will be certainly miserable, but not certainly devout."

They heard his resolution with surprise, but, after a short pause, offered to conduct him to Cairo. He dug up a considerable treasure which he had hid among the rocks, and accompanied them to the city, on which, as he approached it, he gazed with rapture.

Chapter 22. *The Happiness of a Life Led According to Nature*

Rasselas went often to an assembly of learned men, who met at stated times to unbend their minds and compare their opinions. Their manners were somewhat coarse, but their conversation was instructive, and their disputations acute, though sometimes too violent, and often continued till neither controvertist remembered upon what question they began. Some faults were almost general among them; everyone was desirous to dictate to the rest, and everyone was pleased to hear the genius or knowledge of another depreciated.

In this assembly Rasselas was relating his interview with the hermit, and the wonder with which he heard him censure a course of life which he had so deliberately chosen, and so laudably followed. The sentiments of the hearers were various. Some were of opinion that the folly of his choice had been justly punished by condemnation to perpetual perseverance. One of the youngest among them, with great vehemence, pronounced him an hypocrite. Some talked of the right of society to the labor of individuals, and considered retirement as a desertion of duty. Others readily allowed that there was a time when the claims of the public were satisfied, and when a man might properly sequester himself, to review his life and purify his heart.

One, who appeared more affected with the narrative than the rest, thought it likely that the hermit would in a few years go back to his retreat, and perhaps, if shame did not restrain, or death intercept him, return once more from his retreat into the world. "For the hope of happiness," said he, "is so strongly impressed that the longest experience is not able to efface it. Of the present state, whatever it be, we feel and are forced to confess the misery; yet when the same state is again at a distance, imagination paints it as desirable. But the time will surely come when desire will be no longer our torment, and no man shall be wretched but by his own fault."

"This," said a philosopher who had heard him with tokens of great impatience, "is the present condition of a wise man. The time is already come when none are wretched but by their own fault. Nothing is more idle than to inquire after happiness, which nature has kindly placed within our reach. The way to be happy is to live according to nature, in obedience to that universal and unalterable law with which every heart is originally impressed; which is not written on it by precept, but engraven by destiny, not instilled by education, but infused at our nativity. He that lives according to nature will suffer nothing from the delusions of hope, or importunities of desire; he will receive and reject with equability of temper, and act or suffer as the reason of things shall alternately prescribe. Other men may amuse themselves with subtle definitions, or intricate ratiocination. Let them learn to be wise by easier means; let them observe the hind of the forest, and the linnet of the grove; let them consider the life of animals, whose motions are regulated by instinct; they obey their guide, and are happy. Let us therefore, at length, cease to dispute, and learn to live; throw away the encumbrance of precepts, which they who utter them with so much pride and pomp do not understand, and carry with us this simple and intelligible maxim, that deviation from nature is deviation from happiness."

When he had spoken, he looked round him with a placid air, and enjoyed the consciousness of his own beneficence. "Sir," said the prince with great modesty, "as I, like all the rest of mankind, am desirous of felicity, my closest attention has been fixed upon your discourse. I doubt not the truth of a position which a man so learned has so confidently advanced. Let me only know what it is to live according to nature."

"When I find young men so humble and so docile," said the philosopher, "I can deny them no information which my studies have enabled me to afford. To live according to nature, is to act always with due regard to the fitness arising from the relations and qualities of causes and effects; to concur with the great and unchangeable scheme of universal felicity; to cooperate with the general disposition and tendency of the present system of things."

The prince soon found that this was one of the sages whom he should understand less as he heard him longer. He therefore bowed and was silent; and the philosopher, supposing him satisfied, and the rest vanquished, rose up and departed with the air of a man that had co-operated with the present system.[6]

* * *

Chapter 26. The Princess Continues Her Remarks upon Private Life

Nekayah, perceiving her brother's attention fixed, proceeded in her narrative.

"In families where there is or is not poverty, there is commonly discord. If a kingdom be, as Imlac tells us, a great family, a family likewise is a little kingdom, torn with factions and exposed to revolutions. An unpracticed observer expects the love of parents and children to be constant and equal; but this kindness seldom continues beyond the years of infancy: in a short time the children become rivals to their parents. Benefits are allayed[7] by reproaches, and gratitude debased by envy.

"Parents and children seldom act in concert; each child endeavors to appropriate the esteem or fondness of the parents, and the parents, with yet less temptation, betray each other to their children. Thus, some place their confidence in the father, and some in the mother, and by degrees the house is filled with artifices and feuds.

"The opinions of children and parents, of the young and the old, are naturally opposite, by the contrary effects of hope and despondence, of expectation and experience, without crime or folly on either side. The colors of life in youth and age appear different, as the face of nature in spring and winter. And how can children credit the assertions of parents, which their own eyes show them to be false?

"Few parents act in such a manner as much to enforce their maxims by the credit of their lives. The old man trusts wholly to slow contrivance and gradual progression; the youth expects to force his way by genius, vigor, and precipitance. The old man pays regard to riches, and the youth reverences virtue. The old man deifies prudence; the youth commits himself to magnanimity and chance. The young man, who intends no ill, believes that none is intended, and therefore acts with openness and candor; but his father, having suffered the injuries of fraud, is impelled to suspect, and too often allured to practice it. Age looks with anger on the temerity of youth, and youth with contempt on the scrupulosity[8] of age. Thus parents and children, for the greatest part, live on to love less and less; and, if those whom nature has thus closely united are the torments of each other, where shall we look for tenderness and consolation?"

"Surely," said the prince, "you must have been unfortunate in your choice of acquaintance: I am unwilling to believe that the most tender of all relations is thus impeded in its effects by natural necessity."

"Domestic discord," answered she, "is not inevitably and fatally necessary, but yet is not easily avoided. We seldom see that a whole family is virtuous; the good and evil cannot well agree, and the evil can yet less agree with one another. Even the virtuous fall sometimes to variance, when their virtues are

6. In chapters 23–25, Rasselas examines court life; and Nekayah, domestic life. She reports her findings to him.
7. To allay is "to join any thing to another, so as to abate its predominant qualities" (Johnson's Dictionary).
8. "Fear of acting in any manner" (Johnson's Dictionary).

of different kinds, and tending to extremes. In general, those parents have most reverence who most deserve it; for he that lives well cannot be despised.

"Many other evils infest private life. Some are the slaves of servants whom they have trusted with their affairs. Some are kept in continual anxiety to the caprice of rich relations, whom they cannot please, and dare not offend. Some husbands are imperious, and some wives perverse; and, as it is always more easy to do evil than good, though the wisdom or virtue of one can very rarely make many happy, the folly or vice of one may often make many miserable."

"If such be the general effect of marriage," said the prince, "I shall for the future think it dangerous to connect my interest with that of another, lest I should be unhappy by my partner's fault."

"I have met," said the princess, "with many who live single for that reason; but I never found that their prudence ought to raise envy. They dream away their time without friendship, without fondness, and are driven to rid themselves of the day, for which they have no use, by childish amusements, or vicious delights. They act as beings under the constant sense of some known inferiority that fills their minds with rancor, and their tongues with censure. They are peevish at home, and malevolent abroad; and, as the outlaws of human nature, make it their business and their pleasure to disturb that society which debars them from its privileges. To live without feeling or exciting sympathy, to be fortunate without adding to the felicity of others, or afflicted without tasting the balm of pity, is a state more gloomy than solitude; it is not retreat but exclusion from mankind. Marriage has many pains, but celibacy has no pleasures."

"What then is to be done?" said Rasselas; "the more we inquire, the less we can resolve. Surely he is most likely to please himself that has no other inclination to regard."[9]

* * *

Chapter 29. The Debate on Marriage Continued

"The good of the whole," says Rasselas, "is the same with the good of all its parts. If marriage be best for mankind it must be evidently best for individuals, or a permanent and necessary duty must be the cause of evil, and some must be inevitably sacrificed to the convenience of others. In the estimate which you have made of the two states, it appears that the incommodities of a single life are, in a great measure, necessary and certain, but those of the conjugal state accidental and avoidable.

"I cannot forbear to flatter myself that prudence and benevolence will make marriage happy. The general folly of mankind is the cause of general complaint. What can be expected but disappointment and repentance from a choice made in the immaturity of youth, in the ardor of desire, without judgment, without foresight, without inquiry after conformity of opinions, similarity of manners, rectitude of judgment, or purity of sentiment.

"Such is the common process of marriage. A youth and maiden meeting by chance, or brought together by artifice, exchange glances, reciprocate civilities, go home, and dream of one another. Having little to divert atten-

9. In chapters 27–29, Rasselas reports on the unhappiness of court life, and he and Nekayah debate whether marriage leads to happiness or misery.

tion, or diversify thought, they find themselves uneasy when they are apart, and therefore conclude that they shall be happy together. They marry, and discover what nothing but voluntary blindness had before concealed; they wear out life in altercations, and charge nature with cruelty.

"From those early marriages proceeds likewise the rivalry of parents and children: the son is eager to enjoy the world before the father is willing to forsake it, and there is hardly room at once for two generations. The daughter begins to bloom before the mother can be content to fade, and neither can forbear to wish for the absence of the other.

"Surely all these evils may be avoided by that deliberation and delay which prudence prescribes to irrevocable choice. In the variety and jollity of youthful pleasures life may be well enough supported without the help of a partner. Longer time will increase experience, and wider views will allow better opportunities of inquiry and selection: one advantage, at least, will be certain; the parents will be visibly older than their children."

"What reason cannot collect," said Nekayah, "and what experiment has not yet taught, can be known only from the report of others. I have been told that late marriages are not eminently happy. This is a question too important to be neglected, and I have often proposed it to those, whose accuracy of remark, and comprehensiveness of knowledge, made their suffrages[1] worthy of regard. They have generally determined that it is dangerous for a man and woman to suspend their fate upon each other, at a time when opinions are fixed, and habits are established; when friendships have been contracted on both sides, when life has been planned into method, and the mind has long enjoyed the contemplation of its own prospects.

"It is scarcely possible that two traveling through the world under the conduct of chance should have been both directed to the same path, and it will not often happen that either will quit the track which custom has made pleasing. When the desultory levity of youth has settled into regularity, it is soon succeeded by pride ashamed to yield, or obstinacy delighting to contend. And even though mutual esteem produces mutual desire to please, time itself, as it modifies unchangeably the external mien, determines likewise the direction of the passions, and gives an inflexible rigidity to the manners. Long customs are not easily broken: he that attempts to change the course of his own life very often labors in vain; and how shall we do that for others which we are seldom able to do for ourselves?"

"But surely," interposed the prince, "you suppose the chief motive of choice forgotten or neglected. Whenever I shall seek a wife, it shall be my first question, whether she be willing to be led by reason?"

"Thus it is," said Nekayah, "that philosophers are deceived. There are a thousand familiar[2] disputes which reason never can decide; questions that elude investigation, and make logic ridiculous; cases where something must be done, and where little can be said. Consider the state of mankind, and inquire how few can be supposed to act upon any occasions, whether small or great, with all the reasons of action present to their minds. Wretched would be the pair above all names of wretchedness, who should be doomed to adjust by reason every morning all the minute detail of a domestic day.

"Those who marry at an advanced age will probably escape the encroach-

1. Opinions.   2. Domestic.

ments of their children; but, in diminution of this advantage, they will be likely to leave them, ignorant and helpless, to a guardian's mercy: or, if that should not happen, they must at least go out of the world before they see those whom they love best either wise or great.

"From their children, if they have less to fear, they have less also to hope, and they lose, without equivalent, the joys of early love, and the convenience of uniting with manners pliant and minds susceptible of new impressions, which might wear away their dissimilitudes by long cohabitation, as soft bodies, by continual attrition, conform their surfaces to each other.

"I believe it will be found that those who marry late are best pleased with their children, and those who marry early with their partners."

"The union of these two affections," said Rasselas, "would produce all that could be wished. Perhaps there is a time when marriage might unite them, a time neither too early for the father, nor too late for the husband."

"Every hour," answered the princess, "confirms my prejudice in favor of the position so often uttered by the mouth of Imlac, 'That nature sets her gifts on the right hand and on the left.' Those conditions, which flatter hope and attract desire, are so constituted that, as we approach one, we recede from another. There are goods so opposed that we cannot seize both, but, by too much prudence, may pass between them at too great a distance to reach either. This is often the fate of long consideration; he does nothing who endeavors to do more than is allowed to humanity. Flatter not yourself with contrarieties of pleasure. Of the blessings set before you make your choice, and be content. No man can taste the fruits of autumn, while he is delighting his scent with the flowers of the spring: no man can, at the same time, fill his cup from the source and from the mouth of the Nile."[3]

* * *

Chapter 31. They Visit the Pyramids

The resolution being thus taken, they set out the next day. They laid tents upon their camels, being resolved to stay among the pyramids till their curiosity was fully satisfied. They traveled gently, turned aside to everything remarkable, stopped from time to time and conversed with the inhabitants, and observed the various appearances of towns ruined and inhabited, of wild and cultivated nature.

When they came to the great pyramid, they were astonished at the extent of the base, and the height of the top. Imlac explained to them the principles upon which the pyramidal form was chosen for a fabric intended to coextend its duration with that of the world; he showed that its gradual diminution gave it such stability as defeated all the common attacks of the elements, and could scarcely be overthrown by earthquakes themselves, the least resistible of natural violence. A concussion that should shatter the pyramid would threaten the dissolution of the continent.

They measured all its dimensions, and pitched their tents at its foot. Next day they prepared to enter its interior apartments, and having hired the common guides, climbed up to the first passage, when the favorite of the princess, looking into the cavity, stepped back and trembled. "Pekuah," said the prin-

---

3. In chapter 30, Imlac proposes a visit to the pyramids.

cess, "of what art thou afraid?" "Of the narrow entrance," answered the lady, "and of the dreadful gloom. I dare not enter a place which must surely be inhabited by unquiet souls. The original possessors of these dreadful vaults will start up before us, and perhaps shut us in forever." She spoke, and threw her arms round the neck of her mistress.

"If all your fear be of apparitions," said the prince, "I will promise you safety. There is no danger from the dead; he that is once buried will be seen no more."

"That the dead are seen no more," said Imlac, "I will not undertake to maintain, against the concurrent and unvaried testimony of all ages, and of all nations. There is no people, rude or learned, among whom apparitions of the dead are not related and believed. This opinion, which perhaps prevails as far as human nature is diffused, could become universal only by its truth; those that never heard of one another would not have agreed in a tale which nothing but experience can make credible. That it is doubted by single cavilers can very little weaken the general evidence; and some who deny it with their tongues confess it by their fears.

"Yet I do not mean to add new terrors to those which have already seized upon Pekuah. There can be no reason why specters should haunt the pyramid more than other places, or why they should have power or will to hurt innocence and purity. Our entrance is no violation of their privileges; we can take nothing from them, how then can we offend them?"

"My dear Pekuah," said the princess, "I will always go before you, and Imlac shall follow you. Remember that you are the companion of the princess of Abyssinia."

"If the princess is pleased that her servant should die," returned the lady, "let her command some death less dreadful than enclosure in this horrid cavern. You know I dare not disobey you; I must go if you command me, but if I once enter, I never shall come back."

The princess saw that her fear was too strong for expostulation or reproof, and, embracing her, told her that she should stay in the tent till their return. Pekuah was yet not satisfied, but entreated the princess not to pursue so dreadful a purpose as that of entering the recesses of the pyramid. "Though I cannot teach courage," said Nekayah, "I must not learn cowardice, nor leave at last undone what I came hither only to do."

Chapter 32. They Enter the Pyramid

Pekuah descended to the tents, and the rest entered the pyramid. They passed through the galleries, surveyed the vaults of marble, and examined the chest in which the body of the founder is supposed to have been reposited. They then sat down in one of the most spacious chambers to rest a while before they attempted to return.

"We have now," said Imlac, "gratified our minds with an exact view of the greatest work of man, except the wall of China.

"Of the wall it is very easy to assign the motive. It secured a wealthy and timorous nation from the incursions of barbarians, whose unskillfulness in arts made it easier for them to supply their wants by rapine than by industry, and who from time to time poured in upon the habitations of peaceful commerce, as vultures descend upon domestic fowl. Their celerity and fierceness made the wall necessary, and their ignorance made it efficacious.

"But for the pyramids, no reason has ever been given adequate to the cost and labor of the work. The narrowness of the chambers proves that it could afford no retreat from enemies, and treasures might have been reposited at far less expense with equal security. It seems to have been erected only in compliance with that hunger of imagination which preys incessantly upon life, and must be always appeased by some employment. Those who have already all that they can enjoy must enlarge their desires. He that has built for use till use is supplied, must begin to build for vanity, and extend his plan to the utmost power of human performance, that he may not be soon reduced to form another wish.

"I consider this mighty structure as a monument of the insufficiency of human enjoyments. A king, whose power is unlimited, and whose treasures surmount all real and imaginary wants, is compelled to solace, by the erection of a pyramid, the satiety of dominion and tastelessness of pleasures, and to amuse the tediousness of declining life by seeing thousands laboring without end, and one stone, for no purpose, laid upon another. Whoever thou art, that, not content with a moderate condition, imaginest happiness in royal magnificence, and dreamest that command or riches can feed the appetite of novelty with perpetual gratifications, survey the pyramids, and confess thy folly!"[4]

* * *

Chapter 40. The History of a Man of Learning

They returned to Cairo, and were so well pleased at finding themselves together, that none of them went much abroad. The prince began to love learning, and one day declared to Imlac, that he intended to devote himself to science,[5] and pass the rest of his days in literary solitude.

"Before you make your final choice," answered Imlac, "you ought to examine its hazards, and converse with some of those who are grown old in the company of themselves. I have just left the observatory of one of the most learned astronomers in the world, who has spent forty years in unwearied attention to the motions and appearances of the celestial bodies, and has drawn out his soul in endless calculations. He admits a few friends once a month to hear his deductions and enjoy his discoveries. I was introduced as a man of knowledge worthy of his notice. Men of various ideas and fluent conversation are commonly welcome to those whose thoughts have been long fixed upon a single point, and who find the images of other things stealing away. I delighted him with my remarks, he smiled at the narrative of my travels, and was glad to forget the constellations, and descend for a moment into the lower world.

"On the next day of vacation I renewed my visit, and was so fortunate as to please him again. He relaxed from that time the severity of his rule, and permitted me to enter at my own choice. I found him always busy, and always glad to be relieved. As each knew much which the other was desirous of

4. In chapters 33–39, Pekuah—while her friends are in the pyramid—is abducted by a troop of Arabs. The chief is tempted to keep her, but eventually accepts a ransom and returns her unharmed.
5. Knowledge.

learning, we exchanged our notions with great delight. I perceived that I had every day more of his confidence, and always found new cause of admiration in the profundity of his mind. His comprehension is vast, his memory capacious and retentive, his discourse is methodical, and his expression clear.

"His integrity and benevolence are equal to his learning. His deepest researches and most favorite studies are willingly interrupted for any opportunity of doing good by his counsel or his riches. To his closest retreat, at his most busy moments, all are admitted that want his assistance: 'For though I exclude idleness and pleasure, I will never,' says he, 'bar my doors against charity. To man is permitted the contemplation of the skies, but the practice of virtue is commanded.' "

"Surely," said the princess, "this man is happy."

"I visited him," said Imlac, "with more and more frequency, and was every time more enamored of his conversation: he was sublime without haughtiness, courteous without formality, and communicative without ostentation. I was at first, great princess, of your opinion, thought him the happiest of mankind, and often congratulated him on the blessing that he enjoyed. He seemed to hear nothing with indifference but the praises of his condition, to which he always returned a general answer, and diverted the conversation to some other topic.

"Amidst this willingness to be pleased, and labor to please, I had quickly reason to imagine that some painful sentiment pressed upon his mind. He often looked up earnestly towards the sun, and let his voice fall in the midst of his discourse. He would sometimes, when we were alone, gaze upon me in silence with the air of a man who longed to speak what he was yet resolved to suppress. He would often send for me with vehement injunctions of haste, though, when I came to him, he had nothing extraordinary to say. And sometimes, when I was leaving him, he would call me back, pause a few moments and then dismiss me.

Chapter 41. The Astronomer Discovers[6] the Cause of his Uneasiness

"At last the time came when the secret burst his reserve. We were sitting together last night in the turret of his house, watching the emersion of a satellite of Jupiter. A sudden tempest clouded the sky, and disappointed our observation. We sat a while silent in the dark, and then he addressed himself to me in these words: 'Imlac, I have long considered thy friendship as the greatest blessing of my life. Integrity without knowledge is weak and useless, and knowledge without integrity is dangerous and dreadful. I have found in thee all the qualities requisite for trust, benevolence, experience, and fortitude. I have long discharged an office which I must soon quit at the call of nature, and shall rejoice in the hour of imbecility[7] and pain to devolve it upon thee.'

"I thought myself honored by this testimony, and protested that whatever could conduce to his happiness would add likewise to mine.

" 'Hear, Imlac, what thou wilt not without difficulty credit. I have possessed for five years the regulation of weather, and the distribution of the seasons: the sun has listened to my dictates, and passed from tropic to tropic

6. Reveals. 7. Feebleness.

by my direction; the clouds, at my call, have poured their waters, and the Nile has overflowed at my command; I have restrained the rage of the dog-star, and mitigated the fervors of the crab.[8] The winds alone, of all the elemental powers, have hitherto refused my authority, and multitudes have perished by equinoctial tempests which I found myself unable to prohibit or restrain. I have administered this great office with exact justice, and made to the different nations of the earth an impartial dividend of rain and sunshine. What must have been the misery of half the globe, if I had limited the clouds to particular regions, or confined the sun to either side of the equator?'

Chapter 42. *The Opinion of the Astronomer Is Explained and Justified*

"I suppose he discovered in me, through the obscurity of the room, some tokens of amazement and doubt, for, after a short pause, he proceeded thus:

" 'Not to be easily credited will neither surprise nor offend me; for I am, probably, the first of human beings to whom this trust has been imparted. Nor do I know whether to deem this distinction a reward or punishment; since I have possessed it I have been far less happy than before, and nothing but the consciousness of good intention could have enabled me to support the weariness of unremitted vigilance.'

" 'How long, Sir', said I, 'has this great office been in your hands?'

" 'About ten years ago,' said he, 'my daily observations of the changes of the sky led me to consider, whether, if I had the power of the seasons, I could confer greater plenty upon the inhabitants of the earth. This contemplation fastened on my mind, and I sat days and nights in imaginary dominion, pouring upon this country and that the showers of fertility, and seconding every fall of rain with a due proportion of sunshine. I had yet only the will to do good, and did not imagine that I should ever have the power.

" 'One day as I was looking on the fields withering with heat, I felt in my mind a sudden wish that I could send rain on the southern mountains, and raise the Nile to an inundation. In the hurry of my imagination I commanded rain to fall, and, by comparing the time of my command, with that of the inundation, I found that the clouds had listened to my lips.'

" 'Might not some other cause,' said I, 'produce this concurrence? the Nile does not always rise on the same day.'

" 'Do not believe,' said he with impatience, 'that such objections could escape me: I reasoned long against my own conviction, and labored against truth with the utmost obstinacy. I sometimes suspected myself of madness, and should not have dared to impart this secret but to a man like you, capable of distinguishing the wonderful from the impossible, and the incredible from the false.'

" 'Why, Sir,' said I, 'do you call that incredible, which you know, or think you know, to be true?'

" 'Because,' said he, 'I cannot prove it by any external evidence; and I know too well the laws of demonstration to think that my conviction ought to influence another, who cannot, like me, be conscious of its force. I therefore

8. The fourth sign of the zodiac (Cancer). "The dogstar": Sirius was supposed to cause the heat ("dog days") of summer.

shall not attempt to gain credit by disputation. It is sufficient that I feel this power, that I have long possessed, and every day exerted it. But the life of man is short, the infirmities of age increase upon me, and the time will soon come when the regulator of the year must mingle with the dust. The care of appointing a successor has long disturbed me; the night and the day have been spent in comparisons of all the characters which have come to my knowledge, and I have yet found none so worthy as thyself.

Chapter 43. The Astronomer Leaves Imlac His Directions

" 'Hear therefore, what I shall impart, with attention, such as the welfare of a world requires. If the task of a king be considered as difficult, who has the care only of a few millions, to whom he cannot do much good or harm, what must be the anxiety of him, on whom depends the action of the elements, and the great gifts of light and heat!—Hear me therefore with attention.

" 'I have diligently considered the position of the earth and sun, and formed innumerable schemes in which I changed their situation. I have sometimes turned aside the axis of the earth, and sometimes varied the ecliptic of the sun: but I have found it impossible to make a disposition by which the world may be advantaged; what one region gains, another loses by any imaginable alteration, even without considering the distant parts of the solar system with which we are unacquainted. Do not, therefore, in thy administration of the year, indulge thy pride by innovation; do not please thyself with thinking that thou canst make thyself renowned to all future ages, by disordering the seasons. The memory of mischief is no desirable fame. Much less will it become thee to let kindness or interest prevail. Never rob other countries of rain to pour it on thine own. For us the Nile is sufficient.'

"I promised that when I possessed the power, I would use it with inflexible integrity, and he dismissed me, pressing my hand. 'My heart,' said he, 'will be now at rest, and my benevolence will no more destroy my quiet: I have found a man of wisdom and virtue, to whom I can cheerfully bequeath the inheritance of the sun.' "

The prince heard this narration with very serious regard, but the princess smiled, and Pekuah convulsed herself with laughter. "Ladies," said Imlac, "to mock the heaviest of human afflictions is neither charitable nor wise. Few can attain this man's knowledge, and few practice his virtues; but all may suffer his calamity. Of the uncertainties of our present state, the most dreadful and alarming is the uncertain continuance of reason."

The princess was recollected, and the favorite was abashed. Rasselas, more deeply affected, inquired of Imlac, whether he thought such maladies of the mind frequent, and how they were contracted.

Chapter 44. The Dangerous Prevalence[9] of Imagination

"Disorders of intellect," answered Imlac, "happen much more often than superficial observers will easily believe. Perhaps, if we speak with rigorous exactness, no human mind is in its right state. There is no man whose imag-

---

9. Predominance.

ination does not sometimes predominate over his reason, who can regulate his attention wholly by his will, and whose ideas will come and go at his command. No man will be found in whose mind airy notions do not sometimes tyrannize, and force him to hope or fear beyond the limits of sober probability. All power of fancy over reason is a degree of insanity; but while this power is such as we can control and repress, it is not visible to others, nor considered as any depravation of the mental faculties; it is not pronounced madness but when it comes ungovernable, and apparently influences speech or action.

"To indulge the power of fiction, and send imagination out upon the wing, is often the sport of those who delight too much in silent speculation. When we are alone we are not always busy; the labor of excogitation is too violent to last long; the ardor of inquiry will sometimes give way to idleness or satiety. He who has nothing external that can divert him must find pleasure in his own thoughts, and must conceive himself what he is not; for who is pleased with what he is? He then expatiates in boundless futurity, and culls from all imaginable conditions that which for the present moment he should most desire, amuses his desires with impossible enjoyments, and confers upon his pride unattainable dominion. The mind dances from scene to scene, unites all pleasures in all combinations, and riots in delights which nature and fortune, with all their bounty, cannot bestow.

"In time, some particular train of ideas fixes the attention; all other intellectual gratifications are rejected; the mind, in weariness or leisure, recurs constantly to the favorite conception, and feasts on the luscious falsehood, whenever she is offended with the bitterness of truth. By degrees the reign of fancy is confirmed; she grows first imperious, and in time despotic. Then fictions begin to operate as realities, false opinions fasten upon the mind, and life passes in dreams of rapture or of anguish.

"This, sir, is one of the dangers of solitude, which the hermit has confessed not always to promote goodness, and the astronomer's misery has proved to be not always propitious to wisdom."

"I will no more," said the favorite, "imagine myself the queen of Abyssinia. I have often spent the hours which the princess gave to my own disposal, in adjusting ceremonies and regulating the court; I have repressed the pride of the powerful, and granted the petitions of the poor; I have built new palaces in more happy situations, planted groves upon the tops of mountains, and have exulted in the beneficence of royalty, till, when the princess entered, I had almost forgotten to bow down before her."

"And I," said the princess, "will not allow myself any more to play the shepherdess in my waking dreams. I have often soothed my thoughts with the quiet and innocence of pastoral employments, till I have in my chamber heard the winds whistle, and the sheep bleat; sometimes freed the lamb entangled in the thicket, and sometimes with my crook encountered the wolf. I have a dress like that of the village maids, which I put on to help my imagination, and a pipe on which I play softly, and suppose myself followed by my flocks."

"I will confess," said the prince, "an indulgence of fantastic delight more dangerous than yours. I have frequently endeavored to image the possibility of a perfect government, by which all wrong should be restrained, all vice reformed, and all the subjects preserved in tranquility and innocence. This thought produced innumerable schemes of reformation, and dictated many useful regulations and salutary edicts. This has been the sport, and sometimes the labor, of my solitude; and I start, when I think with how little anguish I once supposed the death of my father and my brothers."

"Such," says Imlac, "are the effects of visionary schemes; when we first form them, we know them to be absurd, but familiarize them by degrees, and in time lose sight of their folly."

Chapter 45. They Discourse with an Old Man

The evening was now far past, and they rose to return home. As they walked along the bank of the Nile, delighted with the beams of the moon quivering on the water, they saw at a small distance an old man, whom the prince had often heard in the assembly of the sages. "Yonder," said he, "is one whose years have calmed his passions, but not clouded his reason. Let us close the disquisitions of the night by inquiring what are his sentiments of his own state, that we may know whether youth alone is to struggle with vexation, and whether any better hope remains for the latter part of life."

Here the sage approached and saluted them. They invited him to join their walk, and prattled a while, as acquaintance that had unexpectedly met one another. The old man was cheerful and talkative, and the way seemed short in his company. He was pleased to find himself not disregarded, accompanied them to their house, and, at the prince's request, entered with them. They placed him in the seat of honor, and set wine and conserves before him.

"Sir," said the princess, "an evening walk must give to a man of learning like you pleasures which ignorance and youth can hardly conceive. You know the qualities and the causes of all that you behold, the laws by which the river flows, the periods in which the planets perform their revolutions. Everything must supply you with contemplation, and renew the consciousness of your own dignity."

"Lady," answered he, "let the gay and the vigorous expect pleasure in their excursions; it is enough that age can obtain ease. To me the world has lost its novelty; I look round, and see what I remember to have seen in happier days. I rest against a tree, and consider that in the same shade I once disputed upon the annual overflow of the Nile with a friend who is now silent in the grave. I cast my eyes upward, fix them on the changing moon, and think with pain on the vicissitudes of life. I have ceased to take much delight in physical truth; for what have I to do with those things which I am soon to leave?"

"You may at least recreate[1] yourself," said Imlac, "with the recollection of an honorable and useful life, and enjoy the praise which all agree to give you."

"Praise," said the sage with a sigh, "is to an old man an empty sound. I have neither mother to be delighted with the reputation of her son, nor wife to partake the honors of her husband. I have outlived my friends and my rivals. Nothing is now of much importance; for I cannot extend my interest beyond myself. Youth is delighted with applause, because it is considered as the earnest of some future good, and because the prospect of life is far

---

1. Refresh.

extended; but to me, who am now declining to decrepitude, there is little to be feared from the malevolence of men, and yet less to be hoped from their affection or esteem. Something they may yet take away, but they can give me nothing. Riches would now be useless, and high employment would be pain. My retrospect of life recalls to my view many opportunities of good neglected, much time squandered upon trifles, and more lost in idleness and vacancy. I leave many great designs unattempted, and many great attempts unfinished. My mind is burthened with no heavy crime, and therefore I compose myself to tranquility; endeavor to abstract my thoughts from hopes and cares which, though reason knows them to be vain, still try to keep their old possession of the heart; expect,[2] with serene humility, that hour which nature cannot long delay; and hope to possess, in a better state, that happiness which here I could not find, and that virtue which here I have not attained."

He arose and went away, leaving his audience not much elated with the hope of long life. The prince consoled himself with remarking that it was not reasonable to be disappointed by this account; for age had never been considered as the season of felicity, and if it was possible to be easy in decline and weakness, it was likely that the days of vigor and alacrity might be happy; that the noon of life might be bright, if the evening could be calm.

The princess suspected that age was querulous and malignant, and delighted to repress the expectations of those who had newly entered the world. She had seen the possessors of estates look with envy on their heirs, and known many who enjoy pleasure no longer than they can confine it to themselves.

Pekuah conjectured that the man was older than he appeared, and was willing to impute his complaints to delirious dejection; or else supposed that he had been unfortunate, and was therefore discontented. "For nothing," said she, "is more common than to call our own condition the condition of life."

Imlac, who had no desire to see them depressed, smiled at the comforts which they could so readily procure to themselves, and remembered that, at the same age, he was equally confident of unmingled prosperity, and equally fertile of consolatory expedients. He forbore to force upon them unwelcome knowledge, which time itself would too soon impress. The princess and her lady retired; the madness of the astronomer hung upon their minds, and they desired Imlac to enter upon his office, and delay next morning the rising of the sun.[3]

* * *

Chapter 48. Imlac Discourses on the Nature of the Soul

"What reason," said the prince, "can be given, why the Egyptians should thus expensively preserve those carcasses which some nations consume with fire, others lay to mingle with the earth, and all agree to remove from their sight, as soon as decent rites can be performed?"

"The original of ancient customs," said Imlac, "is commonly unknown; for

2. Await.
3. In chapters 46 and 47, Nekayah, Pekuah, and Rasselas befriend the astronomer and gradually wean him from madness. In search of diversion, all of them visit the catacombs.

the practice often continues when the cause has ceased; and concerning superstitious ceremonies it is vain to conjecture; for what reason did not dictate reason cannot explain. I have long believed that the practice of embalming arose only from tenderness to the remains of relations or friends, and to this opinion I am more inclined, because it seems impossible that this care should have been general: had all the dead been embalmed, their repositories must in time have been more spacious than the dwellings of the living. I suppose only the rich or honorable were secured from corruption, and the rest left to the course of nature.

"But it is commonly supposed that the Egyptians believed the soul to live as long as the body continued undissolved, and therefore tried this method of eluding death."

"Could the wise Egyptians," said Nekayah, "think so grossly of the soul? If the soul could once survive its separation, what could it afterwards receive or suffer from the body?"

"The Egyptians would doubtless think erroneously," said the astronomer, "in the darkness of heathenism, and the first dawn of philosophy. The nature of the soul is still disputed amidst all our opportunities of clearer knowledge: some yet say, that it may be material, who, nevertheless, believe it to be immortal."

"Some," answered Imlac, "have indeed said that the soul is material, but I can scarcely believe that any man has thought it, who knew how to think; for all the conclusions of reason enforce the immateriality of mind, and all the notices of sense and investigations of science concur to prove the unconsciousness of matter.

"It was never supposed that cogitation is inherent in matter, or that every particle is a thinking being. Yet if any part of matter be devoid of thought, what part can we suppose to think? Matter can differ from matter only in form, density, bulk, motion, and direction of motion: to which of these, however varied or combined, can consciousness be annexed? To be round or square, to be solid or fluid, to be great or little, to be moved slowly or swiftly one way or another, are modes of material existence, all equally alien from the nature of cogitation. If matter be once without thought, it can only be made to think by some new modification, but all the modifications which it can admit are equally unconnected with cogitative powers."

"But the materialists," said the astronomer, "urge that matter may have qualities with which we are unacquainted."

"He who will determine," returned Imlac, "against that which he knows, because there may be something which he knows not; he that can set hypothetical possibility against acknowledged certainty, is not to be admitted among reasonable beings. All that we know of matter is, that matter is inert, senseless and lifeless; and if this conviction cannot be opposed but by referring us to something that we know not, we have all the evidence that human intellect can admit. If that which is known may be overruled by that which is unknown, no being, not omniscient, can arrive at certainty."

"Yet let us not," said the astronomer, "too arrogantly limit the Creator's power."

"It is no limitation of omnipotence," replied the poet, "to suppose that one thing is not consistent with another, that the same proposition cannot be at once true and false, that the same number cannot be even and odd, that cogitation cannot be conferred on that which is created incapable of cogitation."

"I know not," said Nekayah, "any great use of this question. Does that immateriality, which, in my opinion, you have sufficiently proved, necessarily include eternal duration?"

"Of immateriality," said Imlac, "our ideas are negative, and therefore obscure. Immateriality seems to imply a natural power of perpetual duration as a consequence of exemption from all causes of decay: whatever perishes, is destroyed by the solution of its contexture,[4] and separation of its parts; nor can we conceive how that which has no parts, and therefore admits no solution, can be naturally corrupted or impaired."

"I know not," said Rasselas, "how to conceive anything without extension: what is extended must have parts, and you allow, that whatever has parts may be destroyed."

"Consider your own conceptions," replied Imlac, "and the difficulty will be less. You will find substance without extension. An ideal form is no less real than material bulk: yet an ideal form has no extension. It is no less certain, when you think on a pyramid, that your mind possesses the idea of a pyramid, than that the pyramid itself is standing. What space does the idea of a pyramid occupy more than the idea of a grain of corn? or how can either idea suffer laceration? As is the effect such is the cause; as thought is, such is the power that thinks; a power impassive and indiscerptible."[5]

"But the Being," said Nekayah, "whom I fear to name, the Being which made the soul, can destroy it."

"He, surely, can destroy it," answered Imlac, "since, however unperishable, it receives from a superior nature its power of duration. That it will not perish by any inherent cause of decay, or principle of corruption, may be shown by philosophy; but philosophy can tell no more. That it will not be annihilated by him that made it, we must humbly learn from higher authority."

The whole assembly stood a while silent and collected. "Let us return," said Rasselas, "from this scene of mortality. How gloomy would be these mansions of the dead to him who did not know that he shall never die; that what now acts shall continue its agency, and what now thinks shall think on for ever. Those that lie here stretched before us, the wise and the powerful of ancient times, warn us to remember the shortness of our present state: they were, perhaps, snatched away while they were busy, like us, in the choice of life."

"To me," said the princess, "the choice of life is become less important; I hope hereafter to think only on the choice of eternity."

They then hastened out of the caverns, and, under the protection of their guard, returned to Cairo.

Chapter 49. The Conclusion, in Which Nothing Is Concluded

It was now the time of the inundation of the Nile: a few days after their visit to the catacombs, the river began to rise.

They were confined to their house. The whole region being under water gave them no invitation to any excursions, and being well supplied with mate-

4. Dissolution of its structure.   5. Not to be separated.

rials for talk, they diverted themselves with comparisons of the different forms of life which they had observed, and with various schemes of happiness which each of them had formed.

Pekuah was never so much charmed with any place as the convent of St. Anthony, where the Arab restored her to the princess, and wished only to fill it with pious maidens, and to be made prioress of the order; she was weary of expectation and disgust,[6] and would gladly be fixed in some unvariable state.

The princess thought that, of all sublunary things, knowledge was the best: she desired first to learn all sciences, and then purposed to found a college of learned women, in which she would preside, that, by conversing with the old and educating the young, she might divide her time between the acquisition and communication of wisdom, and raise up for the next age models of prudence, and patterns of piety.

The prince desired a little kingdom, in which he might administer justice in his own person, and see all the parts of government with his own eyes; but he could never fix the limits of his dominion, and was always adding to the number of his subjects.

Imlac and the astronomer were contented to be driven along the stream of life, without directing their course to any particular port.

Of these wishes that they had formed, they well knew that none could be obtained. They deliberated a while what was to be done, and resolved, when the inundation should cease, to return to Abyssinia.[7]

1759

[A Brief to Free a Slave][1]

It must be agreed that in most ages many countries have had part of their inhabitants in a state of slavery; yet it may be doubted whether slavery can ever be supposed the natural condition of man. It is impossible not to conceive that men in their original state were equal; and very difficult to imagine how one would be subjected to another but by violent compulsion. An individual may, indeed, forfeit his liberty by a crime; but he cannot by that crime forfeit the liberty of his children. What is true of a criminal seems true likewise of a captive. A man may accept life from a conquering enemy on condition of perpetual servitude; but it is very doubtful whether he can entail[2] that servitude on his descendants; for no man can stipulate without commission for another. The condition which he himself accepts, his son or

6. Aversion.
7. Probably not, as is often suggested, to the Happy Valley, which the travelers earlier fled as a prison. Presumably the travelers return, with whatever wisdom they have gained but also with their cherished illusions, to share the common destiny of humankind.
1. Samuel Johnson detested slavery and the owners of slaves. Once, "in company with some very grave men at Oxford, his toast was, 'Here's to the next insurrection of the Negroes in the West Indies,'" and in his pamphlet *Taxation No Tyranny*

(1775), he put the American rebels down with a devastating question: "How is it that we hear the loudest yelps for liberty among the drivers of Negroes?" Although slavery had been abolished in England in 1772, serfdom still existed in Scotland, and the British remained heavily involved in the slave trade. In 1777 a black slave, Joseph Knight, sued for freedom from the Scottish master he had escaped. On his behalf Johnson dictated this argument to Boswell.
2. Settle unalterably.

grandson perhaps would have rejected. If we should admit, what perhaps may with more reason be denied, that there are certain relations between man and man which may make slavery necessary and just,[3] yet it can never be proved that he who is now suing for his freedom ever stood in any of those relations. He is certainly subject by no law, but that of violence, to his present master,[4] who pretends no claim to his obedience, but that he bought him from a merchant of slaves, whose right to sell him never was examined. It is said that, according to the constitutions of Jamaica, he was legally enslaved; these constitutions are merely positive;[5] and apparently injurious to the rights of mankind, because whoever is exposed to sale is condemned to slavery without appeal; by whatever fraud or violence he might have been originally brought into the merchant's power. In our own time princes have been sold, by wretches to whose care they were entrusted, that they might have an European education; but when once they were brought to a market in the plantations, little would avail either their dignity or their wrongs. The laws of Jamaica afford a Negro no redress. His color is considered as a sufficient testimony against him. It is to be lamented that moral right should ever give way to political convenience. But if temptations of interest are sometimes too strong for human virtue, let us at least retain a virtue where there is no temptation to quit it. In the present case there is apparent right on one side, and no convenience on the other. Inhabitants of this island can neither gain riches nor power by taking away the liberty of any part of the human species. The sum of the argument is this:—No man is by nature the property of another: The defendant is, therefore, by nature free: The rights of nature must be some way forfeited before they can be justly taken away: That the defendant has by any act forfeited the rights of nature we require to be proved; and if no proof of such forfeiture can be given, we doubt not but the justice of the court will declare him free.[6]

1777   1792

Rambler No. 4

[ON FICTION]

Saturday, *March* 31, 1750

Simul et jucunda et idonea dicere vitae.
—HORACE, *Art of Poetry*, 334
And join both profit and delight in one.
—CREECH

The works of fiction with which the present generation seems more particularly delighted are such as exhibit life in its true state, diversified only by accidents that daily happen in the world, and influenced by passions and qualities which are really to be found in conversing with mankind.

This kind of writing may be termed, not improperly, the comedy of

---

3. Boswell, who strongly disagreed with Johnson's "prejudice" against slavery, argued that "to abolish a *status,* which in all ages GOD has sanctioned, and man has continued, would not only be *robbery* to an innumerable class of our fellow subjects; but it would be extreme cruelty to the African savages."
4. Knight had been kidnapped as a child.
5. Arbitrarily instituted (opposed to *natural* laws).
6. Knight was set free by the Scottish court.

romance, and is to be conducted nearly by the rules of comic poetry. Its province is to bring about natural events by easy means, and to keep up curiosity without the help of wonder: it is therefore precluded from the machines[1] and expedients of the heroic romance, and can neither employ giants to snatch away a lady from the nuptial rites, nor knights to bring her back from captivity; it can neither bewilder its personages in deserts, nor lodge them in imaginary castles.

I remember a remark made by Scaliger upon Pontanus,[2] that all his writings are filled with the same images; and that if you take from him his lilies and his roses, his satyrs and his dryads, he will have nothing left that can be called poetry. In like manner, almost all the fictions of the last age will vanish if you deprive them of a hermit and a wood, a battle and a shipwreck.

Why this wild strain of imagination found reception so long in polite and learned ages, it is not easy to conceive; but we cannot wonder that while readers could be procured, the authors were willing to continue it; for when a man had by practice gained some fluency of language, he had no further care than to retire to his closet, let loose his invention, and heat his mind with incredibilities; a book was thus produced without fear of criticism, without the toil of study, without knowledge of nature, or acquaintance with life.

The task of our present writers is very different; it requires, together with that learning which is to be gained from books, that experience which can never be attained by solitary diligence, but must arise from general converse and accurate observation of the living world. Their performances have, as Horace expresses it, *plus oneris quanto veniae minus*,[3] little indulgence, and therefore more difficulty. They are engaged in portraits of which everyone knows the original, and can detect any deviation from exactness of resemblance. Other writings are safe, except from the malice of learning, but these are in danger from every common reader; as the slipper ill executed was censured by a shoemaker who happened to stop in his way at the Venus of Apelles.[4]

But the fear of not being approved as just copiers of human manners is not the most important concern that an author of this sort ought to have before him. These books are written chiefly to the young, the ignorant, and the idle, to whom they serve as lectures of conduct, and introductions into life. They are the entertainment of minds unfurnished with ideas, and therefore easily susceptible of impressions; not fixed by principles, and therefore easily following the current of fancy; not informed by experience, and consequently open to every false suggestion and partial account.

That the highest degree of reverence should be paid to youth, and that nothing indecent should be suffered to approach their eyes or ears, are precepts extorted by sense and virtue from an ancient writer by no means eminent for chastity of thought.[5] The same kind, though not the same degree, of caution, is required in everything which is laid before them, to secure

1. The technical term in neoclassical critical theory for the supernatural agents who intervene in human affairs in epic and tragedy.
2. Julius Caesar Scaliger (1484–1558) criticized the Latin poems of the Italian poet Jovianus Pontanus (1426–1503).
3. *Epistles* 2.1.170.
4. According to Pliny the Younger (*Naturalis His-*

toria 35.85), the Greek painter Apelles of Kos (4th century B.C.E.) corrected the drawing of a sandal after hearing a shoemaker criticize it as faulty, but when the flattered artisan dared to find fault with the drawing of a leg, the artist bade him "stick to his last."
5. Juvenal's *Satires* 14.1–58.

them from unjust prejudices, perverse opinions, and incongruous combinations of images.

In the romances formerly written, every transaction and sentiment was so remote from all that passes among men that the reader was in very little danger of making any applications to himself; the virtues and crimes were equally beyond his sphere of activity; and he amused himself with heroes and with traitors, deliverers and persecutors, as with beings of another species, whose actions were regulated upon motives of their own, and who had neither faults nor excellencies in common with himself.

But when an adventurer is leveled with the rest of the world, and acts in such scenes of the universal drama as may be the lot of any other man, young spectators fix their eyes upon him with closer attention, and hope, by observing his behavior and success, to regulate their own practices when they shall be engaged in the like part.

For this reason these familiar histories may perhaps be made of greater use than the solemnities of professed morality, and convey the knowledge of vice and virtue with more efficacy than axioms and definitions. But if the power of example is so great as to take possession of the memory by a kind of violence, and produce effects almost without the intervention of the will, care ought to be taken that when the choice is unrestrained, the best examples only should be exhibited; and that which is likely to operate so strongly should not be mischievous or uncertain in its effects.

The chief advantage which these fictions have over real life is that their authors are at liberty, though not to invent, yet to select objects, and to cull from the mass of mankind those individuals upon which the attention ought most to be employed; as a diamond, though it cannot be made, may be polished by art, and placed in such situation as to display that luster which before was buried among common stones.

It is justly considered as the greatest excellency of art to imitate nature; but it is necessary to distinguish those parts of nature which are most proper for imitation: greater care is still required in representing life, which is so often discolored by passion or deformed by wickedness. If the world be promiscuously[6] described, I cannot see of what use it can be to read the account; or why it may not be as safe to turn the eye immediately upon mankind as upon a mirror which shows all that presents itself without discrimination.

It is therefore not a sufficient vindication of a character that it is drawn as it appears, for many characters ought never to be drawn; nor of a narrative that the train of events is agreeable to observation and experience, for that observation which is called knowledge of the world will be found much more frequently to make men cunning than good. The purpose of these writings is surely not only to show mankind, but to provide that they may be seen hereafter with less hazard; to teach the means of avoiding the snares which are laid by Treachery for Innocence, without infusing any wish for that superiority with which the betrayer flatters his vanity; to give the power of counteracting fraud without the temptation to practice it; to initiate youth by mock encounters in the art of necessary defense, and to increase prudence without impairing virtue.

Many writers, for the sake of following nature, so mingle good and bad

6. Indiscriminately.

qualities in their principal personages that they are both equally conspicuous; and as we accompany them through their adventures with delight, and are led by degrees to interest ourselves in their favor, we lose the abhorrence of their faults because they do not hinder our pleasure, or perhaps regard them with some kindness for being united with so much merit.

There have been men indeed splendidly wicked, whose endowments threw a brightness on their crimes, and whom scarce any villainy made perfectly detestable because they never could be wholly divested of their excellencies; but such have been in all ages the great corrupters of the world, and their resemblance ought no more to be preserved than the art of murdering without pain.

Some have advanced, without due attention to the consequences of this notion, that certain virtues have their correspondent faults, and therefore that to exhibit either apart is to deviate from probability. Thus men are observed by Swift to be "grateful in the same degree as they are resentful." This principle, with others of the same kind, supposes man to act from a brute impulse, and pursue a certain degree of inclination without any choice of the object; for, otherwise, though it should be allowed that gratitude and resentment arise from the same constitution of the passions, it follows not that they will be equally indulged when reason is consulted; yet, unless that consequence be admitted, this sagacious maxim becomes an empty sound, without any relation to practice or to life.

Nor is it evident that even the first motions to these effects are always in the same proportion. For pride, which produces quickness of resentment, will obstruct gratitude by unwillingness to admit that inferiority which obligation implies; and it is very unlikely that he who cannot think he receives a favor will acknowledge or repay it.

It is of the utmost importance to mankind that positions of this tendency should be laid open and confuted; for while men consider good and evil as springing from the same root, they will spare the one for the sake of the other, and in judging, if not of others at least of themselves, will be apt to estimate their virtues by their vices. To this fatal error all those will contribute who confound the colors of right and wrong, and, instead of helping to settle their boundaries, mix them with so much art that no common mind is able to disunite them.

In narratives where historical veracity has no place, I cannot discover why there should not be exhibited the most perfect idea of virtue; of virtue not angelical, nor above probability (for what we cannot credit, we shall never imitate), but the highest and purest that humanity can reach, which, exercised in such trials as the various revolutions of things shall bring upon it, may, by conquering some calamities and enduring others, teach us what we may hope, and what we can perform. Vice (for vice is necessary to be shown) should always disgust; nor should the graces of gaiety, nor the dignity of courage, be so united with it as to reconcile it to the mind. Wherever it appears, it should raise hatred by the malignity of its practices, and contempt by the meanness of its stratagems: for while it is supported by either parts or spirit, it will be seldom heartily abhorred. The Roman tyrant was content to be hated if he was but feared;[7] and there are thousands of the readers of

7. The Emperor Tiberius (see Suetonius's *Lives of the Caesars*).

romances willing to be thought wicked if they may be allowed to be wits. It is therefore to be steadily inculcated that virtue is the highest proof of understanding, and the only solid basis of greatness; and that vice is the natural consequence of narrow thoughts; that it begins in mistake, and ends in ignominy.

Rambler No. 60

[BIOGRAPHY]

Saturday, October 13, 1750

—*Quid sit pulchrum, quid turpe, quid utile, quid non,*
Plenius ac melius Chrysippo et Crantore dicit.
—HORACE, *Epistles,* 1.2. 3–4

Whose works the beautiful and base contain,
Of vice and virtue more instructive rules,
Than all the sober sages of the schools.
—FRANCIS

All joy or sorrow for the happiness or calamities of others is produced by an act of the imagination, that realizes the event, however fictitious, or approximates it, however remote, by placing us, for a time, in the condition of him whose fortune we contemplate; so that we feel, while the deception lasts, whatever motions would be excited by the same good or evil happening to ourselves.

Our passions are therefore more strongly moved, in proportion as we can more readily adopt the pains or pleasure proposed to our minds, by recognizing them as once our own, or considering them as naturally incident to our state of life. It is not easy for the most artful writer to give us an interest in happiness or misery, which we think ourselves never likely to feel, and with which we have never yet been made acquainted. Histories of the downfall of kingdoms, and revolutions of empires, are read with great tranquility; the imperial tragedy pleases common auditors only by its pomp of ornament, and grandeur of ideas; and the man whose faculties have been engrossed by business, and whose heart never fluttered but at the rise or fall of stocks, wonders how the attention can be seized, or the affections agitated, by a tale of love.

Those parallel circumstances, and kindred images to which we readily conform our minds, are, above all other writings, to be found in narratives of the lives of particular persons; and therefore no species of writing seems more worthy of cultivation than biography, since none can be more delightful or more useful, none can more certainly enchain the heart by irresistible interest, or more widely diffuse instruction to every diversity of condition.

The general and rapid narratives of history, which involve a thousand fortunes in the business of a day, and complicate innumerable incidents in one great transaction, afford few lessons applicable to private life, which derives its comforts and its wretchedness from the right or wrong management of things, which nothing but their frequency makes considerable, *Parva si non fiunt quotidie,* says Pliny,[1] and which can have no place in those relations

---

1. Pliny the Younger's *Epistles* 3.1. Johnson translates the phrase in the preceding clause.

which never descend below the consultation of senates, the motions of armies, and the schemes of conspirators.

I have often thought that there has rarely passed a life of which a judicious and faithful narrative would not be useful. For, not only every man has in the mighty mass of the world great numbers in the same condition with himself, to whom his mistakes and miscarriages, escapes and expedients, would be of immediate and apparent use; but there is such an uniformity in the state of man, considered apart from adventitious and separable decorations and disguises, that there is scarce any possibility of good or ill, but is common to humankind. A great part of the time of those who are placed at the greatest distance by fortune, or by temper, must unavoidably pass in the same manner; and though, when the claims of nature are satisfied, caprice, and vanity, and accident, begin to produce discriminations and peculiarities, yet the eye is not very heedful or quick, which cannot discover the same causes still[2] terminating their influence in the same effects, though sometimes accelerated, sometimes retarded, or perplexed by multiplied combinations. We are all prompted by the same motives, all deceived by the same fallacies, all animated by hope, obstructed by danger, entangled by desire, and seduced by pleasure.

It is frequently objected to relations of particular lives, that they are not distinguished by any striking or wonderful vicissitudes. The scholar who passed his life among his books, the merchant who conducted only his own affairs, the priest whose sphere of action was not extended beyond that of his duty, are considered as no proper objects of public regard, however they might have excelled in their several stations, whatever might have been their learning, integrity, and piety. But this notion arises from false measures of excellence and dignity, and must be eradicated by considering, that in the esteem of uncorrupted reason, what is of most use is of most value.

It is, indeed, not improper to take honest advantages of prejudice, and to gain attention by a celebrated name; but the business of the biographer is often to pass slightly over those performances and incidents, which produce vulgar greatness, to lead the thoughts into domestic privacies, and display the minute details of daily life, where exterior appendages are cast aside, and men excel each other only by prudence and by virtue. The account of Thuanus[3] is, with great propriety, said by its author to have been written, that it might lay open to posterity the private and familiar character of that man, *cujus ingenium et candorem ex ipsius scriptis sunt olim semper miraturi,* whose candor and genius will to the end of time be by his writings preserved in admiration.

There are many invisible circumstances which, whether we read as inquirers after natural or moral knowledge, whether we intend to enlarge our science, or increase our virtue, are more important than public occurrences. Thus Sallust, the great master of nature, has not forgot, in his account of Catiline,[4] to remark that *his walk was now quick, and again slow,* as an indication of a mind revolving something with violent commotion. Thus the story of Melancthon[5] affords a striking lecture on the value of time, by informing

---

2. Always.
3. Jacques-Auguste de Thou (1553–1617), an important French historian, of whom Nicholas Rigault wrote a brief biography, a sentence of which Johnson quotes and translates below.

4. Sallust, a Roman historian of the 1st century B.C.E., wrote an account of Catiline's conspiracy against the Roman state.
5. Camerarius wrote a life of Melancthon, a German theologian of the 16th century.

us that when he made an appointment, he expected not only the hour, but the minute to be fixed, that the day might not run out in the idleness of suspense; and all the plans and enterprises of De Witt are now of less importance to the world, than that part of his personal character, which represents him as careful of his health, and negligent of his life.[6]

But biography has often been allotted to writers who seem very little acquainted with the nature of their task, or very negligent about the performance. They rarely afford any other account than might be collected from public papers, but imagine themselves writing a life when they exhibit a chronological series of actions or preferments; and so little regard the manners or behavior of their heroes, that more knowledge may be gained of a man's real character, by a short conversation with one of his servants, than from a formal and studied narrative, begun with his pedigree, and ended with his funeral.

If now and then they condescend to inform the world of particular facts, they are not always so happy as to select the most important. I know not well what advantage posterity can receive from the only circumstance by which Tickell has distinguished Addison from the rest of mankind, the irregularity of his pulse:[7] nor can I think myself overpaid for the time spent in reading the life of Malherbe, by being enabled to relate, after the learned biographer,[8] that Malherbe had two predominant opinions; one, that the looseness of a single woman might destroy all her boast of ancient descent; the other, that the French beggars made use very improperly and barbarously of the phrase *noble gentleman,* because either word included the sense of both.

There are, indeed, some natural reasons why these narratives are often written by such as were not likely to give much instruction or delight, and why most accounts of particular persons are barren and useless. If a life be delayed till interest and envy are at an end, we may hope for impartiality, but must expect little intelligence;[9] for the incidents which give excellence to biography are of a volatile and evanescent kind, such as soon escape the memory, and are rarely transmitted by tradition. We know how few can portray a living acquaintance, except by his most prominent and observable particularities, and the grosser features of his mind; and it may be easily imagined how much of this little knowledge may be lost in imparting it, and how soon a succession of copies will lose all resemblance of the original.

If the biographer writes from personal knowledge, and makes haste to gratify the public curiosity, there is danger lest his interest, his fear, his gratitude, or his tenderness, overpower his fidelity, and tempt him to conceal, if not to invent. There are many who think it an act of piety to hide the faults or failings of their friends, even when they can no longer suffer by their detection; we therefore see whole ranks of characters adorned with uniform panegyric, and not to be known from one another, but by extrinsic and casual circumstances. "Let me remember," says Hale, "when I find myself inclined to pity a criminal, that there is likewise a pity due to the country."[1] If we owe regard to the memory of the dead, there is yet more respect to be paid to knowledge, to virtue, and to truth.

---

6. Sir William Temple, characterizing the Dutch statesman John De Witt.
7. From Thomas Tickell's preface to Addision's *Works* (1721).
8. The life of the French poet François de Mal-

herbe (1555–1628) was written by Honorat de Racan.
9. Information.
1. From Gilbert Burnet's *Life and Death of Sir Matthew Hale* (1682).

A Dictionary of the English Language

Before Johnson, no standard dictionary of the English language existed. The lack had troubled speakers of English for some time, both because Italian and French academies had produced major dictionaries of their own tongues and because, in the absence of any authority, English seemed likely to change utterly from one generation to another. Many eighteenth-century authors feared that their own language would soon become obsolete: as Alexander Pope wrote in *An Essay on Criticism*,

> Our sons their fathers' failing language see,
> And such as Chaucer is, shall Dryden be.

A dictionary could help retard such change, and commercially it would be a book that everyone would need to buy. In 1746 a group of London publishers commissioned Johnson, still an unknown author, to undertake the project. He hoped to finish it in three years; it took him nine. But the quantity and quality of work he accomplished, aided only by six part-time assistants, made him famous as "Dictionary Johnson." The *Dictionary* remained a standard reference book for one hundred years.

Johnson's achievement is notable in three respects: its size (forty thousand words), the wealth of illustrative quotations, and the excellence of the definitions. No earlier English dictionary rivaled the scope of Johnson's two large folio volumes. About 114,000 quotations, gathered from the best English writers from Sidney to the eighteenth century, exemplify the usage of words as well as their meanings. Above all, it was the definitions, however, that established the authority of Johnson's *Dictionary*. A small selection is only too likely to concentrate on a few amusing or notorious definitions, but the great majority are full, clear, and totally free from eccentricity. Indeed, many of them are still repeated in modern dictionaries. Language, Johnson knew, cannot be fixed once and for all; many of the words he defines have radically changed meaning since the eighteenth century. Yet Johnson did more than any person of his time to preserve the ideal of a standard English.

From A Dictionary of the English Language

From *Preface*

* * *

A large work is difficult because it is large, even though all its parts might singly be performed with facility; where there are many things to be done, each must be allowed its share of time and labor, in the proportion only which it bears to the whole; nor can it be expected that the stones which form the dome of a temple should be squared and polished like the diamond of a ring.

Of the event of this work, for which, having labored it with so much application, I cannot but have some degree of parental fondness, it is natural to form conjectures. Those who have been persuaded to think well of my design will require that it should fix our language, and put a stop to those alterations which time and chance have hitherto been suffered to make in it without opposition. With this consequence I will confess that I flattered myself for a while;[1] but now begin to fear that I have indulged expectation which neither

---

1. Johnson's *Plan* (1747) had called for "a dictionary by which the pronunciation of our language may be fixed, and its attainment facilitated; by which its purity may be preserved, its use ascertained, and its duration lengthened."

reason nor experience can justify. When we see men grow old and die at a certain time one after another, from century to century, we laugh at the elixir that promises to prolong life to a thousand years; and with equal justice may the lexicographer be derided, who being able to produce no example of a nation that has preserved their words and phrases from mutability, shall imagine that his dictionary can embalm his language and secure it from corruption and decay, that it is in his power to change sublunary nature, or clear the world at once from folly, vanity, and affectation.

With this hope, however, academies have been instituted, to guard the avenues of their languages, to retain fugitives, and repulse intruders; but their vigilance and activity have hitherto been vain; sounds are too volatile and subtle for legal restraints; to enchain syllables, and to lash the wind, are equally the undertakings of pride, unwilling to measure its desires by its strength. The French language has visibly changed under the inspection of the academy;[2] the style of Amelot's translation of father Paul is observed by Le Courayer to be *un peu passé;*[3] and no Italian will maintain that the diction of any modern writer is not perceptibly different from that of Boccace, Machiavel, or Caro.[4]

Total and sudden transformations of a language seldom happen; conquests and migrations are now very rare: but there are other causes of change, which, though slow in their operation, and invisible in their progress, are perhaps as much superior to human resistance as the revolutions of the sky, or intumescence[5] of the tide. Commerce, however necessary, however lucrative, as it depraves the manners, corrupts the language; they that have frequent intercourse with strangers, to whom they endeavor to accommodate themselves, must in time learn a mingled dialect, like the jargon which serves the traffickers[6] on the Mediterranean and Indian coasts. This will not always be confined to the exchange, the warehouse, or the port, but will be communicated by degrees to other ranks of the people, and be at last incorporated with the current speech.

There are likewise internal causes equally forcible. The language most likely to continue long without alteration would be that of a nation raised a little, and but a little, above barbarity, secluded from strangers, and totally employed in procuring the conveniencies of life; either without books, or, like some of the Mahometan countries, with very few: men thus busied and unlearned, having only such words as common use requires, would perhaps long continue to express the same notions by the same signs. But no such constancy can be expected in a people polished by arts, and classed by subordination, where one part of the community is sustained and accommodated by the labor of the other. Those who have much leisure to think, will always be enlarging the stock of ideas, and every increase of knowledge, whether real or fancied, will produce new words, or combinations of words. When the mind is unchained from necessity, it will range after convenience;

2. The French academy, founded to purify the French language, had produced a dictionary in 1694; but revisions were necessary within a few years.
3. A bit old-fashioned (French). Le Courayer's translation (1736) of Father Paolo Sarpi's *History of the Council of Trent* superseded Amelot's (1683).

4. Like Boccaccio (1313–1375) and Machiavelli (1469–1527), Annibale Caro (1507–1566) was a classic Italian stylist whose work had preceded the dictionary published in 1612 by the Italian academy.
5. Swelling.
6. Traders.

when it is left at large in the fields of speculation, it will shift opinions; as any custom is disused, the words that expressed it must perish with it; as any opinion grows popular, it will innovate speech in the same proportion as it alters practice.

As by the cultivation of various sciences, a language is amplified, it will be more furnished with words deflected from their original sense; the geometrician will talk of a courtier's zenith, or the eccentric virtue of a wild hero, and the physician of sanguine expectations and phlegmatic delays.[7] Copiousness of speech will give opportunities to capricious choice, by which some words will be preferred, and others degraded; vicissitudes of fashion will enforce the use of new, or extend the signification of known terms. The tropes[8] of poetry will make hourly encroachments, and the metaphorical will become the current sense: pronunciation will be varied by levity or ignorance, and the pen must at length comply with the tongue; illiterate writers will at one time or other, by public infatuation, rise into renown, who, not knowing the original import of words, will use them with colloquial licentiousness, confound distinction, and forget propriety. As politeness increases, some expressions will be considered as too gross and vulgar for the delicate, others as too formal and ceremonious for the gay and airy; new phrases are therefore adopted, which must, for the same reasons, be in time dismissed. Swift, in his petty treatise on the English language,[9] allows that new words must sometimes be introduced, but proposes that none should be suffered to become obsolete. But what makes a word obsolete, more than general agreement to forbear it? and how shall it be continued, when it conveys an offensive idea, or recalled again into the mouths of mankind, when it has once by disuse become unfamiliar, and by unfamiliarity unpleasing.

There is another cause of alteration more prevalent than any other, which yet in the present state of the world cannot be obviated. A mixture of two languages will produce a third distinct from both, and they will always be mixed, where the chief part of education, and the most conspicuous accomplishment, is skill in ancient or in foreign tongues. He that has long cultivated another language, will find its words and combinations crowd upon his memory; and haste or negligence, refinement or affectation, will obtrude borrowed terms and exotic expressions.

The great pest of speech is frequency of translation. No book was ever turned from one language into another, without imparting something of its native idiom; this is the most mischievous and comprehensive innovation; single words may enter by thousands, and the fabric of the tongue continue the same, but new phraseology changes much at once; it alters not the single stones of the building, but the order[1] of the columns. If an academy should be established for the cultivation of our style, which I, who can never wish to see dependence multiplied, hope the spirit of English liberty will hinder or destroy, let them, instead of compiling grammars and dictionaries, endeavor with all their influence to stop the license of translators, whose

---

7. "Sanguine" and "phlegmatic" once referred only to the physiological predominance of blood or phlegm. "Zenith" (the point of the sky directly overhead) and "eccentric" (deviating from the center) were originally astronomical and geometrical terms.

8. "A change of a word from its original significa- tion" (Johnson's *Dictionary*).
9. *A Proposal for Correcting, Improving, and Ascertaining the English Tongue* (1712). "Petty": little.
1. Architectural mode (Doric, etc.), which determines the style and proportions of columns.

idleness and ignorance, if it be suffered to proceed, will reduce us to babble a dialect of France.

If the changes that we fear be thus irresistible, what remains but to acquiesce with silence, as in the other insurmountable distresses of humanity? It remains that we retard what we cannot repel, that we palliate what we cannot cure. Life may be lengthened by care, though death cannot be ultimately defeated: tongues, like governments, have a natural tendency to degeneration; we have long preserved our constitution, let us make some struggles for our language.

In hope of giving longevity to that which its own nature forbids to be immortal, I have devoted this book, the labor of years, to the honor of my country, that we may no longer yield the palm of philology without a contest to the nations of the continent. The chief glory of every people arises from its authors: whether I shall add anything by my own writings to the reputation of English literature, must be left to time. Much of my life has been lost under the pressures of disease; much has been trifled away; and much has always been spent in provision for the day that was passing over me; but I shall not think my employment useless or ignoble, if by my assistance foreign nations, and distant ages, gain access to the propagators of knowledge, and understand the teachers of truth; if my labors afford light to the repositories of science, and add celebrity to Bacon, to Hooker, to Milton, and to Boyle.[2]

When I am animated by this wish, I look with pleasure on my book, however defective; and deliver it to the world with the spirit of a man that has endeavored well. That it will immediately become popular I have not promised to myself: a few wild blunders and risible absurdities, from which no work of such multiplicity was ever free, may for a time furnish folly with laughter, and harden ignorance in contempt; but useful diligence will at last prevail, and there never can be wanting some who distinguish desert;[3] who will consider that no dictionary of a living tongue ever can be perfect, since while it is hastening to publication, some words are budding, and some falling away; that a whole life cannot be spent upon syntax and etymology, and that even a whole life would not be sufficient; that he, whose design includes whatever language can express, must often speak of what he does not understand; that a writer will sometimes be hurried by eagerness to the end, and sometimes faint with weariness under a task, which Scaliger compares to the labors of the anvil and the mine;[4] that what is obvious is not always known, and what is known is not always present; that sudden fits of inadvertency will surprise vigilance, slight avocations[5] will reduce attention, and casual eclipses of the mind will darken learning; and that the writer shall often in vain trace his memory at the moment of need, for that which yesterday he knew with intuitive readiness, and which will come uncalled into his thoughts tomorrow.

In this work, when it shall be found that much is omitted, let it not be forgotten that much likewise is performed; and though no book was ever spared out of tenderness to the author, and the world is little solicitous to

---

2. Leading physicist and chemist (1627–1691). "Science": knowledge. Richard Hooker wrote *The Laws of Ecclesiastical Polity* (1594–97), a famous defense of the Church of England.
3. Merit.

4. Joseph Justus Scaliger (1540–1609), a great scholar and lexicographer, wrote Latin verses suggesting that criminals should be condemned to lexicography.
5. Whatever calls one aside.

know whence proceeded the faults of that which it condemns; yet it may gratify curiosity to inform it, that the *English Dictionary* was written with little assistance of the learned, and without any patronage of the great;[6] not in the soft obscurities of retirement, or under the shelter of academic bowers, but amidst inconvenience and distraction, in sickness and in sorrow: and it may repress the triumph of malignant criticism to observe, that if our language is not here fully displayed, I have only failed in an attempt which no human powers have hitherto completed. If the lexicons of ancient tongues, now immutably fixed, and comprised in a few volumes, be yet, after the toil of successive ages, inadequate and delusive; if the aggregated knowledge and cooperating diligence of the Italian academicians did not secure them from the censure of Beni;[7] if the embodied critics of France, when fifty years had been spent upon their work, were obliged to change its economy,[8] and give their second edition another form, I may surely be contented without the praise of perfection, which, if I could obtain, in this gloom of solitude, what would it avail me? I have protracted my work till most of those whom I wished to please have sunk into the grave,[9] and success and miscarriage are empty sounds: I therefore dismiss it with frigid tranquility, having little to fear or hope from censure or from praise.

[SOME DEFINITIONS: A SMALL ANTHOLOGY][1]

ANTHO′LOGY. *n.*

1. A collection of flowers.

To CANT. *v.*

   To talk in the jargon of particular professions, or in any kind of formal affected language, or with a peculiar and studied tone of voice.

>   Men *cant* endlessly about *materia forma;* and hunt chimeras by rules of art, or dress up ignorance in words of bulk or sound, which may stop up the mouth of inquiry.—*Glanville's Scepsis Scientifica.*

ENTHU′SIASM. *n.*

1. A vain belief of private revelation; a vain confidence of divine favor or communication.

>   *Enthusiasm* is founded neither on reason nor divine revelation, but rises from the conceits of a warmed or overweening brain.—*Locke.*

GE′NIUS. *n.*

1. The protecting or ruling power of men, places, or things.

>   And as I awake, sweet music breathe,
>   Sent by some spirit to mortals good,
>   Or th' unseen *genius* of the wood.—*Milton.*

2. A man endowed with superior faculties.

3. Mental power or faculties.

4. Disposition of nature by which anyone is qualified for some peculiar employment.

5. Nature; disposition.

---

6. See Johnson's letter to Lord Chesterfield in Boswell's *Life of Johnson* (p. 1277).
7. Paolo Beni's *L'Anticrusca* (1612) violently attacked the first edition of the *Vocabolario* (the Italian dictionary).

8. Organization.
9. Johnson's wife had died three years earlier.
1. Johnson's definitions include etymologies and illustrative quotations, some of which are omitted in this selection.

IMA'GINATION. *n.*

1. Fancy; the power of forming ideal pictures; the power of representing things absent to one's self or others.

2. Conception; image in the mind; idea.

3. Contrivance; scheme.

LEXICO'GRAPHER. *n.*

A writer of dictionaries; a harmless drudge, that busies himself in tracing the original, and detailing the signification of words.

MELANCHO'LY. *n.*

1. A disease, supposed to proceed from a redundance of black bile.

2. A kind of madness, in which the mind is always fixed on one object.

3. A gloomy, pensive, discontented temper.

NA'TURE. *n.*

1. An imaginary being supposed to preside over the material and animal world.

> Thou, *nature*, art my goddess; to thy law
> My services are bound.—*Shakespeare.*

2. The native state or properties of anything, by which it is discriminated from others.

3. The constitution of an animated body.

4. Disposition of mind; temper.

5. The regular course of things.

6. The compass of natural existence.

7. Natural affection, or reverence; native sensations.

8. The state or operation of the material world.

9. Sort; species.

10. Sentiments or images adapted to nature, or comformable to truth and reality.

11. Physics; the science which teaches the qualities of things.

> *Nature* and *nature's* laws lay hid in night,
> God said, Let Newton be, and all was light.—*Pope.*

NE'TWORK. *n.*

Anything reticulated or decussated, at equal distances, with interstices between the intersections.

OATS. *n.*

A grain, which in England is generally given to horses, but in Scotland supports the people.

PA'STERN. *n.*

1. The knee of an horse.[2]

PA'TRON. *n.*

1. One who countenances, supports, or protects. Commonly a wretch who supports with insolence, and is paid with flattery.

PE'NSION. *n.*

An allowance made to anyone without an equivalent. In England it is generally understood to mean pay given to a state hireling for treason to his country.[3]

---

2. "A lady once asked him how he came to define *Pastern* the *knee* of a horse: instead of making an elaborate defense, as she expected, he at once answered, 'Ignorance, Madam, pure ignorance' " (Boswell).

3. In 1762 Johnson was awarded a pension, but he did not revise the definition in later editions.

SA'TIRE. *n.*

A poem in which wickedness or folly is censured. Proper *satire* is distinguished, by the generality of the reflections, from a *lampoon,* which is aimed against a particular person; but they are too frequently confounded.

TO'RY. *n.*

One who adheres to the ancient constitution of the state, and the apostolical hierarchy of the church of England, opposed to a whig.

The knight is more a *tory* in the country than the town, because it
more advances his interest.—*Addison.*

WHIG. *n.*

2. The name of a faction.

Whoever has a true value for church and state, should avoid the
extremes of *whig* for the sake of the former, and the extremes of tory on
the account of the latter.—*Swift.*

WIT. *n.*

1. The powers of the mind; the mental faculties; the intellects. This is the original signification.
2. Imagination; quickness of fancy.
3. Sentiments produced by quickness of fancy.
4. A man of fancy.
5. A man of genius.
6. Sense; judgment.
7. In the plural. Sound mind; intellect not crazed.
8. Contrivance; stratagem; power of expedients.

1755

The Preface to Shakespeare   This is the finest piece of Shakespeare criticism in the eighteenth century; it culminates a critical tradition that began with John Dryden's remarks on Shakespeare and continued as the plays were edited by Nicholas Rowe, Alexander Pope, Lewis Theobald, and William Warburton. Johnson addresses the standard topics: Shakespeare is the poet of nature, not learning; the creator of characters who spring to life; and a writer whose works express the full range of human passions. But the *Preface* also takes a fresh look not only at the plays but at the first principles of criticism. Resisting "bardolatry"—uncritical worship of Shakespeare—Johnson points out his faults as well as his virtues, yet finds that his truth to life, or "just representations of general nature," surpasses that of all other modern writers. The *Preface* is most original when it attacks the long-standing critical reverence for the unities of time and place. What seems real on the stage, Johnson argues, does not depend on artificial rules but on what the mind is willing to imagine.

Johnson's edition of Shakespeare also contained footnotes and brief introductions to each of the plays. Reprinted here are his afterwords on *Twelfth Night* and *King Lear.*

From The Preface to Shakespeare

[SHAKESPEARE'S EXCELLENCE. GENERAL NATURE]

That praises are without reason lavished on the dead, and that the honors due only to excellence are paid to antiquity, is a complaint likely to be always continued by those who, being able to add nothing to truth, hope for eminence from the heresies of paradox; or those who, being forced by disappointment upon consolatory expedients, are willing to hope from posterity what the present age refuses, and flatter themselves that the regard which is yet denied by envy will be at last bestowed by time.

Antiquity, like every other quality that attracts the notice of mankind, has undoubtedly votaries that reverence it not from reason but from prejudice. Some seem to admire indiscriminately whatever has been long preserved, without considering that time has sometimes cooperated with chance; all perhaps are more willing to honor past than present excellence; and the mind contemplates genius through the shades of age, as the eye surveys the sun through artificial opacity. The great contention of criticism is to find the faults of the moderns and the beauties of the ancients. While an author is yet living we estimate his powers by his worst performance; and when he is dead we rate them by his best.

To works, however, of which the excellence is not absolute and definite, but gradual and comparative; to works not raised upon principles demonstrative and scientific, but appealing wholly to observation and experience, no other test can be applied than length of duration and continuance of esteem. What mankind have long possessed they have often examined and compared; and if they persist to value the possession, it is because frequent comparisons have confirmed opinion in its favor. As among the works of nature no man can properly call a river deep or a mountain high, without the knowledge of many mountains and many rivers; so in the productions of genius, nothing can be styled excellent till it has been compared with other works of the same kind. Demonstration[1] immediately displays its power and has nothing to hope or fear from the flux of years; but works tentative and experimental must be estimated by their proportion to the general and collective ability of man, as it is discovered in a long succession of endeavors. Of the first building that was raised, it might be with certainty determined that it was round or square, but whether it was spacious or lofty must have been referred to time. The Pythagorean scale of numbers[2] was at once discovered to be perfect; but the poems of Homer we yet know not to transcend the common limits of human intelligence, but by remarking that nation after nation, and century after century, has been able to do little more than transpose his incidents, new name his characters, and paraphrase his sentiments.

The reverence due to writings that have long subsisted arises, therefore, not from any credulous confidence in the superior wisdom of past ages, or gloomy persuasion of the degeneracy of mankind, but is the consequence of acknowledged and indubitable positions, that what has been longest known has been most considered, and what is most considered is best understood.

The poet of whose works I have undertaken the revision may now begin to assume the dignity of an ancient and claim the privilege of established fame and prescriptive veneration. He has long outlived his century, the term commonly fixed as the test of literary merit.[3] Whatever advantages he might once derive from personal allusions, local customs, or temporary opinions, have for many years been lost; and every topic of merriment or motive of sorrow which the modes of artificial life afforded him now only obscure the

1. "The highest degree of deducible or argumental evidence" (Johnson's *Dictionary*).
2. Pythagoras discovered the ratios that determine the principal intervals of the musical scale.
3. Horace's *Epistles* 2.1.39.

scenes which they once illuminated. The effects of favor and competition are at an end; the tradition of his friendships and his enmities has perished; his works support no opinion with arguments nor supply any faction with invectives; they can neither indulge vanity nor gratify malignity; but are read without any other reason than the desire of pleasure, and are therefore praised only as pleasure is obtained; yet, thus unassisted by interest or passion, they have passed through variations of taste and changes of manners, and, as they devolved from one generation to another, have received new honors at every transmission.

But because human judgment, though it be gradually gaining upon certainty, never becomes infallible, and approbation, though long continued, may yet be only the approbation of prejudice or fashion, it is proper to inquire by what peculiarities of excellence Shakespeare has gained and kept the favor of his countrymen.

Nothing can please many, and please long, but just representations of general nature. Particular manners can be known to few, and therefore few only can judge how nearly they are copied. The irregular combinations of fanciful invention may delight awhile by that novelty of which the common satiety of life sends us all in quest; but the pleasures of sudden wonder are soon exhausted, and the mind can only repose on the stability of truth.

Shakespeare is, above all writers, at least above all modern writers, the poet of nature, the poet that holds up to his readers a faithful mirror of manners and of life. His characters are not modified by the customs of particular places, unpracticed by the rest of the world; by the peculiarities of studies or professions, which can operate but upon small numbers; or by the accidents of transient fashions or temporary opinions: they are the genuine progeny of common humanity, such as the world will always supply and observation will always find. His persons act and speak by the influence of those general passions and principles by which all minds are agitated and the whole system of life is continued in motion. In the writings of other poets a character is too often an individual: in those of Shakespeare it is commonly a species.

It is from this wide extension of design that so much instruction is derived. It is this which fills the plays of Shakespeare with practical axioms and domestic wisdom. It was said of Euripides[4] that every verse was a precept; and it may be said of Shakespeare that from his works may be collected a system of civil and economical prudence. Yet his real power is not shown in the splendor of particular passages, but by the progress of his fable[5] and the tenor of his dialogue; and he that tries to recommend him by select quotations will succeed like the pedant in Hierocles[6] who, when he offered his house to sale, carried a brick in his pocket as a specimen.

It will not easily be imagined how much Shakespeare excels in accommodating his sentiments to real life but by comparing him with other authors. It was observed of the ancient schools of declamation that the more diligently they were frequented, the more was the student disqualified for the world, because he found nothing there which he should ever meet in any other

4. The Greek tragic poet (ca. 480–406 B.C.E.). The observation is Cicero's.
5. Plot. "The series or contexture of events which constitute a poem epic or dramatic" (Johnson's Dictionary).
6. Hierocles of Alexandria, a Greek philosopher of the 5th century C.E.

place. The same remark may be applied to every stage but that of Shakespeare. The theater, when it is under any other direction, is peopled by such characters as were never seen, conversing in a language which was never heard, upon topics which will never arise in the commerce of mankind. But the dialogue of this author is often so evidently determined by the incident which produces it, and is pursued with so much ease and simplicity, that it seems scarcely to claim the merit of fiction, but to have been gleaned by diligent selection out of common conversation and common occurrences.

Upon every other stage the universal agent is love, by whose power all good and evil is distributed and every action quickened or retarded. To bring a lover, a lady, and a rival into the fable; to entangle them in contradictory obligations, perplex them with oppositions of interest, and harass them with violence of desires inconsistent with each other; to make them meet in rapture, and part in agony; to fill their mouths with hyperbolical joy and outrageous sorrow; to distress them as nothing human ever was distressed; to deliver them as nothing human ever was delivered, is the business of a modern dramatist. For this, probability is violated, life is misrepresented, and language is depraved. But love is only one of many passions; and as it has no great influence upon the sum of life, it has little operation in the dramas of a poet who caught his ideas from the living world and exhibited only what he saw before him. He knew that any other passion, as it was regular or exorbitant, was a cause of happiness or calamity.

Characters thus ample and general were not easily discriminated and preserved; yet perhaps no poet ever kept his personages more distinct from each other. I will not say with Pope that every speech may be assigned to the proper speaker,[7] because many speeches there are which have nothing characteristical; but perhaps though some may be equally adapted to every person, it will be difficult to find that any can be properly transferred from the present possessor to another claimant. The choice is right when there is reason for choice.

Other dramatists can only gain attention by hyperbolical or aggravated characters, by fabulous and unexampled excellence or depravity, as the writers of barbarous romances invigorated the reader by a giant and a dwarf; and he that should form his expectations of human affairs from the play or from the tale would be equally deceived. Shakespeare has no heroes; his scenes are occupied only by men, who act and speak as the reader thinks that he should himself have spoken or acted on the same occasion; even where the agency is supernatural, the dialogue is level with life. Other writers disguise the most natural passions and most frequent incidents so that he who contemplates them in the book will not know them in the world: Shakespeare approximates[8] the remote, and familiarizes the wonderful; the event which he represents will not happen, but, if it were possible, its effects would probably be such as he has assigned; and it may be said that he has not only shown human nature as it acts in real exigencies, but as it would be found in trials to which it cannot be exposed.

This therefore is the praise of Shakespeare, that his drama is the mirror of life; that he who has mazed his imagination in following the phantoms

---

7. In the preface to his edition of Shakespeare's plays (1725).

8. Brings near.

which other writers raise up before him, may here be cured of his delirious ecstasies by reading human sentiments in human language, by scenes from which a hermit may estimate the transactions of the world, and a confessor predict the progress of the passions.

[SHAKESPEARE'S FAULTS. THE THREE DRAMATIC UNITIES]

Shakespeare with his excellencies has likewise faults, and faults sufficient to obscure and overwhelm any other merit. I shall show them in the proportion in which they appear to me, without envious malignity or superstitious veneration. No question can be more innocently discussed than a dead poet's pretensions to renown; and little regard is due to that bigotry which sets candor[9] higher than truth.

His first defect is that to which may be imputed most of the evil in books or in men. He sacrifices virtue to convenience, and is so much more careful to please than to instruct that he seems to write without any moral purpose. From his writings indeed a system of social duty may be selected, for he that thinks reasonably must think morally, but his precepts and axioms drop casually from him; he makes no just distribution of good or evil, nor is always careful to show in the virtuous a disapprobation of the wicked; he carries his persons indifferently through right and wrong, and at the close dismisses them without further care, and leaves their examples to operate by chance. This fault the barbarity of his age cannot extenuate; for it is always a writer's duty to make the world better, and justice is a virtue independent on time or place.

The plots are often so loosely formed that a very slight consideration may improve them, and so carelessly pursued that he seems not always fully to comprehend his own design. He omits opportunities of instructing or delighting which the train of his story seems to force upon him, and apparently rejects those exhibitions which would be more affecting for the sake of those which are more easy.

It may be observed that in many of his plays the latter part is evidently neglected. When he found himself near the end of his work, and in view of his reward, he shortened the labor to snatch the profit. He therefore remits his efforts where he should most vigorously exert them, and his catastrophe is improbably produced or imperfectly represented.

He had no regard to distinction of time or place, but gives to one age or nation, without scruple, the customs, institutions, and opinions of another, at the expense not only of likelihood but of possibility. These faults Pope has endeavored, with more zeal than judgment, to transfer to his imagined interpolators. We need not wonder to find Hector quoting Aristotle, when we see the loves of Theseus and Hippolyta combined with the Gothic mythology of fairies.[1] Shakespeare, indeed, was not the only violator of chronology, for in the same age Sidney, who wanted not the advantages of learning, has, in his *Arcadia*, confounded the pastoral with the feudal times, the days of innocence, quiet, and security with those of turbulence, violence, and adventure.

In his comic scenes he is seldom very successful when he engages his

---

9. Kindness.
1. In *Troilus and Cressida* 2.2.166 and in *Midsummer Night's Dream*, respectively.

characters in reciprocations of smartness and contests of sarcasm; their jests are commonly gross, and their pleasantry licentious; neither his gentlemen nor his ladies have much delicacy, nor are sufficiently distinguished from his clowns by any appearance of refined manners. Whether he represented the real conversation of his time is not easy to determine: the reign of Elizabeth is commonly supposed to have been a time of stateliness, formality, and reserve; yet perhaps the relaxations of that severity were not very elegant. There must, however, have been always some modes of gaiety preferable to others, and a writer ought to choose the best.

In tragedy his performance seems constantly to be worse as his labor is more. The effusions of passion, which exigence forces out, are for the most part striking and energetic; but whenever he solicits his invention, or strains his faculties, the offspring of his throes is tumor,[2] meanness, tediousness, and obscurity.

In narration he affects a disproportionate pomp of diction and a wearisome train of circumlocution, and tells the incident imperfectly in many words which might have been more plainly delivered in few. Narration in dramatic poetry is naturally tedious, as it is unanimated and inactive, and obstructs the progress of the action; it should therefore always be rapid and enlivened by frequent interruption. Shakespeare found it an encumbrance, and instead of lightening it by brevity, endeavored to recommend it by dignity and splendor.

His declamations or set speeches are commonly cold and weak, for his power was the power of nature; when he endeavored, like other tragic writers, to catch opportunities of amplification and, instead of inquiring what the occasion demanded, to show how much his stores of knowledge could supply, he seldom escapes without the pity or resentment of his reader.

It is incident to him to be now and then entangled with an unwieldy sentiment which he cannot well express, and will not reject; he struggles with it awhile, and, if it continues stubborn, comprises it in words such as occur, and leaves it to be disentangled and evolved[3] by those who have more leisure to bestow upon it.

Not that always where the language is intricate the thought is subtle, or the image always great where the line is bulky; the equality of words to things is very often neglected, and trivial sentiments and vulgar[4] ideas disappoint the attention, to which they are recommended by sonorous epithets and swelling figures.

But the admirers of this great poet have most reason to complain when he approaches nearest to his highest excellence, and seems fully resolved to sink them in dejection and mollify them with tender emotions by the fall of greatness, the danger of innocence, or the crosses of love. What he does best, he soon ceases to do. He is not long soft and pathetic without some idle conceit or contemptible equivocation. He no sooner begins to move than he counteracts himself; and terror and pity, as they are rising in the mind, are checked and blasted by sudden frigidity.

A quibble[5] is to Shakespeare what luminous vapors are to the traveler: he follows it at all adventures; it is sure to lead him out of his way, and sure to

---

2. Inflated grandeur, false magnificence.
3. Unfolded.
4. "Mean; low; being of the common rate" (Johnson's *Dictionary*).
5. Pun.

engulf him in the mire. It has some malignant power over his mind, and its fascinations are irresistible. Whatever be the dignity or profundity of his disquisitions, whether he be enlarging knowledge or exalting affection, whether he be amusing[6] attention with incidents, or enchaining it in suspense, let but a quibble spring up before him, and he leaves his work unfinished. A quibble is the golden apple for which he will always turn aside from his career[7] or stoop from his elevation. A quibble, poor and barren as it is, gave him such delight that he was content to purchase it by the sacrifice of reason, propriety, and truth. A quibble was to him the fatal Cleopatra for which he lost the world, and was content to lose it.

It will be thought strange that in enumerating the defects of this writer, I have not yet mentioned his neglect of the unities; his violation of those laws which have been instituted and established by the joint authority of poets and critics.

For his other deviations from the art of writing, I resign him to critical justice without making any other demand in his favor than that which must be indulged to all human excellence: that his virtues be rated with his failings. But from the censure which this irregularity may bring upon him I shall, with due reverence to that learning which I must oppose, adventure to try how I can defend him.

His histories, being neither tragedies nor comedies, are not subject to any of their laws; nothing more is necessary to all the praise which they expect than that the changes of action be so prepared as to be understood; that the incidents be various and affecting, and the characters consistent, natural, and distinct. No other unity is intended, and therefore none is to be sought.

In his other works he has well enough preserved the unity of action. He has not, indeed, an intrigue regularly perplexed and regularly unraveled: he does not endeavor to hide his design only to discover it, for this is seldom the order of real events, and Shakespeare is the poet of nature: but his plan has commonly what Aristotle requires,[8] a beginning, a middle, and an end; one event is concatenated with another, and the conclusion follows by easy consequence. There are, perhaps, some incidents that might be spared, as in other poets there is much talk that only fills up time upon the stage; but the general system makes gradual advances, and the end of the play is the end of expectation.

To the unities of time and place he has shown no regard; and perhaps a nearer view of the principles on which they stand will diminish their value and withdraw from them the veneration which, from the time of Corneille,[9] they have very generally received, by discovering that they have given more trouble to the poet than pleasure to the auditor.

The necessity of observing the unities of time and place arises from the supposed necessity of making the drama credible. The critics hold it impossible that an action of months or years can be possibly believed to pass in three hours; or that the spectator can suppose himself to sit in the theater

6. "To entertain with tranquility; to fill with thoughts that engage the mind, without distracting it" (Johnson's *Dictionary*).
7. Course of action; the ground on which a race is run. In Greek legend Atalanta refused to marry any man who could not defeat her in a foot race. Hippomenes won her by dropping, as he ran, three

of the golden apples of the Hesperides, which she paused to pick up.
8. *Poetics* 7.
9. Pierre Corneille (1606–1684), the French playwright, discussed the unities in his *Discours des trois unités* (1660).

while ambassadors go and return between distant kings, while armies are levied and towns besieged, while an exile wanders and returns, or till he whom they saw courting his mistress shall lament the untimely fall of his son. The mind revolts from evident falsehood, and fiction loses its force when it departs from the resemblance of reality.

From the narrow limitation of time necessarily arises the contraction of place. The spectator who knows that he saw the first act at Alexandria cannot suppose that he sees the next at Rome, at a distance to which not the dragons of Medea[1] could, in so short a time, have transported him; he knows with certainty that he has not changed his place; and he knows that place cannot change itself, that what was a house cannot become a plain, that what was Thebes can never be Persepolis.

Such is the triumphant language with which a critic exults over the misery of an irregular poet, and exults commonly without resistance or reply. It is time, therefore, to tell him by the authority of Shakespeare that he assumes, as an unquestionable principle, a position which, while his breath is forming it into words, his understanding pronounces to be false. It is false that any representation is mistaken for reality; that any dramatic fable in its materiality was ever credible or, for a single moment, was ever credited.

The objection arising from the impossibility of passing the first hour at Alexandria and the next at Rome supposes that when the play opens the spectator really imagines himself at Alexandria, and believes that his walk to the theater has been a voyage to Egypt, and that he lives in the days of Antony and Cleopatra. Surely he that imagines this may imagine more. He that can take the stage at one time for the palace of the Ptolemies may take it in half an hour for the promontory of Actium. Delusion, if delusion be admitted, has no certain limitation; if the spectator can be once persuaded that his old acquaintances are Alexander and Caesar, that a room illuminated with candles is the plain of Pharsalia or the bank of Granicus, he is in a state of elevation above the reach of reason or of truth, and from the heights of empyrean poetry may despise the circumscriptions of terrestrial nature. There is no reason why a mind thus wandering in ecstasy should count the clock, or why an hour should not be a century in that calenture[2] of the brain that can make the stage a field.

The truth is that the spectators are always in their senses, and know, from the first act to the last, that the stage is only a stage, and that the players are only players. They came to hear a certain number of lines recited with just gesture and elegant modulation. The lines relate to some action, and an action must be in some place; but the different actions that complete a story may be in places very remote from each other; and where is the absurdity of allowing that space to represent first Athens, and then Sicily, which was always known to be neither Sicily nor Athens but a modern theater?

By supposition, as place is introduced, time may be extended; the time required by the fable elapses, for the most part, between the acts; for, of so much of the action as is represented, the real and poetical duration is the same. If, in the first act, preparations for war against Mithridates are represented to be made in Rome, the event of the war may, without absurdity,

1. According to legend, Medea fled the scene of her crimes in a chariot drawn by dragons.
2. A delirium produced by tropical heat, which causes sailors to leap into the sea under the delusion that it is a green field.

be represented, in the catastrophe, as happening in Pontus; we know that there is neither war nor preparation for war; we know that we are neither in Rome nor Pontus, that neither Mithridates nor Lucullus are before us. The drama exhibits successive imitations of successive actions; and why may not the second imitation represent an action that happened years after the first, if it be so connected with it that nothing but time can be supposed to intervene? Time is, of all modes of existence, most obsequious[3] to the imagination; a lapse of years is as easily conceived as a passage of hours. In contemplation we easily contract the time of real actions, and therefore willingly permit it to be contracted when we only see their imitation.

It will be asked how the drama moves if it is not credited. It is credited with all the credit due to a drama. It is credited, whenever it moves, as a just picture of a real original; as representing to the auditor what he would himself feel if he were to do or suffer what is there feigned to be suffered or to be done. The reflection that strikes the heart is not that the evils before us are real evils, but that they are evils to which we ourselves may be exposed. If there be any fallacy, it is not that we fancy the players, but that we fancy ourselves, unhappy for a moment; but we rather lament the possibility than suppose the presence of misery, as a mother weeps over her babe when she remembers that death may take it from her. The delight of tragedy proceeds from our consciousness of fiction; if we thought murders and treasons real, they would please no more.

Imitations produce pain or pleasure, not because they are mistaken for realities, but because they bring realities to mind. When the imagination is recreated[4] by a painted landscape, the trees are not supposed capable to give us shade or the fountains coolness; but we consider how we should be pleased with such fountains playing beside us and such woods waving over us. We are agitated in reading the history of *Henry the Fifth;* yet no man takes his book for the field of Agincourt. A dramatic exhibition is a book recited with concomitants that increase or diminish its effect. Familiar comedy is often more powerful on the theater than in the page; imperial tragedy is always less. The humor of Petruchio may be heightened by grimace; but what voice or what gesture can hope to add dignity or force to the soliloquy of Cato?[5]

A play read affects the mind like a play acted. It is therefore evident that the action is not supposed to be real; and it follows that between the acts a longer or shorter time may be allowed to pass, and that no more account of space or duration is to be taken by the auditor of a drama than by the reader of a narrative, before whom may pass in an hour the life of a hero or the revolutions of an empire.

Whether Shakespeare knew the unities and rejected them by design or deviated from them by happy ignorance, it is, I think, impossible to decide and useless to inquire. We may reasonably suppose that, when he rose to notice, he did not want[6] the counsels and admonitions of scholars and critics, and that he at last deliberately persisted in a practice which he might have begun by chance. As nothing is essential to the fable but unity of action, and

3. "Obedient; compliant" (Johnson's *Dictionary*).
4. Delighted.
5. In Addison's tragedy *Cato* (5.1), the hero soliloquizes on immortality shortly before committing

suicide. Petruchio is the hero of Shakespeare's comedy *The Taming of the Shrew*.
6. Lack.

as the unities of time and place arise evidently from false assumptions, and, by circumscribing the extent of the drama, lessen its variety, I cannot think it much to be lamented that they were not known by him, or not observed: nor, if such another poet could arise, should I very vehemently reproach him that his first act passed at Venice and his next in Cyprus.[7] Such violations of rules merely positive[8] become the comprehensive genius of Shakespeare, and such censures are suitable to the minute and slender criticism of Voltaire.

> *Non usque adeo permiscuit imis*
> *Longus summa dies, ut non, si voce Metelli*
> *Serventur leges, malint a Caesare tolli.*[9]

Yet when I speak thus slightly of dramatic rules, I cannot but recollect how much wit and learning may be produced against me; before such authorities I am afraid to stand: not that I think the present question one of those that are to be decided by mere authority, but because it is to be suspected that these precepts have not been so easily received but for better reasons than I have yet been able to find. The result of my inquiries, in which it would be ludicrous to boast of impartiality, is that the unities of time and place are not essential to a just drama, that though they may sometimes conduce to pleasure, they are always to be sacrificed to the nobler beauties of variety and instruction; and that a play written with nice observation of critical rules is to be contemplated as an elaborate curiosity, as the product of superfluous and ostentatious art, by which is shown rather what is possible than what is necessary.

He that without diminution of any other excellence shall preserve all the unities unbroken deserves the like applause with the architect who shall display all the orders of architecture in a citadel without any deduction for its strength; but the principal beauty of a citadel is to exclude the enemy, and the greatest graces of a play are to copy nature and instruct life.* * *

[HENRY IV]

None of Shakespeare's plays are more read than the first and second parts of *Henry the Fourth*. Perhaps no author has ever in two plays afforded so much delight. The great events are interesting, for the fate of kingdoms depends upon them; the slighter occurrences are diverting, and, except one or two, sufficiently probable; the incidents are multiplied with wonderful fertility of invention, and the characters diversified with the utmost nicety of discernment, and the profoundest skill in the nature of man.

The prince, who is the hero both of the comic and tragic part, is a young man of great abilities and violent passions, whose sentiments are right, though his actions are wrong; whose virtues are obscured by negligence, and whose understanding is dissipated by levity. In his idle hours he is rather loose than wicked, and when the occasion forces but his latent qualities, he is great without effort, and brave without tumult. The trifler is roused into a hero, and the hero again reposes in the trifler. This character is great, original, and just.[1]

---

7. As is the case in *Othello*.
8. Arbitrary; not natural.
9. Lucan's *Pharsalia* 3.138–40: "The course of time has not wrought such confusion that the laws

would not rather be trampled on by Caesar than saved by Metellus."
1. Accurate, well grounded.

Percy is a rugged soldier, choleric and quarrelsome, and has only the soldier's virtues, generosity and courage.

But Falstaff, unimitated, unimitable Falstaff, how shall I describe thee? Thou compound of sense and vice; of sense which may be admired but not esteemed, of vice which may be despised, but hardly detested. Falstaff is a character loaded with faults, and with those faults which naturally produce contempt. He is a thief, and a glutton, a coward, and a boaster, always ready to cheat the weak, and prey upon the poor; to terrify the timorous and insult the defenseless. At once obsequious and malignant, he satirizes in their absence those whom he lives by flattering. He is familiar with the prince only as an agent of vice, but of this familiarity he is so proud as not only to be supercilious and haughty with common men, but to think his interest of importance to the duke of Lancaster. Yet the man thus corrupt, thus despicable, makes himself necessary to the prince that despises him, by the most pleasing of all qualities, perpetual gaiety, by an unfailing power of exciting laughter, which is the more freely indulged, as his wit is not of the splendid or ambitious kind, but consists in easy escapes and sallies of levity, which make sport but raise no envy. It must be observed that he is stained with no enourmous or sanguinary crimes, so that his licentiousness is not so offensive but that it may be borne for his mirth.

The moral to be drawn from this representation is that no man is more dangerous than he that with a will to corrupt, hath the power to please; and that neither wit nor honesty ought to think themselves safe with such a companion when they see Henry seduced by Falstaff.

FROM LIVES OF THE POETS

From Milton[1]

[LYCIDAS]

One of the poems on which much praise has been bestowed is *Lycidas;* of which the diction is harsh,[2] the rhymes uncertain, and the numbers unpleasing. What beauty there is, we must therefore seek in the sentiments and images. It is not to be considered as the effusion of real passion; for passion runs not after remote allusions and obscure opinions. Passion plucks no berries from the myrtle and ivy, nor calls upon Arethuse and Mincius, nor tells of "rough satyrs and fauns with cloven heel." Where there is leisure for fiction there is little grief.

In this poem there is no nature, for there is no truth; there is no art, for there is nothing new. Its form is that of a pastoral, easy, vulgar, and therefore disgusting:[3] whatever images it can supply are long ago exhausted; and its inherent improbability always forces dissatisfaction on the mind. When

---

1. Johnson's treatment of Milton as man and poet gave great offense to many ardent Miltonians in his own day and damaged his reputation as a critic in the following century. He did not admire Milton's character, and he detested his politics and religion. But no one has praised *Paradise Lost* more handsomely. Especially offensive in the 19th century was his attack on *Lycidas.* Johnson disliked

modern pastorals, recognizing that the tradition had been worn threadbare. His views on the genre may be read in *Rambler* no. 36 and no. 37.
2. This notorious word does not mean "unmelodious," but "strained, forced, affected, or labored."
3. I.e., displeasing, because its stale conventionality made it "vulgar" by putting it within the reach of the many.

Cowley tells of Hervey that they studied together, it is easy to suppose how much he must miss the companion of his labors and the partner of his discoveries;[4] but what image of tenderness can be excited by these lines!

> We drove afield, and both together heard
> What time the grayfly winds her sultry horn,
> Battening our flocks with the fresh dews of night.

We know that they never drove afield, and that they had no flocks to batten; and though it be allowed that the representation may be allegorical, the true meaning is so uncertain and remote that it is never sought because it cannot be known when it is found.

Among the flocks and copses and flowers appear the heathen deities, Jove and Phoebus, Neptune and Aeolus, with a long train of mythological imagery, such as a college easily supplies. Nothing can less display knowledge or less exercise invention than to tell how a shepherd has lost his companion and must now feed his flocks alone, without any judge of his skill in piping; and how one god asks another god what is become of Lycidas, and how neither god can tell. He who thus grieves will excite no sympathy; he who thus praises will confer no honor.

This poem has yet a grosser fault. With these trifling fictions are mingled the most awful and sacred truths, such as ought never to be polluted with such irreverent combinations. The shepherd likewise is now a feeder of sheep, and afterwards an ecclesiastical pastor, a superintendent of a Christian flock. Such equivocations are always unskillful; but here they are indecent,[5] and at least approach to impiety, of which, however, I believe the writer not to have been conscious.

Such is the power of reputation justly acquired that its blaze drives away the eye from nice examination. Surely no man could have fancied that he read *Lycidas* with pleasure had he not known its author.

[L'ALLEGRO, IL PENSEROSO]

Of the two pieces, *L'Allegro* and *Il Penseroso*, I believe opinion is uniform; every man that reads them, reads them with pleasure. The author's design is not, what Theobald[6] has remarked, merely to show how objects derived their colors from the mind, by representing the operation of the same things upon the gay and the melancholy temper, or upon the same man as he is differently disposed; but rather how, among the successive variety of appearances, every disposition of mind takes hold on those by which it may be gratified.

The *cheerful* man hears the lark in the morning; the *pensive* man hears the nightingale in the evening. The *cheerful* man sees the cock strut, and hears the horn and hounds echo in the wood; then walks "not unseen" to observe the glory of the rising sun or listen to the singing milkmaid, and view the labors of the plowman and the mower; then casts his eyes about him over scenes of smiling plenty, and looks up to the distant tower, the residence of some fair inhabitant: thus he pursues rural gaiety through a day of labor

---

4. Cowley's *On the Death of Mr. William Hervey* (1656).
5. Unbecoming, lacking in decorum.

6. Lewis Theobald (1688–1744), the editor of Shakespeare and the enemy of Pope.

or of play, and delights himself at night with the fanciful narratives of superstitious ignorance.

The *pensive* man at one time walks "unseen" to muse at midnight, and at another hears the sullen curfew. If the weather drives him home he sits in a room lighted only by "glowing embers"; or by a lonely lamp outwatches the North Star to discover the habitation of separate souls, and varies the shades of meditation by contemplating the magnificent or pathetic scenes of tragic and epic poetry. When the morning comes, a morning gloomy with rain and wind, he walks into the dark trackless woods, falls asleep by some murmuring water, and with melancholy enthusiasm expects some dream of prognostication or some music played by aerial performers.

Both Mirth and Melancholy are solitary, silent inhabitants of the breast that neither receive nor transmit communication: no mention is therefore made of a philosophical friend or a pleasant companion. The seriousness does not arise from any participation of calamity, nor the gaiety from the pleasures of the bottle.

The man of *cheerfulness* having exhausted the country tries what "towered cities" will afford, and mingles with scenes of splendor, gay assemblies, and nuptial festivities; but he mingles a mere spectator as, when the learned comedies of Jonson or the wild dramas of Shakespeare are exhibited, he attends the theater.

The *pensive* man never loses himself in crowds, but walks the cloister or frequents the cathedral. Milton probably had not yet forsaken the Church.

Both his characters delight in music; but he seems to think that cheerful notes would have obtained from Pluto a complete dismission of Eurydice, of whom solemn sounds only procured a conditional release.

For the old age of Cheerfulness he makes no provision; but Melancholy he conducts with great dignity to the close of life. His Cheerfulness is without levity, and his Pensiveness without asperity.

Through these two poems the images are properly selected and nicely distinguished, but the colors of the diction seem not sufficiently discriminated. I know not whether the characters are kept sufficiently apart. No mirth can, indeed, be found in his melancholy; but I am afraid that I always meet some melancholy in his mirth. They are two noble efforts of imagination.

[PARADISE LOST]

Those little pieces may be dispatched without much anxiety; a greater work calls for greater care. I am now to examine *Paradise Lost*, a poem which, considered with respect to design, may claim the first place, and with respect to performance the second, among the productions of the human mind.

By the general consent of critics the first praise of genius is due to the writer of an epic poem, as it requires an assemblage of all the powers which are singly sufficient for other compositions. Poetry is the art of uniting pleasure with truth, by calling imagination to the help of reason. Epic poetry undertakes to teach the most important truths by the most pleasing precepts, and therefore relates some great event in the most affecting manner. History must supply the writer with the rudiments of narration, which he must improve and exalt by a nobler art, must animate by dramatic energy, and diversify by retrospection and anticipation; morality must teach him the exact bounds and different shades of vice and virtue; from policy and the practice of life he has to learn the discriminations of character and the tendency of the passions, either single or combined; and physiology must supply him with illustrations and images. To put these materials to poetical use is required an imagination capable of painting nature and realizing fiction. Nor is he yet a poet till he has attained the whole extension of his language, distinguished all the delicacies of phrase, and all the colors of words, and learned to adjust their different sounds to all the varieties of metrical modulation.

Bossu is of opinion that the poet's first work is to find a *moral*, which his fable is afterwards to illustrate and establish.[7] This seems to have been the process only of Milton: the moral of other poems is incidental and consequent; in Milton's only it is essential and intrinsic. His purpose was the most useful and the most arduous: "to vindicate the ways of God to man";[8] to show the reasonableness of religion, and the necessity of obedience to the Divine Law.

To convey this moral there must be a *fable*, a narration artfully constructed, so as to excite curiosity and surprise expectation. In this part of his work Milton must be confessed to have equaled every other poet. He has involved in his account of the Fall of Man the events which preceded, and those that were to follow it: he has interwoven the whole system of theology with such propriety that every part appears to be necessary, and scarcely any recital is wished shorter for the sake of quickening the progress of the main action.

The subject of an epic poem is naturally an event of great importance. That of Milton is not the destruction of a city, the conduct of a colony, or the foundation of an empire. His subject is the fate of worlds, the revolutions of heaven and of earth; rebellion against the Supreme King raised by the highest order of created beings; the overthrow of their host and the punishment of their crime; the creation of a new race of reasonable creatures; their original happiness and innocence, their forfeiture of immortality, and their restoration to hope and peace.

Great events can be hastened or retarded only by persons of elevated dignity. Before the greatness displayed in Milton's poem all other greatness shrinks away. The weakest of his agents are the highest and noblest of human beings, the original parents of mankind; with whose actions the elements consented; on whose rectitude or deviation of will depended the state of terrestrial nature and the condition of all the future inhabitants of the globe.

Of the other agents in the poem, the chief are such as it is irreverence to name on slight occasions. The rest were lower powers;

> of which the least could wield
> Those elements, and arm him with the force
> Of all their regions;[9]

powers which only the control of Omnipotence restrains from laying creation waste, and filling the vast expanse of space with ruin and confusion. To

7. Père le Bossu wrote a treatise on the epic poem, *Traité du Poëme Épique*, 1675, much admired during the late 17th and early 18th centuries.
8. Milton wrote "justify," not "vindicate" (*Paradise*

Lost 1.26). It was Pope, in *An Essay on Man* 1.16, who used "vindicate."
9. *Paradise Lost* 6.221.

display the motives and actions of beings thus superior, so far as human reason can examine them or human imagination represent them, is the task which this mighty poet has undertaken and performed.

In the examination of epic poems much speculation is commonly employed upon the *characters*. The characters in the *Paradise Lost* which admit of examination are those of angels and of man; of angels good and evil, of man in his innocent and sinful state.

Among the angels the virtue of Raphael is mild and placid, of easy condescension and free communication; that of Michael is regal and lofty, and, as may seem, attentive to the dignity of his own nature. Abdiel and Gabriel appear occasionally, and act as every incident requires; the solitary fidelity of Abdiel is very amiably painted.[1]

Of the evil angels the characters are more diversified. To Satan, as Addison observes, such sentiments are given as suit "the most exalted and most depraved being."[2] Milton has been censured by Clarke for the impiety which sometimes breaks from Satan's mouth. For there are thoughts, as he justly remarks, which no observation of character can justify, because no good man would willingly permit them to pass, however transiently, through his own mind.[3] To make Satan speak as a rebel, without any such expressions as might taint the reader's imagination, was indeed one of the great difficulties in Milton's undertaking, and I cannot but think that he has extricated himself with great happiness. There is in Satan's speeches little that can give pain to a pious ear. The language of rebellion cannot be the same with that of obedience. The malignity of Satan foams in haughtiness and obstinacy; but his expressions are commonly general, and no otherwise offensive than as they are wicked.

The other chiefs of the celestial rebellion are very judiciously discriminated in the first and second books; and the ferocious character of Moloch appears, both in the battle and the council, with exact consistency.

To Adam and Eve are given during their innocence such sentiments as innocence can generate and utter. Their love is pure benevolence and mutual veneration; their repasts are without luxury and their diligence without toil. Their addresses to their Maker have little more than the voice of admiration and gratitude. Fruition left them nothing to ask, and Innocence left them nothing to fear.

But with guilt enter distrust and discord, mutual accusation, and stubborn self-defense; they regard each other with alienated minds, and dread their Creator as the avenger of their transgression. At last they seek shelter in his mercy, soften to repentance, and melt in supplication. Both before and after the Fall the superiority of Adam is diligently sustained.

Of the *probable* and the *marvelous*,[4] two parts of a vulgar epic poem which immerge the critic in deep consideration, the *Paradise Lost* requires little to be said. It contains the history of a miracle, of Creation and Redemption; it displays the power and the mercy of the Supreme Being: the probable therefore is marvelous, and the marvelous is probable. The substance of the narrative is truth; and as truth allows no choice, it is, like necessity, superior to rule. To the

---

1. *Paradise Lost* 5.803ff.
2. *Spectator* 303.
3. John Clarke's *Essay upon Study* (1731).

4. Actions in an epic poem that are wonderful because they exceed the probable.

accidental or adventitious parts, as to every thing human, some slight exceptions may be made. But the main fabric is immovably supported.

It is justly remarked by Addison[5] that this poem has, by the nature of its subject, the advantage above all others, that it is universally and perpetually interesting. All mankind will, through all ages, bear the same relation to Adam and to Eve, and must partake of that good and evil which extend to themselves.

Of the *machinery*, so called from *theòs apò mēkhanēs*,[6] by which is meant the occasional interposition of supernatural power, another fertile topic of critical remarks, here is no room to speak, because every thing is done under the immediate and visible direction of Heaven; but the rule is so far observed that no part of the action could have been accomplished by any other means.

Of *episodes*[7] I think there are only two, contained in Raphael's relation of the war in heaven and Michael's prophetic account of the changes to happen in this world. Both are closely connected with the great action; one was necessary to Adam as a warning, the other as a consolation.

To the completeness or *integrity* of the design nothing can be objected; it has distinctly and clearly what Aristotle requires, a beginning, a middle, and an end. There is perhaps no poem of the same length from which so little can be taken without apparent mutilation. Here are no funeral games, nor is there any long description of a shield. The short digressions at the beginning of the third, seventh, and ninth books might doubtless be spared; but superfluities so beautiful who would take away? or who does not wish that the author of the *Iliad* had gratified succeeding ages with a little knowledge of himself? Perhaps no passages are more frequently or more attentively read than those extrinsic paragraphs; and since the end of poetry is pleasure, that cannot be unpoetical with which all are pleased.

The questions, whether the action of the poem be strictly *one*,[8] whether the poem can be properly termed *heroic*, and who is the hero, are raised by such readers as draw their principles of judgment rather from books than from reason. Milton, though he entitled *Paradise Lost* only a "poem," yet calls it himself "heroic song."[9] Dryden, petulantly and indecently, denies the heroism of Adam because he was overcome; but there is no reason why the hero should not be unfortunate except established practice, since success and virtue do not go necessarily together. Cato is the hero of Lucan, but Lucan's authority will not be suffered by Quintilian to decide. However, if success be necessary, Adam's deceiver was at last crushed; Adam was restored to his Maker's favor, and therefore may securely resume his human rank.

After the scheme and fabric of the poem must be considered its component parts, the sentiments, and the diction.

The *sentiments*, as expressive of manners or appropriated to characters, are for the greater part unexceptionably just. Splendid passages containing lessons of morality or precepts of prudence occur seldom. Such is the original formation of this poem that as it admits no human manners till the Fall, it

5. *Spectator* 273.
6. Aristotle's *Poetics* 15.10. *Deus ex machina*, the intervention of supernatural powers into the affairs of humans.
7. Incidental but related narratives within an epic

poem. Johnson is citing *Paradise Lost* 5.577ff. and 11.334ff.
8. I.e., a single action dealing with a single character.
9. *Paradise Lost* 9.25.

can give little assistance to human conduct. Its end is to raise the thoughts above sublunary cares or pleasures. Yet the praise of that fortitude, with which Abdiel maintained his singularity of virtue against the scorn of multitudes, may be accommodated to all times; and Raphael's reproof of Adam's curiosity after the planetary motions, with the answer returned by Adam, may be confidently opposed to any rule of life which any poet has delivered.[1]

The thoughts which are occasionally called forth in the progress are such as could only be produced by an imagination in the highest degree fervid and active, to which materials were supplied by incessant study and unlimited curiosity. The heat of Milton's mind might be said to sublimate his learning, to throw off into his work the spirit of science,[2] unmingled with its grosser parts.

He had considered creation in its whole extent, and his descriptions are therefore learned. He had accustomed his imagination to unrestrained indulgence, and his conceptions therefore were extensive. The characteristic quality of his poem is sublimity. He sometimes descends to the elegant, but his element is the great. He can occasionally invest himself with grace; but his natural port is gigantic loftiness. He can please when pleasure is required; but it is his peculiar power to astonish.

He seems to have been well acquainted with his own genius, and to know what it was that Nature had bestowed upon him more bountifully than upon others; the power of displaying the vast, illuminating the splendid, enforcing the awful, darkening the gloomy, and aggravating the dreadful: he therefore chose a subject on which too much could not be said, on which he might tire his fancy without the censure of extravagance.

* * *

The defects and faults of *Paradise Lost,* for faults and defects every work of man must have, it is the business of impartial criticism to discover. As in displaying the excellence of Milton I have not made long quotations, because of selecting beauties there had been no end, I shall in the same general manner mention that which seems to deserve censure; for what Englishman can take delight in transcribing passages, which, if they lessen the reputation of Milton, diminish in some degree the honor of our country?

* * *

The plan of *Paradise Lost* has this inconvenience, that it comprises neither human actions nor human manners. The man and woman who act and suffer are in a state which no other man or woman can ever know. The reader finds no transaction in which he can be engaged, beholds no condition in which he can by any effort of imagination place himself; he has, therefore, little natural curiosity or sympathy.

We all, indeed, feel the effects of Adam's disobedience; we all sin like Adam, and like him must all bewail our offenses; we have restless and insidious enemies in the fallen angels, and in the blessed spirits we have guardians and friends; in the Redemption of mankind we hope to be included: in the description of heaven and hell we are surely interested, as we are all to reside hereafter either in the regions of horror or of bliss.

1. *Paradise Lost* 8.65ff. 2. Knowledge.

But these truths are too important to be new: they have been taught to our infancy; they have mingled with our solitary thoughts and familiar conversation, and are habitually interwoven with the whole texture of life. Being therefore not new they raise no unaccustomed emotion in the mind: what we knew before, we cannot learn; what is not unexpected, cannot surprise.

Of the ideas suggested by these awful scenes, from some we recede with reverence, except when stated hours require their association; and from others we shrink with horror, or admit them only as salutary inflictions, as counterpoises to our interests and passions. Such images rather obstruct the career of fancy than incite it.

Pleasure and terror are indeed the genuine sources of poetry; but poetical pleasure must be such as human imagination can at least conceive, and poetical terror such as human strength and fortitude may combat. The good and evil of Eternity are too ponderous for the wings of wit; the mind sinks under them in passive helplessness, content with calm belief and humble adoration.

Known truths however may take a different appearance, and be conveyed to the mind by a new train of intermediate images. This Milton has undertaken, and performed with pregnancy and vigor of mind peculiar to himself. Whoever considers the few radical positions which the Scriptures afforded him will wonder by what energetic operation he expanded them to such extent and ramified them to so much variety, restrained as he was by religious reverence from licentiousness of fiction.

Here is a full display of the united force of study and genius; of a great accumulation of materials, with judgment to digest and fancy to combine them: Milton was able to select from nature or from story, from ancient fable or from modern science, whatever could illustrate or adorn his thoughts. An accumulation of knowledge impregnated his mind, fermented by study and exalted by imagination.

* * *

But original deficience cannot be supplied. The want of human interest is always felt. *Paradise Lost* is one of the books which the reader admires and lays down, and forgets to take up again. None ever wished it longer than it is. Its perusal is a duty rather than a pleasure. We read Milton for instruction, retire harassed and overburdened, and look elsewhere for recreation; we desert our master, and seek for companions.

* * *

Dryden remarks that Milton has some flats among his elevations.[3] This is only to say that all the parts are not equal. In every work one part must be for the sake of others; a palace must have passages, a poem must have transitions. It is no more to be required that wit should always be blazing than that the sun should always stand at noon. In a great work there is a vicissitude[4] of luminous and opaque parts, as there is in the world a succession of day and night. Milton, when he has expatiated in the sky, may be allowed sometimes to revisit earth; for what other author ever soared so high or sustained his flight so long?

3. Preface to *Sylvae*; see W. P. Ker (ed.), *Essays* 1.268.   4. Change.

* * *

The highest praise of genius is original invention. Milton cannot be said to have contrived the structure of an epic poem, and therefore owes reverence to that vigor and amplitude of mind to which all generations must be indebted for the art of poetical narration, for the texture of the fable, the variation of incidents, the interposition of dialogue, and all the stratagems that surprise and enchain attention. But of all the borrowers from Homer Milton is perhaps the least indebted. He was naturally a thinker for himself, confident of his own abilities and disdainful of help or hindrance; he did not refuse admission to the thoughts or images of his predecessors, but he did not seek them. From his contemporaries he neither courted nor received support; there is in his writings nothing by which the pride of other authors might be gratified or favor gained, no exchange of praise or solicitation of support. His great works were performed under discountenance and in blindness, but difficulties vanished at his touch; he was born for whatever is arduous; and his work is not the greatest of heroic poems, only because it is not the first.

1779

JAMES BOSWELL
1740–1795

The discovery of a vast number of James Boswell's personal papers (believed until 1925 to have been destroyed by his literary executors) has made it possible to know the author of *The Life of Samuel Johnson* better, perhaps, than we can know any other person, dead or living. His published letters and journals have made modern readers aware of the serious and absurd, the charming and repellent sides of his character. At twenty-three, when he met Johnson, he had already trained himself to listen, to observe, and to remember until he found time to set it all down in writing. Only very rarely, it seems, did he ever take notes of conversations while they were in progress, which might have inhibited the speakers. His unusual memory and disciplined art enabled him to re-create and vividly preserve the many "scenes" that distinguish his journals as they do the *Life*.

Boswell was the elder son of Alexander Boswell of Auchinleck (pronounced *Affléck*) in Ayrshire, a judge who bore the courtesy title of Lord Auchinleck. As a member of an ancient family and heir to its large estate, Boswell was in the technical sense of the term a gentleman, with entrée into the best circles of Edinburgh and London. By temperament he was unstable, emotionally and sexually skittish. By 1769, Boswell was established in what was to prove a successful law practice in Edinburgh and had married his cousin, Margaret Montgomerie. But he kept his ties to London and Johnson. In 1773 he persuaded Johnson to join him in a tour of the Highlands and the Hebrides. Johnson's *Journey to the Western Isles of Scotland* (1775) is a thoughtful account of the way that people live in the Hebrides (though some Scots were offended). Boswell's *Journal of a Tour to the Hebrides* (1785), a preliminary study for the *Life*, is a lively and entertaining diary, approved, at least in part, by Johnson himself.

In 1788, four years after Johnson's death, Boswell abandoned his Scottish practice, moved to London, was admitted to the English bar (but never actually practiced), and often depressed and drunken, began the *Life*. Fortunately he had the help and encouragement of the distinguished literary scholar Edmond Malone, without whose guidance he might never have finished his task. Boswell had an overwhelming amount of material to deal with: his own journals, all of Johnson's letters that he could find, Johnson's voluminous writings, and every scrap of information that his friends would furnish—all of which had to be collected, verified, and somehow reduced to unity.

Although the Johnson of popular legend is largely Boswell's creation, there was much in his life about which Boswell had no firsthand knowledge. At their first meeting, Johnson was fifty-four, a widower, already established as "Dictionary" Johnson and the author of the *Rambler,* and pensioned by the crown. Boswell knew nothing at firsthand of the long, hard years during which Johnson made his way painfully up from obscurity to fame. Hence the *Life* is the portrait of a sage. Its chief glory is conversation: the talk of a man who has experienced broadly, read widely, and observed and reflected on his observations; whose ideas are constantly brought to the test of experience; and whose experience is habitually transmuted into ideas. The book is as large as life and as human as its central character.

From The Life of Samuel Johnson, LL.D.

[PLAN OF THE *LIFE*]

* * * Had Dr. Johnson written his own life, in conformity with the opinion which he has given, that every man's life may be best written by himself;[1] had he employed in the preservation of his own history, that clearness of narration and elegance of language in which he has embalmed so many eminent persons, the world would probably have had the most perfect example of biography that was ever exhibited. But although he at different times, in a desultory manner, committed to writing many particulars of the progress of his mind and fortunes, he never had persevering diligence enough to form them into a regular composition. Of these memorials a few have been preserved; but the greater part was consigned by him to the flames, a few days before his death.

As I had the honor and happiness of enjoying his friendship for upwards of twenty years; as I had the scheme of writing his life constantly in view; as he was well apprised of this circumstance, and from time to time obligingly satisfied my inquiries, by communicating to me the incidents of his early years; as I acquired a facility in recollecting, and was very assiduous in recording, his conversation, of which the extraordinary vigor and vivacity constituted one of the first features of his character; and as I have spared no pains in obtaining materials concerning him, from every quarter where I could discover that they were to be found, and have been favored with the most liberal communications by his friends; I flatter myself that few biographers have entered upon such a work as this with more advantages; independent of literary abilities, in which I am not vain enough to compare myself with some great names who have gone before me in this kind of writing. * * *

Indeed I cannot conceive a more perfect mode of writing any man's life than not only relating all the most important events of it in their order, but interweaving what he privately wrote, and said, and thought; by which mankind are enabled as it were to see him live, and to "live o'er each scene"[2] with

---

1. *Idler* 84. 2. Pope's *Prologue* to Addison's *Cato,* line 4.

him, as he actually advanced through the several stages of his life. Had his other friends been as diligent and ardent as I was, he might have been almost entirely preserved. As it is, I will venture to say that he will be seen in this work more completely than any man who has ever yet lived.

[JOHNSON'S EARLY YEARS. MARRIAGE]

[*1729*] The "morbid melancholy," which was lurking in his constitution, and to which we may ascribe those particularities and that aversion to regular life, which, at a very early period, marked his character, gathered such strength in his twentieth year as to afflict him in a dreadful manner. While he was at Lichfield, in the college vacation of the year 1729, he felt himself overwhelmed with an horrible hypochondria, with perpetual irritation, fretfulness, and impatience; and with a dejection, gloom, and despair, which made existence misery. From this dismal malady he never afterwards was perfectly relieved; and all his labors, and all his enjoyments, were but temporary interruptions of its baleful influence. He told Mr. Paradise[3] that he was sometimes so languid and inefficient that he could not distinguish the hour upon the town-clock. * * *

[*1735*] Though Mrs. Porter was double the age of Johnson, and her person and manner, as described to me by the late Mr. Garrick,[4] were by no means pleasing to others, she must have had a superiority of understanding and talents, as she certainly inspired him with a more than ordinary passion; and she having signified her willingness to accept of his hand, he went to Lichfield to ask his mother's consent to the marriage, which he could not but be conscious was a very imprudent scheme, both on account of their disparity of years and her want of fortune. But Mrs. Johnson knew too well the ardor of her son's temper, and was too tender a parent to oppose his inclinations.

I know not for what reason the marriage ceremony was not performed at Birmingham; but a resolution was taken that it should be at Derby, for which place the bride and bridegroom set out on horseback, I suppose in very good humor. But though Mr. Topham Beauclerk[5] used archly to mention Johnson's having told him, with much gravity, "Sir, it was a love marriage on both sides," I have had from my illustrious friend the following curious account of their journey to church upon the nuptial morn:

9th July: "Sir, she had read the old romances, and had got into her head the fantastical notion that a woman of spirit should use her lover like a dog. So, Sir, at first she told me that I rode too fast, and she could not keep up with me; and, when I rode a little slower, she passed me, and complained that I lagged behind. I was not to be made the slave of caprice; and I resolved to begin as I meant to end. I therefore pushed on briskly, till I was fairly out of her sight. The road lay between two hedges, so I was sure she could not miss it; and I contrived that she should soon come up with me. When she did, I observed her to be in tears." * * *

3. John Paradise, a member of the Essex Head Club, which Johnson founded in 1783.
4. David Garrick (1717–1779), the most famous actor of his day. In 1736 he was one of Johnson's three pupils in an unsuccessful school at Edial.
5. Pronounced *bo-clare*. A descendant of Charles II and the actress Nell Gwynn, he was brilliant and dissolute.

[THE LETTER TO CHESTERFIELD]

[1754] Lord Chesterfield,[6] to whom Johnson had paid the high compliment of addressing to his Lordship the *Plan* of his *Dictionary*, had behaved to him in such a manner as to excite his contempt and indignation. The world has been for many years amused with a story confidently told, and as confidently repeated with additional circumstances, that a sudden disgust was taken by Johnson upon occasion of his having been one day kept long in waiting in his Lordship's antechamber, for which the reason assigned was that he had company with him; and that at last, when the door opened, out walked Colley Cibber;[7] and that Johnson was so violently provoked when he found for whom he had been so long excluded, that he went away in a passion, and never would return. I remember having mentioned this story to George Lord Lyttelton, who told me he was very intimate with Lord Chesterfield; and holding it as a well-known truth, defended Lord Chesterfield, by saying, that Cibber, who had been introduced familiarly by the back stairs, had probably not been there above ten minutes. It may seem strange even to entertain a doubt concerning a story so long and so widely current, and thus implicitly adopted, if not sanctioned, by the authority which I have mentioned; but Johnson himself assured me that there was not the least foundation for it. He told me that there never was any particular incident which produced a quarrel between Lord Chesterfield and him; but that his Lordship's continued neglect was the reason why he resolved to have no connection with him. When the *Dictionary* was upon the eve of publication, Lord Chesterfield, who, it is said, had flattered himself with expectations that Johnson would dedicate the work to him, attempted, in a courtly manner, to soothe, and insinuate himself with the sage, conscious, as it should seem, of the cold indifference with which he had treated its learned author; and further attempted to conciliate him, by writing two papers in *The World*, in recommendation of the work; and it must be confessed that they contain some studied compliments, so finely turned, that if there had been no previous offense, it is probable that Johnson would have been highly delighted. Praise, in general, was pleasing to him; but by praise from a man of rank and elegant accomplishments, he was peculiarly gratified. * * *

This courtly device failed of its effect. Johnson, who thought that "all was false and hollow,"[8] despised the honeyed words, and was even indignant that Lord Chesterfield should, for a moment, imagine that he could be dupe of such an artifice. His expression to me concerning Lord Chesterfield, upon this occasion, was, "Sir, after making great professions, he had, for many years, taken no notice of me; but when my *Dictionary* was coming out, he fell a-scribbling in *The World* about it. Upon which, I wrote him a letter expressed in civil terms, but such as might show him that I did not mind what he said or wrote, and that I had done with him."

This is that celebrated letter of which so much has been said, and about which curiosity has been so long excited, without being gratified. I for many

6. Philip Dormer Stanhope, earl of Chesterfield (1694–1773), statesman, wit, man of fashion. His *Letters,* written for the guidance of his natural son, are famous for their worldly good sense and for their expression of the ideal of an 18th-century gentleman.

7. Colley Cibber (1671–1757), playwright, comic actor, and (after 1730) poet laureate. A fine actor but a very bad poet, Cibber was a constant object of ridicule by the wits of the town. Pope made him king of the Dunces in the *Dunciad* of 1743.
8. *Paradise Lost* 2.112.

years solicited Johnson to favor me with a copy of it, that so excellent a composition might not be lost to posterity. He delayed from time to time to give it me; till at last in 1781, when we were on a visit at Mr. Dilly's,[9] at Southill in Bedfordshire, he was pleased to dictate it to me from memory. He afterwards found among his papers a copy of it, which he had dictated to Mr. Baretti,[1] with its title and corrections, in his own handwriting. This he gave to Mr. Langton; adding that if it were to come into print, he wished it to be from that copy. By Mr. Langton's kindness, I am enabled to enrich my work with a perfect transcript of what the world has so eagerly desired to see.

TO THE RIGHT HONORABLE THE EARL OF CHESTERFIELD

February 7, 1755

MY LORD,

I have been lately informed, by the proprietor of *The World*, that two papers, in which my Dictionary is recommended to the public, were written by your Lordship. To be so distinguished, is an honor, which, being very little accustomed to favors from the great, I know not well how to receive, or in what terms to acknowledge.

When, upon some slight encouragement, I first visited your Lordship, I was overpowered, like the rest of mankind, by the enchantment of your address; and could not forbear to wish that I might boast myself *Le vainqueur du vainqueur de la terre*[2]—that I might obtain that regard for which I saw the world contending; but I found my attendance so little encouraged that neither pride nor modesty would suffer me to continue it. When I had once addressed your Lordship in public, I had exhausted all the art of pleasing which a retired and uncourtly scholar can possess. I had done all that I could; and no man is well pleased to have his all neglected, be it ever so little.

Seven years, my Lord, have now passed since I waited in your outward rooms, or was repulsed from your door; during which time I have been pushing on my work through difficulties of which it is useless to complain, and have brought it, at last, to the verge of publication, without one act of assistance, one word of encouragement, or one smile of favor. Such treatment I did not expect, for I never had a patron before.

The shepherd in Virgil grew at last acquainted with Love, and found him a native of the rocks.[3]

Is not a patron, my Lord, one who looks with unconcern on a man struggling for life in the water, and, when he has reached ground, encumbers him with help? The notice which you have been pleased to take of my labors, had it been early, had been kind; but it has been delayed till I am indifferent, and cannot enjoy it; till I am solitary, and

---

9. Southill was the country home of Charles and Edward Dilly, publishers. The firm published all of Boswell's serious works and shared in the publication of Johnson's *Lives of the Poets* (1779–81).
1. Giuseppe Baretti, an Italian writer and lexicog-
rapher whom Johnson introduced into his circle.
2. The conqueror of the conqueror of the earth (French). From the first line of Scudéry's epic *Alaric* (1654).
3. *Eclogues* 8.44.

cannot impart it; till I am known, and do not want it. I hope it is no very cynical asperity not to confess obligations where no benefit has been received, or to be unwilling that the public should consider me as owing that to a patron which Providence has enabled me to do for myself.

Having carried on my work thus far with so little obligation to any favorer of learning, I shall not be disappointed though I should conclude it, if less be possible, with less; for I have been long wakened from that dream of hope in which I once boasted myself with so much exultation, my Lord, your Lordship's most humble, most obedient servant,

SAM. JOHNSON.

"While this was the talk of the town," says Dr. Adams, in a letter to me, "I happened to visit Dr. Warburton,[4] who finding that I was acquainted with Johnson, desired me earnestly to carry his compliments to him, and to tell him that he honored him for his manly behavior in rejecting these condescensions of Lord Chesterfield, and for resenting the treatment he had received from him, with a proper spirit. Johnson was visibly pleased with this compliment, for he had always a high opinion of Warburton. Indeed, the force of mind which appeared in this letter was congenial with that which Warburton himself amply possessed."

There is a curious minute circumstance which struck me, in comparing the various editions of Johnson's imitations of Juvenal. In the tenth satire, one of the couplets upon the vanity of wishes even for literary distinction stood thus:

> Yet think what ills the scholar's life assail,
> Toil, envy, want, the *garret*, and the jail.

But after experiencing the uneasiness which Lord Chesterfield's fallacious patronage made him feel, he dismissed the word *garret* from the sad group, and in all the subsequent editions the line stands

> Toil, envy, want, the *patron*, and the jail.

[A MEMORABLE YEAR: BOSWELL MEETS JOHNSON]

[1763] This is to me a memorable year; for in it I had the happiness to obtain the acquaintance of that extraordinary man whose memoirs I am now writing; an acquaintance which I shall ever esteem as one of the most fortunate circumstances in my life. * * *

Mr. Thomas Davies the actor, who then kept a bookseller's shop in Russel Street, Covent Garden, told me that Johnson was very much his friend, and came frequently to his house, where he more than once invited me to meet him; but by some unlucky accident or other he was prevented from coming to us. * * *

At last, on Monday the 16th of May, when I was sitting in Mr. Davies's

---

4. William Warburton, bishop of Gloucester, friend and literary executor of Pope, editor of Pope and Shakespeare, theological controversialist.

back parlor, after having drunk tea with him and Mrs. Davies, Johnson unexpectedly came into the shop; and Mr. Davies having perceived him through the glass door in the room in which we were sitting, advancing towards us— he announced his awful approach to me, somewhat in the manner of an actor in the part of Horatio, when he addresses Hamlet on the appearance of his father's ghost, "Look, my Lord, it comes." I found that I had a very perfect idea of Johnson's figure, from the portrait of him painted by Sir Joshua Reynolds soon after he had published his *Dictionary*, in the attitude of sitting in his easy chair in deep meditation, which was the first picture his friend did for him, which Sir Joshua very kindly presented to me, and from which an engraving has been made for this work. Mr. Davies mentioned my name, and respectfully introduced me to him. I was much agitated; and recollecting his prejudice against the Scotch, of which I had heard much, I said to Davies, "Don't tell where I come from."—"From Scotland," cried Davies roguishly. "Mr. Johnson," said I, "I do indeed come from Scotland, but I cannot help it." I am willing to flatter myself that I meant this as light pleasantry to soothe and conciliate him, and not as an humiliating abasement at the expense of my country. But however that might be, this speech was somewhat unlucky; for with that quickness of wit for which he was so remarkable, he seized the expression "come from Scotland," which I used in the sense of being of that country; and, as if I had said that I had come away from it, or left it, retorted, "That, Sir, I find, is what a very great many of your countrymen cannot help." This stroke stunned me a good deal; and when we had sat down, I felt myself not a little embarrassed, and apprehensive of what might come next. He then addressed himself to Davies: "What do you think of Garrick? He has refused me an order for the play for Miss Williams,[5] because he knows the house will be full, and that an order would be worth three shillings." Eager to take any opening to get into conversation with him, I ventured to say, "O Sir, I cannot think Mr. Garrick would grudge such a trifle to you." "Sir," said he, with a stern look, "I have known David Garrick longer than you have done: and I know no right you have to talk to me on the subject." Perhaps I deserved this check; for it was rather presumptuous in me, an entire stranger, to express any doubt of the justice of his animadversion upon his old acquaintance and pupil. I now felt myself much mortified, and began to think that the hope which I had long indulged of obtaining his acquaintance was blasted. And, in truth, had not my ardor been uncommonly strong, and my resolution uncommonly persevering, so rough a reception might have deterred me forever from making any further attempts. Fortunately, however, I remained upon the field not wholly discomfited. * * *

I was highly pleased with the extraordinary vigor of his conversation, and regretted that I was drawn away from it by an engagement at another place. I had, for a part of the evening, been left alone with him, and had ventured to make an observation now and then, which he received very civilly; so that I was satisfied that though there was a roughness in his manner, there was no ill nature in his disposition. Davies followed me to the door, and when I complained to him a little of the hard blows which the great man had given

5. Mrs. Anna Williams (1706–1783), a blind poet and friend of Mrs. Johnson. She continued to live in Johnson's house after his wife's death and habitually sat up to make tea for him whenever he came home.

me, he kindly took upon him to console me by saying, "Don't be uneasy. I can see he likes you very well."

[FEAR OF DEATH]

[1769] When we were alone, I introduced the subject of death, and endeavored to maintain that the fear of it might be got over. I told him that David Hume said to me, he was no more uneasy to think he should *not be* after this life, than that he *had not been* before he began to exist. JOHNSON. "Sir, if he really thinks so, his perceptions are disturbed; he is mad: if he does not think so, he lies. He may tell you, he holds his finger in the flame of a candle, without feeling pain; would you believe him? When he dies, he at least gives up all he has." BOSWELL. "Foote,[6] Sir, told me, that when he was very ill he was not afraid to die." JOHNSON. "It is not true, Sir. Hold a pistol to Foote's breast, or to Hume's breast, and threaten to kill them, and you'll see how they behave." BOSWELL. "But may we not fortify our minds for the approach of death?" Here I am sensible I was in the wrong, to bring before his view what he ever looked upon with horror; for although when in a celestial frame, in his *Vanity of Human Wishes,* he has supposed death to be "kind Nature's signal for retreat," from this stage of being to "a happier seat," his thoughts upon this awful change were in general full of dismal apprehensions. His mind resembled the vast amphitheater, the Colosseum at Rome. In the center stood his judgment, which, like a mighty gladiator, combated those apprehensions that, like the wild beasts of the arena, were all around in cells, ready to be let out upon him. After a conflict, he drove them back into their dens; but not killing them, they were still assailing him. To my question, whether we might not fortify our minds for the approach of death, he answered, in a passion, "No, Sir, let it alone. It matters not how a man dies, but how he lives. The act of dying is not of importance, it lasts so short a time." He added (with an earnest look), "A man knows it must be so, and submits. It will do him no good to whine."

I attempted to continue the conversation. He was so provoked that he said, "Give us no more of this"; and was thrown into such a state of agitation that he expressed himself in a way that alarmed and distressed me; showed an impatience that I should leave him, and when I was going away, called to me sternly, "Don't let us meet tomorrow." * * *

[JOHNSON FACES DEATH]

Death had always been to him an object of terror; so that, though by no means happy, he still clung to life with an eagerness at which many have wondered. At any time when he was ill, he was very much pleased to be told that he looked better. An ingenious member of the Eumelian Club[7] informs me that upon one occasion when he said to him that he saw health returning to his cheek, Johnson seized him by the hand and exclaimed, "Sir, you are one of the kindest friends I ever had." * * *

About eight or ten days before his death, when Dr. Brocklesby paid him

---

6. Samuel Foote, actor and dramatist, famous for his wit and his skill in mimicry.

7. A club to which Boswell and Reynolds belonged.

his morning visit, he seemed very low and desponding, and said, "I have been as a dying man all night." He then emphatically broke out in the words of Shakespeare:

> "Canst thou not minister to a mind diseased;
> Pluck from the memory a rooted sorrow,
> Raze out the written troubles of the brain,
> And with some sweet oblivious antidote
> Cleanse the stuffed bosom of that perilous stuff
> Which weighs upon the heart?"

To which Dr. Brocklesby readily answered, from the same great poet:

> "Therein the patient
> Must minister to himself."[8]

Johnson expressed himself much satisfied with the application. * * *

Dr. Brocklesby, who will not be suspected of fanaticism, obliged me with the following account:

> "For some time before his death, all his fears were calmed and absorbed by the prevalence of his faith, and his trust in the merits and *propitiation* of Jesus Christ." * * *

Johnson having thus in his mind the true Christian scheme, at once rational and consolatory, uniting justice and mercy in the Divinity, with the improvement of human nature, previous to his receiving the Holy Sacrament in his apartment, composed and fervently uttered this prayer:

> "Almighty and most merciful Father, I am now as to human eyes, it seems, about to commemorate, for the last time, the death of thy Son Jesus Christ, our Saviour and Redeemer. Grant, O Lord, that my whole hope and confidence may be in his merits, and thy mercy; enforce and accept my imperfect repentance; make this commemoration available to the confirmation of my faith, the establishment of my hope, and the enlargement of my charity; and make the death of thy Son Jesus Christ effectual to my redemption. Have mercy upon me, and pardon the multitude of my offenses. Bless my friends; have mercy upon all men. Support me, by thy Holy Spirit, in the days of weakness, and at the hour of death; and receive me, at my death, to everlasting happiness, for the sake of Jesus Christ. Amen."

Having * * * made his will on the 8th and 9th of December, and settled all his worldly affairs, he languished till Monday, the 13th of that month, when he expired, about seven o'clock in the evening, with so little apparent pain that his attendants hardly perceived when his dissolution took place. * * *

1791

---

8. *Macbeth* 5.3.40–46.

THOMAS GRAY
1716–1771

The man who wrote the English poem most loved by what Samuel Johnson called "the common reader" was oddly enough a scholarly recluse who lived the quiet life of a university professor in the stagnant atmosphere of mid-eighteenth-century Cambridge, where toward the end of his life he held the professorship of modern history without feeling called on to give a single lecture. He was educated at Eton, where he made intimate friends—Richard West; Thomas Ashton; and Horace Walpole, the son of the prime minister. After four years at Cambridge he left without a degree to make the grand tour of France and Italy as Walpole's guest. The death of West in 1742 desolated Gray, and memories of West haunt much of his verse. He spent the rest of his life in Cambridge, pursuing his studies and writing delightful letters as well as a handful of poems—including two high-flown Pindaric odes, *The Progress of Poesy* (1754) and *The Bard* (1757).

Most of Gray's poems take part in a contemporary reaction against the finish of Pope's couplets; poets sought a new style, at once intimate and prophetic. Gray held that "the language of the age is never the language of poetry," and often uses archaic diction and distorted syntax. But the *Elegy Written in a Country Churchyard* stands alone in his work. It balances Latinate phrases with living English speech, and the learning of a scholar with a common humanity that everyone can share. Johnson, who did not usually like Gray's poetry, acknowledged that the *Elegy* would live forever:

> The Churchyard abounds with images which find a mirror in every mind, and with sentiments to which every bosom returns an echo. The four stanzas beginning "Yet even these bones" are to me original: I have never seen the notions in any other place; yet he that reads them here, persuades himself that he has always felt them. Had Gray written often thus, it had been vain to blame, and useless to praise him.

Ode on the Death of a Favorite Cat[1]
Drowned in a Tub of Goldfishes

'Twas on a lofty vase's side,
Where China's gayest art had dyed
   The azure flowers that blow;°   *bloom*
Demurest of the tabby kind,
5   The pensive Selima reclined,
   Gazed on the lake below.

Her conscious tail her joy declared;
The fair round face, the snowy beard,
   The velvet of her paws,
10 Her coat, that with the tortoise vies,
Her ears of jet, and emerald eyes,
   She saw; and purred applause.

Still had she gazed; but 'midst the tide
Two angel forms were seen to glide,

---

1. Selima, one of Horace Walpole's cats, had recently drowned in a china cistern. Gray wrote this memorial at Walpole's request.

15   The genii of the stream:
    Their scaly armor's Tyrian° hue   *purple*
    Through richest purple to the view
        Betrayed a golden gleam.

    The hapless nymph with wonder saw:
20   A whisker first and then a claw,
        With many an ardent wish,
    She stretched in vain to reach the prize.
    What female heart can gold despise?
        What cat's averse to fish?

25   Presumptuous maid! with looks intent
    Again she stretched, again she bent,
        Nor knew the gulf between.
    (Malignant Fate sat by and smiled)
    The slippery verge her feet beguiled,
30   She tumbled headlong in.

    Eight times emerging from the flood
    She mewed to every watery god,
        Some speedy aid to send.
    No dolphin came, no nereid° stirred: *sea nymph*
35   Nor cruel Tom, nor Susan[2] heard.
        A favorite has no friend!

    From hence, ye beauties, undeceived,
    Know, one false step is ne'er retrieved,
        And be with caution bold.
40   Not all that tempts your wandering eyes
    And heedless hearts is lawful prize;
        Nor all that glisters gold.

1747   1748

Elegy Written in a Country Churchyard

The curfew tolls the knell of parting day,
    The lowing herd wind slowly o'er the lea,
The plowman homeward plods his weary way,
    And leaves the world to darkness and to me.

5   Now fades the glimmering landscape on the sight,
    And all the air a solemn stillness holds,
Save where the beetle wheels his droning flight,
    And drowsy tinklings lull the distant folds;

Save that from yonder ivy-mantled tower
10   The moping owl does to the moon complain

2. "Tom" and "Susan" are servants' names.

Of such, as wandering near her secret bower,
　　Molest her ancient solitary reign.

Beneath those rugged elms, that yew tree's shade,
　　Where heaves the turf in many a moldering heap,
15　Each in his narrow cell forever laid,　　　　　　　　　　　*untaught*
　　The rude° forefathers of the hamlet sleep.

The breezy call of incense-breathing Morn,
　　The swallow twittering from the straw-built shed,
The cock's shrill clarion, or the echoing horn,°　　　　　*hunter's horn*
20　No more shall rouse them from their lowly bed.

For them no more the blazing hearth shall burn,
　　Or busy housewife ply her evening care;
No children run to lisp their sire's return,
　　Or climb his knees the envied kiss to share.

25　Oft did the harvest to their sickle yield,
　　Their furrow oft the stubborn glebe° has broke;　　　　*soil, turf*
How jocund did they drive their team afield!
　　How bowed the woods beneath their sturdy stroke!

Let not Ambition mock their useful toil,
30　Their homely joys, and destiny obscure;
Nor Grandeur hear with a disdainful smile
　　The short and simple annals of the poor.

The boast of heraldry,° the pomp of power,　　　　　　　*noble birth*
　　And all that beauty, all that wealth e'er gave,
35　Awaits alike the inevitable hour.
　　The paths of glory lead but to the grave.

Nor you, ye proud, impute to these the fault,
　　If Memory o'er their tomb no trophies[1] raise,
Where through the long-drawn aisle and fretted[2] vault
40　The pealing anthem swells the note of praise.

Can storied urn[3] or animated° bust　　　　　　　　　　*lifelike*
　　Back to its mansion call the fleeting breath?
Can Honor's voice provoke° the silent dust,　　　　　　*call forth*
　　Or Flattery soothe the dull cold ear of Death?

45　Perhaps in this neglected spot is laid
　　Some heart once pregnant with celestial fire;
Hands that the rod of empire might have swayed,
　　Or waked to ecstasy the living lyre.

---

1. An ornamental or symbolic group of figures
depicting the achievements of the deceased.
2. Decorated with intersecting lines in relief.

3. A funeral urn with an epitaph or pictured story
inscribed on it.

But Knowledge to their eyes her ample page
50   Rich with the spoils of time did ne'er unroll;
Chill Penury repressed their noble rage,
    And froze the genial current of the soul.

Full many a gem of purest ray serene,
    The dark unfathomed caves of ocean bear:
55 Full many a flower is born to blush unseen,
    And waste its sweetness on the desert air.

Some village Hampden,[4] that with dauntless breast
    The little tyrant of his fields withstood;
Some mute inglorious Milton here may rest,
60   Some Cromwell guiltless of his country's blood.

The applause of listening senates to command,
    The threats of pain and ruin to despise,
To scatter plenty o'er a smiling land,
    And read their history in a nation's eyes,

65 Their lot forbade: nor circumscribed alone
    Their growing virtues, but their crimes confined;
Forbade to wade through slaughter to a throne,
    And shut the gates of mercy on mankind,

The struggling pangs of conscious truth to hide,
70   To quench the blushes of ingenuous shame,
Or heap the shrine of Luxury and Pride
    With incense kindled at the Muse's flame.

Far from the madding crowd's ignoble strife,
    Their sober wishes never learned to stray;
75 Along the cool sequestered vale of life
    They kept the noiseless tenor of their way.

Yet even these bones from insult to protect
    Some frail memorial still erected nigh,
With uncouth rhymes and shapeless sculpture decked,[5]
80   Implores the passing tribute of a sigh.

Their name, their years, spelt by the unlettered Muse,
    The place of fame and elegy supply:
And many a holy text around she strews,
    That teach the rustic moralist to die.

85 For who to dumb Forgetfulness a prey,
    This pleasing anxious being e'er resigned,
Left the warm precincts of the cheerful day,
    Nor cast one longing lingering look behind?

---

4. John Hampden (1594–1643), who, both as a
private citizen and as a Member of Parliament,
zealously defended the rights of the people against
the autocratic policies of Charles I.
5. Cf. "the storied urn or animated bust" dedicated inside the church to "the proud" (line 41).

On some fond breast the parting soul relies,
90   Some pious drops the closing eye requires;
Even from the tomb the voice of Nature cries,
    Even in our ashes live their wonted fires.

For thee, who mindful of the unhonored dead
    Dost in these lines their artless tale relate;
95   If chance, by lonely contemplation led,
    Some kindred spirit shall inquire thy fate,

Haply some hoary-headed swain may say,
    "Oft have we seen him at the peep of dawn
Brushing with hasty steps the dews away
100   To meet the sun upon the upland lawn.

"There at the foot of yonder nodding beech
    That wreathes its old fantastic roots so high,
His listless length at noontide would he stretch,
    And pore upon the brook that babbles by.

105   "Hard by yon wood, now smiling as in scorn,
    Muttering his wayward fancies he would rove,
Now drooping, woeful wan, like one forlorn,
    Or crazed with care, or crossed in hopeless love.

"One morn I missed him on the customed hill,
110   Along the heath and near his favorite tree;
Another came; nor yet beside the rill,
    Nor up the lawn, nor at the wood was he;

"The next with dirges due in sad array
    Slow through the churchway path we saw him borne.
115   Approach and read (for thou canst read) the lay,
    Graved on the stone beneath yon aged thorn."

The Epitaph

Here rests his head upon the lap of Earth
    A youth to Fortune and to Fame unknown.
Fair Science° frowned not on his humble birth,   Learning
120   *And Melancholy marked him for her own.*

Large was his bounty, and his soul sincere,
    Heaven did a recompense as largely send:
He gave to Misery all he had, a tear,
    He gained from Heaven ('twas all he wished) a friend.

125   *No farther seek his merits to disclose,*
    Or draw his frailties from their dread abode

(There they alike in trembling hope repose),
  The bosom of his Father and his God.

ca. 1742–50   1751

WILLIAM COLLINS
1721–1759

William Collins was born in Chichester and was educated at Winchester and Oxford. Coming up to London from the university, he tried to establish himself as an author, but he was given rather to planning than to writing books. Samuel Johnson later remembered him affectionately as a man of learning who "loved fairies, genii, giants, and monsters" and who "delighted to rove through the meanders of enchantment." In 1746 Collins published *Odes on Several Descriptive and Allegorical Subjects,* his part in an undertaking, with his friend Joseph Warton, to create a new poetry, more lyrical and fanciful than that of Alexander Pope's generation. Collins's *Odes* address personified abstractions (Fear, Pity, the Passions), which are imagined as vivid presences that overwhelm the poet as he calls them to life. This quest for the sublime has impressed many later readers of Collins, though contemporaries often found his poems obscure. Inheriting some money, the poet traveled for a while, but fits of depression gradually deepened into total debility. He spent his last years in Chichester, forgotten by all but a small circle of loyal friends. By the end of the century, however, his reputation had grown; the Romantics admired his poems and felt akin to him. The *Ode to Evening,* which combines a chaste and cool classicism with a delicate feeling for landscape and mood, is one of the delightful poems of the century.

Ode Written in the Beginning of the Year 1746

> How sleep the brave[1] who sink to rest
> By all their country's wishes blest!
> When Spring, with dewy fingers cold,
> Returns to deck their hallowed mold,
> 5 She there shall dress a sweeter sod
> Than Fancy's feet have ever trod.
>
> By fairy hands their knell is rung,
> By forms unseen their dirge is sung;
> There Honor comes, a pilgrim gray,
> 10 To bless the turf that wraps their clay,
> And Freedom shall awhile repair,
> To dwell a weeping hermit there!

                                                                  1746

---

1. Collins is presumably thinking of those who lost their lives defending England in 1745, when the Scotch Jacobites, led by Bonnie Prince Charlie, penetrated to within 127 miles of London.

Ode to Evening[1]

If aught of oaten stop, or pastoral song,
May hope, chaste Eve, to soothe thy modest ear,
    Like thy own solemn springs,
    Thy springs and dying gales,
5 O nymph reserved, while now the bright-haired sun
Sits in yon western tent, whose cloudy skirts,
    With brede° ethereal wove,   *embroidery*
    O'erhang his wavy bed:
Now air is hushed, save where the weak-eyed bat,
10 With short shrill shriek flits by on leathern wing,
    Or where the beetle winds
    His small but sullen horn,
As oft he rises 'midst the twilight path,
Against the pilgrim borne in heedless hum:
15   Now teach me, maid composed,
    To breathe some softened strain,
Whose numbers,° stealing through thy darkening vale,   *measures*
    May not unseemly with its stillness suit,
    As, musing slow, I hail
20   Thy genial loved return!
For when thy folding-star[2] arising shows
His paly circlet, at his warning lamp
    The fragrant Hours, and elves
    Who slept in flowers the day,
25 And many a nymph who wreaths her brows with sedge,
And sheds the freshening dew, and, lovelier still,
    The pensive Pleasures sweet,
    Prepare thy shadowy car.
Then lead, calm vot'ress, where some sheety lake
30 Cheers the lone heath, or some time-hallowed pile
    Or upland fallows gray
    Reflect its last cool gleam.
But when chill blustering winds, or driving rain,
Forbid my willing feet, be mine the hut
35   That from the mountain's side
    Views wilds, and swelling floods,
And hamlets brown, and dim-discovered spires,
And hears their simple bell, and marks o'er all
    Thy dewy fingers draw
40   The gradual dusky veil.
While Spring shall pour his showers, as oft he wont,
And bathe thy breathing tresses, meekest Eve;
    While Summer loves to sport
    Beneath thy lingering light;
45 While sallow Autumn fills thy lap with leaves;

---

1. Collins borrowed the metrical structure and the rhymeless lines of this ode from Milton's translation of Horace, *Odes* 1.5 (1673). The text printed here is based on the revised version, published in Dodsley's *Miscellany* (1748).

2. The evening star, which signals the hour for herding the sheep into the sheepfold.

Or Winter, yelling through the troublous air,
    Affrights thy shrinking train,
    And rudely rends thy robes;
So long, sure-found beneath the sylvan shed,
50   Shall Fancy, Friendship, Science, rose-lipped Health,
    Thy gentlest influence own,
    And hymn thy favorite name!

                        1746, 1748

WILLIAM COWPER
1731–1800

There are no saner poems in the language than William Cowper's, yet they were written by a man who was periodically insane and who, for forty years, lived day to day with the possibility of madness. After attempting suicide in 1763, he believed that he was damned for having committed the unforgivable sin, the "sin against the Holy Ghost." From then on, a refugee from life, he looked for hope in Evangelicalism; and found shelter, first in the pious family of the clergyman, Morley Unwin, and after Unwin's death, with his widow, Mary Unwin, who cared for Cowper until her death in 1796. Their move to rural Olney (pronounced Own-y) in 1768 brought them under the influence of the Evangelical minister John Newton; with him Cowper wrote the famous *Olney Hymns*. But another attack of madness, in 1773, not only frustrated his planned marriage to Mary Unwin but left him convinced for the rest of his life that he had been cast out by God. He never again attended services, and the main purpose of his life thereafter was to divert his mind from numb despair by every possible innocent device. He gardened, he kept pets, he walked, he wrote letters (some of the best of the century), he conversed, he read—and he wrote poetry. When his work was published, it brought him a measure of fame that his modest nature could never have hoped for. In the small world and gentle musings of Cowper's major work, *The Task* (1785), contemporaries recognized their own heartfelt concerns. No poet of the century was more beloved.

The Castaway

Obscurest night involved the sky,
    The Atlantic billows roared,
When such a destined wretch as I,
    Washed headlong from on board,
5   Of friends, of hope, of all bereft,
    His floating home forever left.

No braver chief[1] could Albion boast
    Than he with whom he went,

---

1. George, Lord Anson (1697–1762), in whose *Voyage* (1748), Cowper, years before writing this poem, had read the story of the sailor washed overboard in a storm.

Nor ever ship left Albion's coast,
10   With warmer wishes sent.
He loved them both, but both in vain,
Nor him beheld, nor her again.

Not long beneath the whelming brine,
      Expert to swim, he lay;
15 Nor soon he felt his strength decline,
      Or courage die away;
But waged with death a lasting strife,
Supported by despair of life.

He shouted; nor his friends had failed
20   To check the vessel's course,
But so the furious blast prevailed,
      That, pitiless perforce,
They left their outcast mate behind,
And scudded still before the wind.

25 Some succor yet they could afford;
      And, such as storms allow,
The cask, the coop, the floated cord,
      Delayed not to bestow.
But he (they knew) nor ship, nor shore,
30 Whate'er they gave, should visit more.

Nor, cruel as it seemed, could he
      Their haste himself condemn,
Aware that flight, in such a sea,
      Alone could rescue them;
35 Yet bitter felt it still to die
Deserted, and his friends so nigh.

He long survives, who lives an hour
      In ocean, self-upheld;
And so long he, with unspent power,
40   His destiny repelled;
And ever, as the minutes flew,
Entreated help, or cried, "Adieu!"

At length, his transient respite past,
      His comrades, who before
45 Had heard his voice in every blast,
      Could catch the sound no more.
For then, by toil subdued, he drank
The stifling wave, and then he sank.

No poet wept him; but the page
50   Of narrative sincere,
That tells his name, his worth, his age,
      Is wet with Anson's tear.

And tears by bards or heroes shed
Alike immortalize the dead.

55 I therefore purpose not, or dream,
 Descanting on his fate,
To give the melancholy theme
 A more enduring date:
But misery still delights to trace
60 Its semblance in another's case.

No voice divine the storm allayed,
 No light propitious shone,
When, snatched from all effectual aid,
 We perished, each alone;
65 But I beneath a rougher sea,
 And whelmed in deeper gulfs than he.

1799   1803

OLAUDAH EQUIANO
ca. 1745–1797

The Interesting Narrative of the Life of Olaudah Equiano, or Gustavus Vassa, the African, Written by Himself, published in 1789, is the classic story of an eighteenth-century African's descent into slavery and rise to freedom. Raised in an Ibo village (in modern Nigeria), Olaudah Equiano was kidnapped by African raiders and sold into slavery. He survived the horrors of the Middle Passage to the New World, where an English naval officer bought him to serve as a cabin boy and renamed him Gustavus Vassa, after a sixteenth-century Swedish hero who freed his people from the Danes (such names concealed the status of a slave, because slavery was frowned on by the British Navy). During years at sea, as well as a period at a London school, Equiano acquired a basic education. He was also baptized, which many slaves expected to make them free. But his hopes were cruelly disappointed when, after six years' service, he was suddenly sold and shipped to the West Indies. There a Quaker merchant, Robert King, purchased him, employed him as a clerk and seaman, and eventually allowed him, in 1766, to buy his freedom. Equiano went back to England, working first as a hairdresser and later voyaging all over the world, even taking part in an effort to find a passage to India by way of the North Pole. In the 1780s he became involved in the abolitionist movement. The story of his life was an important contribution to that movement, not only for its explicit arguments against the slave trade but also for its demonstration that someone born in Africa could be humane, intelligent, a good Christian, and a free and eloquent British subject. The book went through many editions and made Equiano famous. He married an Englishwoman, fathered two daughters, and died in London in 1797.

The Life of Equiano combines several literary genres. It is a captivity narrative, a spiritual autobiography, a travel memoir, an adventure story, and an abolitionist tract. The early chapters describe the healthy, cheerful, and virtuous life of Africans, contrasted with European inhumanity, and the later chapters show how much a black man can achieve, when given a chance. Equiano does not disguise the strains of his

position as he is pulled between different identities anddifferent worlds. His main-
purpose, however, is clearly to force his readers to face the ordeals a slave must
endure—to live in his skin. If *Oroonoko* taught Europeans to sympathize with
Africans, Equiano taught them that a black man could speak for himself.

From The Interesting Narrative of the Life of Olaudah Equiano, or Gustavus Vassa, the African, Written by Himself

[THE MIDDLE PASSAGE][1]

The first object which saluted my eyes when I arrived on the coast was the
sea, and a slave ship, which was then riding at anchor, and waiting for its
cargo. These filled me with astonishment, which was soon converted into
terror when I was carried on board. I was immediately handled and tossed
up to see if I were sound by some of the crew; and I was now persuaded that
I had gotten into a world of bad spirits, and that they were going to kill me.
Their complexions too differing so much from ours, their long hair, and the
language they spoke, (which was very different from any I had ever heard)
united to confirm me in this belief. Indeed such were the horrors of my views
and fears at the moment, that, if ten thousand worlds had been my own, I
would have freely parted with them all to have exchanged my condition with
that of the meanest slave in my own country. When I looked round the ship
too and saw a large furnace of copper boiling, and a multitude of black people
of every description chained together, every one of their countenances
expressing dejection and sorrow, I no longer doubted of my fate; and, quite
overpowered with horror and anguish, I fell motionless on the deck and
fainted. When I recovered a little I found some black people about me, who
I believe were some of those who brought me on board, and had been receiving their pay; they talked to me in order to cheer me, but all in vain. I asked
them if we were not to be eaten by those white men with horrible looks, red
faces, and loose hair. They told me I was not; and one of the crew brought
me a small portion of spirituous liquor in a wine glass; but, being afraid of
him, I would not take it out of his hand. One of the blacks therefore took it
from him and gave it to me, and I took a little down my palate, which, instead
of reviving me, as they thought it would, threw me into the greatest consternation at the strange feeling it produced, having never tasted any such
liquor before. Soon after this the blacks who brought me on board went off,
and left me abandoned to despair. I now saw myself deprived of all chance
of returning to my native country, or even the least glimpse of hope of gaining
the shore, which I now considered as friendly; and I even wished for my
former slavery in preference to my present situation, which was filled with
horrors of every kind, still heightened by my ignorance of what I was to
undergo. I was not long suffered to indulge my grief; I was soon put down
under the decks, and there I received such a salutation in my nostrils as I
had never experienced in my life; so that, with the loathsomeness of the
stench, and crying together, I became so sick and low that I was not able to
eat, nor had I the least desire to taste any thing. I now wished for the last

1. After his kidnapping, young Equiano passes
from one African master to another. The last of
these, a merchant, treats him like a member of the
family, until one morning the boy is suddenly wakened and hurried away to the seacoast.

friend, death, to relieve me; but soon, to my grief, two of the white men offered me eatables; and, on my refusing to eat, one of them held me fast by the hands, and laid me across I think the windlass, and tied my feet, while the other flogged me severely. I had never experienced any thing of this kind before; and although, not being used to the water, I naturally feared that element the first time I saw it, yet nevertheless, could I have got over the nettings,[2] I would have jumped over the side, but I could not; and, besides, the crew used to watch us very closely who were not chained down to the decks, lest we should leap into the water; and I have seen some of these poor African prisoners most severely cut for attempting to do so, and hourly whipped for not eating. This indeed was often the case with myself. In a little time after, amongst the poor chained men, I found some of my own nation, which in a small degree gave ease to my mind. I inquired of these what was to be done with us; they gave me to understand we were to be carried to these white people's country to work for them. I then was a little revived, and thought, if it were no worse than working, my situation was not so desperate: but still I feared I should be put to death, the white people looked and acted, as I thought, in so savage a manner; for I had never seen among any people such instances of brutal cruelty; and this not only shewn towards us blacks, but also to some of the whites themselves. One white man in particular I saw, when we were permitted to be on deck, flogged so unmercifully with a large rope near the foremast, that he died in consequence of it; and they tossed him over the side as they would have done a brute. This made me fear these people the more; and I expected nothing less than to be treated in the same manner. I could not help expressing my fears and apprehensions to some of my countrymen: I asked them if these people had no country, but lived in this hollow place (the ship): they told me they did not, but came from a distant one. "Then," said I, "how comes it in all our country we never heard of them?" They told me because they lived so very far off. I then asked where were their women? had they any like themselves? I was told they had: "and why," said I, "do we not see them?" they answered, because they were left behind. I asked how the vessel could go? they told me they could not tell; but that there were cloths put upon the masts by the help of the ropes I saw, and then the vessel went on; and the white men had some spell or magic they put in the water when they liked in order to stop the vessel. I was exceedingly amazed at this account, and really thought they were spirits. I therefore wished much to be from amongst them, for I expected they would sacrifice me: but my wishes were vain; for we were so quartered that it was impossible for any of us to make our escape. While we stayed on the coast I was mostly on deck; and one day, to my great astonishment, I saw one of these vessels coming in with the sails up. As soon as the whites saw it, they gave a great shout, at which we were amazed; and the more so as the vessel appeared larger by approaching nearer. At last she came to an anchor in my sight, and when the anchor was let go I and my countrymen who saw it were lost in astonishment to observe the vessel stop; and were now convinced it was done by magic. Soon after this the other ship got her boats out, and they came on board of us, and the people of both ships seemed very glad to see each other. Several of the strangers also shook hands

2. A network of small ropes around the ship kept slaves from jumping overboard.

with us black people, and made motions with their hands, signifying I suppose we were to go to their country; but we did not understand them. At last, when the ship we were in had got in all her cargo, they made ready with many fearful noises, and we were all put under deck, so that we could not see how they managed the vessel. But this disappointment was the least of my sorrow. The stench of the hold while we were on the coast was so intolerably loathsome, that it was dangerous to remain there for any time, and some of us had been permitted to stay on the deck for the fresh air; but now that the whole ship's cargo were confined together, it became absolutely pestilential. The closeness of the place, and the heat of the climate, added to the number in the ship, which was so crowded that each had scarcely room to turn himself, almost suffocated us. This produced copious perspirations, so that the air soon became unfit for respiration, from a variety of loathsome smells, and brought on a sickness among the slaves, of which many died, thus falling victims to the improvident avarice, as I may call it, of their purchasers. This wretched situation was again aggravated by the galling of the chains, now become insupportable; and the filth of the necessary tubs,[3] into which the children often fell, and were almost suffocated. The shrieks of the women, and the groans of the dying, rendered the whole a scene of horror almost inconceivable. Happily perhaps for myself I was soon reduced so low here that it was thought necessary to keep me almost always on deck; and from[4] my extreme youth I was not put in fetters. In this situation I expected every hour to share the fate of my companions, some of whom were almost daily brought upon deck at the point of death, which I began to hope would soon put an end to my miseries. Often did I think many of the inhabitants of the deep much more happy than myself. I envied them the freedom they enjoyed, and as often wished I could change my condition for theirs. Every circumstance I met with served only to render my state more painful, and heighten my apprehensions, and my opinion of the cruelty of the whites. One day they had taken a number of fishes; and when they had killed and satisfied themselves with as many as they thought fit, to our astonishment who were on the deck, rather than give any of them to us to eat as we expected, they tossed the remaining fish into the sea again, although we begged and prayed for some as well as we could, but in vain; and some of my countrymen, being pressed by hunger, took an opportunity, when they thought no one saw them, of trying to get a little privately; but they were discovered, and the attempt procured them some very severe floggings.

One day, when we had a smooth sea and moderate wind, two of my wearied countrymen who were chained together (I was near them at the time), preferring death to such a life of misery, somehow made through the nettings and jumped into the sea; immediately another quite dejected fellow, who, on account of his illness, was suffered to be out of irons, also followed their example; and I believe many more would very soon have done the same if they had not been prevented by the ship's crew, who were instantly alarmed. Those of us that were the most active were in a moment put down under the deck, and there was such a noise and confusion amongst the people of the ship as I never heard before, to stop her, and get the boat out to go after the slaves. However two of the wretches were drowned, but they got the other,

---

3. Latrines.　　　　　　　　　　　　4. Because of.

and afterwards flogged him unmercifully for thus attempting to prefer death to slavery. In this manner we continued to undergo more hardships than I can now relate, hardships which are inseparable from this accursed trade. Many a time we were near suffocation from the want of fresh air, which we were often without for whole days together. This, and the stench of the necessary tubs, carried off many. During our passage I first saw flying fishes, which surprised me very much: they used frequently to fly across the ship, and many of them fell on the deck. I also now first saw the use of the quadrant; I had often with astonishment seen the mariners make observations with it, and I could not think what it meant. They at last took notice of my surprise; and one of them, willing to increase it, as well as to gratify my curiosity, made me one day look through it. The clouds appeared to me to be land, which disappeared as they passed along. This heightened my wonder; and I was now more persuaded than ever that I was in another world, and that every thing about me was magic. At last we came in sight of the island of Barbados,[5] at which the whites on board gave a great shout, and made many signs of joy to us. We did not know what to think of this; but as the vessel drew nearer we plainly saw the harbor, and other ships of different kinds and sizes; and we soon anchored amongst them off Bridge Town. Many merchants and planters now came on board, though it was in the evening. They put us in separate parcels,[6] and examined us attentively. They also made us jump, and pointed to the land, signifying we were to go there. We thought by this we should be eaten by these ugly men, as they appeared to us; and, when soon after we were all put down under the deck again, there was much dread and trembling among us, and nothing but bitter cries to be heard all the night from these apprehensions, insomuch that at last the white people got some old slaves from the land to pacify us. They told us we were not to be eaten, but to work, and were soon to go on land, where we should see many of our country people. This report eased us much; and sure enough, soon after we were landed, there came to us Africans of all languages. We were conducted immediately to the merchant's yard, where we were pent up altogether like so many sheep in a fold, without regard to sex or age. As every object was new to me, every thing I saw filled me with surprise. What struck me first was that the houses were built with stories, and in every other respect different from those in Africa; but I was still more astonished on seeing people on horseback. I did not know what this could mean; and indeed I thought these people were full of nothing but magical arts. While I was in this astonishment one of my fellow prisoners spoke to a countryman of his about the horses, who said they were the same kind they had in their country. I understood them, though they were from a distant part of Africa, and I thought it odd I had not seen any horses there; but afterwards, when I came to converse with different Africans, I found they had many horses amongst them, and much larger than those I then saw. We were not many days in the merchant's custody before we were sold after their usual manner, which is this:—On a signal given (as the beat of a drum) the buyers rush at once into the yard where the slaves are confined, and make a choice of that parcel they like best. The noise and clamor with which this is attended, and the eager-

---

5. The easternmost Caribbean island, then an important center for the trade of sugar and slaves.

6. Groups sorted to be sold as one lot.

ness visible in the countenances of the buyers, serve not a little to increase the apprehensions of the terrified Africans, who may well be supposed to consider them as the ministers of that destruction to which they think themselves devoted.[7] In this manner, without scruple, are relations and friends separated, most of them never to see each other again. I remember in the vessel in which I was brought over, in the men's apartment, there were several brothers, who, in the sale, were sold in different lots; and it was very moving on this occasion to see and hear their cries at parting. O, ye nominal Christians! might not an African ask you, learned you this from your God, who says unto you, Do unto all men as you would men should do unto you? Is it not enough that we are torn from our country and friends to toil for your luxury and lust of gain? Must every tender feeling be likewise sacrificed to your avarice? Are the dearest friends and relations, now rendered more dear by their separation from their kindred, still to be parted from each other, and thus prevented from cheering the gloom of slavery with the small comfort of being together and mingling their sufferings and sorrows? Why are parents to lose their children, brothers their sisters, or husbands their wives? Surely this is a new refinement in cruelty, which, while it has no advantage to atone for it, thus aggravates distress, and adds fresh horrors even to the wretchedness of slavery.

* * *

[A FREE MAN][8]

Every day now brought me nearer my freedom, and I was impatient till we proceeded again to sea, that I might have an opportunity of getting a sum large enough to purchase it. I was not long ungratified; for, in the beginning of the year 1766, my master bought another sloop, named the *Nancy*, the largest I had ever seen. She was partly laden, and was to proceed to Philadelphia; our Captain had his choice of three, and I was well pleased he chose this, which was the largest; for, from his having a large vessel, I had more room, and could carry a larger quantity of goods with me. Accordingly, when we had delivered our old vessel, the *Prudence*, and completed the lading of the *Nancy*, having made near three hundred per cent, by four barrels of pork I brought from Charlestown, I laid in as large a cargo as I could, trusting to God's providence to prosper my undertaking. With these views I sailed for Philadelphia. On our passage, when we drew near the land, I was for the first time surprised at the sight of some whales, having never seen any such large sea monsters before; and as we sailed by the land one morning I saw a puppy whale close by the vessel; it was about the length of a wherry boat, and it followed us all the day till we got within the Capes. We arrived safe and in good time at Philadelphia, and I sold my goods there chiefly to the Quakers. They always appeared to be a very honest discreet sort of people, and never attempted to impose on me; I therefore liked them, and ever after chose to deal with them in preference to any others.

7. Doomed.

8. Frustrated in his hope to be set free in England, Equiano is shipped to Montserrat, a British colony in the Leeward Islands of the West Indies. Robert King, a prosperous Quaker merchant from Philadelphia, buys him, treats him kindly, and values

him as a reliable worker. By being useful to a friendly sea captain, Thomas Farmer, Equiano has opportunities to travel and trade goods for money. Eventually King promises to let him purchase his freedom for his original cost: forty pounds sterling.

One Sunday morning while I was here, as I was going to church, I chanced to pass a meeting house. The doors being open, and the house full of people, it excited my curiosity to go in. When I entered the house, to my great surprise, I saw a very tall woman standing in the midst of them, speaking in an audible voice something which I could not understand. Having never seen anything of this kind before, I stood and stared about me for some time, wondering at this odd scene. As soon as it was over I took an opportunity to make inquiry about the place and people, when I was informed they were called Quakers.[9] I particularly asked what that woman I saw in the midst of them had said, but none of them were pleased to satisfy me; so I quitted them, and soon after, as I was returning, I came to a church crowded with people; the church-yard was full likewise, and a number of people were even mounted on ladders, looking in at the windows. I thought this a strange sight, as I had never seen churches, either in England or the West Indies, crowded in this manner before. I therefore made bold to ask some people the meaning of all this, and they told me the Rev. Mr. George Whitfield[1] was preaching. I had often heard of this gentleman, and had wished to see and hear him; but I had never before had an opportunity. I now therefore resolved to gratify myself with the sight, and I pressed in amidst the multitude. When I got into the church I saw this pious man exhorting the people with the greatest fervor and earnestness, and sweating as much as I ever did while in slavery on Montserrat beach. I was very much struck and impressed with this; I thought it strange I had never seen divines exert themselves in this manner before, and I was no longer at a loss to account for the thin congregations they preached to.

When we had discharged our cargo here, and were loaded again, we left this fruitful land once more, and set sail for Montserrat. My traffic had hitherto succeeded so well with me, that I thought, by selling my goods when we arrived at Montserrat, I should have enough to purchase my freedom. But, as soon as our vessel arrived there, my master came on board, and gave orders for us to go to St. Eustatia,[2] and discharge our cargo there, and from thence proceed for Georgia. I was much disappointed at this; but thinking, as usual, it was of no use to murmur at the decrees of fate, I submitted without repining, and we went to St. Eustatia. After we had discharged our cargo there we took in a live cargo, as we call a cargo of slaves. Here I sold my goods tolerably well; but, not being able to lay out all my money in this small island to as much advantage as in many other places, I laid out only part, and the remainder I brought away with me neat.[3] We sailed from hence for Georgia, and I was glad when we got there, though I had not much reason to like the place from my last adventure in Savannah;[4] but I longed to get back to Montserrat and procure my freedom, which I expected to be able to purchase when I returned. As soon as we arrived here I waited on my careful doctor, Mr. Brady, to whom I made the

---

9. Quaker meetings are not led by clergy; any male or female worshiper who felt inspired by God could rise to speak.
1. Whitefield (1714–1770), a famous evangelist who helped found Methodism, was in Britain, not Philadelphia, in 1766. It is possible that Equiano had heard him preach the previous year, in Savannah, Georgia. Equiano's later conversion to Meth-

odism will become a dominant theme of his life story.
2. An island in the Netherlands Antilles (West Indies).
3. Intact.
4. The year before, a drunken slave owner and his servant had beaten Equiano so brutally that he nearly died.

most grateful acknowledgments in my power for his former kindness and attention during my illness.

While we were here an odd circumstance happened to the Captain and me, which disappointed us both a good deal. A silversmith, whom we had brought to this place some voyages before, agreed with the Captain to return with us to the West Indies, and promised at the same time to give the Captain a great deal of money, having pretended to take a liking to him, and being, as we thought, very rich. But while we stayed to load our vessel this man was taken ill in a house where he worked, and in a week's time became very bad. The worse he grew the more he used to speak of giving the Captain what he had promised him, so that he expected something considerable from the death of this man, who had no wife or child, and he attended him day and night. I used also to go with the Captain, at his own desire, to attend him; especially when we saw there was no appearance of his recovery; and, in order to recompense me for my trouble, the Captain promised me ten pounds, when he should get the man's property. I thought this would be of great service to me, although I had nearly money enough to purchase my freedom, if I should get safe this voyage to Montserrat. In this expectation I laid out above eight pounds of my money for a suit of superfine clothes to dance with at my freedom, which I hoped was then at hand. We still contin-ued to attend this man, and were with him even on the last day he lived, till very late at night, when we went on board. After we were got to bed, about one or two o'clock in the morning, the Captain was sent for, and informed the man was dead. On this he came to my bed, and, waking me, informed me of it, and desired me to get up and procure a light, and immediately go to him. I told him I was very sleepy, and wished he would take somebody else with him, or else, as the man was dead, and could want no farther attendance, to let all things remain as they were till next morning. "No, no," said he, "we will have the money tonight, I cannot wait till tomorrow; so let us go." Accordingly I got up and struck a light, and away we both went and saw the man as dead as we could wish. The Captain said he would give him a grand burial, in gratitude for the promised treasure; and desired that all the things belonging to the deceased might be brought forth. Among others, there was a nest of trunks of which he had kept the keys whilst the man was ill, and when they were produced we opened them with no small eagerness and expectation; and as there were a great number within one another, with much impatience we took them one out of the other. At last, when we came to the smallest, and had opened it, we saw it was full of papers, which we supposed to be notes; at the sight of which our hearts leapt for joy; and that instant the Captain, clapping his hands, cried out, "Thank God, here it is." But when we took up the trunk, and began to examine the supposed treasure and long-looked-for bounty, (alas! alas! how uncertain and deceitful are all human affairs!) what had we found! While we were embracing a substance we grasped an empty nothing. The whole amount that was in the nest of trunks was only one dollar and a half; and all that the man possessed would not pay for his coffin. Our sudden and exquisite joy was now succeeded by as sudden and exquisite pain; and my Captain and I exhibited, for some time, most ridiculous figures—pictures of chagrin and disappointment! We went away greatly mortified, and left the deceased to do as well as he could for himself, as we had taken so good care of him when alive for nothing. We set sail once more for Montserrat, and arrived there safe; but much out of humor with our friend the silversmith. When we had unladen the vessel, and I had sold my venture, finding myself master of about forty-seven pounds, I consulted my true friend, the Captain, how I should proceed in offering my master the money for my freedom. He told me to come on a certain morning, when he and my master would be at breakfast together. Accordingly, on that morning I went, and met the Captain there, as he had appointed. When I went in I made my obeisance to my master, and with my money in my hand, and many fears in my heart, I prayed him to be as good as his offer to me, when he was pleased to promise me my freedom as soon as I could purchase it. This speech seemed to confound him; he began to recoil; and my heart that instant sank within me. "What," said he, "give you your freedom? Why, where did you get the money? Have you got forty pounds sterling?" "Yes, sir," I answered. "How did you get it?" replied he. I told him, very honestly. The Captain then said he knew I got the money very honestly and with much industry, and that I was particularly careful. On which my master replied, I got money much faster than he did; and said he would not have made me the promise he did if he had thought I should have got money so soon. "Come, come," said my worthy Captain, clapping my master on the back, "Come, Robert" (which was his name), "I think you must let him have his freedom; you have laid your money out very well; you have received good interest for it all this time, and here is now the principal at last. I know Gustavus has earned you more than an hundred a-year, and he will still save you money, as he will not leave you:—Come, Robert, take the money." My master then said, he would not be worse than his promise; and, taking the money, told me to go to the Secretary at the Register Office, and get my manumission[5] drawn up. These words of my master were like a voice from heaven to me: in an instant all my trepidation was turned into unutterable bliss; and I most reverently bowed myself with gratitude, unable to express my feelings, but by the overflowing of my eyes, while my true and worthy friend, the Captain, congratulated us both with a peculiar degree of heartfelt pleasure. As soon as the first transports of my joy were over, and that I had expressed my thanks to these my worthy friends in the best manner I was able, I rose with a heart full of affection and reverence, and left the room, in order to obey my master's joyful mandate of going to the Register Office. As I was leaving the house I called to mind the words of the Psalmist, in the 126th Psalm, and like him, "I glorified God in my heart, in whom I trusted." These words had been impressed on my mind from the very day I was forced from Deptford[6] to the present hour, and I now saw them, as I thought, fulfilled and verified. My imagination was all rapture as I flew to the Register Office, and in this respect, like the apostle Peter[7] (whose deliverance from prison was so sudden and extraordinary, that he thought he was in a vision), I could scarcely believe I was awake. Heavens! who could do justice to my feelings at this moment! Not conquering heroes themselves, in the midst of a triumph—Not the tender mother who had just regained her long-lost infant, and presses it to her heart—Not the weary hungry mariner, at the sight of the desired friendly port—Not the lover, when he once more

5. Release from slavery.
6. The port near London from which Equiano was sold by his English master.
7. Acts, chap. xii, ver. 9 [Equiano's note].

embraces his beloved mistress, after she had been ravished from his arms!—All within my breast was tumult, wildness, and delirium! My feet scarcely touched the ground, for they were winged with joy, and, like Elijah, as he rose to Heaven,[8] they "were with lightning sped as I went on." Every one I met I told of my happiness, and blazed about the virtue of my amiable master and captain.

When I got to the office and acquainted the Register with my errand he congratulated me on the occasion, and told me he would draw up my manumission for half price, which was a guinea. I thanked him for his kindness; and having received it and paid him, I hastened to my master to get him to sign it, that I might be fully released. Accordingly he signed the manumission that day, so that, before night, I who had been a slave in the morning, trembling at the will of another, was become my own master, and completely free. I thought this was the happiest day I had ever experienced; and my joy was still heightened by the blessings and prayers of the sable race, particularly the aged, to whom my heart had ever been attached with reverence.

As the form of my manumission has something peculiar in it, and expresses the absolute power and dominion one man claims over his fellow, I shall beg leave to present it before my readers at full length:

Montserrat.—To all men unto whom these presents shall come: I Robert King, of the parish of St. Anthony in the said island, merchant, send greeting: Know ye, that I the aforesaid Robert King, for and in consideration of the sum of seventy pounds current money of the said island,[9] to me in hand paid, and to the intent that a negro man-slave, named Gustavus Vassa, shall and may become free, have manumitted, emancipated, enfranchised, and set free, and by these presents do manumit, emancipate, enfranchise, and set free, the aforesaid negro man-slave, named Gustavus Vassa, for ever, hereby giving, granting, and releasing unto him, the said Gustavus Vassa, all right, title, dominion, sovereignty, and property, which, as lord and master over the aforesaid Gustavus Vassa, I had, or now I have, or by any means whatsoever I may or can hereafter possibly have over him the aforesaid negro, for ever. In witness whereof I the above-said Robert King have unto these presents set my hand and seal, this tenth day of July, in the year of our Lord one thousand seven hundred and sixty-six.

ROBERT KING

Signed, sealed, and delivered in the presence of Terrylegay, Montserrat.

Registered the within manumission at full length, this eleventh day of July, 1766, in liber D.[1]

TERRYLEGAY, REGISTER.

In short, the fair as well as black people immediately styled me by a new appellation, to me the most desirable in the world, which was Freeman, and

---

8. 2 Kings 2.11.
9. The equivalent of forty pounds in British money.
1. Book or register D.

at the dances I gave my Georgia superfine blue clothes made no indifferent appearance, as I thought.

* * *

1789

FRANCES BURNEY
1752–1840

People have often made the mistake of underestimating Frances Burney. In person, as in her writing, she seemed a proper, self-effacing lady. Many readers still call her "Fanny," as if familiarity could make her harmless. But she saw through such poses. Sir Joshua Reynolds said that "if he was conscious to himself of any trick, or any affectation, there is nobody he should so much fear as this little Burney!" And Samuel Johnson teased her by claiming that "your shyness, & slyness, & pretending to know nothing, never took *me* in, whatever you may do with others. *I* always knew you for a *toadling!*" (according to legend, little toads may look submissive but actually carry poison). Although her writing crackles with humor, it can be relentless—and sometimes cruel—in exposing bad manners or a selfish heart.

She learned quite young how to hide in a crowd. Devoted daughter of Charles Burney, a popular teacher and historian of music, Frances grew up in a large family that gave her many opportunities to study character and mix discreetly in society. Her first novel, *Evelina, or A Young Lady's Entrance into the World* (1778), was written in secret and published anonymously. But delighted readers, including Johnson, Burke, and Hester Thrale, soon found her out and sang her praises; and a second novel, *Cecilia* (1782), confirmed her reputation. Her home life was less happy, however; she and her stepmother disliked each other, and she fell in love with a young clergyman who never got around to proposing. In 1786, to please her father, she accepted a place as a lady-in-waiting at court, where the paralyzing etiquette and lack of independence tormented her for the next five years, until she finally managed to resign. At forty-one she married a French émigré, General Alexandre Gabriel-Jean-Baptiste d'Arblay. Despite the disapproval of her father—d'Arblay was penniless, Catholic, and politically liberal—the marriage was happy. Madame d'Arblay soon bore a son, and her novel *Camilla* (1796) brought in good money. When she joined her husband in France, in 1802, the Napoleonic wars prevented them from returning to England for ten years; the pain of an outcast dominates her last novel, *The Wanderer, or Female Difficulties* (1814). But she never stopped writing, producing a doctored version of her father's *Memoirs* (1832) and more of the diaries and letters that, edited after her death by a niece, made her famous again.

Burney wrote all her life—not only novels and plays but perpetual letters and journals, recording whatever she saw for friends and family as well as herself. Even the most informal pages display her gifts: a knack for catching character, a wonderful ear for dialogue, wry humor, and a swift pace that carries the reader along from moment to moment. Her special subject is embarrassment—often her own. In scenes like her flight from the king, where she is torn between opposite notions of the right thing to do, shame and comedy mingle. But these trepidations can also be incredibly painful, as in her gripping account of a mastectomy. Despite her propriety, Burney looks at the world and its institutions with the clear eyes of an outsider, aware of the gaps between what people say and what they do. She frees herself to write with utter honesty by pretending, at first, that nobody is going to read her. But her private thoughts are reported so fully and faithfully that, in the end, every reader can share them.

From The Journal and Letters

[FIRST JOURNAL ENTRY]

Poland Street, London, March 27, 1768[1]

To have some account of my thoughts, manners, acquaintance & actions, when the hour arrives in which time is more nimble than memory, is the reason which induces me to keep a journal: a journal in which I must confess my *every* thought, must open my whole heart! But a thing of this kind ought to be addressed to somebody—I must imagine myself to be talking—talking to the most intimate of friends—to one in whom I should take delight in confiding, & remorse in concealment: but who must this friend be?—to make choice of one to whom I can but *half* rely, would be to frustrate entirely the intention of my plan. The only one I could wholly, totally confide in, lives in the same house with me, & not only never *has*, but never *will*, leave me one secret *to* tell her.[2] To whom, then, *must* I dedicate my wonderful, surprising & interesting adventures?—to *whom* dare I reveal my private opinion of my nearest relations? the secret thoughts of my dearest friends? my own hopes, fears, reflections & dislikes?—Nobody!

To Nobody, then, will I write my journal! since to Nobody can I be wholly unreserved—to Nobody can I reveal every thought, every wish of my heart, with the most unlimited confidence, the most unremitting sincerity to the end of my life! For what chance, what accident can end my connections with Nobody? No secret *can* I conceal from No—body, & to No—body can I be *ever* unreserved. Disagreement cannot stop our affection, time itself has no power to end our friendship. The love, the esteem I entertain for Nobody, No-body's self has not power to destroy. From Nobody I have nothing to fear, the secrets sacred to friendship, Nobody will not reveal, when the affair is doubtful, Nobody will not look towards the side least favorable—.

I will suppose you, then, to be my best friend; tho' God forbid you ever should! my dearest companion—& a romantick girl, for mere oddity may perhaps be more sincere—more *tender*—than if you were a friend in propria personæ[3]—in as much as imagination often exceeds reality. In your breast my errors may create pity without exciting contempt; may raise your compassion, without eradicating your love.

From this moment, then, my dear girl—but why, permit me to ask, must a *female* be made Nobody? Ah! my dear, what were this world good for, *were* Nobody a female? And now I have done with *preambulation*.

---

1. This is the first page of Burney's first journal, begun when she was fifteen.
2. Burney's younger sister, Susanna. In 1773, when Burney spent the summer away from home, she began a journal for her sister, and continued it off and on until 1800, when Susanna died.
3. In your own person.

["DOWN WITH HER, BURNEY!"]

Streatham, September 15, 1778[4]

I was then looking over the Life of Cowley, which he had himself given me to read, at the same time that he gave to Mrs. Thrale that of Waller.— They are now *printed,* though they will not be *published* for some time. But he bid me put it away.—"Do," cried he, "put away that now, & *prattle* with us;—I can't make this little Burney prattle,—& I am *sure* she prattles well.— but I shall teach her another lesson than to sit thus silent, before I have done with her."

"To *talk*," cried I, "is the *only* lesson I shall be backward to learn from you, sir."

Mrs. T. Tomorrow, sir, Mrs. Montagu[5] dines here! & then you will have talk enough.

Dr. Johnson began to seesaw, with a countenance strongly expressive of *inward fun,*—&, after enjoying it some time in silence, he suddenly, & with great animation, turned to me, & cried "*Down* with her, Burney!—*down* with her!—spare her not! attack her, fight her, & *down* with her at once!—*You* are a *rising* wit,—*she* is at the *top*,—& when *I* was beginning the world, & was nothing & nobody, the joy of my life was to fire at all the established wits!—& then, every body loved to hallow[6] me on;—but there is no game *now*, & *now*, every body would be glad to see me *conquered*: but *then*, when I was *new*,—to vanquish the great ones was all the delight of my poor little dear soul!—So at her, Burney!—at her, & *down* with her!"

O how we all hollowed![7] By the way, I must tell you that Mrs. Montagu is in very great estimation here, even with Dr. Johnson himself, when others do not praise her *improperly*: Mrs. Thrale ranks her as the *first of women*, in the literary way.

I should have told you, that Miss Gregory, daughter of the Gregory who wrote the letters, or *Legacy* of advice,[8] lives with Mrs. Montagu, & was invited to accompany her.

"Mark, now," said Dr. Johnson, "if I *contradict* her tomorrow; I am determined, let her say what she will, that I will *not* contradict her."

Mrs. T. Why, to be sure, Sir, you *did* put her a little out of countenance last time she came,—yet you were neither rough, nor cruel, nor ill-natured,— but still, when a lady *changes color*, we imagine her feelings are not quite *composed*.

Dr. J. Why, madam, I won't answer that I sha'n't contradict her again, if she provokes me as she did then; but a *less* provocation I will withstand. I believe I am not high in her good graces already, & I begin (added he, laughing heartily) to tremble for my admission into her new house! I doubt I shall never see the inside of it!

Mrs. Montagu is building a most superb house.

---

4. *Evelina* was published in January 1778 and enthusiastically received. After her authorship became known, Burney was invited to Streatham Park, the country house of Hector and Hester Lynch Thrale. Johnson spent much of his time there and was then writing his *Lives of the Poets*. He and Hester Thrale became fond of Burney.
5. Elizabeth Montagu, known as "Queen of the Blues" (or bluestockings), a group of intellectual women, was probably the most respected literary woman in England; she had written the famous *Essay on Shakespear* (1769).
6. A cry inciting hunters to the chase.
7. "To shout; to hoot" (Johnson's *Dictionary*).
8. John Gregory, *A Father's Legacy to His Daughters* (1774).

Mrs. T. O, I warrant you! she *fears* you, indeed, but that, you know, is nothing uncommon: & dearly I love to hear your *disquisitions*,—for certainly she is the first woman, for literary knowledge, in England,—& if in *England* I hope I may say in the *world!*

Dr. J. I believe you may, Madam. She diffuses more knowledge in her conversation than any woman I know,—or, indeed, *almost* any man.

Mrs. T. I declare *I* know *no* man equal to her, take away yourself & Burke, for *that* art.—And *you*, who love magnificence, won't quarrel with her, as everybody else does, for her love of finery.

Dr. J. No, I shall not quarrel with her upon that topic. (then, looking earnestly at *me*) "Nay," he added, "it's very handsome."

"What, sir?" cried I, amazed.

"Why your cap:—I have looked at it some time, & I like it much. It has not that vile *bandeau*[9] across it, which I have so often cursed."

Did you ever hear any thing so strange? *Nothing* escapes him. My Daddy Crisp[1] is not more minute in his attentions: nay, I think he is even *less* so.

Mrs. T. Well, sir, that bandeau you quarreled with was worn by every woman at court the last Birth Day,[2]—& I observed that *all* the men found fault with it.

Dr. J. The truth is,—women,—take them in general,—have *no* idea of grace!—Fashion is *all* they think of;—I don't mean Mrs. Thrale & Miss Burney, when I talk of *women!*—*they* are goddesses!—& therefore I except them.

Mrs. T. Lady Ladd never wore the bandeau, & said she never would, because it is unbecoming.

Dr. J. (*laughing*) Did not she? then is Lady Ladd a charming woman, & I have yet hopes of entering into engagements with her!

Mrs. T. Well, as to that, I can't say,—but, to be sure, the only similitude *I* have yet discovered in you, *is* in *size: there* you agree mighty well.

Dr. J. Why if *any* body could have worn the bandeau, it must have been Lady Ladd, for there is *enough* of her to carry it off; but *you* are too *little* for any thing ridiculous; that which seems *nothing* upon a Patagonian,[3] will become very *conspicuous* upon a Lilliputian; & of *you* there is so little in *all*, that one single absurdity would swallow up *half* of you.

Some time after,—when we had all been a few minutes wholly silent, he turned to me, & said "Come, Burney,—shall you & I *study our parts* against[4] Mrs. Montagu comes?"

How would you be entertained, my dear Susy, if I could give you the *manner*, as well as *matter*, of the conversation of this greatest of men.

[ENCOUNTERING THE KING]

Kew Palace, Monday February 2, 1789

What an adventure had I this morning! one that has occasioned me the severest personal terror I ever experienced in my life.

Sir Lucas Pepys still persisting that exercise and air were absolutely necessary to save me from illness, I have continued my walks, varying my gardens

---

9. A narrow headband.
1. Samuel Crisp, an old family friend, had been a mentor to Burney.
2. June 4, the king's birthday.

3. The Indians of Patagonia, whose average height was more than six feet, were commonly thought to be giants.
4. Before.

from Richmond to Kew, according to the accounts I received of the movements of the king. For this I had her majesty's permission, on the representation of Sir Lucas.

This morning, when I received my intelligence of the king from Dr. John Willis,[5] I begged to know where I might walk in safety? "In Kew gardens," he said, "as the king would be in Richmond."

"Should any unfortunate circumstance," I cried, "at any time, occasion my being seen by his majesty, do not mention my name, but let me run off without call or notice."

This he promised. Everybody, indeed, is ordered to keep out of sight.

Taking, therefore, the time I had most at command, I strolled into the gardens. I had proceeded, in my quick way, nearly half the round, when I suddenly perceived, through some trees, two or three figures. Relying on the instructions of Dr. John, I concluded them to be workmen and gardeners; yet tried to look sharp, and in so doing, as they were less shaded, I thought I saw the person of his majesty!

Alarmed past all possible expression, I waited not to know more, but turning back, ran off with all my might. But what was my terror to hear myself pursued!—to hear the voice of the king himself loudly and hoarsely calling after me, "Miss Burney! Miss Burney!"

I protest I was ready to die. I knew not in what state he might be at the time; I only knew the orders to keep out of his way were universal; that the queen would highly disapprove any unauthorized meeting, and that the very action of my running away might deeply, in his present irritable state, offend him. Nevertheless, on I ran, too terrified to stop, and in search of some short passage, for the garden is full of little labyrinths, by which I might escape.

The steps still pursued me, and still the poor hoarse and altered voice rang in my ears:—more and more footsteps resounded frightfully behind me,—the attendants all running, to catch their eager master, and the voices of the two Doctor Willises loudly exhorting him not to heat himself so unmercifully.

Heavens, how I ran! I do not think I should have felt the hot lava from Vesuvius—at least not the hot cinders—had I so run during its eruption. My feet were not sensible that they even touched the ground.

Soon after, I heard other voices, shriller, though less nervous, call out "Stop! stop! stop!"

I could by no means consent; I knew not what was purposed, but I recollected fully my agreement with Dr. John that very morning, that I should decamp if surprised, and not be named.

My own fears and repugnance, also, after a flight and disobedience like this, were doubled in the thought of not escaping; I knew not to what I might be exposed, should the malady be then high, and take the turn of resentment. Still, therefore, on I flew; and such was my speed, so almost incredible to relate or recollect, that I fairly believe no one of the whole party could have overtaken me, if these words, from one of the attendants, had not reached me: "Doctor Willis begs you to stop!"

"I cannot! I cannot!" I answered, still flying on, when he called out "You must, ma'am; it hurts the king to run."

Then, indeed, I stopped—in a state of fear really amounting to agony. I

5. In 1788, two years after Burney joined the court, George III began to have fits of delirium or madness (today diagnosed as porphyria, a hereditary disease). He was kept in isolation at Kew, under the control of two physicians, Francis and John Willis.

turned round, I saw the two doctors had got the king between them, and three attendants of Dr. Willis's were hovering about. They all slackened their pace, as they saw me stand still; but such was the excess of my alarm, that I was wholly insensible to the effects of a race which, at any other time, would have required an hour's recruit.[6]

As they approached, some little presence of mind happily came to my command; it occurred to me that, to appease the wrath of my flight, I must now show some confidence. I therefore faced them as undauntedly as I was able, only charging the nearest of the attendants to stand by my side.

When they were within a few yards of me, the king called out, "Why did you run away?"

Shocked at a question impossible to answer, yet a little assured by the mild tone of his voice, I instantly forced myself forward, to meet him, though the internal sensation, which satisfied me this was a step the most proper to appease his suspicions and displeasure, was so violently combated by the tremor of my nerves, that I fairly think I may reckon it the greatest effort of personal courage I have ever made.

The effort answered: I looked up, and met all his wonted benignity of countenance, though something still of wildness in his eyes. Think, however, of my surprise, to feel him put both his hands round my two shoulders, and then kiss my cheek!

I wonder I did not really sink, so exquisite was my affright when I saw him spread out his arms! Involuntarily, I concluded he meant to crush me; but the Willises, who have never seen him till this fatal illness, not knowing how very extraordinary an action this was from him, simply smiled and looked pleased, supposing, perhaps, it was his customary salutation!

I believe, however, it was but the joy of a heart unbridled, now, by the forms and proprieties of established custom and sober reason. To see any of his household thus by accident, seemed such a near approach to liberty and recovery, that who can wonder it should serve rather to elate than lessen what yet remains of his disorder!

He now spoke in such terms of his pleasure in seeing me, that I soon lost the whole of my terror; astonishment to find him so nearly well, and gratification to see him so pleased, removed every uneasy feeling, and the joy that succeeded, in my conviction of his recovery, made me ready to throw myself at his feet to express it . . .

What a scene! how variously was I affected by it! but, upon the whole, how inexpressibly thankful to see him so nearly himself—so little removed from recovery!

[A MASTECTOMY]

Paris, March 22, 1812[7]

Separated as I have now so long—long been from my dearest father—brothers—sisters—nieces, & native friends, I would spare, at least, their kind hearts any grief for me but what they must inevitably feel in reflecting upon the sorrow of such an absence to one so tenderly attached to all her first and

6. Renewal of strength.
7. Burney (now Madame d'Arblay) sent this letter to Esther Burney, her sister, describing an operation performed the previous September.

forever so dear & regretted ties—nevertheless, if they should hear that I have been dangerously ill from any hand but my own, they might have doubts of my perfect recovery which my own alone can obviate. And how can I hope they will escape hearing what has reached Seville to the south, and Constantinople to the east? from both I have had messages—yet nothing could urge me to this communication till I heard that M. de Boinville had written it to his wife, without any precaution, because in ignorance of my plan of silence.[8] Still I must hope it may never travel to my dearest father—But to you, my beloved Esther, who, living more in the world, will surely hear it ere long, to you I will write the whole history, certain that, from the moment you know any evil has befallen me your kind kind heart will be constantly anxious to learn its extent, & its circumstances, as well as its termination.

About August, in the year 1810, I began to be annoyed by a small pain in my breast, which went on augmenting from week to week, yet, being rather heavy than acute, without causing me any uneasiness with respect to the consequences: Alas, *"what was the ignorance?"* The most sympathizing of partners, however, was more disturbed: not a start, not a wry face, not a movement that indicated pain was unobserved, & he early conceived apprehensions to which I was a stranger. He pressed me to see some surgeon; I revolted from the idea, & hoped, by care & warmth, to make all succor unnecessary. Thus passed some months, during which Madame de Maisonneuve, my particularly intimate friend, joined with M. d'Arblay to press me to consent to an examination. I thought their fears groundless, and could not make so great a conquest over my repugnance. I relate this false confidence, now, as a warning to my dear Esther—my sisters & nieces, should any similar sensations excite similar alarm. M. d'A. now revealed his uneasiness to another of our kind friends, Mme. de Tracy, who wrote to me a long & eloquent letter upon the subject, that began to awaken very unpleasant surmises; & a conference with her ensued, in which her urgency & representations, aided by her long experience of disease, & most miserable existence by art, subdued me, and, most painfully & reluctantly, I ceased to object, & M. d'A. summoned a physician—M. Bourdois? Maria will cry;— No, my dear Maria, I would not give your beau frere[9] that trouble; not him, but Dr. Jouart, the physician of Miss Potts. Thinking but slightly of my statement, he gave me some directions that produced no fruit—on the contrary, I grew worse, & M. d'A. now would take no denial to my consulting M. Dubois, who had already attended & cured me in an abscess of which Maria, my dearest Esther, can give you the history. M. Dubois, the most celebrated surgeon of France, was then appointed accoucheur to the empress, & already lodged in the Tuilleries,[1] & in constant attendance: but nothing could slacken the ardor of M. d'A. to obtain the first advice. Fortunately for his kind wishes, M. Dubois had retained a partial regard for me from the time of his former attendance, &, when applied to through a third person, he took the first moment of liberty, granted by a *promenade* taken by the empress, to come to me. It was now I began to perceive my real danger. M. Dubois

8. Because Chastel de Boinville's wife was English, it was likely that news of the illness would spread to the Burney family in England.
9. Brother-in-law. Maria (or Marianne), Esther Burney's daughter, had married Antoine Bourdois, whose brother was a prominent French physician.
1. The royal palace in Paris. "Accoucheur": obstetrician.

gave me a prescription to be pursued for a month, during which time he could not undertake to see me again, & pronounced nothing—but uttered so many charges to me to be tranquil, & to suffer no uneasiness, that I could not but suspect there was room for terrible inquietude. My alarm was increased by the nonappearance of M. d'A. after his departure. They had remained together some time in the book room, & M. d'A. did not return— till, unable to bear the suspense, I begged him to come back. He, also, sought then to tranquilize me—but in words only; his looks were shocking! his features, his whole face displayed the bitterest woe. I had not, therefore, much difficulty in telling myself what he endeavored not to tell me—that a small operation would be necessary to avert evil consequences!—Ah, my dearest Esther, for this I felt no courage—my dread & repugnance, from a thousand reasons *besides* the pain, almost shook all my faculties, &, for some time, I was rather confounded & stupified than affrighted.—Direful, however, was the effect of this interview; the pains became quicker & more violent, & the hardness of the spot affected increased. I took, but vainly, my prescription, & every symptom grew more serious. * * * A physician was now called in, Dr. Moreau, to hear if he could suggest any new means: but Dr. Larrey had left him no resources untried.[2] A formal consultation now was held, of Larrey, Ribe, & Moreau—&, in fine, I was formally condemned to an operation by all three. I was as much astonished as disappointed—for the poor breast was no where discolored, & not much larger than its healthy neighbor. Yet I felt the evil to be deep, so deep, that I often thought if it could not be dissolved, it could only with life be extirpated. I called up, however, all the reason I possessed, or could assume, & told them—that if they saw no other alternative, I would not resist their opinion & experience:—the good Dr. Larrey, who, during his long attendance had conceived for me the warmest friendship, had now tears in his eyes; from my dread he had expected resistance.[3] * * * Sundry necessary works & orders filled up my time entirely till one o'clock. When all was ready——but Dr. Moreau then arrived, with news that M. Dubois could not attend till three. Dr. Aumont went away—& the coast was clear. This, indeed, was a dreadful interval. I had no longer any thing to do—I had only to think—TWO HOURS thus spent seemed never-ending. I would fain have written to my dearest father—to you, my Esther— to Charlotte, James, Charles—Amelia Lock—but my arm prohibited me. I strolled to the salon—I saw it fitted with preparations, & I recoiled—But I soon returned; to what effect disguise from myself what I must so soon know?—yet the sight of the immense quantity of bandages, compresses, sponges, lint——made me a little sick.—I walked backwards & forwards till I quieted all emotion, & became, by degrees, nearly stupid—torpid, without sentiment or consciousness;—& thus I remained till the clock struck three. A sudden spirit of exertion then returned—I defied my poor arm, no longer worth sparing, & took my long banished pen to write a few words to M. d'A.—& a few more for Alex, in case of a fatal result. These short billets I could only deposit safely, when the cabriolets[4]—one—two—three—four— succeeded rapidly to each other in stopping at the door. Dr. Moreau instantly

---

2. Dominique-Jean Larrey, "Napoleon's surgeon," is still remembered for his courage on the battlefield and his innovative procedures.
3. One morning, three weeks later, Burney was

suddenly informed that her operation was scheduled for that afternoon. Operations were then performed at home and without anesthetics.
4. Carriages.

entered my room, to see if I were alive. He gave me a wine cordial, & went to the salon. I rang for my maid & nurses—but before I could speak to them, my room, without previous message, was entered by 7 men in black, Dr. Larrey, M. Dubois, Dr. Moreau, Dr. Aumont, Dr. Ribe, & a pupil of Dr. Larrey, & another of M. Dubois. I was now awakened from my stupor—& by a sort of indignation—Why so many? & without leave?—But I could not utter a syllable. M. Dubois acted as commander in chief. Dr. Larrey kept out of sight; M. Dubois ordered a bedstead into the middle of the room. Astonished, I turned to Dr. Larrey, who had promised that an armchair would suffice; but he hung his head, & would not look at me. Two *old mattresses* M. Dubois then demanded, & an old sheet. I now began to tremble violently, more with distaste & horror of the preparations even than of the pain. These arranged to his liking, he desired me to mount the bedstead. I stood suspended, for a moment, whether I should not abruptly escape—I looked at the door, the windows—I felt desperate—but it was only for a moment, my reason then took the command, & my fears & feelings struggled vainly against it. I called to my maid—she was crying, & the two nurses stood, transfixed, at the door. "Let those women all go!" cried M. Dubois. This order recovered me my voice—"No," I cried, "let them stay! *qu'elles restent!*" This occasioned a little dispute, that re-animated me. The maid, however, & one of the nurses ran off—I charged the other to approach, & she obeyed. M. Dubois now tried to issue his commands *en militaire*,[5] but I resisted all that were resistible—I was compelled, however, to submit to taking off my long robe de chambre,[6] which I had meant to retain—Ah, then, how did I think of my sisters!—not one, at so dreadful an instant, at hand, to protect—adjust—guard me—I regretted that I had refused Mme de Maisonneuve– Mme Chastel—no one upon whom I could rely—my departed angel![7]—how did I think of her!—how did I long—long for my Esther—my Charlotte!— My distress was, I suppose, apparent, though not my wishes, for M. Dubois himself now softened, & spoke soothingly. "Can *you*," I cried, "feel for an operation that, to *you*, must seem so trivial?"—"Trivial?" he repeated—taking up a bit of paper, which he tore, unconsciously, into a million of pieces, "*oui—c'est peu de chose—mais—*"[8] he stammered, & could not go on. No one else attempted to speak, but I was softened myself, when I saw even M. Dubois grow agitated, while Dr. Larrey kept always aloof, yet a glance showed me he was pale as ashes. I knew not, positively, then, the immediate danger, but everything convinced me danger was hovering about me, & that this experiment could alone save me from its jaws. I mounted, therefore, unbidden, the bedstead—& M. Dubois placed me upon the mattress, & spread a cambric handkerchief upon my face. It was transparent, however, & I saw, through it, that the bedstead was instantly surrounded by the 7 men & my nurse. I refused to be held; but when, bright through the cambric, I saw the glitter of polished steel—I closed my eyes. I would not trust to convulsive fear the sight of the terrible incision. A silence the most profound ensued, which lasted for some minutes, during which, I imagine, they took their orders by signs, & made their examination—Oh what a horrible suspension!—I did not breathe—& M. Dubois tried vainly to find any pulse. This

---

5. In military fashion. Most of the attending physicians had been army surgeons.
6. Dressing gown.

7. Susanna, Burney's favorite sister, had died in 1800.
8. Yes—it is not much—but— (French).

pause, at length, was broken by Dr. Larrey, who, in a voice of solemn melancholy, said "Qui me tiendra ce sein?—"[9]

No one answered; at least not verbally; but this aroused me from my passively submissive state, for I feared they imagined the whole breast infected—feared it too justly—for, again through the cambric, I saw the hand of M. Dubois held up, while his forefinger first described a straight line from top to bottom of the breast, secondly a cross, & thirdly a circle; intimating that the WHOLE was to be taken off. Excited by this idea, I started up, threw off my veil, &, in answer to the demand "Qui me tiendra ce sein?" cried "C'est moi, monsieur!"[1] & I held my hand under it, & explained the nature of my sufferings, which all sprang from one point, though they darted into every part. I was heard attentively, but in utter silence, & M. Dubois then re-placed me as before, &, as before, spread my veil over my face. How vain, alas, my representation! immediately again I saw the fatal finger describe the cross—& the circle. Hopeless, then, desperate, & self-given up, I closed once more my eyes, relinquishing all watching, all resistance, all interference, & sadly resolute to be wholly resigned.

My dearest Esther, & all my dears to whom she communicates this doleful ditty, will rejoice to hear that this resolution once taken, was firmly adhered to, in defiance of a terror that surpasses all description, & the most torturing pain. Yet—when the dreadful steel was plunged into the breast—cutting through veins—arteries—flesh—nerves—I needed no injunctions not to restrain my cries. I began a scream that lasted uninterruptedly during the whole time of the incision—& I almost marvel that it rings not in my ears still! so excruciating was the agony. When the wound was made, & the instrument was withdrawn, the pain seemed undiminished, for the air that suddenly rushed into those delicate parts felt like a mass of minute but sharp & forked poniards,[2] that were tearing the edges of the wound—but when again I felt the instrument—describing a curve—cutting against the grain, if I may so say, while the flesh resisted in a manner so forcible as to oppose & tire the hand of the operator, who was forced to change from the right to the left—then, indeed, I thought I must have expired. I attempted no more to open my eyes,—they felt as if hermetically shut, & so firmly closed, that the eyelids seemed indented into the cheeks. The instrument this second time withdrawn, I concluded the operation over. Oh no! presently the terrible cutting was renewed—& worse than ever, to separate the bottom, the foundation of this dreadful gland from the parts to which it adhered. Again all description would be baffled—yet again all was not over.—Dr. Larrey rested but his own hand, &—Oh heaven!—I then felt the knife rackling[3] against the breast bone—scraping it!—This performed, while I yet remained in utterly speechless torture, I heard the voice of Mr. Larrey (all others guarded a dead silence) in a tone nearly tragic, desire every one present to pronounce if any thing more remained to be done. The general voice was Yes—but the finger of Mr. Dubois—which I literally *felt* elevated over the wound, though I saw nothing, & though he touched nothing, so indescribably sensitive was the spot—pointed to some further requisition[4]—& again began the scraping!—and, after this, Dr. Moreau thought he discerned a peccant atom—

9. Who will hold this breast for me? (French).
1. *I* will! (French).
2. Daggers.
3. Raking (?).

4. Necessity. Surgical practice of the time dictated that "the whole diseased structure" be cut out, no matter how long or painful the operation.

and still, & still, M. Dubois demanded atom after atom. My dearest Esther, not for days, not for weeks, but for months I could not speak of this terrible business without nearly again going through it! I could not *think* of it with impunity! I was sick, I was disordered by a single question—even now, 9 months after it is over, I have a headache from going on with the account! & this miserable account, which I began 3 months ago, at least, I dare not revise, nor read, the recollection is still so painful.

To conclude, the evil was so profound, the case so delicate, & the precautions necessary for preventing a return so numerous, that the operation, including the treatment & the dressing, lasted 20 minutes! a time, for sufferings so acute, that was hardly supportable. However, I bore it with all the courage I could exert, & never moved, nor stopped them, nor resisted, nor remonstrated, nor spoke—except once or twice, during the dressings, to say "Ah Messieurs! que je vous plains!—"[5] for indeed I was sensible to the feeling concern with which they all saw what I endured, though my speech was principally—*very* principally meant for Dr. Larrey. Except this, I uttered not a syllable, save, when so often they recommenced, calling out "Avertissez moi,[6] Messieurs! avertissez moi!—" Twice, I believe, I fainted; at least, I have two total chasms in my memory of this transaction, that impede my tying together what passed. When all was done, & they lifted me up that I might be put to bed, my strength was so totally annihilated, that I was obliged to be carried, & could not even sustain my hands & arms, which hung as if I had been lifeless; while my face, as the nurse has told me, was utterly colorless. This removal made me open my eyes—& I then saw my good Dr. Larrey, pale nearly as myself, his face streaked with blood, & its expression depicting grief, apprehension, & almost horror.

When I was in bed, my poor M. d'Arblay—who ought to write you himself his own history of this morning—was called to me—& afterwards our Alex.—

[M. D'ARBLAY'S POSTSCRIPT]

No! No my dearest & ever more dear friends, I shall not make a fruitless attempt. No language could convey what I felt in the deadly course of these seven hours. Nevertheless, every one *of you, my dearest dearest friends*, can guess, must even know it. Alexander had no less feeling, but showed more fortitude. He, perhaps, will be more able to describe to you, nearly at least, the torturing state of my poor heart & soul. Besides, I must own, to you, that these details which were, till just now, quite unknown to me, have almost killed me, & I am only able to thank God that this more than half angel has had the sublime courage to deny herself the comfort I might have offered her, to spare me, not the sharing of her excruciating pains, that was impossible, but the witnessing so terrific a scene, & perhaps the remorse to have rendered it more tragic. For I don't flatter myself I could have got through it—I must confess it.

Thank heaven! She is now surprisingly well, & in good spirits, & we hope to have many many still happy days. May that of peace soon arrive, and enable me to embrace better than with my pen my beloved & ever ever more dear friends of the town & country. Amen. Amen![7]

5. How I pity you! (French).
6. Give me warning! (French).
7. The wound healed without infection. Burney returned to England later in 1812 and lived for twenty-eight years.

The Romantic Period
1785–1830

1789–1815:   Revolutionary and Napoleonic period in France.—1789: The Revolution begins with the assembly of the States-General in May and the storming of the Bastille on July 14.—1793: King Louis XVI executed; England joins the alliance against France.—1793–94: The Reign of Terror under Robespierre. 1804: Napoleon crowned emperor.—1815: Napoleon defeated at Waterloo

1807:   British slave trade outlawed (slavery abolished throughout the empire, including the West Indies, twenty-six years later)

1811–20:   The Regency—George, Prince of Wales, acts as regent for George III, who has been declared incurably insane

1820:   Accession of George IV

The British Romantic period is at least as complex and diverse as any other period in literary history. For many decades of the twentieth century, scholars singled out five poets—Wordsworth, Coleridge, Byron, Percy Shelley, and Keats, adding Blake belatedly to make a sixth—and constructed notions of a unified Romanticism on the basis of their works. But there were problems all along: even the two closest collaborators of the 1790s, Wordsworth and Coleridge, interacting on a daily basis, would fit no single definition; Byron despised both Coleridge's metaphysics and Wordsworth's theory and practice of poetry; Shelley and Keats were at opposite poles from each other stylistically and philosophically; Blake was not at all like any of the other five.

Nowadays, although the six poets are still the principal canonical figures by any measure of canonicity, we recognize a much greater range of activities and accomplishments, literary and otherwise. In 1798, the year of Wordsworth and Coleridge's first *Lyrical Ballads,* neither of the authors had much of a reputation; Wordsworth was not even included among the 1112 entries in David Rivers's *Literary Memoirs of Living Authors of Great Britain* of that year, and *Lyrical Ballads* was published anonymously because, as Coleridge told the publisher, "Wordsworth's name is nothing—to a large number of persons mine *stinks.*" Some of the best-regarded poets of the time were women—Anna Barbauld, Charlotte Smith, Mary Robinson—and Wordsworth and Coleridge (both of whom were junior colleagues of Robinson when she was poetry editor of the *Morning Post* in the late 1790s) looked up to them and learned some of their craft from them. The rest of the then-established figures were the later eighteenth-century poets who are printed at the end of volume 1 of this anthology—Gray, Collins, Crabbe, and Cowper

1313

in particular. Only Byron, among the principal poets, was instantly famous; and Felicia Hemans and Letitia Landon ran him a close race as best-sellers. The Romantic period had a great many more participants than the six canonical poets and was interinvolved with a multitude of political, social, and economic changes.

REVOLUTION AND REACTION

Following a widespread practice of historians of English literature, we denote by the "Romantic period" the span between the year 1785, the mid-point of the decade in which Samuel Johnson died and Blake and Burns published their first poems, and 1830, by which time the major writers of the preceding century were either dead or no longer productive. This was a turbulent period, during which England experienced the ordeal of change from a primarily agricultural society, where wealth and power had been concentrated in the landholding aristocracy, to a modern industrial nation, in which the balance of economic power shifted to large-scale employers, who found themselves ranged against an immensely enlarging and increasingly restive working class. And this change occurred in a context of revolution—first the American and then the much more radical French—and of wars, of economic cycles of inflation and depression, and of the constant threat to the social structure from imported revolutionary ideologies to which the ruling classes responded by the repression of traditional liberties.

The early period of the French Revolution, marked by the Declaration of the Rights of Man and the storming of the Bastille to release imprisoned political offenders, evoked enthusiastic support from English liberals and radicals alike. Three important books epitomize the radical social thinking stimulated by the Revolution. Mary Wollstonecraft's A Vindication of the Rights of Men (1790) justified the French Revolution against Edmund Burke's attack in his Reflections on the Revolution in France (1790). Tom Paine's Rights of Man (1791–92) also advocated for England a democratic republic that was to be achieved, if lesser pressures failed, by popular revolution. More important as an influence on Wordsworth, Percy Shelley, and other poets was William Godwin's Inquiry Concerning Political Justice (1793), which foretold an inevitable but peaceful evolution of society to a final stage in which all property would be equally distributed and all government would wither away. But English sympathizers dropped off as the Revolution followed its increasingly grim and violent course: the accession to power by Jacobin extremists; the "September Massacres" of the imprisoned and helpless nobility in 1792, followed by the execution of the king and queen; the invasion by the French Republic of the Rhineland and Netherlands, and its offer of armed assistance to all countries desiring to overthrow their governments, which brought England into the war against France; the guillotining of thousands in the Reign of Terror under Robespierre; and, after the execution in their turn of the men who had directed the Terror, the emergence of Napoleon first as dictator and then as emperor of France. As Wordsworth wrote in The Prelude (11.206–09),

> become Oppressors in their turn,
> Frenchmen had changed a war of self-defence
> For one of Conquest, losing sight of all
> Which they had struggled for. . . .

For Wordsworth and other English observers of liberal inclinations, these events posed a dilemma that became familiar again after the 1920s, in a parallel era of wars, revolutions, and the struggle by competing social ideologies—liberals had no side they could wholeheartedly espouse. Napoleon, the child and champion of the French Revolution, had become an archaggressor, a despot, and the founder of a new dynasty; yet almost all those who opposed him did so for the wrong reasons, with the result that his final defeat at Waterloo in 1815 proved to be the triumph, not of progress and reform, but of reactionary despotisms throughout continental Europe.

In England this was a period of harsh, repressive measures. Public meetings were prohibited, habeas corpus was suspended for the first time in over a hundred years, and advocates of even moderate political change were charged with high treason in time of war. The outlook of the Napoleonic wars put an end to reform for nearly three decades.

Yet this was the very time when profound economic and social changes were creating a desperate need for corresponding changes in political arrangements, and new classes—manufacturing, rather than agricultural— were beginning to demand a voice in government proportionate to their wealth. The "Industrial Revolution"—the shift in manufacturing that resulted from the invention of power-driven machinery to replace hand labor—had begun in the mid-eighteenth century with improvements in machines for processing textiles, and was given immense impetus when James Watt perfected the steam engine in 1765. In the succeeding decades steam replaced wind and water as the primary source of power in one after another type of manufacturing, and after centuries of almost imperceptibly slow change, there began that ever-accelerating alteration in economic and social conditions which shows no signs of slowing down in the foreseeable future. A new laboring population massed in the sprawling mill towns that burgeoned in central and northern England. In rural communities the destruction of home industry was accompanied by a rapid growth of the process—lamented by Oliver Goldsmith in *The Deserted Village* as early as 1770—of enclosing open fields and communally worked farms into privately owned agricultural holdings. Enclosure was by and large necessary for the more efficient methods of agriculture and animal breeding required to supply a growing population (although some of the land thus acquired was turned into vast private estates); in any case, it created a new landless class that either migrated to the industrial towns or remained as farm laborers, subsisting on starvation wages eked out by an inadequate dole. The landscape of England began to take on its modern appearance—the hitherto open rural areas subdivided into a checkerboard of fields enclosed by hedges and stone walls, with the factories of the industrial and trading cities casting a pall of smoke over vast areas of jerry-built houses and slum tenements. Meanwhile, the population was becoming increasingly polarized into what Disraeli later called the "Two Nations"—the two classes of capital and labor, the large owner or trader and the possessionless wageworker, the rich and the poor.

No attempt was made to regulate this shift from the old economic world to the new, not only because of inertia and the power of vested interests but because even liberal reformers were dominated by the social philosophy of laissez-faire. This theory of "let alone" holds that the general welfare can be ensured only by the free operation of economic laws; the government should maintain a policy of strict noninterference and leave people to pursue their private interests. For the great majority of the laboring class the results of this policy were inadequate wages, long hours of work under harsh discipline in sordid conditions, and the large-scale employment of women and children for tasks that destroyed both the body and the spirit. Reports by investigating committees on the coal mines, where male and female children of ten or even five years of age were harnessed to heavy coal-sledges that they dragged by crawling on their hands and knees, read like scenes from Dante's *Inferno*. In 1815 the conclusion of the French war, when the enlargement of the working force by demobilized troops coincided with the fall in the wartime demand for goods, brought on the first modern industrial depression. Since the workers had no vote and were prevented by law from unionizing, their only recourses were petitions, protest meetings, agitation, and hunger riots, which only frightened the ruling class into more repressive measures. In addition the introduction of new machines resulted in further loss of jobs, and this provoked sporadic attempts by dispossessed workers to destroy the machines. After one such outbreak, the House of Lords—despite Lord Byron's eloquent protest—passed a bill (1812) making death the penalty for destroying the frames used for weaving in the stocking industry. In 1819 meetings of workers were organized to demand parliamentary reform. In August of that year, a huge but orderly assembly at St. Peter's Fields, Manchester, was charged by troops, who killed nine and severely injured hundreds more; this was the notorious "Peterloo Massacre," so named with ironic reference to the Battle of Waterloo. The event incited Percy Shelley to write his poems for the working class, *England in 1819, A Song: "Men of England,"* and *To Sidmouth and Castlereagh*.

Suffering was largely confined to the poor, however, for all this while the landed classes, the industrialists, and many of the merchants prospered. The British Empire expanded aggressively both westward and eastward, becoming the most powerful colonial presence in the world. The British East India Company ruled the entire Indian subcontinent at this time, and black slave labor in the West Indies generated great wealth for British plantation owners and their overseers. In London the Regency period (1811–20) was for the leisure class a time of lavish display and moral laxity. In the provinces the gentry in their country houses carried on their family and social concerns— reflected in the novels of Jane Austen—almost untouched by great national and international events.

As in earlier English history, women constituted a deprived class that cut across social classes, for they were widely regarded as inferior to men in intellect and in all but domestic talents. They were therefore provided limited schooling and no facilities for higher education, had only lowly vocations open to them, were subjected to a rigid code of sexual behavior, and possessed (especially after marriage) almost no legal rights. In spite of these disabilities, this was the first era in British literature in which women writers began to rival men in their numbers, their success in sales, their literary reputations—and as poets and social commentators as well as novelists; just in the category of poetry, some nine hundred women are listed in J. R. de J. Jackson's recent bibliography, *Romantic Poetry by Women*. Unlike the men, they had, as a class, much in the way of deprivation and prejudice to contend with. In the revolutionary period, women finally acquired a strong and eloquent champion. Mary Wollstonecraft, who had written an early defense of the French Revolution, *A Vindication of the Rights of Men* (1790), followed this two years later with *A Vindication of the Rights of Woman*, a founding classic of the women's movement. Wollstonecraft asserted that women possess equal intellectual capacity and talents as men and demanded for them a greater share of social, educational, and vocational privileges. The cause of women's rights, however, was not taken up by effective proponents until the Victorian era, and even partial achievement of its aims was delayed until well along in the twentieth century.

But the pressures for reform in the privileges of men, as distinct from women, could not be eliminated in the early nineteenth century, especially since political disabilities were not limited to laborers. Gradually the working-class reformers acquired the support of the middle classes and the liberal Whigs. Finally, at a time of acute economic distress, and after unprecedented agitation and disorders that threatened to break out into revolution, the first Reform Bill was passed in 1832, amid widespread rejoicing. It eliminated the rotten boroughs (depopulated areas whose seats in Commons were at the disposal of a nobleman), redistributed parliamentary representation to include the new industrial cities, and extended the vote. Although about half the middle class, almost all the working class, and all women remained still without a franchise, the principle of the peaceful adjustment of conflicting interests by parliamentary majority had been firmly established, and reform was to go on, by stages, until England acquired universal adult suffrage in 1928.

THE "SPIRIT OF THE AGE"

Writers in Wordsworth's lifetime did not think of themselves as "Romantic"; the word was not applied until half a century later, by English historians. Contemporary critics and reviewers treated them as independent individuals, or else grouped them (often invidiously, but with some basis in fact) into a number of separate schools: "the Lake School" of Wordsworth, Coleridge, and Robert Southey; "the Cockney School," a derogatory term for the Londoners Leigh Hunt, William Hazlitt, and associated writers, including Keats; and "the Satanic School" of Byron, Percy Shelley, and their followers.

Many of the writers, however, did feel that there was something distinctive about their time—not a shared doctrine or literary quality, but a pervasive intellectual and imaginative climate, which some of them called "the spirit of the age." They had the sense that (as Keats said in one of his sonnets) "Great spirits now on earth are sojourning," and that there was evidence of a release of energy, experimental boldness, and creative power that marks a literary renaissance. In his *Defence of Poetry* Shelley claimed that the literature of the age "has arisen as it were from a new birth," and that "an electric life burns" within the words of its best writers which is "less their spirit than the spirit of the age." Shelley explained this literary spirit as an accompaniment of political and social revolution, and other writers agreed. Francis Jeffrey, the foremost conservative reviewer of the day, connected "the revolution in our literature" with "the agitations of the French Revolution, and the discussions as well as the hopes and terrors to which it gave occasion." Hazlitt, who published a book of essays called *The Spirit of the Age*, described how in his early youth the French Revolution had seemed "the dawn of a new era, a new impulse had been given to men's minds." The new poetry of the school of Wordsworth, he maintained, "had its origin in the French Revolution. . . . It was a time of promise, a renewal of the world—and of letters."

The imagination of many Romantic writers was, indeed, preoccupied with the fact and idea of revolution. In the early period of the French Revolution all the leading English writers except Edmund Burke were in sympathy with it, and Robert Burns, William Blake, Wordsworth, Coleridge, Southey, and Mary Wollstonecraft were among its fervent adherents. Later, even after the first boundless expectations had been disappointed by the events in France, the younger writers, including Hazlitt, Hunt, Shelley, and Byron, felt that its example, when purged of its errors, still constituted humanity's best hope. The Revolution generated a pervasive feeling that this was an age of new beginnings when, by discarding traditional procedures and outworn customs, everything was possible, and not only in the political and social realm but in intellectual and literary enterprises as well. In his *Prelude* Wordsworth wrote the classic description of the spirit of the early 1790s, with "France standing on the top of golden hours, / And human nature seeming born again," so that "the whole Earth, / The beauty wore of promise." Something of this sense of limitless possibilities survived the shock of first disappointment at events in France and carried over to the year 1797, when Wordsworth and Coleridge, in excited daily communion, revolutionized, on grounds analogous to the politics of democracy, the theory and practice of poetry. The product of these discussions was the *Lyrical Ballads* of 1798.

POETIC THEORY AND POETIC PRACTICE

Wordsworth undertook to justify the new poetry by a critical manifesto, or statement of poetic principles, first as a short Advertisement in the original *Lyrical Ballads*, then in the form of an extended Preface to the second edition in 1800, which he enlarged still further in the third edition of 1802. In it he set himself in opposition to the literary *ancien régime*, those writers of the eighteenth century who, in his view, had imposed on poetry artificial conventions that distorted its free and natural expression. Many of Wordsworth's later critical writings were attempts to clarify, buttress, or qualify points made in his first declaration. Coleridge said that the Preface was "half a child of my own brain"; and although he soon developed doubts about some of Wordsworth's unguarded statements, and undertook to correct them in *Biographia Literaria* (1817), he did not question the rightness of Wordsworth's attempt to overturn the reigning tradition. In the course of the eighteenth century there had been increasing opposition to the tradition of Dryden, Pope, and Johnson; and especially in the 1740s and later there had emerged many of the critical concepts, as well as a number of the poetic subjects and forms, that were later exploited by Wordsworth and his contemporaries. Wordsworth's Preface nevertheless deserves its reputation as a turning point in English literature, for Wordsworth gathered up isolated ideas, organized them into a coherent theory based on explicit critical principles, and made them the rationale for his own achievements as a poet. We can conveniently use the concepts in this influential essay as points of departure for a survey of distinctive elements that are widespread in the theory and poetry of the Romantic period.

1. The Concept of Poetry and the Poet

Representative eighteenth-century theorists had regarded poetry as primarily an imitation of human life—in a frequent figure, "a mirror held up to nature"—that the poet artfully renders and puts into an order designed to instruct and give artistic pleasure to the reader. Wordsworth, on the other hand, repeatedly described all good poetry as, at the moment of composition, "the spontaneous overflow of powerful feelings." Reversing earlier theory, he thus located the source of a poem not in the outer world, but in the individual poet, and specified that the essential materials of a poem were not external people and events, but the inner feelings of the author, or external objects only after these have been transformed or irradiated by the author's feelings. Other Romantic theories, however diverse in other aspects, concurred by referring primarily to the mind, emotions, and imagination of the poet, instead of to the outer world as perceived by the senses, for the origin, content, and defining attributes of a poem. Many writers, such as Charlotte Smith, identified poetry (in metaphors parallel to Wordsworth's "overflow") as the "expression" or "utterance" or "exhibition" of emotion. Blake and Shelley described a poem as an embodiment of the poet's imaginative vision, which they opposed to the ordinary world of common experience. Coleridge, following German precedents, introduced into English criticism an organic theory, based on the model of the growth of a plant. That is, he conceived a great work of literature to be a self-originating and self-organizing process that begins with a seedlike idea in the poet's imagination, grows by assimilating both the poet's feelings and the diverse materials of sense-experience, and evolves into an organic whole in which the parts are integrally related to each other and to the whole.

In accord with the view that poetry expresses the poet's own feelings and temperament, the lyric poem written in the first person, earlier regarded as a minor kind, became a major Romantic form, and was often described as the most essentially poetic of all the genres. And in the Romantic lyric the "I" often is not a conventionally typical lyric speaker, such as the Petrarchan lover or Cavalier gallant of Elizabethan and seventeenth-century love poems, but has recognizable traits of the poet's own person and circumstances. In the poems of Wordsworth, Coleridge, Shelley, Keats, Smith, Letitia Landon, and others, the experiences and states of mind expressed by the lyric speaker often accord closely with the known facts of the poet's life and with the personal confessions in the poet's letters and journals. Even in his ostensibly fictional writings (narrative and dramatic), Byron usually invites his readers to identify the hero with the author, whether the hero is presented romantically (as in *Childe Harold, Manfred,* and the Oriental tales) or in an ironic perspective (as in *Don Juan*). An extreme instance of this tendency to self-reference is Wordsworth's *Prelude*, which is a poem of epic length and epic seriousness about the growth of the poet's own mind.

The *Prelude* exemplifies two other important tendencies in the period. Like Blake, Coleridge in his early poems, and later on Shelley, Wordsworth presents himself as what he calls "a chosen son," or "Bard." That is, he assumes the persona and voice of a poet-prophet, modeled on Milton and the prophets in the Bible, and puts himself forward as a spokesman for traditional Western civilization at a time of profound crisis—a time, as Wordsworth said in book 2 of *The Prelude*, "of dereliction and dismay" and the "melancholy waste of hopes o'erthrown." (*Son* and *spokesman* are appropriate here; almost always, the bardic poet-prophet was a distinctively male persona.) As bards, Wordsworth and the other visionary poets set out to revise the biblical promise of divine redemption by reconstituting the grounds of hope and pronouncing the coming of a time in which a renewed humanity will inhabit a renovated earth on which men and women will feel thoroughly at home. *The Prelude* also is an instance of a central literary form of English, as of European, Romanticism—a long work about the formation of the self, often centering on a crisis, and presented in the radical metaphor of an interior journey in quest of one's true identity and destined spiritual home. Other English examples of this form are Blake's *Milton*, the crucial episode of Asia's underground journey in Shelley's *Prometheus Unbound*, Keats's *Endymion* and *The Fall of Hyperion*, and, in Victorian poetry, Elizabeth Barrett Browning's *Aurora Leigh*. There are equivalent developments in contemporary prose: the self-revelation in the personal essays of Lamb, Hazlitt, and Leigh Hunt and the currency of spiritual autobiography, whether fictionalized (Thomas Carlyle's *Sartor Resartus*) or presented as fact (Coleridge's *Biographia Literaria*, Thomas De Quincey's *Confessions of an English Opium Eater* and *Autobiographic Sketches*).

2. Poetic Spontaneity and Freedom

Wordsworth defined good poetry not merely as the overflow but as "the *spontaneous* overflow" of feelings. In traditional aesthetic theory, poetry had been regarded as supremely an art—an art that in modern times is practiced by poets who have assimilated classical precedents, are aware of the "rules" governing the kind of poem they are writing, and (except for the felicities that, as Pope said, are "beyond the reach of art") deliberately employ tested means to achieve foreknown effects upon an audience. But to Wordsworth, although the composition of a poem originates from "emotion recollected in tranquillity" and may be preceded and followed by reflection, the immediate act of composition must be spontaneous—that is, arising from impulse, and free from all rules and the artful manipulation of means to foreseen ends. Other important Romantic critics also voiced declarations of artistic independence from inherited precepts. Keats listed as an "axiom" that "if poetry comes not as naturally as the leaves to a tree it had better not come at all." Blake insisted that he wrote from "Inspiration and Vision" and that his long "prophetic" poem *Milton* was given to him by an agency not himself and "produced without Labor or Study." Shelley also thought it "an error to assert that the finest passages of poetry are produced by labor and study," and suggested instead that they are the products of an unconscious creativity: "A great statue or picture grows under the power of the artist as a child in the mother's womb." "The definition of genius," Hazlitt remarked, "is that it acts unconsciously." The surviving manuscripts of the Romantic poets, however, as well as the testimony of observers, show that they worked and reworked their texts no less arduously—if perhaps more immediately under the impetus of first conception—than the poets of earlier ages. Coleridge, who believed that truth lies in a union of opposites, came closer to the facts of Romantic practice when he claimed that the act of composing poetry involves the psychological contraries "of passion and of will, of *spontaneous* impulse and of *voluntary* purpose."

The emphasis in this period on the free activity of the imagination is related to an insistence on the essential role of instinct, intuition, and the feelings of "the heart" to supplement the judgments of the purely logical faculty, "the head," whether in the province of artistic beauty, philosophical and religious truth, or moral goodness. "Deep thinking," Coleridge wrote, "is attainable only by a man of deep feeling, and all truth is a species of revelation"; hence, "a metaphysical solution that does not tell you something in the heart is grievously to be suspected as apocryphal."

3. Romantic "Nature Poetry"

In his Preface, Wordsworth wrote that "I have at all times endeavored to look steadily at my subject," and in a supplementary Essay he complained that from Dryden through Pope there is scarcely an image from external nature "from which it can be inferred that the eye of the poet had been steadily fixed on his object." A glance at the table of contents of any collection of Romantic poems will show the degree to which the natural scene has become a primary poetic subject, while Wordsworth, Shelley, and even more Coleridge and Keats, described natural phenomena with an accuracy of observation that had no earlier match in its ability to capture the sensuous nuance.

Because of the prominence of landscape in this period, "Romantic poetry" has to the popular mind become almost synonymous with "nature poetry." Neither Romantic theory nor practice, however, justifies the opinion that the aim of this poetry was description for its own sake. Wordsworth in fact insisted that the ability to observe and describe objects accurately, although a necessary, is not at all a sufficient condition for poetry, "as its exercise supposes all the higher qualities of the mind to be passive, and in a state of subjection to external objects." And while many of the great Romantic lyrics—Wordsworth's *Tintern Abbey* and *Ode: Intimations of Immortality*, Coleridge's *Frost at Midnight* and *Dejection*, Shelley's *Ode to the West Wind*, Keats's *Nightingale*—begin with an aspect or change of aspect in the natural scene, this serves only as stimulus to the most characteristic human activity, that of thinking. The longer Romantic "nature poems" are in fact usually meditative poems, in which the presented scene serves to raise an emotional problem or personal crisis whose development and resolution constitute the organizing principle of the poem. As Wordsworth said in his Prospectus to *The Recluse*, not nature but "the Mind of Man" is "my haunt, and the main region of my song."

In addition, Romantic poems habitually endow the landscape with human life, passion, and expressiveness. In part such descriptions represent the poetic equivalent of the metaphysical concept of nature, which had developed in deliberate revolt against the worldviews of the scientific philosophers of the seventeenth and eighteenth centuries, who represented the ultimate reality as a mechanical world consisting of physical particles in motion. What is needed in philosophy, Coleridge wrote, is "the substitution of life and intelligence . . . for the philosophy of mechanism, which, in everything that is most worthy of the human intellect, strikes *Death*." But for many Romantic poets it was a matter of immediate experience to respond to the outer universe as a living entity that participates in the feelings of the observer. James Thomson and other descriptive poets of the preceding century had depicted the created universe as giving direct access to God, and even as itself possessing the attributes of divinity. In *Tintern Abbey* and other poems Wordsworth exhibits toward the landscape attitudes and sentiments that human beings had earlier felt not only for God, but also for a father, a mother, or a beloved. Elsewhere, as in the great passage on crossing Simplon Pass (*The Prelude* 6.625ff.), Wordsworth also revives the ancient theological concept that God's creation constitutes a symbol system, a physical revelation parallel to the written Apocalypse, the Book of Revelation in the Bible—

> Characters of the great Apocalypse,
> The types and symbols of Eternity,
> Of first, and last, and midst, and without end.

This view that natural objects correspond to an inner or a spiritual world underlay a tendency, especially in Blake and Percy Shelley, to write a symbolist poetry in which a rose, a sunflower, a mountain, a cave, or a cloud is presented as an object imbued with a significance beyond itself. "I always seek in what I see," Shelley said, "the likeness of something beyond the present and tangible object." And by Blake mere nature, as perceived by the physical eye and unhumanized by the imagination, was spurned "as the dirt upon my feet, no part of me."

4. The Glorification of the Ordinary and the Outcast

In two lectures on Wordsworth, Hazlitt declared that the school of poetry founded by Wordsworth was the literary equivalent of the French Revolution, translating political changes into poetical experiments. "Kings and queens were dethroned from their rank and station in legitimate tragedy or epic poetry, as they were decapitated elsewhere. . . . The paradox [these poets] set out with was that all things are by nature equally fit subjects for poetry; or that if there is any preference to be given, those that are the meanest and most unpromising are the best."

Hazlitt had in mind Wordsworth's statement that the aim of *Lyrical Ballads* was "to choose incidents and situations from common life" and to use a "selection of language really spoken by men," for which the source and model is "humble and rustic life." As Hazlitt shrewdly saw, this was a social rather than a distinctively literary definition of the proper materials and language for poetry. Versifiers of the later decades of the eighteenth century had experimented with the simple treatment of simple subjects, and Robert Burns—like Wordsworth, a sympathizer with the French Revolution—had achieved great poetic success in the serious representation of humble life in a language really spoken by rustics; the women poets especially—Barbauld, Robinson, Baillie—assimilated to their poems the subject matter of everyday life. But

Wordsworth underwrote his poetic practice with a theory that inverted the traditional hierarchy of poetic genres, subjects, and style by elevating humble and rustic life and the plain style, which in earlier theory were appropriate only to the lowly pastoral, into the principal subject and medium for poetry in general. And in his own practice, as Hazlitt also noted, Wordsworth went even further and turned for the subjects of his serious poems not only to humble people but to the ignominious, the outcast, the delinquent—to "convicts, female vagrants, gypsies . . . idiot boys and mad mothers," as well as to "peasants, peddlers, and village barbers." Hence the outrage of Lord Byron, who alone among his major contemporaries insisted that Dryden and Pope had laid out the proper road for poetry, and who—in spite of his liberalism in politics—maintained his literary allegiance both to aristocratic proprieties and to traditional poetic decorum:

> "Peddlers," and "Boats," and "Wagons"! Oh! ye shades
> Of Pope and Dryden, are we come to this?

Hazlitt also insisted that, in his democratization of poetry, Wordsworth was "the most original poet now living." Certainly Wordsworth in *Lyrical Ballads* was, in this respect, more radical than any of his contemporaries. He enlarged greatly his readers' imaginative sympathies and brought into the province of serious literature a range of materials and interests which are still being explored by writers of the present day.

It should be noted, however, that Wordsworth's aim in *Lyrical Ballads* was not simply to represent the world as it is but, as he announced in his Preface, to throw over "situations from common life . . . a certain coloring of imagination, whereby ordinary things should be presented to the mind in an unusual aspect." As this passage indicates, Wordsworth's concern in his poetry was not only with "common life" but with "ordinary *things*"; no one can read his poems without noticing the extraordinary reverence with which he invests words that in earlier writers had been derogatory—words like "common," "ordinary," "everyday," "humble," whether applied to people or to objects in the visible scene. His aim throughout is to shatter the lethargy of custom so as to refresh our sense of wonder—indeed, of divinity—in the everyday, the commonplace, the trivial, and the lowly.

Samuel Johnson had said that "wonder is a pause of reason" and that "all wonder is the effect of novelty upon ignorance." But for many Romantic writers, to arouse in the sophisticated mind that sense of wonder presumed to be felt by the ignorant and the innocent was a primary power of imagination and a major function of poetry. Commenting on the special imaginative quality of Wordsworth's early poetry (*Biographia Literaria*, chapter 6), Coleridge remarked: "To combine the child's sense of wonder and novelty with the appearances, which every day for perhaps forty years had rendered familiar . . . this is the character and privilege of genius," and its prime service is to awaken in the reader "freshness of sensation" in the representation of "familiar objects." Poetry, said Shelley in his *Defense of Poetry*, "reproduces the common universe" but "purges from our inward sight the film of familiarity which obscures from us the wonder of our being," and "creates anew the universe, after it has been blunted by reiteration." And in Carlyle's *Sartor Resartus* (1833–34), the chief—indeed the only—effect of the conversion of the protagonist from despairing unbelief is that he is able to sustain a

sense of the "Natural Supernaturalism" in ordinary experience and so overcome the "custom" which "blinds us to the miraculousness of daily-recurring
miracles." The great power of the imagination, according to all these writers,
is that it makes the old world new again.

5. The Supernatural and "Strangeness in Beauty"

In most of his poems Coleridge, like Wordsworth, dealt with the everyday
things of this world, and in *Frost at Midnight* he showed how well he too
could achieve the effect of wonder in the familiar. But Coleridge tells us
(*Biographia Literaria*, chapter 14) that according to the division of labor in
Lyrical Ballads, his special function was to achieve wonder by a frank violation of natural laws and the ordinary course of events in poems of which
"the incidents and agents were to be, in part at least, supernatural." And in
The Rime of the Ancient Mariner, Christabel, and *Kubla Khan*, Coleridge
opened up to poets in the modern world the realm of mystery and magic, in
which materials from ancient folklore, superstition, and demonology are
used to impress upon the reader the sense of occult powers and unknown
modes of being. Such poems are usually set in the distant past or in faraway
places, or both; the milieu of *Kubla Khan*, for example, exploits the exoticism
both of the Middle Ages and of the Orient. Next to Coleridge, the greatest
master of this Romantic mode—in which supernatural events have a deep
psychological import—was John Keats. In *La Belle Dame sans Merci* and *The
Eve of St. Agnes* he adapted the old forms of ballad and romance to modern
sophisticated use and, like Coleridge, established a medieval setting for
events that violate our sense of realism and the natural order. Hence the
term *medieval revival,* frequently attached to the Romantic period, which
comprehends also the ballad imitations and some of the verse tales and historical novels of Sir Walter Scott.

Another side of the tendency that Walter Pater later called "the addition
of strangeness to beauty" was the Romantic interest in unusual modes of
experience, of a kind that earlier writers had largely ignored as either too
trivial or too aberrant for serious literary concern. Blake, Wordsworth, and
Coleridge in their poetry explored visionary states of consciousness that are
common among children but violate the standard categories of adult judgment. Coleridge was interested in mesmerism (what we now call hypnotism)
and, like Blake and Shelley, studied the literature of the occult and the
esoteric. Coleridge also shared with De Quincey a concern with dreams and
nightmares; both authors exploited in their writings the altered consciousness and distorted perceptions they experienced under their addiction to
opium. Byron made repeated use of the fascination with the forbidden and
the appeal of the terrifying Satanic hero. And Keats was extraordinarily sensitive to the ambivalences of human experience—to the mingling, at their
highest intensity, of pleasure and pain, to destructive aspects of sexuality,
and to the erotic quality of the longing for death. These phenomena had
already been explored by eighteenth-century writers of terror tales and
Gothic fiction, and later in the nineteenth century all of them, sometimes
exaggerated to perversity, became the special literary province of Charles
Baudelaire, Algernon Charles Swinburne, and writers of the European
"Decadence."

INDIVIDUALISM, INFINITE STRIVING,
AND NONCONFORMITY

Through the greater part of the eighteenth century, humans had for the most part been viewed as limited beings in a strictly ordered and essentially unchanging world. A variety of philosophical and religious systems in that century coincided in a distrust of radical innovation, a respect for the precedents established through the ages by the common sense of humanity, and the recommendation to set accessible goals and to avoid extremes, whether in politics, intellect, morality, or art. Many of the great literary works of the period joined in attacking what was called "pride," or aspirations beyond the limits natural to our species. "The bliss of man," Pope wrote in *An Essay on Man*, "(could pride that blessing find) / Is not to act or think beyond mankind":

> This kind, this due degree
> Of blindness, weakness, Heaven bestows on thee.
> Submit.

The Romantic period, the age of unfettered free enterprise, industrial expansion, and boundless revolutionary hope, was also an age of radical individualism in which both the philosophers and poets put an extraordinarily high estimate on human potentialities and powers. In German post-Kantian philosophy, which generated many of the characteristic ideas of European Romanticism, the human mind—what was called the "Subject" or "Ego"— took over various functions that had hitherto been the sole prerogative of Divinity. Most prominent was the rejection by philosophers of a central eighteenth-century concept of the mind as a mirrorlike recipient of a universe already created, and its replacement by a new concept of the mind as itself creating of the universe it perceives. In a parallel fashion, the poets of the new period also described the mind as creating its own experience. According to Blake, the mind creates its proper milieu only if it totally rejects the material world; in Coleridge and Wordsworth, however, the mind creates in collaboration with something given to it from without. Mind, wrote Coleridge in 1801, is "not passive" but "made in God's Image, and that too in the sublimest sense—the Image of the *Creator*." And Wordsworth declared in *The Prelude* (2.258–61) that the individual mind

> Doth, like an Agent of the one great Mind,
> Create, creator and receiver both,
> Working but in alliance with the works
> Which it beholds.

Many Romantic writers also agreed that the mind has access beyond sense to the transcendant and the infinite, through a special faculty they called either Reason or Imagination. In *The Prelude* (6.600ff.) Wordsworth describes a flash of imagination "that has revealed / The invisible world," and affirms:

> Our destiny, our being's heart and home,
> Is with infinitude, and only there;
> With hope it is, hope that can never die,

> Effort, and expectation, and desire,
> And something evermore about to be.

The desire beyond human limits that, to the moralists of the preceding age, had been an essential sin, or tragic error, now becomes a glory and a triumph: the human being refuses to submit to limitations and, though finite, persists in setting infinite, hence inaccessible, goals. Wordsworth characteristically goes on to declare that "under such banners militant, the soul / Seeks for no trophies, struggles for no spoils"; for him, the infinite striving ends in physical quietism and moral fortitude. But for other writers, especially in Germany, the proper human aim is ceaseless activity—a *"Streben nach dem Unendlichen,"* a striving for the infinite. This view is epitomized by Goethe's Faust, who in his quest for the unattainable violates ordinary moral limits, yet wins salvation by his very insatiability, which never stoops to contentment with the possibilities offered by this finite world. Infinite longing—in Shelley's phrase, "the desire of the moth for a star"—was a recurrent theme also in the English literature of the day. "Less than everything," Blake announced, "cannot satisfy man." Shelley's *Alastor* and Keats's *Endymion* both represent the quest for an indefinable and inaccessible goal, and Byron's *Manfred* has for its hero a man whose "powers and will" reach beyond the limits of that human clay "which clogs the ethereal essence," so that "his aspirations / Have been beyond the dwellers of the earth."

In a parallel fashion, Romantic theorists of art rejected the neoclassic ideal of a limited intention, perfectly accomplished, in favor of "the glory of the imperfect," in which the very failures of artists attest the unlimited reach of their aims. And in their own work, Romantic writers deliberately put themselves in competition with the greatest of their predecessors and experimented boldly in poetic language, versification, and design. Especially in their longer poems they struck out in new directions, and in the space of a few decades produced an astonishing variety of forms constructed on novel principles of organization and style. Blake's symbolic lyrics and visionary "prophetic" poems; Coleridge's haunting ballad-narrative of sin and retribution, *The Rime of the Ancient Mariner;* Wordsworth's epiclike spiritual autobiography, *The Prelude;* Shelley's cosmic symbolic drama, *Prometheus Unbound;* Keats's sequence of odes on the irreconcilable conflict in basic human desires; Byron's satiric survey of all European civilization, *Don Juan*—one can say of each of them, as Shelley said of Byron's poem, that it was "something wholly new and relative to the age."

The great eighteenth-century writers had typically dealt with men and women as members of an organized, and usually an urban, society. Literary authors regarded themselves as integral parts of this society, addressed their works to it, and undertook to express its highest ideals and its collective traditional wisdom. Some Romantic writers, on the other hand, deliberately isolated themselves from society to give scope to their individual vision. Wordsworth titled his masterwork *The Recluse*, and he described himself as "musing in solitude" on its subject, "the individual Mind that keeps her own / Inviolate retirement." And in almost all Wordsworth's poems, long or short, the words *single, solitary, by oneself, alone* constitute a leitmotif; typically, his imagination is released by the sudden apparition of a single figure or object, stark against a natural background. Coleridge also, and still more strikingly Byron and Shelley, represented a solitary protagonist who is separated from society because he has rejected it, or because it has rejected him. These last three poets introduced what became a persistent theme in many Victorian and modern writers—the theme of exile, of the disinherited mind that cannot find a spiritual home in its native land and society or anywhere in the modern world. The solitary Romantic nonconformist was sometimes represented as also a great sinner. Male writers of that time were fascinated by the outlaws of myth, legend, or history—Cain, Satan, Faust, the Wandering Jew, or the great, flawed figure of Napoleon—on whom they modeled a number of their villains or their heroes. In Coleridge's *Ancient Mariner* (as in Wordsworth's *Guilt and Sorrow* and *Peter Bell*) the guilty outcast—"alone, alone, all, all alone"—is made to realize and expiate his sin against the community of living things so that he may reassume his place in the social order. But in Byron the violator of conventional laws and limits remains proudly unrepentant. His hero Manfred, a compound of guilt and superhuman greatness, cannot be defeated by death, successfully defying the demons who, in the tradition of Marlowe's *Dr. Faustus*, have come to drag his soul to hell: "I . . . was my own destroyer, and will be / My own hereafter.—Back, ye baffled fiends!" A more reputable Romantic hero, who turns up frequently in Byron and other writers and is made the protagonist of Shelley's great lyrical drama, is the Prometheus of Greek mythology. He shares with Satan the status of superlative nonconformity, since he sets himself in opposition to deity itself; unlike Satan, however, he is the champion rather than the enemy of the human race. Mary Shelley makes ironic use of this figure in her subtitle of 1818: *Frankenstein; or, The Modern Prometheus*—Victor Frankenstein is decidedly not the champion of humankind.

MILLENNIAL EXPECTATIONS

Nowhere is the Romantic combination of boundless aspiration and the reliance on the power of the individual mind and imagination more evident than in the literary treatment of the ultimate hope of humanity. The French Revolution had aroused in many sympathizers the millennial expectations that are profoundly rooted in Hebrew and Christian tradition. "Few persons but those who have lived in it," Robert Southey reminisced in 1824, "can conceive or comprehend what the memory of the French Revolution was, nor what a visionary world seemed to open upon those who were just entering it. Old things seemed passing away, and nothing was dreamt of but the regeneration of the human race." Southey's language—like that of Wordsworth, Coleridge, Hazlitt, and other writers when they described their early Revolutionary fervor—is biblical; and it reflects the extent to which, in England, the Revolution was championed by members of radical Protestant sects, who envisioned it on the model of biblical prophecy.

The Bible ends with the book of Apocalypse (literally, "Revelation"), prophesying a return of human beings to their lost Edenic felicity, first in the millennium ("a thousand years") of an earthly kingdom, then in the eternity of "a new heaven and a new earth"; this consummation of history is symbolized by a marriage between the New Jerusalem and Christ the Lamb. At the outbreak of the French Revolution, Joseph Priestley and other Unitarian leaders hailed that event as the stage preceding the millennium prophesied in Revelation. Coleridge and Wordsworth, in their early poems, also interpreted the Revolution as the violent preliminary to the new earth and heaven of apocalyptic prophecy. And Blake's *The French Revolution* (1791) and *America, a Prophecy* (1793) represented both these revolutions as apocalyptic portents of the last days of the fallen world.

When the later events in France dashed their faith in political revolution as a means to the millennium, a number of Romantic writers salvaged their apocalyptic hope by giving it a new interpretation. They transferred the agency of apocalypse from mass action to the individual mind—from a political to a spiritual revolution—and proposed that "the new earth and new heaven" of Revelation is available here, now, to all of us, if only we can make our visionary imagination triumph over our senses and sensebound understanding. Hence the extraordinary Romantic emphasis on a new way of *seeing* (which is regarded as the restoration of a lost earlier way of seeing) as the chief aim in life. Blake's "Prophetic Books," for example, all deal with some aspects of the Fall and Redemption, and represent apocalypse as the recovery of the imaginative vision of things as they really are, seen "through and not with the eye." "The Nature of my Work," Blake wrote, "is Visionary or Imaginative; it is an Endeavor to Restore what the Ancients called the Golden Age." This concept of the imaginative re-creation of the old earth continues to be expressed by Romantic poets in the original biblical metaphor of a marriage—although now it is not a marriage of the New Jerusalem with the Lamb but a conjunction of the inner faculties into spiritual unity, or else a marriage between the mind and the external world. Coleridge put this latter version succinctly in *Dejection: An Ode*; it is the inner condition of "Joy," at life's highest moments, "Which, wedding nature to us, gives in dower / A new earth and new heaven." Wordsworth announced as his "high argument" in the Prospectus to *The Recluse* (the same theme serves as underpattern for *The Prelude*) that "Paradise, and groves Elysian" are not "a history only of departed things"—

> For the discerning intellect of Man
> When wedded to this goodly universe
> In love and holy passion, shall find these
> A simple produce of the common day.

In Shelley's *Prometheus Unbound*, Prometheus represents archetypal humanity whose total change in moral being frees the imaginative capacity to envision, and to achieve, a regenerate world; the fourth act symbolizes this event in the mode of a marriage festival in which the whole cosmos participates.

Carlyle's *Sartor Resartus,* to mention one other example, is the history of an individual's violent spiritual crisis and conversion, which turns out to be the achievement of an individual apocalypse: "And I awoke to a new Heaven and a new Earth." But, as Carlyle goes on to indicate, this new earth is the old earth, seen by his protagonist as though miraculously re-created, because he has learned to substitute the "Imaginative" faculty for what Carlyle represents as the chief faculty of the eighteenth-century Enlightenment, the "Logical, Mensurative faculty," or "Understanding." Writing in 1830–31, at the close of the period historians have labeled "Romantic," Carlyle thus summed up the tendency of a generation of writers to retain the ancient faith in apocalypse, but to interpret it not as a change of the world, but as a change in our worldview.

OTHER FORMS: THE FAMILIAR ESSAY

This was also, along with its apocalyptic expectations, the period when literature for the first time became big business. Enlightenment-inspired educational reform and a rapid growth in population produced an explosion of potential readership. A new aesthetics of valuing art and literature "as such" emphasized reading for pleasure (as opposed to strictly moral and utilitarian ends); and people in general had more leisure in which to read, as well as more disposable income with which to purchase reading materials. Technological improvements in printing facilitated production and distribution, and commercial and public lending libraries were established. Hence the provision of more literature of all kinds to satisfy the needs of a greatly enlarged literate public.

At the close of the eighteenth century, reviews and magazines were written largely by hacks who acceded to the political bias and financial interests of the publisher and advertisers. The essays they included were weak imitations of the type established nearly a century earlier by single-essay periodicals such as the *Tatler* and the *Spectator*. In 1802, however, the *Edinburgh Review* inaugurated the modern type of periodical publication. It allowed considerable latitude to its writers, set its literary standards high, and was able to meet these standards by paying its contributors rates good enough to command the best talents of the day.

The success of this new enterprise stimulated the founding of rival reviews and magazines. (A "review," usually issued four times yearly, consisted primarily of essays on important books and discussions of contemporary issues; a "magazine" was a monthly publication that printed more miscellaneous materials, including a high proportion of original essays, poems, and stories.) In 1820 appeared the *London Magazine*, liberal in politics and contemporary in literary interests; in its short but notable career until 1829 it printed the work of a group of brilliant writers, including the three men who soon established themselves as the greatest essayists of the age—Lamb, Hazlitt, and De Quincey. These new periodicals not only elevated the essay in literary dignity and quality but revolutionized its form and substance. They competed strenuously for talent, paying well enough so that an author (at least one as prolific as Hazlitt) could earn a living as a freelance essayist. And writers were treated as serious practitioners who were competent, within broad limits, to write as they pleased.

Under these new conditions the "familiar essay"—a commentary on a nontechnical subject written in a relaxed and intimate manner—flourished, and in a fashion that to some degree paralleled the course of Romantic poetry. Each of the three major essayists was in fact closely associated with important poets and supported at least some of the new poetic developments in critical commentaries whose perceptiveness and discrimination render them durably valuable. Like the poets, these essayists were personal and subjective; their essays are often candidly autobiographical, reminiscent, self-analytic; and when the writers treated other matters than themselves, they tended to do so impressionistically, so that the material is seen reflected in the temperament of the essayist. The subject matter of the essays, like that of the poetry, exhibits an extension of range and sympathy far beyond the earlier limits of the leisure class and its fashionable concerns; the essays now dealt with clerks, chimney sweeps, poor relations, handball players, prize-fighters, and murderers. Most strikingly, the essayists resemble the poets in rebelling against eighteenth-century conventions by reviving prose forms long disused and developing new prose styles and structural principles. The result was a notable variety of achievements, ranging from Hazlitt's hard-hitting plain style and seemingly casual order of topics, through Lamb's delicately contrived rhetoric and meticulously controlled organization, to De Quincey's elaborate experiments in applying to prose the rhythms, harmonies, and thematic structure of musical compositions.

THE DRAMA

Although favorable to the essay, literary conditions in the early nineteenth century were unfavorable in the extreme to writing for the stage. By a licensing act that was not repealed until 1843, only the Drury Lane and Covent Garden theaters had the right to produce "legitimate"—that is to say, spoken—drama; the other theaters were restricted by law to entertainments in which there could be no dialogue except to music, and so put on mainly dancing, pantomime, and various types of musical plays. The two monopoly theaters were vast and ill-lighted, and their audiences were noisy and unruly; as a result, actors played in a grandiose and orotund style. To succeed under such conditions, plays had to be blatant and magniloquent, so that the drama of that period (fettered also by rigid moral and political censorship) tended to the extremes of either farce or melodrama. None of the plays written by the professional playwrights of the time is read nowadays; they survive mainly in the limbo of scholarly monographs on the history of the theater.

Nonetheless, attracted irresistibly by the example of their idolized Shakespeare, all the major Romantic poets, and many minor ones, tried their hand at poetic plays. Some of these were written as closet drama—Byron's *Manfred* and Shelley's *Prometheus Unbound*, for example, and most of Joanna Baillie's widely read *Plays on the Passions*—but others were expressly written for the stage. The poets, however, lacked experience with the hard necessities of the practical theater, and they were for the most part unable to throw off the artifice of an archaic style dominated by Elizabethan and Jacobean models.

Above all, the genius of an age that excelled in subjective or visionary literary forms was ill adapted to the theater, which is a peculiarly social genre representing a variety of credible characters. Even Byron, the only important poet of his generation to produce major work in a literary kind that requires a highly developed social sensibility—satire—did not succeed as a practical dramatist. His stage plays, while readable, mainly exhibit various aspects of the Byronic hero; they lack theatrical vigor and variety, and their thin-skinned author wisely refused to let them be put on before the merciless and demonstrative audiences of his day. Coleridge achieved a minor hit with his tragedy *Remorse*, which ran for twenty nights at the Drury Lane in 1813. The most capable Romantic dramatist was, surprisingly, Shelley. In *The Cenci* (1820) Shelley, with great tact and genuine theatrical acumen, converts a true story of the Italian Renaissance—of a monstrous father who violates his daughter and is in turn murdered by her—into a powerful version of his own central fable of the instinctive desire of evil to destroy, by degrading, the defiant individual, and of the moral triumph of the unconquerable single spirit, even in death. The play was not staged, however, until long after Shelley's death.

THE NOVEL

Two new types of fiction were prominent in the late eighteenth century. One was the "Gothic novel," which had been inaugurated in 1764 by Horace Walpole's *The Castle of Otranto: A Gothic Story*, and continued by Clara Reeve in *The Champion of Virtue: A Gothic Story* (1777). The term derives from the frequent setting of these tales in a gloomy castle of the Middle Ages, but it has been extended to a larger group of novels, set somewhere in the past, that exploit the possibilities of mystery and terror in sullen, craggy landscapes; decaying mansions with dank dungeons, secret passages, and stealthy ghosts; chilling supernatural phenomena; and often, sexual persecution of a beautiful maiden by an obsessed and haggard villain. These novels opened up to later fiction the dark, irrational side of human nature—the savage egoism, the perverse impulses, and the nightmarish terrors that lie beneath the controlled and ordered surface of the conscious mind. Some of the most powerful and influential writings in the mode were by women— they doubtless afforded a fictional release for the submerged desires and compensatory fantasies of that rigidly restricted and disadvantaged class. In *The Mysteries of Udolpho* (1794), and better still in *The Italian* (1797), Ann Radcliffe developed the figure of the mysterious and solitary *homme fatal*, torturing others because he is himself tortured by unspeakable guilt, who, though a villain, usurps the place of the hero in the reader's interest. Matthew Gregory Lewis in *The Monk* (1797), which he wrote at the age of twenty, has a similar protagonist and brings to the fore the elements of diabolism, sensuality, and sadistic perversion that were pungent but submerged components in Radcliffe's Gothic formula. Gothicism is apparent also in Romantic poetry: in Coleridge's medieval terror poem *Christabel*, in Byron's recurrent hero-villain, in the setting and descriptive passages of Keats's *Eve of St. Agnes*, and in Shelley's inclinations (fostered by his early love for Gothic tales and his own youthful trials in that form) toward the fantastic, the macabre, and the exploration of the unconscious mind and of such aberrations as incest.

The second fictional mode popular at the turn of the century was the novel of purpose, often written to propagate the new social and political theories current in the period of the French Revolution. The best examples combine didactic intention with elements of Gothic terror. William Godwin, the political philosopher, wrote *Caleb Williams* (1794) to illustrate the thesis that the lower classes are helplessly subject to the power and privilege of the ruling class, but he did so in the form of a chilling story about the relentless pursuit and persecution by a wealthy squire of his young secretary, who has come upon evidence that the squire has committed murder. Mary Shelley—Percy Shelley's wife and the daughter of Mary Wollstonecraft, author of *A Vindication of the Rights of Woman*—wrote a thematic novel of terror that not only is a literary classic but has become a popular myth. Her *Frankenstein* (1818) transforms a story about a fabricated monster into a powerful representation of the moral distortion imposed on an individual who, because he diverges from the norm, is rejected by society. Maria Edgeworth's *Castle Rackrent* (1800), admired by Walter Scott, initiated what he later developed—the British regional novel and the British historical novel—and Hannah More's *Coelebs in Search of a Wife* (1808), a hugely successful novel about marriage and religion, was influential in both Britain and the United States.

The Romantic period produced, in addition to Mary Shelley, two novelists whose renown is worldwide, Jane Austen and Sir Walter Scott. Jane Austen (1775–1817) is the only major author who seems to be untouched by the political, intellectual, and artistic revolutions of her age. Charlotte Brontë, speaking for the Romantic sensibility, complained that Jane Austen's novels lack warmth, enthusiasm, energy; "she ruffles her reader by nothing vehement, disturbs him by nothing profound. The passions are perfectly unknown to her." But Austen deliberately elected to work within the circumference of her own experience—the life of provincial English gentlefolk—and to maintain the decorum of the novel of manners, based on such literary antecedents as the comedy of manners of William Congreve and Richard Brinsley Sheridan and the novels of the earlier women authors Fanny Burney and Maria Edgeworth. Within these elected limits both of subject and form, Austen achieved a fully particularized setting within which to examine and criticize the values men and women live by in their everyday social lives.

Sense and Sensibility and *Northanger Abbey* gently ridicule two later eighteenth-century deviations from the humanistic norm: the cult of sensibility and the taste for Gothic terrors. Austen's other novels, published between 1813 and 1818—*Mansfield Park, Persuasion*, and best of all, *Pride and Prejudice* and *Emma*—all deal with the subject of getting married. This was in fact a central preoccupation and problem for the young leisure-class lady of that age, who had no career open to her outside of domesticity; Austen, however, chose the subject because it provided her with the best realistic opportunities for testing her heroines' practical sense and moral integrity, their degree of knowledge of the world and of themselves, and their capacity to demonstrate grace under social and financial pressure.

Sir Walter Scott (1771–1832) was contemporary with Jane Austen, and admired her greatly, but his work in fiction was at an extreme from hers. In 1814, with the anonymous *Waverley*, he turned from narrative verse (in which Byron had displaced him in popularity) to narrative prose and managed to write almost thirty long works of fiction in the eighteen years before he died. They are in the mode that he himself defined as romance, "the interest of which turns upon marvelous and uncommon incidents," in contrast to the novel such as Jane Austen wrote, in which "the events are accommodated to the ordinary train of human events, and the modern state of society." Scott's originality lay in opening up to fiction the rich and lively realm of history; he sometimes alters the order of events for novelistic purposes, yet he maintains fidelity to the spirit of the past and a meticulous accuracy in antiquarian detail. His series of Scottish novels, including *Guy Mannering, The Antiquary, Old Mortality, Rob Roy,* and (most enduringly) *The Heart of Midlothian,* are rooted in historical events from the seventeenth century up to his own time; *Ivanhoe* is set in thirteenth-century England; *Kenilworth* takes place in the age of Elizabeth; and *Quentin Durward,* the best of his Continental romances, has for its background the French court of the fifteenth century.

Like Byron, Scott wrote with dash and grandiosity in a kind of sustained improvisation; his plotting is often loose, his romantic lovers pallid, and his kings and chieftains large-scale puppets. But in his great scenes of action there are a scope and sweep not to be exceeded in fiction for several decades. And although, unlike his liberal Romantic contemporaries, Scott's political sympathies were aristocratic and feudal, his most vivid and convincing characters are members of the middle and lower classes. His tradesmen, servants, peasantry, social outcasts, and demented old women, speaking a rich Scottish vernacular (Scott's language, like Robert Burns's in verse, tended to become stilted and conventional when he wrote in standard English), make up a populous world in which each person is an individual, rooted in the circumstances of time, place, class, and occupation.

Scott had an immense international vogue, equaling that of Byron and Goethe, and became the acknowledged master of some of the greatest nineteenth-century novelists, including Balzac and Tolstoy. Jane Austen, on the other hand, during her lifetime was admired only by a limited group of English readers. Her novels have, however, demonstrated greater staying power. Scott's combination of casualness in design and prodigality in detail puts off many readers who have formed their sensibilities on the fiction of the present century. But even after the achievements of such masters in the form as Henry James, Jane Austen remains the sovereign of the intricate, spare, and ironic art of the novel of manners.

THE ROMANTIC PERIOD

TEXTS	CONTEXTS
1774 J. W. von Goethe, *The Sorrows of Young Werther*	
	1775 American War of Independence (1775–83)
1776 Adam Smith, *The Wealth of Nations*	
1778 Frances Burney, *Evelina*	
1779 Samuel Johnson, *Lives of the English Poets* (1779–81)	
	1780 Gordon Riots in London
1781 Immanuel Kant, *Critique of Pure Reason*. Jean-Jacques Rousseau, *Confessions*. J. C. Friedrich Schiller, *The Robbers*	
	1783 William Pitt becomes prime minister (serving until 1801 and again in 1804–06)
1784 Charlotte Smith, *Elegiac Sonnets*	1784 Death of Samuel Johnson
1785 William Cowper, *The Task*	
1786 William Beckford, *Vathek*. Robert Burns, *Poems, Chiefly in the Scottish Dialect*	
	1787 W. A. Mozart, *Don Giovanni*
1789 Jeremy Bentham, *Principles of Morals and Legislation*. William Blake, *Songs of Innocence*	1789 Fall of the Bastille (beginning of the French Revolution)
1790 Joanna Baillie, *Poems*. Blake, *The Marriage of Heaven and Hell*. Edmund Burke, *Reflections on the Revolution in France*	1790 Henry James Pye succeeds Thomas Warton as poet laureate. J. M. W. Turner first exhibits at the Royal Academy
1791 William Gilpin, *Observations on the River Wye*. Thomas Paine, *Rights of Man*. Ann Radcliffe, *The Romance of the Forest*	
1792 Mary Wollstonecraft, *A Vindication of the Rights of Woman*	1792 September Massacres in Paris. First gas lights in Britain
1793 William Godwin, *Political Justice*	1793 Execution of Louis XVI and Marie Antoinette. France declares war against Britain (and then Britain against France). The Reign of Terror
1794 Blake, *Songs of Experience*. Godwin, *Caleb Williams*. Radcliffe, *The Mysteries of Udolpho*	1794 The fall of Robespierre
1796 Matthew Gregory Lewis, *The Monk*	
1798 Joanna Baillie, *Plays on the Passions*, volume 1. Bentham, *Political Economy*. Thomas Malthus, *An Essay on the Principle of Population*. William Wordsworth and Samuel Taylor Coleridge, *Lyrical Ballads*	
1800 Maria Edgeworth, *Castle Rackrent*. Mary Robinson, *Lyrical Tales*	

TEXTS	CONTEXTS
	1802 Treaty of Amiens. *Edinburgh Review* founded. John Constable first exhibits at the Royal Academy
	1804 Napoleon crowned emperor
	1805 The French fleet defeated by the British at Trafalgar
1807 Wordsworth, *Poems in Two Volumes*	1807 Abolition of the slave trade in Britain
1808 Goethe, *Faust,* part 1	1808 Ludwig van Beethoven, *Symphonies* 5 and 6
	1811 The Prince of Wales becomes regent for George III, who is declared incurably insane
1812 Lord Byron, *Childe Harold's Pilgrimage,* cantos 1 and 2. Felicia Hemans, *The Domestic Affections*	1812 War between Britain and the United States (1812–15)
1813 Jane Austen, *Price and Prejudice*	1813 Robert Southey succeeds Pye as poet laureate
1814 Walter Scott, *Waverley.* Wordsworth, *The Excursion*	
	1815 Napoleon defeated at Waterloo
1816 Byron, *Childe Harold,* cantos 3 and 4. Coleridge, *Christabel, Kubla Khan.* Percy Shelley, *Alastor*	
1817 Byron, *Manfred.* Coleridge, *Biographia Literaria* and *Sibylline Leaves.* John Keats, *Poems*	1817 *Blackwood's Edinburgh Magazine* founded. Death of Princess Charlotte
1818 Austen, *Northanger Abbey.* Keats, *Endymion.* Thomas Love Peacock, *Nightmare Abbey.* Mary Shelley, *Frankenstein*	
1819 Byron, *Don Juan,* cantos 1 and 2	1819 "Peterloo Massacre" in Manchester
1820 John Clare, *Poems Descriptive of Rural Life.* Keats, *Lamia, Isabella, The Eve of St. Agnes, and Other Poems.* Percy Shelley, *Prometheus Unbound*	1820 Death of George III; accession of George IV. *London Magazine* founded
1821 Thomas De Quincey, *Confessions of an English Opium-Eater.* Percy Shelley, *Adonais*	1821 Deaths of Keats in Rome and Napoleon at St. Helena
	1822 Franz Schubert, *Unfinished Symphony.* Death of Percy Shelley in the Bay of Spezia, near Lerici, Italy
1824 Letitia Landon, *The Improvisatrice*	1824 Death of Byron in Missolonghi
1827 Clare, *The Shepherd's Calendar*	
1828 Hemans, *Records of Woman*	
1830 Charles Lyell, *Principles of Geology* (1830–33). Alfred Tennyson, *Poems, Chiefly Lyrical*	1830 Death of George IV; accession of William IV
	1832 First Reform Bill

ANNA LETITIA BARBAULD
1743–1825

Anna Barbauld, born Anna Letitia Aiken, received an unusual education from her father, a nonconformist minister and schoolmaster, that enabled her to read English before she was three and to master French and Italian, and then both Latin and Greek, while still a child. She made her literary debut with *Poems*, a work that went through five editions between 1773 and 1777 and immediately established her as a leading poet. In 1774 she married Rochemont Barbauld, a dissenting minister, and with him co-managed a school at Palgrave, in Suffolk. Thereafter, becoming increasingly famous and respected in literary circles as (according to the custom of the day) "Mrs. Barbauld," she divided her time between the teaching of younger pupils at Palgrave and a series of writings focused on education, politics, and literature. She published *Devotional Pieces* (1775), three volumes of *Lessons for Children* (1778–79), and *Hymns in Prose for Children* (1781), all of which were reprinted many times. William Hazlitt records a common experience in recalling that he read her works "before those of any other author, male or female, when I was learning to spell words of one syllable in her story-books for children."

She wrote political pamphlets in the 1790s, defending dissenters, democratic government, and popular education and opposing Britain's declaration of war against France; she attacked the slave trade in a verse *Epistle to William Wilberforce* (1791). In the next decade she turned to editing, producing the *Correspondence of Samuel Richardson* (six volumes, 1804), *The British Novelists* (fifty volumes, beginning in 1810), and a popular anthology of poetry and prose for young women called *The Female Speaker* (1811). Her work *The British Novelists* was the first attempt to establish a national canon in fiction paralleling the multivolume collections of British poets (such as the one associated with Samuel Johnson's prefaces) that had been appearing since the 1770s. Her introductory essay, *On the Origin and Progress of Novel-Writing*, is a pioneering statement concerning the educational value of novels.

Barbauld's last major work in poetry was *Eighteen Hundred and Eleven* (1812), a 334-line tirade against contemporary Britain lamenting the war with France (then in its seventeenth year), the poverty of leadership, the fallen economy, colonialism, and the failure of genius (at the conclusion, the Spirit of Genius emigrates to South America). The critical response was anguished and unanimously negative, even from the more liberal critics; and Barbauld seems not to have attempted another long work after this (she was, by this time, in her late sixties). She continued to write shorter pieces, such as the sprightly *Life,* on into the 1820s.

A Summer Evening's Meditation[1]

> 'Tis past! The sultry tyrant of the south
> Has spent his short-lived rage; more grateful hours
> Move silent on; the skies no more repel
> The dazzled sight, but with mild maiden beams
> 5   Of tempered lustre court the cherished eye
> To wander o'er their sphere; where, hung aloft,
> Dian's bright crescent, like a silver bow

---

1. The excursion-and-return structure of this poem anticipates the high flights (and returns) of later lyrics by Coleridge, Percy Shelley, and Keats, among others. But Barbauld's journey, beginning with "mild maiden beams" in line 4 and continuing with Diana's crescent (line 7), Venus's sweetest beam (lines 10 and 11), and "meekened Eve" (line 14), is specifically gendered throughout: it is clearly a woman who is launching "into the trackless deeps of space" (line 82).

New strung in heaven, lifts high its beamy horns
Impatient for the night, and seems to push
10   Her brother down the sky. Fair Venus shines
Even in the eye of day; with sweetest beam
Propitious shines, and shakes a trembling flood
Of softened radiance from her dewy locks.
The shadows spread apace; while meekened[2] Eve,
15   Her cheek yet warm with blushes, slow retires
Through the Hesperian gardens of the west,
And shuts the gates of day. 'Tis now the hour
When Contemplation from her sunless haunts,
The cool damp grotto, or the lonely depth
20   Of unpierced woods, where wrapt in solid shade
She mused away the gaudy hours of noon,
And fed on thoughts unripened by the sun,
Moves forward; and with radiant finger points
To yon blue concave swelled by breath divine,
25   Where, one by one, the living eyes of heaven
Awake, quick kindling o'er the face of ether
One boundless blaze; ten thousand trembling fires,
And dancing lustres, where the unsteady eye,
Restless and dazzled, wanders unconfined
30   O'er all this field of glories; spacious field,
And worthy of the Master: he, whose hand
With hieroglyphics elder than the Nile
Inscribed the mystic tablet, hung on high
To public gaze, and said, "Adore, O man!
35   The finger of thy God." From what pure wells
Of milky light, what soft o'erflowing urn,
Are all these lamps so fill'd? these friendly lamps,
For ever streaming o'er the azure deep
To point our path, and light us to our home.
40   How soft they slide along their lucid spheres!
And silent as the foot of Time, fulfill
Their destined courses: Nature's self is hushed,
And, but a scattered leaf, which rustles through
The thick-wove foliage, not a sound is heard
45   To break the midnight air; though the raised ear,
Intensely listening, drinks in every breath.
How deep the silence, yet how loud the praise!
But are they silent all? or is there not
A tongue in every star, that talks with man,
50   And woos him to be wise? nor woos in vain:
This dead of midnight is the noon of thought,
And Wisdom mounts her zenith with the stars.
At this still hour the self-collected soul
Turns inward, and beholds a stranger there
55   Of high descent, and more than mortal rank;
An embryo God; a spark of fire divine,
Which must burn on for ages, when the sun,—

---

2. Softened, made meek.

Fair transitory creature of a day!—
Has closed his golden eye, and wrapt in shades
60 Forgets his wonted journey through the east.

Ye citadels of light, and seats of Gods!
Perhaps my future home, from whence the soul,
Revolving periods past, may oft look back
With recollected tenderness on all
65 The various busy scenes she left below,
Its deep-laid projects and its strange events,
As on some fond and doting tale that soothed
Her infant hours—O be it lawful now
To tread the hallowed circle of your courts,
70 And with mute wonder and delighted awe
Approach your burning confines. Seized in thought,
On Fancy's wild and roving wing I sail,
From the green borders of the peopled Earth,
And the pale Moon, her duteous fair attendant;
75 From solitary Mars; from the vast orb
Of Jupiter, whose huge gigantic bulk
Dances in ether like the lightest leaf;
To the dim verge, the suburbs of the system,
Where cheerless Saturn 'midst his watery moons
80 Girt with a lucid zone, in gloomy pomp,
Sits like an exiled monarch: fearless thence
I launch into the trackless deeps of space,
Where, burning round, ten thousand suns appear,
Of elder beam, which ask no leave to shine
85 Of our terrestrial star, nor borrow light
From the proud regent of our scanty day;
Sons of the morning, first-born of creation,
And only less than Him who marks their track,
And guides their fiery wheels. Here must I stop,
90 Or is there aught beyond? What hand unseen
Impels me onward through the glowing orbs
Of habitable nature, far remote,
To the dread confines of eternal night,
To solitudes of vast unpeopled space,
95 The deserts of creation, wide and wild;
Where embryo systems and unkindled suns
Sleep in the womb of chaos? fancy droops,
And thought astonished stops her bold career.
But O thou mighty mind! whose powerful word
100 Said, thus let all things be, and thus they were,
Where shall I seek thy presence? how unblamed
Invoke thy dread perfection?
Have the broad eyelids of the morn beheld thee?
Or does the beamy shoulder of Orion
105 Support thy throne? O look with pity down
On erring, guilty man! not in thy names
Of terror clad; not with those thunders armed

That conscious Sinai felt, when fear appalled
The scattered tribes;[3]—thou hast a gentler voice,
110   That whispers comfort to the swelling heart,
Abashed, yet longing to behold her Maker.

But now my soul, unused to stretch her powers
In flight so daring, drops her weary wing,
And seeks again the known accustomed spot,
115   Drest up with sun, and shade, and lawns, and streams,
A mansion fair, and spacious for its guest,
And full replete with wonders. Let me here,
Content and grateful, wait the appointed time,
And ripen for the skies: the hour will come
120   When all these splendours bursting on my sight
Shall stand unveiled, and to my ravished sense
Unlock the glories of the world unknown.

1773

The Rights of Woman[1]

Yes, injured Woman! rise, assert thy right!
Woman! too long degraded, scorned, opprest;
O born to rule in partial Law's despite,
Resume thy native empire o'er the breast!

5   Go forth arrayed in panoply divine;
That angel pureness which admits no stain;
Go, bid proud Man his boasted rule resign,
And kiss the golden sceptre of thy reign.

Go, gird thyself with grace; collect thy store
10   Of bright artillery glancing from afar;
Soft melting tones thy thundering cannon's roar,
Blushes and fears thy magazine of war.

Thy rights are empire: urge no meaner claim,—
Felt, not defined, and if debated, lost;
15   Like sacred mysteries, which withheld from fame,
Shunning discussion, are revered the most.

Try all that wit and art suggest to bend
Of thy imperial foe the stubborn knee;
Make treacherous Man thy subject, not thy friend;
20   Thou mayst command, but never canst be free.

3. When God came down to deliver the Ten Commandments "there were thunders and lightnings
. . . so that all the people . . . trembled" (Exodus
19.16).

1. A response—seemingly favorable until the last
two stanzas—to Mary Wollstonecraft's A Vindication of the Rights of Woman (1792).

Awe the licentious, and restrain the rude;
Soften the sullen, clear the cloudy brow:
Be, more than princes' gifts, thy favours sued;—
She hazards all, who will the least allow.

25 But hope not, courted idol of mankind,
On this proud eminence secure to stay;
Subduing and subdued, thou soon shalt find
Thy coldness soften, and thy pride give way.

Then, then, abandon each ambitious thought,
30 Conquest or rule thy heart shall feebly move,
In Nature's school, by her soft maxims taught,
That separate rights are lost in mutual love.

ca. 1792–95   1825

To a Little Invisible Being
Who Is Expected Soon to Become Visible

Germ of new life, whose powers expanding slow
For many a moon their full perfection wait,—
Haste, precious pledge of happy love, to go
Auspicious borne through life's mysterious gate.

5 What powers lie folded in thy curious frame,—
Senses from objects locked, and mind from thought!
How little canst thou guess thy lofty claim
To grasp at all the worlds the Almighty wrought!

And see, the genial season's warmth to share,
10 Fresh younglings shoot, and opening roses glow!
Swarms of new life exulting fill the air,—
Haste, infant bud of being, haste to blow!°   bloom

For thee the nurse prepares her lulling songs,
The eager matrons count the lingering day;
15 But far the most thy anxious parent longs
On thy soft cheek a mother's kiss to lay.

She only asks to lay her burden down,
That her glad arms that burden may resume;
And nature's sharpest pangs her wishes crown,
20 That free thee living from thy living tomb.

She longs to fold to her maternal breast
Part of herself, yet to herself unknown;
To see and to salute the stranger guest,
Fed with her life through many a tedious moon.

25 Come, reap thy rich inheritance of love!
  Bask in the fondness of a Mother's eye!
  Nor wit nor eloquence her heart shall move
  Like the first accents of thy feeble cry.

  Haste, little captive, burst thy prison doors!
30 Launch on the living world, and spring to light!
  Nature for thee displays her various stores,
  Opens her thousand inlets of delight.

  If charmed verse or muttered prayers had power,
  With favouring spells to speed thee on thy way,
35 Anxious I'd bid my beads° each passing hour,   offer a prayer
  Till thy wished smile thy mother's pangs o'erpay.°   more than compensate

ca. 1795?   1825

Washing-Day

. . . and their voice,
Turning again towards childish treble, pipes
And whistles in its sound.[1]

  The Muses are turned gossips; they have lost
  The buskined° step, and clear high-sounding phrase,   *tragic, elevated*
  Language of gods, Come then, domestic Muse,
  In slipshod measure loosely prattling on
5 Of farm or orchard, pleasant curds and cream,
  Or drowning flies, or shoe lost in the mire
  By little whimpering boy, with rueful face;
  Come, Muse; and sing the dreaded Washing-Day.
  Ye who beneath the yoke of wedlock bend,
10 With bowed soul, full well ye ken the day
  Which week, smooth sliding after week, brings on
  Too soon;—for to that day nor peace belongs
  Nor comfort;—ere the first gray streak of dawn,
  The red-armed washers come and chase repose.
15 Nor pleasant smile, nor quaint device of mirth,
  E'er visited that day: the very cat,
  From the wet kitchen scared and reeking hearth,
  Visits the parlour,—an unwonted guest.
  The silent breakfast-meal is soon dispatched;
20 Uninterrupted, save by anxious looks
  Cast at the lowering sky, if sky should lower.
  From that last evil, O preserve us, heavens!
  For should the skies pour down, adieu to all
  Remains of quiet: then expect to hear
25 Of sad disasters,—dirt and gravel stains
  Hard to efface, and loaded lines at once

1. Loosely quoted from Shakespeare's *As You Like It* 2.7.160–62.

Snapped short,—and linen-horse° by dog thrown down,   *drying rack*
And all the petty miseries of life.
Saints have been calm while stretched upon the rack,
30 And Guatimozin² smiled on burning coals;
But never yet did housewife notable
Greet with a smile a rainy washing-day.
—But grant the welkin° fair, require not thou   *sky*
Who call'st thyself perchance the master there,
35 Or study swept or nicely dusted coat,
Or usual 'tendance;—ask not, indiscreet,
Thy stockings mended, though the yawning rents
Gape wide as Erebus;° nor hope to find   *the underworld*
Some snug recess impervious: shouldst thou try
40 The 'customed garden walks, shine eye shall rue
The budding fragrance of thy tender shrubs,
Myrtle or rose, all crushed beneath the weight
Of coarse checked apron,—with impatient hand
Twitched off when showers impend: or crossing lines
45 Shall mar thy musings, as the wet cold sheet
Flaps in thy face abrupt. Woe to the friend
Whose evil stars have urged him forth to claim
On such a day the hospitable rites!
Looks, blank at best, and stinted courtesy,
50 Shall he receive. Vainly he feeds his hopes
With dinner of roast chicken, savoury pie,
Or tart or pudding:—pudding he nor tart
That day shall eat; nor, though the husband try,
Mending what can't be helped, to kindle mirth
55 From cheer deficient, shall his consort's brow
Clear up propitious:—the unlucky guest
In silence dines, and early slinks away.
I well remember, when a child, the awe
This day struck into me; for then the maids,
60 I scarce knew why, looked cross, and drove me from them:
Nor soft caress could I obtain, nor hope
Usual indulgencies; jelly or creams,
Relic of costly suppers, and set by
For me, their petted one; or buttered toast,
65 When butter was forbid; or thrilling tale
Of ghost or witch, or murder—so I went
And sheltered me beside the parlour fire:
There my dear grandmother, eldest of forms,
Tended the little ones, and watched from harm,
70 Anxiously fond, though oft her spectacles
With elfin cunning hid, and oft the pins
Drawn from her ravelled stocking, might have soured
One less indulgent.—
At intervals my mother's voice was heard,
75 Urging dispatch: briskly the work went on,

2. The last of the Aztec emperors (Cuanhtémoc, d. 1525), who was tortured and executed by the Spanish conquistadors.

All hands employed to wash, to rinse, to wring,
To fold, and starch, and clap,° and iron, and plait.   *flatten*
Then would I sit me down, and ponder much
Why washings were. Sometimes through hollow bowl
80 Of pipe amused we blew, and sent aloft
The floating bubbles; little dreaming then
To see, Mongolfier,[3] thy silken ball
Ride buoyant through the clouds—so near approach
The sports of children and the toils of men.
85 Earth, air, and sky, and ocean, hath its bubbles,[4]
And verse is one of them—this most of all.

1797

Life

Animula, vagula, blandula.[1]

Life! I know not what thou art,
But know that thou and I must part;
And when, or how, or where we met,
I own to me's a secret yet.
5   But this I know, when thou art fled,
Where'er they lay these limbs, this head,
No clod so valueless shall be,
As all that then remains of me.
O whither, whither dost thou fly,
10   Where bend unseen thy trackless course,
And in this strange divorce,
Ah tell where I must seek this compound I?

To the vast ocean of empyreal flame,
From whence thy essence came,
15   Dost thou thy flight pursue, when freed
From matter's base encumbering weed?
Or dost thou, hid from sight,
Wait, like some spell-bound knight,
Through blank oblivious years th' appointed hour,
20   To break thy trance and reassume thy power?
Yet canst thou without thought or feeling be?
O say what art thou, when no more thou 'rt thee?

Life! we've been long together,
Through pleasant and through cloudy weather;
25   'Tis hard to part when friends are dear;
Perhaps 't will cost a sigh, a tear;
Then steal away, give little warning,

---

3. Brothers Joseph-Michel and Jacques-Étienne
Mongolfier successfully launched the first hot-air
balloon, at Annonay, France, in 1783.
4. Cf. *Macbeth* 1.3.77: "The earth hath bubbles,
as the water has."

1. From Aelius Spartianus's *Life of Hadrian* 25—
the first line of a poem supposedly composed by
the emperor Hadrian on his deathbed: "Charming
little soul, hastening away."

Choose thine own time;
Say not Good night, but in some brighter clime
30   Bid me Good morning.

1825

WILLIAM BLAKE
1757–1827

What William Blake called his "Spiritual Life" was as varied, free, and dramatic as his "Corporeal Life" was simple, limited, and unadventurous. His father was a London haberdasher. His only formal education was in art: at the age of ten he entered a drawing school and later studied for a time at the school of the Royal Academy of Arts. At fourteen he entered an apprenticeship for seven years to a well-known engraver, James Basire, and began reading widely in his free time and trying his hand at poetry. At twenty-four he married Catherine Boucher, daughter of a market gardener. She was then illiterate, but Blake taught her to read and to help him in his engraving and printing. In the early and somewhat sentimentalized biographies, Catherine is represented as an ideal wife for an unorthodox and impecunious genius. Blake, however, must have been a trying domestic partner, and his vehement attacks on the torment caused by a possessive, jealous female will, which reached their height in 1793 and remained prominent in his writings for another decade, probably reflect a troubled period at home. The couple was childless.

The Blakes for a time enjoyed a moderate prosperity while Blake gave drawing lessons, illustrated books, and engraved designs made by other artists. When the demand for his work slackened, Blake in 1800 moved to a cottage at Felpham, on the Sussex seacoast, to take advantage of the patronage of the wealthy poetaster, biographer, and amateur of the arts William Hayley, who with the best of narrow intentions tried to transform Blake into a conventional artist and breadwinner. But the caged eagle soon rebelled. Hayley, Blake wrote, "is the Enemy of my Spiritual Life while he pretends to be the Friend of my Corporeal."

At Felpham in 1803 occurred an event that left a permanent mark on Blake's mind and art—an altercation with one John Schofield, a private in the Royal Dragoons. Blake ordered the soldier out of his garden and, when Schofield replied with threats and curses against Blake and his wife, pushed him the fifty yards to the inn where he was quartered. Schofield brought charges that Blake had uttered seditious statements about king and country. Since England was at war with France, sedition was a hanging offense. Blake was acquitted—an event, according to a newspaper account, "which so gratified the auditory that the court was . . . thrown into an uproar by their noisy exultations." Nevertheless Schofield, his fellow soldier Cock, and other participants in the trial haunted Blake's imagination and were enlarged to demonic characters who play a sinister role in *Jerusalem*. The event exacerbated Blake's sense that ominous forces were at work in the contemporary world and led him to complicate the symbolic and allusive style by which he veiled the radical religious, moral, and political opinions that he expressed in his poems.

After three years at Felpham, Blake moved back to London, determined to follow his "Divine Vision," though it meant a life of isolation, misunderstanding, and poverty. When his single bid for public recognition, a one-man show put on in 1809, proved a total failure, Blake passed into almost complete obscurity. Only when he was in his sixties did he finally attract a small but devoted group of young painters who served as an audience for his work and his talk. Blake's old age was serene and self-confident, largely free from the bursts of irascibility with which he had earlier responded to what he viewed as the shallowness and blindness of the English public. He died in his seventieth year.

Blake's first book of poems, *Poetical Sketches*, which he had printed when he was twenty-six years old, showed his dissatisfaction with the reigning poetic tradition and his restless quest for new forms and techniques. For lyric models he turned back to the Elizabethan and early seventeenth-century poets, to the Ossianic poems, and to Collins, Thomas Chatterton, and other eighteenth-century writers outside the tradition of Pope; he also experimented with partial rhymes and novel rhythms and employed bold figures of speech that at times approximate symbols. In 1788 he began to experiment with relief etching, a method that he called "illuminated printing" and used to produce most of his books of poems. Working directly on a copper plate with pens, brushes, and an acid-resistant medium, he wrote the text in reverse (so that it would print in the normal order) and also drew the illustration; he then etched the plate in acid to eat away the untreated copper and leave the design standing in relief. The pages printed from such plates were colored by hand in water colors and stitched together to make up a volume. This process was laborious and time-consuming, and Blake printed very few copies of his books; for example, of *Songs of Innocence and of Experience* only twenty-eight copies (some of them incomplete) are known to exist; of *The Book of Thel*, sixteen; of *The Marriage of Heaven and Hell*, nine; and of *Jerusalem*, five.

It must be remembered that to read a Blake poem in a printed text without the illustrations is to see only an abstraction from an integral and mutually enlightening combination of words and design. In this mode of relief etching, he published *Songs of Innocence* (1789), then added supplementary poems and printed *Songs of Innocence and of Experience* in 1794. The two groups of poems represent the world as it is envisioned by what he calls "two contrary states of the human soul." In the best of the songs of experience, such as *The Tyger* and *London*, Blake achieved his mature lyric technique of compressed metaphor and symbol that explode into a multiplicity of references.

Gradually Blake's thinking about human history and his experience of life and suffering articulated themselves in the "Giant Forms" and their actions, which came to constitute a complete mythology. As Blake's mythical character Los said, speaking for all imaginative artists, "I must Create a System or be enslaved by another Man's." This coherent but constantly altering and enlarging system composed the subject matter first of Blake's "minor prophecies," completed by 1795, and then of the major prophetic books on which he continued working until about 1820: *The Four Zoas*, *Milton*, and *Jerusalem*.

In his sixties Blake gave up poetry to devote himself to pictorial art. In the course of his life he produced hundreds of paintings and engravings, many of them illustrations for the work of other poets, including a representation of Chaucer's Canterbury pilgrims, a superb set of designs for the Book of Job, and a series of illustrations of Dante, on which he was still hard at work when he died. At the time of his death Blake was little known as an artist and almost entirely unknown as a poet. In the mid-nineteenth century he acquired a group of admirers among the Pre-Raphaelites, who regarded him as a precursor. Since the mid-1920s, Blake has finally come into his own, both in poetry and in painting, as one of the most dedicated, intellectually challenging, and astonishingly original of artists. His marked influence ranges from William Butler Yeats, who edited Blake's writings and modeled his own system of mythology on Blake's, to Allen Ginsberg and other Beat and counterculture writers, beginning in the 1950s, who admired Blake's stress on a visionary poetry and his rebellious stance against the conventional life and pieties of his day.

The explication of Blake's cryptic prophetic books has been the preoccupation of many scholars. Blake wrote them in the persona, or "voice," of "the Bard! / Who Present, Past, & Future sees"—that is, as a British poet who follows Spenser, and especially Milton, in a lineage going back to the prophets of the Bible. "The Nature of my Work," he said, "is Visionary or Imaginative." What Blake meant by the key terms *vision* and *imagination,* however, is often misinterpreted by taking literally what he, speaking the traditional language of his great predecessors, intended in a figurative sense. "That which can be made Explicit to the Idiot," Blake declared, "is not worth my care." Blake was a born ironist who enjoyed mystifying his well-meaning but literal-minded friends and who took a defiant pleasure in shocking the dull and complacent "angels" of his day by being deliberately outrageous in representing his work and opinions.

Blake declared that "all he knew was in the Bible" and that "The Old & New Testaments are the Great Code of Art." This is an exaggeration of the truth that all his prophetic writings deal, in various formulations, with some aspects of the overall biblical plot of the creation and the Fall, the history of the generations of humanity in the fallen world, redemption, and the promise of a recovery of Eden and of a New Jerusalem. These events, however, Blake interprets in what he calls "the spiritual sense." For such a procedure he had considerable precedent, not in the neoplatonic and occult thinkers with whom some modern commentators align him, but in the "spiritual" interpreters of the Bible among the radical Protestant sects in seventeenth- and eighteenth-century England. In *The French Revolution, America: A Prophecy, Europe: A Prophecy,* and the trenchant prophetic satire *The Marriage of Heaven and Hell*—all of which Blake wrote in the early 1790s while he was an ardent supporter of the French Revolution—he, like Wordsworth, Coleridge, Southey, and a number of radical English theologians, represented the contemporary Revolution as the purifying violence that, according to biblical prophecy, portended the imminent redemption of humanity and the world. In Blake's later poems, Orc, the fiery spirit of violent revolution, gives way as a central personage to Los, the type of the visionary imagination in the fallen world. Even in his early writings, however, Blake had represented political and social revolution as correlative with a radical change within the mind and imagination of the individual, so that the replacement of Orc by Los does not indicate Blake's recantation of former beliefs, but a shift of emphasis from an apocalypse by revolution to an apocalypse by imagination.

BLAKE'S MATURE MYTH

Blake's first attempt to articulate his full myth of humanity's present, past, and future was *The Four Zoas,* begun in 1796 or 1797. A passage from the opening statement of its theme exemplifies the long verse line (what Blake called "the march of long resounding strong heroic verse") in which he wrote his Prophetic Books and will serve also to outline the visualizable imaginative form in which Blake's thought embodied itself:

> Four Mighty Ones are in every Man; a Perfect Unity
> Cannot Exist, but from the Universal Brotherhood of Eden,
> The Universal Man. To Whom be Glory Evermore, Amen. . . .
> Los was the fourth immortal starry one, & in the Earth
> Of a bright Universe Empery attended day & night
> Days & nights of revolving joy, Urthona was his name
> In Eden; in the Auricular Nerves of Human life
> Which is the Earth of Eden, he his Emanations propagated. . . .
>   Daughter of Beulah, Sing
> His fall into Division & his Resurrection to Unity.

Blake's mythical premise, or starting point, is not a transcendent God but the "Universal Man" who is himself God and who incorporates the cosmos as well. (Blake elsewhere describes this founding image as "the Human Form Divine" and names him "Albion.") The fall, in this myth, is not the fall of humanity away from God but a falling apart of primal people, a "fall into Division." In this event the original sin is what Blake calls "Selfhood," the attempt of an isolated part to be self-sufficient. The breakup of the all-inclusive Universal Man in Eden into exiled parts, it is evident, serves to identify the Fall with the creation—the creation not only of man and of nature as we ordinarily know them but also of a separate sky god who is alien from humanity. Universal Man divides first into the "Four Mighty Ones" who are the Zoas, or chief powers and component aspects of humanity, and these in turn divide sexually into male Spectres and female Emanations. (Thus in the quoted passage the Zoa known in the unfallen state of Eden as Urthona, the imaginative power, separates into the form of Los in the fallen world.) In addition to Eden there are three successively lower "states" of being in the fallen world, which Blake calls Beulah (a pastoral condition of easy and relaxed innocence, without clash of "contraries"), Generation (the realm of common human experience, suffering, and conflicting contraries), and Ulro (Blake's hell, the lowest state, or limit, of bleak rationality, tyranny, static negation, and isolated Selfhood). The fallen world moves through the cycles of its history, successively approaching and falling away from redemption, until, by the agency of the Redeemer (who is equated with the human imagination and is most potently operative in the prophetic poet), it will culminate in an apocalypse. In terms of his controlling image of the Universal Man, Blake describes this apocalypse as a return to the original, undivided condition, "his Resurrection to Unity."

What is confusing to many readers is that Blake alternates this representation of the Fall (as a fragmentation of the one Primal Man into separate parts) with a different kind of representation, in terms of two sharply opposed ways of seeing the universe. In this latter mode, the Fall is a catastrophic change from imaginative insight (which sees the cosmos as unified and humanized) to sight by the physical eye (which sees the cosmos as a multitude of isolated individuals in an inhuman and alien nature). In terms of this distinction, the apocalypse toward which Blake as imaginative artist strives unceasingly will enable men and women once again to envision all beings as participant in the individual life that he calls "the Universal Brotherhood of Eden"— that is, a humanized world in which all individuals, in familial union, can feel at home.

Although Blake did not know it, he shared with a number of contemporary German philosophers the point of view—it has in our own time become the prevailing point of view—that our fall (that is, the malaise of modern culture) is essentially a mode of psychic disintegration and of resultant alienation from oneself, one's world, and one's fellow human beings, and that our hope of recovery lies in a process of reintegration. As a poet, however, Blake does not present this view in abstract conceptual terms, but embodies it in picturable agents acting out an epic plot.

The text for Blake's writings is that of *The Complete Poetry and Prose of William Blake*, edited by David V. Erdman and Harold Bloom (revised edition, Berkeley, 1982). Blake's erratic spelling and punctuation have been altered when the original form might mislead the reader. The editors are grateful for the expert advice of Joseph Viscomi and Robert Essick in editing the selections from Blake.

There Is No Natural Religion[1]

[a]

The Argument. Man has no notion of moral fitness but from Education. Naturally he is only a natural organ subject to Sense.

1. This and the following selection are early illuminated works, probably etched in 1788. They are directed against 18th century Deism. or " natural religion," which bases its religious beliefs on the evidences for the existence and intentions of God that are said to be evident in the natural, or

I. Man cannot naturally Percieve but through his natural or bodily organs.

II. Man by his reasoning power can only compare & judge of what he has already perciev'd.

III. From a perception of only 3 senses or 3 elements none could deduce a fourth or fifth.

IV. None could have other than natural or organic thoughts if he had none but organic perceptions.

V. Man's desires are limited by his perceptions; none can desire what he has not perciev'd.

VI. The desires & perceptions of man, untaught by any thing but organs of sense, must be limited to objects of sense.

Conclusion. If it were not for the Poetic or Prophetic character the Philosophic & Experimental would soon be at the ratio of all things, & stand still unable to do other than repeat the same dull round over again.

1788

There Is No Natural Religion[1]

[b]

I. Man's perceptions are not bounded by organs of perception; he percieves more than sense (tho' ever so acute) can discover.

II. Reason, or the ratio[2] of all we have already known, is not the same that it shall be when we know more.

[III lacking]

IV. The bounded is loathed by its possessor. The same dull round even of a universe would soon become a mill with complicated wheels.

V. If the many become the same as the few when possess'd, More! More! is the cry of a mistaken soul. Less than All cannot satisfy Man.

VI. If any could desire what he is incapable of possessing, despair must be his eternal lot.

VII. The desire of Man being Infinite, the possession is Infinite & himself Infinite.

Application. He who sees the Infinite in all things sees God. He who sees the Ratio only sees himself only.

Therefore God becomes as we are, that we may be as he is.

1788

"organic" world. In this first selection. Blake presents his version of English empiricism, which derives all mental content (including the evidences from which, in "natural religion," reason is held to prove the existence of God) from perceptions by the physical senses.

1. In this second document, Blake asserts his own convictions (in opposition to the empirical and deistic tenets in the preceding tract) that knowledge is not limited to the physical senses, but is as unbounded as the infinite desires of humankind and its godlike capacity for infinite vision.

2. In Latin *ratio* signifies both "reason" and "calculation." Blake applies the term derogatorily to the 18th-century concept of reason as a calculating faculty whose operations are limited to sense-perceptions.

FROM SONGS OF INNOCENCE AND OF EXPERIENCE[1]

SHEWING THE TWO CONTRARY STATES OF THE HUMAN SOUL

FROM SONGS OF INNOCENCE

Introduction

Piping down the valleys wild
Piping songs of pleasant glee
On a cloud I saw a child,
And he laughing said to me,

5   "Pipe a song about a Lamb";
So I piped with merry chear;
"Piper pipe that song again"—
So I piped, he wept to hear.

"Drop thy pipe thy happy pipe
10   Sing thy songs of happy chear";
So I sung the same again
While he wept with joy to hear.

"Piper sit thee down and write
In a book that all may read"—
15   So he vanish'd from my sight.
And I pluck'd a hollow reed,

And I made a rural pen,
And I stain'd the water clear,
And I wrote my happy songs
20   Every child may joy to hear.

1789

The Ecchoing Green

The Sun does arise,
And make happy the skies.
The merry bells ring
To welcome the Spring.

---

1. *Songs of Innocence* was etched in 1789, and in 1794 was combined with additional poems under the title *Songs of Innocence and of Experience;* this collection was reprinted at various later times with varying arrangements of the poems. In his songs of innocence Blake assumes the stance that he is writing "happy songs / Every child may joy to hear," but they do not all depict an innocent and happy world; many of them incorporate injustice, evil, and suffering. These aspects of the fallen world, however, are represented as they appear to a "state" of the human soul that Blake calls "innocence" and that he expresses in a simple pastoral language, in the tradition of Isaac Watts's widely read *Divine Songs for Children* (1715). The vision of the same world, as it appears to the "contrary" state of the soul that Blake calls "experience," is an ugly and terrifying one of poverty, disease, prostitution, war, and social, institutional, and sexual repression, epitomized in the ghastly representation of modern London. Though each stands as an independent poem, a number of the songs of innocence have a matched counterpart, or "contrary," in the songs of experience. Thus *Infant Joy* is paired with *Infant Sorrow,* and the meek *Lamb* reveals its other aspect of divinity in the flaming, wrathful *Tyger.*

Title page for *Songs of Innocence*
(1789)

5   The sky-lark and thrush,
     The birds of the bush,
     Sing louder around,
     To the bells' chearful sound.
     While our sports shall be seen
10   On the Ecchoing Green.

     Old John with white hair
     Does laugh away care,
     Sitting under the oak,
     Among the old folk.
15   They laugh at our play,
     And soon they all say:
     "Such, such were the joys.
     When we all, girls & boys,
     In our youth-time were seen,
20   On the Ecchoing Green."

     Till the little ones weary
     No more can be merry
     The sun does descend,
     And our sports have an end:
25   Round the laps of their mothers,

Many sisters and brothers,
Like birds in their nest,
Are ready for rest;
And sport no more seen,
30   On the darkening Green.

1789

The Lamb

Little Lamb, who made thee?
Dost thou know who made thee?
Gave thee life & bid thee feed,
By the stream & o'er the mead;
5   Gave thee clothing of delight,
Softest clothing wooly bright;
Gave thee such a tender voice,
Making all the vales rejoice!
Little Lamb who made thee?
10   Dost thou know who made thee?

Little Lamb I'll tell thee,
Little Lamb I'll tell thee!
He is callèd by thy name,
For he calls himself a Lamb;
15   He is meek & he is mild,
He became a little child;
I a child & thou a lamb,
We are callèd by his name.
Little Lamb God bless thee.
20   Little Lamb God bless thee.

1789

The Little Black Boy

My mother bore me in the southern wild,
And I am black, but O! my soul is white;
White as an angel is the English child,
But I am black as if bereav'd of light.

5   My mother taught me underneath a tree,
And sitting down before the heat of day,
She took me on her lap and kissèd me,
And pointing to the east, began to say:

"Look on the rising sun: there God does live
10   And gives his light, and gives his heat away;
And flowers and trees and beasts and men receive
Comfort in morning, joy in the noon day.

"And we are put on earth a little space,
That we may learn to bear the beams of love,
15 And these black bodies and this sun-burnt face
Is but a cloud, and like a shady grove.

"For when our souls have learn'd the heat to bear,
The cloud will vanish; we shall hear his voice,
Saying: 'Come out from the grove, my love & care,
20 And round my golden tent like lambs rejoice.' "

Thus did my mother say, and kissèd me;
And thus I say to little English boy:
When I from black and he from white cloud free,
And round the tent of God like lambs we joy,

25 I'll shade him from the heat till he can bear
To lean in joy upon our father's knee.
And then I'll stand and stroke his silver hair,
And be like him, and he will then love me.

1789

The Chimney Sweeper

When my mother died I was very young,
And my father sold me while yet my tongue
Could scarcely cry " 'weep! 'weep! 'weep! 'weep!"[1]
So your chimneys I sweep & in soot I sleep.

5 There's little Tom Dacre, who cried when his head
That curl'd like a lamb's back, was shav'd, so I said,
"Hush, Tom! never mind it, for when your head's bare,
You know that the soot cannot spoil your white hair."

And so he was quiet, & that very night,
10 As Tom was a-sleeping he had such a sight!
That thousands of sweepers, Dick, Joe, Ned, & Jack,
Were all of them lock'd up in coffins of black;

And by came an Angel who had a bright key,
And he open'd the coffins & set them all free;
15 Then down a green plain, leaping, laughing they run,
And wash in a river and shine in the Sun.

Then naked & white, all their bags left behind,
They rise upon clouds, and sport in the wind.
And the Angel told Tom, if he'd be a good boy,
20 He'd have God for his father & never want joy.

1. The child's lisping attempt at the chimney sweeper's street cry, "Sweep! Sweep!"

And so Tom awoke; and we rose in the dark
And got with our bags & our brushes to work.
Tho' the morning was cold, Tom was happy & warm;
So if all do their duty, they need not fear harm.

1789

The Divine Image

To Mercy, Pity, Peace, and Love,
All pray in their distress,
And to these virtues of delight
Return their thankfulness.

5 For Mercy, Pity, Peace, and Love,
Is God, our father dear:
And Mercy, Pity, Peace, and Love,
Is Man, his child and care.

For Mercy has a human heart,
10 Pity, a human face,
And Love, the human form divine,
And Peace, the human dress.

Then every man of every clime,
That prays in his distress,
15 Prays to the human form divine,
Love, Mercy, Pity, Peace.

And all must love the human form,
In heathen, Turk, or Jew.
Where Mercy, Love, & Pity dwell,
20 There God is dwelling too.

1789

Holy Thursday[1]

'Twas on a Holy Thursday, their innocent faces clean,
The children walking two & two, in red & blue & green;
Grey headed beadles[2] walkd before with wands as white as snow,
Till into the high dome of Paul's they like Thames' waters flow.

5 O what a multitude they seemd, these flowers of London town!
Seated in companies they sit with radiance all their own.
The hum of multitudes was there, but multitudes of lambs,
Thousands of little boys & girls raising their innocent hands.

1. In the Anglican Church, the Thursday celebrating the ascension of Jesus (thirty-nine days
after Easter). It was the custom on this day to
march the poor (frequently orphaned) children
from the charity schools of London to a service at
St. Paul's Cathedral.
2. Lower church officers, one of whose duties is
to keep order.

Now like a mighty wind they raise to heaven the voice of song,
10 Or like harmonious thunderings the seats of heaven among.
Beneath them sit the agèd men, wise guardians of the poor;
Then cherish pity, lest you drive an angel from your door.[3]

ca. 1784   1789

Nurse's Song

When the voices of children are heard on the green
And laughing is heard on the hill,
My heart is at rest within my breast
And everything else is still.

5 "Then come home my children, the sun is gone down
And the dews of night arise;
Come, come, leave off play, and let us away
Till the morning appears in the skies."

"No, no, let us play, for it is yet day
10 And we cannot go to sleep;
Besides, in the sky, the little birds fly
And the hills are all coverd with sheep."

"Well, well, go & play till the light fades away
And then go home to bed."
15 The little ones leaped & shouted & laugh'd
And all the hills ecchoèd.

ca. 1784   1789

Infant Joy

"I have no name,
I am but two days old."
What shall I call thee?
"I happy am,
5 Joy is my name."
Sweet joy befall thee!

Pretty joy!
Sweet joy but two days old,
Sweet joy I call thee;
10 Thou dost smile,
I sing the while—
Sweet joy befall thee.

1789

3. Cf. Hebrews 13.2: "Be not forgetful to entertain strangers: for thereby some have entertained angels unawares."

From Songs of Experience

Introduction

Hear the voice of the Bard!
Who Present, Past, & Future sees;
Whose ears have heard
The Holy Word
5   That walk'd among the ancient trees;[1]

Calling the lapsèd Soul[2]
And weeping in the evening dew,
That might controll[3]
The starry pole,
10   And fallen, fallen light renew!

Separate title page for *Songs of Experience* (1794)

1. Genesis 3.8: "And [Adam and Eve] heard the voice of the Lord God walking in the garden in the cool of the day." The Bard, or poet-prophet, whose imagination is not bound by time, has heard the voice of the Lord in Eden.
2. The syntax leaves it ambiguous whether it is "the Bard" or "the Holy Word" who calls to the fallen ("lapsèd") soul and to the fallen earth to stop the natural cycle of light and darkness.
3. The likely syntax is that "Soul" is the subject of "might controll."

"O Earth, O Earth, return!
Arise from out the dewy grass;
Night is worn,
And the morn
15   Rises from the slumberous mass.

"Turn away no more;
Why wilt thou turn away?
The starry floor
The watry shore[4]
20   Is giv'n thee till the break of day."

1794

Earth's Answer[1]

Earth rais'd up her head,
From the darkness dread & drear.
Her light fled:
Stony dread!
5   And her locks cover'd with grey despair.

"Prison'd on watry shore
Starry Jealousy does keep my den,
Cold and hoar
Weeping o'er
10   I hear the Father of the ancient men.[2]

"Selfish father of men,
Cruel, jealous, selfish fear!
Can delight
Chain'd in night
15   The virgins of youth and morning bear?

"Does spring hide its joy
When buds and blossoms grow?
Does the sower
Sow by night,
20   Or the plowman in darkness plow?

"Break this heavy chain
That does freeze my bones around;
Selfish! vain!
Eternal bane!
25   That free Love with bondage bound."

1794

---

4. In Blake's recurrent symbolism the starry sky ("floor") signifies rigid rational order, and the sea signifies chaos.
1. The Earth's answer explains why she, the natural world, cannot by her unaided endeavors renew the fallen light.

2. This is the character that Blake later named "Urizen" in his prophetic works. He is the tyrant who binds the mind to the natural world and also imposes a moral bondage on sexual desire and other modes of human energy.

The Clod & the Pebble

"Love seeketh not Itself to please,
Nor for itself hath any care;
But for another gives its ease,
And builds a Heaven in Hell's despair."

5   So sang a little Clod of Clay,
Trodden with the cattle's feet;
But a Pebble of the brook,
Warbled out these metres meet:

"Love seeketh only Self to please,
10   To bind another to its delight;
Joys in another's loss of ease,
And builds a Hell in Heaven's despite."

1794

Holy Thursday

Is this a holy thing to see,
In a rich and fruitful land,
Babes reduced to misery,
Fed with cold and usurous hand?

5   Is that trembling cry a song?
Can it be a song of joy?
And so many children poor?
It is a land of poverty!

And their sun does never shine,
10 And their fields are bleak & bare,
And their ways are fill'd with thorns;
It is eternal winter there.

For where-e'er the sun does shine,
And where-e'er the rain does fall,
15 Babe can never hunger there,
Nor poverty the mind appall.

1794

The Chimney Sweeper

A little black thing among the snow
Crying " 'weep, 'weep," in notes of woe!
"Where are thy father & mother? say?"
"They are both gone up to the church to pray.

5   "Because I was happy upon the heath,
     And smil'd among the winter's snow;
     They clothed me in the clothes of death,
     And taught me to sing the notes of woe.

     "And because I am happy, & dance & sing,
10   They think they have done me no injury,
     And are gone to praise God & his Priest & King,
     Who make up a heaven of our misery."

1790–92   1794

Nurse's Song

When the voices of children are heard on the green
And whisperings are in the dale,
The days of my youth rise fresh in my mind,
My face turns green and pale.

5   Then come home my children, the sun is gone down
     And the dews of night arise;
     Your spring & your day are wasted in play,
     And your winter and night in disguise.

                                                       1794

The Sick Rose

O Rose, thou art sick.
The invisible worm
That flies in the night
In the howling storm

5   Has found out thy bed
     Of crimson joy,
     And his dark secret love
     Does thy life destroy.

                                                       1794

The invisible worm.
That flies in the night
In the howling storm:

Has found out thy bed
Of crimson joy:
And his dark secret love
Does thy life destroy.

The Sick Rose

The Tyger[1]

Tyger! Tyger! burning bright
In the forests of the night,
What immortal hand or eye
Could frame thy fearful symmetry?

5   In what distant deeps or skies
Burnt the fire of thine eyes?
On what wings dare he aspire?
What the hand dare seize the fire?

And what shoulder, & what art,
10 Could twist the sinews of thy heart?
And when thy heart began to beat,
What dread hand? & what dread feet?

1. For the author's revisions while composing *The Tyger*, see "Poems in Process," in the appendices to this volume.

The Tyger

What the hammer? what the chain?
In what furnace was thy brain?
15   What the anvil? what dread grasp
Dare its deadly terrors clasp?

When the stars threw down their spears[2]
And water'd heaven with their tears,
Did he smile his work to see?
20   Did he who made the Lamb make thee?

Tyger! Tyger! burning bright
In the forests of the night,
What immortal hand or eye
Dare frame thy fearful symmetry?

1790–92   1794

---

2. "Threw down" is ambiguous and may signify that the stars either "surrendered" or "hurled down" their spears.

My Pretty Rose Tree

A flower was offerd to me;
Such a flower as May never bore,
But I said, "I've a Pretty Rose-tree,"
And I passed the sweet flower o'er.

5 Then I went to my Pretty Rose-tree,
To tend her by day and by night.
But my Rose turnd away with jealousy,
And her thorns were my only delight.

1794

Ah Sun-flower

Ah Sun-flower! weary of time,
Who countest the steps of the Sun,
Seeking after that sweet golden clime
Where the traveller's journey is done;

5 Where the Youth pined away with desire,
And the pale Virgin shrouded in snow,
Arise from their graves and aspire,
Where my Sun-flower wishes to go.

1794

The Garden of Love

I went to the Garden of Love,
And saw what I never had seen:
A Chapel was built in the midst,
Where I used to play on the green.

5 And the gates of this Chapel were shut,
And "Thou shalt not" writ over the door;
So I turn'd to the Garden of Love,
That so many sweet flowers bore,

And I saw it was filled with graves,
10 And tomb-stones where flowers should be;
And Priests in black gowns were walking their rounds,
And binding with briars my joys & desires.

1794

London

I wander thro' each charter'd[1] street,
Near where the charter'd Thames does flow,
And mark in every face I meet
Marks of weakness, marks of woe.

5 In every cry of every Man,
In every Infant's cry of fear,

---

1. "Given liberty," but also, ironically, "preempted as private property, and rented out."

In every voice, in every ban,[2]
The mind-forg'd manacles I hear:

How the Chimney-sweeper's cry
10 Every blackning Church appalls,
And the hapless Soldier's sigh
Runs in blood down Palace walls.

But most thro' midnight streets I hear
How the youthful Harlot's curse
15 Blasts the new-born Infant's tear,[3]
And blights with plagues the Marriage hearse.[4]

1794

The Human Abstract[1]

Pity would be no more,
If we did not make somebody Poor;
And Mercy no more could be,
If all were as happy as we;

5 And mutual fear brings peace,
Till the selfish loves increase;
Then Cruelty knits a snare,
And spreads his baits with care.

He sits down with holy fears,
10 And waters the ground with tears;
Then Humility takes its root
Underneath his foot.

Soon spreads the dismal shade
Of Mystery over his head;
15 And the Catterpiller and Fly
Feed on the Mystery.

And it bears the fruit of Deceit,
Ruddy and sweet to eat;
And the Raven his nest has made
20 In its thickest shade.

The Gods of the earth and sea,
Sought thro' Nature to find this Tree,
But their search was all in vain:
There grows one in the Human Brain.

1790–92   1794

2. The various meanings of *ban* are relevant (political and legal prohibition, curse, public condemnation) as well as "banns" (marriage proclamation).
3. Most critics read this line as implying prenatal blindness, resulting from a parent's venereal disease (the "plagues" of line 16) by earlier infection from the harlot.
4. In the older sense: "converts the marriage bed into a bier." Or possibly, because the current sense of the word had also come into use in Blake's day, "converts the marriage coach into a funeral hearse."
1. The matched contrary to *The Divine Image* in *Songs of Innocence*. The virtues of the earlier poem, "Mercy, Pity, Peace, and Love," are now represented as possible marks for exploitation, cruelty, conflict, and hypocritical humility.

Infant Sorrow

My mother groand! my father wept.
Into the dangerous world I leapt,
Helpless, naked, piping loud;
Like a fiend hid in a cloud.

5 Struggling in my father's hands,
Striving against my swadling bands;
Bound and weary I thought best
To sulk upon my mother's breast.

1794

A Poison Tree

I was angry with my friend:
I told my wrath, my wrath did end.
I was angry with my foe:
I told it not, my wrath did grow.

5 And I waterd it in fears,
Night & morning with my tears;
And I sunnèd it with smiles,
And with soft deceitful wiles.

And it grew both day and night,
10 Till it bore an apple bright.
And my foe beheld it shine,
And he knew that it was mine,

And into my garden stole,
When the night had veild the pole;
15 In the morning glad I see
My foe outstretchd beneath the tree.

1794

To Tirzah[1]

Whate'er is Born of Mortal Birth
Must be consumèd with the Earth
To rise from Generation free;
Then what have I to do with thee?[2]

1. Tirzah was the capital of the northern kingdom of Israel and is conceived by Blake in opposition to Jerusalem, capital of the southern kingdom of Judah, whose tribes had been redeemed from captivity. In this poem, which was added to late versions of *Songs of Experience*, Tirzah is represented as the mother—in the realm of material nature and "Generation"—of the mortal body, with its restrictive senses.
2. Echoing the words of Christ to his mother at the marriage in Cana, John 2.4: "Woman, what have I to do with thee? mine hour is not yet come."

5   The Sexes sprung from Shame & Pride,
    Blow'd° in the morn, in evening died;   *blossomed*
    But Mercy changd Death into Sleep;
    The Sexes rose to work & weep.

    Thou, Mother of my Mortal part,
10 With cruelty didst mould my Heart,
    And with false self-deceiving tears
    Didst bind my Nostrils, Eyes, & Ears.

    Didst close my Tongue in senseless clay
    And me to Mortal Life betray.
15 The Death of Jesus set me free;
    Then what have I to do with thee?

ca. 1805

A Divine Image[1]

    Cruelty has a Human Heart
    And Jealousy a Human Face,
    Terror, the Human Form Divine,
    And Secrecy, the Human Dress.

5   The Human Dress is forgèd Iron,
    The Human Form, a fiery Forge,
    The Human Face, a Furnace seal'd,
    The Human Heart, its hungry Gorge.°   *maw, stomach*

1790–91

The Book of Thel   Although Blake dated the etched poem 1789, its composition probably extended to 1791, so that he was working on it at the time he was writing the *Songs of Innocence* and some of the *Songs of Experience. The Book of Thel* treats the same two "states"; now, however, Blake employs the narrative instead of the lyrical mode and embodies aspects of the developing myth that was fully enacted in his later prophetic books. And like the major prophecies, this poem is written in the fourteener, a long line of seven stresses.

    The name *Thel* possibly derives from the Greek word for "wish" or "will" and may be intended to suggest the failure of desire, because of timidity, to fulfill itself. Thel is represented as a virgin dwelling in the Vales of Har, which seems equivalent to the sheltered state of pastoral peace and innocence in Blake's *Songs of Innocence.* Here, however, Thel feels useless and unfulfilled, and appeals for comfort, unavailingly, to various beings who are contented with their roles in Har. Finally, the Clay invites Thel to try the experiment of assuming embodied life. Part 4 (plate 6) expresses the brutal shock of the revelation to Thel of the world of sexual Generation and Experi-

---

1. Blake omitted this poem from all but one copy of *Songs of Experience,* probably because *The Human Abstract* served as a more comprehensive and subtle contrary to *The Divine Image* in *Songs of Innocence.*

ence—a revelation from which she flees in terror back to her sheltered, if unsatisfying, existence in Har.

Some commentators propose that Thel is an unborn soul who rejects the ordeal of an embodied life in the material world. Others propose that Thel is a human virgin who shrinks from experiencing a life of adult sexuality. It is possible, however, to read Blake's little myth as comprehending both these areas of significance. The reader does not need to be an adept in Blake's mythology to recognize the broad symbolic reach of this poem in ordinary human experience—the elemental failure of nerve to meet the challenge of life as it is, the timid incapacity to risk the conflict, physicality, pain, and loss without which there is no possibility either of growth or of creativity.

The Book of Thel

PLATE i[1]

Thel's Motto

Does the Eagle know what is in the pit?
Or wilt thou go ask the Mole?
Can Wisdom be put in a silver rod?
Or Love in a golden bowl?[2]

PLATE 1

1

The daughters of Mne[3] Seraphim led round their sunny flocks,
All but the youngest; she in paleness sought the secret air,
To fade away like morning beauty from her mortal day;
Down by the river of Adona[4] her soft voice is heard,
5   And thus her gentle lamentation falls like morning dew:

"O life of this our spring! why fades the lotus of the water?
Why fade these children of the spring? born but to smile & fall.
Ah! Thel is like a watry bow, and like a parting cloud,
Like a reflection in a glass, like shadows in the water,
10   Like dreams of infants, like a smile upon an infant's face,
Like the dove's voice, like transient day, like music in the air.
Ah! gentle may I lay me down, and gentle rest my head,
And gentle sleep the sleep of death, and gentle hear the voice
Of him that walketh in the garden in the evening time."[5]

15   The Lilly of the valley breathing in the humble grass
Answer'd the lovely maid and said: "I am a watry weed,

1. The plate numbers identify the page, each with its own pictorial design, as originally printed by Blake. These numbers are reproduced here because they are frequently used in references to Blake's writings.
2. Ecclesiastes 12.5–6 describes a time when "fears shall be in the way . . . and desire shall fail: because man goeth to his long home, and the mourners go about the streets: Or ever the silver cord be loosed, or the golden bowl be broken." Blake presumably changed the silver cord to a rod to make it, with the golden bowl, a sexual symbol.

3. There has been much speculation about this curious term. It may be an abbreviation for the name "Mnetha," the goddess of the Vales of Har in Blake's earlier poem *Tiriel*.
4. Possibly suggesting an equation of the Vales of Har to Spenser's Garden of Adonis in *The Faerie Queene* 3.6, as well as to the paradisal garden in Genesis (in line 14).
5. Genesis 3.8: "And they heard the voice of the Lord God walking in the garden in the cool of the day."

Title page for *The Book of Thel* (1789),
plate ii. Copy N, ca. 1815

And I am very small, and love to dwell in lowly vales;
So weak, the gilded butterfly scarce perches on my head;
Yet I am visited from heaven, and he that smiles on all
20 Walks in the valley and each morn over me spreads his hand,
Saying: 'Rejoice, thou humble grass, thou new-born lilly flower,
Thou gentle maid of silent valleys and of modest brooks;
For thou shalt be clothed in light, and fed with morning manna,
Till summer's heat melts thee beside the fountains and the springs
25 To flourish in eternal vales.' Then why should Thel complain?

PLATE 2

Why should the mistress of the vales of Har utter a sigh?"

She ceasd & smild in tears, then sat down in her silver shrine.

Thel answered: "O thou little virgin of the peaceful valley,
Giving to those that cannot crave, the voiceless, the o'ertired;
5 Thy breath doth nourish the innocent lamb, he smells thy milky
    garments,
He crops thy flowers, while thou sittest smiling in his face,
Wiping his mild and meekin° mouth from all contagious taints.   *humble*
Thy wine doth purify the golden honey; thy perfume,
Which thou dost scatter on every little blade of grass that springs,
10 Revives the milkèd cow, & tames the fire-breathing steed.
But Thel is like a faint cloud kindled at the rising sun:
I vanish from my pearly throne, and who shall find my place?"

"Queen of the vales," the Lilly answered, "ask the tender cloud,
And it shall tell thee why it glitters in the morning sky,
15 And why it scatters its bright beauty thro' the humid air.
Descend, O little cloud, & hover before the eyes of Thel."

The Cloud descended, and the Lilly bowd her modest head,
And went to mind her numerous charge among the verdant grass.

PLATE 3

2

"O little Cloud," the virgin said, "I charge thee tell to me,
Why thou complainest not when in one hour thou fade away:
Then we shall seek thee but not find; ah, Thel is like to Thee.
I pass away, yet I complain, and no one hears my voice."

5 The Cloud then shew'd his golden head & his bright form emerg'd,
Hovering and glittering on the air before the face of Thel.

"O virgin, know'st thou not our steeds drink of the golden springs
Where Luvah[6] doth renew his horses? Look'st thou on my youth,
And fearest thou because I vanish and am seen no more,
10 Nothing remains? O maid, I tell thee, when I pass away,
It is to tenfold life, to love, to peace, and raptures holy:
Unseen descending, weigh my light wings upon balmy flowers,
And court the fair eyed dew, to take me to her shining tent;
The weeping virgin trembling kneels before the risen sun,
15 Till we arise link'd in a golden band, and never part,
But walk united, bearing food to all our tender flowers."

"Dost thou O little Cloud? I fear that I am not like thee;
For I walk through the vales of Har and smell the sweetest flowers,
But I feed not the little flowers; I hear the warbling birds,
20 But I feed not the warbling birds; they fly and seek their food;
But Thel delights in these no more, because I fade away,
And all shall say, 'Without a use this shining woman liv'd,
Or did she only live to be at death the food of worms?' "

The Cloud reclind upon his airy throne and answer'd thus:

25 "Then if thou art the food of worms, O virgin of the skies,
How great thy use, how great thy blessing! Every thing that lives
Lives not alone, nor for itself; fear not, and I will call
The weak worm from its lowly bed, and thou shalt hear its voice.
Come forth, worm of the silent valley, to thy pensive queen."

30 The helpless worm arose, and sat upon the Lilly's leaf,
And the bright Cloud saild on, to find his partner in the vale.

6. The earliest mention in Blake's work of one of his "Giant Forms," the Zoas. Luvah is the mythical embodiment of the passional and sexual aspect of humankind. He is represented here, like the Greek Phoebus Apollo, as the driver of the chariot of the sun; he repairs to the Vales of Har simply to rest and water his horses. The cloud in this passage describes the cycle of water, from cloud to rain and (by the vaporizing action of the sun on water) back to the cloud.

PLATE 4

3

Then Thel astonish'd view'd the Worm upon its dewy bed.

"Art thou a Worm? Image of weakness, art thou but a Worm?
I see thee like an infant wrapped in the Lilly's leaf;
Ah, weep not, little voice, thou can'st not speak, but thou can'st weep.
5   Is this a Worm? I see thee lay helpless & naked, weeping,
And none to answer, none to cherish thee with mother's smiles."

The Clod of Clay heard the Worm's voice, & raisd her pitying head;
She bow'd over the weeping infant, and her life exhal'd
In milky fondness; then on Thel she fix'd her humble eyes.

10 "O beauty of the vales of Har! we live not for ourselves;
Thou seest me the meanest thing, and so I am indeed;
My bosom of itself is cold, and of itself is dark,

PLATE 5

But he that loves the lowly, pours his oil upon my head,
And kisses me, and binds his nuptial bands around my breast,
And says: 'Thou mother of my children, I have lovèd thee,
And I have given thee a crown that none can take away.'
5   But how this is, sweet maid, I know not, and I cannot know;
I ponder, and I cannot ponder; yet I live and love."

The daughter of beauty wip'd her pitying tears with her white veil,
And said: "Alas! I knew not this, and therefore did I weep.
That God would love a Worm, I knew, and punish the evil foot
10 That, wilful, bruis'd its helpless form; but that he cherish'd it
With milk and oil I never knew; and therefore did I weep,
And I complaind in the mild air, because I fade away,
And lay me down in thy cold bed, and leave my shining lot."

"Queen of the vales," the matron Clay answered, "I heard thy sighs,
15 And all thy moans flew o'er my roof, but I have call'd them down.
Wilt thou, O Queen, enter my house? 'tis given thee to enter
And to return; fear nothing, enter with thy virgin feet."

PLATE 6

4

The eternal gates' terrific porter lifted the northern bar:[7]
Thel enter'd in & saw the secrets of the land unknown.
She saw the couches of the dead, & where the fibrous roots
Of every heart on earth infixes deep its restless twists:
5   A land of sorrows & of tears where never smile was seen.

---

7. Homer, in *Odyssey* 13, described the Cave of the Naiades, of which the northern gate is for mortals and the southern gate for gods. The neopla-tonist Porphyro had allegorized it as an account of the descent of the soul into matter and then its return.

She wanderd in the land of clouds thro' valleys dark, listning
Dolours & lamentations; waiting oft beside a dewy grave,
She stood in silence, listning to the voices of the ground,
Till to her own grave plot she came, & there she sat down,
10 And heard this voice of sorrow breathed from the hollow pit:

"Why cannot the Ear be closed to its own destruction?
Or the glistning Eye to the poison of a smile?
Why are Eyelids stord with arrows ready drawn,
Where a thousand fighting men in ambush lie?
15 Or an Eye of gifts & graces, show'ring fruits & coinèd gold?
Why a Tongue impress'd with honey from every wind?
Why an Ear, a whirlpool fierce to draw creations in?
Why a Nostril wide inhaling terror, trembling, & affright?
Why a tender curb upon the youthful burning boy?
20 Why a little curtain of flesh on the bed of our desire?"[8]

The Virgin started from her seat, & with a shriek
Fled back unhinderd till she came into the vales of Har.

1789–91

Visions of the Daughters of Albion

This work, dated 1793 on the title page, is one of Blake's early illuminated books, and like his later and longer works is written in what Blake called "the long resounding strong heroic verse" of seven-foot lines. Unlike the timid heroine of *The Book of Thel*, the virgin Oothoon dares to break through into adult sexuality (symbolized by her plucking a marigold and placing it between her breasts) and sets out joyously to join her lover Theotormon, whose realm is the Atlantic Ocean. In her flight overseas she is waylaid and raped by Bromion in the figurative mode of a thunderstorm (1.16–17). The jealous Theotormon, condemning the victim as well as the rapist, binds the two "back to back" in a cave and sits weeping on the threshold. The rest of the work consists of monologues by the three characters, who remain fixed in these postures. Throughout this stage tableau the Daughters of Albion serve as the chorus who, in a recurrent refrain, echo the "woes" and "sighs" of Oothoon, but not her call to rebellion.

This simple drama is densely significant, for as Blake's compressed allusions indicate, the characters, events, and monologues have diverse areas of application. Blake's abrupt opening word, which he etched in very large letters, is *Enslav'd*, and the work as a whole embodies his view that contemporary men, and even more women, in a spiritual parallel to shackled black slaves, are in bondage to oppressive concepts and codes in all aspects of perception, thought, social institutions, and actions. As indicated by the refrain of the Daughters of Albion (that is, contemporary Englishwomen), Oothoon in one aspect represents the sexual disabilities and slavelike status of all women in a male-dominated society. But as "the soft soul of America" (1.3) she is also the revolutionary nation that had recently won political emancipation, yet continued to tolerate an agricultural system that involved black slavery and to acquiesce in the crass economic exploitation of her "soft American plains." At the same time, Oothoon is herself represented in the situation of a black female slave who has been branded, whipped, raped, and impregnated by her master.

8. This catalog of the life of Generation and Experience runs through the various senses to end with touch, the primary sexual sense.

Correlatively, the speeches of the boastful Bromion show him to be not only a sexual exploiter of women and a cruel and acquisitive slave owner but also a general proponent of the use of force to achieve mastery in wars, in an oppressive legal system, and in a religious morality based on the fear of hell (4.19–24). Theotormon is represented as even more contemptible. Broken and paralyzed by the prohibitions of a puritanical religion, he denies any possibility of achieving "joys" in this life, despairs of the power of intellect and imagination to improve the human condition and, rationalizing his own incapacity, bewails Oothoon's daring to think and act other than he does.

Oothoon's long and passionate oration that concludes the poem (plates 5–8) celebrates a free sexual life for both women and men. Blake, however, uses this open and unpossessive sexuality to typify the realization of all human potentialities and to represent an outgoing altruism, as opposed to an enclosed self-centeredness, "the self-love that envies all." To such a suspicious egotism, as her allusions indicate, Oothoon attributes the tyranny of uniform moral laws imposed on variable individuals, a rigidly institutional religion, the acquisitiveness that drives the system of commerce, and the property rights in another person that are established by the marriage contract.

Blake's poem reflects some prominent circumstances of the years of its composition, 1791–93. This was not only the time when the revolutionary spirit had moved from America to France and effected reverberations in England, but also the time of sporadic rebellions by black slaves in the Western Hemisphere and of widespread debate in England about the abolition of the slave trade. Blake himself, while composing the *Visions*, had illustrated the sadistic punishments inflicted on rebellious slaves in his engravings for J. G. Stedman's *A Narrative, of a Five Years' Expedition, against the Revolted Negroes of Surinam* (see David Erdman, *Blake: Prophet against Empire*, chapter 10). Blake's championing of women's liberation parallels some of the views expressed in the *Vindication of the Rights of Woman* published in 1792 by Mary Wollstonecraft, whom Blake knew and admired, and for whom he had illustrated a book the year before.

Visions of the Daughters of Albion

The Eye sees more than the Heart knows.

PLATE iii

The Argument

I loved Theotormon
And I was not ashamed
I trembled in my virgin fears
And I hid in Leutha's[1] vale!

5 I plucked Leutha's flower,
And I rose up from the vale;
But the terrible thunders tore
My virgin mantle in twain.

---

1. In some poems by Blake, Leutha is represented as a female figure who is beautiful and seductive, but treacherous.

Frontispiece, *Visions of the Daughters of Albion* (1793), plate i. Copy P, ca. 1815

PLATE 1

Visions

ENSLAV'D, the Daughters of Albion weep: a trembling lamentation
Upon their mountains; in their valleys, sighs toward America.

For the soft soul of America, Oothoon[2] wandered in woe,
Along the vales of Leutha seeking flowers to comfort her;
5 And thus she spoke to the bright Marygold of Leutha's vale:

"Art thou a flower! art thou a nymph! I see thee now a flower,
Now a nymph! I dare not pluck thee from thy dewy bed!"

The Golden nymph replied: "Pluck thou my flower Oothoon the mild.
Another flower shall spring, because the soul of sweet delight
10 Can never pass away." She ceas'd & closd her golden shrine.

Then Oothoon pluck'd the flower saying, "I pluck thee from thy bed,
Sweet flower, and put thee here to glow between my breasts,
And thus I turn my face to where my whole soul seeks."

Over the waves she went in wing'd exulting swift delight;
15 And over Theotormon's reign took her impetuous course.

2. The name is adapted by Blake from a character in James Macpherson's pretended translations, in the 1760s, from the ancient British bard Ossian.

Bromion rent her with his thunders. On his stormy bed
Lay the faint maid, and soon her woes appalld his thunders hoarse.

Bromion spoke: "Behold this harlot here on Bromion's bed,
And let the jealous dolphins sport around the lovely maid;
20 Thy soft American plains are mine, and mine thy north & south:
Stampt with my signet³ are the swarthy children of the sun:
They are obedient, they resist not, they obey the scourge:
Their daughters worship terrors and obey the violent.

PLATE 2

Now thou maist marry Bromion's harlot, and protect the child
Of Bromion's rage, that Oothoon shall put forth in nine moons' time."⁴

Then storms rent Theotormon's limbs; he rolld his waves around,
And folded his black jealous waters round the adulterate pair;
5 Bound back to back in Bromion's caves terror & meekness dwell.

At entrance Theotormon sits wearing the threshold hard
With secret tears; beneath him sound like waves on a desart shore
The voice of slaves beneath the sun, and children bought with money,
That shiver in religious caves beneath the burning fires
10 Of lust, that belch incessant from the summits of the earth.

Oothoon weeps not: she cannot weep! her tears are locked up;
But she can howl incessant, writhing her soft snowy limbs,
And calling Theotormon's Eagles to prey upon her flesh.⁵

"I call with holy voice! kings of the sounding air,
15 Rend away this defiled bosom that I may reflect
The image of Theotormon on my pure transparent breast."

The Eagles at her call descend & rend their bleeding prey;
Theotormon severely smiles; her soul reflects the smile,
As the clear spring mudded with feet of beasts grows pure & smiles.

20 The Daughters of Albion hear her woes, & eccho back her sighs.

"Why does my Theotormon sit weeping upon the threshold,
And Oothoon hovers by his side, perswading him in vain?
I cry, 'Arise O Theotormon, for the village dog
Barks at the breaking day, the nightingale has done lamenting,
25 The lark does rustle in the ripe corn, and the Eagle returns
From nightly prey, and lifts his golden beak to the pure east,
Shaking the dust from his immortal pinions to awake
The sun that sleeps too long. Arise my Theotormon, I am pure;
Because the night is gone that clos'd me in its deadly black.'
30 They told me that the night & day were all that I could see;

3. A small seal or stamp. The allusion is to the branding of black slaves by their owners.
4. Pregnancy enhanced the market value of a female slave in America.

5. The implied parallel is to Zeus's punishment of Prometheus for befriending the human race, by setting an eagle to devour his liver.

They told me that I had five senses to inclose me up,
And they inclos'd my infinite brain into a narrow circle,
And sunk my heart into the Abyss, a red round globe hot burning,
Till all from life I was obliterated and erased.
35 Instead of morn arises a bright shadow, like an eye
In the eastern cloud,[6] instead of night a sickly charnel house,
That Theotormon hears me not! to him the night and morn
Are both alike: a night of sighs, a morning of fresh tears;

PLATE 3

And none but Bromion can hear my lamentations.

"With what sense is it that the chicken shuns the ravenous hawk?
With what sense does the tame pigeon measure out the expanse?
With what sense does the bee form cells? have not the mouse & frog
5 Eyes and ears and sense of touch? yet are their habitations
And their pursuits as different as their forms and as their joys.
Ask the wild ass why he refuses burdens, and the meek camel
Why he loves man; is it because of eye, ear, mouth, or skin,
Or breathing nostrils? No, for these the wolf and tyger have.
10 Ask the blind worm the secrets of the grave, and why her spires
Love to curl round the bones of death; and ask the rav'nous snake
Where she gets poison, & the wing'd eagle why he loves the sun,
And then tell me the thoughts of man, that have been hid of old.[7]

"Silent I hover all the night, and all day could be silent,
15 If Theotormon once would turn his loved eyes upon me.
How can I be defild when I reflect thy image pure?
Sweetest the fruit that the worm feeds on, & the soul prey'd on by woe,
The new wash'd lamb ting'd with the village smoke, & the bright swan
By the red earth of our immortal river:[8] I bathe my wings,
20 And I am white and pure to hover round Theotormon's breast."

Then Theotormon broke his silence, and he answered:

"Tell me what is the night or day to one o'erflowd with woe?
Tell me what is a thought? & of what substance is it made?
Tell me what is a joy? & in what gardens do joys grow?
25 And in what rivers swim the sorrows? and upon what mountains

PLATE 4

Wave shadows of discontent? and in what houses dwell the wretched
Drunken with woe, forgotten, and shut up from cold despair?

6. The contrast is between the physical sun perceived by the constricted ("inclos'd," line 32) sensible eye and "the breaking day" (line 24) of a new
era perceived by Oothoon's liberated vision.
7. Oothoon implies that "thoughts" (powers of
conceiving a liberated life in a better world) are as
innate to human beings as instinctual patterns of
behavior are to other species of living things.
8. "Red earth" is the etymological meaning of the
Hebrew name "Adam" (cf. *The Marriage of Heaven
and Hell* 2.13, p. 1380). The "immortal river,"
accordingly, may refer to the "river" that "went out
of Eden" (Genesis 2.10).

"Tell me where dwell the thoughts, forgotten till thou call them forth?
Tell me where dwell the joys of old! & where the ancient loves?
5 And when will they renew again & the night of oblivion past?
That I might traverse times & spaces far remote and bring
Comforts into a present sorrow and a night of pain.
Where goest thou, O thought? to what remote land is thy flight?
If thou returnest to the present moment of affliction
10 Wilt thou bring comforts on thy wings and dews and honey and balm,
Or poison from the desart wilds, from the eyes of the envier?"

Then Bromion said, and shook the cavern with his lamentation:

"Thou knowest that the ancient trees seen by thine eyes have fruit;
But knowest thou that trees and fruits flourish upon the earth
15 To gratify senses unknown? trees beasts and birds unknown:
Unknown, not unpercievd, spread in the infinite microscope,
In places yet unvisited by the voyager, and in worlds
Over another kind of seas, and in atmospheres unknown?
Ah! are there other wars, beside the wars of sword and fire?
20 And are there other sorrows, beside the sorrows of poverty?
And are there other joys, beside the joys of riches and ease?
And is there not one law for both the lion and the ox?[9]
And is there not eternal fire, and eternal chains?
To bind the phantoms of existence from eternal life?"

25 Then Oothoon waited silent all the day and all the night,

PLATE 5

But when the morn arose, her lamentation renewd.
The Daughters of Albion hear her woes, & eccho back her sighs.

"O Urizen![1] Creator of men! mistaken Demon of heaven:
Thy joys are tears! thy labour vain, to form men to thine image.
5 How can one joy absorb another? are not different joys
Holy, eternal, infinite! and each joy is a Love.

"Does not the great mouth laugh at a gift? & the narrow eyelids mock
At the labour that is above payment? and wilt thou take the ape
For thy councellor? or the dog for a schoolmaster to thy children?
10 Does he who contemns poverty, and he who turns with
     abhorrence
From usury, feel the same passion, or are they moved alike?
How can the giver of gifts experience the delights of the merchant?
How the industrious citizen the pains of the husbandman?
How different far the fat fed hireling with hollow drum,
15 Who buys whole corn fields into wastes,[2] and sings upon the
     heath:

9. The last line of *The Marriage of Heaven and Hell* proclaims: "One Law for the Lion & Ox is Oppression."
1. This is the first occurrence of the name "Urizen" in Blake. Oothoon's liberated vision recognizes the error in the way God is conceived in conventional religion.
2. Probably a compressed allusion both to the wealthy landowner who converts fertile fields into a game preserve and to the recruiting officer ("with hollow drum") who strips the land of its agricultural laborers.

How different their eye and ear! how different the world to them!
With what sense does the parson claim the labour of the farmer?
What are his nets & gins° & traps? & how does he surround him   snares
With cold floods of abstraction, and with forests of solitude,
20   To build him castles and high spires, where kings & priests may dwell?
Till she who burns with youth, and knows no fixed lot, is bound
In spells of law to one she loaths; and must she drag the chain
Of life, in weary lust? must chilling murderous thoughts obscure
The clear heaven of her eternal spring? to bear the wintry rage
25   Of a harsh terror, driv'n to madness, bound to hold a rod
Over her shrinking shoulders all the day, & all the night
To turn the wheel of false desire, and longings that wake her womb
To the abhorred birth of cherubs in the human form
That live a pestilence & die a meteor & are no more;
30   Till the child dwell with one he hates, and do the deed he loaths,
And the impure scourge force his seed into its unripe birth
E'er yet his eyelids can behold the arrows of the day?[3]

"Does the whale worship at thy footsteps as the hungry dog?
Or does he scent the mountain prey, because his nostrils wide
35   Draw in the ocean? does his eye discern the flying cloud
As the raven's eye? or does he measure the expanse like the vulture?
Does the still spider view the cliffs where eagles hide their young?
Or does the fly rejoice because the harvest is brought in?
Does not the eagle scorn the earth & despise the treasures beneath?
40   But the mole knoweth what is there, & the worm shall tell it thee.
Does not the worm erect a pillar in the mouldering church yard,

PLATE 6

And a palace of eternity in the jaws of the hungry grave?
Over his porch these words are written: 'Take thy bliss O Man!
And sweet shall be thy taste & sweet thy infant joys renew!'

"Infancy, fearless, lustful, happy! nestling for delight
5   In laps of pleasure; Innocence! honest, open, seeking
The vigorous joys of morning light, open to virgin bliss,
Who taught thee modesty, subtil modesty? Child of night & sleep,
When thou awakest wilt thou dissemble all thy secret joys,
Or wert thou not awake when all this mystery was disclos'd?
10   Then com'st thou forth a modest virgin, knowing to dissemble,
With nets found under thy night pillow to catch virgin joy,
And brand it with the name of whore, & sell it in the night,
In silence, ev'n without a whisper, and in seeming sleep.[4]
Religious dreams and holy vespers light thy smoky fires;
15   Once were thy fires lighted by the eyes of honest morn.
And does my Theotormon seek this hypocrite modesty,
This knowing, artful, secret, fearful, cautious, trembling hypocrite?
Then is Oothoon a whore indeed! and all the virgin joys

3. The reference is to the begetting of children, both in actual slavery and in the metaphoric slavery of a loveless marriage, from generation to generation.

4. Oothoon contrasts the natural, innocent sensuality of an infant to the socially acquired, hypocritical modesty of the adult virgin; the latter is Theotormon's concept of female virtue.

Of life are harlots, and Theotormon is a sick man's dream,
20 And Oothoon is the crafty slave of selfish holiness.

"But Oothoon is not so; a virgin fill'd with virgin fancies
Open to joy and to delight where ever beauty appears.
If in the morning sun I find it, there my eyes are fix'd

PLATE 7

In happy copulation; if in evening mild, wearied with work,
Sit on a bank and draw the pleasures of this free born joy.

"The moment of desire! the moment of desire! The virgin
That pines for man shall awaken her womb to enormous joys
5 In the secret shadows of her chamber; the youth shut up from
The lustful joy shall forget to generate & create an amorous image
In the shadows of his curtains and in the folds of his silent pillow.
Are not these the places of religion? the rewards of continence?
The self enjoyings of self denial? Why dost seek religion?
10 Is it because acts are not lovely, that thou seekest solitude,
Where the horrible darkness is impressed with reflections of desire?

"Father of Jealousy,[5] be thou accursed from the earth!
Why hast thou taught my Theotormon this accursed thing?
Till beauty fades from off my shoulders, darken'd and cast out,
15 A solitary shadow wailing on the margin of non-entity.

"I cry, Love! Love! Love! happy happy Love! free as the mountain wind!
Can that be Love, that drinks another as a sponge drinks water?
That clouds with jealousy his nights, with weepings all the day,
To spin a web of age around him, grey and hoary! dark!
20 Till his eyes sicken at the fruit that hangs before his sight.
Such is self-love that envies all! a creeping skeleton
With lamplike eyes watching around the frozen marriage bed.

"But silken nets and traps of adamant[6] will Oothoon spread,
And catch for thee girls of mild silver, or of furious gold;
25 I'll lie beside thee on a bank & view their wanton play
In lovely copulation bliss on bliss with Theotormon:
Red as the rosy morning, lustful as the first born beam,
Oothoon shall view his dear delight, nor e'er with jealous cloud
Come in the heaven of generous love; nor selfish blightings bring.

30 "Does the sun walk in glorious raiment on the secret floor

PLATE 8

Where the cold miser spreads his gold? or does the bright cloud drop
On his stone threshold? does his eye behold the beam that brings
Expansion to the eye of pity? or will he bind himself

---

5. I.e., Urizen (5.3), the false conceived God who
prohibits the satisfaction of human desires.
6. A legendary stone believed to be unbreakable.

(The name is derived from the Greek word for diamond.)

Beside the ox to thy hard furrow? does not that mild beam blot
5   The bat, the owl, the glowing tyger, and the king of night?
The sea fowl takes the wintry blast for a cov'ring to her limbs,
And the wild snake the pestilence to adorn him with gems & gold.
And trees & birds & beasts & men behold their eternal joy.
Arise you little glancing wings, and sing your infant joy!
10   Arise and drink your bliss, for every thing that lives is holy!"[7]

Thus every morning wails Oothoon, but Theotormon sits
Upon the margind ocean conversing with shadows dire.

The Daughters of Albion hear her woes, & eccho back her sighs.

1791–93   1793

The Marriage of Heaven and Hell

This, the most immediately accessible of Blake's longer works, is a vigorous, deliberately outrageous, and at times comic onslaught against timidly conventional and self-righteous members of society as well as against stock opinions of orthodox Christian piety and morality. The seeming simplicity of Blake's satiric attitude, however, is deceptive.

Initially, Blake accepts the terminology of standard Christian morality ("what the religious call Good & Evil") but reverses its values. In this conventional use Evil, which is manifested by the class of beings called Devils and which consigns wrongdoers to the orthodox Hell, is everything associated with the body and its desires and consists essentially of energy, abundance, actions, and freedom. Conventional Good, which is manifested by Angels and guarantees its adherents a place in the orthodox Heaven, is associated with the Soul (regarded as entirely separate from the body) and consists of the contrary qualities of reason, restraint, passivity, and prohibition. Blandly adopting these conventional oppositions, Blake elects to assume the diabolic persona—what he calls "the voice of the Devil"—and to utter "Proverbs of Hell."

But this stance is only a first stage in Blake's complex irony, designed to startle the reader into recognizing the inadequacy of conventional moral categories. As he also says in the opening summary, "Without Contraries is no progression," and "Reason and Energy" are both "necessary to Human existence." It turns out that Blake subordinates his reversal of conventional values under a more inclusive point of view, according to which the real Good, as distinguished from the merely ironic Good, is not abandonment of all restraints but a "marriage," or union of the contraries, of desire and restraint, energy and reason, the promptings of Hell and the denials of Heaven—or as Blake calls these contraries in plate 16, "the Prolific" and "the Devouring." These two classes, he adds, "should be enemies," and "whoever tries to reconcile them seeks to destroy existence." Implicit in Blake's satire is the view that the good and abundant life consists in the sustained tension, without victory or suppression, of co-present oppositions.

Blake was stimulated to write this unique work in response to the writings of the visionary Swedish theologian Emanuel Swedenborg, whom he had at first admired but then had come to recognize as a conventional Angel in the disguise of a radical Devil. In plate 3 the writings of Swedenborg are described as the winding clothes Blake discards as he is resurrected from the tomb of his past self, as a poet-prophet who heralds the apocalyptic promise of his age. Blake wrote *The Marriage of Heaven and Hell* in the early 1790s, during the early years of the French Revolution, when

7. This last phrase is also the concluding line of "A Song of Liberty," appended to *The Marriage of Heaven and Hell.*

he shared the expectations of a number of radical English writers, including the young poets Wordsworth, Coleridge, and Southey, that the revolution was the violent stage that, as the biblical prophets foresaw, immediately preceded the millennium. The double role of *The Marriage* as both satire and revolutionary prophecy is made explicit in *A Song of Liberty*, which Blake etched in 1792 and added as a coda.

The Marriage of Heaven and Hell

PLATE 2

The Argument

Rintrah[1] roars & shakes his fires in the burdend air;
Hungry clouds swag on the deep.

Once meek, and in a perilous path,
The just man kept his course along
5   The vale of death.
Roses are planted where thorns grow,
And on the barren heath
Sing the honey bees.

Then the perilous path was planted,
10 And a river, and a spring,
On every cliff and tomb;
And on the bleached bones
Red clay[2] brought forth;

Till the villain left the paths of ease,
15 To walk in perilous paths, and drive
The just man into barren climes.

Now the sneaking serpent walks
In mild humility,
And the just man rages in the wilds
20 Where lions roam.

Rintrah roars & shakes his fires in the burdend air;
Hungry clouds swag on the deep.

PLATE 3

As a new heaven is begun, and it is now thirty-three years since its advent, the Eternal Hell revives. And lo! Swedenborg[3] is the Angel sitting at the tomb;

---

1. Rintrah plays the role of the angry Old Testament prophet Elijah as well as of John the Baptist, the voice "crying in the wilderness" (Matthew 3), preparing the way for Christ the Messiah. It has been plausibly suggested that stanzas 2–5 summarize the course of biblical history to the present time. "Once" (line 3) refers to Old Testament history after the Fall; "Then" (line 9) is the time of the birth of Christ. "Till" (line 14) identifies the era when Christianity was perverted into an institutional religion. "Now" (line 17) is the time of the

wrathful portent of the French Revolution. In this final era, the hypocritical serpent represents the priest of the "angels" in the poem, while "the just man" is embodied in Blake himself, a raging poet and prophet in the guise of a devil. "Swag" (line 2): sag, hang down.
2. In Hebrew, the literal meaning of "Adam," or created man. The probable reference is to the birth of the Redeemer, the new Adam.
3. Emanuel Swedenborg (1688–1772), Swedish scientist and religious philosopher, had predicted,

his writings are the linen clothes folded up. Now is the dominion of Edom, & the return of Adam into Paradise; see Isaiah xxxiv & XXXV Chap.[4]

Without Contraries is no progression. Attraction and Repulsion, Reason and Energy, Love and Hate, are necessary to Human existence.

From these contraries spring what the religious call Good & Evil. Good is the passive that obeys Reason. Evil is the active springing from Energy.

Good is Heaven. Evil is Hell.

PLATE 4

The Voice of the Devil

All Bibles or sacred codes have been the causes of the following Errors:

1. That Man has two real existing principles; Viz: a Body & a Soul.

2. That Energy, calld Evil, is alone from the Body, & that Reason, calld Good, is alone from the Soul.

3. That God will torment Man in Eternity for following his Energies.

But the following Contraries to these are True:

1. Man has no Body distinct from his Soul; for that calld Body is a portion of Soul discernd by the five Senses, the chief inlets of Soul in this age.

2. Energy is the only life, and is from the Body; and Reason is the bound or outward circumference of Energy.

3. Energy is Eternal Delight.

PLATE 5

Those who restrain desire, do so because theirs is weak enough to be restrained; and the restrainer or reason usurps its place & governs the unwilling.

And being restraind, it by degrees becomes passive, till it is only the shadow of desire.

The history of this is written in *Paradise Lost*,[5] & the Governor or Reason is call'd Messiah.

And the original Archangel, or possessor of the command of the heavenly host, is calld the Devil or Satan, and his children are call'd Sin & Death.[6]

But in the Book of Job, Milton's Messiah is call'd Satan.[7]

on the basis of his visions, that the Last Judgment and the coming of the Kingdom of Heaven would occur in 1757. This was precisely the year of Blake's birth. Now, in 1790, Blake is thirty-three, the age at which Christ had been resurrected from the tomb; correspondingly, Blake rises from the tomb of his past life in his new role as imaginative artist who will redeem his age. But, Blake ironically comments, the works he will engrave in his resurrection will constitute the Eternal Hell, the contrary brought into simultaneous being by Swedenborg's limited New Heaven.

4. Isaiah 34 prophesies "the day of the Lord's vengeance," a time of violent destruction and bloodshed; Isaiah 35 prophesies the redemption to follow, in which "the desert shall . . . blossom as the rose," "in the wilderness shall waters break out, and streams in the desert," and "no lion shall be there," but "an highway shall be there . . . and it shall be called The way of holiness" (cf. "The Argument," lines 3–11, 20). Blake combines with these chapters Isaiah 63, in which "Edom" is the place

from which comes the man whose garments are red with the blood he has spilled; for as he says, "the day of vengeance is in mine heart, and the year of my redeemed is come." Blake interprets this last phrase as predicting the time when Adam would regain his lost Paradise.

With reference to affairs in 1790, Edom can be taken to represent France, and the red man coming from Edom (to England) to be the spirit of the French Revolution, which Blake interprets as a portent of apocalyptic redemption and the recovery of Paradise.

5. What follows, to the end of this section, is Blake's "diabolical" reading of *Paradise Lost*.

6. Satan's giving birth to Sin and then incestuously begetting Death upon her is described in *Paradise Lost* 2.745ff.; the war in heaven, referred to three lines below, in which the Messiah defeated Satan and drove him out of heaven, is described in 6.824ff.

7. In the Book of Job, Satan plays the role of Job's moral accuser and physical tormentor.

For this history has been adopted by both parties.

It indeed appear'd to Reason as if Desire was cast out; but the Devil's account is, that the Messi[PLATE 6]ah fell, & formed a heaven of what he stole from the Abyss.

This is shewn in the Gospel, where he prays to the Father to send the comforter or Desire that Reason may have Ideas to build on;[8] the Jehovah of the Bible being no other than he who dwells in flaming fire. Know that after Christ's death, he became Jehovah.

But in Milton, the Father is Destiny, the Son, a Ratio[9] of the five senses, & the Holy-ghost, Vacuum!

Note. The reason Milton wrote in fetters when he wrote of Angels & God, and at liberty when of Devils & Hell, is because he was a true Poet and of the Devil's party without knowing it.

A Memorable Fancy[1]

As I was walking among the fires of hell, delighted with the enjoyments of Genius, which to Angels look like torment and insanity, I collected some of their Proverbs; thinking that as the sayings used in a nation mark its character, so the Proverbs of Hell shew the nature of Infernal wisdom better than any description of buildings or garments.

When I came home, on the abyss of the five senses, where a flat sided steep frowns over the present world, I saw a mighty Devil folded in black clouds, hovering on the sides of the rock; with cor[PLATE 7]roding fires he wrote the following sentence[2] now perceived by the minds of men, & read by them on earth:

How do you know but ev'ry Bird that cuts the airy way,
Is an immense world of delight, clos'd by your senses five?

Proverbs of Hell[3]

In seed time learn, in harvest teach, in winter enjoy.
Drive your cart and your plow over the bones of the dead.
The road of excess leads to the palace of wisdom.
Prudence is a rich ugly old maid courted by Incapacity.
5 He who desires but acts not, breeds pestilence.
The cut worm forgives the plow.
Dip him in the river who loves water.
A fool sees not the same tree that a wise man sees.
He whose face gives no light, shall never become a star.
10 Eternity is in love with the productions of time.
The busy bee has no time for sorrow.
The hours of folly are measur'd by the clock; but of wisdom, no clock can
    measure.

8. Possibly John 14.16–17, where Christ says he "will pray the Father, and he shall give you another Comforter . . . Even the Spirit of truth."
9. The Latin *ratio* means both "reason" and "sum." Blake applies the term to the 18th-century view, following the empirical philosophy of John Locke, that the content of the mind, on which the faculty of reason operates, is limited to the sum of the experience acquired by the five senses.

1. A parody of what Swedenborg called "memorable relations" of his literal-minded visions of the eternal world.
2. The "mighty Devil" is Blake, as he sees himself reflected in the shiny plate on which he is etching this very passage with "corroding fires," i.e., acid. See also the third from last sentence in plate 14.
3. A "diabolic" version of the Book of Proverbs in the Old Testament.

All wholsom food is caught without a net or a trap.
Bring out number, weight, & measure in a year of dearth.
15 No bird soars too high, if he soars with his own wings.
A dead body revenges not injuries.
The most sublime act is to set another before you.
If the fool would persist in his folly he would become wise.
Folly is the cloke of knavery.
20 Shame is Pride's cloke.

PLATE 8

Prisons are built with stones of Law, Brothels with bricks of Religion.
The pride of the peacock is the glory of God.
The lust of the goat is the bounty of God.
The wrath of the lion is the wisdom of God.
5 The nakedness of woman is the work of God.
Excess of sorrow laughs. Excess of joy weeps.
The roaring of lions, the howling of wolves, the raging of the stormy sea,
    and the destructive sword, are portions of eternity too great for the
    eye of man.
The fox condemns the trap, not himself.
Joys impregnate. Sorrows bring forth.
10 Let man wear the fell of the lion, woman the fleece of the sheep.
The bird a nest, the spider a web, man friendship.
The selfish smiling fool & the sullen frowning fool shall be both thought
    wise, that they may be a rod.
What is now proved was once only imagin'd.
The rat, the mouse, the fox, the rabbit watch the roots; the lion, the tyger,
    the horse, the elephant, watch the fruits.
15 The cistern contains; the fountain overflows.
One thought fills immensity.
Always be ready to speak your mind, and a base man will avoid you.
Every thing possible to be believ'd is an image of truth.
The eagle never lost so much time as when he submitted to learn of the
    crow.

PLATE 9

The fox provides for himself, but God provides for the lion.
Think in the morning, Act in the noon, Eat in the evening, Sleep in the
    night.
He who has sufferd you to impose on him knows you.
As the plow follows words, so God rewards prayers.
5 The tygers of wrath are wiser than the horses of instruction.
Expect poison from the standing water.
You never know what is enough unless you know what is more than
    enough.
Listen to the fool's reproach! it is a kingly title!
The eyes of fire, the nostrils of air, the mouth of water, the beard of earth.
10 The weak in courage is strong in cunning.
The apple tree never asks the beech how he shall grow, nor the lion the
    horse, how he shall take his prey.
The thankful reciever bears a plentiful harvest.
If others had not been foolish, we should be so.

The soul of sweet delight can never be defil'd.
15 When thou seest an Eagle, thou seest a portion of Genius; lift up thy head!
As the catterpiller chooses the fairest leaves to lay her eggs on, so the
        priest lays his curse on the fairest joys.
To create a little flower is the labour of ages.
Damn braces; Bless relaxes.
The best wine is the oldest, the best water the newest.
20 Prayers plow not! Praises reap not!
Joys laugh not! Sorrows weep not!

PLATE 10

The head Sublime, the heart Pathos, the genitals Beauty, the hands & feet
        Proportion.
As the air to a bird or the sea to a fish, so is contempt to the contemptible.
The crow wish'd every thing was black, the owl that every thing was white.
Exuberance is Beauty.
5 If the lion was advised by the fox, he would be cunning.
Improvement makes strait roads, but the crooked roads without
        Improvement are roads of Genius.
Sooner murder an infant in its cradle than nurse unacted desires.
Where man is not, nature is barren.
Truth can never be told so as to be understood, and not be believ'd.
10   Enough! or Too much.

PLATE 11

    The ancient Poets animated all sensible objects with Gods or Geniuses,
calling them by the names and adorning them with the properties of woods,
rivers, mountains, lakes, cities, nations, and whatever their enlarged &
numerous senses could perceive.
    And particularly they studied the genius of each city & country, placing it
under its mental deity.
    Till a system was formed, which some took advantage of & enslav'd the
vulgar by attempting to realize or abstract the mental deities from their
objects; thus began Priesthood,
    Choosing forms of worship from poetic tales.
    And at length they pronounced that the Gods had ordered such things.
    Thus men forgot that All deities reside in the human breast.

PLATE 12

A Memorable Fancy[4]

    The Prophets Isaiah and Ezekiel dined with me, and I asked them how
they dared so roundly to assert that God spake to them; and whether they
did not think at the time that they would be misunderstood, & so be the
cause of imposition.
    Isaiah answer'd: "I saw no God, nor heard any, in a finite organical per-
ception; but my senses discover'd the infinite in every thing, and as I was

4. Blake parodies Swedenborg's accounts, in his *Memorable Relations*, of his conversations with the inhabitants during his spiritual trips to heaven.

then perswaded, & remain confirm'd, that the voice of honest indignation is the voice of God, I cared not for consequences, but wrote."

Then I asked: "Does a firm perswasion that a thing is so, make it so?"

He replied: "All poets believe that it does, & in ages of imagination this firm perswasion removed mountains; but many are not capable of a firm perswasion of any thing."

Then Ezekiel said: "The philosophy of the East taught the first principles of human perception. Some nations held one principle for the origin & some another; we of Israel taught that the Poetic Genius (as you now call it) was the first principle and all the others merely derivative, which was the cause of our despising the Priests & Philosophers of other countries, and prophecying that all Gods [PL 13] would at last be proved to originate in ours & to be the tributaries of the Poetic Genius; it was this that our great poet, King David, desired so fervently & invokes so pathetically, saying by this he conquers enemies & governs kingdoms; and we so loved our God, that we cursed in his name all the deities of surrounding nations, and asserted that they had rebelled; from these opinions the vulgar came to think that all nations would at last be subject to the Jews."

"This," said he, "like all firm perswasions, is come to pass, for all nations believe the Jews' code and worship the Jews' god, and what greater subjection can be?"

I heard this with some wonder, & must confess my own conviction. After dinner I ask'd Isaiah to favour the world with his lost works; he said none of equal value was lost. Ezekiel said the same of his.

I also asked Isaiah what made him go naked and barefoot three years? He answered, "the same that made our friend Diogenes,[5] the Grecian."

I then asked Ezekiel why he eat dung, & lay so long on his right & left side?[6] He answered, "the desire of raising other men into a perception of the infinite; this the North American tribes practise, & is he honest who resists his genius or conscience only for the sake of present ease or gratification?"

PLATE 14

The ancient tradition that the world will be consumed in fire at the end of six thousand years is true, as I have heard from Hell.

For the cherub with his flaming sword is hereby commanded to leave his guard at the tree of life;[7] and when he does, the whole creation will be consumed, and appear infinite and holy, whereas it now appears finite & corrupt.

This will come to pass by an improvement of sensual enjoyment.

But first the notion that man has a body distinct from his soul is to be expunged; this I shall do, by printing in the infernal method, by corrosives, which in Hell are salutary and medicinal, melting apparent surfaces away, and displaying the infinite which was hid.[8]

5. Greek Cynic (4th century), whose extreme repudiation of civilized customs gave rise to anecdotes that he had renounced clothing. In Isaiah 20.2–3, the prophet, at the command of the Lord, walked "naked and barefoot" for three years.
6. The Lord gave these instructions to the prophet

Ezekiel (4.4–6).
7. In Genesis 3.24, when the Lord drove Adam and Eve from the Garden of Eden, he had placed Cherubim and a flaming sword at the eastern end "to keep the way of the tree of life."
8. See n. 2, p. 1382.

If the doors of perception were cleansed every thing would appear to man as it is, infinite.

For man has closed himself up, till he sees all things thro' narrow chinks of his cavern.

PLATE 15

A Memorable Fancy

I was in a Printing house in Hell & saw the method in which knowledge is transmitted from generation to generation.

In the first chamber was a Dragon-Man, clearing away the rubbish from a cave's mouth; within, a number of Dragons were hollowing the cave.

In the second chamber was a Viper folding round the rock & the cave, and others adorning it with gold, silver, and precious stones.

In the third chamber was an Eagle with wings and feathers of air; he caused the inside of the cave to be infinite; around were numbers of Eagle-like men, who built palaces in the immense cliffs.

In the fourth chamber were Lions of flaming fire, raging around & melting the metals into living fluids.

In the fifth chamber were Unnam'd forms, which cast the metals into the expanse.

There they were receiv'd by Men who occupied the sixth chamber, and took the forms of books & were arranged in libraries.[9]

PLATE 16

The Giants[1] who formed this world into its sensual existence, and now seem to live in it in chains, are in truth the causes of its life & the sources of all activity; but the chains are the cunning of weak and tame minds which have power to resist energy; according to the proverb, the weak in courage is strong in cunning.

Thus one portion of being is the Prolific, the other, the Devouring; to the Devourer it seems as if the producer was in his chains, but it is not so; he only takes portions of existence and fancies that the whole.

But the Prolific would cease to be Prolific unless the Devourer as a sea received the excess of his delights.

Some will say, "Is not God alone the Prolific?" I answer, "God only Acts & Is, in existing beings or Men."

These two classes of men are always upon earth, & they should be enemies; whoever tries [PLATE 17] to reconcile them seeks to destroy existence.

Religion is an endeavour to reconcile the two.

Note. Jesus Christ did not wish to unite but to separate them, as in the Parable of sheep and goats! & he says, "I came not to send Peace but a Sword."[2]

Messiah or Satan or Tempter was formerly thought to be one of the Antediluvians[3] who are our Energies.

---

9. In this "Memorable Fancy," Blake allegorizes his procedure in designing, etching, printing, and binding his works of imaginative genius.
1. In this section, human creative energies, called "the Prolific," in their relation to their indispen-

sable contrary, "the Devourer."
2. Matthew 10.34. The parable of the sheep and the goats is in Matthew 25.32–33.
3. Those who lived before Noah's Flood.

A Memorable Fancy

An Angel came to me and said: "O pitiable foolish young man! O horrible! O dreadful state! consider the hot burning dungeon thou art preparing for thyself to all eternity, to which thou art going in such career."

I said: "Perhaps you will be willing to shew me my eternal lot, & we will contemplate together upon it and see whether your lot or mine is most desirable."

So he took me thro' a stable & thro' a church & down into the church vault at the end of which was a mill; thro' the mill we went, and came to a cave; down the winding cavern we groped our tedious way till a void boundless as a nether sky appeared beneath us, & we held by the roots of trees and hung over this immensity, but I said: "If you please, we will commit ourselves to this void, and see whether Providence is here also, if you will not I will." But he answered: "Do not presume, O young man, but as we here remain, behold thy lot which will soon appear when the darkness passes away."[4]

So I remaind with him sitting in the twisted [PLATE 18] root of an oak; he was suspended in a fungus which hung with the head downward into the deep.

By degrees we beheld the infinite Abyss, fiery as the smoke of a burning city; beneath us at an immense distance was the sun, black but shining; round it were fiery tracks on which revolv'd vast spiders, crawling after their prey, which flew, or rather swum in the infinite deep, in the most terrific shapes of animals sprung from corruption; & the air was full of them, & seemed composed of them; these are Devils, and are called Powers of the air. I now asked my companion which was my eternal lot? He said, "Between the black & white spiders."

But now, from between the black & white spiders a cloud and fire burst and rolled thro the deep, blackning all beneath, so that the nether deep grew black as a sea & rolled with a terrible noise. Beneath us was nothing now to be seen but a black tempest, till looking east between the clouds & the waves, we saw a cataract of blood mixed with fire, and not many stones' throw from us appeared and sunk again the scaly fold of a monstrous serpent. At last to the east, distant about three degrees, appeared a fiery crest above the waves. Slowly it reared like a ridge of golden rocks till we discovered two globes of crimson fire, from which the sea fled away in clouds of smoke. And now we saw it was the head of Leviathan; his forehead was divided into streaks of green & purple like those on a tyger's forehead; soon we saw his mouth & red gills hang just above the raging foam, tinging the black deep with beams of blood, advancing toward [PLATE 19] us with all the fury of a spiritual existence.

My friend the Angel climb'd up from his station into the mill. I remain'd alone, & then this appearance was no more, but I found myself sitting on a

4. The "stable" is that where Jesus was born, which, allegorically, leads to the "church" founded in his name and to the "vault" where this institution effectually buried him. The "mill" in Blake is a symbol of mechanical and analytic philosophy; through this the pilgrims pass into the twisting cave of rationalistic theology and descend to an underworld that is an empty abyss. The point of this Blakean equivalent of a carnival funhouse is that only after you have thoroughly confused yourself by this tortuous approach, and only if you then (as in the next two paragraphs) stare at this topsy-turvy emptiness long enough, will the void gradually assume the semblance of the comic horrors of the fantasied Hell of angelic orthodoxy.

pleasant bank beside a river by moon light, hearing a harper who sung to the harp, & his theme was: "The man who never alters his opinion is like standing water, & breeds reptiles of the mind."

But I arose, and sought for the mill, & there I found my Angel, who surprised asked me how I escaped?

I answered: "All that we saw was owing to your metaphysics: for when you ran away, I found myself on a bank by moonlight hearing a harper. But now we have seen my eternal lot, shall I shew you yours? He laughd at my proposal; but I by force suddenly caught him in my arms, & flew westerly thro' the night, til we were elevated above the earth's shadow; then I flung myself with him directly into the body of the sun. Here I clothed myself in white, & taking in my hand Swedenborg's volumes, sunk from the glorious clime, and passed all the planets till we came to Saturn. Here I staid to rest & then leap'd into the void between Saturn & the fixed stars.[5]

"Here," said I, "is your lot, in this space, if space it may be calld." Soon we saw the stable and the church, & I took him to the altar and open'd the Bible, and lo! it was a deep pit, into which I descended, driving the Angel before me. Soon we saw seven houses of brick;[6] one we enterd; in it were a [PLATE 20] number of monkeys, baboons, & all of that species, chaind by the middle, grinning and snatching at one another, but withheld by the shortness of their chains. However, I saw that they sometimes grew numerous, and then the weak were caught by the strong, and with a grinning aspect, first coupled with & then devourd, by plucking off first one limb and then another till the body was left a helpless trunk. This, after grinning & kissing it with seeming fondness, they devourd too; and here & there I saw one savourily picking the flesh off of his own tail. As the stench terribly annoyd us both, we went into the mill, & I in my hand brought the skeleton of a body, which in the mill was Aristotle's Analytics.[7]

So the Angel said: "Thy phantasy has imposed upon me, & thou oughtest to be ashamed."

I answered: "We impose on one another, & it is but lost time to converse with you whose works are only Analytics."

Opposition is true Friendship.

PLATE 21

I have always found that Angels have the vanity to speak of themselves as the only wise; this they do with a confident insolence sprouting from systematic reasoning.

Thus Swedenborg boasts that what he writes is new; tho' it is only the Contents or Index of already publish'd books.

A man carried a monkey about for a shew, & because he was a little wiser than the monkey, grew vain, and conceiv'd himself as much wiser than seven men. It is so with Swedenborg; he shews the folly of churches & exposes

---

5. In the Ptolemaic world picture Saturn was in the outermost planetary sphere; beyond it was the sphere of the fixed stars.
6. The "seven churches which are in Asia," to which John addresses the Book of Revelation 1.4.

Blake now forces on the angel his own diabolic view of angelic biblical exegesis, theological speculation and disputation, and Hell.
7. Aristotle's treatises on logic.

hypocrites, till he imagines that all are religious, & himself the single [PLATE 22] one on earth that ever broke a net.

Now hear a plain fact: Swedenborg has not written one new truth. Now hear another: he has written all the old falsehoods.

And now hear the reason: He conversed with Angels who are all religious, & conversed not with Devils, who all hate religion, for he was incapable thro' his conceited notions.

Thus Swedenborg's writings are a recapitulation of all superficial opinions, and an analysis of the more sublime, but no further.

Have now another plain fact: Any man of mechanical talents may from the writings of Paracelsus or Jacob Behmen[8] produce ten thousand volumes of equal value with Swedenborg's, and from those of Dante or Shakespear, an infinite number.

But when he has done this, let him not say that he knows better than his master, for he only holds a candle in sunshine.

A Memorable Fancy

Once I saw a Devil in a flame of fire, who arose before an Angel that sat on a cloud, and the Devil utterd these words:

"The worship of God is, Honouring his gifts in other men, each according to his genius, and loving the [PLATE 23] greatest men best. Those who envy or calumniate great men hate God, for there is no other God."

The Angel hearing this became almost blue; but mastering himself, he grew yellow, & at last white, pink, & smiling, and then replied:

"Thou Idolater, is not God One? & is not he visible in Jesus Christ? and has not Jesus Christ given his sanction to the law of ten commandments, and are not all other men fools, sinners, & nothings?"

The Devil answer'd; "Bray a fool in a mortar with wheat, yet shall not his folly be beaten out of him.[9] If Jesus Christ is the greatest man, you ought to love him in the greatest degree. Now hear how he has given his sanction to the law of ten commandments: did he not mock at the sabbath, and so mock the sabbath's God?[1] murder those who were murderd because of him? turn away the law from the woman taken in adultery?[2] steal the labor of others to support him? bear false witness when he omitted making a defence before Pilate?[3] covet when he pray'd for his disciples, and when he bid them shake off the dust of their feet against such as refused to lodge them?[4] I tell you, no virtue can exist without breaking these ten commandments. Jesus was all virtue, and acted from im[PLATE 24]pulse, not from rules."

When he had so spoken, I beheld the Angel, who stretched out his arms embracing the flame of fire, & he was consumed and arose as Elijah.[5]

8. Jakob Boehme (1575–1624), a German shoemaker who developed a theosophical system that has had persisting influence both on theological and on metaphysical speculation. Paracelsus (1493–1541), a Swiss physician and a pioneer in empirical medicine, was also a prominent theorist of the occult.

9. Proverbs 27.22: "Though thou shouldst bray a fool in a mortar among wheat with a pestle, yet will not his foolishness depart from him." "Bray": pound into small pieces.

1. Mark 2.27: "The sabbath was made for man."
2. Cf. John 8.2–11.
3. Cf. Matthew 27.13–14.
4. Matthew 10.14: "Whosoever shall not receive you . . . when ye depart . . . shake off the dust of your feet."
5. In 2 Kings 2.11 the prophet Elijah "went up by a whirlwind into heaven," borne by "a chariot of fire."

Note. This Angel, who is now become a Devil, is my particular friend; we often read the Bible together in its infernal or diabolical sense, which the world shall have if they behave well.

I have also The Bible of Hell,[6] which the world shall have whether they will or no.

One Law for the Lion & Ox is Oppression.

1790–93   1790–93

6. I.e., the poems and designs that Blake is working on.

ROBERT BURNS
1759–1796

A favorite myth of later eighteenth-century primitivists was that there exist natural poets who warble their native woodnotes wild, independent of art or literary tradition. These artless poets were sought among peasants and proletarians, whose caste or rural habitation, it was thought, protected them from the artificialities of civilized life and culture. When Robert Burns published his first volume of *Poems* in 1786, he was at once hailed by the literati of Edinburgh as an instance of the natural genius, a "Heaven-taught plowman" whose poems were the spontaneous overflow of his native feelings. Burns rather enjoyed playing the role of the poet by instinct. But in fact he was a well-read (although largely self-educated) man whose quick intelligence and sensibility enabled him to make the most of limited opportunities. And although he broke clear of the contemporary conventions of decayed English neoclassicism, he did so not by instinct but as a deliberate craftsman who turned to two earlier traditions for his models. One of these was the oral tradition of Scottish folklore and folk song; the other was the highly developed literary tradition of poems written in the Scots dialect of English.

His father—William Burnes, as he spelled his name—was a God-fearing and hard-working farmer of Ayrshire, a county in southwestern Scotland, who, unable to make a go of it in a period of hard times and high rents, died in 1784 broken in body and spirit. Robert, with his brother Gilbert, was forced to do the toil of a man while still a boy and began to show signs of the heart trouble of which he was to die when only thirty-seven. Although his father had the Scottish esteem for education and saw to it that his sons attended school whenever they could, Burns's education in literature, theology, politics, and philosophy came mainly from his own reading. At the age of fifteen he fell in love, and was inspired by that event to write his first song. "Thus," he said, "with me began Love and Poesy." After he reached maturity, he cultivated assiduously both these propensities. He began a series of amorous affairs, fathering in 1785 the first of a number of illegitimate children; he also extended greatly the range and quantity of his attempts at poetry. So rapid was his development that by the time he published the Kilmarnock edition, at the age of twenty-seven, he had written all but a few of his greatest long poems.

The Kilmarnock volume (so named from the town in which it was published) is one of the most remarkable first volumes by any British poet, and it had a great and immediate success. Burns was acclaimed "Caledonia's Bard" and lionized by the intellectuals and gentlefolk when he visited Edinburgh soon after his book came out. The peasant-poet demonstrated that he could more than hold his own as a brilliant conversationalist and debater. But he was also wise enough to realize that once the novelty wore off, his eminence in this society would not endure. He had a fierce pride that was quick to resent any hint of contempt or condescension toward himself as a man of low degree. His sympathies were democratic, and he was an outspoken admirer of the republican revolutions in America and France. In religion, too, he was a radical, professing "the Religion of Sentiment and Reason" in opposition to the strict Calvinism in which he had been raised, and he offended many pious Presbyterians by his devastating satires against the rigid tenets and the moral authoritarianism of the Scottish kirk. Furthermore, his sexual irregularities were notorious, less because they were out of the common order at that time than because he flaunted them before the "unco guid"—as his biographer DeLancey Ferguson has said, "it was not so much that he was conspicuously sinful as that he sinned conspicuously." Most of Burns's friends in high station quickly fell away, and his later visits to Edinburgh did not repeat the social success of the first.

In 1788 Burns was given a commission as excise officer, or tax inspector, and he settled down with Jean Armour, a former lover, now his wife, at Ellisland, near Dumfries, combining his official duties with farming. This was the fourth farm on which Burns had worked; and when it, like the others, failed, he moved his family to the lively country town of Dumfries. Here he was fairly happy, despite recurrent illness and a chronic shortage of money. He performed his official duties efficiently and was respected by his fellow townspeople and esteemed by his superiors; he was a devoted family man and father; and he accumulated a circle of intimates to whom he could repair for conversation and conviviality. In 1787 James Johnson, an engraver, had enlisted Burns's aid in collecting Scottish folk songs for an anthology called *The Scots Musical Museum*. Burns soon became the real editor for several volumes of this work, devoting all of his free time to collecting, editing, restoring, and imitating traditional songs, and to writing verses of his own to traditional dance tunes. Almost all of his creative work during the last twelve years of his life went into the writing of songs for the *Musical Museum* and for George Thomson's *Select Collection of Original Scottish Airs*. This was for Burns a devoted labor of love and patriotism, done anonymously, for which he refused to accept any pay, although badly in need of money; and he continued the work when he was literally on his deathbed.

Burns's best poetry was written in Scots, a northern dialect of English spoken by rural people and (on other than formal occasions) by most eighteenth-century Scottish gentlefolk as well. When Burns attempted to write in standard English, the result—except in an occasional lyric such as the lucid and graceful *Afton Water*—tended to be stilted and conventional, with the stock phrasing, sententiousness, and sentimentality of the genteel poetic tradition of his day. He is often considered a "pre-Romantic" who, anticipating Wordsworth, revived the lyric, exploited the literary forms and legends of folk culture, and wrote in the language really spoken by the common people. This reputation is based primarily on his songs. By far the major portion of the poems that Burns published under his own name are concerned with men and manners and are written in the literary forms that had been favored by earlier eighteenth-century poets; they include brilliant satire in a variety of modes, a number of fine verse epistles to friends and fellow poets, and one masterpiece of mock-heroic (or at any rate seriocomic) narrative, *Tam o' Shanter*. The claim could be supported that, next to Pope, Burns is the greatest eighteenth-century master of these literary types. Yet his writings in satire, epistle, and mock-heroic are very remote from Pope's in their heartiness and verve, no less than in their dialect and intricate stanza forms. The reason for the difference is that Burns turned for his models not to Horace and the English neoclassic tradition but to the native tradition that had been established in the golden age of Scottish poetry by Robert Henryson, William Dunbar, Gavin Douglas, and other Scottish Chaucerians of the fifteenth and sixteenth centuries. He knew this literature through his eighteenth-century Scottish predecessors, especially Allan Ramsay and Robert Fergusson, who had collected some of the old poems and written new ones based on the old models. Burns improved greatly on these predecessors, but he derived from them much that is characteristic in his literary forms, subjects, diction, and stanzas.

Burns's songs, however, are more widely known than his longer works and have in themselves been adequate to sustain his poetic reputation. He wrote over three hundred of them, in unequaled abundance and variety. In his songs he gives himself over wholeheartedly to the emotion of the moment, evoked by all the standard lyric subjects: love, drink, work, friendship, patriotism, and bawdry. His poetic character is hearty, generous, rollicking, tender, with a sympathy that encompasses humans of all types, from national heroes to tavern roarers. Burns is not only the national poet of Scotland but a song writer for all English-speaking people. Wherever in the world they may be on New Year's Eve, when, helped by drink and the reminder of their bondage to time, men and women indulge their instinct of a common humanity, they join hands and sing a song of Burns.

The texts printed here are based on *The Poems and Songs of Robert Burns,* ed. James Kinsley, 3 vols. (Oxford, 1968).

Holy Willie's Prayer[1]

And send the Godly in a pet to pray—

POPE

Argument

Holy Willie was a rather oldish batchelor Elder in the parish of Mauchline, and much and justly famed for that polemical chattering which ends in tippling Orthodoxy, and for that Spiritualized Bawdry which refines to Liquorish Devotion.—In a Sessional process with a gentleman in Mauchline, a Mr. Gavin Hamilton, Holy Willie, and his priest, Father Auld, after full hearing in the Presbytry of Ayr, came off but second best; owing partly to the oratorical powers of Mr. Robt. Aiken, Mr. Hamilton's Counsel; but chiefly to Mr. Hamilton's being one of the most irreproachable and truly respectable characters in the country.—On losing his Process, the Muse overheard him at his devotions as follows—

> O thou that in the heavens does dwell!
> Wha, as it pleases best thysel,
> Sends ane to heaven and ten to h-ll,
>   A' for thy glory!
> 5 And no for ony gude or ill
>   They've done before thee.
>
> I bless and praise thy matchless might,
> When thousands thou has left in night,
> That I am here before thy sight,

---

1. This satire, in the form of a dramatic monologue, was inspired by one William Fisher, a self-righteous elder in the parish of Mauchline, and is directed against a basic Calvinist tenet of the old Scottish kirk. Holy Willie assumes that he is one of a small minority, God's "elect"—in other words that he has been predestined for grace, no matter what works he does in this vale of tears. The epigraph is from *The Rape of the Lock.*

10   For gifts and grace,
  A burning and a shining light
     To a' this place.

  What was I, or my generation,
  That I should get such exaltation?
15 I, wha deserv'd most just damnation,
     For broken laws
  Sax° thousand years ere my creation,   *six*
     Thro' Adam's cause!

  When from my mother's womb I fell,
20 Thou might hae plunged me deep in hell,
  To gnash my gooms, and weep, and wail,
     In burning lakes,
  Where damned devils roar and yell
     Chain'd to their stakes.

25 Yet I am here, a chosen sample,
  To shew thy grace is great and ample:
  I'm here, a pillar o' thy temple
     Strong as a rock,
  A guide, a ruler and example
30   To a' thy flock.

  O Lord thou kens what zeal I bear,
  When drinkers drink, and swearers swear,
  And singin' there, and dancin' here,
     Wi' great an' sma';
35 For I am keepet by thy fear,
     Free frae them a'.

  But yet—O Lord—confess I must—
  At times I'm fash'd° wi' fleshly lust;   *troubled*
  And sometimes too, in warldly trust
40   Vile Self gets in;
  But thou remembers we are dust,
     Defil'd wi' sin.

  O Lord—yestreen—thou kens—wi' Meg—
  Thy pardon I sincerely beg!
45 O may't ne'er be a living plague,
     To my dishonor!
  And I'll ne'er lift a lawless leg
     Again upon her.

  Besides, I farther maun° avow,   *must*
50 Wi' Leezie's lass, three times—I trow°—   *believe*
  But Lord, that Friday I was fou°   *drunk*
     When I cam near her;
  Or else, thou kens, thy servant true
     Wad never steer° her.   *molest*

55　Maybe thou lets this fleshly thorn
　　Buffet thy servant e'en and morn,
　　Lest he o'er proud and high should turn,
　　　　That he's sae gifted;
　　If sae, thy hand maun e'en be borne
60　　　　Untill thou lift it.

　　Lord bless thy Chosen in this place,
　　For here thou has a chosen race:
　　But God, confound their stubborn face,
　　　　And blast their name,
65　Wha bring thy rulers to disgrace
　　　　And open shame.

　　Lord mind Gaun Hamilton's² deserts!
　　He drinks, and swears, and plays at cartes,°　　　　　　cards
　　Yet has sae mony taking arts
70　　　　Wi' Great and Sma',
　　Frae God's ain priest the people's hearts
　　　　He steals awa.

　　And when we chasten'd him therefore,
　　Thou kens how he bred sic a splore,°　　　　　　disturbance
75　And set the warld in a roar
　　　　O' laughin at us:
　　Curse thou his basket and his store,
　　　　Kail° and potatoes.　　　　　　broth

　　Lord hear my earnest cry and prayer
80　Against that Presbytry of Ayr!
　　Thy strong right hand, Lord, make it bare
　　　　Upon their heads!
　　Lord visit them, and dinna spare,
　　　　For their misdeeds!

85　O Lord my God, that glib-tongu'd Aiken!
　　My very heart and flesh are quaking
　　To think how I sat, sweating, shaking,
　　　　And piss'd wi' dread,
　　While Auld wi' hingin° lip gaed sneaking　　　　　　hanging
90　　　　And hid his head!

　　Lord, in thy day o'vengeance try him!
　　Lord visit him that did employ him!
　　And pass not in thy mercy by them,
　　　　Nor hear their prayer;
95　But for thy people's sake destroy them,
　　　　And dinna spare!

2. Burns's friend Gavin Hamilton, whom Holy
Willie had brought up on moral charges before the
Kirk Session of the Presbytery of Ayr. As Burns
explains in the Argument, Hamilton was successfully defended by his counsel, Robert Aiken
(referred to in line 85).

But Lord, remember me and mine
Wi' mercies temporal and divine!
That I for grace and gear° may shine,   *wealth*
100   Excell'd by nane!
And a' the glory shall be thine!
          Amen! Amen!

1789   1789

To a Mouse

On Turning Her up in Her Nest with the Plough, November, 1785[1]

Wee, sleeket,° cowran, tim'rous beastie,   *sleek*
O, what a panic's in thy breastie!
Thou need na start awa sae hasty,
          Wi' bickering brattle![2]
5   I wad be laith° to rin an' chase thee   *loath*
          Wi' murd'ring pattle!°   *plowstaff*

I'm truly sorry Man's dominion
Has broken Nature's social union,
An' justifies that ill opinion,
10   Which makes thee startle,
At me, thy poor, earth-born companion,
          An' fellow mortal!

I doubt na, whyles,° but thou may thieve;   *sometimes*
What then? poor beastie, thou maun° live!   *must*
15   A daimen-icker in a thrave[3]
          'S a sma' request:
I'll get a blessin wi' the lave,°   *remainder*
          An' never miss 't!

Thy wee-bit housie, too, in ruin!
20   It's silly° wa's the win's are strewin!   *feeble*
An' naething, now, to big° a new ane,   *build*
          O' foggage° green!   *coarse grass*
An' bleak December's winds ensuin,
          Baith snell° an' keen!   *bitter*

25   Thou saw the fields laid bare an' waste,
An' weary Winter comin fast,
An' cozie here, beneath the blast,
          Thou thought to dwell,
Till crash! the cruel coulter° past   *cutter blade*
30   Out thro' thy cell.

1. Burns's brother claimed that this poem was composed while the poet was actually holding the plow.
2. With headlong scamper.
3. An occasional ear in twenty-four sheaves.

That wee-bit heap o' leaves an' stibble°   *stubble*
Has cost thee monie a weary nibble!
Now thou 's turn'd out, for a' thy trouble,
       But° house or hald,[4]   *without*
35   To thole° the Winter's sleety dribble,   *endure*
       An' cranreuch° cauld!   *hoarfrost*

But Mousie, thou art no thy-lane,°   *not alone*
In proving foresight may be vain:
The best laid schemes o' Mice an' Men
40   Gang aft agley,[5]
An' lea'e us nought but grief an' pain,
       For promis'd joy!

Still, thou art blest, compar'd wi' me!
The present only toucheth thee:
45   But Och! I backward cast my e'e,
       On prospects drear!
An' forward tho' I canna see,
       I guess an' fear!

1785   1786

To a Louse

On Seeing One on a Lady's Bonnet at Church

Ha! whare ye gaun, ye crowlan° ferlie!°   *crawling / wonder*
Your impudence protects you sairly:°   *sorely*
I canna say but ye strunt° rarely,   *strut*
       Owre gawze and lace;
5   Tho' faith, I fear ye dine but sparely,
       On sic a place.

Ye ugly, creepan, blastet wonner,°   *wonder*
Detested, shunn'd, by saunt an' sinner,
How daur ye set your fit° upon her,   *foot*
10   Sae fine a Lady!
Gae somewhere else and seek your dinner,
       On some poor body.

Swith,° in some beggar's haffet° squattle;°   *swift / locks / sprawl*
There ye may creep, and sprawl, and sprattle,°   *struggle*
15   Wi' ither kindred, jumping cattle,
       In shoals and nations;
Whare horn nor bane[1] ne'er daur unsettle,
       Your thick plantations.

Now haud you there, ye're out o' sight,
20   Below the fatt'rels,° snug and tight,   *ribbon ends*

---

4. Hold, holding (i.e., land).
5. Go oft awry.

1. I.e., fine-tooth comb made of horn or bone ("bane").

Na faith ye yet!² ye'll no be right,
　　　Till ye've got on it,
The vera tapmost, towrin height
　　　O' Miss's bonnet.

25　My sooth! right bauld ye set your nose out,
　　As plump an' gray as onie grozet:°　　　　　gooseberry
　　O for some rank, mercurial rozet,°　　　　　rosin
　　　　Or fell,° red smeddum,°　　　　sharp / powder
　　I'd gie you sic a hearty dose o't,
30　　　　Wad dress your droddum!°　　　　buttocks

　　I wad na been surpriz'd to spy
　　You on an auld wife's flainen toy,°　　　　flannel cap
　　Or aiblins° some bit duddie° boy,　　perhaps / ragged
　　　　On 's wylecoat;°　　　　　undershirt
35　But Miss's fine Lunardi,³ fye!
　　　　How daur ye do 't?

　　O Jenny dinna toss your head,
　　An' set your beauties a' abread!°　　　　　abroad
　　Ye little ken what cursed speed
40　　　　The blastie's° makin!　　　　creature's
　　Thae° winks and finger-ends, I dread,　　those
　　　　Are notice takin!

　　O wad some Pow'r the giftie gie us
　　To see oursels as others see us!
45　It wad frae monie a blunder free us
　　　　An' foolish notion:
　　What airs in dress an' gait wad lea'e us,
　　　　And ev'n Devotion!⁴

1785　　　　　　　　　　　　　　　　　1786

Tam o' Shanter: A Tale¹

Of Brownyis and of Bogillis full is this buke.
　　　　　　　　　GAWIN DOUGLAS.

When chapman billies² leave the street,
And drouthy° neebors neebors meet,　　　thirsty

2. Confound you!
3. A balloon-shaped bonnet, named after Vincenzo Lunardi, who made a number of balloon flights in the mid-1780s.
4. I.e., even pretended piety.
1. This poem, written to order for a book on Scottish antiquities, is based on a witch story told about Alloway Kirk, an old ruin near Burns's house in Ayr. As a mock-heroic rendering of folk material, *Tam o' Shanter* is comparable to *The Nun's Priest's Tale* of Chaucer. Burns recognized that the poem was his most sustained and finished artistic performance; it discovers "a spice of roguish waggery" but also shows "a force of genius and a finishing

polish that I despair of ever excelling." The verve and seriocomic sympathy with which Burns manages this misadventure of a confirmed tippler won Wordsworth, a water drinker, to passionate advocacy against the moralists who objected to Burns's ribaldry: "Who, but some impenetrable dunce or narrow-minded puritan in works of art, ever read without delight the picture which he has drawn of the convivial exaltation of the rustic adventurer, Tam o' Shanter? . . . I pity him who cannot perceive that, in all this, though there was no moral purpose, there is a moral effect" (*Letter to a Friend of Burns*, 1816).
2. Peddler fellows.

As market-days are wearing late,
An' folk begin to tak the gate;°   *road*
5   While we sit bousing at the nappy,°   *strong ale*
And getting fou° and unco° happy,   *drunk / very*
We think na on the lang Scots miles,
The mosses, waters, slaps,° and styles,   *gaps (in walls)*
That lie between us and our hame,
10 Whare sits our sulky sullen dame,
Gathering her brows like gathering storm,
Nursing her wrath to keep it warm.

      This truth fand° honest Tam o' Shanter,   *found*
As he frae Ayr ae night did canter,
15 (Auld Ayr, wham ne'er a town surpasses,
For honest men and bonny lasses).

      O Tam! hadst thou but been sae wise,
As ta'en thy ain wife Kate's advice!
She tauld thee weel thou was a skellum,°   *good-for-nothing*
20 A blethering,° blustering, drunken blellum;°   *chattering / babbler*
That frae November till October,
Ae market-day thou was nae sober;
That ilka° melder,³ wi' the miller,   *every*
Thou sat as lang as thou had siller;°   *silver, money*
25 That every naig° was ca'd° a shoe on,   *nag / driven*
The smith and thee gat roaring fou on;
That at the Lord's house, even on Sunday,
Thou drank wi' Kirkton Jean till Monday.
She prophesied that late or soon,
30 Thou would be found deep drown'd in Doon;
Or catch'd wi' warlocks° in the mirk,°   *wizards / night*
By Alloway's auld haunted kirk.

      Ah, gentle dames! it gars° me greet°   *makes / weep*
To think how mony counsels sweet,
35 How mony lengthen'd sage advices,
The husband frae the wife despises!

      But to our tale: Ae market-night,
Tam had got planted unco right;
Fast by an ingle,° bleezing° finely,   *fireplace / blazing*
40 Wi' reaming swats,° that drank divinely;   *foaming new ale*
And at his elbow, Souter° Johnny,   *Cobbler*
His ancient, trusty, drouthy crony;
Tam lo'ed him like a vera brither;
They had been fou for weeks thegither.
45 The night drave on wi' sangs and clatter;
And ay the ale was growing better:
The landlady and Tam grew gracious,
Wi' favours secret, sweet, and precious:

3. The amount of corn processed at a single grinding.

The Souter tauld his queerest stories;
50 The landlord's laugh was ready chorus:
    The storm without might rair° and rustle,   roar
    Tam did na mind the storm a whistle.

    Care, mad to see a man sae happy,
    E'en drown'd himsel amang the nappy:
55 As bees flee hame wi' lades o' treasure,
    The minutes wing'd their way wi' pleasure:
    Kings may be blest, but Tam was glorious,
    O'er a' the ills o' life victorious!

    But pleasures are like poppies spread,
60 You seize the flower, its bloom is shed;
    Or like the snow falls in the river,
    A moment white—then melts for ever;
    Or like the borealis race,
    That flit ere you can point their place;
65 Or like the rainbow's lovely form
    Evanishing amid the storm.—
    Nae man can tether time or tide;
    The hour approaches Tam maun° ride;   must
    That hour, o' night's black arch the key-stane,
70 That dreary hour, he mounts his beast in;
    And sic a night he taks the road in,
    As ne'er poor sinner was abroad in.

    The wind blew as 'twad blawn its last;
    The rattling showers rose on the blast;
75 The speedy gleams the darkness swallow'd;
    Loud, deep, and lang, the thunder bellow'd:
    That night, a child might understand,
    The Deil had business on his hand.

    Weel mounted on his gray mare, Meg,
80 A better never lifted leg,
    Tam skelpit° on thro' dub° and mire,   slapped / puddle
    Despising wind, and rain, and fire;
    Whiles holding fast his gude blue bonnet;
    Whiles crooning o'er some auld Scots sonnet;
85 Whiles glowring° round wi' prudent cares,   staring
    Lest bogles° catch him unawares.   hobgoblins
    Kirk-Alloway was drawing nigh,
    Whare ghaists° and houlets° nightly cry.—   ghosts / owls

    By this time he was cross the ford,
90 Whare in the snaw, the chapman smoor'd;⁴
    And past the birks° and meikle stane,°   birches / big stone
    Whare drunken Charlie brak's neck-bane;
    And thro' the whins, and by the cairn,⁵

---

4. The peddler smothered.
5. Stones heaped up as a memorial. "Whins": furze (an evergreen shrub).

Whare hunters fand the murder'd bairn;
95 And near the thorn, aboon the well,
Where Mungo's mither hang'd hersel.—
Before him Doon pours all his floods;
The doubling storm roars thro' the woods;
The lightnings flash from pole to pole;
100 Near and more near the thunders roll:
When, glimmering thro' the groaning trees,
Kirk-Alloway seemed in a bleeze;°   *blaze*
Thro' ilka bore° the beams were glancing;   *hole*
And loud resounded mirth and dancing.—

105   Inspiring bold John Barleycorn!
What dangers thou canst make us scorn!
Wi' tippeny,[6] we fear nae evil;
Wi' usquabae,° we'll face the devil!—   *whisky*
The swats sae ream'd in Tammie's noddle,
110 Fair play, he car'd na deils a boddle.[7]
But Maggie stood right sair astonish'd,
Till, by the heel and hand admonish'd,
She ventured forward on the light;
And, vow! Tam saw an unco° sight!   *strange*
115 Warlocks and witches in a dance;
Nae cotillion brent° new frae France,   *brand*
But hornpipes, jigs, strathspeys,[8] and reels,
Put life and mettle in their heels.
A winnock-bunker° in the east,   *window seat*
120 There sat auld Nick, in shape o' beast;
A touzie tyke,° black, grim, and large,   *shaggy dog*
To gie them music was his charge:
He screw'd the pipes and gart° them skirl,°   *made / screech*
Till roof and rafters a' did dirl.°—   *rattle*
125 Coffins stood round, like open presses,
That shaw'd the dead in their last dresses;
And by some devilish cantraip° slight   *charm, trick*
Each in its cauld hand held a light.—
By which heroic Tam was able
130 To note upon the haly° table,   *holy*
A murderer's banes in gibbet airns;°   *irons*
Twa span-lang,[9] wee, unchristened bairns;
A thief, new-cutted frae a rape,°   *rope*
Wi' his last gasp his gab° did gape;   *mouth*
135 Five tomahawks, wi' blude red-rusted;
Five scymitars, wi' murder crusted;
A garter, which a babe had strangled;
A knife, a father's throat had mangled,
Whom his ain son o' life bereft,
140 The grey hairs yet stack to the heft;
Wi' mair o' horrible and awefu',
Which even to name wad be unlawfu'.

---

6. Twopenny (of drink).
7. I.e., he didn't care a farthing about devils (a "boddle" is a very small copper coin).
8. Slow Highland dance.
9. Two spans long (a span is the distance from outstretched thumb to little finger).

As Tammie glowr'd, amaz'd, and curious,
The mirth and fun grew fast and furious:
145 The piper loud and louder blew;
The dancers quick and quicker flew;
They reel'd, they set, they cross'd, they cleekit,°   *joined hands*
Till ilka carlin° swat and reekit,   *old woman*
And coost her duddies to the wark,[1]
150 And linket° at it in her sark!°   *tripped lightly / shirt*

Now, Tam, O Tam! had thae been queans,°   *girls*
A' plump and strapping in their teens,
Their sarks, instead o' creeshie flannen,°   *greasy flannel*
Been snaw-white seventeen hunder linnen![2]
155 Thir° breeks o' mine, my only pair,   *these*
That ance were plush, o' gude blue hair,
I wad hae gi'en them off my hurdies,°   *buttocks*
For ae blink o' the bonie burdies!°   *maidens*

But wither'd beldams, auld and droll,
160 Rigwoodie° hags wad spean° a foal,   *bony / wean*
Lowping° and flinging on a crummock,°   *leaping / staff*
I wonder didna turn thy stomach.

But Tam kend what was what fu' brawlie,°   *finely*
There was ae winsome wench and wawlie°   *strapping*
165 That night enlisted in the core,°   *corps*
(Lang after kend on Carrick shore;
For mony a beast to dead she shot,
And perish'd mony a bony boat,
And shook baith meikle corn and bear,°   *barley*
170 And kept the country-side in fear:)
Her cutty° sark, o' Paisley harn,°   *short / yarn*
That while a lassie she had worn,
In longitude tho' sorely scanty,
It was her best, and she was vauntie.°—   *proud*
175 Ah! little kend thy reverend grannie,
That sark she coft° for her wee Nannie,   *bought*
Wi' twa pund Scots ('twas a' her riches),
Wad ever grac'd a dance of witches!

But here my Muse her wing maun cour;°   *lower*
180 Sic flights are far beyond her pow'r;
To sing how Nannie lap and flang,
(A souple jade she was, and strang),
And how Tam stood, like ane bewitch'd,
And thought his very een° enrich'd;   *eyes*
185 Even Satan glowr'd, and fidg'd fu' fain,[3]
And hotch'd° and blew wi' might and main: *jerked*
Till first ae caper, syne° anither,   *then*
Tam tint° his reason a' thegither,   *lost*

1. Cast off her clothes for the work.
2. Very fine linen, woven on a loom with seven-   teen hundred strips.
3. Fidgeted with pleasure.

And roars out, 'Weel done, Cutty-sark!'
190 And in an instant all was dark:
And scarcely had he Maggie rallied,
When out the hellish legion sallied.

As bees bizz out wi' angry fyke,°   *fuss*
When plundering herds° assail their byke;° *herdsmen / hive*
195 As open° pussie's mortal foes,   *begin to bark*
When, pop! she starts before their nose;
As eager runs the market-crowd,
When 'Catch the thief!' resounds aloud;
So Maggie runs the witches follow,
200 Wi' mony an eldritch° skreech and hollow.   *unearthly*

Ah, Tam! Ah, Tam! thou'll get thy fairin'!°   *deserts*
In hell they'll roast thee like a herrin!
In vain thy Kate awaits thy comin!
Kate soon will be a woefu' woman!
205 Now, do thy speedy utmost, Meg,
And win the key-stane of the brig;°   *bridge*
There at them thou thy tail may toss,
A running stream they dare na cross.
But ere the key-stane she could make,
210 The fient a tail she had to shake!⁴
For Nannie, far before the rest,
Hard upon noble Maggie prest,
And flew at Tam wi' furious ettle;°   *intent*
But little wist she Maggie's mettle—
215 Ae spring brought off her master hale,°   *whole*
But left behind her ain gray tail:
The carlin claught° her by the rump,   *clutched*
And left poor Maggie scarce a stump.

Now, wha this tale o' truth shall read,
220 Ilk man and mother's son, take heed:
Whene'er to drink you are inclin'd,
Or cutty-sarks run in your mind,
Think, ye may buy the joys o'er dear,
Remember Tam o' Shanter's mare.

1790   1791

Robert Bruce's March to Bannockburn¹

[SCOTS, WHA HAE]

Scots, wha hae wi' Wallace² bled,
Scots, wham Bruce has aften led,

---

4. I.e., she had no tail left at all.
1. In this best-known of Burns's patriotic songs Robert Bruce is addressing his army before the great victory at Bannockburn (1314), at which the

English were driven from Scotland.
2. Sir William Wallace (ca. 1272–1305), the great Scottish warrior in the wars against the English.

Welcome to your gory bed,—
    Or to victorie.—

5   Now's the day, and now's the hour;
    See the front o' battle lour;
    See approach proud Edward's power,
        Chains and Slaverie.—

    Wha will be a traitor-knave?
10 Wha can fill a coward's grave?
    Wha sae base as be a Slave?
        —Let him turn and flie:—

    Wha for Scotland's king and law,
    Freedom's sword will strongly draw,
15 Free-man stand, or Free-man fa',
        Let him follow me.—

    By Oppression's woes and pains!
    By your Sons in servile chains!
    We will drain our dearest veins,
20   But they *shall* be free!

    Lay the proud Usurpers low!
    Tyrants fall in every foe!
    Liberty's in every blow!
        Let us Do—or Die!!!

1793   1794, 1815

A Red, Red Rose[1]

    O my Luve's like a red, red rose,
        That's newly sprung in June;
    O my Luve's like the melodie
        That's sweetly played in tune.

5   As fair art thou, my bonie lass,
        So deep in luve am I;
    And I will love thee still, my Dear,
        Till a' the seas gang dry.

    Till a' the seas gang dry, my Dear,
10   And the rocks melt wi' the sun:
    O I will love thee still, my Dear,
        While the sands o' life shall run.

    And fare thee weel, my only Luve!
        And fare thee weel, a while!

1. Like many of Burns's lyrics, this one incorporates elements from several current folk songs.

15 And I will come again, my Luve,
Tho' it were ten thousand mile!

1794   1796

Song: For a' that and a' that

Is there, for honest Poverty
   That hangs his head, and a' that;
The coward-slave, we pass him by,
   We dare be poor for a' that!
5   For a' that, and a' that,
      Our toils obscure, and a' that,
The rank is but the guinea's stamp,
   The Man's the gowd° for a' that.   gold

What though on hamely fare we dine,
10   Wear hodden grey,[1] and a' that.
Gie fools their silks, and knaves their wine,
   A Man's a Man for a' that.
For a' that, and a' that,
   Their tinsel show, and a' that;
15 The honest man, though e'er sae poor,
   Is king o' men for a' that.

Ye see yon birkie° ca'd a lord,   brisk young fellow
   Wha struts, and stares, and a' that,
Though hundreds worship at his word,
20   He's but a coof° for a' that.   dolt
For a' that, and a' that,
   His ribband, star and a' that,
The man of independant mind,
   He looks and laughs at a' that.

25 A prince can mak a belted knight,
   A marquis, duke, and a' that;
But an honest man's aboon° his might,   above
   Guid faith he mauna fa' that![2]
For a' that, and a' that,
30   Their dignities, and a' that,
The pith o' Sense, and pride o' Worth,
   Are higher rank than a' that.

Then let us pray that come it may,
   As come it will for a' that,
35 That Sense and Worth, o'er a' the earth
   Shall bear the gree,[3] and a' that.
For a' that, and a' that,
   It's coming yet for a' that,
That Man to Man the warld o'er,
40   Shall brothers be for a' that.

1795   1795

---

1. A coarse cloth of undyed wool.   3. Win the prize.
2. Must not claim that.

MARY WOLLSTONECRAFT
1759–1797

Mary Wollstonecraft's father inherited a substantial fortune and set himself up as a gentleman farmer. He was, however, both extravagant and incompetent, and as one farm after another failed, he became moody and violent and sought solace in heavy bouts of drinking and in tyrannizing over his submissive wife. Mary was the second of five children and the oldest daughter. She later told her husband, William Godwin, that she used to throw herself in front of her mother to protect her from her husband's blows. The solace of Mary's early life was her fervent attachment to Fanny Blood, an accomplished girl two years her senior.

At the age of nineteen Mary Wollstonecraft took a position as companion to a well-to-do widow living in Bath, where she for the first time had the opportunity to observe—and scorn—the social life of the upper classes at the most fashionable of English resort cities. Having left her job in 1780 to nurse her dying mother through a long and harrowing illness, Wollstonecraft next went to live with the Bloods, where her work helped to sustain the struggling family. Her sister Eliza meanwhile had married and, in 1784, after the birth of a daughter, suffered a nervous breakdown. Convinced that her sister's collapse was the result of her husband's cruelty and abuse, Wollstonecraft persuaded her to abandon husband and child and flee to London; because a divorce at that time was not commonly available, and a fugitive wife could be forced to return to her husband, the two women hid in secret quarters while awaiting the grant of a legal separation. The infant, automatically given into the father's custody, died before she was a year old.

The penniless women, together with Fanny Blood and Wollstonecraft's other sister, Everina, established a girls' school at Newington Green, near London. Blood, although already ill with tuberculosis, went to Lisbon to marry her longtime suitor, Hugh Skeys, and quickly became pregnant. Wollstonecraft rushed to Lisbon to attend her friend's childbirth, only to have Fanny die in her arms; the infant died soon afterward. The loss threw Wollstonecraft (already subject to bouts of depression) into black despair, which was heightened when she found that the school at Newington was in bad financial straits and had to be closed. Tormented by creditors, she rallied her energies to write her first book, *Thoughts on the Education of Daughters* (1786), a conventional and pious series of essays, and took up a position as governess for several daughters in the Anglo-Irish family of Viscount Kingsborough, a man of wealth whose seat was in County Cork, Ireland.

The ambiguity of Woolstonescraft's social position as governess, halfway between a servant and member of the family, was galling to her. An antagonism developed between Wollstonecraft and Lady Kingsborough, in part because the children feared their mother and adored their governess, and Wollstonecraft was dismissed. She returned to London, where Joseph Johnson in 1788 published her first novel, *Mary, a Fiction,* a partly autobiographical but conventionally sentimental novel written while she was in Ireland, as well as a book for children, *Original Stories from Real Life.,* which achieved commercial success. Wollstonecraft was befriended and subsidized by Johnson, the major publisher in England of radical and reformist books, and she took a prominent place among the notable writers whom he regularly entertained at his rooms in St. Paul's Churchyard. She published translations from French and German (she had taught herself both languages) and began reviewing books for John-son's newly founded journal, the *Analytical Review.* Though still in straitened circumstances, she helped support her two sisters and her improvident and importunate father, and was also generous with funds—and with advice—to one of her brothers and to the indigent family of Fanny Blood.

In 1790 Edmund Burke's *Reflections on the Revolution in France*—an eloquent and powerful attack on the French Revolution and its English sympathizers—quickly evoked Wollstonecraft's response, *A Vindication of the Rights of Men*. This was a formidable piece of argumentation; its most potent passages are those that represent the disabilities and sufferings of the English lower classes and impugn the motives and sentiments of Burke. This work, the first book-length reply to Burke, scored an immediate success. In 1792 Wollstonecraft focused her defense of the underprivileged on her own sex and wrote, in six weeks of intense effort, *A Vindication of the Rights of Woman*.

Earlier writers both in France and England had proposed that, given an equivalence in education, women would equal men in achievement. Wollstonecraft was particularly indebted to Catharine Macaulay's *Letters on Education* (1790), of which she had written an enthusiastic review. But Wollstonecraft's *Vindication* was unprecedented in its firsthand observations of the disabilities and indignities suffered by women and in the articulateness and passion with which it exposed and decried this injustice. Wollstonecraft's views were conspicuously radical at a time when women had no political rights; were limited to a few lowly vocations as servants, nurses, governesses, and petty shopkeepers; and were legally nonpersons who lost their property to their husbands at marriage and were incapable of instituting an action in the courts of law. An impressive feature of her book, for all its vehemence, is the clear-sightedness and balance of her analysis of the social conditions of the time, as they affect men as well as women. She perceives that women constitute an oppressed class that cuts across the standard hierarchy of social classes; she shows that women, because they are denied political and domestic privileges, have been forced to seek their ends by means of coquetry and cunning; and she also recognizes that men, no less than women, inherit their roles, and that the wielding of irresponsible power corrupts the oppressor no less than it deforms the oppressed. Hence her surprising and telling comparisons between women on the one hand and men of the nobility and military on the other as classes whose values and behavior have been distorted because their social roles prevent them from becoming fully human. In writing this pioneering work, Wollstonecraft found the cause that she was to pursue the rest of her life.

In December 1792, Wollstonecraft went to Paris to observe the French Revolution at firsthand. In Paris she joined a group of English, American, and European expatriates sympathetic to the Revolution and fell in love with Gilbert Imlay, a personable American who played the role in Paris of an American frontiersman and child of nature, but was in fact an adventurer who had left America to avoid prosecution for debt and for freewheeling speculations in Kentucky land. The two became lovers, and Wollstonecraft bore a daughter, Fanny Imlay, in May 1794. Imlay, who was often absent on mysterious business deals, left mother and daughter for a visit to London that he kept protracting. After the publication of her book *An Historical and Moral View of the Origin and Progress of the French Revolution* (1795), Wollstonecraft followed Imlay to London, where, persuaded that he no longer loved her, she tried to commit suicide; the attempt, however, was discovered and prevented by Imlay. To get her out of the way, he persuaded her to take a trip as his business envoy to the Scandinavian countries. Although this was then a region of poor or impassible roads and primitive accommodations, the intrepid Wollstonecraft traveled there for four months, sometimes in the wilds, accompanied by the year-old Fanny and a French nurse.

Back in London, Wollstonecraft discovered that Imlay was living with a new mistress, a strolling actress. Finally convinced he was lost to her, she hurled herself from a bridge into the Thames but was rescued by a passerby. Imlay departed with his actress to Paris. Wollstonecraft, resourceful as always, used the letters she had written to Imlay to compose a book, *Letters Written during a Short Residence in Sweden, Norway, and Denmark* (1796), full of sharp observations of human character, the conditions of Scandinavian women, and the austere northern landscape.

In the same year Wollstonecraft renewed an earlier acquaintance with the philosopher William Godwin. His *Inquiry Concerning Political Justice* (1793), the most drastic proposal for restructuring the political and social order yet published in England, together with his novel of terror, *Caleb Williams* (1794), which embodies his social views, had made him the most famed radical writer of his time. The austerely rationalistic philosopher, then forty years of age, had an unexpected capacity for deep feeling, and what began as a flirtation soon ripened into affection and (as their letters show) passionate physical love. She wrote Godwin, with what was for the time remarkable outspokenness on the part of a woman: "Now by these presents [i.e., this document] let me assure you that you are not only in my heart, but my veins, this morning. I turn from you half abashed—yet you haunt me, and some look, word or touch thrills through my whole frame. Wollstonecraft was soon again with child, and Godwin (who had in his *Inquiry* attacked the institution of marriage as a base form of property rights in human beings) braved the ridicule of his radical friends and conservative enemies by marrying her.

They set up a household together, salvaged their principles by agreeing to live separate social lives. Wollstonecraft was happy for a brief six months. On August 30 she gave birth to a daughter, Mary Wollstonecraft Godwin, later the author of *Frankenstein* and wife of Percy Shelley. The delivery was not difficult, but resulted in massive blood poisoning. After ten days of agony, she lapsed into a coma and died. Her last whispered words were about her husband: "He is the kindest, best man in the world." Godwin wrote to a friend, announcing her death: "I firmly believe that there does not exist her equal in the world. I know from experience we were formed to make each other happy."

To distract himself in his grief Godwin published in 1798 *Memoirs of the Author of "A Vindication of the Rights of Woman"* in which he told, with the total candor on which he prided himself, of her affairs with Imlay and himself, her attempts at suicide, and her free thinking in matters of religion and sexual relationships; in four companion volumes of her *Posthumous Works* he included her outspoken love letters to Imlay. The unintended result was to saddle Wollstonecraft with a scandalous reputation so enduring that through the Victorian era advocates of the equality of women circumspectly avoided references to her *Vindication*; even John Stuart Mill, in his *Subjection of Women* (1869), neglected to mention the work. It was only in the twentieth century, and especially in the later decades, that Wollstonecraft's *Vindication* gained widespread recognition as a classic in the literature not only of women's rights but of the general analysis of the role played by class and gender in the structure of power and domination in modern society.

From A Vindication of the Rights of Woman[1]

Introduction

After considering the historic page, and viewing the living world with anxious solicitude, the most melancholy emotions of sorrowful indignation have depressed my spirits, and I have sighed when obliged to confess, that either nature has made a great difference between man and man, or that the civilization which has hitherto taken place in the world has been very partial. I have turned over various books written on the subject of education, and patiently observed the conduct of parents and the management of schools; but what has been the result?—a profound conviction that the neglected education of my fellow-creatures is the grand source of the mis-

1. The text is from the second revised edition of 1792, as edited by Carol H. Poston for the Norton Critical Edition of *A Vindication* (1975). The editors gratefully acknowledge Poston's permission to use the information in her annotations.

ery I deplore; and that women, in particular, are rendered weak and wretched by a variety of concurring causes, originating from one hasty conclusion. The conduct and manners of women, in fact, evidently prove that their minds are not in a healthy state; for, like the flowers which are planted in too rich a soil, strength and usefulness are sacrificed to beauty; and the flaunting leaves, after having pleased a fastidious eye, fade, disregarded on the stalk, long before the season when they ought to have arrived at maturity.—One cause of this barren blooming I attribute to a false system of education, gathered from the books written on this subject by men who, considering females rather as women than human creatures, have been more anxious to make them alluring mistresses than affectionate wives and rational mothers; and the understanding of the sex has been so bubbled[2] by this specious homage, that the civilized women of the present century, with a few exceptions, are only anxious to inspire love, when they ought to cherish a nobler ambition, and by their abilities and virtues exact respect.

In a treatise, therefore, on female rights and manners, the works which have been particularly written for their improvement must not be overlooked; especially when it is asserted, in direct terms, that the minds of women are enfeebled by false refinement; that the books of instruction, written by men of genius, have had the same tendency as more frivolous productions; and that, in the true style of Mahometanism, they are treated as a kind of subordinate beings, and not as a part of the human species,[3] when improvable reason is allowed to be the dignified distinction which raises men above the brute creation, and puts a natural sceptre in a feeble hand.

Yet, because I am a woman, I would not lead my readers to suppose that I mean violently to agitate the contested question respecting the equality or inferiority of the sex; but as the subject lies in my way, and I cannot pass it over without subjecting the main tendency of my reasoning to misconstruction, I shall stop a moment to deliver, in a few words, my opinion.—In the government of the physical world it is observable that the female in point of strength is, in general, inferior to the male. This is the law of nature; and it does not appear to be suspended or abrogated in favor of woman. A degree of physical superiority cannot, therefore, be denied—and it is a noble prerogative! But not content with this natural pre-eminence, men endeavor to sink us still lower, merely to render us alluring objects for a moment; and women, intoxicated by the adoration which men, under the influence of their senses, pay them, do not seek to obtain a durable interest in their hearts, or to become the friends of the fellow creatures who find amusement in their society.

I am aware of an obvious inference:—from every quarter have I heard exclamations against masculine women; but where are they to be found? If by this appellation men mean to inveigh against their ardor in hunting, shooting, and gaming, I shall most cordially join in the cry; but if it be against the imitation of manly virtues, or, more properly speaking, the attainment of those talents and virtues, the exercise of which ennobles the human character, and which raise females in the scale of animal being, when they are

2. In an archaic sense, deluded, cheated.
3. It was a common but mistaken opinion among

Europeans that the Koran, the sacred text of Islam, teaches that women have no souls.

comprehensively termed mankind;—all those who view them with a philosophic eye must, I should think, wish with me, that they may every day grow
more and more masculine.

This discussion naturally divides the subject. I shall first consider women
in the grand light of human creatures, who, in common with men, are placed
on this earth to unfold their faculties; and afterwards I shall more particularly
point out their peculiar designation.

I wish also to steer clear of an error which many respectable writers have
fallen into; for the instruction which has hitherto been addressed to women,
has rather been applicable to *ladies*, if the little indirect advice, that is scattered through Sandford and Merton,[4] be excepted; but, addressing my sex in
a firmer tone, I pay particular attention to those in the middle class, because
they appear to be in the most natural state.[5] Perhaps the seeds of false refinement, immorality, and vanity, have ever been shed by the great. Weak, artificial beings, raised above the common wants and affections of their race, in
a premature unnatural manner, undermine the very foundation of virtue,
and spread corruption through the whole mass of society! As a class of mankind they have the strongest claim to pity; the education of the rich tends to
render them vain and helpless, and the unfolding mind is not strengthened
by the practice of those duties which dignify the human character.—They
only live to amuse themselves, and by the same law which in nature invariably
produces certain effects, they soon only afford barren amusement.

But as I purpose taking a separate view of the different ranks of society,
and of the moral character of women, in each, this hint is, for the present,
sufficient, and I have only alluded to the subject, because it appears to me
to be the very essence of an introduction to give a cursory account of the
contents of the work it introduces.

My own sex, I hope, will excuse me, if I treat them like rational creatures,
instead of flattering their *fascinating* graces, and viewing them as if they were
in a state of perpetual childhood, unable to stand alone. I earnestly wish to
point out in what true dignity and human happiness consists—I wish to
persuade women to endeavor to acquire strength, both of mind and body,
and to convince them that the soft phrases, susceptibility of heart, delicacy
of sentiment, and refinement of taste, are almost synonymous with epithets
of weakness, and that those beings who are only the objects of pity and that
kind of love, which has been termed its sister, will soon become objects of
contempt.

Dismissing then those pretty feminine phrases, which the men conde-
scendingly use to soften our slavish dependence, and despising that weak
elegancy of mind, exquisite sensibility, and sweet docility of manners, supposed to be the sexual characteristics of the weaker vessel, I wish to shew
that elegance is inferior to virtue, that the first object of laudable ambition
is to obtain a character as a human being, regardless of the distinction of
sex; and that secondary views should be brought to this simple touchstone.

This is a rough sketch of my plan; and should I express my conviction

4. *The History of Sandford and Merton,* by Thomas
Day, was a very popular story for children, published in three volumes (1786–89). In it a tutor,
the Reverend Mr. Barlow, frequently cites the
superiority in moral principles of Harry Sandford,
the son of a poor farmer, over Tommy Merton, the
spoiled son of a rich family.
5. The middle class is viewed as more "natural"
than the upper classes because it is uncorrupted
by the artificialities of leisure-class life.

with the energetic emotions that I feel whenever I think of the subject, the dictates of experience and reflection will be felt by some of my readers. Animated by this important object, I shall disdain to cull[6] my phrases or polish my style;—I aim at being useful, and sincerity will render me unaffected; for, wishing rather to persuade by the force of my arguments, than dazzle by the elegance of my language, I shall not waste my time in rounding periods,[7] or in fabricating the turgid bombast of artificial feelings, which, coming from the head, never reach the heart. I shall be employed about things, not words!—and, anxious to render my sex more respectable members of society, I shall try to avoid that flowery diction which has slided from essays into novels, and from novels into familiar letters and conversation.

These pretty superlatives, dropping glibly from the tongue, vitiate the taste, and create a kind of sickly delicacy that turns away from simple unadorned truth; and a deluge of false sentiments and over-stretched feelings, stifling the natural emotions of the heart, render the domestic pleasures insipid, that ought to sweeten the exercise of those severe duties, which educate a rational and immortal being for a nobler field of action.

The education of women has, of late, been more attended to than formerly; yet they are still reckoned a frivolous sex, and ridiculed or pitied by the writers who endeavour by satire or instruction to improve them. It is acknowledged that they spend many of the first years of their lives in acquiring a smattering of accomplishments; meanwhile strength of body and mind are sacrificed to libertine notions of beauty, to the desire of establishing themselves,—the only way women can rise in the world,—by marriage. And this desire making mere animals of them, when they marry they act as such children may be expected to act:—they dress; they paint, and nickname God's creatures.[8]— Surely these weak beings are only fit for a seraglio![9]—Can they be expected to govern a family with judgment, or take care of the poor babes whom they bring into the world?

If then it can be fairly deduced from the present conduct of the sex, from the prevalent fondness for pleasure which takes place of ambition and those nobler passions that open and enlarge the soul; that the instruction which women have hitherto received has only tended, with the constitution of civil society, to render them insignificant objects of desire— mere propagators of fools!—if it can be proved that in aiming to accomplish them, without cultivating their understandings, they are taken out of their sphere of duties, and made ridiculous and useless when the short-lived bloom of beauty is over,[1] I presume that *rational* men will excuse me for endeavoring to persuade them to become more masculine and respectable.

Indeed the word masculine is only a bugbear: there is little reason to fear

---

6. Be selective in.
7. I.e., in rounding out elaborate sentences. "Period": a formal sentence composed of balanced clauses.
8. Hamlet, charging Ophelia with the faults characteristic of women, says: "You jig, you amble, and you lisp, and / nickname God's creatures, and make your wantonness your ignorance" (*Hamlet* 3.1.143–45).
9. Harem, the women's quarters in a Muslim

household.
1. A lively writer, I cannot recollect his name, asks what business women turned of forty have to do in the world? [Wollstonecraft's note]. Poston, in her edition of the *Vindication*, suggests that Wollstonecraft is recalling a passage in Fanny Burney's novel *Evelina* (1778), where the licentious Lord Merton exclaims: "I don't know what the devil a woman lives for after thirty; she is only in other folks' way."

that women will acquire too much courage or fortitude; for their apparent inferiority with respect to bodily strength, must render them, in some degree, dependent on men in the various relations of life; but why should it be increased by prejudices that give a sex to virtue, and confound simple truths with sensual reveries?

Women are, in fact, so much degraded by mistaken notions of female excellence, that I do not mean to add a paradox when I assert, that this artificial weakness produces a propensity to tyrannize, and gives birth to cunning, the natural opponent of strength, which leads them to play off those contemptible infantine airs that undermine esteem even whilst they excite desire. Let men become more chaste and modest, and if women do not grow wiser in the same ratio it will be clear that they have weaker understandings. It seems scarcely necessary to say, that I now speak of the sex in general. Many individuals have more sense than their male relatives; and, as nothing preponderates where there is a constant struggle for an equilibrium, without[2] it has naturally more gravity, some women govern their husbands without degrading themselves, because intellect will always govern.

Chap. 2. The Prevailing Opinion of a Sexual Character Discussed

To account for, and excuse the tyranny of man, many ingenious arguments have been brought forward to prove, that the two sexes, in the acquirement of virtue, ought to aim at attaining a very different character: or, to speak explicitly, women are not allowed to have sufficient strength of mind to acquire what really deserves the name of virtue. Yet it should seem, allowing them to have souls, that there is but one way appointed by Providence to lead *mankind* to either virtue or happiness.

If then women are not a swarm of ephemeron[3] triflers, why should they be kept in ignorance under the specious name of innocence? Men complain, and with reason, of the follies and caprices of our sex, when they do not keenly satirize our headstrong passions and groveling vices.—Behold, I should answer, the natural effect of ignorance! The mind will ever be unstable that has only prejudices to rest on, and the current will run with destructive fury when there are no barriers to break its force. Women are told from their infancy, and taught by the example of their mothers, that a little knowledge of human weakness, justly termed cunning, softness of temper, *outward* obedience, and a scrupulous attention to a puerile kind of propriety, will obtain for them the protection of man; and should they be beautiful, every thing else is needless, for, at least, twenty years of their lives.

Thus Milton describes our first frail mother; though when he tells us that women are formed for softness and sweet attractive grace,[4] I cannot comprehend his meaning, unless, in the true Mahometan strain, he meant to deprive us of souls, and insinuate that we were beings only designed by sweet attractive grace, and docile blind obedience, to gratify the senses of man when he can no longer soar on the wing of contemplation.

How grossly do they insult us who thus advise us only to render ourselves

2. Unless.
3. A flying insect that lives only one day.
4. Milton asserts the authority of man over woman, on the grounds that "for contemplation he and valor formed, / For softness she and sweet attractive grace; / He for God only, she for God in him" (*Paradise Lost* 4.298ff.).

gentle, domestic brutes! For instance, the winning softness so warmly, and frequently, recommended, that governs by obeying. What childish expressions, and how insignificant is the being—can it be an immortal one? who will condescend to govern by such sinister methods! "Certainly," says Lord Bacon, "man is of kin to the beasts by his body; and if he be not of kin to God by his spirit, he is a base and ignoble creature!"[5] Men, indeed, appear to me to act in a very unphilosophical manner when they try to secure the good conduct of women by attempting to keep them always in a state of childhood. Rousseau[6] was more consistent when he wished to stop the progress of reason in both sexes, for if men eat of the tree of knowledge, women will come in for a taste; but, from the imperfect cultivation which their understandings now receive, they only attain a knowledge of evil.

Children, I grant, should be innocent; but when the epithet is applied to men, or women, it is but a civil term for weakness. For if it be allowed that women were destined by Providence to acquire human virtues, and by the exercise of their understandings, that stability of character which is the firmest ground to rest our future hopes upon, they must be permitted to turn to the fountain of light, and not forced to shape their course by the twinkling of a mere satellite. Milton, I grant, was of a very different opinion; for he only bends to the indefeasible right of beauty, though it would be difficult to render two passages which I now mean to contrast, consistent. But into similar inconsistencies are great men often led by their senses.

> To whom thus Eve with *perfect beauty* adorn'd.
> My Author and Disposer, what thou bidst
> *Unargued* I obey; So God ordains;
> God is *thy law, thou mine*: to know no more
> Is Woman's *happiest* knowledge and her *praise*.[7]

These are exactly the arguments that I have used to children; but I have added, your reason is now gaining strength, and, till it arrives at some degree of maturity, you must look up to me for advice—then you ought to *think*, and only rely on God.

Yet in the following lines Milton seems to coincide with me; when he makes Adam thus expostulate with his Maker.

> Hast thou not made me here thy substitute,
> And these inferior far beneath me set?
> Among *unequals* what society
> Can sort, what harmony or true delight?
> Which must be mutual, in proportion due
> Giv'n and receiv'd; but in *disparity*
> The one intense, the other still remiss
> Cannot well suit with either, but soon prove
> Tedious alike: of *fellowship* I speak
> Such as I seek, fit to participate
> All rational delight[8]—

5. Francis Bacon's *Of Atheism* (1597).
6. Jean-Jacques Rousseau (1712–1778), who proposed limiting the role of rationality, as opposed to reliance on intuition and instinct. Rousseau's opinions about women and their appropriate education, as alluded to in this chapter, are expressed in

his treatise *Émile* (1762), especially book 5, "Sophy, or Woman."
7. *Paradise Lost* 4.634–38 (Wollstonecraft's italics).
8. *Paradise Lost* 8.381–91 (Wollstonecraft's italics).

In treating, therefore, of the manners of women, let us, disregarding sensual arguments, trace what we should endeavor to make them in order to co-operate, if the expression be not too bold, with the supreme Being.

By individual education, I mean, for the sense of the word is not precisely defined, such an attention to a child as will slowly sharpen the senses, form the temper,[9] regulate the passions as they begin to ferment, and set the understanding to work before the body arrives at maturity; so that the man may only have to proceed, not to begin, the important task of learning to think and reason.

To prevent any misconstruction, I must add, that I do not believe that a private education can work the wonders which some sanguine writers have attributed to it. Men and women must be educated, in a great degree, by the opinions and manners of the society they live in. In every age there has been a stream of popular opinion that has carried all before it, and given a family character, as it were, to the century. It may then fairly be inferred, that, till society be differently constituted, much cannot be expected from education. It is, however, sufficient for my present purpose to assert, that, whatever effect circumstances have on the abilities, every being may become virtuous by the exercise of its own reason; for if but one being was created with vicious inclinations, that is positively bad, what can save us from atheism? or if we worship a God, is not that God a devil?

Consequently, the most perfect education, in my opinion, is such an exercise of the understanding as is best calculated to strengthen the body and form the heart. Or, in other words, to enable the individual to attain such habits of virtue as will render it independent. In fact, it is a farce to call any being virtuous whose virtues do not result from the exercise of its own reason. This was Rousseau's opinion respecting men: I extend it to women, and confidently assert that they have been drawn out of their sphere by false refinement, and not by an endeavour to acquire masculine qualities. Still the regal homage which they receive is so intoxicating, that till the manners of the times are changed, and formed on more reasonable principles, it may be impossible to convince them that the illegitimate power, which they obtain, by degrading themselves, is a curse, and that they must return to nature and equality, if they wish to secure the placid satisfaction that unsophisticated affections impart. But for this epoch we must wait—wait, perhaps, till kings and nobles, enlightened by reason, and, preferring the real dignity of man to childish state,[1] throw off their gaudy hereditary trappings: and if then women do not resign the arbitrary power of beauty—they will prove that they have *less* mind than man.

I may be accused of arrogance; still I must declare what I firmly believe, that all the writers who have written on the subject of female education and manners from Rousseau to Dr. Gregory,[2] have contributed to render women more artificial, weak characters, than they would otherwise have been; and, consequently, more useless members of society. I might have expressed this conviction in a lower key; but I am afraid it would have been the whine of affectation, and not the faithful expression of my feelings, of the clear result, which experience and reflection have led me to draw. When I come to that

9. Temperament, character.
1. Pomp, costly display.
2. John Gregory, Scottish author of a widely read book on the education of women, *A Father's Legacy to His Daughters* (1774).

division of the subject, I shall advert to the passages that I more particularly disapprove of, in the works of the authors I have just alluded to; but it is first necessary to observe, that my objection extends to the whole purport of those books, which tend, in my opinion, to degrade one half of the human species, and render women pleasing at the expense of every solid virtue.

Though, to reason on Rousseau's ground, if man did attain a degree of perfection of mind when his body arrived at maturity, it might be proper, in order to make a man and his wife *one*, that she should rely entirely on his understanding; and the graceful ivy, clasping the oak that supported it, would form a whole in which strength and beauty would be equally conspicuous. But, alas! husbands, as well as their helpmates, are often only overgrown children; nay, thanks to early debauchery, scarcely men in their outward form—and if the blind lead the blind, one need not come from heaven to tell us the consequence.

Many are the causes that, in the present corrupt state of society, contribute to enslave women by cramping their understandings and sharpening their senses. One, perhaps, that silently does more mischief than all the rest, is their disregard of order.

To do every thing in an orderly manner, is a most important precept, which women, who, generally speaking, receive only a disorderly kind of education, seldom attend to with that degree of exactness that men, who from their infancy are broken into method, observe. This negligent kind of guess-work, for what other epithet can be used to point out the random exertions of a sort of instinctive common sense, never brought to the test of reason? prevents their generalizing matters of fact—so they do to-day, what they did yesterday, merely because they did it yesterday.

This contempt of the understanding in early life has more baneful consequences than is commonly supposed; for the little knowledge which women of strong minds attain, is, from various circumstances, of a more desultory kind than the knowledge of men, and it is acquired more by sheer observations on real life, than from comparing what has been individually observed with the results of experience generalized by speculation. Led by their dependent situation and domestic employments more into society, what they learn is rather by snatches; and as learning is with them, in general, only a secondary thing, they do not pursue any one branch with that persevering ardour necessary to give vigor to the faculties, and clearness to the judgment. In the present state of society, a little learning is required to support the character of a gentleman; and boys are obliged to submit to a few years of discipline. But in the education of women, the cultivation of the understanding is always subordinate to the acquirement of some corporeal accomplishment; even while enervated by confinement and false notions of modesty, the body is prevented from attaining that grace and beauty which relaxed half-formed limbs never exhibit. Besides, in youth their faculties are not brought forward by emulation; and having no serious scientific study, if they have natural sagacity it is turned too soon on life and manners. They dwell on effects, and modifications, without tracing them back to causes; and complicated rules to adjust behaviour are a weak substitute for simple principles.

As a proof that education gives this appearance of weakness to females, we may instance the example of military men, who are, like them, sent into the world before their minds have been stored with knowledge or fortified by principles. The consequences are similar; soldiers acquire a little superficial knowledge, snatched from the muddy current of conversation, and, from continually mixing with society, they gain, what is termed a knowledge of the world; and this acquaintance with manners and customs has frequently been confounded with a knowledge of the human heart. But can the crude fruit of casual observation, never brought to the test of judgment, formed by comparing speculation and experience, deserve such a distinction? Soldiers, as well as women, practice the minor virtues with punctilious politeness. Where is then the sexual difference, when the education has been the same? All the difference that I can discern, arises from the superior advantage of liberty, which enables the former to see more of life.

It is wandering from my present subject, perhaps, to make a political remark; but, as it was produced naturally by the train of my reflections, I shall not pass it silently over.

Standing armies can never consist of resolute, robust men; they may be well disciplined machines, but they will seldom contain men under the influence of strong passions, or with very vigorous faculties. And as for any depth of understanding, I will venture to affirm, that it is as rarely to be found in the army as amongst women; and the cause, I maintain, is the same. It may be further observed, that officers are also particularly attentive to their persons, fond of dancing, crowded rooms, adventures, and ridicule.[3] Like the *fair* sex, the business of their lives is gallantry.—They were taught to please, and they only live to please. Yet they do not lose their rank in the distinction of sexes, for they are still reckoned superior to women, though in what their superiority consists, beyond what I have just mentioned, it is difficult to discover.

The great misfortune is this, that they both acquire manners before morals, and a knowledge of life before they have, from reflection, any acquaintance with the grand ideal outline of human nature. The consequence is natural; satisfied with common nature, they become a prey to prejudices, and taking all their opinions on credit, they blindly submit to authority. So that, if they have any sense, it is a kind of instinctive glance, that catches proportions, and decides with respect to manners; but fails when arguments are to be pursued below the surface, or opinions analyzed.

May not the same remark be applied to women? Nay, the argument may be carried still further, for they are both thrown out of a useful station by the unnatural distinctions established in civilized life. Riches and hereditary honours have made cyphers of women to give consequence to the numerical figure; and idleness has produced a mixture of gallantry and despotism into society, which leads the very men who are the slaves of their mistresses to tyrannize over their sisters, wives, and daughters. This is only keeping them in rank and file, it is true. Strengthen the female mind by enlarging it, and there will be an end to blind obedience; but, as blind obedience is ever sought for by power, tyrants and sensualists are in the right when they endeavour to keep women in the dark, because the former only want slaves, and the latter a play-thing. The sensualist, indeed, has been the most dangerous of

---

3. Why should women be censured with petulant acrimony, because they seem to have a passion for a scarlet coat? Has not education placed them more on a level with soldiers than any other class of men? [Wollstonecraft's note].

tyrants, and women have been duped by their lovers, as princes by their ministers, whilst dreaming that they reigned over them.

I now principally allude to Rousseau, for his character of Sophia[4] is, undoubtedly, a captivating one, though it appears to me grossly unnatural; however it is not the superstructure, but the foundation of her character, the principles on which her education was built, that I mean to attack; nay, warmly as I admire the genius of that able writer, whose opinions I shall often have occasion to cite, indignation always takes place of admiration, and the rigid frown of insulted virtue effaces the smile of complacency, which his eloquent periods are wont to raise, when I read his voluptuous reveries. Is this the man, who, in his ardor for virtue, would banish all the soft arts of peace, and almost carry us back to Spartan discipline? Is this the man who delights to paint the useful struggles of passion, the triumphs of good dispositions, and the heroic flights which carry the glowing soul out of itself?—How are these mighty sentiments lowered when he describes the pretty foot and enticing airs of his little favorite! But, for the present, I waive the subject, and, instead of severely reprehending the transient effusions of overweening sensibility, I shall only observe, that whoever has cast a benevolent eye on society, must often have been gratified by the sight of a humble mutual love, not dignified by sentiment, or strengthened by a union in intellectual pursuits. The domestic trifles of the day have afforded matters for cheerful converse, and innocent caresses have softened toils which did not require great exercise of mind or stretch of thought: yet, has not the sight of this moderate felicity excited more tenderness than respect? An emotion similar to what we feel when children are playing, or animals sporting,[5] whilst the contemplation of the noble struggles of suffering merit has raised admiration, and carried our thoughts to that world where sensation will give place to reason.

Women are, therefore, to be considered either as moral beings, or so weak that they must be entirely subjected to the superior faculties of men.

Let us examine this question. Rousseau declares that a woman should never, for a moment, feel herself independent, that she should be governed by fear to exercise her natural cunning, and made a coquetish slave in order to render her a more alluring object of desire, a *sweeter* companion to man, whenever he chooses to relax himself. He carries the arguments, which he pretends to draw from the indications of nature, still further, and insinuates that truth and fortitude, the corner stones of all human virtue, should be cultivated with certain restrictions, because, with respect to the female character, obedience is the grand lesson which ought to be impressed with unrelenting rigor.[6]

What nonsense! when will a great man arise with sufficient strength of

4. The title of book 5 of Rousseau's *Émile*.
5. Similar feelings has Milton's pleasing picture of paradisiacal happiness ever raised in my mind; yet, instead of envying the lovely pair, I have, with conscious dignity, or Satanic pride, turned to hell for sublimer objects. In the same style, when viewing some noble monument of human art, I have traced the emanation of the Deity in the order I admired, till, descending from that giddy height, I have caught myself contemplating the grandest of all human sights;—for fancy quickly placed, in some

solitary recess, an outcast of fortune, rising superior to passion and discontent [Wollstonecraft's note].
6. Rousseau had written in *Émile*: "What is most wanted in a woman is gentleness; formed to obey a creature so imperfect as man, a creature often vicious and always faulty, she should early learn to submit to injustice and to suffer the wrongs inflicted on her by her husband without complaint."

mind to puff away the fumes which pride and sensuality have thus spread over the subject! If women are by nature inferior to men, their virtues must be the same in quality, if not in degree, or virtue is a relative idea; consequently, their conduct should be founded on the same principles, and have the same aim.

Connected with man as daughters, wives, and mothers, their moral character may be estimated by their manner of fulfilling those simple duties; but the end, the grand end of their exertions should be to unfold their own faculties and acquire the dignity of conscious virtue. They may try to render their road pleasant; but ought never to forget, in common with man, that life yields not the felicity which can satisfy an immortal soul. I do not mean to insinuate, that either sex should be so lost in abstract reflections or distant views, as to forget the affections and duties that lie before them, and are, in truth, the means appointed to produce the fruit of life; on the contrary, I would warmly recommend them, even while I assert, that they afford most satisfaction when they are considered in their true, sober light.

Probably the prevailing opinion, that woman was created for man, may have taken its rise from Moses's poetical story;[7] yet, as very few, it is presumed, who have bestowed any serious thought on the subject, ever supposed that Eve was, literally speaking, one of Adam's ribs, the deduction must be allowed to fall to the ground; or, only be so far admitted as it proves that man, from the remotest antiquity, found it convenient to exert his strength to subjugate his companion, and his invention to shew that she ought to have her neck bent under the yoke, because the whole creation was only created for his convenience or pleasure.

Let it not be concluded that I wish to invert the order of things; I have already granted, that, from the constitution of their bodies, men seem to be designed by Providence to attain a greater degree of virtue.[8] I speak collectively of the whole sex; but I see not the shadow of a reason to conclude that their virtues should differ in respect to their nature. In fact, how can they, if virtue has only one eternal standard? I must therefore, if I reason consequentially, as strenuously maintain that they have the same simple direction, as that there is a God.

It follows then that cunning should not be opposed to wisdom, little cares to great exertions, or insipid softness, varnished over with the name of gentleness, to that fortitude which grand views alone can inspire.

I shall be told that woman would then lose many of her peculiar graces, and the opinion of a well known poet might be quoted to refute my unqualified assertion. For Pope has said, in the name of the whole male sex,

> Yet ne'er so sure our passion to create,
> As when she touch'd the brink of all we hate.[9]

In what light this sally places men and women, I shall leave to the judicious to determine; meanwhile I shall content myself with observing, that I cannot discover why, unless they are mortal, females should always be degraded by being made subservient to love or lust.

7. The story of the creation of Eve from the rib of Adam (Genesis 2.21–22). Traditionally, the first five books of the Old Testament were attributed to the authorship of Moses.
8. In the third paragraph of her Introduction, Wollstonecraft had said that men are, in general, physically stronger than women.
9. Alexander Pope's Moral Essays 2, Of the Characters of Women, lines 51–52.

To speak disrespectfully of love is, I know, high treason against sentiment and fine feelings; but I wish to speak the simple language of truth, and rather to address the head than the heart. To endeavor to reason love out of the world, would be to out-Quixote Cervantes,[1] and equally offend against common sense; but an endeavor to restrain this tumultuous passion, and prove that it should not be allowed to dethrone superior powers, or to usurp the sceptre which the understanding should ever coolly wield, appears less wild.

Youth is the season for love in both sexes; but in those days of thoughtless enjoyment provision should be made for the more important years of life, when reflection takes place of sensation. But Rousseau, and most of the male writers who have followed his steps, have warmly inculcated that the whole tendency of female education ought to be directed to one point:—to render them pleasing.

Let me reason with the supporters of this opinion who have any knowledge of human nature, do they imagine that marriage can eradicate the habitude of life? The woman who has only been taught to please will soon find that her charms are oblique sunbeams, and that they cannot have much effect on her husband's heart when they are seen every day, when the summer is passed and gone. Will she then have sufficient native energy to look into herself for comfort, and cultivate her dormant faculties? or, is it not more rational to expect that she will try to please other men; and, in the emotions raised by the expectation of new conquests, endeavor to forget the mortification her love or pride has received? When the husband ceases to be a lover—and the time will inevitably come, her desire of pleasing will then grow languid, or become a spring of bitterness; and love, perhaps, the most evanescent of all passions, gives place to jealousy or vanity.

I now speak of women who are restrained by principle or prejudice; such women, though they would shrink from an intrigue with real abhorrence, yet, nevertheless, wish to be convinced by the homage of gallantry that they are cruelly neglected by their husbands; or, days and weeks are spent in dreaming of the happiness enjoyed by congenial souls till their health is undermined and their spirits broken by discontent. How then can the great art of pleasing be such a necessary study? it is only useful to a mistress; the chaste wife, and serious mother, should only consider her power to please as the polish of her virtues, and the affection of her husband as one of the comforts that render her task less difficult and her life happier.—But, whether she be loved or neglected, her first wish should be to make herself respectable,[2] and not to rely for all her happiness on a being subject to like infirmities with herself.

The worthy Dr. Gregory fell into a similar error. I respect his heart; but entirely disapprove of his celebrated Legacy to his Daughters.

He advises them to cultivate a fondness for dress, because a fondness for dress, he asserts, is natural to them. I am unable to comprehend what either he or Rousseau mean, when they frequently use this indefinite term.[3] If they told us that in a pre-existent state the soul was fond of dress, and brought this inclination with it into a new body, I should listen to them with a half smile, as I often do when I hear a rant about innate elegance.—But if he

---

1. I.e., to outdo the hero of Cervantes's *Don Quix-*
ote (1605) in trying to accomplish the impossible.

2. I.e., morally worthy of respect.

3. I.e., "natural."

only meant to say that the exercise of the faculties will produce this fondness—I deny it.—It is not natural; but arises, like false ambition in men, from a love of power.

Dr. Gregory goes much further; he actually recommends dissimulation, and advises an innocent girl to give the lie to her feelings, and not dance with spirit, when gaiety of heart would make her feel eloquent without making her gestures immodest. In the name of truth and common sense, why should not one woman acknowledge that she can take more exercise than another? or, in other words, that she has a sound constitution; and why, to damp innocent vivacity, is she darkly to be told that men will draw conclusions which she little thinks of?[4]—Let the libertine draw what inference he pleases; but, I hope, that no sensible mother will restrain the natural frankness of youth by instilling such indecent cautions. Out of the abundance of the heart the mouth speaketh;[5] and a wiser than Solomon hath said, that the heart should be made clean,[6] and not trivial ceremonies observed, which is not very difficult to fulfill with scrupulous exactness when vice reigns in the heart.

Women ought to endeavor to purify their heart; but can they do so when their uncultivated understandings make them entirely dependent on their senses for employment and amusement, when no noble pursuit sets them above the little vanities of the day, or enables them to curb the wild emotions that agitate a reed over which every passing breeze has power? To gain the affections of a virtuous man is affectation necessary? Nature has given woman a weaker frame than man; but, to ensure her husband's affections, must a wife, who by the exercise of her mind and body whilst she was discharging the duties of a daughter, wife, and mother, has allowed her constitution to retain its natural strength, and her nerves a healthy tone, is she, I say, to condescend to use art and feign a sickly delicacy in order to secure her husband's affection? Weakness may excite tenderness, and gratify the arrogant pride of man; but the lordly caresses of a protector will not gratify a noble mind that pants for, and deserves to be respected. Fondness is a poor substitute for friendship!

In a seraglio, I grant, that all these arts are necessary; the epicure must have his palate tickled, or he will sink into apathy; but have women so little ambition as to be satisfied with such a condition? Can they supinely dream life away in the lap of pleasure, or the languor of weariness, rather than assert their claim to pursue reasonable pleasures and render themselves conspicuous by practising the virtues which dignify mankind? Surely she has not an immortal soul who can loiter life away merely employed to adorn her person, that she may amuse the languid hours, and soften the cares of a fellow-creature who is willing to be enlivened by her smiles and tricks, when the serious business of life is over.

Besides, the woman who strengthens her body and exercises her mind will, by managing her family and practising various virtues, become the friend, and not the humble dependent of her husband; and if she, by possessing

4. In *A Father's Legacy to His Daughters*, Gregory had advised a girl, when she dances, not "to forget the delicacy of [her] sex," lest she be "thought to discover a spirit she little dreams of."
5. Matthew 12.34.

6. Psalm 24 (attributed to David, the "wiser than Solomon"), 3–4: "Who shall ascend into the hill of the Lord? or who shall stand in his holy place? He that hath clean hands, and a pure heart."

such substantial qualities, merit his regard, she will not find it necessary to conceal her affection, nor to pretend to an unnatural coldness of constitution to excite her husband's passions. In fact, if we revert to history, we shall find that the women who have distinguished themselves have neither been the most beautiful nor the most gentle of their sex.

Nature, or, to speak with strict propriety, God, has made all things right; but man has sought him out many inventions to mar the work. I now allude to that part of Dr. Gregory's treatise, where he advises a wife never to let her husband know the extent of her sensibility or affection. Voluptuous precaution, and as ineffectual as absurd.—Love, from its very nature, must be transitory. To seek for a secret that would render it constant, would be as wild a search as for the philosopher's stone, or the grand panacea:[7] and the discovery would be equally useless, or rather pernicious to mankind. The most holy band of society is friendship. It has been well said, by a shrewd satirist, "that rare as true love is, true friendship is still rarer."[8]

This is an obvious truth, and the cause not lying deep, will not elude a slight glance of inquiry.

Love, the common passion, in which chance and sensation take place of choice and reason, is, in some degree, felt by the mass of mankind; for it is not necessary to speak, at present, of the emotions that rise above or sink below love. This passion, naturally increased by suspense and difficulties, draws the mind out of its accustomed state, and exalts the affections; but the security of marriage, allowing the fever of love to subside, a healthy temperature is thought insipid, only by those who have not sufficient intellect to substitute the calm tenderness of friendship, the confidence of respect, instead of blind admiration, and the sensual emotions of fondness.

This is, must be, the course of nature.—Friendship or indifference inevitably succeeds love.—And this constitution seems perfectly to harmonize with the system of government which prevails in the moral world. Passions are spurs to action, and open the mind; but they sink into mere appetites, become a personal and momentary gratification, when the object is gained, and the satisfied mind rests in enjoyment. The man who had some virtue whilst he was struggling for a crown, often becomes a voluptuous tyrant when it graces his brow; and, when the lover is not lost in the husband, the dotard, a prey to childish caprices, and fond jealousies, neglects the serious duties of life, and the caresses which should excite confidence in his children are lavished on the overgrown child, his wife.

In order to fulfil the duties of life, and to be able to pursue with vigour the various employments which form the moral character, a master and mistress of a family ought not to continue to love each other with passion. I mean to say, that they ought not to indulge those emotions which disturb the order of society, and engross the thoughts that should be otherwise employed. The mind that has never been engrossed by one object wants vigor—if it can long be so, it is weak.

A mistaken education, a narrow, uncultivated mind, and many sexual prejudices, tend to make women more constant than men; but, for the present, I shall not touch on this branch of the subject. I will go still further, and

7. A medicine reputed to cure all diseases. "The philosopher's stone," in alchemy, had the power of transmuting base metals into gold.

8. Maxim 473 of La Rochefoucauld (1613–1680), the great French writer of epigrams.

advance, without dreaming of a paradox, that an unhappy marriage is often very advantageous to a family, and that the neglected wife is, in general, the best mother.[9] And this would almost always be the consequence if the female mind were more enlarged: for, it seems to be the common dispensation of Providence, that what we gain in present enjoyment should be deducted from the treasure of life, experience; and that when we are gathering the flowers of the day and revelling in pleasure, the solid fruit of toil and wisdom should not be caught at the same time. The way lies before us, we must turn to the right or left; and he who will pass life away in bounding from one pleasure to another, must not complain if he acquire neither wisdom nor respectability of character.

Supposing, for a moment, that the soul is not immortal, and that man was only created for the present scene,—I think we should have reason to complain that love, infantine fondness, ever grew insipid and palled upon the sense. Let us eat, drink, and love for to-morrow we die, would be, in fact, the language of reason, the morality of life; and who but a fool would part with a reality for a fleeting shadow? But, if awed by observing the improbable[1] powers of the mind, we disdain to confine our wishes or thoughts to such a comparatively mean field of action; that only appears grand and important, as it is connected with a boundless prospect and sublime hopes, what necessity is there for falsehood in conduct, and why must the sacred majesty of truth be violated to detain a deceitful good that saps the very foundation of virtue? Why must the female mind be tainted by coquetish arts to gratify the sensualist, and prevent love from subsiding into friendship, or compassionate tenderness, when there are not qualities on which friendship can be built? Let the honest heart shew itself, and *reason* teach passion to submit to necessity; or, let the dignified pursuit of virtue and knowledge raise the mind above those emotions which rather imbitter than sweeten the cup of life, when they are not restrained within due bounds.

I do not mean to allude to the romantic passion, which is the concomitant of genius.—Who can clip its wing? But that grand passion not proportioned to the puny enjoyments of life, is only true to the sentiment, and feeds on itself. The passions which have been celebrated for their durability have always been unfortunate. They have acquired strength by absence and constitutional melancholy.—The fancy has hovered around a form of beauty dimly seen—but familiarity might have turned admiration into disgust; or, at least, into indifference, and allowed the imagination leisure to start fresh game. With perfect propriety, according to his view of things, does Rousseau make the mistress of his soul, Eloisa, love St. Preux, when life was fading before her;[2] but this is no proof of the immortality of the passion.

Of the same complexion is Dr. Gregory's advice respecting delicacy of sentiment,[3] which he advises a woman not to acquire, if she have determined to marry. This determination, however, perfectly consistent with his former

9. Wollstonecraft's point is that a woman who is not preoccupied with her husband (and his attentions to her) has more time and attention for her children.

1. Poston points out that this may be a misprint in the second edition for "improvable," which occurs in the first edition.

2. In Rousseau's *Julie, ou la Nouvelle Héloise* (1761), Julie, after a life of fidelity to her husband, reveals on her deathbed that she has never lost her passion for St. Preux, her lover when she was young. Wollstonecraft accepts the common opinion that Julie represents Madame d'Houdetot, with whom Rousseau was in love when he wrote the novel.

3. I.e., too elevated and refined a notion of what to expect in a man.

advice, he calls *indelicate*, and earnestly persuades his daughters to conceal it, though it may govern their conduct;—as if it were indelicate to have the common appetites of human nature.

Noble morality! and consistent with the cautious prudence of a little soul that cannot extend its views beyond the present minute division of existence. If all the faculties of woman's mind are only to be cultivated as they respect her dependence on man; if, when a husband be obtained, she have arrived at her goal, and meanly proud rests satisfied with such a paltry crown, let her grovel contentedly, scarcely raised by her employments above the animal kingdom; but, if, struggling for the prize of her high calling, she look beyond the present scene, let her cultivate her understanding without stopping to consider what character the husband may have whom she is destined to marry. Let her only determine, without being too anxious about present happiness, to acquire the qualities that ennoble a rational being, and a rough inelegant husband may shock her taste without destroying her peace of mind. She will not model her soul to suit the frailties of her companion, but to bear with them: his character may be a trial, but not an impediment to virtue.

If Dr. Gregory confined his remark to romantic expectations of constant love and congenial feelings, he should have recollected that experience will banish what advice can never make us cease to wish for, when the imagination is kept alive at the expence of reason.

I own it frequently happens that women who have fostered a romantic unnatural delicacy of feeling, waste their[4] lives in *imagining* how happy they should have been with a husband who could love them with a fervid increasing affection every day, and all day. But they might as well pine married as single—and would not be a jot more unhappy with a bad husband than longing for a good one. That a proper education; or, to speak with more precision, a well stored mind, would enable a woman to support a single life with dignity, I grant; but that she should avoid cultivating her taste, lest her husband should occasionally shock it, is quitting a substance for a shadow. To say the truth, I do not know of what use is an improved taste, if the individual be not rendered more independent of the casualties of life; if new sources of enjoyment, only dependent on the solitary operations of the mind, are not opened. People of taste, married or single, without distinction, will ever be disgusted by various things that touch not less observing minds. On this conclusion the argument must not be allowed to hinge; but in the whole sum of enjoyment is taste to be denominated a blessing?

The question is, whether it procures most pain or pleasure? The answer will decide the propriety of Dr. Gregory's advice, and shew how absurd and tyrannic it is thus to lay down a system of slavery; or to attempt to educate moral beings by any other rules than those deduced from pure reason, which apply to the whole species.

Gentleness of manners, forbearance, and long-suffering, are such amiable Godlike qualities, that in sublime poetic strains the Deity has been invested with them; and, perhaps, no representation of his goodness so strongly fastens on the human affections as those that represent him abundant in mercy and willing to pardon. Gentleness, considered in this point of view, bears on

---

4. For example, the herd of Novelists [Wollstonecraft's note]. The author's reference is to women who have formed their expectations of love as it is misrepresented in the sentimental novels of their time.

its front all the characteristics of grandeur, combined with the winning graces of condescension; but what a different aspect it assumes when it is the submissive demeanour of dependence, the support of weakness that loves, because it wants protection; and is forbearing, because it must silently endure injuries; smiling under the lash at which it dare not snarl. Abject as this picture appears, it is the portrait of an accomplished woman, according to the received opinion of female excellence, separated by specious reasoners from human excellence. Or, they[5] kindly restore the rib, and make one moral being of a man and woman; not forgetting to give her all the "submissive charms."[6] How women are to exist in that state where there is to be neither marrying nor giving in marriage,[7] we are not told. For though moralists have agreed that the tenor of life seems to prove that *man* is prepared by various circumstances for a future state, they constantly concur in advising *woman* only to provide for the present. Gentleness, docility, and a spaniel-like affection are, on this ground, consistently recommended as the cardinal virtues of the sex; and, disregarding the arbitrary economy of nature, one writer has declared that it is masculine for a woman to be melancholy. She was created to be the toy of man, his rattle, and it must jingle in his ears whenever, dismissing reason, he chooses to be amused.

To recommend gentleness, indeed, on a broad basis is strictly philosophical. A frail being should labor to be gentle. But when forbearance confounds right and wrong, it ceases to be a virtue; and, however convenient it may be found in a companion—that companion will ever be considered as an inferior, and only inspire a vapid tenderness, which easily degenerates into contempt. Still, if advice could really make a being gentle, whose natural disposition admitted not of such a fine polish, something towards the advancement of order would be attained; but if, as might quickly be demonstrated, only affectation be produced by this indiscriminate counsel, which throws a stumbling-block in the way of gradual improvement, and true melioration of temper, the sex is not much benefited by sacrificing solid virtues to the attainment of superficial graces, though for a few years they may procure the individuals regal sway.

As a philosopher, I read with indignation the plausible epithets which men use to soften their insults; and, as a moralist, I ask what is meant by such heterogeneous associations, as fair defects, amiable weaknesses, &c.?[8] If there be but one criterion of morals, but one archetype of man, women appear to be suspended by destiny, according to the vulgar tale of Mahomet's coffin;[9] they have neither the unerring instinct of brutes, nor are allowed to fix the eye of reason on a perfect model. They were made to be loved, and must not aim at respect, lest they should be hunted out of society as masculine.

But to view the subject in another point of view. Do passive indolent

---

5. *Vide* [see] Rousseau and Swedenborg [Wollstonecraft's note]. Rousseau's view was that a wife constituted an integral moral being only in concert with her husband. Emanuel Swedenborg (1688–1772), the Swedish theosophist, held that in the married state in heaven male and female are embodied in a single angelic form.
6. Milton says of Adam and Eve in *Paradise Lost* 4.497–99 that "he in delight / Both of her beauty and submissive charms / Smiled with superior love."
7. "For in the resurrection they neither marry, nor are given in marriage, but are as the angels of God in heaven" (Matthew 22.30).
8. In *Paradise Lost* 10.891–92 the fallen Adam refers to Eve as "this fair defect / Of Nature"; and in *Moral Essays* 2.43 Pope describes women as "Fine by defect, and delicately weak."
9. A legend has it that Mohammed's coffin hovers suspended in his tomb.

women make the best wives? Confining our discussion to the present moment of existence, let us see how such weak creatures perform their part. Do the women who, by the attainment of a few superficial accomplishments, have strengthened the prevailing prejudice, merely contribute to the happiness of their husbands? Do they display their charms merely to amuse them? And have women, who have early imbibed notions of passive obedience, sufficient character to manage a family or educate children? So far from it, that, after surveying the history of woman, I cannot help, agreeing with the severest satirist, considering the sex as the weakest as well as the most oppressed half of the species. What does history disclose but marks of inferiority, and how few women have emancipated themselves from the galling yoke of sovereign man?—So few, that the exceptions remind me of an ingenious conjecture respecting Newton: that he was probably a being of a superior order, accidentally caged in a human body.[1] Following the same train of thinking, I have been led to imagine that the few extraordinary women who have rushed in eccentrical directions out of the orbit prescribed to their sex, were *male* spirits, confined by mistake in female frames. But if it be not philosophical to think of sex when the soul is mentioned, the inferiority must depend on the organs; or the heavenly fire, which is to ferment the clay, is not given in equal portions.

But avoiding, as I have hitherto done, any direct comparison of the two sexes collectively, or frankly acknowledging the inferiority of woman, according to the present appearance of things, I shall only insist that men have increased that inferiority till women are almost sunk below the standard of rational creatures. Let their faculties have room to unfold, and their virtues to gain strength, and then determine where the whole sex must stand in the intellectual scale. Yet let it be remembered, that for a small number of distinguished women I do not ask a place.

It is difficult for us purblind mortals to say to what height human discoveries and improvements may arrive when the gloom of despotism subsides, which makes us stumble at every step; but, when morality shall be settled on a more solid basis, then, without being gifted with a prophetic spirit, I will venture to predict that woman will be either the friend or slave of man. We shall not, as at present, doubt whether she is a moral agent, or the link which unites man with brutes.[2] But, should it then appear, that like the brutes they were principally created for the use of man, he will let them patiently bite the bridle, and not mock them with empty praise; or, should their rationality be proved, he will not impede their improvement merely to gratify his sensual appetites. He will not, with all the graces of rhetoric, advise them to submit implicitly their understanding to the guidance of man. He will not, when he treats of the education of women, assert that they ought never to have the free use of reason, nor would he recommend cunning and dissimulation to beings who are acquiring, in like manner as himself, the virtues of humanity.

1. A possible reminiscence of Pope's *An Essay on Man* 2.31–34: "Superior beings [i.e., angels] . . . / Admired such wisdom in an earthly shape, / And showed a Newton as we show an ape."
2. Rousseau doubted that a woman, of herself, was a moral agent. There had been a long dispute about the question of woman being part of humankind. In the *Summa Theologica* (Question XVII, Art. 1) St. Thomas Aquinas concedes, with Aris-

totle, that the "production of woman comes from a defect in the active power, or from some material indisposition, or even from some external influence, such as that of a south wind, which is moist" (English Dominican translation of St. Thomas, edited by Anton C. Pegis, *The Basic Writings of Saint Thomas Aquinas* [New York, 1945], I, 880) [Poston's note].

Surely there can be but one rule of right, if morality has an eternal foundation, and whoever sacrifices virtue, strictly so called, to present convenience, or whose *duty* it is to act in such a manner, lives only for the passing day, and cannot be an accountable creature.

The poet then should have dropped his sneer when he says,

> If weak women go astray,
> The stars are more in fault than they.[3]

For that they are bound by the adamantine chain of destiny is most certain, if it be proved that they are never to exercise their own reason, never to be independent, never to rise above opinion, or to feel the dignity of a rational will that only bows to God, and often forgets that the universe contains any being but itself and the model of perfection to which its ardent gaze is turned, to adore attributes that, softened into virtues, may be imitated in kind, though the degree overwhelms the enraptured mind.

If, I say, for I would not impress by declamation when Reason offers her sober light, if they be really capable of acting like rational creatures, let them not be treated like slaves; or, like the brutes who are dependent on the reason of man, when they associate with him; but cultivate their minds, give them the salutary, sublime curb of principle, and let them attain conscious dignity by feeling themselves only dependent on God. Teach them, in common with man, to submit to necessity, instead of giving, to render them more pleasing, a sex to morals.

Further, should experience prove that they cannot attain the same degree of strength of mind, perseverance, and fortitude, let their virtues be the same in kind, though they may vainly struggle for the same degree; and the superiority of man will be equally clear, if not clearer; and truth, as it is a simple principle, which admits of no modification, would be common to both. Nay, the order of society as it is at present regulated would not be inverted, for woman would then only have the rank that reason assigned her, and arts could not be practised to bring the balance even, much less to turn it.

These may be termed Utopian dreams.—Thanks to that Being who impressed them on my soul, and gave me sufficient strength of mind to dare to exert my own reason, till, becoming dependent only on him for the support of my virtue, I view, with indignation, the mistaken notions that enslave my sex.

I love man as my fellow; but his scepter, real or usurped, extends not to me, unless the reason of an individual demands my homage; and even then the submission is to reason, and not to man. In fact, the conduct of an accountable being must be regulated by the operations of its own reason; or on what foundation rests the throne of God?

It appears to me necessary to dwell on these obvious truths, because females have been insulated, as it were; and, while they have been stripped of the virtues that should clothe humanity, they have been decked with artificial graces that enable them to exercise a short-lived tyranny. Love, in their bosoms, taking place of every nobler passion, their sole ambition is to be fair, to raise emotion instead of inspiring respect; and this ignoble desire, like the servility in absolute monarchies, destroys all strength of character. Liberty

3. Matthew Prior, *Hans Carvel*, lines 11–12, alluding to *Julius Caesar* 1.2.141–42: "The fault, dear Brutus, is not in our stars, / But in ourselves."

is the mother of virtue, and if women be, by their very constitution, slaves, and not allowed to breathe the sharp invigorating air of freedom, they must ever languish like exotics, and be reckoned beautiful flaws in nature.

As to the argument respecting the subjection in which the sex has ever been held, it retorts on man. The many have always been enthralled by the few; and monsters, who scarcely have shewn any discernment of human excellence, have tyrannized over thousands of their fellow-creatures. Why have men of superiour endowments submitted to such degradation? For, is it not universally acknowledged that kings, viewed collectively, have ever been inferior, in abilities and virtue, to the same number of men taken from the common mass of mankind—yet, have they not, and are they not still treated with a degree of reverence that is an insult to reason? China is not the only country where a living man has been made a God.[4] *Men* have submitted to superior strength to enjoy with impunity the pleasure of the moment—*women* have only done the same, and therefore till it is proved that the courtier, who servilely resigns the birthright of a man, is not a moral agent, it cannot be demonstrated that woman is essentially inferior to man because she has always been subjugated.

Brutal force has hitherto governed the world, and that the science of politics is in its infancy, is evident from philosophers scrupling to give the knowledge most useful to man that determinate distinction.

I shall not pursue this argument any further than to establish an obvious inference, that as sound politics diffuse liberty, mankind, including woman, will become more wise and virtuous.

1792

4. The emperors of China were regarded as deities.

WILLIAM WORDSWORTH
1770–1850

William Wordsworth was born in Cockermouth in West Cumberland, just on the northern fringe of the English Lake District. When his mother died, the eight-year-old boy was sent to school at Hawkshead, near Esthwaite Lake, in the heart of that thinly settled region that he and Coleridge were to transform into one of the poetic centers of England. William and his three brothers boarded in the cottage of Ann Tyson, who gave the boys simple comfort, ample affection, and freedom to roam the countryside at will. A vigorous, unruly, and sometimes moody boy, William spent his free days and occasionally "half the night" in the sports and rambles described in the first two books of *The Prelude*, "drinking in" (to use one of his favorite metaphors) the natural sights and sounds, and getting to know the cottagers, shepherds, and solitary wanderers who moved through his imagination into his later poetry. He also found time to read voraciously in the books owned by his young headmaster, William Taylor, who encouraged him in his inclination to poetry.

John Wordsworth, the poet's father, died suddenly when William was thirteen, leaving to his five children mainly the substantial sum owed him by Lord Lonsdale, whom he had served as attorney and as steward of the huge Lonsdale estate. That harsh and litigious nobleman managed to keep from paying the debt until he died in

1802. Wordsworth was nevertheless able to enter St. John's College, Cambridge, in 1787, where he found little in the limited curriculum of that time to appeal to him. He took his degree in 1791 without distinction.

During the summer vacation of his third year at Cambridge (1790), Wordsworth and his closest college friend, the Welshman Robert Jones, journeyed on foot through France and the Alps (described in *The Prelude* 6) at the time when the French were joyously celebrating the first anniversary of the fall of the Bastille. Upon completing his course at Cambridge, Wordsworth spent four months in London, set off on another walking tour with Robert Jones through Wales (the time of the memorable ascent of Mount Snowdon in *The Prelude* 14), and then went back alone to France to master the language and qualify as a traveling tutor.

During his year in France (November 1791 to December 1792) Wordsworth became a fervent "democrat" and proselyte of the French Revolution—which seemed to him, as to many other generous spirits, to promise a "glorious renovation"—and he fell in love with Annette Vallon, the impetuous and warm-hearted daughter of a French surgeon at Blois. It is clear that the two planned to marry, despite their differences in religion and political inclinations (Annette belonged to an old Catholic family whose sympathies were Royalist). But almost immediately after a daughter, Caroline, was born, lack of funds forced Wordsworth to return to England. The outbreak of war between England and France made it impossible for him to rejoin Annette until they had drifted so far apart in sympathies that a permanent union no longer seemed desirable. Wordsworth's agonies of guilt, his divided loyalties between England and France, his gradual disillusion with the course of the Revolution in France—according to his account in *The Prelude* 10 and 11—brought him to the verge of an emotional breakdown, when "sick, wearied out with contrarieties," he "yielded up moral questions in despair." His suffering, his near-collapse, and the successful effort, after his break with his past, to reestablish "a saving intercourse with my true self," are the experiences that underlie many of his greatest poems.

At this critical point a young friend, Raisley Calvert, died and left Wordsworth a sum of money just sufficient to enable him to live by his poetry. He settled in a rent-free house at Racedown, Dorsetshire, with his beloved sister, Dorothy, who now began her long career as confidante, inspirer, and secretary. At that same time Wordsworth met Samuel Taylor Coleridge; two years later he moved to Alfoxden House, Somersetshire, to be near Coleridge, who lived four miles away at Nether Stowey. Here he entered at the age of twenty-seven on the delayed springtime of his poetic career.

Even while he had been an undergraduate at Cambridge, Coleridge claimed that he had detected signs of genius in Wordsworth's rather conventional poem about his tour in the Alps, *Descriptive Sketches*, published in 1793. Now he hailed Wordsworth unreservedly as "the best poet of the age." The two men met almost daily, talked for hours about poetry, and composed prolifically. So close was their association that we find the same phrases occurring in poems by Wordsworth and Coleridge, as well as in the remarkable journals that Dorothy kept at the time; the two poets collaborated in some writings and freely traded thoughts and passages for others; and Coleridge even undertook to complete a few poems that Wordsworth had left unfinished.

The result of their joint efforts was a small volume, published anonymously in 1798, *Lyrical Ballads, with a Few Other Poems*. It opened with Coleridge's *Ancient Mariner;* included three other poems by Coleridge, a number of Wordsworth's verse anecdotes and psychological studies of humble people, and some lyrics in which Wordsworth celebrated impulses from a vernal wood; and closed with Wordsworth's great descriptive and meditative poem in blank verse (not a "lyrical ballad," but one of the "other poems" of the title), *Tintern Abbey*. In this last poem, Wordsworth inaugurated what some critics call his "myth of nature"; that is, his presentation of the "growth" of his mind to maturity, and the development of his emotional and moral life, as an interaction between his mind and the outer world. The volume of *Lyrical Ballads* clearly announces a new literary departure. William Hazlitt said that when he heard Coleridge read some of these newly written poems aloud, "the sense of a new style and a new spirit in poetry came over me," with something of the effect "that arises from the turning up of the fresh soil, or of the first welcome breath of spring." The professional reviewers were less enthusiastic. Nevertheless *Lyrical Ballads* sold out in two years, and Wordsworth published under his own name a new edition, dated 1800, to which he added a second volume of poems, many of them written in homesickness during a long, cold, and friendless winter that he and Dorothy had spent in Goslar, Germany, 1798–99. In his famous Preface to this edition, planned, like so many of the poems, in close consultation with Coleridge, Wordsworth enunciated the principles of the new criticism that served as rationale for the new poetry. Notable among the other works written in this prolific period is his austere and powerful tragic poem *The Ruined Cottage*.

Late in 1799 Wordsworth and Dorothy moved back permanently to their native lakes, settling at Grasmere in the little house later named Dove Cottage. Coleridge, following them, rented Greta Hall at Keswick, thirteen miles away. In 1802 Wordsworth finally came into his father's inheritance and, after an amicable settlement with Annette Vallon, married Mary Hutchinson, a Lake Country woman whom he had known since childhood. The course of his existence after that time was broken by various disasters: the drowning in 1805 of his favorite brother, John, a sea captain whose ship was wrecked in a storm; the death of two of his five children in 1812; a growing estrangement from Coleridge, culminating in a bitter quarrel (1810) from which they were not completely reconciled for almost two decades; and from the 1830s on, the physical and mental decline of his sister, Dorothy. The life of his middle age, however, was one of steadily increasing prosperity and reputation, as well as of political and religious conservatism. In 1813 an appointment as Stamp Distributor (that is, revenue collector) for Westmorland was concrete evidence of his recognition as a national poet. Gradually his residences, as he moved into more and more commodious quarters, became standard stops for tourists; he was awarded honorary degrees and, in 1843, was appointed poet laureate. He died in 1850 at the age of eighty; only then did his executors publish his masterpiece, *The Prelude*, the autobiographical poem that he had written in two parts in 1799, expanded to its full length in 1805, and then continued to revise almost to the last decade of his long life.

Most of Wordsworth's greatest poetry had been written by 1807, when he published *Poems in Two Volumes;* and after *The Excursion* (1814) and the first collected edition of his poems (1815), although he continued to write voluminously, there is an overall decline in his powers. The causes of the decline have been much debated; an important one seems to be inherent in the very nature of his most characteristic writing. Wordsworth is above all the poet of the remembrance of things past, or as he himself put it, of "emotion recollected in tranquillity." Some object or event in the present triggers a sudden renewal of feelings he had experienced in youth; the result is a poem exhibiting the sharp discrepancy between what Wordsworth called "two consciousnesses": himself as he is now and himself as he once was. But the memory of one's early emotional experience is not an inexhaustible resource for poetry, as Wordsworth himself recognized. He said in *The Prelude* 12, while describing the recurrence of "spots of time" from his memories of childhood:

> The days gone by
> Return upon me almost from the dawn
> Of life: the hiding places of Man's power
> Open; I would approach them, but they close.
> I see by glimpses now; when age comes on,
> May scarcely see at all.

The past that Wordsworth recollected was one of moments of intense experience, and of emotional turmoil which is ordered, in the calmer present, into a hard-won equilibrium. As time went on, however, he gained what, in the *Ode to Duty* (composed in 1804), he longed for, "a repose which ever is the same"—but at the expense of the agony and excitation which, under the calm surface, empowers his best and most characteristic poems.

Occasionally, in his middle and later life a jolting experience would revive the intensity of Wordsworth's remembered emotion, and also his earlier poetic strength. The moving sonnet *Surprised by Joy,* for example, was written in his forties at the abrupt realization that time was beginning to diminish his grief at the death some years earlier of his little daughter Catherine. And when Wordsworth was sixty-five years old, the sudden report of the death of James Hogg called up the memory of other and greater poets whom Wordsworth had loved and outlived; the result was his *Extempore Effusion,* written in a return to the simple quatrains of the early *Lyrical Ballads* and with a recovery of the elegiac voice that had uttered the dirges to Lucy, thirty-five years before.

From Lyrical Ballads

We Are Seven[1]

"Twelve steps or more from my mother's door,

————A simple Child,
That lightly draws its breath,
And feels its life in every limb,
What should it know of death?

5   I met a little cottage Girl:
She was eight years old, she said;
Her hair was thick with many a curl
That clustered round her head.

She had a rustic, woodland air,
10   And she was wildly clad:
Her eyes were fair, and very fair;
—Her beauty made me glad.

"Sisters and brothers, little Maid,
How many may you be?"
15   "How many? Seven in all," she said,
And wondering looked at me.

"And where are they? I pray you tell."
She answered, "Seven are we;
And two of us at Conway[2] dwell,
20   And two are gone to sea.

"Two of us in the church-yard lie,
My sister and my brother;

1. Written at Alfoxden in the spring of 1798. . . . The little girl who is the heroine I met within the area of Goodrich Castle [in the Wye Valley north of Tintern Abbey] in the year 1793 [Wordsworth's note]. Wordsworth also tells us that he composed the last line of the last stanza first, and that Coleridge contributed the initial stanza.
2. A seaport town in north Wales.

And, in the church-yard cottage, I
Dwell near them with my mother."

25   "You say that two at Conway dwell,
And two are gone to sea,
Yet ye are seven! I pray you tell,
Sweet Maid, how this may be."

Then did the little Maid reply,
30   "Seven boys and girls are we;
Two of us in the church-yard lie,
Beneath the church-yard tree."

"You run about, my little Maid,
Your limbs they are alive;
35   If two are in the church-yard laid,
Then ye are only five."

"Their graves are green, they may be seen,"
The little Maid replied,
"Twelve steps or more from my mother's door,
40   And they are side by side.

"My stockings there I often knit,
My kerchief there I hem;
And there upon the ground I sit,
And sing a song to them.

45   "And often after sun-set, Sir,
When it is light and fair,
I take my little porringer,[3]
And eat my supper there.

"The first that died was sister Jane;
50   In bed she moaning lay,
Till God released her of her pain;
And then she went away.

"So in the church-yard she was laid;
And, when the grass was dry,
55   Together round her grave we played,
My brother John and I.

"And when the ground was white with snow,
And I could run and slide,
My brother John was forced to go,
60   And he lies by her side."

3. Bowl for porridge.

"How many are you, then," said I,
"If they two are in heaven?"
Quick was the little Maid's reply,
"O Master! we are seven."

65   "But they are dead; those two are dead!
Their spirits are in heaven!"
'Twas throwing words away; for still
The little Maid would have her will,
And said, "Nay, we are seven!"

1798   1798

Lines Written in Early Spring

I heard a thousand blended notes,
While in a grove I sate reclined,
In that sweet mood when pleasant thoughts
Bring sad thoughts to the mind.

5   To her fair works did Nature link
The human soul that through me ran;
And much it grieved my heart to think
What man has made of man.

Through primrose tufts, in that green bower,
10   The periwinkle[1] trailed its wreaths,
And 'tis my faith that every flower
Enjoys the air it breathes.

The birds around me hopped and played,
Their thoughts I cannot measure:—
15   But the least motion which they made,
It seemed a thrill of pleasure.

The budding twigs spread out their fan,
To catch the breezy air;
And I must think, do all I can,
20   That there was pleasure there.

If this belief from heaven be sent,
If such be Nature's holy plan,[2]
Have I not reason to lament
What man has made of man?

1798   1798

1. A trailing evergreen plant with small blue flowers (U.S. myrtle).
2. The version of these two lines in the *Lyrical Ballads* of 1798 reads: "If I these thoughts may not prevent, / If such be of my creed the plan."

Expostulation and Reply[1]

"Why, William, on that old grey stone,
Thus for the length of half a day,
Why, William, sit you thus alone,
And dream your time away?

5 "Where are your books?—that light bequeathed
To Beings else forlorn and blind!
Up! up! and drink the spirit breathed
From dead men to their kind.

"You look round on your Mother Earth,
10 As if she for no purpose bore you;
As if you were her first-born birth,
And none had lived before you!"

One morning thus, by Esthwaite lake,
When life was sweet, I knew not why,
15 To me my good friend Matthew spake,
And thus I made reply.

"The eye—it cannot choose but see;
We cannot bid the ear be still;
Our bodies feel, where'er they be,
20 Against or with our will.

"Nor less I deem that there are Powers
Which of themselves our minds impress;
That we can feed this mind of ours
In a wise passiveness.

25 "Think you, 'mid all this mighty sum
Of things for ever speaking,
That nothing of itself will come,
But we must still be seeking?

"—Then ask not wherefore, here, alone,
30 Conversing[2] as I may,
I sit upon this old grey stone,
And dream my time away."

Spring 1798   1798

---

1. This and the following companion poem have often been attacked—and defended—as Wordsworth's solemn deliverance on the comparative merits of nature and of books. But they are a dialogue between two friends who rally one another by the usual device of overstating parts of a whole truth. Wordsworth said that the pieces originated in a conversation "with a friend who was somewhat unreasonably attached to modern books of moral philosophy," and also that the lore of "a wise passiveness" made the poem a favorite among Quakers.
2. In the old sense of "communing" (with the "things for ever speaking").

The Tables Turned

An Evening Scene on the Same Subject

Up! up! my Friend, and quit your books;
Or surely you'll grow double:
Up! up! my Friend, and clear your looks;
Why all this toil and trouble?

5 The sun, above the mountain's head,
A freshening lustre mellow
Through all the long green fields has spread,
His first sweet evening yellow.

Books! 'tis a dull and endless strife:
10 Come, hear the woodland linnet,°   *small finch*
How sweet his music! on my life,
There's more of wisdom in it.

And hark! how blithe the throstle° sings!   *song thrush*
He, too, is no mean preacher:
15 Come forth into the light of things,
Let Nature be your Teacher.

She has a world of ready wealth,
Our minds and hearts to bless—
Spontaneous wisdom breathed by health,
20 Truth breathed by cheerfulness.

One impulse from a vernal wood
May teach you more of man,
Of moral evil and of good,
Than all the sages can.

25 Sweet is the lore which Nature brings;
Our meddling intellect
Mis-shapes the beauteous forms of things:—
We murder to dissect.

Enough of Science and of Art;
30 Close up those barren leaves;
Come forth, and bring with you a heart
That watches and receives.

1798   1798

Lines[1]

Composed a Few Miles above Tintern Abbey, on Revisiting the Banks of the Wye during a Tour, July 13, 1798

Five years have past; five summers, with the length
Of five long winters! and again I hear
These waters, rolling from their mountain-springs
With a soft inland murmur.—Once again
5   Do I behold these steep and lofty cliffs,
That on a wild secluded scene impress
Thoughts of more deep seclusion; and connect
The landscape with the quiet of the sky.
The day is come when I again repose
10 Here, under this dark sycamore, and view
These plots of cottage-ground, these orchard-tufts,
Which at this season, with their unripe fruits,
Are clad in one green hue, and lose themselves
'Mid groves and copses. Once again I see
15 These hedge-rows, hardly hedge-rows, little lines
Of sportive wood run wild: these pastoral farms,
Green to the very door; and wreaths of smoke
Sent up, in silence, from among the trees!
With some uncertain notice, as might seem
20 Of vagrant dwellers in the houseless woods,
Or of some Hermit's cave, where by his fire
The Hermit sits alone.

                  These beauteous forms,
Through a long absence, have not been to me
As is a landscape to a blind man's eye:
25 But oft, in lonely rooms, and 'mid the din
Of towns and cities, I have owed to them
In hours of weariness, sensations sweet,
Felt in the blood, and felt along the heart;
And passing even into my purer mind,
30 With tranquil restoration:—feelings too
Of unremembered pleasure: such, perhaps,
As have no slight or trivial influence
On that best portion of a good man's life,
His little, nameless, unremembered, acts
35 Of kindness and of love. Nor less, I trust,
To them I may have owed another gift,

1. No poem of mine was composed under circumstances more pleasant for me to remember than this. I began it upon leaving Tintern, after crossing the Wye, and concluded it just as I was entering Bristol in the evening, after a ramble of 4 or 5 days, with my sister. Not a line of it was altered, and not any part of it written down till I reached Bristol [Wordsworth's note]. The poem was printed as the last item in *Lyrical Ballads*.

Wordsworth had first visited the Wye valley and the ruins of Tintern Abbey, in Monmouthshire, while on a solitary walking tour in August 1793, when he was twenty-three years old. The puzzling difference between the present landscape and the remembered "picture of the mind" (line 61) gives rise to an intricately organized meditation, in which the poet reviews his past, evaluates the present, and (through his sister as intermediary) anticipates the future; he ends by rounding back quietly on the scene that had been his point of departure.

Of aspect more sublime; that blessed mood,
In which the burthen of the mystery,
In which the heavy and the weary weight
40 Of all this unintelligible world,
Is lightened:—that serene and blessed mood,
In which the affections gently lead us on,—
Until, the breath of this corporeal frame
And even the motion of our human blood
45 Almost suspended, we are laid asleep
In body, and become a living soul:
While with an eye made quiet by the power
Of harmony, and the deep power of joy,
We see into the life of things.

                                        If this
50 Be but a vain belief, yet, oh! how oft—
In darkness and amid the many shapes
Of joyless daylight; when the fretful stir
Unprofitable, and the fever of the world,
Have hung upon the beatings of my heart—
55 How oft, in spirit, have I turned to thee,
O sylvan Wye! thou wanderer thro' the woods,
How often has my spirit turned to thee!

     And now, with gleams of half-extinguished thought,
With many recognitions dim and faint,
60 And somewhat of a sad perplexity,
The picture of the mind revives again:
While here I stand, not only with the sense
Of present pleasure, but with pleasing thoughts
That in this moment there is life and food
65 For future years. And so I dare to hope,
Though changed, no doubt, from what I was when first
I came among these hills; when like a roe
I bounded o'er the mountains, by the sides
Of the deep rivers, and the lonely streams,
70 Wherever nature led: more like a man
Flying from something that he dreads, than one
Who sought the thing he loved. For nature then
(The coarser pleasures of my boyish days,
And their glad animal movements all gone by)
75 To me was all in all.—I cannot paint
What then I was. The sounding cataract
Haunted me like a passion: the tall rock,
The mountain, and the deep and gloomy wood,
Their colours and their forms, were then to me
80 An appetite; a feeling and a love,
That had no need of a remoter charm,
By thought supplied, nor any interest
Unborrowed from the eye.—That time is past,
And all its aching joys are now no more,

85　And all its dizzy raptures.[2] Not for this
　　Faint° I, nor mourn nor murmur; other gifts　　　　　　　　*lose heart*
　　Have followed; for such loss, I would believe,
　　Abundant recompense. For I have learned
　　To look on nature, not as in the hour
90　Of thoughtless youth; but hearing oftentimes
　　The still, sad music of humanity,
　　Nor harsh nor grating, though of ample power
　　To chasten and subdue. And I have felt
　　A presence that disturbs me with the joy
95　Of elevated thoughts; a sense sublime
　　Of something far more deeply interfused,
　　Whose dwelling is the light of setting suns,
　　And the round ocean and the living air,
　　And the blue sky, and in the mind of man:
100　A motion and a spirit, that impels
　　All thinking things, all objects of all thought,
　　And rolls through all things. Therefore am I still
　　A lover of the meadows and the woods,
　　And mountains; and of all that we behold
105　From this green earth; of all the mighty world
　　Of eye, and ear,—both what they half create,[3]
　　And what perceive; well pleased to recognise
　　In nature and the language of the sense,
　　The anchor of my purest thoughts, the nurse,
110　The guide, the guardian of my heart, and soul
　　Of all my moral being.

　　　　　　　　　　　　Nor perchance,
　　If I were not thus taught, should I the more
　　Suffer my genial spirits[4] to decay:
　　For thou art with me here upon the banks
115　Of this fair river; thou my dearest Friend,[5]
　　My dear, dear Friend; and in thy voice I catch
　　The language of my former heart, and read
　　My former pleasures in the shooting lights
　　Of thy wild eyes. Oh! yet a little while
120　May I behold in thee what I was once,
　　My dear, dear Sister! and this prayer I make,
　　Knowing that Nature never did betray
　　The heart that loved her; 'tis her privilege,
　　Through all the years of this our life, to lead
125　From joy to joy: for she can so inform
　　The mind that is within us, so impress
　　With quietness and beauty, and so feed

---

2. Lines 66ff. contain Wordsworth's famed description of the three stages of his growing up, defined in terms of his evolving relations to the natural scene: the young boy's purely physical responsiveness (lines 73–74); the postadolescent's aching, dizzy, and equivocal passions—a love that is more like dread (lines 67–72, 75–85: this was his state of mind on the occasion of his first visit);

his present state (lines 85ff.), in which for the first time he adds thought to sense.
3. This view that the "creative sensibility" contributes to its own perceptions is often reiterated in *The Prelude*.
4. Creative powers. ("Genial" is here the adjectival form of the noun "genius.")
5. His sister, Dorothy.

With lofty thoughts, that neither evil tongues,
Rash judgments, nor the sneers of selfish men,
130 Nor greetings where no kindness is, nor all
The dreary intercourse of daily life,
Shall e'er prevail against us, or disturb
Our cheerful faith, that all which we behold
Is full of blessings. Therefore let the moon
135 Shine on thee in thy solitary walk;
And let the misty mountain-winds be free
To blow against thee: and, in after years,
When these wild ecstasies shall be matured
Into a sober pleasure; when thy mind
140 Shall be a mansion for all lovely forms,
Thy memory be as a dwelling-place
For all sweet sounds and harmonies; oh! then,
If solitude, or fear, or pain, or grief,
Should be thy portion, with what healing thoughts
145 Of tender joy wilt thou remember me,
And these my exhortations! Nor, perchance—
If I should be where I no more can hear
Thy voice, nor catch from thy wild eyes these gleams
Of past existence[6]—wilt thou then forget
150 That on the banks of this delightful stream
We stood together; and that I, so long
A worshipper of Nature, hither came
Unwearied in that service; rather say
With warmer love—oh! with far deeper zeal
155 Of holier love. Nor wilt thou then forget,
That after many wanderings, many years
Of absence, these steep woods and lofty cliffs,
And this green pastoral landscape, were to me
More dear, both for themselves and for thy sake!

July 1798   1798

Preface to *Lyrical Ballads* (1802)

To the first edition of *Lyrical Ballads*, published jointly with Coleridge in 1798, Wordsworth prefixed an "advertisement" asserting that the majority of the poems were "to be considered as experiments" to determine "how far the language of conversation in the middle and lower classes of society is adapted to the purposes of poetic pleasure." In the second, two-volume edition of 1800 Wordsworth, aided by frequent conversations with Coleridge, expanded the Advertisement into a preface that justified the new poetry not as experiments, but as exemplifying the principles of all good poetry. The Preface was enlarged for the third edition of *Lyrical Ballads*, published two years later; this last version of 1802 is the one that is reprinted here.

Although some of its individual ideas had antecedents in the later eighteenth century, the Preface as a whole deserves its reputation as a revolutionary manifesto about the nature of poetry. Like many radical statements, however, it claims to go back to

6. I.e., reminders of his own "past existence" five years earlier (see lines 116–19).

the implicit principles that governed the great poetry of the past but have been perverted in recent practice. Most discussions of the Preface, following the lead of Coleridge in his *Biographia Literaria*, have focused on Wordsworth's assertions about the valid language of poetry, on which he bases his attack on the "poetic diction" of eighteenth-century poets. As Coleridge pointed out, Wordsworth's argument about this issue is far from clear. It is apparent, however, that Wordsworth undertook to overthrow the basic theory, as well as the reigning practice, of neoclassic poetry. That is, his Preface implicitly denies the traditional assumption that the poetic genres constitute a hierarchy, from epic and tragedy at the top down through comedy, satire, pastoral, to the short lyric at the lowest reaches of the poetic scale; he also rejects the traditional principle of "decorum," according to which the subject matter (especially the social class of the protagonists) and the level of diction are contrived by the poet to conform to the status of the literary kind on the poetic scale.

When Wordsworth asserted in the Preface that he deliberately chose to represent "incidents and situations from common life," he translated his democratic sympathies into critical terms, justifying his use of peasants, children, outcasts, criminals, and idiot boys as serious subjects of poetic and even tragic concern. He also undertook to write in "a selection of language really used by men," on the grounds that there can be no "essential difference between the language of prose and metrical composition." In making this claim, Wordsworth subverted the neoclassic principle that, in many kinds of poem, the language must be elevated over standard speech by a special diction and by artful figures of speech, to match the language to the height and dignity of a particular genre. Wordsworth's own views about the valid language of poetry are based on the new premise that "all good poetry is the spontaneous overflow of powerful feelings"—spontaneous, that is, at the moment of composition, even though the process is influenced by prior thought and acquired poetic skill.

Wordsworth's assertions about the materials and diction of poetry have been greatly influential in expanding the range of serious literature to include the common people and ordinary things and events, as well as in justifying a poetry of sincerity rather than of artifice, expressed in the ordinary language of its time. But in the long view, other aspects of his Preface have been no less significant in establishing its importance, not only as a turning point in English criticism but also as a central document in modern culture. Wordsworth attributed to imaginative literature the primary role in keeping human beings emotionally alive and morally sensitive—that is, keeping them essentially human—in the modern era of a technological and increasingly urban society, with its mass media and mass culture that threaten, in his view, to blunt the mind's "discriminatory powers" and to "reduce it to a state of almost savage torpor."

From Preface to *Lyrical Ballads, with Pastoral and Other Poems* (1802)

[THE SUBJECT AND LANGUAGE OF POETRY]

The first volume of these poems has already been submitted to general perusal. It was published, as an experiment, which, I hoped, might be of some use to ascertain, how far, by fitting to metrical arrangement a selection of the real language of men in a state of vivid sensation, that sort of pleasure and that quantity of pleasure may be imparted, which a poet may rationally endeavour to impart.

I had formed no very inaccurate estimate of the probable effect of those poems: I flattered myself that they who should be pleased with them would read them with more than common pleasure: and, on the other hand, I was well aware, that by those who should dislike them they would be read with more than common dislike. The result has differed from my expectation in this only, that I have pleased a greater number than I ventured to hope I should please.

For the sake of variety, and from a consciousness of my own weakness, I was induced to request the assistance of a friend, who furnished me with the poems of the *Ancient Mariner*, the *Foster-Mother's Tale*, the *Nightingale*, and the poem entitled *Love*. I should not, however, have requested this assistance, had I not believed that the poems of my friend[1] would in a great measure have the same tendency as my own, and that, though there would be found a difference, there would be found no discordance in the colours of our style; as our opinions on the subject of poetry do almost entirely coincide.

Several of my friends are anxious for the success of these poems from a belief, that, if the views with which they were composed were indeed realized, a class of poetry would be produced, well adapted to interest mankind permanently, and not unimportant in the multiplicity, and in the quality of its moral relations: and on this account they have advised me to prefix a systematic defence of the theory upon which the poems were written. But I was unwilling to undertake the task, because I knew that on this occasion the reader would look coldly upon my arguments, since I might be suspected of having been principally influenced by the selfish and foolish hope of *reasoning* him into an approbation of these particular poems: and I was still more unwilling to undertake the task, because, adequately to display my opinions, and fully to enforce my arguments, would require a space wholly disproportionate to the nature of a preface. For to treat the subject with the clearness and coherence of which I believe it susceptible, it would be necessary to give a full account of the present state of the public taste in this country, and to determine how far this taste is healthy or depraved; which, again, could not be determined, without pointing out, in what manner language and the human mind act and re-act on each other, and without retracing the revolutions, not of literature alone, but likewise of society itself. I have therefore altogether declined to enter regularly upon this defence; yet I am sensible, that there would be some impropriety in abruptly obtruding upon the public, without a few words of introduction, poems so materially different from those upon which general approbation is at present bestowed.

It is supposed, that by the act of writing in verse an author makes a formal engagement that he will gratify certain known habits of association; that he not only thus apprizes the reader that certain classes of ideas and expressions will be found in his book, but that others will be carefully excluded. This exponent or symbol held forth by metrical language must in different eras of literature have excited very different expectations: for example, in the age of Catullus, Terence, and Lucretius and that of Statius or Claudian,[2] and in

1. The "friend" of course is Coleridge. When he read this *Preface* and the new poems included in the 1802 edition of *Lyrical Ballads,* Coleridge wrote to Robert Southey that although Wordsworth's Preface of 1800 had been "half a child of my own brain," he now suspects that "there is a radical difference in our theoretical opinions respecting poetry—this I shall endeavour to go to the bottom of." The results of this endeavor are Coleridge's discussions, fifteen years later, of Wordsworth's Preface in *Biographia Literaria,* chaps. 14 and 17.
2. Wordsworth's implied contrast is between the naturalness and simplicity of the first three Roman poets (who wrote in the last two centuries B.C.E.) and the elaborate artifice of the last two Roman poets (Statius wrote in the 1st and Claudian in the 4th century C.E.).

our own country, in the age of Shakespeare and Beaumont and Fletcher, and that of Donne and Cowley, or Dryden, or Pope. I will not take upon me to determine the exact import of the promise which by the act of writing in verse an author, in the present day, makes to his reader; but I am certain, it will appear to many persons that I have not fulfilled the terms of an engagement thus voluntarily contracted. They who have been accustomed to the gaudiness and inane phraseology of many modern writers, if they persist in reading this book to its conclusion, will, no doubt, frequently have to struggle with feelings of strangeness and awkwardness: they will look round for poetry, and will be induced to inquire by what species of courtesy these attempts can be permitted to assume that title. I hope therefore the reader will not censure me, if I attempt to state what I have proposed to myself to perform; and also (as far as the limits of a preface will permit) to explain some of the chief reasons which have determined me in the choice of my purpose: that at least he may be spared any unpleasant feeling of disappointment, and that I myself may be protected from the most dishonorable accusation which can be brought against an author, namely, that of an indolence which prevents him from endeavouring to ascertain what is his duty, or, when this duty is ascertained, prevents him from performing it.

The principal object, then, which I proposed to myself in these poems was to choose incidents and situations from common life, and to relate or describe them, throughout, as far as was possible, in a selection of language really used by men; and, at the same time, to throw over them a certain colouring of imagination, whereby ordinary things should be presented to the mind in an unusual way; and, further, and above all, to make these incidents and situations interesting by tracing in them, truly though not ostentatiously, the primary laws of our nature: chiefly, as far as regards the manner in which we associate ideas in a state of excitement.[3] Low and rustic life was generally chosen, because in that condition, the essential passions of the heart find a better soil in which they can attain their maturity, are less under restraint, and speak a plainer and more emphatic language; because in that condition of life our elementary feelings co-exist in a state of greater simplicity, and, consequently, may be more accurately contemplated, and more forcibly communicated; because the manners of rural life germinate from those elementary feelings; and, from the necessary character of rural occupations, are more easily comprehended; and are more durable; and lastly, because in that condition the passions of men are incorporated with the beautiful and permanent forms of nature. The language, too, of these men is adopted (purified indeed from what appear to be its real defects, from all lasting and rational causes of dislike or disgust) because such men hourly communicate with the best objects from which the best part of language is originally derived; and because, from their rank in society and the sameness and narrow circle of their intercourse, being less under the influence of social vanity they convey their feelings and notions in simple and unelaborated expressions. Accordingly, such a language, arising out of repeated experience and regular feelings, is a more permanent, and a far more philosophical language, than that which is frequently substituted for it by poets, who think that they are conferring honour upon themselves and their art, in proportion

3. Cf. Coleridge's account of their plan in *Biographia Literaria,* the beginning of chap. 14.

as they separate themselves from the sympathies of men, and indulge in arbitrary and capricious habits of expression, in order to furnish food for fickle tastes, and fickle appetites, of their own creation.[4]

I cannot, however, be insensible of the present outcry against the triviality and meanness both of thought and language, which some of my contemporaries have occasionally introduced into their metrical compositions; and I acknowledge, that this defect, where it exists, is more dishonorable to the writer's own character than false refinement or arbitrary innovation, though I should contend at the same time that it is far less pernicious in the sum of its consequences. From such verses the poems in these volumes will be found distinguished at least by one mark of difference, that each of them has a worthy *purpose*. Not that I mean to say, that I always began to write with a distinct purpose formally conceived; but I believe that my habits of meditation have so formed my feelings, as that my descriptions of such objects as strongly excite those feelings, will be found to carry along with them a *purpose*. If in this opinion I am mistaken, I can have little right to the name of a poet. For all good poetry is the spontaneous overflow of powerful feelings: but though this be true, poems to which any value can be attached, were never produced on any variety of subjects but by a man who, being possessed of more than usual organic sensibility, had also thought long and deeply. For our continued influxes of feeling are modified and directed by our thoughts, which are indeed the representatives of all our past feelings; and, as by contemplating the relation of these general representatives to each other we discover what is really important to men, so, by the repetition and continuance of this act, our feelings will be connected with important subjects, till at length, if we be originally possessed of much sensibility, such habits of mind will be produced, that, by obeying blindly and mechanically the impulses of those habits, we shall describe objects, and utter sentiments, of such a nature and in such connection with each other, that the understanding of the being to whom we address ourselves, if he be in a healthful state of association, must necessarily be in some degree enlightened, and his affections ameliorated.

I have said that each of these poems has a purpose. I have also informed my reader what this purpose will be found principally to be: namely, to illustrate the manner in which our feelings and ideas are associated in a state of excitement. But, speaking in language somewhat more appropriate, it is to follow the fluxes and refluxes of the mind when agitated by the great and simple affections of our nature. This object I have endeavored in these short essays to attain by various means; by tracing the maternal passion through many of its more subtile windings, as in the poems of the *Idiot Boy* and the *Mad Mother*; by accompanying the last struggles of a human being, at the approach of death, cleaving in solitude to life and society, as in the poem of the *Forsaken Indian*; by shewing, as in the stanzas entitled *We Are Seven*, the perplexity and obscurity which in childhood attend our notion of death, or rather our utter inability to admit that notion; or by displaying the strength of fraternal, or to speak more philosophically, of moral attachment when early associated with the great and beautiful objects of nature, as in *The*

4. It is worth while here to observe that the affecting parts of Chaucer are almost always expressed in language pure and universally intelligible even to this day [Wordsworth's note].

Brothers; or, as in the Incident of *Simon Lee*, by placing my reader in the way of receiving from ordinary moral sensations another and more salutary impression than we are accustomed to receive from them. It has also been part of my general purpose to attempt to sketch characters under the influence of less impassioned feelings, as in the *Two April Mornings, The Fountain, The Old Man Travelling, The Two Thieves*, &c., characters of which the elements are simple, belonging rather to nature than to manners, such as exist now, and will probably always exist, and which from their constitution may be distinctly and profitably contemplated. I will not abuse the indulgence of my reader by dwelling longer upon this subject; but it is proper that I should mention one other circumstance which distinguishes these poems from the popular poetry of the day; it is this, that the feeling therein developed gives importance to the action and situation, and not the action and situation to the feeling. My meaning will be rendered perfectly intelligible by referring my reader to the poems entitled *Poor Susan* and the *Childless Father*, particularly to the last stanza of the latter poem.

I will not suffer a sense of false modesty to prevent me from asserting, that I point my reader's attention to this mark of distinction, far less for the sake of these particular poems than from the general importance of the subject. The subject is indeed important! For the human mind is capable of being excited without the application of gross and violent stimulants; and he must have a very faint perception of its beauty and dignity who does not know this, and who does not further know, that one being is elevated above another, in proportion as he possesses this capability. It has therefore appeared to me, that to endeavour to produce or enlarge this capability is one of the best services in which, at any period, a writer can be engaged; but this service, excellent at all times, is especially so at the present day. For a multitude of causes, unknown to former times, are now acting with a combined force to blunt the discriminating powers of the mind, and, unfitting it for all voluntary exertion, to reduce it to a state of almost savage torpor. The most effective of these causes are the great national events which are daily taking place, and the increasing accumulation of men in cities, where the uniformity of their occupations produces a craving for extraordinary incident, which the rapid communication of intelligence hourly gratifies.[5] To this tendency of life and manners the literature and theatrical exhibitions of the country have conformed themselves. The invaluable works of our elder writers, I had almost said the works of Shakespeare and Milton, are driven into neglect by frantic novels, sickly and stupid German tragedies,[6] and deluges of idle and extravagant stories in verse.—When I think upon this degrading thirst after outrageous stimulation, I am almost ashamed to have spoken of the feeble effort with which I have endeavoured to counteract it; and, reflecting upon the magnitude of the general evil, I should be oppressed with no dishonorable melancholy, had I not a deep impression of certain inherent and indestructible qualities of the human mind, and likewise of certain powers in the great and permanent objects that act upon it which are equally inherent and indestructible; and did I not further add to this

5. This was the period of the wars against France, of industrial urbanization, and of the rapid proliferation in England of daily newspapers.
6. Wordsworth had in mind the "Gothic" terror novels by writers such as Ann Radcliffe and Matthew Gregory Lewis and the sentimental melodrama, then immensely popular in England, of August von Kotzebue and his German contemporaries.

impression a belief, that the time is approaching when the evil will be systematically opposed, by men of greater powers, and with far more distinguished success.

Having dwelt thus long on the subjects and aim of these poems, I shall request the reader's permission to apprize him of a few circumstances relating to their *style*, in order, among other reasons, that I may not be censured for not having performed what I never attempted. The reader will find that personifications of abstract ideas rarely occur in these volumes; and, I hope, are utterly rejected as an ordinary device to elevate the style, and raise it above prose. I have proposed to myself to imitate, and, as far as is possible, to adopt the very language of men; and assuredly such personifications do not make any natural or regular part of that language. They are, indeed, a figure of speech occasionally prompted by passion, and I have made use of them as such; but I have endeavoured utterly to reject them as a mechanical device of style, or as a family language which writers in metre seem to lay claim to by prescription. I have wished to keep my reader in the company of flesh and blood, persuaded that by so doing I shall interest him. I am, however, well aware that others who pursue a different track may interest him likewise; I do not interfere with their claim, I only wish to prefer a different claim of my own. There will also be found in these volumes little of what is usually called poetic diction;[7] I have taken as much pains to avoid it as others ordinarily take to produce it; this I have done for the reason already alleged, to bring my language near to the language of men, and further, because the pleasure which I have proposed to myself to impart is of a kind very different from that which is supposed by many persons to be the proper object of poetry. I do not know how, without being culpably particular, I can give my reader a more exact notion of the style in which I wished these poems to be written than by informing him that I have at all times endeavoured to look steadily at my subject, consequently, I hope that there is in these poems little falsehood of description, and that my ideas are expressed in language fitted to their respective importance. Something I must have gained by this practice, as it is friendly to one property of all good poetry, namely, good sense; but it has necessarily cut me off from a large portion of phrases and figures of speech which from father to son have long been regarded as the common inheritance of poets. I have also thought it expedient to restrict myself still further, having abstained from the use of many expressions, in themselves proper and beautiful, but which have been foolishly repeated by bad poets, till such feelings of disgust are connected with them as it is scarcely possible by any art of association to overpower.

If in a poem there should be found a series of lines, or even a single line, in which the language, though naturally arranged and according to the strict laws of metre, does not differ from that of prose, there is a numerous class of critics, who, when they stumble upon these prosaisms as they call them, imagine that they have made a notable discovery, and exult over the poet as over a man ignorant of his own profession. Now these men would establish a canon of criticism which the reader will conclude he must utterly reject, if he wishes to be pleased with these volumes. And it would be a most easy task to prove to him, that not only the language of a large portion of every

---

7. In the sense of words, phrases, and figures of speech not commonly used in conversation or prose that are regarded as especially appropriate to poetry.

good poem, even of the most elevated character, must necessarily, except with reference to the metre, in no respect differ from that of good prose, but likewise that some of the most interesting parts of the best poems will be found to be strictly the language of prose, when prose is well written. The truth of this assertion might be demonstrated by innumerable passages from almost all the poetical writings, even of Milton himself. I have not space for much quotation; but, to illustrate the subject in a general manner, I will here adduce a short composition of Gray, who was at the head of those who by their reasonings have attempted to widen the space of separation betwixt prose and metrical composition, and was more than any other man curiously elaborate in the structure of his own poetic diction.[8]

> In vain to me the smiling mornings shine,
> And reddening Phoebus lifts his golden fire:
> The birds in vain their amorous descant join,
> Or cheerful fields resume their green attire:
> These ears, alas! for other notes repine;
> *A different object do these eyes require;*
> *My lonely anguish melts no heart but mine;*
> *And in my breast the imperfect joys expire;*
> Yet Morning smiles the busy race to cheer,
> And new-born pleasure brings to happier men;
> The fields to all their wonted tribute bear;
> To warm their little loves the birds complain.
> *I fruitless mourn to him that cannot hear*
> *And weep the more because I weep in vain.*

It will easily be perceived that the only part of this sonnet which is of any value is the lines printed in italics: it is equally obvious, that, except in the rhyme, and in the use of the single word "fruitless" for fruitlessly, which is so far a defect, the language of these lines does in no respect differ from that of prose.

By the foregoing quotation I have shewn that the language of prose may yet be well adapted to poetry; and I have previously asserted that a large portion of the language of every good poem can in no respect differ from that of good prose. I will go further. I do not doubt that it may be safely affirmed, that there neither is, nor can be, any essential difference between the language of prose and metrical composition. We are fond of tracing the resemblance between poetry and painting, and, accordingly, we call them sisters: but where shall we find bonds of connection sufficiently strict to typify the affinity betwixt metrical and prose composition? They both speak by and to the same organs; the bodies in which both of them are clothed may be said to be of the same substance, their affections are kindred and almost identical, not necessarily differing even in degree; poetry[9] sheds no

---

8. Thomas Gray had written, in a letter to Richard West, that "the language of the age is never the language of poetry." The poem that follows is Gray's *Sonnet on the Death of Richard West*.
9. I here use the word "poetry" (though against my own judgment) as opposed to the word "prose," and synonymous with metrical composition. But much confusion has been introduced into criticism by this contradistinction of poetry and prose, instead of the more philosophical one of poetry and matter of fact, or science. The only strict antithesis to prose is metre; nor is this, in truth, a *strict* antithesis; because lines and passages of metre so naturally occur in writing prose, that it would be scarcely possible to avoid them, even were it desirable [Wordsworth's note].

tears "such as Angels weep,"[1] but natural and human tears; she can boast of no celestial ichor[2] that distinguishes her vital juices from those of prose; the same human blood circulates through the veins of them both.

* * *

["WHAT IS A POET?"]

Taking up the subject, then, upon general grounds, I ask what is meant by the word "poet"? What is a poet? To whom does he address himself? And what language is to be expected from him? He is a man speaking to men: a man, it is true, endued with more lively sensibility, more enthusiasm and tenderness, who has a greater knowledge of human nature, and a more comprehensive soul, than are supposed to be common among mankind; a man pleased with his own passions and volitions, and who rejoices more than other men in the spirit of life that is in him; delighting to contemplate similar volitions and passions as manifested in the goings-on of the universe, and habitually impelled to create them where he does not find them. To these qualities he has added a disposition to be affected more than other men by absent things as if they were present; an ability of conjuring up in himself passions, which are indeed far from being the same as those produced by real events, yet (especially in those parts of the general sympathy which are pleasing and delightful) do more nearly resemble the passions produced by real events, than any thing which, from the motions of their own minds merely, other men are accustomed to feel in themselves; whence, and from practice, he has acquired a greater readiness and power in expressing what he thinks and feels, and especially those thoughts and feelings which, by his own choice, or from the structure of his own mind, arise in him without immediate external excitement.

But, whatever portion of this faculty we may suppose even the greatest poet to possess, there cannot be a doubt but that the language which it will suggest to him, must, in liveliness and truth, fall far short of that which is uttered by men in real life, under the actual pressure of those passions, certain shadows of which the poet thus produces, or feels to be produced, in himself. However exalted a notion we would wish to cherish of the character of a poet, it is obvious, that, while he describes and imitates passions, his situation is altogether slavish and mechanical, compared with the freedom and power of real and substantial action and suffering. So that it will be the wish of the poet to bring his feelings near to those of the persons whose feelings he describes, nay, for short spaces of time perhaps, to let himself slip into an entire delusion, and even confound and identify his own feelings with theirs; modifying only the language which is thus suggested to him, by a consideration that he describes for a particular purpose, that of giving pleasure. Here, then, he will apply the principle on which I have so much insisted, namely, that of selection; on this he will depend for removing what would otherwise be painful or disgusting in the passion; he will feel that there is no necessity to trick out or to elevate nature: and, the more industriously he applies this principle, the deeper will be his faith that no

1. *Paradise Lost* 1.620.
2. In Greek mythology, the fluid in the veins of the gods.

words, which his fancy or imagination can suggest, will be to be compared with those which are the emanations of reality and truth.

But it may be said by those who do not object to the general spirit of these remarks, that, as it is impossible for the poet to produce upon all occasions language as exquisitely fitted for the passion as that which the real passion itself suggests, it is proper that he should consider himself as in the situation of a translator, who deems himself justified when he substitutes excellences of another kind for those which are unattainable by him; and endeavours occasionally to surpass his original, in order to make some amends for the general inferiority to which he feels that he must submit. But this would be to encourage idleness and unmanly despair. Further, it is the language of men who speak of what they do not understand; who talk of poetry as a matter of amusement and idle pleasure; who will converse with us as gravely about a *taste* for poetry, as they express it, as if it were a thing as indifferent as a taste for rope-dancing, or Frontiniac[3] or sherry. Aristotle, I have been told, hath said, that poetry is the most philosophic of all writing;[4] it is so: its object is truth, not individual and local, but general, and operative; not standing upon external testimony, but carried alive into the heart by passion; truth which is its own testimony, which gives strength and divinity to the tribunal to which it appeals, and receives them from the same tribunal. Poetry is the image of man and nature. The obstacles which stand in the way of the fidelity of the biographer and historian, and of their consequent utility, are incalculably greater than those which are to be encountered by the poet who has an adequate notion of the dignity of his art. The poet writes under one restriction only, namely, that of the necessity of giving immediate pleasure to a human being possessed of that information which may be expected from him, not as a lawyer, a physician, a mariner, an astronomer or a natural philosopher, but as a man. Except this one restriction, there is no object standing between the poet and the image of things; between this, and the biographer and historian there are a thousand.

Nor let this necessity of producing immediate pleasure be considered as a degradation of the poet's art. It is far otherwise. It is an acknowledgment of the beauty of the universe, an acknowledgment the more sincere because it is not formal, but indirect; it is a task light and easy to him who looks at the world in the spirit of love: further, it is a homage paid to the native and naked dignity of man, to the grand elementary principle of pleasure, by which he knows, and feels, and lives, and moves.[5] We have no sympathy but what is propagated by pleasure: I would not be misunderstood; but wherever we sympathize with pain it will be found that the sympathy is produced and carried on by subtle combinations with pleasure. We have no knowledge, that is, no general principles drawn from the contemplation of particular facts, but what has been built up by pleasure, and exists in us by pleasure alone. The man of science, the chemist and mathematician, whatever difficulties and disgusts they may have had to struggle with, know and feel this. However painful may be the objects with which the anatomist's knowledge is connected, he feels that his knowledge is pleasure; and where he has no

---

3. A sweet wine made from muscat grapes.
4. Aristotle in fact said that "poetry is more philosophic than history, since its statements are of the nature of universals, whereas those of history are

singulars" (*Poetics* 1451b).
5. A bold echo of the words of St. Paul, that in God "we live, and move, and have our being" (Acts 17.28).

pleasure he has no knowledge. What then does the poet? He considers man and the objects that surround him as acting and re-acting upon each other, so as to produce an infinite complexity of pain and pleasure; he considers man in his own nature and in his ordinary life as contemplating this with a certain quantity of immediate knowledge, with certain convictions, intuitions, and deductions which by habit become of the nature of intuitions; he considers him as looking upon this complex scene of ideas and sensations, and finding every where objects that immediately excite in him sympathies which, from the necessities of his nature, are accompanied by an overbalance of enjoyment.

To this knowledge which all men carry about with them, and to these sympathies in which without any other discipline than that of our daily life we are fitted to take delight, the poet principally directs his attention. He considers man and nature as essentially adapted to each other,[6] and the mind of man as naturally the mirror of the fairest and most interesting qualities of nature. And thus the poet, prompted by this feeling of pleasure which accompanies him through the whole course of his studies, converses with general nature with affections akin to those, which, through labour and length of time, the man of science has raised up in himself, by conversing with those particular parts of nature which are the objects of his studies. The knowledge both of the poet and the man of science is pleasure; but the knowledge of the one cleaves to us as a necessary part of our existence, our natural and unalienable inheritance; the other is a personal and individual acquisition, slow to come to us, and by no habitual and direct sympathy connecting us with our fellow-beings. The man of science seeks truth as a remote and unknown benefactor; he cherishes and loves it in his solitude: the poet, singing a song in which all human beings join with him, rejoices in the presence of truth as our visible friend and hourly companion. Poetry is the breath and finer spirit of all knowledge; it is the impassioned expression which is in the countenance of all science. Emphatically may it be said of the poet, as Shakespeare hath said of man, "that he looks before and after."[7] He is the rock of defence of human nature; an upholder and preserver, carrying everywhere with him relationship and love. In spite of difference of soil and climate, of language and manners, of laws and customs, in spite of things silently gone out of mind and things violently destroyed, the poet binds together by passion and knowledge the vast empire of human society, as it is spread over the whole earth, and over all time. The objects of the poet's thoughts are every where; though the eyes and senses of man are, it is true, his favorite guides, yet he will follow wheresoever he can find an atmosphere of sensation in which to move his wings. Poetry is the first and last of all knowledge—it is as immortal as the heart of man. If the labours of men of science should ever create any material revolution, direct or indirect, in our condition, and in the impressions which we habitually receive, the poet will sleep then no more than at present, but he will be ready to follow the steps of the man of science, not only in those general indirect effects, but he will be at his side, carrying sensation into the midst of the objects of the science itself. The remotest discoveries of the chemist, the botanist, or mineralogist,

6. On the mutual adaptation of man's mind and nature, see Wordsworth's Prospectus to *The* *Recluse*, p. 1494, lines 63–71.
7. *Hamlet* 4.4.37.

will be as proper objects of the poet's art as any upon which it can be employed, if the time should ever come when these things shall be familiar to us, and the relations under which they are contemplated by the followers of these respective sciences shall be manifestly and palpably material to us as enjoying and suffering beings.[8] If the time should ever come when what is now called science, thus familiarized to men, shall be ready to put on, as it were, a form of flesh and blood, the poet will lend his divine spirit to aid the transfiguration, and will welcome the being thus produced, as a dear and genuine inmate of the household of man.—It is not, then, to be supposed that any one, who holds that sublime notion of poetry which I have attempted to convey, will break in upon the sanctity and truth of his pictures by transitory and accidental ornaments, and endeavour to excite admiration of himself by arts, the necessity of which must manifestly depend upon the assumed meanness of his subject.

What I have thus far said applies to poetry in general; but especially to those parts of composition where the poet speaks through the mouth of his characters; and upon this point it appears to have such weight that I will conclude, there are few persons, of good sense, who would not allow that the dramatic parts of composition are defective, in proportion as they deviate from the real language of nature, and are coloured by a diction of the poet's own, either peculiar to him as an individual poet, or belonging simply to poets in general, to a body of men who, from the circumstance of their compositions being in metre, it is expected will employ a particular language.

It is not, then, in the dramatic parts of composition that we look for this distinction of language; but still it may be proper and necessary where the poet speaks to us in his own person and character. To this I answer by referring my reader to the description which I have before given of a poet. Among the qualities which I have enumerated as principally conducing to form a poet, is implied nothing differing in kind from other men, but only in degree. The sum of what I have there said is, that the poet is chiefly distinguished from other men by a greater promptness to think and feel without immediate external excitement, and a greater power in expressing such thoughts and feelings as are produced in him in that manner. But these passions and thoughts and feelings are the general passions and thoughts and feelings of men. And with what are they connected? Undoubtedly with our moral sentiments and animal sensations, and with the causes which excite these; with the operations of the elements and the appearances of the visible universe; with storm and sun-shine, with the revolutions of the seasons, with cold and heat, with loss of friends and kindred, with injuries and resentments, gratitude and hope, with fear and sorrow. These, and the like, are the sensations and objects which the poet describes, as they are the sensations of other men, and the objects which interest them. The poet thinks and feels in the spirit of the passions of men. How, then, can his language differ in any material degree from that of all other men who feel vividly and see clearly? It might be *proved* that it is impossible. But supposing that this were not the case, the poet might then be allowed to use a peculiar language, when expressing his feelings for his own gratification, or that of

8. Wordsworth is at least right in anticipating the poetry of the machine; he himself wrote an early instance, the sonnet *Steamboats, Viaducts, and Railways*.

men like himself. But poets do not write for poets alone, but for men. Unless therefore we are advocates for that admiration which depends upon ignorance, and that pleasure which arises from hearing what we do not understand, the poet must descend from this supposed height, and, in order to excite rational sympathy, he must express himself as other men express themselves. * * *

["EMOTION RECOLLECTED IN TRANQUILLITY"]

I have said that poetry is the spontaneous overflow of powerful feelings: it takes its origin from emotion recollected in tranquillity: the emotion is contemplated till by a species of reaction the tranquillity gradually disappears, and an emotion, kindred to that which was before the subject of contemplation, is gradually produced, and does itself actually exist in the mind. In this mood successful composition generally begins, and in a mood similar to this it is carried on; but the emotion, of whatever kind and in whatever degree, from various causes is qualified by various pleasures, so that in describing any passions whatsoever, which are voluntarily described, the mind will upon the whole be in a state of enjoyment. Now, if nature be thus cautious in preserving in a state of enjoyment a being thus employed, the poet ought to profit by the lesson thus held forth to him, and ought especially to take care, that whatever passions he communicates to his reader, those passions, if his reader's mind be sound and vigorous, should always be accompanied with an overbalance of pleasure. Now the music of harmonious metrical language, the sense of difficulty overcome, and the blind association of pleasure which has been previously received from works of rhyme or metre of the same or similar construction, an indistinct perception perpetually renewed of language closely resembling that of real life, and yet, in the circumstance of metre, differing from it so widely, all these imperceptibly make up a complex feeling of delight, which is of the most important use in tempering the painful feeling which will always be found intermingled with powerful descriptions of the deeper passions. This effect is always produced in pathetic and impassioned poetry; while, in lighter compositions, the ease and gracefulness with which the poet manages his numbers are themselves confessedly a principal source of the gratification of the reader. I might perhaps include all which it is *necessary* to say upon this subject by affirming, what few persons will deny, that, of two descriptions, either of passions, manners, or characters, each of them equally well executed, the one in prose and the other in verse, the verse will be read a hundred times where the prose is read once. * * *

I know that nothing would have so effectually contributed to further the end which I have in view, as to have shewn of what kind the pleasure is, and how the pleasure is produced, which is confessedly produced by metrical composition essentially different from that which I have here endeavoured to recommend: for the reader will say that he has been pleased by such composition; and what can I do more for him? The power of any art is limited; and he will suspect, that, if I propose to furnish him with new friends, it is only upon condition of his abandoning his old friends. Besides, as I have said, the reader is himself conscious of the pleasure which he has received from such composition, composition to which he has peculiarly attached the endearing name of poetry; and all men feel an habitual gratitude, and something of an honorable bigotry for the objects which have long continued to please them: we not only wish to be pleased, but to be pleased in that particular way in which we have been accustomed to be pleased. There is a host of arguments in these feelings; and I should be the less able to combat them successfully, as I am willing to allow, that, in order entirely to enjoy the poetry which I am recommending, it would be necessary to give up much of what is ordinarily enjoyed. But, would my limits have permitted me to point out how this pleasure is produced, I might have removed many obstacles, and assisted my reader in perceiving that the powers of language are not so limited as he may suppose; and that it is possible that poetry may give other enjoyments, of a purer, more lasting, and more exquisite nature. This part of my subject I have not altogether neglected; but it has been less my present aim to prove, that the interest excited by some other kinds of poetry is less vivid, and less worthy of the nobler powers of the mind, than to offer reasons for presuming, that, if the object which I have proposed to myself were adequately attained, a species of poetry would be produced, which is genuine poetry; in its nature well adapted to interest mankind permanently, and likewise important in the multiplicity and quality of its moral relations.

From what has been said, and from a perusal of the poems, the reader will be able clearly to perceive the object which I have proposed to myself: he will determine how far I have attained this object; and, what is a much more important question, whether it be worth attaining; and upon the decision of these two questions will rest my claim to the approbation of the public.

1800, 1802

Strange fits of passion have I known[1]

> Strange fits of passion have I known:
> And I will dare to tell,
> But in the Lover's ear alone,
> What once to me befel.
>
> 5   When she I loved looked every day
> Fresh as a rose in June,
> I to her cottage bent my way,
> Beneath an evening moon.
>
> Upon the moon I fixed my eye,
> 10 All over the wide lea;
> With quickening pace my horse drew nigh
> Those paths so dear to me.

---

1. This and the four following pieces are often grouped by editors as the "Lucy poems," even though *A slumber did my spirit seal* does not identify the "she" who is the subject of that poem. All but the last were written in 1799, while Words- worth and his sister were in Germany, and homesick. There has been diligent speculation about the identity of Lucy, but it remains speculation. The one certainty is that she is not the girl of Wordsworth's *Lucy Gray*.

And now we reached the orchard-plot;
And, as we climbed the hill,
15 The sinking moon to Lucy's cot
Came near, and nearer still.

In one of those sweet dreams I slept,
Kind Nature's gentlest boon!
And all the while my eyes I kept
20 On the descending moon.

My horse moved on; hoof after hoof
He raised, and never stopped:
When down behind the cottage roof,
At once, the bright moon dropped.

25 What fond and wayward thoughts will slide
Into a Lover's head!
"O mercy!" to myself I cried,
"If Lucy should be dead!"[2]

1799   1800

She dwelt among the untrodden ways[1]

She dwelt among the untrodden ways
    Beside the springs of Dove,[2]
A Maid whom there were none to praise
    And very few to love:

5 A violet by a mossy stone
    Half hidden from the eye!
—Fair as a star, when only one
    Is shining in the sky.

She lived unknown, and few could know
10   When Lucy ceased to be;
But she is in her grave, and, oh,
    The difference to me!

1799   1800

Three years she grew

Three years she grew in sun and shower,
Then Nature said, "A lovelier flower

---

2. An additional stanza in an earlier manuscript version demonstrates how a poem can be improved by omission of a passage that is, in itself, excellent poetry: "I told her this: her laughter light / Is ringing in my ears; / And when I think upon that night/ My eyes are dim with tears."

1. For the author's revisions while composing this poem, see "Poems in Process," in the appendices to this volume.
2. There are several rivers by this name in England, including one in the Lake District.

On earth was never sown;
This Child I to myself will take;
5   She shall be mine, and I will make
A Lady of my own.[1]

"Myself will to my darling be
Both law and impulse: and with me
The Girl, in rock and plain,
10   In earth and heaven, in glade and bower,
Shall feel an overseeing power
To kindle or restrain.

"She shall be sportive as the fawn
That wild with glee across the lawn
15   Or up the mountain springs;
And hers shall be the breathing balm,
And hers the silence and the calm
Of mute insensate things.

"The floating clouds their state shall lend
20   To her; for her the willow bend;
Nor shall she fail to see
Even in the motions of the Storm
Grace that shall mould the Maiden's form
By silent sympathy.

25   "The stars of midnight shall be dear
To her; and she shall lean her ear
In many a secret place
Where rivulets dance their wayward round,
And beauty born of murmuring sound
30   Shall pass into her face.

"And vital feelings of delight
Shall rear her form to stately height,
Her virgin bosom swell;
Such thoughts to Lucy I will give
35   While she and I together live
Here in this happy dell."

Thus Nature spake—the work was done—
How soon my Lucy's race was run!
She died, and left to me
40   This heath, this calm, and quiet scene;
The memory of what has been,
And never more will be.

1799   1800

---

1. I.e., Lucy was three years old at the time when Nature made this promise; line 37 makes clear that Lucy
had reached the maturity foretold in the sixth stanza when she died.

A slumber did my spirit seal

A slumber did my spirit seal;
  I had no human fears:
She seemed a thing that could not feel
  The touch of earthly years.

5 No motion has she now, no force;
  She neither hears nor sees;
Rolled round in earth's diurnal° course,   *daily*
  With rocks, and stones, and trees.

1799   1800

I travelled among unknown men

I travelled among unknown men,
  In lands beyond the sea;
Nor, England! did I know till then
  What love I bore to thee.

5 'Tis past, that melancholy dream!
  Nor will I quit thy shore
A second time; for still I seem
  To love thee more and more.

Among thy mountains did I feel
10 The joy of my desire;
And she I cherished turned her wheel
  Beside an English fire.

Thy mornings showed, thy nights concealed
  The bowers where Lucy played;
15 And thine too is the last green field
  That Lucy's eyes surveyed.

ca. 1801   1807

Nutting[1]

————————It seems a day
(I speak of one from many singled out)
One of those heavenly days that cannot die;
When, in the eagerness of boyish hope,
5 I left our cottage-threshold, sallying forth
With a huge wallet o'er my shoulder slung,

1. Wordsworth said that these lines, written in Germany in 1798, were "intended as part of a poem on my own mind [*The Prelude*], but struck out as not being wanted there." He published them in the second edition of *Lyrical Ballads*, 1800.

A nutting-crook in hand; and turned my steps
Tow'rd some far-distant wood, a Figure quaint,
Tricked out in proud disguise of cast-off weeds°   *clothes*
10 Which for that service had been husbanded,
By exhortation of my frugal Dame[2]—
Motley accoutrement, of power to smile
At thorns, and brakes, and brambles,—and, in truth,
More ragged than need was! O'er pathless rocks,
15 Through beds of matted fern, and tangled thickets,
Forcing my way, I came to one dear nook
Unvisited, where not a broken bough
Drooped with its withered leaves, ungracious sign
Of devastation; but the hazels rose
20 Tall and erect, with tempting clusters hung,
A virgin scene!—A little while I stood,
Breathing with such suppression of the heart
As joy delights in; and, with wise restraint
Voluptuous, fearless of a rival, eyed
25 The banquet;—or beneath the trees I sate
Among the flowers, and with the flowers I played;
A temper known to those, who, after long
And weary expectation, have been blest
With sudden happiness beyond all hope.
30 Perhaps it was a bower beneath whose leaves
The violets of five seasons re-appear
And fade, unseen by any human eye;
Where fairy water-breaks[3] do murmur on
For ever; and I saw the sparkling foam,
35 And—with my cheek on one of those green stones
That, fleeced with moss, under the shady trees,
Lay round me, scattered like a flock of sheep—
I heard the murmur and the murmuring sound,
In that sweet mood when pleasure loves to pay
40 Tribute to ease; and, of its joy secure,
The heart luxuriates with indifferent things,
Wasting its kindliness on stocks[4] and stones,
And on the vacant air. Then up I rose,
And dragged to earth both branch and bough, with crash
45 And merciless ravage: and the shady nook
Of hazels, and the green and mossy bower,
Deformed and sullied, patiently gave up
Their quiet being: and, unless I now
Confound my present feelings with the past,
50 Ere from the mutilated bower I turned
Exulting, rich beyond the wealth of kings,
I felt a sense of pain when I beheld
The silent trees, and saw the intruding sky.—
Then, dearest Maiden,[5] move along these shades

---

2. Ann Tyson, with whom Wordsworth lodged
while at Hawkshead grammar school.
3. Places where the flow of a stream is broken by
rocks.

4. Tree stumps. ("Stocks and stones" is a conventional expression for "inanimate things.")
5. In a manuscript passage originally intended to
lead up to *Nutting*, the maiden is called Lucy.

55 In gentleness of heart; with gentle hand
   Touch—for there is a spirit in the woods.

1798   1800

The Ruined Cottage[1]

First Part

'Twas summer and the sun was mounted high.
Along the south the uplands feebly glared
Through a pale steam, and all the northern downs
In clearer air ascending shewed far off
5 Their surfaces with shadows dappled o'er
Of deep embattled clouds: far as the sight
Could reach those many shadows lay in spots
Determined and unmoved, with steady beams
Of clear and pleasant sunshine interposed;
10 Pleasant to him who on the soft cool moss
Extends his careless limbs beside the root
Of some huge oak whose aged branches make
A twilight of their own, a dewy shade
Where the wren warbles while the dreaming man,
15 Half-conscious of that soothing melody,
With side-long eye looks out upon the scene,
By those impending branches made more soft,
More soft and distant. Other lot was mine.
Across a bare wide Common I had toiled
20 With languid feet which by the slipp'ry ground
Were baffled still, and when I stretched myself
On the brown earth my limbs from very heat
Could find no rest nor my weak arm disperse
The insect host which gathered round my face
25 And joined their murmurs to the tedious noise
Of seeds of bursting gorse that crackled round.
I rose and turned towards a group of trees
Which midway in that level stood alone,
And thither come at length, beneath a shade
30 Of clustering elms that sprang from the same root
I found a ruined house, four naked walls
That stared upon each other. I looked round
And near the door I saw an aged Man,

1. Wordsworth wrote *The Ruined Cottage* in 1797–98, then revised it several times before he finally published an expanded version of the story as book 1 of *The Excursion*, in 1814. *The Ruined Cottage* was not published as an independent poem until 1949, when it appeared in the fifth volume of *The Poetical Works of William Wordsworth*, edited by Ernest de Selincourt and Helen Darbishire, who printed a version known as "MS. B." The text reprinted here is from "MS. D," dated 1799, as transcribed by James Butler in the Cornell Wordsworth volume, *"The Ruined Cottage" and*

"*The Pedlar*" (1979).

   This version is one of Wordsworth's earliest successes in verse narrative. The story presents the bleak facts of "a tale of silent suffering"—suffering that is undeserved, unrationalized, and irremissive. The event is "a common tale," and it poses the implicit question, What are we to make of human life, in which such things happen? The narrator confronts the fact of human suffering without reference to the creed of a beneficent power, whether in or out of nature.

Alone, and stretched upon the cottage bench;
35 An iron-pointed staff lay at his side.
With instantaneous joy I recognized
That pride of nature and of lowly life,
The venerable Armytage, a friend
As dear to me as is the setting sun.
40   Two days before
We had been fellow-travellers. I knew
That he was in this neighbourhood and now
Delighted found him here in the cool shade.
He lay, his pack of rustic merchandize
45 Pillowing his head—I guess he had no thought
Of his way-wandering life. His eyes were shut;
The shadows of the breezy elms above
Dappled his face. With thirsty heat oppress'd
At length I hailed him, glad to see his hat
50 Bedewed with water-drops, as if the brim
Had newly scoop'd a running stream. He rose
And pointing to a sun-flower bade me climb
The [   ]² wall where that same gaudy flower
Looked out upon the road. It was a plot
55 Of garden-ground, now wild, its matted weeds
Marked with the steps of those whom as they pass'd,
The goose-berry trees that shot in long lank slips,
Or currants hanging from their leafless stems
In scanty strings, had tempted to o'erleap
60 The broken wall. Within that cheerless spot,
Where two tall hedgerows of thick willow boughs
Joined in a damp cold nook, I found a well
Half-choked [with willow flowers and weeds.]³
I slaked my thirst and to the shady bench
65 Returned, and while I stood unbonneted
To catch the motion of the cooler air
The old Man said, "I see around me here
Things which you cannot see: we die, my Friend,
Nor we alone, but that which each man loved
70 And prized in his peculiar nook of earth
Dies with him or is changed, and very soon
Even of the good is no memorial left.
The Poets in their elegies and songs
Lamenting the departed call the groves,
75 They call upon the hills and streams to mourn,
And senseless rocks, nor idly; for they speak
In these their invocations with a voice
Obedient to the strong creative power
Of human passion. Sympathies there are
80 More tranquil, yet perhaps of kindred birth,
That steal upon the meditative mind
And grow with thought. Beside yon spring I stood

---

2. The brackets here and in later lines mark blank spaces left unfilled in the manuscript.

3. Wordsworth penciled the bracketed phrase into a gap left in the manuscript.

And eyed its waters till we seemed to feel
One sadness, they and I. For them a bond
85 Of brotherhood is broken: time has been
When every day the touch of human hand
Disturbed their stillness, and they ministered
To human comfort. When I stooped to drink,
A spider's web hung to the water's edge,
90 And on the wet and slimy foot-stone lay
The useless fragment of a wooden bowl;
It moved my very heart. The day has been
When I could never pass this road but she
Who lived within these walls, when I appeared,
95 A daughter's welcome gave me, and I loved her
As my own child. O Sir! the good die first,
And they whose hearts are dry as summer dust
Burn to the socket. Many a passenger
Has blessed poor Margaret for her gentle looks
100 When she upheld the cool refreshment drawn
From that forsaken spring, and no one came
But he was welcome, no one went away
But that it seemed she loved him. She is dead,
The worm is on her cheek, and this poor hut,
105 Stripp'd of its outward garb of household flowers,
Of rose and sweet-briar, offers to the wind
A cold bare wall whose earthy top is tricked
With weeds and the rank spear-grass. She is dead,
And nettles rot and adders sun themselves
110 Where we have sate together while she nurs'd
Her infant at her breast. The unshod Colt,
The wandring heifer and the Potter's ass,
Find shelter now within the chimney-wall
Where I have seen her evening hearth-stone blaze
115 And through the window spread upon the road
Its chearful light.—You will forgive me, Sir,
But often on this cottage do I muse
As on a picture, till my wiser mind
Sinks, yielding to the foolishness of grief.
120   She had a husband, an industrious man,
Sober and steady; I have heard her say
That he was up and busy at his loom
In summer ere the mower's scythe had swept
The dewy grass, and in the early spring
125 Ere the last star had vanished. They who pass'd
At evening, from behind the garden-fence
Might hear his busy spade, which he would ply
After his daily work till the day-light
Was gone and every leaf and flower were lost
130 In the dark hedges. So they pass'd their days
In peace and comfort, and two pretty babes
Were their best hope next to the God in Heaven.
—You may remember, now some ten years gone,
Two blighting seasons when the fields were left

135   With half a harvest.[4] It pleased heaven to add
        A worse affliction in the plague of war:
        A happy land was stricken to the heart;
        'Twas a sad time of sorrow and distress:
        A wanderer among the cottages,
140   I with my pack of winter raiment saw
        The hardships of that season: many rich
        Sunk down as in a dream among the poor,
        And of the poor did many cease to be,
        And their place knew them not. Meanwhile, abridg'd
145   Of daily comforts, gladly reconciled
        To numerous self-denials, Margaret
        Went struggling on through those calamitous years
        With chearful hope: but ere the second autumn
        A fever seized her husband. In disease
150   He lingered long, and when his strength returned
        He found the little he had stored to meet
        The hour of accident or crippling age
        Was all consumed. As I have said, 'twas now
        A time of trouble; shoals of artisans
155   Were from their daily labour turned away
        To hang for bread on parish charity,
        They and their wives and children—happier far
        Could they have lived as do the little birds
        That peck along the hedges or the kite
160   That makes her dwelling in the mountain rocks.
        Ill fared it now with Robert, he who dwelt
        In this poor cottage; at his door he stood
        And whistled many a snatch of merry tunes
        That had no mirth in them, or with his knife
165   Carved uncouth figures on the heads of sticks,
        Then idly sought about through every nook
        Of house or garden any casual task
        Of use or ornament, and with a strange,
        Amusing but uneasy novelty
170   He blended where he might the various tasks
        Of summer, autumn, winter, and of spring.
        But this endured not; his good-humour soon
        Became a weight in which no pleasure was,
        And poverty brought on a petted° mood   *ill-tempered*
175   And a sore temper: day by day he drooped,
        And he would leave his home, and to the town
        Without an errand would he turn his steps
        Or wander here and there among the fields.
        One while he would speak lightly of his babes
180   And with a cruel tongue: at other times
        He played with them wild freaks of merriment:
        And 'twas a piteous thing to see the looks

4. As James Butler points out in his introduction, Wordsworth is purposely distancing his story in time. The "two blighting seasons" in fact occurred in 1794–95, only a few years before Wordsworth wrote *The Ruined Cottage,* when a bad harvest was followed by one of the worst winters on record. Much of the seed grain was destroyed in the ground, and the price of wheat nearly doubled.

Of the poor innocent children. 'Every smile,'
Said Margaret to me here beneath these trees,
185 'Made my heart bleed,' At this the old Man paus'd
And looking up to those enormous elms
He said, " 'Tis now the hour of deepest noon,
At this still season of repose and peace,
This hour when all things which are not at rest
190 Are chearful, while this multitude of flies
Fills all the air with happy melody,
Why should a tear be in an old man's eye?
Why should we thus with an untoward mind
And in the weakness of humanity
195 From natural wisdom turn our hearts away,
To natural comfort shut our eyes and ears,
And feeding on disquiet thus disturb
The calm of Nature with our restless thoughts?"

it's a nice dor, why pity Margaret.

END OF THE FIRST PART

Second Part

— main narrator

He spake with somewhat of a solemn tone:
200 But when he ended there was in his face
Such easy chearfulness, a look so mild
That for a little time it stole away
All recollection, and that simple tale
Passed from my mind like a forgotten sound.
205 A while on trivial things we held discourse,
To me soon tasteless. In my own despite
I thought of that poor woman as of one
Whom I had known and loved. He had rehearsed
Her homely tale with such familiar power,
210 With such a[n active]⁵ countenance, an eye
So busy, that the things of which he spake
Seemed present, and, attention now relaxed,
There was a heartfelt chillness in my veins.
I rose, and turning from that breezy shade
215 Went out into the open air and stood
To drink the comfort of the warmer sun.
Long time I had not stayed ere, looking round
Upon that tranquil ruin, I returned
And begged of the old man that for my sake
220 He would resume his story. He replied,
"It were a wantonness and would demand
Severe reproof, if we were men whose hearts
Could hold vain dalliance with the misery
Even of the dead, contented thence to draw
225 A momentary pleasure never marked
By reason, barren of all future good.
But we have known that there is often found
In mournful thoughts, and always might be found,

---

5. Wordsworth penciled the bracketed phrase into a gap left in the manuscript.

A power to virtue friendly; were't not so,
230 I am a dreamer among men, indeed
An idle dreamer. 'Tis a common tale,
By moving accidents[6] uncharactered,
A tale of silent suffering, hardly clothed
In bodily form, and to the grosser sense
235 But ill adapted, scarcely palpable
To him who does not think. But at your bidding
I will proceed.
                    While thus it fared with them
To whom this cottage till that hapless year
Had been a blessed home, it was my chance
240 To travel in a country far remote,
And glad I was when, halting by yon gate
That leads from the green lane, again I saw
These lofty elm-trees. Long I did not rest:
With many pleasant thoughts I cheer'd my way
245 O'er the flat common. At the door arrived,
I knocked, and when I entered with the hope
Of usual greeting, Margaret looked at me
A little while, then turned her head away
Speechless, and sitting down upon a chair
250 Wept bitterly. I wist not what to do
Or how to speak to her. Poor wretch! at last
She rose from off her seat—and then, oh Sir!
I cannot tell how she pronounced my name:
With fervent love, and with a face of grief
255 Unutterably helpless, and a look
That seem'd to cling upon me, she enquir'd
If I had seen her husband. As she spake
A strange surprize and fear came to my heart,
Nor had I power to answer ere she told
260 That he had disappeared—just two months gone.
He left his house; two wretched days had passed,
And on the third by the first break of light,
Within her casement full in view she saw
A purse of gold.[7] 'I trembled at the sight,'
265 Said Margaret, 'for I knew it was his hand
That placed it there, and on that very day
By one, a stranger, from my husband sent,
The tidings came that he had joined a troop
Of soldiers going to a distant land.
270 He left me thus—Poor Man! he had not heart
To take a farewell of me, and he feared
That I should follow with my babes, and sink
Beneath the misery of a soldier's life.'
This tale did Margaret tell with many tears:

6. Othello speaks "of most disastrous chances, / Of moving accidents by flood and field, / Of hair-breadth 'scapes" (*Othello* 1.3.133–35).
7. The "bounty" that her husband had been paid for enlisting in the militia. The shortage of volun-teers and England's sharply rising military needs had in some counties forced the bounty up from about £1 in 1757 to more than £16 in 1796 (J. R. Western, *English Militia in the Eighteenth Century*, 1965, p. 276).

275 And when she ended I had little power
To give her comfort, and was glad to take
Such words of hope from her own mouth as serv'd
To cheer us both: but long we had not talked
Ere we built up a pile of better thoughts,
280 And with a brighter eye she looked around
As if she had been shedding tears of joy.
We parted. It was then the early spring;
I left her busy with her garden tools;
And well remember, o'er that fence she looked,
285 And while I paced along the foot-way path
Called out, and sent a blessing after me
With tender chearfulness and with a voice
That seemed the very sound of happy thoughts.
    I roved o'er many a hill and many a dale
290 With this my weary load, in heat and cold,
Through many a wood, and many an open ground,
In sunshine or in shade, in wet or fair,
Now blithe, now drooping, as it might befal,
My best companions now the driving winds
295 And now the 'trotting brooks'[8] and whispering trees
And now the music of my own sad steps,
With many a short-lived thought that pass'd between
And disappeared. I came this way again
Towards the wane of summer, when the wheat
300 Was yellow, and the soft and bladed grass
Sprang up afresh and o'er the hay-field spread
Its tender green. When I had reached the door
I found that she was absent. In the shade
Where now we sit I waited her return.
305 Her cottage in its outward look appeared
As chearful as before; in any shew
Of neatness little changed, but that I thought
The honeysuckle crowded round the door
And from the wall hung down in heavier wreathes,
310 And knots of worthless stone-crop[9] started out
Along the window's edge, and grew like weeds
Against the lower panes. I turned aside
And stroll'd into her garden.—It was chang'd:
The unprofitable bindweed spread his bells
315 From side to side and with unwieldy wreaths
Had dragg'd the rose from its sustaining wall
And bent it down to earth; the border-tufts—
Daisy and thrift and lowly camomile
And thyme—had straggled out into the paths
320 Which they were used to deck. Ere this an hour
Was wasted. Back I turned my restless steps,
And as I walked before the door it chanced
A stranger passed, and guessing whom I sought

---

8. From Robert Burns (*To William Simpson*, line 87).

9. A plant with yellow flowers that grows on walls and rocks.

He said that she was used to ramble far.
325 The sun was sinking in the west, and now
I sate with sad impatience. From within
Her solitary infant cried aloud.
The spot though fair seemed very desolate,
The longer I remained more desolate.
330 And, looking round, I saw the corner-stones,
Till then unmark'd, on either side the door
With dull red stains discoloured and stuck o'er
With tufts and hairs of wool, as if the sheep
That feed upon the commons thither came
335 Familiarly and found a couching-place
Even at her threshold.—The house-clock struck eight;
I turned and saw her distant a few steps.
Her face was pale and thin, her figure too
Was chang'd. As she unlocked the door she said,
340 'It grieves me you have waited here so long,
But in good truth I've wandered much of late
And sometimes, to my shame I speak, have need
Of my best prayers to bring me back again.'
While on the board she spread our evening meal
345 She told me she had lost her elder child,
That he for months had been a serving-boy
Apprenticed by the parish. 'I perceive
You look at me, and you have cause. Today
I have been travelling far, and many days
350 About the fields I wander, knowing this
Only, that what I seek I cannot find.
And so I waste my time: for I am changed;
And to myself,' said she, 'have done much wrong,
And to this helpless infant. I have slept
355 Weeping, and weeping I have waked; my tears
Have flow'd as if my body were not such
As others are, and I could never die.
But I am now in mind and in my heart
More easy, and I hope,' said she, 'that heaven
360 Will give me patience to endure the things
Which I behold at home.' It would have grieved
Your very heart to see her. Sir, I feel
The story linger in my heart. I fear
'Tis long and tedious, but my spirit clings
365 To that poor woman: so familiarly
Do I perceive her manner, and her look
And presence, and so deeply do I feel
Her goodness, that not seldom in my walks
A momentary trance comes over me;
370 And to myself I seem to muse on one
By sorrow laid asleep or borne away,
A human being destined to awake
To human life, or something very near
To human life, when he shall come again
375 For whom she suffered. Sir, it would have griev'd

Your very soul to see her: evermore
Her eye-lids droop'd, her eyes were downward cast;
And when she at her table gave me food
She did not look at me. Her voice was low,
380 Her body was subdued. In every act
Pertaining to her house-affairs appeared
The careless stillness which a thinking mind
Gives to an idle matter—still she sighed,
But yet no motion of the breast was seen,
385 No heaving of the heart. While by the fire
We sate together, sighs came on my ear;
I knew not how, and hardly whence they came.
I took my staff, and when I kissed her babe
The tears stood in her eyes. I left her then
390 With the best hope and comfort I could give;
She thanked me for my will, but for my hope
It seemed she did not thank me.
                                        I returned
And took my rounds along this road again
Ere on its sunny bank the primrose flower
395 Had chronicled the earliest day of spring.
I found her sad and drooping; she had learn'd
No tidings of her husband: if he lived
She knew not that he lived; if he were dead
She knew not he was dead. She seemed the same
400 In person [or][1] appearance, but her house
Bespoke a sleepy hand of negligence;
The floor was neither dry nor neat, the hearth
Was comfortless [   ],
The windows too were dim, and her few books,
405 Which, one upon the other, heretofore
Had been piled up against the corner-panes
In seemly order, now with straggling leaves
Lay scattered here and there, open or shut
As they had chanced to fall. Her infant babe
410 Had from its mother caught the trick of grief
And sighed among its playthings. Once again
I turned towards the garden-gate and saw
More plainly still that poverty and grief
Were now come nearer to her: the earth was hard,
415 With weeds defaced and knots of withered grass;
No ridges there appeared of clear black mould,
No winter greenness; of her herbs and flowers
It seemed the better part were gnawed away
Or trampled on the earth; a chain of straw
420 Which had been twisted round the tender stem
Of a young apple-tree lay at its root;
The bark was nibbled round by truant sheep.
Margaret stood near, her infant in her arms,
And seeing that my eye was on the tree

1. The word *or* was erased here; later manuscripts read "and."

425 She said, 'I fear it will be dead and gone
Ere Robert come again.' Towards the house
Together we returned, and she inquired
If I had any hope. But for her Babe
And for her little friendless Boy, she said,
430 She had no wish to live, that she must die
Of sorrow. Yet I saw the idle loom
Still in its place. His Sunday garments hung
Upon the self-same nail, his very staff
Stood undisturbed behind the door. And when
435 I passed this way beaten by Autumn winds
She told me that her little babe was dead
And she was left alone. That very time,
I yet remember, through the miry lane
She walked with me a mile, when the bare trees
440 Trickled with foggy damps, and in such sort
That any heart had ached to hear her begg'd
That wheresoe'er I went I still would ask
For him whom she had lost. We parted then,
Our final parting, for from that time forth
445 Did many seasons pass ere I returned
Into this tract again.
                              Five tedious years
She lingered in unquiet widowhood,
A wife and widow. Needs must it have been
A sore heart-wasting. I have heard, my friend,
450 That in that broken arbour she would sit
The idle length of half a sabbath day—
There, where you see the toadstool's lazy head—
And when a dog passed by she still would quit
The shade and look abroad. On this old Bench
455 For hours she sate, and evermore her eye
Was busy in the distance, shaping things
Which made her heart beat quick. Seest thou that path?
(The green-sward now has broken its grey line)
There to and fro she paced through many a day
460 Of the warm summer, from a belt of flax
That girt her waist spinning the long-drawn thread
With backward steps.—Yet ever as there passed
A man whose garments shewed the Soldier's red,
Or crippled Mendicant in Sailor's garb,
465 The little child who sate to turn the wheel
Ceased from his toil, and she with faltering voice,
Expecting still to learn her husband's fate,
Made many a fond inquiry; and when they
Whose presence gave no comfort were gone by,
470 Her heart was still more sad. And by yon gate
Which bars the traveller's road she often stood
And when a stranger horseman came, the latch
Would lift, and in his face look wistfully,
Most happy if from aught discovered there
475 Of tender feeling she might dare repeat

The same sad question. Meanwhile her poor hut
Sunk to decay, for he was gone whose hand
At the first nippings of October frost
Closed up each chink and with fresh bands of straw
480 Chequered the green-grown thatch. And so she lived
Through the long winter, reckless and alone,
Till this reft house by frost, and thaw, and rain
Was sapped; and when she slept the nightly damps
Did chill her breast, and in the stormy day
485 Her tattered clothes were ruffled by the wind
Even at the side of her own fire. Yet still
She loved this wretched spot, nor would for worlds
Have parted hence; and still that length of road
And this rude bench one torturing hope endeared,
490 Fast rooted at her heart, and here, my friend,
In sickness she remained, and here she died,
Last human tenant of these ruined walls."
    The old Man ceased: he saw that I was mov'd;
From that low Bench, rising instinctively,
495 I turned aside in weakness, nor had power
To thank him for the tale which he had told.
I stood, and leaning o'er the garden-gate
Reviewed that Woman's suff'rings, and it seemed
To comfort me while with a brother's love
500 I blessed her in the impotence of grief.
At length [towards] the [Cottage I returned][2]
Fondly, and traced with milder interest
That secret spirit of humanity
Which, 'mid the calm oblivious tendencies
505 Of nature, 'mid her plants, her weeds, and flowers,
And silent overgrowings, still survived.
The old man, seeing this, resumed and said,
"My Friend, enough to sorrow have you given,
The purposes of wisdom ask no more;
510 Be wise and chearful, and no longer read
The forms of things with an unworthy eye.
She sleeps in the calm earth, and peace is here.
I well remember that those very plumes,
Those weeds, and the high spear-grass on that wall,
515 By mist and silent rain-drops silver'd o'er,
As once I passed did to my heart convey
So still an image of tranquillity,
So calm and still, and looked so beautiful
Amid the uneasy thoughts which filled my mind,
520 That what we feel of sorrow and despair
From ruin and from change, and all the grief
The passing shews of being leave behind,
Appeared an idle dream that could not live
Where meditation was. I turned away
525 And walked along my road in happiness."

2. The words inside the brackets were added in MS. E.

He ceased. By this the sun declining shot
A slant and mellow radiance which began
To fall upon us where beneath the trees
We sate on that low bench, and now we felt,
530   Admonished thus, the sweet hour coming on.
A linnet warbled from those lofty elms,
A thrush sang loud, and other melodies,
At distance heard, peopled the milder air.
The old man rose and hoisted up his load.
535   Together casting then a farewell look
Upon those silent walls, we left the shade
And ere the stars were visible attained
A rustic inn, our evening resting-place.

THE END

1797–ca.1799   1949

Michael[1]

A Pastoral Poem

If from the public way you turn your steps
Up the tumultuous brook of Green-head Ghyll,[2]
You will suppose that with an upright path
Your feet must struggle; in such bold ascent
5   The pastoral mountains front you, face to face.
But, courage! for around that boisterous brook
The mountains have all opened out themselves,
And made a hidden valley of their own.
No habitation can be seen; but they
10   Who journey thither find themselves alone
With a few sheep, with rocks and stones, and kites°   *hawks*
That overhead are sailing in the sky.
It is in truth an utter solitude;
Nor should I have made mention of this Dell
15   But for one object which you might pass by,
Might see and notice not. Beside the brook
Appears a straggling heap of unhewn stones!
And to that simple object appertains
A story—unenriched with strange events,
20   Yet not unfit, I deem, for the fireside,
Or for the summer shade. It was the first
Of those domestic tales that spake to me

---

1. This poem is founded on the actual misfortunes of a family at Grasmere. For the account of the sheepfold, see Dorothy Wordsworth's *Grasmere Journals,* October 11, 1800 (p. 1561). Wordsworth wrote to Thomas Poole, on April 9, 1801, that he had attempted to picture a mail "agitated by two of the most powerful affections of the human heart; the parental affection, and the love of property, *landed* property, including the feelings of inheri-

tance, home, and personal and family independence." The subtitle shows Wordsworth's shift of the term "pastoral" from aristocratic make-believe to the tragic suffering of people in what he called "humble and rustic life."
2. A ravine forming the bed of a stream. Green-head Ghyll is not far from Wordsworth's cottage at Grasmere. The other places named in the poem are also in that vicinity.

Of Shepherds, dwellers in the valleys, men
Whom I already loved;—not verily
25   For their own sakes, but for the fields and hills
Where was their occupation and abode.
And hence this Tale, while I was yet a Boy
Careless of books, yet having felt the power
Of Nature, by the gentle agency
30   Of natural objects, led me on to feel
For passions that were not my own, and think
(At random and imperfectly indeed)
On man, the heart of man, and human life.
Therefore, although it be a history
35   Homely and rude, I will relate the same
For the delight of a few natural hearts;
And, with yet fonder feeling, for the sake
Of youthful Poets, who among these hills
Will be my second self when I am gone.

40   Upon the forest-side in Grasmere Vale
There dwelt a Shepherd, Michael was his name;
An old man, stout of heart, and strong of limb.
His bodily frame had been from youth to age
Of an unusual strength: his mind was keen,
45   Intense, and frugal, apt for all affairs,
And in his shepherd's calling he was prompt
And watchful more than ordinary men.
Hence had he learned the meaning of all winds,
Of blasts of every tone; and, oftentimes,
50   When others heeded not, he heard the South
Make subterraneous music, like the noise
Of bagpipers on distant Highland hills.
The Shepherd, at such warning, of his flock
Bethought him, and he to himself would say,
55   "The winds are now devising work for me!"
And, truly, at all times, the storm, that drives
The traveller to a shelter, summoned him
Up to the mountains: he had been alone
Amid the heart of many thousand mists,
60   That came to him, and left him, on the heights.
So lived he till his eightieth year was past.
And grossly that man errs, who should suppose
That the green valleys, and the streams and rocks,
Were things indifferent to the Shepherd's thoughts.
65   Fields, where with cheerful spirits he had breathed
The common air; hills, which with vigorous step
He had so often climbed; which had impressed
So many incidents upon his mind
Of hardship, skill or courage, joy or fear;
70   Which, like a book, preserved the memory
Of the dumb animals, whom he had saved,
Had fed or sheltered, linking to such acts

The certainty of honourable gain;
Those fields, those hills—what could they less? had laid
75 Strong hold on his affections, were to him
A pleasurable feeling of blind love,
The pleasure which there is in life itself.

His days had not been passed in singleness.
His Helpmate was a comely matron, old—
80 Though younger than himself full twenty years.
She was a woman of a stirring life,
Whose heart was in her house: two wheels she had
Of antique form; this large, for spinning wool;
That small, for flax; and if one wheel had rest,
85 It was because the other was at work.
The Pair had but one inmate in their house,
An only Child, who had been born to them
When Michael, telling o'er his years, began
To deem that he was old,—in shepherd's phrase,
90 With one foot in the grave. This only Son,
With two brave sheep-dogs tried in many a storm,
The one of an inestimable worth,
Made all their household. I may truly say,
That they were as a proverb in the vale
95 For endless industry. When day was gone,
And from their occupations out of doors
The Son and Father were come home, even then,
Their labour did not cease; unless when all
Turned to the cleanly supper-board, and there,
100 Each with a mess of pottage and skimmed milk,
Sat round the basket piled with oaten cakes,
And their plain home-made cheese. Yet when the meal
Was ended, Luke (for so the Son was named)
And his old Father both betook themselves
105 To such convenient work as might employ
Their hands by the fire-side; perhaps to card
Wool for the Housewife's spindle, or repair
Some injury done to sickle, flail, or scythe,
Or other implement of house or field.

110   Down from the ceiling, by the chimney's edge,
That in our ancient uncouth country style
With huge and black projection overbrowed
Large space beneath, as duly as the light
Of day grew dim the Housewife hung a lamp;
115 An aged utensil, which had performed
Service beyond all others of its kind.
Early at evening did it burn—and late,
Surviving comrade of uncounted hours,
Which, going by from year to year, had found,
120 And left the couple neither gay perhaps
Nor cheerful, yet with objects and with hopes,
Living a life of eager industry.

And now, when Luke had reached his eighteenth year,
There by the light of his old lamp they sate,
125   Father and Son, while far into the night
The Housewife plied her own peculiar work,
Making the cottage through the silent hours
Murmur as with the sound of summer flies.
This light was famous in its neighbourhood,
130   And was a public symbol of the life
That thrifty Pair had lived. For, as it chanced,
Their cottage on a plot of rising ground
Stood single, with large prospect, north and south,
High into Easedale, up to Dunmail-Raise,
135   And westward to the village near the lake;
And from this constant light, so regular
And so far seen, the House itself, by all
Who dwelt within the limits of the vale,
Both old and young, was named THE EVENING STAR.

140   Thus living on through such a length of years,
The Shepherd, if he loved himself, must needs
Have loved his Helpmate; but to Michael's heart
This son of his old age was yet more dear—
Less from instinctive tenderness, the same
145   Fond spirit that blindly works in the blood of all—
Than that a child, more than all other gifts
That earth can offer to declining man,
Brings hope with it, and forward-looking thoughts,
And stirrings of inquietude, when they
150   By tendency of nature needs must fail.
Exceeding was the love he bare to him,
His heart and his heart's joy! For oftentimes
Old Michael, while he was a babe in arms,
Had done him female service, not alone
155   For pastime and delight, as is the use
Of fathers, but with patient mind enforced
To acts of tenderness; and he had rocked
His cradle, as with a woman's gentle hand.

    And, in a later time, ere yet the Boy
160   Had put on boy's attire, did Michael love,
Albeit of a stern unbending mind,
To have the Young-one in his sight, when he
Wrought in the field, or on his shepherd's stool
Sate with a fettered sheep before him stretched
165   Under the large old oak, that near his door
Stood single, and, from matchless depth of shade,
Chosen for the Shearer's covert from the sun,
Thence in our rustic dialect was called
The CLIPPING TREE, a name which yet it bears.
170   There, while they two were sitting in the shade,
With others round them, earnest all and blithe,
Would Michael exercise his heart with looks

Of fond correction and reproof bestowed
Upon the Child, if he disturbed the sheep
175 By catching at their legs, or with his shouts
Scared them, while they lay still beneath the shears.

And when by Heaven's good grace the boy grew up
A healthy Lad, and carried in his cheek
Two steady roses that were five years old;
180 Then Michael from a winter coppice³ cut
With his own hand a sapling, which he hooped
With iron, making it throughout in all
Due requisites a perfect shepherd's staff,
And gave it to the Boy; wherewith equipt
185 He as a watchman oftentimes was placed
At gate or gap, to stem or turn the flock;
And, to his office prematurely called,
There stood the urchin, as you will divine,
Something between a hindrance and a help;
190 And for this cause not always, I believe,
Receiving from his Father hire of praise;
Though nought was left undone which staff, or voice,
Or looks, or threatening gestures, could perform.

But soon as Luke, full ten years old, could stand
195 Against the mountain blasts; and to the heights,
Not fearing toil, nor length of weary ways,
He with his Father daily went, and they
Were as companions, why should I relate
That objects which the Shepherd loved before
200 Were dearer now? that from the Boy there came
Feelings and emanations—things which were
Light to the sun and music to the wind;
And that the old Man's heart seemed born again?

Thus in his Father's sight the Boy grew up:
205 And now, when he had reached his eighteenth year,
He was his comfort and his daily hope.

While in this sort the simple household lived
From day to day, to Michael's ear there came
Distressful tidings. Long before the time
210 Of which I speak, the Shepherd had been bound
In surety for his brother's son, a man
Of an industrious life, and ample means;
But unforeseen misfortunes suddenly
Had prest upon him; and old Michael now
215 Was summoned to discharge the forfeiture,
A grievous penalty, but little less
Than half his substance. This unlooked-for claim,
At the first hearing, for a moment took
More hope out of his life than he supposed

3. Grove of small trees.

220　That any old man ever could have lost.
　　As soon as he had armed himself with strength
　　To look his trouble in the face, it seemed
　　The Shepherd's sole resource to sell at once
　　A portion of his patrimonial fields.
225　Such was his first resolve; he thought again,
　　And his heart failed him. "Isabel," said he,
　　Two evenings after he had heard the news,
　　"I have been toiling more than seventy years,
　　And in the open sunshine of God's love
230　Have we all lived; yet if these fields of ours
　　Should pass into a stranger's hand, I think
　　That I could not lie quiet in my grave.
　　Our lot is a hard lot; the sun himself
　　Has scarcely been more diligent than I;
235　And I have lived to be a fool at last
　　To my own family. An evil man
　　That was, and made an evil choice, if he
　　Were false to us; and if he were not false,
　　There are ten thousand to whom loss like this
240　Had been no sorrow. I forgive him;—but
　　'Twere better to be dumb than to talk thus.

　　　"When I began, my purpose was to speak
　　Of remedies and of a cheerful hope.
　　Our Luke shall leave us, Isabel; the land
245　Shall not go from us, and it shall be free;
　　He shall possess it, free as is the wind
　　That passes over it. We have, thou know'st,
　　Another kinsman—he will be our friend
　　In this distress. He is a prosperous man,
250　Thriving in trade—and Luke to him shall go,
　　And with his kinsman's help and his own thrift
　　He quickly will repair this loss, and then
　　He may return to us. If here he stay,
　　What can be done? Where every one is poor,
　　What can be gained?"
255　　　　　　　　　　　At this the old Man paused,
　　And Isabel sat silent, for her mind
　　Was busy, looking back into past times.
　　There's Richard Bateman,[4] thought she to herself,
　　He was a parish-boy—at the church-door
260　They made a gathering for him, shillings, pence
　　And halfpennies, wherewith the neighbours bought
　　A basket, which they filled with pedlar's wares;
　　And, with this basket on his arm, the lad
　　Went up to London, found a master there,
265　Who, out of many, chose the trusty boy
　　To go and overlook his merchandise
　　Beyond the seas; where he grew wondrous rich,
　　And left estates and monies to the poor,

---

4. The story alluded to here is well known in the country. The chapel is called Ings Chapel and is on the road leading from Kendal to Ambleside [Wordsworth's note].

And, at his birth-place, built a chapel floored
270 With marble, which he sent from foreign lands.
These thoughts, and many others of like sort,
Passed quickly through the mind of Isabel,
And her face brightened. The old Man was glad,
And thus resumed:—"Well, Isabel! this scheme
275 These two days, has been meat and drink to me.
Far more than we have lost is left us yet.
—We have enough—I wish indeed that I
Were younger;—but this hope is a good hope.
Make ready Luke's best garments, of the best
280 Buy for him more, and let us send him forth
To-morrow, or the next day, or to-night:
—If he *could* go, the Boy should go to-night."

      Here Michael ceased, and to the fields went forth
With a light heart. The Housewife for five days
285 Was restless morn and night, and all day long
Wrought on with her best fingers to prepare
Things needful for the journey of her son.
But Isabel was glad when Sunday came
To stop her in her work: for, when she lay
290 By Michael's side, she through the last two nights
Heard him, how he was troubled in his sleep:
And when they rose at morning she could see
That all his hopes were gone. That day at noon
She said to Luke, while they two by themselves
295 Were sitting at the door, "Thou must not go:
We have no other Child but thee to lose,
None to remember—do not go away,
For if thou leave thy Father he will die."
The Youth made answer with a jocund voice;
300 And Isabel, when she had told her fears,
Recovered heart. That evening her best fare
Did she bring forth, and all together sat
Like happy people round a Christmas fire.

      With daylight Isabel resumed her work;
305 And all the ensuing week the house appeared
As cheerful as a grove in Spring: at length
The expected letter from their kinsman came,
With kind assurances that he would do
His utmost for the welfare of the Boy;
310 To which, requests were added, that forthwith
He might be sent to him. Ten times or more
The letter was read over; Isabel
Went forth to show it to the neighbours round;
Nor was there at that time on English land
315 A prouder heart than Luke's. When Isabel
Had to her house returned, the old Man said,
"He shall depart to-morrow." To this word
The Housewife answered, talking much of things
Which, if at such short notice he should go,

320   Would surely be forgotten. But at length
      She gave consent, and Michael was at ease.

          Near the tumultuous brook of Green-head Ghyll,
      In that deep valley, Michael had designed
      To build a Sheep-fold;[5] and, before he heard
325   The tidings of his melancholy loss,
      For this same purpose he had gathered up
      A heap of stones, which by the streamlet's edge
      Lay thrown together, ready for the work.
      With Luke that evening thitherward he walked:
330   And soon as they had reached the place he stopped,
      And thus the old Man spake to him:—"My Son,
      To-morrow thou wilt leave me: with full heart
      I look upon thee, for thou art the same
      That wert a promise to me ere thy birth,
335   And all thy life hast been my daily joy.
      I will relate to thee some little part
      Of our two histories; 'twill do thee good
      When thou art from me, even if I should touch
      On things thou canst not know of.——After thou
340   First cam'st into the world—as oft befals
      To new-born infants—thou didst sleep away
      Two days, and blessings from thy Father's tongue
      Then fell upon thee. Day by day passed on,
      And still I loved thee with increasing love.
345   Never to living ear came sweeter sounds
      Than when I heard thee by our own fire-side
      First uttering, without words, a natural tune;
      While thou, a feeding babe, didst in thy joy
      Sing at thy Mother's breast. Month followed month,
350   And in the open fields my life was passed
      And on the mountains; else I think that thou
      Hadst been brought up upon thy Father's knees.
      But we were playmates, Luke: among these hills,
      As well thou knowest, in us the old and young
355   Have played together, nor with me didst thou
      Lack any pleasure which a boy can know."
      Luke had a manly heart; but at these words
      He sobbed aloud. The old Man grasped his hand,
      And said, "Nay, do not take it so—I see
360   That these are things of which I need not speak.
      —Even to the utmost I have been to thee
      A kind and a good Father: and herein
      I but repay a gift which I myself
      Received at others' hands; for, though now old
365   Beyond the common life of man, I still
      Remember them who loved me in my youth.
      Both of them sleep together: here they lived,
      As all their Forefathers had done; and when
      At length their time was come, they were not loth

----

5. A sheepfold [pen for sheep] in these mountains is an unroofed building of stone walls, with different divisions [Wordsworth's note].

370   To give their bodies to the family mould.
I wished that thou should'st live the life they lived:
But, 'tis a long time to look back, my Son,
And see so little gain from threescore years.
These fields were burthened° when they came to me;   *mortgaged*
375   Till I was forty years of age, not more
Than half of my inheritance was mine.
I toiled and toiled; God blessed me in my work,
And till these three weeks past the land was free.
—It looks as if it never could endure
380   Another Master. Heaven forgive me, Luke,
If I judge ill for thee, but it seems good
That thou should'st go."
                            At this the old Man paused;
Then, pointing to the stones near which they stood,
Thus, after a short silence, he resumed:
385   "This was a work for us; and now, my Son,
It is a work for me. But, lay one stone—
Here, lay it for me, Luke, with thine own hands.
Nay, Boy, be of good hope;—we both may live
To see a better day. At eighty-four
390   I still am strong and hale;—do thou thy part;
I will do mine.—I will begin again
With many tasks that were resigned to thee:
Up to the heights, and in among the storms,
Will I without thee go again, and do
395   All works which I was wont to do alone,
Before I knew thy face.—Heaven bless thee, Boy!
Thy heart these two weeks has been beating fast
With many hopes; it should be so—yes—yes—
I knew that thou could'st never have a wish
400   To leave me, Luke: thou hast been bound to me
Only by links of love: when thou art gone,
What will be left to us!—But, I forget
My purposes. Lay now the corner-stone,
As I requested; and hereafter, Luke,
405   When thou art gone away, should evil men
Be thy companions, think of me, my Son,
And of this moment; hither turn thy thoughts,
And God will strengthen thee: amid all fear
And all temptation, Luke, I pray that thou
410   May'st bear in mind the life thy Fathers lived,
Who, being innocent, did for that cause
Bestir them in good deeds. Now, fare thee well—
When thou return'st, thou in this place wilt see
A work which is not here: a covenant
415   'Twill be between us; but, whatever fate
Befal thee, I shall love thee to the last,
And bear thy memory with me to the grave."

    The Shepherd ended here; and Luke stooped down,
And, as his Father had requested, laid

420 The first stone of the Sheep-fold. At the sight
     The old Man's grief broke from him; to his heart
     He pressed his Son, he kissèd him and wept;
     And to the house together they returned.
     —Hushed was that House in peace, or seeming peace,
425 Ere the night fell:—with morrow's dawn the Boy
     Began his journey, and when he had reached
     The public way, he put on a bold face;
     And all the neighbours, as he passed their doors,
     Came forth with wishes and with farewell prayers,
430 That followed him till he was out of sight.

        A good report did from their Kinsman come,
     Of Luke and his well-doing: and the Boy
     Wrote loving letters, full of wondrous news,
     Which, as the Housewife phrased it, were throughout
435 "The prettiest letters that were ever seen."
     Both parents read them with rejoicing hearts.
     So, many months passed on: and once again
     The Shepherd went about his daily work
     With confident and cheerful thoughts; and now
440 Sometimes when he could find a leisure hour
     He to that valley took his way, and there
     Wrought at the Sheep-fold. Meantime Luke began
     To slacken in his duty; and, at length,
     He in the dissolute city gave himself
445 To evil courses: ignominy and shame
     Fell on him, so that he was driven at last
     To seek a hiding-place beyond the seas.

        There is a comfort in the strength of love;
     'Twill make a thing endurable, which else
450 Would overset the brain, or break the heart:
     I have conversed with more than one who well
     Remember the old Man, and what he was
     Years after he had heard this heavy news.
     His bodily frame had been from youth to age
455 Of an unusual strength. Among the rocks
     He went, and still looked up to sun and cloud,
     And listened to the wind; and, as before
     Performed all kinds of labour for his sheep,
     And for the land, his small inheritance.
460 And to that hollow dell from time to time
     Did he repair, to build the Fold of which
     His flock had need. 'Tis not forgotten yet
     The pity which was then in every heart
     For the old Man—and 'tis believed by all
465 That many and many a day he thither went,
     And never lifted up a single stone.

        There, by the Sheep-fold, sometimes was he seen
     Sitting alone, or with his faithful Dog,

Then old, beside him, lying at his feet.
470 The length of full seven years, from time to time,
He at the building of this Sheep-fold wrought,
And left the work unfinished when he died.
Three years, or little more, did Isabel
Survive her Husband: at her death the estate
475 Was sold, and went into a stranger's hand.
The Cottage which was named the EVENING STAR
Is gone—the ploughshare has been through the ground
On which it stood; great changes have been wrought
In all the neighbourhood:—yet the oak is left
480 That grew beside their door; and the remains
Of the unfinished Sheep-fold may be seen
Beside the boisterous brook of Green-head Ghyll.

Oct. 11–Dec. 9, 1800   1800

Resolution and Independence[1]

1

There was a roaring in the wind all night;
The rain came heavily and fell in floods;
But now the sun is rising calm and bright;
The birds are singing in the distant woods;
5 Over his own sweet voice the Stock-dove broods;
The Jay makes answer as the Magpie chatters;
And all the air is filled with pleasant noise of waters.

2

All things that love the sun are out of doors;
The sky rejoices in the morning's birth;
10 The grass is bright with rain-drops;—on the moors
The hare is running races in her mirth;
And with her feet she from the plashy earth
Raises a mist; that, glittering in the sun,
Runs with her all the way, wherever she doth run.

3

15 I was a Traveller then upon the moor;
I saw the hare that raced about with joy;
I heard the woods and distant waters roar;
Or heard them not, as happy as a boy:
The pleasant season did my heart employ:
20 My old remembrances went from me wholly;
And all the ways of men, so vain and melancholy.

1. For the meeting with the old leech gatherer, see Dorothy Wordsworth's *Grasmere Journals*, October 3, 1800 (p. 1560). Wordsworth himself tells us that "I was in the state of feeling described in the beginning of the poem, while crossing over Barton Fell from Mr. Clarkson's, at the foot of Ullswater, towards Askam. The image of the hare I then observed on the ridge of the Fell." He wrote the poem eighteen months after this event (see *Grasmere Journals*, May 4 and 7, 1802; pp. 1566 and 1567).

4

But, as it sometimes chanceth, from the might
Of joy in minds that can no further go,
As high as we have mounted in delight
25 In our dejection do we sink as low;
To me that morning did it happen so;
And fears and fancies thick upon me came;
Dim sadness—and blind thoughts, I knew not, nor could name.

5

I heard the sky-lark warbling in the sky;
30 And I bethought me of the playful hare:
Even such a happy Child of earth am I;
Even as these blissful creatures do I fare;
Far from the world I walk, and from all care;
But there may come another day to me—
35 Solitude, pain of heart, distress, and poverty.

6

My whole life I have lived in pleasant thought,
As if life's business were a summer mood;
As if all needful things would come unsought
To genial faith, still rich in genial good;
40 But how can He expect that others should
Build for him, sow for him, and at his call
Love him, who for himself will take no heed at all?

7

I thought of Chatterton,[2] the marvellous Boy,
The sleepless Soul that perished in his pride;
45 Of Him[3] who walked in glory and in joy
Following his plough, along the mountain-side:
By our own spirits are we deified:
We Poets in our youth begin in gladness;
But thereof come in the end despondency and madness.

8

50 Now, whether it were by peculiar grace,
A leading from above, a something given,
Yet it befel, that, in this lonely place,
When I with these untoward thoughts had striven,
Beside a pool bare to the eye of heaven
55 I saw a Man before me unawares: *present!*
The oldest man he seemed that ever wore grey hairs.

9

As a huge stone is sometimes seen to lie
Couched on the bald top of an eminence;

---

2. Thomas Chatterton (1752–1770), a poet of
great talent who, in his loneliness and dire poverty,
poisoned himself at the age of seventeen and so
became the prime Romantic symbol of neglected
young genius.
3. Robert Burns, also considered at that time as a
natural poet who died young and poor, without
adequate recognition.

Wonder to all who do the same espy,
60 By what means it could thither come, and whence;
So that it seems a thing endued with sense:
Like a sea-beast crawled forth, that on a shelf
Of rock or sand reposeth, there to sun itself;

10

Such seemed this Man,[4] not all alive nor dead,
65 Nor all asleep—in his extreme old age:
His body was bent double, feet and head
Coming together in life's pilgrimage;
As if some dire constraint of pain, or rage
Of sickness felt by him in times long past,
70 A more than human weight upon his frame had cast.

11

Himself he propped, limbs, body, and pale face,
Upon a long grey staff of shaven wood:
And, still as I drew near with gentle pace,
Upon the margin of that moorish flood
75 Motionless as a cloud the old Man stood,
That heareth not the loud winds when they call;
And moveth all together, if it move at all.

12

At length, himself unsettling, he the pond
Stirred with his staff, and fixedly did look
80 Upon the muddy water, which he conned,
As if he had been reading in a book:
And now a stranger's privilege I took;
And, drawing to his side, to him did say,
"This morning gives us promise of a glorious day."

13

85 A gentle answer did the old Man make,
In courteous speech which forth he slowly drew:
And him with further words I thus bespake,
"What occupation do you there pursue?
This is a lonesome place for one like you."
90 Ere he replied, a flash of mild surprise
Broke from the sable orbs of his yet-vivid eyes.

14

His words came feebly, from a feeble chest,
But each in solemn order followed each,

---

4. In Wordsworth's own analysis of this passage he says that the stone is endowed with something of life, the sea beast is stripped of some of its life to assimilate it to the stone, and the old man divested of enough life and motion to make "the two objects unite and coalesce in just comparison." He used the passage to demonstrate his theory of how the "conferring, the abstracting, and the modifying powers of the Imagination . . . are all brought into conjunction" (Preface to the *Poems* of 1815). Cf. Coleridge's brief definitions of the imagination in *Biographia Literaria,* chap. 13 (p. 1627).

With something of a lofty utterance drest—
95   Choice word and measured phrase, above the reach
Of ordinary men; a stately speech;
Such as grave Livers[5] do in Scotland use,
Religious men, who give to God and man their dues.

15

He told, that to these waters he had come
100   To gather leeches,[6] being old and poor:
Employment hazardous and wearisome!
And he had many hardships to endure:
From pond to pond he roamed, from moor to moor;
Housing, with God's good help, by choice or chance;
105   And in this way he gained an honest maintenance.

16

The old Man still stood talking by my side;
But now his voice to me was like a stream
Scarce heard; nor word from word could I divide;
And the whole body of the Man did seem
110   Like one whom I had met with in a dream;
Or like a man from some far region sent,
To give me human strength, by apt admonishment.

17

My former thoughts returned: the fear that kills;
And hope that is unwilling to be fed;
115   Cold, pain, and labour, and all fleshly ills;
And mighty Poets in their misery dead.
—Perplexed, and longing to be comforted,
My question eagerly did I renew,
"How is it that you live, and what is it you do?"

18

120   He with a smile did then his words repeat;
And said, that, gathering leeches, far and wide
He travelled; stirring thus about his feet
The waters of the pools where they abide.
"Once I could meet with them on every side;
125   But they have dwindled long by slow decay;
Yet still I persevere, and find them where I may."

19

While he was talking thus, the lonely place,
The old Man's shape, and speech—all troubled me:
In my mind's eye I seemed to see him pace
130   About the weary moors continually,
Wandering about alone and silently.

---

5. Those who live gravely.
6. Used to draw blood for curative purposes. A
leech gatherer, bare legged in shallow water,
stirred the water to attract them and, when they
fastened themselves to his legs, picked them off.

While I these thoughts within myself pursued,
He, having made a pause, the same discourse renewed.

20

And soon with this he other matter blended,
135 Cheerfully uttered, with demeanour kind,
But stately in the main; and when he ended,
I could have laughed myself to scorn to find
In that decrepit Man so firm a mind.
"God," said I, "be my help and stay[7] secure;
140 I'll think of the Leech-gatherer on the lonely moor!"

May 3–July 4, 1802   1807

I wandered lonely as a cloud[1]

I wandered lonely as a cloud
That floats on high o'er vales and hills,
When all at once I saw a crowd,
A host, of golden daffodils;
5   Beside the lake, beneath the trees,
Fluttering and dancing in the breeze.

Continuous as the stars that shine
And twinkle on the milky way,
They stretched in never-ending line
10   Along the margin of a bay:
Ten thousand saw I at a glance,
Tossing their heads in sprightly dance.

The waves beside them danced; but they
Out-did the sparkling waves in glee:
15   A poet could not but be gay,
In such a jocund company:
I gazed—and gazed—but little thought
What wealth the show to me had brought:

For oft, when on my couch I lie
20   In vacant or in pensive mood,
They flash upon that inward eye
Which is the bliss of solitude;
And then my heart with pleasure fills,
And dances with the daffodils.

1804   1807

My heart leaps up

My heart leaps up when I behold
A rainbow in the sky:

---

7. Support (a noun).
1. For the original experience, two years earlier,

see Dorothy Wordsworth's *Grasmere Journals*,
April 15, 1802 (p. 1563).

So was it when my life began;
So is it now I am a man;
So be it when I shall grow old,
      Or let me die!
The Child is father of the Man;
And I could wish my days to be
Bound each to each by natural piety.[1]

Mar. 26, 1802   1807

Ode: Intimations of Immortality

In 1843, Wordsworth said about this *Ode* to Isabella Fenwick:

> This was composed during my residence at Town End, Grasmere; two years at least passed between the writing of the four first stanzas and the remaining part. To the attentive and competent reader the whole sufficiently explains itself; but there may be no harm in adverting here to particular feelings or *experiences* of my own mind on which the structure of the poem partly rests. Nothing was more difficult for me in childhood than to admit the notion of death as a state applicable to my own being. I have said elsewhere [in the opening stanza of *We Are Seven*]:
>
>> —A simple child,
>> That lightly draws its breath,
>> And feels its life in every limb,
>> What should it know of death!—
>
> But it was not so much from [feelings] of animal vivacity that *my* difficulty came as from a sense of the indomitableness of the spirit within me. I used to brood over the stories of Enoch and Elijah [Genesis 5.22–24; 2 Kings 2.11], and almost to persuade myself that, whatever might become of others, I should be translated, in something of the same way, to heaven. With a feeling congenial to this, I was often unable to think of external things as having external existence, and I communed with all that I saw as something not apart from, but inherent in, my own immaterial nature. Many times while going to school have I grasped at a wall or tree to recall myself from this abyss of idealism to the reality. At that time I was afraid of such processes. In later periods of life I have deplored, as we have all reason to do, a subjugation of an opposite character, and have rejoiced over the remembrances, as is expressed in the lines—
>
>> Obstinate questionings
>> Of sense and outward things,
>> Fallings from us, vanishings; etc.
>
> To that dreamlike vividness and splendor which invest objects of sight in childhood, everyone, I believe, if he would look back, could bear testimony, and I need not dwell upon it here: but having in the Poem regarded it as presumptive evidence of a prior state of existence, I think it right to protest against a conclusion, which has given pain to some good and pious persons, that I meant to inculcate such a belief. It is far too shadowy a notion to be recommended to faith, as more than an element in our instincts of immortality. But let us bear in mind that, though the idea is not advanced in revelation, there is nothing there to

1. As distinguished from piety based on the Scriptures, in which God makes the rainbow the token of his covenant with Noah and all his descendants (Genesis 9.12–17). The religious sentiment that binds Wordsworth's mature self to that of his childhood is a continuing responsiveness to the miracle of ordinary things.

contradict it, and the fall of Man presents an analogy in its favor. Accordingly, a pre-existent state has entered into the popular creeds of many nations; and, among all persons acquainted with classic literature, is known as an ingredient in Platonic philosophy. Archimedes said that he could move the world if he had a point whereon to rest his machine. Who has not felt the same aspirations as regards the world of his own mind? Having to wield some of its elements when I was impelled to write this Poem on the 'Immortality of the Soul,' I took hold of the notion of pre-existence as having sufficient foundation in humanity for authorizing me to make for my purpose the best use of it I could as a Poet.

Plato, to whom Wordsworth refers, held the doctrine that the soul is immortal and exists separately from the body both before birth and after death. But while the *Ode* proposes that the soul only gradually loses "the vision splendid" after birth, Plato maintained the contrary: that the knowledge of the eternal Ideas, which the soul had acquired by direct acquaintance, is totally lost at the instant of birth and must be gradually "recollected" by philosophical discipline in the course of this life (*Phaedo* 73–77). Wordsworth's metaphorical use of the concept of preexistence in his poem resembles more closely the view of some neoplatonists that the glory of the unborn soul is gradually quenched by its descent into the darkness of matter.

When he dictated this long note to Isabella Fenwick, at the age of seventy-two or seventy-three, Wordsworth was troubled by objections that his apparent claim for the preexistence of the soul violated the Christian belief that the soul, although it survives after death, does not exist before the birth of an individual. His claim in the note is that he used preexistence not as a doctrine but only as a postulate enabling him to deal "as a poet" with a general human experience: that the passing of youth involves the loss of a freshness and radiance investing everything one sees. Coleridge's *Dejection: An Ode,* which he wrote (in its earliest version) after he had heard the first four stanzas of Wordsworth's poem, employs a similar figurative technique for a comparable, though more devastating, experience of loss.

The original published text of this poem (in 1807) had as its title only "Ode," and then as epigraph *"Paulo maiora canamus"* ("Let us sing of somewhat higher things") from Virgil's *Eclogue 4.*

Ode

Intimations of Immortality from Recollections of Early Childhood

The Child is Father of the Man;
And I could wish my days to be
Bound each to each by natural piety.[1]

I

There was a time when meadow, grove, and stream,
The earth, and every common sight,
        To me did seem
      Apparelled in celestial light,
5   The glory and the freshness of a dream.
It is not now as it hath been of yore;—
        Turn wheresoe'er I may,
            By night or day,
The things which I have seen I now can see no more.

---

1. The concluding lines of Wordsworth's *My heart leaps up.*

2

10   The Rainbow comes and goes,
        And lovely is the Rose,
        The Moon doth with delight
Look round her when the heavens are bare,
        Waters on a starry night
15   Are beautiful and fair;
        The sunshine is a glorious birth;
        But yet I know, where'er I go,
That there hath past away a glory from the earth.

3

        Now, while the birds thus sing a joyous song,
20   And while the young lambs bound
            As to the tabor's[2] sound,
To me alone there came a thought of grief:
A timely utterance[3] gave that thought relief,
            And I again am strong:
25   The cataracts blow their trumpets from the steep;
No more shall grief of mine the season wrong;
I hear the Echoes through the mountains throng,
The Winds come to me from the fields of sleep,[4]
            And all the earth is gay;
30   Land and sea
        Give themselves up to jollity,
            And with the heart of May
        Doth every Beast keep holiday;—
            Thou Child of Joy,
35   Shout round me, let me hear thy shouts, thou happy
        Shepherd-boy!

4

        Ye blessed Creatures, I have heard the call
            Ye to each other make; I see
        The heavens laugh with you in your jubilee;
            My heart is at your festival,
40   My head hath its coronal,[5]
        The fulness of your bliss, I feel—I feel it all.
            Oh evil day! if I were sullen
            While Earth herself is adorning,
                This sweet May-morning,
45   And the Children are culling
                On every side,
            In a thousand valleys far and wide,
            Fresh flowers; while the sun shines warm,
And the Babe leaps up on his Mother's arm:—

2. A small drum often used to beat time for dancing.
3. Perhaps *My heart leaps up*, perhaps *Resolution
and Independence*, perhaps not a poem at all.
4. Of the many suggested interpretations, the simplest is "from the fields where they were sleeping."

Wordsworth often associated a rising wind with the
revival of spirit and of poetic inspiration (see, e.g.,
the opening passage of *The Prelude*, p. 1499).
5. Circlet of wildflowers, with which the shepherd
boys trimmed their hats in May.

50 I hear, I hear, with joy I hear!
            —But there's a Tree, of many, one,
    A single Field which I have looked upon,
    Both of them speak of something that is gone:
            The Pansy at my feet
55   Doth the same tale repeat:
    Whither is fled the visionary gleam?
    Where is it now, the glory and the dream?

5

    Our birth is but a sleep and a forgetting:
    The Soul that rises with us, our life's Star,[6]
60   Hath had elsewhere its setting,
            And cometh from afar:
            Not in entire forgetfulness,
            And not in utter nakedness,
    But trailing clouds of glory do we come
65   From God, who is our home:
    Heaven lies about us in our infancy!
    Shades of the prison-house begin to close
            Upon the growing Boy,
    But He beholds the light, and whence it flows,
70   He sees it in his joy;
    The Youth, who daily farther from the east
            Must travel, still is Nature's Priest,
            And by the vision splendid
            Is on his way attended;
75 At length the Man perceives it die away,
    And fade into the light of common day.

6

    Earth fills her lap with pleasures of her own;
    Yearnings she hath in her own natural kind,
    And, even with something of a Mother's mind,
80   And no unworthy aim,
            The homely[7] Nurse doth all she can
    To make her Foster-child, her Inmate Man,
            Forget the glories he hath known,
    And that imperial palace whence he came.

7

85 Behold the Child among his new-born blisses,
    A six years' Darling of a pigmy size!
    See, where 'mid work of his own hand he lies,
    Fretted[8] by sallies of his mother's kisses,
    With light upon him from his father's eyes!
90 See, at his feet, some little plan or chart,
    Some fragment from his dream of human life,
    Shaped by himself with newly-learnèd art;

6. The sun, as metaphor for the soul.
7. In the old sense: simple and friendly.

8. Irritated; or possibly in the old sense: checkered over.

A wedding or a festival,
A mourning or a funeral;
95   And this hath now his heart,
And unto this he frames his song:
Then will he fit his tongue
To dialogues of business, love, or strife;
But it will not be long
100   Ere this be thrown aside,
And with new joy and pride
The little Actor cons another part;
Filling from time to time his "humorous stage"[9]
With all the Persons, down to palsied Age,
105   That Life brings with her in her equipage;
As if his whole vocation
Were endless imitation.

8

Thou, whose exterior semblance doth belie
Thy Soul's immensity;
110   Thou best Philosopher, who yet dost keep
Thy heritage, thou Eye among the blind,
That, deaf and silent, read'st the eternal deep,
Haunted for ever by the eternal mind,—
Mighty Prophet! Seer blest!
115   On whom those truths do rest,
Which we are toiling all our lives to find,
In darkness lost, the darkness of the grave;
Thou, over whom thy Immortality
Broods like the Day, a Master o'er a Slave,
120   A Presence which is not to be put by;
Thou little Child, yet glorious in the might
Of heaven-born freedom on thy being's height,
Why with such earnest pains dost thou provoke
The years to bring the inevitable yoke,
125   Thus blindly with thy blessedness at strife?
Full soon thy Soul shall have her earthly freight,
And custom lie upon thee with a weight,
Heavy as frost, and deep almost as life!

9

O joy! that in our embers
130   Is something that doth live,
That nature yet remembers
What was so fugitive!
The thought of our past years in me doth breed
Perpetual benediction: not indeed
135   For that which is most worthy to be blest;
Delight and liberty, the simple creed

9. From a sonnet by the Elizabethan poet Samuel
Daniel. In Daniel's age *humorous* meant "capricious" and also referred to the various characters
and temperaments ("humors") represented in
drama.

Of Childhood, whether busy or at rest,
With new-fledged hope still fluttering in his breast:—
   Not for these I raise
140   The song of thanks and praise;
   But for those obstinate questionings
   Of sense and outward things,
   Fallings from us, vanishings;
   Blank misgivings of a Creature
145 Moving about in worlds not realised,[1]
High instincts before which our mortal Nature
Did tremble like a guilty Thing surprised:
   But for those first affections,
   Those shadowy recollections,
150   Which, be they what they may,
Are yet the fountain light of all our day,
Are yet a master light of all our seeing;
  Uphold us, cherish, and have power to make
Our noisy years seem moments in the being
155 Of the eternal Silence: truths that wake,
   To perish never;
Which neither listlessness, nor mad endeavour,
   Nor Man nor Boy,
Nor all that is at enmity with joy,
160 Can utterly abolish or destroy!
  Hence in a season of calm weather
   Though inland far we be,
Our Souls have sight of that immortal sea
   Which brought us hither,
165 Can in a moment travel thither,
And see the Children sport upon the shore,
And hear the mighty waters rolling evermore.

       10

Then sing, ye Birds, sing, sing a joyous song!
   And let the young Lambs bound
170   As to the tabor's sound!
We in thought will join your throng,
   Ye that pipe and ye that play,
   Ye that through your hearts to-day
   Feel the gladness of the May!
175 What though the radiance which was once so bright
Be now for ever taken from my sight,
   Though nothing can bring back the hour
Of splendour in the grass, of glory in the flower;
   We will grieve not, rather find
180   Strength in what remains behind;
   In the primal sympathy
   Which having been must ever be;
   In the soothing thoughts that spring

---

1. Not seeming real (see Wordsworth's comment in the headnote on p. 1479).

Out of human suffering;
185   In the faith that looks through death,
In years that bring the philosophic mind.

11

And O, ye Fountains, Meadows, Hills, and Groves,
Forebode not any severing of our loves!
Yet in my heart of hearts I feel your might;
190   I only have relinquished one delight
To live beneath your more habitual sway.
I love the Brooks which down their channels fret,
Even more than when I tripped lightly as they;
The innocent brightness of a new-born Day
195   Is lovely yet;
The Clouds that gather round the setting sun
Do take a sober colouring from an eye
That hath kept watch o'er man's mortality;
Another race hath been, and other palms are won.[2]
200   Thanks to the human heart by which we live,
Thanks to its tenderness, its joys, and fears,
To me the meanest flower that blows can give
Thoughts that do often lie too deep for tears.

1802–04   1807

Ode to Duty[1]

*Jam non consilio bonus, sed more eò perductus, ut non tantum rectè
facere possim, sed nisi rectè facere non possim.*[2]

Stern Daughter of the Voice of God![3]
O Duty! if that name thou love
Who art a light to guide, a rod
To check the erring, and reprove;
5   Thou, who art victory and law

2. In Greece foot races were often run for the prize of a branch or wreath of palm. Wordsworth's line echoes Paul, 1 Corinthians 9.24, who uses such races as a metaphor for life: "Know ye not that they which run in a race run all, but one receiveth the prize?"

1. "This Ode . . . is on the model of Gray's *Ode to Adversity* which is copied from Horace's *Ode to Fortune*. Many and many a time have I been twitted by my wife and sister for having forgotten this dedication of myself to the stern lawgiver" [Wordsworth's note].

In this poem, a striking departure from his earlier forms and ideas, Wordsworth abandons the descriptive-meditative pattern of his *Tintern Abbey* and *Ode: Intimations of Immortality* and reverts to the standard 18th-century form of an ode addressed to a personified abstraction. The poem also represents Wordsworth's reversion from his

youthful reliance on natural impulse to a more orthodox ethical and religious tradition. It makes no reference to that "Nature" which earlier had constituted for Wordsworth "both law and impulse" and, in *Tintern Abbey,* had been called "The guide, the guardian of my heart, and soul / Of all my moral being" (lines 110–11).

2. Now I am not good by conscious intent, but have been so trained by habit that I not only can act rightly but am unable to act other than rightly (Latin). Added in 1837, this epigraph is an adaptation from *Moral Epistles* 120.10 by Seneca (4 B.C.E.–65 C.E.), Stoic philosopher and writer of tragedies.

3. Cf. *Paradise Lost* 9.652–54: "God so commanded, and left that Command / Sole Daughter of his voice; the rest, we live / Law to ourselves, our Reason is our Law."

When empty terrors overawe;
From vain temptations dost set free;
And calm'st the weary strife of frail humanity!

There are who ask not if thine eye
10 Be on them; who, in love and truth,
Where no misgiving is, rely
Upon the genial sense[4] of youth:
Glad Hearts! without reproach or blot;
Who do thy work, and know it not:
15 Oh! if through confidence misplaced
They fail, thy saving arms, dread Power! around them cast.

Serene will be our days and bright,
And happy will our nature be,
When love is an unerring light,
20 And joy its own security.
And they a blissful course may hold
Even now, who, not unwisely bold,
Live in the spirit of this creed;
Yet seek thy firm support, according to their need.

25 I, loving freedom, and untried;
No sport of every random gust,
Yet being to myself a guide,
Too blindly have reposed my trust:
And oft, when in my heart was heard
30 Thy timely mandate, I deferred
The task, in smoother walks to stray;
But thee I now would serve more strictly, if I may.

Through no disturbance of my soul,
Or strong compunction[5] in me wrought,
35 I supplicate for thy control;
But in the quietness of thought:
Me this unchartered freedom tires;
I feel the weight of chance-desires:
My hopes no more must change their name,
40 I long for a repose that ever is the same.

Stern Lawgiver! yet thou dost wear
The Godhead's most benignant grace;
Nor know we any thing so fair
As is the smile upon thy face:
45 Flowers laugh before thee on their beds
And fragrance in thy footing treads;
Thou dost preserve the stars from wrong;
And the most ancient heavens, through Thee, are fresh and strong.

4. Innate vitality.
5. In the older sense: sting of conscience, or remorse.

To humbler functions, awful Power!
50 I call thee: I myself commend
Unto thy guidance from this hour;
Oh, let my weakness have an end!
Give unto me, made lowly wise,[6]
The spirit of self-sacrifice;
55 The confidence of reason give;
And in the light of truth thy Bondman let me live!

1804   1807

The Solitary Reaper[1]

Behold her, single in the field,
Yon solitary Highland Lass!
Reaping and singing by herself;
Stop here, or gently pass!
5   Alone she cuts and binds the grain,
And sings a melancholy strain;
O listen! for the Vale profound
Is overflowing with the sound.

No Nightingale did ever chaunt
10   More welcome notes to weary bands
Of travellers in some shady haunt,
Among Arabian sands:
A voice so thrilling ne'er was heard
In spring-time from the Cuckoo-bird,
15   Breaking the silence of the seas
Among the farthest Hebrides.

Will no one tell me what she sings?[2]—
Perhaps the plaintive numbers flow
For old, unhappy, far-off things,
20   And battles long ago:
Or is it some more humble lay,
Familiar matter of to-day?
Some natural sorrow, loss, or pain,
That has been, and may be again?

25   Whate'er the theme, the Maiden sang
As if her song could have no ending;
I saw her singing at her work,

6. Another echo from Milton, whose Christian-humanist ethic pervades this ode. The angel Raphael had advised Adam (*Paradise Lost* 8.173–74), "Be lowly wise: / Think only what concerns thee and thy being."
1. One of the rare poems not based on Wordsworth's own experience. The poet tells us that it was suggested by a passage in Thomas Wilkinson's *Tours to the British Mountains* (1824), which he had seen in manuscript: "Passed a female who was reaping alone: she sung in Erse [the Gaelic language of Scotland] as she bended over her sickle; the sweetest human voice I ever heard: her strains were tenderly melancholy, and felt delicious, long after they were heard no more."
2. The poet does not understand Erse, the language in which she sings.

And o'er the sickle bending;—
I listened, motionless and still;
30   And, as I mounted up the hill,
The music in my heart I bore,
Long after it was heard no more.

Nov. 5, 1805   1807

Elegiac Stanzas

Suggested by a Picture of Peele Castle, in a Storm,
Painted by Sir George Beaumont[1]

I was thy neighbour once, thou rugged Pile!
Four summer weeks I dwelt in sight of thee:
I saw thee every day; and all the while
Thy Form was sleeping on a glassy sea.

5   So pure the sky, so quiet was the air!
So like, so very like, was day to day!
Whene'er I looked, thy Image still was there;
It trembled, but it never passed away.

How perfect was the calm! it seemed no sleep;
10   No mood, which season takes away, or brings:
I could have fancied that the mighty Deep
Was even the gentlest of all gentle Things.

Ah! THEN, if mine had been the Painter's hand,
To express what then I saw; and add the gleam,
15   The light that never was, on sea or land,
The consecration, and the Poet's dream;

I would have planted thee, thou hoary Pile
Amid a world how different from this!
Beside a sea that could not cease to smile;
20   On tranquil land, beneath a sky of bliss.

Thou shouldst have seemed a treasure-house divine
Of peaceful years; a chronicle of heaven;—
Of all the sunbeams that did ever shine
The very sweetest had to thee been given.

25   A Picture had it been of lasting ease,
Elysian[2] quiet, without toil or strife;

---

1. A wealthy landscape painter who was Wordsworth's patron and close friend. Peele Castle is on an island opposite Rampside, Lancashire, where Wordsworth had spent a month in 1794, twelve years before he saw Beaumont's painting. The poem has been interpreted as an expression of Wordsworth's loss of faith in nature. It should be noted, however, that the focus of the poem is not on an altered view of nature but on an altered knowledge of human life and on the moral values necessary to manage the inevitability of loss and suffering.
2. Referring to Elysium, in classical mythology the peaceful place where those favored by the gods dwelled after death.

No motion but the moving tide, a breeze,
Or merely silent Nature's breathing life.

Such, in the fond illusion of my heart,
30   Such Picture would I at that time have made:
And seen the soul of truth in every part,
A stedfast peace that might not be betrayed.

So once it would have been,—'tis so no more;
I have submitted to a new control:
35   A power is gone, which nothing can restore;
A deep distress hath humanised my Soul.[3]

Not for a moment could I now behold
A smiling sea, and be what I have been:
The feeling of my loss will ne'er be old;
40   This, which I know, I speak with mind serene.

Then, Beaumont, Friend! who would have been the Friend,
If he had lived, of Him whom I deplore,°   *mourn*
This work of thine I blame not, but commend;
This sea in anger, and that dismal shore.

45   O 'tis a passionate Work!—yet wise and well,
Well chosen is the spirit that is here;
That Hulk which labours in the deadly swell,
This rueful sky, this pageantry of fear!

And this huge Castle, standing here sublime,
50   I love to see the look with which it braves,
Cased in the unfeeling armour of old time,
The lightning, the fierce wind, and trampling waves.

Farewell, farewell the heart that lives alone,
Housed in a dream, at distance from the Kind!°   *humankind*
55   Such happiness, wherever it be known,
Is to be pitied; for 'tis surely blind.

But welcome fortitude, and patient cheer,
And frequent sights of what is to be borne!
Such sights, or worse, as are before me here.—
60   Not without hope we suffer and we mourn.

Summer 1806   1807

---

3. Captain John Wordsworth, William's brother, had been drowned in a shipwreck on February 5, 1805.
He is referred to in lines 41–42.

SONNETS

Composed upon Westminster Bridge,
September 3, 1802[1]

Earth has not any thing to show more fair:
Dull would he be of soul who could pass by
A sight so touching in its majesty:
This City now doth, like a garment, wear
5   The beauty of the morning; silent, bare,
Ships, towers, domes, theatres, and temples lie
Open unto the fields, and to the sky;
All bright and glittering in the smokeless air.
Never did sun more beautifully steep
10   In his first splendour, valley, rock, or hill;
Ne'er saw I, never felt, a calm so deep!
The river glideth at his own sweet will:
Dear God! the very houses seem asleep;
And all that mighty heart is lying still!

1802   1807

It is a beauteous evening

It is a beauteous evening, calm and free,
The holy time is quiet as a Nun
Breathless with adoration; the broad sun
Is sinking down in its tranquillity;
5   The gentleness of heaven broods o'er the Sea:
Listen! the mighty Being is awake,
And doth with his eternal motion make
A sound like thunder—everlastingly.
Dear Child! dear Girl! that walkest with me here,[2]
10   If thou appear untouched by solemn thought,
Thy nature is not therefore less divine:
Thou liest in Abraham's bosom[3] all the year;
And worshipp'st at the Temple's inner shrine,
God being with thee when we know it not.

Aug. 1802   1807

---

1. The date of this experience was not September 3, but July 31, 1802. Its occasion was a trip to France (see Dorothy Wordsworth's *Grasmere Journals,* July 1802, p. 1567). The conflict of feelings attending Wordsworth's brief return to France, where he had once been a revolutionist and the lover of Annette Vallon, evoked a number of personal and political sonnets, among them the two that follow.

2. The girl walking with Wordsworth is Caroline, his daughter by Annette Vallon. For the event described, see Dorothy Wordsworth's *Grasmere Journals,* July 1802 (p. 1567).
3. Where the souls destined for heaven rest after death. Luke 16.22: "And it came to pass, that the beggar died, and was carried by the angels into Abraham's bosom."

London, 1802[4]

Milton! thou should'st be living at this hour:
England hath need of thee: she is a fen
Of stagnant waters: altar, sword, and pen,
Fireside, the heroic wealth of hall and bower,
5 Have forfeited their ancient English dower
Of inward happiness. We are selfish men;
Oh! raise us up, return to us again;
And give us manners, virtue, freedom, power.
Thy soul was like a Star, and dwelt apart:
10 Thou hadst a voice whose sound was like the sea:
Pure as the naked heavens, majestic, free,
So didst thou travel on life's common way,
In cheerful godliness; and yet thy heart
The lowliest duties on herself did lay.

Sept. 1802   1807

The world is too much with us

The world is too much with us; late and soon,
Getting and spending, we lay waste our powers:
Little we see in Nature that is ours;
We have given our hearts away, a sordid boon![5]
5 This Sea that bares her bosom to the moon;
The winds that will be howling at all hours,
And are up-gathered now like sleeping flowers;
For this, for every thing, we are out of tune;
It moves us not.—Great God! I'd rather be
10 A Pagan suckled in a creed outworn;
So might I, standing on this pleasant lea,
Have glimpses that would make me less forlorn;
Have sight of Proteus rising from the sea;
Or hear old Triton[6] blow his wreathèd horn.

1802–04   1807

Surprised by joy[7]

Surprised by joy—impatient as the Wind
I turned to share the transport—Oh! with whom

4. One of a series "written immediately after my
return from France to London, when I could not
but be struck, as here described, with the vanity
and parade of our own country . . . as contrasted
with the quiet, and I may say the desolation, that
the revolution had produced in France" [Words-
worth's note].
5. Gift. It is the act of giving the heart away that
is sordid.
6. A sea deity, usually represented as blowing on
a conch shell. Proteus was an old man of the sea

who (in the *Odyssey*) could assume a variety of
shapes. The description of Proteus echoes *Paradise
Lost* 3.603–04, and that of Triton echoes Spenser's
Colin Clouts Come Home Againe, lines 244–45.
Milton and Spenser are the two English poets with
whom Wordsworth most closely allied himself.
7. This was in fact suggested by my daughter
Catherine, long after her death [Wordsworth's
note]. Catherine Wordsworth died June 4, 1812,
at the age of four.

But Thee, deep buried in the silent tomb,
That spot which no vicissitude can find?
5 Love, faithful love, recalled thee to my mind—
But how could I forget thee? Through what power,
Even for the least division of an hour,
Have I been so beguiled as to be blind
To my most grievous loss!—That thought's return
10 Was the worst pang that sorrow ever bore,
Save one, one only, when I stood forlorn,
Knowing my heart's best treasure was no more;
That neither present time, nor years unborn
Could to my sight that heavenly face restore.

1813–14   1815

Mutability[8]

From low to high doth dissolution climb,
And sink from high to low, along a scale
Of awful notes, whose concord shall not fail;
A musical but melancholy chime,
5 Which they can hear who meddle not with crime,
Nor avarice, nor over-anxious care.
Truth fails not; but her outward forms that bear
The longest date do melt like frosty rime,
That in the morning whitened hill and plain
10 And is no more; drop like the tower sublime
Of yesterday, which royally did wear
His crown of weeds, but could not even sustain
Some casual shout that broke the silent air,
Or the unimaginable touch of Time.

1821   1822

Steamboats, Viaducts, and Railways[9]

Motions and Means, on land and sea at war
With old poetic feeling, not for this,
Shall ye, by Poets even, be judged amiss!
Nor shall your presence, howsoe'er it mar
5 The loveliness of Nature, prove a bar
To the Mind's gaining that prophetic sense
Of future change, that point of vision, whence
May be discovered what in soul ye are.
In spite of all that beauty may disown

8. This sonnet was included in an otherwise rather
pedestrian sequence, *Ecclesiastical Sonnets,* dealing with the history and ceremonies of the Church
of England.
9. In late middle age Wordsworth demonstrates,
as he had predicted in the Preface to *Lyrical Bal-*

lads, that the poet will assimilate to his subject
matter the "material revolution" produced by science. Unlike most poets, furthermore, he boldly
accepts as evidences of human progress even the
unlovely encroachments of technology on his
beloved natural scene.

10 In your harsh features, Nature doth embrace
Her lawful offspring in Man's art; and Time,
Pleased with your triumphs o'er his brother Space,
Accepts from your bold hands the proffered crown
Of hope, and smiles on you with cheer sublime.

1833   1835

Extempore Effusion upon the Death of James Hogg[1]

When first, descending from the moorlands,
I saw the Stream of Yarrow[2] glide
Along a bare and open valley,
The Ettrick Shepherd[3] was my guide.

5   When last along its banks I wandered,
Through groves that had begun to shed
Their golden leaves upon the pathways,
My steps the Border-minstrel[4] led.

The mighty Minstrel breathes no longer,
10   'Mid mouldering ruins low he lies;
And death upon the braes[5] of Yarrow,
Has closed the Shepherd-poet's eyes:

Nor has the rolling year twice measured,
From sign to sign, its stedfast course,
15   Since every mortal power of Coleridge
Was frozen at its marvellous source;

The rapt One, of the godlike forehead,
The heaven-eyed creature sleeps in earth:
And Lamb, the frolic and the gentle,
20   Has vanished from his lonely hearth.

Like clouds that rake the mountain-summits,
Or waves that own no curbing hand,
How fast has brother followed brother,
From sunshine to the sunless land!

25   Yet I, whose lids from infant slumber
Were earlier raised, remain to hear

1. Wordsworth's niece relates how he was deeply moved by finding unexpectedly in a newspaper an account of the death of the poet James Hogg. "Half an hour afterwards he came into the room where the ladies were sitting and asked Miss Hutchinson [his sister-in-law] to write down some lines which he had just composed." All the poets named here, several of Wordsworth's closest friends among them, had died between 1832 and 1835.
2. A river in the southeast of Scotland.
3. I.e., Hogg, who was born in Ettrick Forest and worked as a shepherd. He was discovered as a writer by Sir Walter Scott and became well known as a poet, essayist, and editor.
4. Sir Walter Scott.
5. The sloping banks of a stream.

A timid voice, that asks in whispers,
"Who next will drop and disappear?"

Our haughty life is crowned with darkness,
30 Like London with its own black wreath,
On which with thee, O Crabbe![6] forth-looking,
I gazed from Hampstead's breezy heath.

As if but yesterday departed,
Thou too art gone before; but why,
35 O'er ripe fruit, seasonably gathered,
Should frail survivors heave a sigh?

Mourn rather for that holy Spirit,
Sweet as the spring, as ocean deep;
For Her[7] who, ere her summer faded,
40 Has sunk into a breathless sleep.

No more of old romantic sorrows,
For slaughtered Youth or love-lorn Maid!
With sharper grief is Yarrow smitten,
And Ettrick mourns with her their Poet dead.

Nov. 21, 1835   1835

Prospectus to *The Recluse*[1]

On Man, on Nature, and on Human Life,
Musing in solitude, I oft perceive
Fair trains of imagery before me rise,
Accompanied by feelings of delight
5 Pure, or with no unpleasing sadness mixed;
And I am conscious of affecting thoughts
And dear remembrances, whose presence soothes
Or elevates the Mind, intent to weigh

6. George Crabbe, the poet of rural and village life.
7. The poet Felicia Hemans, who died at forty-two.
1. Through most of his poetic life Wordsworth labored intermittently at a long philosophic poem called *The Recluse*, which he intended to be his masterwork. As he described this project in the Preface to *The Excursion* (1814), it was to consist of an autobiographical introduction (the poem now called *The Prelude*) and three long parts; of these three he completed only book 1 of part 1 (*Home at Grasmere*) and part 2, called *The Excursion*. In the Preface to *The Excursion*, Wordsworth printed this long extract (the concluding section of *Home at Grasmere*) "as a kind of *Prospectus* of the design and scope of the whole Poem"—i.e., of the entire *Recluse*.
   The first version of this Prospectus may have been drafted as early as 1798 or 1800. In language resonant with echoes of *Paradise Lost*, Wordsworth announces an undertaking that he conceives to be no less inspired and sublime than Milton's. In it he will move higher than Milton's heaven and deeper than Milton's hell, past scenes evoking greater fear than hell and greater awe than Jehovah; but without ever leaving "the Mind of Man— / My haunt, and the main region of my song" (lines 40–41). And his "high argument" is that Paradise can be regained; not, however, as in Revelation 21 and in Milton, by the marriage between the New Jerusalem and Christ the Lamb, but by a marriage between the "intellect of Man" and "this goodly universe," and the resulting new "creation . . . which they with blended might / Accomplish" (lines 52–71). In no other passage does Wordsworth reveal so clearly the extent to which he assimilates in his poetry the biblical scheme of Milton's epic—assigning, however, the active role, from creation to redemption, to the human faculties, in their interaction with the external universe.

The good and evil of our mortal state.
10 —To these emotions, whencesoe'er they come,
Whether from breath of outward circumstance,
Or from the Soul—an impulse to herself—
I would give utterance in numerous verse.[2]
Of Truth, of Grandeur, Beauty, Love, and Hope,
15 And melancholy Fear subdued by Faith;
Of blessed consolations in distress;
Of moral strength, and intellectual Power;
Of joy in widest commonalty spread;
Of the individual Mind that keeps her own
20 Inviolate retirement, subject there
To Conscience only, and the law supreme
Of that Intelligence which governs all—
I sing:—"fit audience let me find though few!"[3]

    So prayed, more gaining than he asked, the Bard—
25 In holiest mood. Urania,[4] I shall need
Thy guidance, or a greater Muse, if such
Descend to earth or dwell in highest heaven!
For I must tread on shadowy ground, must sink
Deep—and, aloft ascending, breathe in worlds
30 To which the heaven of heavens[5] is but a veil.
All strength—all terror, single or in bands,
That ever was put forth in personal form—
Jehovah—with his thunder, and the choir
Of shouting Angels, and the empyreal thrones[6]—
35 I pass them unalarmed. Not Chaos, not
The darkest pit of lowest Erebus,[7]
Nor aught of blinder vacancy, scooped out
By help of dreams—can breed such fear and awe
As fall upon us often when we look
40 Into our Minds, into the Mind of Man—
My haunt, and the main region of my song.
—Beauty—a living Presence of the earth,
Surpassing the most fair ideal Forms
Which craft of delicate Spirits hath composed
45 From earth's materials—waits upon my steps;
Pitches her tents before me as I move,
An hourly neighbour. Paradise, and groves
Elysian,[8] Fortunate Fields—like those of old
Sought in the Atlantic Main—why should they be
50 A history only of departed things,
Or a mere fiction of what never was?

---

2. Harmonious verse; an echo of *Paradise Lost* 5.150. The inspiring "breath of outward circumstance" (line 11) parallels the "correspondent breeze" in the opening lines of *The Prelude*.
3. *Paradise Lost* 7.31.
4. The Muse whom Milton had invoked in *Paradise Lost* 7.1–39.
5. In *Paradise Lost* the dwelling place, beyond the visible heaven, of God and His angels.
6. Cf. *Paradise Lost* 2.430: "O progeny of Heaven, empyreal thrones!"
7. In classical myth, a dark region of the underworld; often used as a name for hell by Christian writers.
8. Elysium, in Greek myth, was the place where mortals favored by the gods live a happy life after death. It was sometimes identified with the "Islands of the Blessed," reputed to be located far out in the western sea—hence "sought in the Atlantic Main" (line 49). See Horace, *Epodes* 16.

For the discerning intellect of Man,
When wedded to this goodly universe
In love and holy passion, shall find these
55   A simple produce of the common day.
—I, long before the blissful hour arrives,
Would chant, in lonely peace, the spousal[9] verse
Of this great consummation:—and, by words
Which speak of nothing more than what we are,
60   Would I arouse the sensual from their sleep
Of Death, and win the vacant and the vain
To noble raptures; while my voice proclaims
How exquisitely the individual Mind
(And the progressive powers perhaps no less
65   Of the whole species) to the external World
Is fitted:—and how exquisitely, too—
Theme this but little heard of among men—
The external World is fitted to the Mind;
And the creation (by no lower name
70   Can it be called) which they with blended might
Accomplish:—this is our high argument.[1]
—Such grateful haunts foregoing, if I oft
Must turn elsewhere—to travel near the tribes
And fellowships of men, and see ill sights
75   Of madding passions mutually inflamed;
Must hear Humanity in fields and groves
Pipe solitary anguish; or must hang
Brooding above the fierce confederate storm
Of sorrow, barricadoed[2] evermore
80   Within the walls of cities—may these sounds
Have their authentic comment; that even these
Hearing, I be not downcast or forlorn!—
Descend, prophetic Spirit! that inspir'st
The human Soul of universal earth,
85   Dreaming on things to come;[3] and dost possess
A metropolitan temple[4] in the hearts
Of mighty Poets; upon me bestow
A gift of genuine insight; that my Song
With star-like virtue in its place may shine,
90   Shedding benignant influence, and secure,
Itself, from all malevolent effect
Of those mutations that extend their sway
Throughout the nether sphere![5]—And if with this
I mix more lowly matter; with the thing
95   Contemplated, describe the Mind and Man
Contemplating; and who, and what he was—

---

9. Marital. Hence a "spousal verse" is an epithalamion—a poem written to celebrate a marriage.
1. Theme, as in *Paradise Lost* 1.24: "the height of this great argument."
2. Barricaded, as in *Paradise Lost* 8.241: "Fast we found, fast shut / The dismal gates, and barricadoed strong."
3. Cf. Shakespeare's *Sonnet 107*: "the prophetic soul / Of the wide world dreaming on things to come."
4. The primary church of a religion.
5. In the Ptolemaic world picture, the spheres of the heavenly bodies were immutable, and only the earth (the "nether sphere," or region below the sphere of the moon) was subject to change. Cf. *Paradise Lost* 7.375 and 10.656–64.

The transitory Being that beheld
This Vision; when and where, and how he lived;[6]—
Be not this labour useless. If such theme
100 May sort with highest objects, then—dread Power!
Whose gracious favour is the primal source
Of all illumination—may my Life
Express the image of a better time,
More wise desires, and simpler manners;—nurse
105 My Heart in genuine freedom:—all pure thoughts
Be with me;—so shall thy unfailing love
Guide, and support, and cheer me to the end!

ca. 1798–1814   1814

The Prelude

The Prelude, now regarded as Wordsworth's crowning achievement, was unknown to the public at the time of his death in April 1850. When, three months later, *The Prelude* was published from manuscript by Wordsworth's literary executors, its title was given to it by the poet's wife. Wordsworth himself had referred to it variously as "the poem to Coleridge," "the poem on the growth of my own mind," and "the poem on my own poetical education."

For some seventy-five years this posthumous publication of 1850 was the only known text. Then in 1926 Ernest de Selincourt, working from manuscripts, printed an earlier version of the poem that Wordsworth had completed in 1805. Since that time other scholars have established the existence of a still earlier and much shorter version of *The Prelude*, in two parts, that Wordsworth had composed in 1798–99. The following seems to have been the process of composition that produced the three principal versions of the poem:

1. The *Two-Part Prelude* of 1799. Wordsworth originally planned, early in 1798, to include an account of his own development as a poet in his projected but never-completed philosophical poem *The Recluse* (see the Prospectus to *The Recluse*, n. 1, p. 301). While living in Germany during the autumn and winter of 1798–99, he composed a number of passages about his early experiences with nature. What had been intended to be part of *The Recluse*, however, quickly evolved into an independent autobiographical poem, and by late 1799, when Wordsworth settled with his sister, Dorothy, at Grasmere, he had written a poem in two parts, 978 lines in length, which takes his life from infancy, through his years at Hawkshead School, to the age of seventeen. This poem corresponds, by and large, to the contents of books 1 and 2 of the later versions of *The Prelude*.

2. The 1805 *Prelude*. Late in 1801 Wordsworth began to expand the poem on his poetic life, and in 1804 he set to work intensively on the project. His initial plan was to write it in five books, but he soon decided to enlarge it to incorporate an account of his experiences in France and of his mental crisis after the failure of his hopes in the French Revolution, and to end the poem with his settlement at Grasmere and his taking up the great task of *The Recluse*. He completed the poem, in thirteen books, in May 1805. This is the version that Wordsworth read to Coleridge after the latter's return from Malta (see Coleridge's *To William Wordsworth*, p. 1620).

3. The 1850 *Prelude*. For the next thirty-five years Wordsworth tinkered with the text, polishing the style and qualifying some of its radical statements about the divine sufficiency of the human mind in its communion with nature; he did not, however,

---

6. Wordsworth thus justifies *The Prelude* and the autobiographical sections of *The Recluse*.

in any essential way alter its subject matter or overall design. *The Prelude* that was published in July 1850 is in fourteen books and was printed from a fair copy; it incorporated Wordsworth's latest revisions, which had been made in 1839, as well as some alterations introduced by his literary executors. The selections printed here— from W. J. B. Owen's Cornell Wordsworth volume, *The Fourteen-Book Prelude* (1985)—are from the manuscript of this final version. Our reasons for choosing this version are set forth in Jack Stillinger's "Textual Primitivism and the Editing of Wordsworth," *Studies in Romanticism* 28 (1989): 3–28.

When Wordsworth enlarged the two-part *Prelude* of 1799, he not only made it a poem of epic length but also heightened the style and introduced various thematic parallels with earlier epics, especially *Paradise Lost*. (For a central example, see Wordsworth's version of Milton's enterprise to "justify the ways of God to men," in 14.162–70, p. 1553 and 14.384–89, p. 1555.) The expanded poem, however, is a personal history that turns on a mental crisis and recovery, and for such a narrative design the chief prototype is not the classical or Christian epic but the spiritual autobiography of crisis. St. Augustine's *Confessions* established this central Christian form late in the fourth century, and it has had an uninterrupted history in European literature ever since.

As in Augustine's *Confessions* and many later versions of spiritual autobiography, Wordsworth's persistent metaphor is that of life as a circular journey whose end (as T. S. Eliot put it in *Four Quartets*, his adaptation of the traditional form) is "to arrive where we started / And know the place for the first time" (*Little Gidding*, lines 241– 42). Wordsworth's *Prelude* opens with a literal journey whose chosen goal (1.72, 106– 07) is "a known Vale whither my feet should turn"—that is, the Vale of Grasmere. *The Prelude* narrates a number of later journeys, most notably the crossing of the Alps in book 6 and, at the beginning of the final book, the climactic ascent of Mount Snowdon. In the course of the poem, such literal journeys become the metaphoric vehicle for an interior, spiritual journey in the quest, within the poet's memory, and in the very process of composing his poem, for his lost early self and his proper spiritual home. At its end the poem, adverting to its beginning, leaves the poet at home in the Vale of Grasmere, ready finally to begin his great project *The Recluse* (14.302–11, 374–85).

Throughout *The Prelude*, Wordsworth formulates the course of his life in accordance with an intricate artistic pattern and narrates it in a deliberately traditional voice. Although its episodes are recognizable events in his experience, they are interpreted in retrospect, reordered in sequence, retold as primarily a transaction between mind and nature, and shaped into the inherited design of crisis and recovery, from which the protagonist emerges as a new self in a transformed world, confirmed in his vocation as a poet. And although the narrator is recognizably William Wordsworth, addressing the entire poem as a communication to his friend Coleridge, he adopts the prophetic persona, modeled on the poet-prophets of the Bible, which John Milton had adopted in narrating *Paradise Lost* (13.300–11). In this way Wordsworth, like his great English predecessor, assumes the authority to speak as a national poet whose function is to reconstitute the grounds of hope in a dark time of postrevolutionary reaction and despair. As Wordsworth describes it (2.433–42), he speaks out

> in these times of fear,
> This melancholy waste of hopes overthrown,
> . . . 'mid indifference and apathy
> And wicked exultation, when good men,
> On every side, fall off, we know not how,
> To selfishness, disguised in gentle names
> Of peace and quiet and domestic love
> . . . this time
> Of dereliction and dismay. . . .

FROM THE PRELUDE
OR
GROWTH OF A POET'S MIND

AN AUTOBIOGRAPHICAL POEM

Book First
Introduction, Childhood, and School-time

O there is blessing in this gentle breeze,
A visitant that, while he fans my cheek,
Doth seem half-conscious of the joy he brings
From the green fields, and from yon azure sky.
5   Whate'er his mission, the soft breeze can come
To none more grateful than to me; escaped
From the vast City,[1] where I long have pined
A discontented Sojourner—Now free,
Free as a bird to settle where I will.
10 What dwelling shall receive me? in what vale
Shall be my harbour? underneath what grove
Shall I take up my home? and what clear stream
Shall with its murmur lull me into rest?
The earth is all before me:[2] with a heart
15 Joyous, nor scared at its own liberty,
I look about; and should the chosen guide
Be nothing better than a wandering cloud,
I cannot miss my way. I breathe again;
Trances of thought and mountings of the heart
20 Come fast upon me: it is shaken off,
That burthen of my own unnatural self,
The heavy weight of many a weary day
Not mine, and such as were not made for me.
Long months of peace (if such bold word accord
25 With any promises of human life),
Long months of ease and undisturbed delight
Are mine in prospect; whither shall I turn,
By road or pathway, or through trackless field,
Up hill or down, or shall some floating thing
30 Upon the River point me out my course?
Dear Liberty! Yet what would it avail,
But for a gift that consecrates the joy?
For I, methought, while the sweet breath of heaven
Was blowing on my body, felt, within,
35 A correspondent breeze, that gently moved
With quickening virtue,[3] but is now become
A tempest, a redundant° energy,   abundant

---

1. London. Wordsworth uses this city as a type representing a place of spiritual bondage from which he has finally escaped.
2. One of many echoes from *Paradise Lost*, where the line is applied to Adam and Eve as, at the con- clusion of the poem, they begin their new life after being expelled from Eden: "The world was all before them" (12.646).
3. Revivifying power. ("To quicken" is to give or restore life.)

Vexing its own creation. Thanks to both,
And their congenial° powers that, while they join   kindred
40   In breaking up a long continued frost,
Bring with them vernal promises, the hope
Of active days urged on by flying hours;
Days of sweet leisure taxed with patient thought
Abstruse, nor wanting punctual service high,
45   Matins and vespers, of harmonious verse![4]
        Thus far, O Friend![5] did I, not used to make
A present joy the matter of a Song,[6]
Pour forth, that day, my soul in measured strains,
That would not be forgotten, and are here
50   Recorded:—to the open fields I told
A prophecy:—poetic numbers came
Spontaneously, to clothe in priestly robe
A renovated Spirit singled out,
Such hope was mine, for holy services:
55   My own voice cheered me, and, far more, the mind's
Internal echo of the imperfect sound;
To both I listened, drawing from them both
A chearful confidence in things to come.
        Content, and not unwilling now to give
60   A respite to this passion, I paced on
With brisk and eager steps; and came at length
To a green shady place where down I sate
Beneath a tree, slackening my thoughts by choice,
And settling into gentler happiness.
65   'Twas Autumn, and a clear and placid day,
With warmth, as much as needed, from a sun
Two hours declined towards the west, a day
With silver clouds, and sunshine on the grass,
And, in the sheltered and the sheltering grove,
70   A perfect stillness. Many were the thoughts
Encouraged and dismissed, till choice was made
Of a known Vale[7] whither my feet should turn,
Nor rest till they had reached the very door

4. I.e., verses equivalent to morning prayers (matins) and evening prayers (vespers). The opening passage (lines 1–45), which Wordsworth calls in book 7, line 4, a "glad preamble," replaces the traditional epic device, such as Milton had adopted in *Paradise Lost,* of an opening prayer to the Muse for inspiration. To be "inspired," in the literal sense, is to be breathed or blown into by a divinity (in Latin *spirare* means both "to breathe" and "to blow"). Wordsworth begins his poem with a "blessing" from an outer "breeze," which (lines 34–45) is called the "breath of heaven" and evokes in him a correspondent inner breeze that signalizes a springlike revival of his spirit after a wintry season, and also a burst of poetic power that he goes on to equate (lines 50–54) with the utterances of biblical prophets when inspired by the Holy Spirit. The revivifying breeze and breath, at once material and spiritual, recurs later in *The Prelude* as a kind of leitmotif. It also serves as the radical metaphor of

other Romantic poems such as Coleridge's *The Eolian Harp* and *Dejection: An Ode,* and Shelley's *Ode to the West Wind.*
5. Samuel Taylor Coleridge, to whom Wordsworth addresses the whole of the *Prelude.* For Coleridge's response, after the poem was read to him, see *To William Wordsworth* (p. 1620).
6. In the Preface to *Lyrical Ballads* Wordsworth says that his poetry usually originates in "emotion recollected in tranquillity"; hence not, as in the preceding preamble, during the experience that it records.
7. Grasmere, where Wordsworth settled with his sister, Dorothy, in December 1799. Wordsworth uses his walk to that "Vale" to symbolize a new stage in the journey of his life—a stage in which he returns to what he calls (in the title of the opening book of *The Recluse,* designed to follow *The Prelude*) "Home at Grasmere."

Of the one Cottage which methought I saw.
75 No picture of mere memory ever looked
So fair; and while upon the fancied scene
I gazed with growing love, a higher power
Than Fancy gave assurance of some work
Of glory, there forthwith to be begun,
80 Perhaps too there performed.[8] Thus long I mused,
Nor e'er lost sight of what I mused upon,
Save where, amid the stately grove of Oaks,
Now here—now there—an acorn, from its cup
Dislodged, through sere leaves rustled, or at once
85 To the bare earth dropped with a startling sound.
    From that soft couch I rose not, till the sun
Had almost touched the horizon; casting then
A backward glance upon the curling cloud
Of city smoke, by distance ruralized,
90 Keen as a Truant or a Fugitive,
But as a Pilgrim resolute, I took,
Even with the chance equipment of that hour,
The road that pointed tow'rd the chosen Vale.
    It was a splendid evening: and my Soul
95 Once more made trial of her strength, nor lacked
Eolian visitations;[9] but the harp
Was soon defrauded, and the banded host
Of harmony dispersed in straggling sounds;
And lastly utter silence! "Be it so;
100 Why think of any thing but present good?"
So, like a Home-bound Labourer, I pursued
My way, beneath the mellowing sun, that shed
Mild influence;[1] nor left in me one wish
Again to bend the sabbath of that time[2]
105 To a servile yoke. What need of many words?
A pleasant loitering journey, through three days
Continued, brought me to my hermitage.
I spare to tell of what ensued, the life
In common things,—the endless store of things
110 Rare, or at least so seeming, every day
Found all about me in one neighbourhood;
The self-congratulation,° and from morn   *self-rejoicing*
To night unbroken cheerfulness serene.
But speedily an earnest longing rose
115 To brace myself to some determined aim,
Reading or thinking; either to lay up
New stores, or rescue from decay the old
By timely interference: and therewith
Came hopes still higher, that with outward life

8. I.e., *The Recluse*, which Wordsworth planned
to be his major poetic work.
9. Influences to which his soul responded as an
Eolian harp responds to gusts of a breeze. For a
description of this instrument, see Coleridge's *The
Eolian Harp*, n. 1, p. 1576.

1. An astrological term for the effect of stars on
human life. *Paradise Lost* 7.374–75: "The Pleiades
[a cluster of stars] before him danced / Shedding
sweet influence."
2. That time of rest.

120 I might endue some airy phantasies
     That had been floating loose about for years;
     And to such Beings temperately deal forth
     The many feelings that oppressed my heart.
     That hope hath been discouraged; welcome light
125 Dawns from the East, but dawns—to disappear
     And mock me with a sky that ripens not
     Into a steady morning: if my mind,
     Remembering the bold promise of the past,
     Would gladly grapple with some noble theme,
130 Vain is her wish: where'er she turns, she finds
     Impediments from day to day renewed.
          And now it would content me to yield up
     Those lofty hopes awhile for present gifts
     Of humbler industry. But, O dear Friend!
135 The Poet, gentle Creature as he is,
     Hath, like the Lover, his unruly times,
     His fits when he is neither sick nor well,
     Though no distress be near him but his own
     Unmanageable thoughts: his mind, best pleas'd
140 While she, as duteous as the Mother Dove,
     Sits brooding,³ lives not always to that end,
     But, like the innocent Bird, hath goadings on
     That drive her, as in trouble, through the groves:
     With me is now such passion, to be blamed
145 No otherwise than as it lasts too long.
          When as becomes a Man who would prepare
     For such an arduous Work, I through myself
     Make rigorous inquisition, the report
     Is often chearing; for I neither seem
150 To lack that first great gift, the vital Soul,
     Nor general Truths, which are themselves a sort
     Of Elements and Agents, Under-powers,
     Subordinate helpers of the living Mind:
     Nor am I naked of external things,
155 Forms, images, nor numerous other aids
     Of less regard, though won perhaps with toil,
     And needful to build up a Poet's praise.
     Time, place, and manners do I seek, and these
     Are found in plenteous store, but no where such
160 As may be singled out with steady choice:
     No little band of yet remembered names
     Whom I in perfect confidence might hope
     To summon back from lonesome banishment,
     And make them dwellers in the hearts of men
165 Now living, or to live in future years.
     Sometimes the ambitious Power of choice, mistaking
     Proud spring-tide swellings for a regular sea,

---

3. An echo of Milton's reference in *Paradise Lost*   the vast Abyss / And mad'st it pregnant" (1.21–
to the original act of creation in his invocation to   22).
the Holy Spirit: Thou "Dovelike satst brooding on

Will settle on some British theme, some old
Romantic Tale by Milton left unsung:[4]
170 More often turning to some gentle place
Within the groves of Chivalry, I pipe
To Shepherd Swains, or seated, harp in hand,
Amid reposing knights by a River side
Or fountain, listen to the grave reports
175 Of dire enchantments faced, and overcome
By the strong mind, and Tales of warlike feats
Where spear encountered spear, and sword with sword
Fought, as if conscious of the blazonry
That the shield bore, so glorious was the strife;
180 Whence inspiration for a song that winds
Through ever changing scenes of votive quest,[5]
Wrongs to redress, harmonious tribute paid
To patient courage and unblemished truth,
To firm devotion, zeal unquenchable,
185 And Christian meekness hallowing faithful loves.[6]
Sometimes, more sternly moved, I would relate
How vanquished Mithridates northward passed,
And, hidden in the cloud of years, became
Odin, the Father of a Race by whom
190 Perished the Roman Empire;[7] how the friends
And followers of Sertorius, out of Spain
Flying, found shelter in the Fortunate Isles;
And left their usages, their arts, and laws
To disappear by a slow gradual death;
195 To dwindle and to perish, one by one,
Starved in those narrow bounds: but not the soul
Of Liberty, which fifteen hundred years
Survived, and, when the European came
With skill and power that might not be withstood,
200 Did, like a pestilence, maintain its hold,
And wasted down by glorious death that Race
Of natural Heroes;[8]—or I would record
How, in tyrannic times, some high-souled Man,
Unnamed among the chronicles of Kings,
205 Suffered in silence for truth's sake: or tell
How that one Frenchman, through continued force
Of meditation on the inhuman deeds
Of those who conquered first the Indian isles,

4. In *Paradise Lost* 9.24–41 Milton relates that, in
seeking a subject for his epic poem, he rejected
"fabled Knights" and medieval romance.
5. A quest undertaken to fulfill a vow.
6. An echo of the prefatory statement to Spenser's
Faerie Queene, line 9: "Fierce warres and faithfull
loves shall moralize my song."
7. Mithridates VI, king of Pontus, was defeated by
the Roman Pompey in 66 B.C.E. In chap. 10 of his
Decline and Fall of the Roman Empire, Edward
Gibbon associates him with Odin, a chieftain of
the Goths, who hoped to produce descendants who

would wreak revenge on the conquering Romans.
All the protagonists that Wordsworth considered
for his poem were heroes in fights against tyranny.
8. Sertorius, a Roman general allied with Mithridates, fought off the armies of Pompey and others
until he was assassinated in 72 B.C.E. There is a
legend that after his death his followers, to escape
Roman tyranny, fled from Spain to the Canary
Islands (known in ancient times as "the Fortunate
Isles," line 192), where their descendants flourished until subjugated and decimated by invading
Spaniards late in the 15th century.

Went, single in his ministry, across
210 The Ocean;—not to comfort the Oppressed,
But, like a thirsty wind, to roam about,
Withering the Oppressor:⁹—how Gustavus sought
Help at his need in Dalecarlia's mines:¹
How Wallace² fought for Scotland, left the name
215 Of Wallace to be found, like a wild flower,
All over his dear Country, left the deeds
Of Wallace, like a family of Ghosts,
To people the steep rocks and river banks,
Her natural sanctuaries, with a local soul
220 Of independence and stern liberty.
Sometimes it suits me better to invent
A Tale from my own heart, more near akin
To my own passions, and habitual thoughts,
Some variegated Story, in the main
225 Lofty, but the unsubstantial Structure melts
Before the very sun that brightens it,
Mist into air dissolving! Then, a wish,
My last and favourite aspiration, mounts,
With yearning, tow'rds some philosophic Song
230 Of Truth³ that cherishes our daily life;
With meditations passionate, from deep
Recesses in man's heart, immortal verse
Thoughtfully fitted to the Orphean lyre;⁴
But from this awful burthen I full soon
235 Take refuge, and beguile myself with trust
That mellower years will bring a riper mind
And clearer insight. Thus my days are passed
In contradiction; with no skill to part
Vague longing, haply bred by want of power,
240 From paramount impulse—not to be withstood;
A timorous capacity from prudence;
From circumspection, infinite delay.⁵
Humility and modest awe themselves
Betray me, serving often for a cloke
245 To a more subtile selfishness; that now
Locks every function up in blank° reserve,°   *absolute / inaction*
Now dupes me, trusting to an anxious eye
That with intrusive restlessness beats off
Simplicity, and self-presented truth.
250   Ah! better far than this, to stray about
Voluptuously,° through fields and rural walks,   *luxuriously*

---

9. Dominique de Gourges, a French gentleman who went in 1568 to Florida to avenge the massacre of the French by the Spaniards there [footnote in *The Prelude* of 1850].
1. In the 16th century Gustavus I of Sweden mustered supporters in Dalecarlia, a mining district, to help free Sweden from the tyranny of Denmark.
2. William Wallace, Scottish national hero, fought against the English until captured and executed in 1305.
3. I.e., *The Recluse*.

4. The lyre of Orpheus. In Greek myth Orpheus was able to enchant not only human listeners but the natural world by his singing and playing.
5. The syntax is complex and inverted; in outline, the sense of lines 238–42 seems to be, to put it shortly: "With no ability ('skill') to distinguish between vague desire (perhaps resulting from lack of power) and ruling impulse; between timidity and prudence; between endless delay and carefulness ('circumspection')."

And ask no record of the hours, resigned
To vacant musing, unreproved neglect
Of all things, and deliberate holiday:
255 Far better never to have heard the name
Of zeal and just ambition, than to live
Baffled and plagued by a mind that every hour
Turns recreant to her task, takes heart again,
Then feels immediately some hollow thought
260 Hang like an interdict° upon her hopes.   *prohibition*
This is my lot; for either still I find
Some imperfection in the chosen theme;
Or see of absolute accomplishment
Much wanting, so much wanting, in myself
265 That I recoil and droop, and seek repose
In listlessness from vain perplexity;
Unprofitably travelling toward the grave,
Like a false Steward who hath much received,
And renders nothing back.[6]
                                   Was it for this[7]
270 That one, the fairest of all rivers, loved
To blend his murmurs with my Nurse's song;
And, from his alder shades and rocky falls,
And from his fords and shallows, sent a voice
That flowed along my dreams? For this didst Thou,
275 O Derwent! winding among grassy holms[8]
Where I was looking on, a Babe in arms,
Make ceaseless music, that composed my thoughts
To more than infant softness, giving me,
Amid the fretful dwellings of mankind,
280 A foretaste, a dim earnest, of the calm
That Nature breathes among the hills and groves?
   When he had left the mountains, and received
On his smooth breast the shadow of those Towers
That yet survive, a shattered Monument
285 Of feudal sway, the bright blue River passed
Along the margin of our Terrace Walk;[9]
A tempting Playmate whom we dearly loved.
O many a time have I, a five years' Child,
In a small mill-race severed from his stream,
290 Made one long bathing of a summer's day;
Basked in the sun, and plunged, and basked again,
Alternate all a summer's day, or scoured[1]
The sandy fields, leaping through flow'ry groves
Of yellow ragwort; or when rock and hill,
295 The woods and distant Skiddaw's[2] lofty height,
Were bronzed with deepest radiance, stood alone
Beneath the sky, as if I had been born

6. The reference is to the parable of the false steward in Matthew 25.14–30.
7. The two-part *Prelude* that Wordsworth wrote in
1798–99 begins at this point.
8. Flat ground next to a river.
9. The Derwent River flows by Cockermouth

Castle and then past the garden terrace behind
Wordsworth's father's house in Cockermouth,
Cumberland.
1. Run swiftly over.
2. A mountain nine miles east of Cockermouth.

On Indian plains, and from my Mother's hut
Had run abroad in wantonness, to sport,
300 A naked Savage, in the thunder shower.
    Fair seed-time had my soul, and I grew up
Fostered alike by beauty and by fear;[3]
Much favoured in my birth-place, and no less
In that beloved Vale[4] to which erelong
305 We were transplanted—there were we let loose
For sports of wider range. Ere I had told
Ten birth-days, when among the mountain slopes
Frost, and the breath of frosty wind, had snapped
The last autumnal Crocus, 'twas my joy,
310 With store of Springes° o'er my Shoulder slung,   *bird snares*
To range the open heights where woodcocks ran
Along the smooth green turf. Through half the night,
Scudding away from snare to snare, I plied
That anxious visitation;—moon and stars
315 Were shining o'er my head; I was alone,
And seemed to be a trouble to the peace
That dwelt among them. Sometimes it befel,
In these night-wanderings, that a strong desire
O'erpowered my better reason, and the Bird
320 Which was the Captive of another's toil[5]
Became my prey; and when the deed was done
I heard, among the solitary hills,
Low breathings coming after me, and sounds
Of undistinguishable motion, steps
325 Almost as silent as the turf they trod.
    Nor less, when Spring had warmed the cultured° Vale,   *cultivated*
Roved we as plunderers where the Mother-bird
Had in high places built her lodge; though mean
Our object, and inglorious, yet the end°   *outcome*
330 Was not ignoble. Oh! when I have hung
Above the Raven's nest, by knots of grass
And half-inch fissures in the slippery rock
But ill-sustained; and almost (so it seemed)
Suspended by the blast that blew amain,
335 Shouldering the naked crag; Oh, at that time,
While on the perilous ridge I hung alone,
With what strange utterance did the loud dry wind
Blow through my ears! the sky seemed not a sky
Of earth, and with what motion moved the clouds!
340 Dust as we are, the immortal Spirit grows
Like harmony in music; there is a dark
Inscrutable workmanship that reconciles

3. Wordsworth introduces here a dialectic that plays a central role in the evolution of *The Prelude.* He represents his mind, confronting nature, as fostered in its growth by two antithetic principles, one associated with love and the other with fear. These principles correspond to the two main categories, "the beautiful" and "the sublime," into which theorists of the landscape during the preceding century had classified the antithetic aspects of the natural scene (see, e.g., 1.351–56, 466–75, 546). In the concluding book (in 14.162–70), this antithesis is finally resolved (see n. 3, p. 1553).
4. The valley of Esthwaite, the location of Hawkshead, where Wordsworth attended school.
5. Snare or labor.

Discordant elements, makes them cling together
In one society. How strange that all
345 The terrors, pains, and early miseries,
Regrets, vexations, lassitudes, interfused
Within my mind, should e'er have borne a part,
And that a needful part, in making up
The calm existence that is mine when I
350 Am worthy of myself! Praise to the end!
Thanks to the means which Nature deigned to employ!
Whether her fearless visitings or those
That came with soft alarm like hurtless lightning
Opening the peaceful clouds, or she would use
355 Severer interventions, ministry
More palpable, as best might suit her aim.[6]
    One summer evening (led by her) I found
A little Boat tied to a Willow-tree
Within a rocky cave, its usual home.
360 Straight I unloosed her chain, and, stepping in,
Pushed from the shore. It was an act of stealth
And troubled pleasure, nor without the voice
Of mountain-echoes did my Boat move on,
Leaving behind her still, on either side,
365 Small circles glittering idly in the moon,
Until they melted all into one track!
Of sparkling light. But now, like one who rows
(Proud of his skill) to reach a chosen point
With an unswerving line, I fixed my view
370 Upon the summit of a craggy ridge,
The horizon's utmost boundary; for above
Was nothing but the stars and the grey sky.
She was an elfin Pinnace;° lustily   *small boat*
I dipped my oars into the silent lake;
375 And, as I rose upon the stroke, my boat
Went heaving through the Water like a swan:
When, from behind that craggy Steep, till then
The horizon's bound, a huge peak, black and huge,
As if with voluntary power instinct,°   *endowed*
380 Upreared its head.[7]—I struck, and struck again,
And, growing still in stature, the grim Shape
Towered up between me and the stars, and still,
For so it seemed, with purpose of its own
And measured motion, like a living Thing
385 Strode after me. With trembling oars I turned,
And through the silent water stole my way
Back to the Covert of the Willow-tree;
There, in her mooring-place, I left my Bark,—
And through the meadows homeward went, in grave

---

6. A restatement of the double ministry of nature described in line 302. What follows is a second example of discipline by fear.
7. To direct his boat in a straight line, the rower (sitting facing the stern of the boat) has fixed his eye on a point on the ridge above the nearby shore, which blocks out the landscape behind. As he moves farther out, the black peak rises into his altering angle of vision and seems to stride closer with each stroke of the oars.

390 And serious mood; but after I had seen
That spectacle, for many days, my brain
Worked with a dim and undetermined sense
Of unknown modes of being; o'er my thoughts
There hung a darkness, call it solitude
395 Or blank desertion. No familiar Shapes
Remained, no pleasant images of trees,
Of sea or Sky, no colours of green fields,
But huge and mighty Forms, that do not live
Like living men, moved slowly through the mind
400 By day, and were a trouble to my dreams.
    Wisdom and Spirit of the Universe!
Thou Soul that art the eternity of thought,
That giv'st to forms and images a breath
And everlasting Motion! not in vain,
405 By day or star-light, thus from my first dawn
Of Childhood didst thou intertwine for me
The passions that build up our human Soul,
Not with the mean and vulgar° works of man,   *commonplace*
But with high objects, with enduring things,
410 With life and nature, purifying thus
The elements of feeling and of thought,
And sanctifying, by such discipline,
Both pain and fear; until we recognize
A grandeur in the beatings of the heart.
415   Nor was this fellowship vouchsafed to me
With stinted kindness. In November days
When vapours, rolling down the valley, made
A lonely scene more lonesome; among woods
At noon, and 'mid the calm of summer nights,
420 When, by the margin of the trembling Lake,
Beneath the gloomy hills homeward I went
In solitude, such intercourse was mine:
Mine was it, in the fields both day and night,
And by the waters, all the summer long.
425 —And in the frosty season, when the sun
Was set, and visible for many a mile,
The cottage windows blazed through twilight gloom,
I heeded not their summons,—happy time
It was indeed for all of us; for me
430 It was a time of rapture!—Clear and loud
The village Clock toll'd six—I wheeled about,
Proud and exulting like an untired horse
That cares not for his home.—All shod with steel,
We hissed along the polished ice, in games
435 Confederate, imitative of the chase
And woodland pleasures,—the resounding horn,
The Pack loud-chiming and the hunted hare.
So through the darkness and the cold we flew,
And not a voice was idle: with the din
440 Smitten, the precipices rang aloud;
The leafless trees and every icy crag

Tinkled like iron; while far distant hills
Into the tumult sent an alien sound
Of melancholy, not unnoticed while the stars,
445 Eastward, were sparkling clear, and in the west
The orange sky of evening died away.
Not seldom from the uproar I retired
Into a silent bay,—or sportively
Glanced sideway,[8] leaving the tumultous throng
450 To cut across the reflex° of a star   reflection
That fled, and, flying still before me, gleamed
Upon the glassy plain: and oftentimes,
When we had given our bodies to the wind,
And all the shadowy banks on either side
455 Came sweeping through the darkness, spinning still
The rapid line of motion, then at once
Have I, reclining back upon my heels,
Stopped short; yet still the solitary cliffs
Wheeled by me—even as if the earth had rolled
460 With visible motion her diurnal° round!   daily
Behind me did they stretch in solemn train,°   succession
Feebler and feebler, and I stood and watched
Till all was tranquil as a dreamless sleep.
    Ye presences of Nature, in the sky,
465 And on the earth! Ye visions of the hills!
And Souls[9] of lonely places! can I think
A vulgar hope was yours when ye employed
Such ministry, when ye, through many a year,
Haunting me thus among my boyish sports,
470 On caves and trees, upon the woods and hills,
Impressed upon all forms the characters°   signs
Of danger or desire; and thus did make
The surface of the universal earth
With triumph and delight, with hope and fear,
Work° like a sea?   seethe
475   Not uselessly employed,
Might I pursue this theme through every change
Of exercise and play, to which the year
Did summon us in his delightful round.
    —We were a noisy crew; the sun in heaven
480 Beheld not vales more beautiful than ours,
Nor saw a Band in happiness and joy
Richer, or worthier of the ground they trod.
I could record with no reluctant voice
The woods of Autumn, and their hazel bowers
485 With milk-white clusters hung; the rod and line,
True symbol of hope's foolishness, whose strong
And unreproved enchantment led us on,
By rocks and pools shut out from every star
All the green summer, to forlorn cascades

8. Moved off obliquely.
9. Wordsworth refers both to a single "Spirit" or "Soul" of the universe as a whole (e.g., lines 401–

02) and to plural "Presences" and "Souls" inanimating the various parts of the universe.

490   Among the windings hid of mountain brooks.
      —Unfading recollections! at this hour
      The heart is almost mine with which I felt,
      From some hill-top on sunny afternoons,
      The paper-Kite, high among fleecy clouds,
495   Pull at her rein, like an impatient Courser;
      Or, from the meadows sent on gusty days,
      Beheld her breast the wind, then suddenly
      Dashed headlong, and rejected by the storm.
          Ye lowly Cottages in which we dwelt,
500   A ministration of your own was yours!
      Can I forget you, being as ye were
      So beautiful among the pleasant fields
      In which ye stood? or can I here forget
      The plain and seemly countenance with which
505   Ye dealt out your plain Comforts? Yet had ye
      Delights and exultations of your own.
      Eager and never weary, we pursued
      Our home-amusements by the warm peat-fire
      At evening, when with pencil, and smooth slate
510   In square divisions parcelled out, and all
      With crosses and with cyphers scribbled o'er,
      We schemed and puzzled, head opposed to head,
      In strife too humble to be named in verse;[1]
      Or round the naked table, snow-white deal,°   *pine or fir*
515   Cherry, or maple, sate in close array,
      And to the Combat, Lu or Whist, led on
      A thick-ribbed Army, not as in the world
      Neglected and ungratefully thrown by
      Even for the very service they had wrought,
520   But husbanded through many a long campaign.
      Uncouth assemblage was it, where no few
      Had changed their functions; some, plebeian cards
      Which Fate, beyond the promise of their birth,
      Had dignified, and called to represent
525   The Persons of departed Potentates.
      Oh, with what echoes on the board they fell!
      Ironic diamonds; Clubs, Hearts, Diamonds, Spades,
      A congregation piteously akin!
      Cheap matter offered they to boyish wit,
530   Those sooty Knaves, precipitated down
      With scoffs and taunts like Vulcan[2] out of heaven;
      The paramount Ace, a moon in her eclipse,
      Queens gleaming through their Splendor's last decay,
      And Monarchs surly at the wrongs sustained
535   By royal visages.[3] Meanwhile abroad
      Incessant rain was falling, or the frost

---

1. I.e., ticktacktoe. By his phrasing in this passage, Wordsworth pokes fun at 18th-century poetic diction, which avoided homely terms by using circumlocutions.
2. Roman god of fire and forge. His mother, Juno, when he was born lame, threw him down from Olympus, the abode of the gods.
3. Wordsworth implicitly parallels the boys' card games to the mock-epic description of the aristocratic game of ombre in Pope's *The Rape of the Lock* 3.37–98.

Raged bitterly, with keen and silent tooth;
And, interrupting oft that eager game,
From under Esthwaite's splitting fields of ice
540 The pent-up air, struggling to free itself,
Gave out to meadow-grounds and hills, a loud
Protracted yelling, like the noise of wolves
Howling in Troops along the Bothnic Main.[4]
  Nor, sedulous° as I have been to trace   *diligent*
545 How Nature by extrinsic passion first
Peopled the mind with forms sublime or fair[5]
And made me love them, may I here omit
How other pleasures have been mine, and joys
Of subtler origin; how I have felt,
550 Not seldom even in that tempestuous time,
Those hallowed and pure motions of the sense
Which seem, in their simplicity, to own
An intellectual[6] charm;—that calm delight
Which, if I err not, surely must belong
555 To those first-born° affinities that fit   *innate*
Our new existence to existing things,
And, in our dawn of being, constitute
The bond of union between life and joy.
  Yes, I remember when the changeful earth
560 And twice five summers on my mind had stamped
The faces of the moving year, even then
I held unconscious intercourse with beauty
Old as creation, drinking in a pure
Organic pleasure from the silver wreaths
565 Of curling mist, or from the level plain
Of waters, colored by impending° clouds.   *overhanging*
  The sands of Westmorland, the creeks and bays
Of Cumbria's° rocky limits, they can tell   *Cumberland's*
How, when the Sea threw off his evening shade,
570 And to the Shepherd's hut on distant hills
Sent welcome notice of the rising moon,
How I have stood, to fancies such as these
A Stranger, linking with the Spectacle
No conscious memory of a kindred sight,
575 And bringing with me no peculiar sense
Of quietness or peace, yet have I stood,
Even while mine eye hath moved o'er many a league[7]
Of shining water, gathering, as it seemed,
Through every hair-breadth in that field of light,
580 New pleasure, like a bee among the flowers.
  Thus oft amid those fits of vulgar[8] joy
Which, through all seasons, on a Child's pursuits
Are prompt Attendants; 'mid that giddy bliss

---

4. A northern gulf of the Baltic Sea.
5. The passion at first was "extrinsic" because it was felt not for nature itself but for nature as associated with the outdoor activities he loved. Wordsworth now goes on to distinguish other "subtler" pleasures, felt in the very process of sensing the natural objects.
6. Spiritual, as opposed to sense perceptions.
7. A measure equal to approximately three miles.
8. Ordinary, commonplace.

Which like a tempest works along the blood
585 And is forgotten: even then I felt
Gleams like the flashing of a shield,—the earth
And common face of Nature spake to me
Rememberable things; sometimes, 'tis true,
By chance collisions and quaint accidents
590 (Like those ill-sorted unions, work supposed
Of evil-minded fairies), yet not vain
Nor profitless, if haply they impressed
Collateral[9] objects and appearances,
Albeit lifeless then, and doomed to sleep
595 Until maturer seasons called them forth
To impregnate and to elevate the mind.
—And, if the vulgar joy by its own weight
Wearied itself out of the memory,
The scenes which were a witness of that joy
600 Remained, in their substantial lineaments
Depicted on the brain, and to the eye
Were visible, a daily sight: and thus
By the impressive discipline of fear,
By pleasure and repeated happiness,
605 So frequently repeated, and by force
Of obscure feelings representative
Of things forgotten; these same scenes so bright,
So beautiful, so majestic in themselves,
Though yet the day was distant, did become
610 Habitually dear; and all their forms
And changeful colours by invisible links
Were fastened to the affections.°   feelings
                                        I began
My Story early, not misled, I trust,
By an infirmity of love for days
615 Disowned by memory,[1] fancying flowers where none,
Not even the sweetest, do or can survive
For him at least whose dawning day they cheered;
Nor will it seem to Thee, O Friend! so prompt
In sympathy, that I have lengthened out,
620 With fond and feeble tongue, a tedious tale.
Meanwhile, my hope has been, that I might fetch
Invigorating thoughts from former years;
Might fix the wavering balance of my mind,
And haply meet reproaches too, whose power
625 May spur me on, in manhood now mature,
To honorable toil. Yet should these hopes
Prove vain, and thus should neither I be taught
To understand myself, nor thou to know
With better knowledge how the heart was framed
630 Of him thou lovest, need I dread from thee
Harsh judgments, if the Song be loth to quit

9. Accompanying but subordinate.
1. I.e., he hopes that he has not mistakenly attributed his later thoughts and feelings to a time of life
he can no longer remember.

Those recollected hours that have the charm
Of visionary things, those lovely forms
And sweet sensations that throw back our life,
635 And almost make remotest infancy
A visible scene, on which the sun is shining?
     One end at least hath been attained—my mind
Hath been revived; and, if this genial² mood
Desert me not, forthwith shall be brought down
640 Through later years the story of my life:
The road lies plain before me,—'tis a theme
Single, and of determined bounds; and hence
I chuse it rather, at this time, than work
Of ampler or more varied argument,
645 Where I might be discomfited and lost;
And certain hopes are with me that to thee
This labour will be welcome, honoured Friend!

Book Second
School-time continued

Thus far, O Friend! have we, though leaving much
Unvisited, endeavoured to retrace
The simple ways in which my childhood walked,
Those chiefly, that first led me to the love
5 Of rivers, woods, and fields. The passion yet
Was in its birth, sustained, as might befal,
By nourishment that came unsought; for still,
From week to week, from month to month, we lived
A round of tumult. Duly° were our games   *appropriately*
10 Prolonged in summer till the day-light failed;
No chair remained before the doors, the bench
And threshold steps were empty; fast asleep
The Labourer, and the old Man who had sate,
A later Lingerer, yet the revelry
15 Continued, and the loud uproar; at last,
When all the ground was dark, and twinkling stars
Edged the black clouds, home and to bed we went,
Feverish, with weary joints and beating minds.
Ah! is there One who ever has been young
20 Nor needs a warning voice to tame the pride
Of intellect, and virtue's self-esteem?
One is there,¹ though the wisest and the best
Of all mankind, who covets not at times
Union that cannot be; who would not give,
25 If so he might, to duty and to truth
The eagerness of infantine desire?
A tranquillizing spirit presses now
On my corporeal frame, so wide appears
The vacancy between me and those days,

2. Productive, creative.   1. I.e., "Is there anyone . . . ?"

30 Which yet have such self-presence° in my mind,   *actuality*
    That, musing on them, often do I seem
    Two consciousnesses, conscious of myself
    And of some other Being. A rude mass
    Of native rock, left midway in the Square
35 Of our small market Village, was the goal
    Or centre of these sports; and, when, returned
    After long absence, thither I repaired,
    Gone was the old grey stone, and in its place
    A smart Assembly-room usurped the ground
40 That had been ours.² There let the fiddle scream,
    And be ye happy! Yet, my Friends,³ I know
    That more than one of you will think with me
    Of those soft starry nights, and that old Dame
    From whom the Stone was named, who there had sate
45 And watched her table with its huckster's wares
    Assiduous, through the length of sixty years.
    —We ran a boisterous course, the year span round
    With giddy motion. But the time approached
    That brought with it a regular desire
50 For calmer pleasures, when the winning forms
    Of Nature were collaterally attached⁴
    To every scheme of holiday delight,
    And every boyish sport, less grateful° else   *pleasing*
    And languidly pursued.
                        When summer came,
55 Our pastime was, on bright half-holidays,
    To sweep along the plain of Windermere
    With rival oars; and the selected bourne°   *destination*
    Was now an Island musical with birds
    That sang and ceased not; now a sister isle,
60 Beneath the oaks' umbrageous° covert, sown   *shaded*
    With lilies of the valley like a field;
    And now a third small island,⁵ where survived,
    In solitude, the ruins of a shrine
    Once to our Lady dedicate, and served
65 Daily with chaunted rites. In such a race,
    So ended, disappointment could be none,
    Uneasiness, or pain, or jealousy;
    We rested in the Shade, all pleased alike,
    Conquered and Conqueror. Thus the pride of strength,
70 And the vain-glory of superior skill,
    Were tempered, thus was gradually produced
    A quiet independence of the heart:
    And, to my Friend who knows me, I may add,
    Fearless of blame, that hence, for future days,
75 Ensued a diffidence and modesty;
    And I was taught to feel, perhaps too much,

2. The Hawkshead Town Hall, built in 1790.
3. Coleridge and John Wordsworth (William's brother), who had visited Hawkshead together with William in November 1799.

4. Associated as an accompaniment.
5. The island of Lady Holm, former site of a chapel dedicated to the Virgin Mary.

The self-sufficing power of solitude.
   Our daily meals were frugal, Sabine fare![6]
More than we wished we knew the blessing then
80   Of vigorous hunger—hence corporeal strength
Unsapped by delicate viands; for, exclude
A little weekly stipend,[7] and we lived
Through three divisions of the quartered year
In pennyless poverty. But now, to school
85   From the half-yearly holidays returned,
We came with weightier purses, that sufficed
To furnish treats more costly than the Dame
Of the old grey stone, from her scanty board, supplied.
Hence rustic dinners on the cool green ground,
90   Or in the woods, or by a river side,
Or shady fountains,° while among the leaves   *springs, streams*
Soft airs were stirring, and the mid-day sun
Unfelt shone brightly round us in our joy.
   Nor is my aim neglected if I tell
95   How sometimes, in the length of those half years,
We from our funds drew largely—proud to curb,
And eager to spur on, the gallopping Steed:
And with the cautious Inn-keeper, whose Stud
Supplied our want, we haply might employ
100   Sly subterfuges, if the Adventure's bound
Were distant, some famed Temple[8] where of yore
The Druids worshipped, or the antique Walls
Of that large Abbey which within the Vale
Of Nightshade, to St Mary's honour built,
105   Stands yet, a mouldering Pile, with fractured arch,
Belfry, and Images, and living Trees;
A holy Scene![9]—Along the smooth green Turf
Our Horses grazed:—to more than inland peace
Left by the west wind sweeping overhead
110   From a tumultuous ocean, trees and towers
In that sequestered Valley may be seen
Both silent and both motionless alike;
Such the deep shelter that is there, and such
The safeguard for repose and quietness.
115   Our Steeds remounted, and the summons given,
With whip and spur we through the Chauntry[1] flew
In uncouth race, and left the cross-legged Knight
And the Stone-abbot, and that single Wren
Which one day sang so sweetly in the Nave
120   Of the old Church, that, though from recent Showers
The earth was comfortless, and, touched by faint
Internal breezes, sobbings of the place

6. Like the meals of the Roman poet Horace on his Sabine farm.
7. In his last year at school Wordsworth had an allowance of sixpence a week, and his younger brother Christopher, threepence. After the Midsummer and Christmas holidays (line 85), the boys received a larger sum, ranging up to a guinea.
8. The stone circle at Swinside, on the lower Duddon River, mistakenly believed at the time to have been a Druid temple.
9. Furness Abbey, some twenty miles south of Hawkshead.
1. A chapel endowed for masses to be sung to the donor.

And respirations, from the roofless walls
The shuddering ivy dripped large drops, yet still
125 So sweetly 'mid the gloom the invisible Bird
Sang to herself, that there I could have made
My dwelling-place, and lived for ever there
To hear such music. Through the Walls we flew,
And down the Valley, and, a circuit made
130 In wantonness of heart, through rough and smooth
We scampered homewards. Oh, ye rocks and streams,
And that still Spirit shed from evening air!
Even in this joyous time I sometimes felt
Your presence, when with slackened step we breathed[2]
135 Along the sides of the steep hills, or when,
Lighted by gleams of moonlight from the sea,
We beat with thundering hoofs the level sand.
    Midway on long Winander's Eastern shore,
Within the crescent of a pleasant Bay,
140 A Tavern[3] stood, no homely-featured House,
Primeval like its neighbouring Cottages;
But 'twas a splendid place, the door beset
With Chaises, Grooms, and Liveries,—and within
Decanters, Glasses, and the blood-red Wine.
145 In ancient times, or ere the Hall was built
On the large Island,[4] had this Dwelling been
More worthy of a Poet's love, a Hut
Proud of its one bright fire and sycamore shade.
But, though the rhymes were gone that once inscribed
150 The threshold, and large golden characters
Spread o'er the spangled sign-board had dislodged
The old Lion, and usurped his place in slight
And mockery of the rustic Painter's hand,
Yet to this hour the spot to me is dear
155 With all its foolish pomp. The garden lay
Upon a slope surmounted by the plain
Of a small Bowling-green: beneath us stood
A grove, with gleams of water through the trees
And over the tree-tops; nor did we want
160 Refreshment, strawberries, and mellow cream.
There, while through half an afternoon we played
On the smooth platform, whether skill prevailed
Or happy blunder triumphed, bursts of glee
Made all the mountains ring. But ere night-fall,
165 When in our pinnace we returned, at leisure
Over the shadowy Lake, and to the beach
Of some small Island steered our course with one,
The Minstrel of our Troop,[5] and left him there,
And rowed off gently, while he blew his flute
170 Alone upon the rock,—Oh then the calm

2. Stopped to let the horses catch their breath.
3. The White Lion at Bowness.
4. The Hall on Belle Isle in Lake Windermere had been built in the early 1780s.

5. Identified by Christopher Wordsworth, *Memoirs* (1857), as Robert Greenwood, who became senior fellow of Trinity College, Cambridge.

And dead still water lay upon my mind
Even with a weight of pleasure, and the sky,
Never before so beautiful, sank down
Into my heart, and held me like a dream!
175   Thus were my sympathies enlarged, and thus
Daily the common range of visible things
Grew dear to me: already I began
To love the sun; a boy I loved the sun,
Not as I since have loved him, as a pledge
180 And surety of our earthly life, a light
Which we behold, and feel we are alive;
Nor for his bounty to so many worlds,
But for this cause, that I had seen him lay
His beauty on the morning hills, had seen
185 The western mountain touch his setting orb,
In many a thoughtless hour, when, from excess
Of happiness, my blood appear'd to flow
For its own pleasure, and I breathed with joy;
And from like feelings, humble though intense,
190 To patriotic and domestic love
Analogous, the moon to me was dear;
For I would dream away my purposes,
Standing to gaze upon her while she hung
Midway between the hills, as if she knew
195 No other region; but belonged to thee,
Yea, appertained by a peculiar right
To thee, and thy grey huts,[6] thou one dear Vale!
    Those incidental charms which first attached
My heart to rural objects, day by day
200 Grew weaker, and I hasten on to tell
How Nature, intervenient[7] till this time
And secondary, now at length was sought
For her own sake. But who shall[8] parcel out
His intellect, by geometric rules,
205 Split like a province into round and square?
Who knows the individual hour in which
His habits were first sown, even as a seed?
Who that shall point, as with a wand, and say,
"This portion of the river of my mind
210 Came from yon fountain"? Thou, my friend! art one
More deeply read in thy own thoughts; to thee
Science[9] appears but what in truth she is,
Not as our glory and our absolute boast,
But as a succedaneum,[1] and a prop
215 To our infirmity. No officious slave
Art thou of that false secondary power[2]
By which we multiply distinctions, then

6. Cottages built of gray stones.
7. I.e., entering incidentally into his other concerns.
8. Is able to.
9. In the old sense: learning.

1. In medicine, a drug substituted for a different drug. Wordsworth, however, uses the term to signify a remedy, or palliative.
2. The analytic faculty, as opposed to the power to apprehend "the unity of all" (line 221).

Deem that our puny boundaries are things
That we perceive, and not that we have made.
220 To thee, unblinded by these formal arts,
The unity of all hath been revealed;
And thou wilt doubt with me, less aptly skilled
Than many are to range the faculties
In scale and order, class the cabinet[3]
225 Of their sensations, and in voluble phrase[4]
Run through the history and birth of each
As of a single independent thing.
Hard task, vain hope, to analyse the mind,
If each most obvious and particular thought,
230 Not in a mystical and idle sense,
But in the words of reason deeply weighed,
Hath no beginning.
                              Blest the infant Babe,
(For with my best conjecture I would trace
Our Being's earthly progress) blest the Babe,
235 Nursed in his Mother's arms, who sinks to sleep
Rocked on his Mother's breast; who, when his soul
Claims manifest kindred with a human soul,
Drinks in the feelings of his Mother's eye![5]
For him, in one dear Presence, there exists
240 A virtue which irradiates and exalts
Objects through widest intercourse of sense.
No outcast he, bewildered and depressed;
Along his infant veins are interfused
The gravitation and the filial bond
245 Of nature that connect him with the world.
Is there a flower to which he points with hand
Too weak to gather it, already love
Drawn from love's purest earthly fount for him
Hath beautified that flower; already shades
250 Of pity cast from inward tenderness
Do fall around him upon aught that bears
Unsightly marks of violence or harm.
Emphatically such a Being lives,
Frail Creature as he is, helpless as frail,
255 An inmate of this active universe.
For feeling has to him imparted power
That through the growing faculties of sense
Doth, like an Agent of the one great Mind,
Create, creator and receiver both,
260 Working but in alliance with the works
Which it beholds.[6]—Such, verily, is the first
Poetic spirit of our human life,

3. To classify, as if arranged in a display case.
4. In fluent phraseology.
5. Like the modern psychologist, Wordsworth recognized the importance of earliest infancy in the development of the individual mind, although he had then to invent the terms with which to analyze the process.

6. The infant, in the sense of security and love shed by his mother's presence on outer things, perceives what would otherwise be an alien world as a place to which he has a relationship like that of a son to a mother (lines 239–45). On such grounds Wordsworth asserts that the mind partially creates, by altering, the world it seems simply to perceive.

By uniform control of after years
In most abated or suppressed, in some,
265 Through every change of growth and of decay,
Preeminent till death.
                              From early days,
Beginning not long after that first time
In which, a Babe, by intercourse of touch,
I held mute dialogues with my Mother's heart,[7]
270 I have endeavoured to display the means
Whereby this infant sensibility,
Great birth-right of our being, was in me
Augmented and sustained. Yet is a path
More difficult before me, and I fear
275 That, in its broken windings, we shall need
The chamois'[8] sinews, and the eagle's wing:
For now a trouble came into my mind
From unknown causes. I was left alone,
Seeking the visible world, nor knowing why.
280 The props of my affections were removed,[9]
And yet the building stood, as if sustained
By its own spirit! All that I beheld
Was dear, and hence to finer influxes°   *influences*
The mind lay open, to a more exact
285 And close communion. Many are our joys
In youth, but Oh! what happiness to live
When every hour brings palpable access
Of knowledge, when all knowledge is delight,
And sorrow is not there! The seasons came,
290 And every season, wheresoe'er I moved,
Unfolded transitory qualities
Which, but for this most watchful power of love,
Had been neglected, left a register
Of permanent relations, else unknown.[1]
295 Hence life, and change, and beauty; solitude
More active even than "best society,"[2]
Society made sweet as solitude
By inward concords, silent, inobtrusive;
And gentle agitations of the mind
300 From manifold distinctions, difference
Perceived in things where, to the unwatchful eye,
No difference is, and hence, from the same source,
Sublimer joy: for I would walk alone
Under the quiet stars, and at that time
305 Have felt whate'er there is of power in sound

7. I.e., both infant and mother feel the pulse of the other's heart.
8. An agile species of antelope inhabiting mountainous regions of Europe.
9. Wordsworth's mother had died the month before his eighth birthday. It is unclear from the context whether the "trouble" that came into his mind (line 277) refers to the loss of his mother, in whose arms he had established his initial relationship to the natural world, or to the mysterious pro-

cesses of the continued development and diversification of this relationship.
1. I.e., had it not been for the watchful power of love (line 292), the "transitory qualities" (291) would have been neglected, and the "permanent relations" now recorded in his memory would have been unknown.
2. A partial quotation of a line spoken by Adam to Eve in *Paradise Lost* 9.249: "For solitude sometimes is best society."

To breathe an elevated mood, by form
Or Image unprofaned: and I would stand,
If the night blackened with a coming storm,
Beneath some rock, listening to notes that are
310 The ghostly° language of the ancient earth,   *disembodied*
Or make their dim abode in distant winds.
Thence did I drink the visionary power;
And deem not profitless those fleeting moods
Of shadowy exultation: not for this,
315 That they are kindred to our purer mind
And intellectual life;³ but that the soul,
Remembering how she felt, but what she felt
Remembering not, retains an obscure sense
Of possible sublimity, whereto
320 With growing faculties she doth aspire,
With faculties still growing, feeling still
That, whatsoever point they gain, they yet
Have something to pursue.⁴
                        And not alone
'Mid gloom and tumult, but no less 'mid fair
325 And tranquil scenes, that universal power
And fitness in the latent qualities
And essences of things, by which the mind
Is moved with feelings of delight, to me
Came strengthened with a superadded soul,
330 A virtue not its own.—My morning walks
Were early;—oft before the hours of School
I travelled round our little Lake, five miles
Of pleasant wandering; happy time! more dear
For this, that One was by my side, a Friend⁵
335 Then passionately loved; with heart how full
Would he peruse these lines! for many years
Have since flowed in between us, and, our minds
Both silent to each other, at this time
We live as if those hours had never been.
340 Nor seldom did I lift our Cottage latch
Far earlier, and ere one smoke-wreath had risen
From human dwelling, or the thrush, high perched,
Piped to the woods his shrill *reveillé*,⁶ sate
Alone upon some jutting eminence
345 At the first gleam of dawn-light, when the Vale,
Yet slumbering, lay in utter solitude.
How shall I seek the origin, where find
Faith in the marvellous things which then I felt?
Oft in those moments such a holy calm
350 Would overspread my soul, that bodily eyes
Were utterly forgotten, and what I saw
Appeared like something in myself, a dream,

3. I.e., not because they are related to the non-sensuous ("intellectual") aspect of our life.
4. Cf. the revelation, while crossing Simplon Pass, that our destiny is with "something evermore about

to be" (6.605–09, p. 1531).
5. Identified as John Fleming in a note to the edition of 1850.
6. Military parlance for a signal call.

A prospect° in the mind.   *scene*
                                ’Twere long to tell
What spring and autumn, what the winter snows,
355 And what the summer shade, what day and night,
Evening and morning, sleep and waking thought,
From sources inexhaustible, poured forth
To feed the spirit of religious love,
In which I walked with Nature. But let this
360 Be not forgotten, that I still retained
My first creative sensibility,[7]
That by the regular action of the world
My soul was unsubdued. A plastic° power   *shaping*
Abode with me, a forming hand, at times
365 Rebellious, acting in a devious mood,
A local Spirit of his own, at war
With general tendency, but, for the most,
Subservient strictly to external things
With which it communed. An auxiliar light
370 Came from my mind which on the setting sun
Bestowed new splendor; the melodious birds,
The fluttering breezes, fountains that ran on
Murmuring so sweetly in themselves, obeyed
A like dominion; and the midnight storm
375 Grew darker in the presence of my eye;
Hence my obeisance, my devotion hence,
And hence my transport.°   *exaltation*
                           Nor should this, perchance,
Pass unrecorded, that I still° had loved   *always*
The exercise and produce of a toil
380 Than analytic industry to me
More pleasing, and whose character I deem
Is more poetic, as resembling more
Creative agency. The Song would speak
Of that interminable building reared
385 By observation of affinities
In objects where no brotherhood exists
To passive minds. My seventeenth year was come;
And, whether from this habit rooted now
So deeply in my mind, or from excess
390 Of the great social principle of life
Coercing all things into sympathy,
To unorganic Natures were transferred
My own enjoyments; or the Power of truth,
Coming in revelation, did converse
395 With things that really are;[8] I, at this time,
Saw blessings spread around me like a sea.
Thus while the days flew by and years passed on,

---

7. I.e., the creative perception manifested by the babe in his mother's arms (lines 235ff.).

8. Wordsworth is careful to indicate that there are alternative explanations for his sense that life pervades the inorganic as well as the organic world: it may be the result either of a way of perceiving that has been habitual since infancy or of a projection of his own inner life or else it may be the perception of an objective truth.

From Nature overflowing on my soul
I had received so much, that every thought
400 Was steeped in feeling; I was only then
Contented when with bliss ineffable
I felt the sentiment of Being spread
O'er all that moves, and all that seemeth still;
O'er all that, lost beyond the reach of thought
405 And human knowledge, to the human eye
Invisible, yet liveth to the heart;
O'er all that leaps, and runs, and shouts, and sings,
Or beats the gladsome air; o'er all that glides
Beneath the wave, yea, in the wave itself,
410 And mighty depth of waters. Wonder not
If high the transport, great the joy I felt,
Communing in this sort through earth and Heaven
With every form of Creature, as it looked
Towards the Uncreated with a countenance
415 Of adoration, with an eye of love.[9]
One song they sang, and it was audible,
Most audible, then, when the fleshly ear,
O'ercome by humblest prelude of that strain,
Forgot her functions and slept undisturbed.
420   If this be error, and another faith
Find easier access to the pious mind,[1]
Yet were I grossly destitute of all
Those human sentiments that make this earth
So dear, if I should fail with grateful voice
425 To speak of you, Ye Mountains, and Ye Lakes,
And sounding Cataracts, Ye Mists and Winds
That dwell among the Hills where I was born.
If in my Youth I have been pure in heart,
If, mingling with the world, I am content
430 With my own modest pleasures, and have lived,
With God and Nature communing, removed
From little enmities and low desires,
The gift is yours: if in these times of fear,
This melancholy waste° of hopes o'erthrown,   *wasteland*
435 If, 'mid indifference and apathy
And wicked exultation, when good men,
On every side, fall off, we know not how,
To selfishness, disguised in gentle names
Of peace and quiet and domestic love,
440 Yet mingled, not unwillingly, with sneers
On visionary minds; if, in this time
Of dereliction and dismay,[2] I yet
Despair not of our Nature, but retain
A more than Roman confidence, a faith

9. Wordsworth did not add lines 412–14, giving a Christian frame to his experience of the "one life," until the last revision of *The Prelude*, in 1839.
1. With lines 416–21 cf. *Tintern Abbey*, lines 43–50 (p. 1433).

2. The era, some ten years after the outbreak of the French Revolution, was one of violent reaction, in which many earlier sympathizers were recanting their radical beliefs.

445 That fails not, in all sorrow my support,
The blessing of my life, the gift is yours,
Ye Winds and sounding Cataracts, 'tis yours,
Ye Mountains! thine, O Nature! Thou hast fed
My lofty speculations; and in thee,
450 For this uneasy heart of ours, I find
A never-failing principle of joy
And purest passion.
                              Thou, my Friend! wert reared
In the great City, 'mid far other scenes;[3]
But we, by different roads, at length have gained
455 The self-same bourne. And for this cause to Thee
I speak, unapprehensive of contempt,
The insinuated scoff of coward tongues,
And all that silent language which so oft,
In conversation between Man and Man,
460 Blots from the human countenance all trace
Of beauty and of love. For Thou hast sought
The truth in solitude, and, since the days
That gave thee liberty, full long desired,
To serve in Nature's Temple, thou hast been
465 The most assiduous of her Ministers,[4]
In many things my Brother, chiefly here
In this our deep devotion.
                              Fare Thee well!
Health, and the quiet of a healthful mind,
Attend Thee! seeking oft the haunts of Men,
470 And yet more often living with thyself
And for thyself, so haply shall thy days
Be many, and a blessing to mankind.

From Book Third
Residence at Cambridge[1]

[A WALK IN THE FIELDS. WORDSWORTH'S "HEROIC ARGUMENT"]

   —A track pursuing, not untrod before,
From strict analogies by thought supplied,
Or consciousnesses not to be subdued,
130 To every natural form, rock, fruit or flower,
Even the loose stones that cover the high-way,
I gave a moral life; I saw them feel,
Or linked them to some feeling: the great mass
Lay bedded in a quickening° soul, and all   *life-giving*
135 That I beheld respired with inward meaning.

3. A reminiscence of Coleridge's *Frost at Midnight*, lines 51–52: "For I was reared / In the great city, pent 'mid cloisters dim."
4. Wordsworth may be recalling the conclusion of Coleridge's *France: An Ode* (1798), where, disillusioned about the promise of liberty by the French Revolution, he writes that, while standing on a "sea-cliff's verge," "O Liberty! my spirit felt thee

there." Wordsworth added lines 461–64 some years after Coleridge's death in 1834.
1. In this Book, Wordsworth recounts some of his early experiences as a callow country boy at St. John's College, Cambridge University. He goes on to describe his experience while walking alone in the fields outside of Cambridge.

Add, that whate'er of Terror or of Love
Or Beauty, Nature's daily face put on
From transitory passion, unto this
I was as sensitive as waters are
140　To the sky's influence: in a kindred mood
Of passion, was obedient as a lute
That waits upon the touches of the wind.[2]
Unknown, unthought of, yet I was most rich;
I had a world about me; 'twas my own,
145　I made it; for it only lived to me,
And to the God who sees into the heart.
Such sympathies, though rarely, were betrayed
By outward gestures and by visible looks:
Some called it madness—so, indeed, it was,
150　If child-like fruitfulness in passing joy,
If steady moods of thoughtfulness, matured
To inspiration, sort with such a name;
If prophecy be madness; if things viewed
By Poets in old time, and higher up
155　By the first men, earth's first inhabitants,
May in these tutored days no more be seen
With undisordered sight. But, leaving this,
It was no madness: for the bodily eye
Amid my strongest workings evermore
160　Was searching out the lines of difference
As they lie hid in all external forms,
Near or remote, minute or vast, an eye
Which from a tree, a stone, a withered leaf,
To the broad ocean, and the azure heavens
165　Spangled with kindred multitudes of Stars,
Could find no surface where its power might sleep;
Which spake perpetual logic to my Soul,
And by an unrelenting agency
Did bind my feelings, even as in a chain.
170　　And here, O friend! have I retraced my life
Up to an eminence, and told a tale
Of matters which not falsely may be called
The glory of my Youth. Of genius, power,
Creation, and Divinity itself,
175　I have been speaking, for my theme has been
What passed within me. Not of outward things
Done visibly for other minds; words, signs,
Symbols, or actions, but of my own heart
Have I been speaking, and my youthful mind.
180　O Heavens! how awful is the might of Souls
And what they do within themselves, while yet
The yoke of earth is new to them, the world
Nothing but a wild field where they were sown.
This is, in truth, heroic argument,
185　This genuine prowess, which I wished to touch

2. I.e., as a wind harp.

With hand however weak,[3] but in the main
It lies far hidden from the reach of words.
Points have we, all of us, within our Souls,
Where all stand single: this I feel, and make
190 Breathings for incommunicable powers.[4]
But is not each a memory to himself?
And, therefore, now that we must quit this theme,
I am not heartless;° for there's not a man   *disheartened*
That lives who hath not known his god-like hours,
195 And feels not what an empire we inherit,
As natural Beings, in the strength of Nature.
    No more:—for now into a populous plain
We must descend.—A Traveller I am
Whose tale is only of himself; even so,
200 So be it, if the pure of heart be prompt
To follow, and if Thou, O honored Friend!
Who in these thoughts art ever at my side,
Support, as heretofore, my fainting steps.[5]

*   *   *

Thus in submissive idleness, my Friend,
The laboring time of Autumn, Winter, Spring,
Eight months! rolled pleasingly away—the ninth
635 Came and returned me to my native hills.

From Book Fourth
Summer Vacation[1]

[THE DISCHARGED SOLDIER]

370   Once, when those summer Months
Were flown, and Autumn brought its annual shew
Of oars with oars contending, sails with sails,
Upon Winander's[2] spacious breast, it chanced
That—after I had left a flower-decked room
375 (Whose in-door pastime, lighted-up, survived
To a late hour) and spirits overwrought[3]
Were making night do penance for a day
Spent in a round of strenuous idleness—
My homeward course led up a long ascent
380 Where the road's watery surface, to the top
Of that sharp rising, glittered to the moon
And bore the semblance of another stream

3. Wordsworth describes the innovative epic theme ("heroic argument") for his projected long poem. Cf. his Prospectus to *The Recluse*, lines 25–41 (p. 1495).
4. This obscure assertion may mean that he tries, inadequately, to express the inexpressible.
5. The terms of this behest to Coleridge suggest the relation to Dante of Virgil, his guide in the *Inferno*.

1. Wordsworth returned to Hawkshead for his first summer vacation in 1788.
2. Lake Windermere's.
3. Worked up to a high pitch. Wordsworth is describing a party at which the "pastime" had been dancing. The description of the meeting with the discharged soldier that follows was written in 1798 as an independent poem, which Wordsworth later incorporated in *The Prelude*.

Stealing with silent lapse[4] to join the brook
That murmured in the Vale. All else was still;
385 No living thing appeared in earth or air,
And, save the flowing Water's peaceful voice,
Sound was there none: but lo! an uncouth shape
Shewn by a sudden turning of the road,
So near, that, slipping back into the shade
390 Of a thick hawthorn, I could mark him well,
Myself unseen. He was of stature tall,
A span[5] above man's *common* measure tall.
Stiff, lank, and upright;—a more meagre° man   *emaciated*
Was never seen before by night or day.
395 Long were his arms, pallid his hands;—his mouth
Looked ghastly° in the moonlight. From behind,   *ghostly*
A mile-stone propped him; I could also ken
That he was clothed in military garb,
Though faded, yet entire. Companionless,
400 No dog attending, by no staff sustained
He stood; and in his very dress appeared
A desolation, a simplicity
To which the trappings of a gaudy world
Make a strange background. From his lips erelong
405 Issued low muttered sounds, as if of pain
Or some uneasy thought; yet still his form
Kept the same awful steadiness;—at his feet
His shadow lay and moved not. From self-blame
Not wholly free, I watched him thus; at length
410 Subduing my heart's specious cowardice,[6]
I left the shady nook where I had stood,
And hailed him. Slowly, from his resting-place
He rose; and, with a lean and wasted arm
In measured gesture lifted to his head,
415 Returned my salutation: then resumed
His station as before; and when I asked
His history, the Veteran, in reply,
Was neither slow nor eager; but, unmoved,
And with a quiet uncomplaining voice,
420 A stately air of mild indifference,
He told, in few plain words, a Soldier's tale—
That in the Tropic Islands he had served,
Whence he had landed, scarcely three weeks past,
That on his landing he had been dismissed,[7]
425 And now was travelling towards his native home.
This heard, I said in pity, "Come with me."
He stooped, and straightway from the ground took up
An oaken staff, by me yet unobserved—
A staff which must have dropped from his slack hand

---

4. Flowing. Wordsworth is remembering a description that his sister, Dorothy, had entered into her journal in January 1798, a few days before he composed this passage: "The road to the village of Holford glittered like another stream."
5. About nine inches (the distance between extended thumb and little finger).

6. I.e., he had been deceiving himself in thinking that the motive for his delay was not cowardice.
7. The Tropic Islands are the West Indies. Tens of thousands of British soldiers serving there contracted tropical fevers and died, or else were rendered unfit for further service and discharged.

430 And lay till now neglected in the grass.
    Though weak his step and cautious, he appeared
To travel without pain, and I beheld,
With an astonishment but ill suppressed,
His ghastly figure moving at my side;
435 Nor could I, while we journeyed thus, forbear
To turn from present hardships to the past,
And speak of war, battle, and pestilence,
Sprinkling this talk with questions, better spared,
On what he might himself have seen or felt.
440 He all the while was in demeanour calm,
Concise in answer; solemn and sublime
He might have seemed, but that in all he said
There was a strange half-absence, as of one
Knowing too well the importance of his theme,
445 But feeling it no longer. Our discourse
Soon ended, and together on we passed,
In silence, through a wood, gloomy and still.
Up-turning then along an open field,
We reached a Cottage. At the door I knocked,
450 And earnestly to charitable care
Commended him, as a poor friendless Man
Belated, and by sickness overcome.
Assured that now the Traveller would repose
In comfort, I entreated, that henceforth
455 He would not linger in the public ways,
But ask for timely furtherance and help,
Such as his state required.—At this reproof,
With the same ghastly mildness in his look,
He said, "My trust is in the God of Heaven,
460 And in the eye of him who passes me."
    The Cottage door was speedily unbarred,
And now the Soldier touched his hat once more
With his lean hand; and, in a faltering voice
Whose tone bespake reviving interests
465 Till then unfelt, he thanked me; I returned
The farewell blessing of the patient Man,
And so we parted. Back I cast a look,
And lingered near the door a little space;
Then sought with quiet heart my distant home.
470   This passed, and He who deigns to mark with care
By what rules governed, with what end in view
This Work proceeds, *he* will not wish for more.

From Book Fifth
Books

[THE BOY OF WINANDER]

There was a Boy;[1]—ye knew him well, Ye Cliffs
And Islands of Winander!—many a time

---

1. In an early manuscript version of this passage Wordsworth uses the first-person pronoun. The experience he describes was thus apparently his own.

At evening, when the earliest stars began
To move along the edges of the hills,
370   Rising or setting, would he stand alone,
Beneath the trees, or by the glimmering lake;
And there, with fingers interwoven, both hands
Pressed closely palm to palm and to his mouth
Uplifted, he, as through an instrument,
375   Blew mimic hootings to the silent owls
That they might answer him.—And they would shout
Across the watery Vale, and shout again,
Responsive to his call,—with quivering peals,
And long halloos, and screams, and echoes loud
380   Redoubled and redoubled; concourse wild
Of jocund din! and when a lengthened pause
Of silence came, and baffled his best skill,
Then, sometimes, in that silence, while he hung
Listening, a gentle shock of mild surprize
385   Has carried far into his heart the voice
Of mountain torrents; or the visible scene
Would enter unawares into his mind
With all its solemn imagery, its rocks,
Its woods, and that uncertain heaven, received
390   Into the bosom of the steady lake.[2]
    This Boy was taken from his Mates, and died
In childhood, ere he was full twelve years old.
Fair is the Spot, most beautiful the Vale
Where he was born: the grassy Church-yard hangs
395   Upon a slope above the Village School;
And through that Church-yard when my way has led
On summer evenings, I believe that there
A long half-hour together I have stood
Mute—looking at the grave in which he lies!

From Book Sixth
Cambridge, and the Alps

["HUMAN NATURE SEEMING BORN AGAIN"]

When the third summer freed us from restraint,[1]
A youthful Friend, he too a Mountaineer,
325   Not slow to share my wishes, took his staff,
And, sallying forth, we journeyed, side by side,
Bound to the distant Alps. A hardy slight
Did this unprecedented course imply
Of College studies and their set rewards;[2]

---

2. Coleridge wrote of the last line and a half ("that uncertain heaven . . . lake"): "Had I met these lines running wild in the deserts of Arabia, I should instantly have screamed out, 'Wordsworth.'"
1. After reviewing briefly his second and third years at Cambridge, Wordsworth here describes his trip through France and Switzerland with a college friend, Robert Jones, during the succeeding summer vacation, in 1790. France was then in the

"golden hours" of the early period of the Revolution; the fall of the Bastille had occurred on July 14 of the preceding year.
2. English universities allow much longer vacations than those in the United States, on the optimistic assumption that they will be used primarily for intensive study. Wordsworth is facing his final examinations in the next college year.

330　Nor had, in truth, the scheme been formed by me
　　Without uneasy forethought of the pain,
　　The censures, and ill-omening of those
　　To whom my worldly interests were dear.
　　But Nature then was Sovereign in my mind,
335　And mighty Forms, seizing a youthful fancy,
　　Had given a charter[3] to irregular hopes.
　　In any age of uneventful calm
　　Among the Nations, surely would my heart
　　Have been possessed by similar desire;
340　But Europe at that time was thrilled with joy,
　　France standing on the top of golden hours,
　　And human nature seeming born again.

[CROSSING SIMPLON PASS]

　　* * * That very day,
525　From a bare ridge we also first beheld
　　Unveiled the summit of Mont Blanc, and grieved
　　To have a soulless image on the eye
　　Which had usurped upon a living thought
　　That never more could be.[4] The wondrous Vale
530　Of Chamouny[5] stretched far below, and soon
　　With its dumb cataracts, and streams of ice,
　　A motionless array of mighty waves,
　　Five rivers broad and vast, made rich amends,
　　And reconciled us to realities.
535　There small birds warble from the leafy trees,
　　The eagle soars high in the element;
　　There doth the Reaper bind the yellow sheaf,
　　The Maiden spread the hay-cock in the sun,
　　While Winter like a well-tamed lion walks,
540　Descending from the Mountain to make sport
　　Among the Cottages by beds of flowers.
　　　Whate'er in this wide circuit we beheld,
　　Or heard, was fitted to our unripe state
　　Of intellect and heart. With such a book
545　Before our eyes we could not chuse but read
　　Lessons of genuine brotherhood, the plain
　　And universal reason of mankind,
　　The truths of Young and Old. Nor, side by side
　　Pacing, two social Pilgrims, or alone
550　Each with his humour,[6] could we fail to abound
　　In dreams and fictions pensively composed,
　　Dejection taken up for pleasure's sake,
　　And gilded sympathies; the willow wreath,[7]
　　And sober posies[8] of funereal flowers

3. Privileged freedom.
4. The "image" is the actual sight of Mont Blanc, as against what the poet has imagined the famous Swiss mountain to be.
5. Chamonix, a valley in eastern France, north of Mont Blanc.
6. Temperament, or state of mind.
7. Symbolizing sorrow. "Gilded": laid on like gilt; i.e., superficial.
8. Small bunches of flowers.

555   Gathered, among those solitudes sublime,
From formal gardens of the Lady Sorrow,
Did sweeten many a meditative hour.
    Yet still in me with those soft luxuries
Mixed something of stern mood, an under thirst
560   Of vigor seldom utterly allayed.
And from that source how different a sadness
Would issue, let one incident make known.
When from the Vallais we had turned, and clomb°   *climbed*
Along the Simplon's steep and rugged road,[9]
565   Following a band of Muleteers, we reached
A halting-place where all together took
Their noon-tide meal. Hastily rose our Guide,
Leaving *us* at the Board; awhile we lingered,
Then paced the beaten downward way that led
570   Right to a rough stream's edge and there broke off.
The only track now visible was one
That from the torrent's further brink held forth
Conspicuous invitation to ascend
A lofty mountain. After brief delay
575   Crossing the unbridged stream, that road we took
And clomb with eagerness, till anxious fears
Intruded, for we failed to overtake
Our Comrades gone before. By fortunate chance,
While every moment added doubt to doubt,
580   A Peasant met us, from whose mouth we learned
That to the Spot which had perplexed us first
We must descend, and there should find the road,
Which in the stony channel of the Stream
Lay a few steps, and then along its banks,
585   And that our future course, all plain to sight,
Was downwards, with the current of that Stream.
Loth to believe what we so grieved to hear,
For still we had hopes that pointed to the clouds,
We questioned him again, and yet again;
590   But every word that from the Peasant's lips
Came in reply, translated by our feelings,
Ended in this, *that we had crossed the Alps.*[1]
    Imagination—here the Power so called
Through sad incompetence of human speech—
595   That awful Power rose from the Mind's abyss
Like an unfathered vapour[2] that enwraps
At once some lonely Traveller. I was lost,
Halted without an effort to break through;
But to my conscious soul I now can say,
600   "I recognize thy glory"; in such strength
Of usurpation, when the light of sense

---

9. The Simplon Pass through the Alps.
1. As Dorothy Wordsworth baldly put it later on, "The ambition of youth was disappointed at these tidings." The visionary experience that follows (lines 593–617) occurred not in the Alps but at the time of writing the passage, as the 1805 text explicitly says: "Imagination! lifting up itself / Before the eye and progress of my Song."
2. Sudden vapor from no apparent source.

Goes out, but with a flash that has revealed
The invisible world, doth Greatness make abode,
There harbours, whether we be young or old;
605 Our destiny, our being's heart and home,
Is with infinitude, and only there;
With hope it is, hope that can never die,
Effort, and expectation, and desire,
And something evermore about to be.[3]
610 Under such banners militant the Soul
Seeks for no trophies, struggles for no spoils,
That may attest her prowess, blest in thoughts
That are their own perfection and reward,
Strong in herself, and in beatitude[4]
615 That hides her like the mighty flood of Nile
Poured from his fount of Abyssinian clouds
To fertilize the whole Egyptian plain.
  The melancholy slackening that ensued
Upon those tidings by the Peasant given
620 Was soon dislodged; downwards we hurried fast
And, with the half-shaped road, which we had missed,
Entered a narrow chasm. The brook and road
Were fellow-Travellers in this gloomy Strait,
And with them did we journey several hours
625 At a slow pace. The immeasurable height
Of woods decaying, never to be decayed,
The stationary blasts of waterfalls,
And in the narrow rent at every turn
Winds thwarting winds, bewildered and forlorn,
630 The torrents shooting from the clear blue sky,
The rocks that muttered close upon our ears,
Black drizzling crags that spake by the way-side
As if a voice were in them, the sick sight
And giddy prospect of the raving stream,
635 The unfettered clouds, and region of the Heavens,
Tumult and peace, the darkness and the light—
Were all like workings of one mind, the features
Of the same face, blossoms upon one tree,
Characters of the great Apocalypse,[5]
640 The types and symbols of Eternity,
Of first and last, and midst, and without end.[6]

---

3. At the time, Wordsworth had not been able to understand why he had felt such grievous disappointment at finding that he had already crossed the Alps, while still expecting to climb upward (lines 587–92). Now, a flash of vision reveals the symbolic significance of that experience: that the glory of humankind is to aim infinitely high, even though our capabilities are finite.
4. The ultimate blessedness or happiness.
5. The objects in this natural scene, exhibiting a coincidence of all opposites, are like the written words of the Apocalypse—i.e., of the Book of Revelation, the last book of the New Testament.
6. Cf. Revelation 1.8: "I am Alpha and Omega, the beginning and the ending, saith the Lord." The phrase is repeated in Revelation 21.6, after the fulfillment of the last things. In *Paradise Lost* 5.153–65 Milton says that the things created declare their Creator, and calls on all to extol "him first, him last, him midst, and without end."

From Book Eighth
Retrospect, Love of Nature leading
to Love of Man[1]

[THE SHEPHERD IN THE MIST. MAN STILL SUBORDINATE TO NATURE]

      * * * A rambling School-boy, thus
I felt his presence in his own domain
As of a Lord and Master; or a Power
Or Genius,[2] under Nature, under God
260   Presiding; and severest solitude
Had more commanding looks when he was there.
When up the lonely brooks on rainy days
Angling I went, or trod the trackless hills
By mists bewildered, suddenly mine eyes
265   Have glanced upon him distant a few steps,
In size a Giant, stalking through thick fog,
His sheep like Greenland bears;° or, as he stepped   *polar bears*
Beyond the boundary line of some hill-shadow,
His form hath flashed upon me, glorified
270   By the deep radiance of the setting sun:[3]
Or him have I descried in distant sky,
A solitary object and sublime,
Above all height! like an aerial cross
Stationed alone upon a spiry rock
275   Of the Chartreuse,[4] for worship. Thus was Man
Ennobled outwardly before my sight,
And thus my heart was early introduced
To an unconscious love and reverence
Of human nature; hence the human Form
280   To me became an index of delight,
Of grace, and honor, power, and worthiness.
Meanwhile this Creature, spiritual almost
As those of Books, but more exalted far;
Far more of an imaginative Form
285   Than the gay Corin of the groves, who lives
For his own fancies, or to dance by the hour
In coronal, with Phillis[5] in the midst—
Was, for the purposes of Kind,[6] a Man
With the most common; husband, father; learned,

---

1. In this book Wordsworth reviews the first twenty-one years of his life to trace the transfer of his earlier feelings for nature to shepherds and other humble people who carry on their lonely duties almost as though they were animate parts of the landscape (cf. *Michael*, lines 1–39, pp. 1464–65). Wordsworth's central concern is to describe the early development in his relatively inexperienced mind of an image, or conceptual model, of the largeness, worth, and almost sacred dignity of generic Man (lines 256–81), an image that proved invulnerable to the acid bath of his later experience of the vulgarity, meanness, and evil of which individuals are capable.
2. Presiding spirit.

3. A "glory" is a mountain phenomenon in which the enlarged figure of a person is seen projected by the sun on the mist, with a radiance about its head. Cf. Coleridge's *Dejection: An Ode*, line 54 (p. 1617).
4. In his tour of the Alps, Wordsworth had been deeply impressed by the Chartreuse, a Carthusian monastery in France, with its soaring cross visible against the sky. There is an overtone here of the Christ-like divinity investing the "common" man (line 289).
5. Corin and Phillis, dancing in their coronals, or wreaths of flowers, were stock characters in earlier pastoral literature.
6. I.e., in carrying out the tasks of humankind.

290   Could teach, admonish, suffered with the rest
    From vice and folly, wretchedness and fear;
    Of this I little saw, cared less for it;
    But something must have felt.
                      Call ye these appearances
    Which I beheld of Shepherds in my youth,
295   This sanctity of Nature given to man—
    A shadow, a delusion, ye who pore
    On the dead letter, miss the spirit of things;
    Whose truth is not a motion or a shape
    Instinct with vital functions, but a Block
300   Or waxen image which yourselves have made,
    And ye adore. But blessed be the God
    Of Nature and of Man, that this was so,
    That men before my inexperienced eyes
    Did first present themselves thus purified,
305   Removed, and to a distance that was fit.
    And so we all of us in some degree
    Are led to knowledge, whencesoever led
    And howsoever; were it otherwise,
    And we found evil fast as we find good
310   In our first years, or think that it is found,
    How could the innocent heart bear up and live?

                  *   *   *

340   Yet deem not, Friend, that human-kind with me
    Thus early took a place preeminent;
    Nature herself was at this unripe time
    But secondary to my own pursuits
    And animal activities, and all
345   Their trivial pleasures:[7] and when these had drooped
    And gradually expired, and Nature, prized
    For her own sake, became my joy, even then—
    And upwards through late youth, until not less
    Than two and twenty summers had been told—
350   Was Man in my affections and regards
    Subordinate to her; her visible Forms
    And viewless agencies: a passion she,
    A rapture often, and immediate love
    Ever at hand; *he* only a delight
355   Occasional, an accidental grace,
    His hour being not yet come. *   *   *

---

7. Cf. his account of the stages of his development in lines 65–92 of *Tintern Abbey* (n. 2, p. 1434).

From Book Tenth
France continued[1]

[THE REVOLUTION: PARIS AND ENGLAND]

Cheared with this hope,[2] to Paris I returned;
And ranged, with ardor heretofore unfelt,
50   The spacious City, and in progress passed
The Prison[3] where the unhappy Monarch lay,
Associate with his Children and his Wife,
In Bondage; and the Palace[4] lately stormed,
With roar of Cannon, by a furious Host.
55   I crossed the Square (an empty Area then!)
Of the Carousel, where so late had lain
The Dead, upon the Dying heaped; and gazed
On this and other Spots, as doth a Man
Upon a Volume whose contents he knows
60   Are memorable, but from him locked up,
Being written in a tongue he cannot read;
So that he questions the mute leaves with pain,
And half-upbraids their silence. But, that night,
I felt most deeply in what world I was,
65   What ground I trod on, and what air I breathed.
High was my Room and lonely, near the roof
Of a large Mansion or Hotel,° a Lodge   *town house*
That would have pleased me in more quiet times,
Nor was it wholly without pleasure, then.
70   With unextinguished taper I kept watch,
Reading at intervals; the fear gone by
Pressed on me almost like a fear to come.
I thought of those September massacres,
Divided from me by one little month,
75   Saw them and touched;[5] the rest was conjured up
From tragic fictions, or true history,
Remembrances and dim admonishments.
The Horse is taught his manage,[6] and no Star
Of wildest course but treads back his own steps;
80   For the spent hurricane the air provides
As fierce a Successor; the tide retreats
But to return out of its hiding place
In the great Deep; all things have second birth;
The earthquake is not satisfied at once;
85   And in this way I wrought upon myself

---

1. Wordsworth's second residence in France, while he was twenty-one and twenty-two years of age (1791–92), coincided with a crucial period of the French Revolution. The eighth book of *The Prelude* dealt with his stay at Paris, Orleans, and Blois, during which he developed a passionate commitment to the French people and the cause of revolution. In this tenth book, Wordsworth deals with the period from October 1792 to August 1794.
2. I.e., that the moderates were now taking over

and would eliminate further violence.
3. I.e., the "Temple" (it had once housed the religious Order of Templars), where Louis XVI was held prisoner.
4. The Tuileries. In front of this is the great square of "the Carousel" (line 56), where a number of the mob storming the palace had been killed.
5. I.e., his imagination of the September massacres was so vivid as to be palpable.
6. The French *manège*, the prescribed action and paces of a trained horse.

Until I seemed to hear a voice that cried
To the whole City, "Sleep no more."[7] The Trance
Fled with the Voice to which it had given birth,
But vainly comments of a calmer mind
90 Promised soft peace and sweet forgetfulness.
The place, all hushed and silent as it was,
Appeared unfit for the repose of Night,
Defenceless as a wood where Tygers roam.

* * * In this frame of mind,
Dragged by a chain of harsh necessity,
So seemed it,—now I thankfully acknowledge,
Forced by the gracious providence of Heaven—
225 To England I returned,[8] else (though assured
That I both was, and must be, of small weight,
No better than a Landsman on the deck
Of a ship struggling with a hideous storm)
Doubtless I should have then made common cause
230 With some who perished, haply perished too,[9]
A poor mistaken and bewildered offering,
Should to the breast of Nature have gone back
With all my resolutions, all my hopes,
A Poet only to myself, to Men
235 Useless, and even, belovèd Friend, a Soul
To thee unknown![1]

* * *

What then were my emotions, when in Arms
Britain put forth her free-born strength in league,
265 O pity and shame! with those confederate Powers?[2]
Not in my single self alone I found,
But in the minds of all ingenuous Youth,
Change and subversion from that hour. No shock
Given to my moral nature had I known
270 Down to that very moment; neither lapse
Nor turn of sentiment that might be named
A revolution, save at this one time;
All else was progress on the self-same path
On which, with a diversity of pace,
275 I had been travelling: this a stride at once
Into another region.—As a light
And pliant hare-bell swinging in the breeze
On some gray rock, its birth-place, so had I

---

7. *Macbeth* 2.2.33–34: "Methought I heard a voice cry, 'Sleep no more, / Macbeth does murder sleep.'"
8. Forced by the "harsh necessity" of a lack of money, Wordsworth returned to England late in 1792.
9. Wordsworth had allied his sympathies with the party of the Girondins, almost all of whom were guillotined or committed suicide.
1. Wordsworth did not meet Coleridge, the "beloved Friend," until 1795.

2. England joined the war against France in February 1793. The great moral crisis that almost wrecked Wordsworth's life began with this sudden split between his profound attachments to the English land (the development of which he had described in the early books of *The Prelude*) and his later but heartfelt identification with the cause of the French Revolution. What had seemed a single and coherent development suddenly became split into conflicting parts.

Wantoned, fast rooted on the ancient tower
280 Of my beloved Country, wishing not
A happier fortune than to wither there.
Now was I from that pleasant station torn
And tossed about in whirlwind. I rejoiced,
Yea, afterwards, truth most painful to record!
285 Exulted, in the triumph of my Soul,
When Englishmen by thousands were o'erthrown,
Left without glory on the field, or driven,
Brave hearts, to shameful flight.[3] It was a grief,—
Grief call it not, 'twas any thing but that,—
290 A conflict of sensations without name,
Of which *he* only who may love the sight
Of a Village Steeple as I do can judge,
When, in the Congregation bending all
To their great Father, prayers were offered up,
295 Or praises, for our Country's victories,
And, 'mid the simple Worshippers, perchance
I only, like an uninvited Guest,
Whom no one owned, sate silent, shall I add,
Fed on the day of vengeance yet to come?

* * *

[THE REIGN OF TERROR. NIGHTMARES]

—Domestic carnage now filled the whole year
With Feast-days;[4] old Men from the Chimney-nook,
The Maiden from the bosom of her Love,
The Mother from the Cradle of her Babe,
360 The Warrior from the Field, all perished, all,
Friends, enemies, of all parties, ages, ranks,
Head after head, and never heads enough
For those that bade them fall. They found their joy,
They made it, proudly eager as a Child
365 (If like desires of innocent little ones
May with such heinous appetites be compared),
Pleased in some open field to exercise
A toy that mimics with revolving wings
The motion of a windmill, though the air
370 Do of itself blow fresh and make the Vanes
Spin in his eyesight, *that* contents him not,
But, with the play-thing at arm's length, he sets
His front against the blast, and runs amain
That it may whirl the faster.

* * *

Most melancholy at that time, O Friend!
Were my day-thoughts, my nights were miserable;

3. The French defeated the English in the battle of Hondschoote, September 6, 1793.
4. I.e., festivals celebrated by human slaughter ("carnage"). Lines 356–63 give a description of the height of the Reign of Terror under Robespierre. In 1794, a total of 1,376 people were guillotined in Paris in forty-nine days.

Through months, through years, long after the last beat
400 Of those atrocities, the hour of sleep
To me came rarely charged with natural gifts,
Such ghastly Visions had I of despair
And tyranny, and implements of death,
And innocent victims sinking under fear,
405 And momentary hope, and worn-out prayer,
Each in his separate cell, or penned in crowds
For sacrifice, and struggling with forced mirth
And levity in dungeons where the dust
Was laid with tears. Then suddenly the scene
410 Changed, and the unbroken dream entangled me
In long orations which I strove to plead
Before unjust tribunals—with a voice
Labouring, a brain confounded, and a sense
Death-like of treacherous desertion, felt
415 In the last place of refuge, my own soul.

From Book Eleventh
France, concluded[1]

[RETROSPECT: "BLISS WAS IT IN THAT DAWN." RECOURSE TO
"REASON'S NAKED SELF"]

105   O pleasant exercise of hope and joy![2]
For mighty were the Auxiliars which then stood
Upon our side, we who were strong in Love!
Bliss was it in that dawn to be alive,
But to be young was very Heaven! O times,
110 In which the meagre, stale, forbidding ways
Of custom, law, and statute, took at once
The attraction of a Country in Romance!
When Reason seemed the most to assert her rights,
When most intent on making of herself
115 A prime Enchantress—to assist the work
Which then was going forward in her name!
Not favored spots alone, but the whole earth
The beauty wore of promise—that which sets
(As at some moments might not be unfelt
120 Among the bowers of Paradise itself)
The budding rose above the rose full blown.[3]
What Temper° at the prospect did not wake   *temperament*
To happiness unthought of? The inert
Were roused, and lively natures rapt away![4]
125 They who had fed their Childhood upon dreams,

1. Book 11 deals with the year from August 1794 through September 1795: Wordsworth's growing disillusionment with the French Revolution, his recourse to abstract theories of man and politics, his despair and nervous breakdown, and the beginning of his recovery when he moved from London to Racedown.
2. Wordsworth in this passage turns back to the summer of 1792, when his enthusiasm for the Revolution was at its height.
3. A statement of the Romantic theme of the glory of the imperfect, which sets a higher value on promise than on achievement.
4. Enraptured; carried away by enthusiasm.

The play-fellows of Fancy, who had made
All powers of swiftness, subtilty, and strength
Their ministers,—who in lordly wise had stirred
Among the grandest objects of the Sense,
130 And dealt with whatsoever they found there
As if they had within some lurking right
To wield it;—they, too, who of gentle mood
Had watched all gentle motions, and to these
Had fitted their own thoughts, schemers more mild,
135 And in the region of their peaceful selves;—
Now was it that *both* found, the Meek and Lofty
Did both find helpers to their hearts' desire,
And stuff at hand, plastic° as they could wish,—   malleable
Were called upon to exercise their skill,
140 Not in Utopia,—subterranean Fields,—
Or some secreted Island, Heaven knows where!
But in the very world, which is the world
Of all of us,—the place where in the end
We find our happiness, or not at all!
145   Why should I not confess that Earth was then
To me what an Inheritance new-fallen
Seems, when the first time visited, to one
Who thither comes to find in it his home?
He walks about and looks upon the spot
150 With cordial transport, moulds it and remoulds,
And is half-pleased with things that are amiss,
'Twill be such joy to see them disappear.
      An active partisan, I thus convoked°   called up
From every object pleasant circumstance
155 To suit my ends; I moved among mankind
With genial feelings still° predominant;   always
When erring, erring on the better part,
And in the kinder spirit; placable,
Indulgent, as not uninformed that men
160 See as they have been taught, and that Antiquity[5]
Gives rights to error; and aware no less
That throwing off oppression must be work
As well of licence as of liberty;
And above all, for this was more than all,
165 Not caring if the wind did now and then
Blow keen upon an eminence that gave
Prospect so large into futurity;
In brief, a Child of Nature, as at first,
Diffusing only those affections wider
170 That from the cradle had grown up with me,
And losing, in no other way than light
Is lost in light, the weak in the more strong.
      In the main outline, such, it might be said,
Was my condition, till with open war
175 Britain opposed the Liberties of France;[6]

5. Classical antiquity.
6. On February 11, 1793, England declared war against France.

This threw me first out of the pale° of love,   *enclosure*
Soured, and corrupted, upwards to the source,
My sentiments; was not,[7] as hitherto,
A swallowing up of lesser things in great;
180 But change of them into their contraries;
And thus a way was opened for mistakes
And false conclusions, in degree as gross,
In kind more dangerous. What had been a pride
Was now a shame; my likings and my loves
185 Ran in new channels, leaving old ones dry,
And hence a blow that in maturer age
Would but have touched the judgement, struck more deep
Into sensations near the heart; meantime,
As from the first, wild theories were afloat
190 To whose pretensions sedulously urged[8]
I had but lent a careless ear, assured
That time was ready to set all things right,
And that the multitude so long oppressed
Would be oppressed no more.
                         But when events
195 Brought less encouragement, and unto these
The immediate proof of principles no more
Could be entrusted, while the events themselves,
Worn out in greatness, stripped of novelty,
Less occupied the mind; and sentiments
200 Could through my understanding's natural growth
No longer keep their ground, by faith maintained
Of inward consciousness, and hope that laid
Her hand upon her object; evidence
Safer, of universal application, such
205 As could not be impeached, was sought elsewhere.
    But now, become Oppressors in their turn,
Frenchmen had changed a war of self-defence
For one of Conquest, losing sight of all
Which they had struggled for:[9] and mounted up,
210 Openly in the eye of Earth and Heaven,
The scale of Liberty.[1] I read her doom
With anger vexed, with disappointment sore,
But not dismayed, nor taking to the shame
Of a false Prophet. While resentment rose,
215 Striving to hide, what nought could heal, the wounds
Of mortified presumption, I adhered
More firmly to old tenets, and, to prove[2]
Their temper, strained them more; and thus, in heat
Of contest, did opinions every day
220 Grow into consequence, till round my mind
They clung, as if they were its life, nay more,
The very being of the immortal Soul.

---

7. I.e., there was not (in my sentiments).
8. Diligently argued for.
9. In late 1794 and early 1795 French troops had successes in Spain, Italy, Holland, and Germany—even though, in the constitution written in 1790,

they had renounced all foreign conquest.
1. I.e., the desire for power now outweighed the love of liberty.
2. Test. The figure is that of testing a tempered steel sword.

This was the time when, all things tending fast
To depravation, speculative schemes
225   That promised to abstract the hopes of Man
Out of his feelings, to be fixed thenceforth
For ever in a purer element,
Found ready welcome.[3] Tempting region *that*
For Zeal to enter and refresh herself,
230   Where passions had the privilege to work,
And never hear the sound of their own names:
But, speaking more in charity, the dream
Flattered the young, pleased with extremes, nor least
With that which makes our Reason's naked self
235   The object of its fervour. * * *

[CRISIS, BREAKDOWN, AND RECOVERY]

I summoned my best skill, and toiled, intent
280   To anatomize° the frame of social life,   *analyze*
Yea, the whole body of society
Searched to its heart. Share with me, Friend! the wish
That some dramatic tale indued with shapes
Livelier, and flinging out less guarded words
285   Than suit the Work we fashion, might set forth
What then I learned, or think I learned, of truth,
And the errors into which I fell, betrayed
By present objects, and by reasonings false
From their beginnings, inasmuch as drawn
290   Out of a heart that had been turned aside
From Nature's way by outward accidents,
And which was thus confounded more and more,
Misguided and misguiding. So I fared,
Dragging all precepts, judgments, maxims, creeds,
295   Like culprits to the bar; calling the mind,
Suspiciously, to establish in plain day
Her titles[4] and her honors, now believing,
Now disbelieving, endlessly perplexed
With impulse, motive, right and wrong, the ground
300   Of obligation, what the rule and whence
The sanction, till, demanding formal *proof*
And seeking it in every thing, I lost
All feeling of conviction, and, in fine,°   *the end*
Sick, wearied out with contrarieties,
305   Yielded up moral questions in despair.
    This was the crisis of that strong disease,
This the soul's last and lowest ebb; I drooped,
Deeming our blessed Reason of least use
Where wanted most. * * *

---

3. I.e., schemes that undertook to separate ("abstract") people's hopes for future happiness from reliance on the emotional part of human nature, and instead to ground those hopes on their rational natures ("a purer element"). The allusion is primarily to William Godwin's *Inquiry Concern-* *ing Political Justice* (1793), which attempted to ground ethical and political principles, and the expectation of human progress, exclusively on rational principles.
4. Legal entitlements.

* * * Then it was,
Thanks to the bounteous Giver of all good!
335 That the beloved Woman[5] in whose sight
Those days were passed, now speaking in a voice
Of sudden admonition—like a brook
That does but *cross* a lonely road, and now
Seen, heard, and felt, and caught at every turn,
340 Companion never lost through many a league—
Maintained for me a saving intercourse
With my true self:[6] for, though bedimmed and changed
Both as a clouded and a waning moon,
She whispered still that brightness would return,
345 She in the midst of all preserved me still
A Poet, made me seek beneath that name,
And that alone, my office upon earth.
And lastly, as hereafter will be shewn,
If willing audience fail not, Nature's self,
350 By all varieties of human love
Assisted, led me back through opening day
To those sweet counsels between head and heart
Whence grew that genuine knowledge fraught with peace
Which, through the later sinkings of this cause,
355 Hath still upheld me, and upholds me now
In the catastrophe (for so they dream,
And nothing less), when, finally to close
And rivet down the gains of France, a Pope
Is summoned in, to crown an Emperor:[7]
360 This last opprobrium, when we see a people
That once looked up in faith, as if to Heaven
For manna, take a lesson from the Dog
Returning to his vomit. * * *

Book Twelfth
Imagination and Taste, how impaired and restored[1]

Long time have human ignorance and guilt
Detained us, on what spectacles of woe
Compelled to look, and inwardly oppressed
With sorrow, disappointment, vexing thoughts,
5 Confusion of the judgment, zeal decayed,
And, lastly, utter loss of hope itself
And things to hope for! Not with these began
Our Song, and not with these our Song must end.[2]

---

5. After a long separation, Dorothy Wordsworth
came to live with her brother at Racedown in 1795
and remained a permanent member of his household.
6. Dorothy and the renewed influence of nature
(line 349) healed the inner fracture between his
earlier and later selves, which Wordsworth had
described in 10.268ff.
7. The ultimate blow to liberal hopes for France
occurred when on December 2, 1804, Napoleon

summoned Pope Pius VII to officiate at the ceremony elevating him to emperor. At the last moment,
Napoleon took the crown and donned it himself.
1. Book 12 reviews the "impairment" and gradual
recovery of Wordsworth's creative sensibility in
response to the natural world.
2. The reference is back to the joyous preamble
with which *The Prelude* began. Wordsworth goes
on (line 10) to invoke the breeze described in the
opening line of the poem.

Ye motions of delight, that haunt the sides
10 Of the green hills; ye breezes and soft airs,
Whose subtile intercourse with breathing flowers,
Feelingly watched, might teach Man's haughty race
How without injury to take, to give
Without offence; ye who, as if to shew
15 The wondrous influence of power gently used,
Bend the complying heads of lordly pines,
And with a touch shift the stupendous clouds
Through the whole compass of the sky; ye brooks
Muttering along the stones, a busy noise
20 By day, a quiet sound in silent night;
Ye waves that out of the great deep steal forth
In a calm hour to kiss the pebbly shore,
Not mute, and then retire, fearing no storm;
And you, ye Groves, whose ministry it is
25 To interpose the covert of your shades,
Even as a sleep, between the heart of man
And outward troubles, between man himself,
Not seldom, and his own uneasy heart!
Oh that I had a music and a voice
30 Harmonious as your own, that I might tell
What Ye have done for me! The morning shines,
Nor heedeth Man's perverseness; Spring returns,
I saw the Spring return and could rejoice,
In common with the Children of her love
35 Piping on boughs, or sporting on fresh fields,
Or boldly seeking pleasure nearer heaven
On wings that navigate cerulean skies.
So neither were complacency° nor peace   satisfaction
Nor tender yearnings wanting for my good
40 Through those distracted times;[3] in Nature still
Glorying, I found a counterpoise in her,
Which, when the Spirit of evil reached its height,
Maintained for me a secret happiness.

[THE "SPOTS OF TIME"]

There are in our existence spots of time,[4]
That with distinct pre-eminence retain
210 A renovating virtue, whence, depressed
By false opinion and contentious thought,
Or aught of heavier or more deadly weight,
In trivial occupations, and the round
Of ordinary intercourse, our minds
215 Are nourished and invisibly repaired;
A virtue by which pleasure is inhanced,

---

3. I.e., the period of spiritual crisis that he had described in 11.293–309.
4. Moments of experience in which something ordinary (line 254) suddenly becomes profoundly significant. Because this significance is bestowed by the perceiver, it demonstrates the freedom and creative power of the imaginative mind (lines 220–23, 275–77). The remembrance of such moments nourishes and repairs the mind in periods of depression or distraction when the imagination flags (lines 210–15).

That penetrates, enables us to mount,
When high, more high, and lifts us up when fallen.
This efficacious Spirit chiefly lurks
220 Among those passages of life that give
Profoundest knowledge how and to what point
The mind is lord and master—outward sense
The obedient Servant of her will. Such moments
Are scattered every where, taking their date
225 From our first Childhood. I remember well
That once, while yet my inexperienced hand
Could scarcely hold a bridle, with proud hopes
I mounted, and we journied towards the hills:
An ancient Servant of my Father's house
230 Was with me, my encourager and Guide.
We had not travelled long ere some mischance
Disjoined me from my Comrade, and, through fear
Dismounting, down the rough and stony Moor
I led my horse, and, stumbling on, at length
235 Came to a bottom,° where in former times   *valley*
A Murderer had been hung in iron chains.
The Gibbet mast[5] had mouldered down, the bones
And iron case were gone, but on the turf
Hard by, soon after that fell deed was wrought,
240 Some unknown hand had carved the Murderer's name.
The monumental Letters were inscribed
In times long past, but still from year to year,
By superstition of the neighbourhood,
The grass is cleared away, and to that hour
245 The characters were fresh and visible.
A casual glance had shewn them, and I fled,
Faultering and faint and ignorant of the road:
Then, reascending the bare common, saw
A naked Pool that lay beneath the hills,
250 The Beacon on its summit, and, more near,
A Girl who bore a Pitcher on her head,
And seemed with difficult steps to force her way
Against the blowing wind. It was in truth
An ordinary sight; but I should need
255 Colors and words that are unknown to man
To paint the visionary dreariness
Which, while I looked all round for my lost Guide,
Invested Moorland waste and naked Pool,
The Beacon crowning the lone eminence,
260 The Female and her garments vexed and tossed
By the strong wind.—When, in the blessed hours
Of early love, the loved One[6] at my side,
I roamed, in daily presence of this scene,
Upon the naked Pool and dreary Crags,
265 And on the melancholy Beacon, fell

---

5. The post with a projecting arm used for hanging criminals.

6. Mary Hutchinson.

A spirit of pleasure, and Youth's golden gleam;
And think ye not with radiance more sublime
For these remembrances, and for the power
They had left behind? So feeling comes in aid
270 Of feeling, and diversity of strength
Attends us, if but once we have been strong.
Oh! mystery of Man, from what a depth
Proceed thy honors! I am lost, but see
In simple child-hood something of the base
275 On which thy greatness stands; but this I feel,
That from thyself it comes, that thou must give,
Else never canst receive. The days gone by
Return upon me almost from the dawn
Of life: the hiding-places of Man's power
280 Open; I would approach them, but they close.
I see by glimpses now; when age comes on
May scarcely see at all, and I would give,
While yet we may, as far as words can give,
Substance and life to what I feel, enshrining,
285 Such is my hope, the spirit of the past
For future restoration.—Yet another
Of these memorials.
                    One Christmas-time,[7]
On the glad Eve of its dear holidays,
Feverish, and tired, and restless, I went forth
290 Into the fields, impatient for the sight
Of those led Palfreys[8] that should bear us home,
My Brothers and myself. There rose a Crag
That, from the meeting point of two highways
Ascending, overlooked them both, far stretched;
295 Thither, uncertain on which road to fix
My expectation, thither I repaired,
Scout-like, and gained the summit; 'twas a day
Tempestuous, dark, and wild, and on the grass
I sate, half-sheltered by a naked wall;
300 Upon my right hand couched a single sheep,
Upon my left a blasted hawthorn stood:
With those Companions at my side, I sate,
Straining my eyes intensely, as the mist
Gave intermitting prospect of the copse
305 And plain beneath. Ere we to School returned
That dreary time, ere we had been ten days
Sojourners in my Father's House, he died,[9]
And I and my three Brothers, Orphans then,
Followed his Body to the Grave. The Event,
310 With all the sorrow that it brought, appeared
A chastisement; and when I called to mind
That day so lately passed, when from the Crag
I looked in such anxiety of hope,

---

7. In 1783. Wordsworth, aged thirteen, was at Hawkshead School with two of his brothers.
8. Small saddle horses.

9. John Wordsworth died on December 30, 1783. William's mother had died five years earlier.

With trite reflections of morality,
315 Yet in the deepest passion, I bowed low
To God, who thus corrected my desires;
And afterwards, the wind and sleety rain
And all the business[1] of the Elements,
The single Sheep, and the one blasted tree,
320 And the bleak music of that old stone wall,
The noise of wood and water, and the mist
That on the line of each of those two Roads
Advanced in such indisputable shapes;[2]
All these were kindred spectacles and sounds
325 To which I oft repaired, and thence would drink
As at a fountain; and on winter nights,
Down to this *very* time, when storm and rain
Beat on my roof, or haply at noon-day,
While in a grove I walk whose lofty trees,
330 Laden with summer's thickest foliage, rock
In a strong wind, some working of the spirit,
Some inward agitations, thence are brought,[3]
Whate'er their office, whether to beguile
Thoughts over-busy in the course they took,
335 Or animate an hour of vacant ease.

From Book Thirteenth
Subject concluded

[RETURN TO "LIFE'S FAMILIAR FACE"]

From Nature doth emotion come, and moods
Of calmness equally are Nature's gift:
This is her glory; these two attributes
Are sister horns that constitute her strength.[1]
5 Hence Genius,[2] born to thrive by interchange
Of peace and excitation, finds in her
His best and purest friend, from her receives
That energy by which he seeks the truth,
From her that happy stillness of the mind
10 Which fits him to receive it, when unsought.
Such benefit the humblest intellects
Partake of, each in their degree: 'tis mine
To speak of what myself have known and felt.
Smooth task! for words find easy way, inspired
15 By gratitude and confidence in truth.
Long time in search of knowledge did I range
The field of human life, in heart and mind
Benighted, but the dawn beginning now
To reappear,[3] 'twas proved that not in vain

1. Busy-ness; motions.
2. I.e., shapes one did not dare question.
3. Another instance of Wordsworth's inner response to an outer breeze (cf. 1.33–38, p. 1499).
1. In the Old Testament, the horn of an animal signifies power.
2. A person capable of creativity.
3. I.e., he is beginning to recover from the spiritual crisis recorded in 11.293–309.

20 I had been taught to reverence a Power
That is the visible quality and shape
And image of right reason,[4] that matures
Her processes by steadfast laws, gives birth
To no impatient or fallacious hopes,
25 No heat of passion or excessive zeal,
No vain conceits,—provokes to no quick turns
Of self-applauding intellect,—but trains
To meekness, and exalts by humble faith;[5]
Holds up before the mind, intoxicate
30 With present objects, and the busy dance
Of things that pass away, a temperate shew
Of objects that endure; and by this course
Disposes her, when over-fondly set
On throwing off incumbrances, to seek
35 In Man, and in the frame of social life,
Whate'er there is desireable and good
Of kindred permanence, unchanged in form
And function, or through strict vicissitude
Of life and death revolving. Above all
40 Were re-established now those watchful thoughts
Which (seeing little worthy or sublime
In what the Historian's pen so much delights
To blazon, Power and Energy detached
From moral purpose) early tutored me
45 To look with feelings of fraternal love
Upon the unassuming things that hold
A silent station in this beauteous world.[6]
      Thus moderated, thus composed, I found
Once more in Man an object of delight,
50 Of pure imagination, and of love;
And, as the horizon of my mind enlarged,
Again I took the intellectual eye[7]
For my Instructor, studious more to see
Great Truths, than touch and handle little ones.
55 Knowledge was given accordingly; my trust
Became more firm in feelings that had stood
The test of such a trial; clearer far
My sense of excellence—of right and wrong:
The promise of the present time retired
60 Into its true proportions; sanguine[8] schemes,
Ambitious projects, pleased me less; I sought
For present good in life's familiar face,
And built thereon my hopes of good to come.

4. Wordsworth follows Milton's use of the term "right reason" to denote a human faculty that is inherently attuned to truth.
5. In the text of 1805: "but lifts / The being into magnanimity."
6. Here Wordsworth begins his account of how he came to feel bonds to, and to love, the silent, lowly, common things whose celebration he considers to

be his special vocation as an innovative poet-prophet (see lines 301–08).
7. Perception by the integral mind.
8. Optimistic. Wordsworth apparently refers back to his earlier "ambitious projects" for a long poem, described in 1.166–220, as well as to the optimistic schemes for humankind that had been engendered by his commitment to the French Revolution.

[DISCOVERY OF HIS POETIC SUBJECT.
SIGHT OF "A NEW WORLD"]

220   Here, calling up to mind what then I saw,[9]
A youthful Traveller, and see daily now
In the familiar circuit of my home,
Here might I pause and bend in reverence
To Nature, and the power of human minds,
225   To Men as they are Men within themselves.
How oft high service is performed within,
When all the external Man is rude in shew!
Not like a Temple rich with pomp and gold,
But a mere mountain Chapel that protects
230   Its simple Worshippers from sun and shower.
Of these, said I, shall be my song, of these,
If future years mature me for the task,
Will I record the praises, making Verse
Deal boldly with substantial things; in truth
235   And sanctity of passion speak of these,
That justice may be done, obeisance paid
Where it is due: thus haply shall I teach,
Inspire, through unadulterated° ears   *uncorrupted*
Pour rapture, tenderness, and hope, my theme
240   No other than the very heart of Man
As found among the best of those who live
Not unexalted by religious faith,
Nor uninformed by Books, good books, though few,
In Nature's presence: thence may I select
245   Sorrow, that is not sorrow, but delight,
And miserable love that is not pain
To hear of, for the glory that redounds
Therefrom to human kind and what we are.
Be mine to follow with no timid step
250   Where knowledge leads me; it shall be my pride
That I have dared to tread this holy ground,
Speaking no dream, but things oracular,
Matter not lightly to be heard by those
Who to the letter of the outward promise
255   Do read the invisible Soul,[1] by Men adroit
In speech, and for communion with the world
Accomplished, minds whose faculties are then
Most active when they are most eloquent,
And elevated most, when most admired.
260   Men may be found of other mold than these,
Who are their own Upholders, to themselves

9. Wordsworth has described, as part of his imaginative recovery, his learning to look again with sympathy upon "the unassuming things that hold / A silent station in this beauteous world" (lines 46–47) and his finding again "in Man an object of delight" (line 49). Now he shows how, in reaction against his concern with great actions detached from moral purpose that constituted the French Revolution, he came to embrace the poetic doctrines of the Preface to *Lyrical Ballads*. That is, he will write of simple, lowly people, whose patient endurance of suffering redounds to the glory of humankind and who speak a language that is the spontaneous overflow of powerful feelings (lines 263–64).

1. I.e., this doctrine will not be lightly accepted by those who judge inner worth by exterior seeming.

Encouragement, and energy, and will,
Expressing liveliest thoughts in lively words
As native passion dictates.[2] Others, too,
265 There are, among the walks of homely life,
Still higher, men for contemplation framed,
Shy, and unpractised in the strife of phrase,[3]
Meek men, whose very souls perhaps would sink
Beneath them, summoned to such intercourse:
270 Theirs is the language of the heavens, the power,
The thought, the image, and the silent joy;
Words are but under-agents in their Souls;
When they are grasping with their greatest strength
They do not breathe among them;[4] this I speak
275 In gratitude to God, who feeds our hearts
For his own service; knoweth, loveth us
When we are unregarded by the world.
     Also, about this time did I receive
Convictions still more strong than heretofore
280 Not only that the inner frame is good,
And graciously composed, but that, no less,
Nature for all conditions wants not power
To consecrate, if we have eyes to see,
The outside of her Creatures, and to breathe
285 Grandeur upon the very humblest face
Of human life. I felt that the array
Of act and circumstance, and visible form,
Is mainly, to the pleasure of the mind,
What passion makes them, that meanwhile the forms
290 Of Nature have a passion in themselves
That intermingles with those works of man
To which she summons him; although the works
Be mean, have nothing lofty of their own;
And that the Genius of the Poet hence
295 May boldly take his way among mankind
Wherever Nature leads, that he hath stood
By Nature's side among the Men of old,
And so shall stand for ever. Dearest Friend,
If thou partake the animating faith
300 That Poets, even as Prophets, each with each
Connected in a mighty scheme of truth,
Have each his own peculiar faculty,
Heaven's gift, a sense that fits him to perceive
Objects unseen before, thou wilt not blame
305 The humblest of this band[5] who dares to hope
That unto him hath also been vouchsafed
An insight, that in some sort he possesses
A Privilege, whereby a Work of his,

---

2. In his Preface to *Lyrical Ballads* of 1800, Wordsworth said that he chose characters from low and rustic life because in them "the essential passions of the heart . . . are less under restraint, and speak a plainer and more emphatic language."
3. The rhetoric of controversy.

4. I.e., even in the greatest strength of their intuitive grasp, they do not utter words, which (line 272) are for them merely subsidiary to the fullness of their response to an experience.
5. Wordsworth himself.

Proceeding from a source of untaught things,
310 Creative and enduring, may become
A Power like one of Nature's.

* * *

This for the past, and things that may be viewed
350 Or fancied, in the obscurity of years
From monumental hints:[6] and thou, O Friend!
Pleased with some unpremeditated strains
That served those wanderings to beguile, hast said
That then and there my mind had exercised
355 Upon the vulgar forms of present things,
The actual world of our familiar days,
Yet higher power, had caught from them a tone,
An image, and a character, by books
Not hitherto reflected.[7] Call we this
360 A partial judgement—and yet why? for *then*
We were as Strangers;[8] and I may not speak
Thus wrongfully of verse, however rude,
Which on thy young imagination, trained
In the great City, broke like light from far.
365 Moreover, each man's mind is to herself
Witness and judge; and I remember well
That in Life's every-day appearances
I seemed about this time to gain clear sight
Of a new world, a world, too, that was fit
370 To be transmitted and to other eyes
Made visible, as ruled by those fixed laws
Whence spiritual dignity originates,
Which do both give it being and maintain
A balance, an ennobling interchange
375 Of action from without, and from within;
The excellence, pure function, and best power
Both of the object seen, and eye that sees.

From Book Fourteenth
Conclusion

[THE VISION ON MOUNT SNOWDON. FEAR VS. LOVE RESOLVED.
IMAGINATION]

In one of those Excursions (may they ne'er
Fade from remembrance!), through the Northern tracts
Of Cambria ranging with a youthful Friend,

6. I.e., from suggestions evoked by monuments he had seen in his wanderings.
7. Wordsworth refers to an event that Coleridge narrates in *Biographia Literaria*, chap. 4. In November 1795 Wordsworth had read to Coleridge a manuscript version of his poem *Adventures on Salisbury Plain*. What impressed Coleridge, as he tells us, was Wordsworth's "fine balance of truth in observing with the imaginative faculty in modifying the objects observed, and above all, the orig-

inal gift of spreading . . . the depth and height of the ideal world, around forms, incidents, and situations of which, for the common view, custom had bedimmed all the luster." "This," Coleridge concludes, "is the character and privilege of genius."
8. Though Coleridge and Wordsworth had met in September 1795, they did not become close friends until 1797. "Partial": biased (in Wordsworth's favor).

I left Bethgellert's huts at couching-time,
5 And westward took my way, to see the sun
Rise from the top of Snowdon.[1] To the door
Of a rude Cottage at the Mountain's base
We came, and rouzed the Shepherd who attends
The adventurous Stranger's steps, a trusty Guide;
10 Then, cheered by short refreshment, sallied forth.
—It was a close, warm, breezeless summer night,
Wan, dull, and glaring,[2] with a dripping fog
Low-hung and thick, that covered all the sky.
But, undiscouraged, we began to climb
15 The mountain-side. The mist soon girt us round,
And, after ordinary Travellers' talk
With our Conductor, pensively we sank
Each into commerce with his private thoughts:
Thus did we breast the ascent, and by myself
20 Was nothing either seen or heard that checked
Those musings or diverted, save that once
The Shepherd's Lurcher,[3] who, among the crags,
Had to his joy unearthed a Hedgehog, teased
His coiled-up Prey with barkings turbulent.
25 This small adventure, for even such it seemed
In that wild place, and at the dead of night,
Being over and forgotten, on we wound
In silence as before. With forehead bent
Earthward, as if in opposition set
30 Against an enemy, I panted up
With eager pace, and no less eager thoughts.
Thus might we wear a midnight hour away,
Ascending at loose distance each from each,
And I, as chanced, the foremost of the Band:
35 When at my feet the ground appeared to brighten,
And with a step or two seemed brighter still;
Nor was time given to ask, or learn, the cause;
For instantly a light upon the turf
Fell like a flash; and lo! as I looked up,
40 The Moon hung naked in a firmament
Of azure without cloud, and at my feet
Rested a silent sea of hoary mist.
A hundred hills their dusky backs upheaved
All over this still Ocean;[4] and beyond,
45 Far, far beyond, the solid vapours stretched,
In Headlands, tongues, and promontory shapes.

1. Wordsworth climbed Mount Snowdon—the highest peak in Wales ("Cambria"), and some ten miles from the sea—with Robert Jones, the friend with whom he had also tramped through the Alps (book 6). The climb started from the village of Bethgelert at "couching-time" (line 4), the time of night when the sheep lie down to sleep. This event had taken place in 1791 (or possibly 1793); Wordsworth presents it out of its chronological order to introduce at this point a great natural "type" or "emblem" (lines 66, 70) for the mind, and espe-

cially for the activity of the imagination, whose "restoration" he has described in the two preceding books.
2. In north of England dialect, *glairie,* applied to the weather, means dull, rainy.
3. A crossbred dog used to hunt hares.
4. In Milton's description of the creation of the world, "the mountains huge appear / Emergent, and their broad bare backs upheave / Into the clouds" (*Paradise Lost* 7.285–87).

Into the main Atlantic, that appeared
To dwindle, and give up his majesty,
Usurped upon far as the sight could reach.
50 Not so the ethereal Vault; encroachment none
Was there, nor loss;[5] only the inferior stars
Had disappeared, or shed a fainter light
In the clear presence of the full-orbed Moon;
Who, from her sovereign elevation, gazed
55 Upon the billowy ocean, as it lay
All meek and silent, save that through a rift
Not distant from the shore whereon we stood,
A fixed, abysmal, gloomy breathing-place,
Mounted the roar of waters—torrents—streams
60 Innumerable, roaring with one voice!
Heard over earth and sea, and in that hour,
For so it seemed, felt by the starry heavens.
   When into air had partially dissolved
That Vision, given to Spirits of the night,
65 And three chance human Wanderers, in calm thought
Reflected, it appeared to me the type
Of a majestic Intellect, its acts
And its possessions, what it has and craves,
What in itself it is, and would become.
70 There I beheld the emblem of a Mind
That feeds upon infinity, that broods
Over the dark abyss, intent to hear
Its voices issuing forth to silent light
In one continuous stream; a mind sustained
75 By recognitions of transcendent power
In sense, conducting to ideal form;
In soul, of more than mortal privilege.[6]
One function, above all, of such a mind
Had Nature shadowed there, by putting forth,
80 'Mid circumstances awful and sublime,
That mutual domination which she loves
To exert upon the face of outward things,
So moulded, joined, abstracted; so endowed
With interchangeable supremacy,
85 That Men least sensitive see, hear, perceive,
And cannot chuse but feel. The power which all
Acknowledge when thus moved, which Nature thus
To bodily sense exhibits, is the express
Resemblance of that glorious faculty
90 That higher minds bear with them as their own.[7]
This is the very spirit in which they deal

5. The mist projected in various shapes over the Atlantic Ocean, but did not "encroach" on the heavens overhead.
6. The sense of lines 74–77 seems to be that the mind of someone who is gifted beyond the ordinary lot of mortals recognizes its power to transcend the senses by converting sensory objects into ideal forms.

7. The "glorious faculty" is the imagination, which in its exhibition of mastery over sense—through its power to alter and re-create what is given to it in perception (lines 93–105)—is analogous to that aspect of the outer scene in which the ordinary landscape is transfigured by the moonlit mist. Cf. the mind as "lord and master" of outward sense in 12.219–23 (p. 1543).

With the whole compass of the universe:
They, from their native selves, can send abroad
Kindred mutations; for themselves create
95   A like existence; and whene'er it dawns
Created for them, catch it;—or are caught
By its inevitable mastery,
Like angels stopped upon the wing by sound
Of harmony from heaven's remotest spheres.
100   Them the enduring and the transient both
Serve to exalt; they build up greatest things
From least suggestions; ever on the watch,
Willing to work and to be wrought upon,
They need not extraordinary calls
105   To rouse them, in a world of life they live;
By sensible impressions not enthralled,
But, by their quickening impulse, made more prompt
To hold fit converse with the spiritual world,
And with the generations of mankind
110   Spread over time, past, present, and to come,
Age after age, till Time shall be no more.
Such minds are truly from the Deity,
For they are powers; and hence the highest bliss
That flesh can know is theirs,—the consciousness
115   Of whom they are, habitually infused
Through every image, and through every thought,
And all affections° by communion raised   *emotions*
From earth to heaven, from human to divine.
Hence endless occupation for the Soul,
120   Whether discursive or intuitive;[8]
Hence chearfulness for acts of daily life,
Emotions which best foresight need not fear,
Most worthy then of trust when most intense:
Hence, amid ills that vex, and wrongs that crush
125   Our hearts, if here the words of holy Writ
May with fit reverence be applied, that peace
Which passeth understanding,[9]—that repose
In moral judgements which from this pure source
Must come, or will by Man be sought in vain.
130   Oh! who is he that hath his whole life long
Preserved, enlarged, this freedom in himself?
For this alone is genuine Liberty.
Where is the favoured Being who hath held
That course, unchecked, unerring, and untired,
135   In one perpetual progress smooth and bright?
—A humbler destiny have we retraced,
And told of lapse and hesitating choice,
And backward wanderings along thorny ways:
Yet, compassed round by Mountain Solitudes

8. An echo of *Paradise Lost* 5.488. The "discursive" reason undertakes to reach truths through a logical sequence of premises, observations, and conclusions; the "intuitive" reason comprehends truths immediately.

9. Philippians 4.7: "The peace of God, which passeth all understanding." This passage of Christian piety was added by Wordsworth in a late revision.

140   Within whose solemn temple I received
     My earliest visitations, careless then
     Of what was given me; and which now I range
     A meditative, oft a suffering Man,
     Do I declare, in accents which, from truth
145   Deriving chearful confidence, shall blend
     Their modulation with these vocal streams,
     That, whatsoever falls my better mind
     Revolving[1] with the accidents of life
     May have sustained, that, howsoe'er misled,
150   Never did I, in quest of right and wrong,
     Tamper with conscience from a private aim;
     Nor was in any public hope the dupe
     Of selfish passions; nor did ever yield,
     Wilfully, to mean cares or low pursuits;
155   But shrunk with apprehensive jealousy
     From every combination which might aid
     The tendency, too potent in itself,
     Of use and custom to bow down the Soul
     Under a growing weight of vulgar sense,
160   And substitute a universe of death[2]
     For that which moves with light and life informed,
     Actual, divine, and true. To fear and love,
     To love as prime and chief, for there fear ends,
     Be this ascribed; to early intercourse
165   In presence of sublime or beautiful forms
     With the adverse principles of pain and joy—
     Evil, as one is rashly named by men
     Who know not what they speak. By love subsists
     All lasting grandeur, by pervading love;
170   That gone, we are as dust.[3]—Behold the fields
     In balmy spring-time full of rising flowers
     And joyous Creatures; see that Pair, the lamb
     And the lamb's Mother, and their tender ways
     Shall touch thee to the heart; thou callest this love,
175   And not inaptly so, for love it is,
     Far as it carries thee. In some green Bower
     Rest, and be not alone, but have thou there
     The One who is thy choice of all the world:
     There linger, listening, gazing with delight
180   Impassioned, but delight how pitiable!
     Unless this love by a still higher love
     Be hallowed, love that breathes not without awe;

1. Allusion to the ancient concept of fortune's revolving wheel.

2. Milton's description of hell in *Paradise Lost* 2.622–23: "A universe of death, which God by curse / Created evil."

3. Wordsworth's mind, he had said early in *The Prelude*, had been "fostered alike by beauty and by fear" (1.302 and n. 3, p. 1506); that is, by the opposing but equally necessary principles of the beautiful and the terrifying, or "sublime," aspects of nature. Now, in his conclusion, the principles of fear and pain are said to be mistakenly equated with "evil," and to be ultimately transcended by their "adverse principles" of love and joy. This passage is equivalent to the theodicy of *Paradise Lost*, in which Milton justifies evil and pain ("the ways of God to men," 1.26) by reference to the fall and redemption; Wordsworth, however, translates this into a natural theodicy of the interaction of man's mind with the external world (cf. the Prospectus to *The Recluse*, lines 8–9 and n. 1, pp. 1494–95).

Love that adores, but on the knees of prayer,
By heaven inspired; that frees from chains the soul,
185 Bearing in union with the purest, best
Of earth-born passions, on the wings of praise,
A mutual tribute to the Almighty's Throne.[4]
   This spiritual love acts not, nor can exist
Without Imagination, which in truth
190 Is but another name for absolute power
And clearest insight, amplitude of mind,
And reason, in her most exalted mood.
This faculty hath been the feeding source
Of our long labor: we have traced the stream
195 From the blind cavern whence is faintly heard
Its natal murmur; followed it to light
And open day; accompanied its course
Among the ways of Nature; for a time
Lost sight of it, bewildered and engulphed;
200 Then given it greeting as it rose once more
In strength, reflecting from its placid breast
The works of man, and face of human life;
And lastly, from its progress have we drawn
Faith in life endless, the sustaining thought
205 Of human being, Eternity, and God.[5]
—Imagination having been our theme,
So also hath that intellectual love,
For they are each in each, and cannot stand
Dividually.°—Here must thou be, O Man!   *separately*
210 Power to thyself; no Helper hast thou here;
Here keepest thou in singleness thy state;
No other can divide with thee this work;
No secondary hand can intervene
To fashion this ability; 'tis thine,
215 The prime and vital principle is thine
In the recesses of thy nature, far
From any reach of outward fellowship,
Else is not thine at all. * * *

[CONCLUSION: "THE MIND OF MAN"]

   And now, O Friend![6] this History is brought
To its appointed close: the discipline
And consummation of a Poet's mind
305 In every thing that stood most prominent
Have faithfully been pictured; we have reached
The time (our guiding object from the first)
When we may, not presumptuously, I hope,
Suppose my powers so far confirmed, and such

---

4. In place of lines 182–87, the text of 1805 has: "a love that comes into the heart / With awe and a diffusive sentiment. / Thy love is human merely: this proceeds / More from the brooding soul, and is divine."

5. The 1805 version reads: "The feeling of life endless, the great thought / By which we live, Infinity and God."

6. Coleridge.

310 My knowledge, as to make me capable
Of building up a Work that shall endure.

* * * Having now
Told what best merits mention, further pains
Our present purpose seems not to require,
And I have other tasks. Recall to mind
375 The mood in which this labour was begun.
O Friend! the termination of my course
Is nearer now, much nearer; yet even then,
In that distraction, and intense desire,
I said unto the life which I had lived,
380 Where art thou? Hear I not a voice from thee
Which 'tis reproach to hear?[7] Anon I rose
As if on wings, and saw beneath me stretched
Vast prospect of the world which I had been
And was; and hence this Song, which like a Lark
385 I have protracted, in the unwearied heavens
Singing, and often with more plaintive voice
To earth attempered and her deep-drawn sighs,
Yet centering all in love, and in the end
All gratulant,° if rightly understood.[8]   *congratulatory*

* * *

Oh! yet a few short years of useful life,
And all will be complete, thy[9] race be run,
Thy monument of glory will be raised;
435 Then, though, too weak to tread the ways of truth,
This Age fall back to old idolatry,
Though Men return to servitude as fast
As the tide ebbs, to ignominy and shame
By Nations sink together,[1] we shall still
440 Find solace—knowing what we have learnt to know,
Rich in true happiness if allowed to be
Faithful alike in forwarding a day
Of firmer trust, joint laborers in the Work
(Should Providence such grace to us vouchsafe)
445 Of their deliverance,[2] surely yet to come.
Prophets of Nature, we to them will speak
A lasting inspiration, sanctified
By reason, blest by faith: what we have loved
Others will love, and we will teach them how,
450 Instruct them how the mind of Man becomes

---

7. As he approaches the end, Wordsworth recalls the beginning of *The Prelude*. The reproachful voice is that which asked the question, "Was it for this?" in 1.269ff. This query called forth a vision of his remembered life, which he proceeded to explore in search of both the sources of his poetic powers and the impediments to their fulfillment. The "Song" (line 384) describing this quest, which he then began, is the poem he is now completing.
8. The poet finds that suffering and frustration are justified, when seen as part of the overall design of the life he has just reviewed. The passage echoes

the conclusion of Pope's theodicy (the justification of evil) in *An Essay on Man* 1.291–92: "All discord, harmony not understood; / All partial evil, universal good."
9. Coleridge's.
1. I.e., though men—whole nations of them together—sink to ignominy and shame.
2. In the 1805 text: "redemption." Wordsworth reaffirms his belief in a millennial outcome of human history, though he now bases that belief not on political "revolutions" (cf. line 453) but on a revolution in the mind of man.

> A thousand times more beautiful than the earth
> On which he dwells, above this Frame of things
> (Which 'mid all revolutions in the hopes
> And fears of Men doth still remain unchanged)
> 455   In beauty exalted, as it is itself
> Of quality and fabric more divine.[3]

1798–1839   1850

3. Cf. Wordsworth's assertion that "the Mind of Man" is "My haunt, and the main region of my song" in the Prospectus to *The Recluse*, lines 40–41 (p. 1495).

DOROTHY WORDSWORTH
1771–1855

Dorothy Wordsworth has an enduring place in English literature even though she wrote almost no word for publication. Not until long after her death did scholars gradually retrieve and print her letters, a few poems, and a series of journals that she kept sporadically between 1798 and 1828 because, she wrote, "I shall give William Pleasure by it." It has always been known, from tributes to her by her brother and Coleridge, that she exerted an important influence on the lives and writings of both these men. It is now apparent that she also possessed a power surpassing that of the two poets for precise observation of people and the natural world, together with a genius for terse, luminous, and delicately nuanced description in prose. Her hastily scribbled journals are an incomparable record of what Coleridge, in *Frost at Midnight*, called "all the numberless goings-on of life" in "sea, hill, and wood" as well as in the "populous village," noted by one who lived her life among rural folk.

Dorothy was born on Christmas Day 1771, twenty-one months after William; she was the only girl of five Wordsworth children. From her seventh year, when her mother died, she lived with various relatives—some of them tolerant and affectionate, others rigid and tyrannical—and saw William and her other brothers only occasionally, during the boys' summer vacations from school. In 1795, when she was twenty-four, the bequest to William by Raisley Calvert enabled her to carry out a long-held plan to join her brother in a house at Racedown, and the two spent the rest of their long lives together, first in Dorsetshire and Somersetshire, in the southwest of England, then in their beloved Lake District. She uncomplainingly subordinated her own talents to looking after her brother and his household.

All her adult life she was overworked and troubled by a variety of ailments. Suddenly, after a severe illness in 1835, she suffered a physical and mental collapse. She spent the rest of her existence as an invalid. Hardest for her family to endure was the drastic change in her temperament: from a high-spirited and compassionate woman she became (save for brief intervals of lucidity) querulous, demanding, and at times violent. In this half-life she lingered for twenty years, attended devotedly by William until his death five years before her own in 1855.

The principal selections are from the journal Dorothy kept in 1798 at Alfoxden, Somersetshire, where the Wordsworths had moved from Racedown to be near Coleridge at Nether Stowey, as well as from her journals while at Grasmere (1800–03), with Coleridge residing some thirteen miles away at Greta Hall, Keswick. Her records cover the period when both men emerged as major poets, and in their achievements Dorothy played an indispensable role. In book 11 of *The Prelude* William says that, in the time of his spiritual crisis, Dorothy "maintained for me a saving intercourse / With my true self" and "preserved me still / A Poet"; and in a letter of 1797 Coleridge stressed the delicacy and tact in the responses of William's "exquisite sister" to the world of sense: "Her manners are simple, ardent, impressive. . . . Her information various—her eye watchful in minutest observation of nature—and her taste a perfect electrometer—it bends, protrudes, and draws in, at subtlest beauties & most recondite faults."

The passages from her journals reprinted below include many verbal sketches of natural appearances that recur in Wordsworth's and Coleridge's poems. Of at least equal importance for Wordsworth was her chronicling of the busy wayfaring life of rural England. These were exceedingly hard times for country people, when the suffering caused by the displacement of small farms and of household crafts by large-scale farms and industries was aggravated by the economic distress caused by protracted Continental wars (see Wordsworth's comment in *The Ruined Cottage*, lines 133ff., p. 262). Peddlers, maimed war veterans, leech gatherers, adult and infant beggars, ousted farm families, fugitives, and women abandoned by husbands or lovers streamed along the rural roads and into William's brooding poetic imagination—often by way of Dorothy's prose records.

The journals also show the intensity of Dorothy's love for her brother. Inevitably in our era, the mutual devotion of the orphaned brother and sister has evoked psychoanalytic speculation. It is important to note that Mary Hutchinson, a gentle and open-hearted young woman, had been Dorothy's closest friend ever since childhood, and that Dorothy encouraged William's courtship and marriage, even though she realized that it entailed her own displacement as a focus of her brother's life. All the evidence indicates that their lives in a single household never strained the affectionate relationship between the two women; indeed Dorothy, until she became an invalid, added to her former functions as William's chief support, housekeeper, and scribe a loving ministration to her brother's children.

Because the manuscript of the Alfoxden journal has disappeared, the text printed here is from the transcript published by William Knight in 1897. The selections from the Grasmere journals reproduce Pamela Woof's exact transcription of the manuscripts in the Wordsworth Library at Dove Cottage (Oxford University Press, 1991). Dorothy Wordsworth's poems, written mainly for children in her brother's household and surviving as manuscripts in one or another family commonplace book, were not collected until 1987, when Susan M. Levin edited thirty of them in an appendix ("The Collected Poems of Dorothy Wordsworth") to her *Dorothy Wordsworth and Romanticism*. The two poems included here are reprinted from this source.

From The Alfoxden Journal

Jan. 31, 1798. Set forward to Stowey[1] at half-past five. A violent storm in the wood; sheltered under the hollies. When we left home the moon immensely large, the sky scattered over with clouds. These soon closed in, contracting the dimensions of the moon without concealing her.[2] The sound of the pattering shower, and the gusts of wind, very grand. Left the wood when nothing remained of the storm but the driving wind, and a few scattering drops of rain. Presently all clear, Venus first showing herself between the struggling clouds; afterwards Jupiter appeared. The hawthorn hedges, black and pointed, glittering with millions of diamond drops; the hollies

1. Coleridge's cottage at Nether Stowey, three miles from Alfoxden.

2. Cf. Coleridge's *Christabel*, lines 16–19 (p. 1599).

shining with broader patches of light. The road to the village of Holford glittered like another stream. On our return, the wind high—a violent storm of hail and rain at the Castle of Comfort.[3] All the Heavens seemed in one perpetual motion when the rain ceased; the moon appearing, now half veiled, and now retired behind heavy clouds, the stars still moving, the roads very dirty.

* * *

Feb. 3. A mild morning, the windows open at breakfast, the redbreasts singing in the garden. Walked with Coleridge over the hills. The sea at first obscured by vapour; that vapour afterwards slid in one mighty mass along the sea-shore; the islands and one point of land clear beyond it. The distant country (which was purple in the clear dull air), overhung by straggling clouds that sailed over it, appeared like the darker clouds, which are often seen at a great distance apparently motionless, while the nearer ones pass quickly over them, driven by the lower winds. I never saw such a union of earth, sky, and sea. The clouds beneath our feet spread themselves to the water, and the clouds of the sky almost joined them. Gathered sticks in the wood; a perfect stillness. The redbreasts sang upon the leafless boughs. Of a great number of sheep in the field, only one standing. Returned to dinner at five o'clock. The moonlight still and warm as a summer's night at nine o'clock.

Feb. 4. Walked a great part of the way to Stowey with Coleridge. The morning warm and sunny. The young lasses seen on the hill-tops, in the villages and roads, in their summer holiday clothes—pink petticoats and blue. Mothers with their children in arms, and the little ones that could just walk, tottering by their side. Midges or small flies spinning in the sunshine; the songs of the lark and redbreast; daisies upon the turf; the hazels in blossom; honeysuckles budding. I saw one solitary strawberry flower under a hedge. The furze gay with blossom. The moss rubbed from the pailings by the sheep, that leave locks of wool, and the red marks with which they are spotted, upon the wood.[4]

* * *

Feb. 8. Went up the Park, and over the tops of the hills, till we came to a new and very delicious pathway, which conducted us to the Coombe.[5] Sat a considerable time upon the heath. Its surface restless and glittering with the motion of the scattered piles of withered grass, and the waving of the spiders' threads.[6] On our return the mist still hanging over the sea, but the opposite coast clear, and the rocky cliffs distinguishable. In the deep Coombe, as we stood upon the sunless hill, we saw miles of grass, light and glittering, and the insects passing.

Feb. 9. William gathered sticks.

Feb. 10. Walked to Woodlands, and to the waterfall. The adder's-tongue

---

3. A tavern halfway between Holford and Nether Stowey.
4. Cf. Wordsworth's *The Ruined Cottage,* lines 330–36 (p. 1460).
5. Hodder's Coombe in the Quantock Hills, near

Alfoxden. A combe is a deep valley on the flank of a hill.
6. Cf. Coleridge's *The Rime of the Ancient Mariner,* line 184 (p. 1585).

and the ferns green in the low damp dell. These plants now in perpetual motion from the current of the air; in summer only moved by the drippings of the rocks.[7] A cloudy day.

* * *

Mar. 7. William and I drank tea at Coleridge's. A cloudy sky. Observed nothing particularly interesting—the distant prospect obscured. One only leaf upon the top of a tree—the sole remaining leaf—danced round and round like a rag blown by the wind.[8]

Mar. 8. Walked in the Park in the morning. I sate under the fir trees. Coleridge came after dinner, so we did not walk again. A foggy morning, but a clear sunny day.

Mar. 9. A clear sunny morning, went to meet Mr and Mrs Coleridge. The day very warm.

Mar. 10. Coleridge, Wm, and I walked in the evening to the top of the hill. We all passed the morning in sauntering about the park and gardens, the children playing about, the old man at the top of the hill gathering furze; interesting groups of human creatures, the young frisking and dancing in the sun, the elder quietly drinking in the life and soul of the sun and air.

Mar. 11. A cold day. The children went down towards the sea. William and I walked to the top of the hills above Holford. Met the blacksmith. Pleasant to see the labourer on Sunday jump with the friskiness of a cow upon a sunny day.

* * *

1798   1897

From The Grasmere Journals

1800

May 14 1800 [*Wednesday*]. Wm & John set off into Yorkshire[1] after dinner at ½ past 2 o'clock—cold pork in their pockets. I left them at the turning of the Low-wood bay under the trees. My heart was so full that I could hardly speak to W when I gave him a farewell kiss. I sate a long time upon a stone at the margin of the lake, & after a flood of tears my heart was easier. The lake looked to me I knew not why dull and melancholy, and the weltering on the shores seemed a heavy sound. I walked as long as I could amongst the stones of the shore. The wood rich in flowers. A beautiful yellow, palish yellow flower, that looked thick round & double, & smelt very sweet—I supposed it was a ranunculus—Crowfoot, the grassy-leaved Rabbit-toothed white flower, strawberries, geranium—scentless violet, anemones two kinds, orchises, primroses. The heckberry very beautiful, the crab coming out as a low shrub. Met a blind man, driving a very large beautiful Bull & a cow—he walked with two sticks. Came home by Clappersgate. The valley very green,

---

7. Cf. the description of the dell in Coleridge's *This Lime-Tree Bower My Prison*, lines 13–20 (p. 1578).
8. Cf. *Christabel*, lines 49ff. (p. 1600).

1. William and his younger brother John, on the way to visit Mary Hutchinson, whom William was to marry two and a half years later.

many sweet views up to Rydale head when I could juggle away the fine houses, but they disturbed me even more than when I have been happier— one beautiful view of the Bridge, without Sir Michael's.[2] Sate down very often, tho' it was cold. I resolved to write a journal of the time till W & J return, & I set about keeping my resolve because I will not quarrel with myself, & because I shall give Wm Pleasure by it when he comes home again. At Rydale a woman of the village, stout & well-dressed, begged a halfpenny— she had never she said done it before—but these hard times!—Arrived at home with a bad head-ache, set some slips of privett. The evening cold, had a fire—my face now flame-coloured. It is nine o'clock. I shall soon go to bed. A young woman begged at the door—she had come from Manchester on Sunday morn with two shillings & a slip of paper which she supposed a Bank note—it was a cheat. She had buried her husband & three children within a year & a half—all in one grave—burying very dear—paupers all put in one place—20 shillings paid for as much ground as will bury a man—a stone to be put over it or the right will be lost—11 / 6 each time the ground is opened. Oh! that I had a letter from William!

* * *

Friday 3rd October. Very rainy all the morning—little Sally learning to mark. Wm walked to Ambleside after dinner. I went with him part of the way—he talked much about the object of his Essay for the 2nd volume of LB.[3] I returned expecting the Simpsons—they did not come. I should have met Wm but my teeth ached & it was showery & late—he returned after 10. Amos Cottle's[4] death in the Morning Post. Wrote to S. Lowthian.[5]

N.B. When Wm & I returned from accompanying Jones we met an old man almost double,[6] he had on a coat thrown over his shoulders above his waistcoat & coat. Under this he carried a bundle & had an apron on & a night cap. His face was interesting. He had dark eyes & a long nose—John who afterwards met him at Wythburn took him for a Jew. He was of Scotch parents but had been born in the army. He had had a wife "& a good woman & it pleased God to bless us with ten children"—all these were dead but one of whom he had not heard for many years, a sailor—his trade was to gather leeches, but now leeches are scarce & he had not strength for it—he lived by begging & was making his way to Carlisle where he should buy a few godly books to sell. He said leeches were very scarce partly owing to this dry season, but many years they have been scarce—he supposed it owing to their being much sought after, that they did not breed fast, & were of slow growth. Leeches were formerly 2 / 6 [per] 100; they are now 30 /. He had been hurt in driving a cart his leg broke his body driven over his skull fractured—he felt no pain till he recovered from his first insensibility. It was then late in the evening—when the light was just going away.

* * *

2. Sir Michael le Fleming's estate, Rydal Hall. "Without": outside or beyond.
3. The Preface to the second edition of *Lyrical Ballads,* 1800.
4. The brother of Joseph Cottle, Bristol publisher of the first edition of *Lyrical Ballads.*
5. Sally Lowthian, who had been a servant in the house of the Wordsworths' father.
6. William's *Resolution and Independence,* composed one and a half years later, incorporated various details of Dorothy's description of the leech gatherer. See May 4 and 7, 1802 (pp. 1566–67), for William working on the poem he originally called *The Leech Gatherer.*

Saturday [Oct.] 11th. A fine October morning—sat in the house working all the morning. Wm composing—Sally Ashburner learning to mark. After Dinner we walked up Greenhead Gill in search of a sheepfold.[7] We went by Mr Oliff's & through his woods. It was a delightful day & the views looked excessively chearful & beautiful chiefly that from Mr Oliff's field where our house is to be built. The colours of the mountains soft & rich, with orange fern—The Cattle pasturing upon the hill-tops Kites sailing as in the sky above our heads—Sheep bleating & in lines & chains & patterns scattered over the mountains. They come down & feed on the little green islands in the beds of the torrents & so may be swept away. The Sheepfold is falling away it is built nearly in the form of a heart unequally divided. Look down the brook & see the drops rise upwards & sparkle in the air, at the little falls, the higher sparkles the tallest. We walked along the turf of the mountain till we came to a Cattle track—made by the cattle which come upon the hills. We drank tea at Mr Simpson's returned at about nine—a fine mild night.

Sunday 12th October. Beautiful day. Sate in the house writing in the morning while Wm went into the Wood to compose. Wrote to John in the morning—copied poems for the LB, in the evening wrote to Mrs Rawson. Mary Jameson & Sally Ashburner dined. We pulled apples after dinner, a large basket full. We walked before tea by Bainriggs to observe the many coloured foliage the oaks dark green with yellow leaves—The birches generally still green, some near the water yellowish. The Sycamore crimson & crimson-tufted—the mountain ash a deep orange—the common ash Lemon colour but many ashes still fresh in their summer green. Those that were discoloured chiefly near the water. William composing in the Evening. Went to bed at 12 o'clock.

* * *

1801

Tuesday [Nov.] 24th. A rainy morning. We all were well except that my head ached a little & I took my Breakfast in bed. I read a little of Chaucer, prepared the goose for dinner, & then we all walked out—I was obliged to return for my fur tippet & Spenser[8] it was so cold. We had intended going to Easedale but we shaped our course to Mr Gell's cottage. It was very windy & we heard the wind everywhere about us as we went along the Lane but the walls sheltered us—John Green's house looked pretty under Silver How—as we were going along we were stopped at once, at the distance perhaps of 50 yards from our favorite Birch tree it was yielding to the gusty wind with all its tender twigs, the sun shone upon it & it glanced in the wind like a flying sunshiny shower—it was a tree in shape with stem & branches but it was like a Spirit of water—The sun went in & it resumed its purplish appearance the twigs still yielding to the wind but not so visibly to us. The other Birch trees that were near it looked bright & chearful—but it was a Creature by its own self among them. We could not get into Mr Gell's grounds—the old tree fallen from its undue exaltation above the Gate. A shower came on when we were at Benson's. We went through the wood—it

---

7. The sheepfold in William's *Michael*; lines 1–17 of the poem describe the walk up Greenhead Ghyll.

8. A close-fitting jacket worn by women and children.

became fair, there was a rainbow which spanned the lake from the Island house to the foot of Bainriggs. The village looked populous & beautiful. Catkins are coming out palm trees budding—the alder with its plumb coloured buds. We came home over the stepping stones the Lake was foamy with white waves. I saw a solitary butter flower in the wood. I found it not easy to get over the stepping stones—reached home at dinner time. Sent Peggy Ashburner some goose. She sent me some honey—with a thousand thanks—"alas the gratitude of men has & c"[9] I went in to set her right about this & sate a while with her. She talked about Thomas's having sold his land—"Ay" says she I said many a time "He's not come fra London to buy our Land however" then she told me with what pains & industry they had made up their taxes interest &c &c—how they all got up at 5 o'clock in the morning to spin & Thomas carded, & that they had paid off a hundred pound of the interest. She said she used to take such pleasure in the cattle & sheep—"O how pleased I used to be when they fetched them down, & when I had been a bit poorly I would gang out upon a hill & look over t' fields & see them & it used to do me so much good you cannot think"—Molly said to me when I came in "poor Body! she's very ill but one does not know how long she may last. Many a fair face may gang before her." We sate by the fire without work for some time then Mary read a poem of Daniell upon Learning.[1] After tea Wm read Spenser now & then a little aloud to us. We were making his waistcoat. We had a note from Mrs C., with bad news from poor C very ill. William walked to John's grove—I went to meet him—moonlight but it rained. I met him before I had got as far as John Baty's he had been surprized & terrified by a sudden rushing of winds which seemed to bring earth sky & lake together, as if the whole were going to enclose him in—he was glad he was in a high Road.

In speaking of our walk on Sunday Evening the 22nd November I forgot to notice one most impressive sight—it was the moon & the moonlight seen through hurrying driving clouds immediately behind the Stone man upon the top of the hill on the Forest side. Every tooth & every edge of Rock was visible, & the Man stood like a Giant watching from the Roof of a lofty castle. The hill seemed perpendicular from the darkness below it. It was a sight that I could call to mind at any time it was so distinct.

* * *

1802

Thursday [*Mar. 4*]. Before we had quite finished Breakfast Calvert's man brought the horses for Wm.[2] We had a deal to do to shave—pens to make—poems to put in order for writing, to settle the dress pack up &c &. The man came before the pens were made & he was obliged to leave me with only two—Since he has left me (at ½ past 11) it is now 2 I have been putting the Drawers into order, laid by his clothes which we had thrown here & there & everywhere, filed two months' newspapers & got my dinner 2 boiled eggs & 2 apple tarts. I have set Molly on to clear the garden a little, & I myself have helped. I transplanted some snowdrops—The Bees are busy—Wm has a nice

9. A quotation from William's *Simon Lee*: "Alas! the gratitude of men / Has oft'ner left me mourning."

1. Samuel Daniel's long poem *Musophilus: Containing a General Defense of Learning* (1599).
2. For a journey to Keswick, to visit Coleridge.

bright day. It was hard frost in the night—The Robins are singing sweetly—Now for my walk. I *will* be busy, I *will* look well & be well when he comes back to me. O the Darling! Here is one of his bitten apples! I can hardly find in my heart to throw it into the fire. I must wash myself, then off—I walked round the two Lakes crossed the stepping stones at Rydale Foot. Sate down where we always sit. I was full of thoughts about my darling. Blessings on him. I came home at the foot of our own hill under Loughrigg. They are making sad ravages in the woods—Benson's Wood is going & the wood above the River. The wind has blown down a small fir tree on the Rock that terminates John's path—I suppose the wind of Wednesday night. I read German after my return till tea time. After tea I worked & read the LB, enchanted with the Idiot Boy. Wrote to Wm then went to Bed. It snowed when I went to Bed.

* * *

Monday [*Mar.* 22]. A rainy day—William very poorly. Mr Luff came in after dinner & brought us 2 letters from Sara H. & one from poor Annette. I read Sara's letters while he was here. I finished my letters to M. & S. & wrote to my Br Richard. We talked a good deal about C. & other interesting things. We resolved to see Annette, & that Wm should go to Mary.[3] We wrote to Coleridge not to expect us till Thursday or Friday.

Tuesday [*Mar.* 23]. A mild morning William worked at the Cuckow poem.[4] I sewed beside him. After dinner he slept I read German, & at the closing in of day went to sit in the Orchard—he came to me, & walked backwards & forwards. We talked about C—Wm repeated the poem to me—I left him there & in 20 minutes he came in, rather tired with attempting to write—he is now reading Ben Jonson I am going to read German it is about 10 o'clock, a quiet night. The fire flutters & the watch ticks I hear nothing else save the Breathing of my Beloved & he now & then pushes his book forward & turns over a leaf. Fletcher is not come home. No letter from C.

* * *

Thursday [*Apr.*] 15th. It was a threatening misty morning—but mild. We set off after dinner from Eusemere—Mrs Clarkson went a short way with us but turned back. The wind was furious & we thought we must have returned. We first rested in the large Boat-house, then under a furze Bush opposite Mr Clarksons, saw the plough going in the field. The wind seized our breath the Lake was rough. There was a Boat by itself floating in the middle of the Bay below Water Millock—We rested again in the Water Millock Lane. The hawthorns are black & green, the birches here & there greenish but there is yet more of purple to be seen on the Twigs. We got over into a field to avoid some cows—people working, a few primroses by the roadside, wood-sorrel flower, the anemone, scentless violets, strawberries, & that starry yellow flower which Mrs C calls pile wort. When we were in the woods beyond Gowbarrow park we saw a few daffodils close to the water side.[5] We fancied

3. It had been arranged several months earlier that William was to marry Mary Hutchinson ("Sara H" is Mary's sister, with whom Coleridge had fallen in love). Now the Wordsworths resolve to go to France to settle affairs with Annette Vallon, mother of William's daughter, Caroline. William did not conceal the facts of his early love affair from his family, or from Mary Hutchinson.
4. *To the Cuckoo.*
5. William did not compose his poem on the daffodils, *I wandered lonely as a cloud*, until two years later. Comparison with the poem will show how extensive was his use of Dorothy's prose description (see p. 1478).

that the lake had floated the seeds ashore & that the little colony had so sprung up—But as we went along there were more & yet more & at last under the boughs of the trees, we saw that there was a long belt of them along the shore, about the breadth of a country turnpike road. I never saw daffodils so beautiful they grew among the mossy stones about & about them, some rested their heads upon these stones as on a pillow for weariness & the rest tossed & reeled & danced & seemed as if they verily laughed with the wind that blew upon them over the lake, they looked so gay ever glancing ever changing. This wind blew directly over the lake to them. There was here & there a little knot & a few stragglers a few yards higher up but they were so few as not to disturb the simplicity & unity & life of that one busy high-way—We rested again & again. The Bays were stormy & we heard the waves at different distances & in the middle of the water like the sea—Rain came on, we were wet when we reached Luffs but we called in. Luckily all was chearless & gloomy so we faced the storm—we *must* have been wet if we had waited—put on dry clothes at Dobson's. I was very kindly treated by a young woman, the Landlady looked sour but it is her way. She gave us a goodish supper. Excellent ham & potatoes. We paid 7 / when we came away. William was sitting by a bright fire when I came downstairs. He soon made his way to the Library piled up in a corner of the window. He brought out a volume of Enfield's Speaker,[6] another miscellany, & an odd volume of Congreve's plays. We had a glass of warm rum & water—We enjoyed ourselves & wished for Mary. It rained & blew when we went to bed. NB Deer in Gowbarrow park like skeletons.

Friday 16th April (Good Friday). When I undrew my curtains in the morning, I was much affected by the beauty of the prospect & the change. The sun shone, the wind has passed away, the hills looked chearful, the river was very bright as it flowed into the lake. The Church rises up behind a little knot of Rocks, the steeple not so high as an ordinary 3 story house. Bees, in a row in the garden under the wall. After Wm had shaved we set forward. The valley is at first broken by little rocky woody knolls that make retiring places, fairy valleys in the vale, the river winds along under these hills travelling not in a bustle but not slowly to the lake. We saw a fisherman in the flat meadow on the other side of the water. He came towards us & threw his line over the two arched Bridge. It is a Bridge of a heavy construction, almost bending inwards in the middle, but it is grey & there is a look of ancientry in the architecture of it that pleased me. As we go on the vale opens out more into one vale with somewhat of a cradle Bed. Cottages with groups of trees on the side of the hills. We passed a pair of twin Children 2 years old— & Sate on the next bridge which we crossed a single arch. We rested again upon the Turf & looked at the same Bridge. We observed arches in the water occasioned by the large stones sending it down in two streams—a Sheep came plunging through the river, stumbled up the Bank & passed close to us, it had been frightened by an insignificant little Dog on the other side, its fleece dropped a glittering shower under its belly—Primroses by the road-side, pile wort that shone like stars of gold in the Sun, violets, strawberries, retired & half buried among the grass. When we came to the foot of Brothers water I left William sitting on the Bridge & went along the path on the right side of the Lake through the wood—I was delighted with what I saw. The

---

6. William Enfield's *The Speaker* (1774), a volume of selections suitable for elocution.

water under the boughs of the bare old trees, the simplicity of the mountains & the exquisite beauty of the path. There was one grey cottage. I repeated the Glowworm[7] as I walked along—I hung over the gate, & thought I could have stayed for ever. When I returned I found William writing a poem descriptive of the sights & sounds we saw & heard. There was the gentle flowing of the stream, the glittering lively lake, green fields without a living creature to be seen on them, behind us, a flat pasture with 42 cattle feeding to our left the road leading to the hamlet, no smoke there, the sun shone on the bare roofs. The people were at work ploughing, harrowing & sowing— Lasses spreading dung, a dog's barking now & then, cocks crowing, birds twittering, the snow in patches at the top of the highest hills, yellow palms, purple & green twigs on the Birches, ashes with their glittering spikes quite bare. The hawthorn a bright green with black stems under the oak. The moss of the oak glossy. We then went on, passed two sisters at work, *they first passed us,* one with two pitch forks in her hand. The other had a spade. We had some talk with them. They laughed aloud after we were gone perhaps half in wantonness, half boldness. William finished his poem before we got to the foot of Kirkstone.[8] * * *

Thursday [Apr.] 29. A beautiful morning. The sun shone & all was pleasant. We sent off our parcel to Coleridge by the waggon. Mr Simpson heard the Cuckow today. Before we went out after I had written down the Tinker (which William finished this morning)[9] Luff called. He was very lame, limped into the kitchen—he came on a little Pony. We then went to John's Grove, sate a while at first. Afterwards William lay, & I lay in the trench under the fence—he with his eyes shut & listening to the waterfalls & the Birds. There was no one waterfall above another[1]—it was a sound of waters in the air— the voice of the air. William heard me breathing & rustling now & then but we both lay still, & unseen by one another—he thought that it would be as sweet thus to lie so in the grave, to hear the *peaceful* sounds of the earth & just to know that our dear friends were near. The Lake was still. There was a Boat out. Silver How reflected with delicate purple & yellowish hues as I have seen Spar—Lambs on the island & running races together by the half dozen in the round field near us. The copses greenish, hawthorn green.— Came home to dinner then went to Mr Simpson. We rested a long time under a wall. Sheep & lambs were in the field—cottages smoking. As I lay down on the grass, I observed the glittering silver line on the ridges of the Backs of the sheep, owing to their situation respecting the Sun—which made them look beautiful but with something of strangeness, like animals of another kind—as if belonging to a more splendid world. Met old Mr S at the door—Mrs S poorly—I got mullens & pansies—I was sick & ill & obliged to come home soon. We went to bed immediately—I slept up stairs. The air coldish where it was felt somewhat frosty.

* * *

7. William's poem beginning "Among all lovely things my Love had been," composed four days earlier; "my Love" in this line is Dorothy.
8. The short lyric *Written in March*.

9. William never published his comic poem *The Tinker*. It was first printed in 1897.
1. I.e., no waterfall could be heard individually.

Tuesday May 4th. William had slept pretty well & though he went to bed nervous & jaded in the extreme he rose refreshed. I wrote the Leech Gatherer[2] for him which he had begun the night before & of which he wrote several stanzas in bed this Monday morning. It was very hot, we called at Mr Simpson's door as we passed but did not go in. We rested several times by the way, read & repeated the Leech Gatherer. We were almost melted before we were at the top of the hill. We saw Coleridge on the Wytheburn side of the water. He crossed the Beck to us. Mr Simpson was fishing there. William & I ate a Luncheon, then went on towards the waterfall. It is a glorious wild solitude under that lofty purple crag. It stood upright by itself. Its own self & its shadow below, one mass—all else was sunshine. We went on further. A Bird at the top of the crags was flying round & round & looked in thinness & transparency, shape & motion like a moth. We climbed the hill but looked in vain for a shade except at the foot of the great waterfall, & there we did not like to stay on account of the loose stones above our heads. We came down & rested upon a moss covered Rock, rising out of the bed of the River. There we lay ate our dinner & stayed there till about 4 o'clock or later—Wm & C repeated & read verses. I drank a little Brandy & water & was in Heaven. The Stags horn is very beautiful & fresh springing upon the fells. Mountain ashes, green. We drank tea at a farm house. The woman had not a pleasant countenance, but was civil enough. She had a pretty Boy a year old whom she suckled. We parted from Coleridge at Sara's Crag after having looked at the Letters which C carved in the morning. I kissed them all. Wm deepened the T with C's penknife.[3] We sate afterwards on the wall, seeing the sun go down & the reflections in the still water. C looked well & parted from us chearfully, hopping up upon the side stones. On the Rays we met a woman with 2 little girls one in her arms the other about 4 years old walking by her side, a pretty little thing, but half starved. She had on a pair of slippers that had belonged to some gentleman's child, down at the heels—it was not easy to keep them on—but, poor thing! young as she was, she walked carefully with them. Alas too young for such cares & such travels—The Mother when we accosted her told us that her husband had left her & gone off with another woman & how she *"pursued"* them. Then her fury kindled & her eyes rolled about. She changed again to tears. She was a Cockermouth woman—30 years of age a child at Cockermouth when I was—I was moved & gave her a shilling, I believe 6[d] more than I ought to have given. We had the crescent moon with the "auld moon in her arms."[4]—We rested often:—always upon the Bridges. Reached home at about 10 o'clock. The Lloyds had been here in our absence. We went soon to bed. I repeated verses to William while he was in bed—he was soothed & I left him. "This is the Spot"[5] over & over again.

* * *

2. The poem that was published as *Resolution and Independence*. For its origin, see the entry for October 3, 1800 (p. 1560).

3. The rock, which has since been blasted away to make room for a new road, contained the carved letters: W. W., M. H., D. W., S. T. C., J. W., S. H.

(M. H. and S. H. are Mary and Sara Hutchinson; J. W. is John Wordsworth.)

4. From the *Ballad of Sir Patrick Spens*. Coleridge quoted the stanza, of which this phrase is part, as epigraph to *Dejection: An Ode*.

5. William never completed this poem.

6th May Thursday 1802. A sweet morning we have put the finishing stroke to our Bower & here we are sitting in the orchard. It is one o'clock. We are sitting upon a seat under the wall which I found my Brother building up when I came to him with his apple—he had intended that it should have been done before I came. It is a nice cool shady spot. The small Birds are singing—Lambs bleating, Cuckow calling—The Thrush sings by Fits. Thomas Ashburner's axe is going quietly (without passion) in the orchard—Hens are cackling, Flies humming, the women talking together at their doors—Plumb & pear trees are in Blossom—apple trees greenish—the opposite woods green, the crows are cawing. We have heard Ravens. The ash trees are in blossom, Birds flying all about us. The stitchwort is coming out, there is one budding Lychnis, the primroses are passing their prime. Celandine violets & wood sorrel for ever more little—geraniums & pansies on the wall. We walked in the evening to Tail End to enquire about hurdles for the orchard shed & about Mr Luff's flower—The flower dead—no hurdles. I went to look at the falling wood—Wm also when he had been at Benson's went with me. They have left a good many small oak trees but we dare not hope that they are all to remain. The Ladies are come to Mr Gell's cottage. We saw them as we went & their light when we returned. When we came in we found a Magazine & Review & a letter from Coleridge with verses to Hartley & Sara H. We read the Review,[6] &c. The moon was a perfect Boat a silver Boat when we were out in the evening. The Birch Tree is all over green in *small* leaf more light & elegant than when it is full out. It bent to the breezes as if for the love of its own delightful motions. Sloe thorns & Hawthorns in the hedges.

Friday 7th May. William had slept uncommonly well so, feeling himself strong, he fell to work at the Leech gatherer—He wrote hard at it till dinner time, then he gave over tired to death—he had finished the poem.[7] * * *

* * *

[*July.*] On Thursday morning, 29th, we arrived in London.[8] Wm left me at the Inn—I went to bed &c &c &c—After various troubles and disasters we left London on Saturday morning at ½ past 5 or 6, the 31st of July (I have forgot which). We mounted the Dover Coach at Charing Cross. It was a beautiful morning. The City, St. Paul's, with the River & a multitude of little Boats, made a most beautiful sight as we crossed Westminster Bridge. The houses were not overhung by their cloud of smoke & they were spread out endlessly, yet the sun shone so brightly with such a pure light that there was even something like the purity of one of nature's own grand spectacles.[9] We rode on chearfully now with the Paris Diligence before us, now behind— we walked up the steep hills, beautiful prospects everywhere, till we even reached Dover. * * * We arrived at Calais at 4 o'clock on Sunday morning the 31st of July.[1] We stayed in the vessel till ½ past 7, then Wm went for Letters, at about ½ past 8 or 9. We found out Annette & C chez Madame

---

6. The *Monthly Review* for March 1802.
7. Later entries show, however, that William kept working on the manuscript until July 4.
8. On the way to France to visit Annette Vallon and Caroline (see the entry for March 22, 1802; p. 1563).

9. Cf. William's sonnet *Composed upon Westminster Bridge* (p. 1490).
1. The actual date was August 1. One of the walks by the sea that Dorothy goes on to describe was the occasion for William's sonnet *It is a beauteous evening.*

Avril dans la Rue de la Tête d'or. We lodged opposite two Ladies in tolerably decent-sized rooms but badly furnished, & with large store of bad smells & dirt in the yard, & all about. The weather was very hot. We walked by the sea-shore almost every evening with Annette & Caroline or Wm & I alone. I had a bad cold & could not bathe at first but William did. It was a pretty sight to see as we walked upon the Sands when the tide was low perhaps a hundred people bathing about ¼ of a mile distant from us, and we had delightful walks after the heat of the day was passed away—seeing far off in the west the Coast of England like a cloud crested with Dover Castle, which was but like the summit of the cloud—the Evening star & the glory of the sky. The Reflections in the water were more beautiful than the sky itself, purple waves brighter than precious stones for ever melting away upon the sands. * * *

* * *

[*Sept. 24 and following.*] Mary first met us in the avenue. She looked so fat and well that we were made very happy by the sight of her—then came Sara, & last of all Joanna.[2] Tom was forking corn standing upon the corn cart. We dressed ourselves immediately & got tea—the garden looked gay with asters & sweet peas—I looked at everything with tranquillity & happiness but I was ill both on Saturday & Sunday & continued to be poorly most of the time of our stay. Jack & George came on Friday Evening 1st October. On Saturday 2nd we rode to Hackness, William Jack George & Sara single, I behind Tom. On Sunday 3rd Mary & Sara were busy packing. On Monday 4th October 1802, my Brother William was married to Mary Hutchinson. I slept a good deal of the night & rose fresh & well in the morning—at a little after 8 o'clock I saw them go down the avenue towards the Church. William had parted from me up stairs. I gave him the wedding ring—with how deep a blessing! I took it from my forefinger where I had worn it the whole of the night before—he slipped it again onto my finger and blessed me fervently. When they were absent my dear little Sara prepared the breakfast. I kept myself as quiet as I could, but when I saw the two men running up the walk, coming to tell us it was over, I could stand it no longer & threw myself on the bed where I lay in stillness, neither hearing or seeing any thing, till Sara came upstairs to me & said "They are coming." This forced me from the bed where I lay & I moved I knew not how straight forward, faster than my strength could carry me till I met my beloved William & fell upon his bosom. He & John Hutchinson led me to the house & there I stayed to welcome my dear Mary. As soon as we had breakfasted we departed.[3] It rained when we set off. Poor Mary was much agitated when she parted from her Brothers & Sisters & her home. Nothing particular occurred till we reached Kirby. We had sunshine & showers, pleasant talk, love & chearfulness. * * * It rained very hard when we reached Windermere. We sate in the rain at Wilcock's to change horses, & arrived at Grasmere at about 6 o'clock on Wednesday Evening, the 6th of October 1802. Molly was overjoyed to see us,—for my

2. The Wordsworths have come to Gallow Hill, Yorkshire, for the marriage of William and Mary. The people mentioned are Mary's sisters and brothers (Sara, Joanna, Tom, Jack, and George Hutchinson). Out of consideration for Dorothy's overwrought feelings, only Joanna, Jack, and Tom attended the ceremony at Brampton Church.

3. Dorothy accompanied William and Mary on the three-day journey back to their cottage at Grasmere.

part I cannot describe what I felt, & our dear Mary's feelings would I dare say not be easy to speak of. We went by candle light into the garden & were astonished at the growth of the Brooms, Portugal Laurels, &c &c &—The next day, Thursday, we unpacked the Boxes. On Friday 8th we baked Bread, & Mary & I walked, first upon the Hill side, & then in John's Grove, then in view of Rydale, the first walk that I had taken with my Sister.

* * *

24th December 1802, Christmas Eve. William is now sitting by me at ½ past 10 o'clock. I have been beside him ever since tea running the heel of a stocking, repeating some of his sonnets to him, listening to his own repeating, reading some of Milton's & the Allegro & Penseroso. It is a quiet keen frost. Mary is in the parlour below attending to the baking of cakes & Jenny Fletcher's pies. Sara is in bed in the tooth ache, & so we are—beloved William is turning over the leaves of Charlotte Smith's sonnets, but he keeps his hand to his poor chest pushing aside his breastplate.[4] Mary is well & I am well, & Molly is as blithe as last year at this time. Coleridge came this morning with Wedgwood.[5] We all turned out of Wm's bedroom one by one to meet him—he looked well. We had to tell him of the Birth of his little Girl, born yesterday morning at 6 o'clock.[6] W went with them to Wytheburn in the Chaise, & M & I met Wm on the Rays. It was not an unpleasant morning to the feelings—far from it—the sun shone now & then, & there was no wind, but all things looked chearless & distinct, no meltings of sky into mountains—the mountains like stone-work wrought up with huge hammers.—Last Sunday was as mild a day as I ever remember—We all set off together to walk. I went to Rydale & Wm returned with me. M & S[7] went round the Lakes. There were flowers of various kinds the topmost bell of a fox-glove, geraniums, daisies—a buttercup in the water (but this I saw two or three days before) small yellow flowers (I do not know their name) in the turf a large bunch of strawberry blossoms. Wm sate a while with me, then went to meet M. & S.—Last Saturday I dined at Mr Simpson's also a beautiful mild day. Monday was a frosty day, & it has been frost ever since. On Saturday I dined with Mrs Simpson. It is today Christmas-day Saturday 25th December 1802. I am 31 years of age.—It is a dull frosty day.

* * *

1800–02   1897

Grasmere—A Fragment

Peaceful our valley, fair and green,
And beautiful her cottages,
Each in its nook, its sheltered hold,
Or underneath its tuft of trees.

5 Many and beautiful they are;
But there is *one* that I love best,

4. Probably an undergarment covering the chest.
5. Tom Wedgwood, whose father had founded the famous pottery works, was a friend and generous patron of Coleridge.
6. Coleridge's daughter, Sara (1802–1852).
7. Mary and her sister Sara Hutchinson.

A lowly shed, in truth, it is,
A brother of the rest.

Yet when I sit on rock or hill,
Down looking on the valley fair,
That Cottage with its clustering trees
Summons my heart; it settles there.

Others there are whose small domain
Of fertile fields and hedgerows green
Might more seduce a wanderer's mind
To wish that *there* his home had been.

Such wish be his! I blame him not,
My fancies they perchance are wild
—I love that house because it is
The very Mountains' child.

Fields hath it of its own, green fields,
But they are rocky steep and bare;
Their fence is of the mountain stone,
And moss and lichen flourish there.

And when the storm comes from the North
It lingers near that pastoral spot,
And, piping through the mossy walls,
It seems delighted with its lot.

And let it take its own delight;
And let it range the pastures bare;
Until it reach that group of trees,
—It may not enter there!

A green unfading grove it is,
Skirted with many a lesser tree,
Hazel and holly, beech and oak,
A bright and flourishing company.

Precious the shelter of those trees;
They screen the cottage that I love;
The sunshine pierces to the roof,
And the tall pine-trees tower above.

When first I saw that dear abode,
It was a lovely winter's day:
After a night of perilous storm
The west wind ruled with gentle sway;

A day so mild, it might have been
The first day of the gladsome spring;
The robins warbled, and I heard
One solitary throstle sing.

A Stranger, Grasmere, in thy Vale,
50　All faces then to me unknown,
I left my sole companion-friend
To wander out alone.

Lured by a little winding path,
I quitted soon the public road,
55　A smooth and tempting path it was,
By sheep and shepherds trod.

Eastward, toward the lofty hills,
This pathway led me on
Until I reached a stately Rock,
60　With velvet moss o'ergrown.

With russet oak and tufts of fern
Its top was richly garlanded;
Its sides adorned with eglantine
Bedropp'd with hips of glossy red.

65　There, too, in many a sheltered chink
The foxglove's broad leaves flourished fair,
And silver birch whose purple twigs
Bend to the softest breathing air.

Beneath that Rock my course I stayed,
70　And, looking to its summit high,
"Thou wear'st," said I, "a splendid garb,
Here winter keeps his revelry.

"Full long a dweller on the Plains,
I griev'd when summer days were gone;
75　No more I'll grieve; for Winter here
Hath pleasure gardens of his own.

"What need of flowers? The splendid moss
Is gayer than an April mead;
More rich its hues of various green,
80　Orange, and gold, & glittering red."

—Beside that gay and lovely Rock
There came with merry voice
A foaming streamlet glancing by;
It seemed to say "Rejoice!"

85　My youthful wishes all fulfill'd,
Wishes matured by thoughtful choice,
I stood an Inmate of this vale
How *could* I but rejoice?

ca. 1802–05   1892

Thoughts on My Sick-Bed[1]

And has the remnant of my life
Been pilfered of this sunny Spring?
And have its own prelusive sounds
Touched in my heart no echoing string?

5 Ah! say not so—the hidden life
Couchant° within this feeble frame   *lying*
Hath been enriched by kindred gifts,
That, undesired, unsought-for, came

With joyful heart in youthful days
10 When fresh each season in its Round
I welcomed the earliest Celandine
Glittering upon the mossy ground;

With busy eyes I pierced the lane
In quest of known and *un*known things,
15 —The primrose a lamp on its fortress rock,
The silent butterfly spreading its wings,

The violet betrayed by its noiseless breath,
The daffodil dancing in the breeze,
The carolling thrush, on his naked perch,
20 Towering above the budding trees.

Our cottage-hearth no longer our home,
Companions of Nature were we,
The Stirring, the Still, the Loquacious, the Mute—
To all we gave our sympathy.

25 Yet never in those careless days
When spring-time in rock, field, or bower
Was but a fountain of earthly hope
A promise of fruits & the *splendid* flower.

No! then I never felt a bliss
30 That might with *that* compare
Which, piercing to my couch of rest,
Came on the vernal air.

When loving Friends an offering brought,
The first flowers of the year,
35 Culled from the precincts of our home,
From nooks to Memory dear.

1. In a letter of May 25, 1832, William Words-worth's daughter Dora mentions this as "an affecting poem which she [her aunt Dorothy] has written on the pleasure she received from the first spring flowers that were carried up to her when confined to her sick room." The lines refer to half a dozen or more poems by William, including *I wandered lonely as a cloud* (in line 18) and *Tintern Abbey* (lines 45–52).

With some sad thoughts the work was done,
Unprompted and unbidden,
But joy it brought to my *hidden* life,
40   To consciousness no longer hidden.

I felt a Power unfelt before,
Controlling weakness, languor, pain;
It bore me to the Terrace walk
I trod the Hills again;—

45   No prisoner in this lonely room,
I *saw* the green Banks of the Wye,
Recalling thy prophetic words,
Bard, Brother, Friend from infancy!

No need of motion, or of strength,
50   Or even the breathing air:
—I thought of Nature's loveliest scenes;
And with Memory I was there.

May 1832   1978

SAMUEL TAYLOR COLERIDGE
1772–1834

In *The Prelude* Wordsworth, recording his gratitude to the mountains, lakes, and winds "that dwell among the hills where I was born," commiserates with Coleridge because "thou, my Friend! wert reared / In the great City, 'mid far other scenes." Samuel Taylor Coleridge had in fact been born in the small town of Ottery St. Mary, in rural Devonshire, but on the death of his father he had been sent to school at Christ's Hospital, in London. He was a dreamy, enthusiastic, and extraordinarily precocious schoolboy; Charles Lamb, his schoolmate and lifelong friend, in his essay on Christ's Hospital has given us a vivid sketch of Coleridge's loneliness, his learning, and his eloquence. When in 1791 Coleridge entered Jesus College, Cambridge, he was an accomplished scholar; but he found little intellectual stimulation at the university, fell into idleness, dissoluteness, and debt, then in despair fled to London and enlisted in the Light Dragoons under the alias of Silas Tomkyn Comberbache—one of the most inept cavalrymen in the long history of the British army. Although rescued by his brothers and sent back to Cambridge, he left in 1794 without a degree.

In June 1794 Coleridge met Robert Southey, then a student at Oxford who, like himself, had poetic aspirations, was a radical in religion and politics, and sympathized with the republican experiment in France. Together the two young men planned to establish an ideal democratic community in America for which Coleridge coined the name "Pantisocracy," signifying an equal rule by all. A plausible American real-estate agent persuaded them that the ideal location would be on the banks of the Susquehanna, in Pennsylvania. Twelve men undertook to go; and because perpetuation of the scheme required offspring, hence wives, Coleridge dutifully became engaged to Sara Fricker, conveniently at hand as the sister of Southey's fiancée. The Pantisocracy scheme collapsed, but at Southey's insistence Coleridge went through with the marriage, "resolved," as he said, "but wretched." Later Coleridge's radicalism waned, and he became a conservative in politics—a highly philosophical one—and a staunch Anglican in religion.

In 1795 Coleridge met Wordsworth and at once judged him to be "the best poet of the age." When in 1797 Wordsworth brought his sister, Dorothy, to settle at Alfoxden, only three miles from the Coleridges at Nether Stowey, the period of intimate communication and poetic collaboration began that was the golden time of Coleridge's life. An annuity of £150, granted to Coleridge by Thomas and Josiah Wedgwood, sons of the founder of the famous pottery firm, came just in time to deflect him from assuming a post as a Unitarian minister. After their joint publication of *Lyrical Ballads* in 1798, Coleridge and the Wordsworths spent a winter in Germany, where Coleridge attended the University of Göttingen and began the lifelong study of Kant and the post-Kantian German philosophers and critics that helped alter profoundly his thinking about philosophy, religion, and aesthetics.

Back in England, Coleridge in 1800 followed the Wordsworths to the Lake District, settling at Greta Hall, Keswick. He had become gradually disaffected from his wife, and now he fell helplessly and hopelessly in love with Sara Hutchinson, whose sister, Mary, Wordsworth married in 1802. In accord with the medical prescription of that time, Coleridge had been taking laudanum (opium dissolved in alcohol) to ease the painful physical ailments from which he had suffered from an early age. In 1800–01 heavy dosages during attacks of rheumatism made opium a necessity to him, and Coleridge soon recognized that the drug was a greater evil than the diseases it did not cure. *Dejection: An Ode*, published in 1802, was Coleridge's despairing farewell to health, happiness, and poetic creativity. A two-year sojourn on the Mediterranean island of Malta, intended to restore his health, instead completed his decline. When he returned to England in the late summer of 1806 he was a broken man, an inveterate drug addict, estranged from his wife, suffering from agonies of remorse, and subject to terrifying nightmares of guilt and despair from which his own shrieks awakened him. A bitter quarrel with Wordsworth in 1810 marked the nadir of his life and expectations.

Under these conditions Coleridge's literary efforts, however sporadic and fragmentary, were little short of heroic. In 1808 he gave a course of public lectures in London and, in the next eleven years, followed these with other series on both literary and philosophical topics. He wrote for newspapers and single-handedly undertook to write, publish, and distribute a periodical, *The Friend*, which lasted for some ten months beginning in June 1809. A tragedy, *Remorse*, had in 1813 a successful run of twenty performances at the Drury Lane theater. In 1816 he took up residence at Highgate, a northern suburb of London, under the supervision of the excellent and endlessly forbearing physician James Gillman, who managed to control, although not to eliminate, Coleridge's consumption of opium. The next three years were Coleridge's most sustained period of literary activity: while continuing to lecture and to write for the newspapers on a variety of subjects, he published *Biographia Literaria, Zapolya* (a drama), a book consisting of the essays in *The Friend* (revised and greatly enlarged), two collections of poems, and several important treatises on philosophical and religious subjects. In these last he undertook to establish a philosophical basis for the Trinitarian theology to which he had turned after his youthful period of Unitarianism.

The remaining years of his life, which he spent with Dr. and Mrs. Gillman, were quieter and happier than any he had known since the turn of the century. He came to a peaceful understanding with his wife and was reconciled with Wordsworth, with whom he toured the Rhineland in 1828. His rooms at Highgate became a center for friends, for the London literati, and for a steady stream of pilgrims from England and America. They came to hear one of the wonders of the age, the Sage of Highgate's conversation—or monologue—for even in his decline, Coleridge's talk never lost the almost incantatory power that Hazlitt has immortalized in *My First Acquaintance with*

Poets. When he died, Coleridge left his friends with the sense that an incomparable intellect had vanished from the world. "The most *wonderful* man that I have ever known," Wordsworth declared, his voice breaking; and Charles Lamb wrote, "His great and dear spirit haunts me. . . . Never saw I his likeness, nor probably the world can see again."

Coleridge's friends, however, abetted by his own merciless self-judgments, set current the opinion, still common, that he was great in promise but not in performance. Even in his buoyant youth he described his own character as "indolence capable of energies"; and it is true that while his mind was incessantly active and fertile, he lacked application and staying power. He also manifested early in life a profound sense of guilt and a need for public expiation. After drug addiction sapped his strength and will, he often adapted (or simply adopted) passages from other writers, with little or no acknowledgment, and sometimes in a context that seems designed to reveal that he is reliant on sources that he does not credit. Whatever the tangled motives for his procedure, Coleridge has repeatedly been charged with gross plagiarism, from his day to our own. After *The Rime of the Ancient Mariner*, most of the poems he completed were written, like the first version of *Dejection: An Ode*, in a spasm of intense effort. Writings that required sustained planning and application were either left unfinished or, like *Biographia Literaria*, made up of brilliant sections eked out with filler, sometimes lifted from other writers, in a desperate effort to meet a deadline. Many of his speculations Coleridge merely confided to his notebooks and the ears of his friends, incorporated in letters, and poured out in the margins of his own and other people's books.

Even so, it is only when measured against his own potentialities that Coleridge's achievements appear limited. In opposition to the prevailing British philosophy of empiricism and associationism, Coleridge for most of his mature life expounded his views of the mind as creative in perception, intuitive in its discovery of the first premises of metaphysics and religion, and capable of a poetic re-creation of the world of sense by the fusing and formative power of the imagination. Within the decade after Coleridge died, John Stuart Mill, an acute student of contemporary thought, announced that Coleridge was one of "the two great seminal minds of England," the most important instigator and representative of the conservative intellectual movement of the day. Time has proved Mill's estimate of Coleridge to be just, for his influence is strongly evident in nineteenth-century English and American traditions of philosophical idealism, enlightened political conservatism, and liberal interpretations of Trinitarian theology. By present consensus, Coleridge is also one of the most important and influential of literary theorists; a number of his central ideas were adopted even by some New Critics of the mid-twentieth century who derogated the Romantic poetry for which his criticism provided a rationale. Above all, Coleridge's writings in verse, although small in quantity, are the achievements of a remarkably innovative poet.

In the course of a few years, he wrote his poems of mystery and demonism, *The Rime of the Ancient Mariner, Christabel*, and *Kubla Khan*. No less impressive in their own way are the blank-verse poems of the lonely and meditative mind that, by an extension of Coleridge's term for one of them, are called "Conversation Poems"; in the best of these, *Frost at Midnight*, Coleridge perfected the characteristic pattern of integrally related description and meditation, which Wordsworth immediately used in *Tintern Abbey*. Coleridge himself adapted this pattern to *Dejection: An Ode*, a high achievement in a genre in which few poets have been successful, the irregular English ode. And even when he had mainly given up poetry, after 1805, Coleridge continued to write occasional short lyrics (printed here) that are notable both for their quality and for the extent to which they have been neglected by anthologists.

The Eolian Harp[1]

Composed at Clevedon, Somersetshire

My pensive Sara! thy soft cheek reclined
Thus on mine arm, most soothing sweet it is
To sit beside our cot, our cot o'ergrown
With white-flowered jasmin, and the broad-leaved myrtle,
5   (Meet emblems they of Innocence and Love!)
And watch the clouds, that late were rich with light,
Slow saddening round, and mark the star of eve
Serenely brilliant (such should wisdom be)
Shine opposite! How exquisite the scents
10   Snatched from yon bean-field! and the world so hushed!
The stilly murmur of the distant sea
Tells us of silence.

      And that simplest lute,
Placed length-ways in the clasping casement, hark!
How by the desultory breeze caressed,
15   Like some coy maid half yielding to her lover,
It pours such sweet upbraiding, as must needs
Tempt to repeat the wrong! And now, its strings
Boldlier swept, the long sequacious° notes   *successive*
Over delicious surges sink and rise,
20   Such a soft floating witchery of sound
As twilight Elfins make, when they at eve
Voyage on gentle gales from Fairy-Land,
Where Melodies round honey-dropping flowers,
Footless and wild, like birds of Paradise,[2]
25   Nor pause, nor perch, hovering on untamed wing!
O the one life within us and abroad,
Which meets all motion and becomes its soul,
A light in sound, a sound-like power in light,
Rhythm in all thought, and joyance every where—
30   Methinks, it should have been impossible
Not to love all things in a world so filled;

---

1. Named for Aeolus, god of the winds, the harp has strings stretched over a rectangular sounding box. The strings are tuned in unison. When placed in an opened window, the harp (also called "Eolian lute," "Eolian lyre," "wind harp") responds to the altering wind by sequences of musical chords. This instrument, which seems to voice nature's own music, was a favorite household furnishing in the period and was repeatedly alluded to in Romantic poetry. It served also as one of the recurrent Romantic images for the mind—either the mind in poetic inspiration, as in the last stanza of Shelley's *Ode to the West Wind* (p. 1725), or else the mind in perception, responding to an intellectual breeze by trembling into consciousness, as in this poem, lines 44–48. Coleridge, however, no sooner puts forward this concept than he retracts it, for it comes too close to the heresy of pantheism, which identifies God with the nature that, in the orthodox view, is His creation.

Coleridge wrote this poem to Sara Fricker, whom he married on October 4, 1795, and took to a cottage (the "cot" of lines 3 and 64) at Clevedon, overlooking the Bristol Channel. He later several times expanded and altered the original version; the famous lines 26–29, for example, were not added until 1817. The poem was Coleridge's first achievement in the important Romantic form of the sustained blank-verse lyric of description and meditation, in the mode of conversation addressed to a silent auditor—a form that he perfected in *Frost at Midnight,* and that Wordsworth adopted in *Tintern Abbey.*

2. Brilliantly colored birds found in New Guinea and adjacent islands. The native practice of removing the legs when preparing the skin led Europeans to believe that the birds were footless and spent their lives hovering in the air and feeding on nectar.

Where the breeze warbles, and the mute still air
Is Music slumbering on her instrument.

    And thus, my love! as on the midway slope
35 Of yonder hill I stretch my limbs at noon,
Whilst through my half-closed eye-lids I behold
The sunbeams dance, like diamonds, on the main,
And tranquil muse upon tranquillity;
Full many a thought uncalled and undetained,
40 And many idle flitting phantasies,
Traverse my indolent and passive brain,
As wild and various as the random gales
That swell and flutter on this subject lute!

    And what if all of animated nature
45 Be but organic harps diversely framed,
That tremble into thought, as o'er them sweeps
Plastic and vast, one intellectual breeze,
At once the Soul of each, and God of All?

    But thy more serious eye a mild reproof
50 Darts, O beloved woman! nor such thoughts
Dim and unhallowed dost thou not reject,
And biddest me walk humbly with my God.
Meek daughter in the family of Christ!
Well hast thou said and holily dispraised
55 These shapings of the unregenerate mind;
Bubbles that glitter as they rise and break
On vain Philosophy's aye-babbling spring.
For never guiltless may I speak of him,
The Incomprehensible! save when with awe
60 I praise him, and with Faith that inly feels;
Who with his saving mercies healed me,
A sinful and most miserable man,
Wildered and dark, and gave me to possess
Peace, and this cot, and thee, heart-honored Maid!

1795   1796

This Lime-Tree Bower My Prison

In the June of 1797, some long-expected Friends paid a visit to the author's cottage; and on the morning of their arrival, he met with an accident, which disabled him from walking during the whole time of their stay. One evening, when they had left him for a few hours, he composed the following lines in the garden-bower.[1]

Well, they are gone, and here must I remain,
This lime-tree bower my prison! I have lost
Beauties and feelings, such as would have been
Most sweet to my remembrance even when age
5 Had dimmed mine eyes to blindness! They, meanwhile,
Friends, whom I never more may meet again,
On springy[2] heath, along the hill-top edge,
Wander in gladness, and wind down, perchance,
To that still roaring dell, of which I told;
10 The roaring dell, o'erwooded, narrow, deep,
And only speckled by the mid-day sun;
Where its slim trunk the ash from rock to rock
Flings arching like a bridge;—that branchless ash,
Unsunned and damp, whose few poor yellow leaves
15 Ne'er tremble in the gale, yet tremble still,
Fanned by the water-fall! and there my friends
Behold the dark green file of long lank weeds,
That all at once (a most fantastic sight!)
Still nod and drip beneath the dripping edge
Of the blue clay-stone.[3]

20   Now, my friends emerge
Beneath the wide wide Heaven—and view again
The many-steepled tract magnificent
Of hilly fields and meadows, and the sea,
With some fair bark, perhaps, whose sails light up
25 The slip of smooth clear blue betwixt two Isles
Of purple shadow! Yes! they wander on
In gladness all; but thou, methinks, most glad,
My gentle-hearted Charles! for thou hast pined
And hungered after Nature, many a year,
30 In the great City pent,[4] winning thy way
With sad yet patient soul, through evil and pain

---

1. The time was in fact July 1797; the visiting friends were William and Dorothy Wordsworth and Charles Lamb; the accident was the fault of Mrs. Coleridge—"dear Sara," Coleridge wrote, "accidentally emptied a skillet of boiling milk on my foot"; and the bower consisted of lime (i.e., linden) trees in the garden of Thomas Poole, next door to Coleridge's cottage at Nether Stowey. Coleridge related these facts in a letter to Robert Southey, July 17, 1797, in which he transcribed the first version of this fine "conversation poem."

In the earliest printed text, the title is followed by "Addressed to Charles Lamb, of the India-House, London."
2. *Elastic*, I mean [Coleridge's note].
3. Cf. Dorothy Wordsworth's description of the "low damp dell" in her *Alfoxden Journal*, February 10, 1798 (p. 1558).
4. Despite Coleridge's claim, Charles Lamb eminently preferred London over what he called "dead Nature."

And strange calamity![5] Ah! slowly sink
Behind the western ridge, thou glorious sun!
Shine in the slant beams of the sinking orb,
35 Ye purple heath-flowers! richlier burn, ye clouds!
Live in the yellow light, ye distant groves!
And kindle, thou blue ocean! So my Friend
Struck with deep joy may stand, as I have stood,
Silent with swimming sense; yea, gazing round
40 On the wide landscape, gaze till all doth seem
Less gross than bodily; and of such hues
As veil the Almighty Spirit, when yet he makes
Spirits perceive his presence.

                A delight
Comes sudden on my heart, and I am glad
45 As I myself were there! Nor in this bower,
This little lime-tree bower, have I not marked
Much that has soothed me. Pale beneath the blaze
Hung the transparent foliage; and I watched
Some broad and sunny leaf, and loved to see
50 The shadow of the leaf and stem above
Dappling its sunshine! And that walnut-tree
Was richly tinged, and a deep radiance lay
Full on the ancient ivy, which usurps
Those fronting elms, and now, with blackest mass
55 Makes their dark branches gleam a lighter hue
Through the late twilight: and though now the bat
Wheels silent by, and not a swallow twitters,
Yet still the solitary humble bee
Sings in the bean-flower! Henceforth I shall know
60 That Nature ne'er deserts the wise and pure;
No plot so narrow, be but Nature there,
No waste so vacant, but may well employ
Each faculty of sense, and keep the heart
Awake to Love and Beauty! and sometimes
65 'Tis well to be bereft of promised good,
That we may lift the Soul, and contemplate
With lively joy the joys we cannot share.
My gentle-hearted Charles! when the last rook
Beat its straight path along the dusky air
70 Homewards, I blessed it! deeming its black wing
(Now a dim speck, now vanishing in light)
Had crossed the mighty orb's dilated glory,
While thou stood'st gazing; or when all was still,
Flew creeking o'er thy head, and had a charm
75 For thee, my gentle-hearted Charles, to whom
No sound is dissonant which tells of Life.

1797   1800

5. Some ten months earlier Charles Lamb's sister, Mary, had stabbed their mother to death in a fit of insanity.

The Rime of the Ancient Mariner[1]

IN SEVEN PARTS

Facile credo, plures esse Naturas invisibiles quam visibiles in rerum universitate. Sed horum [sic] omnium familiam quis nobis enarrabit, et gradus et cognationes et discrimina et singulorum munera? Quid agunt? quae loca habitant? Harum rerum notitiam semper ambivit ingenium humanum, nunquam attigit. Juvat, interea, non diffiteor, quandoque in animo, tanquam in tabulâ, majoris et melioris mundi imaginem contemplari: ne mens assuefacta hodiernae vitae minutiis se contrahat nimis, et tota subsidat in pusillas cogitationes. Sed veritati interea invigilandum est, modusque servandus, ut certa ab incertis, diem a nocte, distinguamus.

T. BURNET, *Archaeol. Phil.* p. 68.[2]

Part 1

An ancient Mariner meeteth three gallants bidden to a wedding-feast, and detaineth one.

It is an ancient Mariner
And he stoppeth one of three.
"By thy long grey beard and glittering eye,
Now wherefore stopp'st thou me?

The Bridegroom's doors are opened wide,   5
And I am next of kin;
The guests are met, the feast is set:
May'st hear the merry din."

He holds him with his skinny hand,
"There was a ship," quoth he.   10
"Hold off! unhand me, grey-beard loon!"
Eftsoons[3] his hand dropt he.

The wedding guest is spellbound by the eye of the old sea-faring man, and constrained to hear his tale.

He holds him with his glittering eye—
The wedding-guest stood still,
And listens like a three years' child: 15
The Mariner hath his will.[4]

1. Coleridge describes the origin of this poem in the opening section of chap. 14 of *Biographia Literaria*. In a comment made to the Reverend Alexander Dyce in 1835 and in a note on *We Are Seven* dictated in 1843, Wordsworth added some details. The poem, based on a dream of Coleridge's friend Cruikshank, was originally planned as a collaboration between Coleridge and Wordsworth, to pay the expense of a walking tour they took with Dorothy Wordsworth in November 1797. Before he dropped out of the enterprise, Wordsworth suggested the shooting of the albatross and the navigation of the ship by the dead men; he also contributed lines 13–16 and 226–27.

The version of *The Rime of the Ancient Mariner* printed in *Lyrical Ballads* (1798) contained many archaic words and spellings. In later editions Coleridge greatly improved the poem by pruning the archaisms and by other revisions; he also added the Latin epigraph and the marginal glosses.

2. "I readily believe that there are more invisible than visible Natures in the universe. But who will explain for us the family of all these beings, and the ranks and relations and distinguishing features and functions of each? What do they do? What places do they inhabit? The human mind has always sought the knowledge of these things, but never attained it. Meanwhile I do not deny that it is helpful sometimes to contemplate in the mind, as on a tablet, the image of a greater and better world, lest the intellect, habituated to the petty things of daily life, narrow itself and sink wholly into trivial thoughts. But at the same time we must be watchful for the truth and keep a sense of proportion, so that we may distinguish the certain from the uncertain, day from night." Adapted by Coleridge from Thomas Burnet, *Archaeologiae Philosophicae* (1692).

3. At once.

4. I.e., the Mariner has gained control of the will of the wedding guest by hypnosis—or, as it was called in Coleridge's time, by "mesmerism."

The wedding-guest sat on a stone:
He cannot choose but hear;
And thus spake on that ancient man,
The bright-eyed Mariner.   20

"The ship was cheered, the harbor cleared,
Merrily did we drop
Below the kirk,[5] below the hill,
Below the light house top.

The Mariner tells
how the ship sailed
southward with a
good wind and fair
weather, till it
reached the line.

The sun came up upon the left,   25
Out of the sea came he!
And he shone bright, and on the right
Went down into the sea.

Higher and higher every day,
Till over the mast at noon[6]—"   30
The wedding-guest here beat his breast,
For he heard the loud bassoon.

The Wedding Guest
heareth the bridal
music; but the mari-
ner continueth his
tale.

The bride hath paced into the hall,
Red as a rose is she;
Nodding their heads before her goes   35
The merry minstrelsy.

The wedding-guest he beat his breast,
Yet he cannot choose but hear;
And thus spake on that ancient man,
The bright-eyed Mariner.   40

The ship driven by a
storm toward the
south pole.

"And now the storm-blast came, and he
Was tyrannous and strong:
He struck with his o'ertaking wings,
And chased us south along.

With sloping masts and dipping prow,   45
As who pursued with yell and blow
Still treads the shadow of his foe,
And forward bends his head,
The ship drove fast, loud roared the blast,
And southward aye we fled.   50

And now there came both mist and snow,
And it grew wondrous cold:
And ice, mast-high, came floating by,
As green as emerald.

The land of ice, and
of fearful sounds
where no living thing
was to be seen.

And through the drifts the snowy clifts   55
Did send a dismal sheen:
Nor shapes of men nor beasts we ken—
The ice was all between.

The ice was here, the ice was there,
The ice was all around: 60
It cracked and growled, and roared and howled,
Like noises in a swound![7]

5. Church.
6. The ship had reached the equator.
7. Swoon.

Till a great sea-bird,
called the Albatross,
came through the
snow-fog, and was
received with great
joy and hospitality.

At length did cross an Albatross,
Thorough the fog it came;
As if it had been a Christian soul,
We hailed it in God's name. 65

It ate the food it ne'er had eat,
And round and round it flew.
The ice did split with a thunder-fit;
The helmsman steered us through! 70

And lo! the Albatross
proveth a bird of
good omen, and fol-
loweth the ship as it
returned northward
through fog and
floating ice.

And a good south wind sprung up behind;
The Albatross did follow,
And every day, for food or play,
Came to the mariners' hollo!

In mist or cloud, on mast or shroud,[8] 75
It perched for vespers nine;
Whiles all the night, through fog-smoke white,
Glimmered the white moon-shine."

The ancient Mariner
inhospitably killeth
the pious bird of
good omen.

"God save thee, ancient Mariner!
From the fiends, that plague thee thus!—
Why look'st thou so?"—With my cross-bow 80
I shot the Albatross.

Part 2

The Sun now rose upon the right:[9]
Out of the sea came he,
Still hid in mist, and on the left
Went down into the sea. 85

And the good south wind still blew behind,
But no sweet bird did follow,
Nor any day for food or play
Came to the mariners' hollo! 90

His shipmates cry out
against the ancient
Mariner, for killing
the bird of good luck.

And I had done a hellish thing,
And it would work 'em woe:
For all averred, I had killed the bird
That made the breeze to blow.
Ah wretch! said they, the bird to slay, 95
That made the breeze to blow!

But when the fog
cleared off, they jus-
tify the same, and
thus make themselves
accomplices in the
crime.

Nor dim nor red, like God's own head,
The glorious Sun uprist:
Then all averred, I had killed the bird
That brought the fog and mist. 100
'Twas right, said they, such birds to slay,
That bring the fog and mist.

8. Rope supporting the mast.
9. Having rounded Cape Horn, the ship heads north into the Pacific.

The fair breeze con-
tinues; the ship
enters the Pacific
Ocean, and sails
northward, even till
it reaches the Line.[1]

The fair breeze blew, the white foam flew,
The furrow followed free;
We were the first that ever burst   105
Into that silent sea.

The ship hath been
suddenly becalmed.

Down dropt the breeze, the sails dropt down,
'Twas sad as sad could be;
And we did speak only to break
The silence of the sea!   110

All in a hot and copper sky,
The bloody Sun, at noon,
Right up above the mast did stand,
No bigger than the Moon.

Day after day, day after day,   115
We stuck, nor breath nor motion;
As idle as a painted ship
Upon a painted ocean.

And the Albatross
begins to be avenged.

Water, water, every where,
And all the boards did shrink;   120
Water, water, every where,
Nor any drop to drink.

The very deep did rot: O Christ!
That ever this should be!
Yea, slimy things did crawl with legs   125
Upon the slimy sea.

About, about, in reel and rout
The death-fires[2] danced at night;
The water, like a witch's oils,
Burnt green, and blue and white.   130

A spirit had followed
them; one of the
invisible inhabitants
of this planet, neither
departed souls nor
angels; concerning
whom the learned

And some in dreams assured were
Of the spirit that plagued us so;
Nine fathom deep he had followed us
From the land of mist and snow.

Jew, Josephus, and the Platonic Constantinopolitan, Michael Psellus, may be consulted. They are very
numerous, and there is no climate or element without one or more.

And every tongue, through utter drought,   135
Was withered at the root;
We could not speak, no more than if
We had been choked with soot.

1. I.e., the equator. Unless it is simply an error (Coleridge misreading his own poem), this gloss anticipates the ship's later arrival at the equator, on its trip north from the region of the South Pole, as described in lines 381–84.
2. Usually glossed as the corposant, or St. Elmo's fire—an atmospheric electricity on a ship's mast or rigging—believed by superstitious sailors to portend disaster. Possibly the image is instead a type of oceanic *ignis fatuus* ("foolish fire") resulting from the decomposition of putrescent matter in the sea (see line 123).

The shipmates, in
their sore distress,
would fain throw
the whole guilt on
the ancient Mariner:
in sign whereof they
hang the dead sea
bird round his
neck.

Ah! well-a-day! what evil looks
Had I from old and young!
Instead of the cross, the Albatross
About my neck was hung.

140

Part 3

There passed a weary time. Each throat
Was parched, and glazed each eye.
A weary time! a weary time!
How glazed each weary eye,

145

The ancient Mariner
beholdeth a sign in
the element afar off.

When looking westward, I beheld
A something in the sky.

At first it seemed a little speck,
And then it seemed a mist;
It moved and moved, and took at last
A certain shape, I wist.[3]

150

A speck, a mist, a shape, I wist!
And still it neared and neared:
As if it dodged a water-sprite,[4]
It plunged and tacked and veered.

155

At its nearer
approach, it seemeth
him to be a ship; and
at a dear ransom he
freeth his speech
from the bonds of
thirst.

With throats unslaked, with black lips baked,
We could nor laugh nor wail;
Through utter drought all dumb we stood!
I bit my arm, I sucked the blood,
And cried, A sail! a sail!

160

A flash of joy;

With throats unslaked, with black lips baked,
Agape they heard me call:
Gramercy![5] they for joy did grin,
And all at once their breath drew in,
As they were drinking all.

165

And horror follows.
For can it be a ship
that comes onward
without wind or tide?

See! see! (I cried) she tacks no more!
Hither to work us weal;[6]
Without a breeze, without a tide,
She steadies with upright keel!

170

The western wave was all a-flame.
The day was well nigh done!
Almost upon the western wave
Rested the broad bright Sun;
When that strange shape drove suddenly
Betwixt us and the Sun.

175

It seemeth him but
the skeleton of a
ship.

And straight the Sun was flecked with bars,
(Heaven's Mother send us grace!)
As if through a dungeon-grate he peered
With broad and burning face.

180

Alas! (thought I, and my heart beat loud)
How fast she nears and nears!

3. Knew.
4. A supernatural being that supervises the natural elements (but Coleridge may in fact have been

using the term to mean water-*spout*).
5. Great thanks; from the French *grand-merci*.
6. Benefit.

Are those her sails that glance in the Sun,
Like restless gossameres?[7]

And its ribs are seen
as bars on the face of
the setting Sun. The
specter-woman and
her death-mate, and
no other on board
the skeleton-ship.

Are those her ribs through which the Sun   185
Did peer, as through a grate?
And is that Woman all her crew?
Is that a Death? and are there two?
Is Death that woman's mate?

Like vessel, like
crew!

Her lips were red, her looks were free,   190
Her locks were yellow as gold:
Her skin was as white as leprosy,
The Night-mare Life-in-Death was she,
Who thicks man's blood with cold.

Death and Life-in-
death have diced for
the ship's crew, and
she (the latter) win-
neth the ancient
Mariner.

The naked hulk alongside came,   195
And the twain were casting dice;
"The game is done! I've won! I've won!"
Quoth she, and whistles thrice.

No twilight within
the courts of the sun.

The Sun's rim dips; the stars rush out:
At one stride comes the dark;   200
With far-heard whisper, o'er the sea,
Off shot the spectre-bark.

At the rising of the
Moon,

We listened and looked sideways up!
Fear at my heart, as at a cup,
My life-blood seemed to sip!   205
The stars were dim, and thick the night,
The steersman's face by his lamp gleamed white;
From the sails the dew did drip—
Till clomb above the eastern bar
The horned Moon, with one bright star   210
Within the nether tip.[8]

One after another,

One after one, by the star-dogged Moon,
Too quick for groan or sigh,
Each turned his face with a ghastly pang,
And cursed me with his eye.   215

His shipmates drop
down dead.

Four times fifty living men,
(And I heard nor sigh nor groan)
With heavy thump, a lifeless lump,
They dropped down one by one.

But Life-in-Death
begins her work on
the ancient Mariner.

The souls did from their bodies fly,—   220
They fled to bliss or woe!
And every soul, it passed me by,
Like the whizz of my cross-bow!

---

7. Filmy cobwebs floating in the air.   8. An omen of impending evil.

Part 4

The wedding guest feareth that a spirit is talking to him.

"I fear thee, ancient Mariner!
I fear thy skinny hand!   225
And thou art long, and lank, and brown,
As is the ribbed sea-sand.

I fear thee and thy glittering eye,
And thy skinny hand, so brown."—

But the ancient Mariner assureth him of his bodily life, and proceedeth to relate his horrible penance.

Fear not, fear not, thou wedding-guest!   230
This body drop not down.

Alone, alone, all, all alone,
Alone on a wide wide sea!
And never a saint took pity on
My soul in agony.   235

He despiseth the creatures of the calm,

The many men, so beautiful!
And they all dead did lie:
And a thousand thousand slimy things
Lived on; and so did I.

And envieth that they should live, and so many lie dead.

I looked upon the rotting sea,   240
And drew my eyes away;
I looked upon the rotting deck,
And there the dead men lay.

I looked to heaven, and tried to pray;
But or ever a prayer had gusht,   245
A wicked whisper came, and made
My heart as dry as dust.

I closed my lids, and kept them close,
And the balls like pulses beat;
For the sky and the sea, and the sea and the sky   250
Lay like a load on my weary eye,
And the dead were at my feet.

But the curse liveth for him in the eye of the dead men.

The cold sweat melted from their limbs,
Nor rot nor reek did they:
The look with which they looked on me   255
Had never passed away.

An orphan's curse would drag to hell
A spirit from on high;
But oh! more horrible than that
Is the curse in a dead man's eye!   260
Seven days, seven nights, I saw that curse,
And yet I could not die.

In his loneliness and fixedness he yearneth towards the journeying Moon, and the stars that still sojourn, yet still move onward; and

The moving Moon went up the sky,
And no where did abide:
Softly she was going up,   265
And a star or two beside—

everywhere the blue sky belongs to them, and is their appointed rest, and their native country and their own natural homes, which they enter unannounced, as lords that are certainly expected and yet there is a silent joy at their arrival.

Her beams bemocked the sultry main,
Like April hoar-frost spread;
But where the ship's huge shadow lay,
The charmed water burnt alway   270
A still and awful red.

*By the light of the
Moon he beholdeth
God's creatures of
the great calm.*

Beyond the shadow of the ship,
I watched the water-snakes:
They moved in tracks of shining white,
And when they reared, the elfish light   275
Fell off in hoary flakes.

Within the shadow of the ship
I watched their rich attire:
Blue, glossy green, and velvet black,
They coiled and swam; and every track   280
Was a flash of golden fire.

*Their beauty and
their happiness.*

O happy living things! no tongue
Their beauty might declare:
A spring of love gushed from my heart,

*He blesseth them in
his heart.*

And I blessed them unaware: 285
Sure my kind saint took pity on me,
And I blessed them unaware.

*The spell begins to
break.*

The selfsame moment I could pray;
And from my neck so free
The Albatross fell off, and sank   290
Like lead into the sea.

Part 5

Oh sleep! it is a gentle thing,
Beloved from pole to pole!
To Mary Queen the praise be given!
She sent the gentle sleep from Heaven,   295
That slid into my soul.

*By grace of the holy
Mother, the ancient
Mariner is refreshed
with rain.*

The silly⁹ buckets on the deck,
That had so long remained,
I dreamt that they were filled with dew;
And when I awoke, it rained.   300

My lips were wet, my throat was cold,
My garments all were dank;
Sure I had drunken in my dreams,
And still my body drank.

I moved, and could not feel my limbs: 305
I was so light—almost

9. Simple, homely.

I thought that I had died in sleep,
And was a blessed ghost.

*He heareth sounds
and seeth strange
sights and commo-
tions in the sky and
the element.*

And soon I heard a roaring wind:
It did not come anear;   310
But with its sound it shook the sails,
That were so thin and sere.

The upper air burst into life!
And a hundred fire-flags sheen,[1]
To and fro they were hurried about!   315
And to and fro, and in and out,
The wan stars danced between.

And the coming wind did roar more loud,
And the sails did sigh like sedge;[2]
And the rain poured down from one black cloud;   320
The Moon was at its edge.

The thick black cloud was cleft, and still
The Moon was at its side:
Like waters shot from some high crag,
The lightning fell with never a jag,   325
A river steep and wide.

*The bodies of the
ship's crew are
inspired, and the
ship moves on;*

The loud wind never reached the ship,
Yet now the ship moved on!
Beneath the lightning and the moon
The dead men gave a groan.   330

They groaned, they stirred, they all uprose,
Nor spake, nor moved their eyes;
It had been strange, even in a dream,
To have seen those dead men rise.

The helmsman steered, the ship moved on;   335
Yet never a breeze up blew;
The mariners all 'gan work the ropes,
Where they were wont to do;
They raised their limbs like lifeless tools—
We were a ghastly crew.   340

The body of my brother's son
Stood by me, knee to knee:
The body and I pulled at one rope,
But he said nought to me.

*But not by the souls
of the men, nor by
dæmons[3] of earth or
middle air, but by a
blessed troop of
angelic spirits, sent
down by the invoca-
tion of the guardian
saint.*

"I fear thee, ancient Mariner!"   345
Be calm, thou Wedding-Guest!
'Twas not those souls that fled in pain,
Which to their corses[4] came again,
But a troop of spirits blest:

1. Shone. These fire-flags are probably St. Elmo's
fire (see n. 2, p. 1583), but Coleridge may be
describing the Aurora Australis, or Southern
Lights, and possibly also lightning.
2. A rushlike plant growing in wet soil.

3. Supernatural beings halfway between mortals
and gods (the type of spirit that Coleridge describes
in the gloss beside lines 131–34).
4. Corpses.

For when it dawned—they dropped their arms,   350
And clustered round the mast;
Sweet sounds rose slowly through their mouths,
And from their bodies passed.

Around, around, flew each sweet sound,
Then darted to the Sun;   355
Slowly the sounds came back again,
Now mixed, now one by one.

Sometimes a-dropping from the sky
I heard the sky-lark sing;
Sometimes all little birds that are,   360
How they seemed to fill the sea and air
With their sweet jargoning![5]

And now 'twas like all instruments,
Now like a lonely flute;
And now it is an angel's song,   365
That makes the heavens be mute.

It ceased; yet still the sails made on
A pleasant noise till noon,
A noise like of a hidden brook
In the leafy month of June,   370
That to the sleeping woods all night
Singeth a quiet tune.

Till noon we quietly sailed on,
Yet never a breeze did breathe:
Slowly and smoothly went the ship,   375
Moved onward from beneath.

The lonesome spirit from the south-pole carries on the ship as far as the line, in obedience to the angelic troop, but still requireth vengeance.

Under the keel nine fathom deep,
From the land of mist and snow,
The spirit slid: and it was he
That made the ship to go.   380
The sails at noon left off their tune,
And the ship stood still also.

The Sun, right up above the mast,
Had fixed her to the ocean:
But in a minute she 'gan stir,   385
With a short uneasy motion—
Backwards and forwards half her length
With a short uneasy motion.

Then like a pawing horse let go,
She made a sudden bound: 390
It flung the blood into my head,
And I fell down in a swound.

5. Warbling (Middle English).

The Polar Spirit's fellow dæmons, the invisible inhabitants of the element, take part in his wrong; and two of them relate, one to the other, that penance long and heavy for the ancient Mariner hath been accorded to the Polar Spirit, who returneth southward.

How long in that same fit I lay,
I have not[6] to declare;
But ere my living life returned,   395
I heard and in my soul discerned
Two voices in the air.

"Is it he?" quoth one, "Is this the man?
By him who died on cross,
With his cruel bow he laid full low   400
The harmless Albatross.

The spirit who bideth by himself
In the land of mist and snow,
He loved the bird that loved the man
Who shot him with his bow."   405

The other was a softer voice,
As soft as honey-dew:
Quoth he, "The man hath penance done,
And penance more will do."

Part 6

FIRST VOICE
"But tell me, tell me! speak again,   410
Thy soft response renewing—
What makes that ship drive on so fast?
What is the ocean doing?"

SECOND VOICE
"Still as a slave before his lord,
The ocean hath no blast;   415
His great bright eye most silently
Up to the Moon is cast—

If he may know which way to go;
For she guides him smooth or grim.
See, brother, see! how graciously   420
She looketh down on him."

FIRST VOICE
The Mariner hath been cast into a trance; for the angelic power causeth the vessel to drive northward faster than human life could endure.

"But why drives on that ship so fast,
Without or wave or wind?"

SECOND VOICE
"The air is cut away before,
And closes from behind.   425

Fly, brother, fly! more high, more high!
Or we shall be belated:

---

6. I.e., have not the knowledge.

For slow and slow that ship will go,
When the Mariner's trance is abated."

*The supernatural
motion is retarded;
the Mariner awakes,
and his penance
begins anew.*

I woke, and we were sailing on   430
As in a gentle weather:
'Twas night, calm night, the moon was high;
The dead men stood together.

All stood together on the deck,
For a charnel-dungeon fitter: 435
All fixed on me their stony eyes,
That in the Moon did glitter.

The pang, the curse, with which they died,
Had never passed away:
I could not draw my eyes from theirs,   440
Nor turn them up to pray.

*The curse is finally
expiated.*

And now this spell was snapt: once more
I viewed the ocean green,
And looked far forth, yet little saw
Of what had else been seen—   445

Like one, that on a lonesome road
Doth walk in fear and dread,
And having once turned round walks on,
And turns no more his head;
Because he knows, a frightful fiend   450
Doth close behind him tread.

But soon there breathed a wind on me,
Nor sound nor motion made:
Its path was not upon the sea,
In ripple or in shade.   455

It raised my hair, it fanned my cheek
Like a meadow-gale of spring—
It mingled strangely with my fears,
Yet it felt like a welcoming.

Swiftly, swiftly flew the ship,   460
Yet she sailed softly too:
Sweetly, sweetly blew the breeze—
On me alone it blew.

*And the ancient
Mariner beholdeth
his native country.*

Oh! dream of joy! is this indeed
The light-house top I see?   465
Is this the hill? is this the kirk?
Is this mine own countree?

We drifted o'er the harbour-bar,
And I with sobs did pray—

O let me be awake, my God!　　　　　　　　　　470
Or let me sleep alway.

The harbour-bay was clear as glass,
So smoothly it was strewn!
And on the bay the moonlight lay,
And the shadow of the moon.　　　　　　　　　475

The rock shone bright, the kirk no less,
That stands above the rock:
The moonlight steeped in silentness
The steady weathercock.

And the bay was white with silent light,　　　480
Till rising from the same,

The angelic spirits leave the dead bodies, Full many shapes, that shadows were,
In crimson colours came.

And appear in their own forms of light. A little distance from the prow
Those crimson shadows were:　　　　　　　　485
I turned my eyes upon the deck—
Oh, Christ! what saw I there!

Each corse lay flat, lifeless and flat,
And, by the holy rood!
A man all light, a seraph-man,[7]　　　　　　490
On every corse there stood.

This seraph-band, each waved his hand:
It was a heavenly sight!
They stood as signals to the land,
Each one a lovely light;　　　　　　　　　　495

This seraph-band, each waved his hand,
No voice did they impart—
No voice; but oh! the silence sank
Like music on my heart.

But soon I heard the dash of oars,　　　　　500
I heard the Pilot's cheer;
My head was turned perforce away,
And I saw a boat appear.

The Pilot and the Pilot's boy,
I heard them coming fast:　　　　　　　　　505
Dear Lord in Heaven! it was a joy
The dead men could not blast.

I saw a third—I heard his voice:
It is the Hermit good!
He singeth loud his godly hymns　　　　　　510
That he makes in the wood.

7. A shining celestial being, highest in the ranks of the angels. "Rood": cross.

He'll shrieve my soul, he'll wash away
The Albatross's blood.

Part 7

The Hermit of the wood,

This Hermit good lives in that wood
Which slopes down to the sea.   515
How loudly his sweet voice he rears!
He loves to talk with marineres
That come from a far countree.

He kneels at morn, and noon, and eve—
He hath a cushion plump: 520
It is the moss that wholly hides
The rotted old oak-stump.

The skiff-boat neared: I heard them talk,
"Why, this is strange, I trow!
Where are those lights so many and fair,   525
That signal made but now?"

Approacheth the ship with wonder.

"Strange, by my faith!" the Hermit said—
"And they answered not our cheer!
The planks looked warped! and see those sails,
How thin they are and sere!   530
I never saw aught like to them,
Unless perchance it were

Brown skeletons of leaves that lag
My forest-brook along;
When the ivy-tod[8] is heavy with snow,   535
And the owlet whoops to the wolf below,
That eats the she-wolf's young."

"Dear Lord! it hath a fiendish look"—
(The Pilot made reply)
"I am a-feared"—"Push on, push on!"   540
Said the Hermit cheerily.

The boat came closer to the ship,
But I nor spake nor stirred;
The boat came close beneath the ship,
And straight a sound was heard.   545

The ship suddenly sinketh.

Under the water it rumbled on,
Still louder and more dread:
It reached the ship, it split the bay;
The ship went down like lead.

The ancient Mariner is saved in the Pilot's boat.

Stunned by that loud and dreadful sound,   550
Which sky and ocean smote,
Like one that hath been seven days drowned
My body lay afloat;

---

8. Clump of ivy.

But swift as dreams, myself I found
Within the Pilot's boat.   555

Upon the whirl, where sank the ship,
The boat spun round and round;
And all was still, save that the hill
Was telling of the sound.

I moved my lips—the Pilot shrieked   560
And fell down in a fit;
The holy Hermit raised his eyes,
And prayed where he did sit.

I took the oars: the Pilot's boy,
Who now doth crazy go,   565
Laughed loud and long, and all the while
His eyes went to and fro.
"Ha! ha!" quoth he, "full plain I see,
The Devil knows how to row."

And now, all in my own countree,   570
I stood on the firm land!
The Hermit stepped forth from the boat,
And scarcely he could stand.

The ancient Mariner earnestly entreateth the Hermit to shrieve him; and the penance of life falls on him.

"O shrieve me, shrieve me, holy man!"
The Hermit crossed his brow.⁹   575
"Say quick," quoth he, "I bid thee say—
What manner of man art thou?"

Forthwith this frame of mine was wrenched
With a woful agony,
Which forced me to begin my tale;   580
And then it left me free.

And ever and anon throughout his future life an agony constraineth him to travel from land to land.

Since then, at an uncertain hour,
That agony returns:
And till my ghastly tale is told,
This heart within me burns.   585

I pass, like night, from land to land;
I have strange power of speech;
That moment that his face I see,
I know the man that must hear me:
To him my tale I teach.   590

What loud uproar bursts from that door!
The wedding-guests are there:
But in the garden-bower the bride
And bride-maids singing are:
And hark the little vesper bell,   595
Which biddeth me to prayer!

9. Made the sign of the cross on his forehead. "Shrieve me": hear my confession and grant me absolution.

O Wedding-Guest! this soul hath been
Alone on a wide wide sea:
So lonely 'twas, that God himself
Scarce seemed there to be.   600

O sweeter than the marriage-feast,
'Tis sweeter far to me,
To walk together to the kirk
With a goodly company!—

To walk together to the kirk,   605
And all together pray,
While each to his great Father bends,
Old men, and babes, and loving friends,
And youths and maidens gay!

*And to teach, by
his own example,
love and reverence to
all things that God
made and loveth.*

Farewell, farewell! but this I tell   610
To thee, thou Wedding-Guest!
He prayeth well, who loveth well
Both man and bird and beast.

He prayeth best, who loveth best
All things both great and small;   615
For the dear God who loveth us,
He made and loveth all.[1]

The Mariner, whose eye is bright,
Whose beard with age is hoar,
Is gone: and now the Wedding-Guest   620
Turned from the bridegroom's door.

He went like one that hath been stunned,
And is of sense forlorn:[2]
A sadder and a wiser man,
He rose the morrow morn.   625

1797   1798

---

1. Coleridge said in 1830, answering the objection of the poet Anna Barbauld that the poem "lacked a moral": "I told her that in my own judgment the poem had too much; and that the only, or chief fault, if I might say so, was the obtrusion of the moral sentiment so openly on the reader as a principle or cause of action in a work of pure imagination. It ought to have had no more moral than the *Arabian Nights'* tale of the merchant's sitting down to eat dates by the side of a well and throwing the shells aside, and lo! a genie starts up and says he *must* kill the aforesaid merchant *because* one of the date shells had, it seems, put out the eye of the genie's son."

2. Forsaken.

Kubla Khan

Or, A Vision in a Dream. A Fragment

In[1] the summer of the year 1797, the Author, then in ill health, had retired to a lonely farm house between Porlock and Linton, on the Exmoor confines of Somerset and Devonshire. In consequence of a slight indisposition, an anodyne had been prescribed, from the effect of which he fell asleep in his chair at the moment that he was reading the following sentence, or words of the same substance, in *Purchas's Pilgrimage*: "Here the Khan Kubla commanded a palace to be built, and a stately garden thereunto: and thus ten miles of fertile ground were inclosed with a wall."[2] The author continued for about three hours in a profound sleep, at least of the external senses,[3] during which time he has the most vivid confidence, that he could not have composed less than from two to three hundred lines; if that indeed can be called composition in which all the images rose up before him as things, with a parallel production of the correspondent expressions, without any sensation or consciousness of effort. On awaking he appeared to himself to have a distinct recollection of the whole, and taking his pen, ink, and paper, instantly and eagerly wrote down the lines that are here preserved. At this moment he was unfortunately called out by a person on business from Porlock, and detained by him above an hour, and on his return to his room, found, to his no small surprise and mortification, that though he still retained some vague and dim recollection of the general purport of the vision, yet, with the exception of some eight or ten scattered lines and images, all the rest had passed away like the images on the surface of a stream into which a stone had been cast, but, alas! without the after restoration of the latter:

> Then all the charm
> Is broken—all that phantom-world so fair
> Vanishes, and a thousand circlets spread,
> And each mis-shape[s] the other. Stay awhile,
> Poor youth! who scarcely dar'st lift up thine eyes—
> The stream will soon renew its smoothness, soon
> The visions will return! And lo! he stays,
> And soon the fragments dim of lovely forms
> Come trembling back, unite, and now once more
> The pool becomes a mirror.
>   [From Coleridge's *The Picture; or, the Lover's Resolution,*
>   lines 91–100]

1. In the texts of 1816–29, this note began with an additional short paragraph: "The following fragment is here published at the request of a poet of great and deserved celebrity, and, as far as the Author's own opinions are concerned, rather as a psychological curiosity, than on the ground of any supposed *poetic* merits." The "poet of . . . celebrity" was Lord Byron.
2. "In Xamdu did Cublai Can build a stately Palace, encompassing sixteene miles of plaine ground with a wall, wherein are fertile Meddowes, pleasant Springs, delightfull Streames, and all sorts of beasts of chase and game, and in the middest

thereof a sumptuous house of pleasure, which may be removed from place to place." From Samuel Purchas, *Purchas his Pilgrimage* (1613). The historical Kublai Khan founded the Mongol dynasty in China in the 13th century.
3. In a note on a manuscript copy of *Kubla Khan*, Coleridge gave a more precise account of the nature of this "sleep": "This fragment with a good deal more, not recoverable, composed, in a sort of reverie brought on by two grains of opium, taken to check a dysentery, at a farmhouse between Porlock and Linton, a quarter of a mile from Culbone Church, in the fall of the year, 1797."

Yet from the still surviving recollections in his mind, the Author has frequently purposed to finish for himself what had been originally, as it were, given to him. Αὔριον ἄδιον ἄσω:[4] but the to-morrow is yet to come.

As a contrast to this vision, I have annexed a fragment of a very different character, describing with equal fidelity the dream of pain and disease.[5]—1816.

<blockquote>

In Xanadu did Kubla Khan
A stately pleasure-dome decree:
Where Alph,[6] the sacred river, ran
Through caverns measureless to man

5   Down to a sunless sea.
So twice five miles of fertile ground
With walls and towers were girdled round:
And there were gardens bright with sinuous rills
Where blossomed many an incense-bearing tree;

10 And here were forests ancient as the hills,
Enfolding sunny spots of greenery.

But oh! that deep romantic chasm which slanted
Down the green hill athwart a cedarn cover!
A savage place! as holy and enchanted

15 As e'er beneath a waning moon was haunted
By woman wailing for her demon-lover!
And from this chasm, with ceaseless turmoil seething,
As if this earth in fast thick pants were breathing,
A mighty fountain momently was forced:

20 Amid whose swift half-intermitted burst
Huge fragments vaulted like rebounding hail,
Or chaffy grain beneath the thresher's flail:
And 'mid these dancing rocks at once and ever
It flung up momently the sacred river.

25 Five miles meandering with a mazy motion
Through wood and dale the sacred river ran,
Then reached the caverns measureless to man,
And sank in tumult to a lifeless ocean:
And 'mid this tumult Kubla heard from far

30 Ancestral voices prophesying war!
The shadow of the dome of pleasure
Floated midway on the waves;
Where was heard the mingled measure
From the fountain and the caves.

35 It was a miracle of rare device,
A sunny pleasure-dome with caves of ice!

A damsel with a dulcimer
In a vision once I saw:
</blockquote>

4. I shall sing a sweeter song tomorrow (Greek; recalled from Theocritus's *Idyls* 1.145).

  A number of Coleridge's assertions in this preface have been debated by critics: whether the poem was written in 1797 or later, whether it was actually composed in a "dream" or opium reverie, even whether it is a fragment or in fact complete. All critics agree, however, that this visionary poem

of demonic inspiration is much more than a mere "psychological curiosity."

5. Coleridge refers to *The Pains of Sleep*.
6. Derived probably from the Greek river Alpheus, which flows into the Ionian Sea. Its waters were fabled to rise again in Sicily as the fountain of Arethusa.

It was an Abyssinian maid,
40   And on her dulcimer she played,
Singing of Mount Abora.[7]
Could I revive within me
Her symphony and song,
To such a deep delight 'twould win me,
45   That with music loud and long,
I would build that dome in air,
That sunny dome! those caves of ice!
And all who heard should see them there,
And all should cry, Beware! Beware!
50   His flashing eyes, his floating hair!
Weave a circle round him thrice,[8]
And close your eyes with holy dread,
For he on honey-dew hath fed,
And drunk the milk of Paradise.[9]

ca. 1797–98   1816

Christabel[1]
Preface

The first part of the following poem was written in the year 1797, at Stowey,
in the county of Somerset. The second part, after my return from Germany,
in the year 1800, at Keswick, Cumberland. It is probable, that if the poem
had been finished at either of the former periods, or if even the first and
second part had been published in the year 1800, the impression of its originality would have been much greater than I dare at present expect. But for
this, I have only my own indolence to blame. The dates are mentioned for
the exclusive purpose of precluding charges of plagiarism or servile imitation
from myself. For there is amongst us a set of critics, who seem to hold, that
every possible thought and image is traditional; who have no notion that
there are such things as fountains in the world, small as well as great; and
who would therefore charitably derive every rill they behold flowing, from a
perforation made in some other man's tank. I am confident, however, that
as far as the present poem is concerned, the celebrated poets[2] whose writings
I might be suspected of having imitated, either in particular passages, or in
the tone and the spirit of the whole, would be among the first to vindicate
me from the charge, and who, on any striking coincidence, would permit me
to address them in this doggerel version of two monkish Latin hexameters.

7. Apparently a reminiscence of *Paradise Lost*
4.280–82: "where Abassin Kings their issue guard
/ Mount Amara (though this by some supposed /
True Paradise) under the Ethiop line."
8. A magic ritual, to protect the inspired poet from
intrusion.
9. Lines 50ff. echo in part the description, in
Plato's *Ion* 533–34, of inspired poets, who are "like
Bacchic maidens who draw milk and honey from
the rivers when they are under the influence of
Dionysus but not when they are in their right
mind."
1. Coleridge had planned to publish *Christabel* in
the 2nd edition of *Lyrical Ballads* (1800) but had
not been able to complete the poem. When *Chris-*

tabel was finally published in 1816 in its present
fragmentary state, he still had hopes of finishing it,
for the Preface contained this sentence (deleted in
the edition of 1834): "But as, in my very first conception of the tale, I had the whole present to my
mind, with the wholeness, no less than the liveliness of a vision; I trust that I shall be able to
embody in verse the three parts yet to come, in the
course of the present year."
2. Sir Walter Scott and Lord Byron, who had read
and admired *Christabel* while it circulated in manuscript. Coleridge has in mind Scott's *Lay of the
Last Minstrel* (1805) and Byron's *Siege of Corinth*
(1816), which showed the influence of *Christabel*,
especially in their meter.

Tis mine and it is likewise yours;
But an if this will not do;
Let it be mine, good friend! for I
Am the poorer of the two.

I have only to add, that the metre of the Christabel is not, properly speaking, irregular, though it may seem so from its being founded on a new principle: namely, that of counting in each line the accents, not the syllables.[3] Though the latter may vary from seven to twelve, yet in each line the accents will be found to be only four. Nevertheless this occasional variation in number of syllables is not introduced wantonly, or for the mere ends of convenience, but in correspondence with some transition, in the nature of the imagery or passion.

Part 1

'Tis the middle of night by the castle clock,
And the owls have awakened the crowing cock;
Tu—whit!——Tu—whoo!
And hark, again! the crowing cock,
5   How drowsily it crew.

Sir Leoline, the Baron rich,
Hath a toothless mastiff bitch;
From her kennel beneath the rock
She maketh answer to the clock,
10   Four for the quarters, and twelve for the hour;
Ever and aye, by shine and shower,
Sixteen short howls, not over loud;
Some say, she sees my lady's shroud.

Is the night chilly and dark?
15   The night is chilly, but not dark.
The thin gray cloud is spread on high,
It covers but not hides the sky.
The moon is behind, and at the full;
And yet she looks both small and dull.
20   The night is chill, the cloud is gray:
'Tis a month before the month of May,
And the Spring comes slowly up this way.

The lovely lady, Christabel,
Whom her father loves so well,
25   What makes her in the wood so late,
A furlong from the castle gate?
She had dreams all yesternight
Of her own betrothed knight;
And she in the midnight wood will pray
30   For the weal° of her lover that's far away.   well-being

3. Much of the older English versification, following the example of Anglo-Saxon poetry, had been based on stress, or "accent," and some of it shows as much freedom in varying the number of syllables as does *Christabel*. The poem, however, is a radical departure from the theory and practice of versification in the 18th century, which had been based on a recurrent number of syllables in each line.

She stole along, she nothing spoke,
The sighs she heaved were soft and low,
And naught was green upon the oak,
But moss and rarest mistletoe:[4]
35 She kneels beneath the huge oak tree,
And in silence prayeth she.

The lady sprang up suddenly,
The lovely lady, Christabel!
It moaned as near, as near can be,
40 But what it is, she cannot tell.—
On the other side it seems to be,
Of the huge, broad-breasted, old oak tree.

The night is chill; the forest bare;
Is it the wind that moaneth bleak?
45 There is not wind enough in the air
To move away the ringlet curl
From the lovely lady's cheek—
There is not wind enough to twirl
The one red leaf, the last of its clan,
50 That dances as often as dance it can,
Hanging so light, and hanging so high,
On the topmost twig that looks up at the sky.

Hush, beating heart of Christabel!
Jesu, Maria, shield her well!
55 She folded her arms beneath her cloak,
And stole to the other side of the oak.
        What sees she there?

There she sees a damsel bright,
Drest in a silken robe of white,
60 That shadowy in the moonlight shone:
The neck that made that white robe wan,
Her stately neck, and arms were bare;
Her blue-veined feet unsandal'd were,
And wildly glittered here and there
65 The gems entangled in her hair.
I guess, 'twas frightful there to see
A lady so richly clad as she—
Beautiful exceedingly!

"Mary mother, save me now!"
70 (Said Christabel,) "And who art thou?"

The lady strange made answer meet,
And her voice was faint and sweet:—
"Have pity on my sore distress,

4. In Celtic Britain the mistletoe (a parasitic plant) had been held in veneration when it was found growing—as it rarely does—on an oak tree. (Its usual host is the apple tree.)

I scarce can speak for weariness:
75 Stretch forth thy hand, and have no fear!"
Said Christabel, "How camest thou here?"
And the lady, whose voice was faint and sweet,
Did thus pursue her answer meet:—

"My sire is of a noble line,
80 And my name is Geraldine:
Five warriors seized me yestermorn,
Me, even me, a maid forlorn:
They choked my cries with force and fright,
And tied me on a palfrey white.
85 The palfrey was as fleet as wind,
And they rode furiously behind.
They spurred amain,[5] their steeds were white:
And once we crossed the shade of night.
As sure as Heaven shall rescue me,
90 I have no thought what men they be;
Nor do I know how long it is
(For I have lain entranced I wis[6])
Since one, the tallest of the five,
Took me from the palfrey's back,
95 A weary woman, scarce alive.
Some muttered words his comrades spoke:
He placed me underneath this oak;
He swore they would return with haste;
Whither they went I cannot tell—
100 I thought I heard, some minutes past,
Sounds as of a castle bell.
Stretch forth thy hand" (thus ended she),
"And help a wretched maid to flee."

Then Christabel stretched forth her hand
105 And comforted fair Geraldine:
"O well, bright dame! may you command
The service of Sir Leoline;
And gladly our stout chivalry
Will he send forth and friends withal
110 To guide and guard you safe and free
Home to your noble father's hall."

She rose: and forth with steps they passed
That strove to be, and were not, fast.
Her gracious stars the lady blest,
115 And thus spake on sweet Christabel:
"All our household are at rest,
The hall as silent as the cell;
Sir Leoline is weak in health,
And may not well awakened be,

---

5. At top speed.
6. I believe (Coleridge's misinterpretation of the Middle English adverb *ywis*, meaning "certainly").

120　But we will move as if in stealth,
　　And I beseech your courtesy,
　　This night, to share your couch with me."

　　They crossed the moat, and Christabel
　　Took the key that fitted well;
125　A little door she opened straight,
　　All in the middle of the gate;
　　The gate that was ironed within and without,
　　Where an army in battle array had marched out.
　　The lady sank, belike through pain,
130　And Christabel with might and main
　　Lifted her up, a weary weight,
　　Over the threshold of the gate:[7]
　　Then the lady rose again,
　　And moved, as she were not in pain.

135　So free from danger, free from fear,
　　They crossed the court: right glad they were.
　　And Christabel devoutly cried
　　To the Lady by her side;
　　"Praise we the Virgin all divine
140　Who hath rescued thee from thy distress!"
　　"Alas, alas!" said Geraldine,
　　"I cannot speak for weariness."
　　So free from danger, free from fear,
　　They crossed the court: right glad they were.

145　Outside her kennel the mastiff old
　　Lay fast asleep, in moonshine cold.
　　The mastiff old did not awake,
　　Yet she an angry moan did make!
　　And what can ail the mastiff bitch?
150　Never till now she uttered yell
　　Beneath the eye of Christabel.
　　Perhaps it is the owlet's scritch:
　　For what can ail the mastiff bitch?

　　They passed the hall, that echoes still,
155　Pass as lightly as you will!
　　The brands were flat, the brands were dying,
　　Amid their own white ashes lying;
　　But when the lady passed, there came
　　A tongue of light, a fit of flame;
160　And Christabel saw the lady's eye,
　　And nothing else saw she thereby,
　　Save the boss of the shield of Sir Leoline tall,
　　Which hung in a murky old niche in the wall.
　　"O softly tread," said Christabel,
165　"My father seldom sleepeth well."

7. According to legend, a witch cannot cross the threshold by her own power because it has been blessed against evil spirits.

Sweet Christabel her feet doth bare,
And, jealous of the listening air,
They steal their way from stair to stair,
Now in glimmer, and now in gloom,
170 And now they pass the Baron's room,
As still as death with stifled breath!
And now have reached her chamber door;
And now doth Geraldine press down
The rushes[8] of the chamber floor.

175 The moon shines dim in the open air,
And not a moonbeam enters here.
But they without its light can see
The chamber carved so curiously,
Carved with figures strange and sweet,
180 All made out of the carver's brain,
For a lady's chamber meet:
The lamp with twofold silver chain
Is fastened to an angel's feet.
The silver lamp burns dead and dim;
185 But Christabel the lamp will trim.
She trimmed the lamp, and made it bright,
And left it swinging to and fro,
While Geraldine, in wretched plight,
Sank down upon the floor below.

190 "O weary lady, Geraldine,
I pray you, drink this cordial wine!
It is a wine of virtuous powers;
My mother made it of wild flowers."

"And will your mother pity me,
195 Who am a maiden most forlorn?"
Christabel answered—"Woe is me!
She died the hour that I was born.
I have heard the grey-haired friar tell,
How on her death-bed she did say,
200 That she should hear the castle-bell
Strike twelve upon my wedding day.
O mother dear! that thou wert here!"
"I would," said Geraldine, "she were!"

But soon with altered voice, said she—
205 "Off, wandering mother! Peak and pine!
I have power to bid thee flee."
Alas! what ails poor Geraldine?
Why stares she with unsettled eye?
Can she the bodiless dead espy?
210 And why with hollow voice cries she,
"Off, woman, off! this hour is mine—

8. Often used as a floor covering in the Middle Ages.

Though thou her guardian spirit be,
Off, woman, off! 'tis given to me."

Then Christabel knelt by the lady's side,
215 And raised to heaven her eyes so blue—
"Alas!" said she, "this ghastly ride—
Dear lady! it hath wildered you!"
The lady wiped her moist cold brow,
And faintly said, " 'tis over now!"

220 Again the wild-flower wine she drank:
Her fair large eyes 'gan glitter bright,
And from the floor whereon she sank,
The lofty lady stood upright;
She was most beautiful to see,
225 Like a lady of a far countrée.

And thus the lofty lady spake—
"All they who live in the upper sky,
Do love you, holy Christabel!
And you love them, and for their sake
230 And for the good which me befell,
Even I in my degree will try,
Fair maiden, to requite you well.
But now unrobe yourself; for I
Must pray, ere yet in bed I lie."

235 Quoth Christabel, "So let it be!"
And as the lady bade, did she.
Her gentle limbs did she undress,
And lay down in her loveliness.

But through her brain of weal and woe
240 So many thoughts moved to and fro,
That vain it were her lids to close;
So half-way from the bed she rose,
And on her elbow did recline
To look at the lady Geraldine.

245 Beneath the lamp the lady bowed,
And slowly rolled her eyes around;
Then drawing in her breath aloud,
Like one that shuddered, she unbound
The cincture° from beneath her breast: belt
250 Her silken robe, and inner vest,
Dropt to her feet, and full in view,
Behold! her bosom and half her side——
A sight to dream of, not to tell!
O shield her! shield sweet Christabel!

255 Yet Geraldine nor speaks nor stirs;
Ah! what a stricken look was hers!

Deep from within she seems half-way
To lift some weight with sick assay,°   *attempt*
And eyes the maid and seeks delay;
260   Then suddenly as one defied
Collects herself in scorn and pride,
And lay down by the maiden's side!—
And in her arms the maid she took,
        Ah well-a-day!
265   And with low voice and doleful look
These words did say:
"In the touch of this bosom there worketh a spell,
Which is lord of thy utterance, Christabel!
Thou knowest to-night, and wilt know to-morrow
270   This mark of my shame, this seal of my sorrow;
      But vainly thou warrest,
        For this is alone in
      Thy power to declare,
        That in the dim forest
275   Thou heard'st a low moaning,
And found'st a bright lady, surpassingly fair:
And didst bring her home with thee in love and in charity,
To shield her and shelter her from the damp air."

The Conclusion to Part 1

It was a lovely sight to see
280   The lady Christabel, when she
Was praying at the old oak tree.
      Amid the jagged shadows
      Of mossy leafless boughs,
      Kneeling in the moonlight,
285   To make her gentle vows;
Her slender palms together prest,
Heaving sometimes on her breast;
Her face resigned to bliss or bale°—   *evil, sorrow*
Her face, oh call it fair not pale,
290   And both blue eyes more bright than clear,
Each about to have a tear.

With open eyes (ah woe is me!)
Asleep, and dreaming fearfully,
Fearfully dreaming, yet I wis,
295   Dreaming that alone, which is—
O sorrow and shame! Can this be she,
The lady, who knelt at the old oak tree?
And lo! the worker of these harms,
That holds the maiden in her arms,
300   Seems to slumber still and mild,
As a mother with her child.

A star hath set, a star hath risen,
O Geraldine! since arms of thine

Have been the lovely lady's prison.
305 O Geraldine! one hour was thine—
Thou'st had thy will! By tairn[9] and rill,
The night-birds all that hour were still.
But now they are jubilant anew,
From cliff and tower, tu—whoo! tu—whoo!
310 Tu—whoo! tu—whoo! from wood and fell![1]

And see! the lady Christabel
Gathers herself from out her trance;
Her limbs relax, her countenance
Grows sad and soft; the smooth thin lids
315 Close o'er her eyes; and tears she sheds—
Large tears that leave the lashes bright!
And oft the while she seems to smile
As infants at a sudden light!
Yea, she doth smile, and she doth weep,
320 Like a youthful hermitess,
Beauteous in a wilderness,
Who, praying always, prays in sleep.
And, if she move unquietly,
Perchance, 'tis but the blood so free,
325 Comes back and tingles in her feet.
No doubt, she hath a vision sweet.
What if her guardian spirit 'twere?
What if she knew her mother near?
But this she knows, in joys and woes,
330 That saints will aid if men will call:
For the blue sky bends over all!

Part 2

"Each matin bell," the Baron saith,
"Knells us back to a world of death."
These words Sir Leoline first said,
335 When he rose and found his lady dead:
These words Sir Leoline will say,
Many a morn to his dying day!

And hence the custom and law began,
That still at dawn the sacristan,°   *sexton*
340 Who duly pulls the heavy bell,
Five and forty beads must tell[2]
Between each stroke—a warning knell,
Which not a soul can choose but hear
From Bratha Head to Wyndermere.[3]

345 Saith Bracy the bard, "So let it knell!
And let the drowsy sacristan
Still count as slowly as he can!

9. Tarn, a mountain pool.
1. Elevated moor, or hill.
2. Pray while "telling" (keeping count on) the
beads of a rosary.
3. These and the following names are of localities
in the English Lake District.

There is no lack of such, I ween,
As well fill up the space between.
350 In Langdale Pike° and Witch's Lair,   *Peak*
And Dungeon-ghyll[4] so foully rent,
With ropes of rock and bells of air
Three sinful sextons' ghosts are pent,
Who all give back, one after t'other,
355 The death note to their living brother;
And oft too, by the knell offended,
Just as their one! two! three! is ended,
The devil mocks the doleful tale
With a merry peal from Borodale."

360 The air is still! through mist and cloud
That merry peal comes ringing loud;
And Geraldine shakes off her dread,
And rises lightly from the bed;
Puts on her silken vestments white,
365 And tricks her hair in lovely plight,°   *plait*
And nothing doubting of her spell
Awakens the lady Christabel.
"Sleep you, sweet lady Christabel?
I trust that you have rested well."

370 And Christabel awoke and spied
The same who lay down by her side—
O rather say, the same whom she
Raised up beneath the old oak tree!
Nay, fairer yet! and yet more fair!
375 For she belike hath drunken deep
Of all the blessedness of sleep!
And while she spake, her looks, her air
Such gentle thankfulness declare,
That (so it seemed) her girded vests
380 Grew tight beneath her heaving breasts.
"Sure I have sinned!" said Christabel,
"Now heaven be praised if all be well!"
And in low faltering tones, yet sweet,
Did she the lofty lady greet
385 With such perplexity of mind
As dreams too lively leave behind.

So quickly she rose, and quickly arrayed
Her maiden limbs, and having prayed
That He, who on the cross did groan,
390 Might wash away her sins unknown,
She forthwith led fair Geraldine
To meet her sire, Sir Leoline.

The lovely maid and the lady tall
Are pacing both into the hall,

4. Ravine forming the bed of a stream.

395 And pacing on through page and groom,
Enter the Baron's presence room.

The Baron rose, and while he prest
His gentle daughter to his breast,
With cheerful wonder in his eyes
400 The lady Geraldine espies,
And gave such welcome to the same,
As might beseem so bright a dame!

But when he heard the lady's tale,
And when she told her father's name,
405 Why waxed Sir Leoline so pale,
Murmuring o'er the name again,
Lord Roland de Vaux of Tryermaine?

Alas! they had been friends in youth;
But whispering tongues can poison truth;
410 And constancy lives in realms above;
And life is thorny; and youth is vain;
And to be wroth with one we love,
Doth work like madness in the brain.
And thus it chanced, as I divine,
415 With Roland and Sir Leoline.
Each spake words of high disdain
And insult to his heart's best brother:
They parted—ne'er to meet again!
But never either found another
420 To free the hollow heart from paining—
They stood aloof, the scars remaining,
Like cliffs which had been rent asunder;
A dreary sea now flows between;—
But neither heat, nor frost, nor thunder,
425 Shall wholly do away, I ween,
The marks of that which once hath been.

Sir Leoline, a moment's space,
Stood gazing on the damsel's face:
And the youthful Lord of Tryermaine
430 Came back upon his heart again.

O then the Baron forgot his age,
His noble heart swelled high with rage;
He swore by the wounds in Jesu's side,
He would proclaim it far and wide
435 With trump and solemn heraldry,
That they who thus had wronged the dame,
Were base as spotted infamy!
"And if they dare deny the same,
My herald shall appoint a week,
440 And let the recreant traitors seek
My tourney court—that there and then
I may dislodge their reptile souls

From the bodies and forms of men!"
He spake: his eye in lightning rolls!
445 For the lady was ruthlessly seized; and he kenned
In the beautiful lady the child of his friend!

And now the tears were on his face,
And fondly in his arms he took
Fair Geraldine, who met the embrace,
450 Prolonging it with joyous look.
Which when she viewed, a vision fell
Upon the soul of Christabel,
The vision of fear, the touch and pain!
She shrunk and shuddered, and saw again—
455 (Ah, woe is me! Was it for thee,
Thou gentle maid! such sights to see?)
Again she saw that bosom old,
Again she felt that bosom cold,
And drew in her breath with a hissing sound:
460 Whereat the Knight turned wildly round,
And nothing saw, but his own sweet maid
With eyes upraised, as one that prayed.

The touch, the sight, had passed away,
And in its stead that vision blest,
465 Which comforted her after-rest,
While in the lady's arms she lay,
Had put a rapture in her breast,
And on her lips and o'er her eyes
Spread smiles like light!
                              With new surprise,
470 "What ails then my beloved child?"
The Baron said—His daughter mild
Made answer, "All will yet be well!"
I ween, she had no power to tell
Aught else: so mighty was the spell.

475 Yet he, who saw this Geraldine,
Had deemed her sure a thing divine.
Such sorrow with such grace she blended,
As if she feared, she had offended
Sweet Christabel, that gentle maid!
480 And with such lowly tones she prayed,
She might be sent without delay
Home to her father's mansion.
                                "Nay!
Nay, by my soul!" said Leoline.
"Ho! Bracy, the bard, the charge be thine!
485 Go thou, with music sweet and loud,
And take two steeds with trappings proud,
And take the youth whom thou lov'st best
To bear thy harp, and learn thy song,
And clothe you both in solemn vest,
490 And over the mountains haste along,

Lest wandering folk, that are abroad,
Detain you on the valley road.
And when he has crossed the Irthing flood,
My merry bard! he hastes, he hastes
495 Up Knorren Moor, through Halegarth Wood,
And reaches soon that castle good
Which stands and threatens Scotland's wastes.

"Bard Bracy! bard Bracy! your horses are fleet,
Ye must ride up the hall, your music so sweet,
500 More loud than your horses' echoing feet!
And loud and loud to Lord Roland call,
Thy daughter is safe in Langdale hall!
Thy beautiful daughter is safe and free—
Sir Leoline greets thee thus through me.
505 He bids thee come without delay
With all thy numerous array;
And take thy lovely daughter home:
And he will meet thee on the way
With all his numerous array
510 White with their panting palfreys' foam:
And by mine honour! I will say,
That I repent me of the day
When I spake words of fierce disdain
To Roland de Vaux of Tryermaine!—
515 —For since that evil hour hath flown,
Many a summer's sun hath shone;
Yet ne'er found I a friend again
Like Roland de Vaux of Tryermaine."

The lady fell, and clasped his knees,
520 Her face upraised, her eyes o'erflowing;
And Bracy replied, with faltering voice,
His gracious hail on all bestowing!—
"Thy words, thou sire of Christabel,
Are sweeter than my harp can tell;
525 Yet might I gain a boon of thee,
This day my journey should not be,
So strange a dream hath come to me;
That I had vowed with music loud
To clear yon wood from thing unblest,
530 Warned by a vision in my rest!
For in my sleep I saw that dove,
That gentle bird, whom thou dost love,
And call'st by thy own daughter's name—
Sir Leoline! I saw the same
535 Fluttering, and uttering fearful moan,
Among the green herbs in the forest alone.
Which when I saw and when I heard,
I wonder'd what might ail the bird;
For nothing near it could I see,
540 Save the grass and green herbs underneath the old tree.

"And in my dream methought I went
To search out what might there be found;
And what the sweet bird's trouble meant,
That thus lay fluttering on the ground.
545 I went and peered, and could descry
No cause for her distressful cry;
But yet for her dear lady's sake
I stooped, methought, the dove to take,
When lo! I saw a bright green snake
550 Coiled around its wings and neck,
Green as the herbs on which it couched,
Close by the dove's its head it crouched;
And with the dove it heaves and stirs,
Swelling its neck as she swelled hers!
555 I woke; it was the midnight hour,
The clock was echoing in the tower;
But though my slumber was gone by,
This dream it would not pass away—
It seems to live upon my eye!
560 And thence I vowed this self-same day,
With music strong and saintly song
To wander through the forest bare,
Lest aught unholy loiter there."

Thus Bracy said: the Baron, the while,
565 Half-listening heard him with a smile;
Then turned to Lady Geraldine,
His eyes made up of wonder and love;
And said in courtly accents fine,
"Sweet maid, Lord Roland's beauteous dove,
570 With arms more strong than harp or song,
Thy sire and I will crush the snake!"
He kissed her forehead as he spake,
And Geraldine, in maiden wise,
Casting down her large bright eyes,
575 With blushing cheek and courtesy fine
She turned her from Sir Leoline;
Softly gathering up her train,
That o'er her right arm fell again;
And folded her arms across her chest,
580 And couched her head upon her breast,
And looked askance at Christabel——
Jesu Maria, shield her well!

A snake's small eye blinks dull and shy,
And the lady's eyes they shrunk in her head,
585 Each shrunk up to a serpent's eye,
And with somewhat of malice, and more of dread,
At Christabel she looked askance!—
One moment—and the sight was fled!
But Christabel in dizzy trance
590 Stumbling on the unsteady ground

Shuddered aloud, with a hissing sound;
And Geraldine again turned round,
And like a thing, that sought relief,
Full of wonder and full of grief,
595 She rolled her large bright eyes divine
Wildly on Sir Leoline.

The maid, alas! her thoughts are gone,
She nothing sees—no sight but one!
The maid, devoid of guile and sin,
600 I know not how, in fearful wise
So deeply had she drunken in
That look, those shrunken serpent eyes,
That all her features were resigned
To this sole image in her mind;
605 And passively did imitate
That look of dull and treacherous hate!
And thus she stood, in dizzy trance,
Still picturing that look askance
With forced unconscious sympathy
610 Full before her father's view——
As far as such a look could be,
In eyes so innocent and blue!
And when the trance was o'er, the maid
Paused awhile, and inly prayed:
615 Then falling at the Baron's feet,
"By my mother's soul do I entreat
That thou this woman send away!"
She said: and more she could not say:
For what she knew she could not tell,
620 O'er-mastered by the mighty spell.

Why is thy cheek so wan and wild,
Sir Leoline? Thy only child
Lies at thy feet, thy joy, thy pride,
So fair, so innocent, so mild;
625 The same, for whom thy lady died!
O by the pangs of her dear mother
Think thou no evil of thy child!
For her, and thee, and for no other,
She prayed the moment ere she died:
630 Prayed that the babe for whom she died,
Might prove her dear lord's joy and pride!
That prayer her deadly pangs beguiled,
Sir Leoline!
And wouldst thou wrong thy only child,
635 Her child and thine?

Within the Baron's heart and brain
If thoughts, like these, had any share,
They only swelled his rage and pain,
And did but work confusion there.
640 His heart was cleft with pain and rage,

His cheeks they quivered, his eyes were wild,
Dishonoured thus in his old age;
Dishonoured by his only child,
And all his hospitality
645 To the wrong'd daughter of his friend
By more than woman's jealousy
Brought thus to a disgraceful end—
He rolled his eye with stern regard
Upon the gentle minstrel bard,
650 And said in tones abrupt, austere—
"Why, Bracy! dost thou loiter here?
I bade thee hence!" The bard obeyed;
And turning from his own sweet maid,
The aged knight, Sir Leoline,
655 Led forth the lady Geraldine!

The Conclusion to Part 2

A little child, a limber elf,
Singing, dancing to itself,
A fairy thing with red round cheeks,
That always finds, and never seeks,
660 Makes such a vision to the sight
As fills a father's eyes with light;
And pleasures flow in so thick and fast
Upon his heart, that he at last
Must needs express his love's excess
665 With words of unmeant bitterness.
Perhaps 'tis pretty to force together
Thoughts so all unlike each other;
To mutter and mock a broken charm,
To dally with wrong that does no harm.
670 Perhaps 'tis tender too and pretty
At each wild word to feel within
A sweet recoil of love and pity.
And what, if in a world of sin
(O sorrow and shame should this be true!)
675 Such giddiness of heart and brain
Comes seldom save from rage and pain,
So talks as it's most used to do.

1798–1800   1816

Frost at Midnight[1]

The frost performs its secret ministry,
Unhelped by any wind. The owlet's cry
Came loud—and hark, again! loud as before.
The inmates of my cottage, all at rest,
5   Have left me to that solitude, which suits
Abstruser musings: save that at my side

---

1. The scene is Coleridge's cottage at Nether Stowey; the infant in line 7 is his son Hartley, then aged seventeen months.

My cradled infant slumbers peacefully.
'Tis calm indeed! so calm, that it disturbs
And vexes meditation with its strange
10　And extreme silentness. Sea, hill, and wood,
This populous village! Sea, and hill, and wood,
With all the numberless goings on of life,
Inaudible as dreams! the thin blue flame
Lies on my low burnt fire, and quivers not;
15　Only that film,[2] which fluttered on the grate,
Still flutters there, the sole unquiet thing.
Methinks, its motion in this hush of nature
Gives it dim sympathies with me who live,
Making it a companionable form,
20　Whose puny flaps and freaks the idling Spirit
By its own moods interprets, every where
Echo or mirror seeking of itself,
And makes a toy of Thought.

　　　　　　　　　　　But O! how oft,
How oft, at school, with most believing mind,
25　Presageful, have I gazed upon the bars,
To watch that fluttering stranger! and as oft
With unclosed lids, already had I dreamt
Of my sweet birth-place,[3] and the old church-tower,
Whose bells, the poor man's only music, rang
30　From morn to evening, all the hot Fair-day,
So sweetly, that they stirred and haunted me
With a wild pleasure, falling on mine ear
Most like articulate sounds of things to come!
So gazed I, till the soothing things I dreamt
35　Lulled me to sleep, and sleep prolonged my dreams!
And so I brooded all the following morn,
Awed by the stern preceptor's[4] face, mine eye
Fixed with mock study on my swimming book:
Save if the door half opened, and I snatched
40　A hasty glance, and still my heart leaped up,
For still I hoped to see the stranger's face,
Townsman, or aunt, or sister more beloved,
My play-mate when we both were clothed alike![5]

　　　Dear Babe, that sleepest cradled by my side,
45　Whose gentle breathings, heard in this deep calm,
Fill up the interspersed vacancies
And momentary pauses of the thought!
My babe so beautiful! it thrills my heart
With tender gladness, thus to look at thee,

2. In all parts of the kingdom these films are called
strangers and supposed to portend the arrival of
some absent friend [Coleridge's note]. The "film"
is a piece of soot fluttering on the bar of the grate.
3. Coleridge was born at Ottery St. Mary, Devonshire, but went to school in London, beginning at

the age of nine.
4. The Reverend James Boyer at Coleridge's
school, Christ's Hospital; Coleridge describes him
in *Biographia Literaria*, chap. 1.
5. I.e., when both Coleridge and his sister Ann still
wore infant clothes.

50 And think that thou shalt learn far other lore
And in far other scenes! For I was reared
In the great city, pent 'mid cloisters dim,
And saw nought lovely but the sky and stars.
But thou, my babe! shalt wander like a breeze
55 By lakes and sandy shores, beneath the crags
Of ancient mountain, and beneath the clouds,
Which image in their bulk both lakes and shores
And mountain crags: so shalt thou see and hear
The lovely shapes and sounds intelligible
60 Of that eternal language, which thy God
Utters, who from eternity doth teach
Himself in all, and all things in himself.
Great universal Teacher! he shall mould
Thy spirit, and by giving make it ask.

65   Therefore all seasons shall be sweet to thee,
Whether the summer clothe the general earth
With greenness, or the redbreast sit and sing
Betwixt the tufts of snow on the bare branch
Of mossy apple-tree, while the nigh thatch
70 Smokes in the sun-thaw; whether the eave-drops fall
Heard only in the trances of the blast,
Or if the secret ministry of frost
Shall hang them up in silent icicles,
Quietly shining to the quiet Moon.

Feb. 1798   1798

Dejection: An Ode[1]

> Late, late yestreen I saw the new Moon,
> With the old Moon in her arms;
> And I fear, I fear, my Master dear!
> We shall have a deadly storm.
> *Ballad of Sir Patrick Spence*

I

Well! If the Bard was weather-wise, who made
The grand old ballad of Sir Patrick Spence,
This night, so tranquil now, will not go hence
Unroused by winds, that ply a busier trade

1. This poem originated in a verse letter of 340 lines, called *A Letter to* ———, that Coleridge wrote on the night of April 4, 1802, after hearing the opening stanzas of *Ode: Intimations of Immortality,* which Wordsworth had just composed. The *Letter* was addressed to Sara Hutchinson (whom Coleridge sometimes called "Asra"), the sister of Wordsworth's fiancée, Mary. It picked up the theme of a loss in the quality of perceptual experience that Wordsworth had presented at the beginning of his *Ode.* In his original poem Coleridge lamented at length his unhappy marriage and the hopelessness of his love for Sara Hutchinson. In the next six months Coleridge deleted more than half the original lines, revised and reordered the remaining passages, and so transformed a long verse confession into the compact and dignified *Dejection: An Ode.* He published the *Ode,* in substantially its present form, on October 4, 1802, Wordsworth's wedding day—and also the seventh anniversary of Coleridge's own disastrous marriage to Sara Fricker. Note Coleridge's use of marriage as a metaphor in lines 49 and 67–70.

5 Than those which mould yon cloud in lazy flakes,
 Or the dull sobbing draft, that moans and rakes
  Upon the strings of this Eolian lute,[2]
  Which better far were mute.
 For lo! the New-moon winter-bright!
10 And overspread with phantom light,
 (With swimming phantom light o'erspread
 But rimmed and circled by a silver thread)
 I see the old Moon in her lap, foretelling
  The coming on of rain and squally blast.
15 And oh! that even now the gust were swelling,
  And the slant night-shower driving loud and fast!
 Those sounds which oft have raised me, whilst they awed,
  And sent my soul abroad,
 Might now perhaps their wonted° impulse give,   *customary*
20 Might startle this dull pain, and make it move and live!

2

 A grief without a pang, void, dark, and drear,
  A stifled, drowsy, unimpassioned grief,
  Which finds no natural outlet, no relief,
   In word, or sigh, or tear—
25 O Lady![3] in this wan and heartless mood,
 To other thoughts by yonder throstle woo'd,
  All this long eve, so balmy and serene,
 Have I been gazing on the western sky,
  And its peculiar tint of yellow green:
30 And still I gaze—and with how blank an eye!
 And those thin clouds above, in flakes and bars,
 That give away their motion to the stars;
 Those stars, that glide behind them or between,
 Now sparkling, now bedimmed, but always seen:
35 Yon crescent Moon as fixed as if it grew
 In its own cloudless, starless lake of blue;
 I see them all so excellently fair,
 I see, not feel, how beautiful they are!

3

  My genial[4] spirits fail;
40 And what can these avail
 To lift the smothering weight from off my breast?
  It were a vain endeavour,
  Though I should gaze for ever
 On that green light that lingers in the west:
45 I may not hope from outward forms to win
 The passion and the life, whose fountains are within.

2. A stringed instrument played upon by the wind (see *The Eolian Harp*, n. 1, p. 1576).
3. In the original version "Sara"—i.e., Sara Hutchinson. After intervening versions, in which the poem was addressed first to "William" (Words-worth) and then to "Edmund," Coleridge introduced the noncommittal "Lady" in 1817.
4. In its old use as the adjectival form of *genius*: "My innate powers fail."

4

O Lady! we receive but what we give,
And in our life alone does nature live:
Ours is her wedding-garment, ours her shroud![5]
50   And would we aught behold, of higher worth,
Than that inanimate cold world allowed
To the poor loveless ever-anxious crowd,
    Ah! from the soul itself must issue forth,
A light, a glory,[6] a fair luminous cloud
55   Enveloping the Earth—
And from the soul itself must there be sent
    A sweet and potent voice, of its own birth,
Of all sweet sounds the life and element!

5

O pure of heart! thou need'st not ask of me
60 What this strong music in the soul may be!
What, and wherein it doth exist,
This light, this glory, this fair luminous mist,
This beautiful and beauty-making power.
    Joy,[7] virtuous Lady! Joy that ne'er was given,
65 Save to the pure, and in their purest hour,
Life, and Life's effluence, cloud at once and shower,
Joy, Lady! is the spirit and the power,
Which wedding Nature to us gives in dower,
    A new Earth and new Heaven,[8]
70 Undreamt of by the sensual and the proud—
Joy is the sweet voice, Joy the luminous cloud—
      We in ourselves rejoice!
And thence flows all that charms or ear or sight,
    All melodies the echoes of that voice,
75 All colours a suffusion from that light.

6

There was a time when, though my path was rough,
    This joy within me dallied with distress,
And all misfortunes were but as the stuff
    Whence Fancy made me dreams of happiness:
80 For hope grew round me, like the twining vine,
And fruits, and foliage, not my own, seemed mine.
But now afflictions bow me down to earth:
Nor care I that they rob me of my mirth,

5. I.e., whether nature is experienced as "inanimate" (line 51) or in living interchange with the observer depends on the apathy or joyous vitality of the observer's own spirit.
6. Coleridge commonly used "glory" not in the sense of a halo, merely, but as a term for a mountain phenomenon in which a walker sees his own figure projected by the sun in the mist, enlarged, and with a circle of light around its head.
7. Coleridge often uses "Joy" for a sense of abounding vitality and of harmony between one's inner life and the life of nature. He sometimes calls the contrary "exsiccation," or spiritual dryness.
8. The sense becomes clearer if line 68 is punctuated in the way that Coleridge himself punctuated it when quoting the passage in one of his essays: "Which, wedding Nature to us, gives in dower." The idea is that "Joy" is the condition that (overcoming the alienation between mind and its milieu) marries us to "Nature" and gives by way of wedding portion ("dower") the experience of a renovated world.

But oh! each visitation
85 Suspends what nature gave me at my birth,
      My shaping spirit of Imagination.
For not to think of what I needs must feel,
      But to be still and patient, all I can;
And haply by abstruse research to steal
90   From my own nature all the natural man—
      This was my sole resource, my only plan:
Till that which suits a part infects the whole,
And now is almost grown the habit of my soul.

7

Hence, viper thoughts, that coil around my mind,
95   Reality's dark dream!
I turn from you, and listen to the wind,
      Which long has raved unnoticed. What a scream
Of agony by torture lengthened out
That lute sent forth! Thou Wind, that ravest without,
100   Bare crag, or mountain-tairn,[9] or blasted tree,
Or pine-grove whither woodman never clomb,
Or lonely house, long held the witches' home,
      Methinks were fitter instruments for thee,
Mad Lutanist! who in this month of showers,
105 Of dark brown gardens, and of peeping flowers,
Mak'st Devils' yule,[1] with worse than wintry song,
The blossoms, buds, and timorous leaves among.
      Thou Actor, perfect in all tragic sounds!
Thou mighty Poet, e'en to frenzy bold!
110   What tell'st thou now about?
      'Tis of the rushing of a host in rout,
With groans of trampled men, with smarting wounds—
At once they groan with pain, and shudder with the cold!
But hush! there is a pause of deepest silence!
115   And all that noise, as of a rushing crowd,
With groans, and tremulous shudderings—all is over—
      It tells another tale, with sounds less deep and loud!
      A tale of less affright,
      And tempered with delight,
120 As Otway's[2] self had framed the tender lay,
      'Tis of a little child
      Upon a lonesome wild,
Not far from home, but she hath lost her way:
And now moans low in bitter grief and fear,
125 And now screams loud, and hopes to make her mother hear.

8

'Tis midnight, but small thoughts have I of sleep:
Full seldom may my friend such vigils keep!

9. Tarn, or mountain pool.
1. Christmas as, in a perverted form, it is celebrated by devils.
2. Thomas Otway (1652–1685), a dramatist noted
for the pathos of his tragic passages. The poet originally named was "William," and the allusion was
probably to Wordsworth's *Lucy Gray*.

Visit her, gentle Sleep! with wings of healing,
And may this storm be but a mountain-birth,[3]
130 May all the stars hang bright above her dwelling,
Silent as though they watched the sleeping Earth!
With light heart may she rise,
Gay fancy, cheerful eyes,
Joy lift her spirit, joy attune her voice;
135 To her may all things live, from pole to pole,
Their life the eddying of her living soul!
O simple spirit, guided from above,
Dear Lady! friend devoutest of my choice,
Thus mayest thou ever, evermore rejoice.

Apr. 4, 1802   1802

The Pains of Sleep[1]

Ere on my bed my limbs I lay,
It hath not been my use to pray
With moving lips or bended knees;
But silently, by slow degrees,
5 My spirit I to Love compose,
In humble trust mine eye-lids close,
With reverential resignation,
No wish conceived, no thought exprest,
Only a sense of supplication;
10 A sense o'er all my soul imprest
That I am weak, yet not unblest,
Since in me, round me, every where
Eternal strength and wisdom are.

But yester-night I prayed aloud
15 In anguish and in agony,
Up-starting from the fiendish crowd
Of shapes and thoughts that tortured me:
A lurid light, a trampling throng,
Sense of intolerable wrong,
20 And whom I scorned, those only strong!
Thirst of revenge, the powerless will
Still baffled, and yet burning still!
Desire with loathing strangely mixed
On wild or hateful objects fixed.
25 Fantastic passions! maddening brawl!

3. Probably, "May this be a typical mountain storm, short though violent," although it is possible that Coleridge intended an allusion to Horace's phrase, "the mountain labored and brought forth a mouse."

1. Coleridge included a draft of this poem in a letter to Robert Southey, September 11, 1803, in which he wrote that "my spirits are dreadful, owing entirely to the Horrors of every night—I truly dread to sleep. It is no shadow with me, but substantial Misery foot-thick, that makes me sit by my bedside of a morning, & cry—. I have abandoned all opiates except Ether be one; & that only in *fits.* . . . " The last sentence indicates what Coleridge did not know—that his guilty nightmares were probably withdrawal symptoms from opium. The dreams he describes are very similar to those that De Quincey represents as "The Pains of Opium" in his *Confessions of an English Opium-Eater*.

And shame and terror over all!
Deeds to be hid which were not hid,
Which all confused I could not know,
Whether I suffered, or I did:
30 For all seemed guilt, remorse or woe,
My own or others still the same
Life-stifling fear, soul-stifling shame.

So two nights passed: the night's dismay
Saddened and stunned the coming day.
35 Sleep, the wide blessing, seemed to me
Distemper's worst calamity.
The third night, when my own loud scream
Had waked me from the fiendish dream,
O'ercome with sufferings strange and wild,
40 I wept as I had been a child;
And having thus by tears subdued
My anguish to a milder mood,
Such punishments, I said, were due
To natures deepliest stained with sin,—
45 For aye entempesting anew
The unfathomable hell within,
The horror of their deeds to view,
To know and loathe, yet wish and do!
Such griefs with such men well agree,
50 But wherefore, wherefore fall on me?
To be beloved is all I need,
And whom I love, I love indeed.

1803   1816

To William Wordsworth

*Composed on the Night after His Recitation of a Poem on the Growth of
an Individual Mind*[1]

Friend of the wise! and teacher of the good!
Into my heart have I received that lay
More than historic, that prophetic lay
Wherein (high theme by thee first sung aright)
5 Of the foundations and the building up
Of a Human Spirit thou hast dared to tell
What may be told, to the understanding mind
Revealable; and what within the mind
By vital breathings secret as the soul
10 Of vernal growth, oft quickens in the heart
Thoughts all too deep for words![2]—

1. This was the poem (later called *The Prelude*), addressed to Coleridge, that Wordsworth had completed in 1805. After Coleridge returned from Malta, very low in health and spirits, Wordsworth read the poem aloud to him during the evenings of almost two weeks. Coleridge wrote most of the present response immediately after the reading was completed, on January 7, 1807.

2. Wordsworth had described the effect on his mind of the animating breeze ("vital breathings") in *The Prelude* 1.1–44. "Thoughts . . . words" echoes the last line of Wordsworth's *Intimations* ode. Coleridge goes on to summarize the major themes and events of *The Prelude*.

Theme hard as high!
Of smiles spontaneous, and mysterious fears
(The first-born they of Reason and twin birth),
Of tides obedient to external force,
15 And currents self-determined, as might seem,
Or by some inner power; of moments awful,
Now in thy inner life, and now abroad,
When power streamed from thee, and thy soul received
The light reflected, as a light bestowed—
20 Of fancies fair, and milder hours of youth,
Hyblean³ murmurs of poetic thought
Industrious in its joy, in vales and glens
Native or outland, lakes and famous hills!
Or on the lonely high-road, when the stars
25 Were rising; or by secret mountain-streams,
The guides and the companions of thy way!

　　Of more than Fancy, of the Social Sense
Distending wide, and man beloved as man,
Where France in all her towns lay vibrating
30 Like some becalmed bark beneath the burst
Of Heaven's immediate thunder, when no cloud
Is visible, or shadow on the main.
For thou wert there, thine own brows garlanded,
Amid the tremor of a realm aglow,
35 Amid a mighty nation jubilant,
When from the general heart of human kind
Hope sprang forth like a full-born Deity!
——Of that dear Hope afflicted and struck down,
So summoned homeward, thenceforth calm and sure
40 From the dread watch-tower of man's absolute self,
With light unwaning on her eyes, to look
Far on—herself a glory to behold,
The Angel of the vision! Then (last strain)
Of Duty, chosen laws controlling choice,
45 Action and joy!—An Orphic song⁴ indeed,
A song divine of high and passionate thoughts
To their own music chanted!

　　　　　O great Bard!
Ere yet that last strain dying awed the air,
With steadfast eye I viewed thee in the choir
50 Of ever-enduring men. The truly great
Have all one age, and from one visible space
Shed influence! They, both in power and act,
Are permanent, and Time is not with them,
Save as it worketh for them, they in it.
55 Nor less a sacred roll, than those of old,

---

3. Sweet. Hybla, in ancient Sicily, was famous for its honey.
4. As enchanting and oracular as the song of the legendary Orpheus. There may also be an allusion to the Orphic mysteries, involving spiritual death and rebirth (see lines 61–66). "The Angel of the vision" (line 43) probably alludes to "the great vision of the guarded mount" in Milton's *Lycidas*, line 161.

And to be placed, as they, with gradual fame
Among the archives of mankind, thy work
Makes audible a linked lay of Truth,
Of Truth profound a sweet continuous lay,
60 Not learnt, but native, her own natural notes!
Ah! as I listened with a heart forlorn,
The pulses of my being beat anew:
And even as life returns upon the drowned,[5]
Life's joy rekindling roused a throng of pains—
65 Keen pangs of Love, awakening as a babe
Turbulent, with an outcry in the heart;
And fears self-willed, that shunned the eye of hope;
And hope that scarce would know itself from fear;
Sense of past youth, and manhood come in vain,
70 And genius given, and knowledge won in vain;
And all which I had culled in wood-walks wild,
And all which patient toil had reared, and all,
Commune with thee had opened out—but flowers
Strewed on my corse, and borne upon my bier,
75 In the same coffin, for the self-same grave!

That way no more! and ill beseems it me,
Who came a welcomer in herald's guise,
Singing of glory, and futurity,
To wander back on such unhealthful road,
80 Plucking the poisons of self-harm! And ill
Such intertwine beseems triumphal wreaths
Strewed before thy advancing!

                                Nor do thou,
Sage Bard! impair the memory of that hour
Of thy communion with my nobler mind[6]
85 By pity or grief, already felt too long!
Nor let my words import more blame than needs.
The tumult rose and ceased: for peace is nigh
Where wisdom's voice has found a listening heart.
Amid the howl of more than wintry storms,
90 The halcyon[7] hears the voice of vernal hours
Already on the wing.

                        Eve following eve,[8]
Dear tranquil time, when the sweet sense of Home
Is sweetest! moments for their own sake hailed
And more desired, more precious for thy song,
95 In silence listening, like a devout child,
My soul lay passive, by thy various strain
Driven as in surges now beneath the stars,
With momentary stars of my own birth,

---

5. A death-in-life is also described in, e.g., *Dejection: An Ode* and *Epitaph*.
6. I.e., during the early association between the two poets (1797–98).
7. A fabled bird, able to calm the sea where it nested in winter.
8. The evenings during which Wordsworth read his poem aloud.

Fair constellated foam, still darting off
100   Into the darkness; now a tranquil sea,
Outspread and bright, yet swelling to the moon.

And when—O Friend! my comforter and guide!
Strong in thyself, and powerful to give strength!—
Thy long sustained Song finally closed,
105   And thy deep voice had ceased—yet thou thyself
Wert still before my eyes, and round us both
That happy vision of beloved faces—
Scarce conscious, and yet conscious of its close
I sate, my being blended in one thought
110   (Thought was it? or aspiration? or resolve?)
Absorbed, yet hanging still upon the sound—
And when I rose, I found myself in prayer.

1807   1817

Epitaph[1]

Stop, Christian Passer-by!—Stop, child of God,
And read with gentle breast. Beneath this sod
A poet lies, or that which once seem'd he.—
O, lift one thought in prayer for S. T. C.;
5   That he who many a year with toil of breath
Found death in life, may here find life in death!
Mercy for praise—to be forgiven for[2] fame
He ask'd, and hoped, through Christ. Do thou the same!

1833   1834

Biographia Literaria   In March 1815 Coleridge was preparing a collected edition of his poems and planned to include "a general preface . . . on the principles of philosophic and genial criticism." Characteristically, the materials developed as Coleridge worked on them until, on July 29, he declared that the preface had been extended into a complete work, "an Autobiographia Literaria"; it was to consist of two main parts, "my literary life and opinions, as far as poetry and *poetical* criticism [are] concerned" and a critique of Wordsworth's theory of poetic diction. This work was ready by September 17, 1815, but the *Biographia Literaria,* in two volumes, was not published until July 1817. The delay was caused by a series of miscalculations by his printer, which forced Coleridge to add 150 pages of miscellaneous materials to pad out the length of the second volume.

Coleridge had been planning a detailed critique of Wordsworth's theory of poetic diction ever since 1802, when he had detected "a radical difference in our theoretical opinions respecting poetry." In the selection from chapter 17, Coleridge agrees with

---

1. Written by Coleridge the year before he died. One version that he sent in a letter had as a title: "Epitaph on a Poet little known, yet better known by the Initials of his name than by the Name

Itself."
2. "For" in the sense of "instead of" [Coleridge's note].

Wordsworth's general aim of reforming the artifices of current poetic diction, but he sharply denies Wordsworth's claim that there is no essential difference between the language of poetry and the language spoken by people in real life. The other selections printed here are devoted mainly to the central principle of Coleridge's own critical theory, the distinction between the mechanical "fancy" and the organic "imagination." The biographical section of the *Biographia* (chapters 1 and 4), dealing with the development of his poetic taste and theory, describes his gradual realization, climaxed by his first exposure to Wordsworth's poetry, "that fancy and imagination were two distinct and widely different faculties." The conclusion to chapter 13 tersely summarizes this distinction; and the definition of poetry, at the end of chapter 14, develops at greater length the nature of the process and products of the "synthetic and magical power . . . of imagination." These paragraphs, whose meaning is much disputed, have become a central reference in English literary criticism.

From Biographia Literaria

From *Chapter 4*[1]

[MR. WORDSWORTH'S EARLIER POEMS]

* * * During the last year of my residence at Cambridge, I became acquainted with Mr. Wordsworth's first publication, entitled *Descriptive Sketches*;[2] and seldom, if ever, was the emergence of an original poetic genius above the literary horizon more evidently announced. In the form, style, and manner of the whole poem, and in the structure of the particular lines and periods, there is a harshness and acerbity connected and combined with words and images all a-glow which might recall those products of the vegetable world, where gorgeous blossoms rise out of the hard and thorny rind and shell within which the rich fruit was elaborating. The language was not only peculiar and strong, but at times knotty and contorted, as by its own impatient strength; while the novelty and struggling crowd of images, acting in conjunction with the difficulties of the style, demanded always a greater closeness of attention than poetry (at all events than descriptive poetry) has a right to claim. It not seldom therefore justified the complaint of obscurity. In the following extract I have sometimes fancied that I saw an emblem of the poem itself and of the author's genius as it was then displayed:

'Tis storm; and hid in mist from hour to hour,
All day the floods a deepening murmur pour;
The sky is veiled, and every cheerful sight:
Dark is the region as with coming night;
And yet what frequent bursts of overpowering light!
Triumphant on the bosom of the storm,
Glances the fire-clad eagle's wheeling form;
Eastward, in long perspective glittering, shine
The wood-crowned cliffs that o'er the lake recline;
Wide o'er the Alps a hundred streams unfold,

---

1. Coleridge heads each chapter with a list of topics. In our excerpts from these chapters, we insert the appropriate topic-titles, in brackets, before each selection.

2. Published 1793, the year before Coleridge left

Cambridge; a long descriptive-meditative poem in closed couplets, recounting Wordsworth's walking tour in the Alps in 1790. Wordsworth describes the same tour in *The Prelude*, book 6.

At once to pillars turned that flame with gold;
Behind his sail the peasant strives to shun
The West, that burns like one dilated sun,
Where in a mighty crucible expire
The mountains, glowing hot, like coals of fire.[3]

The poetic Psyche, in its process to full development, undergoes as many changes as its Greek namesake, the butterfly.[4] And it is remarkable how soon genius clears and purifies itself from the faults and errors of its earliest products; faults which, in its earliest compositions, are the more obtrusive and confluent because, as heterogeneous elements which had only a temporary use, they constitute the very *ferment* by which themselves are carried off. Or we may compare them to some diseases, which must work on the humors and be thrown out on the surface in order to secure the patient from their future recurrence. I was in my twenty-fourth year when I had the happiness of knowing Mr. Wordsworth personally;[5] and, while memory lasts, I shall hardly forget the sudden effect produced on my mind by his recitation of a manuscript poem which still remains unpublished, but of which the stanza and tone of style were the same as those of *The Female Vagrant* as originally printed in the first volume of the *Lyrical Ballads*.[6] There was here no mark of strained thought or forced diction, no crowd or turbulence of imagery, and, as the poet hath himself well described in his lines on revisiting the Wye,[7] manly reflection and human associations had given both variety and an additional interest to natural objects which in the passion and appetite of the first love they had seemed to him neither to need or permit. The occasional obscurities, which had risen from an imperfect control over the resources of his native language, had almost wholly disappeared, together with that worse defect of arbitrary and illogical phrases, at once hackneyed and fantastic, which hold so distinguished a place in the *technique* of ordinary poetry and will, more or less, alloy the earlier poems of the truest genius, unless the attention has been specifically directed to their worthlessness and incongruity. I did not perceive anything particular in the mere style of the poem alluded to during its recitation, except indeed such difference as was not separable from the thought and manner; and the Spenserian stanza which always, more or less, recalls to the reader's mind Spenser's own style, would doubtless have authorized in my then opinion a more frequent descent to the phrases of ordinary life than could, without an ill effect, have been hazarded in the heroic couplet. It was not however the freedom from false taste, whether as to common defects or to those more properly his own, which made so unusual an impression on my feelings immediately, and subsequently on my judgment. It was the union of deep feeling with profound thought; the fine balance of truth in observing with the imaginative faculty in modifying the objects observed; and above all the original gift of spreading the tone, the *atmosphere*, and with it the depth and height of the ideal world, around forms, incidents, and situations of which, for the common view, cus-

---

3. *Descriptive Sketches* (1815 version), lines 332ff.
4. In Greek, Psyche is the common name for the soul and the butterfly [Coleridge's note].
5. The meeting occurred in September 1795.
6. *Salisbury Plain* (1793–94), which was left in

manuscript until Wordsworth published a revised version in 1842 under the title *Guilt and Sorrow.* An excerpt from *Salisbury Plain* was printed as *The Female Vagrant*, in *Lyrical Ballads* (1798).
7. Wordsworth's *Tintern Abbey*, lines 76ff.

tom had bedimmed all the luster, had dried up the sparkle and the dewdrops. "To find no contradiction in the union of old and new, to contemplate the Ancient of Days and all his works with feelings as fresh as if all had then sprang forth at the first creative fiat, characterizes the mind that feels the riddle of the world and may help to unravel it. To carry on the feelings of childhood into the powers of manhood; to combine the child's sense of wonder and novelty with the appearances which every day for perhaps forty years had rendered familiar;

> With sun and moon and stars throughout the year,
> And man and woman;[8]

this is the character and privilege of genius, and one of the marks which distinguish genius from talents. And therefore it is the prime merit of genius, and its most unequivocal mode of manifestation, so to represent familiar objects as to awaken in the minds of others a kindred feeling concerning them, and that freshness of sensation which is the constant accompaniment of mental no less than of bodily convalescence. Who has not a thousand times seen snow fall on water? Who has not watched it with a new feeling from the time that he has read Burns' comparison of sensual pleasure

> To snow that falls upon a river
> A moment white—then gone forever![9]

In poems, equally as in philosophic disquisitions, genius produces the strongest impressions of novelty while it rescues the most admitted truths from the impotence caused by the very circumstance of their universal admission. Truths of all others the most awful and mysterious, yet being at the same time of universal interest, are too often considered as *so* true, that they lose all the life and efficiency of truth and lie bedridden in the dormitory of the soul side by side with the most despised and exploded errors." *The Friend*, p. 76, no. 5.[1]

[ON FANCY AND IMAGINATION—THE INVESTIGATION OF THE DISTINCTION IMPORTANT TO THE FINE ARTS]

This excellence, which in all Mr. Wordsworth's writings is more or less predominant and which constitutes the character of his mind, I no sooner felt than I sought to understand. Repeated meditations led me first to suspect (and a more intimate analysis of the human faculties, their appropriate marks, functions, and effects, matured my conjecture into full conviction) that fancy and imagination were two distinct and widely different faculties, instead of being, according to the general belief, either two names with one meaning, or at furthest the lower and higher degree of one and the same power. It is not, I own, easy to conceive a more apposite translation of the Greek *phantasia* than the Latin *imaginatio;* but it is equally true that in all societies there exists an instinct of growth, a certain collective unconscious good sense working progressively to desynonymize those words originally of the same meaning which the conflux of dialects had supplied to the more

8. Altered from Milton's sonnet *To Mr. Cyriack Skinner upon His Blindness.*
9. Altered from Burns's *Tam o' Shanter*, lines 61–62.
1. A periodical published by Coleridge (1809–10).

homogeneous languages, as the Greek and German: and which the same cause, joined with accidents of translation from original works of different countries, occasion in mixed languages like our own. The first and most important point to be proved is, that two conceptions perfectly distinct are confused under one and the same word, and (this done) to appropriate that word exclusively to one meaning, and the synonym (should there be one) to the other. But if (as will be often the case in the arts and sciences) no synonym exists, we must either invent or borrow a word. In the present instance the appropriation had already begun and been legitimated in the derivative adjective: Milton had a highly *imaginative,* Cowley a very *fanciful,* mind. If therefore I should succeed in establishing the actual existence of two faculties generally different, the nomenclature would be at once determined. To the faculty by which I had characterized Milton we should confine the term *imagination;* while the other would be contra-distinguished as *fancy.* Now were it once fully ascertained that this division is no less grounded in nature than that of delirium from mania, or Otway's

> Lutes, lobsters, seas of milk, and ships of amber,[2]

from Shakespeare's

> What! have his daughters brought him to this pass?[3]

or from the preceding apostrophe to the elements, the theory of the fine arts and of poetry in particular could not, I thought, but derive some additional and important light. It would in its immediate effects furnish a torch of guidance to the philosophical critic, and ultimately to the poet himself. In energetic minds truth soon changes by domestication into power; and from directing in the discrimination and appraisal of the product becomes influencive in the production. To admire on principle is the only way to imitate without loss of originality. * * *

From *Chapter 13*

[ON THE IMAGINATION, OR ESEMPLASTIC[4] POWER]

* * * The IMAGINATION, then, I consider either as primary, or secondary. The primary IMAGINATION I hold to be the living power and prime agent of all human perception, and as a repetition in the finite mind of the eternal act of creation in the infinite I AM. The secondary I consider as an echo of the former, coexisting with the conscious will, yet still as identical with the primary in the *kind* of its agency, and differing only in *degree,* and in the *mode* of its operation. It dissolves, diffuses, dissipates, in order to recreate; or where this process is rendered impossible, yet still, at all events, it struggles to idealize and to unify. It is essentially *vital,* even as all objects (*as* objects) are essentially fixed and dead.

FANCY, on the contrary, has no other counters to play with but fixities and definites. The fancy is indeed no other than a mode of memory emancipated from the order of time and space; and blended with, and modified by that

2. Thomas Otway, in *Venice Preserved* (1682), wrote "laurels" in place of "lobsters" (5.2.151).
3. *King Lear* 3.4.59.

4. Coleridge coined this word and used it to mean "molding into unity."

empirical phenomenon of the will which we express by the word CHOICE. But equally with the ordinary memory it must receive all its materials ready made from the law of association.[5] * * *

Chapter 14

OCCASION OF THE *LYRICAL BALLADS*, AND THE OBJECTS ORIGINALLY PROPOSED—PREFACE TO THE SECOND EDITION—THE ENSUING CONTROVERSY, ITS CAUSES AND ACRIMONY—PHILOSOPHIC DEFINITIONS OF A POEM AND POETRY WITH SCHOLIA.[6]

During the first year that Mr. Wordsworth and I were neighbours,[7] our conversations turned frequently on the two cardinal points of poetry, the power of exciting the sympathy of the reader by a faithful adherence to the truth of nature, and the power of giving the interest of novelty by the modifying colors of imagination.[8] The sudden charm which accidents of light and shade, which moonlight or sunset diffused over a known and familiar landscape, appeared to represent the practicability of combining both. These are the poetry of nature. The thought suggested itself (to which of us I do not recollect) that a series of poems might be composed of two sorts. In the one, the incidents and agents were to be, in part at least, supernatural; and the excellence aimed at was to consist in the interesting of the affections by the dramatic truth of such emotions as would naturally accompany such situations, supposing them real. And real in *this* sense they have been to every human being who, from whatever source of delusion, has at any time believed himself under supernatural agency. For the second class, subjects were to be chosen from ordinary life; the characters and incidents were to be such as will be found in every village and its vicinity where there is a meditative and feeling mind to seek after them, or to notice them when they present themselves.

In this idea originated the plan of the *Lyrical Ballads*; in which it was agreed that my endeavours should be directed to persons and characters supernatural, or at least romantic; yet so as to transfer from our inward nature a human interest and a semblance of truth sufficient to procure for these shadows of imagination that willing suspension of disbelief for the moment, which constitutes poetic faith. Mr. Wordsworth, on the other hand, was to propose to himself as his object to give the charm of novelty to things of every day, and to excite a feeling analogous to the supernatural, by awakening the mind's attention from the lethargy of custom and directing it to the loveliness and the wonders of the world before us; an inexhaustible treasure, but for which, in consequence of the film of familiarity and selfish solicitude, we have eyes yet see not, ears that hear not, and hearts that neither feel nor understand.[9]

5. Coleridge conceives God's creation to be a continuing process, which has an analogy in the creative perception ("primary imagination") of all human minds. The creative process is repeated, or "echoed," on still a third level, by the "secondary imagination" of the poet, which dissolves the products of primary perception in order to shape them into a new and unified creation—the imaginative passage or poem. The "fancy," on the other hand, can only manipulate "fixities and definites" that, linked by association, come to it ready-made from perception. Its products, therefore, are not re-creations (echoes of God's original creative process) but mosaic-like reassemblies of existing bits and pieces.

6. Additional remarks, after a philosophic demonstration.

7. At Nether Stowey and Alfoxden, Somerset, in 1797.

8. Cf. Wordsworth's account in his Preface to *Lyrical Ballads* (p. 1436).

9. Cf. Isaiah 6.9–10.

With this view I wrote *The Ancient Mariner,* and was preparing, among other poems, *The Dark Ladie,* and the *Christabel,* in which I should have more nearly realized my ideal than I had done in my first attempt. But Mr. Wordsworth's industry had proved so much more successful and the number of his poems so much greater, that my compositions, instead of forming a balance, appeared rather an interpolation of heterogeneous matter.[1] Mr. Wordsworth added two or three poems written in his own character, in the impassioned, lofty, and sustained diction which is characteristic of his genius. In this form the *Lyrical Ballads* were published; and were presented by him, as an *experiment,*[2] whether subjects which from their nature rejected the usual ornaments and extra-colloquial style of poems in general might not be so managed in the language of ordinary life as to produce the pleasurable interest which it is the peculiar business of poetry to impart. To the second edition[3] he added a preface of considerable length; in which, notwithstanding some passages of apparently a contrary import, he was understood to contend for the extension of this style to poetry of all kinds, and to reject as vicious and indefensible all phrases and forms of style that were not included in what he (unfortunately, I think, adopting an equivocal expression) called the language of *real* life. From this preface, prefixed to poems in which it was impossible to deny the presence of original genius, however mistaken its direction might be deemed, arose the whole long-continued controversy.[4] For from the conjunction of perceived power with supposed heresy I explain the inveteracy and in some instances, I grieve to say, the acrimonious passions with which the controversy has been conducted by the assailants.

Had Mr. Wordsworth's poems been the silly, the childish things which they were for a long time described as being; had they been really distinguished from the compositions of other poets merely by meanness of language and inanity of thought; had they indeed contained nothing more than what is found in the parodies and pretended imitations of them; they must have sunk at once, a dead weight, into the slough of oblivion, and have dragged the preface along with them. But year after year increased the number of Mr. Wordsworth's admirers. They were found too not in the lower classes of the reading public, but chiefly among young men of strong sensibility and meditative minds; and their admiration (inflamed perhaps in some degree by opposition) was distinguished by its intensity, I might almost say, by its *religious* fervor. These facts, and the intellectual energy of the author, which was more or less consciously felt where it was outwardly and even boisterously denied, meeting with sentiments of aversion to his opinions and of alarm at their consequences, produced an eddy of criticism which would of itself have borne up the poems by the violence with which it whirled them round and round. With many parts of this preface, in the sense attributed to them and which the words undoubtedly seem to authorize, I never concurred; but, on the contrary objected to them as erroneous in principle, and as contradictory (in appearance at least) both to other parts of the same preface and to the author's own practice in the greater number of the poems themselves. Mr. Wordsworth in his recent collection[5] has, I find, degraded

1. The first edition of *Lyrical Ballads,* published anonymously in 1798, contained nineteen poems by Wordsworth, four by Coleridge.
2. *Experiments* was the word used by Wordsworth in his *Advertisement* to the first edition.
3. Published in 1800.
4. The controversy over Wordsworth's theory and poetical practice in the literary journals of the day.
5. *Poems,* 2 vols., 1815.

this prefatory disquisition to the end of his second volume, to be read or not at the reader's choice. But he has not, as far as I can discover, announced any change in his poetic creed. At all events, considering it as the source of a controversy in which I have been honored more than I deserve by the frequent conjunction of my name with his, I think it expedient to declare once for all in what points I coincide with his opinions, and in what points I altogether differ. But in order to render myself intelligible I must previously, in as few words as possible, explain my ideas, first, of a POEM; and secondly, of POETRY itself, in *kind* and in *essence*.

The office of philosophical *disquisition* consists in just *distinction*; while it is the privilege of the philosopher to preserve himself constantly aware that distinction is not division. In order to obtain adequate notions of any truth, we must intellectually separate its distinguishable parts; and this is the technical *process* of philosophy. But having so done, we must then restore them in our conceptions to the unity in which they actually coexist; and this is the *result* of philosophy. A poem contains the same elements as a prose composition; the difference therefore must consist in a different combination of them, in consequence of a different object proposed. According to the difference of the object will be the difference of the combination. It is possible that the object may be merely to facilitate the recollection of any given facts or observations by artificial arrangement; and the composition will be a poem, merely because it is distinguished from prose by meter, or by rhyme, or by both conjointly. In this, the lowest sense, a man might attribute the name of a poem to the well-known enumeration of the days in the several months:

> Thirty days hath September,
> April, June, and November, etc.

and others of the same class and purpose. And as a particular pleasure is found in anticipating the recurrence of sounds and quantities, all compositions that have this charm superadded, whatever be their contents, *may* be entitled poems.

So much for the superficial *form*. A difference of object and contents supplies an additional ground of distinction. The immediate purpose may be the communication of truths; either of truth absolute and demonstrable, as in works of science; or of facts experienced and recorded, as in history. Pleasure, and that of the highest and most permanent kind, may *result* from the *attainment* of the end; but it is not itself the immediate end. In other works the communication of pleasure may be the immediate purpose; and though truth, either moral or intellectual, ought to be the *ultimate* end, yet this will distinguish the character of the author, not the class to which the work belongs. Blessed indeed is that state of society in which the immediate purpose would be baffled by the perversion of the proper ultimate end; in which no charm of diction or imagery could exempt the Bathyllus even of an Anacreon, or the Alexis of Virgil,[6] from disgust and aversion!

But the communication of pleasure may be the immediate object of a work not metrically composed; and that object may have been in a high degree

---

6. The reference is to poems of homosexual love. Bathyllus was a beautiful boy praised by Anacreon, a Greek lyric poet (ca. 560–475 B.C.E.); Alexis was a young man loved by the shepherd Corydon in Virgil's *Eclogue* 2.

attained, as in novels and romances. Would then the mere superaddition of meter, with or without rhyme, entitle *these* to the name of poems? The answer is that nothing can permanently please which does not contain in itself the reason why it is so, and not otherwise. If meter be superadded, all other parts must be made consonant with it. They must be such as to justify the perpetual and distinct attention to each part which an exact correspondent recurrence of accent and sound are calculated to excite. The final definition then, so deduced, may be thus worded. A poem is that species of composition which is opposed to works of science by proposing for its *immediate* object pleasure, not truth; and from all other species (having *this* object in common with it) it is discriminated by proposing to itself such delight from the *whole* as is compatible with a distinct gratification from each component *part*.

Controversy is not seldom excited in consequence of the disputants attaching each a different meaning to the same word; and in few instances has this been more striking than in disputes concerning the present subject. If a man chooses to call every composition a poem which is rhyme, or measure, or both, I must leave his opinion uncontroverted. The distinction is at least competent to characterize the writer's intention. If it were subjoined that the whole is likewise entertaining or affecting as a tale or as a series of interesting reflections, I of course admit this as another fit ingredient of a poem and an additional merit. But if the definition sought for be that of a *legitimate* poem, I answer it must be one the parts of which mutually support and explain each other; all in their proportion harmonizing with, and supporting the purpose and known influences of metrical arrangement. The philosophic critics of all ages coincide with the ultimate judgment of all countries in equally denying the praises of a just poem on the one hand to a series of striking lines or distichs,[7] each of which absorbing the whole attention of the reader to itself disjoins it from its context and makes it a separate whole, instead of a harmonizing part; and on the other hand, to an unsustained composition, from which the reader collects rapidly the general result unattracted by the component parts. The reader should be carried forward, not merely or chiefly by the mechanical impulse of curiosity, or by a restless desire to arrive at the final solution; but by the pleasurable activity of mind excited by the attractions of the journey itself. Like the motion of a serpent, which the Egyptians made the emblem of intellectual power; or like the path of sound through the air; at every step he pauses and half recedes, and from the retrogressive movement collects the force which again carries him onward. "*Praecipitandus est* liber *spiritus*,"[8] says Petronius Arbiter most happily. The epithet *liber* here balances the preceding verb; and it is not easy to conceive more meaning condensed in fewer words.

But if this should be admitted as a satisfactory character of a poem, we have still to seek for a definition of poetry. The writings of Plato, and Bishop Taylor, and the *Theoria Sacra* of Burnet,[9] furnish undeniable proofs that poetry of the highest kind may exist without meter, and even without the

---

7. Pairs of lines.
8. "The *free* spirit [of the poet] must be hurled onward." From the *Satyricon*, by the lively Roman satirist Petronius Arbiter (1st century C.E.).
9. Thomas Burnet (1635?–1715), author of *The Sacred Theory of the Earth*. Bishop Jeremy Taylor

(1613–1667), author of *Holy Living* and *Holy Dying*. Coleridge greatly admired the elaborate and sonorous prose of both these writers. He took from a work by Burnet the Latin motto for *The Rime of the Ancient Mariner*.

contradistinguishing objects of a poem. The first chapter of Isaiah (indeed a very large proportion of the whole book) is poetry in the most emphatic sense; yet it would be not less irrational than strange to assert that pleasure, and not truth, was the immediate object of the prophet. In short, whatever *specific* import we attach to the word poetry, there will be found involved in it, as a necessary consequence, that a poem of any length neither can be, nor ought to be, all poetry.[1] Yet if a harmonious whole is to be produced, the remaining parts must be preserved in *keeping* with the poetry; and this can be no otherwise effected than by such a studied selection and artificial arrangement as will partake of *one,* though not a *peculiar,* property of poetry. And this again can be no other than the property of exciting a more continuous and equal attention than the language of prose aims at, whether colloquial or written.

My own conclusions on the nature of poetry, in the strictest use of the word, have been in part anticipated in the preceding disquisition on the fancy and imagination. What is poetry? is so nearly the same question with, what is a poet? that the answer to the one is involved in the solution of the other. For it is a distinction resulting from the poetic genius itself, which sustains and modifies the images, thoughts, and emotions of the poet's own mind.

The poet, described in *ideal* perfection, brings the whole soul of man into activity, with the subordination of its faculties to each other, according to their relative worth and dignity. He diffuses a tone and spirit of unity that blends and (as it were) *fuses,* each into each, by that synthetic and magical power to which we have exclusively appropriated the name of imagination. This power, first put in action by the will and understanding and retained under their irremissive, though gentle and unnoticed, control (*laxis effertur habenis*)[2] reveals itself in the balance or reconciliation of opposite or discordant qualities:[3] of sameness, with difference; of the general, with the concrete; the idea, with the image; the individual, with the representative; the sense of novelty and freshness, with old and familiar objects; a more than usual state of emotion, with more than usual order; judgment ever awake and steady self-possession, with enthusiasm and feeling profound or vehement; and while it blends and harmonizes the natural and the artificial, still subordinates art to nature; the manner to the matter; and our admiration of the poet to our sympathy with the poetry. "Doubtless," as Sir John Davies observes of the soul (and his words may with slight alteration be applied, and even more appropriately, to the poetic IMAGINATION):

> Doubtless this could not be, but that she turns
>   Bodies to spirit by sublimation strange,
> As fire converts to fire the things it burns,
>   As we our food into our nature change.
>
> From their gross matter she abstracts their forms,
>   And draws a kind of quintessence from things;

---

1. Coleridge does not use the word *poetry* in the usual way, as a term for the class of all metrical compositions, or of all "poems," but to designate those passages, whether in verse or prose, produced by the mind of genius in its supreme moments of imaginative activity.

2. Driven with loosened reins (Latin).
3. Here Coleridge introduces the concept that the highest poetry incorporates and reconciles opposite or discordant elements. Under the names of "irony" and "paradox," this concept became a primary criterion of the American New Critics.

Which to her proper nature she transforms,
To bear them light on her celestial wings.

Thus does she, when from individual states
She doth abstract the universal kinds;
Which then reclothed in divers names and fates
Steal access through our senses to our minds.[4]

Finally, GOOD SENSE is the BODY of poetic genius, FANCY its DRAPERY,
MOTION its LIFE, and IMAGINATION the SOUL that is everywhere, and in each;
and forms all into one graceful and intelligent whole.

From *Chapter 17*

[EXAMINATION OF THE TENETS PECULIAR TO MR. WORDSWORTH]

As far then as Mr. Wordsworth in his preface contended, and most ably
contended, for a reformation in our poetic diction, as far as he has envinced
the truth of passion, and the *dramatic* propriety of those figures and metaphors in the original poets which, stripped of their justifying reasons and
converted into mere artifices of connection or ornament, constitute the characteristic falsity in the poetic style of the moderns; and as far as he has, with
equal acuteness and clearness, pointed out the process by which this change
was effected and the resemblances between that state into which the reader's
mind is thrown by the pleasurable confusion of thought from an unaccustomed train of words and images and that state which is induced by
the natural language of impassioned feeling, he undertook a useful task and
deserves all praise, both for the attempt and for the execution. The provo-
cations to this remonstrance in behalf of truth and nature were still of perpetual recurrence before and after the publication of this preface. * * *

My own differences from certain supposed parts of Mr. Wordsworth's theory ground themselves on the assumption that his words had been rightly
interpreted, as purporting that the proper diction for poetry in general consists altogether in a language taken, with due exceptions, from the mouths
of men in real life, a language which actually constitutes the natural conversation of men under the influence of natural feelings.[5] My objection is,
first, that in *any* sense this rule is applicable only to *certain* classes of poetry;
secondly, that even to these classes it is not applicable, except in such a
sense as hath never by anyone (as far as I know or have read) been denied
or doubted; and, lastly, that as far as, and in that degree in which it is
practicable, yet as a *rule* it is useless, if not injurious, and therefore either
need not or ought not to be practiced. * * *

[RUSTIC LIFE (ABOVE ALL, *LOW* AND RUSTIC LIFE) ESPECIALLY
UNFAVORABLE TO THE FORMATION OF A HUMAN DICTION—THE BEST
PARTS OF LANGUAGE THE PRODUCTS OF PHILOSOPHERS, NOT CLOWNS[6]
OR SHEPHERDS]

As little can I agree with the assertion that from the objects with which
the rustic hourly communicates the best part of language is formed. For first,

4. Adapted from John Davies's *Nosce Teipsum*
("Know Thyself"), a philosophical poem (1599).
5. Wordsworth's Preface to *Lyrical Ballads*
(1800): "A selection of the real language of men in

a state of vivid sensation. . . . Low and rustic life
was generally chosen. . . . The language, too, of
these men is adopted."
6. Rustic people.

if to communicate with an object implies such an acquaintance with it, as renders it capable of being discriminately reflected on; the distinct knowledge of an uneducated rustic would furnish a very scanty vocabulary. The few things, and modes of action, requisite for his bodily conveniences, would alone be individualized; while all the rest of nature would be expressed by a small number of confused general terms. Secondly, I deny that the words and combinations of words derived from the objects, with which the rustic is familiar, whether with distinct or confused knowledge, can be justly said to form the *best* part of language. It is more than probable that many classes of the brute creation possess discriminating sounds, by which they can convey to each other notices of such objects as concern their food, shelter, or safety. Yet we hesitate to call the aggregate of such sounds a language, otherwise than metaphorically. The best part of human language, properly so called, is derived from reflection on the acts of the mind itself. It is formed by a voluntary appropriation of fixed symbols to internal acts, to processes and results of imagination, the greater part of which have no place in the consciousness of uneducated man; though in civilized society, by imitation and passive remembrance of what they hear from their religious instructors and other superiors, the most uneducated share in the harvest which they neither sowed or reaped. * * *

[THE LANGUAGE OF MILTON AS MUCH THE LANGUAGE OF *REAL* LIFE, YEA, INCOMPARABLY MORE SO THAN THAT OF THE COTTAGER]

Here let me be permitted to remind the reader that the positions which I controvert are contained in the sentences—"a selection of the REAL language of men"; "the language of these men (i.e., men in low and rustic life) I propose to myself to imitate, and as far as possible to adopt the very language of men." "Between the language of prose and that of metrical composition there neither is, nor can be any essential difference." It is against these exclusively that my opposition is directed.

I object, in the very first instance, to an equivocation in the use of the word "real." Every man's language varies according to the extent of his knowledge, the activity of his faculties, and the depth or quickness of his feelings. Every man's language has, first, its *individualities*; secondly, the common properties of the *class* to which he belongs; and thirdly, words and phrases of *universal* use. The language of Hooker, Bacon, Bishop Taylor, and Burke differs from the common language of the learned class only by the superior number and novelty of the thoughts and relations which they had to convey. The language of Algernon Sidney[7] differs not at all from that which every well-educated gentleman would wish to write, and (with due allowances for the undeliberateness and less connected train of thinking natural and proper to conversation) such as he would wish to talk. Neither one nor the other differ half as much from the general language of cultivated society as the language of Mr. Wordsworth's homeliest composition differs from that of a common peasant. For "real" therefore we must substitute *ordinary*, or *lingua communis*.[8] And this, we have proved, is no more to be found in the phrase-

7. Republican soldier and statesmen (1622– 1683), author of *Discourses Concerning Govern-* *ment*.

8. The common language (Latin).

ology of low and rustic life than in that of any other class. Omit the peculiarities of each, and the result of course must be common to all. And assuredly the omissions and changes to be made in the language of rustics before it could be transferred to any species of poem, except the drama or other professed imitation, are at least as numerous and weighty as would be required in adapting to the same purpose the ordinary language of tradesmen and manufacturers. Not to mention that the language so highly extolled by Mr. Wordsworth varies in every county, nay, in every village, according to the accidental character of the clergyman, the existence or nonexistence of schools; or even, perhaps, as the exciseman, publican, or barber happen to be, or not to be, zealous politicians and readers of the weekly newspaper *pro bono publico*.[9] Anterior to cultivation the *lingua communis* of every country, as Dante has well observed, exists every where in parts and no where as a whole.[1]

Neither is the case rendered at all more tenable by the addition of the words "in a state of excitement."[2] For the nature of a man's words, when he is strongly affected by joy, grief, or anger, must necessarily depend on the number and quality of the general truths, conceptions, and images, and of the words expressing them, with which his mind had been previously stored. For the property of passion is not to *create,* but to set in increased activity. At least, whatever new connections of thoughts or images, or (which is equally, if not more than equally, the appropriate effect of strong excitement) whatever generalizations of truth or experience the heat of passion may produce, yet the terms of their conveyance must have pre-existed in his former conversations, and are only collected and crowded together by the unusual stimulation. It is indeed very possible to adopt in a poem the unmeaning repetitions, habitual phrases, and other blank counters which an unfurnished or confused understanding interposes at short intervals in order to keep hold of his subject which is still slipping from him, and to give him time for recollection; or in mere aid of vacancy, as in the scanty companies of a country stage the same player pops backwards and forwards, in order to prevent the appearance of empty spaces, in the procession of *Macbeth* or *Henry VIIIth.* But what assistance to the poet or ornament to the poem these can supply, I am at a loss to conjecture. Nothing assuredly can differ either in origin or in mode more widely from the apparent tautologies of intense and turbulent feeling in which the passion is greater and of longer endurance than to be exhausted or satisfied by a single representation of the image or incident exciting it. Such repetitions I admit to be a beauty of the highest kind; as illustrated by Mr. Wordsworth himself from the song of Deborah. "At her feet he bowed, he fell, he lay down; at her feet he bowed, he fell; where he bowed, there he fell down dead."[3]

1815   1817

9. For the public welfare (Latin).
1. In *De vulgari eloquentia* (On the speech of the people) Dante discusses—and affirms—the fitness for poetry of the unlocalized Italian vernacular.
2. Wordsworth: "the manner in which we associ-

ate ideas in a state of excitement."
3. Judges 5.27. Cited by Wordsworth in a note to *The Thorn* as an example of the natural tautology of "impassioned feelings."

GEORGE GORDON, LORD BYRON
1788–1824

In his *History of English Literature,* written in the late 1850s, the French critic Hippolyte Taine gave only a few condescending pages to Wordsworth, Coleridge, Percy Shelley, and Keats and then devoted a long chapter to Lord Byron, "the greatest and most English of these artists; he is so great and so English that from him alone we shall learn more truths of his country and of his age than from all the rest together." This comment reflects the fact that Byron had achieved an immense European reputation during his own lifetime, while his English contemporaries were admired only by coteries in England and America. Through much of the nineteenth century he continued to be rated as one of the greatest of English poets and the very prototype of literary Romanticism. His influence was manifested everywhere, not only among minor writers—most European poets struck Byronic attitudes—but among the major poets and novelists (Goethe in Germany, Balzac and Stendhal in France, Pushkin and Dostoevsky in Russia, and Melville in America), painters (especially Delacroix), and composers (including Beethoven and Berlioz).

These facts may surprise the reader who is aware of the recent estimate of Byron as the least consequential of the great Romantic poets, whose achievements have little in common with the distinctive innovations of Wordsworth, Coleridge, Shelley, or Keats. Only Shelley, among these writers, thought highly of either Byron or his work; while Byron spoke slightingly of all of them except Shelley and, in fact, insisted that, measured against the poetic practice of Alexander Pope, he and his contemporaries were "all in the wrong, one as much as another . . . we are upon a wrong revolutionary poetical system, or systems, not worth a damn in itself." Byron's masterpiece, *Don Juan,* is an instance of that favorite neoclassic type, a satire against modern civilization, and shares many of the aims and methods of Pope, Swift, Voltaire, and Sterne. Even Byron's lyrics are old-fashioned: many are in the eighteenth-century gentlemanly mode of witty extemporization and epigram (*Written after Swimming from Sestos to Abydos*) or continue the Cavalier tradition of the elaborate development of a compliment to a lady (*She walks in beauty* and *Stanzas for Music*).

Byron's chief claim to be considered an arch-Romantic is that he provided his age with what Taine called its "ruling personage; that is, the model that contemporaries invest with their admiration and sympathy." This personage is the "Byronic hero." He is first sketched in the opening canto of *Childe Harold,* then recurs in various guises in the verse romances and dramas that followed. In his developed form, as we find it in *Manfred,* he is an alien, mysterious, and gloomy spirit, superior in his passions and powers to the common run of humanity, whom he regards with disdain. He harbors the torturing memory of an enormous, nameless guilt that drives him toward an inevitable doom. He is in his isolation absolutely self-reliant, pursuing his own ends according to his self-generated moral code against any opposition, human or supernatural. And he exerts an attraction on other characters that is the more compelling because it involves their terror at his obliviousness to ordinary human concerns and values. This figure, infusing the archrebel in a nonpolitical form with a strong erotic interest, was imitated in life as well as in art and helped shape the intellectual and the cultural history of the later nineteenth century. The literary descendants of the Byronic hero include Heathcliff in *Wuthering Heights,* Captain Ahab in *Moby-Dick,* and the hero of Pushkin's great poem *Eugene Onegin.* Bertrand Russell, in his *History of Western Philosophy,* gives a chapter to Byron—not because he was a systematic thinker but because "Byronism," the attitude of "Titanic cosmic self-assertion," established a stance toward humanity and the world that entered nineteenth-century philosophy and eventually helped form Nietzsche's concept of the Superman, the hero who is not subject to the ordinary criteria of good and evil.

Byron's contemporaries insisted on identifying the author with his fictional characters. But Byron's letters and the testimony of his friends show that, except for recurrent moods of deep depression, his own temperament was in many respects antithetic to that of his heroes. He was passionate and willful; but when in good humor, he could be very much a man of the world in the eighteenth-century style—gregarious, tolerant, and a witty conversationalist capable of taking an ironic attitude toward his own activities as well as those of others. The aloof hauteur he exhibited in public was largely a mask to hide his diffidence when in a strange company. But although Byronism was largely a fiction, produced by a collaboration between Byron's imagination and that of his public, the fiction was historically more important than the actual person.

Byron was descended from two aristocratic families, both of them colorful, violent, and dissolute. His grandfather was an admiral nicknamed "Foulweather Jack"; his great-uncle was the fifth Baron Byron, known to his rural neighbors as the "Wicked Lord," who was tried by his peers for killing his kinsman William Chaworth in a drunken duel; his father, Captain John Byron, was a rake and fortune hunter who rapidly dissipated the patrimony of two wealthy wives. Byron's mother was a Scotswoman, Catherine Gordon of Gight, the last descendant of a line of lawless Scottish lairds. After her husband died (Byron was then three), she brought up her son in near poverty in Aberdeen, where he was indoctrinated with the Calvinistic morality of Scottish Presbyterianism. Catherine Byron was an ill-educated and extremely irascible woman who nevertheless had an abiding love for her son; they fought violently when together, but corresponded affectionately enough when apart, until her death in 1811.

When Byron was ten, the death of his great-uncle, preceded by that of more immediate heirs to the title, made him the sixth Lord Byron. In a fashion suitable to his new status he was sent to Harrow School, then to Trinity College, Cambridge. He had a deformed foot, made worse by inept surgical treatment, about which he felt acute embarrassment. His lameness made him avid for athletic prowess; he played cricket and made himself an expert boxer, fencer, and horseman and a powerful swimmer. He was also sexually precocious; when only seven, he fell in love with a little cousin, Mary Duff, and so violently that ten years later news of her marriage threw him into convulsions. Both at Cambridge and at his ancestral estate of Newstead, he engaged with more than ordinary zeal in the expensive pursuits and fashionable dissipations of a young Regency lord. As a result, despite a sizable and increasing income, he got into financial difficulties from which he did not entirely extricate himself until late in his life. In the course of his schooling he formed many close and devoted friendships, the most important with John Cam Hobhouse, a sturdy political liberal and commonsense moralist who exerted a steadying influence throughout Byron's turbulent life.

Despite his distractions at the university, Byron found time to try his hand at lyric verse, some of which was published in 1807 in a slim and conventional volume titled *Hours of Idleness*. This was treated so harshly by the pontifical *Edinburgh Review* that Byron was provoked to write in reply his first important poem, *English Bards and Scotch Reviewers*, a vigorous satire in the couplet style of the late-eighteenth-century followers of Pope, in which he incorporated brilliant but tactless ridicule (which he later came to regret) of important poetic contemporaries, including Scott, Wordsworth, and Coleridge.

After attaining his M.A. degree and his majority, Byron set out with Hobhouse in 1809 on a tour through Portugal and Spain to Malta, and then to little-known Albania, Greece, and Asia Minor. In this adventurous two-year excursion, he accumulated materials that he incorporated into many of his important poems, including his last work, *Don Juan*. The first literary product was *Childe Harold*; he wrote the opening two cantos while on the tour that the poem describes; published them in 1812 soon after his return to England; and, in his own oft-quoted phrase, "awoke one morning and found myself famous." He became the celebrity of fashionable London, and increased his literary success by a series of highly readable Near Eastern verse tales; in these the Byronic hero, in various embodiments, flaunts his misanthropy and undergoes a variety of violent and romantic adventures that current gossip attributed to the author himself. In his chronic shortage of money, Byron could well have used the huge income from these publications, but instead maintained his status as an aristocratic amateur by giving the royalties away. Occupying his inherited seat in the House of Lords, he also became briefly active on the extreme liberal side of the Whig party and spoke courageously in defense of the Nottingham weavers who had resorted to smashing the newly invented textile machines that had thrown them out of work. He also supported other liberal measures, including that of Catholic Emancipation.

Byron was extraordinarily handsome—"so beautiful a countenance," Coleridge wrote, "I scarcely ever saw . . . his eyes the open portals of the sun—things of light, and for light." Because of a constitutional tendency to obesity, however, he was able to maintain his looks only by resorting again and again to a starvation diet of biscuits, soda water, and strong cathartics. Often as a result of female initiative rather than his own, Byron entered into a sequence of liaisons with ladies of fashion. One of these, the flamboyant and eccentric young Lady Caroline Lamb, caused him so much distress by her pursuit and public tantrums that Byron turned for relief to marriage with Annabella Milbanke, who was in every way Lady Caroline's opposite, for she was naive, unworldly, intellectual (with a special passion for mathematics), and not a little priggish. This ill-starred marriage produced a daughter (Augusta Ada) and many scenes in which Byron, goaded by financial difficulties, behaved so frantically that his wife suspected his sanity; after only one year, the union ended in a legal separation. The final blow came when Lady Byron discovered her husband's incestuous relations with his half-sister, Augusta Leigh. The two had been raised apart, so that they were almost strangers when they met as adults. Byron's affection for his sister, however guilty, was genuine and endured all through his life. This affair proved a delicious morsel even to the jaded palate of the dissolute Regency society. Byron was ostracized by all but a few friends and was finally forced to leave England forever on April 25, 1816.

Byron now resumed the travels incorporated in the third and fourth cantos of *Childe Harold*. At Geneva he lived for several months in close and intellectually fruitful relation to Percy and Mary Shelley, who were accompanied by Mary's step-sister, Claire Clairmont—a misguided seventeen-year-old who had forced herself on Byron while he was still in England and who in January 1817 bore him a daughter, Allegra. In the fall of 1817 Byron established himself in Venice, where he inaugurated a period of frenzied debauchery that, he estimated, involved more than two hundred women. This period, however, was also one of great literary creativity: often working through the later hours of the night, he finished his tragedy *Manfred*; wrote the fourth canto of *Childe Harold*; and after turning out *Beppo*, a short preview of the narrative style and stanza of *Don Juan*, began the composition of *Don Juan* itself. In the colloquial ottava rima, he finally learned to write poetry as well as he had written the prose of his vivid, informative, and witty letters.

Exhausted and bored by promiscuity, Byron in 1819 settled into a placid and relatively faithful relationship with Teresa Guiccioli, the young wife of the elderly Count Alessandro Guiccioli; according to the Italian upper-class mores of the times, having contracted a marriage of convenience, she could now with propriety attach Byron to herself as a *cavaliere servente*. Through the countess's nationalistic family, the Gambas, Byron became involved in the Carbonari plot against Austrian control over northern Italy. When the Gambas were forced by the authorities to move to Pisa, Byron followed them there and, for the second time, joined the Shelleys. There grew up about them the "Pisan Circle," which in addition to the Gambas included their friends Thomas Medwin and Edward and Jane Williams, as well as the Greek nationalist leader Prince Mavrocordatos, the picturesque Irish Count Taaffe, and the flamboyant and mendacious adventurer Edward Trelawny, who seems to have stepped out of one of Byron's romances. The circle was gradually broken up, first by Shelley's anger over Byron's treatment of his daughter Allegra (Byron had sent the child to be brought up as a Catholic in an Italian convent, where she died of a fever in 1822); then by the expulsion of the Gambas, whom Byron followed to Genoa; and finally by the drowning of Shelley and Williams in July 1822.

Byron meanwhile had been steadily at work on a series of closet tragedies (including *Cain, Sardanapalus,* and *Marino Faliero*) and on his devastating satire on the life and death of George III, *The Vision of Judgment.* But increasingly he devoted himself to the continuation of *Don Juan.* He had always been diffident in his self-judgments and easily swayed by literary advice. But now, confident that he had at last found his métier, he kept on, in spite of persistent objections against the supposed immorality of the poem by the English public, by his publisher John Murray, by his friends and well-wishers, and by his extremely decorous lover, the Countess Guiccioli—by almost everyone, in fact, except the idealist Shelley, who thought *Juan* incomparably better than anything he himself could write and insisted "that every word of it is pregnant with immortality."

Byron finally broke off literature for action when he organized an expedition to assist in the Greek war for independence from the Turks. He knew too well the conditions in Greece, and had too skeptical an estimate of human nature, to entertain hope of success; but, in part because his own writings had helped to kindle European enthusiasm for the Greek cause, he now felt honor-bound to try what could be done. In the dismal, marshy town of Missolonghi he lived a Spartan existence, training troops whom he had himself subsidized and exhibiting practical grasp and a power of leadership amid a chaos of factionalism, intrigue, and military ineptitude. Worn out, he succumbed to a series of feverish attacks and died just after he had reached his thirty-sixth birthday. To this day Byron is revered by the Greek people as a national hero.

Students of Byron still feel, as his friends had felt, the magnetism of his volatile temperament. As Mary Shelley wrote six years after his death, when she read Thomas Moore's edition of his *Letters and Journals:* "The Lord Byron I find there is our Lord Byron—the fascinating—faulty—childish—philosophical being—daring the world—docile to a private circle—impetuous and indolent—gloomy and yet more gay than any other." Of his inner discordances, Byron himself was well aware; he told his friend Lady Blessington: "I am so changeable, being everything by turns and nothing long—I am such a strange *mélange* of good and evil, that it would be difficult to describe me." Yet he remained faithful to his code: a determination to tell the truth as he saw it about the world and about himself (his refusal to suppress or conceal any of his moods is in part what made him seem so contradictory) and a dedication to the freedom of nations and individuals. As he went on to say to Lady Blessington: "There are but two sentiments to which I am constant—a strong love of liberty, and a detestation of cant."

The poetry texts printed here are taken from Jerome J. McGann's edition, *Lord Byron: The Complete Poetical Works* (Oxford, 1980–93).

Written after Swimming from Sestos to Abydos[1]

May 9, 1810

I

If in the month of dark December
Leander, who was nightly wont
(What maid will not the tale remember?)
To cross thy stream, broad Hellespont!

2

5 If when the wintry tempest roared
He sped to Hero, nothing loth,
And thus of old thy current pour'd,
Fair Venus! how I pity both!

3

For *me*, degenerate modern wretch,
10 Though in the genial month of May,
My dripping limbs I faintly stretch,
And think I've done a feat to-day.

4

But since he cross'd the rapid tide,
According to the doubtful story,
15 To woo,—and—Lord knows what beside,
And swam for Love, as I for Glory;

5

'Twere hard to say who fared the best:
Sad mortals! thus the Gods still plague you!
He lost his labour, I my jest:
20 For he was drown'd, and I've the ague.

1810   1812

She walks in beauty[1]

I

She walks in beauty, like the night
Of cloudless climes and starry skies;

---

1. The Hellespont (now called the Dardanelles) is the narrow strait between Europe and Asia. In the ancient story, retold in Christopher Marlowe's *Hero and Leander,* young Leander of Abydos, on the Asian side, swam nightly to visit Hero, a priest-ess of the goddess Venus at Sestos, until he was drowned when he made the attempt in a storm. Byron and a young Lieutenant Ekenhead swam the Hellespont in the reverse direction on May 3, 1810. Byron alternated between complacency and humor in his many references to the event. In a note to the poem, he mentions that the distance was "upwards of four English miles, though the actual breadth is barely one. The rapidity of the current is such that no boat can row directly across. . . . The water was extremely cold, from the melting of the mountain snows."

1. One of the lyrics in *Hebrew Melodies* (1815), written to be set to adaptations of traditional Jew-ish tunes by the young musician Isaac Nathan. Byron wrote the lines the morning after he had met his beautiful young cousin by marriage, Mrs. Rob-ert John Wilmot, who wore a black mourning gown brightened with spangles.

And all that's best of dark and bright
   Meet in her aspect and her eyes:
5 Thus mellow'd to that tender light
   Which heaven to gaudy day denies.

2

One shade the more, one ray the less,
   Had half impair'd the nameless grace
Which waves in every raven tress,
10   Or softly lightens o'er her face;
Where thoughts serenely sweet express
   How pure, how dear their dwelling place.

3

And on that cheek, and o'er that brow,
   So soft, so calm, yet eloquent,
15 The smiles that win, the tints that glow,
   But tell of days in goodness spent,
A mind at peace with all below,
   A heart whose love is innocent!

June 1814   1815

They say that Hope is happiness

Felix qui potuit rerum cognoscere causas.[1]
                      VIRGIL

1

They say that Hope is happiness—
   But genuine Love must prize the past;
And Mem'ry wakes the thoughts that bless:
   They rose the first—they set the last.

2

5 And all that mem'ry loves the most
   Was once our only hope to be:
And all that hope adored and lost
   Hath melted into memory.

3

Alas! it is delusion all—
10   The future cheats us from afar:
Nor can we be what we recall,
   Nor dare we think on what we are.

1814   1829

1. Happy is he who has been able to learn the causes of things (Latin; *Georgics* 2.490).

When we two parted

1

When we two parted
　　In silence and tears,
Half broken-hearted
　　To sever for years,
5　Pale grew thy cheek and cold,
　　Colder thy kiss;
Truly that hour foretold
　　Sorrow to this.

2

The dew of the morning
10　Sunk chill on my brow—
It felt like the warning
　　Of what I feel now.
Thy vows are all broken,
　　And light is thy fame;
15　I hear thy name spoken,
　　And share in its shame.

3

They name thee before me,
　　A knell to mine ear;
A shudder comes o'er me—
20　Why wert thou so dear?
They know not I knew thee,
　　Who knew thee too well:—
Long, long shall I rue thee,
　　Too deeply to tell.

4

25　In secret we met—
　　In silence I grieve,
That thy heart could forget,
　　Thy spirit deceive.
If I should meet thee
30　After long years,
How should I greet thee!—
　　With silence and tears.

1815　　　　　　　　　　　　　　　　　　　　　　　　1815

Darkness[1]

I had a dream, which was not all a dream.
The bright sun was extinguish'd, and the stars

---

1. A powerfully imagined blank-verse description of the end of life on earth—a speculation hardly less common in Byron's time than in ours.

Did wander darkling[2] in the eternal space,
Rayless, and pathless, and the icy earth
5   Swung blind and blackening in the moonless air;
Morn came, and went—and came, and brought no day,
And men forgot their passions in the dread
Of this their desolation; and all hearts
Were chill'd into a selfish prayer for light:
10   And they did live by watchfires—and the thrones,
The palaces of crowned kings—the huts,
The habitations of all things which dwell,
Were burnt for beacons; cities were consumed,
And men were gathered round their blazing homes
15   To look once more into each other's face;
Happy were those who dwelt within the eye
Of the volcanos, and their mountain-torch:
A fearful hope was all the world contain'd;
Forests were set on fire—but hour by hour
20   They fell and faded—and the crackling trunks
Extinguish'd with a crash—and all was black.
The brows of men by the despairing light
Wore an unearthly aspect, as by fits
The flashes fell upon them; some lay down
25   And hid their eyes and wept; and some did rest
Their chins upon their clenched hands, and smiled;
And others hurried to and fro, and fed
Their funeral piles with fuel, and looked up
With mad disquietude on the dull sky,
30   The pall of a past world; and then again
With curses cast them down upon the dust,
And gnash'd their teeth and howl'd: the wild birds shriek'd,
And, terrified, did flutter on the ground,
And flap their useless wings; the wildest brutes
35   Came tame and tremulous; and vipers crawl'd
And twined themselves among the multitude,
Hissing, but stingless—they were slain for food:
And War, which for a moment was no more,
Did glut himself again;—a meal was bought
40   With blood, and each sate sullenly apart
Gorging himself in gloom: no love was left;
All earth was but one thought—and that was death,
Immediate and inglorious; and the pang
Of famine fed upon all entrails—men
45   Died, and their bones were tombless as their flesh;
The meagre by the meagre were devoured,
Even dogs assail'd their masters, all save one,
And he was faithful to a corse, and kept
The birds and beasts and famish'd men at bay,
50   Till hunger clung° them, or the dropping dead   *withered*
Lured their lank jaws; himself sought out no food,
But with a piteous and perpetual moan,

2. In the dark.

And a quick desolate cry, licking the hand
Which answered not with a caress—he died.
55   The crowd was famish'd by degrees; but two
Of an enormous city did survive,
And they were enemies; they met beside
The dying embers of an altar-place,
Where had been heap'd a mass of holy things
60   For an unholy usage; they raked up,
And shivering scraped with their cold skeleton hands
The feeble ashes, and their feeble breath
Blew for a little life, and made a flame
Which was a mockery; then they lifted up
65   Their eyes as it grew lighter, and beheld
Each other's aspects—saw, and shriek'd, and died—
Even of their mutual hideousness they died,
Unknowing who he was upon whose brow
Famine had written Fiend. The world was void,
70   The populous and the powerful—was a lump,
Seasonless, herbless, treeless, manless, lifeless—
A lump of death—a chaos of hard clay.
The rivers, lakes, and ocean all stood still,
And nothing stirred within their silent depths;
75   Ships sailorless lay rotting on the sea,
And their masts fell down piecemeal; as they dropp'd
They slept on the abyss without a surge—
The waves were dead; the tides were in their grave,
The moon their mistress had expired before;
80   The winds were withered in the stagnant air,
And the clouds perish'd; Darkness had no need
Of aid from them—She was the universe.

1816   1816

So, we'll go no more a roving[1]

1

So, we'll go no more a roving
So late into the night,
Though the heart be still as loving,
And the moon be still as bright.

2

5   For the sword outwears its sheath,
And the soul wears out the breast,
And the heart must pause to breathe,
And love itself have rest.

1. Composed in the Lenten aftermath of a spell of feverish dissipation in the Carnival season in Venice, and included in a letter to Thomas Moore, February 28, 1817. Byron wrote, "I find 'the sword wearing out the scabbard,' though I have but just turned the corner of twenty-nine." The poem is based on the refrain of a Scottish song, *The Jolly Beggar:* "And we'll gang nae mair a roving / Sae late into the nicht."

3

Though the night was made for loving,
10   And the day returns too soon,
Yet we'll go no more a roving
By the light of the moon.

1817   1830

When a man hath no freedom to fight for at home[1]

When a man hath no freedom to fight for at home,
Let him combat for that of his neighbors;
Let him think of the glories of Greece and of Rome,
And get knock'd on the head for his labours.

5   To do good to mankind is the chivalrous plan,
And is always as nobly requited;
Then battle for freedom wherever you can,
And, if not shot or hang'd, you'll get knighted.

Nov. 5, 1820   1830

Childe Harold's Pilgrimage

Childe Harold is a travelogue narrated by a melancholy, passionate, well-read, and very eloquent tourist. Byron wrote most of the first two cantos while on the tour through Spain, Portugal, Albania, and Greece that these cantos describe; when he published them, in 1812, they made him at one stroke the best known and most talked about poet in England. Byron took up *Childe Harold* again in 1816, during the European tour he made after the breakup of his marriage. Canto 3, published in 1816, moves through Belgium, up the Rhine, then to Switzerland and the Alps. Canto 4, published in 1818, describes the great cities and monuments of Italy.

Byron chose for his poem the Spenserian stanza, and like James Thomson (in the *Castle of Indolence*) and other eighteenth-century predecessors, he attempted in the first canto to imitate, in a seriocomic fashion, the archaic language of his Elizabethan model. (The word *Childe* itself is the ancient term for a young noble awaiting knighthood.) But he soon dropped the archaisms, and in the last two cantos he adapts Spenser's mellifluous stanza to his own assured and brassy magniloquence.

In the preface to his first two cantos, Byron had insisted that the narrator, Childe Harold, was "a fictitious character," merely "the child of imagination." In the manuscript version of these cantos, however, he had called his hero "Childe Burun," the early form of his own family name. The world insisted on identifying the character as well as the travels of the protagonist with those of the author, and in the fourth canto Byron, abandoning the third-person *dramatis persona*, spoke out frankly in the first person.

Childe Harold achieved a great European reputation, not only because of the character of its protagonist but also because of its high-pitched style, with its abrupt changes in subject, mood, and pace. Goethe applied to the poem the terms *Keckheit*,

---

1. The ironist's attitude toward gratuitous enlistment in a foreign war for national freedom—a cause to which Byron gave his own life less than four years later.

Kühnheit, und Grandiosität: "darling, dash, and grandiosity." Byron converted an accurate tourist's record of scenes, memorials, and museums into a dramatic experience in which everything is presented as it affects the violent sensibility of a new cultural phenomenon, the Romantic Man of Feeling.

From Childe Harold's Pilgrimage

A ROMAUNT[1]

From Canto 1

["SIN'S LONG LABYRINTH"]

1

Oh, thou! in Hellas deem'd of heav'nly birth,
Muse! form'd or fabled at the minstrel's will!
Since sham'd full oft by later lyres on earth,
Mine dares not call thee from thy sacred hill:
5   Yet there I've wander'd by thy vaunted rill;
Yes! sigh'd o'er Delphi's long-deserted shrine,
Where, save that feeble fountain, all is still;
Nor mote° my shell awake the weary Nine[2]   *may*
To grace so plain a tale—this lowly lay of mine.

2

10   Whilome[3] in Albion's° isle there dwelt a youth,   *England's*
Who ne in virtue's ways did take delight;
But spent his days in riot most uncouth,
And vex'd with mirth the drowsy ear of Night.
Ah, me! in sooth he was a shameless wight,
15   Sore given to revel and ungodly glee;
Few earthly things found favour in his sight
Save concubines and carnal companie,
And flaunting wassailers[4] of high and low degree.

3

Childe Harold was he hight:—but whence his name
20   And lineage long, it suits me not to say;
Suffice it, that perchance they were of fame,
And had been glorious in another day:
But one sad losel[5] soils a name for aye,
However mighty in the olden time;
25   Nor all that heralds rake from coffin'd clay,
Nor florid prose, nor honied lies of rhyme
Can blazon evil deeds, or consecrate a crime.

---

1. A romance or narrative of adventure.
2. The Muses, whose "vaunted rill" (line 5) was the Castalian spring. "Shell": lyre. Hermes is fabled to have invented the lyre by stretching strings over the hollow of a tortoise shell.
3. Once upon a time.

4. Noisy, insolent drinkers (Byron is thought to refer to his own youthful carousing with friends at Newstead Abbey).
5. Rascal. Byron's great-uncle, the fifth Lord Byron, had killed a kinsman in a drunken duel.

4

Childe Harold bask'd him in the noon-tide sun,
Disporting there like any other fly;
30 Nor deem'd before his little day was done
One blast might chill him into misery.
But long ere scarce a third of his pass'd by,
Worse than adversity the Childe befell;
He felt the fulness of satiety:
35 Then loath'd he in his native land to dwell,
Which seem'd to him more lone than Eremite's[6] sad cell.

5

For he through Sin's long labyrinth had run,
Nor made atonement when he did amiss,
Had sigh'd to many though he lov'd but one,
40 And that lov'd one, alas! could ne'er be his.
Ah, happy she! to 'scape from him whose kiss
Had been pollution unto aught so chaste;
Who soon had left her charms for vulgar bliss,
And spoil'd her goodly lands to gild his waste,
45 Nor calm domestic peace had ever deign'd to taste.

6

And now Childe Harold was sore sick at heart,
And from his fellow bacchanals would flee;
'Tis said, at times the sullen tear would start,
But Pride congeal'd the drop within his ee:°   eye
50 Apart he stalk'd in joyless reverie,
And from his native land resolv'd to go,
And visit scorching climes beyond the sea;
With pleasure drugg'd he almost long'd for woe,
And e'en for change of scene would seek the shades below.

From Canto 3

["ONCE MORE UPON THE WATERS"]

1

Is thy face like thy mother's, my fair child!
Ada![1] sole daughter of my house and heart?
When last I saw thy young blue eyes they smiled,
And then we parted,—not as now we part,
But with a hope.—
5   Awaking with a start,
The waters heave around me; and on high
The winds lift up their voices: I depart,

---

6. A religious hermit.
1. Byron's daughter Augusta Ada, born in December 1816, a month before her parents separated.

Byron's "hope" (line 5) had been for a reconciliation, but he was never to see Ada again.

Whither I know not; but the hour's gone by,
When Albion's lessening shores could grieve or glad mine eye.

2

10 Once more upon the waters! yet once more!
And the waves bound beneath me as a steed
That knows his rider. Welcome, to their roar!
Swift be their guidance, wheresoe'er it lead!
Though the strain'd mast should quiver as a reed,
15 And the rent canvas fluttering strew the gale,
Still must I on; for I am as a weed,
Flung from the rock, on Ocean's foam, to sail
Where'er the surge may sweep, the tempest's breath prevail.

3

In my youth's summer[2] I did sing of One,
20 The wandering outlaw of his own dark mind;
Again I seize the theme then but begun,
And bear it with me, as the rushing wind
Bears the cloud onwards: in that Tale I find
The furrows of long thought, and dried-up tears,
25 Which, ebbing, leave a sterile track behind,
O'er which all heavily the journeying years
Plod the last sands of life,—where not a flower appears.

4

Since my young days of passion—joy, or pain,
Perchance my heart and harp have lost a string,
30 And both may jar:[3] it may be, that in vain
I would essay as I have sung to sing.
Yet, though a dreary strain, to this I cling;
So that it wean me from the weary dream
Of selfish grief or gladness—so it fling
35 Forgetfulness around me—it shall seem
To me, though to none else, a not ungrateful theme.

5

He, who grown aged in this world of woe,
In deeds, not years, piercing the depths of life,
So that no wonder waits him; nor below
40 Can love, or sorrow, fame, ambition, strife,
Cut to his heart again with the keen knife
Of silent, sharp endurance: he can tell
Why thought seeks refuge in lone caves, yet rife
With airy images, and shapes which dwell
45 Still unimpair'd, though old, in the soul's haunted cell.

6

'Tis to create, and in creating live
A being more intense, that we endow

2. Byron wrote canto 1 at age twenty-one; he is   3. Sound discordant.
now twenty-eight.

With form our fancy, gaining as we give
The life we image, even as I do now.
50 What am I? Nothing; but not so art thou,
Soul of my thought![4] with whom I traverse earth,
Invisible but gazing, as I glow
Mix'd with thy spirit, blended with thy birth,
And feeling still with thee in my crush'd feelings' dearth.

7

55 Yet must I think less wildly:—I *have* thought
Too long and darkly, till my brain became,
In its own eddy boiling and o'erwrought,
A whirling gulf of phantasy and flame:
And thus, untaught in youth my heart to tame,
60 My springs of life were poison'd. 'Tis too late!
Yet am I chang'd; though still enough the same
In strength to bear what time can not abate,
And feed on bitter fruits without accusing Fate.

8

Something too much of this:—but now 'tis past,
65 And the spell closes with its silent seal.[5]
Long absent HAROLD re-appears at last;
He of the breast which fain no more would feel,
Wrung with the wounds which kill not, but ne'er heal;
Yet Time, who changes all, had alter'd him
70 In soul and aspect as in age: years steal
Fire from the mind as vigour from the limb;
And life's enchanted cup but sparkles near the brim.

9

His had been quaff'd too quickly, and he found
The dregs were wormwood; but he fill'd again,
75 And from a purer fount, on holier ground,
And deem'd its spring perpetual; but in vain!
Still round him clung invisibly a chain
Which gall'd for ever, fettering though unseen,
And heavy though it clank'd not; worn with pain,
80 Which pined although it spoke not, and grew keen,
Entering with every step, he took, through many a scene.

10

Secure in guarded coldness, he had mix'd
Again in fancied safety with his kind,
And deem'd his spirit now so firmly fix'd
85 And sheath'd with an invulnerable mind,
That, if no joy, no sorrow lurk'd behind;
And he, as one, might midst the many stand
Unheeded, searching through the crowd to find

4. I.e., Childe Harold, his literary creation.
5. I.e., he sets the seal of silence on his personal tale ("spell").

Fit speculation! such as in strange land
90   He found in wonder-works of God and Nature's hand.

11

But who can view the ripened rose, nor seek
To wear it? who can curiously behold
The smoothness and the sheen of beauty's cheek,
Nor feel the heart can never all grow old?
95   Who can contemplate Fame through clouds unfold
The star which rises o'er her steep, nor climb?
Harold, once more within the vortex, roll'd
On with the giddy circle, chasing Time,
Yet with a nobler aim than in his youth's fond° prime.   *foolish*

12

100   But soon he knew himself the most unfit
Of men to herd with Man; with whom he held
Little in common; untaught to submit
His thoughts to others, though his soul was quell'd
In youth by his own thoughts; still uncompell'd,
105   He would not yield dominion of his mind
To spirits against whom his own rebell'd;
Proud though in desolation; which could find
A life within itself, to breathe without mankind.

13

Where rose the mountains, there to him were friends;
110   Where roll'd the ocean, thereon was his home;
Where a blue sky, and glowing clime, extends,
He had the passion and the power to roam;
The desert, forest, cavern, breaker's foam,
Were unto him companionship; they spake
115   A mutual language, clearer than the tome
Of his land's tongue, which he would oft forsake
For Nature's pages glass'd° by sunbeams on the lake.   *made glassy*

14

Like the Chaldean,[6] he could watch the stars,
Till he had peopled them with beings bright
120   As their own beams; and earth, and earth-born jars,
And human frailties, were forgotten quite:
Could he have kept his spirit to that flight
He had been happy; but this clay will sink
Its spark immortal, envying it the light
125   To which it mounts, as if to break the link
That keeps us from yon heaven which woos us to its brink.

15

But in Man's dwellings he became a thing
Restless and worn, and stern and wearisome,

---

6. A people of ancient Babylonia, expert in astronomy.

Droop'd as a wild-born falcon with clipt wing,
130   To whom the boundless air alone were home:
    Then came his fit again, which to o'ercome,
    As eagerly the barr'd-up bird will beat
    His breast and beak against his wiry dome
    Till the blood tinge his plumage, so the heat
135 Of his impeded soul would through his bosom eat.

16

    Self-exiled Harold wanders forth again,
    With nought of hope left, but with less of gloom;
    The very knowledge that he lived in vain,
    That all was over on this side the tomb,
140   Had made Despair a smilingness assume,
    Which, though 'twere wild,—as on the plundered wreck
    When mariners would madly meet their doom
    With draughts intemperate on the sinking deck,—
Did yet inspire a cheer, which he forbore to check.

[WATERLOO]

17

145 Stop!—for thy tread is on an Empire's dust!
    An Earthquake's spoil is sepulchered below!
    Is the spot mark'd with no colossal bust?
    Nor column trophied for triumphal show?
    None; but the moral's truth tells simpler so,
150   As the ground was before, thus let it be;—
    How that red rain hath made the harvest grow!
    And is this all the world has gained by thee,
Thou first and last of fields! king-making Victory?

18

    And Harold stands upon this place of skulls,
155   The grave of France, the deadly Waterloo![7]
    How in an hour the power which gave annuls
    Its gifts, transferring fame as fleeting too!
    In "pride of place" here last the eagle flew,[8]
    Then tore with bloody talon the rent plain,
160   Pierced by the shaft of banded nations through;
    Ambition's life and labours all were vain;
He wears the shattered links of the world's broken chain.[9]

19

    Fit retribution! Gaul[1] may champ the bit
    And foam in fetters;—but is Earth more free?
165   Did nations combat to make *One* submit;

7. Napoleon's defeat at Waterloo, near Brussels, had occurred only the year before, on June 18, 1815.
8. The eagle was the standard of Napoleon. "Pride of place": from falconry, meaning the highest point of flight (cf. *Macbeth* 2.4.12).
9. Napoleon was then a prisoner at St. Helena.
1. France. Byron, like Shelley and other liberals, saw the defeat of the Napoleonic tyranny as also a victory for tyrannous kings and the forces of extreme reaction throughout Europe.

Or league to teach all kings true sovereignty?
What! shall reviving Thraldom again be
The patched-up idol of enlightened days?
Shall we, who struck the Lion down, shall we
170 Pay the Wolf homage? proffering lowly gaze
And servile knees to thrones? No; *prove*[2] before ye praise!

20

If not, o'er one fallen despot boast no more!
In vain fair cheeks were furrowed with hot tears
For Europe's flowers long rooted up before
175 The trampler of her vineyards; in vain years
Of death, depopulation, bondage, fears,
Have all been borne, and broken by the accord
Of roused-up millions: all that most endears
Glory, is when the myrtle wreathes a sword
180 Such as Harmodius drew on Athens' tyrant lord.[3]

21

There was a sound of revelry by night,[4]
And Belgium's capital had gathered then
Her Beauty and her Chivalry, and bright
The lamps shone o'er fair women and brave men;
185 A thousand hearts beat happily; and when
Music arose with its voluptuous swell,
Soft eyes look'd love to eyes which spake again,
And all went merry as a marriage-bell;
But hush! hark! a deep sound strikes like a rising knell!

22

190 Did ye not hear it?—No; 'twas but the wind,
Or the car rattling o'er the stony street;
On with the dance! let joy be unconfined;
No sleep till morn, when Youth and Pleasure meet
To chase the glowing Hours with flying feet—
195 But, hark!—that heavy sound breaks in once more,
As if the clouds its echo would repeat;
And nearer, clearer, deadlier than before!
Arm! Arm! and out—it is—the cannon's opening roar!

23

Within a windowed niche of that high hall
200 Sate Brunswick's fated chieftain;[5] he did hear
That sound the first amidst the festival,
And caught its tone with Death's prophetic ear;
And when they smiled because he deem'd it near,

---

2. Await the test (proof) of experience.
3. In 514 B.C.E. Harmodius and Aristogeiton, hiding their daggers in myrtle (symbol of love), killed Hipparchus, tyrant of Athens.
4. A famous ball, given by the duchess of Richmond on the eve of the battle of Quatre Bras,

which opened the conflict at Waterloo.
5. The duke of Brunswick, nephew of George III of England, was killed in the battle of Quatre Bras. His father, commanding the Prussian army against Napoleon, had been killed at Auerstedt in 1806 (line 205).

His heart more truly knew that peal too well
205   Which stretch'd his father on a bloody bier,
And roused the vengeance blood alone could quell:
He rush'd into the field, and, foremost fighting, fell.

24

Ah! then and there was hurrying to and fro,
And gathering tears, and tremblings of distress,
210   And cheeks all pale, which but an hour ago
Blush'd at the praise of their own loveliness;
And there were sudden partings, such as press
The life from out young hearts, and choking sighs
Which ne'er might be repeated; who could guess
215   If ever more should meet those mutual eyes,
Since upon nights so sweet such awful morn could rise?

25

And there was mounting in hot haste: the steed,
The mustering squadron, and the clattering car,
Went pouring forward in impetuous speed,
220   And swiftly forming in the ranks of war;
And the deep thunder peal on peal afar;
And near, the beat of the alarming drum
Roused up the soldier ere the morning star;
While throng'd the citizens with terror dumb,
225   Or whispering, with white lips—"The foe! They come! they come!"

26

And wild and high the "Cameron's gathering" rose!
The war-note of Lochiel,[6] which Albyn's° hills   *Scotland's*
Have heard, and heard, too, have her Saxon foes:—
How in the noon of night that pibroch[7] thrills,
230   Savage and shrill! But with the breath which fills
Their mountain-pipe, so fill the mountaineers
With the fierce native daring which instils
The stirring memory of a thousand years,
And Evan's, Donald's[8] fame rings in each clansman's ears!

27

235   And Ardennes[9] waves above them her green leaves,
Dewy with nature's tear-drops, as they pass,
Grieving, if aught inanimate e'er grieves,
Over the unreturning brave,—alas!
Ere evening to be trodden like the grass
240   Which now beneath them, but above shall grow
In its next verdure, when this fiery mass

---

6. "Cameron's gathering" is the clan song of the Camerons, whose chief was called "Lochiel," after his estate.
7. Bagpipe music, usually warlike in character.
8. Sir Evan and Donald Cameron, famous warriors in the Stuart cause in the 17th and 18th centuries.
9. A forested region covering parts of Belgium, France, and Luxembourg.

Of living valour, rolling on the foe
And burning with high hope, shall moulder cold and low.

28

Last noon beheld them full of lusty life,
245 Last eve in Beauty's circle proudly gay,
The midnight brought the signal-sound of strife,
The morn the marshalling in arms,—the day
Battle's magnificently-stern array!
The thunder-clouds close o'er it, which when rent
250 The earth is covered thick with other clay,
Which her own clay shall cover, heaped and pent,
Rider and horse,—friend, foe,—in one red burial blent!

* * *

85

Clear, placid Leman! thy contrasted lake,
With the wild world I dwelt in, is a thing
Which warns me, with its stillness, to forsake
800 Earth's troubled waters for a purer spring.
This quiet sail is as a noiseless wing
To waft me from distraction; once I loved
Torn ocean's roar, but thy soft murmuring
Sounds sweet as if a sister's voice reproved,
805 That I with stern delights should e'er have been so moved.

86

It is the hush of night, and all between
Thy margin and the mountains, dusk, yet clear,
Mellowed and mingling, yet distinctly seen,
Save darken'd Jura,[1] whose capt heights appear
810 Precipitously steep; and drawing near,
There breathes a living fragrance from the shore,
Of flowers yet fresh with childhood; on the ear
Drops the light drip of the suspended oar,
Or chirps the grasshopper one good-night carol more;

87

815 He is an evening reveller, who makes
His life an infancy, and sings his fill;
At intervals, some bird from out the brakes,°   thickets
Starts into voice a moment, then is still.
There seems a floating whisper on the hill,
820 But that is fancy, for the starlight dews
All silently their tears of love instil,
Weeping themselves away, till they infuse
Deep into Nature's breast the spirit of her hues.

88

Ye stars! which are the poetry of heaven!
825 If in your bright leaves we would read the fate

---

1. The mountain range between Switzerland and France, visible from Lake Geneva.

Of men and empires,—'tis to be forgiven,
That in our aspirations to be great,
Our destinies o'erleap their mortal state,
And claim a kindred with you; for ye are
830 A beauty and a mystery, and create
In us such love and reverence from afar,
That fortune, fame, power, life, have named themselves a star.

89

All heaven and earth are still—though not in sleep,
But breathless, as we grow when feeling most;
835 And silent, as we stand in thoughts too deep:—
All heaven and earth are still: From the high host
Of stars, to the lull'd lake and mountain-coast,
All is concentered in a life intense,
Where not a beam, nor air, nor leaf is lost,
840 But hath a part of being, and a sense
Of that which is of all Creator and defence.

90

Then stirs the feeling infinite, so felt
In solitude, where we are *least* alone;
A truth, which through our being then doth melt
845 And purifies from self: it is a tone,
The soul and source of music, which makes known
Eternal harmony, and sheds a charm,
Like to the fabled Cytherea's zone,[2]
Binding all things with beauty;—'twould disarm
850 The spectre Death, had he substantial power to harm.

91

Not vainly did the early Persian make
His altar the high places and the peak
Of earth-o'ergazing mountains, and thus take
A fit and unwall'd temple, there to seek
855 The Spirit, in whose honour shrines are weak,
Uprear'd of human hands. Come, and compare
Columns and idol-dwellings, Goth or Greek,
With Nature's realms of worship, earth and air,
Nor fix on fond abodes to circumscribe thy prayer!

92

860 The sky is changed!—and such a change! Oh night,
And storm, and darkness, ye are wondrous strong,
Yet lovely in your strength, as is the light
Of a dark eye in woman! Far along,
From peak to peak, the rattling crags among
865 Leaps the live thunder! Not from one lone cloud,
But every mountain now hath found a tongue,
And Jura answers, through her misty shroud,
Back to the joyous Alps, who call to her aloud!

---

2. The sash of Venus, which conferred the power to attract love.

93

And this is in the night:—Most glorious night!
870 Thou wert not sent for slumber! let me be
A sharer in thy fierce and far delight,—
A portion of the tempest and of thee!
How the lit lake shines, a phosphoric sea,
And the big rain comes dancing to the earth!
875 And now again 'tis black,—and now, the glee
Of the loud hills shakes with its mountain-mirth,
As if they did rejoice o'er a young earthquake's birth.

94

Now, where the swift Rhone cleaves his way between
Heights which appear as lovers who have parted
880 In hate, whose mining depths so intervene,
That they can meet no more, though broken-hearted;
Though in their souls, which thus each other thwarted,
Love was the very root of the fond rage
Which blighted their life's bloom, and then departed:—
885 Itself expired, but leaving them an age
Of years all winters,—war within themselves to wage.

95

Now, where the quick Rhone thus hath cleft his way,
The mightiest of the storms hath ta'en his stand:
For here, not one, but many, make their play,
890 And fling their thunder-bolts from hand to hand,
Flashing and cast around: of all the band,
The brightest through these parted hills hath fork'd
His lightnings,—as if he did understand,
That in such gaps as desolation work'd,
895 There the hot shaft should blast whatever therein lurk'd.

96

Sky, mountains, river, winds, lake, lightnings! ye!
With night, and clouds, and thunder, and a soul
To make these felt and feeling, well may be
Things that have made me watchful; the far roll
900 Of your departing voices, is the knoll[3]
Of what in me is sleepless,—if I rest.
But where of ye, oh tempests! is the goal?
Are ye like those within the human breast?
Or do ye find, at length, like eagles, some high nest?

97

905 Could I embody and unbosom now
That which is most within me,—could I wreak
My thoughts upon expression, and thus throw
Soul, heart, mind, passions, feelings, strong or weak,

---

3. Knell (old form).

All that I would have sought, and all I seek,
910 Bear, know, feel, and yet breathe—into *one* word,
And that one word were Lightning, I would speak;
But as it is, I live and die unheard,
With a most voiceless thought, sheathing it as a sword.

98

The morn is up again, the dewy morn,
915 With breath all incense, and with cheek all bloom,
Laughing the clouds away with playful scorn,
And living as if earth contain'd no tomb,—
And glowing into day: we may resume
The march of our existence: and thus I,
920 Still on thy shores, fair Leman! may find room
And food for meditation, nor pass by
Much, that may give us pause, if pondered fittingly.

* * *

113

I have not loved the world, nor the world me;[4]
1050 I have not flattered its rank breath, nor bow'd
To its idolatries a patient knee,—
Nor coin'd my cheek to smiles,—nor cried aloud
In worship of an echo; in the crowd
They could not deem me one of such; I stood
1055 Among them, but not of them; in a shroud
Of thoughts which were not their thoughts, and still could,
Had I not filed[5] my mind, which thus itself subdued.

114

I have not loved the world, nor the world me,—
But let us part fair foes; I do believe,
1060 Though I have found them not, that there may be
Words which are things,—hopes which will not deceive,
And virtues which are merciful, nor weave
Snares for the failing: I would also deem
O'er others' griefs that some sincerely grieve;
1065 That two, or one, are almost what they seem,—
That goodness is no name, and happiness no dream.

115

My daughter! with thy name this song begun—
My daughter! with thy name thus much shall end—
I see thee not,—I hear thee not,—but none
1070 Can be so wrapt in thee; thou art the friend
To whom the shadows of far years extend:
Albeit my brow thou never should'st behold,
My voice shall with thy future visions blend,

4. Harold utters this soliloquy as he stands at the summit of an Alpine pass, looking southward on Italy.

5. Defiled. In a note Byron refers to *Macbeth* 3.1.66 ("For Banquo's issue have I filed my mind").

And reach into thy heart,—when mine is cold,—
1075 A token and a tone, even from thy father's mould.

116

To aid thy mind's development,—to watch
Thy dawn of little joys,—to sit and see
Almost thy very growth,—to view thee catch
Knowledge of objects,—wonders yet to thee!
1080 To hold thee lightly on a gentle knee,
And print on thy soft cheek a parent's kiss,—
This, it should seem, was not reserv'd for me;
Yet this was in my nature:—as it is,
I know not what is there, yet something like to this.

117

1085 Yet, though dull Hate as duty should be taught,
I know that thou wilt love me; though my name
Should be shut from thee, as a spell still fraught
With desolation,—and a broken claim:
Though the grave closed between us,—'twere the same,
1090 I know that thou wilt love me; though to drain
My blood from out thy being, were an aim,
And an attainment,—all would be in vain,—
Still thou would'st love me, still that more than life retain.

118

The child of love,—though born in bitterness,
1095 And nurtured in convulsion,—of thy sire
These were the elements,—and thine no less.
As yet such are around thee,—but thy fire
Shall be more tempered, and thy hope far higher.
Sweet be thy cradled slumbers! O'er the sea,
1100 And from the mountains where I now respire,
Fain would I waft such blessing upon thee,
As, with a sigh, I deem thou might'st have been to me!

1812, 1816, 1818

Don Juan   Byron began his masterpiece (pronounced in the English fashion,
Don Joó-un) in July of 1818, published it in installments beginning with cantos 1 and
2 in 1819, and continued working on it almost until his death. He extemporized the
poem from episode to episode. "I *have* no plan," he said, "I *had* no plan; but I had or
have materials." The work was composed with remarkable speed (the 888 lines of
canto 13, for example, were dashed off within a week), and it aims at the effect of
improvisation rather than of artful compression; it asks to be read rapidly, at a conversational pace.

The poem breaks off with the sixteenth canto, but even in its unfinished state *Don
Juan* is the longest satirical poem, and indeed one of the longest poems of any kind,
in English. Its hero, the Spanish libertine, had in the original legend been super-

human in his sexual energy and wickedness. Throughout Byron's version the un-spoken but persistent joke is that this archetypal *homme fatal* of European legend is in fact more acted upon than active. Unfailingly amiable and well intentioned, he is guilty largely of youth, charm, and a courteous and compliant spirit. The women do all the rest.

The chief models for the poem were the Italian seriocomic versions of medieval chivalric romances; the genre had been introduced by Pulci in the fifteenth century and was adopted by Ariosto in his *Orlando Furioso* (1532). From these writers Byron caught the mixed moods and violent oscillations between the sublime and the ridiculous as well as the colloquial management of the complex ottava rima—an eight-line stanza in which the initial interlaced rhymes (*ababab*) build up to the comic turn in the final couplet (*cc*). Byron was influenced in the English use of this Italian form by a mildly amusing poem published in 1817, under the pseudonym of "Whistlecraft," by his friend John Hookham Frere. Other recognizable antecedents of *Don Juan* are Jonathan Swift's *Gulliver's Travels* and Samuel Johnson's *Rasselas*, which had employed the naive traveler as a satiric device, and Laurence Sterne's novel *Tristram Shandy*, with its comic exploitation of a narrative medium blatantly subject to the whimsy of the author. But even the most original literary works play variations on inherited conventions. Shelley at once recognized his friend's poem as "something wholly new and relative to the age."

Byron's literary advisers thought the poem unacceptably immoral, and John Murray took the precaution of printing the first two installments without identifying either Byron as the author or himself as the publisher. But Byron insisted that *Don Juan* is "a satire on abuses of the present state of society" and "the most moral of poems." And the poem is zestfully on the side of life, in its abundant variety. "As to 'Don Juan,' " Byron wrote elatedly to a friend, "confess—confess, you dog—and be candid. . . . it may be profligate—but is it not *life*, is it not *the thing?*"

The controlling element of *Don Juan* is not the narrative but the narrator, and his temperament gives the work its unity. The poem is really a continuous monologue, in the course of which a story manages to be told. It opens with the first-person pronoun and immediately lets us into the storyteller's predicament: "I want a hero. . . ." The voice then goes on, for almost two thousand stanzas, with effortless volubility and shifts of mood, using the occasion of Juan's misadventures to confide to us the speaker's thoughts and devastating judgments on the major institutions, activities, and values of Western society. The poet who in his brilliant successful youth created the gloomy and misanthropic Byronic hero, in his later and sadder life created a character (not the hero, but the narrator of *Don Juan*) who is one of the great comic inventions in English literature.

FROM DON JUAN

Fragment[1]

> I would to Heaven that I were so much Clay—
>   As I am blood—bone—marrow, passion—feeling—
> Because at least the past were past away—
>   And for the future—(but I write this reeling
> 5 Having got drunk exceedingly to day
>   So that I seem to stand upon the ceiling)

---

1. This stanza was written on the back of a page of the manuscript of canto 1. For the author's revisions while composing two stanzas of *Don Juan*, see "Poems in Process," in the appendices to this volume.

I say—the future is a serious matter—
And so—for Godsake—Hock[2] and Soda water.

From Canto 1

[JUAN AND DONNA JULIA]

1

I want a hero: an uncommon want,
    When every year and month sends forth a new one,
Till, after cloying the gazettes with cant,
    The age discovers he is not the true one;
5 Of such as these I should not care to vaunt,
    I'll therefore take our ancient friend Don Juan,
We all have seen him in the pantomime[1]
Sent to the devil, somewhat ere his time.

*   *   *

5

Brave men were living before Agamemnon[2]
    And since, exceeding valorous and sage,
35 A good deal like him too, though quite the same none;
    But then they shone not on the poet's page,
    And so have been forgotten—I condemn none,
    But can't find any in the present age
    Fit for my poem (that is, for my new one);
40 So, as I said, I'll take my friend Don Juan.

6

Most epic poets plunge in *"medias res,"*[3]
    (Horace makes this the heroic turnpike road)
And then your hero tells, whene'er you please,
    What went before—by way of episode,
45 While seated after dinner at his ease,
    Beside his mistress in some soft abode,
Palace, or garden, paradise, or cavern,
Which serves the happy couple for a tavern.

7

That is the usual method, but not mine—
50 My way is to begin with the beginning;
The regularity of my design
    Forbids all wandering as the worst of sinning,
And therefore I shall open with a line
    (Although it cost me half an hour in spinning)

---

2. A white Rhine wine, from the German *Hochheimer.*
1. The Juan legend was a popular subject in English pantomime.
2. In Homer's *Iliad,* the king commanding the Greeks in the siege of Troy. This line is translated from a Latin ode by Horace.
3. Into the middle of things (Latin; Horace's *Art of Poetry* 148).

55   Narrating somewhat of Don Juan's father,
     And also of his mother, if you'd rather.

8

In Seville was he born, a pleasant city,
    Famous for oranges and women—he
Who has not seen it will be much to pity,
60   So says the proverb—and I quite agree;
Of all the Spanish towns is none more pretty,
    Cadiz perhaps—but that you soon may see:—
Don Juan's parents lived beside the river,
A noble stream, and call'd the Guadalquivir.

9

65 His father's name was Jóse[4]—*Don*, of course,
    A true Hidalgo, free from every stain
Of Moor or Hebrew blood, he traced his source
    Through the most Gothic gentlemen of Spain;
A better cavalier ne'er mounted horse,
70   Or, being mounted, e'er got down again,
Than Jóse, who begot our hero, who
Begot—but that's to come——Well, to renew:

10

His mother was a learned lady, famed
    For every branch of every science known—
75 In every christian language ever named,
    With virtues equall'd by her wit alone,
She made the cleverest people quite ashamed,
    And even the good with inward envy groan,
Finding themselves so very much exceeded
80 In their own way by all the things that she did.

11

Her memory was a mine: she knew by heart
    All Calderon and greater part of Lopé,[5]
So that if any actor miss'd his part
    She could have served him for the prompter's copy;
85 For her Feinagle's[6] were an useless art,
    And he himself obliged to shut up shop—he
Could never make a memory so fine as
That which adorn'd the brain of Donna Inez.

12

Her favourite science was the mathematical,
90   Her noblest virtue was her magnanimity,
Her wit (she sometimes tried at wit) was Attic[7] all,

---

4. Normally "José"; Byron transferred the accent to keep his meter.
5. Calderón de la Barca and Lope de Vega, the great Spanish dramatists of the early 17th century.
6. Gregor von Feinagle, a German expert on the art of memory, who had lectured in England in 1811.
7. Athenian. *Attic salt* signifies the famed wit of the Athenians.

Her serious sayings darken'd to sublimity;
In short, in all things she was fairly what I call
A prodigy—her morning dress was dimity,
95   Her evening silk, or, in the summer, muslin,
And other stuffs, with which I won't stay puzzling.

13

She knew the Latin—that is, "the Lord's prayer,"
   And Greek—the alphabet—I'm nearly sure;
She read some French romances here and there,
100   Although her mode of speaking was not pure;
For native Spanish she had no great care,
   At least her conversation was obscure;
Her thoughts were theorems, her words a problem,
As if she deem'd that mystery would ennoble 'em.

*   *   *

22

'Tis pity learned virgins ever wed
170   With persons of no sort of education,
Or gentlemen, who, though well-born and bred,
   Grow tired of scientific conversation:
I don't choose to say much upon this head,
   I'm a plain man, and in a single station,
175 But—Oh! ye lords of ladies intellectual,
Inform us truly, have they not hen-peck'd you all?

23

Don Jóse and his lady quarrell'd—*why,*
   Not any of the many could divine,
Though several thousand people chose to try,
180   'Twas surely no concern of theirs nor mine;
I loathe that low vice curiosity,
   But if there's any thing in which I shine
'Tis in arranging all my friends' affairs.
Not having, of my own, domestic cares.

24

185 And so I interfered, and with the best
   Intentions, but their treatment was not kind;
I think the foolish people were possess'd,
   For neither of them could I ever find,
Although their porter afterwards confess'd—
190   But that's no matter, and the worst's behind,
For little Juan o'er me threw, down stairs,
A pail of housemaid's water unawares.

25

A little curly-headed, good-for-nothing,
   And mischief-making monkey from his birth;
195 His parents ne'er agreed except in doting

Upon the most unquiet imp on earth;
Instead of quarrelling, had they been but both in
   Their senses, they'd have sent young master forth
To school, or had him soundly whipp'd at home,
200   To teach him manners for the time to come.

26

Don Jóse and the Donna Inez led
   For some time an unhappy sort of life,
Wishing each other, not divorced, but dead;
   They lived respectably as man and wife,
205   Their conduct was exceedingly well-bred,
   And gave no outward signs of inward strife,
Until at length the smother'd fire broke out,
And put the business past all kind of doubt.

27

For Inez call'd some druggists and physicians,
210   And tried to prove her loving lord was *mad*,[8]
But as he had some lucid intermissions,
   She next decided he was only *bad*;
Yet when they ask'd her for her depositions,
   No sort of explanation could be had,
215   Save that her duty both to man and God
Required this conduct—which seem'd very odd.

28

She kept a journal, where his faults were noted,
   And open'd certain trunks of books and letters,
All which might, if occasion served, be quoted;
220   And then she had all Seville for abettors,
Besides her good old grandmother (who doted);
   The hearers of her case became repeaters,
Then advocates, inquisitors, and judges,
Some for amusement, others for old grudges.

29

225 And then this best and meekest woman bore
   With such serenity her husband's woes,
Just as the Spartan ladies did of yore,
   Who saw their spouses kill'd, and nobly chose
Never to say a word about them more—
230   Calmly she heard each calumny that rose,
And saw *his* agonies with such sublimity,
That all the world exclaim'd "What magnanimity!"

*   *   *

8. Lady Byron had thought her husband might be insane and sought medical advice on the matter. This and other passages obviously allude to his wife, although Byron insisted that Donna Inez was not intended to be a caricature of Lady Byron.

32

Their friends had tried at reconciliation,
250   Then their relations, who made matters worse;
('Twere hard to say upon a like occasion
    To whom it may be best to have recourse—
I can't say much for friend or yet relation):
    The lawyers did their utmost for divorce,
255 But scarce a fee was paid on either side
Before, unluckily, Don Jóse died.

33

He died: and most unluckily, because,
    According to all hints I could collect
From counsel learned in those kinds of laws,
260   (Although their talk's obscure and circumspect)
His death contrived to spoil a charming cause;
    A thousand pities also with respect
To public feeling, which on this occasion
Was manifested in a great sensation.

*   *   *

37

Dying intestate, Juan was sole heir
290   To a chancery suit, and messuages,[9] and lands,
Which, with a long minority and care,
    Promised to turn out well in proper hands:
Inez became sole guardian, which was fair,
    And answer'd but to nature's just demands;
295 An only son left with an only mother
Is brought up much more wisely than another.

38

Sagest of women, even of widows, she
    Resolved that Juan should be quite a paragon,
And worthy of the noblest pedigree:
300   (His sire was of Castile, his dam from Arragon).
Then for accomplishments of chivalry,
    In case our lord the king should go to war again,
He learn'd the arts of riding, fencing, gunnery,
And how to scale a fortress—or a nunnery.

39

305 But that which Donna Inez most desired,
    And saw into herself each day before all
The learned tutors whom for him she hired,
    Was, that his breeding should be strictly moral;
Much into all his studies she inquired,
310   And so they were submitted first to her, all,

---

9. Houses and the adjoining lands. "Chancery suit": a case in what was then the highest English court, notorious for its delays.

Arts, sciences, no branch was made a mystery
To Juan's eyes, excepting natural history.[1]

40

The languages, especially the dead,
   The sciences, and most of all the abstruse,
315 The arts, at least all such as could be said
   To be the most remote from common use,
In all these he was much and deeply read;
   But not a page of anything that's loose,
Or hints continuation of the species,
320 Was ever suffer'd, lest he should grow vicious.

41

His classic studies made a little puzzle,
   Because of filthy loves of gods and goddesses,
Who in the earlier ages made a bustle,
   But never put on pantaloons or boddices;
325 His reverend tutors had at times a tussle,
   And for their Aeneids, Iliads, and Odysseys,
Were forced to make an odd sort of apology,
For Donna Inez dreaded the mythology.

42

Ovid's a rake, as half his verses show him,
330   Anacreon's morals are a still worse sample,
Catullus scarcely has a decent poem,
   I don't think Sappho's Ode a good example,
Although Longinus[2] tells us there is no hymn
   Where the sublime soars forth on wings more ample;
335 But Virgil's songs are pure, except that horrid one
Beginning with *"Formosum Pastor Corydon."*[3]

43

Lucretius' irreligion[4] is too strong
   For early stomachs, to prove wholesome food;
I can't help thinking Juvenal[5] was wrong,
340   Although no doubt his real intent was good,
For speaking out so plainly in his song,
   So much indeed as to be downright rude;
And then what proper person can be partial
To all those nauseous epigrams of Martial?

44

345 Juan was taught from out the best edition,
   Expurgated by learned men, who place,

1. Includes biology and physiology.
2. The Greek rhetorician Longinus praises a passage from Sappho in *On the Sublime* 10.
3. Virgil's *Eclogue* 2 begins: "The shepherd, Corydon, burned with love for the handsome Alexis."

4. In *De rerum natura* (On the nature of things) Lucretius sets out to show that the universe can be explained without reference to any god.
5. The Latin satires of Juvenal attacked the corruption of Roman society in the 1st century C.E.

Judiciously, from out the schoolboy's vision,
    The grosser parts; but fearful to deface
Too much their modest bard by this omission,
350   And pitying sore his mutilated case,
They only add them all in an appendix,[6]
Which saves, in fact, the trouble of an index.

*   *   *

52

For my part I say nothing—nothing—but
410   *This* I will say—my reasons are my own—
That if I had an only son to put
    To school (as God be praised that I have none)
'Tis not with Donna Inez I would shut
    Him up to learn his catechism alone,
415   No—No—I'd send him out betimes to college,
For there it was I pick'd up my own knowledge.

53

For there one learns—'tis not for me to boast,
    Though I acquired—but I pass over *that,*
As well as all the Greek I since have lost:
420   I say that there's the place—but *"Verbum sat,"*[7]
I think I pick'd up too, as well as most,
    Knowledge of matters—but no matter *what*—
I never married—but, I think, I know
That sons should not be educated so.

54

425   Young Juan now was sixteen years of age,
    Tall, handsome, slender, but well knit; he seem'd
Active, though not so sprightly, as a page;
    And every body but his mother deem'd
Him almost man; but she flew in a rage,
430   And bit her lips (for else she might have scream'd),
If any said so, for to be precocious
Was in her eyes a thing the most atrocious.

55

Amongst her numerous acquaintance, all
    Selected for discretion and devotion,
435   There was the Donna Julia, whom to call
    Pretty were but to give a feeble notion
Of many charms in her as natural
    As sweetness to the flower, or salt to ocean,
Her zone° to Venus, or his bow to Cupid,   *belt, sash*
440   (But this last simile is trite and stupid).

---

6. Fact! There is, or was, such an edition, with all the obnoxious epigrams of Martial placed by themselves at the end [Byron's note].
7. A word [to the wise] is sufficient (Latin).

56

The darkness of her Oriental eye
    Accorded with her Moorish origin;
(Her blood was not all Spanish, by the by;
    In Spain, you know, this is a sort of sin).
445 When proud Grenada fell, and, forced to fly,
    Boabdil wept,[8] of Donna Julia's kin
Some went to Africa, some staid in Spain,
Her great great grandmamma chose to remain.

57

She married (I forget the pedigree)
450   With an Hidalgo,[9] who transmitted down
His blood less noble than such blood should be;
    At such alliances his sires would frown,
In that point so precise in each degree
    That they bred *in and in,* as might be shown,
455 Marrying their cousins—nay, their aunts and nieces,
Which always spoils the breed, if it increases.

58

This heathenish cross restored the breed again,
    Ruin'd its blood, but much improved its flesh;
For, from a root the ugliest in Old Spain
460   Sprung up a branch as beautiful as fresh;
The sons no more were short, the daughters plain:
    But there's a rumour which I fain would hush,
'Tis said that Donna Julia's grandmamma
Produced her Don more heirs at love than law.

59

465 However this might be, the race went on
    Improving still through every generation,
Until it center'd in an only son,
    Who left an only daughter; my narration
May have suggested that this single one
470   Could be but Julia (whom on this occasion
I shall have much to speak about), and she
Was married, charming, chaste,[1] and twenty-three.

60

Her eye (I'm very fond of handsome eyes)
    Was large and dark, suppressing half its fire
475 Until she spoke, then through its soft disguise
    Flash'd an expression more of pride than ire,
And love than either; and there would arise
    A something in them which was not desire,

---

8. The last Moorish king of Granada (then a province in Spain) wept when his capital fell to the Spaniards (1492).

9. A Spanish nobleman of the lower class.
1. I.e., faithful to her husband.

But would have been, perhaps, but for the soul
480 Which struggled through and chasten'd down the whole.

61

Her glossy hair was cluster'd o'er a brow
    Bright with intelligence, and fair and smooth;
Her eyebrow's shape was like the aerial bow,
    Her cheek all purple with the beam of youth,
485 Mounting, at times, to a transparent glow,
    As if her veins ran lightning; she, in sooth,
Possess'd an air and grace by no means common:
Her stature tall—I hate a dumpy woman.

62

Wedded she was some years, and to a man
490   Of fifty, and such husbands are in plenty;
And yet, I think, instead of such a ONE
    'Twere better to have TWO of five and twenty,
Especially in countries near the sun:
    And now I think on't, "mi vien in mente,"[2]
495 Ladies even of the most uneasy virtue
Prefer a spouse whose age is short of thirty.

63

'Tis a sad thing, I cannot choose but say,
    And all the fault of that indecent sun,
Who cannot leave alone our helpless clay,
500   But will keep baking, broiling, burning on,
    That howsoever people fast and pray
    The flesh is frail, and so the soul undone:
What men call gallantry, and gods adultery,
Is much more common where the climate's sultry.

64

505 Happy the nations of the moral north!
    Where all is virtue, and the winter season
Sends sin, without a rag on, shivering forth;
    ('Twas snow that brought St. Francis back to reason);
Where juries cast up what a wife is worth
510   By laying whate'er sum, in mulct,[3] they please on
The lover, who must pay a handsome price,
Because it is a marketable vice.

65

Alfonso was the name of Julia's lord,
    A man well looking for his years, and who
515 Was neither much beloved, nor yet abhorr'd;
    They lived together as most people do,
Suffering each other's foibles by accord,

---

2. It comes to my mind (Italian).   3. By way of a fine or legal penalty.

And not exactly either *one* or *two;*
Yet he was jealous, though he did not show it,
520 For jealousy dislikes the world to know it.

* * *

69

545 Juan she saw, and, as a pretty child,
    Caress'd him often, such a thing might be
Quite innocently done, and harmless styled,
    When she had twenty years, and thirteen he;
But I am not so sure I should have smiled
550   When he was sixteen, Julia twenty-three,
These few short years make wondrous alterations,
Particularly amongst sun-burnt nations.

70

Whate'er the cause might be, they had become
    Changed; for the dame grew distant, the youth shy,
555 Their looks cast down, their greetings almost dumb,
    And much embarrassment in either eye;
There surely will be little doubt with some
    That Donna Julia knew the reason why,
But as for Juan, he had no more notion
560 Than he who never saw the sea of ocean.

71

Yet Julia's very coldness still was kind,
    And tremulously gentle her small hand
Withdrew itself from his, but left behind
    A little pressure, thrilling, and so bland
565 And slight, so very slight, that to the mind
    'Twas but a doubt; but ne'er magician's wand
Wrought change with all Armida's[4] fairy art
Like what this light touch left on Juan's heart.

72

And if she met him, though she smiled no more,
570   She look'd a sadness sweeter than her smile,
As if her heart had deeper thoughts in store
    She must not own, but cherish'd more the while,
For that compression in its burning core;
    Even innocence itself has many a wile,
575 And will not dare to trust itself with truth,
And love is taught hypocrisy from youth.

* * *

75

Poor Julia's heart was in an awkward state;
    She felt it going, and resolved to make

4. The sorceress who seduces Rinaldo in Torquato Tasso's *Jerusalem Delivered.*

595   The noblest efforts for herself and mate,
      For honour's, pride's, religion's, virtue's sake;
    Her resolutions were most truly great,
      And almost might have made a Tarquin[5] quake;
    She pray'd the Virgin Mary for her grace,
600   As being the best judge of a lady's case.

76

    She vow'd she never would see Juan more,
      And next day paid a visit to his mother,
    And look'd extremely at the opening door,
      Which, by the Virgin's grace, let in another;
605   Grateful she was, and yet a little sore—
      Again it opens, it can be no other,
    'Tis surely Juan now—No! I'm afraid
    That night the Virgin was no further pray'd.

77

    She now determined that a virtuous woman
610   Should rather face and overcome temptation,
    That flight was base and dastardly, and no man
      Should ever give her heart the least sensation;
    That is to say, a thought beyond the common
      Preference, that we must feel upon occasion,
615   For people who are pleasanter than others,
    But then they only seem so many brothers.

78

    And even if by chance—and who can tell?
      The devil's so very sly—she should discover
    That all within was not so very well,
620   And, if still free, that such or such a lover
    Might please perhaps, a virtuous wife can quell
      Such thoughts, and be the better when they're over;
    And if the man should ask, 'tis but denial:
    I recommend young ladies to make trial.

79

625   And then there are such things as love divine,
      Bright and immaculate, unmix'd and pure,
    Such as the angels think so very fine,
      And matrons, who would be no less secure,
    Platonic, perfect, "just such love as mine":
630   Thus Julia said—and thought so, to be sure,
    And so I'd have her think, were I the man
    On whom her reveries celestial ran.

*   *   *

---

5. A member of a legendary family of Roman kings noted for tyranny and cruelty; perhaps a reference specifically to Lucius Tarquinus, the villain of Shakespeare's *The Rape of Lucrece*.

86

So much for Julia. Now we'll turn to Juan,
    Poor little fellow! he had no idea
Of his own case, and never hit the true one;
    In feelings quick as Ovid's Miss Medea,[6]
685 He puzzled over what he found a new one,
    But not as yet imagined it could be a
Thing quite in course, and not at all alarming,
Which, with a little patience, might grow charming.

*　*　*

90

Young Juan wander'd by the glassy brooks
    Thinking unutterable things; he threw
715 Himself at length within the leafy nooks
    Where the wild branch of the cork forest grew;
There poets find materials for their books,
    And every now and then we read them through,
So that their plan and prosody are eligible,
720 Unless, like Wordsworth, they prove unintelligible.

91

He, Juan (and not Wordsworth), so pursued
    His self-communion with his own high soul,
Until his mighty heart, in its great mood,
    Had mitigated part, though not the whole
725 Of its disease; he did the best he could
    With things not very subject to control,
And turn'd, without perceiving his condition,
Like Coleridge, into a metaphysician.

92

He thought about himself, and the whole earth,
730   Of man the wonderful, and of the stars,
And how the deuce they ever could have birth;
    And then he thought of earthquakes, and of wars,
How many miles the moon might have in girth,
    Of air-balloons, and of the many bars
735 To perfect knowledge of the boundless skies;
And then he thought of Donna Julia's eyes.

93

In thoughts like these true wisdom may discern
    Longings sublime, and aspirations high,
Which some are born with, but the most part learn
740   To plague themselves withal, they know not why:
'Twas strange that one so young should thus concern
    His brain about the action of the sky;
If *you* think 'twas philosophy that this did,
I can't help thinking puberty assisted.

6. In *Metamorphoses* 7 Ovid tells the story of Medea's mad infatuation for Jason.

94

745 He pored upon the leaves, and on the flowers,
    And heard a voice in all the winds; and then
He thought of wood nymphs and immortal bowers,
    And how the goddesses came down to men:
He miss'd the pathway, he forgot the hours,
750   And when he look'd upon his watch again,
He found how much old Time had been a winner—
He also found that he had lost his dinner.

* * *

103

'Twas on a summer's day—the sixth of June:—
    I like to be particular in dates,
Not only of the age, and year, but moon;
820   They are a sort of post-house, where the Fates
Change horses, making history change its tune,
    Then spur away o'er empires and o'er states,
Leaving at last not much besides chronology,
Excepting the post-obits[7] of theology.

104

825 'Twas on the sixth of June, about the hour
    Of half-past six—perhaps still nearer seven,
When Julia sate within as pretty a bower
    As e'er held houri in that heathenish heaven
Described by Mahomet, and Anacreon Moore,[8]
830   To whom the lyre and laurels have been given,
With all the trophies of triumphant song—
He won them well, and may he wear them long!

105

She sate, but not alone; I know not well
    How this same interview had taken place,
835 And even if I knew, I should not tell—
    People should hold their tongues in any case;
No matter how or why the thing befell,
    But there were she and Juan, face to face—
When two such faces are so, 'twould be wise,
840 But very difficult, to shut their eyes.

106

How beautiful she look'd! her conscious[9] heart
    Glow'd in her cheek, and yet she felt no wrong.
Oh Love! how perfect is thy mystic art,
    Strengthening the weak, and trampling on the strong,

---

7. I.e., postobit bonds (*post obitum*, "after death" [Latin]): loans to an heir that fall due after the death of the person whose estate he or she is to inherit. Byron's meaning is probably that only theology purports to tell us what rewards are due in heaven.

8. Byron's friend the poet Thomas Moore, who had translated the *Odes* of Anacreon. Byron is alluding to the tale of *Paradise and the Peri* in Moore's Oriental poem *Lalla Rookh*.
9. Inwardly aware (of her feelings).

845 How self-deceitful is the sagest part
  Of mortals whom thy lure hath led along—
The precipice she stood on was immense,
  So was her creed° in her own innocence.   *belief*

107

She thought of her own strength, and Juan's youth,
850   And of the folly of all prudish fears,
Victorious virtue, and domestic truth,
  And then of Don Alfonso's fifty years:
I wish these last had not occurr'd, in sooth,
  Because that number rarely much endears,
855 And through all climes, the snowy and the sunny,
Sounds ill in love, whate'er it may in money.

*   *   *

113

The sun set, and up rose the yellow moon:
  The devil's in the moon for mischief; they
Who call'd her CHASTE, methinks, began too soon
900   Their nomenclature; there is not a day,
The longest, not the twenty-first of June,
  Sees half the business in a wicked way
On which three single hours of moonshine smile—
And then she looks so modest all the while.

114

905 There is a dangerous silence in that hour,
  A stillness, which leaves room for the full soul
To open all itself, without the power
  Of calling wholly back its self-control;
The silver light which, hallowing tree and tower,
910   Sheds beauty and deep softness o'er the whole,
Breathes also to the heart, and o'er it throws
A loving languor, which is not repose.

115

And Julia sate with Juan, half embraced
  And half retiring from the glowing arm,
915 Which trembled like the bosom where 'twas placed;
  Yet still she must have thought there was no harm,
Or else 'twere easy to withdraw her waist;
  But then the situation had its charm,
And then—God knows what next—I can't go on;
920 I'm almost sorry that I e'er begun.

116

Oh Plato! Plato! you have paved the way,
  With your confounded fantasies, to more
Immoral conduct by the fancied sway
  Your system feigns o'er the controlless core

925　　Of human hearts, than all the long array
　　　　　Of poets and romancers:—You're a bore,
　　　A charlatan, a coxcomb—and have been,
　　　At best, no better than a go-between.

117

　　　And Julia's voice was lost, except in sighs,
930　　　Until too late for useful conversation;
　　　The tears were gushing from her gentle eyes,
　　　　　I wish, indeed, they had not had occasion,
　　　But who, alas! can love, and then be wise?
　　　　　Not that remorse did not oppose temptation,
935　　A little still she strove, and much repented,
　　　And whispering "I will ne'er consent"—consented.

*　　*　　*

126

　　　'Tis sweet to win, no matter how, one's laurels
　　　　　By blood or ink; 'tis sweet to put an end
　　　To strife; 'tis sometimes sweet to have our quarrels,
　　　　　Particularly with a tiresome friend;
1005　Sweet is old wine in bottles, ale in barrels;
　　　　　Dear is the helpless creature we defend
　　　Against the world; and dear the schoolboy spot
　　　We ne'er forget, though there we are forgot.

127

　　　But sweeter still than this, than these, than all,
1010　　　Is first and passionate love—it stands alone,
　　　Like Adam's recollection of his fall;
　　　　　The tree of knowledge has been pluck'd—all's known—
　　　And life yields nothing further to recall
　　　　　Worthy of this ambrosial sin, so shown,
1015　No doubt in fable, as the unforgiven
　　　Fire which Prometheus[1] filch'd for us from heaven.

*　　*　　*

133

　　　Man's a phenomenon, one knows not what,
　　　　　And wonderful beyond all wondrous measure;
　　　'Tis pity though, in this sublime world, that
1060　　　Pleasure's a sin, and sometimes sin's a pleasure;
　　　Few mortals know what end they would be at,
　　　　　But whether glory, power, or love, or treasure,
　　　The path is through perplexing ways, and when
　　　The goal is gain'd, we die, you know—and then—

134

1065　What then?—I do not know, no more do you—
　　　　　And so good night.—Return we to our story:

---

1. The Titan Prometheus incurred the wrath of Zeus by stealing fire from heaven for humans.

'Twas in November, when fine days are few,
   And the far mountains wax a little hoary,
And clap a white cape on their mantles blue;
1070   And the sea dashes round the promontory,
And the loud breaker boils against the rock,
And sober suns must set at five o'clock.

135

'Twas, as the watchmen say, a cloudy night;
   No moon, no stars, the wind was low or loud
1075 By gusts, and many a sparkling hearth was bright
   With the piled wood, round which the family crowd;
There's something cheerful in that sort of light,
   Even as a summer sky's without a cloud:
I'm fond of fire, and crickets, and all that,
1080 A lobster-salad, and champagne, and chat.

136

'Twas midnight—Donna Julia was in bed,
   Sleeping, most probably—when at her door
Arose a clatter might awake the dead,
   If they had never been awoke before,
1085 And that they have been so we all have read,
   And are to be so, at the least, once more—
The door was fasten'd, but with voice and fist
First knocks were heard, then "Madam—Madam—hist!

137

"For God's sake, Madam—Madam—here's my master,
1090   With more than half the city at his back—
Was ever heard of such a curst disaster!
   'Tis not my fault—I kept good watch—Alack!
Do, pray undo the bolt a little faster—
   They're on the stair just now, and in a crack
1095 Will all be here; perhaps he yet may fly—
Surely the window's not so *very* high!"

138

By this time Don Alfonso was arrived,
   With torches, friends, and servants in great number;
The major part of them had long been wived,
1100   And therefore paused not to disturb the slumber
Of any wicked woman, who contrived
   By stealth her husband's temples to encumber:[2]
Examples of this kind are so contagious,
Were one not punish'd, all would be outrageous.

139

1105 I can't tell how, or why, or what suspicion
   Could enter into Don Alfonso's head;

---

2. Horns growing on the forehead were the traditional emblem of the cuckolded husband.

But for a cavalier of his condition°   rank
    It surely was exceedingly ill-bred
Without a word of previous admonition,
1110   To hold a levee³ round his lady's bed,
And summon lackeys, arm'd with fire and sword,
To prove himself the thing he most abhorr'd.

140

Poor Donna Julia! starting as from sleep,
    (Mind—that I do not say—she had not slept)
1115 Began at once to scream, and yawn, and weep;
    Her maid Antonia, who was an adept,
Contrived to fling the bed-clothes in a heap,
    As if she had just now from out them crept:
I can't tell why she should take all this trouble
1120 To prove her mistress had been sleeping double.

141

But Julia mistress, and Antonia maid,
    Appear'd like two poor harmless women, who
Of goblins, but still more of men afraid,
    Had thought one man might be deterr'd by two,
1125 And therefore side by side were gently laid,
    Until the hours of absence should run through,
And truant husband should return, and say,
"My dear, I was the first who came away."

142

Now Julia found at length a voice, and cried,
1130   "In heaven's name, Don Alfonso, what d'ye mean?
Has madness seized you? would that I had died
    Ere such a monster's victim I had been!
What may this midnight violence betide,
    A sudden fit of drunkenness or spleen?
1135 Dare you suspect me, whom the thought would kill?
Search, then, the room!"—Alfonso said, "I will."

143

He search'd, *they* search'd, and rummaged every where,
    Closet and clothes'-press, chest and window-seat,
And found much linen, lace, and seven pair
1140   Of stockings, slippers, brushes, combs, complete,
With other articles of ladies fair,
    To keep them beautiful, or leave them neat:
Arras⁴ they prick'd and curtains with their swords,
And wounded several shutters, and some boards.

144

1145 Under the bed they search'd, and there they found—
    No matter what—it was not that they sought;

---

3. Morning reception.   4. A tapestry hanging on a wall.

They open'd windows, gazing if the ground
    Had signs or footmarks, but the earth said nought;
And then they stared each others' faces round:
1150   'Tis odd, not one of all these seekers thought,
And seems to me almost a sort of blunder,
Of looking *in* the bed as well as under.

145

During this inquisition Julia's tongue
    Was not asleep—"Yes, search and search," she cried,
1155 "Insult on insult heap, and wrong on wrong!
    It was for this that I became a bride!
For this in silence I have suffer'd long
    A husband like Alfonso at my side;
But now I'll bear no more, nor here remain,
1160 If there be law, or lawyers, in all Spain.

146

"Yes, Don Alfonso! husband now no more,
    If ever you indeed deserved the name,
Is't worthy of your years?—you have threescore,
    Fifty, or sixty—it is all the same—
1165 Is't wise or fitting causeless to explore
    For facts against a virtuous woman's fame?
Ungrateful, perjured, barbarous Don Alfonso,
How dare you think your lady would go on so?"

*   *   *

159

1265 The Senhor Don Alfonso stood confused;
    Antonia bustled round the ransack'd room,
And, turning up her nose, with looks abused
    Her master, and his myrmidons, of whom
Not one, except the attorney, was amused;
1270 He, like Achates,[5] faithful to the tomb,
So there were quarrels, cared not for the cause,
Knowing they must be settled by the laws.

160

With prying snub-nose, and small eyes, he stood,
    Following Antonia's motions here and there,
1275 With much suspicion in his attitude;
    For reputations he had little care;
So that a suit or action were made good,
    Small pity had he for the young and fair,
And ne'er believed in negatives, till these
1280 Were proved by competent false witnesses.

161

But Don Alfonso stood with downcast looks,
    And, truth to say, he made a foolish figure;

5. The *fidus Achates* ("faithful Achates") of Virgil's *Aeneid*, whose loyalty to Aeneas has become proverbial.

When, after searching in five hundred nooks,
   And treating a young wife with so much rigour,
1285 He gain'd no point, except some self-rebukes,
   Added to those his lady with such vigour
Had pour'd upon him for the last half-hour,
   Quick, thick, and heavy—as a thunder-shower.

162

At first he tried to hammer an excuse,
1290   To which the sole reply was tears, and sobs,
And indications of hysterics, whose
   Prologue is always certain throes, and throbs,
Gasps, and whatever else the owners choose:—
   Alfonso saw his wife, and thought of Job's;[6]
1295 He saw too, in perspective, her relations,
   And then he tried to muster all his patience.

163

He stood in act to speak, or rather stammer,
   But sage Antonia cut him short before
The anvil of his speech received the hammer,
1300   With "Pray sir, leave the room, and say no more,
Or madam dies."—Alfonso mutter'd "D—n her,"
   But nothing else, the time of words was o'er;
He cast a rueful look or two, and did,
   He knew not wherefore, that which he was bid.

164

1305 With him retired his *"posse comitatus,"*[7]
   The attorney last, who linger'd near the door,
Reluctantly, still tarrying there as late as
   Antonia let him—not a little sore
At this most strange and unexplain'd *"hiatus"*
1310   In Don Alfonso's facts, which just now wore
An awkward look; as he resolved the case
   The door was fasten'd in his legal face.

165

No sooner was it bolted, than—Oh shame!
   Oh sin! Oh sorrow! and Oh womankind!
1315 How can you do such things and keep your fame,
   Unless this world, and t'other too, be blind?
Nothing so dear as an unfilch'd good name!
   But to proceed—for there is more behind:
With much heart-felt reluctance be it said,
1320 Young Juan slipp'd, half-smother'd, from the bed.

---

6. Job's wife had advised her afflicted husband to "curse God, and die" (Job 2.9).
7. The complete form of the modern word *posse* (*posse comitatus* means literally "power of the county" [Latin], i.e., the body of citizens summoned by a sheriff to preserve order in the county).

166

He had been hid—I don't pretend to say
   How, nor can I indeed describe the where—
Young, slender, and pack'd easily, he lay,
   No doubt, in little compass, round or square;
1325 But pity him I neither must nor may
   His suffocation by that pretty pair;
'Twere better, sure, to die so, than be shut
With maudlin Clarence in his Malmsey butt.[8]

*   *   *

169

1345 What's to be done? Alfonso will be back
   The moment he has sent his fools away.
Antonia's skill was put upon the rack,
   But no device could be brought into play—
And how to parry the renew'd attack?
1350   Besides, it wanted but few hours of day:
Antonia puzzled; Julia did not speak,
But press'd her bloodless lip to Juan's cheek.

170

He turn'd his lip to hers, and with his hand
   Call'd back the tangles of her wandering hair;
1355 Even then their love they could not all command,
   And half forgot their danger and despair:
Antonia's patience now was at a stand—
   "Come, come, 'tis no time now for fooling there,"
She whisper'd, in great wrath—"I must deposit
1360 This pretty gentleman within the closet."

*   *   *

173

Now, Don Alfonso entering, but alone,
   Closed the oration of the trusty maid:
She loiter'd, and he told her to be gone,
1380   An order somewhat sullenly obey'd;
However, present remedy was none,
   And no great good seem'd answer'd if she staid:
Regarding both with slow and sidelong view,
She snuff'd the candle, curtsied, and withdrew.

174

1385 Alfonso paused a minute—then begun
   Some strange excuses for his late proceeding;
He would not justify what he had done,
   To say the best, it was extreme ill-breeding;
But there were ample reasons for it, none
1390   Of which he specified in this his pleading:

---

8. Clarence, brother of Edward IV and of the future Richard III, was reputed to have been assassinated by being drowned in a cask ("butt") of malmsey, a sweet and aromatic wine.

His speech was a fine sample, on the whole,
    Of rhetoric, which the learn'd call *"rigmarole."*[9]

*   *   *

180

Alfonso closed his speech, and begg'd her pardon,
    Which Julia half withheld, and then half granted,
1435 And laid conditions, he thought, very hard on,
    Denying several little things he wanted:
He stood like Adam lingering near his garden,
    With useless penitence perplex'd and haunted,
Beseeching she no further would refuse,
1440 When lo! he stumbled o'er a pair of shoes.

181

A pair of shoes!—what then? not much, if they
    Are such as fit with lady's feet, but these
(No one can tell how much I grieve to say)
    Were masculine; to see them, and to seize,
1445 Was but a moment's act.—Ah! Well-a-day!
    My teeth begin to chatter, my veins freeze—
Alfonso first examined well their fashion,
And then flew out into another passion.

182

He left the room for his relinquish'd sword,
1450   And Julia instant to the closet flew,
"Fly, Juan, fly! for heaven's sake—not a word—
    The door is open—you may yet slip through
The passage you so often have explored—
    Here is the garden-key—Fly—fly—Adieu!
1455 Haste—haste!—I hear Alfonso's hurrying feet—
Day has not broke—there's no one in the street."

183

None can say that this was not good advice,
    The only mischief was, it came too late;
Of all experience 'tis the usual price,
1460   A sort of income-tax laid on by fate:
Juan had reach'd the room-door in a trice,
    And might have done so by the garden-gate,
But met Alfonso in his dressing-gown,
Who threaten'd death—so Juan knock'd him down.

184

1465 Dire was the scuffle, and out went the light,
    Antonia cried out "Rape!" and Julia "Fire!"
But not a servant stirr'd to aid the fight.
    Alfonso, pommell'd to his heart's desire,

---

9. Illogical sequence of vague statements.

Swore lustily he'd be revenged this night;
1470   And Juan, too, blasphemed an octave higher,
His blood was up; though young, he was a Tartar,[1]
And not at all disposed to prove a martyr.

185

Alfonso's sword had dropp'd ere he could draw it,
And they continued battling hand to hand,
1475   For Juan very luckily ne'er saw it;
His temper not being under great command,
If at that moment he had chanced to claw it,
Alfonso's days had not been in the land
Much longer.—Think of husbands', lovers' lives!
1480   And how ye may be doubly widows—wives!

186

Alfonso grappled to detain the foe,
And Juan throttled him to get away,
And blood ('twas from the nose) began to flow;
At last, as they more faintly wrestling lay,
1485   Juan contrived to give an awkward blow,
And then his only garment quite gave way;
He fled, like Joseph,[2] leaving it; but there,
I doubt, all likeness ends between the pair.

187

Lights came at length, and men, and maids, who found
1490   An awkward spectacle their eyes before;
Antonia in hysterics, Julia swoon'd,
Alfonso leaning, breathless, by the door;
Some half-torn drapery scatter'd on the ground,
Some blood, and several footsteps, but no more:
1495   Juan the gate gain'd, turn'd the key about,
And liking not the inside, lock'd the out.

188

Here ends this canto.—Need I sing, or say,
How Juan, naked, favour'd by the night,
Who favours what she should not, found his way,
1500   And reach'd his home in an unseemly plight?
The pleasant scandal which arose next day,
The nine days' wonder which was brought to light,
And how Alfonso sued for a divorce,
Were in the English newspapers, of course.

189

1505   If you would like to see the whole proceedings,
The depositions, and the cause at full,

---

1. A formidable opponent.
2. In Genesis 39.7ff. the chaste Joseph flees from the advances of Potiphar's wife, leaving "his garment in her hand."

The names of all the witnesses, the pleadings
    Of counsel to nonsuit,[3] or to annul,
There's more than one edition, and the readings
1510   Are various, but they none of them are dull,
The best is that in shorthand ta'en by Gurney,[4]
Who to Madrid on purpose made a journey.

190

But Donna Inez, to divert the train
    Of one of the most circulating scandals
1515   That had for centuries been known in Spain,
    Since Roderic's Goths, or older Genseric's Vandals,[5]
First vow'd (and never had she vow'd in vain)
    To Virgin Mary several pounds of candles;
And then, by the advice of some old ladies,
1520   She sent her son to be embark'd at Cadiz.

191

She had resolved that he should travel through
    All European climes, by land or sea,
To mend his former morals, or get new,
    Especially in France and Italy,
1525   (At least this is the thing most people do).
    Julia was sent into a nunnery,
And there, perhaps, her feelings may be better
Shown in the following copy of her letter:

192

"They tell me 'tis decided; you depart:
1530   'Tis wise—'tis well, but not the less a pain;
I have no further claim on your young heart,
    Mine was the victim, and would be again;
To love too much has been the only art
    I used;—I write in haste, and if a stain
1535   Be on this sheet, 'tis not what it appears,
My eyeballs burn and throb, but have no tears.

193

"I loved, I love you, for that love have lost
    State, station, heaven, mankind's, my own esteem,
And yet can not regret what it hath cost,
1540   So dear is still the memory of that dream;
Yet, if I name my guilt, 'tis not to boast,
    None can deem harshlier of me than I deem:
I trace this scrawl because I cannot rest—
I've nothing to reproach, nor to request.

3. Judgment against the plaintiff for failure to establish his case.
4. William B. Gurney (1777–1855), official shorthand writer for the houses of Parliament and a famous court reporter.
5. The Germanic tribes that overran Spain and other parts of southern Europe in the 5th through 8th centuries, notorious for rape and violence.

194

1545 "Man's love is of his life a thing apart,
    'Tis woman's whole existence; man may range
The court, camp, church, the vessel, and the mart,
    Sword, gown, gain, glory, offer in exchange
Pride, fame, ambition, to fill up his heart,
1550   And few there are whom these can not estrange;
Man has all these resources, we but one,
To love again, and be again undone.

195

"My breast has been all weakness, is so yet;
    I struggle, but cannot collect my mind;
1555 My blood still rushes where my spirit's set,
    As roll the waves before the settled wind;
My brain is feminine, nor can forget—
    To all, except your image, madly blind;
As turns the needle[6] trembling to the pole
1560 It ne'er can reach, so turns to you, my soul.

196

"You will proceed in beauty, and in pride,
    Beloved and loving many; all is o'er
For me on earth, except some years to hide
    My shame and sorrow deep in my heart's core;
1565 These I could bear, but cannot cast aside
    The passion which still rends it as before,
And so farewell—forgive me, love me—No,
That word is idle now—but let it go.

197

"I have no more to say, but linger still,
1570   And dare not set my seal upon this sheet,
And yet I may as well the task fulfil,
    My misery can scarce be more complete:
I had not lived till now, could sorrow kill;
    Death flies the wretch who fain the blow would meet,
1575 And I must even survive this last adieu,
And bear with life, to love and pray for you!"

198

This note was written upon gilt-edged paper
    With a neat crow-quill, rather hard, but new;
Her small white fingers scarce could reach the taper,[7]
1580   But trembled as magnetic needles do,
And yet she did not let one tear escape her;
    The seal a sunflower; *"Elle vous suit partout,"*[8]

---

6. Of a compass.
7. The candle (to melt wax to seal the letter).

8. She follows you everywhere (French).

The motto, cut upon a white cornelian;
The wax was superfine, its hue vermilion.

199

1585 This was Don Juan's earliest scrape; but whether
 I shall proceed with his adventures is
Dependent on the public altogether;
 We'll see, however, what they say to this,
Their favour in an author's cap's a feather,
1590 And no great mischief's done by their caprice;
And if their approbation we experience,
Perhaps they'll have some more about a year hence.

200

My poem's epic, and is meant to be
 Divided in twelve books; each book containing,
1595 With love, and war, a heavy gale at sea,
 A list of ships, and captains, and kings reigning,
New characters; the episodes are three:
 A panorama view of hell's in training,
After the style of Virgil and of Homer,
1600 So that my name of Epic's no misnomer.

201

All these things will be specified in time,
 With strict regard to Aristotle's rules,
The *vade mecum*[9] of the true sublime,
 Which makes so many poets, and some fools;
1605 Prose poets like blank-verse, I'm fond of rhyme,
 Good workmen never quarrel with their tools;
I've got new mythological machinery,
And very handsome supernatural scenery.

202

There's only one slight difference between
1610 Me and my epic brethren gone before,
And here the advantage is my own, I ween;
 (Not that I have not several merits more,
But this will more peculiarly be seen)
 They so embellish, that 'tis quite a bore
1615 Their labyrinth of fables to thread through,
Whereas this story's actually true.

203

If any person doubt it, I appeal
 To history, tradition, and to facts,
To newspapers, whose truth all know and feel,
1620 To plays in five, and operas in three acts;

---

9. Go with me (Latin, literal trans.); handbook. Byron is deriding the neoclassic view that Aristotle's *Poetics* proposes "rules" for writing epic and tragedy.

All these confirm my statement a good deal,
    But that which more completely faith exacts
Is, that myself, and several now in Seville,
    Saw Juan's last elopement with the devil.[1]

204

1625 If ever I should condescend to prose,
    I'll write poetical commandments, which
Shall supersede beyond all doubt all those
    That went before; in these I shall enrich
My text with many things that no one knows,
1630   And carry precept to the highest pitch:
I'll call the work "Longinus o'er a Bottle,
Or, Every Poet his *own* Aristotle."

205

Thou shalt believe in Milton, Dryden, Pope;[2]
    Thou shalt not set up Wordsworth, Coleridge, Southey;
1635 Because the first is crazed beyond all hope,
    The second drunk, the third so quaint and mouthey:
With Crabbe it may be difficult to cope,
    And Campbell's Hippocrene[3] is somewhat drouthy:
Thou shalt not steal from Samuel Rogers, nor—
1640 Commit—flirtation with the muse of Moore.

206

Thou shalt not covet Mr. Sotheby's Muse,
    His Pegasus,[4] nor any thing that's his;
Thou shalt not bear false witness like "the Blues,"[5]
    (There's one, at least, is very fond of this);
1645 Thou shalt not write, in short, but what I choose:
    This is true criticism, and you may kiss—
Exactly as you please, or not, the rod,
But if you don't, I'll lay it on, by G—d!

207

If any person should presume to assert
1650   This story is not moral, first I pray
That they will not cry out before they're hurt,
    Then that they'll read it o'er again, and say,
(But, doubtless, nobody will be so pert)
    That this is not a moral tale, though gay;

1. The usual plays on the Juan legend ended with Juan in hell; an early-20th-century version is Bernard Shaw's *Man and Superman*.
2. This is one of many passages, in prose and verse, in which Byron vigorously defended Dryden and Pope against his Romantic contemporaries.
3. Fountain on Mount Helicon whose waters supposedly gave inspiration. George Crabbe, whom Byron admired, was the author of *The Village* and other realistic poems of rural life. Thomas Camp-bell, Samuel Rogers, and Thomas Moore (below) were lesser poets of the Romantic period; the last two were close friends of Byron's.
4. The winged horse symbolizing poetic inspiration. William Sotheby, contemporary poet and translator, was a wealthy man (see line 1642).
5. I.e., bluestockings, a contemporary term for pedantic female intellectuals, among whom Byron numbered his wife (line 1644).

1655   Besides, in canto twelfth, I mean to show
          The very place where wicked people go.

                         *   *   *

                              213
          But now at thirty years my hair is gray—
              (I wonder what it will be like at forty?
          I thought of a peruke° the other day)   wig
1700   My heart is not much greener; and, in short, I
          Have squander'd my whole summer while 'twas May,
              And feel no more the spirit to retort; I
          Have spent my life, both interest and principal,
          And deem not, what I deem'd, my soul invincible.

                              214
1705   No more—no more—Oh! never more on me
              The freshness of the heart can fall like dew,
          Which out of all the lovely things we see
              Extracts emotions beautiful and new,
          Hived in our bosoms like the bag o' the bee:
1710   Think'st thou the honey with those objects grew?
          Alas! 'twas not in them, but in thy power
          To double even the sweetness of a flower.

                              215
          No more—no more—Oh! never more, my heart,
              Canst thou be my sole world, my universe!
1715   Once all in all, but now a thing apart,
              Thou canst not be my blessing or my curse:
          The illusion's gone for ever, and thou art
              Insensible, I trust, but none the worse,
          And in thy stead I've got a deal of judgment,
1720   Though heaven knows how it ever found a lodgement.

                              216
          My days of love are over, me no more
              The charms of maid, wife, and still less of widow,
          Can make the fool of which they made before,
              In short, I must not lead the life I did do;
1725   The credulous hope of mutual minds is o'er,
              The copious use of claret is forbid too,
          So for a good old gentlemanly vice,
          I think I must take up with avarice.

                              217
          Ambition was my idol, which was broken
1730   Before the shrines of Sorrow and of Pleasure;
          And the two last have left me many a token
              O'er which reflection may be made at leisure:
          Now, like Friar Bacon's brazen head, I've spoken,

"Time is, Time was, Time's past,"[6] a chymic treasure[7]
1735 Is glittering youth, which I have spent betimes—
My heart in passion, and my head on rhymes.

218

What is the end of fame? 'tis but to fill
    A certain portion of uncertain paper:
Some liken it to climbing up a hill,
1740   Whose summit, like all hills', is lost in vapour;
For this men write, speak, preach, and heroes kill,
    And bards burn what they call their "midnight taper,"
To have, when the original is dust,
A name, a wretched picture, and worse bust.[8]

219

1745 What are the hopes of man? old Egypt's King
    Cheops erected the first pyramid
And largest, thinking it was just the thing
    To keep his memory whole, and mummy hid;
But somebody or other rummaging,
1750   Burglariously broke his coffin's lid:
Let not a monument give you or me hopes,
Since not a pinch of dust remains of Cheops.

220

But I, being fond of true philosophy,
    Say very often to myself, "Alas!
1755 All things that have been born were born to die,
    And flesh (which Death mows down to hay) is grass;
You've pass'd your youth not so unpleasantly,
    And if you had it o'er again—'twould pass—
So thank your stars that matters are no worse,
1760 And read your Bible, sir, and mind your purse."

221

But for the present, gentle reader! and
    Still gentler purchaser! the bard—that's I—
Must, with permission, shake you by the hand,
    And so your humble servant, and good bye!
1765 We meet again, if we should understand
    Each other; and if not, I shall not try
Your patience further than by this short sample—
'Twere well if others follow'd my example.

222

"Go, little book, from this my solitude!
1770   I cast thee on the waters, go thy ways!

---

6. Spoken by a bronze bust in Robert Greene's comedy *Friar Bacon and Friar Bungay* (1594).
7. "Chymic": alchemic; i.e., the "treasure" is counterfeit gold.

8. Byron was unhappy with the portrait bust of him recently made by the Danish sculptor Thorwaldsen.

And if, as I believe, thy vein be good,
　　The world will find thee after many days."
When Southey's read, and Wordsworth understood,
　　I can't help putting in my claim to praise—
1775　The four first rhymes are Southey's every line:[9]
For God's sake, reader! take them not for mine.

From Canto 2

[JUAN AND HAIDEE][1]

111

How long in his damp trance young Juan lay
　　He knew not, for the earth was gone for him,
And Time had nothing more of night nor day
　　For his congealing blood, and senses dim;
885　And how this heavy faintness pass'd away
　　He knew not, till each painful pulse and limb,
And tingling vein seem'd throbbing back to life,
For Death, though vanquish'd, still retired with strife.

112

His eyes he open'd, shut, again unclosed,
890　For all was doubt and dizziness; methought
He still was in the boat, and had but dozed,
　　And felt again with his despair o'erwrought,
And wish'd it death in which he had reposed,
　　And then once more his feelings back were brought,
895　And slowly by his swimming eyes was seen
A lovely female face of seventeen.

113

'Twas bending close o'er his, and the small mouth
　　Seem'd almost prying into his for breath;
And chafing him, the soft warm hand of youth
900　Recall'd his answering spirits back from death;
And, bathing his chill temples, tried to soothe
　　Each pulse to animation, till beneath
Its gentle touch and trembling care, a sigh
To these kind efforts made a low reply.

114

905　Then was the cordial pour'd, and mantle flung
　　Around his scarce-clad limbs; and the fair arm
Raised higher the faint head which o'er it hung;
　　And her transparent cheek, all pure and warm,
Pillow'd his death-like forehead; then she wrung

9. The lines occur in the last stanza of Southey's
Epilogue to the Lay of the Laureate.
1. Donna Inez has sent her errant son, Juan, off
on a four-year tour. The ship on which he embarks
is wrecked in a savage storm, and Juan, the lone
survivor, half-drowned, is washed ashore on an
island in the Aegean Sea.

910 His dewy curls, long drench'd by every storm;
And watch'd with eagerness each throb that drew
A sigh from his heaved bosom—and hers, too.

115

And lifting him with care into the cave,
The gentle girl, and her attendant,—one
915 Young, yet her elder, and of brow less grave,
And more robust of figure,—then begun
To kindle fire, and as the new flames gave
Light to the rocks that roof'd them, which the sun
Had never seen, the maid, or whatsoe'er
920 She was, appear'd distinct, and tall, and fair.

116

Her brow was overhung with coins of gold,
That sparkled o'er the auburn of her hair,
Her clustering hair, whose longer locks were roll'd
In braids behind, and though her stature were
925 Even of the highest for a female mould,
They nearly reach'd her heel; and in her air
There was a something which bespoke command,
As one who was a lady in the land.

117

Her hair, I said, was auburn; but her eyes
930 Were black as death, their lashes the same hue,
Of downcast length, in whose silk shadow lies
Deepest attraction, for when to the view
Forth from its raven fringe the full glance flies,
Ne'er with such force the swiftest arrow flew;
935 'Tis as the snake late coil'd, who pours his length,
And hurls at once his venom and his strength.

*   *   *

123

And these two tended him, and cheer'd him both
With food and raiment, and those soft attentions,
Which are (as I must own) of female growth,
980 And have ten thousand delicate inventions:
They made a most superior mess of broth,
A thing which poesy but seldom mentions,
But the best dish that e'er was cook'd since Homer's
Achilles order'd dinner for new comers.[2]

124

985 I'll tell you who they were, this female pair,
Lest they should seem princesses in disguise;
Besides, I hate all mystery, and that air

2. A reference to the lavish feast with which Achilles entertained Ajax, Phoenix, and Ulysses (*Iliad* 9.193ff.).

Of clap-trap, which your recent poets prize;
And so, in short, the girls they really were
990 They shall appear before your curious eyes,
Mistress and maid; the first was only daughter
Of an old man, who lived upon the water.

125

A fisherman he had been in his youth,
And still a sort of fisherman was he;
995 But other speculations were, in sooth,
Added to his connection with the sea,
Perhaps not so respectable, in truth:
A little smuggling, and some piracy,
Left him, at last, the sole of many masters
1000 Of an ill-gotten million of piastres.[3]

126

A fisher, therefore, was he—though of men,
Like Peter the Apostle,[4]—and he fish'd
For wandering merchant vessels, now and then,
And sometimes caught as many as he wish'd;
1005 The cargoes he confiscated, and gain
He sought in the slave-market too, and dish'd
Full many a morsel for that Turkish trade,
By which, no doubt, a good deal may be made.

127

He was a Greek, and on his isle had built
1010 (One of the wild and smaller Cyclades)[5]
A very handsome house from out his guilt,
And there he lived exceedingly at ease;
Heaven knows what cash he got, or blood he spilt,
A sad[6] old fellow was he, if you please,
1015 But this I know, it was a spacious building,
Full of barbaric carving, paint, and gilding.

128

He had an only daughter, call'd Haidee,
The greatest heiress of the Eastern Isles;
Besides, so very beautiful was she,
1020 Her dowry was as nothing to her smiles:
Still in her teens, and like a lovely tree
She grew to womanhood, and between whiles
Rejected several suitors, just to learn
How to accept a better in his turn.

129

1025 And walking out upon the beach, below
The cliff, towards sunset, on that day she found,

---

3. Near-Eastern coins.
4. Christ's words to Peter and Andrew, both fishermen: "Follow me, and I will make you fishers of men" (Matthew 4.19).
5. A group of islands in the Aegean Sea.
6. In the playful sense: wicked.

Insensible,—not dead, but nearly so,—
   Don Juan, almost famish'd, and half drown'd;
But being naked, she was shock'd, you know,
1030   Yet deem'd herself in common pity bound,
As far as in her lay, "to take him in,
A stranger"[7] dying, with so white a skin.

130

But taking him into her father's house
   Was not exactly the best way to save,
1035 But like conveying to the cat the mouse,
   Or people in a trance into their grave;
Because the good old man had so much "νοῦς,"[8]
   Unlike the honest Arab thieves so brave,
He would have hospitably cured the stranger,
1040 And sold him instantly when out of danger.

131

And therefore, with her maid, she thought it best
   (A virgin always on her maid relies)
To place him in the cave for present rest:
   And when, at last, he open'd his black eyes,
1045 Their charity increased about their guest;
   And their compassion grew to such a size,
It open'd half the turnpike-gates to heaven—
(St. Paul says 'tis the toll which must be given).[9]

*   *   *

141

And Haidee met the morning face to face;
   Her own was freshest, though a feverish flush
Had dyed it with the headlong blood, whose race
   From heart to cheek is curb'd into a blush,
1125 Like to a torrent which a mountain's base,
   That overpowers some Alpine river's rush,
Checks to a lake, whose waves in circles spread;
Or the Red Sea—but the sea is not red.

142

And down the cliff the island virgin came,
1130   And near the cave her quick light footsteps drew,
While the sun smiled on her with his first flame,
   And young Aurora° kiss'd her lips with dew,   *dawn*
Taking her for a sister; just the same
   Mistake you would have made on seeing the two,
1135 Although the mortal, quite as fresh and fair,
   Had all the advantage too of not being air.

---

7. Cf. Matthew 25.35: "I was a stranger, and ye took me in."
8. *Nous,* "intelligence" (Greek); in England, pronounced so as to rhyme with *mouse.*
9. 1 Corinthians 13.13.

143

And when into the cavern Haidee stepp'd
 All timidly, yet rapidly, she saw
That like an infant Juan sweetly slept;
1140   And then she stopp'd, and stood as if in awe,
(For sleep is awful) and on tiptoe crept
 And wrapt him closer, lest the air, too raw,
Should reach his blood, then o'er him still as death
Bent, with hush'd lips, that drank his scarce-drawn breath.

* * *

148

And she bent o'er him, and he lay beneath,
 Hush'd as the babe upon its mother's breast,
Droop'd as the willow when no winds can breathe,
1180   Lull'd like the depth of ocean when at rest,
Fair as the crowning rose of the whole wreath,
 Soft as the callow° cygnet° in its nest;   *young/swan*
In short, he was a very pretty fellow,
Although his woes had turn'd him rather yellow.

149

1185 He woke and gazed, and would have slept again,
 But the fair face which met his eyes forbade
Those eyes to close, though weariness and pain
 Had further sleep a further pleasure made;
For woman's face was never form'd in vain
1190   For Juan, so that even when he pray'd
He turn'd from grisly saints, and martyrs hairy,
To the sweet portraits of the Virgin Mary.

150

And thus upon his elbow he arose,
 And look'd upon the lady, in whose cheek
1195 The pale contended with the purple rose,
 As with an effort she began to speak;
Her eyes were eloquent, her words would pose,
 Although she told him, in good modern Greek,
With an Ionian accent, low and sweet,
1200 That he was faint, and must not talk, but eat.

* * *

168

And every day by day-break—rather early
 For Juan, who was somewhat fond of rest—
She came into the cave, but it was merely
1340   To see her bird reposing in his nest;
And she would softly stir his locks so curly,
 Without disturbing her yet slumbering guest,
Breathing all gently o'er his cheek and mouth,
As o'er a bed of roses the sweet south.[1]

---

1. The south wind.

169

1345

And every morn his colour freshlier came,
    And every day help'd on his convalescence;
'Twas well, because health in the human frame
    Is pleasant, besides being true love's essence,
For health and idleness to passion's flame
1350
    Are oil and gunpowder; and some good lessons
Are also learnt from Ceres[2] and from Bacchus,
Without whom Venus will not long attack us.

170

While Venus fills the heart (without heart really
    Love, though good always, is not quite so good)
1355
Ceres presents a plate of vermicelli,—
    For love must be sustain'd like flesh and blood,—
While Bacchus pours out wine, or hands a jelly:
    Eggs, oysters too, are amatory food;
But who is their purveyor from above
1360
Heaven knows,—it may be Neptune, Pan, or Jove.

171

When Juan woke he found some good things ready,
    A bath, a breakfast, and the finest eyes
That ever made a youthful heart less steady,
    Besides her maid's, as pretty for their size;
1365
But I have spoken of all this already—
    And repetition's tiresome and unwise,—
Well—Juan, after bathing in the sea,
Came always back to coffee and Haidee.

172

Both were so young, and one so innocent,
1370
    That bathing pass'd for nothing; Juan seem'd
To her, as 'twere, the kind of being sent,
    Of whom these two years she had nightly dream'd,
A something to be loved, a creature meant
    To be her happiness, and whom she deem'd
1375
To render happy; all who joy would win
Must share it,—Happiness was born a twin.

173

It was such pleasure to behold him, such
    Enlargement of existence to partake
Nature with him, to thrill beneath his touch,
1380
    To watch him slumbering, and to see him wake:
To live with him for ever were too much;
    But then the thought of parting made her quake:
He was her own, her ocean-treasure, cast
Like a rich wreck—her first love, and her last.

2. Goddess of the grain.

174

1385　And thus a moon roll'd on, and fair Haidee
　　　　Paid daily visits to her boy, and took
　　　Such plentiful precautions, that still he
　　　　Remain'd unknown within his craggy nook;
　　　At last her father's prows put out to sea,
1390　　For certain merchantmen upon the look,
　　　Not as of yore to carry off an Io,[3]
　　　But three Ragusan vessels, bound for Scio.[4]

175

　　　Then came her freedom, for she had no mother,
　　　　So that, her father being at sea, she was
1395　Free as a married woman, or such other
　　　　Female, as where she likes may freely pass,
　　　Without even the encumbrance of a brother,
　　　　The freest she that ever gazed on glass:
　　　I speak of christian lands in this comparison,
1400　Where wives, at least, are seldom kept in garrison.

176

　　　Now she prolong'd her visits and her talk
　　　　(For they must talk), and he had learnt to say
　　　So much as to propose to take a walk,—
　　　　For little had he wander'd since the day
1405　On which, like a young flower snapp'd from the stalk,
　　　　Drooping and dewy on the beach he lay,—
　　　And thus they walk'd out in the afternoon,
　　　And saw the sun set opposite the moon.

177

　　　It was a wild and breaker-beaten coast,
1410　　With cliffs above, and a broad sandy shore,
　　　Guarded by shoals and rocks as by an host,
　　　　With here and there a creek, whose aspect wore
　　　A better welcome to the tempest-tost;
　　　　And rarely ceas'd the haughty billow's roar,
1415　Save on the dead long summer days, which make
　　　The outstretch'd ocean glitter like a lake.

178

　　　And the small ripple spilt upon the beach
　　　　Scarcely o'erpass'd the cream of your champagne,
　　　When o'er the brim the sparkling bumpers reach,
1420　　That spring-dew of the spirit! the heart's rain!
　　　Few things surpass old wine; and they may preach
　　　　Who please,—the more because they preach in vain,—

3. A mistress of Zeus who was persecuted by his
jealous wife, Hera, and kidnapped by Phoenician
merchants.

4. The Italian name for Chios, an island near Turkey. "Ragusan": Ragusa (or Dubrovnik) is an Adriatic port.

Let us have wine and woman, mirth and laughter,
Sermons and soda water the day after.

179

1425 Man, being reasonable, must get drunk;
   The best of life is but intoxication:
Glory, the grape, love, gold, in these are sunk
   The hopes of all men, and of every nation;
Without their sap, how branchless were the trunk
1430   Of life's strange tree, so fruitful on occasion:
But to return,—Get very drunk; and when
You wake with head-ache, you shall see what then.

180

Ring for your valet—bid him quickly bring
   Some hock and soda-water, then you'll know
1435 A pleasure worthy Xerxes[5] the great king;
   For not the blest sherbet, sublimed with snow,
Nor the first sparkle of the desert-spring,
   Nor Burgundy in all its sunset glow,
After long travel, ennui, love, or slaughter,
1440 Vie with that draught of hock and soda-water.

181

The coast—I think it was the coast that I
   Was just describing—Yes, it *was* the coast—
Lay at this period quiet as the sky,
   The sands untumbled, the blue waves untost,
1445 And all was stillness, save the sea-bird's cry,
   And dolphin's leap, and little billow crost
By some low rock or shelve, that made it fret
Against the boundary it scarcely wet.

182

And forth they wandered, her sire being gone,
1450   As I have said, upon an expedition;
And mother, brother, guardian, she had none,
   Save Zoe, who, although with due precision
She waited on her lady with the sun,
   Thought daily service was her only mission,
1455 Bringing warm water, wreathing her long tresses,
And asking now and then for cast-off dresses.

183

It was the cooling hour, just when the rounded
   Red sun sinks down behind the azure hill,
Which then seems as if the whole earth it bounded,
1460   Circling all nature, hush'd, and dim, and still,

---

5. The 5th-century Persian king was said to have offered a reward to anyone who could discover a new kind of pleasure.

With the far mountain-crescent half surrounded
  On one side, and the deep sea calm and chill
Upon the other, and the rosy sky,
With one star sparkling through it like an eye.

184

1465 And thus they wander'd forth, and hand in hand,
  Over the shining pebbles and the shells,
Glided along the smooth and harden'd sand,
  And in the worn and wild receptacles
Work'd by the storms, yet work'd as it were plann'd,
1470   In hollow halls, with sparry roofs and cells,
They turn'd to rest; and, each clasp'd by an arm,
Yielded to the deep twilight's purple charm.

185

They look'd up to the sky, whose floating glow
  Spread like a rosy ocean, vast and bright;
1475 They gazed upon the glittering sea below,
  Whence the broad moon rose circling into sight;
They heard the wave's splash, and the wind so low,
  And saw each other's dark eyes darting light
Into each other—and, beholding this,
1480 Their lips drew near, and clung into a kiss;

186

A long, long kiss, a kiss of youth and love,
  And beauty, all concentrating like rays
Into one focus, kindled from above;
  Such kisses as belong to early days,
1485 Where heart, and soul, and sense, in concert move,
  And the blood's lava, and the pulse a blaze,
Each kiss a heart-quake,—for a kiss's strength,
I think, it must be reckon'd by its length.

187

By length I mean duration; theirs endured
1490   Heaven knows how long—no doubt they never reckon'd;
And if they had, they could not have secured
  The sum of their sensations to a second:
They had not spoken; but they felt allured,
  As if their souls and lips each other beckon'd,
1495 Which, being join'd, like swarming bees they clung—
Their hearts the flowers from whence the honey sprung.

188

They were alone, but not alone as they
  Who shut in chambers think it loneliness;
The silent ocean, and the starlight bay,
1500   The twilight glow, which momently grew less,
The voiceless sands, and dropping caves, that lay

Around them, made them to each other press,
As if there were no life beneath the sky
Save theirs, and that their life could never die.

189

1505 They fear'd no eyes nor ears on that lone beach,
They felt no terrors from the night, they were
All in all to each other: though their speech
Was broken words, they *thought* a language there,—
And all the burning tongues the passions teach
1510 Found in one sigh the best interpreter
Of nature's oracle—first love,—that all
Which Eve has left her daughters since her fall.

190

Haidee[6] spoke not of scruples, ask'd no vows,
Nor offer'd any; she had never heard
1515 Of plight and promises to be a spouse,
Or perils by a loving maid incurr'd;
She was all which pure ignorance allows,
And flew to her young mate like a young bird;
And, never having dreamt of falsehood, she
1520 Had not one word to say of constancy.

191

She loved, and was beloved—she adored,
And she was worshipp'd; after nature's fashion,
Their intense souls, into each other pour'd,
If souls could die, had perish'd in that passion,—
1525 But by degrees their senses were restored,
Again to be o'ercome, again to dash on;
And, beating 'gainst *his* bosom, Haidee's heart
Felt as if never more to beat apart.

192

Alas! they were so young, so beautiful,
1530 So lonely, loving, helpless, and the hour
Was that in which the heart is always full,
And, having o'er itself no further power,
Prompts deeds eternity can not annul,
But pays off moments in an endless shower
1535 Of hell-fire—all prepared for people giving
Pleasure or pain to one another living.

193

Alas! for Juan and Haidee! they were
So loving and so lovely—till then never,
Excepting our first parents, such a pair

---

6. Byron said, with reference to Haidee: "I was, and am, penetrated with the conviction that women only know evil from men, whereas men have no criterion to judge of purity or goodness but woman."

1540   Had run the risk of being damn'd for ever;
And Haidee, being devout as well as fair,
    Had, doubtless, heard about the Stygian river,[7]
And hell and purgatory—but forgot
Just in the very crisis she should not.

194

1545   They look upon each other, and their eyes
    Gleam in the moonlight; and her white arm clasps
Round Juan's head, and his around hers lies
    Half buried in the tresses which it grasps;
She sits upon his knee, and drinks his sighs,
1550   He hers, until they end in broken gasps;
And thus they form a group that's quite antique,
Half naked, loving, natural, and Greek.

195

And when those deep and burning moments pass'd,
    And Juan sunk to sleep within her arms,
1555   She slept not, but all tenderly, though fast,
    Sustain'd his head upon her bosom's charms;
And now and then her eye to heaven is cast,
    And then on the pale cheek her breast now warms,
Pillow'd on her o'erflowing heart, which pants
1560   With all it granted, and with all it grants.

196

An infant when it gazes on a light,
    A child the moment when it drains the breast,
A devotee when soars the Host[8] in sight,
    An Arab with a stranger for a guest,
1565   A sailor when the prize has struck[9] in fight,
    A miser filling his most hoarded chest,
Feel rapture; but not such true joy are reaping
As they who watch o'er what they love while sleeping.

197

For there it lies so tranquil, so beloved,
1570   All that it hath of life with us is living;
So gentle, stirless, helpless, and unmoved,
    And all unconscious of the joy 'tis giving;
All it hath felt, inflicted, pass'd, and proved,
    Hush'd into depths beyond the watcher's diving;
1575   There lies the thing we love with all its errors
And all its charms, like death without its terrors.

198

The lady watch'd her lover—and that hour
    Of Love's, and Night's, and Ocean's solitude,

---

7. The Styx, which flows through Hades.
8. The Eucharistic wafer.

9. Has lowered its flag in token of surrender.

O'erflow'd her soul with their united power;
1580   Amidst the barren sand and rocks so rude
She and her wave-worn love had made their bower,
    Where nought upon their passion could intrude,
And all the stars that crowded the blue space
Saw nothing happier than her glowing face.

199

1585 Alas! the love of women! it is known
    To be a lovely and a fearful thing;
For all of theirs upon that die is thrown,
    And if 'tis lost, life hath no more to bring
To them but mockeries of the past alone,
1590   And their revenge is as the tiger's spring,
Deadly, and quick, and crushing; yet, as real
Torture is theirs, what they inflict they feel.

200

They are right; for man, to man so oft unjust,
    Is always so to women; one sole bond
1595 Awaits them, treachery is all their trust;
    Taught to conceal, their bursting hearts despond
Over their idol, till some wealthier lust
    Buys them in marriage—and what rests beyond?
A thankless husband, next a faithless lover,
1600 Then dressing, nursing, praying, and all's over.

201

Some take a lover, some take drams or prayers,
    Some mind their household, others dissipation,
Some run away, and but exchange their cares,
    Losing the advantage of a virtuous station;
1605 Few changes e'er can better their affairs,
    Theirs being an unnatural situation,
From the dull palace to the dirty hovel:
Some play the devil, and then write a novel.[1]

202

Haidee was Nature's bride, and knew not this;
1610   Haidee was Passion's child, born where the sun
Showers triple light, and scorches even the kiss
    Of his gazelle-eyed daughters; she was one
Made but to love, to feel that she was his
    Who was her chosen: what was said or done
1615 Elsewhere was nothing—She had nought to fear,
Hope, care, nor love beyond, her heart beat *here*.

203

And oh! that quickening of the heart, that beat!
    How much it costs us! yet each rising throb

---

1. The impetuous Lady Caroline Lamb, having thrown herself at Byron and been after a time rejected, incorporated incidents from the affair in her novel *Glenarvon* (1816).

Is in its cause as its effect so sweet,
1620   That Wisdom, ever on the watch to rob
Joy of its alchymy, and to repeat
    Fine truths, even Conscience, too, has a tough job
To make us understand each good old maxim,
    So good—I wonder Castlereagh[2] don't tax 'em.

204

1625 And now 'twas done—on the lone shore were plighted
    Their hearts; the stars, their nuptial torches, shed
Beauty upon the beautiful they lighted:
    Ocean their witness, and the cave their bed,
By their own feelings hallow'd and united,
1630   Their priest was Solitude, and they were wed:
And they were happy, for to their young eyes
    Each was an angel, and earth paradise.

*   *   *

208

But Juan! had he quite forgotten Julia?
    And should he have forgotten her so soon?
I can't but say it seems to me most truly a
1660   Perplexing question; but, no doubt, the moon
Does these things for us, and whenever newly a
    Strong palpitation rises, 'tis her boon,
Else how the devil is it that fresh features
Have such a charm for us poor human creatures?

209

1665 I hate inconstancy—I loathe, detest,
    Abhor, condemn, abjure the mortal made
Of such quicksilver clay that in his breast
    No permanent foundation can be laid;
Love, constant love, has been my constant guest,
1670   And yet last night, being at a masquerade,
I saw the prettiest creature, fresh from Milan,
    Which gave me some sensations like a villain.

210

But soon Philosophy came to my aid,
    And whisper'd "think of every sacred tie!"
1675 "I will, my dear Philosophy!" I said,
    "But then her teeth, and then, Oh heaven! her eye!
I'll just inquire if she be wife or maid,
    Or neither—out of curiosity."
"Stop!" cried Philosophy, with air so Grecian,
1680 (Though she was masqued then as a fair Venetian).

211

"Stop!" so I stopp'd.—But to return: that which
    Men call inconstancy is nothing more

2. Robert Stewart, Viscount Castlereagh, British foreign secretary (1812–22).

Than admiration due where nature's rich
   Profusion with young beauty covers o'er
1685 Some favour'd object; and as in the niche
   A lovely statue we almost adore,
This sort of adoration of the real
Is but a heightening of the "beau ideal."³

212

'Tis the perception of the beautiful,
1690   A fine extension of the faculties,
Platonic, universal, wonderful,
   Drawn from the stars, and filter'd through the skies,
Without which life would be extremely dull;
   In short, it is the use of our own eyes,
1695 With one or two small senses added, just
To hint that flesh is form'd of fiery dust.

213

Yet 'tis a painful feeling, and unwilling,
   For surely if we always could perceive
In the same object graces quite as killing
1700   As when she rose upon us like an Eve,
'Twould save us many a heart-ache, many a shilling,
   (For we must get them anyhow, or grieve),
Whereas, if one sole lady pleased for ever,
How pleasant for the heart, as well as liver!

       *   *   *

216

In the mean time, without proceeding more
   In this anatomy, I've finish'd now
Two hundred and odd stanzas as before,
   That being about the number I'll allow
1725 Each canto of the twelve, or twenty-four;
   And, laying down my pen, I make my bow,
Leaving Don Juan and Haidee to plead
For them and theirs with all who deign to read.

From Canto 4¹

[JUAN AND HAIDEE]

3

As boy, I thought myself a clever fellow,
   And wish'd that others held the same opinion;
They took it up when my days grew more mellow,
20   And other minds acknowledged my dominion:
Now my sere fancy "falls into the yellow
   Leaf,"² and imagination droops her pinion,

---

3. Ideal beauty (French).
1. Lambor, Haidee's radical father, has been falsely reported to be dead. He returns undetected to find Juan and Haidee asleep in each others arms.
2. Cf. *Macbeth* 5.3.22–24: "My way of life / Is fall'n into the sere, the yellow leaf."

And the sad truth which hovers o'er my desk
Turns what was once romantic to burlesque.

4

25 And if I laugh at any mortal thing,
  'Tis that I may not weep; and if I weep,
'Tis that our nature cannot always bring
  Itself to apathy, for we must steep
Our hearts first in the depths of Lethe's[3] spring
30 Ere what we least wish to behold will sleep:
Thetis baptized her mortal son in Styx;[4]
A mortal mother would on Lethe fix.

5

Some have accused me of a strange design
  Against the creed and morals of the land,
35 And trace it in this poem every line:
  I don't pretend that I quite understand
My own meaning when I would be *very* fine,
  But the fact is that I have nothing plann'd,
Unless it were to be a moment merry,
40 A novel word in my vocabulary.

6

To the kind reader of our sober clime
  This way of writing will appear exotic;
Pulci[5] was sire of the half-serious rhyme,
  Who sang when chivalry was more Quixotic,
45 And revell'd in the fancies of the time,
  True knights, chaste dames, huge giants, kings despotic;
But all these, save the last, being obsolete,
I chose a modern subject as more meet.

7

How I have treated it, I do not know;
50 Perhaps no better than they have treated me
Who have imputed such designs as show
  Not what they saw, but what they wish'd to see;
But if it gives them pleasure, be it so,
  This is a liberal age, and thoughts are free:
55 Meantime Apollo plucks me by the ear,
And tells me to resume my story here.

*   *   *

29

225 Now pillow'd cheek to cheek, in loving sleep,
  Haidee and Juan their siesta took,

---

3. A river in Hades that brings oblivion of life.
4. The river in Hades into which the nymph Thetis dipped Achilles, to make him invulnerable.
5. Author of the *Morgante Maggiore*, prototype of

the Italian seriocomic romance from which Byron derived the stanza and manner of *Don Juan* (see headnote, p. 1659).

A gentle slumber, but it was not deep,
   For ever and anon a something shook
Juan, and shuddering o'er his frame would creep;
230   And Haidee's sweet lips murmur'd like a brook
A wordless music, and her face so fair
Stirr'd with her dream as rose-leaves with the air;

30

Or as the stirring of a deep clear stream
   Within an Alpine hollow, when the wind
235   Walks o'er it, was she shaken by the dream,
   The mystical usurper of the mind—
O'erpowering us to be whate'er may seem
   Good to the soul which we no more can bind;
Strange state of being! (for 'tis still to be)
240   Senseless to feel, and with seal'd eyes to see.

31

She dream'd of being alone on the sea-shore,
   Chain'd to a rock; she knew not how, but stir
She could not from the spot, and the loud roar
   Grew, and each wave rose roughly, threatening her;
245   And o'er her upper lip they seem'd to pour,
   Until she sobb'd for breath, and soon they were
Foaming o'er her lone head, so fierce and high—
Each broke to drown her, yet she could not die.

32

Anon—she was released, and then she stray'd
250   O'er the sharp shingles° with her bleeding feet,   *loose pebbles*
And stumbled almost every step she made;
   And something roll'd before her in a sheet,
Which she must still pursue howe'er afraid;
   'Twas white and indistinct, nor stopp'd to meet
255   Her glance nor grasp, for still she gazed and grasp'd,
And ran, but it escaped her as she clasp'd.

33

The dream changed; in a cave she stood, its walls
   Were hung with marble icicles; the work
Of ages on its water-fretted halls,
260   Where waves might wash, and seals might breed and lurk;
Her hair was dripping, and the very balls
   Of her black eyes seemed turn'd to tears, and murk
The sharp rocks look'd below each drop they caught,
Which froze to marble as it fell, she thought.

34

265   And wet, and cold, and lifeless at her feet,
   Pale as the foam that froth'd on his dead brow,
Which she essay'd in vain to clear, (how sweet

Were once her cares, how idle seem'd they now!)
Lay Juan, nor could aught renew the beat
270　Of his quench'd heart; and the sea dirges low
Rang in her sad ears like a mermaid's song,
And that brief dream appear'd a life too long.

35

And gazing on the dead, she thought his face
　Faded, or alter'd into something new—
275　Like to her father's features, till each trace
　　More like and like to Lambro's aspect grew—
With all his keen worn look and Grecian grace;
　And starting, she awoke, and what to view?
Oh! Powers of Heaven! what dark eye meets she there?
280　'Tis—'tis her father's—fix'd upon the pair!

36

Then shrieking, she arose, and shrieking fell,
　With joy and sorrow, hope and fear, to see
Him whom she deem'd a habitant where dwell
　The ocean-buried, risen from death, to be
285　Perchance the death of one she loved too well:
　Dear as her father had been to Haidee,
It was a moment of that awful kind—
I have seen such—but must not call to mind.

37

Up Juan sprung to Haidee's bitter shriek,
290　And caught her falling, and from off the wall
Snatch'd down his sabre, in hot haste to wreak
　Vengeance on him who was the cause of all:
Then Lambro, who till now forbore to speak,
　Smiled scornfully, and said, "Within my call,
295　A thousand scimitars await the word;
Put up, young man, put up your silly sword."

38

And Haidee clung around him; "Juan, 'tis—
　'Tis Lambro—'tis my father! Kneel with me—
He will forgive us—yes—it must be—yes.
300　Oh! dearest father, in this agony
Of pleasure and of pain—even while I kiss
　Thy garment's hem with transport, can it be
That doubt should mingle with my filial joy?
Deal with me as thou wilt, but spare this boy."

39

305　High and inscrutable the old man stood,
　Calm in his voice, and calm within his eye—
Not always signs with him of calmest mood:
　He look'd upon her, but gave no reply;

Then turn'd to Juan, in whose cheek the blood
310　　Oft came and went, as there resolved to die;
In arms, at least, he stood, in act to spring
On the first foe whom Lambro's call might bring.

40

"Young man, your sword"; so Lambro once more said:
　　Juan replied, "Not while this arm is free."
315　The old man's cheek grew pale, but not with dread,
　　And drawing from his belt a pistol, he
Replied, "Your blood be then on your own head."
　　Then look'd close at the flint, as if to see
'Twas fresh—for he had lately used the lock⁶—
320　And next proceeded quietly to cock.

41

It has a strange quick jar upon the ear,
　　That cocking of a pistol, when you know
A moment more will bring the sight to bear
　　Upon your person, twelve yards off, or so;
325　A gentlemanly distance,⁷ not too near,
　　If you have got a former friend for foe;
But after being fired at once or twice,
The ear becomes more Irish, and less nice.⁸

42

Lambro presented, and one instant more
330　　Had stopp'd this Canto, and Don Juan's breath,
When Haidee threw herself her boy before;
　　Stern as her sire: "On me," she cried, "let death
Descend—the fault is mine; this fatal shore
　　He found—but sought not. I have pledged my faith;
335　I love him—I will die with him: I knew
Your nature's firmness—know your daughter's too."

43

A minute past, and she had been all tears,
　　And tenderness, and infancy: but now
She stood as one who champion'd human fears—
340　　Pale, statue-like, and stern, she woo'd the blow;
And tall beyond her sex, and their compeers,⁹
　　She drew up to her height, as if to show
A fairer mark; and with a fix'd eye scann'd
Her father's face—but never stopp'd his hand.

44

345　He gazed on her, and she on him; 'twas strange
　　How like they look'd! the expression was the same;

---

6. The part of the gun that explodes the charge.
7. I.e., dueling distance.
8. Finicky. Byron alludes to the propensity of hot-
headed young Irishmen to fight duels.
9. I.e., she was the match in height of Lambro and
Juan.

Serenely savage, with a little change
    In the large dark eye's mutual-darted flame;
For she too was as one who could avenge,
350   If cause should be—a lioness, though tame:
Her father's blood before her father's face
Boil'd up, and prov'd her truly of his race.

45

I said they were alike, their features and
    Their stature differing but in sex and years;
355   Even to the delicacy of their hand
    There was resemblance, such as true blood wears;
And now to see them, thus divided, stand
    In fix'd ferocity, when joyous tears,
And sweet sensations, should have welcomed both,
360   Show what the passions are in their full growth.

46

The father paused a moment, then withdrew
    His weapon, and replaced it; but stood still,
And looking on her, as to look her through,
    "Not *I*," he said, "have sought this stranger's ill;
365   Not *I* have made this desolation: few
    Would bear such outrage, and forbear to kill;
But I must do my duty—how thou hast
Done thine, the present vouches for the past.

47

"Let him disarm; or, by my father's head,
370   His own shall roll before you like a ball!"
He raised his whistle, as the word he said,
    And blew; another answer'd to the call,
And rushing in disorderly, though led,
    And arm'd from boot to turban, one and all,
375   Some twenty of his train came, rank on rank;
He gave the word, "Arrest or slay the Frank."[1]

48

Then, with a sudden movement, he withdrew
    His daughter; while compress'd within his clasp,
'Twixt her and Juan interposed the crew;
380   In vain she struggled in her father's grasp—
His arms were like a serpent's coil: then flew
    Upon their prey, as darts an angry asp,
The file of pirates; save the foremost, who
Had fallen, with his right shoulder half cut through.

49

385   The second had his cheek laid open; but
    The third, a wary, cool old sworder, took

---

1. Term used in the Near East to designate a Western European.

The blows upon his cutlass, and then put
   His own well in; so well, ere you could look,
His man was floor'd, and helpless at his foot,
390   With the blood running like a little brook
From two smart sabre gashes, deep and red—
   One on the arm, the other on the head.

50

And then they bound him where he fell, and bore
   Juan from the apartment: with a sign
395 Old Lambro bade them take him to the shore,
   Where lay some ships which were to sail at nine.
They laid him in a boat, and plied the oar
   Until they reach'd some galliots,[2] placed in line;
On board of one of these, and under hatches,
400 They stow'd him, with strict orders to the watches.

51

The world is full of strange vicissitudes,
   And here was one exceedingly unpleasant:
A gentleman so rich in the world's goods,
   Handsome and young, enjoying all the present,
405 Just at the very time when he least broods
   On such a thing is suddenly to sea sent,
Wounded and chain'd, so that he cannot move,
And all because a lady fell in love.

*   *   *

56

Afric is all the sun's, and as her earth
   Her human clay is kindled; full of power
For good or evil, burning from its birth,
   The Moorish blood partakes the planet's hour,
445 And like the soil beneath it will bring forth:
   Beauty and love were Haidée's mother's dower;
But her large dark eye show'd deep Passion's force,
Though sleeping like a lion near a source.

57

Her daughter, temper'd with a milder ray,
450   Like summer clouds all silvery, smooth, and fair,
Till slowly charged with thunder they display
   Terror to earth, and tempest to the air,
Had held till now her soft and milky way;
   But overwrought with passion and despair,
455 The fire burst forth from her Numidian° veins,   *North African*
Even as the Simoom[3] sweeps the blasted plains.

---

2. A small, fast galley, propelled by both oars and sails.   3. A violent, hot, dust-laden desert wind.

58

The last sight which she saw was Juan's gore,
    And he himself o'ermaster'd and cut down;
His blood was running on the very floor
460   Where late he trod, her beautiful, her own;
Thus much she view'd an instant and no more,—
    Her struggles ceased with one convulsive groan;
On her sire's arm, which until now scarce held
Her writhing, fell she like a cedar fell'd.

59

465   A vein had burst, and her sweet lips' pure dyes
    Were dabbled with the deep blood which ran o'er;
And her head droop'd as when the lily lies
    O'ercharged with rain: her summon'd handmaids bore
Their lady to her couch with gushing eyes;
470   Of herbs and cordials they produced their store,
But she defied all means they could employ,
Like one life could not hold, nor death destroy.

60

Days lay she in that state unchanged, though chill
    With nothing livid,[4] still her lips were red;
475   She had no pulse, but death seem'd absent still;
    No hideous sign proclaim'd her surely dead;
Corruption came not in each mind to kill
    All hope; to look upon her sweet face bred
New thoughts of life, for it seem'd full of soul,
480   She had so much, earth could not claim the whole.

           *   *   *

69

545   Twelve days and nights she wither'd thus; at last,
    Without a groan, or sigh, or glance, to show
A parting pang, the spirit from her past:
    And they who watch'd her nearest could not know
The very instant, till the change that cast
550   Her sweet face into shadow, dull and slow,
Glazed o'er her eyes—the beautiful, the black—
Oh! to possess such lustre—and then lack!

70

She died, but not alone; she held within
    A second principle of life, which might
555   Have dawn'd a fair and sinless child of sin;
    But closed its little being without light,
And went down to the grave unborn, wherein
    Blossom and bough lie wither'd with one blight;

---

4. I.e., though she was ashen pale.

In vain the dews of Heaven descend above
560 The bleeding flower and blasted fruit of love.

71

Thus lived—thus died she; never more on her
　　Shall sorrow light, or shame. She was not made
Through years or moons the inner weight to bear,
　　Which colder hearts endure till they are laid
565 By age in earth; her days and pleasures were
　　Brief, but delightful—such as had not staid
Long with her destiny; but she sleeps well
By the sea shore, whereon she loved to dwell.

72

That isle is now all desolate and bare,
570 　　Its dwellings down, its tenants past away;
None but her own and father's grave is there,
　　And nothing outward tells of human clay;
Ye could not know where lies a thing so fair,
　　No stone is there to show, no tongue to say
575 What was; no dirge, except the hollow sea's,
Mourns o'er the beauty of the Cyclades.

73

But many a Greek maid in a loving song
　　Sighs o'er her name; and many an islander
With her sire's story makes the night less long;
580 　　Valour was his, and beauty dwelt with her;
If she loved rashly, her life paid for wrong—
　　A heavy price must all pay who thus err,
In some shape; let none think to fly the danger,
For soon or late Love is his own avenger.

74

585 But let me change this theme, which grows too sad,
　　And lay this sheet of sorrows on the shelf;
I don't much like describing people mad,
　　For fear of seeming rather touch'd myself—
Besides I've no more on this head to add;
590 　　And as my Muse is a capricious elf,
We'll put about, and try another tack
With Juan, left half-kill'd some stanzas back.[5]

1818–23 　　　　　　　　　　　　　　　　　　　　　　1819–24

5. Juan's adventures continue. He is sold as a slave in Constantinople to an enamored sultana; she disguises him as a girl and adds him to her husband's harem for convenience of access. Juan escapes, joins the Russian army that is besieging Ismail, and so distinguishes himself in the capture of the town that he is sent with despatches to St. Petersburg. There he becomes "man-mistress" to the insatiable Catherine the Great. As the result of her assiduous attentions, he falls into a physical decline and, for a salutary change of scene and climate, is sent on a diplomatic mission to England. In canto 16, the last that Byron finished, he is in the middle of an amorous adventure while a guest at the medieval country mansion of an English nobleman, Lord Henry Amundeville, and his very beautiful wife.

PERCY BYSSHE SHELLEY
1792–1822

Percy Bysshe Shelley, a radical nonconformist in every aspect of his life and thought, emerged from a solidly conservative background. His ancestors had been Sussex aristocrats since early in the seventeenth century; his grandfather, Sir Bysshe Shelley, made himself the richest man in Horsham, Sussex; his father, Timothy Shelley, was a hardheaded and conventional Member of Parliament. Percy Shelley himself was in line for a baronetcy and, as befitted his station, was sent to be educated at Eton and Oxford. As a youth he was slight of build, eccentric in manner, and unskilled in sports or fighting and, as a consequence, was mercilessly baited by older and stronger boys. He later said that he saw the petty tyranny of schoolmasters and schoolmates as representative of man's general inhumanity to man, and dedicated his life to a war against injustice and oppression. As he described the experience in the Dedication to *Laon and Cythna*:

> So without shame, I spake:—"I will be wise,
> And just, and free, and mild, if in me lies
> Such power, for I grow weary to behold
> The selfish and the strong still tyrannise
> Without reproach or check." I then controuled
> My tears, my heart grew calm, and I was meek and bold.

At Oxford in the autumn of 1810 Shelley's closest friend was Thomas Jefferson Hogg, a self-centered, self-confident young man who shared Shelley's love of philosophy and scorn of orthodoxy. The two collaborated on a pamphlet, *The Necessity of Atheism,* which claimed that God's existence cannot be proved on empirical grounds, and, provocatively, they mailed it to the bishops and heads of the colleges at Oxford. Shelley refused to repudiate the document and, to his shock and grief, was peremptorily expelled, terminating a university career that had lasted only six months. This event opened a breach between Shelley and his father that widened over the years.

Shelley went to London, where he took up the cause of Harriet Westbrook, the pretty and warmhearted daughter of a well-to-do tavern keeper, whose father, Shelley wrote to Hogg, "has persecuted her in a most horrible way by endeavoring to compel her to go to school." Harriet threw herself on Shelley's protection, and "gratitude and admiration," he wrote, "all demand that I shall love her *forever.*" He eloped with Harriet to Edinburgh and married her, against his conviction that marriage was a tyrannical and degrading social institution. He was then eighteen years of age, and his bride sixteen. The young couple moved restlessly from place to place, living on a small allowance granted reluctantly by their families. In February 1812, accompanied by Harriet's sister Eliza, they traveled to Dublin to distribute Shelley's *Address to the Irish People* and otherwise take part in the movement for Catholic emancipation and for the amelioration of that oppressed and poverty-stricken people.

Back in London, Shelley became a disciple of the radical social philosopher William Godwin, author of the *Inquiry Concerning Political Justice.* In 1813 he printed privately his first important work, *Queen Mab,* a long poem set in the fantastic frame of the journey of a disembodied soul through space, to whom the fairy Mab reveals in visions the woeful past, the dreadful present, and a utopian future. Announcing that "there is no God!" Mab decries institutional religion and codified morality as the roots of social evil, prophesying that all institutions will wither away and humanity will return to its natural condition of goodness and felicity.

In the following spring Shelley, who had drifted apart from Harriet, fell in love with the beautiful Mary Wollstonecraft Godwin, daughter of Mary Wollstonecraft and William Godwin. Convinced that cohabitation without love is immoral, he abandoned

Harriet, fled to France with Mary (taking along her stepsister, Claire Clairmont), and—in accordance with his belief in nonexclusive love—invited Harriet to come live with them in the relationship of a sister. Shelley's elopement with Mary outraged her father, despite the facts that his own views of marriage had been no less radical than Shelley's and that Shelley, himself in financial difficulties, had earlier taken over Godwin's very substantial debts. When he returned to London, Shelley found that the general public, his family, and most of his friends regarded him as not only an atheist and revolutionary but also a gross immoralist. When two years later Harriet, pregnant by an unknown lover, drowned herself in a fit of despair, the courts denied Shelley the custody of their two children. Shelley married Mary Godwin and in 1818 moved to Italy. Thereafter he envisioned himself as an alien and outcast, rejected by the human race to whose welfare he had dedicated his powers and his life.

In Italy he resumed his restless way of life, evading creditors by moving from town to town and house to house. His health was usually bad. Although the death of his grandfather in 1815 had provided a substantial income, he dissipated so much of it by his warmhearted but improvident support of William Godwin, Leigh Hunt, and other needy pensioners that he was constantly short of money and harried by creditors. Within nine months, in 1818–19, Clara and William, children of Percy and Mary Shelley, both died. This tragedy threw Mary into a state of apathy and self-absorption that destroyed the earlier harmony of her relationship with her husband, from which even the birth of another son, Percy Florence, could not entirely rescue her.

In these circumstances, close to despair and knowing that he almost entirely lacked an audience, Shelley wrote his greatest works. In 1819 he completed *Prometheus Unbound* and a tragedy, *The Cenci*. He wrote also numerous lyric poems; a visionary call for a proletarian revolution, *The Mask of Anarchy*; a witty satire on Wordsworth, *Peter Bell the Third*; and a penetrating political essay, *A Philosophical View of Reform*. His works of the next two years include *A Defence of Poetry*; *Epipsychidion*, a rhapsodic vision of love as a spiritual union beyond earthly limits; *Adonais*, his elegy on the death of Keats; and *Hellas*, a lyrical drama evoked by the Greek war for liberation from the Turks. These writings, unlike the early *Queen Mab*, are the products of a mind chastened by tragic experience, deepened by philosophical speculation, and stored with the harvest of his reading—which Shelley carried on, as his friend Hogg said, "in season and out of season, at table, in bed, and especially during a walk," until he became one of the most erudite of poets. His delight in scientific discoveries and speculations continued, but his earlier zest for Gothic terrors and the social theories of the radical eighteenth-century optimists gave way to an absorption in Greek tragedy, Milton's *Paradise Lost*, and the Bible. Although he did not give up his hopes for a millennial future (he wore a ring with the motto *Il buon tempo verrà*—"the good time will come"), he now attributed the evils of society to humanity's own moral failures and grounded the possibility of radical social reform on a reform of the moral and imaginative faculties through the redeeming power of love. Though often represented as a simpleminded doctrinaire, Shelley in fact possessed a complex and energetically inquisitive intelligence that never halted at a fixed mental position; his writings reflect stages in a ceaseless exploration.

The poems of Shelley's maturity also show the influence of his study of Plato and the Neoplatonists. Shelley found congenial the Platonic division of the cosmos into two worlds—the ordinary world of change, mortality, evil, and suffering and an ideal world of perfect and eternal Forms, of which the world of sense-experience is only a distant and illusory reflection. The earlier interpretations of Shelley as a downright Platonic idealist, however, have been drastically modified by modern investigations of his reading and writings. He was a close student of British empirical philosophy, which limits knowledge to valid reasoning on what is given in sense-experience, and within this tradition he felt a special affinity to the radical skepticism of David Hume. A number of Shelley's works, such as *Mont Blanc*, express his view of the narrow limits of what human beings can know with certainty and exemplify his refusal to let his hopes harden into a philosophical or religious creed. To what has been called the "skeptical idealism" of the mature Shelley (see the notes he appended to his lyrics from *Hellas*), hope in a redemption from present social ills is not an intellectual certainty but a moral obligation. Despair is self-fulfilling; we must continue to hope because, by keeping open the possibility of a better future, hope releases the imaginative and creative powers that are the only means of achieving that end.

When in 1820 the Shelleys settled finally at Pisa, he came closer to finding contentment than at any other time in his adult life. A group of friends, Shelley's "Pisan Circle," gathered around them, including for a while Lord Byron and the swashbuckling young Cornishman Edward Trelawny. Chief in Shelley's affections were Edward Williams, a retired lieutenant of a cavalry regiment serving in India, and his charming common-law wife, Jane, with whom Shelley carried on a flirtation and to whom he addressed some of his best lyrics and verse letters. The end came suddenly, and in a way previsioned in the last stanza of *Adonais*, in which he had described his spirit as a ship driven by a violent storm out into the dark unknown. On July 8, 1822, Shelley and Edward Williams were sailing their open boat, the *Don Juan*, on the Gulf of Spezia. A violent squall swamped the boat. When several days later the bodies were washed ashore they were cremated, and Shelley's ashes were buried in the Protestant Cemetery at Rome, near the graves of John Keats and William Shelley, the poet's young son.

Both Shelley's character and his poetry have been the subject of violently contradictory, and often partisan, estimates. His actions according to his deep convictions often led to disastrous consequences for himself and those near to him; and even recent scholars, while repudiating the vicious attacks by Shelley's contemporaries, attribute some of those actions to a self-assured egotism that masked itself as idealism. Yet Byron, who knew Shelley intimately and did not pay moral compliments lightly, wrote to his publisher John Murray, in response to attacks on Shelley at the time of his death: "You are all brutally mistaken about Shelley, who was, without exception, the *best* and least selfish man I ever knew." Shelley's politics, vilified during his lifetime, have made him a literary hero to later political radicals, as well as to the British Labour Party. As a poet, Shelley was greatly admired by Robert Browning, Swinburne, and other Victorians; but in the mid-twentieth century he was repeatedly charged with intellectual and emotional immaturity, shoddy workmanship, and incoherent imagery by such influential writers as F. R. Leavis and his followers in Britain and the New Critics in America. More recently, however, many sympathetic studies have revealed the coherent intellectual understructure of his poems and have confirmed Wordsworth's early recognition that "Shelley is one of the best *artists* of us all: I mean in workmanship of style." Shelley, it has become clear, greatly expanded the metrical and stanzaic resources of English versification. His poems exhibit a broad range of voices, from the high but ordered passion of *Ode to the West Wind*, through the heroic dignity of the utterances of Prometheus, to the approximation of what is inexpressible in the description of Asia's transfiguration and in the visionary conclusion of *Adonais*. Most surprising, for a poet who almost entirely lacked an audience, is the urbanity, the assured command of the tone and language of a cultivated man of the world, exemplified in passages that Shelley wrote all through his mature career and especially in the lyrics and verse letters that he composed during the last year of his life.

The texts printed here are those prepared by Donald H. Reiman and Sharon B. Powers for *Shelley's Poetry and Prose*, a Norton Critical Edition (1977); Reiman has also edited for this anthology a few poems not included in that edition.

Mutability

We are as clouds that veil the midnight moon;
   How restlessly they speed, and gleam, and quiver,
Streaking the darkness radiantly!—yet soon
   Night closes round, and they are lost for ever:

5 Or like forgotten lyres,° whose dissonant strings   *wind harps*
   Give various response to each varying blast,
To whose frail frame no second motion brings
   One mood or modulation like the last.

We rest.—A dream has power to poison sleep;
10   We rise.—One wandering thought pollutes the day;
We feel, conceive or reason, laugh or weep;
   Embrace fond woe, or cast our cares away:

It is the same!—For, be it joy or sorrow,
   The path of its departure still is free:
15 Man's yesterday may ne'er be like his morrow;
   Nought may endure but Mutability.

ca. 1814–15   1816

To Wordsworth[1]

Poet of Nature, thou hast wept to know
That things depart which never may return:
Childhood and youth, friendship and love's first glow,
Have fled like sweet dreams, leaving thee to mourn.
5 These common woes I feel. One loss is mine
Which thou too feel'st, yet I alone deplore.
Thou wert as a lone star, whose light did shine
On some frail bark in winter's midnight roar:
Thou hast like to a rock-built refuge stood
10 Above the blind and battling multitude:
In honoured poverty thy voice did weave
Songs consecrate to truth and liberty,—
Deserting these, thou leavest me to grieve,
Thus having been, that thou shouldst cease to be.

ca. 1814–15   1816

---

1. Shelley's grieved comment on the poet of nature and of social radicalism after his views had become conservative.

Mont Blanc[1]

Lines Written in the Vale of Chamouni

1

The everlasting universe of things
Flows through the mind, and rolls its rapid waves,
Now dark—now glittering—now reflecting gloom—
Now lending splendour, where from secret springs
5   The source of human thought its tribute brings
Of waters,—with a sound but half its own.
Such as a feeble brook will oft assume
In the wild woods, among the mountains lone,
Where waterfalls around it leap forever,
10 Where woods and winds contend, and a vast river
Over its rocks ceaselessly bursts and raves.

2

Thus thou, Ravine of Arve—dark, deep Ravine—
Thou many-coloured, many-voiced vale,
Over whose pines, and crags, and caverns sail
15 Fast cloud shadows and sunbeams: awful° scene,   *awe-inspiring*
Where Power in likeness of the Arve comes down
From the ice gulphs that gird his secret throne,
Bursting through these dark mountains like the flame
Of lightning through the tempest;—thou dost lie,
20 Thy giant brood of pines around thee clinging,
Children of elder time, in whose devotion
The chainless winds still come and ever came
To drink their odours, and their mighty swinging
To hear—an old and solemn harmony;
25 Thine earthly rainbows stretched across the sweep
Of the etherial waterfall, whose veil
Robes some unsculptured[2] image; the strange sleep
Which when the voices of the desart fail
Wraps all in its own deep eternity;—
30 Thy caverns echoing to the Arve's commotion,
A loud, lone sound no other sound can tame;
Thou art pervaded with that ceaseless motion,

1. Mont Blanc, near the French border with Italy, is the highest mountain in the Alps. When he conceived the poem, Shelley was standing on a bridge over the Arve River in the valley of Chamonix, in what is now southeastern France.
   Shelley wrote of this poem: "It was composed under the immediate impression of the deep and powerful feelings excited by the objects which it attempts to describe; and, as an indisciplined over-flowing of the soul, rests its claim to approbation on an attempt to imitate the untamable wildness and inaccessible solemnity from which those feelings sprang."
   Shelley's comment points to two important attributes of *Mont Blanc*. First, he attempts, as in other poems (especially in *Ode to the West Wind*), to make the poem iconic or directly imitative of the alternating "wildness" and "solemnity" of the scene and the consonant thought and feelings it evokes. Second, this work belongs to the genre of the "local" poem, a descriptive-meditative presentation of a precisely identified landscape. In this respect it resembles Wordsworth's *Tintern Abbey*, the major influence on *Mont Blanc*. Shelley's poem, like Wordsworth's, poses the question of the significance of the interchange between nature and the human mind; he proposes, however, a very different answer to that question.
2. I.e., not formed by humans.

Thou art the path of that unresting sound—
Dizzy Ravine! and when I gaze on thee
35 I seem as in a trance sublime and strange
To muse on my own separate phantasy,
My own, my human mind, which passively
Now renders and receives fast influencings,
Holding an unremitting interchange
40 With the clear universe of things around;[3]
One legion of wild thoughts, whose wandering wings
Now float above thy darkness, and now rest
Where that or thou art no unbidden guest,
In the still cave of the witch Poesy,[4]
45 Seeking among the shadows that pass by
Ghosts of all things that are, some shade of thee,
Some phantom, some faint image; till the breast
From which they fled recalls them, thou art there![5]

3

Some say that gleams of a remoter world
50 Visit the soul in sleep,—that death is slumber,
And that its shapes the busy thoughts outnumber
Of those who wake and live.—I look on high;
Has some unknown omnipotence unfurled
The veil of life and death? or do I lie
55 In dream, and does the mightier world of sleep
Spread far around and inaccessibly
Its circles? For the very spirit fails,
Driven like a homeless cloud from steep to steep
That vanishes among the viewless° gales!   *invisible*
60 Far, far above, piercing the infinite sky,
Mont Blanc appears,—still, snowy, and serene—
Its subject mountains their unearthly forms
Pile around it, ice and rock; broad vales between
Of frozen floods, unfathomable deeps,
65 Blue as the overhanging heaven, that spread
And wind among the accumulated steeps;
A desart peopled by the storms alone,
Save when the eagle brings some hunter's bone,
And the wolf tracts° her there—how hideously   *tracks*
70 Its shapes are heaped around! rude, bare, and high,
Ghastly, and scarred, and riven.—Is this the scene
Where the old Earthquake-dæmon[6] taught her young
Ruin? Were these their toys? or did a sea
Of fire, envelope once this silent snow?
75 None can reply—all seems eternal now.

---

3. This passage is remarkably parallel to a passage Shelley could not have read in *The Prelude*, first published in 1850, in which Wordsworth discovers, in the landscape viewed from Mount Snowdon, the "type" or "emblem" of the human mind in its interchange with nature (see *The Prelude* 14.63ff., p. 1551).
4. I.e., in the part of the mind that creates poetry.

5. I.e., the thoughts (line 41) seek, in the poet's creative faculty, some shade, phantom, or image of the Arve; and when the breast, which has forgotten these images, recalls them again—there, suddenly, does the Arve exist.
6. A supernatural being, halfway between mortals and the gods. Here it represents the force that makes earthquakes.

The wilderness has a mysterious tongue
Which teaches awful doubt, or faith so mild,
So solemn, so serene, that man may be
But for such faith[7] with nature reconciled;
80 Thou hast a voice, great Mountain, to repeal
Large codes of fraud and woe; not understood
By all, but which[8] the wise, and great, and good
Interpret, or make felt, or deeply feel.

4

The fields, the lakes, the forests, and the streams,
85 Ocean, and all the living things that dwell
Within the dædal[9] earth; lightning, and rain,
Earthquake, and fiery flood, and hurricane,
The torpor of the year when feeble dreams
Visit the hidden buds, or dreamless sleep
90 Holds every future leaf and flower;—the bound
With which from that detested trance they leap;
The works and ways of man, their death and birth,
And that of him and all that his may be;
All things that move and breathe with toil and sound
95 Are born and die; revolve, subside and swell.
Power dwells apart in its tranquillity
Remote, serene, and inaccessible:
And *this*, the naked countenance of earth,
On which I gaze, even these primæval mountains
100 Teach the adverting mind. The glaciers creep
Like snakes that watch their prey, from their far fountains,
Slow rolling on; there, many a precipice,
Frost and the Sun in scorn of mortal power
Have piled: dome, pyramid, and pinnacle,
105 A city of death, distinct with many a tower
And wall impregnable of beaming ice.
Yet not a city, but a flood of ruin
Is there, that from the boundaries of the sky
Rolls its perpetual stream; vast pines are strewing
110 Its destined path, or in the mangled soil
Branchless and shattered stand: the rocks, drawn down
From yon remotest waste, have overthrown
The limits of the dead and living world,
Never to be reclaimed. The dwelling-place
115 Of insects, beasts, and birds, becomes its spoil;
Their food and their retreat for ever gone,
So much of life and joy is lost. The race
Of man, flies far in dread; his work and dwelling
Vanish, like smoke before the tempest's stream,
120 And their place is not known. Below, vast caves

---

7. I.e., "simply by holding such faith." In Shelley's balance of possibilities, the landscape is equally capable of instilling such a Wordsworthian faith (in the possibility of reconciling humans and nature, lines 78–79) or the "awful" (i.e., "awe-some") doubt (that nature is totally alien to human ends and values).

8. The reference is to "voice," line 80.

9. Intricately formed; derived from Daedalus, builder of the labyrinth in Crete.

Shine in the rushing torrents' restless gleam,
Which from those secret chasms in tumult welling[1]
Meet in the vale, and one majestic River,[2]
The breath and blood of distant lands, for ever
125 Rolls its loud waters to the ocean waves,
Breathes its swift vapours to the circling air.

5

Mont Blanc yet gleams on high:—the power is there,
The still and solemn power of many sights,
And many sounds, and much of life and death.
130 In the calm darkness of the moonless nights,
In the lone glare of day, the snows descend
Upon that Mountain; none beholds them there,
Nor when the flakes burn in the sinking sun,
Or the star-beams dart through them:—Winds contend
135 Silently there, and heap the snow with breath
Rapid and strong, but silently! Its home
The voiceless lightning in these solitudes
Keeps innocently, and like vapour broods
Over the snow. The secret strength of things
140 Which governs thought, and to the infinite dome
Of heaven is as a law, inhabits thee!
And what were thou,° and earth, and stars, and sea,   *Mont Blanc*
If to the human mind's imaginings
Silence and solitude were vacancy?

1816   1817

Hymn to Intellectual Beauty[1]

I

The awful shadow of some unseen Power
    Floats though unseen amongst us,—visiting
    This various world with as inconstant wing
As summer winds that creep from flower to flower.—
5 Like moonbeams that behind some piny mountain shower,[2]
    It visits with inconstant glance
    Each human heart and countenance;
Like hues and harmonies of evening,—
    Like clouds in starlight widely spread,—
10   Like memory of music fled,—
    Like aught that for its grace may be
Dear, and yet dearer for its mystery.

1. This description (as well as that in lines 9–11) seems to be an echo of Coleridge's description of the chasm and sacred river in the recently published *Kubla Khan*, lines 12–24.
2. The Arve, which flows into Lake Geneva.
1. "Intellectual" means "nonsensible." "Intellectual Beauty" is thus beyond access by sense experience. It is simply postulated to account for occasional states of awareness that lend splendor, grace, and truth both to experience of the natural world and to people's moral consciousness. To this mystery (stanzas 5–7) Shelley had, at its early visitation, dedicated his powers, and to it he now prays as he passes the noon of life (stanza 7).
2. Used as a verb.

2

Spirit of BEAUTY, that dost consecrate
    With thine own hues all thou dost shine upon
15   Of human thought or form,—where art thou gone?
Why dost thou pass away and leave our state,
This dim vast vale of tears, vacant and desolate?
        Ask why the sunlight not forever
        Weaves rainbows o'er yon mountain river,
20 Why aught should fail and fade that once is shewn,
        Why fear and dream and death and birth
        Cast on the daylight of this earth
        Such gloom,—why man has such a scope
For love and hate, despondency and hope?

3

25 No voice from some sublimer world hath ever
        To sage or poet these responses given—
        Therefore the name of God and ghosts and Heaven,
Remain the records of their vain endeavour,[3]
Frail spells—whose uttered charm might not avail to sever,
30   From all we hear and all we see,
        Doubt, chance, and mutability.
Thy light alone—like mist o'er mountains driven,
        Or music by the night wind sent
        Through strings of some still instrument,°   *wind harp*
35   Or moonlight on a midnight stream,
Gives grace and truth to life's unquiet dream.

4

Love, Hope, and Self-esteem, like clouds depart
        And come, for some uncertain moments lent.
        Man were immortal, and omnipotent,
40 Didst thou, unknown and awful as thou art,
Keep with thy glorious train firm state within his heart.[4]
        Thou messenger of sympathies,
        That wax and wane in lovers' eyes—
Thou—that to human thought art nourishment,
45   Like darkness to a dying flame!
        Depart not as thy shadow came,
        Depart not—lest the grave should be,
Like life and fear, a dark reality.

5

While yet a boy I sought for ghosts, and sped
50   Through many a listening chamber, cave and ruin,
        And starlight wood, with fearful steps pursuing
Hopes of high talk with the departed dead.

---

3. The names (line 27) are nothing better than
guesses at identifying the mystery by religious philosophers and poets (line 26).

4. I.e., "man would be immortal . . . if thou didst
keep."

I called on poisonous names with which our youth is fed;[5]
   I was not heard—I saw them not—
55   When musing deeply on the lot
Of life, at that sweet time when winds are wooing
    All vital things that wake to bring
    News of buds and blossoming,—
    Sudden, thy shadow fell on me;
60   I shrieked, and clasped my hands in extacy!

6

I vowed that I would dedicate my powers
   To thee and thine—have I not kept the vow?
   With beating heart and streaming eyes, even now
I call the phantoms of a thousand hours
65   Each from his voiceless grave: they have in visioned bowers
    Of studious zeal or love's delight
    Outwatched with me the envious night[6]—
They know that never joy illumed my brow
    Unlinked with hope that thou wouldst free
70   This world from its dark slavery,
    That thou—O awful LOVELINESS,
Wouldst give whate'er these words cannot express.

7

The day becomes more solemn and serene
   When noon is past—there is a harmony
75   In autumn, and a lustre in its sky,
Which through the summer is not heard or seen,
As if it could not be, as if it had not been!
    Thus let thy power, which like the truth
    Of nature on my passive youth
80   Descended, to my onward life supply
    Its calm—to one who worships thee,
    And every form containing thee,
    Whom, SPIRIT fair, thy spells did bind
To fear[7] himself, and love all human kind.

1816   1817

Ozymandias[1]

I met a traveller from an antique land,
Who said—"Two vast and trunkless legs of stone
Stand in the desert. . . . Near them, on the sand,

---

5. Lines 49–52 refer to Shelley's youthful experiments with magic. The "poisonous names" are probably those in the prayers he had been taught as a child.
6. I.e., stayed up until the night, envious of their delight, had reluctantly departed.
7. Probably in the old sense: "to stand in awe of."

1. According to Diodorus Siculus, Greek historian of the 1st century B.C.E., the largest statue in Egypt had the inscription: "I am Ozymandias, king of kings; if anyone wishes to know what I am and where I lie, let him surpass me in some of my exploits." Ozymandias was the Greek name for Ramses II of Egypt, 13th century B.C.E.

Half sunk a shattered visage lies, whose frown,
5   And wrinkled lip, and sneer of cold command,
Tell that its sculptor well those passions read
Which yet survive, stamped on these lifeless things,
The hand that mocked them, and the heart that fed;[2]
And on the pedestal, these words appear:
10   My name is Ozymandias, King of Kings,
Look on my Works, ye Mighty, and despair!
Nothing beside remains. Round the decay
Of that colossal Wreck, boundless and bare
The lone and level sands stretch far away."

1817   1818

A Song: "Men of England"[1]

Men of England, wherefore plough
For the lords who lay ye low?
Wherefore weave with toil and care
The rich robes your tyrants wear?

5   Wherefore feed and clothe and save
From the cradle to the grave
Those ungrateful drones who would
Drain your sweat—nay, drink your blood?

Wherefore, Bees of England, forge
10   Many a weapon, chain, and scourge,
That these stingless drones may spoil
The forced produce of your toil?

Have ye leisure, comfort, calm,
Shelter, food, love's gentle balm?
15   Or what is it ye buy so dear
With your pain and with your fear?

The seed ye sow, another reaps;
The wealth ye find, another keeps;
The robes ye weave, another wears;
20   The arms ye forge, another bears.

Sow seed—but let no tyrant reap:
Find wealth—let no impostor heap:
Weave robes—let not the idle wear:
Forge arms—in your defence to bear.

2. "The hand" is the sculptor's, who had "mocked"
(both imitated and derided) the sculptured passions; "the heart" is the king's, which has "fed" his
passions.
1. This and the two following poems were written
at a time of turbulent unrest, after the return of
troops from the Napoleonic Wars had precipitated
a great economic depression. The *Song*, expressing
Shelley's hope for a proletarian revolution, was
originally planned as one of a series for workers. It
has become, as the poet wished, a hymn of the
British labor movement.

25 Shrink to your cellars, holes, and cells—
In halls ye deck another dwells.
Why shake the chains ye wrought? Ye see
The steel ye tempered glance on ye.

With plough and spade and hoe and loom
30 Trace your grave and build your tomb
And weave your winding-sheet—till fair
England be your Sepulchre.

1819   1839

England in 1819

An old, mad, blind, despised, and dying King;[1]
Princes, the dregs of their dull race, who flow
Through public scorn,—mud from a muddy spring;
Rulers who neither see nor feel nor know,
5 But leechlike to their fainting country cling
Till they drop, blind in blood, without a blow.
A people starved and stabbed in th' untilled field;[2]
An army, whom liberticide and prey
Makes as a two-edged sword to all who wield;
10 Golden and sanguine laws[3] which tempt and slay;
Religion Christless, Godless—a book sealed;
A senate, Time's worst statute, unrepealed[4]—
Are graves from which a glorious Phantom[5] may
Burst, to illumine our tempestuous day.

1819   1839

To Sidmouth and Castlereagh[1]

As from their ancestral oak
    Two empty ravens wind their clarion,
Yell by yell, and croak by croak,
When they scent the noonday smoke
5   Of fresh human carrion:—

As two gibbering night-birds flit
    From their bowers of deadly yew
Through the night to frighten it—

1. George III, who had been declared insane in 1811. He died in 1820.
2. Alluding to the Peterloo Massacre on August 16, 1819. In St. Peter's field, near Manchester, a troop of cavalry had charged into a crowd attending a peaceful rally in support of parliamentary reform. "Peterloo" is an ironic combination of "St. Peter's" and "Waterloo."
3. Laws bought with gold, and leading to bloodshed.
4. The law imposing disabilities on Dissenters and Roman Catholics.

5. I.e., a revolution.
1. Shelley's powerful satire is directed against Viscount Castlereagh, foreign secretary (1812–22), who took a leading part in the European settlement after the Battle of Waterloo, and Viscount Sidmouth (1757–1844), the home secretary, whose cruelly coercive measures (supported by Castlereagh) against unrest in the laboring classes were in large part responsible for the Peterloo Massacre.
    When this poem was reprinted by Mary Shelley in 1839, it was given the title *Similes for Two Political Characters of 1819.*

When the moon is in a fit,
10 And the stars are none, or few:—

As a shark and dogfish wait
 Under an Atlantic isle
For the Negro-ship, whose freight
Is the theme of their debate,
15 Wrinkling their red gills the while—

Are ye—two vultures sick for battle,
 Two scorpions under one wet stone,
Two bloodless wolves whose dry throats rattle,
Two crows perched on the murrained[2] cattle,
20 Two vipers tangled into one.

1819   1832

The Indian Girl's Song[1] [The Indian Serenade]

I arise from dreams of thee
In the first sleep of night—
The winds are breathing low
And the stars are burning bright.
5 I arise from dreams of thee—
And a spirit in my feet
Has borne me—Who knows how?
To thy chamber window, sweet!—

The wandering airs they faint
10 On the dark silent stream—
The champak[2] odours fail
Like sweet thoughts in a dream;
The nightingale's complaint—
It dies upon her heart—
15 As I must die on thine
O beloved as thou art!

O lift me from the grass!
I die, I faint, I fail!
Let thy love in kisses rain
20 On my lips and eyelids pale.
My cheek is cold and white, alas!
My heart beats loud and fast.
Oh press it close to thine again
Where it will break at last.

1819   1822

2. A *murrain* is a malignant disease of domestic animals.
1. Usually headed *The Indian Serenade*. Shelley's title makes it clear that the poem is not a personal utterance but a dramatic lyric, sung by an imagined East Indian girl. It manifests the conventional extravagance of an Oriental love poem.
2. An Indian species of magnolia, bearing fragrant orange flowers.

Ode to the West Wind[1]

1

O wild West Wind, thou breath of Autumn's being,
Thou, from whose unseen presence the leaves dead
Are driven, like ghosts from an enchanter fleeing,

Yellow, and black, and pale, and hectic[2] red,
5 Pestilence-stricken multitudes: O Thou,
Who chariotest to their dark wintry bed

The winged seeds, where they lie cold and low,
Each like a corpse within its grave, until
Thine azure sister of the Spring[3] shall blow

10 Her clarion[4] o'er the dreaming earth, and fill
(Driving sweet buds like flocks to feed in air)
With living hues and odours plain and hill:

Wild Spirit, which art moving everywhere;
Destroyer and Preserver; hear, O hear!

2

15 Thou on whose stream, 'mid the steep sky's commotion,
Loose clouds like Earth's decaying leaves are shed,
Shook from the tangled boughs of Heaven and Ocean,[5]

Angels of rain and lightning: there are spread
On the blue surface of thine aery surge,
20 Like the bright hair uplifted from the head

Of some fierce Mænad,[6] even from the dim verge
Of the horizon to the zenith's height,
The locks of the approaching storm. Thou Dirge

---

1. This poem was conceived and chiefly written in a wood that skirts the Arno, near Florence, and on a day when that tempestuous wind, whose temperature is at once mild and animating, was collecting the vapours which pour down the autumnal rains [Shelley's note]. As in other major Romantic poems—for example, the opening of Wordsworth's *Prelude,* Coleridge's *Dejection: An Ode,* and the conclusion to Shelley's *Adonais*—the rising wind, linked with the cycle of the seasons, is presented as the outer correspondent to an inner change from apathy to spiritual vitality and from imaginative sterility to a burst of creative power that is paralleled to the inspiration of the biblical prophets. In Hebrew, Latin, Greek, and many other languages, the words for *wind, breath, soul,* and *inspiration* are all identical or related. Thus Shelley's west wind is a "spirit" (the Latin *spiritus:* wind, breath, soul, and the root word in "inspiration"), the "breath of Autumn's being," which on earth, sky, and sea destroys in the autumn to revivify in the spring. Around this central image the poem weaves various cycles of death and regeneration— vegetational, human, and divine.

Shelley's sonnet-length stanza, developed from the interlaced three-line units of the Italian *terza rima* (*aba bcb cdc,* etc.), consists of a set of four such tercets, closed by a couplet rhyming with the middle line of the preceding tercet: *aba bcb cdc ded ee.*

2. Referring to the kind of fever that occurs in tuberculosis.

3. The west wind that will blow in the spring.

4. A high, shrill trumpet.

5. The fragmentary clouds ("leaves") are torn by the wind from the larger and higher clouds ("boughs"), which are formed by a union of air with vapor drawn up by the sun from the ocean. "Angels" (line 18) suggests the old sense: "messengers," "harbingers."

6. A female votary who danced frenziedly in the worship of Dionysus (Bacchus), the Greek god of wine and vegetation. As vegetation god, he was fabled to die in the fall and to be resurrected in the spring.

Of the dying year, to which this closing night
25 Will be the dome of a vast sepulchre,
Vaulted with all thy congregated might

Of vapours,° from whose solid atmosphere   clouds
Black rain and fire and hail will burst: O hear!

3

Thou who didst waken from his summer dreams
30 The blue Mediterranean, where he lay,
Lulled by the coil of his chrystalline streams,[7]

Beside a pumice isle in Baiæ's bay,[8]
And saw in sleep old palaces and towers
Quivering within the wave's intenser day,

35 All overgrown with azure moss and flowers
So sweet, the sense faints picturing them! Thou
For whose path the Atlantic's level powers

Cleave themselves into chasms, while far below
The sea-blooms and the oozy woods which wear
40 The sapless foliage of the ocean, know

Thy voice, and suddenly grow grey with fear,
And tremble and despoil themselves:[9] O hear!

4

If I were a dead leaf thou mightest bear;
If I were a swift cloud to fly with thee;
45 A wave to pant beneath thy power, and share

The impulse of thy strength, only less free
Than thou, O Uncontrollable! If even
I were as in my boyhood, and could be

The comrade of thy wanderings over Heaven,
50 As then, when to outstrip thy skiey speed
Scarce seemed a vision; I would ne'er have striven

As thus with thee in prayer in my sore need.
Oh! lift me as a wave, a leaf, a cloud!
I fall upon the thorns of life! I bleed!

55 A heavy weight of hours has chained and bowed
One too like thee: tameless, and swift, and proud.

7. The currents that flow in the Mediterranean
Sea, sometimes with a visible difference in color.
8. West of Naples, the locale of imposing villas
erected by Roman emperors. "Pumice": a porous
volcanic stone.
9. The vegetation at the bottom of the sea . . .
sympathizes with that of the land in the change of
seasons [Shelley's note].

5
Make me thy lyre,[1] even as the forest is:
What if my leaves are falling like its own!
The tumult of thy mighty harmonies

60 Will take from both a deep, autumnal tone,
Sweet though in sadness. Be thou, Spirit fierce,
My spirit! Be thou me, impetuous one!

Drive my dead thoughts over the universe
Like withered leaves to quicken a new birth!
65 And, by the incantation of this verse,

Scatter, as from an unextinguished hearth
Ashes and sparks, my words among mankind!
Be through my lips to unawakened Earth

The trumpet of a prophecy! O Wind,
70 If Winter comes, can Spring be far behind?

1819   1820

Prometheus Unbound   Shelley composed this work in Italy between the
autumn of 1818 and the close of 1819 and published it the following summer. Upon
its completion he wrote in a letter, "It is a drama, with characters and mechanism of
a kind yet unattempted; and I think the execution is better than any of my former
attempts." It is based on the *Prometheus Bound* of Aeschylus, which dramatizes the
sufferings of Prometheus, unrepentant champion of humanity, who, because he had
stolen fire from heaven, was condemned by Zeus to be chained to Mount Caucasus
and to be tortured by a vulture feeding on his liver; in a lost sequel, Aeschylus reconciled Prometheus with his oppressor. Shelley continued Aeschylus's story but transformed it into a symbolic drama about the origin of evil and the possibility of
overcoming it. In such earlier writings as *Queen Mab* Shelley had expressed his belief
that injustice and suffering can be eliminated by an external revolution that will wipe
out or radically reform the causes of evil, attributed to existing social, political, and
religious institutions. Implicit in *Prometheus Unbound*, on the other hand, is the view
that both evil and the possibility of reform are the moral responsibility of men and
women themselves. Social chaos and wars are a gigantic projection of human moral
disorder and inner division and conflict; tyrants are the outer representatives of the
tyranny of our baser over our better elements; hatred for others is a product of self-
contempt; and external political reform is impossible unless we have first reformed
our own nature at its roots, by substituting selfless love for divisive hatred. Shelley
thus incorporates into his secular myth—of universal regeneration by a triumph of
humanity's moral imagination—the ethical teaching of Christ on the Mount, together
with the classical morality represented in the *Prometheus* of Aeschylus. Shelley however, adds the warning (4.562ff.) that even should such a regeneration take place, its
maintenance will depend on an unremitting vigilance, lest the serpent deep in human
nature break loose and start the cycle of evil all over again.
    Shelley writes in his preface that it is a mistake to suppose that the poem contains

1. The Eolian lyre, which responds to the wind with rising and falling musical chords.

"a reasoned system on the theory of human life. Didactic poetry is my abhorrence." *Prometheus Unbound* is not a dramatized philosophical essay or a moral allegory but a large and intricate imaginative construction that involves premises about human nature and the springs of morality and creativity. The non-Christian poet Yeats called it one of "the sacred books of the world," and the Christian critic C. S. Lewis found in it poetic powers matched only by Dante.

FROM PROMETHEUS UNBOUND

A Lyrical Drama in Four Acts

Audisne hæc Amphiarae, sub terram abdite?[1]

Preface

The Greek tragic writers, in selecting as their subject any portion of their national history or mythology, employed in their treatment of it a certain arbitrary discretion. They by no means conceived themselves bound to adhere to the common interpretation or to imitate in story as in title their rivals and predecessors. Such a system would have amounted to a resignation of those claims to preference over their competitors which incited the composition. The Agamemnonian story was exhibited on the Athenian theatre with as many variations as dramas.

I have presumed to employ a similar licence.—The *Prometheus Unbound* of Æschylus, supposed the reconciliation of Jupiter with his victim as the price of the disclosure of the danger threatened to his empire by the consummation of his marriage with Thetis. Thetis, according to this view of the subject, was given in marriage to Peleus, and Prometheus by the permission of Jupiter delivered from his captivity by Hercules.[2]—Had I framed my story on this model I should have done no more than have attempted to restore the lost drama of Æschylus; an ambition, which, if my preference to this mode of treating the subject had incited me to cherish, the recollection of the high comparison such an attempt would challenge, might well abate. But in truth I was averse from a catastrophe so feeble as that of reconciling the Champion with the Oppressor of mankind. The moral interest of the fable which is so powerfully sustained by the sufferings and endurance of Prometheus, would be annihilated if we could conceive of him as unsaying his high language, and quailing before his successful and perfidious adversary. The only imaginary being resembling in any degree Prometheus, is Satan; and Prometheus is, in my judgement, a more poetical character than Satan

1. Cicero, *Tusculan Disputations* 2.60: "Do you hear this, O Amphiaraus, concealed under the earth?" In Greek myth Amphiaraus was a seer. Fleeing from an unsuccessful assault on Thebes, he was saved from his pursuers by Zeus, who by a thunderbolt opened a cleft in the earth that swallowed him up.

  In his *Disputations* Cicero is arguing for the Stoic doctrine of the need to master pain and suffering. He quotes this line (a Latin translation from Aeschylus's lost drama *Epigoni*) in the course of an

anecdote about Dionysius of Heraclea, who, tormented by kidney stones, abjures the doctrine of his Stoic teacher Zeno that pain is not an evil. By way of reproof his fellow-Stoic Cleanthes strikes his foot on the ground and utters this line. Cicero interprets it as an appeal to Zeno the Stoic master (under the name of Amphiaraus).

2. Shelley's description of the subject of Aeschylus's lost drama, *Prometheus Unbound*, is a speculation based on surviving fragments.

because, in addition to courage and majesty and firm and patient opposition to omnipotent force, he is susceptible of being described as exempt from the taints of ambition, envy, revenge, and a desire for personal aggrandisement, which in the Hero of *Paradise Lost,* interfere with the interest. The character of Satan engenders in the mind a pernicious casuistry which leads us to weigh his faults with his wrongs and to excuse the former because the latter exceed all measure. In the minds of those who consider that magnificent fiction with a religious feeling, it engenders something worse. But Prometheus is, as it were, the type of the highest perfection of moral and intellectual nature, impelled by the purest and the truest motives to the best and noblest ends.

This Poem was chiefly written upon the mountainous ruins of the Baths of Caracalla, among the flowery glades, and thickets of odoriferous blossoming trees which are extended in ever winding labyrinths upon its immense platforms and dizzy arches suspended in the air. The bright blue sky of Rome, and the effect of the vigorous awakening of spring in that divinest climate, and the new life with which it drenches the spirits even to intoxication, were the inspiration of this drama.

The imagery which I have employed will be found in many instances to have been drawn from the operations of the human mind, or from those external actions by which they are expressed. This is unusual in modern Poetry; although Dante and Shakespeare are full of instances of the same kind: Dante indeed more than any other poet and with greater success. But the Greek poets, as writers to whom no resource of awakening the sympathy of their contemporaries was unknown, were in the habitual use of this power, and it is the study of their works (since a higher merit would probably be denied me) to which I am willing that my readers should impute this singularity.

One word is due in candour to the degree in which the study of contemporary writings may have tinged my composition, for such has been a topic of censure with regard to poems far more popular, and indeed more deservedly popular than mine. It is impossible that any one who inhabits the same age with such writers as those who stand in the foremost ranks of our own, can conscientiously assure himself, that his language and tone of thought may not have been modified by the study of the productions of those extraordinary intellects. It is true, that, not the spirit of their genius, but the forms in which it has manifested itself, are due, less to the peculiarities of their own minds, than to the peculiarity of the moral and intellectual condition of the minds among which they have been produced. Thus a number of writers possess the form, whilst they want the spirit of those whom, it is alleged, they imitate; because the former is the endowment of the age in which they live, and the latter must be the uncommunicated lightning of their own mind.

The peculiar style of intense and comprehensive imagery which distinguishes the modern literature of England, has not been, as a general power, the product of the imitation of any particular writer. The mass of capabilities remains at every period materially the same; the circumstances which awaken it to action perpetually change. If England were divided into forty republics, each equal in population and extent to Athens, there is no reason to suppose but that, under institutions not more perfect than those of Athens, each would produce philosophers and poets equal to those who (if we except Shakespeare) have never been surpassed. We owe the great writers of the golden age of our literature to that fervid awakening of the public mind which shook to dust the oldest and most oppressive form of the Christian Religion. We owe Milton to the progress and developement of the same spirit; the sacred Milton was, let it ever be remembered, a Republican, and a bold enquirer into morals and religion. The great writers of our own age are, we have reason to suppose, the companions and forerunners of some unimagined change in our social condition or the opinions which cement it. The cloud of mind is discharging its collected lightning, and the equilibrium between institutions and opinions is now restoring, or is about to be restored.[3]

As to imitation; Poetry is a mimetic art. It creates, but it creates by combination and representation. Poetical abstractions are beautiful and new, not because the portions of which they are composed had no previous existence in the mind of man or in nature, but because the whole produced by their combination has some intelligible and beautiful analogy with those sources of emotion and thought, and with the contemporary condition of them: one great poet is a masterpiece of nature, which another not only ought to study but must study. He might as wisely and as easily determine that his mind should no longer be the mirror of all that is lovely in the visible universe, as exclude from his contemplation the beautiful which exists in the writings of a great contemporary. The pretence of doing it would be a presumption in any but the greatest; the effect, even in him, would be strained, unnatural and ineffectual. A Poet, is the combined product of such internal powers as modify the nature of others, and of such external influences as excite and sustain these powers; he is not one, but both. Every man's mind is in this respect modified by all the objects of nature and art, by every word and every suggestion which he ever admitted to act upon his consciousness; it is the mirror upon which all forms are reflected, and in which they compose one form. Poets, not otherwise than philosophers, painters, sculptors and musicians, are in one sense the creators and in another the creations of their age. From this subjection the loftiest do not escape. There is a similarity between Homer and Hesiod, between Æschylus and Euripides, between Virgil and Horace, between Dante and Petrarch, between Shakespeare and Fletcher, between Dryden and Pope; each has a generic resemblance under which their specific distinctions are arranged. If this similarity be the result of imitation, I am willing to confess that I have imitated.

Let this opportunity be conceded to me of acknowledging that I have, what a Scotch philosopher characteristically terms, "a passion for reforming the world:"[4] what passion incited him to write and publish his book, he omits to explain. For my part I had rather be damned with Plato and Lord Bacon, than go to Heaven with Paley and Malthus.[5] But it is a mistake to suppose

3. See Shelley's similar tribute to his great contemporaries in the concluding paragraph of his *Defence of Poetry* (p. 1781).
4. This is the title of chap. 16 in *The Principles of Moral Science* (1805) by the Scottish writer Robert Forsyth.
5. Thomas Malthus's *An Essay on the Principle of Population* (1798) argued that the rate of increase in population will soon exceed the rate of increase in the food supply necessary to sustain it. William Paley wrote *Evidences of Christianity* (1794), which undertakes to prove that the design apparent in natural phenomena, and especially in the human body, entails the existence of God as the great Designer. Shelley ironically expresses his contempt for the doctrines of both these thinkers, which he conceives as arguments for accepting uncomplainingly the present state of the world.

that I dedicate my poetical compositions solely to the direct enforcement of reform, or that I consider them in any degree as containing a reasoned system on the theory of human life. Didactic poetry is my abhorrence; nothing can be equally well expressed in prose that is not tedious and supererogatory in verse. My purpose has hitherto been simply to familiarise the highly refined imagination of the more select classes of poetical readers with beautiful idealisms of moral excellence; aware that until the mind can love, and admire, and trust, and hope, and endure, reasoned principles of moral conduct are seeds cast upon the highway of life which the unconscious passenger tramples into dust, although they would bear the harvest of his happiness. Should I live to accomplish what I purpose, that is, produce a systematical history of what appear to me to be the genuine elements of human society,[6] let not the advocates of injustice and superstition flatter themselves that I should take Æschylus rather than Plato as my model.

The having spoken of myself with unaffected freedom will need little apology with the candid; and let the uncandid consider that they injure me less than their own hearts and minds by misrepresentation. Whatever talents a person may possess to amuse and instruct others, be they ever so inconsiderable, he is yet bound to exert them: if his attempt be ineffectual, let the punishment of an unaccomplished purpose have been sufficient; let none trouble themselves to heap the dust of oblivion upon his efforts; the pile they raise will betray his grave which might otherwise have been unknown.

Prometheus Unbound

From Act 1

SCENE: *A Ravine of Icy Rocks in the Indian Caucasus.* PROMETHEUS *is discovered bound to the Precipice.* PANTHEA *and* IONE *are seated at his feet. Time, Night. During the Scene, Morning slowly breaks.*

PROMETHEUS   Monarch of Gods and Dæmons,[1] and all Spirits
But One, who throng those bright and rolling Worlds
Which Thou and I alone of living things
Behold with sleepless eyes! regard this Earth
5   Made multitudinous with thy slaves, whom thou
Requitest for knee-worship, prayer and praise,
And toil, and hecatombs[2] of broken hearts,
With fear and self contempt and barren hope;
Whilst me, who am thy foe, eyeless° in hate,   *blinded*
10   Hast thou made reign and triumph, to thy scorn,
O'er mine own misery and thy vain revenge.—
Three thousand years of sleep-unsheltered hours
And moments—aye° divided by keen pangs   *always*
Till they seemed years, torture and solitude,
15   Scorn and despair,—these are mine empire:—

6. Shelley did not live to write this history.
1. Demogorgon (see 2.4). "Daemons": supernatural beings, intermediary between gods and mortals. Prometheus is addressing Jupiter.
2. Large sacrificial offerings.

More glorious far than that which thou surveyest
From thine unenvied throne, O Mighty God!
Almighty, had I deigned[3] to share the shame
Of thine ill tyranny, and hung not here
20 Nailed to this wall of eagle-baffling mountain,
Black, wintry, dead, unmeasured; without herb,
Insect, or beast, or shape or sound of life.
Ah me, alas, pain, pain ever, forever!

No change, no pause, no hope!—Yet I endure.
25 I ask the Earth, have not the mountains felt?
I ask yon Heaven—the all-beholding Sun,
Has it not seen? The Sea, in storm or calm,
Heaven's ever-changing Shadow, spread below—
Have its deaf waves not heard my agony?
30 Ah me, alas, pain, pain ever, forever!

The crawling glaciers pierce me with the spears
Of their moon-freezing chrystals; the bright chains
Eat with their burning cold into my bones.
Heaven's winged hound, polluting from thy lips
35 His beak in poison not his own, tears up
My heart;[4] and shapeless sights come wandering by,
The ghastly people of the realm of dream,
Mocking me: and the Earthquake-fiends are charged
To wrench the rivets from my quivering wounds
40 When the rocks split and close again behind;
While from their loud abysses howling throng
The genii of the storm, urging the rage
Of whirlwind, and afflict me with keen hail.
And yet to me welcome is Day and Night,
45 Whether one breaks the hoar frost of the morn,
Or starry, dim, and slow, the other climbs
The leaden-coloured East; for then they lead
Their wingless, crawling Hours,[5] one among whom
—As some dark Priest hales° the reluctant victim—   *drags*
50 Shall drag thee, cruel King, to kiss the blood
From these pale feet,[6] which then might trample thee
If they disdained not such a prostrate slave.
Disdain? Ah no! I pity thee.[7]—What Ruin
Will hunt thee undefended through wide Heaven!
55 How will thy soul, cloven to its depth with terror,
Gape like a Hell within! I speak in grief,

---

3. I.e., you would have been all-powerful, if I had deigned.
4. The vulture, tearing daily at Prometheus's heart, was kissed by Jupiter by way of reward.
5. The Hours were represented in Greek myth and art by human figures with wings.
6. One of a number of implied parallels between

the agony of Prometheus and the passion of Christ.
7. At this early point occurs the crisis of the action: the beginning of Prometheus's change of heart from hate to compassion, consummated in lines 303–05. The rest of the symbolic drama gradually unfolds the consequences of this moral triumph—of which Prometheus himself is unaware.

Not exultation, for I hate no more,
As then, ere misery made me wise.—The Curse
Once breathed on thee I would recall. Ye Mountains,
60 Whose many-voiced Echoes, through the mist
Of cataracts, flung the thunder of that spell!
Ye icy Springs, stagnant with wrinkling frost,
Which vibrated to hear me, and then crept
Shuddering through India! Thou serenest Air,
65 Through which the Sun walks burning without beams!
And ye swift Whirlwinds, who on poised wings
Hung mute and moveless o'er yon hushed abyss,
As thunder louder than your own made rock
The orbed world! If then my words had power
70 —Though I am changed so that aught evil wish
Is dead within, although no memory be
Of what is hate—let them not lose it now!⁸
What was that curse? for ye all heard me speak.⁹

* * *

PHANTASM

Fiend, I defy thee! with a calm, fixed mind,
All that thou canst inflict I bid thee do;
Foul Tyrant both of Gods and Humankind,
265 One only being shalt thou not subdue.
Rain then thy plagues upon me here,
Ghastly disease and frenzying fear;
And let alternate frost and fire
Eat into me, and be thine ire
270 Lightning and cutting hail and legioned forms
Of furies, driving by upon the wounding storms.

Aye, do thy worst. Thou art Omnipotent.
O'er all things but thyself I gave thee power,
And my own will. Be thy swift mischiefs sent
275 To blast mankind, from yon etherial tower.
Let thy malignant spirit move
Its darkness over those I love:
On me and mine I imprecate°   *pray for*
The utmost torture of thy hate
280 And thus devote to sleepless agony
This undeclining head while thou must reign on high.

But thou who art the God and Lord—O thou
Who fillest with thy soul this world of woe,
To whom all things of Earth and Heaven do bow
285 In fear and worship—all-prevailing foe!

---

8. Let my words not lose their power now.
9. In the passage here omitted, none dares, for fear of the god's vengeance, to repeat the curse Prometheus had proclaimed against Jupiter. Pro-

metheus is finally forced to call up the Phantasm of Jupiter himself, who, in the next excerpt, repeats the words of Prometheus's curse.

I curse thee! let a sufferer's curse
Clasp thee, his torturer, like remorse,
Till thine Infinity shall be
A robe of envenomed agony;[1]
290 And thine Omnipotence a crown of pain
To cling like burning gold round thy dissolving brain.

Heap on thy soul by virtue of this Curse
Ill deeds, then be thou damned, beholding good,
Both infinite as is the Universe,
295 And thou, and thy self-torturing solitude.
An awful Image of calm power
Though now thou sittest, let the hour
Come, when thou must appear to be
That which thou art internally.
300 And after many a false and fruitless crime
Scorn track thy lagging fall through boundless space and time.

[The Phantasm vanishes.]

PROMETHEUS   Were these my words, O Parent?
THE EARTH   They were thine.
PROMETHEUS   It doth repent me: words are quick and vain;
Grief for awhile is blind, and so was mine.
305 I wish no living thing to suffer pain.

THE EARTH

Misery, O misery to me,
That Jove at length should vanquish thee.[2]
Wail, howl aloud, Land and Sea,
The Earth's rent heart shall answer ye.
310 Howl, Spirits of the living and the dead,
Your refuge, your defence lies fallen and vanquished.

FIRST ECHO

Lies fallen and vanquished?

SECOND ECHO

Fallen and vanquished!

IONE[3]

Fear not—'tis but some passing spasm,
The Titan is unvanquished still.[4]

*   *   *

1. Like the poisoned shirt of the centaur Nessus, which consumed Hercules' flesh when he put it on. The next two lines allude to the mock crowning of Christ with a crown of thorns.
2. Earth mistakes mercy for submission and, therefore, interprets Prometheus's moral victory as his defeat.
3. Ione, Panthea, and Asia (in the following scene) are sisters and Oceanids—i.e., daughters of Oceanus.

4. In the omitted passage the herald Mercury, at Jupiter's command, brings a group of Furies (in Greek myth, avengers of crimes against the gods) who tempt Prometheus to despair by revealing the loathsome potentialities for evil in humankind's conscious and unconscious mind. In the climactic temptation a Fury tears aside a veil to reveal a representation ("emblem," line 594) of the suffering Christ on the cross.

FURY   Behold, an emblem—those who do endure
595   Deep wrongs for man, and scorn and chains, but heap
        Thousand-fold torment on themselves and him.
PROMETHEUS   Remit the anguish of that lighted stare—
        Close those wan lips—let that thorn-wounded brow
        Stream not with blood—it mingles with thy tears
600   Fix, fix those tortured orbs in peace and death
        So thy sick throes shake not that crucifix,
        So those pale fingers play not with thy gore.—
        O horrible! Thy name I will not speak,
        It hath become a curse.[5] I see, I see
605   The wise, the mild, the lofty and the just,
        Whom thy slaves hate for being like to thee,
        Some hunted by foul lies from their heart's home,
        An early-chosen, late-lamented home,
        As hooded ounces[6] cling to the driven hind,°   *doe*
610   Some linked to corpses in unwholesome cells:
        Some—hear I not the multitude laugh loud?—
        Impaled in lingering fire: and mighty realms
        Float by my feet like sea-uprooted isles
        Whose sons are kneaded down in common blood
615   By the red light of their own burning homes.
FURY   Blood thou canst see, and fire; and canst hear groans;
        Worse things, unheard, unseen, remain behind.
PROMETHEUS   Worse?
FURY   In each human heart terror survives
        The ravin it has gorged:[7] the loftiest fear
620   All that they would disdain to think were true:
        Hypocrisy and custom make their minds
        The fanes° of many a worship, now outworn.   *temples*
        They dare not devise good for man's estate
        And yet they know not that they do not dare.
625   The good want power, but to weep barren tears.
        The powerful goodness want: worse need for them.
        The wise want love, and those who love want wisdom;
        And all best things are thus confused to ill.
        Many are strong and rich,—and would be just,—
630   But live among their suffering fellow men
        As if none felt: they know not what they do.[8]
PROMETHEUS   Thy words are like a cloud of winged snakes
        And yet, I pity those they torture not.
FURY   Thou pitiest them? I speak no more!   [*Vanishes.*]
PROMETHEUS.   Ah woe!

---

5. I.e., the name "Christ" has become, literally, a curse word, and metaphorically, a curse to humankind, in that His religion of love is used to justify religious wars and bloody oppression.
6. Cheetahs, or leopards, used in hunting (hoods were sometimes placed over their eyes to make them easier to control).
7. The prey that it has greedily devoured.

8. The Fury ironically echoes Christ's plea for forgiveness of his crucifiers: "Father, forgive them: for they know not what they do" (Luke 23.34). Lines 625–28 are Shelley's comment on his own age of political reaction and oppression. This passage underlies Yeats's description of the troubled era after World War I in The *Second Coming*, lines 3–8.

635   Ah woe! Alas! pain, pain ever, forever!
      I close my tearless eyes, but see more clear
      Thy works within my woe-illumed mind,
      Thou subtle Tyrant!⁹ . . . Peace is in the grave—
      The grave hides all things beautiful and good—
640   I am a God and cannot find it there,
      Nor would I seek it: for, though dread revenge,
      This is defeat, fierce King, not victory.
      The sights with which thou torturest gird my soul
      With new endurance, till the hour arrives
645   When they shall be no types of things which are.
      PANTHEA   Alas! what sawest thou?
      PROMETHEUS   There are two woes:
      To speak and to behold; thou spare me one.¹
      Names are there, Nature's sacred watchwords—they
      Were borne aloft in bright emblazonry.²
650   The nations thronged around, and cried aloud
      As with one voice, "Truth, liberty and love!"
      Suddenly fierce confusion fell from Heaven
      Among them—there was strife, deceit and fear;
      Tyrants rushed in, and did divide the spoil.
655   This was the shadow of the truth I saw.
      THE EARTH   I felt thy torture, Son, with such mixed joy
      As pain and Virtue give.—To cheer thy state
      I bid ascend those subtle and fair spirits
      Whose homes are the dim caves of human thought
660   And who inhabit, as birds wing the wind,
      Its world-surrounding ether;³ they behold
      Beyond that twilight realm, as in a glass,°   *mirror*
      The future—may they speak comfort to thee!⁴

*   *   *

From *Act 2*

SCENE 4—*The Cave of* DEMOGORGON. ASIA *and* PANTHEA.⁵

PANTHEA   What veiled form sits on that ebon throne?
ASIA   The veil has fallen! . . .
PANTHEA   I see a mighty Darkness

---

9. Jupiter (also addressed as "fierce King," line 642).
1. I.e., spare me the woe of speaking (about what I have beheld).
2. As in a brilliant display of banners.
3. A medium, weightless and infinitely elastic, once supposed to permeate the universe.
4. The speech of the Earth ushers in a troop of spirits representing the noble and virtuous potentialities of the mind, on which rests the hope of a future felicity for humanity.
5. Act 2 has opened with Asia—the feminine principle and embodiment of love, who was separated from Prometheus at the moment of his fall into divisive hate—in a lovely Indian valley at the first hour of the dawn of the spring season of redemption. Asia and her sister Panthea have been led, by

a sweet and irresistible compulsion, first to the portal and then down into the depths of the cave of Demogorgon—the central enigma of Shelley's poem.
Commentators have usually equated Demogorgon with necessity, but the interpretation may be too confining. More flexibly, he can be thought of as process, the inexorable way in which things evolve. But the ultimate mover of that process—the ultimate reason for the way things are—must remain, Shelley skeptically insists, a mystery beyond the limits of accessible knowledge. Demogorgon is ignorant of the principle that controls him and can give merely riddling answers to Asia's questions about the "why" of creation, good, and evil.

Filling the seat of power; and rays of gloom
Dart round, as light from the meridian Sun,
5 Ungazed upon and shapeless—neither limb
Nor form—nor outline;[6] yet we feel it is
A living Spirit.

DEMOGORGON   Ask what thou wouldst know.

ASIA   What canst thou tell?

DEMOGORGON   All things thou dar'st demand.

ASIA   Who made the living world?

DEMOGORGON   God.

ASIA   Who made all
10 That it contains—thought, passion, reason, will,
Imagination?

DEMOGORGON   God, Almighty God.

ASIA   Who made that sense[7] which, when the winds of Spring
In rarest visitation, or the voice
Of one beloved heard in youth alone,
15 Fills the faint eyes with falling tears, which dim
The radiant looks of unbewailing flowers,
And leaves this peopled earth a solitude
When it returns no more?

DEMOGORGON   Merciful God.

ASIA   And who made terror, madness, crime, remorse,
20 Which from the links of the great chain of things
To every thought within the mind of man
Sway and drag heavily—and each one reels
Under the load towards the pit of death;
Abandoned hope, and love that turns to hate;
25 And self-contempt, bitterer to drink than blood;
Pain whose unheeded and familiar speech
Is howling and keen shrieks, day after day;
And Hell, or the sharp fear of Hell?[8]

DEMOGORGON   He reigns.

ASIA   Utter his name—a world pining in pain
30 Asks but his name; curses shall drag him down.

DEMOGORGON   He reigns.

ASIA   I feel, I know it—who?

DEMOGORGON   He reigns.

ASIA   Who reigns? There was the Heaven and Earth at first
And Light and Love;—then Saturn,[9] from whose throne
Time fell, an envious shadow; such the state
35 Of the earth's primal spirits beneath his sway
As the calm joy of flowers and living leaves
Before the wind or sun has withered them
And semivital worms; but he refused

---

6. Echoing Milton's description of Death, *Para-dise Lost* 2.666–73.

7. Presumably the sense by which one is aware of the "unseen Power" that Shelley calls "Intellectual Beauty" (see *Hymn to Intellectual Beauty*, stanza 2, p. 1718).

8. The nouns "hope," "love," etc. (lines 24–28) are

all objects of the verb "made" (line 19).

9. In Greek myth Saturn's reign was the golden age. In Shelley's version Saturn refused to grant mortals knowledge and science, so that it was an age of ignorant innocence in which the deepest human needs remained unfulfilled.

The birthright of their being, knowledge, power,
40 The skill which wields the elements, the thought
Which pierces this dim Universe like light,
Self-empire and the majesty of love,
For thirst of which they fainted. Then Prometheus
Gave wisdom, which is strength, to Jupiter
45 And with this law alone: "Let man be free,"
Clothed him with the dominion of wide Heaven.
To know nor faith nor love nor law, to be
Omnipotent but friendless, is to reign;
And Jove now reigned; for on the race of man
50 First famine, and then toil, and then disease,
Strife, wounds, and ghastly death unseen before,
Fell; and the unseasonable seasons drove,
With alternating shafts of frost and fire,
Their shelterless, pale tribes to mountain caves;
55 And in their desart° hearts fierce wants he sent   *empty*
And mad disquietudes, and shadows idle
Of unreal good, which levied mutual war,
So ruining the lair wherein they raged.
Prometheus saw, and waked the legioned hopes
60 Which sleep within folded Elysian flowers,
Nepenthe, Moly, Amaranth,[1] fadeless blooms;
That they might hide with thin and rainbow wings
The shape of Death; and Love he sent to bind
The disunited tendrils of that vine
65 Which bears the wine of life, the human heart;
And he tamed fire which, like some beast of prey,
Most terrible, but lovely, played beneath
The frown of man, and tortured to his will
Iron and gold, the slaves and signs of power,
70 And gems and poisons, and all subtlest forms,
Hidden beneath the mountains and the waves.
He gave man speech, and speech created thought,
Which is the measure of the Universe;
And Science struck the thrones of Earth and Heaven
75 Which shook, but fell not; and the harmonious mind
Poured itself forth in all-prophetic song,
And music lifted up the listening spirit
Until it walked, exempt from mortal care,
Godlike, o'er the clear billows of sweet sound;
80 And human hands first mimicked and then mocked[2]
With moulded limbs more lovely than its own
The human form, till marble grew divine,
And mothers, gazing, drank the love men see

---

1. These are medicinal drugs and flowers in Greek myth. Asia is describing (lines 59–97) the various sciences and arts given to humans by Prometheus, the culture bringer.

2. I.e., sculptors first merely reproduced but later improved on ("mocked" in the sense of "heightened") the beauty of the human form.

Reflected in their race, behold, and perish.[3]—
He told the hidden power of herbs and springs,   85
And Disease drank and slept—Death grew like sleep.—
He taught the implicated° orbits woven   *intertwined*
Of the wide-wandering stars, and how the Sun
Changes his lair, and by what secret spell
The pale moon is transformed, when her broad eye   90
Gazes not on the interlunar[4] sea;
He taught to rule, as life directs the limbs,
The tempest-winged chariots of the Ocean,
And the Celt knew the Indian.[5] Cities then
Were built, and through their snow-like columns flowed   95
The warm winds, and the azure æther shone,
And the blue sea and shadowy hills were seen . . .
Such the alleviations of his state
Prometheus gave to man—for which he hangs
Withering in destined pain—but who rains down   100
Evil, the immedicable plague, which while
Man looks on his creation like a God
And sees that it is glorious, drives him on,
The wreck of his own will, the scorn of Earth,
The outcast, the abandoned, the alone?—   105
Not Jove: while yet his frown shook Heaven, aye when
His adversary from adamantine chains
Cursed him, he trembled like a slave. Declare
Who is his master? Is he too a slave?

DEMOGORGON   All spirits are enslaved which serve things evil: 110
Thou knowest if Jupiter be such or no.

ASIA   Whom calledst thou God?

DEMOGORGON   I spoke but as ye speak—
For Jove is the supreme of living things.

ASIA   Who is the master of the slave?

DEMOGORGON   —If the Abysm
Could vomit forth its secrets:—but a voice   115
Is wanting, the deep truth is imageless;[6]
For what would it avail to bid thee gaze
On the revolving world? what to bid speak
Fate, Time, Occasion, Chance and Change? To these
All things are subject but eternal Love.   120

ASIA   So much I asked before, and my heart gave
The response thou hast given; and of such truths
Each to itself must be the oracle.—
One more demand . . . and do thou answer me
As my own soul would answer, did it know   125
That which I ask.—Prometheus shall arise

---

3. Expectant mothers looked at the beautiful statues so that their children might, by prenatal influence, be born with the beauty that makes beholders die of love.
4. The phase between old and new moons, when the moon is invisible.
5. The reference is to the ships in which the Celtic (here, non-Greco-Roman) races of Europe were able to sail to India.
6. I.e., ultimate truths can be neither known nor expressed.

Henceforth the Sun of this rejoicing world:
When shall the destined hour arrive?
DEMOGORGON   Behold![7]
ASIA   The rocks are cloven, and through the purple night
130   I see Cars drawn by rainbow-winged steeds
Which trample the dim winds—in each there stands
A wild-eyed charioteer, urging their flight.
Some look behind, as fiends pursued them there
And yet I see no shapes but the keen stars:
135   Others with burning eyes lean forth, and drink
With eager lips the wind of their own speed,
As if the thing they loved fled on before,
And now—even now they clasped it; their bright locks
Stream like a comet's flashing hair: they all
Sweep onward.—
140   DEMOGORGON   These are the immortal Hours
Of whom thou didst demand.—One waits for thee.
ASIA   A Spirit with a dreadful countenance
Checks its dark chariot by the craggy gulph.
Unlike thy brethren, ghastly charioteer,
145   What art thou? whither wouldst thou bear me? Speak!
SPIRIT   I am the shadow of a destiny
More dread than is my aspect—ere yon planet
Has set, the Darkness[8] which ascends with me
Shall wrap in lasting night Heaven's kingless throne.
ASIA   What meanest thou?
150   PANTHEA   That terrible shadow floats
Up from its throne, as may the lurid° smoke   red-glaring
Of earthquake-ruined cities o'er the sea.—
Lo! it ascends the Car . . . the coursers fly
Terrified; watch its path among the stars
Blackening the night!
155   ASIA   Thus I am answered—strange!
PANTHEA   See, near the verge° another chariot stays;   horizon
An ivory shell inlaid with crimson fire
Which comes and goes within its sculptured rim
Of delicate strange tracery—the young Spirit
160   That guides it, has the dovelike eyes of hope.
How its soft smiles attract the soul!—as light
Lures winged insects[9] through the lampless air.

SPIRIT

My coursers are fed with the lightning,
They drink of the whirlwind's stream
165   And when the red morning is brightning
They bathe in the fresh sunbeam;

---

7. Demogorgon's answer is a gesture: he points to
the approaching chariots ("Cars").
8. Demogorgon, who is ascending (lines 150–55)
to effect the dethronement of Jupiter.

9. The ancient image of the soul, or *psyche,* was a
moth. The chariot described here will carry Asia to
a reunion with Prometheus.

They have strength for their swiftness, I deem:
  Then ascend with me, daughter of Ocean.

I desire—and their speed makes night kindle;
170   I fear—they outstrip the Typhoon;
Ere the cloud piled on Atlas[1] can dwindle
We encircle the earth and the moon:
We shall rest from long labours at noon:
  Then ascend with me, daughter of Ocean.

SCENE 5—*The Car pauses within a Cloud on the Top of a snowy Mountain.*
ASIA, PANTHEA, *and the* SPIRIT OF THE HOUR.

SPIRIT

On the brink of the night and the morning
  My coursers are wont to respire,[2]
But the Earth has just whispered a warning
  That their flight must be swifter than fire:
5   They shall drink the hot speed of desire!

ASIA   Thou breathest on their nostrils—but my breath
  Would give them swifter speed.

SPIRIT   Alas, it could not.

PANTHEA   O Spirit! pause and tell whence is the light
  Which fills the cloud? the sun is yet unrisen.

10 SPIRIT   The sun will rise not until noon.[3]—Apollo
  Is held in Heaven by wonder—and the light
  Which fills this vapour, as the aerial hue
  Of fountain-gazing roses fills the water,
  Flows from thy mighty sister.

PANTHEA   Yes, I feel . . .

15 ASIA   What is it with thee, sister? Thou art pale.

PANTHEA   How thou art changed! I dare not look on thee;
  I feel, but see thee not. I scarce endure
  The radiance of thy beauty.[4] Some good change
  Is working in the elements which suffer
20 Thy presence thus unveiled.—The Nereids tell
  That on the day when the clear hyaline°   *glassy sea*
  Was cloven at thy uprise, and thou didst stand
  Within a veined shell,[5] which floated on
  Over the calm floor of the chrystal sea,
25 Among the Ægean isles, and by the shores
  Which bear thy name, love, like the atmosphere

1. A mountain in North Africa that the Greeks regarded as so high that it supported the heavens.
2. Catch their breath.
3. The time of the reunion of Prometheus and Asia.
4. In an earlier scene Panthea had envisioned in a dream the radiant and eternal inner form of Prometheus emerging through his "wound-worn limbs." The corresponding transfiguration of Asia, prepared for by her descent to the underworld, now takes place.
5. The story told by the Nereids (sea nymphs) serves to associate Asia with Aphrodite, goddess of love, emerging (as in Botticelli's painting) from the Mediterranean on a seashell.

Of the sun's fire filling the living world,
Burst from thee, and illumined Earth and Heaven
And the deep ocean and the sunless caves,
30   And all that dwells within them; till grief cast
Eclipse upon the soul from which it came:
Such art thou now, nor is it I alone,
Thy sister, thy companion, thine own chosen one,
But the whole world which seeks thy sympathy.
35   Hearest thou not sounds i' the air which speak the love
Of all articulate beings? Feelest thou not
The inanimate winds enamoured of thee?—List!   [*Music.*]
ASIA   Thy words are sweeter than aught else but his
Whose echoes they are—yet all love is sweet,
40   Given or returned; common as light is love
And its familiar voice wearies not ever.
Like the wide Heaven, the all-sustaining air,
It makes the reptile equal to the God . . .
They who inspire it most are fortunate
45   As I am now; but those who feel it most
Are happier still, after long sufferings
As I shall soon become.
PANTHEA   List! Spirits speak.

VOICE (*in the air, singing*)[6]
Life of Life! thy lips enkindle
With their love the breath between them
50   And thy smiles before they dwindle
Make the cold air fire; then screen them
In those looks where whoso gazes
Faints, entangled in their mazes.

Child of Light! thy limbs are burning
55   Through the vest which seems to hide them
As the radiant lines of morning
Through the clouds ere they divide them,
And this atmosphere divinest
Shrouds thee wheresoe'er thou shinest.

60   Fair are others;—none beholds thee
But thy voice sounds low and tender
Like the fairest, for it folds thee
From the sight, that liquid splendour,
And all feel, yet see thee never
65   As I feel now, lost forever!

Lamp of Earth! where'er thou movest
Its dim shapes are clad with brightness

6. The voice attempts to describe, in a dizzying whirl of optical paradoxes, what it feels like to look on the naked essence of love and beauty.

And the souls of whom thou lovest
    Walk upon the winds with lightness
70 Till they fail, as I am failing,
    Dizzy, lost . . . yet unbewailing!

ASIA

    My soul is an enchanted Boat
    Which, like a sleeping swan, doth float
Upon the silver waves of thy sweet singing,
75   And thine doth like an Angel sit
    Beside the helm conducting it
Whilst all the winds with melody are ringing.
    It seems to float ever—forever—
    Upon that many winding River
80 Between mountains, woods, abysses,
    A Paradise of wildernesses,
Till like one in slumber bound
Borne to the Ocean, I float down, around,
Into a Sea profound, of ever-spreading sound.

85 Meanwhile thy spirit lifts its pinions°   wings
    In Music's most serene dominions,
Catching the winds that fan that happy Heaven.
    And we sail on, away, afar,
    Without a course—without a star—
90 But by the instinct of sweet Music driven
    Till, through Elysian garden islets
    By thee, most beautiful of pilots,
    Where never mortal pinnace° glided,   small boat
    The boat of my desire is guided—
95 Realms where the air we breathe is Love
Which in the winds and on the waves doth move,
Harmonizing this Earth with what we feel above.

    We have past Age's icy caves,
    And Manhood's dark and tossing waves
100 And Youth's smooth ocean, smiling to betray;
    Beyond the glassy gulphs we flee
    Of shadow-peopled Infancy,
Through Death and Birth to a diviner day,[7]
    A Paradise of vaulted bowers
105   Lit by downward-gazing flowers
    And watery paths that wind between
    Wildernesses calm and green,
Peopled by shapes too bright to see,
And rest, having beheld—somewhat like thee,
110 Which walk upon the sea, and chaunt melodiously!

7. Asia is describing what it feels like to be trans-figured—in the image of moving backward in the stream of time, through youth and infancy and birth itself, in order to die to this life and be born again to a "diviner" existence.

From Act 3

SCENE 1—*Heaven.* JUPITER *on his Throne;* THETIS *and the other Deities assembled.*

JUPITER   Ye congregated Powers of Heaven who share
    The glory and the strength of him ye serve,
    Rejoice! henceforth I am omnipotent.
    All else had been subdued to me—alone
5   The soul of man, like unextinguished fire,
    Yet burns towards Heaven with fierce reproach and doubt
    And lamentation and reluctant prayer,
    Hurling up insurrection, which might make
    Our antique empire insecure, though built
10   On eldest faith, and Hell's coeval,[8] fear.
    And though my curses through the pendulous° air   *suspending*
    Like snow on herbless peaks, fall flake by flake
    And cling to it[9]—though under my wrath's night
    It climb the crags of life, step after step,
15   Which wound it, as ice wounds unsandalled feet,
    It yet remains supreme o'er misery,
    Aspiring . . . unrepressed; yet soon to fall:
    Even now have I begotten a strange wonder,
    That fatal Child,[1] the terror of the Earth,
20   Who waits but till the destined Hour arrive,
    Bearing from Demogorgon's vacant throne
    The dreadful might of ever living limbs
    Which clothed that awful spirit unbeheld—
    To redescend, and trample out the spark[2] . . .

25   Pour forth Heaven's wine, Idæan Ganymede,
    And let it fill the dædal[3] cups like fire
    And from the flower-inwoven soil divine
    Ye all triumphant harmonies arise
    As dew from Earth under the twilight stars;
30   Drink! be the nectar circling through your veins
    The soul of joy, ye everliving Gods,
    Till exultation burst in one wide voice
    Like music from Elysian winds.—
                     And thou
    Ascend beside me, veiled in the light
35   Of the desire which makes thee one with me,
    Thetis, bright Image of Eternity!—
    When thou didst cry, "Insufferable might!"[4]
    God! spare me! I sustain not the quick flames,

8. Of the same age.
9. "It" (as also in lines 14 and 16) is "the soul of man" (line 5).
1. The son of Jupiter and Thetis. Jupiter believes that he has begotten a child who will assume the bodily form of the conquered Demogorgon and then return to announce his victory and the defeat of the resistance of Prometheus.

2. Of Prometheus's defiance.
3. Skillfully wrought (from the name of the Greek craftsman Daedalus). Ganymede (line 25) had been seized on Mount Ida by an eagle and carried to heaven to be Jupiter's cupbearer.
4. This description of the sexual union of Jupiter and Thetis is a grotesque parody of the reunion of Prometheus and Asia.

The penetrating presence; all my being,
40 Like him whom the Numidian seps[5] did thaw
Into a dew with poison, is dissolved,
Sinking through its foundations"—even then
Two mighty spirits, mingling, made a third
Mightier than either—which unbodied now
45 Between us, floats, felt although unbeheld,
Waiting the incarnation, which ascends—
Hear ye the thunder of the fiery wheels
Griding[6] the winds?—from Demogorgon's throne.—
Victory! victory! Feel'st thou not, O World,
50 The Earthquake of his chariot thundering up
Olympus?
           [*The Car of the* HOUR *arrives.* DEMOGORGON *descends and moves
           towards the Throne of* JUPITER.]
              Awful Shape, what art thou? Speak!
DEMOGORGON   Eternity—demand no direr name.
Descend, and follow me down the abyss;
I am thy child,[7] as thou wert Saturn's child,
55 Mightier than thee; and we must dwell together
Henceforth in darkness.—Lift thy lightnings not.
The tyranny of Heaven none may retain,
Or reassume, or hold succeeding thee . . .
Yet if thou wilt—as 'tis the destiny
60 Of trodden worms to writhe till they are dead—
Put forth thy might.
JUPITER   Detested prodigy!
Even thus beneath the deep Titanian prisons[8]
I trample thee! . . . thou lingerest?
                              Mercy! mercy!
No pity—no release, no respite! . . . Oh,
65 That thou wouldst make mine enemy my judge.
Even where he hangs, seared by my long revenge
On Caucasus—he would not doom me thus.—
Gentle and just and dreadless, is he not
The monarch of the world?[9] what then art thou? . . .
No refuge! no appeal— . . .
70   Sink with me then—
We two will sink in the wide waves of ruin
Even as a vulture and a snake outspent
Drop, twisted in inextricable fight,[1]
Into a shoreless sea.—Let Hell unlock
75 Its mounded Oceans of tempestuous fire,

5. A serpent of Numidia (North Africa) whose bite was thought to cause putrefaction.
6. Cutting with a rasping sound.
7. Ironically, and in a figurative sense: Demogorgon's function follows from Jupiter's actions.
8. After they overthrew the Titans, Jupiter and the Olympian gods imprisoned them in Tartarus, deep beneath the earth.
9. The ultimate irony: Jupiter appeals to those very qualities of Prometheus for which he has hitherto persecuted him, begging for a mercy that Prometheus has already granted him, but Prometheus's change from vengefulness to mercy is in fact the cause of Jupiter's present downfall.
1. The eagle (or vulture) and the snake locked in equal combat—a favorite Shelleyan image (cf. *Alastor,* lines 227–32).

And whelm on them into the bottomless void
The desolated world and thee and me,
The conqueror and the conquered, and the wreck
Of that for which they combated.
                                   Ai! Ai!
80   The elements obey me not . . . I sink . . .
Dizzily down—ever, forever, down—
And, like a cloud, mine enemy above
Darkens my fall with victory!—Ai! Ai!

From SCENE 4—*A Forest. In the Background a Cave.* PROMETHEUS, ASIA, PAN-
THEA, IONE, *and the* SPIRIT OF THE EARTH.[2]

                    *   *   *

[*The* SPIRIT OF THE HOUR *enters.*]
PROMETHEUS   We feel what thou hast heard and seen—yet speak.
SPIRIT OF THE HOUR   Soon as the sound had ceased whose thunder filled
      The abysses of the sky, and the wide earth,
100   There was a change . . . the impalpable thin air
      And the all-circling sunlight were transformed
      As if the sense of love dissolved in them
      Had folded itself round the sphered world.
      My vision then grew clear and I could see
105   Into the mysteries of the Universe.[3]
      Dizzy as with delight I floated down,
      Winnowing the lightsome air with languid plumes,
      My coursers sought their birthplace in the sun
      Where they henceforth will live exempt from toil,
110   Pasturing flowers of vegetable fire—
      And where my moonlike car will stand within
      A temple, gazed upon by Phidian forms,[4]
      Of thee, and Asia and the Earth, and me
      And you fair nymphs, looking the love we feel,
115   In memory of the tidings it has borne,
      Beneath a dome fretted with graven flowers,
      Poised on twelve columns of resplendent stone
      And open to the bright and liquid sky.
      Yoked to it by an amphisæbnic snake[5]
120   The likeness of those winged steeds will mock[6]
      The flight from which they find repose.—Alas,
      Whither has wandered now my partial[7] tongue

2. After Jupiter's annihilation (described in scene
2), Hercules unbinds Prometheus, who is reunited
with Asia and retires to a cave "where we will sit
and talk of time and change / . . . ourselves
unchanged." In the speech that concludes the act
(reprinted here) the Spirit of the Hour describes
what happened in the human world when he
sounded the apocalyptic trumpet.
3. I.e., the earth's atmosphere clarifies, no longer
refracting the sunlight, and so allows the Spirit of
the Hour to see what is happening on earth.

4. The crescent-shaped ("moonlike") chariot, its
apocalyptic mission accomplished, will be frozen
to stone and will be surrounded by the sculptured
forms of other agents in the drama. Phidias (5th
century B.C.E.) was the noblest of Greek sculptors.
5. A mythical snake with a head at each end; it
serves here as a symbolic warning that a reversal
of the process is always possible.
6. "Imitate" and also, in their immobility, "mock
at" the flight they represent.
7. Biased or, possibly, telling only part of the story.

When all remains untold which ye would hear!—
As I have said, I floated to the Earth:
125 It was, as it is still, the pain of bliss
To move, to breathe, to be; I wandering went
Among the haunts and dwellings of mankind
And first was disappointed not to see
Such mighty change as I had felt within
130 Expressed in outward things; but soon I looked,
And behold! thrones were kingless, and men walked
One with the other even as spirits do,
None fawned, none trampled; hate, disdain or fear,
Self-love or self-contempt on human brows
135 No more inscribed, as o'er the gate of hell,
"All hope abandon, ye who enter here";[8]
None frowned, none trembled, none with eager fear
Gazed on another's eye of cold command
Until the subject of a tyrant's will
140 Became, worse fate, the abject of his own[9]
Which spurred him, like an outspent horse, to death.
None wrought his lips in truth-entangling lines
Which smiled the lie his tongue disdained to speak;
None with firm sneer trod out in his own heart
145 The sparks of love and hope, till there remained
Those bitter ashes, a soul self-consumed,
And the wretch crept, a vampire among men,
Infecting all with his own hideous ill.
None talked that common, false, cold, hollow talk
150 Which makes the heart deny the *yes* it breathes
Yet question that unmeant hypocrisy
With such a self-mistrust as has no name.
And women too, frank, beautiful and kind
As the free Heaven which rains fresh light and dew
155 On the wide earth, past: gentle, radiant forms,
From custom's evil taint exempt and pure;
Speaking the wisdom once they could not think,
Looking emotions once they feared to feel
And changed to all which once they dared not be,
160 Yet being now, made Earth like Heaven—nor pride
Nor jealousy nor envy nor ill shame,
The bitterest of those drops of treasured gall,
Spoilt the sweet taste of the nepenthe,[1] love.

Thrones, altars, judgement-seats and prisons; wherein
165 And beside which, by wretched men were borne
Sceptres, tiaras, swords and chains, and tomes
Of reasoned wrong glozed on[2] by ignorance,

8. The inscription over the gate of hell in Dante's *Inferno* 3.9.
9. I.e., he was so abjectly enslaved that his own will accorded with the tyrant's will.

1. A drug (probably opium) that brings forgetfulness of pain and sorrow.
2. Annotated, explained.

Were like those monstrous and barbaric shapes,
The ghosts of a no more remembered fame,
170　Which from their unworn obelisks[3] look forth
In triumph o'er the palaces and tombs
Of those who were their conquerors, mouldering round.
Those imaged to the pride of Kings and Priests
A dark yet mighty faith, a power as wide
175　As is the world it wasted, and are now
But an astonishment; even so the tools
And emblems of its last captivity
Amid the dwellings of the peopled Earth,
Stand, not o'erthrown, but unregarded now.
180　And those foul shapes, abhorred by God and man—
Which under many a name and many a form
Strange, savage, ghastly, dark and execrable
Were Jupiter,[4] the tyrant of the world;
And which the nations panic-stricken served
185　With blood, and hearts broken by long hope, and love
Dragged to his altars soiled and garlandless
And slain amid men's unreclaiming tears,
Flattering the thing they feared, which fear was hate—
Frown, mouldering fast, o'er their abandoned shrines.
190　The painted veil, by those who were, called life,[5]
Which mimicked, as with colours idly spread,
All men believed and hoped, is torn aside—
The loathsome mask has fallen, the man remains
Sceptreless, free, uncircumscribed—but man:
195　Equal, unclassed, tribeless, and nationless,
Exempt from awe, worship, degree,—the King
Over himself; just, gentle, wise—but man:
Passionless? no—yet free from guilt or pain
Which were, for his will made, or suffered them,
200　Nor yet exempt, though ruling them like slaves,
From chance and death and mutability,
The clogs of that which else might oversoar
The loftiest star of unascended Heaven
Pinnacled dim in the intense inane.[6]

---

3. The Egyptian obelisks (tapering shafts of stone), brought to Rome by its conquering armies, included hieroglyphs that—because they were still undeciphered in Shelley's time—seemed "monstrous and barbaric shapes" (line 168).
4. The "foul shapes" (line 180) were statues of the gods who, whatever their names, were all really manifestations of Jupiter.

5. I.e., which was thought to be life by humans as they were before their regeneration.
6. I.e., a dim point in the extreme of empty space. The sense of lines 198–204 is if regenerate man were to be released from all earthly and biological impediments ("clogs"), he would become what even the stars are not—a pure ideal.

From *Act 4*[7]

SCENE—*A Part of the Forest near the Cave of* PROMETHEUS.

* * *

DEMOGORGON

Man, who wert once a despot and a slave,—
550 A dupe and a deceiver,—a Decay,
A Traveller from the cradle to the grave
  Through the dim night of this immortal Day:

ALL

Speak—thy strong words may never pass away.

DEMOGORGON

This is the Day which down the void Abysm
555 At the Earth-born's spell[8] yawns for Heaven's Despotism,
   And Conquest is dragged Captive through the Deep;[9]
Love from its awful throne of patient power
In the wise heart, from the last giddy hour
  Of dread endurance, from the slippery, steep,
560 And narrow verge of crag-like Agony, springs
And folds over the world its healing wings.

Gentleness, Virtue, Wisdom and Endurance,—
These are the seals of that most firm assurance
  Which bars the pit over Destruction's strength;
565 And if, with infirm hand, Eternity,
Mother of many acts and hours, should free
  The serpent that would clasp her with his length[1]—
These are the spells by which to reassume
An empire o'er the disentangled Doom.[2]

570 To suffer woes which Hope thinks infinite;
To forgive wrongs darker than Death or Night;
  To defy Power which seems Omnipotent;
To love, and bear; to hope, till Hope creates
From its own wreck the thing it contemplates;
575 Neither to change nor falter nor repent:
This, like thy glory, Titan! is to be

---

7. The original drama, completed in the spring of 1819, consisted of three acts. Later that year Shelley added a jubilant fourth act. In Revelation 21, the apocalyptic replacement of the old world by "a new heaven and new earth" had been symbolized by the marriage of the Lamb with the New Jerusalem. Shelley expands this figure into a cosmic marital celebration, in song and dance, in which the reunion of separated elements enacts everywhere the reunion of Prometheus and Asia that is taking place offstage. At the conclusion of the fourth act, Demogorgon calls on all existing things to hear his proclamation of the moral implications of this great drama of humanity's self-betrayal and self-redemption.
8. Prometheus's spell—i.e., his magically effective words of pity, in place of vengefulness.
9. Ephesians 4.8: "When [Christ] ascended up on high, he led captivity captive."
1. A final reminder that the serpent incessantly struggles to break loose and start the cycle of humanity's fall all over again. Felicity must continue to be earned.
2. Shelley's four cardinal virtues (line 562), which seal the serpent in the pit, also constitute the magic formulas ("spells") by which to remaster him, should he again break loose. These virtues are expanded on in the concluding lines (570–75).

Good, great and joyous, beautiful and free;
This is alone Life, Joy, Empire and Victory.

1818–19   1820

The Cloud

I bring fresh showers for the thirsting flowers,
  From the seas and streams;
I bear light shade for the leaves when laid
  In their noon-day dreams.
5   From my wings are shaken the dews that waken
  The sweet buds every one,
When rocked to rest on their mother's° breast,   *earth's*
  As she dances about the Sun.
I wield the flail of the lashing hail,
10   And whiten the green plains under,
And then again I dissolve it in rain,
  And laugh as I pass in thunder.

I sift the snow on the mountains below,
  And their great pines groan aghast;
15   And all the night 'tis my pillow white,
  While I sleep in the arms of the blast.
Sublime on the towers of my skiey bowers,
  Lightning my pilot sits;
In a cavern under is fettered the thunder,
20   It struggles and howls at fits;°   *fitfully*
Over Earth and Ocean, with gentle motion,
  This pilot is guiding me,
Lured by the love of the genii that move
  In the depths of the purple sea;[1]
25   Over the rills, and the crags, and the hills,
  Over the lakes and the plains,
Wherever he dream, under mountain or stream,
  The Spirit he loves remains;
And I all the while bask in Heaven's blue smile,[2]
30   Whilst he is dissolving in rains.

The sanguine Sunrise, with his meteor eyes,
  And his burning plumes outspread,[3]
Leaps on the back of my sailing rack,[4]
  When the morning star shines dead;
35   As on the jag of a mountain crag,
  Which an earthquake rocks and swings,
An eagle alit one moment may sit
  In the light of its golden wings.

---

1. I.e., atmospheric electricity, guiding the cloud (line 18), discharges as lightning when "lured" by the attraction of an opposite charge.
2. The upper part of the cloud remains exposed to the sun.
3. The sun's corona. "Meteor eyes": as bright as a burning meteor.
4. High, broken clouds, driven by the wind.

And when Sunset may breathe, from the lit Sea beneath,
40   Its ardours of rest and of love,
And the crimson pall° of eve may fall   *rich coverlet*
    From the depth of Heaven above,
With wings folded I rest, on mine aëry nest,
    As still as a brooding dove.

45 That orbed maiden with white fire laden
    Whom mortals call the Moon,
Glides glimmering o'er my fleece-like floor,
    By the midnight breezes strewn;
And wherever the beat of her unseen feet,
50   Which only the angels hear,
May have broken the woof,° of my tent's thin roof,   *texture*
    The stars peep behind her, and peer;
And I laugh to see them whirl and flee,
    Like a swarm of golden bees,
55 When I widen the rent in my wind-built tent,
    Till the calm rivers, lakes, and seas,
Like strips of the sky fallen through me on high,
    Are each paved with the moon and these.[5]

I bind the Sun's throne with a burning zone°   *belt, sash*
60   And the Moon's with a girdle of pearl;
The volcanos are dim and the stars reel and swim
    When the whirlwinds my banner unfurl.
From cape to cape, with a bridge-like shape,
    Over a torrent sea,
65 Sunbeam-proof, I hang like a roof—
    The mountains its columns be!
The triumphal arch, through which I march
    With hurricane, fire, and snow,
When the Powers of the Air, are chained to my chair,
70   Is the million-coloured Bow;
The sphere-fire° above its soft colours wove   *sunlight*
    While the moist Earth was laughing below.

I am the daughter of Earth and Water,
    And the nursling of the Sky;
75 I pass through the pores, of the ocean and shores;
    I change, but I cannot die—
For after the rain, when with never a stain
    The pavilion of Heaven is bare,
And the winds and sunbeams, with their convex gleams,
80   Build up the blue dome of Air[6]—
I silently laugh at my own cenotaph,[7]
    And out of the caverns of rain,

5. The stars reflected in the water.
6. The blue color of the sky. The phenomenon, as Shelley indicates, results from the way "sunbeams" are filtered by the earth's atmosphere.

7. The memorial monument of the dead cloud is the cloudless blue dome of the sky. (The point is that a cenotaph is a monument that does not contain a corpse.)

Like a child from the womb, like a ghost from the tomb,
　　I arise, and unbuild it again.—

1820　　　　　　　　　　　　　　　　　　　　　　　　　　　1820

To a Sky-Lark[1]

　　Hail to thee, blithe Spirit!
　　　Bird thou never wert—
　　That from Heaven, or near it,
　　　Pourest thy full heart
5　In profuse strains of unpremeditated art.

　　　Higher still and higher
　　　From the earth thou springest
　　Like a cloud of fire;
　　　The blue deep thou wingest,
10　And singing still dost soar, and soaring ever singest.

　　　In the golden lightning
　　　Of the sunken Sun—
　　O'er which clouds are brightning,
　　　Thou dost float and run;
15　Like an unbodied joy whose race is just begun.

　　　The pale purple even
　　　Melts around thy flight,
　　Like a star of Heaven
　　　In the broad day-light
20　Thou art unseen,—but yet I hear thy shrill delight,

　　　Keen as are the arrows
　　　Of that silver sphere,[2]
　　Whose intense lamp narrows
　　　In the white dawn clear
25　Until we hardly see—we feel that it is there.

　　　All the earth and air
　　　With thy voice is loud,
　　As when Night is bare
　　　From one lonely cloud
30　The moon rains out her beams—and Heaven is overflowed.

　　　What thou art we know not;
　　　What is most like thee?
　　From rainbow clouds there flow not

---

1. The European skylark is a small bird that sings
only in flight, often when it is too high to be visible.
This bird, freed from the bonds of earth and soaring beyond the reach of all the physical senses

except hearing, is made the emblem of a nonma-
terial spirit of pure joy, beyond the possibility of
human experience (see lines 15, 31).
2. The morning star.

Drops so bright to see
35 As from thy presence showers a rain of melody.

Like a Poet hidden
　In the light of thought,
Singing hymns unbidden,
　Till the world is wrought
40 To sympathy with hopes and fears it heeded not:

Like a high-born maiden
　In a palace-tower,
Soothing her love-laden
　Soul in secret hour,
45 With music sweet as love—which overflows her bower:

Like a glow-worm golden
　In a dell of dew,
Scattering unbeholden
　Its aerial hue
50 Among the flowers and grass which screen it from the view:

Like a rose embowered
　In its own green leaves—
By warm winds deflowered—
　Till the scent it gives
55 Makes faint with too much sweet those heavy-winged thieves:[3]

Sound of vernal showers
　On the twinkling grass,
Rain-awakened flowers,
　All that ever was
60 Joyous, and clear and fresh, thy music doth surpass.

Teach us, Sprite° or Bird,　　　　　　　　　　　　*spirit*
　What sweet thoughts are thine;
I have never heard
　Praise of love or wine
65 That panted forth a flood of rapture so divine:

Chorus Hymeneal[4]
　Or triumphal chaunt
Matched with thine would be all
　But an empty vaunt,
70 A thing wherein we feel there is some hidden want.

What objects are the fountains
　Of thy happy strain?
What fields or waves or mountains?
　What shapes of sky or plain?
75 What love of thine own kind? what ignorance of pain?

3. The "warm winds," line 53.　　　　　　4. Marital (from Hymen, Greek god of marriage).

With thy clear keen joyance
    Languor cannot be—
Shadow of annoyance
    Never came near thee;
80 Thou lovest—but ne'er knew love's sad satiety.

Waking or asleep,
    Thou of death must deem
Things more true and deep
    Than we mortals dream,
85 Or how could thy notes flow in such a chrystal stream?

We look before and after,
    And pine for what is not—
Our sincerest laughter
    With some pain is fraught—
90 Our sweetest songs are those that tell of saddest thought.

Yet if we could scorn
    Hate and pride and fear;
If we were things born
    Not to shed a tear,
95 I know not how thy joy we ever should come near.

Better than all measures
    Of delightful sound—
Better than all treasures
    That in books are found—
100 Thy skill to poet were, thou Scorner of the ground!

Teach me half the gladness
    That thy brain must know,
Such harmonious madness
    From my lips would flow
105 The world should listen then—as I am listening now.

1820   1820

To Night[1]

Swiftly walk o'er the western wave,
    Spirit of Night!
Out of the misty eastern cave
Where, all the long and lone daylight
5   Thou wovest dreams of joy and fear,
    Which make thee terrible and dear,
        Swift be thy flight!

1. Night and darkness, as opposed to daylight, are often for Shelley symbols of the primordial powers and revelations of the poetic imagination.

Wrap thy form in a mantle grey,
    Star-inwrought!
10 Blind with thine hair the eyes of day,
Kiss her until she be wearied out—
Then wander o'er City and sea and land,
Touching all with thine opiate wand—
    Come, long-sought!

15 When I arose and saw the dawn
    I sighed for thee;
When Light rode high, and the dew was gone,
And noon lay heavy on flower and tree,
And the weary Day[2] turned to his rest,
20 Lingering like an unloved guest,
    I sighed for thee.

Thy brother Death came, and cried,
    Wouldst thou me?
Thy sweet child Sleep, the filmy-eyed,.
25 Murmured like a noontide bee,
Shall I nestle near thy side?
Wouldst thou me? and I replied,
    No, not thee!

Death will come when thou art dead,
30   Soon, too soon—
Sleep will come when thou art fled;
Of neither would I ask the boon
I ask of thee, beloved Night—
Swift be thine approaching flight,
35   Come soon, soon!

1820   1824

Adonais   John Keats died in Rome on February 23, 1821, and was buried there in the Protestant Cemetery. Shelley had met Keats, had invited him to be his guest at Pisa, and had gradually come to to realize that he was "among the writers of the highest genius who have adorned our age" (Preface to *Adonais*). The name "Adonais" is derived from Adonis, the handsome youth who had been loved by the goddess Venus and slain by a wild boar; the function of the beast in this poem is attributed to the anonymous author of a vituperative review of Keats's *Endymion* in the *Quarterly Review*, April 1818 (now known to be John Wilson Croker), whom Shelley mistakenly believed to be responsible for Keats's illness and death.

    Shelley in a letter described *Adonais*, which he wrote in April to June 1821 and had printed in Pisa in July, as a "highly wrought piece of art." Its artistry consists in part in the care with which it follows the conventions of the pastoral elegy, established more than two thousand years earlier by the Greek Sicilian poets Theocritus, Bion, and Moschus—Shelley had himself translated into English Bion's *Lament for Adonis*

2. Here the "Day" is the male sun, not the female "day" with whom the Spirit of Night dallies in the preceding stanza.

and Moschus's *Lament for Bion*. We recognize the centuries-old poetic ritual in many verbal echoes and in such devices as the mournful and accusing invocation to a muse (stanzas 2–4), the sympathetic participation of nature in the grieving (stanzas 14–17), the procession of appropriate mourners (stanzas 30–35), the denunciation of unworthy practitioners of the pastoral or literary art (stanzas 17, 27–29, 36–37), and above all, in the turn from despair at the finality of human death (lines 1, 64, 190: "*He* will awake no more, oh, never more!") to consolation in the sudden and contradictory discovery that the grave is a gate to a higher existence (line 343: "Peace, peace! he is not dead, he doth not sleep").

The first English publication of *Adonais*, in 1829 in an edition sponsored by the so-called Cambridge Apostles (R. M. Milnes, Alfred Tennyson, and A. H. Hallam) marked the beginning of Keats's posthumous emergence from obscurity as a poet.

Adonais

An Elegy on the Death of John Keats, Author of Endymion, Hyperion, etc.

> [Thou wert the morning star among the living,
> Ere thy fair light had fled—
> Now, having died, thou art as Hesperus, giving
> New splendour to the dead.][1]

1

I weep for Adonais—he is dead!
O, weep for Adonais! though our tears
Thaw not the frost which binds so dear a head!
And thou, sad Hour,[2] selected from all years
5   To mourn our loss, rouse thy obscure compeers,
And teach them thine own sorrow, say: with me
Died Adonais; till the Future dares
Forget the Past, his fate and fame shall be
    An echo and a light unto eternity!

2

10 Where wert thou mighty Mother,[3] when he lay,
When thy Son lay, pierced by the shaft which flies
In darkness?[4] where was lorn° Urania   *abandoned*
When Adonais died? With veiled eyes,
'Mid listening Echoes, in her Paradise
15 She sate, while one,[5] with soft enamoured breath,
Rekindled all the fading melodies,
With which, like flowers that mock the corse° beneath,   *corpse*
    He had adorned and hid the coming bulk of death.

1. Shelley prefixed to *Adonais* a Greek epigram, attributed to Plato; this is Shelley's own translation of the Greek. The planet Venus appears both as the morning star, Lucifer, and as the evening star, Hesperus or Vesper. Shelley makes of this phenomenon a key symbol for Adonais's triumph over death, in stanzas 44–46.
2. Shelley follows the classical mode of personifying the hours, which mark the passage of time and turn of the seasons.
3. Urania. She had originally been the Muse of astronomy, but the name was also an epithet for Venus. Shelley converts Venus Urania, who in Greek myth had been the lover of Adonis, into the mother of Adonais.
4. Alludes to the anonymity of the review of *Endymion*.
5. I.e., the echo of Keats's voice in his poems.

3

O, weep for Adonais—he is dead!
Wake, melancholy Mother, wake and weep!
Yet wherefore? Quench within their burning bed
Thy fiery tears, and let thy loud heart keep
Like his, a mute and uncomplaining sleep;
For he is gone, where all things wise and fair
Descend;—oh, dream not that the amorous Deep°   *abyss*
Will yet restore him to the vital air;
Death feeds on his mute voice, and laughs at our despair.

4

Most musical of mourners, weep again!
Lament anew, Urania!—He[6] died,
Who was the Sire of an immortal strain,
Blind, old, and lonely, when his country's pride,
The priest, the slave, and the liberticide,
Trampled and mocked with many a loathed rite
Of lust and blood; he went, unterrified,
Into the gulph of death; but his clear Sprite°   *spirit*
Yet reigns o'er earth; the third among the sons of light.[7]

5

Most musical of mourners, weep anew!
Not all to that bright station dared to climb;
And happier they their happiness who knew,
Whose tapers yet burn through that night of time
In which suns perished; others more sublime,
Struck by the envious wrath of man or God,
Have sunk, extinct in their refulgent prime;
And some yet live, treading the thorny road,
Which leads, through toil and hate, to Fame's serene abode.

6

But now, thy youngest, dearest one, has perished—
The nursling of thy widowhood, who grew,
Like a pale flower by some sad maiden cherished,
And fed with true love tears, instead of dew;[8]
Most musical of mourners, weep anew!
Thy extreme[9] hope, the loveliest and the last,
The bloom, whose petals nipt before they blew°   *bloomed*
Died on the promise of the fruit, is waste;
The broken lily lies—the storm is overpast.

7

To that high Capital,° where kingly Death   *Rome*
Keeps his pale court in beauty and decay,

---

6. Milton, regarded as precursor of the great poetic tradition in which Keats wrote. He had adopted Urania as the muse of *Paradise Lost*. Lines 31–35 describe Milton's life during the restoration of the Stuart monarchy.
7. The three are Milton and his great predecessors in epic poetry, Homer and Dante. The stanza following describes the lot of other poets, up to Shelley's own time.
8. An allusion to an incident in Keats's *Isabella*.
9. Last, as well as highest.

He came; and bought, with price of purest breath,
A grave among the eternal.—Come away!
Haste, while the vault of blue Italian day
60 Is yet his fitting charnel-roof! while still
He lies, as if in dewy sleep he lay;
Awake him not! surely he takes his fill
Of deep and liquid rest, forgetful of all ill.

8

He will awake no more, oh, never more!—
65 Within the twilight chamber spreads apace,
The shadow of white Death, and at the door
Invisible Corruption waits to trace
His extreme way to her dim dwelling-place;
The eternal Hunger sits, but pity and awe
70 Soothe her pale rage, nor dares she to deface
So fair a prey, till darkness, and the law
Of change, shall 'oer his sleep the mortal curtain draw.

9

O, weep for Adonais!—The quick° Dreams,   *living*
The passion-winged Ministers of thought,
75 Who were his flocks,[1] whom near the living streams
Of his young spirit he fed, and whom he taught
The love which was its music, wander not,—
Wander no more, from kindling brain to brain,
But droop there, whence they sprung; and mourn their lot
80 Round the cold heart, where, after their sweet pain,
They ne'er will gather strength, or find a home again.

10

And one[2] with trembling hands clasps his cold head,
And fans him with her moonlight wings, and cries;
"Our love, our hope, our sorrow, is not dead;
85 See, on the silken fringe of his faint eyes,
Like dew upon a sleeping flower, there lies
A tear some Dream has loosened from his brain."
Lost Angel of a ruined Paradise!
She knew not 'twas her own; as with no stain
90 She faded, like a cloud which had outwept its rain.

11

One from a lucid° urn of starry dew   *luminous*
Washed his light limbs as if embalming them;
Another clipt her profuse locks, and threw
The wreath upon him, like an anadem,°   *rich garland*
95 Which frozen tears instead of pearls begem;
Another in her wilful grief would break
Her bow and winged reeds, as if to stem

1. The products of Keats's imagination, figura- tion) as his sheep.
tively represented (according to pastoral conven- 2. One of the Dreams (line 73).

A greater loss with one which was more weak;
And dull the barbed fire against his frozen cheek.

12

100   Another Splendour on his mouth alit,
That mouth, whence it was wont to draw the breath
Which gave it strength to pierce the guarded wit,[3]
And pass into the panting heart beneath
With lightning and with music: the damp death
105   Quenched its caress upon his icy lips;
And, as a dying meteor stains a wreath
Of moonlight vapour, which the cold night clips,°   *embraces*
It flushed through his pale limbs, and past to its eclipse.

13

And others came . . . Desires and Adorations,
110   Winged Persuasions and veiled Destinies,
Splendours, and Glooms, and glimmering Incarnations
Of hopes and fears, and twilight Phantasies;
And Sorrow, with her family of Sighs,
And Pleasure, blind with tears, led by the gleam
115   Of her own dying smile instead of eyes,
Came in slow pomp;—the moving pomp might seem
Like pageantry of mist on an autumnal stream.

14

All he had loved, and moulded into thought,
From shape, and hue, and odour, and sweet sound,
120   Lamented Adonais. Morning sought
Her eastern watchtower, and her hair unbound,
Wet with the tears which should adorn the ground,
Dimmed the aerial eyes that kindle day;
Afar the melancholy thunder moaned,
125   Pale Ocean in unquiet slumber lay,
And the wild winds flew round, sobbing in their dismay.

15

Lost Echo sits amid the voiceless mountains,
And feeds her grief with his remembered lay,
And will no more reply to winds or fountains,
130   Or amorous birds perched on the young green spray,
Or herdsman's horn, or bell at closing day;
Since she can mimic not his lips, more dear
Than those for whose disdain she pined away
Into a shadow of all sounds:[4]—a drear
135   Murmur, between their songs, is all the woodmen hear.

16

Grief made the young Spring wild, and she threw down
Her kindling buds, as if she Autumn were,

---

3. The cautious intellect (of the listener).
4. Because of her unrequited love for Narcissus, who was enamored of his own reflection (line 141), the nymph Echo pined away until she was only a reflected sound.

Or they dead leaves; since her delight is flown
For whom should she have waked the sullen year?
140 To Phoebus was not Hyacinth so dear[5]
Nor to himself Narcissus, as to both
Thou Adonais: wan they stand and sere[6]
Amid the faint companions of their youth,
With dew all turned to tears; odour, to sighing ruth.°   pity

17

145 Thy spirit's sister, the lorn nightingale[7]
Mourns not her mate with such melodious pain;
Not so the eagle, who like thee could scale
Heaven, and could nourish in the sun's domain
Her mighty youth with morning,[8] doth complain,
150 Soaring and screaming round her empty nest,
As Albion° wails for thee: the curse of Cain   England
Light on his head[9] who pierced thy innocent breast,
And scared the angel soul that was its earthly guest!

18

Ah woe is me! Winter is come and gone,
155 But grief returns with the revolving year;
The airs and streams renew their joyous tone;
The ants, the bees, the swallows reappear;
Fresh leaves and flowers deck the dead Seasons' bier;
The amorous birds now pair in every brake,°   thicket
160 And build their mossy homes in field and brere;°   briar
And the green lizard, and the golden snake,
Like unimprisoned flames, out of their trance awake.

19

Through wood and stream and field and hill and Ocean
A quickening life from the Earth's heart has burst
165 As it has ever done, with change and motion,
From the great morning of the world when first
God dawned on Chaos; in its stream immersed
The lamps of Heaven flash with a softer light;
All baser things pant with life's sacred thirst;
170 Diffuse themselves; and spend in love's delight,
The beauty and the joy of their renewed might.

20

The leprous corpse touched by this spirit tender
Exhales itself in flowers of gentle breath;
Like incarnations of the stars, when splendour
175 Is changed to fragrance, they illumine death

5. Young Hyacinthus was loved by Phoebus Apollo, who accidentally killed him in a game of quoits. Apollo made the hyacinth flower spring from his blood.
6. Dried, withered.
7. To whom Keats had written *Ode to a Nightin-*

gale.
8. In the legend, the aged eagle, to renew his youth, flies toward the sun until his old plumage is burned off and the film cleared from his eyes.
9. The reviewer of *Endymion*.

And mock the merry worm that wakes beneath;
Nought we know, dies. Shall that alone which knows
Be as a sword consumed before the sheath[1]
By sightless° lightning?—th' intense atom glows   *invisible*
180   A moment, then is quenched in a most cold repose.

21

Alas! that all we loved of him should be,
But for our grief, as if it had not been,
And grief itself be mortal! Woe is me!
Whence are we, and why are we? of what scene
185   The actors or spectators? Great and mean
Meet massed in death, who lends what life must borrow.
As long as skies are blue, and fields are green,
Evening must usher night, night urge the morrow,
Month follow month with woe, and year wake year to sorrow.

22

190   *He* will awake no more, oh, never more!
"Wake thou," cried Misery, "childless Mother, rise
Out of thy sleep, and slake,° in thy heart's core,   *assuage*
A wound more fierce than his with tears and sighs."
And all the Dreams that watched Urania's eyes,
195   And all the Echoes whom their sister's song[2]
Had held in holy silence, cried: "Arise!"
Swift as a Thought by the snake Memory stung,
From her ambrosial rest the fading Splendour° sprung.   *Urania*

23

She rose like an autumnal Night, that springs
200   Out of the East, and follows wild and drear
The golden Day, which, on eternal wings,
Even as a ghost abandoning a bier,
Had left the Earth a corpse. Sorrow and fear
So struck, so roused, so rapt Urania;
205   So saddened round her like an atmosphere
Of stormy mist; so swept her on her way
Even to the mournful place where Adonais lay.

24

Out of her secret Paradise she sped,
Through camps and cities rough with stone, and steel,
210   And human hearts, which to her aery tread
Yielding not, wounded the invisible
Palms of her tender feet where'er they fell:
And barbed tongues, and thoughts more sharp than they
Rent the soft Form they never could repel,
215   Whose sacred blood, like the young tears of May,
Paved with eternal flowers that undeserving way.

---

1. The material body. "Sword": the mind that knows.   2. I.e., the Echo in line 127.

25

In the death chamber for a moment Death
Shamed by the presence of that living Might
Blushed to annihilation, and the breath
220   Revisited those lips, and life's pale light
Flashed through those limbs, so late her dear delight.
"Leave me not wild and drear and comfortless,
As silent lightning leaves the starless night!
Leave me not!" cried Urania: her distress
225   Roused Death: Death rose and smiled, and met her vain caress.

26

"Stay yet awhile! speak to me once again;
Kiss me, so long but as a kiss may live;
And in my heartless[3] breast and burning brain
That word, that kiss shall all thoughts else survive
230   With food of saddest memory kept alive,
Now thou art dead, as if it were a part
Of thee, my Adonais! I would give
All that I am to be as thou now art!
But I am chained to Time, and cannot thence depart!

27

235   "Oh gentle child, beautiful as thou wert,
Why didst thou leave the trodden paths of men
Too soon, and with weak hands though mighty heart
Dare the unpastured dragon in his den?[4]
Defenceless as thou wert, oh where was then
240   Wisdom the mirrored shield, or scorn the spear?[5]
Or hadst thou waited the full cycle, when
Thy spirit should have filled its crescent sphere,[6]
The monsters of life's waste had fled from thee like deer.

28

"The herded wolves, bold only to pursue;
245   The obscene ravens, clamorous o'er the dead;
The vultures to the conqueror's banner true
Who feed where Desolation first has fed,
And whose wings rain contagion;—how they fled,
When like Apollo, from his golden bow,
250   The Pythian of the age[7] one arrow sped
And smiled!—The spoilers tempt no second blow,
They fawn on the proud feet that spurn them lying low.

3. Because her heart had been given to Adonais.
4. I.e., the hostile reviewers.
5. The allusion is to Perseus, who had cut off
Medusa's head while avoiding the direct sight of
her (which would have turned him to stone) by
looking only at her reflection in his shield.
6. I.e., when thy spirit, like the full moon, should

have reached its maturity.
7. Byron, who had directed against critics of the
age his satiric poem *English Bards and Scotch
Reviewers* (1809). The allusion is to Apollo, called
"the Pythian" because he had slain the dragon
Python.

29

"The sun comes forth, and many reptiles spawn;
He sets, and each ephemeral insect then
255   Is gathered into death without a dawn,
And the immortal stars awake again;
So is it in the world of living men:
A godlike mind soars forth, in its delight
Making earth bare and veiling heaven,[8] and when
260   It sinks, the swarms that dimmed or shared its light
Leave to its kindred lamps[9] the spirit's awful night."

30

Thus ceased she: and the mountain shepherds came,
Their garlands sere, their magic mantles rent;
The Pilgrim of Eternity,[1] whose fame
265   Over his living head like Heaven is bent,
An early but enduring monument,
Came, veiling all the lightnings of his song
In sorrow; from her wilds Ierne sent
The sweetest lyrist[2] of her saddest wrong,
270   And love taught grief to fall like music from his tongue.

31

Midst others of less note, came one frail Form,[3]
A phantom among men; companionless
As the last cloud of an expiring storm
Whose thunder is its knell; he, as I guess,
275   Had gazed on Nature's naked loveliness,
Actæon-like, and now he fled astray
With feeble steps o'er the world's wilderness,
And his own thoughts, along that rugged way,
Pursued, like raging hounds, their father and their prey.[4]

32

280   A pardlike° Spirit beautiful and swift—   leopardlike
A Love in desolation masked;—a Power
Girt round with weakness;—it can scarce uplift
The weight of the superincumbent hour;[5]
It is a dying lamp, a falling shower,
285   A breaking billow;—even whilst we speak
Is it not broken? On the withering flower
The killing sun smiles brightly: on a cheek
The life can burn in blood, even while the heart may break.

8. As the sun reveals the earth but veils the other stars.
9. The other stars (i.e., creative minds), of lesser brilliance than the sun.
1. Byron, who had referred to his Childe Harold as one of the "wanderers o'er Eternity" (3.669).
2. Thomas Moore (1779–1852), from Ireland ("Ierne"), who had written poems about the oppression of his native land.
3. Shelley himself, represented in one of his aspects—like the Poet in *Alastor,* rather than the author of *Prometheus Unbound.*
4. Actaeon, while hunting, came upon the naked Diana bathing and, as a punishment, was turned into a stag and torn to pieces by his own hounds.
5. The heavy, overhanging hour of Keats's death.

33

His head was bound with pansies overblown,
290   And faded violets, white, and pied, and blue;
And a light spear topped with a cypress cone,
Round whose rude shaft dark ivy tresses grew[6]
Yet dripping with the forest's noonday dew,
Vibrated, as the ever-beating heart
295   Shook the weak hand that grasped it; of that crew
He came the last, neglected and apart;
A herd-abandoned deer struck by the hunter's dart.

34

All stood aloof, and at his partial° moan   *sympathetic*
Smiled through their tears; well knew that gentle band
300   Who in another's fate now wept his own;
As in the accents of an unknown land,
He sung new sorrow; sad Urania scanned
The Stranger's mien, and murmured: "who art thou?"
He answered not, but with a sudden hand
305   Made bare his branded and ensanguined brow,
Which was like Cain's or Christ's[7]—Oh! that it should be so!

35

What softer voice is hushed over the dead?
Athwart what brow is that dark mantle thrown?
What form leans sadly o'er the white death-bed,
310   In mockery of monumental stone,[8]
The heavy heart heaving without a moan?
If it be He,[9] who, gentlest of the wise,
Taught, soothed, loved, honoured the departed one;
Let me not vex, with inharmonious sighs
315   The silence of that heart's accepted sacrifice.

36

Our Adonais has drunk poison—oh!
What deaf and viperous murderer could crown
Life's early cup with such a draught of woe?
The nameless worm[1] would now itself disown:
320   It felt, yet could escape the magic tone
Whose prelude held all envy, hate, and wrong,
But what was howling in one breast alone,
Silent with expectation of the song,[2]
Whose master's hand is cold, whose silver lyre unstrung.

---

6. Like the thyrsus, the leaf-entwined and cone-topped staff carried by Dionysus. The pansies are emblems of sorrowful thought. The cypress is an emblem of mourning.

7. His bloody ("ensanguined") brow bore a mark like that with which God had branded Cain for murdering Abel—or like that left by Christ's crown of thorns.

8. In imitation of a memorial statue.

9. Leigh Hunt, close friend of both Keats and Shelley.

1. Snake—the anonymous reviewer.

2. The promise of later greatness in Keats's early poems "held . . . silent" the expression of all malignant feelings except the reviewer's.

37

325 Live thou, whose infamy is not thy fame!
Live! fear no heavier chastisement from me,
Thou noteless blot on a remembered name!
But be thyself, and know thyself to be!
And ever at thy season be thou free
330 To spill the venom when thy fangs o'erflow:
Remorse and Self-contempt shall cling to thee;
Hot Shame shall burn upon thy secret brow,
And like a beaten hound tremble thou shalt—as now.

38

Nor let us weep that our delight is fled
335 Far from these carrion kites[3] that scream below;
He wakes or sleeps with the enduring dead;
Thou canst not soar where he is sitting now.—
Dust to the dust! but the pure spirit shall flow
Back to the burning fountain whence it came,
340 A portion of the Eternal,[4] which must glow
Through time and change, unquenchably the same,
Whilst thy cold embers choke the sordid hearth of shame.

39

Peace, peace! he is not dead, he doth not sleep—
He hath awakened from the dream of life—
345 'Tis we, who lost in stormy visions, keep
With phantoms an unprofitable strife,
And in mad trance, strike with our spirit's knife
Invulnerable nothings.—*We* decay
Like corpses in a charnel; fear and grief
350 Convulse us and consume us day by day,
And cold hopes swarm like worms within our living clay.

40

He has outsoared the shadow of our night;[5]
Envy and calumny and hate and pain,
And that unrest which men miscall delight,
355 Can touch him not and torture not again;
From the contagion of the world's slow stain
He is secure, and now can never mourn
A heart grown cold, a head grown grey in vain;
Nor, when the spirit's self has ceased to burn,
360 With sparkless ashes load an unlamented urn.

3. Birds of prey; a species of hawk.
4. Shelley adopts for this poem the Neoplatonic view that all life and all forms emanate from the Absolute, the eternal One. The Absolute is imaged as both a radiant light source and an overflowing fountain, which circulates continuously through the dross of matter (stanza 43) and back to its source.
5. He has soared beyond the shadow cast by the earth as it intercepts the sun's light.

41

He lives, he wakes—'tis Death is dead, not he;
Mourn not for Adonais.—Thou young Dawn
Turn all thy dew to splendour, for from thee
The spirit thou lamentest is not gone;
365   Ye caverns and ye forests, cease to moan!
Cease ye faint flowers and fountains, and thou Air
Which like a mourning veil thy scarf hadst thrown
O'er the abandoned Earth, now leave it bare
Even to the joyous stars which smile on its despair!⁶

42

370   He is made one with Nature: there is heard
His voice in all her music, from the moan
Of thunder, to the song of night's sweet bird;⁷
He is a presence to be felt and known
In darkness and in light, from herb and stone,
375   Spreading itself where'er that Power may move
Which has withdrawn his being to its own;
Which wields the world with never wearied love,
Sustains it from beneath, and kindles it above.

43

He is a portion of the loveliness
380   Which once he made more lovely: he doth bear
His part, while the one Spirit's plastic⁸ stress
Sweeps through the dull dense world, compelling there,
All new successions to the forms they wear;
Torturing th' unwilling dross that checks its flight
385   To its own likeness, as each mass may bear;⁹
And bursting in its beauty and its might
From trees and beasts and men into the Heaven's light.

44

The splendours of the firmament of time
May be eclipsed, but are extinguished not;
390   Like stars to their appointed height they climb
And death is a low mist which cannot blot
The brightness it may veil.¹ When lofty thought
Lifts a young heart above its mortal lair,
And love and life contend in it, for what
395   Shall be its earthly doom,° the dead live there²   *destiny*
And move like winds of light on dark and stormy air.

6. Shelley's science is, as usual, accurate: it is the
envelope of air around the earth that, by diffusing
and reflecting sunlight, veils the stars.
7. The nightingale, in allusion to Keats's *Ode to a
Nightingale*.
8. Formative, shaping.
9. I.e., to the degree that a particular substance

will permit.
1. The radiance of stars (i.e., of poets) persists,
even when they are temporarily "eclipsed" by
another heavenly body, or obscured by the veil of
the earth's atmosphere.
2. I.e., in the thought of the "young heart."

45

The inheritors of unfulfilled renown[3]
Rose from their thrones, built beyond mortal thought,
Far in the Unapparent. Chatterton
400 Rose pale, his solemn agony had not
Yet faded from him; Sidney, as he fought
And as he fell and as he lived and loved
Sublimely mild, a Spirit without spot,
Arose; and Lucan, by his death approved:°   *justified*
405 Oblivion as they rose shrank like a thing reproved.

46

And many more, whose names on Earth are dark
But whose transmitted effluence cannot die
So long as fire outlives the parent spark,
Rose, robed in dazzling immortality.
410 "Thou art become as one of us," they cry,
"It was for thee yon kingless sphere has long
Swung blind in unascended majesty,
Silent alone amid an Heaven of song.
Assume thy winged throne, thou Vesper of our throng!"[4]

47

415 Who mourns for Adonais? oh come forth
Fond wretch! and know thyself and him aright.
Clasp with thy panting soul the pendulous[5] Earth;
As from a centre, dart thy spirit's light
Beyond all worlds, until its spacious might
420 Satiate the void circumference: then shrink
Even to a point within our day and night;[6]
And keep thy heart light lest it make thee sink
When hope has kindled hope, and lured thee to the brink.

48

Or go to Rome, which is the sepulchre
425 O, not of him, but of our joy: 'tis nought
That ages, empires, and religions there
Lie buried in the ravage they have wrought;
For such as he can lend,—they[7] borrow not
Glory from those who made the world their prey;
430 And he is gathered to the kings of thought

3. Poets who (like Keats) died young, before achieving their full measure of fame: Thomas Chatterton (1752–1770) committed suicide at seventeen, Sir Philip Sidney (1554–1586) died in battle at thirty-two, and the Roman poet Lucan (39–65 C.E.) killed himself at twenty-six to escape a sentence of death for having plotted against the tyrant Nero.
4. Adonais assumes his place in the sphere of Vesper, the evening star, hitherto unoccupied ("kingless"), hence also "silent" amid the music of the other spheres.

5. Suspended, floating in space.
6. The poet bids the wretch who is foolish ("fond") enough to mourn Adonais to stretch his imagination so as to reach the poet's own cosmic viewpoint and then allow it to contract ("shrink") back to its ordinary vantage point on earth—where, unlike Adonais in his heavenly place, we have an alternation of day and night.
7. Poets like Keats, who can bestow ("lend") glory, as opposed to the Roman conquerors, who borrowed glory from those they conquered.

Who waged contention with their time's decay,
And of the past are all that cannot pass away.

49

    Go thou to Rome,—at once the Paradise,
    The grave, the city, and the wilderness;
435   And where its wrecks like shattered mountains rise,
    And flowering weeds, and fragrant copses[8] dress
    The bones of Desolation's nakedness
    Pass, till the Spirit of the spot shall lead
    Thy footsteps to a slope of green access[9]
440   Where, like an infant's smile, over the dead,
A light of laughing flowers along the grass is spread.

50

    And grey walls moulder round,[1] on which dull Time
    Feeds, like slow fire upon a hoary brand;[2]
    And one keen pyramid with wedge sublime,[3]
445   Pavilioning the dust of him who planned
    This refuge for his memory, doth stand
    Like flame transformed to marble; and beneath,
    A field is spread, on which a newer band
    Have pitched in Heaven's smile their camp of death
450   Welcoming him we lose with scarce extinguished breath.

51

    Here pause: these graves are all too young as yet
    To have outgrown the sorrow which consigned
    Its charge to each; and if the seal is set,
    Here, on one fountain of a mourning mind,[4]
455   Break it not thou! too surely shalt thou find
    Thine own well full, if thou returnest home,
    Of tears and gall. From the world's bitter wind
    Seek shelter in the shadow of the tomb.
What Adonais is, why fear we to become?

52

460   The One remains, the many change and pass;
    Heaven's light forever shines, Earth's shadows fly;
    Life, like a dome of many-coloured glass,
    Stains the white radiance of Eternity,
    Until Death tramples it to fragments.[5]—Die,
465   If thou wouldst be with that which thou dost seek!

8. Undergrowth. In Shelley's time the ruins of ancient Rome were overgrown with weeds and shrubbery.
9. The Protestant Cemetery, Keats's burial place. The next line is a glancing allusion to Shelley's three-year-old son, William, also buried there.
1. The wall of ancient Rome formed one boundary of the cemetery.
2. A burning log.
3. The tomb of Caius Cestius, a Roman tribune,

just outside the cemetery.
4. Shelley's mourning for his son.
5. Earthly life colors ("stains") the pure white light of the One, which is the source of all light (see lines 339–40, n. 4). The azure sky, flowers, etc., of lines 466–68 exemplify earthly colors that, however beautiful, fall far short of the "glory" of the pure Light that they transmit but also refract ("transfuse").

Follow where all is fled!—Rome's azure sky,
Flowers, ruins, statues, music, words, are weak
The glory they transfuse with fitting truth to speak.

53

Why linger, why turn back, why shrink, my Heart?
470 Thy hopes are gone before; from all things here
They have departed; thou shouldst now depart!
A light is past from the revolving year,
And man, and woman; and what still is dear
Attracts to crush, repels to make thee wither.
475 The soft sky smiles,—the low wind whispers near:
'Tis Adonais calls! oh, hasten thither,
No more let Life divide what Death can join together.

54

That Light whose smile kindles the Universe,
That Beauty in which all things work and move,
480 That Benediction which the eclipsing Curse
Of birth can quench not, that sustaining Love
Which through the web of being blindly wove
By man and beast and earth and air and sea,
Burns bright or dim, as each are mirrors of[6]
485 The fire for which all thirst;[7] now beams on me,
Consuming the last clouds of cold mortality.

55

The breath whose might I have invoked in song[8]
Descends on me; my spirit's bark is driven,
Far from the shore, far from the trembling throng
490 Whose sails were never to the tempest given;
The massy earth and sphered skies are riven!
I am borne darkly, fearfully, afar;
Whilst burning through the inmost veil of Heaven,
The soul of Adonais, like a star,
495 Beacons from the abode where the Eternal are.

1821   1821

To Jane[1] (The keen stars were twinkling)

The keen stars were twinkling
And the fair moon was rising among them,
       Dear Jane.
The guitar was tinkling
5   But the notes were not sweet 'till you sung them

---

6. I.e., according to the degree that each reflects.
7. The "thirst" of the human spirit is to return to the fountain and fire (the "burning fountain," line 339) which is its source.
8. Two years earlier Shelley had "invoked" (prayed

to, and also asked for) "the breath of Autumn's being" in his *Ode to the West Wind*.
1. Jane Williams, the common-law wife of Shelley's close friend Edward Williams.

Again.—
As the moon's soft splendour
O'er the faint cold starlight of Heaven
Is thrown—
10   So your voice most tender
To the strings without soul had then given
Its own.

The stars will awaken,
Though the moon sleep a full hour later,
15   Tonight;
No leaf will be shaken
While the dews of your melody scatter
Delight.
Though the sound overpowers
20 Sing again, with your dear voice revealing
A tone
Of some world far from ours,
Where music and moonlight and feeling
Are one.

1822   1832

A Defence of Poetry

In 1820 Shelley's good friend Thomas Love Peacock published an ironic essay, *The Four Ages of Poetry,* implicitly directed against the towering claims for poetry and the poetic imagination made by his Romantic contemporaries. Peacock adopted the premise of Wordsworth and some other Romantic critics—that poetry in its origin was a primitive use of language and mind—but from this premise he proceeded to draw the conclusion that poetry has become a useless anachronism in this age of science and technology. Peacock was himself a poet as well as an excellent prose satirist, and Shelley saw the joke; but he also recognized that the view that Peacock, as a satirist, had assumed was very close to that actually held in his day by Utilitarian philosophers and the material-minded public, who either attacked or contemptuously ignored the imaginative faculty and its achievements. He therefore undertook, as he good-humoredly wrote to Peacock, "to break a lance with you . . . in honor of my mistress Urania," even though he was only "the knight of the shield of shadow and the lance of gossamere." The result was *A Defence of Poetry,* planned to consist of three parts. The last two parts were never written, and even the existing section, written in 1821, remained unpublished until 1840, eighteen years after Shelley's death.

Shelley's emphasis in this essay, like that of Blake in his critical commentaries, is not on the particularity of individual poems but on the universal and permanent qualities and values that, he believes, all great poems, as products of imagination, have in common. Shelley in addition extends the term *poet* to include all creative minds that break out of the conditions of their time and place to envision what he regards as the eternal and general forms of value. This category includes not only writers in prose as well as verse but also artists, legislators, prophets, and the founders of new social and religious institutions.

The *Defence* is an eloquent and enduring claim for the indispensability of the visionary and creative imagination in all the great human concerns. Few later social critics have equaled the cogency of Shelley's attack on our acquisitive society and its narrowly material concepts of utility and progress. Such a bias has opened the way to enormous advances in the physical sciences and our material well-being, but without a proportionate development of our "poetic faculty," the moral imagination. The result, Shelley says, is that "man, having enslaved the elements, remains himself a slave."

From A Defence of Poetry

or Remarks Suggested by an Essay Entitled "The Four Ages of Poetry"

According to one mode of regarding those two classes of mental action, which are called reason and imagination, the former may be considered as mind contemplating the relations borne by one thought to another, however produced; and the latter, as mind acting upon those thoughts so as to colour them with its own light, and composing from them, as from elements, other thoughts, each containing within itself the principle of its own integrity. The one[1] is the *to poiein*,[2] or the principle of synthesis, and has for its objects those forms which are common to universal nature and existence itself; the other is the *to logizein*,[3] or principle of analysis, and its action regards the relations of things, simply as relations; considering thoughts, not in their integral unity, but as the algebraical representations which conduct to certain general results. Reason is the enumeration of quantities already known; imagination is the perception of the value of those quantities, both separately and as a whole. Reason respects the differences, and imagination the similitudes of things. Reason is to Imagination as the instrument to the agent, as the body to the spirit, as the shadow to the substance.

Poetry, in a general sense, may be defined to be "the expression of the Imagination": and poetry is connate with the origin of man. Man is an instrument over which a series of external and internal impressions are driven, like the alternations of an ever-changing wind over an Æolian lyre,[4] which move it by their motion to ever-changing melody. But there is a principle within the human being, and perhaps within all sentient beings, which acts otherwise than in the lyre, and produces not melody, alone, but harmony, by an internal adjustment of the sounds or motions thus excited to the impressions which excite them. It is as if the lyre could accommodate its chords to the motions of that which strikes them, in a determined proportion of sound; even as the musician can accommodate his voice to the sound of the lyre. A child at play by itself will express its delight by its voice and motions; and every inflexion of tone and every gesture will bear exact relation to a corresponding antitype in the pleasurable impressions which awakened it; it will be the reflected image of that impression; and as the lyre trembles and sounds after the wind has died away, so the child seeks, by prolonging in its voice and motions the duration of the effect, to prolong also a consciousness of the cause. In relation to the objects which delight a child, these expres-

---

1. The imagination. "The other" (later in the sentence) is the reason.
2. Making. The Greek word from which the English term *poet* derives means "maker," and "maker" was often used as equivalent to "poet" by Renaissance critics such as Sir Philip Sidney in his

Defence of Poesy, which Shelley had carefully studied.
3. Calculating, reasoning.
4. A wind harp (see Coleridge, *The Eolian Harp*, p. 1576).

sions are, what poetry is to higher objects. The savage (for the savage is to ages what the child is to years) expresses the emotions produced in him by surrounding objects in a similar manner; and language and gesture, together with plastic or pictorial imitation, become the image of the combined effect of those objects, and of his apprehension of them. Man in society, with all his passions and his pleasures, next becomes the object of the passions and pleasures of man; an additional class of emotions produces an augmented treasure of expressions; and language, gesture, and the imitative arts, become at once the representation and the medium, the pencil and the picture, the chisel and the statue, the chord and the harmony. The social sympathies, or those laws from which as from its elements society results, begin to develope themselves from the moment that two human beings coexist; the future is contained within the present as the plant within the seed; and equality, diversity, unity, contrast, mutual dependence, become the principles alone capable of affording the motives according to which the will of a social being is determined to action, inasmuch as he is social; and constitute pleasure in sensation, virtue in sentiment, beauty in art, truth in reasoning, and love in the intercourse of kind. Hence men, even in the infancy of society, observe a certain order in their words and actions, distinct from that of the objects and the impressions represented by them, all expression being subject to the laws of that from which it proceeds. But let us dismiss those more general considerations which might involve an enquiry into the principles of society itself, and restrict our view to the manner in which the imagination is expressed upon its forms.

In the youth of the world, men dance and sing and imitate natural objects, observing[5] in these actions, as in all others, a certain rhythm or order. And, although all men observe a similar, they observe not the same order, in the motions of the dance, in the melody of the song, in the combinations of language, in the series of their imitations of natural objects. For there is a certain order or rhythm belonging to each of these classes of mimetic representation, from which the hearer and the spectator receive an intenser and purer pleasure than from any other: the sense of an approximation to this order has been called taste, by modern writers. Every man in the infancy of art, observes an order which approximates more or less closely to that from which this highest delight results: but the diversity is not sufficiently marked, as that its gradations should be sensible, except in those instances where the predominance of this faculty of approximation to the beautiful (for so we may be permitted to name the relation between this highest pleasure and its cause) is very great. Those in whom it exists in excess are poets, in the most universal sense of the word; and the pleasure resulting from the manner in which they express the influence of society or nature upon their own minds, communicates itself to others, and gathers a sort of reduplication from that community. Their language is vitally metaphorical; that is, it marks the before unapprehended relations of things, and perpetuates their apprehension, until the words which represent them, become through time signs for portions or classes of thoughts[6] instead of pictures of integral thoughts; and then if no new poets should arise to create afresh the associations which have been thus disorganized, language will be dead to all the nobler purposes of

5. Following, obeying.

6. I.e., abstract concepts.

human intercourse. These similitudes or relations are finely said by Lord Bacon to be "the same footsteps of nature impressed upon the various subjects of the world"[7]—and he considers the faculty which perceives them as the storehouse of axioms common to all knowledge. In the infancy of society every author is necessarily a poet, because language itself is poetry; and to be a poet is to apprehend the true and the beautiful, in a word the good which exists in the relation, subsisting, first between existence and perception, and secondly between perception and expression. Every original language near to its source is in itself the chaos of a cyclic poem:[8] the copiousness of lexicography and the distinctions of grammar are the works of a later age, and are merely the catalogue and the form of the creations of Poetry.

But Poets, or those who imagine and express this indestructible order, are not only the authors of language and of music, of the dance and architecture and statuary and painting: they are the institutors of laws, and the founders of civil society and the inventors of the arts of life and the teachers, who draw into a certain propinquity with the beautiful and the true that partial apprehension of the agencies of the invisible world which is called religion.[9] Hence all original religions are allegorical, or susceptible of allegory, and like Janus[1] have a double face of false and true. Poets, according to the circumstances of the age and nation in which they appeared, were called in the earlier epochs of the world legislators or prophets:[2] a poet essentially comprises and unites both these characters. For he not only beholds intensely the present as it is, and discovers those laws according to which present things ought to be ordered, but he beholds the future in the present, and his thoughts are the germs of the flower and the fruit of latest time. Not that I assert poets to be prophets in the gross sense of the word, or that they can foretell the form as surely as they foreknow the spirit of events: such is the pretence of superstition which would make poetry an attribute of prophecy, rather than prophecy an attribute of poetry. A Poet participates in the eternal, the infinite, and the one; as far as relates to his conceptions, time and place and number are not. The grammatical forms which express the moods of time, and the difference of persons and the distinction of place are convertible with respect to the highest poetry without injuring it as poetry, and the choruses of Æschylus, and the book of Job, and Dante's Paradise would afford, more than any other writings, examples of this fact, if the limits of this essay did not forbid citation. The creations of sculpture, painting, and music, are illustrations still more decisive.

Language, colour, form, and religious and civil habits of action are all the instruments and materials of poetry; they may be called poetry by that figure of speech which considers the effect as a synonime of the cause. But poetry in a more restricted sense[3] expresses those arrangements of language, and especially metrical language, which are created by that imperial faculty, whose throne is curtained within the invisible nature of man. And this

7. Francis Bacon's *De Augmentis Scientiarum* (On the enlargement of the sciences) 1.3.
8. A group of poems (e.g., "the Arthurian cycle") that deal with the same subject.
9. Here Shelley enlarges the scope of the term *poetry* to denote all the creative achievements, or imaginative breakthroughs, of humankind, including noninstitutional religious insights.
1. Roman god of beginnings and endings, often represented by two heads facing opposite directions.
2. Sir Philip Sidney had pointed out, in his *Defence of Poesy*, that *vates*, the Roman term for "poet," signifies "a diviner, fore-seer, or Prophet."
3. I.e., restricted to specifically verbal poetry, as against the inclusive sense in which Shelley has been applying the term.

springs from the nature itself of language, which is a more direct representation of the actions and passions of our internal being, and is susceptible of more various and delicate combinations, than colour, form, or motion, and is more plastic and obedient to the controul of that faculty of which it is the creation. For language is arbitrarily produced by the Imagination and has relation to thoughts alone; but all other materials, instruments and conditions of art, have relations among each other, which limit and interpose between conception and expression. The former[4] is as a mirror which reflects, the latter as a cloud which enfeebles, the light of which both are mediums of communication. Hence the fame of sculptors, painters and musicians, although the intrinsic powers of the great masters of these arts, may yield in no degree to that of those who have employed language as the hieroglyphic of their thoughts, has never equalled that of poets in the restricted sense of the term; as two performers of equal skill will produce unequal effects from a guitar and a harp. The fame of legislators and founders of religions, so long as their institutions last, alone seems to exceed that of poets in the restricted sense; but it can scarcely be a question whether, if we deduct the celebrity which their flattery of the gross opinions of the vulgar usually conciliates, together with that which belonged to them in their higher character of poets, any excess will remain.

We have thus circumscribed the meaning of the word Poetry within the limits of that art which is the most familiar and the most perfect expression of the faculty itself. It is necessary however to make the circle still narrower, and to determine the distinction between measured and unmeasured language; for the popular division into prose and verse is inadmissible in accurate philosophy.

Sounds as well as thoughts have relation both between each other and towards that which they represent, and a perception of the order of those relations has always been found connected with a perception of the order of the relations of thoughts. Hence the language of poets has ever affected a certain uniform and harmonious recurrence of sound, without which it were not poetry, and which is scarcely less indispensable to the communication of its influence, than the words themselves, without reference to that peculiar order. Hence the vanity of translation; it were as wise to cast a violet into a crucible that you might discover the formal principle of its colour and odour, as seek to transfuse from one language into another the creations of a poet. The plant must spring again from its seed or it will bear no flower— and this is the burthen of the curse of Babel.[5]

An observation of the regular mode of the recurrence of this harmony in the language of poetical minds, together with its relation to music, produced metre, or a certain system of traditional forms of harmony of language. Yet it is by no means essential that a poet should accommodate his language to this traditional form, so that the harmony which is its spirit, be observed. The practise is indeed convenient and popular, and to be preferred, especially in such composition as includes much form and action: but every great poet must inevitably innovate upon the example of his predecessors in the exact structure of his peculiar versification. The distinction between poets and

---

4. I.e., language, as opposed to the media of sculpture, painting, and music.
5. When the descendants of Noah, who spoke a single language, undertook to build the Tower of Babel that would reach heaven, God cut short the attempt by multiplying languages so that the builders could no longer communicate (see Genesis 11.1–9).

prose writers is a vulgar error. The distinction between philosophers and poets has been anticipated.[6] Plato was essentially a poet—the truth and splendour of his imagery and the melody of his language is the most intense that it is possible to conceive. He rejected the measure of the epic, dramatic, and lyrical forms, because he sought to kindle a harmony in thoughts divested of shape and action, and he forbore to invent any regular plan of rhythm which would include, under determinate forms, the varied pauses of his style. Cicero[7] sought to imitate the cadence of his periods but with little success. Lord Bacon was a poet.[8] His language has a sweet and majestic rhythm, which satisfies the sense, no less than the almost superhuman wisdom of his philosophy satisfies the intellect; it is a strain which distends, and then bursts the circumference of the hearer's mind, and pours itself forth together with it into the universal element with which it has perpetual sympathy. All the authors of revolutions in opinion are not only necessarily poets as they are inventors, nor even as their words unveil the permanent analogy of things by images which participate in the life of truth; but as their periods are harmonious and rhythmical and contain in themselves the elements of verse; being the echo of the eternal music. Nor are those supreme poets, who have employed traditional forms of rhythm on account of the form and action of their subjects, less capable of perceiving and teaching the truth of things, than those who have omitted that form. Shakespeare, Dante and Milton (to confine ourselves to modern writers) are philosophers of the very loftiest power.

A poem is the very image of life expressed in its eternal truth. There is this difference between a story and a poem, that a story is a catalogue of detached facts, which have no other bond of connexion than time, place, circumstance, cause and effect; the other is the creation of actions according to the unchangeable forms of human nature, as existing in the mind of the creator, which is itself the image of all other minds. The one is partial, and applies only to a definite period of time, and a certain combination of events which can never again recur; the other is universal, and contains within itself the germ of a relation to whatever motives or actions have place in the possible varieties of human nature. Time, which destroys the beauty and the use of the story of particular facts, stript of the poetry which should invest them, augments that of Poetry, and for ever develops new and wonderful applications of the eternal truth which it contains. Hence epitomes[9] have been called the moths of just history;[1] they eat out the poetry of it. The story of particular facts is as a mirror which obscures and distorts that which should be beautiful: Poetry is a mirror which makes beautiful that which is distorted.

The parts of a composition may be poetical, without the composition as a whole being a poem. A single sentence may be considered as a whole though it be found in a series of unassimilated portions; a single word even may be a spark of inextinguishable thought. And thus all the great historians, Herodotus, Plutarch, Livy,[2] were poets; and although the plan of these writers,

---

6. I.e., in what Shelley has already said.
7. Marcus Tullius Cicero, the great Roman orator of the 1st century B.C.E.
8. See the *Filium Labyrinthi* and the *Essay on Death* particularly [Shelley's note].
9. Abstracts, summaries.
1. By Bacon in *The Advancement of Learning* 2.2.4.

2. Titus Livius (59 B.C.E.–17 C.E.) wrote an immense history of Rome. Herodotus (ca. 480–ca. 425 B.C.E.) wrote the first systematic history of Greece. Plutarch (ca. 46–ca. 120 C.E.) wrote *Parallel Lives* (of eminent Greeks and Romans).

especially that of Livy, restrained them from developing this faculty in its highest degree, they make copious and ample amends for their subjection, by filling all the interstices of their subjects with living images.

Having determined what is poetry, and who are poets, let us proceed to estimate its effects upon society.

Poetry is ever accompanied with pleasure: all spirits on which it falls, open themselves to receive the wisdom which is mingled with its delight. In the infancy of the world, neither poets themselves nor their auditors are fully aware of the excellence of poetry: for it acts in a divine and unapprehended manner, beyond and above consciousness; and it is reserved for future generations to contemplate and measure the mighty cause and effect in all the strength and splendour of their union. Even in modern times, no living poet ever arrived at the fulness of his fame; the jury which sits in judgement upon a poet, belonging as he does to all time, must be composed of his peers: it must be impanelled by Time from the selectest of the wise of many generations. A Poet is a nightingale, who sits in darkness and sings to cheer its own solitude with sweet sounds; his auditors are as men entranced by the melody of an unseen musician, who feel that they are moved and softened, yet know not whence or why. The poems of Homer and his contemporaries were the delight of infant Greece; they were the elements of that social system which is the column upon which all succeeding civilization has reposed. Homer embodied the ideal perfection of his age in human character; nor can we doubt that those who read his verses were awakened to an ambition of becoming like to Achilles, Hector and Ulysses: the truth and beauty of friendship, patriotism and persevering devotion to an object, were unveiled to the depths in these immortal creations: the sentiments of the auditors must have been refined and enlarged by a sympathy with such great and lovely impersonations, until from admiring they imitated, and from imitation they identified themselves with the objects of their admiration. Nor let it be objected, that these characters are remote from moral perfection, and that they can by no means be considered as edifying patterns for general imitation. Every epoch under names more or less specious has deified its peculiar errors; Revenge is the naked Idol of the worship of a semi-barbarous age; and Self-deceit is the veiled Image of unknown evil before which luxury and satiety lie prostrate. But a poet considers the vices of his contemporaries as the temporary dress in which his creations must be arrayed, and which cover without concealing the eternal proportions of their beauty. An epic or dramatic personage is understood to wear them around his soul, as he may the antient armour or the modern uniform around his body; whilst it is easy to conceive a dress more graceful than either. The beauty of the internal nature cannot be so far concealed by its accidental vesture, but that the spirit of its form shall communicate itself to the very disguise, and indicate the shape it hides from the manner in which it is worn. A majestic form and graceful motions will express themselves through the most barbarous and tasteless costume. Few poets of the highest class have chosen to exhibit the beauty of their conceptions in its naked truth and splendour; and it is doubtful whether the alloy of costume, habit, etc., be not necessary to temper this planetary music[3] for mortal ears.

---

3. The music made by the revolving crystalline spheres of the planets, inaudible to human ears.

The whole objection, however, of the immorality of poetry[4] rests upon a misconception of the manner in which poetry acts to produce the moral improvement of man. Ethical science[5] arranges the elements which poetry has created, and propounds schemes and proposes examples of civil and domestic life: nor is it for want of admirable doctrines that men hate, and despise, and censure, and deceive, and subjugate one another. But Poetry acts in another and diviner manner. It awakens and enlarges the mind itself by rendering it the receptacle of a thousand unapprehended combinations of thought. Poetry lifts the veil from the hidden beauty of the world, and makes familiar objects be as if they were not familiar; it reproduces[6] all that it represents, and the impersonations clothed in its Elysian light stand thenceforward in the minds of those who have once contemplated them, as memorials of that gentle and exalted content[7] which extends itself over all thoughts and actions with which it coexists. The great secret of morals is Love; or a going out of our own nature, and an identification of ourselves with the beautiful which exists in thought, action, or person, not our own. A man, to be greatly good, must imagine intensely and comprehensively; he must put himself in the place of another and of many others; the pains and pleasures of his species must become his own. The great instrument of moral good is the imagination;[8] and poetry administers to the effect by acting upon the cause. Poetry enlarges the circumference of the imagination by replenishing it with thoughts of ever new delight, which have the power of attracting and assimilating to their own nature all other thoughts, and which form new intervals and interstices whose void for ever craves fresh food. Poetry strengthens that faculty which is the organ of the moral nature of man, in the same manner as exercise strengthens a limb. A Poet therefore would do ill to embody his own conceptions of right and wrong, which are usually those of his place and time, in his poetical creations, which participate in neither. By this assumption of the inferior office of interpreting the effect, in which perhaps after all he might acquit himself but imperfectly, he would resign the glory in a participation in the cause.[9] There was little danger that Homer, or any of the eternal Poets, should have so far misunderstood themselves as to have abdicated this throne of their widest dominion. Those in whom the poetical faculty, though great, is less intense, as Euripides, Lucan, Tasso,[1] Spenser, have frequently affected[2] a moral aim, and the effect of their poetry is diminished in exact proportion to the degree in which they compel us to advert to this purpose.[3]

4. In the preceding paragraph Shelley has been implicitly dealing with the charge, voiced by Plato in his *Republic,* that poetry is immoral because it represents evil characters acting evilly.
5. Moral philosophy.
6. Produces anew, re-creates.
7. Contentment.
8. Central to Shelley's theory is the concept (developed by 18th-century philosophers) of the sympathetic imagination—the faculty by which an individual is enabled to identify with the thoughts and feelings of others. Shelley insists that the faculty in poetry that enables us to share the joys and sufferings of invented characters is also the basis of all morality, for it compels us to feel for others as we feel for ourselves.
9. The "effect," or the explicit moral standards

into which imaginative insights are translated at a particular time or place, is contrasted to the "cause" of all morality, the imagination itself.
1. Tasso Torquato (1544–1595), Italian poet, author of *Jerusalem Delivered,* an epic poem about a crusade. Euripides (ca. 484–406 B.C.E.), Greek writer of tragedies. Lucan (39–65 C.E.), Roman poet, author of the *Pharsalia.*
2. Assumed, adopted.
3. In the following omitted passage Shelley reviews the history of drama and poetry in relation to civilization and morality and proceeds to refute the charge that poets are less useful than "reasoners and merchants." He begins by defining *utility* in terms of pleasure and then distinguishes between the lower (physical and material) and the higher (imaginative) pleasures.

* * *

It is difficult to define pleasure in its highest sense; the definition involving a number of apparent paradoxes. For, from an inexplicable defect of harmony in the constitution of human nature, the pain of the inferior is frequently connected with the pleasures of the superior portions of our being. Sorrow, terror, anguish, despair itself are often the chosen expressions of an approximation to the highest good. Our sympathy in tragic fiction depends on this principle; tragedy delights by affording a shadow of the pleasure which exists in pain. This is the source also of the melancholy which is inseparable from the sweetest melody. The pleasure that is in sorrow is sweeter than the pleasure of pleasure itself. And hence the saying, "It is better to go to the house of mourning, than to the house of mirth."[4] Not that this highest species of pleasure is necessarily linked with pain. The delight of love and friendship, the ecstasy of the admiration of nature, the joy of the perception and still more of the creation of poetry is often wholly unalloyed.

The production and assurance of pleasure in this highest sense is true utility. Those who produce and preserve this pleasure are Poets or poetical philosophers.

The exertions of Locke, Hume, Gibbon, Voltaire, Rousseau,[5] and their disciples, in favour of oppressed and deluded humanity, are entitled to the gratitude of mankind. Yet it is easy to calculate the degree of moral and intellectual improvement which the world would have exhibited, had they never lived. A little more nonsense would have been talked for a century or two; and perhaps a few more men, women, and children, burnt as heretics. We might not at this moment have been congratulating each other on the abolition of the Inquisition in Spain.[6] But it exceeds all imagination to conceive what would have been the moral condition of the world if neither Dante, Petrarch, Boccaccio, Chaucer, Shakespeare, Calderon, Lord Bacon, nor Milton, had ever existed; if Raphael and Michael Angelo had never been born; if the Hebrew poetry had never been translated; if a revival of the study of Greek literature had never taken place; if no monuments of antient sculpture had been handed down to us; and if the poetry of the religion of the antient world had been extinguished together with its belief. The human mind could never, except by the intervention of these excitements, have been awakened to the invention of the grosser sciences, and that application of analytical reasoning to the aberrations of society, which it is now attempted to exalt over the direct expression of the inventive and creative faculty itself.

We have more moral, political and historical wisdom, than we know how to reduce into practice; we have more scientific and economical knowledge than can be accommodated to the just distribution of the produce which it multiplies. The poetry in these systems of thought, is concealed by the accumulation of facts and calculating processes. There is no want of knowledge respecting what is wisest and best in morals, government, and political economy, or at least, what is wiser and better than what men now practise and

---

4. Ecclesiastes 7.2.
5. In a note Shelley says that, although Peacock had classified Rousseau with these other thinkers of the 17th and 18th centuries, "he was essentially a poet. The others, even Voltaire, were mere rea-

soners."
6. The Inquisition had been suspended in 1820, the year before Shelley wrote this essay; it was not abolished permanently until 1834.

endure. But we let "*I dare not* wait upon *I would*, like the poor cat i' the adage."[7] We want the creative faculty to imagine that which we know; we want the generous impulse to act that which we imagine; we want the poetry of life: our calculations have outrun conception; we have eaten more than we can digest. The cultivation of those sciences which have enlarged the limits of the empire of man over the external world, has, for want of the poetical faculty, proportionally circumscribed those of the internal world; and man, having enslaved the elements, remains himself a slave. To what but a cultivation of the mechanical arts in a degree disproportioned to the presence of the creative faculty, which is the basis of all knowledge, is to be attributed the abuse of all invention for abridging and combining labour, to the exasperation of the inequality of mankind? From what other cause has it arisen that these inventions which should have lightened, have added a weight to the curse imposed on Adam? Poetry, and the principle of Self, of which money is the visible incarnation, are the God and Mammon of the world.[8]

The functions of the poetical faculty are two-fold; by one it creates new materials of knowledge, and power and pleasure; by the other it engenders in the mind a desire to reproduce and arrange them according to a certain rhythm and order which may be called the beautiful and the good. The cultivation of poetry is never more to be desired than at periods when, from an excess of the selfish and calculating principle, the accumulation of the materials of external life exceed the quantity of the power of assimilating them to the internal laws of human nature. The body has then become too unwieldy for that which animates it.

Poetry is indeed something divine. It is at once the centre and circumference of knowledge; it is that which comprehends all science, and that to which all science must be referred. It is at the same time the root and blossom of all other systems of thought; it is that from which all spring, and that which adorns all; and that which, if blighted, denies the fruit and the seed, and withholds from the barren world the nourishment and the succession of the scions of the tree of life. It is the perfect and consummate surface and bloom of things; it is as the odour and the colour of the rose to the texture of the elements which compose it, as the form and the splendour of unfaded beauty to the secrets of anatomy and corruption. What were Virtue, Love, Patriotism, Friendship etc.—what were the scenery of this beautiful Universe which we inhabit—what were our consolations on this side of the grave—and what were our aspirations beyond it—if Poetry did not ascend to bring light and fire from those eternal regions where the owl-winged faculty of calculation dare not ever soar? Poetry is not like reasoning, a power to be exerted according to the determination of the will. A man cannot say, "I will compose poetry." The greatest poet even cannot say it: for the mind in creation is as a fading coal which some invisible influence, like an inconstant wind, awakens to transitory brightness: this power arises from within, like the colour of a flower which fades and changes as it is developed, and the conscious portions of our natures are unprophetic either of its approach or its departure.[9] Could this influence be durable in its original purity and

7. *Macbeth* 1.7.44–45.
8. Matthew 6.24: "Ye cannot serve God and Mammon."

9. This passage reiterates the ancient belief that the highest poetry is "inspired" and therefore occurs independently of the intention, effort, or

force, it is impossible to predict the greatness of the results; but when com-position begins, inspiration is already on the decline, and the most glorious poetry that has ever been communicated to the world is probably a feeble shadow of the original conception of the poet. I appeal to the greatest Poets of the present day, whether it be not an error to assert that the finest passages of poetry are produced by labour and study. The toil and the delay recom-mended by critics can be justly interpreted to mean no more than a careful observation of the inspired moments, and an artificial connexion of the spaces between their suggestions by the intertexture of conventional expres-sions; a necessity only imposed by the limitedness of the poetical faculty itself. For Milton conceived the Paradise Lost as a whole before he executed it in portions. We have his own authority also for the Muse having "dictated" to him the "unpremeditated song,"[1] and let this be an answer to those who would allege the fifty-six various readings of the first line of the Orlando Furioso.[2] Compositions so produced are to poetry what mosaic is to painting. This instinct and intuition of the poetical faculty is still more observable in the plastic and pictorial arts: a great statue or picture grows under the power of the artist as a child in the mother's womb; and the very mind which directs the hands in formation is incapable of accounting to itself for the origin, the gradations, or the media of the process.

Poetry is the record of the best and happiest[3] moments of the happiest and best minds. We are aware of evanescent visitations of thought and feel-ing sometimes associated with place or person, sometimes regarding our own mind alone, and always arising unforeseen and departing unbidden, but ele-vating and delightful beyond all expression: so that even in the desire and the regret they leave, there cannot but be pleasure, participating as it does in the nature of its object. It is as it were the interpenetration of a diviner nature through our own; but its footsteps are like those of a wind over a sea, where the coming calm erases, and whose traces remain only as on the wrin-kled sand which paves it. These and corresponding conditions of being are experienced principally by those of the most delicate sensibility and the most enlarged imagination; and the state of mind produced by them is at war with every base desire. The enthusiasm of virtue, love, patriotism, and friendship is essentially linked with these emotions; and whilst they last, self appears as what it is, an atom to a Universe. Poets are not only subject to these experiences as spirits of the most refined organization, but they can colour all that they combine with the evanescent hues of this etherial world; a word, or a trait in the representation of a scene or a passion, will touch the enchanted chord, and reanimate, in those who have ever experienced these emotions, the sleeping, the cold, the buried image of the past. Poetry thus makes immortal all that is best and most beautiful in the world; it arrests the vanishing apparitions which haunt the interlunations[4] of life, and veiling them or in language or in form sends them forth among mankind, bearing sweet news of kindred joy to those with whom their sisters abide—abide, because there is no portal of expression from the caverns of the spirit which

consciousness of the poet. Unlike earlier critics, however, Shelley attributes such poetry not to a god or a muse but to the unconscious depths of the poet's own mind.
1. *Paradise Lost* 9.21–24.
2. The epic poem by the 16th-century Italian poet

Ariosto, noted for his care in composition.
3. In the double sense of "most joyous" and "most apt or felicitous in invention."
4. The dark intervals between the old and new moons.

they inhabit into the universe of things. Poetry redeems from decay the visitations of the divinity in man.

Poetry turns all things to loveliness; it exalts the beauty of that which is most beautiful, and it adds beauty to that which is most deformed; it marries exultation and horror, grief and pleasure, eternity and change; it subdues to union under its light yoke all irreconcilable things. It transmutes all that it touches, and every form moving within the radiance of its presence is changed by wondrous sympathy to an incarnation of the spirit which it breathes; its secret alchemy turns to potable gold[5] the poisonous waters which flow from death through life; it strips the veil of familiarity from the world, and lays bare the naked and sleeping beauty which is the spirit of its forms.

All things exist as they are perceived: at least in relation to the percipient. "The mind is its own place, and of itself can make a heaven of hell, a hell of heaven."[6] But poetry defeats the curse which binds us to be subjected to the accident of surrounding impressions. And whether it spreads its own figured curtain or withdraws life's dark veil from before the scene of things, it equally creates for us a being within our being. It makes us the inhabitants of a world to which the familiar world is a chaos. It reproduces the common universe of which we are portions and percipients, and it purges from our inward sight the film of familiarity which obscures from us the wonder of our being. It compels us to feel that which we perceive, and to imagine that which we know. It creates anew the universe after it has been annihilated in our minds by the recurrence of impressions blunted by reiteration.[7] It justifies that bold and true word of Tasso: *Non merita nome di creatore, se non Iddio ed il Poeta.*[8]

A Poet, as he is the author to others of the highest wisdom, pleasure, virtue and glory, so he ought personally to be the happiest, the best, the wisest, and the most illustrious of men. As to his glory, let Time be challenged to declare whether the fame of any other institutor of human life be comparable to that of a poet. That he is the wisest, the happiest, and the best, inasmuch as he is a poet, is equally incontrovertible: the greatest poets have been men of the most spotless virtue, of the most consummate prudence, and, if we could look into the interior of their lives, the most fortunate of men: and the exceptions, as they regard those who possessed the poetic faculty in a high yet inferior degree, will be found on consideration to confirm rather than destroy the rule. Let us for a moment stoop to the arbitration of popular breath, and usurping and uniting in our own persons the incompatible characters of accuser, witness, judge and executioner, let us decide without trial, testimony, or form that certain motives of those who are "there sitting where we dare not soar"[9] are reprehensible. Let us assume that Homer was a drunkard, that Virgil was a flatterer, that Horace was a coward, that Tasso was a madman, that Lord Bacon was a peculator, that Raphael was a libertine, that Spenser was a poet laureate.[1] It is inconsistent with this division of our sub-

---

5. Alchemists aimed to produce a drinkable ("potable") form of gold that would be an elixir of life, curing all diseases.
6. Satan's speech, *Paradise Lost* 1.254–55.
7. Shelley's version of a widespread Romantic doctrine that the poetic imagination transforms the familiar into the miraculous and recreates the old world into a new world. See, e.g., Coleridge's *Biographia Literaria* on "freshness of sensation,"

chap. 4 (p. 1624), and Carlyle's *Sartor Resartus,* "Natural Supernaturalism," book 3, chap. 8.
8. "No one merits the name of Creator except God and the Poet." Quoted by Pierantonio Serassi in his *Life of Torquato Tasso* (1785).
9. *Paradise Lost* 4.829.
1. Charges that had in fact been made against these men. The use of "poet laureate" as a derogatory term was a dig at Robert Southey, who held

ject to cite living poets, but Posterity has done ample justice to the great names now referred to. Their errors have been weighed and found to have been dust in the balance; if their sins "were as scarlet, they are now white as snow";[2] they have been washed in the blood of the mediator and the redeemer Time. Observe in what a ludicrous chaos the imputations of real or fictitious crime have been confused in the contemporary calumnies against poetry and poets;[3] consider how little is, as it appears—or appears, as it is; look to your own motives, and judge not, lest ye be judged.

Poetry, as has been said, in this respect differs from logic, that it is not subject to the controul of the active powers of the mind, and that its birth and recurrence has no necessary connexion with consciousness or will. It is presumptuous to determine that these[4] are the necessary conditions of all mental causation, when mental effects are experienced insusceptible of being referred to them. The frequent recurrence of the poetical power, it is obvious to suppose, may produce in the mind an habit of order and harmony correlative with its own nature and with its effects upon other minds. But in the intervals of inspiration, and they may be frequent without being durable, a poet becomes a man, and is abandoned to the sudden reflux of the influences under which others habitually live. But as he is more delicately organized than other men, and sensible to pain and pleasure, both his own and that of others, in a degree unknown to them, he will avoid the one and pursue the other with an ardour proportioned to this difference. And he renders himself obnoxious to calumny,[5] when he neglects to observe the circumstances under which these objects of universal pursuit and flight have disguised themselves in one another's garments.

But there is nothing necessarily evil in this error, and thus cruelty, envy, revenge, avarice, and the passions purely evil, have never formed any portion of the popular imputations on the lives of poets.

I have thought it most favourable to the cause of truth to set down these remarks according to the order in which they were suggested to my mind, by a consideration of the subject itself, instead of following that of the treatise that excited me to make them public.[6] Thus although devoid of the formality of a polemical reply; if the view they contain be just, they will be found to involve a refutation of the doctrines of the Four Ages of Poetry, so far at least as regards the first division of the subject. I can readily conjecture what should have moved the gall of the learned and intelligent author of that paper; I confess myself, like him, unwilling to be stunned by the Theseids of the hoarse Codri of the day. Bavius and Mævius[7] undoubtedly are, as they ever were, insufferable persons. But it belongs to a philosophical critic to distinguish rather than confound.

The first part of these remarks has related to Poetry in its elements and principles; and it has been shewn, as well as the narrow limits assigned them would permit, that what is called poetry, in a restricted sense, has a common

---

that honor at the time Shelley was writing. "Peculator": a misappropriator of public money. Raphael is the 16th-century Italian painter.

2. Isaiah 1.18.

3. Shelley alludes especially to the charges of immorality by contemporary reviewers against Lord Byron and himself.

4. I.e., consciousness or will. Shelley again pro-

poses that some mental processes are unconscious—outside our control or awareness.

5. Exposed to slander.

6. Peacock's Four Ages of Poetry.

7. Would-be poets satirized by Virgil and Horace. "Theseids": epic poems about Theseus. Codrus (plural "Codri") was the Roman author of a long, dull Theseid attacked by Juvenal and others.

source with all other forms of order and of beauty according to which the materials of human life are susceptible of being arranged, and which is poetry in an universal sense.

The second part[8] will have for its object an application of these principles to the present state of the cultivation of Poetry, and a defence of the attempt to idealize the modern forms of manners and opinions, and compel them into a subordination to the imaginative and creative faculty. For the literature of England, an energetic developement of which has ever preceded or accompanied a great and free developement of the national will, has arisen as it were from a new birth. In spite of the low-thoughted envy which would undervalue contemporary merit, our own will be a memorable age in intellectual achievements, and we live among such philosophers and poets as surpass beyond comparison any who have appeared since the last national struggle for civil and religious liberty.[9] The most unfailing herald, companion, and follower of the awakening of a great people to work a beneficial change in opinion or institution, is Poetry. At such periods there is an accumulation of the power of communicating and receiving intense and impassioned conceptions respecting man and nature. The persons in whom this power resides, may often, as far as regards many portions of their nature, have little apparent correspondence with that spirit of good of which they are the ministers. But even whilst they deny and abjure, they are yet compelled to serve, the Power which is seated upon the throne of their own soul. It is impossible to read the compositions of the most celebrated writers of the present day without being startled with the electric life which burns within their words. They measure the circumference and sound the depths of human nature with a comprehensive and all-penetrating spirit, and they are themselves perhaps the most sincerely astonished at its manifestations, for it is less their spirit than the spirit of the age.[1] Poets are the hierophants[2] of an unapprehended inspiration, the mirrors of the gigantic shadows which futurity casts upon the present, the words which express what they understand not; the trumpets which sing to battle, and feel not what they inspire: the influence which is moved not, but moves.[3] Poets are the unacknowledged legislators of the World.

1821   1840

---

8. Shelley, however, completed only the first part.
9. In the age of Milton and the English Civil Wars.
1. By attributing to the great poets and philosophers of his time a shared "spirit of the age," Shelley anticipates what later historians were to

identify as "the Romantic movement."
2. Priests who are expositors of sacred mysteries.
3. Aristotle had said that God is the "Unmoved Mover" of the universe.

FELICIA DOROTHEA HEMANS
1793–1835

Born in Liverpool and brought up in Wales, Felicia Hemans published her first two volumes—*Poems* and *England and Spain, or Valour and Patriotism*—when she was fifteen. She followed these four years later with *The Domestic Affections and Other*

Poems (1812) and from 1816 on into the 1830s produced new books of poetry almost annually: short sentimental lyrics, tales and "historic scenes," translations, songs for music, sketches of women, hymns for children. She also published literary criticism in the magazines and wrote three plays. Her work was widely read, anthologized, memorized, and set to music throughout the nineteenth century and was especially popular and influential in the United States, where the first of many collected editions of her poems appeared in 1825. When she died, she was eulogized by many poets, including William Wordsworth, Letitia Landon, and Elizabeth Barrett—a sign of the high regard in which she was held by her contemporaries.

A tablet erected by her brothers in the cathedral of St. Asaph, in north Wales, reads in part, "In memory of Felicia Hemans, whose character is best pourtrayed in her writings." But there are several characters in her poems, and some of them seem not entirely compatible with some of the others. She is frequently thought of as the poet (in the nineteenth century as "the poetess") of domestic affections, at the center of a cult of domesticity in which women are subservient to men, who carry on the important business of life, and patriarchy is the acknowledged if not always accepted standard. Among her most popular pieces in this vein, *Evening Prayer, at a Girls' School* depicts the happy ignorance of schoolgirls whose enjoyment of life will end when they reach womanhood, and *Indian Woman's Death-Song* is the lament of a Native American woman whose husband has abandoned her, sung as she plunges in her canoe over a cataract to suicide with an infant in her arms.

Many of Hemans's longer narratives, by contrast, recount the exploits of women warriors who, to avenge personal, family, or national injustice or insult, destroy enemies in a manner not conventionally associated with female behavior. In *The Widow of Crescentius*, Stephania stalks and poisons the German emperor Otho, the murderer of her husband; in *The Wife of Asdrubal*, a mother publicly kills her own children and herself to show contempt for her husband, a betrayer of the Carthaginians whom he governed; the heroine of *The Bride of the Greek Isle*, boarding the ship of the pirates who have killed her husband, annihilates them (and herself) in a conflagration rivaling the monumental explosion described in *Casabianca*. Among the numerous themes of her work, patriotism and military action recur frequently; there may be a biographical basis for these motifs, given that her two oldest brothers distinguished themselves in the Peninsular War and her military husband (who deserted her and their five sons in 1818) had also served in Spain. But some of her most famous patriotic and military poems are now being viewed as critiques of the virtues and ideologies they had been thought by earlier readers to inculcate. *The Homes of England*, for example, has been read as both asserting and undermining the idea that all homes are equal, ancestral estates and cottages alike; and in *Casabianca*, the boy's automatic steadfastness has been interpreted as empty obedience rather than admirable loyalty.

Hemans was the highest paid writer in *Blackwood's* during her day. Her books sold more copies than those of any other contemporary poet except Byron and Walter Scott. She was a shrewd calculator of the literary marketplace and a genius in her negotiations with publishers (which she carried on entirely through the mails). Her self-abasing women of the domestic affections and her scimitar-wielding superwomen of the revenge narratives exist side by side throughout her works. These and other seeming dissonances clearly enhanced the strong appeal of her poems to a wide range of readers, men as well as women.

England's Dead

Son of the ocean isle!
Where sleep your mighty dead?
Show me what high and stately pile
Is rear'd o'er Glory's bed.

5   Go, stranger! track the deep,
     Free, free the white sail spread!
   Wave may not foam, nor wild wind sweep,
     Where rest not England's dead.

     On Egypt's burning plains,
10   By the pyramid o'ersway'd,
   With fearful power the noonday reigns,
     And the palm trees yield no shade.[1]

     But let the angry sun
     From heaven look fiercely red,
15   Unfelt by those whose task is done!—
     There slumber England's dead.

     The hurricane hath might
     Along the Indian shore,
   And far by Ganges' banks at night,
20   Is heard the tiger's roar.

     But let the sound roll on!
     It hath no tone of dread,
   For those that from their toils are gone;—
     There slumber England's dead.

25   Loud rush the torrent floods
     The western wilds among,
   And free, in green Columbia's woods,
     The hunter's bow is strung.

     But let the floods rush on!
30   Let the arrow's flight be sped!
   Why should *they* reck whose task is done?—
     There slumber England's dead!

     The mountain storms rise high
     In the snowy Pyrenees,
35   And toss the pine boughs through the sky,
     Like rose leaves on the breeze.

     But let the storm rage on!
     Let the fresh wreaths be shed!
   For the Roncesvalles' field[2] is won,—
40   *There* slumber England's dead.

     On the frozen deep's repose
     'Tis a dark and dreadful hour,

1. English forces defeated the French at Alexandria in the spring of 1801. The rest of the references—to 18th- and early-19th-century battles in India (lines 17–24), America (lines 25–32), Spain (lines 33–40), and on the sea (lines 41–48)—are more general.
2. Roncesvalles, the mountain pass in the Pyrenees between France and Spain, was a scene of action during the Peninsular War (1808–14).

When round the ship the ice-fields close,
    And the northern night clouds lower.

45 But let the ice drift on!
    Let the cold-blue desert spread!
    Their course with mast and flag is done,—
    Even there sleep England's dead.

    The warlike of the isles,
50 The men of field and wave!
    Are not the rocks their funeral piles,
    The seas and shores their grave?

    Go, stranger! track the deep,
    Free, free the white sail spread!
55 Wave may not foam, nor wild wind sweep,
    Where rest not England's dead.

                                        1822

The Landing of the Pilgrim Fathers in New England

Look now abroad—another race has fill'd
Those populous borders—wide the wood recedes,
And towns shoot up, and fertile realms are till'd;
The land is full of harvests and green meads.
                                        —BRYANT[1]

    The breaking waves dash'd high
        On a stern and rock-bound coast,
    And the woods against a stormy sky
        Their giant branches toss'd;

5   And the heavy night hung dark,
        The hills and waters o'er,
    When a band of exiles moor'd their bark
        On the wild New England shore.

    Not as the conqueror comes,
10   They, the true-hearted, came;
    Not with the roll of the stirring drums,
        And the trumpet that sings of fame;

    Not as the flying come,
        In silence and in fear;—
15 They shook the depths of the desert gloom
        With their hymns of lofty cheer.

    Amidst the storm they sang,
        And the stars heard and the sea;

1. William Cullen Bryant, *The Ages* (1821), lines 280–83.

And the sounding aisles of the dim woods rang
20   To the anthem of the free!

The ocean eagle soar'd
        From his nest by the white wave's foam;
And the rocking pines of the forest roar'd—
        This was their welcome home!

25 There were men with hoary hair
        Amidst that pilgrim band;—
    Why had *they* come to wither there,
        Away from their childhood's land?

    There was woman's fearless eye,
30   Lit by her deep love's truth;
    There was manhood's brow serenely high,
        And the fiery heart of youth.

    What sought they thus afar?
        Bright jewels of the mine?
35 The wealth of seas, the spoils of war?—
        They sought a faith's pure shrine!

    Aye, call it holy ground,
        The soil where first they trod.
    They have left unstain'd what there they found—
40   Freedom to worship God.

                                        1826

Casabianca[1]

    The boy stood on the burning deck
        Whence all but he had fled;
    The flame that lit the battle's wreck
        Shone round him o'er the dead.

5   Yet beautiful and bright he stood,
        As born to rule the storm;
    A creature of heroic blood,
        A proud, though childlike form.

    The flames roll'd on—he would not go
10   Without his father's word;
    That father, faint in death below,
        His voice no longer heard.

1. Young Casabianca, a boy about thirteen years old, son to the Admiral of the *Orient*, remained at his post (in the Battle of the Nile) after the ship had taken fire, and all the guns had been abandoned; and perished in the explosion of the vessel, when the flames had reached the powder [Hemans's note]. The Battle of the Nile, in which Nelson captured and destroyed the French fleet in Aboukir Bay, took place on August 1, 1798.

He call'd aloud:—"Say, Father, say
  If yet my task is done?"
15 He knew not that the chieftain lay
  Unconscious of his son.

"Speak, Father!" once again he cried,
  "If I may yet be gone!"
And but the booming shots replied,
20   And fast the flames roll'd on.

Upon his brow he felt their breath,
  And in his waving hair,
And look'd from that lone post of death
  In still, yet brave despair.

25 And shouted but once more aloud,
  "My Father! must I stay?"
While o'er him fast, through sail and shroud,
  The wreathing fires made way.

They wrapt the ship in splendour wild,
30   They caught the flag on high,
And stream'd above the gallant child,
  Like banners in the sky.

There came a burst of thunder sound—
  The boy—oh! where was he?
35 Ask of the winds that far around
  With fragments strew'd the sea!—

With mast, and helm, and pennon fair,
  That well had borne their part,
But the noblest thing which perish'd there
40   Was that young faithful heart!

                                                    1826

The Homes of England

> Where's the coward that would not dare
> To fight for such a land?
>   —*Marmion*[1]

The stately Homes of England,
  How beautiful they stand!
Amidst their tall ancestral trees,
  O'er all the pleasant land.
5 The deer across their greensward bound
  Through shade and sunny gleam,

---

1. From Sir Walter Scott's long poem *Marmion* (1808), 4.633–34, a tale of betrayal and bloody conflict between the English and the Scots. When she first published the poem, in *Blackwood's*, April 1827, Hemans used as epigraph a passage from the work of another Scottish author, Joanna Baillie's *Ethwald: A Tragedy*, part 2 (1802), 1.2.76–82.

And the swan glides past them with the sound
   Of some rejoicing stream.

The merry Homes of England!
10   Around their hearths by night,
What gladsome looks of household love
   Meet in the ruddy light!
There woman's voice flows forth in song,
   Or childhood's tale is told,
15 Or lips move tunefully along
   Some glorious page of old.

The blessed Homes of England!
   How softly on their bowers
Is laid the holy quietness
20   That breathes from Sabbath-hours!
Solemn, yet sweet, the church-bell's chime
   Floats through their woods at morn;
All other sounds, in that still time,
   Of breeze and leaf are born.

25 The Cottage Homes of England!
   By thousands on her plains,
They are smiling o'er the silvery brooks,
   And round the hamlet-fanes.°   *village churches*
Through glowing orchards forth they peep,
30   Each from its nook of leaves,
And fearless there the lowly sleep,
   As the bird beneath their eaves.

The free, fair Homes of England!
   Long, long, in hut and hall,
35 May hearts of native proof be rear'd
   To guard each hallow'd wall!
And green for ever be the groves,
   And bright the flowery sod,
Where first the child's glad spirit loves
40   Its country and its God!

                                      1827

A Spirit's Return

> "This is to be a mortal,
> And seek the things beyond mortality!"
> —MANFRED[1]

Thy voice prevails—dear friend, my gentle friend!
This long-shut heart for thee shall be unsealed,

1. A remark concerning Manfred's convulsion at the moment the Phantom of his beloved Astarte disappears (*Manfred* 2.4.158–59). Hemans's poem can be read as commentary on Byron's play, Percy Shelley's *Alastor*, and Keats's *Endymion* (see the note to lines 216–17 below), all of which depict a protagonist's problems in communicating with an otherworldly lover.

And though thy soft eye mournfully will bend
Over the troubled stream, yet once revealed
5   Shall its freed waters flow; then rocks must close
For evermore, above their dark repose.

Come while the gorgeous mysteries of the sky
Fused in the crimson sea of sunset lie;
Come to the woods, where all strange wandering sound
10   Is mingled into harmony profound;
Where the leaves thrill with spirit, while the wind
Fills with a viewless being, unconfined,
The trembling reeds and fountains—our own dell,
With its green dimness and Aeolian° breath,   *wind-blown*
15   Shall suit th' unveiling of dark records well—
Hear me in tenderness and silent faith!

Thou knew'st me not in life's fresh vernal morn—
I would thou hadst!—for then my heart on thine
Had poured a worthier love; now, all o'erworn
20   By its deep thirst for something too divine,
It hath but fitful music to bestow,
Echoes of harp-strings broken long ago.

Yet even in youth companionless I stood,
As a lone forest-bird 'midst ocean's foam;
25   For me the silver cords of brotherhood
Were early loosed; the voices from my home
Passed one by one, and melody and mirth
Left me a dreamer by a silent hearth.

But, with the fulness of a heart that burned
30   For the deep sympathies of mind, I turned
From that unanswering spot, and fondly sought
In all wild scenes with thrilling murmurs fraught,
In every still small voice and sound of power,
And flute-note of the wind through cave and bower,
35   A perilous delight!—for then first woke
My life's lone passion, the mysterious quest
Of secret knowledge; and each tone that broke
From the wood-arches or the fountain's breast,
Making my quick soul vibrate as a lyre,
40   But ministered to that strange inborn fire.
'Midst the bright silence of the mountain dells,
In noon-tide hours or golden summer-eves,
My thoughts have burst forth as a gale that swells
Into a rushing blast, and from the leaves
45   Shakes out response. O thou rich world unseen!
Thou curtained realm of spirits!—thus my cry
Hath troubled air and silence—dost thou lie
Spread all around, yet by some filmy screen
Shut from us ever? The resounding woods,
50   Do their depths teem with marvels?—and the floods,

And the pure fountains, leading secret veins
Of quenchless melody through rock and hill,
Have they bright dwellers?—are their lone domains
Peopled with beauty, which may never still
55 *Our* weary thirst of soul?—Cold, weak and cold,
Is earth's vain language, piercing not one fold
Of our deep being! Oh, for gifts more high!
For a seer's glance to rend mortality!
For a charmed rod, to call from each dark shrine
60 The oracles divine!

I woke from those high fantasies, to know
My kindred with the earth—I woke to love:
O gentle friend! to love in doubt and woe,
Shutting the heart the worshipped name above,
65 Is to love deeply—and *my* spirit's dower
Was a sad gift, a melancholy power
Of so adoring—with a buried care,
And with the o'erflowing of a voiceless prayer,
And with a deepening dream, that day by day,
70 In the still shadow of its lonely sway,
Folded me closer, till the world held nought
Save the *one* being to my centred thought.

There was no music but his voice to hear,
No joy but such as with *his* step drew near;
75 Light was but where he looked—life where he moved;
Silently, fervently, thus, thus I loved.
Oh! but such love is fearful!—and I knew
Its gathering doom:—the soul's prophetic sight
Even then unfolded in my breast, and threw
80 O'er all things round a full, strong, vivid light,
Too sorrowfully clear!—an undertone
Was given to Nature's harp, for me alone
Whispering of grief.—Of grief?—be strong, awake,
Hath not thy love been victory, O, my soul?
85 Hath not its conflict won a voice to shake
Death's fastnesses?—a magic to control
Worlds far removed?—from o'er the grave to thee
Love hath made answer; and *thy* tale should be
Sung like a lay of triumph!—Now return,
90 And take thy treasure from its bosomed urn,
And lift it once to light!

        In fear, in pain,
I said I loved—but yet a heavenly strain
Of sweetness floated down the tearful stream,
A joy flashed through the trouble of my dream!
95 I knew myself beloved!—we breathed no vow,
No mingling visions might our fate allow,
As unto happy hearts; but still and deep,
Like a rich jewel gleaming in a grave,

Like golden sand in some dark river's wave,
100   So did my soul that costly knowledge keep
So jealously!—a thing o'er which to shed,
When stars alone beheld the drooping head,
Lone tears! yet ofttimes burdened with the excess
Of our strange nature's quivering happiness.

105   But, oh! sweet friend! we dream not of love's might
Till death has robed with soft and solemn light
The image we enshrine!—Before *that* hour,
We have but glimpses of the o'ermastering power
Within us laid!—*then* doth the spirit-flame
110   With sword-like lightning rend its mortal frame;
The wings of that which pants to follow fast
Shake their clay-bars, as with a prisoned blast—
The sea is in our souls!

He died—*he* died
On whom my lone devotedness was cast!
115   I might not keep one vigil by his side,
I, whose wrung heart watched with him to the last!
I might not once his fainting head sustain,
Nor bathe his parched lips in the hour of pain,
Nor say to him, "Farewell!"—He passed away—
120   Oh! had *my* love been there, its conquering sway
Had won him back from death! but thus removed,
Borne o'er the abyss no sounding-line hath proved,
Joined with the unknown, the viewless—he became
Unto my thoughts another, yet the same—
125   Changed—hallowed—glorified!—and his low grave
Seemed a bright mournful altar—mine, all mine:—
Brother and friend soon left me *that* sole shrine,
The birthright of the faithful!—*their* world's wave
Soon swept them from its brink.—Oh! deem thou not
130   That on the sad and consecrated spot
My soul grew weak!—I tell thee that a power
There kindled heart and lip—a fiery shower
My words were made—a might was given to prayer,
And a strong grasp to passionate despair,
135   And a dead triumph!—Know'st thou what I sought?
For what high boon my struggling spirit wrought?—
Communion with the dead!—I sent a cry,
Through the veiled empires of eternity,
A voice to cleave them! By the mournful truth,
140   By the lost promise of my blighted youth,
By the strong chain a mighty love can bind
On the beloved, the spell of mind o'er mind;
By words, which in themselves are magic high,
Armed and inspired, and winged with agony;
145   By tears, which comfort not, but burn, and seem
To bear the heart's blood in their passion stream;

I summoned, I adjured!—with quickened sense,
With the keen vigil of a life intense,
I watched, an answer from the winds to wring,
150 I listened, if perchance the stream might bring
Token from worlds afar: I taught *one* sound
Unto a thousand echoes—one profound
Imploring accent to the tomb, the sky—
One prayer to night—"Awake, appear, reply!"
155 Hast thou been told that from the viewless bourne,
The dark way never hath allowed return?
That all, which tears can move, with life is fled—
That earthly love is powerless on the dead?
Believe it not!—there is a large lone star
160 Now burning o'er yon western hill afar,
And under its clear light there lies a spot
Which well might utter forth—Believe it not!

I sat beneath that planet—I had wept
My woe to stillness, every night-wind slept;
165 A hush was on the hills; the very streams
Went by like clouds, or noiseless founts in dreams,
And the dark tree o'ershadowing me that hour,
Stood motionless, even as the gray church-tower
Whereon I gazed unconsciously:—there came
170 A low sound, like the tremor of a flame,
Or like the light quick shiver of a wing,
Flitting through twilight woods, across the air;
And I looked up!—Oh! for strong words to bring
Conviction o'er thy thought!—Before me there,
175 He, the departed, stood!—Ay, face to face,
So near, and yet how far!—his form, his mien,
Gave to remembrance back each burning trace
Within:—Yet something awfully serene,
Pure, sculpture-like, on the pale brow, that wore
180 Of the once-beating heart no token more;
And stillness on the lip—and o'er the hair
A gleam, that trembled through the breathless air;
And an unfathomed calm, that seemed to lie
In the grave sweetness of the illumined eye;
185 Told of the gulfs between our beings set,
And, as that unsheathed spirit-glance I met,
Made my soul faint:—with *fear*? Oh! *not* with fear!
With the sick feeling that in *his* far sphere
My love could be as nothing! But he spoke—
190 How shall I tell thee of the startling thrill
In that low voice, whose breezy tones could fill
My bosom's infinite? O, friend! I woke
Then first to heavenly life!—Soft, solemn, clear
Breathed the mysterious accents on mine ear,
195 Yet strangely seemed as if the while they rose
From depths of distance, o'er the wide repose

Of slumbering waters wafted, or the dells
Of mountains, hollow with sweet-echo cells;
But, as they murmured on, the mortal chill
200 Passed from me, like a mist before the morn,
And, to that glorious intercourse upborne
By slow degrees, a calm, divinely still,
Possessed my frame: I sought that lighted eye—
From its intense and searching purity
205 I drank in *soul!*—I questioned of the dead—
Of the hushed, starry shores their footsteps tread,
And I was answered:—if remembrance there,
With dreamy whispers fill the immortal air;
If thought, here piled from many a jewel-heap,
210 Be treasure in that pensive land to keep;
If love, o'ersweeping change, and blight, and blast
Find *there* the music of his home at last;
I asked, and I was answered:—Full and high
Was that communion with eternity,
215 Too rich for aught so fleeting!—Like a knell
Swept o'er my sense its closing words, "Farewell,
On earth we meet no more!"[2]—and all was gone—
The pale bright settled brow—the thrilling tone,
The still and shining eye! and never more
220 May twilight gloom or midnight hush restore
That radiant guest! One full-fraught hour of heaven,
To earthly passion's wild implorings given,
Was made my own—the ethereal fire hath shivered
The fragile censer[3] in whose mould it quivered
225 Brightly, consumingly! What now is left?
A faded world, of glory's hues bereft—
A void, a chain!—I dwell 'midst throngs, apart,
In the cold silence of the stranger's heart;
A fixed, immortal shadow stands between
230 My spirit and life's fast receding scene;
A gift hath severed me from human ties,
A power is gone from all earth's melodies,
Which never may return: their chords are broken,
The music of another land hath spoken—
235 No after-sound is sweet!—this weary thirst!
And I have heard celestial fountains burst!—
What *here* shall quench it?
                                        Dost thou not rejoice,
When the spring sends forth an awakening voice
Through the young woods?—Thou dost!—And in the birth
240 Of early leaves, and flowers, and songs of mirth,
Thousands, like thee, find gladness!—Couldst thou know
How every breeze then summons *me* to go!

---

2. This is the answer to Manfred's question to the Phantom of Astarte (2.4.154): "Say, shall we meet again?" Astarte vanishes, and Nemesis says, "She's gone, and will not be recall'd." Hemans's lines also echo Endymion's renunciation of his dream god-dess at a crucial moment in Keats's *Endymion* (4.657–59): "The hour may come / When we shall meet in pure elysium. / On earth I may not love thee."
3. Container in which incense is burned.

How all the light of love and beauty shed
By those rich hours, but woos me to the dead!
245 The *only* beautiful that change no more—
The only loved!—the dwellers on the shore
Of spring fulfilled!—The dead!—*whom* call we so?
They that breathe purer air, that feel, that know
Things wrapt from us!—Away!—within me pent,
250 That which is barred from its own element
Still droops or struggles!—But the day *will* come—
Over the deep the free bird finds its home,
And the stream lingers 'midst the rocks, yet greets
The sea at last; and the winged flower-seed meets
255 A soil to rest in:—shall not *I*, too, be,
My spirit-love! upborne to dwell with thee?
Yes! by the power whose conquering anguish stirred
The tomb, whose cry beyond the stars was heard,
Whose agony of triumph won thee back
260 Through the dim pass no mortal step may track,
Yet shall we meet!—that glimpse of joy divine
Proved thee for ever and for ever mine!

1830

JOHN KEATS
1795–1821

John Keats's father was head stableman at a London livery stable; he married his employer's daughter and inherited the business. The poet's mother, by all reports, was a strongly sensuous woman and a rather casual but affectionate rearer of her five children—John (the first born), his three brothers (one of whom died in infancy), and a sister. Keats was sent to the Reverend John Clarke's private school at Enfield, where he was a noisy, high-spirited boy; despite his small stature (when full-grown, he was barely over five feet in height), he distinguished himself in sports and fistfights. Here he had the good fortune to have as a mentor Charles Cowden Clarke, son of the headmaster, who later became a writer and editor; he encouraged Keats's passion for reading and, both at school and in the course of their later friendship, introduced him to Spenser and other poets, to music, and to the theater.

When Keats was eight his father was killed by a fall from a horse, and when he was fourteen his mother died of tuberculosis. Although the livery stable had prospered, and £8,000 had been left in trust to the children by Keats's grandmother, the estate remained tied up in the law courts for all of Keats's lifetime. The children's guardian, Richard Abbey, an unimaginative and practical-minded businessman, took Keats out of school at the age of fifteen and bound him apprentice to Thomas Hammond, a surgeon and apothecary at Edmonton. In 1815 Keats carried on his medical studies at Guy's Hospital, London, and the next year qualified to practice as an apothecary-surgeon—but almost immediately, over his guardian's protests, he abandoned medicine for poetry.

This decision was influenced by Keats's friendship with Leigh Hunt, then editor of the *Examiner* and a leading political radical, poet, and prolific writer of criticism and periodical essays. Hunt, the first successful author of Keats's acquaintance, added his enthusiastic encouragement of Keats's poetic efforts to that of Clarke. More important, he introduced him to writers greater than Hunt himself—William Hazlitt, Charles Lamb, and Percy Shelley—as well as to Benjamin Robert Haydon, painter of grandiose historical and religious canvases. Through Hunt, Keats also met John Hamilton Reynolds and then Charles Wentworth Dilke and Charles Brown, who became his intimate friends and provided him with an essential circumstance for a fledgling poet: a sympathetic and appreciative audience.

The rapidity and sureness of Keats's development has no match. He did not even undertake poetry until his eighteenth year and, for the following few years, produced album verse that was at best merely competent and at times manifested an arch sentimentality. Suddenly, in 1816, he spoke out loud and bold in the sonnet *On First Looking into Chapman's Homer*. Later that same year he wrote *Sleep and Poetry*, in which he laid out for himself a program deliberately modeled on the careers of the greatest poets, asking only

> for ten years, that I may overwhelm
> Myself in poesy; so I may do the deed
> That my own soul has to itself decreed.

For even while his health was good, Keats felt a foreboding of early death and applied himself to his art with a desperate urgency. In 1817 he went on to compose *Endymion,* an ambitious undertaking of more than four thousand lines. It is a profuse allegory of a mortal's quest for an ideal feminine counterpart and a flawless happiness beyond earthly possibility; in a number of passages, it already exhibits the sure movement and phrasing of his mature poetic style. But Keats's critical judgment and aspiration exceeded his achievement: long before he completed it, he declared impatiently that he carried on with the "slipshod" *Endymion* only as a "trial of invention" and began to block out *Hyperion,* conceived on the model of Milton's *Paradise Lost* in that most demanding of forms, the epic poem. His success in achieving the Miltonic manner is one of the reasons why Keats abandoned *Hyperion* before it was finished, for he recognized that he was uncommonly susceptible to poetic influences and regarded this as a threat to his individuality. "I will write independently," he insisted. "The Genius of Poetry must work out its own salvation in a man." He had refused the chance of intimacy with Shelley "that I might have my own unfettered scope"; he had broken away from Leigh Hunt's influence lest he get "the reputation of Hunt's *élève* [pupil]"; now he shied away from domination by Milton's powerfully infectious style.

With the year 1818 began a series of troubles that culminated in Keats's mortal illness. Sentimental legend used to fix the blame on two anonymous articles: a scurrilous attack on Keats as a member of the "Cockney School" (that is, Hunt's radical literary circle in London), which appeared in the heavily Tory *Blackwood's Magazine,* and a savage mauling of *Endymion* in the *Quarterly Review.* Shelley gave impetus to this myth by his description of Keats in *Adonais* as "a pale flower," and Byron, who knew even less about him, asserted that he was "snuffed out by an article." But in fact, Keats had the good sense to recognize that the attacks were motivated by Tory bias and class snobbery, and he had already passed his own severe judgment on *Endymion:* "My own domestic criticism," he said, "has given me pain without comparison beyond what *Blackwood* or the *Quarterly* could possibly inflict." More important was the financial distress of his brother George and his young bride, who emigrated to Kentucky and lost their money in an ill-advised investment; Keats, himself short of funds, had now to turn to literary journeywork to eke out the family income. His brother Tom contracted tuberculosis, and the poet, in devoted attendance, helplessly watched him waste away until his death that December. In the summer of that year Keats had taken a strenuous walking tour in the English Lake District, Scotland, and Ireland. It was a glorious adventure but a totally exhausting one in wet, cold weather, and he returned in August with a chronically ulcerated throat made increasingly ominous by the shadow of the tuberculosis that had killed his mother and brother. And in the late fall of that same year Keats fell unwillingly, helplessly in love with Fanny Brawne. This attractive, vivacious, and mildly flirtatious woman of eighteen had little interest in poetry, but she possessed an alert and sensible mind and loved Keats sincerely. They became engaged, but Keats's dedication to poetry, his poverty, and his growing illness made marriage impossible and love a torment.

In this period of acute distress and emotional turmoil, within five years of his first trying his hand at poetry, Keats achieved the culmination of his brief poetic career. Between January and September of 1819, masterpiece followed masterpiece in astonishing succession: *The Eve of St. Agnes, La Belle Dame sans Merci*, all of the "great odes," *Lamia*, and a sufficient number of fine sonnets to make him, with Wordsworth, the major Romantic craftsman in that form. All of these poems possess the distinctive qualities of the work of Keats's maturity: a slow-paced, gracious movement; a concreteness of description in which all the senses—tactile, gustatory, kinetic, visceral, as well as visual and auditory—combine to give the total apprehension of an experience; a delight at the sheer existence of things outside himself, the poet seeming to lose his own identity in a total identification with the object he contemplates; and a concentrated felicity of phrasing that reminded his friends, as it has many critics since, of the language of Shakespeare. Under the richly sensuous surface, we find Keats's characteristic presentation of all experience as a tangle of inseparable but irreconcilable opposites. He finds melancholy in delight and pleasure in pain; he feels the highest intensity of love as an approximation to death; he inclines equally toward a life of indolence and "sensation" and toward a life of thought; he is aware both of the attraction of an imaginative dream world without "disagreeables" and the remorseless pressure of the actual; he aspires at the same time to aesthetic detachment and to social responsibility.

His letters, hardly less remarkable than his poetry, show that Keats felt on his pulses the conflicts he dramatized in his major poems. Above all, they reveal him wrestling with the problem of evil and suffering—what to make of our lives in the discovery that "the world is full of misery and heartbreak, pain, sickness and oppression." To the end of his life, he refused to seek solace for the complexity and contradictions of experience either in the abstractions of inherited philosophical doctrines or in the absolutes of a religious creed. At the close of his poetic career, in the latter part of 1819, Keats began to rework the epic *Hyperion* into the form of a dream vision that he called *The Fall of Hyperion*. In the introductory section of this fragment the poet is told by the prophetess Moneta that he has hitherto been merely a dreamer; he must know that

> The poet and the dreamer are distinct,
> Diverse, sheer opposite, antipodes,

and that the height of poetry can be reached only by

> those to whom the miseries of the world
> Are misery, and will not let them rest.

He was seemingly planning to undertake a new direction and subject matter, when illness and death intervened.

On the night of February 3, 1820, he coughed up blood. As a physician, he refused to evade the truth: "I cannot be deceived in that colour; that drop of blood is my death warrant. I must die." That spring and summer a series of hemorrhages rapidly weakened him. In the autumn he allowed himself to be persuaded to seek the milder climate of Italy in the company of Joseph Severn, a young painter, but these last months were only what he called "a posthumous existence." He died in Rome on February 23, 1821, and was buried in the Protestant Cemetery. At times the agony of his disease, the seeming frustration of his hopes for great poetic achievement, and the despair of his passion for Fanny Brawne compelled even Keats's brave spirit to bitterness, and jealousy, but he always recovered his gallantry. His last letter, written to Charles Brown, concludes: "I can scarcely bid you good bye even in a letter. I always made an awkward bow. God bless you! John Keats."

No one can read Keats's poems and letters without an undersense of the tragic waste of an extraordinary intellect and genius cut off so early. What he might have done is beyond conjecture; what we do know is that his poetry, when he stopped writing at the age of twenty-four, exceeds the accomplishment at the same age of Chaucer, Shakespeare, and Milton.

The texts here are taken from Jack Stillinger's edition, *The Poems of John Keats* (Cambridge, Mass., 1978).

On First Looking into Chapman's Homer[1]

Much have I travell'd in the realms of gold,
    And many goodly states and kingdoms seen;
    Round many western islands have I been
Which bards in fealty to Apollo hold.
5 Oft of one wide expanse had I been told
    That deep-brow'd Homer ruled as his demesne;[2]
    Yet did I never breathe its pure serene[3]
Till I heard Chapman speak out loud and bold:
Then felt I like some watcher of the skies
10   When a new planet swims into his ken;
    Or like stout Cortez when with eagle eyes
    He star'd at the Pacific—and all his men
Look'd at each other with a wild surmise—
    Silent, upon a peak in Darien.

Oct. 1816   1816

From Sleep and Poetry[1]

[O FOR TEN YEARS]

O for ten years, that I may overwhelm
Myself in poesy; so I may do the deed
That my own soul has to itself decreed.
Then will I pass the countries that I see
100 In long perspective, and continually

1. Keats's mentor Charles Cowden Clarke introduced him to the robust translation of Homer by the Elizabethan poet and dramatist George Chapman. They read through the night, and Keats walked home at dawn. This sonnet reached Clarke by the ten o'clock mail that same morning. It was Balboa, not Cortez, who caught his first sight of the Pacific from the heights of Darien, in Panama, but none of Keats's contemporaries noticed the error.
2. Realm, feudal possession.
3. Clear expanse of air.
1. At the early age of twenty-one, Keats set himself a regimen of poetic training modeled on the course followed by the greatest poets. Virgil had established the pattern of beginning with pastoral writing and proceeding gradually to the point at which he was ready to undertake the epic, and this pattern had been deliberately followed by Spenser and Milton. Keats's version of this program, as he describes it here, is to begin with the realm "of Flora, and old Pan" (line 102) and, within ten years, to climb up to the level of poetry dealing with "the agonies, the strife / Of human hearts" (lines 124–25). The latter achievement Keats found best represented among his contemporaries by Wordsworth and, less successfully, Shelley; Keats's vision of the chariot of poesy (lines 125–54) parallels Shelley's allegorical visions. The program Keats set himself is illuminated by his analysis of Wordsworth's progress in his letter to J. H. Reynolds of May 3, 1818 (p. 1848).

Taste their pure fountains. First the realm I'll pass
Of Flora, and old Pan:[2] sleep in the grass,
Feed upon apples red, and strawberries,
And choose each pleasure that my fancy sees;
105 Catch the white-handed nymphs in shady places,
To woo sweet kisses from averted faces,—
Play with their fingers, touch their shoulders white
Into a pretty shrinking with a bite
As hard as lips can make it: till agreed,
110 A lovely tale of human life we'll read.
And one will teach a tame dove how it best
May fan the cool air gently o'er my rest;
Another, bending o'er her nimble tread,
Will set a green robe floating round her head,
115 And still will dance with ever varied ease,
Smiling upon the flowers and the trees:
Another will entice me on, and on
Through almond blossoms and rich cinnamon;
Till in the bosom of a leafy world
120 We rest in silence, like two gems upcurl'd
In the recesses of a pearly shell.

          And can I ever bid these joys farewell?
Yes, I must pass them for a nobler life,
Where I may find the agonies, the strife
125 Of human hearts: for lo! I see afar,
O'er sailing the blue cragginess, a car[3]
And steeds with streamy manes—the charioteer
Looks out upon the winds with glorious fear:
And now the numerous tramplings quiver lightly
130 Along a huge cloud's ridge; and now with sprightly
Wheel downward come they into fresher skies,
Tipt round with silver from the sun's bright eyes.
Still downward with capacious whirl they glide;
And now I see them on a green-hill's side
135 In breezy rest among the nodding stalks.
The charioteer with wond'rous gesture talks
To the trees and mountains; and there soon appear
Shapes of delight, of mystery, and fear,
Passing along before a dusky space
140 Made by some mighty oaks: as they would chase
Some ever-fleeting music on they sweep.
Lo! how they murmur, laugh, and smile, and weep:
Some with upholden hand and mouth severe;
Some with their faces muffled to the ear
145 Between their arms; some, clear in youthful bloom,
Go glad and smilingly athwart the gloom;
Some looking back, and some with upward gaze;

2. I.e., the carefree pastoral world. Flora was the
Roman goddess of flowers. Pan was the Greek god
of pastures, woods, and animal life.
3. This chariot, with its "charioteer" (line 127),

represents the higher poetic imagination, which
bodies forth the matters "of delight, of mystery,
and fear" (line 138) that characterize the grander
poetic genres.

Yes, thousands in a thousand different ways
Flit onward—now a lovely wreath of girls
150 Dancing their sleek hair into tangled curls;
And now broad wings. Most awfully intent,
The driver of those steeds is forward bent,
And seems to listen: O that I might know
All that he writes with such a hurrying glow.

155 The visions all are fled—the car is fled
Into the light of heaven, and in their stead
A sense of real things comes doubly strong,
And, like a muddy stream, would bear along
My soul to nothingness: but I will strive
160 Against all doubtings, and will keep alive
The thought of that same chariot, and the strange
Journey it went.

* * *

Oct.–Dec. 1816   1817

On Seeing the Elgin Marbles[1]

My spirit is too weak—mortality
    Weighs heavily on me like unwilling sleep,
    And each imagined pinnacle and steep
Of godlike hardship tells me I must die
5 Like a sick eagle looking at the sky.
    Yet 'tis a gentle luxury to weep
    That I have not the cloudy winds to keep
Fresh for the opening of the morning's eye.
Such dim-conceived glories of the brain
10   Bring round the heart an undescribable feud;
So do these wonders a most dizzy pain,
    That mingles Grecian grandeur with the rude
Wasting of old time—with a billowy main—
    A sun—a shadow of a magnitude.

Mar. 1 or 2, 1817   1817

---

1. Lord Elgin had brought to England in 1806 the marble statues and friezes that adorned the Parthenon at Athens; in 1816 they were purchased by the government for the British Museum.

From Endymion: A Poetic Romance[1]

"The stretched metre of an antique song"

INSCRIBED TO THE MEMORY OF THOMAS CHATTERTON

Preface

Knowing within myself the manner in which this Poem has been produced, it is not without a feeling of regret that I make it public.

What manner I mean, will be quite clear to the reader, who must soon perceive great inexperience, immaturity, and every error denoting a feverish attempt, rather than a deed accomplished. The two first books, and indeed the two last, I feel sensible are not of such completion as to warrant their passing the press; nor should they if I thought a year's castigation would do them any good;—it will not: the foundations are too sandy. It is just that this youngster should die away: a sad thought for me, if I had not some hope that while it is dwindling I may be plotting, and fitting myself for verses fit to live.

This may be speaking too presumptuously, and may deserve a punishment: but no feeling man will be forward to inflict it: he will leave me alone, with the conviction that there is not a fiercer hell than the failure in a great object. This is not written with the least atom of purpose to forestall criticisms of course, but from the desire I have to conciliate men who are competent to look, and who do look with a zealous eye, to the honour of English literature.

The imagination of a boy is healthy, and the mature imagination of a man is healthy; but there is a space of life between, in which the soul is in a ferment, the character undecided, the way of life uncertain, the ambition thick-sighted: thence proceeds mawkishness, and all the thousand bitters which those men I speak of must necessarily taste in going over the following pages.

I hope I have not in too late a day touched the beautiful mythology of Greece, and dulled its brightness: for I wish to try once more,[2] before I bid it farewell.

Teignmouth, April 10, 1818

From *Book 1*

[A THING OF BEAUTY]

A thing of beauty is a joy for ever:
Its loveliness increases; it will never

---

1. This poem of more than four thousand lines (based on the classical myth of a mortal beloved by the goddess of the moon) tells of Endymion's long and agonized search for an immortal goddess whom he had seen in several visions. In the course of his wanderings he comes upon an Indian maid who had been abandoned by the followers of Bacchus and, to his utter despair, succumbs to a sensual passion for her, in apparent betrayal of his love for his heavenly ideal. In the resolution the Indian maid reveals that she is herself Cynthia (Diana), goddess of the moon, the celestial subject of his earlier visions.

The verse epigraph is adapted from Shakespeare's Sonnet 17, line 12: "And stretchèd metre of an antique song." Thomas Chatterton (1752–1770), to whom *Endymion* is inscribed, wrote a number of brilliant pseudoarchaic poems that he attributed to an imaginary 15th-century poet, Thomas Rowley. Keats described him as "the most English of poets except Shakespeare."

2. In *Hyperion*, which Keats was already planning.

Pass into nothingness; but still will keep
A bower quiet for us, and a sleep
5   Full of sweet dreams, and health, and quiet breathing.
Therefore, on every morrow, are we wreathing
A flowery band to bind us to the earth,
Spite of despondence, of the inhuman dearth
Of noble natures, of the gloomy days,
10 Of all the unhealthy and o'er-darkened ways
Made for our searching: yes, in spite of all,
Some shape of beauty moves away the pall
From our dark spirits. Such the sun, the moon,
Trees old, and young sprouting a shady boon
15 For simple sheep; and such are daffodils
With the green world they live in; and clear rills
That for themselves a cooling covert make
'Gainst the hot season; the mid forest brake,°   thicket
Rich with a sprinkling of fair musk-rose blooms:
20 And such too is the grandeur of the dooms°   judgments
We have imagined for the mighty dead;
All lovely tales that we have heard or read:
An endless fountain of immortal drink,
Pouring unto us from the heaven's brink.[3]

25   Nor do we merely feel these essences
For one short hour; no, even as the trees
That whisper round a temple become soon
Dear as the temple's self, so does the moon,
The passion poesy, glories infinite,
30 Haunt us till they become a cheering light
Unto our souls, and bound to us so fast,
That, whether there be shine, or gloom o'ercast,
They alway must be with us, or we die.

        Therefore, 'tis with full happiness that I
35 Will trace the story of Endymion.
The very music of the name has gone
Into my being, and each pleasant scene
Is growing fresh before me as the green
Of our own vallies. * * *

[THE "PLEASURE THERMOMETER"]

    "Peona![4] ever have I long'd to slake
770 My thirst for the world's praises: nothing base,

---

3. The poet sets up, and seeks to resolve, the basic opposition between the inevitably "mortal" pleasures in this life and the conceived possibility of "immortal" delight. Thus "essences" (line 25) seem to be the things of beauty in this world, purged of the mutability that is inescapable in ordinary experience. The central passage dealing with this theme is in book 1, lines 777ff.
4. The sister to whom Endymion confides his troubles. Of lines 769–857, Keats wrote to his publisher, John Taylor: "When I wrote it, it was the regular stepping of the Imagination towards a Truth. My having written that Argument will per-

haps be of the greatest Service to me of anything I ever did—It set before me at once the gradations of Happiness even like a kind of Pleasure Thermometer, and is my first step towards the chief attempt in the Drama—the playing of different Natures with Joy and Sorrow." The gradations on this "Pleasure Thermometer" mark the stages on the way to what Keats calls "happiness" (line 777)—his secular version of the religious concept of "felicity" that, in the orthodox view, is to be achieved by a surrender of oneself to God. For Keats, the way to happiness lies through a fusion of ourselves, first sensuously, with the lovely

No merely slumberous phantasm, could unlace
The stubborn canvas for my voyage prepar'd—
Though now 'tis tatter'd; leaving my bark bar'd
And sullenly drifting: yet my higher hope
775   Is of too wide, too rainbow-large a scope,
To fret at myriads of earthly wrecks.
Wherein lies happiness? In that which becks
Our ready minds to fellowship divine,
A fellowship with essence; till we shine,
780   Full alchemiz'd,[5] and free of space. Behold
The clear religion of heaven! Fold
A rose leaf round thy finger's taperness,
And soothe thy lips: hist, when the airy stress
Of music's kiss impregnates the free winds,
785   And with a sympathetic touch unbinds
Eolian[6] magic from their lucid wombs:
Then old songs waken from enclouded tombs;
Old ditties sigh above their father's grave;
Ghosts of melodious prophecyings rave
790   Round every spot where trod Apollo's foot;
Bronze clarions awake, and faintly bruit,[7]
Where long ago a giant battle was;
And, from the turf, a lullaby doth pass
In every place where infant Orpheus slept.
795   Feel we these things?—that moment have we stept
Into a sort of oneness, and our state
Is like a floating spirit's. But there are
Richer entanglements, enthralments far
More self-destroying, leading, by degrees,
800   To the chief intensity: the crown of these
Is made of love and friendship, and sits high
Upon the forehead of humanity.
All its more ponderous and bulky worth
Is friendship, whence there ever issues forth
805   A steady splendour; but at the tip-top
There hangs by unseen film, an orbed drop
Of light, and that is love: its influence,
Thrown in our eyes, genders a novel sense,
At which we start and fret; till in the end,
810   Melting into its radiance, we blend,
Mingle, and so become a part of it,—
Nor with aught else can our souls interknit
So wingedly: when we combine therewith,
Life's self is nourish'd by its proper pith,[8]
815   And we are nurtured like a pelican brood.[9]

objects of nature and art (lines 781–97), then on a higher level, with other human beings through "love and friendship" (line 801) and, ultimately, sexual love. By this "self-destroying," or loss of personal identity through our imaginative identification with a beloved person outside ourselves, we escape from the material limits and the self-centered condition of ordinary experience, to achieve a "fellowship with essence," which is a kind of immortality within our mortal existence (line 844).

5. Transformed by alchemy from a base to a precious metal.
6. From Aeolus, god of winds.
7. Make a sound.
8. Its own elemental substance.
9. Young pelicans were once thought to feed on their mother's flesh. In a parallel way, our life is nourished by another's life, with which it fuses in love.

Aye, so delicious is the unsating food,
That men, who might have tower'd in the van
Of all the congregated world, to fan
And winnow from the coming step of time
820   All chaff of custom, wipe away all slime
Left by men-slugs and human serpentry,
Have been content to let occasion die,
Whilst they did sleep in love's elysium.
And, truly, I would rather be struck dumb,
825   Than speak against this ardent listlessness:
For I have ever thought that it might bless
The world with benefits unknowingly;
As does the nightingale, upperched high,
And cloister'd among cool and bunched leaves—
830   She sings but to her love, nor e'er conceives
How tiptoe Night holds back her dark-grey hood.[1]
Just so may love, although 'tis understood
The mere commingling of passionate breath,
Produce more than our searching witnesseth:
835   What I know not: but who, of men, can tell
That flowers would bloom, or that green fruit would swell
To melting pulp, that fish would have bright mail,
The earth its dower of river, wood, and vale,
The meadows runnels, runnels pebble-stones,
840   The seed its harvest, or the lute its tones,
Tones ravishment, or ravishment its sweet,
If human souls did never kiss and greet?

    "Now, if this earthly love has power to make
Men's being mortal, immortal; to shake
845   Ambition from their memories, and brim
Their measure of content; what merest whim,
Seems all this poor endeavour after fame,
To one, who keeps within his stedfast aim
A love immortal, an immortal too.
850   Look not so wilder'd; for these things are true,
And never can be born of atomies°   *mites*
That buzz about our slumbers, like brain-flies,
Leaving us fancy-sick. No, no, I'm sure,
My restless spirit never could endure
855   To brood so long upon one luxury,
Unless it did, though fearfully, espy
A hope beyond the shadow of a dream."

Apr.–Nov. 1817   1818

---

1. I.e., in order to hear better.

On Sitting Down to Read *King Lear* Once Again[1]

O golden-tongued Romance, with serene lute!
   Fair plumed syren, queen of far-away!
   Leave melodizing on this wintry day,
Shut up thine olden pages, and be mute.
5 Adieu! for, once again, the fierce dispute
   Betwixt damnation and impassion'd clay
   Must I burn through; once more humbly assay
The bitter-sweet of this Shakespearean fruit.
Chief Poet! and ye clouds of Albion,[2]
10   Begetters of our deep eternal theme!
When through the old oak forest[3] I am gone,
   Let me not wander in a barren dream:
But, when I am consumed in the fire,
Give me new phoenix[4] wings to fly at my desire.

Jan. 22, 1818   1838

When I have fears that I may cease to be[1]

When I have fears that I may cease to be
   Before my pen has glean'd my teeming brain,
Before high piled books, in charactry,[2]
   Hold like rich garners the full ripen'd grain;
5 When I behold, upon the night's starr'd face,
   Huge cloudy symbols of a high romance,
And think that I may never live to trace
   Their shadows, with the magic hand of chance;
And when I feel, fair creature of an hour,
10   That I shall never look upon thee more,
Never have relish in the fairy power
   Of unreflecting love;—then on the shore
Of the wide world I stand alone, and think
Till love and fame to nothingness do sink.

Jan. 1818   1848

To Homer

Standing aloof in giant ignorance,
   Of thee I hear and of the Cyclades,[1]

1. Keats pauses, while revising *Endymion: A Poetic Romance,* to read again Shakespeare's great tragedy. The word "syren" (line 2) indicates Keats's feeling that "Romance" was enticing him from the poet's prime duty, to deal with "the agonies, the strife / Of human hearts" (*Sleep and Poetry,* lines 124–25).
2. Old name for England. *King Lear* is set in Celtic Britain.
3. A reference either to *King Lear* or to *Endymion.*

4. The fabulous bird that periodically burns itself to death to rise anew from the ashes.
1. The first, and one of the most successful, of Keats's attempts at the sonnet in the Shakespearean rhyme scheme.
2. Characters; printed letters of the alphabet.
1. A group of islands in the Aegean Sea, off Greece. Keats's allusion is to his ignorance of the Greek language.

As one who sits ashore and longs perchance
To visit dolphin-coral in deep seas.
5   So wast thou blind;—but then the veil was rent,
For Jove uncurtain'd heaven to let thee live,
And Neptune made for thee a spumy tent,
And Pan made sing for thee his forest-hive;
Aye on the shores of darkness there is light,
10   And precipices show untrodden green,
There is a budding morrow in midnight,
There is a triple sight in blindness keen;
Such seeing hadst thou, as it once befel
To Dian, Queen of Earth, and Heaven, and Hell.[2]

1818   1848

The Eve of St. Agnes[1]

1

St. Agnes' Eve—Ah, bitter chill it was!
The owl, for all his feathers, was a-cold;
The hare limp'd trembling through the frozen grass,
And silent was the flock in woolly fold:
5   Numb were the Beadsman's[2] fingers, while he told
His rosary, and while his frosted breath,
Like pious incense from a censer old,
Seem'd taking flight for heaven, without a death,
Past the sweet Virgin's picture, while his prayer he saith.

2

10   His prayer he saith, this patient, holy man;
Then takes his lamp, and riseth from his knees,
And back returneth, meagre, barefoot, wan,
Along the chapel aisle by slow degrees:
The sculptur'd dead, on each side, seem to freeze,
15   Emprison'd in black, purgatorial rails:
Knights, ladies, praying in dumb° orat'ries,°   *silent / chapels*
He passeth by; and his weak spirit fails
To think[3] how they may ache in icy hoods and mails.

---

2. In late pagan cults Diana was worshiped as a three-figured goddess, the deity of nature and of the moon as well as the queen of hell. The "triple sight" that blind Homer paradoxically commands is of these three regions and also of heaven, sea, and earth (the realms of Jove, Neptune, and Pan, lines 6–8).

1. St. Agnes, martyred ca. 303 at the age of thirteen, is the patron saint of virgins. Legend has it that if a chaste young woman performs the proper ritual, she will dream of her future husband on the evening before St. Agnes's Day, January 21. Keats combines this superstition with the Romeo and Juliet theme of young love thwarted by feuding families and tells the story in a sequence of evolving Spenserian stanzas. The luxurious product has been called "a colored dream," but it is a complexly meaningful

dream, in which the strong contrasts of heat and cold, crimson and silver, youth and age, revelry and austere penance, sensuality and chastity, life and death, and hell and heaven assume symbolic values. They figure forth the extremes of spirituality and physicality that are involved in sexuality, the difference between the dream and the reality of passion, and the ambivalences at the center of both human love and the imagination. The poem is Keats's first complete success in sustained narrative. For the author's revisions while composing stanzas 26 and 30 of *The Eve of St. Agnes,* see "Poems in Process," in the appendices to the volume.

2. One who is paid to pray for his benefactor. He "tells" (counts) the beads of his rosary, to keep track of his prayers.

3. I.e., when he thinks.

3

Northward he turneth through a little door,
20 And scarce three steps, ere Music's golden tongue
Flatter'd° to tears this aged man and poor;   *beguiled*
But no—already had his deathbell rung;
The joys of all his life were said and sung:
His was harsh penance on St. Agnes' Eve:
25 Another way he went, and soon among
Rough ashes sat he for his soul's reprieve,
And all night kept awake, for sinners' sake to grieve.

4

That ancient Beadsman heard the prelude soft;
And so it chanc'd, for many a door was wide,
30 From hurry to and fro. Soon, up aloft,
The silver, snarling trumpets 'gan to chide:
The level chambers, ready with their pride,°   *ostentation*
Were glowing to receive a thousand guests:
The carved angels, ever eager-eyed,
35 Star'd, where upon their heads the cornice rests,
With hair blown back, and wings put cross-wise on their breasts.

5

At length burst in the argent revelry,[4]
With plume, tiara, and all rich array,
Numerous as shadows haunting fairily
40 The brain, new stuff'd, in youth, with triumphs gay
Of old romance. These let us wish away,
And turn, sole-thoughted, to one Lady there,
Whose heart had brooded, all that wintry day,
On love, and wing'd St. Agnes' saintly care,
45 As she had heard old dames full many times declare.

6

They told her how, upon St. Agnes' Eve,
Young virgins might have visions of delight,
And soft adorings from their loves receive
Upon the honey'd middle of the night,
50 If ceremonies due they did aright;
As, supperless to bed they must retire,
And couch supine their beauties, lily white;
Nor look behind, nor sideways, but require
Of heaven with upward eyes for all that they desire.

7

55 Full of this whim was thoughtful Madeline:
The music, yearning like a god in pain,
She scarcely heard: her maiden eyes divine,
Fix'd on the floor, saw many a sweeping train

4. Silver-adorned revelers.

Pass by—she heeded not at all: in vain
60   Came many a tiptoe, amorous cavalier,
And back retir'd, not cool'd by high disdain;
But she saw not: her heart was otherwhere:
She sigh'd for Agnes' dreams, the sweetest of the year.

8

She danc'd along with vague, regardless eyes,
65   Anxious her lips, her breathing quick and short:
The hallow'd hour was near at hand: she sighs
Amid the timbrels,° and the throng'd resort   *small drums*
Of whisperers in anger, or in sport;
'Mid looks of love, defiance, hate, and scorn,
70   Hoodwink'd with faery fancy; all amort,[5]
Save to St. Agnes and her lambs unshorn,[6]
And all the bliss to be before to-morrow morn.

9

So, purposing each moment to retire,
She linger'd still. Meantime, across the moors,
75   Had come young Porphyro, with heart on fire
For Madeline. Beside the portal doors,
Buttress'd from moonlight,[7] stands he, and implores
All saints to give him sight of Madeline,
But for one moment in the tedious hours,
80   That he might gaze and worship all unseen;
Perchance speak, kneel, touch, kiss—in sooth such things have been.

10

He ventures in: let no buzz'd whisper tell:
All eyes be muffled, or a hundred swords
Will storm his heart, Love's fev'rous citadel:
85   For him, those chambers held barbarian hordes,
Hyena foemen, and hot-blooded lords,
Whose very dogs would execrations howl
Against his lineage: not one breast affords
Him any mercy, in that mansion foul,
90   Save one old beldame,[8] weak in body and in soul.

11

Ah, happy chance! the aged creature came,
Shuffling along with ivory-headed wand,°   *staff*
To where he stood, hid from the torch's flame,
Behind a broad hall-pillar, far beyond
95   The sound of merriment and chorus bland:°   *soft*

5. As though dead. "Hoodwinked": covered by a hood or blindfolded.
6. On St. Agnes's Day it was the custom to offer lambs' wool at the altar, to be made into cloth by nuns.
7. Sheltered from the moonlight by the buttresses (the supports projecting from the wall).
8. Old (and usually, homely) woman; an ironic development in English from the French meaning, "lovely lady."

He startled her; but soon she knew his face,
And grasp'd his fingers in her palsied hand,
Saying, "Mercy, Porphyro! hie thee from this place;
They are all here to-night, the whole blood-thirsty race!

12

100 "Get hence! get hence! there's dwarfish Hildebrand;
He had a fever late, and in the fit
He cursed thee and thine, both house and land:
Then there's that old Lord Maurice, not a whit
More tame for his gray hairs—Alas me! flit!
105 Flit like a ghost away."—"Ah, Gossip⁹ dear,
We're safe enough; here in this arm-chair sit,
And tell me how"—"Good Saints! not here, not here;
Follow me, child, or else these stones will be thy bier."

13

He follow'd through a lowly arched way,
110 Brushing the cobwebs with his lofty plume,
And as she mutter'd "Well-a—well-a-day!"
He found him in a little moonlight room,
Pale, lattic'd, chill, and silent as a tomb.
"Now tell me where is Madeline," said he,
115 "O tell me, Angela, by the holy loom
Which none but secret sisterhood may see,
When they St. Agnes' wool are weaving piously."

14

"St. Agnes! Ah! it is St. Agnes' Eve—
Yet men will murder upon holy days:
120 Thou must hold water in a witch's sieve,¹
And be liege-lord of all the Elves and Fays,
To venture so: it fills me with amaze
To see thee, Porphyro!—St. Agnes' Eve!
God's help! my lady fair the conjuror plays²
125 This very night: good angels her deceive!
But let me laugh awhile, I've mickle° time to grieve."   much

15

Feebly she laugheth in the languid moon,
While Porphyro upon her face doth look,
Like puzzled urchin on an aged crone
130 Who keepeth clos'd a wond'rous riddle-book,
As spectacled she sits in chimney nook.
But soon his eyes grew brilliant, when she told
His lady's purpose; and he scarce could brook°   restrain
Tears, at the thought of those enchantments cold,
135 And Madeline asleep in lap of legends old.

---

9. In the old sense: godmother or old friend.
1. A sieve made to hold water by witchcraft.

2. I.e., in her attempt to evoke the vision of her lover.

16

Sudden a thought came like a full-blown rose,
Flushing his brow, and in his pained heart
Made purple riot: then doth he propose
A stratagem, that makes the beldame start:
140   "A cruel man and impious thou art:
Sweet lady, let her pray, and sleep, and dream
Alone with her good angels, far apart
From wicked men like thee. Go, go!—I deem
Thou canst not surely be the same that thou didst seem."

17

145   "I will not harm her, by all saints I swear,"
Quoth Porphyro: "O may I ne'er find grace
When my weak voice shall whisper its last prayer,
If one of her soft ringlets I displace,
Or look with ruffian passion in her face:
150   Good Angela, believe me by these tears;
Or I will, even in a moment's space,
Awake, with horrid shout, my foemen's ears,
And beard them, though they be more fang'd than wolves and bears."

18

"Ah! why wilt thou affright a feeble soul?
155   A poor, weak, palsy-stricken, churchyard thing,
Whose passing-bell° may ere the midnight toll;   *death knell*
Whose prayers for thee, each morn and evening,
Were never miss'd."—Thus plaining,° doth she bring   *complaining*
A gentler speech from burning Porphyro;
160   So woful, and of such deep sorrowing,
That Angela gives promise she will do
Whatever he shall wish, betide her weal or woe.

19

Which was, to lead him, in close secrecy,
Even to Madeline's chamber, and there hide
165   Him in a closet, of such privacy
That he might see her beauty unespied,
And win perhaps that night a peerless bride,
While legion'd fairies pac'd the coverlet,
And pale enchantment held her sleepy-eyed.
170   Never on such a night have lovers met,
Since Merlin paid his Demon all the monstrous debt.[3]

20

"It shall be as thou wishest," said the Dame:
"All cates° and dainties shall be stored there   *delicacies*
Quickly on this feast-night: by the tambour frame[4]

3. Probably the episode in the Arthurian legends
in which Merlin, the magician, lost his life when
the wily Vivien turned one of his own spells against
him.
4. A drum-shaped embroidery frame.

175   Her own lute thou wilt see: no time to spare,
    For I am slow and feeble, and scarce dare
    On such a catering trust my dizzy head.
    Wait here, my child, with patience; kneel in prayer
    The while: Ah! thou must needs the lady wed,
180   Or may I never leave my grave among the dead."

21

    So saying, she hobbled off with busy fear.
    The lover's endless minutes slowly pass'd;
    The dame return'd, and whisper'd in his ear
    To follow her; with aged eyes aghast
185   From fright of dim espial. Safe at last,
    Through many a dusky gallery, they gain
    The maiden's chamber, silken, hush'd, and chaste;
    Where Porphyro took covert, pleas'd amain.°   *mightily*
His poor guide hurried back with agues in her brain.

22

190   Her falt'ring hand upon the balustrade,
    Old Angela was feeling for the stair,
    When Madeline, St. Agnes' charmed maid,
    Rose, like a mission'd spirit,[5] unaware:
    With silver taper's light, and pious care,
195   She turn'd, and down the aged gossip led
    To a safe level matting. Now prepare,
    Young Porphyro, for gazing on that bed;
She comes, she comes again, like ring-dove fray'd° and fled.   *frightened*

23

    Out went the taper as she hurried in;
200   Its little smoke, in pallid moonshine, died:
    She clos'd the door, she panted, all akin
    To spirits of the air, and visions wide:
    No uttered syllable, or, woe betide!
    But to her heart, her heart was voluble,
205   Paining with eloquence her balmy side;
    As though a tongueless nightingale should swell
Her throat in vain, and die, heart-stifled, in her dell.

24

    A casement high and triple-arch'd there was,
    All garlanded with carven imag'ries
210   Of fruits, and flowers, and bunches of knot-grass,
    And diamonded with panes of quaint device,
    Innumerable of stains and splendid dyes,
    As are the tiger-moth's deep-damask'd wings;
    And in the midst, 'mong thousand heraldries,

5. I.e., like an angel sent on a mission.

215   And twilight saints, and dim emblazonings,
        A shielded scutcheon blush'd with blood of queens and kings.[6]

25

        Full on this casement shone the wintry moon,
        And threw warm gules[7] on Madeline's fair breast,
        As down she knelt for heaven's grace and boon;°   gift, blessing
220   Rose-bloom fell on her hands, together prest,
        And on her silver cross soft amethyst,
        And on her hair a glory, like a saint:
        She seem'd a splendid angel, newly drest,
        Save wings, for heaven:—Porphyro grew faint:
225   She knelt, so pure a thing, so free from mortal taint.

26

        Anon his heart revives: her vespers done,
        Of all its wreathed pearls her hair she frees;
        Unclasps her warmed jewels one by one;
        Loosens her fragrant boddice; by degrees
230   Her rich attire creeps rustling to her knees:
        Half-hidden, like a mermaid in sea-weed,
        Pensive awhile she dreams awake, and sees,
        In fancy, fair St. Agnes in her bed,
        But dares not look behind, or all the charm is fled.

27

235   Soon, trembling in her soft and chilly nest,
        In sort of wakeful swoon, perplex'd[8] she lay,
        Until the poppied warmth of sleep oppress'd
        Her soothed limbs, and soul fatigued away;
        Flown, like a thought, until the morrow-day;
240   Blissfully haven'd both from joy and pain;
        Clasp'd like a missal where swart Paynims pray;[9]
        Blinded alike from sunshine and from rain,
        As though a rose should shut, and be a bud again.

28

        Stol'n to this paradise, and so entranced,
245   Porphyro gazed upon her empty dress,
        And listen'd to her breathing, if it chanced
        To wake into a slumberous tenderness;
        Which when he heard, that minute did he bless,
        And breath'd himself: then from the closet crept,
250   Noiseless as fear in a wide wilderness,
        And over the hush'd carpet, silent, stept,
        And 'tween the curtains peep'd, where, lo!—how fast she slept.

6. I.e., among the genealogical emblems ("heraldries") and other devices ("emblazonings"), a heraldic shield signified by its colors that the family was of royal blood.

7. Red (heraldry).

8. In a confused state between waking and sleeping.

9. Variously interpreted; perhaps: held tightly, cherished (or else kept shut, fastened with a clasp), like a Christian prayer book ("missal") in a land where the religion is that of dark-skinned pagans ("swart Paynims").

29

Then by the bed-side, where the faded moon
Made a dim, silver twilight, soft he set
255   A table, and, half anguish'd, threw thereon
A cloth of woven crimson, gold, and jet:—
O for some drowsy Morphean amulet![1]
The boisterous, midnight, festive clarion,[2]
The kettle-drum, and far-heard clarionet,
260   Affray his ears, though but in dying tone:—
The hall door shuts again, and all the noise is gone.

30

And still she slept an azure-lidded sleep,
In blanched linen, smooth, and lavender'd,
While he from forth the closet brought a heap
265   Of candied apple, quince, and plum, and gourd;°   *melon*
With jellies soother than the creamy curd,
And lucent syrops, tinct with cinnamon;
Manna and dates, in argosy transferr'd
From Fez,[3] and spiced dainties, every one,
270   From silken Samarcand to cedar'd Lebanon.

31

These delicates he heap'd with glowing hand
On golden dishes and in baskets bright
Of wreathed silver: sumptuous they stand
In the retired quiet of the night,
275   Filling the chilly room with perfume light.—
"And now, my love, my seraph[4] fair, awake!
Thou art my heaven, and I thine eremite:[5]
Open thine eyes, for meek St. Agnes' sake,
Or I shall drowse beside thee, so my soul doth ache."

32

280   Thus whispering, his warm, unnerved arm
Sank in her pillow. Shaded was her dream
By the dusk curtains:—'twas a midnight charm
Impossible to melt as iced stream:
The lustrous salvers in the moonlight gleam;
285   Broad golden fringe upon the carpet lies:
It seem'd he never, never could redeem
From such a stedfast spell his lady's eyes;
So mus'd awhile, entoil'd in woofed phantasies.[6]

33

Awakening up, he took her hollow lute,—
290   Tumultuous,—and, in chords that tenderest be,

1. Sleep-producing charm.
2. High-pitched trumpet.
3. I.e., jellies softer ("soother") than the curds of cream, clear ("lucent") syrups tinged with cinnamon, and sweet gums ("manna") and dates trans-ported in a great merchant ship ("argosy") from Fez.
4. One of the highest orders of angels.
5. Hermit, religious solitary.
6. Entangled in a weave of fantasies.

He play'd an ancient ditty, long since mute,
In Provence call'd, "La belle dame sans mercy":[7]
Close to her ear touching the melody;—
Wherewith disturb'd, she utter'd a soft moan:
295   He ceased—she panted quick—and suddenly
Her blue affrayed eyes wide open shone:
Upon his knees he sank, pale as smooth-sculptured stone.

34

Her eyes were open, but she still beheld,
Now wide awake, the vision of her sleep:
300   There was a painful change, that nigh expell'd
The blisses of her dream so pure and deep:
At which fair Madeline began to weep,
And moan forth witless words with many a sigh;
While still her gaze on Porphyro would keep;
305   Who knelt, with joined hands and piteous eye,
Fearing to move or speak, she look'd so dreamingly.

35

"Ah, Porphyro!" said she, "but even now
Thy voice was at sweet tremble in mine ear,
Made tuneable with every sweetest vow;
310   And those sad eyes were spiritual and clear:
How chang'd thou art! how pallid, chill, and drear!
Give me that voice again, my Porphyro,
Those looks immortal, those complainings dear!
Oh leave me not in this eternal woe,
315   For if thou diest, my love, I know not where to go."

36

Beyond a mortal man impassion'd far
At these voluptuous accents, he arose,
Ethereal, flush'd, and like a throbbing star
Seen mid the sapphire heaven's deep repose;
320   Into her dream he melted, as the rose
Blendeth its odour with the violet,—
Solution sweet: meantime the frost-wind blows
Like Love's alarum pattering the sharp sleet
Against the window-panes; St. Agnes' moon hath set.

37

325   'Tis dark: quick pattereth the flaw-blown° sleet: gust-blown
"This is no dream, my bride, my Madeline!"
'Tis dark: the iced gusts still rave and beat:
"No dream, alas! alas! and woe is mine!
Porphyro will leave me here to fade and pine.—
330   Cruel! what traitor could thee hither bring?
I curse not, for my heart is lost in thine,

7. "The Lovely Lady without Pity," title of a work by the medieval poet Alain Chartier. Keats later adopted the title for his own ballad.

Though thou forsakest a deceived thing;—
A dove forlorn and lost with sick unpruned wing."

38

"My Madeline! sweet dreamer! lovely bride!
335   Say, may I be for aye thy vassal blest?
Thy beauty's shield, heart-shap'd and vermeil° dyed?   *vermilion*
Ah, silver shrine, here will I take my rest
After so many hours of toil and quest,
A famish'd pilgrim,—saved by miracle.
340   Though I have found, I will not rob thy nest
Saving of thy sweet self; if thou think'st well
To trust, fair Madeline, to no rude infidel.

39

"Hark! 'tis an elfin-storm from faery land,
Of haggard[8] seeming, but a boon indeed:
345   Arise—arise! the morning is at hand;—
The bloated wassaillers[9] will never heed:—
Let us away, my love, with happy speed;
There are no ears to hear, or eyes to see,—
Drown'd all in Rhenish and the sleepy mead:[1]
350   Awake! arise! my love, and fearless be,
For o'er the southern moors I have a home for thee."

40

She hurried at his words, beset with fears,
For there were sleeping dragons all around,
At glaring watch, perhaps, with ready spears—
355   Down the wide stairs a darkling[2] way they found.—
In all the house was heard no human sound.
A chain-droop'd lamp was flickering by each door;
The arras, rich with horseman, hawk, and hound,
Flutter'd in the besieging wind's uproar;
360   And the long carpets rose along the gusty floor.

41

They glide, like phantoms, into the wide hall;
Like phantoms, to the iron porch, they glide;
Where lay the Porter, in uneasy sprawl,
With a huge empty flaggon by his side:
365   The wakeful bloodhound rose, and shook his hide,
But his sagacious eye an inmate owns:[3]
By one, and one, the bolts full easy slide:—
The chains lie silent on the footworn stones;—
The key turns, and the door upon its hinges groans.

42

370   And they are gone: ay, ages long ago
These lovers fled away into the storm.

---

8. Wild, untamed (originally, a wild hawk).   heavy fermented drink made with honey).
9. Drunken carousers.   2. In the dark.
1. Rhine wine and the sleep-producing mead (a   3. Acknowledges a member of the household.

That night the Baron dreamt of many a woe,
And all his warrior-guests, with shade and form
Of witch, and demon, and large coffin-worm,
375 Were long be-nightmar'd. Angela the old
Died palsy-twitch'd, with meagre face deform;
The Beadsman, after thousand aves[4] told,
For aye° unsought for slept among his ashes cold.   *ever*

Jan.–Feb. 1819   1820

Bright star, would I were stedfast as thou art[1]

Bright star, would I were stedfast as thou art—
Not in lone splendor hung aloft the night,
And watching, with eternal lids apart,
Like nature's patient, sleepless eremite,[2]
5   The moving waters at their priestlike task
Of pure ablution[3] round earth's human shores,
Or gazing on the new soft-fallen mask
Of snow upon the mountains and the moors;
No—yet still stedfast, still unchangeable,
10   Pillow'd upon my fair love's ripening breast,
To feel for ever its soft swell and fall,
Awake for ever in a sweet unrest,
Still, still to hear her tender-taken breath,
And so live ever—or else swoon to death.[4]

1819   1838

La Belle Dame sans Merci: A Ballad[1]

1

O what can ail thee, knight at arms,
   Alone and palely loitering?
The sedge has wither'd from the lake,
   And no birds sing.

2

5   O what can ail thee, knight at arms,
   So haggard and so woe-begone?

4. The prayers beginning *Ave Maria* ("Hail Mary").
1. While on a tour of the Lake District in 1818, Keats had said that the austere scenes "refine one's sensual vision into a sort of north star which can never cease to be open lidded and steadfast over the wonders of the great Power." The thought developed into this sonnet, which Keats drafted in 1819, then copied into his volume of Shakespeare's poems at the end of September or the beginning of October 1820, while on his way to Italy, where he died.
2. Hermit, religious solitary.
3. Washing, as part of a religious rite.
4. In the earlier version: "Half passionless, and so

swoon on to death."
1. The title, though not the subject, was taken from a medieval poem by Alain Chartier and means "The Lovely Lady without Pity." The story of a mortal destroyed by his love for a supernatural femme fatale has been told repeatedly in myth, fairy tale, and ballad. The text printed here is Keats's earlier version of the poem, as transcribed by Charles Brown. The version published in 1820 begins, "Ah, what can ail thee, wretched wight."
   Keats imitates a frequent procedure of folk ballads by casting the poem into the dialogue form. The first three stanzas are addressed to the knight, and the rest of the poem is his reply.

The squirrel's granary is full,
    And the harvest's done.

3

I see a lily on thy brow
10   With anguish moist and fever dew,
And on thy cheeks a fading rose
    Fast withereth too.

4

I met a lady in the meads,
    Full beautiful, a fairy's child;
15 Her hair was long, her foot was light,
    And her eyes were wild.

5

I made a garland for her head,
    And bracelets too, and fragrant zone;[2]
She look'd at me as she did love,
20   And made sweet moan.

6

I set her on my pacing steed,
    And nothing else saw all day long,
For sidelong would she bend, and sing
    A fairy's song.

7

25 She found me roots of relish sweet,
    And honey wild, and manna dew,
And sure in language strange she said—
    I love thee true.

8

She took me to her elfin grot,
30   And there she wept, and sigh'd full sore,
And there I shut her wild wild eyes
    With kisses four.

9

And there she lulled me asleep,
    And there I dream'd—Ah! woe betide!
35 The latest° dream I ever dream'd   *last*
    On the cold hill's side.

10

I saw pale kings, and princes too,
    Pale warriors, death pale were they all;

2. Belt (of flowers).

They cried—"La belle dame sans merci
40   Hath thee in thrall!"

II

I saw their starv'd lips in the gloam
  With horrid warning gaped wide,
And I awoke and found me here
  On the cold hill's side.

12

45 And this is why I sojourn here,
  Alone and palely loitering,
Though the sedge is wither'd from the lake,
  And no birds sing.

Apr. 1819   1820

Sonnet to Sleep

O soft embalmer of the still midnight,
  Shutting with careful fingers and benign
Our gloom-pleas'd eyes, embower'd from the light,
  Enshaded in forgetfulness divine:
5 O soothest° Sleep! if so it please thee, close,   *softest*
  In midst of this thine hymn, my willing eyes,
Or wait the Amen ere thy poppy[1] throws
  Around my bed its lulling charities.
Then save me or the passed day will shine
10 Upon my pillow, breeding many woes:
Save me from curious° conscience, that still hoards   *scrupulous*
  Its strength for darkness, burrowing like the mole;
Turn the key deftly in the oiled wards,[2]
  And seal the hushed casket of my soul.

Apr. 1819   1838

Ode to Psyche[1]

O Goddess! hear these tuneless numbers, wrung
  By sweet enforcement and remembrance dear,

---

1. Opium is made from the dried juice of the opium poppy.
2. The ridges in a lock that correspond to the notches of the key.
1. This poem initiated the sequence of great odes that Keats wrote in the spring of 1819. It is copied into the same journal-letter that included the *Sonnet to Sleep* and several other sonnets as well as a comment about "endeavoring to discover a better sonnet stanza than we have." It is therefore likely that Keats's experiments with sonnet schemes led to the development of the intricate and varied stanzas of his odes and also that he abandoned the sonnet on discovering the richer possibilities of the more spacious form. In his journal-letter, on April 30, he said that of all his recent poems, *Psy-*

che "is the first and the only one with which I have taken even moderate pains. I have for the most part dashed off my lines in a hurry. This I have done leisurely—I think it reads the more richly for it and will I hope encourage me to write other things in even a more peaceable and healthy spirit."

In the story told by the Roman author Apuleius in the 2nd century, Psyche was a lovely mortal beloved by Cupid, "the winged boy," son of Venus. After various tribulations imposed by Venus because she was jealous of Psyche's beauty, Psyche was wedded to Cupid and translated to heaven as an immortal. To this latter-day goddess, Keats in the last two stanzas promises to establish a place of worship within his own mind, with himself as poet-priest and prophet.

And pardon that thy secrets should be sung
Even into thine own soft-conched[2] ear:
5 Surely I dreamt to-day, or did I see
The winged Psyche with awaken'd eyes?[3]
I wander'd in a forest thoughtlessly,
And, on the sudden, fainting with surprise,
Saw two fair creatures, couched side by side
10 In deepest grass, beneath the whisp'ring roof
Of leaves and trembled blossoms, where there ran
A brooklet, scarce espied:
'Mid hush'd, cool-rooted flowers, fragrant-eyed,
Blue, silver-white, and budded Tyrian,[4]
15 They lay calm-breathing on the bedded grass;
Their arms embraced, and their pinions° too;   *wings*
Their lips touch'd not, but had not bade adieu,
As if disjoined by soft-handed slumber,
And ready still past kisses to outnumber
20 At tender eye-dawn of aurorean love:[5]
The winged boy I knew;
But who wast thou, O happy, happy dove?
His Psyche true!

O latest born and loveliest vision far
25 Of all Olympus' faded hierarchy![6]
Fairer than Phoebe's sapphire-region'd star,[7]
Or Vesper,° amorous glow-worm of the sky;   *evening star*
Fairer than these, though temple thou hast none,
Nor altar heap'd with flowers;
30 Nor virgin-choir to make delicious moan
Upon the midnight hours;
No voice, no lute, no pipe, no incense sweet
From chain-swung censer teeming;
No shrine, no grove, no oracle, no heat
35 Of pale-mouth'd prophet dreaming.

O brightest! though too late for antique vows,
Too, too late for the fond believing lyre,
When holy were the haunted forest boughs,
Holy the air, the water, and the fire;
40 Yet even in these days so far retir'd
From happy pieties, thy lucent fans,°   *shining wings*
Fluttering among the faint Olympians,
I see, and sing, by my own eyes inspired.
So let me be thy choir, and make a moan

2. Soft and shaped like a seashell.
3. Another of Keats's inquiries into the relation of dreams to poetic vision; see, e.g., *Sleep and Poetry*, the concluding lines of *Ode to a Nightingale*, and the opening section of *The Fall of Hyperion: A Dream*.
4. The purple dye anciently made in Tyre.
5. Aurora was the goddess of the dawn.
6. The ranks of the classic gods of Mount Olym-

pus. "You must recollect that Psyche was not embodied as a goddess before the time of Apuleius the Platonist who lived after the Augustan age, and consequently the goddess was never worshiped or sacrificed to with any of the ancient fervor—and perhaps never thought of in the old religion" (Keats, journal-letter, April 30, 1819).
7. The moon, supervised by the goddess Phoebe (Diana).

45   Upon the midnight hours;
Thy voice, thy lute, thy pipe, thy incense sweet
    From swinged censer teeming;
Thy shrine, thy grove, thy oracle, thy heat
    Of pale-mouth'd prophet dreaming.

50 Yes, I will be thy priest, and build a fane°   *temple*
    In some untrodden region of my mind,
Where branched thoughts, new grown with pleasant pain,
    Instead of pines shall murmur in the wind:
Far, far around shall those dark-cluster'd trees
55   Fledge the wild-ridged mountains steep by steep;[8]
And there by zephyrs, streams, and birds, and bees,
    The moss-lain Dryads° shall be lull'd to sleep;   *wood nymphs*
And in the midst of this wide quietness
A rosy sanctuary will I dress
60 With the wreath'd trellis of a working brain,
    With buds, and bells, and stars without a name,
With all the gardener Fancy e'er could feign,
    Who breeding flowers, will never breed the same:
And there shall be for thee all soft delight
65   That shadowy thought can win,
A bright torch, and a casement ope at night,
    To let the warm Love[9] in!

Apr. 1819   1820

Ode to a Nightingale[1]

1

My heart aches, and a drowsy numbness pains
    My sense, as though of hemlock[2] I had drunk,
Or emptied some dull opiate to the drains
    One minute past, and Lethe[3]-wards had sunk:
5 'Tis not through envy of thy happy lot,
    But being too happy in thine happiness,—
        That thou, light-winged Dryad of the trees,
        In some melodious plot
Of beechen green, and shadows numberless,
10   Singest of summer in full-throated ease.

2

O, for a draught of vintage! that hath been
    Cool'd a long age in the deep-delved earth,

---

8. I.e., the trees shall stand, rank against rank, like layers of feathers.
9. I.e., Cupid, god of love.
1. Charles Brown, with whom Keats was then living in Hampstead, wrote: "In the spring of 1819 a nightingale had built her nest near my house. Keats felt a tranquil and continual joy in her song; and one morning he took his chair from the breakfast table to the grass plot under a plum tree, where he sat for two or three hours. When he came into the house, I perceived he had some scraps of paper in his hand, and these he was quietly thrusting behind the books. On inquiry, I found those scraps, four or five in number, contained his poetic feeling on the song of our nightingale."
2. A poisonous herb, not the North American evergreen tree.
3. River in Hades whose waters cause forgetfulness.

Tasting of Flora[4] and the country green,
    Dance, and Provençal song,[5] and sunburnt mirth!
15 O for a beaker full of the warm South,
    Full of the true, the blushful Hippocrene,[6]
      With beaded bubbles winking at the brim,
        And purple-stained mouth;
    That I might drink, and leave the world unseen,
20   And with thee fade away into the forest dim:

3

Fade far away, dissolve, and quite forget
    What thou among the leaves hast never known,
The weariness, the fever, and the fret
    Here, where men sit and hear each other groan;
25 Where palsy shakes a few, sad, last gray hairs,
    Where youth grows pale, and spectre-thin, and dies;[7]
      Where but to think is to be full of sorrow
        And leaden-eyed despairs,
    Where Beauty cannot keep her lustrous eyes,
30   Or new Love pine at them beyond to-morrow.

4

Away! away! for I will fly to thee,
    Not charioted by Bacchus and his pards,
But on the viewless wings of Poesy,[8]
    Though the dull brain perplexes and retards:
35 Already with thee! tender is the night,
    And haply the Queen-Moon is on her throne,
      Cluster'd around by all her starry Fays;°   *fairies*
        But here there is no light,
    Save what from heaven is with the breezes blown
40   Through verdurous° glooms and winding mossy ways. *green-foliaged*

5

I cannot see what flowers are at my feet,
    Nor what soft incense hangs upon the boughs,
But, in embalmed° darkness, guess each sweet   *perfumed*
    Wherewith the seasonable month endows
45 The grass, the thicket, and the fruit-tree wild;
    White hawthorn, and the pastoral eglantine;[9]
      Fast fading violets cover'd up in leaves;
        And mid-May's eldest child,
    The coming musk-rose, full of dewy wine,
50   The murmurous haunt of flies on summer eves.

---

4. Roman goddess of flowers, or the flowers themselves.
5. Provence, in southern France, was in the late Middle Ages renowned for its troubadours—writers and singers of love songs.
6. Fountain of the Muses on Mount Helicon, hence the waters of inspiration, here applied metaphorically to a beaker of wine.

7. Keats's brother Tom, wasted by tuberculosis, had died the preceding winter.
8. I.e., by getting drunk not on wine (the "vintage" of stanza 2) but on the invisible ("viewless") wings of the poetic imagination. (Bacchus, god of wine, was sometimes represented in a chariot drawn by "pards"—leopards.)
9. Sweetbrier or honeysuckle.

6

Darkling° I listen; and, for many a time   *in darkness*
    I have been half in love with easeful Death,
    Call'd him soft names in many a mused° rhyme,   *mediated*
    To take into the air my quiet breath;
55   Now more than ever seems it rich to die,
    To cease upon the midnight with no pain,
        While thou art pouring forth thy soul abroad
           In such an ecstasy!
    Still wouldst thou sing, and I have ears in vain—
60   To thy high requiem become a sod.

7

Thou wast not born for death, immortal Bird!
    No hungry generations tread thee down;
    The voice I hear this passing night was heard
    In ancient days by emperor and clown:
65   Perhaps the self-same song that found a path
    Through the sad heart of Ruth,[1] when, sick for home,
        She stood in tears amid the alien corn;°   *wheat*
           The same that oft-times hath
    Charm'd magic casements, opening on the foam
70   Of perilous seas, in faery lands forlorn.

8

Forlorn! the very word is like a bell
    To toll me back from thee to my sole self!
    Adieu! the fancy[2] cannot cheat so well
    As she is fam'd to do, deceiving elf.
75   Adieu! adieu! thy plaintive anthem° fades   *hymn*
    Past the near meadows, over the still stream,
        Up the hill-side; and now 'tis buried deep
           In the next valley-glades:
    Was it a vision, or a waking dream?
80   Fled is that music:—Do I wake or sleep?[3]

May 1819   1819

Ode on a Grecian Urn[1]

I

Thou still unravish'd bride of quietness,
    Thou foster-child of silence and slow time,

---

1. The young widow in the biblical Book of Ruth.
2. I.e., imagination, "the viewless wings of Poesy" of line 33.
3. See n. 3, p. 1817.
1. This urn, with its sculptured reliefs of Dionysian ecstasies, panting young lovers in flight and pursuit, a pastoral piper under spring foliage, and the quiet procession of priest and townspeople, resembles parts of various vases, sculptures, and paintings, but it existed in all its particulars only in

Keats's imagination. In the urn—which captures moments of intense experience in attitudes of grace and immobilizes them in marble—Keats found the perfect correlative for his concern with the longing for permanence in a world of change. The interpretation of the details with which he develops this concept, however, is hotly disputed, all the way from the opening phrase—is "still" an adverb ("as yet") or an adjective ("motionless")?— to the two concluding lines, which have already

Sylvan[2] historian, who canst thus express
    A flowery tale more sweetly than our rhyme:
5 What leaf-fring'd legend haunts about thy shape
    Of deities or mortals, or of both,
        In Tempe or the dales of Arcady?[3]
What men or gods are these? What maidens loth?
What mad pursuit? What struggle to escape?
10   What pipes and timbrels? What wild ecstasy?

2

Heard melodies are sweet, but those unheard
    Are sweeter; therefore, ye soft pipes, play on;
Not to the sensual ear,[4] but, more endear'd,
    Pipe to the spirit ditties of no tone:
15 Fair youth, beneath the trees, thou canst not leave
    Thy song, nor ever can those trees be bare;
        Bold lover, never, never canst thou kiss,
Though winning near the goal—yet, do not grieve;
        She cannot fade, though thou hast not thy bliss,
20 For ever wilt thou love, and she be fair!

3

Ah, happy, happy boughs! that cannot shed
    Your leaves, nor ever bid the spring adieu;
And, happy melodist, unwearied,
    For ever piping songs for ever new;
25 More happy love! more happy, happy love!
    For ever warm and still to be enjoy'd,
        For ever panting, and for ever young;
All breathing human passion far above,
    That leaves a heart high-sorrowful and cloy'd,
30   A burning forehead, and a parching tongue.

4

Who are these coming to the sacrifice?
    To what green altar, O mysterious priest,
Lead'st thou that heifer lowing at the skies,
    And all her silken flanks with garlands drest?
35 What little town by river or sea shore,
    Or mountain-built with peaceful citadel,
        Is emptied of this folk, this pious morn?
And, little town, thy streets for evermore
    Will silent be; and not a soul to tell
40   Why thou art desolate, can e'er return.

---

accumulated as much critical discussion as the "two-handed engine" in Milton's *Lycidas* or the cruxes in Shakespeare's plays. These disputes testify to the enigmatic richness of meaning in the five stanzas, as well as to the fact that the ode has become a central point of reference in the criticism of the English lyric.

2. Rustic, representing a woodland scene.
3. The valleys of Arcadia, a state in ancient Greece often used as a symbol of the pastoral ideal. "Tempe": a beautiful valley in Greece that has come to represent supreme rural beauty.
4. The ear of sense (as opposed to that of the "spirit," or imagination).

5

O Attic[5] shape! Fair attitude! with brede
   Of marble men and maidens overwrought,[6]
With forest branches and the trodden weed;
   Thou, silent form, dost tease us out of thought
45 As doth eternity: Cold Pastoral!
   When old age shall this generation waste,
     Thou shalt remain, in midst of other woe
   Than ours, a friend to man, to whom thou say'st,
"Beauty is truth, truth beauty,"[7]—that is all
50   Ye know on earth, and all ye need to know.

1819   1820

Ode on Melancholy   This is Keats's best-known statement of his recurrent theme of the mingled contrarieties of life. The remarkable last stanza, in which Melancholy becomes a veiled goddess in a mystery religion, implies that it is the tragic human destiny that beauty, joy, and life itself owe not only their quality but their value to the fact that they are transitory and turn into their opposites.

The poem once had the following initial stanza, which Keats canceled in manuscript:

Though you should build a bark of dead men's bones,
   And rear a phantom gibbet for a mast,
Stitch creeds together for a sail, with groans
   To fill it out, bloodstained and aghast;
Although your rudder be a Dragon's tail,
   Long sever'd, yet still hard with agony,
     Your cordage large uprootings from the skull
Of bald Medusa: certes you would fail
   To find the Melancholy, whether she
     Dreameth in any isle of Lethe dull.

Ode on Melancholy

1

No, no, go not to Lethe,[1] neither twist
   Wolf's-bane, tight-rooted, for its poisonous wine;
Nor suffer thy pale forehead to be kiss'd
   By nightshade, ruby grape of Proserpine;[2]

---

5. Greek. Attica was the region of Greece in which Athens was located.
6. Ornamented all over ("overwrought") with an interwoven pattern ("brede").
7. The quotation marks around this phrase are found in the volume of poems Keats published in 1820, but there are no quotation marks in the version printed in *Annals of the Fine Arts* that same year or in the transcripts of the poem made by Keats's friends. This discrepancy has multiplied the diversity of critical interpretations of the last two lines. Critics disagree whether the whole of these lines is said by the urn, or "Beauty is truth,

truth beauty" by the urn and the rest by the lyric speaker; whether the "ye" in the last line is addressed to the lyric speaker, to the readers, to the urn, or to the figures on the urn; whether "all ye know" is that beauty is truth, or this plus the statement in lines 46–48; and whether "beauty is truth" is a profound metaphysical proposition, an overstatement representing the limited point of view of the urn, or simply nonsensical.
1. The waters of forgetfulness in Hades.
2. The wife of Pluto and queen of the infernal regions. "Nightshade" and "wolf's-bane" (line 2) are poisonous plants.

⁵ Make not your rosary of yew-berries,[3]
   Nor let the beetle, nor the death-moth be
     Your mournful Psyche,[4] nor the downy owl
A partner in your sorrow's mysteries;[5]
   For shade to shade will come too drowsily,
¹⁰   And drown the wakeful anguish of the soul.[6]

2

But when the melancholy fit shall fall
   Sudden from heaven like a weeping cloud,
That fosters the droop-headed flowers all,
   And hides the green hill in an April shroud;
¹⁵ Then glut thy sorrow on a morning rose,
   Or on the rainbow of the salt sand-wave,
     Or on the wealth of globed peonies;
Or if thy mistress some rich anger shows,
   Emprison her soft hand, and let her rave,
²⁰   And feed deep, deep upon her peerless eyes.

3

She[7] dwells with Beauty—Beauty that must die;
   And Joy, whose hand is ever at his lips
Bidding adieu; and aching Pleasure nigh,
   Turning to poison while the bee-mouth sips:
²⁵ Ay, in the very temple of Delight
   Veil'd Melancholy has her sovran shrine,
     Though seen of none save him whose strenuous tongue
Can burst Joy's grape against his palate fine;[8]
His soul shall taste the sadness of her might,
³⁰   And be among her cloudy trophies hung.[9]

1819   1820

Ode on Indolence[1]

"They toil not, neither do they spin."[2]

I

One morn before me were three figures seen,
   With bowed necks, and joined hands, side-faced;

3. A symbol of death.
4. In ancient times, Psyche (the soul) was sometimes represented as a butterfly or moth, fluttering out of the mouth of a dying man. The allusion may also be to the death's-head moth, which has skull-like markings on its back. The "beetle" of line 6 refers to replicas of the large black beetle, the scarab, which were often placed by Egyptians in their tombs as a symbol of resurrection.
5. Secret religious rites.
6. I.e., sorrow needs contrast to sustain its intensity.
7. Usually taken to refer to Melancholy rather than to "thy mistress" in line 18.
8. Sensitive, subtly discriminative.

9. A reference to the Greek and Roman practice of hanging trophies in the temples of the gods.
1. On March 19, 1819, Keats wrote to George and Georgiana Keats: "This morning I am in a sort of temper indolent and supremely careless. . . . Neither Poetry, nor Ambition, nor Love have any alertness of countenance as they pass by me: they seem rather like three figures on a greek vase—a Man and two women—whom no one but myself could distinguish in their disguisement. This is the only happiness; and is a rare instance of advantage in the body overpowering the Mind." The ode was probably written soon after this time, but was not published until 1848, long after the poet's death.
2. Matthew 6.28.

And one behind the other stepp'd serene,
　　In placid sandals, and in white robes graced:
5　They pass'd, like figures on a marble urn,
　　　When shifted round to see the other side;
　　　　They came again: as when the urn once more
　　Is shifted round, the first seen shades return;
　　　And they were strange to me, as may betide
10　　　With vases, to one deep in Phidian[3] lore.

2

How is it, shadows, that I knew ye not?
　　How came ye muffled in so hush a masque?
Was it a silent deep-disguised plot
　　To steal away, and leave without a task
15　My idle days? Ripe was the drowsy hour;
　　　The blissful cloud of summer-indolence
　　　　Benumb'd my eyes; my pulse grew less and less;
　　Pain had no sting, and pleasure's wreath no flower.
　　　O, why did ye not melt, and leave my sense
20　　　Unhaunted quite of all but—nothingness?

3

A third time pass'd they by, and, passing, turn'd
　　Each one the face a moment whiles to me;
Then faded, and to follow them I burn'd
　　And ached for wings, because I knew the three:
25　The first was a fair maid, and Love her name;
　　　The second was Ambition, pale of cheek,
　　　　And ever watchful with fatigued eye;
　　The last, whom I love more, the more of blame
　　　Is heap'd upon her, maiden most unmeek,—
30　　　I knew to be my demon Poesy.

4

They faded, and, forsooth! I wanted wings:
　　O folly! What is Love? and where is it?
And for that poor Ambition—it springs
　　From a man's little heart's short fever-fit;
35　For Poesy!—no,—she has not a joy,—
　　　At least for me,—so sweet as drowsy noons,
　　　　And evenings steep'd in honied indolence;
　　O, for an age so shelter'd from annoy,
　　　That I may never know how change the moons,
40　　　Or hear the voice of busy common-sense!

5

A third time came they by;—alas! wherefore?
　　My sleep had been embroider'd with dim dreams;
My soul had been a lawn besprinkled o'er

---

3. Phidias was the great Athenian sculptor of the 5th century B.C.E. who designed the marble sculptures
for the Parthenon.

With flowers, and stirring shades, and baffled beams:
45 The morn was clouded, but no shower fell,
        Though in her lids hung the sweet tears of May;
        The open casement press'd a new-leaved vine,
        Let in the budding warmth and throstle's lay;
    O shadows! 'twas a time to bid farewell!
50   Upon your skirts had fallen no tears of mine.

6

    So, ye three ghosts, adieu! Ye cannot raise
        My head cool-bedded in the flowery grass;
    For I would not be dieted with praise,
        A pet-lamb in a sentimental farce![4]
55 Fade softly from my eyes, and be once more
        In masque-like figures on the dreamy urn;
        Farewell! I yet have visions for the night,
    And for the day faint visions there is store;
        Vanish, ye phantoms, from my idle spright,°   *spirit*
60   Into the clouds, and never more return!

Spring 1819   1848

Lamia

In a note printed at the end of the poem, Keats cited as his source the following story in Robert Burton's *Anatomy of Melancholy* (1621):

One Menippus Lycius, a young man twenty-five years of age, that going betwixt Cenchreas and Corinth, met such a phantasm in the habit of a fair gentlewoman, which, taking him by the hand, carried him home to her house, in the suburbs of Corinth. . . . The young man, a philosopher, otherwise staid and discreet, able to moderate his passions, though not this of love, tarried with her a while to his great content, and at last married her, to whose wedding, amongst other guests, came Apollonius; who, by some probable conjectures, found her out to be a serpent, a lamia; and that all her furniture was, like Tantalus's gold, described by Homer, no substance but mere illusions. When she saw herself descried, she wept, and desired Apollonius to be silent, but he would not be moved, and thereupon she, plate, house, and all that was in it, vanished in an instant: many thousands took notice of this fact, for it was done in the midst of Greece.

In ancient demonology, a "lamia" was a monster in woman's form who preyed on human beings. There are various clues that Keats invested the ancient legend with allegorical significance (see especially 2.229–38). Its interpretation, however, and even the inclination of Keats's own sympathies in the contest between Lamia and Apollonius, have been disputed. Perhaps Keats simply failed to make up his mind or wavered in the course of composition. In any case, the poem presents an inevitably fatal situation, in which no one is entirely blameless or blameworthy and no character monopolizes either our sympathy or antipathy. Lamia is an enchantress, a liar, and a calculating expert in *amour*; but she apparently intends no harm, is genuinely in love, and is very beautiful. And both male protagonists exhibit culpable extremes. Lycius,

---

4. In a letter of June 9, 1819, Keats wrote: "I have been very idle lately, very averse to writing; both from the overpowering idea of our dead poets and from abatement of my love of fame. I hope I am a little more of a Philosopher than I was, conse-quently a little less of a versifying Pet-lamb. . . . You will judge of my 1819 temper when I tell you that the thing I have most enjoyed this year has been writing an ode to Indolence."

though an attractive young lover, is gullible, a slave to his passions, and capable of gratuitous cruelty; while Apollonius, though realistically clear-sighted, is rigid, puritanical, and inhumane.

The poem, written between late June and early September 1819, is a return, after the Spenserian stanzas of *The Eve of St. Agnes,* to the pentameter couplets Keats had used in *Endymion* and other early poems. But Keats had in the meantime been studying John Dryden's closed and strong-paced couplets. The initial lines of Dryden's version of Boccaccio's story *Cymon and Iphigenia* demonstrate the kind of narrative model that helped Keats make the technical transition from the fluent but sprawling gracefulness of the opening of *Endymion* to the vigor and economy of the opening of *Lamia:*

> In that sweet isle where Venus keeps her court,
> And every grace, and all the loves, resort;
> Where either sex is formed of softer earth,
> And takes the bent of pleasure from their birth;
> There lived a Cyprian lord, above the rest
> Wise, wealthy, with a numerous issue blessed. . . .

Lamia

Part 1

Upon a time, before the faery broods
Drove Nymph and Satyr[1] from the prosperous woods,
Before King Oberon's bright diadem,
Sceptre, and mantle, clasp'd with dewy gem,
5 Frighted away the Dryads and the Fauns
From rushes green, and brakes,° and cowslip'd lawns,   *thickets*
The ever-smitten Hermes[2] empty left
His golden throne, bent warm on amorous theft:
From high Olympus had he stolen light,
10 On this side of Jove's clouds, to escape the sight
Of his great summoner, and made retreat
Into a forest on the shores of Crete.
For somewhere in that sacred island dwelt
A nymph, to whom all hoofed Satyrs knelt;
15 At whose white feet the languid Tritons[3] poured
Pearls, while on land they wither'd and adored.
Fast by the springs where she to bathe was wont,
And in those meads where sometime she might haunt,
Were strewn rich gifts, unknown to any Muse,
20 Though Fancy's casket were unlock'd to choose.
Ah, what a world of love was at her feet!
So Hermes thought, and a celestial heat
Burnt from his winged heels to either ear,
That from a whiteness, as the lily clear,
25 Blush'd into roses 'mid his golden hair,
Fallen in jealous curls about his shoulders bare.[4]

---

1. Nymphs and satyrs—like the dryads and fauns in line 5—were minor classical deities of the woods and fields, said here to have been driven off by Oberon, king of the fairies, who were supernatural beings of the postclassical era.
2. Or Mercury; wing-footed messenger at the

summons of Jove (line 11), Hermes was notoriously amorous.
3. Minor sea gods.
4. I.e., the curls clung jealously to his bare shoulders. This line is the first of a number of Alexandrines, a six-foot line, used to vary the metrical

From vale to vale, from wood to wood, he flew,
Breathing upon the flowers his passion new,
And wound with many a river to its head,
30 To find where this sweet nymph prepar'd her secret bed:
In vain; the sweet nymph might nowhere be found,
And so he rested, on the lonely ground,
Pensive, and full of painful jealousies
Of the Wood-Gods, and even the very trees.
35 There as he stood, he heard a mournful voice,
Such as once heard, in gentle heart, destroys
All pain but pity: thus the lone voice spake:
"When from this wreathed tomb shall I awake!
When move in a sweet body fit for life,
40 And love, and pleasure, and the ruddy strife
Of hearts and lips! Ah, miserable me!"
The God, dove-footed,⁵ glided silently
Round bush and tree, soft-brushing, in his speed,
The taller grasses and full-flowering weed,
45 Until he found a palpitating snake,
Bright, and cirque-couchant⁶ in a dusky brake.

   She was a gordian⁷ shape of dazzling hue,
Vermilion-spotted, golden, green, and blue;
Striped like a zebra, freckled like a pard,°   leopard
50 Eyed like a peacock,⁸ and all crimson barr'd;
And full of silver moons, that, as she breathed,
Dissolv'd, or brighter shone, or interwreathed
Their lustres with the gloomier tapestries—
So rainbow-sided, touch'd with miseries,
55 She seem'd, at once, some penanced lady elf,
Some demon's mistress, or the demon's self.
Upon her crest she wore a wannish⁹ fire
Sprinkled with stars, like Ariadne's tiar:¹
Her head was serpent, but ah, bitter-sweet!
60 She had a woman's mouth with all its pearls² complete:
And for her eyes: what could such eyes do there
But weep, and weep, that they were born so fair?
As Proserpine still weeps for her Sicilian air.³
Her throat was serpent, but the words she spake
65 Came, as through bubbling honey, for Love's sake,
And thus; while Hermes on his pinions lay,
Like a stoop'd falcon⁴ ere he takes his prey.

   "Fair Hermes, crown'd with feathers, fluttering light,
I had a splendid dream of thee last night:

---

movement—a device that Keats learned from Dryden. Another such device is the triplet, occurring
first in lines 61–63.
5. I.e., quietly as a dove.
6. Lying in a circular coil.
7. Intricately twisted, like the knot tied by King
Gordius, which no one could undo.
8. Having multicolored spots, like the "eyes" in a
peacock's tail.
9. Rather dark.

1. Ariadne, who was transformed into a constellation, had been represented in a painting by Titian
wearing a symbolic crown, or tiara ("tiar"), of stars.
2. "Pearls" had become almost a synonym for
teeth in Elizabethan love poems.
3. Proserpine had been carried off to Hades by
Pluto from the field of Enna, in Sicily.
4. *Stoop* is the term for the plunge of a falcon on
his prey.

70 I saw thee sitting, on a throne of gold,
 Among the Gods, upon Olympus old,
 The only sad one; for thou didst not hear
 The soft, lute-finger'd Muses chaunting clear,
 Nor even Apollo when he sang alone,
75 Deaf to his throbbing throat's long, long melodious moan.
 I dreamt I saw thee, robed in purple flakes,
 Break amorous through the clouds, as morning breaks,
 And, swiftly as a bright Phœbean dart,[5]
 Strike for the Cretan isle; and here thou art!
80 Too gentle Hermes, hast thou found the maid?"
 Whereat the star of Lethe[6] not delay'd
 His rosy eloquence, and thus inquired:
 "Thou smooth-lipp'd serpent, surely high inspired!
 Thou beauteous wreath, with melancholy eyes,
85 Possess whatever bliss thou canst devise,
 Telling me only where my nymph is fled,—
 Where she doth breathe!" "Bright planet, thou hast said,"
 Return'd the snake, "but seal with oaths, fair God!"
 "I swear," said Hermes, "by my serpent rod,
90 And by thine eyes, and by thy starry crown!"
 Light flew his earnest words, among the blossoms blown.
 Then thus again the brilliance feminine:
 "Too frail of heart! for this lost nymph of thine,
 Free as the air, invisibly, she strays
95 About these thornless wilds; her pleasant days
 She tastes unseen; unseen her nimble feet
 Leave traces in the grass and flowers sweet;
 From weary tendrils, and bow'd branches green,
 She plucks the fruit unseen, she bathes unseen:
100 And by my power is her beauty veil'd
 To keep it unaffronted, unassail'd
 By the love-glances of unlovely eyes,
 Of Satyrs, Fauns, and blear'd Silenus'[7] sighs.
 Pale grew her immortality, for woe
105 Of all these lovers, and she grieved so
 I took compassion on her, bade her steep
 Her hair in weïrd° syrops, that would keep   *magical*
 Her loveliness invisible, yet free
 To wander as she loves, in liberty.
110 Thou shalt behold her, Hermes, thou alone,
 If thou wilt, as thou swearest, grant my boon!"
 Then, once again, the charmed God began
 An oath, and through the serpent's ears it ran
 Warm, tremulous, devout, psalterian.[8]
115 Ravish'd, she lifted her Circean head,
 Blush'd a live damask,[9] and swift-lisping said,

---

5. A ray of Phoebus Apollo, god of the sun.
6. Hermes, when he appeared like a star on the banks of Lethe, in the darkness of Hades. (One of Hermes' offices was to guide the souls of the dead to the lower regions.)
7. Satyr, tutor of Bacchus, usually represented as drunk.
8. Either "like a psalm" or "like the sound of the psaltery" (an ancient stringed instrument).
9. The color of a damask rose (large and fragrant pink rose). "Circean": like that of Circe, the enchantress in the *Odyssey*.

"I was a woman, let me have once more
A woman's shape, and charming as before.
I love a youth of Corinth—O the bliss!
120 Give me my woman's form, and place me where he is.
Stoop, Hermes, let me breathe upon thy brow,
And thou shalt see thy sweet nymph even now."
The God on half-shut feathers sank serene,
She breath'd upon his eyes, and swift was seen
125 Of both the guarded nymph near-smiling on the green.
It was no dream; or say a dream it was,
Real are the dreams of Gods, and smoothly pass
Their pleasures in a long immortal dream.
One warm, flush'd moment, hovering, it might seem
130 Dash'd by the wood-nymph's beauty, so he burn'd;
Then, lighting on the printless verdure, turn'd
To the swoon'd serpent, and with languid arm,
Delicate, put to proof the lythe Caducean charm.[1]
So done, upon the nymph his eyes he bent
135 Full of adoring tears and blandishment,
And towards her stept: she, like a moon in wane,
Faded before him, cower'd, nor could restrain
Her fearful sobs, self-folding like a flower
That faints into itself at evening hour:
140 But the God fostering her chilled hand,
She felt the warmth, her eyelids open'd bland,°   *softly*
And, like new flowers at morning song of bees,
Bloom'd, and gave up her honey to the lees.°   *dregs*
Into the green-recessed woods they flew;
145 Nor grew they pale, as mortal lovers do.

     Left to herself, the serpent now began
To change; her elfin blood in madness ran,
Her mouth foam'd, and the grass, therewith besprent,°   *sprinkled*
Wither'd at dew so sweet and virulent;
150 Her eyes in torture fix'd, and anguish drear,
Hot, glaz'd, and wide, with lid-lashes all sear,
Flash'd phosphor and sharp sparks, without one cooling tear.
The colours all inflam'd throughout her train,
She writh'd about, convuls'd with scarlet pain:
155 A deep volcanian yellow took the place
Of all her milder-mooned body's grace;[2]
And, as the lava ravishes the mead,
Spoilt all her silver mail, and golden brede;[3]
Made gloom of all her frecklings, streaks and bars,
160 Eclips'd her crescents, and lick'd up her stars:
So that, in moments few, she was undrest
Of all her sapphires, greens, and amethyst,
And rubious-argent:° of all these bereft,   *silvery red*
Nothing but pain and ugliness were left.

1. I.e., put to the test the magic of the flexible
Caduceus (Hermes' official staff).
2. I.e., the yellow of sulfur (thrown up by a volcano) replaced her former silvery moon color.
3. Embroidery, interwoven pattern. "Mail": inter-
linked rings, as in a coat of armor.

165　Still shone her crown; that vanish'd, also she
　　　Melted and disappear'd as suddenly;
　　　And in the air, her new voice luting soft,
　　　Cried, "Lycius! gentle Lycius!"—Borne aloft
　　　With the bright mists about the mountains hoar
170　These words dissolv'd: Crete's forests heard no more.

　　　　　Whither fled Lamia, now a lady bright,
　　　A full-born beauty new and exquisite?
　　　She fled into that valley they pass o'er
　　　Who go to Corinth from Cenchreas' shore;[4]
175　And rested at the foot of those wild hills,
　　　The rugged founts of the Peæran rills,
　　　And of that other ridge whose barren back
　　　Stretches, with all its mist and cloudy rack,
　　　South-westward to Cleone. There she stood
180　About a young bird's flutter from a wood,
　　　Fair, on a sloping green of mossy tread,
　　　By a clear pool, wherein she passioned[5]
　　　To see herself escap'd from so sore ills,
　　　While her robes flaunted with the daffodils.

185　　　Ah, happy Lycius!—for she was a maid
　　　More beautiful than ever twisted braid,
　　　Or sigh'd, or blush'd, or on spring-flowered lea°　　　*meadow*
　　　Spread a green kirtle° to the minstrelsy:　　　*gown*
　　　A virgin purest lipp'd, yet in the lore
190　Of love deep learned to the red heart's core:
　　　Not one hour old, yet of sciential brain
　　　To unperplex bliss from its neighbour pain;
　　　Define their pettish limits, and estrange
　　　Their points of contact, and swift counterchange;[6]
195　Intrigue with the specious chaos,[7] and dispart
　　　Its most ambiguous atoms with sure art;
　　　As though in Cupid's college she had spent
　　　Sweet days a lovely graduate, still unshent,°　　　*unspoiled*
　　　And kept his rosy terms[8] in idle languishment.

200　　　Why this fair creature chose so fairily
　　　By the wayside to linger, we shall see;
　　　But first 'tis fit to tell how she could muse
　　　And dream, when in the serpent prison-house,
　　　Of all she list,° strange or magnificent:　　　*wished*
205　How, ever, where she will'd, her spirit went;
　　　Whether to faint Elysium, or where
　　　Down through tress-lifting waves the Nereids[9] fair

4. Cenchrea (Keats's "Cenchreas") was a harbor of Corinth, in southern Greece.
5. Felt intense excitement.
6. I.e., of knowledgeable ("sciential") brain to disentangle ("unperplex") bliss from its closely related pain, to define their quarreled-over ("pettish") limits, and to separate out ("estrange") their points of contact and the swift changes of each condition into its opposite. Cf. Keats's *Ode on Melancholy*, lines 21–26 (p. 1823).
7. I.e., turn to her own artful purpose the seeming ("specious") chaos.
8. The terms spent studying in "Cupid's college."
9. Sea nymphs, of whom Thetis (line 208, the mother of Achilles) was one.

Wind into Thetis' bower by many a pearly stair;
Or where God Bacchus drains his cups divine,
210 Stretch'd out, at ease, beneath a glutinous pine;
Or where in Pluto's gardens palatine°   *palatial*
Mulciber's columns gleam in far piazzian line.[1]
And sometimes into cities she would send
Her dream, with feast and rioting to blend;
215 And once, while among mortals dreaming thus,
She saw the young Corinthian Lycius
Charioting foremost in the envious race,
Like a young Jove with calm uneager face,
And fell into a swooning love of him.
220 Now on the moth-time of that evening dim
He would return that way, as well she knew,
To Corinth from the shore; for freshly blew
The eastern soft wind, and his galley now
Grated the quaystones with her brazen prow
225 In port Cenchreas, from Egina isle
Fresh anchor'd; whither he had been awhile
To sacrifice to Jove, whose temple there
Waits with high marble doors for blood and incense rare.
Jove heard his vows, and better'd his desire;
230 For by some freakful chance he made retire
From his companions, and set forth to walk,
Perhaps grown wearied of their Corinth talk:
Over the solitary hills he fared,
Thoughtless at first, but ere eve's star appeared
235 His phantasy was lost, where reason fades,
In the calm'd twilight of Platonic shades.[2]
Lamia beheld him coming, near, more near—
Close to her passing, in indifference drear,
His silent sandals swept the mossy green;
240 So neighbour'd to him, and yet so unseen
She stood: he pass'd, shut up in mysteries,
His mind wrapp'd like his mantle, while her eyes
Follow'd his steps, and her neck regal white
Turn'd—syllabling thus, "Ah, Lycius bright,
245 And will you leave me on the hills alone?
Lycius, look back! and be some pity shown."
He did; not with cold wonder fearingly,
But Orpheus-like at an Eurydice;[3]
For so delicious were the words she sung,
250 It seem'd he had lov'd them a whole summer long:
And soon his eyes had drunk her beauty up,
Leaving no drop in the bewildering cup,
And still the cup was full,—while he, afraid
Lest she should vanish ere his lip had paid

---

1. I.e., columns made by Mulciber (Vulcan, god of fire and metalworking) gleam in long lines around open courts (piazzas).
2. I.e., he was absorbed in musing about the obscurities of Plato's philosophy.
3. As Orpheus looked at Eurydice in Hades. Orpheus was allowed by Pluto to lead Eurydice back to earth on condition that he not look back at her, but he could not resist doing so, hence lost her once more.

255 Due adoration, thus began to adore;
Her soft look growing coy, she saw his chain so sure:
"Leave thee alone! Look back! Ah, Goddess, see
Whether my eyes can ever turn from thee!
For pity do not this sad heart belie[4]—
260 Even as thou vanishest so I shall die.
Stay! though a Naiad of the rivers, stay!
To thy far wishes will thy streams obey:
Stay! though the greenest woods be thy domain,
Alone they can drink up the morning rain:
265 Though a descended Pleiad,[5] will not one
Of thine harmonious sisters keep in tune
Thy spheres, and as thy silver proxy shine?
So sweetly to these ravish'd ears of mine
Came thy sweet greeting, that if thou shouldst fade
270 Thy memory will waste me to a shade:—
For pity do not melt!"—"If I should stay,"
Said Lamia, "here, upon this floor of clay,
And pain my steps upon these flowers too rough,
What canst thou say or do of charm enough
275 To dull the nice[6] remembrance of my home?
Thou canst not ask me with thee here to roam
Over these hills and vales, where no joy is,—
Empty of immortality and bliss!
Thou art a scholar, Lycius, and must know
280 That finer spirits cannot breathe below
In human climes, and live: Alas! poor youth,
What taste of purer air hast thou to soothe
My essence? What serener palaces,
Where I may all my many senses please,
285 And by mysterious sleights a hundred thirsts appease?
It cannot be—Adieu!" So said, she rose
Tiptoe with white arms spread. He, sick to lose
The amorous promise of her lone complain,
Swoon'd, murmuring of love, and pale with pain.
290 The cruel lady, without any show
Of sorrow for her tender favourite's woe,
But rather, if her eyes could brighter be,
With brighter eyes and slow amenity,
Put her new lips to his, and gave afresh
295 The life she had so tangled in her mesh:
And as he from one trance was wakening
Into another, she began to sing,
Happy in beauty, life, and love, and every thing,
A song of love, too sweet for earthly lyres,
300 While, like held breath, the stars drew in their panting fires.
And then she whisper'd in such trembling tone,
As those who, safe together met alone

4. Be false to.
5. One of the seven sisters composing the constellation Pleiades.
6. Detailed, minutely accurate.

For the first time through many anguish'd days,
Use other speech than looks; bidding him raise
305His drooping head, and clear his soul of doubt,
For that she was a woman, and without
Any more subtle fluid in her veins
Than throbbing blood, and that the self-same pains
Inhabited her frail-strung heart as his.
310And next she wonder'd how his eyes could miss
Her face so long in Corinth, where, she said,
She dwelt but half retir'd, and there had led
Days happy as the gold coin could invent
Without the aid of love; yet in content
315Till she saw him, as once she pass'd him by,
Where 'gainst a column he leant thoughtfully
At Venus' temple porch, 'mid baskets heap'd
Of amorous herbs and flowers, newly reap'd
Late on that eve, as 'twas the night before
320The Adonian feast;[7] whereof she saw no more,
But wept alone those days, for why should she adore?
Lycius from death awoke into amaze,
To see her still, and singing so sweet lays;
Then from amaze into delight he fell
325To hear her whisper woman's lore so well;
And every word she spake entic'd him on
To unperplex'd delight[8] and pleasure known.
Let the mad poets say whate'er they please
Of the sweets of Fairies, Peris,[9] Goddesses,
330There is not such a treat among them all,
Haunters of cavern, lake, and waterfall,
As a real woman, lineal indeed
From Pyrrha's pebbles[1] or old Adam's seed.
Thus gentle Lamia judg'd, and judg'd aright,
335That Lycius could not love in half a fright,
So threw the goddess off, and won his heart
More pleasantly by playing woman's part,
With no more awe than what her beauty gave,
That, while it smote, still guaranteed to save.
340Lycius to all made eloquent reply,
Marrying to every word a twinborn sigh;
And last, pointing to Corinth, ask'd her sweet,
If 'twas too far that night for her soft feet.
The way was short, for Lamia's eagerness
345Made, by a spell, the triple league decrease
To a few paces; not at all surmised
By blinded Lycius, so in her comprized.[2]
They pass'd the city gates, he knew not how,
So noiseless, and he never thought to know.

---

7. The feast of Adonis, beloved by Venus.
8. I.e., delight not mixed with its neighbor, pain
(see line 192).
9. Fairylike creatures in Persian mythology.

1. Descended from the pebbles with which, in
Greek myth, Pyrrha and Deucalion repeopled the
earth after the flood.
2. Bound up, absorbed.

350   As men talk in a dream, so Corinth all,
       Throughout her palaces imperial,
       And all her populous streets and temples lewd,[3]
       Mutter'd, like tempest in the distance brew'd,
       To the wide-spreaded night above her towers.
355   Men, women, rich and poor, in the cool hours,
       Shuffled their sandals o'er the pavement white,
       Companion'd or alone; while many a light
       Flared, here and there, from wealthy festivals,
       And threw their moving shadows on the walls,
360   Or found them cluster'd in the corniced shade
       Of some arch'd temple door, or dusky colonnade.

       Muffling his face, of greeting friends in fear,
       Her fingers he press'd hard, as one came near
       With curl'd gray beard, sharp eyes, and smooth bald crown,
365   Slow-stepp'd, and robed in philosophic gown:
       Lycius shrank closer, as they met and past,
       Into his mantle, adding wings to haste,
       While hurried Lamia trembled: "Ah," said he,
       "Why do you shudder, love, so ruefully?
370   Why does your tender palm dissolve in dew?"—
       "I'm wearied," said fair Lamia: "tell me who
       Is that old man? I cannot bring to mind
       His features:—Lycius! wherefore did you blind
       Yourself from his quick eyes?" Lycius replied,
375   " 'Tis Apollonius sage, my trusty guide
       And good instructor; but to-night he seems
       The ghost of folly haunting my sweet dreams."

       While yet he spake they had arrived before
       A pillar'd porch, with lofty portal door,
380   Where hung a silver lamp, whose phosphor glow
       Reflected in the slabbed steps below,
       Mild as a star in water; for so new,
       And so unsullied was the marble hue,
       So through the crystal polish, liquid fine,
385   Ran the dark veins, that none but feet divine
       Could e'er have touch'd there. Sounds Æolian[4]
       Breath'd from the hinges, as the ample span
       Of the wide doors disclos'd a place unknown
       Some time to any, but those two alone,
390   And a few Persian mutes, who that same year
       Were seen about the markets: none knew where
       They could inhabit; the most curious
       Were foil'd, who watch'd to trace them to their house:
       And but the flitter-winged verse must tell,
395   For truth's sake, what woe afterwards befel,

3. Temples of Venus, whose worship sometimes involved ritual prostitution.
4. Like sounds from the wind harp (Aeolus is god of winds), which responds musically to a current of air.

'Twould humour many a heart to leave them thus,
Shut from the busy world of more incredulous.

Part 2

Love in a hut, with water and a crust,
Is—Love, forgive us!—cinders, ashes, dust;
Love in a palace is perhaps at last
More grievous torment than a hermit's fast:—
5   That is a doubtful tale from faery land,
Hard for the non-elect to understand.
Had Lycius liv'd to hand his story down,
He might have given the moral a fresh frown,
Or clench'd it quite: but too short was their bliss
10   To breed distrust and hate, that make the soft voice hiss.
Besides, there, nightly, with terrific glare,
Love, jealous grown of so complete a pair,
Hover'd and buzz'd his wings, with fearful roar,
Above the lintel of their chamber door,
15   And down the passage cast a glow upon the floor.

    For all this came a ruin: side by side
They were enthroned, in the even tide,
Upon a couch, near to a curtaining
Whose airy texture, from a golden string,
20   Floated into the room, and let appear
Unveil'd the summer heaven, blue and clear,
Betwixt two marble shafts:—there they reposed,
Where use had made it sweet, with eyelids closed,
Saving a tythe which love still open kept,
25   That they might see each other while they almost slept;
When from the slope side of a suburb hill,
Deafening the swallow's twitter, came a thrill
Of trumpets—Lycius started—the sounds fled,
But left a thought, a buzzing in his head.
30   For the first time, since first he harbour'd in
That purple-lined palace of sweet sin,
His spirit pass'd beyond its golden bourn
Into the noisy world almost forsworn.
The lady, ever watchful, penetrant,
35   Saw this with pain, so arguing a want
Of something more, more than her empery°   empire
Of joys; and she began to moan and sigh
Because he mused beyond her, knowing well
That but a moment's thought is passion's passing bell.°   death knell
40   "Why do you sigh, fair creature?" whisper'd he:
"Why do you think?" return'd she tenderly:
"You have deserted me;—where am I now?
Not in your heart while care weighs on your brow:
No, no, you have dismiss'd me; and I go
45   From your breast houseless: ay, it must be so."

He answer'd, bending to her open eyes,
Where he was mirror'd small in paradise,
"My silver planet, both of eve and morn![5]
Why will you plead yourself so sad forlorn,
50 While I am striving how to fill my heart
With deeper crimson, and a double smart?
How to entangle, trammel up and snare
Your soul in mine, and labyrinth you there
Like the hid scent in an unbudded rose?
55 Ay, a sweet kiss—you see your mighty woes.[6]
My thoughts! shall I unveil them? Listen then!
What mortal hath a prize, that other men
May be confounded and abash'd withal,
But lets it sometimes pace abroad majestical,
60 And triumph, as in thee I should rejoice
Amid the hoarse alarm of Corinth's voice.
Let my foes choke, and my friends shout afar,
While through the thronged streets your bridal car
Wheels round its dazzling spokes."—The lady's cheek
65 Trembled; she nothing said, but, pale and meek,
Arose and knelt before him, wept a rain
Of sorrows at his words; at last with pain
Beseeching him, the while his hand she wrung,
To change his purpose. He thereat was stung,
70 Perverse, with stronger fancy to reclaim
Her wild and timid nature to his aim:
Besides, for all his love, in self despite,
Against his better self, he took delight
Luxurious in her sorrows, soft and new.
75 His passion, cruel grown, took on a hue
Fierce and sanguineous as 'twas possible
In one whose brow had no dark veins to swell.
Fine was the mitigated fury, like
Apollo's presence when in act to strike
80 The serpent—Ha, the serpent! certes, she
Was none. She burnt, she lov'd the tyranny,
And, all subdued, consented to the hour
When to the bridal he should lead his paramour.
Whispering in midnight silence, said the youth,
85 "Sure some sweet name thou hast, though, by my truth,
I have not ask'd it, ever thinking thee
Not mortal, but of heavenly progeny,
As still I do. Hast any mortal name,
Fit appellation for this dazzling frame?
90 Or friends or kinsfolk on the citied earth,
To share our marriage feast and nuptial mirth?"
"I have no friends," said Lamia, "no, not one;
My presence in wide Corinth hardly known:
My parents' bones are in their dusty urns

5. The planet Venus, which is both the morning and the evening star.

6. Playfully: "You see how great your troubles were!"

95   Sepulchred, where no kindled incense burns,
Seeing all their luckless race are dead, save me,
And I neglect the holy rite for thee.
Even as you list invite your many guests;
But if, as now it seems, your vision rests
100 With any pleasure on me, do not bid
Old Apollonius—from him keep me hid."
Lycius, perplex'd at words so blind and blank,
Made close inquiry; from whose touch she shrank,
Feigning a sleep; and he to the dull shade
105 Of deep sleep in a moment was betray'd.

     It was the custom then to bring away,
The bride from home at blushing shut of day,
Veil'd, in a chariot, heralded along
By strewn flowers, torches, and a marriage song,
110 With other pageants: but this fair unknown
Had not a friend. So being left alone,
(Lycius was gone to summon all his kin)
And knowing surely she could never win
His foolish heart from its mad pompousness,
115 She set herself, high-thoughted, how to dress
The misery in fit magnificence.
She did so, but 'tis doubtful how and whence
Came, and who were her subtle servitors.
About the halls, and to and from the doors,
120 There was a noise of wings, till in short space
The glowing banquet-room shone with wide-arched grace.
A haunting music, sole perhaps and lone
Supportress of the faery-roof, made moan
Throughout, as fearful the whole charm might fade.
125 Fresh carved cedar, mimicking a glade
Of palm and plantain, met from either side,
High in the midst, in honour of the bride:
Two palms and then two plantains, and so on,
From either side their stems branch'd one to one
130 All down the aisled place; and beneath all
There ran a stream of lamps straight on from wall to wall.
So canopied, lay an untasted feast
Teeming with odours. Lamia, regal drest,
Silently paced about, and as she went,
135 In pale contented sort of discontent,
Mission'd her viewless servants to enrich
The fretted[7] splendour of each nook and niche.
Between the tree-stems, marbled plain at first,
Came jasper pannels; then, anon, there burst
140 Forth creeping imagery of slighter trees,
And with the larger wove in small intricacies.
Approving all, she faded at self-will,
And shut the chamber up, close, hush'd and still,

---

7. Adorned with fretwork (interlaced patterns).

Complete and ready for the revels rude,
145 When dreadful° guests would come to spoil her solitude.   *terrifying*

    The day appear'd, and all the gossip rout.
O senseless Lycius! Madman! wherefore flout
The silent-blessing fate, warm cloister'd hours,
And show to common eyes these secret bowers?
150 The herd approach'd; each guest, with busy brain,
Arriving at the portal, gaz'd amain,°   *intently*
And enter'd marveling: for they knew the street,
Remember'd it from childhood all complete
Without a gap, yet ne'er before had seen
155 That royal porch, that high-built fair demesne;°   *estate*
So in they hurried all, maz'd, curious and keen:
Save one, who look'd thereon with eye severe,
And with calm-planted steps walk'd in austere;
'Twas Apollonius: something too he laugh'd,
160 As though some knotty problem, that had daft°   *baffled*
His patient thought, had now begun to thaw,
And solve and melt:—'twas just as he foresaw.

    He met within the murmurous vestibule
His young disciple. " 'Tis no common rule,
165 Lycius," said he, "for uninvited guest
To force himself upon you, and infest
With an unbidden presence the bright throng
Of younger friends; yet must I do this wrong,
And you forgive me." Lycius blush'd, and led
170 The old man through the inner doors broad-spread;
With reconciling words and courteous mien
Turning into sweet milk the sophist's spleen.

    Of wealthy lustre was the banquet-room,
Fill'd with pervading brilliance and perfume:
175 Before each lucid pannel fuming stood
A censer fed with myrrh and spiced wood,
Each by a sacred tripod held aloft,
Whose slender feet wide-swerv'd upon the soft
Wool-woofed° carpets: fifty wreaths of smoke   *woven*
180 From fifty censers their light voyage took
To the high roof, still mimick'd as they rose
Along the mirror'd walls by twin-clouds odorous.
Twelve sphered tables, by silk seats insphered,
High as the level of a man's breast rear'd
185 On libbard's° paws, upheld the heavy gold   *leopard's*
Of cups and goblets, and the store thrice told
Of Ceres' horn,[8] and, in huge vessels, wine
Come from the gloomy tun with merry shine.
Thus loaded with a feast the tables stood,
190 Each shrining in the midst the image of a God.

8. The horn of plenty, overflowing with the products of Ceres, goddess of grain.

When in an antichamber every guest
Had felt the cold full sponge to pleasure press'd,
By minist'ring slaves, upon his hands and feet,
And fragrant oils with ceremony meet
195 Pour'd on his hair, they all mov'd to the feast
In white robes, and themselves in order placed
Around the silken couches, wondering
Whence all this mighty cost and blaze of wealth could spring.

Soft went the music the soft air along,
200 While fluent Greek a vowel'd undersong
Kept up among the guests, discoursing low
At first, for scarcely was the wine at flow;
But when the happy vintage touch'd their brains,
Louder they talk, and louder come the strains
205 Of powerful instruments:—the gorgeous dyes,
The space, the splendour of the draperies,
The roof of awful richness, nectarous cheer,
Beautiful slaves, and Lamia's self, appear,
Now, when the wine has done its rosy deed,
210 And every soul from human trammels freed,
No more so strange; for merry wine, sweet wine,
Will make Elysian shades not too fair, too divine.

Soon was God Bacchus at meridian height;
Flush'd were their cheeks, and bright eyes double bright:
215 Garlands of every green, and every scent
From vales deflower'd, or forest-trees branch-rent,
In baskets of bright osier'd[9] gold were brought
High as the handles heap'd, to suit the thought
Of every guest; that each, as he did please,
220 Might fancy-fit his brows, silk-pillow'd at his ease.

What wreath for Lamia? What for Lycius?
What for the sage, old Apollonius?
Upon her aching forehead be there hung
The leaves of willow and of adder's tongue;[1]
225 And for the youth, quick, let us strip for him
The thyrsus,[2] that his watching eyes may swim
Into forgetfulness; and, for the sage,
Let spear-grass and the spiteful thistle wage
War on his temples. Do not all charms fly
230 At the mere touch of cold philosophy?[3]
There was an awful° rainbow once in heaven: awe-inspiring
We know her woof, her texture; she is given
In the dull catalogue of common things.

---

9. Plaited. An "osier" is a strip of willow used in weaving baskets.
1. A fern whose spikes resemble a serpent's tongue.
2. The vine-covered staff of Bacchus, used to signify drunkenness.
3. In the sense of "natural philosophy," or science.

Benjamin Haydon tells in his *Autobiography* how, at a hard-drinking and high-spirited dinner party, Keats had agreed with Charles Lamb (to what extent jokingly, it is not clear) that Newton's *Optics* "had destroyed all the poetry of the rainbow by reducing it to the prismatic colors."

Philosophy will clip an Angel's wings,
235 Conquer all mysteries by rule and line,
Empty the haunted air, and gnomed mine[4]—
Unweave a rainbow, as it erewhile made
The tender-person'd Lamia melt into a shade.

By her glad Lycius sitting, in chief place,
240 Scarce saw in all the room another face,
Till, checking his love trance, a cup he took
Full brimm'd, and opposite sent forth a look
'Cross the broad table, to beseech a glance
From his old teacher's wrinkled countenance,
245 And pledge[5] him. The bald-head philosopher
Had fix'd his eye, without a twinkle or stir
Full on the alarmed beauty of the bride,
Brow-beating her fair form, and troubling her sweet pride.
Lycius then press'd her hand, with devout touch,
250 As pale it lay upon the rosy couch:
'Twas icy, and the cold ran through his veins;
Then sudden it grew hot, and all the pains
Of an unnatural heat shot to his heart.
"Lamia, what means this? Wherefore dost thou start?
255 Know'st thou that man?" Poor Lamia answer'd not.
He gaz'd into her eyes, and not a jot
Own'd° they the lovelorn piteous appeal: acknowledged
More, more he gaz'd: his human senses reel:
Some hungry spell that loveliness absorbs;
260 There was no recognition in those orbs.
"Lamia!" he cried—and no soft-toned reply.
The many heard, and the loud revelry
Grew hush; the stately music no more breathes;
The myrtle[6] sicken'd in a thousand wreaths.
265 By faint degrees, voice, lute, and pleasure ceased;
A deadly silence step by step increased,
Until it seem'd a horrid presence there,
And not a man but felt the terror in his hair.
"Lamia!" he shriek'd; and nothing but the shriek
270 With its sad echo did the silence break.
"Begone, foul dream!" he cried, gazing again
In the bride's face, where now no azure vein
Wander'd on fair-spaced temples; no soft bloom
Misted the cheek; no passion to illume
275 The deep-recessed vision:—all was blight;
Lamia, no longer fair, there sat a deadly white.
"Shut, shut those juggling[7] eyes, thou ruthless man!
Turn them aside, wretch! or the righteous ban
Of all the Gods, whose dreadful images
280 Here represent their shadowy presences,
May pierce them on the sudden with the thorn

4. Gnomes were guardians of mines.
5. Drink a toast to.
6. Sacred to Venus, hence an emblem of love.
7. Deceiving, full of trickery.

Of painful blindness; leaving thee forlorn,
In trembling dotage to the feeblest fright
Of conscience, for their long offended might,
285 For all thine impious proud-heart sophistries,
Unlawful magic, and enticing lies.
Corinthians! look upon that gray-beard wretch!
Mark how, possess'd, his lashless eyelids stretch
Around his demon eyes! Corinthians, see!
290 My sweet bride withers at their potency."
"Fool!" said the sophist, in an under-tone
Gruff with contempt; which a death-nighing moan
From Lycius answer'd, as heart-struck and lost,
He sank supine beside the aching ghost.
295 "Fool! Fool!" repeated he, while his eyes still
Relented not, nor mov'd; "from every ill
Of life have I preserv'd thee to this day,
And shall I see thee made a serpent's prey?"
Then Lamia breath'd death breath; the sophist's eye,
300 Like a sharp spear, went through her utterly,
Keen, cruel, perceant,° stinging: she, as well   piercing
As her weak hand could any meaning tell,
Motion'd him to be silent; vainly so,
He look'd and look'd again a level—No!
305 "A Serpent!" echoed he; no sooner said,
Than with a frightful scream she vanished:
And Lycius' arms were empty of delight,
As were his limbs of life, from that same night.
On the high couch he lay!—his friends came round—
310 Supported him—no pulse, or breath they found,
And, in its marriage robe, the heavy body wound.

July–Aug. 1819   1820

To Autumn[1]

I

Season of mists and mellow fruitfulness,
    Close bosom-friend of the maturing sun;
Conspiring with him how to load and bless
    With fruit the vines that round the thatch-eves run;
5   To bend with apples the moss'd cottage-trees,
    And fill all fruit with ripeness to the core;
        To swell the gourd, and plump the hazel shells
    With a sweet kernel; to set budding more,
    And still more, later flowers for the bees,
10   Until they think warm days will never cease,
        For summer has o'er-brimm'd their clammy cells.

1. Two days after this ode was composed, Keats
wrote to J. H. Reynolds: "I never liked stubble
fields so much as now—Aye, better than the chilly
green of the spring. Somehow a stubble plain looks
warm—in the same way that some pictures look
warm—this struck me so much in my Sunday's
walk that I composed upon it." For the author's
revisions while composing To Autumn, see "Poems
in Process," in the appendices to this volume.

2

Who hath not seen thee oft amid thy store?
    Sometimes whoever seeks abroad may find
Thee sitting careless on a granary floor,
15   Thy hair soft-lifted by the winnowing[2] wind;
Or on a half-reap'd furrow sound asleep,
    Drows'd with the fume of poppies, while thy hook°   *scythe*
      Spares the next swath and all its twined flowers:
And sometimes like a gleaner thou dost keep
20   Steady thy laden head across a brook;
Or by a cyder-press, with patient look,
    Thou watchest the last oozings hours by hours.

3

Where are the songs of spring? Ay, where are they?
    Think not of them, thou hast thy music too,—
25   While barred clouds bloom the soft-dying day,
    And touch the stubble-plains with rosy hue;
Then in a wailful choir the small gnats mourn
    Among the river sallows,° borne aloft   *willows*
    Or sinking as the light wind lives or dies;
30   And full-grown lambs loud bleat from hilly bourn;°   *region*
Hedge-crickets sing; and now with treble soft
    The red-breast whistles from a garden-croft;[3]
And gathering swallows twitter in the skies.

Sept. 19, 1819   1820

Letters

Letters   Keats's letters serve as a running commentary on his life, reading, thinking, and writing. His early reputation as a poet of pure luxury, sensation, and art for art's sake has undergone a radical change since, in the twentieth century, critics began to pay close attention to the letters. For Keats thought hard and persistently about life and art, and any seed of an ethical or critical idea that he picked up from his contemporaries (in particular, Hazlitt, Coleridge, Wordsworth) instantly germinated and flourished in the rich soil of his imagination. What T. S. Eliot said about the Metaphysical poets applies to Keats in his letters: his "mode of feeling was directly and freshly altered by [his] reading and thought." And like Donne, he looked not only into the heart but, literally, "into the cerebral cortex, the nervous system, and the digestive tract." A number of Keats's casual comments on the poet and on poetry included here—especially those dealing with "negative capability" and with what we now call empathy—have become standard points of reference in aesthetic theory. But Keats himself regarded nothing that he said as final; each statement constituted only a stage in his continuing exploration into what he called "the mystery."

    The text printed here is that of the edition of the *Letters* by Hyder E. Rollins (1958), which reproduces the original manuscripts precisely.

---

2. To "winnow" is to fan the chaff from the grain.   3. An enclosed plot of farmland.

LETTERS

To Benjamin Bailey[1]

[THE AUTHENTICITY OF THE IMAGINATION]

[November 22, 1817]

My dear Bailey,

* * * O I wish I was as certain of the end of all your troubles as that of your momentary start about the authenticity of the Imagination. I am certain of nothing but of the holiness of the Heart's affections and the truth of Imagination—What the imagination seizes as Beauty must be truth[2]— whether it existed before or not—for I have the same Idea of all our Passions as of Love they are all in their sublime, creative of essential Beauty—In a Word, you may know my favorite Speculation by my first Book and the little song[3] I sent in my last—which is a representation from the fancy of the probable mode of operating in these Matters—The Imagination may be compared to Adam's dream[4]—he awoke and found it truth. I am the more zealous in this affair, because I have never yet been able to perceive how any thing can be known for truth by consequitive reasoning[5]—and yet it must be— Can it be that even the greatest Philosopher ever ~~when~~ arrived at his goal without putting aside numerous objections—However it may be, O for a Life of Sensations[6] rather than of Thoughts! It is "a Vision in the form of Youth" a Shadow of reality to come—and this consideration has further conv[i]nced me for it has come as auxiliary to another favorite Speculation of mine, that we shall enjoy ourselves here after by having what we called happiness on Earth repeated in a finer tone and so repeated[7]—And yet such a fate can only befall those who delight in sensation rather than hunger as you do after Truth—Adam's dream will do here and seems to be a conviction that Imagination and its empyreal reflection is the same as human Life and its spiritual repetition. But as I was saying—the simple imaginative Mind may have its rewards in the repeti[ti]on of its own silent Working coming continually on the spirit with a fine suddenness—to compare great things with small—have you never by being surprised with an old Melody—in a delicious place—by a delicious voice, fe[l]t over again your very speculations and surmises at the time it first operated on your soul—do you not remember forming to yourself the singer's face more beautiful [than] it was possible and yet with the elevation of the Moment you did not think so—even then you were mounted on the Wings of Imagination so high—that the Prototype must be here after—that delicious face you will see—What a time! I am continually run-

---

1. One of Keats's closest friends. Keats had stayed with him the month before at Oxford, where Bailey was an undergraduate.
2. The phrase occurs in a poetic context at the close of *Ode on a Grecian Urn*. Try substituting "real," or "reality," where Keats uses the word *truth*.
3. The song was "O Sorrow," from book 4 of *Endymion*.
4. In *Paradise Lost* 8.452–90, Adam dreams that

Eve has been created, and awakes to find her real. Adam also describes an earlier prefigurative dream in the same work, 8.283–311.
5. Consecutive reasoning—reasoning that moves by logical steps.
6. Probably not only sense experiences but also the intuitive perceptions of truths, as opposed to truth achieved by consecutive reasoning.
7. Cf. the "Pleasure Thermometer" in *Endymion* 1.777ff. (p. 1800).

ning away from the subject—sure this cannot be exactly the case with a complex Mind—one that is imaginative and at the same time careful of its fruits—who would exist partly on sensation partly on thought—to whom it is necessary that years should bring the philosophic Mind[8]—such an one I consider your's and therefore it is necessary to your eternal Happiness that you not only ~~have~~ drink this old Wine of Heaven which I shall call the redigestion of our most ethereal Musings on Earth; but also increase in knowledge and know all things. I am glad to hear you are in a fair Way for Easter—you will soon get through your unpleasant reading and then!—but the world is full of troubles and I have not much reason to think myself pesterd with many—I think Jane or Marianne has a better opinion of me than I deserve—for really and truly I do not think my Brothers illness connected with mine—you know more of the real Cause than they do—nor have I any chance of being rack'd as you have been[9]—you perhaps at one time thought there was such a thing as Worldly Happiness to be arrived at, at certain periods of time marked out—you have of necessity from your disposition been thus led away—I scarcely remember counting upon any Happiness—I look not for it if it be not in the present hour—nothing startles me beyond the Moment. The setting sun will always set me to rights—or if a Sparrow come before my Window I take part in its existence and pick about the Gravel. The first thing that strikes me on hea[r]ing a Misfortune having befalled another is this. "Well it cannot be helped.—he will have the pleasure of trying the resources of his spirit, and I beg now my dear Bailey that hereafter should you observe any thing cold in me not to [put] it to the account of heartlessness but abstraction—for I assure you I sometimes feel not the influence of a Passion or Affection during a whole week—and so long this sometimes continues I begin to suspect myself and the genuiness of my feelings at other times—thinking them a few barren Tragedy-tears.
* * *

Your affectionate friend
John Keats—

To George and Thomas Keats

[NEGATIVE CAPABILITY]

[December 21, 27 (?), 1817]

My dear Brothers

I must crave your pardon for not having written ere this. * * * I spent Friday evening with Wells[1] & went the next morning to see *Death on the Pale horse*. It is a wonderful picture, when West's[2] age is considered; But there is nothing to be intense upon; no women one feels mad to kiss; no face swelling

8. An echo of Wordsworth, *Ode: Intimations of Immortality*, line 187.
9. Keats's friends Jane and Mariane Reynolds feared that his ill health at this time threatened tuberculosis, from which his brother Tom was suffering. Bailey had recently experienced pain (been "racked") because of an unsuccessful love affair.

1. Charles Wells, a former schoolmate of Tom Keats.
2. Benjamin West (1738–1820), painter of historical pictures, was an American who moved to England and became president of the Royal Academy. The *Christ Rejected* mentioned a few sentences farther on is also by West.

into reality. the excellence of every Art is its intensity, capable of making all disagreeables evaporate, from their being in close relationship with Beauty & Truth[3]—Examine King Lear & you will find this examplified throughout; but in this picture we have unpleasantness without any momentous depth of speculation excited, in which to bury its repulsiveness—The picture is larger than Christ rejected—I dined with Haydon[4] the sunday after you left, & had a very pleasant day, I dined too (for I have been out too much lately) with Horace Smith & met his two Brothers with Hill & Kingston & one Du Bois,[5] they only served to convince me, how superior humour is to wit in respect to enjoyment—These men say things which make one start, without making one feel, they are all alike; their manners are alike; they all know fashionables; they have a mannerism in their very eating & drinking, in their mere handling a Decanter—They talked of Kean[6] & his low company— Would I were with that company instead of yours said I to myself! I know such like acquaintance will never do for me & yet I am going to Reynolds, on wednesday—Brown & Dilke[7] walked with me & back from the Christmas pantomime.[8] I had not a dispute but a disquisition with Dilke, on various subjects; several things dovetailed in my mind, & at once it struck me, what quality went to form a Man of Achievement especially in Literature & which Shakespeare possessed so enormously—I mean *Negative Capability*,[9] that is when man is capable of being in uncertainties, Mysteries, doubts, without any irritable reaching after fact & reason—Coleridge, for instance, would let go by a fine isolated verisimilitude caught from the Penetralium[1] of mystery, from being incapable of remaining content with half knowledge. This pursued through Volumes would perhaps take us no further than this, that with a great poet the sense of Beauty overcomes every other consideration, or rather obliterates all consideration.

Shelley's poem[2] is out & there are words about its being objected too, as much as Queen Mab was. Poor Shelley I think he has his Quota of good qualities, in sooth la!! Write soon to your most sincere friend & affectionate Brother

John

---

3. Keats's solution to a problem at least as old as Aristotle's *Poetics*: why do we take pleasure in the aesthetic representation of a subject that in life would be ugly or painful?

4. Keats's close friend Benjamin Haydon, painter of large-scale historical and religious pictures.

5. Smith was one of the best-known literary wits of the day; the others mentioned were men of letters or of literary interests.

6. Edmund Kean, noted Shakespearean actor of the early 19th century.

7. Charles Armitage Brown, John Hamilton Reynolds, and Charles Wentworth Dilke were all writers and friends of Keats. Keats interrupted the writing of this letter after the dash; beginning with "Brown & Dilke" he is writing several days after the preceding sentences.

8. Christmas pantomimes were performed each year at Drury Lane and Covent Garden theaters.

9. This famous and elusive phrase has accumulated a sizable body of commentary. Two points may be offered here: (1) Keats is concerned with a central aesthetic question of his day: to distinguish between what was called the "objective" poet, who simply and impersonally presents material, and the "subjective" or "sentimental" poet, who presents material as it appears when viewed through the writer's personal interests, beliefs, and feelings. The poet of "negative capability" is the objective poet (see the letter to Reynolds, February 3, 1818, p. 1846). (2) Keats goes on to propose that, within a poem, the presentation of subject matter in an artistic form that appeals to our "sense of Beauty" is enough, independently of its truth or falsity when considered outside the poem.

1. The Latin *penetralia* signified the innermost and most secret parts of a temple.

2. *Laon and Cythna* (1817), which dealt with incest and had to be recalled by the author; Shelley revised and republished it as *The Revolt of Islam* (1818). *Queen Mab* (1813) was a youthful poem in which Shelley presented his radical program for the achievement of a millennial earthly state by the elimination of "kings, priests, and statesmen" and the reform of human institutions.

To John Hamilton Reynolds[1]

[Wordsworth's Poetry]

[February 3, 1818]

My dear Reynolds,

* * * It may be said that we ought to read our Contemporaries. that Wordsworth &c should have their due from us. but for the sake of a few fine imaginative or domestic passages, are we to be bullied into a certain Philosophy engendered in the whims of an Egotist[2]—Every man has his speculations, but every man does not brood and peacock over them till he makes a false coinage and deceives himself—Many a man can travel to the very bourne[3] of Heaven, and yet want confidence to put down his halfseeing. Sancho[4] will invent a Journey heavenward as well as any body. We hate poetry that has a palpable design upon us—and if we do not agree, seems to put its hand in its breeches pocket. Poetry should be great & unobtrusive, a thing which enters into one's soul, and does not startle it or amaze it with itself but with its subject.—How beautiful are the retired flowers! how would they lose their beauty were they to throng into the highway crying out, "admire me I am a violet! dote upon me I am a primrose! Modern poets differ from the Elizabethans in this. Each of the moderns like an Elector of Hanover governs his petty state, & knows how many straws are swept daily from the Causeways in all his dominions & has a continual itching that all the Housewives should have their coppers well scoured: the antients were ~~Emperors of large~~ Emperors of vast Provinces, they had only heard of the remote ones and scarcely cared to visit them.—I will cut all this—I will have no more of Wordsworth or Hunt[5] in particular—Why should we be of the tribe of Manasseh, when we can wander with Esau?[6] why should we kick against the Pricks, when we can walk on Roses? Why should we be owls, when we can be Eagles? Why be teased with "nice Eyed wagtails," when we have in sight "the Cherub Contemplation"?[7]—Why with Wordsworths "Matthew with a bough of wilding in his hand" when we can have Jacques "under an oak &c"[8]—The secret of the Bough of Wilding will run through your head faster than I can write it—Old Matthew spoke to him some years ago on some nothing, & because he happens in an Evening Walk to imagine the figure of the old man—he must stamp it down in black & white, and it is henceforth sacred—I don't mean to deny Wordsworth's grandeur & Hunt's merit, but I mean to say we need not be teazed with grandeur & merit—when we can have them uncontaminated & unobtrusive. Let us have the old

1. A close friend who was at this time an insurance clerk and also an able poet and man of letters.
2. Keats immensely admired Wordsworth, as succeeding letters will show, and learned more from him than from any poetic contemporary. He had reservations, however, about the subjective and didactic qualities of Wordsworth's poetry—reservations that, in some moods, he stated in unflattering terms.
3. Boundary.
4. Sancho Panza, the earthy squire in Cervantes's *Don Quixote*.

5. Leigh Hunt, a poet who earlier had strongly influenced Keats's style.
6. I.e., why should we carry on a conventional way of life (as did the tribe of Manasseh in Old Testament history) when we can become adventurers (like Esau, who sold his birthright in Genesis 25.29–34 and became an outlaw).
7. Milton, *Il Penseroso*, line 54. "Nice Eyed wagtails": from Hunt's *Nymphs*.
8. *As You Like It* 2.1.31. The Wordsworth phrase is from his poem *The Two April Mornings*. A "wilding" is a wild apple tree.

Poets, & robin Hood[9] Your letter and its sonnets gave me more pleasure than will the 4th Book of Childe Harold[1] & the whole of any body's life & opinions. * * *

Y[r] sincere friend and Coscribbler
John Keats.

To John Taylor[1]

[KEATS'S AXIOMS IN POETRY]

[February 27, 1818]

My dear Taylor,

Your alteration strikes me as being a great improvement—the page looks much better. * * * It is a sorry thing for me that any one should have to overcome Prejudices in reading my Verses—that affects me more than any hypercriticism on any particular Passage. In *Endymion* I have most likely but moved into the Go-cart from the leading strings. In Poetry I have a few Axioms, and you will see how far I am from their Centre. 1st I think Poetry should surprise by a fine excess and not by Singularity—it should strike the Reader as a wording of his own highest thoughts, and appear almost a Remembrance—2nd Its touches of Beauty should never be half way therby making the reader breathless instead of content: the rise, the progress, the setting of imagery should like the Sun come natural natural too him—shine over him and set soberly although in magnificence leaving him in the Luxury of twilight—but it is easier to think what Poetry should be than to write it— and this leads me on to another axiom. That if Poetry comes not as naturally as the Leaves to a tree it had better not come at all. However it may be with me I cannot help looking into new countries with "O for a Muse of fire to ascend!"[2]—If Endymion serves me as a Pioneer perhaps I ought to be content. I have great reason to be content, for thank God I can read and perhaps understand Shakspeare to his depths, and I have I am sure many friends, who, if I fail, will attribute any change in my Life and Temper to Humbleness rather than to Pride—to a cowering under the Wings of great Poets rather than to a Bitterness that I am not appreciated. I am anxious to get Endymion printed that I may forget it and proceed. * * *

Your sincere and oblig[d] friend
John Keats—

P.S. You shall have a sho[r]t *Preface* in good time—

---

9. A reference to two sonnets on Robin Hood, written by Reynolds, which he had sent to Keats.
1. Canto 4 of Byron's *Childe Harold's Pilgrimage* was being eagerly awaited by English readers.

1. Partner in the publishing firm of Taylor and Hessey, to whom Keats wrote this letter while *Endymion* was being put through the press.
2. Altered from *Henry V*, Prologue, line 1.

To John Hamilton Reynolds

[MILTON, WORDSWORTH, AND THE CHAMBERS OF HUMAN LIFE]

[May 3, 1818]

My dear Reynolds.

* * * Were I to study physic or rather Medicine again,—I feel it would not make the least difference in my Poetry; when the Mind is in its infancy a Bias in is in reality a Bias, but when we have acquired more strength, a Bias becomes no Bias. Every department of knowledge we see excellent and calculated towards a great whole. I am so convinced of this, that I am glad at not having given away my medical Books, which I shall again look over to keep alive the little I know thitherwards; and moreover intend through you and Rice to become a sort of Pip-civilian.[1] An extensive knowledge is needful to thinking people—it takes away the heat and fever; and helps, by widening speculation, to ease the Burden of the Mystery:[2] a thing I begin to understand a little, and which weighed upon you in the most gloomy and true sentence in your Letter. The difference of high Sensations with and without knowledge appears to me this—in the latter case we are falling continually ten thousand fathoms deep and being blown up again without wings and with all [the] horror of a ~~Case~~ bare shoulderd Creature—in the former case, our shoulders are fledged,[3] and we go thro' the same ~~Fir~~ air and space without fear. * * *

You say "I fear there is little chance of any thing else in this life." You seem by that to have been going through with a more painful and acute ~~test~~ zest the same labyrinth that I have—I have come to the same conclusion thus far. My Branchings out therefrom have been numerous: one of them is the consideration of Wordsworth's genius and as a help, in the manner of gold being the meridian Line of worldly wealth,—how he differs from Milton.[4]—And here I have nothing but surmises, from an uncertainty whether Miltons apparently less anxiety for Humanity proceeds from his seeing further or no than Wordsworth: And whether Wordsworth has in truth epic passions, and martyrs himself to the human heart, the main region of his song[5]—In regard to his genius alone—we find what he says true as far as we have experienced and we can judge no further but by larger experience—for axioms in philosophy are not axioms until they are proved upon our pulses: We read fine——things but never feel them to [the] full until we have gone the same steps as the Author.—I know this is not plain; you will know exactly my meaning when I say, that now I shall relish Hamlet more than I ever have done—Or, better—You are sensible no man can set down Venery[6] as a bestial or joyless thing until he is sick of it and therefore all philosophizing on it would be mere wording. Until we are sick, we understand not;—in fine, as

---

1. Apparently "a small-scale layman." James Rice, a lawyer, was one of Keats's favorite friends.
2. Wordsworth, *Tintern Abbey,* line 38. Here begins Keats's insightful expansion of the significance of this and other phrases and passages in Wordsworth.
3. Grow wings.
4. I.e., as gold is the standard of material wealth

(in the way that the meridian line of Greenwich Observatory, England, is the reference for measuring degrees of longitude), so Milton is the standard of poetic value, by which we may measure Wordsworth.
5. Cf. Prospectus to *The Recluse,* line 41 (p. 1495).
6. Sexual indulgence.

Byron says, "Knowledge is Sorrow";[7] and I go on to say that "Sorrow is Wisdom"—and further for aught we can know for certainty! "Wisdom is folly."
* * *

I will return to Wordsworth—whether or no he has an extended vision or a circumscribed grandeur—whether he is an eagle in his nest, or on the wing—And to be more explicit and to show you how tall I stand by the giant, I will put down a simile of human life as far as I now perceive it; that is, to the point to which I say we both have arrived at—Well—I compare human life to a large Mansion of Many Apartments, two of which I can only describe, the doors of the rest being as yet shut upon me—The first we step into we call the infant or thoughtless Chamber, in which we remain as long as we do not think—We remain there a long while, and notwithstanding the doors of the second Chamber remain wide open, showing a bright appearance, we care not to hasten to it; but are at length imperceptibly impelled by the awakening of the thinking principle—within us—we no sooner get into the second Chamber, which I shall call the Chamber of Maiden-Thought,[8] than we become intoxicated with the light and the atmosphere, we see nothing but pleasant wonders, and think of delaying there for ever in delight: However among the effects this breathing is father of is that tremendous one of sharpening one's vision into the head heart and nature of Man—of convincing ones nerves that the World is full of Misery and Heartbreak, Pain, Sickness and oppression—whereby This Chamber of Maiden Thought becomes gradually darken'd and at the same time on all sides of it many doors are set open—but all dark—all leading to dark passages—We see not the ballance of good and evil. We are in a Mist—We are now in that state—We feel the "burden of the Mystery," To this point was Wordsworth come, as far as I can conceive when he wrote "Tintern Abbey" and it seems to me that his Genius is explorative of those dark Passages. Now if we live, and go on thinking, we too shall explore them. he is a Genius and superior [to] us, in so far as he can, more than we, make discoveries, and shed a light in them—Here I must think Wordsworth is deeper than Milton—though I think it has depended more upon the general and gregarious advance of intellect, than individual greatness of Mind—From the Paradise Lost and the other Works of Milton, I hope it is not too presuming, even between ourselves to say, his Philosophy, human and divine, may be tolerably understood by one not much advanced in years, In his time englishmen were just emancipated from a great superstition—and Men had got hold of certain points and resting places in reasoning which were too newly born to be doubted, and too much oppressed opposed by the Mass of Europe not to be thought etherial and authentically divine—who could gainsay his ideas on virtue, vice, and Chastity in Comus, just at the time of the dismissal of Cod-pieces[9] and a hundred other disgraces? who would not rest satisfied with his hintings at good and evil in the Paradise Lost, when just free from the inquisition and burrning in Smithfield?[1] The Reformation produced such immediate and greats benefits, that Protestantism was considered under the immediate eye of heaven, and its

---

7. *Manfred* 1.1.10: "Sorrow is knowledge."
8. I.e., innocent thought, with the implication (as in "maiden voyage") of a first undertaking.
9. In the 15th and 16th centuries, the codpiece was a flap, often ornamental, that covered an open-

ing in the front of men's breeches.
1. An open place northwest of the walls of the City of London where, in the 16th century, heretics were burned.

own remaining Dogmas and superstitions, then, as it were, regenerated, constituted those resting places and seeming sure points of Reasoning—from that I have mentioned, Milton, whatever he may have thought in the sequel,[2] appears to have been content with these by his writings—He did not think into the human heart, as Wordsworth has done—Yet Milton as a Philosop[h]er, had sure as great powers as Wordsworth—What is then to be inferr'd? O many things—It proves there is really a grand march of intellect—, It proves that a mighty providence subdues the mightiest Minds to the service of the time being, whether it be in human Knowledge or Religion— * * * Tom[3] has spit a leetle blood this afternoon, and that is rather a damper—but I know—the truth is there is something real in the World Your third Chamber of Life shall be a lucky and a gentle one—stored with the wine of love—and the Bread of Friendship— * * *

Your affectionate friend
John Keats.

To Richard Woodhouse[1]

[A POET HAS NO IDENTITY]

[October 27, 1818]

My dear Woodhouse,

Your Letter gave me a great satisfaction; more on account of its friendliness, than any relish of that matter in it which is accounted so acceptable in the "genus irritabile"[2] The best answer I can give you is in a clerklike manner to make some observations on two principle points, which seem to point like indices into the midst of the whole pro and con, about genius, and views and atchievements and ambition and cœtera. 1st As to the poetical Character itself, (I mean that sort of which, if I am any thing, I am a Member; that sort distinguished from the wordsworthian or egotistical sublime; which is a thing per se and stands alone) it is not itself—it has no self—it is every thing and nothing—It has no character—it enjoys light and shade; it lives in gusto, be it foul or fair, high or low, rich or poor, mean or elevated—It has as much delight in conceiving an Iago as an Imogen.[3] What shocks the virtuous philosop[h]er, delights the camelion[4] Poet. It does no harm from its relish of the dark side of things any more than from its taste for the bright one; because they both end in speculation.[5] A Poet is the most unpoetical of any thing in existence; because he has no Identity—he is continually in for[6]—and filling some other Body—The Sun, the Moon, the Sea and Men and Women who are creatures of impulse are poetical and have about them

2. Later on.
3. Keats's younger brother, then eighteen, who was dying of tuberculosis.
1. A young lawyer with literary interests who early recognized Keats's talents and prepared, or preserved, manuscript copies of many of his poems and letters.
2. "The irritable race," a phrase Horace had applied to poets (*Epistles* 2.2.102).

3. Iago is the villain in Shakespeare's *Othello* and Imogen the virtuous heroine in his *Cymbeline*.
4. The chameleon is a lizard that camouflages itself by changing its color to match its surroundings.
5. Possibly "in contemplation"—i.e., without affecting our practical judgment or actions.
6. Instead of "in for," Keats may have intended to write "informing."

an unchangeable attribute—the poet has none; no identity—he is certainly the most unpoetical of all God's Creatures. If then he has no self, and if I am a Poet, where is the Wonder that I should say I would ~~right~~ write no more? Might I not at that very instant [have] been cogitating on the Characters of saturn and Ops?[7] It is a wretched thing to confess; but is a very fact that not one word I ever utter can be taken for granted as an opinion growing out of my identical nature—how can it, when I have no nature? When I am in a room with People if I ever am free from speculating on creations of my own brain, then not myself goes home to myself: but the identity of every one in the room begins to to press upon me[8] that, I am in a very little time an[ni]hilated—not only among Men; it would be the same in a Nursery of children: I know not whether I make myself wholly understood: I hope enough so to let you see that no dependence is to be placed on what I said that day.

In the second place I will speak of my views, and of the life I purpose to myself—I am ambitious of doing the world some good: if I should be spared that may be the work of maturer years—in the interval I will assay to reach to as high a summit in Poetry as the nerve[9] bestowed upon me will suffer. The faint conceptions I have of Poems to come brings the blood frequently into my forehead—All I hope is that I may not lose all interest in human affairs—that the solitary indifference I feel for applause even from the finest Spirits, will not blunt any acuteness of vision I may have. I do not think it will—I feel assured I should write from the mere yearning and fondness I have for the Beautiful even if my night's labours should be burnt every morning and no eye ever shine upon them. But even now I am perhaps not speaking from myself; but from some character in whose soul I now live. I am sure however that this next sentence is from myself. I feel your anxiety, good opinion and friendliness in the highest degree, and am

Your's most sincerely
John Keats

To George and Georgiana Keats[1]

[THE VALE OF SOUL-MAKING]

[February 14–May 3, 1819]

My dear Brother & Sister—

* * * I have this moment received a note from Haslam[2] in which he expects the death of his Father who has been for some time in a state of insensibility—his mother bears up he says very well—I shall go to [town] tommorrow to see him. This is the world—thus we cannot expect to give way many hours to pleasure—Circumstances are like Clouds continually gathering and burst-

7. Characters in Keats's *Hyperion*. Woodhouse had recently written Keats to express concern at a remark by the poet that, because former writers had preempted the best poetic materials and styles, there was nothing new left for the modern poet.
8. Perhaps "*so* to press upon me."
9. Sinew.

1. Keats's brother and his wife, who had emigrated to Louisville, Kentucky, in 1818. This is part of a long letter that Keats wrote over a period of several months. The date of this first extract is March 19.
2. William Haslam, a young businessman and close friend.

ing—While we are laughing the seed of some trouble is put into ~~he~~ the wide arable land of events—while we are laughing it sprouts [it] grows and suddenly bears a poison fruit which we must pluck—Even so we have leisure to reason on the misfortunes of our friends; our own touch us too nearly for words. Very few men have ever arrived at a complete disinterestedness of Mind: very few have been influenced by a pure desire of the benefit of others—in the greater part of the Benefactors ~~of~~ & to Humanity some meretricious motive has sullied their greatness—some melodramatic scenery has facinated them—From the manner in which I feel Haslam's misfortune I perceive how far I am from any humble standard of disinterestedness—Yet this feeling ought to be carried to its highest pitch, as there is no fear of its ever injuring society—which it would do I fear pushed to an extremity—For in wild nature the Hawk would loose his Breakfast of Robins and the Robin his of Worms The Lion must starve as well as the swallow—The greater part of Men make their way with the same instinctiveness, the same unwandering eye from their purposes, the same animal eagerness as the Hawk—The Hawk wants a Mate, so does the Man—look at them both they set about it and procure on[e] in the same manner—They want both a nest and they both set about one in the same manner—they get their food in the same manner—The noble animal Man for his amusement smokes his pipe—the Hawk balances about the Clouds—that is the only difference of their leisures. This it is that makes the Amusement of Life—to a speculative Mind. I go among the Feilds and catch a glimpse of a stoat[3] or a fieldmouse peeping out of the withered grass—the creature hath a purpose and its eyes are bright with it—I go amongst the buildings of a city and I see a Man hurrying along—to what? The Creature has a purpose and his eyes are bright with it. But then as Wordsworth says, "we have all one human heart"[4]—there is an ellectric fire in human nature tending to purify—so that among these human creature[s] there is continually some birth of new heroism—The pity is that we must wonder at it: as we should at finding a pearl in rubbish—I have no doubt that thousands of people never heard of have had hearts comp[l]etely disinterested: I can remember but two—Socrates and Jesus—their Histories evince it—What I heard a little time ago, Taylor observe with respect to Socrates, may be said of Jesus—That he was so great as man that though he transmitted no writing of his own to posterity, we have his Mind and his sayings and his greatness handed to us by others. It is to be lamented that the history of the latter was written and revised by Men interested in the pious frauds of Religion. Yet through all this I see his splendour. Even here though I myself am pursueing the same instinctive course as the veriest human animal you can think of—I am however young writing at random— straining at particles of light in the midst of a great darkness—without knowing the bearing of any one assertion of any one opinion. Yet may I not in this be free from sin?[5] May there not be superior beings amused with any graceful, though instinctive attitude my mind [may] fall into, as I am entertained with the alertness of a Stoat or the anxiety of a Deer? Though a quarrel in

3. A weasel.
4. *The Old Cumberland Beggar*, line 153.
5. Keats speculates that though his instinctive course is not, any more than an animal's, "disinterested" (free from selfish interests), it may still, like an animal's, be natural, hence innocent and possessed of an innate grace and beauty. He further supposes that this may be the nature of poetry, also, as distinguished from the deliberate and self-conscious process of philosophical reasoning (cf. the letter to George and Thomas Keats on "Negative Capability," begun on December 21, 1817, p. 1844).

the streets is a thing to be hated, the energies displayed in it are fine; the commonest Man shows a grace in his quarrel—By a superior being our reasoning[s] may take the same tone—though erroneous they may be fine—This is the very thing in which consists poetry; and if so it is not so fine a thing as philosophy—For the same reason that an eagle is not so fine a thing as a truth—Give me this credit—Do you not think I strive—to know myself? Give me this credit—and you will not think that on my own accou[n]t I repeat Milton's lines

> "How charming is divine Philosophy
> Not harsh and crabbed as dull fools suppose
> But musical as is Apollo's lute"—[6]

No—no for myself—feeling grateful as I do to have got into a state of mind to relish them properly—Nothing ever becomes real till it is experienced—Even a Proverb is no proverb to you till your Life has illustrated it— * * *

* * * I have been reading lately two very different books Robertson's America and Voltaire's Siecle De Louis xiv[7] It is like walking arm and arm between Pizarro and the great-little Monarch.[8] In How lementabl[e] a case do we see the great body of the people in both instances: in the first, where Men might seem to inherit quiet of Mind from unsophisticated senses; from uncontamination of civilisation; and especially from their being as it were estranged from the mutual helps of Society and its mutual injuries—and thereby more immediately under the Protection of Providence—even there they had mortal pains to bear as bad; or even worse than Baliffs,[9] Debts and Poverties of civilised Life—The whole appears to resolve into this—that Man is originally "a poor forked creature"[1] subject to the same mischances as the beasts of the forest, destined to hardships and disquietude of some kind or other. If he improves by degrees his bodily accommodations and comforts—at each stage, at each accent there are waiting for him a fresh set of annoyances—he is mortal and there is still a heaven with its Stars abov[e] his head. The most interesting question that can come before us is, How far by the persevering endeavours of a seldom appearing Socrates Mankind may be made happy—I can imagine such happiness carried to an extreme—but what must it end in?—Death—and who could in such a case bear with death—the whole troubles of life which are now frittered away in a series of years, would the[n] be accumulated for the last days of a being who instead of hailing its approach, would leave this world as Eve left Paradise—But in truth I do not at all believe in this sort of perfectibility—the nature of the world will not admit of it—the inhabitants of the world will correspond to itself—Let the fish philosophise the ice away from the Rivers in winter time and they shall be at continual play in the tepid delight of summer. Look at the Poles and at the sands of Africa, Whirlpools and volcanoes—Let men exterminate them and I will say that they may arrive at earthly Happiness—The point at which Man may arrive is as far as the paralel state in inanimate nature and no

---

6. *Comus*, lines 475–77.
7. Voltaire, *Le Siècle de Louis XIV*, 5 vols. (1751); William Robertson, *The History of America* (1777—Keats was reading the 10th ed., 4 vols., 1803). In this second extract from the journal-letter Keats is writing toward the end of April (on the 21st or 28th).
8. Francisco Pizarro, the Spanish explorer whose exploits are described in Robertson's *America*. The "Monarch" is Louis XIV.
9. Bailiffs: officers of the law whose duties included making arrests for bad debts.
1. *King Lear* 3.4.95–97. Lear says: "Unaccommodated man is no more but such a poor, bare, forked animal as thou art."

further—For instance suppose a rose to have sensation, it blooms on a beautiful morning it enjoys itself—but there comes a cold wind, a hot sun—it can not escape it, it cannot destroy its annoyances—they are as native to the world as itself: no more can man be happy in spite, the world[l]y elements will prey upon his nature—The common cognomen of this world among the misguided and superstitious is "a vale of tears" from which we are to be redeemed by a certain arbitrary interposition of God and taken to Heaven— What a little circumscribe[d] straightened notion! Call the world if you Please "The vale of Soul-making" Then you will find out the use of the world (I am speaking now in the highest terms for human nature admitting it to be immortal which I will here take for granted for the purpose of showing a thought which has struck me concerning it) I say *"Soul making"* Soul as distinguished from an Intelligence—There may be intelligences or sparks of the divinity in millions—but they are not Souls ~~the~~ till they acquire identities, till each one is personally itself. I[n]telligences are atoms of perception— they know and they see and they are pure, in short they are God—how then are Souls to be made? How then are these sparks which are God to have identity given them—so as ever to possess a bliss peculiar to each ones individual existence? How, but by the medium of a world like this? This point I sincerely wish to consider because I think it a grander system of salvation than the chrysteain religion—or rather it is a system of Spirit-creation[2]— This is effected by three grand materials acting the one upon the other for a series of years—These three Materials are the *Intelligence*—the *human heart* (as distinguished from intelligence or Mind) and the *World* or *Elemental space* suited for the proper action of *Mind and Heart* on each other for the purpose of forming the *Soul* or *Intelligence destined to possess the sense of Identity*. I can scarcely express what I but dimly perceive—and yet I think I perceive it—that you may judge the more clearly I will put it in the most homely form possible—I will call the *world* a School instituted for the purpose of teaching little children to read—I will call the *human heart* the *horn Book*[3] used in that School—and I will call the *Child able to read, the Soul* made from that *school* and its *hornbook*. Do you not see how necessary a World of Pains and troubles is to school an Intelligence and make it a soul? A Place where the heart must feel and suffer in a thousand diverse ways! Not merely is the Heart a Hornbook, It is the Minds Bible, it is the Minds experience, it is the teat from which the Mind or intelligence sucks its identity—As various as the Lives of Men are—so various become their souls, and thus does God make individual beings, Souls, Identical Souls of the sparks of his own essence—This appears to me a faint sketch of a system of Salvation which does not affront our reason and humanity—I am convinced that many difficulties which christians labour under would vanish before it—There is one wh[i]ch even now Strikes me— the Salvation of Children—In them the Spark or intelligence returns to God

---

2. Keats is struggling for an analogy that will embody his solution to the ancient riddle of evil, as an alternative to what he understands to be the Christian view: that evil exists as a test of the individual's merit of salvation in heaven, and this world is only a proving ground for a later and better life. Keats proposes that the function of the human experience of sorrow and pain is to feed and discipline the formless and unstocked "intelligence" that we possess at birth and thus to shape it into a rich and coherent "identity," or "soul." This result provides a justification ("salvation") for our suffering in terms of our earthly life itself: that is, experience is its own reward. The passage is analogous to what Wordsworth says in the last two stanzas of his *Ode: Intimations of Immortality*.

3. A child's primer, which used to consist of a sheet of paper mounted on thin wood, protected by a sheet of transparent horn.

without any identity—it having had no time to learn of, and be altered by, the heart—or seat of the human Passions—It is pretty generally suspected that the chr[i]stian scheme has been coppied from the ancient persian and greek Philosophers. Why may they not have made this simple thing even more simple for common apprehension by introducing Mediators and Personages in the same manner as in the hethen mythology abstractions are personified—Seriously I think it probable that this System of Soul-making—may have been the Parent of all the more palpable and personal Schemes of Redemption, among the Zoroastrians the Christians and the Hindoos. For as one part of the human species must have their carved Jupiter; so another part must have the palpable and named Mediatior and saviour, their Christ their Oromanes and their Vishnu[4]—If what I have said should not be plain enough, as I fear it may not be, I will [put] you in the place where I began in this series of thoughts—I mean, I began by seeing how man was formed by circumstances—and what are circumstances?—but touchstones of his heart—? and what are touch stones?—but proovings of his hearrt?—and what are proovings of his heart but fortifiers or alterers of his nature? and what is his altered nature but his soul?—and what was his soul before it came into the world and had These provings and alterations and perfectionings?—An intelligences—without Identity—and how is this Identity to be made? Through the medium of the Heart? And how is the heart to become this Medium but in a world of Circumstances?—There now I think what with Poetry and Theology you may thank your Stars that my pen is not very long winded— * * *

This is the 3d of May & every thing is in delightful forwardness; the violets are not withered, before the peeping of the first rose; You must let me know every thing, how parcels go & come, what papers you have, & what Newspapers you want, & other things—God bless you my dear Brother & Sister

Your ever Affectionate Brother
John Keats—

To Fanny Brawne

[FANNY BRAWNE AS KEATS'S "FAIR STAR"]

[July 25, 1819]

My sweet Girl,

I hope you did not blame me much for not obeying your request of a Letter on Saturday: we have had four in our small room playing at cards night and morning leaving me no undisturb'd opportunity to write. Now Rice and Martin are gone I am at liberty. Brown to my sorrow confirms the account you give of your ill health. You cannot conceive how I ache to be with you: how I would die for one hour——for what is in the world? I say you cannot conceive; it is impossible you should look with such eyes upon me as I have upon you: it cannot be. Forgive me if I wander a little this evening, for I have been all day employ'd in a very abstr[a]ct Poem[1] and I am in deep love with

---

4. The deity who creates and preserves the world, in Hindu belief. Oromanes (Ahriman) was the principle of evil, locked in a persisting struggle with Ormazd, the principle of good, in the Zoroastrian religion.

1. Probably *The Fall of Hyperion*.

you—two things which must excuse me. I have, believe me, not been an age in letting you take possession of me; the very first week I knew you I wrote myself your vassal; but burnt the Letter as the very next time I saw you I thought you manifested some dislike to me. If you should ever feel for Man at the first sight what I did for you, I am lost. Yet I should not quarrel with you, but hate myself if such a thing were to happen—only I should burst if the thing were not as fine as a Man as you are as a Woman. Perhaps I am too vehement, then fancy me on my knees, especially when I mention a part of you Letter which hurt me; you say speaking of Mr. Severn[2] "but you must be satisfied in knowing that I admired you much more than your friend." My dear love, I cannot believe there ever was or ever could be any thing to admire in me especially as far as sight goes—I cannot be admired, I am not a thing to be admired. You are, I love you; all I can bring you is a swooning admiration of your Beauty. I hold that place among Men which snub-nos'd brunettes with meeting eyebrows do among women—they are trash to me—unless I should find one among them with a fire in her heart like the one that burns in mine. You absorb me in spite of myself—you alone: for I look not forward with any pleasure to what is call'd being settled in the world; I tremble at domestic cares—yet for you I would meet them, though if it would leave you the happier I would rather die than do so. I have two luxuries to brood over in my walks, your Loveliness and the hour of my death. O that I could have possession of them both in the same minute. I hate the world: it batters too much the wings of my self-will, and would I could take a sweet poison from your lips to send me out of it. From no others would I take it. I am indeed astonish'd to find myself so careless of all cha[r]ms but yours—remembring as I do the time when even a bit of ribband was a matter of interest with me. What softer words can I find for you after this—what it is I will not read. Nor will I say more here, but in a Postscript answer any thing else you may have mentioned in your Letter in so many words—for I am distracted with a thousand thoughts. I will imagine you Venus tonight and pray, pray, pray to your star like a Hethen.[3]

Your's ever, fair Star,

John Keats.

To Percy Bysshe Shelley[1]

[LOAD EVERY RIFT WITH ORE]

[August 16, 1820]

My dear Shelley,

I am very much gratified that you, in a foreign country, and with a mind almost over occupied, should write to me in the strain of the Letter beside me. If I do not take advantage of your invitation it will be prevented by a circumstance I have very much at heart to prophesy[2]—There is no doubt

---

2. Joseph Severn, who later looked after Keats during his final illness in Rome.

3. See Keats's sonnet *Bright star* (p. 1814) for parallels to this and other remarks in the present letter.

1. Written in reply to a letter urging Keats (who was ill) to spend the winter with the Shelleys in Pisa.

2. His own death.

that an english winter would put an end to me, and do so in a lingering
hateful manner, therefore I must either voyage or journey to Italy as a soldier
marches up to a battery. My nerves at present are the worst part of me, yet
they feel soothed when I think that come what extreme may, I shall not be
destined to remain in one spot long enough to take a hatred of any four
particular bed-posts. I am glad you take any pleasure in my poor Poem;[3]—
which I would willingly take the trouble to unwrite, if possible, did I care so
much as I have done about Reputation. I received a copy of the Cenci,[4] as
from yourself from Hunt. There is only one part of it I am judge of; the
Poetry, and dramatic effect, which by many spirits now a days is considered
the mammon. A modern work it is said must have a purpose,[5] which may be
the God—*an artist* must serve Mammon—he must have "self concentration"
selfishness perhaps. You I am sure will forgive me for sincerely remarking
that you might curb your magnanimity and be more of an artist, and "load
every rift"[6] of your subject with ore. The thought of such discipline must fall
like cold chains upon you, who perhaps never sat with your wings furl'd for
six Months together. And is not this extraordina[r]y talk for the writer of
Endymion? whose mind was like a pack of scattered cards—I am pick'd up
and sorted to a pip.[7] My Imagination is a Monastry and I am its Monk—you
must explain my metap^{cs}[8] to yourself. I am in expectation of Prometheus[9]
every day. Could I have my own wish for its interest effected you would have
it still in manuscript—or be but now putting an end to the second act. I
remember you advising me not to publish my first-blights, on Hampstead
heath—I am returning advice upon your hands. Most of the Poems in the
volume I send you[1] have been written above two years, and would never have
been publish'd but from a hope of gain; so you see I am inclined enough to
take your advice now. I must exp[r]ess once more my deep sense of your
kindness, adding my sincere thanks and respects for Mrs Shelley. In the hope
of soon seeing you I remain

> most sincerely yours,
> John Keats—

To Charles Brown[1]

[KEATS'S LAST LETTER]

> Rome. 30 November 1820.

My dear Brown,

'Tis the most difficult thing in the world to me to write a letter. My stomach
continues so bad, that I feel it worse on opening any book,—yet I am much

3. Keats's *Endymion*, Shelley had written, contains treasures, "though treasures poured forth
with indistinct profusion." Keats here responds
with advice in kind.
4. Shelley's blank-verse tragedy, *The Cenci*, had
been published in the spring of 1820.
5. Wordsworth had said this in his Preface to *Lyrical Ballads*. For "Mammon" see Matthew 6.24 and
Luke 16.13: "Ye cannot serve God and mammon."
6. Spenser, *The Faerie Queene* 2.7.28: "With rich
metall loaded every rifte."
7. Perfectly ordered; all the suits in the deck
matched up ("pips" are the conventional spots on

playing cards).
8. Metaphysics.
9. *Prometheus Unbound*, of which Shelley had
promised Keats a copy.
1. Keats's volume of 1820, including *Lamia, The
Eve of St. Agnes*, and the odes. When Shelley
drowned, he had this small book open in his
pocket.
1. Written to Keats's friend Charles Armitage
Brown from the house on the Spanish Stairs, in
the Piazza di Spagna, where Keats was being
tended in his mortal illness by the devoted Joseph
Severn.

better than I was in Quarantine.[2] Then I am afraid to encounter the proing and conning of any thing interesting to me in England. I have an habitual feeling of my real life having past, and that I am leading a posthumous existence. God knows how it would have been—but it appears to me—however, I will not speak of that subject. I must have been at Bedhampton nearly at the time you were writing to me from Chichester—how unfortunate—and to pass on the river too! There was my star predominant![3] I cannot answer any thing in your letter, which followed me from Naples to Rome, because I am afraid to look it over again. I am so weak (in mind) that I cannot bear the sight of any hand writing of a friend I love so much as I do you. Yet I ride the little horse,—and, at my worst, even in Quarantine, summoned up more puns, in a sort of desperation, in one week than in any year of my life. There is one thought enough to kill me—I have been well, healthy, alert &c, walking with her[4]—and now—the knowledge of contrast, feeling for light and shade, all that information (primitive sense) necessary for a poem are great enemies to the recovery of the stomach. There, you rogue, I put you to the torture,—but you must bring your philosophy to bear—as I do mine, really—or how should I be able to live? Dr Clarke is very attentive to me; he says, there is very little the matter with my lungs, but my stomach, he says, is very bad. I am well disappointed in hearing good news from George,—for it runs in my head we shall all die young. I have not written to X X X X X yet,[5] which he must think very neglectful; being anxious to send him a good account of my health, I have delayed it from week to week. If I recover, I will do all in my power to correct the mistakes made during sickness; and if I should not, all my faults will be forgiven. I shall write to X X X to-morrow, or next day. I will write to X X X X X in the middle of next week. Severn is very well, though he leads so dull a life with me. Remember me to all friends, and tell X X X X I should not have left London without taking leave of him, but from being so low in body and mind. Write to George as soon as you receive this, and tell him how I am, as far as you can guess;—and also a note to my sister—who walks about my imagination like a ghost—she is so like Tom.[6] I can scarcely bid you good bye even in a letter. I always made an awkward bow.

God bless you!
John Keats.

2. When it landed at Naples, Keats's ship had been quarantined for ten miserably hot days.
3. *The Winter's Tale* 1.2.202–03: "It is a bawdy planet, that will strike / Where 'tis predominant."
4. Fanny Brawne.
5. Charles Brown, whose manuscript transcription is the only text for this letter, substituted crosses for the names of Keats's friends to conceal their identities.
6. Keats's youngest brother, whom Fanny, his only sister, closely resembled, had died of tuberculosis on December 1, 1818. George was John Keats's younger brother.

The Victorian Age
1830–1901

In 1897 Mark Twain was visiting London during the Diamond Jubilee celebrations honoring the sixtieth anniversary of Queen Victoria's coming to the throne. "British history is two thousand years old," Twain observed, "and yet in a good many ways the world has moved farther ahead since the Queen was born than it moved in all the rest of the two thousand put together." And if the whole world had "moved" during that long lifetime and reign of Victoria's, it was in her own country itself that the change was most marked and dramatic, a change that brought England to its highest point of development as a world power.

In the eighteenth century the pivotal city of Western civilization had been Paris; by the second half of the nineteenth century this center of influence had shifted to London, a city that expanded from about two million inhabitants when Victoria came to the throne to six and a half million at the time of her death. The rapid growth of London is one of the many indications of the most important development of the age: the shift from a way of life based on the ownership of land to a modern urban economy based on trade and manufacturing. "We have been living, as it were, the life of three hundred years in thirty" was the impression formed by Dr. Thomas Arnold during the early stages of England's industrialization. By the end of the century—after the resources of steam power had been more fully exploited for fast railways and iron ships, for looms, printing presses, and farmers' combines, and after the introduction of the telegraph, intercontinental cable, photography, anesthetics, and universal compulsory education—a late Victorian could look back with astonishment on these developments during his or her lifetime. Walter Besant, one of these late Victorians, observed that so completely transformed were "the mind and habits of the ordinary Englishman" by 1897, "that he would not, could he see him, recognize his own grandfather."

Because England was the first country to become industrialized, its transformation was an especially painful one: it experienced a host of social and economic problems consequent to rapid and unregulated industrialization. England also experienced an enormous increase in wealth. An early start enabled England to capture markets all over the globe. Cotton and other manufactured products were exported in English ships, a merchant fleet whose size was without parallel in other countries. The profits gained from trade led also to extensive capital investments in all continents. After England had become the world's workshop, London became, from 1870 on, the world's banker. England gained particular profit from the development of its own colonies, which, by 1890, comprised more than a quarter of all the territory on the surface of the earth; one in four people was a subject of Queen Victoria. By the end of the century England was the world's foremost imperial power.

The reactions of Victorian writers to the fast-paced expansion of England were various. Thomas Babington Macaulay (1800–1859) relished the spectacle with strenuous enthusiasm. During the prosperous 1850s Macaulay's essays and histories, with their recitations of the statistics of industrial growth, constituted a Hymn to Progress as well as a celebration of the superior qualities of the English people—"the greatest and most highly civilized people that ever the world saw." Other writers felt that leadership in commerce and industry was being paid for at a terrible price in human happiness, that a so-called progress had been gained only by abandoning traditional rhythms of life and traditional patterns of human relationships. The melancholy poetry of Matthew Arnold often strikes this note:

> For what wears out the life of mortal men?
> 'Tis that from change to change their being rolls;
> 'Tis that repeated shocks, again, again,
> Exhaust the energy of strongest souls.

Although many Victorians shared a sense of satisfaction in the industrial and political preeminence of England during the period, they also suffered from an anxious sense of something lost, a sense too of being displaced persons in a world made alien by technological changes that had been exploited too quickly for the adaptive powers of the human psyche.

QUEEN VICTORIA AND THE VICTORIAN TEMPER

Queen Victoria's long reign, from 1837 to 1901, defines the historical period that bears her name. The question naturally arises whether the distinctive character of those years justifies the adjective *Victorian*. In part Victoria herself encouraged her own identification with the qualities we associate with the adjective—earnestness, moral responsibility, domestic propriety. As a young wife, as the mother of nine children, and as the black-garbed Widow of Windsor in the forty years after her husband's death in 1861, Victoria represented the domestic fidelities her citizens embraced. After her death Henry James wrote, "I mourn the safe and motherly old middle-class queen, who held the nation warm under the fold of her big, hideous Scotch-plaid shawl." Changes in the reproduction of visual images aided in making her the icon she became. She is the first British monarch of whom we have photographs. These pictures, and the ease and cheapness with which they were reproduced, facilitated her representing her country's sense of itself during her reign.

Victoria came to the throne in a decade that does seem to mark a different historical consciousness among Britain's writers. In 1831 John Stuart Mill asserts, "we are living in an age of transition." In the same year Thomas Carlyle writes, "The Old has passed away, but alas, the New appears not in its stead; the Time is still in pangs of travail with the New." Although the historical changes that created the England of the 1830s had been in progress for many decades, writers of the thirties shared a sharp new sense of modernity, of a break with the past, of historical self-consciousness. They responded to their sense of the historical moment with a strenuous call to action that they self-consciously distinguished from the attitude of the previous generation.

In 1834 Carlyle urged his contemporaries, "Close thy *Byron*; open thy *Goethe*." He was saying, in effect, to abandon the introspection of the Romantics and to turn to the higher moral purpose that he found in Goethe. The popular novelist Edward Bulwer-Lytton (1803–1873) in his *England and the English* made a similar judgment. "When Byron passed away," he wrote, " . . . we turned to the actual and practical career of life: we awoke from the morbid, the dreaming, 'the moonlight and dimness of the mind,' and by a natural reaction addressed ourselves to the active and daily objects which lay before us." This sense of historical self-consciousness, of strenuous social enterprise, and of growing national achievement led writers as early as the 1850s and 1860s to define their age as Victorian. The very fact that Victoria reigned for so long sustained the concept of a distinctive historical period that writers defined even as they lived it.

When Queen Victoria died, a reaction developed against many of the achievements of the previous century; this reinforced the sense that the Victorian age was a distinct period. In the earlier decades of the twentieth century, writers took pains to separate themselves from the Victorians. It was then the fashion for most literary critics to treat their Victorian predecessors as somewhat absurd creatures, stuffily complacent prigs with whose way of life they had little in common. Writers of the Georgian period (1911–36) took great delight in puncturing overinflated Victorian balloons, as Lytton Strachey, a member of Virginia Woolf's circle, did in *Eminent Victorians* (1918). A subtler example occurs in Woolf's *Orlando*, a fictionalized survey of English literature from Elizabethan times to 1928, in which the Victorians are presented in terms of dampness, rain, and proliferating vegetation:

> Ivy grew in unparalleled profusion. Houses that had been of bare stone were smothered in greenery. . . . And just as the ivy and the evergreen rioted in the damp earth outside, so did the same fertility show itself within. The life of the average woman was a succession of childbirths. . . . Giant cauliflowers towered deck above deck till they rivaled . . . the elm trees themselves. Hens laid incessantly eggs of no special tint. . . . The whole sky itself as it spread wide above the British Isles was nothing but a vast feather bed.

This witty description not only identifies a distinguishing quality of Victorian life and literature—a superabundant energy—but reveals the author's distaste for its smothering profusion. Woolf was the daughter of Sir Leslie Stephen (1832–1904), himself an eminent Victorian. In her later life, when assessing her father's powerful personality, Woolf recorded in her diary that she herself could never have become a writer if he had not died when he did. Growing up under such towering shadows, she and her generation mocked their predecessors to make them less intimidating. In his reminiscences *Portraits from Life,* the novelist Ford Madox Ford (1873–1939) recalled his feelings of terror when he confronted the works of Carlyle and Ruskin, which he likened to an overpowering range of high mountains. The mid-Victorians, he wrote, were "a childish nightmare to me."

The Georgian reaction against the Victorians is now only a matter of the history of taste, but its aftereffects still sometimes crop up when the term *Victorian* is employed in an exclusively pejorative sense, as prudish or old-fashioned. Contemporary historians and critics now find the Victorian period a richly complex example of a society struggling with the issues and problems we identify with modernism. But to give the period the single designation *Victorian* reduces its complexity. For a period almost seventy years in length, we can hardly expect generalizations to be uniformly applicable. It is, therefore, helpful to subdivide the age into three phases: Early Victorian (1830–48), Mid-Victorian (1848–70), and Late Victorian (1870–1901). It is also helpful to consider the final decade, the nineties, as a bridge between two centuries.

THE EARLY PERIOD (1830–48): A TIME OF TROUBLES

In the early 1830s, two historical events occurred of momentous conse-quence for England. In 1830 the Liverpool and Manchester Railway opened, becoming the first steam-powered, public railway line in the world. A burst of railway construction followed. By 1850, 6,621 miles of railway line con-nected all of England's major cities. By 1900, England had 15,195 lines of track and an underground railway system beneath London. The train trans-formed England's landscape, supported the growth of its commerce, and shrank the distances between its cities. The opening of England's first railway coincided with the opening of the country's Reform Parliament. The railway had increased the pressure for parliamentary reform. "Parliamentary reform must follow soon after the opening of this road," a Manchester man observed in 1830, when the railway opened. "A million of persons will pass over it in the course of this year, and see that hitherto unseen village of Newton; and they must be convinced of the absurdity of its sending two members to Par-liament while Manchester sends none." Despite the growth of manufactur-ing cities consequent to the Industrial Revolution, England was still governed by an archaic electoral system whereby some of the new industrial cities were unrepresented in Parliament while "rotten boroughs" (communities that had become depopulated) elected the nominees of the local squire to Parliament.

By 1830 a time of economic distress had brought England close to revo-lution. Manufacturing interests, who refused to tolerate their exclusion from the political process any longer, led working men in agitating for reform. Fearing the kind of revolution it had seen in Europe, Parliament passed a Reform Bill in 1832 that transformed England's class structure. The Reform Bill of 1832 extended the right to vote to all males owning property worth £10 or more in annual rent. In effect the voting public thereafter included the lower middle classes but not the working classes, who did not obtain the vote until 1867, when a second reform bill was passed. Even more important than the extension of the franchise was the virtual abolition of the rotten boroughs and the redistribution of parliamentary representation. Because it broke up the monopoly of power that the conservative landowners had so long enjoyed (the Tory party had been in office almost continuously from 1783 to 1830), the Reform Bill represents the beginning of a new age, in which middle-class economic interests gained increasing power.

Yet even the newly constituted Parliament was unable to find legislative solutions to the problems facing the nation. The economic and social difficulties attendant on industrialization were so severe that the 1830s and 1840s became known as the Time of Troubles. After a period of prosperity from 1832 to 1836, a crash in 1837, followed by a series of bad harvests, produced a period of unemployment, desperate poverty, and rioting. Conditions in the new industrial and coal-mining areas were terrible. Workers and their families in the slums of such cities as Manchester lived in horribly crowded, unsanitary housing; and the conditions under which women and children toiled in mines and factories were unimaginably brutal. Elizabeth Barrett's poem *The Cry of the Children* (1843) expresses her horrified response to an official report on child labor, describing five-year-olds dragging heavy tubs of coal through low-ceilinged mine passages for sixteen hours a day.

The owners of mines and factories regarded themselves as innocent of blame for such conditions, for they were wedded to an economic theory of laissez-faire, which assumed that unregulated working conditions would ultimately benefit everyone. A sense of the seemingly hopeless complexity of the situation during the Hungry 1840s is provided by an entry for 1842 in the diary of the statesman Charles Greville, an entry written at the same time that Carlyle was making his contribution to the "Condition of England Question," *Past and Present*. Conditions in the north of England, Greville reports, were "appalling":

> There is an immense and continually increasing population, no adequate demand for labor, . . . no confidence, but a universal alarm, disquietude, and discontent. Nobody can sell anything. . . . Certainly I have never seen . . . so serious a state of things as that which now stares us in the face; and this after thirty years of uninterrupted peace, and the most ample scope afforded for the development of all our resources. . . . One remarkable feature in the present condition of affairs is that nobody can account for it, and nobody pretends to be able to point out any remedy.

In reality many remedies were proposed. One of the most striking was put forward by the Chartists, a large organization of workers. In 1838 the organization drew up a "People's Charter" advocating the extension of the right to vote, the use of secret balloting, and other legislative reforms. For ten years the Chartist leaders engaged in agitation to have their program adopted by Parliament. Their fiery speeches, delivered at conventions designed to collect signatures for petitions to Parliament, created fears of revolution. In *Locksley Hall* Tennyson seems to have had the Chartist demonstrations in mind when he wrote: "Slowly comes a hungry people, as a lion, creeping nigher, / Glares at one that nods and winks behind a slowly-dying fire." Although the Chartist movement had fallen apart by 1848, it succeeded in creating an atmosphere open to reform. One of the most important reforms was the abolition of the high tariffs on imported grains, tariffs known as the Corn Laws (the word *corn* in England refers to wheat and other grains). These high tariffs had been established to protect English farm products from having to compete with low-priced products imported from abroad. Landowners and farmers fought to keep these tariffs in force so that high prices for their wheat would be ensured; but the rest of the population suffered severely from the exorbitant price of bread or, in years of bad crops, from scarcity of food. In 1845 serious crop failures in England and the outbreak of potato blight in Ireland convinced Sir Robert Peel, the Tory prime minister, that traditional protectionism must be abandoned. In 1846 the Corn Laws were repealed by Parliament, and the way was paved for the introduction of a system of Free Trade whereby goods could be imported with the payment of only minimal tariff duties. Although Free Trade did not eradicate the slums of Manchester, it worked well for many years and helped relieve the major crisis of the Victorian economy. In 1848, when revolutions were breaking out all over Europe, England was relatively unaffected. A large Chartist demonstration in London seemed to threaten revolution, but it came to nothing. The next two decades were relatively calm and prosperous.

This Time of Troubles left its mark on some early Victorian literature. "Insurrection is a most sad necessity," Carlyle writes in his *Past and Present*, "and governors who wait for that to instruct them are surely getting into the fatalest courses." A similar refrain runs through Carlyle's history *The French Revolution* (1837). Memories of the French Reign of Terror lasted longer than memories of Trafalgar and Waterloo, memories freshened by later outbreaks of civil strife, "the red fool-fury of the Seine" as Tennyson described one of the violent overturnings of government in France. It is the novelists of the 1840s and early 1850s, however, who show the most marked response to the industrial and political scene. Vivid records of these conditions are to be found in the fiction of Charles Kingsley (1819–1875); Elizabeth Gaskell (1810–1865); and Benjamin Disraeli (1804–1881), a novelist who became prime minister. For his novel *Sybil* (1845) Disraeli chose an appropriate subtitle, *The Two Nations*—a phrase that pointed out the line dividing the England of the rich from the other nation, the England of the poor.

THE MID-VICTORIAN PERIOD (1848–70): ECONOMIC PROSPERITY, THE GROWTH OF EMPIRE, AND RELIGIOUS CONTROVERSY

In the decades following the Time of Troubles some Victorian writers, such as Dickens, continued to make critical attacks on the shortcomings of the Victorian social scene. Even more critical and indignant than Dickens was John Ruskin, who turned from a purely moral and aesthetic criticism of art during this period to denounce the evils of Victorian industry, as in his *The Stones of Venice* (1853), which combines a history of architecture with stern prophecies about the doom of technological culture, or in his attacks on laissez-faire economics in *Unto This Last* (1862). Generally speaking, however, the realistic novels of Anthony Trollope (1815–1882), with their comfortable tolerance and equanimity, are a more characteristic reflection of the mid-Victorian attitude toward the social and political scene than are Ruskin's lamentations. Overall, this second phase of the Victorian period had many harassing problems, but it was a time of prosperity. On the whole its institutions worked well. Even the badly bungled war against Russia in the Crimea (1854–56) did not seriously affect the growing sense of satisfaction that the challenging difficulties of the 1840s had been solved or would be solved by English wisdom and energy. The monarchy was proving its worth in a modern setting. The queen and her husband, Prince Albert, were themselves models of middle-class domesticity and devotion to duty. The aristocracy was discovering that Free Trade was enriching rather than impoverishing their estates; agriculture flourished together with trade and industry. And through a succession of Factory Acts in Parliament, which restricted child labor and limited hours of employment, the condition of the working classes was also being gradually improved. When we speak of Victorian complacency or stability or optimism, we are usually referring to this mid-Victorian phase—"The Age of Improvement," as the historian Asa Briggs has called it. "Of all the decades in our history," writes G. M. Young, "a wise man would choose the eighteen-fifties to be young in."

In 1851 Prince Albert opened the Great Exhibition in Hyde Park, where a gigantic glass greenhouse, the Crystal Palace, had been erected to display the exhibits of modern industry and science. The Crystal Palace was one of the first buildings constructed according to modern architectural principles in which materials such as glass and iron are employed for purely functional ends (much late Victorian furniture, on the other hand, with its fantastic and irrelevant ornamentation, was constructed according to the opposite principle). The building itself, as well as the exhibits, symbolized the triumphant feats of Victorian technology. As Benjamin Disraeli wrote to a friend in 1862: "It is a privilege to live in this age of rapid and brilliant events. What an error to consider it a utilitarian age. It is one of infinite romance."

England's technological progress, together with its prosperity, led to an enormous expansion of its influence throughout the globe. Its annual export of goods nearly trebled in value between 1850 and 1870. Not only the export of goods but that of people and capital increased. Between 1853 and 1880, 2,466,000 emigrants left Britain, many bound for British colonies. By 1870, British capitalists had invested £800 million abroad; in 1850, the total had been only £300 million. This investment, of people, money, and technology, created the British Empire. Important building blocks of the empire were put in place in the mid-Victorian period. In the 1850s and 1860s there was large-scale immigration to Australia; in 1867, Parliament unified the Canadian provinces into the Dominion of Canada. In 1857, Parliament took over the government of India from the private East India Company, which had controlled the country, and started to put in place its civil service government. In 1876, Queen Victoria was named empress of India. Although the competitive scramble for African colonies did not take place until the final decades of the century, the model of empire was created earlier, made possible by technological revolution in communication and transportation. Much as Rome had built roads through Europe in the years of the Roman Empire, Britain built railways and strung telegraph wires. It also put in place a framework for education and government that preserves British influence in former colonies even today. Britain's motives, in creating its empire, were many. It sought wealth, markets for manufactured goods, sources for raw materials, and world power and influence. Many English people also saw the expansion of empire as a moral responsibility, what Kipling termed "the White Man's burden." Queen Victoria herself stated that the imperial mission was "to protect the poor natives and advance civilization." Missionary societies flourished, spreading Christianity in India, Asia, and Africa.

At the same time that the British missionary enterprise was expanding, there was increasing debate about religious belief. By the mid-Victorian period, the Church of England had evolved into three major divisions: Evangelical, or Low Church, Broad Church, and High Church. The Evangelicals emphasized spiritual transformation of the individual by conversion and a strictly moral Christian life. Zealously dedicated to good causes (they were responsible for the emancipation of all slaves in the British Empire as early as 1833), advocates of a strict Puritan code of morality, and righteously censorious of worldliness in others, the Evangelicals became a powerful and active minority in the early part of the nineteenth century. Much of the power of the Evangelicals depended on the fact that their view of life and religion was virtually identical with that of a much larger group external to the Church of England, the Nonconformists, or Dissenters—that is, Baptists, Methodists, Congregationalists, and other Protestant denominations. The High Church was also associated with a group external to the Church of England; it was the "Catholic" side of the church, emphasizing the importance of tradition, ritual, and authority. In the 1830s, a High Church movement took shape, known both as "the Oxford movement," because it originated at Oxford University, and as "Tractarianism," because its leaders developed their arguments in a series of pamphlets or tracts. Led by John Henry Newman, who later converted to Roman Catholicism, Tractarians argued that the Church could maintain its power and authority only by resisting liberal tendencies and holding to its original traditions. The Broad Church resisted the doctrinal and ecclesiastical controversies that separated the High Church and Evangelical divisions. Open to modern advances in thought, its adherents emphasized the broadly inclusive nature of the church.

Some rationalist challenges to religious belief that developed before the Victorian period maintained their influence. The most significant was Utilitarianism, also known as Benthamism or Philosophical Radicalism. Utilitarianism derived from the thought of Jeremy Bentham (1748–1832) and his disciple James Mill (1773–1836), the father of John Stuart Mill. Bentham believed that all human beings seek to maximize pleasure and minimize pain. The criterion by which we should judge a morally correct action, therefore, is the extent to which it provides the greatest pleasure to the greatest number. Measuring religion by this moral arithmetic, Benthamites concluded that it was an outmoded superstition; it did not meet the rationalist test of value. Utilitarianism was widely influential in providing a philosophical basis for political reform, but it aroused considerable opposition on the part of those who felt it failed to recognize people's spiritual needs. Raised according to strict utilitarian principles by his father, John Stuart Mill came to be critical of them. In the mental and spiritual crisis portrayed in his *Autobiography*, Mill describes his realization that his utilitarian upbringing had left him no power to feel. In *Sartor Resartus*, Carlyle describes a similar spiritual crisis in which he struggles to rediscover the springs of religious feeling in the face of his despair at the specter of a universe governed only by utilitarian principles. Later both Dickens, in his portrayal of Thomas Gradgrind in *Hard Times*, "a man of facts and calculations," "ready to weigh and measure any parcel of human nature," and John Ruskin, in his *Unto This Last*, attack utilitarianism.

In mid-Victorian England, however, the challenge to religious belief gradually shifted from the Utilitarians to some of the leaders of science, in particular to Thomas Henry Huxley, who popularized the theories of Charles Darwin. Although many English scientists were themselves individuals of strong religious convictions, the impact of their scientific discoveries seemed consistently damaging to established faiths. Complaining in 1851 about the "flimsiness" of his own religious faith, Ruskin exclaimed: "If only the Geologists would let me alone, I could do very well, but those dreadful hammers! I hear the clink of them at the end of every cadence of the Bible verses."

The damage lamented by Ruskin was effected in two ways. First the scientific attitude of mind was applied toward a study of the Bible itself. This kind of investigation, developed especially in Germany, was known as the "Higher Criticism." Instead of treating the Bible as a sacredly infallible document, scientifically minded scholars examined it as a mere text of history and presented evidence about its composition that believers, especially in Protestant countries, found disconcerting, to say the least. A noteworthy example of such Higher Criticism studies was David Friedrich Strauss's *Das Leben Jesu*, which was translated by George Eliot in 1846 as *The Life of Jesus*. The second kind of damage was effected by the view of humanity implicit in the discoveries of geology and astronomy, the new and "Terrible Muses" of literature, as Tennyson called them in a late poem. Geology, by extending the history of the earth backward millions of years, reduced the stature of the human species in time. John Tyndall, an eminent physicist, said in an address at Belfast in 1874 that in the eighteenth century people had an "unwavering trust" in the "chronology of the Old Testament" but in Victorian times they had to become accustomed to

> the idea that not for six thousand, nor for sixty thousand, nor for six thousand thousand, but for aeons embracing untold millions of years, this earth has been the theater of life and death. The riddle of the rocks has been read by the geologist and paleontologist, from sub-Cambrian depths to the deposits thickening over the sea bottoms of today. And upon the leaves of that stone book are . . . stamped the characters, plainer and surer than those formed by the ink of history, which carry the mind back into abysses of past time.

The discoveries of astronomers, by extending a knowledge of stellar distances to dizzying expanses, were likewise disconcerting. Carlyle's friend John Sterling remarked in a letter of 1837 how geology "gives one the same sort of bewildering view of the abysmal extent of Time that Astronomy does of Space." To Tennyson's speaker in *Maud* (1855) the stars are "innumerable" tyrants of "iron skies." They are "Cold fires, yet with power to burn and brand / His nothingness into man."

In the mid-Victorian period, biology reduced humankind even further into "nothingness." Darwin's great treatise *The Origin of Species* (1859) was interpreted by the nonscientific public in a variety of ways. Some chose to assume that evolution was synonymous with progress, but most readers recognized that Darwin's theory of natural selection conflicted not only with the concept of creation derived from the Bible but also with long-established assumptions of the values attached to humanity's special role in the world. Darwin's later treatise *The Descent of Man* (1871) raised more explicitly the haunting question of our identification with the animal kingdom. If the principle of survival of the fittest was accepted as the key to conduct, there remained the inquiry: fittest for what? As John Fowles writes in his 1968 novel about Victorian England, *The French Lieutenant's Woman,* Darwin's theories made the Victorians feel "infinitely isolated." "By the 1860s the great iron structures of their philosophies, religions, and social stratifications were already beginning to look dangerously corroded to the more perspicacious."

Disputes about evolutionary science, like the disputes about religion, are a reminder that beneath the placidly prosperous surface of the mid-Victorian age there were serious conflicts and anxieties. In the same year as the Great Exhibition, with its celebration of the triumphs of trade and industry, Charles Kingsley wrote, "The young men and women of our day are fast parting from their parents and each other; the more thoughtful are wandering either towards Rome, towards sheer materialism, or towards an unchristian and unphilosophic spiritualism."

THE LATE PERIOD (1870–1901): DECAY OF VICTORIAN VALUES

The third phase of the Victorian age is more difficult to categorize. At first glance its point of view seems merely an extension of mid-Victorianism, whose golden glow lingered on through the Jubilee years of 1887 and 1897 (years celebrating the fiftieth and sixtieth anniversaries of the queen's accession) down to 1914. For many Victorians, this final phase of the century was a time of serenity and security, the age of house parties and long weekends in the country. In the amber of Henry James's prose is immortalized a sense of the comfortable pace of these pleasant, well-fed gatherings. Life in London, too, was for many an exhilarating heyday. In *My Life and Loves* the Irish-American Frank Harris (1854–1931), often a severe critic of the English scene, records his recollections of the gaiety of London in the 1880s: "London: who would give even an idea of its varied delights: London, the center of civilization, the queen city of the world without a peer in the multitude of its attractions, as superior to Paris as Paris is to New York." The exhilarating sense of London's delights reflects in part the proliferation of things: commodities, inventions, products that were changing the texture of modern life. England had become a country committed not only to continuing technological change but also to a culture of consumerism, generating new products for sale.

The wealth of England's empire provided the foundation on which its economy was built. The final decades of the century saw the apex of British imperialism, yet the cost of the empire became increasingly apparent in rebellions, massacres, and bungled wars, such as the Indian Mutiny in 1857; the Jamaica Rebellion in 1865; the massacre of General Gordon and his troops at Khartoum, in the Sudan, in 1885, where he had been sent to evacuate the British in the face of a religiously inspired revolt; and the Boer War, at the end of the century, in which England engaged in a long, bloody, and unpopular struggle to annex two independent republics in the south of Africa controlled by Dutch settlers called Boers. In addition, the "Irish Question," as it was called, became especially divisive in the 1880s when Home Rule for Ireland became a topic of heated debate—a proposed reform that was unsuccessfully advocated by Prime Minister Gladstone and other leaders. And outside of the British Empire, other developments challenged Victorian stability and security. The sudden emergence of Bismarck's Germany after the defeat of France in 1871 was progressively to confront England with powerful threats to its naval and military position and also to its preeminence in trade and industry. The recovery of the United States after the Civil War likewise provided new and serious competition not only in industry but also in agriculture. As the westward expansion of railroads in the United States and Canada opened up the vast, grain-rich prairies, the typical English farmer had to confront lower grain prices and a dramatically different scale of productivity, which England could not match. In 1873 and 1874 such severe economic depressions occurred that the rate of emigration rose to an alarming degree. Another change in the mid-Victorian balance of power was the growth of labor as a political and economic force. In 1867, under Disraeli's guidance, a second Reform Bill had been passed that extended the right to vote to sections of the working classes; and this, together with the subsequent development of trade unions, made labor a powerful political force that included a wide variety of kinds of socialism. Some labor leaders were disciples of the Tory-socialism of John Ruskin and shared his idealistic conviction that the middle-class economic and political system, with its distrust of state interference, was irresponsible and immoral. Other labor leaders had been influenced instead by the revolutionary theories of Karl Marx and Friedrich Engels as expounded in their *Communist Manifesto* of 1847 and in Marx's *Das Kapital* (1867, 1885, 1895). The first English author of note to embrace Marxism was the poet and painter William Morris, who shared with Marx a conviction that utopia could be achieved only after the working classes had, by revolution, taken control of government and industry.

In much of the literature of this final phase of Victorianism we can sense an overall change of attitudes. Some of the late Victorian writers expressed the change openly by simply attacking the major mid-Victorian idols. Samuel Butler (1835–1902), for example, set about demolishing Darwin, Tennyson, and Prime Minister Gladstone, figures whose aura of authority reminded him of his own father. For the more worldly and casual-mannered Prime Minister Disraeli, on the other hand, Butler could express considerable admiration: "Earnestness was his greatest danger, but if he did not quite overcome it (as who indeed can? it is the last enemy that shall be subdued), he managed to veil it with a fair amount of success." In his novel *The Way of All Flesh*, much of which was written in the 1870s, Butler satirized family life, in particular the tyrannical self-righteousness of a Victorian father, his own father (a clergyman) serving as his model. In a different vein Walter Pater and his followers concluded that the striving of their predecessors was ultimately pointless, that the answers to our problems are not to be found, and that our role is to enjoy the fleeting moments of beauty in "this short day of frost and sun." It is symptomatic of this shift in point of view that Edward FitzGerald's beautiful translation of the *Rubáiyát of Omar Khayyám* (1859), with its melancholy theme that life's problems are insoluble, went virtually unnoticed in the 1860s but became a popular favorite in subsequent decades.

THE NINETIES

The changes in attitude that had begun cropping up in the 1870s became much more conspicuous in the final decade of the century and give the nineties a special aura of notoriety. Of course the changes were not in evidence everywhere. Throughout the empire at its outposts in India and Africa, the English were building railways and administering governments with the same strenuous energy as in the mid-Victorian period. The stories of Kipling and Conrad variously record the struggles of such people. Also embodying the task of sustaining an empire were the soldiers and sailors who fought in various colonial wars, most notably in the war against the Boers in South Africa (1899–1902). But back in England, Victorian standards were breaking down on several fronts. One colorful embodiment of changing values was Victoria's son and heir, Edward, Prince of Wales, who was entering his fiftieth year as the nineties began. A pleasure-seeking, easygoing person, Edward was the antithesis of his father, Prince Albert, an earnest-minded intellectual who had devoted his life to hard work and to administrative responsibilities. Edward's carryings-on were a favorite topic for newspaper articles, one of which noted how this father of five children "openly maintained scandalous relations with ballet dancers and chorus singers."

Much of the writing of the decade illustrates a breakdown of a different sort. Melancholy, not gaiety, is characteristic of its spirit. Artists of the nineties, representing the Aesthetic movement, were very much aware of living at the end of a great century and often cultivated a deliberately fin de siècle ("end-of-century") pose. A studied languor, a weary sophistication, a search for new ways of titillating jaded palates can be found in both the poetry and the prose of the period. *The Yellow Book*, a periodical that ran from 1894 to 1897, is generally taken to represent the aestheticism of the nineties. The startling black-and-white drawings and designs of its art editor, Aubrey Beardsley (1872–1898), the prose of George Moore and Max Beerbohm, and the poetry of Ernest Dowson illustrate different aspects of the movement. In 1893 the Austrian critic Max Nordau summed up what seemed to him to be happening, in a book that was as sensational as its title: *Degeneration*.

From the perspective of the twentieth century, however, it is easy to see in the nineties the beginning of the modernist movement in literature; a number of the great writers of the twentieth century—Yeats, Hardy, Conrad, Shaw—were already publishing.

In Dickens's *David Copperfield* (1850) the hero affirms: "I have always been thoroughly in earnest." Forty-five years later Oscar Wilde's comedy *The Importance of Being Earnest* turns this typical mid-Victorian word *earnest* into a pun, a key joke in this comic spectacle of earlier Victorian values being turned upside down. As Richard Le Gallienne (a novelist of the nineties) remarked in *The Romantic Nineties* (1926): "Wilde made dying Victorianism laugh at itself, and it may be said to have died of the laughter."

THE ROLE OF WOMEN

Political and legal reforms in the course of the Victorian period had given citizens many rights. In 1844 Friedrich Engels observed: "England is unquestionably the freest—that is the least unfree—country in the world, North America not excepted." England had indeed done much to extend its citizens' liberties, but women did not share in these freedoms. They could not vote or hold political office. (Although petitions to Parliament advocating women's suffrage were introduced as early as the 1840s, women did not get the vote until 1918.) Until the passage of the Married Women's Property Acts (1870–1908), married women could not own or handle their own property. Although men could divorce their wives for adultery, wives could divorce their husbands only if adultery were combined with cruelty, bigamy, incest, or bestiality. Educational and employment opportunities for women were limited. These inequities stimulated a spirited debate about women's roles known as the "Woman Question." Arguments for women's rights were based on the libertarian principles that had formed the basis of extended rights for men. In Hardy's last novel, *Jude the Obscure* (1895), his heroine justifies leaving her husband by quoting a passage from Mill's *On Liberty*. She might have quoted another work by Mill, *The Subjection of Women*, which, like Mary Wollstonecraft's *A Vindication of the Rights of Women* (1792), challenges long-established assumptions about women's role in society.

The changing conditions of women's work created by the Industrial Revolution posed an equally strong challenge to traditional views of women's roles. The explosive growth of the textile industries brought hundreds of thousands of lower-class women into factory jobs with grueling working conditions, and the need for coal to fuel England's industrial development brought women into the mines. The Factory Acts (1802–78) introduced increasing regulation of the conditions of labor in mines and factories, including reduction of the sixteen-hour day. Other changes in legislation extended women's rights. The Custody Act of 1839 gave a mother the right to petition the court for access to her minor children and custody of children under seven (raised to sixteen in 1878). The Divorce and Matrimonial Causes Act of 1857 established a civil divorce court (divorce previously could be granted only by an ecclesiastical court) and provided a deserted wife the right to apply for a protection order that would allow her rights to her property. Although divorce remained so expensive as to be available only to the rich, these changes in marriage and divorce laws, together with the Married Women's Property Acts, began to establish a basis for the rights of women in marriage.

In addition to pressuring Parliament for legal reform, feminists worked to enlarge educational opportunities for women. In 1837 none of England's three universities was open to women. Tennyson's long poem *The Princess* (1847), with its fantasy of a women's college from whose precincts all males are excluded, was inspired by contemporary discussions of the need for women to obtain an education more advanced than that provided by the popular finishing schools such as Miss Pinkerton's Academy in Thackeray's *Vanity Fair*. Although by the end of the poem, Princess Ida has repented of her Amazonian scheme, she and the prince look forward to a future in which man will be "more of woman, she of man." The poem reflects a climate of opinion that led in 1848 to the establishment of the first women's college in London, an example later recommended by Thomas Henry Huxley, a strong advocate of advanced education for women. By the end of Victoria's reign, women could take degrees at twelve universities or university colleges and could study, although not earn a degree, at Oxford and Cambridge.

There was also agitation for improved employment opportunities for women. Writers as diverse as Charlotte Brontë, Elizabeth Barrett Browning, and Florence Nightingale complained that middle-class women were taught trivial accomplishments to fill up days in which there was nothing important to do. The problem of nothing to do was acute in quite a different way for what contemporary journalists called "surplus" or "redundant" women, that is, the women in the population who remained unmarried because of the imbalance in numbers between the sexes. Such women (of whom there were approximately half a million in mid-Victorian England) had few employment opportunities, none of them attractive or profitable. Emigration was frequently proposed as a solution to the problem, but the number of single female emigrants was never high enough to affect significantly the population imbalance. Bad working conditions and underemployment drove thousands of women into prostitution, which became increasingly professionalized in the nineteenth century. The only occupation at which an unmarried middle-class woman could earn a living and maintain some claim to gentility was that of a governess, but a governess could expect no security of employment, only minimal wages, and an ambiguous status, somewhere between servant and family member, that isolated her within the household. Perhaps because the governess so clearly indicated the precariousness of the unmarried middle-class woman's status in Victorian England, the governess novel, of which the most famous examples are *Jane Eyre* and *Vanity Fair*, became a popular genre through which to explore women's roles in society.

As such novels indicate, Victorian society was preoccupied not only with legal and economic limitations on women's lives but with the very nature of woman. In *The Subjection of Women* John Stuart Mill argues that "what is now called the nature of women is eminently an artificial thing—the result of forced repression in some directions, unnatural stimulation in others." In Tennyson's *The Princess* the king voices a more traditional view of woman's role:

> Man for the field and woman for the hearth:
> Man for the sword and for the needle she:
> Man with the head and woman with the heart:
> Man to command and woman to obey.

The king's relegation of women to the hearth and heart reflects an ideology that claimed that woman had a special nature peculiarly fit for her domestic role. Most aptly epitomized by the title of Coventry Patmore's immensely popular poem *The Angel in the House* (1854–62), this concept of womanhood stressed woman's purity and selflessness. Protected and enshrined within the home, her role was to create a place of peace where man could take refuge from the difficulties of modern life. In *Of Queen's Gardens* John Ruskin writes:

> This is the true nature of home—it is the place of Peace; the shelter, not only from all injury, but from all terror, doubt, and division. In so far as it is not this, it is not home; so far as the anxieties of the outer life penetrate into it, and the inconsistently-minded, unknown, unloved, or hostile society of the outer world is allowed either by husband or wife to cross the threshold, it ceases to be home; it is then only a part of that outer world which you have roofed over, and lighted fire in. But so far as it is a sacred place, a vestal temple, a temple of the hearth watched over by Household Gods, . . . so far it vindicates the name, and fulfills the praise, of home.

Such an exalted conception of home placed great pressure on the woman who ran it to be, in Ruskin's words, "enduringly, incorruptibly good; instinctively, infallibly wise—wise, not for self-development, but for self-renunciation." It is easy to recognize the oppressive aspects of this ideology. Paradoxically, however, it was used not only by antifeminists, eager to keep woman in her place, but by some feminists as well, in justifying the special contribution that woman could make to public life.

In his preface to *The Portrait of a Lady* (1881) Henry James writes: "Millions of presumptuous girls, intelligent or not intelligent, daily affront their destiny, and what is it open to their destiny to *be*, at the most, that we should make an ado about it?" Every major Victorian novelist makes the "ado" that James describes in addressing the question of woman's vocation. Ultimately, as Victorian novels illustrate, the basic problem was not only political, economic, and educational. It was how women were regarded, and regarded themselves, as members of a society.

LITERACY, PUBLICATION, AND READING

Literacy increased significantly during the Victorian period, although precise figures are difficult to calculate. In 1837 about half of the adult male population could read and write to some extent; by the end of the century, basic literacy was almost universal, the product in part of compulsory national education, required by 1880 to the age of ten. There was also an explosion of things to read. Because of technological changes in printing—presses powered by steam, paper made from wood pulp rather than rags, and, toward the end of the century, typesetting machines—publishers could bring out more printed material more cheaply than ever before. The number of newspapers, periodicals, and books increased exponentially during the Victorian period. Books remained fairly expensive, and most readers borrowed them from commercial lending libraries. (There were few public libraries until the final decades of the century.) After the repeal of the stamp tax and duties on advertisements just after midcentury, an extensive popular press developed.

The most significant development in publishing from the point of view of literary culture was the growth of the periodical. In the first thirty years of the Victorian period, 170 new periodicals were started in London alone.

There were magazines for every taste: cheap and popular magazines that published sensational tales; religious monthlys; weekly newspapers; satiric periodicals noted for their political cartoons (the most famous of these was *Punch*); women's magazines; monthly miscellanies publishing fiction, poetry, and articles on current affairs; and reviews and quarterlies, ostensibly reviewing new books but using the reviews, which were always unsigned, as occasions for essays on the subjects in question. The chief reviews and monthly magazines had a great deal of power and influence; they defined issues in public affairs, and they made and broke literary reputations. They also published the major writers of the period: the fiction of Dickens, Thackeray, Eliot, Trollope, and Gaskell; the essays of Carlyle, Mill, Arnold, and Ruskin; the poetry of Tennyson and the Brownings all appeared in monthly magazines.

The circumstances of periodical publication exerted a shaping force on literature. Novels and long works of nonfiction prose were published in serial form. Although serial publication of works began in the late eighteenth century, it was the publication of Dickens's *Pickwick Papers* (1836–37) in individual numbers that established its popularity. All of Dickens's novels and many of those of his contemporaries were published in serial form. Readers therefore read these works in relatively short, discrete installments over a period that could extend more than a year, with time for reflection and interpretation in between. Serial publication encouraged a certain kind of plotting and pacing and allowed writers to take account of their readers' reactions as they constructed subsequent installments. Writers created a continuing world, punctuated by the ends of installments, which served to stimulate the curiosity that would keep readers buying subsequent issues. Serial publication also created a distinctive sense of a community of readers, a sense encouraged by the practice of reading aloud in family gatherings.

As the family reading of novels suggests, the middle-class reading public enjoyed a common reading culture. Poets such as Tennyson and Elizabeth Barrett Browning appealed to a large body of readers; prose writers like Carlyle, Arnold, and Ruskin achieved a status as sages; and the major Victorian novelists were popular writers. Readers shared the expectation that literature would not only delight but instruct, that it would be continuous with the lived world, and that it would illuminate social problems. "Tennyson," one of his college friends warned him, "we cannot live in art." These expectations weighed more heavily on some writers than others. Tennyson wore his public mantle with considerable ambivalence; Arnold abandoned the private mode of lyric poetry in order to speak about public issues in lectures and essays.

By the 1870s the sense of a broad readership, with a shared set of social concerns, had begun to dissolve. Writers had begun to define themselves in opposition to a general public; poets like the Pre-Raphaelites pursued art for art's sake, doing exactly what Tennyson's friend had warned against; mass publication included less and less serious literature. By the end of Victoria's reign, writers could no longer assume a unified reading public.

THE NOVEL

The novel was the dominant form in Victorian literature. Initially published, for the most part, in serial form, novels subsequently appeared in three-volume editions, or "three-deckers." "Large loose baggy monsters," Henry James called them, reflecting his dissatisfaction with their sprawling, panoramic expanse. As their size suggests, Victorian novels seek to represent a large and comprehensive social world, with the variety of classes and social settings that constitute a community. They contain a multitude of characters and a number of plots, setting in motion the kinds of patterns that reveal the author's vision of the deep structures of the social world—how, in George Eliot's words, "the mysterious mixture behaves under the varying experiments of Time." They presents themselves as realistic, that is, as representing a social world that shares the features of the one we inhabit. The French novelist Stendhal (1783–1842) called the novel "a mirror wandering down a road," but the metaphor of the mirror is somewhat deceptive, since it implies that writers exert no shaping force on their material. It would be more accurate to speak not of realism but of realisms, since each novelist presents a specific vision of reality whose representational force he or she seeks to persuade us to acknowledge through a variety of techniques and conventions. The worlds of Dickens, of Trollope, of Eliot, of the Brontës hardly seem continuous with each other, but their authors share the attempt to convince us that the characters and events they imagine resemble those we experience in actual life.

The experience that Victorian novelists most frequently depict is the set of social relationships in the middle-class society developing around them. It is a society where the material conditions of life indicate social position, where money defines opportunity, where social class enforces a powerful sense of stratification, yet where chances for class mobility exist. Pip can aspire to the great expectations that provide the title for Dickens's novel; Jane Eyre can marry her employer, a landed gentleman. Most Victorian novels focus on a protagonist whose effort to define his or her place in society is the main concern of the plot. The novel thus constructs a tension between surrounding social conditions and the aspiration of the hero or heroine, whether it be for love, social position, or a life adequate to his or her imagination. This tension makes the novel the natural form to use in portraying woman's struggle for self-realization in the context of the constraints imposed upon her. For both men and women writers, the heroine is often, therefore, the representative protagonist whose search for fulfillment emblematizes the human condition. The great heroines of Victorian fiction—Jane Eyre, Maggie Tulliver, Dorothea Brooke, Isabel Archer, Tess of the d'Urbervilles, even Becky Sharp—all seem in some way to illustrate George Eliot's judgment, voiced in the Prelude to *Middlemarch*, of "a certain spiritual grandeur ill-matched with meanness of opportunity."

The novel was not only a fertile medium for the portrayal of women; women writers were, for the first time, not figures on the margins but major authors. Jane Austen, the Brontës, Elizabeth Gaskell, George Eliot—all helped define the genre. When Charlotte Brontë screwed up her courage to write to the poet laureate, Robert Southey, to ask his advice about a career as a writer, he warned her, "Literature cannot be the business of a woman's life, and it ought not to be." Charlotte Brontë put this letter, with one other from Southey, in an envelope, with the inscription "Southey's advice to be kept forever. My twenty-first birthday." Brontë's ability ultimately to depart from Southey's advice derived in part from how amenable the novel was to women writers. It concerned the domestic life that women knew well—

courtship, family relationships, marriage. It was a popular form whose market women could enter easily. It did not carry the burden of an august tradition as poetry did, nor did it build on the learning of a university education. In his essay *The Lady Novelists,* George Henry Lewes declared, "The advent of female literature promises woman's view of life, woman's experience." His common-law wife, George Eliot, together with many of her sister novelists, fulfilled his prophecy.

Whether written by women or men, the Victorian novel was extraordinarily various. It encompassed a wealth of styles and genres from the extravagant comedy of Dickens to the Gothic romances of the Brontë sisters, from the satire of Thackeray to the probing psychological fiction of Eliot, from the social and political realism of Trollope to the sensation novels of Wilkie Collins. Later in the century, a number of popular genres developed—crime, mystery, and horror novels, science fiction, detective stories. For the Victorians, the novel was both a principal form of entertainment and a spur to social sympathy. There was not a social topic that the novel did not address. Dickens, Gaskell, and many lesser novelists tried to stimulate efforts for social reform through their depiction of social problems. Writing at the beginning of the twentieth century, Joseph Conrad defined the novel in a way that could speak for the Victorians: "What is a novel if not a conviction of our fellow-men's existence strong enough to take upon itself a form of imagined life clearer than reality and whose accumulated verisimilitude of selected episodes puts to shame the pride of documentary history?"

POETRY

Victorian poetry developed in the context of the novel. As the novel emerged as the dominant form of literature, poets sought new ways of telling stories in verse; examples include Tennyson's *Maud,* Elizabeth Barrett Browning's *Aurora Leigh,* Robert Browning's *The Ring and the Book,* and Arthur Hugh Clough's *Amours de Voyage.* Poets and critics debated what the appropriate subjects of such long narrative poems should be. Some, like Matthew Arnold, held that poets should use the heroic materials of the past; others, like Elizabeth Barrett Browning, felt that poets should represent "their age, not Charlemagne's." Poets also experimented with character and perspective. *Amours de Voyage* is a long epistolary poem that tells the story of a failed romance through letters written by its various characters; *The Ring and the Book* presents its plot—an old Italian murder story—through ten different perspectives.

Victorian poetry also developed in the shadow of Romanticism. By 1837, when Victoria ascended the throne, all of the major Romantic poets, save Wordsworth, were dead, but they had died young, and many readers consequently still regarded them as their contemporaries. Not even twenty years separated the birth dates of Tennyson and Browning from that of Keats, but they lived more than three times as long as he did. All of the Victorian poets show the strong influence of the Romantics, but they cannot sustain the confidence that the Romantics felt in the power of the imagination. The Victorians often rewrite Romantic poems with a sense of belatedness and distance. When, in his poem *Resignation,* Arnold addresses his sister upon revisiting a landscape, much as Wordsworth had addressed his sister in *Tin-*

tern Abbey, he tells her the rocks and sky "seem to bear rather than rejoice." Tennyson frequently represents his muse as an embowered woman, cut off from the world and doomed to death. The speakers of Browning's poems who embrace the visions that their imaginations present are madmen. When Hardy writes *The Darkling Thrush* in December 1900, Keats's nightingale has become "an aged thrush, frail, gaunt, and small."

Victorian poets build upon this sense of belated Romanticism in a number of different ways. Some poets writing in the second half of the century, like Rossetti and Swinburne, embrace an attenuated Romanticism, art pursued for its own sake. Reacting against what he sees as the insufficiency of an allegory of the state of one's own mind as the basis of poetry, Arnold seeks an objective basis for poetic emotion and finally gives up writing poems altogether when he decides that the present age lacks the culture necessary to support great poetry. The more fruitful reaction to the subjectivity of Romantic poetry, however, was not Arnold's but Browning's. Turning from the mode of his early poetry, modeled on Shelley, Browning began writing dramatic monologues, poems, he said, which are "Lyric in expression" but "Dramatic in principle, and so many utterances of so many imaginary persons, not mine." Tennyson simultaneously developed a more lyric form of the dramatic monologue. The idea of creating a lyric poem in the voice of a speaker ironically distinct from the poet is the great achievement of Victorian poetry, one developed extensively in the twentieth century. In *Poetry and the Age* (1953), the modernist poet and critic Randall Jarrell acknowledges this fact: "The dramatic monologue, which once had depended for its effect upon being a departure from the norm of poetry, now became in one form or other the norm."

The formal experimentation of Victorian poetry, both in long narrative and in the dramatic monologue, may make it seem eclectic, but Victorian poetry shares a number of characteristics. It tends to be pictorial, to use detail to construct visual images that represent the emotion or situation the poem concerns. In his review of Tennyson's first volume of poetry, Arthur Henry Hallam defines this kind of poetry as "picturesque," as combining visual impressions in such a way that they create a picture that carries the dominant emotion of the poem. This aesthetic brings poets and painters close together. Contemporary artists frequently illustrated Victorian poems, and poems themselves often present paintings. Victorian poetry also uses sound in a distinctive way. Whether it be the mellifluousness of Tennyson or Swinburne, with its emphasis on beautiful cadences, alliteration, and vowel sounds, or the roughness of Browning or Hopkins, a roughness adopted in part in reaction against Tennyson, the sound of Victorian poetry reflects an attempt to use poetry as a medium with a presence almost independent of sense. The resulting style can become so syntactically elaborate that it is easy to parody, as in Hopkins's description of Browning as a man "bouncing up from table with his mouth full of bread and cheese" or T. S. Eliot's criticism of Swinburne's poetry, where "meaning is merely the hallucination of meaning." Yet it is important to recognize that these poets use sound to convey meaning, to quote Hallam's review of Tennyson once more, "where words would not." "The tone becomes the sign of the feeling." In all of these developments—the experimentation with narrative and perspective, the dramatic monologue, the use of visual detail and sound—Victorian poets seek to represent psychology in a different way. Their most distinctive achievement is a poetry of mood and character. They therefore sat in uneasy relationship to the public expectation that poets be sages with something to teach. Tennyson, Browning, and Arnold showed varying discomfort with this public role; poets beginning to write in the second half of the century distanced themselves from their public by embracing an identity as bohemian rebels. Women poets encountered a different set of difficulties in developing their poetic voice. When, in Barrett Browning's epic about the growth of a woman poet, Aurora Leigh's cousin Romney discourages her poetic ambitions by telling her that women are "weak for art" but "strong for life and duty," he articulates the prejudice of an age. Women poets view their vocation in the context of the constraints and expectations upon their sex. Perhaps because of this, their poems are less complicated by the experiments in perspective than those of their male contemporaries.

VICTORIAN PROSE

Although Victorian poets felt ambivalent about the didactic mission the public expected of the man of letters, writers of nonfiction prose aimed specifically to instruct. Although the term *nonfictional prose* is clumsy and not quite exact (the Victorians themselves did not use the term but instead referred to history, biography, theology, criticism), it has its uses not only to distinguish these prose writers from the novelists but to indicate the centrality of argument and persuasion to Victorian intellectual life. The growth of the periodical press, described earlier, provided the vehicle and marketplace for nonfictional prose. It reflects a vigorous sense of shared intellectual life and the public urgency of social and moral issues. On a wide range of controversial topics—religious, political, and aesthetic—writers seek to convince their readers to share their convictions and values. Such writers seem at times almost secular priests. Indeed, in the fifth lecture of *On Heroes and Hero Worship*, Carlyle defines the writer precisely in these terms: "Men of Letters are a perpetual Priesthood, from age to age, teaching all Men that God is still present in their life. . . . In the true Literary Man, there is thus ever, acknowledged or not by the world, a sacredness." The modern man of letters, Carlyle argues, differs from his earlier counterpart in that he writes for money. "Never, till about a hundred years ago, was there seen any figure of a Great Soul living apart in that anomalous manner; endeavouring to speak forth the inspiration that was in him by Printed Books, and find place and subsistence by what the world would please him for doing that." This combination, of a new market position for nonfictional writing and an exalted sense of the didactic function of the writer, produces the genre we call Victorian prose.

On behalf of nonfictional prose, Walter Pater argued in his essay *Style* (1889) that it was "the special and opportune art of the modern world." He believed not that it was superior to verse but that it more readily conveys the "chaotic variety and complexity" of modern life, the "incalculable" intellectual diversity of the "master currents of the present time." Pater's characterization of prose helps us understand what its writers were attempting to do. Despite the diversity of styles and subjects, Victorian prose writers were engaged in shaping belief in a bewilderingly complex and changing world. Their modes of persuasion differ. Mill and Huxley rely on clear reasoning, logical argument, and the kind of lucid style favored by essayists of the eighteenth century. Carlyle and Ruskin write a prose that is more Romantic in character, that seeks to move readers as well as convince them. Whatever the differences in their rhetorical techniques, however, they share an urgency of exposition. Not only by what they said but by how they said it, Victorian prose writers were claiming a place for literature in a scientific and materialistic culture. Arnold and Pater share this as an explicit aim. Each in his own way argues that culture—the intensely serious appreciation of great works of literature—provides the kind of immanence and meaning that people once found in religion. For Arnold, this is an intensely moral experience; for Pater it is aesthetic. Together they develop the basis for the claims of modern literary criticism.

VICTORIAN DRAMA AND THEATER

If the Victorian age can lay claim to greatness for its poetry, its prose, and its novels, it would be difficult to make such a high claim for its plays, at least until the final decade of the century. Here we must distinguish between play writing on the one hand and theatrical activity on the other. For the theater itself, throughout the period, was a flourishing and popular institution, in which were performed not merely conventional dramas but a rich variety of theatrical entertainments, many with lavish spectacular effects—burlesques, extravaganzas, highly scenic and altered versions of Shakespeare's plays, melodramas, pantomimes, and musicals. Robert Corrigan gives figures that suggest the extent of the popularity of such entertainment: "In the decade between 1850 and 1860 the number of theaters built throughout the country was doubled, and in the middle of the sixties, in London alone, 150,000 would be attending the theater on any given day. Only when we realize that the theatre was to Victorian England what television is to us today will we be able to comprehend both its wide appeal and its limited artistic achievement." The popularity of theatrical entertainment made theater a powerful influence in other genres. Dickens was devoted to the theater and composed many of the scenes of his novels with theatrical techniques. Thackeray represents himself as the puppetmaster of his characters in *Vanity Fair* and employs the stock gestures and expressions of melodramatic acting in his illustrations for the novel. Tennyson, Browning, and Henry James all tried their hands at writing plays, though with no commercial success. Successful plays on stage were written by the lesser lights of literature such as Dion Boucicault (1820–1890), the period's most prolific and popular dramatist. The comic operas of W. S. Gilbert and Arthur Sullivan prove the exception to this judgment. Their satire of Victorian values and institutions, what Gilbert called their "topsyturvydom," and their grave and quasi-respectful treatment of the ridiculous not only make them delightful in themselves but anticipate the techniques of Shaw and Wilde. Around 1890, when the socially controversial plays of the Norwegian dramatist Henrik Ibsen (1828–1906) became known in England, Arthur Pinero (1855–1934) and Bernard Shaw began writing "problem plays" that addressed difficult social issues. In the 1890s Shaw and Oscar Wilde transformed British theater with their comic masterpieces. Although they did not like each other's work, they both created a kind of comedy that took aim at Victorian pretense and hypocrisy.

THE VICTORIAN AGE

TEXTS	CONTEXTS
1830 Alfred Lord Tennyson, *Poems, Chiefly Lyrical*	1830 Opening of Liverpool and Manchester Railway
1832 Sir Charles Lyell, *Principles of Geology*	1832 First Reform Bill
1833 Thomas Carlyle, *Sartor Resartus*	1833 Factory Act. Beginning of Oxford Movement
1836 Charles Dickens, *Pickwick Papers*	1836 First train in London
1837 Carlyle, *The French Revolution*	1837 Victoria becomes queen
	1838 "People's Charter" issued by Chartist Movement
	1840 Queen marries Prince Albert
1842 Tennyson, *Poems*. Robert Browning, *Dramatic Lyrics*	1842 Chartist Riots. Copyright Act. Mudie's Circulating Library
1843 John Ruskin, *Modern Painters* (vol. 1)	1845–46 Potato famine in Ireland. Mass emigration to North America
1846 George Eliot, *The Life of Jesus* (translation)	1846 Repeal of Corn Laws. Browning marries Elizabeth Barrett
1847 Charlotte Brontë, *Jane Eyre*. Emily Brontë, *Wuthering Heights*	1847 Ten Hours Factory Act
1848 Elizabeth Gaskell, *Mary Barton*. William Makepeace Thackeray, *Vanity Fair*	1848 Revolution on the Continent. Second Republic established in France. Founding of Pre-Raphaelite Brotherhood
1850 Tennyson, *In Memoriam*	1850 Tennyson succeeds Wordsworth as Poet Laureate
1851 Ruskin, *Stones of Venice*	1851 Great Exhibition of science and industry at the Crystal Palace
1853 Matthew Arnold, *Poems*	
1854 Dickens, *Hard Times*	1854 Crimean War. Florence Nightingale organizes nurses to care for sick and wounded
1855 R. Browning, *Men and Women*	
1857 Elizabeth Barrett Browning, *Aurora Leigh*	1857 Indian Mutiny. Matrimonial Causes Act
1859 Charles Darwin, *The Origin of Species*. John Stuart Mill, *On Liberty*. Tennyson, *Idylls of the King* (books 1–4)	
1860 Dickens, *Great Expectations*. Eliot, *The Mill on the Floss*	1860 Italian unification
	1861 Death of Prince Albert
	1861–65 American Civil War
1862 Christina Rossetti, *Goblin Market*	
1864 R. Browning, *Dramatis Personae*	

TEXTS	CONTEXTS
1865　Lewis Carroll, *Alice's Adventures in Wonderland*	1865　Jamaica Rebellion
1866　Algernon Charles Swinburne, *Poems and Ballads*	
1867　Karl Marx, *Das Kapital*	1867　Second Reform Bill
	1868　Opening of Suez Canal
1869　Arnold, *Culture and Anarchy*. Mill, *The Subjection of Women*	
	1870　Married Women's Property Act. Victory in Franco-Prussian War makes Germany a world power
1871　Darwin, *Descent of Man*	1871　Newnham College (first women's college) founded at Cambridge
1872　Eliot, *Middlemarch*	
1873　Walter Pater, *Studies in the Renaissance*	
	1877　Queen Victoria made empress of India. Gerard Manley Hopkins joins Jesuit order
	1878　Electric street lighting in London
	1882　Married Women's Property Act
1885　Gilbert and Sullivan, *The Mikado*	1885　Massacre of General Gordon and his forces and fall of Khartoum
1886　Robert Louis Stevenson, *Doctor Jekyll and Mr. Hyde*	
1888　Rudyard Kipling, *Plain Tales from the Hills*	
1889　William Butler Yeats, *Crossways*	
	1890　First subway line in London
1891　Thomas Hardy, *Tess of the D'Urbervilles*. Bernard Shaw, *The Quintessence of Ibsenism*. Oscar Wilde, *The Picture of Dorian Grey*. Arthur Conan Doyle, *Adventures of Sherlock Holmes*	1891　Free elementary education
1893　Shaw, *Mrs. Warren's Profession*	1893　Independent Labour Party
1895　Wilde, *The Importance of Being Earnest*. Hardy, *Jude the Obscure*	1895　Oscar Wilde arrested and imprisoned for homosexuality
1896　A. E. Housman, *A Shropshire Lad*	
1898　Hardy, *Wessex Poems*	1898　Discovery of radium
	1899　Irish Literary Theater founded in Dublin
	1899–1902　Boer War
1900　Joseph Conrad, *Lord Jim*	
	1901　Death of Queen Victoria; succession of Edward VII

THOMAS CARLYLE
1795–1881

Carlyle was forty-one years old when Victoria became queen of England. He had been born in the same year as Keats, yet he is rarely grouped with his contemporaries among the Romantic writers. Instead his name is linked with younger men such as Dickens, Browning, and Ruskin, the early generation of Victorian writers, for whom he became (according to Elizabeth Barrett Browning) "the great teacher of the age." The classification is fitting, for it was Carlyle's role to foresee the problems that were to preoccupy the Victorians and early to report on his experiences in confronting these problems. After 1837 his loud voice began to attract an audience; and he soon became one of the most influential figures of the age, affecting the attitudes of scientists, statesmen, and especially of writers. His wife once complained that Ralph Waldo Emerson had no ideas (except mad ones) that he had not derived from Carlyle. " 'But pray, Mrs. Carlyle,' replied a friend, *who has?'* "

Carlyle was born in Ecclefechan, a village in Scotland, the eldest child of a large family. His mother, at the time of her marriage, was illiterate. His father, James Carlyle, a stonemason and later a farmer, was proudly characterized by his son as a peasant. The key to the character of James Carlyle was the Scottish Calvinism that he instilled into the members of his household. Frugality, hard work, a tender but undemonstrative family loyalty, and a peculiar blend of self-denial and self-righteousness were characteristic features of Carlyle's childhood home.

With his father's aid the young Carlyle was educated at Annan Academy and at Edinburgh University, the subject of his special interest being mathematics; he left without taking a degree. It was his parents' hope that their son would become a clergyman, but in this respect Thomas made a severe break with his ancestry. He was a prodigious reader; and his exposure to such skeptical writers as Hume, Voltaire, and Gibbon had undermined his faith. Gibbon's *Decline and Fall of the Roman Empire,* he told Emerson, was "the splendid bridge from the old world to the new." By the time he was twenty-three Carlyle had crossed the bridge and had abandoned his Christian faith and his proposed career as a clergyman. During the period in which he was thinking through his religious position, he supported himself by teaching school in Scotland and, later, by tutoring private pupils; but from 1824 to the end of his life he relied exclusively on his writings for his livelihood. His early writings consisted of translations, biographies, and critical studies of Goethe and other German authors, to whose view of life he was deeply attracted. The German Romantics (loosely grouped by Carlyle under the label "Mystics") were the second most important influence on his life and character, exceeded only by his early family experiences. Aided by the writings of these German poets and philosophers, he arrived finally at a faith in life that served as a substitute for the Christian faith he had lost.

His most significant early essay, *Characteristics,* appeared in *The Edinburgh Review* in 1831. A year earlier he had begun writing *Sartor Resartus,* an account of the life and opinions of an imaginary philosopher, Professor Diogenes Teufelsdröckh, a work that he had great difficulty in persuading anyone to publish. In book form *Sartor* first appeared in America in 1836, where Carlyle's follower Emerson had prepared an enthusiastic audience for this unusual work. His American following (which was later to become a vast one) did little at first, however, to relieve the poverty in which he still found himself after fifteen years of writing. In 1837 the tide at last turned when he published *The French Revolution.* "O it has been a great success, dear," his wife assured him; but her husband, embittered by the long struggle, was incredulous that the sought-for recognition had at last come to him.

After completing *The French Revolution* he edited, in 1845, the *Letters and*

Speeches of Oliver Cromwell, a Puritan leader of heroic dimensions in Carlyle's eyes, and later wrote a full-length biography, *The History of Friedrich II of Prussia, Called Frederick the Great* (1858–65). Carlyle's pamphleteering is seen at its best in *Past and Present* (1843) and in its most violent phase in his *Latter-Day Pamphlets* (1850). Following the death of his wife, he wrote very little. For the remaining fifteen years of his life he confined himself to reading or to talking to the stream of visitors who called at Cheyne Walk to listen to the "Sage of Chelsea," as he came to be called. In 1874 he accepted the Prussian Order of Merit from Bismarck but declined an English baronetcy offered by Disraeli. In 1881 he died and was buried near his family in Ecclefechan churchyard.

From Past and Present[1]

From *Democracy*

If the Serene Highnesses and Majesties do not take note of that,[2] then, as I perceive, *that* will take note of itself! The time for levity, insincerity, and idle babble and play-acting, in all kinds, is gone by; it is a serious, grave time. Old long-vexed questions, not yet solved in logical words or parliamentary laws, are fast solving themselves in facts, somewhat unblessed to behold! This largest of questions, this question of Work and Wages, which ought, had we heeded Heaven's voice, to have begun two generations ago or more, cannot be delayed longer without hearing Earth's voice. "Labour" will verily need to be somewhat "organized," as they say,—God knows with what difficulty. Man will actually need to have his debts and earnings a little better paid by man; which, let Parliaments speak of them, or be silent of them, are eternally his due from man, and cannot, without penalty and at length not without death-penalty,[3] be withheld. How much ought to cease among us straightway; how much ought to begin straightway, while the hours yet are!

Truly they are strange results to which this of leaving all to "Cash"; of quietly shutting up the God's Temple, and gradually opening wide-open the Mammon's Temple, with "Laissez-faire, and Every man for himself,"—have led us in these days! We have Upper, speaking Classes, who indeed do "speak" as never man spake before; the withered flimsiness, godless baseness and barrenness of whose Speech might of itself indicate what kind of Doing and practical Governing went on under it! For Speech is the gaseous element out of which most kinds of Practice and Performance, especially all kinds of

1. In 1845 there were reputedly one and a half million unemployed in England (out of a population of eighteen million). The closing of factories and the reduction of wages led to severe rioting in the manufacturing districts. Bread-hungry mobs (as well as the Chartist mobs who demanded political reforms) caused many observers to dread that a large-scale revolution was imminent. Carlyle was himself so appalled by the plight of the industrial workers that he postponed his research into the life and times of Cromwell to air his views on the contemporary crisis. *Past and Present,* a book written in seven weeks, was a call for heroic leadership. Cromwell and other historic leaders are cited, but the principal example from the past is Abbot Samson, a medieval monk who established order in the monasteries under his charge. Carlyle hoped that the "Captains of Industry" might provide a com-

parable leadership in 1843. He was aware that the spread of democracy was inevitable, but he had little confidence in it as a method of producing leaders. Nor did he have any confidence, at this time, in the landed aristocracy, who seemed to him preoccupied with fox hunting, preserving their game, and upholding the tariffs on grain (Corn Laws). In place of a "Do nothing Aristocracy" there was need for a "Working Aristocracy." This first selection is from book 3, chap. 13.
2. The previous chapter, *Reward,* had urged that English manufacturers needed the help of everyone and that Parliament should remove the tariffs (Corn Laws) restricting the growth of trade and industry.
3. I.e., by the outbreak of a revolution, as in France.

moral Performance, condense themselves, and take shape; as the one is, so will the other be. Descending, accordingly, into the Dumb Class in its Stockport Cellars and Poor-Law Bastilles,[4] have we not to announce that they are hitherto unexampled in the History of Adam's Posterity?

Life was never a May-game for men: in all times the lot of the dumb millions born to toil was defaced with manifold sufferings, injustices, heavy burdens, avoidable and unavoidable; not play at all, but hard work that made the sinews sore and the heart sore. As bond-slaves, *villani, bordarii, sochemanni,* nay indeed as dukes, earls and kings, men were oftentimes made weary of their life; and had to say, in the sweat of their brow and of their soul, Behold, it is not sport, it is grim earnest, and our back can bear no more! Who knows not what massacrings and harryings there have been; grinding, long-continuing, unbearable injustices,—till the heart had to rise in madness, and some *"Eu Sachsen, nimith euer sachses,* You Saxons, out with your gully-knives, then!" You Saxons, some "arrestment," partial "arrestment of the Knaves and Dastards" has become indispensable!—The page of Dryasdust[5] is heavy with such details.

And yet I well venture to believe that in no time, since the beginnings of Society, was the lot of those same dumb millions of toilers so entirely unbearable as it is even in the days now passing over us. It is not to die, or even to die of hunger, that makes a man wretched; many men have died; all men must die,—the last exit of us all is in a Fire-Chariot of Pain.[6] But it is to live miserable we know not why; to work sore and yet gain nothing; to be heart-worn, weary, yet isolated, unrelated, girt-in with a cold universal Laissez-faire: it is to die slowly all our life long, imprisoned in a deaf, dead, Infinite Injustice, as in the accursed iron belly of a Phalaris' Bull![7] This is and remains for ever intolerable to all men whom God has made. Do we wonder at French Revolutions, Chartisms, Revolts of Three Days? The times, if we will consider them, are really unexampled.

Never before did I hear of an Irish Widow reduced to "prove her sisterhood by dying of typhus-fever and infecting seventeen persons,"—saying in such undeniable way, "You *see,* I was your sister!"[8] Sisterhood, brotherhood, was often forgotten; but not till the rise of these ultimate Mammon and Shotbelt Gospels[9] did I ever see it so expressly denied. If no pious Lord or *Law-ward* would remember it, always some pious Lady ("*Hlaf-dig,*" Benefactress, "*Loaf-giveress,*" they say she is,—blessings on her beautiful heart!) was there, with mild mother-voice and hand, to remember it; some pious thoughtful *Elder,* what we now call "Prester," *Presbyter* or "Priest," was there to put all men in mind of it, in the name of the God who had made all.

Not even in Black Dahomey was it ever, I think, forgotten to the typhus-

---

4. I.e., workhouse for the unemployed. "Stockport Cellars": in a cellar in the slum district of Stockport, an industrial town near Manchester, three children were poisoned by their starving parents, who wanted to collect insurance benefits from a burial society.

5. An imaginary author of dull histories.

6. 2 Kings 2.11.

7. Phalaris was a Sicilian tyrant whose victims were roasted alive by being confined inside the brass figure of a bull under which a fire was lit.

8. An incident referred to several times in *Past and Present.* Dickens in *Bleak House* also showed how indifference to the lack of sanitation in London slums led to the spread of disease to other parts of the city.

9. The attitudes of land-owning aristocracy who were committed to preserving their exclusive right to shoot game birds and animals. "Mammon [gospel]": the pursuit of wealth according to the economic code of laissez-faire, whereby no one took the responsibility of caring for the starving widow.

fever length. Mungo Park,[1] resourceless, had sunk down to die under the Negro Village-Tree, a horrible White object in the eyes of all. But in the poor Black Woman, and her daughter who stood aghast at him, whose earthly wealth and funded capital consisted of one small calabash of rice, there lived a heart richer than *"Laissez-faire"*: they, with a royal munificence, boiled their rice for him; they sang all night to him, spinning assiduous on their cotton distaffs, as he lay to sleep: "Let us pity the poor white man; no mother has he to fetch him milk, no sister to grind him corn!" Thou poor black Noble One,—thou *Lady* too: did not a God make thee too; was there not in thee too something of a God!—

Gurth,[2] born thrall of Cedric the Saxon, has been greatly pitied by Dryasdust and others. Gurth, with the brass collar round his neck, tending Cedric's pigs in the glades of the wood, is not what I call an exemplar of human felicity: but Gurth, with the sky above him, with the free air and tinted boscage and umbrage round him, and in him at least the certainty of supper and social lodging when he came home; Gurth to me seems happy, in comparison with many a Lancashire and Buckinghamshire man, of these days, not born thrall of anybody! Gurth's brass collar did not gall him: Cedric *deserved* to be his Master. The pigs were Cedric's, but Gurth too would get his parings of them. Gurth had the inexpressible satisfaction of feeling himself related indissolubly, though in a rude brass-collar way, to his fellow-mortals in this Earth. He had superiors, inferiors, equals.—Gurth is now "emancipated" long since; has what we call "Liberty." Liberty, I am told, is a Divine thing. Liberty when it becomes the "Liberty to die by starvation" is not so divine!

Liberty? The true liberty of a man, you would say, consisted in his finding out, or being forced to find out, the right path, and to walk thereon. To learn, or to be taught, what work he actually was able for; and then by permission, persuasion, and even compulsion, to set about doing of the same! That is his true blessedness, honour, "liberty" and maximum of wellbeing: if liberty be not that, I for one have small care about liberty. You do not allow a palpable madman to leap over precipices; you violate his liberty, you that are wise; and keep him, were it in strait-waistcoats, away from the precipices! Every stupid, every cowardly and foolish man is but a less palpable madman: his true liberty were that a wiser man, that any and every wiser man, could, by brass collars, or in whatever milder or sharper way, lay hold of him when he was going wrong, and order and compel him to go a little righter. O, if thou really art my *Senior*, Seigneur, my *Elder*, Presbyter or Priest,—if thou art in very deed my *Wiser*, may a beneficent instinct lead and impel thee to "conquer" me, to command me! If thou do know better than I what is good and right, I conjure thee in the name of God, force me to do it; were it by never such brass collars, whips and handcuffs, leave me not to walk over precipices! That I have been called, by all the Newspapers, a "free man" will avail me little, if my pilgrimage have ended in death and wreck. O that the Newspapers had called me slave, coward, fool, or what it pleased their sweet voices to name me, and I had attained not death, but life!—Liberty requires new definitions.

1. Explorer and author of *Travels in the Interior of Africa* (1799); in 1806, he was killed by Africans. "Black Dahomey": a state in west Africa where human sacrifice and cannibalism persisted.
2. A swineherd described in Scott's *Ivanhoe*.

A conscious abhorrence and intolerance of Folly, of Baseness, Stupidity, Poltroonery and all that brood of things, dwells deep in some men: still deeper in others an *unconscious* abhorrence and intolerance, clothed moreover by the beneficent Supreme Powers in what stout appetites, energies, egoisms so-called, are suitable to it;—these latter are your Conquerors, Romans, Normans, Russians, Indo-English; Founders of what we call Aristocracies. Which indeed have they not the most "divine right" to found;—being themselves very truly *Aristoi,* BRAVEST, BEST; and conquering generally a confused rabble of WORST, or at lowest, clearly enough, of WORSE? I think their divine right, tried, with affirmatory verdict, in the greatest Law-Court known to me, was good! A class of men who are dreadfully exclaimed against by Dryasdust; of whom nevertheless beneficent Nature has oftentimes had need; and may, alas, again have need.

When, across the hundredfold poor scepticisms, trivialisms, and constitutional cobwebberies of Dryasdust, you catch any glimpse of a William the Conqueror, a Tancred of Hauteville[3] or such like,—do you not discern veritably some rude outline of a true God-made King; whom not the Champion of England[4] cased in tin, but all Nature and the Universe were calling to the throne? It is absolutely necessary that he get thither. Nature does not mean her poor Saxon children to perish, of obesity, stupor or other malady, as yet: a stern Ruler and Line of Rulers therefore is called in,—a stern but most beneficent *perpetual House-Surgeon* is by Nature herself called in, and even the appropriate *fees* are provided for him! Dryasdust talks lamentably about Hereward and the Fen Counties; fate of earl Waltheof;[5] Yorkshire and the North reduced to ashes; all of which is undoubtedly lamentable. But even Dryasdust apprises me of one fact: "A child, in this William's reign, might have carried a purse of gold from end to end of England." My erudite friend, it is a fact which outweighs a thousand! Sweep away thy constitutional, sentimental, and other cobwebberies; look eye to eye, if thou still have any eye, in the face of this big burly William Bastard: thou wilt see a fellow of most flashing discernment, of most strong lion-heart;—in whom, as it were, within a frame of oak and iron, the gods have planted the soul of "a man of genius"! Dost thou call that nothing? I call it an immense thing!—Rage enough was in this Willelmus Conquaestor, rage enough for his occasions;—and yet the essential element of him, as of all such men, is not scorching *fire,* but shining illuminative *light.* Fire and light are strangely interchangeable; nay, at bottom, I have found them different forms of the same most godlike "elementary substance" in our world: a thing worth stating in these days. The essential element of this Conquaestor is, first of all, the most sun-eyed perception of what *is* really what on this God's-Earth;—which, thou wilt find, does mean at bottom "Justice," and "Virtues" not a few: *Conformity* to what the Maker

---

3. Norman hero of the First Crusade. King William I of England (reigned 1066–87), surnamed *the Conqueror* after the Battle of Hastings in 1066. Being an illegitimate son, he also bore the surname of William the Bastard. Although some historians condemn William as a ruthless ruler, he is ranked by Carlyle as a hero because of his strong and efficient government. William fulfilled the requirements of the kingly hero described by Carlyle in his lectures *On Heroes:* a man fittest "to *command* over us . . . to tell us what we are to *do.*"

4. An official who goes through a formality, at coronation ceremonies, of demanding whether anyone challenges the right of the monarch to ascend the throne. He wears full armor ("cased in tin"). A symbol of outworn feudal customs.

5. His execution in 1075, on a supposedly trumped-up charge, is cited as a blot on William's record as king. Hereward the Wake, an outlaw whose exploits against William the Conqueror made him seem a romantic figure like Robin Hood.

has seen good to make; that, I suppose, will mean Justice and a Virtue or two?—

Dost thou think Willelmus Conquaestor would have tolerated ten years' jargon, one hour's jargon, on the propriety of killing Cotton-manufactures by partridge Corn-Laws?[6] I fancy, this was not the man to knock out of his night's-rest with nothing but a noisy bedlamism in your mouth! "Assist us still better to bush the partridges; strangle Plugson who spins the shirts?"—*"Par la Splendeur de Dieu!"*[7]—Dost thou think Willelmus Conquaestor, in this new time, with Steam-engine Captains of Industry on one hand of him, and Joe-Manton Captains of Idleness[8] on the other, would have doubted which *was* really the BEST; which did deserve strangling, and which not?

I have a certain indestructible regard for Willelmus Conquaestor. A resident House-Surgeon, provided by Nature for her beloved English People, and even furnished with the requisite fees, as I said; for he by no means felt himself doing Nature's work, this Willelmus, but his own work exclusively! And his own work withal it was; informed *"par la Splendeur de Dieu."*—I say, it is necessary to get the work out of such a man, however harsh that be! When a world, not yet doomed for death, is rushing down to ever-deeper Baseness and Confusion, it is a dire necessity of Nature's to bring in her ARISTOCRACIES, her BEST, even by forcible methods. When their descendants or representatives cease entirely to *be* the Best, Nature's poor world will very soon rush down again to Baseness; and it becomes a dire necessity of Nature's to cast them out. Hence French Revolutions, Five-point Charters, Democracies, and a mournful list of *Etceteras,* in these our afflicted times.

* * *

Democracy, the chase of Liberty in that direction, shall go its full course; unrestrained by him of Pferdefuss-Quacksalber,[9] or any of *his* household. The Toiling Millions of Mankind, in most vital need and passionate instinctive desire of Guidance, shall cast away False-Guidance; and hope, for an hour, that No-Guidance will suffice them: but it can be for an hour only. The smallest item of human Slavery is the oppression of man by his Mock-Superiors; the palpablest, but I say at bottom the smallest. Let him shake off such oppression, trample it indignantly under his feet; I blame him not, I pity and commend him. But oppression by your Mock-Superiors well shaken off, the grand problem yet remains to solve: That of finding government by your Real-Superiors! Alas, how shall we ever learn the solution of that, benighted, bewildered, sniffing, sneering, godforgetting unfortunates as we are? It is a work for centuries; to be taught us by tribulations, confusions, insurrections, obstructions; who knows if not by conflagration and despair! It is a lesson inclusive of all other lessons; the hardest of all lessons to learn.

6. See n. 1, p. 1883.
7. By the splendor of God! (French): one of William's oaths. Plugson of Undershot was Carlyle's term to describe the new class of industrial leaders.
8. The idle aristocracy who wasted time shooting partridges with guns made by Joseph Manton, a London gunsmith. This speech sums up the pleas of the High Tariff lobby in Parliament. "Keep the Corn Laws intact so that the aristocratic landlords may continue to enjoy shooting partridges on their estates; subdue the manufacturing leaders by preventing trade."
9. Horse foot quack doctor.

Captains of Industry[1]

If I believed that Mammonism with its adjuncts was to continue henceforth the one serious principle of our existence, I should reckon it idle to solicit remedial measures from any Government, the disease being insusceptible of remedy. Government can do much, but it can in no wise do all. Government, as the most conspicuous object in Society, is called upon to give signal of what shall be done; and, in many ways, to preside over further, and command the doing of it. But the Government cannot do, by all its signalling and commanding, what the Society is radically indisposed to do. In the long-run every Government is the exact symbol of its People, with their wisdom and unwisdom; we have to say, Like People like Government.— The main substance of this immense Problem of Organizing Labour, and first of all of Managing the Working Classes, will, it is very clear, have to be solved by those who stand practically in the middle of it; by those who themselves work and preside over work. Of all that can be enacted by any Parliament in regard to it, the germs must already lie potentially extant in those two Classes, who are to obey such enactment. A Human Chaos *in* which there is no light, you vainly attempt to irradiate by light shed *on* it: order never can arise there.

But it is my firm conviction that the "Hell of England" will *cease* to be that of "not making money"; that we shall get a nobler Hell and a nobler Heaven! I anticipate light *in* the Human Chaos, glimmering, shining more and more; under manifold true signals from without That light shall shine. Our deity no longer being Mammon,—O Heavens, each man will then say to himself: "Why such deadly haste to make money? I shall not go to Hell, even if I do not make money! There is another Hell, I am told!" Competition, at railway-speed, in all branches of commerce and work will then abate:—good felt-hats for the head, in every sense, instead of seven-feet lath-and-plaster hats on wheels,[2] will then be discoverable! Bubble-periods,[3] with their panics and commercial crises, will again become infrequent; steady modest industry will take the place of gambling speculation. To be a noble Master, among noble Workers, will again be the first ambition with some few; to be a rich Master only the second. How the Inventive Genius of England, with the whirr of its bobbins and billy-rollers[4] shoved somewhat into the backgrounds of the brain, will contrive and devise, not cheaper produce exclusively, but fairer distribution of the produce at its present cheapness! By degrees, we shall again have a Society with something of Heroism in it, something of Heaven's Blessing on it; we shall again have, as my German friend[5] asserts, "instead of Mammon-Feudalism with unsold cotton-shirts and Preservation of the Game, noble just Industrialism and Government by the Wisest!"

It is with the hope of awakening here and there a British man to know himself for a man and divine soul, that a few words of parting admonition, to all persons to whom the Heavenly Powers have lent power of any kind in this land, may now be addressed. And first to those same Master-Workers, Leaders of Industry; who stand nearest, and in fact powerfullest, though not

---

1. From book 4, chap. 4.
2. A London hatter's mode of advertising.
3. Periods of violent fluctuation in the stock market caused by unsound speculating.
4. Machines used to prepare cotton or wool for spinning.
5. Teufelsdröckh, the hero of *Sartor Resartus*.

most prominent, being as yet in too many senses a Virtuality rather than an Actuality.

The Leaders of Industry, if Industry is ever to be led, are virtually the Captains of the World; if there be no nobleness in them, there will never be an Aristocracy more. But let the Captains of Industry consider: once again, are they born of other clay than the old Captains of Slaughter; doomed for ever to be not Chivalry, but a mere gold-plated *Doggery,*—what the French well name *Canaille,* "Doggery" with more or less gold carrion at its disposal? Captains of Industry are the true Fighters, henceforth recognizable as the only true ones: Fighters against Chaos, Necessity and the Devils and Jötuns;[6] and lead on Mankind in that great, and alone true, and universal warfare; the stars in their courses fighting for them, and all Heaven and all Earth saying audibly, Well done! Let the Captains of Industry retire into their own hearts, and ask solemnly, If there is nothing but vulturous hunger for fine wines, valet reputation and gilt carriages, discoverable there? Of hearts made by the Almighty God I will not believe such a thing. Deep-hidden under wretchedest god-forgetting Cants, Epicurisms, Dead-Sea Apisms;[7] forgotten as under foullest fat Lethe mud and weeds, there is yet, in all hearts born into this God's-World, a spark of the Godlike slumbering. Awake, O night-mare sleepers; awake, arise, or be for ever fallen! This is not playhouse poetry; it is sober fact. Our England, our world cannot live as it is. It will connect itself with a God again, or go down with nameless throes and fire-consummation to the Devils. Thou who feelest aught of such a Godlike stirring in thee, any faintest intimation of it as through heavy-laden dreams, follow *it,* I conjure thee. Arise, save thyself, be one of those that save thy country.

Bucaniers,[8] Chactaw Indians, whose supreme aim in fighting is that they may get the scalps, the money, that they may amass scalps and money; out of such came no Chivalry, and never will! Out of such came only gore and wreck, infernal rage and misery; desperation quenched in annihilation. Behold it, I bid thee, behold there, and consider! What is it that thou have a hundred thousand-pound bills laid up in thy strong-room, a hundred scalps hung up in thy wigwam? I value not them or thee. Thy scalps and thy thousand-pound bills are as yet nothing, if no nobleness from within irradiate them; if no Chivalry, in action, or in embryo ever struggling towards birth and action, be there.

Love of men cannot be bought by cash-payment; and without love, men cannot endure to be together. You cannot lead a Fighting World without having it regimented, chivalried: the thing, in a day, becomes impossible; all men in it, the highest at first, the very lowest at last, discern consciously, or by a noble instinct, this necessity. And can you any more continue to lead a Working World unregimented, anarchic? I answer, and the Heavens and Earth are now answering, No! The thing becomes not "in a day" impossible; but in some two generations it does. Yes, when fathers and mothers, in Stock-port hunger-cellars, begin to eat their children, and Irish widows have to prove their relationship by dying of typhus-fever; and amid Governing "Cor-

6. Giants of Scandinavian mythology.
7. A reference to a Muslim story in which a tribe living near the Dead Sea was transformed into apes because the people had ignored the prophecies of Moses.
8. Buccaneers.

porations of the Best and Bravest," busy to preserve their game by "bushing," dark millions of God's human creatures start up in mad Chartisms, impracticable Sacred-Months, and Manchester Insurrections;[9]—and there is a virtual Industrial Aristocracy as yet only half-alive, spell-bound amid money-bags and ledgers; and an actual Idle Aristocracy seemingly near dead in somnolent delusions, in trespasses and double-barrels,[1] "sliding," as on inclined-planes, which every new year they *soap* with new Hansard's-jargon[2] under God's sky, and so are "sliding" ever faster, towards a "scale" and balance-scale whereon is written *Thou art found Wanting;*——in such days, after a generation or two, I say, it does become, even to the low and simple, very palpably impossible! No Working World, any more than a Fighting World, can be led on without a noble Chivalry of Work, and laws and fixed rules which follow out of that,—far nobler than any Chivalry of Fighting was. As an anarchic multitude on mere Supply-and-demand, it is becoming inevitable that we dwindle in horrid suicidal convulsion, and self-abrasion, frightful to the imagination, into *Chactaw* Workers. With wigwams and scalps,—with palaces and thousand-pound bills; with savagery, depopulation, chaotic desolation! Good Heavens, will not one French Revolution and Reign of Terror suffice us, but must there be two? There will be two if needed; there will be twenty if needed; there will be precisely as many as needed. The Laws of Nature will have themselves fulfilled. That is a thing certain to me.

Your gallant battle-hosts and work-hosts, as the others did, will need to be made loyally yours; they must and will be regulated, methodically secured in their just share of conquest under you;—joined with you in veritable brotherhood, sonhood, by quite other and deeper ties than those of temporary day's wages! How would mere redcoated regiments, to say nothing of chivalries, fight for you, if you could discharge them on the evening of the battle, on payment of the stipulated shillings,—and they discharge you on the morning of it! Chelsea Hospitals,[3] pensions, promotions, rigorous lasting covenant on the one side and on the other, are indispensable even for a hired fighter. The Feudal Baron, much more,—how could he subsist with mere temporary mercenaries round him, at sixpence a day; ready to go over to the other side, if sevenpence were offered? He could not have subsisted;—and his noble instinct saved him from the necessity of even trying! The Feudal Baron had a Man's Soul in him; to which anarchy, mutiny, and the other fruits of temporary mercenaries, were intolerable: he had never been a Baron otherwise, but had continued a Chactaw and Bucanier. He felt it precious, and at last it became habitual, and his fruitful enlarged existence included it as a necessity, to have men round him who in heart loved him; whose life he watched over with rigour yet with love; who were prepared to give their life for him, if need came. It was beautiful; it was human! Man lives not otherwise, nor can live contented, anywhere or anywhen. Isolation is the sumtotal of wretchedness to man. To be cut off, to be left solitary: to have a world alien, not your world; all a hostile camp for you; not a home at all, of

---

9. In 1819 a large open-air labor meeting in Manchester was broken up by charging cavalry. Thirteen men and women were massacred, and many others were wounded.
1. I.e., the only concern of the landed aristocrats

is to keep trespassers off their game preserves and reserve shooting rights to themselves.
2. Parliamentary oratory, as in Hansard's printed record of debates in the House of Commons.
3. Home for disabled veterans.

hearts and faces who are yours, whose you are! It is the frightfullest enchantment; too truly a work of the Evil One. To have neither superior, nor inferior, nor equal, united manlike to you. Without father, without child, without brother. Man knows no sadder destiny. "How is each of us," exclaims Jean Paul,[4] "so lonely in the wide bosom of the All!" Encased each as in his transparent "ice-palace"; our brother visible in his, making signals and gesticulations to us;—visible, but for ever unattainable: on his bosom we shall never rest, nor he on ours. It was not a God that did this; no!

Awake, ye noble Workers, warriors in the one true war: all this must be remedied. It is you who are already half-alive, whom I will welcome into life; whom I will conjure in God's name to shake off your enchanted sleep, and live wholly! Cease to count scalps, goldpurses; not in these lies your or our salvation. Even these, if you count only these, will not be left. Let bucaniering be put far from you; alter, speedily abrogate all laws of the bucaniers, if you would gain any victory that shall endure. Let God's justice, let pity, nobleness and manly valour, with more gold-purses or with fewer, testify themselves in this your brief Life-transit to all the Eternities, the Gods and Silences. It is to you I call; for ye are not dead, ye are already half-alive: there is in you a sleepless dauntless energy, the prime-matter of all nobleness in man. Honour to you in your kind. It is to you I call: ye know at least this, That the mandate of God to His creature man is: Work! The future Epic of the World rests not with those that are near dead, but with those that are alive, and those that are coming into life.

Look around you. Your world-hosts are all in mutiny, in confusion, destitution; on the eve of fiery wreck and madness! They will not march farther for you, on the sixpence a day and supply-and-demand principle; they will not; nor ought they, nor can they. Ye shall reduce them to order, begin reducing them. To order, to just subordination; noble loyalty in return for noble guidance. Their souls are driven nigh mad; let yours be sane and ever saner. Not as a bewildered bewildering mob; but as a firm regimented mass, with real captains over them, will these men march any more. All human interests, combined human endeavours, and social growths in this world, have, at a certain stage of their development, required organizing: and Work, the grandest of human interests, does now require it.

God knows, the task will be hard: but no noble task was ever easy. This task will wear away your lives, and the lives of your sons and grandsons: but for what purpose, if not for tasks like this, were lives given to men? Ye shall cease to count your thousand-pound scalps, the noble of you shall cease! Nay, the very scalps, as I say, will not long be left if you count on these. Ye shall cease wholly to be barbarous vulturous Chactaws, and become noble European Nineteenth-Century Men. Ye shall know that Mammon, in never such gigs[5] and flunkey "respectabilities," is not the alone God; that of himself he is but a Devil, and even a Brute-god.

Difficult? Yes, it will be difficult. The short-fibre cotton; that too was difficult. The waste cotton-shrub, long useless, disobedient, as the thistle by the wayside,—have ye not conquered it; made it into beautiful bandana webs; white woven shirts for men; bright-tinted air-garments wherein flit

4. Jean Paul Richter (1763–1825), German humorist.

5. Light carriages; to own one was a sign of respectable status comparable with owning certain kinds of automobiles today.

goddesses? Ye have shivered mountains asunder, made the hard iron pliant to you as soft putty: the Forest-giants, Marsh-jötuns bear sheaves of golden grain; Aegir the Seademon[6] himself stretches his back for a sleek highway to you, and on Firehorses and Windhorses ye career. Ye are most strong. Thor red-bearded, with his blue sun-eyes, with his cheery heart and strong thunder-hammer, he and you have prevailed. Ye are most strong, ye Sons of the icy North, of the far East,—far marching from your rugged Eastern Wildernesses, hitherward from the grey Dawn of Time! Ye are Sons of the *Jötunland*; the land of Difficulties Conquered. Difficult? You must try this thing. Once try it with the understanding that it will and shall have to be done. Try it as ye try the paltrier thing, making of money! I will bet on you once more, against all Jötuns, Tailor-gods,[7] Double-barrelled Law-wards, and Denizens of Chaos whatsoever.

1843   1843

6. From Scandinavian mythology.   7. False gods.

ELIZABETH BARRETT BROWNING
1806–1861

During her lifetime, Elizabeth Barrett Browning was England's most famous woman poet. Passionately admired by contemporaries as diverse as Ruskin, Swinburne, and Emily Dickinson for her moral and emotional ardor and her energetic engagement with the issues of her day, she was more famous than her husband, Robert Browning, at the time of her death. Her work fell into disrepute with the modernist reaction against what was seen as the inappropriate didacticism and rhetorical excess of Victorian poetry; but recently scholars interested in her exploration of what it means to be a woman poet have restored her status as a major writer.

Barrett Browning received an unusual education for a woman of her time. Availing herself of her brother's tutor, she studied Latin and Greek. She read voraciously in history, philosophy, and literature and began to write poetry from an early age—her first volume of poetry was published when she was thirteen. But as her intellectual and literary powers matured, her personal life became increasingly circumscribed both by ill health and by a tyrannically protective father, who had forbidden any of his eleven children to marry. By the age of thirty-nine, Elizabeth Barrett was a prominent woman of letters who lived in semiseclusion as an invalid in her father's house, where she occasionally received visitors in her room. One of these visitors was Robert Browning, who, moved by his admiration of her poetry, wrote to tell her "I do as I say, love these books with all my heart—and I love you too." He thereby initiated a courtship that culminated in 1846 in their secret marriage and elopement to Italy, for which her father never forgave her. Once in Italy, she regained much health and strength, bearing and raising a son, Pen, to whom she was ardently devoted, and becoming deeply involved in Italian nationalist politics. She and her husband made their home in Florence, at the house called Casa Guidi, where she died in 1861.

Barrett Browning's poetry is characterized by a fervent moral sensibility. In her early work, she tended to use the visionary modes of Romantic narrative poetry, but she turned increasingly to contemporary topics, particularly liberal causes of her day. For example, in 1843, when government investigations had exposed the exploitation of children employed in coal mines and factories, she wrote *The Cry of the Children,* a powerful indictment of the appalling use of child labor. Like Harriet Beecher Stowe in *Uncle Tom's Cabin,* Barrett Browning uses literature as a tool of social protest and reform. In later poems she took up the cause of the *risorgimento,* the movement to unify Italy as a nation-state, in which Italy's struggle for freedom and identity found resonance with her own.

For many years Elizabeth Barrett Browning was best known for her *Sonnets from the Portuguese,* a sequence of forty-four sonnets presented under the guise of a translation from the Portuguese language, in which she recorded the stages of her love for Robert Browning. But increasingly, her verse novel *Aurora Leigh* (1857) has attracted critical attention. The poem depicts the growth of a woman poet and is thus, as Cora Kaplan observes, the first work in English by a woman writer in which the heroine herself is an author. When Barrett Browning first envisioned the poem, she wrote, "My chief *intention* just now is the writing of a sort of novel-poem . . . running into the midst of our conventions, and rushing into drawing-rooms and the like 'where angels fear to tread'; and so, meeting face to face and without mask the Humanity of the age, and speaking the truth as I conceive of it out plainly." The poem is a female *Prelude* (cf. Wordsworth's *The Prelude*), a portrait of the artist as a young woman committed to a socially inclusive realist art. It is a daring work both in its presentation of social issues concerning women and in its claims for Aurora's poetic vocation; on her twentieth birthday, to pursue her career as a poet, Aurora refuses a proposal of marriage from her cousin Romney, who wants her to be his helpmate in the liberal causes he has embraced. Later in the poem, she rescues a fallen woman and takes her to Italy, where they settle together and confront a chastened Romney.

Immensely popular in its own day, *Aurora Leigh* had extravagant admirers (like Ruskin, who asserted that it was the greatest poem written in English) and critics who found fault with both its poetry and its morality. With its crowded canvas and melodramatic plot, it seems closer to the novel than to poetry, but it is important to view the poem in the context of the debate about appropriate poetic subject that engaged other Victorian poets. Unlike Arnold, who believed that the present age had not produced actions heroic enough to be the subjects of a great poetry, and unlike Tennyson, who used Arthurian legend to represent contemporary concerns, Barrett Browning felt that the present age contained the materials for an epic poetry. Virginia Woolf writes that "Elizabeth Barrett was inspired by a flash of true genius when she rushed into the drawing-room and said that here, where we live and work, is the true place for the poet." And whatever its faults, *Aurora Leigh* succeeds in giving us what Woolf describes as "a sense of life in general, of people who are unmistakably Victorian, wrestling with the problems of their own time, all brightened, intensified, and compacted by the fire of poetry. . . . Aurora Leigh, with her passionate interest in social questions, her conflict as artist and woman, her longing for knowledge and freedom, is the true daughter of her age."

The Cry of the Children[1]

"Φεῦ, φεῦ, τί προσδέρκεσθέ μ' ὄμμασιν, τέκνα;"
—*Medea*[2]

Do ye hear the children weeping, O my brothers,
    Ere the sorrow comes with years?
They are leaning their young heads against their mothers,

---

1. Barrett Browning wrote *The Cry of the Children* in response to the report of a parliamentary commission written by her friend R. H. Horne on the labor of children in mines and factories. Many of the details of Barrett Browning's poem derive from the report.

2. Alas, my children, why do you look at me? (Greek), from Euripides' tragedy *Medea.* Medea speaks these lines when she kills her children in vengeance.

And *that* cannot stop their tears.
5   The young lambs are bleating in the meadows,
      The young birds are chirping in the nest,
    The young fawns are playing with the shadows,
      The young flowers are blowing toward the west—
    But the young, young children, O my brothers,
10   They are weeping bitterly!
    They are weeping in the playtime of the others,
      In the country of the free.

    Do you question the young children in the sorrow
      Why their tears are falling so?
15   The old man may weep for his to-morrow
      Which is lost in Long Ago;
    The old tree is leafless in the forest,
      The old year is ending in the frost,
    The old wound, if stricken, is the sorest,
20   The old hope is hardest to be lost:
    But the young, young children, O my brothers,
      Do you ask them why they stand
    Weeping sore before the bosoms of their mothers,
      In our happy Fatherland?

25   They look up with their pale and sunken faces,
      And their looks are sad to see,
    For the man's hoary anguish draws and presses
      Down the cheeks of infancy;
    "Your old earth," they say, "is very dreary,"
30   "Our young feet," they say, "are very weak;
    Few paces have we taken, yet are weary—
      Our grave-rest is very far to seek:
    Ask the aged why they weep, and not the children,
      For the outside earth is cold,
35   And we young ones stand without, in our bewildering,
      And the graves are for the old."

    "True," say the children, "it may happen
      That we die before our time:
    Little Alice died last year, her grave is shapen
40   Like a snowball, in the rime.
    We looked into the pit prepared to take her:
      Was no room for any work in the close clay!
    From the sleep wherein she lieth none will wake her,
      Crying, 'Get up, little Alice! it is day.'
45   If you listen by that grave, in sun and shower,
      With your ear down, little Alice never cries;
    Could we see her face, be sure we should not know her,
      For the smile has time for growing in her eyes:
    And merry go her moments, lulled and stilled in
50   The shroud by the kirk° chime.   *church*
    It is good when it happens," say the children,
      "That we die before our time."

Alas, alas, the children! they are seeking
        Death in life, as best to have:
55 They are binding up their hearts away from breaking,
        With a ceremen° from the grave.   *shroud*
    Go out, children, from the mine and from the city,
        Sing out, children, as the little thrushes do;
    Pluck your handfuls of the meadow-cowslips pretty,
60   Laugh aloud, to feel your fingers let them through!
    But they answer, "Are your cowslips of the meadows
        Like our weeds anear the mine?
    Leave us quiet in the dark of the coal-shadows,
        From your pleasures fair and fine!

65 "For oh," say the children, "we are weary,
        And we cannot run or leap;
    If we cared for any meadows, it were merely
        To drop down in them and sleep.
    Our knees tremble sorely in the stooping,
70   We fall upon our faces, trying to go;
    And, underneath our heavy eyelids drooping,
        The reddest flower would look as pale as snow.
    For, all day, we drag our burden tiring
        Through the coal-dark, underground;
75 Or, all day, we drive the wheels of iron
        In the factories, round and round.

    "For, all day, the wheels are droning, turning;
        Their wind comes in our faces,
    Till our hearts turn, our heads with pulses burning,
80   And the walls turn in their places:
    Turns the sky in the high window blank and reeling,
        Turns the long light that drops adown the wall,
    Turn the black flies that crawl along the ceiling,
        All are turning, all the day, and we with all.
85 And all day, the iron wheels are droning,
        And sometimes we could pray,
    'O ye wheels,' (breaking out in a mad moaning)
        'Stop! be silent for to-day!' "

    Ay, be silent! Let them hear each other breathing
90   For a moment, mouth to mouth!
    Let them touch each other's hands, in a fresh wreathing
        Of their tender human youth!
    Let them feel that this cold metallic motion
        Is not all the life God fashions or reveals:
95 Let them prove their living souls against the notion
        That they live in you, or under you, O wheels!
    Still, all day, the iron wheels go onward,
        Grinding life down from its mark;
    And the children's souls, which God is calling sunward,
100   Spin on blindly in the dark.

Now tell the poor young children; O my brothers,
    To look up to Him and pray;
So the blessed One who blesseth all the others,
    Will bless them another day.
105 They answer, "Who is God that He should hear us,
    While the rushing of the iron wheels is stirred?
When we sob aloud, the human creatures near us
    Pass by, hearing not, or answer not a word.
And *we* hear not (for the wheels in their resounding)
110   Strangers speaking at the door:
Is it likely God, with angels singing round Him,
    Hears our weeping any more?

Two words, indeed, of praying we remember,
    And at midnight's hour of harm,
115 'Our Father,' looking upward in the chamber,
    We say softly for a charm.
We know no other words except 'Our Father,'
    And we think that, in some pause of angels' song,
God may pluck them with the silence sweet to gather,
120   And hold both within His right hand which is strong.
'Our Father!' If He heard us, He would surely
    (For they call Him good and mild)
Answer, smiling down the steep world very purely,
    'Come and rest with me, my child.'

125 "But, no!" say the children, weeping faster,
    "He is speechless as a stone:
And they tell us, of His image is the master
    Who commands us to work on.
Go to!" say the children,— "up in Heaven,
130   Dark, wheel-like, turning clouds are all we find.
Do not mock us; grief has made us unbelieving:
    We look up for God, but tears have made us blind."
Do you hear the children weeping and disproving,
    O my brothers, what ye preach?
135 For God's possible is taught by His world's loving,
    And the children doubt of each.

And well may the children weep before you!
    They are weary ere they run;
They have never seen the sunshine, nor the glory
140   Which is brighter than the sun.
They know the grief of man, without its wisdom;
    They sink in man's despair, without its calm;
Are slaves, without the liberty in Christdom,
    Are martyrs, by the pang without the palm:
145 Are worn as if with age, yet unretrievingly
    The harvest of its memories cannot reap,—
Are orphans of the earthly love and heavenly.
    Let them weep! let them weep!

They look up with their pale and sunken faces,
150   And their look is dread to see,
For they mind you of their angels in high places,
         With eyes turned on Deity.
"How long," they say, "how long, O cruel nation,
   Will you stand, to move the world, on a child's heart,—
155 Stifle down with a mailed heel its palpitation,
   And tread onward to your throne amid the mart?
Our blood splashes upward, O gold-heaper,
         And your purple shows your path!
But the child's sob in the silence curses deeper
160   Than the strong man in his wrath."

                                                            1843

From Sonnets from the Portuguese

21

Say over again, and yet once over again,
That thou dost love me. Though the word repeated
Should seem "a cuckoo song,"[1] as thou dost treat it,
Remember, never to the hill or plain,
5   Valley and wood, without her cuckoo strain
Comes the fresh Spring in all her green completed.
Belovèd, I, amid the darkness greeted
By a doubtful spirit voice, in that doubt's pain
Cry, "Speak once more—thou lovest!" Who can fear
10 Too many stars, though each in heaven shall roll,
Too many flowers, though each shall crown the year?
Say thou dost love me, love me, love me—toll
The silver iterance!°—only minding, Dear,   *repetition*
To love me also in silence with thy soul.

22

When our two souls stand up erect and strong,
Face to face, silent, drawing nigh and nigher,
Until the lengthening wings break into fire
At either curvèd point—what bitter wrong
5   Can the earth do to us, that we should not long
Be here contented? Think. In mounting higher,
The angels would press on us and aspire
To drop some golden orb of perfect song
Into our deep, dear silence. Let us stay
10 Rather on earth, Belovèd,—where the unfit
Contrarious moods of men recoil away
And isolate pure spirits, and permit
A place to stand and love in for a day,
With darkness and the death-hour rounding it.

---

1. The cuckoo has a repeating call.

32

The first time that the sun rose on thine oath
To love me, I looked forward to the moon
To slacken all those bonds which seemed too soon
And quickly tied to make a lasting troth.
5   Quick-loving hearts, I thought, may quickly loathe;
And, looking on myself, I seemed not one
For such man's love!—more like an out-of-tune
Worn viol, a good singer would be wroth
To spoil his song with, and which, snatched in haste,
10   Is laid down at the first ill-sounding note.
I did not wrong myself so, but I placed
A wrong on *thee*. For perfect strains may float
'Neath master-hands, from instruments defaced—
And great souls, at one stroke, may do and dote.

43

How do I love thee? Let me count the ways.
I love thee to the depth and breadth and height
My soul can reach, when feeling out of sight
For the ends of Being and ideal Grace.
5   I love thee to the level of everyday's
Most quiet need, by sun and candlelight.
I love thee freely, as men strive for Right;
I love thee purely, as they turn from Praise.
I love thee with the passion put to use
10   In my old griefs, and with my childhood's faith.
I love thee with a love I seemed to lose
With my lost saints—I love thee with the breath,
Smiles, tears, of all my life!—and, if God choose,
I shall but love thee better after death.

1845–47   1850

From Aurora Leigh

From *Book 1*

[THE FEMININE EDUCATION OF AURORA LEIGH][1]

Then, land!—then, England! oh, the frosty cliffs[2]
Looked cold upon me. Could I find a home
Among those mean red houses through the fog?
And when I heard my father's language first
255   From alien lips which had no kiss for mine

1. Aurora Leigh, the only child of an Italian mother and an English father, was raised in Italy by her father since her mother's death when Aurora was four years old. When she was thirteen her father also died, and the orphaned girl has been sent to England to live with her father's maiden sister, who is to be responsible for the girl's education.
2. The white chalk cliffs at Dover.

I wept aloud, then laughed, then wept, then wept,
And some one near me said the child was mad
Through much sea-sickness. The train swept us on:
Was this my father's England? the great isle?
260   The ground seemed cut up from the fellowship
Of verdure, field from field,[3] as man from man;
The skies themselves looked low and positive,
As almost you could touch them with a hand,
And dared to do it they were so far off
265   From God's celestial crystals;[4] all things blurred
And dull and vague. Did Shakespeare and his mates
Absorb the light here?—not a hill or stone
With heart to strike a radiant colour up
Or active outline on the indifferent air.

270   I think I see my father's sister stand
Upon the hall-step of her country-house
To give me welcome. She stood straight and calm,
Her somewhat narrow forehead braided tight
As if for taming accidental thoughts
275   From possible pulses;[5] brown hair pricked with gray
By frigid use of life (she was not old,
Although my father's elder by a year),
A nose drawn sharply, yet in delicate lines;
A close mild mouth, a little soured about
280   The ends, through speaking unrequited loves
Or peradventure niggardly half-truths;
Eyes of no colour,—once they might have smiled,
But never, never have forgot themselves
In smiling; cheeks, in which was yet a rose
285   Of perished summers, like a rose in a book,
Kept more for ruth° than pleasure,—if past bloom,   *remorse*
Past fading also.
                She had lived, we'll say,
A harmless life, she called a virtuous life,
A quiet life, which was not life at all
290   (But that, she had not lived enough to know),
Between the vicar and the county squires,
The lord-lieutenant[6] looking down sometimes
From the empyrean to assure their souls
Against chance vulgarisms, and, in the abyss,
295   The apothecary,[7] looked on once a year
To prove their soundness of humility.
The poor-club[8] exercised her Christian gifts
Of knitting stockings, stitching petticoats,
Because we are of one flesh, after all,
300   And need one flannel[9] (with a proper sense

---

3. English fields were separated from each other by hedgerows.
4. Perhaps a reference to the ancient notion that the sky was composed of several crystalline spheres orbiting around the earth.
5. I.e., pulsation in her temples from excitement.

6. Governor of the county.
7. Pharmacist, who in England at the time could prescribe as well as sell medicine.
8. Club devoted to making things for the poor.
9. I.e., flannel petticoat.

Of difference in the quality)—and still
The book-club, guarded from your modern trick
Of shaking dangerous questions from the crease,[1]
Preserved her intellectual. She had lived
305   A sort of cage-bird life, born in a cage,
Accounting that to leap from perch to perch
Was act and joy enough for any bird.
Dear heaven, how silly are the things that live
In thickets, and eat berries!
                                                    I, alas,
310   A wild bird scarcely fledged, was brought to her cage,
And she was there to meet me. Very kind.
Bring the clean water, give out the fresh seed.

She stood upon the steps to welcome me,
Calm, in black garb. I clung about her neck,—
315   Young babes, who catch at every shred of wool
To draw the new light closer, catch and cling
Less blindly. In my ears my father's word
Hummed ignorantly, as the sea in shells,
"Love, love, my child." She, black there with my grief,
320   Might feel my love— she was his sister once—
I clung to her. A moment she seemed moved,
Kissed me with cold lips, suffered me to cling,
And drew me feebly through the hall into
The room she sat in.
                                        There, with some strange spasm
325   Of pain and passion, she wrung loose my hands
Imperiously, and held me at arm's length,
And with two grey-steel naked-bladed eyes
Searched through my face,—ay, stabbed it through and through,
Through brows and cheeks and chin, as if to find
330   A wicked murderer in my innocent face,
If not here, there perhaps. Then, drawing breath,
She struggled for her ordinary calm—
And missed it rather,—told me not to shrink,
As if she had told me not to lie or swear,—
335   "She loved my father and would love me too
As long as I deserved it." Very kind.

I understood her meaning afterward;
She thought to find my mother in my face,
And questioned it for that. For she, my aunt,
340   Had loved my father truly, as she could,
And hated, with the gall of gentle souls,
My Tuscan[2] mother who had fooled away
A wise man from wise courses, a good man
From obvious duties, and, depriving her,
345   His sister, of the household precedence,

---

1. The fold between two pages of a book, which had to be cut to open the pages. Presumably more modern books revealed more dangerous material when the crease was cut.
2. From Tuscany, a region in central Italy.

Had wronged his tenants, robbed his native land,
And made him mad, alike by life and death,
In love and sorrow. She had pored° for years   *pored over*
What sort of woman could be suitable
350   To her sort of hate, to entertain it with,
And so, her very curiosity
Became hate too, and all the idealism
She ever used in life was used for hate,
Till hate, so nourished, did exceed at last
355   The love from which it grew, in strength and heat,
And wrinkled her smooth conscience with a sense
Of disputable virtue (say not, sin)
When Christian doctrine was enforced at church.

And thus my father's sister was to me
360   My mother's hater. From that day she did
Her duty to me (I appreciate it
In her own word as spoken to herself),
Her duty, in large measure, well pressed out
But measured always. She was generous, bland,
365   More courteous than was tender, gave me still
The first place,—as if fearful that God's saints
Would look down suddenly and say "Herein
You missed a point, I think, through lack of love."
Alas, a mother never is afraid
370   Of speaking angerly to any child,
Since love, she knows, is justified of love.
And I, I was a good child on the whole,
A meek and manageable child. Why not?
I did not live, to have the faults of life:
375   There seemed more true life in my father's grave
Than in all England. Since *that* threw me off
Who fain would cleave (his latest will, they say,
Consigned me to his land), I only thought
Of lying quiet there where I was thrown
380   Like sea-weed on the rocks, and suffering her
To prick me to a pattern with her pin,[3]
Fibre from fibre, delicate leaf from leaf,
And dry out from my drowned anatomy
The last sea-salt left in me.
                   So it was.
385   I broke the copious curls upon my head
In braids, because she liked smooth-ordered hair.
I left off saying my sweet Tuscan words
Which still at any stirring of the heart
Came up to float across the English phrase
390   As lilies (*Bene* or *Che che*[4]), because
She liked my father's child to speak his tongue.
I learnt the collects[5] and the catechism,

---

3. As in embroidery.
4. No, no, indeed (Italian). *"Bene"*: it is well (Italian).
5. Seasonal opening prayers in the Anglican Church service.

The creeds,[6] from Athanasius back to Nice,
The Articles, the Tracts *against* the times[7]
395 (By no means Buonaventure's "Prick of Love"[8]),
And various popular synopses of
Inhuman doctrines never taught by John,[9]
Because she liked instructed piety.
I learnt my complement of classic French
400 (Kept pure of Balzac and neologism[1])
And German also, since she liked a range
Of liberal education,—tongues,° not books.   languages
I learnt a little algebra, a little
Of the mathematics,—brushed with extreme flounce
405 The circle of the sciences, because
She misliked women who are frivolous.
I learnt the royal genealogies
Of Oviedo,[2] the internal laws
Of the Burmese empire,—by how many feet
410 Mount Chimborazo outsoars Teneriffe,
What navigable river joins itself
To Lara,[3] and what census of the year five
Was taken at Klagenfurt,[4]—because she liked
A general insight into useful facts.
415 I learnt much music,—such as would have been
As quite impossible in Johnson's day[5]
As still it might be wished—fine sleights of hand
And unimagined fingering, shuffling off
The hearer's soul through hurricanes of notes
420 To a noisy Tophet;° and I drew . . . costumes   Hell
From French engravings, nereids° neatly draped   sea nymphs
(With smirks of simmering godship): I washed in[6]
Landscapes from nature (rather say, washed out).
I danced the polka and Cellarius,[7]
425 Spun glass, stuffed birds, and modeled flowers in wax,
Because she liked accomplishments in girls.
I read a score of books on womanhood
To prove, if women do not think at all,
They may teach thinking (to a maiden aunt
430 Or else the author),—books that boldly assert
Their right of comprehending husband's talk
When not too deep, and even of answering

6. Articles of Christian faith such as those pro-claimed at the early church council held at Nicaea.
7. In the 1830s leaders of the conservative High Church party, such as John Henry Newman, had published *Tracts for the Times*, which expounded arguments against efforts by liberals to modernize the Anglican Church. Aurora's version of the title is hence ironic. "Articles": the thirty-nine articles are the principles of faith of the Church of England.
8. St. Bonaventure's doctrine that the power of the heart to love leads to higher illumination than the power of the mind to reason.
9. I.e., the author of the Gospel.
1. A new word or expression. Balzac (1799–1850),
a French novelist whose realism made him improper reading for a young lady.
2. Spanish historian (16th century), who wrote a book on the genealogies of the grandees of Spain.
3. A town in Spain on the river Arlanza. Mount Chimborazo is one of the highest peaks of the Andes. Teneriffe is a mountain in the Canary Islands.
4. A town in Austria.
5. Allusion to the story about Samuel Johnson, who, when told how difficult a piece of music was that a young lady was playing, replied, "I would it had been impossible."
6. As in painting with watercolors.
7. A kind of waltz.

With pretty "may it please you," or "so it is,"—
Their rapid insight and fine aptitude,
435 Particular worth and general missionariness,
As long as they keep quiet by the fire
And never say "no" when the world says "ay,"
For that is fatal,—their angelic reach
Of virtue, chiefly used to sit and darn,
440 And fatten household sinners,—their, in brief,
Potential faculty in everything
Of abdicating power in it: she owned
She liked a woman to be womanly,
And English women, she thanked God and sighed
445 (Some people always sigh in thanking God),
Were models to the universe. And last
I learnt cross-stitch,[8] because she did not like
To see me wear the night with empty hands
A-doing nothing. So, my shepherdess
450 Was something after all (the pastoral saints
Be praised for't), leaning lovelorn with pink eyes
To match her shoes, when I mistook the silks;
Her head uncrushed by that round weight of hat
So strangely similar to the tortoise shell
Which slew the tragic poet.[9]
455   By the way,
The works of women are symbolical.
We sew, sew, prick our fingers, dull our sight,
Producing what? A pair of slippers, sir,
To put on when you're weary—or a stool
460 To stumble over and vex you . . . "curse that stool!"
Or else at best, a cushion, where you lean
And sleep, and dream of something we are not
But would be for your sake. Alas, alas!
This hurts most, this—that, after all, we are paid
The worth of our work, perhaps.
465   In looking down
Those years of education (to return)
I wonder if Brinvilliers suffered more
In the water-torture[1] . . . flood succeeding flood
To drench the incapable throat and split the veins . . .
470 Than I did. Certain of your feebler souls
Go out in such a process; many pine
To a sick, inodorous light; my own endured:
I had relations in the Unseen, and drew
The elemental nutriment and heat
475 From nature, as earth feels the sun at nights,
Or as a babe sucks surely in the dark.
I kept the life thrust on me, on the outside

---

8. I.e., embroidery.
9. According to tradition, the Greek playwright Aeschylus was killed by an eagle, who, mistaking his bald head for a stone, dropped a tortoise on it to break the shell.

1. Marie Marguerite, Marquise de Brinvilliers, a celebrated criminal who was beheaded in 1676, was tortured by having water forced down her throat.

Of the inner life with all its ample room
For heart and lungs, for will and intellect,
480 Inviolable by conventions. God,
I thank thee for that grace of thine!
                              At first
I felt no life which was not patience,—did
The thing she bade me, without heed to a thing
Beyond it, sat in just the chair she placed,
485 With back against the window, to exclude
The sight of the great lime-tree on the lawn,[2]
Which seemed to have come on purpose from the woods
To bring the house a message,—ay, and walked
Demurely in her carpeted low rooms,
490 As if I should not, harkening my own steps,
Misdoubt I was alive. I read her books,
Was civil to her cousin, Romney Leigh,
Gave ear to her vicar, tea to her visitors,
And heard them whisper, when I changed a cup
495 (I blushed for joy at that),—"The Italian child,
For all her blue eyes and her quiet ways,
Thrives ill in England: she is paler yet
Than when we came the last time; she will die."

From *Book 2*

[AURORA'S ASPIRATIONS][3]

Times followed one another. Came a morn
I stood upon the brink of twenty years,
And looked before and after, as I stood
Woman and artist,—either incomplete,
5 Both credulous of completion. There I held
The whole creation in my little cup,
And smiled with thirsty lips before I drank
"Good health to you and me, sweet neighbour mine,
And all these peoples."
                              I was glad, that day;
10 The June was in me, with its multitudes
Of nightingales all singing in the dark,
And rosebuds reddening where the calyx[4] split.
I felt so young, so strong, so sure of God!
So glad, I could not choose be very wise!
15 And, old at twenty, was inclined to pull
My childhood backward in a childish jest
To see the face of't once more, and farewell!

2. Cf. Coleridge's *This Lime-Tree Bower My Prison*, in which the lime tree becomes the vehicle of a realization that Nature never deserts the wise and pure even when they seem to be cut off from her most beautiful vistas.
3. Stifled by her aunt's oppressive conventionality, Aurora has found three sources of comfort and inspiration: poetic aspirations, fostered by the discovery of her father's library; the beauty of the natural world; and the intellectual companionship of her cousin Romney Leigh, an idealistic young man troubled by the misery of the poor and inspired by contemporary notions of social reform.
4. The protective outer leaves covering a flower or bud.

In which fantastic mood I bounded forth
At early morning,—would not wait so long
20   As even to snatch my bonnet by the strings,
But, brushing a green trail across the lawn
With my gown in the dew, took will and away
Among the acacias of the shrubberies,
To fly my fancies in the open air
25   And keep my birthday, till my aunt awoke
To stop good dreams. Meanwhile I murmured on
As honeyed bees keep humming to themselves,
"The worthiest poets have remained uncrowned
Till death has bleached their foreheads to the bone;
30   And so with me it must be unless I prove
Unworthy of the grand adversity,
And certainly I would not fail so much.
What, therefore, if I crown myself to-day
In sport, not pride, to learn the feel of it,
35   Before my brows be numbed as Dante's own
To all the tender pricking of such leaves?
Such leaves! what leaves?"
                               I pulled the branches down
To choose from.
                  "Not the bay![5] I choose no bay
(The fates deny us if we are overbold),
40   Nor myrtle—which means chiefly love; and love
Is something awful which one dares not touch
So early o' mornings. This verbena strains
The point of passionate fragrance; and hard by,
This guelder-rose,° at far too slight a beck   cranberry bush
45   Of the wind; will toss about her flower-apples.
Ah—there's my choice,—that ivy on the wall,
That headlong ivy! not a leaf will grow
But thinking of a wreath. Large leaves, smooth leaves,
Serrated like my vines, and half as green.
50   I like such ivy, bold to leap a height
'Twas strong to climb; as good to grow on graves
As twist about a thyrsus;[6] pretty too
(And that's not ill) when twisted round a comb."
Thus speaking to myself, half singing it,
55   Because some thoughts are fashioned like a bell
To ring with once being touched, I drew a wreath
Drenched, blinding me with dew, across my brow,
And fastening it behind so, turning faced
. . . My public!—cousin Romney—with a mouth
Twice graver than his eyes.
60   I stood there fixed,—
My arms up, like the caryatid,[7] sole
Of some abolished temple, helplessly

---

5. A type of laurel tree whose leaves the ancient
Greeks used to honor athletic champions; subsequently, a symbol of poetic achievement.
6. Staff twined with ivy, carried by Dionysus in

Greek myth.
7. Classical column in the form of a draped female
figure.

Persistent in a gesture which derides
A former purpose. Yet my blush was flame,
As if from flax, not stone.
65   "Aurora Leigh,
The earliest of Auroras!"[8]
                          Hand stretched out
I clasped, as shipwrecked men will clasp a hand,
Indifferent to the sort of palm. The tide
Had caught me at my pastime, writing down
70   My foolish name too near upon the sea
Which drowned me with a blush as foolish. "You,
My cousin!"
                  The smile died out in his eyes
And dropped upon his lips, a cold dead weight,
For just a moment, "Here's a book I found!
75   No name writ on it—poems, by the form;
Some Greek upon the margin,—lady's Greek
Without the accents. Read it? Not a word.
I saw at once the thing had witchcraft in't,
Whereof the reading calls up dangerous spirits:
I rather bring it to the witch."
80   "My book.
You found it" . . .
                          "In the hollow by the stream
That beech leans down into—of which you said
The Oread in it has a Naiad's[9] heart
And pines for waters."
                          "Thank you."
                                            "Thanks to *you*
85   My cousin! that I have seen you not too much
Witch, scholar, poet, dreamer, and the rest,
To be a woman also."
                          With a glance
The smile rose in his eyes again and touched
The ivy on my forehead, light as air.
90   I answered gravely "Poets needs must be
Or men or women—more's the pity."
                                            "Ah,
But men, and still less women, happily,
Scarce need be poets. Keep to the green wreath,
Since even dreaming of the stone and bronze
95   Brings headaches, pretty cousin, and defiles
The clean white morning dresses."
                                            "So you judge!
Because I love the beautiful I must
Love pleasure chiefly, and be overcharged
For ease and whiteness! well, you know the world,
100 And only miss your cousin, 'tis not much.
But learn this; I would rather take my part

---

8. Dawns; from Aurora, Roman goddess of the
dawn.

9. Water nymph's. "Oread": tree nymph.

With God's Dead, who afford to walk in white
Yet spread His glory, than keep quiet here
And gather up my feet from even a step
105 For fear to soil my gown in so much dust.
I choose to walk at all risks.—Here, if heads
That hold a rhythmic thought, must ache perforce,
For my part I choose headaches,—and to-day's
My birthday,"
        "Dear Aurora, choose instead
To cure them. You have balsams."°   *balms*
110   "I perceive.
The headache is too noble for my sex.
You think the heartache would sound decenter,
Since that's the woman's special, proper ache,
And altogether tolerable, except
115 To a woman."

[AURORA'S REJECTION OF ROMNEY][1]

                    There he glowed on me
With all his face and eyes. "No other help?"
Said he—"no more than so?"
345   "What help?" I asked.
"You'd scorn my help,—as Nature's self, you say,
Has scorned to put her music in my mouth
Because a woman's. Do you now turn round
And ask for what a woman cannot give?"

350 "For what she only can, I turn and ask,"
He answered, catching up my hands in his,
And dropping on me from his high-eaved brow
The full weight of his soul,—"I ask for love,
And that, she can; for life in fellowship
355 Through bitter duties—that, I know she can;
For wifehood—will she?"
                    "Now," I said, "may God
Be witness 'twixt us two!" and with the word,
Meseemed[2] I floated into a sudden light
Above his stature,—"am I proved too weak
360 To stand alone, yet strong enough to bear
Such leaners on my shoulder? poor to think,
Yet rich enough to sympathise with thought?
Incompetent to sing, as blackbirds can,
Yet competent to love, like HIM?"
                  I paused;

---

1. Romney and Aurora have been arguing about whether art, particularly a young woman's poetry, is useful in a world that, according to Romney, is full of human suffering. Romney claims that women have no faculty of generalizing and are, therefore, doomed to be trivial poets and ineffectual social reformers. Aurora is quick to agree that to be merely a poetaster would be intolerable to her, but while she admires Romney's lofty concern for humanity, she remains untempted to join forces with him.
2. It seemed to me.

365 Perhaps I darkened, as the lighthouse will
That turns upon the sea. "It's always so.
Anything does for a wife."
                              "Aurora, dear,
And dearly honoured,"—he pressed in at once
With eager utterance,—"you translate me ill.
370 I do not contradict my thought of you
Which is most reverent, with another thought
Found less so. If your sex is weak for art
(And I, who said so, did but honour you
By using truth in courtship), it is strong
375 For life and duty. Place your fecund heart
In mine, and let us blossom for the world
That wants love's colour in the grey of time.
My talk, meanwhile, is arid to you, ay,
Since all my talk can only set you where
380 You look down coldly on the arena-heaps
Of headless bodies, shapeless, indistinct!
The Judgment-Angel scarce would find his way
Through such a heap of generalised distress
To the individual man with lips and eyes,
385 Much less Aurora. Ah, my sweet, come down,
And hand in hand we'll go where yours shall touch
These victims, one by one! till, one by one,
The formless, nameless trunk of every man
Shall seem to wear a head with hair you know,
390 And every woman catch your mother's face
To melt you into passion."
                              "I am a girl,"
I answered slowly; "you do well to name
My mother's face. Though far too early, alas,
God's hand did interpose 'twixt it and me,
395 I know so much of love as used to shine
In that face and another. Just so much;
No more indeed at all. I have not seen
So much love since, I pray you pardon me,
As answers even to make a marriage with
400 In this cold land of England. What you love
Is not a woman, Romney, but a cause:
You want a helpmate, not a mistress, sir,
A wife to help your ends,—in her no end.
Your cause is noble, your ends excellent,
405 But I, being most unworthy of these and that,
Do otherwise conceive of love. Farewell."

"Farewell, Aurora? you reject me thus?"
He said.
              "Sir, you were married long ago.
You have a wife already whom you love,
410 Your social theory. Bless you both, I say.
For my part, I am scarcely meek enough

To be the handmaid of a lawful spouse.
Do I look a Hagar,[3] think you?"
"So you jest."

"Nay, so, I speak in earnest," I replied.
415   "You treat of marriage too much like, at least,
A chief apostle: you would bear with you
A wife . . . a sister . . . shall we speak it out?
A sister of charity."
"Then, must it be
Indeed farewell? And was I so far wrong
420   In hope and in illusion, when I took
The woman to be nobler than the man,
Yourself the noblest woman, in the use
And comprehension of what love is,—love,
That generates the likeness of itself
425   Through all heroic duties? so far wrong,
In saying bluntly, venturing truth on love,
'Come, human creature, love and work with me,'—
Instead of 'Lady, thou art wondrous fair,
'And, where the Graces walk before, the Muse
430   'Will follow at the lightning of their eyes,
'And where the Muse walks, lovers need to creep:
'Turn round and love me, or I die of love.' "

With quiet indignation I broke in.
"You misconceive the question like a man,
435   Who sees a woman as the complement
Of his sex merely. You forget too much
That every creature, female as the male,
Stands single in responsible act and thought
As also in birth and death. Whoever says
440   To a loyal woman, 'Love and work with me,'
Will get fair answers if the work and love,
Being good themselves, are good for her—the best
She was born for. Women of a softer mood,
Surprised by men when scarcely awake to life,
445   Will sometimes only hear the first word, love,
And catch up with it any kind of work,
Indifferent, so that dear love go with it.
I do not blame such women, though, for love,
They pick much oakum;[4] earth's fanatics make
450   Too frequently heaven's saints. But *me* your work
Is not the best for,—nor your love the best,
Nor able to commend the kind of work
For love's sake merely. Ah, you force me, sir,
To be overbold in speaking of myself:
455   I too have my vocation,—work to do,

---

3. In Genesis 16, Sarah's maidservant, who bore a child, Ishmael, by Sarah's husband, Abraham.

4. Fiber derived by untwisting (picking) old rope, a task frequently assigned to workhouse inmates.

The heavens and earth have set me since I changed
My father's face for theirs, and, though your world
Were twice as wretched as you represent,
Most serious work, most necessary work
460 As any of the economists'. Reform,
Make trade a Christian possibility,
And individual right no general wrong;
Wipe out earth's furrows of the Thine and Mine,
And leave one green for men to play at bowls,[5]
465 With innings for them all! . . . What then, indeed,
If mortals are not greater by the head
Than any of their prosperities? what then,
Unless the artist keep up open roads
Betwixt the seen and unseen,—bursting through
470 The best of your conventions with his best,
The speakable, imaginable best
God bids him speak, to prove what lies beyond
Both speech and imagination? A starved man
Exceeds a fat beast: we'll not barter, sir,
475 The beautiful for barley.—And, even so,
I hold you will not compass your poor ends
Of barley-feeding and material ease,
Without a poet's individualism
To work your universal. It takes a soul,
480 To move a body: it takes a high-souled man,
To move the masses, even to a cleaner stye:
It takes the ideal, to blow a hair's-breadth off
The dust of the actual.—Ah, your Fouriers[6] failed,
Because not poets enough to understand
485 That life develops from within.——For me,
Perhaps I am not worthy, as you say,
Of work like this: perhaps a woman's soul
Aspires, and not creates: yet we aspire,
And yet I'll try out your perhapses, sir,
490 And if I fail . . . why, burn me up my straw[7]
Like other false works—I'll not ask for grace;
Your scorn is better, cousin Romney. I
Who love my art, would never wish it lower
To suit my stature. I may love my art.
495 You'll grant that even a woman may love art,
Seeing that to waste true love on anything
Is womanly, past question."

From *Book 5*

[POETS AND THE PRESENT AGE]

The critics say that epics have died out
140 With Agamemnon and the goat-nursed gods;[8]

---

5. A game of skill played on a smooth lawn with weighted wooden balls.
6. François-Marie-Charles Fourier (1772–1837), a French political theorist who advocated communal property as a basis for social harmony.
7. I.e., destroy my poetry (a deliberate archaism).
8. Zeus was nursed by a goat.

I'll not believe it. I could never deem,
As Payne Knight[9] did (the mythic mountaineer
Who travelled higher than he was born to live,
And showed sometimes the goitre[1] in his throat

145 Discoursing of an image seen through fog),
That Homer's heroes measured twelve feet high.
They were but men:—his Helen's hair turned grey
Like any plain Miss Smith's who wears a front;[2]
And Hector's infant whimpered at a plume[3]

150 As yours last Friday at a turkey-cock.
All actual heroes are essential men,
And all men possible heroes: every age,
Heroic in proportions, double-faced,
Looks backward and before, expects a morn
And claims an epos.°   *epic poem*

155   Ay, but every age
Appears to souls who live in 't (ask Carlyle)[4]
Most unheroic. Ours, for instance, ours:
The thinkers scout it, and the poets abound
Who scorn to touch it with a finger-tip:

160 A pewter age,[5]—mixed metal, silver-washed;
An age of scum, spooned off the richer past,
An age of patches for old gaberdines,°   *coats*
An age of mere transition,[6] meaning nought
Except that what succeeds must shame it quite

165 If God please. That's wrong thinking, to my mind,
And wrong thoughts make poor poems.
                                     Every age,
Through being beheld too close, is ill-discerned
By those who have not lived past it. We'll suppose
Mount Athos carved, as Alexander schemed,

170 To some colossal statue of a man.[7]
The peasants, gathering brushwood in his ear,
Had guessed as little as the browsing goats
Of form or feature of humanity
Up there,—in fact, had travelled five miles off

175 Or ere the giant image broke on them,
Full human profile, nose and chin distinct,
Mouth, muttering rhythms of silence up the sky
And fed at evening with the blood of suns;

9. Richard Payne Knight (1750–1824), a classical philologist, who, upon England's acquisition of the Parthenon marbles, claimed that Lord Elgin had wasted his labor because they were not all Greek.
1. A disease often contracted in high mountain areas because of the low iodine content of the water.
2. A piece of false hair worn over the forehead by women.
3. In an episode in the *Iliad,* Hector tries to take his infant son in his arms; but the child clings to his nurse, frightened of his father's helmet and crest.
4. In *Heroes and Hero-Worship* (1841), Carlyle argues that the present age needs a renewed per-

ception of the heroic.
5. Allusion to the convention, which originates in Hesiod, of describing civilization's decline through a succession of ages named for increasingly less precious materials, i.e., the Golden Age, the Silver Age, the Bronze Age.
6. In *The Spirit of the Age* (1831) John Stuart Mill calls the present age "an age of transition."
7. Dionocrates, a sculptor, is said to have suggested to Alexander that Mount Athos be carved into the statue of a conqueror with a city in his left hand and a basin in his right, where all the waters of the region could be collected and used to water the pasture lands below.

Grand torso,—hand, that flung perpetually
180   The largesse of a silver river down
To all the country pastures. 'Tis even thus
With times we live in,—evermore too great
To be apprehended near.   But poets should
Exert a double vision; should have eyes
185   To see near things as comprehensively
As if afar they took their point of sight,
And distant things as intimately deep
As if they touched them. Let us strive for this.
I do distrust the poet who discerns
190   No character or glory in his times,
And trundles back his soul five hundred years,
Past moat and drawbridge, into a castle-court,
To sing—oh, not of lizard or of toad
Alive i' the ditch there,—'twere excusable,
195   But of some black chief, half knight, half sheep-lifter,
Some beauteous dame, half chattel and half queen,
As dead as must be, for the greater part,
The poems made on their chivalric bones;
And that's no wonder: death inherits death.

200   Nay, if there's room for poets in this world
A little overgrown (I think there is),
Their sole work is to represent the age,
Their age, not Charlemagne's,[8]—this live, throbbing age,
That brawls, cheats, maddens, calculates, aspires,
205   And spends more passion, more heroic heat,
Betwixt the mirrors of its drawing-rooms,
Than Roland[9] with his knights at Roncesvalles.
To flinch from modern varnish, coat or flounce,
Cry out for togas and the picturesque,
210   Is fatal,—foolish too. King Arthur's self
Was commonplace to Lady Guenever;
And Camelot to minstrels seemed as flat
As Fleet Street[1] to our poets.   Never flinch,
But still, unscrupulously epic, catch
215   Upon the burning lava of a song
The full-veined, heaving, double-breasted Age:
That, when the next shall come, the men of that
May touch the impress with reverent hand, and say
"Behold,—behold the paps° we all have sucked!   *breasts*
220   This bosom seems to beat still, or at least
It sets ours beating: this is living art,
Which thus presents and thus records true life."

1853–56   1857

8. Frankish conqueror (742–814), who created a
European empire.
9. Legendary medieval hero, whose adventures

are told in the epic poem *Chanson de Roland*.
1. A center for book shops and newspaper and
publishing offices in London.

Mother and Poet[1]

(Turin, After News from Gaeta, 1861)

1

DEAD! One of them shot by the sea in the east,
  And one of them shot in the west by the sea.
Dead! both my boys! When you sit at the feast
  And are wanting a great song for Italy free,
5   Let none look at *me!*

2

Yet I was a poetess only last year,
  And good at my art, for a woman, men said;
But *this* woman, *this*, who is agonised here,
  —The east sea and west sea rhyme on in her head
10   For ever instead.

3

What art can a woman be good at? Oh, vain!
  What art *is* she good at, but hurting her breast
With the milk-teeth of babes, and a smile at the pain?
  Ah boys, how you hurt! you were strong as you pressed,
15   And I proud, by that test.

4

What art's for a woman? To hold on her knees
  Both darlings! to feel all their arms round her throat,
Cling, strangle a little! to sew by degrees
  And 'broider the long-clothes and neat little coat;
20   To dream and to doat.

5

To teach them . . . It stings there! *I* made them indeed
  Speak plain the word *country.* I taught them, no doubt,
That a country's a thing men should die for at need.
  I prated of liberty, rights, and about
25   The tyrant cast out.

6

And when their eyes flashed . . . O my beautiful eyes! . . .
  I exulted; nay, let them go forth at the wheels
Of the guns, and denied not. But then the surprise
  When one sits quite alone! Then one weeps, then one kneels!
30   God, how the house feels!

---

1. The speaker is the Italian poet and patriot Laura Savio of Turin, both of whose sons were killed in the struggle for the unification of Italy, one in the attack on the fortress at Ancona, the other at the siege of Gaeta, the last stronghold of the Neapolitan government.

7

At first, happy news came, in gay letters moiled°   *moistened*
    With my kisses,—of camp-life and glory, and how
They both loved me; and, soon coming home to be spoiled
    In return would fan off every fly from my brow
35   With their green laurel-bough.[2]

8

Then was triumph at Turin: "Ancona was free!"
    And some one came out of the cheers in the street,
With a face pale as stone, to say something to me.
    My Guido was dead! I fell down at his feet,
40   While they cheered in the street.

9

I bore it; friends soothed me; my grief looked sublime
    As the ransom of Italy. One boy remained
To be leant on and walked with, recalling the time
    When the first grew immortal, while both of us strained
45   To the height he had gained.

10

And letters still came, shorter, sadder, more strong,
    Writ now but in one hand, "I was not to faint,—
One loved me for two—would be with me ere long:
    And *Viva l'Italia!*—he died for, our saint,
50   Who forbids our complaint."

11

My Nanni would add, "he was safe, and aware
    Of a presence that turned off the balls,°—was imprest   *cannonballs*
It was Guido himself, who knew what I could bear,
    And how 'twas impossible, quite dispossessed
55   To live on for the rest."

12

On which, without pause, up the telegraph line
    Swept smoothly the next news from Gaeta:—*Shot.*
Tell his mother. Ah, ah, "his," "their" mother,—not "mine,"
    No voice says *"My* mother" again to me. What!
60   You think Guido forgot?

13

Are souls straight so happy that, dizzy with Heaven,
    They drop earth's affections, conceive not of woe?
I think not. Themselves were too lately forgiven
    Through THAT Love and Sorrow which reconciled so
65   The Above and Below.

2. A laurel crown is the conventional mark of a poet's fame.

14

O Christ of the five wounds, who look'dst through the dark
    To the face of thy mother! consider, I pray,
How we common mothers stand desolate, mark,
    Whose sons, not being Christs, die with eyes turned away
70   And no last word to say!

15

Both boys dead? but that's out of nature. We all
    Have been patriots, yet each house must always keep one.
'Twere imbecile, hewing out roads to a wall;
    And, when Italy's made, for what end is it done
75   If we have not a son?

16

Ah, ah, ah! when Gaeta's taken, what then?
    When the fair wicked queen sits no more at her sport
Of the fire-balls of death crashing souls out of men?
    When the guns of Cavalli[3] with final retort
80   Have cut the game short?

17

When Venice and Rome keep their new jubilee,[4]
    When your flag takes all heaven for its white, green, and red,
When *you* have your country from mountain to sea,
    When King Victor has Italy's crown on his head,
85   (And *I* have my Dead)—

18

What then? Do not mock me. Ah, ring your bells low,
    And burn your lights faintly! *My* country is *there,*
Above the star pricked by the last peak of snow:
    My Italy's THERE, with my brave civic Pair,
90   To disfranchise despair!

19

Forgive me. Some women bear children in strength,
    And bite back the cry of their pain in self-scorn;
But the birth-pangs of nations will wring us at length
    Into wail such as this—and we sit on forlorn
95   When the man-child is born.

20

Dead! One of them shot by the sea in the east,
    And one of them shot in the west by the sea.
Both! both my boys! If in keeping the feast

3. The general commanding the siege of Gaeta. "The fair wicked queen": Maria, wife of Francis II, the last ruler of the Neapolitan government, who retreated to Gaeta.
4. The celebration when they too will have been united with the rest of Italy under King Victor Emmanuel. In 1861, when the poem was written, they were the two cities that were still independent of the new state.

You want a great song for your Italy free,
100   Let none look at *me!*

1861   1862

ALFRED, LORD TENNYSON
1809–1892

Whether or not Alfred Tennyson was the greatest of the Victorian poets, as affirmed by many critics today, there is no doubt that in his own lifetime he was the most popular of poets. On the bookshelves of almost every family of readers in England and the United States, from 1850 onward, were the works of a man who had incontestably gained the title that Walt Whitman longed for: "The Poet of the People" (Whitman, in fact, called Tennyson, colorfully, "the Boss"). Popularity inevitably provided provocation for a reaction in the decades following his death. In the course of repudiating their Victorian predecessors, the Edwardians and Georgians established the fashion of making fun of Tennyson's great achievements. Samuel Butler (1835–1902), who anticipated early twentieth-century tastes, has a characteristic entry in his *Notebooks:* "Talking it over, we agreed that Blake was no good because he learnt Italian at sixty in order to study Dante, and we knew Dante was no good because he was so fond of Virgil, and Virgil was no good because Tennyson ran him, and as for Tennyson—well, Tennyson goes without saying." In the second half of the twentieth century, Butler's flippant dismissal of Tennyson expresses an attitude that is no longer fashionable. The delights to be found in this superb "lord of language"—as Tennyson himself addresses his favorite predecessor, Virgil—have been rediscovered, and Tennyson's stature as one of the major poets of any age has been reestablished.

Like his poetry, Tennyson's life and character have been reassessed in the twentieth century. To many of his contemporaries he seemed a remote wizard, secure in his laureate's robes, a man whose life had been sheltered, marred only by the loss of his best friend in youth. During much of his career Tennyson may have been isolated, but his was not a sheltered life in the real sense of the word. Although he grew up in a parsonage, it was not the kind of parsonage one encounters in the novels of Jane Austen. It was a household dominated by frictions and loyalties and broodings over ancestral inheritances, in which the children showed marked strains of instability and eccentricity.

Alfred was the fourth son in a family of twelve children. One of his brothers had to be confined to an insane asylum for life; another was long addicted to opium; another had violent quarrels with his father, the Reverend Dr. George Tennyson. This father, a man of considerable learning, had himself been born the eldest son of a wealthy landowner and had, therefore, expected to be heir to his family's estates. Instead he was disinherited in favor of his younger brother and had to make his own livelihood by joining the clergy, a profession that he disliked. After George Tennyson had settled in a small rectory in Somersby, his brooding sense of dissatisfaction led to increasingly violent bouts of drunkenness, despite which he was able to serve as tutor for his sons in classical and modern languages to prepare them for entering the university.

Before leaving this strange household for Cambridge, Alfred had already demonstrated a flair for writing verse—precocious exercises in the manner of Milton or Byron or the Elizabethan dramatists. He had even published a volume in 1827, in collaboration with his brother Charles, *Poems by Two Brothers*. This feat drew him to the attention of a group of gifted undergraduates at Cambridge, "the Apostles," who encouraged him to devote his life to poetry. Up until that time, the young man had known scarcely anyone outside the circle of his own family. Despite his massive frame and powerful physique, he was painfully shy; and the friendships he found at Cambridge as well as the intellectual and political discussions in which he participated served to give him confidence and to widen his horizons as a poet. The most important of these friendships was with Arthur Hallam, a leader of the Apostles, who later became engaged to Tennyson's sister. Hallam's sudden death, in 1833, seemed an overwhelming calamity to his friend. Not only the long elegy *In Memoriam* but many of Tennyson's other poems are tributes to this early friendship.

Alfred's career at Cambridge was interrupted and finally broken off in 1831 by family dissensions and financial need, and he returned home to study and practice the craft of poetry. His early volumes (1830 and 1832) were attacked as "obscure" or "affected" by some of the reviewers. Tennyson suffered acutely under hostile criticism, but he also profited from it. His volume of 1842 demonstrated a remarkable advance in taste and technical excellence, and in 1850 he at last attained fame and full critical recognition with *In Memoriam*. In the same year, he became poet laureate in succession to Wordsworth. The struggle during the previous twenty years had been made especially painful by the long postponement of his marriage to Emily Sellwood, whom he had loved since 1836 but could not marry, because of poverty, until 1850.

His life thereafter was a comfortable one. He was as popular as Byron had been. The earnings from his poetry (sometimes exceeding £10,000 a year) enabled him to purchase a house in the country and to enjoy the kind of seclusion he liked. His notoriety was enhanced, like that of Bernard Shaw and Walt Whitman, by his colorful appearance. Huge and shaggy, in cloak and broad-brimmed hat, gruff in manner as a farmer, he impressed everyone as what is called a "character." The pioneering photographer Julia Cameron, who took magnificent portraits of him, called him "the most beautiful old man on earth." Like Dylan Thomas in the twentieth century, he had a booming voice that electrified listeners when he read his poetry, "mouthing out his hollow o's and a's, / Deep-chested music." Moreover, for many Victorian readers, he seemed not only a great poetical phrase maker and a striking individual but also a wise man whose occasional pronouncements on politics or world affairs represented the national voice itself. In 1884 he accepted a peerage. In 1892 he died and was buried in Westminster Abbey.

It is often said that success was bad for Tennyson and that after *In Memoriam* his poetic power seriously declined. That in his last forty-two years certain of his mannerisms became accentuated is true. One of the difficulties of his dignified blank verse was, as he said himself, that it is hard to describe commonplace objects and "at the same time to retain poetical elevation." This difficulty is evident, for example, in *Enoch Arden* (1864), a long blank verse narrative of everyday life in a fishing village, in which a basketful of fish is ornately described as "Enoch's ocean spoil / In ocean-smelling osier." In others of his later poems, those dealing with national affairs, there is also an increased shrillness of tone—a mannerism accentuated by Tennyson's realizing that like Dickens he had a vast public behind him to back up his pronouncements.

It is foolish, however, to try to shelve all of Tennyson's later productions. In 1855 he published his experimental monologue *Maud*, perhaps his finest long poem, in which he displays the bitterness and despair its alienated hero feels toward society. In 1859 he published four books of his *Idylls of the King*, a large-scale epic that occupied most of his energies in the second half of his career. The *Idylls* uses the body of Arthurian legend to construct a vision of the rise and fall of civilization. In this civilization, women at once inspire men's highest efforts and sow the seeds of their destruction. The *Idylls* provides Tennyson's most extensive social vision, one whose concern with medieval ideals of social community, heroism, and courtly love and whose despairing sense of the cycles of historical change typifies much social thought of the age.

W. H. Auden stated that Tennyson had "the finest ear, perhaps, of any English poet." The interesting point is that Tennyson did not "have" such an ear: he developed it. Studies of the original versions of his poems in the 1830 and 1832 volumes demonstrate how hard he worked at his craftsmanship. Like Chaucer or Keats or Pope, Tennyson studied his predecessors assiduously to perfect his technique. Anyone wanting to learn the traditional craft of English verse can study with profit the various stages of revision that such poems as *The Lotos-Eaters* were subjected to by this painstaking and artful poet. Some lines of 1988 by the American poet Karl Shapiro effectively characterize Tennyson's accomplishments in these areas:

> Long-lived, the very image of English Poet,
> Whose songs still break out tears in the generations,
> Whose poetry for practitioners still astounds,
> Who crafted his life and letters like a watch.

Tennyson's early poetry shows other skills as well. One of these was a capacity for linking scenery to states of mind. As early as 1835, J. S. Mill identified the special kind of scene painting to be found in early poems such as *Mariana*: "not the power of producing that rather vapid species of composition usually termed descriptive poetry . . . but the power of *creating* scenery, in keeping with some state of human feeling so fitted to it as to be the embodied symbol of it, and to summon up the state of feeling itself, with a force not to be surpassed by anything but reality."

The state of feeling to which Tennyson was most intensely drawn was a melancholy isolation, often portrayed through the consciousness of an abandoned woman, as in *Mariana*. Tennyson's absorption with such emotions in his early poetry evoked considerable criticism. His friend R. C. Trench warned him, "Tennyson, we cannot live in Art," and Mill urged him to "cultivate, and with no half devotion, philosophy as well as poetry." Advice of this kind Tennyson was already predisposed to heed. The death of Hallam, the religious uncertainties that he had himself experienced, together with his own extensive study of writings by geologists, astronomers, and biologists, led him to confront many of the religious issues that bewildered his and later generations. The result was *In Memoriam* (1850), a long elegy written over a period of seventeen years, embodying the poet's reflections on our relation to God and to nature.

Was Tennyson intellectually equipped to deal with the great questions raised in *In Memoriam*? The answer may depend on a reader's religious and philosophical presuppositions. Some, such as T. H. Huxley, considered Tennyson an intellectual giant, a thinker who had mastered the scientific thought of his century and fully confronted the issues it raised. Others dismissed Tennyson, in this phase, as a lightweight. Auden went so far as to call him the "stupidest" of English poets. He went on to say, "There was little about melancholia that he didn't know; there was little else that he did." Perhaps T. S. Eliot's evaluation of *In Memoriam* is the more accurate: the poem, he wrote, is remarkable not "because of the quality of its faith but because of the quality of its doubt." Tennyson's mind was slow, ponderous, brooding; for the composition of *In Memoriam* such qualities of mind were assets, not liabilities. In these terms we can understand when Tennyson's poetry really fails to measure up: it is when he writes of events of the moment over which his thoughts and feelings have had no time to brood. Several of his poems are what he himself called "newspaper verse." They are letters to the editor, in effect, with the ephemeral heat and simplicity we expect of such productions. *The Charge of the Light Brigade,* inspired by a report in the *Times* of a cavalry charge at Balaclava during the Crimean War, is one of the best of his productions in this category.

Tennyson's poems of contemporary events were inevitably popular in his own day. So too were those poems in which, as in *Locksley Hall,* he dipped into the future.

The technological changes wrought by Victorian inventors and engineers fascinated him. Sometimes they gave him an assurance of human progress as swaggeringly exultant as that of Macaulay. At other times the horrors of industrialism's by-products in the slums, the persistence of barbarity and bloodshed, the greed of the newly rich, destroyed his hopes that humanity was evolving upward. Such a late poem as *The Dawn* embodies an attitude that he found in Virgil: "Thou majestic in thy sadness at the doubtful doom of human kind."

For despite Tennyson's fascination with technological developments, he was essentially a poet of the countryside, a man whose whole being was conditioned by the recurring rhythms of rural rather than urban life. He had the country dweller's awareness of traditional roots and sense of the past. It is appropriate that most of his best poems are about the past, not about the present or future. Even in his childhood, Tennyson said that "the words 'far, far away' had always a strange charm for me"; he was haunted by what he called "the passion of the past." The past became his great theme, whether it be his own past (as in *In the Valley of Cauteretz*), his country's past (as in *The Idylls of the King*), the past of humankind, the past of the world itself:

> There rolls the deep where grew the tree.
> O earth, what changes hast thou seen!
> There where the long street roars hath been
> The stillness of the central sea.

Tennyson is the first major writer to express this awareness of the vast extent of geological time that has haunted human consciousness since Victorian scientists exposed the history of the earth's crust. In his more usual vein, however, it is the recorded past of humankind that inspires him, the classical past in particular. Classical themes, as Douglas Bush has noted, "generally banished from his mind what was timid, parochial, sentimental . . . and evoked his special gifts and most authentic emotions, his rich and wistful sense of the past, his love of nature, and his power of style."

One returns, finally, to the question of language. At the time of his death, a critic complained that Tennyson was merely "a discoverer of words rather than of ideas." The same complaint has been made by Bernard Shaw and others—not about Tennyson but about Shakespeare.

The Kraken[1]

Below the thunders of the upper deep,
Far, far beneath in the abysmal sea,
His ancient, dreamless, uninvaded sleep
The Kraken sleepeth: faintest sunlights flee
5 About his shadowy sides; above him swell
Huge sponges of millennial growth and height;
And far away into the sickly light,
From many a wondrous grot and secret cell
Unnumbered and enormous polypi°   *octopuses*
10 Winnow with giant arms the slumbering green.
There hath he lain for ages, and will lie
Battening upon huge sea worms in his sleep,
Until the latter fire[2] shall heat the deep;

---

1. A mythical sea beast of gigantic size.
2. Fire that would finally consume the world (Revelation 16.8–9).

Then once by man and angels to be seen,
15 In roaring he shall rise and on the surface die.

1830

The Lady of Shalott[1]

Part 1

On either side the river lie
Long fields of barley and of rye,
That clothe the wold° and meet the sky;   rolling plain
And through the field the road runs by
5   To many-towered Camelot;
And up and down the people go,
Gazing where the lilies blow°   bloom
Round an island there below,
          The island of Shalott.

10 Willows whiten, aspens quiver,
Little breezes dusk and shiver
Through the wave that runs forever
By the island in the river
          Flowing down to Camelot.
15 Four gray walls, and four gray towers,
Overlook a space of flowers,
And the silent isle imbowers
          The Lady of Shalott.

By the margin, willow-veiled,
20 Slide the heavy barges trailed
By slow horses; and unhailed
The shallop° flitteth silken-sailed   light open boat
          Skimming down to Camelot:
But who hath seen her wave her hand?
25 Or at the casement seen her stand?
Or is she known in all the land,
          The Lady of Shalott?

Only reapers, reaping early
In among the bearded barley,
30 Hear a song that echoes cheerly
From the river winding clearly,
          Down to towered Camelot;
And by the moon the reaper weary,
Piling sheaves in uplands airy,
35 Listening, whispers " 'Tis the fairy
          Lady of Shalott."

---

1. For the author's revisions while composing this poem, see "Poems in Process," in the appendices to this volume.

Part 2

There she weaves by night and day
A magic web with colors gay.
She has heard a whisper say,
40   A curse is on her if she stay
         To look down to Camelot.
She knows not what the curse may be,
And so she weaveth steadily,
And little other care hath she,
45   The Lady of Shalott.

And moving through a mirror clear[2]
That hangs before her all the year,
Shadows of the world appear.
There she sees the highway near
50   Winding down to Camelot;
There the river eddy whirls,
And there the surly village churls,
And the red cloaks of market girls,
         Pass onward from Shalott.

55 Sometimes a troop of damsels glad,
An abbot on an ambling pad,°   *easy-paced horse*
Sometimes a curly shepherd lad,
Or long-haired page in crimson clad,
         Goes by to towered Camelot;
60 And sometimes through the mirror blue
The knights come riding two and two:
She hath no loyal knight and true,
         The Lady of Shalott.

But in her web she still delights
65 To weave the mirror's magic sights,
For often through the silent nights
A funeral, with plumes and lights
         And music, went to Camelot;
Or when the moon was overhead,
70 Came two young lovers lately wed:
"I am half sick of shadows," said
         The Lady of Shalott.

Part 3

A bowshot from her bower eaves,
He rode between the barley sheaves,
75 The sun came dazzling through the leaves,
And flamed upon the brazen greaves[3]
         Of bold Sir Lancelot.

---

2. Weavers used mirrors, placed facing their looms, to see the progress of their work.   3. Armor protecting the leg below the knee.

A red-cross knight[4] forever kneeled
To a lady in his shield,
80 That sparkled on the yellow field,
        Beside remote Shalott.

The gemmy bridle glittered free,
Like to some branch of stars we see
Hung in the golden Galaxy.
85 The bridle bells rang merrily
        As he rode down to Camelot;
And from his blazoned baldric[5] slung
A mighty silver bugle hung,
And as he rode his armor rung,
90   Beside remote Shalott.

All in the blue unclouded weather
Thick-jeweled shone the saddle leather,
The helmet and the helmet-feather
Burned like one burning flame together,
95   As he rode down to Camelot;
As often through the purple night,
Below the starry clusters bright,
Some bearded meteor, trailing light,
        Moves over still Shalott.

100 His broad clear brow in sunlight glowed;
On burnished hooves his war horse trode;
From underneath his helmet flowed
His coal-black curls as on he rode,
        As he rode down to Camelot.
105 From the bank and from the river
He flashed into the crystal mirror,
"Tirra lirra," by the river
        Sang Sir Lancelot.

She left the web, she left the loom,
110 She made three paces through the room,
She saw the water lily bloom,
She saw the helmet and the plume,
        She looked down to Camelot.
Out flew the web and floated wide;
115 The mirror cracked from side to side;
"The curse is come upon me," cried
        The Lady of Shalott.

Part 4

In the stormy east wind straining,
The pale yellow woods were waning,
120 The broad stream in his banks complaining,

4. Cf. *The Faerie Queene* 1 and 3.2.17–25.
5. A belt worn diagonally from one shoulder to the opposite hip; it supported a sword, bugle, etc.

Heavily the low sky raining
    Over towered Camelot;
Down she came and found a boat
Beneath a willow left afloat,
125 And round about the prow she wrote
    The Lady of Shalott.

And down the river's dim expanse
Like some bold seër in a trance,
Seeing all his own mischance—
130 With a glassy countenance
    Did she look to Camelot.
And at the closing of the day
She loosed the chain, and down she lay;
The broad steam bore her far away,
135   The Lady of Shalott.

Lying, robed in snowy white
That loosely flew to left and right—
The leaves upon her falling light—
Through the noises of the night
140   She floated down to Camelot;
And as the boat-head wound along
The willowy hills and fields among,
They heard her singing her last song,
    The Lady of Shalott.

145 Heard a carol, mournful, holy,
Chanted loudly, chanted lowly,
Till her blood was frozen slowly,
And her eyes were darkened wholly,[6]
    Turned to towered Camelot.
150 For ere she reached upon the tide
The first house by the waterside,
Singing in her song she died,
    The Lady of Shalott.

Under tower and balcony,
155 By garden wall and gallery,
A gleaming shape she floated by,
Dead-pale between the houses high,
    Silent into Camelot.
Out upon the wharfs they came,
160 Knight and burgher, lord and dame,
And round the prow they read her name,
    The Lady of Shalott.

Who is this? and what is here?
And in the lighted palace near
165 Died the sound of royal cheer;

6. In the 1832 version (reproduced in "Poems in Process") this line read: "And her smooth face sharpened
slowly." George Eliot informed Tennyson that she preferred the earlier version.

And they crossed themselves for fear,
　　All the knights at Camelot:
But Lancelot mused a little space;
He said, "She has a lovely face;
170　God in his mercy lend her grace,
　　The Lady of Shalott."

1831–32　　　　　　　　　　　　　　　　　　　　　　1832, 1842

Dante Gabriel Rossetti's 1857 engraving for publisher Edward Moxon's illustrated collection of Tennyson's poetry shows Lancelot musing "a little space" on the Lady of Shalott in her boat.

The Lotos-Eaters[1]

"Courage!" he[2] said, and pointed toward the land,
"This mounting wave will roll us shoreward soon."

1. Based on a short episode from the *Odyssey* (9.82–97) in which the weary Greek veterans of the Trojan War are tempted by a desire to abandon their long voyage homeward. As Odysseus later reported: "On the tenth day we set foot on the land of the lotos-eaters who eat a flowering food.... I sent forth certain of my company [who] ... mixed with the men of the lotos-eaters who gave ... them of the lotos to taste. Now whosoever of them did eat the honey-sweet fruit of the lotos had no more wish to bring tidings nor to come back, but there

he chose to abide ... forgetful of his homeward way."
　Tennyson expands Homer's brief account into an elaborate picture of weariness and the desire for rest and death. The descriptions in the first stanzas are similar to *Faerie Queene* 2.6 and employ the same stanza form. The final section derives, in part, from Lucretius's conception of the gods in *De rerum natura*.
2. Odysseus (or Ulysses).

In the afternoon they came unto a land[3]
In which it seemèd always afternoon.
5   All round the coast the languid air did swoon,
Breathing like one that hath a weary dream.
Full-faced above the valley stood the moon;
And, like a downward smoke, the slender stream
Along the cliff to fall and pause and fall did seem.

10   A land of streams! some, like a downward smoke,
Slow-dropping veils of thinnest lawn,° did go;   *fine, thin linen*
And some through wavering lights and shadows broke,
Rolling a slumbrous sheet of foam below.
They saw the gleaming river seaward flow
15   From the inner land; far off, three mountaintops
Three silent pinnacles of aged snow,
Stood sunset-flushed; and, dewed with showery drops,
Up-clomb the shadowy pine above the woven copse.

The charmèd sunset lingered low adown
20   In the red West; through mountain clefts the dale
Was seen far inland, and the yellow down[4]
Bordered with palm, and many a winding vale
And meadow, set with slender galingale;[5]
A land where all things always seemed the same!
25   And round about the keel with faces pale,
Dark faces pale against that rosy flame,
The mild-eyed melancholy Lotos-eaters came.

Branches they bore of that enchanted stem,
Laden with flower and fruit, whereof they gave
30   To each, but whoso did receive of them
And taste, to him the gushing of the wave
Far far away did seem to mourn and rave
On alien shores; and if his fellow spake,
His voice was thin, as voices from the grave;
35   And deep-asleep he seemed, yet all awake,
And music in his ears his beating heart did make.

They sat them down upon the yellow sand,
Between the sun and moon upon the shore;
And sweet it was to dream of Fatherland,
40   Of child, and wife, and slave; but evermore
Most weary seemed the sea, weary the oar,
Weary the wandering fields of barren foam,
Then some one said, "We will return no more";
And all at once they sang, "Our island home°   *Ithaca*
45   Is far beyond the wave; we will no longer roam."

3. The repetition of "land" from line 1 was deliberate; Tennyson said that this "no rhyme" was
"lazier" in its effect. Cf. "afternoon" (lines 3–4) and
the rhyming of "adown" and "down" (lines 19 and

21).
4. An open plain on high ground.
5. A plant resembling tall coarse grass.

Choric Song[6]

1

There is sweet music here that softer falls
Than petals from blown roses on the grass,
Or night-dews on still waters between walls
Of shadowy granite, in a gleaming pass;
50   Music that gentlier on the spirit lies,
Than tired[7] eyelids upon tired eyes;
Music that brings sweet sleep down from the blissful skies.
Here are cool mosses deep,
And through the moss the ivies creep,
55   And in the stream the long-leaved flowers weep,
And from the craggy ledge the poppy hangs in sleep.

2

Why are we weighed upon with heaviness,
And utterly consumed with sharp distress,
While all things else have rest from weariness?
60   All things have rest: why should we toil alone,
We only toil, who are the first of things,
And make perpetual moan,
Still from one sorrow to another thrown;
Nor ever fold our wings,
65   And cease from wanderings,
Nor steep our brows in slumber's holy balm;
Nor harken what the inner spirit sings,
"There is no joy but calm!"—
Why should we only toil, the roof and crown of things?[8]

3

70   Lo! in the middle of the wood,
The folded leaf is wooed from out the bud
With winds upon the branch, and there
Grows green and broad, and takes no care,
Sun-steeped at noon, and in the moon
75   Nightly dew-fed; and turning yellow
Falls, and floats adown the air.
Lo! sweetened with summer light,
The full-juiced apple, waxing over-mellow,
Drops in a silent autumn night.
80   All its allotted length of days
The flower ripens in its place,
Ripens and fades, and falls, and hath no toil,
Fast-rooted in the fruitful soil.

6. Sung by the mariners.
7. Tennyson wanted the word to be pronounced as *tie-yerd* rather than *tier'd* or *tire-èd*, thus "making the word neither monosyllable or disyllabic, but a dreamy child of the two."

8. Cf. *Faerie Queene* 2.6.17: "Why then dost thou, O man, that of them all / Art Lord, and eke of nature Sovereaine, / Wilfully . . . wast thy joyous houres in needlesse paine?"

4

Hateful is the dark blue sky,
85 Vaulted o'er the dark blue sea.
Death is the end of life; ah, why
Should life all labor be?
Let us alone. Time driveth onward fast,
And in a little while our lips are dumb.
90 Let us alone. What is it that will last?
All things are taken from us, and become
Portions and parcels of the dreadful past.
Let us alone. What pleasure can we have
To war with evil? Is there any peace
95 In ever climbing up the climbing wave?
All things have rest, and ripen toward the grave
In silence—ripen, fall, and cease:
Give us long rest or death, dark death, or dreamful ease.[9]

5

How sweet it were, hearing the downward stream,
100 With half-shut eyes ever to seem
Falling asleep in a half-dream!
To dream and dream, like yonder amber light,
Which will not leave the myrrh-bush on the height;
To hear each other's whispered speech;
105 Eating the Lotos day by day,
To watch the crisping° ripples on the beach,   *curling*
And tender curving lines of creamy spray;
To lend our hearts and spirits wholly
To the influence of mild-minded melancholy;
110 To muse and brood and live again in memory,
With those old faces of our infancy
Heaped over with a mound of grass,
Two handfuls of white dust, shut in an urn of brass!

6

Dear is the memory of our wedded lives,
115 And dear the last embraces of our wives
And their warm tears; but all hath suffered change;
For surely now our household hearths are cold,
Our sons inherit us, our looks are strange,
And we should come like ghosts to trouble joy.
120 Or else the island princes° overbold   *Penelope's suitors*
Have eat our substance, and the minstrel sings
Before them of the ten years' war in Troy,
And our great deeds, as half-forgotten things.
Is there confusion in the little isle?
125 Let what is broken so remain.
The Gods are hard to reconcile;

---

9. Cf. *Faerie Queen* 1.9.40: "Sleepe after toyle, port after stormie seas, / Ease after warre, death after life does greatly please."

'Tis hard to settle order once again.
There *is* confusion worse than death,
Trouble on trouble, pain on pain,
130 Long labor unto aged breath,
Sore tasks to hearts worn out by many wars
And eyes grown dim with gazing on the pilot-stars.

7

But, propped on beds of amaranth and moly,[1]
How sweet—while warm airs lull us, blowing lowly—
135 With half-dropped eyelid still,
Beneath a heaven dark and holy,
To watch the long bright river drawing slowly
His waters from the purple hill—
To hear the dewy echoes calling
140 From cave to cave through the thick-twined vine—
To watch the emerald-colored water falling
Through many a woven acanthus[2] wreath divine!
Only to hear and see the far-off sparkling brine,
Only to hear were sweet, stretched out beneath the pine.

8

145 The Lotos blooms below the barren peak,
The Lotos blows by every winding creek;
All day the wind breathes low with mellower tone;
Through every hollow cave and alley lone
Round and round the spicy downs the yellow Lotos dust is blown.
150 We have had enough of action, and of motion we,
Rolled to starboard, rolled to larboard, when the surge was seething free,
Where the wallowing monster spouted his foam-fountains in the sea.
Let us swear an oath, and keep it with an equal mind,
In the hollow Lotos land to live and lie reclined
155 On the hills like Gods together, careless of mankind.
For they lie beside their nectar, and the bolts° are hurled   thunderbolts
Far below them in the valleys, and the clouds are lightly curled
Round their golden houses, girdled with the gleaming world;
Where they smile in secret, looking over wasted lands,
160 Blight and famine, plague and earthquake, roaring deeps and fiery sands,
Clanging fights, and flaming towns, and sinking ships, and praying hands.
But they smile, they find a music centered in a doleful song
Steaming up, a lamentation and an ancient tale of wrong,
Like a tale of little meaning though the words are strong;
165 Chanted from an ill-used race of men that cleave the soil,
Sow the seed, and reap the harvest with enduring toil,
Storing yearly little dues of wheat, and wine and oil;
Till they perish and they suffer—some, 'tis whispered—down in hell
Suffer endless anguish, others in Elysian valleys dwell,
170 Resting weary limbs at last on beds of asphodel.[3]

1. A flower with magical properties mentioned by
Homer. "Amaranth": a legendary unfading flower.
2. A plant resembling a thistle. Its leaves were the
model for ornaments on Corinthian columns.
3. A yellow lilylike flower supposed to grow in the
Elysian valleys.

Surely, surely, slumber is more sweet than toil, the shore
Than labor in the deep mid-ocean, wind and wave and oar;
O, rest ye, brother mariners, we will not wander more.

1832, 1842

Ulysses[1]

It little profits that an idle king,
By this still hearth, among these barren crags,
Matched with an aged wife, I mete and dole
Unequal laws[2] unto a savage race,
5   That hoard, and sleep, and feed,[3] and know not me.
   I cannot rest from travel; I will drink
Life to the lees. All times I have enjoyed
Greatly, have suffered greatly, both with those
That loved me, and alone; on shore, and when
10 Through scudding drifts the rainy Hyades[4]
Vexed the dim sea. I am become a name;
For always roaming with a hungry heart
Much have I seen and known—cities of men
And manners, climates, councils, governments,
15 Myself not least, but honored of them all—
And drunk delight of battle with my peers,
Far on the ringing plains of windy Troy,
I am a part of all that I have met;
Yet all experience is an arch wherethrough
20 Gleams that untraveled world whose margin fades
Forever and forever when I move.
How dull it is to pause, to make an end,
To rust unburnished, not to shine in use![5]
As though to breathe were life! Life piled on life
25 Were all too little, and of one to me
Little remains; but every hour is saved
From that eternal silence, something more,
A bringer of new things; and vile it were
For some three suns to store and hoard myself,
30 And this gray spirit yearning in desire

1. According to Dante, after the fall of Troy, Ulysses never returned to his island home of Ithaca. Instead he persuaded some of his followers to seek new experiences by a voyage of exploration westward out beyond the Strait of Gibraltar. In his inspiring speech to his aging crew he said: "Consider your origin: you were not made to live as brutes, but to pursue virtue and knowledge" (*Inferno* 26). Tennyson modified Dante's version by combining it with Homer's account (*Odyssey* 19–24). Thus Tennyson has Ulysses make his speech in Ithaca some time after his return home to his reunion with his wife, Penelope, and his son, Telemachus, and, presumably, his resumption of administrative responsibilities involved in governing his kingdom.

Tennyson himself stated that this poem expressed his own "need of going forward and braving the struggle of life" after the death of Hallam.
2. Measure out rewards and punishments.
3. Cf. *Hamlet* 4.4.33–35: "What is a man, / If his chief good . . . / Be but to sleep and feed? a beast, no more."
4. A group of stars whose rising was assumed to be followed by rain. "Scudding drifts": driving showers of spray and rain.
5. Cf. Ulysses' speech in *Troilus and Cressida* 3.3.150–53: "Perseverance, dear my lord, / Keeps honour bright; to have done, is to hang / Quite out of fashion, like a rusty mail / in monumental mockery."

To follow knowledge like a sinking star,
Beyond the utmost bound of human thought.

This is my son, mine own Telemachus,
To whom I leave the scepter and the isle—
35 Well-loved of me, discerning to fulfill
This labor, by slow prudence to make mild
A rugged people, and through soft degrees
Subdue them to the useful and the good.
Most blameless is he, centered in the sphere
40 Of common duties, decent not to fail
In offices of tenderness, and pay
Meet adoration to my household gods,
When I am gone. He works his work, I mine.

There lies the port; the vessel puffs her sail;
45 There gloom the dark, broad seas. My mariners,
Souls that have toiled, and wrought, and thought with me—
That ever with a frolic welcome took
The thunder and the sunshine, and opposed
Free hearts, free foreheads—you and I are old;
50 Old age hath yet his honor and his toil.
Death closes all; but something ere the end,
Some work of noble note, may yet be done,
Not unbecoming men that strove with Gods.
The lights begin to twinkle from the rocks;
55 The long day wanes; the slow moon climbs; the deep
Moans round with many voices. Come, my friends,
'Tis not too late to seek a newer world.
Push off, and sitting well in order smite
The sounding furrows; for my purpose holds
60 To sail beyond the sunset, and the baths
Of all the western stars,[6] until I die.
It may be that the gulfs will wash us down;
It may be we shall touch the Happy Isles,[7]
And see the great Achilles, whom we knew.
65 Though much is taken, much abides; and though
We are not now that strength which in old days
Moved earth and heaven, that which we are, we are—
One equal temper of heroic hearts,
Made weak by time and fate, but strong in will
70 To strive, to seek, to find, and not to yield.

1833   1842

6. The outer ocean or river that, in Greek cosmology, surrounded the flat circle of the earth and into which the stars descended.
7. In Greek myth the Islands of the Blessed, a paradise of perpetual summer, located in the far-western ocean. They were peopled by great heroes who, without having died, had been translated there by the gods and made immortal.

Tithonus[1]

The woods decay, the woods decay and fall,
The vapors weep their burthen to the ground,
Man comes and tills the field and lies beneath,
And after many a summer dies the swan.[2]
5 Me only cruel immortality
Consumes; I wither slowly in thine arms,[3]
Here at the quiet limit of the world,
A white-haired shadow roaming like a dream
The ever-silent spaces of the East,
10 Far-folded mists, and gleaming halls of morn.
      Alas! for this gray shadow, once a man—
So glorious in his beauty and thy choice,
Who madest him thy chosen, that he seemed
To his great heart none other than a God!
15 I asked thee, "Give me immortality."
Then didst thou grant mine asking with a smile,
Like wealthy men who care not how they give.
But thy strong Hours indignant worked their wills,
And beat me down and marred and wasted me,
20 And though they could not end me, left me maimed
To dwell in presence of immortal youth,
Immortal age beside immortal youth,
And all I was in ashes. Can thy love,
Thy beauty, make amends, though even now,
25 Close over us, the silver star,[4] thy guide,
Shines in those tremulous eyes that fill with tears
To hear me? Let me go; take back thy gift.
Why should a man desire in any way
To vary from the kindly race of men,
30 Or pass beyond the goal of ordinance[5]
Where all should pause, as is most meet for all?
      A soft air fans the cloud apart; there comes
A glimpse of that dark world where I was born.
Once more the old mysterious glimmer steals
35 From thy pure brows, and from thy shoulders pure,
And bosom beating with a heart renewed.
Thy cheek begins to redden through the gloom,
Thy sweet eyes brighten slowly close to mine,
Ere yet they blind the stars, and the wild team[6]
40 Which love thee, yearning for thy yoke, arise,
And shake the darkness from their loosened manes,
And beat the twilight into flakes of fire.
      Lo! ever thus thou growest beautiful

1. A Trojan prince loved by the goddess of the dawn, Eos or Aurora, who obtained for him the gift of living forever but neglected to obtain for him the gift of everlasting youth. For the author's revisions while composing this poem, see "Poems in Process," in the appendices to this volume.
2. Some species of swans live for at least fifty years.
3. The arms of Aurora.
4. The morning star that precedes the dawn.
5. What is decreed or ordained as human destiny.
6. The horses that draw Aurora's chariot into the sky at daybreak.

In silence, then before thine answer given
45   Departest, and thy tears are on my cheek.
     Why wilt thou ever scare me with thy tears,
And make me tremble lest a saying learnt,
In days far-off, on that dark earth, be true?
"The Gods themselves cannot recall their gifts."
50   Ay me! ay me! with what another heart
In days far-off, and with what other eyes
I used to watch—if I be he that watched—
The lucid outline forming round thee; saw
The dim curls kindle into sunny rings;
55   Changed with thy mystic change, and felt my blood
Glow with the glow that slowly crimsoned all
Thy presence and thy portals, while I lay,
Mouth, forehead, eyelids, growing dewy-warm
With kisses balmier than half-opening buds
60   Of April, and could hear the lips that kissed
Whispering I knew not what of wild and sweet,
Like that strange song I heard Apollo sing,
While Ilion like a mist rose into towers.[7]
     Yet hold me not forever in thine East;
65   How can my nature longer mix with thine?
Coldly thy rosy shadows bathe me, cold
Are all thy lights, and cold my wrinkled feet
Upon thy glimmering thresholds, when the steam
Floats up from those dim fields about the homes
70   Of happy men that have the power to die,
And grassy barrows of the happier dead.
Release me, and restore me to the ground.
Thou seest all things, thou wilt see my grave;
Thou wilt renew thy beauty morn by morn,
75   I earth in earth forget these empty courts,
And thee returning on thy silver wheels.

1833, 1859   1860

Break, Break, Break

Break, break, break,
     On thy cold gray stones, O Sea!
And I would that my tongue could utter
     The thoughts that arise in me.

5   O, well for the fisherman's boy,
     That he shouts with his sister at play!
O, well for the sailor lad,
     That he sings in his boat on the bay!

And the stately ships go on
10   To their haven under the hill;

---

7. The walls of Troy ("Ilion") were supposed to have been built to the strains of Apollo's music.

But O for the touch of a vanished hand,
And the sound of a voice that is still!

Break, break, break,
At the foot of thy crags, O Sea!
15 But the tender grace of a day that is dead
Will never come back to me.

1834   1842

The Eagle: A Fragment

He clasps the crag with crooked hands;
Close to the sun in lonely lands,
Ringed with the azure world, he stands.

The wrinkled sea beneath him crawls:
5 He watches from his mountain walls,
And like a thunderbolt he falls.

1851

Locksley Hall[1]

Comrades, leave me here a little, while as yet 'tis early morn;
Leave me here, and when you want me, sound upon the bugle horn.

'Tis the place, and all around it, as of old, the curlews call,
Dreary gleams[2] about the moorland flying over Locksley Hall;

5 Locksley Hall, that in the distance overlooks the sandy tracts,
And the hollow ocean-ridges roaring into cataracts.

Many a night from yonder ivied casement, ere I went to rest,
Did I look on great Orion sloping slowly to the west.

Many a night I saw the Pleiads,[3] rising through the mellow shade,
10 Glitter like a swarm of fireflies tangled in a silver braid.

Here about the beach I wandered, nourishing a youth sublime
With the fairy tales of science, and the long result of time;

1. The situation in this poem—of a young man's being jilted by a woman who chose to marry a wealthy landowner—may have been suggested to Tennyson by the experience of his brother Frederick, a hot-tempered man who had fallen in love with his cousin Julia Tennyson and who was similarly unsuccessful. It may also have been inspired by Tennyson's own frustrated courtship of Rosa Baring, who rejected the young poet in favor of a wealthy suitor. Concerning the ranting tone of the speaker (a tone accentuated by the heavily marked trochaic meter), Tennyson said: "The whole poem represents young life, its good side, its deficiencies, and its yearnings."
2. Tennyson stated that "gleams" does not refer to "curlews" flying but to streaks of light.
3. Or the Pleiades, a seven-starred constellation.

When the centuries behind me like a fruitful land reposed;
When I clung to all the present for the promise that it closed°   enclosed

15   When I dipped into the future far as human eye could see,
Saw the vision of the world and all the wonder that would be.—

In the spring a fuller crimson comes upon the robin's breast;
In the spring the wanton lapwing gets himself another crest;

In the spring a livelier iris changes on the burnished dove;[4]
20   In the spring a young man's fancy lightly turns to thoughts of love.

Then her cheek was pale and thinner than should be for one so young,
And her eyes on all my motions with a mute observance hung.

And I said, "My cousin Amy, speak, and speak the truth to me,
Trust me, cousin, all the current of my being sets to thee."

25   On her pallid cheek and forehead came a color and a light,
As I have seen the rosy red flushing in the northern night.

And she turned—her bosom shaken with a sudden storm of sighs—
All the spirit deeply dawning in the dark of hazel eyes—

Saying, "I have hid my feelings, fearing they should do me wrong";
30   Saying, "Dost thou love me, cousin?" weeping, "I have loved thee long."

Love took up the glass of Time, and turned it in his glowing hands;
Every moment, lightly shaken, ran itself in golden sands.

Love took up the harp of Life, and smote on all the chords with might;
Smote the chord of Self, that, trembling, passed in music out of sight.

35   Many a morning on the moorland did we hear the copses ring,
And her whisper thronged my pulses with the fullness of the spring.

Many an evening by the waters did we watch the stately ships,
And our spirits rushed together at the touching of the lips.

O my cousin, shallow-hearted! O my Amy, mine no more!
40   O the dreary, dreary moorland! O the barren, barren shore!

Falser than all fancy fathoms, falser than all songs have sung,
Puppet to a father's threat, and servile to a shrewish tongue!

Is it well to wish thee happy?—having known me—to decline
On a range of lower feelings and a narrower heart than mine!

45   Yet it shall be; thou shalt lower to his level day by day,
What is fine within thee growing coarse to sympathize with clay.

4. The rainbowlike colors of a dove's throat plumage are intensified in the mating season.

As the husband is, the wife is; thou art mated with a clown,°   *boor*
And the grossness of his nature will have weight to drag thee down.

He will hold thee, when his passion shall have spent its novel force,
50   Something better than his dog, a little dearer than his horse.

What is this? his eyes are heavy; think not they are glazed with wine.
Go to him, it is thy duty; kiss him, take his hand in thine.

It may be my lord is weary, that his brain is overwrought;
Soothe him with thy finer fancies, touch him with thy lighter thought.

55   He will answer to the purpose, easy things to understand—
Better thou wert dead before me, though I slew thee with my hand!

Better thou and I were lying, hidden from the heart's disgrace,
Rolled in one another's arms, and silent in a last embrace.

Cursed be the social wants that sin against the strength of youth!
60   Cursed be the social lies that warp us from the living truth!

Cursed be the sickly forms that err from honest Nature's rule!
Cursed be the gold that gilds the straitened° forehead of the fool!   *narrowed*

Well—'tis well that I should bluster!—Hadst thou less unworthy proved—
Would to God—for I had loved thee more than ever wife was loved.

65   Am I mad, that I should cherish that which bears but bitter fruit?
I will pluck it from my bosom, though my heart be at the root.

Never, though my mortal summers to such length of years should come
As the many-wintered crow⁵ that leads the clanging rookery home.

Where is comfort? in division of the records of the mind?
70   Can I part her from herself, and love her, as I knew her, kind?

I remember one that perished; sweetly did she speak and move;
Such a one do I remember, whom to look at was to love.

Can I think of her as dead, and love her for the love she bore?
No—she never loved me truly; love is love for evermore.

75   Comfort? comfort scorned of devils! this is truth the poet⁶ sings,
That a sorrow's crown of sorrow is remembering happier things.

Drug thy memories, lest thou learn it, lest thy heart be put to proof,
In the dead unhappy night, and when the rain is on the roof.

Like a dog, he hunts in dreams, and thou art staring at the wall,
80   Where the dying night-lamp flickers, and the shadows rise and fall.

---

5. A rook, a long-lived bird.   6. Dante's *Inferno* 5.121–23.

Then a hand shall pass before thee, pointing to his drunken sleep,
To thy widowed[7] marriage-pillows, to the tears that thou wilt weep.

Thou shalt hear the "Never, never," whispered by the phantom years.
And a song from out the distance in the ringing of thine ears;

85 And an eye shall vex thee, looking ancient kindness on thy pain.
Turn thee, turn thee on thy pillow; get thee to thy rest again.

Nay, but Nature brings thee solace; for a tender voice will cry.
'Tis a purer life than thine, a lip to drain thy trouble dry.

Baby lips will laugh me down; my latest rival brings thee rest.
90 Baby fingers, waxen touches, press me from the mother's breast.

O, the child too clothes the father with a dearness not his due.
Half is thine and half is his; it will be worthy of the two.

O, I see thee old and formal, fitted to thy petty part,
With a little hoard of maxims preaching down a daughter's heart.

95 "They were dangerous guides the feelings—she herself was not exempt—
Truly, she herself had suffered"—Perish in thy self-contempt!

Overlive it—lower yet—be happy! wherefore should I care?
I myself must mix with action, lest I wither by despair.

What is that which I should turn to, lighting upon days like these?
100 Every door is barred with gold, and opens but to golden keys.

Every gate is thronged with suitors, all the markets overflow.
I have but an angry fancy; what is that which I should do?

I had been content to perish, falling on the foeman's ground,
When the ranks are rolled in vapor, and the winds are laid with sound.[8]

105 But the jingling of the guinea helps the hurt that Honor feels,
And the nations do but murmur, snarling at each other's heels.

Can I but relive in sadness? I will turn that earlier page.
Hide me from my deep emotion, O thou wondrous Mother-Age![9]

Make me feel the wild pulsation that I felt before the strife,
110 When I heard my days before me, and the tumult of my life;

Yearning for the large excitement that the coming years would yield,
Eager-hearted as a boy when first he leaves his father's field,

---

7. Presumably figurative. Her marriage having become a mockery, she is widowed.
8. It was once believed that the firing of artillery stilled the winds.

9. A happier past at life's beginning, which generated a more confident anticipation of the future (see also line 185).

And at night along the dusky highway near and nearer drawn,
Sees in heaven the light of London flaring like a dreary dawn;

115 And his spirit leaps within him to be gone before him then,
Underneath the light he looks at, in among the throngs of men;

Men, my brothers, men the workers, ever reaping something new;
That which they have done but earnest° of the things that they   *pledge*
   shall do.

For I dipped into the future, far as human eye could see,
120 Saw the Vision of the world, and all the wonder that would be;

Saw the heavens fill with commerce, argosies of magic sails,[1]
Pilots of the purple twilight, dropping down with costly bales;

Heard the heavens fill with shouting, and there rained a ghastly dew
From the nations' airy navies grappling in the central blue;

125 Far along the world-wide whisper of the south wind rushing warm,
With the standards of the peoples plunging through the thunderstorm;

Till the war drum throbbed no longer, and the battle flags were furled
In the Parliament of man, the Federation of the world.

There the common sense of most shall hold a fretful realm in awe,
130 And the kindly earth shall slumber, lapped in universal law.

So I triumphed ere my passion sweeping through me left me dry,
Left me with the palsied heart, and left me with the jaundiced eye;

Eye, to which all order festers, all things here are out of joint.
Science moves, but slowly, slowly, creeping on from point to point;

135 Slowly comes a hungry people, as a lion, creeping nigher,
Glares at one that nods and winks behind a slowly-dying fire.

Yet I doubt not through the ages one increasing purpose runs,
And the thoughts of men are widened with the process of the suns.

What is that to him that reaps not harvest of his youthful joys,
140 Though the deep heart of existence beat forever like a boy's?

Knowledge comes, but wisdom lingers, and I linger on the shore,
And the individual withers, and the world is more and more.

Knowledge comes, but wisdom lingers, and he bears a laden breast,
Full of sad experience, moving toward the stillness of his rest.

1. Probably airships, such as balloons.

145   Hark, my merry comrades call me, sounding on the bugle horn,
      They to whom my foolish passion were a target for their scorn.

      Shall it not be scorn to me to harp on such a moldered string?
      I am shamed through all my nature to have loved so slight a thing.

      Weakness to be wroth with weakness! woman's pleasure, woman's pain—
150   Nature made them blinder motions bounded in a shallower brain.

      Woman is the lesser man, and all thy passions, matched with mine,
      Are as moonlight unto sunlight, and as water unto wine—

      Here at least, where nature sickens, nothing. Ah, for some retreat
      Deep in yonder shining Orient, where my life began to beat.

155   Where in wild Mahratta-battle[2] fell my father evil-starred—
      I was left a trampled orphan, and a selfish uncle's ward.

      Or to burst all links of habit—there to wander far away,
      On from island unto island at the gateways of the day.

      Larger constellations burning, mellow moons and happy skies,
160   Breadths of tropic shade and palms in cluster, knots of Paradise.

      Never comes the trader, never floats an European flag,
      Slides the bird o'er lustrous woodland, swings the trailer° from   *vine*
        the crag;

      Droops the heavy-blossomed bower, hangs the heavy-fruited tree—
      Summer isles of Eden lying in dark purple spheres of sea.

165   There methinks would be enjoyment more than in this march of mind,
      In the steamship, in the railway, in the thoughts that shake mankind.

      There the passions cramped no longer shall have scope and breathing space;
      I will take some savage woman, she shall rear my dusky race.

      Iron-jointed, supple-sinewed, they shall dive, and they shall run,
170   Catch the wild goat by the hair, and hurl their lances in the sun;

      Whistle back the parrot's call, and leap the rainbows of the brooks,
      Not with blinded eyesight poring over miserable books—

      Fool, again the dream, the fancy! but I *know* my words are wild,
      But I count the gray barbarian lower than the Christian child.

175   I, to herd with narrow foreheads, vacant of our glorious gains,
      Like a beast with lower pleasures, like a beast with lower pains!

2. Reference to wars waged by a Hindu people against the British forces in India (1803 and 1817).

Mated with a squalid savage—what to me were sun or clime?
I the heir of all the ages, in the foremost files of time—

I that rather held it better men should perish one by one,
180 Than that earth should stand at gaze like Joshua's moon in Ajalon![3]

Not in vain the distance beacons. Forward, forward let us range,
Let the great world spin forever down the ringing grooves[4] of change.

Through the shadow of the globe we sweep into the younger day;
Better fifty years of Europe than a cycle of Cathay.[5]

185 Mother-Age—for mine I knew not—help me as when life begun;
Rift the hills, and roll the waters, flash the lightnings, weigh the sun.

O, I see the crescent promise of my spirit hath not set.
Ancient founts of inspiration well through all my fancy yet.

Howsoever these things be, a long farewell to Locksley Hall!
190 Now for me the woods may wither, now for me the roof-tree fall.

Comes a vapor from the margin, blackening over heath and holt,
Cramming all the blast before it, in its breast a thunderbolt.

Let it fall on Locksley Hall, with rain or hail, or fire or snow;
For the mighty wind arises, roaring seaward, and I go.

1837–38   1842

FROM THE PRINCESS[1]

The Splendor Falls

The splendor falls on castle walls
    And snowy summits old in story;
The long light shakes across the lakes,
    And the wild cataract leaps in glory.
5 Blow, bugle, blow, set the wild echoes flying,
Blow, bugle; answer, echoes, dying, dying, dying.

O, hark, O, hear! how thin and clear,
    And thinner, clearer, farther going!
O, sweet and far from cliff and scar°   mountainside

---

3. At the command of Joshua, the sun and moon stood still while the Israelites completed the slaughter of their enemies in the valley of Ajalon (Joshua 10.12–13).
4. Railroad tracks. Tennyson at one time had the impression that train wheels ran in grooved rails.
5. China, regarded in the 19th century as a static, unprogressive country.

1. *The Princess* (1847), a long narrative poem, contains interludes in which occasional songs are sung. The six songs printed here, some of which first appeared in later editions of the poem, rank among the finest of Tennyson's lyrics, and various 19th- and 20th-century composers have set them to music.

10   The horns of Elfland faintly blowing!
Blow, let us hear the purple glens replying,
Blow, bugle; answer, echoes, dying, dying, dying.

O love, they die in yon rich sky,
    They faint on hill or field or river;
15   Our echoes roll from soul to soul,
    And grow forever and forever.
Blow, bugle, blow, set the wild echoes flying,
And answer, echoes, answer, dying, dying, dying.

1850

Tears, Idle Tears[1]

Tears, idle tears, I know not what they mean,
Tears from the depth of some divine despair
Rise in the heart, and gather to the eyes,
In looking on the happy autumn-fields,
5   And thinking of the days that are no more.

Fresh as the first beam glittering on a sail,
That brings our friends up from the underworld,
Sad as the last which reddens over one
That sinks with all we love below the verge;
10   So sad, so fresh, the days that are no more.

Ah, sad and strange as in dark summer dawns
The earliest pipe of half-awakened birds
To dying ears, when unto dying eyes
The casement slowly grows a glimmering square;
15   So sad, so strange, the days that are no more.

Dear as remembered kisses after death,
And sweet as those by hopeless fancy feigned
On lips that are for others; deep as love,
Deep as first love, and wild with all regret;
20   O Death in Life, the days that are no more!

1847

Now Sleeps the Crimson Petal

Now sleeps the crimson petal, now the white;
Nor waves the cypress in the palace walk;
Nor winks the gold fin in the porphyry font.
The firefly wakens; waken thou with me.

1. Tennyson commented: "This song came to me on the yellowing autumn-tide at Tintern Abbey, full for me of its bygone memories." This locale would be for him associated both with Wordsworth's *Tintern Abbey* and with memories of Hallam, who was buried across the Bristol Channel in this area. "It is what I have always felt even from a boy, and what as a boy I called the 'passion of the past.' And it is so always with me now; it is the distance that charms me in the landscape, the picture and the past, and not the immediate today in which I move."

5   Now droops the milk-white peacock like a ghost,
And like a ghost she glimmers on to me.

Now lies the Earth all Danaë[1] to the stars,
And all thy heart lies open unto me.

Now slides the silent meteor on, and leaves
10 A shining furrow, as thy thoughts in me.

Now folds the lily all her sweetness up,
And slips into the bosom of the lake.
So fold thyself, my dearest, thou, and slip
Into my bosom and be lost in me.

1847

["The Woman's Cause Is Man's"][1]

"Blame not thyself too much," I said, "nor blame
240 Too much the sons of men and barbarous laws;
These were the rough ways of the world till now.
Henceforth thou hast a helper, me, that know
The woman's cause is man's: they rise or sink
Together, dwarfed or godlike, bond or free:
245 For she that out of Lethe scales with man
The shining steps of Nature, shares with man
His nights, his days, moves with him to one goal,
Stays all the fair young planet in her hands—
If she be small, slight-natured, miserable,
250 How shall men grow? but work no more alone!
Our place is much: as far as in us lies
We two will serve them both in aiding her—
Will clear away the parasitic forms
That seem to keep her up but drag her down—
255 Will leave her space to burgeon out of all
Within her—let her make herself her own
To give or keep, to live and learn and be
All that not harms distinctive womanhood.
For woman is not undevelopt man,
260 But diverse: could we make her as the man,
Sweet Love were slain: his dearest bond is this,

1. A Greek princess, who was confined in a metal tower by her father to prevent suitors from coming near her. Zeus, however, succeeded in visiting her in the form of a shower of gold. Their offspring was the hero Perseus.

1. *The Princess* was Tennyson's attempt to address the contemporary debate over woman's proper role. It tells the story of a prince who courts the young and beautiful Princess Ida. She has vowed she will never marry and has established a women's university from which men are excluded. The prince and his two companions dress themselves up in women's clothes to gain entrance to the uni-

versity. When a battle ensues—in which King Gama, the prince's father, invades the university to rescue his son and force Ida to marry him—the university is turned into a hospital and the princess is persuaded of the error of her ways. The prince's final vision, from book 7 (reprinted here), in which he imagines a future of gradual change, by which men and women adopt the strengths of the other while maintaining their distinct natures, has been a key text in discussing Victorian patriarchy. In the operetta *Princess Ida*, Gilbert and Sullivan use Tennyson's story to satirize feminism.

Not like to like, but like in difference.
Yet in the long years liker must they grow;
The man be more of woman, she of man;
265 He gain in sweetness and in moral height,
Nor lose the wrestling thews that throw the world;
She mental breadth, nor fail in childward care,
Nor lose the childlike in the larger mind;
Till at the last she set herself to man,
270 Like perfect music unto noble words;
And so these twain, upon the skirts of Time,
Sit side by side, full-summed in all their powers,
Dispensing harvest, sowing the To-be,
Self-reverent each and reverencing each,
275 Distinct in individualities,
But like each other even as those who love.
Then comes the statelier Eden back to men:
Then reign the world's great bridals, chaste and calm:
Then springs the crowning race of humankind.
May these things be!"
280   Sighing she spoke "I fear
They will not."
                        Dear, but let us type them now
In our own lives, and this proud watchword rest
Of equal; seeing either sex alone
Is half itself, and in true marriage lies
285 Nor equal, nor unequal: each fulfils
Defect in each, and always thought in thought,
Purpose in purpose, will in will, they grow,
The single pure and perfect animal,
The two-celled heart beating, with one full stroke,
Life."
290   And again sighing she spoke: "A dream
That once was mine! what woman taught you this?"

1839–47   1847

In Memoriam A. H. H.

When Arthur Hallam died suddenly at the age of twenty-two, Tennyson felt that his life had been shattered. Hallam was not only Tennyson's closest friend, and his sister's fiancé, but a critic and champion of his poetry. Widely regarded as the most promising young man of his generation, Hallam had written a review of Tennyson's first book of poetry that is still one of the best assessments of it. When Tennyson lost Hallam's love and support, he was overwhelmed with doubts about his own life and vocation and about the meaning of the universe and humankind's place in it, doubts reinforced by his study of geology and other sciences. To express the variety of his feelings and reflections, he began to compose a series of lyrics. Tennyson later arranged these "short swallow-flights of song," as he called them, written at intervals over a period of seventeen years, into one long elegy. Although the resulting poem has many affinities with traditional elegies like Milton's *Lycidas* and Shelley's *Adonais,* its structure is strikingly different. It is made up of individual lyric units that are seemingly self-contained but take their full meaning from their place in the whole. As T. S. Eliot has written, "It is unique: it is a long poem made by putting together lyrics, which have only the unity and continuity of a diary, the concentrated diary of a man confessing himself." Though intensely personal, it expressed the religious doubts of his age. Eliot continues, "It is not religious because of the quality of its faith but because of the quality of its doubt. . . . *In Memoriam* is a poem of despair." It is also a love poem. Like Shakespeare's sonnets, to which the poem alludes, *In Memoriam* vests its most intense emotion in male friendship.

The sections of the poem record a progressive development from despair to some sort of hope. Some of the early sections of the poem resemble traditional pastoral elegies, including those portraying the voyage during which Hallam's body was brought to England for burial (sections 9 to 15 and 19). Other early sections portraying the speaker's loneliness, in which even Christmas festivities seem joyless (sections 28 to 30), are more distinctive. With the passage of time, indicated by anniversaries and by recurring changes of the seasons, the speaker comes to accept the loss and to assert his belief in life and in an afterlife. In particular the recurring Christmases (sections 28, 78, 104) indicate the stages of his development, yet the pattern of progress in the poem is not a simple unimpeded movement upward. Dramatic conflicts recur throughout. Thus the most intense expression of doubt occurs not at the beginning of *In Memoriam* but as late as sections 54, 55, and 56.

The quatrain form in which the whole poem is written is usually called the "*In Memoriam* stanza," although it had been occasionally used by earlier poets. So rigid a form taxed Tennyson's ingenuity in achieving variety, but it is one of several means by which the diverse parts of the poem are knitted together.

The introductory section, consisting of eleven stanzas, is commonly referred to as the "Prologue," although Tennyson did not assign a title to it. It was written in 1849 after the rest of the poem was complete.

FROM IN MEMORIAM A. H. H.

OBIIT MDCCCXXXIII[1]

Strong Son of God, immortal Love,
   Whom we, that have not seen thy face,
   By faith, and faith alone, embrace,
Believing where we cannot prove;[2]

5   Thine are these orbs[3] of light and shade;
   Thou madest Life in man and brute;
   Thou madest Death; and lo, thy foot
Is on the skull which thou hast made.

Thou wilt not leave us in the dust:
10   Thou madest man, he knows not why,
   He thinks he was not made to die;
And thou hast made him: thou art just.

Thou seemest human and divine,
   The highest, holiest manhood, thou.

1. Died 1833.
2. Cf. John 20.24–29, in which Jesus rebukes Thomas for his doubts concerning the Resurrection: "Blessed are they that have not seen, and yet have believed."
3. The sun and moon (according to Tennyson's note).

15 Our wills are ours, we know not how;
　　Our wills are ours, to make them thine.

　　Our little systems⁴ have their day;
　　　They have their day and cease to be;
　　　They are but broken lights of thee,
20 And thou, O Lord, art more than they.

　　We have but faith: we cannot know,
　　　For knowledge is of things we see;
　　　And yet we trust it comes from thee,
　　A beam in darkness: let it grow.

25 Let knowledge grow from more to more,
　　　But more of reverence in us dwell;
　　　That mind and soul, according well,
　　May make one music as before,⁵

　　But vaster. We are fools and slight;
30 　We mock thee when we do not fear:
　　　But help thy foolish ones to bear;
　　Help thy vain worlds to bear thy light.

　　Forgive what seemed my sin in me,
　　　What seemed my worth since I began;
35 　For merit lives from man to man,
　　And not from man, O Lord, to thee.

　　Forgive my grief for one removed,
　　　Thy creature, whom I found so fair.
　　　I trust he lives in thee, and there
40 I find him worthier to be loved.

　　Forgive these wild and wandering cries,
　　　Confusions of a wasted° youth;　　　　　　　　desolated
　　　Forgive them where they fail in truth,
　　And in thy wisdom make me wise.

1849

1

　　I held it truth, with him who sings
　　　To one clear harp in divers tones,⁶
　　　That men may rise on stepping stones
　　Of their dead selves to higher things.

5 　But who shall so forecast the years
　　　And find in loss a gain to match?

---

4. Of religion and philosophy.
5. As in the days of fixed religious faith.

6. Identified by Tennyson as Goethe.

Or reach a hand through time to catch
The far-off interest of tears?

Let Love clasp Grief lest both be drowned,
10 Let darkness keep her raven gloss.
 Ah, sweeter to be drunk with loss,
To dance with Death, to beat the ground,

Than that the victor Hours should scorn
 The long result of love, and boast,
15 "Behold the man that loved and lost,
But all he was is overworn."

2

Old yew, which graspest at the stones
 That name the underlying dead,
 Thy fibers net the dreamless head,
Thy roots are wrapped about the bones.

5 The seasons bring the flower again,
 And bring the firstling to the flock;
 And in the dusk of thee the clock
Beats out the little lives of men.

O, not for thee the glow, the bloom,
10 Who changest not in any gale,
 Nor branding summer suns avail
To touch thy thousand years of gloom[7]

And gazing on thee, sullen tree,
 Sick for° thy stubborn hardihood,   *envying*
15 I seem to fail from out my blood
And grow incorporate into thee.

3

O Sorrow, cruel fellowship,
 O Priestess in the vaults of Death,
 O sweet and bitter in a breath,
What whispers from thy lying lip?

5 "The stars," she whispers, "blindly run;
 A web is woven across the sky;
 From out waste places comes a cry,
And murmurs from the dying sun;

---

7. The ancient yew tree, growing in the grounds near the clock tower and church where Hallam was to be buried, seems neither to blossom in spring nor to change from its dark mournful color in summer. "Thousand years": cf. Book of Common Prayer Psalm 90: "For a thousand years in Thy sight are but as yesterday when it is past, and as a watch in the night."

> "And all the phantom, Nature, stands—
> 10   With all the music in her tone,
>   A hollow echo of my own—
> A hollow form with empty hands."

> And shall I take a thing so blind,
>   Embrace her° as my natural good;   *Sorrow*
> 15   Or crush her, like a vice of blood,
> Upon the threshold of the mind?

4

> To Sleep I give my powers away;
>   My will is bondsman to the dark;
>   I sit within a helmless bark,
> And with my heart I muse and say:

> 5   O heart, how fares it with thee now,
>   That thou should fail from thy desire,
>   Who scarcely darest to inquire,
> "What is it makes me beat so low?"

> Something it is which thou hast lost,
> 10   Some pleasure from thine early years.
>   Break thou deep vase of chilling tears,
> That grief hath shaken into frost![8]

> Such clouds of nameless trouble cross
>   All night below the darkened eyes;
> 15   With morning wakes the will, and cries,
> "Thou shalt not be the fool of loss."

5

> I sometimes hold it half a sin
>   To put in words the grief I feel;
>   For words, like Nature, half reveal
> And half conceal the Soul within.

> 5   But, for the unquiet heart and brain,
>   A use in measured language lies;
>   The sad mechanic exercise,
> Like dull narcotics, numbing pain.

> In words, like weeds,° I'll wrap me o'er,   *garments*
> 10   Like coarsest clothes against the cold;
>   But that large grief which these enfold
> Is given in outline and no more.

8. Water can be brought below freezing-point and not turn into ice—if it be kept still; but if it be moved suddenly it turns into ice and may break a vase [Tennyson's note].

6

One writes, that "Other friends remain,"
    That "Loss is common to the race"—
    And common is the commonplace,
And vacant chaff well meant for grain.

5 That loss is common would not make
    My own less bitter, rather more:
    Too common! Never morning wore
To evening, but some heart did break.

O father, wheresoe'er thou be,
10   Who pledgest° now thy gallant son;   *toasts*
    A shot, ere half thy draft be done,
Hath stilled the life that beat from thee.

O mother, praying God will save
    Thy sailor—while thy head is bowed,
15   His heavy-shotted hammock-shroud
Drops in his vast and wandering grave.

Ye know no more than I who wrought
    At that last hour to please him well;[9]
    Who mused on all I had to tell,
20 And something written, something thought;

Expecting still his advent home;
    And ever met him on his way
    With wishes, thinking, "here today,"
Or "here tomorrow will he come."

25 O somewhere, meek, the unconscious dove,
    That sittest ranging° golden hair;   *arranging*
    And glad to find thyself so fair,
Poor child, that waitest for thy love!

For now her father's chimney glows
30   In expectation of a guest;
    And thinking "this will please him best,"
She takes a riband or a rose;

For he will see them on tonight;
    And with the thought her color burns;
35   And, having left the glass, she turns
Once more to set a ringlet right;

And, even when she turned, the curse
    Had fallen, and her future Lord

9. According to Tennyson's son, his father had discovered that he had been writing a letter to Hallam during the very hour when his friend died.

Was drowned in passing through the ford,
40   Or killed in falling from his horse.

O what to her shall be the end?
    And what to me remains of good?
    To her, perpetual maidenhood,
And unto me no second friend.

7

Dark house,[1] by which once more I stand
    Here in the long unlovely street,
    Doors, where my heart was used to beat
So quickly, waiting for a hand,

5   A hand that can be clasped no more—
    Behold me, for I cannot sleep,
    And like a guilty thing I creep
At earliest morning to the door.

He is not here; but far away
10   The noise of life begins again,
    And ghastly through the drizzling rain
On the bald street breaks the blank day.

8

A happy lover who has come
    To look on her that loves him well,
    Who 'lights and rings the gateway bell,
And learns her gone and far from home;

5   He saddens, all the magic light
    Dies off at once from bower and hall,
    And all the place is dark, and all
The chambers emptied of delight:

So find I every pleasant spot
10   In which we two were wont to meet,
    The field, the chamber, and the street,
For all is dark where thou art not.

Yet as that other, wandering there
    In those deserted walks, may find
15   A flower beat with rain and wind,
Which once she fostered up with care;

1. The house on Wimpole Street, in London, where Hallam had lived.

So seems it in my deep regret,
 O my forsaken heart, with thee
 And this poor flower of poesy
20 Which little cared for fades not yet.

But since it pleased a vanished eye,[2]
 I go to plant it on his tomb,
 That if it can it there may bloom,
Or dying, there at least may die.

9

Fair ship, that from the Italian shore
 Sailest the placid ocean-plains
 With my lost Arthur's loved remains,
Spread thy full wings, and waft him o'er.

5 So draw him home to those that mourn
 In vain; a favorable speed
 Ruffle thy mirrored mast, and lead
Through prosperous floods his holy urn.

All night no ruder air perplex
10 Thy sliding keel, till Phosphor,° bright   *morning star*
 As our pure love, through early light
Shall glimmer on the dewey decks.

Sphere all your lights around, above;
 Sleep, gentle heavens, before the prow;
15 Sleep, gentle winds, as he sleeps now,
My friend, the brother of my love;

My Arthur, whom I shall not see
 Till all my widowed race be run;
 Dear as the mother to the son,
20 More than my brothers are to me.

10

I hear the noise about thy keel;
 I hear the bell struck in the night;
 I see the cabin window bright;
I see the sailor at the wheel.

5 Thou bring'st the sailor to his wife,
 And traveled men from foreign lands;
 And letters unto trembling hands;
And, thy dark freight, a vanished life.

2. Hallam expressed enthusiasm for Tennyson's early poetry in a review written in 1831.

So bring him; we have idle dreams;
10   This look of quiet flatters thus
     Our home-bred fancies. O, to us,
The fools of habit, sweeter seems

To rest beneath the clover sod,
     That takes the sunshine and the rains,
15   Or where the kneeling hamlet drains
The chalice of the grapes of God;[3]

Than if with thee the roaring wells
     Should gulf him fathom-deep in brine,
     And hands so often clasped in mine,
20   Should toss with tangle° and with shells.   *seaweed*

11

Calm is the morn without a sound,
     Calm as to suit a calmer grief,
     And only through the faded leaf
The chestnut pattering to the ground;

5   Calm and deep peace on this high wold,°   *open countryside*
     And on these dews that drench the furze,
     And all the silvery gossamers
That twinkle into green and gold;

Calm and still light on yon great plain
10   That sweeps with all its autumn bowers,
     And crowded farms and lessening towers,
To mingle with the bounding main;

Calm and deep peace in this wide air,
     These leaves that redden to the fall,
15   And in my heart, if calm at all,
If any calm, a calm despair;

Calm on the seas, and silver sleep,
     And waves that sway themselves in rest,
     And dead calm in that noble breast
20   Which heaves but with the heaving deep.[4]

12

Lo, as a dove when up she springs
     To bear through Heaven a tale of woe,

3. Reference to a burial inside a church building rather than in the churchyard.
4. It is now the autumn of 1833, and the poet imagines that Hallam's body was already being brought back by ship to England. The date of the actual voyage seems to have been later in the year.

Some dolorous message knit below
  The wild pulsation of her wings;

5 Like her I go; I cannot stay;
    I leave this mortal ark behind,
    A weight of nerves without a mind,
  And leave the cliffs, and haste away

  O'er ocean-mirrors rounded large,
10   And reach the glow of southern skies,
    And see the sails at distance rise,
  And linger weeping on the marge,

  And saying; "Comes he thus, my friend?
    Is this the end of all my care?"
15   And circle moaning in the air:
  "Is this the end? Is this the end?"

  And forward dart again, and play
    About the prow, and back return
    To where the body sits, and learn
20 That I have been an hour away.

13

Tears of the widower, when he sees
  A late-lost form that sleep reveals,
  And moves his doubtful arms, and feels
Her place is empty, fall like these;

5 Which weep a loss forever new,
    A void where heart on heart reposed;
    And, where warm hands have pressed and closed,
Silence, till I be silent too;

Which weep the comrade of my choice,
10   An awful thought, a life removed,
    The human-hearted man I loved,
A Spirit, not a breathing voice.

Come, Time, and teach me, many years,
  I do not suffer in a dream;
15   For now so strange do these things seem,
Mine eyes have leisure for their tears,

My fancies time to rise on wing,
    And glance about the approaching sails,
    As though they brought but merchants' bales,
20 And not the burthen that they bring.[5]

5. The poet asks Time to teach him to confront the "awful" fact of what has happened (line 10) so that he will not delude himself by fancying the ship is bearing only merchandise and not the body of his friend.

14

If one should bring me this report,
    That thou° hadst touched the land today,   *the ship*
    And I went down unto the quay;[6]
And found thee lying in the port;

5   And standing, muffled round with woe,
    Should see thy passengers in rank
    Come stepping lightly down the plank
And beckoning unto those they know;

And if along with these should come
10   The man I held as half divine,
    Should strike a sudden hand in mine,
And ask a thousand things of home;

And I should tell him all my pain,
    And how my life had drooped of late,
15   And he should sorrow o'er my state
And marvel what possessed my brain;

And I perceived no touch of change,
    No hint of death in all his frame,
    But found him all in all the same,
20   I should not feel it to be strange.

15

Tonight the winds begin to rise
    And roar from yonder dropping day;
    The last red leaf is whirled away,
The rooks are blown about the skies;

5   The forest cracked, the waters curled,
    The cattle huddled on the lea;
    And wildly dashed on tower and tree
The sunbeam strikes along the world:

And but for fancies, which aver
10   That all thy motions gently pass
    Athwart a plane of molten glass,
I scarce could brook the strain and stir

That makes the barren branches loud;
    And but for fear it is not so,
15   The wild unrest that lives in woe
Would dote and pore on yonder cloud

---

6. By 1850 the accepted pronunciation of "quay" would rhyme with *key*, but Tennyson reverts to an earlier pronunciation, *kay*.

That rises upward always higher,
   And onward drags a laboring breast,
   And topples round the dreary west,
20 A looming bastion fringed with fire.

*   *   *

19

The Danube to the Severn[7] gave
   The darkened heart that beat no more;
   They laid him by the pleasant shore,
And in the hearing of the wave.

5 There twice a day the Severn fills;
   The salt sea water passes by,
   And hushes half the babbling Wye,[8]
And makes a silence in the hills.

The Wye is hushed nor moved along,
10   And hushed my deepest grief of all,
   When filled with tears that cannot fall,
I brim with sorrow drowning song.

The tide flows down, the wave again
   Is vocal in its wooded walls;
15   My deeper anguish also falls,
And I can speak a little then.

*   *   *

21

I sing to him that rests below,
   And, since the grasses round me wave,
   I take the grasses of the grave,[9]
And make them pipes whereon to blow.

5 The traveler hears me now and then,
   And sometimes harshly will he speak:
   "This fellow would make weakness weak,
And melt the waxen hearts of men."

---

7. Hallam died at Vienna on the Danube. His burial place is on the banks of the Severn, a tidal river in the southwest of England.

8. The water of the Wye River, a tributary of the Severn, is dammed up as the tide flows in, and its sound is silenced until, with the turn of the tide, its "wave" once more becomes "vocal" (lines 13–14); these stanzas were written at Tintern Abbey in the Wye River country.

9. The poet assumes that the burial was in the churchyard; in fact, Hallam's body was interred in a vault inside St. Andrews church at Clevedon, Somersetshire, on January 3, 1834 (see section 10, lines 11–16).

Another answers: "Let him be,
10   He loves to make parade of pain,
      That with his piping he may gain
The praise that comes to constancy."

A third is wroth: "Is this an hour
      For private sorrow's barren song,
15   When more and more the people throng
The chairs and thrones of civil power?

"A time to sicken and to swoon,
      When Science reaches forth her arms[1]
      To feel from world to world, and charms
20 Her secret from the latest moon?"[2]

Behold, ye speak an idle thing;
      Ye never knew the sacred dust.
      I do but sing because I must,
And pipe but as the linnets sing:

25 And one is glad; her note is gay,
      For now her little ones have ranged;
      And one is sad; her note is changed,
Because her brood is stolen away.

22

The path by which we twain did go,
      Which led by tracts that pleased us well,
      Through four sweet years arose and fell,
From flower to flower, from snow to snow;

5 And we with singing cheered the way,
      And, crowned with all the season lent,
      From April on to April went,
And glad at heart from May to May.

But where the path we walked began
10   To slant the fifth autumnal slope,[3]
      As we descended following Hope,
There sat the Shadow feared of man;

Who broke our fair companionship,
      And spread his mantle dark and cold,
15   And wrapped thee formless in the fold,
And dulled the murmur on thy lip,

1. Astronomical instruments such as telescopes.
2. Probably alluding to the discovery in 1846 of the planet Neptune and one of its moons.

3. Hallam died just before the beginning of autumn (September 15, 1833) in the fifth year of the friendship.

And bore thee where I could not see
  Nor follow, though I walk in haste,
  And think that somewhere in the waste
20 The Shadow sits and waits for me.

23

Now, sometimes in my sorrow shut,
  Or breaking into song by fits,
  Alone, alone, to where he sits,
The Shadow cloaked from head to foot,

5 Who keeps the keys of all the creeds,
  I wander, often falling lame,
  And looking back to whence I came,
Or on to where the pathway leads;

And crying, How changed from where it ran
10 Through lands where not a leaf was dumb,
  But all the lavish hills would hum
The murmur of a happy Pan;

When each by turns was guide to each,
  And Fancy light from Fancy caught,
15 And Thought leapt out to wed with Thought
Ere Thought could wed itself with Speech;

And all we met was fair and good,
  And all was good that Time could bring,
  And all the secret of the Spring
20 Moved in the chambers of the blood;

And many an old philosophy
  On Argive heights[4] divinely sang,
  And round us all the thicket rang
To many a flute of Arcady.[5]

24

And was the day of my delight
  As pure and perfect as I say?
  The very source and fount of day
Is dashed with wandering isles of night.[6]

5 If all was good and fair we met,
  This earth had been the Paradise

4. Argos, a Greek city renowned for its music.
5. A sheep-raising region in Greece associated
with pastoral poetry.
6. Moving spots on the sun.

It never looked to human eyes
Since our first sun arose and set.

And is it that the haze of grief
10   Makes former gladness loom so great?
        The lowness of the present state,
That sets the past in this relief?

Or that the past will always win
        A glory from its being far,
15   And orb into the perfect star
We saw not when we moved therein?[7]

25

I know that this was Life—the track
        Whereon with equal feet we fared;
        And then, as now, the day prepared
The daily burden for the back.

5   But this it was that made me move
        As light as carrier birds in air;
        I loved the weight I had to bear,
Because it needed help of Love;

Nor could I weary, heart or limb,
10   When mighty Love would cleave in twain
        The lading° of a single pain,   burden
And part it, giving half to him.

26

Still onward winds the dreary way;
        I with it, for I long to prove
        No lapse of moons can canker Love,
Whatever fickle tongues may say.

5   And if that eye which watches guilt
        And goodness, and hath power to see
        Within the green the mouldered tree,
And towers fallen as soon as built—

O, if indeed that eye foresee
10   Or see—in Him is no before—
        In more of life true life no more
And Love the indifference to be,

7. The poet speculates whether past experiences seem so much more "pure and perfect" (line 2) than present ones because they are far distant from us in time, just as our planet earth would have the deceptive appearance of being a perfect orb if we viewed it from a great distance in space, as from another planet (cf. *Locksley Hall Sixty Years After*, lines 187–92).

Then might I find, ere yet the morn
Breaks hither over Indian seas,
15   That Shadow waiting with the keys,
To shroud me from my proper scorn.[8]

27

I envy not in any moods
The captive void of noble rage,
The linnet born within the cage,
That never knew the summer woods;

5   I envy not the beast that takes
His license in the field of time,
Unfettered by the sense of crime,
To whom a conscience never wakes;

Nor, what may count itself as blest,
10   The heart that never plighted troth
But stagnates in the weeds of sloth;
Nor any want-begotten rest.[9]

I hold it true, whate'er befall;
I feel it, when I sorrow most;
15   'Tis better to have loved and lost
Than never to have loved at all.

28

The time draws near the birth of Christ.[1]
The moon is hid, the night is still;
The Christmas bells from hill to hill
Answer each other in the mist.

5   Four voices of four hamlets round,
From far and near, on mead and moor,
Swell out and fail, as if a door
Were shut between me and the sound;

Each voice four changes[2] on the wind,
10   That now dilate, and now decrease,
Peace and goodwill, goodwill and peace,
Peace and goodwill, to all mankind.

8. The Deity, being outside time, sees (rather than foresees) whether or not the rest of life ("more of life," line 11) will be pointless. If pointless, then the way for the speaker to deal with his self-scorn ("proper scorn") might be to seek death.
9. Complacency resulting from some deficiency ("want").
1. The first Christmas after Hallam's death (1833); the setting is Tennyson's family home in Lincolnshire.
2. Different sequences in which church bells are pealed.

This year I slept and woke with pain,
   I almost wished no more to wake,
15   And that my hold on life would break
Before I heard those bells again;

But they my troubled spirit rule,
   For they controlled me when a boy;
   They bring me sorrow touched with joy,
20 The merry, merry bells of Yule.

29

With such compelling cause to grieve
   As daily vexes household peace,
   And chains regret to his decease,
How dare we keep our Christmas eve;

5 Which brings no more a welcome guest
   To enrich the threshold of the night
   With showered largess of delight
In dance and song and game and jest?

Yet go, and while the holly boughs
10   Entwine the cold baptismal font,
   Make one wreath more for Use and Wont,[3]
That guard the portals of the house;

Old sisters of a day gone by,
   Gray nurses, loving nothing new;
15   Why should they miss their yearly due
Before their time? They too will die.

30

With trembling fingers did we weave
   The holly round the Christmas hearth;
   A rainy cloud possessed the earth,
And sadly fell our Christmas eve.

5 At our old pastimes in the hall
   We gamboled, making vain pretense
   Of gladness, with an awful sense
Of one mute Shadow watching all.

We paused: the winds were in the beech;
10   We heard them sweep the winter land;
   And in a circle hand-in-hand
Sat silent, looking each at each.

3. Personifying the spirits who expect customary observances of the Christmas season to be followed.

Then echo-like our voices rang;
    We sung, though every eye was dim,
15   A merry song we sang with him
Last year; impetuously we sang.

We ceased; a gentler feeling crept
    Upon us: surely rest is meet.[4]
    "They rest," we said, "their sleep is sweet,"
20   And silence followed, and we wept.

Our voices took a higher range;
    Once more we sang: "They do not die
    Nor lose their mortal sympathy,
Nor change to us, although they change;

25 "Rapt[5] from the fickle and the frail
    With gathered power, yet the same,
    Pierces the keen seraphic flame
From orb to orb,[6] from veil to veil."

Rise, happy morn, rise, holy morn,
30   Draw forth the cheerful day from night:
    O Father, touch the east, and light
The light that shone when Hope was born.

*   *   *

34

My own dim life should teach me this,
    That life shall live forevermore,
    Else earth is darkness at the core,
And dust and ashes all that is;

5 This round of green, this orb of flame,
    Fantastic beauty; such as lurks
    In some wild poet, when he works
Without a conscience or an aim.

What then were God to such as I?
10   'Twere hardly worth my while to choose
    Of things all mortal, or to use
A little patience ere I die;

'Twere best at once to sink to peace,
    Like birds the charming serpent[7] draws,
15   To drop head-foremost in the jaws
Of vacant darkness and to cease.

4. Proper or appropriate.
5. Carried away from.
6. The angelic spirit ("flame") of the dead moves from star to star.
7. Some snakes are reputed to capture their prey by casting a charm.

35

Yet if some voice that man could trust
   Should murmur from the narrow house,
   "The cheeks drop in, the body bows;
Man dies, nor is there hope in dust";

5   Might I not say? "Yet even here,
   But for one hour, O Love, I strive
   To keep so sweet a thing alive."
But I should turn mine ears and hear

The moanings of the homeless sea,
10   The sound of streams that swift or slow
   Draw down Aeonian[8] hills, and sow
The dust of continents to be;

And Love would answer with a sigh,
   "The sound of that forgetful shore
15   Will change my sweetness more and more,
Half-dead to know that I shall die."

O me, what profits it to put
   An idle case? If Death were seen
   At first as Death, Love had not been,
20   Or been in narrowest working shut,

Mere fellowship of sluggish moods,
   Or in his coarsest Satyr-shape
   Had bruised the herb and crushed the grape,
And basked and battened in the woods.[9]

*   *   *

39

Old warder of these buried bones,
   And answering now my random stroke
   With fruitful cloud and living smoke,
Dark yew, that graspest at the stones

5   And dippest toward the dreamless head,
   To thee too comes the golden hour
   When flower is feeling after flower;[1]
But Sorrow—fixed upon the dead,

8. Eons old, seemingly everlasting.
9. Lines 18ff. may be paraphrased: if we knew death to be final and that no afterlife were possible, love could not exist except on a primitive or bestial level.

1. The ancient yew tree in the graveyard was described in section 2 as never changing. Now the poet discovers that in the flowering season, if the tree is struck ("my random stroke"), it gives off a cloud of golden pollen.

And darkening the dark graves of men—
10   What whispered from her lying lips?
Thy gloom is kindled at the tips,[2]
And passes into gloom again.

* * *

47

That each, who seems a separate whole,
    Should move his rounds,[3] and fusing all
    The skirts[4] of self again, should fall
Remerging in the general Soul,

5   Is faith as vague as all unsweet.
    Eternal form shall still divide
    The eternal soul from all beside;
And I shall know him when we meet;

And we shall sit at endless feast,
10   Enjoying each the other's good.
    What vaster dream can hit the mood
Of Love on earth? He seeks at least

Upon the last and sharpest height,
    Before the spirits fade away,
15   Some landing place, to clasp and say,
"Farewell! We lose ourselves in light."

48

If these brief lays, of Sorrow born,
    Were taken to be such as closed
    Grave doubts and answers here proposed,
Then these were such as men might scorn.

5   Her care is not to part and prove;
    She takes, when harsher moods remit,
    What slender shade of doubt may flit,
And makes it vassal unto love;

And hence, indeed, she sports with words,
10   But better serves a wholesome law,
    And holds it sin and shame to draw
The deepest measure from the chords;

Nor dare she trust a larger lay,
    But rather loosens from the lip

---

2. Only the tips of the yew branches are in flower.   4. Outer edges or fringes.
3. I.e., go through the customary circuit of life.

15   Short swallow-flights of song, that dip
          Their wings in tears, and skim away.

50

Be near me when my light is low,
     When the blood creeps, and the nerves prick
     And tingle; and the heart is sick,
And all the wheels of being slow.

5   Be near me when the sensuous frame
     Is racked with pangs that conquer trust;
     And Time, a maniac scattering dust,
And Life, a Fury slinging flame.

Be near me when my faith is dry,
10   And men the flies of latter spring,
     That lay their eggs, and sting and sing
And weave their petty cells and die.

Be near me when I fade away,
     To point the term of human strife,
15   And on the low dark verge of life
The twilight of eternal day.

* * *

54

O, yet we trust that somehow good
     Will be the final goal of ill,
     To pangs of nature, sins of will,
Defects of doubt, and taints of blood;

5   That nothing walks with aimless feet;
     That not one life shall be destroyed,
     Or cast as rubbish to the void,
When God hath made the pile complete;

That not a worm is cloven in vain;
10   That not a moth with vain desire
     Is shriveled in a fruitless fire,
Or but subserves another's gain.

Behold, we know not anything;
     I can but trust that good shall fall
15   At last—far off—at last, to all,
And every winter change to spring.

So runs my dream; but what am I?
  An infant crying in the night;
  An infant crying for the light,
20 And with no language but a cry.

55

The wish, that of the living whole
  No life may fail beyond the grave,
  Derives it not from what we have
The likest God within the soul?

5 Are God and Nature then at strife,
  That Nature lends such evil dreams?
  So careful of the type she seems,
So careless of the single life,

That I, considering everywhere
10 Her secret meaning in her deeds,
  And finding that of fifty seeds
She often brings but one to bear,

I falter where I firmly trod,
  And falling with my weight of cares
15 Upon the great world's altar-stairs
That slope through darkness up to God,

I stretch lame hands of faith, and grope,
  And gather dust and chaff, and call
  To what I feel is Lord of all,
20 And faintly trust the larger hope.[5]

56

"So careful of the type?" but no.
  From scarpèd[6] cliff and quarried stone
  She° cries, "A thousand types are gone;   *i.e., Nature*
I care for nothing, all shall go.

5 "Thou makest thine appeal to me:
  I bring to life, I bring to death;
  The spirit does but mean the breath:
I know no more." And he, shall he,

Man, her last work, who seemed so fair,
10 Such splendid purpose in his eyes,
  Who rolled the psalm to wintry skies,
Who built him fanes° of fruitless prayer,   *temples*

5. As expressed in lines 1 and 2.   6. Cut away so that the strata are exposed.

Who trusted God was love indeed
   And love Creation's final law—
15   Though Nature, red in tooth and claw
With ravine, shrieked against his creed—

Who loved, who suffered countless ills,
   Who battled for the True, the Just,
   Be blown about the desert dust,
20   Or sealed within the iron hills?[7]

No more? A monster then, a dream,
   A discord. Dragons of the prime,
   That tare° each other in their slime,   *tore (archaic)*
Were mellow music matched with° him.   *compared to*

25   O life as futile, then, as frail!
   O for thy voice to soothe and bless!
   What hope of answer, or redress?
Behind the veil, behind the veil.

57

Peace; come away: the song of woe
   Is after all an earthly song.
   Peace; come away: we do him wrong
To sing so wildly: let us go.

5   Come; let us go: your cheeks are pale;
   Methinks my friend is richly shrined;
   But half my life I leave behind.
But I shall pass, my work will fail.

Yet in these ears, till hearing dies,
10   One set slow bell will seem to toll
   The passing of the sweetest soul
That ever looked with human eyes.

I hear it now, and o'er and o'er,
   Eternal greetings to the dead;
15   And "Ave,° Ave, Ave," said,   *Hail (Latin)*
"Adieu, adieu," forevermore.

58

In those sad words I took farewell.
   Like echoes in sepulchral halls,
   As drop by drop the water falls
In vaults and catacombs, they fell;

7. Preserved like fossils in rock.

5   And, falling, idly broke the peace
          Of hearts that beat from day to day,
          Half-conscious of their dying clay,
       And those cold crypts where they shall cease.

       The high Muse answered: "Wherefore grieve
10   Thy brethren with a fruitless tear?
          Abide a little longer here,
       And thou shalt take a nobler leave."

59

       O Sorrow, wilt thou live with me
          No casual mistress, but a wife,
          My bosom friend and half of life;
       As I confess it needs must be?

5   O Sorrow, wilt thou rule my blood,
          Be sometimes lovely like a bride,
          And put thy harsher moods aside,
       If thou wilt have me wise and good?

       My centered passion cannot move,
10   Nor will it lessen from today;
          But I'll have leave at times to play
       As with the creature of my love;

       And set thee forth, for thou art mine,
          With so much hope for years to come,
15   That, howsoe'er I know thee, some
       Could hardly tell what name were thine.

                    *   *   *

64

       Dost thou look back on what hath been,
          As some divinely gifted man,
          Whose life in low estate began
       And on a simple village green;

5   Who breaks his birth's invidious bar,
          And grasps the skirts of happy chance,
          And breasts the blows of circumstance,
       And grapples with his evil star;

       Who makes by force his merit known
10   And lives to clutch the golden keys,[8]

8. Badges of high public office.

To mold a mighty state's decrees,
And shape the whisper of the throne;

And moving up from high to higher,
    Becomes on Fortune's crowning slope
15   The pillar of a people's hope,
The center of a world's desire;

Yet feels, as in a pensive dream,
    When all his active powers are still,
    A distant dearness in the hill,
20 A secret sweetness in the stream,

The limit of his narrower fate,
    While yet beside its vocal springs
    He played at counselors and kings,
With one that was his earliest mate;

25 Who plows with pain his native lea
    And reaps the labor of his hands,
    Or in the furrow musing stands:
"Does my old friend remember me?"

* * *

67

When on my bed the moonlight falls,
    I know that in thy place of rest
    By that broad water[9] of the west
There comes a glory on the walls:

5   Thy marble bright in dark appears,
    As slowly steals a silver flame
    Along the letters of thy name,
And o'er the number of thy years.

The mystic glory swims away,
10   From off my bed the moonlight dies;
    And closing eaves of wearied eyes
I sleep till dusk is dipped in gray;

And then I know the mist is drawn
    A lucid veil from coast to coast,
15   And in the dark church like a ghost
Thy tablet glimmers to the dawn.

* * *

9. The Severn River.

70

I cannot see the features right,
　　When on the gloom I strive to paint
　　The face I know; the hues are faint
And mix with hollow masks of night;

5　Cloud-towers by ghostly masons wrought,
　　A gulf that ever shuts and gapes,
　　A hand that points, and pallèd shapes
In shadowy thoroughfares of thought;

And crowds that stream from yawning doors,
10　And shoals of puckered faces drive;
　　Dark bulks that tumble half alive,
And lazy lengths on boundless shores;

Till all at once beyond the will
　　I hear a wizard music roll,
15　And through a lattice on the soul
Looks thy fair face and makes it still.

71

Sleep, kinsman thou to death and trance
　　And madness, thou has forged at last
　　A night-long present of the past
In which we went through summer France.[1]

5　Hadst thou such credit with the soul?
　　Then bring an opiate trebly strong,
　　Drug down the blindfold sense of wrong,
That so my pleasure may be whole;

While now we talk as once we talked
10　Of men and minds, the dust of change,
　　The days that grow to something strange,
In walking as of old we walked

Beside the river's wooded reach,
　　The fortress, and the mountain ridge,
15　The cataract flashing from the bridge,
The breaker breaking on the beach.

72

Risest thou thus, dim dawn, again,[2]
　　And howlest, issuing out of night,

1. In the summer of 1830 Hallam and Tennyson went through southern France en route to Spain.　　2. September 15, 1834, the first anniversary of Hallam's death.

With blasts that blow the poplar white,
And lash with storm the streaming pane?

5   Day, when my crowned estate[3] begun
      To pine in that reverse of doom,[4]
      Which sickened every living bloom,
    And blurred the splendor of the sun;

    Who usherest in the dolorous hour
10   With thy quick tears that make the rose
      Pull sideways, and the daisy close
    Her crimson fringes to the shower;

    Who mightst have heaved a windless flame
      Up the deep East, or, whispering, played
15   A checker-work of beam and shade
    Along the hills, yet looked the same,

    As wan, as chill, as wild as now;
      Day, marked as with some hideous crime,
      When the dark hand struck down through time,
20   And canceled nature's best: but thou,

    Lift as thou mayst thy burthened brows
      Through clouds that drench the morning star,
      And whirl the ungarnered sheaf afar,
    And sow the sky with flying boughs,

25   And up thy vault with roaring sound
      Climb thy thick noon, disastrous day;
      Touch thy dull goal of joyless gray,
    And hide thy shame beneath the ground.

*   *   *

75

I leave thy praises unexpressed
    In verse that brings myself relief,
    And by the measure of my grief
I leave thy greatness to be guessed.

5   What practice howsoe'er expert
      In fitting aptest words to things,
      Or voice the richest-toned that sings,
    Hath power to give thee as thou wert?

3. State of happiness.
4. The reversal or disaster that doom brought upon him when Hallam died.

I care not in these fading days
10   To raise a cry that lasts not long,
       And round thee with the breeze of song
To stir a little dust of praise.

Thy leaf has perished in the green,
       And, while we breathe beneath the sun,
15   The world which credits what is done
Is cold to all that might have been.

So here shall silence guard thy fame;
       But somewhere, out of human view,
       Whate'er thy hands are set to do
20 Is wrought with tumult of acclaim.

*   *   *

78

Again at Christmas⁵ did we weave
       The holly round the Christmas hearth;
       The silent snow possessed the earth,
And calmly fell our Christmas eve.

5   The yule clog° sparkled keen with frost,   *log*
       No wing of wind the region swept,
       But over all things brooding slept
The quiet sense of something lost.

As in the winters left behind,
10   Again our ancient games had place,
       The mimic picture's⁶ breathing grace,
And dance and song and hoodman-blind.⁷

Who showed a token of distress?
       No single tear, no mark of pain—
15   O sorrow, then can sorrow wane?
O grief, can grief be changed to less?

O last regret, regret can die!
       No—mixed with all this mystic frame,
       Her deep relations are the same,
20 But with long use her tears are dry.

*   *   *

5. The second Christmas (1834) after Hallam's death.
6. A game in which the participants pose in the manner of some famous statue or painting and the spectators try to guess what work of art is being portrayed.
7. The player in the game of blindman's buff who wears a blindfold or hood.

82

I wage not any feud with Death
    For changes wrought on form and face;
    No lower life that earth's embrace
May breed with him can fright my faith.

5   Eternal process moving on,
    From state to state the spirit walks;
    And these are but the shattered stalks,
Or ruined chrysalis of one.

Nor blame I Death, because he bare
10   The use of virtue out of earth;
    I know transplanted human worth
Will bloom to profit, otherwhere.

For this alone on Death I wreak
    The wrath that garners in my heart:
15   He put our lives so far apart
We cannot hear each other speak.

83

Dip down upon the northern shore,
    O sweet new-year° delaying long;   *spring 1835*
    Thou doest expectant Nature wrong;
Delaying long, delay no more.

5   What stays thee from the clouded noons,
    Thy sweetness from its proper place?
    Can trouble live with April days,
Or sadness in the summer moons?

Bring orchis, bring the foxglove spire,
10   The little speedwell's° darling blue,   *spring flower*
    Deep tulips dashed with fiery dew,
Laburnums, dropping-wells of fire.

O thou, new-year, delaying long,
    Delayest the sorrow in my blood,
15   That longs to burst a frozen bud
And flood a fresher throat with song.

84

When I contemplate all alone
    The life that had been thine below,

And fix my thoughts on all the glow
To which thy crescent would have grown,

5   I see thee sitting crowned with good,
        A central warmth diffusing bliss
        In glance and smile, and clasp and kiss,
    On all the branches of thy blood;

    Thy blood, my friend, and partly mine;
10   For now the day was drawing on,
        When thou shouldst link thy life with one
    Of mine own house, and boys of thine

    Had babbled "Uncle" on my knee;
        But that remorseless iron hour
15   Made cypress of her orange flower,[8]
    Despair of hope, and earth of thee.

    I seem to meet their least desire,
        To clap their cheeks, to call them mine.
        I see their unborn faces shine
20   Beside the never-lighted fire.

    I see myself an honored guest,
        Thy partner in the flowery walk
        Of letters, genial table talk,
    Or deep dispute, and graceful jest;

25   While now thy prosperous labor fills
        The lips of men with honest praise,
        And sun by sun the happy days
    Descend below the golden hills

    With promise of a morn as fair;
30   And all the train of bounteous hours
        Conduct, by paths of growing powers,
    To reverence and the silver hair;

    Till slowly worn her earthly robe,
        Her lavish mission richly wrought,
35   Leaving great legacies of thought,
    Thy spirit should fail from off the globe;

    What time mine own might also flee,
        As linked with thine in love and fate,
        And, hovering o'er the dolorous strait
40   To the other shore, involved in thee,

8. Orange blossoms are associated with brides—here the poet's sister Emily Tennyson, to whom Hallam
had been engaged.

Arrive at last the blessed goal,
    And He that died in Holy Land
    Would reach us out the shining hand,
And take us as a single soul.

45 What reed was that on which I leant?
    Ah, backward fancy, wherefore wake
    The old bitterness again, and break
The low beginnings of content?

*   *   *

86

Sweet after showers, ambrosial air,
    That rollest from the gorgeous gloom
    Of evening over brake and bloom
And meadow, slowly breathing bare

5 The round of space,[9] and rapt below
    Through all the dewy-tasseled wood,
    And shadowing down the hornèd flood[1]
In ripples, fan my brows and blow

The fever from my cheek, and sigh
10   The full new life that feeds thy breath
    Throughout my frame, till Doubt and Death,
Ill brethren, let the fancy fly

From belt to belt of crimson seas
    On leagues of odor streaming far,
15   To where in yonder orient star
A hundred spirits whisper "Peace."

87

I passed beside the reverend walls[2]
    In which of old I wore the gown;
    I roved at random through the town,
And saw the tumult of the halls;

5 And heard once more in college fanes
    The storm their high-built organs make,
    And thunder-music, rolling, shake
The prophet blazoned on the panes;

And caught once more the distant shout,
10   The measured pulse of racing oars

---

9. Air that is slowly clearing the clouds from the sky.

1. Between two promontories [Tennyson's note].
2. Of Trinity College, Cambridge University.

Among the willows; paced the shores
And many a bridge, and all about

The same gray flats again, and felt
The same, but not the same; and last
15   Up that long walk of limes I passed
To see the rooms in which he dwelt.

Another name was on the door.
I lingered; all within was noise
Of songs, and clapping hands, and boys
20   That crashed the glass and beat the floor;

Where once we held debate, a band
Of youthful friends,[3] on mind and art,
And labor, and the changing mart,
And all the framework of the land;

25   When one would aim an arrow fair,
But send it slackly from the string;
And one would pierce an outer ring,
And one an inner, here and there;

And last the master bowman, he,
30   Would cleave the mark. A willing ear
We lent him. Who but hung to hear
The rapt oration flowing free

From point to point, with power and grace
And music in the bounds of law,[4]
35   To those conclusions when we saw
The God within him light his face,

And seem to lift the form, and glow
In azure orbits heavenly-wise;
And over those ethereal eyes
40   The bar of Michael Angelo?[5]

88

Wild bird,[6] whose warble, liquid sweet,
Rings Eden through the budded quicks,[7]
O tell me where the senses mix,
O tell me where the passions meet,

3. "The Apostles," an undergraduate club to which Tennyson and Hallam had belonged.
4. An essay presented by Hallam at Cambridge in 1831 provides an example of his skill while still an undergraduate in theological argument (cf. *The Writings of Arthur Hallam*, edited by T. H. V. Mot-ter, 1943, pp. 198–213).
5. Hallam, like Michelangelo, had a prominent ridge of bone above his eyes.
6. Probably a nightingale.
7. Hawthorn hedges.

5 Whence radiate: fierce extremes employ
      Thy spirits in the darkening leaf,
      And in the midmost heart of grief
      Thy passion clasps a secret joy;

      And I—my harp would prelude woe—
10   I cannot all command the strings;
      The glory of the sum of things
      Will flash along the chords and go.

89

Witch elms that counterchange the floor
      Of this flat lawn with dusk and bright;[8]
      And thou, with all thy breadth and height
      Of foliage, towering sycamore;

5 How often, hither wandering down,
      My Arthur found your shadows fair,
      And shook to all the liberal air
      The dust and din and steam of town!

      He brought an eye for all he saw;
10   He mixed in all our simple sports;
      They pleased him, fresh from brawling courts
      And dusty purlieus of the law.[9]

      O joy to him in this retreat,
      Immantled in ambrosial dark,
15   To drink the cooler air, and mark
      The landscape winking through the heat!

      O sound to rout the brood of cares,
      The sweep of scythe in morning dew,
      The gust that round the garden flew,
20 And tumbled half the mellowing pears!

      O bliss, when all in circle drawn
      About him, heart and ear were fed
      To hear him, as he lay and read
      The Tuscan poets on the lawn!

25 Or in the all-golden afternoon
      A guest, or happy sister, sung,
      Or here she brought the harp and flung
      A ballad to the brightening moon.

8. Shadows of the elm tree checker the lawn at
Somersby, the Tennysons' country home.

9. Hallam became a law student in London after
leaving Cambridge.

Nor less it pleased in livelier moods,
30   Beyond the bounding hill to stray,
    And break the livelong summer day
With banquet in the distant woods;

Whereat we glanced from theme to theme,
    Discussed the books to love or hate,
35   Or touched the changes of the state,
Or threaded some Socratic dream;[1]

But if I praised the busy town,
    He loved to rail against it still,
    For "ground in yonder social mill
40 We rub each other's angles down,

"And merge," he said, "in form and gloss
    The picturesque of man and man."
    We talked: the stream beneath us ran,
The wine-flask lying couched in moss,

45 Or cooled within the glooming wave;
    And last, returning from afar,
    Before the crimson-circled star[2]
Had fallen into her father's[3] grave,

And brushing ankle-deep in flowers,
50 We heard behind the woodbine veil
    The milk that bubbled in° the pail,   *into*
And buzzings of the honeyed hours.

* * *

91

When rosy plumelets tuft the larch,
    And rarely° pipes the mounted thrush,   *exquisitely*
    Or underneath the barren bush
Flits by the sea-blue bird° of March;   *kingfisher*

5 Come, wear the form by which I know
    Thy spirit in time among thy peers;
    The hope of unaccomplished years
Be large and lucid round thy brow.

When summer's hourly-mellowing change
10 May breathe, with many roses sweet,

---

1. I.e., worked our way through some discourse of Socrates (as recorded by Plato).
2. Venus, which will sink into the west as the sun has done.
3. According to the nebular hypothesis, planets condensed out of the sun's atmosphere; in this sense the sun is the "father" of planets.

Upon the thousand waves of wheat
That ripple round the lowly grange,

Come; not in watches of the night,
But where the sunbeam broodeth warm,
15   Come, beauteous in thine after form,
And like a finer light in light.

*   *   *

93

I shall not see thee. Dare I say
   No spirit ever brake the band
   That stays him from the native land
Where first he walked when clasped in clay?[4]

5 No visual shade of someone lost,
   But he, the Spirit himself, may come
   Where all the nerve of sense is numb,
Spirit to Spirit, Ghost to Ghost.

Oh, therefore from thy sightless° range   *invisible*
10   With gods in unconjectured bliss,
   Oh, from the distance of the abyss
Of tenfold-complicated change,

Descend, and touch, and enter; hear
   The wish too strong for words to name,
15   That in this blindness of the frame°   *living frame*
My Ghost may feel that thine is near.

94

How pure at heart and sound in head,
   With what divine affections bold
   Should be the man whose thought would hold
An hour's communion with the dead.

5 In vain shalt thou, or any, call
   The spirits from their golden day,
   Except, like them, thou too canst say,
My spirit is at peace with all.

They haunt the silence of the breast,
10   Imaginations calm and fair,
   The memory like a cloudless air,
The conscience as a sea at rest;

---

4. I.e., when he was alive and clothed in flesh.

But when the heart is full of din,
　　And doubt beside the portal waits,
15　　　They can but listen at the gates,
And hear the household jar within.

95

By night we lingered on the lawn,
　　For underfoot the herb was dry;
　　And genial warmth; and o'er the sky
The silvery haze of summer drawn;

5　　And calm that let the tapers burn
　　　Unwavering: not a cricket chirred;
　　　The brook alone far off was heard,
And on the board the fluttering urn.[5]

And bats went round in fragrant skies,
10　　And wheeled or lit the filmy shapes[6]
　　　That haunt the dusk, with ermine capes
And woolly breasts and beaded eyes;

While now we sang old songs that pealed
　　From knoll to knoll, where, couched at ease,
15　　　The white kine° glimmered, and the trees　　　　*cows*
Laid their dark arms[7] about the field.

But when those others, one by one,
　　Withdrew themselves from me and night,
　　And in the house light after light
20　Went out, and I was all alone,

A hunger seized my heart; I read
　　Of that glad year which once had been,
　　In those fallen leaves which kept their green,
The noble letters of the dead.

25　And strangely on the silence broke
　　　The silent-speaking words, and strange
　　　Was love's dumb cry defying change
To test his worth; and strangely spoke

The faith, the vigor, bold to dwell
30　　On doubts that drive the coward back,
　　　And keen through wordy snares to track
Suggestion to her inmost cell.

5. For boiling water for tea or coffee, heated by a
fluttering flame.
6. The white-winged night moths called ermine
moths.
7. Cast the shadows of their branches.

So word by word, and line by line,
  The dead man touched me from the past,
35   And all at once it seemed at last
The[8] living soul was flashed on mine.

And mine in this was wound, and whirled
  About empyreal heights of thought,
  And came on that which is, and caught
40 The deep pulsations of the world,

Aeonian music[9] measuring out
  The steps of Time—the shocks of Chance—
  The blows of Death. At length my trance
Was canceled, stricken through with doubt.[1]

45 Vague words! but ah, how hard to frame
  In matter-molded forms of speech,
  Or even for intellect to reach
Through memory that which I became.

Till now the doubtful dusk revealed
50   The knolls once more where, couched at ease,
  The white kine glimmered, and the trees
Laid their dark arms about the field;

And sucked from out the distant gloom
  A breeze began to tremble o'er
55   The large leaves of the sycamore,
And fluctuate all the still perfume,

And gathering freshlier overhead,
  Rocked the full-foliaged elms, and swung
  The heavy-folded rose, and flung
60 The lilies to and fro, and said,

"The dawn, the dawn," and died away;
  And East and West, without a breath,
  Mixed their dim lights, like life and death,
To broaden into boundless day.

8. It was "His" in the 1st edition, and also in the
1st edition, line 37 read, "And mine in his was
wound."
9. Of the universe, which has pulsated for eons.
1. In a letter of 1874, replying to an inquiry about
his experience of mystical trances, Tennyson
wrote: "A kind of waking trance I have frequently
had, quite up from boyhood, when I have been all
alone. This has generally come upon me through
repeating my own name two or three times to
myself silently, till all at once, as it were out of the
intensity of the consciousness of individuality, the
individuality itself seemed to dissolve and fade
away into boundless being, and this not a confused
state, but the clearest of the clearest, the surest of
the surest, the weirdest of the weirdest, utterly
beyond words, where death was an almost laughable impossibility, the loss of personality (if so it
were) seeming no extinction but the only true life.
. . . This might . . . be the state which St. Paul
describes, 'Whether in the body I cannot tell, or
whether out of the body I cannot tell.' . . . I am
ashamed of my feeble description. Have I not said
the state is utterly beyond words? But in a moment,
when I come back to my normal state of 'sanity,' I
am ready to fight for *mein liebes Ich* [my dear self],
and hold that it will last for aeons of aeons" (*Alfred
Lord Tennyson, A Memoir*, 1897, vol. 1, 320).

96

You say, but with no touch of scorn,
    Sweet-hearted, you,[2] whose light blue eyes
    Are tender over drowning flies,
You tell me, doubt is Devil-born.

5 I know not: one indeed I knew
    In many a subtle question versed,
    Who touched a jarring lyre at first,
But ever strove to make it true;

Perplexed in faith, but pure in deeds,
10   At last he beat his music out.
    There lives more faith in honest doubt,
Believe me, than in half the creeds.

He fought his doubts and gathered strength,
    He would not make his judgment blind,
15   He faced the specters of the mind
And laid them; thus he came at length

To find a stronger faith his own,
    And Power was with him in the night,
    Which makes the darkness and the light,
20 And dwells not in the light alone,

But in the darkness and the cloud,
    As over Sinaï's peaks of old,[3]
    While Israel made their gods of gold,
Although the trumpet blew so loud.

*   *   *

99

Risest thou thus, dim dawn, again,[4]
    So loud with voices of the birds,
    So thick with lowings of the herds,
Day, when I lost the flower of men;

5 Who tremblest through thy darkling red
    On yon swollen brook that bubbles fast[5]
    By meadows breathing of the past,
And woodlands holy to the dead;

Who murmurest in the foliage eaves
10   A song that slights the coming care,[6]

2. A woman of simple faith.
3. Cf. Exodus 19.16–25. After veiling Mount Sinai in a "cloud" of smoke, God addressed Moses from the darkness.
4. September 15, 1835, the second anniversary of Hallam's death.
5. I.e., reflections of the clouded red light of dawn quiver on the surface of the fast-moving water.
6. I.e., disregards future events such as death or the coming of autumn.

And Autumn laying here and there
A fiery finger on the leaves;

Who wakenest with thy balmy breath
To myriads on the genial earth,
15   Memories of bridal, or of birth,[7]
And unto myriads more, of death.

Oh, wheresoever those[8] may be,
Betwixt the slumber of the poles,
Today they count as kindred souls;
20   They know me not, but mourn with me.

*   *   *

103

On that last night before we went
From out the doors where I was bred,[9]
I dreamed a vision of the dead,
Which left my after-morn content.

5   Methought I dwelt within a hall,
And maidens with me; distant hills
From hidden summits fed with rills
A river sliding by the wall.

The hall with harp and carol rang.
10   They sang of what is wise and good
And graceful. In the center stood
A statue veiled, to which they sang;

And which, though veiled, was known to me,
The shape of him I loved, and love
15   Forever. Then flew in a dove
And brought a summons from the sea;

And when they learnt that I must go,
They wept and wailed, but led the way
To where the little shallop° lay   light open boat
20   At anchor in the flood below;

And on by many a level mead,
And shadowing bluff that made the banks,
We glided winding under ranks
Of iris and the golden reed;

---

7. Cf. *Epilogue*, lines 117–28 (p. 1992).
8. I.e., the many who remember death.
9. In 1837 Tennyson and his family moved away from their home in Lincolnshire, which had been closely associated with his friendship with Hallam. In section 104 the move seems to occur in 1835, the year of the third Christmas after Hallam's death.

25　And still as vaster grew the shore
　　　And rolled the floods in grander space,
　　　The maidens gathered strength and grace
　　And presence, lordlier than before;

　　And I myself, who sat apart
30　　And watched them, waxed in every limb;
　　　I felt the thews of Anakim,[1]
　　The pulses of a Titan's[2] heart;

　　As one would sing the death of war,
　　　And one would chant the history
35　　Of that great race which is to be,[3]
　　And one the shaping of a star;

　　Until the forward-creeping tides
　　　Began to foam, and we to draw
　　　From deep to deep, to where we saw
40　A great ship lift her shining sides.[4]

　　The man we loved was there on deck,
　　　But thrice as large as man he bent
　　　To greet us. Up the side I went,
　　And fell in silence on his neck;

45　Whereat those maidens with one mind
　　　Bewailed their lot; I did them wrong:
　　　"We served thee here," they said, "so long,
　　And wilt thou leave us now behind?"

　　So rapt° I was, they could not win　　　　　　　　　　*entranced*
50　　An answer from my lips, but he
　　　Replying, "Enter likewise ye
　　And go with us:" they entered in.

　　And while the wind began to sweep
　　　A music out of sheet and shroud,
55　　We steered her toward a crimson cloud
　　That landlike slept along the deep.

104

　　The time draws near the birth of Christ;[5]
　　　The moon is hid, the night is still;

---

1. Plural of *Anak;* a reference to the giant sons of Anak (cf. Numbers 13.33).
2. Giant of Greek mythology.
3. See the account of the "crowning race" in *Epilogue,* lines 128–44.
4. Cf. *Morte d'Arthur,* lines 255–322, in which Bedivere is left behind as Arthur's barge, the ship of death, sails away. In the present dream vision not only is the speaker taken aboard but also his companions, who represent the creative arts of this world—"all the human powers and talents that do not pass with life but go along with it," as Tennyson said of this passage.
5. See n. 1, p. 1957.

A single church below the hill
Is pealing, folded in the mist.

5   A single peal of bells below,
    That wakens at this hour of rest
    A single murmur in the breast,
That these are not the bells I know.

Like strangers' voices here they sound,
10   In lands where not a memory strays,
    Nor landmark breathes of other days,
But all is new unhallowed ground.

105

Tonight ungathered let us leave
    This laurel, let this holly stand:[6]
    We live within the stranger's land,
And strangely falls our Christmas eve.

5   Our father's dust is left alone
    And silent under other snows:
    There in due time the woodbine blows,
The violet comes, but we are gone.

No more shall wayward grief abuse
10   The genial hour with mask and mime;
    For change of place, like growth of time,
Has broke the bond of dying use.

Let cares that petty shadows cast,
    By which our lives are chiefly proved,
15   A little spare the night I loved,
And hold it solemn to the past.

But let no footstep beat the floor,
    Nor bowl of wassail mantle warm;[7]
    For who would keep an ancient form
20   Through which the spirit breathes no more?

Be neither song, nor game, nor feast;
    Nor harp be touched, nor flute be blown;
    No dance, no motion, save alone
What lightens in the lucid east

25   Of rising worlds[8] by yonder wood.
    Long sleeps the summer in the seed;

6. Cf. section 29, in which the family in their former home still continued to gather holly. In the new home, the customary observances lapse.
7. I.e., no bowl of hot punch warms the mantelpiece.
8. The scintillating motion of the stars that rise [Tennyson's note].

Run out your measured arcs, and lead
The closing cycle rich in good.

106

Ring out, wild bells, to the wild sky,
    The flying cloud, the frosty light:
    The year is dying in the night;
Ring out, wild bells, and let him die.

5   Ring out the old, ring in the new,
    Ring, happy bells, across the snow:
    The year is going, let him go;
Ring out the false, ring in the true.

Ring out the grief that saps the mind,
10   For those that here we see no more;
    Ring out the feud of rich and poor,
Ring in redress to all mankind.

Ring out a slowly dying cause,
    And ancient forms of party strife;
15   Ring in the nobler modes of life,
With sweeter manners, purer laws.

Ring out the want, the care, the sin,
    The faithless coldness of the times:
    Ring out, ring out my mournful rhymes,
20   But ring the fuller minstrel in.

Ring out false pride in place and blood,
    The civic slander and the spite;
    Ring in the love of truth and right,
Ring in the common love of good.

25   Ring out old shapes of foul disease;
    Ring out the narrowing lust of gold;
    Ring out the thousand wars of old,
Ring in the thousand years of peace.

Ring in the valiant man and free,
30   The larger heart, the kindlier hand;
    Ring out the darkness of the land,
Ring in the Christ that is to be.[9]

---

9. These allusions to the second coming of Christ and to the millennium are derived from Revelation 20, but Tennyson has interpreted the biblical account in his own way. He once told his son of his conviction that "the forms of Christian religion would alter; but that the spirit of Christ would still grow from more to more."

107

It is the day when he was born.°   *February 1*
 A bitter day that early sank
 Behind a purple-frosty bank
Of vapor, leaving night forlorn.

5 The time admits not flowers or leaves
 To deck the banquet. Fiercely flies
 The blast of North and East, and ice
Makes daggers at the sharpened eaves,

And bristles all the brakes and thorns
10 To yon hard crescent, as she hangs
 Above the wood which grides[1] and clangs
Its leafless ribs and iron horns

Together, in the drifts[2] that pass
 To darken on the rolling brine
15 That breaks the coast. But fetch the wine,
Arrange the board and brim the glass;

Bring in great logs and let them lie,
 To make a solid core of heat;
 Be cheerful-minded, talk and treat
20 Of all things even as he were by;

We keep the day. With festal cheer,
 With books and music, surely we
 Will drink to him, whate'er he be,
And sing the songs he loved to hear.

108

I will not shut me from my kind,
 And, lest I stiffen into stone,
 I will not eat my heart alone,
Nor feed with sighs a passing wind:

5 What profit lies in barren faith,
 And vacant yearning, though with might
 To scale the heaven's highest height,
Or dive below the wells of Death?

What find I in the highest place,
10 But mine own phantom chanting hymns?
 And on the depths of death there swims
The reflex of a human face.°   *his own face*

1. Clashes with a strident noise.   2. Either cloud-drifts or clouds of snow.

I'll rather take what fruit may be
　　Of sorrow under human skies:
15　'Tis held that sorrow makes us wise,
　　Whatever wisdom sleep with thee.°　　　　　　*Hallam*

109

Heart-affluence in discursive talk
　　From household fountains never dry;
　　The critic clearness of an eye
That saw through all the Muses' walk;[3]

5　Seraphic intellect and force
　　To seize and throw the doubts of man;
　　Impassioned logic, which outran
The hearer in its fiery course;

High nature amorous of the good,
10　But touched with no ascetic gloom;
　　And passion pure in snowy bloom
Through all the years of April blood;

A love of freedom rarely felt,
　　Of freedom in her regal seat
15　Of England; not the schoolboy heat,
The blind hysterics of the Celt;[4]

And manhood fused with female grace
　　In such a sort, the child would twine
　　A trustful hand, unasked, in thine,
20　And find his comfort in thy face;

All these have been, and thee mine eyes
　　Have looked on: if they looked in vain,
　　My shame is greater who remain,
Nor let thy wisdom make me wise.

＊　＊　＊

115

Now fades the last long streak of snow,
　　Now burgeons every maze of quick°　　　*hawthorn hedges*
　　About the flowering squares,° and thick　　　*fields*
By ashen roots the violets blow.

5　Now rings the woodland loud and long,
　　The distance takes a lovelier hue,

3. The realm of art and literature.
4. A member of one of the groups of peoples populating ancient Britain; i.e., a less-civilized people.

And drowned in yonder living blue
The lark becomes a sightless song.

Now dance the lights on lawn and lea,
10   The flocks are whiter down the vale,
And milkier every milky sail
On winding stream or distant sea;

Where now the seamew pipes, or dives
In yonder greening gleam, and fly
15   The happy birds, that change their sky
To build and brood, that live their lives

From land to land; and in my breast
Spring wakens too, and my regret
Becomes an April violet,
20   And buds and blossoms like the rest.

* * *

118

Contèmplate all this work of Time,
The giant laboring in his youth;
Nor dream of human love and truth,
As dying Nature's earth and lime;[5]

5   But trust that those we call the dead
Are breathers of an ampler day
For ever nobler ends. They[6] say,
The solid earth whereon we tread

In tracts of fluent heat began,
10   And grew to seeming-random forms,
The seeming prey of cyclic storms,
Till at the last arose the man;

Who throve and branched from clime to clime,
The herald of a higher race,
15   And of himself in higher place
If so he type[7] this work of time

Within himself, from more to more;
Or, crowned with attributes of woe
Like glories, move his course, and show
20   That life is not as idle ore,

---

5. Alluding to the materialistic analysis of living matter into chemicals and simpler compounds [cited by Susan Shatto].

6. Geologists and astronomers.

7. Emulate, prefigure as a type.

But iron dug from central gloom,
  And heated hot with burning fears,
  And dipped in baths of hissing tears,
And battered with the shocks of doom

25 To shape and use. Arise and fly
  The reeling Faun, the sensual feast;
  Move upward, working out the beast,
And let the ape and tiger die.

119

Doors, where my heart was used to beat
  So quickly, not as one that weeps
  I come once more; the city sleeps;
I smell the meadow in the street;

5 I hear a chirp of birds; I see
  Betwixt the black fronts long-withdrawn
  A light blue lane of early dawn,
And think of early days and thee,

And bless thee, for thy lips are bland,
10 And bright the friendship of thine eye;
  And in my thoughts with scarce a sigh
I take the pressure of thine hand.

120

I trust I have not wasted breath:
  I think we are not wholly brain,
  Magnetic mockeries;[8] not in vain,
Like Paul[9] with beasts, I fought with Death;

5 Not only cunning casts in clay:
  Let Science prove we are, and then
  What matters Science unto men,
At least to me? I would not stay.

Let him, the wiser man who springs
10 Hereafter, up from childhood shape
  His action like the greater ape,
But I was *born* to other things.

---

8. Mechanisms operated by responses to electrical forces.

9. 1 Corinthians 15.32.

121

Sad Hesper° o'er the buried sun   *evening star*
     And ready, thou, to die with him,
     Thou watchest all things ever dim
And dimmer, and a glory done.

5   The team is loosened from the wain,°   *hay wagon*
     The boat is drawn upon the shore;
     Thou listenest to the closing door,
And life is darkened in the brain.

Bright Phosphor,° fresher for the night,   *morning star*
10   By thee the world's great work is heard
     Beginning, and the wakeful bird;
Behind thee comes the greater light.[1]

The market boat is on the stream,
     And voices hail it from the brink;
15   Thou hear'st the village hammer clink,
And see'st the moving of the team.

Sweet Hesper-Phosphor, double name[2]
     For what is one, the first, the last,
     Thou, like my present and my past,
20   Thy place is changed; thou art the same.

                    *   *   *

123

There rolls the deep where grew the tree.
     O earth, what changes hast thou seen!
     There where the long street roars hath been
The stillness of the central sea.[3]

5   The hills are shadows, and they flow
     From form to form, and nothing stands;
     They melt like mist, the solid lands,
Like clouds they shape themselves and go.

But in my spirit will I dwell,
10   And dream my dream, and hold it true;

1. Cf. Genesis 1.16: "The greater light to rule the day."
2. The planet Venus is both evening star and morning star.
3. Cf. a passage from Sir Charles Lyell's *The Principles of Geology* (1832), a book well known to Tennyson. In discussing the "interchange of sea and land" that has occurred "on the surface of our globe" Lyell remarks: "In the Mediterranean alone, many flourishing inland towns and a still greater number of ports now stand where the sea rolled its waves since the era when civilized nations first grew in Europe."

For though my lips may breathe adieu,
I cannot think the thing farewell.

124

That which we dare invoke to bless;
  Our dearest faith; our ghastliest doubt;
  He, They, One, All; within, without;
The Power in darkness whom we guess—

5 I found Him not in world or sun,
  Or eagle's wing, or insect's eye,[4]
  Nor through the questions men may try,
The petty cobwebs we have spun.

If e'er when faith had fallen asleep,
10 I heard a voice, "believe no more,"
  And heard an ever-breaking shore
That tumbled in the Godless deep,

A warmth within the breast would melt
  The freezing reason's colder part,
15 And like a man in wrath the heart
Stood up and answered, "I have felt."[5]

No, like a child in doubt and fear:
  But that blind clamor made me wise;
  Then was I as a child that cries,
20 But, crying, knows his father near;

And what I am beheld again
  What is, and no man understands;
  And out of darkness came the hands
That reach through nature, molding men.

       *   *   *

126

Love is and was my lord and king,
  And in his presence I attend
  To hear the tidings of my friend,
Which every hour his couriers bring.

5 Love is and was my king and lord,
  And will be, though as yet I keep

---

4. He does not discover satisfactory proof of God's existence in the 18th-century argument that because objects in nature are designed there must exist a designer.

5. Cf. Thomas Carlyle's *Sartor Resartus, The Everlasting No.*

Within the court on earth, and sleep
Encompassed by his faithful guard,

And hear at times a sentinel
10   Who moves about from place to place,
        And whispers to the worlds of space,
In the deep night, that all is well.

127

And all is well, though faith and form[6]
    Be sundered in the night of fear;
    Well roars the storm to those that hear
A deeper voice across the storm,

5   Proclaiming social truth shall spread,
        And justice, even though thrice again
        The red fool-fury of the Seine
    Should pile her barricades with dead.[7]

But ill for him that wears a crown,
10   And him, the lazar,[8] in his rags!
        They tremble, the sustaining crags;
    The spires of ice are toppled down,

And molten up, and roar in flood;
        The fortress crashes from on high,
15   The brute earth lightens[9] to the sky,
    And the great Aeon[1] sinks in blood,

And compassed by the fires of hell,
    While thou, dear spirit, happy star,
    O'erlook'st the tumult from afar,
20 And smilest, knowing all is well.

*   *   *

129

Dear friend, far off, my lost desire,
    So far, so near in woe and weal,
    O loved the most, when most I feel
There is a lower and a higher;

---

6. Traditional institutions through which faith was formerly expressed, such as the church.
7. Revolutionary uprisings in France, in each of which a king lost his throne (line 9): in 1789 against Louis XVI, in 1830 against Charles X, and in 1848 against Louis-Philippe. The third (line 6) would have been a prophecy if, as Tennyson rec-ollected, section 127 were finished at a date earlier than 1848.
8. Pauper suffering from disease.
9. Is lit up by fire.
1. A vast tract of time, here perhaps modern Western civilization.

5   Known and unknown, human, divine;
      Sweet human hand and lips and eye;
      Dear heavenly friend that canst not die,
    Mine, mine, forever, ever mine;

    Strange friend, past, present, and to be;
10   Loved deeplier, darklier understood;
      Behold, I dream a dream of good,
    And mingle all the world with thee.

130

    Thy voice is on the rolling air
      I hear thee where the waters run;
      Thou standest in the rising sun,
    And in the setting thou art fair.

5   What art thou then? I cannot guess;
      But though I seem in star and flower
      To feel thee some diffusive power,
    I do not therefore love thee less.

    My love involves the love before;
10   My love is vaster passion now;
      Tho' mix'd with God and Nature thou,
    I seem to love thee more and more.

    Far off thou art, but ever nigh;
      I have thee still, and I rejoice;
15   I prosper, circled with thy voice;
    I shall not lose thee tho' I die.

131

    O living will[2] that shalt endure
      When all that seems shall suffer shock,
      Rise in the spiritual rock,°   *Christ*
    Flow through our deeds and make them pure,

5   That we may lift from out of dust
      A voice as unto him that hears,
      A cry above the conquered years
    To one that with us works, and trust,

    With faith that comes of self-control,
10   The truths that never can be proved

2. Tennyson later commented that he meant here the moral will of humankind.

Until we close with all we loved,
And all we flow from, soul in soul.

From Epilogue[3]

* * *

And rise, O moon, from yonder down,
110   Till over down and over dale
All night the shining vapor sail
And pass the silent-lighted town,

The white-faced halls, the glancing rills,
And catch at every mountain head,
115   And o'er the friths° that branch and spread   *inlets of the sea*
Their sleeping silver through the hills;

And touch with shade the bridal doors,
With tender gloom the roof, the wall;
And breaking let the splendor fall
120   To spangle all the happy shores

By which they rest, and ocean sounds,
And, star and system rolling past,
A soul shall draw from out the vast
And strike his being into bounds,

125   And, moved through life of lower phase,
Result in man,[4] be born and think,
And act and love, a closer link
Betwixt us and the crowning race

Of those that, eye to eye, shall look
130   On knowledge; under whose command
Is Earth and Earth's, and in their hand
Is Nature like an open book;

No longer half-akin to brute,
For all we thought and loved and did,
135   And hoped, and suffered, is but seed
Of what in them is flower and fruit;

Whereof the man that with me trod
This planet was a noble type
Appearing ere the times were ripe,
140   That friend of mine who lives in God,

3. The *Epilogue* describes the wedding day of Tennyson's sister Cecilia to Edmund Lushington. At the conclusion (printed here) the speaker reflects on the moonlit wedding night and the kind of offspring that will result from their union.

4. A child will be conceived and will develop in embryo through various stages. This development is similar to human evolution from the animal to the human level and perhaps to a future higher stage of development.

That God, which ever lives and loves,
   One God, one law, one element,
   And one far-off divine event,
To which the whole creation moves.

1833–50   1850

The Charge of the Light Brigade[1]

1

Half a league, half a league,
Half a league onward,
All in the valley of Death
   Rode the six hundred.
5 "Forward the Light Brigade!
Charge for the guns!" he said.
Into the valley of Death
   Rode the six hundred.[2]

2

"Forward, the Light Brigade!"
10 Was there a man dismayed?
Not though the soldier knew
   Someone had blundered.
Theirs not to make reply,
Theirs not to reason why,
15 Theirs but to do and die.
Into the valley of Death
   Rode the six hundred.

3

Cannon to right of them,
Cannon to left of them,
20 Cannon in front of them
   Volleyed and thundered;
Stormed at with shot and shell,
Boldly they rode and well,
Into the jaws of Death,
25 Into the mouth of hell
   Rode the six hundred.

4

Flashed all their sabers bare,
Flashed as they turned in air
Sab'ring the gunners there,

---

1. During the Crimean War, owing to confusion of orders, a brigade of British cavalry charged some entrenched batteries of Russian artillery. This blunder cost the lives of three-quarters of the six hundred horsemen engaged (see Cecil Woodham-Smith, *The Reason Why*, 1954). Tennyson rapidly composed his "ballad" (as he called the poem) after reading an account of the battle in a newspaper.
2. In the recording Tennyson made of this poem, "hundred" sounds like "hunderd"—a Lincolnshire pronunciation that reinforces the rhyme with "thundered," etc.

30 Charging an army, while
    All the world wondered.
  Plunged in the battery smoke
  Right through the line they broke;
  Cossack and Russian
35 Reeled from the saber stroke
    Shattered and sundered.
  Then they rode back, but not,
    Not the six hundred.

5

  Cannon to right of them,
40 Cannon to left of them,
  Cannon behind them
    Volleyed and thundered;
  Stormed at with shot and shell,
  While horse and hero fell.
45 They that had fought so well
  Came through the jaws of Death,
  Back from the mouth of hell,
  All that was left of them,
    Left of six hundred.

6

50 When can their glory fade?
  O the wild charge they made!
    All the world wondered.
  Honor the charge they made!
  Honor the Light Brigade,
55   Noble six hundred!

1854   1854

Idylls of the King

When John Milton was considering subjects suitable for an epic poem, one of those he entertained was the story of the Christian British king Arthur, a semilegendary leader of about 500 who fought off the heathen Saxon invaders who had swarmed into Britain after the withdrawal of the Roman legions. Tennyson likewise saw that the Arthurian story had epic potential and selected it for his lifework as "the greatest of all poetical subjects." At intervals, during a period of fifty years, he labored over the twelve books that make up his *Idylls of the King*, completing the work in 1888.

The principal source of Tennyson's stories of Arthur and his knights was Sir Thomas Malory's *Morte Darthur*, a version that Malory translated into English prose from French sources in 1470. As Talbot Donaldson has suggested, one basis of the appeal of the Arthurian stories, like the legends of Robin Hood and stories of the American West, is that all three represent the struggle of individuals to restore order in situations of chaos and anarchy, a task performed in the face of seemingly overwhelming odds. The individual stories in Tennyson's *Idylls* have the same basic appeal, but the overall design of the whole poem is more ambitious and impressive. The *Idylls of the King* represent the rise and fall of a civilization. They imply that after two thousand years of Christianity, Western civilization may be going through a cycle in which it must confront the possibilities of a renewal in the future or an apocalyptic extinction. The books move through summer and autumn and culminate in the bleak wintry scene of Arthur's last battle in which his order perishes in a civil war; the leader of the enemy forces is his own nephew, Sir Modred.

Throughout the books of the *Idylls* the forces of opposition grow in strength, and disaffections infect leading figures of the Round Table itself. The most glaring example is the adulterous relationship between Guinevere, Arthur's "sumptuous" queen (as Tennyson once described her), and the king's chief lieutenant and friend, Sir Lancelot. Many other fallings away subsequently come to light, such as the perfidious betrayal by Sir Gawain in the ninth book, *Pelleas and Ettarre,* and the cynical conduct of Sir Tristram, whose story is told in the bitter tenth book, *The Last Tournament.* Even Merlin, Arthur's trusted magician and counselor, becomes corrupted and can perform no further offices for the king (*Merlin and Vivien*). *The Passing of Arthur* depicts the apocalyptic end of this long process of disintegration and decay.

FROM IDYLLS OF THE KING

The Passing of Arthur[1]

That story which the bold Sir Bedivere,[2]
First made and latest left of all the knights,
Told, when the man was no more than a voice
In the white winter of his age, to those
5   With whom he dwelt, new faces, other minds.

For on their march to westward, Bedivere,
Who slowly paced among the slumbering host,
Heard in his tent the moanings of the King:

"I found Him in the shining of the stars,
10   I marked Him in the flowering of His fields,
But in His ways with men I find Him not.
I waged His wars, and now I pass and die.
O me! for why is all around us here
As if some lesser god had made the world,
15   But had not force to shape it as he would,
Till the High God behold it from beyond,
And enter it, and make it beautiful?
Or else as if the world were wholly fair,
But that these eyes of men are dense and dim,
20   And have not power to see it as it is:
Perchance, because we see not to the close;—
For I, being simple, thought to work His will,
And have but stricken with the sword in vain;
And all whereon I leaned in wife and friend

---

1. The principal source for *The Passing of Arthur* was Malory's *Morte Darthur* 21.4–5. Preceding the action of this idyll, Arthur had been in France with his nephew Gawain fighting against the forces of Lancelot. Learning at that time of the gathering of an army against him in England, under the leadership of his nephew, Modred, Arthur re-

turned there to engage in his last battle. Upon landing at Dover, Gawain was slain.
2. A knight who had long been close to the king, described in *The Coming of Arthur:* "Bedivere, the first of all his knights / Knighted by Arthur at his crowning."

25   Is traitor to my peace, and all my realm
     Reels back into the beast, and is no more.
     My God, thou hast forgotten me in my death:[3]
     Nay—God my Christ—I pass but shall not die."

     Then, ere that last weird battle in the west,
30   There came on Arthur sleeping, Gawain killed
     In Lancelot's war, the ghost of Gawain blown
     Along a wandering wind, and past his ear
     Went shrilling. "Hollow, hollow all delight!
     Hail, King! tomorrow thou shalt pass away.
35   Farewell! there is an isle of rest for thee.
     And I am blown along a wandering wind,
     And hollow, hollow, hollow all delight."
     And fainter onward, like wild birds that change
     Their season in the night and wail their way
40   From cloud to cloud, down the long wind the dream
     Shrilled; but in going mingled with dim cries
     Far in the moonlit haze among the hills,
     As of some lonely city sacked by night,
     When all is lost, and wife and child with wail
45   Pass to new lords; and Arthur woke and called,
     "Who spake? A dream. O light upon the wind,
     Thine, Gawain, was the voice—are these dim cries
     Thine? or doth all that haunts the waste and wild
     Mourn, knowing it will go along with me?"

50   This heard the bold Sir Bedivere and spake:
     "O me, my King, let pass whatever will,
     Elves, and the harmless glamor of the field;[4]
     But in their stead thy name and glory cling
     To all high places like a golden cloud
55   Forever: but as yet thou shalt not pass.
     Light was Gawain in life, and light in death
     Is Gawain, for the ghost is as the man;
     And care not thou for dreams from him, but rise—
     I hear the steps of Modred in the west,
60   And with him many of thy people, and knights
     Once thine, whom thou hast loved, but grosser grown
     Than heathen, spitting at their vows and thee.
     Right well in heart they know thee for the King.
     Arise, go forth and conquer as of old."

65   Then spake King Arthur to Sir Bedivere:
     "Far other is this battle in the west
     Whereto we move, than when we strove in youth,
     And brake the petty kings, and fought with Rome,
     Or thrust the heathen from the Roman wall,
70   And shook him through the north. Ill doom is mine
     To war against my people and my knights.

3. Cf. Matthew 27.46: "My God, my God, why
hast thou forsaken me?"
4. Tennyson said the reference is to "the legends

which cluster round the King's name." One legend
told of the elves' bestowing gifts on Arthur as a
child.

The king who fights his people fights himself.
And they thy knights, who loved me once, the stroke
That strikes them dead is as my death to me.
75 Yet let us hence, and find or feel a way
Through this blind haze, which ever since I saw
One lying in the dust at Almesbury,[5]
Hath folded in the passes of the world."

Then rose the King and moved his host by night,
80 And ever pushed Sir Modred, league by league,
Back to the sunset bound of Lyonnesse[6]—
A land of old upheaven from the abyss
By fire, to sink into the abyss again;
Where fragments of forgotten peoples dwelled,
85 And the long mountains ended in a coast
Of ever-shifting sand, and far away
The phantom circle of a moaning sea.
There the pursuer could pursue no more,
And he that fled no further fly the King;
90 And there, that day when the great light of heaven
Burned at his lowest in the rolling year,
On the waste sand by the waste sea they closed.
Nor ever yet had Arthur fought a fight
Like this last, dim, weird battle of the west.
95 A deathwhite mist slept over sand and sea:
Whereof the chill, to him who breathed it, drew
Down with his blood, till all his heart was cold
With formless fear; and even on Arthur fell
Confusion, since he saw not whom he fought.
100 For friend and foe were shadows in the mist,
And friend slew friend not knowing whom he slew;
And some had visions out of golden youth,
And some beheld the faces of old ghosts
Look in upon the battle; and in the mist
105 Was many a noble deed, many a base,
And chance and craft and strength in single fights,
And ever and anon with host to host
Shocks, and the splintering spear, the hard mail hewn,
Shield-breakings, and the clash of brands, the crash
110 Of battleaxes on shattered helms, and shrieks
After the Christ, of those who falling down
Looked up for heaven, and only saw the mist;
And shouts of heathen and the traitor knights,
Oaths, insult, filth, and monstrous blasphemies,
115 Sweat, writhings, anguish, laboring of the lungs
In that close mist, and cryings for the light,
Moans of the dying, and voices of the dead.

Last, as by some one deathbed after wail
Of suffering, silence follows, or through death

---

5. The convent to which Guinevere had withdrawn; during the king's farewell visit to her there,
she had lain in the dust at his feet.

6. Legendary land, extending west from Cornwall,
which sank into the sea.

120 Or deathlike swoon, thus over all that shore,
Save for some whisper of the seething seas,
A dead hush fell; but when the dolorous day
Grew drearier toward twilight falling, came
A bitter wind, clear from the North, and blew
125 The mist aside, and with that wind the tide
Rose, and the pale King glanced across the field
Of battle: but no man was moving there;
Nor any cry of Christian heard thereon,
Nor yet of heathen; only the wan wave
130 Brake in among dead faces, to and fro
Swaying the helpless hands, and up and down
Tumbling the hollow helmets of the fallen,
And shivered brands that once had fought with Rome,
And rolling far along the gloomy shores
135 The voice of days of old and days to be.

Then spake King Arthur to Sir Bedivere,
And whiter than the mist that all day long
Had held the field of battle was the King:

"Hearest thou this great voice that shakes the world,
140 And wastes the narrow realm whereon we move,
And beats upon the faces of the dead,
My dead, as though they had not died for me?—
O Bedivere, for on my heart hath fallen
Confusion, till I know not what I am,
145 Nor whence I am, nor whether I be King.
Behold, I seem but King among the dead."

Then spake the bold Sir Bedivere: "My King,
King everywhere! and so the dead have kings,
There also will I worship thee as King.
150 Yet still thy life is whole, and still I live
Who love thee; but who hates thee, he that brought
The heathen back among us, yonder stands,
Modred, unharmed, the traitor of thine house."

Then spake the King: "My house hath been my doom.
155 But call not thou this traitor of my house
Who hath but dwelled beneath one roof with me.
My house are rather they who sware my vows,
Yea, even while they brake them, owned me King.
And well for thee, saying in my dark hour,
160 When all the purport of my throne hath failed,
That quick or dead thou holdest me for King.
King am I, whatsoever be their cry;
And one last act of kinghood shalt thou see
Yet, ere I pass." And uttering this the King
165 Made at the man: then Modred smote his liege
Hard on that helm which many a heathen sword
Had beaten thin; while Arthur at one blow,

Striking the last stroke with Excalibur,
Slew him, and all but slain himself, he fell.

170   So all day long the noise of battle rolled
Among the mountains by the winter sea;
Until King Arthur's Table, man by man,
Had fallen in Lyonnesse about their lord,
King Arthur. Then, because his wound was deep,
175 The bold Sir Bedivere uplifted him,
And bore him to a chapel nigh the field,
A broken chancel with a broken cross,
That stood on a dark strait of barren land:
On one side lay the Ocean, and on one
180 Lay a great water, and the moon was full.

    Then spake King Arthur to Sir Bedivere:
"The sequel of today unsolders all
The goodliest fellowship of famous knights
Whereof this world holds record. Such a sleep
185 They sleep—the men I loved. I think that we
Shall never more, at any future time,
Delight our souls with talk of knightly deeds,
Walking about the gardens and the halls
Of Camelot, as in the days that were.
190 I perish by this people which I made,—
Though Merlin sware that I should come again
To rule once more;[7] but, let what will be, be,
I am so deeply smitten through the helm
That without help I cannot last til morn.
195 Thou therefore take my brand Excalibur,
Which was my pride: for thou rememberest how
In those old days, one summer noon, an arm
Rose up from out the bosom of the lake,
Clothed in white samite, mystic, wonderful,
200 Holding the sword—and how I rowed across
And took it, and have worn it, like a king;
And, wheresoever I am sung or told
In aftertime, this also shall be known:
But now delay not: take Excalibur,
205 And fling him far into the middle mere:[8]
Watch what thou seëst, and lightly° bring me word."   *quickly*

    To him replied the bold Sir Bedivere:
"It is not meet, Sir King, to leave thee thus,
Aidless, alone, and smitten through the helm—
210 A little thing may harm a wounded man;
Yet I thy hest° will all perform at full,   *command*
Watch what I see, and lightly bring thee word."

---

7. Cf. Malory, *Morte Darthur* 21.7: "Some men yet say in many parts of England that King Arthur is not dead, but by the will of our Lord in another place. And men say that he will come again."
8. Middle of the lake.

So saying, from the ruined shrine he stepped,
And in the moon athwart the place of tombs,
215 Where lay the mighty bones of ancient men,
Old knights, and over them the sea-wind sang
Shrill, chill, with flakes of foam. He, stepping down
By zigzag paths, and juts of pointed rock,
Came on the shining levels of the lake.

220 There drew he forth the brand Excalibur,
And o'er him, drawing it, the winter moon,
Brightening the skirts of a long cloud, ran forth
And sparkled keen with frost against the hilt:
For all the haft twinkled with diamond sparks,
225 Myriads of topaz-lights, and jacinth°-work   red gem
Of subtlest jewelry. He gazed so long
That both his eyes were dazzled as he stood,
This way and that dividing the swift mind,
In act to throw: but at the last it seemed
230 Better to leave Excalibur concealed
There in the many-knotted waterflags,
That whistled stiff and dry about the marge.
So strode he back slow to the wounded King.

Then spake King Arthur to Sir Bedivere:
235 "Hast thou performed my mission which I gave?
What is it thou hast seen? or what hast heard?"
And answer made the bold Sir Bedivere:
"I heard the ripple washing in the reeds,
And the wild water lapping on the crag."

240 To whom replied King Arthur, faint and pale:
"Thou hast betrayed thy nature and thy name.
Not rendering true answer, as beseemed
Thy fëalty, nor like a noble knight:
For surer sign had followed, either hand,
245 Or voice, or else a motion of the mere.
This is a shameful thing for men to lie.
Yet now, I charge thee, quickly go again,
As thou art lief° and dear, and do the thing   beloved
I bade thee, watch, and lightly bring me word."

250 Then went Sir Bedivere the second time
Across the ridge, and paced beside the mere,
Counting the dewy pebbles, fixed in thought;
But when he saw the wonder of the hilt,
How curiously and strangely chased,[9] he smote
255 His palms together, and he cried aloud:

"And if indeed I cast the brand away,
Surely a precious thing, one worthy note,

9. Adorned. "Curiously": skillfully.

Should thus be lost forever from the earth,
Which might have pleased the eyes of many men.
260   What good should follow this, if this were done?
What harm, undone? Deep harm to disobey,
Seeing obedience is the bond of rule.
Were it well to obey then, if a king demand
An act unprofitable, against himself?
265   The King is sick, and knows not what he does.
What record, or what relic of my lord
Should be to aftertime, but empty breath
And rumors of a doubt? But were this kept,
Stored in some treasure-house of mighty kings,
270   Some one might show it at a joust of arms,
Saying, 'King Arthur's sword, Excalibur,
Wrought by the lonely maiden of the Lake.
Nine years she wrought it, sitting in the deeps
Upon the hidden bases of the hills.'
275   So might some old man speak in the aftertime
To all the people, winning reverence.
But now much honor and much fame were lost."

So spake he, clouded with his own conceit,[1]
And hid Excalibur the second time,
280   And so strode back slow to the wounded king.

Then spoke King Arthur, breathing heavily:
"What is it thou hast seen? or what hast heard?"

And answer made the bold Sir Bedivere:
"I heard the water lapping on the crag,
285   And the long ripple washing in the reeds."

To whom replied King Arthur, much in wrath:
"Ah, miserable and unkind, untrue,
Unknightly, traitor-hearted! Woe is me!
Authority forgets a dying king,
290   Laid widowed of the power in his eye
That bowed the will. I see thee what thou art,
For thou, the latest-left of all my knights,
In whom should meet the offices of all,
Thou wouldst betray me for the precious hilt;
295   Either from lust of gold, or like a girl
Valuing the giddy pleasure of the eyes.
Yet, for a man may fail in duty twice,
And the third time may prosper, get thee hence:
But, if thou spare to fling Excalibur,
300   I will arise and slay thee with my hands."

Then quickly rose Sir Bedivere, and ran,
And, leaping down the ridges lightly, plunged

1. Vain and foolish fancies.

Among the bullrush beds, and clutched the sword,
And strongly wheeled and threw it. The great brand
305 Made lightnings in the splendor of the moon,
And flashing round and round and whirled in an arch,
Shot like a streamer of the northern morn,[2]
Seen where the moving isles of winter shock[3]
By night, with noises of the Northern Sea.
310 So flashed and fell the brand Excalibur:
But ere he dipped the surface, rose an arm
Clothed in white samite, mystic, wonderful,
And caught him by the hilt, and brandished him
Three times, and drew him under in the mere.
315 And lightly went the other to the King.

Then spoke King Arthur, drawing thicker breath:
"Now see I by thine eyes that this is done.
Speak out: what is it thou hast heard, or seen?"

And answer made the bold Sir Bedivere:
320 "Sir King, I closed mine eyelids, lest the gems
Should blind my purpose, for I never saw,
Nor shall see, here or elsewhere, till I die,
Not though I live three lives of mortal men,
So great a miracle as yonder hilt.
325 Then with both hands I flung him, wheeling him;
But when I looked again, behold an arm,
Clothed in white samite, mystic, wonderful,
That caught him by the hilt, and brandished him
Three times, and drew him under in the mere."

330 And answer made King Arthur, breathing hard:
"My end draws nigh; 'tis time that I were gone.
Make broad thy shoulders to receive my weight,
And bear me to the margin; yet I fear
My wound hath taken cold, and I shall die."

335 So saying, from the pavement he half rose,
Slowly, with pain, reclining on his arm,
And looking wistfully with wide blue eyes
As in a picture. Him Sir Bedivere
Remorsefully regarded through his tears,
340 And would have spoken, but he found not words;
Then took with care, and kneeling on one knee,
O'er both his shoulders drew the languid hands,
And rising bore him through the place of tombs.

But, as he walked, King Arthur panted hard,
345 Like one that feels a nightmare on his bed
When all the house is mute. So sighed the King,
Muttering and murmuring at his ear, "Quick, quick!
I fear it is too late, and I shall die."

2. The northern lights.   3. Where the icebergs collide.

But the other swiftly strode from ridge to ridge,
350 Clothed with his breath, and looking, as he walked,
Larger than human on the frozen hills.
He heard the deep behind him, and a cry
Before. His own thought drove him like a goad.
Dry clashed his harness in the icy caves
355 And barren chasms, and all to left and right
The bare black cliff clanged round him, as he based
His feet on juts of slippery crag that rang
Sharp-smitten with the dint of armèd heels—
And on a sudden, lo! the level lake,
360 And the long glories of the winter moon.

   Then saw they how there hove a dusky barge,
Dark as a funeral scarf from stem to stern,
Beneath them; and descending they were ware
That all the decks were dense with stately forms,
365 Black-stoled, black-hooded, like a dream—by these
Three Queens with crowns of gold: and from them rose
A cry that shivered to the tingling stars,
And, as it were one voice, an agony
Of lamentation, like a wind that shrills
370 All night in a waste land, where no one comes,
Or hath come, since the making of the world.

   Then murmured Arthur, "Place me in the barge."
So to the barge they came. There those three Queens
Put forth their hands, and took the King, and wept.
375 But she, that rose the tallest of them all
And fairest, laid his head upon her lap,
And loosed the shattered casque,° and chafed his hands,   *helmet*
And called him by his name, complaining loud,
And dropping bitter tears against a brow
380 Striped with dark blood: for all his face was white
And colorless, and like the withered moon
Smote by the fresh beam of the springing east;
And all his greaves and cuisses⁴ dashed with drops
Of onset;⁵ and the light and lustrous curls—
385 That made his forehead like a rising sun
High from the daïs-throne—were parched with dust;
Or, clotted into points and hanging loose,
Mixed with the knightly growth that fringed his lips.
So like a shattered column lay the King;
390 Not like that Arthur who, with lance in rest,
From spur to plume a star of tournament,
Shot through the lists at Camelot, and charged
Before the eyes of ladies and of kings.

   Then loudly cried the bold Sir Bedivere:
395 "Ah! my Lord Arthur, whither shall I go?

---

4. Armor to protect the front of the thighs.   5. Blood from battle.
"Greaves": armor to protect the leg below the knee.

Where shall I hide my forehead and my eyes?
For now I see the true old times are dead,
When every morning brought a noble chance,
And every chance brought out a noble knight.
400 Such times have been not since the light that led
The holy Elders[6] with the gift of myrrh.
But now the whole Round Table is dissolved
Which was an image of the mighty world,
And I, the last, go forth companionless,
405 And the days darken round me, and the years,
Among new men, strange faces, other minds."

    And slowly answered Arthur from the barge:
"The old order changeth, yielding place to new,
And God fulfills himself in many ways,
410 Lest one good custom should corrupt the world.
Comfort thyself: what comfort is in me?
I have lived my life, and that which I have done
May He within himself make pure! but thou,
If thou shouldst never see my face again,
415 Pray for my soul. More things are wrought by prayer
Than this world dreams of. Wherefore, let thy voice
Rise like a fountain for me night and day.
For what are men better than sheep or goats
That nourish a blind life within the brain,
420 If, knowing God, they lift not hands of prayer
Both for themselves and those who call them friend?
For so the whole round earth is every way
Bound by gold chains about the feet of God.
But now farewell. I am going a long way
425 With these thou seëst—if indeed I go
(For all my mind is clouded with a doubt)—
To the island-valley of Avilion;[7]
Where falls not hail, or rain, or any snow,
Nor ever wind blows loudly: but it lies
430 Deep-meadowed, happy, fair with orchard lawns
And bowery hollows crowned with summer sea,
Where I will heal me of my grievous wound."

    So said he, and the barge with oar and sail
Moved from the brink, like some full-breasted swan
435 That, fluting a wild carol ere her death,
Ruffles her pure cold plume, and takes the flood
With swarthy webs. Long stood Sir Bedivere
Revolving many memories, till the hull
Looked one black dot against the verge of dawn,
440 And on the mere the wailing died away.

    But when that moan had passed for evermore,
The stillness of the dead world's winter dawn

---

6. I.e., the star that guided the three kings ("Elders") to the Christ child at Bethlehem.
7. Or Avalon, in Celtic mythology and medieval romance, the Vale of the Blessed where heroes enjoyed life after death.

Amazed him, and he groaned, "The King is gone."
And therewithal came on him the weird rhyme,[8]
445 "From the great deep to the great deep he goes."

Whereat he slowly turned and slowly clomb
The last hard footstep of that iron crag;
Thence marked the black hull moving yet, and cried,
"He passes to be King among the dead,
450 And after healing of his grievous wound
He comes again; but—if he come no more—
O me, be yon dark Queens in yon black boat,
Who shrieked and wailed, the three whereat we gazed
On that high day, when, clothed with living light,
455 They stood before his throne in silence, friends
Of Arthur, who should help him at his need?"

Then from the dawn it seemed there came, but faint
As from beyond the limit of the world,
Like the last echo born of a great cry,
460 Sounds, as if some fair city were one voice
Around a king returning from his wars.

Thereat once more he moved about, and clomb
Even to the highest he could climb, and saw,
Straining his eyes beneath an arch of hand,
465 Or thought he saw, the speck that bare the King,
Down that long water opening on the deep
Somewhere far off, pass on and on, and go
From less to less and vanish into light.
And the new sun rose bringing the new year.

1833–69   1869

Flower in the Crannied Wall

Flower in the crannied wall,
I pluck you out of the crannies,
I hold you here, root and all, in my hand,
Little flower—but if I could understand
5 What you are, root and all, and all in all,
I should know what God and man is.

1869

Crossing the Bar[1]

Sunset and evening star,
And one clear call for me!
And may there be no moaning of the bar,[2]
When I put out to sea,

8. A mysterious prophecy in verse had been spoken by Merlin concerning Arthur's birth; see *The Coming of Arthur,* lines 409–10.
1. Although not the last poem written by Tennyson, *Crossing the Bar* appears, at his request, as the final poem in all collections of his work.
2. Mournful sound of the ocean beating on a sand bar at the mouth of a harbor.

5   But such a tide as moving seems asleep,
     Too full for sound and foam,
   When that which drew from out the boundless deep
     Turns again home.

   Twilight and evening bell,
10   And after that the dark!
   And may there be no sadness of farewell,
     When I embark;

   For though from out our bourne° of Time and Place   *boundary*
     The flood may bear me far,
15   I hope to see my Pilot face to face[3]
     When I have crossed the bar.

1889   1889

---

3. The expression "face to face" also occurs in two lines of section 131 of *In Memoriam* not used but left in manuscript: "And come to look on those we loved / And That which made us, face to face."

ELIZABETH GASKELL
1810–1865

It is ironic that the writer whom contemporaries and future generations knew as "Mrs. Gaskell" once instructed her sister-in-law that it was "a silly piece of bride-like affectation not to sign yourself by your proper name." Despite the wifely identity that the name Mrs. Gaskell connotes, Elizabeth Gaskell, as she always signed herself, wrote fiction on contemporary social topics that stimulated considerable controversy. Her first novel, *Mary Barton* (1848), presents a sympathetic picture of the hardships and the grievances of the working class. Another early novel, *Ruth* (1853), portrays the seduction and rehabilitation of an unwed mother.

Elizabeth Cleghorn Gaskell was born in 1810 in Chelsea, on the outskirts of London, to a Unitarian family. Her mother died when Gaskell was one, and the girl was sent to rural Knutsford, in Cheshire, to be raised by her aunt. At the age of twenty-one, she met and married William Gaskell, a Unitarian minister whose chapel was in the industrial city of Manchester. For the first ten years of her marriage, she led the life of a minister's wife, bearing five children, keeping a house, and helping her husband serve his congregation. When her fourth child and only son, William, died at the age of one year, Gaskell grew despondent. Her husband encouraged her to write as a way of allaying her grief, and so she produced *Mary Barton*, subtitled *A Tale of Manchester Life*. In the preface to the novel she wrote that she was inspired by thinking "how deep might be the romance in the lives of some of those who elbowed me daily in the busy streets of the town in which I resided. I had always felt a deep sympathy with the careworn men, who looked as if doomed to struggle through their lives in strange alternations between work and want." She observes the bitterness of their resentment against the rich and sets herself the task of creating understanding and sympathy for them.

Anonymously published, the novel was widely reviewed and discussed. Elizabeth Gaskell was soon identified as the author; she subsequently developed a wide acquaintance in literary circles. She wrote five more novels and about thirty short stories, many of which were published in Dickens's journal *Household Words*, later titled *All the Year Round*. The contrasting experiences Gaskell's life had given her of the south and the north, of rural Knutsford and industrial Manchester, defined the poles of her fiction. Her second novel, *Cranford* (1853), presents a delicate picture of the small events of country village life, a subject to which she returns with greater range and psychological depth in her last novel, *Wives and Daughters* (1866). In *North and South* (1855), Gaskell brings together the two worlds of her fiction in the story of Margaret Hale, a young woman from the south who moves to a factory town in the north.

One of the writers her literary fame led her to know was Charlotte Brontë, with whom she became friends. When Brontë died in 1855, Gaskell was approached by Patrick Brontë to write the story of his daughter's life. Gaskell's *Life of Charlotte Brontë* (1857) is a masterpiece of English biography and one of Gaskell's finest portrayals of character. Her focus in the *Life* on the relationship between Brontë's identity as a writer and her role as daughter, sister, and wife reflects the balance Gaskell herself sought between the stories she wove and the people she tended. "My dear Scheherazade," Dickens called her, words of praise and affection in which future readers have joined.

The Old Nurse's Story[1]

You know, my dears, that your mother was an orphan, and an only child; and I dare say you have heard that your grandfather was a clergyman up in Westmoreland, where I come from. I was just a girl in the village school, when, one day, your grandmother came in to ask the mistress if there was any scholar there who would do for a nurse-maid; and mighty proud I was, I can tell ye, when the mistress called me up, and spoke to my being a good girl at my needle, and a steady honest girl, and one whose parents were very respectable, though they might be poor. I thought I should like nothing better than to serve the pretty young lady, who was blushing as deep as I was, as she spoke of the coming baby, and what I should have to do with it. However, I see you don't care so much for this part of my story, as for what you think is to come, so I'll tell you at once I was engaged, and settled at the parsonage before Miss Rosamond (that was the baby, who is now your mother) was born. To be sure, I had little enough to do with her when she came, for she was never out of her mother's arms, and slept by her all night long; and proud enough was I sometimes when missis trusted her to me. There never was such a baby before or since, though you've all of you been fine enough in your turns; but for sweet winning ways, you've none of you come up to your mother. She took after her mother, who was a real lady born; a Miss Furnivall, a granddaughter of Lord Furnivall's in Northumberland. I believe she had neither brother nor sister, and had been brought up in my lord's family till she had married your grandfather, who was just a curate, son to a shopkeeper in Carlisle—but a clever fine gentleman as ever was—and one who was a right-down hard worker in his parish, which was very wide, and scattered all abroad over the Westmoreland Fells. When your mother, little Miss Rosamond, was about four or five years old, both her parents died in a fort-

---

1. Originally published anonymously in the 1852 Christmas number of Dickens's journal *Household Words;* it was later republished in Gaskell's *Lizzie Leigh, and Other Tales* (1855).

night—one after the other. Ah! that was a sad time. My pretty young mistress and me was looking for another baby, when my master came home from one of his long rides, wet and tired, and took the fever he died of; and then she never held up her head again, but just lived to see her dead baby, and have it laid on her breast before she sighed away her life. My mistress had asked me, on her death-bed, never to leave Miss Rosamond; but if she had never spoken a word, I would have gone with the little child to the end of the world.

The next thing, and before we had well stilled our sobs, the executors and guardians came to settle the affairs. They were my poor young mistress's own cousin, Lord Furnivall, and Mr. Esthwaite, my master's brother, a shop-keeper in Manchester; not so well to do then, as he was afterwards, and with a large family rising about him. Well! I don't know if it were their settling, or because of a letter my mistress wrote on her death-bed to her cousin, my lord; but somehow it was settled that Miss Rosamond and me were to go to Furnivall Manor House, in Northumberland, and my lord spoke as if it had been her mother's wish that she should live with his family, and as if he had no objections, for that one or two more or less could make no difference in so grand a household. So, though that was not the way in which I should have wished the coming of my bright and pretty pet to have been looked at— who was like a sunbeam in any family, be it never so grand—I was well pleased that all the folks in the Dale should stare and admire, when they heard I was going to be young lady's maid at my Lord Furnivall's at Furnivall Manor.

But I made a mistake in thinking we were to go and live where my lord did. It turned out that the family had left Furnivall Manor House fifty years or more. I could not hear that my poor young mistress had ever been there, though she had been brought up in the family; and I was sorry for that, for I should have liked Miss Rosamond's youth to have passed where her mother's had been.

My lord's gentleman, from whom I asked as many questions as I durst, said that the Manor House was at the foot of the Cumberland Fells, and a very grand place; that an old Miss Furnivall, a great-aunt of my lord's, lived there, with only a few servants; but that it was a very healthy place, and my lord had thought that it would suit Miss Rosamond very well for a few years, and that her being there might perhaps amuse his old aunt.

I was bidden by my lord to have Miss Rosamond's things ready by a certain day. He was a stern, proud man, as they say all the Lord Furnivalls were; and he never spoke a word more than was necessary. Folk did say he had loved my young mistress; but that, because she knew that his father would object, she would never listen to him, and married Mr. Esthwaite; but I don't know. He never married at any rate. But he never took much notice of Miss Rosamond; which I thought he might have done if he had cared for her dead mother. He sent his gentleman with us to the Manor House, telling him to join him at Newcastle that same evening; so there was no great length of time for him to make us known to all the strangers before he, too, shook us off; and we were left, two lonely young things (I was not eighteen), in the great old Manor House. It seems like yesterday that we drove there. We had left our own dear parsonage very early, and we had both cried as if our hearts would break, though we were travelling in my lord's carriage, which I had thought so much of once. And now it was long past noon on a September day, and we stopped to change horses for the last time at a little smoky town, all full of colliers and miners. Miss Rosamond had fallen asleep, but Mr. Henry told me to waken her, that she might see the park and the Manor House as we drove up. I thought it rather a pity; but I did what he bade me, for fear he should complain of me to my lord. We had left all signs of a town or even a village, and were then inside the gates of a large wild park—not like the parks here in the south, but with rocks, and the noise of running water, and gnarled thorn-trees, and old oaks, all white and peeled with age.

The road went up about two miles, and then we saw a great and stately house, with many trees close around it, so close that in some places their branches dragged against the walls when the wind blew; and some hung broken down; for no one seemed to take much charge of the place;—to lop the wood, or to keep the moss-covered carriage-way in order. Only in front of the house all was clear. The great oval drive was without a weed; and neither tree nor creeper was allowed to grow over the long, many-windowed front; at both sides of which a wing projected, which were each the ends of other side fronts; for the house, although it was so desolate, was even grander than I expected. Behind it rose the Fells, which seemed unenclosed and bare enough; and on the left hand of the house as you stood facing it, was a little old-fashioned flower-garden, as I found out afterwards. A door opened out upon it from the west front; it had been scooped out of the thick dark wood for some old Lady Furnivall; but the branches of the great forest trees had grown and overshadowed it again, and there were very few flowers that would live there at that time.

When we drove up to the great front entrance, and went into the hall I thought we should be lost—it was so large, and vast, and grand. There was a chandelier all of bronze, hung down from the middle of the ceiling; and I had never seen one before, and looked at it all in amaze. Then, at one end of the hall, was a great fire-place, as large as the sides of the houses in my country, with massy andirons and dogs to hold the wood; and by it were heavy old-fashioned sofas. At the opposite end of the hall, to the left as you went in—on the western side—was an organ built into the wall, and so large that it filled up the best part of that end. Beyond it, on the same side, was a door; and opposite, on each side of the fire-place, were also doors leading to the east front; but those I never went through as long as I stayed in the house, so I can't tell you what lay beyond.

The afternoon was closing in, and the hall, which had no fire lighted in it, looked dark and gloomy; but we did not stay there a moment. The old servant who had opened the door for us bowed to Mr. Henry, and took us in through the door at the further side of the great organ, and led us through several smaller halls and passages into the west drawing-room, where he said that Miss Furnivall was sitting. Poor little Miss Rosamond held very tight to me, as if she were scared and lost in that great place, and, as for myself, I was not much better. The west drawing-room was very cheerful-looking, with a warm fire in it, and plenty of good comfortable furniture about. Miss Furnivall was an old lady not far from eighty, I should think, but I do not know. She was thin and tall, and had a face as full of fine wrinkles as if they had been drawn all over it with a needle's point. Her eyes were very watchful, to make up, I suppose, for her being so deaf as to be obliged to use a trumpet.[2] Sitting with her, working at the same great piece of tapestry, was Mrs. Stark, her maid and companion, and almost as old as she was. She had lived with Miss Furnivall ever since they both were young, and now she seemed more like a friend than a servant; she looked so cold and grey, and stony, as if she had never loved or cared for any one; and I don't suppose she did care for any one, except her mistress; and, owing to the great deafness of the latter, Mrs. Stark treated her very much as if she were a child. Mr. Henry gave some message from my lord, and then he bowed good-bye to us all,—taking no notice of my sweet little Miss Rosamond's out-stretched hand—and left us standing there, being looked at by the two old ladies through their spectacles.

I was right glad when they rung for the old footman who had shown us in at first, and told him to take us to our rooms. So we went out of that great drawing-room, and into another sitting-room, and out of that, and then up a great flight of stairs, and along a broad gallery—which was something like a library, having books all down one side, and windows and writing-tables all down the other—till we came to our rooms, which I was not sorry to hear were just over the kitchens; for I began to think I should be lost in that wilderness of a house. There was an old nursery, that had been used for all the little lords and ladies long ago, with a pleasant fire burning in the grate, and the kettle boiling on the hob, and tea things spread out on the table; and out of that room was the night-nursery, with a little crib for Miss Rosamond close to my bed. And old James called up Dorothy, his wife, to bid us welcome; and both he and she were so hospitable and kind, that by-and-by Miss Rosamond and me felt quite at home; and by the time tea was over, she was sitting on Dorothy's knee, and chattering away as fast as her little tongue could go. I soon found out that Dorothy was from Westmoreland, and that bound her and me together, as it were; and I would never wish to meet with kinder people than were old James and his wife. James had lived pretty nearly all his life in my lord's family, and thought there was no one so grand as they. He even looked down a little on his wife; because, till he had married her, she had never lived in any but a farmer's household. But he was very fond of her, as well he might be. They had one servant under them, to do all the rough work. Agnes they called her; and she and me, and James and Dorothy, with Miss Furnivall and Mrs. Stark, made up the family; always remembering my sweet little Miss Rosamond! I used to wonder what they had done before she came, they thought so much of her now. Kitchen and drawing-room, it was all the same. The hard, sad Miss Furnivall, and the cold Mrs. Stark, looked pleased when she came fluttering in like a bird, playing and pranking hither and thither, with a continual murmur, and pretty prattle of gladness. I am sure, they were sorry many a time when she flitted away into the kitchen, though they were too proud to ask her to stay with them, and were a little surprised at her taste; though, to be sure, as Mrs. Stark said, it was not to be wondered at, remembering what stock her father had come of. The great, old rambling house, was a famous place for little Miss Rosamond. She made expeditions all over it, with me at her heels; all, except the east wing, which was never opened, and whither we never thought

2. A horn-shaped device used by the hard of hearing to amplify sound.

of going. But in the western and northern part was many a pleasant room; full of things that were curiosities to us, though they might not have been to people who had seen more. The windows were darkened by the sweeping boughs of the trees, and the ivy which had overgrown them: but, in the green gloom, we could manage to see old China jars and carved ivory boxes, and great heavy books, and, above all, the old pictures!

Once, I remember, my darling would have Dorothy go with us to tell us who they all were; for they were all portraits of some of my lord's family, though Dorothy could not tell us the names of every one. We had gone through most of the rooms, when we came to the old state drawing-room over the hall, and there was a picture of Miss Furnivall; or, as she was called in those days, Miss Grace, for she was the younger sister. Such a beauty she must have been! but with such a set, proud look, and such scorn looking out of her handsome eyes, with her eyebrows just a little raised, as if she wondered how any one could have the impertinence to look at her; and her lip curled at us, as we stood there gazing. She had a dress on, the like of which I had never seen before, but it was all the fashion when she was young; a hat of some soft white stuff like beaver, pulled a little over her brows, and a beautiful plume of feathers sweeping round it on one side; and her gown of blue satin was open in front to a quilted white stomacher.[3]

"Well, to be sure!" said I, when I had gazed my fill. "Flesh is grass, they do say; but who would have thought that Miss Furnivall had been such an out-and-out beauty, to see her now?"

"Yes," said Dorothy. "Folks change sadly. But if what my master's father used to say was true, Miss Furnivall, the elder sister, was handsomer than Miss Grace. Her picture is here somewhere; but, if I show it you, you must never let on, even to James, that you have seen it. Can the little lady hold her tongue, think you?" asked she.

I was not so sure, for she was such a little sweet, bold, open-spoken child, so I set her to hide herself; and then I helped Dorothy to turn a great picture, that leaned with its face towards the wall, and was not hung up as the others were. To be sure, it beat Miss Grace for beauty; and, I think, for scornful pride, too, though in that matter it might be hard to choose. I could have looked at it an hour, but Dorothy seemed half frightened of having shown it to me, and hurried it back again, and bade me run and find Miss Rosamond, for that there were some ugly places about the house, where she should like ill for the child to go. I was a brave, high-spirited girl, and thought little of what the old woman said, for I liked hide-and-seek as well as any child in the parish; so off I ran to find my little one.

As winter drew on, and the days grew shorter, I was sometimes almost certain that I heard a noise as if some one was playing on the great organ in the hall. I did not hear it every evening; but, certainly, I did very often; usually when I was sitting with Miss Rosamond, after I had put her to bed, and keeping quite still and silent in the bedroom. Then I used to hear it booming and swelling away in the distance. The first night, when I went down to my supper, I asked Dorothy who had been playing music, and James said very shortly that I was a gowk to take the wind soughing[4] among the trees for

---

3. Ornamental covering for the front of the body.   4. Moaning.
"Beaver": felted wool.

music; but I saw Dorothy look at him very fearfully, and Bessy, the kitchen-maid, said something beneath her breath, and went quite white. I saw they did not like my question, so I held my peace till I was with Dorothy alone, when I knew I could get a good deal out of her. So, the next day, I watched my time, and I coaxed and asked her who it was that played the organ; for I knew that it was the organ and not the wind well enough, for all I had kept silence before James. But Dorothy had had her lesson, I'll warrant, and never a word could I get from her. So then I tried Bessy, though I had always held my head rather above her, as I was evened to James and Dorothy, and she was little better than their servant. So she said I must never, never tell; and, if I ever told, I was never to say *she* had told me; but it was a very strange noise, and she had heard it many a time, but most of all on winter nights, and before storms; and folks did say, it was the old lord playing on the great organ in the hall, just as he used to do when he was alive; but who the old lord was, or why he played, and why he played on stormy winter evenings in particular, she either could not or would not tell me. Well! I told you I had a brave heart; and I thought it was rather pleasant to have that grand music rolling about the house, let who would be the player; for now it rose above the great gusts of wind, and wailed and triumphed just like a living creature, and then it fell to a softness most complete; only it was always music and tunes, so it was nonsense to call it the wind. I thought, at first, it might be Miss Furnivall who played, unknown to Bessy; but, one day when I was in the hall by myself, I opened the organ and peeped all about it, and around it, as I had done to the organ in Crosthwaite Church once before, and I saw it was all broken and destroyed inside, though it looked so brave and fine; and then, though it was noon-day, my flesh began to creep a little, and I shut it up, and ran away pretty quickly to my own bright nursery; and I did not like hearing the music for some time after that, any more than James and Dorothy did. All this time Miss Rosamond was making herself more and more beloved. The old ladies liked her to dine with them at their early dinner; James stood behind Miss Furnivall's chair, and I behind Miss Rosamond's, all in state; and, after dinner, she would play about in a corner of the great drawing-room, as still as any mouse, while Miss Furnivall slept, and I had my dinner in the kitchen. But she was glad enough to come to me in the nursery afterwards; for, as she said, Miss Furnivall was so sad, and Mrs. Stark so dull; but she and I were merry enough; and, by-and-by, I got not to care for that weird rolling music, which did one no harm, if we did not know where it came from.

That winter was very cold. In the middle of October the frosts began, and lasted many, many weeks. I remember, one day at dinner, Miss Furnivall lifted up her sad, heavy eyes, and said to Mrs. Stark, "I am afraid we shall have a terrible winter," in a strange kind of meaning way. But Mrs. Stark pretended not to hear, and talked very loud of something else. My little lady and I did not care for the frost;—not we! As long as it was dry we climbed up the steep brows, behind the house, and went up on the Fells, which were bleak and bare enough, and there we ran races in the fresh, sharp air; and once we came down by a new path that took us past the two old gnarled holly-trees, which grew about half-way down by the east side of the house. But the days grew shorter and shorter; and the old lord, if it was he, played away more and more stormily and sadly on the great organ. One Sunday afternoon,—it must have been towards the end of November—I asked Dorothy to take charge of little Missey when she came out of the drawing-room, after Miss Furnivall had had her nap; for it was too cold to take her with me to church, and yet I wanted to go. And Dorothy was glad enough to promise, and was so fond of the child that all seemed well; and Bessy and I set off very briskly, though the sky hung heavy and black over the white earth, as if the night had never fully gone away; and the air, though still, was very biting and keen.

"We shall have a fall of snow," said Bessy to me. And sure enough, even while we were in church, it came down thick, in great large flakes, so thick it almost darkened the windows. It had stopped snowing before we came out, but it lay soft, thick and deep beneath our feet, as we tramped home. Before we got to the hall the moon rose, and I think it was lighter then,—what with the moon, and what with the white dazzling snow—than it had been when we went to church, between two and three o'clock. I have not told you that Miss Furnivall and Mrs. Stark never went to church: they used to read the prayers together, in their quiet gloomy way; they seemed to feel the Sunday very long without their tapestry-work to be busy at. So when I went to Dorothy in the kitchen, to fetch Miss Rosamond and take her up-stairs with me, I did not much wonder when the old woman told me that the ladies had kept the child with them, and that she had never come to the kitchen, as I had bidden her, when she was tired of behaving pretty in the drawing-room. So I took off my things and went to find her, and bring her to her supper in the nursery. But when I went into the best drawing-room, there sat the two old ladies, very still and quiet, dropping out a word now and then, but looking as if nothing so bright and merry as Miss Rosamond had ever been near them. Still I thought she might be hiding from me; it was one of her pretty ways; and that she had persuaded them to look as if they knew nothing about her; so I went softly peeping under this sofa, and behind that chair, making believe I was sadly frightened at not finding her.

"What's the matter, Hester?" said Mrs. Stark sharply. I don't know if Miss Furnivall had seen me, for, as I told you, she was very deaf, and she sat quite still, idly staring into the fire, with her hopeless face. "I'm only looking for my little Rosy-Posy," replied I, still thinking that the child was there, and near me, though I could not see her.

"Miss Rosamond is not here," said Mrs. Stark. "She went away more than an hour ago to find Dorothy." And she too turned and went on looking into the fire.

My heart sank at this, and I began to wish I had never left my darling. I went back to Dorothy and told her. James was gone out for the day, but she and me and Bessy took lights, and went up into the nursery first and then we roamed over the great large house, calling and entreating Miss Rosamond to come out of her hiding place, and not frighten us to death in that way. But there was no answer; no sound.

"Oh!" said I at last, "Can she have got into the east wing and hidden there?"

But Dorothy said it was not possible, for that she herself had never been in there; that the doors were always locked, and my lord's steward had the keys, she believed; at any rate, neither she nor James had ever seen them: so, I said I would go back and see it, after all, she was not hidden in the drawing-room, unknown to the old ladies; and if I found her there, I would whip her well for the fright she had given me; but I never meant to do it. Well, I went back to the west drawing-room, and I told Mrs. Stark we could not find her anywhere, and asked for leave to look all about the furniture there, for I thought now, that she might have fallen asleep in some warm hidden corner; but no! we looked, Miss Furnivall got up and looked, trembling all over, and she was no where there; then we set off again, every one in the house, and looked in all the places we had searched before, but we could not find her. Miss Furnivall shivered and shook so much, that Mrs. Stark took her back into the warm drawing-room; but not before they had made me promise to bring her to them when she was found. Well-a-day! I began to think she never would be found, when I bethought me to look out into the great front court, all covered with snow. I was up-stairs when I looked out; but, it was such clear moonlight, I could see quite plain two little footprints, which might be traced from the hall door, and round the corner of the east wing. I don't know how I got down, but I tugged open the great, stiff hall door; and, throwing the skirt of my gown over my head for a cloak, I ran out. I turned the east corner, and there a black shadow fell on the snow; but when I came again into the moonlight, there were the little footmarks going up—up to the Fells. It was bitter cold; so cold that the air almost took the skin off my face as I ran, but I ran on, crying to think how my poor little darling must be perished and frightened. I was within sight of the holly-trees, when I saw a shepherd coming down the hill, bearing something in his arms wrapped in his maud.[5] He shouted to me, and asked me if I had lost a bairn;[6] and, when I could not speak for crying, he bore towards me, and I saw my wee bairnie lying still, and white, and stiff, in his arms, as if she had been dead. He told me he had been up the Fells to gather in his sheep, before the deep cold of night came on, and that under the holly-trees (black marks on the hill-side, where no other bush was for miles around) he had found my little lady—my lamb—my queen—my darling—stiff and cold, in the terrible sleep which is frost-begotten. Oh! the joy, and the tears of having her in my arms once again! for I would not let him carry her; but took her, maud and all, into my own arms, and held her near my own warm neck and heart, and felt the life stealing slowly back again into her little gentle limbs. But she was still insensible when we reached the hall, and I had no breath for speech. We went in by the kitchen door.

"Bring the warming-pan," said I; and I carried her up-stairs and began undressing her by the nursery fire, which Bessy had kept up. I called my little lammie all the sweet and playful names I could think of,—even while my eyes were blinded by my tears; and at last, oh! at length she opened her large blue eyes. Then I put her into her warm bed, and sent Dorothy down to tell Miss Furnivall that all was well; and I made up my mind to sit by my darling's bedside the live-long night. She fell away into a soft sleep as soon as her pretty head had touched the pillow, and I watched by her till morning light; when she wakened up bright and clear—or so I thought at first—and, my dears, so I think now.

She said, that she had fancied that she should like to go to Dorothy, for that both the old ladies were asleep, and it was very dull in the drawing-

5. Shawl of gray plaid used by shepherds in the region.   6. Child.

room; and that, as she was going through the west lobby, she saw the snow through the high window falling—falling—soft and steady; but she wanted to see it lying pretty and white on the ground; so she made her way into the great hall; and then, going to the window, she saw it bright and soft upon the drive; but while she stood there, she saw a little girl, not so old as she was, "but so pretty," said my darling, "and this little girl beckoned to me to come out; and oh, she was so pretty and so sweet, I could not choose but go." And then this other little girl had taken her by the hand, and side by side the two had gone round the east corner.

"Now you are a naughty little girl, and telling stories," said I. "What would your good mamma, that is in heaven, and never told a story in her life, say to her little Rosamond, if she heard her—and I dare say she does—telling stories!"

"Indeed, Hester," sobbed out my child; "I'm telling you true. Indeed I am."

"Don't tell me!" said I, very stern. "I tracked you by your foot-marks through the snow; there were only yours to be seen: and if you had had a little girl to go hand-in-hand with you up the hill, don't you think the foot-prints would have gone along with yours?"

"I can't help it, dear, dear Hester," said she, crying, "if they did not; I never looked at her feet, but she held my hand fast and tight in her little one, and it was very, very cold. She took me up the Fell-path, up to the holly trees; and there I saw a lady weeping and crying; but when she saw me, she hushed her weeping, and smiled very proud and grand, and took me on her knees, and began to lull me to sleep; and that's all, Hester—but that is true; and my dear mamma knows it is," said she, crying. So I thought the child was in a fever, and pretended to believe her, as she went over her story—over and over again, and always the same. At last Dorothy knocked at the door with Miss Rosamond's breakfast; and she told me the old ladies were down in the eating-parlour, and that they wanted to speak to me. They had both been into the night-nursery the evening before, but it was after Miss Rosamond was asleep; so they had only looked at her—not asked me any questions.

"I shall catch it," thought I to myself, as I went along the north gallery. "And yet," I thought, taking courage, "it was in their charge I left her; and it's they that's to blame for letting her steal away unknown and unwatched." So I went in boldly, and told my story. I told it all to Miss Furnivall, shouting it close to her ear; but when I came to the mention of the other little girl out in the snow, coaxing and tempting her out, and willing her up to the grand and beautiful lady by the Holly-tree, she threw her arms up—her old and withered arms—and cried aloud, "Oh! Heaven, forgive! Have mercy!"

Mrs. Stark took hold of her; roughly enough, I thought; but she was past Mrs. Stark's management, and spoke to me, in a kind of wild warning and authority.

"Hester! keep her from that child! It will lure her to her death! That evil child! Tell her it is a wicked, naughty child." Then, Mrs. Stark hurried me out of the room; where, indeed, I was glad enough to go; but Miss Furnivall kept shrieking out, "Oh! have mercy! Wilt Thou never forgive! It is many a long year ago——"

I was very uneasy in my mind after that. I durst never leave Miss Rosamond, night or day, for fear lest she might slip off again, after some fancy or other; and all the more, because I thought I could make out that Miss

Furnivall was crazy, from their odd ways about her; and I was afraid lest something of the same kind (which might be in the family, you know) hung over my darling. And the great frost never ceased all this time; and, whenever it was a more stormy night than usual, between the gusts, and through the wind, we heard the old lord playing on the great organ. But, old lord, or not, wherever Miss Rosamond went, there I followed; for my love for her, pretty helpless orphan, was stronger than my fear for the grand and terrible sound. Besides, it rested with me to keep her cheerful and merry, as beseemed her age. So we played together, and wandered together, here and there, and everywhere; for I never dared to lose sight of her again in that large and rambling house. And so it happened, that one afternoon, not long before Christmas day, we were playing together on the billiard-table in the great hall (not that we knew the right way of playing, but she liked to roll the smooth ivory balls with her pretty hands, and I liked to do whatever she did); and, by-and-bye, without our noticing it, it grew dusk indoors, though it was still light in the open air, and I was thinking of taking her back into the nursery, when, all of a sudden, she cried out:

"Look, Hester! look! there is my poor little girl out in the snow!"

I turned towards the long narrow windows, and there, sure enough, I saw a little girl, less than my Miss Rosamond—dressed all unfit to be out-of-doors such a bitter night—crying, and beating against the window-panes, as if, she wanted to be let in. She seemed to sob and wail, till Miss Rosamond could bear it no longer, and was flying to the door to open it, when, all of a sudden, and close upon us, the great organ pealed out so loud and thundering, it fairly made me tremble; and all the more, when I remembered me that, even in the stillness of that dead-cold weather, I had heard no sound of little battering hands upon the window-glass, although the Phantom Child had seemed to put forth all its force; and, although I had seen it wail and cry, no faintest touch of sound had fallen upon my ears. Whether I remembered all this at the very moment, I do not know; the great organ sound had so stunned me into terror; but this I know, I caught up Miss Rosamond before she got the hall-door opened, and clutched her, and carried her away, kicking and screaming, into the large bright kitchen, where Dorothy and Agnes were busy with their mince-pies.

"What is the matter with my sweet one?" cried Dorothy, as I bore in Miss Rosamond, who was sobbing as if her heart would break.

"She won't let me open the door for my little girl to come in; and she'll die if she is out on the Fells all night. Cruel, naughty Hester," she said, slapping me; but she might have struck harder, for I had seen a look of ghastly terror on Dorothy's face, which made my very blood run cold.

"Shut the back kitchen door fast, and bolt it well," said she to Agnes. She said no more; she gave me raisins and almonds to quiet Miss Rosamond: but she sobbed about the little girl in the snow, and would not touch any of the good things. I was thankful when she cried herself to sleep in bed. Then I stole down to the kitchen, and told Dorothy I had made up my mind. I would carry my darling back to my father's house in Applethwaite; where, if we lived humbly, we lived at peace. I said I had been frightened enough with the old lord's organ-playing; but now, that I had seen for myself this little moaning child, all decked out as no child in the neighborhood could be, beating and battering to get in, yet always without any sound or noise—with the dark wound on its right shoulder; and that Miss Rosamond had known it again for the phantom that had nearly lured her to her death (which Dorothy knew was true); I would stand it no longer.

I saw Dorothy change color once or twice. When I had done, she told me she did not think I could take Miss Rosamond with me, for that she was my lord's ward, and I had no right over her; and she asked me, would I leave the child that I was so fond of, just for sounds and sights that could do me no harm; and that they had all had to get used to in their turns? I was all in a hot, trembling passion; and I said it was very well for her to talk, that knew what these sights and noises betokened, and that had, perhaps, had something to do with the Spectre-child while it was alive. And I taunted her so, that she told me all she knew, at last; and then I wished I had never been told, for it only made me more afraid than ever.

She said she had heard the tale from old neighbors, that were alive when she was first married; when folks used to come to the hall sometimes, before it had got such a bad name on the country side: it might not be true, or it might, what she had been told.

The old lord was Miss Furnivall's father—Miss Grace, as Dorothy called her, for Miss Maude was the elder, and Miss Furnivall by rights. The old lord was eaten up with pride. Such a proud man was never seen or heard of; and his daughters were like him. No one was good enough to wed them, although they had choice enough; for they were the great beauties of their day, as I had seen by their portraits, where they hung in the state drawing-room. But, as the old saying is, "Pride will have a fall;" and these two haughty beauties fell in love with the same man, and he no better than a foreign musician, whom their father had down from London to play music with him at the Manor House. For, above all things, next to his pride, the old lord loved music. He could play on nearly every instrument that ever was heard of; and it was a strange thing it did not soften him; but he was a fierce dour old man, and had broken his poor wife's heart with his cruelty, they said. He was mad after music, and would pay any money for it. So he got this foreigner to come; who made such beautiful music, that they said the very birds on the trees stopped their singing to listen. And, by degrees, this foreign gentleman got such a hold over the old lord, that nothing would serve him but that he must come every year; and it was he that had the great organ brought from Holland and built up in the hall, where it stood now. He taught the old lord to play on it; but many and many a time, when Lord Furnivall was thinking of nothing but his fine organ, and his finer music, the dark foreigner was walking abroad in the woods with one of the young ladies; now Miss Maude, and then Miss Grace.

Miss Maude won the day and carried off the prize, such as it was; and he and she were married, all unknown to any one; and before he made his next yearly visit, she had been confined of a little girl at a farm-house on the Moors, while her father and Miss Grace thought she was away at Doncaster Races. But though she was a wife and a mother, she was not a bit softened, but as haughty and as passionate as ever; and perhaps more so, for she was jealous of Miss Grace, to whom her foreign husband paid a deal of court—by way of blinding her—as he told his wife. But Miss Grace triumphed over Miss Maude, and Miss Maude grew fiercer and fiercer, both with her husband and with her sister; and the former—who could easily shake off what was disagreeable, and hide himself in foreign countries—went away a month before his usual time that summer, and half threatened that he would never come back again. Meanwhile, the little girl was left at the farm-house, and her mother used to have her horse saddled and gallop wildly over the hills to see her once every week, at the very least—for where she loved, she loved; and where she hated, she hated. And the old lord went on playing—playing on his organ; and the servants thought the sweet music he made had soothed down his awful temper, of which (Dorothy said) some terrible tales could be told. He grew infirm too, and had to walk with a crutch; and his son—that was the present Lord Furnivall's father—was with the army in America, and the other son at sea; so Miss Maude had it pretty much her own way, and she and Miss Grace grew colder and bitterer to each other every day; till at last they hardly ever spoke, except when the old lord was by. The foreign musician came again the next summer, but it was for the last time; for they led him such a life with their jealously and their passions, that he grew weary, and went away, and never was heard of again. And Miss Maude, who had always meant to have her marriage acknowledged when her father should be dead, was left now a deserted wife—whom nobody knew to have been married—with a child that she dared not own, although she loved it to distraction; living with a father whom she feared, and a sister whom she hated. When the next summer passed over and the dark foreigner never came, both Miss Maude and Miss Grace grew gloomy and sad; they had a haggard look about them, though they looked handsome as ever. But by and by Miss Maude brightened; for her father grew more and more infirm, and more than ever carried away by his music; and she and Miss Grace lived almost entirely apart, having separate rooms, the one on the west side—Miss Maude on the east—those very rooms which were now shut up. So she thought she might have her little girl with her, and no one need ever know except those who dared not speak about it, and were bound to believe that it was, as she said, a cottager's child she had taken a fancy to. All this, Dorothy said, was pretty well known; but what came afterwards no one knew, except Miss Grace, and Mrs. Stark, who was even then her maid, and much more of a friend to her than ever her sister had been. But the servants supposed, from words that were dropped, that Miss Maude had triumphed over Miss Grace, and told her that all the time the dark foreigner had been mocking her with pretended love—he was her own husband; the color left Miss Grace's cheek and lips that very day for ever, and she was heard to say many a time that sooner or later she would have her revenge; and Mrs. Stark was for ever spying about the east rooms.

One fearful night, just after the New Year had come in, when the snow was lying thick and deep, and the flakes were still falling—fast enough to blind any one who might be out and abroad—there was a great and violent noise heard, and the old lord's voice above all, cursing and swearing awfully,—and the cries of a little child,—and the proud defiance of a fierce woman,—and the sound of a blow,—and a dead stillness,—and moans and wailings dying away on the hill-side! Then the old lord summoned all his servants, and told them, with terrible oaths, and words more terrible, that his daughter had disgraced herself, and that he had turned her out of doors,—her, and her child,—and that if ever they gave her help,—or food—

or shelter,—he prayed that they might never enter Heaven. And, all the while, Miss Grace stood by him, white and still as any stone; and when he had ended she heaved a great sigh, as much as to say her work was done, and her end was accomplished. But the old lord never touched his organ again, and died within the year; and no wonder! for, on the morrow of that wild and fearful night, the shepherds, coming down the Fell side, found Miss Maude sitting, all crazy and smiling, under the holly-trees, nursing a dead child,—with a terrible mark on its right shoulder. "But that was not what killed it," said Dorothy; "it was the frost and the cold—every wild creature was in its hole, and every beast in its fold,—while the child and its mother were turned out to wander on the Fells! And now you know all! and I wonder if you are less frightened now?"

I was more frightened than ever; but I said I was not. I wished Miss Rosamond and myself well out of that dreadful house for ever; but I would not leave her, and I dared not take her away. But oh! how I watched her, and guarded her! We bolted the doors, and shut the window-shutters fast, an hour or more before dark, rather than leave them open five minutes too late. But my little lady still heard the weird child crying and mourning; and not all we could do or say, could keep her from wanting to go to her, and let her in from the cruel wind and the snow. All this time, I kept away from Miss Furnivall and Mrs. Stark, as much as ever I could; for I feared them—I knew no good could be about them, with their grey hard faces, and their dreamy eyes, looking back into the ghastly years that were gone. But, even in my fear, I had a kind of pity—for Miss Furnivall, at least. Those gone down to the pit can hardly have a more hopeless look than that which was ever on her face. At last I even got so sorry for her—who never said a word but what was quite forced from her—that I prayed for her; and I taught Miss Rosamond to pray for one who had done a deadly sin; but often when she came to those words, she would listen, and start up from her knees, and say, "I hear my little girl plaining and crying very sad—Oh! let her in, or she will die!"

One night—just after New Year's Day had come at last, and the long winter had taken a turn as I hoped—I heard the west drawing-room bell ring three times, which was the signal for me. I would not leave Miss Rosamond alone, for all she was asleep—for the old lord had been playing wilder than ever— and I feared lest my darling should waken to hear the spectre child; see her I knew she could not, I had fastened the windows too well for that. So, I took her out of her bed and wrapped her up in such outer clothes as were most handy, and carried her down to the drawing-room, where the old ladies sat at their tapestry work as usual. They looked up when I came in, and Mrs. Stark asked, quite astounded, "Why did I bring Miss Rosamond there, out of her warm bed?" I had begun to whisper, "Because I was afraid of her being tempted out while I was away, by the wild child in the snow," when she stopped me short (with a glance at Miss Furnivall) and said Miss Furnivall wanted me to undo some work she had done wrong, and which neither of them could see to unpick. So, I laid my pretty dear on the sofa, and sat down on a stool by them, and hardened my heart against them as I heard the wind rising and howling.

Miss Rosamond slept on sound, for all the wind blew so; and Miss Furnivall said never a word, nor looked round when the gusts shook the windows. All at once she started up to her full height, and put up one hand as if to bid us listen.

"I hear voices!" said she. "I hear terrible screams—I hear my father's voice!"

Just at that moment, my darling wakened with a sudden start: "My little girl is crying, oh, how she is crying!" and she tried to get up and go to her, but she got her feet entangled in the blanket, and I caught her up; for my flesh had begun to creep at these noises, which they heard while we could catch no sound. In a minute or two the noises came, and gathered fast, and filled our ears; we, too, heard voices and screams, and no longer heard the winter's wind that raged abroad. Mrs. Stark looked at me, and I at her, but we dared not speak. Suddenly Miss Furnivall went towards the door, out into the ante-room, through the west lobby, and opened the door into the great hall. Mrs. Stark followed, and I durst not be left, though my heart almost stopped beating for fear. I wrapped my darling tight in my arms, and went out with them. In the hall the screams were louder than ever; they sounded to come from the east wing—nearer and nearer—close on the other side of the locked-up doors—close behind them. Then I noticed that the great bronze chandelier seemed all alight, though the hall was dim, and that a fire was blazing in the vast hearth-place, though it gave no heat; and I shuddered up with terror, and folded my darling closer to me. But as I did so, the east door shook, and she, suddenly struggling to get free from me, cried, "Hester! I must go! My little girl is there; I hear her; she is coming! Hester, I must go!"

I held her tight with all my strength; with a set will, I held her. If I had died, my hands would have grasped her still; I was so resolved in my mind. Miss Furnivall stood listening, and paid no regard to my darling, who had got down to the ground, and whom I, upon my knees now, was holding with both my arms clasped round her neck; she still striving and crying to get free.

All at once, the east door gave way with a thundering crash, as if torn open in a violent passion, and there came into that broad and mysterious light, the figure of a tall old man, with grey hair and gleaming eyes. He drove before him, with many a relentless gesture of abhorrence, a stern and beautiful woman, with a little child clinging to her dress.

"Oh Hester! Hester!" cried Miss Rosamond. "It's the lady! the lady below the holly-trees; and my little girl is with her. Hester! Hester! let me go to her; they are drawing me to them. I feel them—I feel them. I must go!"

Again she was almost convulsed by her efforts to get away; but I held her tighter and tighter; till I feared I should do her a hurt; but rather that than let her go towards those terrible phantoms. They passed along towards the great hall-door, where the winds howled and ravened for their prey; but before they reached that, the lady turned; and I could see that she defied the old man with a fierce and proud defiance; but then she quailed—and then she threw up her arms wildly and piteously to save her child—her little child—from a blow from his uplifted crutch.

And Miss Rosamond was torn as by a power stronger than mine, and writhed in my arms, and sobbed (for by this time the poor darling was growing faint).

"They want me to go with them on to the Fells—they are drawing me to them. Oh, my little girl! I would come, but cruel, wicked Hester holds me very tight." But when she saw the uplifted crutch she swooned away, and I thanked God for it. Just at this moment—when the tall old man, his hair streaming as in the blast of a furnace, was going to strike the little shrinking child—Miss Furnivall, the old woman by my side, cried out, "Oh, father! father! spare the little innocent child!" But just then I saw—we all saw—another phantom shape itself, and grow clear out of the blue and misty light that filled the hall; we had not seen her till now, for it was another lady who stood by the old man, with a look of relentless hate and triumphant scorn. That figure was very beautiful to look upon, with a soft white hat drawn down over the proud brows, and a red and curling lip. It was dressed in an open robe of blue satin. I had seen that figure before. It was the likeness of Miss Furnivall in her youth; and the terrible phantoms moved on, regardless of old Miss Furnivall's wild entreaty,—and the uplifted crutch fell on the right shoulder of the little child, and the younger sister looked on, stony and deadly serene. But at that moment, the dim lights, and the fire that gave no heat, went out of themselves, and Miss Furnivall lay at our feet stricken down by the palsy—death-stricken.

Yes! she was carried to her bed that night never to rise again. She lay with her face to the wall, muttering low but muttering alway: "Alas! alas! what is done in youth can never be undone in age! What is done in youth can never be undone in age!"

1852

ROBERT BROWNING
1812–1889

During the years of his marriage Robert Browning was sometimes referred to as "Mrs. Browning's husband." Elizabeth Barrett was at that time a famous poet, whereas her husband was a relatively unknown experimenter whose poems were greeted with misunderstanding or indifference. Not until the 1860s did he at last gain a public and become recognized as the rival or equal of Tennyson. In the twentieth century his reputation has persisted but in an unusual way: his poetry is admired by two groups of readers widely different in tastes. To one group, among whom are the Browning societies that have flourished in England and America, Browning is a wise philosopher and religious teacher who resolved the doubts that had troubled Arnold and Tennyson.

The second group of readers enjoy Browning less for his attempt to solve problems of religious doubt than for his attempt to solve the problems of how poetry should be written. Such poets as Ezra Pound and Robert Lowell have recognized that more than any other nineteenth-century poet, it was Browning who energetically hacked through a trail that has subsequently become the main road of twentieth-century poetry. In *Poetry and the Age* (1953) Randall Jarrell remarked how "the dramatic monologue, which once had depended for its effect upon being a departure from the norm of poetry, now became in one form or another the norm."

The dramatic monologue, as Browning uses it, separates the speaker from the poet in such a way that the reader must work through the words of the speaker to discover the meaning of the poet. For example, in the well-known early monologue *My Last Duchess*, we listen to the duke as he speaks of his dead wife. From his one-sided conversation we piece together the situation, both past and present, and we infer what sort of woman the duchess really was and what sort of man the duke is. Ultimately, we may also infer what the poet himself thinks of the speaker he has created. In this poem, it is fairly easy to reach such a judgment, although the pleasure of the poem results from our reconstruction of a story quite different from the one the duke thinks he is telling. Many of Browning's poems are far less stable, and it is difficult to discern the relationship of the poet to his speaker. In reading *A Grammarian's Funeral*, for example, can we be sure that the central character is a hero? Or is he merely a fool? In *"Childe Roland to the Dark Tower Came"* is the speaker describing a phantasmagoric landscape of his own paranoid imagining or is the poem a fable of courage and defiance in a modern wasteland?

In addition to his experiments with the dramatic monologue, Browning also experimented with language and syntax. The grotesque rhymes and jaw-breaking diction that he often employs have been repugnant to some critics; George Santayana, for instance, dismissed him as a clumsy barbarian. But to those who appreciate Browning, the incongruities of language are a humorous and appropriate counterpart to an imperfect world. Ezra Pound's tribute to "Old Hippety-Hop o' the accents," as he addresses Browning, is both affectionate and memorable:

> Heart that was big as the bowels of Vesuvius
> Words that were winged as her sparks in eruption,
> Eagled and thundered as Jupiter Pluvius
> Sound in your wind past all signs o' corruption.

Robert Browning was born in Camberwell, a London suburb. His father, a bank clerk, was a learned man with an extensive library. His mother was a kindly, religious-minded woman, interested in music, whose love for her brilliant son was warmly reciprocated. Until the time of his marriage, at the age of thirty-four, Browning was rarely absent from his parents' home. He attended a boarding school near Camberwell, traveled a little (to Russia and Italy), and was a student at the University of London for a short period, but he preferred to pursue his education at home, where he was tutored in foreign languages, music, boxing, and horsemanship and where he read omnivorously. From this unusual education he acquired a store of knowledge on which to draw for the background of his poems.

The "obscurity" of which his contemporaries complained in his earlier poetry may be partly accounted for by the circumstances of Browning's education, but it also reflects his anxious desire to avoid exposing himself too explicitly before his readers. His first poem, *Pauline,* published when he was twenty-one, had been modeled on the example of Shelley, the most personal of poets. When an otherwise admiring review by John Stuart Mill noted that the young author was afflicted with an "intense and morbid self-consciousness," Browning was overwhelmed with embarrassment. He resolved to avoid confessional writings thereafter.

One way of reducing the personal element in his poetry was to write plays instead of soul-searching narratives or lyrics. In 1836, encouraged by the actor W. C. Macready, Browning began work on his first play, *Strafford*, a historical tragedy that lasted only four nights when it was produced in London in 1837. For ten years, the young writer struggled to write for the theater, but all his stage productions remained failures. Nevertheless, writing dialogue for actors led him to explore another form more congenial to his genius, the dramatic monologue, a form that enabled him through imaginary speakers to avoid explicit autobiography. His first collection of such monologues, *Dramatic Lyrics*, appeared in 1842; but it received no more critical enthusiasm than did his plays.

Browning's resolution to avoid the subjective manner of Shelley did not preclude his being influenced by the earlier poet in other ways. At fourteen, when he first discovered Shelley's works, he became an atheist and liberal. Although he grew away from the atheism, after a struggle, and also the extreme phases of his liberalism, he retained from Shelley's influence something permanent and more difficult to define: an ardent dedication to ideals (often undefined ideals) and an energetic striving toward goals (often undefined goals).

Browning's ardent romanticism also found expression in his love affair with Elizabeth Barrett, which had the dramatic ingredients of Browning's own favorite story of St. George rescuing the maiden from the dragon. Almost everything seemed unpropitious when Browning met Elizabeth Barrett in 1845. She was six years older than he was, a semi-invalid, jealously guarded by her possessively tyrannical father. But love, as the poet was to say later, is best; and love swept aside all obstacles. After their elopement to Italy, the former semi-invalid was soon enjoying good health and a full life. The husband likewise seemed to thrive during the years of this remarkable marriage. His most memorable volume of poems, *Men and Women* (1855), reflects his enjoyment of Italy: its picturesque landscapes and lively street scenes as well as its monuments from the past—its Renaissance past in particular.

The happy fifteen-year sojourn in Italy ended in 1861 with Elizabeth's death. The widower returned to London with his son. During the twenty-eight years remaining to him, the quantity of verse he produced did not diminish. Nor, during the first decade, did it decrease in quality. *Dramatis Personae* (1864) is a volume containing some of his finest monologues, such as *Caliban upon Setebos*. And in 1868 he published his greatest single poem, *The Ring and the Book,* which was inspired by his discovery of an old book of legal records concerning a murder trial in seventeenth-century Rome. His poem tells the story of a brutally sadistic husband, Count Guido Franceschini. The middle-aged Guido grows dissatisfied with his young wife, Pompilia, and accuses her of having adulterous relations with a handsome priest who, like St. George, had tried to rescue her from the dragon's den in which her husband confined her. Eventually Guido stabs his wife to death and is himself executed. In a series of twelve books, Browning retells this tale of violence, presenting it from the contrasting points of view of participants and spectators. Because of its vast scale, *The Ring and the Book* is like a Victorian novel, but in its experiments with multiple points of view it anticipates later novels such as Conrad's *Lord Jim* (1900).

After *The Ring and the Book* several more volumes appeared. In general, Browning's writings during the last two decades of his life suffer from a certain mechanical repetition of mannerism and an excess of argumentation—faults into which he may have been led by the unqualified enthusiasm of his admirers, for it was during this period that he gained his great following. When he died, in 1889, he was buried in Westminster Abbey.

During the London years, Browning became abundantly fond of social life. He dined at the homes of friends and at clubs, where he enjoyed port wine and conversation. He would talk loudly and emphatically about many topics—except his own poetry, about which he was usually reticent.

Despite his bursts of outspokenness, Browning's character seemed, in Hardy's words, "*the* literary puzzle of the nineteenth century." Like Yeats, he was a poet preoccupied with masks. On the occasion of his burial, his friend Henry James reflected that many oddities and many great writers have been buried in Westminster Abbey, "but none of the odd ones have been so great and none of the great ones been so odd."

Just as Browning's character is hard to identify so also are his poems difficult to relate to the age in which they were written. Bishops and painters of the Renaissance, physicians of the Roman Empire, musicians of eighteenth-century Germany—as we explore this gallery of talking portraits we seem to be in a world of time long past, remote from the world of steam engines and disputes about human beings' descent from the ape.

Yet our first impression is misleading. Many of these portraits explore problems that confronted Browning's contemporaries, especially problems of faith and doubt, good and evil, and problems of the function of the artist in modern life. *Caliban upon Setebos,* for example, is a highly topical critique of Darwinism and of natural (as opposed to supernatural) religions. Browning's own attitude toward these topics is partially concealed because of his use of speakers and of settings from earlier ages, yet we do encounter certain recurrent religious assumptions that we can safely assign to the poet himself. The most recurrent is that God has created an imperfect world as a kind of testing ground, a "vale of soul-making," as Keats had said. It followed, for Browning's purposes, that the human soul must be immortal and that heaven itself be perfect. As Abt Vogler affirms: "On the earth the broken arcs; in the heaven, a perfect round." Armed with such a faith, Browning sometimes gives the impression that he was himself untroubled by the doubts that gnawed at the hearts of Arnold and Clough and Tennyson. Yet Browning's apparent optimism is consistently being tested by his bringing to light the evils of human nature. His gallery of villains— murderers, sadistic husbands, mean and petty manipulators—is an extraordinary one. Few writers, in fact, seem to have been more aware of the existence of evil.

A second aspect of Browning's poetry that separates it from the Victorian age is its style. The most representative Victorian poets such as Tennyson and Dante Gabriel Rossetti write in the manner of Keats, Milton, Spenser, and of classical poets such as Virgil. Theirs is the central stylistic tradition in English poetry, one that favors smoothly polished texture, elevated diction and subjects, and pleasing liquidity of sound. Browning draws from a different tradition, more colloquial and discordant, a tradition that includes the poetry of John Donne, the soliloquies of Shakespeare, and certain features of the narrative style of Chaucer. Of most significance are Browning's affinities with Donne. Both poets sacrifice, on occasion, the pleasures of harmony and of a consistent elevation of tone by using a harshly discordant style and unexpected juxtapositions that startle us into an awareness of a world of everyday realities and trivialities. Readers who dislike this kind of poetry in Browning or in Donne argue that it suffers from prosiness. Oscar Wilde once described the novelist George Meredith as "a prose Browning." And so, he added, was Browning. Wilde's joke may help us to relate Browning to his contemporaries. For if Browning seems out of step with other Victorian poets, he is by no means out of step with his contemporaries in prose. The grotesque, which plays such a prominent role in the style and subject matter of Carlyle and Dickens and in the aesthetic theories of John Ruskin, is equally prominent in Browning's verse:

> Fee, faw, fum! bubble and squeak!
> Blessedest Thursday's the fat of the week.
> Rumble and tumble, sleek and rough,
> Stinking and savory, smug and gruff.

Like Carlyle's *Sartor Resartus* these lines from *Holy-Cross Day* present a situation of grave seriousness with noisy jocularity. It was fitting that Browning and Carlyle remained good friends, even though the elder writer kept urging Browning to give up verse in favor of prose.

The link between Browning and the Victorian prose writers is not limited to style. With the later generation of Victorian novelists, George Eliot, George Meredith, and Henry James, Browning shares a central preoccupation. Like Eliot in particular, he was interested in exposing the devious ways in which our minds work and the complexity of our motives. "My stress lay on incidents in the development of a human soul," he wrote; "little else is worth study." His psychological insights can be illustrated in such poems as *The Bishop Orders His Tomb* and *Andrea del Sarto.* Although these are spoken monologues, not inner monologues in the manner of James Joyce, the insight into the workings of the mind is similarly acute. As in reading Joyce, we must be on our guard to follow the rapid shifts of the speakers' mental processes as jumps are made from one cluster of associations to another. A further challenge for the reader of Browning is to identify what has been left out. As was remarked in a letter by the 1890s poet Ernest Dowson, Browning's "masterpieces in verse" demonstrate both "subtlety" and "the tact of omission." *My Last Duchess,* he added, "is pure Henry James."

But Browning's role as a forerunner of twentieth-century literature should not blind us to his essential Victorianism. Energy is the most characteristic aspect of his writing and of the man (Turgenev compared Browning's handshake to an electric shock). Gerard Manley Hopkins described Browning as "a man bouncing up from table with his mouth full of bread and cheese and saying that he meant to stand no blasted nonsense." This buoyancy imparts a creative vitality to all of Browning's writings.

Porphyria's Lover[1]

The rain set early in tonight,
    The sullen wind was soon awake,
It tore the elm-tops down for spite,
    And did its worst to vex the lake:
5   I listened with heart fit to break.
When glided in Porphyria; straight
    She shut the cold out and the storm,
And kneeled and made the cheerless grate
    Blaze up, and all the cottage warm;
10   Which done, she rose, and from her form
Withdrew the dripping cloak and shawl,
    And laid her soiled gloves by, untied
Her hat and let the damp hair fall,
    And, last, she sat down by my side
15   And called me. When no voice replied,
She put my arm about her waist,
    And made her smooth white shoulder bare,
And all her yellow hair displaced,
    And, stooping, made my cheek lie there,
20   And spread, o'er all, her yellow hair,
Murmuring how she loved me—she
    Too weak, for all her heart's endeavor,
To set its struggling passion free
    From pride, and vainer ties dissever,
25   And give herself to me forever.
But passion sometimes would prevail,
    Nor could tonight's gay feast restrain
A sudden thought of one so pale
    For love of her, and all in vain:
30   So, she was come through wind and rain.
Be sure I looked up at her eyes
    Happy and proud; at last I knew
Porphyria worshiped me: surprise
    Made my heart swell, and still it grew
35   While I debated what to do.

---

1. One of a pair of monologues originally published under the title *Madhouse Cells,* a title that emphasized the abnormal state of mind of the speaker.

That moment she was mine, mine, fair,
    Perfectly pure and good: I found
A thing to do, and all her hair
    In one long yellow string I wound
40   Three times her little throat around,
And strangled her. No pain felt she;
    I am quite sure she felt no pain.
As a shut bud that holds a bee,
    I warily oped her lids: again
45   Laughed the blue eyes without a stain.
And I untightened next the tress
    About her neck; her cheek once more
Blushed bright beneath my burning kiss:
    I propped her head up as before,
50   Only, this time my shoulder bore
Her head, which droops upon it still:
    The smiling rosy little head,
So glad it has its utmost will,
    That all it scorned at once is fled,
55   And I, its love, am gained instead!
Porphyria's love: she guessed not how
    Her darling one wish would be heard.
And thus we sit together now,
    And all night long we have not stirred,
60   And yet God has not said a word!

1834   1836, 1842

Soliloquy of the Spanish Cloister

1

Gr-r-r—there go, my heart's abhorrence!
    Water your damned flowerpots, do!
If hate killed men, Brother Lawrence,
    God's blood, would not mine kill you!
5 What? your myrtle bush wants trimming?
    Oh, that rose has prior claims—
Needs its leaden vase filled brimming?
    Hell dry you up with its flames!

2

At the meal we sit together:
10   *Salve tibi!*[1] I must hear
Wise talk of the kind of weather,
    Sort of season, time of year:
Not a plenteous cork crop: scarcely
    Dare we hope oak-galls,[2] *I doubt:*

1. Hail to thee! (Latin). This and other speeches
in italics in this stanza are the words of Brother
Lawrence.

2. Abnormal outgrowths on oak trees, used for
tanning.

15 *What's the Latin name for "parsley"?*
      What's the Greek name for Swine's Snout?[3]

                              3

Whew! We'll have our platter burnished,
      Laid with care on our own shelf!
With a fire-new spoon we're furnished,
20   And a goblet for ourself,
Rinsed like something sacrificial
      Ere 'tis fit to touch our chaps°   jaws
Marked with L. for our initial!
      (He-he! There his lily snaps!)

                              4

25 *Saint*, forsooth! While brown Dolores
      Squats outside the Convent bank
With Sanchicha, telling stories,
      Steeping tresses in the tank,
Blue-black, lustrous, thick like horsehairs,
30   —Can't I see his dead eye glow,
Bright as 'twere a Barbary corsair's?[4]
      (That is, if he'd let it show!)

                              5

When he finishes refection,°   dinner
      Knife and fork he never lays
35 Cross-wise, to my recollection,
      As do I, in Jesu's praise.
I the Trinity illustrate,
      Drinking watered orange pulp—
In three sips the Arian[5] frustrate;
40   While he drains his at one gulp.

                              6

Oh, those melons? If he's able
      We're to have a feast! so nice!
One goes to the Abbot's table,
      All of us get each a slice.
45 How go on your flowers? None double?
      Not one fruit-sort can you spy?
Strange!—And I, too, at such trouble,
      Keep them close-nipped on the sly!

                              7

There's a great text in Galatians,[6]
50   Once you trip on it, entails

3. Dandelion (19th-century use).
4. Pirate of the Barbary Coast of northern Africa, renowned for fierceness and lechery.
5. Heretical follower of Arius (256–336), who denied the doctrine of the Trinity.
6. The speaker hopes to obtain Lawrence's damnation by luring him into a heresy, this to be

accomplished by exposing him to the difficult task of interpreting "Galatians" in an unswervingly orthodox way. In Galatians 5.15–23, St. Paul specifies an assortment of "works of the flesh" that lead to damnation, which could make up a total of "twenty-nine" (line 51).

Twenty-nine distinct damnations,
    One sure, if another fails:
If I trip him just a-dying,
    Sure of heaven as sure can be,
55 Spin him round and send him flying
    Off to hell, a Manichee?[7]

8

Or, my scrofulous French novel
    On gray paper with blunt type!
Simply glance at it, you grovel
60   Hand and foot in Belial's gripe:
If I double down its pages
    At the woeful sixteenth print,
When he gathers his greengages,
    Ope a sieve and slip it in't?

9

65 Or, there's Satan!—one might venture
    Pledge one's soul to him, yet leave
Such a flaw in the indenture
    As he'd miss till, past retrieve,
Blasted lay that rose-acacia[8]
70   We're so proud of! *Hy, Zy, Hine*[9]
'St, there's Vespers! *Plena gratiâ
Ave, Virgo!*[1] Gr-r-r—you swine!

ca. 1839   1842

My Last Duchess[1]

Ferrara

That's my last Duchess painted on the wall,
Looking as if she were alive. I call
That piece a wonder, now: Frà Pandolf's[2] hands
Worked busily a day, and there she stands.
5 Will 't please you sit and look at her? I said
"Frà Pandolf" by design, for never read
Strangers like you that pictured countenance,
The depth and passion of its earnest glance,
But to myself they turned (since none puts by
10 The curtain I have drawn for you, but I)

---

7. A heretic, a follower of Mani (3rd century), Persian prophet.
8. The speaker would pledge his own soul to Satan in return for blasting Lawrence and his "rose-acacia," but the pledge would be so cleverly worded that the speaker himself would not have to pay his debt to Satan. There would be an escape clause ("flaw in the indenture") for himself.
9. Perhaps the opening of a mysterious curse against Lawrence.
1. Full of grace, Hail, Virgin! (Latin). The speaker's twisted state of mind may be reflected in his mixed-up version of the prayer to Mary: "Ave, Maria, gratia plena."
1. The poem is based on incidents in the life of Alfonso II, duke of Ferrara in Italy, whose first wife, Lucrezia, a young woman, died in 1561 after three years of marriage. Following her death, the duke negotiated through an agent to marry a niece of the count of Tyrol. Browning represents the duke as addressing this agent.
2. Brother Pandolf, an imaginary painter.

And seemed as they would ask me, if they durst,
How such a glance came there; so, not the first
Are you to turn and ask thus. Sir, 'twas not
Her husband's presence only, called that spot
15 Of joy into the Duchess' cheek: perhaps
Frà Pandolf chanced to say "Her mantle laps
Over my lady's wrist too much," or "Paint
Must never hope to reproduce the faint
Half-flush that dies along her throat": such stuff
20 Was courtesy, she thought, and cause enough
For calling up that spot of joy. She had
A heart—how shall I say?—too soon made glad,
Too easily impressed; she liked whate'er
She looked on, and her looks went everywhere.
25 Sir, 'twas all one! My favor at her breast,
The dropping of the daylight in the West,
The bough of cherries some officious fool
Broke in the orchard for her, the white mule
She rode with round the terrace—all and each
30 Would draw from her alike the approving speech,
Or blush, at least. She thanked men—good! but thanked
Somehow—I know not how—as if she ranked
My gift of a nine-hundred-years-old name
With anybody's gift. Who'd stoop to blame
35 This sort of trifling? Even had you skill
In speech—(which I have not)—to make your will
Quite clear to such an one, and say, "Just this
Or that in you disgusts me; here you miss,
Or there exceed the mark"—and if she let
40 Herself be lessoned so, nor plainly set
Her wits to yours, forsooth, and made excuse
—E'en then would be some stooping; and I choose
Never to stoop. Oh sir, she smiled, no doubt,
Whene'er I passed her; but who passed without
45 Much the same smile? This grew; I gave commands;
Then all smiles stopped together. There she stands
As if alive. Will 't please you rise? We'll meet
The company below, then. I repeat,
The Count your master's known munificence
50 Is ample warrant that no just pretense
Of mine for dowry will be disallowed;
Though his fair daughter's self, as I avowed
At starting, is my object. Nay, we'll go
Together down, sir. Notice Neptune, though,
55 Taming a sea horse, thought a rarity,
Which Claus of Innsbruck³ cast in bronze for me!

1842   1842

---

3. An unidentified or imaginary sculptor. The count of Tyrol had his capital at Innsbruck.

Home-Thoughts, from Abroad

1

Oh, to be in England
Now that April's there,
And whoever wakes in England
Sees, some morning, unaware,
5   That the lowest boughs and the brushwood sheaf
Round the elm-tree bole are in tiny leaf,
While the chaffinch sings on the orchard bough
In England—now!

2

And after April, when May follows,
10   And the whitethroat builds, and all the swallows!
Hark, where my blossomed peartree in the hedge
Leans to the field and scatters on the clover
Blossoms and dewdrops—at the bent spray's edge—
That's the wise thrush; he sings each song twice over,
15   Lest you should think he never could recapture
The first fine careless rapture!
And though the fields look rough with hoary dew,
All will be gay when noontide wakes anew
The buttercups, the little children's dower
20   —Far brighter than this gaudy melon-flower!

ca. 1845   1845

The Bishop Orders His Tomb at Saint Praxed's Church[1]

Rome, 15—

Vanity, saith the preacher, vanity![2]
Draw round my bed: is Anselm keeping back?
Nephews—sons mine . . . ah God, I know not! Well—
She, men would have to be your mother once,
5   Old Gandolf envied me, so fair she was!
What's done is done, and she is dead beside,
Dead long ago, and I am Bishop since,

1. In *Fra Lippo Lippi*, Browning represents the dawn of the Renaissance in Italy, with its fresh zest for human experiences in this world. In this monologue, he portrays a later stage of the Renaissance when such worldliness, full-blown, had infected some of the leading clergy of Italy. Browning's portrait of the dying bishop is, however, not primarily a satire against corruption in the church. It is a brilliant exposition of the workings of a mind, a mind that has been conditioned by special historical circumstances. The Victorian historian of art John Ruskin said of this poem:

I know of no other piece of modern English, prose or poetry, in which there is so much told,

as in these lines, of the Renaissance spirit—its worldliness, inconsistency, pride, hypocrisy, ignorance of itself, love of art, of luxury, and of good Latin. It is nearly all that I have said of the central Renaissance in thirty pages of the *Stones of Venice*, put into as many lines, Browning's also being the antecedent work.

St. Praxed's Church was named in honor of St. Praxedes, a Roman virgin of the 2nd century who gave her riches to poor Christians. Both the bishop and his predecessor, Gandolf, are imaginary persons.
2. Cf. Ecclesiastes 1.2.

And as she died so must we die ourselves,
And thence ye may perceive the world's a dream.
10   Life, how and what is it? As here I lie
In this state chamber, dying by degrees,
Hours and long hours in the dead night, I ask
"Do I live, am I dead?" Peace, peace seems all.
Saint Praxed's ever was the church for peace;
15   And so, about this tomb of mine. I fought
With tooth and nail to save my niche, ye know:
—Old Gandolf cozened° me, despite my care;   *cheated*
Shrewd was that snatch from out the corner south
He graced his carrion with, God curse the same!
20   Yet still my niche is not so cramped but thence
One sees the pulpit o' the epistle side,³
And somewhat of the choir, those silent seats,
And up into the aery dome where live
The angels, and a sunbeam's sure to lurk:
25   And I shall fill my slab of basalt⁴ there,
And 'neath my tabernacle⁵ take my rest,
With those nine columns round me, two and two,
The odd one at my feet where Anselm stands:
Peach-blossom marble all, the rare, the ripe
30   As fresh-poured red wine of a mighty pulse.⁶
—Old Gandolf with his paltry onion-stone,⁷
Put me where I may look at him! True peach,
Rosy and flawless: how I earned the prize!
Draw close: that conflagration of my church
35   —What then? So much was saved if aught were missed!
My sons, ye would not be my death? Go dig
The white-grape vineyard where the oil-press stood,
Drop water gently till the surface sink,
And if ye find . . . Ah God, I know not, I! . . .
40   Bedded in store of rotten fig leaves soft,
And corded up in a tight olive-frail,⁸
Some lump, ah God, of *lapis lazuli*,⁹
Big as a jew's head cut off at the nape,¹
Blue as a vein o'er the Madonna's breast . . .
45   Sons, all have I bequeathed you, villas, all,
That brave Frascati² villa with its bath,
So, let the blue lump poise between my knees,
Like God the Father's globe on both his hands
Ye worship in the Jesu Church³ so gay,
50   For Gandolf shall not choose but see and burst!
Swift as a weaver's shuttle fleet our years:⁴

---

3. The Epistles of the New Testament are read from the right-hand side of the altar (as one faces it).
4. Dark-colored igneous rock.
5. Stone canopy or tentlike roof, presumably supported by the "nine columns" under which the sculptured effigy of the bishop would lie on the "slab of basalt."
6. Browning uses "pulse" in the special sense of a pulpy mash of fermented grapes from which a strong wine might be poured off.
7. An inferior marble that peels in layers.
8. Basket for holding olives.
9. Valuable bright blue stone.
1. Perhaps a reference to the head of John the Baptist, cut off at the request of Salomé.
2. Suburb of Rome, used as a resort by wealthy Italians.
3. Il Gesù, a Jesuit church in Rome. In a chapel in this church the figure of an angel (rather than God) holds a huge lump of lapis lazuli in his hands.
4. Cf. Job 7.6.

Man goeth to the grave, and where is he?
Did I say basalt for my slab, sons? Black[5]—
'Twas ever antique-black I meant! How else
55   Shall ye contrast my frieze[6] to come beneath?
The bas-relief[7] in bronze ye promised me,
Those Pans and Nymphs ye wot of, and perchance
Some tripod, thyrsus, with a vase or so,
The Saviour at his sermon on the mount,
60   Saint Praxed in a glory, and one Pan
Ready to twitch the Nymph's last garment off,
And Moses with the tables[8] . . . but I know
Ye mark me not! What do they whisper thee,
Child of my bowels, Anselm? Ah, ye hope
65   To revel down my villas while I gasp
Bricked o'er with beggar's moldy travertine°   *Italian limestone*
Which Gandolf from his tomb-top chuckles at!
Nay, boys, ye love me—all of jasper, then!
'Tis jasper ye stand pledged to, lest I grieve
70   My bath must needs be left behind, alas!
One block, pure green as a pistachio nut,
There's plenty jasper somewhere in the world—
And have I not Saint Praxed's ear to pray
Horses for ye, and brown Greek manuscripts,
75   And mistresses with great smooth marbly limbs?
—That's if ye carve my epitaph aright,
Choice Latin, picked phrase, Tully's[9] every word,
No gaudy ware like Gandolf's second line—
Tully, my masters? Ulpian[1] serves his need!
80   And then how I shall lie through centuries,
And hear the blessed mutter of the mass,
And see God made and eaten all day long,[2]
And feel the steady candle flame, and taste
Good strong thick stupefying incense-smoke!
85   For as I lie here, hours of the dead night,
Dying in state and by such slow degrees,
I fold my arms as if they clasped a crook,°   *bishop's staff*
And stretch my feet forth straight as stone can point,
And let the bedclothes, for a mortcloth,[3] drop
90   Into great laps and folds of sculptor's-work:
And as yon tapers dwindle, and strange thoughts
Grow, with a certain humming in my ears,
About the life before I lived this life,

---

5. I.e., black marble.
6. Continuous band of sculpture.
7. Sculpture in which the figures do not project far from the background surface.
8. Sculpture in which the figures do not project far from the background surface. The sculpture would consist of a mixture of pagan and Christian iconography. "Tripod": seat on which the Oracle of Delphi made prophecies. "Thyrsus": a long staff carried in processions in honor of Bacchus, the god of wine. "Glory": halo. "Tables": the stone tablets on which the Ten Commandments were written.

Such intermingling of pagan and Christian traditions, characteristic of the Renaissance, had been attacked in 1841 in *Contrasts*, a book on architecture by A. W. Pugin, a Roman Catholic.
9. I.e., Marcus Tullius Cicero, whose writing was the model, during the Renaissance, of classical Latin prose.
1. Late Latin prose writer, not a model of good style.
2. Reference to the doctrine of transubstantiation.
3. Rich cloth spread over a dead body or coffin.

And this life too, popes, cardinals, and priests,
95 Saint Praxed at his sermon on the mount,[4]
Your tall pale mother with her talking eyes,
And new-found agate urns as fresh as day,
And marble's language, Latin pure, discreet
—Aha, ELUCESCEBAT[5] quoth our friend?
100 No Tully, said I, Ulpian at the best!
Evil and brief hath been my pilgrimage.[6]
All *lapis*, all, sons! Else I give the Pope
My villas! Will ye ever eat my heart?
Ever your eyes were as a lizard's quick,
105 They glitter like your mother's for my soul,
Or ye would heighten my impoverished frieze,
Pierce out its starved design, and fill my vase
With grapes, and add a vizor and a Term,[7]
And to the tripod ye would tie a lynx
110 That in his struggle throws the thyrsus down,
To comfort me on my entablature[8]
Whereon I am to lie till I must ask
"Do I live, am I dead?" There, leave me, there!
For ye have stabbed me with ingratitude
115 To death—ye wish it—God, ye wish it! Stone—
Gritstone,[9] a-crumble! Clammy squares which sweat
As if the corpse they keep were oozing through—
And no more *lapis* to delight the world!
Well go! I bless ye. Fewer tapers there,
120 But in a row: and, going, turn your backs
—Aye, like departing altar-ministrants,
And leave me in my church, the church for peace,
That I may watch at leisure if he leers—
Old Gandolf, at me, from his onion-stone,
125 As still he envied me, so fair she was!

1844   1845

Meeting at Night[1]

I

The gray sea and the long black land;
And the yellow half-moon large and low;
And the startled little waves that leap
In fiery ringlets from their sleep,
5 As I gain the cove with pushing prow,
And quench its speed i' the slushy sand.

---

4. The bishop is confusing St. Praxed (a woman) with Christ—an indication that his mind is wandering.
5. He was illustrious (Latin); word from Gandolf's epitaph. The bishop considers the form of the verb to be in "gaudy" bad taste (line 78). If the epitaph had been copied from Cicero instead of from Ulpian, the word would have been *elucebat*.
6. Cf. Genesis 47.9.

7. Statue of Terminus, the Roman god of boundaries, usually represented without arms. "Vizor": part of a helmet, often represented in sculpture.
8. Horizontal platform supporting a statue or effigy.
9. Coarse sandstone.
1. This poem and the one that follows it appeared originally under the single title *Night and Morning*. The speaker in both is a man.

2

Then a mile of warm sea-scented beach;
Three fields to cross till a farm appears;
A tap at the pane, the quick sharp scratch
10   And blue spurt of a lighted match,
And a voice less loud, through its joys and fears,
Than the two hearts beating each to each!

1845

Parting at Morning

Round the cape of a sudden came the sea,
And the sun looked over the mountain's rim:
And straight was a path of gold for him,°   *the sun*
And the need of a world of men for me.

1845

Love among the Ruins[1]

1

Where the quiet-colored end of evening smiles,
        Miles and miles
On the solitary pastures where our sheep
        Half-asleep
5   Tinkle homeward through the twilight, stray or stop
        As they crop—
Was the site once of a city great and gay
        (So they say),
Of our country's very capital, its prince
10   Ages since
Held his court in, gathered councils, wielding far
        Peace or war.

2

Now—the country does not even boast a tree,
        As you see,
15   To distinguish slopes of verdure, certain rills
        From the hills
Intersect and give a name to (else they run
        Into one),
Where the domed and daring palace shot its spires
20   Up like fires
O'er the hundred-gated circuit of a wall
        Bounding all,
Made of marble, men might march on nor be pressed,
        Twelve abreast.

---

1. The ruins may be those of such cities as Babylon and Nineveh or the site of the Circus Maximus
in Rome. The unusual stanza used in this poem
was invented by Browning. The contrast between
past and present, which is the core of the poem, is
reinforced by devoting one half of each stanza to
the past and the other half to the present.

3

25   And such plenty and perfection, see, of grass
         Never was!
    Such a carpet as, this summertime, o'erspreads
         And embeds
    Every vestige of the city, guessed alone,
30   Stock or stone—
    Where a multitude of men breathed joy and woe
         Long ago;
    Lust of glory pricked their hearts up, dread of shame
         Struck them tame;
35   And that glory and that shame alike, the gold
         Bought and sold.

4

    Now—the single little turret that remains
         On the plains,
    By the caper overrooted, by the gourd
40   Overscored,
    While the patching houseleek's[2] head of blossom winks
         Through the chinks—
    Marks the basement whence a tower in ancient time
         Sprang sublime,
45   And a burning ring, all round, the chariots traced
         As they raced,
    And the monarch and his minions and his dames
         Viewed the games.

5

    And I know, while thus the quiet-colored eve
50   Smiles to leave
    To their folding, all our many-tinkling fleece
         In such peace,
    And the slopes and rills in undistinguished gray
         Melt away—
55   That a girl with eager eyes and yellow hair
         Waits me there
    In the turret whence the charioteers caught soul
         For the goal,
    When the king looked, where she looks now, breathless, dumb
60   Till I come.

6

    But he looked upon the city, every side,
         Far and wide,
    All the mountains topped with temples, all the glades'
         Colonnades,
65   All the causeys,[3] bridges, aqueducts—and then,
         All the men!
    When I do come, she will speak not, she will stand,

---

2. Common European plant, with petals clustered in the shape of rosettes.   3. Causeways or roads raised above low ground.

Either hand
On my shoulder, give her eyes the first embrace
70   Of my face,
Ere we rush, ere we extinguish sight and speech
Each on each.

7

In one year they sent a million fighters forth
South and north,
75 And they built their gods a brazen pillar high
As the sky,
Yet reserved a thousand chariots in full force—
Gold, of course.
Oh heart! oh blood that freezes, blood that burns!
80   Earth's returns
For whole centuries of folly, noise, and sin!
Shut them in,
With their triumphs and their glories and the rest!
Love is best.

1853   1855

"Childe Roland to the Dark Tower Came"[1]

(See Edgar's Song in "Lear")

1

My first thought was, he lied in every word,
That hoary cripple, with malicious eye
Askance° to watch the working of his lie   squinting sidewise
On mine, and mouth scarce able to afford
5 Suppression of the glee, that pursed and scored
Its edge, at one more victim gained thereby.

2

What else should he be set for, with his staff?
What, save to waylay with his lies, ensnare
All travelers who might find him posted there,
10 And ask the road? I guessed what skull-like laugh
Would break, what crutch 'gin write my epitaph
For pastime in the dusty thoroughfare,

---

1. Browning stated that this poem "came upon me as a kind of dream," and that it was written in one day. Although the poem was among those of his own writings that pleased him most, he was reluctant to explain what the dream (or nightmare) signified. He once agreed with a friend's suggestion that the meaning might be expressed in the statement: "He that endureth to the end shall be saved." Most readers have responded to the poem in this way, finding in the story of Roland's quest an inspiring expression of defiance and courage. Other readers find the poem to be more expressive of despair than of enduring hope, and it is at least true that the landscape is as grim and nightmare-

like as in such 20th-century writings as T. S. Eliot's *Hollow Men* or Franz Kafka's *Penal Colony*. It has been said of *"Childe Roland"* that every reader can be his own allegorist.

The lines from Shakespeare's *King Lear* 3.4 (lines 163–65), from which the title is taken, are spoken when Lear is about to enter a hovel on the heath, and Edgar, feigning madness, chants the fragment of a song reminiscent of quests and challenges in fairy tales: "Child Rowland to the dark tower came, / His word was still,—Fie, foh, and fum, / I smell the blood of a British man." "Childe": a youth of gentle birth, usually a candidate for knighthood.

3

If at his counsel I should turn aside
    Into that ominous tract which, all agree,
15   Hides the Dark Tower. Yet acquiescingly
I did turn as he pointed: neither pride
Nor hope rekindling at the end descried,
    So much as gladness that some end might be.

4

For, what with my whole world-wide wandering,
    What with my search drawn out through years, my hope
20   Dwindled into a ghost not fit to cope
With that obstreperous joy success would bring,
I hardly tried now to rebuke the spring
    My heart made, finding failure in its scope.

5

25 As when a sick man very near to death
    Seems dead indeed, and feels begin and end
    The tears and takes the farewell of each friend,
And hears one bid the other go, draw breath
Freelier outside ("since all is o'er," he saith,
30   "And the blow fallen no grieving can amend"),

6

While some discuss if near the other graves
    Be room enough for this, and when a day
    Suits best for carrying the corpse away,
With care about the banners, scarves and staves:
35 And still the man hears all, and only craves
    He may not shame such tender love and stay.

7

Thus, I had so long suffered in this quest,
    Heard failure prophesied so oft, been writ
    So many times among "The Band"—to wit,
40 The knights who to the Dark Tower's search addressed
Their steps—that just to fail as they, seemed best,
    And all the doubt was now—should I be fit?

8

So, quiet as despair, I turned from him,
    That hateful cripple, out of his highway
45   Into the path he pointed. All the day
Had been a dreary one at best, and dim
Was settling to its close, yet shot one grim
    Red leer to see the plain catch its estray.[2]

---

2. Literally, a domestic animal that has strayed away from its home.

9

For mark! no sooner was I fairly found
50   Pledged to the plain, after a pace or two,
        Than, pausing to throw backward a last view
O'er the safe road, 'twas gone; gray plain all round:
Nothing but plain to the horizon's bound.
        I might go on; naught else remained to do.

10

55 So, on I went. I think I never saw
        Such starved ignoble nature; nothing throve:
        For flowers—as well expect a cedar grove!
But, cockle, spurge,³ according to their law
Might propagate their kind, with none to awe,
60   You'd think; a burr had been a treasure trove.

11

No! penury, inertness and grimace,
        In some strange sort, were the land's portion. "See
        Or shut your eyes," said Nature peevishly,
"It nothing skills: I cannot help my case;
65 'Tis the Last Judgment's fire must cure this place,
        Calcine⁴ its clods and set my prisoners free."

12

If there pushed any ragged thistle stalk
        Above its mates, the head was chopped; the bents⁵
        Were jealous else. What made those holes and rents
70 In the dock's° harsh swarth leaves, bruised as to balk   *coarse plant*
All hope of greenness? 'tis a brute must walk
        Pashing their life out, with a brute's intents.

13

As for the grass, it grew as scant as hair
        In leprosy; thin dry blades pricked the mud
75   Which underneath looked kneaded up with blood.
One stiff blind horse, his every bone a-stare,
Stood stupefied, however he came there:
        Thrust out past service from the devil's stud!

14

Alive? he might be dead for aught I know,
80   With that red gaunt and colloped° neck a-strain,   *ridged*
        And shut eyes underneath the rusty mane;
Seldom went such grotesqueness with such woe;
I never saw a brute I hated so;
        He must be wicked to deserve such pain.

---

3. A bitter-juiced weed. "Cockle": a weed that
bears burrs.

4. Turn to powder by heat.

5. Coarse, stiff grasses.

15

85   I shut my eyes and turned them on my heart.
      As a man calls for wine before he fights,
      I asked one draught of earlier, happier sights,
  Ere fitly I could hope to play my part.
  Think first, fight afterwards—the soldier's art:
90   One taste of the old time sets all to rights.

16

  Not it! I fancied Cuthbert's reddening face
      Beneath its garniture of curly gold,
      Dear fellow, till I almost felt him fold
  An arm in mine to fix me to the place,
95   That way he used. Alas, one night's disgrace!
      Out went my heart's new fire and left it cold.

17

  Giles then, the soul of honor—there he stands
      Frank as ten years ago when knighted first.
      What honest man should dare (he said) he durst.
100   Good—but the scene shifts—faugh! what hangman hands
  Pin to his breast a parchment? His own bands
      Read it. Poor traitor, spit upon and cursed!

18

  Better this present than a past like that;
      Back therefore to my darkening path again!
105   No sound, no sight as far as eye could strain.
  Will the night send a howlet° or a bat?   *owl*
  I asked: when something on the dismal flat
      Came to arrest my thoughts and change their train.

19

  A sudden little river crossed my path
110   As unexpected as a serpent comes.
      No sluggish tide congenial to the glooms;
  This, as it frothed by, might have been a bath
  For the fiend's glowing hoof—to see the wrath
      Of its black eddy bespate° with flakes and spumes.   *bespattered*

20

115   So petty yet so spiteful! All along,
      Low scrubby alders kneeled down over it;
      Drenched willows flung them headlong in a fit
  Of mute despair, a suicidal throng:
  The river which had done them all the wrong,
120   Whate'er that was, rolled by, deterred no whit.

21

  Which, while I forded—good saints, how I feared
      To set my foot upon a dead man's cheek,

Each step, or feel the spear I thrust to seek
For hollows, tangled in his hair or beard!
125 —It may have been a water rat I speared,
But, ugh! it sounded like a baby's shriek.

22

Glad was I when I reached the other bank.
Now for a better country. Vain presage!
Who were the strugglers, what war did they wage,
130 Whose savage trample thus could pad the dank
Soil to a plash? Toads in a poisoned tank,
Or wild cats in a red-hot iron cage—

23

The fight must so have seemed in that fell cirque.°   *dreadful arena*
What penned them there, with all the plain to choose?
135 No footprint leading to that horrid mews,[6]
None out of it. Mad brewage set to work
Their brains, no doubt, like galley slaves the Turk
Pits for his pastime, Christians against Jews.

24

And more than that—a furlong on—why, there!
140 What bad use was that engine for, that wheel,
Or brake,[7] not wheel—that harrow fit to reel
Men's bodies out like silk? with all the air
Of Tophet's° tool, on earth left unaware,   *Hell's*
Or brought to sharpen its rusty teeth of steel.

25

145 Then came a bit of stubbed ground, once a wood,
Next a marsh, it would seem, and now mere earth
Desperate and done with; (so a fool finds mirth,
Makes a thing and then mars it, till his mood
Changes and off he goes!) within a rood[8]
150 Bog, clay and rubble, sand and stark black dearth.

26

Now blotches rankling, colored gay and grim,
Now patches where some leanness of the soil's
Broke into moss or substances like boils;
Then came some palsied oak, a cleft in him
155 Like a distorted mouth that splits its rim
Gaping at death, and dies while it recoils.

27

And just as far as ever from the end!
Naught in the distance but the evening, naught

6. Enclosed stable yard.
7. A toothed machine used for separating the fibers of flax or hemp; here an instrument of torture.
8. Quarter acre of land.

160　To point my footstep further! At the thought,
　　　A great black bird, Apollyon's[9] bosom friend,
　　　Sailed past, nor beat his wide wing dragon-penned[1]
　　　　That brushed my cap—perchance the guide I sought.

28

　　　For, looking up, aware I somehow grew,
　　　　'Spite of the dusk, the plain had given place
165　　　All round to mountains—with such name to grace
　　　Mere ugly heights and heaps now stolen in view.
　　　How thus they had surprised me—solve it, you!
　　　　How to get from them was no clearer case.

29

　　　Yet half I seemed to recognize some trick
170　　　Of mischief happened to me, God knows when—
　　　　In a bad dream perhaps. Here ended, then,
　　　Progress this way. When, in the very nick
　　　Of giving up, one time more, came a click
　　　　As when a trap shuts—you're inside the den!

30

175　Burningly it came on me all at once,
　　　　This was the place! those two hills on the right,
　　　　Crouched like two bulls locked horn in horn in fight;
　　　While to the left, a tall scalped mountain . . . Dunce,
　　　Dotard, a-dozing at the very nonce,°　　　　　　　*moment*
180　　　After a life spent training for the sight!

31

　　　What in the midst lay but the Tower itself?
　　　　The round squat turret, blind as the fool's heart,[2]
　　　　Built of brown stone, without a counterpart
　　　In the whole world. The tempest's mocking elf
185　　　Points to the shipman thus the unseen shelf
　　　　He strikes on, only when the timbers start.

32

　　　Not see? because of night perhaps?—why, day
　　　　Came back again for that! before it left,
　　　　The dying sunset kindled through a cleft:
190　　　The hills, like giants at a hunting, lay,
　　　Chin upon hand, to see the game at bay—
　　　　"Now stab and end the creature—to the heft!"[3]

33

　　　Not hear? when noise was everywhere! it tolled
　　　　Increasing like a bell. Names in my ears

9. In Revelation 9.11 Apollyon is "the angel of the bottomless pit." In Bunyan's *Pilgrim's Progress*, he is a hideous "monster"; "he had wings like a dragon."

1. With wings or pinions like those of a dragon.
2. Cf. Psalm 14.1: "The fool hath said in his heart, There is no God."
3. Handle of dagger or sword.

195   Of all the lost adventurers my peers—
How such a one was strong, and such was bold,
     And such was fortunate, yet each of old
       Lost, lost! one moment knelled the woe of years.

34

     There they stood, ranged along the hillsides, met
200   To view the last of me, a living frame
       For one more picture! in a sheet of flame
     I saw them and I knew them all. And yet
Dauntless the slug-horn⁴ to my lips I set,
       And blew. *"Childe Roland to the Dark Tower came."*

1852   1855

Fra Lippo Lippi¹

I am poor brother Lippo, by your leave!
You need not clap your torches to my face.
Zooks,² what's to blame? you think you see a monk!
What, 'tis past midnight, and you go the rounds,
5   And here you catch me at an alley's end
Where sportive ladies leave their doors ajar?
The Carmine's³ my cloister: hunt it up,
Do—harry out, if you must show your zeal,
Whatever rat, there, haps on his wrong hole,
10   And nip each softling of a wee white mouse,
Weke, weke, that's crept to keep him company!
Aha, you know your betters! Then, you'll take
Your hand away that's fiddling on my throat,
And please to know me likewise. Who am I?
15   Why, one, sir, who is lodging with a friend
Three streets off—he's a certain . . . how d'ye call?
Master—a . . . Cosimo of the Medici,⁴
I' the house that caps the corner. Boh! you were best!
Remember and tell me, the day you're hanged,
20   How you affected such a gullet's gripe!⁵
But you,⁶ sir, it concerns you that your knaves
Pick up a manner nor discredit you:
Zooks, are we pilchards,° that they sweep the streets   *small fish*

4. The war cry or slogan of a clan about to engage in battle (Scottish). In 1770, however, the poet Chatterton was misled into using it to mean a kind of trumpet or horn. Browning followed Chatterton's example, although the original meaning would also be relevant here.

1. This monologue portrays the dawn of the Renaissance in Italy at a point when the medieval attitude toward life and art was about to be displaced by a fresh appreciation of earthly pleasures. It was from Giorgio Vasari's *Lives of the Painters* that Browning derived most of his information about the life of the Florentine painter and friar Lippo Lippi (1406–1469), but the theory of art propounded by Lippi in the poem was developed by the poet himself.

2. A shortened version of *Gadzooks,* a mild oath now obscure in meaning but perhaps resembling a phrase still in use: "God's truth."

3. Santa Maria del Carmine, a church and cloister of the Carmelite order of friars to which Lippi belonged.

4. Lippi's patron, banker and virtual ruler of Florence.

5. I.e., how you had the arrogance to choke the gullet of someone with my connections.

6. The officer in charge of the patrol of policemen or watchmen.

And count fair prize what comes into this net?
25 He's Judas to a tittle, that man is![7]
Just such a face! Why, sir, you make amends.
Lord, I'm not angry! Bid your hangdogs go
Drink out this quarter-florin to the health
Of the munificent House that harbors me
30 (And many more beside, lads! more beside!)
And all's come square again. I'd like his face—
His, elbowing on his comrade in the door
With the pike and lantern—for the slave that holds
John Baptist's head a-dangle by the hair
35 With one hand ("Look you, now," as who should say)
And his weapon in the other, yet unwiped!
It's not your chance to have a bit of chalk,
A wood-coal or the like? or you should see!
Yes, I'm the painter, since you style me so.
40 What, brother Lippo's doings, up and down,
You know them and they take you? like enough!
I saw the proper twinkle in your eye—
'Tell you, I liked your looks at very first.
Let's sit and set things straight now, hip to haunch.
45 Here's spring come, and the nights one makes up bands
To roam the town and sing out carnival,[8]
And I've been three weeks shut within my mew,°   *private den*
A-painting for the great man, saints and saints
And saints again. I could not paint all night—
50 Ouf! I leaned out of window for fresh air.
There came a hurry of feet and little feet,
A sweep of lute-strings, laughs, and whiffs of song—
Flower o' the broom,
Take away love, and our earth is a tomb!
55 *Flower o' the quince,*
I let Lisa go, and what good in life since?[9]
Flower o' the thyme—and so on. Round they went.
Scarce had they turned the corner when a titter
Like the skipping of rabbits by moonlight—three slim shapes,
60 And a face that looked up . . . zooks, sir, flesh and blood,
That's all I'm made of! Into shreds it went,
Curtain and counterpane and coverlet,
All the bed-furniture—a dozen knots,
There was a ladder! Down I let myself,
65 Hands and feet, scrambling somehow, and so dropped,
And after them. I came up with the fun
Hard by Saint Laurence,[1] hail fellow, well met—
Flower o' the rose,
If I've been merry, what matter who knows!
70 And so as I was stealing back again
To get to bed and have a bit of sleep

---

7. I.e., one of the watchmen has a face that would serve as a model for a painting of Judas.
8. Season of revelry before the commencement of Lent.

9. This and other interspersed flower songs are called *stornelli* in Italy.
1. San Lorenzo, a church in Florence.

Ere I rise up tomorrow and go work
On Jerome knocking at his poor old breast
With his great round stone to subdue the flesh,[2]
75 You snap me of the sudden. Ah, I see!
Though your eye twinkles still, you shake your head—
Mine's shaved—a monk, you say—the sting's in that!
If Master Cosimo announced himself,
Mum's the word naturally; but a monk!
80 Come, what am I a beast for? tell us, now!
I was a baby when my mother died
And father died and left me in the street.
I starved there, God knows how, a year or two
On fig skins, melon parings, rinds and shucks,
85 Refuse and rubbish. One fine frosty day,
My stomach being empty as your hat,
The wind doubled me up and down I went.
Old Aunt Lapaccia trussed me with one hand
(Its fellow was a stinger as I knew),
90 And so along the wall, over the bridge,
By the straight cut to the convent. Six words there,
While I stood munching my first bread that month:
"So, boy, you're minded," quoth the good fat father
Wiping his own mouth, 'twas refection time°— mealtime
95 "To quit this very miserable world?
Will you renounce" . . . "the mouthful of bread?" thought I;
By no means! Brief, they made a monk of me;
I did renounce the world, its pride and greed,
Palace, farm, villa, shop, and banking house,
100 Trash, such as these poor devils of Medici
Have given their hearts to—all at eight years old.
Well, sir, I found in time, you may be sure,
'Twas not for nothing—the good bellyful,
The warm serge and the rope that goes all round,
105 And day-long blessed idleness beside!
"Let's see what the urchin's fit for"—that came next.
Not overmuch their way, I must confess.
Such a to-do! They tried me with their books:
Lord, they'd have taught me Latin in pure waste!
110 *Flower o' the clove,*
All the Latin I construe is "amo," I love!
But, mind you, when a boy starves in the streets
Eight years together, as my fortune was,
Watching folk's faces to know who will fling
115 The bit of half-stripped grape bunch he desires,
And who will curse or kick him for his pains—
Which gentleman processional and fine,
Holding a candle to the Sacrament,
Will wink and let him lift a plate and catch
120 The droppings of the wax to sell again,

2. A picture of Saint Jerome (ca. 340–420), whose ascetic observances were hardly a congenial subject for such a painter as Lippi.

Or holla for the Eight° and have him whipped—   *Florentine magistrates*
How say I?—nay, which dog bites, which lets drop
His bone from the heap of offal in the street—
Why, soul and sense of him grow sharp alike,
125 He learns the look of things, and none the less
For admonition from the hunger-pinch.
I had a store of such remarks, be sure,
Which, after I found leisure, turned to use.
I drew men's faces on my copybooks,
130 Scrawled them within the antiphonary's marge,³
Joined legs and arms to the long music-notes,
Found eyes and nose and chin for A's and B's,
And made a string of pictures of the world
Betwixt the ins and outs of verb and noun,
135 On the wall, the bench, the door. The monks looked black.
"Nay," quoth the Prior,⁴ "turn him out, d' ye say?
In no wise. Lose a crow and catch a lark.
What if at last we get our man of parts,
We Carmelites, like those Camaldolese
140 And Preaching Friars,⁵ to do our church up fine
And put the front on it that ought to be!"
And hereupon he bade me daub away.
Thank you! my head being crammed, the walls a blank,
Never was such prompt disemburdening.
145 First, every sort of monk, the black and white,
I drew them, fat and lean: then, folk at church,
From good old gossips waiting to confess
Their cribs of barrel droppings, candle ends—
To the breathless fellow at the altar-foot,
150 Fresh from his murder, safe and sitting there
With the little children round him in a row
Of admiration, half for his beard and half
For that white anger of his victim's son
Shaking a fist at him with one fierce arm,
155 Signing himself with the other because of Christ
(Whose sad face on the cross sees only this
After the passion° of a thousand years)   *sufferings* .
Till some poor girl, her apron o'er her head
(Which the intense eyes looked through), came at eve
160 On tiptoe, said a word, dropped in a loaf,
Her pair of earrings and a bunch of flowers
(The brute took growling), prayed, and so was gone.
I painted all, then cried " 'Tis ask and have;
Choose, for more's ready!"—laid the ladder flat,
165 And showed my covered bit of cloister wall.
The monks closed in a circle and praised loud
Till checked, taught what to see and not to see,
Being simple bodies—"That's the very man!
Look at the boy who stoops to pat the dog!

---

3. Margin of music book used for choral singing.
4. Head of a Carmelite convent.

5. Benedictine and Dominican religious orders, respectively.

170   That woman's like the Prior's niece who comes
     To care about his asthma: it's the life!"
     But there my triumph's straw-fire flared and funked;[6]
     Their betters took their turn to see and say:
     The Prior and the learned pulled a face
175   And stopped all that in no time. "How? what's here?
     Quite from the mark of painting, bless us all!
     Faces, arms, legs and bodies like the true
     As much as pea and pea! it's devil's game!
     Your business is not to catch men with show,
180   With homage to the perishable clay,
     But lift them over it, ignore it all,
     Make them forget there's such a thing as flesh.
     Your business is to paint the souls of men—
     Man's soul, and it's a fire, smoke . . . no, it's not . . .
185   It's vapor done up like a newborn babe—
     (In that shape when you die it leaves your mouth)
     It's . . . well, what matters talking, it's the soul!
     Give us no more of body than shows soul!
     Here's Giotto,[7] with his Saint a-praising God,
190   That sets us praising—why not stop with him?
     Why put all thoughts of praise out of our head
     With wonder at lines, colors, and what not?
     Paint the soul, never mind the legs and arms!
     Rub all out, try at it a second time.
195   Oh, that white smallish female with the breasts,
     She's just my niece . . . Herodias,[8] I would say—
     Who went and danced and got men's heads cut off!
     Have it all out!" Now, is this sense, I ask?
     A fine way to paint soul, by painting body
200   So ill, the eye can't stop there, must go further
     And can't fare worse! Thus, yellow does for white
     When what you put for yellow's simply black,
     And any sort of meaning looks intense
     When all beside itself means and looks naught.
205   Why can't a painter lift each foot in turn,
     Left foot and right foot, go a double step,
     Make his flesh liker and his soul more like,
     Both in their order? Take the prettiest face,
     The Prior's niece . . . patron-saint—is it so pretty
210   You can't discover if it means hope, fear,
     Sorrow or joy? won't beauty go with these?
     Suppose I've made her eyes all right and blue,
     Can't I take breath and try to add life's flash,
     And then add soul and heighten them threefold?
215   Or say there's beauty with no soul at all—

6. Went up in smoke.
7. Great Florentine painter (1276–1337), whose stylized pictures of religious subjects were admired as models of pre-Renaissance art.
8. Also called Salomé, had the same name as her mother (Herodias), sister-in-law of King Herod. The daughter's dance coincided with the beheading of John the Baptist, who had aroused her mother's displeasure (Matthew 14.6–11).

(I never saw it—put the case the same—)
If you get simple beauty and naught else,
You get about the best thing God invents:
That's somewhat: and you'll find the soul you have missed,
220 Within yourself, when you return him thanks.
"Rub all out!" Well, well, there's my life, in short,
And so the thing has gone on ever since.
I'm grown a man no doubt, I've broken bounds:
You should not take a fellow eight years old
225 And make him swear to never kiss the girls.
I'm my own master, paint now as I please—
Having a friend, you see, in the Corner-house![9]
Lord, it's fast holding by the rings in front—
Those great rings serve more purposes than just
230 To plant a flag in, or tie up a horse!
And yet the old schooling sticks, the old grave eyes
Are peeping o'er my shoulder as I work,
The heads shake still—"It's art's decline, my son!
You're not of the true painters, great and old;
235 Brother Angelico's the man, you'll find;
Brother Lorenzo[1] stands his single peer:
Fag on at flesh, you'll never make the third!"
Flower o' the pine,
You keep your mistr . . . manners, and I'll stick to mine!
240 I'm not the third, then: bless us, they must know!
Don't you think they're the likeliest to know,
They with their Latin? So, I swallow my rage,
Clench my teeth, suck my lips in tight, and paint
To please them—sometimes do and sometimes don't;
245 For, doing most, there's pretty sure to come
A turn, some warm eve finds me at my saints—
A laugh, a cry, the business of the world—
(*Flower o' the peach,*
Death for us all, and his own life for each!)
250 And my whole soul revolves, the cup runs over,
The world and life's too big to pass for a dream,
And I do these wild things in sheer despite,
And play the fooleries you catch me at,
In pure rage! The old mill-horse, out at grass
255 After hard years, throws up his stiff heels so,
Although the miller does not preach to him
The only good of grass is to make chaff.°   straw
What would men have? Do they like grass or no—
May they or mayn't they? all I want's the thing
260 Settled forever one way. As it is,
You tell too many lies and hurt yourself:
You don't like what you only like too much,
You do like what, if given you at your word,

9. The Medici palace.
1. Fra Angelico (1387–1455) and Lorenzo Mon-   aco (1370–1425), whose paintings were in the
approved traditional manner.

You find abundantly detestable.
265 For me, I think I speak as I was taught;
I always see the garden and God there
A-making man's wife: and, my lesson learned,
The value and significance of flesh,
I can't unlearn ten minutes afterwards.

270   You understand me: I'm a beast, I know.
But see, now—why, I see as certainly
As that the morning star's about to shine,
What will hap some day. We've a youngster here
Comes to our convent, studies what I do,
275 Slouches and stares and lets no atom drop:
His name is Guidi[2]—he'll not mind the monks—
They call him Hulking Tom, he lets them talk—
He picks my practice up—he'll paint apace,
I hope so—though I never live so long,
280 I know what's sure to follow. You be judge!
You speak no Latin more than I, belike;
However, you're my man, you've seen the world
—The beauty and the wonder and the power,
The shapes of things, their colors, lights and shades,
285 Changes, surprises—and God made it all!
—For what? Do you feel thankful, aye or no,
For this fair town's face, yonder river's line,
The mountain round it and the sky above,
Much more the figures of man, woman, child,
290 These are the frame to? What's it all about?
To be passed over, despised? or dwelt upon,
Wondered at? oh, this last of course!—you say.
But why not do as well as say—paint these
Just as they are, careless what comes of it?
295 God's works—paint any one, and count it crime
To let a truth slip. Don't object, "His works
Are here already; nature is complete:
Suppose you reproduce her—(which you can't)
There's no advantage! You must beat her, then."
300 For, don't you mark? we're made so that we love
First when we see them painted, things we have passed
Perhaps a hundred times nor cared to see;
And so they are better, painted—better to us,
Which is the same thing. Art was given for that;
305 God uses us to help each other so,
Lending our minds out. Have you noticed, now,
Your cullion's° hanging face? A bit of chalk,   *rascal's*
And trust me but you should, though! How much more,
If I drew higher things with the same truth!

---

2. Guidi or Masaccio (1401–1428), a painter who
may have been Lippi's master rather than his pupil,
although Browning, in a letter to the press in 1870,
argued that Lippi had been born earlier. Like
Lippi, Masaccio was in revolt against the medieval
theory of art. His frescoes in the chapel of Santa
Maria del Carmine are considered his masterpiece.

310   That were to take the Prior's pulpit-place,
      Interpret God to all of you! Oh, oh,
      It makes me mad to see what men shall do
      And we in our graves! This world's no blot for us,
      Nor blank; it means intensely, and means good:
315   To find its meaning is my meat and drink.
      "Aye, but you don't so instigate to prayer!"
      Strikes in the Prior: "when your meaning's plain
      It does not say to folk—remember matins,
      Or, mind you fast next Friday!" Why, for this
320   What need of art at all? A skull and bones,
      Two bits of stick nailed crosswise, or, what's best,
      A bell to chime the hour with, does as well.
      I painted a Saint Laurence[3] six months since
      At Prato, splashed the fresco[4] in fine style:
325   "How looks my painting, now the scaffold's down?"
      I ask a brother: "Hugely," he returns—
      "Already not one phiz of your three slaves
      Who turn the Deacon off his toasted side,
      But it's scratched and prodded to our heart's content,
330   The pious people have so eased their own
      With coming to say prayers there in a rage:
      We get on fast to see the bricks beneath.
      Expect another job this time next year,
      For pity and religion grow i' the crowd—
335   Your painting serves its purpose!" Hang the fools!

      —That is—you'll not mistake an idle word
      Spoke in a huff by a poor monk, God wot,
      Tasting the air this spicy night which turns
      The unaccustomed head like Chianti wine!
340   Oh, the church knows! don't misreport me, now!
      It's natural a poor monk out of bounds
      Should have his apt word to excuse himself:
      And hearken how I plot to make amends.
      I have bethought me: I shall paint a piece
345   . . . There's for you! Give me six months, then go, see
      Something in Sant' Ambrogio's![5] Bless the nuns!
      They want a cast o' my office.[6] I shall paint
      God in the midst, Madonna and her babe,
      Ringed by a bowery flowery angel brood,
350   Lilies and vestments and white faces, sweet
      As puff on puff of grated orris-root[7]
      When ladies crowd to Church at midsummer.
      And then i' the front, of course a saint or two—
      Saint John, because he saves the Florentines,

---

3. A scene representing the fiery martyrdom of
Saint Laurence.
4. Painted on a freshly plastered surface. It must
be painted quickly before the plaster dries. Prato
is a town near Florence
5. A convent church in Florence.

6. Sample of my work. The completed painting,
which Browning saw in Florence, is Lippi's *Coronation of the Virgin.*
7. Powder (like talcum) made from sweet-smelling
roots of a flower.

355 Saint Ambrose, who puts down in black and white
The convent's friends and gives them a long day,
And Job, I must have him there past mistake,
The man of Uz (and Us without the z,
Painters who need his patience). Well, all these
360 Secured at their devotion, up shall come
Out of a corner when you least expect,
As one by a dark stair into a great light,
Music and talking, who but Lippo! I!—
Mazed, motionless and moonstruck—I'm the man!
365 Back I shrink—what is this I see and hear?
I, caught up with my monk's things by mistake,
My old serge gown and rope that goes all round,
I, in this presence, this pure company!
Where's a hole, where's a corner for escape?
370 Then steps a sweet angelic slip of a thing
Forward, puts out a soft palm—"Not so fast!"
—Addresses the celestial presence, "nay—
He made you and devised you, after all,
Though he's none of you! Could Saint John there draw—
375 His camel-hair[8] make up a painting-brush?
We come to brother Lippo for all that,
Iste perfecit opus!"[9] So, all smile—
I shuffle sideways with my blushing face
Under the cover of a hundred wings
380 Thrown like a spread of kirtles° when you're gay   skirts
And play hot cockles,[1] all the doors being shut,
Till, wholly unexpected, in there pops
The hothead husband! Thus I scuttle off
To some safe bench behind, not letting go
385 The palm of her, the little lily thing
That spoke the good word for me in the nick,
Like the Prior's niece . . . Saint Lucy, I would say.
And so all's saved for me, and for the church
A pretty picture gained. Go, six months hence!
390 Your hand, sir, and good-by: no lights, no lights!
The street's hushed, and I know my own way back,
Don't fear me! There's the gray beginning. Zooks!

ca. 1853   1855

---

8. Cf. Mark 1.6: "And John was clothed with camel's hair."
9. This man made the work! (Latin). In this painting, as later completed, these words appear beside a figure that Browning took to be Lippi's self-portrait.
1. A game in which a player wears a blindfold.

Andrea del Sarto[1]

(called "The Faultless Painter")

But do not let us quarrel any more,
No, my Lucrezia; bear with me for once:
Sit down and all shall happen as you wish.
You turn your face, but does it bring your heart?
5   I'll work then for your friend's friend, never fear,
Treat his own subject after his own way,
Fix his own time, accept too his own price,
And shut the money into this small hand
When next it takes mine. Will it? tenderly?
10   Oh, I'll content him—but tomorrow, Love!
I often am much wearier than you think,
This evening more than usual, and it seems
As if—forgive now—should you let me sit
Here by the window with your hand in mine
15   And look a half-hour forth on Fiesole,[2]
Both of one mind, as married people use,
Quietly, quietly the evening through,
I might get up tomorrow to my work
Cheerful and fresh as ever. Let us try.
20   Tomorrow, how you shall be glad for this!
Your soft hand is a woman of itself,
And mine the man's bared breast she curls inside.
Don't count the time lost, neither; you must serve
For each of the five pictures we require:
25   It saves a model. So! keep looking so—
My serpentining beauty, rounds on rounds![3]
—How could you ever prick those perfect ears,
Even to put the pearl there! oh, so sweet—
My face, my moon, my everybody's moon,
30   Which everybody looks on and calls his,
And, I suppose, is looked on by in turn,
While she looks—no one's: very dear, no less.[4]
You smile? why, there's my picture ready made,
There's what we painters call our harmony!

---

1. This portrait of Andrea del Sarto (1486–1531) was derived from a biography written by his pupil Giorgio Vasari, author of *The Lives of the Painters*. Vasari's account seeks to explain why his Florentine master, one of the most skillful painters of the Renaissance, never altogether fulfilled the promise he had shown early in his career and why he had never arrived (in Vasari's opinion) at the level of such artists as Raphael. Vasari noted that Andrea suffered from "a certain timidity of mind . . . which rendered it impossible that those evidences of ardor and animation, which are proper to the more exalted character, should ever appear in him."

Browning also follows Vasari's account of Andrea's marriage to a beautiful widow, Lucrezia, "an artful woman who made him do as she pleased in all things." Vasari reports that Andrea's "immoderate love for her soon caused him to neglect the studies demanded by his art" and that this infatuation had "more influence over him than the glory and honor towards which he had begun to make such hopeful advances."

Browning's poem has often been praised for its exposition of a paradoxical theory of success and failure, but it has other qualities as well. Its slow-paced, enervated blank verse, its setting of a quiet evening in autumn, its comparative lack of the movement and noise that we expect in Browning's energetic verse create a unity of impression that is unobtrusive yet effective.

2. A suburb on the hills overlooking Florence.
3. Coils of hair like the coils of a serpent.
4. Her affections are centered on no one person, not even on her husband, yet she is nevertheless dear to him.

35 A common grayness silvers everything[5]—
 All in a twilight, you and I alike
 —You, at the point of your first pride in me
 (That's gone you know)—but I, at every point;
 My youth, my hope, my art, being all toned down
40 To yonder sober pleasant Fiesole.
 There's the bell clinking from the chapel top;
 That length of convent wall across the way
 Holds the trees safer, huddled more inside;
 The last monk leaves the garden; days decrease,
45 And autumn grows, autumn in everything.
 Eh? the whole seems to fall into a shape
 As if I saw alike my work and self
 And all that I was born to be and do,
 A twilight-piece. Love, we are in God's hand.
50 How strange now, looks the life he makes us lead;
 So free we seem, so fettered fast we are!
 I feel he laid the fetter: let it lie!
 This chamber for example—turn your head—
 All that's behind us! You don't understand
55 Nor care to understand about my art,
 But you can hear at least when people speak:
 And that cartoon,° the second from the door   *drawing*
 —It is the thing, Love! so such things should be—
 Behold Madonna!—I am bold to say.
60 I can do with my pencil what I know,
 What I see, what at bottom of my heart
 I wish for, if I ever wish so deep—
 Do easily, too—when I say, perfectly,
 I do not boast, perhaps: yourself are judge,
65 Who listened to the Legate's[6] talk last week,
 And just as much they used to say in France.
 At any rate 'tis easy, all of it!
 No sketches first, no studies, that's long past:
 I do what many dream of, all their lives,
70 —Dream? strive to do, and agonize to do,
 And fail in doing. I could count twenty such
 On twice your fingers, and not leave this town,
 Who strive—you don't know how the others strive
 To paint a little thing like that you smeared
75 Carelessly passing with your robes afloat—
 Yet do much less, so much less, Someone[7] says
 (I know his name, no matter)—so much less!
 Well, less is more, Lucrezia: I am judged.
 There burns a truer light of God in them,
80 In their vexed beating stuffed and stopped-up brain,
 Heart, or whate'er else, than goes on to prompt
 This low-pulsed forthright craftsman's hand of mine.
 Their works drop groundward, but themselves, I know,

---

5. The predominant color in many of Andrea's paintings is silver gray.

6. A deputy of the pope.

7. Probably Michelangelo (1475–1564).

Reach many a time a heaven that's shut to me,
85 Enter and take their place there sure enough,
Though they come back and cannot tell the world.
My works are nearer heaven, but I sit here.
The sudden blood of these men! at a word—
Praise them, it boils, or blame them, it boils too.
90 I, painting from myself and to myself,
Know what I do, am unmoved by men's blame
Or their praise either. Somebody remarks
Morello's[8] outline there is wrongly traced,
His hue mistaken; what of that? or else,
95 Rightly traced and well ordered; what of that?
Speak as they please, what does the mountain care?
Ah, but a man's reach should exceed his grasp,
Or what's a heaven for? All is silver-gray
Placid and perfect with my art: the worse!
100 I know both what I want and what might gain,
And yet how profitless to know, to sigh
"Had I been two, another and myself,
Our head would have o'erlooked the world!" No doubt.
Yonder's a work now, of that famous youth
105 The Urbinate[9] who died five years ago.
('Tis copied,[1] George Vasari sent it me.)
Well, I can fancy how he did it all,
Pouring his soul, with kings and popes to see,
Reaching, that heaven might so replenish him,
110 Above and through his art—for it gives way;
That arm is wrongly put—and there again—
A fault to pardon in the drawing's lines,
Its body, so to speak: its soul is right,
He means right—that, a child may understand.
115 Still, what an arm! and I could alter it:
But all the play, the insight and the stretch—
Out of me, out of me! And wherefore out?
Had you enjoined them on me, given me soul,
We might have risen to Rafael, I and you!
120 Nay, Love, you did give all I asked, I think—
More than I merit, yes, by many times.
But had you—oh, with the same perfect brow,
And perfect eyes, and more than perfect mouth,
And the low voice my soul hears, as a bird
125 The fowler's pipe,[2] and follows to the snare—
Had you, with these the same, but brought a mind!
Some women do so. Had the mouth there urged
"God and the glory! never care for gain.
The present by the future, what is that?
130 Live for fame, side by side with Agnolo!°   *Michelangelo*
Rafael is waiting: up to God, all three!"

---

8. A mountain peak outside Florence.   from selling it.
9. Raphael (1483–1520), born at Urbino.   2. Whistle or call used by hunters to lure wild fowl
1. In saying that the painting is a copy, Andrea   into range.
may perhaps be concerned to prevent Lucrezia

I might have done it for you. So it seems:
Perhaps not. All is as God overrules.
Beside, incentives come from the soul's self;
135   The rest avail not. Why do I need you?
What wife had Rafael, or has Agnolo?
In this world, who can do a thing, will not;
And who would do it, cannot, I perceive:
Yet the will's somewhat—somewhat, too, the power—
140   And thus we half-men struggle. At the end,
God, I conclude, compensates, punishes.
'Tis safer for me, if the award be strict,
That I am something underrated here.
Poor this long while, despised, to speak the truth.
145   I dared not, do you know, leave home all day,
For fear of chancing on the Paris lords.
The best is when they pass and look aside;
But they speak sometimes; I must bear it all.
Well may they speak! That Francis,[3] that first time,
150   And that long festal year at Fontainebleau!
I surely then could sometimes leave the ground,
Put on the glory, Rafael's daily wear,
In that humane great monarch's golden look—
One finger in his beard or twisted curl
155   Over his mouth's good mark that made the smile,
One arm about my shoulder, round my neck,
The jingle of his gold chain in my ear,
I painting proudly with his breath on me,
All his court round him, seeing with his eyes,
160   Such frank French eyes, and such a fire of souls
Profuse, my hand kept plying by those hearts—
And, best of all, this, this, this face beyond,
This in the background, waiting on my work,
To crown the issue with a last reward!
165   A good time, was it not, my kingly days?
And had you not grown restless . . . but I know—
'Tis done and past; 'twas right, my instinct said;
Too live the life grew, golden and not gray,
And I'm the weak-eyed bat no sun should tempt
170   Out of the grange whose four walls make his world.
How could it end in any other way?
You called me, and I came home to your heart.
The triumph was—to reach and stay there; since
I reached it ere the triumph, what is lost?
175   Let my hands frame your face in your hair's gold,
You beautiful Lucrezia that are mine!
"Rafael did this, Andrea painted that;
The Roman's is the better when you pray,
But still the other's Virgin was his wife—"

3. King Francis I of France had invited Andrea to his court at Fontainebleau and warmly encouraged him in his painting. On returning to Florence, however, Andrea is reputed to have stolen some funds entrusted to him by Francis; and to please Lucrezia he built a house with the money. Now he is afraid of being insulted by "Paris lords" on the streets.

180   Men will excuse me. I am glad to judge
       Both pictures in your presence; clearer grows
       My better fortune, I resolve to think.
       For, do you know, Lucrezia, as God lives,
       Said one day Agnolo, his very self,
185   To Rafael . . . I have known it all these years . . .
       (When the young man was flaming out his thoughts
       Upon a palace wall for Rome to see,
       Too lifted up in heart because of it)
       "Friend, there's a certain sorry little scrub
190   Goes up and down our Florence, none cares how,
       Who, were he set to plan and execute
       As you are, pricked on by your popes and kings,
       Would bring the sweat into that brow of yours!"
       To Rafael's—And indeed the arm is wrong.
195   I hardly dare . . . yet, only you to see,
       Give the chalk here—quick, thus the line should go!
       Aye, but the soul! he's Rafael! rub it out!
       Still, all I care for, if he spoke the truth,
       (What he? why, who but Michel Agnolo?
200   Do you forget already words like those?)
       If really there was such a chance, so lost—
       Is, whether you're—not grateful—but more pleased.
       Well, let me think so. And you smile indeed!
       This hour has been an hour! Another smile?
205   If you would sit thus by me every night
       I should work better, do you comprehend?
       I mean that I should earn more, give you more.
       See, it is settled dusk now; there's a star;
       Morello's gone, the watch-lights show the wall,
210   The cue-owls[4] speak the name we call them by.
       Come from the window, love—come in, at last,
       Inside the melancholy little house
       We built to be so gay with. God is just.
       King Francis may forgive me: oft at nights
215   When I look up from painting, eyes tired out,
       The walls become illumined, brick from brick
       Distinct, instead of mortar, fierce bright gold,
       That gold of his I did cement them with!
       Let us but love each other. Must you go?
220   That Cousin here again? he waits outside?
       Must see you—you, and not with me? Those loans?
       More gaming debts to pay?[5] you smiled for that?
       Well, let smiles buy me! have you more to spend?
       While hand and eye and something of a heart
225   Are left me, work's my ware, and what's it worth?
       I'll pay my fancy. Only let me sit
       The gray remainder of the evening out,

---

4. A kind of owl named for its cry, which sounds like *cue*.
5. Lucrezia's "Cousin" (or lover or friend) owes gambling debts to a creditor. Andrea has already contracted (lines 5–10) to pay off these debts by painting some pictures according to the creditor's specifications. Now he agrees to pay off further debts.

Idle, you call it, and muse perfectly
How I could paint, were I but back in France,
230 One picture, just one more—the Virgin's face,
Not yours this time! I want you at my side
To hear them—that is, Michel Agnolo—
Judge all I do and tell you of its worth.
Will you? Tomorrow, satisfy your friend.
235 I take the subjects for his corridor,
Finish the portrait out of hand—there, there,
And throw him in another thing or two
If he demurs; the whole should prove enough
To pay for this same Cousin's freak. Beside,
240 What's better and what's all I care about,
Get you the thirteen scudi° for the ruff!   *Italian coins*
Love, does that please you? Ah, but what does he,
The Cousin! What does he to please you more?

    I am grown peaceful as old age tonight.
245 I regret little, I would change still less.
Since there my past life lies, why alter it?
The very wrong to Francis!—it is true
I took his coin, was tempted and complied,
And built this house and sinned, and all is said.
250 My father and my mother died of want.[6]
Well, had I riches of my own? you see
How one gets rich! Let each one bear his lot.
They were born poor, lived poor, and poor they died:
And I have labored somewhat in my time
255 And not been paid profusely. Some good son
Paint my two hundred pictures—let him try!
No doubt, there's something strikes a balance. Yes,
You loved me quite enough, it seems tonight.
This must suffice me here. What would one have?
260 In heaven, perhaps, new chances, one more chance—
Four great walls in the New Jerusalem,[7]
Meted on each side by the angel's reed,°   *measuring rod*
For Leonard,[8] Rafael, Agnolo and me
To cover—the three first without a wife,
265 While I have mine! So—still they overcome
Because there's still Lucrezia—as I choose.

    Again the Cousin's whistle! Go, my Love.

ca. 1853   1855

---

6. According to Vasari, Andrea's infatuation for Lucrezia prompted him to stop supporting his poverty-stricken parents.

7. Cf. Revelation 21.10–21.
8. Leonardo da Vinci (1452–1519).

A Grammarian's Funeral[1]

Shortly after the Revival of Learning in Europe

Let us begin and carry up this corpse,
    Singing together.
Leave we the common crofts,[2] the vulgar thorpes°   *villages*
    Each in its tether[3]
5 Sleeping safe on the bosom of the plain,
    Cared for till cock-crow:
Look out if yonder be not day again
    Rimming the rock-row!
That's the appropriate country; there, man's thought,
10   Rarer, intenser,
Self-gathered for an outbreak, as it ought,
    Chafes in the censer.
Leave we the unlettered plain[4] its herd and crop;
    Seek we sepulture°   *burial place*
15 On a tall mountain, citied to the top,
    Crowded with culture!
All the peaks soar, but one the rest excels;
    Clouds overcome it;
No! yonder sparkle is the citadel's
20   Circling its summit.
Thither our path lies; wind we up the heights:
    Wait ye the warning?
Our low life was the level's and the night's;
    He's for the morning.
25 Step to a tune, square chests, erect each head,
    'Ware° the beholders!   *beware*
This is our master, famous, calm, and dead,
    Borne on our shoulders.

Sleep, crop and herd! sleep, darkling thorpe and croft,
30   Safe from the weather!
He, whom we convoy to his grave aloft,
    Singing together,
He was a man born with thy face and throat,
    Lyric Apollo![5]
35 Long he lived nameless: how should spring take note
    Winter would follow?
Till lo, the little touch, and youth was gone!
    Cramped and diminished,

---

1. The speaker is one of the students who are bearing the body of their scholarly master to the mountaintop for burial. The student's defense of the dead grammarian's idealistic dedication to knowledge and faith in a future life is expressed in some of the harshest-sounding and most laborious verse ever written by Browning. It is this grotesque combination of opposites (soaring idealism in conjunction with harsh or petty realities) that gives *A Grammarian's Funeral* its distinctive tone.
  No model for the grammarian has been specifi-

cally identified. Browning seems to have had in mind the kind of early Renaissance scholar whose devotion to the Greek language made it possible for others to enjoy the more recognizably significant aspects of the revival of learning.
2. Small tracts of land farmed by peasants.
3. Restricted to a narrow sphere like an animal tied to a stake.
4. Flatlands at the base of the mountain that are populated by illiterate shepherds and peasants.
5. God of music and embodiment of male beauty.

Moaned he, "New measures, other feet anon!
40   My dance is finished?"
No, that's the world's way: (keep the mountain-side,
        Make for the city!)
He knew the signal, and stepped on with pride
        Over men's pity;
45 Left play for work, and grappled with the world
        Bent on escaping:
"What's in the scroll," quoth he, "thou keepest furled?
        Show me their shaping,
Theirs who most studied man, the bard and sage—
50   Give!"—So, he gowned him,[6]
Straight got by heart that book to its last page:
        Learned, we found him.
Yea, but we found him bald too, eyes like lead,
        Accents uncertain:
55 "Time to taste life," another would have said,
        "Up with the curtain!"
This man said rather, "Actual life comes next?
        Patience a moment!
Grant I have mastered learning's crabbed text,
60   Still there's the comment.[7]
Let me know all! Prate not of most or least,
        Painful or easy!
Even to the crumbs I'd fain eat up the feast,
        Aye, nor feel queasy."
65 Oh, such a life as he resolved to live,
        When he had learned it,
When he had gathered all books had to give!
        Sooner, he spurned it.
Image the whole, then execute the parts—
70   Fancy the fabric
Quite, ere you build, ere steel strike fire from quartz,
        Ere mortar dab brick!

(Here's the town gate reached: there's the market place
        Gaping before us.)
75 Yea, this in him was the peculiar grace
        (Hearten our chorus!)
That before living he'd learn how to live—
        No end to learning:
Earn the means first—God surely will contrive
80   Use for our earning.
Others mistrust and say, "But time escapes:
        Live now or never!"
He said, "What's time? Leave Now for dogs and apes!
        Man has Forever."
85 Back to his book then: deeper drooped his head:
        Calculus[8] racked him:

6. Dressed in academic gown; became a scholar.   8. A stone such as a gallstone.
7. Commentaries or annotations on a text.

Leaden before, his eyes grew dross of lead:
  Tussis° attacked him.   *a cough*
"Now, master, take a little rest!"—not he!
90   (Caution redoubled,
 Step two abreast, the way winds narrowly!)
  Not a whit troubled
Back to his studies, fresher than at first,
  Fierce as a dragon
95 He (soul-hydroptic° with a sacred thirst)
  Sucked at the flagon.
Oh, if we draw a circle premature,
  Heedless of far gain,
Greedy for quick returns of profit, sure
100   Bad is our bargain!
Was it not great? did not he throw on God
  (He loves the burthen)—
God's task to make the heavenly period
  Perfect the earthen?
105 Did not he magnify the mind, show clear
  Just what it all meant?
He would not discount life, as fools do here,
  Paid by installment.
He ventured neck or nothing—heaven's success
110   Found, or earth's failure:
"Wilt thou trust death or not?" He answered "Yes:
  Hence with life's pale lure!"
That low man seeks a little thing to do,
  Sees it and does it:
115 This high man, with a great thing to pursue,
  Dies ere he knows it.
That low man goes on adding one to one,
  His hundred's soon hit:
This high man, aiming at a million,
120   Misses an unit.[1]
That, has the world here—should he need the next,
  Let the world mind him!
This, throws himself on God, and unperplexed
  Seeking shall find him.
125 So, with the throttling hands of death at strife,
  Ground he at grammar;
Still, through the rattle, parts of speech were rife:
  While he could stammer
He settled *Hoti's* business—let it be!—
130   Properly based *Oun*—
Gave us the doctrine of the enclitic *De*,[2]
  Dead from the waist down.
Well, here's the platform, here's the proper place:

9. Insatiably soul thirsty.
1. A small item such as some trifling worldly pleasure.
2. "*Hoti*," "*Oun*," and "*De*": Greek particles meaning "that," "then," and "toward." An unaccented word such as *de* is "enclitic" when it affects the accentuation of a word adjacent to it. In a letter of 1863, Browning commented to Tennyson that he wanted his grammarian to have been working on "the biggest of the littlenesses."

<pre>
          Hail to your purlieus,
135   All ye highfliers of the feathered race,
          Swallows and curlews!
      Here's the top peak; the multitude below
          Live, for they can, there:
      This man decided not to Live but Know—
140   Bury this man there?
      Here—here's his place, where meteors shoot, clouds form,
          Lightnings are loosened,
      Stars come and go! Let joy break with the storm,
          Peace let the dew send!
145   Lofty designs must close in like effects:
          Loftily lying,
      Leave him—still loftier than the world suspects,
          Living and dying.
</pre>

ca. 1854   1855

Caliban upon Setebos Two closely related controversies of the Victorian period led Browning to write this poem (the title of which means "Caliban's thoughts about Setebos"). The first, stimulated by Darwin, was concerned with humanity's origins and our relation to other animals (the poem teems with animal life; in 295 lines, as Park Honan has shown, there are sixty-three references to animals). Caliban, the half-man and half-monster of Shakespeare's *Tempest,* provided the poet with a model of how the mind of a primitive creature may operate. The second controversy concerned the nature of God and God's responsibility for the existence of suffering in the world. Like many humans, Caliban thinks of God's nature as similar to his own. His anthropomorphic conception of the deity, whom he calls Setebos, is confined to what he has observed of life on his island and to what he has observed of himself. From the former derives his "natural theology," that is, his identifying the character of God from evidences provided by nature rather than from the evidence of supernatural revelation. From the latter, his observation of his own character, derives Caliban's conception of God's willful power. Caliban himself admires power and thinks of God in Calvinistic terms as a being who selects at random some creatures who are to be saved and others who are to be condemned to suffer.

An obstacle for the reader is Caliban's use of the third-person pronoun to refer to himself. Thus " 'Will sprawl" means "Caliban will sprawl" (an apostrophe before the verb usually indicates that Caliban himself is the implied subject). The deity is also referred to in the third person but with an initial capital letter ("He").

Caliban upon Setebos

Or Natural Theology in the Island

"Thou thoughtest that I was altogether such a one as thyself."[1]

['Will sprawl, now that the heat of day is best,
Flat on his belly in the pit's much mire,

---

1. Psalm 50.21. The speaker is God.

With elbows wide, fists clenched to prop his chin.
And, while he kicks both feet in the cool slush,
5   And feels about his spine small eft-things° course,   *water lizards*
Run in and out each arm, and make him laugh:
And while above his head a pompion° plant,   *pumpkin*
Coating the cave-top as a brow its eye,
Creeps down to touch and tickle hair and beard,
10 And now a flower drops with a bee inside,
And now a fruit to snap at, catch and crunch—
He looks out o'er yon sea which sunbeams cross
And recross till they weave a spider web
(Meshes of fire, some great fish breaks at times)
15 And talks to his own self, howe'er he please,
Touching that other, whom his dam² called God.
Because to talk about Him, vexes—ha,
Could He but know! and time to vex is now,
When talk is safer than in wintertime.
20 Moreover Prosper and Miranda³ sleep
In confidence he drudges at their task,
And it is good to cheat the pair, and gibe,
Letting the rank tongue blossom into speech.]

Setebos, Setebos, and Setebos!
25 'Thinketh, He dwelleth i' the cold o' the moon.

'Thinketh He made it, with the sun to match,
But not the stars; the stars came otherwise;
Only made clouds, winds, meteors, such as that:
Also this isle, what lives and grows thereon,
30 And snaky sea which rounds and ends the same.

'Thinketh, it came of being ill at ease:
He hated that He cannot change His cold,
Nor cure its ache. 'Hath spied an icy fish
That longed to 'scape the rock-stream where she lived,
35 And thaw herself within the lukewarm brine
O' the lazy sea her stream thrusts far amid,
A crystal spike 'twixt two warm walls of wave;⁴
Only, she ever sickened, found repulse
At the other kind of water, not her life,
40 (Green-dense and dim-delicious, bred o' the sun)
Flounced back from bliss she was not born to breathe,
And in her old bounds buried her despair,
Hating and loving warmth alike: so He.

'Thinketh, He made thereat the sun, this isle,
45 Trees and the fowls here, beast and creeping thing.
Yon otter, sleek-wet, black, lithe as a leech;
Yon auk,° one fire-eye in a ball of foam,   *sea bird*

2. Caliban's mother, Sycorax.
3. The daughter of Prospero, the magician, who is
Caliban's master in *The Tempest*.

4. I.e., the thin stream of cold water that is driven
into the warm ocean like a spike between walls.

That floats and feeds; a certain badger brown
He hath watched hunt with that slant white-wedge eye
50 By moonlight; and the pie° with the long tongue   *magpie*
That pricks deep into oakwarts for a worm,
And says a plain word when she finds her prize,
But will not eat the ants; the ants themselves
That build a wall of seeds and settled stalks
55 About their hole—He made all these and more,
Made all we see, and us, in spite: how else?
He could not, Himself, make a second self
To be His mate; as well have made Himself:
He would not make what he mislikes or slights,
60 An eyesore to Him, or not worth His pains:
But did, in envy, listlessness, or sport,
Make what Himself would fain, in a manner, be—
Weaker in most points, stronger in a few,
Worthy, and yet mere playthings all the while,
65 Things He admires and mocks too—that is it.
Because, so brave, so better though they be,
It nothing skills if He begin to plague.[5]
Look now, I melt a gourd-fruit into mash,
Add honeycomb and pods, I have perceived,
70 Which bite like finches when they bill and kiss—
Then, when froth rises bladdery,° drink up all,   *bubbly*
Quick, quick, till maggots scamper through my brain;
Last, throw me on my back i' the seeded thyme,
And wanton, wishing I were born a bird.
75 Put case, unable to be what I wish,
I yet could make a live bird out of clay:
Would not I take clay, pinch my Caliban
Able to fly?—for, there, see, he hath wings,
And great comb like the hoopoe's[6] to admire,
80 And there, a sting to do his foes offense,
There, and I will that he begin to live,
Fly to yon rock-top, nip me off the horns
Of griggs° high up that make the merry din,   *grasshoppers*
Saucy through their veined wings, and mind me not.
85 In which feat, if his leg snapped, brittle clay,
And he lay stupid-like—why, I should laugh;
And if he, spying me, should fall to weep,
Beseech me to be good, repair his wrong,
Bid his poor leg smart less or grow again—
90 Well, as the chance were, this might take or else
Not take my fancy: I might hear his cry,
And give the mankin three sound legs for one,
Or pluck the other off, leave him like an egg,
And lessoned he was mine and merely clay.
95 Were this no pleasure, lying in the thyme,
Drinking the mash, with brain become alive,

5. I.e., our superior virtues are of no help to us if
God elects to inflict plagues on us.

6. Bird with bright plumage.

Making and marring clay at will? So He.
'Thinketh, such shows nor right nor wrong in Him,
Nor kind, nor cruel: He is strong and Lord.
100 'Am strong myself compared to yonder crabs
That march now from the mountain to the sea;
'Let twenty pass, and stone the twenty-first,
Loving not, hating not, just choosing so.
'Say, the first straggler that boasts purple spots
105 Shall join the file, one pincer twisted off;
'Say, this bruised fellow shall receive a worm,
And two worms he whose nippers end in red;
As it likes me each time, I do: so He.

Well then, 'supposeth He is good i' the main,
110 Placable if His mind and ways were guessed,
But rougher than His handiwork, be sure!
Oh, He hath made things worthier than Himself,
And envieth that, so helped, such things do more
Than He who made them! What consoles but this?
115 That they, unless through Him, do naught at all,
And must submit: what other use in things?
'Hath cut a pipe of pithless elder-joint
That, blown through, gives exact the scream o' the jay
When from her wing you twitch the feathers blue:
120 Sound this, and little birds that hate the jay
Flock within stone's throw, glad their foe is hurt:
Put case such pipe could prattle and boast forsooth,
"I catch the birds, I am the crafty thing,
I make the cry my maker cannot make
125 With his great round mouth; he must blow through mine!"
Would not I smash it with my foot? So He.

But wherefore rough, why cold and ill at ease?
Aha, that is a question! Ask, for that,
What knows—the something over Setebos
130 That made Him, or He, may be, found and fought,
Worsted, drove off and did to nothing,° perchance.   *completely overcame*
There may be something quiet o'er His head,
Out of His reach, that feels nor joy nor grief,
Since both derive from weakness in some way.
135 I joy because the quails come; would not joy
Could I bring quails here when I have a mind:
This Quiet, all it hath a mind to, doth.
'Esteemeth stars the outposts of its couch,
But never spends much thought nor care that way.
140 It may look up, work up—the worse for those
It works on! 'Careth but for Setebos[7]
The many-handed as a cuttlefish,
Who, making Himself feared through what He does,
Looks up, first, and perceives he cannot soar

7. Caliban's concern is to appease only Setebos, not the other deity—the Quiet.

145 To what is quiet and hath happy life;
Next looks down here, and out of very spite
Makes this a bauble-world to ape yon real,
These good things to match those as hips[8] do grapes.
'Tis solace making baubles, aye, and sport.

150 Himself peeped late, eyed Prosper at his books
Careless and lofty, lord now of the isle:
Vexed, 'stitched a book of broad leaves, arrow-shaped,
Wrote thereon, he knows what, prodigious words;
Has peeled a wand and called it by a name;

155 Weareth at whiles for an enchanter's robe
The eyed skin of a supple oncelot;[9]
And hath an ounce[1] sleeker than youngling mole,
A four-legged serpent he makes cower and couch,
Now snarl, now hold its breath and mind his eye,

160 And saith she is Miranda and my wife:
'Keeps for his Ariel[2] a tall pouch-bill crane
He bids go wade for fish and straight disgorge;
Also a sea beast, lumpish, which he snared,
Blinded the eyes of, and brought somewhat tame,

165 And split its toe-webs, and now pens the drudge
In a hole o' the rock and calls him Caliban;
A bitter heart that bides its time and bites.
'Plays thus at being Prosper in a way,
Taketh his mirth with make-believes: so He.

170 His dam held that the Quiet made all things
Which Setebos vexed only: 'holds not so.
Who made them weak, meant weakness He might vex.
Had He meant other, while His hand was in,
Why not make horny eyes no thorn could prick,

175 Or plate my scalp with bone against the snow,
Or overscale my flesh 'neath joint and joint,
Like an orc's° armor? Aye—so spoil His sport!   *sea monster's*
He is the One now: only He doth all.

'Saith, He may like, perchance, what profits Him.
180 Aye, himself loves what does him good; but why?
'Gets good no otherwise. This blinded beast
Loves whoso places flesh-meat on his nose,
But, had he eyes, would want no help, but hate
Or love, just as it liked him: He hath eyes.

185 Also it pleaseth Setebos to work,
Use all His hands, and exercise much craft,
By no means for the love of what is worked.
'Tasteth, himself, no finer good i' the world
When all goes right, in this safe summertime,

190 And he wants little, hungers, aches not much,

8. Hard fruits produced by wild roses.
9. Browning may have invented this term from the Spanish *oncela* or from the French *ocelot*. Both words signify a leopard or spotted wildcat.

1. A large, ferocious leopard, six or seven feet in length.
2. In *The Tempest*, a spirit who serves Prospero.

Than trying what to do with wit and strength.
'Falls to make something: 'piled yon pile of turfs,
And squared and stuck there squares of soft white chalk,
And, with a fish-tooth, scratched a moon on each,
195 And set up endwise certain spikes of tree,
And crowned the whole with a sloth's skull a-top,
Found dead i' the woods, too hard for one to kill.
No use at all i' the work, for work's sole sake;
'Shall some day knock it down again: so He.

200 'Saith He is terrible: watch His feats in proof!
One hurricane will spoil six good months' hope.
He hath a spite against me, that I know,
Just as He favors Prosper, who knows why?
So it is, all the same, as well I find.
205 'Wove wattles half the winter, fenced them firm
With stone and stake to stop she-tortoises
Crawling to lay their eggs here: well, one wave,
Feeling the foot of Him upon its neck,
Gaped as a snake does, lolled out its large tongue,
210 And licked the whole labor flat; so much for spite.
'Saw a ball° flame down late (yonder it lies)   *meteorite*
Where, half an hour before, I slept i' the shade:
Often they scatter sparkles: there is force!
'Dug up a newt He may have envied once
215 And turned to stone, shut up inside a stone.
Please Him and hinder this?—What Prosper does?[3]
Aha, if He would tell me how! Not He!
There is the sport: discover how or die!
All need not die, for of the things o' the isle
220 Some flee afar, some dive, some run up trees;
Those at His mercy—why, they please Him most
When . . . when . . . well, never try the same way twice!
Repeat what act has pleased, He may grow wroth.
You must not know His ways, and play Him off,
225 Sure of the issue. 'Doth the like himself:
'Spareth a squirrel that it nothing fears
But steals the nut from underneath my thumb,
And when I threat, bites stoutly in defense:
'Spareth an urchin° that contrariwise   *hedgehog*
230 Curls up into a ball, pretending death
For fright at my approach: the two ways please.
But what would move my choler more than this,
That either creature counted on its life
Tomorrow and next day and all days to come,
235 Saying, forsooth, in the inmost of its heart,
"Because he did so yesterday with me,
And otherwise with such another brute,
So must he do henceforth and always."—Aye?

3. I.e., shall I please Setebos, as Prospero does, and thus prevent my being punished as the newt was
punished?

Would teach the reasoning couple what "must" means!
240   'Doth as he likes, or wherefore Lord? So He.

'Conceiveth all things will continue thus,
And we shall have to live in fear of Him
So long as He lives, keeps His strength: no change,
If He have done His best, make no new world
245   To please Him more, so leave off watching this—
If He surprise not even the Quiet's self
Some strange day—or, suppose, grow into it
As grubs grow butterflies: else, here are we,
And there is He, and nowhere help at all.
250   'Believeth with the life, the pain shall stop.
His dam held different, that after death
He both plagued enemies and feasted friends:
Idly![4] He doth His worst in this our life,
Giving just respite lest we die through pain,
255   Saving last pain for worst—with which, an end.
Meanwhile, the best way to escape His ire
Is, not to seem too happy. 'Sees, himself,
Yonder two flies, with purple films and pink,
Bask on the pompion-bell above: kills both.
260   'Sees two black painful beetles roll their ball
On head and tail as if to save their lives:
Moves them the stick away they strive to clear.

Even so, 'would have Him misconceive, suppose
This Caliban strives hard and ails no less,
265   And always, above all else, envies Him;
Wherefore he mainly dances on dark nights,
Moans in the sun, gets under holes to laugh,
And never speaks his mind save housed as now:
Outside, 'groans, curses. If He caught me here,
270   O'erheard this speech, and asked "What chucklest at?"
'Would, to appease Him, cut a finger off,
Or of my three kid yearlings burn the best,
Or let the toothsome apples rot on tree,
Or push my tame beast for the orc to taste:
275   While myself lit a fire, and made a song
And sung it, *"What I hate, be consecrate*
To celebrate Thee and Thy state, no mate
For Thee; what see for envy in poor me?"
Hoping the while, since evils sometimes mend,
280   Warts rub away and sores are cured with slime,
That some strange day, will either the Quiet catch
And conquer Setebos, or likelier He
Decrepit may doze, doze, as good as die.

---

4. I.e., Caliban thinks his mother's opinion was wrong or idle. God's sport with humankind is confined to this world: there is no afterlife.

[What, what? A curtain o'er the world at once!
285 Crickets stop hissing; not a bird—or, yes,
There scuds His raven that has told Him all!
It was fool's play this prattling! Ha! The wind
Shoulders the pillared dust, death's house o' the move,[5]
And fast invading fires begin! White blaze—
290 A tree's head snaps—and there, there, there, there, there,
His thunder follows! Fool to gibe at Him!
Lo! 'Lieth flat and loveth Setebos!
'Maketh his teeth meet through his upper lip,
Will let those quails fly, will not eat this month
295 One little mess of whelks,° so he may 'scape!]   *shellfish*

ca. 1860   1864

Prospice[1]

Fear death?—to feel the fog in my throat,
    The mist in my face,
When the snows begin, and the blasts denote
    I am nearing the place,
5   The power of the night, the press of the storm,
        The post of the foe;
Where he stands, the Arch Fear in a visible form,
        Yet the strong man must go:
For the journey is done and the summit attained,
10   And the barriers fall,
Though a battle's to fight ere the guerdon be gained,
        The reward of it all.
I was ever a fighter, so—one fight more,
        The best and the last!
15 I would hate that death bandaged my eyes, and forbore,
        And bade me creep past.
No! let me taste the whole of it, fare like my peers
        The heroes of old,
Bear the brunt, in a minute pay glad life's arrears
20   Of pain, darkness, and cold.
For sudden the worst turns the best to the brave,
        The black minute's at end,
And the elements' rage, the fiend-voices that rave,
        Shall dwindle, shall blend,
25 Shall change, shall become first a peace out of pain,
        Then a light, then thy breast,
O thou soul of my soul![2] I shall clasp thee again,
        And with God be the rest!

ca. 1861   1864

---

5. The whirlwind stirs up a column of dust that
Caliban associates with a house of death.

1. The title means "Look forward."
2. Browning's wife.

Rabbi Ben Ezra[1]

1

Grow old along with me!
The best is yet to be,
The last of life, for which the first was made:
    Our times are in His hand
5   Who saith, "A whole I planned,
Youth shows but half; trust God: see all nor be afraid!"

2

    Not that, amassing flowers,
    Youth sighed, "Which rose make ours,
Which lily leave and then as best recall?"
10   Not that, admiring stars,
    It yearned, "Nor Jove, nor Mars;
Mine be some figured flame which blends, transcends them all!"

3

    Not for such hopes and fears
    Annulling youth's brief years,
15 Do I remonstrate: folly wide the mark!
    Rather I prize the doubt
    Low kinds exist without,
Finished and finite clods, untroubled by a spark.

4

    Poor vaunt of life indeed,
20   Were man but formed to feed
On joy, to solely seek and find and feast:
    Such feasting ended, then
    As sure an end to men;
Irks care the crop-full bird? Frets doubt the maw-crammed beast?[2]

5

25   Rejoice we are allied
    To That which doth provide
And not partake, effect and not receive!
    A spark disturbs our clod;
    Nearer we hold of God
30 Who gives, than of His tribes that take, I must believe.

6

    Then, welcome each rebuff
    That turns earth's smoothness rough,

---

1. The speaker, Abraham Ibn Ezra (ca. 1092–1167), was an eminent biblical scholar of Spain, but Browning makes little attempt to present him as a distinct individual or to relate him to the age in which he lived. Unlike the more characteristic monologues, *Rabbi Ben Ezra* is not dramatic but declamatory.

2. I.e., does care disturb a bird whose gullet ("crop") is full of food? Does doubt trouble an animal whose stomach ("maw") is full?

Each sting that bids nor sit nor stand but go!
  Be our joys three parts pain!
35   Strive, and hold cheap the strain;
Learn, nor account the pang; dare, never grudge the throe!°   *anguish*

7

  For thence—a paradox
  Which comforts while it mocks—
Shall life succeed in that it seems to fail:
40   What I aspired to be,
  And was not, comforts me:
A brute I might have been, but would not sink i' the scale.

8

  What is he but a brute
  Whose flesh has soul to suit,
45 Whose spirit works lest arms and legs want play?
   To man, propose this test—
  Thy body at its best,
How far can that project thy soul on its lone way?

9

  Yet gifts should prove their use:
50   I own the Past profuse
Of power each side, perfection every turn:
   Eyes, ears took in their dole,
  Brain treasured up the whole;
Should not the heart beat once, "How good to live and learn"?

10

55   Not once beat, "Praise be Thine!
  I see the whole design,
I, who saw power, see now love perfect too:
   Perfect I call Thy plan:
  Thanks that I was a man!
60 Maker, remake, complete—I trust what Thou shalt do!"

11

  For pleasant is this flesh;
  Our soul, in its rose-mesh[3]
Pulled ever to the earth, still yearns for rest;
   Would we some prize might hold
65   To match those manifold
Possessions of the brute—gain most, as we did best!

12

  Let us not always say,
  "Spite of this flesh today
I strove, made head, gained ground upon the whole!"

---

3. The body, which holds the soul in its net.

70   As the bird wings and sings,
            Let us cry, "All good things
Are ours, nor soul helps flesh more, now, than flesh helps soul!"

13

        Therefore I summon age
        To grant youth's heritage,
75 Life's struggle having so far reached its term:
        Thence shall I pass, approved
        A man, for aye removed
From the developed brute; a god though in the germ.

14

        And I shall thereupon
80   Take rest, ere I be gone
Once more on my adventure brave and new;[4]
        Fearless and unperplexed,
        When I wage battle next,
What weapons to select, what armor to indue.°   *put on*

15

85   Youth ended, I shall try
        My gain or loss thereby;
Leave the fire ashes,[5] what survives is gold:
        And I shall weigh the same,
        Give life its praise or blame:
90 Young, all lay in dispute; I shall know, being old.

16

        For note, when evening shuts,
        A certain moment cuts
The deed off, calls the glory from the gray:
        A whisper from the west
95   Shoots—"Add this to the rest,
Take it and try its worth: here dies another day."

17

        So, still within this life,
        Though lifted o'er its strife,
Let me discern, compare, pronounce at last,
100   "This rage was right i' the main,
        That acquiescence vain:
The Future I may face now I have proved the Past."

18

        For more is not reserved
        To man, with soul just nerved
105 To act tomorrow what he learns today:

---

4. In the next life.   5. If the fire leaves ashes.

Here, work enough to watch
The Master work, and catch
Hints of the proper craft, tricks of the tool's true play.

19

As it was better, youth
110   Should strive, through acts uncouth,
Toward making, than repose on aught found made:
So, better, age, exempt
From strife, should know, than tempt°   *attempt*
Further. Thou waitedst age: wait death nor be afraid!

20

115   Enough now, if the Right
And Good and Infinite
Be named here, as thou callest thy hand thine own,
With knowledge absolute,
Subject to no dispute
120   From fools that crowded youth, nor let thee feel alone.

21

Be there, for once and all,
Severed great minds from small,
Announced to each his station in the Past!
Was I, the world arraigned,[6]
125   Were they, my soul disdained,
Right? Let age speak the truth and give us peace at last![7]

22

Now, who shall arbitrate?
Ten men love what I hate,
Shun what I follow, slight what I receive;
130   Ten, who in ears and eyes
Match me: we all surmise,
They this thing, and I that: whom shall my soul believe?

23

Not on the vulgar mass
Called "work," must sentence pass,
135   Things done, that took the eye and had the price;
O'er which, from level stand,
The low world laid its hand,
Found straightway to its mind, could value in a trice:

24

But all, the world's coarse thumb
140   And finger failed to plumb,

6. I.e., was I, whom the world arraigned.
7. Stanzas 20 and 21 affirm that in age we can more readily think independently than in youth.

Maturity enables us to ignore the pressure of having to conform to the thinking of the crowd of small-minded people.

So passed in making up the main account;
    All instincts immature,
    All purposes unsure,
That weighed not as his work, yet swelled the man's amount:

25

145   Thoughts hardly to be packed
    Into a narrow act,
Fancies that broke through language and escaped;
    All I could never be,
    All, men ignored in me,
150 This, I was worth to God, whose wheel the pitcher shaped.[8]

26

    Aye, note that Potter's wheel,
    That metaphor! and feel
Why time spins fast, why passive lies our clay—
    Thou, to whom fools propound,[9]
155   When the wine makes its round,
"Since life fleets, all is change; the Past gone, seize today!"

27

    Fool! All that is, at all,
    Lasts ever, past recall;
Earth changes, but thy soul and God stand sure:
160   What entered into thee,
    That was, is, and shall be:
Time's wheel runs back or stops: Potter and clay endure.

28

    He fixed thee 'mid this dance
    Of plastic circumstance,
165 This Present, thou, forsooth, wouldst fain arrest:[1]
    Machinery just meant
    To give thy soul its bent,
Try thee and turn thee forth, sufficiently impressed.

29

    What though the earlier grooves
170   Which ran the laughing loves
Around thy base,[2] no longer pause and press?
    What though, about thy rim,
    Skull-things in order grim
Grow out, in graver mood, obey the sterner stress?

---

8. The speaker's highest qualities of soul were shaped on a potting wheel into an enduring "pitcher" by God. Cf. Isaiah 64.8.
9. Perhaps addressed to Omar Khayyám, whose poem, *The Rubáiyát*, urged men to eat, drink, and be merry. Edward FitzGerald's translation of Omar's poem had appeared in 1859.
1. I.e., you would be glad to stop ("arrest") time at this present point of your life.
2. Of the clay pitcher.

30

175 　　　　Look not thou down but up!
　　　　To uses of a cup,
　　The festal board, lamp's flash, and trumpet's peal,
　　　　The new wine's foaming flow,
　　　　The Master's lips a-glow!
180 Thou, heaven's consummate cup, what need'st thou with earth's wheel?

31

　　　　But I need, now as then,
　　　　Thee, God, who moldest men;
　　And since, not even while the whirl was worst,
　　　　Did I—to the wheel of life
185 　　　　With shapes and colors rife,
　　Bound dizzily—mistake my end, to slake Thy thirst:

32

　　　　So, take and use Thy work:
　　　　Amend what flaws may lurk,
　　What strain o' the stuff, what warpings past the aim!
190 　　　　My times be in Thy hand!
　　　　Perfect the cup as planned!
　　Let age approve of youth, and death complete the same!

ca. 1862　　　　　　　　　　　　　　　　　　　　　　　　　　1864

MATTHEW ARNOLD
1822–1888

How is a full and enjoyable life to be lived in a modern industrial society? This was the recurrent topic in the poetry and prose of Matthew Arnold. In his poetry the question itself is raised; in his prose some answers are attempted. "The misapprehensiveness of his age is exactly what a poet is sent to remedy," wrote Browning. Oddly enough it is to Arnold's work rather than to Browning's that the statement seems more appropriate. And its applicability to Arnold has persisted from Victorian times to ours, in part because the "misapprehensiveness" has also persisted.

　　Matthew Arnold was born in Laleham, a village in the valley of the Thames. That his childhood was spent in the vicinity of a river seems appropriate, for clear-flowing streams were later to appear in his poems as symbols of serenity. At six, Arnold was moved to Rugby School, where his father, Dr. Thomas Arnold, had become headmaster. As a clergyman Dr. Arnold was a leader of the liberal or Broad Church and hence one of the principal opponents of John Henry Newman. As a headmaster he became famous as an educational reformer, a teacher who instilled into his pupils an earnest preoccupation with moral and social issues and also an awareness of the connection between liberal studies and modern life. At Rugby his eldest son, Matthew, was directly exposed to the powerful force of the father's mind and character. The son's attitude toward this force was a mixture of attraction and repulsion. That he was permanently influenced by his father is evident in his poems and in his writings on religion and politics, but like many sons of clergymen, he made a determined effort in his youth to be different. At Oxford he behaved like a character from one of Evelyn Waugh's early novels. Elegantly and colorfully dressed, alternately languid or merry in manner, he attracted attention as a dandy whose irreverent jokes irritated his more solemn undergraduate friends and acquaintances. "His manner displeases, from its seeming foppery," wrote Charlotte Brontë after talking with the young man. "The shade of Dr. Arnold," she added, "seemed to me to frown on his young representative." Thus with Rugby School's standards of earnestness the son of Dr. Arnold appeared to have no connection. Even his studies did not seem to occupy him seriously. By a session of cramming, he managed to earn second-class honors in his final examinations, a near disaster that was redeemed by his election to a fellowship at Oriel College.

Arnold's biographers usually dismiss his youthful frivolity of spirit as a temporary pose or mask, but it was more. It remained to color his prose style, brightening his most serious criticism with geniality and wit. For most readers the jauntiness of his prose is a virtue, although for others it is offensive. Anyone suspicious of urbanity and irony would applaud Whitman's sour comment that Arnold is "one of the dudes of literature." A more appropriate estimate of his manner is provided by Arnold's own description of Sainte-Beuve as a critic: "a critic of measure, not exuberant; of the center, not provincial . . . with gay and amiable temper, his manner as good as his matter—the 'critique souriant' [smiling critic]."

Unlike Tennyson or Carlyle, Arnold had to confine his writing and reading to his spare time. In 1847 he took the post of private secretary to Lord Lansdowne, and in 1851, the year of his marriage, he became an inspector of schools, a position that he held for thirty-five years. Although his work as an inspector may have reduced his output as a writer, it had several advantages. His extensive traveling in England took him to the homes of the more ardently Protestant middle classes, and when he criticized the dullness of middle-class life (as he often did), Arnold knew his subject intimately. His position also led to travel on the Continent to study the schools of Europe. As a critic of English education, he was thus able to make helpful comparisons and to draw on a stock of fresh ideas in the same way as in his literary criticism he used his knowledge of French, German, Italian, and classical literatures to measure the achievements of English writers. Despite the monotony of much of his work as an inspector, Arnold became convinced of its importance. It was work that contributed to what he regarded as the most important need of his century: the development of a satisfactory system of education for the middle classes.

In 1849, Arnold published *The Strayed Reveler,* the first of his volumes of poetry. Eight years later, as a tribute to his poetic achievement, he was elected to the professorship of poetry at Oxford, a part-time position that he held for ten years. Later, like Dickens and Thackeray before him, Arnold toured America to make money by lecturing. The reception accorded his lectures was varied. Sometimes his audiences were indifferent, but it is of interest to learn from the *Washington Post* of his stunning success in that city, where, following a two-hour address, the great African American leader Frederick Douglass "moved that a tremendous vote of thanks be tendered to the speaker." For his two visits (1883 and 1886), there was the further inducement of seeing his daughter Lucy, who had married an American. Two years after his second visit to the United States, Arnold died of a sudden heart attack.

Arnold's career as a writer can be divided roughly into four periods. In the 1850s most of his poems appeared; in the 1860s, his literary criticism and social criticism; in the 1870s, his religious and educational writings; and in the 1880s, his second set of essays in literary criticism.

About his career as a poet, two questions are repeatedly asked. The first is whether his poetry is as effective as or better than his prose; the second is why he virtually stopped writing poetry after 1860. The first has, of course, been variously answered.

Many would endorse Tennyson's request in a letter: "Tell Mat not to write any more of those prose things like *Literature and Dogma,* but to give us something like his *Thyrsis, Scholar Gypsy,* or *Forsaken Merman.*" At the opposite extreme is a recent critic, J. D. Jump, who has a high regard for Arnold's prose but considers only one of the poems (*Dover Beach*) to have merit. Such readers complain, and with good cause, of Arnold's bad habits as a poet: for example, his excessive reliance on italics instead of on meter as a method of emphasizing the meaning of a line. Or they cite the prosy flatness of some of his lines. Contrariwise, when Arnold leaves the flat plane of versified reflections and attempts to scale the heights of what he called "the grand style," there is a different kind of uncertainty that becomes evident, as in *Sohrab and Rustum,* in the overelaborated similes. Yet the success of such lovely poems as *Thyrsis* is more than enough to overcome the indictments of the critics. Often, as in *Thyrsis,* he is at his best as a poet of nature. Settings of seashore or river or mountaintop provide something more than picturesque backdrops for these poems; they function to draw the meaning together. A concern for rendering outdoor nature may seem a curious accomplishment for so sophisticated a writer, but as his contemporaries noted, Arnold is in this respect, as in several others, similar to Thomas Gray.

Arnold's own verdict on the qualities of his poetry is a reasonable one. In a letter to his mother, in 1869, he writes:

> My poems represent, on the whole, the main movement of mind of the last quarter of a century, and thus they will probably have their day as people become conscious to themselves of what that movement of mind is, and interested in the literary productions which reflect it. It might be fairly urged that I have less poetical sentiment than Tennyson, and less intellectual vigor and abundance than Browning; yet, because I have perhaps more of a fusion of the two than either of them, and have more regularly applied that fusion to the main line of modern development, I am likely enough to have my turn, as they have had theirs.

The emphasis in the letter on "movement of mind" suggests that Arnold's poetry and prose should be studied together. Such an approach can be fruitful provided that it does not obscure the important difference between Arnold the poet and Arnold the critic. T. S. Eliot once said of his own writings that "in one's prose reflections one may be legitimately occupied with ideals, whereas in the writing of verse, one can deal only with actuality." Arnold's writings provide a nice verification of Eliot's seeming paradox. As a poet he usually records his own experiences, his own feelings of loneliness and isolation as a lover, his longing for a serenity that he cannot find, his melancholy sense of the passing of youth (more than for many men, Arnold's thirtieth birthday was an awesome landmark after which he felt, he said, "three parts iced over"). Above all he records his despair in a universe in which humanity's role seemed as incongruous as it was later to seem to Thomas Hardy. In a memorable passage of his *Stanzas from the Grande Chartreuse,* he describes himself as "wandering between two worlds, one dead, / The other powerless to be born." And addressing the representatives of a faith that seems to him dead, he cries: "Take me, cowled forms, and fence me round, / Till I possess my soul again."

As a poet, then, like T. S. Eliot and W. H. Auden, Arnold provides a record of a sick individual in a sick society. This was "actuality" as he experienced it—an actuality, like Eliot's and Auden's, representative of his era. As a prose writer, a formulator of "ideals," he seeks a different role. It is the role of what Auden calls the "healer" of a sick society, or as he himself called Goethe, the "Physician of the iron age." And in this difference we have a clue to the question previously raised: why did Arnold virtually abandon the writing of poetry and shift into criticism? Among other reasons, he abandoned it because he was dissatisfied with the kind of poetry he himself was writing.

In one of his excellent letters to his friend Arthur Hugh Clough in the 1850s (letters that provide the best insight we have into Arnold's mind and tastes) this note of dissatisfaction is struck: "I am glad you like the *Gypsy Scholar*—but what does it *do* for you? Homer *animates*—Shakespeare *animates*—in its poor way I think *Sohrab and Rustum animates*—the *Gypsy Scholar* at best awakens a pleasing melancholy. But this is not what we want." It is evident that early in his career Arnold had evolved a theory of what poetry should do for its readers, a theory based, in part, on his impression of what classical poetry had achieved. To help make life bearable, poetry, in Arnold's view, must bring joy. As he says in the preface to his *Poems* in 1853, it must "inspirit and rejoice the reader"; it must "convey a charm, and infuse delight." Such a demand does not exclude tragic poetry but does exclude works "in which suffering finds no vent in action; in which a continual state of mental distress is prolonged." Of Charlotte Brontë's novel *Villette* he says witheringly: "The writer's mind contains nothing but hunger, rebellion, and rage. . . . No fine writing can hide this thoroughly, and it will be fatal to her in the long run." Judged by such a standard, most nineteenth-century poems, including *Empedocles on Etna* and others by Arnold, were unsatisfactory. And when Arnold tried himself to write poems that would meet his own requirements—*Sohrab and Rustum* or *Balder Dead*—he was not at his best. By the late 1850s he thus found himself at a dead end. By turning aside to literary criticism he was able partially to escape the dilemma. In his prose his melancholy and "morbid" personality was subordinated to the resolutely cheerful and purposeful character he had created for himself by an effort of will.

Arnold's two volumes of *Essays in Criticism* (1865 and 1888) repeatedly show how authors as different as Marcus Aurelius, Tolstoy, Homer, and Wordsworth provide the virtues he sought in his reading. Among these virtues was plainness of style. Although he could on occasion recommend the richness of language of such poets as Keats or Tennyson—their "natural magic" as he himself called it—Arnold's usual preference was for literature that was unadorned. And beyond stylistic excellences the principal virtue he admired as a critic was what he called the quality of "high seriousness." Given a world in which formal religion appeared to be of subordinate importance, it became increasingly important to Arnold that the poet must be a serious thinker who could offer guidance for his readers. Arnold's attitude toward religion helps to account for his finally asking perhaps too much from literature. Excessive expectations underlie his most glaring blunder as a critic: his solemnly inadequate discussion of Chaucer's lack of high seriousness in *The Study of Poetry*.

In *The Function of Criticism,* it is apparent that Arnold regarded good literary criticism, as he regarded literature itself, as a potent force in producing what he conceived as a civilized society. From a close study of this basic essay one could forecast the third stage of his career: his excursion into the criticism of society that was to culminate in *Culture and Anarchy* (1869) and *Friendship's Garland* (1871).

Arnold's starting point as a critic of society is different from that of Carlyle and John Ruskin. The older prophets attacked the Victorian middle classes on the grounds of their materialism, their selfish indifference to the sufferings of the poor—their immorality, in effect. Arnold argued instead that the "Philistines," as he called them, were not so much wicked as ignorant, narrow-minded, and suffering from the dullness of their private lives. This novel analysis was reinforced by Arnold's conviction that the world of the future, both in England and America, would be a middle-class world, a world dominated therefore by a class inadequately equipped for leadership and inadequately equipped to enjoy civilized living.

To establish this point, Arnold employed cajolery, satire, and even quotations from the newspapers with considerable effect. He also employed memorable catchwords (such as "sweetness and light") that sometimes pose an obstacle to understanding the complexities of his position. His view of civilization, for example, was pared down to a four-point formula of the four "powers": conduct, intellect and knowledge, beauty, social life and manners. The formula was simple and workable. Applying it to French or American civilizations, he had a scale by which to show up the virtues of different countries as well as their inadequacies. Applying the formula to his own country, Arnold usually awarded the Victorian middle classes an A in the first category (of conduct) but a failing grade in the other three categories.

Arnold's relentless exposure of middle-class narrow-mindedness eventually led him into the arena of religious controversy. As a critic of religious institutions he was arguing, in effect, that just as the middle classes did not know how to lead full lives, so also did they not know how to read the Bible intelligently or attend church intelligently. Of the Christian religion, he remarked that there are two things "that surely must be clear to anybody with eyes in his head. One is, that men cannot do without it; the other that they cannot do with it as it is." His three full-length studies of the Bible, including *Literature and Dogma* (1873), are best considered in this way as a postscript to his social criticism. The Bible, to Arnold, was a great work of literature like the *Odyssey,* and the Church of England was a great national institution like Parliament. Both Bible and church must be preserved not because historical Christianity was credible but because both, when properly understood, were agents of what he called "culture"—they contributed to making humanity more civilized.

The term *culture* is perhaps Arnold's most familiar catchword, although what he meant by it has sometimes been misunderstood. For him the term connotes the qualities of an open-minded intelligence (as described in *The Function of Criticism*)—a refusal to take things on authority. In this respect, Arnold appears close to T. H. Huxley and J. S. Mill. But the word also connotes a full awareness of humanity's past and a capacity to enjoy the best works of art, literature, history, and philosophy that have come down to us from that past. As a way of viewing life in all its aspects, including the social, political, and religious, culture represents for Arnold the most effective way of curing the ills of a sick society. It is his principal prescription.

To attempt to define culture brings one to a final aspect of Arnold's career as a critic: his writings on education, in which he sought to make cultural values, as he said, "prevail." Most obviously these writings comprise his reply to Huxley in his admirably reasoned essay *Literature and Science,* and his volumes of official reports written as an inspector of schools. Less obviously, they comprise all his prose. At the core of these writings is his belief that good education is *the* crucial need. Arnold was essentially a great teacher. He has the faults of a teacher: a tendency to repeat himself, to lean too hard on formulated phrases, and he displays something of the lectern manner at times. He also has the great teacher's virtues, in particular the virtue of skillfully conveying to us the conviction on which all his arguments are based. This conviction is that the humanist tradition of which he is the expositor can enable the individual man or woman to live life more fully and to change the course of society. He believes that a democratic society can thrive only if its citizens become educated in what he saw as the great Western tradition, "the best that is known and thought." These values, which some readers find elitist, make Arnold both timely and controversial. It is for these values Arnold fought. He boxed with the gloves on—kid gloves, his opponents used to say—and he provided a lively exhibition of footwork that is a pleasure in itself for us to witness. Yet the gracefulness of the display should not obscure the fact that he is landing hard blows squarely on his opponents.

Although his lifelong attacks against the inadequacies of puritanism make Arnold one of the most anti-Victorian figures of the Victorian age, there is an assumption behind his attacks that is itself characteristically Victorian. This assumption is that the puritan middle classes *can* be changed, that they are, as we would more clumsily say, educable. In 1852, writing to Clough on the subject of equality (a political objective in which he believed by conviction if not by instinct), he observed: "I am more and more convinced that the world tends to become more comfortable for the mass, and more uncomfortable for those of any natural gift or distinction—and it is as well perhaps that it should be so—for hitherto the gifted have astonished and delighted the world, but not trained or inspired or in any real way changed it." Arnold's gifts as a poet and critic enabled him to do both: to delight the world and also to change it.

The Forsaken Merman

Come, dear children, let us away;
Down and away below!
Now my brothers call from the bay,
Now the great winds shoreward blow,
5   Now the salt tides seaward flow;
Now the wild white horses play,
Champ and chafe and toss in the spray.
Children dear, let us away!
This way, this way!

10   Call her once before you go—
Call once yet!
In a voice that she will know:
"Margaret! Margaret!"
Children's voices should be dear
15   (Call once more) to a mother's ear;
Children's voices, wild with pain—
Surely she will come again!
Call her once and come away;
This way, this way!
20   "Mother dear, we cannot stay!
The wild white horses foam and fret."
Margaret! Margaret!

Come, dear children, come away down;
Call no more!
25   One last look at the white-walled town,
And the little gray church on the windy shore,
Then come down!
She will not come though you call all day;
Come away, come away!

30   Children dear, was it yesterday
We heard the sweet bells over the bay?
In the caverns where we lay,
Through the surf and through the swell,
The far-off sound of a silver bell?
35   Sand-strewn caverns, cool and deep,
Where the winds are all asleep;
Where the spent lights quiver and gleam,
Where the salt weed sways in the stream,
Where the sea beasts, ranged all round,
40   Feed in the ooze of their pasture ground;
Where the sea snakes coil and twine,
Dry their mail and bask in the brine;
Where great whales come sailing by,

Sail and sail, with unshut eye,
45 Round the world for ever and aye?
When did music come this way?
Children dear, was it yesterday?

Children dear, was it yesterday
(Call yet once) that she went away?
50 Once she sate with you and me,
On a red gold throne in the heart of the sea,
And the youngest sate on her knee.
She combed its bright hair, and she tended it well,
When down swung the sound of a far-off bell.
55 She sighed, she looked up through the clear green sea;
She said: "I must go, for my kinsfolk pray
In the little gray church on the shore today.
'Twill be Easter time in the world—ah me!
And I lose my poor soul, Merman! here with thee."
60 I said: "Go up, dear heart, through the waves;
Say thy prayer, and come back to the kind sea-caves!"
She smiled, she went up through the surf in the bay.
Children dear, was it yesterday?

Children dear, were we long alone?
65 "The sea grows stormy, the little ones moan;
Long prayers," I said, "in the world they say;
Come!" I said; and we rose through the surf in the bay.
We went up the beach, by the sandy down
Where the sea-stocks bloom, to the white-walled town;
70 Through the narrow paved streets, where all was still,
To the little gray church on the windy hill.
From the church came a murmur of folk at their prayers,
But we stood without in the cold blowing airs.
We climbed on the graves, on the stones worn with rains,
75 And we gazed up the aisle through the small leaded panes.
She sate by the pillar; we saw her clear:
"Margaret, hist! come quick, we are here!
Dear heart," I said, "we are long alone;
The sea grows stormy, the little ones moan."
80 But, ah, she gave me never a look,
For her eyes were sealed to the holy book!
Loud prays the priest; shut stands the door.
Come away, children, call no more!
Come away, come down, call no more!

85   Down, down, down!
Down to the depths of the sea!
She sits at her wheel in the humming town,
Singing most joyfully.
Hark what she sings: "O joy, O joy,
90 For the humming street, and the child with its toy!
For the priest, and the bell, and the holy well;
For the wheel where I spun,

And the blessed light of the sun!"
And so she sings her fill,
95 Singing most joyfully,
Till the spindle drops from her hand,
And the whizzing wheel stands still.
She steals to the window, and looks at the sand,
And over the sand at the sea;
100 And her eyes are set in a stare;
And anon there breaks a sigh,
And anon there drops a tear,
From a sorrow-clouded eye,
And a heart sorrow-laden,
105 A long, long sigh;
For the cold strange eyes of a little Mermaiden
And the gleam of her golden hair.

    Come away, away children;
Come children, come down!
110 The hoarse wind blows coldly;
Lights shine in the town.
She will start from her slumber
When gusts shake the door;
She will hear the winds howling,
115 Will hear the waves roar.
We shall see, while above us
The waves roar and whirl,
A ceiling of amber,
A pavement of pearl.
120 Singing: "Here came a mortal,
But faithless was she!
And alone dwell forever
The kings of the sea."

    But, children, at midnight,
125 When soft the winds blow,
When clear falls the moonlight,
When spring tides are low;
When sweet airs come seaward
From heaths starred with broom,
130 And high rocks throw mildly
On the blanched sands a gloom;
Up the still, glistening beaches,
Up the creek we will hie,
Over banks of bright seaweed
135 The ebb-tide leaves dry.
We will gaze, from the sand-hills,
At the white, sleeping town;
At the church on the hillside—
And then come back down.
140 Singing: "There dwells a loved one,
But cruel is she!

She left lonely forever
The kings of the sea."

1849

To Marguerite—Continued

Yes! in the sea of life enisled,
With echoing straits between us thrown,
Dotting the shoreless watery wild,
We mortal millions live *alone*.
5 The islands feel the enclasping flow,
And then their endless bounds they know.
But when the moon their hollows lights,
And they are swept by balms of spring,
And in their glens, on starry nights,
10 The nightingales divinely sing;
And lovely notes, from shore to shore,
Across the sounds and channels pour—

Oh! then a longing like despair
Is to their farthest caverns sent;
15 For surely once, they feel, we were
Parts of a single continent!
Now round us spreads the watery plain—
Oh might our marges meet again!

Who ordered that their longing's fire
20 Should be, as soon as kindled, cooled?
Who renders vain their deep desire?—
A God, a God their severance ruled!
And bade betwixt their shores to be
The unplumbed, salt, estranging sea.

1849   1852

The Buried Life

Light flows our war of mocking words, and yet,
Behold, with tears mine eyes are wet!
I feel a nameless sadness o'er me roll.
Yes, yes, we know that we can jest,
5 We know, we know that we can smile!
But there's a something in this breast,
To which thy light words bring no rest,
And thy gay smiles no anodyne.
Give me thy hand, and hush awhile,
10 And turn those limpid eyes on mine,
And let me read there, love! thy inmost soul.

Alas! is even love too weak
To unlock the heart, and let it speak?
Are even lovers powerless to reveal
15   To one another what indeed they feel?
I knew the mass of men concealed
Their thoughts, for fear that if revealed
They would by other men be met
With blank indifference, or with blame reproved;
20   I knew they lived and moved
Tricked in disguises, alien to the rest
Of men, and alien to themselves—and yet
The same heart beats in every human breast!

But we, my love!—doth a like spell benumb
25   Our hearts, our voices?—must we too be dumb?
Ah! well for us, if even we,
Even for a moment, can get free
Our heart, and have our lips unchained;
For that which seals them hath been deep-ordained!

30   Fate, which foresaw
How frivolous a baby man would be—
By what distractions he would be possessed,
How he would pour himself in every strife,
And well-nigh change his own identity—
35   That it might keep from his capricious play
His genuine self, and force him to obey
Even in his own despite his being's law,
Bade through the deep recesses of our breast
The unregarded river of our life
40   Pursue with indiscernible flow its way;
And that we should not see
The buried stream, and seem to be
Eddying at large in blind uncertainty,
Though driving on with it eternally.

45   But often, in the world's most crowded streets,[1]
But often, in the din of strife,
There rises an unspeakable desire
After the knowledge of our buried life;
A thirst to spend our fire and restless force
50   In tracking out our true, original course;
A longing to inquire
Into the mystery of this heart which beats
So wild, so deep in us—to know
Whence our lives come and where they go.
55   And many a man in his own breast then delves,
But deep enough, alas! none ever mines.
And we have been on many thousand lines,

---

1. This passage, like many others in Arnold's poetry, illustrates Wordsworth's effect on his writings. In this instance cf. Wordsworth's *Tintern Abbey* 25–27: "But oft, in lonely rooms, and 'mid the din / Of towns and cities, I have owed to them, / In hours of weariness, sensations sweet."

And we have shown, on each, spirit and power;
But hardly have we, for one little hour,
60 Been on our own line, have we been ourselves—
Hardly had skill to utter one of all
The nameless feelings that course through our breast,
But they course on forever unexpressed.
And long we try in vain to speak and act
65 Our hidden self, and what we say and do
Is eloquent, is well—but 'tis not true!
And then we will no more be racked
With inward striving, and demand
Of all the thousand nothings of the hour
70 Their stupefying power;
Ah yes, and they benumb us at our call!
Yet still, from time to time, vague and forlorn,
From the soul's subterranean depth upborne
As from an infinitely distant land,
75 Come airs, and floating echoes, and convey
A melancholy into all our day.[2]

Only—but this is rare—
When a beloved hand is laid in ours,
When, jaded with the rush and glare
80 Of the interminable hours,
Our eyes can in another's eyes read clear,
When our world-deafened ear
Is by the tones of a loved voice caressed—
A bolt is shot back somewhere in our breast,
85 And a lost pulse of feeling stirs again.
The eye sinks inward, and the heart lies plain,
And what we mean, we say, and what we would, we know.
A man becomes aware of his life's flow,
And hears its winding murmur; and he sees
90 The meadows where it glides, the sun, the breeze.

And there arrives a lull in the hot race
Wherein he doth forever chase
That flying and elusive shadow, rest.
An air of coolness plays upon his face,
95 And an unwonted calm pervades his breast.
And then he thinks he knows
The hills where his life rose,
And the sea where it goes.

1852

---

2. Cf. Wordworth's *Ode: Intimations of Immortality*, lines 149–51: "Those shadowy recollections,/Which,
be they what they may,/Are yet the fountain light of all our day."

The Scholar Gypsy The story of a seventeenth-century student who left Oxford and joined a band of gypsies had made a strong impression on Arnold. In the poem he wistfully imagines that the spirit of this scholar is still to be encountered in the Cumner countryside near Oxford, having achieved immortality by a serene pursuit of the secret of human existence. Like Keats's nightingale, the scholar has escaped "the weariness, the fever, and the fret" of modern life.

At the outset, the poet addresses a shepherd who has been helping him in his search for traces of the scholar. The shepherd is addressed as *you*. After line 61, with the shift to *thou* and *thy*, the person addressed is the scholar himself, and the poet thereafter sometimes uses the pronoun *we* to indicate he is speaking for all humanity of later generations.

About the setting Arnold wrote to his brother Tom on May 15, 1857: "You alone of my brothers are associated with that life at Oxford, the *freest* and most delightful part, perhaps, of my life, when with you and Clough and Walrond I shook off all the bonds and formalities of the place, and enjoyed the spring of life and that unforgotten Oxfordshire and Berkshire country. Do you remember a poem of mine called 'The Scholar Gipsy'? It was meant to fix the remembrance of those delightful wanderings of ours in the Cumner Hills."

The passage from Joseph Glanvill's *Vanity of Dogmatizing* (1661) that inspired the poem was included by Arnold as a note:

> There was very lately a lad in the University of Oxford, who was by his poverty forced to leave his studies there; and at last to join himself to a company of vagabond gypsies. Among these extravagant people, by the insinuating subtilty of his carriage, he quickly got so much of their love and esteem as that they discovered to him their mystery. After he had been a pretty while exercised in the trade, there chanced to ride by a couple of scholars, who had formerly been of his acquaintance. They quickly spied out their old friend among the gypsies; and he gave them an account of the necessity which drove him to that kind of life, and told them that the people he went with were not such imposters as they were taken for, but that they had a traditional kind of learning among them, and could do wonders by the power of imagination, their fancy binding that of others: that himself had learned much of their art, and when he had compassed the whole secret, he intended, he said, to leave their company, and give the world an account of what he had learned.

The Scholar Gypsy

Go, for they call you, shepherd, from the hill;
  Go, shepherd, and untie the wattled cotes![1]
    No longer leave thy wistful flock unfed,
    Nor let thy bawling fellows rack their throats,
5   Nor the cropped herbage shoot another head.
      But when the fields are still,
  And the tired men and dogs all gone to rest,
    And only the white sheep are sometimes seen
    Cross and recross the strips of moon-blanched green,
10 Come, shepherd, and again begin the quest!

Here, where the reaper was at work of late—
  In this high field's dark corner, where he leaves
    His coat, his basket, and his earthen cruse,[2]

---

1. Sheepfolds woven from sticks.   2. Pot or jug for carrying his drink.

And in the sun all morning binds the sheaves,
15   Then here, at noon, comes back his stores to use—
        Here will I sit and wait,
    While to my ear from uplands far away
        The bleating of the folded° flocks is borne,   *penned up*
        With distant cries of reapers in the corn[3]—
20   All the live murmur of a summer's day.

    Screened is this nook o'er the high, half-reaped field,
        And here till sundown, shepherd! will I be.
        Through the thick corn the scarlet poppies peep,
    And round green roots and yellowing stalks I see
25   Pale pink convolvulus in tendrils creep;
          And air-swept lindens yield
    Their scent, and rustle down their perfumed showers
        Of bloom on the bent grass[4] where I am laid,
        And bower me from the August sun with shade;
30   And the eye travels down to Oxford's towers.

    And near me on the grass lies Glanvill's book—
        Come, let me read the oft-read tale again!
        The story of the Oxford scholar poor,
    Of pregnant parts[5] and quick inventive brain,
35   Who, tired of knocking at preferment's door,
          One summer morn forsook
    His friends, and went to learn the gypsy lore,
        And roamed the world with that wild brotherhood,
        And came, as most men deemed, to little good,
40   But came to Oxford and his friends no more.

    But once, years after, in the country lanes,
        Two scholars, whom at college erst he knew,
        Met him, and of his way of life inquired;
    Whereat he answered, that the gypsy crew,
45   His mates, had arts to rule as they desired
          The workings of men's brains,
    And they can bind them to what thoughts they will.
        "And I," he said, "the secret of their art,
        When fully learned, will to the world impart;
50   But it needs heaven-sent moments for this skill."

    This said, he left them, and returned no more.—
        But rumors hung about the countryside,
        That the lost Scholar long was seen to stray,
    Seen by rare glimpses, pensive and tongue-tied,
55   In hat of antique shape, and cloak of grey,
          The same the gypsies wore.
    Shepherds had met him on the Hurst[6] in spring;
        At some lone alehouse in the Berkshire moors,
        On the warm ingle-bench, the smock-frocked boors[7]
60   Had found him seated at their entering,

3. Grain or wheat.
4. A stiff kind of grass.
5. Teeming with ideas.
6. A hill near Oxford. All the place names in the poem (except those in the final two stanzas) refer to the countryside near Oxford.
7. Rustics. "Ingle-bench": fireside bench.

But, 'mid their drink and clatter, he would fly.
   And I myself seem half to know thy looks,
     And put the shepherds, wanderer! on thy trace;
     And boys who in lone wheatfields scare the rooks[8]
65   I ask if thou hast passed their quiet place;
        Or in my boat I lie
   Moored to the cool bank in the summer heats,
     'Mid wide grass meadows which the sunshine fills,
     And watch the warm, green-muffled Cumner hills,
70   And wonder if thou haunt'st their shy retreats.

For most, I know, thou lov'st retired ground!
   Thee at the ferry Oxford riders blithe,
     Returning home on summer nights, have met
     Crossing the stripling Thames[9] at Bab-lock-hithe,
75   Trailing in the cool stream thy fingers wet,
        As the punt's rope chops round;[1]
   And leaning backward in a pensive dream,
     And fostering in thy lap a heap of flowers
     Plucked in shy fields and distant Wychwood bowers,
80   And thine eyes resting on the moonlit stream.

And then they land, and thou art seen no more!—
   Maidens, who from the distant hamlets come
     To dance around the Fyfield elm in May,
     Oft through the darkening fields have seen thee roam,
85   Or cross a stile into the public way.
        Oft thou hast given them store
   Of flowers—the frail-leafed, white anemone,
     Dark bluebells drenched with dews of summer eves,
     And purple orchises with spotted leaves—
90   But none hath words she can report of thee.

And, above Godstow Bridge, when hay time's here
   In June, and many a scythe in sunshine flames,
     Men who through those wide fields of breezy grass
     Where black-winged swallows haunt the glittering Thames,
95   To bathe in the abandoned lasher pass,[2]
        Have often passed thee near
   Sitting upon the river bank o'ergrown;
     Marked thine outlandish garb, thy figure spare,
     Thy dark vague eyes, and soft abstracted air—
100   But, when they came from bathing, thou wast gone!

At some lone homestead in the Cumner hills,
   Where at her open door the housewife darns,
     Thou hast been seen, or hanging on a gate
     To watch the threshers in the mossy barns.

---

8. Boys hired to frighten crows away from eating wheat grains.
9. The narrow upper reaches of the river before it broadens out to its full width.
1. The scholar's flat-bottomed boat ("punt") is tied up by a rope at the riverbank near the ferry crossing like the speaker's boat (in the previous stanza), which was "moored to the cool bank." The motion of the boat as it is stirred by the current of the river causes the chopping sound of the rope in the water.
2. Water that spills over a dam or weir.

105　　Children, who early range these slopes and late
　　　　　For cresses from the rills,
　　　Have known thee eying, all an April day,
　　　　　The springing pastures and the feeding kine;
　　　　　And marked thee, when the stars come out and shine,
110　　Through the long dewy grass move slow away.

　　　In autumn, on the skirts of Bagley Wood—
　　　　　Where most the gypsies by the turf-edged way
　　　　　Pitch their smoked tents, and every bush you see
　　　With scarlet patches tagged and shreds of grey,
115　　　　Above the forest ground called Thessaly—
　　　　　The blackbird, picking food,
　　　Sees thee, nor stops his meal, nor fears at all;
　　　　　So often has he known thee past him stray,
　　　　　Rapt, twirling in thy hand a withered spray,
120　　And waiting for the spark from heaven to fall.

　　　And once, in winter, on the causeway chill
　　　　　Where home through flooded fields foot-travelers go,
　　　　　Have I not passed thee on the wooden bridge,
　　　Wrapped in thy cloak and battling with the snow,
125　　　　Thy face tow'rd Hinksey and its wintry ridge?
　　　　　And thou hast climbed the hill,
　　　And gained the white brow of the Cumner range;
　　　　　Turned once to watch, while thick the snowflakes fall,
　　　　　The line of festal light in Christ Church hall[3]—
130　　Then sought thy straw in some sequestered grange.

　　　But what—I dream! Two hundred years are flown
　　　　　Since first thy story ran through Oxford halls,
　　　　　And the grave Glanvill did the tale inscribe
　　　That thou wert wandered from the studious walls
135　　　　To learn strange arts, and join a gypsy tribe;
　　　　　And thou from earth art gone
　　　Long since, and in some quiet churchyard laid—
　　　　　Some country nook, where o'er thy unknown grave
　　　　　Tall grasses and white flowering nettles wave,
140　　Under a dark, red-fruited yew tree's shade.

　　　—No, no, thou hast not felt the lapse of hours!
　　　　　For what wears out the life of mortal men?
　　　　　'Tis that from change to change their being rolls;
　　　'Tis that repeated shocks, again, again,
145　　　　Exhaust the energy of strongest souls
　　　　　And numb the elastic powers.
　　　Till having used our nerves with bliss and teen,°　　　　　*vexation*
　　　　　And tired upon a thousand schemes our wit,
　　　　　To the just-pausing Genius[4] we remit
150　　Our worn-out life, and are—what we have been.

3. The dining hall of an Oxford college.
4. Perhaps the spirit of the universe, which pauses briefly to receive back the life given to us.

Thou hast not lived, why should'st thou perish, so?
   Thou hadst *one* aim, *one* business, *one* desire;
     Else wert thou long since numbered with the dead!
   Else hadst thou spent, like other men, thy fire!
155   The generations of thy peers are fled,
        And we ourselves shall go;
   But thou possessest an immortal lot,
     And we imagine thee exempt from age
     And living as thou liv'st on Glanvill's page,
160   Because thou hadst—what we, alas! have not.

For early didst thou leave the world, with powers
   Fresh, undiverted to the world without,
     Firm to their mark, not spent on other things;
   Free from the sick fatigue, the languid doubt,
165   Which much to have tried, in much been baffled, brings.
        O life unlike to ours!
   Who fluctuate idly without term or scope,
     Of whom each strives, nor knows for what he strives,
     And each half[5] lives a hundred different lives;
170   Who wait like thee, but not, like thee, in hope.

Thou waitest for the spark from heaven! and we,
   Light half-believers of our casual creeds,
     Who never deeply felt, nor clearly willed,
   Whose insight never has borne fruit in deeds,
175   Whose vague resolves never have been fulfilled;
        For whom each year we see
   Breeds new beginnings, disappointments new;
     Who hesitate and falter life away,
     And lose tomorrow the ground won today—
180   Ah! do not we, wanderer! await it too?

Yes, we await it!—but it still delays,
   And then we suffer! and amongst us one,[6]
     Who most has suffered, takes dejectedly
   His seat upon the intellectual throne;
185   And all his store of sad experience he
        Lays bare of wretched days;
   Tells us his misery's birth and growth and signs,
     And how the dying spark of hope was fed,
     And how the breast was soothed, and how the head,
190   And all his hourly varied anodynes.

This for our wisest! and we others pine,
   And wish the long unhappy dream would end,
     And waive all claim to bliss, and try to bear;
   With close-lipped patience for our only friend,
195   Sad patience, too near neighbor to despair—

---

5. An adverb modifying "lives."
6. Probably Goethe, although possibly referring to

Tennyson, whose *In Memoriam* had appeared in 1850.

But none has hope like thine!
 Thou through the fields and through the woods dost stray,
  Roaming the countryside, a truant boy,
  Nursing thy project in unclouded joy,
200 And every doubt long blown by time away.

O born in days when wits were fresh and clear,
 And life ran gaily as the sparkling Thames;
  Before this strange disease of modern life,
  With its sick hurry, its divided aims,
205 Its heads o'ertaxed, its palsied hearts, was rife—
   Fly hence, our contact fear!
 Still fly, plunge deeper in the bowering wood!
  Averse, as Dido did with gesture stern
  From her false friend's approach in Hades turn,[7]
210 Wave us away, and keep thy solitude!

Still nursing the unconquerable hope,
 Still clutching the inviolable shade,
  With a free, onward impulse brushing through,
  By night, the silvered branches of the glade—
215 Far on the forest skirts, where none pursue.
   On some mild pastoral slope
 Emerge, and resting on the moonlit pales
  Freshen thy flowers as in former years
  With dew, or listen with enchanted ears,
220 From the dark dingles,° to the nightingales!   *small deep valleys*

But fly our paths, our feverish contact fly!
 For strong the infection of our mental strife,
  Which, though it gives no bliss, yet spoils for rest;
 And we should win thee from thy own fair life,
225 Like us distracted, and like us unblest.
   Soon, soon thy cheer would die,
 Thy hopes grow timorous, and unfixed thy powers,
  And thy clear aims be cross and shifting made;
  And then thy glad perennial youth would fade,
230 Fade, and grow old at last, and die like ours.

Then fly our greetings, fly our speech and smiles!
 —As some grave Tyrian trader, from the sea,
  Descried at sunrise an emerging prow
 Lifting the cool-haired creepers stealthily,
235 The fringes of a southward-facing brow
   Among the Aegean isles;
 And saw the merry Grecian coaster come,
  Freighted with amber grapes, and Chian wine,
  Green, bursting figs, and tunnies° steeped in brine— *tuna fish*
240 And knew the intruders on his ancient home,

7. Dido committed suicide after her lover, Aeneas, deserted her. When he later encountered her in Hades, she turned sternly away from him.

The young lighthearted masters of the waves—
    And snatched his rudder, and shook out more sail;
      And day and night held on indignantly
    O'er the blue Midland waters with the gale,
245   Betwixt the Syrtes[8] and soft Sicily,
        To where the Atlantic raves
    Outside the western straits; and unbent sails
      There, where down cloudy cliffs, through sheets of foam,
      Shy traffickers, the dark Iberians[9] come;
250 And on the beach undid his corded bales.[1]

                                    1853

Dover Beach

The sea is calm tonight.
The tide is full, the moon lies fair
Upon the straits—on the French coast the light
Gleams and is gone; the cliffs of England stand,
5 Glimmering and vast, out in the tranquil bay.
Come to the window, sweet is the night air!
Only, from the long line of spray
Where the sea meets the moon-blanched land,
Listen! you hear the grating roar[1]
10 Of pebbles which the waves draw back, and fling,
At their return, up the high strand,
Begin, and cease, and then again begin,
With tremulous cadence slow, and bring
The eternal note of sadness in.

15 Sophocles long ago
Heard it on the Aegean, and it brought
Into his mind the turbid ebb and flow
Of human misery;[2] we

---

8. Shoals off the coast of North Africa.
9. Dark inhabitants of Spain and Portugal—perhaps associated with gypsies.
1. The elaborate simile of the final two stanzas has been variously interpreted. The trader from Tyre is disconcerted when, peering out through the foliage ("fringes," line 235) that screens his hiding place, he sees noisy intruders entering his harbor. Like the Scholar Gypsy, when similarly intruded on by hearty extroverts, he resolves to flee and seek a new home.
    The reference (line 249) to the Iberians as *"shy traffickers"* (traders) is explained by Kenneth Allott as having been derived from Herodotus's *History* (4.196). Herodotus describes a distinctive method of selling goods established by Carthaginian merchants who used to sail through the Strait of Gibraltar to trade with the inhabitants of the coast of West Africa. The Carthaginians would leave bales of their merchandise on display along the beaches and, without having seen their prospective customers, would return to their ships. The shy natives would then come down from their inland hiding places and set gold beside the bales they wished to buy. When the natives withdrew in their turn, the Carthaginians would return to the beach and decide whether payments were adequate, a process repeated until agreement was reached. On the Atlantic coasts this method of bargaining persisted into the 19th century. As William Beloe, a translator of Herodotus, noted in 1844: "In this manner they transact their exchange without seeing one another, or without the least instance of dishonesty . . . on either side." For the solitary Tyrian trader such a procedure, with its avoidance of "contact" (line 221), would have been especially appropriate.
1. Cf. Wordsworth's *It Is a Beauteous Evening*, lines 6–8: "Listen! the mighty Being is awake, / And doth with his eternal motion make / A sound like thunder—everlastingly."
2. A reference to a chorus in *Antigone*, which compares human sorrow to the sound of the waves moving the sand beneath them (lines 585–91).

Find also in the sound a thought,
20 Hearing it by this distant northern sea.

The Sea of Faith
Was once, too, at the full, and round earth's shore
Lay like the folds of a bright girdle furled.[3]
But now I only hear
25 Its melancholy, long, withdrawing roar,
Retreating, to the breath
Of the night wind, down the vast edges drear
And naked shingles[4] of the world.

Ah, love, let us be true
30 To one another! for the world, which seems
To lie before us like a land of dreams,
So various, so beautiful, so new,
Hath really neither joy, nor love, nor light,
Nor certitude, nor peace, nor help for pain;
35 And we are here as on a darkling plain
Swept with confused alarms of struggle and flight,
Where ignorant armies[5] clash by night.

ca. 1851   1867

Stanzas from the Grande Chartreuse[1]

Through Alpine meadows soft-suffused
With rain, where thick the crocus blows,
Past the dark forges long disused,
The mule track from Saint Laurent goes.
5 The bridge is crossed, and slow we ride,
Through forest, up the mountainside.

The autumnal evening darkens round,
The wind is up, and drives the rain;
While, hark! far down, with strangled sound
10 Doth the Dead Guier's[2] stream complain,

3. This difficult line means, in general, that at high tide the sea envelops the land closely. Its forces are "gathered" up (to use Wordsworth's term for it) like the "folds" of bright clothing ("girdle") that have been compressed ("furled"). At ebb tide, as the sea retreats, it is unfurled and spread out. It still surrounds the shoreline but not as an "enclasping flow" (as in To Marguerite—Continued).
4. Beaches covered with pebbles.
5. Perhaps alluding to conflicts in Arnold's own time such as occurred during the revolutions of 1848 in Europe, or at the Siege of Rome by the French in 1849 (the date of composition of the poem is unknown, although generally assumed to be 1851.) But the passage also refers back to another battle, one that occurred more than two thousand years earlier when an Athenian army was attempting an invasion of Sicily at nighttime. As this "night battle" was described by Thucydides in his History of the Peloponnesian War (7, chap.44), the invaders became confused by darkness and slaughtered many of their own men. Hence "ignorant armies."
1. A monastery situated high in the French Alps. It was established in 1084 by Saint Bruno, founder of the Carthusians (line 30), whose austere regimen of solitary contemplation, fasting, and religious exercises (lines 37–44) had remained virtually unchanged for centuries. Arnold visited the site on September 7, 1851, accompanied by his bride. His account may be compared with that by Wordsworth (Prelude 6.416–88), who had made a similar visit in 1790.
2. The Guiers Mort River flows down from the monastery and joins the Guiers Vif in the valley below. Wordsworth speaks of the two rivers as "the sister streams of Life and Death."

Where that wet smoke, among the woods,
Over his boiling cauldron broods.

Swift rush the spectral vapors white
Past limestone scars° with ragged pines,   *precipices*
15   Showing—then blotting from our sight!—
Halt—through the cloud-drift something shines!
High in the valley, wet and drear,
The huts of Courrerie appear.

Strike leftward! cries our guide; and higher
20   Mounts up the stony forest way.
At last the encircling trees retire;
Look! through the showery twilight grey
What pointed roofs are these advance?—
A palace of the Kings of France?

25   Approach, for what we seek is here!
Alight, and sparely sup, and wait
For rest in this outbuilding near;
Then cross the sward and reach that gate.
Knock; pass the wicket! Thou art come
30   To the Carthusians' world-famed home.

The silent courts, where night and day
Into their stone-carved basins cold
The splashing icy fountains play—
The humid corridors behold!
35   Where, ghostlike in the deepening night,
Cowled forms brush by in gleaming white.

The chapel, where no organ's peal
Invests the stern and naked prayer—
With penitential cries they kneel
40   And wrestle; rising then, with bare
And white uplifted faces stand,
Passing the Host from hand to hand;[3]

Each takes, and then his visage wan
Is buried in his cowl once more.
45   The cells!—the suffering Son of Man
Upon the wall—the knee-worn floor—
And where they sleep, that wooden bed,
Which shall their coffin be, when dead![4]

The library, where tract and tome
50   Not to feed priestly pride are there,

---

3. Arnold, during his short visit, may not actually have witnessed the service of the Mass in the monastery. The consecrated wafer ("the Host") is not passed from the hand of the officiating priest to the hands of the communicant (as is the practice in Arnold's own Anglican Church) but placed, instead, on the tongue of the communicant (who kneels rather than stands).
4. A Carthusian is buried on a wooden plank but does not sleep in a coffin.

To hymn the conquering march of Rome,
Nor yet to amuse, as ours are!
They paint of souls the inner strife,
Their drops of blood, their death in life.

55   The garden, overgrown—yet mild,
See, fragrant herbs[5] are flowering there!
Strong children of the Alpine wild
Whose culture is the brethren's care;
Of human tasks their only one,
60   And cheerful works beneath the sun.

Those halls, too, destined to contain
Each its own pilgrim-host of old,
From England, Germany, or Spain—
All are before me! I behold
65   The House, the Brotherhood austere!
—And what am I, that I am here?

For rigorous teachers seized my youth,
And purged its faith, and trimmed its fire,
Showed me the high, white star of Truth,
70   There bade me gaze, and there aspire.
Even now their whispers pierce the gloom:
What dost thou in this living tomb?

Forgive me, masters of the mind![6]
At whose behest I long ago
75   So much unlearnt, so much resigned—
I come not here to be your foe!
I seek these anchorites, not in ruth,[7]
To curse and to deny your truth;

Not as their friend, or child, I speak!
80   But as, on some far northern strand,
Thinking of his own Gods, a Greek
In pity and mournful awe might stand
Before some fallen Runic stone[8]—
For both were faiths, and both are gone.

85   Wandering between two worlds, one dead,
The other powerless to be born,
With nowhere yet to rest my head,
Like these, on earth I wait forlorn.

Their faith, my tears, the world deride—
90 I come to shed them at their side.

Oh, hide me in your gloom profound,
Ye solemn seats of holy pain!
Take me, cowled forms, and fence me round,
Till I possess my soul again;
95 Till free my thoughts before me roll,
Not chafed by hourly false control!

For the world cries your faith is now
But a dead time's exploded dream;
My melancholy, sciolists[9] say,
100 Is a passed mode, an outworn theme—
As if the world had ever had
A faith, or sciolists been sad!

Ah, if it *be* passed, take away,
At least, the restlessness, the pain;
105 Be man henceforth no more a prey
To these out-dated stings again!
The nobleness of grief is gone—
Ah, leave us not the fret alone!

But—if you[1] cannot give us ease—
110 Last of the race of them who grieve
Here leave us to die out with these
Last of the people who believe!
Silent, while years engrave the brow;
Silent—the best are silent now.

115 Achilles[2] ponders in his tent,
The kings of modern thought[3] are dumb;
Silent they are, though not content,
And wait to see the future come.
They have the grief men had of yore,
120 But they contend and cry no more.

Our fathers[4] watered with their tears
This sea of time whereon we sail,
Their voices were in all men's ears
Who passed within their puissant hail.
125 Still the same ocean round us raves,
But we stand mute, and watch the waves.

9. Superficial-minded persons who pretend to know the answers to all questions.
1. It is not clear whether the speaker has resumed addressing his "rigorous teachers" (line 67) or (as would seem more likely) a combination of the sciolists, who scorn the speaker's melancholy, and the worldly, who scorn the faith of the monks. See his address to the "sons of the world" (lines 161–68).
2. Until the death of Patroclus, he refused to participate in the Trojan war, hence similar to modern

intellectual leaders who refuse to speak out about their frustrated sense of alienation.
3. Variously but never satisfactorily identified as Newman or Carlyle (the latter was said to have preached the gospel of silence in forty volumes). Another advocate of stoical silence was the French poet Alfred de Vigny (1797–1863).
4. Predecessors among the Romantic writers such as Byron.

For what availed it, all the noise
And outcry of the former men?—
Say, have their sons achieved more joys,
130   Say, is life lighter now than then?
The sufferers died, they left their pain—
The pangs which tortured them remain.

What helps it now, that Byron bore,
With haughty scorn which mocked the smart,
135   Through Europe to the Aetolian shore[5]
The pageant of his bleeding heart?
That thousands counted every groan,
And Europe made his woe her own?

What boots it, Shelley! that the breeze
140   Carried thy lovely wail away,
Musical through Italian trees
Which fringe thy soft blue Spezzian bay?[6]
Inheritors of thy distress
Have restless hearts one throb the less?

145   Or are we easier, to have read,
O Obermann![7] the sad, stern page,
Which tells us how thou hidd'st thy head
From the fierce tempest of thine age
In the lone brakes of Fontainebleau,
150   Or chalets near the Alpine snow?

Ye slumber in your silent grave!
The world, which for an idle day
Grace to your mood of sadness gave,
Long since hath flung her weeds° away.   *mourning clothes*
155   The eternal trifler[8] breaks your spell;
But we—we learnt your lore too well!

Years hence, perhaps, may dawn an age,
More fortunate, alas! than we,
Which without hardness will be sage,
160   And gay without frivolity.
Sons of the world, oh, speed those years;
But, while we wait, allow our tears!

Allow them! We admire with awe
The exulting thunder of your race;
165   You give the universe your law,
You triumph over time and space!
Your pride of life, your tireless powers,
We laud them, but they are not ours.

---

5. Region in Greece where Byron died.
6. The Gulf of Spezia in Italy, where Shelley was drowned.
7. Melancholy hero of *Obermann* (1804), a novel by the French writer Senancour.
8. The sciolist, as in line 99.

We are like children reared in shade
170 Beneath some old-world abbey wall,
Forgotten in a forest glade,
And secret from the eyes of all.
Deep, deep the greenwood round them waves,
Their abbey, and its close° of graves!   *enclosure*

175 But, where the road runs near the stream,
Oft through the trees they catch a glance
Of passing troops in the sun's beam—
Pennon, and plume, and flashing lance!
Forth to the world those soldiers fare,
180 To life, to cities, and to war!

And through the wood, another way,
Faint bugle notes from far are borne,
Where hunters gather, staghounds bay,[9]
Round some fair forest-lodge at morn.
185 Gay dames are there, in sylvan green;
Laughter and cries—those notes between!

The banners flashing through the trees
Make their blood dance and chain their eyes;
That bugle music on the breeze
190 Arrests them with a charmed surprise.
Banner by turns and bugle woo:
Ye shy recluses, follow too!

O children, what do ye reply?—
"Action and pleasure, will ye roam
195 Through these secluded dells to cry
And call us?—but too late ye come!
Too late for us your call ye blow,
Whose bent was taken long ago.

"Long since we pace this shadowed nave;
200 We watch those yellow tapers shine,
Emblems of hope over the grave,
In the high altar's depth divine;
The organ carries to our ear
Its accents of another sphere.[1]

205 "Fenced early in this cloistral round
Of reverie, of shade, of prayer,
How should we grow in other ground?
How can we flower in foreign air?

9. Cf. the contrast between recluses and hunters in *The Scholar Gypsy*, lines 71–81 (p. 2086).
1. The organ music is from the abbey in the green- wood (line 174), as contrasted with the monastery on the mountaintop in which there is no organ (line 37).

—Pass, banners, pass, and bugles, cease;
210 And leave our desert to its peace!"

1852(?)   1855

Thyrsis[1]

A Monody, to Commemorate the Author's Friend, Arthur Hugh Clough,
Who Died at Florence, 1861

How changed is here each spot man makes or fills!
In the two Hinkseys[2] nothing keeps the same;
    The village street its haunted mansion lacks,
And from the sign is gone Sibylla's[3] name,
5   And from the roofs the twisted chimney stacks—
    Are ye too changed, ye hills?
See, 'tis no foot of unfamiliar men
    Tonight from Oxford up your pathway strays!
Here came I often, often, in old days—
10 Thyrsis and I; we still had Thyrsis then.

Runs it not here, the track by Childsworth Farm,
Past the high wood, to where the elm tree crowns
    The hill behind whose ridge the sunset flames?
The signal-elm, that looks on Ilsley Downs,
15   The Vale, the three lone weirs, the youthful Thames?—
    This winter eve is warm,
Humid the air! leafless, yet soft as spring,
    The tender purple spray on copse and briers!
And that sweet city with her dreaming spires,
20 She needs not June for beauty's heightening,

Lovely all times she lies, lovely tonight!—
Only, methinks, some loss of habit's power
    Befalls me wandering through this upland dim.
Once passed I blindfold here, at any hour;
25   Now seldom come I, since I came with him.
    That single elm tree bright
Against the west—I miss it! is it gone?
    We prized it dearly; while it stood, we said,

---

1. In the 1840s, at Oxford, Clough had been one of Arnold's closest friends. After the death of this fellow poet twenty years later, Arnold revisited the Thames valley countryside that they had explored together. The familiar scenes prompted him to review the changes wrought by time on the ideals shared in his Oxford days with Clough, ideals symbolized, in part, by a distant elm and by the story of the Scholar Gypsy. The survival of these ideals in the face of the difficulties of modern life is the subject of this elegy. Unlike Tennyson in such elegies as *In Memoriam*, Arnold rarely touches here on other kinds of immortality.

As a framework for his elegy, Arnold draws on the same Greek and Latin pastoral tradition from which Milton's *Lycidas* and Shelley's *Adonais* were derived. Hence Clough is referred to by one of the traditional names for a shepherd poet, Thyrsis, and Arnold himself as Corydon. The sense of distancing that results from this traditional elegiac mode is reduced considerably by the realism of the setting with its bleak wintry landscape at twilight, a landscape that is brightened, in turn, by evocations of the return of hopeful springtime.
2. The villages of North Hinksey and South Hinksey.
3. Sibylla Kerr had been the proprietress of a tavern in South Hinksey.

Our friend, the Gypsy Scholar, was not dead;
30 While the tree lived, he in these fields lived on.

Too rare, too rare, grow now my visits here,
But once I knew each field, each flower, each stick;
And with the countryfolk acquaintance made
By barn in threshing time, by new-built rick.
35 Here, too, our shepherd pipes we first assayed.
Ah me! this many a year
My pipe is lost, my shepherd's holiday!
Needs must I lose them, needs with heavy heart
Into the world and wave of men depart;
40 But Thyrsis of his own will went away.[4]

It irked him to be here, he could not rest.
He loved each simple joy the country yields,
He loved his mates; but yet he could not keep,°   stay
For that a shadow loured on the fields,
45 Here with the shepherds and the silly° sheep.   innocent
Some life of men unblest
He knew, which made him droop, and filled his head.
He went; his piping took a troubled sound
Of storms[5] that rage outside our happy ground;
50 He could not wait their passing, he is dead.

So, some tempestuous morn in early June,
When the year's primal burst of bloom is o'er,
Before the roses and the longest day—
When garden walks and all the grassy floor
55 With blossoms red and white of fallen May
And chestnut flowers are strewn—
So have I heard the cuckoo's parting cry,
From the wet field, through the vexed garden trees,
Come with the volleying rain and tossing breeze:
60 *The bloom is gone, and with the bloom go I!*

Too quick despairer, wherefore wilt thou go?
Soon will the high Midsummer pomps come on,
Soon will the musk carnations break and swell,
Soon shall we have gold-dusted snapdragon,
65 Sweet-William with his homely cottage-smell,
And stocks in fragrant blow;
Roses that down the alleys shine afar,
And open, jasmine-muffled lattices,
And groups under the dreaming garden trees,
70 And the full moon, and the white evening star.

He hearkens not! light comer, he is flown!
What matters it? next year he will return,

---

4. Arnold left Oxford out of the necessity for earning a living; Clough left as a matter of principle when in 1848 he resigned a fellowship rather than subscribe to the doctrines of the Church of England.
5. Religious and political controversies.

And we shall have him in the sweet spring days,
With whitening hedges, and uncrumpling fern,
75   And bluebells trembling by the forest ways,
      And scent of hay new-mown.
But Thyrsis never more we swains shall see,
    See him come back, and cut a smoother reed,
    And blow a strain the world at last shall heed—
80   For Time, not Corydon, hath conquered thee!

Alack, for Corydon no rival now!—
    But when Sicilian shepherds lost a mate,
    Some good survivor with his flute would go,
    Piping a ditty sad for Bion's fate;[6]
85   And cross the unpermitted ferry's flow,[7]
      And relax Pluto's brow,
And make leap up with joy the beauteous head
    Of Proserpine, among whose crownèd hair
    Are flowers first opened on Sicilian air,[8]
90   And flute his friend, like Orpheus,[9] from the dead.

O easy access to the hearer's grace
    When Dorian shepherds[1] sang to Proserpine!
    For she herself had trod Sicilian fields,
    She knew the Dorian water's gush divine,
95   She knew each lily white which Enna[2] yields,
      Each rose with blushing face;
She loved the Dorian pipe, the Dorian strain.
    But ah, of our poor Thames she never heard!
    Her foot the Cumner cowslips never stirred;
100   And we should tease her with our plaint in vain!

Well! wind-dispersed and vain the words will be,
    Yet, Thyrsis, let me give my grief its hour
    In the old haunt, and find our tree-topped hill!
Who, if not I, for questing here hath power?
105   I know the wood which hides the daffodil,
      I know the Fyfield tree,
I know what white, what purple fritillaries[3]
    The grassy harvest of the river fields,
    Above by Ensham, down by Sandford, yields,
110   And what sedged brooks are Thames's tributaries;

I know these slopes; who knows them if not I?—
    But many a dingle[4] on the loved hillside,
    With thorns once studded, old, white-blossomed trees,

6. Moschus, a Greek poet, composed a pastoral elegy upon the death of the poet Bion in Sicily.
7. The river Styx across which the dead were ferried to the underworld.
8. Pluto ruled the underworld with his queen, Proserpine. In spring, Proserpine's returning above ground in Sicily would cause the flowers to blossom.
9. His music enabled him to enter the "unpermit-
ted" realms of the dead and to bring his wife, Eurydice, back with him to the land of the living.
1. Greeks who colonized Sicily, the home of pastoral poetry.
2. From a meadow near the Sicilian town of Enna, Proserpine had been carried off to the underworld by Pluto (or Dis).
3. Flowers commonly found in moist meadows.
4. Small deep valley.

Where thick the cowslips grew, and far descried
115   High towered the spikes of purple orchises,
        Hath since our day put by
    The coronals of that forgotten time;
     Down each green bank hath gone the plowboy's team,
     And only in the hidden brookside gleam
120   Primroses, orphans of the flowery prime.

Where is the girl, who by the boatman's door,
    Above the locks, above the boating throng,
     Unmoored our skiff when through the Wytham flats,
    Red loosestrife[5] and blond meadowsweet among
125   And darting swallows and light water-gnats,
     We tracked the shy Thames shore?
    Where are the mowers, who, as the tiny swell
     Of our boat passing heaved the river grass,
     Stood with suspended scythe to see us pass?—
130   They all are gone, and thou art gone as well!

Yes, thou art gone! and round me too the night
    In ever-nearing circle weaves her shade.
     I see her veil draw soft across the day,
    I feel her slowly chilling breath invade
135   The cheek grown thin, the brown hair sprent° with grey;   *sprinkled*
     I feel her finger light
    Laid pausefully upon life's headlong train;
     The foot less prompt to meet the morning dew,
     The heart less bounding at emotion new,
140   And hope, once crushed, less quick to spring again.

And long the way appears, which seemed so short
    To the less practiced eye of sanguine youth;
     And high the mountaintops, in cloudy air,
    The mountaintops where is the throne of Truth,
145   Tops in life's morning sun so bright and bare!
     Unbreachable the fort
    Of the long-battered world uplifts its wall;
     And strange and vain the earthly turmoil grows,
     And near and real the charm of thy repose,
150   And night as welcome as a friend would fall.

But hush! the upland hath a sudden loss
    Of quiet!—Look, adown the dusk hillside,
     A troop of Oxford hunters going home,
    As in old days, jovial and talking, ride!
155   From hunting with the Berkshire hounds they come.
     Quick! let me fly, and cross
    Into yon farther field!—'Tis done; and see,
     Backed by the sunset, which doth glorify
     The orange and pale violet evening sky,
160   Bare on its lonely ridge, the Tree! the Tree!

5. Flowers that grow on banks of streams.

I take the omen! Eve lets down her veil,
The white fog creeps from bush to bush about,
The west unflushes, the high stars grow bright,
And in the scattered farms the lights come out.
165 I cannot reach the signal-tree tonight,
Yet, happy omen, hail!
Hear it from thy broad lucent Arno vale[6]
(For there thine earth-forgetting eyelids keep
The morningless and unawakening sleep
170 Under the flowery oleanders pale),

Hear it, O Thyrsis, still our tree is there!—
Ah, vain! These English fields, this upland dim,
These brambles pale with mist engarlanded,
That lone, sky-pointing tree, are not for him;
175 To a boon southern country he is fled,
And now in happier air,
Wandering with the great Mother's train divine[7]
(And purer or more subtle soul than thee,
I trow, the mighty Mother doth not see)
180 Within a folding of the Apennine,[8]

Thou hearest the immortal chants[9] of old!—
Putting his sickle to the perilous grain
In the hot cornfield of the Phrygian king,[1]
For thee the Lityerses song again
185 Young Daphnis with his silver voice doth sing;
Sings his Sicilian fold,
His sheep, his hapless love, his blinded eyes—
And how a call celestial round him rang,
And heavenward from the fountain brink he sprang,
190 And all the marvel of the golden skies.

There thou art gone, and me thou leavest here
Sole in these fields! yet will I not despair.
Despair I will not, while I yet descry
'Neath the mild canopy of English air
195 That lonely tree against the western sky.
Still, still these slopes, 'tis clear,
Our Gypsy Scholar haunts, outliving thee!
Fields where soft sheep from cages pull the hay,

6. Clough was buried in Florence, which is situated in the valley of the Arno River.
7. Followers of Demeter (whose name may mean Earth Mother), who was worshiped as the goddess of agriculture.
8. Mountains near Florence.
9. Sung in Demeter's honor.
1. Daphnis, the ideal Sicilian shepherd of Greek pastoral poetry, was said to have followed into Phrygia his mistress Piplea, who had been carried off by robbers, and to have found her in the power of the king of Phrygia, Lityerses. Lityerses used to make strangers try a contest with him in reaping corn, and to put them to death if he overcame them. Hercules arrived in time to save Daphnis,

took upon himself the reaping contest with Lityerses, overcame him, and slew him. The Lityerses song connected with this tradition was, like the Linus song, one of the early plaintive strains of Greek popular poetry, and used to be sung by corn reapers. Other traditions represented Daphnis as beloved by a nymph who exacted from him an oath to love no one else. He fell in love with a princess, and was struck blind by the jealous nymph. Mercury, who was his father, raised him to heaven, and made a fountain spring up in the place from which he ascended. At this fountain the Sicilians offered yearly sacrifices [from Servius's commentary on Virgil's Ecologues; Arnold's note].

Woods with anemones in flower till May,
200   Know him a wanderer still; then why not me?

A fugitive and gracious light he seeks,
        Shy to illumine; and I seek it too.
        This does not come with houses or with gold,
        With place, with honor, and a flattering crew;
205   'Tis not in the world's market bought and sold—
                But the smooth-slipping weeks
        Drop by, and leave its seeker still untired;
            Out of the heed of mortals he is gone,
            He wends unfollowed, he must house alone;
210   Yet on he fares, by his own heart inspired.

Thou too, O Thyrsis, on like quest wast bound;
        Thou wanderedst with me for a little hour!
        Men gave thee nothing; but this happy quest,
        If men esteemed thee feeble, gave thee power,
215   If men procured thee trouble, gave thee rest.
                And this rude Cumner ground,
        Its fir-topped Hurst, its farms, its quiet fields,
            Here cam'st thou in thy jocund youthful time,
            Here was thine height of strength, thy golden prime!
220   And still the haunt beloved a virtue yields.

What though the music of thy rustic flute
        Kept not for long its happy, country tone;
            Lost it too soon, and learnt a stormy note[2]
        Of men contention-tossed, of men who groan,
225   Which tasked thy pipe too sore, and tired thy throat—
                It failed, and thou wast mute!
        Yet hadst thou always visions of our light,
            And long with men of care thou couldst not stay,
            And soon thy foot resumed its wandering way,
230   Left human haunt, and on alone till night.

Too rare, too rare, grow now my visits here!
        'Mid city noise, not, as with thee of yore,
            Thyrsis! in reach of sheep-bells is my home.
        —Then through the great town's harsh, heart-wearying roar,
235   Let in thy voice a whisper often come,
                To chase fatigue and fear:
        Why faintest thou? I wandered till I died.
            Roam on! The light we sought is shining still.
            Dost thou ask proof? Our tree yet crowns the hill,
240   *Our Scholar travels yet the loved hillside.*

                                                    1866

2. Clough's poetry often dealt with contemporary religious problems.

From The Function of Criticism at the Present Time[1]

Many objections have been made to a proposition which, in some remarks of mine on translating Homer,[2] I ventured to put forth; a proposition about criticism, and its importance at the present day. I said: "Of the literature of France and Germany, as of the intellect of Europe in general, the main effort, for now many years, has been a critical effort; the endeavor, in all branches of knowledge, theology, philosophy, history, art, science, to see the object as in itself it really is." I added, that owing to the operation in English literature of certain causes, "almost the last thing for which one would come to English literature is just that very thing which now Europe most desires—criticism"; and that the power and value of English literature was thereby impaired. More than one rejoinder declared that the importance I here assigned to criticism was excessive, and asserted the inherent superiority of the creative effort of the human spirit over its critical effort. And the other day, having been led by a Mr. Shairp's excellent notice of Wordsworth[3] to turn again to his biography, I found, in the words of this great man, whom I, for one, must always listen to with the profoundest respect, a sentence passed on the critic's business, which seems to justify every possible disparagement of it. Wordsworth says in one of his letters:

> The writers in these publications (the Reviews), while they prosecute their inglorious employment, cannot be supposed to be in a state of mind very favorable for being affected by the finer influences of a thing so pure as genuine poetry.

And a trustworthy reporter of his conversation quotes a more elaborate judgment to the same effect:

> Wordsworth holds the critical power very low, infinitely lower than the inventive; and he said today that if the quantity of time consumed in writing critiques on the works of others were given to original composition, of whatever kind it might be, it would be much better employed; it would make a man find out sooner his own level, and it would do infinitely less mischief. A false or malicious criticism may do much injury to the minds of others; a stupid invention, either in prose or verse, is quite harmless.

1. This essay served as an introduction to *Essays in Criticism* (1865). As a declaration of intentions it can serve as a standard for measuring his total accomplishment in criticism. The essay makes us aware that criticism, for Arnold, meant a great deal more than casual book reviewing or mere censoriousness. He was not a Utilitarian, yet his object in this essay is to show that good criticism is useful. Creative writers, he argues, can profit in a special way from good criticism, but all of us can also derive from it benefits of the greatest value. In particular, we may develop a civilized attitude of mind in which to examine the social, political, aesthetic, and religious problems that confront us.
2. *On Translating Homer* (1861).
3. J. C. Shairp's essay *Wordsworth: The Man and the Poet* was published in 1864. Arnold comments in a footnote:

> I cannot help thinking that a practice, common in England during the last century, and still followed in France, of printing a notice of this kind—a notice by a competent critic—to serve as an introduction to an eminent author's works, might be revived among us with advantage. To introduce all succeeding editions of Wordsworth, Mr. Shairp's notice might, it seems to me, excellently serve; it is written from the point of view of an admirer, nay, of a disciple, and that is right; but then the disciple must be also, as in this case he is, a critic, a man of letters, not, as too often happens, some relation or friend with no qualification for his task except affection for his author.

It is almost too much to expect of poor human nature, that a man capable of producing some effect in one line of literature, should, for the greater good of society, voluntarily doom himself to impotence and obscurity in another. Still less is this to be expected from men addicted to the composition of the "false or malicious criticism" of which Wordsworth speaks. However, everybody would admit that a false or malicious criticism had better never have been written. Everybody, too, would be willing to admit, as a general proposition, that the critical faculty is lower than the inventive. But is it true that criticism is really, in itself, a baneful and injurious employment; is it true that all time given to writing critiques on the works of others would be much better employed if it were given to original composition, of whatever kind this may be? Is it true that Johnson had better have gone on producing more *Irenes*[4] instead of writing his *Lives of the Poets*; nay, is it certain that Wordsworth himself was better employed in making his Ecclesiastical Sonnets than when he made his celebrated Preface[5] so full of criticism, and criticism of the works of others? Wordsworth was himself a great critic, and it is to be sincerely regretted that he has not left us more criticism; Goethe was one of the greatest of critics, and we may sincerely congratulate ourselves that he has left us so much criticism. Without wasting time over the exaggeration which Wordsworth's judgment on criticism clearly contains, or over an attempt to trace the causes—not difficult, I think, to be traced—which may have led Wordsworth to this exaggeration, a critic may with advantage seize an occasion for trying his own conscience, and for asking himself of what real service, at any given moment, the practice of criticism either is or may be made to his own mind and spirit, and to the minds and spirits of others.

The critical power is of lower rank than the creative. True; but in assenting to this proposition, one or two things are to be kept in mind. It is undeniable that the exercise of a creative power, that a free creative activity, is the highest function of man; it is proved to be so by man's finding in it his true happiness. But it is undeniable, also, that men may have the sense of exercising this free creative activity in other ways than in producing great works of literature or art; if it were not so, all but a very few men would be shut out from the true happiness of all men. They may have it in well-doing, they may have it in learning, they may have it even in criticizing. This is one thing to be kept in mind. Another is, that the exercise of the creative power in the production of great works of literature or art, however high this exercise of it may rank, is not at all epochs and under all conditions possible; and that therefore labor may be vainly spent in attempting it, which might with more fruit be used in preparing for it, in rendering it possible. This creative power works with elements, with materials; what if it has not those materials, those elements, ready for its use? In that case it must surely wait till they are ready. Now, in literature—I will limit myself to literature, for it is about literature that the question arises—the elements with which the creative power works are ideas; the best ideas on every matter which literature touches, current at the time. At any rate we may lay it down as certain that in modern literature no manifestation of the creative power not working with these can be very

4. *Irene* is the name of a clumsy play by Samuel Johnson.
5. To *Lyrical Ballads* (1800). "Ecclesiastical Son-

nets": a sonnet sequence by Wordsworth, usually regarded as minor verse.

important or fruitful. And I say *current* at the time, not merely accessible at the time; for creative literary genius does not principally show itself in discovering new ideas, that is rather the business of the philosopher. The grand work of literary genius is a work of synthesis and exposition, not of analysis and discovery; its gift lies in the faculty of being happily inspired by a certain intellectual and spiritual atmosphere, by a certain order of ideas, when it finds itself in them; of dealing divinely with these ideas, presenting them in the most effective and attractive combinations—making beautiful works with them, in short. But it must have the atmosphere, it must find itself amidst the order of ideas, in order to work freely; and these it is not so easy to command. This is why great creative epochs in literature are so rare, this is why there is so much that is unsatisfactory in the productions of many men of real genius; because, for the creation of a masterwork of literature two powers must concur, the power of the man and the power of the moment, and the man is not enough without the moment; the creative power has, for its happy exercise, appointed elements, and those elements are not in its own control.

Nay, they are more within the control of the critical power. It is the business of the critical power, as I said in the words already quoted, "in all branches of knowledge, theology, philosophy, history, art, science, to see the object as in itself it really is." Thus it tends, at last, to make an intellectual situation of which the creative power can profitably avail itself. It tends to establish an order of ideas, if not absolutely true, yet true by comparison with that which it displaces; to make the best ideas prevail. Presently these new ideas reach society, the touch of truth is the touch of life, and there is a stir and growth everywhere; out of this stir and growth come the creative epochs of literature.

Or, to narrow our range, and quit these considerations of the general march of genius and of society—considerations which are apt to become too abstract and impalpable—everyone can see that a poet, for instance, ought to know life and the world before dealing with them in poetry; and life and the world being in modern times very complex things, the creation of a modern poet, to be worth much, implies a great critical effort behind it; else it must be a comparatively poor, barren, and short-lived affair. This is why Byron's poetry had so little endurance in it, and Goethe's so much; both Byron and Goethe had a great productive power, but Goethe's was nourished by a great critical effort providing the true materials for it, and Byron's was not; Goethe knew life and the world, the poet's necessary subjects, much more comprehensively and thoroughly than Byron. He knew a great deal more of them, and he knew them much more as they really are.

It has long seemed to me that the burst of creative activity in our literature, through the first quarter of this century, had about it in fact something premature; and that from this cause its productions are doomed, most of them, in spite of the sanguine hopes which accompanied and do still accompany them, to prove hardly more lasting than the productions of far less splendid epochs. And this prematureness comes from its having proceeded without having its proper data, without sufficient materials to work with. In other words, the English poetry of the first quarter of this century, with plenty of energy, plenty of creative force, did not know enough. This makes Byron so empty of matter, Shelley so incoherent, Wordsworth even, profound as he is, yet so wanting in completeness and variety. Wordsworth cared little for books, and disparaged Goethe. I admire Wordsworth, as he is, so much that I cannot wish him different; and it is vain, no doubt, to imagine such a man different from what he is, to suppose that he *could* have been different. But surely the one thing wanting to make Wordsworth an even greater poet than he is—his thought richer, and his influence of wider application—was that he should have read more books, among them, no doubt, those of that Goethe whom he disparaged without reading him.

But to speak of books and reading may easily lead to a misunderstanding here. It was not really books and reading that lacked to our poetry at this epoch: Shelley had plenty of reading, Coleridge had immense reading. Pindar and Sophocles—as we all say so glibly, and often with so little discernment of the real import of what we are saying—had not many books; Shakespeare was no deep reader. True; but in the Greece of Pindar and Sophocles, in the England of Shakespeare, the poet lived in a current of ideas in the highest degree animating and nourishing to the creative power; society was, in the fullest measure, permeated by fresh thought, intelligent and alive. And this state of things is the true basis for the creative power's exercise, in this it finds its data, its materials, truly ready for its hand; all the books and reading in the world are only valuable as they are helps to this. Even when this does not actually exist, books and reading may enable a man to construct a kind of semblance of it in his own mind, a world of knowledge and intelligence in which he may live and work. This is by no means an equivalent to the artist for the nationally diffused life and thought of the epochs of Sophocles or Shakespeare; but, besides that it may be a means of preparation for such epochs, it does really constitute, if many share in it, a quickening and sustaining atmosphere of great value. Such an atmosphere the many-sided learning and the long and widely combined critical effort of Germany formed for Goethe, when he lived and worked. There was no national glow of life and thought there as in the Athens of Pericles[6] or the England of Elizabeth. That was the poet's weakness. But there was a sort of equivalent for it in the complete culture and unfettered thinking of a large body of Germans. That was his strength. In the England of the first quarter of this century there was neither a national glow of life and thought, such as we had in the age of Elizabeth, nor yet a culture and a force of learning and criticism such as were to be found in Germany. Therefore the creative power of poetry wanted, for success in the highest sense, materials and a basis; a thorough interpretation of the world was necessarily denied to it.

At first sight it seems strange that out of the immense stir of the French Revolution and its age should not have come a crop of works of genius equal to that which came out of the stir of the great productive time of Greece, or out of that of the Renascence, with its powerful episode the Reformation. But the truth is that the stir of the French Revolution took a character which essentially distinguished it from such movements as these. These were, in the main, disinterestedly intellectual and spiritual movements; movements in which the human spirit looked for its satisfaction in itself and in the increased play of its own activity. The French Revolution took a political, practical character. The movement, which went on in France under the old

---

6. The leading statesman of Athens (d. 429 B.C.E.) during a period of the city's most outstanding achievements in art, literature, and politics.

régime, from 1700 to 1789, was far more really akin than that of the Revolution itself to the movement of the Renascence; the France of Voltaire and Rousseau told far more powerfully upon the mind of Europe than the France of the Revolution. Goethe reproached this last expressly with having "thrown quiet culture back." Nay, and the true key to how much in our Byron, even in our Wordsworth, is this!—that they had their source in a great movement of feeling, not in a great movement of mind. The French Revolution, however— that object of so much blind love and so much blind hatred—found undoubtedly its motive power in the intelligence of men, and not in their practical sense; this is what distinguishes it from the English Revolution of Charles the First's time. This is what makes it a more spiritual event than our Revolution, an event of much more powerful and worldwide interest, though practically less successful; it appeals to an order of ideas which are universal, certain, permanent. 1789 asked of a thing, Is it rational? 1642 asked of a thing, Is it legal? or, when it went furthest, Is it according to conscience? This is the English fashion, a fashion to be treated, within its own sphere, with the highest respect; for its success, within its own sphere, has been prodigious. But what is law in one place is not law in another; what is law here today is not law even here tomorrow; and as for conscience, what is binding on one man's conscience is not binding on another's. The old woman who threw her stool at the head of the surpliced minister in St. Giles's Church at Edinburgh[7] obeyed an impulse to which millions of the human race may be permitted to remain strangers. But the prescriptions of reason are absolute, unchanging, of universal validity; *to count by tens is the easiest way of counting*—that is a proposition of which everyone, from here to the Antipodes, feels the force; at least I should say so if we did not live in a country where it is not impossible that any morning we may find a letter in the *Times* declaring that a decimal coinage is an absurdity.[8] That a whole nation should have been penetrated with an enthusiasm for pure reason, and with an ardent zeal for making its prescriptions triumph, is a very remarkable thing, when we consider how little of mind, or anything so worthy and quickening as mind, comes into the motives which alone, in general, impel great masses of men. In spite of the extravagant direction given to this enthusiasm, in spite of the crimes and follies in which it lost itself, the French Revolution derives from the force, truth, and universality of the ideas which it took for its law, and from the passion with which it could inspire a multitude for these ideas, a unique and still living power; it is—it will probably long remain—the greatest, the most animating event in history. And as no sincere passion for the things of the mind, even though it turn out in many respects an unfortunate passion, is ever quite thrown away and quite barren of good, France has reaped from hers one fruit—the natural and legitimate fruit though not precisely the grand fruit she expected: she is the country in Europe where *the people* is most alive.

But the mania for giving an immediate political and practical application to all these fine ideas of the reason was fatal. Here an Englishman is in his element: on this theme we can all go on for hours. And all we are in the

---

7. In 1637 rioting broke out in Scotland against a new kind of church service prescribed by Charles I. The riot was started by an old woman hurling a stool at a clergyman.
8. In 1863 a proposal in Parliament to introduce the French decimal system for weights and measures had provoked articles in the *Times* defending the English system (of ounces and pounds or inches and feet) as more practical.

habit of saying on it has undoubtedly a great deal of truth. Ideas cannot be too much prized in and for themselves, cannot be too much lived with; but to transport them abruptly into the world of politics and practice, violently to revolutionize this world to their bidding—that is quite another thing. There is the world of ideas and there is the world of practice; the French are often for suppressing the one and the English the other; but neither is to be suppressed. A member of the House of Commons said to me the other day: "That a thing is an anomaly, I consider to be no objection to it whatever." I venture to think he was wrong; that a thing is an anomaly *is* an objection to it, but absolutely and in the sphere of ideas: it is not necessarily, under such and such circumstances, or at such and such a moment, an objection to it in the sphere of politics and practice. Joubert[9] has said beautifully: *"C'est la force et le droit qui règlent toutes choses dans le monde; la force en attendant le droit."*—"Force and right are the governors of this world; force till right is ready." *Force till right is ready;* and till right is ready, force, the existing order of things, is justified, is the legitimate ruler. But right is something moral, and implies inward recognition, free assent of the will; we are not ready for right—*right,* so far as we are concerned, is *not ready*—until we have attained this sense of seeing it and willing it. The way in which for us it may change and transform force, the existing order of things, and become, in its turn, the legitimate ruler of the world, should depend on the way in which, when our time comes, we see it and will it. Therefore for other people enamored of their own newly discerned right, to attempt to impose it upon us as ours, and violently to substitute their right for our force, is an act of tyranny, and to be resisted. It sets at nought the second great half of our maxim, *force till right is ready.* This was the grand error of the French Revolution; and its movement of ideas, by quitting the intellectual sphere and rushing furiously into the political sphere, ran, indeed a prodigious and memorable course, but produced no such intellectual fruit as the movement of ideas of the Renascence, and created, in opposition to itself, what I may call an *epoch of concentration.* The great force of that epoch of concentration was England; and the great voice of that epoch of concentration was Burke.[1] It is the fashion to treat Burke's writings on the French Revolution as superannuated and conquered by the event; as the eloquent but unphilosophical tirades of bigotry and prejudice. I will not deny that they are often disfigured by the violence and passion of the moment, and that in some directions Burke's view was bounded, and his observation therefore at fault. But on the whole, and for those who can make the needful corrections, what distinguishes these writings is their profound, permanent, fruitful, philosophical truth, They contain the true philosophy of an epoch of concentration, dissipate the heavy atmosphere which its own nature is apt to engender round it, and make its resistance rational instead of mechanical.

But Burke is so great because, almost alone in England, he brings thought to bear upon politics, he saturates politics with thought. It is his accident that his ideas were at the service of an epoch of concentration, not of an epoch of expansion; it is his characteristic that he so lived by ideas, and had

9. Joseph Joubert (1754–1824), French moralist about whom Arnold wrote one of his *Essays in Criticism.*
1. Edmund Burke (1729–1797), prominent statesman and author of *Reflections on the French Revolution* (1790), which expressed the conservative opposition to revolutionary theories.

such a source of them welling up within him, that he could float even an epoch of concentration and English Tory politics with them. It does not hurt him that Dr. Price[2] and the Liberals were enraged with him; it does not even hurt him that George the Third and the Tories were enchanted with him. His greatness is that he lived in a world which neither English Liberalism nor English Toryism is apt to enter—the world of ideas, not the world of catchwords and party habits. So far is it from being really true of him that he "to party gave up what was meant for mankind,"[3] that at the very end of his fierce struggle with the French Revolution, after all his invectives against its false pretensions, hollowness, and madness, with his sincere convictions of its mischievousness, he can close a memorandum on the best means of combating it, some of the last pages he ever wrote[4]—the *Thoughts on French Affairs*, in December 1791—with these striking words:

> The evil is stated, in my opinion, as it exists. The remedy must be where power, wisdom, and information, I hope, are more united with good intentions than they can be with me. I have done with this subject, I believe, forever. It has given me many anxious moments for the last two years. *If a great change is to be made in human affairs, the minds of men will be fitted to it; the general opinions and feelings will draw that way. Every fear, every hope will forward it; and then they who persist in opposing this mighty current in human affairs, will appear rather to resist the decrees of Providence itself, than the mere designs of men. They will not be resolute and firm, but perverse and obstinate.*

That return of Burke upon himself has always seemed to me one of the finest things in English literature, or indeed in any literature. That is what I call living by ideas: when one side of a question has long had your earnest support, when all your feelings are engaged, when you hear all round you no language but one, when your party talks this language like a steam engine and can imagine no other—still to be able to think, still to be irresistibly carried, if so it be, by the current of thought to the opposite side of the question, and, like Balaam, to be unable to speak anything *but what the Lord has put in your mouth.*[5] I know nothing more striking, and I must add that I know nothing more un-English.

For the Englishman in general is like my friend the Member of Parliament, and believes, point-blank, that for a thing to be an anomaly is absolutely no objection to it whatever. He is like the Lord Auckland of Burke's day, who, in a memorandum on the French Revolution, talks of certain "miscreants, assuming the name of philosophers, who have presumed themselves capable of establishing a new system of society." The Englishman has been called a political animal, and he values what is political and practical so much that ideas easily become objects of dislike in his eyes, and thinkers, "miscreants," because ideas and thinkers have rashly meddled with politics and practice. This would be all very well if the dislike and neglect confined themselves to ideas transported out of their own sphere, and meddling rashly with practice;

2. Richard Price (1723–1791), a prorevolutionary clergyman who was an opponent of Burke's.
3. From Oliver Goldsmith's poem *Retaliation* (1774).
4. Arnold was mistaken; Burke continued to write for another six years after 1791. According to Arnold's editor, R. H. Super, the mistake was caused by misunderstanding a passage in one of Burke's letters.
5. Cf. Numbers 22.38.

but they are inevitably extended to ideas as such, and to the whole life of intelligence; practice is everything, a free play of the mind is nothing. The notion of the free play of the mind upon all subjects being a pleasure in itself, being an object of desire, being an essential provider of elements without which a nation's spirit, whatever compensations it may have for them, must, in the long run, die of inanition, hardly enters into an Englishman's thoughts. It is noticeable that the word *curiosity,* which in other languages is used in a good sense, to mean, as a high and fine quality of man's nature, just this disinterested love of a free play of the mind on all subjects, for its own sake— it is noticeable, I say, that this word has in our language no sense of the kind, no sense but a rather bad and disparaging one. But criticism, real criticism, is essentially the exercise of this very quality. It obeys an instinct prompting it to try to know the best that is known and thought in the world, irrespectively of practice, politics, and everything of the kind; and to value knowledge and thought as they approach this best, without the intrusion of any other considerations whatever. This is an instinct for which there is, I think, little original sympathy in the practical English nature, and what there was of it has undergone a long benumbing period of blight and suppression in the epoch of concentration which followed the French Revolution.

But epochs of concentration cannot well endure forever; epochs of expansion, in the due course of things, follow them. Such an epoch of expansion seems to be opening in this country. In the first place all danger of a hostile forcible pressure of foreign ideas upon our practice has long disappeared; like the traveler in the fable, therefore, we begin to wear our cloak a little more loosely.[6] Then, with a long peace, the ideas of Europe steal gradually and amicably in, and mingle, though in infinitesimally small quantities at a time, with our own notions. Then, too, in spite of all that is said about the absorbing and brutalizing influence of our passionate material progress, it seems to me indisputable that this progress is likely, though not certain, to lead in the end to an apparition of intellectual life; and that man, after he has made himself perfectly comfortable and has now to determine what to do with himself next, may begin to remember that he has a mind, and that the mind may be made the source of great pleasure. I grant it is mainly the privilege of faith, at present, to discern this end to our railways, our business, and our fortune-making; but we shall see if, here as elsewhere, faith is not in the end the true prophet. Our ease, our traveling, and our unbounded liberty to hold just as hard and securely as we please to the practice to which our notions have given birth, all tend to beget an inclination to deal a little more freely with these notions themselves, to canvass them a little, to penetrate a little into their real nature. Flutterings of curiosity, in the foreign sense of the word, appear amongst us, and it is in these that criticism must look to find its account. Criticism first; a time of true creative activity, perhaps—which, as I have said, must inevitably be preceded amongst us by a time of criticism—hereafter, when criticism has done its work.

It is of the last importance that English criticism should clearly discern what rule for its course, in order to avail itself of the field now opening to it,

6. See Aesop's fable of the wind and the sun, in which the wind and the sun compete to see who is more powerful. The sun wins because he causes the traveler to take off his coat, whereas the wind makes him hold it closely.

and to produce fruit for the future, it ought to take. The rule may be summed up in one word—*disinterestedness*.[7] And how is criticism to show disinterestedness? By keeping aloof from what is called "the practical view of things"; by resolutely following the law of its own nature, which is to be a free play of the mind on all subjects which it touches. By steadily refusing to lend itself to any of those ulterior, political, practical considerations about ideas, which plenty of people will be sure to attach to them, which perhaps ought often to be attached to them, which in this country at any rate are certain to be attached to them quite sufficiently, but which criticism has really nothing to do with. Its business is, as I have said, simply to know the best that is known and thought in the world, and by in its turn making this known, to create a current of true and fresh ideas. Its business is to do this with inflexible honesty, with due ability; but its business is to do no more, and to leave alone all questions of practical consequences and applications, questions which will never fail to have due prominence given to them. Else criticism, besides being really false to its own nature, merely continues in the old rut which it has hitherto followed in this country, and will certainly miss the chance now given to it. For what is at present the bane of criticism in this country? It is that practical considerations cling to it and stifle it. It subserves interests not its own. Our organs of criticism are organs of men and parties having practical ends to serve, and with them those practical ends are the first thing and the play of mind the second; so much play of mind as is compatible with the prosecution of those practical ends is all that is wanted. An organ like the *Revue des Deux Mondes*,[8] having for its main function to understand and utter the best that is known and thought in the world, existing, it may be said, as just an organ for a free play of the mind, we have not. But we have the *Edinburgh Review*, existing as an organ of the old Whigs, and for as much play of mind as may suit its being that; we have the *Quarterly Review*, existing as an organ of the Tories, and for as much play of mind as may suit its being that; we have the *British Quarterly Review*, existing as an organ of the political Dissenters, and for as much play of mind as may suit its being that; we have the *Times*, existing as an organ of the common, satisfied, well-to-do Englishman, and for as much play of mind as may suit its being that. And so on through all the various fractions, political and religious, of our society; every fraction has, as such, its organ of criticism, but the notion of combining all fractions in the common pleasure of a free disinterested play of mind meets with no favor. Directly this play of mind wants to have more scope, and to forget the pressure of practical considerations a little, it is checked, it is made to feel the chain. We saw this the other day in the extinction, so much to be regretted, of the *Home and Foreign Review*.[9] Perhaps in no organ of criticism in this country was there so much knowledge, so much play of mind; but these could not save it. The *Dublin Review* subordinates play of mind to the practical business of English and Irish Catholicism, and lives. It must needs be that men should act in sects and parties, that each of these sects and parties should have its organ, and should

---

7. This key word in Arnold's argument connotes independence and objectivity of mind. It means not having an interest, in the sense of an ax to grind. It does not mean lack of interest.

8. An international magazine of exceptionally high quality, founded in Paris in 1829.
9. A liberal Catholic periodical, founded in 1862, which ceased publication in 1864.

make this organ subserve the interests of its action; but it would be well, too, that there should be a criticism, not the minister of these interests, not their enemy, but absolutely and entirely independent of them. No other criticism will ever attain any real authority or make any real way towards its end—the creating a current of true and fresh ideas.

It is because criticism has so little kept in the pure intellectual sphere, has so little detached itself from practice, has been so directly polemical and controversial, that it has so ill accomplished, in this country, its best spiritual work, which is to keep man from a self-satisfaction which is retarding and vulgarizing, to lead him towards perfection, by making his mind dwell upon what is excellent in itself, and the absolute beauty and fitness of things. A polemical practical criticism makes men blind even to the ideal imperfection of their practice, makes them willingly assert its ideal perfection, in order the better to secure it against attack; and clearly this is narrowing and baneful for them. If they were reassured on the practical side, speculative considerations of ideal perfection they might be brought to entertain, and their spiritual horizon would thus gradually widen. Sir Charles Adderley[1] says to the Warwickshire farmers:

> Talk of the improvement of breed! Why, the race we ourselves represent, the men and women, the old Anglo-Saxon race, are the best breed in the whole world. . . . The absence of a too enervating climate, too unclouded skies, and a too luxurious nature, has produced so vigorous a race of people, and has rendered us so superior to all the world.

Mr. Roebuck[2] says to the Sheffield cutlers:

> I look around me and ask what is the state of England? Is not property safe? Is not every man able to say what he likes? Can you not walk from one end of England to the other in perfect security? I ask you whether, the world over or in past history, there is anything like it? Nothing. I pray that our unrivaled happiness may last.

Now obviously there is a peril for poor human nature in words and thoughts of such exuberant self-satisfaction, until we find ourselves safe in the streets of the Celestial City.

> *Das wenige verschwindet leicht dem Blicke*
> *Der vorwärts sieht, wie viel noch übrig bleibt—*[3]

says Goethe; "the little that is done seems nothing when we look forward and see how much we have yet to do." Clearly this is a better line of reflection for weak humanity, so long as it remains on this earthly field of labor and trial.

But neither Sir Charles Adderley nor Mr. Roebuck is by nature inaccessible to considerations of this sort. They only lose sight of them owing to the controversial life we all lead, and the practical form which all speculation takes with us. They have in view opponents whose aim is not ideal, but practical; and in their zeal to uphold their own practice against these innovators, they go so far as even to attribute to this practice an ideal perfection.

1. Conservative politician and wealthy landowner (1814–1905).
2. John Arthur Roebuck (1801–1879), radical politician and representative in Parliament for the industrial city of Sheffield.
3. Goethe's *Iphigenie auf Tauris* 1.2.91–92.

Somebody has been wanting to introduce a six-pound franchise, or to abolish church-rates,[4] or to collect agricultural statistics by force, or to diminish local self-government. How natural, in reply to such proposals, very likely improper or ill-timed, to go a little beyond the mark and to say stoutly, "Such a race of people as we stand, so superior to all the world! The old Anglo-Saxon race, the best breed in the whole world! I pray that our unrivaled happiness may last! I ask you whether, the world over or in past history, there is anything like it?" And so long as criticism answers this dithyramb by insisting that the old Anglo-Saxon race would be still more superior to all others if it had no church-rates, or that our unrivaled happiness would last yet longer with a six-pound franchise, so long will the strain, "The best breed in the whole world!" swell louder and louder, everything ideal and refining will be lost out of sight, and both the assailed and their critics will remain in a sphere, to say the truth, perfectly unvital, a sphere in which spiritual progression is impossible. But let criticism leave church-rates and the franchise alone, and in the most candid spirit, without a single lurking thought of practical innovation, confront with our dithyramb this paragraph on which I stumbled in a newspaper immediately after reading Mr. Roebuck:

> A shocking child murder has just been committed at Nottingham. A girl named Wragg left the workhouse there on Saturday morning with her young illegitimate child. The child was soon afterwards found dead on Mapperly Hills, having been strangled. Wragg is in custody.

Nothing but that; but, in juxtaposition with the absolute eulogies of Sir Charles Adderley and Mr. Roebuck, how eloquent, how suggestive are those few lines! "Our old Anglo-Saxon breed, the best in the whole world!"—how much that is harsh and ill-favored there is in this best! *Wragg!* If we are to talk of ideal perfection, of "the best in the whole world," has anyone reflected what a touch of grossness in our race, what an original shortcoming in the more delicate spiritual perceptions, is shown by the natural growth amongst us of such hideous names—Higginbottom, Stiggins, Bugg! In Ionia and Attica they were luckier in this respect than "the best race in the world"; by the Ilissus[5] there was no Wragg, poor thing! And "our unrivaled happiness"— what an element of grimness, bareness, and hideousness mixes with it and blurs it; the workhouse, the dismal Mapperly Hills[6]—how dismal those who have seen them will remember—the gloom, the smoke, the cold, the strangled illegitimate child! "I ask you whether, the world over or in past history, there is anything like it?" Perhaps not, one is inclined to answer; but at any rate, in that case, the world is very much to be pitied. And the final touch— short, bleak and inhuman: *Wragg is in custody.* The sex lost in the confusion of our unrivaled happiness; or (shall I say?) the superfluous Christian name lopped off by the straightforward vigor of our old Anglo-Saxon breed! There is profit for the spirit in such contrasts as this; criticism serves the cause of perfection by establishing them. By eluding sterile conflict, by refusing to remain in the sphere where alone narrow and relative conceptions have any worth and validity, criticism may diminish its momentary importance, but

---

4. Taxes supporting the Church of England. "Six-pound franchise": a radical proposal to extend the right to vote to anyone owning land worth £6 annual rent.

5. A stream in Attica, Greece.
6. Adjacent to the coal-mining and industrial area of Nottingham (later associated with the writings of D. H. Lawrence).

only in this way has it a chance of gaining admittance for those wider and more perfect conceptions to which all its duty is really owed. Mr. Roebuck will have a poor opinion of an adversary who replies to his defiant songs of triumph only by murmuring under his breath, *Wragg is in custody;* but in no other way will these songs of triumph be induced gradually to moderate themselves, to get rid of what in them is excessive and offensive, and to fall into a softer and truer key.

It will be said that it is a very subtle and indirect action which I am thus prescribing for criticism, and that, by embracing in this manner the Indian virtue of detachment and abandoning the sphere of practical life, it condemns itself to a slow and obscure work. Slow and obscure it may be, but it is the only proper work of criticism. The mass of mankind will never have any ardent zeal for seeing things as they are; very inadequate ideas will always satisfy them. On these inadequate ideas reposes, and must repose, the general practice of the world. That is as much as saying that whoever sets himself to see things as they are will find himself one of a very small circle; but it is only by this small circle resolutely doing its own work that adequate ideas will ever get current at all. The rush and roar of practical life will always have a dizzying and attracting effect upon the most collected spectator, and tend to draw him into its vortex; most of all will this be the case where that life is so powerful as it is in England. But it is only by remaining collected, and refusing to lend himself to the point of view of the practical man, that the critic can do the practical man any service, and it is only by the greatest sincerity in pursuing his own course, and by at last convincing even the practical man of his sincerity, that he can escape misunderstandings which perpetually threaten him.

For the practical man is not apt for fine distinctions, and yet in these distinctions truth and the highest culture greatly find their account. But it is not easy to lead a practical man—unless you reassure him as to your practical intentions, you have no chance of leading him—to see that a thing which he has always been used to look at from one side only, which he greatly values, and which, looked at from that side, quite deserves, perhaps, all the prizing and admiring which he bestows upon it—that this thing, looked at from another side, may appear much less beneficent and beautiful, and yet retain all its claims to our practical allegiance. Where shall we find language innocent enough, how shall we make the spotless purity of our intentions evident enough, to enable us to say to the political Englishman that the British Constitution itself, which, seen from the practical side, looks such a magnificent organ of progress and virtue, seen from the speculative side— with its compromises, its love of facts, its horror of theory, its studied avoidance of clear thoughts—that, seen from this side, our august Constitution sometimes looks—forgive me, shade of Lord Somers!—a colossal machine for the manufacture of Philistines?[7] How is Cobbett[8] to say this and not be misunderstood, blackened as he is with the smoke of a lifelong conflict in the field of political practice? how is Mr. Carlyle to say it and not be mis-

7. The unenlightened middle classes, whose opposition to the defenders of culture is parallel to the biblical tribe that fought against the people of Israel, "the children of light." Arnold's repeated use of this parallel has established the term in our language. John Somers (1651–1716), statesman

responsible for formulating the Declaration of Rights.
8. William Cobbett (1762–1835), vehement reformer whose political position anticipated that of Dickens.

understood, after his furious raid into this field with his *Latter-day Pamphlets*? how is Mr. Ruskin, after his pugnacious political economy?[9] I say, the critic must keep out of the region of immediate practice in the political, social, humanitarian sphere if he wants to make a beginning for that more free speculative treatment of things, which may perhaps one day make its benefits felt even in this sphere, but in a natural and thence irresistible manner.

* * *

If I have insisted so much on the course which criticism must take where politics and religion are concerned, it is because, where these burning matters are in question, it is most likely to go astray. I have wished, above all, to insist on the attitude which criticism should adopt towards things in general; on its right tone and temper of mind. But then comes another question as to the subject matter which literary criticism should most seek. Here, in general, its course is determined for it by the idea which is the law of its being; the idea of a disinterested endeavor to learn and propagate the best that is known and thought in the world, and thus to establish a current of fresh and true ideas. By the very nature of things, as England is not all the world, much of the best that is known and thought in the world cannot be of English growth, must be foreign; by the nature of things, again, it is just this that we are least likely to know, while English thought is streaming in upon us from all sides, and takes excellent care that we shall not be ignorant of its existence. The English critic of literature, therefore, must dwell much on foreign thought, and with particular heed on any part of it, which, while significant and fruitful in itself, is for any reason specially likely to escape him. Again, judging is often spoken of as the critic's one business, and so in some sense it is; but the judgment which almost insensibly forms itself in a fair and clear mind, along with fresh knowledge, is the valuable one; and thus knowledge, and ever fresh knowledge, must be the critic's great concern for himself. And it is by communicating fresh knowledge, and letting his own judgment pass along with it—but insensibly, and in the second place, not the first, as a sort of companion and clue, not as an abstract lawgiver—that the critic will generally do most good to his readers. Sometimes, no doubt, for the sake of establishing an author's place in literature, and his relation to a central standard (and if this is not done, how are we to get at our *best in the world*?) criticism may have to deal with a subject matter so familiar that fresh knowledge is out of the question, and then it must be all judgment; an enunciation and detailed application of principles. Here the great safeguard is never to let oneself become abstract, always to retain an intimate and lively consciousness of the truth of what one is saying, and, the moment this fails us, to be sure that something is wrong. Still under all circumstances, this mere judgment and application of principles is, in itself, not the most satisfactory work to the critic; like mathematics, it is tautological, and cannot well give us, like fresh learning, the sense of creative activity.

But stop, some one will say; all this talk is of no practical use to us whatever; this criticism of yours is not what we have in our minds when we speak

---

9. Reference to *Unto This Last* (1862), in which Ruskin shifted from art criticism to an attack on traditional theories of economics.

of criticism; when we speak of critics and criticism, we mean critics and criticism of the current English literature of the day; when you offer to tell criticism its function, it is to this criticism that we expect you to address yourself. I am sorry for it, for I am afraid I must disappoint these expectations. I am bound by my own definition of criticism: *a disinterested endeavor to learn and propagate the best that is known and thought in the world.* How much of current English literature comes into this "best that is known and thought in the world"? Not very much I fear; certainly less, at this moment, than of the current literature of France or Germany. Well, then, am I to alter my definition of criticism, in order to meet the requirements of a number of practicing English critics, who, after all, are free in their choice of a business? That would be making criticism lend itself just to one of those alien practical considerations, which, I have said, are so fatal to it. One may say, indeed, to those who have to deal with the mass—so much better disregarded—of current English literature, that they may at all events endeavor, in dealing with this, to try it, so far as they can, by the standard of the best that is known and thought in the world; one may say, that to get anywhere near this standard, every critic should try and possess one great literature, at least, besides his own; and the more unlike his own, the better. But, after all, the criticism I am really concerned with—the criticism which alone can much help us for the future, the criticism which, throughout Europe, is at the present day meant, when so much stress is laid on the importance of criticism and the critical spirit—is a criticism which regards Europe as being, for intellectual and spiritual purposes, one great confederation, bound to a joint action and working to a common result, and whose members have, for their proper outfit, a knowledge of Greek, Roman, and Eastern antiquity, and of one another. Special, local, and temporary advantages being put out of account, that modern nation will in the intellectual and spiritual sphere make most progress, which most thoroughly carries out this program. And what is that but saying that we too, all of us, as individuals, the more thoroughly we carry it out, shall make the more progress?

There is so much inviting us!—what are we to take? what will nourish us in growth towards perfection? That is the question which, with the immense field of life and of literature lying before him, the critic has to answer; for himself first, and afterwards for others. In this idea of the critic's business the essays brought together in the following pages have had their origin; in this idea, widely different as are their subjects, they have, perhaps, their unity.

I conclude with what I said at the beginning: to have the sense of creative activity is the great happiness and the great proof of being alive, and it is not denied to criticism to have it; but then criticism must be sincere, simple, flexible, ardent, ever widening its knowledge. Then it may have, in no contemptible measure, a joyful sense of creative activity; a sense which a man of insight and conscience will prefer to what he might derive from a poor, starved, fragmentary, inadequate creation. And at some epochs no other creation is possible.

Still, in full measure, the sense of creative activity belongs only to genuine creation; in literature we must never forget that. But what true man of letters ever can forget it? It is no such common matter for a gifted nature to come into possession of a current of true and living ideas, and to produce amidst the inspiration of them, that we are likely to underrate it. The epochs of Aeschylus and Shakespeare make us feel their pre-eminence. In an epoch like those is, no doubt, the true life of literature; there is the promised land, towards which criticism can only beckon. That promised land it will not be ours to enter, and we shall die in the wilderness: but to have desired to enter it, to have saluted it from afar, is already, perhaps, the best distinction among contemporaries; it will certainly be the best title to esteem with posterity.

1864, 1865

From Culture and Anarchy[1]

From Chapter 1. Sweetness and Light

The impulse of the English race towards moral development and self-conquest has nowhere so powerfully manifested itself as in Puritanism. Nowhere has Puritanism found so adequate an expression as in the religious organization of the Independents.[2] The modern Independents have a newspaper, the *Nonconformist*, written with great sincerity and ability. The motto, the standard, the profession of faith which this organ of theirs carries aloft, is: "The Dissidence of Dissent and the Protestantism of the Protestant religion." There is sweetness and light, and an ideal of complete harmonious human perfection! One need not go to culture and poetry to find language to judge it. Religion, with its instinct for perfection, supplies language to judge it, language, too, which is in our mouths every day. "Finally, be of one mind, united in feeling," says St. Peter.[3] There is an ideal which judges the Puritan ideal: "The Dissidence of Dissent and the Protestantism of the Protestant religion!" And religious organizations like this are what people believe in, rest in, would give their lives for! Such, I say, is the wonderful virtue of even the beginnings of perfection, of having conquered even the plain faults of our animality, that the religious organization which has helped us to do it can seem to us something precious, salutary, and to be propagated, even when it wears such a brand of imperfection on its forehead as this. And men have got such a habit of giving to the language of religion a special application, of making it a mere jargon, that for the condemnation which religion itself passes on the shortcomings of their religious organizations they have

1. Arnold began *Culture and Anarchy* in the context of the turbulent political debate that preceded the passage of the second Reform Bill in 1867. The political climate seemed to some to threaten anarchy, to which Arnold opposed culture. A characteristic quality of the cultured state of mind is summed up, for his purposes, in his formula "sweetness and light," a phrase suggesting reasonableness of temper and intellectual insight. Arnold derived the phrase from a fable contrasting the spider with the bee in Swift's *Battle of the Books*. The spider (representing a narrow, self-centered, and uncultured mind) spins out of itself "nothing at all but flybane and cobweb." The bee (representing a cultured mind that has drawn nourishment from the humanist tradition) ranges far and wide and brings to its hive honey and also wax out of which candles may be made. Therefore, the bee, Swift says, furnishes humankind "with the two noblest

of things, which are sweetness and light."

The selections printed here illustrate aspects of Arnold's indictment of the middle classes for their lack of sweetness and light. The first and third expose the narrowness and dullness of middle-class Puritan religious institutions in both the 17th and 19th centuries. The second, *Doing As One Likes*, shows the limitations of the middle-class political bias and the irresponsibility of laissez-faire. Here Arnold is most close to Carlyle and Ruskin. These three extracts indicate why it has been said that Matthew Arnold discovered the foibles of Main Street fifty years before Sinclair Lewis exposed them in his novels of American life.

2. A 17th-century Puritan group (of which Cromwell was an adherent), allied with the Congregationalists.

3. Cf. 1 Peter 3.8.

no ear; they are sure to cheat themselves and to explain this condemnation away. They can only be reached by the criticism which culture, like poetry, speaking of language not to be sophisticated, and resolutely testing these organizations by the ideal of a human perfection complete on all sides, applies to them.

But men of culture and poetry, it will be said, are again and again failing, and failing conspicuously, in the necessary first stage to a harmonious perfection, in the subduing of the great obvious faults of our animality, which it is the glory of these religious organizations to have helped us to subdue. True, they do often so fail. They have often been without the virtues as well as the faults of the Puritan; it has been one of their dangers that they so felt the Puritan's faults that they too much neglected the practice of his virtues. I will not, however, exculpate them at the Puritan's expense. They have often failed in morality, and morality is indispensable. And they have been punished for their failure, as the Puritan has been rewarded for his performance. They have been punished wherein they erred; but their ideal of beauty, of sweetness and light, and a human nature complete on all its sides, remains the true ideal of perfection still; just as the Puritan's ideal of perfection remains narrow and inadequate, although for what he did well he has been richly rewarded. Notwithstanding the mighty results of the Pilgrim Fathers' voyage, they and their standard of perfection are rightly judged when we figure to ourselves Shakespeare or Virgil—souls in whom sweetness and light, and all that in human nature is most humane, were eminent—accompanying them on their voyage, and think what intolerable company Shakespeare and Virgil would have found them! In the same way let us judge the religious organizations which we see all around us. Do not let us deny the good and the happiness which they have accomplished; but do not let us fail to see clearly that their idea of human perfection is narrow and inadequate, and that the Dissidence of Dissent and the Protestantism of the Protestant religion will never bring humanity to its true goal. As I said with regard to wealth: Let us look at the life of those who live in and for it—so I say with regard to the religious organizations. Look at the life imaged in such a newspaper as the *Nonconformist*—a life of jealousy of the Establishment,[4] disputes, tea-meetings, openings of chapels, sermons; and then think of it as an ideal of a human life completing itself on all sides, and aspiring with all its organs after sweetness, light, and perfection!

From *Chapter 2. Doing As One Likes*

* * *

When I began to speak of culture, I insisted on our bondage to machinery, on our proneness to value machinery as an end in itself, without looking beyond it to the end for which alone, in truth, it is valuable. Freedom, I said, was one of those things which we thus worshiped in itself, without enough regarding the ends for which freedom is to be desired. In our common notions and talk about freedom, we eminently show our idolatry of machinery. Our prevalent notion is—and I quoted a number of instances to prove it—that it is a most happy and important thing for a man merely to be able

4. The Church of England or the Established Church.

to do as he likes. On what he is to do when he is thus free to do as he likes, we do not lay so much stress. Our familiar praise of the British Constitution under which we live, is that it is a system of checks—a system which stops and paralyzes any power in interfering with the free action of individuals. To this effect Mr. Bright,[5] who loves to walk in the old ways of the Constitution, said forcibly in one of his great speeches, what many other people are every day saying less forcibly, that the central idea of English life and politics is *the assertion of personal liberty.* Evidently this is so; but evidently, also, as feudalism, which with its ideas, and habits of subordination was for many centuries silently behind the British Constitution, dies out, and we are left with nothing but our system of checks, and our notion of its being the great right and happiness of an Englishman to do as far as possible what he likes, we are in danger of drifting towards anarchy. We have not the notion, so familiar on the Continent and to antiquity, of *the State*—the nation in its collective and corporate character, entrusted with stringent powers for the general advantage, and controlling individual wills in the name of an interest wider than that of individuals. We say, what is very true, that this notion is often made instrumental to tyranny; we say that a State is in reality made up of the individuals who compose it, and that every individual is the best judge of his own interests. Our leading class is an aristocracy, and no aristocracy likes the notion of a State-authority greater than itself, with a stringent administrative machinery superseding the decorative inutilities of lord-lieutenancy, deputy-lieutenancy, and the *posse comitatus,*[6] which are all in its own hands. Our middle class, the great representative of trade and Dissent, with its maxims of every man for himself in business, every man for himself in religion, dreads a powerful administration which might somehow interfere with it; and besides, it has its own decorative inutilities of vestry-manship and guardianship, which are to this class what lord-lieutenancy and the county magistracy are to the aristocratic class, and a stringent administration might either take these functions out of its hands, or prevent its exercising them in its own comfortable, independent manner, as at present.

Then as to our working class. This class, pressed constantly by the hard daily compulsion of material wants, is naturally the very center and stronghold of our national idea, that it is man's ideal right and felicity to do as he likes. I think I have somewhere related how M. Michelet[7] said to me of the people of France, that it was "a nation of barbarians civilized by the conscription." He meant that through their military service the idea of public duty and of discipline was brought to the mind of these masses, in other respects so raw and uncultivated. Our masses are quite as raw and uncultivated as the French; and so far from their having the idea of public duty and of discipline, superior to the individual's self-will, brought to their mind by a universal obligation of military service, such as that of the conscription—so far from their having this, the very idea of a conscription is so at variance with our English notion of the prime right and blessedness of doing as one likes, that I remember the manager of the Clay Cross works in Derbyshire told me during the Crimean war, when our want of soldiers was much felt and some people were talking of a conscription, that sooner than submit to

---

5. John Bright (19th century), orator and reformer.
6. Power of the county (Latin); a feudal method

of enforcing law by local authorities instead of by agencies of the central government.
7. Jules Michelet (1798–1874), French historian.

a conscription the population of that district would flee to the mines, and lead a sort of Robin Hood life underground.

For a long time, as I have said, the strong feudal habits of subordination and deference continued to tell upon the working class. The modern spirit has now almost entirely dissolved those habits, and the anarchical tendency of our worship of freedom in and for itself, of our superstitious faith, as I say, in machinery, is becoming very manifest. More and more, because of this our blind faith in machinery, because of our want of light to enable us to look beyond machinery to the end for which machinery is valuable, this and that man, and this and that body of men, all over the country, are beginning to assert and put in practice an Englishman's right to do what he likes; his right to march where he likes, meet where he likes, enter where he likes, hoot as he likes, threaten as he likes, smash as he likes.[8] All this, I say, tends to anarchy; and though a number of excellent people, and particularly my friends of the Liberal or progressive party, as they call themselves, are kind enough to reassure us by saying that these are trifles, that a few transient outbreaks of rowdyism signify nothing, that our system of liberty is one which itself cures all the evils which it works, that the educated and intelligent classes stand in overwhelming strength and majestic repose, ready, like our military force in riots, to act at a moment's notice—yet one finds that one's Liberal friends generally say this because they have such faith in themselves and their nostrums, when they shall return, as the public welfare requires, to place and power. But this faith of theirs one cannot exactly share, when one has so long had them and their nostrums at work, and see that they have not prevented our coming to our present embarrassed condition. And one finds, also, that the outbreaks of rowdyism tend to become less and less of trifles, to become more frequent rather than less frequent; and that meanwhile our educated and intelligent classes remain in their majestic repose, and somehow or other, whatever happens, their overwhelming strength, like our military force in riots, never does act.

How indeed, *should* their overwhelming strength act, when the man who gives an inflammatory lecture, or breaks down the park railings, or invades a Secretary of State's office, is only following an Englishman's impulse to do as he likes; and our own conscience tells us that we ourselves have always regarded this impulse as something primary and sacred? Mr. Murphy[9] lectures at Birmingham, and showers on the Catholic population of that town "words," says the Home Secretary, "only fit to be addressed to thieves or murderers." What then? Mr. Murphy has his own reasons of several kinds. He suspects the Roman Catholic Church of designs upon Mrs. Murphy; and he says if mayors and magistrates do not care for their wives and daughters, he does. But, above all, he is doing as he likes; or, in worthier language, asserting his personal liberty. "I will carry out my lectures if they walk over my body as a dead corpse, and I say to the Mayor of Birmingham that he is my servant while I am in Birmingham, and as my servant he must do his duty and protect me." Touching and beautiful words, which find a sympathetic chord in every British bosom! The moment it is plainly put before us that a man is asserting his personal liberty, we are half disarmed; because

8. A reference to the riots of 1866 in which a London mob demolished the iron railings enclosing Hyde Park.

9. An orator whose inflammatory anti-Catholic public speech *The Errors of the Roman Church* led to rioting in Birmingham and other cities in 1867.

we are believers in freedom, and not in some dream of a right reason to which the assertion of our freedom is to be subordinated. Accordingly, the Secretary of State had to say that although the lecturer's language was "only fit to be addressed to thieves or murderers," yet, "I do not think he is to be deprived, I do not think that anything I have said could justify the inference that he is to be deprived, of the right of protection in a place built by him for the purpose of these lectures; because the language was not language which afforded grounds for a criminal prosecution." No, nor to be silenced by Mayor, or Home Secretary, or any administrative authority on earth, simply on their notion of what is discreet and reasonable! This is in perfect consonance with our public opinion, and with our national love for the assertion of personal liberty.

* * *

From *Chapter* 5. Porro Unum Est Necessarium[1]

* * *

* * * Sweetness and light evidently have to do with the bent or side in humanity which we call Hellenic. Greek intelligence has obviously for its essence the instinct for what Plato calls the true, firm, intelligible law of things; the law of light, of seeing things as they are. Even in the natural sciences, where the Greeks had not time and means adequately to apply this instinct, and where we have gone a great deal further than they did, it is this instinct which is the root of the whole matter and the ground of all our success; and this instinct the world has mainly learnt of the Greeks, inasmuch as they are humanity's most signal manifestation of it. Greek art, again, Greek beauty, have their root in the same impulse to see things as they really are, inasmuch as Greek art and beauty rest on fidelity to nature—the *best* nature—and on a delicate discrimination of what this best nature is. To say we work for sweetness and light, then, is only another way of saying that we work for Hellenism. But, oh! cry many people, sweetness and light are not enough; you must put strength or energy along with them, and make a kind of trinity of strength, sweetness and light, and then, perhaps, you may do some good. That is to say, we are to join Hebraism, strictness of the moral conscience, and manful walking by the best light we have, together with Hellenism, inculcate both, and rehearse the praises of both.

Or, rather, we may praise both in conjunction, but we must be careful to praise Hebraism most. "Culture," says an acute, though somewhat rigid critic, Mr. Sidgwick,[2] "diffuses sweetness and light. I do not undervalue these blessings, but religion gives fire and strength, and the world wants fire and strength even more than sweetness and light." By religion, let me explain, Mr. Sidgwick here means particularly that Puritanism on the insufficiency of which I have been commenting and to which he says I am unfair. Now, no doubt, it is possible to be a fanatical partisan of light and the instincts which push us to it, a fanatical enemy of strictness of moral conscience and

---

1. But one thing is needful (Latin; Luke 10.42). This chapter develops a contrast established in chap. 4 between *Hebraism* (Puritan morality and energetic devotion to work) and *Hellenism* (cultivation of the aesthetic and intellectual understanding of life). The Puritan middle classes, according to Arnold, think that the "one thing needful" is the Hebraic form of virtue.

2. Henry Sidgwick (1838–1900), philosopher, whose article on Arnold appeared in *Macmillan's Magazine* (Aug. 1867).

the instincts which push us to it. A fanaticism of this sort deforms and vulgarizes the well-known work, in some respects so remarkable, of the late Mr. Buckle.[3] Such a fanaticism carries its own mark with it, in lacking sweetness; and its own penalty, in that, lacking sweetness, it comes in the end to lack light too. And the Greeks—the great exponents of humanity's bent for sweetness and light united, of its perception that the truth of things must be at the same time beauty—singularly escaped the fanaticism which we moderns, whether we Hellenize or whether we Hebraize, are so apt to show. They arrived—though failing, as has been said, to give adequate practical satisfaction to the claims of man's moral side—at the idea of a comprehensive adjustment of the claims of both the sides in man, the moral as well as the intellectual, of a full estimate of both, and of a reconciliation of both; an idea which is philosophically of the greatest value, and the best of lessons for us moderns. So we ought to have no difficulty in conceding to Mr. Sidgwick that manful walking by the best light one has—fire and strength as he calls it—has its high value as well as culture, the endeavor to see things in their truth and beauty, the pursuit of sweetness and light. But whether at this or that time, and to this or that set of persons, one ought to insist most on the praises of fire and strength, or on the praises of sweetness and light, must depend, one would think, on the circumstances and needs of that particular time and those particular persons. And all that we have been saying, and indeed any glance at the world around us, shows that with us, with the most respectable and strongest part of us, the ruling force is now, and long has been, a Puritan force—the care for fire and strength, strictness of conscience, Hebraism, rather than the care for sweetness and light, spontaneity of consciousness, Hellenism.

Well, then, what is the good of our now rehearsing the praises of fire and strength to ourselves, who dwell too exclusively on them already? When Mr. Sidgwick says so broadly, that the world wants fire and strength even more than sweetness and light, is he not carried away by a turn for broad generalization? does he not forget that the world is not all of one piece, and every piece with the same needs at the same time? It may be true that the Roman world at the beginning of our era, or Leo the Tenth's Court at the time of the Reformation, or French society in the eighteenth century,[4] needed fire and strength even more than sweetness and light. But can it be said that the Barbarians who overran the empire needed fire and strength even more than sweetness and light; or that the Puritans needed them more; or that Mr. Murphy, the Birmingham lecturer, and the Rev. W. Cattle[5] and his friends, need them more?

The Puritan's great danger is that he imagines himself in possession of a rule telling him the *unum necessarium,* or one thing needful, and that he then remains satisfied with a very crude conception of what this rule really is and what it tells him, thinks he has now knowledge and henceforth needs only to act, and, in this dangerous state of assurance and self-satisfaction, proceeds to give full swing to a number of the instincts of his ordinary self. Some of the instincts of his ordinary self he has, by the help of his rule of

---

3. Henry Thomas Buckle (1821–1862), author of *A History of Civilization.*
4. Societies representing an excess of sophisticated worldliness as at the courts of such a Roman emperor as Nero (54–68 C.E.) or Pope Leo X (1513–1521) or Louis XV (1715–1774), respectively.
5. A Nonconformist clergyman who was chairman of the anti-Catholic meeting addressed by Murphy in 1867 (see *Chapter 2. Doing As One Likes,* p. 2120).

life, conquered; but others which he has not conquered by this help he is so far from perceiving to need subjugation, and to be instincts of an inferior self, that he even fancies it to be his right and duty, in virtue of having conquered a limited part of himself, to give unchecked swing to the remainder. He is, I say, a victim of Hebraism, of the tendency to cultivate strictness of conscience rather than spontaneity of consciousness. And what he wants is a larger conception of human nature, showing him the number of other points at which his nature must come to its best, besides the points which he himself knows and thinks of. There is no *unum necessarium,* or one thing needful, which can free human nature from the obligation of trying to come to its best at all these points. The real *unum necessarium* for us is to come to our best at all points. Instead of our "one thing needful," justifying in us vulgarity, hideousness, ignorance, violence—our vulgarity, hideousness, ignorance, violence, are really so many touchstones which try our one thing needful, and which prove that in the state, at any rate, in which we ourselves have it, it is not all we want. And as the force which encourages us to stand staunch and fast by the rule and ground we have is Hebraism, so the force which encourages us to go back upon this rule, and to try the very ground on which we appear to stand, is Hellenism—a turn for giving our consciousness free play and enlarging its range. And what I say is, not that Hellenism is always for everybody more wanted than Hebraism, but that for the Rev. W. Cattle at this particular moment, and for the great majority of us his fellow countrymen, it is more wanted.

*   *   *

1868, 1869

From The Study of Poetry[1]

"The future of poetry is immense, because in poetry, where it is worthy of its high destinies, our race, as time goes on, will find an ever surer and surer stay. There is not a creed which is not shaken, not an accredited dogma which is not shown to be questionable, not a received tradition which does not threaten to dissolve. Our religion has materialized itself in the fact, in the supposed fact; it has attached its emotion to the fact, and now the fact is failing it. But for poetry the idea is everything; the rest is a world of illusion, of divine illusion. Poetry attaches its emotion to the idea; the idea *is* the fact. The strongest part of our religion today is its unconscious poetry."

Let me be permitted to quote these words of my own, as uttering the thought which should, in my opinion, go with us and govern us in all our study of poetry. In the present work[2] it is the course of one great contributory stream to the world-river of poetry that we are invited to follow. We are here

---

1. Aside from its vindication of the importance of literature, this essay is an interesting example of the variety of Arnold's own reading. To know literature in only one language seemed to him not to know literature. His personal *Notebooks* show that throughout his active life he continued to read books in French, German, Italian, Latin, and Greek. His favorite authors in these languages are used by him as a means of testing English poetry. The testing is sometimes a severe one. Readers may also protest that despite Arnold's own wit, his essay is limited by an incomplete recognition of the values of comic literature, a shortcoming abundantly evident in the discussion of Chaucer. Nevertheless, whether we agree or disagree with some of Arnold's verdicts, we can be attracted by the combination of traditionalism and impressionism on which these verdicts are based, and we can enjoy the memorable phrasemaking in which the verdicts are expressed. *The Study of Poetry* has been extraordinarily potent in shaping literary tastes in England and in America.

2. An anthology of English poetry for which this essay served as the introduction.

invited to trace the stream of English poetry. But whether we set ourselves, as here, to follow only one of the several streams that make the mighty river of poetry, or whether we seek to know them all, our governing thought should be the same. We should conceive of poetry worthily, and more highly than it has been the custom to conceive of it. We should conceive of it as capable of higher uses, and called to higher destinies, than those which in general men have assigned to it hitherto. More and more mankind will discover that we have to turn to poetry to interpret life for us, to console us, to sustain us. Without poetry, our science will appear incomplete; and most of what now passes with us for religion and philosophy will be replaced by poetry. Science, I say, will appear incomplete without it. For finely and truly does Wordsworth call poetry "the impassioned expression which is in the countenance of all science";[3] and what is a countenance without its expression? Again, Wordsworth finely and truly calls poetry "the breath and finer spirit of all knowledge": our religion, parading evidences such as those on which the popular mind relies now; our philosophy, pluming itself on its reasonings about causation and finite and infinite being; what are they but the shadows and dreams and false shows of knowledge? The day will come when we shall wonder at ourselves for having trusted to them, for having taken them seriously; and the more we perceive their hollowness, the more we shall prize "the breath and finer spirit of knowledge" offered to us by poetry.

But if we conceive thus highly of the destinies of poetry, we must also set our standard for poetry high, since poetry, to be capable of fulfilling such high destinies, must be poetry of a high order of excellence. We must accustom ourselves to a high standard and to a strict judgment. * * *

The best poetry is what we want; the best poetry will be found to have a power of forming, sustaining, and delighting us, as nothing else can. A clearer, deeper sense of the best in poetry, and of the strength and joy to be drawn from it, is the most precious benefit which we can gather from a poetical collection such as the present. And yet in the very nature and conduct of such a collection there is inevitably something which tends to obscure in us the consciousness of what our benefit should be, and to distract us from the pursuit of it. We should therefore steadily set it before our minds at the outset, and should compel ourselves to revert constantly to the thought of it as we proceed.

Yes; constantly in reading poetry, a sense for the best, the really excellent, and of the strength and joy to be drawn from it, should be present in our minds and should govern our estimate of what we read. But this real estimate, the only true one, is liable to be superseded, if we are not watchful, by two other kinds of estimate, the historic estimate and the personal estimate, both of which are fallacious. A poet or a poem may count to us historically, they may count to us on grounds personal to ourselves, and they may count to us really. They may count to us historically. The course of development of a nation's language, thought, and poetry, is profoundly interesting; and by regarding a poet's work as a stage in this course of development we may easily bring ourselves to make it of more importance as poetry than in itself it really is, we may come to use a language of quite exaggerated praise in criticizing it; in short, to overrate it. So arises in our poetic judg-

---

3. Preface to *Lyrical Ballads*.

ments the fallacy caused by the estimate which we may call historic. Then, again, a poet or a poem may count to us on grounds personal to ourselves. Our personal affinities, likings, and circumstances, have great power to sway our estimate of this or that poet's work, and to make us attach more importance to it as poetry than in itself it really possesses, because to us it is, or has been, of high importance. Here also we overrate the object of our interest, and apply to it a language of praise which is quite exaggerated. And thus we get the source of a second fallacy in our poetic judgments—the fallacy caused by an estimate which we may call personal.

* * *

* * * The historic estimate is likely in especial to affect our judgment and our language when we are dealing with ancient poets; the personal estimate when we are dealing with poets our contemporaries, or at any rate modern. The exaggerations due to the historic estimate are not in themselves, perhaps, of very much gravity. Their report hardly enters the general ear; probably they do not always impose even on the literary men who adopt them. But they lead to a dangerous abuse of language. So we hear Caedmon,[4] amongst our own poets, compared to Milton. I have already noticed the enthusiasm of one accomplished French critic for "historic origins."[5] Another eminent French critic, M. Vitet, comments upon that famous document of the early poetry of his nation, the *Chanson de Roland*.[6] It is indeed a most interesting document. The *joculator* or *jongleur*[7] Taillefer, who was with William the Conqueror's army at Hastings, marched before the Norman troops, so said the tradition, singing "of Charlemagne and of Roland and of Oliver, and of the vassals who died at Roncevaux"; and it is suggested that in the *Chanson de Roland* by one Turoldus or *Théroulde*, a poem preserved in a manuscript of the twelfth century in the Bodleian Library at Oxford, we have certainly the matter, perhaps even some of the words, of the chant which Taillefer sang. The poem has vigor and freshness; it is not without pathos. But M. Vitet is not satisfied with seeing in it a document of some poetic value, and of very high historic and linguistic value; he sees in it a grand and beautiful work, a monument of epic genius. In its general design he finds the grandiose conception, in its details he finds the constant union of simplicity with greatness, which are the marks, he truly says, of the genuine epic, and distinguish it from the artificial epic of literary ages. One thinks of Homer; this is the sort of praise which is given to Homer, and justly given. Higher praise there cannot well be, and it is the praise due to epic poetry of the highest order only, and to no other. Let us try, then, the *Chanson de Roland* at its best. Roland, mortally wounded, lays himself down under a pine tree, with his face turned towards Spain and the enemy—

> *De plusurs choses à remembrer li prist,*
> *De tantes teres cume li bers cunquist,*

---

4. A 7th-century Old English poet.
5. Charles d'Héricault, a critic cited earlier in a passage omitted here. Arnold had mildly reprimanded him for his "historical" bias in praising a 15th-century poet, Clement Marot, at the expense of such classical 17th-century poets as Racine.

6. An 11th-century epic poem in Old French that tells of the wars of Charlemagne against the Moors in Spain and of the bravery of the French leaders Roland and Oliver.
7. Minstrel.

De dulce France, des humes de sun lign,
De Carlemagne sun seignor ki l'nurrit.[8]

That is primitive work, I repeat, with an undeniable poetic quality of its own. It deserves such praise, and such praise is sufficient for it. But now turn to Homer—

Ὣς φάτο, τοὺς δ᾽ ἤδη κάτεχεν φυσίζοος αἶα
ἐν Λακεδαίμονι αὖθι, φίλῃ ἐν πατρίδι γαίῃ.[9]

We are here in another world, another order of poetry altogether; here is rightly due such supreme praise as that which M. Vitet gives to the *Chanson de Roland.* If our words are to have any meaning, if our judgments are to have any solidity, we must not heap that supreme praise upon poetry of an order immeasurably inferior.

Indeed there can be no more useful help for discovering what poetry belongs to the class of the truly excellent, and can therefore do us most good, than to have always in one's mind lines and expressions of the great masters, and to apply them as a touchstone to other poetry. Of course we are not to require this other poetry to resemble them; it may be very dissimilar. But if we have any tact we shall find them, when we have lodged them well in our minds, an infallible touchstone for detecting the presence or absence of high poetic quality, and also the degree of this quality, in all other poetry which we may place beside them. Short passages, even single lines, will serve our turn quite sufficiently. Take the two lines which I have just quoted from Homer, the poet's comment on Helen's mention of her brothers—or take his

Ἀ δειλώ, τί σφῶϊ δόμεν Πηλῆϊ ἄνακτι
θνητῷ; ὑμεῖς δ᾽ ἐστὸν ἀγήρω τ᾽ ἀθανάτω τε.
ἦ ἵνα δυστήνοισι μετ᾽ ἀνδράσιν ἄλγε᾽ ἔχητον;[1]

the address of Zeus to the horses of Peleus—or take finally his

Καὶ σέ, γέρον, τὸ πρὶν μὲν ἀκούομεν ὄλβιον εἶναι·[2]

the words of Achilles to Priam, a suppliant before him. Take that incomparable line and a half of Dante, Ugolino's tremendous words—

Io no piangeva; sì dentro impietrai.
Piangevan elli . . .[3]

take the lovely words of Beatrice to Virgil—

Io son fatta da Dio, sua mercè, tale,
Che la vostra miseria non mi tange,
Nè fiamma d'esto incendio non m'assale . . .[4]

---

8. "Then began he to call many things to remembrance—all the lands which his valor conquered and pleasant France, and the men of his lineage, and Charlemagne his liege lord who nourished him." *Chanson de Roland* 3.939–42 [Arnold's note].
9. "So said she; they long since in Earth's soft arms were reposing, / There, in their own dear land, their fatherland, Lacedaemon." *Iliad* 3.243–44 (translated by Dr. Hawtrey) [Arnold's note].
1. "Ah, unhappy pair, why gave we you to King Peleus, to a mortal? but ye are without old age, and

immortal. Was it that with men born to misery ye might have sorrow?" *Iliad* 17.443–45 [Arnold's note].
2. "Nay, and thou too, old man, in former days wast, as we hear, happy." *Iliad* 24.543 [Arnold's note].
3. "I wailed not, so of stone I grew within; *they* wailed." *Inferno* 33.49–50 [Arnold's note].
4. "Of such sort hath God, thanked be His mercy, made me, that your misery toucheth me not, neither doth the flame of this fire strike me." *Inferno* 2.91–93 [Arnold's note].

take the simple, but perfect, single line—

> *In la sua volontade è nostra pace.*[5]

Take of Shakespeare a line or two of Henry the Fourth's expostulation with sleep—

> Wilt thou upon the high and giddy mast
> Seal up the shipboy's eyes, and rock his brains
> In cradle of the rude imperious surge . . .[6]

and take, as well, Hamlet's dying request to Horatio—

> If thou didst ever hold me in thy heart,
> Absent thee from felicity awhile,
> And in this harsh world draw thy breath in pain,
> To tell my story . . .[7]

Take of Milton that Miltonic passage—

> Darkened so, yet shone
> Above them all the archangel; but his face
> Deep scars of thunder had intrenched, and care
> Sat on his faded cheek . . .[8]

add two such lines as—

> And courage never to submit or yield
> And what is else not to be overcome . . .[9]

and finish with the exquisite close to the loss of Proserpine, the loss

> . . . which cost Ceres all that pain
> To seek her through the world.[1]

These few lines, if we have tact and can use them, are enough even of themselves to keep clear and sound our judgments about poetry, to save us from fallacious estimates of it, to conduct us to a real estimate.

The specimens I have quoted differ widely from one another, but they have in common this: the possession of the very highest poetical quality. If we are thoroughly penetrated by their power, we shall find that we have acquired a sense enabling us, whatever poetry may be laid before us, to feel the degree in which a high poetical quality is present or wanting there. Critics give themselves great labor to draw out what in the abstract constitutes the characters of a high quality of poetry. It is much better simply to have recourse to concrete examples—to take specimens of poetry of the high, the very highest quality, and to say: The characters of a high quality of poetry are what is expressed *there*. They are far better recognized by being felt in the verse of the master, than by being perused in the prose of the critic. Nevertheless if we are urgently pressed to give some critical account of them, we may safely, perhaps, venture on laying down, not indeed how and why the characters arise, but where and in what they arise. They are in the matter and substance of the poetry, and they are in its manner and style. Both of

---

5. "In His will is our peace." *Paradiso* 3.85 [Arnold's note].
6. *2 Henry IV* 3.1.18–20.
7. *Hamlet* 5.2.357–60.
8. *Paradise Lost* 1.599–602.
9. *Paradise Lost* 1.108–9.
1. *Paradise Lost* 4.271–72.

these, the substance and matter on the one hand, the style and manner on the other, have a mark, an accent, of high beauty, worth, and power. But if we are asked to define this mark and accent in the abstract, our answer must be: No, for we should thereby be darkening the question, not clearing it. The mark and accent are as given by the substance and matter of that poetry, by the style and manner of that poetry, and of all other poetry which is akin to it in quality.

Only one thing we may add as to the substance and matter of poetry, guiding ourselves by Aristotle's profound observation that the superiority of poetry over history consists in its possessing a higher truth and a higher seriousness (φιλοσοφώτερον καὶ σπουδαιότερον).[2] Let us add, therefore, to what we have said, this: that the substance and matter of the best poetry acquire their special character from possessing, in an eminent degree, truth and seriousness. We may add yet further, what is in itself evident, that to the style and manner of the best poetry their special character, their accent, is given by their diction, and, even yet more, by their movement. And though we distinguish between the two characters, the two accents, of superiority, yet they are nevertheless vitally connected one with the other. The superior character of truth and seriousness, in the matter and substance of the best poetry, is inseparable from the superiority of diction and movement marking its style and manner. The two superiorities are closely related, and are in steadfast proportion one to the other. So far as high poetic truth and seriousness are wanting to a poet's matter and substance, so far also, we may be sure, will a high poetic stamp of diction and movement be wanting to his style and manner. In proportion as this high stamp of diction and movement, again, is absent from a poet's style and manner, we shall find, also, that high poetic truth and seriousness are absent from his substance and matter.

So stated, these are but dry generalities; their whole force lies in their application. And I could wish every student of poetry to make the application of them for himself. Made by himself, the application would impress itself upon his mind far more deeply than made by me. Neither will my limits allow me to make any full application of the generalities above propounded; but in the hope of bringing out, at any rate, some significance in them, and of establishing an important principle more firmly by their means, I will, in the space which remains to me, follow rapidly from the commencement the course of our English poetry with them in my view.

* * *

Chaucer's * * * poetical importance does not need the assistance of the historic estimate; it is real. He is a genuine source of joy and strength, which is flowing still for us and will flow always. He will be read, as time goes on, far more generally than he is read now. His language is a cause of difficulty for us; but so also, and I think in quite as great a degree, is the language of Burns. In Chaucer's case, as in that of Burns, it is a difficulty to be unhesitatingly accepted and overcome.

If we ask ourselves wherein consists the immense superiority of Chaucer's poetry over the romance poetry—why it is that in passing from this to Chaucer we suddenly feel ourselves to be in another world, we shall find that his

2. Aristotle's *Poetics* 9.

superiority is both in the substance of his poetry and in the style of his poetry. His superiority in substance is given by his large, free, simple, clear yet kindly view of human life—so unlike the total want, in the romance poets, of all intelligent command of it. Chaucer has not their helplessness; he has gained the power to survey the world from a central, a truly human point of view. We have only to call to mind the Prologue to *The Canterbury Tales*. The right comment upon it is Dryden's: "It is sufficient to say, according to the proverb, that *here is God's plenty*." And again: "He is a perpetual fountain of good sense."[3] It is by a large, free, sound representation of things, that poetry, this high criticism of life, has truth of substance; and Chaucer's poetry has truth of substance.

Of his style and manner, if we think first of the romance poetry and then of Chaucer's divine liquidness of diction, his divine fluidity of movement, it is difficult to speak temperately. They are irresistible, and justify all the rapture with which his successors speak of his "gold dewdrops of speech."[4] Johnson misses the point entirely when he finds fault with Dryden for ascribing to Chaucer the first refinement of our numbers, and says that Gower[5] also can show smooth numbers and easy rhymes. The refinement of our numbers means something far more than this. A nation may have versifiers with smooth numbers and easy rhymes, and yet may have no real poetry at all. Chaucer is the father of our splendid English poetry; he is our "well of English undefiled,"[6] because by the lovely charm of his diction, the lovely charm of his movement, he makes an epoch and founds a tradition. In Spenser, Shakespeare, Milton, Keats, we can follow the tradition of the liquid diction, the fluid movement, of Chaucer; at one time it is his liquid diction of which in these poets we feel the virtue, and at another time it is his fluid movement. And the virtue is irresistible.

Bounded as is my space, I must yet find room for an example of Chaucer's virtue, as I have given examples to show the virtue of the great classics. I feel disposed to say that a single line is enough to show the charm of Chaucer's verse; that merely one line like this—

O martyr souded[7] in virginitee!

has a virtue of manner and movement such as we shall not find in all the verse of romance poetry—but this is saying nothing. The virtue is such as we shall not find, perhaps, in all English poetry, outside the poets whom I have named as the special inheritors of Chaucer's tradition. A single line, however, is too little if we have not the strain of Chaucer's verse well in our memory; let us take a stanza. It is from *The Prioress's Tale*, the story of the Christian child murdered in a Jewry—

My throte is cut unto my nekke-bone
Saidè this child, and as by way of kinde
I should have deyd, yea, longè time agone;
But Jesu Christ, as ye in bookès finde,

3. Both quotations are from Dryden's preface to his *Fables Ancient and Modern* (1700).
4. *The Life of Our Lady*, a poem by John Lydgate (ca. 1370–ca.1451).
5. John Gower (ca. 1325–1408), friend of Chaucer and author of the *Confessio Amantis*, a long poem in octosyllabic couplets.

6. Said of Chaucer by Spenser in *Faerie Queene* 4.2.32.
7. The French *soudé*: soldered, fixed fast [Arnold's note]. From *The Canterbury Tales*, *The Prioress's Tale* (line 127); Chaucer wrote "souded to" rather than "souded in."

Will that his glory last and be in minde,
And for the worship of his mother dere
Yet may I sing O *Alma* loud and clere.

Wordsworth has modernized this Tale, and to feel how delicate and evanescent is the charm of verse, we have only to read Wordsworth's first three lines of this stanza after Chaucer's—

My throat is cut unto the bone, I trow,
Said this young child, and by the law of kind
I should have died, yea, many hours ago.

The charm is departed. It is often said that the power of liquidness and fluidity in Chaucer's verse was dependent upon a free, a licentious dealing with language, such as is now impossible; upon a liberty, such as Burns too enjoyed, of making words like *neck, bird,* into a dissyllable by adding to them, and words like *cause, rhyme,* into a dissyllable by sounding the *e* mute. It is true that Chaucer's fluidity is conjoined with this liberty, and is admirably served by it; but we ought not to say that it was dependent upon it. It was dependent upon his talent. Other poets with a like liberty do not attain to the fluidity of Chaucer; Burns himself does not attain to it. Poets, again, who have a talent akin to Chaucer's, such as Shakespeare or Keats, have known how to attain to his fluidity without the like liberty.

And yet Chaucer is not one of the great classics. His poetry transcends and effaces, easily and without effort, all the romance poetry of Catholic Christendom; it transcends and effaces all the English poetry contemporary with it, it transcends and effaces all the English poetry subsequent to it down to the age of Elizabeth. Of such avail is poetic truth of substance, in its natural and necessary union with poetic truth of style. And yet, I say, Chaucer is not one of the great classics. He has not their accent. What is wanting to him is suggested by the mere mention of the name of the first great classic of Christendom, the immortal poet who died eighty years before Chaucer—Dante. The accent of such verse as

In la sua volontade è nostra pace . . .

is altogether beyond Chaucer's reach; we praise him, but we feel that this accent is out of the question for him. It may be said that it was necessarily out of the reach of any poet in the England of that stage of growth. Possibly; but we are to adopt a real, not a historic, estimate of poetry. However we may account for its absence, something is wanting, then, to the poetry of Chaucer, which poetry must have before it can be placed in the glorious class of the best. And there is no doubt what that something is. It is the spoudaiotes, the high and excellent seriousness, which Aristotle assigns as one of the grand virtues of poetry. The substance of Chaucer's poetry, his view of things and his criticism of life, has largeness, freedom, shrewdness, benignity; but it has not this high seriousness. Homer's criticism of life has it, Dante's has it, Shakespeare's has it. It is this chiefly which gives to our spirits what they can rest upon; and with the increasing demands of our modern ages upon poetry, this virtue of giving us what we can rest upon will be more and more highly esteemed. A voice from the slums of Paris, fifty or sixty years after Chaucer, the voice of poor Villon[8] out of his life of riot and

8. François Villon (1431–1484), French poet and vagabond.

crime, has at its happy moments (as, for instance, in the last stanza of *La Belle Heaulmière*)[9] more of this important poetic virtue of seriousness than all the productions of Chaucer. But its apparition in Villon, and in men like Villon, is fitful; the greatness of the great poets, the power of their criticism of life, is that their virtue is sustained.

To our praise, therefore, of Chaucer as a poet there must be this limitation: he lacks the high seriousness of the great classics, and therewith an important part of their virtue. Still, the main fact for us to bear in mind about Chaucer is his sterling value according to that real estimate which we firmly adopt for all poets. He has poetic truth of substance, though he has not high poetic seriousness, and corresponding to his truth of substance he has an exquisite virtue of style and manner. With him is born our real poetry.

For my present purpose I need not dwell on our Elizabethan poetry, or on the continuation and close of this poetry in Milton. We all of us profess to be agreed in the estimate of this poetry; we all of us recognize it as great poetry, our greatest, and Shakespeare and Milton as our poetical classics. The real estimate, here, has universal currency. With the next age of our poetry divergency and difficulty begin. An historic estimate of that poetry has established itself; and the question is, whether it will be found to coincide with the real estimate.

The age of Dryden, together with our whole eighteenth century which followed it, sincerely believed itself to have produced poetical classics of its own, and even to have made advance, in poetry, beyond all its predecessors. Dryden regards as not seriously disputable the opinion "that the sweetness of English verse was never understood or practiced by our fathers."[1] Cowley[2] could see nothing at all in Chaucer's poetry. Dryden heartily admired it, and, as we have seen, praised its matter admirably; but of its exquisite manner and movement all he can find to say is that "there is the rude sweetness of a Scotch tune in it, which is natural and pleasing, though not perfect."[3] Addison, wishing to praise Chaucer's numbers, compares them with Dryden's own. And all through the eighteenth century, and down even into our own times, the stereotyped phrase of approbation for good verse found in our early poetry has been, that it even approached the verse of Dryden, Addison, Pope, and Johnson.

Are Dryden and Pope poetical classics? Is the historic estimate, which represents them as such, and which has been so long established that it cannot easily give way, the real estimate? Wordsworth and Coleridge, as is well known, denied it; but the authority of Wordsworth and Coleridge does not weigh much with the young generation, and there are many signs to show that the eighteenth century and its judgments are coming into favor again. Are the favorite poets of the eighteenth century classics?

It is impossible within my present limits to discuss the question fully. And what man of letters would not shrink from seeming to dispose dictatorially

9. The name *Heaulmière* is said to be derived from a headdress (helm) worn as a mask by courtesans. In Villon's ballad, a poor old creature of this class laments her days of youth and beauty. The last stanza of the ballad runs thus—"*Ainsi le bon temps regretons / Entrenous, pauvres vieilles sottes, / Assises bas, à croppetons, / Tout en ung tas comme pelottes; / A petit feu de chenevottes / Tost allumeés, tost estaincles, / Et jadis fusmes si mignottes! / Ainsi en prend à maintz et maintes.*" [It may be trans- lated:] "Thus amongst ourselves we regret the good time, poor silly old things, low-seated on our heels, all in a heap like so many balls; by a little fire of hemp stalks, soon lighted, soon spent. And once we were such darlings! So fares it with many and many a one" [Arnold's note].
1. *Essay on Dramatic Poesy.*
2. Abraham Cowley (1618–1667), English poet.
3. Preface to his *Fables*.

of the claims of two men who are, at any rate, such masters in letters as Dryden and Pope; two men of such admirable talent, both of them, and one of them, Dryden, a man, on all sides, of such energetic and genial power? And yet, if we are to gain the full benefit from poetry, we must have the real estimate of it. I cast about for some mode of arriving, in the present case, at such an estimate without offense. And perhaps the best way is to begin, as it is easy to begin, with cordial praise.

When we find Chapman, the Elizabethan translator of Homer, expressing himself in his preface thus: "Though truth in her very nakedness sits in so deep a pit, that from Gades to Aurora and Ganges few eyes can sound her, I hope yet those few here will so discover and confirm that, the date being out of her darkness in this morning of our poet, he shall now gird his temples with the sun," we pronounce that such a prose is intolerable. When we find Milton writing: "And long it was not after, when I was confirmed in this opinion, that he, who would not be frustrate of his hope to write well hereafter in laudable things, ought himself to be a true poem"[4]—we pronounce that such a prose has its own grandeur, but that it is obsolete and inconvenient. But when we find Dryden telling us: "What Virgil wrote in the vigor of his age, in plenty and at ease, I have undertaken to translate in my declining years; struggling with wants, oppressed with sickness, curbed in my genius, liable to be misconstrued in all I write"[5]—then we exclaim that here at last we have the true English prose, a prose such as we would all gladly use if we only knew how. Yet Dryden was Milton's contemporary.

But after the Restoration the time had come when our nation felt the imperious need of a fit prose. So, too, the time had likewise come when our nation felt the imperious need of freeing itself from the absorbing preoccupation which religion in the Puritan age had exercised. It was impossible that this freedom should be brought about without some negative excess, without some neglect and impairment of the religious life of the soul; and the spiritual history of the eighteenth century shows us that the freedom was not achieved without them. Still, the freedom was achieved; the preoccupation, an undoubtedly baneful and retarding one if it had continued, was got rid of. And as with religion amongst us at that period, so it was also with letters. A fit prose was a necessity; but it was impossible that a fit prose should establish itself amongst us without some touch of frost to the imaginative life of the soul. The needful qualities for a fit prose are regularity, uniformity, precision, balance. The men of letters, whose destiny it may be to bring their nation to the attainment of a fit prose, must of necessity, whether they work in prose or in verse, give a predominating, an almost exclusive attention to the qualities of regularity, uniformity, precision, balance. But an almost exclusive attention to these qualities involves some repression and silencing of poetry.

We are to regard Dryden as the puissant and glorious founder, Pope as the splendid high priest, of our age of prose and reason, of our excellent and indispensable eighteenth century. For the purposes of their mission and destiny their poetry, like their prose, is admirable. Do you ask me whether Dryden's verse, take it almost where you will, is not good?

4. *Apology for Smectymnuus.*
5. *Postscript to the Reader* in his translation of Virgil.

> A milk-white Hind, immortal and unchanged,
> Fed on the lawns and in the forest ranged.[6]

I answer: Admirable for the purposes of the inaugurator of an age of prose and reason. Do you ask me whether Pope's verse, take it almost where you will, is not good?

> To Hounslow Heath I point, and Banstead Down;
> Thence comes your mutton, and these chicks my own.[7]

I answer: Admirable for the purposes of the high priest of an age of prose and reason. But do you ask me whether such verse proceeds from men with an adequate poetic criticism of life, from men whose criticism of life has a high seriousness, or even, without that high seriousness, has poetic largeness, freedom, insight, benignity? Do you ask me whether the application of ideas to life in the verse of these men, often a powerful application, no doubt, is a powerful *poetic* application? Do you ask me whether the poetry of these men has either the matter or the inseparable manner of such an adequate poetic criticism; whether it has the accent of

> Absent thee from felicity awhile . . .

or of

> And what is else not to be overcome . . .

or of

> O martyr souded in virginitee!

I answer: It has not and cannot have them; it is the poetry of the builders of an age of prose and reason. Though they may write in verse, though they may in a certain sense be masters of the art of versification, Dryden and Pope are not classics of our poetry, they are classics of our prose.

Gray is our poetical classic of that literature and age; the position of Gray is singular, and demands a word of notice here. He has not the volume or the power of poets who, coming in times more favorable, have attained to an independent criticism of life. But he lived with the great poets, he lived, above all, with the Greeks, through perpetually studying and enjoying them; and he caught their poetic point of view for regarding life, caught their poetic manner. The point of view and the manner are not self-sprung in him, he caught them of others; and he had not the free and abundant use of them. But whereas Addison and Pope never had the use of them, Gray had the use of them at times. He is the scantiest and frailest of classics in our poetry, but he is a classic.[8]

* * *

At any rate the end to which the method and the estimate are designed to lead, and from leading to which, if they do lead to it, they get their whole value—the benefit of being able clearly to feel and deeply to enjoy the best, the truly classic, in poetry—is an end, let me say it once more at parting, of

---

6. *The Hind and the Panther* 1.1–2.
7. *Imitations of Horace*, Satire 2.2.143–144.
8. After Gray, the only other poet discussed by Arnold is Burns (not printed here). Arnold concludes that "Burns, like Chaucer, comes short of the high seriousness of the great classics."

supreme importance. We are often told that an era is opening in which we are to see multitudes of a common sort of readers, and masses of a common sort of literature; that such readers do not want and could not relish anything better than such literature, and that to provide it is becoming a vast and profitable industry. Even if good literature entirely lost currency with the world, it would still be abundantly worth while to continue to enjoy it by oneself. But it never will lose currency with the world, in spite of momentary appearances; it never will lose supremacy. Currency and supremacy are insured to it, not indeed by the world's deliberate and conscious choice, but by something far deeper—by the instinct of self-preservation in humanity.

1880

CHRISTINA ROSSETTI
1830–1894

Referring to the title of George Gissing's novel about women who choose not to marry, the critic Jerome McGann calls Christina Rossetti "one of nineteenth-century England's greatest 'Odd Women.' " Her life had little apparent incident. She was the youngest child in the Rossetti family. Her father was an exiled Italian patriot who wrote poetry and commentaries on Dante that tried to show evidence in his poems of mysterious ancient conspiracies; her mother was an Anglo-Italian who had worked as a governess. Their household was a lively gathering place for Italian exiles, full of conversation of politics and culture, which encouraged Christina, like her brothers Dante Gabriel and William Michael, to develop an early love for art and literature and to draw and write poetry from a very early age. When she was an adolescent, her life changed dramatically: her father became a permanent invalid, the family's economic situation worsened, and her own health deteriorated. At this point, she, her mother, and her sister became intensely involved with the Anglo-Catholic movement within the Church of England. For the rest of her life, Christina Rossetti governed herself by strict religious principles, giving up theater, opera, and chess; on two occasions, she canceled plans for marriage because of religious scruples, breaking her first engagement when her fiancé reverted to Roman Catholicism and ultimately refusing to marry a second suitor because he seemed insufficiently concerned with religion. She lived a quiet life, occupying herself with charitable work—including ten years of volunteer service at a penitentiary for fallen women—with caring for her family, and with writing poetry.

Christina Rossetti's first volume of poetry, *Goblin Market and Other Poems* (1862), contains all the different poetic modes that mark her achievement—pure lyric, narrative fable, ballad, and the devotional verse to which she increasingly turned in her later years. The most remarkable poem in the book is the title piece, which early established its popularity as a seemingly simple moral fable for children. Later readers have likened it to Coleridge's *Rime of the Ancient Mariner* and have detected in it a complex representation of the religious themes of temptation and sin, and of redemption by vicarious suffering; the fruit that tempts Laura, however, is clearly not from the Tree of Knowledge but from an orchard of sensual delights. In its deceptively simple style, *Goblin Market,* like many of her poems, demonstrates her affinity with the early aims of the Pre-Raphaelite group, but her work as a whole resists this classification. A consciousness of gender often leads her to criticize the conventional representation of women in Pre-Raphaelite art, as in her sonnet *In An Artist's Studio,* and a stern religious vision controls the sensuous impulses typical of Pre-Raphaelite poetry and painting. Virginia Woolf has described the distinctive combination of sensuousness and religious severity in Rossetti's work.

> Your poems are full of gold dust and "sweet geraniums' varied brightness"; your eye noted incessantly how rushes are "velvet headed," and lizards have a "strange metallic mail"—your eye, indeed, observed with a sensual pre-Raphaelite intensity that must have surprised Christina the Anglo-Catholic. But to her you owed perhaps the fixity and sadness of your muse. . . . No sooner have you feasted on beauty with your eyes than your mind tells you that beauty is vain and beauty passes. Death, oblivion, and rest lap round your songs with their dark wave.

William Michael Rossetti wrote of his sister, "She was replete with the spirit of self-postponement." Christina Rossetti was a poet who created, in Sandra M. Gilbert and Susan Gubar's term, "an aesthetics of renunciation." She writes a poetry of deferral, of deflection, of negation, whose very denials and constraints give her a powerful way to articulate a poetic self in critical relationship to the little that the world offers. Like Emily Dickinson, she often, as in *Winter: My Secret,* uses a coy playfulness and sardonic wit to reduce the self but at the same time to preserve for it a secret inner space. And like Dickinson, she wrote many poems of an extraordinarily pure lyric beauty that made Virginia Woolf remark, "Your instinct was so sure, so direct, so intense that it produced poems that sing like music in one's ears—like a melody by Mozart or an air by Gluck."

Song

She sat and sang alway
    By the green margin of a stream,
Watching the fishes leap and play
    Beneath the glad sunbeam.

5   I sat and wept away
    Beneath the moon's most shadowy beam,
Watching the blossoms of the May
    Weep leaves into the stream.

I wept for memory;
10   She sang for hope that is so fair:
My tears were swallowed by the sea;
    Her songs died on the air.

1848   1862

Song

When I am dead, my dearest,
    Sing no sad songs for me;
Plant thou no roses at my head,

Nor shady cypress tree:
5   Be the green grass above me
     With showers and dewdrops wet;
     And if thou wilt, remember,
     And if thou wilt, forget.

     I shall not see the shadows,
10   I shall not feel the rain;
     I shall not hear the nightingale
     Sing on, as if in pain:
     And dreaming through the twilight
     That doth not rise nor set,
15   Haply I may remember,
     And haply may forget.

1848   1862

After Death

The curtains were half drawn, the floor was swept
    And strewn with rushes, rosemary and may[1]
Lay thick upon the bed on which I lay,
Where thro' the lattice ivy-shadows crept.
5   He leaned above me, thinking that I slept
    And could not hear him; but I heard him say:
"Poor child, poor child": and as he turned away
Came a deep silence, and I knew he wept.
He did not touch the shroud, or raise the fold
10   That hid my face, or take my hand in his,
    Or ruffle the smooth pillows for my head:
    He did not love me living; but once dead
He pitied me; and very sweet it is
To know he still is warm tho' I am cold.

1849   1862

Dead before Death

Ah! changed and cold, how changed and very cold!
    With stiffened smiling lips and cold calm eyes:
    Changed, yet the same; much knowing, little wise;
This was the promise of the days of old!
5   Grown hard and stubborn in the ancient mould,
    Grown rigid in the sham of lifelong lies:
    We hoped for better things as years would rise,
But it is over as a tale once told.
All fallen the blossom that no fruitage bore,
10   All lost the present and the future time,
    All lost, all lost, the lapse that went before:

---

1. Flowers associated with death.

So lost till death shut-to the opened door,
    So lost from chime to everlasting chime,
So cold and lost for ever evermore.

1854   1862

Cobwebs

It is a land with neither night nor day,
    Nor heat nor cold, nor any wind, nor rain,
    Nor hills nor valleys; but one even plain
Stretches thro' long unbroken miles away:
5   While thro' the sluggish air a twilight grey
    Broodeth; no moons or seasons wax and wane,
    No ebb and flow are there along the main,
No bud-time no leaf-falling, there for aye:—
No ripple on the sea, no shifting sand,
10   No beat of wings to stir the stagnant space,
No pulse of life thro' all the loveless land:
And loveless sea; no trace of days before,
    No guarded home, no toil-won resting place,
No future hope no fear for evermore.

1855   1896

A Triad

Three sang of love together: one with lips
    Crimson, with cheeks and bosom in a glow,
Flushed to the yellow hair and finger tips;
    And one there sang who soft and smooth as snow
5   Bloomed like a tinted hyacinth at a show;
And one was blue with famine after love,
    Who like a harpstring snapped rang harsh and low
The burden of what those were singing of.
One shamed herself in love; one temperately
10   Grew gross in soulless love, a sluggish wife;
One famished died for love. Thus two of three
    Took death for love and won him after strife;
One droned in sweetness like a fattened bee:
    All on the threshold, yet all short of life.

1856   1862

In an Artist's Studio[1]

One face looks out from all his canvases,
    One selfsame figure sits or walks or leans;

---

1. William Michael Rossetti, the younger of Christina's older brothers, noted, "The reference is apparently to our brother's studio, and to his constantly repeated heads of the lady whom he afterwards married, Miss Siddal."

We found her hidden just behind those screens,
That mirror gave back all her loveliness.
5 A queen in opal or in ruby dress,
   A nameless girl in freshest summer-greens,
   A saint, an angel;—every canvass means
The same one meaning, neither more nor less.
He feeds upon her face by day and night,
10 And she with true kind eyes looks back on him
Fair as the moon and joyful as the light:
   Not wan with waiting, not with sorrow dim;
Not as she is, but was when hope shone bright;
   Not as she is, but as she fills his dream.

1856   1896

A Birthday

My heart is like a singing bird
   Whose nest is in a watered shoot;
My heart is like an apple tree
   Whose boughs are bent with thickset fruit;
5 My heart is like a rainbow shell
   That paddles in a halcyon° sea;   *tranquil*
My heart is gladder than all these
   Because my love is come to me.

Raise me a dais of silk and down;
10 Hang it with vair° and purple dyes;   *squirrel fur*
Carve it in doves and pomegranates,
   And peacocks with a hundred eyes;
Work it in gold and silver grapes,
   In leaves and silver fleurs-de-lys;
15 Because the birthday of my life
   Is come, my love is come to me.

1857   1862

An Apple-Gathering

I plucked pink blossoms from mine apple tree
   And wore them all that evening in my hair:
Then in due season when I went to see
   I found no apples there.

5 With dangling basket all along the grass
   As I had come I went the selfsame track:
My neighbours mocked me while they saw me pass
   So empty-handed back.

Lilian and Lilias smiled in trudging by,
10 Their heaped-up basket teazed me like a jeer;

Sweet-voiced they sang beneath the sunset sky,
    Their mother's home was near.

Plump Gertrude passed me with her basket full,
    A stronger hand than hers helped it along;
15 A voice talked with her thro' the shadows cool
    More sweet to me than song.

Ah Willie, Willie, was my love less worth
    Than apples with their green leaves piled above?
I counted rosiest apples on the earth
20   Of far less worth than love.

So once it was with me you stooped to talk
    Laughing and listening in this very lane:
To think that by this way we used to walk
    We shall not walk again!

25 I let my neighbours pass me, ones and twos
    And groups; the latest said the night grew chill,
And hastened: but I loitered, while the dews
    Fell fast I loitered still.

1857   1862

Up-Hill

Does the road wind up-hill all the way?
    Yes, to the very end.
Will the day's journey take the whole long day?
    From morn to night, my friend.

5 But is there for the night a resting-place?
    A roof for when the slow dark hours begin.
May not the darkness hide it from my face?
    You cannot miss that inn.

Shall I meet other wayfarers at night?
10   Those who have gone before.
Then must I knock, or call when just in sight?
    They will not keep you standing at that door.

Shall I find comfort, travel-sore and weak?
    Of labour you shall find the sum.
15 Will there be beds for me and all who seek?
    Yea, beds for all who come.

1858   1862

Goblin Market

Morning and evening
Maids heard the goblins cry:
"Come buy our orchard fruits,
Come buy, come buy:
5   Apples and quinces,
Lemons and oranges,
Plump unpecked cherries,
Melons and raspberries,
Bloom-down-cheeked peaches,
10   Swart-headed mulberries,
Wild free-born cranberries,
Crab-apples, dewberries,
Pine-apples, blackberries,
Apricots, strawberries;—
15   All ripe together
In summer weather,—
Morns that pass by,
Fair eves that fly;
Come buy, come buy:
20   Our grapes fresh from the vine,
Pomegranates full and fine,
Dates and sharp bullaces,
Rare pears and greengages,
Damsons[1] and bilberries,
25   Taste them and try:
Currants and gooseberries,
Bright-fire-like barberries,
Figs to fill your mouth,
Citrons from the South,
30   Sweet to tongue and sound to eye;
Come buy, come buy."

Evening by evening
Among the brookside rushes,
Laura bowed her head to hear,
35   Lizzie veiled her blushes:
Crouching close together
In the cooling weather,
With clasping arms and cautioning lips,
With tingling cheeks and finger tips.
40   "Lie close," Laura said,
Pricking up her golden head:
"We must not look at goblin men,
We must not buy their fruits:
Who knows upon what soil they fed
45   Their hungry thirsty roots?"
"Come buy," call the goblins

---

1. "Bullaces," "greengages," and "damsons" are varieties of plums.

Hobbling down the glen.
"Oh," cried Lizzie, "Laura, Laura,
You should not peep at goblin men."
50 Lizzie covered up her eyes,
Covered close lest they should look;
Laura reared her glossy head,
And whispered like the restless brook:
"Look, Lizzie, look, Lizzie,
55 Down the glen tramp little men.
One hauls a basket,
One bears a plate,
One lugs a golden dish
Of many pounds weight.
60 How fair the vine must grow
Whose grapes are so luscious;
How warm the wind must blow
Thro' those fruit bushes."
"No," said Lizzie: "No, no, no;
65 Their offers should not charm us,
Their evil gifts would harm us."
She thrust a dimpled finger
In each ear, shut eyes and ran:
Curious Laura chose to linger
70 Wondering at each merchant man.
One had a cat's face,
One whisked a tail,
One tramped at a rat's pace,
One crawled like a snail,
75 One like a wombat prowled obtuse and furry,
One like a ratel[2] tumbled hurry skurry.
She heard a voice like voice of doves
Cooing all together:
They sounded kind and full of loves
80 In the pleasant weather.

Laura stretched her gleaming neck
Like a rush-imbedded swan,
Like a lily from the beck,°   *small brook*
Like a moonlit poplar branch,
85 Like a vessel at the launch
When its last restraint is gone.

Backwards up the mossy glen
Turned and trooped the goblin men,
With their shrill repeated cry,
90 "Come buy, come buy."
When they reached where Laura was
They stood stock still upon the moss,
Leering at each other,
Brother with queer brother;

---

2. South African mammal resembling a badger (pronounced *ray-tell*).

95   Signalling each other,
        Brother with sly brother.
        One set his basket down,
        One reared his plate;
        One began to weave a crown
100   Of tendrils, leaves and rough nuts brown
        (Men sell not such in any town);
        One heaved the golden weight
        Of dish and fruit to offer her:
        "Come buy, come buy," was still their cry.
105   Laura stared but did not stir,
        Longed but had no money:
        The whisk-tailed merchant bade her taste
        In tones as smooth as honey,
        The cat-faced purr'd,
110   The rat-paced spoke a word
        Of welcome, and the snail-paced even was heard;
        One parrot-voiced and jolly
        Cried "Pretty Goblin" still for "Pretty Polly;"—
        One whistled like a bird.

115   But sweet-tooth Laura spoke in haste:
        "Good folk, I have no coin;
        To take were to purloin:
        I have no copper in my purse,
        I have no silver either,
120   And all my gold is on the furze
        That shakes in windy weather
        Above the rusty heather."
        "You have much gold upon your head,"
        They answered all together:
125   "Buy from us with a golden curl."
        She clipped a precious golden lock,
        She dropped a tear more rare than pearl,
        Then sucked their fruit globes fair or red:
        Sweeter than honey from the rock.
130   Stronger than man-rejoicing wine,
        Clearer than water flowed that juice;
        She never tasted such before,
        How should it cloy with length of use?
        She sucked and sucked and sucked the more
135   Fruits which that unknown orchard bore;
        She sucked until her lips were sore;
        Then flung the emptied rinds away
        But gathered up one kernel-stone,
        And knew not was it night or day
140   As she turned home alone.

        Lizzie met her at the gate
        Full of wise upbraidings:
        "Dear, you should not stay so late,
        Twilight is not good for maidens;

145 Should not loiter in the glen
In the haunts of goblin men.
Do you not remember Jeanie,
How she met them in the moonlight,
Took their gifts both choice and many,
150 Ate their fruits and wore their flowers
Plucked from bowers
Where summer ripens at all hours?
But ever in the noonlight
She pined and pined away;
155 Sought them by night and day,
Found them no more but dwindled and grew grey;
Then fell with the first snow,
While to this day no grass will grow
Where she lies low:
160 I planted daisies there a year ago
That never blow.
You should not loiter so."
"Nay, hush," said Laura:
"Nay, hush, my sister:
165 I ate and ate my fill,
Yet my mouth waters still;
Tomorrow night I will
Buy more:" and kissed her:
"Have done with sorrow;
170 I'll bring you plums tomorrow
Fresh on their mother twigs,
Cherries worth getting;
You cannot think what figs
My teeth have met in,
175 What melons icy-cold
Piled on a dish of gold
Too huge for me to hold,
What peaches with a velvet nap,
Pellucid grapes without one seed:
180 Odorous indeed must be the mead
Whereon they grow, and pure the wave they drink
With lilies at the brink,
And sugar-sweet their sap."

Golden head by golden head,
185 Like two pigeons in one nest
Folded in each other's wings,
They lay down in their curtained bed:
Like two blossoms on one stem,
Like two flakes of new-fall'n snow,
190 Like two wands of ivory
Tipped with gold for awful° kings.   awe-inspiring
Moon and stars gazed in at them,
Wind sang to them lullaby,
Lumbering owls forbore to fly,
195 Not a bat flapped to and fro

This frontispiece is one of the two illustrations that Dante Gabriel Rossetti provided for his sister's first volume of poetry in 1862.

Round their rest:
Cheek to cheek and breast to breast
Locked together in one nest.

Early in the morning
200   When the first cock crowed his warning,
Neat like bees, as sweet and busy,
Laura rose with Lizzie:
Fetched in honey, milked the cows,
Aired and set to rights the house,
205   Kneaded cakes of whitest wheat,
Cakes for dainty mouths to eat,
Next churned butter, whipped up cream,
Fed their poultry, sat and sewed;
Talked as modest maidens should:
210   Lizzie with an open heart,
Laura in an absent dream,
One content, one sick in part;
One warbling for the mere bright day's delight,
One longing for the night.

215   At length slow evening came:
They went with pitchers to the reedy brook;

Lizzie most placid in her look,
Laura most like a leaping flame.
They drew the gurgling water from its deep;
220 Lizzie plucked purple and rich golden flags,
Then turning homewards said: "The sunset flushes
Those furthest loftiest crags;
Come, Laura, not another maiden lags,
No wilful squirrel wags,
225 The beasts and birds are fast asleep."
But Laura loitered still among the rushes
And said the bank was steep.

And said the hour was early still,
The dew not fall'n, the wind not chill:
230 Listening ever, but not catching
The customary cry,
"Come buy, come buy,"
With its iterated jingle
Of sugar-baited words:
235 Not for all her watching
Once discerning even one goblin
Racing, whisking, tumbling, hobbling;
Let alone the herds
That used to tramp along the glen,
240 In groups or single,
Of brisk fruit-merchant men.

Till Lizzie urged, "O Laura, come;
I hear the fruit-call but I dare not look:
You should not loiter longer at this brook:
245 Come with me home.
The stars rise, the moon bends her arc,
Each glowworm winks her spark,
Let us get home before the night grows dark:
For clouds may gather
250 Tho' this is summer weather,
Put out the lights and drench us thro';
Then if we lost our way what should we do?"

Laura turned cold as stone
To find her sister heard that cry alone,
255 That goblin cry,
"Come buy our fruits, come buy."
Must she then buy no more such dainty fruit?
Must she no more such succous° pasture find,   *juicy, succulent*
Gone deaf and blind?
260 Her tree of life drooped from the root:
She said not one word in her heart's sore ache;
But peering thro' the dimness, nought discerning,
Trudged home, her pitcher dripping all the way;
So crept to bed, and lay
265 Silent till Lizzie slept;

Then sat up in a passionate yearning,
And gnashed her teeth for baulked desire, and wept
As if her heart would break.

Day after day, night after night,
270 Laura kept watch in vain
In sullen silence of exceeding pain.
She never caught again the goblin cry:
"Come buy, come buy;"—
She never spied the goblin men
275 Hawking their fruits along the glen:
But when the noon waxed bright
Her hair grew thin and gray;
She dwindled, as the fair full moon doth turn
To swift decay and burn
280 Her fire away.

One day remembering her kernel-stone
She set it by a wall that faced the south;
Dewed it with tears, hoped for a root,
Watched for a waxing shoot,
285 But there came none;
It never saw the sun,
It never felt the trickling moisture run:
While with sunk eyes and faded mouth
She dreamed of melons, as a traveller sees
290 False waves in desert drouth
With shade of leaf-crowned trees,
And burns the thirstier in the sandful breeze.

She no more swept the house,
Tended the fowls or cows,
295 Fetched honey, kneaded cakes of wheat,
Brought water from the brook:
But sat down listless in the chimney-nook
And would not eat.

Tender Lizzie could not bear
300 To watch her sister's cankerous care
Yet not to share.
She night and morning
Caught the goblins' cry:
"Come buy our orchard fruits,
305 Come buy, come buy:"—
Beside the brook, along the glen,
She heard the tramp of goblin men,
The voice and stir
Poor Laura could not hear;
310 Longed to buy fruit to comfort her,
But feared to pay too dear.
She thought of Jeanie in her grave,
Who should have been a bride;
But who for joys brides hope to have

315　Fell sick and died
　　In her gay prime,
　　In earliest Winter time,
　　With the first glazing rime,
　　With the first snow-fall of crisp Winter time.

320　Till Laura dwindling
　　Seemed knocking at Death's door:
　　Then Lizzie weighed no more
　　Better and worse;
　　But put a silver penny in her purse,
325　Kissed Laura, crossed the heath with clumps of furze
　　At twilight, halted by the brook:
　　And for the first time in her life
　　Began to listen and look.

　　Laughed every goblin
330　When they spied her peeping:
　　Came towards her hobbling,
　　Flying, running, leaping,
　　Puffing and blowing,
　　Chuckling, clapping, crowing,
335　Clucking and gobbling,
　　Mopping and mowing,
　　Full of airs and graces,
　　Pulling wry faces,
　　Demure grimaces,
340　Cat-like and rat-like,
　　Ratel- and wombat-like,
　　Snail-paced in a hurry,
　　Parrot-voiced and whistler,
　　Helter skelter, hurry skurry,
345　Chattering like magpies,
　　Fluttering like pigeons,
　　Gliding like fishes,—
　　Hugged her and kissed her,
　　Squeezed and caressed her:
350　Stretched up their dishes,
　　Panniers, and plates:
　　"Look at our apples
　　Russet and dun,
　　Bob at our cherries,
355　Bite at our peaches,
　　Citrons and dates,
　　Grapes for the asking,
　　Pears red with basking
　　Out in the sun,
360　Plums on their twigs;
　　Pluck them and suck them,
　　Pomegranates, figs."—

　　"Good folk," said Lizzie,
　　Mindful of Jeanie:

365   "Give me much and many:"—
    Held out her apron,
    Tossed them her penny.
    "Nay, take a seat with us,
    Honour and eat with us,"
370   They answered grinning:
    "Our feast is but beginning.
    Night yet is early,
    Warm and dew-pearly,
    Wakeful and starry:
375   Such fruits as these
    No man can carry;
    Half their bloom would fly,
    Half their dew would dry,
    Half their flavour would pass by.
380   Sit down and feast with us,
    Be welcome guest with us,
    Cheer you and rest with us."—
    "Thank you," said Lizzie: "But one waits
    At home alone for me:
385   So without further parleying,
    If you will not sell me any
    Of your fruits tho' much and many,
    Give me back my silver penny
    I tossed you for a fee."—
390   They began to scratch their pates,
    No longer wagging, purring,
    But visibly demurring,
    Grunting and snarling.
    One called her proud,
395   Cross-grained, uncivil;
    Their tones waxed loud,
    Their looks were evil.
    Lashing their tails
    They trod and hustled her,
400   Elbowed and jostled her,
    Clawed with their nails,
    Barking, mewing, hissing, mocking,
    Tore her gown and soiled her stocking,
    Twitched her hair out by the roots,
405   Stamped upon her tender feet,
    Held her hands and squeezed their fruits
    Against her mouth to make her eat.

    White and golden Lizzie stood,
    Like a lily in a flood,—
410   Like a rock of blue-veined stone
    Lashed by tides obstreperously,—
    Like a beacon left alone
    In a hoary roaring sea,
    Sending up a golden fire,—
415   Like a fruit-crowned orange-tree

White with blossoms honey-sweet
Sore beset by wasp and bee,—
Like a royal virgin town
Topped with gilded dome and spire
420   Close beleaguerred by a fleet
Mad to tug her standard down.

One may lead a horse to water,
Twenty cannot make him drink.
Tho' the goblins cuffed and caught her,
425   Coaxed and fought her,
Bullied and besought her,
Scratched her, pinched her black as ink,
Kicked and knocked her,
Mauled and mocked her,
430   Lizzie uttered not a word;
Would not open lip from lip
Lest they should cram a mouthful in:
But laughed in heart to feel the drip
Of juice that syruped all her face,
435   And lodged in dimples of her chin,
And streaked her neck which quaked like curd.
At last the evil people
Worn out by her resistance
Flung back her penny, kicked their fruit
440   Along whichever road they took,
Not leaving root or stone or shoot;
Some writhed into the ground,
Some dived into the brook
With ring and ripple,
445   Some scudded on the gale without a sound,
Some vanished in the distance.

In a smart, ache, tingle,
Lizzie went her way;
Knew not was it night or day;
450   Sprang up the bank, tore thro' the furze,
Threaded copse and dingle,
And heard her penny jingle
Bouncing in her purse,
Its bounce was music to her ear.
455   She ran and ran
As if she feared some goblin man
Dogged her with gibe or curse
Or something worse:
But not one goblin skurried after,
460   Nor was she pricked by fear;
The kind heart made her windy-paced
That urged her home quite out of breath with haste
And inward laughter.

She cried "Laura," up the garden,
465   "Did you miss me?

Come and kiss me.
Never mind my bruises,
Hug me, kiss me, suck my juices
Squeezed from goblin fruits for you,
470 Goblin pulp and goblin dew.
Eat me, drink me, love me;
Laura, make much of me:
For your sake I have braved the glen
And had to do with goblin merchant men."

475 Laura started from her chair,
Flung her arms up in the air,
Clutched her hair:
"Lizzie, Lizzie, have you tasted
For my sake the fruit forbidden?
480 Must your light like mine be hidden,
Your young life like mine be wasted,
Undone in mine undoing
And ruined in my ruin,
Thirsty, cankered, goblin-ridden?"—
485 She clung about her sister,
Kissed and kissed and kissed her:
Tears once again
Refreshed her shrunken eyes,
Dropping like rain
490 After long sultry drouth;
Shaking with aguish fear, and pain,
She kissed and kissed her with a hungry mouth.

Her lips began to scorch,
That juice was wormwood to her tongue,
495 She loathed the feast:
Writhing as one possessed she leaped and sung,
Rent all her robe, and wrung
Her hands in lamentable haste,
And beat her breast.
500 Her locks streamed like the torch
Borne by a racer at full speed,
Or like the mane of horses in their flight,
Or like an eagle when she stems³ the light
Straight toward the sun,
505 Or like a caged thing freed,
Or like a flying flag when armies run.

Swift fire spread thro' her veins, knocked at her heart,
Met the fire smouldering there
And overbore its lesser flame:
510 She gorged on bitterness without a name:
Ah! fool, to choose such part
Of soul-consuming care!

3. Makes headway against.

Sense failed in the mortal strife:
Like the watch-tower of a town
515 Which an earthquake shatters down,
Like a lightning-stricken mast,
Like a wind-uprooted tree
Spun about,
Like a foam-topped waterspout
520 Cast down headlong in the sea,
She fell at last;
Pleasure past and anguish past,
Is it death or is it life?

Life out of death.
525 That night long Lizzie watched by her,
Counted her pulse's flagging stir,
Felt for her breath,
Held water to her lips, and cooled her face
With tears and fanning leaves:
530 But when the first birds chirped about their eaves,
And early reapers plodded to the place
Of golden sheaves,
And dew-wet grass
Bowed in the morning winds so brisk to pass,
535 And new buds with new day
Opened of cup-like lilies on the stream,
Laura awoke as from a dream,
Laughed in the innocent old way,
Hugged Lizzie but not twice or thrice;
540 Her gleaming locks showed not one thread of grey,
Her breath was sweet as May
And light danced in her eyes.

Days, weeks, months, years
Afterwards, when both were wives
545 With children of their own;
Their mother-hearts beset with fears,
Their lives bound up in tender lives;
Laura would call the little ones
And tell them of her early prime,
550 Those pleasant days long gone
Of not-returning time:
Would talk about the haunted glen,
The wicked, quaint fruit-merchant men,
Their fruits like honey to the throat
555 But poison in the blood;
(Men sell not such in any town:)
Would tell them how her sister stood
In deadly peril to do her good,
And win the fiery antidote:
560 Then joining hands to little hands
Would bid them cling together,
"For there is no friend like a sister

In calm or stormy weather;
To cheer one on the tedious way,
565　To fetch one if one goes astray,
To lift one if one totters down,
To strengthen whilst one stands."

1859　　　　　　　　　　　　　　　　　　　　　　　　　1862

"No, Thank You, John"

I never said I loved you, John:
　　Why will you teaze me day by day,
And wax a weariness to think upon
　　With always "do" and "pray"?

5　You know I never loved you, John;
　　No fault of mine made me your toast:
Why will you haunt me with a face as wan
　　As shows an hour-old ghost?

I dare say Meg or Moll would take
10　Pity upon you, if you'd ask:
And pray don't remain single for my sake
　　Who can't perform that task.

I have no heart?—Perhaps I have not;
　　But then you're mad to take offence
15　That I don't give you what I have not got:
　　Use your own common sense.

Let bygones be bygones:
　　Don't call me false, who owed not to be true:
I'd rather answer "No" to fifty Johns
20　Than answer "Yes" to you.

Let's mar our pleasant days no more,
　　Song-birds of passage, days of youth:
Catch at today, forget the days before:
　　I'll wink at your untruth.

25　Let us strike hands as hearty friends;
　　No more, no less; and friendship's good:
Only don't keep in view ulterior ends,
　　And points not understood

In open treaty. Rise above
30　Quibbles and shuffling off and on:
Here's friendship for you if you like; but love,—
　　No, thank you, John.

1860　　　　　　　　　　　　　　　　　　　　　　　　　1862

Promises Like Pie-Crust

Promise me no promises,
   So will I not promise you:
Keep we both our liberties,
   Never false and never true:
5 Let us hold the die uncast,
   Free to come as free to go:
For I cannot know your past,
   And of mine what can you know?

You, so warm, may once have been
10   Warmer towards another one:
I, so cold, may once have seen
   Sunlight, once have felt the sun:
Who shall show us if it was
   Thus indeed in time of old?
15 Fades the image from the glass,
   And the fortune is not told.

If you promised, you might grieve
   For lost liberty again:
If I promised, I believe
20   I should fret to break the chain.
Let us be the friends we were,
   Nothing more but nothing less:
Many thrive on frugal fare
   Who would perish of excess.

1861   1896

In Progress

Ten years ago it seemed impossible
   That she should ever grow so calm as this,
   With self-remembrance in her warmest kiss
And dim dried eyes like an exhausted well.
5 Slow-speaking when she has some fact to tell,
   Silent with long-unbroken silences,
   Centred in self yet not unpleased to please,
Gravely monotonous like a passing bell.
Mindful of drudging daily common things,
10   Patient at pastime, patient at her work,
    Wearied perhaps but strenuous certainly.
    Sometimes I fancy we may one day see
Her head shoot forth seven stars from where they lurk
And her eyes lightnings and her shoulders wings.

1862   1896

A Life's Parallels

Never on this side of the grave again,
   On this side of the river,
On this side of the garner of the grain,
   Never,—

5 Ever while time flows on and on and on,
   That narrow noiseless river,
Ever while corn bows heavy-headed, wan,
   Ever,—

Never despairing, often fainting, rueing,
10   But looking back, ah never!
Faint yet pursuing, faint yet still pursuing
   Ever.

                                         1881

From Later Life

17

Something this foggy day, a something which
  Is neither of this fog nor of today,
  Has set me dreaming of the winds that play
Past certain cliffs, along one certain beach,
5   And turn the topmost edge of waves to spray:
  Ah pleasant pebbly strand so far away,
So out of reach while quite within my reach,
  As out of reach as India or Cathay!
I am sick of where I am and where I am not,
10   I am sick of foresight and of memory,
  I am sick of all I have and all I see,
   I am sick of self, and there is nothing new;
Oh weary impatient patience of my lot!—
   Thus with myself: how fares it, Friends, with you?

                                         1881

Cardinal Newman[1]

In the grave, whither thou goest[2]

O weary Champion of the Cross, lie still:
  Sleep thou at length the all-embracing sleep:
  Long was thy sowing-day, rest now and reap:
Thy fast was long, feast now thy spirit's fill.

---

1. Written on the occasion of the death of John   2. Ecclesiastes 9.10.
Henry Newman.

5   Yea, take thy fill of love, because thy will
       Chose love not in the shallows but the deep:
       Thy tides were springtides, set against the neap[3]
       Of calmer souls: thy flood rebuked their rill.
       Now night has come to thee—please God, of rest:
10   So some time must it come to every man;
       To first and last, where many last are first.
       Now fixed and finished thine eternal plan,
       Thy best has done its best, thy worst its worst:
Thy best its best, Please God, thy best its best.

                                                              1890

Sleeping at Last

Sleeping at last, the trouble & tumult over,
   Sleeping at last, the struggle & horror past,
Cold & white out of sight of friend & of lover
      Sleeping at last.

5   No more a tired heart downcast or overcast,
No more pangs that wring or shifting fears that hover,
Sleeping at last in a dreamless sleep locked fast.

Fast asleep.   Singing birds in their leafy cover
   Cannot wake her, nor shake her the gusty blast.
10   Under the purple thyme and the purple clover
      Sleeping at last.

                                                              1896

3. Tides that do not rise to the high-water mark of the spring tides.

GERARD MANLEY HOPKINS
1844–1889

It has been said that the most important date in Gerard Manley Hopkins's career was 1918, twenty-nine years after his death, for it was then that the first publication of his poems made them accessible to the world of readers. During his lifetime, these remarkable poems, most of them celebrating the wonders of God's creation, had been known only to a small circle of friends, including his literary executor, the poet Robert Bridges, who waited until 1918 before releasing them to a publisher. Partly because his work was first made public in a twentieth-century volume, but especially because of his striking experiments in meter and diction, Hopkins was widely hailed as a pioneering figure of "modern" literature, miraculously unconnected with his fellow Victorian poets (who during the 1920s and 1930s were largely out of fashion among critical readers). And this way of classifying and evaluating his writings has long persisted. In 1936 a substantial selection of his poems led off *The Faber Book of Modern Verse,* one of the most influential anthologies of the century, featuring poets such as W. H. Auden, Dylan Thomas, and T. S. Eliot (the only one whose selections occupy more pages than those allotted to Hopkins). And the first four editions of *The Norton Anthology of English Literature* (1962–79) grouped Hopkins with these same twentieth-century poets. To reclassify him is not to repudiate his earlier reputation as a "modern" but rather to suggest that his work can be better understood and appreciated if it is restored to the Victorian world out of which it developed.

Hopkins was born near London into a large and cultivated family in comfortable circumstances. After a brilliant career at Highgate School, he entered Oxford in 1863, where he was exposed to a variety of Victorian ways of thinking, both secular and religious. Among influential leaders at Oxford was Matthew Arnold, professor of poetry, but more important for Hopkins was his tutor, Walter Pater, an aesthetician whose emphasis on the intense apprehension of sensuous beauty struck a responsive chord in Hopkins. At Oxford he was also exposed to the Broad Church theology of one of the tutors at his college (Balliol), Benjamin Jowett. But Hopkins became increasingly attracted first to the High Church movement represented at Oxford by Edward Pusey, and then to Roman Catholicism. Profoundly influenced by John Henry Newman's conversion to Rome and by subsequent conversations with Newman himself, Hopkins entered the Roman Catholic Church in 1866. The estrangement from his family that resulted from his conversion was very painful for him; his parents' letters to him were so "terrible" (he reported to Newman) that he could not bear to "read them twice." And this alienation was heightened by his decision not only to become a Roman Catholic but to become a priest and, in particular, a Jesuit priest, for in the eyes of many Victorian Protestants, the Jesuit order was regarded with a special distrust. For the rest of his life, Hopkins served as a priest and teacher in various places, among them Oxford, Liverpool, and Lancashire. In 1884 he was appointed professor of classics at University College in Dublin, where Newman had served as rector in the 1850s and where James Joyce would be enrolled as a student at the turn of the century.

At school and at Oxford in the early 1860s, Hopkins had written poems in the vein of Keats. He burned most of these early writings after his conversion (although drafts survive), for he believed that his vocation must require renouncing such personal satisfactions as the writing of poems. Only after his superiors in the church encouraged him to do so did he resume writing poetry, but during the seven years of silence, as his letters show, he had been thinking about experimenting with what he called a "new rhythm." The result, in 1876, was his rhapsodic lyric-narrative, *The Wreck of the Deutschland,* a long ode about the wreck of a ship in which five Franciscan nuns were drowned. The style of the poem was so distinctive that the editor of the Jesuit magazine to which he had submitted it "dared not print it," as Hopkins himself reported. During the remaining fourteen years of his life, Hopkins continued to write poems but seldom submitted them for publication, partly because he was convinced that poetic fame was incompatible with his religious vocation but also because of a fear that readers would be discouraged by the eccentricity of his work.

Hopkins's sense of his own singularity gives us an indication of the organizing structure of his poetry. Drawing on the theology of Duns Scotus, a medieval philosopher, he felt that everything in the universe was characterized by what he called *inscape,* the distinctive design that constitutes individual identity. This identity is not static but dynamic. Each being in the universe "selves," that is, enacts its identity. And the human being, the most highly selved, the most individually distinctive being in the universe, recognizes the inscape of other beings in an act that Hopkins calls *instress,* the apprehension of an object in an intense thrust of energy toward it that enables one to realize its specific distinctiveness. Ultimately, the instress of inscape leads one to Christ, for the individual identity of any object is the stamp of divine creation on it. In the act of instress, therefore, the human being becomes a celebrant of the divine, at once recognizing God's creation and enacting his or her own God-given identity within it.

Poetry for Hopkins enacts this celebration. It is instress, and it realizes the inscape of its subject in its own distinctive design. Hopkins wrote, "But as air, melody, is what strikes me most of all in music and design in painting, so design, pattern or what I am in the habit of calling 'inscape' is what I above all aim at in poetry." To create inscape, Hopkins seeks to give each poem a unique design that captures the initial inspiration when he is "caught" by his subject. Many of the characteristics of Hopkins's style—his disruption of conventional syntax, his coining and compounding of words, his use of ellipsis and repetition—can be understood as ways of representing the stress and action of the brain in moments of inspiration. He creates compounds to represent the unique interlocking of the characteristics of an object—"piece-bright," "dapple-dawn-drawn," "blue-bleak." He omits syntactical connections to fuse qualities more intensely—"the dearest freshness deep down things." He creates puns to suggest how God's creation rhymes and chimes in a divine patterning. He violates conventional syntactic order to represent the shape of mental experience. In the act of imaginative apprehension, a language particular to the moment generates itself.

Hopkins also uses a new rhythm to give each poem its distinctive design. In the new metric system he created, which he called *sprung rhythm*, lines have a given number of stresses, but the number and placement of unstressed syllables is highly variable. Hopkins rarely marks all the intended stresses, only those that readers might not anticipate. To indicate stressed syllables, Hopkins often uses both the stress (´) and the "great stress" (˝). A curved line marks an "outride"—one or more syllables added to a foot but not counted in the scansion of the line; they indicate a stronger stress on the preceding syllable and a short pause after the outride. Here, for example, is the scansion for the first three lines of *The Windhover*:

> I caúght this mórning mórning's mínion, kíng-
> dom of dáylight's daúphin, dapple-dawn-drawn Fálcon, in his ríding
> Of the rólling level underneáth him steady aír, and stríding

Hopkins argued that sprung rhythm was the natural rhythm of common speech and written prose, as well as of music. He found a model for it in Old English poetry and in nursery rhymes, but he claimed that it had not been used in English poetry since the Elizabethan Age.

The density and difficulty that result from Hopkins's unconventional rhythm and syntax make his poetry seem modern, but his concern with the imagination's shaping of the natural world puts him very much in the Romantic tradition, and his creation of a rough and difficult style, designed to capture the mind's own motion, resembles the style of Browning. "A horrible thing has happened to me," Hopkins wrote in 1864, "I have begun to *doubt* Tennyson." He goes on to criticize Tennyson for using the grand style as a smooth and habitual poetic speech. Like Swinburne, Pater, and Henry James as well as Browning, Hopkins displays a new mannerism, characteristic of the latter part of the nineteenth century, which paradoxically combines an elaborate aestheticism with a more complex representation of consciousness.

In Hopkins's early poetry, his singular apprehension of the beauty of individual objects always brings him to an ecstatic illumination of the presence of God. But in his late poems, the so-called terrible sonnets, his distinctive individuality comes to isolate him from the God who made him thus. Hopkins wrote, "To me there is no resemblance: searching nature, I taste *self* but at one tankard, that of my own being." In the terrible sonnets, Hopkins confronts the solipsism to which his own stress on individuality seems to lead him. Like the mad speakers of so many Victorian dramatic monologues, he cannot escape a world solely of his own imagining. Yet even these poems of despair, which seem so distinctively modern, reflect a traditional religious vision, the dark night of the soul as described by the Spanish mystic Saint John of the Cross.

In his introduction to *The Oxford Book of Modern Verse*, Yeats calls Hopkins's poetry "a last development of poetical diction." Yeats's remark indicates the anomaly that Hopkins's work poses. Perhaps it is only appropriate for a writer who stressed the uniqueness of inscape to strike us with the individuality of his achievement.

God's Grandeur

The world is charged with the grandeur of God.
　　It will flame out, like shining from shook foil;[1]
　　It gathers to a greatness, like the ooze of oil
Crushed.[2] Why do men then now not reck his rod?
5　Generations have trod, have trod, have trod;
　　And all is seared with trade; bleared, smeared with toil;
　　And wears man's smudge and shares man's smell: the soil
Is bare now, nor can foot feel, being shod.

And for° all this, nature is never spent; 　　　　　　　*despite*
10　There lives the dearest freshness deep down things;
　　And though the last lights off the black West went
　　Oh, morning, at the brown brink eastward, springs—
Because the Holy Ghost over the bent
　　World broods with warm breast and with ah! bright wings.

1877　　　　　　　　　　　　　　　　　　　　　　　　　　1918

The Starlight Night

Look at the stars! look, look up at the skies!
　　O look at all the fire-folk sitting in the air!
　　The bright boroughs, the circle-citadels there!
Down in dim woods the diamond delves!° the elves'-eyes! 　*quarries*
5　The grey lawns cold where gold, where quickgold;[1] lies!
　　Wind-beat whitebeam! airy abeles° set on a flare! 　*white poplars*
　　Flake-doves sent floating forth at a farmyard scare!—
Ah well! it is all a purchase, all is a prize.

Buy then! bid then!—What?—Prayer, patience, alms, vows.
10　Look, look: a May-mess,[2] like on orchard boughs!
　　Look! March-bloom, like on mealed-with-yellow sallows![3]
These are indeed the barn; withindoors house
　　The shocks. This piece-bright paling[4] shuts the spouse
Christ home, Christ and his mother and all his hallows.° 　*saints*

1877　　　　　　　　　　　　　　　　　　　　　　　　　　1918

---

1. Hopkins explained this image in a letter: "I mean foil in its sense of leaf or tinsel. . . . Shaken goldfoil gives off broad glares like sheet lightning and also, and this is true of nothing else, owing to its zigzag dints and creasings and network of small many cornered facets, a sort of fork lightning too."
2. I.e., from the crushing of olives.

1. Coined by analogy with quicksilver. The starlight night resembles the lawns below it where the dew, reflecting the starlight, looks like gold.
2. A profusion of growing things such as May blossoms.
3. Willows, here with yellow spots like meal.
4. Picket fence. "Shocks": sheaves of grain.

As Kingfishers Catch Fire

As kingfishers catch fire, dragonflies draw flame;
　　As tumbled over rim in roundy wells
　　Stones ring; like each tucked° string tells, each hung bell's　　*plucked*
Bow swung finds tongue to fling out broad its name;
5　Each mortal thing does one thing and the same:
　　Deals out that being indoors° each one dwells;　　*within*
　　Selves[1]—goes itself; *myself* it speaks and spells,
Crying *What I do is me: for that I came.*

I say more: the just man justices;[2]
10　　Keeps gráce: thát keeps all his goings graces;
Acts in God's eye what in God's eye he is—
　　Chríst. For Christ plays in ten thousand places,
Lovely in limbs, and lovely in eyes not his
　　To the Father through the features of men's faces.

1877　　　　　　　　　　　　　　　　　　　　　　　　1918

Spring

Nothing is so beautiful as Spring—
　　When weeds, in wheels, shoot long and lovely and lush;
　　Thrush's eggs look little low heavens, and thrush
Through the echoing timber does so rinse and wring
5　The ear, it strikes like lightnings to hear him sing;
　　The glassy peartree leaves and blooms, they brush
　　The descending blue; that blue is all in a rush
With richness; the racing lambs too have fair their fling.

What is all this juice and all this joy?
10　　A strain of the earth's sweet being in the beginning
In Eden garden.—Have, get, before it cloy,
　　Before it cloud, Christ, lord, and sour with sinning,
Innocent mind and Mayday in girl and boy,
　　Most, O maid's child,[1] thy choice and worthy the winning.

1877　　　　　　　　　　　　　　　　　　　　　　　　1918

The Windhover[1]

To Christ our Lord

I caught this morning morning's minion,° king-　　　　　　　　*darling*
　　dom of daylight's dauphin,[2] dapple-dawn-drawn Falcon, in his riding
　　Of the rolling level underneath him steady air, and striding

1. Fulfills its individuality.
2. Acts in a just manner.
1. Jesus, son of the Virgin Mary.

1. Kestrel, a small falcon noted for hovering in the air.
2. A prince who is heir to the French throne.

High there, how he rung upon the rein of a wimpling[3] wing
5 In his ecstasy! then off, off forth on swing,
        As a skate's heel sweeps smooth on a bow-bend: the hurl and gliding
        Rebuffed the big wind. My heart in hiding
Stirred for a bird,—the achieve of, the mastery of the thing!

Brute beauty and valour and act, oh, air, pride, plume, here
10   Buckle![4] AND the fire that breaks from thee then, a billion
Times told lovelier, more dangerous, O my chevalier!°   *knight*

No wonder of it: shéer plód makes plough down sillion[5]
Shine, and blue-bleak embers, ah my dear,
        Fall, gall[6] themselves, and gash gold-vermilion.

1877   1918

Pied[1] Beauty

Glory be to God for dappled things—
    For skies of couple-colour as a brinded[2] cow;
        For rose-moles all in stipple upon trout that swim;
Fresh-firecoal chestnut-falls,[3] finches' wings;
5   Landscape plotted and pieced—fold, fallow, and plough;[4]
        And áll trádes, their gear and tackle and trim.°   *equipment*

All things counter, original, spare,[5] strange;
    Whatever is fickle, freckled (who knows how?)
        With swift, slow; sweet, sour; adazzle, dim;
10 He fathers-forth whose beauty is past change:
                    Praise him.

1877   1918

Hurrahing in Harvest

Summer ends now; now, barbarous in beauty, the stooks[1] rise
Around; up above, what wind-walks! what lovely behavior
Of silk-sack clouds! has wilder, wilful-wavier
Meal-drift moulded ever and melted across skies?

5 I walk, I lift up, I lift up heart, eyes,
Down all that glory in the heavens to glean our Saviour;
And, éyes, heárt, what looks, what lips yet gave you a
Rapturous love's greeting of realer, of rounder replies?

And the azurous hung hills are his world-wielding shoulder
10   Majestic—as a stallion stalwart, very-violet-sweet!—

3. Rippling. "Rung upon the rein": circled at the end of a rein.
4. The verb can be read as imperative or indicative. All three meanings are relevant: to prepare for action, to fasten together, to collapse.
5. The ridge between two furrows of a plowed field.
6. Break the surface of.

1. Of two or more colors in blotches, variegated.
2. Brownish orange in color with streaks of gray.
3. I.e., freshly fallen chestnuts, bright as coals.
4. Divided into fields used as pastures ("fold"), lying fallow, or plowed for cultivation. The landscape thus appears like patches of different colors.
5. Rare. "Counter": contrary.
1. Sheaves of grain.

These things, these things were here and but the beholder
Wanting; which two when they once meet,
The heart rears wings bold and bolder
And hurls for him, O half hurls earth for him off under his feet.

1877   1918

Binsey Poplars

felled 1879

My aspens dear, whose airy cages quelled,
Quelled or quenched in leaves the leaping sun,
All felled, felled, are all felled;
    Of a fresh and following folded rank
5   Not spared, not one
          That dandled a sandalled
        Shadow that swam or sank
On meadow and river and wind-wandering
       weed-winding bank.

10   O if we but knew what we do
         When we delve° or hew—   *dig*
      Hack and rack° the growing green!   *torture*
        Since country is so tender
      To touch, her being só slender,
15   That, like this sleek and seeing ball°   *the eye*
    But a prick will make no eye at all,

    Where we, even where we mean
        To mend her we end her,
      When we hew or delve:
20   After-comers cannot guess the beauty been.
    Ten or twelve, only ten or twelve
      Strokes of havoc únselve[1]
        The sweet especial scene,
      Rural scene, a rural scene,
25   Sweet especial rural scene.

1879   1918

Duns Scotus's Oxford[1]

Towery city and branchy between towers;
Cuckoo-echoing, bell-swarmèd, lark-charmèd, rook-racked, river-rounded;
The dapple-eared lily below thee; that country and town did
Once encounter in, here coped[2] and poisèd powers;

---

1. Rob it of self.
1. Duns Scotus, the medieval theologian, lectured at Oxford about 1301. His idea that individuality is the final perfection of any creature influenced Hopkins's conception of inscape. When Hopkins came on two of Scotus's commentaries in 1872, he wrote that he was immediately "flush with a new stroke of enthusiasm . . . when I took in any inscape of the sky or sea I thought of Scotus."
2. Set off against one another.

5   Thou hast a base and brickish skirt[3] there, sours
That neighbour-nature thy grey beauty is grounded
Best in; graceless growth, thou hast confounded
Rural rural keeping[4]—folk, flocks, and flowers.

Yet ah! this air I gather and I release
10 He lived on; these weeds and waters, these walls are what
He haunted who of all men most sways my spirits to peace;

Of realty° the rarest-veinèd unraveller; a not   *reality*
Rivalled insight, be rival Italy or Greece;
Who fired France for Mary without spot.[5]

1879   1918

Felix Randal

Felix Randal the farrier,° O is he dead then? my duty   *blacksmith*
   all ended,
Who have watched his mould of man, big-boned and hardy-handsome
Pining, pining, till time when reason rambled in it and some
Fatal four disorders, fleshed there, all contended?

5   Sickness broke him. Impatient, he cursed at first, but mended
Being anointed[1] and all; though a heavenlier heart began some
Months earlier, since I had our sweet reprieve and ransom[2]
Tendered to him. Ah well, God rest him all road ever[3] he offended!

This seeing the sick endears them to us, us too it endears.
10 My tongue had taught thee comfort, touch had quenched thy tears,
Thy tears that touched my heart, child, Felix, poor Felix Randal;
How far from then forethought of, all thy more boisterous years,
When thou at the random[4] grim forge, powerful amidst peers,
Didst fettle° for the great grey drayhorse his bright and battering   *prepare*
   sandal!

1880   1918

Spring and Fall:

to a young child

Márgarét, áre you gríeving
Over Goldengrove unleaving?
Leáves, líke the things of man, you

3. Redbrick housing developments and industrial complexes, built in the 19th century on the north edge of Oxford, are in marked contrast with the "gray" stone buildings of the medieval city.
4. The "brickish skirt" has destroyed the way in which the rural landscape and the old city have tended and preserved each other.
5. In Paris, Scotus was the first to defend the doc-trine of the Immaculate Conception, that Mary was born without original sin.
1. In Extreme Unction, the sacrament for the dying.
2. Holy Communion preceded by confession and absolution.
3. In whatever way.
4. Built with stones of irregular size and shape.

With your fresh thoughts care for, can you?
5　Áh! ás the heart grows older
It will come to such sights colder
By and by, nor spare a sigh
Though worlds of wanwood leafmeal[1] lie;
And yet you *will* weep and know why.
10　Now no matter, child, the name:
Sórrow's spríngs áre the same.
Nor mouth had, no nor mind, expressed
What heart heard of, ghost° guessed:　　　　　　　*spirit*
It ís the blight man was born for,
15　It is Margaret you mourn for.

1880　　　　　　　　　　　　　　　　　　　　　　　　1918

[Carrion Comfort][1]

Not, I'll not, carrion comfort, Despair, not feast on thee,[2]
Not untwist—slack they may be—these last strands of man
In me ór, most weary, cry *I can no more*. I can;
Can something, hope, wish day come, not choose not to be.

5　But ah, but O thou terrible, why wouldst thou rude on me
Thy wring-world right foot rock?[3] lay a lionlimb against me?
　　scan
With darksome devouring eyes my bruisèd bones? and fan,
O in turns of tempest, me heaped there; me frantic to avoid
　　thee and flee?

Why? That my chaff might fly; my grain lie, sheer and clear.
10　Nay in all that toil, that coil,° since (seems) I kissed the rod,　　*tumult*
Hand rather,[4] my heart lo! lapped strength, stole joy, would
　　laugh, chéer.
Cheer whom though? The Hero whose heaven-handling
　　flung me, fóot tród
Me? or me that fought him? O which one? is it each one?
　　That night, that year
Of now done darkness I wretch lay wrestling with (my God!)
　　my God.

1885　　　　　　　　　　　　　　　　　　　　　　　　1918

No Worst, There Is None

No worst, there is none. Pitched past pitch of grief,
More pangs will, schooled at forepangs, wilder wring.

1. Coined by analogy with piecemeal. "Wan-wood": pale or dim; the forest may be pale because of light-colored autumn leaves or dim because light is filtered through the leaves.
1. The title of this poem was supplied by Bridges. It is one of the "terrible sonnets," as are the three following poems.

2. The satisfaction of giving in to despair as a kind of "comfort" is implicitly likened to a vulture's satisfaction in feasting on dead flesh.
3. I.e., why wouldst thou roughly against me rock thy right foot that wrings the world?
4. I.e., the hand that wields the rod.

Comforter, where, where is your comforting?
Mary, mother of us, where is your relief?

5 My cries heave, herds-long;[1] huddle in a main, a chief-
woe, world-sorrow; on an age-old anvil wince and sing—
Then lull, then leave off. Fury had shrieked "No ling-
ering! Let me be fell: force[2] I must be brief."
O the mind, mind has mountains; cliffs of fall
10 Frightful, sheer, no-man-fathomed. Hold them cheap
May who ne'er hung there. Nor does long our small
Durance° deal with that steep or deep. Here! creep,   endurance
Wretch, under a comfort serves in a whirlwind: all
Life death does end and each day dies with sleep.

1885   1918

I Wake and Feel the Fell of Dark, Not Day

I wake and feel the fell° of dark, not day.   bitterness
What hours, O what black hoürs we have spent
This night! what sights you, heart, saw; ways you went!
And more must, in yet longer light's delay.

5 With witness I speak this. But where I say
Hours I mean years, mean life. And my lament
Is cries countless, cries like dead letters[1] sent
To dearest him that lives alas! away.

I am gall, I am heartburn. God's most deep decree
10 Bitter would have me taste: my taste was me;
Bones built in me, flesh filled, blood brimmed the curse.

Selfyeast of spirit a dull dough sours. I see
The lost are like this, and their scourge to be
As I am mine, their sweating selves; but worse.

1885   1918

Thou Art Indeed Just, Lord

*Justus quidem tu es, Domine, si disputem tecum; verumtamen
justa loquar ad te: Quare via impiorum prosperatur? &c.*[1]

Thou art indeed just, Lord, if I contend
With thee; but, sir, so what I plead is just.
Why do sinners' ways prosper? and why must
Disappointment all I endeavour end?

---

1. Like the succession of cries made by cattle that
have been following one another in a long line.
2. Perforce. "Fell": fierce.
1. Letters undelivered or returned to the sender
by the post office.

1. "Righteous art thou, O Lord, when I plead with
thee: yet let me talk with thee of thy judgments:
Wherefore doth the way of the wicked prosper?"
(Jeremiah 12.1). The Latin was Hopkins's title.

5 Wert thou my enemy, O thou my friend,
How wouldst thou worse, I wonder, than thou dost
Defeat, thwart me? Oh, the sots and thralls of lust
Do in spare hours more thrive than I that spend,

Sir, life upon thy cause. See, banks and brakes°   thickets
10 Now, leavèd how thick! lacèd they are again
With fretty chervil,[2] look, and fresh wind shakes

Them; birds build—but not I build; no, but strain,
Time's eunuch, and not breed one work that wakes.
Mine, O thou lord of life, send my roots rain.

1889   1918

2. A kind of herb, related to parsley.

OSCAR WILDE
1854–1900

In Oscar Wilde's comedy *The Importance of Being Earnest* (1895) there is an account of a rakish character, Ernest Worthing, whose death in a Paris hotel is reported by the manager. Five years later, Wilde himself died in Paris (where he was living in exile) attended by a hotel manager. The coincidence seems a curious paradigm of Wilde's whole career, for with him the connections between his life and his art were unusually close. Indeed, in his last years, he told André Gide that he seemed to have put his genius into his life and only his talent into his writings.

His father, Sir William, was a distinguished surgeon in Dublin, where Wilde was born and grew up. After majoring in classical studies at Trinity College, Dublin, he won a scholarship to Oxford and there established a brilliant academic record. At Oxford he came under the influence of the aesthetic theories of John Ruskin (who was at the time professor of fine arts) and, more important, of Walter Pater. With characteristic hyperbole, Wilde affirmed of Pater's *Renaissance:* "It is my golden book; I never travel anywhere without it. But it is the very flower of decadence; the last trumpet should have sounded the moment it was written."

After graduating in 1878, Wilde settled in London, where his fellow Irishmen, Bernard Shaw and William Butler Yeats, were also to settle. Here Wilde quickly established himself both as a writer and as a spokesperson for the school of "art for art's sake." In Wilde's view this school included not only French poets and critics but also a line of English poets going back through Rossetti and the Pre-Raphaelites to Keats. In 1882 he visited America for a lengthy (and successful) lecture tour during which he startled audiences by airing the gospel of the "aesthetic movement." In one of these lectures, he asserted that "to disagree with three fourths of all England on all points of view is one of the first elements of sanity."

For his role as a spokesperson for aestheticism, Wilde had many gifts. From all accounts he was a dazzling conversationalist. Yeats reported, after first listening to him: "I never before heard a man talking with perfect sentences, as if he had written them all overnight with labor and yet all spontaneous." Wilde delighted his listeners not only by his polished wordplay but also by uttering opinions that were both out-rageous and incongruous, as for example, his solemn affirmation that Queen Victoria was one of the three women he most admired and whom he would have married "with pleasure" (the other two were Sarah Bernhardt, the actress, and Lillie Langtry, reput-edly a mistress of Victoria's son Edward, prince of Wales).

In addition to his mastery of witty conversation, Wilde had the gifts of an actor who delights in gaining attention. Pater had been a most shy and reticent man, but there was nothing reticent about his disciple who had discovered, early, that a flam-boyant style of dress was one of the most effective means of gaining attention. Like the dandies of the earlier decades of the nineteenth century (including Benjamin Disraeli and Charles Dickens), Wilde favored colorful costumes in marked contrast to the sober black suits of the late-Victorian middle classes. A green carnation in his buttonhole and velvet knee breeches became for Wilde badges of his youthful icon-oclasm, and even when he approached middle age, he continued to emphasize the gap between generations. In a letter written when he was forty-two years old, he remarks: "The opinions of the old on matters of Art are, of course, of no value what-ever."

Wilde's campaign early prompted an amused response from middle-class quarters. In 1881, Gilbert and Sullivan staged their comic opera *Patience*, which mocked the affectations of the aesthetes in the character of Bunthorne, especially in his song, "If You're Anxious for to Shine in the High Aesthetic Line."

Wilde's successes for seventeen years in England and America were, of course, not limited to his self-advertising stunts as a dandy. In his writings, he excelled in a variety of genres: as a critic of literature and of society (*The Decay of Lying*, 1889, and *The Soul of Man under Socialism*, 1891) and also as a novelist, poet, and dramatist. Much of his prose, including *The Critic as Artist*, develops Pater's aestheticism, particularly its sense of the superiority of art to life and its lack of obligation to any standards of mimesis. His novel *The Picture of Dorian Gray*, which created a sensation when it was published in 1891, takes a somewhat different perspective. The novel is a strik-ingly ingenious story of a handsome young man and his selfish pursuit of sensual pleasures. Until the end of the book he himself remains fresh and healthy in appear-ance while his portrait mysteriously changes into a horrible image of his corrupted soul. Although the preface to the novel (reprinted here) emphasizes that art and morality are totally separate, in the novel itself, at least in its later chapters, Wilde seems to be portraying the evils of self-regarding hedonism.

As a poet Wilde felt overshadowed by the Victorian predecessors whom he admired—Robert Browning, D. G. Rossetti, and Swinburne—and had trouble finding his own voice. Many of the poems in his first volume (1881) are highly derivative, but such pieces as *The Harlot's House* and *Impression du Matin* offer a distinctive perspective on city streets that seems to anticipate early poems by T. S. Eliot. His most outstanding success, however, was as a writer of comedies, which were staged in London and New York from 1892 through 1895, including *Lady Windermere's Fan*, *A Woman of No Importance*, *An Ideal Husband*, and *The Importance of Being Earnest*.

By the spring of 1895 this triumphant success suddenly crumbled when Wilde was arrested and sentenced to jail, with hard labor, for two years. Although Wilde was married and the father of two children, he did not hide his homosexual relationships. When he began a romance (in 1891) with the handsome young poet Lord Alfred Douglas, he set in motion the events that brought about his ruin. In 1895, Lord Alfred's father, the marquis of Queensberry, accused Wilde of homosexuality; Wilde recklessly sued for libel, lost the case, and was thereupon arrested and convicted for what was then on the statute books a serious criminal offense. The revulsion of feeling against him in England and in America was violent, and the aesthetic movement itself suffered a severe setback not only with the public but among writers as well.

His two years in jail led Wilde to write two sober and emotionally high-pitched works, his poem *The Ballad of Reading Gaol* (1898) and his prose confession *De Profundis* (1905). After leaving jail, Wilde, a ruined man, emigrated to France, where he lived out the last three years of his life under an assumed name. Before his departure from England he had been divorced and declared a bankrupt, and in France he had to rely on friends for financial support. Wilde is buried in Paris in the Père Lachaise cemetery.

E Tenebris[1]

Come down, O Christ, and help me! reach thy hand,
    For I am drowning in a stormier sea
    Than Simon on thy lake of Galilee:[2]
The wine of life is spilt upon the sand,
5 My heart is as some famine-murdered land
    Whence all good things have perished utterly,
    And well I know my soul in Hell must lie
If I this night before God's throne should stand.
"He sleeps perchance, or rideth to the chase,
10   Like Baal, when his prophets howled that name
    From morn to noon on Carmel's smitten height."[3]
Nay, peace, I shall behold, before the night,
    The feet of brass,[4] the robe more white than flame,
The wounded hands, the weary human face.

                                      1881

The Harlot's House

We caught the tread of dancing feet,
We loitered down the moonlit street,
And stopped beneath the Harlot's house.

Inside, above the din and fray,
5 We heard the loud musicians play
The "Treues Liebes Herz" of Strauss.[1]

Like strange mechanical grotesques,
Making fantastic arabesques,
The shadows raced across the blind.

10 We watched the ghostly dancers spin
To sound of horn and violin,
Like black leaves wheeling in the wind.

1. Out of darkness (Latin).
2. Simon Peter, one of the twelve apostles, came close to drowning in a storm until rescued by Christ (Matthew 14.28–31).
3. The poet imagines an ironic voice discouraging him; it uses the language of Elijah when he mocked the priests of Baal for their god's impotence by suggesting that perhaps Baal was on a journey or asleep (1 Kings 18.19–40).
4. Cf. Revelation 1.13–16, where the "Son of man" is seen in a vision, "his feet like unto fine brass, as if they burned in a furnace."
1. *Heart of True Love*, a waltz by the Austrian composer and "Waltz King" Johann Strauss (1825–1899).

Like wire-pulled automatons,
Slim silhouetted skeletons
15   Went sidling through the slow quadrille,[2]

Then took each other by the hand,
And danced a stately saraband;[3]
Their laughter echoed thin and shrill.

Sometimes a clockwork puppet pressed
20   A phantom lover to her breast,
Sometimes they seemed to try to sing,

Sometimes a horrible marionette
Came out, and smoked its cigarette
Upon the steps like a live thing.[4]

25   Then turning to my love I said,
"The dead are dancing with the dead,
The dust is whirling with the dust."

But she, she heard the violin,
And left my side, and entered in;
30   Love passed into the house of Lust.

Then suddenly the tune went false,
The dancers wearied of the waltz,
The shadows ceased to wheel and whirl,

And down the long and silent street,
35   The dawn, with silver-sandaled feet,
Crept like a frightened girl.

1885, 1908

From The Critic as Artist[1]
[CRITICISM ITSELF AN ART]

ERNEST   Gilbert, you sound too harsh a note. Let us go back to the more gracious fields of literature. What was it you said? That it was more difficult to talk about a thing than to do it?

GILBERT   [*after a pause*] Yes: I believe I ventured upon that simple truth. Surely you see now that I am right? When man acts he is a puppet. When

2. Intricate dance involving four couples facing each other in a square.
3. A slow and stately dance, originating in Spain.
4. In an illustration for the poem by Althea Gyles (approved by Wilde), the marionette is pictured as a man in evening dress.
1. In "the library of a house in Piccadilly," Gilbert and Ernest, two sophisticated young men, are talking about the use and function of criticism. Earlier in the dialogue, Ernest had complained that criticism is officious and useless: "Why should the artist be troubled by the shrill clamor of criticism?

Why should those who cannot create take upon themselves to estimate the value of creative work?" Gilbert, in his reply, argues that criticism is creative in its own right. He digresses to compare the life of action unfavorably with the life of art: actions are dangerous and their results unpredictable; "if we lived long enough to see the results of our actions it may be that those who call themselves good would be sickened by a dull remorse, and those whom the world calls evil stirred by a noble joy." The excerpt printed here begins immediately following this digression.

he describes he is a poet. The whole secret lies in that. It was easy enough on the sandy plains by windy Ilion[2] to send the notched arrow from the painted bow, or to hurl against the shield of hide and flamelike brass the long ash-handled spear. It was easy for the adulterous queen[3] to spread the Tyrian carpets for her lord, and then, as he lay couched in the marble bath, to throw over his head the purple net, and call to her smooth-faced lover to stab through the meshes at the heart that should have broken at Aulis.[4] For Antigone[5] even, with Death waiting for her as her bridegroom, it was easy to pass through the tainted air at noon, and climb the hill, and strew with kindly earth the wretched naked corse that had no tomb. But what of those who wrote about these things? What of those who gave them reality, and made them live forever? Are they not greater than the men and women they sing of? "Hector that sweet knight is dead."[6] And Lucian[7] tells us how in the dim underworld Menippus saw the bleaching skull of Helen, and marveled that it was for so grim a favor that all those horned ships were launched, those beautiful mailed men laid low, those towered cities brought to dust. Yet, every day the swanlike daughter of Leda comes out on the battlements, and looks down at the tide of war. The graybeards wonder at her loveliness, and she stands by the side of the king.[8] In his chamber of stained ivory lies her leman.[9] He is polishing his dainty armor, and combing the scarlet plume. With squire and page, her husband passes from tent to tent. She can see his bright hair, and hears, or fancies that she hears, that clear cold voice. In the courtyard below, the son of Priam is buckling on his brazen cuirass. The white arms of Andromache[1] are around his neck. He sets his helmet on the ground, lest their babe should be frightened. Behind the embroidered curtains of his pavilion sits Achilles,[2] in perfumed raiment, while in harness of gilt and silver the friend of his soul[3] arrays himself to go forth to fight. From a curiously carven chest that his mother Thetis had brought to his shipside, the Lord of the Myrmidons takes out that mystic chalice that the lip of man had never touched, and cleanses it with brimstone, and with fresh water cools it, and, having washed his hands, fills with black wine its burnished hollow, and spills the thick grape-blood upon the ground in honor of Him whom at Dodona[4] barefooted prophets worshiped, and prays to Him, and knows not that he prays in vain, and that by the hands of two knights from Troy, Panthous' son, Euphorbus, whose love-locks were looped with gold, and the Priamid,[5] the lion-hearted, Patroclus, the comrade of comrades, must meet his doom. Phantoms, are they? Heroes of mist and mountain? Shadows in a song? No: they

---

2. Troy. Gilbert is referring to Homer's *Iliad*.

3. Clytemnestra, whose murder of her husband, Agamemnon, provides the plot for Aeschylus's tragedy of that name.

4. Where Agamemnon sacrificed his daughter Iphigenia, thus incurring Clytemnestra's wrath.

5. Antigone defied Creon, king of Thebes, by burying the body of her brother, an act that Creon had forbidden, and was punished by death; see Sophocles' play *Antigone*.

6. Cf. Shakespeare's *Love's Labour's Lost* 5.2.663: "The sweet war-man [Hector] is dead and rotten."

7. Late Greek satirical writer, influenced by the earlier Greek seriocomic writer Menippus.

8. Priam. Homer in the *Iliad* describes the old

men of Troy admiring the beauty of Helen, "swanlike daughter of Leda" and of Zeus (Zeus came to Leda in the form of a swan).

9. Lover (i.e., Paris).

1. Wife of Hector, one of the sons of Priam.

2. Son of Peleus and of the sea nymph Thetis; Achilles was the Greek hero, opposite of Hector, the Trojan hero, in the Trojan war. The scene set here is a tissue of recollections from the *Iliad*.

3. I.e., Patroclus.

4. Seat of a very ancient oracle of Zeus.

5. "Son of Priam," i.e., Hector. With the help of Euphorbus, one of the bravest of the Trojans, he slew Patroclus and was in turn slain by Achilles.

are real. Action! What is action? It dies at the moment of its energy. It is a base concession to fact. The world is made by the singer for the dreamer.

ERNEST   While you talk it seems to me to be so.

GILBERT   It is so in truth. On the moldering citadel of Troy lies the lizard like a thing of green bronze. The owl has built her nest in the palace of Priam. Over the empty plain wander shepherd and goatherd with their flocks, and where, on the wine-surfaced, oily sea, οἶνοψ πόντος,[6] as Homer calls it, copper-prowed and streaked with vermilion, the great galleys of the Danaoi[7] came in their gleaming crescent, the lonely tunny-fisher sits in his little boat and watches the bobbing corks of his net. Yet, every morning the doors of the city are thrown open, and on foot, or in horse-drawn chariot, the warriors go forth to battle, and mock their enemies from behind their iron masks. All day long the fight rages, and when night comes the torches gleam by the tents, and the cresset[8] burns in the hall. Those who live in marble or on painted panel know of life but a single exquisite instant, eternal indeed in its beauty, but limited to one note of passion or one mood of calm. Those whom the poet makes live have their myriad emotions of joy and terror, of courage and despair, of pleasure and of suffering. The seasons come and go in glad or saddening pageant, and with winged or leaden feet the years pass by before them. They have their youth and their manhood, they are children, and they grow old. It is always dawn for St. Helena, as Veronese saw her at the window.[9] Through the still morning air the angels bring her the symbol of God's pain. The cool breezes of the morning lift the gilt threads from her brow. On that little hill by the city of Florence, where the lovers of Giorgione[1] are lying, it is always the solstice of noon, made so languorous by summer suns that hardly can the slim naked girl dip into the marble tank the round bubble of clear glass, and the long fingers of the lute player rest idly upon the chords. It is twilight always for the dancing nymphs whom Corot[2] set free among the silver poplars of France. In eternal twilight they move, those frail diaphanous figures, whose tremulous white feet seem not to touch the dew-drenched grass they tread on. But those who walk in epos,[3] drama, or romance, see through the laboring months the young moons wax and wane, and watch the night from evening unto morning star, and from sunrise unto sunsetting can note the shifting day with all its gold and shadow. For them, as for us, the flowers bloom and wither, and the Earth, that Green-tressed Goddess as Coleridge calls her, alters her raiment for their pleasure. The statue is concentrated to one moment of perfection. The image stained upon the canvas possesses no spiritual element of growth or change. If they know nothing of death, it is because they know little of life, for the secrets of life and death belong to those, and those only, whom the sequence of time affects, and who possess not merely the present but the future, and can rise or fall from a past of glory or of shame. Move-

---

6. Wine-dark sea (Greek).
7. Greeks.
8. Metal basket holding fuel burned for illumination, often hung from the ceiling.
9. One of the best-known paintings of the 16th-century Italian Paolo Veronese is *Helena's Vision*.

1. Italian painter (ca. 1477–1511), the most brilliant colorist of his time.
2. Jean-Baptiste-Camille Corot, 19th-century French painter, best-known for his shimmering trees.
3. Epic poetry.

ment, that problem of the visible arts, can be truly realized by Literature alone. It is Literature that shows us the body in its swiftness and the soul in its unrest.

ERNEST   Yes; I see now what you mean. But, surely, the higher you place the creative artist, the lower must the critic rank.

GILBERT   Why so?

ERNEST   Because the best that he can give us will be but an echo of rich music, a dim shadow of clear-outlined form. It may, indeed, be that life is chaos, as you tell me that it is; that its martyrdoms are mean and its heroisms ignoble; and that it is the function of Literature to create, from the rough material of actual existence, a new world that will be more marvelous, more enduring, and more true than the world that common eyes look upon, and through which common natures seek to realize their perfection. But surely, if this new world has been made by the spirit and touch of a great artist, it will be a thing so complete and perfect that there will be nothing left for the critic to do. I quite understand now, and indeed admit most readily, that it is far more difficult to talk about a thing than to do it. But it seems to me that this sound and sensible maxim, which is really extremely soothing to one's feelings, and should be adopted as its motto by every Academy of Literature all over the world, applies only to the relations that exist between Art and Life, and not to any relations that there may be between Art and Criticism.

GILBERT   But, surely, Criticism is itself an art. And just as artistic creation implies the working of the critical faculty, and, indeed, without it cannot be said to exist at all, so Criticism is really creative in the highest sense of the word. Criticism is, in fact, both creative and independent.

ERNEST   Independent?

GILBERT   Yes; independent. Criticism is no more to be judged by any low standard of imitation or resemblance than is the work of poet or sculptor. The critic occupies the same relation to the work of art that he criticizes as the artist does to the visible world of form and color, or the unseen world of passion and of thought. He does not even require for the perfection of his art the finest materials. Anything will serve his purpose. And just as out of the sordid and sentimental amours of the silly wife of a small country doctor in the squalid village of Yonville-l'Abbaye, near Rouen, Gustave Flaubert[4] was able to create a classic, and make a masterpiece of style, so, from subjects of little or of no importance, such as the pictures in this year's Royal Academy, or in any year's Royal Academy for that matter, Mr. Lewis Morris's poems, M. Ohnet's novels, or the plays of Mr. Henry Arthur Jones,[5] the true critic can, if it be his pleasure so to direct or waste his faculty of contemplation, produce work that will be flawless in beauty and instinct with intellectual subtlety. Why not? Dullness is always an irresistible temptation for brilliancy, and stupidity is the permanent *Bestia Trionfans*[6] that calls wisdom from its cave. To an artist so creative as the critic, what does subject matter signify? No

---

4. French novelist (1821–1880); the reference is to his novel *Madame Bovary* (1857).
5. Wilde is mischievously suggesting his low opinion of the contemporary writers just named. Morris was a Welsh poet and essayist often ridiculed by the critics. Georges Ohnet was a French novelist

and dramatist. Jones was one of the leading English playwrights of his time.
6. Triumphant beast (Latin). A reference to *Spaccio della Bestia Trionfante* (Expulsion of the triumphant beast, 1584), a philosophical allegory by the Italian philosopher Giordano Bruno.

more and no less than it does to the novelist and the painter. Like them, he can find his motives everywhere. Treatment is the test. There is nothing that has not in it suggestion or challenge.

ERNEST   But is Criticism really a creative art?

GILBERT   Why should it not be? It works with materials, and puts them into a form that is at once new and delightful. What more can one say of poetry? Indeed, I would call criticism a creation within a creation. For just as the great artists, from Homer and Aeschylus, down to Shakespeare and Keats, did not go directly to life for their subject matter, but sought for it in myth, and legend, and ancient tale, so the critic deals with materials that others have, as it were, purified for him, and to which imaginative form and color have been already added. Nay, more, I would say that the highest Criticism, being the purest form of personal impression, is in its way more creative than creation, as it has least reference to any standard external to itself, and is, in fact, its own reason for existing, and, as the Greeks would put it, in itself, and to itself, an end. Certainly, it is never trammeled by any shackles of verisimilitude. No ignoble considerations of probability, that cowardly concession to the tedious repetitions of domestic or public life, affect it ever. One may appeal from fiction unto fact. But from the soul there is no appeal.

ERNEST   From the soul?

GILBERT   Yes, from the soul. That is what the highest criticism really is, the record of one's own soul. It is more fascinating than history, as it is concerned simply with oneself. It is more delightful than philosophy, as its subject is concrete and not abstract, real and not vague. It is the only civilized form of autobiography, as it deals not with the events, but with the thoughts of one's life, not with life's physical accidents of deed or circumstance, but with the spiritual moods and imaginative passions of the mind. I am always amused by the silly vanity of those writers and artists of our day who seem to imagine that the primary function of the critic is to chatter about their second-rate work. The best that one can say of most modern creative art is that it is just a little less vulgar than reality, and so the critic, with his fine sense of distinction and sure instinct of delicate refinement, will prefer to look into the silver mirror or through the woven veil, and will turn his eyes away from the chaos and clamor of actual existence, though the mirror be tarnished and the veil be torn. His sole aim is to chronicle his own impressions. It is for him that pictures are painted, books written, and marble hewn into form.

ERNEST   I seem to have heard another theory of Criticism.

GILBERT   Yes: it has been said by one whose gracious memory we all revere,[7] and the music of whose pipe once lured Proserpina from her Sicilian fields, and made those white feet stir, and not in vain, the Cumnor cowslips, that the proper aim of Criticism is to see the object as in itself it really is. But this is a very serious error, and takes no cognizance of Criticism's most perfect form, which is in its essence purely subjective,

---

7. I.e., Matthew Arnold, whose poem *Thyrsis* (lines 91–100) evokes the legend of Proserpina, a goddess associated with the pastoral landscapes of Sicily. Arnold believed that it would be "in vain" to summon Proserpina to visit the Cumnor hills landscape (near Oxford), but Wilde's speaker here flatters Arnold that the summons was so beautiful that it was "not in vain." For the prose passage about the "aim of Criticism," see Arnold's *The Function of Criticism at the Present Time* (para. 1, p. 2103).

and seeks to reveal its own secret and not the secret of another. For the highest Criticism deals with art not as expressive but as impressive purely.

ERNEST   But is that really so?

GILBERT   Of course it is. Who cares whether Mr. Ruskin's views on Turner[8] are sound or not? What does it matter? That mighty and majestic prose of his, so fervid and so fiery-colored in its noble eloquence, so rich in its elaborate symphonic music, so sure and certain, at its best, in subtle choice of word and epithet, is at least as great a work of art as any of those wonderful sunsets that bleach or rot on their corrupted canvases in England's Gallery; greater indeed, one is apt to think at times, not merely because its equal beauty is more enduring, but on account of the fuller variety of its appeal, soul speaking to soul in those long-cadenced lines, not through form and color alone, though through these, indeed, completely and without loss, but with intellectual and emotional utterance, with lofty passion and with loftier thought, with imaginative insight, and with poetic aim; greater, I always think, even as Literature is the greater art. Who, again, cares whether Mr. Pater has put into the portrait of Mona Lisa[9] something that Leonardo never dreamed of? The painter may have been merely the slave of an archaic smile, as some have fancied, but whenever I pass into the cool galleries of the Palace of the Louvre, and stand before that strange figure "set in its marble chair in that cirque of fantastic rocks, as in some faint light under sea," I murmur to myself, "She is older than the rocks among which she sits; like the vampire, she has been dead many times, and learned the secrets of the grave; and has been a diver in deep seas, and keeps their fallen day about her: and trafficked for strange webs with Eastern merchants; and, as Leda, was the mother of Helen of Troy, and, as St. Anne, the mother of Mary; and all this has been to her but as the sound of lyres and flutes, and lives only in the delicacy with which it has molded the changing lineaments, and tinged the eyelids and the hands." And I say to my friend, "The presence that thus so strangely rose beside the waters is expressive of what in the ways of a thousand years man had come to desire"; and he answers me, "Hers is the head upon which all 'the ends of the world are come,' and the eyelids are a little weary."

And so the picture becomes more wonderful to us than it really is, and reveals to us a secret of which, in truth, it knows nothing, and the music of the mystical prose is as sweet in our ears as was that flute-player's music that lent to the lips of La Gioconda[1] those subtle and poisonous curves. Do you ask me what Leonardo would have said had any one told him of this picture that "all the thoughts and experience of the world had etched and molded therein that which they had of power to refine and make expressive the outward form, the animalism of Greece, the lust of Rome, the reverie of the Middle Age with its spiritual ambition and imaginative loves, the return of the Pagan world, the sins of the Borgias?" He would probably have answered that he had contemplated none of

---

8. For Ruskin's defense of the paintings of Turner, see *Modern Painters*, especially his praise of Turner's *The Slave Ship*.
9. All remaining references in this paragraph are to Pater's essay *La Gioconda*.
1. I.e., the *Mona Lisa* (she was the wife of Francesco del Gioconda—hence "La Gioconda").

these things, but had concerned himself simply with certain arrangements of lines and masses, and with new and curious color-harmonies
of blue and green. And it is for this very reason that the criticism which
I have quoted is criticism of the highest kind. It treats the work of art
simply as a starting point for a new creation. It does not confine itself—
let us at least suppose so for the moment—to discovering the real intention of the artist and accepting that as final. And in this it is right, for
the meaning of any beautiful created thing is, at least, as much in the
soul of him who looks at it, as it was in his soul who wrought it. Nay, it
is rather the beholder who lends to the beautiful thing its myriad meanings, and makes it marvelous for us, and sets it in some new relation to
the age, so that it becomes a vital portion of our lives, and symbol of
what we pray for, or perhaps of what, having prayed for, we fear that we
may receive. The longer I study, Ernest, the more clearly I see that the
beauty of the visible arts is, as the beauty of music, impressive[2] primarily,
and that it may be marred, and indeed often is so, by any excess of
intellectual intention on the part of the artist. For when the work is
finished it has, as it were, an independent life of its own, and may deliver
a message far other than that which was put into its lips to say. Sometimes, when I listen to the overture to *Tannhäuser*,[3] I seem indeed to see
that comely knight treading delicately on the flower-strewn grass, and to
hear the voice of Venus calling to him from the caverned hill. But at
other times it speaks to me of a thousand different things, of myself, it
may be, and my own life, or of the lives of others whom one has loved
and grown weary of loving, or of the passions that man has known, or of
the passions that man has not known, and so has sought for. Tonight it
may fill one with that ΕΡΩΣ ΤΩΝ ΑΔΥΝΑΤΩΝ, that *amour de l'impossible*,[4]
which falls like a madness on many who think they live securely and out
of reach of harm, so that they sicken suddenly with the poison of unlimited desire, and, in the infinite pursuit of what they may not obtain, grow
faint and swoon or stumble. Tomorrow, like the music of which Aristotle
and Plato tell us, the noble Dorian music of the Greek, it may perform
the office of a physician, and give us an anodyne against pain, and
heal the spirit that is wounded, and "bring the soul into harmony with
all right things." And what is true about music is true about all the
arts. Beauty has as many meanings as man has moods. Beauty is the
symbol of symbols. Beauty reveals everything, because it expresses
nothing. When it shows us itself, it shows us the whole fiery-colored
world.

ERNEST   But is such work as you have talked about really criticism?

GILBERT   It is the highest Criticism, for it criticizes not merely the individual work of art, but Beauty itself, and fills with wonder a form which
the artist may have left void, or not understood, or understood incom-
pletely.

ERNEST   The highest Criticism, then, is more creative than creation, and

2. I.e., designed to create an impression of the
senses.
3. An opera by Richard Wagner (1845) based on
the legend of a 14th-century German poet who fell
under the spell of Venus and lived with her in the
Venusberg.
4. Love of the impossible, in Greek (in capital letters, perhaps to give the effect of an inscription)
and in French.

the primary aim of the critic is to see the object as in itself it really is not; that is your theory, I believe?

GILBERT Yes, that is my theory. To the critic the work of art is simply a suggestion for a new work of his own, that need not necessarily bear any obvious resemblance to the thing it criticizes. The one characteristic of a beautiful form is that one can put into it whatever one wishes, and see in it whatever one chooses to see; and the Beauty, that gives to creation its universal and aesthetic element, makes the critic a creator in his turn, and whispers of a thousand different things which were not present in the mind of him who carved the statue or painted the panel or graved the gem.

It is sometimes said by those who understand neither the nature of the highest Criticism nor the charm of the highest Art, that the pictures that the critic loves most to write about are those that belong to the anecdotage of painting, and that deal with scenes taken out of literature or history. But this is not so. Indeed, pictures of this kind are far too intelligible. As a class, they rank with illustrations, and even considered from this point of view are failures, as they do not stir the imagination, but set definite bounds to it. For the domain of the painter is, as I suggested before, widely different from that of the poet. To the latter belongs life in its full and absolute entirety; not merely the beauty that men look at, but the beauty that men listen to also; not merely the momentary grace of form or the transient gladness of color, but the whole sphere of feeling, the perfect cycle of thought. The painter is so far limited that it is only through the mask of the body that he can show us the mystery of the soul; only through conventional images that he can handle ideas; only through its physical equivalents that he can deal with psychology. And how inadequately does he do it then, asking us to accept the torn turban of the Moor for the noble rage of Othello, or a dotard in a storm for the wild madness of Lear! Yet it seems as if nothing could stop him. Most of our elderly English painters spend their wicked and wasted lives in poaching upon the domain of the poets, marring their motives by clumsy treatment, and striving to render, by visible form or color, the marvel of what is invisible, the splendor of what is not seen. Their picures are, as a natural consequence, insufferably tedious. They have degraded the invisible arts into the obvious arts, and the one thing not worth looking at is the obvious. I do not say that poet and painter may not treat of the same subject. They have always done so, and will always do so. But while the poet can be pictorial or not, as he chooses, the painter must be pictorial always. For a painter is limited, not to what he sees in nature, but to what upon canvas may be seen.

And so, my dear Ernest, pictures of this kind will not really fascinate the critic. He will turn from them to such works as make him brood and dream and fancy, to works that possess the subtle quality of suggestion, and seem to tell one that even from them there is an escape into a wider world. It is sometimes said that the tragedy of an artist's life is that he cannot realize his ideal. But the true tragedy that dogs the steps of most artists is that they realize their ideal too absolutely. For, when the ideal is realized, it is robbed of its wonder and its mystery, and becomes simply a new starting point for an ideal that is other than itself. This is the reason why music is the perfect type of art. Music can never reveal its ultimate secret. This, also, is the explanation of the value of limitations in art. The sculptor gladly surrenders imitative color, and the painter the actual dimensions of form, because by such renunciations they are able to avoid too definite a presentation of the Real, which would be mere imitation, and too definite a realization of the Ideal, which would be too purely intellectual. It is through its very incompleteness that Art becomes complete in beauty, and so addresses itself, not to the faculty of recognition nor to the faculty of reason, but to the aesthetic sense alone, which, while accepting both reason and recognition as stages of apprehension, subordinates them both to a pure synthetic impression of the work of art as a whole, and, taking whatever alien emotional elements the work may possess, uses their very complexity as a means by which a richer unity may be added to the ultimate impression itself. You see, then, how it is that the aesthetic critic rejects these obvious modes of art that have but one message to deliver, and having delivered it become dumb and sterile, and seeks rather for such modes as suggest reverie and mood, and by their imaginative beauty make all interpretations true, and no interpretation final. Some resemblance, no doubt, the creative work of the critic will have to the work that has stirred him to creation, but it will be such resemblance as exists, not between Nature and the mirror that the painter of landscape or figure may be supposed to hold up to her, but between Nature and the work of the decorative artist. Just as on the flowerless carpets of Persia, tulip and rose blossom indeed and are lovely to look on, though they are not reproduced in visible shape or line; just as the pearl and purple of the sea shell is echoed in the church of St. Mark at Venice; just as the vaulted ceiling of the wondrous chapel at Ravenna is made gorgeous by the gold and green and sapphire of the peacock's tail, though the birds of Juno fly not across it; so the critic reproduces the work that he criticizes in a mode that is never imitative, and part of whose charm may really consist in the rejection of resemblance, and shows us in this way not merely the meaning but also the mystery of Beauty, and, by transforming each art into literature, solves once for all the problem of Art's unity.

But I see it is time for supper. After we have discussed some Chambertin and a few ortolans,[5] we will pass on to the question of the critic considered in the light of the interpreter.

ERNEST   Ah! you admit, then, that the critic may occasionally be allowed to see the object as in itself it really is.

GILBERT   I am not quite sure. Perhaps I may admit it after supper. There is a subtle influence in supper.

1890, 1891

Preface to *The Picture of Dorian Gray*

The artist is the creator of beautiful things.
To reveal art and conceal the artist is art's aim.

---

5. Birds esteemed by epicures for their delicate flavor. "Chambertin": one of the finest wines of Burgundy.

The critic is he who can translate into another manner or a new material his impression of beautiful things.

   The highest, as the lowest, form of criticism is a mode of auto-biography.

Those who find ugly meanings in beautiful things are corrupt without being charming. This is a fault.

   Those who find beautiful meanings in beautiful things are the cultivated. For these there is hope.

  They are the elect to whom beautiful things mean only Beauty.

  There is no such thing as a moral or an immoral book.

  Books are well written, or badly written. That is all.

The nineteenth-century dislike of Realism is the rage of Caliban[1] seeing his own face in a glass.

   The nineteenth-century dislike of Romanticism is the rage of Caliban not seeing his own face in a glass.

The moral life of man forms part of the subject matter of the artist, but the morality of art consists in the perfect use of an imperfect medium. No artist desires to prove anything. Even things that are true can be proved.

  No artist has ethical sympathies. An ethical sympathy in an artist is an unpardonable mannerism of style.

   No artist is ever morbid. The artist can express everything.

Thought and language are to the artist instruments of an art.

  Vice and Virtue are to the artist materials for an art.

From the point of view of form, the type of all the arts is the art of the musician. From the point of view of feeling, the actor's craft is the type.

  All art is at once surface and symbol.

  Those who go beneath the surface do so at their peril.

  Those who read the symbol do so at their peril.

It is the spectator, and not life, that art really mirrors.

  Diversity of opinion about a work of art shows that the work is new, complex, and vital.

  When critics disagree the artist is in accord with himself. We can forgive a man for making a useful thing as long as he does not admire it. The only excuse for making a useless thing is that one admires it intensely.

  All art is quite useless.

1891

The Importance of Being Earnest

Of the four stage comedies by Wilde, his last, *The Importance of Being Earnest,* is generally regarded as his masterpiece. It was first staged in February 1895 and was an immediate hit. Only one critic failed to find it delightful; curiously, this was Wilde's fellow playwright from Ireland, Bernard Shaw, who, though amused, found Wilde's wit "hateful" and "sinister," and thought the play exhibited "real degeneracy." Despite Shaw's complaints, the first London production ran for eighty-six performances, but when Wilde was sentenced to prison, production ceased for several years. Shortly before his death it was revived in London and New York, and has subsequently become a classic of the theater.

---

1. The character in Shakespeare's *Tempest* is half-human, half-monster.

In its original version, the play was in four acts. At the request of the stage producer, Wilde reduced it to three acts—the version almost always used in performances and therefore the version reprinted here. A few of the notes in the text cite passages from the four-act version.

The play was first published in 1899. Earlier, in an interview, Wilde had described his overall aim in writing it: "It has as its philosophy . . . that we should treat all the trivial things of life seriously, and all the serious things of life with sincere and studied triviality." Just before his death he remarked that although he was pleased with the "bright and happy" tone and temper of his play, he wished it might have had a "higher seriousness of intent." Later critics have found this seriousness of intent in the play's deconstruction of Victorian moral and social values. Like another Victorian master-piece of the absurd, *Alice's Adventures in Wonderland*, *The Importance of Being Earnest* empties manners and morals of their underlying sense to create a nominalist world where earnest is not a quality of character but a name, where words, to para-phrase Humpty Dumpty in *Through the Looking-Glass*, mean what you choose them to mean, neither more nor less.

The literary ancestry of Wilde's play has been variously identified. In its witty word-play and worldly attitudes it has been likened to comedies of the Restoration period such as Congreve's *Love for Love*. In its genial and lighthearted tone, it has some affinities with the festive comedies of Shakespeare, such as *Twelfth Night*, and with Goldsmith's *She Stoops to Conquer*. A more immediate predecessor was *Engaged* (1877), a comic play by W. S. Gilbert that anticipated some of the burlesque effects exploited by Wilde, such as the interrupting of sentimental scenes by the consumption of food, and the inviolable imperturbability of the speakers. Gilbert's advice to the actors who were putting on his *Engaged* is worth citing as a clue to how *The Impor-tance of Being Earnest* may be most effectively imagined as a stage representation:

> It is absolutely essential to the success of this piece that it should be played with the most perfect earnestness and gravity throughout. . . . Directly the actors show that they are conscious of the absurdity of their utterances the piece begins to drag.

The Importance of Being Earnest

First Act

SCENE—*Morning room in* ALGERNON's *flat in Half-Moon Street.*[1]

The room is luxuriously and artistically furnished. The sound of a piano is heard in the adjoining room.

[LANE *is arranging afternoon tea on the table, and after the music has ceased,* ALGERNON *enters.*]

ALGERNON   Did you hear what I was playing, Lane?

LANE   I didn't think it polite to listen, sir.

ALGERNON   I'm sorry for that, for your sake. I don't play accurately—any-one can play accurately—but I play with wonderful expression. As far as the piano is concerned, sentiment is my forte. I keep science for Life.

LANE   Yes, sir.

---

1. A highly fashionable location (at the time of the play) in the West End of London.

ALGERNON   And, speaking of the science of Life, have you got the cucumber sandwiches cut for Lady Bracknell?[2]

LANE   Yes, sir. [*Hands them on a salver.*]

ALGERNON [*Inspects them, takes two, and sits down on the sofa.*]   Oh! . . . by the way, Lane, I see from your book[3] that on Thursday night, when Lord Shoreham and Mr. Worthing were dining with me, eight bottles of champagne are entered as having been consumed.

LANE   Yes, sir; eight bottles and a pint.

ALGERNON   Why is it that at a bachelor's establishment the servants invariably drink the champagne? I ask merely for information.

LANE   I attribute it to the superior quality of the wine, sir. I have often observed that in married households the champagne is rarely of a first-rate brand.

ALGERNON   Good Heavens! Is marriage so demoralizing as that?

LANE   I believe it *is* a very pleasant state, sir. I have had very little experience of it myself up to the present. I have only been married once. That was in consequence of a misunderstanding between myself and a young person.

ALGERNON [*Languidly.*]   I don't know that I am much interested in your family life, Lane.

LANE   No, sir; it is not a very interesting subject. I never think of it myself.

ALGERNON   Very natural, I am sure. That will do, Lane, thank you.

LANE   Thank you, sir.   [LANE *goes out.*]

ALGERNON   Lane's views on marriage seem somewhat lax. Really, if the lower orders don't set us a good example, what on earth is the use of them? They seem, as a class, to have absolutely no sense of moral responsibility.

        [*Enter* LANE.]

LANE   Mr. Ernest Worthing.

        [*Enter* JACK.]   [LANE *goes out.*]

ALGERNON   How are you, my dear Ernest? What brings you up to town?

JACK   Oh, pleasure, pleasure! What else should bring one anywhere? Eating as usual, I see, Algy!

ALGERNON [*Stiffly.*]   I believe it is customary in good society to take some slight refreshment at five o'clock. Where have you been since last Thursday?

JACK [*Sitting down on the sofa.*]   In the country.

ALGERNON   What on earth do you do there?

JACK [*Pulling off his gloves.*]   When one is in town one amuses oneself. When one is in the country one amuses other people. It is excessively boring.

ALGERNON   And who are the people you amuse?

JACK [*Airily.*]   Oh, neighbors, neighbors.

ALGERNON   Got nice neighbors in your part of Shropshire?

JACK   Perfectly horrid! Never speak to one of them.

ALGERNON   How immensely you must amuse them! [*Goes over and takes sandwich.*] By the way, Shropshire is your county, is it not?

2. The name of a place in Berkshire where the mother of Lord Alfred Douglas had her summer home, which Wilde had visited.

3. Cellar book, in which records were kept of wines.

JACK   Eh? Shropshire?[4] Yes, of course. Hallo! Why all these cups? Why cucumber sandwiches? Why such reckless extravagance in one so young? Who is coming to tea?

ALGERNON   Oh! merely Aunt Augusta and Gwendolen.

JACK   How perfectly delightful!

ALGERNON   Yes, that is all very well; but I am afraid Aunt Augusta won't quite approve of your being here.

JACK   May I ask why?

ALGERNON   My dear fellow, the way you flirt with Gwendolen is perfectly disgraceful. It is almost as bad as the way Gwendolen flirts with you.

JACK   I am in love with Gwendolen. I have come up to town expressly to propose to her.

ALGERNON   I thought you had come up for pleasure? . . . I call that business.

JACK   How utterly unromantic you are!

ALGERNON   I really don't see anything romantic in proposing. It is very romantic to be in love. But there is nothing romantic about a definite proposal. Why, one may be accepted. One usually is, I believe. Then the excitement is all over. The very essence of romance is uncertainty. If ever I get married, I'll certainly try to forget the fact.

JACK   I have no doubt about that, dear Algy. The Divorce Court was specially invented for people whose memories are so curiously constituted.

ALGERNON   Oh! there is no use speculating on that subject. Divorces are made in Heaven—[JACK *puts out his hand to take a sandwich.* ALGERNON *at once interferes.*] Please don't touch the cucumber sandwiches. They are ordered specially for Aunt Augusta. [*Takes one and eats it.*]

JACK   Well, you have been eating them all the time.

ALGERNON   That is quite a different matter. She is my aunt. [*Takes plate from below.*] Have some bread and butter. The bread and butter is for Gwendolen. Gwendolen is devoted to bread and butter.

JACK [*Advancing to table and helping himself.*]   And very good bread and butter it is too.

ALGERNON   Well, my dear fellow, you need not eat as if you were going to eat it all. You behave as if you were married to her already. You are not married to her already, and I don't think you ever will be.

JACK   Why on earth do you say that?

ALGERNON   Well, in the first place, girls never marry the men they flirt with. Girls don't think it right.

JACK   Oh, that is nonsense!

ALGERNON   It isn't. It is a great truth. It accounts for the extraordinary number of bachelors that one sees all over the place. In the second place, I don't give my consent.

JACK   Your consent!

ALGERNON   My dear fellow, Gwendolen is my first cousin. And before I allow you to marry her, you will have to clear up the whole question of Cecily. [*Rings bell.*]

---

4. As we learn later, the estate is in Hertfordshire, a very long distance from Shropshire. In the four-act version of the play, when this discrepancy is pointed out by Algernon, Jack replies: "My dear fellow! Surely you don't expect me to be accurate about geography? No gentleman is accurate about geography. Why, I got a prize for geography when I was at school. I can't be expected to know anything about it now."

JACK   Cecily! What on earth do you mean? What do you mean, Algy, by Cecily? I don't know anyone of the name of Cecily.
    [*Enter* LANE.]
ALGERNON   Bring me that cigarette case Mr. Worthing left in the smoking-room the last time he dined here.
LANE   Yes, sir.   [LANE *goes out.*]
JACK   Do you mean to say you have had my cigarette case all this time? I wish to goodness you had let me know. I have been writing frantic letters to Scotland Yard[5] about it. I was very nearly offering a large reward.
ALGERNON   Well, I wish you would offer one. I happen to be more than usually hard up.
JACK   There is no good offering a large reward now that the thing is found.
    [*Enter* LANE *with the cigarette case on a salver.* ALGERNON *takes it at once.* LANE *goes out.*]
ALGERNON   I think that is rather mean of you, Ernest, I must say. [*Opens case and examines it.*] However, it makes no matter, for, now that I look at the inscription inside, I find that the thing isn't yours after all.
JACK   Of course it's mine. [*Moving to him.*] You have seen me with it a hundred times, and you have no right whatsoever to read what is written inside. It is a very ungentlemanly thing to read a private cigarette case.
ALGERNON   Oh! it is absurd to have a hard-and-fast rule about what one should read and what one shouldn't. More than half of modern culture depends on what one shouldn't read.
JACK   I am quite aware of the fact, and I don't propose to discuss modern culture. It isn't the sort of thing one should talk of in private. I simply want my cigarette case back.
ALGERNON   Yes; but this isn't your cigarette case. This cigarette case is a present from someone of the name of Cecily, and you said you didn't know anyone of that name.
JACK   Well, if you want to know, Cecily happens to be my aunt.
ALGERNON   Your aunt!
JACK   Yes. Charming old lady she is, too. Lives at Tunbridge Wells.[6] Just give it back to me, Algy.
ALGERNON [*retreating to back of sofa.*]   But why does she call herself little Cecily if she is your aunt and lives at Tunbridge Wells? [*Reading.*] "From little Cecily with her fondest love."
JACK [*Moving to sofa and kneeling upon it.*]   My dear fellow, what on earth is there in that? Some aunts are tall, some aunts are not tall. That is a matter that surely an aunt may be allowed to decide for herself. You seem to think that every aunt should be exactly like your aunt! That is absurd! For Heaven's sake give me back my cigarette case. [*Follows Algy round the room.*]
ALGERNON   Yes. But why does your aunt call you her uncle? "From little Cecily, with her fondest love to her dear Uncle Jack." There is no objection, I admit, to an aunt being a small aunt, but why an aunt, no matter what her size may be, should call her own nephew her uncle, I can't quite make out. Besides, your name isn't Jack at all; it is Ernest.
JACK   It isn't Ernest; it's Jack.
ALGERNON   You have always told me it was Ernest. I have introduced you

---

5. Police headquarters in London.   6. A fashionable resort town south of London.

to everyone as Ernest. You answer to the name of Ernest. You look as if your name was Ernest. You are the most earnest looking person I ever saw in my life. It is perfectly absurd your saying that your name isn't Ernest. It's on your cards. Here is one of them. [*Taking it from case.*] "Mr. Ernest Worthing, B. 4, The Albany."⁷ I'll keep this as a proof that your name is Ernest if ever you attempt to deny it to me, or to Gwendolen, or to anyone else. [*Puts the card in his pocket.*]

JACK   Well, my name is Ernest in town and Jack in the country, and the cigarette case was given to me in the country.

ALGERNON   Yes, but that does not account for the fact that your small Aunt Cecily, who lives at Tunbridge Wells, calls you her dear uncle. Come, old boy, you had much better have the thing out at once.

JACK   My dear Algy, you talk exactly as if you were a dentist. It is very vulgar to talk like a dentist when one isn't a dentist. It produces a false impression.

ALGERNON   Well, that is exactly what dentists always do. Now, go on! Tell me the whole thing. I may mention that I have always suspected you of being a confirmed and secret Bunburyist; and I am quite sure of it now.

JACK   Bunburyist? What on earth do you mean by a Bunburyist?

ALGERNON   I'll reveal to you the meaning of that incomparable expression as soon as you are kind enough to inform me why you are Ernest in town and Jack in the country.

JACK   Well, produce my cigarette case first.

ALGERNON   Here it is. [*Hands cigarette case.*] Now produce your explanation, and pray make it improbable. [*Sits on sofa.*]

JACK   My dear fellow, there is nothing improbable about my explanation at all. In fact it's perfectly ordinary. Old Mr. Thomas Cardew, who adopted me when I was a little boy, made me in his will guardian to his granddaughter, Miss Cecily Cardew. Cecily, who addresses me as her uncle from motives of respect that you could not possibly appreciate, lives at my place in the country under the charge of her admirable governess, Miss Prism.

ALGERNON   Where is that place in the country, by the way?

JACK   That is nothing to you, dear boy. You are not going to be invited. . . . I may tell you candidly that the place is not in Shropshire.

ALGERNON   I suspected that, my dear fellow! I have Bunburyed all over Shropshire on two separate occasions. Now, go on. Why are you Ernest in town and Jack in the country?

JACK   My dear Algy, I don't know whether you will be able to understand my real motives. You are hardly serious enough. When one is placed in the position of guardian, one has to adopt a very high moral tone on all subjects. It's one's duty to do so. And as a high moral tone can hardly be said to conduce very much to either one's health or one's happiness, in order to get up to town I have always pretended to have a younger brother of the name of Ernest, who lives in the Albany, and gets into the most dreadful scrapes. That, my dear Algy, is the whole truth pure and simple.

ALGERNON   The truth is rarely pure and never simple. Modern life would

7. A former residence of the duke of Albany (brother of George IV) near Piccadilly that had been converted into elegant apartments often rented by country gentry for visits to London.

be very tedious if it were either, and modern literature a complete impossibility!

JACK   That wouldn't be at all a bad thing.

ALGERNON   Literary criticism is not your forte, my dear fellow. Don't try it. You should leave that to people who haven't been at a University. They do it so well in the daily papers. What you really are is a Bunburyist. I was quite right in saying you were a Bunburyist. You are one of the most advanced Bunburyists I know.

JACK   What on earth do you mean?

ALGERNON   You have invented a very useful young brother called Ernest, in order that you may be able to come up to town as often as you like. I have invented an invaluable permanent invalid called Bunbury, in order that I may be able to go down into the country whenever I choose. Bunbury is perfectly invaluable. If it wasn't for Bunbury's extraordinary bad health, for instance, I wouldn't be able to dine with you at Willis's tonight, for I have been really engaged[8] to Aunt Augusta for more than a week.

JACK   I haven't asked you to dine with me anywhere tonight.

ALGERNON   I know. You are absurdly careless about sending out invitations. It is very foolish of you. Nothing annoys people so much as not receiving invitations.

JACK   You had much better dine with your Aunt Augusta.

ALGERNON   I haven't the smallest intention of doing anything of the kind. To begin with, I dined there on Monday, and once a week is quite enough to dine with one's own relations. In the second place, whenever I do dine there I am always treated as a member of the family, and sent down with[9] either no woman at all, or two. In the third place, I know perfectly well whom she will place me next to, tonight. She will place me next Mary Farquhar, who always flirts with her own husband across the dinner table. That is not very pleasant. Indeed, it is not even decent . . . and that sort of thing is enormously on the increase. The amount of women in London who flirt with their own husbands is perfectly scandalous. It looks so bad. It is simply washing one's clean linen in public. Besides, now that I know you to be a confirmed Bunburyist, I naturally want to talk to you about Bunburying. I want to tell you the rules.

JACK   I'm not a Bunburyist at all. If Gwendolen accepts me, I am going to kill my brother, indeed I think I'll kill him in any case. Cecily is a little too much interested in him. It is rather a bore. So I am going to get rid of Ernest. And I strongly advise you to do the same with Mr. . . . with your invalid friend who has the absurd name.

ALGERNON   Nothing will induce me to part with Bunbury, and if you ever get married, which seems to me extremely problematic, you will be very glad to know Bunbury. A man who marries without knowing Bunbury has a very tedious time of it.

JACK   That is nonsense. If I marry a charming girl like Gwendolen, and she is the only girl I ever saw in my life that I would marry, I certainly won't want to know Bunbury.

8. I.e., committed to attend her dinner party. "Willis's": a first-class restaurant in the vicinity of St. James's Street.

9. I.e., required to escort, as a dinner partner.

ALGERNON   Then your wife will. You don't seem to realize, that in married life three is company and two is none.

JACK [*Sententiously.*]   That, my dear young friend, is the theory that the corrupt French Drama has been propounding for the last fifty years.[1]

ALGERNON   Yes; and that the happy English home has proved in half the time.

JACK   For heaven's sake, don't try to be cynical. It's perfectly easy to be cynical.

ALGERNON   My dear fellow, it isn't easy to be anything nowadays. There's such a lot of beastly competition about. [*The sound of an electric bell is heard.*] Ah! that must be Aunt Augusta. Only relatives, or creditors, ever ring in that Wagnerian manner.[2] Now, if I get her out of the way for ten minutes, so that you can have an opportunity for proposing to Gwendolen, may I dine with you tonight at Willis's?

JACK   I suppose so, if you want to.

ALGERNON   Yes, but you must be serious about it. I hate people who are not serious about meals. It is so shallow of them.

　　　　　[*Enter* LANE.]

LANE   Lady Bracknell and Miss Fairfax.

　　　　　[ALGERNON *goes forward to meet them. Enter* LADY BRACKNELL *and* GWENDOLEN.]

LADY BRACKNELL   Good afternoon, dear Algernon, I hope you are behaving very well.

ALGERNON   I'm feeling very well, Aunt Augusta.

LADY BRACKNELL   That's not quite the same thing. In fact the two things rarely go together. [*Sees* JACK *and bows to him with icy coldness.*]

ALGERNON [*To* GWENDOLEN.]   Dear me, you are smart![3]

GWENDOLEN   I am always smart! Aren't I, Mr. Worthing?

JACK   You're quite perfect, Miss Fairfax.

GWENDOLEN   Oh! I hope I am not that. It would leave no room for developments, and I intend to develop in many directions. [GWENDOLEN *and* JACK *sit down together in the corner.*]

LADY BRACKNELL   I'm sorry if we are a little late, Algernon, but I was obliged to call on dear Lady Harbury. I hadn't been there since her poor husband's death. I never saw a woman so altered; she looks quite twenty years younger. And now I'll have a cup of tea, and one of those nice cucumber sandwiches you promised me.

ALGERNON   Certainly, Aunt Augusta. [*Goes over to teatable.*]

LADY BRACKNELL   Won't you come and sit here, Gwendolen?

GWENDOLEN   Thanks, mamma,[4] I'm quite comfortable where I am.

ALGERNON [*Picking up empty plate in horror.*]   Good heavens! Lane! Why are there no cucumber sandwiches? I ordered them specially.

LANE [*Gravely.*]   There were no cucumbers in the market this morning, sir. I went down twice.

ALGERNON   No cucumbers!

---

1. Almost all the plays by the leading French playwrights of the second half of the 19th century (Alexandre Dumas *fils*, Émile Augier, and Victorien Sardou) focus on the topic of marital infidelity. As Brander Matthews, an American critic, noted in 1882, "the trio—husband, wife, and lover" had become "almost universal" in the French theater.

2. Insistently loud, like some of the music in Richard Wagner's large-scale operas.

3. Elegantly fashionable.

4. Pronounced with the accent on the second syllable.

LANE No, sir. Not even for ready money.

ALGERNON That will do, Lane, thank you.

LANE Thank you, sir.

ALGERNON I am greatly distressed, Aunt Augusta, about there being no cucumbers, not even for ready money.

LADY BRACKNELL It really makes no matter, Algernon. I had some crumpets[5] with Lady Harbury, who seems to me to be living entirely for pleasure now.

ALGERNON I hear her hair has turned quite gold from grief.

LADY BRACKNELL It certainly has changed its color. From what cause I, of course, cannot say. [ALGERNON *crosses and hands tea.*] Thank you. I've quite a treat for you tonight, Algernon. I am going to send you down with Mary Farquhar. She is such a nice woman, and so attentive to her husband. It's delightful to watch them.

ALGERNON I am afraid, Aunt Augusta, I shall have to give up the pleasure of dining with you tonight after all.

LADY BRACKNELL [*Frowning.*] I hope not, Algernon. It would put my table completely out. Your uncle would have to dine upstairs. Fortunately he is accustomed to that.

ALGERNON It is a great bore, and, I need hardly say, a terrible disappointment to me, but the fact is I have just had a telegram to say that my poor friend Bunbury is very ill again. [*Exchanges glances with* JACK.] They seem to think I should be with him.

LADY BRACKNELL It is very strange. This Mr. Bunbury seems to suffer from curiously bad health.

ALGERNON Yes; poor Bunbury is a dreadful invalid.

LADY BRACKNELL Well, I must say, Algernon, that I think it is high time that Mr. Bunbury made up his mind whether he was going to live or to die. This shilly-shallying with the question is absurd. Nor do I in any way approve of the modern sympathy with invalids. I consider it morbid. Illness of any kind is hardly a thing to be encouraged in others. Health is the primary duty of life. I am always telling that to your poor uncle, but he never seems to take much notice . . . as far as any improvement in his ailments goes. I should be obliged if you would ask Mr. Bunbury, from me, to be kind enough not to have a relapse on Saturday, for I rely on you to arrange my music for me. It is my last reception, and one wants something that will encourage conversation, particularly at the end of the season[6] when everyone has practically said whatever they had to say, which, in most cases, was probably not much.

ALGERNON I'll speak to Bunbury, Aunt Augusta, if he is still conscious, and I think I can promise you he'll be all right by Saturday. Of course the music is a great difficulty. You see, if one plays good music, people don't listen, and if one plays bad music, people don't talk. But I'll run over the program I've drawn out, if you will kindly come into the next room for a moment.

LADY BRACKNELL Thank you, Algernon. It is very thoughtful of you. [*Rising, and following* ALGERNON.] I'm sure the program will be delightful,

5. A kind of toasted muffin.

6. The social season, extending from May through July, when people of fashion came into London from their country estates for entertainments and parties.

after a few expurgations. French songs I cannot possibly allow. People always seem to think that they are improper, and either look shocked, which is vulgar, or laugh, which is worse. But German sounds a thoroughly respectable language, and indeed, I believe is so. Gwendolen, you will accompany me.

GWENDOLEN   Certainly, mamma.

[LADY BRACKNELL *and* ALGERNON *go into the music room,* GWENDOLEN *remains behind.*]

JACK   Charming day it has been, Miss Fairfax.

GWENDOLEN   Pray don't talk to me about the weather, Mr. Worthing. Whenever people talk to me about the weather, I always feel quite certain that they mean something else. And that makes me so nervous.

JACK   I do mean something else.

GWENDOLEN   I thought so. In fact, I am never wrong.

JACK   And I would like to be allowed to take advantage of Lady Bracknell's temporary absence . . .

GWENDOLEN   I would certainly advise you to do so. Mamma has a way of coming back suddenly into a room that I have often had to speak to her about.

JACK [*Nervously.*]   Miss Fairfax, ever since I met you I have admired you more than any girl . . . I have ever met since . . . I met you.

GWENDOLEN   Yes, I am quite aware of the fact. And I often wish that in public, at any rate, you had been more demonstrative. For me you have always had an irresistible fascination. Even before I met you I was far from indifferent to you. [JACK *looks at her in amazement.*] We live, as I hope you know, Mr. Worthing, in an age of ideals. The fact is constantly mentioned in the more expensive monthly magazines, and has reached the provincial pulpits, I am told: and my ideal has always been to love someone of the name of Ernest. There is something in that name that inspires absolute confidence. The moment Algernon first mentioned to me that he had a friend called Ernest, I knew I was destined to love you.

JACK   You really love me, Gwendolen?

GWENDOLEN   Passionately!

JACK   Darling! You don't know how happy you've made me.

GWENDOLEN   My own Ernest!

JACK   But you don't really mean to say that you couldn't love me if my name wasn't Ernest?

GWENDOLEN   But your name is Ernest.

JACK   Yes, I know it is. But supposing it was something else? Do you mean to say you couldn't love me then?

GWENDOLEN [*Glibly.*]   Ah! that is clearly a metaphysical speculation, and like most metaphysical speculations has very little reference at all to the actual facts of real life, as we know them.

JACK   Personally, darling, to speak quite candidly, I don't much care about the name of Ernest . . . I don't think the name suits me at all.

GWENDOLEN   It suits you perfectly. It is a divine name. It has a music of its own. It produces vibrations.

JACK   Well, really, Gwendolen, I must say that I think there are lots of other much nicer names. I think Jack, for instance, a charming name.

GWENDOLEN   Jack? . . . No, there is very little music in the name Jack, if any at all, indeed. It does not thrill. It produces absolutely no vibrations. . . . I have known several Jacks, and they all, without exception, were more than usually plain. Besides, Jack is a notorious domesticity for John! And I pity any woman who is married to a man called John. She would probably never be allowed to know the entrancing pleasure of a single moment's solitude. The only really safe name is Ernest.

JACK Gwendolen, I must get christened at once—I mean we must get married at once. There is no time to be lost.

GWENDOLEN Married, Mr. Worthing?

JACK [*Astounded.*] Well . . . surely. You know that I love you, and you led me to believe, Miss Fairfax, that you were not absolutely indifferent to me.

GWENDOLEN I adore you. But you haven't proposed to me yet. Nothing has been said at all about marriage. The subject has not even been touched on.

JACK Well . . . may I propose to you now?

GWENDOLEN I think it would be an admirable opportunity. And to spare you any possible disappointment, Mr. Worthing, I think it only fair to tell you quite frankly beforehand that I am fully determined to accept you.

JACK Gwendolen!

GWENDOLEN Yes, Mr. Worthing, what have you got to say to me?

JACK You know what I have got to say to you.

GWENDOLEN Yes, but you don't say it.

JACK Gwendolen, will you marry me? [*Goes on his knees.*]

GWENDOLEN Of course I will, darling. How long you have been about it! I am afraid you have had very little experience in how to propose.

JACK My own one, I have never loved anyone in the world but you.

GWENDOLEN Yes, but men often propose for practice. I know my brother Gerald does. All my girlfriends tell me so. What wonderfully blue eyes you have, Ernest! They are quite, quite blue. I hope you will always look at me just like that, especially when there are other people present.

        [*Enter* LADY BRACKNELL.]

LADY BRACKNELL Mr. Worthing! Rise, sir, from this semi-recumbent posture. It is most indecorous.

GWENDOLEN Mamma! [*He tries to rise; she restrains him.*] I must beg you to retire. This is no place for you. Besides, Mr. Worthing has not quite finished yet.

LADY BRACKNELL Finished what, may I ask?

GWENDOLEN I am engaged to Mr. Worthing, mamma.

        [*They rise together.*]

LADY BRACKNELL Pardon me, you are not engaged to anyone. When you do become engaged to someone, I, or your father, should his health permit him, will inform you of the fact. An engagement should come on a young girl as a surprise, pleasant or unpleasant, as the case may be. It is hardly a matter that she could be allowed to arrange for herself. . . . And now I have a few questions to put to you, Mr. Worthing. While I am making these inquiries, you, Gwendolen, will wait for me below in the carriage.

GWENDOLEN [*Reproachfully.*] Mamma!

LADY BRACKNELL   In the carriage, Gwendolen! [GWENDOLEN *goes to the door. She and* JACK *blow kisses to each other behind* LADY BRACKNELL'*s back.* LADY BRACKNELL *looks vaguely about as if she could not understand what the noise was. Finally turns round.*] Gwendolen, the carriage!

GWENDOLEN   Yes, mamma. [*Goes out, looking back at* JACK.]

LADY BRACKNELL [*Sitting down.*]   You can take a seat, Mr. Worthing.
    [*Looks in her pocket for notebook and pencil.*]

JACK   Thank you, Lady Bracknell, I prefer standing.

LADY BRACKNELL [*Pencil and notebook in hand.*]   I feel bound to tell you that you are not down on my list of eligible young men, although I have the same list as the dear Duchess of Bolton has. We work together, in fact. However, I am quite ready to enter your name, should your answers be what a really affectionate mother requires. Do you smoke?

JACK   Well, yes, I must admit I smoke.

LADY BRACKNELL   I am glad to hear it. A man should always have an occupation of some kind. There are far too many idle men in London as it is. How old are you?

JACK   Twenty-nine.

LADY BRACKNELL   A very good age to be married at. I have always been of opinion that a man who desires to get married should know either everything or nothing. Which do you know?

JACK [*After some hesitation.*]   I know nothing, Lady Bracknell.

LADY BRACKNELL   I am pleased to hear it. I do not approve of anything that tampers with natural ignorance. Ignorance is like a delicate exotic fruit; touch it and the bloom is gone. The whole theory of modern education is radically unsound. Fortunately in England, at any rate, education produces no effect whatsoever. If it did, it would prove a serious danger to the upper classes, and probably lead to acts of violence in Grosvenor Square.[7] What is your income?

JACK   Between seven and eight thousand a year.

LADY BRACKNELL [*Makes a note in her book.*]   In land, or in investments?

JACK   In investments, chiefly.

LADY BRACKNELL   That is satisfactory. What between the duties expected of one during one's lifetime, and the duties exacted from one after one's death,[8] land has ceased to be either a profit or a pleasure. It gives one position, and prevents one from keeping it up. That's all that can be said about land.

JACK   I have a country house with some land, of course, attached to it, about fifteen hundred acres, I believe; but I don't depend on that for my real income. In fact, as far as I can make out, the poachers are the only people who make anything out of it.

LADY BRACKNELL   A country house! How many bedrooms? Well, that point can be cleared up afterwards. You have a town house, I hope? A girl with a simple, unspoiled nature, like Gwendolen, could hardly be expected to reside in the country.

JACK   Well, I own a house in Belgrave Square,[9] but it is let by the year to

---

7. A fashionable residential area in the West End of London.
8. The wordplay is on "death duties"—i.e., inheritance taxes.
9. Another fashionable residential area in the West End known as Belgravia.

Lady Bloxham. Of course, I can get it back whenever I like, at six months' notice.

LADY BRACKNELL Lady Bloxham? I don't know her.

JACK Oh, she goes about very little. She is a lady considerably advanced in years.

LADY BRACKNELL Ah, nowadays that is no guarantee of respectability of character. What number in Belgrave Square?

JACK 149.

LADY BRACKNELL [*Shaking her head.*] The unfashionable side. I thought there was something. However, that could easily be altered.

JACK Do you mean the fashion, or the side?

LADY BRACKNELL [*Sternly.*] Both, if necessary, I presume. What are your politics?

JACK Well, I am afraid I really have none. I am a Liberal Unionist.[1]

LADY BRACKNELL Oh, they count as Tories. They dine with us. Or come in the evening, at any rate. Now to minor matters. Are your parents living?

JACK I have lost both my parents.

LADY BRACKNELL Both? To lose one parent may be regarded as a misfortune—to lose *both* seems like carelessness. Who was your father? He was evidently a man of some wealth. Was he born in what the Radical papers call the purple of commerce, or did he rise from the ranks of aristocracy?

JACK I am afraid I really don't know. The fact is, Lady Bracknell, I said I had lost my parents. It would be nearer the truth to say that my parents seem to have lost me. . . . I don't actually know who I am by birth. I was . . . well, I was found.

LADY BRACKNELL Found!

JACK The late Mr. Thomas Cardew, an old gentleman of a very charitable and kindly disposition, found me, and gave me the name of Worthing, because he happened to have a first-class ticket for Worthing in his pocket at the time. Worthing is a place in Sussex. It is a seaside resort.

LADY BRACKNELL Where did the charitable gentleman who had a first-class ticket for this seaside resort find you?

JACK [*Gravely.*] In a handbag.

LADY BRACKNELL A handbag?

JACK [*Very seriously.*] Yes, Lady Bracknell. I was in a handbag—a somewhat large, black leather handbag, with handles to it—an ordinary handbag, in fact.

LADY BRACKNELL In what locality did this Mr. James, or Thomas, Cardew come across this ordinary handbag?

JACK In the cloak room at Victoria Station. It was given to him in mistake for his own.[2]

LADY BRACKNELL The cloak room at Victoria Station?

JACK Yes. The Brighton line.

---

1. A splinter group of members of the Liberal Party who, in 1886, led by Joseph Chamberlain, joined forces with the Conservative Party (the "Tories") in opposing Home Rule for Ireland.

2. In the four-act version of the play, Jack explains

further what happened to Mr. Cardew: "He did not discover the error till he arrived at his own house. All subsequent efforts to ascertain who I was were unavailing."

LADY BRACKNELL   The line is immaterial. Mr. Worthing, I confess I feel somewhat bewildered by what you have just told me. To be born, or at any rate, bred in a handbag, whether it had handles or not, seems to me to display a contempt for the ordinary decencies of family life that reminds one of the worst excesses of the French Revolution. And I presume you know what that unfortunate movement led to? As for the particular locality in which the handbag was found, a cloak room at a railway station might serve to conceal a social indiscretion—has probably, indeed, been used for that purpose before now—but it could hardly be regarded as an assured basis for a recognized position in good society.

JACK   May I ask you then what you would advise me to do? I need hardly say I would do anything in the world to ensure Gwendolen's happiness.

LADY BRACKNELL   I would strongly advise you, Mr. Worthing, to try and acquire some relations as soon as possible, and to make a definite effort to produce at any rate one parent, of either sex, before the season is quite over.[3]

JACK   Well, I don't see how I could possibly manage to do that. I can produce the handbag at any moment, it is in my dressing room at home. I really think that should satisfy you, Lady Bracknell.

LADY BRACKNELL   Me, sir! What has it to do with me? You can hardly imagine that I and Lord Bracknell would dream of allowing our only daughter—a girl brought up with the utmost care—to marry into a cloak room, and form an alliance with a parcel? Good morning, Mr. Worthing!

[LADY BRACKNELL *sweeps out in majestic indignation.*]

JACK   Good morning! [ALGERNON, *from the other room, strikes up the Wedding March.* JACK *looks perfectly furious, and goes to the door.*] For goodness' sake don't play that ghastly tune, Algy! How idiotic you are!

[*The music stops, and* ALGERNON *enters cheerily.*]

ALGERNON   Didn't it go off all right, old boy? You don't mean to say Gwendolen refused you? I know it is a way she has. She is always refusing people. I think it is most ill-natured of her.

JACK   Oh, Gwendolen is as right as a trivet.[4] As far as she is concerned, we are engaged. Her mother is perfectly unbearable. Never met such a Gorgon[5] . . . I don't really know what a Gorgon is like, but I am quite sure that Lady Bracknell is one. In any case, she is a monster, without being a myth, which is rather unfair . . . I beg your pardon, Algy, I suppose I shouldn't talk about your own aunt in that way before you.

ALGERNON   My dear boy, I love hearing my relations abused. It is the only thing that makes me put up with them at all. Relations are simply a tedious pack of people who haven't got the remotest knowledge of how to live, nor the smallest instinct about when to die.

JACK   Oh, that is nonsense!

ALGERNON   It isn't!

---

3. In the four-act version of the play, Jack later comments to Algernon about Lady Bracknell's demands about locating parents: "After all what does it matter whether a man has ever had a father and mother or not? Mothers, of course, are all right. They pay a chap's bills and don't bother him. But fathers bother a chap and never pay his bills. I don't know a single chap at the club who speaks to his father." And Algernon remarks: "Yes. Fathers are certainly not popular just at present. . . . They are like these chaps, the minor poets. They are never quoted."

4. Proverbial expression meaning reliably steady, like a tripod ("trivet") used to support pots over a fire.

5. A mythical female creature, like Medusa, whose look turned into stone anyone beholding her.

JACK   Well, I won't argue about the matter. You always want to argue about things.

ALGERNON   That is exactly what things were originally made for.

JACK   Upon my word, if I thought that, I'd shoot myself . . . [*A pause.*] You don't think there is any chance of Gwendolen becoming like her mother in about a hundred and fifty years, do you, Algy?

ALGERNON   All women become like their mothers. That is their tragedy. No man does. That's his.

JACK   Is that clever?

ALGERNON   It is perfectly phrased! and quite as true as any observation in civilized life should be.

JACK   I am sick to death of cleverness. Everybody is clever nowadays. You can't go anywhere without meeting clever people. The thing has become an absolute public nuisance. I wish to goodness we had a few fools left.

ALGERNON   We have.

JACK   I should extremely like to meet them. What do they talk about?

ALGERNON   The fools? Oh! about the clever people, of course.

JACK   What fools!

ALGERNON   By the way, did you tell Gwendolen the truth about your being Ernest in town, and Jack in the country?

JACK [*In a very patronizing manner.*]   My dear fellow, the truth isn't quite the sort of thing one tells to a nice sweet refined girl. What extraordinary ideas you have about the way to behave to a woman!

ALGERNON   The only way to behave to a woman is to make love to her, if she is pretty, and to someone else if she is plain.

JACK   Oh, that is nonsense.

ALGERNON   What about your brother? What about the profligate Ernest?

JACK   Oh, before the end of the week I shall have got rid of him. I'll say he died in Paris of apoplexy. Lots of people die of apoplexy, quite suddenly, don't they?

ALGERNON   Yes, but it's hereditary, my dear fellow. It's a sort of thing that runs in families. You had much better say a severe chill.

JACK   You are sure a severe chill isn't hereditary, or anything of that kind?

ALGERNON   Of course it isn't!

JACK   Very well, then. My poor brother Ernest is carried off suddenly in Paris, by a severe chill. That gets rid of him.[6]

ALGERNON   But I thought you said that . . . Miss Cardew was a little too much interested in your poor brother Ernest? Won't she feel his loss a good deal?

JACK   Oh, that is all right. Cecily is not a silly romantic girl, I am glad to say. She has got a capital appetite, goes on long walks, and pays no attention at all to her lessons.

ALGERNON   I would rather like to see Cecily.

JACK   I will take very good care you never do. She is excessively pretty, and she is only just eighteen.

ALGERNON   Have you told Gwendolen yet that you have an excessively pretty ward who is only just eighteen?

---

6. In the four-act version of the play Jack explains further: "I'll wear mourning for him, of course; that would be only decent. I don't at all mind wearing mourning. I think that all black, with a good pearl pin, rather smart. Then I'll go down home and break the news to my household."

JACK   Oh! one doesn't blurt these things out to people. Cecily and Gwendolen are perfectly certain to be extremely great friends. I'll bet you anything you like that half an hour after they have met, they will be calling each other sister.

ALGERNON   Women only do that when they have called each other a lot of other things first. Now, my dear boy, if we want to get a good table at Willis's, we really must go and dress. Do you know it is nearly seven?

JACK   [*Irritably.*] Oh! it always is nearly seven.

ALGERNON   Well, I'm hungry.

JACK   I never knew you when you weren't. . . .

ALGERNON   What shall we do after dinner? Go to the theater?

JACK   Oh no! I loathe listening.

ALGERNON   Well, let us go to the club?

JACK   Oh, no! I hate talking.

ALGERNON   Well, we might trot around to the Empire[7] at ten?

JACK   Oh no! I can't bear looking at things. It is so silly.

ALGERNON   Well, what shall we do?

JACK   Nothing!

ALGERNON   It is awfully hard work doing nothing. However, I don't mind hard work where there is no definite object of any kind.

[*Enter* LANE.]

LANE   Miss Fairfax.

[*Enter* GWENDOLEN. LANE *goes out.*]

ALGERNON   Gwendolen, upon my word!

GWENDOLEN   Algy, kindly turn your back. I have something very particular to say to Mr. Worthing.

ALGERNON   Really, Gwendolen, I don't think I can allow this at all.

GWENDOLEN   Algy, you always adopt a strictly immoral attitude towards life. You are not quite old enough to do that. [ALGERNON *retires to the fireplace.*]

JACK   My own darling!

GWENDOLEN   Ernest, we may never be married. From the expression on mamma's face I fear we never shall. Few parents nowadays pay any regard to what their children say to them. The old-fashioned respect for the young is fast dying out. Whatever influence I ever had over mamma, I lost at the age of three. But although she may prevent us from becoming man and wife, and I may marry someone else, and marry often, nothing that she can possibly do can alter my eternal devotion to you.

JACK   Dear Gwendolen!

GWENDOLEN   The story of your romantic origin, as related to me by mamma, with unpleasing comments, has naturally stirred the deeper fibers of my nature. Your Christian name has an irresistible fascination. The simplicity of your character makes you exquisitely incomprehensible to me. Your town address at the Albany I have. What is your address in the country?

JACK   The Manor House, Woolton, Hertfordshire.

---

7. A music hall in Leicester Square that featured light entertainment.

[ALGERNON, *who has been carefully listening, smiles to himself, and writes the address on his shirt-cuff.*[8] *Then picks up the Railway Guide.*]

GWENDOLEN   There is a good postal service, I suppose? It may be necessary to do something desperate. That of course will require serious consideration. I will communicate with you daily.

JACK   My own one!

GWENDOLEN   How long do you remain in town?

JACK   Till Monday.

GWENDOLEN   Good! Algy, you may turn round now.

ALGERNON   Thanks, I've turned round already.

GWENDOLEN   You may also ring the bell.

JACK   You will let me see you to your carriage, my own darling?

GWENDOLEN   Certainly.

JACK [*To* LANE, *who now enters.*]   I will see Miss Fairfax out.

LANE   Yes, sir. [JACK *and* GWENDOLEN *go off.*]

[LANE *presents several letters on a salver to* ALGERNON. *It is to be surmised that they are bills, as* ALGERNON *after looking at the envelopes, tears them up.*]

ALGERNON   A glass of sherry, Lane.

LANE   Yes, sir.

ALGERNON   Tomorrow, Lane, I'm going Bunburying.

LANE   Yes, sir.

ALGERNON   I shall probably not be back till Monday. You can put up my dress clothes, my smoking jacket,[9] and all the Bunbury suits . . .

LANE   Yes, sir. [*Handing sherry.*]

ALGERNON   I hope tomorrow will be a fine day, Lane.

LANE   It never is, sir.

ALGERNON   Lane, you're a perfect pessimist.

LANE   I do my best to give satisfaction, sir.

[*Enter* JACK. LANE *goes off.*]

JACK   There's a sensible, intellectual girl! the only girl I ever cared for in my life. [ALGERNON *is laughing immoderately.*] What on earth are you so amused at?

ALGERNON   Oh, I'm a little anxious about poor Bunbury, that is all.

JACK   If you don't take care, your friend Bunbury will get you into a serious scrape some day.

ALGERNON   I love scrapes. They are the only things that are never serious.

JACK   Oh, that's nonsense, Algy. You never talk anything but nonsense.

ALGERNON   Nobody ever does.

[JACK *looks indignantly at him, and leaves the room.* ALGERNON *lights a cigarette, reads his shirt-cuff, and smiles.*]

ACT-DROP[1]

---

8. Because shirt cuffs were heavily starched they provided a good surface on which to make notes.
9. Coat worn when gentlemen assembled in a room designated for smoking. The object was to avoid contaminating their regular clothing with the smell of cigars or pipes, which was considered offensive to ladies.
1. A special curtain lowered during theatrical performances to denote intervals between acts or scenes.

Second Act

SCENE—*Garden at the Manor House. A flight of gray stone steps leads up to the house. The garden, an old-fashioned one, full of roses. Time of year, July. Basket chairs, and a table covered with books, are set under a large yew tree.*

[MISS PRISM[2] *discovered seated at the table.* CECILY *is at the back watering flowers.*]

MISS PRISM [*Calling.*] Cecily, Cecily! Surely such a utilitarian occupation as the watering of flowers is rather Moulton's duty than yours? Especially at a moment when intellectual pleasures await you. Your German grammar is on the table. Pray open it at page fifteen. We will repeat yesterday's lesson.

CECILY [*Coming over very slowly.*] But I don't like German. It isn't at all a becoming language. I know perfectly well that I look quite plain after my German lesson.

MISS PRISM Child, you know how anxious your guardian is that you should improve yourself in every way. He laid particular stress on your German, as he was leaving for town yesterday. Indeed, he always lays stress on your German when he is leaving for town.

CECILY Dear Uncle Jack is so very serious! Sometime he is so serious that I think he cannot be quite well.

MISS PRISM [*Drawing herself up.*] Your guardian enjoys the best of health, and his gravity of demeanor is especially to be commended in one so comparatively young as he is. I know no one who has a higher sense of duty and responsibility.

CECILY I suppose that is why he often looks a little bored when we three are together.

MISS PRISM Cecily! I am surprised at you. Mr. Worthing has many troubles in his life. Idle merriment and triviality would be out of place in his conversation. You must remember his constant anxiety about that unfortunate young man his brother.

CECILY I wish Uncle Jack would allow that unfortunate young man, his brother, to come down here sometimes. We might have a good influence over him, Miss Prism. I am sure you certainly would. You know German, and geology, and things of that kind influence a man very much. [CECILY *begins to write in her diary.*]

MISS PRISM [*Shaking her head.*] I do not think that even I could produce any effect on a character that according to his own brother's admission is irretrievably weak and vacillating. Indeed I am not sure that I would desire to reclaim him. I am not in favor of this modern mania for turning bad people into good people at a moment's notice. As a man sows so let him reap.[3] You must put away your diary, Cecily. I really don't see why you should keep a diary at all.

CECILY I keep a diary in order to enter the wonderful secrets of my life. If I didn't write them down I should probably forget all about them.

---

2. The name has connotations with the expression "prunes and prism" from Dickens's *Little Dorrit*, in which Mrs. General, a prim and proper teacher of manners for young ladies, trains them to repeat "prunes and prism" aloud because this exercise "gives a pretty form to the lips."
3. Cf. Galatians 6.7.

MISS PRISM   Memory, my dear Cecily, is the diary that we all carry about with us.

CECILY   Yes, but it usually chronicles the things that have never happened, and couldn't possibly have happened. I believe that Memory is responsible for nearly all the three-volume novels that Mudie[4] sends us.

MISS PRISM   Do not speak slightingly of the three-volume novel, Cecily. I wrote one myself in earlier days.

CECILY   Did you really, Miss Prism? How wonderfully clever you are! I hope it did not end happily? I don't like novels that end happily. They depress me so much.

MISS PRISM   The good ended happily, and the bad unhappily. That is what Fiction means.

CECILY   I suppose so. But it seems very unfair. And was your novel ever published?

MISS PRISM   Alas! no. The manuscript unfortunately was abandoned. I use the word in the sense of lost or mislaid. To your work, child, these speculations are profitless.

CECILY [*Smiling.*]   But I see dear Dr. Chasuble coming up through the garden.

MISS PRISM [*Rising and advancing.*]   Dr. Chasuble! This is indeed a pleasure.

[*Enter* CANON CHASUBLE.]

CHASUBLE   And how are we this morning? Miss Prism, you are, I trust, well?

CECILY   Miss Prism has just been complaining of a slight headache. I think it would do her so much good to have a short stroll with you in the Park, Dr. Chasuble.

MISS PRISM   Cecily, I have not mentioned anything about a headache.

CECILY   No, dear Miss Prism, I know that, but I felt instinctively that you had a headache. Indeed I was thinking about that, and not about my German lesson, when the Rector came in.

CHASUBLE   I hope, Cecily, you are not inattentive.

CECILY   Oh, I am afraid I am.

CHASUBLE   That is strange. Were I fortunate enough to be Miss Prism's pupil, I would hang upon her lips. [MISS PRISM *glares.*] I spoke metaphorically.—My metaphor was drawn from bees. Ahem! Mr. Worthing, I suppose, has not returned from town yet?

MISS PRISM   We do not expect him till Monday afternoon.

CHASUBLE   Ah yes, he usually likes to spend his Sunday in London. He is not one of those whose sole aim is enjoyment, as, by all accounts, that unfortunate young man his brother seems to be. But I must not disturb Egeria[5] and her pupil any longer.

MISS PRISM   Egeria? My name is Laetitia, Doctor.

CHASUBLE [*Bowing.*]   A classical allusion merely, drawn from the Pagan authors. I shall see you both no doubt at Evensong?[6]

---

4. Mudie's Circulating Library lent copies of new three-volume novels (usually sentimental tales) to subscribers for a moderate fee. Mudie's power in controlling the book market, especially for novels, was on the wane by 1895.

5. Roman goddess of fountains. Her name was also used as an epithet for a woman who provides guidance for other women.
6. Evening church services.

MISS PRISM I think, dear Doctor, I will have a stroll with you. I find I have a headache after all, and a walk might do it good.

CHASUBLE With pleasure, Miss Prism, with pleasure. We might go as far as the schools and back.

MISS PRISM That would be delightful. Cecily, you will read your Political Economy[7] in my absence. The chapter on the Fall of the Rupee[8] you may omit. It is somewhat too sensational. Even these metallic problems have their melodramatic side. [*Goes down the garden with* DR. CHASUBLE.]

CECILY [*Picks up books and throws them back on table.*] Horrid Political Economy! Horrid Geography! Horrid, horrid German!

[*Enter* MERRIMAN *with a card on a salver.*]

MERRIMAN Mr. Ernest Worthing has just driven over from the station. He has brought his luggage with him.

CECILY [*Takes the card and reads it.*] "Mr. Ernest Worthing, B. 4, The Albany, W." Uncle Jack's brother! Did you tell him Mr. Worthing was in town?

MERRIMAN Yes, Miss. He seemed very much disappointed. I mentioned that you and Miss Prism were in the garden. He said he was anxious to speak to you privately for a moment.

CECILY. Ask Mr. Ernest Worthing to come here. I suppose you had better talk to the housekeeper about a room for him.

MERRIMAN Yes, Miss.   [MERRIMAN *goes off.*]

CECILY I have never met any really wicked person before. I feel rather frightened. I am so afraid he will look just like everyone else. [*Enter* ALGERNON, *very gay and debonair.*] He does!

ALGERNON [*Raising his hat.*] You are my little cousin Cecily, I'm sure.

CECILY You are under some strange mistake. I am not little. In fact, I believe I am more than usually tall for my age. [ALGERNON *is rather taken aback.*] But I am your cousin Cecily. You, I see from your card, are Uncle Jack's brother, my cousin Ernest, my wicked cousin Ernest.

ALGERNON Oh! I am not really wicked at all, cousin Cecily. You mustn't think that I am wicked.

CECILY If you are not, then you have certainly been deceiving us all in a very inexcusable manner. I hope you have not been leading a double life, pretending to be wicked and being really good all the time. That would be hypocrisy.

ALGERNON [*Looks at her in amazement.*] Oh! Of course I have been rather reckless.

CECILY I am glad to hear it.

ALGERNON In fact, now you mention the subject, I have been very bad in my own small way.

CECILY I don't think you should be so proud of that, though I am sure it must have been very pleasant.

ALGERNON It is much pleasanter being here with you.

CECILY I can't understand how you are here at all. Uncle Jack won't be back till Monday afternoon.

ALGERNON That is a great disappointment. I am obliged to go up by the

7. I.e., book about economics.
8. The basic unit of currency in India. British civil servants who worked in India were paid in rupees and would suffer from its fall in value.

first train on Monday morning. I have a business appointment that I am anxious . . . to miss.

CECILY   Couldn't you miss it anywhere but in London?

ALGERNON   No: the appointment is in London.

CECILY   Well, I know, of course, how important it is not to keep a business engagement, if one wants to retain any sense of the beauty of life, but still I think you had better wait till Uncle Jack arrives. I know he wants to speak to you about your emigrating.

ALGERNON   About my what?

CECILY   Your emigrating. He has gone up to buy your outfit.

ALGERNON   I certainly wouldn't let Jack buy my outfit. He has no taste in neckties at all.

CECILY   I don't think you will require neckties. Uncle Jack is sending you to Australia.[9]

ALGERNON   Australia? I'd sooner die.

CECILY   Well, he said at dinner on Wednesday night, that you would have to choose between this world, the next world, and Australia.

ALGERNON   Oh, well! The accounts I have received of Australia and the next world are not particularly encouraging. This world is good enough for me, cousin Cecily.

CECILY   Yes, but are you good enough for it?

ALGERNON   I'm afraid I'm not that. That is why I want you to reform me. You might make that your mission, if you don't mind, cousin Cecily.

CECILY   I'm afraid I've no time, this afternoon.

ALGERNON   Well, would you mind my reforming myself this afternoon?

CECILY   It is rather Quixotic of you. But I think you should try.

ALGERNON   I will. I feel better already.

CECILY   You are looking a little worse.

ALGERNON   That is because I am hungry.

CECILY   How thoughtless of me. I should have remembered that when one is going to lead an entirely new life, one requires regular and wholesome meals. Won't you come in?

ALGERNON   Thank you. Might I have a buttonhole[1] first? I never have any appetite unless I have a buttonhole first.

CECILY   A Maréchal Niel?[2] [Picks up scissors.]

ALGERNON   No, I'd sooner have a pink rose.

CECILY   Why? [Cuts a flower.]

ALGERNON   Because you are like a pink rose, cousin Cecily.

CECILY   I don't think it can be right for you to talk to me like that. Miss Prism never says such things to me.

ALGERNON   Then Miss Prism is a shortsighted old lady. [CECILY puts the rose in his buttonhole.] You are the prettiest girl I ever saw.

CECILY   Miss Prism says that all good looks are a snare.

ALGERNON   They are a snare that every sensible man would like to be caught in.

9. Although Australia had originally been a place to which criminals were banished, it was, by this time, like Canada, a place to which families might send harmless but useless members, who would be paid an allowance to remain abroad.

1. I.e., a flower worn in the buttonhole of a man's coat lapel.
2. A chrome yellow variety of rose named after one of the generals of Napoleon III.

CECILY   Oh! I don't think I would care to catch a sensible man. I shouldn't know what to talk to him about.

[*They pass into the house.* MISS PRISM *and* DR. CHASUBLE *return.*]

MISS PRISM   You are too much alone, dear Dr. Chasuble. You should get married. A misanthrope I can understand—a womanthrope, never!

CHASUBLE [*With a scholar's shudder.*][3]   Believe me, I do not deserve so neologistic a phrase. The precept as well as the practice of the Primitive Church was distinctly against matrimony.

MISS PRISM [*Sententiously.*]   That is obviously the reason why the Primitive Church has not lasted up to the present day. And you do not seem to realize, dear Doctor, that by persistently remaining single, a man converts himself into a permanent public temptation. Men should be more careful; this very celibacy leads weaker vessels astray.

CHASUBLE   But is a man not equally attractive when married?

MISS PRISM   No married man is ever attractive except to his wife.

CHASUBLE   And often, I've been told, not even to her.

MISS PRISM   That depends on the intellectual sympathies of the woman. Maturity can always be depended on. Ripeness can be trusted. Young women are green. [DR. CHASUBLE *starts.*] I spoke horticulturally. My metaphor was drawn from fruits. But where is Cecily?

CHASUBLE   Perhaps she followed us to the schools.

[*Enter* JACK *slowly from the back of the garden. He is dressed in the deepest mourning, with crape hat-band and black gloves.*]

MISS PRISM   Mr. Worthing!

CHASUBLE   Mr. Worthing?

MISS PRISM   This is indeed a surprise. We did not look for you till Monday afternoon.

JACK [*Shakes* MISS PRISM'*s hand in a tragic manner.*]   I have returned sooner than I expected. Dr. Chasuble, I hope you are well?

CHASUBLE   Dear Mr. Worthing, I trust this garb of woe does not betoken some terrible calamity?

JACK   My brother.

MISS PRISM   More shameful debts and extravagance?

CHASUBLE   Still leading his life of pleasure?

JACK [*Shaking his head.*]   Dead!

CHASUBLE   Your brother Ernest dead?

JACK   Quite dead.

MISS PRISM   What a lesson for him! I trust he will profit by it.

CHASUBLE   Mr. Worthing, I offer you my sincere condolence. You have at least the consolation of knowing that you were always the most generous and forgiving of brothers.

JACK   Poor Ernest! He had many faults, but it is a sad, sad blow.

CHASUBLE   Very sad indeed. Were you with him at the end?

JACK   No. He died abroad; in Paris, in fact. I had a telegram last night from the manager of the Grand Hotel.

CHASUBLE   Was the cause of death mentioned?

JACK   A severe chill, it seems.

---

3. He shudders because instead of using the correct word for woman hater, *misogynist*, she has coined her own expression.

MISS PRISM As a man sows, so shall he reap.

CHASUBLE [*Raising his hand.*] Charity, dear Miss Prism, charity! None of us are perfect. I myself am peculiarly susceptible to drafts. Will the interment take place here?

JACK No. He seemed to have expressed a desire to be buried in Paris.

CHASUBLE In Paris! [*Shakes his head.*] I fear that hardly points to any very serious state of mind at the last. You would no doubt wish me to make some slight allusion to this tragic domestic affliction next Sunday. [JACK *presses his hand convulsively.*] My sermon on the meaning of the manna in the wilderness can be adapted to almost any occasion, joyful, or, as in the present case, distressing. [*All sigh.*] I have preached it at harvest celebrations, christenings, confirmations, on days of humiliation and festal days. The last time I delivered it was in the Cathedral, as a charity sermon on behalf of the Society for the Prevention of Discontent among the Upper Orders. The Bishop, who was present, was much struck by some of the analogies I drew.

JACK Ah! That reminds me, you mentioned christenings, I think, Dr. Chasuble? I suppose you know how to christen all right? [DR. CHASUBLE *looks astounded.*] I mean, of course, you are continually christening, aren't you?

MISS PRISM It is, I regret to say, one of the Rector's most constant duties in this parish. I have often spoken to the poorer classes on the subject. But they don't seem to know what thrift is.

CHASUBLE But is there any particular infant in whom you are interested, Mr. Worthing? Your brother was, I believe, unmarried, was he not?

JACK Oh yes.

MISS PRISM [*Bitterly.*] People who live entirely for pleasure usually are.

JACK But it is not for any child, dear Doctor. I am very fond of children. No! the fact is, I would like to be christened myself, this afternoon, if you have nothing better to do.

CHASUBLE But surely, Mr. Worthing, you have been christened already?

JACK I don't remember anything about it.

CHASUBLE But have you any grave doubts on the subject?

JACK I certainly intend to have. Of course I don't know if the thing would bother you in any way, or if you think I am a little too old now.

CHASUBLE Not at all. The sprinkling, and, indeed, the immersion of adults is a perfectly canonical practice.

JACK Immersion!

CHASUBLE You need have no apprehensions. Sprinkling is all that is necessary, or indeed I think advisable. Our weather is so changeable. At what hour would you wish the ceremony performed?

JACK Oh, I might trot round about five if that would suit you.

CHASUBLE Perfectly, perfectly! In fact I have two similar ceremonies to perform at that time. A case of twins that occurred recently in one of the outlying cottages on your own estate. Poor Jenkins the carter, a most hard-working man.

JACK Oh! I don't see much fun in being christened along with other babies. It would be childish. Would half-past five do?

CHASUBLE Admirably! Admirably! [*Takes out watch.*] And now, dear Mr.

2200 / OSCAR WILDE

Worthing, I will not intrude any longer into a house of sorrow. I would merely beg you not to be too much bowed down by grief. What seem to us bitter trials are often blessings in disguise.

MISS PRISM   This seems to me a blessing of an extremely obvious kind.

[*Enter* CECILY *from the house.*]

CECILY   Uncle Jack! Oh, I am pleased to see you back. But what horrid clothes you have got on! Do go and change them.

MISS PRISM   Cecily!

CHASUBLE   My child! my child! [CECILY *goes towards* JACK; *he kisses her brow in a melancholy manner.*]

CECILY   What is the matter, Uncle Jack? Do look happy! You look as if you had toothache, and I have got such a surprise for you. Who do you think is in the dining room? Your brother!

JACK   Who?

CECILY   Your brother Ernest. He arrived about half an hour ago.

JACK   What nonsense! I haven't got a brother!

CECILY   Oh, don't say that. However badly he may have behaved to you in the past he is still your brother. You couldn't be so heartless as to disown him. I'll tell him to come out. And you will shake hands with him, won't you, Uncle Jack? [*Runs back into the house.*]

CHASUBLE   These are very joyful tidings.

MISS PRISM   After we had all been resigned to his loss, his sudden return seems to me peculiarly distressing.

JACK   My brother is in the dining room? I don't know what it all means. I think it is perfectly absurd.

[*Enter* ALGERNON *and* CECILY *hand in hand. They come slowly up to* JACK.]

JACK   Good heavens! [*Motions* ALGERNON *away.*]

ALGERNON   Brother John, I have come down from town to tell you that I am very sorry for all the trouble I have given you, and that I intend to lead a better life in the future. [JACK *glares at him and does not take his hand.*]

CECILY   Uncle Jack, you are not going to refuse your own brother's hand?

JACK   Nothing will induce me to take his hand. I think his coming down here disgraceful. He knows perfectly well why.

CECILY   Uncle Jack, do be nice. There is some good in everyone. Ernest has just been telling me about his poor invalid friend Mr. Bunbury whom he goes to visit so often. And surely there must be much good in one who is kind to an invalid, and leaves the pleasures of London to sit by a bed of pain.

JACK   Oh! he has been talking about Bunbury, has he?

CECILY   Yes, he has told me all about poor Mr. Bunbury, and his terrible state of health.

JACK   Bunbury! Well, I won't have him talk to you about Bunbury or about anything else. It is enough to drive one perfectly frantic.

ALGERNON   Of course I admit that the faults were all on my side. But I must say that I think that Brother John's coldness to me is peculiarly painful. I expected a more enthusiastic welcome, especially considering it is the first time I have come here.

CECILY   Uncle Jack, if you don't shake hands with Ernest, I will never forgive you.

JACK   Never forgive me?

CECILY   Never, never, never!

JACK   Well, this is the last time I shall ever do it. [*Shakes hands with* ALGERNON *and glares.*]

CHASUBLE   It's pleasant, is it not, to see so perfect a reconciliation? I think we might leave the two brothers together.

MISS PRISM   Cecily, you will come with us.

CECILY   Certainly, Miss Prism. My little task of reconciliation is over.

CHASUBLE   You have done a beautiful action today, dear child.

MISS PRISM   We must not be premature in our judgments.

CECILY   I feel very happy. [*They all go off.*]

JACK   You young scoundrel, Algy, you must get out of this place as soon as possible. I don't allow any Bunburying here.

[*Enter* MERRIMAN.]

MERRIMAN   I have put Mr. Ernest's things in the room next to yours, sir. I suppose that is all right?

JACK   What?

MERRIMAN   Mr. Ernest's luggage, sir. I have unpacked it and put it in the room next to your own.

JACK   His luggage?

MERRIMAN   Yes, sir. Three portmanteaus, a dressing case, two hat-boxes, and a large luncheon basket.[4]

ALGERNON   I am afraid I can't stay more than a week this time.

JACK   Merriman, order the dogcart[5] at once. Mr. Ernest has been suddenly called back to town.

MERRIMAN   Yes, sir.   [*Goes back into the house.*]

ALGERNON   What a fearful liar you are, Jack. I have not been called back to town at all.

JACK   Yes, you have.

ALGERNON   I haven't heard anyone call me.

JACK   Your duty as a gentleman calls you back.

ALGERNON   My duty as a gentleman has never interfered with my pleasures in the smallest degree.

JACK   I can quite understand that.

ALGERNON   Well, Cecily is a darling.

JACK   You are not to talk of Miss Cardew like that. I don't like it.

ALGERNON   Well, I don't like your clothes. You look perfectly ridiculous in them. Why on earth don't you go up and change? It is perfectly childish to be in deep mourning for a man who is actually staying for a whole week with you in your house as a guest. I call it grotesque.

---

4. According to *Cassell's Domestic Dictionary*, "a convenient little receptacle in which gentlemen who are going out shooting for the day, or artists who wish to sketch, can carry their luncheon with them." "Portmanteaus": large leather suitcases. A "dressing case" (also according to *Cassell's*) was "ordinarily made of rosewood, mahogany or cormandel wood." It was supposed to include "scent bottles, jars for pomade and tooth-powders, hair brushes and combs, shaving, nail and tooth brushes, razors and strop, nail scissors, buttonhook, tweezer, nail file and penknife" [noted by Russell Jackson].

5. A horse-drawn cart with seats, originally designed to carry hunters and their hunting dogs.

JACK   You are certainly not staying with me for a whole week as a guest or anything else. You have got to leave . . . by the four-five train.

ALGERNON   I certainly won't leave you so long as you are in mourning. It would be most unfriendly. If I were in mourning you would stay with me, I suppose. I should think it very unkind if you didn't.

JACK   Well, will you go if I change my clothes?

ALGERNON   Yes, if you are not too long. I never saw anybody take so long to dress, and with such little result.

JACK   Well, at any rate, that is better than being always overdressed as you are.

ALGERNON   If I am occasionally a little overdressed, I make up for it by being always immensely overeducated.

JACK   Your vanity is ridiculous, your conduct an outrage, and your presence in my garden utterly absurd. However, you have got to catch the four-five, and I hope you will have a pleasant journey back to town. This Bunburying, as you call it, has not been a great success for you. [Goes into the house.]

ALGERNON   I think it has been a great success. I'm in love with Cecily, and that is everything.

[Enter CECILY at the back of the garden. She picks up the can and begins to water the flowers.]

But I must see her before I go, and make arrangements for another Bunbury. Ah, there she is.

CECILY   Oh, I merely came back to water the roses. I thought you were with Uncle Jack.

ALGERNON   He's gone to order the dogcart for me.

CECILY   Oh, is he going to take you for a nice drive?

ALGERNON   He's going to send me away.

CECILY   Then have we got to part?

ALGERNON   I am afraid so. It's very painful parting.

CECILY   It is always painful to part from people whom one has known for a very brief space of time. The absence of old friends one can endure with equanimity. But even a momentary separation from anyone to whom one has just been introduced is almost unbearable.

ALGERNON   Thank you.

[Enter MERRIMAN.]

MERRIMAN   The dogcart is at the door, sir. [ALGERNON looks appealingly at CECILY.]

CECILY   It can wait, Merriman . . . for . . . five minutes.

MERRIMAN   Yes, Miss.   [Exit MERRIMAN.]

ALGERNON   I hope, Cecily, I shall not offend you if I state quite frankly and openly that you seem to me to be in every way the visible personification of absolute perfection.

CECILY   I think your frankness does you great credit, Ernest. If you will allow me I will copy your remarks into my diary. [Goes over to table and begins writing in diary.]

ALGERNON   Do you really keep a diary? I'd give anything to look at it. May I?

CECILY   Oh no. [Puts her hand over it.] You see, it is simply a very young girl's record of her own thoughts and impressions, and consequently meant for publication. When it appears in volume form I hope you will order a copy. But pray, Ernest, don't stop. I delight in taking down from dictation. I have reached "absolute perfection." You can go on. I am quite ready for more.

ALGERNON [*Somewhat taken aback.*]   Ahem! Ahem!

CECILY   Oh, don't cough, Ernest. When one is dictating one should speak fluently and not cough. Besides, I don't know how to spell a cough. [*Writes as* ALGERNON *speaks.*]

ALGERNON [*Speaking very rapidly.*]   Cecily, ever since I first looked upon your wonderful and incomparable beauty, I have dared to love you wildly, passionately, devotedly, hopelessly.

CECILY   I don't think that you should tell me that you love me wildly, passionately, devotedly, hopelessly. Hopelessly doesn't seem to make much sense, does it?

ALGERNON   Cecily!

[*Enter* MERRIMAN.]

MERRIMAN   The dogcart is waiting, sir.

ALGERNON   Tell it to come round next week, at the same hour.

MERRIMAN [*Looks at* CECILY, *who makes no sign.*]   Yes, sir.

[MERRIMAN *retires.*]

CECILY   Uncle Jack would be very much annoyed if he knew you were staying on till next week, at the same hour.

ALGERNON   Oh, I don't care about Jack. I don't care for anybody in the whole world but you. I love you, Cecily. You will marry me, won't you?

CECILY   You silly boy! Of course. Why, we have been engaged for the last three months.

ALGERNON   For the last three months?

CECILY   Yes, it will be exactly three months on Thursday.

ALGERNON   But how did we become engaged?

CECILY   Well, ever since dear Uncle Jack first confessed to us that he had a younger brother who was very wicked and bad, you of course have formed the chief topic of conversation between myself and Miss Prism. And of course a man who is much talked about is always very attractive. One feels there must be something in him after all. I daresay it was foolish of me, but I fell in love with you, Ernest.

ALGERNON   Darling! And when was the engagement actually settled?

CECILY   On the 14th of February last. Worn out by your entire ignorance of my existence, I determined to end the matter one way or the other, and after a long struggle with myself I accepted you under this dear old tree here. The next day I bought this little ring in your name, and this is the little bangle with the true lovers' knot I promised you always to wear.

ALGERNON   Did I give you this? It's very pretty, isn't it?

CECILY   Yes, you've wonderfully good taste, Ernest. It's the excuse I've always given for your leading such a bad life. And this is the box in which I keep all your dear letters. [*Kneels at table, opens box, and produces letters tied up with blue ribbon.*]

ALGERNON   My letters! But my own sweet Cecily, I have never written you any letters.

CECILY You need hardly remind me of that, Ernest. I remember only too well that I was forced to write your letters for you. I always wrote three times a week, and sometimes oftener.

ALGERNON Oh, do let me read them, Cecily?

CECILY Oh, I couldn't possibly. They would make you far too conceited. [*Replaces box.*] The three you wrote me after I had broken off the engagement are so beautiful, and so badly spelled, that even now I can hardly read them without crying a little.

ALGERNON But was our engagement ever broken off?

CECILY Of course it was. On the 22nd of last March. You can see the entry if you like. [*Shows diary.*] "Today I broke off my engagement with Ernest. I feel it is better to do so. The weather still continues charming."

ALGERNON But why on earth did you break if off? What had I done? I had done nothing at all. Cecily, I am very much hurt indeed to hear you broke it off. Particularly when the weather was so charming.

CECILY It would hardly have been a really serious engagement if it hadn't been broken off at least once. But I forgave you before the week was out.

ALGERNON [*Crossing to her, and kneeling.*] What a perfect angel you are, Cecily.

CECILY You dear romantic boy. [*He kisses her, she puts her fingers through his hair.*] I hope your hair curls naturally, does it?

ALGERNON Yes, darling, with a little help from others.

CECILY I am so glad.

ALGERNON You'll never break off our engagement again, Cecily?

CECILY I don't think I could break it off now that I have actually met you. Besides, of course, there is the question of your name.

ALGERNON Yes, of course. [*Nervously.*]

CECILY You must not laugh at me, darling, but it had always been a girlish dream of mine to love someone whose name was Ernest. [ALGERNON *rises,* CECILY *also.*] There is something in that name that seems to inspire absolute confidence. I pity any poor married woman whose husband is not called Ernest.

ALGERNON But, my dear child, do you mean to say you could not love me if I had some other name?

CECILY But what name?

ALGERNON Oh, any name you like—Algernon—for instance . . .

CECILY But I don't like the name of Algernon.

ALGERNON Well, my own dear, sweet, loving little darling, I really can't see why you should object to the name of Algernon. It is not at all a bad name. In fact, it is rather an aristocratic name. Half of the chaps who get into the Bankruptcy Court are called Algernon. But seriously, Cecily . . . [*Moving to her.*] . . . if my name was Algy, couldn't you love me?

CECILY [*Rising.*] I might respect you, Ernest, I might admire your character, but I fear that I should not be able to give you my undivided attention.

ALGERNON Ahem! Cecily! [*Picking up hat.*] Your Rector here is, I suppose, thoroughly experienced in the practice of all the rites and ceremonials of the Church?

CECILY Oh, yes. Dr. Chasuble is a most learned man. He has never written a single book, so you can imagine how much he knows.

ALGERNON   I must see him at once on a most important christening—I mean on most important business.

CECILY   Oh!

ALGERNON   I shan't be away more than half an hour.

CECILY   Considering that we have been engaged since February the 14th, and that I only met you today for the first time, I think it is rather hard that you should leave me for so long a period as half an hour. Couldn't you make it twenty minutes?

ALGERNON   I'll be back in no time. [*Kisses her and rushes down the garden.*]

CECILY   What an impetuous boy he is! I like his hair so much. I must enter his proposal in my diary.

[*Enter* MERRIMAN.]

MERRIMAN   A Miss Fairfax has just called to see Mr. Worthing. On very important business, Miss Fairfax states.

CECILY   Isn't Mr. Worthing in his library?

MERRIMAN   Mr. Worthing went over in the direction of the Rectory some time ago.

CECILY   Pray ask the lady to come out here; Mr. Worthing is sure to be back soon. And you can bring tea.

MERRIMAN   Yes, Miss.   [*Goes out.*]

CECILY   Miss Fairfax! I suppose one of the many good elderly women who are associated with Uncle Jack in some of his philanthropic work in London. I don't quite like women who are interested in philanthropic work. I think it is so forward of them.

[*Enter* MERRIMAN.]

MERRIMAN   Miss Fairfax.

[*Enter* GWENDOLEN.]   [*Exit* MERRIMAN.]

CECILY [*Advancing to meet her.*]   Pray let me introduce myself to you. My name is Cecily Cardew.

GWENDOLEN   Cecily Cardew? [*Moving to her and shaking hands.*] What a very sweet name! Something tells me that we are going to be great friends. I like you already more than I can say. My first impressions of people are never wrong.

CECILY   How nice of you to like me so much after we have known each other such a comparatively short time. Pray sit down.

GWENDOLEN [*Still standing up.*]   I may call you Cecily, may I not?

CECILY   With pleasure!

GWENDOLEN   And you will always call me Gwendolen, won't you?

CECILY   If you wish.

GWENDOLEN   Then that is all quite settled, is it not?

CECILY   I hope so. [*A pause. They both sit down together.*]

GWENDOLEN   Perhaps this might be a favorable opportunity for my mentioning who I am. My father is Lord Bracknell. You have never heard of papa, I suppose?

CECILY   I don't think so.

GWENDOLEN   Outside the family circle, papa, I am glad to say, is entirely unknown. I think that is quite as it should be. The home seems to me to be the proper sphere for the man. And certainly once a man begins to neglect his domestic duties he becomes painfully effeminate, does he not? And I don't like that. It makes men so very attractive. Cecily, mamma, whose views on education are remarkably strict, has brought me up to be extremely shortsighted; it is part of her system; so do you mind my looking at you through my glasses?

CECILY   Oh! not at all, Gwendolen. I am very fond of being looked at.

GWENDOLEN [*After examining* CECILY *carefully through a lorgnette.*]   You are here on a short visit, I suppose.

CECILY   Oh no! I live here.

GWENDOLEN [*Severely.*]   Really? Your mother, no doubt, or some female relative of advanced years, resides here also?

CECILY   Oh no! I have no mother, nor, in fact, any relations.

GWENDOLEN   Indeed?

CECILY   My dear guardian, with the assistance of Miss Prism, has the arduous task of looking after me.

GWENDOLEN   Your guardian?

CECILY   Yes, I am Mr. Worthing's ward.

GWENDOLEN   Oh! It is strange he never mentioned to me that he had a ward. How secretive of him! He grows more interesting hourly. I am not sure, however, that the news inspires me with feelings of unmixed delight. [*Rising and going to her.*] I am very fond of you, Cecily; I have liked you ever since I met you! But I am bound to state that now that I know that you are Mr. Worthing's ward, I cannot help expressing a wish you were—well just a little older than you seem to be—and not quite so very alluring in appearance. In fact, if I may speak candidly——

CECILY   Pray do! I think that whenever one has anything unpleasant to say, one should always be quite candid.

GWENDOLEN   Well, to speak with perfect candor, Cecily, I wish that you were fully forty-two, and more than usually plain for your age. Ernest has a strong upright nature. He is the very soul of truth and honor. Disloyalty would be as impossible to him as deception. But even men of the noblest possible moral character are extremely susceptible to the influence of the physical charms of others. Modern, no less than Ancient History, supplies us with many most painful examples of what I refer to. If it were not so, indeed, History would be quite unreadable.

CECILY   I beg your pardon, Gwendolen, did you say Ernest?

GWENDOLEN   Yes.

CECILY   Oh, but it is not Mr. Ernest Worthing who is my guardian. It is his brother—his elder brother.

GWENDOLEN [*Sitting down again.*]   Ernest never mentioned to me that he had a brother.

CECILY   I am sorry to say they have not been on good terms for a long time.

GWENDOLEN   Ah! that accounts for it. And now that I think of it I have never heard any man mention his brother. The subject seems distasteful to most men. Cecily, you have lifted a load from my mind. I was growing almost anxious. It would have been terrible if any cloud had come across a friendship like ours, would it not? Of course you are quite, quite sure that it is not Mr. Ernest Worthing who is your guardian?

CECILY   Quite sure. [*A pause.*] In fact, I am going to be his.

GWENDOLEN [*Inquiringly.*]   I beg your pardon?

CECILY [*Rather shy and confidingly.*]   Dearest Gwendolen, there is no reason why I should make a secret of it to you. Our little county newspaper is sure to chronicle the fact next week. Mr. Ernest Worthing and I are engaged to be married.

GWENDOLEN [*Quite politely, rising.*] My darling Cecily, I think there must be some slight error. Mr. Ernest Worthing is engaged to me. The announcement will appear in the *Morning Post*[6] on Saturday at the latest.

CECILY [*Very politely, rising.*] I am afraid you must be under some misconception. Ernest proposed to me exactly ten minutes ago. [*Shows diary.*]

GWENDOLEN [*Examines diary through her lorgnette carefully.*] It is certainly very curious, for he asked me to be his wife yesterday afternoon at 5:30. If you would care to verify the incident, pray do so. [*Produces diary of her own.*] I never travel without my diary. One should always have something sensational to read in the train. I am so sorry, dear Cecily, if it is any disappointment to you, but I am afraid *I* have the prior claim.

CECILY It would distress me more than I can tell you, dear Gwendolen, if it caused you any mental or physical anguish, but I feel bound to point out that since Ernest proposed to you he clearly has changed his mind.

GWENDOLEN [*Meditatively.*] If the poor fellow has been entrapped into any foolish promise I shall consider it my duty to rescue him at once, and with a firm hand.

CECILY [*Thoughtfully and sadly.*] Whatever unfortunate entanglement my dear boy may have got into, I will never reproach him with it after we are married.

GWENDOLEN Do you allude to me, Miss Cardew, as an entanglement? You are presumptuous. On an occasion of this kind it becomes more than a moral duty to speak one's mind. It becomes a pleasure.

CECILY Do you suggest, Miss Fairfax, that I entrapped Ernest into an engagement? How dare you? This is no time for wearing the shallow mask of manners. When I see a spade I call it a spade.

GWENDOLEN [*Satirically.*] I am glad to say that I have never seen a spade. It is obvious that our social spheres have been widely different.

[*Enter* MERRIMAN, *followed by the footman. He carries a salver, tablecloth, and plate stand.* CECILY *is about to retort. The presence of the servants exercises a restraining influence, under which both girls chafe.*]

MERRIMAN Shall I lay tea here as usual, Miss?

CECILY [*Sternly, in a calm voice.*] Yes, as usual.

[MERRIMAN *begins to clear table and lay cloth. A long pause.* CECILY *and* GWENDOLEN *glare at each other.*]

GWENDOLEN Are there many interesting walks in the vicinity, Miss Cardew?

CECILY Oh! yes! a great many. From the top of one of the hills quite close one can see five counties.

GWENDOLEN Five counties! I don't think I should like that. I hate crowds.

CECILY [*Sweetly.*] I suppose that is why you live in town?

[GWENDOLEN *bites her lip, and beats her foot nervously with her parasol.*]

6. A popular journal featuring society gossip and also announcements of engagements and marriages.

GWENDOLEN [*Looking round.*]   Quite a well-kept garden this is, Miss Cardew.

CECILY   So glad you like it, Miss Fairfax.

GWENDOLEN   I had no idea there were any flowers in the country.

CECILY   Oh, flowers are as common here, Miss Fairfax, as people are in London.

GWENDOLEN   Personally I cannot understand how anybody manages to exist in the country, if anybody who is anybody does. The country always bores me to death.

CECILY   Ah! This is what the newspapers call agricultural depression, is it not? I believe the aristocracy are suffering very much from it just at present.[7] It is almost an epidemic amongst them, I have been told. May I offer you some tea, Miss Fairfax?

GWENDOLEN [*With elaborate politeness.*]   Thank you. [*Aside.*] Detestable girl! But I require tea!

CECILY [*Sweetly.*]   Sugar?

GWENDOLEN [*Superciliously.*]   No, thank you. Sugar is not fashionable any more. [CECILY *looks angrily at her, takes up the tongs and puts four lumps of sugar into the cup.*]

CECILY [*Severely.*]   Cake or bread and butter?

GWENDOLEN [*In a bored manner.*]   Bread and butter, please. Cake is rarely seen at the best houses nowadays.

CECILY [*Cuts a very large slice of cake, and puts it on the tray.*]   Hand that to Miss Fairfax.

> [MERRIMAN *does so, and goes out with footman.* GWENDOLEN *drinks the tea and makes a grimace. Puts down cup at once, reaches out her hand to the bread and butter, looks at it, and finds it is cake. Rises in indignation.*]

GWENDOLEN   You have filled my tea with lumps of sugar, and though I asked most distinctly for bread and butter, you have given me cake. I am known for the gentleness of my disposition, and the extraordinary sweetness of my nature, but I warn you, Miss Cardew, you may go too far.

CECILY [*Rising.*]   To save my poor, innocent, trusting boy from the machinations of any other girl there are no lengths to which I would not go.

GWENDOLEN   From the moment I saw you I distrusted you. I felt that you were false and deceitful. I am never deceived in such matters. My first impressions of people are invariably right.

CECILY   It seems to me, Miss Fairfax, that I am trespassing on your valuable time. No doubt you have many other calls of a similar character to make in the neighborhood.

> [*Enter* JACK.]

GWENDOLEN [*Catching sight of him.*]   Ernest! My own Ernest!

JACK   Gwendolen! Darling! [*Offers to kiss her.*]

GWENDOLEN [*Drawing back.*]   A moment! May I ask if you are engaged to be married to this young lady? [*Points to* CECILY.]

JACK [*Laughing.*]   To dear little Cecily! Of course not! What could have put such an idea into your pretty little head?

---

7. From the 1870s on, landowners (including aristocrats) had been suffering severe losses because of adverse economic conditions.

GWENDOLEN   Thank you. You may! [*Offers her cheek.*]

CECILY [*Very sweetly.*]   I knew there must be some misunderstanding, Miss Fairfax. The gentleman whose arm is at present round your waist is my dear guardian, Mr. John Worthing.

GWENDOLEN   I beg your pardon?

CECILY   This is Uncle Jack.

GWENDOLEN [*Receding.*]   Jack! Oh!

[*Enter* ALGERNON.]

CECILY   Here is Ernest.

ALGERNON [*Goes straight over to* CECILY *without noticing anyone else.*]   My own love! [*Offers to kiss her.*]

CECILY [*Drawing back.*]   A moment, Ernest! May I ask you—are you engaged to be married to this young lady?

ALGERNON [*Looking round.*]   To what young lady? Good heavens! Gwendolen!

CECILY   Yes! to good heavens, Gwendolen, I mean to Gwendolen.

ALGERNON [*Laughing.*]   Of course not! What could have put such an idea into your pretty little head?

CECILY   Thank you. [*Presenting her cheek to be kissed.*] You may. [ALGERNON *kisses her.*]

GWENDOLEN   I felt there was some slight error, Miss Cardew. The gentleman who is now embracing you is my cousin, Mr. Algernon Moncrieff.

CECILY. [*Breaking away from* ALGERNON.] Algernon Moncrieff! Oh! [*The two girls move towards each other and put their arms round each other's waists as if for protection.*]

CECILY   Are you called Algernon?

ALGERNON   I cannot deny it.

CECILY   Oh!

GWENDOLEN   Is your name really John?

JACK [*Standing rather proudly.*]   I could deny it if I liked, I could deny anything if I liked. But my name certainly is John. It has been John for years.

CECILY [*To* GWENDOLEN.]   A gross deception has been practiced on both of us.

GWENDOLEN   My poor wounded Cecily!

CECILY   My sweet wronged Gwendolen!

GWENDOLEN [*Slowly and seriously.*]   You will call me sister, will you not? [*They embrace.* JACK *and* ALGERNON *groan and walk up and down.*]

CECILY [*Rather brightly.*]   There is just one question I would like to be allowed to ask my guardian.

GWENDOLEN   An admirable idea! Mr. Worthing, there is just one question I would like to be permitted to put to you. Where is your brother Ernest? We are both engaged to be married to your brother Ernest, so it is a matter of some importance to us to know where your brother Ernest is at present.

JACK [*Slowly and hesitatingly.*]   Gwendolen—Cecily—it is very painful for me to be forced to speak the truth. It is the first time in my life that I have ever been reduced to such a painful position, and I am really quite inexperienced in doing anything of the kind. However I will tell you quite frankly that I have no brother Ernest. I have no brother at all. I never had a brother in my life, and I certainly have not the smallest intention of ever having one in the future.

CECILY [*Surprised.*]   No brother at all?

JACK [*Cheerily.*]   None!

GWENDOLEN [*Severely.*]   Had you never a brother of any kind?

JACK [*Pleasantly.*]   Never. Not even of any kind.

GWENDOLEN   I am afraid it is quite clear, Cecily, that neither of us is engaged to be married to anyone.

CECILY   It is not a very pleasant position for a young girl suddenly to find herself in. Is it?

GWENDOLEN   Let us go into the house. They will hardly venture to come after us there.

CECILY   No, men are so cowardly, aren't they?

[*They retire into the house with scornful looks.*]

JACK   This ghastly state of things is what you call Bunburying, I suppose?

ALGERNON   Yes, and a perfectly wonderful Bunbury it is. The most wonderful Bunbury I have ever had in my life.

JACK   Well, you've no right whatsoever to Bunbury here.

ALGERNON   That is absurd. One has a right to Bunbury anywhere one chooses. Every serious Bunburyist knows that.

JACK   Serious Bunburyist! Good heavens!

ALGERNON   Well, one must be serious about something, if one wants to have any amusement in life. I happen to be serious about Bunburying. What on earth you are serious about I haven't got the remotest idea. About everything, I should fancy. You have such an absolutely trivial nature.

JACK   Well, the only small satisfaction I have in the whole of this wretched business is that your friend Bunbury is quite exploded. You won't be able to run down to the country quite so often as you used to do, dear Algy. And a very good thing too.

ALGERNON   Your brother is a little off-color, isn't he, dear Jack? You won't be able to disappear to London quite so frequently as your wicked custom was. And not a bad thing either.

JACK   As for your conduct towards Miss Cardew, I must say that your taking in a sweet, simple, innocent girl like that is quite inexcusable. To say nothing of the fact that she is my ward.

ALGERNON   I can see no possible defense at all for your deceiving a brilliant, clever, thoroughly experienced young lady like Miss Fairfax. To say nothing of the fact that she is my cousin.

JACK   I wanted to be engaged to Gwendolen, that is all. I love her.

ALGERNON   Well, I simply wanted to be engaged to Cecily. I adore her.

JACK   There is certainly no chance of your marrying Miss Cardew.

ALGERNON   I don't think there is much likelihood, Jack, of you and Miss Fairfax being united.

JACK   Well, that is no business of yours.

ALGERNON   If it was my business, I wouldn't talk about it. [*Begins to eat muffins.*] It is very vulgar to talk about one's business. Only people like stockbrokers do that, and then merely at dinner parties.

JACK   How can you sit there, calmly eating muffins when we are in this horrible trouble, I can't make out. You seem to me to be perfectly heartless.

ALGERNON   Well, I can't eat muffins in an agitated manner. The butter would probably get on my cuffs. One should always eat muffins quite calmly. It is the only way to eat them.

JACK   I say it's perfectly heartless your eating muffins at all, under the circumstances.

ALGERNON   When I am in trouble, eating is the only thing that consoles me. Indeed, when I am in really great trouble, as anyone who knows me intimately will tell you, I refuse everything except food and drink. At the present moment I am eating muffins because I am unhappy. Besides, I am particularly fond of muffins. [*Rising.*]

JACK [*Rising.*]   Well, that is no reason why you should eat them all in that greedy way. [*Takes muffins from* ALGERNON.]

ALGERNON [*Offering tea cake.*]   I wish you would have tea cake instead. I don't like tea cake.

JACK   Good heavens! I suppose a man may eat his own muffins in his own garden.

ALGERNON   But you have just said it was perfectly heartless to eat muffins.

JACK   I said it was perfectly heartless of you, under the circumstances. That is a very different thing.

ALGERNON   That may be. But the muffins are the same. [*He seizes the muffin dish from* JACK.]

JACK   Algy, I wish to goodness you would go.

ALGERNON   You can't possibly ask me to go without having some dinner. It's absurd. I never go without my dinner. No one ever does, except vegetarians and people like that. Besides I have just made arrangements with Dr. Chasuble to be christened at a quarter to six under the name of Ernest.

JACK   My dear fellow, the sooner you give up that nonsense the better. I made arrangements this morning with Dr. Chasuble to be christened myself at 5:30, and I naturally will take the name of Ernest. Gwendolen would wish it. We can't both be christened Ernest. It's absurd. Besides, I have a perfect right to be christened if I like. There is no evidence at all that I ever have been christened by anybody. I should think it extremely probable I never was, and so does Dr. Chasuble. It is entirely different in your case. You have been christened already.

ALGERNON   Yes, but I have not been christened for years.

JACK   Yes, but you have been christened. That is the important thing.

ALGERNON   Quite so. So I know my constitution can stand it. If you are not quite sure about your ever having been christened, I must say I think it rather dangerous your venturing on it now. It might make you very unwell. You can hardly have forgotten that someone very closely connected with you was very nearly carried off this week in Paris by a severe chill.

JACK   Yes, but you said yourself that a severe chill was not hereditary.

ALGERNON   It usen't to be, I know—but I daresay it is now. Science is always making wonderful improvements in things.

JACK [*Picking up the muffin dish.*]   Oh, that is nonsense; you are always talking nonsense.

ALGERNON   Jack, you are at the muffins again! I wish you wouldn't. There are only two left. [*Takes them.*] I told you I was particularly fond of muffins.

JACK   But I hate tea cake.

ALGERNON   Why on earth then do you allow tea cake to be served up for your guests? What ideas you have of hospitality!

JACK   Algernon! I have already told you to go. I don't want you here. Why don't you go!

ALGERNON   I haven't quite finished my tea yet! and there is still one muffin left. [*Jack groans, and sinks into a chair.* ALGERNON *still continues eating.*]

ACT-DROP

Third Act

SCENE—*Morning room*[8] *at the Manor House.*

[GWENDOLEN *and* CECILY *are at the window, looking out into the garden.*]

GWENDOLEN   The fact that they did not follow us at once into the house, as anyone else would have done, seems to me to show that they have some sense of shame left.

CECILY   They have been eating muffins. That looks like repentance.

GWENDOLEN [*After a pause.*]   They don't seem to notice us at all. Couldn't you cough?

CECILY   But I haven't got a cough.

GWENDOLEN   They're looking at us. What effrontery!

CECILY   They're approaching. That's very forward of them.

GWENDOLEN   Let us preserve a dignified silence.

CECILY   Certainly. It's the only thing to do now.

[*Enter* JACK *followed by* ALGERNON. *They whistle some dreadful popular air from a British Opera.*[9]]

GWENDOLEN   This dignified silence seems to produce an unpleasant effect.

CECILY   A most distasteful one.

GWENDOLEN   But we will not be the first to speak.

CECILY   Certainly not.

GWENDOLEN   Mr. Worthing, I have something very particular to ask you. Much depends on your reply.

CECILY   Gwendolen, your common sense is invaluable. Mr. Moncrieff, kindly answer me the following question. Why did you pretend to be my guardian's brother?

ALGERNON   In order that I might have an opportunity of meeting you.

CECILY [*To* GWENDOLEN.]   That certainly seems a satisfactory explanation, does it not?

GWENDOLEN   Yes, dear, if you can believe him.

CECILY   I don't. But that does not affect the wonderful beauty of his answer.

GWENDOLEN   True. In matters of grave importance, style, not sincerity is the vital thing. Mr. Worthing, what explanation can you offer to me for

8. A relatively informally furnished room for receiving visitors making morning calls (usually close friends of the host or hostess). Afternoon visitors, on the other hand, would be received in the drawing room, a much more formal and elegant setting.

9. Probably a reference to one of the operas of Gilbert and Sullivan.

pretending to have a brother? Was it in order that you might have an opportunity of coming up to town to see me as often as possible?

JACK Can you doubt it, Miss Fairfax?

GWENDOLEN I have the gravest doubts upon the subject. But I intend to crush them. This is not the moment for German skepticism.[1] [*Moving to* CECILY.] Their explanations appear to be quite satisfactory, especially Mr. Worthing's. That seems to me to have the stamp of truth upon it.

CECILY I am more than content with what Mr. Moncrieff said. His voice alone inspires one with absolute credulity.

GWENDOLEN Then you think we should forgive them?

CECILY Yes. I mean no.

GWENDOLEN True! I had forgotten. There are principles at stake that one cannot surrender. Which of us should tell them? The task is not a pleasant one.

CECILY Could we not both speak at the same time?

GWENDOLEN An excellent idea! I nearly always speak at the same time as other people. Will you take the time from me?

CECILY Certainly. [GWENDOLEN *beats time with uplifted finger.*]

GWENDOLEN AND CECILY [*Speaking together.*] Your Christian names are still an insuperable barrier. That is all!

JACK AND ALGERNON [*Speaking together.*] Our Christian names! Is that all? But we are going to be christened this afternoon.

GWENDOLEN [*To* JACK.] For my sake you are prepared to do this terrible thing?

JACK I am.

CECILY [*To* ALGERNON.] To please me you are ready to face this fearful ordeal?

ALGERNON I am!

GWENDOLEN How absurd to talk of the equality of the sexes! Where questions of self-sacrifice are concerned, men are infinitely beyond us.

JACK We are. [*Clasps hands with* ALGERNON.]

CECILY They have moments of physical courage of which we women know absolutely nothing.

GWENDOLEN [*To* JACK.] Darling!

ALGERNON [*To* CECILY.] Darling. [*They fall into each other's arms.*]

[*Enter* MERRIMAN. *When he enters he coughs loudly, seeing the situation.*]

MERRIMAN Ahem! Ahem! Lady Bracknell!

JACK Good heavens!

[*Enter* LADY BRACKNELL. *The couples separate in alarm. Exit* MERRIMAN.]

LADY BRACKNELL Gwendolen! What does this mean?

GWENDOLEN Merely that I am engaged to be married to Mr. Worthing, mamma.

LADY BRACKNELL Come here. Sit down. Sit down immediately. Hesitation of any kind is a sign of mental decay in the young, of physical weakness

---

1. Many 19th-century German scholars (e.g., D. F. Strauss) seemed, in England, to be notoriously skeptical in their analyses of religious texts.

in the old. [*Turns to* JACK.] Apprised, sir, of my daughter's sudden flight by her trusty maid, whose confidence I purchased by means of a small coin, I followed her at once by a luggage train. Her unhappy father is, I am glad to say, under the impression that she is attending a more than usually lengthy lecture by the University Extension Scheme on the Influence of a Permanent Income on Thought. I do not propose to undeceive him. Indeed I have never undeceived him on any question. I would consider it wrong. But of course, you will clearly understand that all communication between yourself and my daughter must cease immediately from this moment. On this point, as indeed on all points, I am firm.

JACK   I am engaged to be married to Gwendolen, Lady Bracknell!

LADY BRACKNELL   You are nothing of the kind, sir. And now, as regards Algernon! . . . Algernon!

ALGERNON   Yes, Aunt Augusta.

LADY BRACKNELL   May I ask if it is in this house that your invalid friend Mr. Bunbury resides?

ALGERNON [*Stammering.*]   Oh! No! Bunbury doesn't live here. Bunbury is somewhere else at present. In fact, Bunbury is dead.

LADY BRACKNELL   Dead! When did Mr. Bunbury die? His death must have been extremely sudden.

ALGERNON [*Airily.*]   Oh! I killed Bunbury this afternoon. I mean poor Bunbury died this afternoon.

LADY BRACKNELL   What did he die of?

ALGERNON   Bunbury? Oh, he was quite exploded.

LADY BRACKNELL   Exploded! Was he the victim of a revolutionary outrage? I was not aware that Mr. Bunbury was interested in social legislation. If so, he is well punished for his morbidity.

ALGERNON   My dear Aunt Augusta, I mean he was found out! The doctors found out that Bunbury could not live, that is what I mean—so Bunbury died.

LADY BRACKNELL   He seems to have had great confidence in the opinion of his physicians. I am glad, however, that he made up his mind at the last to some definite course of action, and acted under proper medical advice. And now that we have finally got rid of this Mr. Bunbury, may I ask, Mr. Worthing, who is that young person whose hand my nephew Algernon is now holding in what seems to me a peculiarly unnecessary manner?

JACK   That lady is Miss Cecily Cardew, my ward.

[LADY BRACKNELL *bows coldly to* CECILY.]

ALGERNON   I am engaged to be married to Cecily, Aunt Augusta.

LADY BRACKNELL   I beg your pardon?

CECILY   Mr. Moncrieff and I are engaged to be married, Lady Bracknell.

LADY BRACKNELL [*With a shiver, crossing to the sofa and sitting down.*]   I do not know whether there is anything peculiarly exciting in the air of this particular part of Hertfordshire, but the number of engagements that go on seems to me considerably above the proper average that statistics have laid down for our guidance. I think some preliminary inquiry on my part would not be out of place. Mr. Worthing, is Miss Cardew at all connected with any of the larger railway stations in London? I merely desire information. Until yesterday I had no idea that there were any families or persons whose origin was a Terminus.[2] [JACK *looks perfectly furious, but restrains himself.*]

JACK [*In a clear, cold voice.*]   Miss Cardew is the granddaughter of the late Mr. Thomas Cardew of 149, Belgrave Square, S.W.; Gervase Park, Dorking, Surrey; and the Sporran, Fifeshire, N.B.[3]

LADY BRACKNELL   That sounds not unsatisfactory. Three addresses always inspire confidence, even in tradesmen. But what proof have I of their authenticity?

JACK   I have carefully preserved the Court Guides of the period. They are open to your inspection, Lady Bracknell.

LADY BRACKNELL [*Grimly.*]   I have known strange errors in that publication.

JACK   Miss Cardew's family solicitors are Messrs. Markby, Markby, and Markby.

LADY BRACKNELL   Markby, Markby, and Markby? A firm of the very highest position in their profession. Indeed I am told that one of the Mr. Markbys is occasionally to be seen at dinner parties. So far I am satisfied.

JACK [*Very irritably.*]   How extremely kind of you, Lady Bracknell! I have also in my possession, you will be pleased to hear, certificates of Miss Cardew's birth, baptism, whooping cough, registration, vaccination, confirmation, and the measles; both the German and the English variety.

LADY BRACKNELL   Ah! A life crowded with incident, I see; though perhaps somewhat too exciting for a young girl. I am not myself in favor of premature experiences. [*Rises, looks at her watch.*] Gwendolen! the time approaches for our departure. We have not a moment to lose. As a matter of form, Mr. Worthing, I had better ask you if Miss Cardew has any little fortune?

JACK   Oh! about a hundred and thirty thousand pounds in the Funds.[4] That is all. Good-bye, Lady Bracknell. So pleased to have seen you.

LADY BRACKNELL [*Sitting down again.*]   A moment, Mr. Worthing. A hundred and thirty thousand pounds! And in the Funds! Miss Cardew seems to me a most attractive young lady, now that I look at her. Few girls of the present day have any really solid qualities, any of the qualities that last, and improve with time. We live, I regret to say, in an age of surfaces. [*To* CECILY.] Come over here, dear. [CECILY *goes across.*] Pretty child! your dress is sadly simple, and your hair seems almost as Nature might have left it. But we can soon alter all that. A thoroughly experienced French maid produces a really marvelous result in a very brief space of time. I remember recommending one to young Lady Lancing, and after three months her own husband did not know her.

JACK [*Aside.*]   And after six months nobody knew her.

LADY BRACKNELL [*Glares at* JACK *for a few moments. Then bends, with a practiced smile, to* CECILY.]   Kindly turn round, sweet child. [CECILY *turns completely round.*] No, the side view is what I want. [CECILY *presents her profile.*] Yes, quite as I expected. There are distinct social possibilities in your profile. The two weak points in our age are its want of principle and its want of profile. The chin a little higher, dear. Style

---

2. Station at the end of a railway line.
3. Presumably North Britain, i.e., Scotland.

4. Interest-bearing government bonds.

largely depends on the way the chin is worn. They are worn very high, just at present. Algernon!

ALGERNON   Yes, Aunt Augusta!

LADY BRACKNELL   There are distinct social possibilities in Miss Cardew's profile.

ALGERNON   Cecily is the sweetest, dearest, prettiest girl in the whole world. And I don't care twopence about social possibilities.

LADY BRACKNELL   Never speak disrespectfully of Society, Algernon. Only people who can't get into it do that. [*To* CECILY.] Dear child, of course you know that Algernon has nothing but his debts to depend upon. But I do not approve of mercenary marriages. When I married Lord Bracknell I had no fortune of any kind. But I never dreamed for a moment of allowing that to stand in my way. Well, I suppose I must give my consent.

ALGERNON   Thank you, Aunt Augusta.

LADY BRACKNELL   Cecily, you may kiss me!

CECILY [*Kisses her.*]   Thank you, Lady Bracknell.

LADY BRACKNELL. You may also address me as Aunt Augusta for the future.

CECILY   Thank you, Aunt Augusta.

LADY BRACKNELL   The marriage, I think, had better take place quite soon.

ALGERNON   Thank you, Aunt Augusta.

CECILY   Thank you, Aunt Augusta.

LADY BRACKNELL   To speak frankly, I am not in favor of long engagements. They give people the opportunity of finding out each other's character before marriage, which I think is never advisable.

JACK   I beg your pardon for interrupting you, Lady Bracknell, but this engagement is quite out of the question. I am Miss Cardew's guardian, and she cannot marry without my consent until she comes of age. That consent I absolutely decline to give.

LADY BRACKNELL   Upon what grounds may I ask? Algernon is an extremely, I may almost say an ostentatiously, eligible young man. He has nothing, but he looks everything. What more can one desire?

JACK   It pains me very much to have to speak frankly to you, Lady Bracknell, about your nephew, but the fact is that I do not approve at all of his moral character. I suspect him of being untruthful. [ALGERNON *and* CECILY *look at him in indignant amazement.*]

LADY BRACKNELL   Untruthful! My nephew Algernon? Impossible! He is an Oxonian.[5]

JACK   I fear there can be no possible doubt about the matter. This afternoon, during my temporary absence in London on an important question of romance, he obtained admission to my house by means of the false pretense of being my brother. Under an assumed name he drank, I've just been informed by my butler, an entire pint bottle of my Perrier-Jouet, Brut, '89;[6] a wine I was specially reserving for myself. Continuing his disgraceful deception, he succeeded in the course of the afternoon in alienating the affections of my only ward. He subsequently stayed to tea, and devoured every single muffin. And what makes his conduct all the more heartless is, that he was perfectly well aware from the first that

---

5. I.e., he had been a student at Oxford (originally spelled *Oxenford*).

6. An outstanding brand and year of dry champagne.

I have no brother, that I never had a brother, and that I don't intend to have a brother, not even of any kind. I distinctly told him so myself yesterday afternoon.

LADY BRACKNELL Ahem! Mr. Worthing, after careful consideration I have decided entirely to overlook my nephew's conduct to you.

JACK That is very generous of you, Lady Bracknell. My own decision, however, is unalterable. I decline to give my consent.

LADY BRACKNELL [*To* CECILY.] Come here, sweet child. [CECILY *goes over.*] How old are you, dear?

CECILY Well, I am really only eighteen, but I always admit to twenty when I go to evening parties.

LADY BRACKNELL You are perfectly right in making some slight alteration. Indeed, no woman should ever be quite accurate about her age. It looks so calculating. . . . [*In a meditative manner.*] Eighteen, but admitting to twenty at evening parties. Well, it will not be very long before you are of age and free from the restraints of tutelage. So I don't think your guardian's consent is, after all, a matter of any importance.

JACK Pray excuse me, Lady Bracknell, for interrupting you again, but it is only fair to tell you that according to the terms of her grandfather's will Miss Cardew does not come legally of age till she is thirty-five.

LADY BRACKNELL That does not seem to me to be a grave objection. Thirty-five is a very attractive age. London society is full of women of the very highest birth who have, of their own free choice, remained thirty-five for years. Lady Dumbleton is an instance in point. To my own knowledge she has been thirty-five ever since she arrived at the age of forty, which was many years ago now. I see no reason why our dear Cecily should not be even still more attractive at the age you mention than she is at present. There will be a large accumulation of property.

CECILY Algy, could you wait for me till I was thirty-five?

ALGERNON Of course I could, Cecily. You know I could.

CECILY Yes, I felt it instinctively, but I couldn't wait all that time. I hate waiting even five minutes for anybody. It always makes me rather cross. I am not punctual myself, I know, but I do like punctuality in others, and waiting, even to be married, is quite out of the question.

ALGERNON Then what is to be done, Cecily?

CECILY I don't know, Mr. Moncrieff.

LADY BRACKNELL My dear Mr. Worthing, as Miss Cardew states positively that she cannot wait till she is thirty-five—a remark which I am bound to say seems to me to show a somewhat impatient nature—I would beg of you to reconsider your decision.

JACK But my dear Lady Bracknell, the matter is entirely in your own hands. The moment you consent to my marriage with Gwendolen, I will most gladly allow your nephew to form an alliance with my ward.

LADY BRACKNELL [*Rising and drawing herself up.*] You must be quite aware that what you propose is out of the question.

JACK Then a passionate celibacy is all that any of us can look forward to.

LADY BRACKNELL This is not the destiny I propose for Gwendolen. Algernon, of course, can choose for himself. [*Pulls out her watch.*] Come, dear; [GWENDOLEN *rises.*] we have already missed five, if not six, trains. To miss any more might expose us to comment on the platform.

[*Enter* DR. CHASUBLE.]

CHASUBLE   Everything is quite ready for the christenings.

LADY BRACKNELL   The christenings, sir! Is not that somewhat premature!

CHASUBLE [*Looking rather puzzled, and pointing to* JACK *and* ALGERNON.]   Both these gentlemen have expressed a desire for immediate baptism.

LADY BRACKNELL   At their age? The idea is grotesque and irreligious! Algernon, I forbid you to be baptized. I will not hear of such excesses. Lord Bracknell would be highly displeased if he learned that that was the way in which you wasted your time and money.

CHASUBLE   Am I to understand then that there are to be no christenings at all this afternoon?

JACK   I don't think that, as things are now, it would be of much practical value to either of us, Dr. Chasuble.

CHASUBLE   I am grieved to hear such sentiments from you, Mr. Worthing. They savor of the heretical views of the Anabaptists,[7] views that I have completely refuted in four of my unpublished sermons. However, as your present mood seems to be one peculiarly secular, I will return to the church at once. Indeed, I have just been informed by the pew-opener[8] that for the last hour and a half Miss Prism has been waiting for me in the vestry.

LADY BRACKNELL [*Starting.*]   Miss Prism! Did I hear you mention a Miss Prism?

CHASUBLE   Yes, Lady Bracknell. I am on my way to join her.

LADY BRACKNELL   Pray allow me to detain you for a moment. This matter may prove to be one of vital importance to Lord Bracknell and myself. Is this Miss Prism a female of repellent aspect, remotely connected with education?

CHASUBLE [*Somewhat indignantly.*]   She is the most cultivated of ladies, and the very picture of respectability.

LADY BRACKNELL   It is obviously the same person. May I ask what position she holds in your household?

CHASUBLE [*Severely.*]   I am a celibate, madam.

JACK [*Interposing.*]   Miss Prism, Lady Bracknell, has been for the last three years Miss Cardew's esteemed governess and valued companion.

LADY BRACKNELL   In spite of what I hear of her, I must see her at once. Let her be sent for.

CHASUBLE [*Looking off.*]   She approaches; she is nigh.

[*Enter* MISS PRISM *hurriedly.*]

MISS PRISM   I was told you expected me in the vestry, dear Canon. I have been waiting for you there for an hour and three quarters. [*Catches sight of* LADY BRACKNELL *who has fixed her with a stony glare.* MISS PRISM *grows pale and quails. She looks anxiously round as if desirous to escape.*]

LADY BRACKNELL [*In a severe, judicial voice.*]   Prism! [MISS PRISM *bows her head in shame.*] Come here, Prism! [MISS PRISM *approaches in a humble manner.*] Prism! Where is that baby? [*General consternation.* THE CANON *starts back in horror.* ALGERNON *and* JACK *pretend to be anxious to shield*

---

7. A radical Protestant sect of the 17th century, whose views about baptism were regarded as heretical by Anglicans.

8. A person employed at church services to usher worshipers to their pews and open the doors for them.

CECILY *and* GWENDOLEN *from hearing the details of a terrible public scandal.*] Twenty-eight years ago, Prism, you left Lord Bracknell's house, Number 104, Upper Grosvenor Street, in charge of a perambulator that contained a baby, of the male sex. You never returned. A few weeks later, through the elaborate investigations of the Metropolitan police, the perambulator was discovered at midnight, standing by itself in a remote corner of Bayswater.[9] It contained the manuscript of a three-volume novel of more than usually revolting sentimentality. [MISS PRISM *starts in involuntary indignation.*] But the baby was not there! [*Everyone looks at* MISS PRISM.] Prism! Where is that baby? [*A pause.*]

MISS PRISM Lady Bracknell, I admit with shame that I do not know. I only wish I did. The plain facts of the case are these. On the morning of the day you mention, a day that is forever branded on my memory, I prepared as usual to take the baby out in its perambulator. I had also with me a somewhat old, but capacious handbag, in which I had intended to place the manuscript of a work of fiction that I had written during my few unoccupied hours. In a moment of mental abstraction, for which I never can forgive myself, I deposited the manuscript in the bassinette, and placed the baby in the handbag.

JACK [*Who has been listening attentively.*] But where did you deposit the handbag?

MISS PRISM. Do not ask me, Mr. Worthing.

JACK Miss Prism, this is a matter of no small importance to me. I insist on knowing where you deposited the handbag that contained that infant.

MISS PRISM I left it in the cloak room of one of the larger railway stations in London.

JACK What railway station?

MISS PRISM [*Quite crushed.*] Victoria. The Brighton line. [*Sinks into a chair.*]

JACK I must retire to my room for a moment. Gwendolen, wait here for me.

GWENDOLEN If you are not too long, I will wait here for you all my life.

[*Exit* JACK *in great excitement.*]

CHASUBLE What do you think this means, Lady Bracknell?

LADY BRACKNELL I dare not even suspect, Dr. Chasuble. I need hardly tell you that in families of high position strange coincidences are not supposed to occur. They are hardly considered the thing.

[*Noises heard overhead as if someone was throwing trunks about. Everyone looks up.*]

CECILY Uncle Jack seems strangely agitated.

CHASUBLE Your guardian has a very emotional nature.

LADY BRACKNELL This noise is extremely unpleasant. It sounds as if he was having an argument. I dislike arguments of any kind. They are always vulgar, and often convincing.

CHASUBLE [*Looking up.*] It has stopped now. [*The noise is redoubled.*]

LADY BRACKNELL I wish he would arrive at some conclusion.

GWENDOLEN This suspense is terrible. I hope it will last.

[*Enter* JACK *with a handbag of black leather in his hand.*]

9. A once fashionable locality in the West End near Kensington Gardens.

JACK [*Rushing over to* MISS PRISM.] Is this the handbag, Miss Prism? Examine it carefully before you speak. The happiness of more than one life depends on your answer.

MISS PRISM [*Calmly.*] It seems to be mine. Yes, here is the injury it received through the upsetting of a Gower Street omnibus in younger and happier days. Here is the stain on the lining caused by the explosion of a temperance beverage, an incident that occurred at Leamington. And here, on the lock, are my initials. I had forgotten that in an extravagant mood I had had them placed there. The bag is undoubtedly mine. I am delighted to have it so unexpectedly restored to me. It has been a great inconvenience being without it all these years.

JACK [*In a pathetic voice.*] Miss Prism, more is restored to you than this handbag. I was the baby you placed in it.

MISS PRISM [*Amazed.*] You!

JACK [*Embracing her.*] Yes . . . mother!

MISS PRISM [*Recoiling in indignant astonishment.*] Mr. Worthing! I am unmarried!

JACK Unmarried! I do not deny that is a serious blow. But after all, who has the right to cast a stone against one who has suffered? Cannot repentance wipe out an act of folly? Why should there be one law for men, and another for women? Mother, I forgive you. [*Tries to embrace her again.*]

MISS PRISM [*Still more indignant.*] Mr. Worthing, there is some error. [*Pointing to* LADY BRACKNELL.] There is the lady who can tell you who you really are.

JACK [*After a pause.*] Lady Bracknell, I hate to seem inquisitive, but would you kindly inform me who I am?

LADY BRACKNELL I am afraid that the news I have to give you will not altogether please you. You are the son of my poor sister, Mrs. Moncrieff, and consequently Algernon's elder brother.

JACK Algy's elder brother! Then I have a brother after all. I knew I had a brother! I always said I had a brother! Cecily—how could you have ever doubted that I had a brother? [*Seizes hold of* ALGERNON.] Dr. Chasuble, my unfortunate brother. Miss Prism, my unfortunate brother. Gwendolen, my unfortunate brother. Algy, you young scoundrel, you will have to treat me with more respect in the future. You have never behaved to me like a brother in all your life.

ALGERNON Well, not till today, old boy, I admit. I did my best, however, though I was out of practice. [*Shakes hands.*]

GWENDOLEN [*To* JACK.] My own! But what own are you? What is your Christian name, now that you have become someone else?

JACK Good heavens! . . . I had quite forgotten that point. Your decision on the subject of my name is irrevocable, I suppose?

GWENDOLEN I never change, except in my affections.

CECILY What a noble nature you have, Gwendolen!

JACK Then the question had better be cleared up at once. Aunt Augusta, a moment. At the time when Miss Prism left me in the handbag, had I been christened already?

LADY BRACKNELL Every luxury that money could buy, including christening, had been lavished on you by your fond and doting parents.

JACK   Then I was christened! That is settled. Now, what name was I given? Let me know the worst.

LADY BRACKNELL   Being the eldest son you were naturally christened after your father.

JACK [*Irritably.*]   Yes, but what was my father's Christian name?

LADY BRACKNELL [*Meditatively.*]   I cannot at the present moment recall what the General's Christian name was. But I have no doubt he had one. He was eccentric, I admit. But only in later years. And that was the result of the Indian climate, and marriage, and indigestion, and other things of that kind.

JACK   Algy! Can't you recollect what our father's Christian name was?

ALGERNON   My dear boy, we were never even on speaking terms. He died before I was a year old.

JACK   His name would appear in the Army Lists of the period, I suppose, Aunt Augusta?

LADY BRACKNELL   The General was essentially a man of peace, except in his domestic life. But I have no doubt his name would appear in any military directory.

JACK   The Army Lists of the last forty years are here. These delightful records should have been my constant study. [*Rushes to bookcase and tears the books out.*] M. Generals . . . Mallam, Maxbohm,[1] Magley, what ghastly names they have—Markby, Migsby, Mobbs, Moncrieff! Lieutenant 1840, Captain, Lieutenant Colonel, Colonel, General 1869, Christian names, Ernest John. [*Puts book very quietly down and speaks quite calmly.*] I always told you, Gwendolen, my name was Ernest, didn't I? Well it is Ernest after all. I mean it naturally is Ernest.

LADY BRACKNELL   Yes, I remember now that the General was called Ernest. I knew I had some particular reason for disliking the name.

GWENDOLEN   Ernest! My own Ernest! I felt from the first that you could have no other name!

JACK   Gwendolen, it is a terrible thing for a man to find out suddenly that all his life he has been speaking nothing but the truth. Can you forgive me?

GWENDOLEN   I can. For I feel that you are sure to change.

JACK   My own one!

CHASUBLE [*To* MISS PRISM.]   Laetitia! [*Embraces her.*]

MISS PRISM [*Enthusiastically.*]   Frederick! At last!

ALGERNON   Cecily! [*Embraces her.*] At last!

JACK   Gwendolen! [*Embraces her.*] At last!

LADY BRACKNELL   My nephew, you seem to be displaying signs of triviality.

JACK   On the contrary, Aunt Augusta, I've now realized for the first time in my life the vital Importance of Being Earnest.

CURTAIN

performed 1895   1899

---

1. A play on the name of Max Beerbohm (1872–1956), English essayist, caricaturist, and parodist.

BERNARD SHAW
1856–1950

Winston Churchill described Bernard Shaw as a "bright, nimble, fierce, and comprehending being, Jack Frost dancing bespangled in the sunshine." Churchill's words not only name essential qualities of the man but also suggest how long his life and historical reach were. Born and raised in the Victorian period, Shaw continued an important public figure until his death in 1950. His experience encompassed the momentous historical changes of the last half of the nineteenth century and the first half of the twentieth. Shaw made it his business to pronounce on them all in the witty epigrammatic style that characterizes his plays. He was an engaged public intellectual, who created himself as a remarkable public character.

Like Oscar Wilde, the other playwright whose work changed the course of British drama, Shaw was an Irishman. He was born in Dublin, in Shaw's own words, "the fruit of an unsuitable marriage between two quite amiable people who finally separated in the friendliest fashion." His mother, an aspiring singer, went to London to pursue her musical career; Shaw followed five years later, in 1876, quitting the job he had held since the age of fifteen at a land agent's office. His intention was to become a novelist. He spent much of his time in the Reading Room of the British Museum, where a young journalist named William Archer introduced himself because he was so intrigued by the combination of things Shaw was studying—Marx's *Das Kapital* and the score of Wagner's opera, *Tristan and Isolde*.

These two works indicate the main involvements of Shaw's life in London. *Das Kapital* convinced him that socialism was the answer to society's problems. With the socialist economist Sidney Webb and his wife, also a socialist economist, Beatrice Webb, Shaw joined the Fabian Society, a socialist organization that had committed itself to gradual reform rather than revolution. Shaw quickly became a leader in the group and its principal spokesman. His pronouncements and tracts had a wit absent from most political writing. *In Fabian Tract No. 2*, for example, he argued that nineteenth-century capitalism had divided society "into hostile classes, with large appetites and no dinners at one extreme and large dinners and no appetites at the other." Though painfully shy, he disciplined himself to become an accomplished public speaker. Accepting fees from no one, he spoke everywhere, stipulating only that he could speak on whatever subject he liked.

Meanwhile, his acquaintance with William Archer led him to journalism. He worked first as an art critic, then as a music critic, championing the operas of Richard Wagner and introducing a new standard of wit and judgment to music reviewing, writing of a hapless soprano who "fell fearlessly on Mozart and was defeated with heavy loss to the hearers," a corps de ballet, that "wandered about in the prompt corner as if some vivisector had removed from their heads that portion of the brain which enables us to find our way out the door," or Schubert's "Death and the Maiden" quartet, which makes one "reconciled to Death and indifferent to the Maiden." Shaw then turned to drama criticism, where he later described his work as "a siege laid to the theater of the XIXth Century by an author who had to cut his own way into it at the point of the pen, and throw some of its defenders into the moat." Just as he championed the music of Wagner, he now championed the plays of the Norwegian dramatist, Henrik Ibsen. In 1891 he published *The Quintessence of Ibsenism*, in which, in setting out the reasons for his admiration of Ibsen, he defined the kind of drama he wanted to write.

In the first ten years of his life in London, Shaw had written five unsuccessful novels. When he turned to drama in the 1890s, he found his medium. Shaw's first play, *Widowers' Houses* (1892), dealt with the problem of slum landlords. Though it ran only two performances, Shaw's career as a dramatist was launched. In the course of his career he wrote more than fifty plays. Among the most famous are *Mrs. Warren's Profession* (1893), *Arms and the Man* (1894), *Candida* (1894), *The Devil's Disciple* (1896), *Caesar and Cleopatra* (1898), *Man and Superman* (1903), *Major Barbara* (1905), *Androcles and the*

Lion (1912), *Pygmalion* (1912; later the basis of the musical *My Fair Lady*), *Heartbreak House* (1919), *Back to Methuselah* (1920), and *Saint Joan* (1923). (Because the production and publication history of Shaw's plays is so complex, this list gives the date of composition.) Shaw at first had difficulty getting his plays performed. Therefore, in 1898 he decided to publish them in book form as *Plays Pleasant and Unpleasant,* for which he wrote a didactic preface, the first of many that he provided his plays. Then in 1904, the producer and Shakespearean Harley Granville-Barker put on *Candida* at the Royal Court Theater, which he was managing. The play was a success, and Shaw went on to work with Barker in making the Royal Court the center for avant-garde drama in London.

In *The Quintessence of Ibsenism,* Shaw defines the elements of the kind of theater he aspired to create:

> first, the introduction of the discussion and its development until it so over-spreads and interpenetrates the action that it finally assimilates it, making play and discussion practically identical; and second, as a consequence of making the spectators themselves the persons of the drama, and the incidents of their own lives its incidents, the disuse of the old stage tricks by which audiences had to be induced to take an interest in unreal people and improbable circumstances, and the substitution of a forensic technique of recrimination, disillusion, and penetration through ideals to the truth, with a free use of all the rhetorical and lyrical arts of the orator, the preacher, the pleader, and the rhapsodist.

Shaw created a drama of ideas, in which his characters strenuously argue points of view that justify their social positions—the prostitute in *Mrs. Warren's Profession*, the munitions manufacturer in *Major Barbara*. His object is to attack the complacencies and conventional moralism of his audience. By the rhetorical brilliance of his dialogue and by surprising reversals of plot conventions, Shaw manipulates his audience into a position of uncomfortable sympathy with points of view and characters that violate traditional assumptions.

By the end of the first decade of the twentieth century, as a result of the success of his plays at the Royal Court Theater, Shaw had become a literary celebrity. Like Oscar Wilde, he had worked to develop a public persona, but with a substantial difference in aim. Whereas Wilde used his public image to define an aesthetic point of view, Shaw used his public personality—iconoclastic, clownish, argumentative— to advocate social ideas. He was radical in many respects. He was a vegetarian, a nonsmoker, and a nondrinker. He was courageous enough to be a pacifist in World War I. He championed the reform of English spelling and punctuation. He believed in women's rights and the abolition of private property. He also believed in the Life Force and progressive evolution, driven by the power of the human will, a point of view that led to sympathy with Mussolini and other dictators before World War II. Shaw's insistent rationality made some of his contemporaries view him as bloodless. After seeing *Arms and the Man,* Yeats described a nightmare in which he was haunted by a sewing machine, "that clicked and shone, but the incredible thing was that the machine smiled, smiled perpetually." However, Yeats goes on to say, "Yet I delighted in Shaw the formidable man. He could hit my enemies and the enemies of all I loved, as I could never hit, as no living author that was dear to me could ever hit."

Shaw wrote *Mrs. Warren's Profession* in 1893, but though it was published in *Plays Pleasant and Unpleasant* in 1898, public performance was long prohibited by British censors. In 1902, the Stage Society, technically a private club and so not under the jurisdiction of the censors, gave performances for its own members. The play was produced in New York in 1905; but it was closed down by the police, and the producer and his company were arrested. They were eventually acquitted, and the play was allowed to continue. Legal public performance in England did not take place until 1926, the year after Shaw won the Nobel Prize.

Shaw's preface to the play attacks the confusions and contradictions involved in the censorship of plays and contains an eloquent plea for the recognition of the seriousness and morality of *Mrs. Warren's Profession*. The play was written, he tells us, "to draw attention to the truth that prostitution is caused, not by female depravity and male licentiousness, but simply by underpaying, undervaluing, and overworking women so shamefully that the poorest of them are forced to resort to prostitution to keep body and soul together. He argues that Mrs. Warren's defense of herself in the play is "valid and unanswerable." Shaw's discussion of Mrs. Warren's self-justification continues:

> But it is no defense at all of the vice which she organizes. It is no defense of an immoral life to say that the alternative offered by society collectively to poor women is a miserable life, starved, overworked, fetid, ailing, ugly. Though it is quite natural and *right* for Mrs. Warren to choose what is, according to her lights, the least immoral alternative, it is none the less infamous of society to offer such alternatives. For the alternatives offered are not morality and immorality but two sorts of immorality. The man who cannot see that starvation, overwork, dirt, and disease are as anti-social as prostitution—that they are the vices and crimes of a nation, and not merely its misfortunes—is (to put it as politely as possible) a hopelessly Private Person.

This is Shaw's way of saying that such a man is a hopeless idiot; the word *idiot* comes from the Greek *idiotes*, "a private person," as distinct from one interested in public affairs.

Shaw's belief in spelling reform led him to introduce simplifications in his own texts that he insisted on his publishers retaining. These simplifications (omission of the apostrophe in a number of contractions, and the use of widely spaced letters rather than italics to indicate emphasis, for example) are retained in the selection reprinted here.

Mrs. Warren's Profession

Act 1

Summer afternoon in a cottage garden on the eastern slope of a hill a little south of Haslemere in Surrey. Looking up the hill, the cottage is seen in the left hand corner of the garden, with its thatched roof and porch, and a large latticed window to the left of the porch. A paling completely shuts in the garden, except for a gate on the right. The common rises uphill beyond the paling to the sky line. Some folded canvas garden chairs are leaning against the side bench in the porch. A lady's bicycle is propped against the wall, under the window. A little to the right of the porch a hammock is slung from two posts. A big canvas umbrella, stuck in the ground, keeps the sun off the hammock, in which a young lady lies reading and making notes, her head towards the cottage and her feet towards the gate. In front of the hammock, and within reach of her hand, is a common kitchen chair, with a pile of serious-looking books and a supply of writing paper on it.

A gentleman walking on the common comes into sight from behind the cottage. He is hardly past middle age, with something of the artist about him, unconventionally but carefully dressed, and clean-shaven except for a moustache, with an eager susceptible face and very amiable and considerate manners. He has silky black hair, with waves of grey and white in it. His eyebrows are white, his moustache black. He seems not certain of his way. He looks over the paling; takes stock of the place; and sees the young lady.

THE GENTLEMAN [*Taking off his hat.*] I beg your pardon. Can you direct me to Hindhead View—Mrs Alison's?

THE YOUNG LADY [*Glancing up from her book.*] This is Mrs Alison's. [*She resumes her work.*]

THE GENTLEMAN Indeed! Perhaps—may I ask are you Miss Vivie Warren?

THE YOUNG LADY [*Sharply, as she turns on her elbow to get a good look at him.*] Yes.

THE GENTLEMAN [*Daunted and conciliatory.*] I'm afraid I appear intrusive. My name is Praed. [VIVIE *at once throws her books upon the chair, and gets out of the hammock.*] Oh, pray dont let me disturb you.

VIVIE [*Striding to the gate and opening it for him.*] Come in, Mr Praed. [*He comes in.*] Glad to see you. [*She proffers her hand and takes his with a resolute and hearty grip. She is an attractive specimen of the sensible, able, highly-educated young middle-class Englishwoman. Age 22. Prompt, strong, confident, self-possessed. Plain business-like dress, but not dowdy. She wears a chatelaine[1] at her belt, with a fountain pen and a paper knife among its pendants.*]

PRAED Very kind of you indeed, Miss Warren. [*She shuts the gate with a vigorous slam. He passes in to the middle of the garden, exercising his fingers, which are slightly numbed by her greeting.*] Has your mother arrived?

VIVIE [*Quickly, evidently scenting aggression.*] Is she coming?

PRAED [*Surprised.*] Didnt you expect us?

VIVIE No.

PRAED Now, goodness me, I hope Ive not mistaken the day. That would be just like me, you know. Your mother arranged that she was to come down from London and that I was to come over from Horsham to be introduced to you.

VIVIE [*Not at all pleased.*] Did she? Hm! My mother has rather a trick of taking me by surprise—to see how I behave myself when she's away, I suppose. I fancy I shall take my mother very much by surprise one of these days, if she makes arrangements that concern me without consulting me beforehand. She hasnt come.

PRAED [*Embarrassed.*] I'm really very sorry.

VIVIE [*Throwing off her displeasure.*] It's not your fault, Mr Praed, is it? And I'm very glad youve come. You are the only one of my mother's friends I have ever asked her to bring to see me.

PRAED [*Relieved and delighted.*] Oh, now this is really very good of you, Miss Warren!

VIVIE Will you come indoors; or would you rather sit out here and talk?

PRAED It will be nicer out here, dont you think?

VIVIE Then I'll go and get you a chair. [*She goes to the porch for a garden chair.*]

1. Clasp or hook.

PRAED [*Following her.*]   Oh, pray, pray! Allow me. [*He lays hands on the chair.*]

VIVIE [*Letting him take it.*]   Take care of your fingers: theyre rather dodgy things, those chairs. [*She goes across to the chair with the books on it; pitches them into the hammock; and brings the chair forward with one swing.*]

PRAED [*Who has just unfolded his chair.*]   Oh, now d o let me take that hard chair. I like hard chairs.

VIVIE   So do I. Sit down, Mr Praed. [*This invitation she gives with genial peremptoriness, his anxiety to please her clearly striking her as a sign of weakness of character on his part. But he does not immediately obey.*]

PRAED   By the way, though, hadnt we better go to the station to meet your mother?

VIVIE [*Coolly.*]   Why? She knows the way.

PRAED [*Disconcerted.*]   Er—I suppose she does. [*He sits down.*]

VIVIE   Do you know, you are just like what I expected. I hope you are disposed to be friends with me.

PRAED [*Again beaming.*]   Thank you, my d e a r Miss Warren: thank you. Dear me! I'm glad your mother hasnt spoilt you!

VIVIE   How?

PRAED   Well, in making you too conventional. You know, my dear Miss Warren, I am a born anarchist. I hate authority. It spoils the relations between parent and child: even between mother and daughter. Now I was always afraid that your mother would strain her authority to make you very conventional. It's such a relief to find that she hasnt.

VIVIE   Oh! have I been behaving unconventionally?

PRAED   Oh no; oh dear no. At least not conventionally unconventionally, you understand. [*She nods and sits down. He goes on, with a cordial outburst.*] But it was so charming of you to say that you were disposed to be friends with me! You modern young ladies are splendid: perfectly splendid!

VIVIE [*Dubiously.*]   Eh? [*Watching him with dawning disappointment as to the quality of his brains and character.*]

PRAED   When I was your age, young men and women were afraid of each other: there was no good fellowship. Nothing real. Only gallantry copied out of novels, and as vulgar and affected as it could be. Maidenly reserve! gentlemanly chivalry! always saying no when you meant yes! simple purgatory for shy and sincere souls.

VIVIE   Yes, I imagine there must have been a frightful waste of time. Especially women's time.

PRAED   Oh, waste of life, waste of everything. But things are improving. Do you know, I have been in a positive state of excitement about meeting you ever since your magnificent achievements at Cambridge: a thing unheard of in my day. It was perfectly splendid, you tieing with the third wrangler.[2] Just the right place, you know. The first wrangler is always a dreamy, morbid fellow, in whom the thing is pushed to the length of a disease.

---

2. A unique Cambridge term denoting distinction in the final honors examination (known as the tripos) leading to an A.B. in mathematics. The person who achieved the top mark was the senior wrangler; then came the junior wrangler, and then third wrangler.

VIVIE   It doesnt pay. I wouldnt do it again for the same money.

PRAED [*Aghast.*]   The same money!

VIVIE   I did it for £50.

PRAED   Fifty pounds!

VIVIE   Yes. Fifty pounds. Perhaps you dont know how it was. Mrs. Latham, my tutor at Newnham,[3] told my mother that I could distinguish myself in the mathematical tripos if I went in for it in earnest. The papers were full just then of Phillipa Summers beating the senior wrangler. You remember about it, of course.

PRAED [*Shakes his head energetically.*]!!!

VIVIE   Well anyhow she did; and nothing would please my mother but that I should do the same thing. I said flatly it was not worth my while to face the grind since I was not going in for teaching; but I offered to try for fourth wrangler, or thereabouts, for £50. She closed with me at that, after a little grumbling; and I was better than my bargain. But I wouldn't do it again for that. Two hundred pounds would have been nearer the mark.

PRAED [*Much damped.*]   Lord bless me! Thats a very practical way of looking at it.

VIVIE   Did you expect to find me an unpractical person?

PRAED   But surely it's practical to consider not only the work these honors cost, but also the culture they bring.

VIVIE   Culture! My dear Mr Praed: do you know what the mathematical tripos means? It means grind, grind, grind for six to eight hours a day at mathematics, and nothing but mathematics. I'm supposed to know something about science; but I know nothing except the mathematics it involves. I can make calculations for engineers, electricians, insurance companies, and so on; but I know next to nothing about engineering or electricity or insurance. I dont even know arithmetic well. Outside mathematics, lawn-tennis, eating, sleeping, cycling, and walking, I'm a more ignorant barbarian than any woman could possibly be who hadnt gone in for the tripos.

PRAED [*Revolted.*]   What a monstrous, wicked, rascally system! I knew it! I felt at once that it meant destroying all that makes womanhood beautiful.

VIVIE   I dont object to it on that score in the least. I shall turn it to very good account, I assure you.

PRAED   Pooh! In what way?

VIVIE   I shall set up in chambers in the City, and work at actuarial calculations and conveyancing. Under cover of that I shall do some law, with one eye on the Stock Exchange all the time. Ive come down here by myself to read law: not for a holiday, as my mother imagines. I hate holidays.

PRAED   You make my blood run cold. Are you to have no romance, no beauty in your life?

VIVIE   I don't care for either, I assure you.

PRAED   You cant mean that.

VIVIE   Oh yes I do. I like working and getting paid for it. When I'm tired

---

3. Women's college at Cambridge University.

of working, I like a comfortable chair, a cigar, a little whisky, and a novel with a good detective story in it.

PRAED [*Rising in a frenzy of repudiation.*] I dont believe it. I am an artist; and I cant believe it: I refuse to believe it. It's only that you havnt discovered yet what a wonderful world art can open up to you.

VIVIE Yes I have. Last May I spent six weeks in London with Honoria Fraser. Mamma thought we were doing a round of sightseeing together; but I was really at Honoria's chambers in Chancery Lane[4] every day, working away at actuarial calculations for her, and helping her as well as a greenhorn could. In the evenings we smoked and talked, and never dreamt of going out except for exercise. And I never enjoyed myself more in my life. I cleared all my expenses, and got initiated into the business without a fee into the bargain.

PRAED But bless my heart and soul, Miss Warren, do you call that discovering art?

VIVIE Wait a bit. That wasnt the beginning. I went up to town on an invitation from some artistic people in Fitzjohn's Avenue: one of the girls was a Newnham chum. They took me to the National Gallery—

PRAED [*Approving.*] Ah!! [*He sits down, much relieved.*]

VIVIE [*Continuing.*]—to the Opera—

PRAED [*Still more pleased.*] Good!

VIVIE—and to a concert where the band played all the evening: Beethoven and Wagner and so on. I wouldnt go through that experience again for anything you could offer me. I held out for civility's sake until the third day; and then I said, plump out, that I couldnt stand any more of it, and went off to Chancery Lane. N o w you know the sort of perfectly splendid modern young lady I am. How do you think I shall get on with my mother?

PRAED [*Startled.*] Well, I hope—er—

VIVIE It's not so much what you hope as what you believe, that I want to know.

PRAED Well, frankly, I am afraid your mother will be a little disappointed. Not from any shortcoming on your part, you know: I dont mean that. But you are so different from her ideal.

VIVIE Her what?!

PRAED Her ideal.

VIVIE Do you mean her ideal of ME?

PRAED Yes.

VIVIE What on earth is it like?

PRAED Well, you must have observed, Miss Warren, that people who are dissatisfied with their own bringing-up generally think that the world would be all right if everybody were to be brought up quite differently. Now your mother's life has been—er—I suppose you know—

VIVIE Dont suppose anything, Mr Praed. I hardly know my mother. Since I was a child I have lived in England, at school or college, or with people paid to take charge of me. I have been boarded out all my life. My mother has lived in Brussels or Vienna and never let me go to her. I only see her when she visits England for a few days. I dont complain: it's been very

4. I.e., office in the legal quarter of London.

pleasant; for people have been very good to me; and there has always been plenty of money to make things smooth. But dont imagine I know anything about my mother. I know far less than you do.

PRAED [*Very ill at ease.*]   In that case—[*He stops, quite at a loss. Then, with a forced attempt at gaiety*] But what nonsense we are talking! Of course you and your mother will get on capitally. [*He rises, and looks abroad at the view.*] What a charming little place you have here!

VIVIE [*Unmoved.*]   Rather a violent change of subject, Mr Praed. Why wont my mother's life bear being talked about?

PRAED   Oh, you really mustnt say that. Isnt it natural that I should have a certain delicacy in talking to my old friend's daughter about her behind her back? You and she will have plenty of opportunity of talking about it when she comes.

VIVIE   No: s h e wont talk about it either. [*Rising.*] However, I daresay you have good reasons for telling me nothing. Only, mind this, Mr Praed. I expect there will be a battle royal when my mother hears of my Chancery Lane project.

PRAED [*Ruefully.*]   I'm afraid there will.

VIVIE   Well, I shall win, because I want nothing but my fare to London to start there to-morrow earning my own living by devilling[5] for Honoria. Besides, I have no mysteries to keep up; and it seems she has. I shall use that advantage over her if necessary.

PRAED [*Greatly shocked.*]   Oh no! No, pray. Youd not do such a thing.

VIVIE   Then tell me why not.

PRAED   I really cannot. I appeal to your good feeling. [*She smiles at his sentimentality.*] Besides you may be too bold. Your mother is not to be trifled with when she's angry.

VIVIE   You cant frighten me, Mr Praed. In that month at Chancery Lane I had opportunities of taking the measure of one or two women v e r y like my mother. You may back me to win. But if I hit harder in my ignorance than I need, remember that it is you who refuse to enlighten me. Now, let us drop the subject. [*She takes her chair and replaces it near the hammock with the same vigorous swing as before.*]

PRAED [*Taking a desperate resolution.*]   One word, Miss Warren. I had better tell you. It's very difficult; but—

[MRS WARREN *and* SIR GEORGE CROFTS *arrive at the gate.* MRS WARREN *is between 40 and 50, formerly pretty, showily dressed in a brilliant hat and a gay blouse fitting tightly over her bust and flanked by fashionable sleeves, Rather spoilt and domineering, and decidedly vulgar, but, on the whole, a genial and fairly presentable old blackguard of a woman.*

CROFTS *is a tall powerfully-built man of about 50, fashionably dressed in the style of a young man. Nasal voice, reedier than might be expected from his strong frame. Clean-shaven bulldog jaws, large flat ears, and thick neck: gentlemanly combination of the most brutal types of city man, sporting man, and man about town.*]

VIVIE   Here they are. [*Coming to them as they enter the garden.*] How do, mater? Mr Praed's been here this half hour waiting for you.

MRS WARREN   Well, if youve been waiting, Praddy, it's your own fault: I

---

5. Acting as assistant to a barrister (trial lawyer) as a way of gaining legal experience.

thought youd have the gumption to know I was coming by the 3.10 train. Vivie: put your hat on, dear: youll get sunburnt. Oh, I forgot to introduce you. Sir George Crofts: my little Vivie.

[CROFTS *advances to* VIVIE *with his most courtly manner. She nods, but makes no motion to shake hands.*]

CROFTS   May I shake hands with a young lady whom I have known by reputation very long as the daughter of one of my oldest friends?

VIVIE [*Who has been looking him up and down sharply.*]   If you like. [*She takes his tenderly proffered hand and gives it a squeeze that makes him open his eyes; then turns away, and says to her mother*] Will you come in, or shall I get a couple more chairs? [*She goes into the porch for the chairs.*]

MRS WARREN   Well George, what do you think of her?

CROFTS [*Ruefully.*]   She has a powerful fist. Did you shake hands with her, Praed?

PRAED   Yes: it will pass off presently.

CROFTS   I hope so. [VIVIE *reappears with two more chairs. He hurries to her assistance.*] Allow me.

MRS WARREN [*Patronizingly.*]   Let Sir George help you with the chairs, dear.

VIVIE [*Pitching them into his arms.*]   Here you are. [*She dusts her hands and turns to* MRS WARREN.] Youd like some tea, wouldnt you?

MRS WARREN [*Sitting in* PRAED's *chair and fanning herself.*]   I'm dying for a drop to drink.

VIVIE   I'll see about it. [*She goes into the cottage.*]

[SIR GEORGE *has by this time managed to unfold a chair and plant it beside* MRS WARREN, *on her left. He throws the other on the grass and sits down, looking dejected and rather foolish, with the handle of his stick in his mouth.* PRAED, *still very uneasy, fidgets about the garden on their right.*]

MRS WARREN [*To* PRAED, *looking at* CROFTS.]   Just look at him, Praddy: he looks cheerful, dont he? He's been worrying my life out these three years to have that little girl of mine shewn to him; and now that Ive done it, he's quite out of countenance. [*Briskly.*] Come! sit up, George; and take your stick out of your mouth. [CROFTS *sulkily obeys.*]

PRAED   I think, you know—if you dont mind my saying so—that we had better get out of the habit of thinking of her as a little girl. You see she has really distinguished herself; and I'm not sure, from what I have seen of her, that she is not older than any of us.

MRS WARREN [*Greatly amused.*]   Only listen to him, George! Older than any of us! Well, she has been stuffing you nicely with her importance.

PRAED   But young people are particularly sensitive about being treated in that way.

MRS WARREN   Yes; and young people have to get all that nonsense taken out of them, and a good deal more besides. Dont you interfere, Praddy: I know how to treat my own child as well as you do. [PRAED, *with a grave shake of his head, walks up the garden with his hands behind his back.* MRS WARREN *pretends to laugh, but looks after him with perceptible concern. Then she whispers to* CROFTS] Whats the matter with him? What does he take it like that for?

CROFTS [*Morosely.*]   Youre afraid of Praed.

MRS WARREN   What! Me! Afraid of dear old Praddy! Why, a fly wouldnt be afraid of him.

CROFTS   Y o u r e afraid of him.

MRS WARREN [*Angry.*]   I'll trouble you to mind your own business, and not try any of your sulks on me. I'm not afraid of y o u, anyhow. If you cant make yourself agreeable, youd better go home. [*She gets up, and turning her back on him, finds herself face to face with* PRAED.] Come, Praddy, I know it was only your tender-heartedness. Youre afraid I'll bully her.

PRAED   My dear Kitty: you think I'm offended. Dont imagine that: pray dont. But you know I often notice things that escape you; and though you never take my advice, you sometimes admit afterwards that you ought to have taken it.

MRS WARREN   Well, what do you notice now?

PRAED   Only that Vivie is a grown woman. Pray, Kitty, treat her with every respect.

MRS WARREN [*With genuine amazement.*]   Respect! Treat my own daughter with respect! What next, pray!

VIVIE [*Appearing at the cottage door and calling to* MRS WARREN.]   Mother: will you come to my room before tea?

MRS WARREN   Yes, dearie. [*She laughs indulgently at* PRAED's *gravity, and pats him on the cheek as she passes him on her way to the porch.*] Dont be cross, Praddy. [*She follows* VIVIE *into the cottage.*]

CROFTS [*Furtively.*]   I say, Praed.

PRAED   Yes.

CROFTS   I want to ask you a rather particular question.

PRAED   Certainly. [*He takes* MRS WARREN's *chair and sits close to* CROFTS.]

CROFTS   Thats right: they might hear us from the window. Look here: did Kitty ever tell you who that girl's father is?

PRAED   Never.

CROFTS   Have you any suspicion of who it might be?

PRAED   None.

CROFTS [*Not believing him.*]   I know, of course, that you perhaps might feel bound not to tell if she had said anything to you. But it's very awkward to be uncertain about it now that we shall be meeting the girl every day. We dont exactly know how we ought to feel towards her.

PRAED   What difference can that make? We take her on her own merits. What does it matter who her father was?

CROFTS [*Suspiciously.*]   Then you know who he was?

PRAED [*With a touch of temper.*]   I said no just now. Did you not hear me?

CROFTS   Look here, Praed. I ask you as a particular favor. If you do know [*Movement of protest from* PRAED.]—I only say, if you know you might at least set my mind at rest about her. The fact is, I feel attracted.

PRAED [*Sternly.*]   What do you mean?

CROFTS   Oh, dont be alarmed: it's quite an innocent feeling. Thats what puzzles me about it. Why, for all I know, I might be her father.

PRAED   You! Impossible!

CROFTS [*Catching him up cunningly.*]   You know for certain that I'm not?

PRAED   I know nothing about it, I tell you, any more than you. But really, Crofts—oh no, it's out of the question. Theres not the least resemblance.

CROFTS As to that, theres no resemblance between her and her mother that I can see. I suppose she's not y o u r daughter, is she?

PRAED [*Rising indignantly.*] Really, Crofts—!

CROFTS No offence, Praed. Quite allowable as between two men of the world.

PRAED [*Recovering himself with an effort and speaking gently and gravely.*] Now listen to me, my dear Crofts. [*He sits down again.*] I have nothing to do with that side of Mrs Warren's life, and never had. She has never spoken to me about it; and of course I have never spoken to her about it. Your delicacy will tell you that a handsome woman needs s o m e friends who are not—well, not on that footing with her. The effect of her own beauty would become a torment to her if she could not escape from it occasionally. You are probably on much more confidential terms with Kitty than I am. Surely you can ask her the question yourself.

CROFTS I have asked her, often enough. But she's so determined to keep the child all to herself that she would deny that it ever had a father if she could. [*Rising.*] I'm thoroughly uncomfortable about it, Praed.

PRAED [*Rising also.*] Well, as you are, at all events, old enough to be her father, I dont mind agreeing that we both regard Miss Vivie in a parental way, as a young girl whom we are bound to protect and help. What do you say?

CROFTS [*Aggressively.*] I'm no older than you, if you come to that.

PRAED Yes you are, my dear fellow: you were born old. I was born a boy: Ive never been able to feel the assurance of a grown-up man in my life. [*He folds his chair and carries it to the porch.*]

MRS WARREN [*Calling from within the cottage.*] Prad-dee! George! Tea-ea-ea-ea!

CROFTS [*Hastily.*] She's calling us. [*He hurries in.*]

[PRAED *shakes his head bodingly, and is following* CROFTS *when he is hailed by a young gentleman who has just appeared on the common, and is making for the gate. He is pleasant, pretty, smartly dressed, cleverly good-for-nothing, not long turned 20, with a charming voice and agreeably disrespectful manners. He carries a light sporting magazine rifle.*]

THE YOUNG GENTLEMAN Hallo! Praed!

PRAED Why, Frank Gardner! [FRANK *comes in and shakes hands cordially.*] What on earth are you doing here?

FRANK Staying with my father.

PRAED The Roman father?[6]

FRANK He's rector here. I'm living with my people this autumn for the sake of economy. Things came to a crisis in July: the Roman father had to pay my debts. He's stony broke in consequence; and so am I. What are you up to in these parts? Do you know the people here?

PRAED Yes: I'm spending the day with a Miss Warren.

FRANK [*Enthusiastically.*] What! Do you know Vivie? Isnt she a jolly girl? I'm teaching her to shoot with this. [*Putting down the rifle.*] I'm so glad she knows you: youre just the sort of fellow she ought to know. [*He smiles,*

---

6. Not "Roman Catholic" (he is a Church of England priest) but a father with a Roman sense of duty. The word is used ironically.

and raises the charming voice almost to a singing tone as he exclaims]
It's e v e r so jolly to find you here, Praed.

PRAED   I'm an old friend of her mother. Mrs Warren brought me over to make her daughter's acquaintance.

FRANK   The mother! Is s h e here?

PRAED   Yes: inside, at tea.

MRS WARREN [*Calling from within.*]   Prad-dee-ee-ee-eee! The tea-cake'll be cold.

PRAED [*Calling.*]   Yes, Mrs Warren. In a moment. Ive just met a friend here.

MRS WARREN   A what?

PRAED [*Louder.*]   A friend.

MRS WARREN   Bring him in.

PRAED   All right. [*to* FRANK] Will you accept the invitation?

FRANK [*Incredulous, but immensely amused.*]   Is that Vivie's mother?

PRAED   Yes.

FRANK   By jove! What a lark! Do you think she'll like me?

PRAED   Ive no doubt youll make yourself popular, as usual. Come in and try. [*Moving towards the house.*]

FRANK   Stop a bit. [*Seriously.*] I want to take you into my confidence.

PRAED   Pray dont. It's only some fresh folly, like the barmaid at Redhill.

FRANK   It's ever so much more serious than that. You say youve only just met Vivie for the first time?

PRAED   Yes.

FRANK [*Rhapsodically.*]   Then you can have no idea what a girl she is. Such character! Such sense! And her cleverness! Oh, my eye, Praed, but I can tell you she is clever! And—need I add?—she loves me.

CROFTS [*Putting his head out of the window.*]   I say, Praed: what are you about? D o come along. [*He disappears.*]

FRANK   Hallo! Sort of chap that would take a prize at a dog show, aint he? Who's he?

PRAED   Sir George Crofts, an old friend of Mrs Warren's. I think we had better come in.

[*On their way to the porch they are interrupted by a call from the gate. Turning, they see an elderly clergyman looking over it.*]

THE CLERGYMAN [*Calling.*]   Frank!

FRANK   Hallo! [*To* PRAED.] The Roman father. [*To the clergyman.*] Yes, gov'nor: all right: presently. [*To* PRAED.] Look here, Praed: youd better go in to tea. I'll join you directly.

PRAED   Very good. [*He goes into the cottage.*]

[*The clergyman remains outside the gate, with his hands on the top of it. The* REV. SAMUEL GARDNER, *a beneficed clergyman of the Established Church, is over 50. Externally he is pretentious, booming, noisy, important. Really he is that obsolescent social phenomenon the fool of the family dumped on the Church by his father, the patron, clamorously asserting himself as father and clergyman without being able to command respect in either capacity.*]

REV. SAMUEL   Well, sir. Who are your friends here, if I may ask?

FRANK   Oh, it's all right, gov'nor! Come in.

REV. SAMUEL   No sir; not until I know whose garden I am entering.

FRANK   It's all right. It's Miss Warren's.

REV. SAMUEL   I have not seen her at church since she came.

FRANK   Of course not: she's a third wrangler. Ever so intellectual. Took a higher degree than you did; so why should she go to hear you preach?

REV. SAMUEL   Dont be disrespectful, sir.

FRANK   Oh, it dont matter: nobody hears us. Come in. [*He opens the gate, unceremoniously pulling his father with it into the garden.*] I want to introduce you to her. Do you remember the advice you gave me last July, gov'nor?

REV. SAMUEL   [*Severely.*]   Yes, I advised you to conquer your idleness and flippancy, and to work your way into an honorable profession and live on it and not upon me.

FRANK   No; thats what you thought of afterwards. What you actually said was that since I had neither brains nor money, I'd better turn my good looks to account by marrying somebody with both. Well, look here. Miss Warren has brains: you cant deny that.

REV. SAMUEL   Brains are not everything.

FRANK   No, of course not: theres the money—

REV. SAMUEL   [*Interrupting him austerely.*]   I was not thinking of money, sir. I was speaking of higher things. Social position, for instance.

FRANK   I dont care a rap about that.

REV. SAMUEL   But I do, sir.

FRANK   Well, nobody wants you to marry her. Anyhow, she has what amounts to a high Cambridge degree; and she seems to have as much money as she wants.

REV. SAMUEL   [*Sinking into a feeble vein of humor.*]   I greatly doubt whether she has as much money as y o u will want.

FRANK   Oh, come; I havnt been so very extravagant. I live ever so quietly; I dont drink; I dont bet much; and I never go regularly on the razzle-dazzle as you did when you were my age.

REV. SAMUEL   [*Booming hollowly.*]   Silence, sir.

FRANK   Well, you told me yourself, when I was making ever such an ass of myself about the barmaid at Redhill, that you once offered a woman £50 for the letters you wrote to her when—

REV. SAMUEL   [*Terrified.*]   Sh-sh-sh, Frank, for heaven's sake! [*He looks round apprehensively. Seeing no one within earshot he plucks up courage to boom again, but more subduedly.*] You are taking an ungentlemanly advantage of what I confided to you for your own good, to save you from an error you would have repented all your life long. Take warning by your father's follies, sir; and dont make them an excuse for your own.

FRANK   Did you ever hear the story of the Duke of Wellington and his letters?

REV. SAMUEL   No, sir; and I dont want to hear it.

FRANK   The old Iron Duke didnt throw away £50: not he. He just wrote: "Dear Jenny: publish and be damned! Yours affectionately, Wellington." Thats what you should have done.

REV. SAMUEL   [*Piteously.*]   Frank, my boy: when I wrote those letters I put myself into that woman's power. When I told you about them I put myself, to some extent, I am sorry to say, in your power. She refused my money with these words, which I shall never forget. "Knowledge is power" she said; "and I never sell power." Thats more than twenty years ago; and she has never made use of her power or caused me a moment's uneasiness. You are behaving worse to me than she did, Frank.

FRANK   Oh yes I dare say! Did you ever preach at her the way you preach at me every day?

REV. SAMUEL [*Wounded almost to tears.*]   I leave you sir. You are incorrigible. [*He turns towards the gate.*]

FRANK [*Utterly unmoved.*]   Tell them I shant be home to tea, will you, gov'nor, like a good fellow? [*He moves towards the cottage door and is met by* PRAED *and* VIVIE *coming out.*]

VIVIE. [*To* FRANK.] Is that your father, Frank? I do so want to meet him.

FRANK   Certainly. [*Calling after his father.*] Gov'nor. Youre wanted. [*The parson turns at the gate, fumbling nervously at his hat.* PRAED *crosses the garden to the opposite side, beaming in anticipation of civilities.*] My father: Miss Warren.

VIVIE [*Going to the clergyman and shaking his hand.*]   Very glad to see you here, Mr Gardner. [*Calling to the cottage.*] Mother: come along: youre wanted.

> [MRS WARREN *appears on the threshold, and is immediately transfixed recognizing the clergyman.*]

VIVIE [*Continuing.*]   Let me introduce—

MRS WARREN [*Swooping on the* REVEREND SAMUEL.]   Why, it's Sam Gardner, gone into the Church! Well, I never! Dont you know us, Sam? This is George Crofts, as large as life and twice as natural. Dont you remember me?

REV. SAMUEL [*Very red.*]   I really—er—

MRS WARREN   Of course you do. Why, I have a whole album of your letters still: I came across them only the other day.

REV. SAMUEL [*Miserably confused.*]   Miss Vavasour, I believe.

MRS WARREN [*Correcting him quickly in a loud whisper.*]   Tch! Nonsense! Mrs Warren: dont you see my daughter there?

Act 2

Inside the cottage after nightfall. Looking eastward from within instead of westward from without, the latticed window, with its curtains drawn, is now seen in the middle of the front wall of the cottage, with the porch door to the left of it. In the left-hand side wall is the door leading to the kitchen. Farther back against the same wall is a dresser with a candle and matches on it, and FRANK's *rifle standing beside them, with the barrel resting in the plate-rack. In the centre a table stands with a lighted lamp on it.* VIVIE's *books and writing materials are on a table to the right of the window, against the wall. The fireplace is on the right, with a settle: there is no fire. Two of the chairs are set right and left of the table. The cottage door opens, shewing a fine starlit night without; and* MRS WARREN, *her shoulders wrapped in a shawl borrowed from* VIVIE, *enters, followed by* FRANK, *who throws his cap on the window seat. She has had enough of walking, and gives a gasp of relief as she unpins her hat; takes it off; sticks the pin through the crown; and puts it on the table.*

MRS WARREN   O Lord! I dont know which is the worst of the country, the walking or the sitting at home with nothing to do. I could do with a whisky and soda now very well, if only they had such a thing in this place.

FRANK   Perhaps Vivie's got some.

MRS WARREN   Nonsense! What would a young girl like her be doing with such things! Never mind: it dont matter. I wonder how she passes her time here! I'd a good deal rather be in Vienna.

FRANK   Let me take you there. [*He helps her to take off her shawl, gallantly giving her shoulders a very perceptible squeeze as he does so.*]

MRS WARREN   Ah! would you? I'm beginning to think youre a chip of the old block.

FRANK   Like the gov'nor, eh? [*He hangs the shawl on the nearest chair, and sits down.*]

MRS WARREN   Never you mind. What do you know about such things? Youre only a boy. [*She goes to the hearth, to be farther from temptation.*]

FRANK   Do come to Vienna with me? It'd be ever such larks.

MRS WARREN   No, thank you. Vienna is no place for you—at least not until youre a little older. [*She nods at him to emphasize this piece of advice. He makes a mock-piteous face, belied by his laughing eyes. She looks at him; then comes back to him.*] Now, look here, little boy [*taking his face in her hands and turning it up to her*]; I know you through and through by your likeness to your father, better than you know yourself. Dont you go taking any silly ideas into your head about me. Do you hear?

FRANK [*Gallantly wooing her with his voice.*]   Cant help it, my dear Mrs Warren: it runs in the family.

> [*She pretends to box his ears; then looks at the pretty laughing upturned face for a moment, tempted. At last she kisses him, and immediately turns away, out of patience with herself.*]

MRS WARREN   There! I shouldnt have done that. I am wicked. Never you mind, my dear: it's only a motherly kiss. Go and make love to Vivie.

FRANK   So I have.

MRS WARREN [*Turning on him with a sharp note of alarm in her voice.*]   What!

FRANK   Vivie and I are ever such chums.

MRS WARREN   What do you mean? Now see here: I wont have any young scamp tampering with my little girl. Do you hear? I wont have it.

FRANK [*Quite unabashed.*]   My dear Mrs Warren: dont you be alarmed. My intentions are honorable: ever so honorable; and your little girl is jolly well able to take care of herself. She dont need looking after half so much as her mother. She aint so handsome, you know.

MRS WARREN [*Taken aback by his assurance.*]   Well, you have got a nice healthy two inches thick of cheek all over you. I dont know where you got it. Not from your father, anyhow.

CROFTS [*In the garden.*]   The gipsies, I suppose?

REV. SAMUEL [*Replying.*]   The broomsquires[7] are far worse.

MRS WARREN [*To FRANK.*]   S-sh! Remember! youve had your warning.

> [CROFTS *and the* REVEREND SAMUEL *come in from the garden, the clergyman continuing his conversation as he enters.*]

---

7. Small country landowners.

REV. SAMUEL   The perjury at the Winchester assizes[8] is deplorable.

MRS WARREN   Well? What became of you two? And wheres Praddy and Vivie?

CROFTS [*Putting his hat on the settle and his stick in the chimney corner.*]   They went up the hill. We went to the village. I wanted a drink. [*He sits down on the settle, putting his legs up along the seat.*]

MRS WARREN   Well, she oughtnt to go off like that without telling me. [*To* FRANK.] Get your father a chair, Frank: where are your manners? [FRANK *springs up and gracefully offers his father his chair; and then takes another from the wall and sits down at the table, in the middle, with his father on his right and* MRS WARREN *on his left.*] George: where are you going to stay to-night? You cant stay here. And whats Praddy going to do?

CROFTS   Gardner'll put me up.

MRS WARREN   Oh no doubt youve taken care of yourself! But what about Praddy?

CROFTS   Dont know. I suppose he can sleep at the inn.

MRS WARREN   Havnt you room for him, Sam?

REV. SAMUEL   Well—er—you see, as rector here, I am not free to do as I like. Er—what is Mr Praed's social position?

MRS. WARREN   Oh, he's all right: he's an architect. What an old stick-in-the-mud you are, Sam!

FRANK   Yes, it's all right, gov'nor. He built that place down in Wales for the Duke. Caernarvon Castle they call it. You must have heard of it. [*He winks with lightning smartness at* MRS WARREN, *and regards his father blandly.*]

REV. SAMUEL   Oh, in that case, of course we shall only be too happy. I suppose he knows the Duke personally.

FRANK   Oh, ever so intimately! We can stick him in Georgina's old room.

MRS WARREN   Well, thats settled. Now if those two would only come in and let us have supper. Theyve no right to stay out after dark like this.

CROFTS [*Aggressively.*]   What harm are they doing you?

MRS WARREN   Well, harm or not, I dont like it.

FRANK   Better not wait for them, Mrs Warren. Praed will stay out as long as possible. He has never known before what it is to stray over the heath on a summer night with my Vivie.

CROFTS [*Sitting up in some consternation.*]   I say, you know! Come!

REV. SAMUEL [*Rising, startled out of his professional manner into real force and sincerity.*]   Frank, once for all, it's out of the question. Mrs Warren will tell you that it's not to be thought of.

CROFTS   Of course not.

FRANK [*With enchanting placidity.*]   Is that so, Mrs Warren?

MRS WARREN [*Reflectively.*]   Well, Sam, I dont know. If the girl wants to get married, no good can come of keeping her unmarried.

REV. SAMUEL [*Astounded.*]   But married to him!—your daughter to my son! Only think: it's impossible.

CROFTS   Of course it's impossible. Dont be a fool, Kitty.

MRS WARREN [*Nettled.*]   Why not? Isnt my daughter good enough for your son?

REV. SAMUEL   But surely, my dear Mrs Warren, you know the reasons—

8. Law courts.

MRS WARREN [*Defiantly.*] I know no reasons. If you know any, you can tell them to the lad, or to the girl, or to your congregation, if you like.

REV. SAMUEL [*Collapsing helplessly into his chair.*] You know very well that I couldnt tell anyone the reasons. But my boy will believe me when I tell him there a r e reasons.

FRANK Quite right, Dad: he will. But has your boy's conduct ever been influenced by your reasons?

CROFTS You cant marry her: and thats all about it. [*He gets up and stands on the hearth, with his back to the fireplace, frowning determinedly.*]

MRS WARREN [*Turning on him sharply.*] What have you got to do with it, pray?

FRANK [*With his prettiest lyrical cadence.*] Precisely what I was going to ask, myself, in my own graceful fashion.

CROFTS [*To* MRS WARREN.] I suppose you dont want to marry the girl to a man younger than herself and without either a profession or twopence to keep her on. Ask Sam, if you dont believe me. [*To the parson.*] How much more money are you going to give him?

REV. SAMUEL Not another penny. He has had his patrimony; and he spent the last of it in July. [MRS WARREN's *face falls.*]

CROFTS [*Watching her.*] There! I told you. [*He resumes his place on the settle and puts up his legs on the seat again, as if the matter were finally disposed of.*]

FRANK [*Plaintively.*] This is ever so mercenary. Do you suppose Miss Warren's going to marry for money? If we love one another—

MRS WARREN Thank you. Your love's a pretty cheap commodity, my lad. If you have no means of keeping a wife, that settles it: you cant have Vivie.

FRANK [*Much amused.*] What do y o u say, gov'nor, eh?

REV. SAMUEL I agree with Mrs Warren.

FRANK And good old Crofts has already expressed his opinion.

CROFTS [*Turning angrily on his elbow.*] Look here: I want none of y o u r cheek.

FRANK [*Pointedly.*] I'm ever so sorry to surprise you, Crofts, but you allowed yourself the liberty of speaking to me like a father a moment ago. One father is enough, thank you.

CROFTS [*Contemptuously.*] Yah! [*He turns away again.*]

FRANK [*Rising.*] Mrs Warren: I cannot give my Vivie up, even for your sake.

MRS WARREN [*Muttering.*] Young scamp!

FRANK [*Continuing.*] And as you no doubt intend to hold out other prospects to her, I shall lose no time in placing my case before her. [*They stare at him; and he begins to declaim gracefully*]

> He either fears his fate too much,
> Or his deserts are small,
> That dares not put it to the touch
> To gain or lose it all.[9]

9. From the poem *My Dear and Only Love*, by the marquis of Montrose (1612–1650).

[*The cottage door opens whilst he is reciting; and* VIVIE *and* PRAED *come in. He breaks off.* PRAED *puts his hat on the dresser. There is an immediate improvement in the company's behavior.* CROFTS *takes down his legs from the settle and pulls himself together as* PRAED *joins him at the fireplace.* MRS WARREN *loses her ease of manner and takes refuge in querulousness.*]

MRS WARREN Wherever have you been, Vivie?

VIVIE [*Taking off her hat and throwing it carelessly on the table.*] On the hill.

MRS WARREN Well, you shouldnt go off like that without letting me know. How could I tell what had become of you? And night coming on too!

VIVIE [*Going to the door of the kitchen and opening it, ignoring her mother.*] Now, about supper? [*All rise except* MRS WARREN.] We shall be rather crowded in here, I'm afraid.

MRS WARREN Did you hear what I said, Vivie?

VIVIE [*Quietly.*] Yes, mother. [*Reverting to the supper difficulty.*] How many are we? [*Counting.*] One, two, three, four, five, six. Well, two will have to wait until the rest are done: Mrs Alison has only plates and knives for four.

PRAED Oh, it doesnt matter about me. I—

VIVIE You have had a long walk and are hungry, Mr Praed: you shall have your supper at once. I can wait myself. I want one person to wait with me. Frank: are you hungry?

FRANK Not the least in the world. Completely off my peck, in fact.

MRS WARREN [*To* CROFTS.] Neither are you, George. You can wait.

CROFTS Oh, hang it. Ive eaten nothing since tea-time. Cant Sam do it?

FRANK Would you starve my poor father?

REV. SAMUEL [*Testily.*] Allow me to speak for myself, sir. I am perfectly willing to wait.

VIVIE [*Decisively.*] Theres no need. Only two are wanted. [*She opens the door of the kitchen.*] Will you take my mother in, Mr Gardner. [*The parson takes* MRS WARREN; *and they pass into the kitchen.* PRAED *and* CROFTS *follow. All except* PRAED *clearly disapprove of the arrangement, but do not know how to resist it.* VIVIE *stands at the door looking in at them.*] Can you squeeze past to that corner, Mr Praed: it's rather a tight fit. Take care of your coat against the white-wash: thats right. Now, are you all comfortable?

PRAED [*Within.*] Quite, thank you.

MRS WARREN [*Within.*] Leave the door open, dearie. [VIVIE *frowns; but* FRANK *checks her with a gesture, and steals to the cottage door, which he softly sets wide open.*] Oh Lor, what a draught! Youd better shut it, dear.

[VIVIE *shuts it with a slam, and then, noting with disgust that her mother's hat and shawl are lying about, takes them tidily to the window seat, whilst* FRANK *noiselessly shuts the cottage door.*]

FRANK [*Exulting.*] Aha! Got rid of em. Well, Vivvums: what do you think of my guvernor?

VIVIE [*Preoccupied and serious.*] Ive hardly spoken to him. He doesnt strike me as being a particularly able person.

FRANK Well, you know, the old man is not altogether such a fool as he looks. You see, he was shoved into the Church rather; and in trying to live up to it he makes a much bigger ass of himself than he really is. I dont dislike him as much as you might expect. He means well. How do you think youll get on with him?

VIVIE [*Rather grimly.*]   I dont think my future life will be much concerned with him, or with any of that old circle of my mother's, except perhaps Praed. [*She sits down on the settle.*] What do you think of my mother?

FRANK   Really and truly?

VIVIE   Yes, really and truly.

FRANK   Well, she's ever so jolly. But she's rather a caution, isn't she? And Crofts! Oh my eye, Crofts! [*He sits beside her.*]

VIVIE   What a lot, Frank!

FRANK   What a crew!

VIVIE [*With intense contempt for them.*]   If I thought that I was like that—that I was going to be a waster, shifting along from one meal to another with no purpose, and no character, and no grit in me, I'd open an artery and bleed to death without one moment's hesitation.

FRANK   Oh no, you wouldnt. Why should they take any grind when they can afford not to? I wish I had their luck. No: what I object to is their form. It isnt the thing: it's slovenly, ever so slovenly.

VIVIE   Do you think your form will be any better when youre as old as Crofts, if you dont work?

FRANK   Of course I do. Ever so much better. Vivvums mustnt lecture: her little boy's incorrigible. [*He attempts to take her face caressingly in his hands.*]

VIVIE [*Striking his hands down sharply.*]   Off with you: Vivvums is not in a humor for petting her little boy this evening. [*She rises and comes forward to the other side of the room.*]

FRANK [*Following her.*]   How unkind!

VIVIE [*Stamping at him.*]   Be serious. I'm serious.

FRANK   Good. Let us talk learnedly. Miss Warren: do you know that all the most advanced thinkers are agreed that half the diseases of modern civilization are due to starvation of the affections in the young. Now, I—

VIVIE [*Cutting him short.*]   You are very tiresome. [*She opens the inner door.*] Have you room for Frank there? He's complaining of starvation.

MRS WARREN [*Within.*]   Of course there is. [*Clatter of knives and glasses as she moves the things on the table.*] Here! theres room now beside me. Come along, Mr Frank.

FRANK   Her little boy will be ever so even with his Vivvums for this. [*He passes into the kitchen.*]

MRS WARREN [*Within.*]   Here, Vivie: come on you too, child. You must be famished. [*She enters, followed by* CROFTS, *who holds the door open for* VIVIE *with marked deference. She goes out without looking at him; and he shuts the door after her.*] Why, George, you cant be done: youve eaten nothing. Is there anything wrong with you?

CROFTS   Oh, all I wanted was a drink. [*He thrusts his hands in his pockets, and begins prowling about the room, restless and sulky.*]

MRS WARREN   Well, I like enough to eat. But a little of that cold beef and cheese and lettuce goes a long way. [*With a sigh of only half repletion she sits down lazily on the settle.*]

CROFTS   What do you go encouraging that young pup for?

MRS WARREN [*On the alert at once.*]   Now see here, George: what are you up to about that girl? Ive been watching your way of looking at her. Remember: I know you and what your looks mean.

CROFTS   Theres no harm in looking at her, is there?

MRS WARREN   I'd put you out and pack you back to London pretty soon if I saw any of your nonsense. My girl's little finger is more to me than your whole body and soul. [CROFTS *receives this with a sneering grin.* MRS WARREN, *flushing a little at her failure to impose on him in the character of a theatrically devoted mother, adds in a lower key*] Make your mind easy: the young pup has no more chance than you have.

CROFTS   Maynt a man take an interest in a girl?

MRS WARREN   Not a man like you.

CROFTS   How old is she?

MRS WARREN   Never you mind how old she is.

CROFTS   Why do you make such a secret of it?

MRS WARREN   Because I choose.

CROFTS   Well, I'm not fifty yet; and my property is as good as ever it was—

MRS WARREN [*Interrupting him.*]   Yes; because youre as stingy as youre vicious.

CROFTS [*Continuing.*]   And a baronet isnt to be picked up every day. No other man in my position would put up with you for a mother-in-law. Why shouldnt she marry me?

MRS WARREN   You!

CROFTS   We three could live together quite comfortably. I'd die before her and leave her a bouncing widow with plenty of money. Why not? It's been growing in my mind all the time Ive been walking with that fool inside there.

MRS WARREN [*Revolted.*]   Yes; it's the sort of thing that would grow in your mind.

> [*He halts in his prowling; and the two look at one another, she steadfastly, with a sort of awe behind her contemptuous disgust: he stealthily, with a carnal gleam in his eye and a loose grin.*]

CROFTS [*Suddenly becoming anxious and urgent as he sees no sign of sympathy in her.*]   Look here, Kitty: youre a sensible woman: you neednt put on any moral airs. I'll ask no more questions; and you need answer none. I'll settle the whole property on her; and if you want a cheque for yourself on the wedding day, you can name any figure you like—in reason.

MRS WARREN   So it's come to that with you, George, like all the other worn-out old creatures!

CROFTS [*Savagely.*]   Damn you!

> [*Before she can retort the door of the kitchen is opened; and the voices of the others are heard returning.* CROFTS, *unable to recover his presence of mind, hurries out of the cottage. The clergyman appears at the kitchen door.*]

REV. SAMUEL [*Looking around.*]   Where is Sir George?

MRS WARREN   Gone out to have a pipe. [*The clergyman takes his hat from the table, and joins* MRS WARREN *at the fireside. Meanwhile* VIVIE *comes in, followed by* FRANK, *who collapses into the nearest chair with an air of extreme exhaustion.* MRS WARREN *looks round at* VIVIE *and says, with her affectation of maternal patronage even more forced than usual*] Well, dearie: have you had a good supper?

VIVIE   You know what Mrs Alison's suppers are. [*She turns to* FRANK *and pets him.*] Poor Frank! was all the beef gone? did it get nothing but bread and cheese and ginger beer? [*Seriously, as if she had done quite enough trifling for one evening.*] Her butter is really awful. I must get some down from the stores.

FRANK   Do, in heaven's name!

> [VIVIE *goes to the writing-table and makes a memorandum to order the butter.* PRAED *comes in from the kitchen, putting up his handkerchief, which he has been using as a napkin.*]

REV. SAMUEL   Frank, my boy: it is time for us to be thinking of home. Your mother does not know yet that we have visitors.

PRAED   I'm afraid we're giving trouble.

FRANK [*Rising.*]   Not the least in the world; my mother will be delighted to see you. She's a genuinely intellectual artistic woman; and she sees nobody here from one year's end to another except the gov'nor; so you can imagine how jolly dull it pans out for her. [*To his father.*] Y o u r e not intellectual or artistic are you, pater? So take Praed home at once; and I'll stay here and entertain Mrs Warren. Youll pick up Crofts in the garden. He'll be excellent company for the bull-pup.

PRAED [*Taking his hat from the dresser, and coming close to* FRANK.]   Come with us, Frank. Mrs Warren has not seen Miss Vivie for a long time; and we have prevented them from having a moment together yet.

FRANK [*Quite softened, and looking at* PRAED *with romantic admiration.*]   Of course. I forgot. Ever so thanks for reminding me. Perfect gentleman, Praddy. Always were. My ideal through life. [*He rises to go, but pauses a moment between the two older men, and puts his hand on* PRAED's *shoulder.*] Ah, if you had only been my father instead of this unworthy old man! [*He puts his other hand on his father's shoulder.*]

REV. SAMUEL [*Blustering.*]   Silence, sir, silence; you are profane.

MRS WARREN [*Laughing heartily.*]   You should keep him in better order, Sam. Goodnight. Here: take George his hat and stick with my compliments.

REV. SAMUEL [*Taking them.*]   Goodnight. [*They shake hands. As he passes* VIVIE *he shakes hands with her also and bids her goodnight. Then, in booming command, to* FRANK.] Come along, sir, at once. [*He goes out.*]

MRS WARREN   Byebye, Praddy.

PRAED   Byebye, Kitty.

> [*They shake hands affectionately and go out together, she accompanying him to the garden gate.*]

FRANK [*To* VIVIE.]   Kissums?

VIVIE [*Fiercely.*]   No. I hate you. [*She takes a couple of books and some paper from the writing-table, and sits down with them at the middle table, at the end next the fireplace.*]

FRANK [*Grimacing.*]   Sorry. [*He goes for his cap and rifle.* MRS WARREN *returns. He takes her hand.*] Goodnight, d e a r Mrs Warren. [*He kisses her hand. She snatches it away, her lips tightening, and looks more than half disposed to box his ears. He laughs mischievously and runs off, clapping-to the door behind him.*]

MRS WARREN [*Resigning herself to an evening of boredom now that the men are gone.*]   Did you ever in your life hear anyone rattle on so? Isnt he a tease? [*She sits at the table.*] Now that I think of it, dearie, dont you go on encouraging him. I'm sure he's a regular good-for-nothing.

VIVIE [*Rising to fetch more books.*]   I'm afraid so. Poor Frank! I shall have to get rid of him; but I shall feel sorry for him, though he's not worth it. That man Crofts does not seem to me to be good for much either: is he? [*She throws the books on the table rather roughly.*]

MRS WARREN [*Galled by* VIVIE's *indifference.*]   What do you know of men, child, to talk that way about them? Youll have to make up your mind to see a good deal of Sir George Crofts, as he's a friend of mine.

VIVIE [*Quite unmoved.*]   Why? [*She sits down and opens a book.*] Do you expect that we shall be much together? You and I, I mean?

MRS WARREN [*Staring at her.*]   Of course: until youre married. Youre not going back to college again.

VIVIE   Do you think my way of life would suit you? I doubt it.

MRS WARREN   Y o u r way of life! What do you mean?

VIVIE [*Cutting a page of her book with the paper knife on her chatelaine.*]   Has it really never occurred to you, mother, that I have a way of life like other people?

MRS WARREN   What nonsense is this youre trying to talk? Do you want to shew your independence, now that youre a great little person at school? Dont be a fool, child.

VIVIE [*Indulgently.*]   Thats all you have to say on the subject, is it, mother?

MRS WARREN [*Puzzled, then angry.*]   Dont you keep on asking me questions like that. [*Violently.*] Hold your tongue. [VIVIE *works on, losing no time, and saying nothing.*] You and your way of life, indeed! What next? [*She looks at* VIVIE *again. No reply.*] Your way of life will be what I please, so it will. [*Another pause.*] Ive been noticing these airs in you ever since you got that tripos or whatever you call it. If you think I'm going to put up with them youre mistaken; and the sooner you find it out, the better. [*Muttering.*] All I have to say on the subject, indeed! [*Again raising her voice angrily.*] Do you know who youre speaking to, Miss?

VIVIE [*Looking across at her without raising her head from her book.*]   No. Who are you? What are you?

MRS WARREN [*Rising breathless.*]   You young imp!

VIVIE   Everybody knows my reputation, my social standing, and the profession I intend to pursue. I know nothing about you. What is that way of life which you invite me to share with you and Sir George Crofts, pray?

MRS WARREN   Take care. I shall do something I'll be sorry for after, and you too.

VIVIE [*Putting aside her books with cool decision.*]   Well, let us drop the subject until you are better able to face it. [*Looking critically at her mother.*] You want some good walks and a little lawn tennis to set you up. You are shockingly out of condition: you were not able to manage twenty yards uphill today without stopping to pant; and your wrists are mere rolls of fat. Look at mine. [*She holds out her wrists.*]

MRS WARREN [*After looking at her helplessly, begins to whimper.*]   Vivie—

VIVIE [*Springing up sharply.*]   Now pray dont begin to cry. Anything but that. I really cannot stand whimpering. I will go out of the room if you do.

MRS WARREN [*Piteously.*]   Oh, my darling, how can you be so hard on me?
Have I no rights over you as your mother?

VIVIE   Are you my mother?

MRS WARREN [*Appalled.*]   Am I your mother! Oh, Vivie!

VIVIE   Then where are our relatives? my father? our family friends? You
claim the rights of a mother: the right to call me fool and child; to speak
to me as no woman in authority over me at college dare speak to me; to
dictate my way of life; and to force on me the acquaintance of a brute
whom anyone can see to be the most vicious sort of London man about
town. Before I give myself the trouble to resist such claims, I may as well
find out whether they have any real existence.

MRS WARREN [*Distracted, throwing herself on her knees.*]   Oh no, no. Stop,
stop. I am your mother: I swear it. Oh, you cant mean to turn on me—
my own child! It's not natural. You believe me, dont you? Say you believe
me.

VIVIE   Who was my father?

MRS WARREN   You dont know what youre asking. I cant tell you.

VIVIE [*Determinedly.*]   Oh yes you can, if you like. I have a right to know;
and you know very well that I have that right. You can refuse to tell me,
if you please; but if you do, you will see the last of me tomorrow morning.

MRS WARREN   Oh, it's too horrible to hear you talk like that. You
wouldnt—you c o u l d n t leave me.

VIVIE [*Ruthlessly.*]   Yes, without a moment's hesitation, if you trifle with
me about this. [*Shivering with disgust.*] How can I feel sure that I may
not have the contaminated blood of that brutal waster in my veins?

MRS WARREN   No, no. On my oath it's not he, nor any of the rest that you
have ever met. I'm certain of that, at least.

    [VIVIE's *eyes fasten sternly on her mother as the significance of this flashes
    on her.*]

VIVIE [*Slowly.*]   You are certain of that, a t l e a s t. Ah! You mean that
that is all you are certain of. [*Thoughtfully.*] I see. [MRS WARREN *buries
her face in her hands.*] Dont do that, mother: you know you dont feel it
a bit. [MRS WARREN *takes down her hands and looks up deplorably at* VIVIE,
who takes out her watch and says] Well, that is enough for tonight. At
what hour would you like breakfast? Is half-past eight too early for you?

MRS WARREN [*Wildly.*]   My God, what sort of woman are you?

VIVIE [*Coolly.*]   The sort the world is mostly made of, I should hope. Otherwise I dont understand how it gets its business done. Come [*taking her
mother by the wrist, and pulling her up pretty resolutely*]: pull yourself
together. Thats right.

MRS WARREN [*Querulously.*]   Youre very rough with me, Vivie.

VIVIE   Nonsense. What about bed? It's past ten.

MRS WARREN [*Passionately.*]   Whats the use of my going to bed? Do you
think I could sleep?

VIVIE   Why not? I shall.

MRS WARREN   You! youve no heart. [*She suddenly breaks out vehemently
in her natural tongue—the dialect of a woman of the people—with all her
affectations of maternal authority and conventional manners gone, and an
overwhelming inspiration of true conviction and scorn in her.*] Oh, I wont
bear it: I wont put up with the injustice of it. What right have you to set

yourself up above me like this? You boast of what you are to me—to m e, who gave you the chance of being what you are. What chance had I! Shame on you for a bad daughter and a stuck-up prude!

VIVIE [*Sitting down with a shrug, no longer confident; for her replies, which have sounded sensible and strong to her so far, now begin to ring rather woodenly and even priggishly against the new tone of her mother.*] Dont think for a moment I set myself above you in any way. You attacked me with the conventional authority of a mother: I defended myself with the conventional superiority of a respectable woman. Frankly, I am not going to stand any of your nonsense; and when you drop it I shall not expect you to stand any of mine. I shall always respect your right to your own opinions and your own way of life.

MRS WARREN My own opinions and my own way of life! Listen to her talking! Do you think I was brought up like you? able to pick and choose my own way of life? Do you think I did what I did because I liked it, or thought it right, or wouldnt rather have gone to college and been a lady if I'd had the chance?

VIVIE Everybody has some choice, mother. The poorest girl alive may not be able to choose between being Queen of England or Principal of Newnham; but she can choose between ragpicking and flower-selling, according to her taste. People are always blaming their circumstances for what they are. I dont believe in circumstances. The people who get on in this world are the people who get up and look for the circumstances they want, and, if they cant find them, make them.

MRS WARREN Oh, it's easy to talk, very easy, isnt it? Here! would you like to know what my circumstances were?

VIVIE Yes: you had better tell me. Wont you sit down?

MRS WARREN Oh, I'll sit down: dont you be afraid. [*She plants her chair farther forward with brazen energy, and sits down.* VIVIE *is impressed in spite of herself.*] D'you know what your gran'mother was?

VIVIE No.

MRS WARREN No you dont. I do. She called herself a widow and had a fried-fish shop down by the Mint, and kept herself and four daughters out of it. Two of us were sisters: that was me and Liz; and we were both good-looking and well made. I suppose our father was a well-fed man: mother pretended he was a gentleman; but I dont know. The other two were only half sisters: undersized, ugly, starved looking, hard working, honest poor creatures: Liz and I would have half-murdered them if mother hadnt half-murdered us to keep our hands off them. They were the respectable ones. Well, what did they get by their respectability? I'll tell you. One of them worked in a whitelead factory twelve hours a day for nine shillings a week until she died of lead poisoning. She only expected to get her hands a little paralyzed; but she died. The other was always held up to us as a model because she married a Government laborer in the Deptford victualling yard, and kept his room and the three children neat and tidy on eighteen shillings a week—until he took to drink. That was worth being respectable for, wasnt it?

VIVIE [*Now thoughtfully attentive.*] Did you and your sister think so?

MRS WARREN Liz didnt, I can tell you: she had more spirit. We both went to a church school—that was part of the ladylike airs we gave ourselves

to be superior to the children that knew nothing and went nowhere—
and we stayed there until Liz went out one night and never came back.
I know the school-mistress thought I'd soon follow her example; for the
clergyman was always warning me that Lizzie'd end by jumping off
Waterloo Bridge. Poor fool: that was all he knew about it! But I was more
afraid of the whitelead factory than I was of the river; and so would you
have been in my place. That clergyman got me a situation as a scullery
maid in a temperance restaurant where they sent out for anything you
liked. Then I was waitress; and then I went to the bar at Waterloo station:
fourteen hours a day serving drinks and washing glasses for four shillings
a week and my board. That was considered a great promotion for me.
Well, one cold, wretched night, when I was so tired I could hardly keep
myself awake, who should come up for a half of Scotch but Lizzie, in a
long fur cloak, elegant and comfortable, with a lot of sovereigns in her
purse.

VIVIE [*Grimly.*]   My aunt Lizzie!

MRS WARREN. Yes; and a very good aunt to have, too. She's living down at
Winchester now, close to the cathedral, one of the most respectable
ladies there. Chaperones girls at the county ball, if you please. No river
for Liz, thank you! You remind me of Liz a little: she was a first-rate
business woman—saved money from the beginning—never let herself
look too like what she was—never lost her head or threw away a chance.
When she saw I'd grown up good-looking she said to me across the bar
"What are you doing there, you little fool? wearing out your health and
your appearance for other people's profit!" Liz was saving money then to
take a house for herself in Brussels; and she thought we two could save
faster than one. So she lent me some money and gave me a start; and I
saved steadily and first paid her back, and then went into business with
her as her partner. Why shouldnt I have done it? The house in Brussels
was real high class: a much better place for a woman to be in than the
factory where Anne Jane got poisoned. None of our girls were ever
treated as I was treated in the scullery of that temperance place, or at
the Waterloo bar, or at home. Would you have had me stay in them and
become a worn out old drudge before I was forty?

VIVIE [*Intensely interested by this time.*]   No; but why did you choose that
business? Saving money and good management will succeed in any business.

MRS WARREN   Yes, saving money. But where can a woman get the money
to save in any other business? Could you save out of four shillings a week
and keep yourself dressed as well? Not you. Of course, if youre a plain
woman and cant earn anything more; or if you have a turn for music, or
the stage, or newspaper writing; thats different. But neither Liz nor I had
any turn for such things: all we had was our appearance and our turn
for pleasing men. Do you think we were such fools as to let other people
trade in our good looks by employing us as shopgirls, or barmaids, or
waitresses, when we could trade in them ourselves and get all the profits
instead of starvation wages? Not likely.

VIVIE   You were certainly quite justified—from the business point of view.

MRS WARREN   Yes; or any other point of view. What is any respectable girl
brought up to do but to catch some rich man's fancy and get the benefit

of his money by marrying him?—as if a marriage ceremony could make any difference in the right or wrong of the thing! Oh! the hypocrisy of the world makes me sick! Liz and I had to work and save and calculate just like other people; elseways we should be as poor as any good-for-nothing drunken waster of a woman that thinks her luck will last for ever. [*With great energy.*] I despise such people: theyve no character; and if theres a thing I hate in a woman, it's want of character.

VIVIE   Come now, mother: frankly! Isnt it part of what you call character in a woman that she should greatly dislike such a way of making money?

MRS WARREN   Why, of course. Everybody dislikes having to work and make money; but they have to do it all the same. I'm sure Ive often pitied a poor girl; tired out and in low spirits, having to try to please some man that she doesnt care two straws for—some half-drunken fool that thinks he's making himself agreeable when he's teasing and worrying and disgusting a woman so that hardly any money could pay her for putting up with it. But she has to bear with disagreeables and take the rough with the smooth, just like a nurse in a hospital or anyone else. It's not work that any woman would do for pleasure, goodness knows; though to hear the pious people talk you would suppose it was a bed of roses.

VIVIE   Still, you consider it worth while. It pays.

MRS WARREN   Of course it's worth while to a poor girl, if she can resist temptation and is good-looking and well conducted and sensible. It's far better than any other employment open to her. I always thought that oughtnt to be. It c a n t be right, Vivie, that there shouldnt be better opportunities for women. I stick to that: it's wrong. But it's so, right or wrong; and a girl must make the best of it. But of course it's not worth while for a lady. If you took to it youd be a fool; but I should have been a fool if I'd taken to anything else.

VIVIE [*More and more deeply moved.*]   Mother; suppose we were both as poor as you were in those wretched old days, are you quite sure that you wouldnt advise me to try the Waterloo bar, or marry a laborer, or even go into the factory?

MRS WARREN [*Indignantly.*]   Of course not. What sort of mother do you take me for! How could you keep your self-respect in such starvation and slavery? And whats a woman worth? whats life worth? without self-respect! Why am I independent and able to give my daughter a first-rate education, when other women that had just as good opportunities are in the gutter? Because I always knew how to respect myself and control myself. Why is Liz looked up to in a cathedral town? The same reason. Where would we be now if we'd minded the clergyman's foolishness? Scrubbing floors for one and sixpence a day and nothing to look forward to but the workhouse infirmary. Dont you be led astray by people who dont know the world, my girl. The only way for a woman to provide for herself decently is for her to be good to some man that can afford to be good to her. If she's in his own station of life, let her make him marry her; but if she's far beneath him she cant expect it: why should she? it wouldn't be for her own happiness. Ask any lady in London society that has daughters; and she'll tell you the same, except that I tell you straight and she'll tell you crooked. Thats all the difference.

VIVIE [*Fascinated, gazing at her.*]   My dear mother; you are a wonderful woman: you are stronger than all England. And are you really and truly not one wee bit doubtful—or—or—ashamed?

MRS WARREN   Well, of course, dearie, it's only good manners to be ashamed of it; it's expected from a woman. Women have to pretend to feel a great deal that they dont feel. Liz used to be angry with me for plumping out the truth about it. She used to say that when every woman could learn enough from what was going on in the world before her eyes, there was no need to talk about it to her. But then Liz was such a perfect lady! She had the true instinct of it; while I was always a bit of a vulgarian. I used to be so pleased when you sent me your photos to see that you were growing up like Liz: youve just her ladylike, determined way. But I cant stand saying one thing when everyone knows I mean another. Whats the use in such hypocrisy? If people arrange the world that way for women, theres no good pretending it's arranged the other way. No: I never was a bit ashamed really. I consider I had a right to be proud of how we managed everything so respectably, and never had a word against us, and how the girls were so well taken care of. Some of them did very well: one of them married an ambassador. But of course now I darent talk about such things: whatever would they think of us! [*She yawns.*] Oh dear! I do believe I'm getting sleepy after all. [*She stretches herself lazily, thoroughly relieved by her explosion, and placidly ready for her night's rest.*]

VIVIE   I believe it is I who will not be able to sleep now. [*She goes to the dresser and lights the candle. Then she extinguishes the lamp, darkening the room a good deal.*] Better let in some fresh air before locking up. [*She opens the cottage door, and finds that it is broad moonlight.*] What a beautiful night! Look! [*She draws aside the curtains of the window. The landscape is seen bathed in the radiance of the harvest moon rising over Blackdown.*]

MRS WARREN [*With a perfunctory glance at the scene.*]   Yes, dear; but take care you dont catch your death of cold from the night air.

VIVIE [*Contemptuously.*]   Nonsense.

MRS WARREN [*Querulously.*]   Oh yes: everything I say is nonsense, according to you.

VIVIE [*Turning to her quickly.*]   No: really that is not so, mother. You have got completely the better of me tonight, though I intended it to be the other way. Let us be good friends now.

MRS WARREN [*Shaking her head a little ruefully.*]   So it has been the other way. But I suppose I must give in to it. I always got the worst of it from Liz; and now I suppose it'll be the same with you.

VIVIE   Well, never mind. Come: goodnight, dear old mother. [*She takes her mother in her arms.*]

MRS WARREN [*Fondly.*]   I brought you up well, didnt I, dearie?

VIVIE   You did.

MRS WARREN   And youll be good to your poor old mother for it, wont you?

VIVIE   I will, dear. [*Kissing her.*] Goodnight.

MRS WARREN [*With unction.*]   Blessings on my own dearie darling! a mother's blessing!

[*She embraces her daughter protectingly, instinctively looking upward for divine sanction.*]

Act 3

In the Rectory garden next morning, with the sun shining from a cloudless sky. The garden wall has a five-barred wooden gate, wide enough to admit a carriage, in the middle. Beside the gate hangs a bell on a coiled spring, communicating with a pull outside. The carriage drive comes down the middle of the garden and then swerves to its left, where it ends in a little gravelled circus opposite the Rectory porch. Beyond the gate is seen the dusty high road, parallel with the wall, bounded on the farther side by a strip of turf and an unfenced pine wood. On the lawn, between the house and the drive, is a clipped yew tree, with a garden bench in its shade. On the opposite side the garden is shut in by a box hedge; and there is a sundial on the turf, with an iron chair near it. A little path leads off through the box hedge, behind the sundial.

FRANK, seated on the chair near the sundial, on which he has placed the morning papers, is reading The Standard. *His father comes from the house, red-eyed and shivery, and meets* FRANK's *eye with misgiving.*

FRANK [*Looking at his watch.*]   Half-past eleven. Nice hour for a rector to come down to breakfast!

REV. SAMUEL   Dont mock, Frank: dont mock. I am a little—er—[*Shivering.*]—

FRANK   Off color?

REV. SAMUEL [*Repudiating the expression.*]   No, sir: u n w e l l this morning. Wheres your mother?

FRANK   Dont be alarmed: she's not here. Gone to town by the 11.13 with Bessie. She left several messages for you. Do you feel equal to receiving them now, or shall I wait til youve breakfasted?

REV. SAMUEL   I h a v e breakfasted, sir. I am surprised at your mother going to town when we have people staying with us. Theyll think it very strange.

FRANK   Possibly she has considered that. At all events, if Crofts is going to stay here, and you are going to sit up every night with him until four, recalling the incidents of your fiery youth, it is clearly my mother's duty, as a prudent housekeeper, to go up to the stores and order a barrel of whisky and few hundred siphons.

REV. SAMUEL   I did not observe that Sir George drank excessively.

FRANK   You were not in a condition to, gov'nor.

REV. SAMUEL   Do you mean to say that I—?

FRANK [*Calmly.*]   I never saw a beneficed clergyman less sober. The anecdotes you told about your past career were so awful that I really dont think Praed would have passed the night under your roof if it hadnt been for the way my mother and he took to one another.

REV. SAMUEL   Nonsense, sir. I am Sir George Crofts' host. I must talk to him about something; and he has only one subject. Where is Mr Praed now?

FRANK   He is driving my mother and Bessie to the station.

REV. SAMUEL   Is Crofts up yet?

FRANK   Oh, long ago. He hasnt turned a hair: he's in much better practice
than you. Has kept it up ever since, probably. He's taken himself off
somewhere to smoke.

[FRANK *resumes his paper. The parson turns disconsolately towards the*
gate; then comes back irresolutely.]

REV. SAMUEL   Er—Frank.

FRANK   Yes.

REV. SAMUEL   Do you think the Warrens will expect to be asked here after
yesterday afternoon?

FRANK   Theyve been asked already.

REV. SAMUEL [*Appalled.*]   What!!!

FRANK   Crofts informed us at breakfast that you told him to bring Mrs
Warren and Vivie over here today, and to invite them to make this house
their home. My mother then found she must go to town by the 11.13
train.

REV. SAMUEL [*With despairing vehemence.*]   I never gave any such invitation. I never thought of such a thing.

FRANK [*Compassionately.*]   How do you know, gov'nor, what you said and
thought last night?

PRAED [*Coming in through the hedge.*]   Good morning.

REV. SAMUEL   Good morning. I must apologize for not having met you at
breakfast. I have a touch of—of—

FRANK   Clergyman's sore throat, Praed. Fortunately not chronic.

PRAED [*Changing the subject.*]   Well, I must say your house is in a charming spot here. Really most charming.

REV. SAMUEL   Yes: it is indeed. Frank will take you for a walk, Mr Praed,
if you like. I'll ask you to excuse me: I must take the opportunity to write
my sermon while Mrs Gardner is away and you are all amusing yourselves. You wont mind, will you?

PRAED   Certainly not. Dont stand on the slightest ceremony with me.

REV. SAMUEL   Thank you. I'll—er—er—[*He stammers his way to the porch*
and vanishes into the house.]

PRAED   Curious thing it must be writing a sermon every week.

FRANK   Ever so curious, if he did it. He buys em. He's gone for some soda
water.

PRAED   My dear boy: I wish you would be more respectful to your father.
You know you can be so nice when you like.

FRANK   My dear Praddy: you forget that I have to live with the governor.
When two people live together—it doesnt matter whether theyre father
and son or husband and wife or brother and sister—they cant keep up
the polite humbug thats so easy for ten minutes on an afternoon call.
Now the governor, who unites to many admirable domestic qualities the
irresoluteness of a sheep and the pompousness and aggressiveness of a
jackass—

PRAED   No, pray, pray, my dear Frank, remember! He is your father.

FRANK   I give him due credit for that. [*Rising and flinging down his paper.*]
But just imagine his telling Crofts to bring the Warrens over here! He
must have been ever so drunk. You know, my dear Praddy, my mother
wouldnt stand Mrs Warren for a moment. Vivie mustnt come here until
she's gone back to town.

PRAED   But your mother doesnt know anything about Mrs Warren, does she? [*He picks up the paper and sits down to read it.*]

FRANK   I don't know. Her journey to town looks as if she did. Not that my mother would mind in the ordinary way: she has stuck like a brick to lots of women who had got into trouble. But they were all nice women. Thats what makes the real difference. Mrs Warren, no doubt, has her merits; but she's ever so rowdy; and my mother simply wouldnt put up with her. So—hallo! [*This exclamation is provoked by the reappearance of the clergyman, who comes out of the house in haste and dismay.*]

REV. SAMUEL   Frank: Mrs Warren and her daughter are coming across the heath with Crofts: I saw them from the study windows. What am I to say about your mother?

FRANK   Stick on your hat and go out and say how delighted you are to see them; and that Frank's in the garden; and that mother and Bessie have been called to the bedside of a sick relative, and were ever so sorry they couldnt stop; and that you hope Mrs Warren slept well; and—and—say any blessed thing except the truth, and leave the rest to Providence.

REV. SAMUEL   But how are we to get rid of them afterwards?

FRANK   Theres no time to think of that now. Here! [*He bounds into the house.*]

REV. SAMUEL   He's so impetuous. I dont know what to do with him, Mr Praed.

FRANK [*Returning with clerical felt hat, which he claps on his father's head.*]   Now: off with you. [*Rushing him through the gate.*] Praed and I'll wait here, to give the thing an unpremeditated air. [*The clergyman, dazed but obedient, hurries off.*]

FRANK   We must get the old girl back to town somehow, Praed. Come! Honestly, dear Praddy, do you like seeing them together?

PRAED   Oh, why not?

FRANK [*His teeth on edge.*]   Dont it make your flesh creep ever so little? that wicked old devil, up to every villainy under the sun, I'll swear, and Vivie—ugh!

PRAED   Hush, pray. Theyre coming.

[*The clergyman and* CROFTS *are seen coming along the road, followed by* MRS WARREN *and* VIVIE *walking affectionately together.*]

FRANK   Look: she actually has her arm round the old woman's waist. It's her right arm: she began it. She's gone sentimental, by God! Ugh! ugh! Now do you feel the creeps? [*The clergyman opens the gate; and* MRS WARREN *and* VIVIE *pass him and stand in the middle of the garden looking at the house.* FRANK, *in an ecstasy of dissimulation, turns gaily to* MRS WARREN, *exclaiming*] Ever so delighted to see you, Mrs Warren. This quiet old rectory garden becomes you perfectly.

MRS WARREN   Well, I never! Did you hear that, George? He says I look well in a quiet old rectory garden.

REV. SAMUEL [*Still holding the gate for* CROFTS, *who loafs through it, heavily bored.*]   You look well everywhere, Mrs Warren.

FRANK   Bravo, gov'nor! Now look here: lets have a treat before lunch. First lets see the church. Everyone has to do that. It's a regular old thirteenth century church, you know: the gov'nor's ever so fond of it, because he got up a restoration fund and had it completely rebuilt six years ago. Praed will be able to shew its points.

PRAED [*Rising.*]   Certainly, if the restoration has left any to shew.

REV. SAMUEL [*Mooning hospitably at them.*]   I shall be pleased, I'm sure, if Sir George and Mrs Warren really care about it.

MRS WARREN   Oh, come along and get it over.

CROFTS [*Turning back towards the gate.*]   Ive no objection.

REV. SAMUEL   Not that way. We go through the fields, if you dont mind. Round here. [*He leads the way by the little path through the box hedge.*]

CROFTS   Oh, all right. [*He goes with the parson.*]

   [PRAED *follows with* MRS WARREN. VIVIE *does not stir: she watches them until they have gone, with all the lines of purpose in her face marking it strongly.*]

FRANK   Aint you coming?

VIVIE   No. I want to give you a warning, Frank. You were making fun of my mother just now when you said that about the rectory garden. That is barred in future. Please treat my mother with as much respect as you treat your own.

FRANK   My dear Viv: she wouldnt appreciate it: the two cases require different treatment. But what on earth has happened to you? Last night we were perfectly agreed as to your mother and her set. This morning I find you attitudinizing sentimentally with your arm round your parent's waist.

VIVIE [*Flushing.*]   Attitudinizing!

FRANK   That was how it struck me. First time I ever saw you do a second-rate thing.

VIVIE [*Controlling herself.*]   Yes, Frank: there has been a change; but I dont think it a change for the worse. Yesterday I was a little prig.

FRANK   And today?

VIVIE [*Wincing; then looking at him steadily.*]   Today I know my mother better than you do.

FRANK   Heaven forbid!

VIVIE   What do you mean?

FRANK   Viv: theres a freemasonry among thoroughly immoral people that you know nothing of. Youve too much character. T h a t s the bond between your mother and me: thats why I know her better than youll ever know her.

VIVIE   You are wrong: you know nothing about her. If you knew the circumstances against which my mother had to struggle—

FRANK [*Adroitly finishing the sentence for her.*]   I should know why she is what she is, shouldnt I? What difference would that make? Circumstances or no circumstances, Viv, you wont be able to stand your mother.

VIVIE [*Very angrily.*]   Why not?

FRANK   Because she's an old wretch, Viv. If you ever put your arm round her waist in my presence again, I'll shoot myself there and then as a protest against an exhibition which revolts me.

VIVIE   Must I choose between dropping your acquaintance and dropping my mother's?

FRANK [*Gracefully.*]   That would put the old lady at ever such a disadvantage. No, Viv: your infatuated little boy will have to stick to you in any case. But he's all the more anxious that you shouldnt make mistakes. It's no use, Viv: your mother's impossible. She may be a good sort; but she's a bad lot, a very bad lot.

VIVIE [*Hotly.*] Frank—! [*He stands his ground. She turns away and sits down on the bench under the yew tree, struggling to recover her self-command. Then she says*] Is she to be deserted by all the world because she's what you call a bad lot? Has she no right to live?

FRANK No fear of that, Viv: s h e wont ever be deserted. [*He sits on the bench beside her.*]

VIVIE But I am to desert her, I suppose.

FRANK [*Babyishly, lulling her and making love to her with his voice.*] Mustnt go live with her. Little family group of mother and daughter wouldnt be a success. Spoil our little group.

VIVIE [*Falling under the spell.*] What little group?

FRANK The babes in the wood: Vivie and little Frank. [*He nestles against her like a weary child.*] Lets go and get covered up with leaves.

VIVIE [*Rhythmically, rocking him like a nurse.*] Fast asleep, hand in hand, under the trees.

FRANK The wise little girl with her silly little boy.

VIVIE The dear little boy with his dowdy little girl.

FRANK Ever so peaceful, and relieved from the imbecility of the little boy's father and the questionableness of the little girl's—

VIVIE [*Smothering the word against her breast.*] Sh-sh-sh-sh! little girl wants to forget all about her mother. [*They are silent for some moments, rocking one another. Then* VIVIE *wakes up with a shock, exclaiming*] What a pair of fools we are! Come: sit up. Gracious! your hair. [*She smoothes it.*] I wonder do all grown up people play in that childish way when nobody is looking. I never did it when I was a child.

FRANK Neither did I. You are my first playmate. [*He catches her hand to kiss it, but checks himself to look round first. Very unexpectedly, he sees* CROFTS *emerging from the box hedge.*] Oh damn!

VIVIE Why damn, dear?

FRANK [*Whispering.*] Sh! Here's this brute Crofts. [*He sits farther away from her with an unconcerned air.*]

CROFTS. Could I have a few words with you, Miss Vivie?

VIVIE Certainly.

CROFTS [*To* FRANK.] Youll excuse me, Gardner. Theyre waiting for you in the church, if you don't mind.

FRANK [*Rising.*] Anything to oblige you, Crofts—except church. If you should happen to want me, Vivvums, ring the gate bell. [*He goes into the house with unruffled suavity.*]

CROFTS [*Watching him with a crafty air as he disappears, and speaking to* VIVIE *with an assumption of being on privileged terms with her.*] Pleasant young fellow that, Miss Vivie. Pity he has no money, isnt it?

VIVIE Do you think so?

CROFTS Well, whats he to do? No profession. No property. Whats he good for?

VIVIE I realize his disadvantages, Sir George.

CROFTS [*A little taken aback at being so precisely interpreted.*] Oh, it's not that. But while we're in this world we're in it; and money's money. [*Vivie does not answer.*] Nice day, isnt it?

VIVIE [*With scarcely veiled contempt for this effort at conversation.*] Very.

CROFTS [*With brutal good humor, as if he liked her pluck.*] Well, thats not what I came to say. [*Sitting down beside her.*] Now listen, Miss Vivie. I'm quite aware that I'm not a young lady's man.

VIVIE Indeed, Sir George?

CROFTS No; and to tell you the honest truth I dont want to be either. But when I say a thing I mean it; when I feel a sentiment I feel it in earnest; and what I value I pay hard money for. Thats the sort of man I am.

VIVIE It does you great credit, I'm sure.

CROFTS Oh, I dont mean to praise myself. I have my faults, Heaven knows: no man is more sensible of that than I am. I know I'm not perfect: thats one of the disadvantages of being a middle-aged man; for I'm not a young man, and I know it. But my code is a simple one, and, I think, a good one. Honor between man and man; fidelity between man and woman; and no cant about this religion or that religion, but an honest belief that things are making for good on the whole.

VIVIE [*With biting irony.*] "A power, not ourselves, that makes for righteousness," eh?

CROFTS [*Taking her seriously.*] Oh certainly. Not ourselves, of course. You understand what I mean. Well, now as to practical matters. You may have an idea that Ive flung my money about; but I havnt: I'm richer today than when I first came into the property. Ive used my knowledge of the world to invest my money in ways that other men have overlooked; and whatever else I may be, I'm a safe man from the money point of view.

VIVIE It's very kind of you to tell me all this.

CROFTS Oh well, come, Miss Vivie: you neednt pretend you dont see what I'm driving at. I want to settle down with a Lady Crofts. I suppose you think me very blunt, eh?

VIVIE Not at all: I am much obliged to you for being so definite and business-like. I quite appreciate the offer: the money, the position, L a d y C r o f t s, and so on. But I think I will say no, if you don't mind. I'd rather not. [*She rises, and strolls across to the sundial to get out of his immediate neighborhood.*]

CROFTS [*Not at all discouraged, and taking advantage of the additional room left him on the seat to spread himself comfortably, as if a few preliminary refusals were part of the inevitable routine of courtship.*] I'm in no hurry. It was only just to let you know in case young Gardner should try to trap you. Leave the question open.

VIVIE [*Sharply.*] My no is final. I wont go back from it.

[*CROFTS is not impressed. He grins; leans forward with his elbows on his knees to prod with his stick at some unfortunate insect in the grass; and looks cunningly at her. She turns away impatiently.*]

CROFTS I'm a good deal older than you. Twenty-five years; quarter of a century. I shant live for ever; and I'll take care that you shall be well off when I'm gone.

VIVIE I am proof against even that inducement, Sir George. Dont you think youd better take your answer? There is not the slightest chance of my altering it.

CROFTS [*Rising after a final slash at a daisy, and coming nearer to her.*] Well, no matter. I could tell you some things that would change your mind fast enough; but I wont, because I'd rather win you by honest affection. I was a good friend to your mother: ask her whether I wasnt. She'd never have made the money that paid for your education if it hadnt been for my advice and help, not to mention the money I advanced her. There are not many men would have stood by her as I have. I put not less than £40,000 into it, from first to last.

VIVIE [*Staring at him.*]   Do you mean to say you were my mother's business partner?

CROFTS   Yes. Now just think of all the trouble and the explanations it would save if we were to keep the whole thing in the family, so to speak. Ask your mother whether she'd like to have to explain all her affairs to a perfect stranger.

VIVIE   I see no difficulty, since I understand that the business is wound up, and the money invested.

CROFTS [*Stopping short, amazed.*]   Wound up! Wind up a business thats paying 35 per cent in the worst years! Not likely. Who told you that?

VIVIE [*Her color quite gone.*]   Do you mean that it is still—? [*She stops abruptly, and puts her hand on the sundial to support herself. Then she gets quickly to the iron chair and sits down.*] What business are you talking about?

CROFTS   Well, the fact is it's not what would be considered exactly a high-class business in my set—the county set, you know—our set it will be if you think better of my offer. Not that theres any mystery about it: dont think that. Of course you know by your mother's being in it that it's perfectly straight and honest. Ive known her for many years; and I can say of her that she'd cut off her hands sooner than touch anything that was not what it ought to be. I'll tell you all about it if you like. I dont know whether youve found in travelling how hard it is to find a really comfortable private hotel.

VIVIE [*Sickened, averting her face.*]   Yes: go on.

CROFTS   Well, thats all it is. Your mother has a genius for managing such things. We've got two in Brussels, one in Ostend, one in Vienna, and two in Budapest. Of course there are others besides ourselves in it; but we hold most of the capital; and your mother's indispensable as managing director. Youve noticed, I daresay, that she travels a good deal. But you see you cant mention such things in society. Once let out the word hotel and everybody says you keep a public-house. You wouldnt like people to say that of your mother, would you? Thats why we're so reserved about it. By the way, youll keep it to yourself, wont you? Since it's been a secret so long, it had better remain so.

VIVIE   And this is the business you invite me to join you in?

CROFTS   Oh, no. My wife shant be troubled with business. Youll not be in it more than youve always been.

VIVIE   I always been! What do you mean?

CROFTS   Only that youve always lived on it. It paid for your education and the dress you have on your back. Dont turn up your nose at business, Miss Vivie: where would your Newnhams and Girtons[1] be without it?

VIVIE [*Rising, almost beside herself.*]   Take care. I know what this business is.

CROFTS [*Staring, with a suppressed oath.*]   Who told you?

---

1. Girton, like Newnham, is a women's college at Cambridge University.

VIVIE   Your partner. My mother.

CROFTS [*Black with rage.*]   The old—

VIVIE   Just so.

> [*He swallows the epithet and stands for a moment swearing and raging foully to himself. But he knows that his cue is to be sympathetic. He takes refuge in generous indignation.*]

CROFTS   She ought to have had more consideration for you. I'd never have told you.

VIVIE   I think you would probably have told me when we were married; it would have been a convenient weapon to break me in with.

CROFTS [*Quite sincerely.*]   I never intended that. On my word as a gentleman I didnt.

> [VIVIE *wonders at him. Her sense of the irony of his protest cools and braces her. She replies with contemptuous self-possession.*]

VIVIE   It does not matter. I suppose you understand that when we leave here today our acquaintance ceases.

CROFTS   Why? Is it for helping your mother?

VIVIE   My mother was a very poor woman who had no reasonable choice but to do as she did. You were a rich gentleman; and you did the same for the sake of 35 per cent. You are a pretty common sort of scoundrel, I think. That is my opinion of you.

CROFTS [*After a stare: not at all displeased, and much more at ease on these frank terms than on their former ceremonious ones.*]   Ha! ha! ha! ha! Go it, little missie, go it: it doesnt hurt me and it amuses you. Why the devil shouldnt I invest my money that way? I take the interest on my capital like other people: I hope you dont think I dirty my own hands with the work. Come! you wouldnt refuse the acquaintance of my mother's cousin the Duke of Belgravia because some of the rents he gets are earned in queer ways. You wouldnt cut the Archbishop of Canterbury, I suppose, because the Ecclesiastical Commissioners have a few publicans and sinners among their tenants. Do you remember your Crofts scholarship at Newnham? Well, that was founded by my brother the M.P.[2] He gets his 22 per cent out of a factory with 600 girls in it, and not one of them getting wages enough to live on. How d'ye suppose they manage when they have no family to fall back on? Ask your mother. And do you expect me to turn my back on 35 per cent when all the rest are pocketing what they can, like sensible men? No such fool! If youre going to pick and choose your acquaintances on moral principles, youd better clear out of this country, unless you want to cut yourself out of all decent society.

VIVIE [*Conscience stricken.*]   You might go on to point out that I myself never asked where the money I spent came from. I believe I am just as bad as you.

CROFTS [*Greatly reassured.*]   Of course you are; and a very good thing too! What harm does it do after all? [*Rallying her jocularly.*] So you dont think me such a scoundrel now you come to think it over. Eh?

VIVIE   I have shared profits with you; and I admitted you just now to the familiarity of knowing what I think of you.

CROFTS [*With serious friendliness.*]   To be sure you did. You wont find me

2. Member of Parliament.

a bad sort: I dont go in for being superfine intellectually; but Ive plenty
of honest human feeling; and the old Crofts breed comes out in a sort
of instinctive hatred of anything low, in which I'm sure youll sympathize
with me. Believe me, Miss Vivie, the world isnt such a bad place as the
croakers make out. As long as you dont fly openly in the face of society,
society doesnt ask any inconvenient questions; and it makes precious
short work of the cads who do. There are no secrets better kept than the
secrets everybody guesses. In the class of people I can introduce you to,
no lady or gentleman would so far forget themselves as to discuss my
business affairs or your mother's. No man can offer you a safer position.

VIVIE [*Studying him curiously.*]   I suppose you really think youre getting
on famously with me.

CROFTS   Well, I hope I may flatter myself that you think better of me than
you did at first.

VIVIE [*Quietly.*]   I hardly find you worth thinking about at all now. When
I think of the society that tolerates you, and the laws that protect you!
when I think of how helpless nine out of ten young girls would be in the
hands of you and my mother! the unmentionable woman and her capitalist bully—

CROFTS [*Livid.*]   Damn you!

VIVIE   You need not. I feel among the damned already.

   [*She raises the latch of the gate to open it and go out. He follows her
   and puts his hand heavily on the top bar to prevent its opening.*]

CROFTS [*Panting with fury.*]   Do you think I'll put up with this from you,
you young devil?

VIVIE [*Unmoved.*]   Be quiet. Some one will answer the bell. [*Without
flinching a step she strikes the bell with the back of her hand. It clangs
harshly; and he starts back involuntarily. Almost immediately* FRANK
appears at the porch with his rifle.]

FRANK [*With cheerful politeness.*]   Will you have the rifle, Viv; or shall I
operate?

VIVIE   Frank: have you been listening?

FRANK [*Coming down into the garden.*]   Only for the bell, I assure you; so
that you shouldn't have to wait. I think I shewed great insight into your
character Crofts.

CROFTS   For two pins I'd take that gun from you and break it across your
head.

FRANK [*Stalking him cautiously.*]   Pray dont. I'm ever so careless in handling firearms. Sure to be a fatal accident, with a reprimand from the
coroner's jury for my negligence.

VIVIE   Put the rifle away, Frank: it's quite unnecessary.

FRANK   Quite right, Viv. Much more sportsmanlike to catch him in a trap.
[CROFTS, *understanding the insult, makes a threatening movement.*]
Crofts: there are fifteen cartridges in the magazine here; and I am a dead
shot at the present distance and at an object of your size.

CROFTS   Oh, you neednt be afraid. I'm not going to touch you.

FRANK   Ever so magnanimous of you under the circumstances! Thank you!

CROFTS   I'll tell you this before I go. It may interest you, since youre so
fond of one another. Allow me, Mister Frank, to introduce you to your
half-sister, the eldest daughter of the Reverend Samuel Gardner. Miss

Vivie: your half-brother. Good morning. [*He goes out through the gate and along the road.*]

FRANK [*After a pause of stupefaction, raising the rifle.*]   Youll testify before the coroner that it's an accident, Viv. [*He takes aim at the retreating figure of* CROFTS. VIVIE *seizes the muzzle and pulls it round against her breast.*]

VIVIE   Fire now. You may.

FRANK [*Dropping his end of the rifle hastily.*]   Stop! take care. [*She lets go. It falls on the turf.*] Oh, youve given your little boy such a turn. Suppose it had gone off! ugh! [*He sinks on the garden seat, overcome.*]

VIVIE   Suppose it had: do you think it would not have been a relief to have some sharp physical pain tearing through me?

FRANK [*Coaxingly.*]   Take it ever so easy, dear Viv. Remember; even if the rifle scared that fellow into telling the truth for the first time in his life, that only makes us the babes in the wood in earnest. [*He holds out his arms to her.*] Come and be covered up with leaves again.

VIVIE [*With a cry of disgust.*]   Ah, not that, not that. You make all my flesh creep.

FRANK   Why, whats the matter?

VIVIE   Goodbye. [*She makes for the gate.*]

FRANK [*Jumping up.*]   Hallo! Stop! Viv! Viv! [*She turns in the gateway.*] Where are you going to? Where shall we find you?

VIVIE   At Honoria Fraser's chambers, 67 Chancery Lane, for the rest of my life. [*She goes off quickly in the opposite direction to that taken by* CROFTS.]

FRANK   But I say—wait—dash it! [*He runs after her.*]

Act 4

HONORIA FRASER's *chambers in Chancery Lane. An office at the top of New Stone Buildings, with a plate-glass window, distempered walls, electric light, and a patent stove. Saturday afternoon. The chimneys of Lincoln's Inn*[3] *and the western sky beyond are seen through the window. There is a double writing table in the middle of the room, with a cigar box, ash pans, and a portable electric reading lamp almost snowed up in heaps of papers and books. This table has knee holes and chairs right and left and is very untidy. The clerk's desk, closed and tidy, with its high stool, is against the wall, near a door communicating with the inner rooms. In the opposite wall is the door leading to the public corridor. Its upper panel is of opaque glass, lettered in black on the outside,* FRASER AND WARREN. *A baize screen hides the corner between this door and the window.*

FRANK, *in a fashionable light-colored coaching suit, with his stick, gloves, and white hat in his hands, is pacing up and down the office. Somebody tries the door with a key.*

FRANK [*Calling.*]   Come in. It's not locked.

[VIVIE *comes in, in her hat and jacket. She stops and stares at him.*]

VIVIE [*Sternly.*]   What are you doing here?

FRANK   Waiting to see you. Ive been here for hours. Is this the way you attend to your business? [*He puts his hat and stick on the table, and*

---

3. One of the four legal societies in London collectively known as the Inns of Court.

perches himself with a vault on the clerk's stool, looking at her with every appearance of being in a specially restless, teasing flippant mood.]

VIVIE   Ive been away exactly twenty minutes for a cup of tea. [*She takes off her hat and jacket and hangs them up behind the screen.*] How did you get in?

FRANK   The staff had not left when I arrived. He's gone to play cricket on Primrose Hill.[4] Why dont you employ a woman, and give your sex a chance?

VIVIE   What have you come for?

FRANK   [*Springing off the stool and coming close to her.*]   Viv: lets go and enjoy the Saturday half-holiday somewhere, like the staff. What do you say to Richmond,[5] and then a music hall, and a jolly supper?

VIVIE   Cant afford it. I shall put in another six hours work before I go to bed.

FRANK   Cant afford it, cant we? Aha! Look here. [*He takes out a handful of sovereigns and makes them chink.*] Gold, Viv: gold!

VIVIE   Where did you get it?

FRANK   Gambling, Viv: gambling. Poker.

VIVIE   Pah! It's meaner than stealing it. No: I'm not coming. [*She sits down to work at the table, with her back to the glass door, and begins turning over the papers.*]

FRANK   [*Remonstrating piteously.*]   But, my dear Viv, I want to talk to you ever so seriously.

VIVIE   Very well: sit down in Honoria's chair and talk here. I like ten minutes chat after tea. [*He murmurs.*] No use groaning: I'm inexorable. [*He takes the opposite seat disconsolately.*] Pass that cigar box, will you?

FRANK   [*Pushing the cigar box across.*]   Nasty womanly habit. Nice men dont do it any longer.

VIVIE   Yes: they object to the smell in the office; and weve had to take to cigarets. See! [*She opens the box and takes out a cigaret, which she lights. She offers him one; but he shakes his head with a wry face. She settles herself comfortably in her chair, smoking.*] Go ahead.

FRANK   Well, I want to know what youve done—what arrangements youve made.

VIVIE   Everything was settled twenty minutes after I arrived here. Honoria has found the business too much for her this year; and she was on the point of sending for me and proposing a partnership when I walked in and told her I hadnt a farthing in the world. So I installed myself and packed her off for a fortnight's holiday. What happened at Haslemere when I left?

FRANK   Nothing at all. I said youd gone to town on particular business.

VIVIE   Well?

FRANK   Well, either they were too flabbergasted to say anything, or else Crofts had prepared your mother. Anyhow, she didnt say anything; and Crofts didnt say anything; and Praddy only stared. After tea they got up and went; and Ive not seen them since.

VIVIE   [*Nodding placidly with one eye on a wreath of smoke.*]   Thats all right.

4. A park in northwest London.   5. A residential suburb in southwest London.

FRANK [*Looking round disparagingly.*]   Do you intend to stick in this confounded place?

VIVIE [*Blowing the wreath decisively away, and sitting straight up.*]   Yes. These two days have given me back all my strength and self-possession. I will never take a holiday again as long as I live.

FRANK [*With a very wry face.*]   Mps! You look quite happy. And as hard as nails.

VIVIE [*Grimly.*]   Well for me that I am!

FRANK [*Rising.*]   Look here, Viv: we must have an explanation. We parted the other day under a complete misunderstanding. [*He sits on the table, close to her.*]

VIVIE [*Putting away the cigaret.*]   Well: clear it up.

FRANK   You remember what Crofts said?

VIVIE   Yes.

FRANK   That revelation was supposed to bring about a complete change in the nature of our feeling for one another. It placed us on the footing of brother and sister.

VIVIE   Yes.

FRANK   Have you ever had a brother?

VIVIE   No.

FRANK   Then you dont know what being brother and sister feels like? Now I have lots of sisters; and the fraternal feeling is quite familiar to me. I assure you my feeling for you is not the least in the world like it. The girls will go their way; I will go mine; and we shant care if we never see one another again. Thats brother and sister. But as to you, I cant be easy if I have to pass a week without seeing you. Thats not brother and sister. It's exactly what I felt an hour before Crofts made his revelation. In short, dear Viv, it's love's young dream.

VIVIE [*Bitingly.*]   The same feeling, Frank, that brought your father to my mother's feet. Is that it?

FRANK [*So revolted that he slips off the table for a moment.*]   I very strongly object, Viv, to have my feelings compared to any which the Reverend Samuel is capable of harboring; and I object still more to a comparison of you to your mother. [*Resuming his perch.*] Besides, I dont believe the story. I have taxed my father with it, and obtained from him what I consider tantamount to a denial.

VIVIE   What did he say?

FRANK   He said he was sure there must be some mistake.

VIVIE   Do you believe him?

FRANK   I am prepared to take his word as against Crofts'.

VIVIE   Does it make any difference? I mean in your imagination or conscience; for of course it makes no real difference.

FRANK [*Shaking his head.*]   None whatever to m e.

VIVIE   Nor to me.

FRANK [*Staring.*]   But this is ever so surprising! [*He goes back to his chair.*] I thought our whole relations were altered in your imagination and conscience, as you put it, the moment those words were out of the brute's muzzle.

VIVIE   No: it was not that. I didnt believe him. I only wish I could.

FRANK   Eh?

VIVIE   I think brother and sister would be a very suitable relation for us.

FRANK   You really mean that?

VIVIE   Yes. It's the only relation I care for, even if we could afford any other. I mean that.

FRANK [*Raising his eyebrows like one on whom a new light has dawned, and rising with quite an effusion of chivalrous sentiment.*]   My dear Viv: why didnt you say so before? I am ever so sorry for persecuting you. I understand, of course.

VIVIE [*Puzzled.*]   Understand what?

FRANK   Oh, I'm not a fool in the ordinary sense: only in the Scriptural sense of doing all the things the wise man declared to be folly, after trying them himself on the most extensive scale. I see I am no longer Vivvum's little boy. Dont be alarmed: I shall never call you Vivvums again—at least unless you get tired of your new little boy, whoever he may be.

VIVIE   My new little boy!

FRANK [*With conviction.*]   Must be a new little boy. Always happens that way. No other way, in fact.

VIVIE   None that you know of, fortunately for you.

[*Someone knocks at the door.*]

FRANK   My curse upon yon caller, whoe'er he be!

VIVIE   It's Praed. He's going to Italy and wants to say goodbye. I asked him to call this afternoon. Go and let him in.

FRANK   We can continue our conversation after his departure for Italy. I'll stay him out. [*He goes to the door and opens it.*] How are you, Praddy? Delighted to see you. Come in.

[PRAED, *dressed for travelling, comes in, in high spirits.*]

PRAED   How do you do, Miss Warren? [*She presses his hand cordially, though a certain sentimentality in his high spirits jars on her.*] I start in an hour from Holborn Viaduct.[6] I wish I could persuade you to try Italy.

VIVIE   What for?

PRAED   Why, to saturate yourself with beauty and romance, of course.

[VIVIE, *with a shudder, turns her chair to the table, as if the work waiting for her were a support to her.* PRAED *sits opposite to her.* FRANK *places a chair near* VIVIE, *and drops lazily and carelessly into it, talking at her over his shoulder.*]

FRANK   No use, Praddy. Viv is a little Philistine. She is indifferent to my romance, and insensible to my beauty.

VIVIE   Mr Praed: once for all, there is no beauty and no romance in life for me. Life is what it is; and I am prepared to take it as it is.

PRAED [*Enthusiastically.*]   You will not say that if you come with me to Verona and on to Venice. You will cry with delight at living in such a beautiful world.

FRANK   This is most eloquent, Praddy. Keep it up.

PRAED   Oh, I assure you I have cried—I shall cry again, I hope—at fifty! At your age, Miss Warren, you would not need to go so far as Verona. Your spirits would absolutely fly up at the mere sight of Ostend. You would be charmed with the gaiety, the vivacity, the happy air of Brussels.

VIVIE [*Springing up with an exclamation of loathing.*]   Agh!

6. A road bridge in the City of London.

PRAED [*Rising.*]   Whats the matter?

FRANK [*Rising.*]   Hallo, Viv!

VIVIE [*To* PRAED, *with deep reproach.*]   Can you find no better example of your beauty and romance than Brussels to talk to me about?

PRAED [*Puzzled.*]   Of course it's very different from Verona. I dont suggest for a moment that—

VIVIE [*Bitterly.*]   Probably the beauty and romance come to much the same in both places.

PRAED [*Completely sobered and much concerned.*]   My dear Miss Warren: I—[*Looking inquiringly at* FRANK.] Is anything the matter?

FRANK   She thinks your enthusiasm frivolous, Praddy. She's had ever such a serious call.

VIVIE [*Sharply.*]   Hold your tongue, Frank. Dont be silly.

FRANK [*Sitting down.*]   Do you call this good manners, Praed?

PRAED [*Anxious and considerate.*]   Shall I take him away, Miss Warren? I feel sure we have disturbed you at your work.

VIVIE   Sit down: I'm not ready to go back to work yet. [PRAED *sits.*] You both think I have an attack of nerves. Not a bit of it. But there are two subjects I want dropped, if you dont mind. One of them [*To* FRANK.] is love's young dream in any shape or form: the other [*To* PRAED.] is the romance and beauty of life, especially Ostend and the gaiety of Brussels. You are welcome to any illusions you may have left on these subjects: I have none. If we three are to remain friends, I must be treated as a woman of business, permanently single [*To* FRANK.] and permanently unromantic [*to* PRAED].

FRANK   I also shall remain permanently single until you change your mind. Praddy: change the subject. Be eloquent about something else.

PRAED [*Diffidently.*]   I'm afraid theres nothing else in the world that I c a n talk about. The Gospel of Art is the only one I can preach. I know Miss Warren is a great devotee of the Gospel of Getting On; but we cant discuss that without hurting your feelings, Frank, since you are determined not to get on.

FRANK   Oh, dont mind my feelings. Give me some improving advice by all means: it does me ever so much good. Have another try to make a successful man of me, Viv. Come; lets have it all: energy, thrift, foresight, self-respect, character. Dont you hate people who have no character, Viv?

VIVIE [*Wincing.*]   Oh, stop, stop: let us have no more of that horrible cant. Mr Praed: if there are really only those two gospels in the world, we had better all kill ourselves; for the same taint is in both, through and through.

FRANK [*Looking critically at her.*]   There is a touch of poetry about you today, Viv, which has hitherto been lacking.

PRAED [*Remonstrating.*]   My dear Frank: arnt you a little unsympathetic?

VIVIE [*Merciless to herself.*]   No: it's good for me. It keeps me from being sentimental.

FRANK [*Bantering her.*]   Checks your strong natural propensity that way, dont it?

VIVIE [*Almost hysterically.*]   Oh yes; go on: dont spare me. I was sentimental for one moment in my life—beautifully sentimental—by moonlight; and now—

FRANK [*Quickly.*]   I say, Viv: take care. Dont give yourself away.

VIVIE   Oh, do you think Mr Praed does not know all about my mother? [*Turning on* PRAED.] You had better have told me that morning, Mr Praed. You are very old fashioned in your delicacies, after all.

PRAED   Surely it is you who are a little old fashioned in your prejudices, Miss Warren, I feel bound to tell you, speaking as an artist, and believing that the most intimate human relationships are far beyond and above the scope of the law, that though I know that your mother is an unmarried woman, I do not respect her the less on that account. I respect her more.

FRANK [*Airily.*]   Hear! Hear!

VIVIE [*Staring at him.*]   Is that a l l you know?

PRAED   Certainly that is all.

VIVIE   Then you neither of you know anything. Your guesses are innocence itself compared to the truth.

PRAED [*Rising, startled and indignant, and preserving his politeness with an effort.*]   I hope not. [*More emphatically.*] I hope not, Miss Warren.

FRANK [*Whistles.*]   Whew!

VIVIE   You are not making it easy for me to tell you, Mr Praed.

PRAED [*His chivalry drooping before their conviction.*]   If there is anything worse—that is, anything else—are you sure you are right to tell us, Miss Warren?

VIVIE   I am sure that if I had the courage I should spend the rest of my life in telling everybody—stamping and branding it into them until they all felt their part in its abomination as I feel mine. There is nothing I despise more than the wicked convention that protects these things by forbidding a woman to mention them. And yet I cant tell you. The two infamous words that describe what my mother is are ringing in my ears and struggling on my tongue; but I cant utter them: the shame of them is too horrible for me. [*She buries her face in her hands. The two men, astonished, stare at one another and then at her. She raises her head again desperately and snatches a sheet of paper and a pen.*] Here: let me draft you a prospectus.

FRANK   Oh, she's mad. Do you hear, Viv? mad. Come! pull yourself together.

VIVIE   You shall see. [*She writes.*] "Paid up capital: not less than £40,000 standing in the name of Sir George Crofts, Baronet, the chief shareholder. Premises at Brussels, Ostend, Vienna and Budapest. Managing director: Mrs Warren"; and now dont let us forget her qualifications: the two words. [*She writes the words and pushes the paper to them.*] There! Oh no: dont read it: dont! [*She snatches it back and tears it to pieces; then seizes her head in her hands and hides her face on the table.*]

> [FRANK, *who has watched the writing over his shoulder, and opened his eyes very widely at it, takes a card from his pocket; scribbles the two words on it; and silently hands it to* PRAED, *who reads it with amazement, and hides it hastily in his pocket.*]

FRANK [*Whispering tenderly.*]   Viv, dear: thats all right. I read what you wrote: so did Praddy. We understand. And we remain, as this leaves us at present, yours ever so devotedly.

PRAED   We do indeed, Miss Warren. I declare you are the most splendidly courageous woman I ever met.

[*This sentimental compliment braces* VIVIE. *She throws it away from her with an impatient shake, and forces herself to stand up, though not without some support from the table.*]

FRANK   Dont stir, Viv, if you dont want to. Take it easy.

VIVIE   Thank you. You can always depend on me for two things: not to cry and not to faint. [*She moves a few steps towards the door of the inner room, and stops close to* PRAED *to say.*] I shall need much more courage than that when I tell my mother that we have come to the parting of the ways. Now I must go into the next room for a moment to make myself neat again, if you dont mind.

PRAED   Shall we go away?

VIVIE   No; I shall be back presently. Only for a moment. [*She goes into the other room,* PRAED *opening the door for her.*]

PRAED   What an amazing revelation! I'm extremely disappointed in Crofts: I am indeed.

FRANK   I'm not in the least. I feel he's perfectly accounted for at last. But what a facer for me, Praddy! I cant marry her now.

PRAED [*Sternly.*]   Frank! [*The two look at one another,* FRANK *unruffled,* PRAED *deeply indignant.*] Let me tell you, Gardner, that if you desert her now you will behave very despicably.

FRANK   Good old Praddy! Ever chivalrous! But you mistake: it's not the moral aspect of the case: it's the money aspect. I really cant bring myself to touch the old woman's money now.

PRAED   And was that what you were going to marry on?

FRANK   What else? *I* havnt any money, nor the smallest turn for making it. If I married Viv now she would have to support me; and I should cost her more than I am worth.

PRAED   But surely a clever bright fellow like you can make something by your own brains.

FRANK   Oh yes, a little. [*He takes out his money again.*] I made all that yesterday in an hour and a half. But I made it in a highly speculative business. No, dear Praddy: even if Bessie and Georgina marry millionaires and the governor dies after cutting them off with a shilling, I shall have only four hundred a year. And he wont die until he's three score and ten: he hasnt originality enough. I shall be on short allowance for the next twenty years. No short allowance for Viv, if I can help it. I withdraw gracefully and leave the field to the gilded youth of England. So thats settled. I shant worry her about it: I'll just send her a little note after we're gone. She'll understand.

PRAED [*Grasping his hand.*]   Good fellow, Frank! I heartily beg your pardon. But must you never see her again?

FRANK   Never see her again! Hang it all, be reasonable. I shall come along as often as possible, and be her brother. I can n o t understand the absurd consequences you romantic people expect from the most ordinary transactions. [*A knock at the door.*] I wonder who this is. Would you mind opening the door? If it's a client it will look more respectable than if I appeared.

PRAED   Certainly. [*He goes to the door and opens it.* FRANK *sits down in* VIVIE's *chair to scribble a note.*] My dear Kitty: come in: come in.

[MRS WARREN *comes in, looking apprehensively round for* VIVIE. *She has done her best to make herself matronly and dignified. The brilliant hat is replaced by a sober bonnet, and the gay blouse covered by a costly black silk mantle. She is pitiably anxious and ill at ease: evidently panic-stricken.*]

MRS WARREN [*To* FRANK.] What! Y o u r e here, are you?

FRANK [*Turning in his chair from his writing, but not rising.*] Here, and charmed to see you. You come like a breath of spring.

MRS WARREN Oh, get out with your nonsense. [*In a low voice.*] Wheres Vivie?

[FRANK *points expressively to the door of the inner room, but says nothing.*]

MRS WARREN [*Sitting down suddenly and almost beginning to cry.*] Praddy: wont she see me, dont you think?

PRAED My dear Kitty: dont distress yourself. Why should she not?

MRS WARREN Oh, you never can see why not: youre too innocent. Mr Frank: did she say anything to you?

FRANK [*Folding his note.*] She m u s t see you, if [*very expressively*] you wait til she comes in.

MRS WARREN [*Frightened.*] Why shouldnt I wait?

[FRANK *looks quizzically at her; puts his note carefully on the inkbottle, so that* VIVIE *cannot fail to find it when next she dips her pen; then rises and devotes his attention entirely to her.*]

FRANK My dear Mrs Warren: suppose you were a sparrow—ever so tiny and pretty a sparrow hopping in the roadway—and you saw a steam roller coming in your direction, would you wait for it?

MRS WARREN Oh, dont bother me with your sparrows. What did she run away from Haslemere like that for?

FRANK I'm afraid she'll tell you if you rashly await her return.

MRS WARREN Do you want me to go away?

FRANK No: I always want you to stay. But I a d v i s e you to go away.

MRS WARREN What! and never see her again!

FRANK Precisely.

MRS WARREN [*Crying again.*] Praddy: dont let him be cruel to me. [*She hastily checks her tears and wipes her eyes.*] She'll be so angry if she sees Ive been crying.

FRANK [*With a touch of real compassion in his airy tenderness.*] You know that Praddy is the soul of kindness, Mrs Warren. Praddy: what do y o u say? Go or stay?

PRAED [*To* MRS WARREN.] I really should be very sorry to cause you unnecessary pain; but I think perhaps you had better not wait. The fact is— [VIVIE *is heard at the inner door.*]

FRANK Sh! Too late. She's coming.

MRS WARREN Dont tell her I was crying. [VIVIE *comes in. She stops gravely on seeing* MRS WARREN, *who greets her with hysterical cheerfulness.*] Well, dearie. So here you are at last.

VIVIE I am glad you have come: I want to speak to you. You said you were going, Frank, I think.

FRANK Yes. Will you come with me, Mrs Warren? What do you say to a trip to Richmond, and the theatre in the evening? There is safety in Richmond. No steam roller there.

VIVIE   Nonsense, Frank. My mother will stay here.

MRS WARREN [*Scared.*]   I dont know: perhaps I'd better go. We're disturbing you at your work.

VIVIE [*With quiet decision.*]   Mr. Praed: please take Frank away. Sit down,
mother. [MRS WARREN *obeys helplessly.*]

PRAED   Come, Frank. Goodbye, Miss Vivie.

VIVIE [*Shaking hands.*]   Goodbye. A pleasant trip.

PRAED   Thank you: thank you. I hope so.

FRANK [*To* MRS WARREN.]   Goodbye: youd ever so much better have taken
my advice. [*He shakes hands with her. Then airily to* VIVIE] Byebye, Viv.

VIVIE   Goodbye. [*He goes out gaily without shaking hands with her.*]

PRAED [*Sadly.*]   Goodbye, Kitty.

MRS WARREN [*Sniveling.*]   —oobye!

> [PRAED *goes.* VIVIE, *composed and extremely grave, sits down in Hono-
> ria's chair, and waits for her mother to speak.* MRS WARREN, *dreading a
> pause, loses no time in beginning.*]

MRS WARREN   Well, Vivie, what did you go away like that for without saying a word to me? How could you do such a thing! And what have you
done to poor George? I wanted him to come with me; but he shuffled
out of it. I could see that he was quite afraid of you. Only fancy: he
wanted me not to come. As if [*Trembling.*] I should be afraid of you,
dearie. [VIVIE's *gravity deepens.*] But of course I told him it was all settled
and comfortable between us, and that we were on the best of terms. [*She
breaks down.*] Vivie: whats the meaning of this? [*She produces a commercial envelope, and fumbles at the enclosure with trembling fingers.*] I
got it from the bank this morning.

VIVIE   It is my month's allowance. They sent it to me as usual the other
day. I simply sent it back to be placed to your credit, and asked them to
send you the lodgment receipt. In future I shall support myself.

MRS WARREN [*Not daring to understand.*]   Wasnt it enough? Why didnt
you tell me? [*With a cunning gleam in her eye.*] I'll double it: I was
intending to double it. Only let me know how much you want.

VIVIE   You know very well that that has nothing to do with it. From this
time I go my own way in my own business and among my own friends.
And you will go yours. [*She rises.*] Goodbye.

MRS WARREN [*Rising, appalled.*]   Goodbye?

VIVIE   Yes: Goodbye. Come: dont let us make a useless scene: you understand perfectly well. Sir George Crofts has told me the whole business.

MRS WARREN [*Angrily.*]   Silly old— [*She swallows an epithet, and turns
white at the narrowness of her escape from uttering it.*]

VIVIE   Just so.

MRS WARREN   He ought to have his tongue cut out. But I thought it was
ended: you said you didnt mind.

VIVIE [*Steadfastly.*]   Excuse me: I d o mind.

MRS WARREN   But I explained—

VIVIE   You explained how it came about. You did not tell me that it is still
going on. [*She sits.*]

> [MRS WARREN, *silenced for a moment, looks forlornly at* VIVIE, *who waits,
> secretly hoping that the combat is over. But the cunning expression
> comes back into* MRS WARREN's *face; and she bends across the table, sly
> and urgent, half whispering.*]

MRS WARREN   Vivie: do you know how rich I am?

VIVIE   I have no doubt you are very rich.

MRS WARREN   But you dont know all that that means: youre too young. It means a new dress every day; it means theatres and balls every night; it means having the pick of all the gentlemen in Europe at your feet; it means a lovely house and plenty of servants; it means the choicest of eating and drinking; it means everything you like, everything you want, everything you can think of. And what are you here? A mere drudge, toiling and moiling early and late for your bare living and two cheap dresses a year. Think over it. [*Soothingly.*] Youre shocked, I know. I can enter into your feelings; and I think they do you credit; but trust me, nobody will blame you: you may take my word for that. I know what young girls are; and I know youll think better of it when youve turned it over in your mind.

VIVIE   So thats how it's done, is it? You must have said all that to many a woman, mother, to have it so pat.

MRS WARREN [*Passionately.*]   What harm am I asking you to do? [VIVIE *turns away contemptuously.* MRS WARREN *continues desperately.*] Vivie: listen to me: you dont understand: youve been taught wrong on purpose: you dont know what the world is really like.

VIVIE [*Arrested.*]   Taught wrong on purpose! What do you mean?

MRS WARREN   I mean that youre throwing away all your chances for nothing. You think that people are what they pretend to be: that the way you were taught at school and college to think right and proper is the way things really are. But it's not: it's all only a pretence, to keep the cowardly slavish common run of people quiet. Do you want to find that out, like other women, at forty, when youve thrown yourself away and lost your chances; or wont you take it in good time now from your own mother, that loves you and swears to you that it's truth: gospel truth? [*urgently*] Vivie: the big people, the clever people, the managing people, all know it. They do as I do, and think what I think. I know plenty of them. I know them to speak to, to introduce you to, to make friends of for you. I dont mean anything wrong; thats what you dont understand: your head is full of ignorant ideas about me. What do the people that taught you know about life or about people like me? When did they ever meet me, or speak to me, or let anyone tell them about me? the fools! Would they ever have done anything for you if I hadnt paid them? Havnt I told you that I want you to be respectable? Havnt I brought you up to be respectable? And how can you keep it up without my money and my influence and Lizzie's friends? Cant you see that youre cutting your own throat as well as breaking my heart in turning your back on me?

VIVIE   I recognize the Crofts philosophy of life, mother. I heard it all from him that day at the Gardners'.

MRS WARREN   You think I want to force that played-out old sot on you! I dont, Vivie: on my oath I dont.

VIVIE   It would not matter if you did: you would not succeed. [MRS WARREN *winces, deeply hurt by the implied indifference towards her affectionate intention.* VIVIE, *neither understanding this nor concerning herself about it, goes on calmly.*] Mother: you dont at all know the sort of person I am. I dont object to Crofts more than to any other coarsely built man of his class. To tell you the truth, I rather admire him for being strong-minded enough to enjoy himself in his own way and make plenty of money instead of living the usual shooting, hunting, dining-out, tailoring, loafing life of his set merely because all the rest do it. And I'm perfectly aware that if I'd been in the same circumstances as my aunt Liz, I'd have done exactly what she did. I dont think I'm more prejudiced or straitlaced than you: I think I'm less. I'm certain I'm less sentimental. I know very well that fashionable morality is all a pretence, and that if I took your money and devoted the rest of my life to spending it fashionably, I might be as worthless and vicious as the silliest woman could possibly want to be without having a word said to me about it. But I dont want to be worthless. I shouldnt enjoy trotting about the park to advertize my dressmaker and carriage builder, or being bored at the opera to shew off a shopwindowful of diamonds.

MRS WARREN [*Bewildered.*]   But—

VIVIE   Wait a moment: Ive not done. Tell me why you continue your business now that you are independent of it. Your sister, you told me, has left all that behind her. Why dont you do the same?

MRS WARREN   Oh, it's all very easy for Liz: she likes good society, and has the air of being a lady. Imagine me in a cathedral town! Why, the very rooks in the trees would find me out even if I could stand the dulness of it. I must have work and excitement, or I should go melancholy mad. And what else is there for me to do? The life suits me: I'm fit for it and not for anything else. If I didnt do it somebody else would; so I dont do any real harm by it. And then it brings in money; and I like making money. No; it's no use: I cant give it up—not for anybody. But what need you know about it? I'll never mention it. I'll keep Crofts away. I'll not trouble you much: you see I have to be constantly running about from one place to another. Youll be quit of me altogether when I die.

VIVIE   No: I am my mother's daughter. I am like you: I must have work, and must make more money than I spend. But my work is not your work, and my way not your way. We must part. It will not make much difference to us: instead of meeting one another for perhaps a few months in twenty years we shall never meet: thats all.

MRS WARREN [*Her voice stifled in tears.*]   Vivie: I meant to have been more with you: I did indeed.

VIVIE   It's no use, mother: I am not to be changed by a few cheap tears and entreaties any more than you are, I daresay.

MRS WARREN [*Wildly.*]   Oh, you call a mother's tears cheap.

VIVIE   They cost you nothing; and you ask me to give you the peace and quietness of my whole life in exchange for them. What use would my company be to you if you could get it? What have we two in common that could make either of us happy together?

MRS WARREN [*Lapsing recklessly into her dialect.*]   We're mother and daughter. I want my daughter. Ive a right to you. Who is to care for me when I'm old? Plenty of girls have taken to me like daughters and cried at leaving me; but I let them all go because I had you to look forward to. I kept myself lonely for you. Youve no right to turn on me now and refuse to do your duty as a daughter.

VIVIE [*Jarred and antagonized by the echo of the slums in her mother's voice.*]   My duty as a daughter! I thought we should come to that pres-

ently. Now once for all, mother, you want a daughter and Frank wants
a wife. I dont want a mother; and I dont want a husband. I have spared
neither Frank nor myself in sending him about his business. Do you think
I will spare y o u ?

MRS WARREN [*Violently.*]   Oh, I know the sort you are: no mercy for yourself or anyone else. *I* know. My experience has done that for me anyhow:
I can tell the pious, canting, hard, selfish woman when I meet her. Well,
keep yourself to yourself: *I* dont want you. But listen to this. Do you
know what I would do with you if you were a baby again? aye, as sure as
there's a Heaven above us.

VIVIE   Strangle me, perhaps.

MRS WARREN   No: I'd bring you up to be a real daughter to me, and not
what you are now, with your pride and your prejudices and the college
education you stole from me: yes, stole: deny it if you can: what was it
but stealing? I'd bring you up in my own house, I would.

VIVIE [*Quietly.*]   In one of your own houses.

MRS WARREN [*Screaming.*]   Listen to her! listen to how she spits on her
mother's grey hairs! Oh, may you live to have your own daughter tear
and trample on you as you have trampled on me. And you will: you will.
No woman ever had luck with a mother's curse on her.

VIVIE   I wish you wouldnt rant, mother. It only hardens me. Come: I suppose I am the only young woman you ever had in your power that you
did good to. Dont spoil it all now.

MRS WARREN   Yes, Heaven forgive me, it's true; and you are the only one
that ever turned on me. Oh, the injustice of it! the injustice! the injustice!
I always wanted to be a good woman. I tried honest work; and I was
slave-driven until I cursed the day I ever heard of honest work. I was a
good mother; and because I made my daughter a good woman she turns
me out as if I was a leper. Oh, if I only had my life to live over again! I'd
talk to that lying clergyman in the school. From this time forth, so help
me Heaven in my last hour, I'll do wrong and nothing but wrong. And
I'll prosper on it.

VIVIE   Yes: it's better to choose your line and go through with it. If I had
been you, mother, I might have done as you did; but I should not have
lived one life and believed in another. You are a conventional woman at
heart. That is why I am bidding you goodbye now. I am right, am I not?

MRS WARREN [*Taken aback.*]   Right to throw away all my money?

VIVIE   No: right to get rid of you? I should be a fool not to! Isnt that so?

MRS WARREN [*Sulkily.*]   Oh well, yes, if you come to that, I suppose you
are. But Lord help the world if everybody took to doing the right thing!
And now I'd better go than stay where I'm not wanted. [*She turns to the
door.*]

VIVIE [*Kindly.*]   Wont you shake hands?

MRS WARREN [*After looking at her fiercely for a moment with a savage
impulse to strike her.*]   No, thank you. Goodbye.

VIVIE [*Matter-of-factly.*]   Goodbye. [MRS WARREN *goes out, slamming the
door behind her. The strain on* VIVIE's *face relaxes; her grave expression
breaks up into one of joyous content; her breath goes out in a half sob, half
laugh of intense relief. She goes buoyantly to her place at the writing-table;
pushes the electric lamp out of the way; pulls over a great sheaf of papers;*

and is in the act of dipping her pen in the ink when she finds FRANK's *note. She opens it unconcernedly and reads it quickly, giving a little laugh at some quaint turn of expression in it.*] And goodbye, Frank. [*She tears the note up and tosses the pieces into the wastepaper basket without a second thought. Then she goes at her work with a plunge, and soon becomes absorbed in its figures.*]

1893   1898

The Twentieth Century

HISTORICAL BACKGROUND

The modern period, which for convenience we call "the twentieth century," begins really with the late nineteenth, when the sense of the passing of a major phase of English history was already in the air. Queen Victoria's Jubilee in 1887 and, even more, her Diamond Jubilee in 1897 were felt even by contemporaries to mark the end of an era. As the nineteenth century drew to a close, there were many manifestations of a weakening of traditional stabilities. The aesthetic movement, with its insistence on "art for art's sake," assaulted the assumptions about the nature and function of art held by ordinary middle-class readers, deliberately, provocatively. It helped to widen the breach between artists and writers on the one hand and the "Philistine" public on the other—a breach an earlier symptom of which was Matthew Arnold's war on the Philistines in *Culture and Anarchy* and that was later to result in the "alienation of the artist," which has since become a commonplace of criticism. This breach was more than a purely English matter. From France came the tradition of the bohemian life that scorned the limits imposed by conventional ideas of respectability, together with other notions of the artist as rejecting and rejected by ordinary society, which in different ways fostered the view of the alienated artist. The life and work of the French symbolist poets and James Joyce's *Portrait of the Artist as a Young Man* (1916) show some of the very different ways in which this attitude revealed itself in literature all over Europe. In England, the growth of popular education as a result of the Education Act of 1870, which finally made elementary education compulsory and universal, led to the rapid emergence of a large, unsophisticated literary public at whom new kinds of journalism, in particular the cheap "yellow press," were directed. A public that was literate increased steadily throughout the nineteenth century, and one result of this was the splitting up of the audience for literature into "highbrows," "lowbrows," and "middlebrows." Although in earlier periods there had been different kinds of audience for different kinds of writing, the split now developed with unprecedented speed and to an unprecedented degree because of the mass production of popular literature for the newly literate. The fragmentation of the reading public now merged with the artist's war on the Philistine (and indeed was one of the causes of that war in the first place) to widen the gap between popular art and art esteemed only by the sophisticated and the expert.

Another manifestation—or at least accompaniment—of the end of the Victorian Age was the rise of various kinds of pessimism and stoicism. The novels and poetry of Thomas Hardy show one kind of pessimism (and it *was* pessimism, even if Hardy himself repudiated the term), and the poems of A. E. Housman show another variety, while a real or affected stoicism is to be found not only in these writers but also in many minor writers of the last decade of the nineteenth century and the first decade of the twentieth. Examples of this stoicism—the determination to stand for human dignity by enduring bravely, with a stiff upper lip, whatever fate may bring—range from Robert Louis Stevenson's essays and the rhetorically assertive poems of the editor and journalist W. E. Henley, to Rudyard Kipling's *Jungle Books* and many of his short stories, and the last stanza of Housman's *The Chestnut Casts His Flambeaux* ("Bear them we can, and if we can we must").

Although the high tide of anti-Victorianism was marked by the publication in 1918 of that classic of ironic debunking, *Eminent Victorians* by Lytton Strachey (1880–1932), the criticism of the normal attitudes and preconceptions of the Victorian middle classes first became really violent in the last two decades of the nineteenth century. No one could have been more savage in attacks on the Victorian conceptions of the family, education, and religion than Samuel Butler, whose novel *The Way of All Flesh* (completed in 1884, posthumously published in 1903) is still the bitterest indictment in English literature of the Victorian way of life. The chorus of those calling in question Victorian assumptions grew ever louder as the century drew to an end; sounding prominently in it was the voice of the young Bernard Shaw, one of Butler's greatest admirers. The position of women, too, was rapidly changing during this period. The Married Woman's Property Act of 1882, which allowed married women to own property in their own right; the admission of women to the universities at different times during the latter part of the century; the fight for women's suffrage, which was not won until 1918 (and not fully won until 1928)—these events marked a change in the attitude toward women and in the part they played in the national life as well as in the relation between the sexes, which is reflected in a variety of ways in the literature of the period.

The Boer War (1899–1902), fought by the British to establish political and economic control over the Boer republics (self-governing states) of South Africa, marked both the high point of and the reaction against British imperialism. It was a war against which many British intellectuals protested and one that the British in the end were slightly ashamed of having won. The development of the British Empire into the British Commonwealth (an association of self-governing countries) continued in fits and starts throughout the first half of the twentieth century, with imperialist and anti-imperialist sentiment often meeting head on in Parliament and the press; writers as far apart as Kipling and E. M. Forster occupied themselves with the problem. The Irish question also caused a great deal of excitement from the beginning of the period until well into the 1920s. A steadily rising Irish nationalism protested with increasing violence against the cultural, economic, and political subordination of Ireland to the British Crown and government. In World War I some Irish nationalists sought German help in rebelling against Britain, and this exacerbated feelings on both sides. No one can fully understand Yeats or Joyce without some awareness of the Irish struggle for independence, the feelings of Anglo-Irish literary people on this burning topic, and the way in which the Irish literary revival of the late nineteenth and early twentieth centuries (with which Yeats was much concerned) reflected a determination to achieve a vigorous national life culturally even if the road seemed blocked politically.

Edwardian England (1901–10) was very conscious of being no longer Victorian. Edward VII stamped his extrovert and self-indulgent character on the decade in which he reigned. It was a vulgar age of conspicuous enjoyment by those who could afford it, and writers and artists kept well away from involvement in high society (although there were some important exceptions): in general, there was no equivalent in this period to Queen Victoria's interest in Tennyson. The alienation of artists and intellectuals was proceeding apace. From 1910 (when George V came to the throne) until war broke out in August 1914, Britain achieved a temporary equilibrium between Victorian earnestness and Edwardian flashiness; in retrospect that Georgian period seems peculiarly golden, the last phase of assurance and stability before the old order throughout Europe broke up in violence with results that are still with us. Yet even then, under the surface, there was restlessness and experimentation. If this was the age of Rupert Brooke, it was also the age of T. S. Eliot's first experiments in a radically new kind of poetry.

The postwar disillusion of the 1920s was, it might be said, a spiritual matter, just as Eliot's Waste Land was a spiritual and not a literal wasteland. Depression and unemployment in the early 1930s, followed by the rise of Hitler and the cruel shadow of Fascism and Nazism over Europe, with its threat of another war, represented another sort of wasteland that produced another sort of effect on poets and novelists. While Eliot, Lawrence, Wyndham Lewis, Yeats, and others of the older generation turned to the political right, the impotence of capitalist governments in the face of Hitlerism combined with economic dislocation to turn the majority of young intellectuals (and not only intellectuals) in the 1930s to the political Left. The 1930s were the red decade, because only the Left seemed to offer any solution. The early poetry of W. H. Auden and his contemporaries cried out for "the death of the old gang" (in Auden's phrase)and a clean sweep politically and economically, while the right-wing army's rebellion against the left-wing republican government in Spain, which started in the summer of 1936 and soon led to full-scale civil war, was regarded as a rehearsal for an inevitable second world war and thus further emphasized the inadequacy of politicians. Yet though all this is reflected passionately in the literature of the period, particularly in the poetry, it was not accompanied by any interesting developments in technique; many younger writers were more anxious to express their attitudes than to construct new kinds of works of art. The outbreak of World War II in September 1939, following very shortly on Hitler's pact with the Soviet Union, which shocked and disillusioned so many of the young left-wing writers, marked the sudden end of the red decade; the concern of writers in Britain now was to maintain their integrity and indeed their existence in what was from the beginning expected to be a long and destructive war. This they did surprisingly well, but nevertheless the struggle brought inevitable exhaustion, and winning a war, Great Britain lost an empire. India, long the jewel in the imperial Crown, came to independence in 1947 and, although India and the newly formed Muslim state of Pakistan elected to remain within the British Commonwealth, other former dominions did not. The Irish Republic withdrew from the Commonwealth in 1949, and the Republic of South Africa in 1961. While Britain was engaged in a painful reappraisal of its place in the world, countries that had lost the war—West Germany and Japan—were, in economic terms, winning the peace that followed.

Less obvious, but no less significant for English literature, were changes on the national scene. London, as the capital of the empire, had long dominated the culture as well as the politics and the economy of the British Isles. London spoke for Britain in the impeccable southern English intonations of the radio announcers of the state-owned British Broadcasting Corporation (known as the BBC), but from the 1960s this changed. Regional dialects and, then, multicultural accents were admitted to the airwaves. Regional radio and television stations sprang up. The Arts Council, which had subsidized the nation's drama, literature, music, painting, and plastic arts from London, delegated much of its grant-giving responsibility to regional arts councils. This gave a new confidence to writers and artists outside London— the Beatles were launched from Liverpool—and has since contributed to a notable renaissance of regional literature. At its best, this builds on the native tradition of Hardy and Yeats, transcending the narrowly provincial to achieve a true universality. These decentralizing developments also encouraged the efflorescence of black British and postcolonial writing, a different vision of the destiny and cultural significance of English literature, that would add such names as Wole Soyinka and Derek Walcott (both Nobel Prize winners), Chinua Achebe, Anita Desai, Hanif Kureishi, and V. S. Naipaul to the annals of that literature.

From the 1960s, London ceased to be essentially the sole cultural stage of the United Kingdom, and though its Parliament remained the sole political stage, successive governments came under increasing pressure from the regions and the wider world. The Labour government of Harold Wilson (1964–70) so capitulated to the demands of powerful labor unions that inflation spiraled out of control and the Labour Party lost the next election. Wilson's government was succeeded by that of the Conservative Edward Heath (1970–74), who negotiated Britain's entry into the European Common Market but, trying to break a militant miners' strike, called a general election and was defeated. The following Labour government, elected with the crucial support of the unions, again tried to resist their demands and again failed. In the general election of 1979, Margaret Thatcher led the Conservatives to power, becoming thereby the country's first woman to hold the office of prime minister, an office she was to hold for an unprecedented twelve years. Pursuing a vision of a "new," more productive Britain, she curbed the power of the unions and began to dismantle the "welfare state," privatizing nationalized industries and utilities in the interests of an aggressive free-market economy. Initially, her policies had a bracing effect on a nation still sunk in postwar, postimperial torpor, but increasingly they widened the gap between rich and poor, black and white, north and south (in both England and Ireland), and between the constituent parts of the United Kingdom.

Thatcher was deposed by her own party in 1990, but the Conservatives had run out of energy and ideas, and they were routed in the election of 1997. The electorate's message was clear, and Tony Blair, the new Labour prime minister, moved at once to restore the rundown Health Service and system of state education. Honoring other of his campaign pledges, he offered Scotland its own parliament and Wales its own assembly, each with tax-raising powers and a substantial budget for the operation of its social services.

The Labour government also made significant progress toward solving the bitter and bloody problems of Northern Ireland. Since the mid-1980s, it had been clear that neither the British Army nor the Provisional IRA could achieve a decisive military victory. Within both the IRA and its political wing, Sinn Fein (Ourselves Alone), recognition of this fact led to internal discussion about achieving an alternative to a purely militarist approach to securing a united Ireland. This internal dialogue ultimately resulted in the declaration of a first ceasefire in 1994, which was broken, and a second in 1997. Though Sinn Fein still cannot be described as a wholly constitutional party, available evidence seems to show that politics have now taken precedence over violent struggle in the republican movement. Since the outbreak of the present troubles in the late 1960s, there have been many peace initiatives, none of them successful, but with the Labour victory of 1997, the most significant opportunity for peace has arisen from a redirection of IRA/Sinn Fein policy toward abandoning armed struggle. This shift in direction should also be seen in the light of greater London-Dublin cooperation, which culminated in the Downing Street Declaration of December 1993. The declaration attempted to create a framework for political cooperation within the context of the European Community and greater North-South cooperation on the island of Ireland. This most promising initiative culminated in elections to a Northern Ireland Assembly, which met for the first time in July 1998. That October, John Hume, leader of the (Roman Catholic) Social Democratic and Labour Party, and David Trimble, leader of the (Protestant) Ulster Unionist Party, were jointly awarded the Nobel Peace Prize, and the business of politics, after an absence of nearly three decades, returned from the streets to the floor of a parliament in Northern Ireland.

POETRY

The years leading up to World War I saw the start of a poetic revolution. The imagist movement, influenced by the philosopher-poet T. E. Hulme's insistence on hard, clear, precise images and encouraged by the modernist American poet Ezra Pound, who was then living in London, fought against romantic fuzziness and facile emotionalism in poetry. Imagists insisted on "direct treatment of the 'thing,' whether subjective or objective," on the avoidance of all words "that did not contribute to the presentation," and on a freer metrical movement than a strict adherence to "the sequence of a metronome" could allow. All this encouraged precision in imagery and freedom of rhythmic movement, but more was required for the production of poetry of any real scope and interest. Imagism went in for the short, sharply etched, descriptive lyric, but it had no technique for the production of longer and more complex poems. Other new ideas about poetry helped to provide this technique. Sir Herbert Grierson's great edition of the poems of John Donne in 1912 both reflected and helped to encourage a new enthusiasm for seventeenth-century Metaphysical poetry. The revival of interest in Metaphysical wit brought with it a desire on the part of some pioneering poets to introduce into their poetry a much higher degree of intellectual complexity than had been found among the Victorians or the Georgians. The full subtlety of French symbolist poetry also now came to be appreciated; it had been admired in the 1890s, but for its dreamy suggestiveness rather than for its imagistic precision and complexity. At the same time a need was felt to bring poetic language and rhythms closer to those of conversation or at least to spice the formalities of poetic utterance with echoes of the colloquial and even the slangy. Irony, which made possible several levels of discourse simultaneously, and wit, with the use of puns (banished from serious poetry for more than two hundred years), helped to achieve that union of thought and passion that T. S. Eliot, in his review of Grierson's anthology of Metaphysical poetry (1921), saw as characteristic of the Metaphysicals and wished to bring back into modern poetry. A new critical and a new creative movement in poetry went hand in hand, with Eliot the high priest of both. It was Eliot who extended the scope of Imagism by bringing the English Metaphysicals and the French symbolists (as well as the English Jacobean dramatists) to the rescue, thus adding new criteria of complexity and allusiveness to the criteria of concreteness and precision stressed by the Imagists. It was Eliot, too, who introduced into modern English and American poetry the kind of irony achieved by shifting suddenly from the formal to the colloquial or by oblique allusions to objects or ideas that contrasted sharply with those carried by the surface meaning of the poem. Thus between, say, 1911 (the first year of the Georgian poets) and 1922 (the year of the publication of *The Waste Land*) a major revolution occurred in English—and for that matter American—poetic theory and practice, one that determined the way in which most serious poets and critics now think about their art. This revolution was by no means an isolated literary phenomenon. Writers on both sides of the English Channel were influenced by the French impressionist, postimpressionist, and cubist painters' radical reexamination of the nature of reality. Pound wrote books about the French sculptor Henri Gaudier-Brzeska and the American composer George Antheil. Wilfred Owen wrote in 1918: "I suppose I am doing in poetry what the advanced composers are doing in music"; and Eliot, while writing *The Waste Land* three years later, was so impressed by a performance of the composer Igor Stravinsky's *Le Sacre du Printemps* (The Rite of Spring) that he stood up at the end and cheered.

The posthumous publication by Robert Bridges in 1918 of the poetry of Gerard Manley Hopkins encouraged experimentation in language and rhythms. Hopkins combined absolute precision of the individual image with a complex ordering of images and a new kind of metrical patterning. The young poets of the early 1930s—Auden, Stephen Spender, C. Day Lewis—were much influenced by Hopkins as well as by Eliot (then the presiding genius of modern English and American poetry) and by a variety of other poets from the sixteenth-century John Skelton to Wilfred Owen.

Meanwhile the remarkable career of Yeats, stretching across the whole modern period, showed how a truly great poet can reflect the varying developments of his or her age yet maintain an unmistakably individual accent. Beginning among the aesthetes of the 1890s, turning later to a more tough and spare ironic language without losing his characteristic verbal magic, working out his own notions of symbolism and bringing them in different ways into his poetry, developing in his full maturity a rich symbolic and Metaphysical poetry with its own curiously haunting cadences and its imagery both shockingly realistic and movingly suggestive, Yeats's work is itself a history of English poetry between 1890 and 1939. Yet he is always Yeats, unique and inimitable—without doubt the greatest English-speaking poet of his age.

In his poem *Remembering the 'Thirties*, Donald Davie declared: "A neutral tone is nowadays preferred." That tone—the coolly clinical tone of Auden— dominated the poetry of the decade, but as it ended and World War II began, a neutral tone gave way to the vehemence of what came to be known as the New Apocalypse. The poets of this movement, the most notable of whom was Dylan Thomas, owed something of their audacity and violence to the example of the French surrealist poets and painters, who sought to express, often by free association, the operation of the subconscious mind. Many of these, such as Salvador Dali and Pablo Picasso, were both poets and painters, whose poetry was introduced to English readers in translations and in *A Short History of Surrealism* (1936) by David Gascoyne, one of the poets of the New Apocalypse. With the coming of the 1950s, however, the pendulum swung back again. A new generation of poets that included Donald Davie, Thom Gunn, and Philip Larkin reacted against what seemed to them the verbal excesses of Dylan Thomas, Edith Sitwell, and others. "The Movement," as this new group came to be called, aimed once again for a neutral tone, a purity of diction, in which to render an unpretentious fidelity to experience. Larkin, its most notable exponent, explicitly rejected the imported modernism of Pound and Eliot in favor of a native tradition represented in this century by Hardy. That tradition now flourishes in the work of Tony Harrison.

The last quarter century has seen no poetic movement or school of comparable originality and importance, but such groupings—and "isms" (modernism, symbolism, surrealism) in the arts generally—have never flourished on British soil as they have in France and America. In 1994, the New Generation Poets were launched by their publishers but, though individually lively, they lacked any unifying program, and the marketing of their work belongs (as F. R. Leavis famously said of the Sitwells) "to the history of publicity rather than of poetry." Public relations, however, have had a measurable impact on what has long—at least since the Middle Ages—been thought of as an essentially private art. An expanding poetry industry, with a network of well-publicized, well-attended public readings, has encouraged the development of "performance poetry." Written for the stage, these poems tend to be more accessible, informal, loosely textured, loosely structured, and lighter in tone than those written for the page. The future of such poems, which do not always "work" on the page (any more than those written for the page always work on the stage), may well lie with electronic media rather than with what Craig Raine's Martian calls "Caxtons . . . mechanical birds with many wings."

A century that began with a springtime of poetic innovation drew to its close with the full flowering of such older poets as Heaney, Hill, Hughes, and Walcott, and welcome signs of new growth wherever English is spoken.

FICTION

Novels—Henry James's "loose baggy monsters"—can be and do and include anything at all. The form defies prescriptions and limits. But its variety can be thought of as always converging energetically on the main and normal focuses of western literary endeavor, namely, constructing the self, reproducing what appears to be the nature of the real, and wrestling with the difficulties and intransigencies of the words one is compelled to use in these writing struggles. What characterizes twentieth-century fiction making is that these ancient problems of literary idea and practice become matters of intense reflection and debate as never before: for all writers, of course, but especially for novelists.

The century's novels may be divided roughly into three main strata: the period of high modernism through the 1920s, celebrating personal and textual inwardness; the reaction against modernism, involving a return to social realism and assorted documentary endeavors, which particularly characterizes the 1930s; the messy half century or so after World War II, in which the fictional claims of various realisms—urban, proletarian, provincial English, regional (especially Scottish and Irish), immigrant, postcolonial, feminist, gay—are asserted alongside, but also through, a continuing self-consciousness about language and form and meaning which is, in effect, the enduring legacy of modernism. By the end of the century, the modernist impulse had turned thus, amidst the vast array of possible subjects and styles, into the striking pluralism of postmodernism: a challenging mix of possibilities oddly reminiscent of the early part of the century when a Pole, Joseph Conrad, an Irishman, James Joyce, and an American, Henry James, were the most instrumental inventors of the modernist "English" novel.

The high modernists—the later James, Conrad, Joyce, plus the home-produced D. H. Lawrence and Virginia Woolf—wrote in the wake of the shattering of confidence in the great old certainties about the deity and the Christian faith, about the person, knowledge, materialism, history, the old Grand Narratives, which had, more or less, sustained the western novel through the nineteenth century. Into this general shaking of belief in the novel's founding assumptions—that the world, things, selves, were knowable, that language was a usefully revelatory instrument created under the aegis of the Divine Word, that the Divine Author and His story gave history meaning and moral shape and sanctioned the ordering of narratives into morally telling beginnings, middles, and endings—the modernists bravely ventured, trying all at once to be true to the new skepticisms and hesitations, and also to construct credible new alternatives to the old belief systems.

The once-prevailing nineteenth-century notions of ordinary reality came under serious attack. Virginia Woolf's explicit assault (in her famous 1919 essay *Modern Fiction*) on the "materialism" of the realistic Edwardian heirs of Victorian naturalist confidence, Arnold Bennett, H. G. Wells, and John Galsworthy, set the current tone. What was knowable, and thus writable, was not out there as some given, fixed, transcribable essence. Reality existed,

rather, only as it was perceived. Hence the introduction of the impressionistic, flawed, even utterly unreliable narration, represented very commonly
in some not-to-be-relied-on narrator ("reflectors" James called them)—a substitute for the classic nineteenth-century authoritative narrating voice (usually the voice of the author or some close substitute for that). Conrad's
Marlow, the main narrating voice of *Heart of Darkness* as of other central
Conrad fictions, with his large rhetoric of the invisible, inaudible, impossible,
unintelligible, and so unsayable, came to seem foundational. The real was
offered, thus, only, or mainly, as refracted and reflected in the novel's representative consciousnesses. "Look within," Virginia Woolf urged the novelist. Reality and its truth had gone inward.

Woolf's subject would be "an ordinary mind on an ordinary day." The life
that mattered most would now be mental life. And so the modernist novel
turned resolutely inward, its large concern being now with consciousness—a
flow of reflections, momentary impressions, disjunctive bits of recall and
half-memory, simultaneously revealing both the past and the way the past is
repressed, though who can tell how much exactly? This concentration was
mightily assisted by the great contemporary drive of the psychoanalytic movement led by Sigmund Freud, to narrate the reality of persons as the life
primarily of the mind in all its expanding dimensions of investigation—consciousness, subconsciousness, unconsciousness, id, libido, and so on. And
the apparent truths of this inward life were, of course, utterly tricky, scattered, fragmentary, spotty, now illuminated, now twilit, now quite occluded.
Virginia Woolf was right to perceive Joyce's *Ulysses* as a prime expression of
this desired impressionistic agenda ("he is concerned at all costs to reveal
the flickerings of that innermost flame which flashes its messages through
the brain").

The characters of Joyce and Woolf are caught, then, as they are immersed
in the so-called "stream of consciousness"; and some version of an interior
flow of thought becomes the main modernist access to "character." The
reader overhears the characters speaking, so to say, from within their particular consciousnesses, but not always directly. The modernists felt free also
to enter their characters' minds to speak as it were on their behalf in the
technique known as *free indirect style* (*style indirect libre* in French).

A marked feature of the new fictional selfhood was a fraught condition of
existential loneliness. Conrad's Lord Jim, Joyce's Leopold Bloom and Stephen Dedalus, Lawrence's Paul Morel or his Birkin, and Woolf's Mrs. Dalloway were people on their own, choosing individuals, but bereft of the old
props, Church, Bible, ideological consensus, and so doomed to make their
own puzzled way through life's labyrinths without much confidence in tele-
ology or ontology, in means and ends, in the knowable solidity of the world,
above all in language as a tool of knowledge about self and other. Episte-
mological confidence leaked dramatically away from the novel. The old conclusive tendency of plots (everything resolved on the novel's last page, on the
model of the detective story) gave place to irresolute open endings—the
unending vista of the last paragraph of D. H. Lawrence's *Sons and Lovers*,
the circularity by which the last sentence of James Joyce's *Finnegans Wake*
hooks back to be completed in the novel's own first word, so that reading
simply starts all over again.

Not surprisingly, novelists became central to the building of modern myths on the dry bones of the old Christian ones. In his review of *Ulysses* ("*Ulysses,* Order, and Myth," 1921), T. S. Eliot famously praised the novel for replacing old "narrative method" by a new "mythical method" (he meant particularly the way Joyce's Irish Jew Bloom is mythicized as a modern Ulysses, his life's odyssey a revival of old episodes from the Homeric *Odyssey*). This manipulation of "a continuous parallel between contemporaneity and antiquity" was, Eliot thought, "a step toward making the modern world possible for art," much in keeping with the new anthropology and psychology as well as with what Yeats was doing in verse. Such private myth-making could, of course, take worrying turns. The "religion of the blood" that D. H. Lawrence celebrated led directly to the fascist sympathies of his *Aaron's Rod* and the revived Aztec blood-cult of *The Plumed Serpent*. And the new centrality of the linguistic and textual subject, the now central business of reading and writing in these highly metafictional novels (all about writers and artists, and surrogates for artists, such as Woolf's Mrs. Ramsay with her dinners and Mrs. Dalloway with her party, all those producers of what Woolf called the "unpublished works of women"), was not necessarily more consoling either. The greatest modernist example of linguisticity rampant as such, *Finnegans Wake,* verges on unreadability.

And, of course, though the skeptical modernist linguistic turn, the rejection of materialist externality and of the realist project of the Victorians, did leave ineradicable traces on twentieth-century fiction, its revolutions never became absolute or permanent. *Ulysses* was simply unrepeatable and *Finnegans Wake* a monumental dead end. But even within the greatest modernist fictions the worldly subject, politics, moral questions, never quite dried up. Woolf and Joyce are, for example, great celebrators of the perplexities of urban life in London and Dublin. (Modernist fiction is everywhere an art of the great city.) Lawrence was greatly preoccupied with the condition of England, industrialism, provincial life. Satire was one of modernism's recurrent notes. So it was not odd for the novelists who came through in the 1920s—for instance, the right-wing Wyndham Lewis and Evelyn Waugh— to resort to the social subject and the satiric stance, nor for their left-leaning contemporaries who developed alongside them and came to be seen as even more characteristic of the 1930s Red Decade—Graham Greene, it might be, or George Orwell—to engage with the *condition humaine* in ways that Dickens or Balzac, let alone Bennett-Wells-Galsworthy, would have recognized as not all that distant from their own spirit. (Woolf's denigrated trio all lived on into the 1930s; Wells, whose *Time Machine* and *War of the Worlds* helped pioneer the SciFi genre at the end of the nineteenth century, was still producing scary prognostications of apocalyptic war in the 1930s, for instance *The Shape of Things to Come,* and did not die until 1946.)

Linguistic self-consciousness would remain high on the novel's agenda— the modernist lessons ran deep—but the documentarists who dominated the 1930s indicated just how much the linguistic subject would rely on politicization for its survival: the estranging grammar of Henry Green's *Living* is a part of his proletarian people's West Midland's discourse; the lexicography of Walter Greenwood's *Love on the Dole* is a key part of his radical protest on behalf of Manchester's unemployed; the comically chaotic meeting of English and German languages in Christopher Isherwood's Berlin stories is central to a fiction of dire warning about Anglo-German politics; George

Orwell's Newspeak in *Nineteen-Eighty-Four* is the culmination of nearly two decades of politically motivated engagement with the ways of English speakers at home and abroad. In this politicized aftermath of the modernist experiment, Huxley's *Eyeless in Gaza*, say, is as much a matter of satirical engagement with the socio-politico-moral matter of the 1930s as are the reflections on modern linguistic corruptions in the Year of Our Ford in Huxley's even more obviously satirical *Brave New World*.

Where World War I was a great engine of modernism, a prime endorser of the chaos of belief and the fragility of language and the human subject, the impact of the Spanish Civil War and then World War II was to confirm the English novel in its return to registering the social scene and the historical event. World War II provoked whole series of more or less realist fictions: Evelyn Waugh's *Sword of Honour* trilogy, Anthony Powell's *A Dance to the Music of Time* sequence, Olivia Manning's *Balkan Trilogy*, as well as powerful singletons such as Greene's *The Ministry of Fear*, Waugh's *Brideshead Revisited*, and H. E. Bates's *Fair Stood the Wind for France*. C. P. Snow's long *Strangers and Brothers* sequence is central to the English novel's mid-century role as concerned assessor of the War and its human aftermaths.

The new fictions of the post–World War II period speak with the satirical energies of the young demobilized officer class (Kingsley Amis's *Lucky Jim* set the tone of a whole generation of disgruntled awkward-squad jokers), and of the ordinary provincial citizen finding a fictional voice yet again in the new Welfare State atmosphere of the 1950s (as Alan Sillitoe's proletarian Nottingham novel *Saturday Night and Sunday Morning*, for instance, or John Wain's graduating scholarship-boy's protest against the educational poshocracy, *Hurry on Down*).

Two undoubtedly major careers were launched in 1954 in this atmosphere of questing for new moral bases for the post-Holocaust nuclear age—William Golding, with *The Lord of the Flies*, and Iris Murdoch, with *Under the Net*. Both writers produced large numbers of novels carrying on where their first novels began: intense post-Christian moral fables in Golding's case, moral philosophy in Murdoch's. Murdoch and Golding were consciously retrospective (as were the important group of contemporary Roman Catholics—Greene, Waugh, and Muriel Spark) in their investment in moral form. But such conscious retro-determinations were not enough to hold back or calm the anxiety that all belatedness inevitably entails. And as the century drew on, British fiction's main effort was a coming to terms with the many palpably disconcerting features of a pervasive sense of posteriority—postwar flatness; postimperial diminutions of power and influence; and the sense of the Grand Narratives really now losing their force as never before.

Younger novelists, such as Anita Brookner, Martin Amis, Graham Swift, Sebastian Faulks, and Ian McEwan, became massively obsessed with Germany (the now accusingly prosperous old foe), and with the still haunting ghosts of the *Hitlerzeit*—and not least after 1989, when the Berlin Wall came down and wartime European horrors stirred once more into vivid focus. Meanwhile, the postimperial dereliction of the once-grand center of London became a main topic of the later Kingsley Amis, of ex-Rhodesian Doris Lessing, of Ian McEwan, as well as of Kingsley Amis's son Martin (especially in his greatly important *London Fields* and *The Information*). Where earlier in the century Conrad and E. M. Forster (*A Passage to India*) had been harshly accusatory about Britain's overseas behavior, now it was nostalgia for old imperial days that energized the pages of Lawrence Durrell's *Alexandrian Quartet,* Paul Scott's *Raj Quartet* and *Staying On,* and J. G. Farrell's *The Siege of Krishnapur* and *Singapore Grip.* At the same time, there was a widespread sense that what was mainly left now for English fiction was merely a rehashing of old stories (critics often accuse the late-century English novel of being far too obsessed with the past, much too content with the historical subject). The modernist, Joycean notion that resurrecting ancient narratives was a way of revitalizing present consciousness had given way to a fear that the postmodern present was under condemnation to a rather disabled career of simply parroting old stuff (*on est parle,* "one is spoken," rather than speaking for oneself, thinks the main character of Julian Barnes's *Flaubert's Parrot,* reflecting in some dismay on this dilemma). Ventriloquial reproduction of old voices became Peter Ackroyd's trademark. Like the subject of A. S. Byatt's *Possession,* which is about the magnetism of past (Victorian) writers and writings, all this comes to seem central to late-century times. And being merely possessed by the past revives all the old orthodox worries about mediumistic, even demonic, possession, which Yeats managed to avoid and which Peter Ackroyd's encounters with London mediums (as in his *English Music*) and A. S. Byatt's stories about raising the dead in seances, in *Angels and Insects,* do not.

Of course there are many energetic new end-of-century voices, particularly ones from assorted margins, eager to fight off and against prevalent moods of enervation at the English center. Women's voices (like Beryl Bainbridge, dark historicizer of male as well as female plights; Jeanette Winterson, great word-mongering celebrator of women's arts and bodiliness; Michele Roberts, lusty reviver of repressed female stories; above all, Angela Carter, feminist neomythographer, reviser of fairy tales, rewriter of Sade, espouser of raucously bad-mouthing girls). And regional voices (especially Irish ones, as Brian Moore, John Banville, Bernard MacLaverty; and Scottish ones, not least the so-called Glasgow School of Alasdair Gray, A. L. Kennedy, and James Kelman). And "genre" voices (that is, novelists pushing their way into the mainstream from the generic edge, especially of science fiction—a movement fathered, or grandfathered, by J. G. Ballard, author of the influential *Crash* and *The Atrocity Exhibition,* and guru of Martin Amis and Will Self). And male-gay voices (Alan Hollinghurst, pioneer of the openly male-homosexual literary novel of the post–World War II period; Adam Mars-Jones, short-story chronicler of the AIDS crisis among gay men). And, of course, immigrant, postcolonial voices. Where once Jean Rhys, V. S. Naipaul, and Doris Lessing led a distinct but limited phalanx of old Commonwealth novelists residing in Britain, late-century English fiction would look startlingly thin and poverty-stricken indeed were it not for the huge presence of writers of overseas, mainly Commonwealth, origin—the likes of Wilson Harris, Fred d'Aguiar, David Dabydeen, Alice Munro, Christopher Hope, Caryl Phillips, Adam Zameenzad, Abdulrazak Gurnah, Hanif Kureishi, Kazuo Ishiguro, and, above all, Salman Rushdie, Indian-born importer of South American and German (Gunther Grass–type) magic realism, many-voiced satirist of Indian, Pakistani, and British life (the latter especially in his masterpiece, *The Satanic Verses*). Among such novelists, and in particular Rushdie, the English novel deploys its postmodernistic energies with little anxiety about belatedness, no fright over parroting, and no neomodernist worries about attempting realistic encounters with the world.

Energetic such postcolonialist writings undoubtedly are. They do not, however, manage to keep quite at bay the prevailing sense of strain infecting end-of-century (and end-of-millennium) British fiction—the rather desperate attempt by the best of the younger novelists to ward off a general failure of British cultural nerve and particular fears about the British novel's contemporary sterility, that is to be witnessed in their rather hectic investment in what Martin Amis has called the gimmick, and J. G. Ballard for his part has welcomed as "ransacking the library of extreme metaphors": efforts, important in their way, but tellingly overdone, such as Martin Amis's stylistic and formal extremes (including the backward narration of his Holocaust novel, *Time's Arrow*); Julian Barnes's persistent risky investment in the essayistic; Patrick McGrath's dark revival of the gothic; Will Self's showy parade of urban criminals and degenerates. Grimly attractive as these are, they are desperate measures nonetheless.

DRAMA

Modern drama begins in a sense with the witty drawing-room comedies of Oscar Wilde; yet Wilde founded no dramatic school. His wit was combative and generative of paradoxes, but beneath the glitter of his verbal play it is possible to see serious—if heavily coded—reflections on social, political, and even feminist issues. Bernard Shaw brought still another kind of wit into drama—not Wilde's lighthearted sparkle but the provocative paradox that was meant to tease and disturb, to challenge the complacency of the audience. Shaw's discussion plays were given dramatic life through the mastery of theatrical techniques, which he learned during his years as a drama critic.

Wilde and Shaw were both born in Ireland, and it was in Dublin that the century's first major theatrical movement originated. The Irish Literary Theatre was founded in 1899, with Yeats's early play *The Countess Cathleen* as its first production. The founders—Yeats, Lady Gregory, George Moore, and Edward Martyn—wanted to make a contribution to an Irish literary revival, but they were influenced also by the Independent Theatre in London, founded in 1891 by J. T. Grein in order to encourage new developments in the drama. In 1902 the Irish Literary Theatre was able to maintain a permanent all-Irish company and changed its name to the Irish National Theatre, which moved in 1904 to the Abbey Theatre, by which name it has since been known. J. M. Synge's use of the speech and imagination of Irish country people, Yeats's powerful symbolic use of themes from old Irish legend, and Sean O'Casey's use of the Irish civil war as a background for plays combining tragic melodrama, humor of character, and irony of circumstance brought new kinds of vitality to the theater. In England, T. S. Eliot attempted with considerable success to revive a ritual poetic drama with his *Murder in the Cathedral* (1935). His later attempts to combine religious symbolism with the box-office appeal of an entertaining society comedy (as in *The Cocktail Party*, 1950), although impressive technical achievements, were not wholly successful: the combination of contemporary social chatter with profound religious symbolism produces both an unevenness of tone and disturbing shifts in levels of realism.

In spite of the achievements of Shaw, Yeats, and Eliot, it cannot be said of the drama, as it can of poetry and fiction in the first half of the century, that a technical revolution occurred that changed the whole course of literary history with respect to that particular literary form. The reformers of the 1890s invoked the name of the Norwegian playwright Ibsen: like Shaw they saw him as essentially a critic of middle-class society rather than (as critics tend to see him today) as an essentially poetic dramatist experimenting with symbolic modes of expression. This may be the reason why the influence of Ibsen soon petered out in run-of-the-mill plays of humanitarian social concern. The staple of the London West End theater remained social comedy stiffened by occasional irony and sweetened by sentimentality (Noel Coward [1899–1973] was one of the best, as well as most successful, purveyors of this sort of fare though his work was often underpinned by a frisson of sexual innuendo). The cleverly contrived sentimentalities of J. M. Barrie (1860–1937) were highly popular in their day; Barrie's plays showed a great theatrical skill and a determined cunning in the exploitation of the audience's reaction.

The course of British and Irish drama during the first half of the century may have been less revolutionary than developments in poetry and fiction over the same period, but its revolution was to come in the decade following the end of World War II. Wartime verse plays, commissioned by the BBC and written for radio by Louis MacNeice and other poets, helped prepare the audience that in the late 1940s and early 1950s rapturously received the verse plays of Christopher Fry. It seemed that these were about to bring a new kind of poetic life into English drama. But Fry's exuberant use of metaphor—often more pyrotechnic than functional—soon lost its appeal, and by the late 1950s a very different kind of drama brought vitality to the British theater.

While Brecht, Ionesco, and Sartre straddled the stages of Europe in the postwar years, and English followers of "absurd" drama like N. F. Simpson presented a rather anemic version of European existentialism, Samuel Beckett changed the history of drama with his first play, written in French in 1948 and translated by the author himself as *Waiting for Godot* (1953). *Godot*'s apparent lack of plot ("nothing happens—twice") throws the theatrical focus onto its language, which George Steiner has described as "the main instrument of man's refusal to accept the world as it is." The theatrical tremors caused by *Godot* and such of Beckett's later plays as *Not I* (1973) and *That Time* (1976) gave impetus to a seismic shift in British writing for the theater.

The epicenter of this new movement was the Royal Court Theatre, symbolically located a little away from London's West End "theater land." From 1956, the Royal Court was the home of the English Stage Company. Together they provided a venue and a vision that provoked and enabled a new wave of writers, many of whom had learned their stagecraft as actors in provincial repertory theaters and touring companies throughout Britain and Ireland. John Osborne's *Look Back in Anger* (1956) was the hit of the ESCs first season (significantly helped by its broadcast on television in the autumn of 1956). Osborne offered his audience what he called "lessons in feeling" through his searing depiction of the emotional cruelty and directionless angst of Jimmy Porter, described by one puzzled contemporary critic as a "Wolverhampton Hamlet." *Look Back in Anger* is technically a rather traditional play, but its novelty lay in its nonmetropolitan setting and in the arias of discontent of its very English rebel without a cause. Osborne explored issues and injustices with a tone of savage indignation, and his later plays, *The Entertainer* (1957) and *Luther* (1960), are technically more adventurous. The former explores the changes in English society through the elegant and challenging allegory of Archie Rice's declining fortunes as a music-hall artist, while the latter studies a historical rebel with a very tangible cause (and chronic constipation).

The changes in British theater in the 1950s and 1960s were in part a response to the new challenges of technicolor cinema and increasing public access to television. Many landmark social dramas of the 1950s were subsequently filmed (often under the imaginative direction of Tony Richardson). Theater had to rediscover and redefine what was distinctive about the experience it offered in the face of the large budgets and technical resources of the new media. Indeed, in the middle to late 1960s (generally considered a dry period in British theater) a generation of talented writers, such as David Mercer and David Rudkin, worked almost exclusively for television, where the stand-alone single play became a hallmark of high-class scheduling. But they built on the foundations laid by the naturalism of the so-called "kitchen sink" dramatists of the 1950s, like Arnold Wesker, a would-be English Arthur Miller, whose trilogy *Chicken Soup with Barley* (1958) showed that the personal was the political by confronting social, cultural, and psychological issues in the family arena. While naturalistic plays were one response to social and cultural changes of the postwar period, another group of Royal Court writers was refocusing theater on language and symbolism. Harold Pinter's "comedies of menace" map out a social trajectory from his early study of working-class stress and inarticulate anxiety, *The Room* (1957), through the film-noirish black farce of *The Dumb Waiter* (1960) and the emotional power plays of *The Caretaker* (1960), to the savagely comic study of middle-class escape from working-class mores in *The Homecoming* (1965). Later plays reflect on patrician suspicion and betrayal, though in the 1980s his work acquired a more overtly political voice.

The political was always close to the surface of John Arden. His *Sergeant Musgrave's Dance* (1959) explores colonial oppression, communal guilt for wartime atrocities, and pacifism in the stylized setting of an isolated mining town. Using songs, ballads, dance, and proverbs, Arden makes a dramatic and vivid synthesis of popular cultural forms to highlight the universality of his political and social analyses. More experimentally, Joan Littlewood's Theatre Workshop pioneered the use of improvisation and group work to develop shows made up of filmlike collage of numerous small scenes: distinctive examples are Shelagh Delaney's *A Taste of Honey* (1958) and *O, What a Lovely War* (1963), both subsequently filmed.

In the theater of the 1960s, the black comedies of Joe Orton shocked bourgeois sentiment in a series of classically precise and sexually ambiguous parodies of other forms of theater: his farce *What the Butler Saw* (1969) even ends with a *deus ex machina*. The cerebral fireworks of Tom Stoppard were supported by an unusually high degree of technical virtuosity in his stage-craft. While Orton reads like Pinter on fast-forward, early Stoppard pays parodic homage to the verbal texture and theatrical technique of Beckett. This enjoyment and exploitation of self-conscious theatricality arises partly out of the desire to show theater as different from film and television and is everywhere apparent in the drama of the 1970s. The liturgical stylization of Peter Shaffer's *Equus* (1973) and the bleak mental landscape of his Salieri in *Amadeus* emphasize the stage as battleground and site of struggle (an effect lost in their naturalistic film versions), while Stoppard's time-slips and memory lapses in *Travesties* (1974) allow a nonnaturalistic study of the role of memory and imagination in the creative process, a theme he returns to more recently in *Arcadia* (1995), a stunning double-exposure account of a Romantic poet and his modern critical commentators occupying the same physical space but never reaching intellectual common ground. Alan Ayck-bourn's work at Scarborough has explored and extended the technical pos-sibilities of "theater in the round" in a prolific and highly successful series of social tragicomedies.

The Lord Chamberlain's abolition in 1968 of state censorship of plays permitted mainstream theaters to commission and perform for the first time work that addressed and presented controversial political, social, and sexual issues. Challenging studies of violence, social deprivation, and political and sexual aggression have characterized the work of Howard Brenton, Howard Barker, and Edward Bond. They often use mythical settings and epic stories to construct austerely sweeping critiques and striking tableaux of power and oppression. Bond's *Lear* (1971) typifies his ambitious combination of soaring lyrical language and alienatingly realistic violence. The post-1968 liberali-zation coincided with the collapse of the postwar liberal humanist consensus and encouraged the emergence of new theater groups addressing specific political agendas. Companies such as John McGrath's 7:84; Monstrous Reg-iment; Gay Sweatshop and Joint Stock worked collaboratively with drama-tists who were invited in to help devise and develop shows. Increasingly in the 1970s, published plays are either transcriptions of the first production or "blueprints for the alchemy of live performance" (Micheline Wandor). In Ireland, the foundation of the Field Day Theatre Company in 1980 by the well-established playwright Brian Friel and actor Stephen Rea had similar motives of collaborative cultural catalysis. Their first production, Friel's *Translations* (1980), exploring linguistic colonialism and the fragility of cul-tural identity in nineteenth-century Ireland, achieved huge international success.

It may not be accidental that this ethos of collaboration and group devel-opment produced the first major cohort of women dramatists to break through onto mainstream stages. Caryl Churchill, whose *Top Girls* (1982) and *Serious Money* (1987) anatomize the market-driven ethos of the 1980s, explores modern society with the wit and detachment of Restoration comedy. Like David Mamet in the United States, she carefully transcribes and over-laps the speech of her characters to create a seamlessly interlocking web of discourse that aspires to reproduce a streamlined version of the ebb and flow of normal speech. Pam Gems studies the social and sexual politics of misog-yny and feminism in her campy theatrical explorations of strong women—*Queen Cristina* (1977), *Piaf* (1978), *Camille* (1984)—while Sarah Daniels reinterprets the naturalism of kitchen-sink drama by adding to it the linguistic stylization of Churchill.

In retrospect, the opening of the new National Theatre complex on London's South Bank in 1976 may represent the high-water mark in postwar British theater. The 1980s and 1990s have seen recession and shrinking subsidy close companies and theaters. As in the 1920s and 1930s, musical theater has offered an escapist perspective, while the globalization of television has seen a retreat from new and challenging work into the synthetic world of soap opera, costume drama, and the classic serial.

THE TWENTIETH CENTURY

TEXTS	CONTEXTS
	1901–10 Reign of Edward VII
1902 Joseph Conrad, *Heart of Darkness*	1902 End of the Anglo-Boer War
	1903 Henry Ford founds Ford Motor Company. Wright Brothers make the first successful airplane flight
	1905 Albert Einstein, theory of special relativity. Impressionist exhibition, London
	1910 Post-Impressionist exhibition, London
	1910–36 Reign of George V
1910 Bernard Shaw, *Pygmalion*	
1914 James Joyce, *Dubliners*. Thomas Hardy, *Satires of Circumstance*	1914–18 World War I
1916 Joyce, *A Portrait of the Artist as a Young Man*	1916 Easter Uprising in Dublin
1917 T. S. Eliot, *The Love Song of J. Alfred Prufrock*	
1918 Gerard Manley Hopkins, *Poems*	1918 Armistice. Franchise Act grants vote to women over thirty
1920 D. H. Lawrence, *Women in Love*	1920 Treaty of Versailles. League of Nations formed
1921 William Butler Yeats, *Michael Robartes and the Dancer*	1921 Formation of Irish Free State with Northern Ireland (Ulster) remaining part of Great Britain
1922 Katherine Mansfield, *The Garden Party and Other Stories*. Joyce, *Ulysses*. Eliot, *The Waste Land.*	
1924 Forster, *A Passage to India*	
1927 Virginia Woolf, *To the Lighthouse*	
1928 Yeats, *The Tower*	
1929 Woolf, *A Room of One's Own*. Robert Graves, *Goodbye to All That*	1929 Stock market crash; the Great Depression begins
1930 Siegfried Sassoon, *Memoirs of an Infantry Officer*	
	1933 Hitler comes to power in Germany
1935 Eliot, *Murder in the Cathedral*	1936–39 Spanish Civil War
	1936 Edward VIII succeeds George V but abdicates in favor of his brother, crowned as George VI
1937 David Jones, *In Parenthesis*	
1939 Joyce, *Finnegans Wake*. Yeats, *Last Poems and Two Plays*	1939–45 World War II
	1940 Fall of France. Battle of Britain
	1941–45 The Holocaust

TEXTS	CONTEXTS
1944 Eliot, *Four Quartets*	
1945 W. H. Auden, *Collected Poems.* George Orwell, *Animal Farm*	1945 First atomic bombs dropped, on Japan
1946 Dylan Thomas, *Deaths and Entrances*	
	1947 India and Pakistan become independent nations
1949 Orwell, *Nineteen Eighty-Four*	
	1950 Apartheid laws passed in South Africa
1955 Samuel Beckett, *Waiting for Godot*	
	1956 Suez Crisis
	1961 Berlin Wall erected
1962 Doris Lessing, *The Golden Notebook*	1962 Cuban missile crisis
1964 Philip Larkin, *The Whitsun Weddings*	
	1965 U.S. troops land in South Vietnam
1966 Nadine Gordimer, *The Late Bourgeois World.* Tom Stoppard, *Rosencrantz and Guildenstern Are Dead*	
1969 Jean Rhys, *Wide Sargasso Sea*	1969 Apollo moon landing
1971 V. S. Naipaul, *In a Free State*	1971 Indo-Pakistan War, leading to creation of Bangladesh
1972 Seamus Heaney, *North*	1972 Britain enters European Common Market
	1973 U.S. troops leave Vietnam
1979 Craig Raine, *A Martian Sends a Postcard Home*	1979 Islamic Revolution in Iran; the Shah flees. Soviets invade Afghanistan
1980 J. M. Coetzee, *Waiting for the Barbarians*	1980–88 Iran-Iraq War
1981 Salman Rushdie, *Midnight's Children*	
	1982 Falklands War
1988 Rushdie, *The Satanic Verses*	
	1989 Fall of the Berlin Wall. Tieneman Square, Beijing, demonstration and massacre
1991 Derek Walcott, *Omeros*	1991 Collapse of the Soviet Union
1992 Thom Gunn, *The Man with Night Sweats*	
	1994 Democracy comes to South Africa
	1997 Labour Party victory in the UK ends eighteen years of Conservative government
1998 Ted Hughes, *Birthday Letters*	1998 Anglo-American bombing of Iraq. British handover of Hong Kong to China. Northern Ireland Assembly established

THOMAS HARDY
1840–1928

Thomas Hardy was born near Dorchester, in that area of southwest England that he was to make the "Wessex" of his novels. He attended local schools until the age of fifteen, when he was apprenticed to a Dorchester architect with whom he worked for six years. In 1861 he went to London to continue his studies and to practice as an architect. Meanwhile he was completing his general education informally through his own erratic reading and was becoming more and more interested in both fiction and poetry. After some early attempts at writing both short stories and poems, he decided to concentrate on fiction. His first novel was rejected by the publishers in 1868 on the recommendation of George Meredith, who nevertheless advised Hardy to write another. The result was *Desperate Remedies,* published anonymously in 1871, followed the next year by his first real success (also published anonymously), *Under the Greenwood Tree.* Hardy's career as a novelist was now well launched; he gave up his architectural work and produced a series of novels that ended with *Jude the Obscure* in 1896. The hostile reception of this novel sent him back to poetry. His remarkable epic-drama of the Napoleonic Wars, *The Dynasts,* came out in three parts between 1903 and 1908; after this he wrote mostly lyric poetry.

His later work explores the bitter ironies of life with sometimes an almost malevolent staging of coincidence to emphasize the disparity between human desire and ambition on the one hand and what fate has in store for the characters on the other. But fate is not a wholly external force. Men and women are driven by the demands of their own nature as much as by anything from outside them.

Hardy himself denied that he was a pessimist, calling himself a "meliorist," that is, one who believes that the world may be made better by human effort. But there is little sign of meliorism in either his most important novels or his lyric poetry. In the poems, many of his characteristic attitudes and ideas and many of his favorite situations can be found. A number of his poems are verse anecdotes illustrating the perversity of fate, the disastrous or ironic coincidence. But his best poems go beyond this mood to present with quiet gravity and a carefully controlled elegiac feeling some aspect of human sorrow or loss or frustration or regret, always projected through a particular, fully realized situation. *Hap* shows Hardy in the characteristic mood of complaining about the irony of human destiny in a universe ruled by chance, but the group of poems written after the death of his first wife in 1912 gives, with remarkable power, concrete embodiment to a sense of loss. That power—we see it also in *A Broken Appointment*—is achieved through a kind of verbal as well as an emotional integrity. Hardy's poetry, like his prose, often has a self-taught air about it; both can seem odd or, on first reading, clumsy. But at their best both his poetry and his prose have an air of persuasive authenticity. The association of a given emotion with particular visual memories in *Neutral Tones,* for example, is impressive because it carries such extraordinary conviction, and it carries that conviction because the rhythms and rhymes are handled so as to suggest the kind of utterance actually wrung from the poet (consider, e.g., the curious dead fall of "They had fallen from an ash, and were gray"). At the same time, Hardy will use an antique or a poetic word or phrase ("thereby," "a-wing") if it fits in with the movement of the poem and keeps him from having to stop and search for something more deft: the result is an effect not of artificiality but of spontaneity. Hardy's use of ballad rhythms often helps to give an elemental quality to his poetry, suggesting that this incident or situation, carefully particularized though it is, nevertheless stands for some profound and recurring themes in human experience.

The sadness in Hardy—his inability to believe in the government of the world by a benevolent God, his sense of the waste and frustration involved in human life, his insistent irony when faced with moral or metaphysical questions—is part of the late Victorian mood. What has been termed "the disappearance of God" affected him more deeply than many of his contemporaries, because until he was twenty-five he seriously considered entering the church. Yet his characteristic themes and attitudes cannot be related simply to the reaction to new scientific and philosophical ideas (Darwin's theory of evolution, for example) that we see in so many forms in late-nineteenth-century literature. The favorite poetic mood of both Tennyson and Arnold was also an elegiac one (e.g., in Tennyson's *Break, Break, Break* and Arnold's *Dover Beach*), but this is not Hardy's mood. The sad-sweet cadences of Victorian self-pity are not to be found in Hardy's poetry, which is sterner, as though braced by a long look at the worst. It is this sternness—sometimes amounting to ruggedness—together with his verbal and emotional integrity, his refusal ever to surrender to mere poetic fashion, his quietly searching individual accent, that has helped to bring about the steady rise in Hardy's poetic reputation, so that today he is regarded not only as a distinguished novelist but also as a great English poet. He appears as the major figure—with more poems than either Yeats or Eliot—in Philip Larkin's influential *Oxford Book of Twentieth-Century English Verse* (1973).

Hap[1]

If but some vengeful god would call to me
From up the sky, and laugh: "Thou suffering thing,
Know that thy sorrow is my ecstasy,
That thy love's loss is my hate's profiting!"

5 Then would I bear it, clench myself, and die,
Steeled by the sense of ire° unmerited;   *anger*
Half-eased in that a Powerfuller than I
Had willed and meted° me the tears I shed.   *allotted, given*

But not so. How arrives it joy lies slain,
10 And why unblooms the best hope ever sown?
—Crass Casualty obstructs the sun and rain,
And dicing Time for gladness casts a moan . . . .
These purblind Doomsters[2] had as readily strown
Blisses about my pilgrimage as pain.

1866   1898

The Impercipient[1]

(At a Cathedral Service)

That with this bright believing band
I have no claim to be,
That faiths by which my comrades stand
Seem fantasies to me,
5 And mirage-mists their Shining Land,
Is a strange destiny.

1. I.e., chance (as also "Casualty," line 11).
2. Half-blind judges.

1. An unperceiving person.

Why thus my soul should be consigned
    To infelicity,
Why always I must feel as blind
10   To sights my brethren see,
Why joys they have found I cannot find,
    Abides a mystery.

Since heart of mine knows not that ease
    Which they know; since it be
15 That He who breathes All's Well to these
    Breathes no All's-Well to me,
My lack might move their sympathies
    And Christian charity!

I am like a gazer who should mark
20   An inland company
Standing upfingered, with, "Hark! hark!
    The glorious distant sea!"
And feel, "Alas, 'tis but yon dark
    And wind-swept pine to me!"

25 Yet I would bear my shortcomings
    With meet tranquillity,
But for the charge that blessed things
    I'd liefer² not have be.
O, doth a bird beshorn of wings
30   Go earth-bound wilfully!

. . .

Enough. As yet disquiet clings
    About us. Rest shall we.

1898

Neutral Tones

We stood by a pond that winter day,
And the sun was white, as though chidden of° God,   *rebuked by*
And a few leaves lay on the starving sod°   *turf*
  —They had fallen from an ash, and were grey.

5 Your eyes on me were as eyes that rove
Over tedious riddles of years ago;
And some words played between us to and fro
  On which lost the more by our love.

The smile on your mouth was the deadest thing
10 Alive enough to have strength to die;

2. I would prefer.

And a grin of bitterness swept thereby
 Like an ominous bird a-wing . . .

Since then, keen lessons that love deceives,
And wrings with wrong, have shaped to me
15 Your face, and the God-curst sun, and a tree,
 And a pond edged with greyish leaves.

1867   1898

I Look into My Glass[1]

I look into my glass,
And view my wasting skin,
And say, "Would God it came to pass
My heart had shrunk as thin!"

5 For then, I, undistrest
By hearts grown cold to me,
Could lonely wait my endless rest
With equanimity.

But Time, to make me grieve,
10 Part steals, lets part abide;
And shakes this fragile frame at eve
With throbbings of noontide.

1898

A Broken Appointment

You did not come.
And marching Time drew on, and wore me numb.—
Yet less for loss of your dear presence there
Than that I thus found lacking in your make
5 That high compassion which can overbear
Reluctance for pure lovingkindness' sake
Grieved I, when, as the hope-hour stroked its sum,
 You did not come.

You love not me,
10 And love alone can lend you loyalty;
—I know and knew it. But, unto the store
Of human deeds divine in all but name,
Was it not worth a little hour or more
To add yet this: Once you, a woman, came

1. Mirror.

15 To soothe a time-torn man; even though it be
        You love not me?

1902

Drummer Hodge

1

They throw in Drummer Hodge, to rest
    Uncoffined—just as found:
His landmark is a kopje-crest
    That breaks the veldt[1] around;
5 And foreign constellations[2] west°   set
    Each night above his mound.

2

Young Hodge the Drummer never knew—
    Fresh from his Wessex home—
The meaning of the broad Karoo,[3]
10   The Bush,[4] the dusty loam,
And why uprose to nightly view
    Strange stars amid the gloam.

3

Yet portion of that unknown plain
    Will Hodge for ever be;
15 His homely Northern breast and brain
    Grow to some Southern tree,
And strange-eyed constellations reign
    His stars eternally.

1899   1902

The Darkling[1] Thrush

I leant upon a coppice gate[2]
    When Frost was spectre-grey,
And Winter's dregs made desolate
    The weakening eye of day.
5 The tangled bine-stems[3] scored the sky
    Like strings of broken lyres,
And all mankind that haunted nigh°   near
    Had sought their household fires.

1. South African Dutch (Afrikaans) word for a
plain or prairie. "Kopje-crest": Afrikaans for a small
hill. The poem is a lament for an English soldier
killed in the Boer War (1899–1902).
2. Those visible only in the Southern Hemisphere.
3. A dry tableland region in South Africa (usually

spelled "Karroo").
4. British colonial word for an uncleared area of
land.
1. In the dark.
2. Gate leading to a small wood or thicket.
3. Twining stems of shrubs.

The land's sharp features seemed to be
10   The Century's corpse outleant,[4]
His crypt the cloudy canopy,
        The wind his death-lament.
The ancient pulse of germ and birth
        Was shrunken hard and dry,
15 And every spirit upon earth
        Seemed fervourless as I.

At once a voice arose among
        The bleak twigs overhead
In a full-hearted evensong
20   Of joy illimited;
An aged thrush, frail, gaunt, and small,
        In blast-beruffled plume,
Had chosen thus to fling his soul
        Upon the growing gloom.

25 So little cause for carolings
        Of such ecstatic sound
Was written on terrestrial things
        Afar or nigh around,
That I could think there trembled through
30   His happy good-night air
Some blessed Hope, whereof he knew
        And I was unaware.

1900   1901

The Ruined Maid

"O 'Melia,[1] my dear, this does everything crown!
Who could have supposed I should meet you in Town?
And whence such fair garments, such prosperi-ty?"—
"O didn't you know I'd been ruined?" said she.

5   —"You left us in tatters, without shoes or socks,
Tired of digging potatoes, and spudding up docks;[2]
And now you've gay bracelets and bright feathers three!"—
"Yes: that's how we dress when we're ruined," said she.

—"At home in the barton° you said 'thee' and 'thou,'   farmyard
10 And 'thik oon,' and 'theäs oon,' and 't'other'; but now
Your talking quite fits 'ee for high compa-ny!"—
"Some polish is gained with one's ruin," said she.

—"Your hands were like paws then, your face blue and bleak
But now I'm bewitched by your delicate cheek,

---

4. Leaning out (of its coffin); i.e., the 19th century
was dead. This poem was written on December 31,
1900.

1. Diminutive form of Amelia.
2. Digging up a species of thick-rooted weed.

15　And your little gloves fit as on any la-dy!"—
　　"We never do work when we're ruined," said she.

　　—"You used to call home-life a hag-ridden dream,
　　And you'd sigh, and you'd sock;° but at present you seem   *sigh*
　　To know not of megrims° or melancho-ly!"—   *low spirits*
20　"True. One's pretty lively when ruined," said she.

　　—"I wish I had feathers, a fine sweeping gown,
　　And a delicate face, and could strut about Town!"—
　　"My dear—a raw country girl, such as you be,
　　Cannot quite expect that. You ain't ruined," said she.

1866   1901

Channel Firing[1]

　　That night your great guns, unawares,
　　Shook all our coffins as we lay,
　　And broke the chancel[2] window-squares,
　　We thought it was the Judgement-day

5　And sat upright. While drearisome
　　Arose the howl of wakened hounds:
　　The mouse let fall the altar-crumb,
　　The worms drew back into the mounds,

　　The glebe cow[3] drooled. Till God called, "No;
10　It's gunnery practise out at sea
　　Just as before you went below;
　　The world is as it used to be:

　　"All nations striving strong to make
　　Red war yet redder. Mad as hatters[4]
15　They do no more for Christès[5] sake
　　Than you who are helpless in such matters.

　　"That this is not the judgement-hour
　　For some of them's a blessed thing,
　　For if it were they'd have to scour
20　Hell's floor for so much threatening. . . .

　　"Ha, ha. It will be warmer when
　　I blow the trumpet (if indeed
　　I ever do; for you are men,
　　And rest eternal sorely need)."

1. Written in April 1914, when Anglo-German naval rivalry was growing steadily more acute; the title refers to gunnery practice in the English Channel. Four months later (August 4), World War I broke out.
2. Part of church nearest to the altar.

3. I.e., cow on a small plot of land belonging to a church (a "glebe" is a small field).
4. Cf. the Mad Hatter in Lewis Carroll's *Alice's Adventures in Wonderland* (1865).
5. The archaic spelling and pronunciation suggest a ballad note of doom.

25 So down we lay again. "I wonder,
Will the world ever saner be,"
Said one, "than when He sent us under
In our indifferent century!"

And many a skeleton shook his head.
30 "Instead of preaching forty year,"
My neighbour Parson Thirdly said,
"I wish I had stuck to pipes and beer."

Again the guns disturbed the hour,
Roaring their readiness to avenge,
35 As far inland as Stourton Tower,
And Camelot, and starlit Stonehenge.[6]

1914   1914

The Convergence of the Twain

(Lines on the Loss of the Titanic)[1]

I

In a solitude of the sea
Deep from human vanity,
And the Pride of Life that planned her, stilly couches she.

2

Steel chambers, late the pyres
5 Of her salamandrine fires,[2]
Cold currents thrid,[3] and turn to rhythmic tidal lyres.

3

Over the mirrors meant
To glass the opulent
The sea-worm crawls—grotesque, slimed, dumb, indifferent.

4

10 Jewels in joy designed
To ravish the sensuous mind
Lie lightless, all their sparkles bleared and black and blind.

6. The sound of guns preparing for war across the Channel reaches Alfred's ("Stourten") Tower (near Stourton in Dorset), commemorating King Alfred's defeat of a Danish invasion in 879; also the site of King Arthur's court at Camelot (supposedly near Glastonbury) and the famous prehistoric stone circle of Stonehenge on Salisbury Plain.

1. The *Titanic* was the largest and most luxurious ocean liner of the day. Considered unsinkable, it sank with great loss of life on April 15, 1912, on the ship's maiden voyage, from Southampton to the United States, after colliding with an iceberg. Twain: two.

2. Probably "fires in which nothing could survive" (although, since the salamander is a lizardlike animal supposed to be able to live in fire, "salamandrine" usually means "able to resist or to live in fire").

3. A variant form of the verb *thread*.

5

Dim moon-eyed fishes near
Gaze at the gilded gear
15   And query: "What does this vaingloriousness down here?" . . .

6

Well: while was fashioning
This creature of cleaving wing,
The Immanent Will[4] that stirs and urges everything

7

Prepared a sinister mate
20   For her—so gaily great—
A Shape of Ice, for the time far and dissociate.

8

And as the smart ship grew
In stature, grace, and hue,
In shadowy silent distance grew the Iceberg too.

9

25   Alien they seemed to be:
No mortal eye could see
The intimate welding of their later history,

10

Or sign that they were bent
By paths coincident
30   On being anon° twin halves of one august° event,   *soon / important*

11

Till the Spinner of the Years
Said "Now!" And each one hears,
And consummation comes, and jars two hemispheres.

1912   1912, 1914

Ah, Are You Digging on My Grave?

"Ah, are you digging on my grave
       My loved one?—planting rue?"[1]
—"No: yesterday he went to wed
One of the brightest wealth has bred.
5   'It cannot hurt her now,' he said,
       'That I should not be true.' "

"Then who is digging on my grave?
       My nearest dearest kin?"

---

4. The force (blind, but slowly gaining consciousness throughout history) that drives the world,
according to Hardy's philosophy.

1. A yellow-flowered herb, traditionally an
emblem of sorrow (*rue* is also an archaic word for
"sorrow").

—"Ah, no; they sit and think, 'What use!
10   What good will planting flowers produce?
No tendance of her mound can loose
    Her spirit from Death's gin.' "°   *trap*

"But some one digs upon my grave?
    My enemy?—prodding sly?"
15 —"Nay: when she heard you had passed the Gate
That shuts on all flesh soon or late,
She thought you no more worth her hate,
    And cares not where you lie."

"Then, who is digging on my grave?
20   Say—since I have not guessed!"
—"O it is I, my mistress dear,
Your little dog, who still lives near,
And much I hope my movements here
    Have not disturbed your rest?"

25   "Ah, yes! *You* dig upon my grave . . .
    Why flashed it not on me
That one true heart was left behind!
What feeling do we ever find
To equal among human kind
30   A dog's fidelity!"

"Mistress, I dug upon your grave
    To bury a bone, in case
I should be hungry near this spot
When passing on my daily trot.
35 I am sorry, but I quite forgot
    It was your resting-place."

                      1914

The Workbox

"See, here's the workbox, little wife,
    That I made of polished oak."
He was a joiner,° of village life;   *carpenter*
    She came of borough folk.°   *townspeople*

5   He holds the present up to her
    As with a smile she nears
And answers to the profferer,
    " 'Twill last all my sewing years!"

"I warrant it will. And longer too.
10   'Tis a scantling¹ that I got

1. Small piece of wood.

Off poor John Wayward's coffin, who
 Died of they knew not what.

"The shingled pattern that seems to cease
 Against your box's rim
15 Continues right on in the piece
 That's underground with him.

"And while I worked it made me think
 Of timber's varied doom;
One inch where people eat and drink,
20 The next inch in a tomb.

"But why do you look so white, my dear,
 And turn aside your face?
You knew not that good lad, I fear,
 Though he came from your native place?"

25 "How could I know that good young man,
 Though he came from my native town,
When he must have left far earlier than
 I was a woman grown?"

"Ah, no. I should have understood!
30 It shocked you that I gave
To you one end of a piece of wood
 Whose other is in a grave?"

"Don't, dear, despise my intellect,
 Mere accidental things
35 Of that sort never have effect
 On my imaginings."

Yet still her lips were limp and wan,
 Her face still held aside,
As if she had known not only John,
40 But known of what he died.

1914

In Time of "The Breaking of Nations"[1]

I

Only a man harrowing clods
 In a slow silent walk
With an old horse that stumbles and nods
 Half asleep as they stalk.

---

1. Cf. "Thou art my battle axe and weapon of war: for with thee will I break in pieces the nations" (Jeremiah 51.20). The poem was written during World War I.

2

5 Only thin smoke without flame
From the heaps of couch-grass;
Yet this will go onward the same
Though Dynasties pass.

3

Yonder a maid and her wight°   man
10 Come whispering by:
War's annals will cloud into night
Ere their story die.

1915   1916

He Never Expected Much

[or]

A Consideration

[*A reflection*] *on My Eighty-Sixth Birthday*

Well, World, you have kept faith with me,
Kept faith with me;
Upon the whole you have proved to be
Much as you said you were.
5 Since as a child I used to lie
Upon the leaze° and watch the sky,   pasture
Never, I own, expected I
That life would all be fair.

'Twas then you said, and since have said,
10   Times since have said,
In that mysterious voice you shed
From clouds and hills around:
"Many have loved me desperately,
Many with smooth serenity,
15 While some have shown contempt of me
Till they dropped underground.

"I do not promise overmuch,
Child; overmuch;
Just neutral-tinted haps° and such,"   happenings
20   You said to minds like mine.
Wise warning for your credit's sake!
Which I for one failed not to take,
And hence could stem such strain and ache
As each year might assign.

1926   1928

JOSEPH CONRAD
1857–1924

Joseph Conrad was born Jozef Teodor Konrad Nalecz Korzeniowski in Poland (then under Russian rule), son of a Polish patriot who suffered exile in Russia for his Polish nationalist activities and died in 1869, leaving Conrad to be brought up by a maternal uncle. At the age of fifteen he amazed his family and friends by announcing his passionate desire to go to sea; he was eventually allowed to go to Marseilles in 1874, and from there he made a number of voyages on French merchant ships to Martinique and the West Indies. In 1878 he signed on an English ship that brought him to the east coast English port of Lowestoft, where (still as an ordinary seaman) he joined the crew of a small coasting vessel plying between Lowestoft and Newcastle. In six voyages between these two ports he learned English. Thus launched on a career in the British merchant service, Conrad sailed on a variety of British ships to the East and elsewhere and eventually gained his master's certificate in 1886, the year when he became a naturalized British subject. He received his first command in 1888, and in 1890 took a steamboat up the Congo River in nightmarish circumstances (described in *Heart of Darkness*) that produced severe illness and permanently haunted his imagination. In the early 1890s he was already thinking of turning some of his Malayan experiences into English fiction, and in 1892–93, when serving as first mate on the *Torrens* sailing from London to Adelaide, he revealed to a sympathetic passenger that he had begun a novel (*Almayer's Folly*), while on the return journey he impressed the young John Galsworthy, who was on board, with his conversation. Although possessed of a master's certificate, Conrad found it difficult to get the kind of job as master that he wished, and occasionally he had to serve in lesser capacities. His difficulty in obtaining a command, together with the interest aroused by *Almayer's Folly* when it was published in 1895, helped to turn him away from the sea to a career as a writer. He settled in London and in 1896 married an English woman; this son of a Polish patriot turned merchant seaman turned writer was henceforth an English novelist.

Conrad was for a long time regarded as a sea writer whose exotic descriptions of eastern landscapes and exploitation of the romantic atmosphere of Malaya and other unfamiliar regions gave his work a special kind of richness and splendor. But this is only one, and not in the last analysis the most important, aspect of his work. More and more Conrad used the sea and the circumstances of life on shipboard or in remote eastern settlements as means of exploring certain profound moral ambiguities in human experience. The use of intermediate narrators and multiple points of view is common in Conrad; it is his favorite way of suggesting the complexity of experience and the difficulty of judging human actions. This notion of the difficulty of true communion, coupled with the idea that communion can be unexpectedly forced on us—sometimes with someone who may be on the surface our moral opposite, so that we can at times be compelled into a mysterious recognition of our opposite as our true self—is found in many of Conrad's works.

Several stories and novels explore the ways in which the codes we live by are tested in moments of crisis, revealing either their inadequacy or our own. Imagination can corrupt (as with Lord Jim) or save (as in *The Shadow-Line*, 1917), and there are times when total lack of it can see a man through (Captain MacWhirr in *Typhoon*, 1902), though a similar lack in other circumstances can render a man comically ridiculous (Captain Mitchell in *Nostromo*, 1904).

Nostromo, a profound and subtle study of the corrupting effects of politics and "material interests" on personal relationships (set in an imaginary Latin American republic), is often regarded as Conrad's greatest work. He wrote two other political novels—*The Secret Agent* (1906) and *Under Western Eyes* (1911). Conrad was as much a pessimist as Hardy, but he projected his pessimism in subtler ways. He was also a great master of English prose, an astonishing fact when we realize that he was twenty-one before he learned any English, and that to the end of his life he spoke English with a thick foreign accent.

Heart of Darkness

This story is derived from Conrad's personal experience in the Congo in 1890. Like Marlow, the narrator of the story, Conrad had as a child determined one day to visit the heart of Africa. "It was in 1868, when nine years old or thereabouts, that while looking at a map of Africa at the time and putting my finger on the blank space then representing the unsolved mystery of that continent, I said to myself with absolute assurance and an amazing audacity which are no longer in my character now: 'When I grow up I shall go *there*' " (*A Personal Record*, 1912).

Conrad was promised a job as a Congo River pilot through the influence of his distant cousin Marguerite Poradowska, who lived in Brussels and knew important officials of the Belgian company that exploited the Congo. At this time the Congo, although nominally an independent state, the Congo Free State (État Indépendent du Congo), was virtually the personal property of Leopold II, king of the Belgians, who made a fortune out of it. Later, the appalling abuses involved in the naked colonial exploitation that went on in the Congo were exposed to public view, and international criticism compelled the setting up of a committee of inquiry in 1904. What Conrad saw in 1890 shocked him profoundly and shook his view of the moral basis of all exploring and trading in newly discovered countries and indeed of civilization in general. "*Heart of Darkness* is experience, too," Conrad wrote in his 1917 "Author's Note," "but it is experience pushed a little (and only very little) beyond the actual facts of the case for the perfectly legitimate, I believe, purpose of bringing it home to the minds and bosoms of the readers." And later he told Edward Garnett: "Before the Congo I was just a mere animal."

Conrad arrived in Africa in May 1890 and made his way up the Congo River very much as described in *Heart of Darkness*. At Kinshasa (which Conrad spells Kinchassa) on Stanley Pool, which he reached after an exhausting two-hundred-mile trek from Matadi, near the mouth of the river, Conrad was much taken aback to learn that the steamer of which he was to be captain had been damaged and was undergoing repairs. He was sent as supernumerary on another steamer to learn the river. This other steamer was sent to Stanley Falls to collect and bring back to Kinshasa one Georges Antoine Klein, an agent of the company who had fallen gravely ill and who in fact died on board. Klein was the original of Kurtz. Conrad himself then fell seriously ill and eventually returned to London in January 1891 without ever having actually served as a Congo River pilot, the job for which he went out to Africa. The Congo experience permanently impaired his health: it also permanently haunted his imagination. The nightmare atmosphere of *Heart of Darkness* is an accurate reflection of Conrad's own response to his traumatic experience.

The theme of the story is partly the "choice of nightmares" facing the white man in the Congo—either to become like the wholly commercially minded manager, who sees Africa, its people, and its resources solely as instruments of financial gain, or to become like Kurtz, the self-tortured and corrupted idealist. The manager is a "hollow man" (T. S. Eliot quoted from this story in his poem of that title); his only objections to Kurtz are commercial, not moral; Kurtz's methods are "unsound" and would therefore lose the company money. At the last, he seems to recognize the moral horror of his having succumbed to the dark temptations that African life posed for the white man. "He had summed up—he had judged." But the story also has other levels of meaning, and the counterpointing of Western civilization in Europe with what that civilization has done in Africa (see the concluding interview between Marlow and Kurtz's "intended"—based on a real interview between Conrad and the dead Klein's fiancée) throws out several of these.

Heart of Darkness

1

The *Nellie*, a cruising yawl,[1] swung to her anchor without a flutter of the sails, and was at rest. The flood had made, the wind was nearly calm, and being bound down the river, the only thing for it was to come to and wait for the turn of the tide.

The sea-reach of the Thames stretched before us like the beginning of an interminable waterway. In the offing the sea and the sky were welded together without a joint, and in the luminous space the tanned sails of the barges drifting up with the tide seemed to stand still in red clusters of canvas sharply peaked, with gleams of varnished sprits. A haze rested on the low shores that ran out to sea in vanishing flatness. The air was dark above Gravesend,[2] and farther back still seemed condensed into a mournful gloom, brooding motionless over the biggest, and the greatest, town on earth.

The Director of Companies was our captain and our host. We four affectionately watched his back as he stood in the bows looking to seaward. On the whole river there was nothing that looked half so nautical. He resembled a pilot, which to a seaman is trustworthiness personified. It was difficult to realise his work was not out there in the luminous estuary, but behind him, within the brooding gloom.

Between us there was, as I have already said somewhere, the bond of the sea. Besides holding our hearts together through long periods of separation, it had the effect of making us tolerant of each other's yarns—and even convictions. The Lawyer—the best of old fellows—had, because of his many years and many virtues, the only cushion on deck, and was lying on the only rug. The Accountant had brought out already a box of dominoes, and was toying architecturally with the bones. Marlow sat cross-legged right aft, leaning against the mizzenmast. He had sunken cheeks, a yellow complexion, a straight back, an ascetic aspect, and, with his arms dropped, the palms of hands outwards, resembled an idol. The Director, satisfied the anchor had good hold, made his way aft and sat down amongst us. We exchanged a few words lazily. Afterwards there was silence on board the yacht. For some reason or other we did not begin that game of dominoes. We felt meditative, and fit for nothing but placid staring. The day was ending in a serenity of still and exquisite brilliance. The water shone pacifically; the sky, without a speck, was a benign immensity of unstained light; the very mist on the Essex marshes was like a gauzy and radiant fabric, hung from the wooded rises inland, and draping the low shores in diaphanous folds. Only the gloom to the west, brooding over the upper reaches, became more sombre every minute, as if angered by the approach of the sun.

And at last, in its curved and imperceptible fall, the sun sank low, and

1. Two-masted boat.
2. River port on the south bank of the Thames twenty-four miles east (downriver) of London.

from glowing white changed to a dull red without rays and without heat, as if about to go out suddenly, stricken to death by the touch of that gloom brooding over a crowd of men.

Forthwith a change came over the waters, and the serenity became less brilliant but more profound. The old river in its broad reach rested unruffled at the decline of day, after ages of good service done to the race that peopled its banks, spread out in the tranquil dignity of a waterway leading to the uttermost ends of the earth. We looked at the venerable stream not in the vivid flush of a short day that comes and departs for ever, but in the august light of abiding memories. And indeed nothing is easier for a man who has, as the phrase goes, "followed the sea" with reverence and affection, than to evoke the great spirit of the past upon the lower reaches of the Thames. The tidal current runs to and fro in its unceasing service, crowded with memories of men and ships it has borne to the rest of home or to the battles of the sea. It had known and served all the men of whom the nation is proud, from Sir Francis Drake to Sir John Franklin,[3] knights all, titled and untitled—the great knights-errant of the sea. It had borne all the ships whose names are like jewels flashing in the night of time, from the *Golden Hind* returning with her round flanks full of treasure, to be visited by the Queen's Highness and thus pass out of the gigantic tale, to the *Erebus* and *Terror,* bound on other conquests—and that never returned. It had known the ships and the men. They had sailed from Deptford, from Greenwich, from Erith—the adventurers and the settlers; kings' ships and the ships of men on 'Change; captains, admirals, the dark "interlopers"[4] of the Eastern trade, and the commissioned "generals" of East India fleets. Hunters for gold or pursuers of fame, they all had gone out on that stream, bearing the sword, and often the torch, messengers of the might within the land, bearers of a spark from the sacred fire. What greatness had not floated on the ebb of that river into the mystery of an unknown earth! . . . The dreams of men, the seed of commonwealths, the germs of empires.

The sun set; the dusk fell on the stream, and lights began to appear along the shore. The Chapman lighthouse, a three-legged thing erect on a mudflat, shone strongly. Lights of ships moved in the fairway[5]—a great stir of lights going up and going down. And farther west on the upper reaches the place of the monstrous town was still marked ominously on the sky, a brooding gloom in sunshine, a lurid glare under the stars.

"And this also," said Marlow suddenly, "has been one of the dark places of the earth."

He was the only man of us who still "followed the sea." The worst that could be said of him was that he did not represent his class. He was a seaman, but he was a wanderer too, while most seamen lead, if one may so express

---

3. Sir John Franklin (1786–1847), Arctic explorer who in 1845 commanded an expedition consisting of the ships *Erebus* and *Terror* in search of the Northwest Passage. The ships never returned. Sir Francis Drake (ca. 1540–1596), Elizabethan naval hero and explorer, sailed around the world on his ship *The Golden Hind*. Queen Elizabeth knighted Drake on board his ship, loaded with captured Spanish treasure, on his return.
4. Private ships muscling in on the monopoly of the East India Company, which was founded in 1600, lost its trading monopoly in 1813, and transferred its governmental functions to the Crown in 1858. Deptford, on the south bank of the Thames, on the eastern edge of London, was once an important dockyard. Greenwich is on the south bank of the Thames immediately east of Deptford. Erith is eight miles farther east. " 'Change": the Stock Exchange.
5. Navigable part of a river, through which ships enter and depart.

it, a sedentary life. Their minds are of the stay-at-home order, and their home is always with them—the ship; and so is their country—the sea. One ship is very much like another, and the sea is always the same. In the immutability of their surroundings the foreign shores, the foreign faces, the changing immensity of life, glide past, veiled not by a sense of mystery but by a slightly disdainful ignorance; for there is nothing mysterious to a seaman unless it be the sea itself, which is the mistress of his existence and as inscrutable as Destiny. For the rest, after his hours of work, a casual stroll or a casual spree on shore suffices to unfold for him the secret of a whole continent, and generally he finds the secret not worth knowing. The yarns of seamen have a direct simplicity, the whole meaning of which lies within the shell of a cracked nut. But Marlow was not typical (if his propensity to spin yarns be excepted), and to him the meaning of an episode was not inside like a kernel but outside, enveloping the tale which brought it out only as a glow brings out a haze, in the likeness of one of these misty halos that sometimes are made visible by the spectral illumination of moonshine.

His remark did not seem at all surprising. It was just like Marlow. It was accepted in silence. No one took the trouble to grunt even; and presently he said, very slow:

"I was thinking of very old times, when the Romans first came here, nineteen hundred years ago—the other day. . . . Light came out of this river since—you say Knights? Yes; but it is like a running blaze on a plain, like a flash of lightning in the clouds. We live in the flicker—may it last as long as the old earth keeps rolling! But darkness was here yesterday. Imagine the feelings of a commander of a fine—what d'ye call 'em?—trireme[6] in the Mediterranean, ordered suddenly to the north; run overland across the Gauls in a hurry; put in charge of one of these craft the legionaries—a wonderful lot of handy men they must have been too—used to build, apparently by the hundred, in a month or two, if we may believe what we read. Imagine him here—the very end of the world, a sea the colour of lead, a sky the colour of smoke, a kind of ship about as rigid as a concertina—and going up this river with stores, or orders, or what you like. Sandbanks, marshes, forests, savages—precious little to eat fit for a civilised man, nothing but Thames water to drink. No Falernian wine[7] here, no going ashore. Here and there a military camp lost in a wilderness, like a needle in a bundle of hay—cold, fog, tempests, disease, exile, and death—death skulking in the air, in the water, in the bush. They must have been dying like flies here. Oh yes—he did it. Did it very well, too, no doubt, and without thinking much about it either, except afterwards to brag of what he had gone through in his time, perhaps. They were men enough to face the darkness. And perhaps he was cheered by keeping his eye on a chance of promotion to the fleet at Ravenna[8] by and by, if he had good friends in Rome and survived the awful climate. Or think of a decent young citizen in a toga—perhaps too much dice, you know—coming out here in the train of some prefect, or tax-gatherer, or trader, even, to mend his fortunes. Land in a swamp, march through the woods, and in some inland post feel the savagery, the utter savagery, had closed round

6. Ancient Greek and Roman galley with three ranks of oars.
7. Wine from a famed wine-making district in Campania (Italy).

8. A city in northern Italy once directly on the Adriatic Sea and an important naval station in Roman times. It is now about six miles from the sea, connected with it by a canal.

him—all that mysterious life of the wilderness that stirs in the forest, in the jungles, in the hearts of wild men. There's no initiation either into such mysteries. He has to live in the midst of the incomprehensible, which is also detestable. And it has a fascination, too, that goes to work upon him. The fascination of the abomination—you know. Imagine the growing regrets, the longing to escape, the powerless disgust, the surrender, the hate."

He paused.

"Mind," he began again, lifting one arm from the elbow, the palm of the hand outwards, so that, with his legs folded before him, he had the pose of a Buddha preaching in European clothes and without a lotus-flower—"Mind, none of us would feel exactly like this. What saves us is efficiency—the devotion to efficiency. But these chaps were not much account, really. They were no colonists; their administration was merely a squeeze, and nothing more, I suspect. They were conquerors, and for that you want only brute force—nothing to boast of, when you have it, since your strength is just an accident arising from the weakness of others. They grabbed what they could get for the sake of what was to be got. It was just robbery with violence, aggravated murder on a great scale, and men going at it blind—as is very proper for those who tackle a darkness. The conquest of the earth, which mostly means the taking it away from those who have a different complexion or slightly flatter noses than ourselves, is not a pretty thing when you look into it too much. What redeems it is the idea only. An idea at the back of it; not a sentimental pretence but an idea; and an unselfish belief in the idea—something you can set up, and bow down before, and offer a sacrifice to. . . ."

He broke off. Flames glided in the river, small green flames, red flames, white flames, pursuing, overtaking, joining, crossing each other—then separating slowly or hastily. The traffic of the great city went on in the deepening night upon the sleepless river. We looked on, waiting patiently—there was nothing else to do till the end of the flood; but it was only after a long silence, when he said, in a hesitating voice, "I suppose you fellows remember I did once turn fresh-water sailor for a bit," that we knew we were fated, before the ebb began to run, to hear about one of Marlow's inconclusive experiences.

"I don't want to bother you much with what happened to me personally," he began, showing in this remark the weakness of many tellers of tales who seem so often unaware of what their audience would best like to hear; "yet to understand the effect of it on me you ought to know how I got out there, what I saw, how I went up that river to the place where I first met the poor chap. It was the farthest point of navigation and the culminating point of my experience. It seemed somehow to throw a kind of light on everything about me—and into my thoughts. It was sombre enough too—and pitiful—not extraordinary in any way—not very clear either. No, not very clear. And yet it seemed to throw a kind of light.

"I had then, as you remember, just returned to London after a lot of Indian Ocean, Pacific, China Seas—a regular dose of the East—six years or so, and I was loafing about, hindering you fellows in your work and invading your homes, just as though I had got a heavenly mission to civilise you. It was very fine for a time, but after a bit I did get tired of resting. Then I began to look for a ship—I should think the hardest work on earth. But the ships wouldn't even look at me. And I got tired of that game too.

"Now when I was a little chap I had a passion for maps. I would look for hours at South America, or Africa, or Australia, and lose myself in all the glories of exploration. At that time there were many blank spaces on the earth, and when I saw one that looked particularly inviting on a map (but they all look that) I would put my finger on it and say, When I grow up I will go there. The North Pole was one of these places, I remember. Well, I haven't been there yet, and shall not try now. The glamour's off. Other places were scattered about the Equator, and in every sort of latitude all over the two hemispheres. I have been in some of them, and . . . well, we won't talk about that. But there was one yet—the biggest, the most blank, so to speak—that I had a hankering after.

"True, by this time it was not a blank space any more. It had got filled since my boyhood with rivers and lakes and names. It had ceased to be a blank space of delightful mystery—a white patch for a boy to dream gloriously over. It had become a place of darkness. But there was in it one river especially, a mighty big river, that you could see on the map, resembling an immense snake uncoiled, with its head in the sea, its body at rest curving afar over a vast country, and its tail lost in the depths of the land. And as I looked at the map of it in a shop-window, it fascinated me as a snake would a bird—a silly little bird. Then I remembered there was a big concern, a Company for trade on that river. Dash it all! I thought to myself, they can't trade without using some kind of craft on that lot of fresh water—steamboats! Why shouldn't I try to get charge of one? I went on along Fleet Street, but could not shake off the idea. The snake had charmed me.

"You understand it was a Continental concern, that Trading Society; but I have a lot of relations living on the Continent, because it's cheap and not so nasty as it looks, they say.

"I am sorry to own I began to worry them. This was already a fresh departure for me. I was not used to get things that way, you know. I always went my own road and on my own legs where I had a mind to go. I wouldn't have believed it of myself; but, then—you see—I felt somehow I must get there by hook or by crook. So I worried them. The men said, 'My dear fellow,' and did nothing. Then—would you believe it?—I tried the women. I, Charlie Marlow, set the women to work—to get a job. Heavens! Well, you see, the notion drove me. I had an aunt, a dear enthusiastic soul. She wrote: 'It will be delightful. I am ready to do anything, anything for you. It is a glorious idea. I know the wife of a very high personage in the Administration, and also a man who has lots of influence with,' etc. etc. She was determined to make no end of fuss to get me appointed skipper of a river steamboat, if such was my fancy.

"I got my appointment—of course; and I got it very quick. It appears the Company had received news that one of their captains had been killed in a scuffle with the natives. This was my chance, and it made me the more anxious to go. It was only months and months afterwards, when I made the attempt to recover what was left of the body, that I heard the original quarrel arose from a misunderstanding about some hens. Yes, two black hens. Fresleven—that was the fellow's name, a Dane—thought himself wronged somehow in the bargain, so he went ashore and started to hammer the chief of the village with a stick. Oh, it didn't surprise me in the least to hear this, and at the same time to be told that Fresleven was the gentlest, quietest creature that ever walked on two legs. No doubt he was; but he had been a couple of years already out there engaged in the noble cause, you know, and he probably felt the need at last of asserting his self-respect in some way. Therefore he whacked the old nigger mercilessly, while a big crowd of his people watched him, thunderstruck, till some man—I was told the chief's son—in desperation at hearing the old chap yell, made a tentative jab with a spear at the white man—and of course it went quite easy between the shoulder-blades. Then the whole population cleared into the forest, expecting all kinds of calamities to happen, while, on the other hand, the steamer Fresleven commanded left also in a bad panic, in charge of the engineer, I believe. Afterwards nobody seemed to trouble much about Fresleven's remains, till I got out and stepped into his shoes. I couldn't let it rest, though; but when an opportunity offered at last to meet my predecessor, the grass growing through his ribs was tall enough to hide his bones. They were all there. The supernatural being had not been touched after he fell. And the village was deserted, the huts gaped black, rotting, all askew within the fallen enclosures. A calamity had come to it, sure enough. The people had vanished. Mad terror had scattered them, men, women, and children, through the bush, and they had never returned. What became of the hens I don't know either. I should think the cause of progress got them, anyhow. However, through this glorious affair I got my appointment, before I had fairly begun to hope for it.

"I flew around like mad to get ready, and before forty-eight hours I was crossing the Channel to show myself to my employers, and sign the contract. In a very few hours I arrived in a city that always makes me think of a whited sepulchre. Prejudice no doubt. I had no difficulty in finding the Company's offices. It was the biggest thing in the town, and everybody I met was full of it. They were going to run an oversea empire, and make no end of coin by trade.

"A narrow and deserted street in deep shadow, high houses, innumerable windows with venetian blinds, a dead silence, grass sprouting between the stones, imposing carriage archways right and left, immense double doors standing ponderously ajar. I slipped through one of these cracks, went up a swept and ungarnished staircase, as arid as a desert, and opened the first door I came to. Two women, one fat and the other slim, sat on straw-bottomed chairs, knitting black wool. The slim one got up and walked straight at me—still knitting with downcast eyes—and only just as I began to think of getting out of her way, as you would for a somnambulist, stood still, and looked up. Her dress was as plain as an umbrella-cover, and she turned round without a word and preceded me into a waiting-room. I gave my name, and looked about. Deal table in the middle, plain chairs all round the walls, on one end a large shining map, marked with all the colours of a rainbow. There was a vast amount of red—good to see at any time, because one knows that some real work is done in there, a deuce of a lot of blue, a little green, smears of orange, and, on the East Coast, a purple patch, to show where the jolly pioneers of progress drink the jolly lager-beer. However, I wasn't going into any of these. I was going into the yellow. Dead in the centre. And the river was there—fascinating—deadly—like a snake. Ough! A door opened, a white-haired secretarial head, but wearing a compassionate expression, appeared, and a skinny forefinger beckoned me into the sanctuary. Its light was dim, and a heavy writing desk squatted in the middle. From behind that structure came out an impression of pale plumpness in a frockcoat. The great man himself. He was five feet six, I should judge, and had his grip on the handle-end of ever so many millions. He shook hands, I fancy, murmured vaguely, was satisfied with my French. *Bon voyage.*

"In about forty-five seconds I found myself again in the waiting-room with the compassionate secretary, who, full of desolation and sympathy, made me sign some document. I believe I undertook amongst other things not to disclose any trade secrets. Well, I am not going to.

"I began to feel slightly uneasy. You know I am not used to such ceremonies, and there was something ominous in the atmosphere. It was just as though I had been let into some conspiracy—I don't know—something not quite right; and I was glad to get out. In the outer room the two women knitted black wool feverishly. People were arriving, and the younger one was walking back and forth introducing them. The old one sat on her chair. Her flat cloth slippers were propped up on a foot-warmer, and a cat reposed on her lap. She wore a starched white affair on her head, had a wart on one cheek, and silver-rimmed spectacles hung on the tip of her nose. She glanced at me above the glasses. The swift and indifferent placidity of that look troubled me. Two youths with foolish and cheery countenances were being piloted over, and she threw at them the same quick glance of unconcerned wisdom. She seemed to know all about them and about me too. An eerie feeling came over me. She seemed uncanny and fateful. Often far away there I thought of these two, guarding the door of Darkness, knitting black wool as for a warm pall, one introducing, introducing continuously to the unknown, the other scrutinising the cheery and foolish faces with unconcerned old eyes. *Ave!* Old knitter of black wool. *Morituri te salutant.*[9] Not many of those she looked at ever saw her again—not half, by a long way.

"There was yet a visit to the doctor. 'A simple formality,' assured me the secretary, with an air of taking an immense part in all my sorrows. Accordingly a young chap wearing his hat over the left eyebrow, some clerk I suppose—there must have been clerks in the business, though the house was as still as a house in a city of the dead—came from somewhere upstairs, and led me forth. He was shabby and careless, with ink-stains on the sleeves of his jacket, and his cravat was large and billowy, under a chin shaped like the toe of an old boot. It was a little too early for the doctor, so I proposed a drink, and thereupon he developed a vein of joviality. As we sat over our vermuths he glorified the Company's business, and by and by I expressed casually my surprise at him not going out there. He became very cool and collected all at once. 'I am not such a fool as I look, quoth Plato to his disciples,' he said sententiously, emptied his glass with great resolution, and we rose.

"The old doctor felt my pulse, evidently thinking of something else the while. 'Good, good for there,' he mumbled, and then with a certain eagerness asked me whether I would let him measure my head. Rather surprised, I said Yes, when he produced a thing like callipers and got the dimensions back and front and every way, taking notes carefully. He was an unshaven little

---

9. "Hail! . . . Those who are about to die salute you" (Latin). The Roman gladiators' salute to the emperor on entering the arena.

man in a threadbare coat like a gaberdine, with his feet in slippers, and I thought him a harmless fool. 'I always ask leave, in the interests of science, to measure the crania of those going out there,' he said. 'And when they come back too?' I asked. 'Oh, I never see them,' he remarked; 'and, moreover, the changes take place inside, you know.' He smiled, as if at some quiet joke. 'So you are going out there. Famous. Interesting too.' He gave me a searching glance, and made another note. 'Ever any madness in your family?' he asked, in a matter-of-fact tone. I felt very annoyed. 'Is that question in the interests of science too?' 'It would be,' he said, without taking notice of my irritation, 'interesting for science to watch the mental changes of individuals, on the spot, but . . . ' 'Are you an alienist?'[1] I interrupted. 'Every doctor should be—a little,' answered that original[2] imperturbably. 'I have a little theory which you Messieurs who go out there must help me to prove. This is my share in the advantages my country shall reap from the possession of such a magnificent dependency. The mere wealth I leave to others. Pardon my questions, but you are the first Englishman coming under my observation . . . ' I hastened to assure him I was not in the least typical. 'If I were,' said I, 'I wouldn't be talking like this with you.' 'What you say is rather profound, and probably erroneous,' he said, with a laugh. 'Avoid irritation more than exposure to the sun. Adieu. How do you English say, eh? Good-bye. Ah! Good-bye. Adieu. In the tropics one must before everything keep calm.' . . . He lifted a warning forefinger. . . . 'Du calme, du calme. Adieu.'

"One thing more remained to do—say good-bye to my excellent aunt. I found her triumphant. I had a cup of tea—the last decent cup of tea for many days—and in a room that most soothingly looked just as you would expect a lady's drawing-room to look, we had a long quiet chat by the fireside. In the course of these confidences it became quite plain to me I had been represented to the wife of the high dignitary, and goodness knows to how many more people besides, as an exceptional and gifted creature—a piece of good fortune for the Company—a man you don't get hold of every day. Good heavens! and I was going to take charge of a two-penny-halfpenny river-steamboat with a penny whistle attached! It appeared, however, I was also one of the Workers, with a capital—you know. Something like an emissary of light, something like a lower sort of apostle. There had been a lot of such rot let loose in print and talk just about that time, and the excellent woman, living right in the rush of all that humbug, got carried off her feet. She talked about 'weaning those ignorant millions from their horrid ways,' till, upon my word, she made me quite uncomfortable. I ventured to hint that the Company was run for profit.

" 'You forget, dear Charlie, that the labourer is worthy of his hire,' she said brightly. It's queer how out of touch with truth women are. They live in a world of their own, and there had never been anything like it, and never can be. It is too beautiful altogether, and if they were to set it up it would go to pieces before the first sunset. Some confounded fact we men have been living contentedly with ever since the day of creation would start up and knock the whole thing over.

"After this I got embraced, told to wear flannel, be sure to write often, and

1. Doctor who treats mental diseases. (The term has now been replaced by *psychiatrist*.) 2. Eccentric person.

so on—and I left. In the street—I don't know why—a queer feeling came to me that I was an impostor. Odd thing that I, who used to clear out for any part of the world at twenty-four hours' notice, with less thought than most men give to the crossing of a street, had a moment—I won't say of hesitation, but of startled pause, before this commonplace affair. The best way I can explain it to you is by saying that, for a second or two, I felt as though, instead of going to the centre of a continent, I were about to set off for the centre of the earth.

"I left in a French steamer, and she called in every blamed port they have out there, for, as far as I could see, the sole purpose of landing soldiers and custom-house officers. I watched the coast. Watching a coast as it slips by the ship is like thinking about an enigma. There it is before you—smiling, frowning, inviting, grand, mean, insipid, or savage, and always mute with an air of whispering, Come and find out. This one was almost featureless, as if still in the making, with an aspect of monotonous grimness. The edge of a colossal jungle, so dark green as to be almost black, fringed with white surf, ran straight, like a ruled line, far, far away along a blue sea whose glitter was blurred by a creeping mist. The sun was fierce, the land seemed to glisten and drip with steam. Here and there greyish-whitish specks showed up clustered inside the white surf, with a flag flying above them perhaps—settlements some centuries old, and still no bigger than pin-heads on the untouched expanse of their background. We pounded along, stopped, landed soldiers; went on, landed custom-house clerks to levy toll in what looked like a God-forsaken wilderness, with a tin shed and a flag-pole lost in it; landed more soldiers—to take care of the custom-house clerks presumably. Some, I heard, got drowned in the surf; but whether they did or not, nobody seemed particularly to care. They were just flung out there, and on we went. Every day the coast looked the same, as though we had not moved; but we passed various places—trading places—with names like Gran' Bassam, Little Popo; names that seemed to belong to some sordid farce acted in front of a sinister back-cloth. The idleness of a passenger, my isolation amongst all these men with whom I had no point of contact, the oily and languid sea, the uniform sombreness of the coast, seemed to keep me away from the truth of things, within the toil of a mournful and senseless delusion. The voice of the surf heard now and then was a positive pleasure, like the speech of a brother. It was something natural, that had its reason, that had a meaning. Now and then a boat from the shore gave one a momentary contact with reality. It was paddled by black fellows. You could see from afar the white of their eyeballs glistening. They shouted, sang; their bodies streamed with perspiration; they had faces like grotesque masks—these chaps; but they had bone, muscle, a wild vitality, an intense energy of movement, that was as natural and true as the surf along their coast. They wanted no excuse for being there. They were a great comfort to look at. For a time I would feel I belonged still to a world of straightforward facts; but the feeling would not last long. Something would turn up to scare it away. Once, I remember, we came upon a man-of-war anchored off the coast. There wasn't even a shed there, and she was shelling the bush. It appears the French had one of their wars going on thereabouts. Her ensign dropped limp like a rag; the muzzles of the long six-inch guns stuck out all over the low hull; the greasy, slimy swell swung her up lazily and let her down, swaying her thin masts. In the empty immensity of earth, sky, and water, there she was, incomprehensible, firing into a continent. Pop, would go one of the six-inch guns; a small flame would dart and vanish, a little white smoke would disappear, a tiny projectile would give a feeble screech—and nothing happened. Nothing could happen. There was a touch of insanity in the proceeding, a sense of lugubrious drollery in the sight; and it was not dissipated by somebody on board assuring me earnestly there was a camp of natives—he called them enemies!—hidden out of sight somewhere.

"We gave her her letters (I heard the men in that lonely ship were dying of fever at the rate of three a day) and went on. We called at some more places with farcical names, where the merry dance of death and trade goes on in a still and earthy atmosphere as of an overheated catacomb; all along the formless coast bordered by dangerous surf, as if Nature herself had tried to ward off intruders; in and out of rivers, streams of death in life, whose banks were rotting into mud, whose waters, thickened into slime, invaded the contorted mangroves, that seemed to writhe at us in the extremity of an impotent despair. Nowhere did we stop long enough to get a particularised impression, but the general sense of vague and oppressive wonder grew upon me. It was like a weary pilgrimage amongst hints for nightmares.

"It was upward of thirty days before I saw the mouth of the big river. We anchored off the seat of the government. But my work would not begin till some two hundred miles farther on. So as soon as I could I made a start for a place thirty miles higher up.

"I had my passage on a little sea-going steamer. Her captain was a Swede, and knowing me for a seaman, invited me on the bridge. He was a young man, lean, fair, and morose, with lanky hair and a shuffling gait. As we left the miserable little wharf, he tossed his head contemptuously at the shore. 'Been living there?' he asked. I said, 'Yes.' 'Fine lot these government chaps—are they not?' he went on, speaking English with great precision and considerable bitterness. 'It is funny what some people will do for a few francs a month. I wonder what becomes of that kind when it goes up country?' I said to him I expected to see that soon. 'So-o-o!' he exclaimed. He shuffled athwart, keeping one eye ahead vigilantly. 'Don't be too sure,' he continued. 'The other day I took up a man who hanged himself on the road. He was a Swede, too.' 'Hanged himself! Why, in God's name?' I cried. He kept on looking out watchfully. 'Who knows? The sun too much for him, or the country perhaps.'

"At last we opened a reach. A rocky cliff appeared, mounds of turned-up earth by the shore, houses on a hill, others with iron roofs, amongst a waste of excavations, or hanging to the declivity. A continuous noise of the rapids above hovered over this scene of inhabited devastation. A lot of people, mostly black and naked, moved about like ants. A jetty projected into the river. A blinding sunlight drowned all this at times in a sudden recrudescence of glare. 'There's your Company's station,' said the Swede, pointing to three wooden barrack-like structures on the rocky slope. 'I will send your things up. Four boxes did you say? So. Farewell.'

"I came upon a boiler wallowing in the grass, then found a path leading up the hill. It turned aside for the boulders, and also for an undersized railway truck lying there on its back with its wheels in the air. One was off. The thing looked as dead as the carcass of some animal. I came upon more pieces of decaying machinery, a stack of rusty nails. To the left a clump of trees made a shady spot, where dark things seemed to stir feebly. I blinked, the path was steep. A horn tooted to the right, and I saw the black people run. A heavy and dull detonation shook the ground, a puff of smoke came out of the cliff, and that was all. No change appeared on the face of the rock. They were building a railway. The cliff was not in the way or anything; but this objectless blasting was all the work going on.

"A slight clinking behind me made me turn my head. Six black men advanced in a file, toiling up the path. They walked erect and slow, balancing small baskets full of earth on their heads, and the clink kept time with their footsteps. Black rags were wound round their loins, and the short ends behind waggled to and fro like tails. I could see every rib, the joints of their limbs were like knots in a rope; each had an iron collar on his neck, and all were connected together with a chain whose bights swung between them, rhythmically clinking. Another report from the cliff made me think suddenly of that ship of war I had seen firing into a continent. It was the same kind of ominous voice; but these men could by no stretch of imagination be called enemies. They were called criminals, and the outraged law, like the bursting shells, had come to them, an insoluble mystery from the sea. All their meagre breasts panted together, the violently dilated nostrils quivered, the eyes stared stonily uphill. They passed me within six inches, without a glance, with that complete, deathlike indifference of unhappy savages. Behind this raw matter one of the reclaimed, the product of the new forces at work, strolled despondently, carrying a rifle by its middle. He had a uniform jacket with one button off, and seeing a white man on the path, hoisted his weapon to his shoulder with alacrity. This was simple prudence, white men being so much alike at a distance that he could not tell who I might be. He was speedily reassured, and with a large, white, rascally grin, and a glance at his charge, seemed to take me into partnership in his exalted trust. After all, I also was a part of the great cause of these high and just proceedings.

"Instead of going up, I turned and descended to the left. My idea was to let that chain-gang get out of sight before I climbed the hill. You know I am not particularly tender; I've had to strike and to fend off. I've had to resist and to attack sometimes—that's only one way of resisting—without counting the exact cost, according to the demands of such sort of life as I had blundered into. I've seen the devil of violence, and the devil of greed, and the devil of hot desire; but, by all the stars! these were strong, lusty, red-eyed devils, that swayed and drove men—men, I tell you. But as I stood on this hillside, I foresaw that in the blinding sunshine of that land I would become acquainted with a flabby, pretending, weak-eyed devil of a rapacious and pitiless folly. How insidious he could be, too, I was only to find out several months later and a thousand miles farther. For a moment I stood appalled, as though by a warning. Finally I descended the hill, obliquely, towards the trees I had seen.

"I avoided a vast artificial hole somebody had been digging on the slope, the purpose of which I found it impossible to divine. It wasn't a quarry or a sandpit, anyhow. It was just a hole. It might have been connected with the philanthropic desire of giving the criminals something to do. I don't know. Then I nearly fell into a very narrow ravine, almost no more than a scar in the hillside. I discovered that a lot of imported drainage-pipes for the settlement had been tumbled in there. There wasn't one that was not broken. It was a wanton smash-up. At last I got under the trees. My purpose was to stroll into the shade for a moment; but no sooner within than it seemed to me I had stepped into the gloomy circle of some Inferno. The rapids were near, and an uninterrupted, uniform, headlong, rushing noise filled the mournful stillness of the grove, where not a breath stirred, not a leaf moved, with a mysterious sound—as though the tearing pace of the launched earth had suddenly become audible.

"Black shapes crouched, lay, sat between the trees, leaning against the trunks, clinging to the earth, half coming out, half effaced within the dim light, in all the attitudes of pain, abandonment, and despair. Another mine on the cliff went off, followed by a slight shudder of the soil under my feet. The work was going on. The work! And this was the place where some of the helpers had withdrawn to die.

"They were dying slowly—it was very clear. They were not enemies, they were not criminals, they were nothing earthly now—nothing but black shadows of disease and starvation, lying confusedly in the greenish gloom. Brought from all the recesses of the coast in all the legality of time contracts, lost in uncongenial surroundings, fed on unfamiliar food, they sickened, became inefficient, and were then allowed to crawl away and rest. These moribund shapes were free as air—and nearly as thin. I began to distinguish the gleam of eyes under the trees. Then, glancing down, I saw a face near my hand. The black bones reclined at full length with one shoulder against the tree, and slowly the eyelids rose and the sunken eyes looked up at me, enormous and vacant, a kind of blind, white flicker in the depths of the orbs, which died out slowly. The man seemed young—almost a boy—but you know with them it's hard to tell. I found nothing else to do but to offer him one of my good Swede's ship's biscuits I had in my pocket. The fingers closed slowly on it and held—there was no other movement and no other glance. He had tied a bit of white worsted[3] round his neck—Why? Where did he get it? Was it a badge—an ornament—a charm—a propitiatory act? Was there any idea at all connected with it? It looked startling round his black neck, this bit of white thread from beyond the seas.

"Near the same tree two more bundles of acute angles sat with their legs drawn up. One, with his chin propped on his knees, stared at nothing, in an intolerable and appalling manner: his brother phantom rested its forehead, as if overcome with a great weariness; and all about others were scattered in every pose of contorted collapse, as in some picture of a massacre or a pestilence. While I stood horror-struck, one of these creatures rose to his hands and knees, and went off on all-fours towards the river to drink. He lapped out of his hand, then sat up in the sunlight, crossing his shins in front of him, and after a time let his woolly head fall on his breastbone.

"I didn't want any more loitering in the shade, and I made haste towards the station. When near the buildings I met a white man, in such an unexpected elegance of get-up that in the first moment I took him for a sort of vision. I saw a high starched collar, white cuffs, a light alpaca[4] jacket, snowy trousers, a clear necktie, and varnished boots. No hat. Hair parted, brushed,

---

3. Fine wool fabric.
4. Made from the wool of a South American animal.

oiled, under a green-lined parasol held in a big white hand. He was amazing, and had a penholder behind his ear.

"I shook hands with this miracle, and I learned he was the Company's chief accountant, and that all the book-keeping was done at this station. He had come out for a moment, he said, 'to get a breath of fresh air.' The expression sounded wonderfully odd, with its suggestion of sedentary desk-life. I wouldn't have mentioned the fellow to you at all, only it was from his lips that I first heard the name of the man who is so indissolubly connected with the memories of that time. Moreover, I respected the fellow. Yes; I respected his collars, his vast cuffs, his brushed hair. His appearance was certainly that of a hairdresser's dummy; but in the great demoralisation of the land he kept up his appearance. That's backbone. His starched collars and got-up shirt-fronts were achievements of character. He had been out nearly three years; and, later, I could not help asking him how he managed to sport such linen. He had just the faintest blush, and said modestly, 'I've been teaching one of the native women about the station. It was difficult. She had a distaste for the work.' Thus this man had verily accomplished something. And he was devoted to his books, which were in apple-pie order.

"Everything else in the station was in a muddle,—heads, things, buildings. Strings of dusty niggers with splay feet arrived and departed; a stream of manufactured goods, rubbishy cottons, beads, and brass-wire sent into the depths of darkness, and in return came a precious trickle of ivory.

"I had to wait in the station for ten days—an eternity. I lived in a hut in the yard, but to be out of the chaos I would sometimes get into the accountant's office. It was built of horizontal planks, and so badly put together that, as he bent over his high desk, he was barred from neck to heels with narrow strips of sunlight. There was no need to open the big shutter to see. It was hot there too; big flies buzzed fiendishly, and did not sting, but stabbed. I sat generally on the floor, while, of faultless appearance (and even slightly scented), perching on a high stool, he wrote, he wrote. Sometimes he stood up for exercise. When a truckle-bed with a sick man (some invalided agent from up country) was put in there, he exhibited a gentle annoyance. 'The groans of this sick person' he said, 'distract my attention. And without that it is extremely difficult to guard against clerical errors in this climate.'

"One day he remarked, without lifting his head, 'In the interior you will no doubt meet Mr Kurtz.' On my asking who Mr Kurtz was, he said he was a first-class agent; and seeing my disappointment at this information, he added slowly, laying down his pen, 'He is a very remarkable person.' Further questions elicited from him that Mr Kurtz was at present in charge of a trading-post, a very important one, in the true ivory-country, at 'the very bottom of there. Sends in as much ivory as all the others put together . . .' He began to write again. The sick man was too ill to groan. The flies buzzed in a great peace.

"Suddenly there was a growing murmur of voices and a great tramping of feet. A caravan had come in. A violent babble of uncouth sounds burst out on the other side of the planks. All the carriers were speaking together, and in the midst of the uproar the lamentable voice of the chief agent was heard 'giving it up' tearfully for the twentieth time that day. . . . He rose slowly. 'What a frightful row,' he said. He crossed the room gently to look at the sick man, and returning, said to me, 'He does not hear.' 'What! Dead?' I asked, startled. 'No, not yet,' he answered, with great composure. Then, alluding with a toss of the head to the tumult in the station-yard, 'When one has got to make correct entries, one comes to hate those savages—hate them to the death.' He remained thoughtful for a moment. 'When you see Mr Kurtz,' he went on, 'tell him from me that everything here'—he glanced at the desk— 'is very satisfactory. I don't like to write to him—with those messengers of ours you never know who may get hold of your letter—at that Central Station.' He stared at me for a moment with his mild, bulging eyes. 'Oh, he will go far, very far,' he began again. 'He will be a somebody in the Administration before long. They, above—the Council in Europe, you know—mean him to be.'

"He turned to his work. The noise outside had ceased, and presently in going out I stopped at the door. In the steady buzz of flies the homeward-bound agent was lying flushed and insensible; the other, bent over his books, was making correct entries of perfectly correct transactions; and fifty feet below the doorstep I could see the still tree-tops of the grove of death.

"Next day I left that station at last, with a caravan of sixty men, for a two-hundred-mile tramp.

"No use telling you much about that. Paths, paths, everywhere; a stamped-in network of paths spreading over the empty land, through long grass, through burnt grass, through thickets, down and up chilly ravines, up and down stony hills ablaze with heat; and a solitude, a solitude, nobody, not a hut. The population had cleared out a long time ago. Well, if a lot of mysterious niggers armed with all kinds of fearful weapons suddenly took to travelling on the road between Deal and Gravesend, catching the yokels right and left to carry heavy loads for them, I fancy every farm and cottage thereabouts would get empty very soon. Only here the dwellings were gone too. Still, I passed through several abandoned villages. There's something pathetically childish in the ruins of grass walls. Day after day, with the stamp and shuffle of sixty pair of bare feet behind me, each pair under a 60-lb. load. Camp, cook, sleep, strike camp, march. Now and then a carrier dead in harness, at rest in the long grass near the path, with an empty water-gourd and his long staff lying by his side. A great silence around and above. Perhaps on some quiet night the tremor of far-off drums, sinking, swelling, a tremor vast, faint; a sound weird, appealing, suggestive, and wild—and perhaps with as profound a meaning as the sound of bells in a Christian country. Once a white man in an unbuttoned uniform, camping on the path with an armed escort of lank Zanzibaris,[5] very hospitable and festive—not to say drunk. Was looking after the upkeep of the road, he declared. Can't say I saw any road or any upkeep, unless the body of a middle-aged negro, with a bullet-hole in the forehead, upon which I absolutely stumbled three miles farther on, may be considered as a permanent improvement. I had a white companion too, not a bad chap, but rather too fleshy and with the exasperating habit of fainting on the hot hillsides, miles away from the least bit of shade and water. Annoying, you know, to hold your own coat like a parasol over a man's head while he is coming-to. I couldn't help asking him once what he meant by coming there at all. 'To make money, of course. What do you think?' he said

5. Natives of Zanzibar, an island off the east coast of Africa, once part of the sultanate of Zanzibar and a British protectorate, now part of the independent state of Tanzania. Zanzibaris were used as mercenaries throughout Africa.

scornfully. Then he got fever, and had to be carried in a hammock slung under a pole. As he weighed sixteen stone[6] I had no end of rows with the carriers. They jibbed, ran away, sneaked off with their loads in the night— quite a mutiny. So, one evening, I made a speech in English with gestures, not one of which was lost to the sixty pairs of eyes before me, and the next morning I started the hammock off in front all right. An hour afterwards I came upon the whole concern wrecked in a bush—man, hammock, groans, blankets, horrors. The heavy pole had skinned his poor nose. He was very anxious for me to kill somebody, but there wasn't the shadow of a carrier near. I remembered the old doctor—'It would be interesting for science to watch the mental changes of individuals, on the spot.' I felt I was becoming scientifically interesting. However, all that is to no purpose. On the fifteenth day I came in sight of the big river again, and hobbled into the Central Station. It was on a back water surrounded by scrub and forest, with a pretty border of smelly mud on one side, and on the three others enclosed by a crazy fence of rushes. A neglected gap was all the gate it had, and the first glance at the place was enough to let you see the flabby devil was running that show. White men with long staves in their hands appeared languidly from amongst the buildings, strolling up to take a look at me, and then retired out of sight somewhere. One of them, a stout, excitable chap with black moustaches, informed me with great volubility and many digressions, as soon as I told him who I was, that my steamer was at the bottom of the river. I was thunderstruck. What, how, why? Oh, it was 'all right.' The 'manager himself' was there. All quite correct. 'Everybody had behaved splendidly! splendidly!'—'You must,' he said in agitation, 'go and see the general manager at once. He is waiting!'

"I did not see the real significance of that wreck at once. I fancy I see it now, but I am not sure—not at all. Certainly the affair was too stupid—when I think of it—to be altogether natural. Still . . . But at the moment it presented itself simply as a confounded nuisance. The steamer was sunk. They had started two days before in a sudden hurry up the river with the manager on board, in charge of some volunteer skipper, and before they had been out three hours they tore the bottom out of her on stones, and she sank near the south bank. I asked myself what I was to do there, now my boat was lost. As a matter of fact, I had plenty to do in fishing my command out of the river. I had to set about it the very next day. That, and the repairs when I brought the pieces to the station, took some months.

"My first interview with the manager was curious. He did not ask me to sit down after my twenty-mile walk that morning. He was commonplace in complexion, in feature, in manners, and in voice. He was of middle size and of ordinary build. His eyes, of the usual blue, were perhaps remarkably cold, and he certainly could make his glance fall on one as trenchant and heavy as an axe. But even at these times the rest of his person seemed to disclaim the intention. Otherwise there was only an indefinable, faint expression of his lips, something stealthy—a smile—not a smile—I remember it, but I can't explain. It was unconscious, this smile was, though just after he had said something it got intensified for an instant. It came at the end of his speeches like a seal applied on the words to make the meaning of the com-

6. One stone equals 14 pounds. The man weighed 224 pounds.

monest phrase appear absolutely inscrutable. He was a common trader, from his youth up employed in these parts—nothing more. He was obeyed, yet he inspired neither love nor fear, nor even respect. He inspired uneasiness. That was it! Uneasiness. Not a definite mistrust—just uneasiness—nothing more. You have no idea how effective such a . . . a . . . faculty can be. He had no genius for organising, for initiative, or for order even. That was evident in such things as the deplorable state of the station. He had no learning, and no intelligence. His position had come to him—why? Perhaps because he was never ill . . . He had served three terms of three years out there . . . Because triumphant health in the general rout of constitutions is a kind of power in itself. When he went home on leave he rioted on a large scale— pompously. Jack ashore—with a difference—in externals only. This one could gather from his casual talk. He originated nothing, he could keep the routine going—that's all. But he was great. He was great by this little thing that it was impossible to tell what could control such a man. He never gave that secret away. Perhaps there was nothing within him. Such a suspicion made one pause—for out there there were no external checks. Once when various tropical diseases had laid low almost every 'agent' in the station, he was heard to say, 'Men who come out here should have no entrails.' He sealed the utterance with that smile of his, as though it had been a door opening into a darkness he had in his keeping. You fancied you had seen things— but the seal was on. When annoyed at meal-times by the constant quarrels of the white men about precedence, he ordered an immense round table to be made, for which a special house had to be built. This was the station's mess-room. Where he sat was the first place—the rest were nowhere. One felt this to be his unalterable conviction. He was neither civil nor uncivil. He was quiet. He allowed his 'boy'—an overfed young negro from the coast— to treat the white men, under his very eyes, with provoking insolence.

"He began to speak as soon as he saw me. I had been very long on the road. He could not wait. Had to start without me. The up-river stations had to be relieved. There had been so many delays already that he did not know who was dead and who was alive, and how they got on—and so on, and so on. He paid no attention to my explanations, and, playing with a stick of sealing-wax, repeated several times that the situation was 'very grave, very grave.' There were rumours that a very important station was in jeopardy, and its chief, Mr Kurtz, was ill. Hoped it was not true. Mr Kurtz was . . . I felt weary and irritable. Hang Kurtz, I thought. I interrupted him by saying I had heard of Mr Kurtz on the coast. 'Ah! So they talk of him down there,' he murmured to himself. Then he began again, assuring me Mr Kurtz was the best agent he had, an exceptional man, of the greatest importance to the Company; therefore I could understand his anxiety. He was, he said, 'very, very uneasy.' Certainly he fidgeted on his chair a good deal, exclaimed, 'Ah, Mr Kurtz!' broke the stick of sealing-wax and seemed dumbfounded by the accident. Next thing he wanted to know 'how long it would take to' . . . I interrupted him again. Being hungry, you know, and kept on my feet too, I was getting savage. 'How can I tell?' I said, 'I haven't even seen the wreck yet—some months, no doubt.' All this talk seemed to me so futile. 'Some months,' he said. 'Well, let us say three months before we can make a start. Yes. That ought to do the affair.' I flung out of his hut (he lived all alone in a clay hut with a sort of verandah) muttering to myself my opinion of him.

He was a chattering idiot. Afterwards I took it back when it was borne in upon me startlingly with what extreme nicety he had estimated the time requisite for the 'affair.'

"I went to work the next day, turning, so to speak, my back on that station. In that way only it seemed to me I could keep my hold on the redeeming facts of life. Still, one must look about sometimes; and then I saw this station, these men strolling aimlessly about in the sunshine of the yard. I asked myself sometimes what it all meant. They wandered here and there with their absurd long staves in their hands, like a lot of faithless pilgrims bewitched inside a rotten fence. The word 'ivory' rang in the air, was whispered, was sighed. You would think they were praying to it. A taint of imbecile rapacity blew through it all, like a whiff from some corpse. By Jove! I've never seen anything so unreal in my life. And outside, the silent wilderness surrounding this cleared speck on the earth struck me as something great and invincible, like evil or truth, waiting patiently for the passing away of this fantastic invasion.

"Oh, these months! Well, never mind. Various things happened. One evening a grass shed full of calico, cotton prints, beads, and I don't know what else, burst into a blaze so suddenly that you would have thought the earth had opened to let an avenging fire consume all that trash. I was smoking my pipe quietly by my dismantled steamer, and saw them all cutting capers in the light, with their arms lifted high, when the stout man with moustaches came tearing down to the river, a tin pail in his hand, assured me that everybody was 'behaving splendidly, splendidly,' dipped about a quart of water and tore back again. I noticed there was a hole in the bottom of his pail.

"I strolled up. There was no hurry. You see the thing had gone off like a box of matches. It had been hopeless from the very first. The flame had leaped high, driven everybody back, lighted up everything—and collapsed. The shed was already a heap of embers glowing fiercely. A nigger was being beaten near by. They said he had caused the fire in some way; be that as it may, he was screeching most horribly. I saw him, later, for several days, sitting in a bit of shade looking very sick and trying to recover himself: afterwards he arose and went out—and the wilderness without a sound took him into its bosom again. As I approached the glow from the dark I found myself at the back of two men, talking. I heard the name of Kurtz pronounced, then the words, 'take advantage of this unfortunate accident.' One of the men was the manager. I wished him a good evening. 'Did you ever see anything like it—eh? it is incredible,' he said, and walked off. The other man remained. He was a first-class agent, young, gentlemanly, a bit reserved, with a forked little beard and a hooked nose. He was standoffish with the other agents, and they on their side said he was the manager's spy upon them. As to me, I had hardly ever spoken to him before. We got into talk, and by and by we strolled away from the hissing ruins. Then he asked me to his room, which was in the main building of the station. He struck a match, and I perceived that this young aristocrat had not only a silver-mounted dressing-case but also a whole candle all to himself. Just at that time the manager was the only man supposed to have any right to candles. Native mats covered the clay walls; a collection of spears, assegais,[7] shields, knives, was hung up in tro-

7. Slender iron-tipped spears.

phies. The business entrusted to this fellow was the making of bricks—so I had been informed; but there wasn't a fragment of a brick anywhere in the station, and he had been there more than a year—waiting. It seems he could not make bricks without something, I don't know what—straw maybe. Anyway, it could not be found there, and as it was not likely to be sent from Europe, it did not appear clear to me what he was waiting for. An act of special creation perhaps. However, they were all waiting—all the sixteen or twenty pilgrims of them—for something; and upon my word it did not seem an uncongenial occupation, from the way they took it, though the only thing that ever came to them was disease—as far as I could see. They beguiled the time by backbiting and intriguing against each other in a foolish kind of way. There was an air of plotting about that station, but nothing came of it, of course. It was as unreal as everything else—as the philanthropic pretence of the whole concern, as their talk, as their government, as their show of work. The only real feeling was a desire to get appointed to a trading-post where ivory was to be had, so that they could earn percentages. They intrigued and slandered and hated each other only on that account—but as to effectually lifting a little finger—oh no. By heavens! there is something after all in the world allowing one man to steal a horse while another must not look at a halter. Steal a horse straight out. Very well. He has done it. Perhaps he can ride. But there is a way of looking at a halter that would provoke the most charitable of saints into a kick.

"I had no idea why he wanted to be sociable, but as we chatted in there it suddenly occurred to me the fellow was trying to get at something—in fact, pumping me. He alluded constantly to Europe, to the people I was supposed to know there—putting leading questions as to my acquaintances in the sepulchral city, and so on. His little eyes glittered like mica[8] discs—with curiosity—though he tried to keep up a bit of superciliousness. At first I was astonished, but very soon I became awfully curious to see what he would find out from me. I couldn't possibly imagine what I had in me to make it worth his while. It was very pretty to see how he baffled himself, for in truth my body was full only of chills, and my head had nothing in it but that wretched steamboat business. It was evident he took me for a perfectly shameless prevaricator. At last he got angry, and, to conceal a movement of furious annoyance, he yawned. I rose. Then I noticed a small sketch in oils, on a panel, representing a woman, draped and blindfolded, carrying a lighted torch. The background was sombre—almost black. The movement of the woman was stately, and the effect of the torchlight on the face was sinister.

"It arrested me, and he stood by civilly, holding an empty half-pint champagne bottle (medical comforts) with the candle stuck in it. To my question he said Mr Kurtz had painted this—in this very station more than a year ago—while waiting for means to go to his trading-post. 'Tell me, pray,' said I, 'who is this Mr Kurtz?'

"'The chief of the Inner Station,' he answered in a short tone, looking away. 'Much obliged,' I said, laughing. 'And you are the brickmaker of the Central Station. Every one knows that.' He was silent for a while. 'He is a prodigy,' he said at last. 'He is an emissary of pity, and science, and progress, and devil knows what else. We want,' he began to declaim suddenly, 'for the

8. Glassy mineral.

guidance of the cause entrusted to us by Europe, so to speak, higher intelligence, wide sympathies, a singleness of purpose.' 'Who says that?' I asked. 'Lots of them,' he replied. 'Some even write that; and so *he* comes here, a special being, as you ought to know.' 'Why ought I to know?' I interrupted, really surprised. He paid no attention. 'Yes. To-day he is chief of the best station, next year he will be assistant-manager, two years more and . . . but I daresay you know what he will be in two years' time. You are of the new gang—the gang of virtue. The same people who sent him specially also recommended you. Oh, don't say no. I've my own eyes to trust.' Light dawned upon me. My dear aunt's influential acquaintances were producing an unexpected effect upon that young man. I nearly burst into a laugh. 'Do you read the Company's confidential correspondence?' I asked. He hadn't a word to say. It was great fun. 'When Mr Kurtz,' I continued severely, 'is General Manager, you won't have the opportunity.'

"He blew the candle out suddenly, and we went outside. The moon had risen. Black figures strolled about listlessly, pouring water on the glow, whence proceeded a sound of hissing; steam ascended in the moonlight; the beaten nigger groaned somewhere. 'What a row the brute makes!' said the indefatigable man with the moustaches, appearing near us. 'Serve him right. Transgression—punishment—bang! Pitiless, pitiless. That's the only way. This will prevent all conflagrations for the future. I was just telling the manager . . .' He noticed my companion, and became crestfallen all at once. 'Not in bed yet,' he said, with a kind of servile heartiness; 'it's so natural. Ha! Danger—agitation.' He vanished. I went on to the river-side, and the other followed me. I heard a scathing murmur at my ear, 'Heap of muffs—go to.' The pilgrims could be seen in knots gesticulating, discussing. Several had still their staves in their hands. I verily believe they took these sticks to bed with them. Beyond the fence the forest stood up spectrally in the moonlight, and through the dim stir, through the faint sounds of that lamentable courtyard, the silence of the land went home to one's very heart—its mystery, its greatness, the amazing reality of its concealed life. The hurt nigger moaned feebly somewhere near by, and then fetched a deep sigh that made me mend my pace away from there. I felt a hand introducing itself under my arm. 'My dear sir,' said the fellow, 'I don't want to be misunderstood, and especially by you, who will see Mr Kurtz long before I can have that pleasure. I wouldn't like him to get a false idea of my disposition. . . .'

"I let him run on, this papier-mâché Mephistopheles, and it seemed to me that if I tried I could poke my forefinger through him, and would find nothing inside but a little loose dirt, maybe. He, don't you see, had been planning to be assistant-manager by and by under the present man, and I could see that the coming of that Kurtz had upset them both not a little. He talked precipitately, and I did not try to stop him. I had my shoulders against the wreck of my steamer, hauled up on the slope like a carcass of some big river animal. The smell of mud, of primeval mud, by Jove! was in my nostrils, the high stillness of primeval forest was before my eyes; there were shiny patches on the black creek. The moon had spread over everything a thin layer of silver— over the rank grass, over the mud, upon the wall of matted vegetation standing higher than the wall of a temple, over the great river I could see through a sombre gap glittering, glittering, as it flowed broadly by without a murmur. All this was great, expectant, mute, while the man jabbered about himself. I wondered whether the stillness on the face of the immensity looking at us two were meant as an appeal or as a menace. What were we who had strayed in here? Could we handle that dumb thing, or would it handle us? I felt how big, how confoundedly big, was that thing that couldn't talk and perhaps was deaf as well. What was in there? I could see a little ivory coming out from there, and I had heard Mr Kurtz was in there. I had heard enough about it too—God knows! Yet somehow it didn't bring any image with it—no more than if I had been told an angel or a fiend was in there. I believed it in the same way one of you might believe there are inhabitants in the planet Mars. I knew once a Scotch sailmaker who was certain, dead sure, there were people in Mars. If you asked him for some idea how they looked and behaved, he would get shy and mutter something about 'walking on all-fours.' If you as much as smiled, he would—though a man of sixty—offer to fight you. I would not have gone so far as to fight for Kurtz, but I went for him near enough to a lie. You know I hate, detest, and can't bear a lie, not because I am straighter than the rest of us, but simply because it appals me. There is a taint of death, a flavour of mortality in lies—which is exactly what I hate and detest in the world—what I want to forget. It makes me miserable and sick, like biting something rotten would do. Temperament, I suppose. Well, I went near enough to it by letting the young fool there believe anything he liked to imagine as to my influence in Europe. I became in an instant as much of a pretence as the rest of the bewitched pilgrims. This simply because I had a notion it somehow would be of help to that Kurtz whom at the time I did not see—you understand. He was just a word for me. I did not see the man in the name any more than you do. Do you see him? Do you see the story? Do you see anything? It seems to me I am trying to tell you a dream— making a vain attempt, because no relation of a dream can convey the dream-sensation, that commingling of absurdity, surprise, and bewilderment in a tremor of struggling revolt, that notion of being captured by the incredible which is of the very essence of dreams. . . ."

He was silent for a while.

". . . No, it is impossible; it is impossible to convey the life-sensation of any given epoch of one's existence—that which makes its truth, its mean-ing—its subtle and penetrating essence. It is impossible. We live, as we dream—alone. . . ."

He paused again as if reflecting, then added:

"Of course in this you fellows see more than I could then. You see me, whom you know. . . ."

It had become so pitch dark that we listeners could hardly see one another. For a long time already he, sitting apart, had been no more to us than a voice. There was not a word from anybody. The others might have been asleep, but I was awake. I listened, I listened on the watch for the sentence, for the word, that would give me the clue to the faint uneasiness inspired by this narrative that seemed to shape itself without human lips in the heavy night-air of the river.

". . . Yes—I let him run on," Marlow began again, "and think what he pleased about the powers that were behind me. I did! And there was nothing behind me! There was nothing but that wretched, old, mangled steamboat I was leaning against, while he talked fluently about 'the necessity for every man to get on.' 'And when one comes out here, you conceive, it is not to gaze at the moon.' Mr Kurtz was a 'universal genius,' but even a genius would find it easier to work with 'adequate tools—intelligent men.' He did not make bricks—why, there was a physical impossibility in the way—as I was well aware; and if he did secretarial work for the manager, it was because 'no sensible man rejects wantonly the confidence of his superiors.' Did I see it? I saw it. What more did I want? What I really wanted was rivets, by heaven! Rivets. To get on with the work—to stop the hole. Rivets I wanted. There were cases of them down at the coast—cases—piled up—burst—split! You kicked a loose rivet at every second step in that station yard on the hillside. Rivets had rolled into the grove of death. You could fill your pockets with rivets for the trouble of stooping down—and there wasn't one rivet to be found where it was wanted. We had plates that would do, but nothing to fasten them with. And every week the messenger, a lone negro, letter-bag on shoulder and staff in hand, left our station for the coast. And several times a week a coast caravan came in with trade goods—ghastly glazed calico that made you shudder only to look at it, glass beads value about a penny a quart, confounded spotted cotton handkerchiefs. And no rivets. Three carriers could have brought all that was wanted to set that steamboat afloat.

"He was becoming confidential now, but I fancy my unresponsive attitude must have exasperated him at last, for he judged it necessary to inform me he feared neither God nor devil, let alone any mere man. I said I could see that very well, but what I wanted was a certain quantity of rivets—and rivets were what really Mr Kurtz wanted, if he had only known it. Now letters went to the coast every week. . . . 'My dear sir,' he cried, 'I write from dictation.' I demanded rivets. There was a way—for an intelligent man. He changed his manner; became very cold, and suddenly began to talk about a hippopotamus; wondered whether sleeping on board the steamer (I stuck to my salvage night and day) I wasn't disturbed. There was an old hippo that had the bad habit of getting out on the bank and roaming at night over the station grounds. The pilgrims used to turn out in a body and empty every rifle they could lay hands on at him. Some even had sat up o' nights for him. All this energy was wasted, though. 'That animal has a charmed life,' he said; 'but you can say this only of brutes in this country. No man—you apprehend me?—no man here bears a charmed life.' He stood there for a moment in the moonlight with his delicate hooked nose set a little askew, and his mica eyes glittering without a wink, then, with a curt Good-night, he strode off. I could see he was disturbed and considerably puzzled, which made me feel more hopeful than I had been for days. It was a great comfort to turn from that chap to my influential friend, the battered, twisted, ruined, tinpot steamboat. I clambered on board. She rang under my feet like an empty Huntley & Palmer biscuit-tin kicked along a gutter; she was nothing so solid in make, and rather less pretty in shape, but I had expended enough hard work on her to make me love her. No influential friend would have served me better. She had given me a chance to come out a bit—to find out what I could do. No, I don't like work. I had rather laze about and think of all the fine things that can be done. I don't like work—no man does—but I like what is in the work—the chance to find yourself. Your own reality—for yourself, not for others—what no other man can ever know. They can only see the mere show, and never can tell what it really means.

"I was not surprised to see somebody sitting aft, on the deck, with his legs dangling over the mud. You see I rather chummed with the few mechanics there were in that station, whom the other pilgrims naturally despised—on account of their imperfect manners, I suppose. This was the foreman—a boiler-maker by trade—a good worker. He was a lank, bony, yellow-faced man, with big intense eyes. His aspect was worried, and his head was as bald as the palm of my hand; but his hair in falling seemed to have stuck to his chin, and had prospered in the new locality, for his beard hung down to his waist. He was a widower with six young children (he had left them in charge of a sister of his to come out there), and the passion of his life was pigeon-flying. He was an enthusiast and a connoisseur. He would rave about pigeons. After work hours he used sometimes to come over from his hut for a talk about his children and his pigeons; at work, when he had to crawl in the mud under the bottom of the steamboat, he would tie up that beard of his in a kind of white serviette[9] he brought for the purpose. It had loops to go over his ears. In the evening he could be seen squatted on the bank rinsing that wrapper in the creek with great care, then spreading it solemnly on a bush to dry.

"I slapped him on the back and shouted 'We shall have rivets!' He scrambled to his feet exclaiming 'No! Rivets!' as though he couldn't believe his ears. Then in a low voice, 'You . . . eh?' I don't know why we behaved like lunatics. I put my finger to the side of my nose and nodded mysteriously. 'Good for you!' he cried, snapped his fingers above his head, lifting one foot. I tried a jig. We capered on the iron deck. A frightful clatter came out of that hulk, and the virgin forest on the other bank of the creek sent it back in a thundering roll upon the sleeping station. It must have made some of the pilgrims sit up in their hovels. A dark figure obscured the lighted doorway of the manager's hut, vanished, then, a second or so after, the doorway itself vanished too. We stopped, and the silence driven away by the stamping of our feet flowed back again from the recesses of the land. The great wall of vegetation, an exuberant and entangled mass of trunks, branches, leaves, boughs, festoons, motionless in the moonlight, was like a rioting invasion of soundless life, a rolling wave of plants, piled up, crested, ready to topple over the creek, to sweep every little man of us out of his little existence. And it moved not. A deadened burst of mighty splashes and snorts reached us from afar, as though an ichthyosaurus[1] had been taking a bath of glitter in the great river. 'After all,' said the boiler-maker in a reasonable tone, 'why shouldn't we get the rivets?' Why not, indeed! I did not know of any reason why we shouldn't. 'They'll come in three weeks,' I said confidently.

"But they didn't. Instead of rivets there came an invasion, an infliction, a visitation. It came in sections during the next three weeks, each section headed by a donkey carrying a white man in new clothes and tan shoes, bowing from that elevation right and left to the impressed pilgrims. A quarrelsome band of footsore sulky niggers trod on the heels of the donkey; a lot of tents, camp-stools, tin boxes, white cases, brown bales would be shot down in the courtyard, and the air of mystery would deepen a little over the muddle of the station. Five such instalments came, with their absurd air of disorderly flight with the loot of innumerable outfit shops and provision stores, that, one would think, they were lugging, after a raid, into the wilderness for

9. Table napkin.   1. Large prehistoric marine creature.

equitable division. It was an inextricable mess of things decent in themselves but that human folly made look like the spoils of thieving.

"This devoted band called itself the Eldorado[2] Exploring Expedition, and I believe they were sworn to secrecy. Their talk, however, was the talk of sordid buccaneers: it was reckless without hardihood, greedy without audacity, and cruel without courage; there was not an atom of foresight or of serious intention in the whole batch of them, and they did not seem aware these things are wanted for the work of the world. To tear treasure out of the bowels of the land was their desire, with no more moral purpose at the back of it than there is in burglars breaking into a safe. Who paid the expenses of the noble enterprise I don't know; but the uncle of our manager was leader of that lot.

"In exterior he resembled a butcher in a poor neighbourhood, and his eyes had a look of sleepy cunning. He carried his fat paunch with ostentation on his short legs, and during the time his gang infested the station spoke to no one but his nephew. You could see these two roaming about all day long with their heads close together in an everlasting confab.[3]

"I had given up worrying myself about the rivets. One's capacity for that kind of folly is more limited than you would suppose. I said Hang!—and let things slide. I had plenty of time for meditation, and now and then I would give some thought to Kurtz. I wasn't very interested in him. No. Still, I was curious to see whether this man, who had come out equipped with moral ideas of some sort, would climb to the top after all, and how he would set about his work when there."

2

"One evening as I was lying flat on the deck of my steamboat, I heard voices approaching—and there were the nephew and the uncle strolling along the bank. I laid my head on my arm again, and had nearly lost myself in a doze, when somebody said in my ear, as it were: 'I am as harmless as a little child, but I don't like to be dictated to. Am I the manager—or am I not? I was ordered to send him there. It's incredible.' . . . I became aware that the two were standing on the shore alongside the forepart of the steamboat, just below my head. I did not move; it did not occur to me to move: I was sleepy. 'It *is* unpleasant,' grunted the uncle. 'He has asked the Administration to be sent there,' said the other, 'with the idea of showing what he could do; and I was instructed accordingly. Look at the influence that man must have. Is it not frightful?' They both agreed it was frightful, then made several bizarre remarks: 'Make rain and fine weather—one man—the Council—by the nose'—bits of absurd sentences that got the better of my drowsiness, so that I had pretty near the whole of my wits about me when the uncle said, 'The climate may do away with this difficulty for you. Is he alone there?' 'Yes,' answered the manager; 'he sent his assistant down the river with a note to me in these terms: "Clear this poor devil out of the country, and don't bother sending more of that sort. I had rather be alone than have the kind of men you can dispose of with me." It was more than a year ago. Can

2. Fabled laud of gold (*el dorado*, Spanish for "the gilded") imagined by the Spanish conquistadors to exist in South America.
3. Confabulation, talk.

you imagine such impudence?' 'Anything since then?' asked the other hoarsely. 'Ivory,' jerked the nephew; 'lots of it—prime sort—lots—most annoying, from him.' 'And with that?' questioned the heavy rumble. 'Invoice,' was the reply fired out, so to speak. Then silence. They had been talking about Kurtz.

"I was broad awake by this time, but, lying perfectly at ease, remained still, having no inducement to change my position. 'How did that ivory come all this way?' growled the elder man, who seemed very vexed. The other explained that it had come with a fleet of canoes in charge of an English half-caste clerk Kurtz had with him; that Kurtz had apparently intended to return himself, the station being by that time bare of goods and stores, but after coming three hundred miles, had suddenly decided to go back, which he started to do alone in a small dugout with four paddlers, leaving the half-caste to continue down the river with the ivory. The two fellows there seemed astounded at anybody attempting such a thing. They were at a loss for an adequate motive. As for me, I seemed to see Kurtz for the first time. It was a distinct glimpse: the dugout, four paddling savages, and the lone white man turning his back suddenly on the headquarters, on relief, on thoughts of home—perhaps; setting his face towards the depths of the wilderness, towards his empty and desolate station. I did not know the motive. Perhaps he was just simply a fine fellow who stuck to his work for its own sake. His name, you understand, had not been pronounced once. He was 'that man.' The half-caste, who, as far as I could see, had conducted a difficult trip with great prudence and pluck, was invariably alluded to as 'that scoundrel.' The 'scoundrel' had reported that the 'man' had been very ill—had recovered imperfectly. . . . The two below me moved away then a few paces, and strolled back and forth at some little distance. I heard: 'Military post—doc-tor—two hundred miles—quite alone now—unavoidable delays—nine months—no news—strange rumours.' They approached again, just as the manager was saying, 'No one, as far as I know, unless a species of wandering trader—a pestilential fellow, snapping ivory from the natives.' Who was it they were talking about now? I gathered in snatches that this was some man supposed to be in Kurtz's district, and of whom the manager did not approve. 'We will not be free from unfair competition till one of these fellows is hanged for an example,' he said. 'Certainly,' grunted the other; 'get him hanged! Why not? Anything—anything can be done in this country. That's what I say; nobody here, you understand, *here*, can endanger your position. And why? You stand the climate—you outlast them all. The danger is in Europe; but there before I left I took care to—' They moved off and whis-pered, then their voices rose again. 'The extraordinary series of delays is not my fault. I did my possible.'[4] The fat man sighed, 'Very sad.' 'And the pestif-erous absurdity of his talk,' continued the other; 'he bothered me enough when he was here. "Each station should be like a beacon on the road towards better things, a centre for trade of course, but also for humanising, improv-ing, instructing." Conceive you—that ass! And he wants to be manager! No, it's—' Here he got choked by excessive indignation, and I lifted my head the

4. Literal rendering of the French *J'ai fait mon possible* (I have done all I could). Conrad sprinkles the conversation of his Belgian characters with Gallicisms to remind us that their words, though reported in English, were spoken in French. Other examples are "a species of wandering trader" (above), "Conceive you" (below), "I would be des-olated" (p. 2335).

least bit. I was surprised to see how near they were—right under me. I could have spat upon their hats. They were looking on the ground, absorbed in thought. The manager was switching his leg with a slender twig: his sagacious relative lifted his head. 'You have been well since you came out this time?' he asked. The other gave a start. 'Who? I? Oh! Like a charm—like a charm. But the rest—oh, my goodness! All sick. They die so quick, too, that I haven't the time to send them out of the country—it's incredible!' 'H'm. Just so,' grunted the uncle. 'Ah! my boy, trust to this—I say, trust to this.' I saw him extend his short flipper of an arm for a gesture that took in the forest, the creek, the mud, the river—seemed to beckon with a dishonouring flourish before the sunlit face of the land a treacherous appeal to the lurking death, to the hidden evil, to the profound darkness of its heart. It was so startling that I leaped to my feet and looked back at the edge of the forest, as though I had expected an answer of some sort to that black display of confidence. You know the foolish notions that come to one sometimes. The high stillness confronted these two figures with its ominous patience, waiting for the passing away of a fantastic invasion.

"They swore aloud together—out of sheer fright, I believe—then, pretending not to know anything of my existence, turned back to the station. The sun was low; and leaning forward side by side, they seemed to be tugging painfully uphill their two ridiculous shadows of unequal length, that trailed behind them slowly over the tall grass without bending a single blade.

"In a few days the Eldorado Expedition went into the patient wilderness, that closed upon it as the sea closes over a diver. Long afterwards the news came that all the donkeys were dead. I know nothing as to the fate of the less valuable animals. They, no doubt, like the rest of us, found what they deserved. I did not inquire. I was then rather excited at the prospect of meeting Kurtz very soon. When I say very soon I mean it comparatively. It was just two months from the day we left the creek when we came to the bank below Kurtz's station.

"Going up that river was like travelling back to the earliest beginnings of the world, when vegetation rioted on the earth and the big trees were kings. An empty stream, a great silence, an impenetrable forest. The air was warm, thick, heavy, sluggish. There was no joy in the brilliance of sunshine. The long stretches of the waterway ran on, deserted, into the gloom of overshadowed distances. On silvery sandbanks hippos and alligators sunned themselves side by side. The broadening waters flowed through a mob of wooded islands; you lost your way on that river as you would in a desert, and butted all day long against shoals, trying to find the channel, till you thought yourself bewitched and cut off for ever from everything you had known once—somewhere—far away—in another existence perhaps. There were moments when one's past came back to one, as it will sometimes when you have not a moment to spare to yourself; but it came in the shape of an unrestful and noisy dream, remembered with wonder amongst the overwhelming realities of this strange world of plants, and water, and silence. And this stillness of life did not in the least resemble a peace. It was the stillness of an implacable force brooding over an inscrutable intention. It looked at you with a vengeful aspect. I got used to it afterwards; I did not see it any more; I had no time. I had to keep guessing at the channel; I had to discern, mostly by inspiration, the signs of hidden banks; I watched for sunken stones; I was learning to clap my teeth smartly before my heart flew out, when I shaved by a fluke some infernal sly old snag that would have ripped the life out of the tin-pot steamboat and drowned all the pilgrims; I had to keep a look-out for the signs of dead wood we could cut up in the night for next day's steaming. When you have to attend to things of that sort, to the mere incidents of the surface, the reality—the reality, I tell you— fades. The inner truth is hidden—luckily, luckily. But I felt it all the same; I felt often its mysterious stillness watching me at my monkey tricks, just as it watches you fellows performing on your respective tight-ropes for—what is it? half a crown a tumble—"

"Try to be civil, Marlow," growled a voice, and I knew there was at least one listener awake besides myself.

"I beg your pardon. I forgot the heartache which makes up the rest of the price. And indeed what does the price matter, if the trick be well done? You do your tricks very well. And I didn't do badly either, since I managed not to sink that steamboat on my first trip. It's a wonder to me yet. Imagine a blindfolded man set to drive a van over a bad road. I sweated and shivered over that business considerably, I can tell you. After all, for a seaman, to scrape the bottom of the thing that's supposed to float all the time under his care is the unpardonable sin. No one may know of it, but you never forget the thump—eh? A blow on the very heart. You remember it, you dream of it, you wake up at night and think of it—years after—and go hot and cold all over. I don't pretend to say that steamboat floated all the time. More than once she had to wade for a bit, with twenty cannibals splashing around and pushing. We had enlisted some of these chaps on the way for a crew. Fine fellows—cannibals—in their place. They were men one could work with, and I am grateful to them. And, after all, they did not eat each other before my face: they had brought along a provision of hippo-meat which went rotten, and made the mystery of the wilderness stink in my nostrils. Phoo! I can sniff it now. I had the manager on board and three or four pilgrims with their staves—all complete. Sometimes we came upon a station close by the bank, clinging to the skirts of the unknown, and the white men rushing out of a tumble-down hovel, with great gestures of joy and surprise and welcome, seemed very strange—had the appearance of being held there captive by a spell. The word 'ivory' would ring in the air for a while—and on we went again into the silence, along empty reaches, round the still bends, between the high walls of our winding way, reverberating in hollow claps the ponderous beat of the stern-wheel. Trees, trees, millions of trees, massive, immense, running up high; and at their foot, hugging the bank against the stream, crept the little begrimed steamboat, like a sluggish beetle crawling on the floor of a lofty portico. It made you feel very small, very lost, and yet it was not altogether depressing, that feeling. After all, if you were small, the grimy beetle crawled on—which was just what you wanted it to do. Where the pilgrims imagined it crawled to I don't know. To some place where they expected to get something, I bet! For me it crawled towards Kurtz—exclusively; but when the steam-pipes started leaking we crawled very slow. The reaches opened before us and closed behind, as if the forest had stepped leisurely across the water to bar the way for our return. We penetrated deeper and deeper into the heart of darkness. It was very quiet there. At night sometimes the roll of drums behind the curtain of trees would run up the river and remain sustained faintly, as if hovering in the air high over our heads, till the first break of day. Whether it meant war, peace, or prayer we could not tell. The dawns were heralded by the descent of a chill stillness; the woodcutters slept, their fires burned low; the snapping of a twig would make you start. We were wanderers on a prehistoric earth, on an earth that wore the aspect of an unknown planet. We could have fancied ourselves the first of men taking possession of an accursed inheritance, to be subdued at the cost of profound anguish and of excessive toil. But suddenly, as we struggled round a bend, there would be a glimpse of rush walls, of peaked grass-roofs, a burst of yells, a whirl of black limbs, a mass of hands clapping, of feet stamping, of bodies swaying, of eyes rolling, under the droop of heavy and motionless foliage. The steamer toiled along slowly on the edge of a black and incomprehensible frenzy. The prehistoric man was cursing us, praying to us, welcoming us—who could tell? We were cut off from the comprehension of our surroundings; we glided past like phantoms, wondering and secretly appalled, as sane men would be before an enthusiastic outbreak in a madhouse. We could not understand because we were too far and could not remember, because we were travelling in the night of first ages, of those ages that are gone, leaving hardly a sign—and no memories.

"The earth seemed unearthly. We are accustomed to look upon the shackled form of a conquered monster, but there—there you could look at a thing monstrous and free. It was unearthly, and the men were— No, they were not inhuman. Well, you know, that was the worst of it—this suspicion of their not being inhuman. It would come slowly to one. They howled and leaped, and spun, and made horrid faces; but what thrilled you was just the thought of their humanity—like yours—the thought of your remote kinship with this wild and passionate uproar. Ugly. Yes, it was ugly enough; but if you were man enough you would admit to yourself that there was in you just the faintest trace of a response to the terrible frankness of that noise, a dim suspicion of there being a meaning in it which you—you so remote from the night of first ages—could comprehend. And why not? The mind of man is capable of anything—because everything is in it, all the past as well as all the future. What was there after all? Joy, fear, sorrow, devotion, valour, rage—who can tell?—but truth—truth stripped of its cloak of time. Let the fool gape and shudder—the man knows, and can look on without a wink. But he must at least be as much of a man as these on the shore. He must meet that truth with his own true stuff—with his own inborn strength. Principles? Principles won't do. Acquisitions, clothes, pretty rags—rags that would fly off at the first good shake. No; you want a deliberate belief. An appeal to me in this fiendish row—is there? Very well; I hear; I admit, but I have a voice too, and for good or evil mine is the speech that cannot be silenced. Of course, a fool, what with sheer fright and fine sentiments, is always safe. Who's that grunting? You wonder I didn't go ashore for a howl and a dance? Well, no—I didn't. Fine sentiments, you say? Fine sentiments be hanged! I had no time. I had to mess about with white-lead and strips of woollen blanket helping to put bandages on those leaky steam-pipes—I tell you. I had to watch the steering, and circumvent those snags, and get the tin-pot along by hook or by crook. There was surface-truth enough in these things to save a wiser man. And between whiles I had to look after the savage who was fireman. He was an improved specimen; he could fire up a vertical boiler. He was there below me, and, upon my word, to look at him was as edifying as seeing a dog in a parody of breeches and a feather hat, walking on his hind legs. A few months of training had done for that really fine chap. He squinted at the steam-gauge and at the water-gauge with an evident effort of intrepidity—and he had filed teeth too, the poor devil, and the wool of his pate shaved into queer patterns, and three ornamental scars on each of his cheeks. He ought to have been clapping his hands and stamping his feet on the bank, instead of which he was hard at work, a thrall to strange witchcraft, full of improving knowledge. He was useful because he had been instructed; and what he knew was this—that should the water in that transparent thing disappear, the evil spirit inside the boiler would get angry through the greatness of his thirst, and take a terrible vengeance. So he sweated and fired up and watched the glass fearfully (with an impromptu charm, made of rags, tied to his arm, and a piece of polished bone, as big as a watch, stuck flatways through his lower lip), while the wooded banks slipped past us slowly, the short noise was left behind, the interminable miles of silence—and we crept on, towards Kurtz. But the snags were thick, the water was treacherous and shallow, the boiler seemed indeed to have a sulky devil in it, and thus neither that fireman nor I had any time to peer into our creepy thoughts.

"Some fifty miles below the Inner Station we came upon a hut of reeds, an inclined and melancholy pole, with the unrecognisable tatters of what had been a flag of some sort flying from it, and a neatly stacked wood-pile. This was unexpected. We came to the bank, and on the stack of firewood found a flat piece of board with some faded pencil-writing on it. When deciphered it said: 'Wood for you. Hurry up. Approach cautiously.' There was a signature, but it was illegible—not Kurtz—a much longer word. Hurry up. Where? Up the river? 'Approach cautiously.' We had not done so. But the warning could not have been meant for the place where it could be only found after approach. Something was wrong above. But what—and how much? That was the question. We commented adversely upon the imbecility of that telegraphic style. The bush around said nothing, and would not let us look very far, either. A torn curtain of red twill hung in the doorway of the hut, and flapped sadly in our faces. The dwelling was dismantled; but we could see a white man had lived there not very long ago. There remained a rude table—a plank on two posts; a heap of rubbish reposed in a dark corner, and by the door I picked up a book. It had lost its covers, and the pages had been thumbed into a state of extremely dirty softness; but the back had been lovingly stitched afresh with white cotton thread, which looked clean yet. It was an extraordinary find. Its title was, *An Inquiry into some Points of Seamanship*, by a man Towser, Towson—some such name—Master in His Majesty's Navy. The matter looked dreary reading enough, with illustrative diagrams and repulsive tables of figures, and the copy was sixty years old. I handled this amazing antiquity with the greatest possible tenderness, lest it should dissolve in my hands. Within, Towson or Towser was inquiring earnestly into the breaking strain of ships' chains and tackle, and other such matters. Not a very enthralling book; but at the first glance you could see there a singleness of intention, an honest concern for the right way of going to work, which made these humble pages, thought out so many years ago, luminous with another than a professional light. The simple old sailor, with his talk of chains and purchases, made me forget the jungle and the pilgrims in a delicious sensation of having come upon something unmistakably real. Such a book being there was wonderful enough; but still more astounding were the notes pencilled in the margin, and plainly referring to the text. I couldn't believe my eyes! They were in cipher! Yes, it looked like cipher. Fancy a man lugging with him a book of that description into this nowhere and studying it—and making notes—in cipher at that! It was an extravagant mystery.

"I had been dimly aware for some time of a worrying noise, and when I lifted my eyes I saw the wood-pile was gone, and the manager, aided by all the pilgrims, was shouting at me from the river-side. I slipped the book into my pocket. I assure you to leave off reading was like tearing myself away from the shelter of an old and solid friendship.

"I started the lame engine ahead. 'It must be this miserable trader—this intruder,' exclaimed the manager, looking back malevolently at the place we had left. 'He must be English,' I said. 'It will not save him from getting into trouble if he is not careful,' muttered the manager darkly. I observed with assumed innocence that no man was safe from trouble in this world.

"The current was more rapid now, the steamer seemed at her last gasp, the stern-wheel flopped languidly, and I caught myself listening on tiptoe for the next beat of the float,[5] for in sober truth I expected the wretched thing to give up every moment. It was like watching the last flickers of a life. But still we crawled. Sometimes I would pick out a tree a little way ahead to measure our progress towards Kurtz by, but I lost it invariably before we got abreast. To keep the eyes so long on one thing was too much for human patience. The manager displayed a beautiful resignation. I fretted and fumed and took to arguing with myself whether or no I would talk openly with Kurtz; but before I could come to any conclusion it occurred to me that my speech or my silence, indeed any action of mine, would be a mere futility. What did it matter what any one knew or ignored? What did it matter who was manager? One gets sometimes such a flash of insight. The essentials of this affair lay deep under the surface, beyond my reach, and beyond my power of meddling.

"Towards the evening of the second day we judged ourselves about eight miles from Kurtz's station. I wanted to push on; but the manager looked grave, and told me the navigation up there was so dangerous that it would be advisable, the sun being very low already, to wait where we were till next morning. Moreover, he pointed out that if the warning to approach cautiously were to be followed, we must approach in daylight—not at dusk, or in the dark. This was sensible enough. Eight miles meant nearly three hours' steaming for us, and I could also see suspicious ripples at the upper end of the reach. Nevertheless, I was annoyed beyond expression at the delay, and most unreasonably too, since one night more could not matter much after so many months. As we had plenty of wood, and caution was the word, I brought up in the middle of the stream. The reach was narrow, straight, with high sides like a railway cutting. The dusk came gliding into it long before the sun had set. The current ran smooth and swift, but a dumb immobility sat on the banks. The living trees, lashed together by the creepers and every living bush of the undergrowth, might have been changed into stone, even

5. Automatic water-level regulator opening and closing a water-supply valve.

to the slenderest twig, to the lightest leaf. It was not sleep—it seemed unnatural, like a state of trance. Not the faintest sound of any kind could be heard. You looked on amazed, and began to suspect yourself of being deaf—then the night came suddenly, and struck you blind as well. About three in the morning some large fish leaped, and the loud splash made me jump as though a gun had been fired. When the sun rose there was a white fog, very warm and clammy, and more blinding than the night. It did not shift or drive; it was just there, standing all round you like something solid. At eight or nine, perhaps, it lifted as a shutter lifts. We had a glimpse of the towering multitude of trees, of the immense matted jungle, with the blazing little ball of the sun hanging over it—all perfectly still—and then the white shutter came down again, smoothly, as if sliding in greased grooves. I ordered the chain, which we had begun to heave in, to be paid out again. Before it stopped running with a muffled rattle, a cry, a very loud cry, as of infinite desolation, soared slowly in the opaque air. It ceased. A complaining clamour, modulated in savage discords, filled our ears. The sheer unexpectedness of it made my hair stir under my cap. I don't know how it struck the others: to me it seemed as though the mist itself had screamed, so suddenly, and apparently from all sides at once, did this tumultuous and mournful uproar arise. It culminated in a hurried outbreak of almost intolerably excessive shrieking, which stopped short, leaving us stiffened in a variety of silly attitudes, and obstinately listening to the nearly as appalling and excessive silence. 'Good God! What is the meaning—?' stammered at my elbow one of the pilgrims—a little fat man, with sandy hair and red whiskers, who wore side-spring boots, and pink pyjamas tucked into his socks. Two others remained open-mouthed a whole minute, then dashed into the little cabin, to rush out incontinently and stand darting scared glances, with Winchesters at 'ready' in their hands. What we could see was just the steamer we were on, her outlines blurred as though she had been on the point of dissolving, and a misty strip of water, perhaps two feet broad, around her—and that was all. The rest of the world was nowhere, as far as our eyes and ears were concerned. Just nowhere. Gone, disappeared; swept off without leaving a whisper or a shadow behind.

"I went forward, and ordered the chain to be hauled in short, so as to be ready to trip the anchor and move the steamboat at once if necessary. 'Will they attack?' whispered an awed voice. 'We will all be butchered in this fog,' murmured another. The faces twitched with the strain, the hands trembled slightly, the eyes forgot to wink. It was very curious to see the contrast of expressions of the white men and of the black fellows of our crew, who were as much strangers to that part of the river as we, though their homes were only eight hundred miles away. The whites, of course greatly discomposed, had besides a curious look of being painfully shocked by such an outrageous row. The others had an alert, naturally interested expression; but their faces were essentially quiet, even those of the one or two who grinned as they hauled at the chain. Several exchanged short, grunting phrases, which seemed to settle the matter to their satisfaction. Their headman, a young, broad-chested black, severely draped in dark-blue fringed cloths, with fierce nostrils and his hair all done up artfully in oily ringlets, stood near me. 'Aha!' I said, just for good fellowship's sake. 'Catch 'im,' he snapped, with a blood-shot widening of his eyes and a flash of sharp teeth—'catch 'im. Give 'im to us.' 'To you, eh?' I asked; 'what would you do with them?' 'Eat 'im!' he said curtly, and, leaning his elbow on the rail, looked out into the fog in a dignified and profoundly pensive attitude. I would no doubt have been properly horrified, had it not occurred to me that he and his chaps must be very hungry: that they must have been growing increasingly hungry for at least this month past. They had been engaged for six months (I don't think a single one of them had any clear idea of time, as we at the end of countless ages have. They still belonged to the beginnings of time—had no inherited experience to teach them, as it were), and of course, as long as there was a piece of paper written over in accordance with some farcical law or other made down the river, it didn't enter anybody's head to trouble how they would live. Certainly they had brought with them some rotten hippo-meat, which couldn't have lasted very long, anyway, even if the pilgrims hadn't, in the midst of a shocking hullabaloo, thrown a considerable quantity of it overboard. It looked like a high-handed proceeding; but it was really a case of legitimate self-defence. You can't breathe dead hippo waking, sleeping, and eating, and at the same time keep your precarious grip on existence. Besides that, they had given them every week three pieces of brass wire, each about nine inches long; and the theory was they were to buy their provisions with that currency in river-side villages. You can see how *that* worked. There were either no villages, or the people were hostile, or the director, who like the rest of us fed out of tins, with an occasional old he-goat thrown in, didn't want to stop the steamer for some more or less recondite reasons. So, unless they swallowed the wire itself, or made loops of it to snare the fishes with, I don't see what good their extravagant salary could be to them. I must say it was paid with a regularity worthy of a large and honourable trading company. For the rest, the only thing to eat—though it didn't look eatable in the least—I saw in their possession was a few lumps of some stuff like half-cooked dough, of a dirty lavender colour, they kept wrapped in leaves, and now and then swallowed a piece of, but so small that it seemed done more for the look of the thing than for any serious purpose of sustenance. Why in the name of all the gnawing devils of hunger they didn't go for us—they were thirty to five—and have a good tuck-in for once, amazes me now when I think of it. They were big powerful men, with not much capacity to weigh the consequences, with courage, with strength, even yet, though their skins were no longer glossy and their muscles no longer hard. And I saw that something restraining, one of those human secrets that baffle probability, had come into play there. I looked at them with a swift quickening of interest—not because it occurred to me I might be eaten by them before very long, though I own to you that just then I perceived—in a new light, as it were—how unwholesome the pilgrims looked, and I hoped, yes, I positively hoped, that my aspect was not so—what shall I say?—so—unappetising: a touch of fantastic vanity which fitted well with the dream-sensation that pervaded all my days at that time. Perhaps I had a little fever too. One can't live with one's finger everlastingly on one's pulse. I had often 'a little fever,' or a little touch of other things—the playful paw-strokes of the wilderness, the preliminary trifling before the more serious onslaught which came in due course. Yes; I looked at them as you would on any human being, with a curiosity of their impulses, motives, capacities, weaknesses, when brought to the test of an inexorable physical necessity. Restraint! What possible restraint? Was it superstition, disgust, patience, fear—or some kind of primitive honour? No fear can stand up to hunger, no patience can wear it out, disgust simply does not exist where hunger is; and as to superstition, beliefs, and what you may call principles, they are less than chaff in a breeze. Don't you know the devilry of lingering starvation, its exasperating torment, its black thoughts, its sombre and brooding ferocity? Well, I do. It takes a man all his inborn strength to fight hunger properly. It's really easier to face bereavement, dishonour, and the perdition of one's soul—than this kind of prolonged hunger. Sad, but true. And these chaps too had no earthly reason for any kind of scruple. Restraint! I would just as soon have expected restraint from a hyena prowling amongst the corpses of a battlefield. But there was the fact facing me—the fact dazzling, to be seen, like the foam on the depths of the sea, like a ripple on an unfathomable enigma, a mystery greater—when I thought of it—than the curious, inexplicable note of desperate grief in this savage clamour that had swept by us on the river-bank, behind the blind whiteness of the fog.

"Two pilgrims were quarrelling in hurried whispers as to which bank. 'Left.' 'No, no; how can you? Right, right, of course.' 'It is very serious,' said the manager's voice behind me; 'I would be desolated if anything should happen to Mr. Kurtz before we came up.' I looked at him, and had not the slightest doubt he was sincere. He was just the kind of man who would wish to preserve appearances. That was his restraint. But when he muttered something about going on at once, I did not even take the trouble to answer him. I knew, and he knew, that it was impossible. Were we to let go our hold of the bottom, we would be absolutely in the air—in space. We wouldn't be able to tell where we were going to—whether up or down stream, or across—till we fetched against one bank or the other—and then we wouldn't know at first which it was. Of course I made no move. I had no mind for a smashup. You couldn't imagine a more deadly place for a shipwreck. Whether drowned at once or not, we were sure to perish speedily in one way or another. 'I authorise you to take all the risks,' he said, after a short silence. 'I refuse to take any,' I said shortly; which was just the answer he expected, though its tone might have surprised him. 'Well, I must defer to your judgment. You are captain,' he said, with marked civility. I turned my shoulder to him in sign of my appreciation, and looked into the fog. How long would it last? It was the most hopeless look-out. The approach to this Kurtz grubbing for ivory in the wretched bush was beset by as many dangers as though he had been an enchanted princess sleeping in a fabulous castle. 'Will they attack, do you think?' asked the manager, in a confidential tone.

"I did not think they would attack, for several obvious reasons. The thick fog was one. If they left the bank in their canoes they would get lost in it, as we would be if we attempted to move. Still, I had also judged the jungle of both banks quite impenetrable—and yet eyes were in it, eyes that had seen us. The river-side bushes were certainly very thick; but the undergrowth behind was evidently penetrable. However, during the short lift I had seen no canoes anywhere in the reach—certainly not abreast of the steamer. But what made the idea of attack inconceivable to me was the nature of the noise—of the cries we had heard. They had not the fierce character boding of immediate hostile intention. Unexpected, wild, and violent as they had been, they had given me an irresistible impression of sorrow. The glimpse of the steamboat had for some reason filled those savages with unrestrained grief. The danger, if any, I expounded, was from our proximity to a great human passion let loose. Even extreme grief may ultimately vent itself in violence—but more generally takes the form of apathy. . . .

"You should have seen the pilgrims stare! They had no heart to grin, or even to revile me; but I believe they thought me gone mad—with fright, maybe. I delivered a regular lecture. My dear boys, it was no good bothering. Keep a look-out? Well, you may guess I watched the fog for the signs of lifting as a cat watches a mouse; but for anything else our eyes were of no more use to us than if we had been buried miles deep in a heap of cotton-wool. It felt like it too—choking, warm, stifling. Besides, all I said, though it sounded extravagant, was absolutely true to fact. What we afterwards alluded to as an attack was really an attempt at repulse. The action was very far from being aggressive—it was not even defensive, in the usual sense: it was undertaken under the stress of desperation, and in its essence was purely protective.

"It developed itself, I should say, two hours after the fog lifted, and its commencement was at a spot, roughly speaking, about a mile and a half below Kurtz's station. We had just floundered and flopped round a bend, when I saw an islet, a mere grassy hummock of bright green, in the middle of the stream. It was the only thing of the kind; but as we opened the reach more, I perceived it was the head of a long sandbank, or rather of a chain of shallow patches stretching down the middle of the river. They were discoloured, just awash, and the whole lot was seen just under the water, exactly as a man's backbone is seen running down the middle of his back under the skin. Now, as far as I did see, I could go to the right or to the left of this. I didn't know either channel, of course. The banks looked pretty well alike, the depth appeared the same; but as I had been informed the station was on the west side, I naturally headed for the western passage.

"No sooner had we fairly entered it than I became aware it was much narrower than I had supposed. To the left of us there was the long uninter-rupted shoal, and to the right a high steep bank heavily overgrown with bushes. Above the bush the trees stood in serried ranks. The twigs overhung the current thickly, and from distance to distance a large limb of some tree projected rigidly over the stream. It was then well on in the afternoon, the face of the forest was gloomy, and a broad strip of shadow had already fallen on the water. In this shadow we steamed up—very slowly, as you may imag-ine. I sheered her well inshore—the water being deepest near the bank, as the sounding-pole informed me.

"One of my hungry and forbearing friends was sounding in the bows just below me. This steamboat was exactly like a decked scow. On the deck there were two little teak-wood houses, with doors and windows. The boiler was in the fore-end, and the machinery right astern. Over the whole there was a light roof, supported on stanchions. The funnel projected through that roof, and in front of the funnel a small cabin built of light planks served for a pilot-house. It contained a couch, two camp-stools, a loaded Martini-Henry[6] leaning in one corner, a tiny table, and the steering-wheel. It had a wide door in front and a broad shutter at each side. All these were always thrown open, of course. I spent my days perched up there on the extreme fore-end

---

6. Rifle combining the seven-grooved barrel of the Scottish gunmaker A. Henry with the block-action breech mechanism introduced by the Swiss inventor F. Martini.

of that roof, before the door. At night I slept, or tried to, on the couch. An athletic black belonging to some coast tribe, and educated by my poor predecessor, was the helmsman. He sported a pair of brass earrings, wore a blue cloth wrapper from the waist to the ankles, and thought all the world of himself. He was the most unstable kind of fool I had ever seen. He steered with no end of a swagger while you were by; but if he lost sight of you, he became instantly the prey of an abject funk, and would let that cripple of a steamboat get the upper hand of him in a minute.

"I was looking down at the sounding-pole, and feeling much annoyed to see at each try a little more of it stick out of that river, when I saw my poleman give up the business suddenly, and stretch himself flat on the deck, without even taking the trouble to haul his pole in. He kept hold on it though, and it trailed in the water. At the same time the fireman, whom I could also see below me, sat down abruptly before his furnace and ducked his head. I was amazed. Then I had to look at the river mighty quick, because there was a snag in the fairway. Sticks, little sticks, were flying about—thick; they were whizzing before my nose, dropping below me, striking behind me against my pilot-house. All this time the river, the shore, the woods, were very quiet—perfectly quiet. I could only hear the heavy splashing thump of the stern-wheel and the patter of these things. We cleared the snag clumsily. Arrows, by Jove! We were being shot at! I stepped in quickly to close the shutter on the land-side. That fool-helmsman, his hands on the spokes, was lifting his knees high, stamping his feet, champing his mouth, like a reined-in horse. Confound him! And we were staggering within ten feet of the bank. I had to lean right out to swing the heavy shutter, and I saw a face amongst the leaves on the level with my own, looking at me very fierce and steady; and then suddenly, as though a veil had been removed from my eyes, I made out, deep in the tangled gloom, naked breasts, arms, legs, glaring eyes—the bush was swarming with human limbs in movement, glistening, of bronze colour. The twigs shook, swayed, and rustled, the arrows flew out of them, and then the shutter came to. 'Steer her straight,' I said to the helmsman. He held his head rigid, face forward; but his eyes rolled, he kept on lifting and setting down his feet gently, his mouth foamed a little. 'Keep quiet!' I said in a fury. I might just as well have ordered a tree not to sway in the wind. I darted out. Below me there was a great scuffle of feet on the iron deck; confused exclamations; a voice screamed, 'Can you turn back?' I caught sight of a V-shaped ripple on the water ahead. What? Another snag! A fusillade burst out under my feet. The pilgrims had opened with their Winchesters, and were simply squirting lead into that bush. A deuce of a lot of smoke came up and drove slowly forward. I swore at it. Now I couldn't see the ripple or the snag either. I stood in the doorway, peering, and the arrows came in swarms. They might have been poisoned, but they looked as though they wouldn't kill a cat. The bush began to howl. Our wood-cutters raised a warlike whoop; the report of a rifle just at my back deafened me. I glanced over my shoulder, and the pilot-house was yet full of noise and smoke when I made a dash at the wheel. The fool-nigger had dropped everything, to throw the shutter open and let off that Martini-Henry. He stood before the wide opening, glaring, and I yelled at him to come back, while I straightened the sudden twist out of that steamboat. There was no room to turn even if I had wanted to, the snag was somewhere very near ahead in that confounded smoke, there was no time to lose, so I just crowded her into the bank—right into the bank, where I knew the water was deep.

"We tore slowly along the overhanging bushes in a whirl of broken twigs and flying leaves. The fusillade below stopped short, as I had foreseen it would when the squirts got empty. I threw my head back to a glinting whizz that traversed the pilot-house, in at one shutter-hole and out at the other. Looking past that mad helmsman, who was shaking the empty rifle and yelling at the shore, I saw vague forms of men running bent double, leaping, gliding, distinct, incomplete, evanescent. Something big appeared in the air before the shutter, the rifle went overboard, and the man stepped back swiftly, looked at me over his shoulder in an extraordinary, profound, familiar manner, and fell upon my feet. The side of his head hit the wheel twice, and the end of what appeared a long cane clattered round and knocked over a little camp-stool. It looked as though after wrenching that thing from somebody ashore he had lost his balance in the effort. The thin smoke had blown away, we were clear of the snag, and looking ahead I could see that in another hundred yards or so I would be free to sheer off, away from the bank; but my feet felt so very warm and wet that I had to look down. The man had rolled on his back and stared straight up at me; both his hands clutched that cane. It was the shaft of a spear that, either thrown or lunged through the opening, had caught him in the side just below the ribs; the blade had gone in out of sight, after making a frightful gash; my shoes were full; a pool of blood lay very still, gleaming dark-red under the wheel; his eyes shone with an amazing lustre. The fusillade burst out again. He looked at me anxiously, gripping the spear like something precious, with an air of being afraid I would try to take it away from him. I had to make an effort to free my eyes from his gaze and attend to the steering. With one hand I felt above my head for the line of the steam whistle, and jerked out screech after screech hurriedly. The tumult of angry and warlike yells was checked instantly, and then from the depths of the woods went out such a tremulous and prolonged wail of mournful fear and utter despair as may be imagined to follow the flight of the last hope from the earth. There was a great commotion in the bush; the shower of arrows stopped, a few dropping shots rang out sharply—then silence, in which the languid beat of the stern-wheel came plainly to my ears. I put the helm hard a-starboard at the moment when the pilgrim in pink pyjamas, very hot and agitated, appeared in the doorway. 'The manager sends me—' he began in an official tone, and stopped short. 'Good God!' he said, glaring at the wounded man.

"We two whites stood over him, and his lustrous and inquiring glance enveloped us both. I declare it looked as though he would presently put to us some question in an understandable language; but he died without uttering a sound, without moving a limb, without twitching a muscle. Only in the very last moment, as though in response to some sign we could not see, to some whisper we could not hear, he frowned heavily, and that frown gave to his black death-mask an inconceivably sombre, brooding, and menacing expression. The lustre of inquiring glance faded swiftly into vacant glassiness. 'Can you steer?' I asked the agent eagerly. He looked very dubious; but I made a grab at his arm, and he understood at once I meant him to steer whether or no. To tell you the truth, I was morbidly anxious to change my shoes and socks. 'He is dead,' murmured the fellow, immensely impressed.

'No doubt about it,' said I, tugging like mad at the shoe-laces. 'And by the way, I suppose Mr Kurtz is dead as well by this time.'

"For the moment that was the dominant thought. There was a sense of extreme disappointment, as though I had found out I had been striving after something altogether without a substance. I couldn't have been more disgusted if I had travelled all this way for the sole purpose of talking with Mr Kurtz. Talking with . . . I flung one shoe overboard, and became aware that that was exactly what I had been looking forward to—a talk with Kurtz. I made the strange discovery that I had never imagined him as doing, you know, but as discoursing. I didn't say to myself, 'Now I will never see him,' or 'Now I will never shake him by the hand,' but, 'Now I will never hear him.' The man presented himself as a voice. Not of course that I did not connect him with some sort of action. Hadn't I been told in all the tones of jealousy and admiration that he had collected, bartered, swindled, or stolen more ivory than all the other agents together? That was not the point. The point was in his being a gifted creature, and that of all his gifts the one that stood out pre-eminently, that carried with it a sense of real presence, was his ability to talk, his words—the gift of expression, the bewildering, the illuminating, the most exalted and the most contemptible, the pulsating stream of light, or the deceitful flow from the heart of an impenetrable darkness.

"The other shoe went flying unto the devil-god of that river. I thought, By Jove! it's all over. We are too late; he has vanished—the gift has vanished, by means of some spear, arrow, or club. I will never hear that chap speak after all—and my sorrow had a startling extravagance of emotion, even such as I had noticed in the howling sorrow of these savages in the bush. I couldn't have felt more of lonely desolation somehow, had I been robbed of a belief or had missed my destiny in life. . . . Why do you sigh in this beastly way, somebody? Absurd? Well, absurd. Good Lord! mustn't a man ever— Here, give me some tobacco." . . .

There was a pause of profound stillness, then a match flared, and Marlow's lean face appeared, worn, hollow, with downward folds and dropped eyelids, with an aspect of concentrated attention; and as he took vigorous draws at his pipe, it seemed to retreat and advance out of the night in the regular flicker of the tiny flame. The match went out.

"Absurd!" he cried. "This is the worst of trying to tell . . . Here you all are, each moored with two good addresses, like a hulk with two anchors, a butcher round one corner, a policeman round another, excellent appetites, and temperature normal—you hear—normal from year's end to year's end. And you say, Absurd! Absurd be—exploded! Absurd! My dear boys, what can you expect from a man who out of sheer nervousness had just flung overboard a pair of new shoes? Now I think of it, it is amazing I did not shed tears. I am, upon the whole, proud of my fortitude. I was cut to the quick at the idea of having lost the inestimable privilege of listening to the gifted Kurtz. Of course I was wrong. The privilege was waiting for me. Oh yes, I heard more than enough. And I was right, too. A voice. He was very little more than a voice. And I heard—him—it—this voice—other voices—all of them were so little more than voices—and the memory of that time itself lingers around me, impalpable, like a dying vibration of one immense jabber, silly, atrocious, sordid, savage, or simply mean, without any kind of sense. Voices, voices— even the girl herself—now—"

He was silent for a long time.

"I laid the ghost of his gifts at last with a lie," he began suddenly. "Girl! What? Did I mention a girl? Oh, she is out of it—completely. They—the women I mean—are out of it—should be out of it. We must help them to stay in that beautiful world of their own, lest ours gets worse. Oh, she had to be out of it. You should have heard the disinterred body of Mr Kurtz saying, 'My Intended.' You would have perceived directly then how completely she was out of it. And the lofty frontal bone of Mr Kurtz! They say the hair goes on growing sometimes, but this—ah—specimen was impressively bald. The wilderness had patted him on the head, and, behold, it was like a ball—an ivory ball; it had caressed him, and—lo!—he had withered; it had taken him, loved him, embraced him, got into his veins, consumed his flesh, and sealed his soul to its own by the inconceivable ceremonies of some devilish initiation. He was its spoiled and pampered favourite. Ivory? I should think so. Heaps of it, stacks of it. The old mud shanty was bursting with it. You would think there was not a single tusk left either above or below the ground in the whole country. 'Mostly fossil,' the manager had remarked disparagingly. It was no more fossil than I am; but they call it fossil when it is dug up. It appears these niggers do bury the tusks sometimes—but evidently they couldn't bury this parcel deep enough to save the gifted Mr Kurtz from his fate. We filled the steamboat with it, and had to pile a lot on the deck. Thus he could see and enjoy as long as he could see, because the appreciation of this favour had remained with him to the last. You should have heard him say, 'My ivory.' Oh yes, I heard him. 'My Intended, my ivory, my station, my river, my—' everything belonged to him. It made me hold my breath in expectation of hearing the wilderness burst into a prodigious peal of laughter that would shake the fixed stars in their places. Everything belonged to him—but that was a trifle. The thing was to know what he belonged to, how many powers of darkness claimed him for their own. That was the reflection that made you creepy all over. It was impossible—it was not good for one either—trying to imagine. He had taken a high seat amongst the devils of the land—I mean literally. You can't understand. How could you?—with solid pavement under your feet, surrounded by kind neighbours ready to cheer you or to fall on you, stepping delicately between the butcher and the policeman, in the holy terror of scandal and gallows and lunatic asylums—how can you imagine what particular region of the first ages a man's untrammelled feet may take him into by the way of solitude—utter solitude without a policeman—by the way of silence—utter silence, where no warning voice of a kind neighbour can be heard whispering of public opinion? These little things make all the great difference. When they are gone you must fall back upon your own innate strength, upon your own capacity for faithfulness. Of course you may be too much of a fool to go wrong—too dull even to know you are being assaulted by the powers of darkness. I take it, no fool ever made a bargain for his soul with the devil: the fool is too much of a fool, or the devil too much of a devil—I don't know which. Or you may be such a thunderingly exalted creature as to be altogether deaf and blind to anything but heavenly sights and sounds. Then the earth for you is only a standing place—and whether to be like this is your loss or your gain I won't pretend to say. But most of us are neither one nor the other. The earth for us is a place to live in, where we must put up with sights, with sounds, with smells, too, by Jove!—breathe dead hippo, so to speak, and not be contaminated. And there, don't you see? your strength comes in, the faith in your ability for the digging of unostentatious holes to bury the stuff in—your power of devotion, not to yourself, but to an obscure, back-breaking business. And that's difficult enough. Mind, I am not trying to excuse or even explain—I am trying to account to myself for—for—Mr Kurtz—for the shade of Mr Kurtz. This initiated wraith from the back of Nowhere honoured me with its amazing confidence before it vanished altogether. This was because it could speak English to me. The original Kurtz had been educated partly in England, and—as he was good enough to say himself—his sympathies were in the right place. His mother was half-English, his father was half-French. All Europe contributed to the making of Kurtz; and by and by I learned that, most appropriately, the International Society for the Suppression of Savage Customs had entrusted him with the making of a report, for its future guidance. And he had written it too. I've seen it. I've read it. It was eloquent, vibrating with eloquence, but too high-strung, I think. Seventeen pages of close writing he had found time for! But this must have been before his— let us say—nerves went wrong, and caused him to preside at certain midnight dances ending with unspeakable rites, which—as far as I reluctantly gathered from what I heard at various times—were offered up to him—do you understand?—to Mr Kurtz himself. But it was a beautiful piece of writing. The opening paragraph, however, in the light of later information, strikes me now as ominous. He began with the argument that we whites, from the point of development we had arrived at, 'must necessarily appear to them [savages] in the nature of supernatural beings—we approach them with the might as of a deity,' and so on, and so on. 'By the simple exercise of our will we can exert a power for good practically unbounded,' etc. etc. From that point he soared and took me with him. The peroration was magnificent, though difficult to remember, you know. It gave me the notion of an exotic Immensity ruled by an august Benevolence. It made me tingle with enthusiasm. This was the unbounded power of eloquence—of words—of burning noble words. There were no practical hints to interrupt the magic current of phrases, unless a kind of note at the foot of the last page, scrawled evidently much later, in an unsteady hand, may be regarded as the exposition of a method. It was very simple, and at the end of that moving appeal to every altruistic sentiment it blazed at you, luminous and terrifying, like a flash of lightning in a serene sky: 'Exterminate all the brutes!' The curious part was that he had apparently forgotten all about that valuable postscriptum, because, later on, when he in a sense came to himself, he repeatedly entreated me to take good care of 'my pamphlet' (he called it), as it was sure to have in the future a good influence upon his career. I had full information about all these things, and, besides, as it turned out, I was to have the care of his memory. I've done enough for it to give me the indisputable right to lay it, if I choose, for an everlasting rest in the dust-bin of progress, amongst all the sweepings and, figuratively speaking, all the dead cats of civilisation. But then, you see, I can't choose. He won't be forgotten. Whatever he was, he was not common. He had the power to charm or frighten rudimentary souls into an aggravated witchdance in his honour; he could also fill the small souls of the pilgrims with bitter misgivings: he had one devoted friend at least, and he had conquered one soul in the world that was neither rudimentary nor tainted with self-seeking. No; I can't forget him, though I am not prepared to affirm the fellow was exactly worth the life we lost in getting to him. I missed my late helmsman awfully—I missed him even while his body was still lying in the pilot-house. Perhaps you will think it passing strange this regret for a savage who was no more account than a grain of sand in a black Sahara. Well, don't you see, he had done something, he had steered; for months I had him at my back—a help—an instrument. It was a kind of partnership. He steered for me—I had to look after him, I worried about his deficiencies, and thus a subtle bond had been created, of which I only became aware when it was suddenly broken. And the intimate profundity of that look he gave me when he received his hurt remains to this day in my memory—like a claim of distant kinship affirmed in a supreme moment.

"Poor fool! If he had only left that shutter alone. He had no restraint, no restraint—just like Kurtz—a tree swayed by the wind. As soon as I had put on a dry pair of slippers, I dragged him out, after first jerking the spear out of his side, which operation I confess I performed with my eyes shut tight. His heels leaped together over the little doorstep; his shoulders were pressed to my breast; I hugged him from behind desperately. Oh! he was heavy, heavy; heavier than any man on earth, I should imagine. Then without more ado I tipped him overboard. The current snatched him as though he had been a wisp of grass, and I saw the body roll over twice before I lost sight of it for ever. All the pilgrims and the manager were then congregated on the awning-deck about the pilot-house, chattering at each other like a flock of excited magpies, and there was a scandalised murmur at my heartless promptitude. What they wanted to keep that body hanging about for I can't guess. Embalm it, maybe. But I had also heard another, and a very ominous, murmur on the deck below. My friends the wood-cutters were likewise scandalised, and with a better show of reason—though I admit that the reason itself was quite inadmissible. Oh, quite! I had made up my mind that if my late helmsman was to be eaten, the fishes alone should have him. He had been a very second-rate helmsman while alive, but now he was dead he might have become a first-class temptation, and possibly cause some startling trouble. Besides, I was anxious to take the wheel, the man in pink pyjamas showing himself a hopeless duffer at the business.

"This I did directly the simple funeral was over. We were going half-speed, keeping right in the middle of the stream, and I listened to the talk about me. They had given up Kurtz, they had given up the station; Kurtz was dead, and the station had been burnt—and so on—and so on. The red-haired pilgrim was beside himself with the thought that at least this poor Kurtz had been properly revenged. 'Say! We must have made a glorious slaughter of them in the bush. Eh? What do you think? Say?' He positively danced, the bloodthirsty little gingery beggar.[7] And he had nearly fainted when he saw the wounded man! I could not help saying, 'You made a glorious lot of smoke, anyhow.' I had seen, from the way the tops of the bushes rustled and flew, that almost all the shots had gone too high. You can't hit anything unless you take aim and fire from the shoulder; but these chaps fired from the hip

7. Redheaded rascal.

with their eyes shut. The retreat, I maintained—and I was right—was caused by the screeching of the steam-whistle. Upon this they forgot Kurtz, and began to howl at me with indignant protests.

"The manager stood by the wheel murmuring confidentially about the necessity of getting well away down the river before dark at all events, when I saw in the distance a clearing on the river-side and the outlines of some sort of building. 'What's this?' I asked. He clapped his hands in wonder. 'The station!' he cried. I edged in at once, still going half-speed.

"Through my glasses I saw the slope of a hill interspersed with rare trees and perfectly free from undergrowth. A long decaying building on the summit was half buried in the high grass; the large holes in the peaked roof gaped black from afar; the jungle and the woods made a background. There was no enclosure or fence of any kind; but there had been one apparently, for near the house half a dozen slim posts remained in a row, roughly trimmed, and with their upper ends ornamented with round carved balls. The rails, or whatever there had been between, had disappeared. Of course the forest surrounded all that. The river-bank was clear, and on the water side I saw a white man under a hat like a cart-wheel beckoning persistently with his whole arm. Examining the edge of the forest above and below, I was almost certain I could see movements—human forms gliding here and there. I steamed past prudently, then stopped the engines and let her drift down. The man on the shore began to shout, urging us to land. 'We have been attacked,' screamed the manager. 'I know—I know. It's all right,' yelled back the other, as cheerful as you please. 'Come along. It's all right. I am glad.'

"His aspect reminded me of something I had seen—something funny I had seen somewhere. As I manœuvred to get alongside, I was asking myself, 'What does this fellow look like?' Suddenly I got it. He looked like a harlequin.[8] His clothes had been made of some stuff that was brown holland[9] probably, but it was covered with patches all over, with bright patches, blue, red, and yellow—patches on the back, patches on the front, patches on elbows, on knees; coloured binding round his jacket, scarlet edging at the bottom of his trousers; and the sunshine made him look extremely gay and wonderfully neat withal, because you could see how beautifully all this patching had been done. A beardless, boyish face, very fair, no features to speak of, nose peeling, little blue eyes, smiles and frowns chasing each other over that open countenance like sunshine and shadow on a wind-swept plain. 'Look out, captain!' he cried; 'there's a snag lodged in here last night.' What! Another snag? I confess I swore shamefully. I had nearly holed my cripple, to finish off that charming trip. The harlequin on the bank turned his little pug nose up to me. 'You English?' he asked, all smiles. 'Are you?' I shouted from the wheel. The smiles vanished, and he shook his head as if sorry for my disappointment. Then he brightened up. 'Never mind!' he cried encouragingly. 'Are we in time?' I asked. 'He is up there,' he replied, with a toss of the head up the hill, and becoming gloomy all of a sudden. His face was like the autumn sky, overcast one moment and bright the next.

"When the manager, escorted by the pilgrims, all of them armed to the teeth, had gone to the house, this chap came on board. 'I say, I don't like

8. Character from Italian comedy traditionally dressed in multicolored clothes.   9. Coarse linen fabric.

this. These natives are in the bush,' I said. He assured me earnestly it was all right. 'They are simple people,' he added; 'well, I am glad you came. It took me all my time to keep them off.' 'But you said it was all right,' I cried. 'Oh, they meant no harm,' he said; and as I stared he corrected himself, 'Not exactly.' Then vivaciously, 'My faith, your pilot-house wants a clean up!' In the next breath he advised me to keep enough steam on the boiler to blow the whistle in case of any trouble. 'One good screech will do more for you than all your rifles. They are simple people,' he repeated. He rattled away at such a rate he quite overwhelmed me. He seemed to be trying to make up for lots of silence, and actually hinted, laughing, that such was the case. 'Don't you talk with Mr Kurtz?' I said. 'You don't talk with that man—you listen to him,' he exclaimed with severe exaltation. 'But now—' He waved his arm, and in the twinkling of an eye was in the uttermost depths of despondency. In a moment he came up again with a jump, possessed himself of both my hands, shook them continuously, while he gabbled: 'Brother sailor . . . honour . . . pleasure . . . delight . . . introduce   myself . . . Russian . . . son of an arch-priest . . . Government of Tambov . . . What? Tobacco! English tobacco; the excellent English tobacco! Now, that's brotherly. Smoke? Where's a sailor that does not smoke?'

"The pipe soothed him, and gradually I made out he had run away from school, had gone to sea in a Russian ship; ran away again; served some time in English ships; was now reconciled with the arch-priest. He made a point of that. 'But when one is young one must see things, gather experience, ideas; enlarge the mind.' 'Here!' I interrupted. 'You can never tell! Here I met Mr Kurtz,' he said, youthfully solemn and reproachful. I held my tongue after that. It appears he had persuaded a Dutch trading-house on the coast to fit him out with stores and goods, and had started for the interior with a light heart, and no more idea of what would happen to him than a baby. He had been wandering about that river for nearly two years alone, cut off from everybody and everything. 'I am not so young as I look. I am twenty-five,' he said. 'At first old Van Shuyten would tell me to go to the devil,' he narrated with keen enjoyment; 'but I stuck to him, and talked and talked, till at last he got afraid I would talk the hind-leg off his favourite dog, so he gave me some cheap things and a few guns, and told me he hoped he would never see my face again. Good old Dutchman, Van Shuyten. I sent him one small lot of ivory a year ago, so that he can't call me a little thief when I get back. I hope he got it. And for the rest I don't care. I had some wood stacked for you. That was my old house. Did you see?'

"I gave him Towson's book. He made as though he would kiss me, but restrained himself. 'The only book I had left, and I thought I had lost it,' he said, looking at it ecstatically. 'So many accidents happen to a man going about alone, you know. Canoes get upset sometimes—and sometimes you've got to clear out so quick when the people get angry.' He thumbed the pages. 'You made notes in Russian?' I asked. He nodded. 'I thought they were written in cipher,' I said. He laughed, then became serious. 'I had lots of trouble to keep these people off,' he said. 'Did they want to kill you?' I asked. 'Oh no!' he cried, and checked himself. 'Why did they attack us?' I pursued. He hesitated, then said shamefacedly, 'They don't want him to go.' 'Don't they?' I said curiously. He nodded a nod full of mystery and wisdom. 'I tell you,' he cried, 'this man has enlarged my mind.' He opened his arms wide, staring at me with his little blue eyes that were perfectly round."

3

"I looked at him, lost in astonishment. There he was before me, in motley, as though he had absconded from a troupe of mimes, enthusiastic, fabulous. His very existence was improbable, inexplicable, and altogether bewildering. He was an insoluble problem. It was inconceivable how he had existed, how he had succeeded in getting so far, how he had managed to remain—why he did not instantly disappear. 'I went a little farther,' he said, 'then still a little farther—till I had gone so far that I don't know how I'll ever get back. Never mind. Plenty time. I can manage. You take Kurtz away quick—quick—I tell you.' The glamour of youth enveloped his particoloured rags, his destitution, his loneliness, the essential desolation of his futile wanderings. For months—for years—his life hadn't been worth a day's purchase; and there he was gallantly, thoughtlessly alive, to all appearance indestructible solely by the virtue of his few years and of his unreflecting audacity. I was seduced into something like admiration—like envy. Glamour urged him on, glamour kept him unscathed. He surely wanted nothing from the wilderness but space to breathe in and to push on through. His need was to exist, and to move onwards at the greatest possible risk, and with a maximum of privation. If the absolutely pure, uncalculating, unpractical spirit of adventure had ever ruled a human being, it ruled this be-patched youth. I almost envied him the possession of this modest and clear flame. It seemed to have consumed all thought of self so completely, that, even while he was talking to you, you forgot that it was he—the man before your eyes—who had gone through these things. I did not envy him his devotion to Kurtz, though. He had not meditated over it. It came to him, and he accepted it with a sort of eager fatalism. I must say that to me it appeared about the most dangerous thing in every way he had come upon so far.

"They had come together unavoidably, like two ships becalmed near each other, and lay rubbing sides at last. I suppose Kurtz wanted an audience, because on a certain occasion, when encamped in the forest, they had talked all night, or more probably Kurtz had talked. 'We talked of everything,' he said, quite transported at the recollection. 'I forgot there was such a thing as sleep. The night did not seem to last an hour. Everything! Everything! . . . Of love too.' 'Ah, he talked to you of love!' I said, much amused. 'It isn't what you think,' he cried, almost passionately. 'It was in general. He made me see things—things.'

"He threw his arms up. We were on deck at the time, and the head-man of my wood-cutters, lounging near by, turned upon him his heavy and glittering eyes. I looked around, and I don't know why, but I assure you that never, never before, did this land, this river, this jungle, the very arch of this blazing sky, appear to me so hopeless and so dark, so impenetrable to human thought, so pitiless to human weakness. 'And, ever since, you have been with him, of course?' I said.

"On the contrary. It appears their intercourse had been very much broken by various causes. He had, as he informed me proudly, managed to nurse Kurtz through two illnesses (he alluded to it as you would to some risky feat), but as a rule Kurtz wandered alone, far in the depths of the forest. 'Very often coming to this station, I had to wait days and days before he would turn up,' he said. 'Ah, it was worth waiting for!—sometimes.' 'What was he doing? exploring or what?' I asked. 'Oh yes, of course'; he had discovered lots of villages, a lake too—he did not know exactly in what direction; it was dangerous to inquire too much—but mostly his expeditions had been for ivory. 'But he had no goods to trade with by that time,' I objected. 'There's a good lot of cartridges left even yet,' he answered, looking away. 'To speak plainly, he raided the country,' I said. He nodded. 'Not alone, surely!' He muttered something about the villages round that lake. 'Kurtz got the tribe to follow him, did he?' I suggested. He fidgeted a little. 'They adored him,' he said. The tone of these words was so extraordinary that I looked at him searchingly. It was curious to see his mingled eagerness and reluctance to speak of Kurtz. The man filled his life, occupied his thoughts, swayed his emotions. 'What can you expect?' he burst out; 'he came to them with thunder and lightning, you know—and they had never seen anything like it—and very terrible. He could be very terrible. You can't judge Mr Kurtz as you would an ordinary man. No, no, no! Now—just to give you an idea—I don't mind telling you, he wanted to shoot me too one day—but I don't judge him.' 'Shoot you!' I cried. 'What for?' 'Well, I had a small lot of ivory the chief of that village near my house gave me. You see I used to shoot game for them. Well, he wanted it, and wouldn't hear reason. He declared he would shoot me unless I gave him the ivory and then cleared out of the country, because he could do so, and had a fancy for it, and there was nothing on earth to prevent him killing whom he jolly well pleased. And it was true too. I gave him the ivory. What did I care! But I didn't clear out. No, no. I couldn't leave him. I had to be careful, of course, till we got friendly again for a time. He had his second illness then. Afterwards I had to keep out of the way; but I didn't mind. He was living for the most part in those villages on the lake. When he came down to the river, sometimes he would take to me, and sometimes it was better for me to be careful. This man suffered too much. He hated all this, and somehow he couldn't get away. When I had a chance I begged him to try and leave while there was time; I offered to go back with him. And he would say yes, and then he would remain; go off on another ivory hunt; disappear for weeks; forget himself amongst these people—forget himself—you know.' 'Why! he's mad,' I said. He protested indignantly. Mr Kurtz couldn't be mad. If I had heard him talk, only two days ago, I wouldn't dare hint at such a thing. . . . I had taken up my binoculars while we talked, and was looking at the shore, sweeping the limit of the forest at each side and at the back of the house. The consciousness of there being people in that bush, so silent, so quiet—as silent and quiet as the ruined house on the hill—made me uneasy. There was no sign on the face of nature of this amazing tale that was not so much told as suggested to me in desolate exclamations, completed by shrugs, in interrupted phrases, in hints ending in deep sighs. The woods were unmoved, like a mask—heavy, like the closed door of a prison—they looked with their air of hidden knowledge, of patient expectation, of unapproachable silence. The Russian was explaining to me that it was only lately that Mr Kurtz had come down to the river, bringing along with him all the fighting men of that lake tribe. He had been absent for several months—getting himself adored, I suppose—and had come down unexpectedly, with the intention to all appearance of making a raid either across the river or down stream. Evidently the appetite for more ivory had got the better of the—what shall I say?—less material aspirations. However, he had got much worse suddenly. 'I heard he was lying helpless, and so I came up—took my chance,' said the Russian. 'Oh, he is bad, very bad.' I directed my glass to the house. There were no signs of life, but there was the ruined roof, the long mud wall peeping above the grass, with three little square window-holes, no two of the same size; all this brought within reach of my hand, as it were. And then I made a brusque movement, and one of the remaining posts of that vanished fence leaped up in the field of my glass. You remember I told you I had been struck at the distance by certain attempts at ornamentation, rather remarkable in the ruinous aspect of the place. Now I had suddenly a nearer view, and its first result was to make me throw my head back as if before a blow. Then I went carefully from post to post with my glass, and I saw my mistake. These round knobs were not ornamental but symbolic; they were expressive and puzzling, striking and disturbing—food for thought and also for the vultures if there had been any looking down from the sky; but at all events for such ants as were industrious enough to ascend the pole. They would have been even more impressive, those heads on the stakes, if their faces had not been turned to the house. Only one, the first I had made out, was facing my way. I was not so shocked as you may think. The start back I had given was really nothing but a movement of surprise. I had expected to see a knob of wood there, you know. I returned deliberately to the first I had seen—and there it was, black, dried, sunken, with closed eyelids—a head that seemed to sleep at the top of that pole, and, with the shrunken dry lips showing a narrow white line of the teeth, was smiling too, smiling continuously at some endless and jocose dream of that eternal slumber.

"I am not disclosing any trade secrets. In fact the manager said afterwards that Mr Kurtz's methods had ruined the district. I have no opinion on that point, but I want you clearly to understand that there was nothing exactly profitable in these heads being there. They only show that Mr Kurtz lacked restraint in the gratification of his various lusts, that there was something wanting in him—some small matter which, when the pressing need arose, could not be found under his magnificent eloquence. Whether he knew of this deficiency himself I can't say. I think the knowledge came to him at last—only at the very last. But the wilderness had found him out early, and had taken on him a terrible vengeance for the fantastic invasion. I think it had whispered to him things about himself which he did not know, things of which he had no conception till he took counsel with this great solitude—and the whisper had proved irresistibly fascinating. It echoed loudly within him because he was hollow at the core. . . . I put down the glass, and the head that had appeared near enough to be spoken to seemed at once to have leaped away from me into inaccessible distance.

"The admirer of Mr Kurtz was a bit crestfallen. In a hurried, indistinct voice he began to assure me he had not dared to take these—say, symbols—down. He was not afraid of the natives; they would not stir till Mr Kurtz gave the word. His ascendancy was extraordinary. The camps of these people surrounded the place, and the chiefs came every day to see him. They would crawl . . . 'I don't want to know anything of the ceremonies used when approaching Mr Kurtz,' I shouted. Curious, this feeling that came over me that such details would be more intolerable than those heads drying on the stakes under Mr Kurtz's windows. After all, that was only a savage sight, while I seemed at one bound to have been transported into some lightless region of subtle horrors, where pure, uncomplicated savagery was a positive relief, being something that had a right to exist—obviously—in the sunshine. The young man looked at me with surprise. I suppose it did not occur to him that Mr Kurtz was no idol of mine. He forgot I hadn't heard any of these splendid monologues on, what was it? on love, justice, conduct of life—or what not. If it had come to crawling before Mr Kurtz, he crawled as much as the veriest savage of them all. I had no idea of the conditions, he said: these heads were the heads of rebels. I shocked him excessively by laughing. Rebels! What would be the next definition I was to hear? There had been enemies, criminals, workers—and these were rebels. Those rebellious heads looked very subdued to me on their sticks. 'You don't know how such a life tries a man like Kurtz,' cried Kurtz's last disciple. 'Well, and you?' I said. 'I! I! I am a simple man. I have no great thoughts. I want nothing from anybody. How can you compare me to . . . ?' His feelings were too much for speech, and suddenly he broke down. 'I don't understand,' he groaned. 'I've been doing my best to keep him alive, and that's enough. I had no hand in all this. I have no abilities. There hasn't been a drop of medicine or a mouthful of invalid food for months here. He was shamefully abandoned. A man like this, with such ideas. Shamefully! Shamefully! I—I—haven't slept for the last ten nights. . . .'

"His voice lost itself in the calm of the evening. The long shadows of the forest had slipped down hill while we talked, had gone far beyond the ruined hovel, beyond the symbolic row of stakes. All this was in the gloom, while we down there were yet in the sunshine, and the stretch of the river abreast of the clearing glittered in a still and dazzling splendour, with a murky and overshadowed bend above and below. Not a living soul was seen on the shore. The bushes did not rustle.

"Suddenly round the corner of the house a group of men appeared, as though they had come up from the ground. They waded waist-deep in the grass, in a compact body, bearing an improvised stretcher in their midst. Instantly, in the emptiness of the landscape, a cry arose whose shrillness pierced the still air like a sharp arrow flying straight to the very heart of the land; and, as if by enchantment, streams of human beings—of naked human beings—with spears in their hands, with bows, with shields, with wild glances and savage movements, were poured into the clearing by the dark-faced and pensive forest. The bushes shook, the grass swayed for a time, and then everything stood still in attentive immobility.

" 'Now, if he does not say the right thing to them we are all done for,' said the Russian at my elbow. The knot of men with the stretcher had stopped too, half-way to the steamer, as if petrified. I saw the man on the stretcher sit up, lank and with an uplifted arm, above the shoulders of the bearers. 'Let us hope that the man who can talk so well of love in general will find some particular reason to spare us this time,' I said. I resented bitterly the absurd danger of our situation, as if to be at the mercy of that atrocious phantom had been a dishonouring necessity. I could not hear a sound, but through my glasses I saw the thin arm extended commandingly, the lower jaw moving, the eyes of that apparition shining darkly far in its bony head that nodded with grotesque jerks. Kurtz—Kurtz—that means 'short' in German—don't it? Well, the name was as true as everything else in his life—and death. He looked at least seven feet long. His covering had fallen off, and his body emerged from it pitiful and appalling as from a winding-sheet. I could see the cage of his ribs all astir, the bones of his arm waving. It was as though an animated image of death carved out of old ivory had been shaking its hand with menaces at a motionless crowd of men made of dark and glittering bronze. I saw him open his mouth wide—it gave him a weirdly voracious aspect, as though he had wanted to swallow all the air, all the earth, all the men before him. A deep voice reached me faintly. He must have been shouting. He fell back suddenly. The stretcher shook as the bearers staggered forward again, and almost at the same time I noticed that the crowd of savages was vanishing without any perceptible movement of retreat, as if the forest that had ejected these beings so suddenly had drawn them in again as the breath is drawn in a long aspiration.

"Some of the pilgrims behind the stretcher carried his arms—two shot-guns, a heavy rifle, and a light revolver-carbine—the thunderbolts of that pitiful Jupiter. The manager bent over him murmuring as he walked beside his head. They laid him down in one of the little cabins—just a room for a bedplace and a camp-stool or two, you know. We had brought his belated correspondence, and a lot of torn envelopes and open letters littered his bed. His hand roamed feebly amongst these papers. I was struck by the fire of his eyes and the composed languor of his expression. It was not so much the exhaustion of disease. He did not seem in pain. This shadow looked satiated and calm, as though for the moment it had had its fill of all the emotions.

"He rustled one of the letters, and looking straight in my face said, 'I am glad.' Somebody had been writing to him about me. These special recommendations were turning up again. The volume of tone he emitted without effort, almost without the trouble of moving his lips, amazed me. A voice! a voice! It was grave, profound, vibrating, while the man did not seem capable of a whisper. However, he had enough strength in him—factitious no doubt—to very nearly make an end of us, as you shall hear directly.

"The manager appeared silently in the doorway; I stepped out at once and he drew the curtain after me. The Russian, eyed curiously by the pilgrims, was staring at the shore. I followed the direction of his glance.

"Dark human shapes could be made out in the distance, flitting indistinctly against the gloomy border of the forest, and near the river two bronze figures, leaning on tall spears, stood in the sunlight under fantastic head-dresses of spotted skins, warlike and still in statuesque repose. And from right to left along the lighted shore moved a wild and gorgeous apparition of a woman.

"She walked with measured steps, draped in striped and fringed cloths, treading the earth proudly, with a slight jingle and flash of barbarous ornaments. She carried her head high; her hair was done in the shape of a helmet; she had brass leggings to the knee, brass wire gauntlets to the elbow, a crimson spot on her tawny cheek, innumerable necklaces of glass beads on her neck; bizarre things, charms, gifts of witch-men, that hung about her, glittered and trembled at every step. She must have had the value of several elephant tusks upon her. She was savage and superb, wild-eyed and magnificent; there was something ominous and stately in her deliberate progress. And in the hush that had fallen suddenly upon the whole sorrowful land, the immense wilderness, the colossal body of the fecund and mysterious life seemed to look at her, pensive, as though it had been looking at the image of its own tenebrous and passionate soul.

"She came abreast of the steamer, stood still, and faced us. Her long shadow fell to the water's edge. Her face had a tragic and fierce aspect of wild sorrow and of dumb pain mingled with the fear of some struggling, half-shaped resolve. She stood looking at us without a stir, and like the wilderness itself, with an air of brooding over an inscrutable purpose. A whole minute passed, and then she made a step forward. There was a low jingle, a glint of yellow metal, a sway of fringed draperies, and she stopped as if her heart had failed her. The young fellow by my side growled. The pilgrims murmured at my back. She looked at us all as if her life had depended upon the unswerving steadiness of her glance. Suddenly she opened her bared arms and threw them up rigid above her head, as though in an uncontrollable desire to touch the sky, and at the same time the swift shadows darted out on the earth, swept around on the river, gathering the steamer into a shadowy embrace. A formidable silence hung over the scene.

"She turned away slowly, walked on, following the bank, and passed into the bushes to the left. Once only her eyes gleamed back at us in the dusk of the thickets before she disappeared.

" 'If she had offered to come aboard I really think I would have tried to shoot her,' said the man of patches nervously. 'I had been risking my life every day for the last fortnight to keep her out of the house. She got in one day and kicked up a row about those miserable rags I picked up in the store-room to mend my clothes with. I wasn't decent. At least it must have been that, for she talked like a fury to Kurtz for an hour, pointing at me now and then. I don't understand the dialect of this tribe. Luckily for me, I fancy Kurtz felt too ill that day to care, or there would have been mischief. I don't understand. . . . No—it's too much for me. Ah, well, it's all over now.'

"At this moment I heard Kurtz's deep voice behind the curtain: 'Save me!—save the ivory, you mean. Don't tell me. Save *me*! Why, I've had to save you. You are interrupting my plans now. Sick! Sick! Not so sick as you would like to believe. Never mind. I'll carry my ideas out yet—I will return. I'll show you what can be done. You with your little peddling notions—you are interfering with me. I will return. I . . . .'

"The manager came out. He did me the honour to take me under the arm and lead me aside. 'He is very low, very low,' he said. He considered it necessary to sigh, but neglected to be consistently sorrowful. 'We have done all we could for him—haven't we? But there is no disguising the fact, Mr Kurtz has done more harm than good to the Company. He did not see the time was not ripe for vigorous action. Cautiously, cautiously—that's my principle. We must be cautious yet. The district is closed to us for a time. Deplorable! Upon the whole, the trade will suffer. I don't deny there is a remarkable quantity of ivory—mostly fossil. We must save it, at all events—but look how precarious the position is—and why? Because the method is unsound.' 'Do you,' said I, looking at the shore, 'call it "unsound method"?' 'Without doubt,' he exclaimed hotly, 'Don't you?' . . . 'No method at all,' I murmured after a while. 'Exactly,' he exulted. 'I anticipated this. Shows a complete want of judgment. It is my duty to point it out in the proper quarter.' 'Oh,' said I, 'that fellow—what's his name?—the brickmaker, will make a readable report for you.' He appeared confounded for a moment. It seemed to me I had never breathed an atmosphere so vile, and I turned mentally to Kurtz for relief—positively for relief. 'Nevertheless, I think Mr Kurtz is a remarkable man,' I said with emphasis. He started, dropped on me a cold heavy glance, said very quietly, 'He *was*,' and turned his back on me. My hour of favour was over; I found myself lumped along with Kurtz as a partisan of methods for which the time was not ripe: I was unsound! Ah! but it was something to have at least a choice of nightmares.

"I had turned to the wilderness really, not to Mr Kurtz, who, I was ready to admit, was as good as buried. And for a moment it seemed to me as if I also were buried in a vast grave full of unspeakable secrets. I felt an intolerable weight oppressing my breast, the smell of the damp earth, the unseen presence of victorious corruption, the darkness of an impenetrable night. . . . The Russian tapped me on the shoulder. I heard him mumbling and stammering something about 'brother seaman—couldn't conceal—knowledge of matters that would affect Mr Kurtz's reputation.' I waited. For him evidently Mr Kurtz was not in his grave; I suspect that for him Mr Kurtz was one of the immortals. 'Well!' said I at last, 'speak out. As it happens, I am Mr Kurtz's friend—in a way.'

"He stated with a good deal of formality that had we not been 'of the same profession,' he would have kept the matter to himself without regard to consequences. He suspected 'there was an active ill-will towards him on the part of these white men that—' 'You are right,' I said, remembering a certain conversation I had overheard. 'The manager thinks you ought to be hanged.' He showed a concern at this intelligence which amused me at first. 'I had better get out of the way quietly,' he said earnestly. 'I can do no more for Kurtz now, and they would soon find some excuse. What's to stop them? There's a military post three hundred miles from here.' 'Well, upon my word,' said I, 'perhaps you had better go if you have any friends amongst the savages near by.' 'Plenty,' he said. 'They are simple people—and I want nothing, you know.' He stood biting his lip, then: 'I don't want any harm to happen to these whites here, but of course I was thinking of Mr Kurtz's reputation—but you are a brother seaman and—' 'All right,' said I, after a time. 'Mr Kurtz's reputation is safe with me.' I did not know how truly I spoke.

"He informed me, lowering his voice, that it was Kurtz who had ordered the attack to be made on the steamer. 'He hated sometimes the idea of being taken away—and then again . . . But I don't understand these matters. I am a simple man. He thought it would scare you away—that you would give it up, thinking him dead. I could not stop him. Oh, I had an awful time of it this last month.' 'Very well,' I said. 'He is all right now.' 'Ye-e-es,' he muttered, not very convinced apparently. 'Thanks,' said I; 'I shall keep my eyes open.' 'But quiet—eh?' he urged anxiously. 'It would be awful for his reputation if anybody here—' I promised a complete discretion with great gravity. 'I have a canoe and three black fellows waiting not very far. I am off. Could you give me a few Martini-Henry cartridges?' I could, and did, with proper secrecy. He helped himself, with a wink at me, to a handful of my tobacco. 'Between sailors—you know—good English tobacco.' At the door of the pilot-house he turned round—'I say, haven't you a pair of shoes you could spare?' He raised one leg. 'Look.' The soles were tied with knotted strings sandal-wise under his bare feet. I rooted out an old pair, at which he looked with admiration before tucking it under his left arm. One of his pockets (bright red) was bulging with cartridges, from the other (dark blue) peeped 'Towson's Inquiry,' etc. etc. He seemed to think himself excellently well equipped for a renewed encounter with the wilderness. 'Ah! I'll never, never meet such a man again. You ought to have heard him recite poetry—his own too it was, he told me. Poetry!' He rolled his eyes at the recollection of these delights. 'Oh, he enlarged my mind!' 'Good-bye,' said I. He shook hands and vanished in the night. Sometimes I ask myself whether I had ever really seen him—whether it was possible to meet such a phenomenon! . . .

"When I woke up shortly after midnight his warning came to my mind with its hint of danger that seemed, in the starred darkness, real enough to make me get up for the purpose of having a look round. On the hill a big fire burned, illuminating fitfully a crooked corner of the station-house. One of the agents with a picket of a few of our blacks, armed for the purpose, was keeping guard over the ivory; but deep within the forest, red gleams that wavered, that seemed to sink and rise from the ground amongst confused columnar shapes of intense blackness, showed the exact position of the camp where Mr Kurtz's adorers were keeping their uneasy vigil. The monotonous beating of a big drum filled the air with muffled shocks and a lingering vibration. A steady droning sound of many men chanting each to himself some weird incantation came out from the black, flat wall of the woods as the humming of bees comes out of a hive, and had a strange narcotic effect upon my half-awake senses. I believe I dozed off leaning over the rail, till an abrupt burst of yells, an overwhelming outbreak of a pent-up and mysterious frenzy, woke me up in a bewildered wonder. It was cut short all at once, and the low droning went on with an effect of audible and soothing silence. I glanced casually into the little cabin. A light was burning within, but Mr Kurtz was not there.

"I think I would have raised an outcry if I had believed my eyes. But I didn't believe them at first—the thing seemed so impossible. The fact is I was completely unnerved by a sheer blank fright, pure abstract terror, unconnected with any distinct shape of physical danger. What made this emotion so overpowering was—how shall I define it?—the moral shock I received, as if something altogether monstrous, intolerable to thought and odious to the soul, had been thrust upon me unexpectedly. This lasted of course the merest fraction of a second, and then the usual sense of commonplace, deadly danger, the possibility of a sudden onslaught and massacre, or something of the kind, which I saw impending, was positively welcome and composing. It pacified me, in fact, so much that I did not raise an alarm.

"There was an agent buttoned up inside an ulster[1] and sleeping on a chair on deck within three feet of me. The yells had not awakened him; he snored very slightly; I left him to his slumbers and leaped ashore. I did not betray Mr Kurtz—it was ordered I should never betray him—it was written I should be loyal to the nightmare of my choice. I was anxious to deal with this shadow by myself alone—and to this day I don't know why I was so jealous of sharing with any one the peculiar blackness of that experience.

"As soon as I got on the bank I saw a trail—a broad trail through the grass. I remember the exultation with which I said to myself, 'He can't walk—he is crawling on all-fours—I've got him.' The grass was wet with dew. I strode rapidly with clenched fists. I fancy I had some vague notion of falling upon him and giving him a drubbing. I don't know. I had some imbecile thoughts.

---

1. Long overcoat.

The knitting old woman with the cat obtruded herself upon my memory as a most improper person to be sitting at the other end of such an affair. I saw a row of pilgrims squirting lead in the air out of Winchesters held to the hip. I thought I would never get back to the steamer, and imagined myself living alone and unarmed in the woods to an advanced age. Such silly things—you know. And I remember I confounded the beat of the drum with the beating of my heart, and was pleased at its calm regularity.

"I kept to the track though—then stopped to listen. The night was very clear; a dark blue space, sparkling with dew and starlight, in which black things stood very still. I thought I could see a kind of motion ahead of me. I was strangely cocksure of everything that night. I actually left the track and ran in a wide semicircle (I verily believe chuckling to myself) so as to get in front of that stir, of that motion I had seen—if indeed I had seen anything. I was circumventing Kurtz as though it had been a boyish game.

"I came upon him, and, if he had not heard me coming, I would have fallen over him too, but he got up in time. He rose, unsteady, long, pale, indistinct, like a vapour exhaled by the earth, and swayed slightly, misty and silent before me; while at my back the fires loomed between the trees, and the murmur of many voices issued from the forest. I had cut him off cleverly; but when actually confronting him I seemed to come to my senses, I saw the danger in its right proportion. It was by no means over yet. Suppose he began to shout? Though he could hardly stand, there was still plenty of vigour in his voice. 'Go away—hide yourself,' he said, in that profound tone. It was very awful. I glanced back. We were within thirty yards of the nearest fire. A black figure stood up, strode on long black legs, waving long black arms, across the glow. It had horns—antelope horns, I think—on its head. Some sorcerer, some witch-man no doubt: it looked fiend-like enough. 'Do you know what you are doing?' I whispered. 'Perfectly,' he answered, raising his voice for that single word: it sounded to me far off and yet loud, like a hail through a speaking-trumpet. If he makes a row we are lost, I thought to myself. This clearly was not a case for fisticuffs, even apart from the very natural aversion I had to beat that Shadow—this wandering and tormented thing. 'You will be lost,' I said—'utterly lost.' One gets sometimes such a flash of inspiration, you know. I did say the right thing, though indeed he could not have been more irretrievably lost than he was at this very moment, when the foundations of our intimacy were being laid—to endure—to endure—even to the end—even beyond.

" 'I had immense plans,' he muttered irresolutely. 'Yes,' said I; 'but if you try to shout I'll smash your head with—' There was not a stick or a stone near. 'I will throttle you for good,' I corrected myself. 'I was on the threshold of great things,' he pleaded, in a voice of longing, with a wistfulness of tone that made my blood run cold. 'And now for this stupid scoundrel—' 'Your success in Europe is assured in any case,' I affirmed steadily. I did not want to have the throttling of him, you understand—and indeed it would have been very little use for any practical purpose. I tried to break the spell—the heavy, mute spell of the wilderness—that seemed to draw him to its pitiless breast by the awakening of forgotten and brutal instincts, by the memory of gratified and monstrous passions. This alone, I was convinced, had driven him out to the edge of the forest, to the bush, towards the gleam of fires, the throb of drums, the drone of weird incantations; this alone had beguiled his unlawful soul beyond the bounds of permitted aspirations. And, don't you see, the terror of the position was not in being knocked on the head—though I had a very lively sense of that danger too—but in this, that I had to deal with a being to whom I could not appeal in the name of anything high or low. I had, even like the niggers, to invoke him—himself—his own exalted and incredible degradation. There was nothing either above or below him, and I knew it. He had kicked himself loose of the earth. Confound the man! he had kicked the very earth to pieces. He was alone, and I before him did not know whether I stood on the ground or floated in the air. I've been telling you what we said—repeating the phrases we pronounced—but what's the good? They were common everyday words—the familiar, vague sounds exchanged on every waking day of life. But what of that? They had behind them, to my mind, the terrific suggestiveness of words heard in dreams, of phrases spoken in nightmares. Soul! If anybody had ever struggled with a soul, I am the man. And I wasn't arguing with a lunatic either. Believe me or not, his intelligence was perfectly clear—concentrated, it is true, upon himself with horrible intensity, yet clear; and therein was my only chance—barring, of course, the killing him there and then, which wasn't so good, on account of unavoidable noise. But his soul was mad. Being alone in the wilderness, it had looked within itself, and, by heavens! I tell you, it had gone mad. I had—for my sins, I suppose, to go through the ordeal of looking into it myself. No eloquence could have been so withering to one's belief in mankind as his final burst of sincerity. He struggled with himself too. I saw it—I heard it. I saw the inconceivable mystery of a soul that knew no restraint, no faith, and no fear, yet struggling blindly with itself. I kept my head pretty well; but when I had him at last stretched on the couch, I wiped my forehead, while my legs shook under me as though I had carried half a ton on my back down that hill. And yet I had only supported him, his bony arm clasped round my neck—and he was not much heavier than a child.

"When next day we left at noon, the crowd, of whose presence behind the curtain of trees I had been acutely conscious all the time, flowed out of the woods again, filled the clearing, covered the slope with a mass of naked, breathing, quivering, bronze bodies. I steamed up a bit, then swung downstream, and two thousand eyes followed the evolutions of the splashing, thumping, fierce river-demon beating the water with its terrible tail and breathing black smoke into the air. In front of the first rank, along the river, three men, plastered with bright red earth from head to foot, strutted to and fro restlessly. When we came abreast again, they faced the river, stamped their feet, nodded their horned heads, swayed their scarlet bodies; they shook towards the fierce river-demon a bunch of black feathers, a mangy skin with a pendent tail—something that looked like a dried gourd; they shouted periodically together strings of amazing words that resembled no sounds of human language; and the deep murmurs of the crowd, interrupted suddenly, were like the responses of some satanic litany.

"We had carried Kurtz into the pilot-house: there was more air there. Lying on the couch, he stared through the open shutter. There was an eddy in the mass of human bodies, and the woman with helmeted head and tawny cheeks rushed out to the very brink of the stream. She put out her hands, shouted something, and all that wild mob took up the shout in a roaring chorus of articulated, rapid, breathless utterance.

" 'Do you understand this?' I asked.

"He kept on looking out past me with fiery, longing eyes, with a mingled expression of wistfulness and hate. He made no answer, but I saw a smile, a smile of indefinable meaning, appear on his colourless lips that a moment after twitched convulsively. 'Do I not?' he said slowly, gasping, as if the words had been torn out of him by a supernatural power.

"I pulled the string of the whistle, and I did this because I saw the pilgrims on deck getting out their rifles with an air of anticipating a jolly lark. At the sudden screech there was a movement of abject terror through that wedged mass of bodies. 'Don't! don't you frighten them away,' cried some one on deck disconsolately. I pulled the string time after time. They broke and ran, they leaped, they crouched, they swerved, they dodged the flying terror of the sound. The three red chaps had fallen flat, face down on the shore, as though they had been shot dead. Only the barbarous and superb woman did not so much as flinch, and stretched tragically her bare arms after us over the sombre and glittering river.

"And then that imbecile crowd down on the deck started their little fun, and I could see nothing more for smoke.

"The brown current ran swiftly out of the heart of darkness, bearing us down towards the sea with twice the speed of our upward progress; and Kurtz's life was running swiftly too, ebbing, ebbing out of his heart into the sea of inexorable time. The manager was very placid, he had no vital anxieties now, he took us both in with a comprehensive and satisfied glance: the 'affair' had come off as well as could be wished. I saw the time approaching when I would be left alone of the party of 'unsound method.' The pilgrims looked upon me with disfavour. I was, so to speak, numbered with the dead. It is strange how I accepted this unforeseen partnership, this choice of nightmares forced upon me in the tenebrous land invaded by these mean and greedy phantoms.

"Kurtz discoursed. A voice! a voice! It rang deep to the very last. It survived his strength to hide in the magnificent folds of eloquence the barren darkness of his heart. Oh, he struggled! he struggled! The wastes of his weary brain were haunted by shadowy images now—images of wealth and fame revolving obsequiously round his unextinguishable gift of noble and lofty expression. My Intended, my station, my career, my ideas—these were the subjects for the occasional utterances of elevated sentiments. The shade of the original Kurtz frequented the bedside of the hollow sham, whose fate it was to be buried presently in the mould of primeval earth. But both the diabolic love and the unearthly hate of the mysteries it had penetrated fought for the possession of that soul satiated with primitive emotions, avid of lying fame, of sham distinction, of all the appearances of success and power.

"Sometimes he was contemptibly childish. He desired to have kings meet him at railway stations on his return from some ghastly Nowhere, where he intended to accomplish great things. 'You show them you have in you something that is really profitable, and then there will be no limits to the recognition of your ability,' he would say. 'Of course you must take care of the motives—right motives—always.' The long reaches that were like one and the same reach, monotonous bends that were exactly alike, slipped past the steamer with their multitude of secular[2] trees looking patiently after this grimy fragment of another world, the forerunner of change, of conquest, of

2. Centuries old.

trade, of massacres, of blessings. I looked ahead—piloting. 'Close the shutter,' said Kurtz suddenly one day; 'I can't bear to look at this.' I did so. There was a silence. 'Oh, but I will wring your heart yet!' he cried at the invisible wilderness.

"We broke down—as I had expected—and had to lie up for repairs at the head of an island. This delay was the first thing that shook Kurtz's confidence. One morning he gave me a packet of papers and a photograph—the lot tied together with a shoe-string. 'Keep this for me,' he said. 'This noxious fool' (meaning the manager) 'is capable of prying into my boxes when I am not looking.' In the afternoon I saw him. He was lying on his back with closed eyes, and I withdrew quietly, but I heard him mutter, 'Live rightly, die, die . . . ' I listened. There was nothing more. Was he rehearsing some speech in his sleep, or was it a fragment of a phrase from some newspaper article? He had been writing for the papers and meant to do so again, 'for the furthering of my ideas. It's a duty.'

"His was an impenetrable darkness. I looked at him as you peer down at a man who is lying at the bottom of a precipice where the sun never shines. But I had not much time to give him, because I was helping the engine-driver to take to pieces the leaky cylinders, to straighten a bent connecting-rod, and in other such matters. I lived in an infernal mess of rust, filings, nuts, bolts, spanners, hammers, ratchet-drills—things I abominate, because I don't get on with them. I tended the little forge we fortunately had aboard; I toiled wearily in a wretched scrap-heap—unless I had the shakes too bad to stand.

"One evening coming in with a candle I was startled to hear him say a little tremulously, 'I am lying here in the dark waiting for death.' The light was within a foot of his eyes. I forced myself to murmur, 'Oh, nonsense!' and stood over him as if transfixed.

"Anything approaching the change that came over his features I have never seen before, and hope never to see again. Oh, I wasn't touched. I was fascinated. It was as though a veil had been rent. I saw on that ivory face the expression of sombre pride, of ruthless power, of craven terror—of an intense and hopeless despair. Did he live his life again in every detail of desire, temptation, and surrender during that supreme moment of complete knowledge? He cried in a whisper at some image, at some vision—he cried out twice, a cry that was no more than a breath:

" 'The horror! The horror!'

"I blew the candle out and left the cabin. The pilgrims were dining in the mess-room, and I took my place opposite the manager, who lifted his eyes to give me a questioning glance, which I successfully ignored. He leaned back, serene, with that peculiar smile of his sealing the unexpressed depths of his meanness. A continuous shower of small flies streamed upon the lamp, upon the cloth, upon our hands and faces. Suddenly the manager's boy put his insolent black head in the doorway, and said in a tone of scathing contempt:

" 'Mistah Kurtz—he dead.'

"All the pilgrims rushed out to see. I remained, and went on with my dinner. I believe I was considered brutally callous. However, I did not eat much. There was a lamp in there—light, don't you know—and outside it was so beastly, beastly dark. I went no more near the remarkable man who had pronounced a judgement upon the adventures of his soul on this earth. The voice was gone. What else had been there? But I am of course aware that next day the pilgrims buried something in a muddy hole.

"And then they very nearly buried me.

"However, as you see, I did not go to join Kurtz there and then. I did not. I remained to dream the nightmare out to the end, and to show my loyalty to Kurtz once more. Destiny. My destiny! Droll thing life is—that mysterious arrangement of merciless logic for a futile purpose. The most you can hope from it is some knowledge of yourself—that comes too late—a crop of unextinguishable regrets. I have wrestled with death. It is the most unexciting contest you can imagine. It takes place in an impalpable greyness, with nothing underfoot, with nothing around, without spectators, without clamour, without glory, without the great desire of victory, without the great fear of defeat, in a sickly atmosphere of tepid scepticism, without much belief in your own right, and still less in that of your adversary. If such is the form of ultimate wisdom, then life is a greater riddle than some of us think it to be. I was within a hair's-breadth of the last opportunity for pronouncement, and I found with humiliation that probably I would have nothing to say. This is the reason why I affirm that Kurtz was a remarkable man. He had something to say. He said it. Since I had peeped over the edge myself, I understand better the meaning of his stare, that could not see the flame of the candle, but was wide enough to embrace the whole universe, piercing enough to penetrate all the hearts that beat in the darkness. He had summed up—he had judged. 'The horror!' He was a remarkable man. After all, this was the expression of some sort of belief; it had candour, it had conviction, it had a vibrating note of revolt in its whisper, it had the appalling face of a glimpsed truth—the strange commingling of desire and hate. And it is not my own extremity I remember best—a vision of greyness without form filled with physical pain, and a careless contempt for the evanescence of all things— even of this pain itself. No! It is his extremity that I seem to have lived through. True, he had made that last stride, he had stepped over the edge, while I had been permitted to draw back my hesitating foot. And perhaps in this is the whole difference; perhaps all the wisdom, and all truth, and all sincerity, are just compressed into that inappreciable moment of time in which we step over the threshold of the invisible. Perhaps! I like to think my summing-up would not have been a word of careless contempt. Better his cry—much better. It was an affirmation, a moral victory paid for by innumerable defeats, by abominable terrors, by abominable satisfactions. But it was a victory! That is why I have remained loyal to Kurtz to the last, and even beyond, when a long time after I heard once more, not his own voice, but the echo of his magnificent eloquence thrown to me from a soul as translucently pure as a cliff of crystal.

"No, they did not bury me, though there is a period of time which I remember mistily, with a shuddering wonder, like a passage through some inconceivable world that had no hope in it and no desire. I found myself back in the sepulchral city resenting the sight of people hurrying through the streets to filch a little money from each other, to devour their infamous cookery, to gulp their unwholesome beer, to dream their insignificant and silly dreams. They trespassed upon my thoughts. They were intruders whose knowledge of life was to me an irritating pretence, because I felt so sure they could not possibly know the things I knew. Their bearing, which was simply the bearing of commonplace individuals going about their business in the assurance of perfect safety, was offensive to me like the outrageous flauntings of folly in the face of a danger it is unable to comprehend. I had no particular desire to enlighten them, but I had some difficulty in restraining myself from laughing in their faces, so full of stupid importance. I daresay I was not very well at that time. I tottered about the streets—there were various affairs to settle—grinning bitterly at perfectly respectable persons. I admit my behaviour was inexcusable, but then my temperature was seldom normal in these days. My dear aunt's endeavours to 'nurse up my strength' seemed altogether beside the mark. It was not my strength that wanted nursing, it was my imagination that wanted soothing. I kept the bundle of papers given me by Kurtz, not knowing exactly what to do with it. His mother had died lately, watched over, as I was told, by his Intended. A clean-shaven man, with an official manner and wearing gold-rimmed spectacles, called on me one day and made inquiries, at first circuitous, afterwards suavely pressing, about what he was pleased to denominate certain 'documents.' I was not surprised, because I had had two rows with the manager on the subject out there. I had refused to give up the smallest scrap out of that package, and I took the same attitude with the spectacled man. He became darkly menacing at last, and with much heat argued that the Company had the right to every bit of information about its 'territories.' And, said he, 'Mr Kurtz's knowledge of unexplored regions must have been necessarily extensive and peculiar—owing to his great abilities and to the deplorable circumstances in which he had been placed: therefore—' I assured him Mr Kurtz's knowledge, however extensive, did not bear upon the problems of commerce or administration. He invoked then the name of science. 'It would be an incalculable loss if,' etc. etc. I offered him the report on the 'Suppression of Savage Customs,' with the postscriptum torn off. He took it up eagerly, but ended by sniffing at it with an air of contempt. 'This is not what we had a right to expect,' he remarked. 'Expect nothing else,' I said. 'There are only private letters.' He withdrew upon some threat of legal proceedings, and I saw him no more; but another fellow, calling himself Kurtz's cousin, appeared two days later, and was anxious to hear all the details about his dear relative's last moments. Incidentally he gave me to understand that Kurtz had been essentially a great musician. 'There was the making of an immense success,' said the man, who was an organist, I believe, with lank grey hair flowing over a greasy coat-collar. I had no reason to doubt his statement; and to this day I am unable to say what was Kurtz's profession, whether he ever had any—which was the greatest of his talents. I had taken him for a painter who wrote for the papers, or else for a journalist who could paint—but even the cousin (who took snuff during the interview) could not tell me what he had been—exactly. He was a universal genius—on that point I agreed with the old chap, who thereupon blew his nose noisily into a large cotton handkerchief and withdrew in senile agitation, bearing off some family letters and memoranda without importance. Ultimately a journalist anxious to know something of the fate of his 'dear colleague' turned up. This visitor informed me Kurtz's proper sphere ought to have been politics 'on the popular side.' He had furry straight eyebrows, bristly hair cropped short, an eyeglass on a broad ribbon, and, becoming expansive, confessed his opinion that Kurtz really couldn't write a bit—'but heavens! how that man could talk! He electrified large meetings. He had faith—don't you see?—he had the faith. He could get himself to believe anything—anything. He would have been a splendid leader of an extreme party.' 'What party?' I asked. 'Any party,' answered the other. 'He was an—an—extremist.' Did I not think so? I assented. Did I know, he asked, with a sudden flash of curiosity, 'what it was that had induced him to go out there?' 'Yes,' said I, and forthwith handed him the famous Report for publication, if he thought fit. He glanced through it hurriedly, mumbling all the time, judged 'it would do,' and took himself off with this plunder.

"Thus I was left at last with a slim packet of letters and the girl's portrait. She struck me as beautiful—I mean she had a beautiful expression. I know that the sunlight can be made to lie too, yet one felt that no manipulation of light and pose could have conveyed the delicate shade of truthfulness upon those features. She seemed ready to listen without mental reservation, without suspicion, without a thought for herself. I concluded I would go and give her back her portrait and those letters myself. Curiosity? Yes; and also some other feeling perhaps. All that had been Kurtz's had passed out of my hands: his soul, his body, his station, his plans, his ivory, his career. There remained only his memory and his Intended—and I wanted to give that up too to the past, in a way—to surrender personally all that remained of him with me to that oblivion which is the last word of our common fate. I don't defend myself. I had no clear perception of what it was I really wanted. Perhaps it was an impulse of unconscious loyalty, or the fulfilment of one of those ironic necessities that lurk in the facts of human existence. I don't know. I can't tell. But I went.

"I thought his memory was like the other memories of the dead that accumulate in every man's life—a vague impress on the brain of shadows that had fallen on it in their swift and final passage; but before the high and ponderous door, between the tall houses of a street as still and decorous as a well-kept alley in a cemetery, I had a vision of him on the stretcher, opening his mouth voraciously, as if to devour all the earth with all its mankind. He lived then before me; he lived as much as he had ever lived—a shadow insatiable of splendid appearances, of frightful realities; a shadow darker than the shadow of the night, and draped nobly in the folds of a gorgeous eloquence. The vision seemed to enter the house with me—the stretcher, the phantom-bearers, the wild crowd of obedient worshippers, the gloom of the forests, the glitter of the reach between the murky bends, the beat of the drum, regular and muffled like the beating of a heart—the heart of a conquering darkness. It was a moment of triumph for the wilderness, an invading and vengeful rush which, it seemed to me, I would have to keep back alone for the salvation of another soul. And the memory of what I had heard him say afar there, with the horned shapes stirring at my back, in the glow of fires, within the patient woods, those broken phrases came back to me, were heard again in their ominous and terrifying simplicity. I remembered his abject pleading, his abject threats, the colossal scale of his vile desires, the meanness, the torment, the tempestuous anguish of his soul. And later on I seemed to see his collected languid manner, when he said one day, 'This lot of ivory now is really mine. The Company did not pay for it. I collected it myself at a very great personal risk. I am afraid they will try to claim it as theirs though. H'm. It is a difficult case. What do you think I ought to do—resist? Eh? I want no more than justice.' . . . He wanted no more than justice—no more than justice. I rang the bell before a mahogany door on the first floor, and while I waited he seemed to stare at me out of the glossy panel—stare with that wide and immense stare embracing, condemning, loathing all the universe. I seemed to hear the whispered cry, 'The horror! The horror!'

"The dusk was falling. I had to wait in a lofty drawing-room with three long windows from floor to ceiling that were like three luminous and be-draped columns. The bent gilt legs and backs of the furniture shone in indistinct curves. The tall marble fireplace had a cold and monumental whiteness. A grand piano stood massively in a corner; with dark gleams on the flat surfaces like a sombre and polished sarcophagus. A high door opened—closed. I rose.

"She came forward, all in black, with a pale head, floating towards me in the dusk. She was in mourning. It was more than a year since his death, more than a year since the news came; she seemed as though she would remember and mourn for ever. She took both my hands in hers and murmured, 'I had heard you were coming.' I noticed she was not very young—I mean not girlish. She had a mature capacity for fidelity, for belief, for suffering. The room seemed to have grown darker, as if all the sad light of the cloudy evening had taken refuge on her forehead. This fair hair, this pale visage, this pure brow, seemed surrounded by an ashy halo from which the dark eyes looked out at me. Their glance was guileless, profound, confident, and trustful. She carried her sorrowful head as though she were proud of that sorrow, as though she would say, I—I alone know how to mourn for him as he deserves. But while we were still shaking hands, such a look of awful desolation came upon her face that I perceived she was one of those creatures that are not the playthings of Time. For her he had died only yesterday. And, by Jove! the impression was so powerful that for me too he seemed to have died only yesterday—nay, this very minute. I saw her and him in the same instant of time—his death and her sorrow—I saw her sorrow in the very moment of his death. Do you understand? I saw them together—I heard them together. She had said, with a deep catch of the breath, 'I have survived'; while my strained ears seemed to hear distinctly, mingled with her tone of despairing regret, the summing-up whisper of his eternal condemnation. I asked myself what I was doing there, with a sensation of panic in my heart as though I had blundered into a place of cruel and absurd mysteries not fit for a human being to behold. She motioned me to a chair. We sat down. I laid the packet gently on the little table, and she put her hand over it. . . . 'You knew him well,' she murmured, after a moment of mourning silence.

" 'Intimacy grows quickly out there,' I said. 'I knew him as well as it is possible for one man to know another.'

" 'And you admired him,' she said. 'It was impossible to know him and not to admire him. Was it?'

" 'He was a remarkable man,' I said unsteadily. Then before the appealing fixity of her gaze, that seemed to watch for more words on my lips, I went on, 'It was impossible not to—'

" 'Love him,' she finished eagerly, silencing me into an appalled dumbness.
'How true! how true! But when you think that no one knew him so well as
I! I had all his noble confidence. I knew him best.'

" 'You knew him best,' I repeated. And perhaps she did. But with every
word spoken the room was growing darker, and only her forehead, smooth
and white, remained illumined by the unextinguishable light of belief and
love.

" 'You were his friend,' she went on. 'His friend,' she repeated, a little
louder. 'You must have been, if he had given you this, and sent you to me. I
feel I can speak to you—and oh! I must speak. I want you—you who have
heard his last words—to know I have been worthy of him. . . . It is not pride.
. . . Yes! I am proud to know I understood him better than any one on earth—
he told me so himself. And since his mother died I have had no one—no
one—to—to—'

"I listened. The darkness deepened. I was not even sure whether he had
given me the right bundle. I rather suspect he wanted me to take care of
another batch of his papers which, after his death, I saw the manager examining under the lamp. And the girl talked, easing her pain in the certitude
of my sympathy; she talked as thirsty men drink. I had heard that her engagement with Kurtz had been disapproved by her people. He wasn't rich enough
or something. And indeed I don't know whether he had not been a pauper
all his life. He had given me some reason to infer that it was his impatience
of comparative poverty that drove him out there.

" '. . . Who was not his friend who had heard him speak once?' she was
saying. 'He drew men towards him by what was best in them.' She looked at
me with intensity. 'It is the gift of the great,' she went on, and the sound of
her low voice seemed to have the accompaniment of all the other sounds,
full of mystery, desolation, and sorrow, I had ever heard—the ripple of the
river, the soughing of the trees swayed by the wind, the murmurs of the
crowds, the faint ring of incomprehensible words cried from afar, the whisper
of a voice speaking from beyond the threshold of an eternal darkness. 'But
you have heard him! You know!' she cried.

" 'Yes, I know,' I said with something like despair in my heart, but bowing
my head before the faith that was in her, before that great and saving illusion
that shone with an unearthly glow in the darkness, in the triumphant darkness from which I could not have defended her—from which I could not
even defend myself.

" 'What a loss to me—to us!'—she corrected herself with beautiful generosity; then added in a murmur, 'To the world.' By the last gleams of twilight
I could see the glitter of her eyes, full of tears—of tears that would not fall.

" 'I have been very happy—very fortunate—very proud,' she went on. 'Too
fortunate. Too happy for a little while. And now I am unhappy for—for life.'

"She stood up; her fair hair seemed to catch all the remaining light in a
glimmer of gold. I rose too.

" 'And of all this,' she went on mournfully, 'of all his promise, and of all
his greatness, of his generous mind, of his noble heart, nothing remains—
nothing but a memory. You and I—'

" 'We shall always remember him,' I said hastily.

" 'No!' she cried. 'It is impossible that all this should be lost—that such a
life should be sacrificed to leave nothing—but sorrow. You know what vast

plans he had. I knew of them too—I could not perhaps understand—but others knew of them. Something must remain. His words, at least, have not died.'

" 'His words will remain,' I said.

" 'And his example,' she whispered to herself. 'Men looked up to him—his goodness shone in every act. His example—'

" 'True,' I said; 'his example too. Yes, his example. I forgot that.'

" 'But I do not. I cannot—I cannot believe—not yet. I cannot believe that I shall never see him again, that nobody will see him again, never, never, never.'

"She put out her arms as if after a retreating figure, stretching them black and with clasped pale hands across the fading and narrow sheen of the window. Never see him! I saw him clearly enough then. I shall see this eloquent phantom as long as I live, and I shall see her too, a tragic and familiar Shade, resembling in this gesture another one, tragic also, and bedecked with powerless charms, stretching bare brown arms over the glitter of the infernal stream, the stream of darkness. She said suddenly very low, 'He died as he lived.'

" 'His end,' said I, with dull anger stirring in me, 'was in every way worthy of his life.'

" 'And I was not with him,' she murmured. My anger subsided before a feeling of infinite pity.

" 'Everything that could be done—' I mumbled.

" 'Ah, but I believed in him more than any one on earth—more than his own mother, more than—himself. He needed me! Me! I would have treasured every sigh, every word, every sign, every glance.'

"I felt like a chill grip on my chest. 'Don't,' I said, in a muffled voice.

" 'Forgive me. I—I—have mourned so long in silence—in silence. . . . You were with him—to the last? I think of his loneliness. Nobody near to understand him as I would have understood. Perhaps no one to hear. . . . '

" 'To the very end,' I said shakily. 'I heard his very last words. . . . ' I stopped in a fright.

" 'Repeat them,' she murmured in a heart-broken tone. 'I want—I want—something—something—to—to live with.'

"I was on the point of crying at her, 'Don't you hear them?' The dusk was repeating them in a persistent whisper all around us, in a whisper that seemed to swell menacingly like the first whisper of a rising wind. 'The horror! The horror!'

" 'His last word—to live with,' she insisted. 'Don't you understand I loved him—I loved him—I loved him!'

"I pulled myself together and spoke slowly.

" 'The last word he pronounced was—your name.'

"I heard a light sigh and then my heart stood still, stopped dead short by an exulting and terrible cry, by the cry of inconceivable triumph and of unspeakable pain. 'I knew it—I was sure!' . . . She knew. She was sure. I heard her weeping; she had hidden her face in her hands. It seemed to me that the house would collapse before I could escape, that the heavens would fall upon my head. But nothing happened. The heavens do not fall for such a trifle. Would they have fallen, I wonder, if I had rendered Kurtz that justice which was his due? Hadn't he said he wanted only justice? But

I couldn't. I could not tell her. It would have been too dark—too dark altogether. . . ."[3]

Marlow ceased, and sat apart, indistinct and silent, in the pose of a meditating Buddha. Nobody moved for a time. "We have lost the first of the ebb," said the Director suddenly. I raised my head. The offing was barred by a black bank of clouds, and the tranquil waterway leading to the uttermost ends of the earth flowed sombre under an overcast sky—seemed to lead into the heart of an immense darkness.

1899   1902

3. Writing to William Blackwood (editor of *Blackwood's Magazine*, where the story first appeared) in May 1902, Conrad referred to "the last pages of Heart of Darkness where the interview of the man and the girl locks in—as it were—the whole 30,000 words of narrative description into one suggestive view of a whole phase of life, and makes of that story something quite on another plane than an anecdote of a man who went mad in the Centre of Africa" (Joseph Conrad, *Letters to William Blackwood and David S. Meldrum*, ed. William Blackburn, 1958).

WILLIAM BUTLER YEATS
1865–1939

William Butler Yeats was born in Sandymount, Dublin. His father's family, of English stock, had been in Ireland for at least two hundred years; his mother's, the Pollexfens, hailing originally from Devon, had been for some generations in Sligo, in the west of Ireland. J. B. Yeats, his father, had abandoned law to take up painting, at which he made a somewhat precarious living. The Yeatses were in London from 1874 until 1883, when they returned to Ireland—to Howth, a few miles from Dublin. On leaving high school in Dublin in 1883 Yeats decided to be an artist, with poetry as his avocation, and attended art school; but he soon left, to concentrate on poetry. His first published poems appeared in the *Dublin University Review* in 1885.

Yeats's father was a religious skeptic, but he believed in the "religion of art." Yeats himself, religious by temperament but unable to believe in Christian orthodoxy, sought all his life for traditions of esoteric thought that would compensate for a lost religion. This search led him to various kinds of mysticism, to folklore, theosophy, spiritualism, and neoplatonism—not in any strict chronological order, for he kept returning to and reworking earlier aspects of his thought. In middle life he elaborated a symbolic system of his own, based on a variety of sources, that enabled him to strengthen the pattern and coherence of his poetic imagery. The student of Yeats is constantly coming up against this willful and sometimes baffling esotericism that he cultivated sometimes playfully, sometimes earnestly, sometimes treating it as though it were a body of truths and sometimes as though it were a convenient language of symbols. Modern scholarship has traced most of Yeats's mystical and quasi-mystical ideas to sources that were common to William Blake and Percy Shelley and that sometimes go far back into pre-Platonic beliefs and traditions. But his greatness as a poet lies in his ability to communicate the power and significance of his symbols, by the way he expresses and organizes them, even to readers who know nothing of his system.

Yeats's childhood and young manhood were spent between Dublin, London, and Sligo; and each of these places contributed something to his poetic development. In London in the 1890s he met the important poets of the day; and in 1891 was one of the founders of the Rhymers' Club, whose members included Lionel Johnson, Ernest Dowson, and many other characteristic figures of the 1890s. Here he acquired ideas of poetry that were vaguely Pre-Raphaelite: he believed, in this early stage of his career, that a poet's language should be dreamy, evocative, and ethereal. From the countryside around Sligo he got something much more vigorous and earthy—a knowledge of the life of the peasantry and of their folklore. In Dublin he was influenced by the currents of Irish nationalism and, although often in disagreement with those who wished to use literature for crude political ends, he nevertheless learned to see his poetry as a contribution to a rejuvenated Irish culture. The three influences of Dublin, London, and Sligo did not develop in chronological order—he was going to and fro among these places throughout his early life—and we sometimes find a poem based on Sligo folklore in the midst of a group of dreamy poems written under the influence of the Rhymers' Club or an echo of Irish nationalist feeling in a lyric otherwise wholly Pre-Raphaelite in tone.

We can distinguish quite clearly, however, the main periods into which Yeats's poetic career falls. He began in the tradition of self-conscious Romanticism, which he learned from the London poets of the 1890s. Edmund Spenser and Shelley, and a little later Blake, were also important influences. About the same time he was writing poems (e.g., *The Stolen Child*) deriving from his Sligo experience, with a quiet precision of natural imagery, country place names, and themes from folklore. A little later—i.e., in the latter part of his first period—Dublin literary circles sent him to Standish O'Grady's *History of Ireland: Heroic Period,* where he found the great stories of the heroic age of Irish history, and to George Sigerson's and Douglas Hyde's translations of Gaelic poetry into "that dialect which gets from Gaelic its syntax and keeps its still partly Tudor vocabulary." Even when he plays with Neoplatonic ideas, as in *The Rose of the World* (also the product of the latter part of his early period), he can link them with Irish heroic themes and so give a dignity and a *style* to his imagery not normally associated with this sort of poetic dreaminess. Thus the heroic legends of old Ireland and the folk traditions of the modern Irish countryside provided Yeats with a stiffening for his early dreamlike imagery, which is why even his first, "nineties" phase is productive of interesting poems. *The Lake Isle of Innisfree,* spoiled for some by overanthologizing, is nevertheless a fine poem of its kind: it is the clarity and control shown in the handling of the imagery that keeps all romantic fuzziness out of it and gives it its haunting quality. In *The Man Who Dreamed of Faeryland* he makes something peculiarly effective out of the contrast between human activities and the strangeness of nature. In *The Madness of King Goll* the disturbing sense of the *otherness* of the natural world drives the king mad. (Such contrasts are common in the early Yeats; in his later poetry he tries to resolve what he called these "antinomies" in inclusive symbols; e.g., *Crazy Jane Talks with the Bishop.*)

It is important to realize that Yeats had a habit of revising his earlier poems in later printings, tightening up the language and getting rid of the more self-indulgent romantic imagery. The revised versions are found in his *Collected Poems,* which, therefore, present a somewhat muted picture of his poetic development. For the complete picture one should consult *The Variorum Edition* edited by Peter Allt and Russell K. Alspach (1957).

It was Irish nationalism that first sent Yeats in search of a consistently simpler and more popular style. He tells in one of his autobiographical essays how he sought for a style in which to express the elemental facts about Irish life and aspirations. This led him to the concrete image, as did Hyde's translations from Gaelic folk songs, in which "nothing . . . was abstract, nothing worn-out." But other forces were also working on him. In 1902 a friend gave him the works of the German philosopher Friedrich Nietzsche, to which he responded with great excitement, and it would seem that, in persuading Yeats, the passive love-poet, to get off his knees, Nietzsche's books prompted his search for a more active stance, a more masculine style. Looking back in 1906, he found that he had mistaken the poetic ideal. "Without knowing it, I had come to care for nothing but impersonal beauty. . . . We should ascend out of common interests, the thoughts of the newspapers, of the market place, but only so far as we can carry the normal, passionate, reasoning self, the personality as a whole." The result of the abandonment of "impersonal beauty," and of the desire to "carry the normal, passionate, reasoning self" into his poetry, is seen in the volumes of collected poems, *In the Seven Woods* (1903) and *The Green Helmet and Other Poems* (1910). *The Folly of Being Comforted* and *Adam's Curse* are from the former of these, and one can see immediately how Yeats here combines the colloquial with the formal. This is characteristic of his "second period."

By this time Yeats had met the beautiful actress and violent Irish nationalist Maud Gonne, with whom he was desperately in love for many years, but who persistently refused to marry him. The affair is reflected in many of the poems of his second period, notably *No Second Troy,* published in *The Green Helmet.* He had also met Lady Gregory, Irish writer and promoter of Irish literature, in 1896, and she invited him to spend the following summer at her country house, Coole Park, in Galway. Yeats spent many holidays with Lady Gregory and discovered the attractiveness of the "country house ideal," seeing in an aristocratic life of elegance and leisure in a great house a method of imposing order on chaos and a symbol of the Neoplatonic dance of life. He expresses this view many times in his poetry—e.g., at the end of *A Prayer for My Daughter*—and it became an important part of his complex of attitudes. The middle classes, with their Philistine money grubbing, he detested, and for his ideal characters he looked either below them, to peasants and beggars, or above them, to the aristocracy, for each of these had their own traditions and lived according to them.

It was under Lady Gregory's influence that Yeats became involved in the founding of the Irish National Theatre in 1899. This led to his active participation in problems of play production, which included political problems of censorship, economic problems of paying carpenters and actors, and other aspects of "theater business, management of men." All this had an effect on his style. The reactions of Dublin audiences did not encourage Yeats's trust in popular judgment, and his bitterness with the "Paudeens," middle-class shopkeepers—who seemed to him to be without any dignity, or understanding, or nobility of spirit—produced some of the most effective poems of his third or middle period. He was now becoming more and more of a national figure. Three public controversies had moved him to anger and to poetry; the first over the hounding of Parnell (*To a Shade*), the second over Synge's play *The Playboy of the Western World* in 1907, and the third over the Lane pictures (*September 1913*). In each, the cause for which he fought was defeated by representatives of the Roman Catholic middle class, and at last, bitterly turning his back on Ireland, Yeats moved to England. Then came the Easter Rising (*Easter 1916*), mounted by members of the class and religion that had so long opposed him. Persuaded by Gonne (whose estranged husband was one of the executed leaders of the rising) that "tragic dignity had returned to Ireland," Yeats himself returned. To mark his new commitment, he refurbished, occupied, and renamed "Thoor Ballylee" the Norman tower on Lady Gregory's land that was to become one of the central symbols of his later poetry. In 1922 he was appointed a senator of the recently established Irish Free State and served until 1928, playing an active part not only in promoting the arts but also in general political affairs, in which he supported the views of the Protestant landed class.

Meanwhile Yeats was responding in his own way to the change in poetic taste represented in the poetry and criticism of Ezra Pound and T. S. Eliot immediately before World War I. A gift for epigram had already begun to emerge in his poetry; in the volume titled *The Wild Swans at Coole* (1919) he has a poem citing Walter Savage Landor (the nineteenth-century poet who wrote some fine lapidary verse) and John Donne as masters. To the precision, and the combination of colloquial and formal, that he had achieved early in the century, he now added a metaphysical as well as an epigrammatic element, and this is seen in the later poems of his third period. He also continued his experiments with different kinds of rhythm. At the same time he was continuing his search for a language of symbols and pursuing his esoteric studies. Yeats married in 1917, and his wife proved so sympathetic to his imaginative needs that the automatic writing which for several years she produced (believed by Yeats to have been dictated by spirits) gave him the elements of a symbolic system that he later worked out in his book *A Vision* (1925, 1937) and that he used in all sorts of ways in much of his later poetry. Some of Yeats's poetry is unintelligible without a knowledge of *A Vision*, but the better poems, such as the two on Byzantium, can be appreciated without such knowledge by the experienced reader who responds sensitively to the patterning of the imagery reinforced by the incantatory effect of the rhythms. Some criticism decries attempts by those who are not experts in the background of Yeats's esoteric thought to discuss his poetry and insists that only a detailed knowledge of Yeats's sources can yield his poetic meaning; but while it is true that some particular images do not yield all their significance to those who are ignorant of the background, it is also true that too literal a paraphrase of the symbolism in the light of the sources robs the poems of their power by reducing them to mere exercises in the use of a code.

The Tower (1928) and *The Winding Stair* (1933), from which the poems from *Sailing to Byzantium* through *After Long Silence* have been here selected, represent the mature Yeats at his very best—a realist-symbolist-Metaphysical poet with an uncanny power over words. These volumes represent his fourth and greatest period. Here, in his poems of the 1920s and 1930s, winding stairs, spinning tops, "gyres," spirals of all kinds, are important symbols; not only are they connected with Yeats's philosophy of history and of personality but they also serve as a means of resolving some of those contraries that had arrested him from the beginning. Life is a journey up a spiral staircase; as we grow older we cover the ground we have covered before, only higher up; as we look down the winding stair below us we measure our progress by the number of places where we were but no longer are. The journey is both repetitious and progressive; we go both round and upward. Through symbolic images of this kind Yeats explores the paradoxes of time and change, of growth and identity, of love and age, of life and art, of madness and wisdom.

The Byzantium poems show him trying to escape from the turbulence of life to the calm eternity of art. But in his fifth and final period he returned to the turbulence after (if only partly as a result of) undergoing the Steinach operation to increase his sexual potency in 1934, and his last poems have a controlled yet startling wildness. Yeats's return to life, to "the foul rag-and-bone shop of the heart," is one of the most impressive final phases of any poet's career. "I shall be a sinful man to the end, and think upon my deathbed of all the nights I wasted in my youth," he wrote in old age to a correspondent, and in one of his last letters he wrote: "When I try to put all into a phrase I say, 'Man can embody truth but he cannot know it.' . . . The abstract is not life and everywhere draws out its contradictions. You can refute Hegel but not the Saint or the Song of Sixpence." When he died in January 1939, he left a body of verse that, in variety and power, makes him beyond question the greatest twentieth-century poet of the English language.

The Stolen Child

Where dips the rocky highland
Of Sleuth Wood[1] in the lake,
There lies a leafy island

---

1. This and other places mentioned in the poem are in County Sligo, in northwestern Ireland, where Yeats spent much of his childhood.

Where flapping herons wake
5   The drowsy water-rats;
There we've hid our faery vats,
Full of berries
And of reddest stolen cherries.
Come away, O human child!
10 *To the waters and the wild*
With a faery, hand in hand,
For the world's more full of weeping than you can understand.

Where the wave of moonlight glosses
The dim grey sands with light,
15 Far off by furthest Rosses
We foot it all the night,
Weaving olden dances,
Mingling hands and mingling glances
Till the moon has taken flight;
20 To and fro we leap
And chase the frothy bubbles,
While the world is full of troubles
And is anxious in its sleep.
Come away, O human child!
25 *To the waters and the wild*
With a faery, hand in hand,
For the world's more full of weeping than you can understand.

Where the wandering water gushes
From the hills above Glen-Car,
30 In pools among the rushes
That scarce could bathe a star,
We seek for slumbering trout
And whispering in their ears
Give them unquiet dreams;
35 Leaning softly out
From ferns that drop their tears
Over the young streams.
Come away, O human child!
To the waters and the wild
40 *With a faery, hand in hand,*
For the world's more full of weeping than you can understand.

Away with us he's going,
The solemn-eyed:
He'll hear no more the lowing
45 Of the calves on the warm hillside
Or the kettle on the hob
Sing peace into his breast,
Or see the brown mice bob
Round and round the oatmeal-chest.
50 *For he comes, the human child,*
To the waters and the wild

With a faery, hand in hand,
From a world more full of weeping than he can understand.

1886, 1889

The Rose of the World[1]

Who dreamed that beauty passes like a dream?
For these red lips, with all their mournful pride,
Mournful that no new wonder may betide,
Troy passed away in one high funeral gleam,
5 And Usna's children died.[2]

We and the labouring world are passing by:
Amid men's souls, that waver and give place
Like the pale waters in their wintry race,
Under the passing stars, foam of the sky,
10 Lives on this lonely face.

Bow down, archangels, in your dim abode:
Before you were, or any hearts to beat,
Weary and kind one lingered by His seat;
He made the world to be a grassy road
15 Before her wandering feet.

1892

The Lake Isle of Innisfree[1]

I will arise and go now, and go to Innisfree,
And a small cabin build there, of clay and wattles[2] made;
Nine bean-rows will I have there, a hive for the honey-bee,
And live alone in the bee-loud glade.

5 And I shall have some peace there, for peace comes dropping slow,
Dropping from the veils of the morning to where the cricket sings;
There midnight's all a glimmer, and noon a purple glow,
And evening full of the linnet's wings.

I will arise and go now, for always night and day
10 I hear lake water lapping with low sounds by the shore;
While I stand on the roadway, or on the pavements grey,
I hear it in the deep heart's core.

1890   1890, 1892

---

1. The platonic idea of eternal beauty. "I notice upon reading these poems for the first time for several years that the quality symbolized as The Rose differs from the Intellectual Beauty of Shelley and of Spenser in that I have imagined it as suffering with man and not as something pursued and seen from afar" [Yeats, in 1925].
2. In Old Irish legend the Ulster warrior Naoise, son of Usna or Usnach (pronounced *Úskna*) carried off the beautiful Deirdre, whom King Con-

chubar of Ulster had intended to marry, and with his two brothers took her to Scotland. Eventually Conchubar lured the four of them back to Ireland and killed the three brothers.
1. Island in Lough Gill, County Sligo. "My father had read to me some passage out of [Thoreau's] *Walden*, and I planned to live some day in a cottage on a little island called Innisfree."
2. Stakes interwoven with twigs or branches.

The Sorrow of Love[1]

The brawling of a sparrow in the eaves,
The brilliant moon and all the milky sky,
And all that famous harmony of leaves,
Had blotted out man's image and his cry.

5 A girl arose that had red mournful lips
And seemed the greatness of the world in tears,
Doomed like Odysseus and the labouring ships
And proud as Priam murdered with his peers;[2]

Arose, and on the instant clamorous eaves,
10 A climbing moon upon an empty sky,
And all that lamentation of the leaves,
Could but compose man's image and his cry.

1891   1892, 1925

When You Are Old[1]

When you are old and grey and full of sleep,
And nodding by the fire, take down this book,
And slowly read, and dream of the soft look
Your eyes had once, and of their shadows deep;

5 How many loved your moments of glad grace,
And loved your beauty with love false or true,
But one man loved the pilgrim soul in you,
And loved the sorrows of your changing face;

And bending down beside the glowing bars,[2]
10 Murmur, a little sadly, how Love fled
And paced upon the mountains overhead
And hid his face amid a crowd of stars.

1891   1892

Who Goes with Fergus?[1]

Who will go drive with Fergus now,
And pierce the deep wood's woven shade,

---

1. For the author's revisions while composing this poem, see "Poems in Process," in the appendices to this volume.
2. Odysseus (whom the Romans called Ulysses), hero of Homer's *Odyssey*, which describes how, after having fought in the siege of Troy, he wandered for ten years before reaching his home, the Greek island of Ithaca. Priam was king of Troy at the time of the siege and was killed when the Greeks captured the city.
1. A poem suggested by a sonnet of the 16th-

century French poet Pierre de Ronsard; it begins *"Quand vous serez bien vieille, au soir, à la chandelle"* ("When you are old, sitting at evening by candle light") but ends very differently from Yeats's poem.
2. I.e., of the grate.
1. In a late version of this Irish heroic legend, Fergus, "king of the proud Red Branch Kings," gave up his throne voluntarily to King Conchubar of Ulster to learn by dreaming and meditating the bitter wisdom of the poet and philosopher.

And dance upon the level shore?
Young man, lift up your russet brow,
5   And lift your tender eyelids, maid,
And brood on hopes and fear no more.

And no more turn aside and brood
Upon love's bitter mystery;
For Fergus rules the brazen cars,°   bronze chariots
10   And rules the shadows of the wood,
And the white breast of the dim sea
And all dishevelled wandering stars.

1893

The Man Who Dreamed of Faeryland

He stood among a crowd at Dromahair;[1]
His heart hung all upon a silken dress,
And he had known at last some tenderness,
Before earth took him to her stony care;
5   But when a man poured fish into a pile,
It seemed they raised their little silver heads,
And sang what gold morning or evening sheds
Upon a woven world-forgotten isle
Where people love beside the ravelled[2] seas;
10   That Time can never mar a lover's vows
Under that woven changeless roof of boughs:
The singing shook him out of his new ease.

He wandered by the sands of Lissadell;
His mind ran all on money cares and fears,
15   And he had known at last some prudent years
Before they heaped his grave under the hill;
But while he passed before a plashy place,
A lug-worm with its grey and muddy mouth
Sang that somewhere to north or west or south
20   There dwelt a gay, exulting, gentle race
Under the golden or the silver skies;
That if a dancer stayed his hungry foot
It seemed the sun and moon were in the fruit:
And at that singing he was no more wise.

25   He mused beside the well of Scanavin,
He mused upon his mockers: without fail
His sudden vengeance were a country tale,
When earthy night had drunk his body in;
But one small knot-grass growing by the pool
30   Sang where—unnecessary cruel voice—
Old silence bids its chosen race rejoice,
Whatever ravelled waters rise and fall

1. This and other place names in the poem refer
to places in County Sligo.

2. Tangled; here turbulent.

Or stormy silver fret the gold of day,
And midnight there enfold them like a fleece
35 And lover there by lover be at peace.
The tale drove his fine angry mood away.

He slept under the hill of Lugnagall;
And might have known at last unhaunted sleep
Under that cold and vapour-turbaned steep,
40 Now that the earth had taken man and all:
Did not the worms that spired about his bones
Proclaim with that unwearied, reedy cry
That God has laid His fingers on the sky,
That from those fingers glittering summer runs
45 Upon the dancer by the dreamless wave.
Why should those lovers that no lovers miss
Dream, until God burn Nature with a kiss?
The man has found no comfort in the grave.

1891, 1892

The Secret Rose[1]

Far-off, most secret, and inviolate Rose,
Enfold me in my hour of hours; where those
Who sought thee in the Holy Sepulchre,
Or in the wine-vat, dwell beyond the stir
5   And tumult of defeated dreams; and deep
Among pale eyelids, heavy with the sleep
Men have named beauty. Thy great leaves enfold
The ancient beards, the helms of ruby and gold
Of the crowned Magi;[2] and the king whose eyes
10 Saw the Pierced Hands and Rood° of elder rise   the Cross
In Druid vapour and make the torches dim;
Till vain frenzy awoke and he died;[3] and him
Who met Fand walking among the flaming dew

1. The Rose is a symbol of beauty (see *The Rose of the World*, p. 2368). Yeats reveals in an interesting note how he used his sources: "I find that I have unintentionally changed the old story of Conchubar's death. He did not see the Crucifixion in a vision but was told of it . . . I have imagined Cuchulain meeting Fand 'walking among the flaming dew,' because, I think, of something in Mr. Standish O'Grady's books. [See headnote, p. 2364.] I have founded the man 'who drove the gods out of their liss,' or fort, upon something I have read about Caoilte after the battle of Gabhra, when almost all his companions were killed, driving the gods out of their liss, . . . I have founded 'the proud dreaming kind' upon Fergus, the son of Rogh, but when I wrote my poem here, and in the song in my early book, 'Who will drive with Fergus now?' I only knew him in Mr. Standish O'Grady, . . . I have founded 'him who sold tillage, and house, and goods,' upon something in 'The Red Pony,' a folktale in Mr. Larminie's *West Irish Folk Tales*. A young man 'saw a light before him on the high-road. When he came as far, there was an open box on the road, and a light coming up out of it. He took up the box. There was a lock of hair in it. Presently he had to go to become the servant of a king for his living. There were eleven boys. When they were going out into the stable at ten o'clock, each of them took a light but he. He took no candle at all with him. Each of them went into his own stable. When he went into his stable he opened the box. He left it in a hole in the wall. The light was great. It was twice as much as in the other stables.' The king hears of it, and makes him show him the box. The king says, 'You must go and bring me the woman to whom the hair belongs.' In the end the young man, and not the king, marries the woman."
2. The wise men from the east who came to do homage to the infant Jesus.
3. King Conchubar, in early Christian legend, is said to have died on the day of Christ's crucifixion in a fit of rage at hearing the news. Yeats makes Conchubar see the crucifixion in a vision raised by the magic of the ancient Celtic priests, or Druids (see n. 1). "Pierced Hands": Christ's.

By a grey shore where the wind never blew,
15　And lost the world and Emer for a kiss;[4]
And him[5] who drove the gods out of their liss,°   *fort*
And till a hundred morns had flowered red
Feasted, and wept the barrows of his dead;
And the proud dreaming king[6] who flung the crown
20　And sorrow away, and calling bard and clown
Dwelt among wine-stained wanderers in deep woods;
And him who sold tillage, and house, and goods,
And sought through lands and islands numberless years,
Until he found, with laughter and with tears,
25　A woman of so shining loveliness
That men threshed corn at midnight by a tress,
A little stolen tress.[7] I, too, await
The hour of thy great wind of love and hate.
When shall the stars be blown about the sky,
30　Like the sparks blown out of a smithy, and die?
Surely thine hour has come, thy great wind blows,
Far-off, most secret, and inviolate Rose?

1896, 1897

The Folly of Being Comforted

One that is ever kind said yesterday:
"Your well-belovèd's hair has threads of grey,
And little shadows come about her eyes;
Time can but make it easier to be wise
5　Though now it seem impossible, and so
All that you need is patience."

                  Heart cries, "No,
I have not a crumb of comfort, not a grain.
Time can but make her beauty over again:
Because of that great nobleness of hers
10　The fire that stirs about her, when she stirs,
When all the wild summer was in her gaze."

O heart! O heart! if she'd but turn her head,
You'd know the folly of being comforted.

1902, 1903

Adam's Curse[1]

We sat together at one summer's end,
That beautiful mild woman, your close friend,

---

4. The ancient Irish hero Cuchulain was seduced by Fand away from his wife, Emer.
5. Legendary Irish hero and companion of Oisin, son of Finn, poet and warrior.
6. I.e., Fergus (see 3rd n. 1, p. 2369).
7. See n. 1, p. 2371.

1. To work for a living was the curse imposed by God on Adam after the Fall (Genesis 3.17–19). The poem reflects an incident in Yeats's passionate but hopeless love for the beautiful revolutionary Maud Gonne (see A. N. Jeffares, *W. B. Yeats: Man and Poet*, 1949, pp. 128–29).

And you and I, and talked of poetry.
I said: "A line will take us hours maybe;
5 Yet if it does not seem a moment's thought,
Our stitching and unstitching has been naught.
Better go down upon your marrow-bones
And scrub a kitchen pavement, or break stones
Like an old pauper, in all kinds of weather;
10 For to articulate sweet sounds together
Is to work harder than all these, and yet
Be thought an idler by the noisy set
Of bankers, schoolmasters, and clergymen
The martyrs call the world."

And thereupon
15 That beautiful mild woman for whose sake
There's many a one shall find out all heartache
On finding that her voice is sweet and low
Replied: "To be born woman is to know—
Although they do not talk of it at school—
20 That we must labour to be beautiful."

I said: "It's certain there is no fine thing
Since Adam's fall but needs much labouring.
There have been lovers who thought love should be
So much compounded of high courtesy
25 That they would sigh and quote with learned looks
Precedents out of beautiful old books;
Yet now it seems an idle trade enough."

We sat grown quiet at the name of love;
We saw the last embers of daylight die,
30 And in the trembling blue-green of the sky
A moon, worn as if it had been a shell
Washed by time's waters as they rose and fell
About the stars and broke in days and years.

I had a thought for no one's but your ears:
35 That you were beautiful, and that I strove
To love you in the old high way of love;
That it had all seemed happy, and yet we'd grown
As weary-hearted as that hollow moon.

Nov. 1902   1902, 1903

No Second Troy

Why should I blame her[1] that she filled my days
With misery, or that she would of late
Have taught to ignorant men most violent ways,

1. Maud Gonne.

Or hurled the little streets upon the great,
5 Had they but courage equal to desire?
What could have made her peaceful with a mind
That nobleness made simple as a fire,
With beauty like a tightened bow, a kind
That is not natural in an age like this,
10 Being high and solitary and most stern?
Why, what could she have done, being what she is?
Was there another Troy for her to burn?[2]

Dec. 1908   1910

The Fascination of What's Difficult[1]

The fascination of what's difficult
Has dried the sap out of my veins, and rent
Spontaneous joy and natural content
Out of my heart. There's something ails our colt
5 That must, as if it had not holy blood
Nor on Olympus leaped from cloud to cloud,
Shiver under the lash, strain, sweat and jolt
As though it dragged road-metal. My curse on plays
That have to be set up in fifty ways,
10 On the day's war with every knave and dolt,
Theatre business, management of men.
I swear before the dawn comes round again
I'll find the stable and pull out the bolt.

Sept. 1909–Mar. 1910   1910

September 1913[1]

What need you,[2] being come to sense,
But fumble in a greasy till
And add the halfpence to the pence
And prayer to shivering prayer, until
5 You have dried the marrow from the bone?
For men were born to pray and save:
Romantic Ireland's dead and gone,
It's with O'Leary[3] in the grave.

2. Helen of Troy was the cause of the destruction of the first Troy.
1. Written when Yeats was director-manager of the Abbey Theatre. "Subject. To complain of the fascination of what's difficult. It spoils spontaneity and pleasure, and wastes time. Repeat the line ending difficult three times and rhyme on bolt, exalt, colt, jolt" [Yeats's diary for September 1909].
1. Originally titled Romance in Ireland (On Reading Much of the Correspondence against the Art Gallery) and published in the Irish Times of Sept. 8, 1913. Sir Hugh Lane, Lady Gregory's nephew, had offered his collection of French impressionist paintings to the city of Dublin, provided they were permanently housed in a suitable gallery. Fierce abuse of the paintings and of the proposed design

of the gallery in the Dublin nationalist press caused Lane to send the pictures to the London National Gallery. (Lane was drowned in the Lusitania in 1915; after years of bitter court dispute over an unwitnessed codicil to his will bequeathing the paintings to Dublin, an arrangement was reached in 1959 for the pictures to hang first in Dublin and then in London, for five years at a time.)
2. I.e., members of the new and predominantly Roman Catholic middle class.
3. John O'Leary (1830–1907), Irish nationalist of great courage and integrity who, returning to Dublin in 1885 after five years' imprisonment and fifteen years' exile, drew Yeats and others to the nationalist cause.

Yet they were of a different kind,
10 The names that stilled your childish play,
They have gone about the world like wind,
But little time had they to pray
For whom the hangman's rope was spun,
And what, God help us, could they save?
15 Romantic Ireland's dead and gone,
It's with O'Leary in the grave.

Was it for this the wild geese[4] spread
The grey wing upon every tide;
For this that all that blood was shed,
20 For this Edward Fitzgerald died,
And Robert Emmet and Wolfe Tone,[5]
All that delirium of the brave?
Romantic Ireland's dead and gone,
It's with O'Leary in the grave.

25 Yet could we turn the years again,
And call those exiles as they were
In all their loneliness and pain,
You'd cry, "Some woman's yellow hair
Has maddened every mother's son":
30 They weighed so lightly what they gave.
But let them be, they're dead and gone,
They're with O'Leary in the grave.

Sept. 1913   1913

To a Shade[1]

If you have revisited the town, thin Shade,
Whether to look upon your monument
(I wonder if the builder has been paid)
Or happier-thoughted when the day is spent
5 To drink of that salt breath out of the sea
When grey gulls flit about instead of men,
And the gaunt houses put on majesty:
Let these content you and be gone again;
For they are at their old tricks yet.
                                          A man[2]
10 Of your own passionate serving kind who had brought
In his full hands what, had they only known,
Had given their children's children loftier thought,
Sweeter emotion, working in their veins

---

4. Popular name for the Irishmen who, because of the penal laws against Catholics, were forced to flee to the Continent from 1691 until Catholic Emancipation in 1829. One hundred and twenty thousand fought in the armies of France, Spain, and Austria.
5. Theobald Wolfe Tone (1763–1798), one of the chief founders of the United Irishmen (an Irish nationalist organization), committed suicide in prison in Dublin. Lord Edward Fitzgerald (1763–1798), British officer who, after being dismissed from the army for disloyal activities, joined the United Irishmen, was arrested, and died in prison. Emmet (1778–1803), also an Irish patriot, was executed for treason after a heroic career.
1. The spirit of the great Irish nationalist leader Charles Stewart Parnell (1846–1891).
2. Sir Hugh Lane (see 2nd n. 1, p. 2374).

Like gentle blood, has been driven from the place,
15   And insult heaped upon him for his pains,
And for his open-handedness, disgrace;
Your enemy, an old foul mouth, had set
The pack upon him.[3]
                    Go, unquiet wanderer,
And gather the Glasnevin[4] coverlet
20   About your head till the dust stops your ear,
The time for you to taste of that salt breath
And listen at the corners has not come;
You had enough of sorrow before death—
Away, away! You are safer in the tomb.

Sept. 1913   1913

A Coat

I made my song a coat
Covered with embroideries
Out of old mythologies[1]
From heel to throat;
5   But the fools caught it,[2]
Wore it in the world's eyes
As though they'd wrought it.
Song, let them take it,
For there's more enterprise
10   In walking naked.

1912   1914

The Wild Swans at Coole[1]

The trees are in their autumn beauty,
The woodland paths are dry,
Under the October twilight the water
Mirrors a still sky;
5   Upon the brimming water among the stones
Are nine-and-fifty swans.

The nineteenth autumn has come upon me
Since I first made my count;[2]
I saw, before I had well finished,
10   All suddenly mount

3. William Martin Murphy, proprietor of the *Irish Independent* and *Evening Herald*. He had opposed the Lane benefaction and had earlier supported those who led the attack on Parnell.
4. The cemetery where Parnell is buried.
1. Gaelic legends, which Yeats had read in such translations as those of Standish O'Grady and James Clarence Mangan.

2. Probably a reference to the protégés of Æ [George William Russell], among them Seamus O'Sullivan. Cf. *To a poet who would have me Praise certain Bad Poets, Imitators of His and Mine*.
1. Coole Park, Lady Gregory's country estate, where Yeats was a frequent guest.
2. His first visit had been in 1897 (nineteen years earlier).

And scatter wheeling in great broken rings
Upon their clamorous wings.

I have looked upon those brilliant creatures,
And now my heart is sore.
15 All's changed since I, hearing at twilight,
The first time on this shore,
The bell-beat of their wings above my head,
Trod with a lighter tread.

Unwearied still, lover by lover,[3]
20 They paddle in the cold
Companionable streams or climb the air;
Their hearts have not grown old;
Passion or conquest, wander where they will,
Attend upon them still.

25 But now they drift on the still water,
Mysterious, beautiful;
Among what rushes will they build,
By what lake's edge or pool
Delight men's eyes when I awake some day
30 To find they have flown away?

Oct. 1916   1917

In Memory of Major Robert Gregory[1]

1

Now that we're almost settled in our house[2]
I'll name the friends that cannot sup with us
Beside a fire of turf° in th' ancient tower,   peat
And having talked to some late hour
5 Climb up the narrow winding stair to bed:
Discoverers of forgotten truth[3]
Or mere companions of my youth,
All, all are in my thoughts to-night being dead.

2

Always we'd have the new friend meet the old
10 And we are hurt if either friend seem cold,
And there is salt to lengthen out the smart
In the affections of our heart,
And quarrels are blown up upon that head;
But not a friend that I would bring

3. In Irish legend, the lovers Baile and Aillinn had been changed into swans; also, the subject of Yeats's poem *Baile and Aillinn* (1903).
1. Robert Gregory (1881–1918), the only child of Lady Gregory, Yeats's friend, patron, and codirector of the Abbey Theatre. At its first printing, this elegy carried the following note: "(Major Robert Gregory, R.F.C. [Royal Flying Corps], M.C. [Military Cross], Legion of Honour, was killed in action on the Italian Front, January 23, 1918)."
2. Thoor Ballylee, the Norman tower and adjoining cottages Yeats had purchased for himself and his wife.
3. Those interested in the occult tradition.

15 This night can set us quarrelling,
For all that come into my mind are dead.

3

Lionel Johnson[4] comes the first to mind,
That loved his learning better than mankind,
Though courteous to the worst; much falling he
20 Brooded upon sanctity
Till all his Greek and Latin learning seemed
A long blast upon the horn that brought
A little nearer to his thought
A measureless consummation that he dreamed.

4

25 And that enquiring man John Synge[5] comes next,
That dying chose the living world for text
And never could have rested in the tomb
But that, long travelling, he had come
Towards nightfall upon certain set apart
30 In a most desolate stony place,[6]
Towards nightfall upon a race
Passionate and simple like his heart.

5

And then I think of old George Pollexfen,[7]
In muscular youth well known to Mayo[8] men
35 For horsemanship at meets or at racecourses,
That could have shown how pure-bred horses
And solid men, for all their passion, live
But as the outrageous stars incline
By opposition, square and trine;[9]
40 Having grown sluggish and contemplative.

6

They were my close companions many a year,
A portion of my mind and life, as it were,
And now their breathless faces seem to look
Out of some old picture-book;
45 I am accustomed to their lack of breath,
But not that my dear friend's dear son,
Our Sidney[1] and our perfect man,
Could share in that discourtesy of death.

---

4. English poet and scholar (1867–1902).
5. Irish poet and playwright (1871–1909), who was codirector—with Yeats and Lady Gregory—of the Abbey Theatre.
6. The Aran Islands off the west coast of Ireland, the setting of such Synge plays as *The Playboy of the Western World* (1907).
7. Yeats's maternal uncle (1839–1910), with whom he had spent holidays in Sligo as a young man.

8. Irish county north of Galway.
9. Terms from astrology, a pseudoscience in which both Pollexfen and Yeats were interested.
1. Robert Gregory had an Elizabethan versatility like that of Sir Philip Sidney (1554–1586), poet, scholar, and soldier, who died young and in battle overseas. Yeats's admiration for Gregory was more qualified than his elegy suggests (see n. 7, p. 2380).

7

For all things the delighted eye now sees
50 Were loved by him;[2] the old storm-broken trees
That cast their shadows upon road and bridge;
The tower set on the stream's edge;
The ford where drinking cattle make a stir
Nightly, and startled by that sound
55 The water-hen must change her ground;
He might have been your heartiest welcomer.

8

When with the Galway foxhounds he would ride
From Castle Taylor to the Roxborough side[3]
Or Esserkelly plain, few kept his pace;
60 At Mooneen he had leaped a place
So perilous that half the astonished meet
Had shut their eyes; and where was it
He rode a race without a bit?
And yet his mind outran the horses' feet.

9

65 We dreamed that a great painter had been born[4]
To cold Clare[5] rock and Galway rock and thorn,
To that stern colour and that delicate line
That are our secret discipline
Wherein the gazing heart doubles her might.
70 Soldier, scholar, horseman, he,
And yet he had the intensity
To have published all to be a world's delight.

10

What other could so well have counselled us
In all lovely intricacies of a house
75 As he that practised or that understood
All work in metal or in wood,
In moulded plaster or in carven stone?
Soldier, scholar, horseman, he,
And all he did done perfectly
80 As though he had but that one trade alone.

11

Some burn damp faggots,[6] others may consume
The entire combustible world in one small room
As though dried straw, and if we turn about
The bare chimney is gone black out
85 Because the work had finished in that flare.

---

2. Thoor Ballylee had formerly been owned by the Gregory family.
3. Big country houses in County Galway. Roxborough was Lady Gregory's childhood home.
4. "Robert Gregory painted the Burren Hills and thereby found what promised to grow into a great style, but he had hardly found it before he was killed" (Yeats, *Essays and Introductions*, p. 209).
5. A county south of County Galway.
6. Bundle of sticks or small branches used for fuel.

Soldier, scholar, horseman, he,
As 'twere all life's epitome,[7]
What made us dream that he could comb grey hair?

12

I had thought, seeing how bitter is that wind
90   That shakes the shutter, to have brought to mind
All those that manhood tried, or childhood loved
Or boyish intellect approved,
With some appropriate commentary on each;
Until imagination brought
95   A fitter welcome; but a thought
Of that late death took all my heart for speech.

June 1918   1918

Easter 1916[1]

I have met them at close of day
Coming with vivid faces
From counter or desk among grey
Eighteenth-century houses.
5   I have passed with a nod of the head
Or polite meaningless words,
Or have lingered awhile and said
Polite meaningless words,
And thought before I had done
10   Of a mocking tale or a gibe
To please a companion
Around the fire at the club,
Being certain that they and I
But lived where motley[2] is worn:
15   All changed, changed utterly:
A terrible beauty is born.

That woman's days were spent
In ignorant good-will,
Her nights in argument
20   Until her voice grew shrill.
What voice more sweet than hers
When, young and beautiful,
She rode to harriers?[3]

7. Cf. Dryden's scathingly satirical portrait of George Villiers (1628–1687), second duke of Buckingham, *Absalom and Achitophel: A Poem*, lines 544–52.

1. This title, with its resemblance to *September 1913*, suggests that the poem is a palinode (one in which the author retracts something said in a former poem). On Easter Monday of 1916, Irish nationalists launched a heroic but unsuccessful revolt against the British government; the week of street fighting that followed is known as the Easter Rebellion. As a result, a number of the nationalists were executed: Britain, at war with Germany, was in no mood to tolerate Irish agitation for independence—which was supported, for obvious reasons, by Germany. Yeats knew the chief rebels personally.

2. Jester's parti-colored costume.

3. Constance Gore-Booth (afterward Countess Markiewicz), a member of the Sligo county aristocracy. A gay and beautiful woman, she had annoyed Yeats by becoming an embittered nationalist.

This man had kept a school
25 And rode our wingèd horse;[4]
This other his helper and friend[5]
Was coming into his force;
He might have won fame in the end,
So sensitive his nature seemed,
30 So daring and sweet his thought.
This other man I had dreamed
A drunken, vainglorious lout.[6]
He had done most bitter wrong
To some who are near my heart,
35 Yet I number him in the song;
He, too, has resigned his part
In the casual comedy;
He, too, has been changed in his turn,
Transformed utterly:
40 A terrible beauty is born.

Hearts with one purpose alone
Through summer and winter seem
Enchanted to a stone
To trouble the living stream.
45 The horse that comes from the road,
The rider, the birds that range
From cloud to tumbling cloud,
Minute by minute they change;
A shadow of cloud on the stream
50 Changes minute by minute;
A horse-hoof slides on the brim,
And a horse plashes within it;
The long-legged moor-hens dive,
And hens to moor-cocks call;
55 Minute by minute they live:
The stone's in the midst of all.

Too long a sacrifice
Can make a stone of the heart.
O when may it suffice?
60 That is Heaven's part, our part
To murmur name upon name,
As a mother names her child
When sleep at last has come
On limbs that had run wild.
65 What is it but nightfall?
No, no, not night but death;
Was it needless death after all?
For England may keep faith
For all that is done and said.

---

4. Padraic Pearse, a schoolmaster, a leader in the movement to restore the Gaelic language in Ireland, and a poet (hence the reference to "our wingèd horse"—Pegasus, the horse of the Muses).

5. Thomas MacDonagh.
6. Major John MacBride. Gonne, to Yeats's great disgust, had married MacBride in 1903, only to be separated from him after two years.

70   We know their dream; enough
        To know they dreamed and are dead;
        And what if excess of love
        Bewildered them till they died?
        I write it out in a verse—
75   MacDonagh and MacBride
        And Connolly[7] and Pearse
        Now and in time to be,
        Wherever green is worn,
        Are changed, changed utterly:
80   A terrible beauty is born.

May–Sept. 1916   1916, 1920

The Second Coming[1]

Turning and turning in the widening gyre
The falcon cannot hear the falconer;
Things fall apart; the center cannot hold;
Mere anarchy is loosed upon the world,
5   The blood-dimmed tide is loosed, and everywhere
The ceremony of innocence is drowned;
The best lack all conviction, while the worst
Are full of passionate intensity.[2]
Surely some revelation is at hand;
10   Surely the Second Coming is at hand.
The Second Coming! Hardly are those words out
When a vast image out of *Spiritus Mundi*[3]
Troubles my sight: somewhere in sands of the desert
A shape with lion body and the head of a man,
15   A gaze blank and pitiless as the sun,
Is moving its slow thighs, while all about it
Reel shadows of the indignant desert birds.
The darkness drops again; but now I know
That twenty centuries of stony sleep
20   Were vexed to nightmare by a rocking cradle,[4]
And what rough beast, its hour come round at last,
Slouches towards Bethlehem to be born?

Jan. 1919   1920, 1921

---

7. James Connolly, Pearse's partner in leading the insurrection. Like the other rebels named here, he was executed by firing squad.
1. This poem expresses Yeats's sense of the dissolution of the civilization of his time, the end of one cycle of history and the approach of another. He called each cycle of history a "gyre" (line 1)–literally a circular or spiral turn (Yeats pronounced it with a hard g). The birth of Christ brought to an end the cycle that had lasted from what Yeats called the "Babylonian mathematical starlight" (2000 B.C.E.) to the dissolution of Greco-Roman culture. "What if the irrational return?" Yeats asked in his prose work *A Vision.* "What if the circle begin again?" He speculates that "we may be

about to accept the most implacable authority the world has known."
2. Lines 4–8 refer to the Russian Revolution of 1917. "The ceremony of innocence" suggests Yeats's view of ritual as the basis of civilized living. Cf. the last stanza of *A Prayer for My Daughter* (p. 2384).
3. The spirit or soul of the universe, with which all individual souls are connected through the "Great Memory," which Yeats held to be a universal subconscious in which the human race preserves its past memories. It is thus a source of symbolic images for the poet.
4. I.e., the cradle of the infant Christ.

A Prayer for My Daughter[1]

Once more the storm is howling, and half hid
Under this cradle-hood and coverlid
My child sleeps on. There is no obstacle
But Gregory's wood[2] and one bare hill
5   Whereby the haystack- and roof-levelling wind,
Bred on the Atlantic, can be stayed;
And for an hour I have walked and prayed
Because of the great gloom that is in my mind.

I have walked and prayed for this young child an hour
10   And heard the sea-wind scream upon the tower,
And under the arches of the bridge, and scream
In the elms above the flooded stream;
Imagining in excited reverie
That the future years had come,
15   Dancing to a frenzied drum,
Out of the murderous innocence of the sea.[3]

May she be granted beauty and yet not
Beauty to make a stranger's eye distraught,
Or hers before a looking-glass, for such,
20   Being made beautiful overmuch,
Consider beauty a sufficient end,
Lose natural kindness and maybe
The heart-revealing intimacy
That chooses right, and never find a friend.

25   Helen being chosen found life flat and dull
And later had much trouble from a fool,[4]
While that great Queen, that rose out of the spray,[5]
Being fatherless could have her way
Yet chose a bandy-leggèd smith for man.
30   It's certain that fine women eat
A crazy salad with their meat
Whereby the Horn of Plenty is undone.

In courtesy I'd have her chiefly learned;
Hearts are not had as a gift but hearts are earned
35   By those that are not entirely beautiful;
Yet many, that have played the fool
For beauty's very self, has charm made wise,
And many a poor man that has roved,

---

1. Yeats's daughter, Anne Butler, was born on February 26, 1919, in Dublin and brought home to the refitted Norman tower of Thoor Ballylee (Ballylee Castle) in Galway, where Yeats lived; it is not far from Coole Park.
2. Originally part of the Gregory estate, which had once also included Thoor Ballylee.

3. A reference to Yeats's visions of the future (cf. *The Second Coming*, p. 2382).
4. Menelaus, the husband of Helen, whom she deserted in favor of Paris.
5. Venus, wife (in the *Odyssey* and later accounts) of Vulcan, "bandy-leggèd" god of fire and forge (line 29).

Loved and thought himself beloved,
40 From a glad kindness cannot take his eyes.

May she become a flourishing hidden tree
That all her thoughts may like the linnet° be,   *songbird*
And have no business but dispensing round
Their magnanimities of sound,
45 Not but in merriment begin a chase,
Nor but in merriment a quarrel.
O may she live like some green laurel
Rooted in one dear perpetual place.

My mind, because the minds that I have loved,
50 The sort of beauty that I have approved,
Prosper but little, has dried up of late,
Yet knows that to be choked with hate
May well be of all evil chances chief.
If there's no hatred in a mind
55 Assault and battery of the wind
Can never tear the linnet from the leaf.

An intellectual hatred is the worst,
So let her think opinions are accursed.
Have I not seen the loveliest woman[6] born
60 Out of the mouth of Plenty's horn,
Because of her opinionated mind
Barter that horn and every good
By quiet natures understood
For an old bellows full of angry wind?

65 Considering that, all hatred driven hence,
The soul recovers radical innocence
And learns at last that it is self-delighting,
Self-appeasing, self-affrighting,
And that its own sweet will is Heaven's will;
70 She can, though every face should scowl
And every windy quarter howl
Or every bellows burst, be happy still.

And may her bridegroom bring her to a house
Where all's accustomed, ceremonious;
75 For arrogance and hatred are the wares
Peddled in the thoroughfares.
How but in custom and in ceremony
Are innocence and beauty born?
Ceremony's a name for the rich horn,
80 And custom for the spreading laurel tree.

Feb.–June 1919   1919, 1921

6. Maud Gonne.

Sailing to Byzantium[1]

I

That is no country for old men. The young
In one another's arms, birds in the trees
—Those dying generations—at their song,
The salmon-falls, the mackerel-crowded seas,
5   Fish, flesh, or fowl, commend all summer long
Whatever is begotten, born, and dies.
Caught in that sensual music all neglect
Monuments of unageing intellect.

2

An aged man is but a paltry thing,
10   A tattered coat upon a stick, unless
Soul clap its hands and sing, and louder sing
For every tatter in its mortal dress,
Nor is there singing school but studying
Monuments of its own magnificence;
15   And therefore I have sailed the seas and come
To the holy city of Byzantium.

3

O sages standing in God's holy fire
As in the gold mosaic of a wall,[2]
Come from the holy fire, perne in a gyre,[3]
20   And be the singing-masters of my soul.
Consume my heart away; sick with desire
And fastened to a dying animal
It knows not what it is; and gather me
Into the artifice of eternity.

4

25   Once out of nature I shall never take
My bodily form from any natural thing,
But such a form as Grecian goldsmiths make
Of hammered gold and gold enamelling
To keep a drowsy Emperor awake;[4]

---

1. Yeats wrote in *A Vision:* "I think that if I could be given a month of antiquity and leave to spend it where I chose, I would spend it in Byzantium [modern Istanbul] a little before Justinian opened St. Sophia and closed the Academy of Plato [i.e., ca. 535 C.E.]. . . . I think that in early Byzantium, maybe never before or since in recorded history, religious, aesthetic, and practical life were one, that architects and artificers . . . spoke to the multitude in gold and silver. The painter, the mosaic worker, the worker in gold and silver, the illuminator of sacred books were almost impersonal, almost perhaps without the consciousness of individual design, absorbed in their subject matter and that the vision of a whole people."

2. Yeats had in mind the mosaic frieze of the holy martyrs in the church of San Apollinare Nuovo at Ravenna, which he had visited in 1907.
3. I.e., whirl round in a spiral motion. "Perne": or pirn; literally a bobbin, reel, or spool, on which something is wound. It became a favorite word of Yeats's, used as a verb meaning "to spin round"; he associated the spinning with the spinning of fate.
4. "I have read somewhere," Yeats wrote, "that in the Emperor's palace at Byzantium was a tree made of gold and silver, and artificial birds that sang." Cf. also Hans Christian Andersen's *Emperor's Nightingale,* which may have been in Yeats's mind at the time.

30 Or set upon a golden bough to sing
To lords and ladies of Byzantium
Of what is past, or passing, or to come.

Sept. 1926   1927

Leda and the Swan[1]

A sudden blow: the great wings beating still
Above the staggering girl, her thighs caressed
By the dark webs, her nape caught in his bill,
He holds her helpless breast upon his breast.

5   How can those terrified vague fingers push
The feathered glory from her loosening thighs?
And how can body, laid in that white rush,
But feel the strange heart beating where it lies?

A shudder in the loins engenders there
10 The broken wall, the burning roof and tower[2]
And Agamemnon dead.
                                        Being so caught up,
So mastered by the brute blood of the air,
Did she put on his knowledge with his power
Before the indifferent beak could let her drop?

Sept. 1923   1924, 1928

Among School Children

I

I walk through the long schoolroom questioning;
A kind old nun in a white hood replies;
The children learn to cipher and to sing,
To study reading-books and history,
5   To cut and sew, be neat in everything
In the best modern way—the children's eyes
In momentary wonder stare upon
A sixty-year-old smiling public man.

1. In Greek mythology Zeus visited Leda in the form of a swan. As a result of the union Leda gave birth to Helen and to Clytemnestra (wife of Agamemnon). Yeats saw Zeus's visit to Leda as an "annunciation," marking the beginning of Greek civilization: "I imagine the annunciation that founded Greece as made to Leda, remembering that they showed in a Spartan temple, strung up to the roof as a holy relic, an unhatched egg of hers, and that from one of her eggs came love and from the other war" (*A Vision*). In the original Cuala Press edition Yeats noted: "I wrote *Leda and the Swan* because the editor of a political review asked me for a poem. I thought, 'After the individualist, demagogic movement, founded by Hobbes and popularized by the Encyclopedists and the French Revolution, we have a soil so exhausted that it cannot grow that crop again for centuries.' Then I thought, 'Nothing is now possible but some movement from above preceded by some violent annunciation.' My fancy began to play with Leda and the Swan for metaphor, and I began this poem; but as I wrote, bird and lady took such possession of the scene that all politics went out of it, and my friend tells me that his 'conservative readers would misunderstand the poem.'" For the author's revisions while composing this poem, see "Poems in Process," in the appendices to this volume.
2. I.e., the destruction of Troy, caused by Helen's elopement with the Trojan Paris. Agamemnon was murdered by his wife, Clytemnestra, the other daughter of Leda and the Swan.

2

I dream of a Ledaean[1] body, bent
10   Above a sinking fire, a tale that she
Told of a harsh reproof, or trivial event
That changed some childish day to tragedy—
Told, and it seemed that our two natures blent
Into a sphere from youthful sympathy,
15   Or else, to alter Plato's parable,
Into the yolk and white of the one shell.[2]

3

And thinking of that fit of grief or rage
I look upon one child or t'other there
And wonder if she stood so at that age—
20   For even daughters of the swan can share
Something of every paddler's heritage—
And had that colour upon cheek or hair,
And thereupon my heart is driven wild:
She stands before me as a living child.

4

25   Her present image floats into the mind—
Did Quattrocento[3] finger fashion it
Hollow of cheek as though it drank the wind
And took a mess of shadows for its meat?
And I though never of Ledaean kind
30   Had pretty plumage once—enough of that,
Better to smile on all that smile, and show
There is a comfortable kind of old scarecrow.

5

What youthful mother, a shape upon her lap
Honey of generation had betrayed,
35   And that must sleep, shriek, struggle to escape
As recollection or the drug decide,[4]
Would think her son, did she but see that shape
With sixty or more winters on its head,
A compensation for the pang of his birth,
40   Or the uncertainty of his setting forth?

1. Adjective from "Leda," meaning "like Helen of Troy" (Leda's daughter). The reference is to Maud Gonne (as also in lines 19–28).
2. In Plato's *Symposium* Aristophanes explains love by supposing that "the primeval man was round and had four hands and four feet, back and sides forming a circle, one head with two faces," and was subsequently divided into two. "After the division, the two parts of man, each desiring his other half, came together, and threw their arms about one another eager to grow into one." The fact that Helen was born from an egg (as the daughter of Leda and the Swan) suggests Yeats's image for such a union.
3. I.e., 15th century; a reference to Italian pain-ters the period.
4. I have taken the 'honey of generation' from Por-phyry's essay on 'The Cave of the Nymphs,' but find no warrant in Porphyry for considering it the 'drug' that destroys the 'recollection' of prenatal freedom [Yeats's note]. Porphyry was a Neopla-tonic philosopher of the 3rd century C.E. "Honey of generation," by blotting out the memory of pre-natal happiness, "betrays" an infant to be born into this world. The infant will either "sleep" or "strug-gle to escape" (from this world), depending on whether the drug works or the recollection of bliss-ful prenatal life overcomes the oblivion caused by the drug.

6

Plato thought nature but a spume that plays
Upon a ghostly paradigm of things;
Solider Aristotle played the taws
Upon the bottom of a king of kings;[5]
45   World-famous golden-thighed Pythagoras[6]
Fingered upon a fiddle-stick or strings
What a star sang and careless Muses heard:
Old clothes upon old sticks to scare a bird.[7]

7

Both nuns and mothers worship images,[8]
50   But those the candles light are not as those
That animate a mother's reveries,
But keep a marble or a bronze repose.
And yet they too break hearts—O Presences
That passion, piety or affection knows,
55   And that all heavenly glory symbolise—
O self-born mockers of man's enterprise;

8

Labour is blossoming or dancing where
The body is not bruised to pleasure soul,
Nor beauty born out of its own despair,
60   Nor blear-eyed wisdom out of midnight oil.
O chestnut tree, great-rooted blossomer,
Are you the leaf, the blossom, or the bole?
O body swayed to music, O brightening glance,
How can we know the dancer from the dance?

June 1926   1927

A Dialogue of Self and Soul[1]

1

MY SOUL. I summon to the winding ancient stair;
Set all your mind upon the steep ascent,
Upon the broken, crumbling battlement,
Upon the breathless starlit air,
5   Upon the star that marks the hidden pole;
Fix every wandering thought upon

5. I.e., Plato thought nature was a mere appearance ("spume") veiling the ultimate spiritual and mathematical reality ("ghostly paradigm"). Aristotle was "solider" in that he believed that form really inhered in the matter of nature and thus that nature itself had reality. Aristotle was tutor to Alexander the Great and disciplined him by applying the "taws" or strap.
6. Greek philosopher (early 6th century B.C.E.), interested in mathematics and the mathematical study of acoustics and music. His disciples, the Pythagoreans, developed a mystical philosophy of numerical relations and united the notions of astronomical and mathematical relations in the

theory of the music of the spheres. Pythagoreans regarded their master with veneration as a god with a golden thigh.
7. A contemptuous description of the philosophies of Plato, Aristotle, and Pythagoras.
8. Nuns worship images of Christ or the Virgin; mothers worship their own inward images of their children.
1. In a letter of Oct. 2, 1923, Yeats wrote, "I am writing a new tower poem 'Sword and Tower,' which is a choice of rebirth rather than deliverance from birth. I make the Japanese sword and its silk covering my symbol of life." The sword was a present from a friend, Junzo Sato.

That quarter where all thought is done:
Who can distinguish darkness from the soul?

MY SELF. The consecrated blade upon my knees
10   Is Sato's ancient blade, still as it was,
Still razor-keen, still like a looking-glass
Unspotted by the centuries;
That flowering, silken, old embroidery, torn
From some court-lady's dress and round
15   The wooden scabbard bound and wound,
Can, tattered, still protect, faded adorn.

MY SOUL. Why should the imagination of a man
Long past his prime remember things that are
Emblematical of love and war?
20   Think of ancestral night that can,
If but imagination scorn the earth
And intellect its wandering
To this and that and t'other thing,
Deliver from the crime of death and birth.

25   MY SELF. Montashigi, third of his family, fashioned it
Five hundred years ago, about it lie
Flowers from I know not what embroidery—
Heart's purple—and all these I set
For emblems of the day against the tower
30   Emblematical of the night,
And claim as by a soldier's right
A charter to commit the crime once more.

MY SOUL. Such fullness in that quarter overflows
And falls into the basin of the mind
35   That man is stricken deaf and dumb and blind,
For intellect no longer knows
Is from *Ought*, or *Knower* from the *Known*—
That is to say, ascends to Heaven;
Only the dead can be forgiven;
40   But when I think of that my tongue's a stone.

2

MY SELF. A living man is blind and drinks his drop.
What matter if the ditches are impure?
What matter if I live it all once more?
Endure that toil of growing up;
45   The ignominy of boyhood; the distress
Of boyhood changing into man;
The unfinished man and his pain
Brought face to face with his own clumsiness;

The finished man among his enemies?—
50   How in the name of Heaven can he escape
That defiling and disfigured shape

The mirror of malicious eyes
Casts upon his eyes until at last
He thinks that shape must be his shape?
55 And what's the good of an escape
If honour find him in the wintry blast?

I am content to live it all again
And yet again, if it be life to pitch
Into the frog-spawn of a blind man's ditch,
60 A blind man battering blind men;
Or into that most fecund ditch of all,
The folly that man does
Or must suffer, if he woos
A proud woman not kindred of his soul.

65 I am content to follow to its source
Every event in action or in thought;
Measure the lot; forgive myself the lot!
When such as I cast out remorse
So great a sweetness flows into the breast
70 We must laugh and we must sing,
We are blest by everything,
Everything we look upon is blest.

July–Dec. 1927   1929

For Anne Gregory

"Never shall a young man,
Thrown into despair
By those great honey-coloured
Ramparts at your ear,
5 Love you for yourself alone
And not your yellow hair."

"But I can get a hair-dye
And set such colour there,
Brown, or black, or carrot,
10 That young men in despair
May love me for myself alone
And not my yellow hair."

"I heard an old religious man
But yesternight declare
15 That he had found a text to prove
That only God, my dear,
Could love you for yourself alone
And not your yellow hair."

Sept. 1930   1931, 1932

Byzantium[1]

The unpurged images of day recede;
The Emperor's drunken soldiery are abed;
Night resonance recedes, night-walkers' song
After great cathedral gong;
5 A starlit or a moonlit dome[2] disdains
All that man is,
All mere complexities,
The fury and the mire° of human veins.   *deep mud*

Before me floats an image, man or shade,
10 Shade more than man, more image than a shade;
For Hades'[3] bobbin bound in mummy-cloth
May unwind the winding path;[4]
A mouth that has no moisture and no breath
Breathless mouths may summon;
15 I hail the superhuman;
I call it death-in-life and life-in-death.[5]

Miracle, bird or golden handiwork,
More miracle than bird or handiwork,
Planted on the star-lit golden bough,[6]
20 Can like the cocks of Hades crow,
Or, by the moon embittered, scorn aloud
In glory of changeless metal
Common bird or petal
And all complexities of mire or blood.

25 At midnight on the Emperor's pavement flit
Flames that no faggot feeds, nor steel has lit,
Nor storm disturbs, flames begotten of flame,
Where blood-begotten spirits come
And all complexities of fury leave,
30 Dying into a dance,
An agony of trance,
An agony of flame[7] that cannot singe a sleeve.

1. On October 4, 1930, Yeats sent his friend Sturge Moore a copy of *Byzantium,* saying, "The poem originates from a criticism of yours. You objected to the last verse of 'Sailing to Byzantium' because a bird made by a goldsmith was just as natural as anything else. That showed me that the idea needed exposition." The previous April, Yeats had noted in his diary: "Subject for a poem / Describe Byzantium as it is in the system towards the end of the first Christian millennium. A walking mummy; flames at the street corners where the soul is purified. Birds of hammered gold singing in the golden trees. In the harbour [dolphins] offering their backs to the wailing dead that they may carry them to paradise."
2. Of the great church of St. Sophia.
3. Hell in Greek mythology.
4. The spool of people's fate, which spins their destiny and which is symbolized by the wrappings around a mummy, may lead people, as it unwinds, to the realm of pure spirit.
5. Cf. Coleridge's *The Rime of the Ancient Mariner,* line 193: "The Night-mare LIFE-IN-DEATH was she."
6. Part of the death-world of artifice and eternity; it is opposed to a real, living bough, which would be lighted by the sun or the moon. Reminiscent of the golden bough that guides Aeneas through the underworld in Virgil's *Aeneid,* it is also associated with the mystical tree of the esoteric Hebrew doctrine of the cabala, in whose branches "the birds lodge and build their nests; that is, the souls or angels have their place." The cock, that crows at dawn, appears on Roman tombstones as a herald of rebirth (line 20).
7. This phrase was suggested to Yeats by a Japanese Nō play, *Motomezuka,* wherein a young girl suffers from perpetual burning, which is a sense of

Astraddle on the dolphin's mire and blood,[8]
Spirit after spirit! The smithies break the flood,
35 The golden smithies of the Emperor!
Marbles of the dancing floor
Break bitter furies of complexity,
Those images that yet
Fresh images beget,
40 That dolphin-torn, that gong-tormented sea.

Sept. 1930   1932

Crazy Jane Talks with the Bishop[1]

I met the Bishop on the road
And much said he and I.
"Those breasts are flat and fallen now,
Those veins must soon be dry;
5 Live in a heavenly mansion,
Not in some foul sty."

"Fair and foul are near of kin,
And fair needs foul," I cried.[2]
"My friends are gone, but that's a truth
10 Nor grave nor bed denied,
Learned in bodily lowliness
And in the heart's pride.

"A woman can be proud and stiff
When on love intent;
15 But Love has pitched his mansion in
The place of excrement;
For nothing can be sole or whole
That has not been rent."

Nov. 1931   1932

After Long Silence[1]

Speech after long silence; it is right,
All other lovers being estranged or dead,
Unfriendly lamplight hid under its shade,
The curtains drawn upon unfriendly night,
5 That we descant and yet again descant
Upon the supreme theme of Art and Song:

---

her own guilt. A priest tells her that the flames will cease if she no longer believes in their reality; she finds herself incapable of disbelief, however, and the play ends in "the dance of her agony."
8. The dolphin, in ancient art, was a symbol of the soul in transit from one state to another.
1. One of a series of poems dealing with the paradox that wisdom may reside with fools and beg-

gars (such as Jane) rather than with the respectable representatives of orthodoxy (such as the bishop).
2. Cf. Shakespeare's Macbeth 1.1.10: "Fair is foul, and foul is fair."
1. For the author's revisions while composing this poem, see "Poems in Process," in the appendices to this volume.

Bodily decrepitude is wisdom; young
We loved each other and were ignorant.

Nov. 1929   1932

Lapis Lazuli[1]

(*For Harry Clifton*)

I have heard that hysterical women say
They are sick of the palette and fiddle-bow,
Of poets that are always gay,
For everybody knows or else should know
5   That if nothing drastic is done
Aeroplane and Zeppelin will come out,
Pitch like King Billy[2] bomb-balls in
Until the town lie beaten flat.

All perform their tragic play,
10 There struts Hamlet, there is Lear,
That's Ophelia, that Cordelia;
Yet they, should the last scene be there,
The great stage curtain about to drop,
If worthy their prominent part in the play,
15 Do not break up their lines to weep.
They know that Hamlet and Lear are gay;
Gaiety transfiguring all that dread.
All men have aimed at, found and lost;
Black out; Heaven blazing into the head:
20 Tragedy wrought to its uttermost.
Though Hamlet rambles and Lear rages,
And all the drop-scenes drop at once
Upon a hundred thousand stages,
It cannot grow by an inch or an ounce.

25 On their own feet they came, or on shipboard,
Camel-back, horse-back, ass-back, mule-back,
Old civilisations put to the sword.
Then they and their wisdom went to rack:
No handiwork of Callimachus,[3]

1. A deep blue stone. "I notice that you have much lapis lazuli; someone has sent me a present of a great piece carved by some Chinese sculptor into the semblance of a mountain with temple, trees, paths, and an ascetic and pupil about to climb the mountain. Ascetic, pupil, hard stone, eternal theme of the sensual east. The heroic cry in the midst of despair. But no, I am wrong, the east has its solutions always and therefore knows nothing of tragedy. It is we, not the east, that must raise the heroic cry" [Yeats to Dorothy Wellesley, July 6, 1935].
2. King William III (William of Orange), who defeated the army of King James II at the Battle of the Boyne in 1690. "Zeppelin": a cigar-shaped airship invented by a German, Count F. von Zeppelin.
3. Greek sculptor (5th century B.C.E.), supposedly the originator of the Corinthian column and of the use of the running drill to imitate folds in drapery in statues. Yeats wrote of him: "With Callimachus pure Ionic revives again . . . and upon the only example of his work known to us, a marble chair, a Persian is represented, and may one not discover a Persian symbol in that bronze lamp, shaped like a palm . . . ? But he was an archaistic workman, and those who set him to work brought back public life to an older form" (*A Vision*).

30 Who handled marble as if it were bronze,
Made draperies that seemed to rise
When sea-wind swept the corner, stands;
His long lamp-chimney shaped like the stem
Of a slender palm, stood but a day;
35 All things fall and are built again,
And those that build them again are gay.

Two Chinamen, behind them a third,
Are carved in lapis lazuli,
Over them flies a long-legged bird,
40 A symbol of longevity;
The third, doubtless a serving-man,
Carries a musical instrument.

Every discolouration of the stone,
Every accidental crack or dent,
45 Seems a water-course or an avalanche,
Or lofty slope where it still snows
Though doubtless plum or cherry-branch
Sweetens the little half-way house
Those Chinamen climb towards, and I
50 Delight to imagine them seated there;
There, on the mountain and the sky,
On all the tragic scene they stare.
One asks for mournful melodies;
Accomplished fingers begin to play.
55 Their eyes mid many wrinkles, their eyes,
Their ancient, glittering eyes, are gay.

July 1936   1938

Long-Legged Fly

That civilisation may not sink,
Its great battle lost,
Quiet the dog, tether the pony
To a distant post;
5 Our master Caesar[1] is in the tent
Where the maps are spread,
His eye fixed upon nothing,
A hand under his head.
Like a long-legged fly upon the stream
10 *His mind moves upon silence.*

That the topless towers be burnt
And men recall that face,
Move most gently if move you must
In this lonely place.
15 She[2] thinks, part woman, three parts a child,

1. Emperor of Rome.
2. Helen of Troy, who precipitated the Trojan War. Cf. Marlowe, *Dr. Faustus*: "Was this the face that launched a thousand ships / And burnt the topless towers of Ilium?"

That nobody looks; her feet
Practice a tinker shuffle
Picked up on a street.
Like a long-legged fly upon the stream
20 *Her mind moves upon silence.*

That girls at puberty may find
The first Adam in their thought,
Shut the door of the Pope's chapel,
Keep those children out.
25 There on that scaffolding reclines
Michael Angelo.[3]
With no more sound than the mice make
His hand moves to and fro.
Like a long-legged fly upon the stream
30 *His mind moves upon silence.*

Nov. 1937   1939

The Circus Animals' Desertion

1

I sought a theme and sought for it in vain,
I sought it daily for six weeks or so.
Maybe at last, being but a broken man,
I must be satisfied with my heart, although
5 Winter and summer till old age began
My circus animals were all on show,
Those stilted boys, that burnished chariot,
Lion and woman and the Lord knows what.[1]

2

What can I but enumerate old themes?
10 First that sea-rider Oisin[2] led by the nose
Through three enchanted islands, allegorical dreams,
Vain gaiety, vain battle, vain repose,
Themes of the embittered heart, or so it seems,
That might adorn old songs or courtly shows;
15 But what cared I that set him on to ride,
I, starved for the bosom of his faery bride?

And then a counter-truth filled out its play,
The Countess Cathleen[3] was the name I gave it;

3. Michelangelo (1475–1564) is painting *The Creation of Man* on the Sistine Chapel ceiling in the Vatican. Cf. *Under Ben Bulben* (p. 2396).
1. Yeats refers to the ancient Irish heroes of his early work ("those stilted boys"), the gilded carriage of his play *The Unicorn from the Stars* (1908), and "A Sphinx with woman breast and lion paw" in his poem *The Double Vision of Michael Robartes*.
2. In the long title-poem of Yeats's first book, *The Wanderings of Oisin and Other Poems* (1889), the legendary poet-warrior Oisin (pronounced *Ushēēn*)

is bewitched by the beautiful fairy woman Niamh (pronounced *Neeve*). He returns 150 years later to find his friends dead and Ireland Christian.
3. A play (1892) about an Irish countess who sells her soul to the devil to buy food for the starving peasantry but is taken up to heaven (for God "Looks always on the motive, not the deed"). It was dedicated to Maud Gonne ("my dear," line 21) and inspired by her work on behalf of evicted peasants in the West of Ireland.

She, pity-crazed, had given her soul away,
20 But masterful Heaven had intervened to save it.
I thought my dear must her own soul destroy,
So did fanaticism and hate enslave it,
And this brought forth a dream and soon enough
This dream itself had all my thought and love.

25 And when the Fool and Blind Man stole the bread
Cuchulain fought the ungovernable sea;[4]
Heart-mysteries there, and yet when all is said
It was the dream itself enchanted me:
Character isolated by a deed
30 To engross the present and dominate memory.
Players and painted stage took all my love,
And not those things that they were emblems of.

3

Those masterful images because complete
Grew in pure mind, but out of what began?
35 A mound of refuse or the sweepings of a street,
Old kettles, old bottles, and a broken can,
Old iron, old bones, old rags, that raving slut
Who keeps the till. Now that my ladder's gone,
I must lie down where all the ladders start,
40 In the foul rag-and-bone shop of the heart.

1939

Under Ben Bulben[1]

1

Swear by what the sages spoke
Round the Mareotic Lake[2]
That the Witch of Atlas knew,
Spoke and set the cocks a-crow.

5 Swear by those horsemen, by those women
Complexion and form prove superhuman,[3]
That pale, long-visaged company
That air in immortality
Completeness of their passions won;

---

4. In Yeats's play *On Baile's Strand* (1904).
1. Mountain in Country Sligo that Yeats had often climbed as a boy. Nine years after he died in the south of France, his body was brought home to Ireland and buried in Drumcliff churchyard at the foot of Ben Bulben.
2. Lake Mareotis, bordering the city of Alexandria, Egypt, where a school of neo-Pythagorean philosophers flourished in the 1st century C.E. By Lake Mareotis also flourished (3rd century C.E.) the Christian Neoplatonists, in whom Yeats was much

interested. The lake is mentioned in Shelley's poem *The Witch of Atlas*, a poem that Yeats admired and interpreted in his own way, seeing the witch as a symbol of timeless, absolute beauty; hence what she "knew" and "spoke" and what "set the cocks a-crow" can be related to the "miracle" that "can like the cocks of Hades crow" in *Byzantium* (lines 17–20, p. 2391).
3. The *sidhe*, or fairy folk, who were believed to ride through the countryside near Ben Bulben.

10   Now they ride the wintry dawn
      Where Ben Bulben sets the scene.

      Here's the gist of what they mean.

2

      Many times man lives and dies
      Between his two eternities,
15   That of race and that of soul,
      And ancient Ireland knew it all.
      Whether man die in his bed
      Or the rifle knocks him dead,
      A brief parting from those dear
20   Is the worst man has to fear.
      Though grave-diggers' toil is long,
      Sharp their spades, their muscles strong,
      They but thrust their buried men
      Back in the human mind again.

3

25   You that Mitchel's prayer have heard,
      "Send war in our time, O Lord!"[4]
      Know that when all words are said
      And a man is fighting mad,
      Something drops from eyes long blind,
30   He completes his partial mind,
      For an instant stands at ease,
      Laughs aloud, his heart at peace.
      Even the wisest man grows tense
      With some sort of violence
35   Before he can accomplish fate,
      Know his work or choose his mate.

4

      Poet and sculptor, do the work,
      Nor let the modish painter shirk
      What his great forefathers did,
40   Bring the soul of man to God.
      Make him fill the cradles right.

      Measurement began our might:
      Forms a stark Egyptian thought,
      Forms that gentler Phidias[5] wrought

4. John Mitchel (1815–1875), an Irish patriot imprisoned for his activities, wrote in his *Jail Journal:* "Give us war in our time, O Lord!"
5. Greek sculptor (5th century B.C.), generally thought to have raised the classical ideal in art to its highest culmination. Yeats here itemizes steps in his history of knowledge and the arts, beginning with Babylonian mathematics ("measurement"), through "stark Egyptian thought," to the Renaissance of Michelangelo. Each of these steps is related to Yeats's cyclical theory of history.

45   Michael Angelo left a proof
On the Sistine Chapel roof,
Where but half-awakened Adam
Can disturb globe-trotting Madam
Till her bowels are in heat,[6]
50   Proof that there's a purpose set
Before the secret working mind:
Profane perfection of mankind.

Quattrocento[7] put in paint
On backgrounds for a God or Saint
55   Gardens where a soul's at ease;
Where everything that meets the eye,
Flowers and grass and cloudless sky,
Resemble forms that are or seem
When sleepers wake and yet still dream,
60   And when it's vanished still declare,
With only bed and bedstead there,
That heavens had opened.
               Gyres[8] run on;
When that greater dream had gone
Calvert and Wilson, Blake and Claude,[9]
65   Prepared a rest for the people of God,
Palmer's phrase, but after that
Confusion fell upon our thought.

5

Irish poets, learn your trade,
Sing whatever is well made,
70   Scorn the sort now growing up
All out of shape from toe to top,
Their unremembering hearts and heads
Base-born products of base beds.
Sing the peasantry, and then
75   Hard-riding country gentlemen,
The holiness of monks, and after
Porter-drinkers'[1] randy laughter;
Sing the lords and ladies gay
That were beaten into the clay
80   Through seven heroic centuries;
Cast your mind on other days
That we in coming days may be
Still the indomitable Irishry.

---

6. Cf. *Long-Legged Fly*, stanza 3, p. 2395.
7. 15th-century Italian art.
8. See n. 1, p. 2382.
9. Works by the five artists all provided images for Yeats's poetry. Edward Calvert, 19th-century wood engraver. Richard Wilson, 18th-century landscape painter. William Blake, "one of the great myth-

makers and mask-makers." Claude Lorrain, 17th-century landscape painter. Samuel Palmer (line 66), 19th-century landscape painter and etcher, one of whose works was *The Lonely Tower*. Calvert, Blake, and Palmer knew one another and shared a view of the holiness of art.
1. Drinkers of dark brown bitter beer.

6

Under bare Ben Bulben's head
85   In Drumcliff churchyard Yeats is laid.
An ancestor was rector there[2]
Long years ago, a church stands near,
By the road an ancient cross.
No marble, no conventional phrase;
90   On limestone quarried near the spot
By his command these words are cut:
        Cast a cold eye
        On life, on death.
        Horseman, pass by!

Sept. 1938   1939

From Reveries over Childhood and Youth[1]

[THE YEATS FAMILY]

Some six miles off towards Ben Bulben and beyond the Channel,[2] as we call the tidal river between Sligo and the Rosses, and on top of a hill there was a little square two-storied house covered with creepers and looking out upon a garden where the box borders were larger than any I had ever seen, and where I saw for the first time the crimson streak of the gladiolus and awaited its blossom with excitement. Under one gable a dark thicket of small trees made a shut-in mysterious place, where one played and believed that something was going to happen. My great-aunt Micky lived there. Micky was not her right name for she was Mary Yeats and her father had been my great-grandfather, John Yeats, who had been Rector of Drumcliffe, a few miles further off, and died in 1847. She was a spare, high-coloured, elderly woman and had the oldest-looking cat I had ever seen, for its hair had grown into matted locks of yellowy white. She farmed and had one old man-servant, but could not have farmed at all, had not neighbouring farmers helped to gather in the crops, in return for the loan of her farm implements and "out of respect for the family," for as Johnny MacGurk, the Sligo barber said to me, "The Yeats's were always very respectable." She was full of family history; all her dinner-knives were pointed like daggers through much cleaning, and there was a little James the First cream-jug with the Yeats motto and crest, and on her dining-room mantel-piece a beautiful silver cup that had belonged to my great-great-grandfather, who had married a certain Mary Butler. It had upon it the Butler crest and had been already old at the date 1534, when the initials of some bride and bridegroom were engraved under the lip. All its history for generations was rolled up inside it upon a piece of paper yellow with age, until some caller took the paper to light his pipe.

Another family of Yeats, a widow and her two children on whom I called

---

2. The Reverend John Yeats (1774–1847) was rector of Drumcliff from 1805.
1. Yeats wrote a variety of autobiographical essays between 1914 and 1928; these were originally published separately and later collected as *The Autobiography of W. B. Yeats* (1936, 1953). The

selections given here are from *Reveries over Childhood and Youth,* first published in 1915, and *The Trembling of the Veil,* first published in 1922.
2. Yeats's favorite County Sligo landscape. Cf. the places named in *The Stolen Child* (p. 2366).

sometimes with my grandmother, lived near in a long low cottage, and owned a very fierce turkey-cock that did battle with their visitors; and some miles away lived the secretary to the Grand Jury and Land Agent, my great-uncle Mat Yeats and his big family of boys and girls; but I think it was only in later years that I came to know them well. I do not think any of these liked the Pollexfens, who were well off and seemed to them purse-proud, whereas they themselves had come down in the world. I remember them as very well-bred and very religious in the Evangelical way and thinking a good deal of Aunt Micky's old histories. There had been among our ancestors a King's County soldier, one of Marlborough's[3] generals, and when his nephew came to dine he gave him boiled pork, and when the nephew said he disliked boiled pork he had asked him to dine again and promised him something he would like better. However, he gave him boiled pork again and the nephew took the hint in silence. The other day as I was coming home from America, I met one of his descendants whose family has not another discoverable link with ours, and he too knew the boiled pork story and nothing else. We have the General's portrait, and he looks very fine in his armour and his long curly wig, and underneath it, after his name, are many honours that have left no tradition among us. Were we country people, we could have summarised his life in a legend. Other ancestors or great-uncles bore a part in Irish history; one saved the life of Sarsfield[4] at the battle of Sedgmoor; another, taken prisoner by King James's army, owed his to Sarsfield's gratitude; another, a century later, roused the gentlemen of Meath[5] against some local Jacquerie,[6] and was shot dead upon a country road, and yet another "chased the United Irishmen[7] for a fortnight, fell into their hands and was hanged." The notorious Major Sirr, who arrested Lord Edward Fitzgerald[8] and gave him the bullet wound he died of in the jail, was godfather to several of my great-great-grandfather's children; while to make a balance, my great-grandfather had been Robert Emmett's[9] friend and was suspected and imprisoned though but for a few hours. One great-uncle fell at New Orleans in 1813, while another, who became Governor of Penang, led the forlorn hope at the taking of Rangoon,[1] and even in the last generation of all there had been lives of some power and pleasure. An old man who had entertained many famous people, in his eighteenth-century house, where battlement and tower showed the influence of Horace Walpole,[2] had but lately, after losing all his money, drowned himself, first taking off his rings and chain and watch as became a collector of many beautiful things; and once to remind us of more passionate life, a gunboat put into Rosses, commanded by the illegitimate son of some great-uncle or other. Now that I can look at their miniatures, turning them

---

3. John Churchill, duke of Marlborough (1650–1722) English general in the War of the Spanish Succession (1702–13).

4. Patrick Sarsfield (d. 1693), Irish Jacobite general who served in the battle of Sedgemoor (1685) when the duke of Monmouth, illegitimate son of Charles II who was claiming the throne from his uncle James II, was defeated and captured.

5. Maritime county in province of Leinster, in the east of Ireland.

6. Peasant revolutionary. The "Jacquerie" was a peasants' revolt (1358) against the nobles in northern France (the term derived from *Jacques Bonhomme*, the nobility's contemptuous name for a peasant).

7. The Irish society founded in 1791 by Theobald Wolfe Tone that later was influential in causing the Irish rebellion of 1798.

8. A British officer (1763–1798), who, after dismissal from the army for disloyal activities, joined the United Irishmen. Cf. *September 1913*, lines 19–22 (p. 2375).

9. An Irish patriot, (1778–1803), hanged at Dublin for treason.

1. Capital of Burma, which was taken by the British in 1824. Penang is an island in Malaya.

2. The 18th-century English author whose pseudo-Gothic house, Strawberry Hill, much influenced subsequent Gothic architecture in England and elsewhere.

over to find the name of soldier, or lawyer, or Castle official,[3] and wondering if they cared for good books or good music, I am delighted with all that joins my life to those who had power in Ireland or with those anywhere that were good servants and poor bargainers, but I cared nothing as a child for Micky's tales. I could see my grandfather's ships come up the bay or the river, and his sailors treated me with deference, and a ship's carpenter made and mended my toy boats and I thought that nobody could be so important as my grandfather. Perhaps, too, it is only now that I can value those more gentle natures so unlike his passion and violence. An old Sligo priest has told me how my great-grandfather John Yeats always went into his kitchen rattling the keys, so much did he fear finding some one doing wrong, and of a speech of his when the agent of the great landowner of his parish brought him from cottage to cottage to bid the women send their children to the Protestant school. All promised till they came to one who cried, "Child of mine will never darken your door." "Thank you, my woman," he said, "you are the first honest woman I have met to-day." My uncle, Mat Yeats, the Land Agent, had once waited up every night for a week to catch some boys who stole his apples and when he caught them had given them six-pence and told them not to do it again. Perhaps it is only fancy or the softening touch of the miniaturist that makes me discover in their faces some courtesy and much gentleness. Two eighteenth-century faces interest me the most, one that of a great-great-grandfather, for both have under their powdered curling wigs a half-feminine charm, and as I look at them I discover a something clumsy and heavy in myself. Yet it was a Yeats who spoke the only eulogy that turns my head: "We have ideas and no passions, but by marriage with a Pollexfen we have given a tongue to the sea cliffs."

Among the miniatures there is a larger picture, an admirable drawing by I know not what master, that is too harsh and merry for its company. He was a connection and close friend of my great-grandmother Corbet, and though we spoke of him as "Uncle Beattie" in our childhood, no blood relation. My great-grandmother who died at ninety-three had many memories of him. He was the friend of Goldsmith and was accustomed to boast, clergyman though he was, that he belonged to a hunt-club of which every member but himself had been hanged or transported for treason, and that it was not possible to ask him a question he could not reply to with a perfectly appropriate blasphemy or indecency.

[AN IRISH LITERATURE]

From these debates, from O'Leary's[4] conversation, and from the Irish books he lent or gave me has come all I have set my hand to since. I had begun to know a great deal about the Irish poets who had written in English. I read with excitement books I should find unreadable to-day, and found romance in lives that had neither wit nor adventure. I did not deceive myself, I knew how often they wrote a cold and abstract language, and yet I who had never wanted to see the houses where Keats and Shelley lived would ask

---

3. Official at Dublin Castle, where the viceroy (representing the British Crown) lived with his staff before Irish independence was achieved in 1922.

4. John O'Leary (d. 1907), an Irish nationalist, for whom Yeats had great respect. Cf. *September 1913* (p. 2374), lines 7–8: "Romantic Ireland's dead and gone, / It's with O'Leary in the grave."

everybody what sort of place Inchedony was, because Callanan had named after it a bad poem in the manner of *Childe Harold*.[5] Walking home from a debate, I remember saying to some college student, "Ireland cannot put from her the habits learned from her old military civilisation and from a church that prays in Latin. Those popular poets have not touched her heart, her poetry when it comes will be distinguished and lonely." O'Leary had once said to me, "Neither Ireland nor England knows the good from the bad in any art, but Ireland unlike England does not hate the good when it is pointed out to her." I began to plot and scheme how one might seal with the right image the soft wax before it began to harden. I had noticed that Irish Catholics among whom had been born so many political martyrs had not the good taste, the household courtesy and decency of the Protestant Ireland I had known, yet Protestant Ireland seemed to think of nothing but getting on in the world. I thought we might bring the halves together if we had a national literature that made Ireland beautiful in the memory, and yet had been freed from provincialism by an exacting criticism, an European pose.

1915

5. *Childe Harold's Pilgrimage*. Jeremiah John Callanan, Anglo-Irish poet, published *The Recluse of Inchedony and Other Poems* in 1830.

VIRGINIA WOOLF
1882–1941

Virginia Woolf was born in London, daughter of Leslie (later Sir Leslie) Stephen, the Victorian critic, philosopher, biographer, and scholar. She grew up as a member of a large and talented family, educating herself in her father's magnificent library, meeting in childhood many eminent Victorians, learning Greek from Walter Pater's sister. After her father's death in 1904 she settled with her sister and two brothers in Bloomsbury, that district of London which later was to become associated with her and the group among whom she moved. The "Bloomsbury Group" included Lytton Strachey, the biographer; J. M. Keynes, the celebrated economist; Roger Fry, an art critic; and E. M. Forster. When her sister, Vanessa, a notable painter, married Clive Bell, an art critic, in 1907, she and her brother took together another house in Bloomsbury, and there they entertained their literary and artistic friends at evening gatherings where the conversation sparkled. Their intelligence was equaled by their frankness, notably on sexual topics, and the sexual life of Bloomsbury provided ample material for discussion. Virginia was herself bisexual; and thirteen years after her marriage to the journalist and essayist Leonard Woolf, she fell passionately in love with the poet Vita [Victoria] Sackville-West, wife of the bisexual diplomat and author Harold Nicolson. Woolf's relationship with this aristocratic lesbian was to produce the most light-hearted and scintillating of her books, *Orlando* (1928). She was fortunate to have a husband as supportive emotionally as he was intellectually, and their marriage withstood this and other strains. Together they founded the Hogarth Press in 1917—a press that published some of the most interesting literature of our time, including Eliot's *Poems* (1919) and *Homage to John Dryden* (1924), the English translations of Freud, as well as her own novels. Her suicide in March 1941, resulting from her dread of World War II and her fear that she was about to lose her mind and become a burden on her husband, first revealed to the public that she had been subject to periods of nervous depression, particularly after finishing a book, and that underneath the liveliness and wit so well known among the Bloomsbury Group lay disturbing psychological tensions.

Woolf came naturally into the profession of writing. She moved among writers and artists, and her world was from the beginning the cultured world of the middle-class and upper-middle-class London intelligentsia. She rebelled against what she called the "materialism" of such novelists as Arnold Bennett and John Galsworthy and sought a more delicate rendering of those aspects of consciousness in which she felt that the truth of human experience really lay. After two novels cast in traditional form, she developed her own style, which handled the stream of consciousness with a carefully modulated poetic flow and brought into prose fiction something of the rhythms and the imagery of lyric poetry. The sketches in which she explored the possibilities of moving between action and contemplation, between specific external events in time and delicate tracings of the flow of consciousness where the mind moves between retrospect and anticipation, were collected in *Monday or Tuesday* (1921). These were technical experiments, and they made possible those later novels in which her characteristic method is fully developed—*Jacob's Room* (1922); *Mrs. Dalloway* (1925), the first completely successful novel in her "new" style; *To the Lighthouse* (1927); *The Waves* (1931), the most stylized of her novels; and *Between the Acts* (1941), published after her death. She was a skilled exponent of the stream of consciousness technique in her novels, exploring with great subtlety problems of personal identity and personal relationships as well as the significance of time, change, and memory for human personality.

Woolf was increasingly concerned with the position of women, especially professional women, and the constrictions they suffered under. She wrote several cogent essays on the subject, notably in *A Room of One's Own* (1929) and *Three Guineas* (1938). Her novel *The Years* (1937) was originally to have included reflections on the position of women interspersed amid the action, but she later decided to publish them as a separate book, which became *Three Guineas*.

She also wrote a great many reviews and critical essays, collected in *The Common Reader* (1925) and *The Second Common Reader* (1932); informal and personal in tone, her criticism is suggestive rather than authoritative and has an engaging air of spontaneity. She is equally concerned with her own craft as a writer and with what it was like to be a quite different person living in a different age. At once more informal and more revealing are the six volumes of her *Letters* (1975–80) and five volumes of her *Diary* (1977–84). These, with their running commentary on her life and work, resemble the sketchbooks of a great painter and serve as a reminder that her writings, for all their variety, have the coherence found only in the work of the greatest writers.

The Mark on the Wall

Perhaps it was the middle of January in the present year that I first looked up and saw the mark on the wall. In order to fix a date it is necessary to remember what one saw. So now I think of the fire; the steady film of yellow light upon the page of my book; the three chrysanthemums in the round glass bowl on the mantelpiece. Yes, it must have been the winter time, and we had just finished our tea, for I remember that I was smoking a cigarette when I looked up and saw the mark on the wall for the first time. I looked up through the smoke of my cigarette and my eye lodged for a moment upon the burning coals, and that old fancy of the crimson flag flapping from the castle tower came into my mind, and I thought of the cavalcade of red knights riding up the side of the black rock. Rather to my relief the sight of the mark interrupted the fancy, for it is an old fancy, an automatic fancy, made as a child perhaps. The mark was a small round mark, black upon the white wall, about six or seven inches above the mantelpiece.

How readily our thoughts swarm upon a new object, lifting it a little way, as ants carry a blade of straw so feverishly, and then leave it. . . . If that mark was made by a nail, it can't have been for a picture, it must have been for a miniature—the miniature of a lady with white powdered curls, powder-dusted cheeks, and lips like red carnations. A fraud of course, for the people who had this house before us would have chosen pictures in that way—an old picture for an old room. That is the sort of people they were—very interesting people, and I think of them so often, in such queer places, because one will never see them again, never know what happened next. They wanted to leave this house because they wanted to change their style of furniture, so he said, and he was in process of saying that in his opinion art should have ideas behind it when we were torn asunder, as one is torn from the old lady about to pour out tea and the young man about to hit the tennis ball in the back garden of the suburban villa as one rushes past in the train.

But for that mark, I'm not sure about it; I don't believe it was made by a nail after all; it's too big, too round, for that. I might get up, but if I got up and looked at it, ten to one I shouldn't be able to say for certain; because once a thing's done, no one ever knows how it happened. Oh! dear me, the mystery of life; the inaccuracy of thought! The ignorance of humanity! To show how very little control of our possessions we have—what an accidental affair this living is after all our civilisation—let me just count over a few of the things lost in one lifetime, beginning, for that seems always the most mysterious of losses—what cat would gnaw, what rat would nibble—three pale blue canisters of book-binding tools? Then there were the bird cages, the iron hoops, the steel skates, the Queen Anne coal-scuttle, the bagatelle board, the hand organ—all gone, and jewels, too. Opals and emeralds, they lie about the roots of turnips. What a scraping paring affair it is to be sure! The wonder is that I've any clothes on my back, that I sit surrounded by solid furniture at this moment. Why, if one wants to compare life to anything, one must liken it to being blown through the Tube[1] at fifty miles an hour—landing at the other end without a single hairpin in one's hair! Shot out at the feet of God entirely naked! Tumbling head over heels in the asphodel meadows[2] like brown paper parcels pitched down a shoot in the post office! With one's hair flying back like the tail of a race-horse. Yes, that seems to express the rapidity of life, the perpetual waste and repair; all so casual, all so haphazard. . . .

But after life. The slow pulling down of thick green stalks so that the cup of the flower, as it turns over, deluges one with purple and red light. Why, after all, should one not be born there as one is born here, helpless, speech-less, unable to focus one's eyesight, groping at the roots of the grass, at the toes of the Giants? As for saying which are trees, and which are men and

1. The London underground railway, or subway.
2. I.e., heaven, the next world (in Greek mythology, asphodel flowers grow in the Elysian fields).

women, or whether there are such things, that one won't be in a condition to do for fifty years or so. There will be nothing but spaces of light and dark, intersected by thick stalks, and rather higher up perhaps, rose-shaped blots of an indistinct colour—dim pinks and blues—which will, as time goes on, become more definite, become—I don't know what. . . .

And yet that mark on the wall is not a hole at all. It may even be caused by some round black substance, such as a small rose leaf, left over from the summer, and I, not being a very vigilant housekeeper—look at the dust on the mantelpiece, for example, the dust which, so they say, buried Troy three times over, only fragments of pots utterly refusing annihilation, as one can believe.

The tree outside the window taps very gently on the pane. . . . I want to think quietly, calmly, spaciously, never to be interrupted, never to have to rise from my chair, to slip easily from one thing to another, without any sense of hostility, or obstacle. I want to sink deeper and deeper, away from the surface, with its hard separate facts. To steady myself, let me catch hold of the first idea that passes . . . Shakespeare. . . . Well, he will do as well as another. A man who sat himself solidly in an arm-chair, and looked into the fire, so— A shower of ideas fell perpetually from some very high Heaven down through his mind. He leant his forehead on his hand, and people, looking in through the open door—for this scene is supposed to take place on a summer's evening— But how dull this is, this historical fiction! It doesn't interest me at all. I wish I could hit upon a pleasant track of thought, a track indirectly reflecting credit upon myself, for those are the pleasantest thoughts, and very frequent even in the minds of modest mouse-coloured people, who believe genuinely that they dislike to hear their own praises. They are not thoughts directly praising oneself; that is the beauty of them; they are thoughts like this:

"And then I came into the room. They were discussing botany. I said how I'd seen a flower growing on a dust heap on the site of an old house in Kingsway.[3] The seed, I said, must have been sown in the reign of Charles the First. What flowers grew in the reign of Charles the First?" I asked— (But I don't remember the answer.) Tall flowers with purple tassels to them perhaps. And so it goes on. All the time I'm dressing up the figure of myself in my own mind, lovingly, stealthily, not openly adoring it, for if I did that, I should catch myself out, and stretch my hand at once for a book in self-protection. Indeed, it is curious how instinctively one protects the image of oneself from idolatry or any other handling that could make it ridiculous, or too unlike the original to be believed in any longer. Or is it not so very curious after all? It is a matter of great importance. Suppose the looking-glass smashes, the image disappears, and the romantic figure with the green of forest depths all about it is there no longer, but only that shell of a person which is seen by other people—what an airless, shallow, bald, prominent world it becomes! A world not to be lived in. As we face each other in omnibuses and underground railways we are looking into the mirror; that accounts for the vagueness, the gleam of glassiness, in our eyes. And the novelists in future will realise more and more the importance of these reflections, for of course there is not one reflection but an almost infinite number; those are

3. Street in London.

the depths they will explore, those the phantoms they will pursue, leaving the description of reality more and more out of their stories, taking a knowledge of it for granted, as the Greeks did and Shakespeare perhaps—but these generalisations are very worthless. The military sound of the word is enough. It recalls leading articles, cabinet ministers—a whole class of things indeed which, as a child, one thought the thing itself, the standard thing, the real thing, from which one could not depart save at the risk of nameless damnation. Generalisations bring back somehow Sunday in London, Sunday afternoon walks, Sunday luncheons, and also ways of speaking of the dead, clothes, and habits—like the habit of sitting all together in one room until a certain hour, although nobody liked it. There was a rule for everything. The rule for tablecloths at that particular period was that they should be made of tapestry with little yellow compartments marked upon them, such as you may see in photographs of the carpets in the corridors of the royal palaces. Tablecloths of a different kind were not real tablecloths. How shocking, and yet how wonderful it was to discover that these real things, Sunday luncheons, Sunday walks, country houses, and tablecloths were not entirely real, were indeed half phantoms, and the damnation which visited the disbeliever in them was only a sense of illegitimate freedom. What now takes the place of those things I wonder, those real standard things? Men perhaps, should you be a woman; the masculine point of view which governs our lives, which sets the standard, which establishes Whitaker's Table of Precedency,[4] which has become, I suppose, since the war, half a phantom to many men and women, which soon, one may hope, will be laughed into the dustbin where the phantoms go, the mahogany sideboards and the Landseer[5] prints, Gods and Devils, Hell and so forth, leaving us all with an intoxicating sense of illegitimate freedom—if freedom exists. . . .

In certain lights that mark on the wall seems actually to project from the wall. Nor is it entirely circular. I cannot be sure, but it seems to cast a perceptible shadow, suggesting that if I ran my finger down that strip of the wall it would, at a certain point, mount and descend a small tumulus, a smooth tumulus like those barrows on the South Downs[6] which are, they say, either tombs or camps. Of the two I should prefer them to be tombs, desiring melancholy like most English people, and finding it natural at the end of a walk to think of the bones stretched beneath the turf. . . . There must be some book about it. Some antiquary must have dug up those bones and given them a name. . . . What sort of a man is an antiquary, I wonder? Retired Colonels for the most part, I daresay, leading parties of aged labourers to the top here, examining clods of earth and stone, and getting into correspondence with the neighbouring clergy, which, being opened at breakfast time, gives them a feeling of importance, and the comparison of arrowheads necessitates cross-country journeys to the country towns, an agreeable necessity both to them and to their elderly wives, who wish to make plum jam or to clean out the study, and have every reason for keeping that great question of the camp or the tomb in perpetual suspension, while the Colonel

---

4. *Whitaker's Almanack*, an annual compendium of information, prints a "Table of Precedency," which shows the order in which the various ranks in public life and society proceed on formal occasions.

5. Edwin Henry Landseer, 19th-century animal painter, reproductions of whose *Stag at Bay, Monarch of the Glen*, and similar paintings were often found in Victorian homes.

6. A range of low hills in southeastern England. "Barrows": mounds of earth or stones erected by prehistoric peoples, usually as burial places.

himself feels agreeably philosophic in accumulating evidence on both sides of the question. It is true that he does finally incline to believe in the camp; and, being opposed, indites a pamphlet which he is about to read at the quarterly meeting of the local society when a stroke lays him low, and his last conscious thoughts are not of wife or child, but of the camp and that arrow-head there, which is now in the case at the local museum, together with the foot of a Chinese murderess, a handful of Elizabethan nails, a great many Tudor clay pipes, a piece of Roman pottery, and the wineglass that Nelson drank out of—proving I really don't know what.

No, no, nothing is proved, nothing is known. And if I were to get up at this very moment and ascertain that the mark on the wall is really—what shall we say?—the head of a gigantic old nail, driven in two hundred years ago, which has now, owing to the patient attrition of many generations of housemaids, revealed its head above the coat of paint, and is taking its first view of modern life in the sight of a white-walled fire-lit room, what should I gain?—Knowledge? Matter for further speculation? I can think sitting still as well as standing up. And what is knowledge? What are our learned men save the descendants of witches and hermits who crouched in caves and in woods brewing herbs, interrogating shrew-mice and writing down the language of the stars? And the less we honour them as our superstitions dwindle and our respect for beauty and health of mind increases. . . . Yes, one could imagine a very pleasant world. A quiet, spacious world, with the flowers so red and blue in the open fields. A world without professors or specialists or house-keepers with the profiles of policemen, a world which one could slice with one's thought as a fish slices the water with his fin, grazing the stems of the water-lilies, hanging suspended over nests of white sea eggs. . . . How peaceful it is down here, rooted in the centre of the world and gazing up through the grey waters, with their sudden gleams of light, and their reflections—if it were not for Whitaker's Almanack—if it were not for the Table of Precedency!

I must jump up and see for myself what that mark on the wall really is— a nail, a rose-leaf, a crack in the wood?

Here is nature once more at her old game of self-preservation. This train of thought, she perceives, is threatening mere waste of energy, even some collision with reality, for who will ever be able to lift a finger against Whitaker's Table of Precedency? The Archbishop of Canterbury is followed by the Lord High Chancellor; the Lord High Chancellor is followed by the Archbishop of York. Everybody follows somebody, such is the philosophy of Whitaker; and the great thing is to know who follows whom. Whitaker knows, and let that, so Nature counsels, comfort you, instead of enraging you; and if you can't be comforted, if you must shatter this hour of peace, think of the mark on the wall.

I understand Nature's game—her prompting to take action as a way of ending any thought that threatens to excite or to pain. Hence, I suppose, comes our slight contempt for men of action—men, we assume, who don't think. Still, there's no harm in putting a full stop to one's disagreeable thoughts by looking at a mark on the wall.

Indeed, now that I have fixed my eyes upon it, I feel that I have grasped a plank in the sea; I feel a satisfying sense of reality which at once turns the two Archbishops and the Lord High Chancellor to the shadows of shades.

Here is something definite, something real. Thus, waking from a midnight dream of horror, one hastily turns on the light and lies quiescent, worshipping the chest of drawers, worshipping solidity, worshipping reality, worshipping the impersonal world which is a proof of some existence other than ours. That is what one wants to be sure of. . . . Wood is a pleasant thing to think about. It comes from a tree; and trees grow, and we don't know how they grow. For years and years they grow, without paying any attention to us, in meadows, in forests, and by the side of rivers—all things one likes to think about. The cows swish their tails beneath them on hot afternoons; they paint rivers so green that when a moorhen dives one expects to see its feathers all green when it comes up again. I like to think of the fish balanced against the stream like flags blown out; and of water-beetles slowly raising domes of mud upon the bed of the river. I like to think of the tree itself: first of the close dry sensation of being wood; then the grinding of the storm; then the slow, delicious ooze of sap; I like to think of it, too, on winter's nights standing in the empty field with all leaves close-furled, nothing tender exposed to the iron bullets of the moon, a naked mast upon an earth that goes tumbling, tumbling, all night long. The song of birds must sound very loud and strange in June; and how cold the feet of insects must feel upon it, as they make laborious progresses up the creases of the bark, or sun themselves upon the thin green awning of the leaves, and look straight in front of them with diamond-cut red eyes. . . . One by one the fibres snap beneath the immense cold pressure of the earth, then the last storm comes and, falling, the highest branches drive deep into the ground again. Even so, life isn't done with; there are a million patient, watchful lives still for a tree, all over the world, in bedrooms, in ships, on the pavement, living rooms, where men and women sit after tea, smoking cigarettes. It is full of peaceful thoughts, happy thoughts, this tree. I should like to take each one separately—but something is getting in the way. . . . Where was I? What has it all been about? A tree? A river? The Downs? Whitaker's Almanack? The fields of asphodel? I can't remember a thing. Everything's moving, falling, slipping, vanishing. . . . There is a vast upheaval of matter. Someone is standing over me and saying:

"I'm going out to buy a newspaper."

"Yes?"

"Though it's no good buying newspapers. . . . Nothing ever happens. Curse this war; God damn this war! . . . All the same, I don't see why we should have a snail on our wall."

Ah, the mark on the wall! It was a snail.

1921

Modern Fiction

In making any survey, even the freest and loosest, of modern fiction, it is difficult not to take it for granted that the modern practice of the art is somehow an improvement upon the old. With their simple tools and primitive materials, it might be said, Fielding[1] did well and Jane Austen even

1. Henry Fielding (1707–1754), novelist.

better, but compare their opportunities with ours! Their masterpieces certainly have a strange air of simplicity. And yet the analogy between literature and the process, to choose an example, of making motor cars scarcely holds good beyond the first glance. It is doubtful whether in the course of the centuries, though we have learnt much about making machines, we have learnt anything about making literature. We do not come to write better; all that we can be said to do is to keep moving, now a little in this direction, now in that, but with a circular tendency should the whole course of the track be viewed from a sufficiently lofty pinnacle. It need scarcely be said that we make no claim to stand, even momentarily, upon that vantage-ground. On the flat, in the crowd, half blind with dust, we look back with envy to those happier warriors, whose battle is won and whose achievements wear so serene an air of accomplishment that we can scarcely refrain from whispering that the fight was not so fierce for them as for us. It is for the historian of literature to decide; for him to say if we are now beginning or ending or standing in the middle of a great period of prose fiction, for down in the plain little is visible. We only know that certain gratitudes and hostilities inspire us; that certain paths seem to lead to fertile land, others to the dust and the desert; and of this perhaps it may be worth while to attempt some account.

Our quarrel, then, is not with the classics, and if we speak of quarrelling with Mr Wells, Mr Bennett, and Mr Galsworthy;[2] it is partly that by the mere fact of their existence in the flesh their work has a living, breathing, everyday imperfection which bids us take what liberties with it we choose. But it is also true, that, while we thank them for a thousand gifts, we reserve our unconditional gratitude for Mr Hardy, for Mr Conrad, and in much lesser degree for the Mr Hudson of *The Purple Land, Green Mansions,* and *Far Away and Long Ago.*[3] Mr Wells, Mr Bennett, and Mr Galsworthy have excited so many hopes and disappointed them so persistently that our gratitude largely takes the form of thanking them for having shown us what they might have done but have not done; what we certainly could not do, but as certainly, perhaps, do not wish to do. No single phrase will sum up the charge or grievance which we have to bring against a mass of work so large in its volume and embodying so many qualities, both admirable and the reverse. If we tried to formulate our meaning in one word we should say that these three writers are materialists. It is because they are concerned not with the spirit but with the body that they have disappointed us, and left us with the feeling that the sooner English fiction turns its back upon them, as politely as may be, and marches, if only into the desert, the better for its soul. Naturally, no single word reaches the centre of three separate targets. In the case of Mr Wells it falls notably wide of the mark. And yet even with him it indicates to our thinking the fatal alloy in his genius, the great clod of clay that has got itself mixed up with the purity of his inspiration. But Mr Bennett is perhaps the worst culprit of the three, inasmuch as he is by far the best workman. He can make a book so well constructed and solid in its craftsmanship that it is difficult for the most exacting of critics to see through what chink or crevice decay can creep in. There is not so much as a draught

2. H. G. Wells (1866–1946), Arnold Bennett (1867–1931), John Galsworthy (1867–1933), novelists.
3. W. H. Hudson (1841–1922), naturalist and writer, was born in Argentina, although he later lived in London. *The Purple Land* (1885) is about South America; *Green Mansions* (1904), a novel set in South America, was his first real success.

between the frames of the windows, or a crack in the boards. And yet—if life should refuse to live there? That is a risk which the creator of *The Old Wives' Tale*, George Cannon, Edwin Clayhanger,[4] and hosts of other figures, may well claim to have surmounted. His characters live abundantly, even unexpectedly, but it remains to ask how do they live, and what do they live for? More and more they seem to us, deserting even the well-built villa in the Five Towns,[5] to spend their time in some softly padded first-class railway carriage, pressing bells and buttons innumerable; and the destiny to which they travel so luxuriously becomes more and more unquestionably an eternity of bliss spent in the very best hotel in Brighton.[6] It can scarcely be said of Mr Wells that he is a materialist in the sense that he takes too much delight in the solidity of his fabric. His mind is too generous in its sympathies to allow him to spend much time in making things shipshape and substantial. He is a materialist from sheer goodness of heart, taking upon his shoulders the work that ought to have been discharged by Government officials, and in the plethora of his ideas and facts scarcely having leisure to realize, or forgetting to think important, the crudity and coarseness of his human beings. Yet what more damaging criticism can there be both of his earth and of his Heaven than that they are to be inhabited here and hereafter by his Joans and his Peters? Does not the inferiority of their natures tarnish whatever institutions and ideals may be provided for them by the generosity of their creator? Nor, profoundly though we respect the integrity and humanity of Mr Galsworthy, shall we find what we seek in his pages.

If we fasten, then, one label on all these books, on which is one word, materialists, we mean by it that they write of unimportant things; that they spend immense skill and immense industry making the trivial and the transitory appear the true and the enduring.

We have to admit that we are exacting, and, further, that we find it difficult to justify our discontent by explaining what it is that we exact. We frame our question differently at different times. But it reappears most persistently as we drop the finished novel on the crest of a sigh—Is it worth while? What is the point of it all? Can it be that, owing to one of those little deviations which the human spirit seems to make from time to time, Mr Bennett has come down with his magnificent apparatus for catching life just an inch or two on the wrong side? Life escapes; and perhaps without life nothing else is worth while. It is a confession of vagueness to have to make use of such a figure as this, but we scarcely better the matter by speaking, as critics are prone to do, of reality. Admitting the vagueness which afflicts all criticism of novels, let us hazard the opinion that for us at this moment the form of fiction most in vogue more often misses than secures the thing we seek. Whether we call it life or spirit, truth or reality, this, the essential thing, has moved off, or on, and refuses to be contained any longer in such ill-fitting vestments as we provide. Nevertheless, we go on perseveringly, conscientiously, constructing our two and thirty chapters after a design which more and more ceases to resemble the vision in our minds. So much of the enormous labour of proving the solidity, the likeness to life, of the story is not merely labour thrown away but labour misplaced to the extent of obscuring

---

4. Characters in Arnold Bennett's novels; *The Old Wives' Tale* (1908) is the best known.
5. The pottery towns of Staffordshire in which

many of Bennett's novels and stories were set.
6. One-time fashionable seaside resort on the southwest coast of England.

and blotting out the light of the conception. The writer seems constrained, not by his own free will but by some powerful and unscrupulous tyrant who has him in thrall, to provide a plot, to provide comedy, tragedy, love interest, and an air of probability embalming the whole so impeccable that if all his figures were to come to life they would find themselves dressed down to the last button of their coats in the fashion of the hour. The tyrant is obeyed; the novel is done to a turn. But sometimes, more and more often as time goes by, we suspect a momentary doubt, a spasm of rebellion, as the pages fill themselves in the customary way. Is life like this? Must novels be like this?

Look within and life, it seems, is very far from being "like this." Examine for a moment an ordinary mind on an ordinary day. The mind receives a myriad impressions—trivial, fantastic, evanescent, or engraved with the sharpness of steel. From all sides they come, an incessant shower of innumerable atoms; and as they fall, as they shape themselves into the life of Monday or Tuesday,[7] the accent falls differently from of old; the moment of importance came not here but there; so that, if a writer were a free man and not a slave, if he could write what he chose, not what he must, if he could base his work upon his own feeling and not upon convention, there would be no plot, no comedy, no tragedy, no love interest or catastrophe in the accepted style, and perhaps not a single button sewn on as the Bond Street[8] tailors would have it. Life is not a series of gig-lamps[9] symmetrically arranged; life is a luminous halo, a semi-transparent envelope surrounding us from the beginning of consciousness to the end. Is it not the task of the novelist to convey this varying, this unknown and uncircumscribed spirit, whatever aberration or complexity it may display, with as little mixture of the alien and external as possible? We are not pleading merely for courage and sincerity; we are suggesting that the proper stuff of fiction is a little other than custom would have us believe it.

It is, at any rate, in some such fashion as this that we seek to define the quality which distinguishes the work of several young writers, among whom Mr James Joyce is the most notable, from that of their predecessors. They attempt to come closer to life, and to preserve more sincerely and exactly what interests and moves them, even if to do so they must discard most of the conventions which are commonly observed by the novelist. Let us record the atoms as they fall upon the mind in the order in which they fall, let us trace the pattern, however disconnected and incoherent in appearance, which each sight or incident scores upon the consciousness. Let us not take it for granted that life exists more fully in what is commonly thought big than in what is commonly thought small. Anyone who has read *The Portrait of the Artist as a Young Man* or, what promises to be a far more interesting work, *Ulysses*,[1] now appearing in the *Little Review*, will have hazarded some theory of this nature as to Mr Joyce's intention. On our part, with such a fragment before us, it is hazarded rather than affirmed; but whatever the intention of the whole, there can be no question but that it is of the utmost sincerity and that the result, difficult or unpleasant as we may judge it, is undeniably important. In contrast with those whom we have called materi-

---

7. *Monday or Tuesday* was the title of the collection of experimental stories and sketches that Woolf brought out in 1921.

8. Fashionable shopping street in London.
9. Carriage lamps.
1. Written April, 1919 [Woolf's note].

alists, Mr Joyce is spiritual; he is concerned at all costs to reveal the flickerings of that innermost flame which flashes its messages through the brain, and in order to preserve it he disregards with complete courage whatever seems to him adventitious, whether it be probability, or coherence, or any other of these signposts which for generations have served to support the imagination of a reader when called upon to imagine what he can neither touch nor see. The scene in the cemetery,[2] for instance, with its brilliancy, its sordidity, its incoherence, its sudden lightning flashes of significance, does undoubtedly come so close to the quick of the mind that, on a first reading at any rate, it is difficult not to acclaim a masterpiece. If we want life itself, here surely we have it. Indeed, we find ourselves fumbling rather awkwardly if we try to say what else we wish, and for what reason a work of such originality yet fails to compare, for we must take high examples, with *Youth* or *The Mayor of Casterbridge*.[3] It fails because of the comparative poverty of the writer's mind, we might say simply and have done with it. But it is possible to press a little further and wonder whether we may not refer our sense of being in a bright yet narrow room, confined and shut in, rather than enlarged and set free, to some limitation imposed by the method as well as by the mind. Is it the method that inhibits the creative power? Is it due to the method that we feel neither jovial nor magnanimous, but centred in a self which, in spite of its tremor of susceptibility, never embraces or creates what is outside itself and beyond? Does the emphasis laid, perhaps didactically, upon indecency contribute to the effect of something angular and isolated? Or is it merely that in any effort of such originality it is much easier, for contemporaries especially, to feel what it lacks than to name what it gives? In any case it is a mistake to stand outside examining "methods". Any method is right, every method is right, that expresses what we wish to express, if we are writers; that brings us closer to the novelist's intention if we are readers. This method has the merit of bringing us closer to what we were prepared to call life itself; did not the reading of *Ulysses* suggest how much of life is excluded or ignored, and did it not come with a shock to open *Tristram Shandy* or even *Pendennis*[4] and be by them convinced that there are not only other aspects of life, but more important ones into the bargain.

However this may be, the problem before the novelist at present, as we suppose it to have been in the past, is to contrive means of being free to set down what he chooses. He has to have the courage to say that what interests him is no longer "this" but "that": out of "that" alone must he construct his work. For the moderns "that", the point of interest, lies very likely in the dark places of psychology. At once, therefore, the accent falls a little differently; the emphasis is upon something hitherto ignored; at once a different outline of form becomes necessary, difficult for us to grasp, incomprehensible to our predecessors. No one but a modern, no one perhaps but a Russian, would have felt the interest of the situation which Tchekov[5] has made into the short story which he calls "Gusev." Some Russian soldiers lie ill on board a ship which is taking them back to Russia. We are given a few scraps of their talk

---

2. The sixth episode ("Hades") of *Ulysses*, where Bloom goes to Paddy Dignam's funeral.
3. Stories by, respectively, Joseph Conrad and Thomas Hardy.

4. Novels by, respectively, Laurence Sterne (1713–1768) and William Makepeace Thackeray (1811–1863).
5. Anton Pavlovich Chekhov (1860–1904).

and some of their thoughts; then one of them dies and is carried away; the talk goes on among the others for a time, until Gusev himself dies, and looking "like a carrot or a radish" is thrown overboard. The emphasis is laid upon such unexpected places that at first it seems as if there were no emphasis at all; and then, as the eyes accustom themselves to twilight and discern the shapes of things in a room we see how complete the story is, how profound, and how truly in obedience to his vision Tchekov has chosen this, that, and the other, and placed them together to compose something new. But it is impossible to say "this is comic," or "that is tragic," nor are we certain, since short stories, we have been taught, should be brief and conclusive, whether this, which is vague and inconclusive, should be called a short story at all.

The most elementary remarks upon modern English fiction can hardly avoid some mention of the Russian influence, and if the Russians are mentioned one runs the risk of feeling that to write of any fiction save theirs is waste of time. If we want understanding of the soul and heart where else shall we find it of comparable profundity? If we are sick of our own materialism the least considerable of their novelists has by right of birth a natural reverence for the human spirit. "Learn to make yourself akin to people. . . . But let this sympathy be not with the mind—for it is easy with the mind— but with the heart, with love towards them." In every great Russian writer we seem to discern the features of a saint, if sympathy for the sufferings of others, love towards them, endeavour to reach some goal worthy of the most exacting demands of the spirit constitute saintliness. It is the saint in them which confounds us with a feeling of our own irreligious triviality, and turns so many of our famous novels to tinsel and trickery. The conclusions of the Russian mind, thus comprehensive and compassionate, are inevitably, perhaps, of the utmost sadness. More accurately indeed we might speak of the inconclusiveness of the Russian mind. It is the sense that there is no answer, that if honestly examined life presents question after question which must be left to sound on and on after the story is over in hopeless interrogation that fills us with a deep, and finally it may be with a resentful, despair. They are right perhaps; unquestionably they see further than we do and without our gross impediments of vision. But perhaps we see something that escapes them, or why should this voice of protest mix itself with our gloom? The voice of protest is the voice of another and an ancient civilisation which seems to have bred in us the instinct to enjoy and fight rather than to suffer and understand. English fiction from Sterne to Meredith[6] bears witness to our natural delight in humour and comedy, in the beauty of earth, in the activities of the intellect, and in the splendour of the body. But any deductions that we may draw from the comparison of two fictions so immeasurably far apart are futile save indeed as they flood us with a view of the infinite possibilities of the art and remind us that there is no limit to the horizon, and that nothing—no "method," no experiment, even of the wildest—is forbidden, but only falsity and pretence. "The proper stuff of fiction" does not exist; everything is the proper stuff of fiction, every feeling, every thought; every quality of brain and spirit is drawn upon; no perception comes amiss.

---

6. George Meredith (1828–1909), novelist.

And if we can imagine the art of fiction come alive and standing in our midst, she would undoubtedly bid us break her and bully her, as well as honour and love her, for so her youth is renewed and her sovereignty assured.

1925

A Room of One's Own[1]

Chapter One

But, you may say, we asked you to speak about women and fiction—what has that got to do with a room of one's own? I will try to explain. When you asked me to speak about women and fiction I sat down on the banks of a river and began to wonder what the words meant. They might mean simply a few remarks about Fanny Burney; a few more about Jane Austen; a tribute to the Brontës and a sketch of Haworth Parsonage under snow; some witticisms if possible about Miss Mitford; a respectful allusion to George Eliot; a reference to Mrs. Gaskell[2] and one would have done. But at second sight the words seemed not so simple. The title women and fiction might mean, and you may have meant it to mean, women and what they are like; or it might mean women and the fiction that they write; or it might mean women and the fiction that is written about them; or it might mean that somehow all three are inextricably mixed together and you want me to consider them in that light. But when I began to consider the subject in this last way, which seemed the most interesting, I soon saw that it had one fatal drawback. I should never be able to come to a conclusion. I should never be able to fulfil what is, I understand, the first duty of a lecturer—to hand you after an hour's discourse a nugget of pure truth to wrap up between the pages of your notebooks and keep on the mantelpiece for ever. All I could do was to offer you an opinion upon one minor point—a woman must have money and a room of her own if she is to write fiction; and that, as you will see, leaves the great problem of the true nature of woman and the true nature of fiction unsolved. I have shirked the duty of coming to a conclusion upon these two questions—women and fiction remain, so far as I am concerned, unsolved problems. But in order to make some amends I am going to do what I can to show you how I arrived at this opinion about the room and the money. I am going to develop in your presence as fully and freely as I can the train of thought which led me to think this. Perhaps if I lay bare the ideas, the prejudices, that lie behind this statement you will find that they have some bearing upon women and some upon fiction. At any rate, when a subject is highly controversial—and any question about sex is that—one cannot hope to tell the truth. One can only show how one came to hold whatever opinion one does hold. One can only give one's audience the chance of drawing their own conclusions as they observe the limitations, the prejudices, the idiosyncrasies

---

1. This essay is based upon two papers read to the Arts Society at Newnham and the Odtaa at Girton in October 1928. The papers were too long to be read in full, and have since been altered and expanded [Woolf's note]. Newnham and Girton are women's colleges at Cambridge. Odtaa, or "One Damn Thing After Another," was an elite literary society.

2. All British writers: Frances Burney (1752–1840); Jane Austen (1775–1817); Charlotte (1816–1855), Emily (1818–1848), and Anne (1820–1849) Brontë, who grew up in the parsonage in Haworth (Yorkshire), where their father was curate; Mary Russell Mitford (1787–1855); George Eliot (pseudonym of Marian Evans, 1819–1880); and Elizabeth Gaskell (1810–1865).

of the speaker. Fiction here is likely to contain more truth than fact. Therefore I propose, making use of all the liberties and licences of a novelist, to tell you the story of the two days that preceded my coming here—how, bowed down by the weight of the subject which you have laid upon my shoulders, I pondered it, and made it work in and out of my daily life. I need not say that what I am about to describe has no existence; Oxbridge[3] is an invention; so is Fernham; "I" is only a convenient term for somebody who has no real being. Lies will flow from my lips, but there may perhaps be some truth mixed up with them; it is for you to seek out this truth and to decide whether any part of it is worth keeping. If not, you will of course throw the whole of it into the wastepaper basket and forget all about it.

Here then was I (call me Mary Beton, Mary Seton, Mary Carmichael or by any name you please—it is not a matter of any importance) sitting on the banks of a river a week or two ago in fine October weather, lost in thought. That collar I have spoken of, women and fiction, the need of coming to some conclusion on a subject that raises all sorts of prejudices and passions, bowed my head to the ground. To the right and left bushes of some sort, golden and crimson, glowed with the colour, even it seemed burnt with the heat, of fire. On the further bank the willows wept in perpetual lamentation, their hair about their shoulders. The river reflected whatever it chose of sky and bridge and burning tree, and when the undergraduate had oared his boat through the reflections they closed again, completely, as if he had never been. There one might have sat the clock round lost in thought. Thought—to call it by a prouder name than it deserved—had let its line down into the stream. It swayed, minute after minute, hither and thither among the reflections and the weeds, letting the water lift it and sink it, until—you know the little tug—the sudden conglomeration of an idea at the end of one's line: and then the cautious hauling of it in, and the careful laying of it out? Alas, laid on the grass how small, how insignificant this thought of mine looked; the sort of fish that a good fisherman puts back into the water so that it may grow fatter and be one day worth cooking and eating. I will not trouble you with that thought now, though if you look carefully you may find it for yourselves in the course of what I am going to say.

But however small it was, it had, nevertheless, the mysterious property of its kind—put back into the mind, it became at once very exciting, and important; and as it darted and sank, and flashed hither and thither, set up such a wash and tumult of ideas that it was impossible to sit still. It was thus that I found myself walking with extreme rapidity across a grass plot. Instantly a man's figure rose to intercept me. Nor did I at first understand that the gesticulations of a curious-looking object, in a cut-away coat and evening shirt, were aimed at me. His face expressed horror and indignation. Instinct rather than reason came to my help; he was a Beadle; I was a woman. This was the turf; there was the path. Only the Fellows and Scholars are allowed here; the gravel is the place for me. Such thoughts were the work of a moment. As I regained the path the arms of the Beadle sank, his face assumed its usual repose, and though turf is better walking than gravel, no very great harm was done. The only charge I could bring against the Fellows

3. A common term blending Oxford and Cambridge.

and Scholars of whatever the college might happen to be was that in protection of their turf, which has been rolled for 300 years in succession, they had sent my little fish into hiding.

What idea it had been that had sent me so audaciously trespassing I could not now remember. The spirit of peace descended like a cloud from heaven, for if the spirit of peace dwells anywhere, it is in the courts and quadrangles of Oxbridge on a fine October morning. Strolling through those colleges past those ancient halls the roughness of the present seemed smoothed away; the body seemed contained in a miraculous glass cabinet through which no sound could penetrate, and the mind, freed from any contact with facts (unless one trespassed on the turf again), was at liberty to settle down upon whatever meditation was in harmony with the moment. As chance would have it, some stray memory of some old essay about revisiting Oxbridge in the long vacation brought Charles Lamb to mind—Saint Charles, said Thackeray,[4] putting a letter of Lamb's to his forehead. Indeed, among all the dead (I give you my thoughts as they came to me), Lamb is one of the most congenial; one to whom one would have liked to say, Tell me then how you wrote your essays? For his essays are superior even to Max Beerbohm's,[5] I thought, with all their perfection, because of that wild flash of imagination, that lightning crack of genius in the middle of them which leaves them flawed and imperfect, but starred with poetry. Lamb then came to Oxbridge perhaps a hundred years ago. Certainly he wrote an essay—the name escapes me[6]— about the manuscript of one of Milton's poems which he saw here. It was *Lycidas* perhaps, and Lamb wrote how it shocked him to think it possible that any word in *Lycidas* could have been different from what it is. To think of Milton changing the words in that poem seemed to him a sort of sacrilege. This led me to remember what I could of *Lycidas* and to amuse myself with guessing which word it could have been that Milton had altered, and why. It then occurred to me that the very manuscript itself which Lamb had looked at was only a few hundred yards away, so that one could follow Lamb's footsteps across the quadrangle to that famous library[7] where the treasure is kept. Moreover, I recollected, as I put this plan into execution, it is in this famous library that the manuscript of Thackeray's *Esmond* is also preserved. The critics often say that *Esmond* is Thackeray's most perfect novel. But the affectation of the style, with its imitation of the eighteenth century, hampers one, so far as I remember; unless indeed the eighteenth-century style was natural to Thackeray—a fact that one might prove by looking at the manuscript and seeing whether the alterations were for the benefit of the style or of the sense. But then one would have to decide what is style and what is meaning, a question which—but here I was actually at the door which leads into the library itself. I must have opened it, for instantly there issued, like a guardian angel barring the way with a flutter of black gown instead of white wings, a deprecating, silvery, kindly gentleman, who regretted in a low voice as he waved me back that ladies are only admitted to the library if accompanied by a Fellow of the College or furnished with a letter of introduction.

That a famous library has been cursed by a woman is a matter of complete

4. William Makepeace Thackeray (1811–1863), English novelist, was author of *The History of Henry Esmond, Esquire* (1852), mentioned later. Charles Lamb (1775–1834), English writer.

5. Beerbohm (1872–1956), English essayist and parodist.
6. *Oxford in the Vacation.*
7. The library at Trinity College, Cambridge.

indifference to a famous library. Venerable and calm, with all its treasures safe locked within its breast, it sleeps complacently and will, so far as I am concerned, so sleep for ever. Never will I wake those echoes, never will I ask for that hospitality again, I vowed as I descended the steps in anger. Still an hour remained before luncheon, and what was one to do? Stroll on the meadows? sit by the river? Certainly it was a lovely autumn morning; the leaves were fluttering red to the ground; there was no great hardship in doing either. But the sound of music reached my ear. Some service or celebration was going forward. The organ complained magnificently as I passed the chapel door. Even the sorrow of Christianity sounded in that serene air more like the recollection of sorrow than sorrow itself; even the groanings of the ancient organ seemed lapped in peace. I had no wish to enter had I the right, and this time the verger might have stopped me, demanding perhaps my baptismal certificate, or a letter of introduction from the Dean. But the outside of these magnificent buildings is often as beautiful as the inside. Moreover, it was amusing enough to watch the congregation assembling, coming in and going out again, busying themselves at the door of the chapel like bees at the mouth of a hive. Many were in cap and gown; some had tufts of fur on their shoulders; others were wheeled in bath-chairs; others, though not past middle age, seemed creased and crushed into shapes so singular that one was reminded of those giant crabs and crayfish who heave with difficulty across the sand of an aquarium. As I leant against the wall the University indeed seemed a sanctuary in which are preserved rare types which would soon be obsolete if left to fight for existence on the pavement of the Strand.[8] Old stories of old deans and old dons came back to mind, but before I had summoned up courage to whistle—it used to be said that at the sound of a whistle old Professor ——— instantly broke into a gallop—the venerable congregation had gone inside. The outside of the chapel remained. As you know, its high domes and pinnacles can be seen, like a sailing-ship always voyaging never arriving, lit up at night and visible for miles, far away across the hills. Once, presumably, this quadrangle with its smooth lawns, its massive buildings, and the chapel itself was marsh too, where the grasses waved and the swine rootled. Teams of horses and oxen, I thought, must have hauled the stone in wagons from far countries, and then with infinite labour the grey blocks in whose shade I was now standing were poised in order one on top of another, and then the painters brought their glass for the windows, and the masons were busy for centuries up on that roof with putty and cement, spade and trowel.[9] Every Saturday somebody must have poured gold and silver out of a leathern purse into their ancient fists, for they had their beer and skittles presumably of an evening. An unending stream of gold and silver, I thought, must have flowed into this court perpetually to keep the stones coming and the masons working; to level, to ditch, to dig and to drain. But it was then the age of faith, and money was poured liberally to set these stones on a deep foundation, and when the stones were raised, still more money was poured in from the coffers of kings and queens and great nobles to ensure that hymns should be sung here and scholars taught. Lands were granted; tithes were paid. And when the age of faith was

8. A busy thoroughfare in London.
9. King's College Chapel, Cambridge, was built from 1446 to 1547.

over and the age of reason had come, still the same flow of gold and silver went on; fellowships were founded; lectureships endowed; only the gold and silver flowed now, not from the coffers of the king, but from the chests of merchants and manufacturers, from the purses of men who had made, say, a fortune from industry, and returned, in their wills, a bounteous share of it to endow more chairs, more lectureships, more fellowships in the university where they had learnt their craft. Hence the libraries and laboratories; the observatories; the splendid equipment of costly and delicate instruments which now stands on glass shelves, where centuries ago the grasses waved and the swine rootled. Certainly, as I strolled round the court, the foundation of gold and silver seemed deep enough; the pavement laid solidly over the wild grasses. Men with trays on their heads went busily from staircase to staircase. Gaudy blossoms flowered in window-boxes. The strains of the gramophone blared out from the rooms within. It was impossible not to reflect—the reflection whatever it may have been was cut short. The clock struck. It was time to find one's way to luncheon.

It is a curious fact that novelists have a way of making us believe that luncheon parties are invariably memorable for something very witty that was said, or for something very wise that was done. But they seldom spare a word for what was eaten. It is part of the novelist's convention not to mention soup and salmon and ducklings, as if soup and salmon and ducklings were of no importance whatsoever, as if nobody ever smoked a cigar or drank a glass of wine. Here, however, I shall take the liberty to defy that convention and to tell you that the lunch on this occasion began with soles, sunk in a deep dish, over which the college cook had spread a counterpane of the whitest cream, save that it was branded here and there with brown spots like the spots on the flanks of a doe. After that came the partridges, but if this suggests a couple of bald, brown birds on a plate you are mistaken. The partridges, many and various, came with all their retinue of sauces and salads, the sharp and the sweet, each in its order; their potatoes, thin as coins but not so hard; their sprouts, foliated as rosebuds but more succulent. And no sooner had the roast and its retinue been done with than the silent serving-man, the Beadle himself perhaps in a milder manifestation, set before us, wreathed in napkins, a confection which rose all sugar from the waves. To call it pudding and so relate it to rice and tapioca would be an insult. Meanwhile the wineglasses had flushed yellow and flushed crimson; had been emptied; had been filled. And thus by degrees was lit, halfway down the spine, which is the seat of the soul, not that hard little electric light which we call brilliance, as it pops in and out upon our lips, but the more profound, subtle and subterranean glow, which is the rich yellow flame of rational intercourse. No need to hurry. No need to sparkle. No need to be anybody but oneself. We are all going to heaven and Vandyck[1] is of the company—in other words, how good life seemed, how sweet its rewards, how trivial this grudge or that grievance, how admirable friendship and the society of one's kind, as, lighting a good cigarette, one sunk among the cushions in the window-seat.

If by good luck there had been an ash-tray handy, if one had not knocked the

1. Sir Anthony Van Dyck (1599–1641), born in Antwerp but lived for some years in England. He painted many grand portraits of the English royal family and court.

ash out of the window in default, if things had been a little different from what they were, one would not have seen, presumably, a cat without a tail. The sight of that abrupt and truncated animal padding softly across the quadrangle changed by some fluke of the subconscious intelligence the emotional light for me. It was as if some one had let fall a shade. Perhaps the excellent hock was relinquishing its hold. Certainly, as I watched the Manx cat pause in the middle of the lawn as if it too questioned the universe, something seemed lacking, something seemed different. But what was lacking, what was different, I asked myself, listening to the talk. And to answer that question I had to think myself out of the room, back into the past, before the war indeed, and to set before my eyes the model of another luncheon party held in rooms not very far distant from these; but different. Everything was different. Meanwhile the talk went on among the guests, who were many and young, some of this sex, some of that; it went on swimmingly, it went on agreeably, freely, amusingly. And as it went on I set it against the background of that other talk, and as I matched the two together I had no doubt that one was the descendant, the legitimate heir of the other. Nothing was changed; nothing was different save only—here I listened with all my ears not entirely to what was being said, but to the murmur or current behind it. Yes, that was it—the change was there. Before the war at a luncheon party like this people would have said precisely the same things but they would have sounded different, because in those days they were accompanied by a sort of humming noise, not articulate, but musical, exciting, which changed the value of the words themselves. Could one set that humming noise to words? Perhaps with the help of the poets one could. A book lay beside me and, opening it, I turned casually enough to Tennyson. And here I found Tennyson was singing:

> There has fallen a splendid tear
>   From the passion-flower at the gate.
> She is coming, my dove, my dear;
>   She is coming, my life, my fate;
> The red rose cries, "She is near, she is near";
>   And the white rose weeps, "She is late";
> The larkspur listens, "I hear, I hear";
>   And the lily whispers, "I wait."[2]

Was that what men hummed at luncheon parties before the war? And the women?

> My heart is like a singing bird
>   Whose nest is in a water'd shoot;
> My heart is like an apple tree
>   Whose boughs are bent with thick-set fruit;
> My heart is like a rainbow shell
>   That paddles in a halcyon sea;
> My heart is gladder than all these
>   Because my love is come to me.[3]

Was that what women hummed at luncheon parties before the war?

There was something so ludicrous in thinking of people humming such things even under their breath at luncheon parties before the war that I burst

2. *Maud* 1.22.10.

3. Christina Rossetti's *A Birthday*, first stanza.

out laughing, and had to explain my laughter by pointing at the Manx cat, who did look a little absurd, poor beast, without a tail, in the middle of the lawn. Was he really born so, or had he lost his tail in an accident? The tailless cat, though some are said to exist in the Isle of Man, is rarer than one thinks. It is a queer animal, quaint rather than beautiful. It is strange what a difference a tail makes—you know the sort of things one says as a lunch party breaks up and people are finding their coats and hats.

This one, thanks to the hospitality of the host, had lasted far into the afternoon. The beautiful October day was fading and the leaves were falling from the trees in the avenue as I walked through it. Gate after gate seemed to close with gentle finality behind me. Innumerable beadles were fitting innumerable keys into well-oiled locks; the treasure-house was being made secure for another night. After the avenue one comes out upon a road—I forget its name—which leads you, if you take the right turning, along to Fernham. But there was plenty of time. Dinner was not till half-past seven. One could almost do without dinner after such a luncheon. It is strange how a scrap of poetry works in the mind and makes the legs move in time to it along the road. Those words—

> There has fallen a splendid tear
> From the passion-flower at the gate.
> She is coming, my dove, my dear—

sang in my blood as I stepped quickly along towards Headingley. And then, switching off into the other measure, I sang, where the waters are churned up by the weir:

> My heart is like a singing bird
> Whose nest is in a water'd shoot;
> My heart is like an apple tree . . .

What poets, I cried aloud, as one does in the dusk, what poets they were!

In a sort of jealousy, I suppose, for our own age, silly and absurd though these comparisons are, I went on to wonder if honestly one could name two living poets now as great as Tennyson and Christina Rossetti were then. Obviously it is impossible, I thought, looking into those foaming waters, to compare them. The very reason why the poetry excites one to such abandonment, such rapture, is that it celebrates some feeling that one used to have (at luncheon parties before the war perhaps), so that one responds easily, familiarly, without troubling to check the feeling, or to compare it with any that one has now. But the living poets express a feeling that is actually being made and torn out of us at the moment. One does not recognize it in the first place; often for some reason one fears it; one watches it with keenness and compares it jealously and suspiciously with the old feeling that one knew. Hence the difficulty of modern poetry; and it is because of this difficulty that one cannot remember more than two consecutive lines of any good modern poet. For this reason—that my memory failed me—the argument flagged for want of material. But why, I continued, moving on towards Headingley, have we stopped humming under our breath at luncheon parties? Why has Alfred ceased to sing

> She is coming, my dove, my dear?

Why has Christina ceased to respond

> *My heart is gladder than all these*
> *Because my love is come to me?*

Shall we lay the blame on the war? When the guns fired in August 1914, did the faces of men and women show so plain in each other's eyes that romance was killed? Certainly it was a shock (to women in particular with their illusions about education, and so on) to see the faces of our rulers in the light of the shell-fire. So ugly they looked—German, English, French—so stupid. But lay the blame where one will, on whom one will, the illusion which inspired Tennyson and Christina Rossetti to sing so passionately about the coming of their loves is far rarer now than then. One has only to read, to look, to listen, to remember. But why say "blame"? Why, if it was an illusion, not praise the catastrophe, whatever it was, that destroyed illusion and put truth in its place? For truth . . . those dots mark the spot where, in search of truth, I missed the turning up to Fernham. Yes indeed, which was truth and which was illusion, I asked myself. What was the truth about these houses, for example, dim and festive now with their red windows in the dusk, but raw and red and squalid, with their sweets and their boot-laces, at nine o'clock in the morning? And the willows and the river and the gardens that run down to the river, vague now with the mist stealing over them, but gold and red in the sunlight—which was the truth, which was the illusion about them? I spare you the twists and turns of my cogitations, for no conclusion was found on the road to Headingley, and I ask you to suppose that I soon found out my mistake about the turning and retraced my steps to Fernham.

As I have said already that it was an October day, I dare not forfeit your respect and imperil the fair name of fiction by changing the season and describing lilacs hanging over garden walls, crocuses, tulips and other flowers of spring. Fiction must stick to facts, and the truer the facts the better the fiction—so we are told. Therefore it was still autumn and the leaves were still yellow and falling, if anything, a little faster than before, because it was now evening (seven twenty-three to be precise) and a breeze (from the southwest to be exact) had risen. But for all that there was something odd at work:

> *My heart is like a singing bird*
> *Whose nest is in a water'd shoot;*
> *My heart is like an apple tree*
> *Whose boughs are bent with thick-set fruit—*

perhaps the words of Christina Rossetti were partly responsible for the folly of the fancy—it was nothing of course but a fancy—that the lilac was shaking its flowers over the garden walls, and the brimstone butterflies were scudding hither and thither, and the dust of the pollen was in the air. A wind blew, from what quarter I know not, but it lifted the half-grown leaves so that there was a flash of silver grey in the air. It was the time between the lights when colours undergo their intensification and purples and golds burn in window-panes like the beat of an excitable heart; when for some reason the beauty of the world revealed and yet soon to perish (here I pushed into the garden, for, unwisely, the door was left open and no beadles seemed about), the beauty of the world which is so soon to perish, has two edges, one of laughter, one of anguish, cutting the heart asunder. The gardens of Fernham lay before me in the spring twilight, wild and open, and in the long grass, sprinkled and carelessly flung, were daffodils and bluebells, not orderly perhaps at the best of times, and now wind-blown and waving as they tugged at their roots. The windows of the building, curved like ships' windows among generous waves of red brick, changed from lemon to silver under the flight of the quick spring clouds. Somebody was in a hammock, somebody, but in this light they were phantoms only, half guessed, half seen, raced across the grass—would no one stop her?—and then on the terrace, as if popping out to breathe the air, to glance at the garden, came a bent figure, formidable yet humble, with her great forehead and her shabby dress—could it be the famous scholar, could it be J—— H—— herself?[4] All was dim, yet intense too, as if the scarf which the dusk had flung over the garden were torn asunder by star or sword—the flash of some terrible reality leaping, as its way is, out of the heart of the spring. For youth——

Here was my soup. Dinner was being served in the great dining-hall. Far from being spring it was in fact an evening in October. Everybody was assembled in the big dining-room. Dinner was ready. Here was the soup. It was a plain gravy soup. There was nothing to stir the fancy in that. One could have seen through the transparent liquid any pattern that there might have been on the plate itself. But there was no pattern. The plate was plain. Next came beef with its attendant greens and potatoes—a homely trinity, suggesting the rumps of cattle in a muddy market, and sprouts curled and yellowed at the edge, and bargaining and cheapening, and women with string bags on Monday morning. There was no reason to complain of human nature's daily food, seeing that the supply was sufficient and coal-miners doubtless were sitting down to less. Prunes and custard followed. And if any one complains that prunes, even when mitigated by custard, are an uncharitable vegetable (fruit they are not), stringy as a miser's heart and exuding a fluid such as might run in misers' veins who have denied themselves wine and warmth for eighty years and yet not given to the poor, he should reflect that there are people whose charity embraces even the prune. Biscuits and cheese came next, and here the water-jug was liberally passed round, for it is the nature of biscuits to be dry, and these were biscuits to the core. That was all. The meal was over. Everybody scraped their chairs back; the swing-doors swung violently to and fro; soon the hall was emptied of every sign of food and made ready no doubt for breakfast next morning. Down corridors and up staircases the youth of England went banging and singing. And was it for a guest, a stranger (for I had no more right here in Fernham than in Trinity or Somerville or Girton or Newnham or Christchurch), to say, "The dinner was not good," or to say (we were now, Mary Seton and I, in her sitting-room), "Could we not have dined up here alone?" for if I had said anything of the kind I should have been prying and searching into the secret economies of a house which to the stranger wears so fine a front of gaiety and courage. No, one could say nothing of the sort. Indeed, conversation for a moment flagged. The human frame being what it is, heart, body and brain all mixed together, and not contained in separate compartments as they will be no doubt in another

---

4. Jane Harrison (1850–1928), fellow and lecturer in classical archaeology at Newnham College, Cambridge; author of *Ancient Art and Ritual* (1913) and other influential books.

million years, a good dinner is of great importance to good talk. One cannot think well, love well, sleep well, if one has not dined well. The lamp in the spine does not light on beef and prunes. We are all *probably* going to heaven, and Vandyck is, we *hope,* to meet us round the next corner—that is the dubious and qualifying state of mind that beef and prunes at the end of the day's work breed between them. Happily my friend, who taught science, had a cupboard where there was a squat bottle and little glasses—(but there should have been sole and partridge to begin with)—so that we were able to draw up to the fire and repair some of the damages of the day's living. In a minute or so we were slipping freely in and out among all those objects of curiosity and interest which form in the mind in the absence of a particular person, and are naturally to be discussed on coming together again—how somebody has married, another has not; one thinks this, another that; one has improved out of all knowledge, the other most amazingly gone to the bad—with all those speculations upon human nature and the character of the amazing world we live in which spring naturally from such beginnings. While these things were being said, however, I became shamefacedly aware of a current setting in of its own accord and carrying everything forward to an end of its own. One might be talking of Spain or Portugal, of book or racehorse, but the real interest of whatever was said was none of those things, but a scene of masons on a high roof some five centuries ago. Kings and nobles brought treasure in huge sacks and poured it under the earth. This scene was for ever coming alive in my mind and placing itself by another of lean cows and a muddy market and withered greens and the stringy hearts of old men—these two pictures, disjointed and disconnected and nonsensical as they were, were for ever coming together and combating each other and had me entirely at their mercy. The best course, unless the whole talk was to be distorted, was to expose what was in my mind to the air, when with good luck it would fade and crumble like the head of the dead king when they opened the coffin at Windsor. Briefly, then, I told Miss Seton about the masons who had been all those years on the roof of the chapel, and about the kings and queens and nobles bearing sacks of gold and silver on their shoulders, which they shovelled into the earth; and then how the great financial magnates of our own time came and laid cheques and bonds, I suppose, where the others had laid ingots and rough lumps of gold. All that lies beneath the colleges down there, I said; but this college, where we are now sitting, what lies beneath its gallant red brick and the wild unkempt grasses of the garden? What force is behind the plain china off which we dined, and (here it popped out of my mouth before I could stop it) the beef, the custard and the prunes?

Well, said Mary Seton, about the year 1860—Oh, but you know the story, she said, bored, I suppose, by the recital. And she told me—rooms were hired. Committees met. Envelopes were addressed. Circulars were drawn up. Meetings were held; letters were read out; so-and-so has promised so much; on the contrary, Mr ——— won't give a penny. The *Saturday Review* has been very rude. How can we raise a fund to pay for offices? Shall we hold a bazaar? Can't we find a pretty girl to sit in the front row? Let us look up what John Stuart Mill said on the subject. Can any one persuade the editor of the ——— to print a letter? Can we get Lady ——— to sign it? Lady ——— is out of town. That was the way it was done, presumably, sixty years ago, and it was a prodigious effort, and a great deal of time was spent on it. And it was only after a long struggle and with the utmost difficulty that they got thirty thousand pounds together.[5] So obviously we cannot have wine and partridges and servants carrying tin dishes on their heads, she said. We cannot have sofas and separate rooms. "The amenities," she said, quoting from some book or other, "will have to wait."[6]

At the thought of all those women working year after year and finding it hard to get two thousand pounds together, and as much as they could do to get thirty thousand pounds, we burst out in scorn at the reprehensible poverty of our sex. What had our mothers been doing then that they had no wealth to leave us? Powdering their noses? Looking in at shop windows? Flaunting in the sun at Monte Carlo? There were some photographs on the mantel-piece. Mary's mother—if that was her picture—may have been a wastrel in her spare time (she had thirteen children by a minister of the church), but if so her gay and dissipated life had left too few traces of its pleasures on her face. She was a homely body; an old lady in a plaid shawl which was fastened by a large cameo; and she sat in a basket-chair, encouraging a spaniel to look at the camera, with the amused, yet strained expression of one who is sure that the dog will move directly the bulb is pressed. Now if she had gone into business; had become a manufacturer of artificial silk or a magnate on the Stock Exchange; if she had left two or three hundred thousand pounds to Fernham, we could have been sitting at our ease tonight and the subject of our talk might have been archaeology, botany, anthropology, physics, the nature of the atom, mathematics, astronomy, relativity, geography. If only Mrs Seton and her mother and her mother before her had learnt the great art of making money and had left their money, like their fathers and their grandfathers before them, to found fellowships and lectureships and prizes and scholarships appropriated to the use of their own sex, we might have dined very tolerably up here alone off a bird and a bottle of wine; we might have looked forward without undue confidence to a pleasant and honourable lifetime spent in the shelter of one of the liberally endowed professions. We might have been exploring or writing; mooning about the venerable places of the earth; sitting contemplative on the steps of the Parthenon, or going at ten to an office and coming home comfortably at half-past four to write a little poetry. Only, if Mrs Seton and her like had gone into business at the age of fifteen, there would have been—that was the snag in the argument—no Mary. What, I asked, did Mary think of that? There between the curtains was the October night, calm and lovely, with a star or two caught in the yellowing trees. Was she ready to resign her share of it and her memories (for they had been a happy family, though a large one) of games and quarrels up in Scotland, which she is never tired of praising for the fineness of its air and the quality of its cakes, in order that Fernham might have been endowed with fifty thousand pounds or so by a stroke of the pen? For, to endow a college would neces-

---

5. "We are told that we ought to ask for £30,000 at least. . . . It is not a large sum, considering that there is to be but one college of this sort for Great Britain, Ireland and the Colonies, and considering how easy it is to raise immense sums for boys' schools. But considering how few people really wish women to be educated, it is a good deal."— Lady Stephen, *Life of Miss Emily Davies* [Woolf's note].

6. "Every penny which could be scraped together was set aside for building, and the amenities had to be postponed."—R. Strachey, *The Cause* [Woolf's note].

sitate the suppression of families altogether. Making a fortune and bearing thirteen children—no human being could stand it. Consider the facts, we said. First there are nine months before the baby is born. Then the baby is born. Then there are three or four months spent in feeding the baby. After the baby is fed there are certainly five years spent in playing with the baby. You cannot, it seems, let children run about the streets. People who have seen them running wild in Russia say that the sight is not a pleasant one. People say, too, that human nature takes its shape in the years between one and five. If Mrs Seton, I said, had been making money, what sort of memories would you have had of games and quarrels? What would you have known of Scotland, and its fine air and cakes and all the rest of it? But it is useless to ask these questions, because you would never have come into existence at all. Moreover, it is equally useless to ask what might have happened if Mrs Seton and her mother and her mother before her had amassed great wealth and laid it under the foundations of college and library, because, in the first place, to earn money was impossible for them, and in the second, had it been possible, the law denied them the right to possess what money they earned. It is only for the last forty-eight years that Mrs Seton has had a penny of her own. For all the centuries before that it would have been her husband's property—a thought which, perhaps, may have had its share in keeping Mrs Seton and her mothers off the Stock Exchange. Every penny I earn, they may have said, will be taken from me and disposed of according to my husband's wisdom—perhaps to found a scholarship or to endow a fellowship in Balliol or Kings,[7] so that to earn money, even if I could earn money, is not a matter that interests me very greatly. I had better leave it to my husband.

At any rate, whether or not the blame rested on the old lady who was looking at the spaniel, there could be no doubt that for some reason or other our mothers had mismanaged their affairs very gravely. Not a penny could be spared for "amenities"; for partridges and wine, beadles and turf, books and cigars, libraries and leisure. To raise bare walls out of the bare earth was the utmost they could do.

So we talked standing at the window and looking, as so many thousands look every night, down on the domes and towers of the famous city beneath us. It was very beautiful, very mysterious in the autumn moonlight. The old stone looked very white and venerable. One thought of all the books that were assembled down there; of the pictures of old prelates and worthies hanging in the panelled rooms; of the painted windows that would be throwing strange globes and crescents on the pavement; of the tablets and memorials and inscriptions; of the fountains and the grass; of the quiet rooms looking across the quiet quadrangles. And (pardon me the thought) I thought, too, of the admirable smoke and drink and the deep armchairs and the pleasant carpets: of the urbanity, the geniality, the dignity which are the offspring of luxury and privacy and space. Certainly our mothers had not provided us with anything comparable to all this—our mothers who found it difficult to scrape together thirty thousand pounds, our mothers who bore thirteen children to ministers of religion at St Andrews.[8]

7. Colleges at Oxford and Cambridge, respectively.
8. Perhaps St. Andrew Holborn, a church in London designed by Sir Christopher Wren (1632–1723).

So I went back to my inn, and as I walked through the dark streets I pondered this and that, as one does at the end of the day's work. I pondered why it was that Mrs Seton had no money to leave us; and what effect poverty has on the mind; and what effect wealth has on the mind; and I thought of the queer old gentlemen I had seen that morning with tufts of fur upon their shoulders; and I remembered how if one whistled one of them ran; and I thought of the organ booming in the chapel and of the shut doors of the library; and I thought how unpleasant it is to be locked out; and I thought how it is worse perhaps to be locked in; and, thinking of the safety and prosperity of the one sex and of the poverty and insecurity of the other and of the effect of tradition and of the lack of tradition upon the mind of a writer, I thought at last that it was time to roll up the crumpled skin of the day, with its arguments and its impressions and its anger and its laughter, and cast it into the hedge. A thousand stars were flashing across the blue wastes of the sky. One seemed alone with an inscrutable society. All human beings were laid asleep—prone, horizontal, dumb. Nobody seemed stirring in the streets of Oxbridge. Even the door of the hotel sprang open at the touch of an invisible hand—not a boots was sitting up to light me to bed, it was so late.

Chapter Two

The scene, if I may ask you to follow me, was now changed. The leaves were still falling, but in London now, not Oxbridge; and I must ask you to imagine a room, like many thousands, with a window looking across people's hats and vans and motor-cars to other windows, and on the table inside the room a blank sheet of paper on which was written in large letters WOMEN AND FICTION, but no more. The inevitable sequel to lunching and dining at Oxbridge seemed, unfortunately, to be a visit to the British Museum. One must strain off what was personal and accidental in all these impressions and so reach the pure fluid, the essential oil of truth. For that visit to Oxbridge and the luncheon and the dinner had started a swarm of questions. Why did men drink wine and women water? Why was one sex so prosperous and the other so poor? What effect has poverty on fiction? What conditions are necessary for the creation of works of art?—a thousand questions at once suggested themselves. But one needed answers, not questions; and an answer was only to be had by consulting the learned and the unprejudiced, who have removed themselves above the strife of tongue and the confusion of body and issued the result of their reasoning and research in books which are to be found in the British Museum. If truth is not to be found on the shelves of the British Museum, where, I asked myself, picking up a notebook and a pencil, is truth?

Thus provided, thus confident and enquiring, I set out in the pursuit of truth. The day, though not actually wet, was dismal, and the streets in the neighbourhood of the Museum were full of open coal-holes, down which sacks were showering; four-wheeled cabs were drawing up and depositing on the pavement corded boxes containing, presumably, the entire wardrobe of some Swiss or Italian family seeking fortune or refuge or some other desirable commodity which is to be found in the boarding-houses of Bloomsbury in the winter. The usual hoarse-voiced men paraded the streets with plants on barrows. Some shouted; others sang. London was like a workshop. London was like a machine. We were all being shot backwards and forwards on this plain foundation to make some pattern. The British Museum was another department of the factory. The swing-doors swung open; and there one stood under the vast dome, as if one were a thought in the huge bald forehead which is so splendidly encircled by a band of famous names. One went to the counter; one took a slip of paper; one opened a volume of the catalogue, and . . . . . the five dots here indicate five separate minutes of stupefaction, wonder and bewilderment. Have you any notion how many books are written about women in the course of one year? Have you any notion how many are written by men? Are you aware that you are, perhaps, the most discussed animal in the universe? Here had I come with a notebook and a pencil proposing to spend a morning reading, supposing that at the end of the morning I should have transferred the truth to my notebook. But I should need to be a herd of elephants, I thought, and a wilderness of spiders, desperately referring to the animals that are reputed longest lived and most multitudinously eyed, to cope with all this. I should need claws of steel and beak of brass even to penetrate the husk. How shall I ever find the grains of truth embedded in all this mass of paper, I asked myself, and in despair began running my eye up and down the long list of titles. Even the names of the books gave me food for thought. Sex and its nature might well attract doctors and biologists; but what was surprising and difficult of explanation was the fact that sex—woman, that is to say—also attracts agreeable essayists, light-fingered novelists, young men who have taken the M.A. degree; men who have taken no degree; men who have no apparent qualification save that they are not women. Some of these books were, on the face of it, frivolous and facetious; but many, on the other hand, were serious and prophetic, moral and hortatory. Merely to read the titles suggested innumerable schoolmasters, innumerable clergymen mounting their platforms and pulpits and holding forth with a loquacity which far exceeded the hour usually allotted to such discourse on this one subject. It was a most strange phenomenon; and apparently—here I consulted the letter M—one confined to male sex. Women do not write books about men—a fact that I could not help welcoming with relief, for if I had first to read all that men have written about women, then all that women have written about men, the aloe that flowers once in a hundred years would flower twice before I could set pen to paper. So, making a perfectly arbitrary choice of a dozen volumes or so, I sent my slips of paper to lie in the wire tray, and waited in my stall, among the other seekers for the essential oil of truth.

What could be the reason, then, of this curious disparity, I wondered, drawing cart-wheels on the slips of paper provided by the British taxpayer for other purposes. Why are women, judging from this catalogue, so much more interesting to men than men are to women? A very curious fact it seemed, and my mind wandered to picture the lives of men who spend their time in writing books about women; whether they were old or young, married or unmarried, red-nosed or hump-backed—anyhow, it was flattering, vaguely, to feel oneself the object of such attention, provided that it was not entirely bestowed by the crippled and the infirm—so I pondered until all such frivolous thoughts were ended by an avalanche of books sliding down on to the desk in front of me. Now the trouble began. The student who has been trained in research at Oxbridge has no doubt some method of shepherding his question past all distractions till it runs into its answer as a sheep runs into its pen. The student by my side, for instance, who was copying assiduously from a scientific manual was, I felt sure, extracting pure nuggets of the essential ore every ten minutes or so. His little grunts of satisfaction indicated so much. But if, unfortunately, one has had no training in a university, the question far from being shepherded to its pen flies like a frightened flock hither and thither, helter-skelter, pursued by a whole pack of hounds. Professors, schoolmasters, sociologists, clergymen, novelists, essayists, journalists, men who had no qualification save that they were not women, chased my simple and single question— Why are women poor?—until it became fifty questions; until the fifty questions leapt frantically into mid-stream and were carried away. Every page in my notebook was scribbled over with notes. To show the state of mind I was in, I will read you a few of them, explaining that the page was headed quite simply, WOMEN AND POVERTY, in block letters; but what followed was something like this:

> Condition in Middle Ages of,
> Habits in the Fiji Islands of,
> Worshipped as goddesses by,
> Weaker in moral sense than,
> Idealism of,
> Greater conscientiousness of,
> South Sea Islanders, age of puberty among,
> Attractiveness of,
> Offered as sacrifice to,
> Small size of brain of,
> Profounder sub-consciousness of,
> Less hair on the body of,
> Mental, moral and physical inferiority of,
> Love of children of,
> Greater length of life of,
> Weaker muscles of,
> Strength of affections of,
> Vanity of,
> Higher education of,
> Shakespeare's opinion of,
> Lord Birkenhead's opinion of,
> Dean Inge's opinion of,
> La Bruyère's opinion of,
> Dr Johnson's opinion of,
> Mr Oscar Browning's[9] opinion of, . . .

Here I drew breath and added, indeed, in the margin, Why does Samuel Butler[1] say, "Wise men never say what they think of women"? Wise men never say anything else apparently. But, I continued, leaning back in my

9. F. E. Smith, earl of Birkenhead (1872–1930), was lord chancellor (1919–22) and an opponent of women's suffrage. William Ralph Inge (1860–1954), dean of St. Paul's Cathedral in London (1911–34). Woolf quotes the opinions of the French moralist Jean de La Bruyère (1645–1696) and of the English writer Samuel Johnson (1609–1784) below. Oscar Browning (1837–1923) was a famous history lecturer at King's College, Cambridge.
1. British writer (1835–1902).

chair and looking at the vast dome in which I was a single but by now some-what harassed thought, what is so unfortunate is that wise men never think the same thing about women. Here is Pope:

Most women have no character at all.

And here is La Bruyère:

Les femmes sont extrêmes; elles sont meilleures ou pires que les hommes—[2]

a direct contradiction by keen observers who were contemporary. Are they capable of education or incapable? Napoleon thought them incapable. Dr Johnson thought the opposite.[3] Have they souls or have they not souls? Some savages say they have none. Others, on the contrary, maintain that women are half divine and worship them on that account.[4] Some sages hold that they are shallower in the brain; others that they are deeper in the conscious-ness. Goethe honoured them; Mussolini[5] despises them. Wherever one looked men thought about women and thought differently. It was impossible to make head or tail of it all, I decided, glancing with envy at the reader next door who was making the neatest abstracts, headed often with an A or a B or a C, while my own notebook rioted with the wildest scribble of contradic-tory jottings. It was distressing, it was bewildering, it was humiliating. Truth had run through my fingers. Every drop had escaped.

I could not possibly go home, I reflected, and add as a serious contribution to the study of women and fiction that women have less hair on their bodies than men, or that the age of puberty among the South Sea Islanders is nine— or is it ninety?—even the handwriting had become in its distraction indeci-pherable. It was disgraceful to have nothing more weighty or respectable to show after a whole morning's work. And if I could not grasp the truth about W. (as for brevity's sake I had come to call her) in the past, why bother about W. in the future? It seemed pure waste of time to consult all those gentlemen who specialise in woman and her effect on whatever it may be—politics, children, wages, morality—numerous and learned as they are. One might as well leave their books unopened.

But while I pondered I had unconsciously, in my listlessness, in my des-peration, been drawing a picture where I should, like my neighbour, have been writing a conclusion. I had been drawing a face, a figure. It was the face and the figure of Professor von X. engaged in writing his monumental work entitled *The Mental, Moral, and Physical Inferiority of the Female Sex.* He was not in my picture a man attractive to women. He was heavily built; he had a great jowl; to balance that he had very small eyes; he was very red in the face. His expression suggested that he was labouring under some emotion that made him jab his pen on the paper as if he were killing some noxious insect as he wrote, but even when he had killed it that did not satisfy him; he must go on killing it; and even so, some cause for anger and irritation remained. Could it be his wife, I asked, looking at my picture. Was she in love with a cavalry officer? Was the cavalry officer slim and elegant and dressed in astrachan? Had he been laughed at, to adopt the Freudian theory, in his cradle by a pretty girl? For even in his cradle the professor, I thought, could not have been an attractive child. Whatever the reason, the professor was made to look very angry and very ugly in my sketch, as he wrote his great book upon the mental, moral and physical inferiority of women. Drawing pictures was an idle way of finishing an unprofitable morning's work. Yet it is in our idleness, in our dreams, that the submerged truth sometimes comes to the top. A very elementary exercise in psychology, not to be dignified by the name of psycho-analysis, showed me, on looking at my notebook, that the sketch of the angry professor had been made in anger. Anger had snatched my pencil while I dreamt. But what was anger doing there? Interest, confusion, amusement, boredom—all these emotions I could trace and name as they succeeded each other throughout the morning. Had anger, the black snake, been lurking among them? Yes, said the sketch, anger had. It referred me unmistakably to the one book, to the one phrase, which had roused the demon; it was the professor's statement about the mental, moral and physical inferiority of women. My heart had leapt. My cheeks had burnt. I had flushed with anger. There was nothing specially remarkable, however foolish, in that. One does not like to be told that one is naturally the inferior of a little man— I looked at the student next me—who breathes hard, wears a ready-made tie, and has not shaved this fortnight. One has certain foolish vanities. It is only human nature, I reflected, and began drawing cartwheels and circles over the angry professor's face till he looked like a burning bush or a flaming comet—anyhow, an apparition without human semblance or significance. The professor was nothing now but a faggot burning on the top of Hampstead Heath.[6] Soon my own anger was explained and done with; but curiosity remained. How explain the anger of the professors? Why were they angry? For when it came to analysing the impression left by these books there was always an element of heat. This heat took many forms; it showed itself in satire, in sentiment, in curiosity, in reprobation. But there was another element which was often present and could not immediately be identified. Anger, I called it. But it was anger that had gone underground and mixed itself with all kinds of other emotions. To judge from its odd effects, it was anger disguised and complex, not anger simple and open.

Whatever the reason, all these books, I thought, surveying the pile on the desk, are worthless for my purposes. They were worthless scientifically, that is to say, though humanly they were full of instruction, interest, boredom, and very queer facts about the habits of the Fiji Islanders. They had been written in the red light of emotion and not in the white light of truth. Therefore they must be returned to the central desk and restored each to his own cell in the enormous honeycomb. All that I had retrieved from that morning's work had been the one fact of anger. The professors—I lumped them together thus—were angry. But why, I asked myself, having returned the books, why, I repeated, standing under the colonnade among the pigeons and the prehistoric canoes, why are they angry? And, asking myself this ques-

6. An extensive area of open land on a hill overlooking London. "Faggot": a bundle of sticks.

tion, I strolled off to find a place for luncheon. What is the real nature of what I call for the moment their anger? I asked. Here was a puzzle that would last all the time that it takes to be served with food in a small restaurant somewhere near the British Museum. Some previous luncher had left the lunch edition of the evening paper on a chair, and, waiting to be served, I began idly reading the headlines. A ribbon of very large letters ran across the page. Somebody had made a big score in South Africa. Lesser ribbons announced that Sir Austen Chamberlain was at Geneva.[7] A meat axe with human hair on it had been found in a cellar. Mr Justice ——— commented in the Divorce Courts upon the Shamelessness of Women. Sprinkled about the paper were other pieces of news. A film actress had been lowered from a peak in California and hung suspended in mid-air. The weather was going to be foggy. The most transient visitor to this planet, I thought, who picked up this paper could not fail to be aware, even from this scattered testimony, that England is under the rule of a patriarchy. Nobody in their senses could fail to detect the dominance of the professor. His was the power and the money and the influence. He was the proprietor of the paper and its editor and sub-editor. He was the Foreign Secretary and the Judge. He was the cricketer; he owned the racehorses and the yachts. He was the director of the company that pays two hundred per cent to its shareholders. He left millions to charities and colleges that were ruled by himself. He suspended the film actress in mid-air. He will decide if the hair on the meat axe is human; he it is who will acquit or convict the murderer, and hang him, or let him go free. With the exception of the fog he seemed to control every-thing. Yet he was angry. I knew that he was angry by this token. When I read what he wrote about women I thought, not of what he was saying, but of himself. When an arguer argues dispassionately he thinks only of the argu-ment; and the reader cannot help thinking of the argument too. If he had written dispassionately about women, had used indisputable proofs to estab-lish his argument and had shown no trace of wishing that the result should be one thing rather than another, one would not have been angry either. One would have accepted the fact, as one accepts the fact that a pea is green or a canary yellow. So be it, I should have said. But I had been angry because he was angry. Yet it seemed absurd, I thought, turning over the evening paper, that a man with all this power should be angry. Or is anger, I won-dered, somehow, the familiar, the attendant sprite on power? Rich people, for example, are often angry because they suspect that the poor want to seize their wealth. The professors, or patriarchs, as it might be more accurate to call them, might be angry for that reason partly, but partly for one that lies a little less obviously on the surface. Possibly they were not "angry" at all; often, indeed, they were admiring, devoted, exemplary in the relations of private life. Possibly when the professor insisted a little too emphatically upon the inferiority of women, he was concerned not with their inferiority, but with his own superiority. That was what he was protecting rather hot-headedly and with too much emphasis, because it was a jewel to him of the rarest price. Life for both sexes—and I looked at them, shouldering their way along the pavement—is arduous, difficult, a perpetual struggle. It calls

7. Headquarters of the League of Nations. Chamberlain (1863–1937) was a British statesman and brother of Neville Chamberlain, British prime minister (1937–40).

for gigantic courage and strength. More than anything, perhaps, creatures of illusion as we are, it calls for confidence in oneself. Without self-confidence we are as babes in the cradle. And how can we generate this imponderable quality, which is yet so invaluable, most quickly? By thinking that other people are inferior to oneself. By feeling that one has some innate superiority—it may be wealth, or rank, a straight nose, or the portrait of a grandfather by Romney[8]—for there is no end to the pathetic devices of the human imagination—over other people. Hence the enormous importance to a patriarch who has to conquer, who has to rule, of feeling that great numbers of people, half the human race indeed, are by nature inferior to himself. It must indeed be one of the chief sources of his power. But let me turn the light of this observation on to real life, I thought. Does it help to explain some of those psychological puzzles that one notes in the margin of daily life? Does it explain my astonishment the other day when Z, most humane, most modest of men, taking up some book by Rebecca West[9] and reading a passage in it, exclaimed, "The arrant feminist! She says that men are snobs!" The exclamation, to me so surprising—for why was Miss West an arrant feminist for making a possibly true if uncomplimentary statement about the other sex?—was not merely the cry of wounded vanity; it was a protest against some infringement of his power to believe in himself. Women have served all these centuries as looking-glasses possessing the magic and delicious power of reflecting the figure of man at twice its natural size. Without that power probably the earth would still be swamp and jungle. The glories of all our wars would be unknown. We should still be scratching the outlines of deer on the remains of mutton bones and bartering flints for sheepskins or whatever simple ornament took our unsophisticated taste. Supermen and Fingers of Destiny would never have existed. The Czar and the Kaiser[1] would never have worn their crowns or lost them. Whatever may be their use in civilised societies, mirrors are essential to all violent and heroic action. That is why Napoleon and Mussolini[2] both insist so emphatically upon the inferiority of women, for if they were not inferior, they would cease to enlarge. That serves to explain in part the necessity that women so often are to men. And it serves to explain how restless they are under her criticism; how impossible it is for her to say to them this book is bad, this picture is feeble, or whatever it may be, without giving far more pain and rousing far more anger than a man would do who gave the same criticism. For if she begins to tell the truth, the figure in the looking-glass shrinks; his fitness for life is diminished. How is he to go on giving judgement, civilising natives, making laws, writing books, dressing up and speechifying at banquets, unless he can see himself at breakfast and at dinner at least twice the size he really is? So I reflected, crumbling my bread and stirring my coffee and now and again looking at the people in the street. The looking-glass vision is of supreme importance because it charges the vitality; it stimulates the nervous system. Take it away and man may die, like the drug fiend deprived of his cocaine. Under the spell of that illusion, I thought, looking out of the window, half the people on the pavement are striding to work. They put on their hats and coats in the morning under its agreeable rays. They start the day confident,

---

8. George Romney (1734–1802), fashionable portrait painter.
9. Adopted name of Cecily Isabel Fairfield (1892–

1983), feminist, journalist, and novelist.
1. Rulers of Russia and Germany, respectively.
2. I.e., dictators.

braced, believing themselves desired at Miss Smith's tea party; they say to themselves as they go into the room, I am the superior of half the people here, and it is thus that they speak with that self-confidence, that self-assurance, which have had such profound consequences in public life and lead to such curious notes in the margin of the private mind.

But these contributions to the dangerous and fascinating subject of the psychology of the other sex—it is one, I hope, that you will investigate when you have five hundred a year of your own—were interrupted by the necessity of paying the bill. It came to five shillings and ninepence. I gave the waiter a ten-shilling note and he went to bring me change. There was another ten-shilling note in my purse; I noticed it, because it is a fact that still takes my breath away—the power of my purse to breed ten-shillings notes automatically. I open it and there they are. Society gives me chicken and coffee, bed and lodging, in return for a certain number of pieces of paper which were left me by an aunt, for no other reason than that I share her name.

My aunt, Mary Beton, I must tell you, died by a fall from her horse when she was riding out to take the air in Bombay. The news of my legacy reached me one night about the same time that the act was passed that gave votes to women. A solicitor's letter fell into the post-box and when I opened it I found that she had left me five hundred pounds a year for ever. Of the two—the vote and the money—the money, I own, seemed infinitely the more important. Before that I had made my living by cadging odd jobs from newspapers, by reporting a donkey show here or a wedding there; I had earned a few pounds by addressing envelopes, reading to old ladies, making artificial flowers, teaching the alphabet to small children in a kindergarten. Such were the chief occupations that were open to women before 1918. I need not, I am afraid, describe in any detail the hardness of the work, for you know perhaps women who have done it; nor the difficulty of living on the money when it was earned, for you may have tried. But what still remains with me as a worse infliction than either was the poison of fear and bitterness which those days bred in me. To begin with, always to be doing work that one did not wish to do, and to do it like a slave, flattering and fawning, not always necessarily perhaps, but it seemed necessary and the stakes were too great to run risks; and then the thought of that one gift which it was death to hide—a small one but dear to the possessor—perishing and with it myself, my soul—all this became like a rust eating away the bloom of the spring, destroying the tree at its heart. However, as I say, my aunt died; and whenever I change a ten-shilling note a little of that rust and corrosion is rubbed off; fear and bitterness go. Indeed, I thought, slipping the silver into my purse, it is remarkable, remembering the bitterness of those days, what a change of temper a fixed income will bring about. No force in the world can take from me my five hundred pounds. Food, house and clothing are mine for ever. Therefore not merely do effort and labour cease, but also hatred and bitterness. I need not hate any man; he cannot hurt me. I need not flatter any man; he has nothing to give me. So imperceptibly I found myself adopting a new attitude towards the other half of the human race. It was absurd to blame any class or any sex, as a whole. Great bodies of people are never responsible for what they do. They are driven by instincts which are not within their control. They too, the patriarchs, the professors, had endless difficulties, terrible drawbacks to contend with. Their education had been in some ways as faulty as my own. It had bred in them defects as great. True, they had money and power, but only at the cost of harbouring in their breasts an eagle, a vulture, for ever tearing the liver out and plucking at the lungs—the instinct for possession, the rage for acquisition which drives them to desire other people's fields and goods perpetually; to make frontiers and flags; battleships and poison gas; to offer up their own lives and their children's lives. Walk through the Admiralty Arch[3] (I had reached that monument), or any other avenue given up to trophies and cannon, and reflect upon the kind of glory celebrated there. Or watch in the spring sunshine the stockbroker and the great barrister going indoors to make money and more money and more money when it is a fact that five hundred pounds a year will keep one alive in the sunshine. These are unpleasant instincts to harbour, I reflected. They are bred of the conditions of life; of the lack of civilisation, I thought, looking at the statue of the Duke of Cambridge, and in particular at the feathers in his cocked hat, with a fixity that they have scarcely ever received before. And, as I realised these drawbacks, by degrees fear and bitterness modified themselves into pity and toleration; and then in a year or two, pity and toleration went, and the greatest release of all came, which is freedom to think of things in themselves. That building, for example, do I like it or not? Is that picture beautiful or not? Is that in my opinion a good book or a bad? Indeed my aunt's legacy unveiled the sky to me, and substituted for the large and imposing figure of a gentleman, which Milton recommended for my perpetual adoration, a view of the open sky.

So thinking, so speculating, I found my way back to my house by the river. Lamps were being lit and an indescribable change had come over London since the morning hour. It was as if the great machine after labouring all day had made with our help a few yards of something very exciting and beautiful—a fiery fabric flashing with red eyes, a tawny monster roaring with hot breath. Even the wind seemed flung like a flag as it lashed the houses and rattled the hoardings.

In my little street, however, domesticity prevailed. The house painter was descending his ladder; the nursemaid was wheeling the perambulator carefully in and out back to nursery tea; the coal-heaver was folding his empty sacks on top of each other; the woman who keeps the green-grocer's shop was adding up the day's takings with her hands in red mittens. But so engrossed was I with the problem you have laid upon my shoulders that I could not see even these usual sights without referring them to one centre. I thought how much harder it is now than it must have been even a century ago to say which of these employments is the higher, the more necessary. Is it better to be a coal-heaver or a nursemaid; is the charwoman who has brought up eight children of less value to the world than the barrister who has made a hundred thousand pounds? It is useless to ask such questions; for nobody can answer them. Not only do the comparative values of char-women and lawyers rise and fall from decade to decade, but we have no rods with which to measure them even as they are at the moment. I had been foolish to ask my professor to furnish me with "indisputable proofs" of this or that in his argument about women. Even if one could state the value of

3. Between the Mall and Trafalgar Square in London, constructed 1906–11 to commemorate Britain's imperial successes.

any one gift at the moment, those values will change; in a century's time very possibly they will have changed completely. Moreover, in a hundred years, I thought, reaching my own doorstep, women will have ceased to be the protected sex. Logically they will take part in all the activities and exertions that were once denied them. The nursemaid will heave coal. The shop-woman will drive an engine. All assumptions founded on the facts observed when women were the protected sex will have disappeared—as, for example (here a squad of soldiers marched down the street), that women and clergymen and gardeners live longer than other people. Remove that protection, expose them to the same exertions and activities, make them soldiers and sailors and engine-drivers and dock labourers, and will not women die off so much younger, so much quicker, than men that one will say, "I saw a woman today," as one used to say, "I saw an aeroplane." Anything may happen when womanhood has ceased to be a protected occupation, I thought, opening the door. But what bearing has all this upon the subject of my paper, Women and Fiction? I asked, going indoors.

Chapter Three

It was disappointing not to have brought back in the evening some important statement, some authentic fact. Women are poorer than men because— this or that. Perhaps now it would be better to give up seeking for the truth, and receiving on one's head an avalanche of opinion hot as lava, discoloured as dish-water. It would be better to draw the curtains; to shut out distractions; to light the lamp; to narrow the enquiry and to ask the historian, who records not opinions but facts, to describe under what conditions women lived, not throughout the ages, but in England, say in the time of Elizabeth.

For it is a perennial puzzle why no woman wrote a word of that extraordinary literature when every other man, it seemed, was capable of song or sonnet. What were the conditions in which women lived, I asked myself; for fiction, imaginative work that is, is not dropped like a pebble upon the ground, as science may be; fiction is like a spider's web, attached ever so lightly perhaps, but still attached to life at all four corners. Often the attachment is scarcely perceptible; Shakespeare's plays, for instance, seem to hang there complete by themselves. But when the web is pulled askew, hooked up at the edge, torn in the middle, one remembers that these webs are not spun in midair by incorporeal creatures, but are the work of suffering human beings, and are attached to grossly material things, like health and money and the houses we live in.

I went, therefore, to the shelf where the histories stand and took down one of the latest, Professor Trevelyan's *History of England*.[4] Once more I looked up Women, found "position of," and turned to the pages indicated. "Wife-beating," I read, "was a recognised right of man, and was practised without shame by high as well as low. . . . Similarly," the historian goes on, "the daughter who refused to marry the gentleman of her parents' choice was liable to be locked up, beaten and flung about the room, without any shock being inflicted on public opinion. Marriage was not an affair of per-

4. G. M. Trevelyan's *History of England* (1926) long held its place as the standard one-volume history of the country.

sonal affection, but of family avarice, particularly in the 'chivalrous' upper classes. . . . Betrothal often took place while one or both of the parties was in the cradle, and marriage when they were scarcely out of the nurses' charge." That was about 1470, soon after Chaucer's time. The next reference to the position of women is some two hundred years later, in the time of the Stuarts. "It was still the exception for women of the upper and middle class to choose their own husbands, and when the husband had been assigned, he was lord and master, so far at least as law and custom could make him. Yet even so," Professor Trevelyan concludes, "neither Shakespeare's women nor those of authentic seventeenth-century memoirs, like the Verneys and the Hutchinsons,[5] seem wanting in personality and character." Certainly, if we consider it, Cleopatra must have had a way with her; Lady Macbeth, one would suppose, had a will of her own; Rosalind,[6] one might conclude, was an attractive girl. Professor Trevelyan is speaking no more than the truth when he remarks that Shakespeare's women do not seem wanting in personality and character. Not being a historian, one might go even further and say that women have burnt like beacons in all the works of all the poets from the beginning of time—Clytemnestra, Antigone, Cleopatra, Lady Macbeth, Phèdre, Cressida, Rosalind, Desdemona, the Duchess of Malfi, among the dramatists; then among the prose writers: Millamant, Clarissa, Becky Sharp, Anna Karenina, Emma Bovary, Madame de Guermantes[7]—the names flock to mind, nor do they recall women "lacking in personality and character." Indeed, if woman had no existence save in the fiction written by men, one would imagine her a person of the utmost importance, very various; heroic and mean; splendid and sordid; infinitely beautiful and hideous in the extreme; as great as a man, some think even greater.[8] But this is woman in fiction. In fact, as Professor Trevelyan points out, she was locked up, beaten and flung about the room.

A very queer, composite being thus emerges. Imaginatively she is of the highest importance; practically she is completely insignificant. She pervades poetry from cover to cover; she is all but absent from history. She dominates the lives of kings and conquerors in fiction; in fact she was the slave of any boy whose parents forced a ring upon her finger. Some of the most inspired

---

5. "The ideal family life of the period [1640–50] that ended in such tragic political division has been recorded once for all in the *Memoirs of the Verney Family*" (Trevelyan, *History of England*). Lucy Hutchinson (b. 1628) wrote the biography of her husband, Col. John Hutchinson (1616–1684); it was first published in 1806.

6. These three Shakespearean heroines are, respectively, in *Antony and Cleopatra, Macbeth,* and *As You Like It*.

7. Characters in, respectively, Aeschylus's *Agamemnon*; Sophocles' *Antigone*; Shakespeare's *Antony and Cleopatra* and *Macbeth*; Racine's *Phèdre*; Shakespeare's *Troilus and Cressida, As You Like It,* and *Othello*; Webster's *The Duchess of Malfi*; Congreve's *Way of the World*; Richardson's *Clarissa*; Thackeray's *Vanity Fair*; Tolstoy's *Anna Karenina*; Flaubert's *Madame Bovary*; and Proust's *A la recherche du temps perdu*.

8. "It remains a strange and almost inexplicable fact that in Athena's city, where women were kept in almost Oriental suppression as odalisques or drudges, the stage should yet have produced figures like Clytemnestra and Cassandra, Atossa and Antigone, Phèdre and Medea, and all the other heroines who dominate play after play of the 'misogynist' Euripides. But the paradox of this world where in real life a respectable woman could hardly show her face alone in the street, and yet on the stage woman equals or surpasses man, has never been satisfactorily explained. In modern tragedy the same predominance exists. At all events, a very cursory survey of Shakespeare's work (similarly with Webster, though not with Marlowe or Jonson) suffices to reveal how this dominance, this initiative of women, persists from Rosalind to Lady Macbeth. So too in Racine; six of his tragedies bear their heroines' names; and what male characters of his shall we set against Hermione and Andromaque, Bérénice and Roxane, Phèdre and Athalie? So again with Ibsen; what men shall we match with Solveig and Nora, Hedda and Hilda Wangel and Rebecca West?"—F. L. Lucas, *Tragedy*, pp. 114–15 [Woolf's note].

words, some of the most profound thoughts in literature fall from her lips;
in real life she could hardly read, could scarcely spell, and was the property
of her husband.

It was certainly an odd monster that one made up by reading the historians
first and the poets afterwards—a worm winged like an eagle; the spirit of life
and beauty in a kitchen chopping up suet. But these monsters, however
amusing to the imagination, have no existence in fact. What one must do to
bring her to life was to think poetically and prosaically at one and the same
moment, thus keeping in touch with fact—that she is Mrs Martin, aged
thirty-six, dressed in blue, wearing a black hat and brown shoes; but not
losing sight of fiction either—that she is a vessel in which all sorts of spirits
and forces are coursing and flashing perpetually. The moment, however,
that one tries this method with the Elizabethan woman, one branch of
illumination fails; one is held up by the scarcity of facts. One knows
nothing detailed, nothing perfectly true and substantial about her. History
scarcely mentions her. And I turned to Professor Trevelyan again to see what
history meant to him. I found by looking at his chapter headings that it
meant—

"The Manor Court and the Methods of Open-field Agriculture . . . The
Cistercians and Sheep-farming . . . The Crusades . . . The University . . .
The House of Commons . . . The Hundred Years' War . . . The Wars of the
Roses . . . The Renaissance Scholars . . . The Dissolution of the Monasteries
. . . Agrarian and Religious Strife . . . The Origin of English Sea-power . . .
The Armada . . ." and so on. Occasionally an individual woman is mentioned,
an Elizabeth, or a Mary; a queen or a great lady. But by no possible means
could middle-class women with nothing but brains and character at their
command have taken part in any one of the great movements which, brought
together, constitute the historian's view of the past. Nor shall we find her in
any collection of anecdotes. Aubrey[9] hardly mentions her. She never writes
her own life and scarcely keeps a diary; there are only a handful of her letters
in existence. She left no plays or poems by which we can judge her. What
one wants, I thought—and why does not some brilliant student at Newnham
or Girton supply it?—is a mass of information; at what age did she marry;
how many children had she as a rule; what was her house like; had she a
room to herself; did she do the cooking; would she be likely to have a servant?
All these facts lie somewhere, presumably, in parish registers and account
books; the life of the average Elizabethan woman must be scattered about
somewhere, could one collect it and make a book of it. It would be ambitious
beyond my daring, I thought, looking about the shelves for books that were
not there, to suggest to the students of those famous colleges that they should
re-write history, though I own that it often seems a little queer as it is, unreal,
lop-sided; but why should they not add a supplement to history? calling it,
of course, by some inconspicuous name so that women might figure there
without impropriety? For one often catches a glimpse of them in the lives of
the great, whisking away into the background, concealing, I sometimes think,
a wink, a laugh, perhaps a tear. And, after all, we have lives enough of Jane
Austen; it scarcely seems necessary to consider again the influence of the
tragedies of Joanna Baillie[1] upon the poetry of Edgar Allan Poe; as for myself,

9. John Aubrey (1626–1697), diarist.   1. Baillie (1762–1851), poet and dramatist.

I should not mind if the homes and haunts of Mary Russell Mitford[2] were closed to the public for a century at least. But what I find deplorable, I continued, looking about the bookshelves again, is that nothing is known about women before the eighteenth century. I have no model in my mind to turn about this way and that. Here am I asking why women did not write poetry in the Elizabethan age, and I am not sure how they were educated; whether they were taught to write; whether they had sitting-rooms to themselves; how many women had children before they were twenty-one; what, in short, they did from eight in the morning till eight at night. They had no money evidently; according to Professor Trevelyan they were married whether they liked it or not before they were out of the nursery, at fifteen or sixteen very likely. It would have been extremely odd, even upon this showing, had one of them suddenly written the plays of Shakespeare, I concluded, and I thought of that old gentleman, who is dead now, but was a bishop, I think, who declared that it was impossible for any woman, past, present, or to come, to have the genius of Shakespeare. He wrote to the papers about it. He also told a lady who applied to him for information that cats do not as a matter of fact go to heaven, though they have, he added, souls of a sort. How much thinking those old gentlemen used to save one! How the borders of ignorance shrank back at their approach! Cats do not go to heaven. Women cannot write the plays of Shakespeare.

Be that as it may, I could not help thinking, as I looked at the works of Shakespeare on the shelf, that the bishop was right at least in this; it would have been impossible, completely and entirely, for any woman to have written the plays of Shakespeare in the age of Shakespeare. Let me imagine, since facts are so hard to come by, what would have happened had Shakespeare had a wonderfully gifted sister, called Judith, let us say. Shakespeare himself went, very probably—his mother was an heiress—to the grammar school, where he may have learnt Latin—Ovid, Virgil and Horace—and the elements of grammar and logic. He was, it is well known, a wild boy who poached rabbits, perhaps shot a deer, and had, rather sooner than he should have done, to marry a woman in the neighbourhood, who bore him a child rather quicker than was right. That escapade sent him to seek his fortune in London. He had, it seemed, a taste for the theatre; he began by holding horses at the stage door. Very soon he got work in the theatre, became a successful actor, and lived at the hub of the universe, meeting everybody, knowing everybody, practising his art on the boards, exercising his wits in the streets, and even getting access to the palace of the queen. Meanwhile his extraordinarily gifted sister, let us suppose, remained at home. She was as adventurous, as imaginative, as agog to see the world as he was. But she was not sent to school. She had no chance of learning grammar and logic, let alone of reading Horace and Virgil. She picked up a book now and then, one of her brother's perhaps, and read a few pages. But then her parents came in and told her to mend the stockings or mind the stew and not moon about with books and papers. They would have spoken sharply but kindly, for they were substantial people who knew the conditions of life for a woman and loved their daughter—indeed, more likely than not she was the apple of her father's eye. Perhaps she scribbled some pages up in an apple loft on the

---

2. Mitford (1787–1855), poet and novelist, best known for her sketches of country life.

sly, but was careful to hide them or set fire to them. Soon, however, before she was out of her teens, she was to be betrothed to the son of a neighbouring wool-stapler.[3] She cried out that marriage was hateful to her, and for that she was severely beaten by her father. Then he ceased to scold her. He begged her instead not to hurt him, not to shame him in this matter of her marriage. He would give her a chain of beads or a fine petticoat, he said; and there were tears in his eyes. How could she disobey him? How could she break his heart? The force of her own gift alone drove her to it. She made up a small parcel of her belongings, let herself down by a rope one summer's night and took the road to London. She was not seventeen. The birds that sang in the hedge were not more musical than she was. She had the quickest fancy, a gift like her brother's, for the tune of words. Like him, she had a taste for the theatre. She stood at the stage door; she wanted to act, she said. Men laughed in her face. The manager—a fat, loose-lipped man—guffawed. He bellowed something about poodles dancing and women acting—no woman, he said, could possibly be an actress. He hinted—you can imagine what. She could get no training in her craft. Could she even seek her dinner in a tavern or roam the streets at midnight? Yet her genius was for fiction and lusted to feed abundantly upon the lives of men and women and the study of their ways. At last—for she was very young, oddly like Shakespeare the poet in her face, with the same grey eyes and rounded brows—at last Nick Greene the actor-manager took pity on her; she found herself with child by that gentleman and so—who shall measure the heat and violence of the poet's heart when caught and tangled in a woman's body?—killed herself one winter's night and lies buried at some cross-roads where the omnibuses now stop outside the Elephant and Castle.[4]

That, more or less, is how the story would run, I think, if a woman in Shakespeare's day had had Shakespeare's genius. But for my part, I agree with the deceased bishop, if such he was—it is unthinkable that any woman in Shakespeare's day should have had Shakespeare's genius. For genius like Shakespeare's is not born among labouring, uneducated, servile people. It was not born in England among the Saxons and the Britons. It is not born today among the working classes. How, then, could it have been born among women whose work began, according to Professor Trevelyan, almost before they were out of the nursery, who were forced to it by their parents and held to it by all the power of law and custom? Yet genius of a sort must have existed among women as it must have existed among the working classes. Now and again an Emily Brontë or a Robert Burns blazes out and proves its presence. But certainly it never got itself on to paper. When, however, one reads of a witch being ducked, of a woman possessed by devils, of a wise woman selling herbs, or even of a very remarkable man who had a mother, then I think we are on the track of a lost novelist, a suppressed poet, of some mute and inglorious[5] Jane Austen, some Emily Brontë who dashed her brains out on the moor or mopped and mowed about the highways crazed with the torture that her gift had put her to. Indeed, I would venture to guess that

3. A stapler is a dealer in staple goods (i.e., established goods in trade and marketing); hence a wool-stapler is a dealer in wool (one of the "staple" products of 16th-century England).
4. Suicides were buried at crossroads. The Elephant and Castle was a tavern south of the Thames where roads went off to different parts of southern England.
5. An echo of Thomas Gray's famous line about "some mute inglorious Milton" in *Elegy Written in a Country Churchyard* (1751), line 59.

Anon, who wrote so many poems without signing them, was often a woman. It was a woman Edward Fitzgerald,[6] I think, suggested who made the ballads and the folk-songs, crooning them to her children, beguiling her spinning with them, or the length of the winter's night.

This may be true or it may be false—who can say?—but what is true in it, so it seemed to me, reviewing the story of Shakespeare's sister as I had made it, is that any woman born with a great gift in the sixteenth century would certainly have gone crazed, shot herself, or ended her days in some lonely cottage outside the village, half witch, half wizard, feared and mocked at. For it needs little skill in psychology to be sure that a highly gifted girl who had tried to use her gift for poetry would have been so thwarted and hindered by other people, so tortured and pulled asunder by her own contrary instincts, that she must have lost her health and sanity to a certainty. No girl could have walked to London and stood at a stage door and forced her way into the presence of actor-managers without doing herself a violence and suffering an anguish which may have been irrational—for chastity may be a fetish invented by certain societies for unknown reasons—but were none the less inevitable. Chastity had then, it has even now, a religious importance in a woman's life, and has so wrapped itself round with nerves and instincts that to cut it free and bring it to the light of day demands courage of the rarest. To have lived a free life in London in the sixteenth century would have meant for a woman who was poet and playwright a nervous stress and dilemma which might well have killed her. Had she survived, whatever she had written would have been twisted and deformed, issuing from a strained and morbid imagination. And undoubtedly, I thought, looking at the shelf where there are no plays by women, her work would have gone unsigned. That refuge she would have sought certainly. It was the relic of the sense of chastity that dictated anonymity to women even so late as the ninteeenth century. Currer Bell, George Eliot, George Sand,[7] all the victims of inner strife as their writings prove, sought ineffectively to veil themselves by using the name of a man. Thus they did homage to the convention, which if not implanted by the other sex was liberally encouraged by them (the chief glory of a woman is not to be talked of, said Pericles,[8] himself a much-talked-of man), that publicity in women is detestable. Anonymity runs in their blood. The desire to be veiled still possesses them. They are not even now as concerned about the health of their fame as men are, and, speaking generally, will pass a tombstone or a signpost without feeling an irresistible desire to cut their names on it, as Alf, Bert or Chas. must do in obedience to their instinct, which murmurs if it sees a fine woman go by, or even a dog, Ce chien est à moi.[9] And, of course, it may not be a dog, I thought, remembering Parliament Square, the Sieges Allee[1] and other avenues; it may be a piece of land or a man with curly black hair. It is one of the great advantages of being a woman that one can pass even a very fine negress without wishing to make an Englishwoman of her.

That woman, then, who was born with a gift of poetry in the sixteenth century, was an unhappy woman, a woman at strife against herself. All the

6. Poet and translator (1809–1883).
7. Male pseudonyms, respectively, of Charlotte Brontë, Marian Evans, and Amandine-Aurore-Lucie Dupin.

8. Athenian statesman (ca. 495–429 B.C.E.).
9. This dog is mine (French).
1. Avenue of Victory, a busy thoroughfare in Berlin.

conditions of her life, all her own instincts, were hostile to the state of mind which is needed to set free whatever is in the brain. But what is the state of mind that is most propitious to the act of creation, I asked. Can one come by any notion of the state that furthers and makes possible that strange activity? Here I opened the volume containing the Tragedies of Shakespeare. What was Shakespeare's state of mind, for instance, when he wrote *Lear* and *Antony and Cleopatra*? It was certainly the state of mind most favourable to poetry that there has ever existed. But Shakespeare himself said nothing about it. We only know casually and by chance that he "never blotted a line."[2] Nothing indeed was ever said by the artist himself about his state of mind until the eighteenth century perhaps. Rousseau[3] perhaps began it. At any rate, by the nineteenth century self-consciousness had developed so far that it was the habit for men of letters to describe their minds in confessions and autobiographies. Their lives also were written, and their letters were printed after their deaths. Thus, though we do not know what Shakespeare went through when he wrote *Lear,* we do know what Carlyle went through when he wrote the *French Revolution;* what Flaubert went through when he wrote *Madame Bovary;* what Keats was going through when he tried to write poetry against the coming of death and the indifference of the world.

And one gathers from this enormous modern literature of confession and self-analysis that to write a work of genius is almost always a feat of prodigious difficulty. Everything is against the likelihood that it will come from the writer's mind whole and entire. Generally material circumstances are against it. Dogs will bark; people will interrupt; money must be made; health will break down. Further, accentuating all these difficulties and making them harder to bear is the world's notorious indifference. It does not ask people to write poems and novels and histories; it does not need them. It does not care whether Flaubert finds the right word or whether Carlyle scrupulously verifies this or that fact. Naturally, it will not pay for what it does not want. And so the writer, Keats, Flaubert, Carlyle, suffers, especially in the creative years of youth, every form of distraction and discouragement. A curse, a cry of agony, rises from those books of analysis and confession. "Mighty poets in their misery dead"[4]—that is the burden of their song. If anything comes through in spite of all this, it is a miracle, and probably no book is born entire and uncrippled as it was conceived.

But for women, I thought, looking at the empty shelves, these difficulties were infinitely more formidable. In the first place, to have a room of her own, let alone a quiet room or a sound-proof room, was out of the question, unless her parents were exceptionally rich or very noble, even up to the beginning of the nineteenth century. Since her pin money, which depended on the good will of her father, was only enough to keep her clothed, she was debarred from such alleviations as came even to Keats or Tennyson or Carlyle, all poor men, from a walking tour, a little journey to France, from the separate lodging which, even if it were miserable enough, sheltered them from the claims and tyrannies of their families. Such material difficulties were formidable; but much worse were the immaterial. The indifference of

2. Ben Jonson, in *Timber,* writes, "I remember, the players have often mentioned it as an honour to Shakespeare that in his writing (whatsoever he penned) he never blotted out a line."

3. Jean-Jacques Rousseau (1712–1778), early Romantic French philosopher and writer.
4. From Wordsworth's *Resolution and Independence.*

the world which Keats and Flaubert and other men of genius have found so hard to bear was in her case not indifference but hostility. The world did not say to her as it said to them, Write if you choose; it makes no difference to me. The world said with a guffaw, Write? What's the good of your writing? Here the psychologists of Newnham and Girton might come to our help, I thought, looking again at the blank spaces on the shelves. For surely it is time that the effect of discouragement upon the mind of the artist should be measured, as I have seen a dairy company measure the effect of ordinary milk and Grade A milk upon the body of the rat. They set two rats in cages side by side, and of the two one was furtive, timid and small, and the other was glossy, bold and big. Now what food do we feed women as artists upon? I asked, remembering, I suppose, that dinner of prunes and custard. To answer that question I had only to open the evening paper and to read that Lord Birkenhead is of opinion—but really I am not going to trouble to copy out Lord Birkenhead's opinion upon the writing of women. What Dean Inge says I will leave in peace. The Harley Street specialist[5] may be allowed to rouse the echoes of Harley Street with his vociferations without raising a hair on my head. I will quote, however, Mr Oscar Browning, because Mr Oscar Browning was a great figure in Cambridge at one time, and used to examine the students at Girton and Newnham. Mr Oscar Browning was wont to declare "that the impression left on his mind, after looking over any set of examination papers, was that, irrespective of the marks he might give, the best woman was intellectually the inferior of the worst man." After saying that Mr Browning went back to his rooms—and it is this sequel that endears him and makes him a human figure of some bulk and majesty—he went back to his rooms and found a stable-boy lying on the sofa—"a mere skeleton, his cheeks were cavernous and sallow, his teeth were black, and he did not appear to have the full use of his limbs. . . . 'That's Arthur' [said Mr Browning]. 'He's a dear boy really and most high-minded.' " The two pictures always seem to me to complete each other. And happily in this age of biography the two pictures often do complete each other, so that we are able to interpret the opinions of great men not only by what they say, but by what they do.

But though this is possible now, such opinions coming from the lips of important people must have been formidable enough even fifty years ago. Let us suppose that a father from the highest motives did not wish his daughter to leave home and become writer, painter or scholar. "See what Mr Oscar Browning says," he would say; and there was not only Mr Oscar Browning; there was the *Saturday Review*; there was Mr Greg[6]—the "essentials of a woman's being," said Mr Greg emphatically, "are that *they are supported by, and they minister to, men*"—there was an enormous body of masculine opinion to the effect that nothing could be expected of women intellectually. Even if her father did not read out loud these opinions, any girl could read them for herself; and the reading, even in the nineteenth century, must have lowered her vitality, and told profoundly upon her work. There would always have been that assertion—you cannot do this, you are incapable of doing that—to protest against, to overcome. Probably for a novelist this germ is no longer of much effect; for there have been women novelists of merit. But for

5. On Harley Street in London many medical specialists have their consulting rooms.

6. Sir W. W. Greg (1875–1959), bibliographer and literary scholar.

painters it must still have some sting in it; and for musicians, I imagine, is even now active and poisonous in the extreme. The woman composer stands where the actress stood in the time of Shakespeare. Nick Greene, I thought, remembering the story I had made about Shakespeare's sister, said that a woman acting put him in mind of a dog dancing. Johnson repeated the phrase two hundred years later of women preaching. And here, I said, opening a book about music, we have the very words used again in this year of grace, 1928, of women who try to write music. "Of Mlle Germaine Tailleferre one can only repeat Dr Johnson's dictum concerning a woman preacher, transposed into terms of music. 'Sir, a woman's composing is like a dog's walking on his hind legs. It is not done well, but you are surprised to find it done at all.' "[7] So accurately does history repeat itself.

Thus, I concluded, shutting Mr Oscar Browning's life and pushing away the rest, it is fairly evident that even in the nineteenth century a woman was not encouraged to be an artist. On the contrary, she was snubbed, slapped, lectured and exhorted. Her mind must have been strained and her vitality lowered by the need of opposing this, of disproving that. For here again we come within range of that very interesting and obscure masculine complex which has had so much influence upon the woman's movement; that deep-seated desire, not so much that *she* shall be inferior as that *he* shall be superior, which plants him wherever one looks, not only in front of the arts, but barring the way to politics too, even when the risk to himself seems infinitesimal and the suppliant humble and devoted. Even Lady Bessborough, I remembered, with all her passion for politics, must humbly bow herself and write to Lord Granville Leveson-Gower:[8] ". . . notwithstanding all my violence in politics and talking so much on that subject, I perfectly agree with you that no woman has any business to meddle with that or any other serious business, farther than giving her opinion (if she is ask'd)." And so she goes on to spend her enthusiasm where it meets with no obstacle whatsoever upon that immensely important subject, Lord Granville's maiden speech in the House of Commons. The spectacle is certainly a strange one, I thought. The history of men's opposition to women's emancipation is more interesting perhaps than the story of that emancipation itself. An amusing book might be made of it if some young student at Girton or Newnham would collect examples and deduce a theory—but she would need thick gloves on her hands, and bars to protect her of solid gold.

But what is amusing now, I recollected, shutting Lady Bessborough, had to be taken in desperate earnest once. Opinions that one now pastes in a book labelled cock-a-doodle-dum and keeps for reading to select audiences on summer nights once drew tears, I can assure you. Among your grandmothers and great-grandmothers there were many that wept their eyes out. Florence Nightingale shrieked loud in her agony.[9] Moreover, it is all very well for you, who have got yourselves to college and enjoy sitting-rooms—or is it only bed-sitting-rooms?—of your own to say that genius should disregard such opinions; that genius should be above caring what is said of it. Unfortunately, it is precisely the men or women of genius who mind most what is

7. *A Survey of Contemporary Music*, Cecil Gray, p. 246 [Woolf's note].
8. Leveson-Gower (1773–1846). Lady Bessborough is Henrietta, countess of Bessborough (1761–1821).
9. See *Cassandra*, by Florence Nightingale, printed in *The Cause*, by R. Strachey [Woolf's note].

said of them. Remember Keats. Remember the words he had cut on his tombstone.[1] Think of Tennyson; think—but I need hardly multiply instances of the undeniable, if very unfortunate, fact that it is the nature of the artist to mind excessively what is said about him. Literature is strewn with the wreckage of men who have minded beyond reason the opinions of others.

And this susceptibility of theirs is doubly unfortunate, I thought, returning again to my original enquiry into what state of mind is most propitious for creative work, because the mind of an artist, in order to achieve the prodigious effort of freeing whole and entire the work that is in him, must be incandescent, like Shakespeare's mind, I conjectured, looking at the book which lay open at *Antony and Cleopatra*. There must be no obstacle in it, no foreign matter unconsumed.

For though we say that we know nothing about Shakespeare's state of mind, even as we say that, we are saying something about Shakespeare's state of mind. The reason perhaps why we know so little of Shakespeare— compared with Donne or Ben Jonson or Milton—is that his grudges and spites and antipathies are hidden from us. We are not held up by some "revelation" which reminds us of the writer. All desire to protest, to preach, to proclaim an injury, to pay off a score, to make the world the witness of some hardship or grievance was fired out of him and consumed. Therefore his poetry flows from him free and unimpeded. If ever a human being got his work expressed completely, it was Shakespeare. If ever a mind was incandescent, unimpeded, I thought, turning again to the bookcase, it was Shakespeare's mind.

Chapter Four

That one would find any woman in that state of mind in the sixteenth century was obviously impossible. One has only to think of the Elizabethan tombstones with all those children kneeling with clasped hands; and their early deaths; and to see their houses with their dark, cramped rooms, to realise that no woman could have written poetry then. What one would expect to find would be that rather later perhaps some great lady would take advantage of her comparative freedom and comfort to publish something with her name to it and risk being thought a monster. Men, of course, are not snobs, I continued, carefully eschewing "the arrant feminism" of Miss Rebecca West; but they appreciate with sympathy for the most part the efforts of a countess to write verse. One would expect to find a lady of title meeting with far greater encouragement than an unknown Miss Austen or a Miss Brontë at that time would have met with. But one would also expect to find that her mind was disturbed by alien emotions like fear and hatred and that her poems showed traces of that disturbance. Here is Lady Winchilsea,[2] for example, I thought, taking down her poems. She was born in the year 1661; she was noble both by birth and by marriage; she was childless; she wrote poetry, and one has only to open her poetry to find her bursting out in indignation against the position of women:

1. Here lies one whose name was writ in water.
2. Anne Finch, countess of Winchilsea (1661–

1720); the quotations are from her poem *The Introduction*.

> *How are we fallen! fallen by mistaken rules,*
> *And Education's more than Nature's fools;*
> *Debarred from all improvements of the mind,*
> *And to be dull, expected and designed;*
> *And if some one would soar above the rest,*
> *With warmer fancy, and ambition pressed,*
> *So strong the opposing faction still appears,*
> *The hopes to thrive can ne'er outweigh the fears.*

Clearly her mind has by no means "consumed all impediments and become incandescent." On the contrary, it is harrassed and distracted with hates and grievances. The human race is split up for her into two parties. Men are the "opposing faction"; men are hated and feared, because they have the power to bar her way to what she wants to do—which is to write.

> *Alas! a woman that attempts the pen,*
> *Such a presumptuous creature is esteemed,*
> *The fault can by no virtue be redeemed.*
> *They tell us we mistake our sex and way;*
> *Good breeding, fashion, dancing, dressing, play,*
> *Are the accomplishments we should desire;*
> *To write, or read, or think, or to enquire,*
> *Would cloud our beauty, and exhaust our time,*
> *And interrupt the conquests of our prime,*
> *Whilst the dull manage of a servile house*
> *Is held by some our utmost art and use.*

Indeed she has to encourage herself to write by supposing that what she writes will never be published; to soothe herself with the sad chant:

> *To some few friends, and to thy sorrows sing,*
> *For groves of laurel thou wert never meant;*
> *Be dark enough thy shades, and be thou there content.*

Yet it is clear that could she have freed her mind from hate and fear and not heaped it with bitterness and resentment, the fire was hot within her. Now and again words issue of pure poetry:

> *Nor will in fading silks compose,*
> *Faintly the inimitable rose.*

—they are rightly praised by Mr Murry,[3] and Pope, it is thought, remembered and appropriated those others:

> *Now the jonquille o'ercomes the feeble brain;*
> *We faint beneath the aromatic pain.*

It was a thousand pities that the woman who could write like that, whose mind was turned to nature and reflection, should have been forced to anger and bitterness. But how could she have helped herself? I asked, imagining the sneers and the laughter, the adulation of the toadies, the scepticism of the professional poet. She must have shut herself up in a room in the country

---

3. John Middleton Murry (1889–1957), English literary critic.

to write, and been torn asunder by bitterness and scruples perhaps, though her husband was of the kindest, and their married life perfection. She "must have," I say, because when one comes to seek out the facts about Lady Winchilsea, one finds, as usual, that almost nothing is known about her. She suffered terribly from melancholy, which we can explain at least to some extent when we find her telling us how in the grip of it she would imagine:

> My lines decried, and my employment thought,
> An useless folly or presumptuous fault:

The employment, which was thus censured, was, as far as one can see, the harmless one of rambling about the fields and dreaming:

> My hand delights to trace unusual things,
> And deviates from the known and common way,
> Nor will in fading silks compose,
> Faintly the inimitable rose.

Naturally, if that was her habit and that was her delight, she could only expect to be laughed at; and, accordingly, Pope or Gay[4] is said to have satirised her "as a blue-stocking with an itch for scribbling." Also it is thought that she offended Gay by laughing at him. She said that his *Trivia* showed that "he was more proper to walk before a chair than to ride in one." But this is all "dubious gossip" and, says Mr Murry, "uninteresting." But there I do not agree with him, for I should have liked to have had more even of dubious gossip so that I might have found out or made up some image of this melancholy lady, who loved wandering in the fields and thinking about unusual things and scorned, so rashly, so unwisely, "the dull manage of a servile house." But she became diffuse, Mr Murry says. Her gift is all grown about with weeds and bound with briars. It had no chance of showing itself for the fine distinguished gift it was. And so, putting her back on the shelf, I turned to the other great lady, the Duchess whom Lamb loved, hare-brained, fantastical Margaret of Newcastle,[5] her elder, but her contemporary. They were very different, but alike in this that both were noble and both childless, and both were married to the best of husbands. In both burnt the same passion for poetry and both are disfigured and deformed by the same causes. Open the Duchess and one finds the same outburst of rage, "Women live like Bats or Owls, labour like Beasts, and die like Worms. . . ." Margaret too might have been a poet; in our day all that activity would have turned a wheel of some sort. As it was, what could bind, tame or civilise for human use that wild, generous, untutored intelligence? It poured itself out, higgledy-piggledy, in torrents of rhyme and prose, poetry and philosophy which stand congealed in quartos and folios that nobody ever reads. She should have had a microscope put in her hand. She should have been taught to look at the stars and reason scientifically. Her wits were turned with solitude and freedom. No one checked her. No one taught her. The professors fawned on her. At Court they jeered at her. Sir Egerton Brydges[6] complained of her

---

4. John Gay (1685–1732), English poet and playwright, author of the poem *Trivia, or The Art of Walking the Streets of London* (1716), mentioned below.

5. Margaret Lucas Cavendish, duchess of Newcastle (1623–1673), author of *Female Orations*, quoted below.

6. English writer (1762–1837).

coarseness—"as flowing from a female of high rank brought up in the Courts." She shut herself up at Welbeck alone.

What a vision of loneliness and riot the thought of Margaret Cavendish brings to mind! as if some giant cucumber had spread itself over all the roses and carnations in the garden and choked them to death. What a waste that the woman who wrote "the best bred women are those whose minds are civilest" should have frittered her time away scribbling nonsense and plunging ever deeper into obscurity and folly till the people crowded round her coach when she issued out. Evidently the crazy Duchess became a bogey to frighten clever girls with. Here, I remembered, putting away the Duchess and opening Dorothy Osborne's[7] letters, is Dorothy writing to Temple about the Duchess's new book. "Sure the poore woman is a little distracted, shee could never bee soe rediculous else as to venture at writeing book's and in verse too, if I should not sleep this fortnight I should not come to that."

And so, since no woman of sense and modesty could write books, Dorothy, who was sensitive and melancholy, the very opposite of the Duchess in temper, wrote nothing. Letters did not count. A woman might write letters while she was sitting by her father's sick-bed. She could write them by the fire whilst the men talked without disturbing them. The strange thing is, I thought, turning over the pages of Dorothy's letters, what a gift that untaught and solitary girl had for the framing of a sentence, for the fashioning of a scene. Listen to her running on:

"After dinner wee sitt and talk till Mr B. com's in question and then I am gon. the heat of the day is spent in reading or working and about sixe or seven a Clock, I walke out into a Common that lyes hard by the house where a great many young wenches keep Sheep and Cow's and sitt in the shades singing of Ballads; I goe to them and compare their voyces and Beauty's to some Ancient Shepherdesses that I have read of and finde a vaste difference there, but trust mee I think these are as innocent as those could bee. I talke to them, and finde they want nothing to make them the happiest People in the world, but the knoledge that they are soe. most commonly when we are in the middest of our discourse one looks aboute her and spyes her Cow's goeing into the Corne and then away they all run, as if they had wing's at theire heels. I that am not soe nimble stay behinde, and when I see them driveing home theire Cattle I think tis time for mee to retyre too. when I have supped I goe into the Garden and soe to the syde of a small River that runs by it where I sitt downe and wish you with mee. . . ."

One could have sworn that she had the makings of a writer in her. But "if I should not sleep this fortnight I should not come to that"—one can measure the opposition that was in the air to a woman writing when one finds that even a woman with a great turn for writing has brought herself to believe that to write a book was to be ridiculous, even to show oneself distracted. And so we come, I continued, replacing the single short volume of Dorothy Osborne's letters upon the shelf, to Mrs Behn.[8]

And with Mrs Behn we turn a very important corner on the road. We leave behind, shut up in their parks among their folios, those solitary great ladies who wrote without audience or criticism, for their own delight alone. We

---

7. Later, Lady Temple (1627–1695), famous for her letters to her future husband.

8. Aphra Behn (ca. 1640–1689), English poet and playwright, and author of *Oroonoko*.

come to town and rub shoulders with ordinary people in the streets. Mrs Behn was a middle-class woman with all the plebeian virtues of humour, vitality and courage; a woman forced by the death of her husband and some unfortunate adventures of her own to make her living by her wits. She had to work on equal terms with men. She made, by working very hard, enough to live on. The importance of that fact outweighs anything that she actually wrote, even the splendid "A Thousand Martyrs I have made," or "Love in Fantastic Triumph sat," for here begins the freedom of the mind, or rather the possibility that in the course of time the mind will be free to write what it likes. For now that Aphra Behn had done it, girls could go to their parents and say, You need not give me an allowance; I can make money by my pen. Of course the answer for many years to come was, Yes, by living the life of Aphra Behn! Death would be better! and the door was slammed faster than ever. That profoundly interesting subject, the value that men set upon women's chastity and its effect upon their education, here suggests itself for discussion, and might provide an interesting book if any student at Girton or Newnham cared to go into the matter. Lady Dudley, sitting in diamonds among the midges of a Scottish moor, might serve for frontispiece. Lord Dudley, *The Times* said when Lady Dudley died the other day, "a man of cultivated taste and many accomplishments, was benevolent and bountiful, but whimsically despotic. He insisted upon his wife's wearing full dress, even at the remotest shooting-lodge in the Highlands; he loaded her with gorgeous jewels," and so on, "he gave her everything—always excepting any measure of responsibility." Then Lord Dudley had a stroke and she nursed him and ruled his estates with supreme competence for ever after. That whimsical despotism was in the nineteenth century too.

But to return. Aphra Behn proved that money could be made by writing at the sacrifice, perhaps, of certain agreeable qualities; and so by degrees writing became not merely a sign of folly and a distracted mind, but was of practical importance. A husband might die, or some disaster overtake the family. Hundreds of women began as the eighteenth century drew on to add to their pin money, or to come to the rescue of their families by making translations or writing the innumerable bad novels which have ceased to be recorded even in text-books, but are to be picked up in the fourpenny boxes in the Charing Cross Road.[9] The extreme activity of mind which showed itself in the later eighteenth century among women—the talking, and the meeting, the writing of essays on Shakespeare, the translating of the classics—was founded on the solid fact that women could make money by writing. Money dignifies what is frivolous if unpaid for. It might still be well to sneer at "blue stockings with an itch for scribbling," but it could not be denied that they could put money in their purses. Thus, towards the end of the eighteenth century a change came about which, if I were rewriting history, I should describe more fully and think of greater importance than the Crusades or the Wars of the Roses. The middle-class woman began to write. For if *Pride and Prejudice* matters, and *Middlemarch* and *Villette* and *Wuthering Heights*[1] matter, then it matters far more than I can prove in an hour's discourse that women generally, and not merely the lonely aristocrat shut

9. A street in London famed for its bookshops.
1. Novels by, respectively, Jane Austen, George Eliot, Charlotte Brontë, and Emily Brontë.

up in her country house among her folios and her flatterers, took to writing. Without those forerunners, Jane Austen and the Brontës and George Eliot could no more have written than Shakespeare could have written without Marlowe, or Marlowe without Chaucer, or Chaucer without those forgotten poets who paved the ways and tamed the natural savagery of the tongue. For masterpieces are not single and solitary births; they are the outcome of many years of thinking in common, of thinking by the body of the people, so that the experience of the mass is behind the single voice. Jane Austen should have laid a wreath upon the grave of Fanny Burney, and George Eliot done homage to the robust shade of Eliza Carter[2]—the valiant old woman who tied a bell to her bedstead in order that she might wake early and learn Greek. All women together ought to let flowers fall upon the tomb of Alphra Behn which is, most scandalously but rather appropriately, in Westminster Abbey, for it was she who earned them the right to speak their minds. It is she— shady and amorous as she was—who makes it not quite fantastic for me to say to you tonight: Earn five hundred a year by your wits.

Here, then, one had reached the early nineteenth century. And here, for the first time, I found several shelves given up entirely to the works of women. But why, I could not help asking, as I ran my eyes over them, were they, with very few exceptions, all novels? The original impulse was to poetry. The "supreme head of song" was a poetess. Both in France and in England the women poets precede the women novelists. Moreover, I thought, looking at the four famous names, what had George Eliot in common with Emily Brontë? Did not Charlotte Brontë fail entirely to understand Jane Austen? Save for the possibly relevant fact that not one of them had a child, four more incongruous characters could not have met together in a room—so much so that it is tempting to invent a meeting and a dialogue between them. Yet by some strange force they were all compelled, when they wrote, to write novels. Had it something to do with being born of the middle class, I asked; and with the fact, which Miss Emily Davies[3] a little later was so strikingly to demonstrate, that the middle-class family in the early nineteenth century was possessed only of a single sitting-room between them? If a woman wrote, she would have to write in the common sitting-room. And, as Miss Nightingale was so vehemently to complain,—"women never have an half hour . . . that they can call their own"—she was always interrupted. Still it would be easier to write prose and fiction there than to write poetry or a play. Less concentration is required. Jane Austen wrote like that to the end of her days. "How she was able to effect all this," her nephew writes in his Memoir, "is surprising, for she had no separate study to repair to, and most of the work must have been done in the general sitting-room, subject to all kinds of casual interruptions. She was careful that her occupation should not be suspected by servants or visitors or any persons beyond her own family party."[4] Jane Austen hid her manuscripts or covered them with a piece of blotting-paper. Then, again, all the literary training that a woman had in the early nineteenth century was training in the observation of character, in the analysis of emotion. Her sensibility had been educated for centuries by the influences of the common sitting-room. People's feelings were impressed

2. English poet and translator. (1717–1806).
3. English educator (1830–1921), who established what was to become Girton College.

4. *Memoir of Jane Austen*, by her nephew, James Edward Austen-Leigh [Woolf's note].

on her; personal relations were always before her eyes. Therefore, when the middle-class woman took to writing, she naturally wrote novels, even though, as seems evident enough, two of the four famous women here named were not by nature novelists. Emily Brontë should have written poetic plays; the overflow of George Eliot's capacious mind should have spread itself when the creative impulse was spent upon history or biography. They wrote novels, however; one may even go further, I said, taking *Pride and Prejudice* from the shelf, and say that they wrote good novels. Without boasting or giving pain to the opposite sex, one may say that *Pride and Prejudice* is a good book. At any rate, one would not have been ashamed to have been caught in the act of writing *Pride and Prejudice*. Yet Jane Austen was glad that a hinge creaked, so that she might hide her manuscript before any one came in. To Jane Austen there was something discreditable in writing *Pride and Prejudice*. And, I wondered, would *Pride and Prejudice* have been a better novel if Jane Austen had not thought it necessary to hide her manuscript from visitors? I read a page or two to see; but I could not find any signs that her circumstances had harmed her work in the slightest. That, perhaps, was the chief miracle about it. Here was a woman about the year 1800 writing without hate, without bitterness, without fear, without protest, without preaching. That was how Shakespeare wrote, I thought, looking at *Antony and Cleopatra*; and when people compare Shakespeare and Jane Austen, they may mean that the minds of both had consumed all impediments; and for that reason we do not know Jane Austen and we do not know Shakespeare, and for that reason Jane Austen pervades every word that she wrote, and so does Shakespeare. If Jane Austen suffered in any way from her circumstances it was in the narrowness of life that was imposed upon her. It was impossible for a woman to go about alone. She never travelled; she never drove through London in an omnibus or had luncheon in a shop by herself. But perhaps it was the nature of Jane Austen not to want what she had not. Her gift and her circumstances matched each other completely. But I doubt whether that was true of Charlotte Brontë, I said, opening *Jane Eyre* and laying it beside *Pride and Prejudice*.

I opened it at chapter twelve and my eye was caught by the phrase, "Anybody may blame me who likes." What were they blaming Charlotte Brontë for, I wondered? And I read how Jane Eyre used to go up on to the roof when Mrs. Fairfax was making jellies and looked over the fields at the distant view. And then she longed—and it was for this that they blamed her—that "then I longed for a power of vision which might overpass that limit; which might reach the busy world, towns, regions full of life I had heard of but never seen: that then I desired more of practical experience than I possessed; more of intercourse with my kind, of acquaintance with variety of character than was here within my reach. I valued what was good in Mrs. Fairfax, and what was good in Adèle; but I believed in the existence of other and more vivid kinds of goodness, and what I believed in I wished to behold.

"Who blames me? Many, no doubt, and I shall be called discontented. I could not help it: the restlessness was in my nature; it agitated me to pain sometimes . . . .

"It is vain to say human beings ought to be satisfied with tranquillity: they must have action; and they will make it if they cannot find it. Millions are condemned to a stiller doom than mine, and millions are in silent revolt against their lot. Nobody knows how many rebellions ferment in the masses of life which people earth. Women are supposed to be very calm generally: but women feel just as men feel; they need exercise for their faculties and a field for their efforts as much as their brothers do; they suffer from too rigid a restraint, too absolute a stagnation, precisely as men would suffer; and it is narrow-minded in their more privileged fellow-creatures to say that they ought to confine themselves to making puddings and knitting stockings, to playing on the piano and embroidering bags. It is thoughtless to condemn them, or laugh at them, if they seek to do more or learn more than custom has pronounced necessary for their sex.

"When thus alone I not unfrequently heard Grace Poole's laugh. . . ."

That is an awkward break, I thought. It is upsetting to come upon Grace Poole all of a sudden. The continuity is disturbed. One might say, I continued, laying the book down beside *Pride and Prejudice,* that the woman who wrote those pages had more genius in her than Jane Austen; but if one reads them over and marks that jerk in them, that indignation, one sees that she will never get her genius expressed whole and entire. Her books will be deformed and twisted. She will write in a rage where she should write calmly. She will write foolishly where she should write wisely. She will write of herself where she should write of her characters. She is at war with her lot. How could she help but die young, cramped and thwarted?

One could not but play for a moment with the thought of what might have happened if Charlotte Brontë had possessed say three hundred a year—but the foolish woman sold the copyright of her novels outright for fifteen hundred pounds; had somehow possessed more knowledge of the busy world, and towns and regions full of life; more practical experience, and intercourse with her kind and acquaintance with a variety of character. In those words she puts her finger exactly not only upon her own defects as a novelist but upon those of her sex at that time. She knew, no one better, how enormously her genius would have profited if it had not spent itself in solitary visions over distant fields; if experience and intercourse and travel had been granted her. But they were not granted; they were withheld; and we must accept the fact that all those good novels, *Villette, Emma, Wuthering Heights, Middlemarch,* were written by women without more experience of life than could enter the house of a respectable clergyman; written too in the common sitting-room of that respectable house and by women so poor that they could not afford to buy more than a few quires of paper at a time upon which to write *Wuthering Heights* or *Jane Eyre.* One of them, it is true, George Eliot, escaped after much tribulation, but only to a secluded villa in St John's Wood.[5] And there she settled down in the shadow of the world's disapproval. "I wish it to be understood," she wrote, "that I should never invite any one to come and see me who did not ask for the invitation"; for was she not living in sin with a married man and might not the sight of her damage the chastity of Mrs Smith or whoever it might be that chanced to call? One must submit to the social convention, and be "cut off from what is called the world." At the same time, on the other side of Europe, there was a young man living freely with this gipsy or with that great lady; going to the wars; picking up unhindered and uncensored all that varied experience of human life which

5. A suburb in northwest London that developed in the 1840s.

served him so splendidly later when he came to write his books. Had Tolstoi lived at the Priory in seclusion with a married lady "cut off from what is called the world," however edifying the moral lesson, he could scarcely, I thought, have written *War and Peace*.

But one could perhaps go a little deeper into the question of novel-writing and the effect of sex upon the novelist. If one shuts one's eyes and thinks of the novel as a whole, it would seem to be a creation owning a certain looking-glass likeness to life, though of course with simplifications and distortions innumerable. At any rate, it is a structure leaving a shape on the mind's eye, built now in squares, now pagoda shaped, now throwing out wings and arcades, now solidly compact and domed like the Cathedral of Saint Sofia at Constantinople. This shape, I thought, thinking back over certain famous novels, starts in one the kind of emotion that is appropriate to it. But that emotion at once blends itself with others, for the "shape" is not made by the relation of stone to stone, but by the relation of human being to human being. Thus a novel starts in us all sorts of antagonistic and opposed emotions. Life conflicts with something that is not life. Hence the difficulty of coming to any agreement about novels, and the immense sway that our private prejudices have upon us. On the one hand, we feel You—John the hero—must live, or I shall be in the depths of despair. On the other, we feel, Alas, John, you must die, because the shape of the book requires it. Life conflicts with something that is not life. Then since life it is in part, we judge it as life. James is the sort of man I most detest, one says. Or, This is a farrago of absurdity. I could never feel anything of the sort myself. The whole structure, it is obvious, thinking back on any famous novel, is one of infinite complexity, because it is thus made up of so many different judgments, of so many different kinds of emotion. The wonder is that any book so composed holds together for more than a year or two, or can possibly mean to the English reader what it means for the Russian or the Chinese. But they do hold together occasionally very remarkably. And what holds them together in these rare instances of survival (I was thinking of *War and Peace*) is something that one calls integrity, though it has nothing to do with paying one's bills or behaving honourably in an emergency. What one means by integrity, in the case of the novelist, is the conviction that he gives one that this is the truth. Yes, one feels, I should never have thought that this could be so; I have never known people behaving like that. But you have convinced me that so it is, so it happens. One holds every phrase, every scene to the light as one reads—for Nature seems, very oddly, to have provided us with an inner light by which to judge of the novelist's integrity or disintegrity. Or perhaps it is rather that Nature, in her most irrational mood, has traced in invisible ink on the walls of the mind a premonition which these great artists confirm; a sketch which only needs to be held to the fire of genius to become visible. When one so exposes it and sees it come to life one exclaims in rapture, But this is what I have always felt and known and desired! And one boils over with excitement, and, shutting the book even with a kind of reverence as if it were something very precious, a stand-by to return to as long as one lives, one puts it back on the shelf, I said, taking *War and Peace* and putting it back in its place. If, on the other hand, these poor sentences that one takes and tests rouse first a quick and eager response with their bright colouring and their dashing gestures but there they stop: something seems to check them in their development: or if they bring to light only a faint scribble in that corner and a blot over there, and nothing appears whole and entire, then one heaves a sigh of disappointment and says, Another failure. This novel has come to grief somewhere.

And for the most part, of course, novels do come to grief somewhere. The imagination falters under the enormous strain. The insight is confused; it can no longer distinguish between the true and the false; it has no longer the strength to go on with the vast labour that calls at every moment for the use of so many different faculties. But how would all this be affected by the sex of the novelist, I wondered, looking at *Jane Eyre* and the others. Would the fact of her sex in any way interfere with the integrity of a woman novelist—that integrity which I take to be the backbone of the writer? Now, in the passages I have quoted from *Jane Eyre,* it is clear that anger was tampering with the integrity of Charlotte Brontë the novelist. She left her story, to which her entire devotion was due, to attend to some personal grievance. She remembered that she had been starved of her proper due of experience— she had been made to stagnate in a parsonage mending stockings when she wanted to wander free over the world. Her imagination swerved from indignation and we feel it swerve. But there were many more influences than anger tugging at her imagination and deflecting it from its path. Ignorance, for instance. The portrait of Rochester is drawn in the dark. We feel the influence of fear in it; just as we constantly feel an acidity which is the result of oppression, a buried suffering smouldering beneath her passion, a rancour which contracts those books, splendid as they are, with a spasm of pain.

And since a novel has this correspondence to real life, its values are to some extent those of real life. But it is obvious that the values of women differ very often from the values which have been made by the other sex; naturally, this is so. Yet it is the masculine values that prevail. Speaking crudely, football and sport are "important"; the worship of fashion, the buying of clothes "trivial." And these values are inevitably transferred from life to fiction. This is an important book, the critic assumes, because it deals with war. This is an insignificant book because it deals with the feelings of women in a drawing-room. A scene in a battlefield is more important than a scene in a shop—everywhere and much more subtly the difference of value persists. The whole structure, therefore, of the early nineteenth-century novel was raised, if one was a woman, by a mind which was slightly pulled from the straight, and made to alter its clear vision in deference to external authority. One has only to skim those old forgotten novels and listen to the tone of voice in which they are written to divine that the writer was meeting criticism; she was saying this by way of aggression, or that by way of conciliation. She was admitting that she was "only a woman," or protesting that she was "as good as a man." She met that criticism as her temperament dictated, with docility and diffidence, or with anger and emphasis. It does not matter which it was; she was thinking of something other than the thing itself. Down comes her book upon our heads. There was a flaw in the centre of it. And I thought of all the women's novels that lie scattered, like small pock-marked apples in an orchard, about the secondhand book shops of London. It was the flaw in the centre that had rotted them. She had altered her values in deference to the opinion of others.

But how impossible it must have been for them not to budge either to the right or to the left. What genius, what integrity it must have required in face of all that criticism, in the midst of that purely patriarchal society, to hold fast to the thing as they saw it without shrinking. Only Jane Austen did it and Emily Brontë. It is another feather, perhaps the finest, in their caps. They wrote as women write, not as men write. Of all the thousand women who wrote novels then, they alone entirely ignored the perpetual admonitions of the eternal pedagogue—write this, think that. They alone were deaf to that persistent voice, now grumbling, now patronising, now domineering, now grieved, now shocked, now angry, now avuncular, that voice which cannot let women alone, but must be at them, like some too conscientious governess, adjuring them, like Sir Egerton Brydges, to be refined; dragging even into the criticism of poetry criticism of sex;[6] admonishing them, if they would be good and win, as I suppose, some shiny prize, to keep within certain limits which the gentleman in question thinks suitable: ". . . female novelists should only aspire to excellence by courageously acknowledging the limitations of their sex."[7] That puts the matter in a nutshell, and when I tell you, rather to your surprise, that this sentence was written not in August 1828 but in August 1928, you will agree, I think, that however delightful it is to us now, it represents a vast body of opinion—I am not going to stir those old pools, I take only what chance has floated to my feet—that was far more vigorous and far more vocal a century ago. It would have needed a very stalwart young woman in 1828 to disregard all those snubs and chidings and promises of prizes. One must have been something of a firebrand to say to oneself, Oh, but they can't buy literature too. Literature is open to everybody. I refuse to allow you, Beadle though you are, to turn me off the grass. Lock up your libraries if you like; but there is no gate, no lock, no bolt that you can set upon the freedom of my mind.

But whatever effect discouragement and criticism had upon their writing— and I believe that they had a very great effect—that was unimportant compared with the other difficulty which faced them (I was still considering those early nineteenth-century novelists) when they came to set their thoughts on paper—that is that they had no tradition behind them, or one so short and partial that it was of little help. For we think back through our mothers if we are women. It is useless to go to the great men writers for help, however much one may go to them for pleasure. Lamb, Browne, Thackeray, Newman, Sterne, Dickens, De Quincey—whoever it may be—never helped a woman yet, though she may have learnt a few tricks of them and adapted them to her use. The weight, the pace, the stride of a man's mind are too unlike her own for her to lift anything substantial from him successfully. The ape is too distant to be sedulous. Perhaps the first thing she would find, setting pen to paper, was that there was no common sentence ready for her use. All the great novelists like Thackeray and Dickens and Balzac have written a natural prose, swift but not slovenly, expressive but not precious, taking their own tint without ceasing to be common property. They have based it on the sentence that was current at the time. The sentence that was current at the

6. "[She] has a metaphysical purpose, and that is a dangerous obsession, especially with a woman, for women rarely possess men's healthy love of rhetoric. It is a strange lack in the sex which is in other things more primitive and more materialistic."—*New Criterion*, June 1928 [Woolf's note].

7. "If, like the reporter, you believe that female novelists should only aspire to excellence by courageously acknowledging the limitations of their sex (Jane Austen [has] demonstrated how gracefully this gesture can be accomplished). . . ."—*Life and Letters*, August 1928 [Woolf's note].

beginning of the nineteenth century ran something like this perhaps: "The grandeur of their works was an argument with them, not to stop short, but to proceed. They could have no higher excitement or satisfaction than in the exercise of their art and endless generations of truth and beauty. Success prompts to exertion; and habit facilitates success." That is a man's sentence; behind it one can see Johnson, Gibbon and the rest. It was a sentence that was unsuited for a woman's use. Charlotte Brontë, with all her splendid gift for prose, stumbled and fell with that clumsy weapon in her hands. George Eliot committed atrocities with it that beggar description. Jane Austen looked at it and laughed at it and devised a perfectly natural, shapely sentence proper for her own use and never departed from it. Thus, with less genius for writing than Charlotte Brontë, she got infinitely more said. Indeed, since freedom and fullness of expression are of the essence of the art, such a lack of tradition, such a scarcity and inadequacy of tools, must have told enormously upon the writing of women. Moreover, a book is not made of sentences laid end to end, but of sentences built, if an image helps, into arcades or domes. And this shape too has been made by men out of their own needs for their own uses. There is no reason to think that the form of the epic or of the poetic play suits a woman any more than the sentence suits her. But all the older forms of literature were hardened and set by the time she became a writer. The novel alone was young enough to be soft in her hands—another reason, perhaps, why she wrote novels. Yet who shall say that even now "the novel" (I give it inverted commas to mark my sense of the words' inadequacy), who shall say that even this most pliable of all forms is rightly shaped for her use? No doubt we shall find her knocking that into shape for herself when she has the free use of her limbs; and providing some new vehicle, not necessarily in verse, for the poetry in her. For it is the poetry that is still denied outlet. And I went on to ponder how a woman nowadays would write a poetic tragedy in five acts—would she use verse—would she not use prose rather?

But these are difficult questions which lie in the twilight of the future. I must leave them, if only because they stimulate me to wander from my subject into trackless forests where I shall be lost and, very likely, devoured by wild beasts. I do not want, and I am sure that you do not want me, to broach that very dismal subject, the future of fiction, so that I will only pause here one moment to draw your attention to the great part which must be played in that future so far as women are concerned by physical conditions. The book has somehow to be adapted to the body, and at a venture one would say that women's books should be shorter, more concentrated, than those of men, and framed so that they do not need long hours of steady and uninterrupted work. For interruptions there will always be. Again, the nerves that feed the brain would seem to differ in men and women, and if you are going to make them work their best and hardest, you must find out what treatment suits them—whether these hours of lectures, for instance, which the monks devised, presumably, hundreds of years ago, suit them—what alternations of work and rest they need, interpreting rest not as doing nothing but as doing something but something that is different; and what should that difference be? All this should be discussed and discovered; all this is part of the question of women and fiction. And yet, I continued, approaching the bookcase again, where shall I find that elaborate study of the psychology of women by a woman? If through their incapacity to play football women are not going to be allowed to practise medicine——

Happily my thoughts were now given another turn.

Chapter Five

I had come at last, in the course of this rambling, to the shelves which hold books by the living; by women and by men; for there are almost as many books written by women now as by men. Or if that is not yet quite true, if the male is still the voluble sex, it is certainly true that women no longer write novels solely. There are Jane Harrison's books on Greek archaeology; Vernon Lee's books on aesthetics; Gertrude Bell's[8] books on Persia. There are books on all sorts of subjects which a generation ago no woman could have touched. There are poems and plays and criticism; there are histories and biographies, books of travel and books of scholarship and research; there are even a few philosophies and books about science and economics. And though novels predominate, novels themselves may very well have changed from association with books of a different feather. The natural simplicity, the epic age of women's writing, may have gone. Reading and criticism may have given her a wider range, a greater subtlety. The impulse towards auto-biography may be spent. She may be beginning to use writing as an art, not as a method of self-expression. Among these new novels one might find an answer to several such questions.

I took down one of them at random. It stood at the very end of the shelf, was called *Life's Adventure*, or some such title, by Mary Carmichael,[9] and was published in this very month of October. It seems to be her first book, I said to myself, but one must read it as if it were the last volume in a fairly long series, continuing all those other books that I have been glancing at— Lady Winchilsea's poems and Aphra Behn's plays and the novels of the four great novelists. For books continue each other, in spite of our habit of judging them separately. And I must also consider her—this unknown woman—as the descendant of all those other women whose circumstances I have been glancing at and see what she inherits of their characteristics and restrictions. So, with a sigh, because novels so often provide an anodyne and not an antidote, glide one into torpid slumbers instead of rousing one with a burning brand, I settled down with a notebook and a pencil to make what I could of Mary Carmichael's first novel, *Life's Adventure*.

To begin with, I ran my eye up and down the page. I am going to get the hang of her sentences first, I said, before I load my memory with blue eyes and brown and the relationship that there may be between Chloe and Roger. There will be time for that when I have decided whether she has a pen in her hand or a pickaxe. So I tried a sentence or two on my tongue. Soon it was obvious that something was not quite in order. The smooth gliding of sentence after sentence was interrupted. Something tore, something scratched; a single word here and there flashed its torch in my eyes. She was

---

8. English archaeologist and writer (1868–1926). Harrison (1850–1928), scholar and lecturer at Cambridge. Lee (1856–1935), essayist and art critic.
9. A work titled *Love's Creation* was published in London in 1928 under the name Marie Carmichael, the pseudonym for Marie Stopes, a crusader for birth control. The plot and characters resemble those mentioned by Woolf.

"unhanding" herself as they say in the old plays. She is like a person striking a match that will not light, I thought. But why, I asked her as if she were present, are Jane Austen's sentences not of the right shape for you? Must they all be scrapped because Emma and Mr Woodhouse are dead? Alas, I sighed, that it should be so. For while Jane Austen breaks from melody to melody as Mozart from song to song, to read this writing was like being out at sea in an open boat. Up one went, down one sank. This terseness, this shortwindedness, might mean that she was afraid of something; afraid of being called "sentimental" perhaps; or she remembers that women's writing has been called flowery and so provides a superfluity of thorns; but until I have read a scene with some care, I cannot be sure whether she is being herself or some one else. At any rate, she does not lower one's vitality, I thought, reading more carefully. But she is heaping up too many facts. She will not be able to use half of them in a book of this size. (It was about half the length of *Jane Eyre*.) However, by some means or other she succeeded in getting us all—Roger, Chloe, Olivia, Tony and Mr Bigham—in a canoe up the river. Wait a moment, I said, leaning back in my chair, I must consider the whole thing more carefully before I go any further.

I am almost sure, I said to myself, that Mary Carmichael is playing a trick on us. For I feel as one feels on a switchback railway when the car, instead of sinking, as one has been led to expect, swerves up again. Mary is tampering with the expected sequence. First she broke the sentence; now she has broken the sequence. Very well, she has every right to do both these things if she does them not for the sake of breaking, but for the sake of creating. Which of the two it is I cannot be sure until she has faced herself with a situation. I will give her every liberty, I said, to choose what that situation shall be; she shall make it of tin cans and old kettles if she likes; but she must convince me that she believes it to be a situation; and then when she has made it she must face it. She must jump. And, determined to do my duty by her as reader if she would do her duty by me as writer, I turned the page and read . . . I am sorry to break off so abruptly. Are there no men present? Do you promise me that behind that red curtain over there the figure of Sir Chartres Biron is not concealed? We are all women, you assure me? Then I may tell you that the very next words I read were these—"Chloe liked Olivia . . ." Do not start. Do not blush. Let us admit in the privacy of our own society that these things sometimes happen. Sometimes women do like women.

"Chloe liked Olivia," I read. And then it struck me how immense a change was there. Chloe liked Olivia perhaps for the first time in literature. Cleopatra did not like Octavia. And how completely *Antony and Cleopatra* would have been altered had she done so! As it is, I thought, letting my mind, I am afraid, wander a little from *Life's Adventure,* the whole thing is simplified, conventionalised, if one dared say it, absurdly. Cleopatra's only feeling about Octavia is one of jealousy. Is she taller than I am? How does she do her hair? The play, perhaps, required no more. But how interesting it would have been if the relationship between the two women had been more complicated. All these relationships between women, I thought, rapidly recalling the splendid gallery of fictitious women, are too simple. So much has been left out, unattempted. And I tried to remember any case in the course of my reading where two women are represented as friends. There is an attempt at it in *Diana of the Crossways.* They are confidantes, of course, in Racine[1] and the Greek tragedies. They are now and then mothers and daughters. But almost without exception they are shown in their relation to men. It was strange to think that all the great women of fiction were, until Jane Austen's day, not only seen by the other sex, but seen only in relation to the other sex. And how small a part of a woman's life is that; and how little can a man know even of that when he observes it through the black or rosy spectacles which sex puts upon his nose. Hence, perhaps, the peculiar nature of woman in fiction; the astonishing extremes of her beauty and horror; her alternations between heavenly goodness and hellish depravity—for so a lover would see her as his love rose or sank, was prosperous or unhappy. This is not so true of the nineteenth-century novelists, of course. Woman becomes much more various and complicated there. Indeed it was the desire to write about women perhaps that led men by degrees to abandon the poetic drama which, with its violence, could make so little use of them, and to devise the novel as a more fitting receptacle. Even so it remains obvious, even in the writing of Proust,[2] that a man is terribly hampered and partial in his knowledge of women, as a woman in her knowledge of men.

Also, I continued, looking down at the page again, it is becoming evident that women, like men, have other interests besides the perennial interests of domesticity. "Chloe liked Olivia. They shared a laboratory together. . . ." I read on and discovered that these two young women were engaged in mincing liver, which is, it seems, a cure for pernicious anaemia: although one of them was married and had—I think I am right in stating—two small children. Now all that, of course, has had to be left out, and thus the splendid portrait of the fictitious woman is much too simple and much too monotonous. Suppose, for instance, that men were only represented in literature as the lovers of women, and were never the friends of men, soldiers, thinkers, dreamers; how few parts in the plays of Shakespeare could be allotted to them; how literature would suffer! We might perhaps have most of Othello; and a good deal of Antony; but no Caesar, no Brutus, no Hamlet, no Lear, no Jaques— literature would be incredibly impoverished, as indeed literature is impoverished beyond our counting by the doors that have been shut upon women. Married against their will, kept in one room, and to one occupation, how could a dramatist give a full or interesting or truthful account of them? Love was the only possible interpreter. The poet was forced to be passionate or bitter, unless indeed he chose to "hate women," which meant more often than not that he was unattractive to them.

Now if Chloe likes Olivia and they share a laboratory, which of itself will make their friendship more varied and lasting because it will be less personal; if Mary Carmichael knows how to write, and I was beginning to enjoy some quality in her style; if she has a room to herself, of which I am not quite sure; if she has five hundred a year of her own—but that remains to be proved—then I think that something of great importance has happened.

For if Chloe likes Olivia and Mary Carmichael knows how to express it she will light a torch in that vast chamber where nobody has yet been. It is all half lights and profound shadows like those serpentine caves where one

---

1. Jean Racine (1639–1699), French dramatist. *"Diana of the Crossways":* (1885) novel by the English author George Meredith (1828–1909).

2. Marcel Proust (1871–1922), French novelist and author of the seven-volume *A la recherche du temps perdu* (1913–27).

goes with a candle peering up and down, not knowing where one is stepping. And I began to read the book again, and read how Chloe watched Olivia put a jar on a shelf and say how it was time to go home to her children. That is a sight that has never been seen since the world began, I exclaimed. And I watched too, very curiously. For I wanted to see how Mary Carmichael set to work to catch those unrecorded gestures, those unsaid or half-said words, which form themselves, no more palpably than the shadows of moths on the ceiling, when women are alone, unlit by the capricious and coloured light of the other sex. She will need to hold her breath, I said, reading on, if she is to do it; for women are so suspicious of any interest that has not some obvious motive behind it, so terribly accustomed to concealment and suppression, that they are off at the flicker of an eye turned observingly in their direction. The only way for you to do it, I thought, addressing Mary Carmichael as if she were there, would be to talk of something else, looking steadily out of the window, and thus note, not with a pencil in a notebook, but in the shortest of shorthand, in words that are hardly syllabled yet, what happens when Olivia—this organism that has been under the shadow of the rock these million years—feels the light fall on it, and sees coming her way a piece of strange food—knowledge, adventure, art. And she reaches out for it, I thought, again raising my eyes from the page, and has to devise some entirely new combination of her resources, so highly developed for their purposes, so as to absorb the new into the old without disturbing the infinitely intricate and elaborate balance of the whole.

But, alas, I had done what I had determined not to do; I had slipped unthinkingly into praise of my own sex. "Highly developed"—"infinitely intricate"—such are undeniably terms of praise, and to praise one's own sex is always suspect, often silly; moreover, in this case, how could one justify it? One could not go to the map and say Columbus discovered America and Columbus was a woman; or take an apple and remark, Newton discovered the laws of gravitation and Newton was a woman; or look into the sky and say aeroplanes are flying overhead and aeroplanes were invented by women. There is no mark on the wall to measure the precise height of women. There are no yard measures, neatly divided into the fractions of an inch, that one can lay against the qualities of a good mother or the devotion of a daughter, or the fidelity of a sister, or the capacity of a housekeeper. Few women even now have been graded at the universities; the great trials of the professions, army and navy, trade, politics and diplomacy have hardly tested them. They remain even at this moment almost unclassified. But if I want to know all that a human being can tell me about Sir Hawley Butts, for instance, I have only to open Burke or Debrett[3] and I shall find that he took such and such a degree; owns a hall; has an heir; was Secretary to a Board; represented Great Britain in Canada; and has received a certain number of degrees, offices, medals and other distinctions by which his merits are stamped upon him indelibly. Only Providence can know more about Sir Hawley Butts than that.

When, therefore, I say "highly developed," "infinitely intricate," of women, I am unable to verify my words either in Whitaker, Debrett or the University

---

3. Annual reference works of genealogy and the peerage. Sir Hawley Butts, however, seems to be Woolf's invention.

Calendar. In this predicament what can I do? And I looked at the bookcase again. There were the biographies: Johnson and Goethe and Carlyle and Sterne and Cowper and Shelley and Voltaire and Browning and many others. And I began thinking of all those great men who have for one reason or another admired, sought out, lived with, confided in, made love to, written of, trusted in, and shown what can only be described as some need of and dependence upon certain persons of the opposite sex. That all these relationships were absolutely Platonic I would not affirm, and Sir William Joynson Hicks[4] would probably deny. But we should wrong these illustrious men very greatly if we insisted that they got nothing from these alliances but comfort, flattery and the pleasures of the body. What they got, it is obvious, was something that their own sex was unable to supply; and it would not be rash, perhaps, to define it further, without quoting the doubtless rhapsodical words of the poets, as some stimulus, some renewal of creative power which is in the gift only of the opposite sex to bestow. He would open the door of drawing-room or nursery, I thought, and find her among her children perhaps, or with a piece of embroidery on her knee—at any rate, the centre of some different order and system of life, and the contrast between this world and his own, which might be the law courts or the House of Commons, would at once refresh and invigorate; and there would follow, even in the simplest talk, such a natural difference of opinion that the dried ideas in him would be fertilised anew; and the sight of her creating in a different medium from his own would so quicken his creative power that insensibly his sterile mind would begin to plot again, and he would find the phrase or the scene which was lacking when he put on his hat to visit her. Every Johnson has his Thrale,[5] and holds fast to her for some such reasons as these, and when the Thrale marries her Italian music master Johnson goes half mad with rage and disgust, not merely that he will miss his pleasant evenings at Streatham, but that the light of his life will be "as if gone out."

And without being Dr Johnson or Goethe or Carlyle or Voltaire, one may feel, though very differently from these great men, the nature of this intricacy and the power of this highly developed creative faculty among women. One goes into the room—but the resources of the English language would be much put to the stretch, and whole flights of words would need to wing their way illegitimately into existence before a woman could say what happens when she goes into a room. The rooms differ so completely; they are calm or thunderous; open on to the sea, or, on the contrary, give on to a prison yard; are hung with washing; or alive with opals and silks; are hard as horsehair or soft as feathers—one has only to go into any room in any street for the whole of that extremely complex force of femininity to fly in one's face. How should it be otherwise? For women have sat indoors all these millions of years, so that by this time the very walls are permeated by their creative force, which has, indeed, so overcharged the capacity of bricks and mortar that it must needs harness itself to pens and brushes and business and politics. But this creative power differs greatly from the creative power of men. And one must conclude that it would be a thousand pities if it were hindered or wasted, for it was won by centuries of the most drastic discipline,

4. Hicks (1865–1932), English Conservative politician and evangelical religious figure.
5. Hester Lynch Thrale (1741–1821), who with her husband, Henry, was for many years friend and hostess to Samuel Johnson at their home in Streatham Place. After Henry's death, she married an Italian musician, much to Johnson's distress; his reaction helped end their friendship.

and there is nothing to take its place. It would be a thousand pities if women wrote like men, or lived like men, or looked like men, for if two sexes are quite inadequate, considering the vastness and variety of the world, how should we manage with one only? Ought not education to bring out and fortify the differences rather than the similarities? For we have too much likeness as it is, and if an explorer should come back and bring word of other sexes looking through the branches of other trees at other skies, nothing would be of greater service to humanity; and we should have the immense pleasure into the bargain of watching Professor X rush for his measuring-rods to prove himself "superior."

Mary Carmichael, I thought, still hovering at a little distance above the page, will have her work cut out for her merely as an observer. I am afraid indeed that she will be tempted to become, what I think the less interesting branch of the species—the naturalist-novelist, and not the contemplative. There are so many new facts for her to observe. She will not need to limit herself any longer to the respectable houses of the upper middle classes. She will go without kindness or condescension, but in the spirit of fellowship into those small, scented rooms where sit the courtesan, the harlot and the lady with the pug dog. There they still sit in the rough and ready-made clothes that the male writer has had perforce to clap upon their shoulders. But Mary Carmichael will have out her scissors and fit them close to every hollow and angle. It will be a curious sight, when it comes, to see these women as they are, but we must wait a little, for Mary Carmichael will still be encumbered with that self-consciousness in the presence of "sin" which is the legacy of our sexual barbarity. She will still wear the shoddy old fetters of class on her feet.

However, the majority of women are neither harlots nor courtesans; nor do they sit clasping pug dogs to dusty velvet all through the summer afternoon. But what do they do then? and there came to my mind's eye one of those long streets somewhere south of the river whose infinite rows are innumerably populated. With the eye of the imagination I saw a very ancient lady crossing the street on the arm of a middle-aged woman, her daughter, perhaps, both so respectably booted and furred that their dressing in the afternoon must be a ritual, and the clothes themselves put away in cupboards with camphor, year after year, throughout the summer months. They cross the road when the lamps are being lit (for the dusk is their favourite hour), as they must have done year after year. The elder is close on eighty; but if one asked her what her life has meant to her, she would say that she remembered the streets lit for the battle of Balaclava, or had heard the guns fire in Hyde Park for the birth of King Edward the Seventh.[6] And if one asked her, longing to pin down the moment with date and season, but what were you doing on the fifth of April 1868, or the second of November 1875, she would look vague and say that she could remember nothing. For all the dinners are cooked; the plates and cups washed; the children set to school and gone out into the world. Nothing remains of it all. All has vanished. No biography or history has a word to say about it. And the novels, without meaning to, inevitably lie.

All these infinitely obscure lives remain to be recorded, I said, addressing

6. In 1841 (since Woolf is writing in 1928, Edward's birth would actually have been before the birth of a woman "close on eighty"). The "battle of Balaclava," famous for the charge of the Light Brigade, occurred in 1854.

Mary Carmichael as if she were present; and went on in thought through the streets of London feeling in imagination the pressure of dumbness, the accumulation of unrecorded life, whether from the women at the street corners with their arms akimbo, and the rings embedded in their fat swollen fingers, talking with a gesticulation like the swing of Shakespeare's words; or from the violet-sellers and match-sellers and old crones stationed under doorways; or from drifting girls whose faces, like waves in sun and cloud, signal the coming of men and women and the flickering lights of shop windows. All that you will have to explore, I said to Mary Carmichael, holding your torch firm in your hand. Above all, you must illumine your own soul with its profundities and its shallows, and its vanities and its generosities, and say what your beauty means to you or your plainness, and what is your relation to the everchanging and turning world of gloves and shoes and stuffs swaying up and down among the faint scents that come through chemists' bottles down arcades of dress material over a floor of pseudo-marble. For in imagination I had gone into a shop; it was laid with black and white paving; it was hung, astonishingly beautifully, with coloured ribbons. Mary Carmichael might well have a look at that in passing, I thought, for it is a sight that would lend itself to the pen as fittingly as any snowy peak or rocky gorge in the Andes. And there is the girl behind the counter too—I would as soon have her true history as the hundred and fiftieth life of Napoleon or seventieth study of Keats and his use of Miltonic inversion when old Professor Z and his like are now inditing. And then I went on very warily, on the very tips of my toes (so cowardly am I, so afraid of the lash that was once almost laid on my own shoulders), to murmur that she should also learn to laugh, without bitterness, at the vanities—say rather at the peculiarities, for it is a less offensive word—of the other sex. For there is a spot the size of a shilling at the back of the head which one can never see for oneself. It is one of the good offices that sex can discharge for sex—to describe that spot the size of a shilling at the back of the head. Think how much women have profited by the comments of Juvenal; by the criticism of Strindberg.[7] Think with what humanity and brilliancy men, from the earliest ages, have pointed out to women that dark place at the back of the head! And if Mary were very brave and very honest, she would go behind the other sex and tell us what she found there. A true picture of man as a whole can never be painted until a woman has described that spot the size of a shilling. Mr Woodhouse and Mr Casaubon[8] are spots of that size and nature. Not of course that any one in their senses would counsel her to hold up to scorn and ridicule of set purpose—literature shows the futility of what is written in that spirit. Be truthful, one would say, and the result is bound to be amazingly interesting. Comedy is bound to be enriched. New facts are bound to be discovered.

However, it was high time to lower my eyes to the page again. It would be better, instead of speculating what Mary Carmichael might write and should write, to see what in fact Mary Carmichael did write. So I began to read again. I remembered that I had certain grievances against her. She had broken up Jane Austen's sentence, and thus given me no chance of pluming myself upon my impeccable taste, my fastidious ear. For it was useless to say, "Yes, yes, this is very nice; but Jane Austen wrote much better than you do," when I had to admit that there was no point of likeness between them. Then she had gone further and broken the sequence—the expected order. Perhaps she had done this unconsciously, merely giving things their natural order, as a woman would, if she wrote like a woman. But the effect was somehow baffling; one could not see a wave heaping itself, a crisis coming round the next corner. Therefore I could not plume myself either upon the depths of my feelings and my profound knowledge of the human heart. For whenever I was about to feel the usual things in the usual places, about love, about death, the annoying creature twitched me away, as if the important point were just a little further on. And thus she made it impossible for me to roll out my sonorous phrases about "elemental feelings," the "common stuff of humanity," "depths of the human heart," and all those other phrases which support us in our belief that, however clever we may be on top, we are very serious, very profound and very humane underneath. She made me feel, on the contrary, that instead of being serious and profound and humane, one might be—and the thought was far less seductive—merely lazy minded and conventional into the bargain.

But I read on, and noted certain other facts. She was no "genius"—that was evident. She had nothing like the love of Nature, the fiery imagination, the wild poetry, the brilliant wit, the brooding wisdom of her great predecessors, Lady Winchilsea, Charlotte Brontë, Jane Austen and George Eliot; she could not write with the melody and the dignity of Dorothy Osborne— indeed she was no more than a clever girl whose books will no doubt be pulped by the publishers in ten years' time. But, nevertheless, she had certain advantages which women of far greater gift lacked even half a century ago. Men were no longer to her "the opposing faction"; she need not waste her time railing against them; she need not climb on to the roof and ruin her peace of mind longing for travel, experience and a knowledge of the world and character that were denied her. Fear and hatred were almost gone, or traces of them showed only in a slight exaggeration of the joy of freedom, a tendency to the caustic and satirical, rather than to the romantic, in her treatment of the other sex. Then there could be no doubt that as a novelist she enjoyed some natural advantages of a high order. She had a sensibility that was very wide, eager and free. It responded to an almost imperceptible touch on it. It feasted like a plant newly stood in the air on every sight and sound that came its way. It ranged, too, very subtly and curiously, among almost unknown or unrecorded things; it lighted on small things and showed that perhaps they were not small after all. It brought buried things to light and made one wonder what need there had been to bury them. Awkward though she was and without the unconscious bearing of long descent which makes the least turn of the pen of a Thackeray or a Lamb delightful to the ear, she had—I began to think—mastered the first great lesson; she wrote as a woman, but as a woman who has forgotten that she is a woman, so that her pages were full of that curious sexual quality which comes only when sex is unconscious of itself.

All this was to the good. But no abundance of sensation or fineness of perception would avail unless she could build up out of the fleeting and the personal the lasting edifice which remains unthrown. I had said that I would wait until she faced herself with "a situation." And I meant by that until she proved by summoning, beckoning and getting together that she was not a skimmer of surfaces merely, but had looked beneath into the depths. Now is the time, she would say to herself at a certain moment, when without doing anything violent I can show the meaning of all this. And she would begin—how unmistakable that quickening is!—beckoning and summoning, and there would rise up in memory, half forgotten, perhaps quite trivial things in other chapters dropped by the way. And she would make their presence felt while some one sewed or smoked a pipe as naturally as possible, and one would feel, as she went on writing, as if one had gone to the top of the world and seen it laid out, very majestically, beneath.

At any rate, she was making the attempt. And as I watched her lengthening out for the test, I saw, but hoped that she did not see, the bishops and the deans, the doctors and the professors, the patriarchs and the pedagogues all at her shouting warning and advice. You can't do this and you shan't do that! Fellows and scholars only allowed on the grass! Ladies not admitted without a letter of introduction! Aspiring and graceful female novelists this way! So they kept at her like the crowd at a fence on the race-course, and it was her trial to take her fence without looking to right or left. If you stop to curse you are lost, I said to her; equally, if you stop to laugh. Hesitate or fumble and you are done for. Think only of the jump, I implored her, as if I had put the whole of my money on her back; and she went over it like a bird. But there was a fence beyond that and a fence beyond that. Whether she had the staying power I was doubtful, for the clapping and the crying were fraying to the nerves. But she did her best. Considering that Mary Carmichael was no genius, but an unknown girl writing her first novel in a bed-sitting-room, without enough of those desirable things, time, money and idleness, she did not do so badly, I thought.

Give her another hundred years, I concluded, reading the last chapter— people's noses and bare shoulders showed naked against a starry sky, for some one had twitched the curtain in the drawing-room—give her a room of her own and five hundred a year, let her speak her mind and leave out half that she now puts in, and she will write a better book one of these days. She will be a poet, I said, putting *Life's Adventure*, by Mary Carmichael, at the end of the shelf, in another hundred years' time.

Chapter Six

Next day the light of the October morning was falling in dusty shafts through the uncurtained windows, and the hum of traffic rose from the street. London then was winding itself up again; the factory was astir; the machines were beginning. It was tempting, after all this reading, to look out of the window and see what London was doing on the morning of the twenty-sixth of October 1928. And what was London doing? Nobody, it seemed, was reading *Antony and Cleopatra*. London was wholly indifferent, it appeared, to Shakespeare's plays. Nobody cared a straw—and I do not blame them—for the future of fiction, the death of poetry or the development by the average woman of a prose style completely expressive of her mind. If opinions upon any of these matters had been chalked on the pavement, nobody would have stooped to read them. The nonchalance of the hurrying feet would have rubbed them out in half an hour. Here came an errand-boy;

here a woman with a dog on a lead. The fascination of the London street is that no two people are ever alike; each seems bound on some private affair of his own. There were the business-like, with their little bags; there were the drifters rattling sticks upon area railings; there were affable characters to whom the streets serve for clubroom, hailing men in carts and giving information without being asked for it. Also there were funerals to which men, thus suddenly reminded of the passing of their own bodies, lifted their hats. And then a very distinguished gentleman came slowly down a doorstep and paused to avoid collision with a bustling lady who had, by some means or other, acquired a splendid fur coat and a bunch of Parma violets. They all seemed separate, self-absorbed, on business of their own.

At this moment, as so often happens in London, there was a complete lull and suspension of traffic. Nothing came down the street; nobody passed. A single leaf detached itself from the plane tree at the end of the street, and in that pause and suspension fell. Somehow it was like a signal falling, a signal pointing to a force in things which one had overlooked. It seemed to point to a river, which flowed past, invisibly, round the corner, down the street, and took people and eddied them along, as the stream at Oxbridge had taken the undergraduate in his boat and the dead leaves. Now it was bringing from one side of the street to the other diagonally a girl in patent leather boots, and then a young man in a maroon overcoat; it was also bringing a taxi-cab; and it brought all three together at a point directly beneath my window; where the taxi stopped; and the girl and the young man stopped; and they got into the taxi; and then the cab glided off as if it were swept on by the current elsewhere.

The sight was ordinary enough; what was strange was the rhythmical order with which my imagination had invested it; and the fact that the ordinary sight of two people getting into a cab had the power to communicate something of their own seeming satisfaction. The sight of two people coming down the street and meeting at the corner seems to ease the mind of some strain, I thought, watching the taxi turn and make off. Perhaps to think, as I had been thinking these two days, of one sex as distinct from the other is an effort. It interferes with the unity of the mind. Now that effort had ceased and that unity had been restored by seeing two people come together and get into a taxi-cab. The mind is certainly a very mysterious organ, I reflected, drawing my head in from the window, about which nothing whatever is known, though we depend upon it so completely. Why do I feel that there are severances and oppositions in the mind, as there are strains from obvious causes on the body? What does one mean by "the unity of the mind," I pondered, for clearly the mind has so great a power of concentrating at any point at any moment that it seems to have no single state of being. It can separate itself from the people in the street, for example, and think of itself as apart from them, at an upper window looking down on them. Or it can think with other people spontaneously, as, for instance, in a crowd waiting to hear some piece of news read out. It can think back through its fathers or through its mothers, as I have said that a woman writing thinks back through her mothers. Again if one is a woman one is often surprised by a sudden splitting off of consciousness, say in walking down Whitehall,[9] when

9. London thoroughfare along which are located the chief offices of the British government.

from being the natural inheritor of that civilisation, she becomes, on the contrary, outside of it, alien and critical. Clearly the mind is always altering its focus, and bringing the world into different perspectives. But some of these states of mind seem, even if adopted spontaneously, to be less comfortable than others. In order to keep oneself continuing in them one is unconsciously holding something back, and gradually the repression becomes an effort. But there may be some state of mind in which one could continue without effort because nothing is required to be held back. And this perhaps, I thought, coming in from the window, is one of them. For certainly when I saw the couple get into the taxi-cab the mind felt as if, after being divided, it had come together again in a natural fusion. The obvious reason would be that it is natural for the sexes to co-operate. One has a profound, if irrational, instinct in favour of the theory that the union of man and woman makes for the greatest satisfaction, the most complete happiness. But the sight of the two people getting into the taxi and the satisfaction it gave me made me also ask whether there are two sexes in the mind corresponding to the two sexes in the body, and whether they also require to be united in order to get complete satisfaction and happiness. And I went on amateurishly to sketch a plan of the soul so that in each of us two powers preside, one male, one female; and in the man's brain, the man predominates over the woman, and in the woman's brain, the woman predominates over the man. The normal and comfortable state of being is that when the two live in harmony together, spiritually cooperating. If one is a man, still the woman part of the brain must have effect; and a woman also must have intercourse with the man in her. Coleridge perhaps meant this when he said that a great mind is androgynous. It is when this fusion takes place that the mind is fully fertilised and uses all its faculties. Perhaps a mind that is purely masculine cannot create, any more than a mind that is purely feminine, I thought. But it would be well to test what one meant by man-womanly, and conversely by woman-manly, by pausing and looking at a book or two.

Coleridge certainly did not mean, when he said that a great mind is androgynous, that it is a mind that has any special sympathy with women; a mind that takes up their cause or devotes itself to their interpretation. Perhaps the androgynous mind is less apt to make these distinctions than the single-sexed mind. He meant, perhaps, that the androgynous mind is resonant and porous; that it transmits emotion without impediment; that it is naturally creative, incandescent and undivided. In fact one goes back to Shakespeare's mind as the type of the androgynous, of the man-womanly mind, though it would be impossible to say what Shakespeare thought of women. And if it be true that it is one of the tokens of the fully developed mind that it does not think specially or separately of sex, how much harder it is to attain that condition now than ever before. Here I came to the books by living writers, and there paused and wondered if this fact were not at the root of something that had long puzzled me. No age can ever have been as stridently sex-conscious as our own; those innumerable books by men about women in the British Museum are a proof of it. The Suffrage campaign was no doubt to blame. It must have roused in men an extraordinary desire for self-assertion; it must have made them lay an emphasis upon their own sex and its characteristics which they would not have troubled to think about had they not been challenged. And when one is challenged, even by a few women in black bonnets, one retaliates, if one has never been challenged before, rather excessively. That perhaps accounts for some of the characteristics that I remember to have found here, I thought, taking down a new novel by Mr A, who is in the prime of life and very well thought of, apparently, by the reviewers. I opened it. Indeed, it was delightful to read a man's writing again. It was so direct, so straightforward after the writing of women. It indicated such freedom of mind, such liberty of person, such confidence in himself. One had a sense of physical well-being in the presence of this well-nourished, well-educated, free mind, which had never been thwarted or opposed, but had had full liberty from birth to stretch itself in whatever way it liked. All this was admirable. But after reading a chapter or two a shadow seemed to lie across the page. It was a straight dark bar, a shadow shaped something like the letter "I." One began dodging this way and that to catch a glimpse of the landscape behind it. Whether that was indeed a tree or a woman walking I was not quite sure. Back one was always hailed to the letter "I." One began to be tired of "I." Not but what this "I" was a most respectable "I"; honest and logical; as hard as a nut, and polished for centuries by good teaching and good feeding. I respect and admire that "I" from the bottom of my heart. But—here I turned a page or two, looking for something or other— the worst of it is that in the shadow of the letter "I" all is shapeless as mist. Is that a tree? No, it is a woman. But . . . she has not a bone in her body, I thought, watching Phoebe, for that was her name, coming across the beach. Then Alan got up and the shadow of Alan at once obliterated Phoebe. For Alan had views and Phoebe was quenched in the flood of his views. And then Alan, I thought, had passions; and here I turned page after page very fast, feeling that the crisis was approaching, and so it was. It took place on the beach under the sun. It was done very openly. It was done very vigorously. Nothing could have been more indecent. But . . . I had said "but" too often. One cannot go on saying "but." One must finish the sentence somehow, I rebuked myself. Shall I finish it, "But—I am bored!" But why was I bored? Partly because of the dominance of the letter "I" and the aridity, which, like the giant beech tree, it casts within its shade. Nothing will grow there. And partly for some more obscure reason. There seemed to be some obstacle, some impediment of Mr A's mind which blocked the fountain of creative energy and shored it within narrow limits. And remembering the lunch party at Oxbridge, and the cigarette ash and the Manx cat and Tennyson and Christina Rossetti all in a bunch, it seemed possible that the impediment lay there. As he no longer hums under his breath, "There has fallen a splendid tear from the passion-flower at the gate," when Phoebe crosses the beach, and she no longer replies, "My heart is like a singing bird whose nest is in a water'd shoot," when Alan approaches what can he do? Being honest as the day and logical as the sun, there is only one thing he can do. And that he does, to do him justice, over and over (I said, turning the pages) and over again. And that, I added, aware of the awful nature of the confession, seems somehow dull. Shakespeare's indecency uproots a thousand other things in one's mind, and is far from being dull. But Shakespeare does it for pleasure; Mr A, as the nurses say, does it on purpose. He does it in protest. He is protesting against the equality of the other sex by asserting his own superiority. He is therefore impeded and inhibited and self-conscious as Shakespeare might have been if he too had known Miss Clough and Miss Davies.

Doubtless Elizabethan literature would have been very different from what it is if the woman's movement had begun in the sixteenth century and not in the nineteenth.

What, then, it amounts to, if this theory of the two sides of the mind holds good, is that virility has now become self-conscious—men, that is to say, are now writing only with the male side of their brains. It is a mistake for a woman to read them, for she will inevitably look for something that she will not find. It is the power of suggestion that one most misses, I thought, taking Mr B the critic in my hand and reading, very carefully and very dutifully, his remarks upon the art of poetry. Very able they were, acute and full of learning; but the trouble was, that his feelings no longer communicated; his mind seemed separated into different chambers; not a sound carried from one to the other. Thus, when one takes a sentence of Mr B into the mind it falls plump to the ground—dead; but when one takes a sentence of Coleridge into the mind, it explodes and gives birth to all kinds of other ideas, and that is the only sort of writing of which one can say that it has the secret of perpetual life.

But whatever the reason may be, it is a fact that one must deplore. For it means—here I had come to rows of books by Mr Galsworthy and Mr Kipling[1]—that some of the finest works of our greatest living writers fall upon deaf ears. Do what she will a woman cannot find in them that fountain of perpetual life which the critics assure her is there. It is not only that they celebrate male virtues, enforce male values and describe the world of men; it is that the emotion with which these books are permeated is to a woman incomprehensible. It is coming, it is gathering, it is about to burst on one's head, one begins saying long before the end. That picture will fall on old Jolyon's head; he will die of the shock; the old clerk will speak over him two or three obituary words; and all the swans on the Thames will simultaneously burst out singing. But one will rush away before that happens and hide in the gooseberry bushes, for the emotion which is so deep, so subtle, so symbolical to a man moves a woman to wonder. So with Mr Kipling's officers who turn their backs; and his Sowers who sow the Seed; and his Men who are alone with their Work; and the Flag—one blushes at all these capital letters as if one had been caught eavesdropping at some purely masculine orgy. The fact is that neither Mr Galsworthy nor Mr Kipling has a spark of the woman in him. Thus all their qualities seem to a woman, if one may generalise, crude and immature. They lack suggestive power. And when a book lacks suggestive power, however hard it hits the surface of the mind it cannot penetrate within.

And in that restless mood in which one takes books out and puts them back again without looking at them I began to envisage an age to come of pure, of self-assertive virility, such as the letters of professors (take Sir Walter Raleigh's letters, for instance) seem to forebode, and the rulers of Italy have already brought into being. For one can hardly fail to be impressed in Rome by the sense of unmitigated masculinity; and whatever the value of unmitigated masculinity upon the state, one may question the effect of it upon the art of poetry. At any rate, according to the newspapers, there is a certain anxiety about fiction in Italy. There has been a meeting of academicians

1. John Galsworthy (1867–1933) and Rudyard Kipling (1865–1936), English novelists.

whose object it is "to develop the Italian novel." "Men famous by birth, or in finance, industry or the Fascist corporations" came together the other day and discussed the matter, and a telegram was sent to the Duce[2] expressing the hope "that the Fascist era would soon give birth to a poet worthy of it." We may all join in that pious hope, but it is doubtful whether poetry can come out of an incubator. Poetry ought to have a mother as well as a father. The Fascist poem, one may fear, will be a horrid little abortion such as one sees in a glass jar in the museum of some county town. Such monsters never live long, it is said; one has never seen a prodigy of that sort cropping grass in a field. Two heads on one body do not make for length of life.

However, the blame for all this, if one is anxious to lay blame, rests no more upon one sex than upon the other. All seducers and reformers are responsible, Lady Bessborough when she lied to Lord Granville; Miss Davies when she told the truth to Mr Greg. All who have brought about a state of sex-consciousness are to blame, and it is they who drive me, when I want to stretch my faculties on a book, to seek it in that happy age, before Miss Davies and Miss Clough were born, when the writer used both sides of his mind equally. One must turn back to Shakespeare then, for Shakespeare was androgynous; and so was Keats and Sterne and Cowper and Lamb and Coleridge. Shelley perhaps was sexless. Milton and Ben Jonson had a dash too much of the male in them. So had Wordsworth and Tolstoi. In our time Proust was wholly androgynous, if not perhaps a little too much of a woman. But that failing is too rare for one to complain of it, since without some mixture of the kind the intellect seems to predominate and the other faculties of the mind harden and become barren. However, I consoled myself with the reflection that this is perhaps a passing phase; much of what I have said in obedience to my promise to give you the course of my thoughts will seem out of date; much of what flames in my eyes will seem dubious to you who have not yet come of age.

Even so, the very first sentence that I would write here, I said, crossing over to the writing-table and taking up the page headed Women and Fiction, is that it is fatal for any one who writes to think of their sex. It is fatal to be a man or woman pure and simple; one must be woman-manly or man-womanly. It is fatal for a woman to lay the least stress on any grievance; to plead even with justice any cause; in any way to speak consciously as a woman. And fatal is no figure of speech; for anything written with that conscious bias is doomed to death. It ceases to be fertilised. Brilliant and effective, powerful and masterly, as it may appear for a day or two, it must wither at nightfall; it cannot grow in the minds of others. Some collaboration has to take place in the mind between the woman and the man before the act of creation can be accomplished. Some marriage of opposites has to be consummated. The whole of the mind must lie wide open if we are to get the sense that the writer is communicating his experience with perfect fullness. There must be freedom and there must be peace. Not a wheel must grate, not a light glimmer. The curtains must be close drawn. The writer, I thought, once his experience is over, must lie back and let his mind celebrate its nuptials in darkness. He must not look or question what is being done. Rather, he must pluck the petals from a rose or watch the swans float calmly

2. "The leader," i.e., Mussolini.

down the river. And I saw again the current which took the boat and the undergraduate and the dead leaves; and the taxi took the man and the woman, I thought, seeing them come together across the street, and the current swept them away, I thought, hearing far off the roar of London's traffic, into that tremendous stream.

Here, then, Mary Beton ceases to speak. She has told you how she reached the conclusion—the prosaic conclusion—that it is necessary to have five hundred a year and a room with a lock on the door if you are to write fiction or poetry. She has tried to lay bare the thoughts and impressions that led her to think this. She has asked you to follow her flying into the arms of a Beadle, lunching here, dining there, drawing pictures in the British Museum, taking books from the shelf, looking out of the window. While she has been doing all these things, you no doubt have been observing her failings and foibles and deciding what effect they have had on her opinions. You have been contradicting her and making whatever additions and deductions seem good to you. That is all as it should be, for in a question like this truth is only to be had by laying together many varieties of error. And I will end now in my own person by anticipating two criticisms, so obvious that you can hardly fail to make them.

No opinion has been expressed, you may say, upon the comparative merits of the sexes even as writers. That was done purposely, because, even if the time had come for such a valuation—and it is far more important at the moment to know how much money women had and how many rooms than to theorise about their capacities—even if the time had come I do not believe that gifts, whether of mind or character, can be weighed like sugar and butter, not even in Cambridge, where they are so adept at putting people into classes and fixing caps on their heads and letters after their names. I do not believe that even the Table of Precedency which you will find in Whitaker's *Almanac* represents a final order of values, or that there is any sound reason to suppose that a Commander of the Bath will ultimately walk in to dinner behind a Master in Lunacy. All this pitting of sex against sex, of quality against quality; all this claiming of superiority and imputing of inferiority, belong to the private-school stage of human existence where there are "sides," and it is necessary for one side to beat another side, and of the utmost importance to walk up to a platform and receive from the hands of the Headmaster himself a highly ornamental pot. As people mature they cease to believe in sides or in Headmasters or in highly ornamental pots. At any rate, where books are concerned, it is notoriously difficult to fix labels of merit in such a way that they do not come off. Are not reviews of current literature a perpetual illustration of the difficulty of judgement? "This great book," "this worthless book," the same book is called by both names. Praise and blame alike mean nothing. No, delightful as the pastime of measuring may be, it is the most futile of all occupations, and to submit to the decrees of the measurers the most servile of attitudes. So long as you write what you wish to write, that is all that matters; and whether it matters for ages or only for hours, nobody can say. But to sacrifice a hair of the head of your vision, a shade of its colour, in deference to some Headmaster with a silver pot in his hand or to some professor with a measuring-rod up his sleeve, is the most abject treachery, and the sacrifice of wealth and chastity which used to be said to be the greatest of human disasters, a mere flea-bite in comparison.

Next I think that you may object that in all this I have made too much of the importance of material things. Even allowing a generous margin for symbolism, that five hundred a year stands for the power to contemplate, that a lock on the door means the power to think for oneself, still you may say that the mind should rise above such things; and that great poets have often been poor men. Let me then quote to you the words of your own Professor of Literature, who knows better than I do what goes to the making of a poet. Sir Arthur Quiller-Couch writes:[3]

"What are the great poetical names of the last hundred years or so? Coleridge, Wordsworth, Byron, Shelley, Landor, Keats, Tennyson, Browning, Arnold, Morris, Rossetti, Swinburne—we may stop there. Of these, all but Keats, Browning, Rossetti were University men; and of these three, Keats, who died young, cut off in his prime, was the only one not fairly well to do. It may seem a brutal thing to say, and it is a sad thing to say: but, as a matter of hard fact, the theory that poetical genius bloweth where it listeth, and equally in poor and rich, holds little truth. As a matter of hard fact, nine out of those twelve were University men: which means that somehow or other they procured the means to get the best education England can give. As a matter of hard fact, of the remaining three you know that Browning was well to do, and I challenge you that, if he had not been well to do, he would no more have attained to write *Saul* or *The Ring and the Book* than Ruskin would have attained to writing *Modern Painters* if his father had not dealt prosperously in business. Rossetti had a small private income; and, moreover, he painted. There remains but Keats; whom Atropos[4] slew young, as she slew John Clare in a mad-house, and James Thomson by the laudanum he took to drug disappointment. These are dreadful facts, but let us face them. It is—however dishonouring to us as a nation—certain that, by some fault in our commonwealth, the poor poet has not in these days, nor has had for two hundred years, a dog's chance. Believe me—and I have spent a great part of ten years in watching some three hundred and twenty elementary schools—we may prate of democracy, but actually, a poor child in England has little more hope than had the son of an Athenian slave to be emancipated into that intellectual freedom of which great writings are born."

Nobody could put the point more plainly. "The poor poet has not in these days, nor has had for two hundred years, a dog's chance . . . a poor child in England has little more hope than had the son of an Athenian slave to be emancipated into that intellectual freedom of which great writings are born." That is it. Intellectual freedom depends upon material things. Poetry depends upon intellectual freedom. And women have always been poor, not for two hundred years merely, but from the beginning of time. Women have had less intellectual freedom than the sons of Athenian slaves. Women, then, have not had a dog's chance of writing poetry. That is why I have laid so much stress on money and a room of one's own. However, thanks to the toils of those obscure women in the past, of whom I wish we knew more, thanks, curiously enough, to two wars, the Crimean which let Florence Nightingale out of her drawing-room, and the European War which opened the doors to the average woman some sixty years later, these evils are in the way to be bettered. Otherwise you would not be here tonight, and your chance of earn-

---

3. *The Art of Writing*, by Sir Arthur Quiller-Couch [Woolf's note].

4. In Greek mythology, the Fate who cut the thread of life.

ing five hundred pounds a year, precarious as I am afraid that it still is, would be minute in the extreme.

Still, you may object, why do you attach so much importance to this writing of books by women when, according to you, it requires so much effort, leads perhaps to the murder of one's aunts, will make one almost certainly late for luncheon, and may bring one into very grave disputes with certain very good fellows? My motives, let me admit, are partly selfish. Like most uneducated Englishwomen, I like reading—I like reading books in the bulk. Lately my diet has become a trifle monotonous; history is too much about wars; biography too much about great men; poetry has shown, I think, a tendency to sterility, and fiction—but I have sufficiently exposed my disabilities as a critic of modern fiction and will say no more about it. Therefore I would ask you to write all kinds of books, hesitating at no subject however trivial or however vast. By hook or by crook, I hope that you will possess yourselves of money enough to travel and to idle, to contemplate the future or the past of the world, to dream over books and loiter at street corners and let the line of thought dip deep into the stream. For I am by no means confining you to fiction. If you would please me—and there are thousands like me—you would write books of travel and adventure, and research and scholarship, and history and biography, and criticism and philosophy and science. By so doing you will certainly profit the art of fiction. For books have a way of influencing each other. Fiction will be much the better for standing cheek by jowl with poetry and philosophy. Moreover, if you consider any great figure of the past, like Sappho, like the Lady Murasaki,[5] like Emily Brontë, you will find that she is an inheritor as well as an originator, and has come into existence because women have come to have the habit of writing naturally; so that even as a prelude to poetry such activity on your part would be invaluable.

But when I look back through these notes and criticise my own train of thought as I made them, I find that my motives were not altogether selfish. There runs through these comments and discursions the conviction—or is it the instinct?—that good books are desirable and that good writers, even if they show every variety of human depravity, are still good human beings. Thus when I ask you to write more books I am urging you to do what will be for your good and for the good of the world at large. How to justify this instinct or belief I do not know, for philosophic words, if one has not been educated at a university, are apt to play one false. What is meant by "reality"? It would seem to be something very erratic, very undependable—now to be found in a dusty road, now in a scrap of newspaper in the street, now in a daffodil in the sun. It lights up a group in a room and stamps some casual saying. It overwhelms one walking home beneath the stars and makes the silent world more real than the world of speech—and then there it is again in an omnibus in the uproar of Piccadilly. Sometimes, too, it seems to dwell in shapes too far away for us to discern what their nature is. But whatever it touches, it fixes and makes permanent. That is what remains over when the skin of the day has been cast into the hedge; that is what is left of past time and of our loves and hates. Now the writer, as I think, has the chance

5. Japanese writer, (978?–?1026) author of *The Tale of Genji*. Sappho (7th century B.C.E.), Greek lyric poet.

to live more than other people in the presence of this reality. It is his business to find it and collect it and communicate it to the rest of us. So at least I infer from reading *Lear* or *Emma* or *La Recherche du Temps Perdu*. For the reading of these books seems to perform a curious couching operation on the senses; one sees more intensely afterwards; the world seems bared of its covering and given an intenser life. Those are the enviable people who live at enmity with unreality; and those are the pitiable who are knocked on the head by the thing done without knowing or caring. So that when I ask you to earn money and have a room of your own, I am asking you to live in the presence of reality, an invigorating life, it would appear, whether one can impart it or not.

Here I would stop, but the pressure of convention decrees that every speech must end with a peroration. And a peroration addressed to women should have something, you will agree, particularly exalting and ennobling about it. I should implore you to remember your responsibilities, to be higher, more spiritual; I should remind you how much depends upon you, and what an influence you can exert upon the future. But those exhortations can safely, I think, be left to the other sex, who will put them, and indeed have put them, with far greater eloquence than I can compass. When I rummage in my own mind I find no noble sentiments about being companions and equals and influencing the world to higher ends. I find myself saying briefly and prosaically that it is much more important to be oneself than anything else. Do not dream of influencing other people, I would say, if I knew how to make it sound exalted. Think of things in themselves.

And again I am reminded by dipping into newspapers and novels and biographies that when a woman speaks to women she should have something very unpleasant up her sleeve. Women are hard on women. Women dislike women. Women—but are you not sick to death of the word? I can assure you that I am. Let us agree, then, that a paper read by a woman to women should end with something particularly disagreeable.

But how does it go? What can I think of? The truth is, I often like women. I like their unconventionality. I like their subtlety. I like their anonymity. I like—but I must not run on in this way. That cupboard there,—you say it holds clean table-napkins only; but what if Sir Archibald Bodkin were concealed among them? Let me then adopt a sterner tone. Have I, in the preceding words, conveyed to you sufficiently the warnings and reprobation of mankind? I have told you the very low opinion in which you were held by Mr Oscar Browning. I have indicated what Napoleon once thought of you and what Mussolini thinks now. Then, in case any of you aspire to fiction, I have copied out for your benefit the advice of the critic about courageously acknowledging the limitations of your sex. I have referred to Professor X and given prominence to his statement that women are intellectually, morally and physically inferior to men. I have handed on all that has come my way without going in search of it, and here is a final warning—from Mr John Langdon Davies.[6] Mr John Langdon Davies warns women "that when children cease to be altogether desirable, women cease to be altogether necessary." I hope you will make a note of it.

How can I further encourage you to go about the business of life? Young

6. *A Short History of Women*, by John Langdon Davies [Woolf's note].

women, I would say, and please attend, for the peroration is beginning, you are, in my opinion, disgracefully ignorant. You have never made a discovery of any sort of importance. You have never shaken an empire or led an army into battle. The plays of Shakespeare are not by you, and you have never introduced a barbarous race to the blessings of civilisation. What is your excuse? It is all very well for you to say, pointing to the streets and squares and forests of the globe swarming with black and white and coffee-coloured inhabitants, all busily engaged in traffic and enterprise and love-making, we have had other work on our hands. Without our doing, those seas would be unsailed and those fertile lands a desert. We have borne and bred and washed and taught, perhaps to the age of six or seven years, the one thousand six hundred and twenty-three million human beings who are, according to statistics, at present in existence, and that, allowing that some had help, takes time.

There is truth in what you say—I will not deny it. But at the same time may I remind you that there have been at least two colleges for women in existence in England since the year 1866; that after the year 1880 a married woman was allowed by law to possess her own property; and that in 1919—which is a whole nine years ago—she was given a vote? May I also remind you that the most of the professions have been open to you for close on ten years now? When you reflect upon these immense privileges and the length of time during which they have been enjoyed, and the fact that there must be at this moment some two thousand women capable of earning over five hundred a year in one way or another, you will agree that the excuse of lack of opportunity, training, encouragement, leisure and money no longer holds good. Moreover, the economists are telling us that Mrs Seton has had too many children. You must, of course, go on bearing children, but, so they say, in twos and threes, not in tens and twelves.

Thus, with some time on your hands and with some book learning in your brains—you have had enough of the other kind, and are sent to college partly, I suspect, to be uneducated—surely you should embark upon another stage of your very long, very laborious and highly obscure career. A thousand pens are ready to suggest what you should do and what effect you will have. My own suggestion is a little fantastic, I admit; I prefer, therefore, to put it in the form of fiction.

I told you in the course of this paper that Shakespeare had a sister; but do not look for her in Sir Sidney Lee's[7] life of the poet. She died young—alas, she never wrote a word. She lies buried where the omnibuses now stop, opposite the Elephant and Castle. Now my belief is that this poet who never wrote a word and was buried at the crossroads still lives. She lives in you and in me, and in many other women who are not here tonight, for they are washing up the dishes and putting the children to bed. But she lives; for great poets do not die; they are continuing presences; they need only the opportunity to walk among us in the flesh. This opportunity, as I think, it is now coming within your power to give her. For my belief is that if we live another century or so—I am talking of the common life which is the real life and not of the little separate lives which we live as individuals—and have five hundred a year each of us and rooms of our own; if we have the habit

7. Biographer and Shakespeare scholar (1859–1926), author of *Life of William Shakespeare* (1898).

of freedom and the courage to write exactly what we think; if we escape a little from the common sitting-room and see human beings not always in their relation to each other but in relation to reality; and the sky, too, and the trees or whatever it may be in themselves; if we look past Milton's bogey,[8] for no human being should shut out the view; if we face the fact, for it is a fact, that there is no arm to cling to, but that we go alone and that our relation is to the world of reality and not only to the world of men and women, then the opportunity will come and the dead poet who was Shakespeare's sister will put on the body which she has so often laid down. Drawing her life from the lives of the unknown who were her forerunners, as her brother did before her, she will be born. As for her coming without that preparation, without that effort on our part, without that determination that when she is born again she shall find it possible to live and write her poetry, that we cannot expect, for that would be impossible. But I maintain that she would come if we worked for her, and that so to work, even in poverty and obscurity, is worth while.

1929

Professions for Women[1]

When your secretary invited me to come here, she told me that your Society is concerned with the employment of women and she suggested that I might tell you something about my own professional experiences. It is true I am a woman; it is true I am employed; but what professional experiences have I had? It is difficult to say. My profession is literature; and in that profession there are fewer experiences for women than in any other, with the exception of the stage—fewer, I mean, that are peculiar to women. For the road was cut many years ago—by Fanny Burney, by Aphra Behn, by Harriet Martineau,[2] by Jane Austen, by George Eliot—many famous women, and many more unknown and forgotten, have been before me, making the path smooth, and regulating my steps. Thus, when I came to write, there were very few material obstacles in my way. Writing was a reputable and harmless occupation. The family peace was not broken by the scratching of a pen. No demand was made upon the family purse. For ten and sixpence one can buy paper enough to write all the plays of Shakespeare—if one has a mind that way. Pianos and models, Paris, Vienna, and Berlin, masters and mistresses, are not needed by a writer. The cheapness of writing paper is, of course, the reason why women have succeeded as writers before they have succeeded in the other professions.

But to tell you my story—it is a simple one. You have only got to figure to yourselves a girl in a bedroom with a pen in her hand. She had only to move that pen from left to right—from ten o'clock to one. Then it occurred to her

---

8. Milton, with his unhappy first marriage, his campaign for freedom of divorce, and his deliberate subordination of Eve to Adam in *Paradise Lost*, was and often still is held to be (not altogether accurately) an example of what the present age calls a male chauvinist.

1. A paper read to the Women's Service League [Woolf's note].
2. Economist, moralist, journalist, and novelist (1802–1876). Burney (1752–1840), author of *Evelina* and other novels. Behn (1640–1689), writer of romances and plays.

to do what is simple and cheap enough after all—to slip a few of those pages into an envelope, fix a penny stamp in the corner, and drop the envelope into the red box at the corner. It was thus that I became a journalist; and my effort was rewarded on the first day of the following month—a very glorious day it was for me—by a letter from an editor containing a cheque for one pound ten shillings and sixpence. But to show you how little I deserve to be called a professional woman, how little I know of the struggles and difficulties of such lives, I have to admit that instead of spending that sum upon bread and butter, rent, shoes and stockings, or butcher's bills, I went out and bought a cat—a beautiful cat, a Persian cat, which very soon involved me in bitter disputes with my neighbours.

What could be easier than to write articles and to buy Persian cats with the profits? But wait a moment. Articles have to be about something. Mine, I seem to remember, was about a novel by a famous man. And while I was writing this review, I discovered that if I were going to review books I should need to do battle with a certain phantom. And the phantom was a woman, and when I came to know her better I called her after the heroine of a famous poem, The Angel in the House.[3] It was she who used to come between me and my paper when I was writing reviews. It was she who bothered and wasted my time and so tormented me that at last I killed her. You who come of a younger and happier generation may not have heard of her—you may not know what I mean by The Angel in the House. I will describe her as shortly as I can. She was intensely sympathetic. She was immensely charming. She was utterly unselfish. She excelled in the difficult arts of family life. She sacrificed herself daily. If there was chicken, she took the leg; if there was a draught she sat in it—in short she was so constituted that she never had a mind or a wish of her own, but preferred to sympathise always with the minds and wishes of others. Above all—I need not say it—she was pure. Her purity was supposed to be her chief beauty—her blushes, her great grace. In those days—the last of Queen Victoria—every house had its Angel. And when I came to write I encountered her with the very first words. The shadow of her wings fell on my page; I heard the rustling of her skirts in the room. Directly, that is to say, I took my pen in my hand to review that novel by a famous man, she slipped behind me and whispered: 'My dear, you are a young woman. You are writing about a book that has been written by a man. Be sympathetic; be tender; flatter; deceive; use all the arts and wiles of our sex. Never let anybody guess that you have a mind of your own. Above all, be pure.' And she made as if to guide my pen. I now record the one act for which I take some credit to myself, though the credit rightly belongs to some excellent ancestors of mine who left me a certain sum of money—shall we say five hundred pounds a year?—so that it was not necessary for me to depend solely on charm for my living. I turned upon her and caught her by the throat. I did my best to kill her. My excuse, if I were to be had up in a court of law, would be that I acted in self-defence. Had I not killed her she would have killed me. She would have plucked the heart out of my writing. For, as I found, directly I put pen to paper, you cannot review even a novel without having a mind of your own, without expressing what you think to be the truth about human relations, morality, sex. And all these questions,

---

3. By Coventry Patmore (1823–1896), published 1854–62.

according to the Angel of the House, cannot be dealt with freely and openly by women; they must charm, they must conciliate, they must—to put it bluntly—tell lies if they are to succeed. Thus, whenever I felt the shadow of her wing or the radiance of her halo upon my page, I took up the inkpot and flung it at her. She died hard. Her fictitious nature was of great assistance to her. It is far harder to kill a phantom than a reality. She was always creeping back when I thought I had despatched her. Though I flatter myself that I killed her in the end, the struggle was severe; it took much time that had better have been spent upon learning Greek grammar; or in roaming the world in search of adventures. But it was a real experience; it was an experience that was bound to befall all women writers at that time. Killing the Angel in the House was part of the occupation of a woman writer.

But to continue my story. The Angel was dead; what then remained? You may say that what remained was a simple and common object—a young woman in a bedroom with an inkpot. In other words, now that she had rid herself of falsehood, that young woman had only to be herself. Ah, but what is 'herself'? I mean, what is a woman? I assure you, I do not know. I do not believe that you know. I do not believe that anybody can know until she has expressed herself in all the arts and professions open to human skill. That indeed is one of the reasons why I have come here—out of respect for you, who are in process of showing us by your experiments what a woman is, who are in process of providing us, by your failures and successes, with that extremely important piece of information.

But to continue the story of my professional experiences. I made one pound ten and six by my first review; and I bought a Persian cat with the proceeds. Then I grew ambitious. A Persian cat is all very well, I said; but a Persian cat is not enough. I must have a motor-car. And it was thus that I became a novelist—for it is a very strange thing that people will give you a motor-car if you will tell them a story. It is a still stranger thing that there is nothing so delightful in the world as telling stories. It is far pleasanter than writing reviews of famous novels. And yet, if I am to obey your secretary and tell you my professional experiences as a novelist, I must tell you about a very strange experience that befell me as a novelist. And to understand it you must try first to imagine a novelist's state of mind. I hope I am not giving away professional secrets if I say that a novelist's chief desire is to be as unconscious as possible. He has to induce in himself a state of perpetual lethargy. He wants life to proceed with the utmost quiet and regularity. He wants to see the same faces, to read the same books, to do the same things day after day, month after month, while he is writing, so that nothing may break the illusion in which he is living—so that nothing may disturb or disquiet the mysterious nosings about, feelings round, darts, dashes, and sudden discoveries of that very shy and illusive spirit, the imagination. I suspect that this state is the same both for men and women. Be that as it may, I want you to imagine me writing a novel in a state of trance. I want you to figure to yourselves a girl sitting with a pen in her hand, which for minutes, and indeed for hours, she never dips into the inkpot. The image that comes to my mind when I think of this girl is the image of a fisherman lying sunk in dreams on the verge of a deep lake with a rod held out over the water. She was letting her imagination sweep unchecked round every rock and cranny of the world that lies submerged in the depths of our unconscious being. Now came the experience that I believe to be far commoner with women writers than with men. The line raced through the girl's fingers. Her imagination had rushed away. It had sought the pools, the depths, the dark places where the largest fish slumber. And then there was a smash. There was an explosion. There was foam and confusion. The imagination had dashed itself against something hard. The girl was roused from her dream. She was indeed in a state of the most acute and difficult distress. To speak without figure, she had thought of something, something about the body, about the passions which it was unfitting for her as a woman to say. Men, her reason told her, would be shocked. The consciousness of what men will say of a woman who speaks the truth about her passions had roused her from her artist's state of unconsciousness. She could write no more. The trance was over. Her imagination could work no longer. This I believe to be a very common experience with women writers—they are impeded by the extreme conventionality of the other sex. For though men sensibly allow themselves great freedom in these respects, I doubt that they realize or can control the extreme severity with which they condemn such freedom in women.

These then were two very genuine experiences of my own. These were two of the adventures of my professional life. The first—killing the Angel in the House—I think I solved. She died. But the second, telling the truth about my own experiences as a body, I do not think I solved. I doubt that any woman has solved it yet. The obstacles against her are still immensely powerful— and yet they are very difficult to define. Outwardly, what is simpler than to write books? Outwardly, what obstacles are there for a woman rather than for a man? Inwardly, I think, the case is very different; she has still many ghosts to fight, many prejudices to overcome. Indeed it will be a long time still, I think, before a woman can sit down to write a book without finding a phantom to be slain, a rock to be dashed against. And if this is so in literature, the freest of all professions for women, how is it in the new professions which you are now for the first time entering?

Those are the questions that I should like, had I time, to ask you. And indeed, if I have laid stress upon these professional experiences of mine, it is because I believe that they are, though in different forms, yours also. Even when the path is nominally open—when there is nothing to prevent a woman from being a doctor, a lawyer, a civil servant—there are many phantoms and obstacles, as I believe, looming in her way. To discuss and define them is I think of great value and importance; for thus only can the labour be shared, the difficulties be solved. But besides this, it is necessary also to discuss the ends and the aims for which we are fighting, for which we are doing battle with these formidable obstacles. Those aims cannot be taken for granted; they must be perpetually questioned and examined. The whole position, as I see it—here in this hall surrounded by women practising for the first time in history I know not how many different professions—is one of extraordinary interest and importance. You have won rooms of your own in the house hitherto exclusively owned by men. You are able, though not without great labour and effort, to pay the rent. You are earning your five hundred pounds a year. But this freedom is only a beginning; the room is your own, but it is still bare. It has to be furnished; it has to be decorated; it has to be shared. How are you going to furnish it, how are you going to decorate it? With whom are you going to share it, and upon what terms? These, I think are questions of the utmost importance and interest. For the first time in history you are able to ask them; for the first time you are able to decide for yourselves what the answers should be. Willingly would I stay and discuss those questions and answers—but not tonight. My time is up; and I must cease.

1942

From A Sketch of the Past[1]

[MOMENTS OF BEING AND NON-BEING]

—I begin: the first memory.

This was of red and purple flowers on a black ground—my mother's dress; and she was sitting either in a train or in an omnibus, and I was on her lap. I therefore saw the flowers she was wearing very close; and can still see purple and red and blue, I think, against the black; they must have been anemones, I suppose. Perhaps we were going to St Ives; more probably, for from the light it must have been evening, we were coming back to London. But it is more convenient artistically to suppose that we were going to St Ives, for that will lead to my other memory, which also seems to be my first memory, and in fact it is the most important of all my memories. If life has a base that it stands upon, if it is a bowl that one fills and fills and fills— then my bowl without a doubt stands upon this memory. It is of lying half asleep, half awake, in bed in the nursery at St Ives. It is of hearing the waves breaking, one, two, one, two, and sending a splash of water over the beach; and then breaking, one, two, one, two, behind a yellow blind. It is of hearing the blind draw its little acorn[2] across the floor as the wind blew the blind out. It is of lying and hearing this splash and seeing this light, and feeling, it is almost impossible that I should be here; of feeling the purest ecstasy I can conceive.

I could spend hours trying to write that as it should be written, in order to give the feeling which is even at this moment very strong in me. But I should fail (unless I had some wonderful luck); I dare say I should only succeed in having the luck if I had begun by describing Virginia herself.

Here I come to one of the memoir writer's difficulties—one of the reasons why, though I read so many, so many are failures. They leave out the person to whom things happened. The reason is that it is so difficult to describe any human being. So they say: "This is what happened"; but they do not say what the person was like to whom it happened. And the events mean very little unless we know first to whom they happened. Who was I then? Adeline Virginia Stephen, the second daughter of Leslie and Julia Prinsep Stephen, born on 25th January 1882, descended from a great many people, some famous, others obscure; born into a large connection, born not of rich parents, but of well-to-do parents, born into a very communicative, literate,

1. The autobiographical essay from which this extract is taken was published in Moments of Being, ed. Jeanne Schulkind (1976). Woolf began it on April 18, 1939, as a relief from the labor of writing Roger Fry: A Biography (1940). The last date entered in the manuscript is November 17, 1940, some four months before her death. Under the shadow of approaching war, she gropes back for the bright memories of childhood, especially those associated with the Stephens' summer home, Talland House, at St. Ives in Cornwall, the setting for her novel To the Lighthouse.
2. I.e., the acorn-shaped button on the end of the blind cord.

letter writing, visiting, articulate, late nineteenth century world; so that I could if I liked to take the trouble, write a great deal here not only about my mother and father but about uncles and aunts, cousins and friends. But I do not know how much of this, or what part of this, made me feel what I felt in the nursery at St Ives. I do not know how far I differ from other people. That is another memoir writer's difficulty. Yet to describe oneself truly one must have some standard of comparison; was I clever, stupid, good looking, ugly, passionate, cold—? Owing partly to the fact that I was never at school, never competed in any way with children of my own age, I have never been able to compare my gifts and defects with other people's. But of course there was one external reason for the intensity of this first impression: the impression of the waves and the acorn on the blind; the feeling, as I describe it sometimes to myself, of lying in a grape and seeing through a film of semi-transparent yellow—it was due partly to the many months we spent in London. The change of nursery was a great change. And there was the long train journey; and the excitement. I remember the dark; the lights; the stir of the going up to bed.

But to fix my mind upon the nursery—it had a balcony; there was a partition, but it joined the balcony of my father's and mother's bedroom. My mother would come out onto her balcony in a white dressing gown. There were passion flowers growing on the wall; they were great starry blossoms, with purple streaks, and large green buds, part empty, part full.

If I were a painter I should paint these first impressions in pale yellow, silver, and green. There was the pale yellow blind; the green sea; and the silver of the passion flowers. I should make a picture that was globular; semi-transparent. I should make a picture of curved petals; of shells; of things that were semi-transparent; I should make curved shapes, showing the light through, but not giving a clear outline. Everything would be large and dim; and what was seen would at the same time be heard; sounds would come through this petal or leaf—sounds indistinguishable from sights. Sound and sight seem to make equal parts of these first impressions. When I think of the early morning in bed I also hear the caw of rooks[3] falling from a great height. The sound seems to fall through an elastic, gummy air; which holds it up; which prevents it from being sharp and distinct. The quality of the air above Talland House seemed to suspend sound, to let it sink down slowly, as if it were caught in a blue gummy veil. The rooks cawing is part of the waves breaking—one, two, one, two—and the splash as the wave drew back and then it gathered again, and I lay there half awake, half asleep, drawing in such ecstasy as I cannot describe.

The next memory—all these colour-and-sound memories hang together at St Ives—was much more robust; it was highly sensual. It was later. It still makes me feel warm; as if everything were ripe; humming; sunny; smelling so many smells at once; and all making a whole that even now makes me stop—as I stopped then going down to the beach; I stopped at the top to look down at the gardens. They were sunk beneath the road. The apples were on a level with one's head. The gardens gave off a murmur of bees; the apples were red and gold; there were also pink flowers; and grey and silver leaves. The buzz, the croon, the smell, all seemed to press voluptuously against some

---

3. Black crows.

membrane; not to burst it; but to hum round one such a complete rapture of pleasure that I stopped, smelt; looked. But again I cannot describe that rapture. It was rapture rather than ecstasy.

The strength of these pictures—but sight was always then so much mixed with sound that picture is not the right word—the strength anyhow of these impressions makes me again digress. Those moments—in the nursery, on the road to the beach—can still be more real than the present moment. This I have just tested. For I got up and crossed the garden. Percy was digging the asparagus bed; Louie was shaking a mat in front of the bedroom door.[4] But I was seeing them through the sight I saw here—the nursery and the road to the beach. At times I can go back to St Ives more completely than I can this morning. I can reach a state where I seem to be watching things happen as if I were there. That is, I suppose, that my memory supplies what I had forgotten, so that it seems as if it were happening independently, though I am really making it happen. In certain favourable moods, memories—what one has forgotten—come to the top. Now if this is so, is it not possible—I often wonder—that things we have felt with great intensity have an existence independent of our minds; are in fact still in existence? And if so, will it not be possible, in time, that some device will be invented by which we can tap them? I see it—the past—as an avenue lying behind; a long ribbon of scenes, emotions. There at the end of the avenue still, are the garden and the nursery. Instead of remembering here a scene and there a sound, I shall fit a plug into the wall;[5] and listen in to the past. I shall turn up August 1890. I feel that strong emotion must leave its trace; and it is only a question of discovering how we can get ourselves again attached to it, so that we shall be able to live our lives through from the start.

But the peculiarity of these two strong memories is that each was very simple. I am hardly aware of myself, but only of the sensation. I am only the container of the feeling of ecstasy, of the feeling of rapture. Perhaps this is characteristic of all childhood memories; perhaps it accounts for their strength. Later we add to feelings much that makes them more complex; and therefore less strong; or if not less strong, less isolated, less complete. But instead of analysing this, here is an instance of what I mean—my feeling about the looking-glass in the hall.

There was a small looking-glass in the hall at Talland House. It had, I remember, a ledge with a brush on it. By standing on tiptoe I could see my face in the glass. When I was six or seven perhaps, I got into the habit of looking at my face in the glass. But I only did this if I was sure that I was alone. I was ashamed of it. A strong feeling of guilt seemed naturally attached to it. But why was this so? One obvious reason occurs to me—Vanessa and I were both what was called tomboys; that is, we played cricket, scrambled over rocks, climbed trees, were said not to care for clothes and so on. Perhaps therefore to have been found looking in the glass would have been against our tomboy code. But I think that my feeling of shame went a great deal deeper. I am almost inclined to drag in my grandfather—Sir James, who once smoked a cigar, liked it, and so threw away his cigar and never smoked another. I am almost inclined to think that I inherited a streak of the puritan,

4. The gardener and "daily help," respectively, at Monks House, the Woolfs' country home in Rod-mell, Sussex.
5. I.e., as if plugging in a radio.

of the Clapham Sect.[6] At any rate, the looking-glass shame has lasted all my life, long after the tomboy phase was over. I cannot now powder my nose in public. Everything to do with dress—to be fitted, to come into a room wearing a new dress—still frightens me; at least makes me shy, self-conscious, uncomfortable. "Oh to be able to run, like Julian Morrell,[7] all over the garden in a new dress", I thought not many years ago at Garsington; when Julian undid a parcel and put on a new dress and scampered round and round like a hare. Yet femininity was very strong in our family. We were famous for our beauty—my mother's beauty, Stella's beauty, gave me as early as I can remember, pride and pleasure. What then gave me this feeling of shame, unless it were that I inherited some opposite instinct? My father was spartan, ascetic, puritanical. He had I think no feeling for pictures; no ear for music; no sense of the sound of words. This leads me to think that my—I would say 'our' if I knew enough about Vanessa, Thoby and Adrian[8]—but how little we know even about brothers and sisters—this leads me to think that my natural love for beauty was checked by some ancestral dread. Yet this did not prevent me from feeling ecstasies and raptures spontaneously and intensely and without any shame or the least sense of guilt, so long as they were disconnected with my own body. I thus detect another element in the shame which I had in being caught looking at myself in the glass in the hall. I must have been ashamed or afraid of my own body. Another memory, also of the hall, may help to explain this. There was a slab outside the dining room door for standing dishes upon. Once when I was very small Gerald Duckworth lifted me onto this, and as I sat there he began to explore my body.[9] I can remember the feel of his hand going under my clothes; going firmly and steadily lower and lower. I remember how I hoped that he would stop; how I stiffened and wriggled as his hand approached my private parts. But it did not stop. His hand explored my private parts too. I remember resenting, disliking it—what is the word for so dumb and mixed a feeling? It must have been strong, since I still recall it. This seems to show that a feeling about certain parts of the body; how they must not be touched; how it is wrong to allow them to be touched; must be instinctive. It proves that Virginia Stephen was not born on the 25th January 1882, but was born many thousands of years ago; and had from the very first to encounter instincts already acquired by thousands of ancestresses in the past.

And this throws light not merely on my own case, but upon the problem that I touched on the first page; why it is so difficult to give any account of the person to whom things happen. The person is evidently immensely complicated. Witness the incident of the looking-glass. Though I have done my best to explain why I was ashamed of looking at my own face I have only been able to discover some possible reasons; there may be others; I do not suppose that I have got at the truth; yet this is a simple incident; and it

6. In marrying Jane Catherine Venn, Woolf's grandfather, James Stephen, had allied himself with the heart of the so-called Clapham sect. John and Henry Venn, respectively rector and curate of Clapham in south London, were prominent members of this evangelical society that, in the early 19th century, was instrumental in bringing about the abolition of the slave trade.

7. Daughter of Philip Morrell, Member of Parlia-

ment, and his wife, Ottoline, the celebrated literary hostess. Garsington Manor was their house in Oxfordshire.

8. Woolf's brothers and sister.

9. Woolf's half-brother and the subject of her autobiographical essay 22 Hyde Park Gate, written in 1920 and published in Moments of Being (1978).

happened to me personally; and I have no motive for lying about it. In spite of all this, people write what they call "lives" of other people; that is, they collect a number of events, and leave the person to whom it happened unknown. Let me add a dream; for it may refer to the incident of the looking-glass. I dreamt that I was looking in a glass when a horrible face—the face of an animal—suddenly showed over my shoulder. I cannot be sure if this was a dream, or if it happened. Was I looking in the glass one day when something in the background moved, and seemed to me alive? I cannot be sure. But I have always remembered the other face in the glass, whether it was a dream or a fact, and that it frightened me.

These then are some of my first memories. But of course as an account of my life they are misleading, because the things one does not remember are as important; perhaps they are more important. If I could remember one whole day I should be able to describe, superficially at least, what life was like as a child. Unfortunately, one only remembers what is exceptional. And there seems to be no reason why one thing is exceptional and another not. Why have I forgotten so many things that must have been, one would have thought, more memorable than what I do remember? Why remember the hum of bees in the garden going down to the beach, and forget completely being thrown naked by father into the sea? (Mrs Swanwick says she saw that happen.)[1]

This leads to a digression, which perhaps may explain a little of my own psychology; even of other people's. Often when I have been writing one of my so-called novels I have been baffled by this same problem; that is, how to describe what I call in my private shorthand—"non-being." Every day includes much more non-being than being. Yesterday for example, Tuesday the 18th of April, was [as] it happened a good day; above the average in "being." It was fine; I enjoyed writing these first pages; my head was relieved of the pressure of writing about Roger; I walked over Mount Misery[2] and along the river; and save that the tide was out, the country, which I notice very closely always, was coloured and shaded as I like—there were the willows, I remember, all plumy and soft green and purple against the blue. I also read Chaucer with pleasure; and began a book—the memoirs of Madame de la Fayette—which interested me. These separate moments of being were however embedded in many more moments of non-being. I have already forgotten what Leonard and I talked about at lunch; and at tea; although it was a good day the goodness was embedded in a kind of non-descript cotton wool. This is always so. A great part of every day is not lived consciously. One walks, eats, sees things, deals with what has to be done; the broken vacuum cleaner; ordering dinner; writing orders to Mabel;[3] washing; cooking dinner; bookbinding. When it is a bad day the proportion of non-being is much larger. I had a slight temperature last week; almost the whole day was non-being. The real novelist can somehow convey both sorts of being. I think Jane Austen can; and Trollope; perhaps Thackeray and Dickens and Tolstoy. I have never been able to do both. I tried—in *Night*

1. In Mrs. Swanwick's autobiography, *I Have Been Young* (1935), she recalls having known Leslie Stephen at St. Ives: "We watched with delight his naked babies running about the beach or being towed into the sea between his legs, and their beautiful mother."
2. Two cottages on the hillside between Southease and Piddinghoe known locally as Mount Misery.
3. Instructions to the Woolfs' maid.

and Day; and in *The Years*.[4] But I will leave the literary side alone for the moment.

As a child then, my days, just as they do now, contained a large proportion of this cotton wool, this non-being. Week after week passed at St Ives and nothing made any dint upon me. Then, for no reason that I know about, there was a sudden violent shock; something happened so violently that I have remembered it all my life. I will give a few instances. The first: I was fighting with Thoby on the lawn. We were pommelling each other with our fists. Just as I raised my fist to hit him, I felt: why hurt another person? I dropped my hand instantly, and stood there, and let him beat me. I remember the feeling. It was a feeling of hopeless sadness. It was as if I became aware of something terrible; and of my own powerlessness. I slunk off alone, feeling horribly depressed. The second instance was also in the garden at St Ives. I was looking at the flower bed by the front door; "That is the whole," I said. I was looking at a plant with a spread of leaves; and it seemed suddenly plain that the flower itself was a part of the earth; that a ring enclosed what was the flower; and that was the real flower; part earth; part flower. It was a thought I put away as being likely to be very useful to me later. The third case was also at St Ives. Some people called Valpy had been staying at St Ives, and had left. We were waiting at dinner one night, when somehow I overheard my father or my mother say that Mr Valpy had killed himself. The next thing I remember is being in the garden at night and walking on the path by the apple tree. It seemed to me that the apple tree was connected with the horror of Mr Valpy's suicide. I could not pass it. I stood there looking at the grey-green creases of the bark—it was a moonlit night—in a trance of horror. I seemed to be dragged down, hopelessly, into some pit of absolute despair from which I could not escape. My body seemed paralysed.

These are three instances of exceptional moments. I often tell them over, or rather they come to the surface unexpectedly. But now that for the first time I have written them down, I realise something that I have never realised before. Two of these moments ended in a state of despair. The other ended, on the contrary, in a state of satisfaction. When I said about the flower "That is the whole," I felt that I had made a discovery. I felt that I had put away in my mind something that I should go back [to], to turn over and explore. It strikes me now that this was a profound difference. It was the difference in the first place between despair and satisfaction. This difference I think arose from the fact that I was quite unable to deal with the pain of discovering that people hurt each other; that a man I had seen had killed himself. The sense of horror held me powerless. But in the case of the flower I found a reason; and was thus able to deal with the sensation. I was not powerless. I was conscious—if only at a distance—that I should in time explain it. I do not know if I was older when I saw the flower than I was when I had the other two experiences. I only know that many of these exceptional moments brought with them a peculiar horror and a physical collapse; they seemed dominant; myself passive. This suggests that as one gets older one has a greater power through reason to provide an explanation; and that this explanation blunts the sledge-hammer force of the blow. I think this is true, because though I still have the peculiarity that I receive these sudden shocks,

---

4. Novels published in 1919 and 1938, respectively.

they are now always welcome; after the first surprise, I always feel instantly that they are particularly valuable. And so I go on to suppose that the shock-receiving capacity is what makes me a writer. I hazard the explanation that a shock is at once in my case followed by the desire to explain it. I feel that I have had a blow; but it is not, as I thought as a child, simply a blow from an enemy hidden behind the cotton wool of daily life; it is or will become a revelation of some order; it is a token of some real thing behind appearances; and I make it real by putting it into words. It is only by putting it into words that I make it whole; this wholeness means that it has lost its power to hurt me; it gives me, perhaps because by doing so I take away the pain, a great delight to put the severed parts together. Perhaps this is the strongest pleasure known to me. It is the rapture I get when in writing I seem to be discovering what belongs to what; making a scene come right; making a character come together. From this I reach what I might call a philosophy; at any rate it is a constant idea of mine; that behind the cotton wool is hidden a pattern; that we—I mean all human beings—are connected with this; that the whole world is a work of art; that we are parts of the work of art. *Hamlet* or a Beethoven quartet is the truth about this vast mass that we call the world. But there is no Shakespeare, there is no Beethoven; certainly and emphatically there is no God; we are the words; we are the music; we are the thing itself. And I see this when I have a shock.

This intuition of mine—it is so instinctive that it seems given to me, not made by me—has certainly given its scale to my life ever since I saw the flower in the bed by the front door at St Ives. If I were painting myself I should have to find some—rod, shall I say—something that would stand for the conception. It proves that one's life is not confined to one's body and what one says and does; one is living all the time in relation to certain background rods or conceptions. Mine is that there is a pattern hid behind the cotton wool. And this conception affects me every day. I prove this, now, by spending the morning writing, when I might be walking, running a shop, or learning to do something that will be useful if war comes. I feel that by writing I am doing what is far more necessary than anything else.

All artists I suppose feel something like this. It is one of the obscure elements in life that has never been much discussed. It is left out in almost all biographies and autobiographies, even of artists. Why did Dickens spend his entire life writing stories? What was his conception? I bring in Dickens partly because I am reading *Nicholas Nickleby* at the moment; also partly because it struck me, on my walk yesterday, that these moments of being of mine were scaffolding in the background; were the invisible and silent part of my life as a child. But in the foreground there were of course people; and these people were very like characters in Dickens. They were caricatures; they were very simple; they were immensely alive. They could be made with three strokes of the pen, if I could do it. Dickens owes his astonishing power to make characters alive to the fact that he saw them as a child sees them; as I saw Mr Wolstenholme; C. B. Clarke, and Mr Gibbs.

I name these three people because they all died when I was a child. Therefore they have never been altered. I see them exactly as I saw them then. Mr Wolstenholme was a very old gentleman who came every summer to stay with us. He was brown; he had a beard and very small eyes in fat cheeks; and he fitted into a brown wicker beehive chair as if it had been his nest. He used to sit in this beehive chair smoking and reading. He had only one characteristic—that when he ate plum tart he spurted the juice through his nose so that it made a purple stain on his grey moustache. This seemed enough to cause us perpetual delight. We called him "The Woolly One." By way of shading him a little I remember that we had to be kind to him because he was not happy at home; that he was very poor, yet once gave Thoby half a crown; that he had a son who was drowned in Australia; and I know too that he was a great mathematician. He never said a word all the time I knew him. But he still seems to me a complete character; and whenever I think of him I begin to laugh.

Mr Gibbs was perhaps less simple. He wore a tie ring; had a bald, benevolent head; was dry; neat; precise; and had folds of skin under his chin. He made father groan—"why can't you go—why can't you go?" And he gave Vanessa and myself two ermine skins, with slits down the middle out of which poured endless wealth—streams of silver. I also remember him lying in bed, dying; husky; in a night shirt; and showing us drawings by Retzsch.[5] The character of Mr Gibbs also seems to me complete and amuses me very much.

As for C. B. Clarke, he was an old botanist; and he said to my father "All you young botanists like Osmunda."[6] He had an aunt aged eighty who went for a walking tour in the New Forest. That is all—that is all I have to say about these three old gentlemen. But how real they were! How we laughed at them! What an immense part they played in our lives!

One more caricature comes into my mind; though pity entered into this one. I am thinking of Justine Nonon. She was immensely old. Little hairs sprouted on her long bony chin. She was a hunchback; and walked like a spider, feeling her way with her long dry fingers from one chair to another. Most of the time she sat in the arm-chair beside the fire. I used to sit on her knee; and her knee jogged up and down; and she sang in a hoarse cracked voice "Ron ron ron—et plon plon plon—" and then her knee gave and I was tumbled onto the floor. She was French; she had been with the Thackerays. She only came to us on visits. She lived by herself at Shepherd's Bush; and used to bring Adrian a glass jar of honey. I got the notion that she was extremely poor; and it made me uncomfortable that she brought this honey, because I felt she did it by way of making her visit acceptable. She said too: "I have come in my carriage and pair"—which meant the red omnibus. For this too I pitied her; also because she began to wheeze; and the nurses said she would not live much longer; and soon she died. That is all I know about her; but I remember her as if she were a completely real person, with nothing left out, like the three old men.

Apr. 1939–Nov. 1940   1978

---

5. Friedrich Retzsch (1779–1857), German engraver.   6. Flowering ferns.

JAMES JOYCE
1882–1941

James Joyce was born in Dublin, son of a talented but feckless father who is accurately described by Stephen Dedalus in *A Portrait of the Artist as a Young Man* as a man who had in his time been "a medical student, an oarsman, a tenor, an amateur actor, a shouting politician, a small landlord, a small investor, a drinker, a good fellow, a storyteller, somebody's secretary, something in a distillery, a tax-gatherer, a bankrupt, and at present a praiser of his own past." The elder Joyce drifted steadily down the financial and social scale, his family moving from house to house, each one less genteel and more shabby than the previous. James Joyce's whole education was Catholic, from the age of six to the age of nine at Clongowes Wood College and from eleven to sixteen at Belvedere College, Dublin. Both were Jesuit institutions and were normal roads to the priesthood. He then studied modern languages at University College, Dublin.

From a comparatively early age Joyce regarded himself as a rebel against the shabbiness and Philistinism of Dublin. In his early youth he was very religious, but in his last year at Belvedere he began to reject his Catholic faith in favor of a literary mission that he saw as involving rebellion and exile. He refused to play any part in the nationalist or other popular activities of his fellow students, and he created some stir by his outspoken articles. By 1902, when he received his A.B. degree, he was already committed to a career as exile and writer. For Joyce, as for his character Stephen Dedalus, the latter implied the former. To preserve his integrity, to avoid involvement in popular sentimentalities and dishonesties, and above all to be able to re-create with both total understanding and total objectivity the Dublin life he knew so well, he felt that he had to go abroad.

Joyce went to Paris after graduation, was recalled to Dublin by his mother's fatal illness, had a short spell there as a schoolteacher, then returned to the Continent in 1904 to teach English at Trieste and then at Zurich. He took with him Nora Barnacle, an uneducated Galway girl with no interest in literature; her native vivacity and peasant wit charmed Joyce, and the two lived in devoted companionship until Joyce's death, although they were not married until 1931. In 1920 Joyce settled in Paris, where he lived until December 1940, when the war forced him to take refuge in Switzerland; he died in Zurich a few weeks later.

Proud, obstinate, absolutely convinced of his genius, given to fits of sudden gaiety and of sudden silence, Joyce was not always an easy person to get along with, yet he never lacked friends, and throughout his thirty-six years on the Continent he was always the center of a literary circle. Life was hard at first. At Trieste he had very little money, and he did not improve matters by drinking heavily, a habit checked somewhat by his brother Stanislaus, who came out from Dublin to act (as Stanislaus put it much later) as his "brother's keeper." His financial position was much improved by the patronage of Mrs. Harold McCormick (Edith Rockefeller), who provided him with a monthly stipend from March 1917 until September 1919, when they quarreled, apparently because Joyce refused to submit to psychoanalysis by Carl Jung, who had been heavily endowed by her. The New York lawyer and art patron John Quinn, steered in Joyce's direction by Ezra Pound, also helped Joyce financially in 1917. A more permanent benefactor was the English feminist and editor Harriet Shaw Weaver, who not only subsidized Joyce generously from 1917 to the end of his life but occupied herself indefatigably with arrangements for publishing his work.

Joyce's almost lifelong exile from his native Ireland has something paradoxical about it. No writer has ever been more soaked in Dublin, its atmosphere, its history, its topography; in spite of doing most of his writing in Trieste, Zurich, and Paris, he wrote only and always about Dublin. He devised ways of expanding his accounts of

Dublin, however, so that they became microcosms, small-scale models, of all human life, of all history, and of all geography. Indeed that was his life's work: to write about Dublin in such a way that he was writing about all of human experience.

Joyce began his career by writing a series of stories etching with extraordinary clarity aspects of Dublin life. But these stories—published as *Dubliners* in 1914—are more than sharp realistic sketches. In each, the detail is so chosen and organized that carefully interacting symbolic meanings are set up, and as a result, *Dubliners* is a book about human fate as well as a series of sketches of Dublin. Furthermore, the stories are presented in a particular order so that new meanings arise from the relation between them.

The last story in *Dubliners, The Dead,* was not part of the original draft of the book but was added later, at a time when Joyce was preoccupied with the nature of artistic objectivity. A series of jolting events frees the protagonist, Gabriel, from his possessiveness and egotism; the view he attains at the end is the mood of supreme neutrality that Joyce saw as the beginning of artistic awareness. It is the view of art developed by Stephen Dedalus in *A Portrait of the Artist as a Young Man*. *Dubliners* represents Joyce's first phase: he had to come directly to terms with the life he had rejected, to see it for what it was and for what it meant. Next, he had to come to terms with the meaning of his own development as a man dedicated to writing. He did this by weaving his autobiography into a novel so finely chiseled and carefully organized, so stripped of everything superfluous, that each word contributes to the presentation of the theme: the parallel movement toward art and toward exile.

In the *Portrait* Stephen worked out a theory of art that considers that art moves from the lyrical form—which is the simplest, the personal expression of an instant of emotion—through the narrative form—no longer purely personal—to the dramatic— the highest and most nearly perfect form, where "the artist, like the God of creation, remains within or behind or beyond or above his handiwork, invisible, refined out of existence, indifferent, paring his fingernails." This view of art, which involves the objectivity, even the exile, of the artist (even though the artist uses only the materials provided for him or her by his or her own life), is related to that held by the poets of the 1890s. More widely, it is related to the rejection by the artist of the ordinary world of middle-class values and activities that we see equally, though in different ways, in Matthew Arnold's war against the Philistines and in the concept (very un-Arnoldian) of the artist as bohemian. Joyce's career belongs to that long chapter in the history of the arts in Western civilization that begins with the artist's declaring independence and ends with his or her feeling inevitable alienation. But if Joyce was alienated, as in certain ways he clearly was, he made his alienation serve his art: the kinds of writing represented by *Ulysses* and *Finnegans Wake* represent the most consummate craftsmanship put at the service of a humanely comic vision of all life. Some of Joyce's innovations in organization and style have been imitated by other writers, but these books are, and will probably remain, unique in our literature.

From the beginning, Joyce had trouble with the Philistines. Publication of *Dubliners* was held up for many years while he fought with both English and Irish publishers about certain words and phrases that they wished to eliminate. (It was one of the former who finally published the book.) His masterpiece *Ulysses* was banned in both Britain and America on its first appearance in 1922; its earlier serialization in an American magazine, *The Little Review* (March 1918–December 1920), had had to stop abruptly when the U.S. Post Office brought a charge of obscenity against it. Fortunately, Judge Woolsey's history-making decision in favor of *Ulysses* in a U.S. district court on December 6, 1933, resulted in the lifting of the ban and the free circulation of the work first in America and soon afterward in Britain.

ULYSSES

Ulysses is an account of one day in the lives of citizens of Dublin in the year 1904; it is thus the description of a limited number of events involving a limited number of people in a limited environment. Yet Joyce's ambition—which took him seven years to realize—is to make his action into a microcosm of all human experience. The events are not, therefore, told on a single level; the story is presented in such a manner that depth and implication are given to them and they become symbolic of the activity of the Individual in the World. The most obvious of the devices that Joyce employs to make clear the microcosmic aspect of his story is the parallel with Homer's *Odyssey;* every episode in *Ulysses* corresponds in some way to an episode in the *Odyssey.* Joyce regarded Homer's Ulysses as the most "complete" man in literature, a man who is shown in all his aspects—both coward and hero, cautious and reckless, weak and strong, husband and philanderer, father and son, dignified and ridiculous; so he makes his hero, Leopold Bloom, an Irish Jew, into a modern Ulysses and by so doing helps make him Everyman and make Dublin the world.

The book opens at eight o'clock on the morning of June 16, 1904. Stephen Dedalus (the same character we saw in the *Portrait,* but this is two years after our last glimpse of him there) had been summoned back to Dublin by his mother's fatal illness and now lives in an old military tower on the shore with Buck Mulligan, a rollicking medical student, and an Englishman called Haines. In the first three episodes of *Ulysses,* which concentrate on Stephen, he is built up as an aloof, uncompromising artist, rejecting all advances by representatives of the normal world, the incomplete man, to be contrasted later with the complete Leopold Bloom, who is much more "normal" and conciliatory. After tracing Stephen through his early-morning activities and learning the main currents of his mind, we go, in the fourth episode, to the home of Bloom. We follow closely his every activity: attending a funeral, transacting his business, eating his lunch, walking through the Dublin streets, worrying about his wife's infidelity with Blazes Boylan—and at each point the contents of his mind, including retrospect and anticipation, are presented to the reader, until all his past history is revealed. Finally, Bloom and Stephen, who have been just missing each other all day, get together. By this time it is late, and Stephen, who has been drinking with some medical students, is the worse for liquor. Bloom, moved by a paternal feeling toward Stephen (his own son had died in infancy and in a symbolic way Stephen takes his place), follows him during subsequent adventures in the role of protector. The climax of the book comes when Stephen, far gone in drink, and Bloom, worn out with fatigue, succumb to a series of hallucinations where their subconscious and unconscious come to the surface in dramatic form and their whole personalities are revealed with a completeness and a frankness unique in literature. Then Bloom takes the unresponsive Stephen home and gives him a meal. After Stephen's departure Bloom retires to bed—it is now two in the morning on June 17—while his wife, Molly, representing the principles of sex and reproduction on which all human life is based, closes the book with a long monologue in which her experiences as woman are remembered.

On the level of realistic description, *Ulysses* pulses with life and can be enjoyed for its evocation of early twentieth-century Dublin. On the level of psychological exploration, it gives a profound and moving presentation of the personality and consciousness of Leopold Bloom and (to a lesser extent) Stephen Dedalus. On the level of style, it exhibits the most fascinating linguistic virtuosity. On a deeper symbolic level, the novel explores the paradoxes of human loneliness and sociability (for Bloom is both Jew and Dubliner, both exile and citizen, just as all of us are in a sense both exiles and citizens), and it explores the problems posed by the relations between parent and child, between the generations, and between the sexes. At the same time, through its use of themes from Homer, Dante, and Shakespeare and from literature, philosophy, and history, the book weaves a subtle pattern of allusion and suggestion that illuminates many aspects of human experience. The more one reads *Ulysses* the more one finds in it, but at the same time one does not need to probe into the symbolic meaning to relish both its literary artistry and its human feeling. At the forefront stands Leopold Bloom, from one point of view, a frustrated and confused outsider in the society in which he moves, from another, a champion of kindness and justice whose humane curiosity about his fellows redeems him from mere vulgarity and gives the book its positive human foundation.

Readers who come to *Ulysses* with expectations about the way the story is to be presented derived from their reading of Victorian novels or even of such twentieth-century novelists as Conrad and Lawrence will find much that is at first puzzling. Joyce presents the consciousness of his characters directly, without any explanatory comment that tells the reader whose consciousness is being rendered (this is the stream of consciousness method). He may move, in the same paragraph and without any sign that he is making such a transition, from a description of a character's action—e.g., Stephen walking along the shore or Bloom entering a restaurant—to an evocation of the character's mental response to this action. That response is always multiple: it derives partly from the character's immediate situation and partly from the whole complex of attitudes that his past history has created in him. To suggest this multiplicity, Joyce may vary his style, from the flippant to the serious or from a realistic description to a suggestive set of images that indicate what might be called the general tone of the character's consciousness. Past and present mingle in the texture of the prose because they mingle in the texture of consciousness, and this mingling can be indicated by puns, by sudden breaks into a new kind of style or a new kind of subject matter, or by some other device for keeping the reader constantly in sight of the shifting, kaleidoscopic nature of human awareness. With a little experience, the reader learns to follow the implications of Joyce's shifts in manner and content—even to follow that at first sight bewildering passage in the "Proteus" episode in which Stephen does not go to visit his uncle and aunt but, passing the road that leads to their house, imagines the kind of conversation that would take place in his home *if* he had gone to visit his uncle and had then returned home and reported that he had done so. *Ulysses* must not be approached as though it were a novel written in a traditional manner; all preconceptions must be set aside and we must follow wherever the author leads us and let the language tell us what it has to say without our troubling whether language is being used "properly" or not.

FINNEGANS WAKE

Joyce's last work, *Finnegans Wake*, was published in 1939; it took more than fourteen years to write, and Joyce considered it his masterpiece. In *Ulysses* he had made the symbolic aspect of the novel at least as important as the realistic aspect, but in *Finnegans Wake* he gave up realism altogether. This vast story of a symbolic Irish-man's cosmic dream develops by enormous reverberating puns a continuous expansion of meaning, the elements in the puns deriving from every conceivable source in history, literature, mythology, and Joyce's personal experience. The whole book being (on one level at least) a dream, Joyce invents his own dream language in which words are combined, distorted, created by fitting together bits of other words, used with several different meanings at once, often drawn from several different languages at once, and fused in all sorts of ways to achieve whole clusters of meaning simultaneously. In fact, so many echoing suggestions can be found in every word or phrase that a full annotation of even a few pages would require a large book. It has taken the cooperative work of a number of devoted readers to make clear the complex interactions of the multiple puns and pun clusters through which the ideas are projected, and every rereading reveals new meanings. It is true that many readers find the efforts of explication demanded by *Finegans Wake* too arduous; some, indeed, feel that the law of diminishing returns has now begun to operate, and that the effort of both author and reader is disproportionate. Nevertheless, the book has great beauty and fascination even for the casual reader. Students are advised to read aloud—or to listen to the record of Joyce reading aloud—the extract printed here to appreciate the degree to which the rhythms of the prose assist in conveying the meaning.

To an even greater extent than *Ulysses*, *Finnegans Wake* aims at embracing all of human history. The title is from an Irish-American ballad about Tom Finnegan, a hod carrier who falls off a ladder when drunk and is apparently killed, but who revives when during the wake (the watch by the dead body) someone spills whiskey on him. The theme of death and resurrection, of cycles of change coming round in the course of history, is central to *Finnegans Wake*, which derives one of its main principles of organization from the cyclical theory of history put forward in 1725 by the Italian philosopher Giambattista Vico. Vico held that history passes through four phases: the divine or theocratic, when people are governed by their awe of the supernatural; the aristocratic (the "heroic age" reflected in Homer and in *Beowulf*); the democratic and individualistic; and the final stage of chaos, a fall into confusion startles humanity back into supernatural reverence and starts the process once again. Joyce, like Yeats, saw his own generation as in the final stage awaiting the shock that will bring humans back to the first.

A mere account of the narrative line of *Finnegans Wake* cannot, of course, give any idea of the content of the work. If one explains that it opens with Finnegan's fall, then introduces his successor Humphrey Chimpden Earwicker, who is Everyman, and whose dream constitutes the novel; that he is presented as having guilt feelings about an indecency he committed (or may have committed) in Phoenix Park, Dublin; that his wife, Anna Livia Plurabelle or ALP (who is also Eve, Iseult, Ireland, the river Liffey), changes her role just as he does; that he has two sons, Shem and Shaun (or Jerry and Kevin), who represent introvert and extrovert, artist and practical man, creator and popularizer, and symbolize this basic dichotomy in human nature by all kinds of metamorphoses; and if one adds that, in the four books into which *Finnegans Wake* is divided (after Vico's pattern), actions comic or grotesque or sad or tender or desperate or passionate or terribly ordinary (and very often several of these things at the same time) take place with all the shifting meanings of a dream, so that characters change into others or into inanimate objects and the setting keeps shifting—if we explain all this, we still have said very little about what makes *Finnegans Wake* what it is. The dreamer, whose initials HCE indicate his universality ("Here Comes Everybody"), is at the same time a particular person, who keeps a pub in Chapelizod, a Dublin suburb on the river Liffey near Phoenix Park. His mysterious misdemeanor in Phoenix Park is in a sense Original Sin: Earwicker is Adam as well as a primeval giant, the Hill of Howth, the Great Parent ("Haveth Childers Everywhere" is another expansion of HCE), and Man in History. Other characters who flit and change through the book, such as the Twelve Customers (who are also twelve jurymen and public opinion) and the Four Old Men (who are also judges, the authors of the four Gospels, and the four elements), help weave the texture of multiple significance so characteristic of the work. But always it is the punning language, extending significance downward—rather than the plot, developing it lengthwise—that bears the main load of meaning.

Araby[1]

North Richmond Street, being blind, was a quiet street except at the hour when the Christian Brothers' School[2] set the boys free. An uninhabited house of two storeys stood at the blind end, detached from its neighbours in a square ground. The other houses of the street, conscious of decent lives within them, gazed at one another with brown imperturbable faces.

The former tenant of our house, a priest, had died in the back drawing-room. Air, musty from having been long enclosed, hung in all the rooms, and the waste room behind the kitchen was littered with old useless papers. Among these I found a few paper-covered books, the pages of which were curled and damp: *The Abbot*, by Walter Scott, *The Devout Communicant* and *The Memoirs of Vidocq*.[3] I liked the last best because its leaves were yellow. The wild garden behind the house contained a central apple-tree and a few straggling bushes under one of which I found the late tenant's rusty bicycle-pump. He had been a very charitable priest; in his will he had left all his money to institutions and the furniture of his house to his sister.

When the short days of winter came dusk fell before we had well eaten our dinners. When we met in the street the houses had grown sombre. The space of sky above us was the colour of ever-changing violet and towards it the lamps of the street lifted their feeble lanterns. The cold air stung us and we played till our bodies glowed. Our shouts echoed in the silent street. The career of our play brought us through the dark muddy lanes behind the houses where we ran the gantlet of the rough tribes from the cottages, to the back doors of the dark dripping gardens where odours arose from the ashpits, to the dark odorous stables where a coachman smoothed and combed the horse or shook music from the buckled harness. When we returned to the street light from the kitchen windows had filled the areas. If my uncle was seen turning the corner we hid in the shadow until we had seen him safely housed. Or if Mangan's sister came out on the doorstep to call her brother in to his tea we watched her from our shadow peer up and down the street. We waited to see whether she would remain or go in and, if she remained, we left our shadow and walked up to Mangan's steps resignedly. She was waiting for us, her figure defined by the light from the half-opened door. Her brother always teased her before he obeyed and I stood by the railings looking at her. Her dress swung as she moved her body and the soft rope of her hair tossed from side to side.

Every morning I lay on the floor in the front parlour watching her door. The blind was pulled down to within an inch of the sash so that I could not be seen. When she came out on the doorstep my heart leaped. I ran to the hall, seized my books and followed her. I kept her brown figure always in my eye and, when we came near the point at which our ways diverged, I quickened my pace and passed her. This happened morning after morning. I had never spoken to her, except for a few casual words, and yet her name was like a summons to all my foolish blood.

Her image accompanied me even in places the most hostile to romance. On Saturday evenings when my aunt went marketing I had to go to carry some of the parcels. We walked through the flaring streets, jostled by drunken men and bargaining women, amid the curses of labourers, the shrill litanies of shop-boys who stood on guard by the barrels of pigs' cheeks, the

3. François Eugène Vidocq (1775–1857) had an extraordinary career as soldier, thief, chief of the French detective force, and private detective. *The* *Abbot* is a historical novel dealing with Mary, Queen of Scots. *The Devout Communicant* is a Catholic religious manual.

nasal chanting of street-singers, who sang a *come-all-you*[4] about O'Donovan Rossa, or a ballad about the troubles in our native land. These noises converged in a single sensation of life for me: I imagined that I bore my chalice safely through a throng of foes. Her name sprang to my lips at moments in strange prayers and praises which I myself did not understand. My eyes were often full of tears (I could not tell why) and at times a flood from my heart seemed to pour itself out into my bosom. I thought little of the future. I did not know whether I would ever speak to her or not or, if I spoke to her, how I could tell her of my confused adoration. But my body was like a harp and her words and gestures were like fingers running upon the wires.

One evening I went into the back drawing-room in which the priest had died. It was a dark rainy evening and there was no sound in the house. Through one of the broken panes I heard the rain impinge upon the earth, the fine incessant needles of water playing in the sodden beds. Some distant lamp or lighted window gleamed below me. I was thankful that I could see so little. All my senses seemed to desire to veil themselves and, feeling that I was about to slip from them, I pressed the palms of my hands together until they trembled, murmuring: *O love! O love!* many times.

At last she spoke to me. When she addressed the first words to me I was so confused that I did not know what to answer. She asked me was I going to *Araby*.[5] I forgot whether I answered yes or no. It would be a splendid bazaar, she said; she would love to go.

—And why can't you? I asked.

While she spoke she turned a silver bracelet round and round her wrist. She could not go, she said, because there would be a retreat that week in her convent.[6] Her brother and two other boys were fighting for their caps and I was alone at the railings. She held one of the spikes, bowing her head towards me. The light from the lamp opposite our door caught the white curve of her neck, lit up her hair that rested there and, falling, lit up the hand upon the railing. It fell over one side of her dress and caught the white border of a petticoat, just visible as she stood at ease.

—It's well for you, she said.

—If I go, I said, I will bring you something.

What innumerable follies laid waste my waking and sleeping thoughts after that evening! I wished to annihilate the tedious intervening days. I chafed against the work of school. At night in my bedroom and by day in the classroom her image came between me and the page I strove to read. The syllables of the word *Araby* were called to me through the silence in which my soul luxuriated and cast an Eastern enchantment over me. I asked for leave to go to the bazaar on Saturday night. My aunt was surprised and hoped it was not some Freemason affair.[7] I answered few questions in class. I watched my master's face pass from amiability to sternness; he hoped I was not beginning to idle. I could not call my wandering thoughts together. I had hardly any patience with the serious work of life which, now that it stood

---

4. Street ballad, so called from its opening words. This one was about the 19th-century Irish nationalist Jeremiah Donovan, popularly known as O'Donovan Rossa.
5. The bazaar, described by its "official catalogue" as a "Grand Oriental Fête," was actually held in Dublin on May 14–19, 1894.

6. I.e., her convent school. "Retreat": period of seclusion from ordinary activities devoted to religious exercises.
7. His aunt shares her church's distrust of the Freemasons, an old European secret society, reputedly anti-Catholic.

between me and my desire, seemed to me child's play, ugly monotonous child's play.

On Saturday morning I reminded my uncle that I wished to go to the bazaar in the evening. He was fussing at the hallstand, looking for the hat-brush, and answered me curtly:

—Yes, boy, I know.

As he was in the hall I could not go into the front parlour and lie at the window. I left the house in bad humour and walked slowly towards the school. The air was pitilessly raw and already my heart misgave me.

When I came home to dinner my uncle had not yet been home. Still it was early. I sat staring at the clock for some time and, when its ticking began to irritate me, I left the room. I mounted the staircase and gained the upper part of the house. The high cold empty gloomy rooms liberated me and I went from room to room singing. From the front window I saw my companions playing below in the street. Their cries reached me weakened and indistinct and, leaning my forehead against the cool glass, I looked over at the dark house where she lived. I may have stood there for an hour, seeing nothing but the brown-clad figure cast by my imagination, touched discreetly by the lamplight at the curved neck, at the hand upon the railings and at the border below the dress.

When I came downstairs again I found Mrs Mercer sitting at the fire. She was an old garrulous woman, a pawn-broker's widow, who collected used stamps for some pious purpose. I had to endure the gossip of the tea-table. The meal was prolonged beyond an hour and still my uncle did not come. Mrs Mercer stood up to go: she was sorry she couldn't wait any longer, but it was after eight o'clock and she did not like to be out late, as the night air was bad for her. When she had gone I began to walk up and down the room, clenching my fists. My aunt said:

—I'm afraid you may put off your bazaar for this night of Our Lord.

At nine o'clock I heard my uncle's latchkey in the halldoor. I heard him talking to himself and heard the hallstand rocking when it had received the weight of his overcoat. I could interpret these signs. When he was midway through his dinner I asked him to give me the money to go to the bazaar. He had forgotten.

—The people are in bed and after their first sleep now, he said.

I did not smile. My aunt said to him energetically:

—Can't you give him the money and let him go? You've kept him late enough as it is.

My uncle said he was very sorry he had forgotten. He said he believed in the old saying: *All work and no play makes Jack a dull boy*. He asked me where I was going and, when I had told him a second time he asked me did I know *The Arab's Farewell to his Steed*.[8] When I left the kitchen he was about to recite the opening lines of the piece to my aunt.

I held a florin[9] tightly in my hand as I strode down Buckingham Street towards the station. The sight of the streets thronged with buyers and glaring with gas recalled to me the purpose of my journey. I took my seat in a third-

8. Once-popular sentimental poem by Caroline Norton.

9. A silver coin, now obsolete, worth two shillings.

class carriage of a deserted train. After an intolerable delay the train moved out of the station slowly. It crept onward among ruinous houses and over the twinkling river. At Westland Row Station a crowd of people pressed to the carriage doors; but the porters moved them back, saying that it was a special train for the bazaar. I remained alone in the bare carriage. In a few minutes the train drew up beside an improvised wooden platform. I passed out on to the road and saw by the lighted dial of a clock that it was ten minutes to ten. In front of me was a large building which displayed the magical name.

I could not find any sixpenny entrance and, fearing that the bazaar would be closed, I passed in quickly through a turnstile, handing a shilling to a weary-looking man. I found myself in a big hall girdled at half its height by a gallery. Nearly all the stalls were closed and the greater part of the hall was in darkness. I recognized a silence like that which pervades a church after a service. I walked into the centre of the bazaar timidly. A few people were gathered about the stalls which were still open. Before a curtain, over which the words *Café Chantant*[1] were written in coloured lamps, two men were counting money on a salver. I listened to the fall of the coins.

Remembering with difficulty why I had come I went over to one of the stalls and examined porcelain vases and flowered tea-sets. At the door of the stall a young lady was talking and laughing with two young gentlemen. I remarked their English accents and listened vaguely to their conversation.

—O, I never said such a thing!

—O, but you did!

—O, but I didn't!

—Didn't she say that?

—Yes. I heard her.

—O, there's a . . . fib![2]

Observing me the young lady came over and asked me did I wish to buy anything. The tone of her voice was not encouraging; she seemed to have spoken to me out of a sense of duty. I looked humbly at the great jars that stood like eastern guards at either side of the dark entrance to the stall and murmured:

—No, thank you.

The young lady changed the position of one of the vases and went back to the two young men. They began to talk of the same subject. Once or twice the young lady glanced at me over her shoulder.

I lingered before her stall, though I knew my stay was useless, to make my interest in her wares seem the more real. Then I turned away slowly and walked down the middle of the bazaar. I allowed the two pennies to fall against the sixpence in my pocket. I heard a voice call from one end of the gallery that the light was out. The upper part of the hall was now completely dark.

Gazing up into the darkness I saw myself as a creature driven and derided by vanity; and my eyes burned with anguish and anger.

1905   1914

---

1. Singing café (French; literal trans.); a café that provided musical entertainment, popular early in the 20th century.

2. A lie.

The Dead

Lily, the caretaker's daughter, was literally run off her feet. Hardly had she brought one gentleman into the little pantry behind the office on the ground floor and helped him off with his overcoat than the wheezy hall-door bell clanged again and she had to scamper along the bare hallway to let in another guest. It was well for her she had not to attend to the ladies also. But Miss Kate and Miss Julia had thought of that and had converted the bathroom upstairs into a ladies' dressing-room. Miss Kate and Miss Julia were there, gossiping and laughing and fussing, walking after each other to the head of the stairs, peering down over the banisters and calling down to Lily to ask her who had come.

It was always a great affair, the Misses Morkan's annual dance. Everybody who knew them came to it, members of the family, old friends of the family, the members of Julia's choir, any of Kate's pupils that were grown up enough and even some of Mary Jane's pupils too. Never once had it fallen flat. For years and years it had gone off in splendid style as long as anyone could remember; ever since Kate and Julia, after the death of their brother Pat, had left the house in Stoney Batter and taken Mary Jane, their only niece, to live with them in the dark gaunt house on Usher's Island, the upper part of which they had rented from Mr Fulham, the cornfactor[1] on the ground floor. That was a good thirty years ago if it was a day. Mary Jane, who was then a little girl in short clothes, was now the main prop of the household for she had the organ in Haddington Road. She had been through the Academy and gave a pupils' concert every year in the upper room of the Antient Concert Rooms.[2] Many of her pupils belonged to better-class families on the Kingstown and Dalkey line. Old as they were, her aunts also did their share. Julia, though she was quite grey, was still the leading soprano in Adam and Eve's, and Kate, being too feeble to go about much, gave music lessons to beginners on the old square piano in the back room. Lily, the caretaker's daughter, did housemaid's work for them. Though their life was modest they believed in eating well; the best of everything: diamond-bone sirloins, three-shilling tea and the best bottled stout.[3] But Lily seldom made a mistake in the orders so that she got on well with her three mistresses. They were fussy, that was all. But the only thing they would not stand was back answers.

Of course they had good reason to be fussy on such a night. And then it was long after ten o'clock and yet there was no sign of Gabriel and his wife. Besides they were dreadfully afraid that Freddy Malins might turn up screwed. They would not wish for worlds that any of Mary Jane's pupils should see him under the influence; and when he was like that it was sometimes very hard to manage him. Freddy Malins always came late but they wondered what could be keeping Gabriel: and that was what brought them every two minutes to the banisters to ask Lily had Gabriel or Freddy come.

—O, Mr Conroy, said Lily to Gabriel when she opened the door for him, Miss Kate and Miss Julia thought you were never coming. Good-night, Mrs Conroy.

---

1. Grain merchant.
2. Concert hall in Dublin. The academy was the Royal Irish Academy of Music.
3. A dark brown malt liquor, akin to beer.

—I'll engage they did, said Gabriel, but they forget that my wife here takes three mortal hours to dress herself.

He stood on the mat, scraping the snow from his goloshes, while Lily led his wife to the foot of the stairs and called out:

—Miss Kate, here's Mrs Conroy.

Kate and Julia came toddling down the dark stairs at once. Both of them kissed Gabriel's wife, said she must be perished alive and asked was Gabriel with her.

—Here I am as right as the mail, Aunt Kate! Go on up. I'll follow, called out Gabriel from the dark.

He continued scraping his feet vigorously while the three women went upstairs, laughing, to the ladies' dressing-room. A light fringe of snow lay like a cape on the shoulders of his overcoat and like toecaps on the toes of his goloshes; and, as the buttons of his overcoat slipped with a squeaking noise through the snow-stiffened frieze,[4] a cold fragrant air from out-of-doors escaped from crevices and folds.

—Is it snowing again, Mr Conroy? asked Lily.

She had preceded him into the pantry to help him off with his overcoat. Gabriel smiled at the three syllables she had given his surname and glanced at her. She was a slim, growing girl, pale in complexion and with hay-coloured hair. The gas in the pantry made her look still paler. Gabriel had known her when she was a child and used to sit on the lowest step nursing a rag doll.

—Yes, Lily, he answered, and I think we're in for a night of it.

He looked up at the pantry ceiling, which was shaking with the stamping and shuffling of feet on the floor above, listened for a moment to the piano and then glanced at the girl, who was folding his overcoat carefully at the end of a shelf.

—Tell me, Lily, he said in a friendly tone, do you still go to school?

—O no, sir, she answered. I'm done schooling this year and more.

—O, then, said Gabriel gaily, I suppose we'll be going to your wedding one of these fine days with your young man, eh?

The girl glanced back at him over her shoulder and said with great bitterness:

—The men that is now is only all palaver and what they can get out of you.

Gabriel coloured as if he felt he had made a mistake and, without looking at her, kicked off his goloshes and flicked actively with his muffler at his patent-leather shoes.

He was a stout tallish young man. The high colour of his cheeks pushed upwards even to his forehead where it scattered itself in a few formless patches of pale red; and on his hairless face there scintillated restlessly the polished lenses and the bright gilt rims of the glasses which screened his delicate and restless eyes. His glossy black hair was parted in the middle and brushed in a long curve behind his ears where it curled slightly beneath the groove left by his hat.

When he had flicked lustre into his shoes he stood up and pulled his

4. A kind of coarse woolen cloth.

waistcoat down more tightly on his plump body. Then he took a coin rapidly from his pocket.

—O Lily, he said, thrusting it into her hands, it's Christmas-time, isn't it? Just . . . here's a little. . . .

He walked rapidly towards the door.

—O no, sir! cried the girl, following him. Really, sir, I wouldn't take it.

—Christmas-time! Christmas-time! said Gabriel, almost trotting to the stairs and waving his hand to her in deprecation.

The girl, seeing that he had gained the stairs, called out after him:

—Well, thank you, sir.

He waited outside the drawing-room door until the waltz should finish, listening to the skirts that swept against it and to the shuffling of feet. He was still discomposed by the girl's bitter and sudden retort. It had cast a gloom over him which he tried to dispel by arranging his cuffs and the bows of his tie. Then he took from his waistcoat pocket a little paper and glanced at the headings he had made for his speech. He was undecided about the lines from Robert Browning for he feared they would be above the heads of his hearers. Some quotation that they could recognise from Shakespeare or from the Melodies[5] would be better. The indelicate clacking of the men's heels and the shuffling of their soles reminded him that their grade of culture differed from his. He would only make himself ridiculous by quoting poetry to them which they could not understand. They would think that he was airing his superior education. He would fail with them just as he had failed with the girl in the pantry. He had taken up a wrong tone. His whole speech was a mistake from first to last, an utter failure.

Just then his aunts and his wife came out of the ladies' dressing-room. His aunts were two small plainly dressed old women. Aunt Julia was an inch or so taller. Her hair, drawn low over the tops of her ears, was grey; and grey also, with darker shadows, was her large flaccid face. Though she was stout in build and stood erect her slow eyes and parted lips gave her the appearance of a woman who did not know where she was or where she was going. Aunt Kate was more vivacious. Her face, healthier than her sister's, was all puckers and creases, like a shrivelled red apple, and her hair, braided in the same old-fashioned way, had not lost its ripe nut colour.

They both kissed Gabriel frankly. He was their favourite nephew, the son of their dead elder sister, Ellen, who had married T. J. Conroy of the Port and Docks.

—Gretta tells me you're not going to take a cab back to Monkstown to-night, Gabriel, said Aunt Kate.

—No, said Gabriel, turning to his wife, we had quite enough of that last year, hadn't we. Don't you remember, Aunt Kate, what a cold Gretta got out of it? Cab windows rattling all the way, and the east wind blowing in after we passed Merrion. Very jolly it was. Gretta caught a dreadful cold.

Aunt Kate frowned severely and nodded her head at every word.

—Quite right, Gabriel, quite right, she said. You can't be too careful.

—But as for Gretta there, said Gabriel, she'd walk home in the snow if she were let.

5. *Irish Melodies* by Dublin-born Thomas Moore (1779–1852), a collection of songs—words and music—that was extremely popular in late-19th- and early-20th-century Ireland.

Mrs Conroy laughed.

—Don't mind him, Aunt Kate, she said. He's really an awful bother, what with green shades for Tom's eyes at night and making him do the dumb-bells, and forcing Eva to eat the stirabout.[6] The poor child! And she simply hates the sight of it! . . . O, but you'll never guess what he makes me wear now!

She broke out into a peal of laughter and glanced at her husband, whose admiring and happy eyes had been wandering from her dress to her face and hair. The two aunts laughed heartily too, for Gabriel's solicitude was a stand-ing joke with them.

—Goloshes! said Mrs Conroy. That's the latest. Whenever it's wet under-foot I must put on my goloshes. To-night even he wanted me to put them on, but I wouldn't. The next thing he'll buy me will be a diving suit.

Gabriel laughed nervously and patted his tie reassuringly while Aunt Kate nearly doubled herself, so heartily did she enjoy the joke. The smile soon faded from Aunt Julia's face and her mirthless eyes were directed towards her nephew's face. After a pause she asked:

—And what are goloshes, Gabriel?

—Goloshes, Julia! exclaimed her sister. Goodness me, don't you know what goloshes are? You wear them over your . . . over your boots, Gretta, isn't it?

—Yes, said Mrs Conroy. Guttapercha things. We both have a pair now. Gabriel says everyone wears them on the continent.

—O, on the continent, murmured Aunt Julia, nodding her head slowly.

Gabriel knitted his brows and said, as if he were slightly angered:

—It's nothing very wonderful but Gretta thinks it very funny because she says the word reminds her of Christy Minstrels.[7]

—But tell me, Gabriel, said Aunt Kate, with brisk tact. Of course, you've seen about the room. Gretta was saying . . .

—O, the room is all right, replied Gabriel. I've taken one in the Gresham.[8]

—To be sure, said Aunt Kate, by far the best thing to do. And the children, Gretta, you're not anxious about them?

—O, for one night, said Mrs Conroy. Besides, Bessie will look after them.

—To be sure, said Aunt Kate again. What a comfort it is to have a girl like that, one you can depend on! There's that Lily, I'm sure I don't know what has come over her lately. She's not the girl she was at all.

Gabriel was about to ask his aunt some questions on this point but she broke off suddenly to gaze after her sister who had wandered down the stairs and was craning her neck over the banisters.

—Now, I ask you, she said, almost testily, where is Julia going? Julia! Julia! Where are you going?

Julia, who had gone halfway down one flight, came back and announced blandly:

—Here's Freddy.

At the same moment a clapping of hands and a final flourish of the pianist

6. Porridge made by stirring oatmeal in boiling milk or water.
7. Originally the name of a troupe of entertainers imitating African Americans, founded by George Christy of New York. By Joyce's time the meaning had become extended to any group with blackened faces who sang what were known as Negro melo-dies to banjo accompaniment, interspersed with jokes.
8. The Gresham Hotel, still one of the best hotels in Dublin.

told that the waltz had ended. The drawing-room door was opened from within and some couples came out. Aunt Kate drew Gabriel aside hurriedly and whispered into his ear:

—Slip down, Gabriel, like a good fellow and see if he's all right, and don't let him up if he's screwed. I'm sure he's screwed. I'm sure he is.

Gabriel went to the stairs and listened over the banisters. He could hear two persons talking in the pantry. Then he recognised Freddy Malins' laugh. He went down the stairs noisily.

—It's such a relief, said Aunt Kate to Mrs Conroy, that Gabriel is here. I always feel easier in my mind when he's here. . . . Julia, there's Miss Daly and Miss Power will take some refreshment. Thanks for your beautiful waltz, Miss Daly. It made lovely time.

A tall wizen-faced man, with a stiff grizzled moustache and swarthy skin, who was passing out with his partner said:

—And may we have some refreshment, too, Miss Morkan?

—Julia, said Aunt Kate summarily, and here's Mr Browne and Miss Furlong. Take them in, Julia, with Miss Daly and Miss Power.

—I'm the man for the ladies, said Mr Browne, pursing his lips until his moustache bristled and smiling in all his wrinkles. You know, Miss Morkan, the reason they are so fond of me is—

He did not finish his sentence, but, seeing that Aunt Kate was out of earshot, at once led the three young ladies into the back room. The middle of the room was occupied by two square tables placed end to end, and on these Aunt Julia and the caretaker were straightening and smoothing a large cloth. On the sideboard were arrayed dishes and plates, and glasses and bundles of knives and forks and spoons. The top of the closed square piano served also as a sideboard for viands and sweets. At a smaller sideboard in one corner two young men were standing, drinking hop-bitters.

Mr Browne led his charges thither and invited them all, in jest, to some ladies' punch, hot, strong and sweet. As they said they never took anything strong he opened three bottles of lemonade for them. Then he asked one of the young men to move aside, and, taking hold of the decanter, filled out for himself a goodly measure of whisky. The young men eyed him respectfully while he took a trial sip.

—God help me, he said, smiling, it's the doctor's orders.

His wizened face broke into a broader smile, and the three young ladies laughed in musical echo to his pleasantry, swaying their bodies to and fro, with nervous jerks of their shoulders. The boldest said:

—O, now, Mr Browne, I'm sure the doctor never ordered anything of the kind.

Mr Browne took another sip of his whisky and said, with sidling mimicry:

—Well, you see, I'm like the famous Mrs Cassidy, who is reported to have said: *Now, Mary Grimes, if I don't take it, make me take it, for I feel I want it.*

His hot face had leaned forward a little too confidentially and he had assumed a very low Dublin accent so that the young ladies, with one instinct, received his speech in silence. Miss Furlong, who was one of Mary Jane's pupils, asked Miss Daly what was the name of the pretty waltz she had played; and Mr Browne, seeing that he was ignored, turned promptly to the two young men who were more appreciative.

A red-faced young woman, dressed in pansy, came into the room, excitedly clapping her hands and crying:

—Quadrilles![9] Quadrilles!

Close on her heels came Aunt Kate, crying:

—Two gentlemen and three ladies, Mary Jane!

—O, here's Mr Bergin and Mr Kerrigan, said Mary Jane. Mr Kerrigan, will you take Miss Power? Miss Furlong, may I get you a partner, Mr Bergin. O, that'll just do now.

—Three ladies, Mary Jane, said Aunt Kate.

The two young gentlemen asked the ladies if they might have the pleasure, and Mary Jane turned to Miss Daly.

—O, Miss Daly, you're really awfully good, after playing for the last two dances, but really we're so short of ladies to-night.

—I don't mind in the least, Miss Morkan.

—But I've a nice partner for you, Mr Bartell D'Arcy, the tenor. I'll get him to sing later on. All Dublin is raving about him.

—Lovely voice, lovely voice! said Aunt Kate.

As the piano had twice begun the prelude to the first figure Mary Jane led her recruits quickly from the room. They had hardly gone when Aunt Julia wandered slowly into the room, looking behind her at something.

—What is the matter, Julia? asked Aunt Kate anxiously. Who is it?

Julia, who was carrying in a column of table-napkins, turned to her sister and said, simply, as if the question had surprised her:

—It's only Freddy, Kate, and Gabriel with him.

In fact right behind her Gabriel could be seen piloting Freddy Malins across the landing. The latter, a young man of about forty, was of Gabriel's size and build, with very round shoulders. His face was fleshy and pallid, touched with colour only at the thick hanging lobes of his ears and at the wide wings of his nose. He had coarse features, a blunt nose, a convex and receding brow, tumid and protruded lips. His heavy-lidded eyes and the disorder of his scanty hair made him look sleepy. He was laughing heartily in a high key at a story which he had been telling Gabriel on the stairs and at the same time rubbing the knuckles of his left fist backwards and forwards into his left eye.

—Good-evening, Freddy, said Aunt Julia.

Freddy Malins bade the Misses Morkan good-evening in what seemed an offhand fashion by reason of the habitual catch in his voice and then, seeing that Mr Browne was grinning at him from the sideboard, crossed the room on rather shaky legs and began to repeat in an undertone the story he had just told to Gabriel.

—He's not so bad, is he? said Aunt Kate to Gabriel.

Gabriel's brows were dark but he raised them quickly and answered:

—O no, hardly noticeable.

—Now, isn't he a terrible fellow! she said. And his poor mother made him take the pledge[1] on New Year's Eve. But come on, Gabriel, into the drawing-room.

Before leaving the room with Gabriel she signalled to Mr Browne by frown-

---

9. A square dance usually performed by four couples.

1. Sign a solemn promise not to drink alcohol.

ing and shaking her forefinger in warning to and fro. Mr Browne nodded in answer and, when she had gone, said to Freddy Malins:

—Now, then, Teddy, I'm going to fill you out a good glass of lemonade just to buck you up.

Freddy Malins, who was nearing the climax of his story, waved the offer aside impatiently but Mr Browne, having first called Freddy Malins' attention to a disarray in his dress, filled out and handed him a full glass of lemonade. Freddy Malins' left hand accepted the glass mechanically, his right hand being engaged in the mechanical readjustment of his dress. Mr Browne, whose face was once more wrinkling with mirth, poured out for himself a glass of whisky while Freddy Malins exploded, before he had well reached the climax of his story, in a kink of high-pitched bronchitic laughter and, setting down his untasted and overflowing glass, began to rub the knuckles of his left fist backwards and forwards into his left eye, repeating words of his last phrase as well as his fit of laughter would allow him.

Gabriel could not listen while Mary Jane was playing her Academy piece, full of runs and difficult passages, to the hushed drawing-room. He liked music but the piece she was playing had no melody for him and he doubted whether it had any melody for the other listeners, though they had begged Mary Jane to play something. Four young men, who had come from the refreshment-room to stand in the door-way at the sound of the piano, had gone away quietly in couples after a few minutes. The only persons who seemed to follow the music were Mary Jane herself, her hands racing along the key-board or lifted from it at the pauses like those of a priestess in momentary imprecation, and Aunt Kate standing at her elbow to turn the page.

Gabriel's eyes, irritated by the floor, which glittered with beeswax under the heavy chandelier, wandered to the wall above the piano. A picture of the balcony scene in *Romeo and Juliet* hung there and beside it was a picture of the two murdered princes in the Tower which Aunt Julia had worked in red, blue and brown wools when she was a girl. Probably in the school they had gone to as girls that kind of work had been taught, for one year his mother had worked for him as a birthday present a waistcoat of purple tabinet,[2] with little foxes' heads upon it, lined with brown satin and having round mulberry buttons. It was strange that his mother had had no musical talent though Aunt Kate used to call her the brains carrier of the Morkan family. Both she and Julia had always seemed a little proud of their serious and matronly sister. Her photograph stood before the pierglass.[3] She held an open book on her knees and was pointing out something in it to Constantine who, dressed in a man-o'-war suit,[4] lay at her feet. It was she who had chosen the names for her sons for she was very sensible of the dignity of family life. Thanks to her, Constantine was now senior curate[5] in Balbriggan and, thanks to her, Gabriel himself had taken his degree in the Royal University. A shadow passed over his face as he remembered her sullen opposition to his marriage. Some slighting phrases she had used still rankled in his memory; she had once spoken of Gretta as being country cute and that was not true

2. A kind of poplin made chiefly in Ireland.
3. Large tall mirror.
4. Sailor suit, favorite wear for children of both sexes early in the 20th century.
5. Clergyman appointed to assist a parish priest.

of Gretta at all. It was Gretta who had nursed her during all her last long illness in their house at Monkstown.

He knew that Mary Jane must be near the end of her piece for she was playing again the opening melody with runs of scales after every bar and while he waited for the end the resentment died down in his heart. The piece ended with a trill of octaves in the treble and a final deep octave in the bass. Great applause greeted Mary Jane as, blushing and rolling up her music nervously, she escaped from the room. The most vigorous clapping came from the four young men in the doorway who had gone away to the refreshment-room at the beginning of the piece but had come back when the piano had stopped.

Lancers[6] were arranged. Gabriel found himself partnered with Miss Ivors. She was a frank-mannered talkative young lady, with a freckled face and prominent brown eyes. She did not wear a low-cut bodice and the large brooch which was fixed in the front of her collar bore on it an Irish device.

When they had taken their places she said abruptly:

—I have a crow to pluck with you.

—With me? said Gabriel.

She nodded her head gravely.

—What is it? asked Gabriel, smiling at her solemn manner.

—Who is G. C.? answered Miss Ivors, turning her eyes upon him.

Gabriel coloured and was about to knit his brows, as if he did not understand, when she said bluntly:

—O, innocent Amy! I have found out that you write for *The Daily Express.* Now, aren't you ashamed of yourself?

—Why should I be ashamed of myself? asked Gabriel, blinking his eyes and trying to smile.

—Well, I'm ashamed of you, said Miss Ivors frankly. To say you'd write for a rag like that. I didn't think you were a West Briton.[7]

A look of perplexity appeared on Gabriel's face. It was true that he wrote a literary column every Wednesday in *The Daily Express,* for which he was paid fifteen shillings. But that did not make him a West Briton surely. The books he received for review were almost more welcome than the paltry cheque. He loved to feel the covers and turn over the pages of newly printed books. Nearly every day when his teaching in the college was ended he used to wander down the quays to the second-hand booksellers, to Hickey's on Bachelor's Walk, to Webb's, or Massey's on Aston's Quay, or to O'Clohissey's in the by-street. He did not know how to meet her charge. He wanted to say that literature was above politics. But they were friends of many years' standing and their careers had been parallel, first at the University and then as teachers: he could not risk a grandiose phrase with her. He continued blinking his eyes and trying to smile and murmured lamely that he saw nothing political in writing reviews of books.

When their turn to cross had come he was still perplexed and inattentive. Miss Ivors promptly took his hand in a warm grasp and said in a soft friendly tone:

—Of course, I was only joking. Come, we cross now.

6. A square dance for four or more couples.
7. One who denies a separate Irish nationality and

sees Ireland as simply a western extension of Great Britain.

When they were together again she spoke of the University question and Gabriel felt more at ease. A friend of hers had shown her his review of Browning's poems. That was how she had found out the secret: but she liked the review immensely. Then she said suddenly:

—O, Mr Conroy, will you come for an excursion to the Aran Isles[8] this summer? We're going to stay there a whole month. It will be splendid out in the Atlantic. You ought to come. Mr Clancy is coming, and Mr Kilkelly and Kathleen Kearney. It would be splendid for Gretta too if she'd come. She's from Connacht,[9] isn't she?

—Her people are, said Gabriel shortly.

—But you will come, won't you? said Miss Ivors, laying her warm hand eagerly on his arm.

—The fact is, said Gabriel, I have already arranged to go—

—Go where? asked Miss Ivors.

—Well, you know, every year I go for a cycling tour with some fellows and so—

—But where? asked Miss Ivors.

—Well, we usually go to France or Belgium or perhaps Germany, said Gabriel awkwardly.

—And why do you go to France and Belgium, said Miss Ivors, instead of visiting your own land?

—Well, said Gabriel, it's partly to keep in touch with the languages and partly for a change.

—And haven't you your own language to keep in touch with—Irish? asked Miss Ivors.

—Well, said Gabriel, if it comes to that, you know, Irish is not my language.

Their neighbours had turned to listen to the cross-examination. Gabriel glanced right and left nervously and tried to keep his good humour under the ordeal which was making a blush invade his forehead.

—And haven't you your own land to visit, continued Miss Ivors, that you know nothing of, your own people, and your own country?

—O, to tell you the truth, retorted Gabriel suddenly, I'm sick of my own country, sick of it!

—Why? asked Miss Ivors.

Gabriel did not answer for his retort had heated him.

—Why? repeated Miss Ivors.

They had to go visiting together and, as he had not answered her, Miss Ivors said warmly:

—Of course, you've no answer.

Gabriel tried to cover his agitation by taking part in the dance with great energy. He avoided her eyes for he had seen a sour expression on her face. But when they met in the long chain he was surprised to feel his hand firmly pressed. She looked at him from under her brows for a moment quizzically[1] until he smiled. Then, just as the chain was about to start again, she stood on tiptoe and whispered into his ear:

—West Briton!

8. Three small islands lying across the entrance to Galway Bay, on the west coast of Ireland.
9. Connacht (or Connaught) is a region in the

west of Ireland containing largely a poor peasant population.
1. Teasingly.

When the lancers were over Gabriel went away to a remote corner of the room where Freddy Malins' mother was sitting. She was a stout feeble old woman with white hair. Her voice had a catch in it like her son's and she stuttered slightly. She had been told that Freddy had come and that he was nearly all right. Gabriel asked her whether she had had a good crossing. She lived with her married daughter in Glasgow and came to Dublin on a visit once a year. She answered placidly that she had had a beautiful crossing and that the captain had been most attentive to her. She spoke also of the beautiful house her daughter kept in Glasgow, and of all the nice friends they had there. While her tongue rambled on Gabriel tried to banish from his mind all memory of the unpleasant incident with Miss Ivors. Of course the girl or woman, or whatever she was, was an enthusiast but there was a time for all things. Perhaps he ought not to have answered her like that. But she had no right to call him a West Briton before people, even in joke. She had tried to make him ridiculous before people, heckling him and staring at him with her rabbit's eyes.

He saw his wife making her way towards him through the waltzing couples. When she reached him she said into his ear:

—Gabriel, Aunt Kate wants to know won't you carve the goose as usual. Miss Daly will carve the ham and I'll do the pudding.

—All right, said Gabriel.

—She's sending in the younger ones first as soon as this waltz is over so that we'll have the table to ourselves.

—Were you dancing? asked Gabriel.

—Of course I was. Didn't you see me? What words had you with Molly Ivors?

—No words. Why? Did she say so?

—Something like that. I'm trying to get that Mr D'Arcy to sing. He's full of conceit, I think.

—There were no words, said Gabriel moodily, only she wanted me to go for a trip to the west of Ireland and I said I wouldn't.

His wife clasped her hands excitedly and gave a little jump.

—O, do go, Gabriel, she cried. I'd love to see Galway again.

—You can go if you like, said Gabriel coldly.

She looked at him for a moment, then turned to Mrs Malins and said:

—There's a nice husband for you, Mrs Malins.

While she was threading her way back across the room Mrs Malins, without adverting to the interruption, went on to tell Gabriel what beautiful places there were in Scotland and beautiful scenery. Her son-in-law brought them every year to the lakes and they used to go fishing. Her son-in-law was a splendid fisher. One day he caught a fish, a beautiful big big fish, and the man in the hotel boiled it for their dinner.

Gabriel hardly heard what she said. Now that supper was coming near he began to think again about his speech and about the quotation. When he saw Freddy Malins coming across the room to visit his mother Gabriel left the chair free for him and retired into the embrasure of the window. The room had already cleared and from the back room came the clatter of plates and knives. Those who still remained in the drawing-room seemed tired of dancing and were conversing quietly in little groups. Gabriel's warm trembling fingers tapped the cold pane of the window. How cool it must be outside! How pleasant it would be to walk out alone, first along by the river and then through the park! The snow would be lying on the branches of the trees and forming a bright cap on the top of the Wellington Monument. How much more pleasant it would be there than at the supper-table!

He ran over the headings of his speech: Irish hospitality, sad memories, the Three Graces,[2] Paris, the quotation from Browning. He repeated to himself a phrase he had written in his review: *One feels that one is listening to a thought-tormented music.* Miss Ivors had praised the review. Was she sincere? Had she really any life of her own behind all her propagandism? There had never been any ill-feeling between them until that night. It unnerved him to think that she would be at the supper-table, looking up at him while he spoke with her critical quizzing eyes. Perhaps she would not be sorry to see him fail in his speech. An idea came into his mind and gave him courage. He would say, alluding to Aunt Kate and Aunt Julia: *Ladies and Gentlemen, the generation which is now on the wane among us may have had its faults but for my part I think it had certain qualities of hospitality, of humour, of humanity, which the new and very serious and hypereducated generation that is growing up around us seems to me to lack.* Very good: that was one for Miss Ivors. What did he care that his aunts were only two ignorant old women?

A murmur in the room attracted his attention. Mr Browne was advancing from the door, gallantly escorting Aunt Julia, who leaned upon his arm, smiling and hanging her head. An irregular musketry of applause escorted her also as far as the piano and then, as Mary Jane seated herself on the stool, and Aunt Julia, no longer smiling, half turned so as to pitch her voice fairly into the room, gradually ceased. Gabriel recognised the prelude. It was that of an old song of Aunt Julia's—*Arrayed for the Bridal.*[3] Her voice, strong and clear in tone, attacked with great spirit the runs which embellish the air and though she sang very rapidly she did not miss even the smallest of the grace notes. To follow the voice, without looking at the singer's face, was to feel and share the excitement of swift and secure flight. Gabriel applauded loudly with all the others at the close of the song and loud applause was borne in from the invisible supper-table. It sounded so genuine that a little colour struggled into Aunt Julia's face as she bent to replace in the music-stand the old leather-bound songbook that had her initials on the cover. Freddy Malins, who had listened with his head perched sideways to hear her better, was still applauding when everyone else had ceased and talking animatedly to his mother who nodded her head gravely and slowly in acquiescence. At last, when he could clap no more, he stood up suddenly and hurried across the room to Aunt Julia whose hand he seized and held in both his hands, shaking it when words failed him or the catch in his voice proved too much for him.

—I was just telling my mother, he said, I never heard you sing so well, never. No, I never heard your voice so good as it is to-night. Now! Would you believe that now? That's the truth. Upon my word and honour that's the truth I never heard your voice sound so fresh and so . . . so clear and fresh, never.

2. In Greek mythology, three goddesses—Aglaia, splendor; Euphrosyne, festivity; and Thalia, rejoicing—who together represented loveliness and joy. Gabriel is making a mental note to refer to his two aunts and Mary Jane in this complimentary way.
3. This old song (beginning "Arrayed for the bri-dal, in beauty behold her") "is replete with long and complicated runs, requiring a sophisticated and gifted singer" (Bowen, *Musical Allusions in the Works of James Joyce,* 1974); the suggestion is that Aunt Julia was a really accomplished singer.

Aunt Julia smiled broadly and murmured something about compliments as she released her hand from his grasp. Mr Browne extended his open hand towards her and said to those who were near him in the manner of a show-man introducing a prodigy to an audience:

—Miss Julia Morkan, my latest discovery!

He was laughing very heartily at this himself when Freddy Malins turned to him and said:

—Well, Browne, if you're serious you might make a worse discovery. All I can say is I never heard her sing half so well as long as I am coming here. And that's the honest truth.

—Neither did I, said Mr Browne. I think her voice has greatly improved.

Aunt Julia shrugged her shoulders and said with meek pride:

—Thirty years ago I hadn't a bad voice as voices go.

—I often told Julia, said Aunt Kate emphatically, that she was simply thrown away in that choir. But she never would be said by me.

She turned as if to appeal to the good sense of the others against a refractory child while Aunt Julia gazed in front of her, a vague smile of reminiscence playing on her face.

—No, continued Aunt Kate, she wouldn't be said or led by anyone, slaving there in that choir night and day, night and day. Six o'clock on Christmas morning! And all for what?

—Well, isn't it for the honour of God, Aunt Kate? asked Mary Jane, twisting round on the piano-stool and smiling.

Aunt Kate turned fiercely on her niece and said:

—I know all about the honour of God, Mary Jane, but I think it's not at all honourable for the pope to turn out the women out of the choirs that have slaved there all their lives and put little whipper-snappers of boys over their heads. I suppose it is for the good of the Church if the pope does it. But it's not just, Mary Jane, and it's not right.

She had worked herself into a passion and would have continued in defence of her sister for it was a sore subject with her but Mary Jane, seeing that all the dancers had come back, intervened pacifically:

—Now, Aunt Kate, you're giving scandal to Mr Browne who is of the other persuasion.[4]

Aunt Kate turned to Mr Browne, who was grinning at this allusion to his religion, and said hastily:

—O, I don't question the pope's being right. I'm only a stupid old woman and I wouldn't presume to do such a thing. But there's such a thing as common everyday politeness and gratitude. And if I were in Julia's place I'd tell that Father Healy straight up to his face . . .

—And besides, Aunt Kate, said Mary Jane, we really are all hungry and when we are hungry we are all very quarrelsome.

—And when we are thirsty we are also quarrelsome, added Mr Browne.

—So that we had better go to supper, said Mary Jane, and finish the discussion afterwards.

On the landing outside the drawing-room Gabriel found his wife and Mary Jane trying to persuade Miss Ivors to stay for supper. But Miss Ivors, who had put on her hat and was buttoning her cloak, would not stay. She did not feel in the least hungry and she had already overstayed her time.

4. I.e., Protestant.

—But only for ten minutes, Molly, said Mrs Conroy. That won't delay you.

—To take a pick itself, said Mary Jane, after all your dancing.

—I really couldn't, said Miss Ivors.

—I am afraid you didn't enjoy yourself at all, said Mary Jane hopelessly.

—Ever so much, I assure you, said Miss Ivors, but you really must let me run off now.

—But how can you get home? asked Mrs Conroy.

—O, it's only two steps up the quay.

Gabriel hesitated a moment and said:

—If you will allow me, Miss Ivors, I'll see you home if you really are obliged to go.

But Miss Ivors broke away from them.

—I won't hear of it, she cried. For goodness sake go in to your suppers and don't mind me. I'm quite well able to take care of myself.

—Well, you're the comical girl, Molly, said Mrs Conroy frankly.

—Beannacht libh,[5] cried Miss Ivors, with a laugh, as she ran down the staircase.

Mary Jane gazed after her, a moody puzzled expression on her face, while Mrs Conroy leaned over the banisters to listen for the hall-door. Gabriel asked himself was he the cause of her abrupt departure. But she did not seem to be in ill humour: she had gone away laughing. He stared blankly down the staircase.

At that moment Aunt Kate came toddling out of the supper-room, almost wringing her hands in despair.

—Where is Gabriel? she cried. Where on earth is Gabriel? There's everyone waiting in there, stage to let, and nobody to carve the goose!

—Here I am, Aunt Kate! cried Gabriel, with sudden animation, ready to carve a flock of geese, if necessary.

A fat brown goose lay at one end of the table and at the other end, on a bed of creased paper strewn with sprigs of parsley, lay a great ham, stripped of its outer skin and peppered over with crust crumbs, a neat paper frill round its shin and beside this was a round of spiced beef. Between these rival ends ran parallel lines of side-dishes: two little minsters of jelly, red and yellow; a shallow dish full of blocks of blancmange and red jam, a large green leaf-shaped dish with a stalk-shaped handle, on which lay bunches of purple raisins and peeled almonds, a companion dish on which lay a solid rectangle of Smyrna figs, a dish of custard topped with grated nutmeg, a small bowl full of chocolates and sweets wrapped in gold and silver papers and a glass vase in which stood some tall celery stalks. In the centre of the table there stood, as sentries to a fruit-stand which upheld a pyramid of oranges and American apples, two squat old-fashioned decanters of cut glass, one containing port and the other dark sherry. On the closed square piano a pudding in a huge yellow dish lay in waiting and behind it were three squads of bottles of stout and ale and minerals, drawn up according to the colours of their uniforms, the first two black, with brown and red labels, the third and smallest squad white, with transverse green sashes.

Gabriel took his seat boldly at the head of the table and, having looked to the edge of the carver, plunged his fork firmly into the goose. He felt quite

5. Blessing on you (Gaelic; literal trans.); good-bye.

at ease now for he was an expert carver and liked nothing better than to find himself at the head of a well-laden table.

—Miss Furlong, what shall I send you? he asked. A wing or a slice of the breast?

—Just a small slice of the breast.

—Miss Higgins, what for you?

—O, anything at all, Mr Conroy.

While Gabriel and Miss Daly exchanged plates of goose and plates of ham and spiced beef Lily went from guest to guest with a dish of hot floury potatoes wrapped in a white napkin. This was Mary Jane's idea and she had also suggested apple sauce for the goose but Aunt Kate had said that plain roast goose without apple sauce had always been good enough for her and she hoped she might never eat worse. Mary Jane waited on her pupils and saw that they got the best slices and Aunt Kate and Aunt Julia opened and carried across from the piano bottles of stout and ale for the gentlemen and bottles of minerals for the ladies. There was a great deal of confusion and laughter and noise, the noise of orders and counter-orders, of knives and forks, of corks and glass-stoppers. Gabriel began to carve second helpings as soon as he had finished the first round without serving himself. Everyone protested loudly so that he compromised by taking a long draught of stout for he had found the carving hot work. Mary Jane settled down quietly to her supper but Aunt Kate and Aunt Julia were still toddling round the table, walking on each other's heels, getting in each other's way and giving each other unheeded orders. Mr Browne begged of them to sit down and eat their suppers and so did Gabriel but they said there was time enough so that, at last, Freddy Malins stood up and, capturing Aunt Kate, plumped her down on her chair amid general laughter.

When everyone had been well served Gabriel said, smiling:

—Now, if anyone wants a little more of what vulgar people call stuffing let him or her speak.

A chorus of voices invited him to begin his own supper and Lily came forward with three potatoes which she had reserved for him.

—Very well, said Gabriel amiably, as he took another preparatory draught, kindly forget my existence, ladies and gentlemen, for a few minutes.

He set to his supper and took no part in the conversation with which the table covered Lily's removal of the plates. The subject of talk was the opera company which was then at the Theatre Royal. Mr Bartell D'Arcy, the tenor, a dark-complexioned young man with a smart moustache, praised very highly the leading contralto of the company but Miss Furlong thought she had a rather vulgar style of production. Freddy Malins said there was a negro chieftain singing in the second part of the Gaiety pantomime who had one of the finest tenor voices he had every heard.

—Have you heard him? he asked Mr Bartell D'Arcy across the table.

—No, answered Mr Bartell D'Arcy carelessly.

—Because, Freddy Malins explained, now I'd be curious to hear your opinion of him. I think he has a grand voice.

—It takes Teddy to find out the really good things, said Mr Browne familiarly to the table.

—And why couldn't he have a voice too? asked Freddy Malins sharply. Is it because he's only a black?

Nobody answered this question and Mary Jane led the table back to the legitimate opera. One of her pupils had given her a pass for *Mignon*.[6] Of course it was very fine, she said, but it made her think of poor Georgina Burns. Mr Browne could go back farther still, to the old Italian companies that used to come to Dublin—Tietjens, Ilma de Murzka, Campanini, the great Trebelli, Giuglini, Ravelli, Aramburo. Those were the days, he said, when there was something like singing to be heard in Dublin. He told too of how the top gallery of the old Royal used to be packed night after night, of how one night an Italian tenor had sung five encores to *Let Me Like a Soldier Fall*,[7] introducing a high C every time, and of how the gallery boys would sometimes in their enthusiasm unyoke the horses from the carriage of some great *prima donna* and pull her themselves through the streets to her hotel. Why did they never play the grand old operas now, he asked, *Dinorah, Lucrezia Borgia*?[8] Because they could not get the voices to sing them: that was why.

—O, well, said Mr Bartell D'Arcy, I presume there are as good singers today as there were then.

—Where are they? asked Mr Browne defiantly.

—In London, Paris, Milan, said Mr Bartell d'Arcy warmly. I suppose Caruso,[9] for example, is quite as good, if not better than any of the men you have mentioned.

—Maybe so, said Mr Browne. But I may tell you I doubt it strongly.

—O, I'd give anything to hear Caruso sing, said Mary Jane.

—For me, said Aunt Kate, who had been picking a bone, there was only one tenor. To please me, I mean. But I suppose none of you ever heard of him.

—Who was he, Miss Morkan? asked Mr Bartell D'Arcy politely.

—His name, said Aunt Kate, was Parkinson. I heard him when he was in his prime and I think he had then the purest tenor voice that was ever put into a man's throat.

—Strange, said Mr Bartell d'Arcy. I never even heard of him.

—Yes, yes, Miss Morkan is right, said Mr Browne. I remember hearing of old Parkinson but he's too far back for me.

—A beautiful pure sweet mellow English tenor, said Aunt Kate with enthusiasm.

Gabriel having finished, the huge pudding was transferred to the table. The clatter of forks and spoons began again. Gabriel's wife served out spoonfuls of the pudding and passed the plates down the table. Midway down they were held up by Mary Jane, who replenished them with raspberry or orange jelly or with blancmange and jam. The pudding was of Aunt Julia's making and she received praises for it from all quarters. She herself said that it was not quite brown enough.

—Well, I hope, Miss Morkan, said Mr Browne, that I'm brown enough for you because, you know, I'm all brown.

---

6. Opera by Ambroise Thomas first produced in Paris in 1866 and in London in 1870.
7. This song, from the opera *Maritana* by W. Wallace (it actually begins "Yes! let me like a soldier fall"), ends on middle C; it would be a piece of exhibitionism to end on a high C, as Joyce's father, who had a good voice, used to do. Joyce's brother Stanislaus remembered the song as insufferable

rubbish. Mr. Browne is not to be taken seriously as a music critic.
8. An opera by Donizetti, first produced at La Scala, Milan, in 1833. *Dinorah* is an opera by Meyerbeer, first produced in Paris in 1859.
9. Enrico Caruso (1873–1921), the great Italian dramatic tenor.

All the gentlemen, except Gabriel, ate some of the pudding out of compliment to Aunt Julia. As Gabriel never ate sweets the celery had been left for him. Freddy Malins also took a stalk of celery and ate it with his pudding. He had been told that celery was a capital thing for the blood and he was just then under doctor's care. Mrs Malins, who had been silent all through the supper, said that her son was going down to Mount Melleray in a week or so. The table then spoke of Mount Melleray, how bracing the air was down there, how hospitable the monks were and how they never asked for a penny-piece from their guests.

—And do you mean to say, asked Mr Browne incredulously, that a chap can go down there and put up there as if it were a hotel and live on the fat of the land and then come away without paying a farthing?

—O, most people give some donation to the monastery when they leave, said Mary Jane.

—I wish we had an institution like that in our Church, said Mr Browne candidly.

He was astonished to hear that the monks never spoke, got up at two in the morning and slept in their coffins. He asked what they did it for.

—That's the rule of the order, said Aunt Kate firmly.

—Yes, but why? asked Mr Browne.

Aunt Kate repeated that it was the rule, that was all. Mr Browne still seemed not to understand. Freddy Malins explained to him, as best he could, that the monks were trying to make up for the sins committed by all the sinners in the outside world. The explanation was not very clear for Mr Browne grinned and said:

—I like that idea very much but wouldn't a comfortable spring bed do them as well as a coffin?

—The coffin, said Mary Jane, is to remind them of their last end.

As the subject had grown lugubrious it was buried in a silence of the table during which Mrs Malins could be heard saying to her neighbour in an indistinct undertone:

—They are very good men, the monks, very pious men.

The raisins and almonds and figs and apples and oranges and chocolates and sweets were now passed about the table and Aunt Julia invited all the guests to have either port or sherry. At first Mr Bartell D'Arcy refused to take either but one of his neighbours nudged him and whispered something to him upon which he allowed his glass to be filled. Gradually as the last glasses were being filled the conversation ceased. A pause followed, broken only by the noise of the wine and by unsettlings of chairs. The Misses Morkan, all three, looked down at the tablecloth. Someone coughed once or twice and then a few gentlemen patted the table gently as a signal for silence. The silence came and Gabriel pushed back his chair and stood up.

The patting at once grew louder in encouragement and then ceased altogether. Gabriel leaned his ten trembling fingers on the tablecloth and smiled nervously at the company. Meeting a row of upturned faces he raised his eyes to the chandelier. The piano was playing a waltz tune and he could hear the skirts sweeping against the drawing-room door. People, perhaps, were standing in the snow on the quay outside, gazing up at the lighted windows and listening to the waltz music. The air was pure there. In the distance lay the park where the trees were weighted with snow. The Wellington Monument wore a gleaming cap of snow that flashed westward over the white field of Fifteen Acres.

He began:

—Ladies and Gentlemen.

—It has fallen to my lot this evening, as in years past, to perform a very pleasing task but a task for which I am afraid my poor powers as a speaker are all too inadequate.

—No, no! said Mr Browne.

—But, however that may be, I can only ask you to-night to take the will for the deed and to lend me your attention for a few moments while I endeavour to express to you in words what my feelings are on this occasion.

—Ladies and Gentlemen. It is not the first time that we have gathered together under this hospitable roof, around this hospitable board. It is not the first time that we have been the recipients—or perhaps, I had better say, the victims—of the hospitality of certain good ladies.

He made a circle in the air with his arm and paused. Everyone laughed or smiled at Aunt Kate and Aunt Julia and Mary Jane who all turned crimson with pleasure. Gabriel went on more boldly:

—I feel more strongly with every recurring year that our country has no tradition which does it so much honour and which it should guard so jealously as that of its hospitality. It is a tradition that is unique as far as my experience goes (and I have visited not a few places abroad) among the modern nations. Some would say, perhaps, that with us it is rather a failing than anything to be boasted of. But granted even that, it is, to my mind, a princely failing, and one that I trust will long be cultivated among us. Of one thing, at least, I am sure. As long as this one roof shelters the good ladies aforesaid—and I wish from my heart it may do so for many and many a long year to come—the tradition of genuine warm-hearted courteous Irish hospitality, which our forefathers have handed down to us and which we in turn must hand down to our descendants, is still alive among us.

A hearty murmur of assent ran round the table. It shot through Gabriel's mind that Miss Ivors was not there and that she had gone away discourteously: and he said with confidence in himself:

—Ladies and Gentlemen.

—A new generation is growing up in our midst, a generation actuated by new ideas and new principles. It is serious and enthusiastic for these new ideas and its enthusiasm, even when it is misdirected, is, I believe, in the main sincere. But we are living in a sceptical and, if I may use the phrase, a thought-tormented age: and sometimes I fear that this new generation, educated or hypereducated as it is, will lack those qualities of humanity, of hospitality, of kindly humour which belonged to an older day. Listening to-night to the names of all those great singers of the past it seemed to me, I must confess, that we were living in a less spacious age. Those days might, without exaggeration, be called spacious days: and if they are gone beyond recall let us hope, at least, that in gatherings such as this we shall still speak of them with pride and affection, still cherish in our hearts the memory of those dead and gone great ones whose fame the world will not willingly let die.

—Hear, hear! said Mr Browne loudly.

—But yet, continued Gabriel, his voice falling into a softer inflection, there are always in gatherings such as this sadder thoughts that will recur to our minds: thoughts of the past, of youth, of changes, of absent faces that we miss here to-night. Our path through life is strewn with many such sad memories: and were we to brood upon them always we could not find the heart to go on bravely with our work among the living. We have all of us living duties and living affections which claim, and rightly claim, our strenuous endeavours.

—Therefore, I will not linger on the past. I will not let any gloomy moralising intrude upon us here to-night. Here we are gathered together for a brief moment from the bustle and rush of our everyday routine. We are met here as friends, in the spirit of good-fellowship, as colleagues, also to a certain extent, in the true spirit of *camaraderie*, and as the guests of—what shall I call them?—the Three Graces of the Dublin musical world.

The table burst into applause and laughter at this sally. Aunt Julia vainly asked each of her neighbours in turn to tell her what Gabriel had said.

—He says we are the Three Graces, Aunt Julia, said Mary Jane.

Aunt Julia did not understand but she looked up, smiling, at Gabriel, who continued in the same vein:

—Ladies and Gentlemen.

—I will not attempt to play to-night the part that Paris played on another occasion. I will not attempt to choose between them. The task would be an invidious one and one beyond my poor powers. For when I view them in turn, whether it be our chief hostess herself, whose good heart, whose too good heart, has become a byword with all who know her, or her sister, who seems to be gifted with perennial youth and whose singing must have been a surprise and a revelation to us all to-night, or, last but not least, when I consider our youngest hostess, talented, cheerful, hard-working and the best of nieces, I confess, Ladies and Gentlemen, that I do not know to which of them I should award the prize.

Gabriel glanced down at his aunts and, seeing the large smile on Aunt Julia's face and the tears which had risen to Aunt Kate's eyes, hastened to his close. He raised his glass of port gallantly, while every member of the company fingered a glass expectantly, and said loudly:

—Let us toast them all three together. Let us drink to their health, wealth, long life, happiness and prosperity and may they long continue to hold the proud and self-won position which they hold in their profession and the position of honour and affection which they hold in our hearts.

All the guests stood up, glass in hand, and, turning towards the three seated ladies, sang in unison, with Mr Browne as leader:

> *For they are jolly gay fellows,*
> *For they are jolly gay fellows,*
> *For they are jolly gay fellows,*
> *Which nobody can deny.*

Aunt Kate was making frank use of her handkerchief and even Aunt Julia seemed moved. Freddy Malins beat time with his pudding-fork and the singers turned towards one another, as if in melodious conference, while they sang, with emphasis:

> *Unless he tells a lie,*
> *Unless he tells a lie.*

Then, turning once more towards their hostesses, they sang:

> *For they are jolly gay fellows,*
> *For they are jolly gay fellows,*
> *For they are jolly gay fellows,*
> *Which nobody can deny.*

The acclamation which followed was taken up beyond the door of the supper-room by many of the other guests and renewed time after time, Freddy Malins acting as officer with his fork on high.

The piercing morning air came into the hall where they were standing so that Aunt Kate said:

—Close the door, somebody. Mrs Malins will get her death of cold.

—Browne is out there, Aunt Kate, said Mary Jane.

—Browne is everywhere, said Aunt Kate, lowering her voice.

Mary Jane laughed at her tone.

—Really, she said archly, he is very attentive.

—He has been laid on here like the gas, said Aunt Kate in the same tone, all during the Christmas.

She laughed herself this time good-humouredly and then added quickly:

—But tell him to come in, Mary Jane, and close the door. I hope to goodness he didn't hear me.

At that moment the hall-door was opened and Mr Browne came in from the doorstep, laughing as if his heart would break. He was dressed in a long green overcoat with mock astrakhan cuffs and collar and wore on his head an oval fur cap. He pointed down the snow-covered quay from where the sound of shrill prolonged whistling was borne in.

—Teddy will have all the cabs in Dublin out, he said.

Gabriel advanced from the little pantry behind the office, struggling into his overcoat and, looking round the hall, said:

—Gretta not down yet?

—She's getting on her things, Gabriel, said Aunt Kate.

—Who's playing up there? asked Gabriel.

—Nobody. They're all gone.

—O no, Aunt Kate, said Mary Jane. Bartell D'Arcy and Miss O'Callaghan aren't gone yet.

—Someone is strumming at the piano, anyhow, said Gabriel.

Mary Jane glanced at Gabriel and Mr Browne and said with a shiver:

—It makes me feel cold to look at you two gentlemen muffled up like that. I wouldn't like to face your journey home at this hour.

—I'd like nothing better this minute, said Mr Browne stoutly, than a rattling fine walk in the country or a fast drive with a good spanking goer between the shafts.

—We used to have a very good horse and trap[1] at home, said Aunt Julia sadly.

—The never-to-be-forgotten Johnny, said Mary Jane, laughing.

Aunt Kate and Gabriel laughed too.

—Why, what was wonderful about Johnny? asked Mr Browne.

—The late lamented Patrick Morkan, our grandfather, that is, explained Gabriel, commonly known in his later years as the old gentleman, was a glue-boiler.

---

1. A two-wheeled horse-drawn carriage on springs.

—O, now, Gabriel, said Aunt Kate, laughing, he had a starch mill.

—Well, glue or starch, said Gabriel, the old gentleman had a horse by the name of Johnny. And Johnny used to work in the old gentleman's mill, walking round and round in order to drive the mill. That was all very well; but now comes the tragic part about Johnny. One fine day the old gentleman thought he'd like to drive out with the quality[2] to a military review in the park.

—The Lord have mercy on his soul, said Aunt Kate compassionately.

—Amen, said Gabriel. So the old gentleman, as I said, harnessed Johnny and put on his very best tall hat and his very best stock collar and drove out in grand style from his ancestral mansion somewhere near Back Lane, I think.

Everyone laughed, even Mrs Malins, at Gabriel's manner and Aunt Kate said:

—O now, Gabriel, he didn't live in Back Lane, really. Only the mill was there.

—Out from the mansion of his forefathers, continued Gabriel, he drove with Johnny. And everything went on beautifully until Johnny came in sight of King Billy's statue: and whether he fell in love with the horse King Billy sits on or whether he thought he was back again in the mill, anyhow he began to walk round the statue.

Gabriel paced in a circle round the hall in his goloshes amid the laughter of the others.

—Round and round he went, said Gabriel, and the old gentleman, who was a very pompous old gentleman, was highly indignant. *Go on, sir! What do you mean, sir? Johnny! Johnny! Most extraordinary conduct! Can't understand the horse!*

The peals of laughter which followed Gabriel's imitation of the incident were interrupted by a resounding knock at the hall-door. Mary Jane ran to open it and let in Freddy Malins. Freddy Malins, with his hat well back on his head and his shoulders humped with cold, was puffing and steaming after his exertions.

—I could only get one cab, he said.

—O, we'll find another along the quay, said Gabriel.

—Yes, said Aunt Kate. Better not keep Mrs Malins standing in the draught.

Mrs Malins was helped down the front steps by her son and Mr Browne and, after many manœuvres, hoisted into the cab. Freddy Malins clambered in after her and spent a long time settling her on the seat, Mr Browne helping him with advice. At last she was settled comfortably and Freddy Malins invited Mr Browne into the cab. There was a good deal of confused talk, and then Mr Browne got into the cab. The cabman settled his rug over his knees, and bent down for the address. The confusion grew greater and the cabman was directed differently by Freddy Malins and Mr Browne, each of whom had his head out through a window of the cab. The difficulty was to know where to drop Mr Browne along the route and Aunt Kate, Aunt Julia and Mary Jane helped the discussion from the doorstep with cross-directions and contradictions and abundance of laughter. As for Freddy Malins he was speechless with laughter. He popped his head in and out of the window every moment, to the great danger of his hat, and told his mother how the discus-

2. People of rank or high social position.

sion was progressing till at last Mr Browne shouted to the bewildered cabman above the din of everybody's laughter:

—Do you know Trinity College?

—Yes, sir, said the cabman.

—Well, drive bang up against Trinity College gates, said Mr Browne, and then we'll tell you where to go. You understand now?

—Yes, sir, said the cabman.

—Make like a bird for Trinity College.

—Right, sir, cried the cabman.

The horse was whipped up and the cab rattled off along the quay amid a chorus of laughter and adieus.

Gabriel had not gone to the door with the others. He was in a dark part of the hall gazing up the staircase. A woman was standing near the top of the first flight, in the shadow also. He could not see her face but he could see the terracotta and salmonpink panels of her skirt which the shadow made appear black and white. It was his wife. She was leaning on the banisters, listening to something. Gabriel was surprised at her stillness and strained his ear to listen also. But he could hear little save the noise of laughter and dispute on the front steps, a few chords struck on the piano and a few notes of a man's voice singing.

He stood still in the gloom of the hall, trying to catch the air that the voice was singing and gazing up at his wife. There was grace and mystery in her attitude as if she were a symbol of something. He asked himself what is a woman standing on the stairs in the shadow, listening to distant music, a symbol of. If he were a painter he would paint her in that attitude. Her blue felt hat would show off the bronze of her hair against the darkness and the dark panels of her skirt would show off the light ones. *Distant Music* he would call the picture if he were a painter.

The hall-door was closed; and Aunt Kate, Aunt Julia and Mary Jane came down the hall, still laughing.

—Well, isn't Freddy terrible? said Mary Jane. He's really terrible.

Gabriel said nothing but pointed up the stairs towards where his wife was standing. Now that the hall-door was closed the voice and the piano could be heard more clearly. Gabriel held up his hand for them to be silent. The song seemed to be in the old Irish tonality and the singer seemed uncertain both of his words and of his voice. The voice, made plaintive by distance and by the singer's hoarseness, faintly illuminated the cadence of the air with words expressing grief:

> *O, the rain falls on my heavy locks*
> *And the dew wets my skin,*
> *My babe lies cold . . .*

—O, exclaimed Mary Jane. It's Bartell D'Arcy singing and he wouldn't sing all the night. O, I'll get him to sing a song before he goes.

—O do, Mary Jane, said Aunt Kate.

Mary Jane brushed past the others and ran to the staircase but before she reached it the singing stopped and the piano was closed abruptly.

—O, what a pity! she cried. Is he coming down, Gretta?

Gabriel heard his wife answer yes and saw her come down towards them. A few steps behind her were Mr Bartell D'Arcy and Miss O'Callaghan.

—O, Mr D'Arcy, cried Mary Jane, it's downright mean of you to break off like that when we were all in raptures listening to you.

—I have been at him all the evening, said Miss O'Callaghan, and Mrs Conroy too and he told us he had a dreadful cold and couldn't sing.

—O, Mr D'Arcy, said Aunt Kate, now that was a great fib to tell.

—Can't you see that I'm as hoarse as a crow? said Mr D'Arcy roughly.

He went into the pantry hastily and put on his overcoat. The others, taken aback by his rude speech, could find nothing to say. Aunt Kate wrinkled her brows and made signs to the others to drop the subject. Mr D'Arcy stood swathing his neck carefully and frowning.

—It's the weather, said Aunt Julia, after a pause.

—Yes, everybody has colds, said Aunt Kate readily, everybody.

—They say, said Mary Jane, we haven't had snow like it for thirty years; and I read this morning in the newspapers that the snow is general all over Ireland.

—I love the look of snow, said Aunt Julia sadly.

—So do I, said Miss O'Callaghan. I think Christmas is never really Christmas unless we have the snow on the ground.

—But poor Mr D'Arcy doesn't like the snow, said Aunt Kate, smiling.

Mr D'Arcy came from the pantry, full swathed and buttoned, and in a repentant tone told them the history of his cold. Everyone gave him advice and said it was a great pity and urged him to be very careful of his throat in the night air. Gabriel watched his wife who did not join in the conversation. She was standing right under the dusty fanlight and the flame of the gas lit up the rich bronze of her hair which he had seen her drying at the fire a few days before. She was in the same attitude and seemed unaware of the talk about her. At last she turned towards them and Gabriel saw that there was colour on her cheeks and that her eyes were shining. A sudden tide of joy went leaping out of his heart.

—Mr D'Arcy, she said, what is the name of that song you were singing?

—It's called *The Lass of Aughrim*,[3] said Mr D'Arcy, but I couldn't remember it properly. Why? Do you know it?

—*The Lass of Aughrim*, she repeated. I couldn't think of the name.

—It's a very nice air, said Mary Jane. I'm sorry you were not in voice tonight.

—Now, Mary Jane, said Aunt Kate, don't annoy Mr D'Arcy. I won't have him annoyed.

Seeing that all were ready to start she shepherded them to the door where good-night was said:

—Well, good-night, Aunt Kate, and thanks for the pleasant evening.

—Good-night, Gabriel. Good-night, Gretta!

—Good-night, Aunt Kate, and thanks ever so much. Good-night, Aunt Julia.

—O, good-night, Gretta, I didn't see you.

—Good-night, Mr D'Arcy. Good-night, Miss O'Callaghan.

—Good-night, Miss Morkan.

—Good-night, again.

3. An Irish version of a ballad about a girl deserted by her lover whom she later tries to find, bringing the baby she had by him. Other versions are called *Love Gregory* and *Lord Gregory* (the name of the deserting lover), *The Lass of Lochryan*, and *The Lass of Ocram*.

—Good-night, all. Safe home.

—Good-night. Good-night.

The morning was still dark. A dull yellow light brooded over the houses and the river; and the sky seemed to be descending. It was slushy underfoot; and only streaks and patches of snow lay on the roofs, on the parapets of the quay and on the area railings. The lamps were still burning redly in the murky air and, across the river, the palace of the Four Courts stood out menacingly against the heavy sky.

She was walking on before him with Mr Bartell D'Arcy, her shoes in a brown parcel tucked under one arm and her hands holding her skirt up from the slush. She had no longer any grace of attitude but Gabriel's eyes were still bright with happiness. The blood went bounding along his veins; and the thoughts went rioting through his brain, proud, joyful, tender, valorous.

She was walking on before him so lightly and so erect that he longed to run after her noiselessly, catch her by the shoulders and say something foolish and affectionate into her ear. She seemed to him so frail that he longed to defend her against something and then to be alone with her. Moments of their secret life together burst like stars upon his memory. A heliotrope envelope was lying beside his breakfast-cup and he was caressing it with his hand. Birds were twittering in the ivy and the sunny web of the curtain was shimmering along the floor: he could not eat for happiness. They were standing on the crowded platform and he was placing a ticket inside the warm palm of her glove. He was standing with her in the cold, looking in through a grated window at a man making bottles in a roaring furnace. It was very cold. Her face, fragrant in the cold air, was quite close to his; and suddenly she called out to the man at the furnace:

—Is the fire hot, sir?

But the man could not hear her with the noise of the furnace. It was just as well. He might have answered rudely.

A wave of yet more tender joy escaped from his heart and went coursing in warm flood along his arteries. Like the tender fires of stars moments of their life together, that no one knew of or would ever know of, broke upon and illumined his memory. He longed to recall to her those moments, to make her forget the years of their dull existence together and remember only their moments of ecstasy. For the years, he felt, had not quenched his soul or hers. Their children, his writing, her household cares had not quenched all their souls' tender fire. In one letter that he had written to her then he had said: *Why is it that words like these seem to me so dull and cold? Is it because there is no word tender enough to be your name?*

Like distant music these words that he had written years before were borne towards him from the past. He longed to be alone with her. When the others had gone away, when he and she were in their room in the hotel, then they would be alone together. He would call her softly:

—Gretta!

Perhaps she would not hear at once: she would be undressing. Then something in his voice would strike her. She would turn and look at him. . . .

At the corner of Winetavern Street they met a cab. He was glad of its rattling noise as it saved him from conversation. She was looking out of the window and seemed tired. The others spoke only a few words, pointing out some building or street. The horse galloped along wearily under the murky morning sky, dragging his old rattling box after his heels, and Gabriel was again in a cab with her, galloping to catch the boat, galloping to their honeymoon.

As the cab drove across O'Connell[4] Bridge Miss O'Callaghan said:

—They say you never cross O'Connell Bridge without seeing a white horse.

—I see a white man this time, said Gabriel.

—Where? asked Mr Bartell D'Arcy.

Gabriel pointed to the statue, on which lay patches of snow. Then he nodded familiarly to it and waved his hand.

—Good-night, Dan, he said gaily.

When the cab drew up before the hotel Gabriel jumped out and, in spite of Mr Bartell D'Arcy's protest, paid the driver. He gave the man a shilling over his fare. The man saluted and said:

—A prosperous New Year to you, sir.

—The same to you, said Gabriel cordially.

She leaned for a moment on his arm in getting out of the cab and while standing at the curbstone, bidding the others good-night. She leaned lightly on his arm, as lightly as when she had danced with him a few hours before. He had felt proud and happy then, happy that she was his, proud of her grace and wifely carriage. But now, after the kindling again of so many memories, the first touch of her body, musical and strange and perfumed, sent through him a keen pang of lust. Under cover of her silence he pressed her arm closely to his side; and, as they stood at the hotel door, he felt that they had escaped from their lives and duties, escaped from home and friends and run away together with wild and radiant hearts to a new adventure.

An old man was dozing in a great hooded chair in the hall. He lit a candle in the office and went before them to the stairs. They followed him in silence, their feet falling in soft thuds on the thickly carpeted stairs. She mounted the stairs behind the porter, her head bowed in the ascent, her frail shoulders curved as with a burden, her skirt girt tightly about her. He could have flung his arms about her hips and held her still for his arms were trembling with desire to seize her and only the stress of his nails against the palms of his hands held the wild impulse of his body in check. The porter halted on the stairs to settle his guttering candle. They halted too on the steps below him. In the silence Gabriel could hear the falling of the molten wax into the tray and the thumping of his own heart against his ribs.

The porter led them along a corridor and opened a door. Then he set his unstable candle down on a toilet-table and asked at what hour they were to be called in the morning.

—Eight, said Gabriel.

The porter pointed to the tap of the electric-light and began a muttered apology but Gabriel cut him short.

—We don't want any light. We have light enough from the street. And I say, he added, pointing to the candle, you might remove that handsome article, like a good man.

The porter took up his candle again, but slowly for he was surprised by

---

4. Daniel O'Connell (1775–1847), Irish nationalist, statesman, and orator. His statue stands by O'Connell Bridge in Dublin.

such a novel idea. Then he mumbled good-night and went out. Gabriel shot the lock to.

A ghostly light from the street lamp lay in a long shaft from one window to the door. Gabriel threw his overcoat and hat on a couch and crossed the room towards the window. He looked down into the street in order that his emotion might calm a little. Then he turned and leaned against a chest of drawers with his back to the light. She had taken off her hat and cloak and was standing before a large swinging mirror, unhooking her waist.[5] Gabriel paused for a few moments, watching her, and then said:

—Gretta!

She turned away from the mirror slowly and walked along the shaft of light towards him. Her face looked so serious and weary that the words would not pass Gabriel's lips. No, it was not the moment yet.

—You looked tired, he said.

—I am a little, she answered.

—You don't feel ill or weak?

—No, tired: that's all.

She went on to the window and stood there, looking out. Gabriel waited again and then, fearing that diffidence was about to conquer him, he said abruptly:

—By the way, Gretta!

—What is it?

—You know that poor fellow Malins? he said quickly.

—Yes. What about him?

—Well, poor fellow, he's a decent sort of chap after all, continued Gabriel in a false voice. He gave me back that sovereign I lent him and I didn't expect it really. It's a pity he wouldn't keep away from that Browne, because he's not a bad fellow at heart.

He was trembling now with annoyance. Why did she seem so abstracted? He did not know how he could begin. Was she annoyed, too, about something? If she would only turn to him or come to him of her own accord! To take her as she was would be brutal. No, he must see some ardour in her eyes first. He longed to be master of her strange mood.

—When did you lend him the pound? she asked, after a pause.

Gabriel strove to restrain himself from breaking out into brutal language about the sottish Malins and his pound. He longed to cry to her from his soul, to crush her body against his, to overmaster her. But he said:

—O, at Christmas, when he opened that little Christmas-card shop in Henry Street.

He was in such a fever of rage and desire that he did not hear her come from the window. She stood before him for an instant, looking at him strangely. Then, suddenly raising herself on tiptoe and resting her hands lightly on his shoulders, she kissed him.

—You are a very generous person, Gabriel, she said.

Gabriel, trembling with delight at her sudden kiss and at the quaintness of her phrase, put his hands on her hair and began smoothing it back, scarcely touching it with his fingers. The washing had made it fine and brilliant. His heart was brimming over with happiness. Just when he was wishing

---

5. Shirtwaist; a tailored blouse.

for it she had come to him of her own accord. Perhaps her thoughts had been running with his. Perhaps she had felt the impetuous desire that was in him and then the yielding mood had come upon her. Now that she had fallen to him so easily he wondered why he had been so diffident.

He stood, holding her head between his hands. Then, slipping one arm swiftly about her body and drawing her towards him, he said softly:

—Gretta dear, what are you thinking about?

She did not answer nor yield wholly to his arm. He said again, softly:

—Tell me what it is, Gretta. I think I know what is the matter. Do I know?

She did not answer at once. Then she said in an outburst of tears:

—O, I am thinking about that song, *The Lass of Aughrim*.

She broke loose from him and ran to the bed and, throwing her arms across the bed-rail, hid her face. Gabriel stood stock-still for a moment in astonishment and then followed her. As he passed in the way of the cheval-glass he caught sight of himself in full length, his broad, well-filled shirt-front, the face whose expression always puzzled him when he saw it in a mirror and his glimmering gilt-rimmed eyeglasses. He halted a few paces from her and said:

—What about the song? Why does that make you cry?

She raised her head from her arms and dried her eyes with the back of her hand like a child. A kinder note than he had intended went into his voice.

—Why, Gretta? he asked.

—I am thinking about a person long ago who used to sing that song.

—And who was the person long ago? asked Gabriel, smiling.

—It was a person I used to know in Galway when I was living with my grandmother, she said.

The smile passed away from Gabriel's face. A dull anger began to gather again at the back of his mind and the dull fires of his lust began to glow angrily in his veins.

—Someone you were in love with? he asked ironically.

—It was a young boy I used to know, she answered, named Michael Furey. He used to sing that song, *The Lass of Aughrim*. He was very delicate.

Gabriel was silent. He did not wish her to think that he was interested in this delicate boy.

—I can see him so plainly, she said after a moment. Such eyes as he had: big dark eyes! And such an expression in them—an expression!

—O then, you were in love with him? said Gabriel.

—I used to go out walking with him, she said, when I was in Galway.

A thought flew across Gabriel's mind.

—Perhaps that was why you wanted to go to Galway with that Ivors girl? he said coldly.

She looked at him and asked in surprise:

—What for?

Her eyes made Gabriel feel awkward. He shrugged his shoulders and said:

—How do I know! To see him perhaps.

She looked away from him along the shaft of light towards the window in silence.

—He is dead, she said at length. He died when he was only seventeen. Isn't it a terrible thing to die so young as that?

—What was he? asked Gabriel, still ironically.

—He was in the gasworks, she said.

Gabriel felt humiliated by the failure of his irony and by the evocation of this figure from the dead, a boy in the gasworks. While he had been full of memories of their secret life together, full of tenderness and joy and desire, she had been comparing him in her mind with another. A shameful consciousness of his own person assailed him. He saw himself as a ludicrous figure, acting as a pennyboy for his aunts, a nervous well-meaning sentimentalist, orating to vulgarians and idealising his own clownish lusts, the pitiable fatuous fellow he had caught a glimpse of in the mirror. Instinctively he turned his back more to the light lest she might see the shame that burned upon his forehead.

He tried to keep up his tone of cold interrogation but his voice when he spoke was humble and indifferent.

—I suppose you were in love with this Michael Furey, Gretta, he said.

—I was great with him at that time, she said.

Her voice was veiled and sad. Gabriel, feeling now how vain it would be to try to lead her whither he had purposed, caressed one of her hands and said, also sadly:

—And what did he die of so young, Gretta? Consumption, was it?

—I think he died for me, she answered.

A vague terror seized Gabriel at this answer as if, at that hour when he had hoped to triumph, some impalpable and vindictive being was coming against him, gathering forces against him in its vague world. But he shook himself free of it with an effort of reason and continued to caress her hand. He did not question her again for he felt that she would tell him of herself. Her hand was warm and moist: it did not respond to his touch but he continued to caress it just as he had caressed her first letter to him that spring morning.

—It was in the winter, she said, about the beginning of the winter when I was going to leave my grandmother's and come up here to the convent. And he was ill at the time in his lodgings in Galway and wouldn't be let out and his people in Oughterard were written to. He was in decline, they said, or something like that. I never knew rightly.

She paused for a moment and sighed.

—Poor fellow, she said. He was very fond of me and he was such a gentle boy. We used to go out together, walking, you know, Gabriel, like the way they do in the country. He was going to study singing only for his health. He had a very good voice, poor Michael Furey.

—Well; and then? asked Gabriel.

—And then when it came to the time for me to leave Galway and come up to the convent he was much worse and I wouldn't be let see him so I wrote a letter saying I was going up to Dublin and would be back in the summer and hoping he would be better then.

She paused for a moment to get her voice under control and then went on:

—Then the night before I left I was in my grandmother's house in Nuns' Island, packing up, and I heard gravel thrown up against the window. The window was so wet I couldn't see so I ran downstairs as I was and slipped out the back into the garden and there was the poor fellow at the end of the garden, shivering.

—And did you not tell him to go back? asked Gabriel.

—I implored him to go home at once and told him he would get his death in the rain. But he said he did not want to live. I can see his eyes as well as well! He was standing at the end of the wall where there was a tree.

—And did he go home? asked Gabriel.

—Yes, he went home. And when I was only a week in the convent he died and he was buried in Oughterard where his people came from. O, the day I heard that, that he was dead!

She stopped, choking with sobs, and overcome by emotion, flung herself face downward on the bed, sobbing in the quilt. Gabriel held her hand for a moment longer, irresolutely, and then, shy of intruding on her grief, let it fall gently and walked quietly to the window.

She was fast asleep.

Gabriel, leaning on his elbow, looked for a few moments unresentfully on her tangled hair and half-open mouth, listening to her deep-drawn breath. So she had had that romance in her life: a man had died for her sake. It hardly pained him now to think how poor a part he, her husband, had played in her life. He watched her while she slept as though he and she had never lived together as man and wife. His curious eyes rested long upon her face and on her hair: and, as he thought of what she must have been then, in that time of her first girlish beauty, a strange friendly pity for her entered his soul. He did not like to say even to himself that her face was no longer beautiful but he knew that it was no longer the face for which Michael Furey had braved death.

Perhaps she had not told him all the story. His eyes moved to the chair over which she had thrown some of her clothes. A petticoat string dangled to the floor. One boot stood upright, its limp upper fallen down: the fellow of it lay upon its side. He wondered at his riot of emotions of an hour before. From what had it proceeded? From his aunt's supper, from his own foolish speech, from the wine and dancing, the merry-making when saying good-night in the hall, the pleasure of the walk along the river in the snow. Poor Aunt Julia! She, too, would soon be a shade with the shade of Patrick Morkan and his horse. He had caught that haggard look upon her face for a moment when she was singing *Arrayed for the Bridal*. Soon, perhaps, he would be sitting in that same drawing-room, dressed in black, his silk hat on his knees. The blinds would be drawn down and Aunt Kate would be sitting beside him, crying and blowing her nose and telling him how Julia had died. He would cast about in his mind for some words that might console her, and would find only lame and useless ones. Yes, yes: that would happen very soon.

The air of the room chilled his shoulders. He stretched himself cautiously along under the sheets and lay down beside his wife. One by one they were all becoming shades. Better pass boldly into that other world, in the full glory of some passion, than fade and wither dismally with age. He thought of how she who lay beside him had locked in her heart for so many years that image of her lover's eyes when he had told her that he did not wish to live.

Generous tears filled Gabriel's eyes. He had never felt like that himself towards any woman but he knew that such a feeling must be love. The tears gathered more thickly in his eyes and in the partial darkness he imagined he saw the form of a young man standing under a dripping tree. Other forms were near. His soul had approached that region where dwell the vast hosts of the dead. He was conscious of, but could not apprehend, their wayward and flickering existence. His own identity was fading out into a grey impalpable world: the solid world itself which these dead had one time reared and lived in was dissolving and dwindling.

A few light taps upon the pane made him turn to the window. It had begun to snow again. He watched sleepily the flakes, silver and dark, falling obliquely against the lamplight. The time had come for him to set out on his journey westward. Yes, the newspapers were right: snow was general all over Ireland. It was falling on every part of the dark central plain, on the treeless hills, falling softly upon the Bog of Allen[6] and, farther westward, softly falling into the dark mutinous Shannon waves. It was falling, too, upon every part of the lonely churchyard on the hill where Michael Furey lay buried. It lay thickly drifted on the crooked crosses and headstones, on the spears of the little gate, on the barren thorns. His soul swooned slowly as he heard the snow falling faintly through the universe and faintly falling, like the descent of their last end, upon all the living and the dead.

1914

From Ulysses[1]

[PROTEUS][2]

Ineluctable modality of the visible: at least that if no more, thought through my eyes.[3] Signatures of all things[4] I am here to read, seaspawn and seawrack, the nearing tide, that rusty boot. Snotgreen, bluesilver, rust: coloured signs. Limits of the diaphane.[5] But he adds: in bodies. Then he was aware of them bodies before of them coloured. How? By knocking his sconce

6. The name given to many separate peat bogs between the rivers Liffey (which runs through Dublin) and Shannon (which runs through the central plain of Ireland).

1. *Ulysses* was first published in book form on Feb. 2, 1922, Joyce's fortieth birthday. The text given here has been collated with the 1932 Odyssey Press edition.

2. *Proteus* is so titled because of the deliberate analogies that exist between it and the description of Proteus in *Odyssey* 4. (Joyce did not title any of the episodes in *Ulysses*, but the names are his; he used them in correspondence and in talk with friends.)

In Homer's *Odyssey*, Proteus is the changing sea god who continually alters his shape: when Telemachus, the son of Ulysses, asks Menelaus for help in finding his father, Menelaus tells him that he encountered Proteus by the seashore on the island of Pharos "in front of Egypt," and that, by holding on to him while he changed from one shape to another, he was able to force him to tell what had happened to Ulysses and the other Greek heroes of the Trojan war. In Joyce's narrative, Stephen Dedalus (who, like Homer's Telemachus, is looking for a father, but not in the literal "consubstantial" sense) is walking by the Dublin shore alone, "along Sandymount strand," speculating on the shifting shapes of things and the possibility of knowing truth by mere appearances.

First Stephen meditates on the "modality of the visible" and on the mystical notion that God writes his signature on all His works; then on the "modality of the audible," closing his eyes and trying to know reality simply through the sense of hearing. As he continues his walk, the people and objects he sees mingle in his thoughts with memories of his past relations with his family, of his schooldays, his residence in Paris from where he was recalled by his mother's fatal illness, his feeling of guilt about his mother's death (he had refused to kneel down and pray at her bedside, because he considered it would be a betrayal of his integrity as an unbeliever), and a variety of speculations about life and reality often derived from mystical works he had read "in the stagnant bay of Marsh's library" (in Dublin). The highly theoretical, inquiring, musing, speculating mind of Stephen is in sharp contrast to the practical, humane, sensual, concrete imagination of the book's real hero, Leopold Bloom, but there are also significant parallels between the streams of consciousness of the two. Some of the more important themes that emerge in Stephen's reverie are pointed out in the footnotes.

3. I.e., the sense of sight provides an unavoidable way ("ineluctable modality") of knowing reality, the knowledge thus provided being a kind of "thought through [the] eyes."

4. From Jakob Böhme (1575–1624), German mystic.

5. Transparency. Stephen is speculating on Aristotle's view of perception as developed in his *De Anima*.

against them, sure. Go easy. Bald he was and a millionaire, *maestro di color che sanno.*[6] Limit of the diaphane in. Why in? Diaphane, adiaphane.[7] If you can put your five fingers through it, it is a gate, if not a door. Shut your eyes and see.

Stephen closed his eyes to hear his boots crush crackling wrack and shells. You are walking through it howsomever. I am, a stride at a time. A very short space of time through very short times of space. Five, six: the *Nacheinander.*[8] Exactly: and that is the ineluctable modality of the audible. Open your eyes. No. Jesus! If I fell over a cliff that beetles o'er his base,[9] fell through the *Nebeneinander*[1] ineluctably. I am getting on nicely in the dark. My ash sword hangs at my side. Tap with it: they do.[2] My two feet in his boots[3] are at the ends of my legs, *nebeneinander.* Sounds solid: made by the mallet of *Los demiurgos.*[4] Am I walking into eternity along Sandymount strand? Crush, crack, crik, crick. Wild sea money. Dominie[5] Deasy kens them a'.

> *Won't you come to Sandymount,*
> *Madeline the mare?*

Rhythm begins, you see. I hear. A catalectic tetrameter[6] of iambs marching. No, agallop: *deline the mare.*

Open your eyes now. I will. One moment. Has all vanished since? If I open and am for ever in the black adiaphane. *Basta!*[7] I will see if I can see.

See now. There all the time without you: and ever shall be, world without end.

They came down the steps from Leahy's terrace prudently, *Frauenzimmer:*[8] and down the shelving shore flabbily, their splayed feet sinking in the silted sand. Like me, like Algy,[9] coming down to our mighty mother. Number one swung lourdily[1] her midwife's bag, the other's gamp[2] poked in the beach. From the liberties, out for the day. Mrs Florence MacCabe, relict of the late Patk MacCabe,[3] deeply lamented, of Bride Street. One of her sisterhood

6. There was a tradition that Aristotle was bald, with thin legs, small eyes, and a lisp. Aristotle is also traditionally supposed to have inherited considerable wealth and to have been presented with a fortune by his former pupil Alexander the Great. The Italian phrase is Dante's description of Aristotle in the *Inferno,* and means "the master of them that know."

7. What is not transparent (opposite of "diaphane").

8. "After one another." Stephen, with eyes shut, is now sensing reality through the sense of sound only: unlike sight, sound falls on the sense of hearing in chronological sequence, one sound after another.

9. "What if it tempt you toward the flood, my lord. / Or to the dreadful summit of the cliff / That beetles o'er his base into the sea" (*Hamlet* 1.4.69–71).

1. Beside one another.

2. Stephen is still walking with his eyes shut, tapping with his "ash sword" (the walking stick of ash wood he always carried), as "they" (i.e., blind people) do.

3. I.e., Buck Mulligan's. Stephen, lacking boots of his own, had borrowed a castoff pair of Mulligan's.

4. The Demiurge, or demiurgos, supernatural being who, according to the Gnostic philosophy, made the world in subordination to God. The mystical notion of the Demiurge who created the world haunts Stephen's mind; it is the Demiurge who writes his signature on created objects and whose

mallet fashioned them. The world, sensed by the ear only, "sounds solid," as though made by the Demiurge's hammer. The ending *-os* gives the word the appearance of a Spanish plural, so Joyce whimsically writes "Los demiurgos," which in Spanish would be "the demiurges."

5. Schoolmaster. Mr. Deasy was the headmaster of the school where Stephen taught (the previous episode has shown Stephen teaching). "Kens them a' ": knows them all; Stephen is putting Deasy into a mock-Scottish folk song.

6. The first of the two lines of popular verse that have come into Stephen's head consists metrically of four iambic feet ("tetrameter") with the last foot unlike the first, not defective ("catalectic").

7. Enough! (Italian).

8. Here, midwives. Stephen sees them coming from Leahy's Terrace, which runs by the beach.

9. Algernon Charles Swinburne, who wrote: "I will go back to the great sweet mother, / Mother and lover of men, the sea. / I will go down to her, I and none other" (*The Triumph of Time,* lines 1–3).

1. Heavily (coined by Stephen from the French *lourd*). Stephen, like Joyce, had studied modern languages at University College, Dublin, and his preoccupation with words and languages is part of his character as potential literary artist.

2. Umbrella; and perhaps reference to Mrs. Gamp, the nurse in Dickens's *Martin Chuzzlewit.*

3. Stephen imagines the first midwife is called Mrs. MacCabe. "Relict": widow.

lugged me squealing into life. Creation from nothing. What has she in the bag? A misbirth with a trailing navelcord, hushed in ruddy wool. The cords of all link back, strandentwining cable of all flesh. That is why mystic monks. Will you be as gods? Gaze in your *omphalos.* Hello. Kinch here. Put me on to Edenville. Aleph, alpha: nought, nought, one.[4]

Spouse and helpmate of Adam Kadmon: Heva,[5] naked Eve. She had no navel. Gaze. Belly without blemish, bulging big, a buckler of taut vellum, no, whiteheaped corn, orient and immortal, standing from everlasting to everlasting. Womb of sin.[6]

Wombed in sin darkness I was too, made not begotten. By them, the man with my voice and my eyes and a ghostwoman with ashes on her breath.[7] They clasped and sundered, did the coupler's will. From before the ages He willed me and now may not will me away or ever. A *lex eterna*[8] stays about Him. Is that then the divine substance wherein Father and Son are consubstantial? Where is poor dear Arius[9] to try conclusions? Warring his life long on the contransmagnificandjewbangtantiality.[1] Illstarred heresiarch.[2] In a Greek watercloset he breathed his last: *euthanasia.* With beaded mitre and with crozier, stalled upon his throne, widower of a widowed see, with upstiffed omophorion, with clotted hinderparts.

Airs romped round him, nipping and eager airs. They are coming, waves. The whitemaned seahorses, champing, brightwindbridled, the steeds of Mananaan.[3]

I mustn't forget his letter for the press. And after? The Ship, half twelve. By the way go easy with that money like a good young imbecile. Yes, I must.[4]

---

4. Stephen is speculating on the mystical significance of the navel cord, seeing it as linking the generations, the combined navel cords stretching back to Adam and Eve. A mystic gazed in his *omphalos* (navel) to make contact with the first man. Stephen thinks of himself ("Kinch," his nickname) calling up Adam in "Edenville" through his navel, using the line of linked navel cords as a telephone line. Adam's telephone number, "Aleph, alpha: nought, nought, one," begins with the first letters of the Hebrew and of the Greek alphabet to suggest the great primeval number.

5. Hebrew for Eve. Because she was not born in the regular way, but created from Adam's rib, she had no navel. "Adam Kadman": Adam the Beginner, so called in Hebrew cabalistic literature of the Middle Ages.

6. Stephen is led, through reflection on Eve's navelless "belly without blemish," to a recollection of the description of the original Eden (Paradise) by Thomas Traherne (ca. 1637–1674), from whose prose *Centuries of Meditation* he quotes: "The corn was orient and immortal wheat, which should never be reaped, nor was ever sown. I thought it had stood from everlasting to everlasting." But immediately afterward Stephen reflects that such language is inappropriate to Eve's body, as hers was the "womb of sin"—i.e., she first ate the fatal apple and brought forth sin.

7. Stephen is haunted by thoughts of his mother in this guise.

8. Eternal law. God's eternal law, Stephen reflects, willed his birth from the beginning. He then goes on to speculate on the nature of the divine substance and whether God the Father and

God the Son are of the same substance ("consubstantial").

9. Third-century theologian who "tried conclusions" on this matter, maintaining that Christ was less divine than God (Arius's views were condemned as heretical by the Council of Nicaea in 325).

1. Ironic "portmanteau word" made up of terms connected with the Arian controversy—"consubstantial," "transubstantial" (of a substance that changes into another)—and with the facts of Christ's nature (e.g., "Jew"; Jesus was a Jew, as Leopold Bloom in a later episode reminds an anti-Semitic Irishman).

2. Arch-heretic. Arius died suddenly in Constantinople in 336. He was never a bishop, and Stephen's image of him at the moment of death in full episcopal attire seems to combine recollections of other early "heresiarchs." In an earlier reverie Stephen had conjured up in his mind "a horde of heresies fleeing with mitres awry." These heretics are connected in Stephen's mind with argument about the relation between God the Father and God the Son and so with the problem of the true nature of paternity, which haunts him constantly.

3. Mananaan MacLir, Celtic sea god; his steeds are the "whitemaned seahorses." ("White horses" is still the name in Britain for the white foam on top of waves.)

4. Mr. Deasy had given Stephen a letter to the press to be taken to the newspaper office. After that he has an appointment with Mulligan at The Ship, a tavern. "That money" is Mr. Deasy's last payment to him.

His pace slackened. Here. Am I going to aunt Sara's or not? My consubstantial father's voice. Did you see anything of your artist brother Stephen lately? No? Sure he's not down in Strasburg terrace with his aunt Sally? Couldn't he fly a bit higher than that, eh? And and and and tell us Stephen, how is uncle Si? O weeping God, the things I married into. De boys up in de hayloft. The drunken little costdrawer and his brother, the cornet player. Highly respectable gondoliers. And skeweyed Walter sirring his father, no less. Sir. Yes, sir. No, sir. Jesus wept: and no wonder, by Christ.[5]

I pull the wheezy bell of their shuttered cottage: and wait. They take me for a dun, peer out from a coign of vantage.[6]

—It's Stephen, sir.

—Let him in. Let Stephen in.

A bolt drawn back and Walter welcomes me.

—We thought you were someone else.

In his broad bed nuncle Richie, pillowed and blanketed, extends over the hillock of his knees a sturdy forearm. Cleanchested. He has washed the upper moiety.

—Morrow, nephew.

He lays aside the lapboard whereon he drafts his bills of costs for the eyes of master Goff and master Shapland Tandy, filing consents and common searches and a writ of *Duces Tecum.*[7] A bogoak frame over his bald head: Wilde's *Requiescat.*[8] The drone of his misleading whistle brings Walter back.

—Yes, sir?

—Malt[9] for Richie and Stephen, tell mother. Where is she?

—Bathing Crissie, sir.

Papa's little bedpal. Lump of love.

—No, uncle Richie . . .

—Call me Richie. Damn your lithia water. It lowers. Whusky!

—Uncle Richie, really. . . .

—Sit down or by the law Harry I'll knock you down.

Walter squints vainly for a chair.

—He has nothing to sit down on, sir.

—He has nowhere to put it, you mug. Bring in our chippendale chair. Would you like a bite of something? None of your damned lawdeedaw air here: the rich of a rasher fried with a herring? Sure? So much the better. We have nothing in the house but backache pills.

All'erta![1] He drones bars of Ferrando's *aria di sortita.* The grandest number, Stephen, in the whole opera. Listen.

His tuneful whistle sounds again, finely shaded, with rushes of the air, his fists bigdrumming on his padded knees.

This wind is sweeter.

5. Stephen has been wondering whether to call on his uncle and aunt, Richie and Sara Goulding. He imagines his father interrogating him about the visit as if he had gone; he then pictures his cousins asking after his father, Simon Dedalus (his cousins' "uncle Si"). Simon is contemptuous of his wife's relations (Sara Goulding is his wife's sister). Stephen knows that any mention of them will bring on the familiar abuse of "the things I married into"—at best "highly respectable gondoliers" (from Gilbert and Sullivan's opera *The Gondoliers*). The scene that follows is also Stephen's purely imaginary picture of what the visit would be like.

6. Favorable corner.

7. You shall take with you. Opening words of a search warrant. Goulding was a law clerk with Messrs. Goff and Tandy.

8. Poem by Oscar Wilde.

9. Whiskey.

1. Look out! The first words of the *aria di sortita* (aria sung by a character about to leave the stage) sung by Ferrando, captain of the guard, in Verdi's opera *Il Trovatore.*

Houses of decay, mine, his and all. You told the Clongowes gentry you had an uncle a judge and an uncle a general in the army.[2] Come out of them, Stephen. Beauty is not there. Nor in the stagnant bay of Marsh's library where you read the fading prophecies of Joachim Abbas.[3] For whom? The hundredheaded rabble of the cathedral close.[4] A hater of his kind ran from them to the wood of madness, his mane foaming in the moon, his eyeballs stars. Houyhnhnm, horsenostrilled.[5] The oval equine faces, Temple, Buck Mulligan, Foxy Campbell. Lantern jaws. Abbas[6] father, furious dean, what offence laid fire to their brains? Paff! *Descende, calve, ut nimium decalveris.*[7] A garland of grey hair on his comminated head see him me clambering down to the footpace (*descende*), clutching a monstrance, basiliskeyed. Get down, bald poll! A choir gives back menace and echo, assisting about the altar's horns, the snorted Latin of jackpriests moving burly in their albs, tonsured and oiled and gelded, fat with the fat of kidneys of wheat.

And at the same instant perhaps a priest round the corner is elevating it. Dringdring! And two streets off another locking it into a pyx.[8] Dringadring! And in a ladychapel another taking housel all to his own cheek. Dringdring! Down, up, forward, back. Dan Occam[9] thought of that, invincible doctor. A misty English morning the imp hypostasis tickled his brain. Bringing his host down and kneeling he heard twine with his second bell the first bell in the transept (he is lifting his) and, rising, heard (now I am lifting) their two bells (he is kneeling) twang in diphthong.

Cousin Stephen, you will never be a saint.[1] Isle of saints.[2] You were awfully holy, weren't you? You prayed to the Blessed Virgin that you might not have a red nose. You prayed to the devil in Serpentine avenue that the fubsy widow in front might lift her clothes still more from the wet street. *O si, certo!*[3] Sell your soul for that, do, dyed rags pinned round a squaw. More tell me, more still! On the top of the Howth tram alone crying to the rain: *Naked women!* What about that, eh?

What about what? What else were they invented for?

Reading two pages apiece of seven books every night, eh? I was young. You bowed to yourself in the mirror, stepping forward to applause earnestly, striking face. Hurray for the Goddamned idiot! Hray! No-one saw: tell no-one. Books you were going to write with letters for titles. Have you read his

2. Stephen, reflecting on the steady social decline of his family, is remembering that, while at school at Clongowes Wood College, he had pretended to have important relations.

3. Abbot Joachim of Floris (the monastery of San Giovanni in Fiore, Italy), 12th-century mystic and theologian, whose prophetic work *Expositio in Apocalypsin* Stephen (i.e., Joyce) had read in Marsh's Library.

4. I.e., the precinct of a cathedral (Marsh's Library is in the close of St. Patrick's Cathedral).

5. St. Patrick's Close has recalled Jonathan Swift (who was dean of St. Patrick's). Stephen remembers Swift's misanthropy (he was "a hater of his kind") and his creation of the Houyhnhnms (noble horses) in book 4 of *Gulliver's Travels*. Then he thinks of people he knew who have horse faces.

6. Literally: father.

7. Go down, bald-head, lest you become even balder. This sentence, from Joachim's *Concordia* of the Old and New Testaments, is based on the mocking cry of the children to the prophet Elisha

(2 Kings 2.23: "Go up, thou bald head"); Joachim saw Elisha as a forerunner of St. Benedict—both had shaven or baldish heads. Stephen goes on to imagine the "comminated" (threatened) head of Joachim descending, clutching a "monstrance" (receptacle in which the Host [consecrated bread or wafer] is exposed for adoration), in the midst of a nightmare church service.

8. Vessel in which the Host is kept. Stephen is imagining such a service, with himself officiating (he almost became a priest).

9. William of Occam or Ockham ("Dan" means "master"), 14th-century English theologian, who held that the individual thing is the reality and its name, the universal, an abstraction; he was concerned with hypostasis—the essential part of a thing as distinct from its attributes.

1. A parody of the words of Dryden to his distant relative Swift: Cousin, you will never make a poet.

2. Ireland was called "*insula sanctorum*," (isle of saints) in the Middle Ages.

3. Oh yes, certainly!

F? O yes, but I prefer Q. Yes, but W is wonderful. O yes, W. Remember your epiphanies[4] on green oval leaves, deeply deep, copies to be sent if you died to all the great libraries of the world, including Alexandria? Someone was to read them there after a few thousand years, a mahamanvantara.[5] Pico della Mirandola[6] like. Ay, very like a whale.[7] When one reads these strange pages of one long gone one feels that one is at one with one who once . . .

The grainy sand had gone from under his feet. His boots trod again a damp crackling mast, razorshells, squeaking pebbles, that on the unnumbered pebbles beats, wood sieved by the shipworm, lost Armada. Unwholesome sandflats waited to suck his treading soles, breathing upward sewage breath. He coasted them, walking warily. A porterbottle stood up, stogged to its waist, in the cakey sand dough. A sentinel: isle of dreadful thirst.[8] Broken hoops on the shore; at the land a maze of dark cunning nets; farther away chalkscrawled backdoors and on the higher beach a dryingline with two crucified shirts. Ringsend: wigwams of brown steersmen and master mariners. Human shells.

He halted. I have passed the way to aunt Sara's. Am I not going there? Seems not. No-one about. He turned northeast and crossed the firmer sand towards the Pigeonhouse.[9]

—*Qui vous a mis dans cette fichue position?*

—*C'est le pigeon, Joseph.*

Patrice, home on furlough, lapped warm milk with me in the bar MacMahon. Son of the wild goose, Kevin Egan of Paris. My father's a bird, he lapped the sweet *lait chaud* with pink young tongue, plump bunny's face. Lap, *lapin.* He hopes to win in the *gros lots.* About the nature of women he read in Michelet. But he must send me *La Vie de Jésus* by M. Léo Taxil. Lent it to his friend.[1]

—*C'est tordant, vous savez. Moi, je suis socialiste. Je ne crois pas en l'existence de Dieu. Faut pas le dire à mon père.*

—*Il croit?*

—*Mon père, oui.*

---

4. Joyce's term for the prose poems he wrote as a young man. An epiphany, he said, was the sudden "revelation of the whatness of a thing"—of a gesture, a phrase, or a thought which he had experienced; he attempted to express, in the writing, the moment at which "the soul of the commonest object . . . seems to us radiant." Stephen's recollection of early and exotic literary ambitions is drawn directly from Joyce's own ambitions at the same age.
5. Cycle of change and recurrence, in Indian mystical thought. It is connected in Stephen's mind with the constant ebb and flow of the sea by which he is walking.
6. Fifteenth-century mystical philosopher; his *Heptaplus* is a mystical account of the creation, much influenced by Jewish cabalistic thought.
7. Polonius to Hamlet (*Hamlet* 3.2.399) with reference to the changing shape of a cloud. The Protean theme of constant change, of ebb and flow, and of metempsychosis (i.e., transmigration of souls: a major theme in *Ulysses*), is working in Stephen's mind. The following sentence is a parody of an elegant, condescending modern essay on Pico or some other early mystic.
8. The atmosphere of the sandflats reminds Stephen of a desert island where people die of thirst. (The island of Pharos, where Menelaus found Proteus, was an "island of dreadful hunger.")
9. The Pigeon House in Ringsend, an old structure built on a breakwater in Dublin Bay and which in the course of time has served a great variety of purposes, suggests to Stephen the Dove, which is the symbol of the Holy Spirit, and this in turn suggests an irreverent dialogue (supposedly between Joseph and Mary when Mary is found to be pregnant: "Who has got you into this wretched condition?" "It was the pigeon [i.e., the Holy Dove], Joseph"). This he had picked up in Paris from the blasphemous M. Léo Taxil, whose book *La Vie de Jésus* ("The Life of Jesus") is mentioned in the next paragraph.
1. Stephen had first met Léo Taxil through Patrice, the son of "Kevin Egan of Paris," who in real life was the exiled nationalist Joseph Casey. The phrase "my father's a bird" comes from *The Song of the Cheerful Jesus,* a blasphemous poem by Buck Mulligan (actually Oliver Gogarty, who really wrote the poem); Stephen recalls Patrice reciting it as he drank warm milk ("*lait chaud*"), lapping it like a "*lapin*" (rabbit), and expressing the hope that he would win something substantial in the French national lottery (*gros lot:* "first prize"). Jules Michelet (1798–1874), French historian.

Schluss.[2] He laps.

My Latin quarter hat. God, we simply must dress the character. I want puce gloves. You were a student, weren't you? Of what in the other devil's name? Paysayenn. P. C. N., you know: *physiques, chimiques et naturelles.*[3] Aha. Eating your groatsworth of *mou en civet,*[4] fleshpots of Egypt, elbowed by belching cabmen. Just say in the most natural tone: when I was in Paris, *boul'Mich',*[5] I used to. Yes, used to carry punched tickets to prove an alibi if they arrested you for murder somewhere. Justice. On the night of the seventeenth of February 1904 the prisoner was seen by two witnesses. Other fellow did it: other me. Hat, tie, overcoat, nose. *Lui, c'est moi.*[6] You seem to have enjoyed yourself.

Proudly walking. Whom were you trying to walk like? Forget: a dispossessed. With mother's money order, eight shillings, the banging door of the post office slammed in your face by the usher. Hunger toothache. *Encore deux minutes.* Look clock. Must get. *Fermé.* Hired dog! Shoot him to bloody bits with a bang shotgun, bits man spattered walls all brass buttons. Bits all khrrrrklak in place clack back. Not hurt? O, that's all right. Shake hands. See what I meant, see? O, that's all right. Shake a shake. O, that's all only all right.[7]

You were going to do wonders, what? Missionary to Europe after fiery Columbanus. Fiacre and Scotus on their creepystools[8] in heaven spilt from their pintpots, loudlatinlaughing: *Euge! Euge!*[9] Pretending to speak broken English as you dragged your valise, porter threepence, across the slimy pier at Newhaven. *Comment?* Rich booty you brought back; *Le Tutu,* five tattered numbers of *Pantalon Blanc et Culotte Rouge,*[1] a blue French telegram, curiosity to show:

—Mother dying come home father.[2]

The aunt thinks you killed your mother. That's why she won't.[3]

> *Then here's a health to Mulligan's aunt*
> *And I'll tell you the reason why.*
> *She always kept things decent in*
> *The Hannigan famileye.*

His feet marched in sudden proud rhythm over the sand furrows, along by the boulders of the south wall. He stared at them proudly, piled stone

2. End. Conversation between Stephen and Patrice: "It's screamingly funny, you know. I'm a socialist myself. I don't believe in the existence of God. Mustn't tell my father." "He is a believer?" "My father, yes."

3. I.e., the faculty of physics, chemistry, and biology at the École de Médecine in Paris, where Stephen, like Joyce, took a premedical course for a short time. The faculty was popularly known as "P. C. N." (pronounced "Paysayenn").

4. Stew.

5. Popular Parisian abbreviation for the Boulevard Saint Michel.

6. "He is me"—a parody of Louis XIV's remark "*L'état c'est moi*" (I am the state).

7. A recollection of the occasion when, desperate for money, Stephen had received a money order for eight shillings from his mother. Afflicted with both hunger and toothache, he had gone to cash it at the post office—which was closed, even though, as he expostulated with the man at the

door, there were still two minutes (*"encore deux minutes"*) until the official closing time. In his retrospective rage he imagines himself shooting the "hired dog" to bits, and then in a revulsion of feeling has a mental reconciliation with him.

8. Low stools. "Columbanus": 6th-century Irish missionary on the Continent. Fiacre was a 6th-century Irish saint. Duns Scotus (ca. 1265–1308), scholastic theologian and philosopher.

9. Well done!

1. Like the preceding name, name of French popular periodical.

2. This telegram was actually received by Joyce in Paris.

3. Stephen recalls Buck Mulligan's telling him that his (Mulligan's) aunt disapproved of Stephen because, by refusing to pray at his dying mother's bedside, he had hastened her death. Stephen then tries to laugh away his feeling of guilt by quoting mentally a (slightly parodied) verse of a popular song.

mammoth skulls. Gold light on sea, on sand, on boulders. The sun is there, the slender trees, the lemon houses.

Paris rawly waking, crude sunlight on her lemon streets. Moist pith of farls[4] of bread, the froggreen wormwood, her matin incense, court the air. Belluomo rises from the bed of his wife's lover's wife, the kerchiefed housewife is astir, a saucer of acetic acid in her hand. In Rodot's Yvonne and Madeleine newmake their tumbled beauties, shattering with gold teeth *chaussons* of pastry, their mouths yellowed with the *pus* of *flan breton*.[5] Faces of Paris men go by, their wellpleased pleasers, curled *conquistadores*.[6]

Noon slumbers. Kevin Egan rolls gunpowder cigarettes through fingers smeared with printer's ink,[7] sipping his green fairy as Patrice his white. About us gobblers fork spiced beans down their gullets. *Un demi setier!*[8] A jet of coffee steam from the burnished caldron. She serves me at his beck. *Il est irlandais. Hollandais? Non fromage. Deux irlandais, nous, Irlande, vous savez? Ah, oui!*[9] She thought you wanted a cheese *hollandais*. Your postprandial, do you know that word? Postprandial. There was a fellow I knew once in Barcelona, queer fellow, used to call it his postprandial. Well: *slainte!*[1] Around the slabbed tables the tangle of wined breaths and grumbling gorges. His breath hangs over our saucestained plates, the green fairy's fang thrusting between his lips. Of Ireland, the Dalcassians, of hopes, conspiracies, of Arthur Griffith now.[2] To yoke me as his yokefellow, our crimes our common cause. You're your father's son. I know the voice. His fustian shirt, sanguineflowered, trembles its Spanish tassels at his secrets. M. Drumont,[3] famous journalist, Drumont, know what he called queen Victoria? Old hag with the yellow teeth. *Vieille ogresse* with the *dents jaunes*. Maud Gonne, beautiful woman, *la Patrie*, M. Millevoye, Félix Faure,[4] know how he died? Licentious men. The *froeken, bonne à tout faire*,[5] who rubs male nakedness in the bath at Upsala. *Moi faire*, she said, *tous les messieurs*.[6] Not this *monsieur*, I said. Most licentious custom. Bath a most private thing. I wouldn't let my brother, not even my own brother, most lascivious thing. Green eyes, I see you. Fang, I feel. Lascivious people.

The blue fuse burns deadly between hands and burns clear. Loose tobacco shreds catch fire: a flame and acrid smoke light our corner. Raw facebones under his peep of day boy's hat. How the head centre got away, authentic version. Got up as a young bride, man, veil, orangeblossoms, drove out the road to Malahide. Did, faith. Of lost leaders, the betrayed, wild escapes. Disguises, clutched at, gone not here.[7]

Spurned lover. I was a strapping young gossoon[8] at that time, I tell you.

4. Thin circular cakes.
5. Memories of a restaurant in Paris. "*Chaussons*": pastry turnovers. "*Flan breton*": pastry filled with custard.
6. Conquerors (Spanish).
7. Egan (i.e., Joseph Casey) became a typesetter for the Parisian edition of the *New York Herald*.
8. Abusive Parisian slang for a liquid measure (about one-fourth of a liter)—here, presumably, of wine or beer.
9. He is Irish. Dutch? Not cheese. We are two Irishmen, Ireland, you understand? Oh, yes!
1. Your health! (Gaelic).
2. Two extremes of Irish history. From the Dalcassian line came the early kings of Munster (from 300 C.E. on). Arthur Griffith (1872–1922) was an Irish revolutionary leader, founder of the Sinn Fein ("Ourselves Alone") movement.
3. Edouard Drumont (1844–1917), French politician and bitter anti-Semite.
4. Nineteenth-century French statesman. Maud Gonne, the beautiful actress and violent Irish nationalist whom Yeats loved. "*La Patrie*": journal edited by Lucien Millevoye, French nationalist deputy and Maud Gonne's lover.
5. Maid-of-all-work (French). "*Froeken*": *fröken*, unmarried woman or Miss (Swedish).
6. I do all the gentlemen (in broken French).
7. Another Protean theme of change. Egan had told Stephen of his cousin James Stephens's escape from prison disguised as a bride (Stephens was really the cousin of Casey, the original of Egan in this episode).
8. Boy.

I'll show you my likeness one day. I was, faith. Lover, for her love he prowled with colonel Richard Burke, tanist of his sept,[9] under the walls of Clerken-well[1] and, crouching, saw a flame of vengeance hurl them upward in the fog. Shattered glass and toppling masonry. In gay Paree he hides, Egan of Paris, unsought by any save by me. Making his day's stations, the dingy printing-case, his three taverns, the Montmartre lair he sleeps short night in, *rue de la Goutte-d'Or*, damascened with flyblown faces of the gone. Loveless, land-less, wifeless. She is quite nicey comfy without her outcast man,[2] madame in *rue Gît-le-Cœur*, canary and two buck lodgers. Peachy cheeks, a zebra skirt, frisky as a young thing's. Spurned and undespairing. Tell Pat[3] you saw me, won't you? I wanted to get poor Pat a job one time. *Mon fils*, soldier of France. I taught him to sing *The boys of Kilkenny are stout roaring blades.* Know that old lay? I taught Patrice that. Old Kilkenny: saint Canice, Strong-bow's castle on the Nore.[4] Goes like this. O, O. He takes me, Napper Tandy,[5] by the hand.

> O, O the boys of
> Kilkenny . . .

Weak wasting hand on mine. They have forgotten Kevin Egan, not he them. Remembering thee, O Sion.[6]

He had come nearer the edge of the sea and wet sand slapped his boots. The new air greeted him, harping in wild nerves, wind of wild air of seeds of brightness. Here, I am not walking out to the Kish lightship, am I? He stood suddenly, his feet beginning to sink slowly in the quaking soil. Turn back.

Turning, he scanned the shore south, his feet sinking again slowly in new sockets. The cold domed room of the tower[7] waits. Through the barbicans[8] the shafts of light are moving ever, slowly ever as my feet are sinking, creep-ing duskward over the dial floor. Blue dusk, nightfall, deep blue night. In the darkness of the dome they wait, their pushedback chairs, my obelisk valise, around a board of abandoned platters. Who to clear it? He has the key.[9] I will not sleep there when this night comes. A shut door of a silent tower, entombing their blind bodies, the panthersahib and his pointer.[1] Call: no answer. He lifted his feet up from the suck and turned back by the mole of boulders. Take all, keep all. My soul walks with me, form of forms. So in the moon's midwatches I pace the path above the rocks, in sable silvered, hearing Elsinore's tempting flood.[2]

9. Clan. "Tanist": successor-apparent to a Celtic chief.
1. District in east-central London. Stephen is recalling Egan's conversation about the Fenian vio-lence in London that necessitated his fleeing to France.
2. I.e., Egan's wife, who is "quite nicey comfy" in the metaphorical "rue Gît-le-Cœur" (i.e., the street where the heart lies dead) back home in Ireland.
3. Patrice, Egan's son.
4. Kilkenny is called after the Irish Saint Canice (its Irish name is Cill Chainnigh), on the river Nore, where Strongbow (the second earl of Pem-broke, who invaded Ireland in the 12th century), had his stronghold.
5. James Napper Tandy (1740–1803), Irish revo-lutionary hero of the song "The Wearing of the Green."
6. Cf. Psalm 137.1 (in the King James Bible): "we

wept, when we remembered Zion." But "Zion" in the Douay (Roman Catholic) Bible, is spelled "Sion," and the Book of Common Prayer has "When we remembered thee, O Sion."
7. Where Stephen lived with Buck Mulligan.
8. Outworks of a castle.
9. In the preceding episode, Mulligan asked for and got the key of the tower from Stephen.
1. I.e., Mulligan and the Englishman Haines, who lived with Stephen in the tower. Stephen thinks of them as calling for him in vain, because he has decided not to return.
2. Cf. *Hamlet* 1.2.242, where the ghost of Ham-let's murdered father is described as having a beard of "sable silver'd." Allusions to *Hamlet* occur often in *Ulysses*; in a later episode Stephen expounds the theory that Shakespeare is to be identified not with Hamlet himself but with his betrayed father.

The flood is following me. I can watch it flow past from here. Get back then by the Poolbeg road to the strand there. He climbed over the sedge and eely oarweeds and sat on a stool of rock, resting his ashplant in a grike.[3]

A bloated carcass of a dog lay lolled on bladderwrack. Before him the gunwale of a boat, sunk in sand. *Un coche ensablé*[4] Louis Veuillot called Gautier's[5] prose. These heavy sands are language tide and wind have silted here. And there, the stoneheaps of dead builders, a warren of weasel rats. Hide gold there. Try it. You have some. Sands and stones. Heavy of the past. Sir Lout's toys. Mind you don't get one bang on the ear. I'm the bloody well gigant rolls all them bloody well boulders, bones for my steppingstones. Fee-fawfum. I zmellz de bloodz oldz an Iridzman.[6]

A point, live dog, grew into sight running across the sweep of sand. Lord, is he going to attack me? Respect his liberty. You will not be master of others or their slave. I have my stick. Sit tight. From farther away, walking shore-ward across from the crested tide, figures, two. The two maries. They have tucked it safe mong the bulrushes. Peekaboo. I see you. No, the dog. He is running back to them. Who?

Galleys of the Lochlanns[7] ran here to beach, in quest of prey, their blood-beaked prows riding low on a molten pewter surf. Dane vikings, torcs of tomahawks aglitter on their breasts when Malachi wore the collar of gold. A school of turlehide whales stranded in hot noon, spouting, hobbling in the shallows. Then from the starving cagework city a horde of jerkined dwarfs, my people, with flayers' knives, running, scaling, hacking in green blubbery whalemeat. Famine, plague and slaughters. Their blood is in me, their lusts my waves. I moved among them on the frozen Liffey, that I, a changeling, among the spluttering resin fires. I spoke to no-one: none to me.

The dog's bark ran towards him, stopped, ran back.[8] Dog of my enemy. I just simply stood pale, silent, bayed about. *Terribilia meditans.*[9] A primrose doublet, fortune's knave, smiled on my fear. For that are you pining, the bark of their applause? Pretenders: live their lives. The Bruce's brother, Thomas Fitzgerald, silken knight, Perkin Warbeck, York's false scion, in breeches of silk of whiterose ivory, wonder of a day, and Lambert Simnel, with a tail of nans and sutlers, a scullion crowned.[1] All kings' sons. Paradise of pretenders then and now. He saved men from drowning[2] and you shake at a cur's yelp-ing. But the courtiers who mocked Guido in Or san Michele were in their own house. House of . . . We don't want any of your medieval abstrusiosities. Would you do what he did? A boat would be near, a lifebuoy. *Natürlich,*[3] put there for you. Would you or would you not? The man that was drowned nine days ago off Maiden's rock. They are waiting for him now. The truth, spit it out. I would want to. I would try. I am not a strong swimmer. Water cold

3. Chink, crevice.
4. A coach embedded in the sand.
5. Théophile Gautier, 19th-century French poet, novelist, and critic. Veuillot, 19th-century French journalist.
6. Stephen is thinking of the boulders on the shore as the work of a large but clumsy giant ("Sir Lout"). "They [Sir Lout and his family] were giants right enough. . . . My Sir Lout has rocks in his mouth instead of teeth. He articulates badly" (Joyce to Frank Budgen, reported in Budgen's *James Joyce and the Making of Ulysses,* 1934).
7. Scandinavians (Gaelic). Stephen is meditating

on the Vikings who settled Dublin; it was here that they came ashore, he thinks.
8. The dog in this and subsequent paragraphs keeps changing in appearance; he "is the mummer among beasts—the Protean animal" (Joyce to Budgen). Joyce himself was afraid of dogs.
9. Meditating terrible things.
1. Stephen is meditating on pretenders (i.e., false claimants): the names here are those of pretenders who have figured in English history. This is the Proteus theme again—disguises and changes.
2. Mulligan had saved a man from drowning.
3. Of course.

soft. When I put my face into it in the basin at Clongowes. Can't see! Who's behind me? Out quickly, quickly! Do you see the tide flowing quickly in on all sides, sheeting the lows of sands quickly, shellcocoacoloured? If I had land under my feet. I want his life still to be his, mine to be mine. A drowning man. His human eyes scream to me out of horror of his death. I . . . With him together down . . . I could not save her.[4] Waters: bitter death: lost.

A woman and a man. I see her skirties. Pinned up, I bet.

Their dog ambled about a bank of dwindling sand, trotting, sniffing on all sides. Looking for something lost in a past life. Suddenly he made off like a bounding hare, ears flung back, chasing the shadow of a lowskimming gull. The man's shrieked whistle struck his limp ears. He turned, bounded back, came nearer, trotted on twinkling shanks. On a field tenney a buck, trippant, proper, unattired.[5] At the lacefringe of the tide he halted with stiff forehoofs, seawardpointed ears. His snout lifted barked at the wavenoise, herds of seamorse. They serpented towards his feet, curling, unfurling many crests, every ninth, breaking, plashing, from far, from farther out, waves and waves.

Cocklepickers.[6] They waded a little way in the water and, stooping, soused their bags, and, lifting them again, waded out. The dog yelped running to them, reared up and pawed them, dropping on all fours, again reared up at them with mute bearish fawning. Unheeded he kept by them as they came towards the drier sand, a rag of wolf's tongue redpanting from his jaws. His speckled body ambled ahead of them and then loped off at a calf's gallop. The carcass lay on his path. He stopped, sniffed, stalked round it, brother, nosing closer, went round it, sniffing rapidly like a dog all over the dead dog's bedraggled fell. Dogskull, dogsniff, eyes on the ground, moves to one great goal. Ah, poor dogsbody. Here lies poor dogsbody's body.

—Tatters! Outofthat, you mongrel.

The cry brought him skulking back to his master and a blunt bootless kick sent him unscathed across a spit of sand, crouched in flight. He slunk back in a curve. Doesn't see me. Along by the edge of the mole he lolloped, dawdled, smelt a rock and from under a cocked hindleg pissed against it. He trotted forward and, lifting his hindleg, pissed quick short at an unsmelt rock. The simple pleasures of the poor. His hindpaws then scattered sand: then his forepaws dabbled and delved. Something he buried there, his grandmother.[7] He rooted in the sand, dabbling, delving and stopped to listen to the air, scraped up the sand again with a fury of his claws, soon ceasing, a pard,[8] a panther, got in spousebreach,[9] vulturing the dead.

After he woke me last night same dream or was it? Wait. Open hallway.

---

4. A man had been drowned off the coast, and his body had not yet been recovered. As Stephen thinks of the horror of drowning he recalls once again his mother's death.

5. At this point in its constantly changing appearance the dog looks like a heraldic animal and is described in the language of heraldry. This sentence means: "On an orange-brown (tawny) background, a buck, tripping, in natural colors, without horns."

6. Stephen recognizes the man and woman on the beach as gypsy cockle pickers (cockles are edible shellfish, like mussels).

7. Reference to a joke Stephen had made to his pupils in school that morning about "the fox burying his grandmother under a hollybush." This has many symbolic reverberations throughout Ulysses. The buried grandmother suggests Stephen's mother, the church, and Ireland (the "Poor old Woman"), while the hollybush, evergreen tree of life, represents resurrection in which, in spite of his religious disbelief, Stephen is much interested and about which (as about metempsychosis) he is continually brooding.

8. Leopard or panther.

9. I.e., begotten in adultery.

Street of harlots. Remember. Haroun al Raschid.[1] I am almosting it. That man led me, spoke. I was not afraid. The melon he had he held against my face. Smiled: creamfruit smell. That was the rule, said. In. Come. Red carpet spread. You will see who.

Shouldering their bags they trudged, the red Egyptians.[2] His blued feet out of turnedup trousers slapped the clammy sand, a dull brick muffler strangling his unshaven neck. With woman steps she followed: the ruffian and his strolling mort. Spoils[3] slung at her back. Loose sand and shellgrit crusted her bare feet. About her windraw face her hair trailed. Behind her lord his helpmate, bing awast, to Romeville.[4] When night hides her body's flaws calling under her brown shawl from an archway where dogs have mired. Her fancyman is treating two Royal Dublins in O'Loughlin's of Blackpitts. Buss her, wap in rogues' rum lingo, for, O, my dimber wapping dell.[5] A shefiend's whiteness under her rancid rags. Fumbally's lane that night: the tanyard smells.

> *White thy fambles, red thy gan*
> *And thy quarrons dainty is.*
> *Couch a hogshead with me then.*
> *In the darkmans clip and kiss.*[6]

Morose delectation Aquinas tunbelly calls this, *frate porcospino*.[7] Unfallen Adam rode and not rutted. Call away let him:[8] *thy quarrons dainty is.* Language no whit worse than his. Monkwords, marybeads jabber on their girdles: roguewords, tough nuggets patter in their pockets.

Passing now.

A side-eye at my Hamlet hat. If I were suddenly naked here as I sit? I am not. Across the sands of all the world, followed by the sun's flaming sword, to the west, trekking to evening lands. She trudges, schlepps, trains, drags, trascines her load.[9] A tide westering, moondrawn, in her wake. Tides, myriad-islanded, within her, blood not mine, *oinopa ponton*,[1] a winedark sea. Behold the handmaid of the moon. In sleep the wet sign calls her hour, bids her rise. Bridebed, childbed, bed of death, ghostcandled.[2] *Omnis caro ad te veniet.* He comes, pale vampire, through storm his eyes, his bat sails bloodying the sea, mouth to her mouth's kiss.[3]

Here. Put a pin in that chap, will you? My tablets.[4] Mouth to her kiss. No. Must be two of em. Glue 'em well. Mouth to her mouth's kiss.

---

1. Stephen's dream of the famous Caliph of Baghdad, of the "street of harlots" and of his meeting a man with a melon, foreshadows his meeting later in the day with Leopold Bloom and his visit to the brothel area of Dublin.
2. I.e., gypsies. As Stephen watches the gypsy cockle pickers with their dog he imagines their vagabond life and recalls fragments of gypsy speech and of thieves' slang.
3. The association of gypsy ("Mort": free gypsy woman; harlot) with Egyptian reminds Stephen of the Israelites "spoiling the Egyptians" (Exodus 12.36).
4. Go away to London.
5. Seventeenth-century thieves' slang. "Buss": kiss. "Wap": copulate with. "Rum": good. "Dimber": pretty. "Wapping dell": whore.
6. More thieves' slang. "Fambles": hands. "Gan": mouth. "Quarrons": body. "Couch a hogshead":

come to bed. "Darkmans": night. "Clip": kiss. These four lines and some of the phrases in the preceding paragraph are quoted from a song of the period, "The Rogue's Delight in Praise of His Strolling Mort" (cf. 1st n. 2 and n. 3, this page).
7. Brother porcupine (Italian), a reference to the fat ("tunbelly") but prickly philosopher, St. Thomas Aquinas.
8. The gypsy is calling his dog.
9. All words suggesting moving or dragging. " 'I like that crescendo of verbs,' he [Joyce] said. 'The irresistible tug of the tides' " (Budgen).
1. Winedark sea (Homer).
2. He is thinking of his mother again. The following Latin (from the burial service) means: All flesh will come to thee.
3. Death comes like the Flying Dutchman in a phantom ship to give the fatal kiss.
4. Cf. *Hamlet* 1.5.107: "My tables!"

His lips lipped and mouthed fleshless lips of air: mouth to her womb. Oomb, allwombing tomb.[5] His mouth moulded issuing breath, unspeeched: ooeeehah: roar of cataractic planets, globed, blazing, roaring wayawayaway-awayawayaway. Paper. The banknotes, blast them. Old Deasy's letter. Here. Thanking you for the hospitality tear the blank end off. Turning his back to the sun he bent over far to a table of rock and scribbled words.[6] That's twice I forgot to take slips from the library counter.

His shadow lay over the rocks as he bent, ending. Why not endless till the farthest star? Darkly they are there behind this light, darkness shining in the brightness, delta of Cassiopeia, worlds. Me sits there with his augur's rod of ash, in borrowed sandals, by day beside a livid sea, unbeheld, in violet night walking beneath a reign of uncouth stars.[7] I throw this ended shadow from me, manshape ineluctable, call it back. Endless, would it be mine, form of my form? Who watches me here? Who ever anywhere will read these written words? Signs on a white field. Somewhere to someone in your flutiest voice. The good bishop of Cloyne[8] took the veil of the temple out of his shovel hat: veil of space with coloured emblems hatched on its field. Hold hard. Coloured on a flat: yes, that's right. Flat I see, then think distance, near, far, flat I see, east, back. Ah, see now. Falls back suddenly, frozen in stereoscope. Click does the trick. You find my words dark. Darkness is in our souls, do you not think? Flutier. Our souls, shamewounded by our sins, cling to us yet more, a woman to her lover clinging, the more the more.

She trusts me, her hand gentle, the longlashed eyes. Now where the blue hell am I bringing her beyond the veil?[9] Into the ineluctable modality of the ineluctable visuality. She, she, she. What she? The virgin at Hodges Figgis' window on Monday looking in for one of the alphabet books you were going to write. Keen glance you gave her. Wrist through the braided jess of her sunshade. She lives in Leeson park with a grief and kickshaws, a lady of letters. Talk that to some else, Stevie: a pickmeup. Bet she wears those curse of God stays suspenders and yellow stockings, darned with lumpy wool. Talk about apple dumplings, *piuttosto*.[1] Where are your wits?

Touch me. Soft eyes. Soft soft soft hand. I am lonely here. O, touch me soon, now. What is that word known to all men? I am quiet here alone. Sad too. Touch, touch me.

He lay back at full stretch over the sharp rocks, cramming the scribbled note and pencil into a pocket, his hat tilted down on his eyes. That is Kevin Egan's movement I made, nodding for his nap, sabbath sleep. *Et vidit Deus. Et erant valde bona.*[2] Alo! *Bonjour.* Welcome as the flowers in May. Under

5. Our understanding of Stephen's consciousness here can be illuminated with reference to Blake's poem *The Gates of Paradise,* which concludes: "The door of death I open found / And the worm weaving in the ground: / Thou'rt my mother from the womb, / Wife, sister, daughter, to the tomb." Cf. also *Romeo and Juliet* 2.3.9–10: "the earth that's nature's mother is her tomb. / What is her burying ground that is her womb."
6. Stephen tears off the blank end of Mr. Deasy's letter to the press and writes a poem that will be quoted later in the novel.
7. He imagines himself as the constellation Cassiopeia, supposed to represent the wife of Cepheus (an Ethiopian king) seated in a chair and holding up her arms. His ash walking stick he thinks of as

an "augur's [Roman soothsayer's] rod of ash."
8. George Berkeley (1685–1753), bishop of Cloyne (in Ireland), who argued that the external world has no objective reality but exists only in the mind of the perceiver. Stephen (as at the opening of this episode) is experimenting again with ways of sensing reality.
9. "She" is Psyche, the soul, whom he is bringing from "beyond the veil." But from metaphysical speculations on reality and the soul Stephen is led (by the Psyche association) to think of "the virgin at Hodges Figgis' [a bookseller's] window."
1. Rather, sooner.
2. Connecting two phrases from the Vulgate: "And God saw" (Genesis 1.4) and "And they were very good" (Genesis 1.31).

its leaf he watched through peacocktwittering lashes the southing sun. I am caught in this burning scene. Pan's hour, the faunal noon. Among gumheavy serpentplants, milkoozing fruits, where on the tawny waters leaves lie wide. Pain is far.

And no more turn aside and brood.[3]

His gaze brooded on his broadtoed boots, a buck's castoffs, *nebeneinander*. He counted the creases of rucked leather wherein another's foot had nested warm. The foot that beat the ground in tripudium, foot I dislove. But you were delighted when Esther Osvalt's shoe went on you: girl I knew in Paris. *Tiens, quel petit pied!*[4] Staunch friend, a brother soul: Wilde's love that dare not speak its name. He now will leave me. And the blame? As I am. As I am. All or not at all.

In long lassoes from the Cock lake the water flowed full, covering green-goldenly lagoons of sand, rising, flowing. My ashplant will float away. I shall wait. No, they will pass on, passing chafing against the low rocks, swirling, passing. Better get this job over quick. Listen: a fourworded wavespeech: seesoo, hrss, rsseeiss ooos. Vehement breath of waters amid seasnakes, rearing horses, rocks. In cups of rocks it slops: flop, slop, slap: bounded in barrels. And, spent, its speech ceases. It flows purling, widely flowing, floating foampool, flower unfurling.

Under the upswelling tide he saw the writhing weeds lift languidly and sway reluctant arms, hising up their petticoats,[5] in whispering water swaying and upturning coy silver fronds. Day by day: night by night: lifted, flooded and let fall. Lord, they are weary: and, whispered to, they sigh. Saint Ambrose heard it, sigh of leaves and waves, waiting, awaiting the fullness of their times, *diebus ac noctibus iniurias patiens ingemiscit.*[6] To no end gathered; vainly then released, forthflowing, wending back: loom of the moon. Weary too in sight of lovers, lascivious men, a naked woman shining in her courts, she draws a toil of waters.

Five fathoms out there. Full fathom five thy father lies.[7] At one he said. Found drowned. High water at Dublin bar. Driving before it a loose drift of rubble, fanshoals of fishes, silly shells. A corpse rising salt-white from the undertow, bobbing landward a pace a pace a porpoise. There he is. Hook it quick. Sunk though he be beneath the watery floor. We have him. Easy now.

Bag of corpsegas sopping in foul brine. A quiver of minnows, fat of a spongy titbit, flash through the slits of his buttoned trouserfly. God becomes man becomes fish becomes barnacle goose becomes featherbed mountain. Dead breaths I living breathe, tread dead dust, devour a urinous offal from all dead. Hauled stark over the gunwhale he breathes upward the stench of his green grave, his leprous nosehole snoring to the sun.

A seachange[8] this, brown eyes saltblue. Seadeath, mildest of all deaths

---

3. The first line of the second (and last) stanza of Yeats's poem *Who Goes with Fergus?* which is often in Stephen's mind. The line expresses for him the mood of noontide stillness and of lotos eating in a lush Asian scene that overcomes him momentarily when he realizes that it is twelve o'clock, the hour of the Greek nature god Pan, "faunal noon." This Asian lotos-eating theme, which is associated also with Bloom, is important in the *Odyssey*.
4. Look, what a little foot!

5. A phrase from a vulgar song sung by Mulligan earlier that morning.
6. Night and day he patiently groaned forth his wrongs (St. Ambrose).
7. From Ariel's song (*The Tempest* 1.2.396). The theme of the drowned man is important in this episode (cf. the drowned sailor in Eliot's *Waste Land*).
8. Another quotation from Ariel's song (*The Tempest*).

known to man. Old Father Ocean. *Prix de Paris:*[9] beware of imitations. Just you give it a fair trial. We enjoyed ourselves immensely.

Come. I thirst. Clouding over. No black clouds anywhere, are there?[1] Thunderstorm. Allbright he falls, proud lightning of the intellect, *Lucifer, dico, qui nescit occasum.*[2] No. My cockle hat and staff and hismy sandal shoon.[3] Where? To evening lands. Evening will find itself.

He took the hilt of his ashplant, lunging with it softly, dallying still. Yes, evening will find itself in me, without me. All days make their end. By the way next when is it? Tuesday will be the longest day. Of all the glad new year, mother,[4] the rum tum tiddledy tum. Lawn Tennyson,[5] gentleman poet. *Già.*[6] For the old hag with the yellow teeth. And Monsieur Drumont, gentleman journalist. *Già.* My teeth are very bad. Why, I wonder? Feel. That one is going too. Shells. Ought I go to a dentist, I wonder, with what money? That one. Toothless Kinch, the superman. Why is that, I wonder, or does it mean something perhaps?

My handkerchief. He threw it. I remember. Did I not take it up?

His hand groped vainly in his pockets. No, I didn't. Better buy one.

He laid the dry snot picked from his nostril on a ledge of rock, carefully. For the rest let look who will.

Behind. Perhaps there is someone.

He turned his face over a shoulder, rere regardant.[7] Moving through the air high spars of a threemaster, her sails brailed up on the crosstrees,[8] homing, upstream, silently moving, a silent ship.

[LESTRYGONIANS][9]

Pineapple rock, lemon platt, butter scotch. A sugarsticky girl shovelling scoopfuls of creams for a christian brother. Some school treat. Bad for their

---

9. Prize of Paris. The reference is probably to the Paris Exposition of 1889, where prizes were awarded in various categories of food, etc.; the prize-winning commodities bear the seal of the prize on the label (hence, "beware of imitations"). Stephen mentally awards the prize to death by drowning.

1. Stephen is looking up to make sure the sky does not threaten a thunderstorm; like Joyce, he hates thunder.

2. Lucifer, I say, who knows not his fall. Thunder and lightning recall the fall of Lucifer.

3. From Ophelia's mad song (*Hamlet* 4.5.23–26): "How should I your true-love know / From another one? / By his cockle hat and staff / And his sandal shoon." Ophelia, too, was drowned.

4. Cf. Tennyson, *The May Queen:* "You must wake and call me early, call me early, mother dear; / Tomorrow 'ill be the happiest time of all the glad New Year."

5. Alfred, Lord Tennyson. A parody of the poet's name, punning on "lawn tennis," attributed to W. B. Yeats.

6. Of course!

7. Looking behind him (heraldic terminology). Stephen, as we leave him sitting by the shore, is described in a highly stylized, heraldic language.

8. When Budgen pointed out to Joyce that *crosstrees* was not the proper nautical term for the spars to which the sails are bent, Joyce thanked him but added: "But the word 'crosstrees' is essential. It comes in later on and I can't change it. After all, a yard is also a crosstree for the onlooking landlubber." Joyce later uses *crosstree* in a reference to the crucifixion of Christ, so that the suggestion here is of Stephen as both artist and martyr (as his name implies). But the ship is also a real ship, which arrived in Dublin on June 16, 1904.

9. It is lunchtime in Dublin and Leopold Bloom, as he walks through the city in no great hurry (for he likes to linger and watch what goes on around him), thinks of food. The Lestrygonians in book 10 of the *Odyssey* are cannibals, and throughout this episode there are suggestions of the slaughter of living creatures for food or of food as something disgusting, which make somewhat tenuous contact with Homer's description of the cannibals spearing Ulysses' men for food; the parallel is not, however, profound or very important. What is most important about this episode is that it shows us Bloom's consciousness responding to the sights and sounds of Dublin. His humane curiosity, his desire to learn and to improve the human lot, his sympathetic concern for Mrs. Breen and Mrs. Purefoy, his feeding the gulls, his recollections of a happier time when his daughter was a baby and his relations with his wife, Molly, were thoroughly satisfactory, his interest in opera, his continuous shying away from thoughts of his wife's rendezvous with the dashing Blazes Boylan—all this helps to build up his character in depth and to differentiate him sharply from Stephen. Unlike Stephen, Bloom's

tummies. Lozenge and comfit manufacturer to His Majesty the King. God. Save. Our. Sitting on his throne sucking red jujubes white.

A sombre Y. M. C. A. young man, watchful among the warm sweet fumes of Graham Lemon's, placed a throwaway in a hand of Mr Bloom.

Heart to heart talks.

Bloo . . . Me? No.

Blood of the Lamb.[1]

His slow feet walked him riverward, reading. Are you saved? All are washed in the blood of the lamb. God wants blood victim. Birth, hymen, martyr, war, foundation of a building, sacrifice, kidney burntoffering, druids' altars. Elijah is coming. Dr John Alexander Dowie,[2] restorer of the church in Zion, is coming.

Is coming! Is coming!! Is coming!!!
All heartily welcome.

Paying game. Torry and Alexander last year. Polygamy. His wife will put the stopper on that. Where was that ad some Birmingham firm the luminous crucifix. Our Saviour. Wake up in the dead of night and see him on the wall, hanging. Pepper's ghost idea.[3] Iron Nails Ran In.

Phosphorus it must be done with. If you leave a bit of codfish for instance. I could see the bluey silver over it. Night I went down to the pantry in the kitchen. Don't like all the smells in it waiting to rush out. What was it she[4] wanted? The Malaga raisins. Thinking of Spain. Before Rudy[5] was born. The phosphorescence, that bluey greeny. Very good for the brain.

From Butler's monument house corner he glanced along Bachelor's walk. Dedalus' daughter there still outside Dillon's auctionrooms. Must be selling off some old furniture. Knew her eyes at once from the father. Lobbing about waiting for him. Home always breaks up when the mother goes. Fifteen children he had. Birth every year almost. That's in their theology or the priest won't give the poor woman the confession, the absolution. Increase and multiply. Did you ever hear such an idea? Eat you out of house and home. No families themselves to feed. Living on the fat of the land. Their butteries and larders. I'd like to see them do the black fast Yom Kippur.[6] Crossbuns. One meal and a collation for fear he'd collapse on the altar. A housekeeper of one of those fellows if you could pick it out of her. Never pick it out of her. Like getting L s. d.[7] out of him. Does himself well. No guests. All for number one.

interest in language is confined to simple puns and translations; his interest in poetry is obvious and sentimental; his interest in the nature of reality takes the form of half-forgotten fragments of science remaining in his mind from school days. Everything about him is concrete, practical, sensual, and middlebrow or lowbrow, as distinct from the abstract, theoretical, esoteric speculations of Stephen in the *Proteus* episode. For example, when Stephen saw seagulls, he speculated on Daedalus and on flying as a symbol of the artist going into exile; when Bloom sees them, he thinks they must be hungry and buys a bun to feed them. There are parallels between their two streams of consciousness. Bloom's thoughts, in a sense, include Stephen's but in a popularized and even vulgarized form.

1. Bloom has been handed a religious leaflet

("throwaway") containing the phrase "Blood of the Lamb." He at first mistakes "Blood" for "Bloom."
2. Dowie (1847–1907), Scottish-American evangelist who established the "Christian Catholic Apostolic Church in Zion" (i.e., Zion City, IL) in 1901.
3. A dramatic troupe advertising themselves as "The original Pepper's Ghost! and Spectral Opera Company" was popular in the late 19th century; they seem to have specialized in ghostly special effects, possibly achieved through the use of phosphorescent material on their costumes.
4. I.e., Bloom's wife, Molly, born in Gibraltar.
5. Their son, who had died in infancy eleven years before.
6. Jewish Day of Atonement.
7. I.e., cash: L, s., d. are the abbreviations, respectively, for pounds, shillings, and pence.

Watching his water. Bring your own bread and butter. His reverence. Mum's the word.

Good Lord, that poor child's dress is in flitters. Underfed she looks too. Potatoes and marge, marge and potatoes. It's after they feel it. Proof of the pudding. Undermines the constitution.

As he set foot on O'Connell bridge a puffball of smoke plumed up from the parapet. Brewery barge with export stout. England. Sea air sours it, I heard. Be interesting some day get a pass through Hancock to see the brewery. Regular world in itself. Vats of porter, wonderful. Rats get in too. Drink themselves bloated as big as a collie floating. Dead drunk on the porter. Drink till they puke again like christians. Imagine drinking that! Rats: vats. Well of course if we knew all the things.

Looking down he saw flapping strongly, wheeling between the gaunt quay-walls, gulls. Rough weather outside. If I threw myself down? Reuben J's son must have swallowed a good bellyful of that sewage.[8] One and eightpence too much. Hhhhm. It's the droll way he comes out with the things. Knows how to tell a story too.

They wheeled lower. Looking for grub. Wait.

He threw down among them a crumpled paper ball. Elijah thirtytwo feet per sec is com.[9] Not a bit. The ball bobbed unheeded on the wake of swells, floated under by the bridgepiers. Not such damn fools. Also the day I threw that stale cake out of the Erin's King picked it up in the wake fifty yards astern. Live by their wits. They wheeled, flapping.

> *The hungry famished gull*
> *Flaps o'er the waters dull.*

That is how poets write, the similar sounds. But then Shakespeare has no rhymes: blank verse. The flow of the language it is. The thoughts. Solemn.

> *Hamlet, I am thy father's spirit*
> *Doomed for a certain time to walk the earth.*[1]

—Two apples a penny! Two for a penny!

His gaze passed over the glazed apples serried on her stand. Australians they must be this time of year. Shiny peels: polishes them up with a rag or a handkerchief.

Wait. Those poor birds.

He halted again and bought from the old applewoman two Banbury cakes for a penny and broke the brittle paste and threw its fragments down into the Liffey. See that? The gulls swooped silently two, then all from their heights, pouncing on prey. Gone. Every morsel.

Aware of their greed and cunning he shook the powdery crumb from his hands. They never expected that. Manna.[2] Live on fishy flesh they have to, all seabirds, gulls, seagoose. Swans from Anna Liffey[3] swim down here some-

---

8. Reuben J. Dodd, Dublin solicitor (lawyer), whose son had been rescued from the Liffey River by a man to whom Reuben J. had given two shillings as a reward—"one and eightpence too much," as Simon Dedalus had remarked to Bloom earlier that morning when they were discussing the incident. It is Dedalus's comment that Bloom is thinking of in the following sentences.

9. I.e., Elijah is coming, accelerating at the rate of

thirty-two feet per second per second, the acceleration rate of falling bodies. ("Elijah is coming" is the legend on the handbill Bloom is tossing away).

1. *Hamlet* 1.5.9–10 (slightly misquoted).

2. The divine food (small, round, and white) that the children of Israel ate in the wilderness (Exodus 16.14–15).

3. The Liffey flows from the Wicklow Mountains northeast and east to Dublin Bay.

times to preen themselves. No accounting for tastes. Wonder what kind is swanmeat. Robinson Crusoe had to live on them.

They wheeled, flapping weakly. I'm not going to throw any more. Penny quite enough. Lot of thanks I get. Not even a caw. They spread foot and mouth disease too. If you cram a turkey, say, on chestnutmeal it tastes like that. Eat pig like pig. But then why is it that saltwater fish are not salty? How is that?

His eyes sought answer from the river and saw a rowboat rock at anchor on the treacly swells lazily its plastered board.

Kino's
11/—
Trousers[4]

Good idea that. Wonder if he pays rent to the corporation. How can you own water really? It's always flowing in a stream, never the same, which in the stream of life we trace. Because life is a stream. All kinds of places are good for ads. That quack doctor for the clap used to be stuck up in all the greenhouses. Never see it now. Strictly confidential. Dr Hy Franks. Didn't cost him a red like Maginni the dancing master self advertisement. Got fellows to stick them up or stick them up himself for that matter on the q.t. running in to loosen a button. Flybynight. Just the place too. POST NO BILLS. POST NO PILLS.[5] Some chap with a dose burning him.

If he . . .

O!

Eh?

No . . . No.

No, no. I don't believe it. He wouldn't surely?

No, no.[6]

Mr Bloom moved forward, raising his troubled eyes. Think no more about that. After one. Timeball on the ballastoffice is down. Dunsink time. Fascinating little book that is of Sir Robert Ball's. Parallax. I never exactly understood.[7] There's a priest. Could ask him. Par it's Greek: parallel, parallax. Met him pike hoses[8] she called it till I told her about the transmigration. O rocks!

Mr Bloom smiled O rocks at two windows of the ballastoffice. She's right after all. Only big words for ordinary things on account of the sound. She's not exactly witty. Can be rude too. Blurt out what I was thinking. Still I don't know. She used to say Ben Dollard had a base barreltone voice. He has legs like barrels and you'd think he was singing into a barrel. Now isn't that wit?

---

4. I.e., eleven shillings ("11/-") for Kino's Trousers. Bloom is a canvasser for advertisements: he receives commissions from newspapers for getting tradesmen to place advertisements with them.

5. The revised text edited by John Kidd (1993) reads, POST NO BILLS. POST 110 PILLS. "Post no bills" can mean either "do not affix any posters" or "mail no accounts." Bloom is punning to himself on the quack doctor's advertising (by posting bills), collecting his money (by mailing accounts), and sending pills to patients by mail.

6. Blazes Boylan, flashy philanderer, is due to call on Molly Bloom that afternoon, to discuss the program of a concert that he is managing for her (Molly is a singer). Bloom knows that Boylan and his wife will commit adultery together. Here it suddenly occurs to him that Boylan might give Molly

a "dose" of veneral disease, but he puts the thought from him as incredible.

7. The "timeball on the ballastoffice" registers the official time of the observatory at Dunsink. Noticing that the timeball is down, which means that it is after one o'clock, Bloom is reminded of the observatory, then of the Irish astronomer Sir Robert Ball's popular book on astronomy, The Story of the Heavens (1886), and of the astronomical term "parallax" he found in the book but "never exactly understood."

8. Molly's way of pronouncing metempsychosis. When Bloom had explained metempsychosis to her that morning, she had exclaimed "O rocks" at the pretentious term. He now mentally repeats "O rocks!" at the thought of the word parallax.

They used to call him big Ben. Not half as witty as calling him base barrel-tone. Appetite like an albatross. Get outside of a baron of beef. Powerful man he was at stowing away number one Bass.[9] Barrel of Bass. See? It all works out.

A procession of whitesmocked men marched slowly towards him along the gutter, scarlet sashes across their boards. Bargains. Like that priest they are this morning: we have sinned: we have suffered. He read the scarlet letters on their five tall white hats: H. E. L. Y. S. Wisdom Hely's. Y lagging behind drew a chunk of bread from under his foreboard, crammed it into his mouth and munched as he walked. Our staple food. Three bob a day, walking along the gutters, street after street. Just keep skin and bone together, bread and skilly. They are not Boyl: no: M'Glade's men. Doesn't bring in any business either. I suggested to him about a transparent showcart with two smart girls sitting inside writing letters, copybooks, envelopes, blottingpaper. I bet that would have caught on. Smart girls writing something catch the eye at once. Everyone dying to know what she's writing. Get twenty of them round you if you stare at nothing. Have a finger in the pie. Women too. Curiosity. Pillar of salt. Wouldn't have it of course because he didn't think of it himself first. Or the inkbottle I suggested with a false stain of black celluloid. His ideas for ads like Plumtree's potted under the obituaries, cold meat department. You can't lick 'em. What? Our envelopes. Hello! Jones, where are you going? Can't stop, Robinson, I am hastening to purchase the only reliable inkeraser *Kansell,* sold by Hely's Ltd, 85 Dame street. Well out of that ruck I am. Devil of a job it was collecting accounts of those convents. Tranquilla convent. That was a nice nun there, really sweet face. Wimple suited her small head. Sister? Sister? I am sure she was crossed in love by her eyes. Very hard to bargain with that sort of a woman. I disturbed her at her devotions that morning. But glad to communicate with the outside world. Our great day, she said. Feast of Our Lady of Mount Carmel. Sweet name too: caramel. She knew, I think she knew by the way she. If she had married she would have changed. I suppose they really were short of money. Fried everything in the best butter all the same. No lard for them. My heart's broke eating dripping. They like buttering themselves in and out. Molly tasting it, her veil up. Sister? Pat Claffey, the pawnbroker's daughter. It was a nun they say invented barbed wire.

He crossed Westmoreland street when apostrophe S had plodded by. Rover cycleshop. Those races are on today. How long ago is that? Year Phil Gilligan died. We were in Lombard street west. Wait, was in Thom's. Got the job in Wisdom Hely's year we married. Six years. Ten years ago: ninety-four he died, yes that's right the big fire at Arnott's. Val Dillon was lord mayor. The Glencree dinner. Alderman Robert O'Reilly emptying the port into his soup before the flag fell, Bobbob lapping it for the inner alderman. Couldn't hear what the band played. For what we have already received may the Lord make us. Milly[1] was a kiddy then. Molly had that elephantgrey dress with the braided frogs. Mantailored with selfcovered buttons. She didn't like it because I sprained my ankle first day she wore choir picnic at the Sugarloaf. As if that. Old Goodwin's tall hat done up with some sticky stuff. Flies' picnic

---

9. A popular British ale.

1. Bloom's fifteen-year-old daughter.

too. Never put a dress on her back like it. Fitted her like a glove, shoulder and hips. Just beginning to plump it out well. Rabbitpie we had that day. People looking after her.

Happy. Happier then. Snug little room that was with the red wallpaper, Dockrell's, one and ninepence a dozen. Milly's tubbing night. American soap I bought: elderflower. Cosy smell of her bathwater. Funny she looked soaped all over. Shapely too. Now photography.[2] Poor papa's daguerreotype atelier he told me of. Hereditary taste.

He walked along the curbstone.

Stream of life. What was the name of that priestlylooking chap was always squinting in when he passed? Weak eyes, woman. Stopped in Citron's saint Kevin's parade. Pen something. Pendennis? My memory is getting. Pen . . . ? Of course it's years ago. Noise of the trams probably. Well, if he couldn't remember the dayfather's name that he sees every day.

Bartell d'Arcy was the tenor, just coming out then. Seeing her home after practice. Conceited fellow with his waxedup moustache. Gave her that song *Winds that blow from the south.*

Windy night that was I went to fetch her there was that lodge meeting on about those lottery tickets after Goodwin's concert in the supperroom or oakroom of the Mansion house. He and I behind. Sheet of her music blew out of my hand against the High school railings. Lucky it didn't. Thing like that spoils the effect of a night for her. Professor Goodwin linking her in front. Shaky on his pins, poor old sot. His farewell concerts. Positively last appearance on any stage. May be for months and may be for never. Remember her laughing at the wind, her blizzard collar up. Corner of Harcourt road remember that gust. Brrfoo! Blew up all her skirts and her boa nearly smothered old Goodwin. She did get flushed in the wind. Remember when we got home raking up the fire and frying up those pieces of lap of mutton for her supper with the Chutney sauce she liked. And the mulled rum. Could see her in the bedroom from the hearth unclamping the busk of her stays: white.

Swish and soft flop her stays made on the bed. Always warm from her. Always liked to let her self out. Sitting there after till near two taking out her hairpins. Milly tucked up in beddyhouse. Happy. Happy. That was the night . . .

—O, Mr Bloom, how do you do?

—O, how do you do, Mrs Breen?[3]

—No use complaining. How is Molly those times? Haven't seen her for ages.

—In the pink, Mr Bloom said gaily, Milly has a position down in Mullingar, you know.

—Go away! Isn't that grand for her?

—Yes, in a photographer's there. Getting on like a house on fire. How are all your charges?

—All on the baker's list, Mrs Breen said.

How many has she? No other in sight.

—You're in black I see. You have no . . .

2. Milly is working at a photographer's.
3. Mrs. Breen had been an old sweetheart of Bloom's.

—No, Mr. Bloom said. I have just come from a funeral.

Going to crop up all day, I foresee. Who's dead, when and what did he die of? Turn up like a bad penny.

—O dear me, Mrs Breen said, I hope it wasn't any near relation.

May as well get her sympathy.

—Dignam, Mr Bloom said. An old friend of mine. He died quite suddenly, poor fellow. Heart trouble, I believe. Funeral was this morning.

> Your funeral's tomorrow
> While you're coming through the rye.
> Diddlediddle dumdum
> Diddlediddle . . .

—Sad to lose the old friends, Mrs Breen's womaneyes said melancholily.

Now that's quite enough about that. Just quietly: husband.

—And your lord and master?

Mrs Breen turned up her two large eyes. Hasn't lost them anyhow.

—O, don't be talking, she said. He's a caution to rattlesnakes. He's in there now with his lawbooks finding out the law of libel. He has me heart-scalded. Wait till I show you.

Hot mockturtle vapour and steam of newbaked jampuffs rolypoly poured out from Harrison's. The heavy noonreek tickled the top of Mr Bloom's gullet. Want to make good pastry, butter, best flour, Demerara sugar, or they'd taste it with the hot tea. Or is it from her? A barefoot arab stood over the grating, breathing in the fumes. Deaden the gnaw of hunger that way. Pleasure or pain is it? Penny dinner. Knife and fork chained to the table.

Opening her handbag, chipped leather, hatpin: ought to have a guard on those things. Stick it in a chap's eye in the tram. Rummaging. Open. Money. Please take one. Devils if they lose sixpence. Raise Cain. Husband barging. Where's the ten shillings I gave you on Monday? Are you feeding your little brother's family? Soiled handkerchief: medicinebottle. Pastille that was fell. What is she? . . .

—There must be a new moon out, she said. He's always bad then.[4] Do you know what he did last night?

Her hand ceased to rummage. Her eyes fixed themselves on him, wide in alarm, yet smiling.

—What? Mr. Bloom asked.

Let her speak. Look straight in her eyes. I believe you. Trust me.

—Woke me up in the night, she said. Dream he had, a nightmare.

Indiges.

—Said the ace of spades[5] was walking up the stairs.

—The ace of spades! Mr Bloom said.

She took a folded postcard from her handbag.

—Read that, she said. He got it this morning.

—What is it? Mr Bloom asked, taking the card. U. P.?

—U.p.: up, she said. Someone taking a rise out of him. It's a great shame for them whoever he is.

—Indeed it is, Mr Bloom said.

She took back the card, sighing.

---

4. Mr. Breen is mentally disturbed.   5. Symbol of death.

—And now he's going round to Mr Menton's office. He's going to take an action for ten thousand pounds, he says.

She folded the card into her untidy bag and snapped the catch.

Same blue serge dress she had two years ago, the nap bleaching. Seen its best days. Wispish hair over her ears. And that dowdy toque: three old grapes to take the harm out of it. Shabby genteel. She used to be a tasty dresser. Lines round her mouth. Only a year or so older than Molly.

See the eye that woman gave her, passing. Cruel. The unfair sex.

He looked still at her, holding back behind his look his discontent. Pungent mockturtle oxtail mulligatawny. I'm hungry too. Flakes of pastry on the gusset of her dress: daub of sugary flour stuck to her cheek. Rhubarb tart with liberal fillings, rich fruit interior. Josie Powell that was. In Luke Doyle's long ago, Dolphin's Barn, the charades. U.p.: up.

Change the subject.

—Do you ever see anything of Mrs Beaufoy, Mr Bloom asked.

—Mina Purefoy? she said.

Philip Beaufoy I was thinking. Playgoers' Club[6] Matcham often thinks of the masterstroke. Did I pull the chain? Yes. The last act.

—Yes.

—I just called to ask on the way in is she over it. She's in the lying-in hospital in Holles street. Dr Horne got her in. She's three days bad now.

—O, Mr Bloom said. I'm sorry to hear that.

—Yes, Mrs Breen said. And a houseful of kids at home. It's a very stiff birth, the nurse told me.

—O, Mr Bloom said.

His heavy pitying gaze absorbed her news. His tongue clacked in compassion. Dth! Dth!

—I'm sorry to hear that, he said. Poor thing! Three days! That's terrible for her.

Mrs Breen nodded.

—She was taken bad on the Tuesday . . . .

Mr Bloom touched her funnybone gently, warning her.

—Mind! Let this man pass.

A bony form strode along the curbstone from the river, staring with a rapt gaze into the sunlight through a heavystringed glass. Tight as a skullpiece a tiny hat gripped his head. From his arm a folded dustcoat, a stick and an umbrella dangled to his stride.

—Watch him, Mr Bloom said. He always walks outside the lampposts. Watch!

—Who is he if it's a fair question? Mrs Breen asked. Is he dotty?

—His name is Cashel Boyle O'Connor Fitzmaurice Tisdall Farrell, Mr Bloom said smiling. Watch!

—He has enough of them, she said. Denis will be like that one of these days.

She broke off suddenly.

—There he is, she said. I must go after him. Goodbye. Remember me to Molly, won't you?

6. Bloom is thinking of the story *Matcham's Masterstroke*, by "Mr. Philip Beaufoy, Playgoers' Club, London," which he had read in the toilet that morning. He then mentally quotes the opening sentence.

—I will, Mr Bloom said.

He watched her dodge through passers towards the shopfronts. Denis Breen in skimpy frockcoat and blue canvas shoes shuffled out of Harrison's hugging two heavy tomes to his ribs. Blown in from the bay. Like old times. He suffered her to overtake him without surprise and thrust his dull grey beard towards her, his loose jaw wagging as he spoke earnestly.

Meshuggah.[7] Off his chump.

Mr Bloom walked on again easily, seeing ahead of him in sunlight the tight skullpiece, the dangling stick, umbrella, dustcoat. Going the two days. Watch him! Out he goes again. One way of getting on in the world. And that other old mosey lunatic in those duds. Hard time she must have with him.

U.p.: up. I'll take my oath that's Alf Bergan or Richie Goulding. Wrote it for a lark in the Scotch house, I bet anything. Round to Menton's office. His oyster eyes staring at the postcard. Be a feast for the gods.

He passed the *Irish Times*. There might be other answers lying there. Like to answer them all. Good system for criminals. Code. At their lunch now. Clerk with the glasses there doesn't know me. O, leave them there to simmer. Enough bother wading through fortyfour of them. Wanted smart lady typist to aid gentleman in literary work. I called you naughty darling because I do not like that other world. Please tell me what is the meaning. Please tell me what perfume does your wife. Tell me who made the world.[8] The way they spring those questions on you. And the other one Lizzie Twigg.[9] My literary efforts have had the good fortune to meet with the approval of the eminent poet A. E. (Mr Geo. Russell).[1] No time to do her hair drinking sloppy tea with a book of poetry.

Best paper by long chalks for a small ad. Got the provinces now. Cook and general, exc cuisine, housemaid kept. Wanted live man for spirit counter. Resp. girl (R. C.) wishes to hear of post in fruit or pork shop. James Carlisle made that. Six and a half per cent dividend. Made a big deal on Coates's shares. Ca' canny. Cunning old Scotch hunks. All the toady news. Our gracious and popular vicereine.[2] Bought the *Irish Field* now. Lady Mountcashel has quite recovered after her confinement and rode out with the Ward Union staghounds at the enlargement yesterday at Rathoath. Uneatable fox. Pothunters too. Fear injects juices make it tender enough for them. Riding astride. Sit her horse like a man. Weightcarrying huntress. No sidesaddle or pillion for her, not for Joe. First to the meet and in at the death. Strong as a broodmare some of those horsey women. Swagger around livery stables. Toss off a glass of brandy neat while you'd say knife. That one at the Grosvenor this morning. Up with her on the car: wishswish. Stonewall or fivebarred gate put her mount to it. Think that pugnosed driver did it out of spite. Who is this she was like? O yes! Mrs Miriam Dandrade that sold me

---

7. Mad (Yiddish).
8. Cf. Marlowe's *The Tragical History of Doctor Faustus* 5, lines 237–44:
FAUSTUS. . . . Tell me who made the world?
MEPHASTOPHILIS. I will not.
. . . Think on hell Faustus, for thou art damned.
FAUSTUS. Think, Faustus, upon God, that made the world.
9. Bloom is mentally quoting a letter written to him by the typist Martha Clifford, with whom he is carrying on a purely epistolary love affair (she had misspelled *word* as *world*: "I do not like that

other world"). Lizzie Twigg was one of the other typists who had answered his advertisement for a secretary "to aid gentleman in literary work" (Bloom's pretext for beginning such an affair).
1. Æ (George Russell, 1867–1935), the Irish poet mentioned as a reference by Lizzie Twigg when she answered Bloom's advertisement, is later encountered by Bloom with a woman who Bloom speculates might be Lizzie.
2. Wife of the viceroy, who represented the British Crown in Ireland; Bloom is thinking of the society column in the *Irish Times*.

her old wraps and black underclothes in the Shelbourne hotel. Divorced Spanish American. Didn't take a feather out of her my handling them. As if I was her clotheshorse. Saw her in the viceregal party when Stubbs the park ranger got me in with Whelan of the *Express*. Scavenging what the quality left. High tea. Mayonnaise I poured on the plums thinking it was custard. Her ears ought to have tingled for a few weeks after. Want to be a bull for her. Born courtesan. No nursery work for her, thanks.

Poor Mrs Purefoy! Methodist husband. Method in his madness. Saffron bun and milk and soda lunch in the educational dairy. Eating with a stopwatch, thirtytwo chews to the minute. Still his muttonchop whiskers grew. Supposed to be well connected. Theodore's cousin in Dublin Castle. One tony relative in every family. Hardy annuals he presents her with. Saw him out at the Three Jolly Topers marching along bareheaded and his eldest boy carrying one in a marketnet. The squallers. Poor thing! Then having to give the breast year after year all hours of the night. Selfish those t.t's[3] are. Dog in the manger. Only one lump of sugar in my tea, if you please.

He stood at Fleet street crossing. Luncheon interval a sixpenny at Rowe's? Must look up that ad in the national library.[4] An eightpenny in the Burton. Better. On my way.

He walked on past Bolton's Westmoreland house. Tea. Tea. Tea. I forgot to tap Tom Kernan.[5]

Sss. Dth, dth, dth! Three days imagine groaning on a bed with a vinegared handkerchief round her forehead, her belly swollen out. Phew! Dreadful simply! Child's head too big: forceps. Doubled up inside her trying to butt its way out blindly, groping for the way out. Kill me that would. Lucky Molly got over hers lightly. They ought to invent something to stop that. Life with hard labour. Twilightsleep idea: queen Victoria was given that. Nine she had. A good layer. Old woman that lived in a shoe she had so many children. Suppose he was consumptive. Time someone thought about it instead of gassing about the what was it the pensive bosom of the silver effulgence. Flapdoddle to feed fools on. They could easily have big establishments. Whole thing quite painless out of all the taxes give every child born five quid at compound interest up to twentyone, five per cent is a hundred shillings and five tiresome pounds, multiply by twenty decimal system, encourage people to put by money save hundred and ten and a bit twentyone years want to work it out on paper come to a tidy sum, more than you think.

Not stillborn of course. They are not even registered. Trouble for nothing.

Funny sight two of them together, their bellies out. Molly and Mrs Moisel. Mothers' meeting. Phthisis retires for the time being, then returns. How flat they look after all of a sudden! Peaceful eyes. Weight off their mind. Old Mrs Thornton was a jolly old soul. All my babies, she said. The spoon of pap in her mouth before she fed them. O, that's nyumyum. Got her hand crushed by old Tom Wall's son. His first bow to the public. Head like a prize pumpkin. Snuffy Dr Murren. People knocking them up at all hours. For God's sake doctor. Wife in her throes. Then keep them waiting months for their fee. To

---

3. Abbreviation of "teetotalers," total abstainers from alcohol.
4. Bloom's goal, on his walk through Dublin, is the National Library, where he wants to look up an advertisement in a back number of the *Kilkenny*

People.
5. A Dublin tea merchant and friend of Bloom's, whom Bloom had earlier intended to ask ("tap") for some tea.

attendance on your wife. No gratitude in people. Humane doctors, most of them.

Before the huge high door of the Irish house of parliament a flock of pigeons flew. Their little frolic after meals. Who will we do it on? I pick the fellow in black. Here goes. Here's good luck. Must be thrilling from the air. Apjohn, myself and Owen Goldberg up in the trees near Goose green playing the monkeys. Mackerel they called me.

A squad of constables debouched from College street, marching in Indian file. Goosestep. Foodheated faces, sweating helmets, patting their truncheons. After their feed with a good load of fat soup under their belts. Policeman's lot is oft a happy one.[6] They split up into groups and scattered, saluting towards their beats. Let out to graze. Best moment to attack one in pudding time. A punch in his dinner. A squad of others, marching irregularly, rounded Trinity railings, making for the station. Bound for their troughs. Prepare to receive cavalry. Prepare to receive soup.

He crossed under Tommy Moore's roguish finger. They did right to put him up over a urinal: meeting of the waters.[7] Ought to be places for women. Running into cakeshops. Settle my hat straight. *There is not in this wide world a vallee.* Great song of Julia Morkan's. Kept her voice up to the very last. Pupil of Michael Balfe's wasn't she?

He gazed after the last broad tunic. Nasty customers to tackle. Jack Power could a tale unfold: father a G man. If a fellow gave them trouble being lagged they let him have it hot and heavy in the bridewell.[8] Can't blame them after all with the job they have especially the young hornies. That horsepoliceman the day Joe Chamberlain was given his degree in Trinity he got a run for his money.[9] My word he did! His horse's hoofs clattering after us down Abbey street. Luck I had the presence of mind to dive into Manning's or I was souped. He did come a wallop, by George. Must have cracked his skull on the cobblestones. I oughtn't to have got myself swept along with those medicals. And the Trinity jibs[1] in their mortarboards. Looking for trouble. Still I got to know that young Dixon who dressed that sting for me in the Mater and now he's in Holles street where Mrs Purefoy. Wheels within wheels. Police whistle in my ears still. All skedaddled. Why he fixed on me. Give me in charge. Right here it began.

—Up the Boers!

—Three cheers for De Wet![2]

—We'll hang Joe Chamberlain on a sourapple tree.

Silly billies: mob of young cubs yelling their guts out. Vinegar hill. The Butter exchange band. Few years' time half of them magistrates and civil servants. War comes on: into the army helterskelter: same fellows used to. Whether on the scaffold high.

Never know who you're talking to. Corny Kelleher he has Harvey Duff in his eye. Like that Peter or Denis or James Carey that blew the gaff on the

---

6. Cf. W. S. Gilbert, *Pirates of Penzance:* "The policeman's lot is not a happy one."
7. *The Meeting of the Waters* was a famous poem by the much-loved Irish poet Thomas Moore (1779–1852), whose statue Bloom now passes.
8. Prison.
9. When Joseph Chamberlain, the British colonial

secretary, came to Dublin to receive an honorary degree from Trinity College, a group of medical students rioted against him and against the Boer War.
1. Trinity College students.
2. Boer general.

invincibles. Member of the corporation too. Egging raw youths on to get in the know. All the time drawing secret service pay from the castle.[3] Drop him like a hot potato. Why those plainclothes men are always courting slaveys. Easily twig a man used to uniform. Squarepushing up against a backdoor. Maul her a bit. Then the next thing on the menu. And who is the gentleman does be visiting there? Was the young master saying anything? Peeping Tom through the keyhole. Decoy duck. Hotblooded young student fooling round her fat arms ironing.

—Are those yours, Mary?

—I don't wear such things . . . Stop or I'll tell the missus on you. Out half the night.

—There are great times coming, Mary. Wait till you see.

—Ah, get along with your great times coming.

Barmaids too. Tobaccoshopgirls.

James Stephens'[4] idea was the best. He knew them. Circles of ten so that a fellow couldn't round on more than his own ring. Sinn Fein.[5] Back out you get the knife. Hidden hand. Stay in. The firing squad. Turnkey's daughter got him out of Richmond, off from Lusk. Putting up in the Buckingham Palace hotel under their very noses. Garibaldi.[6]

You must have a certain fascination: Parnell. Arthur Griffith[7] is a square-headed fellow but he has no go in him for the mob. Want to gas about our lovely land. Gammon and spinach. Dublin Bakery Company's tearoom. Debating societies. That republicanism is the best form of government. That the language question should take precedence of the economic question. Have your daughters inveigling them to your house. Stuff them up with meat and drink. Michaelmas goose. Here's a good lump of thyme seasoning under the apron for you. Have another quart of goosegrease before it gets too cold. Halffed enthusiasts. Penny roll and a walk with the band. No grace for the carver. The thought that the other chap pays best sauce in the world. Make themselves thoroughly at home. Show us over those apricots, meaning peaches. The not far distant day. Home Rule sun rising up in the northwest.[8]

His smile faded as he walked, a heavy cloud hiding the sun slowly, shadowing Trinity's surly front. Trams passed one another, ingoing, outgoing, clanging. Useless words. Things go on same; day after day: squads of police marching out, back: trams in, out. Those two loonies mooching about. Dignam carted off. Mina Purefoy swollen belly on a bed groaning to have a child tugged out of her. One born every second somewhere. Other dying every second. Since I fed the birds five minutes. Three hundred kicked the bucket. Other three hundred born, washing the blood off, all are washed in the blood of the lamb, bawling maaaaaa.

Cityful passing away, other cityful coming, passing away too: other coming on, passing on. Houses, lines of houses, streets, miles of pavements, piledup

3. I.e., from the British government, whose representative lived at Dublin Castle.
4. Irish nationalist revolutionary.
5. Irish revolutionary movement. The Gaelic words mean "Ourselves Alone."
6. Bloom is thinking of a variety of nationalist conspirators who escaped from danger, among them the 19th-century Italian patriot and general Giu-

seppe Garibaldi.
7. Founder of the Sinn Fein (1872–1922). Charles Stewart Parnell (1846–1891), Irish nationalist political leader.
8. Reference to Griffith's comment on the *Freeman* masthead, which showed the sun rising in the northwest from behind the Bank of Ireland. Bloom has a *Freeman* in his pocket.

bricks, stones. Changing hands. This owner, that. Landlord never dies they say. Other steps into his shoes when he gets his notice to quit. They buy the place up with gold and still they have all the gold. Swindle in it somewhere. Piled up in cities, worn away age after age. Pyramids in sand. Built on bread and onions. Slaves Chinese wall. Babylon. Big stones left. Round towers. Rest rubble, sprawling suburbs, jerrybuilt, Kerwan's mushroom houses built of breeze. Shelter for the night.

No-one is anything.

This is the very worst hour of the day. Vitality. Dull, gloomy: hate this hour. Feel as if I had been eaten and spewed.

Provost's house. The reverend Dr Salmon: tinned salmon. Well tinned in there. Wouldn't live in it if they paid me. Hope they have liver and bacon today. Nature abhors a vacuum.

The sun freed itself slowly and lit glints of light among the silverware in Walter Sexton's window opposite by which John Howard Parnell[9] passed, unseeing.

There he is: the brother. Image of him. Haunting face. Now that's a coincidence. Course hundreds of times you think of a person and don't meet him. Like a man walking in his sleep. No-one knows him. Must be a corporation meeting today. They say he never put on the city marshal's uniform since he got the job. Charley Beulger used to come out on his high horse, cocked hat, puffed, powdered and shaved. Look at the woebegone walk of him. Eaten a bad egg. Poached eyes on ghost. I have a pain. Great man's brother: his brother's brother. He'd look nice on the city charger. Drop into the D. B. C. probably for his coffee, play chess there. His brother used men as pawns. Let them all go to pot. Afraid to pass a remark on him. Freeze them up with that eye of his. That's the fascination: the name. All a bit touched. Mad Fanny and his other sister Mrs Dickinson driving about with scarlet harness. Bolt upright like surgeon M'Ardle. Still David Sheehy beat him for south Meath. Apply for the Chiltern Hundreds[1] and retire into public life. The patriot's banquet. Eating orangepeels in the park. Simon Dedalus said when they put him in parliament that Parnell would come back from the grave and lead him out of the House of Commons by the arm.

—Of the twoheaded octopus, one of whose heads is the head upon which the ends of the world have forgotten to come while the other speaks with a Scotch accent. The tentacles . . .

They passed from behind Mr Bloom along the curbstone. Beard and bicycle. Young woman.

And there he is too. Now that's really a coincidence: second time. Coming events cast their shadows before. With the approval of the eminent poet, Mr Geo Russell. That might be Lizzie Twigg with him.[2] A. E.: what does that mean? Initials perhaps. Albert Edward, Arthur Edmund, Alphonsus Eb Ed El Esquire. What was he saying? The ends of the world with a Scotch accent.

9. Parnell's brother.
1. The Stewardship of the Chiltern Hundreds (a tract of land in central England owned by the British Crown) is by a legal figment held to be an office of profit under the Crown and is conferred on any Member of Parliament wishing to resign his seat, which by law he cannot do, so long as he is duly qualified. A Member of Parliament who accepts an office of profit under the Crown must vacate his seat.

2. Bloom wonders whether the woman with A. E. might be Lizzie Twigg and then goes on to speculate on the meaning of "A. E." and on Russell's mystical ideas.

Tentacles: octopus. Something occult: symbolism. Holding forth. She's taking it all in. Not saying a word. To aid gentleman in literary work.

His eyes followed the high figure in homespun, beard and bicycle, a listening woman at his side. Coming from the vegetarian. Only weggebobbles and fruit. Don't eat a beefsteak. If you do the eyes of that cow will pursue you through all eternity. They say it's healthier. Wind and watery though. Tried it. Keep you on the run all day. Bad as a bloater. Dreams all night. Why do they call that thing they gave me nutsteak? Nutarians. Fruitarians. To give you the idea you are eating rumpsteak. Absurd. Salty too. They cook in soda. Keep you sitting by the tap all night.

Her stockings are loose over her ankles. I detest that: so tasteless. Those literary etherial people they are all. Dreamy, cloudy, symbolistic. Esthetes they are. I wouldn't be surprised if it was that kind of food you see produces the like waves of the brain the poetical. For example one of those policemen sweating Irish stew into their shirts; you couldn't squeeze a line of poetry out of him. Don't know what poetry is even. Must be in a certain mood.

> The dreamy cloudy gull
> Waves o'er the waters dull.

He crossed at Nassau street corner and stood before the window of Yeates and Son, pricing the fieldglasses. Or will I drop into old Harris's and have a chat with young Sinclair? Wellmannered fellow. Probably at his lunch. Must get those old glasses of mine set right. Gœrz lenses six guineas. Germans making their way everywhere. Sell on easy terms to capture trade. Undercutting. Might chance on a pair in the railway lost property office. Astonishing the things people leave behind them in trains and cloakrooms. What do they be thinking about? Women too. Incredible. Last year travelling to Ennis had to pick up that farmer's daughter's bag and hand it to her at Limerick junction. Unclaimed money too. There's a little watch up there on the roof of the bank to test those glasses by.

His lids came down on the lower rims of his irides. Can't see it. If you imagine it's there you can almost see it. Can't see it.

He faced about and, standing between the awnings, held out his right hand at arm's length towards the sun. Wanted to try that often. Yes: completely. The tip of his little finger blotted out the sun's disk. Must be the focus where the rays cross. If I had black glasses. Interesting. There was a lot of talk about those sunspots when we were in Lombard street west. Terrific explosions they are. There will be a total eclipse this year: autumn some time.

Now that I come to think of it, that ball falls at Greenwich time. It's the clock is worked by an electric wire from Dunsink. Must go out there some first Saturday of the month. If I could get an introduction to professor Joly or learn up something about his family. That would do to: man always feels complimented. Flattery where least expected. Nobleman proud to be descended from some king's mistress. His foremother. Lay it on with a trowel. Cap in hand goes through the land. Not go in and blurt out what you know you're not to: what's parallax? Show this gentleman the door.

Ah.

His hand fell again to his side.

Never know anything about it. Waste of time. Gasballs spinning about, crossing each other, passing. Same old dingdong always. Gas, then solid, then world, then cold, then dead shell drifting around, frozen rock like that pineapple rock. The moon. Must be a new moon out, she said. I believe there is.

He went on by la maison Claire.

Wait. The full moon was the night we were Sunday fortnight exactly there is a new moon. Walking down by the Tolka. Not bad for a Fairview moon. She was humming. The young May moon she's beaming, love. He other side of her. Elbow, arm. He. Glowworm's la-amp is gleaming, love. Touch. Fingers. Asking. Answer. Yes.

Stop. Stop. If it was it was.[3] Must.

Mr Bloom, quickbreathing, slowlier walking passed Adam court.

With deep quiet relief, his eyes took note: this is street here middle of the day Bob Doran's bottle shoulders. On his annual bend, M'Coy said. They drink in order to say or do something or *cherchez la femme*.[4] Up in the Coombe with chummies and streetwalkers and then the rest of the year as sober as a judge.

Yes. Thought so. Sloping into the Empire. Gone. Plain soda would do him good. Where Pat Kinsella had his Harp theatre before Whitbread ran the Queen's.[5] Broth of a boy. Dion Boucicault[6] business with his harvestmoon face in a poky bonnet. Three Purty Maids from School. How time flies eh? Showing long red pantaloons under his skirts. Drinkers, drinking, laughed spluttering, their drink against their breath. More power, Pat. Coarse red: fun for drunkards: guffaw and smoke. Take off that white hat. His parboiled eyes. Where is he now? Beggar somewhere. The harp that once did starve us all.[7]

I was happier then. Or was that I? Or am I now I? Twentyeight I was. She twentythree when we left Lombard street west something changed. Could never like it again after Rudy. Can't bring back time. Like holding water in your hand. Would you go back to then? Just beginning then. Would you? Are you not happy in your home, you poor little naughty boy? Wants to sew on buttons for me. I must answer. Write it in the library.

Grafton street gay with housed awnings lured his senses. Muslin prints silk, dames and dowagers, jingle of harnesses, hoofthuds lowringing in the baking causeway. Thick feet that woman has in the white stockings. Hope the rain mucks them up on her. Countrybred chawbacon. All the beef to the heels were in. Always gives a woman clumsy feet. Molly looks out of plumb.

He passed, dallying, the windows of Brown Thomas, silk mercers. Cascades of ribbons. Flimsy China silks. A tilted urn poured from its mouth a flood of bloodhued poplin: lustrous blood. The huguenots brought that here. *La causa è santa!*[8] *Tara tara*. Great chorus that. *Tara*. Must be washed in rainwater. Meyerbeer. *Tara: bom bom bom*.

---

3. Bloom is thinking again of his wife's infidelity.
4. Look for the woman (in the case).
5. The Queen's Theatre.
6. Irish-born American dramatist, manager, and actor.
7. A reference to the lack of financial success of the Harp Theatre through a punning reworking

(almost worthy of Stephen Dedalus) of Moore's famous *Harp That Once Through Tara's Halls*.
8. "The cause is sacred," chorus from Meyerbeer's opera *Les Huguenots*, which Bloom is recalling. The Huguenots were 16th- and 17th-century French Protestants, many of whom fled to Britain to escape persecution.

Pincushions. I'm a long time threatening to buy one. Stick them all over the place. Needles in window curtains.

He bared slightly his left forearm. Scrape: nearly gone. Not today anyhow. Must go back for that lotion. For her birthday perhaps. Junejuly augseptember eighth. Nearly three months off. Then she mightn't like it. Women won't pick up pins. Say it cuts lo.

Gleaming silks, petticoats on slim brass rails, rays of flat silk stockings. Useless to go back. Had to be. Tell me all.

High voices. Sunwarm silk. Jingling harnesses. All for a woman, home and houses, silkwebs, silver, rich fruits, spicy from Jaffa. Agendath Netaim.[9] Wealth of the world.

A warm human plumpness settled down on his brain. His brain yielded. Perfume of embraces all him assailed. With hungered flesh obscurely, he mutely craved to adore.

Duke street. Here we are. Must eat. The Burton. Feel better then.

He turned Combridge's corner, still pursued. Jingling hoofthuds. Perfumed bodies, warm, full. All kissed, yielded: in deep summer fields, tangled pressed grass, in trickling hallways of tenements, along sofas, creaking beds.

—Jack, love!

—Darling!

—Kiss me, Reggy!

—My boy!

—Love![1]

His heart astir he pushed in the door of the Burton restaurant. Stink gripped his trembling breath: pungent meatjuice, slop of greens. See the animals feed.

Men, men, men.

Perched on high stools by the bar, hats shoved back, at the tables calling for more bread no charge, swilling, wolfing gobfuls of sloppy food, their eyes bulging, wiping wetted moustaches. A pallid suetfaced young man polished his tumbler knife fork and spoon with his napkin. New set of microbes. A man with an infant's saucestained napkin tucked round him shovelled gurgling soup down his gullet. A man spitting back on his plate: halfmasticated gristle: no teeth to chewchewchew it. Chump chop from the grill. Bolting to get it over. Sad booser's eyes. Bitten off more than he can chew. Am I like that? See ourselves as others see us. Hungry man is an angry man. Working tooth and jaw. Don't! O! A bone! That last pagan king of Ireland Cormac in the schoolpoem choked himself at Sletty southward of the Boyne.[2] Wonder what he was eating. Something galoptious. Saint Patrick converted him to Christianity. Couldn't swallow it all however.

—Roast beef and cabbage.

—One stew.

Smells of men. His gorge rose. Spaton sawdust, sweetish warmish cigarettesmoke, reek of plug, spilt beer, men's beery piss, the stale of ferment.

---

9. Planters' Company (Hebrew). Bloom recalls a leaflet, which he had seen that morning and is still carrying in his pocket, advertising an early Zionist settlement
1. Sensual images are leading Bloom to imagine love scenes from a sentimental novel. The Lestrygonians had used "the handsome daughter of Les-

trygonian Antiphates" as a decoy to lure Ulysses' men to her father, and Bloom is drawn by his sensual and sexual imagination to enter Burton's restaurant—only to be disgusted by the grossness of the atmosphere.
2. Bloom is recalling a "schoolpoem" about a legendary incident in Irish history.

Couldn't eat a morsel here. Fellow sharpening knife and fork, to eat all before him, old chap picking his tootles. Slight spasm, full, chewing the cud. Before and after. Grace after meals. Look on this picture then on that. Scoffing up stewgravy with sopping sippets of bread. Lick it off the plate, man! Get out of this.

He gazed round the stooled and tabled eaters, tightening the wings of his nose.

—Two stouts here.

—One corned and cabbage.

That fellow ramming a knifeful of cabbage down as if his life depended on it. Good stroke. Give me the fidgets to look. Safer to eat from his three hands. Tear it limb from limb. Second nature to him. Born with a silver knife in his mouth. That's witty, I think. Or no. Silver means born rich. Born with a knife. But then the allusion is lost.

An illgirt server gathered sticky clattering plates. Rock, the bailiff, standing at the bar blew the foamy crown from his tankard. Well up: it splashed yellow near his boot. A diner, knife and fork upright, elbows on table, ready for a second helping stared towards the food-lift across his stained square of newspaper. Other chap telling him something with his mouth full. Sympathetic listener. Table talk. I munched hum un thu Unchster Bunk un Munchday. Ha? Did you, faith?

Mr Bloom raised two fingers doubtfully to his lips. His eyes said:

—Not here. Don't see him.[3]

Out. I hate dirty eaters.

He backed towards the door. Get a light snack in Davy Byrne's. Stopgap. Keep me going. Had a good breakfast.

—Roast and mashed here.

—Pint of stout.

Every fellow for his own, tooth and nail. Gulp. Grub. Gulp. Gobstuff.

He came out into clearer air and turned back towards Grafton street. Eat or be eaten. Kill! Kill!

Suppose that communal kitchen years to come perhaps. All trotting down with porringers and tommycans to be filled. Devour contents in the street. John Howard Parnell example the provost of Trinity every mother's son don't talk of your provosts and provost of Trinity women and children, cabmen, priests, parsons, fieldmarshals, archbishops. From Ailesbury road, Clyde road, artisans' dwellings north Dublin union, lord mayor in his gingerbread coach, old queen in a bathchair. My plate's empty. After you with our incorporated drinking cup. Like sir Philip Crampton's fountain. Rub off the microbes with your handkerchief. Next chap rubs on a new batch with his. Father O'Flynn would make hares of them all. Have rows all the same. All for number one. Children fighting for the scrapings of the pot. Want a souppot as big as the Phoenix park. Harpooning flitches and hindquarters out of it. Hate people all round you. City Arms hotel *table d'hôte* she called it. Soup, joint and sweet. Never know whose thoughts you're chewing. Then who'd wash up all the plates and forks? Might be all feeding on tabloids that time. Teeth getting worse and worse.

3. He pretends he is looking for someone he cannot see, so that he has an excuse to leave without eating.

After all there's a lot in that vegetarian fine flavour of things from the earth garlic, of course, it stinks Italian organgrinders crisp of onions mushrooms truffles. Pain to animal too. Pluck and draw fowl. Wretched brutes there at the cattlemarket waiting for the poleaxe to split their skulls open. Moo. Poor trembling calves. Meh. Staggering bob. Bubble and squeak. Butchers' buckets wobble lights. Give us that brisket off the hook. Plup. Rawhead and bloody bones. Flayed glasseyed sheep hung from their haunches, sheepsnouts bloodypapered snivelling nosejam on sawdust. Top and lashers going out. Don't maul them pieces, young one.

Hot fresh blood they prescribe for decline. Blood always needed. Insidious. Lick it up smokinghot, thick sugary. Famished ghosts.

Ah, I'm hungry.

He entered Davy Byrne's. Moral pub. He doesn't chat. Stands a drink now and then. But in leapyear once in four. Cashed a cheque for me once.

What will I take now? He drew his watch. Let me see now. Shandygaff?

—Hello, Bloom, Nosey Flynn said from his nook.

—Hello, Flynn.

—How's things?

—Tiptop . . . Let me see. I'll take a glass of burgundy and . . . let me see.

Sardines on the shelves. Almost taste them by looking. Sandwich? Ham and his descendants mustered and bred there. Potted meats. What is home without Plumtree's potted meat? Incomplete. What a stupid ad! Under the obituary notices they stuck it. All up a plumtree. Dignam's potted mat. Cannibals would with lemon and rice. White missionary too salty. Like pickled pork. Expect the chief consumes the parts of honour. Ought to be tough from exercise. His wives in a row to watch the effect. *There was a right royal old nigger. Who ate or something the somethings of the reverend Mr MacTrigger.* With it an abode of bliss. Lord knows what concoction. Cauls mouldy tripes windpipes faked and minced up. Puzzle find the meat. Kosher. No meat and milk together. Hygiene that was what they call now, Yom Kippur fast spring cleaning of inside. Peace and war depend on some fellow's digestion. Religions. Christmas turkeys and geese. Slaughter of innocents. Eat, drink and be merry. Then casual wards full after. Heads bandaged. Cheese digests all but itself. Mighty cheese.

—Have you a cheese sandwich?

—Yes, sir.

Like a few olives too if they had them. Italian I prefer. Good glass of burgundy; take away that. Lubricate. A nice salad, cool as a cucumber. Tom Kernan can dress. Puts gusto into it. Pure olive oil. Milly served me that cutlet with a sprig of parsley. Take one Spanish onion. God made food, the devil the cooks. Devilled crab.

—Wife well?

—Quite well, thanks . . . A cheese sandwich, then. Gorgonzola, have you?

—Yes, sir.

Nosey Flynn sipped his grog.

—Doing any singing those times?

Look at his mouth. Could whistle in his own ear. Flap ears to match. Music. Knows as much about it as my coachman. Still better tell him. Does no harm. Free ad.

—She's engaged for a big tour end of this month. You may have heard perhaps.

—No. O, that's the style. Who's getting it up?

The curate[4] served.

—How much is that?

—Seven d., sir . . . Thank you, sir.

Mr Bloom cut his sandwich into slender strips. *Mr MacTrigger.* Easier than the dreamy creamy stuff. *His five hundred wives. Had the time of their lives.*

—Mustard, sir?

—Thank you.

He studded under each lifted strip yellow blobs. *Their lives.* I have it. *It grew bigger and bigger and bigger.*

—Getting it up? he said. Well, it's like a company idea, you see. Part shares and part profits.

—Ay, now I remember, Nosey Flynn said, putting his hand in his pocket to scratch his groin. Who is this was telling me? Isn't Blazes Boylan mixed up in it?

A warm shock of air heat of mustard hanched on Mr Bloom's heart. He raised his eyes and met the stare of a bilious clock. Two. Pub clock five minutes fast. Time going on. Hands moving. Two. Not yet.[5]

His midriff yearned then upward, sank within him, yearned more longly, longingly.

Wine.

He smellsipped the cordial juice and, bidding his throat strongly to speed it, set his wineglass delicately down.

—Yes, he said. He's the organiser in point of fact.

No fear: no brains.

Nosey Flynn snuffled and scratched. Flea having a good square meal.

—He had a good slice of luck, Jack Mooney was telling me, over that boxing match Myler Keogh won again that soldier in the Portobello barracks. By God, he had the little kipper down in the country Carlow he was telling me....

Hope that dewdrop doesn't come down into his glass. No, snuffled it up.

—For near a month, man, before it came off. Sucking duck eggs by God till further orders. Keep him off the boose, see? O, by God, Blazes is a hairy chap.

Davy Byrne came forward from the hindbar in tuckstitched shirtsleeves, cleaning his lips with two wipes of his napkin. Herring's blush. Whose smile upon each feature plays with such and such replete. Too much fat on the parsnips.

—And here's himself and pepper on him, Nosey Flynn said. Can you give us a good one for the Gold cup?

—I'm off that, Mr Flynn, Davy Byrne answered. I never put anything on a horse.

—You're right there, Nosey Flynn said.

Mr Bloom ate his strips of sandwich, fresh clean bread, with relish of disgust, pungent mustard, the feety savour of green cheese. Sips of his wine

4. Bartender.   5. I.e., not yet time for Boylan to visit Molly.

soothed his palate. Not logwood that. Tastes fuller this weather with the chill off.

Nice quiet bar. Nice piece of wood in that counter. Nicely planed. Like the way it curves there.

—I wouldn't do anything at all in that line, Davy Byrne said. It ruined many a man, the same horses.

Vintners' sweepstake. Licensed for the sale of beer, wine and spirits for consumption on the premises. Heads I win tails you lose.

—True for you, Nosey Flynn said. Unless you're in the know. There's no straight sport going now. Lenehan gets some good ones. He's giving Sceptre today. Zinfandel's the favourite, lord Howard de Walden's, won at Epsom. Morny Cannon is riding him. I could have got seven to one against Saint Amant a fortnight before.

—That so? Davy Byrne said. . . .

He went towards the window and, taking up the petty cash book, scanned its pages.

—I could, faith, Nosey Flynn said, snuffling. That was a rare bit of horseflesh. Saint Frusquin was her sire. She won in a thunderstorm, Rothschild's filly, with wadding in her ears. Blue jacket and yellow cap. Bad luck to big Ben Dollard and his John O'Gaunt. He put me off it. Ay.

He drank resignedly from his tumbler, running his fingers down the flutes.

—Ay, he said, sighing.

Mr Bloom, champing standing, looked upon his sigh. Nosey numbskull. Will I tell him that horse Lenehan?[6] He knows already. Better let him forget. Go and lose more. Fool and his money. Dewdrop coming down again. Cold nose he'd have kissing a woman. Still they might like. Prickly beards they like. Dogs' cold noses. Old Mrs Riordan with the rumbling stomach's Skye terrier in the City Arms hotel. Molly fondling him in her lap. O, the big doggybowwowsywowsy!

Wine soaked and softened rolled pith of bread mustard a moment mawkish cheese. Nice wine it is. Taste it better because I'm not thirsty. Bath of course does that. Just a bite or two. Then about six o'clock I can. Six. Six. Time will be gone then. She . . .

Mild fire of wine kindled his veins. I wanted that badly. Felt so off colour. His eyes unhungrily saw shelves of tins, sardines, gaudy lobsters' claws. All the odd things people pick up for food. Out of shells, periwinkles with a pin, off trees, snails out of the ground the French eat, out of the sea with bait on a hook. Silly fish learn nothing in a thousand years. If you didn't know risky putting anything into your mouth. Poisonous berries. Johnny Magories. Roundness you think good. Gaudy colour warns you off. One fellow told another and so on. Try it on the dog first. Led on by the smell or the look. Tempting fruit. Ice cones. Cream. Instinct. Orangegroves for instance. Need artificial irrigation. Bleibtreustrasse.[7] Yes but what about oysters. Unsightly like a clot of phlegm. Filthy shells. Devil to open them too. Who found them out? Garbage, sewage they feed on. Fizz and Red bank oysters. Effect on the sexual. Aphrodis. He was in the Red bank this morning. Was he oyster old fish at table. Perhaps he young flesh in bed. No. June has no ar no oysters.

---

6. Bloom is wondering whether to pass on a tip from Lenehan, who wrote for the racing paper *Sport*.

7. The Berlin street that contained the offices of the "Planters' Company."

But there are people like tainted game. Jugged hare. First catch your hare. Chinese eating eggs fifty years old, blue and green again. Dinner of thirty courses. Each dish harmless might mix inside. Idea for a poison mystery. That archduke Leopold was it. No. Yes, or was it Otto one of those Habsburgs? Or who was it used to eat the scruff off his own head? Cheapest lunch in town. Of course, aristocrats, then the others copy to be in the fashion. Milly too rock oil and flour. Raw pastry I like myself. Half the catch of oysters they throw back in the sea to keep up the price. Cheap. No-one would buy. Caviare. Do the grand. Hock in green glasses. Swell blowout. Lady this. Powdered bosom pearls. The élite. Crème de la crème.⁸ They want special dishes to pretend they're. Hermit with a platter of pulse keep down the stings of the flesh. Know me come eat with me. Royal sturgeon. High sheriff, Coffey, the butcher, right to venisons of the forest from his ex.⁹ Send him back the half of a cow. Spread I saw down in the Master of the Rolls' kitchen area. Whitehatted Chef like a rabbi. Combustible duck. Curly cabbage à la duchesse de Parme. Just as well to write it on the bill of fare so you can know what you've eaten too many drugs spoil the broth. I know it myself. Dosing it with Edwards' desicated soup. Geese stuffed silly for them. Lobsters boiled alive. Do ptake some ptarmigan. Wouldn't mind being a waiter in a swell hotel. Tips, evening dress, halfnaked ladies. May I tempt you to a little more filleted lemon sole, miss Dubedat? Yes, do bedad. And she did bedad. Huguenot name I expect that. A miss Dubedat lived in Killiney, I remember. Du, de la, French. Still it's the same fish, perhaps old Micky Hanlon of Moore street ripped the guts out of making money, hand over fist, finger in fishes' gills, can't write his name on a cheque, think he was painting the landscape with his mouth twisted. Moooikill A Aitcha Ha. Ignorant as a kish of brogues,¹ worth fifty thousand pounds.

Stuck on the pane two flies buzzed, stuck.

Glowing wine on his palate lingered swallowed. Crushing in the winepress grapes of Burgundy. Sun's heat it is. Seems to a secret touch telling me memory. Touched his sense moistened remembered. Hidden under wild ferns on Howth. Below us bay sleeping sky. No sound. The sky. The bay purple by the Lion's head. Green by Drumleck. Yellowgreen towards Sutton. Fields of undersea, the lines faint brown in grass, buried cities. Pillowed on my coat she had her hair, earwigs in the heather scrub my hand under her nape, you'll toss me all. O wonder! Coolsoft with ointments her hand touched me, caressed: her eyes upon me did not turn away. Ravished over her I lay, full lips full open, kissed her mouth. Yum. Softly she gave me in my mouth the seedcake warm and chewed. Mawkish pulp her mouth had mumbled sweet and sour with spittle. Joy: I ate it: joy. Young life, her lips that gave me pouting. Soft, warm, sticky gumjelly lips. Flowers her eyes were, take me, willing eyes. Pebbles fell. She lay still. A goat. No-one. High on Ben Howth rhododendrons a nannygoat walking surefooted, dropping currants. Screened under ferns she laughed warmfolded. Wildly I lay on her, kissed her, eyes, her lips, her stretched neck, beating, woman's breasts full in her

---

8. Cream of the cream (i.e., the very best, socially).
9. All sturgeon caught in or off Britain were the property of the king, according to the ancient traditional rights to certain kinds of fish or game.

Bloom goes on to imagine a Dublin butcher having a "right to venisons of the forest from his ex[cellency]"—i.e., the viceroy.
1. A basket of shoes.

blouse of nun's veiling, fat nipples upright. Hot I tongued her. She kissed me. I was kissed. All yielding she tossed my hair. Kissed, she kissed me.[2]

Me. And me now.

Stuck, the flies buzzed.

His downcast eyes followed the silent veining of the oaken slab. Beauty: it curves: curves are beauty. Shapely goddesses, Venus, Juno: curves the world admires. Can see them library museum standing in the round hall, naked goddesses. Aids to digestion. They don't care what man looks. All to see. Never speaking, I mean to say to fellows like Flynn. Suppose she did Pygmalion and Galatea[3] what would she say first? Mortal! Put you in your proper place. Quaffing nectar at mess with gods, golden dishes, all ambrosial. Not like a tanner lunch we have, boiled mutton, carrots and turnips, bottle of Allsop. Nectar, imagine it drinking electricity: god's food. Lovely forms of women sculped Junonian. Immortal lovely. And we stuffing food in one hole and out behind: food, chyle, blood, dung, earth, food: have to feed it like stoking an engine. They have no. Never looked. I'll look today. Keeper won't see. Bend down let something see if she.

Dribbling a quiet message from his bladder came to go to do not to do there to do. A man and ready he drained his glass to the lees and walked, to men too they gave themselves, manly conscious, lay with men lovers, a youth enjoyed her, to the yard.

When the sound of his boots had ceased Davy Byrne said from his book:

—What is this he is? Isn't he in the insurance line?

—He's out of that long ago, Nosey Flynn said. He does canvassing for the *Freeman.*

—I know him well to see, Davy Byrne said. Is he in trouble?

—Trouble? Nosey Flynn said. Not that I heard of. Why?

—I noticed he was in mourning.

—Was he? Nosey Flynn said. So he was, faith. I asked him how was all at home. You're right, by God. So he was.

—I never broach the subject, Davy Byrne said humanely, if I see a gentleman is in trouble that way. It only brings it up fresh in their minds.

—It's not the wife anyhow, Nosey Flynn said. I met him the day before yesterday and he coming out of that Irish farm dairy John Wyse Nolan's wife has in Henry street with a jar of cream in his hand taking it home to his better half. She's well nourished, I tell you. Plovers on toast.

—And is he doing for the *Freeman?* Davy Byrne said.

Nosey Flynn pursed his lips.

—He doesn't buy cream on the ads he picks up. You can make bacon of that.

—How so? Davy Byrne asked, coming from his book.

Nosey Flynn made swift passes in the air with juggling fingers. He winked.

—He's in the craft,[4] he said.

2. Bloom is remembering when he first proposed to Molly, on the Hill of Howth, near Dublin, Molly also recalls this in the final "Penelope" episode, which is her soliloquy: "we were lying among the rhododendrons on Howth head in the gray tweed suit and his straw hat the day I got him to propose to me yes . . . my God after that long kiss I near lost my breath . . . I saw he understood or felt what a woman is and I knew I could always get round him and I gave him all the pleasure I could leading him on."

3. Pygmalion was the sculptor whose statue of Galatea came alive.

4. I.e., in the "free and accepted order" of Freemasons, one of the oldest European secret societies; it was not in good repute in predominantly Roman Catholic countries like Ireland.

—Do you tell me so? Davy Byrne said.

—Very much so, Nosey Flynn said. Ancient free and accepted order. Light, life and love, by God. They give him a leg up. I was told that by a, well, I won't say who.

—Is that a fact?

—O, it's a fine order, Nosey Flynn said. They stick to you when you're down. I know a fellow was trying to get into it, but they're as close as damn it. By God they did right to keep the women out of it.

Davy Byrne smiledyawnednodded all in one:

—Iiiiiichaaaaaaach!

—There was one woman, Nosey Flynn said, hid herself in a clock to find out what they do be doing. But be damned but they smelt her out and swore her in on the spot a master mason. That was one of the Saint Legers of Doneraile.

Davy Byrne, sated after his yawn, said with tearwashed eyes:

—And is that a fact? Decent quiet man he is. I often saw him in here and I never once saw him, you know, over the line.

—God Almighty couldn't make him drunk, Nosey Flynn said firmly. Slips off when the fun gets too hot. Didn't you see him look at his watch? Ah, you weren't there. If you ask him to have a drink first thing he does he outs with the watch to see what he ought to imbibe. Declare to God he does.

—There are some like that, Davy Byrne said. He's a safe man, I'd say.

—He's not too bad, Nosey Flynn said, snuffling it up. He has been known to put his hand down too to help a fellow. Give the devil his due. O, Bloom has his good points. But there's one thing he'll never do.

His hand scrawled a dry pen signature beside his grog.

—I know, Davy Byrne said.

—Nothing in black and white, Nosey Flynn said.

Paddy Leonard and Bantam Lyons came in. Tom Rochford followed frowning, a plaining hand on his claret waistcoat.

—Day, Mr Byrne.

—Day, gentlemen.

They paused at the counter.

—Who's standing? Paddy Leonard asked.

—I'm sitting anyhow, Nosey Flynn answered.

—Well, what'll it be? Paddy Leonard asked.

—I'll take a stone ginger, Bantam Lyons said.

—How much? Paddy Leonard cried. Since when, for God's sake? What's yours, Tom?

—How is the main drainage? Nosey Flynn asked, sipping.

For answer Tom Rochford pressed his hand to his breastbone and hiccupped.

—Would I trouble you for a glass of fresh water, Mr Byrne? he said.

—Certainly, sir.

Paddy Leonard eyed his alemates.

—Lord love a duck, he said, look at what I'm standing drinks to! Cold water and gingerpop! Two fellows that would suck whisky off a sore leg. He has some bloody horse up his sleeve for the Gold cup. A dead snip.

—Zinfandel is it? Nosey Flynn asked.

Tom Rochford spilt powder from a twisted paper into the water set before him.

—That cursed dyspepsia, he said before drinking.

—Breadsoda is very good, Davy Byrne said.

Tom Rochford nodded and drank.

—Is it Zinfandel?

—Say nothing, Bantam Lyons winked. I'm going to plunge five bob on my own.

—Tell us if you're worth your salt and be damned to you, Paddy Leonard said. Who gave it to you?

Mr Bloom on his way out raised three fingers in greeting.

—So long, Nosey Flynn said.

The others turned.

—That's the man now that gave it to me, Bantam Lyons whispered.

—Prrwht! Paddy Leonard said with scorn. Mr Byrne, sir, we'll take two of your small Jamesons[5] after that and a . . .

—Stone ginger, Davy Byrne added civilly.

—Ay, Paddy Leonard said. A suckingbottle for the baby.

Mr Bloom walked towards Dawson street, his tongue brushing his teeth smooth. Something green it would have to be: spinach say. Then with those Röntgen rays searchlight you could.

At Duke lane a ravenous terrier choked up a sick knuckly cud on the cobblestones and lapped it with new zest. Surfeit. Returned with thanks having fully digested the contents. First sweet then savoury. Mr Bloom coasted warily. Ruminants. His second course. Their upper jaw they move. Wonder if Tom Rochford will do anything with that invention of his. Wasting time explaining it to Flynn's mouth. Lean people long mouths. Ought to be a hall or a place where inventors could go in and invent free. Course then you'd have all the cranks pestering.

He hummed, prolonging in solemn echo, the closes of the bars:

> *Don Giovanni, a cenar teco*
> *M'invitasti.*[6]

Feel better. Burgundy. Good pick me up. Who distilled first? Some chap in the blues. Dutch courage. That *Kilkenny People* in the national library now I must.

Bare clean closestools, waiting, in the window of William Miller, plumber, turned back his thoughts. They could: and watch it all the way down, swallow a pin sometimes come out of the ribs years after, tour round the body, changing biliary duct, spleen squirting liver, gastric juice coils of intestines like pipes. But the poor buffer would have to stand all the time with his insides entrails on show. Science.

---

5. Brand of Irish whiskey.
6. Because Molly is a singer, Bloom is familiar with opera. Here he recalls the song sung by the Commendatore's statue in Mozart's *Don Giovanni* and translates accurately the Italian words he quotes, except for *"teco"* (with thee). This opera supplies some of the key themes in *Ulysses*, and the famous duet between Don Giovanni and Zerlina. *"Là ci darèm la mano"* (There we will join hands), haunts Bloom's mind continually throughout the day. It is on the program of Molly's concert that she is discussing with Boylan that afternoon, and Bloom associates it with her adultery with Boylan.

—*A cenar teco.*

What does that *teco* mean? Tonight perhaps.

> *Don Giovanni, thou hast me invited*
> *To come to supper tonight,*
> *The rum the rumdum.*

Doesn't go properly.

Keyes: two months if I get Nannetti[7] to. That'll be two pounds ten, about two pounds eight. Three Hynes owes me. Two eleven. Prescott's ad. Two fifteen. Five guineas about. On the pig's back.

Could buy one of those silk petticoats for Molly, colour of her new garters. Today. Today. Not think.[8]

Tour the south then. What about English wateringplaces? Brighton, Margate. Piers by moonlight. Her voice floating out. Those lovely seaside girls. Against John Long's a drowsing loafer lounged in heavy thought, gnawing a crusted knuckle. Handy man wants job. Small wages. Will eat anything.

Mr Bloom turned at Gray's confectioner's window of unbought tarts and passed the reverend Thomas Connellan's bookstore. *Why I left the church of Rome? Birds' Nest.* Women run him. They say they used to give pauper children soup to change to protestants in the time of the potato blight. Society over the way papa went to for the conversion of poor jews. Same bait. *Why we left the church of Rome?*

A blind stripling stood tapping the curbstone with his slender cane. No tram in sight. Wants to cross.

—Do you want to cross? Mr Bloom asked.

The blind stripling did not answer. His wallface frowned weakly. He moved his head uncertainly.

—You're in Dawson street, Mr Bloom said. Molesworth street is opposite. Do you want to cross? There's nothing in the way.

The cane moved out trembling to the left. Mr Bloom's eye followed its line and saw again the dyeworks' van drawn up before Drago's. Where I saw his brillantined hair just when I was. Horse drooping. Driver in John Long's. Slaking his drouth.

—There's a van there, Mr Bloom said, but it's not moving. I'll see you across. Do you want to go to Molesworth street?

—Yes, the stripling answered. South Frederick street.

—Come, Mr Bloom said.

He touched the thin elbow gently: then took the limp seeing hand to guide it forward.

Say something to him. Better not do the condescending. They mistrust what you tell them. Pass a common remark.

—The rain kept off.

No answer.

Stains on his coat. Slobbers his food, I suppose. Tastes all different for

---

7. Proofreader and business manager of the *Freeman's Journal* and in charge of the advertising Bloom is trying to get for the paper. If he will add a complimentary reference to Keyes, a grocer, in a gossip column, Keyes promises to renew his advertisement, which means a commission for Bloom.
8. I.e., of Molly and Boylan.

him. Have to be spoonfed first. Like a child's hand, his hand. Like Milly's was. Sensitive. Sizing me up I daresay from my hand. Wonder if he has a name. Van. Keep his cane clear of the horse's legs tired drudge get his doze. That's right. Clear. Behind a bull: in front of a horse.

—Thanks, sir.

Knows I'm a man. Voice.

—Right now? First turn to the left.

The blind stripling tapped the curbstone and went on his way, drawing his cane back, feeling again.

Mr Bloom walked behind the eyeless feet, a flatcut suit of herringbone tweed. Poor young fellow! How on earth did he know that van was there? Must have felt it. See things in their foreheads perhaps. Kind of sense of volume. Weight would he feel it if something was removed. Feel a gap. Queer idea of Dublin he must have, tapping his way round by the stones. Could he walk in a beeline if he hadn't that cane? Bloodless pious face like a fellow going in to be a priest.

Penrose! That was that chap's name.

Look at all the things they can learn to do. Read with their fingers. Tune pianos. Or we are surprised they have any brains. Why we think a deformed person or a hunchback clever if he says something we might say. Of course the other senses are more. Embroider. Plait baskets. People ought to help. Workbasket I could buy Molly's birthday. Hates sewing. Might take an objection. Dark men they call them.

Sense of smell must be stronger too. Smells on all sides bunched together. Each person too. Then the spring, the summer: smells. Tastes. They say you can't taste wines with your eyes shut or a cold in the head. Also smoke in the dark they say get no pleasure.

And with a woman, for instance. More shameless not seeing. That girl passing the Stewart institution, head in the air. Look at me. I have them all on. Must be strange not to see her. Kind of a form in his mind's eye. The voice temperature when he touches her with fingers must almost see the lines, the curves. His hands on her hair, for instance. Say it was black for instance. Good. We call it black. Then passing over her white skin. Different feel perhaps. Feeling of white.

Postoffice. Must answer.[9] Fag[1] today. Send her a postal order two shillings half a crown. Accept my little present. Stationer's just here too. Wait. Think over it.

With a gentle finger he felt ever so slowly the hair combed back above his ears. Again. Fibres of fine fine straw. Then gently his finger felt the skin of his right cheek. Downy hair there too. Not smooth enough. The belly is the smoothest. No-one about. There he goes into Frederick street. Perhaps to Levenston's dancing academy piano. Might be settling my braces.

Walking by Doran's public house he slid his hand between waistcoat and trousers and, pulling aside his shirt gently, felt a slack fold of his belly. But I know it's whitey yellow. Want to try in the dark to see.

He withdrew his hand and pulled his dress to.

Poor fellow! Quite a boy. Terrible. Really terrible. What dreams would he

9. Martha Clifford's letter.   1. Nuisance.

have, not seeing. Life a dream for him. Where is the justice being born that way. All those women and children excursion beanfeast burned and drowned in New York.[2] Holocaust. Karma they call that transmigration for sins you did in a past life the reincarnation met him pike hoses.[3] Dear, dear, dear. Pity of course: but somehow you can't cotton on to them someway.

Sir Frederick Falkiner going into the freemasons' hall. Solemn as Troy. After his good lunch in Earlsfort terrace. Old legal cronies cracking a magnum. Tales of the bench and assizes and annals of the bluecoat school.[4] I sentenced him to ten years. I suppose he'd turn up his nose at that stuff I drank. Vintage wine for them, the year marked on a dusty bottle. Has his own ideas of justice in the recorder's court. Wellmeaning old man. Police charge sheets crammed with cases get their percentage manufacturing crime. Sends them to the rightabout. The devil on moneylenders. Gave Reuben J. a great strawcalling. Now he's really what they call a dirty jew. Power those judges have. Crusty old topers in wigs. Bear with a sore paw. And may the Lord have mercy on your soul.

Hello, placard. Mirus bazaar. His excellency the lord lieutenant. Sixteenth today it is. In aid of funds for Mercer's hospital. The *Messiah* was first given for that. Yes. Handel. What about going out there. Ballsbridge. Drop in on Keyes. No use sticking to him like a leech. Wear out my welcome. Sure to know someone on the gate.

Mr Bloom came to Kildare street. First I must. Library.

Straw hat in sunlight. Tan shoes. Turnedup trousers. It is. It is.[5]

His heart quopped softly. To the right. Museum. Goddesses. He swerved to the right.

Is it? Almost certain. Won't look. Wine in my face. Why did I? Too heady. Yes, it is. The walk. Not see. Not see. Get on.

Making for the museum gate with long windy strides he lifted his eyes. Handsome building. Sir Thomas Deane designed. Not following me?

Didn't see me perhaps. Light in his eyes.

The flutter of his breath came forth in short sighs. Quick. Cold statues: quiet there. Safe in a minute.

No, didn't see me. After two. Just at the gate.

My heart!

His eyes beating looked steadfastly at cream curves of stone. Sir Thomas Deane was the Greek architecture.

Look for something I.

His hasty hand went quick into a pocket, took out, read unfolded Agendath Netaim. Where did I?

Busy looking for.

He thrust back quickly Agendath.

Afternoon she said.

I am looking for that. Yes, that. Try all pockets. Handker. *Freeman*. Where did I? Ah, yes. Trousers. Purse. Potato. Where did I?

2. This terrible disaster on an excursion steamer on a New York City river took place on June 15, 1904, and was reported in the Dublin papers on June 16.

3. I.e., metempsychosis. Bloom is remembering again their morning conversation on this subject, when Molly exclaimed, "O rocks!"

4. Sir Frederick Falkiner wrote the history of the "bluecoat school" in Oxmantown, Dublin. The Dublin bluecoat school was founded by Charles II for poor children.

5. Bloom catches a glimpse of Boylan and tries to avoid an encounter.

Hurry. Walk quietly. Moment more. My heart.

His hand looking for the where did I put found in his hip pocket soap lotion have to call tepid paper stuck. Ah, soap there! Yes. Gate.[6]

Safe!

1914–21   1922

Finnegans Wake

Because the meanings in *Finnegans Wake* are developed not by action but by language—a great network of multiple puns that echo themes back and forth throughout the book—the careful reading of a single passage, even out of context, will convey more than any summary of the "plot" (some discussion of the general plan of the work is given in the Joyce headnote). The particular passage printed here was one of Joyce's favorites, and there exists a phonograph recording of it made by him. It consists of the closing pages of chapter 8 of book 1; the chapter was published separately as *Anna Livia Plurabelle* in 1928 and 1930, although the finished book omits this title.

The entire chapter is a dialogue, and the scene is the river Liffey: two washerwomen are washing in public the dirty linen of HCE and ALP (the "hero" and "heroine"; see headnote p. 2491) and gossiping as they work. As this excerpt opens, it is growing dark; things become gradually less and less distinct, so that the washerwomen cannot be sure what the objects seen in the dusk really are. As it grows darker, the river becomes wider (we get nearer its mouth) and the wind rises, so that the women have more and more difficulty hearing each other. At last, as night falls, they become part of the landscape, an elm tree and a stone on the river bank. Toward the end of the dialogue they ask to hear a tale of Shem and Shaun (HCE's two sons), and this question points the way to book 2, which opens with the two boys (metamorphosed for the moment into Glugg and Chuff) playing in front of the tavern in the evening.

A complete annotation of even this brief passage is, of course, a physical impossibility in this anthology. The notes that are provided are intended to indicate the nature of what Joyce does with language and to enable the reader to see what is going on. But there are all sorts of suggestions built up in the language that are not referred to in the notes: all readers will find some for themselves.

From Finnegans Wake

From *Anna Livia Plurabelle*

* * * Well, you know or don't you kennet[1] or haven't I told you every telling has a taling and that's the he and the she of it. Look, look, the dusk is growing! My branches lofty are taking root. And my cold cher's gone ashley.[2]

---

6. Anxious to avoid Boylan, Bloom pretends to admire the architecture of the Museum and National Library building and then pretends to be looking for something in his pockets, where he finds the "Agendath Netaim" leaflet. He continues to search desperately in his pockets to avoid looking up and seeing Boylan, discovers the potato he carries as a remedy against rheumatism and a cake of soap he had bought that morning (the soap reminds him that he must call at the chemist's to collect a face lotion he had ordered for Molly). At last he goes through the National Library gate and feels safe.

1. Ken it ("know it") + Kennet (river in England). Rivers in *Finnegans Wake* symbolize the flow of life, and thousands of river names are suggested

throughout the book in allusive pun combinations, as here.

2. "Cold cher": cold cheer (i.e., cold comfort) + cold chair + (perhaps) culture. "Gone ashley": gone to ashes. Going to ashes suggests the fiery death and rebirth of the mythical phoenix: from the ashes of the dead phoenix rises a new one. Modern culture, which can provide only cold cheer, is in the state of decay, the "going to ashes," which precedes the stage of rebirth into a new cultural cycle (according to Giambattista Vico's cyclical theory of history, which is important to *Finnegans Wake*). "Gone ashley" also means "turned into an ash tree" (i.e., it is so cold that the speaker feels herself turning into a tree).

Fieluhr? Filou![3] What age is at? It saon[4] is late. 'Tis endless now senne[5] eye or erewone[6] last saw Waterhouse's clogh.[7] They took it asunder, I hurd thum sigh. When will they reassemble it? O, my back, my back, my bach![8] I'd want to go to Aches-les-Pains.[9] Pingpong! There's the Belle for Sexaloitez![10]And Concepta de Send-us-pray! Pang! Wring out the Clothes! Wring in the dew![11] Godavari,[12] vert the showers![13] And grant thaya grace! Aman. Will we spread them here now? Ay, we will. Flip! Spread on your bank and I'll spread mine on mine. Flep! It's what I'm doing. Spread! It's churning chill. Der went[14] is rising. I'll lay a few stones on the hostel sheets. A man and his bride embraced between them. Else I'd have sprinkled and folded them only. And I'll tie my butcher's apron here. It's suety yet. The strollers will pass it by. Six shifts, ten kerchiefs, nine to hold to the fire and this for the code,[15] the convent napkins, twelve, one baby's shawl. Good mother Jossiph[16] knows, she said. Whose head? Mutter snores? Deataceas![17] Wharnow are alle her childer, say? In kingdome gone or power to come or gloria be to them farther? Allalivial, allalluvial![18] Some here, more no more, more again lost alla stranger.[19] I've heard tell that same brooch of the Shannons[20] was married into a family in Spain. And all the Dunders de Dunnes[21] in Markland's[22] Vineland beyond the Brendan's herring pool[23] takes number nine in yangsee's[24] hats. And one of Biddy's[25] beads went bobbing till she rounded up lost histereve[26] with a marigold and a cobbler's candle in a side strain of a main drain of a manzin-ahurries[27] off Bachelor's Walk. But all that's left to the last of the Meaghers[28] in the loup[29] of the years prefixed and between is one kneebuckle and two hooks in the front. Do you tell me that now? I do in troth. Orara por Orbe

3. Pickpocket; thief (French). "Fieluhr": *Viel Uhr?* (What's the time? German). From an old anecdote of a German soldier and a French soldier shouting at each other across the Rhine. They mishear each other as the washerwomen will later.
4. Soon + Saône (river in France).
5. Since + Senne (river in Belgium).
6. E'er a one + *Erewhon* (novel by Samuel Butler—an anagram for *Nowhere*).
7. Waterhouse's clock, a well-known clock on Dame Street, Dublin.
8. "Brook" (German) + "dear" (Welsh).
9. Cf. Aix-les-Bains, France.
10. "Sachselüte," a Zurich fertility rite (literally, the ringing of six o'clock), which celebrates the burial of winter.
11. Tennyson, *In Memoriam:* "Ring out the old, ring in the new."
12. God of Eire + the name of a river in India.
13. "Vert": avert + *vert* ("green," French), for "the showers" make grass green.
14. *Der Wind* ("the wind," German) + Derwent (river in England).
15. Cold + code (i.e., the code in which the book is written). The numbers in this sentence have special meanings indicated in other episodes.
16. Joseph + *joss* ("God," pidgin English) + gossip (which derives from "god-sib," Middle English, "godparent").
17. A play on Deo gratias ("thanks be to God") and on Dea Tacita ("silent-goddess"), a name from Roman mythology.
18. Multiple punning—Anna Livia + all alive + *la lluvia* ("rain," Spanish) + alluvial—suggesting the mother-river-fertility associations of ALP. At least two other meanings are also present: All alive O! (street cry of shellfish vendors) + Alleluia (Vulgate Latin form of "Hallelujah").
19. Cf. *à l'étranger* (abroad, French).
20. Ornament and branch of the Shannons (family and river).
21. The form of the name suggests an aristocratic Anglo-Norman family. "Dunder" suggests thunder. *Dun* is an Irish word meaning "hill," "fort on a hill."
22. Borderland + land of the mark (i.e., land of money, or America; Markland's Vineland was one of Leif Ericson's names for America). Both King Mark of Cornwall (a character in the Tristan and Iseult story) and Mark of the Gospels are primary symbolic characters in *Finnegans Wake.*
23. The Atlantic Ocean. St. Brendan was an Irish monk who sailed out into the Atlantic to find the terrestrial paradise.
24. Yankees' + Yangtze (river in China). The de Dunnes have swollen heads now that they have emigrated to America.
25. Diminutive form of the name Bridget. St. Brigid (or Bridget) is a patron saint of Ireland. "Biddy" is also a term for an Irish maidservant.
26. Yester eve (last night) + eve of history. The sentence may be paraphrased: "Irish history got lost when she went off in a side branch of the main Roman Catholic church, and Biddy (i.e., Ireland) landed herself in the dirt." There are also Freudian implications here.
27. A urinal + Manzanares (river in Spain).
28. Thomas Francis Meagher, Irish patriot and revolutionary, who was transported to Van Diemen's Land in 1849 and escaped to America in 1852.
29. Loop + *loup* ("wolf" and also "solitary man," French). Cf. Wolfe Tone, the ill-fated Irish revolutionist.

and poor Las Animals![30] Ussa, Ulla, we're umbas[31] all! Mezha, didn't you hear it a deluge of times, ufer[32] and ufer, respund to spond?[33] You deed, you deed! I need, I need! It's that irrawaddyng[34] I've stoke in my aars. It all but husheth the lethest zswound. Oronoko![35] What's your trouble? Is that the great Finn-leader[36] himself in his joakimono[37] on his statue riding the high horse there forehengist?[38] Father of Otters,[39] it is himself! Yonne there! Isset that? On Fallareen Common? You're thinking of Astley's Amphitheayter where the bobby restrained you making sugarstuck pouts to the ghostwhite horse of the Peppers.[40] Throw the cobwebs from your eyes, woman, and spread your washing proper! It's well I know your sort of slop. Flap! Ireland sober is Ireland stiff.[41] Lord help you, Maria, full of grease, the load is with me! Your prayers. I sonht zo![42] Madammangut! Were you lifting your elbow, tell us, glazy cheeks, in Conway's Carrigacurra canteen? Was I what, hob-bledyhips?[43] Flop! Your rere gait's creakorheuman bitts your butts dis-agrees.[44] Amn't I up since the damp dawn, marthared mary allacook, with Corrigan's pulse and varicoarse veins, my pramaxle smashed, Alice Jane in decline and my oneeyed mongrel twice run over, soaking and bleaching boiler rags, and sweating cold, a widow like me, for to deck my tennis champion son, the laundryman with the lavandier flannels? You won your limpopo[45] limp from the husky[46] hussars when Collars and Cuffs was heir to the town and your slur gave the stink to Carlow.[47] Holy Scamander,[48] I sar[49] it again! Near the golden falls. Icis on us! Seints of light! Zezere![50] Subdue your noise, you hamble creature! What is it but a blackburry growth or the dwyergray ass them four old codgers[51] owns. Are you meanam[52] Tarpey and Lyons and Gregory?[53] I meyne now, thank all, the four of them, and the roar of them, that draves[54] that stray in the mist and old Johnny MacDougal along with them. Is that the Poolbeg flasher beyant,[55] pharphar,

---

30. Souls (Spanish) + the name of a river in Colorado. *Ora pro nobis* (pray for us; Latin) + Orara (river in New South Wales) + *pro orbe* (for the world; Latin) + Orbe (river in France). The entire sentence may be read: "Pray for us and for all souls."

31. *Umbra* (shade; Latin) + Umba (river in Africa). "Ussa," "Ulla," and "Mezha" are also river names; each contains a number of other meanings.

32. Bank (of river).

33. *Spund* (bung; German).

34. A multiple pun: Irrawady (river in Burma) + irritating + wadding. This and the following sentence may be paraphrased: "It's that wadding I've stuck in my ears. It hushes the least sound."

35. *Oroonoko* (novel by Aphra Behn about a "noble savage," published ca. 1678) + Orinoco (river in Venezuela).

36. Fionn mac Cumhail (Finn MacCool), legendary hero of ancient Ireland.

37. Comic kimono. *Joki* is the Finnish word for river; the name Joachim is perhaps also implied.

38. According to tradition, Hengist was the Jute invader of England (with Horsa), ca. 449; he founded the kingdom of Kent.

39. Father of Waters (i.e., the Mississippi) + Father of Orders (i.e., Saint Patrick).

40. Philip Astley's Royal Amphitheatre was a famous late 18th-century English circus, specializing in trained horses. "Pepper's Ghost" was a popular circus act. One of the washerwomen has been reproving the other, who thought she saw the great

Finn himself riding his high horse, by telling her that once before she had to be restrained by a policeman for making "sugarstuck pouts" at a circus horse.

41. The temperance reformer Father Matthew had as his slogan "Ireland sober is Ireland free."

42. I thought so + Izonzo (river in Italy).

43. Hobbledehoy + wobbly hips.

44. The sentence is a punning discussion of her hard work and ailments.

45. A river in south Africa.

46. Cf. *uisge* (whiskey, but literally "water [of life]," Gaelic).

47. I.e., "You got a slur on your reputation carrying on with soldiers in the Age of Elegance, and the scandal was all over Ireland" (ALP is being addressed and some of her many lovers are mentioned). "Carlow": a county in Ireland.

48. River near Troy, famous in classical legend.

49. I saw + Isar (river in Germany).

50. See there + Zezere (river in Portugal).

51. The Four Old Men, who represent, among other things, the authors of the Gospels, and the four elements.

52. Meaning + Menam (river in Thailand).

53. Tarpey, Lyons, Gregory, and MacDougal (next sentence) are the "four old codgers."

54. Drives + Drave (river in Hungary).

55. I.e., the Poolbeg Lighthouse beyond (this lighthouse is in Dublin Bay). "Pharphar": far far + Pharphar (river in Damascus) + *pharos* (lighthouse; Greek).

or a fireboat coasting nyar[56] the Kishtna[57] or a glow I behold within a hedge or my Garry come back from the Indes? Wait till the honeying of the lune,[58] love! Die eve, little eve, die![59] We see that wonder in your eye. We'll meet again, we'll part once more. The spot I'll seek if the hour you'll find. My chart shines high where the blue milk's upset. Forgivemequick. I'm going! Bubye! And you, pluck your watch, forgetmenot. Your evenlode.[60] So save to jurna's[61] end! My sights are swimming thicker on me by the shadows to this place. I sow[62] home slowly now by own way, moyvalley way. Towy[63] I too, rathmine.

Ah, but she was the queer old skeowsha[64] anyhow, Anna Livia, trinket-toes! And sure he was the quare old buntz too, Dear Dirty Dumpling,[65] foostherfather of fingalls[66] and dottergills. Gammer and gaffer we're all their gangsters. Hadn't he seven dams to wive him? And every dam had her seven crutches. And every crutch had its seven hues.[67] And each hue had a differing cry. Sudds[68] for me and supper for you and the doctor's bill for Joe John. Befor! Bifur![69] He married his markets, cheap by foul, I know, like any Etrurian Catholic Heathen, in their pinky limony creamy birnies[70] and their turkiss indienne mauves. But at milkidmass[71] who was the spouse? Then all that was was fair. Tys Elvenland![72] Teems of times and happy returns. The seim anew.[73] Ordovico or viricordo. Anna was, Livia is, Plura-belle's to be.[74] Northmen's thing made southfolk's place but howmulty plur-ators made each one in person?[75] Latin me that, my trinity scholard, out of eure sanscreed into oure eryan![76] *Hircus Civis Eblanensis!*[77] He had buckgoat paps on him, soft ones for orphans. Ho,[78] Lord! Twins of his bosom. Lord

56. Near + Nyar (river in India).
57. City in ancient Mesopotamia, traditionally the ruling city after the Flood + Krishna (Hindu god of joy) + Kistna (river in India) + the Kish lightship (in Dublin Bay).
58. Loon (boy; Scottish) + *luna* (moon; Latin). "Honeying of the lune": honeymoon, etc.
59. From a children's game in which a swing is allowed to slow down to the refrain "She's dead, little Eva, little Eva, she's dead."
60. Evening load + Evenlode (river in England).
61. Journey + Jurna (river in Brazil).
62. Sow (river in England).
63. Name of a river in Wales. Moy is the name of an Irish river, and Moyvalley and Rathmine are names of Dublin suburbs.
64. Old timer, in Dublin.
65. "Dumpling" suggests Humpty Dumpty, whose fall is one of the many involved in the vastly symbolic fall of Finnegan. The phrase "Dear Dirty Dublin" occurs in *Ulysses*.
66. Blond and dark Scandinavian invaders of Ireland.
67. Colors of the rainbow (suggested a few lines later by "pinky limony creamy" and "turkiss indienne mauves"). In these sentences Joyce is parodying the nursery rhyme, "As I was going to St. Ives / I met a man with seven wives."
68. Suds (slang for beer) + soap suds + sudd (the floating vegetable matter that often obstructs navigation on the White Nile).
69. Bifurcated creature! This image of man as a forked being suggests HCE (cf. "Etrurian Catholic Heathen"). HCE's marital history, in his role as the Great Parent or generator, is one of the themes in this passage.
70. Coats of mail.

71. Milking time + Michaelmas (September 29).
72. 'Tis the land of Elves + Tys Elv (Norway).
73. The same again + Seim (river in Ireland).
74. The Ordovices were an ancient British tribe in northern Wales, and Ordovician is a term for a geological period. "Ordovico" is also a pun on Vico and his order of historical phases. Joyce is suggesting the cyclical nature of history: the marital history of HCE is the history of ever-renewing life ("the seim anew"), and HCE's bride is Everywoman, past, present, and future ("Anna was, Livia is, Plurabelle's to be"). "Viricordo" is another verbal twist to Vico and his cycles, suggesting his *ricorso* ("recurrence," i.e., the fourth stage of the cycle that brings back the first), as well as overtones from the Latin *vir* (man) and *cor* (heart): the heart of the individual beats on, through all phases of civilization.
75. This sentence may be paraphrased: "The Northmen's assembly (thing) is now in Suffolk Place, but how many ancestors went into the making of each one of us?"
76. I.e., out of your Sanskrit into your Aryan. "Sanscreed" has further punning meanings: *sans* screed (without script) + *sans* creed (without faith). Thus the phrase can read: "out of your illiteracy or faithlessness into Irish" (Eire-an). I.e., the greatest skeptic must pause in reverence before the endless flow of life, represented by Irish history.
77. The Goat-Citizen of Dublin! (Latin). The goat is the symbol of lust and so of fecundity; "*Eblanensis*" is the adjective form of Eblana, the name given by the 3rd-century Alexandrian geographer Ptolemy to what may have been the site of the modern Dublin.
78. River (Chinese).

save us! And ho! Hey? What all men. Hot? His tittering daughters of. Whawk?

Can't hear with the waters of. The chittering waters of. Flittering bats, fieldmice bawk talk. Ho! Are you not gone ahome? What Thom Malone? Can't hear with bawk of bats, all thim liffeying waters of. Ho, talk save us! My foos won't moos.[79] I feel as old as yonder elm. A tale told of Shaun or Shem? All Livia's daughter-sons. Dark hawks hear us. Night! Night! My ho head halls. I feel as heavy as yonder stone. Tell me of John or Shaun? Who were Shem and Shaun the living sons or daughters of? Night now! Tell me, tell me, tell me, elm! Night night! Telmetale of stem or stone.[80] Beside the rivering waters of, hitherandthithering waters of. Night!

1923–38   1939

---

79. Move + *Moos* (moss, German). Her foot ("foos") won't move; it is also turning to moss.
80. Stone and elm tree are important symbols in *Finnegans Wake*. Signifying permanence and change, time and space, mercy and justice, they undergo many changes of symbolic meaning throughout the book.

D. H. LAWRENCE
1885–1930

David Herbert Lawrence was born in the Midland mining village of Eastwood, Nottinghamshire. His father was a miner; his mother, better educated than her husband and self-consciously genteel, fought all her married life to lift her children out of the working class. Lawrence was aware from an early age of the struggle between his parents; he was very much on his mother's side during his childhood, resenting his father's coarse and sometimes drunken behavior and allying himself with his mother's delicacy and refinement. After the death of an elder brother he became the center of his mother's emotional life and played in his own relation to her a loving and protective role. His mother's claims on him kept frustrating his relationships with women, and the personal problems and conflicts that resulted are presented in his first really distinguished novel, *Sons and Lovers* (1913), where, against a background of paternal coarseness and vitality conflicting with maternal refinement and gentility, he sets the theme of the demanding mother who has given up the prospect of achieving a true emotional life with her husband and turns to her sons with a stultifying and possessive love. Many years later Lawrence came to feel that he had misjudged his father, whose coarseness represented after all a genuine vitality and some wholeness of personality, even if these qualities were impoverished and distorted by the civilization in which he lived.

Spurred on by his mother, Lawrence escaped through education from the mining world of his father. He won a scholarship to Nottingham high school and later, after working first as a clerk and then as an elementary-school teacher (1902–6), studied for two years at Nottingham University College, where he obtained his teacher's certificate in 1908. Meanwhile he was reading on his own a great deal of literature and some philosophy and was working on his first novel, encouraged (as he was in all his early writing) by Jessie Chambers, the "Miriam" of *Sons and Lovers*. His first published work was a group of poems that appeared in the *English Review* for November 1909. The following February the same periodical published his first short story. He was now regarded in London literary circles as a promising young writer; his first novel, *The White Peacock* (1910), was received with respect. From 1908 to 1912 he taught school in Croydon, a southern suburb of London, but he gave this up after falling in love with Frieda von Richthofen, the German wife of a professor of French at Nottingham. They went to Germany together and married in 1914, after Frieda had been divorced by her first husband.

Abroad with Frieda, Lawrence finished *Sons and Lovers,* the autobiographical novel at which he had been working off and on for years. The war brought them back to England, where Frieda's German origins and Lawrence's fierce objection to the war gave him trouble with the authorities. More and more—especially after the banning of his next novel, *The Rainbow,* in 1915—Lawrence came to feel that the forces of modern civilization were arrayed against him. As soon as he could leave England after the war he sought refuge in Italy, Australia, Mexico, then again in Italy, and finally in the south of France, often desperately ill, restlessly searching for an ideal, or at least a tolerable, community in which to live. He died of tuberculosis in the south of France on March 2, 1930, at the age of forty-four.

Lawrence was at home with cosmic images as no other English writer except Blake has ever been; he was at home, one might say, with the universe, with all that is deep-rooted and elemental in the Individual and Nature, and at constant war with the mechanical and artificial, with the constraints and hypocrisies that civilization imposes on our fundamental selves. His most characteristic writings are essentially a record in symbolic terms of his explorations of human individuality and of all that hindered it and all that might fulfill it, whether in the natural world or in the world of other individuals.

This is not what the English novel is generally supposed to do, and Lawrence, with new things to say and a new way of using the novel form, was not easily or quickly appreciated. His early novels, *The White Peacock, The Trespasser,* and even the original and impressive *Sons and Lovers,* were more conventional in style and treatment; they aroused contemporary interest and even acclaim, and it appeared that he might be on his way to becoming one of the acknowledged and popular Georgian novelists. But with the publication of *The Rainbow* in 1915 the true, original Lawrence first emerged clearly, and the critics turned away in bewilderment and condemnation. *The Rainbow* was suppressed as indecent a month after its publication, and the war between Lawrence and the world of timid convention was on. The rest of his life, during which he produced about a dozen more novels and many poems, short stories, sketches, and miscellaneous articles, was, in his own words, "a savage enough pilgrimage," marked by incessant struggle and by moments of frustration and despair. Lawrence was one of those artists who had to create the taste by which they could be appreciated. He had no gift for explaining his attitude and literary technique in simple expository prose. He could explain himself only by performing, by operating in his own way as an artist, letting the work of art speak with its own voice and pulse with its own life. When he tried to talk *about* his ideas, instead of projecting them symbolically in art, he was often irritatingly and vaguely rhetorical. "Sense of truth," "supreme impulse" are phrases characteristic of Lawrence's belief in intuition, in the dark forces of the inner self, that must not be allowed to be swamped by the rational faculties but must be brought into a harmonious relation with them. It was a point of view—or rather, a perception, a passionate insight—that could not be convincingly expressed in argument but demanded direct projection in art.

The genteel culture of Lawrence's mother came more and more to represent death for Lawrence. In much of his later work, and especially in some of his short stories, he sets the deadening restrictiveness of middle-class conventional living against the forces of liberation that are often represented by an outsider—a peasant, a gypsy, a worker, a primitive of some kind, someone free by circumstance or personal effort. The recurring theme of his short stories—which contain some of his best work—is the distortion of love by possessiveness or gentility or a false romanticism or a false conception of the life of the artist and the achievement of a living relation between a man and a woman against the pressure of class-feeling or tradition or habit or prejudice.

His two masterpieces, *The Rainbow* and *Women in Love* (both of which developed out of what was originally conceived as a single novel to be called *The Sisters*), are to be read as symbolic and dramatic poems in prose. In these novels Lawrence probes with both subtlety and power into various aspects of relationship—the relationship between humans and their environment, the relationship between the generations, the relationship between man and woman, the relationship between instinct and intellect, and above all the proper basis for the marriage relationship as he conceived it. Lawrence's view of marriage as a struggle derived from his own relationship with his strong-minded German-born wife, Frieda. There are more and bitterer lovers' quarrels in Lawrence's novels than anywhere else in English literature. Lawrence's "crockery-throwing" view of love could become tedious, except that, as he presents it, it is bound up with the deepest rhythms and most profound instincts of the man-woman relationship.

In *The Rainbow* and *Women in Love* Lawrence is developing a radically new kind of novel in which he explores kinds of human relationships with a combination of uncanny psychological precision and intense poetic feeling. They have an acute surface realism, a sharp sense of time and place, and brilliant topographical detail; and at the same time their high poetic symbolism, both of the total pattern of action and of incidents and objects within it, establishes a rhythm of meaning that is missed by those who read the novels with the conventional categories of "plot" and "characters" in mind. His next novel, *Aaron's Rod* (1922), is more uneven; in it Lawrence, employing many of his own experiences, explores problems of human relations under the question of moral and political leadership, which for a time obsessed him. He was concerned with the struggle for leadership in marriage as well as in politics. Two other novels on the theme of leadership, *Kangaroo* (1923), set in Australia, and *The Plumed Serpent* (1926), set in Mexico, similarly uneven, show him trying to give symbolic fictional form to his own problems and preoccupations. But *Kangaroo* in particular has its moments of uncanny perceptiveness, and it is extraordinary how Lawrence, drawing on his experiences during a short stay in Australia, was able to get beneath the skin of the country and evoke so much of the essential reality of both place and people.

It is hard to think of another English novelist whose best and most characteristic work makes such a disquieting assault on our normal patterns of thought and feeling. It is not simply that Lawrence is a rebel against convention—many writers have been that—or that his views are startling, though they sometimes are. It is rather that the whole response to life, and in particular to the problems posed by human relationships, that emerges from his novels and stories seems to come so profoundly from the deepest recesses of his being and, therefore, assault the deepest recesses of *our* being, that the challenge seems to go beyond that which is normally asserted by a work of art. It is difficult to escape the challenge; to make any attempt to respond fully to what he is saying is to be drawn into his world, forced to share his vision.

Although there are complex critical reasons for the posthumous triumph of this writer who was so much reviled in his lifetime, there is also a simple and striking reason that must not be forgotten. Lawrence had vision; he had a poetic sense of life; he had a keen ear and a piercing eye for every kind of vitality and color and sound in the world, for landscape—be it of England or Italy or New Mexico—for the individuality and concreteness of things in nature, and for the individuality and concreteness of people. His travel sketches are as impressive in their way as his novels; he seizes both on the symbolic incident and on the concrete reality, and each is interpreted in terms of the other. He looked at the world freshly, with his own eyes, avoiding formulas and clichés; and he forged for himself a kind of utterance that, at his best, was able to convey powerfully and vividly what his fresh, original vision showed him. This kind of originality has its drawbacks; he was sometimes shrill, sometimes repetitive, sometimes almost hysterical; some scenes in his novels are murky with unachieved symbolism or splutter with unresolved passion. But the great Lawrence remains.

This restless pilgrim with his uncanny perceptions into the depths of physical things, with his uncompromising honesty and originality in his view of human beings and the world, cannot be dismissed as merely a great eccentric. Nor is he a great prophet. He is essentially an artist; it is his *rendering* of life in his art, not his preaching about life's meaning, that matters.

Odour of Chrysanthemums

I

The small locomotive engine, Number 4, came clanking, stumbling down from Selston with seven full wagons. It appeared round the corner with loud threats of speed, but the colt that it startled from among the gorse,[1] which still flickered indistinctly in the raw afternoon, out-distanced it at a canter. A woman, walking up the railway line to Underwood, drew back into the hedge, held her basket aside, and watched the footplate of the engine advancing. The trucks[2] thumped heavily past, one by one, with slow inevitable movement, as she stood insignificantly trapped between the jolting black wagons and the hedge; then they curved away towards the coppice[3] where the withered oak leaves dropped noiselessly, while the birds, pulling at the scarlet hips beside the track, made off into the dusk that had already crept into the spinney.[4] In the open, the smoke from the engine sank and cleaved to the rough grass. The fields were dreary and forsaken, and in the marshy strip that led to the whimsey,[5] a reedy pit-pond, the fowls had already abandoned their run among the alders, to roost in the tarred fowl-house. The pit-bank loomed up beyond the pond, flames like red sores licking its ashy sides, in the afternoon's stagnant light. Just beyond rose the tapering chimneys and the clumsy black headstocks of Brinsley Colliery.[6] The two wheels were spinning fast up against the sky, and the winding engine rapped out its little spasms. The miners were being turned up.

The engine whistled as it came into the wide bay of railway lines beside the colliery, where rows of trucks stood in harbour.

Miners, single, trailing and in groups, passed like shadows diverging home. At the edge of the ribbed level of sidings squat a low cottage, three steps down from the cinder track. A large bony vine clutched at the house, as if to claw down the tiled roof. Round the bricked yard grew a few wintry primroses. Beyond, the long garden sloped down to a bush-covered brook course. There were some twiggy apple trees, winter-crack trees, and ragged cabbages. Beside the path hung disheveled pink chrysanthemums, like pink cloths hung on bushes. A woman came stooping out of the felt-covered fowl-house, half-way down the garden. She closed and padlocked the door, then drew herself erect, having brushed some bits from her white apron.

She was a tall woman of imperious mien, handsome, with definite black eyebrows. Her smooth black hair was parted exactly. For a few moments she

---

1. Also known as furze or whin, a prickly bush with yellow flowers common on heaths, moors, and hillsides all over Britain.
2. Open freight cars.
3. A wood of small trees or shrubs.
4. Copse, thicket.
5. Machine for raising ore or water from a mine.
6. Coal mine. "Headstocks" support revolving parts of a machine.

stood steadily watching the miners as they passed along the railway: then she turned towards the brook course. Her face was calm and set, her mouth was closed with disillusionment. After a moment she called:

"John!" There was no answer. She waited, and then said distinctly:

"Where are you?"

"Here!" replied a child's sulky voice from among the bushes. The woman looked piercingly through the dusk.

"Are you at that brook?" she asked sternly.

For answer the child showed himself before the raspberry-canes that rose like whips. He was a small, sturdy boy of five. He stood quite still, defiantly.

"Oh!" said the mother, conciliated. "I thought you were down at that wet brook—and you remember what I told you——"

The boy did not move or answer.

"Come, come on in," she said more gently, "it's getting dark. There's your grandfather's engine coming down the line!"

The lad advanced slowly, with resentful, taciturn movement. He was dressed in trousers and waistcoat of cloth that was too thick and hard for the size of the garments. They were evidently cut down from a man's clothes.

As they went slowly towards the house he tore at the ragged wisps of chrysanthemums and dropped the petals in handfuls along the path.

"Don't do that—it does look nasty," said his mother. He refrained, and she, suddenly pitiful, broke off a twig with three or four wan flowers and held them against her face. When mother and son reached the yard her hand hesitated, and instead of laying the flower aside, she pushed it in her apron-band. The mother and son stood at the foot of the three steps looking across the bay of lines at the passing home of the miners. The trundle of the small train was imminent. Suddenly the engine loomed past the house and came to a stop opposite the gate.

The engine-driver, a short man with round grey beard, leaned out of the cab high above the woman.

"Have you got a cup of tea?" he said in a cheery, hearty fashion.

It was her father. She went in, saying she would mash.[7] Directly, she returned.

She's angry he's marrying...

"I didn't come to see you on Sunday," began the little grey-bearded man.

"I didn't expect you," said his daughter.

The engine-driver winced; then, reassuming his cheery, airy manner, he said:

"Oh, have you heard then? Well, and what do you think——?"

"I think it is soon enough," she replied.

At her brief censure the little man made an impatient gesture, and said coaxingly, yet with dangerous coldness:

"Well, what's a man to do? It's no sort of life for a man of my years, to sit at my own hearth like a stranger. And if I'm going to marry again it may as well be soon as late—what does it matter to anybody?"

The woman did not reply, but turned and went into the house. The man in the engine-cab stood assertive, till she returned with a cup of tea and a piece of bread and butter on a plate. She went up the steps and stood near the footplate of the hissing engine.

"You needn't 'a' brought me bread an' butter," said her father. "But a cup

7. Steep the tea.

of tea"—he sipped appreciatively—"it's very nice." He sipped for a moment or two, then: "I hear as Walter's got another bout[8] on," he said.

"When hasn't he?" said the woman bitterly.

"I heerd tell of him in the 'Lord Nelson' braggin' as he was going to spend that b—— afore he went: half a sovereign[9] that was."

"When?" asked the woman.

"A' Sat'day night—I know that's true."

"Very likely," she laughed bitterly. "He gives me twenty-three shillings."

"Aye, it's a nice thing, when a man can do nothing with his money but make a beast of himself!" said the grey-whiskered man. The woman turned her head away. Her father swallowed the last of his tea and handed her the cup.

"Aye, he sighed, wiping his mouth. "It's a settler,[1] it is——"

He put his hand on the lever. The little engine strained and groaned, and the train rumbled towards the crossing. The woman again looked across the metals. Darkness was settling over the spaces of the railway and trucks: the miners, in grey somber groups, were still passing home. The winding engine pulsed hurriedly, with brief pauses. Elizabeth Bates looked at the dreary flow of men, then she went indoors. Her husband did not come.

The kitchen was small and full of firelight; red coals piled glowing up the chimney mouth. All the life of the room seemed in the white, warm hearth and the steel fender reflecting the red fire. The cloth was laid for tea; cups glinted in the shadows. At the back, where the lowest stairs protruded into the room, the boy sat struggling with a knife and a piece of white wood. He was almost hidden in the shadow. It was half-past four. They had but to await the father's coming to begin tea. As the mother watched her son's sullen little struggle with the wood, she saw herself in his silence and pertinacity; she saw the father in her child's indifference to all but himself. She seemed to be occupied by her husband. He had probably gone past his home, slunk past his own door, to drink before he came in, while his dinner spoiled and wasted in waiting. She glanced at the clock, then took the potatoes to strain them in the yard. The garden and fields beyond the brook were closed in uncertain darkness. When she rose with the saucepan, leaving the drain steaming into the night behind her, she saw the yellow lamps were lit along the high road that went up the hill away beyond the space of the railway lines and the field.

Then again she watched the men trooping home, fewer now and fewer.

Indoors the fire was sinking and the room was dark red. The woman put her saucepan on the hob, and set a batter-pudding near the mouth of the oven. Then she stood unmoving. Directly, gratefully, came quick young steps to the door. Someone hung on the latch a moment, then a little girl entered and began pulling off her outdoor things, dragging a mass of curls, just ripening from gold to brown, over her eyes with her hat.

Her mother chid her for coming late from school, and said she would have to keep her at home the dark winter days.

"Why, mother, it's hardly a bit dark yet. The lamp's not lighted, and my father's not home."

"No, he isn't. But it's a quarter to five! Did you see anything of him?"

8. Session; i.e., bout of drinking.
9. Gold coin worth twenty shillings. Half a sovereign is worth ten. Lord Nelson is the name of a public house (pub).
1. Crushing (or final) blow.

The child became serious. She looked at her mother with large, wistful blue eyes.

"No, mother, I've never seen him. Why? Has he come up an' gone past, to Old Brinsley? He hasn't, mother, 'cos I never saw him."

"He'd watch that," said the mother bitterly, "he'd take care as you didn't see him. But you may depend upon it, he's seated in the 'Prince o' Wales.'[2] He wouldn't be this late."

The girl looked at her mother piteously.

"Let's have our teas, mother, should we?" said she.

The mother called John to table. She opened the door once more and looked out across the darkness of the lines. All was deserted: she could not hear the winding-engines.

"Perhaps," she said to herself, "he's stopped to get some ripping[3] done."

They sat down to tea. John, at the end of the table near the door, was almost lost in the darkness. Their faces were hidden from each other. The girl crouched against the fender slowly moving a thick piece of bread before the fire. The lad, his face a dusky mark on the shadow, sat watching her who was transfigured in the red glow.

"I do think it's beautiful to look in the fire," said the child.

"Do you?" said her mother. "Why?"

"It's so red, and full of little caves—and it feels so nice, and you can fair smell it."

"It'll want mending directly," replied her mother, "and then if your father comes he'll carry on and say there never is a fire when a man comes home sweating from the pit. A public-house is always warm enough."

There was silence till the boy said complainingly: "Make haste, our Annie."

"Well, I am doing! I can't make the fire do it no faster, can I?"

"She keeps wafflin' it about so's to make 'er slow," grumbled the boy.

"Don't have such an evil imagination, child," replied the mother.

Soon the room was busy in the darkness with the crisp sound of crunching. The mother ate very little. She drank her tea determinedly, and sat thinking. When she rose her anger was evident in the stern unbending of her head. She looked at the pudding in the fender, and broke out:

"It is a scandalous thing as a man can't even come home to his dinner! If it's crozzled up to a cinder I don't see why I should care. Past his very door he goes to get to a public-house, and here I sit with his dinner waiting for him——"

She went out. As she dropped piece after piece of coal on the red fire, the shadows fell on the walls, till the room was almost in total darkness.

"I canna see," grumbled the invisible John. In spite of herself, the mother laughed.

"You know the way to your mouth," she said. She set the dust pan outside the door. When she came again like a shadow on the hearth, the lad repeated, complaining sulkily:

"I canna see."

"Good gracious!" cried the mother irritably, "you're as bad as your father if it's a bit dusk!"

Nevertheless, she took a paper spill from a sheaf on the mantelpiece and proceeded to light the lamp that hung from the ceiling in the middle of the room. As she reached up, her figure displayed itself just rounding with maternity.

"Oh, mother——!" exclaimed the girl.

"What?" said the woman, suspended in the act of putting the lamp-glass over the flame. The copper reflector shone handsomely on her, as she stood with uplifted arm, turning to face her daughter.

"You've got a flower in your apron!" said the child, in a little rapture at this unusual event.

"Goodness me!" exclaimed the woman, relieved. "One would think the house was afire." She replaced the glass and waited a moment before turning up the wick. A pale shadow was seen floating vaguely on the floor.

"Let me smell!" said the child, still rapturously, coming forward and putting her face to her mother's waist.

"Go along, silly!" said the mother, turning up the lamp. The light revealed their suspense so that the woman felt it almost unbearable. Annie was still bending at her waist. Irritably, the mother took the flowers out from her apron-band.

"Oh, mother—don't take them out!" Annie cried, catching her hand and trying to replace the sprig.

"Such nonsense!" said the mother, turning away. The child put the pale chrysanthemums to her lips, murmuring:

"Don't they smell beautiful!"

Her mother gave a short laugh.

"No," she said, "not to me. It was chrysanthemums when I married him, and chrysanthemums when you were born, and the first time they ever brought him home drunk, he'd got brown chrysanthemums in his buttonhole."

She looked at the children. Their eyes and their parted lips were wondering. The mother sat rocking in silence for some time. Then she looked at the clock.

"Twenty minutes to six!" In a tone of fine bitter carelessness she continued: "Eh, he'll not come now till they bring him. There he'll stick! But he needn't come rolling in here in his pit-dirt, for *I* won't wash him. He can lie on the floor——Eh, what a fool I've been, what a fool! And this is what I came here for, to this dirty hole, rats and all, for him to slink past his very door. Twice last week—he's begun now——"

She silenced herself and rose to clear the table.

While for an hour or more the children played, subduedly intent, fertile of imagination, united in fear of the mother's wrath, and in dread of their father's home-coming, Mrs Bates sat in her rocking chair making a "singlet" of thick cream-coloured flannel, which gave a dull wounded sound as she tore off the grey edge. She worked at her sewing with energy, listening to the children, and her anger wearied itself, lay down to rest, opening its eyes from time to time and steadily watching, its ears raised to listen. Sometimes even her anger quailed and shrank, and the mother suspended her sewing, tracing the footsteps that thudded along the sleepers outside; she would lift her head sharply to bid the children "hush," but she recovered herself in time, and the footsteps went past the gate, and the children were not flung out of their play-world.

But at last Annie sighed, and gave in. She glanced at her wagon of slippers, and loathed the game. She turned plaintively to her mother.

"Mother!"—but she was inarticulate.

John crept out like a frog from under the sofa. His mother glanced up.

"Yes," she said, "just look at those shirt-sleeves!"

The boy held them out to survey them, saying nothing. Then somebody called in a hoarse voice away down the line, and suspense bristled in the room, till two people had gone by outside, talking.

"It is time for bed," said the mother.

"My father hasn't come," wailed Annie plaintively. But her mother was primed with courage.

"Never mind. They'll bring him when he does come—like a log." She meant there would be no scene. "And he may sleep on the floor till he wakes himself. I know he'll not go to work to-morrow after this!"

The children had their hands and faces wiped with a flannel. They were very quiet. When they had put on their night-dresses, they said their prayers, the boy mumbling. The mother looked down at them, at the brown silken bush of intertwining curls in the nape of the girl's neck, at the little black head of the lad, and her heart burst with anger at their father, who caused all three such distress. The children hid their faces in her skirts for comfort.

When Mrs Bates came down, the room was strangely empty, with a tension of expectancy. She took up her sewing and stitched for some time without raising her head. Meantime her anger was tinged with fear.

II

The clock struck eight and she rose suddenly, dropping her sewing on her chair. She went to the stair-foot door, opened it, listening. Then she went out, locking the door behind her.

Something scuffled in the yard, and she started, though she knew it was only the rats with which the place was over-run. The night was very dark. In the great bay of railway lines, bulked with trucks, there was no trace of light, only away back she could see a few yellow lamps at the pit-top, and the red smear of the burning pit-bank on the night. She hurried along the edge of the track, then, crossing the converging lines, came to the stile by the white gates, whence she emerged on the road. Then the fear which had led her shrank. People were walking up to New Brinsley; she saw the lights in the houses; twenty yards farther on were the broad windows of the "Prince of Wales," very warm and bright, and the loud voices of men could be heard distinctly. What a fool she had been to imagine that anything had happened to him! He was merely drinking over there at the "Prince of Wales." She faltered. She had never yet been to fetch him, and she never would go. So she continued her walk towards the long straggling line of houses, standing back on the highway. She entered a passage between the dwellings.

"Mr Rigley?—Yes! Did you want him? No, he's not in at this minute."

The raw-boned woman leaned forward from her dark scullery and peered at the other, upon whom fell a dim light through the blind of the kitchen window.

"Is it Mrs Bates?" she asked in a tone tinged with respect.

"Yes. I wondered if your Master was at home. Mine hasn't come yet."

" 'Asn't 'e! Oh, Jack's been 'ome an' 'ad 'is dinner an' gone out. 'E's just gone for 'alf an hour afore bed-time. Did you call at the 'Prince of Wales'?"

"No——"

"No, you didn't like——! It's not very nice." The other woman was indulgent. There was an awkward pause. "Jack never said nothink about—about your Master," she said.

"No!—I expect he's stuck in there!"

Elizabeth Bates said this bitterly, and with recklessness. She knew that the woman across the yard was standing at her door listening, but she did not care. As she turned:

"Stop a minute! I'll just go an' ask Jack if 'e knows anythink," said Mrs Rigley.

"Oh no—I wouldn't like to put——!"

"Yes, I will, if you'll just step inside an' see as th' childer doesn't come downstairs and set theirselves afire."

Elizabeth Bates, murmuring a remonstrance, stepped inside. The other woman apologised for the state of the room.

The kitchen needed apology. There were little frocks and trousers and childish undergarments on the squab[4] and on the floor, and a litter of playthings everywhere. On the black American cloth[5] of the table were pieces of bread and cake, crusts, slops, and a teapot with cold tea.

"Eh, ours is just as bad," said Elizabeth Bates, looking at the woman, not at the house. Mrs Rigley put a shawl over her head and hurried out, saying:

"I shanna be a minute."

The other sat, noting with faint disapproval the general untidiness of the room. Then she fell to counting the shoes of various sizes scattered over the floor. There were twelve. She sighed and said to herself: "No wonder!"—glancing at the litter. There came the scratching of two pairs of feet on the yard, and the Rigleys entered. Elizabeth Bates rose. Rigley was a big man, with very large bones. His head looked particularly bony. Across his temple was a blue scar, caused by a wound got in the pit, a wound in which the coal dust remained blue like tattooing.

" 'Asna 'e come whoam yit?" asked the man, without any form of greeting, but with deference and sympathy. "I couldna say wheer he is—'e's non ower theer!"—he jerked his head to signify the "Prince of Wales."

" 'E's 'appen gone up to th' Yew,"[6] said Mrs Rigley.

There was another pause. Rigley had evidently something to get off his mind:

"Ah left 'im finishin' a stint," he began. "Loose-all[7] 'ad bin gone about ten minutes when we com'n away, an' I shouted: 'Are ter comin', Walt?' an' 'e said: 'Go on, Ah shanna be but a'ef a minnit,' so we com'n ter th' bottom, me an' Bowers, thinkin' as 'e wor just behint, an' 'ud come up i' th' next bantle[8]——"

He stood perplexed, as if answering a charge of deserting his mate. Elizabeth Bates, now again certain of disaster, hastened to reassure him:

"I expect 'e's gone up to th' 'Yew Tree,' as you say. It's not the first time. I've fretted myself into a fever before now. He'll come home when they carry him."

4. Couch.
5. Oilcloth.
6. I.e., the Yew Tree (a pub).
7. Signal for end of work.
8. Group.

"Ay, isn't it too bad!" deplored the other woman.

"I'll just step up to Dick's an' see if 'e *is* theer," offered the man, afraid of appearing alarmed, afraid of taking liberties.

"Oh, I wouldn't think of bothering you that far," said Elizabeth Bates, with emphasis, but he knew she was glad of his offer.

As they stumbled up the entry, Elizabeth Bates heard Rigley's wife run across the yard and open her neighbour's door. At this, suddenly all the blood in her body seemed to switch away from her heart.

"Mind!" warned Rigley. "Ah've said many a time as Ah'd fill up them ruts in this entry, sumb'dy 'll be breakin' their legs yit."

She recovered herself and walked quickly along with the miner.

"I don't like leaving the children in bed, and nobody in the house," she said.

"No, you dunna!" he replied courteously. They were soon at the gate of the cottage.

"Well, I shanna be many minnits. Dunna you be frettin' now, 'e'll be all right," said the butty.[9]

"Thank you very much, Mr Rigley," she replied.

"You're welcome!" he stammered, moving away. "I shanna be many minnits."

The house was quiet. Elizabeth Bates took off her hat and shawl, and rolled back the rug. When she had finished, she sat down. It was a few minutes past nine. She was startled by the rapid chuff of the winding-engine at the pit, and the sharp whirr of the brakes on the rope as it descended. Again she felt the painful sweep of her blood, and she put her hand to her side, saying aloud: "Good gracious!—it's only the nine o'clock deputy[1] going down," rebuking herself.

She sat still, listening. Half an hour of this, and she was wearied out.

"What am I working myself up like this for?" she said pitiably to herself, "I s'll only be doing myself some damage."

She took out her sewing again.

At a quarter to ten there were footsteps. One person! She watched for the door to open. It was an elderly woman, in a black bonnet and a black woollen shawl—his mother. She was about sixty years old, pale, with blue eyes, and her face all wrinkled and lamentable. She shut the door and turned to her daughter-in-law peevishly.

"Eh, Lizzie, whatever shall we do, whatever shall we do!" she cried.

Elizabeth drew back a little, sharply.

"What is it, mother?" she said.

The elder woman seated herself on the sofa.

"I don't know, child, I can't tell you!"—she shook her head slowly. Elizabeth sat watching her, anxious and vexed.

"I don't know," replied the grandmother, sighing very deeply. "There's no end to my troubles, there isn't. The things I've gone through, I'm sure it's enough——!" She wept without wiping her eyes, the tears running.

"But, mother," interrupted Elizabeth, "what do you mean? What is it?"

The grandmother slowly wiped her eyes. The fountains of her tears were stopped by Elizabeth's directness. She wiped her eyes slowly.

---

9. Workmate (cf. "buddy"). Among English coal miners it has the meaning of "a supervisor inter-

mediary between the employers and the men."
1. Minor coal-mine official.

"Poor child! Eh, you poor thing!" she moaned. "I don't know what we're going to do, I don't—and you as you are—it's a thing, it is indeed!"

Elizabeth waited.

"Is he dead?" she asked, and at the words her heart swung violently, though she felt a slight flush of shame at the ultimate extravagance of the question. Her words sufficiently frightened the old lady, almost brought her to herself.

"Don't say so, Elizabeth! We'll hope it's not as bad as that; no, may the Lord spare us that, Elizabeth. Jack Rigley came just as I was sittin' down to a glass afore going to bed, an' 'e said: ' 'Appen you'll go down th' line, Mrs. Bates. Walt's had an accident. 'Appen you'll go an' sit wi' 'er till we can get him home.' I hadn't time to ask him a word afore he was gone. An' I put my bonnet on an' come straight down, Lizzie. I thought to myself: 'Eh, that poor blessed child, if anybody should come an' tell her of a sudden, there's no knowin' what'll 'appen to 'er.' You mustn't let it upset you, Lizzie—or you know what to expect. How long is it, six months—or is it five, Lizzie? Ay!"— the old woman shook her head—"time slips on, it slips on! Ay!"

Elizabeth's thoughts were busy elsewhere. If he was killed—would she be able to manage on the little pension and what she could earn?—she counted up rapidly. If he was hurt—they wouldn't take him to the hospital—how tiresome he would be to nurse!—but perhaps she'd be able to get him away from the drink and his hateful ways. She would—while he was ill. The tears offered to come to her eyes at the picture. But what sentimental luxury was this she was beginning? She turned to consider the children. At any rate she was absolutely necessary for them. They were her business.

"Ay!" repeated the old woman, "it seems but a week or two since he brought me his first wages. Ay—he was a good lad, Elizabeth, he was, in his way. I don't know why he got to be such a trouble, I don't. He was a happy lad at home, only full of spirits. But there's no mistake he's been a handful of trouble, he has! I hope the Lord'll spare him to mend his ways. I hope so, I hope so. You've had a sight o' trouble with him, Elizabeth, you have indeed. But he was a jolly enough lad wi' me, he was, I can assure you. I don't know how it is . . . ."

The old woman continued to muse aloud, a monotonous irritating sound, while Elizabeth thought concentratedly, startled once, when she heard the winding-engine chuff quickly, and the brakes skirr with a shriek. Then she heard the engine more slowly, and the brakes made no sound. The old woman did not notice. Elizabeth waited in suspense. The mother-in-law talked, with lapses into silence.

"But he wasn't your son, Lizzie, an' it makes a difference. Whatever he was, I remember him when he was little, an' I learned to understand him and to make allowances. You've got to make allowances for them——"

It was half-past ten, and the old woman was saying: "But it's trouble from beginning to end; you're never too old for trouble, never too old for that——" when the gate banged back, and there were heavy feet on the steps.

"I'll go, Lizzie, let me go," cried the old woman, rising. But Elizabeth was at the door. It was a man in pit-clothes.

"They're bringin' 'im, Missis," he said. Elizabeth's heart halted a moment. Then it surged on again, almost suffocating her.

"Is he—is it bad?" she asked.

The man turned away, looking at the darkness:

"The doctor says 'e'd been dead hours. 'E saw 'im i' th' lamp-cabin."

The old woman, who stood just behind Elizabeth, dropped into a chair, and folded her hands, crying: "Oh, my boy, my boy!"

"Hush!" said Elizabeth, with a sharp twitch of a frown. "Be still, mother, don't waken th' children: I wouldn't have them down for anything!"

The old woman moaned softly, rocking herself. The man was drawing away. Elizabeth took a step forward.

"How was it?" she asked.

"Well, I couldn't say for sure," the man replied, very ill at ease. " 'E wor finishin' a stint an' th' butties 'ad gone, an' a lot o' stuff come down atop 'n 'im."

"And crushed him?" cried the widow, with a shudder.

"No," said the man, "it fell at th' back of 'im. 'E wor under th' face an' it niver touched 'im. It shut 'im in. It seems 'e wor smothered."

Elizabeth shrank back. She heard the old woman behind her cry:

"What?—what did 'e say it was?"

The man replied, more loudly: " 'E wor smothered!"

Then the old woman wailed aloud, and this relieved Elizabeth.

"Oh, mother," she said, putting her hand on the old woman, "don't waken th' children, don't waken th' children."

She wept a little, unknowing, while the old mother rocked herself and moaned. Elizabeth remembered that they were bringing him home, and she must be ready. "They'll lay him in the parlour," she said to herself, standing a moment pale and perplexed.

Then she lighted a candle and went into the tiny room. The air was cold and damp, but she could not make a fire, there was no fireplace. She set down the candle and looked round. The candlelight glittered on the lustre-glasses, on the two vases that held some of the pink chrysanthemums, and on the dark mahogany. There was a cold, deathly smell of chrysanthemums in the room. Elizabeth stood looking at the flowers. She turned away, and calculated whether there would be room to lay him on the floor, between the couch and the chiffonier. She pushed the chairs aside. There would be room to lay him down and to step round him. Then she fetched the old red tablecloth, and another old cloth, spreading them down to save her bit of carpet. She shivered on leaving the parlour; so, from the dresser drawer she took a clean shirt and put it at the fire to air. All the time her mother-in-law was rocking herself in the chair and moaning.

"You'll have to move from there, mother," said Elizabeth. "They'll be bringing him in. Come in the rocker."

The old mother rose mechanically, and seated herself by the fire, continuing to lament. Elizabeth went into the pantry for another candle, and there, in the little pent-house under the naked tiles, she heard them coming. She stood still in the pantry doorway, listening. She heard them pass the end of the house, and come awkwardly down the three steps, a jumble of shuffling footsteps and muttering voices. The old woman was silent. The men were in the yard.

Then Elizabeth heard Matthews, the manager of the pit, say: "You go in first, Jim. Mind!"

The door came open, and the two women saw a collier backing into the room, holding one end of a stretcher, on which they could see the nailed pitboots of the dead man. The two carriers halted, the man at the head stooping to the lintel of the door.

"Wheer will you have him?" asked the manager, a short, white-bearded man.

Elizabeth roused herself and came from the pantry carrying the unlighted candle.

"In the parlour," she said.

"In there, Jim!" pointed the manager, and the carriers backed round into the tiny room. The coat with which they had covered the body fell off as they awkwardly turned through the two doorways, and the women saw their man, naked to the waist, lying stripped for work. The old woman began to moan in a low voice of horror.

"Lay th' stretcher at th' side," snapped the manager, "an' put 'im on th' cloths. Mind now, mind! Look you now——!"

One of the men had knocked off a vase of chrysanthemums. He stared awkwardly, then they set down the stretcher. Elizabeth did not look at her husband. As soon as she could get in the room, she went and picked up the broken vase and the flowers.

"Wait a minute!" she said.

The three men waited in silence while she mopped up the water with a duster.

"Eh, what a job, what a job, to be sure!" the manager was saying, rubbing his brow with trouble and perplexity. "Never knew such a thing in my life, never! He'd no business to ha' been left. I never knew such a thing in my life! Fell over him clean as a whistle, an' shut him in. Not four foot of space, there wasn't—yet it scarce bruised him."

He looked down at the dead man, lying prone, half naked, all grimed with coal-dust.

" ' 'Sphyxiated,' the doctor said. It *is* the most terrible job I've ever known Seems as if it was done o' purpose. Clean over him, an' shut 'im in, like a mouse-trap"—he made a sharp, descending gesture with his hand.

The colliers standing by jerked aside their heads in hopeless comment.

The horror of the thing bristled upon them all.

Then they heard the girl's voice upstairs calling shrilly: "Mother, mother—who is it? Mother, who is it?"

Elizabeth hurried to the foot of the stairs and opened the door:

"Go to sleep!" she commanded sharply. "What are you shouting about? Go to sleep at once—there's nothing——"

Then she began to mount the stairs. They could hear her on the boards, and on the plaster floor of the little bedroom. They could hear her distinctly:

"What's the matter now?—what's the matter with you, silly thing?"—her voice was much agitated, with an unreal gentleness.

"I thought it was some men come," said the plaintive voice of the child. "Has he come?"

"Yes, they've brought him. There's nothing to make a fuss about. Go to sleep now, like a good child."

They could hear her voice in the bedroom, they waited whilst she covered the children under the bedclothes.

"Is he drunk?" asked the girl, timidly, faintly.

"No! No—he's not! He—he's asleep."

"Is he asleep downstairs?"

"Yes—and don't make a noise."

There was silence for a moment, then the men heard the frightened child again:

"What's that noise?"

"It's nothing, I tell you, what are you bothering for?"

The noise was the grandmother moaning. She was oblivious of everything, sitting on her chair rocking and moaning. The manager put his hand on her arm and bade her "Sh—sh! !"

The old woman opened her eyes and looked at him. She was shocked by this interruption, and seemed to wonder.

"What time is it?" the plaintive thin voice of the child, sinking back unhappily into sleep, asked this last question.

"Ten o'clock," answered the mother more softly. Then she must have bent down and kissed the children.

Matthews beckoned to the men to come away. They put on their caps and took up the stretcher. Stepping over the body, they tiptoed out of the house. None of them spoke till they were far from the wakeful children.

When Elizabeth came down she found her mother alone on the parlour floor, leaning over the dead man, the tears dropping on him.

"We must lay him out," the wife said. She put on the kettle, then returning knelt at the feet, and began to unfasten the knotted leather laces. The room was clammy and dim with only one candle, so that she had to bend her face almost to the floor. At last she got off the heavy boots and put them away.

"You must help me now," she whispered to the old woman. Together they stripped the man.

When they arose, saw him lying in the naïve dignity of death, the women stood arrested in fear and respect. For a few moments they remained still, looking down, the old mother whimpering. Elizabeth felt countermanded. She saw him, how utterly inviolable he lay in himself. She had nothing to do with him. She could not accept it. Stooping, she laid her hand on him, in claim. He was still warm, for the mine was hot where he had died. His mother had his face between her hands, and was murmuring incoherently. The old tears fell in succession as drops from wet leaves; the mother was not weeping, merely her tears flowed. Elizabeth embraced the body of her husband, with cheek and lips. She seemed to be listening, inquiring, trying to get some connection. But she could not. She was driven away. He was impregnable.

She rose, went into the kitchen where she poured warm water into a bowl, brought soap and flannel and a soft towel. "I must wash him," she said.

Then the old mother rose stiffly, and watched Elizabeth as she carefully washed his face, carefully brushing his big blond moustache from his mouth with the flannel. She was afraid with a bottomless fear, so she ministered to him. The old woman, jealous, said:

"Let me wipe him!"—and she kneeled on the other side drying slowly as Elizabeth washed, her big black bonnet sometimes brushing the dark head of her daughter-in-law. They worked thus in silence for a long time. They never forgot it was death, and the touch of the man's dead body gave them strange emotions, different in each of the women; a great dread possessed them both, the mother felt the lie was given to her womb, she was denied;

the wife felt the utter isolation of the human soul, the child within her was a weight apart from her.

At last it was finished. He was a man of handsome body, and his face showed no traces of drink. He was blond, full-fleshed, with fine limbs. But he was dead.

"Bless him," whispered his mother, looking always at his face, and speaking out of sheer terror. "Dear lad—bless him!" She spoke in a faint, sibilant ecstasy of fear and mother love.

Elizabeth sank down again to the floor, and put her face against his neck, and trembled and shuddered. But she had to draw away again. He was dead, and her living flesh had no place against his. A great dread and weariness held her: she was so unavailing. Her life was gone like this.

"White as milk he is, clear as a twelve-month baby, bless him, the darling!" the old mother murmured to herself. "Not a mark on him, clear and clean and white, beautiful as ever a child was made," she murmured with pride. Elizabeth kept her face hidden.

"He went peaceful, Lizzie—peaceful as sleep. Isn't he beautiful, the lamb? Ay—he must ha' made his peace, Lizzie. 'Appen he made it all right, Lizzie, shut in there. He'd have time. He wouldn't look like this if he hadn't made his peace. The lamb, the dear lamb. Eh, but he had a hearty laugh. I loved to hear it. He had the heartiest laugh, Lizzie, as a lad——"

Elizabeth looked up. The man's mouth was fallen back, slightly open under the cover of the moustache. The eyes, half shut, did not show glazed in the obscurity. Life with its smoky burning gone from him, had left him apart and utterly alien to her. And she knew what a stranger he was to her. In her womb was ice of fear, because of this separate stranger with whom she had been living as one flesh. Was this what it all meant—utter, intact separateness, obscured by heat of living? In dread she turned her face away. The fact was too deadly. There had been nothing between them, and yet they had come together, exchanging their nakedness repeatedly. Each time he had taken her, they had been two isolated beings, far apart as now. He was no more responsible than she. The child was like ice in her womb. For as she looked at the dead man, her mind, cold and detached, said clearly: "Who am I? What have I been doing? I have been fighting a husband who did not exist. *He* existed all the time. What wrong have I done? What was that I have been living with? There lies the reality, this man." And her soul died in her for fear: she knew she had never seen him, he had never seen her, they had met in the dark and had fought in the dark, not knowing whom they met or whom they fought. And now she saw, and turned silent in seeing. For she had been wrong. She had said he was something he was not; she had felt familiar with him. Whereas he was apart all the while, living as she never lived, feeling as she never felt.

In fear and shame she looked at his naked body, that she had known falsely. And he was the father of her children. Her soul was torn from her body and stood apart. She looked at his naked body and was ashamed, as if she had denied it. After all, it was itself. It seemed awful to her. She looked at his face, and she turned her own face to the wall. For his look was other than hers, his way was not her way. She had denied him what he was—she saw it now. She had refused him as himself. And this had been her life, and his life. She was grateful to death, which restored the truth. And she knew she was not dead.

And all the while her heart was bursting with grief and pity for him. What had he suffered? What stretch of horror for this helpless man! She was rigid with agony. She had not been able to help him. He had been cruelly injured, this naked man, this other being, and she could make no reparation. There were the children—but the children belonged to life. This dead man had nothing to do with them. He and she were only channels through which life had flowed to issue in the children. She was a mother—but how awful she knew it now to have been a wife. And he, dead now, how awful he must have felt it to be a husband. She felt that in the next world he would be a stranger to her. If they met there, in the beyond, they would only be ashamed of what had been before. The children had come, for some mysterious reason, out of both of them. But the children did not unite them. Now he was dead, she knew how eternally he was apart from her, how eternally he had nothing more to do with her. She saw this episode of her life closed. They had denied each other in life. Now he had withdrawn. An anguish came over her. It was finished then: it had become hopeless between them long before he died. Yet he had been her husband. But how little!

"Have you got his shirt, 'Lizabeth?"

Elizabeth turned without answering, though she strove to weep and behave as her mother-in-law expected. But she could not, she was silenced. She went into the kitchen and returned with the garment.

"It is aired," she said, grasping the cotton shirt here and there to try. She was almost ashamed to handle him; what right had she or anyone to lay hands on him; but her touch was humble on his body. It was hard work to clothe him. He was so heavy and inert. A terrible dread gripped her all the while: that he could be so heavy and utterly inert, unresponsive, apart. The horror of the distance between them was almost too much for her—it was so infinite a gap she must look across.

At last it was finished. They covered him with a sheet and left him lying, with his face bound. And she fastened the door of the little parlour, lest the children should see what was lying there. Then, with peace sunk heavy on her heart, she went about making tidy the kitchen. She knew she submitted to life, which was her immediate master. But from death, her ultimate master, she winced with fear and shame.

1911, 1914

The Horse Dealer's Daughter

"Well, Mabel, and what are you going to do with yourself?" asked Joe, with foolish flippancy. He felt quite safe himself. Without listening for an answer, he turned aside, worked a grain of tobacco to the tip of his tongue, and spat it out. He did not care about anything, since he felt safe himself.

The three brothers and the sister sat round the desolate breakfast-table, attempting some sort of desultory consultation. The morning's post had given the final tap to the family fortunes, and all was over. The dreary dining-room itself, with its heavy mahogany furniture, looked as if it were waiting to be done away with.

But the consultation amounted to nothing. There was a strange air of ineffectuality about the three men, as they sprawled at table, smoking and reflecting vaguely on their own condition. The girl was alone, a rather short, sullen-looking young woman of twenty-seven. She did not share the same life as her brothers. She would have been good-looking, save for the impressive fixity of her face, "bull-dog," as her brothers called it.

There was a confused tramping of horses' feet outside. The three men all sprawled round in their chairs to watch. Beyond the dark holly bushes that separated the strip of lawn from the high-road, they could see a cavalcade of shire horses swinging out of their own yard, being taken for exercise. This was the last time. These were the last horses that would go through their hands. The young men watched with critical, callous look. They were all frightened at the collapse of their lives, and the sense of disaster in which they were involved left them no inner freedom.

Yet they were three fine, well-set fellows enough. Joe, the eldest, was a man of thirty-three, broad and handsome in a hot, flushed way. His face was red, he twisted his black moustache over a thick finger, his eyes were shallow and restless. He had a sensual way of uncovering his teeth when he laughed, and his bearing was stupid. Now he watched the horses with a glazed look of helplessness in his eyes, a certain stupor of downfall.

The great draught horses swung past. They were tied head to tail, four of them, and they heaved along to where a lane branched off from the high-road, planting their great hoofs floutingly in the fine black mud, swinging their great rounded haunches sumptuously, and trotting a few sudden steps as they were led into the lane, round the corner. Every movement showed a massive, slumbrous strength, and a stupidity which held them in subjection. The groom at the head looked back, jerking the leading rope. And the cavalcade moved out of sight up the lane, the tail of the last horse, bobbed up tight and stiff, held out taut from the swinging great haunches as they rocked behind the hedges in a motion-like sleep.

Joe watched with glazed hopeless eyes. The horses were almost like his own body to him. He felt he was done for now. Luckily he was engaged to a woman as old as himself, and therefore her father, who was steward of a neighbouring estate, would provide him with a job. He would marry and go into harness. His life was over, he would be a subject animal now.

He turned uneasily aside, the retreating steps of the horses echoing in his ears. Then, with foolish restlessness, he reached for the scraps of bacon-rind from the plates, and making a faint whistling sound, flung them to the terrier that lay against the fender. He watched the dog swallow them, and waited till the creature looked into his eyes. Then a faint grin came on his face, and in a high, foolish voice he said:

"You won't get much more bacon, shall you, you little b——?"

The dog faintly and dismally wagged its tail, then lowered its haunches, circled round, and lay down again.

There was another helpless silence at the table. Joe sprawled uneasily in his seat, not willing to go till the family conclave was dissolved. Fred Henry, the second brother, was erect, clean-limbed, alert. He had watched the passing of the horses with more *sang-froid*.[1] If he was an animal, like Joe, he was an animal which controls, not one which is controlled. He was master of any

---

1. Cold blood (French, literal trans.); here, calm detachment.

horse, and he carried himself with a well-tempered air of mastery. But he was not master of the situations of life. He pushed his coarse brown moustache upwards, off his lip, and glanced irritably at his sister, who sat impassive and inscrutable.

"You'll go and stop with Lucy for a bit, shan't you?" he asked. The girl did not answer.

"I don't see what else you can do," persisted Fred Henry.

"Go as a skivvy,"[2] Joe interpolated laconically.

The girl did not move a muscle.

"If I was her, I should go in for training for a nurse," said Malcolm, the youngest of them all. He was the baby of the family, a young man of twenty-two, with a fresh, jaunty *museau*.[3]

But Mabel did not take any notice of him. They had talked at her and round her for so many years, that she hardly heard them at all.

The marble clock on the mantelpiece softly chimed the half-hour, the dog rose uneasily from the hearth-rug and looked at the party at the breakfast-table. But still they sat in an ineffectual conclave.

"Oh, all right," said Joe suddenly, apropos of nothing. "I'll get a move on."

He pushed back his chair, straddled his knees with a downward jerk, to get them free, in horsey fashion, and went to the fire. Still he did not go out of the room; he was curious to know what the others would do or say. He began to charge his pipe, looking down at the dog and saying in a high, affected voice:

"Going wi' me? Going wi' me are ter? Tha'rt goin' further than tha counts on just now, dost hear?"

The dog faintly wagged his tail, the man stuck out his jaw and covered his pipe with his hands, and puffed intently, losing himself in the tobacco, looking down all the while at the dog with an absent brown eye. The dog looked up at him in mournful distrust. Joe stood with his knees stuck out, in real horsey fashion.

"Have you had a letter from Lucy?" Fred Henry asked of his sister.

"Last week," came the neutral reply.

"And what does she say?"

There was no answer.

"Does she *ask* you to go and stop there?" persisted Fred Henry.

"She says I can if I like."

"Well, then, you'd better. Tell her you'll come on Monday."

This was received in silence.

"That's what you'll do then, is it?" said Fred Henry, in some exasperation.

But she made no answer. There was a silence of futility and irritation in the room. Malcolm grinned fatuously.

"You'll have to make up your mind between now and next Wednesday," said Joe loudly, "or else find yourself lodgings on the kerbstone."

The face of the young woman darkened, but she sat on immutable.

"Here's Jack Ferguson!" exclaimed Malcolm, who was looking aimlessly out of the window.

"Where?" exclaimed Joe loudly.

"Just gone past."

---

2. Servant girl.   3. Muzzle (French); here, face.

"Coming in?"

Malcolm craned his neck to see the gate.

"Yes," he said.

There was a silence. Mabel sat on like one condemned, at the head of the table. Then a whistle was heard from the kitchen. The dog got up and barked sharply. Joe opened the door and shouted:

"Come on."

After a moment a young man entered. He was muffled up in overcoat and a purple woollen scarf, and his tweed cap, which he did not remove, was pulled down on his head. He was of medium height, his face was rather long and pale, his eyes looked tired.

"Hello, Jack! Well, Jack!" exclaimed Malcolm and Joe. Fred Henry merely said: "Jack."

"What's doing?" asked the newcomer, evidently addressing Fred Henry.

"Same. We've got to be out by Wednesday. Got a cold?"

"I have—got it bad, too."

"Why don't you stop in?"

"*Me* stop in? When I can't stand on my legs, perhaps I shall have a chance." The young man spoke huskily. He had a slight Scotch accent.

"It's a knock-out, isn't it," said Joe, boisterously, "if a doctor goes round croaking with a cold. Looks bad for the patients, doesn't it?"

The young doctor looked at him slowly.

"Anything the matter with *you,* then?" he asked sarcastically.

"Not as I know of. Damn your eyes, I hope not. Why?"

"I thought you were very concerned about the patients, wondered if you might be one yourself."

"Damn it, no, I've never been patient to no flaming doctor, and hope I never shall be," returned Joe.

At this point Mabel rose from the table, and they all seemed to become aware of her existence. She began putting the dishes together. The young doctor looked at her, but did not address her. He had not greeted her. She went out of the room with the tray, her face impassive and unchanged.

"When are you off then, all of you?" asked the doctor.

"I'm catching the eleven-forty," replied Malcolm. "Are you goin' down wi' th' trap, Joe?"

"Yes, I've told you I'm going down wi' th' trap, haven't I?"

"We'd better be getting her in then. So long Jack, if I don't see you before I go," said Malcolm, shaking hands.

He went out, followed by Joe, who seemed to have his tail between his legs.

"Well, this is the devil's own," exclaimed the doctor, when he was left alone with Fred Henry. "Going before Wednesday, are you?"

"That's the orders," replied the other.

"Where, to Northampton?"

"That's it."

"The devil!" exclaimed Ferguson, with quiet chagrin.

And there was silence between the two.

"All settled up, are you?" asked Ferguson.

"About."

There was another pause.

"Well, I shall miss yer, Freddy, boy," said the young doctor.

"And I shall miss thee, Jack," returned the other.

"Miss you like hell," mused the doctor.

Fred Henry turned aside. There was nothing to say. Mabel came in again, to finish clearing the table.

"What are *you* going to do, then, Miss Pervin?" asked Ferguson. "Going to your sister's, are you?"

Mabel looked at him with her steady, dangerous eyes, that always made him uncomfortable, unsettling his superficial ease.

"No," she said.

"Well, what in the name of fortune *are* you going to do? Say what you mean to do," cried Fred Henry, with futile intensity.

But she only averted her head, and continued her work. She folded the white table-cloth, and put on the chenille cloth.

"The sulkiest bitch that ever trod!" muttered her brother.

But she finished her task with perfectly impassive face, the young doctor watching her interestedly all the while. Then she went out.

Fred Henry stared after her, clenching his lips, his blue eyes fixing in sharp antagonism, as he made a grimace of sour exasperation.

"You could bray[4] her into bits, and that's all you'd get out of her," he said, in a small, narrowed tone.

The doctor smiled faintly.

"What's she *going* to do, then?" he asked.

"Strike me if *I* know!" returned the other.

There was a pause. Then the doctor stirred.

"I'll be seeing you tonight, shall I?" he said to his friend.

"Ay—where's it to be? Are we going over to Jessdale?"

"I don't know. I've got such a cold on me. I'll come round to the 'Moon and Stars,'[5] anyway."

"Let Lizzie and May miss their night for once, eh?"

"That's it—if I feel as I do now."

"All's one——"

The two young men went through the passage and down to the back door together. The house was large, but it was servantless now, and desolate. At the back was a small bricked house-yard and beyond that a big square, gravelled fine and red, and having stables on two sides. Sloping, dank, winter-dark fields stretched away on the open sides.

But the stables were empty. Joseph Pervin, the father of the family, had been a man of no education, who had become a fairly large horse dealer. The stables had been full of horses, there was a great turmoil and come-and-go of horses and of dealers and grooms. Then the kitchen was full of servants. But of late things had declined. The old man had married a second time, to retrieve his fortunes. Now he was dead and everything was gone to the dogs,[6] there was nothing but debt and threatening.

For months, Mabel had been servantless in the big house, keeping the home together in penury for her ineffectual brothers. She had kept house for ten years. But previously it was with unstinted means. Then, however

4. Grind.
5. Name of a public house (pub).
6. Gone wrong (slang).

brutal and coarse everything was, the sense of money had kept her proud, confident. The men might be foul-mouthed, the women in the kitchen might have had reputations, her brothers might have illegitimate children. But so long as there was money, the girl felt herself established, and brutally proud, reserved.

No company came to the house, save dealers and coarse men. Mabel had no associates of her own sex, after her sister went away. But she did not mind. She went regularly to church, she attended to her father. And she lived in the memory of her mother, who had died when she was fourteen, and whom she had loved. She had loved her father, too, in a different way, depending upon him, and feeling secure in him, until at the age of fifty-four, he married again. And then she had set hard against him. Now he had died and left them all hopelessly in debt.

She had suffered badly during the period of poverty. Nothing, however, could shake the curious, sullen, animal pride that dominated each member of the family. Now, for Mabel, the end had come. Still she would not cast about her. She would follow her own way just the same. She would always hold the keys of her own situation. Mindless and persistent, she endured from day to day. Why should she think? Why should she answer anybody? It was enough that this was the end, and there was no way out. She need not pass any more darkly along the main street of the small town, avoiding every eye. She need not demean herself any more, going into the shops and buying the cheapest food. This was at an end. She thought of nobody, not even of herself. Mindless and persistent, she seemed in a sort of ecstasy to be coming nearer to her fulfilment, her own glorification, approaching her dead mother, who was glorified.

In the afternoon, she took a little bag, with shears and sponge and a small scrubbing-brush, and went out. It was a grey, wintry day, with saddened, dark green fields and an atmosphere blackened by the smoke of foundries not far off. She went quickly, darkly along the causeway, heeding nobody, through the town to the churchyard.

There she always felt secure, as if no one could see her, although as a matter of fact she was exposed to the stare of everyone who passed along under the churchyard wall. Nevertheless, once under the shadow of the great looming church, among the graves, she felt immune from the world, reserved within the thick churchyard wall as in another country.

Carefully she clipped the grass from the grave, and arranged the pinky-white, small chrysanthemums in the tin cross. When this was done, she took an empty jar from a neighbouring grave, brought water, and carefully, most scrupulously sponged the marble headstone and the coping-stone.

It gave her sincere satisfaction to do this. She felt in immediate contact with the world of her mother. She took minute pains, went through the park in a state bordering on pure happiness, as if in performing this task she came into a subtle, intimate connection with her mother. For the life she followed here in the world was far less real than the world of death she inherited from her mother.

The doctor's house was just by the church. Ferguson, being a mere hired assistant, was slave to the country-side. As he hurried now to attend to the out-patients in the surgery, glancing across the graveyard with his quick eye, he saw the girl at her task at the grave. She seemed so intent and remote, it was like looking into another world. Some mystical element was touched in him. He slowed down as he walked, watching her as if spellbound.

She lifted her eyes, feeling him looking. Their eyes met. And each looked away again at once, each feeling, in some way, found out by the other. He lifted his cap and passed on down the road. There remained distinct in his consciousness, like a vision, the memory of her face, lifted from the tombstone in the churchyard, and looking at him with slow, large, portentous eyes. It *was* portentous, her face. It seemed to mesmerise him. There was a heavy power in her eyes which laid hold of his whole being, as if he had drunk some powerful drug. He had been feeling weak and done before. Now the life came back into him, he felt delivered from his own fretted, daily self.

He finished his duties at the surgery as quickly as might be, hastily filling up the bottles of the waiting people with cheap drugs. Then, in perpetual haste, he set off again to visit several cases in another part of his round, before tea-time. At all times he preferred to walk if he could, but particularly when he was not well. He fancied the motion restored him.

The afternoon was falling. It was grey, deadened, and wintry, with a slow, moist, heavy coldness sinking in and deadening all the faculties. But why should he think or notice? He hastily climbed the hill and turned across the dark green fields, following the black cinder-track. In the distance, across a shallow dip in the country, the small town was clustered like smouldering ash, a tower, a spire, a heap of low, raw, extinct houses. And on the nearest fringe of the town, sloping into the dip, was Oldmeadow, the Pervins' house. He could see the stables and the outbuildings distinctly, as they lay towards him on the slope. Well, he would not go there many more times! Another resource would be lost to him, another place gone: the only company he cared for in the alien, ugly little town he was losing. Nothing but work, drudgery, constant hastening from dwelling to dwelling among the colliers and the iron-workers. It wore him out, but at the same time he had a craving for it. It was a stimulant to him to be in the homes of the working people, moving, as it were, through the innermost body of their life. His nerves were excited and gratified. He could come so near, into the very lives of the rough, inarticulate, powerfully emotional men and women. He grumbled, he said he hated the hellish hole. But as a matter of fact it excited him, the contact with the rough, strongly-feeling people was a stimulant applied direct to his nerves.

Below Oldmeadow, in the green, shallow, soddened hollow of fields, lay a square, deep pond. Roving across the landscape, the doctor's quick eye detected a figure in black passing through the gate of the field, down towards the pond. He looked again. It would be Mabel Pervin. His mind suddenly became alive and attentive.

Why was she going down there? He pulled up on the path on the slope above, and stood staring. He could just make sure of the small black figure moving in the hollow of the failing day. He seemed to see her in the midst of such obscurity, that he was like a clairvoyant, seeing rather with the mind's eye than with ordinary sight. Yet he could see her positively enough, whilst he kept his eye attentive. He felt, if he looked away from her, in the thick, ugly falling dusk, he would lose her altogether.

He followed her minutely as she moved, direct and intent, like something transmitted rather than stirring in voluntary activity, straight down the field towards the pond. There she stood on the bank for a moment. She never raised her head. Then she waded slowly into the water.

He stood motionless as the small black figure walked slowly and deliberately towards the centre of the pond, very slowly, gradually moving deeper into the motionless water, and still moving forward as the water got up to her breast. Then he could see her no more in the dusk of the dead afternoon.

"There!" he exclaimed. "Would you believe it?"

And he hastened straight down, running over the wet, soddened fields, pushing through the hedges, down into the depression of callous wintry obscurity. It took him several minutes to come to the pond. He stood on the bank, breathing heavily. He could see nothing. His eyes seemed to penetrate the dead water. Yes, perhaps that was the dark shadow of her black clothing beneath the surface of the water.

He slowly ventured into the pond. The bottom was deep, soft clay, he sank in, and the water clasped dead cold round his legs. As he stirred he could smell the cold, rotten clay that fouled up into the water. It was objectionable in his lungs. Still, repelled and yet not heeding, he moved deeper into the pond. The cold water rose over his thighs, over his loins, upon his abdomen. The lower part of his body was all sunk in the hideous cold element. And the bottom was so deeply soft and uncertain, he was afraid of pitching with his mouth underneath. He could not swim, and was afraid.

He crouched a little, spreading his hands under the water and moving them round, trying to feel for her. The dead cold pond swayed upon his chest. He moved again, a little deeper, and again, with his hands underneath, he felt all around under the water. And he touched her clothing. But it evaded his fingers. He made a desperate effort to grasp it.

And so doing he lost his balance and went under, horribly, suffocating in the foul earthy water, struggling madly for a few moments. At last, after what seemed an eternity, he got his footing, rose again into the air and looked around. He gasped, and knew he was in the world. Then he looked at the water. She had risen near him. He grasped her clothing, and drawing her nearer, turned to take his way to land again.

He went very slowly, carefully, absorbed in the slow progress. He rose higher, climbing out of the pond. The water was now only about his legs; he was thankful, full of relief to be out of the clutches of the pond. He lifted her and staggered on to the bank, out of the horror of wet, grey clay.

He laid her down on the bank. She was quite unconscious and running with water. He made the water come from her mouth, he worked to restore her. He did not have to work very long before he could feel the breathing begin again in her; she was breathing naturally. He worked a little longer. He could feel her live beneath his hands; she was coming back. He wiped her face, wrapped her in his overcoat, looked round into the dim, dark grey world, then lifted her and staggered down the bank and across the fields.

It seemed an unthinkably long way, and his burden so heavy he felt he would never get to the house. But at last he was in the stable-yard, and then in the house-yard. He opened the door and went into the house. In the kitchen he laid her down on the hearth-rug and called. The house was empty. But the fire was burning in the grate.

Then again he kneeled to attend to her. She was breathing regularly, her eyes were wide open and as if conscious, but there seemed something missing in her look. She was conscious in herself, but unconscious of her surroundings.

He ran upstairs, took blankets from a bed, and put them before the fire to warm. Then he removed her saturated, earthy-smelling clothing, rubbed her dry with a towel, and wrapped her naked in the blankets. Then he went into the dining room, to look for spirits. There was a little whisky. He drank a gulp himself, and put some into her mouth.

The effect was instantaneous. She looked full into his face, as if she had been seeing him for some time, and yet had only just become conscious of him.

"Dr. Ferguson?" she said.

"What?" he answered.

He was divesting himself of his coat, intending to find some dry clothing upstairs. He could not bear the smell of the dead, clayey water, and he was mortally afraid for his own health.

"What did I do?" she asked.

"Walked into the pond," he replied. He had begun to shudder like one sick, and could hardly attend to her. Her eyes remained full on him, he seemed to be going dark in his mind, looking back at her helplessly. The shuddering became quieter in him, his life came back to him, dark and unknowing, but strong again.

"Was I out of my mind?" she asked, while her eyes were fixed on him all the time.

"Maybe, for the moment," he replied. He felt quiet, because his strength had come back. The strange fretful strain had left him.

"Am I out of my mind now?" she asked.

"Are you?" he reflected a moment. "No," he answered truthfully. "I don't see that you are." He turned his face aside. He was afraid now, because he felt dazed, and felt dimly that her power was stronger than his, in this issue. And she continued to look at him fixedly all the time. "Can you tell me where I shall find some dry things to put on?" he asked.

"Did you dive into the pond for me?" she asked.

"No," he answered. "I walked in. But I went in overhead as well."

There was silence for a moment. He hesitated. He very much wanted to go upstairs to get into dry clothing. But there was another desire in him. And she seemed to hold him. His will seemed to have gone to sleep, and left him, standing there slack before her. But he felt warm inside himself. He did not shudder at all, though his clothes were sodden on him.

"Why did you?" she asked.

"Because I didn't want you to do such a foolish thing," he said.

"It wasn't foolish," she said, still gazing at him as she lay on the floor, with a sofa cushion under her head. "It was the right thing to do. I knew best, then."

"I'll go and shift these wet things," he said. But still he had not the power to move out of her presence, until she sent him. It was as if she had the life of his body in her hands, and he could not extricate himself. Or perhaps he did not want to.

Suddenly she sat up. Then she became aware of her own immediate condition. She felt the blankets about her, she knew her own limbs. For a moment it seemed as if her reason were going. She looked round, with wild eye, as if seeking something. He stood still with fear. She saw her clothing lying scattered.

"Who undressed me?" she asked, her eyes resting full and inevitable on his face.

"I did," he replied, "to bring you round."

For some moments she sat and gazed at him awfully, her lips parted.

"Do you love me, then?" she asked.

He only stood and stared at her, fascinated. His soul seemed to melt.

She shuffled forward on her knees, and put her arms round him, round his legs, as he stood there, pressing her breasts against his knees and thighs, clutching him with strange, convulsive certainty, pressing his thighs against her, drawing him to her face, her throat, as she looked up at him with flaring, humble eyes of transfiguration, triumphant in first possession.

"You love me," she murmured, in strange transport, yearning and triumphant and confident. "You love me. I know you love me, I know."

And she was passionately kissing his knees, through the wet clothing, passionately and indiscriminately kissing his knees, his legs, as if unaware of everything.

He looked down at the tangled wet hair, the wild, bare, animal shoulders. He was amazed, bewildered, and afraid. He had never thought of loving her. He had never wanted to love her. When he rescued her and restored her, he was a doctor, and she was a patient. He had had no single personal thought of her. Nay, this introduction of the personal element was very distasteful to him, a violation of his professional honour. It was horrible to have her there embracing his knees. It was horrible. He revolted from it, violently. And yet— and yet—he had not the power to break away.

She looked at him again, with the same supplication of powerful love, and that same transcendent, frightening light of triumph. In view of the delicate flame which seemed to come from her face like a light, he was powerless. And yet he had never intended to love her. He had never intended. And something stubborn in him could not give way.

"You love me," she repeated, in a murmur of deep, rhapsodic assurance. "You love me."

Her hands were drawing him, drawing him down to her. He was afraid, even a little horrified. For he had, really, no intention of loving her. Yet her hands were drawing him towards her. He put out his hand quickly to steady himself, and grasped her bare shoulder. A flame seemed to burn the hand that grasped her soft shoulder. He had no intention of loving her: his whole will was against his yielding. It was horrible. And yet wonderful was the touch of her shoulders, beautiful the shining of her face. Was she perhaps mad? He had a horror of yielding to her. Yet something in him ached also.

He had been staring away at the door, away from her. But his hand remained on her shoulder. She had gone suddenly very still. He looked down at her. Her eyes were now wide with fear, with doubt, the light was dying from her face, a shadow of terrible greyness was returning. He could not bear the touch of her eyes' question upon him, and the look of death behind the question.

With an inward groan he gave way, and let his heart yield towards her. A sudden gentle smile came on his face. And her eyes, which never left his face, slowly, slowly filled with tears. He watched the strange water rise in her eyes, like some slow fountain coming up. And his heart seemed to burn and melt away in his breast.

He could not bear to look at her any more. He dropped on his knees and caught her head with his arms and pressed her face against his throat. She was very still. His heart, which seemed to have broken, was burning with a kind of agony in his breast. And he felt her slow, hot tears wetting his throat. But he could not move.

He felt the hot tears wet his neck and the hollows of his neck, and he remained motionless, suspended through one of man's eternities. Only now it had become indispensable to him to have her face pressed close to him; he could never let her go again. He could never let her head go away from the close clutch of his arm. He wanted to remain like that for ever, with his heart hurting him in a pain that was also life to him. Without knowing, he was looking down on her damp, soft brown hair.

Then, as it were suddenly, he smelt the horrid stagnant smell of that water. And at the same moment she drew away from him and looked at him. Her eyes were wistful and unfathomable. He was afraid of them, and he fell to kissing her, not knowing what he was doing. He wanted her eyes not to have that terrible, wistful, unfathomable look.

When she turned her face to him again, a faint delicate flush was glowing, and there was again dawning that terrible shining of joy in her eyes, which really terrified him, and yet which he now wanted to see, because he feared the look of doubt still more.

"You love me?" she said, rather faltering.

"Yes." The word cost him a painful effort. Not because it wasn't true. But because it was too newly true, the *saying* seemed to tear open again his newly-torn heart. And he hardly wanted it to be true, even now.

She lifted her face to him, and he bent forward and kissed her on the mouth, gently, with the one kiss that is an eternal pledge. And as he kissed her his heart strained again in his breast. He never intended to love her. But now it was over. He had crossed over the gulf to her, and all that he had left behind had shrivelled and become void.

After the kiss, her eyes again slowly filled with tears. She sat still, away from him, with her face drooped aside, and her hands folded in her lap. The tears fell very slowly. There was complete silence. He too sat there motionless and silent on the hearth-rug. The strange pain of his heart that was broken seemed to consume him. That he should love her? That this was love! That he should be ripped open in this way! Him, a doctor! How they would all jeer if they knew! It was agony to him to think they might know.

In the curious naked pain of the thought he looked again to her. She was sitting there drooped into a muse. He saw a tear fall, and his heart flared hot. He saw for the first time that one of her shoulders was quite uncovered, one arm bare, he could see one of her small breasts; dimly, because it had become almost dark in the room.

"Why are you crying?" he asked, in an altered voice.

She looked up at him, and behind her tears the consciousness of her situation for the first time brought a dark look of shame to her eyes.

"I'm not crying, really," she said, watching him, half frightened.

He reached his hand, and softly closed it on her bare arm.

"I love you! I love you!" he said in a soft, low vibrating voice, unlike himself.

She shrank, and dropped her head. The soft, penetrating grip of his hand on her arm distressed her. She looked up at him.

"I want to go," she said. "I want to go and get you some dry things."

"Why?" he said. "I'm all right."

"But I want to go," she said. "And I want you to change your things."

He released her arm, and she wrapped herself in the blanket, looking at him, rather frightened. And still she did not rise.

"Kiss me," she said wistfully.

He kissed her, but briefly, half in anger.

Then, after a second, she rose nervously, all mixed up in the blanket. He watched her in her confusion as she tried to extricate herself and wrap herself up so that she could walk. He watched her relentlessly, as she knew. And as she went, the blanket trailing, and as he saw a glimpse of her feet and her white leg, he tried to remember her as she was when he had wrapped her in the blanket. But then he didn't want to remember, because she had been nothing to him then, and his nature revolted from remembering her as she was when she was nothing to him.

A tumbling muffled noise from within the dark house startled him. Then he heard her voice: "There are clothes." He rose and went to the foot of the stairs, and gathered up the garments she had thrown down. Then he came back to the fire, to rub himself down and dress. He grinned at his own appearance when he had finished.

The fire was sinking, so he put on coal. The house was now quite dark, save for the light of a street-lamp that shone in faintly from beyond the holly trees. He lit the gas with matches he found on the mantelpiece. Then he emptied the pockets of his own clothes, and threw all his wet things in a heap into the scullery. After which he gathered up her sodden clothes, gently, and put them in a separate heap on the copper-top in the scullery.

It was six o'clock on the clock. His own watch had stopped. He ought to go back to the surgery. He waited, and still she did not come down. So he went to the foot of the stairs and called:

"I shall have to go."

Almost immediately he heard her coming down. She had on her best dress of black voile, and her hair was tidy, but still damp. She looked at him—and in spite of herself, smiled.

"I don't like you in those clothes," she said.

"Do I look a sight?" he answered.

They were shy of one another.

"I'll make you some tea," she said.

"No, I must go."

"Must you?" And she looked at him again with the wide, strained, doubtful eyes. And again, from the pain of his breast, he knew how he loved her. He went and bent to kiss her, gently, passionately, with his heart's painful kiss.

"And my hair smells so horrible," she murmured in distraction. "And I'm so awful, I'm so awful! Oh no, I'm too awful." And she broke into bitter, heart-broken sobbing. "You can't want to love me, I'm horrible."

"Don't be silly, don't be silly," he said, trying to comfort her, kissing her, holding her in his arms. "I want you, I want to marry you, we're going to be married, quickly, quickly—to-morrow if I can."

But she only sobbed terribly, and cried:

"I feel awful. I feel awful. I feel I'm horrible to you."

"No, I want you, I want you," was all he answered, blindly, with that terrible intonation which frightened her almost more than her horror lest he should *not* want her.

1922

Why the Novel Matters

We have curious ideas of ourselves. We think of ourselves as a body with a spirit in it, or a body with a soul in it, or a body with a mind in it. *Mens sana in corpore sano*.[1] The years drink up the wine, and at last throw the bottle away, the body, of course, being the bottle.

It is a funny sort of superstition. Why should I look at my hand, as it so cleverly writes these words, and decide that it is a mere nothing compared to the mind that directs it? Is there really any huge difference between my hand and my brain? Or my mind? My hand is alive, it flickers with a life of its own. It meets all the strange universe in touch, and learns a vast number of things, and knows a vast number of things. My hand, as it writes these words, slips gaily along, jumps like a grasshopper to dot an *i*, feels the table rather cold, gets a little bored if I write too long, has its own rudiments of thought, and is just as much *me* as is my brain, my mind, or my soul. Why should I imagine that there is a *me* which is more *me* than my hand is? Since my hand is absolutely alive, me alive.

Whereas, of course, as far as I am concerned, my pen isn't alive at all. My pen *isn't* me alive. Me alive ends at my finger tips.

Whatever is me alive is me. Every tiny bit of my hands is alive, every little freckle and hair and fold of skin. And whatever is me alive is me. Only my finger-nails, those ten little weapons between me and an inanimate universe, they cross the mysterious Rubicon[2] between me alive and things like my pen, which are not alive, in my own sense.

So, seeing my hand is all alive, and me alive, wherein is it just a bottle, or a jug, or a tin can, or a vessel of clay, or any of the rest of that nonsense? True, if I cut it it will bleed, like a can of cherries. But then the skin that is cut, and the veins that bleed, and the bones that should never be seen, they are all just as alive as the blood that flows. So the tin can business, or vessel of clay, is just bunk.

And that's what you learn, when you're a novelist. And that's what you are very liable *not* to know, if you're a parson, or a philosopher, or a scientist, or a stupid person. If you're a parson, you talk about souls in heaven. If you're a novelist, you know that paradise is in the palm of your hand, and on the end of your nose, because both are alive; and alive, and man alive, which is more than you can say, for certain, of paradise. Paradise is after life, and I for one am not keen on anything that is *after* life. If you are a philosopher, you talk about infinity, and the pure spirit which knows all things. But if you

1. A healthy mind in a healthy body (Latin).
2. When Julius Caesar crossed the river Rubicon (near Rimini, Italy) in 49 B.C.E., in defiance of the Senate, he indicated his intention of advancing against Pompey and thus involving the country in civil war. Hence to "cross the Rubicon" means to take an important and irrevocable decision.

pick up a novel, you realise immediately that infinity is just a handle to this self-same jug of a body of mine; while as for knowing, if I find my finger in the fire, I know that fire burns, with a knowledge so emphatic and vital, it leaves Nirvana[3] merely a conjecture. Oh, yes, my body, me alive, *knows,* and knows intensely. And as for the sum of all knowledge, it can't be anything more than an accumulation of all the things I know in the body, and you, dear reader, know in the body.

These damned philosophers, they talk as if they suddenly went off in steam, and were then much more important than they are when they're in their shirts. It is nonsense. Every man, philosopher included, ends in his own finger-tips. That's the end of his man alive. As for the words and thoughts and sighs and aspirations that fly from him, they are so many tremulations in the ether, and not alive at all. But if the tremulations reach another man alive, he may receive them into his life, and his life may take on a new colour, like a chameleon creeping from a brown rock on to a green leaf. All very well and good. It still doesn't alter the fact that the so-called spirit, the message or teaching of the philosopher or the saint, isn't alive at all, but just a tremulation upon the ether, like a radio message. All this spirit stuff is just tremulations upon the ether. If you, as man alive, quiver from the tremulation of the ether into new life, that is because you are man alive, and you take sustenance and stimulation into your alive man in a myriad ways. But to say that the message, or the spirit which is communicated to you, is more important than your living body, is nonsense. You might as well say that the potato at dinner was more important.

Nothing is important but life. And for myself, I can absolutely see life nowhere but in the living. Life with a capital L is only man alive. Even a cabbage in the rain is cabbage alive. All things that are alive are amazing. And all things that are dead are subsidiary to the living. Better a live dog than a dead lion. But better a live lion than a live dog. *C'est la vie!*

It seems impossible to get a saint, or a philosopher, or a scientist, to stick to this simple truth. They are all, in a sense, renegades. The saint wishes to offer himself up as spiritual food for the multitude. Even Francis of Assisi turns himself into a sort of angel-cake, of which anyone may take a slice. But an angel-cake is rather less than man alive. And poor St Francis might well apologise to his body, when he is dying: "Oh, pardon me, my body, the wrong I did you through the years!" It was no wafer, for others to eat.

The philosopher, on the other hand, because he can think, decides that nothing but thoughts matter. It is as if a rabbit, because he can make little pills, should decide that nothing but little pills matter. As for the scientist, he has absolutely no use for me so long as I am man alive. To the scientist, I am dead. He puts under the microscope a bit of dead me, and calls it me. He takes me to pieces, and says first one piece, and then another piece, is me. My heart, my liver, my stomach have all been scientifically me, according to the scientist; and nowadays I am either a brain, or nerves, or glands, or something more up-to-date in the tissue line.

Now I absolutely flatly deny that I am a soul, or a body, or a mind, or an intelligence, or a brain, or a nervous system, or a bunch of glands, or any of the rest of these bits of me. The whole is greater than the part. And therefore,

3. In Buddhist theology, the extinction of the self and its desires and the attainment of perfect beatitude.

I, who am man alive, am greater than my soul, or spirit, or body, or mind, or consciousness, or anything else that is merely a part of me. I am a man, and alive. I am man alive, and as long as I can, I intend to go on being man alive.

For this reason I am a novelist. And being a novelist, I consider myself superior to the saint, the scientist, the philosopher, and the poet, who are all great masters of different bits of man alive, but never get the whole hog.

The novel is the one bright book of life. Books are not life. They are only tremulations on the ether. But the novel as a tremulation can make the whole man alive tremble. Which is more than poetry, philosophy, science, or any other book-tremulation can do.

The novel is the book of life. In this sense, the Bible is a great confused novel. You may say, it is about God. But it is really about man alive. Adam, Eve, Sarai, Abraham, Isaac, Jacob, Samuel, David, Bath-Sheba, Ruth, Esther, Solomon, Job, Isaiah, Jesus, Mark, Judas, Paul, Peter: what is it but man alive, from start to finish? Man alive, not mere bits. Even the Lord is another man alive, in a burning bush, throwing the tablets of stone at Moses's head.

I do hope you begin to get my idea, why the novel is supremely important, as a tremulation on the ether. Plato makes the perfect ideal being tremble in me. But that's only a bit of me. Perfection is only a bit, in the strange make-up of man alive. The Sermon on the Mount makes the selfless spirit of me quiver. But that, too, is only a bit of me. The Ten Commandments set the old Adam shivering in me, warning me that I am a thief and a murderer, unless I watch it. But even the old Adam is only a bit of me.

I very much like all these bits of me to be set trembling with life and the wisdom of life. But I do ask that the whole of me shall tremble in its whole-ness, some time or other.

And this, of course, must happen in me, living.

But as far as it can happen from a communication, it can only happen when a whole novel communicates itself to me. The Bible—but *all* the Bible—and Homer, and Shakespeare: these are the supreme old novels. These are all things to all men. Which means that in their wholeness they affect the whole man alive, which is the man himself, beyond any part of him. They set the whole tree trembling with a new access of life, they do not just stimulate growth in one direction.

I don't want to grow in any one direction any more. And, if I can help it, I don't want to stimulate anybody else into some particular direction. A par-ticular direction ends in a *cul-de-sac*. We're in a *cul-de-sac* at present.

I don't believe in any dazzling revelation, or in any supreme Word. "The grass withereth, the flower fadeth, but the Word of the Lord shall stand for ever." That's the kind of stuff we've drugged ourselves with. As a matter of fact, the grass withereth, but comes up all the greener for that reason, after the rains. The flower fadeth, and therefore the bud opens. But the Word of the Lord, being man-uttered and a mere vibration on the ether, becomes staler and staler, more and more boring, till at last we turn a deaf ear and it ceases to exist, far more finally than any withered grass. It is grass that renews its youth like the eagle, not any Word.

We should ask for no absolutes, or absolute. Once and for all and for ever, let us have done with the ugly imperialism of any absolute. There is no absolute good, there is nothing absolutely right. All things flow and change, and even change is not absolute. The whole is a strange assembly of apparently incongruous parts, slipping past one another.

Me, man alive, I am a very curious assembly of incongruous parts. My yea! of today is oddly different from my yea! of yesterday. My tears of to-morrow will have nothing to do with my tears of a year ago. If the one I love remains unchanged and unchanging, I shall cease to love her. It is only because she changes and startles me into change and defies my inertia, and is herself staggered in her inertia by my changing, that I can continue to love her. If she stayed put, I might as well love the pepper pot.

In all this change, I maintain a certain integrity. But woe betide me if I try to put my finger on it. If I say of myself, I am this, I am that!—then, if I stick to it, I turn into a stupid fixed thing like a lamp-post. I shall never know wherein lies my integrity, my individuality, my me. I *can* never know it. It is useless to talk about my ego. That only means that I have made up an *idea* of myself, and that I am trying to cut myself out to pattern. Which is no good. You can cut your cloth to fit your coat, but you can't clip bits off your living body, to trim it down to your idea. True, you can put yourself into ideal corsets. But even in ideal corsets, fashions change.

Let us learn from the novel. In the novel, the characters can do nothing but *live*. If they keep on being good, according to pattern, or bad, according to pattern, or even volatile, according to pattern, they cease to live, and the novel falls dead. A character in a novel has got to live, or it is nothing.

We, likewise, in life have got to live, or we are nothing.

What we mean by living is, of course, just as indescribable as what we mean by *being*. Men get ideas into their heads, of what they mean by Life, and they proceed to cut life out to pattern. Sometimes they go into the desert to seek God, sometimes they go into the desert to seek cash, sometimes it is wine, woman, and song, and again it is water, political reform, and votes. You never know what it will be next: from killing your neighbour with hideous bombs and gas that tears the lungs, to supporting a Foundlings' Home[4] and preaching infinite Love, and being co-respondent in a divorce.

In all this wild welter, we need some sort of guide. It's no good inventing Thou Shalt Nots!

What then? Turn truly, honourably to the novel, and see wherein you are man alive, and wherein you are dead man in life. You may love a woman as man alive, and you may be making love to a woman as sheer dead man in life. You may eat your dinner as man alive, or as a mere masticating corpse. As man alive you may have shot at your enemy. But as a ghastly simulacrum of life you may be firing bombs into men who are neither your enemies nor your friends, but just things you are dead to. Which is criminal, when the things happen to be alive.

To be alive, to be man alive, to be whole man alive: that is the point. And at its best, the novel, and the novel supremely, can help you. It can help you not to be dead man in life. So much of a man walks about dead and a carcass in the street and house, to-day: so much of women is merely dead. Like a pianoforte with half the notes mute.

But the novel you can see, plainly, when the man goes dead, the woman

4. Orphanage.

goes inert. You can develop an instinct for life, if you will, instead of a theory of right and wrong, good and bad.

In life, there is right and wrong, good and bad, all the time. But what is right in one case is wrong in another. And in the novel you see one man becoming a corpse, because of his so-called goodness, another going dead because of his so-called wickedness. Right and wrong is an instinct: but an instinct of the whole consciousness in a man, bodily, mental, spiritual at once. And only in the novel are *all* things given full play, or at least, they may be given full play, when we realize that life itself, and not inert safety, is the reason for living. For out of the full play of all things emerges the only thing that is anything, the wholeness of a man, the wholeness of a woman, man live, and live woman.

1936

Piano[1]

Softly, in the dusk, a woman is singing to me;
Taking me back down the vista of years, till I see
A child sitting under the piano, in the boom of the tingling strings
And pressing the small, poised feet of a mother who smiles as she sings.

5   In spite of myself, the insidious mastery of song
Betrays me back, till the heart of me weeps to belong
To the old Sunday evenings at home, with winter outside
And hymns in the cozy parlour, the tinkling piano our guide.

So now it is vain for the singer to burst into clamour
10 With the great black piano appassionato. The glamour
Of childish days is upon me, my manhood is cast
Down in the flood of remembrance, I weep like a child for the past.

1918

Bavarian Gentians[1]

Not every man has gentians in his house
in soft September, at slow, sad Michaelmas.

Bavarian gentians, big and dark, only dark
darkening the daytime torchlike with the smoking blueness of Pluto's[2]
      gloom,
5   ribbed and torchlike, with their blaze of darkness spread blue
down flattening into points, flattened under the sweep of white day
torch-flower of the blue-smoking darkness, Pluto's dark-blue daze,

---

1. For an earlier version of this poem, see "Poems in Process," in the appendices to this volume.
1. Keith Sagar challenges the accepted view that this is the final version of the poem in "The Genesis of 'Bavarian Gentians,'" *The D. H. Lawrence Review* (Spring 1975): 47–53. He prefers the

longer version printed in *The Collected Poems of D. H. Lawrence* (1964), ed. Vivian de Sola Pinto and Warren Roberts, 975.
2. God of the underworld in classical mythology. He was also called "Dis" (line 8).

black lamps from the halls of Dis, burning dark blue,
giving off darkness, blue darkness, as Demeter's pale lamps give off light,
10 lead me then, lead me the way.

Reach me a gentian, give me a torch
let me guide myself with the blue, forked torch of this flower
down the darker and darker stairs, where blue is darkened on blueness.
even where Persephone[3] goes, just now, from the frosted September
15 to the sightless realm where darkness was awake upon the dark
and Persephone herself is but a voice
or a darkness invisible enfolded in the deeper dark
of the arms Plutonic, and pierced with the passion of dense gloom,
among the splendour of torches of darkness, shedding darkness on the lost
    bride and her groom.

1923

Snake

A snake came to my water-trough
On a hot, hot day, and I in pyjamas for the heat,
To drink there.

In the deep, strange-scented shade of the great dark carob-tree
5   I came down the steps with my pitcher
And must wait, must stand and wait, for there he was at the trough before
    me.

He reached down from a fissure in the earth-wall in the gloom
And trailed his yellow-brown slackness soft-bellied down, over the edge of
    the stone trough
And rested his throat upon the stone bottom,
10 And where the water had dripped from the tap, in a small clearness,
He sipped with his straight mouth,
Softly drank through his straight gums, into his slack long body,
Silently.

Someone was before me at my water-trough,
15 And I, like a second comer, waiting.

He lifted his head from his drinking, as cattle do,
And looked at me vaguely, as drinking cattle do,
And flickered his two-forked tongue from his lips, and mused a moment,
And stooped and drank a little more,
20 Being earth-brown, earth-golden from the burning bowels of the earth
On the day of Sicilian July, with Etna smoking.

3. Bride of Pluto, who abducted her from the earth, and daughter of Demeter, goddess of the fruits of the earth (line 9). She was allowed to return to earth every spring but had to descend again to Hades in the autumn, "the frosted Sep- tember." Demeter and Persephone were central figures in ancient fertility myths, where Persephone's annual descent and return were linked with the death and rebirth of vegetation.

The voice of my education said to me
He must be killed,
For in Sicily the black, black snakes are innocent, the gold are venomous.

25   And voices in me said, If you were a man
You would take a stick and break him now, and finish him off.

But must I confess how I liked him,
How glad I was he had come like a guest in quiet, to drink at my water-
    trough
And depart peaceful, pacified, and thankless
30   Into the burning bowels of this earth?

Was it cowardice, that I dared not kill him?
Was it perversity, that I longed to talk to him?
Was it humility, to feel so honoured?
I felt so honoured.

35   And yet those voices:
If you were not afraid, you would kill him!

And truly I was afraid, I was most afraid,
But even so, honoured still more
That he should seek my hospitality
40   From out the dark door of the secret earth.

He drank enough
And lifted his head, dreamily, as one who has drunken,
And flickered his tongue like a forked night on the air, so black;
Seeming to lick his lips,
45   And looked around like a god, unseeing, into the air,
And slowly turned his head,
And slowly, very slowly, as if thrice adream
Proceeded to draw his slow length curving round
And climb the broken bank of my wall-face.

50   And as he put his head into that dreadful hole,
And as he slowly drew up, snake-easing his shoulders, and entered farther,
A sort of horror, a sort of protest against his withdrawing into that horrid
    black hole,
Deliberately going into the blackness, and slowly drawing himself after,
Overcame me now his back was turned.

55   I looked round, I put down my pitcher,
I picked up a clumsy log
And threw it at the water-trough with a clatter.

I think it did not hit him;
But suddenly that part of him that was left behind convulsed in undigni-
    fied haste,
60   Writhed like lightning, and was gone

Into the black hole, the earth-lipped fissure in the wall-front
At which, in the intense still noon, I stared with fascination.

And immediately I regretted it.
I thought how paltry, how vulgar, what a mean act!
65 I despised myself and the voices of my accursed human education.

And I thought of the albatross,[1]
And I wished he would come back, my snake.

For he seemed to me again like a king,
Like a king in exile, uncrowned in the underworld,
70 Now due to be crowned again.

And so, I missed my chance with one of the lords
Of life.
And I have something to expiate;
A pettiness.

1923

1. In Coleridge's *Ancient Mariner.*

T. S. ELIOT
1888–1965

Thomas Stearns Eliot was born in St. Louis, Missouri, of New England stock. He
entered Harvard in 1906 and was influenced there by the anti-Romanticism of Irving
Babbitt and the philosophical and critical interests of George Santayana, as well as
by the enthusiasm that prevailed in certain Harvard circles for Elizabethan and Jacobean literature, the Italian Renaissance, and Indian mystical philosophy. His philosophical studies included intensive work on the English idealist philosopher F. H.
Bradley, on whom he eventually wrote his Harvard dissertation. (Bradley's emphasis
on the private nature of individual experience, "a circle enclosed on the outside," had
considerable influence on the private imagery of Eliot's poetry and on the view of the
relation between the individual and other individuals reflected in much of his poetry.)
Later, Eliot studied literature and philosophy in France and Germany, before going
to England shortly after the outbreak of World War I in 1914. He studied Greek
philosophy at Oxford, taught school in London, and then obtained a position with
Lloyd's Bank. In 1915 he married an English writer, Vivienne Haigh-Wood, but the
marriage was not a success. She was highly neurotic and in increasingly bad health.
The strain told on Eliot, too. By November 1921 distress and worry had brought him
to the verge of a nervous breakdown, and on medical advice, he went to recuperate
in a Swiss sanitorium. Two months later he returned, pausing in Paris long enough
to give Ezra Pound the manuscript of *The Waste Land.* Eliot left his wife in 1933;
and she was eventually committed to a mental home, where she died in 1947. Ten
years later he married again and, for the eight years that remained to him, at last
knew happiness.
  Eliot started writing literary and philosophical reviews soon after settling in Lon-

don. He wrote for the *Athenaeum* and the *Times Literary Supplement,* among other periodicals, and was assistant editor of the *Egoist* from 1917 to 1919. In 1922 he founded the influential quarterly *Criterion,* which he edited until it ceased publication in 1939. His poetry first appeared in 1915, when *The Love Song of J. Alfred Prufrock* was printed in *Poetry* magazine (Chicago) and a few other short poems were published in the short-lived periodical *Blast.* His first published collection of poems was *Prufrock and Other Observations,* 1917; two other small collections followed in 1919 and 1920; in 1922 *The Waste Land* appeared, first in the *Criterion* in October, then in the *Dial* (in America) in November, and finally in book form. *Poems 1909–25* (1925) collected these earlier poems. Meanwhile he was also publishing collections of his critical essays, notably *The Sacred Wood* in 1920 and *Homage to John Dryden* in 1924. *For Lancelot Andrewes* followed in 1928 and in 1932 he included most of these earlier essays with some new ones in *Selected Essays.* In 1925 he joined the London publishing firm of Faber and Gwyer, becoming a director when the firm became Faber & Faber. He became a British subject and joined the Church of England in 1927.

"Our civilization comprehends great variety and complexity, and this variety and complexity, playing upon a refined sensibility, must produce various and complex results. The poet must become more and more comprehensive, more allusive, more indirect, in order to force, to dislocate if necessary, language into his meaning." This remark, from Eliot's essay *The Metaphysical Poets* (1921), gives one clue to his poetic method from *Prufrock* through *The Waste Land.* In the tradition of the Georgian poets who were active when he settled in London, he saw an exhausted poetic mode being employed, with no verbal excitement or original craftsmanship. He sought to make poetry more subtle, more suggestive, and at the same time more precise. He had learned from the imagists the necessity of clear and precise images, and he learned, too, from the philosopher-poet T. E. Hulme and from his early supporter and adviser Ezra Pound to fear romantic softness and to regard the poetic medium rather than the poet's personality as the important factor. At the same time, the "hard, dry" images advocated by Hulme were not enough for him; he wanted wit, allusiveness, irony. He saw in the Metaphysical poets how wit and passion could be combined, and he saw in the French symbolists how an image could be both absolutely precise in what it referred to physically and at the same time endlessly suggestive in the meanings it set up because of its relationship to other images. The combination of precision, symbolic suggestion, and ironic mockery in the poetry of the late-nineteenth-century French poet Jules Laforgue attracted and influenced him, and he was influenced too by other nineteenth-century French poets: by Théophile Gautier's artful carving of impersonal shapes of meaning; by Charles Baudelaire's strangely evocative explorations of the symbolic suggestions of objects and images; by the symbolist poets Paul Verlaine, Arthur Rimbaud, and Stéphane Mallarmé. He also found in the Jacobean dramatists a flexible blank verse with overtones of colloquial movement: Middleton, Tourneur, Webster, and others, taught him as much—in the way of verse movement, imagery, the counterpointing of the accent of conversation and the note of terror—as either the Metaphysicals or the French symbolists.

Hulme's protests against the Romantic concept of poetry fitted in well enough with what Eliot had learned from Irving Babbitt at Harvard; yet for all his severity with such poets as Shelley, for all his conscious cultivation of a classical viewpoint and his insistence on order and discipline rather than on mere self-expression in art, one side of Eliot's poetic genius is, in one sense of the word, Romantic. The symbolist influence on his imagery, his interest in the evocative and the suggestive, such lines as "And fiddled whisper music on those strings / And bats with baby faces in the violet light / Whistled, and beat their wings," and such recurring images as the hyacinth girl and the rose garden, all show what could be called a Romantic element in his poetry. But it is combined with a dry ironic allusiveness, a play of wit, and a colloquial element, which are not normally found in poets of the Romantic tradition.

Eliot's real novelty—and the cause of much bewilderment when his poems first appeared—was his deliberate elimination of all merely connective and transitional passages, his building up of the total pattern of meaning through the immediate juxtaposition of images without overt explanation of what they are doing, together with his use of oblique references to other works of literature (some of them quite obscure to most readers of his time). *Prufrock* presents a symbolic landscape where the meaning emerges from the mutual interaction of the images, and that meaning is enlarged by echoes, often ironic, of Hesiod and Dante and Shakespeare. *The Waste Land* is a series of scenes and images with no author's voice intervening to tell us where we are but with the implications developed through multiple contrasts and through analogies with older literary works often referred to in a distorted quotation or half-concealed allusion. Furthermore, the works referred to are not necessarily works that are central in the Western literary tradition: besides Dante and Shakespeare there are pre-Socratic philosophers; minor (as well as major) seventeenth-century poets and dramatists; works of anthropology, history, and philosophy; and other echoes of the poet's private reading. In a culture where there is no longer any assurance on the part of the poet that his or her public has a common cultural heritage, a common knowledge of works of the past, Eliot felt it necessary to build up his own body of references. It is this that marks the difference between Eliot's use of earlier literature and, say, Milton's. Both poets are difficult for the modern reader, who needs editorial assistance in recognizing and understanding many of the allusions—but Milton was drawing on a body of knowledge common to educated people in his day. Nevertheless, this aspect of Eliot can be exaggerated: the fact remains that the nature of his imagery together with the movement of his verse generally succeed in setting the tone he requires, in establishing the area of meaning to be developed, so that even a reader ignorant of most of the literary allusions can often get the feel of the poem and achieve some understanding of what it says.

Eliot's early poetry, until at least the middle 1920s, is mostly concerned in one way or another with the Waste Land, with aspects of the decay of culture in the modern Western world. After his formal acceptance of Anglican Christianity we find a penitential note in much of his verse, a note of quiet searching for spiritual peace, with considerable allusion to biblical, liturgical, and mystical religious literature and to Dante. *Ash Wednesday* (1930), a poem in six parts, much less fiercely concentrated in style than the earlier poetry, explores with gentle insistence a mood both penitential and questioning. The so-called *Ariel* poems (the title has nothing to do with their form or content) present or explore aspects of religious doubt or discovery or revelation, sometimes, as in *Marina*, using a purely secular imagery and sometimes, as in *Journey of the Magi*, drawing on biblical incident. In *Four Quartets* (of which the first, *Burnt Norton*, appeared in the *Collected Poems* of 1935, though all four were not completed until 1943, when they were published together) Eliot further explored essentially religious moods, dealing with the relation between time and eternity and the cultivation of that selfless passivity that can yield the moment of timeless revelation in the midst of time. The mocking irony, the savage humor, the deliberately startling juxtaposition of the sordid and the romantic give way in these later poems to a quieter poetic idiom, often still complexly allusive but never deliberately shocking.

Eliot's criticism was the criticism of a practicing poet who worked out in relation to his reading of older literature what he needed to hold and to admire. He lent the growing weight of his authority to that shift in literary taste that replaced Milton by Donne as the great seventeenth-century English poet and replaced Tennyson in the nineteenth century by Hopkins. His often-quoted description of the late seventeenth-century "dissociation of sensibility"—keeping wit and passion in separate compartments—which he saw as determining the course of English poetry throughout the eighteenth and nineteenth centuries, is both a contribution to the rewriting of English literary history and an explanation of what he was aiming at in his own poetry: the reestablishment of that *unified* sensibility he found in Donne and other early seventeenth-century poets and dramatists. His view of tradition, his dislike of the poetic exploitation of the author's own personality, his advocacy of what he called "orthodoxy," made him suspicious of what he considered eccentric geniuses such as Blake and D. H. Lawrence. On the other side, his dislike of the grandiloquent and his insistence on complexity and on the mingling of the formal with the conversational made him distrustful of the influence of Milton on English poetry. He considered himself "classicist in literature, royalist in politics, and Anglo-Catholic in religion" (*For Lancelot Andrewes*, 1928), in favor of order against chaos, tradition against eccentricity, authority against rampant individualism; yet his own poetry is in many respects untraditional and certainly highly individual in tone. His conservative and even authoritarian habit of mind alienated some who admire—and some whose own poetry has been much influenced by—his poetry.

Eliot's plays have all been, directly or indirectly, on religious themes. *Murder in the Cathedral* (1935) deals with the murder of Archbishop Thomas à Becket in an appropriately ritual manner, with much use of a chorus and with the central speech in the form of a sermon by the archbishop in his cathedral shortly before his murder. *The Family Reunion* (1939) deals with the problem of guilt and redemption in a modern upper-class English family; it makes a deliberate attempt to combine choric devices from Greek tragedy with a poetic idiom subdued to the accents of drawing-room conversation. In his three later plays, all written in the 1950s, *The Cocktail Party, The Confidential Clerk,* and *The Elder Statesman,* he achieved popular success by casting a serious religious theme in the form of a sophisticated modern social comedy, using a verse that is so conversational in movement that when spoken in the theater it does not sound like verse at all.

Critics differ on the degree to which Eliot succeeded in his last plays in combining box-office success with dramatic effectiveness. But there is no disagreement on his importance as one of the great renovators of the English poetic dialect, whose influence on a whole generation of poets, critics, and intellectuals generally was enormous. His range as a poet is limited, and his interest in the great middle ground of human experience (as distinct from the extremes of saint and sinner) deficient: but when in 1948 he was awarded the rare honor of the Order of Merit by King George VI and also gained the Nobel Prize in literature, his positive qualities were widely and fully recognized—his poetic cunning, his fine craftsmanship, his original accent, his historical and representative importance as *the* poet of the modern symbolist-Metaphysical tradition.

The Love Song of J. Alfred Prufrock[1]

*S'io credesse che mia risposta fosse
a persona che mai tornasse al mondo,
questa fiamma staria senza più scosse.
Ma per cio cche giammai di questo fondo
non torno vivo alcun, s'i'odo il vero,
senza tema d'infamia ti rispondo.*[2]

Let us go then, you and I,
When the evening is spread out against the sky

---

1. The title implies an ironic contrast between the romantic suggestions of "love song" and the dully prosaic name "J. Alfred Prufrock."
2. "If I thought that my reply would be to one who would ever return to the world, this flame would stay without further movement; but since none has ever returned alive from this depth, if what I hear is true, I answer you without fear of infamy" (Dante, *Inferno* 27.61–66). Guido da Montefeltro, shut up in his flame (the punishment given to false counselors), tells the shame of his evil life to Dante because he believes Dante will never return to earth to report it.

Like a patient etherised upon a table;
Let us go, through certain half-deserted streets,
5   The muttering retreats
Of restless nights in one-night cheap hotels
And sawdust restaurants with oyster shells:
Streets that follow like a tedious argument
Of insidious intent
10   To lead you to an overwhelming question. . .
Oh, do not ask, 'What is it?'
Let us go and make our visit.

    In the room the women come and go
Talking of Michelangelo.

= cat

15   The yellow fog that rubs its back upon the window-panes,
The yellow smoke that rubs its muzzle on the window-panes
Licked its tongue into the corners of the evening,
Lingered upon the pools that stand in drains,
Let fall upon its back the soot that falls from chimneys,
20   Slipped by the terrace, made a sudden leap,
And seeing that it was a soft October night,
Curled once about the house, and fell asleep.

    And indeed there will be time[3]
For the yellow smoke that slides along the street,
25   Rubbing its back upon the window-panes;
There will be time, there will be time
To prepare a face to meet the faces that you meet;
There will be time to murder and create,
And time for all the works and days of hands[4]
30   That lift and drop a question on your plate;
Time for you and time for me,
And time yet for a hundred indecisions,
And for a hundred visions and revisions,
Before the taking of a toast and tea.

35   In the room the women come and go
Talking of Michelangelo.

    And indeed there will be time
To wonder, 'Do I dare?' and, 'Do I dare?'
Time to turn back and descend the stair,
40   With a bald spot in the middle of my hair—
(They will say: 'How his hair is growing thin!')
My morning coat, my collar mounting firmly to the chin,
My necktie rich and modest, but asserted by a simple pin—
(They will say: 'But how his arms and legs are thin!')
45   Do I dare

3. Cf. Andrew Marvell, *To His Coy Mistress*, line
1: "Had we but world enough, and time."
4. *Works and Days* is a poem about the farming
year by Hesiod (8th century B.C.E.), Greek poet.

Eliot's contrast is between useful agricultural labor
and the futile "works and days of hands" engaged
in meaningless social gesturing.

how do you know that? busk!

Disturb the universe?
In a minute there is time
For decisions and revisions which a minute will reverse.

50 For I have known them all already, known them all—
Have known the evenings, mornings, afternoons,
I have measured out my life with coffee spoons;
I know the voices dying with a dying fall[5]
Beneath the music from a farther room.
    So how should I presume?

55 And I have known the eyes already, known them all—
The eyes that fix you in a formulated phrase,
And when I am formulated, sprawling on a pin,
When I am pinned and wriggling on the wall,
Then how should I begin
60 To spit out all the butt-ends of my days and ways?
    And how should I presume?

And I have known the arms already, known them all—
Arms that are braceleted and white and bare
(But in the lamplight, downed with light brown hair!)
65 Is it perfume from a dress
That makes me so digress?
Arms that lie along a table, or wrap about a shawl.
    And should I then presume?
    And how should I begin?

            . . .

70 Shall I say, I have gone at dusk through narrow streets
And watched the smoke that rises from the pipes
Of lonely men in shirt-sleeves, leaning out of windows? . . .
  I should have been a pair of ragged claws
Scuttling across the floors of silent seas.[6]

him compared to that creature (not Hamlet...)

            . . .

75 And the afternoon, the evening, sleeps so peacefully!
Smoothed by long fingers,
Asleep . . . tired . . . or it malingers,
Stretched on the floor, here beside you and me.
Should I, after tea and cakes and ices,
80 Have the strength to force the moment to its crisis?
But though I have wept and fasted, wept and prayed,
Though I have seen my head (grown slightly bald) brought in upon a
    platter,[7]

---

5. Ironic recollection of Orsino's speech in *Twelfth Night* 1.1.4: "That strain again! It had a dying fall."
6. I.e., he would have been better as a crab on the ocean bed. Perhaps, too, the motion of a crab sug-

gests futility and growing old. Cf. *Hamlet* 2.2.205–206: "for you yourself, sir, should be old as I am, if, like a crab, you could go backward."
7. Like that of John the Baptist. See Mark 6.17–28 and Matthew 14.3–11.

I am no prophet—and here's no great matter;
I have seen the moment of my greatness flicker,
85 And I have seen the eternal Footman hold my coat, and snicker,
And in short, I was afraid.

And would it have been worth it, after all,
After the cups, the marmalade, the tea,
Among the porcelain, among some talk of you and me,
90 Would it have been worth while,
To have bitten off the matter with a smile,
To have squeezed the universe into a ball[8]
To roll it toward some overwhelming question,
To say: 'I am Lazarus,[9] come from the dead,
95 Come back to tell you all, I shall tell you all'—
If one, settling a pillow by her head,
    Should say: 'That is not what I meant at all.
    That is not it, at all.'

And would it have been worth it, after all,
100 Would it have been worth while,
After the sunsets and the dooryards and the sprinkled streets,
After the novels, after the teacups, after the skirts that trail along the floor—
And this, and so much more?—
It is impossible to say just what I mean!
105 But as if a magic lantern threw the nerves in patterns on a screen:
Would it have been worth while
If one, settling a pillow or throwing off a shawl,
And turning toward the window, should say:
    'That is not it at all,
110   That is not what I meant, at all.'

• • •

No! I am not Prince Hamlet, nor was meant to be;
Am an attendant lord, one that will do
To swell a progress,[1] start a scene or two,
Advise the prince; no doubt, an easy tool,
115 Deferential, glad to be of use,
Politic, cautious, and meticulous;
Full of high sentence,[2] but a bit obtuse;
At times, indeed, almost ridiculous—
Almost, at times, the Fool.

120   I grow old . . . I grow old . . .
I shall wear the bottoms of my trousers rolled.

---

8. Cf., Marvell, *To His Coy Mistress*, lines 41–44: "Let us roll all our strength and all / Our sweetness up into one ball, / And tear our pleasures with rough strife / Thorough the iron gates of life."
9. Cf. Luke 16.19–31 and John 11.1–44.
1. In the Elizabethan sense of a state journey

made by a royal or noble person. Elizabethan plays sometimes showed such "progresses" crossing the stage. Cf. Chaucer's *General Prologue* to *The Canterbury Tales*, line 308.
2. In its older meanings: "opinions," "sententiousness."

Shall I part my hair behind? Do I dare to eat a peach?
I shall wear white flannel trousers, and walk upon the beach.
I have heard the mermaids singing, each to each.

125 I do not think that they will sing to me.

I have seen them riding seaward on the waves
Combing the white hair of the waves blown back
When the wind blows the water white and black.

We have lingered in the chambers of the sea
130 By sea-girls wreathed with seaweed red and brown
Till human voices wake us, and we drown.

1910–11   1915, 1917

Sweeney Among the Nightingales

ὤμοι, πέπληγμαι καιρίαν πληγὴν ἔσω.[1]

Apeneck Sweeney spreads his knees
Letting his arms hang down to laugh,
The zebra stripes along his jaw
Swelling to maculate° giraffe.   spotted, stained

5   The circles of the stormy moon
Slide westward toward the River Plate,[2]
Death and the Raven drift above
And Sweeney guards the hornèd gate.[3]

Gloomy Orion and the Dog
10   Are veiled;[4] and hushed the shrunken seas;
The person in the Spanish cape
Tries to sit on Sweeney's knees

Slips and pulls the table cloth
Overturns a coffee-cup,
15   Reorganized upon the floor
She yawns and draws a stocking up;

The silent man in mocha brown
Sprawls at the window-sill and gapes;

---

1. "Alas, I am struck with a mortal blow within" (Aeschylus, *Agamemnon*, line 1343). The voice of Agamemnon heard crying out from the palace as he is murdered by his wife, Clytemnestra.
2. Estuary on the South American coast between Argentina and Uruguay, formed by the Uruguay and Paraná rivers.

3. The gates of horn, in Hades, through which true dreams come to the upper world.
4. "Orion" and "the Dog" are the constellations. For Sweeney and his lady friend, the gate of vision is blocked and the great myth-making constellations are "veiled."

The waiter brings in oranges
20   Bananas figs and hothouse grapes;

The silent vertebrate in brown
Contracts and concentrates, withdraws;
Rachel *née* Rabinovitch
Tears at the grapes with murderous paws;

25   She and the lady in the cape
Are suspect, thought to be in league;
Therefore the man with heavy eyes
Declines the gambit, shows fatigue,

Leaves the room and reappears
30   Outside the window, leaning in,
Branches of wistaria
Circumscribe a golden grin;

The host with someone indistinct
Converses at the door apart,
35   The nightingales are singing near
The Convent of the Sacred Heart,

And sang within the bloody wood
When Agamemnon cried aloud[5]
And let their liquid siftings fall
40   To stain the stiff dishonoured shroud.

                                          1918, 1919

The Waste Land   This is a poem about spiritual dryness, about the kind of existence in which no regenerating belief gives significance and value to people's daily activities, sex brings no fruitfulness, and death heralds no resurrection. Eliot himself gives one of the main clues to the theme and structure of the poem in a general note, in which he stated that "not only the title, but the plan and a good deal of the symbolism of the poem were suggested by Miss Jessie L. Weston's book on the Grail legend: *From Ritual to Romance*" (1920). He further acknowledged a general indebtedness to Sir James Frazer's *Golden Bough* (13 volumes, 1890–1915), "especially the . . . volumes *Adonis, Attis, Osiris,*" in which Frazer deals with ancient vegetation myths and fertility ceremonies. Weston's study, drawing on material from Frazer and other anthropologists, traced the relationship of these myths and rituals to Christianity and most especially to the legend of the Holy Grail. She found an archetypal fertility myth in the story of the Fisher King whose death, infirmity, or impotence (there are many forms of the myth) brought drought and desolation to the land and failure of the power to reproduce themselves among both humans and beasts. This symbolic Waste Land can be revived only if a "questing knight" goes to

5. Agamemnon was not murdered in a "bloody wood," but in his bath. Eliot is here telescoping Agamemnon's murder with the wood where Philomela, in Greek myth, was ravished by her sister's husband, Terens (she was subsequently turned into a nightingale), and also with the "bloody wood" of Nemi, where in ancient times the old priest was slain by his successor (as described in the first chapter of Sir James Frazer's *Golden Bough*).

the Chapel Perilous, situated in the heart of it, and there asks certain ritual questions about the Grail (or Cup) and the Lance—originally fertility symbols, female and male, respectively. The proper asking of these questions revives the king and restores fertility to the land. The relation of this original Grail myth to fertility cults and rituals found in many different civilizations, and represented by stories of a dying god who is later resurrected (e.g., Tammuz, Adonis, Attis), shows their common origin in a response to the cyclical movement of the seasons, with vegetation dying in winter to be resurrected again in the spring. Christianity, according to Weston, gave its own spiritual meaning to the myth; it "did not hesitate to utilize the already existing medium of instruction, but boldly identified the Deity of Vegetation, regarded as Life Principle, with the God of the Christian Faith." The Fisher King is related to the use of the fish symbol in early Christianity. Weston states "with certainty that the Fish is a Life symbol of immemorial antiquity, and that the title of Fisher has, from the earliest ages, been associated with the Deities who were held to be specially connected with the origin and preservation of Life." Eliot, following Weston, thus uses a great variety of mythological and religious material, both Occidental and Oriental, to paint a symbolic picture of the modern Waste Land and the need for regeneration. The terror of that life—its loneliness, emptiness, and irrational apprehensions—as well as its misuse of sexuality are vividly presented, but paradoxically, the poem ends with a benediction. Another significant general source for the poem is the composer Richard Wagner, some of whose operas (*Götterdämmerung* ["Twilight of the Gods"], *Parsifal, Das Rheingold,* and *Tristan und Isolde*) are drawn on.

The poem as published owed a great deal to the severe pruning of Ezra Pound; the original manuscript, with Pound's excisions and comments, provides fascinating information about the genesis and development of the poem. It was reproduced in facsimile in 1971, edited by Eliot's widow, Valerie Eliot, who also supplied notes supplementing those that Eliot himself added when the poem was first published in book form in 1925 and that are included with the present editors' footnotes to the poem.

The Waste Land

"Nam Sibyllam quidem Cumis ego ipse oculis meis vidi in ampulla pendere, et cum illi pueri dicerent: Σίβυλλα τί θέλεις; respondebat illa: ἀποθανεῖν θέλω."[1]

FOR EZRA POUND
il miglior fabbro[2]

I. The Burial of the Dead[3]

April is the cruellest month, breeding
Lilacs out of the dead land, mixing
Memory and desire, stirring

1. From the *Satyricon* of Petronius (1st century C.E.): "For once I myself saw with my own eyes the Sibyl at Cumae hanging in a cage, and when the boys said to her 'Sibyl, what do you want?' she replied, 'I want to die.' " (The Greek may be transliterated, "Síbylla tí théleis?" and "apothanéin thélo.") The Cumaean Sibyl was the most famous of the Sibyls, the prophetic old women of Greek mythology; she guided Aeneas through Hades in the *Aeneid*. She had been granted immortality by Apollo, but because she forgot to ask for perpetual youth, she shrank into withered old age and her authority declined.

2. "The better craftsman," a tribute originally paid to the Provençal poet Arnaut Daniel in Dante's *Purgatorio* 26.117. Ezra Pound (1885–1972), American expatriate poet who was a key figure in the modern movement in poetry, helped Eliot with the final revisions.

3. The title comes from the Anglican burial service.

Dull roots with spring rain.
5   Winter kept us warm, covering
Earth in forgetful snow, feeding
A little life with dried tubers.
Summer surprised us, coming over the Starnbergersee[4]
With a shower of rain; we stopped in the colonnade,
10   And went on in sunlight, into the Hofgarten,[5]
And drank coffee, and talked for an hour.
Bin gar keine Russin, stamm' aus Litauen, echt deutsch.[6]
And when we were children, staying at the arch-duke's,
My cousin's, he took me out on a sled,
15   And I was frightened. He said, Marie,
Marie, hold on tight. And down we went.
In the mountains, there you feel free.
I read, much of the night, and go south in the winter.

        What are the roots that clutch, what branches grow
20   Out of this stony rubbish? Son of man,[7]
You cannot say, or guess, for you know only
A heap of broken images, where the sun beats,
And the dead tree gives no shelter, the cricket no relief,[8]
And the dry stone no sound of water. Only
25   There is shadow under this red rock,[9]
(Come in under the shadow of this red rock),
And I will show you something different from either
Your shadow at morning striding behind you
Or your shadow at evening rising to meet you;
30   I will show you fear in a handful of dust.
                Frisch weht der Wind
                Der Heimat zu
                Mein Irisch Kind,
                Wo weilest du?[1]
35   'You gave me hyacinths first a year ago;
They called me the hyacinth girl.'
—Yet when we came back, late, from the Hyacinth garden,
Yours arms full, and your hair wet, I could not
Speak, and my eyes failed, I was neither

---

4. Lake a few miles south of Munich, where the "mad" King Ludwig II of Bavaria drowned in 1886 in mysterious circumstances. This romantic, melancholy king was a passionate admirer of Richard Wagner and especially of Wagner's opera *Tristan und Isolde,* which plays a significant part in *The Waste Land.* Ludwig's suffering of "death by water" in the Starnbergersee thus evokes a cluster of themes central to the poem. Eliot had met King Ludwig's second cousin Countess Marie Larisch and talked with her. Although he had probably not read the countess's book *My Past,* which discusses King Ludwig at length, he got information about her life and times from her in person, and the remarks made in lines 7–17 are hers. They distill a sense of romantic decadence that Eliot associates with this period of European history. Line 17 is a translation of the opening of a Bavarian folksong celebrating King Ludwig and lamenting his drowning.

5. A small public park in Munich.
6. I am not Russian at all; I come from Lithuania, a true German
7. Cf. Ezekiel 2.1 [Eliot's note]. Here God is addressing Ezekiel. God continues, "stand upon thy feet, and I will speak unto thee."
8. Cf. Ecclesiastes 12.5 [Eliot's note]. The verse cited by Eliot is part of the preacher's picture of the desolation of old age, "when they shall be afraid of that which is high, and fears shall be in the way, and the almond tree shall flourish, and the grasshopper shall be a burden, and desire shall fail."
9. Cf. Isaiah 32.2: the "righteous king" "shall be . . . as rivers of water in a dry place, as the shadow of a great rock in a weary land."
1. V. [see] *Tristan und Isolde,* 1, verses 5–8 [Eliot's note]. In Wagner's opera, a sailor recalls the girl he has left behind: "Fresh blows the wind to the homeland; my Irish child, where are you waiting?"

40   Living nor dead, and I knew nothing,
      Looking into the heart of light, the silence.
      Oed' und leer das Meer.[2]

      Madame Sosostris,[3] famous clairvoyante,
      Had a bad cold, nevertheless
45   Is known to be the wisest woman in Europe,
      With a wicked pack of cards.[4] Here, said she,
      Is your card, the drowned Phoenician Sailor,[5]
      (Those are pearls that were his eyes. Look!)
      Here is Belladonna,[6] the Lady of the Rocks,
50   The lady of situations.
      Here is the man with three staves,[7] and here the Wheel,[8]
      And here is the one-eyed merchant,[9] and this card,
      Which is blank, is something he carries on his back,
      Which I am forbidden to see. I do not find
55   The Hanged Man.[1] Fear death by water.
      I see crowds of people, walking round in a ring.
      Thank you. If you see dear Mrs Equitone,
      Tell her I bring the horoscope myself:
      One must be so careful these days.

60   Unreal City,[2]
      Under the brown fog of a winter dawn,

2. Id. [Ibid] 3, verse 24 [Eliot's note]. In act 3 of *Tristan und Isolde,* Tristan lies dying. He is waiting for Isolde to come to him from Cornwall, but a shepherd, appointed to watch for her sail, can only report, "Waste and empty is the sea."

3. A mock Egyptian name (suggested to Eliot by "Sesostris, the Sorceress of Ecbatana," the name assumed by a character in Aldous Huxley's novel *Crome Yellow* who dresses up as a gypsy to tell fortunes at a fair).

4. A.e., the deck of Tarot cards. The four suits of the Tarot pack, discussed by Jessie Weston in *From Ritual to Romance,* are the cup, lance, sword, and dish—the life symbols found in the Grail story. Weston noted that "today the Tarot has fallen somewhat into disrepute, being principally used for purposes of divination." Some of the cards mentioned in lines 46–56 are discussed by Eliot in his note to this passage: "I am not familiar with the exact constitution of the Tarot pack of cards, from which I have obviously departed to suit my own convenience. The Hanged Man, a member of the traditional pack, fits my purpose in two ways: because he is associated in my mind with the Hanged God of Frazer, and because I associate him with the hooded figure in the passage of the disciples to Emmaus in part 5. The Phoenician Sailor and the Merchant appear later; also the 'crowds of people,' and Death by Water is executed in part 4. The Man with Three Staves (an authentic member of the Tarot pack) I associate, quite arbitrarily, with the Fisher King himself."

5. See part 4. Phlebas the Phoenician and Mr. Eugenides, the Smyrna merchant—both of whom appear later in the poem—are different phases of the same symbolic character, here identified as the "Phoenician Sailor." Mr. Eugenides exports "currants" (line 210); the drowned Phlebas floats in the "current" (line 315). The line that follows is from

Shakespeare's *Tempest* (1.2.398). Ariel's song to the shipwrecked Ferdinand, who was "sitting on a bank / Weeping again the King my father's wrack," when "this music crept by me on the waters." The song is about the supposed drowning of Ferdinand's father, Alonso. *The Waste Land* contains many references to *The Tempest.* Ferdinand is associated with Phlebas and Mr. Eugenides and, therefore, with the "drowned Phoenician Sailor."

6. Beautiful lady. The word also suggests Madonna (the Virgin Mary) and, therefore, the Madonna of the Rocks (as in Leonardo da Vinci's painting); the rocks symbolize the church. Belladonna is also an eye cosmetic and a poison—the deadly nightshade. In the next line, the woman figure of the Virgin becomes "the lady of situations," foreshadowing the neurasthenic lady of intrigue in part 2.

7. Life-force symbol, associated by Eliot with the Fisher King.

8. I.e., the wheel of fortune, whose turning represents the reversals of human life.

9. I.e., Mr. Eugenides, "one-eyed" because the figure is in profile on the card and also as a suggestion of evil or crookedness.

1. On his card in the Tarot pack he is shown hanging from one foot from a T-shaped cross. He symbolizes the self-sacrifice of the fertility god who is killed in order that his resurrection may bring fertility once again to land and people.

2. Cf. Baudelaire: *'Fourmillante cité, cité pleine de rêves, / Où le spectre en plein jour raccroche le passant'* [Eliot's note]. The lines are quoted from *Les Sept Vieillards* ("The Seven Old Men") by Charles Baudelaire (1821–67); it is poem 93 of *Les Fleurs du Mal* ("The Flowers of Evil"). The lines may be translated: "Swarming city, city full of dreams, / Where the specter in broad daylight accosts the passerby."

A crowd flowed over London Bridge, so many,[3]
I had not thought death had undone so many.
Sighs, short and infrequent, were exhaled,[4]
65 And each man fixed his eyes before his feet.
Flowed up the hill and down King William Street,
To where Saint Mary Woolnoth kept the hours
With a dead sound on the final stroke of nine.[5]
There I saw one I knew, and stopped him, crying: 'Stetson![6]
70 'You who were with me in the ships at Mylae![7]
'That corpse you planted last year in your garden,
'Has it begun to sprout?[8] Will it bloom this year?
'Or has the sudden frost disturbed its bed?
'Oh keep the Dog far hence, that's friend to men,
75 'Or with his nails he'll dig it up again![9]
'You! hypocrite lecteur!—mon semblable—mon frère!'[1]

II. A Game of Chess[2]

The Chair she sat in, like a burnished throne,[3]
Glowed on the marble, where the glass
Held up by standards wrought with fruited vines
80 From which a golden Cupidon peeped out
(Another hid his eyes behind his wing)
Doubled the flames of sevenbranched candelabra
Reflecting light upon the table as
The glitter of her jewels rose to meet it,
85 From satin cases poured in rich profusion.
In vials of ivory and coloured glass
Unstoppered, lurked her strange synthetic perfumes,
Unguent, powdered, or liquid—troubled, confused

3. Cf. Inferno 3.55–57 [Eliot's note]. The note goes on to quote Dante's lines, which may be translated: "So long a train of people, / that I should never have believed / That death had undone so many." Dante, just outside the gate of hell, has seen "the wretched souls of those who lived without disgrace and without praise." In his essay on Baudelaire, Eliot argued that in a sense it was better to be positively evil than to be neither good nor evil.
4. Cf. Inferno 4.25–27 [Eliot's note]. In Limbo, the first circle of hell, Dante has found the virtuous heathens, who lived before Christianity and are, therefore, eternally unable to achieve their desire of seeing God. Dante's lines, cited by Eliot, mean "Here, so far as I could tell by listening, / there was no lamentation except sighs, / which caused the eternal air to tremble."
5. A phenomenon which I have often noticed [Eliot's note]. St. Mary Woolnoth is a church in the "Unreal City" of London (the financial district); the crowd is flowing across London Bridge to work in the City.
6. Presumably representing the "average businessman."
7. The battle of Mylae (260 B.C.E.) in the First Punic War, which, in some measure like World War I, was fought for economic reasons.
8. A distortion of the ritual death of the fertility god.
9. Cf. the Dirge in Webster's White Devil [Eliot's note]. In the play by John Webster (d. 1625), the

dirge, sung by Cornelia, has the lines "But keep the wolf far thence, that's foe to men, / For with his nails he'll dig them up again." Eliot makes the "wolf" into a "dog," which is not a foe but a friend to humans. There may be a reference to Sirius, the Dog Star, which is important in Egyptian mythology as heralding the fertilizing floods of the Nile (this is discussed by Weston).
1. V. Baudelaire, Preface to Fleurs du Mal [Eliot's note]. The passage is the last line of the introductory poem Au Lecteur ("To the Reader") in Baudelaire's Fleurs du Mal; it may be translated: "Hypocrite reader!—my likeness—my brother!" Au Lecteur describes man as sunk in stupidity, sin, and evil, but the worst in "each man's foul menagerie of sin" is boredom, the "monstre délicat"— "You know him, reader."
2. The title suggests two plays by Thomas Middleton (1580–1627): A Game at Chess and, more significant, Women Beware Women, which has a scene in which a mother-in-law is distracted by a game of chess while her daughter-in-law is seduced: every move in the chess game represents a move in the seduction.
3. Cf. Antony and Cleopatra, 2.2.190 [Eliot's note]. In Shakespeare's play, Enobarbus's famous description of the first meeting of Antony and Cleopatra begins, "The barge she sat in, like a burnish'd throne, / Burn'd on the water." Eliot's language in the opening lines of part 2 is full of ironic distortions of Enobarbus's speech.

And drowned the sense in odours; stirred by the air
90 That freshened from the window, these ascended
In fattening the prolonged candle-flames,
Flung their smoke into the laquearia,⁴
Stirring the pattern on the coffered ceiling.
Huge sea-wood fed with copper
95 Burned green and orange, framed by the coloured stone,
In which sad light a carvèd dolphin swam.
Above the antique mantel was displayed
As though a window gave upon the sylvan scene⁵
The change of Philomel,⁶ by the barbarous king
100 So rudely forced; yet there the nightingale
Filled all the desert with inviolable voice
And still she cried, and still the world pursues,
'Jug Jug'⁷ to dirty ears.
And other withered stumps of time
105 Were told upon the walls; staring forms
Leaned out, leaning, hushing the room enclosed.
Footsteps shuffled on the stair.
Under the firelight, under the brush, her hair
Spread out in fiery points
110 Glowed into words, then would be savagely still.

'My nerves are bad tonight. Yes, bad. Stay with me.
'Speak to me. Why do you never speak. Speak.
'What are you thinking of? What thinking? What?
'I never know what you are thinking. Think.'

115 I think we are in rats' alley⁸
Where the dead men lost their bones.

'What is that noise?'
                                    The wind under the door.⁹
'What is that noise now? What is the wind doing?'
120   Nothing again nothing.

                                                    'Do
'You know nothing? Do you see nothing? Do you remember
'Nothing?'

        I remember
125 Those are pearls that were his eyes.
"Are you alive, or not? Is there nothing in your head?"
                                                    But

---

4. Laquearia. V. *Aeneid*, 1. 726 [Eliot's note]. *Laquearia* means "a paneled ceiling," and Eliot's note quotes the passage in the *Aeneid* that was his source for the word. The passage may be translated: "Blazing torches hang from the gold-paneled ceiling [*laquearibus aureis*], and torches conquer the night with flames." Virgil is describing the banquet given by Dido, queen of Carthage, for Aeneas, with whom she fell in love.
5. Sylvan scene. V. Milton, *Paradise Lost*, 4.140 [Eliot's note]. The phrase is part of the first description of Eden, which we see through Satan's eyes.

6. V. Ovid, *Metamorphoses*, 6, Philomela [Eliot's note]. The note is a reference to Ovid's version of the Greek myth of the rape of Philomela by "the barbarous king" Tereus, husband of her sister Procne. Philomela was transformed into a nightingale. Eliot's note for line 100 refers ahead to his elaboration of the nightingale's song.
7. Conventional representation of nightingale's song in Elizabethan poetry.
8. Cf. part 3, line 195 [Eliot's note].
9. Cf. Webster: 'Is the wind in that door still?' [Eliot's note]. The line cited in the note is from John Webster, *The Devil's Law Case* 3.2.162.

O O O O that Shakespeherian Rag[1]—
It's so elegant
130 So intelligent
'What shall I do now? What shall I do?'
'I shall rush out as I am, and walk the street
'With my hair down, so. What shall we do tomorrow?
'What shall we ever do?'
135   The hot water at ten.
And if it rains, a closed car at four.
And we shall play a game of chess,[2]
Pressing lidless eyes and waiting for a knock upon the door.

      When Lil's husband got demobbed,[3] I said—
140 I didn't mince my words, I said to her myself,
HURRY UP PLEASE ITS TIME[4]
Now Albert's coming back, make yourself a bit smart.
He'll want to know what you done with that money he gave you
To get yourself some teeth. He did, I was there.
145 You have them all out, Lil, and get a nice set,
He said, I swear, I can't bear to look at you.
And no more can't I, I said, and think of poor Albert,
He's been in the army four years, he wants a good time,
And if you don't give it him, there's others will, I said.
150 Oh is there, she said. Something o' that, I said.
Then I'll know who to thank, she said, and give me a straight look.
HURRY UP PLEASE ITS TIME
If you don't like it you can get on with it, I said.
Others can pick and choose if you can't.
155 But if Albert makes off, it won't be for lack of telling.
You ought to be ashamed, I said, to look so antique.
(And her only thirty-one.)
I can't help it, she said, pulling a long face,
It's them pills I took, to bring it off, she said.
160 (She's had five already, and nearly died of young George.)
The chemist[5] said it would be all right, but I've never been the same
You *are* a proper fool, I said.
Well, if Albert won't leave you alone, there it is, I said,
What you get married for if you don't want children?
165 HURRY UP PLEASE ITS TIME
Well, that Sunday Albert was home, they had a hot gammon,°   ham, bacon
And they asked me in to dinner, to get the beauty of it hot—
HURRY UP PLEASE ITS TIME
HURRY UP PLEASE ITS TIME
170 Goonight Bill. Goonight Lou. Goonight May. Goonight.
Ta ta. Goonight. Goonight.
Good night, ladies, good night, sweet ladies, good night, good night.[6]

1. American ragtime song, which was a hit of Zieg-
feld's Follies in 1912.
2. Cf. the game of chess in Middleton's *Women
Beware Women* [Eliot's note]. The significance of
this chess game is discussed in n. 2, p. 2616.
3. British slang for "demobilized" (discharged
from the army).
4. The traditional call of the British bartender at
closing time.
5. Druggist. "To bring it off": to cause an abortion.
6. Cf. the mad Ophelia's departing words (*Hamlet*
4.5.72). Ophelia, too, met "death by water."

III. The Fire Sermon[7]

The river's tent is broken: the last fingers of leaf
Clutch and sink into the wet bank. The wind
175 Crosses the brown land, unheard. The nymphs are departed.
Sweet Thames, run softly, till I end my song.[8]
The river bears no empty bottles, sandwich papers,
Silk handkerchiefs, cardboard boxes, cigarette ends
Or other testimony of summer nights. The nymphs are departed.
180 And their friends, the loitering heirs of city directors;
Departed, have left no addresses.
By the waters of Leman I sat down and wept[9] . . .
Sweet Thames, run softly till I end my song,
Sweet Thames, run softly, for I speak not loud or long.
185 But at my back in a cold blast I hear[1]
The rattle of the bones, and chuckle spread from ear to ear.

A rat crept softly through the vegetation
Dragging its slimy belly on the bank
While I was fishing in the dull canal
190 On a winter evening round behind the gashouse
Musing upon the king my brother's wreck[2]
And on the king my father's death before him.
White bodies naked on the low damp ground
And bones cast in a little low dry garret,
195 Rattled by the rat's foot only, year to year.
But at my back from time to time I hear[3]
The sound of horns and motors, which shall bring
Sweeney to Mrs Porter in the spring.[4]
O the moon shone bright on Mrs Porter
200 And on her daughter
They wash their feet in soda water[5]
Et O ces voix d'enfants, chantant dans la coupole![6]

Twit twit twit
Jug jug jug jug jug jug

---

7. The Fire Sermon was preached by the Buddha against the fires of lust and other passions that destroy people and prevent their regeneration (see also n. 7, p. 2623).

8. V. Spenser, *Prothalamion* [Eliot's note]. Eliot's line is the refrain from Spenser's marriage song, which is also set by the Thames in London—but a very different Thames from the modern littered river.

9. Cf. Psalms 137.1, in which the exiled Hebrews mourn for their homeland: "By the rivers of Babylon, there we sat down, yea, we wept, when we remembered Zion." Lake Leman is another name for Lake Geneva; Eliot wrote *The Waste Land* in Lausanne, by that lake. The common noun *leman* is an archaic word meaning a lover, sweetheart, or mistress.

1. An ironic distortion of Andrew Marvell's *To His Coy Mistress*, lines 21–22: "But at my back I always hear / Time's winged chariot hurrying near." Cf. line 196.

2. Cf. *The Tempest*, 1.2 [Eliot's note]. See line 48.

3. Cf. Marvell, *To His Coy Mistress* [Eliot's note].

4. Cf. Day, *Parliament of Bees*: 'When of the sudden, listening, you shall hear, / A noise of horns and hunting, which shall bring / Actaeon to Diana in the spring, / Where all shall see her naked skin' [Eliot's note]. Actaeon was changed to a stag and hunted to death after he saw Diana, the goddess of chastity, bathing with her nymphs.

5. I do not know the origin of the ballad from which these lines are taken: it was reported to me from Sydney, Australia [Eliot's note]. One of the less bawdy versions of the song, which was popular among Australian troops in World War I, went as follows: "O the moon shines bright on Mrs Porter / And on the daughter / Of Mrs. Porter. / They wash their feet in soda water / And so they oughter / To keep them clean."

6. V. Verlaine, *Parsifal* [Eliot's note]. The line is translated, "And O those children's voices singing in the dome!" Verlaine's sonnet describes Parsifal, the questing knight, resisting all sensual temptations to keep himself pure for the Grail; Wagner's Parsifal had his feet washed before entering the castle of the Grail.

205 So rudely forc'd.
Tereu[7]

Unreal City
Under the brown fog of a winter noon
Mr Eugenides, the Smyrna[8] merchant
210 Unshaven, with a pocket full of currants
C.i.f.[9] London: documents at sight,
Asked me in demotic° French   *popular*
To luncheon at the Cannon Street Hotel[1]
Followed by a weekend at the Metropole.

215 At the violet hour, when the eyes and back
Turn upward from the desk, when the human engine waits
Like a taxi throbbing waiting,
I Tiresias,[2] though blind, throbbing between two lives,
Old man with wrinkled female breasts, can see
220 At the violet hour, the evening hour that strives
Homeward, and brings the sailor home from sea,[3]
The typist home at teatime, clears her breakfast, lights
Her stove, and lays out food in tins.
Out of the window perilously spread
225 Her drying combinations touched by the sun's last rays,
On the divan are piled (at night her bed)
Stockings, slippers, camisoles, and stays.
I Tiresias, old man with wrinkled dugs
Perceived the scene, and foretold the rest—
230 I too awaited the expected guest.
He, the young man carbuncular,° arrives,   *pimply*
A small house agent's clerk, with one bold stare,

---

7. A reference to Tereus, who "rudely forc'd" Philomela; it was also one of the conventional words for a nightingale's song inElizabethan poetry. Cf. the song from John Lyly's *Alexander and Campaspe* (1564): "Oh, 'tis the ravished nightingale. / Jug, jug, jug, jug, tereu! she cries," and lines 100ff.
8. Seaport in western Turkey; here associated with Carthage and the ancient Phoenician and Syrian merchants (unlike those of modern Smyrna), who spread the old mystery cults. The sort of cult spread by Mr. Eugenides is indicated by his suggestion of "a weekend at the Metropole" (a luxury hotel at Brighton).
9. The currants were quoted at a price 'carriage and insurance free to London'; and the Bill of Lading etc. were to be handed to the buyer upon payment of the sight draft [Eliot's note].
1. Located near the station that was then chief terminus for travelers to the Continent, hence a favorite meeting place for businesspeople going or coming from abroad.
2. Tiresias, although a mere spectator and not indeed a 'character', is yet the most important personage in the poem, uniting all the rest. Just as the one-eyed merchant, seller of currants, melts into the Phoenician Sailor, and the latter is not wholly distinct from Ferdinand Prince of Naples, so all the women are one woman, and the two sexes meet in Tiresias. What Tiresias *sees*, in fact, is the substance of the poem. The whole passage from Ovid is of great anthropological interest [Eliot's note]. The note then quotes the Latin text of Ovid's *Metamorphoses* that tells the story of Tiresias's change

of sex. The Latin may be translated: "[The story goes that once Jove, having drunk a great deal,] jested with Juno. He said, 'Your pleasure in love is really greater than that enjoyed by men.' She denied it; so they decided to seek the opinion of the wise Tiresias, for he knew both aspects of love. For once, with a blow of his staff, he had committed violence on two huge snakes as they copulated in the green forest; and—wonderful to tell—was turned from a man into a woman and thus spent seven years. In the eighth year he saw the same snakes again and said: 'If a blow struck at you is so powerful that it changes the sex of the giver, I will now strike at you again.' With these words she struck the snakes, and again became a man. So he was appointed arbitrator in the playful quarrel, and supported Jove's statement. It is said that Saturnia [i.e., Juno] was quite disproportionately upset, and condemned the arbitrator to perpetual blindness. But the almighty father (for no god may undo what has been done by another god), in return for the sight that was taken away, gave him the power to know the future and so lightened the penalty paid by the honor."
3. This may not appear as exact as Sappho's lines, but I had in mind the 'longshore' or 'dory' fisherman, who returns at nightfall [Eliot's note]. Sappho's poem addressed Hesperus, the evening star, as the star that brings everyone home from work to evening rest; her poem is here distorted by Eliot. There is also an echo of Robert Louis Stevenson's *Requiem*, line 221: "Home is the sailor, home from sea".

One of the low on whom assurance sits
As a silk hat on a Bradford[4] millionaire.
235   The time is now propitious, as he guesses,
The meal is ended, she is bored and tired,
Endeavours to engage her in caresses
Which still are unreproved, if undesired.
Flushed and decided, he assaults at once;
240   Exploring hands encounter no defence;
His vanity requires no response,
And makes a welcome of indifference.
(And I Tiresias have foresuffered all
Enacted on this same divan or bed;
245   I who have sat by Thebes[5] below the wall
And walked among the lowest of the dead.)
Bestows one final patronising kiss,
And gropes his way, finding the stairs unlit . . .

She turns and looks a moment in the glass,
250   Hardly aware of her departed lover;
Her brain allows one half-formed thought to pass:
'Well now that's done: and I'm glad it's over.'
When lovely woman stoops to folly and
Paces about her room again, alone,
255   She smoothes her hair with automatic hand,
And puts a record on the gramophone.[6]

'This music crept by me upon the waters'[7]
And along the Strand, up Queen Victoria Street.
O City city, I can sometimes hear
260   Beside a public bar in Lower Thames Street,
The pleasant whining of a mandoline
And a clatter and a chatter from within
Where fishmen lounge at noon: where the walls
Of Magnus Martyr hold
265   Inexplicable splendour of Ionian white and gold.[8]

The river sweats[9]
Oil and tar

4. Either the Yorkshire woolen manufacturing town, where many fortunes were made in World War I, or the pioneer oil town of Bradford, Pennsylvania, the home of one of Eliot's wealthy Harvard contemporaries, T. E. Hanley.
5. Tiresias lived in Thebes for many generations, where he witnessed the tragic fates of Oedipus and Creon; he prophesied in the marketplace by the wall of Thebes.
6. V. Goldsmith, the song in *The Vicar of Wakefield* [Eliot's note]. Olivia, a character in Oliver Goldsmith's novel, sings the following song when she returns to the place where she was seduced: "When lovely woman stoops to folly / And finds too late that men betray / What charm can soothe her melancholy, / What art can wash her guilt away? / The only art her guilt to cover, / To hide her shame from every eye, / To give repentance to her lover / And wring his bosom—is to die."
7. V. *The Tempest*, as above [Eliot's note]. Cf. line 48. The line is from Ferdinand's speech, continu-

ing after "weeping again the King my father's wrack."
8. The interior of St Magnus Martyr is to my mind one of the finest among [Sir Christopher] Wren's interiors [Eliot's note]. In these lines, the "pleasant" music, the "fishmen" resting after labor, and the splendor of the church interior all suggest a world of true values, where work and relaxation are both real and take place in a context of religious meaning. It is but a momentary glimpse of an almost lost world.
9. The Song of the (three) Thames-daughters begins here. From line 292 to 306 inclusive they speak in turn. V. *Götterdämmerung*, 3.1: the Rhine-daughters [Eliot's note]. Eliot parallels the Thames-daughters with the Rhinemaidens in Wagner's opera *Götterdämmerung* ("The Twilight of the Gods") who lament that, with the gold of the Rhine stolen, the beauty of the river is gone. The refrain in lines 277–78 is borrowed from Wagner.

The barges drift
With the turning tide
270   Red sails
Wide
To leeward, swing on the heavy spar.
The barges wash
Drifting logs
275   Down Greenwich reach
Past the Isle of Dogs.[1]
      Weialala leia
      Wallala leialala

Elizabeth and Leicester[2]
280   Beating oars
The stern was formed
A gilded shell
Red and gold
The brisk swell
285   Rippled both shores
Southwest wind
Carried down stream
The peal of bells
White towers
290   Weialala leia
      Wallala leialala

'Trams and dusty trees.
Highbury bore me. Richmond and Kew
Undid me.[3] By Richmond I raised my knees
295   Supine on the floor of a narrow canoe.'

'My feet are at Moorgate,[4] and my heart
Under my feet. After the event
He wept. He promised "a new start."
I made no comment. What should I resent?'

300   'On Margate[5] Sands.
I can connect
Nothing with nothing.
The broken fingernails of dirty hands.

1. Greenwich is a borough in London on the south side of the Thames; opposite is the Isle of Dogs (a peninsula): Eliot presumably intends a reference to the earlier theme of the Dog.
2. The fruitless love of Queen Elizabeth and the earl of Leicester (Robert Dudley) is recalled in Eliot's note: "V. [J. A.] Froude, *Elizabeth*, Vol. 1, ch. 4, letter of De Quadra to Philip of Spain: 'In the afternoon we were in a barge, watching the games on the river. (The queen) was alone with Lord Robert and myself on the poop, when they began to talk nonsense, and went so far that Lord Robert at last said, as I was on the spot there was no reason why they should not be married if the queen pleased.' " Queen Elizabeth was born in the old Greenwich House, by the river, where Greenwich Hospital now stands.
3. Cf. *Purgatorio*, 5.133 [Eliot's note]. The *Purgatorio* lines, which Eliot here parodies, may be translated: "Remember me, who am La Pia. / Siena made me, Maremma undid me." "Highbury": a residential London suburb. "Richmond": a pleasant part of London westward up the Thames, with boating and riverside hotels. "Kew": adjoining Richmond, has the famous Kew Gardens.
4. Underground (subway) station Eliot used daily while working at Lloyds Bank.
5. Popular seaside resort on Thames estuary.

My people humble people who expect
305 Nothing.'
        la la

To Carthage then I came[6]

Burning burning burning burning[7]
O Lord Thou pluckest me out[8]
310 O Lord Thou pluckest

burning

IV. Death by Water[9]

Phlebas the Phoenician, a fortnight dead,
Forgot the cry of gulls, and the deep sea swell
And the profit and loss.
315   A current under sea
Picked his bones in whispers. As he rose and fell
He passed the stages of his age and youth
Entering the whirlpool.
                Gentile or Jew
320 O you who turn the wheel and look to windward,
consider Phlebas, who was once handsome and tall as you.

V. What the Thunder Said[1]

  After the torchlight red on sweaty faces
After the frosty silence in the gardens
After the agony in stony places
325 The shouting and the crying
Prison and palace and reverberation
Of thunder of spring over distant mountains

6. V. St Augustine's *Confessions*: 'to Carthage then I came, where a caldron of unholy loves sang all about mine ears' [Eliot's note]. The passage from the *Confessions* quoted here occurs in St. Augustine's account of his youthful life of lust. Cf. line 92 and its note.

7. The complete text of the Buddha's Fire Sermon (which corresponds in importance to the Sermon on the Mount) from which these words are taken, will be found translated in the late Henry Clarke Warren's *Buddhism in Translation* (Harvard Oriental Series) [Eliot's note]. In the sermon, the Buddha instructs his priests that all things "are on fire. . . . The eye . . . is on fire; forms are on fire; eye-consciousness is on fire; impressions received by the eye are on fire; and whatever sensation, pleasant, unpleasant, or indifferent, originates in dependence on impressions received by the eye, that also is on fire. And with what are these on fire? With the fire of passion, say I, with the fire of hatred, with the fire of infatuation." For Christ's Sermon on the Mount see Matthew 5–7.

8. "From St. Augustine's *Confessions* again. The collocation of these two representatives of eastern and western asceticism, as the culmination of this part of the poem, is not an accident" [Eliot's note].

Cf. also Zechariah 3.2, where God, rebuking Satan, speaks of Joshua the high priest as "a brand plucked out of the fire."

9. This section has been interpreted in two ways: either it signifies death by water without resurrection (water *misused*) or it symbolizes the sacrificial death that precedes rebirth. It is true that Phlebas is purged of his commercial interests and vanities when he suffers a sea change, and Weston tells of the annual casting into the sea at Alexandria of an effigy of the head of Adonis—to be taken out after seven days by jubilant celebrators of the cult. The majority of interpreters, however, see Phlebas's drowning as a death by water that brings no resurrection, although there is a strange sense of peace in the death. Cf. line 47 and n. 5, p. 2615.

1. In the first part of part 5 three themes are employed: the journey to Emmaus, the approach to the Chapel Perilous (see Miss Weston's book), and the present decay of eastern Europe [Eliot's note]. The journey to Emmaus (see line 360 and n. 5, p. 2624) is a significant feature in the story of Christ, and in this section the Waste Land is more clearly related to that story. Christ is associated with the slain fertility god, but there is still no resurrection.

He who was living is now dead[2]
We who were living are now dying
330   With a little patience

Here is no water but only rock
Rock and no water and the sandy road
The road winding above among the mountains
Which are mountains of rock without water
335   If there were water we should stop and drink
Amongst the rock one cannot stop or think
Sweat is dry and feet are in the sand
If there were only water amongst the rock
Dead mountain mouth of carious teeth that cannot spit
340   Here one can neither stand nor lie nor sit
There is not even silence in the mountains
But dry sterile thunder without rain
There is not even solitude in the mountains
But red sullen faces sneer and snarl
345   From doors of mudcracked houses
                                    If there were water
        And no rock
        If there were rock
        And also water
350   And water
        A spring
        A pool among the rock
        If there were the sound of water only
        Not the cicada[3]
355   And dry grass singing
        But sound of water over a rock
        Where the hermit thrush[4] sings in the pine trees
        Drip drop drip drop drop drop drop
        But there is no water

360   Who is the third who walks always beside you?[5]
When I count, there are only you and I together
But when I look ahead up the white road
There is always another one walking beside you
Gliding wrapped in a brown mantle, hooded
365   I do not know whether a man or a woman
—But who is that on the other side of you?

2. These lines, containing allusions to Christ's imprisonment and trial and to Gethsemane and Golgotha, suggest the hopeless day between Good Friday and Easter, between the Crucifixion and the Resurrection—associated with the death of the Fisher King.
3. Grasshopper. Cf. the prophecy of Ecclesiastes, "the grasshopper shall be a burden, and desire shall fail." Cf. also line 23 and n. 8, p. 2614.
4. This is . . . the hermit thrush which I have heard in Quebec County . . . Its 'water-dripping song' is justly celebrated [Eliot's note].
5. The following lines were stimulated by the account of one of the Antarctic expeditions (I forget which, but I think one of Shackleton's): it was related that the party of explorers, at the extremity of their strength, had the constant delusion that there was *one more member* than could actually be counted [Eliot's note]. This reminiscence is associated with the journey of Christ's disciples to Emmaus given in Luke 24.13–16: "And it came to pass, that, while they communed together and reasoned, Jesus himself drew near, and went with them. But their eyes were holden that they should not know him."

What is that sound high in the air[6]
Murmur of maternal lamentation
Who are those hooded hordes swarming
370 Over endless plains, stumbling in cracked earth
Ringed by the flat horizon only
What is the city over the mountains
Cracks and reforms and bursts in the violet air
Falling towers
375 Jerusalem Athens Alexandria
Vienna London
Unreal

A woman drew her long black hair out tight
And fiddled whisper music on those strings
380 And bats with baby faces in the violet light
Whistled, and beat their wings
And crawled head downward down a blackened wall
And upside down in air were towers
Tolling reminiscent bells, that kept the hours
385 And voices singing out of empty cisterns and exhausted wells.

In this decayed hole among the mountains
In the faint moonlight, the grass is singing
Over the tumbled graves, about the chapel
There is the empty chapel, only the wind's home.[7]
390 It has no windows, and the door swings,
Dry bones can harm no one.
Only a cock stood on the rooftree
Co co rico co co rico[8]
In a flash of lightning. Then a damp gust
395 Bringing rain

Ganga° was sunken, and the limp leaves   *Ganges River*
Waited for rain, while the black clouds
Gathered far distant, over Himavant.[9]
The jungle crouched, humped in silence.
400 Then spoke the thunder
Da[1]
Datta: what have we given?
My friend, blood shaking my heart

6. Eliot's note for lines 367–377 is: "Cf. Herman Hesse, *Blick ins Chaos* ["A Glimpse into Chaos"]." The note then quotes a passage from the German text, which is translated: "Already half of Europe, already at least half of Eastern Europe, on the way to Chaos, drives drunk in sacred infatuation along the edge of the precipice, sings drunkenly, as though hymn singing, as Dmitri Karamazov [in Dostoyevski's *Brothers Karamazov*] sang. The offended bourgeois laughs at the songs; the saint and the seer hear them with tears."
7. Suggesting the moment of near despair before the Chapel Perilous, when the questing knight sees nothing there but decay. This illusion of nothingness is the knight's final test.
8. The crowing of the cock signals the departure of ghosts and evil spirits. Cf. *Hamlet* 1.1.157ff.

9. I.e., snowy mountain; the name of a peak in the Himalayas.
1. 'Datta, dayadhvam, damyata' (Give, sympathize, control). The fable of the meaning of the Thunder is found in the *Brihadaranyaka—Upanishad*, 5, 1 [Eliot's note]. The Hindu fable referred to is that of gods, men, and demons each in turn asking of their father Prajapati, "Speak to us, O Lord." To each he replied with the one syllable "*DA*," and each group interpreted it in a different way: "*Datta,*" to give alms; "*Dayadhvam,*" to have compassion; "*Damyata,*" to practice self-control. The fable concludes, "This is what the divine voice, the Thunder, repeats when he says: *DA, DA, DA:* 'Control yourselves; give alms; be compassionate.' Therefore one should practice these three things: self-control, alms-giving, and compassion."

The awful daring of a moment's surrender
405 Which an age of prudence can never retract
By this, and this only, we have existed
Which is not to be found in our obituaries
Or in memories draped by the beneficent spider[2]
Or under seals broken by the lean solicitor°   *lawyer*
410 In our empty rooms
DA
Dayadhvam: I have heard the key[3]
Turn in the door once and turn once only
We think of the key, each in his prison
415 Thinking of the key, each confirms a prison
Only at nightfall, æthereal rumors
Revive for a moment a broken Coriolanus[4]
DA
Damyata: The boat responded
420 Gaily, to the hand expert with sail and oar
The sea was calm, your heart would have responded
Gaily, when invited, beating obedient
To controlling hands

                        I sat upon the shore
425 Fishing,[5] with the arid plain behind me
Shall I at least set my lands in order?[6]
London Bridge is falling down falling down falling down[7]
Poi s'ascose nel foco che gli affina[8]
Quando fiam uti chelidon[9]—O swallow swallow[1]

2. Cf. Webster, *The White Devil,* 5.6: '. . . they'll remarry / Ere the worm pierce your winding-sheet, ere the spider / Make a thin curtain for your epitaphs' [Eliot's note].
3. Cf. *Inferno,* 33.46 [Eliot's note]. In this passage from the *Inferno* Ugolino recalls his imprisonment in the tower with his children, where they starved to death: "And I heard below the door of the horrible tower being locked up." Eliot implies that we cannot obey the command to sympathize because we are imprisoned within the circle of our own egotism. Eliot's note for this line goes on to quote F. H. Bradley, *Appearance and Reality,* p. 346, as follows: " 'My external sensations are no less private to myself than are my thoughts or my feelings. In either case my experience falls within my own circle, a circle closed on the outside; and, with all its elements alike, every sphere is opaque to the others which surround it. . . . In brief, regarded as an existence which appears in a soul, the whole world for each is peculiar and private to that soul.' "
4. Coriolanus, who acted out of pride rather than duty, is an obvious example of a man locked in the prison of his own self. He led the enemy against his native city out of injured pride (cf. Shakespeare, *Coriolanus*).
5. V. Weston: *From Ritual to Romance;* chapter on the Fisher King [Eliot's note].
6. Cf. Isaiah 38.1: "Thus saith the Lord, Set thine house in order, for thou shalt die, and not live." The inclusive "I," who sits in the symbolic act of fishing (seeking salvation, regeneration, eternity) with the Waste Land behind him, wonders how far he can order his affairs.

7. One of the later lines of this nursery rhyme is "Take the key and lock her up, my fair lady."
8. V. *Purgatorio,* 26.148 [Eliot's note]. The note goes on to quote lines 145–148 of the *Purgatorio,* in which Arnaut Daniel, the Provençal poet, addresses Dante: " 'Now I pray you, by that virtue which guides you to the summit of the stairway, be mindful in due time of my pain.' " Then (in the line Eliot quotes here) "he hid himself in the fire which refines them." The purgatorial vision of refining fire—as distinct from the fires of lust—represents one of the hopeful fragments shored up by the seeker for regeneration and order.
9. V. *Pervigilium Veneris.* Cf. Philomela in parts 2 and 3 [Eliot's note]. The Latin phrase in the text means, "When shall I be as the swallow?" It comes from the *Pervigilium Veneris* ("Vigil of Venus"), an anonymous late Latin poem combining a hymn to Venus with a description of spring. In the last two stanzas of the *Pervigilium* occurs a recollection of the Tereus-Procne-Philomela myth (except that in this version the swallow is identified with Philomela); the anonymous poet's mood changes to one of sadness, combined with hope for renewal: "The maid of Tereus sings under the poplar shade, so that you would think musical trills of love came from her mouth and not a sister's complaint of a barbarous husband. . . . She sings, we are silent. When will my spring come? When shall I be as the swallow that I may cease to be silent? I have lost the Muse in silence, and Apollo regards me not."
1. Cf. Swinburne's *Itylus,* which begins, "Swallow, my sister, O sister swallow, / How can thine heart be full of spring?" and Tennyson's lyric in *The Princess:* "O Swallow, Swallow, flying, flying south."

430   *Le Prince d'Aquitaine à la tour abolie*[2]
    These fragments I have shored against my ruins[3]
    Why then Ile fit you. Hieronymo's mad againe.[4]
    Datta. Dayadhvam. Damyata.
          Shantih   shantih   shantih[5]

1921   1922

The Hollow Men

Mistah Kurtz—he dead.[1]
A penny for the Old Guy[2]

I

    We are the hollow men
    We are the stuffed men
    Leaning together
    Headpiece filled with straw. Alas!
5   Our dried voices, when
    We whisper together
    Are quiet and meaningless
    As wind in dry glass
    Or rats' feet over broken glass
10 In our dry cellar[3]

    Shape without form, shade without colour,
    Paralysed force, gesture without motion;

    Those who have crossed
    With direct eyes, to death's other Kingdom
15 Remember us—if at all—not as lost
    Violent souls, but only
    As the hollow men
    The stuffed men.

2. V. Gerard de Nerval, Sonnet *El Desdichado* [Eliot's note]. The French line may be translated, "The Prince of Aquitaine in the ruined tower." One of the cards in the Tarot pack is "the tower struck by lightning."
3. This may refer to the whole poem—fragments assembled by the speaker in the attempt to come to terms with his situation.
4. V. Kyd's *Spanish Tragedy* [Eliot's note]. Subtitled "Hieronymo's Mad Againe," Kyd's play (1594) is an early example of the Elizabethan tragedy of revenge. Hieronymo, driven mad by the murder of his son, has his revenge when he is asked to write a court entertainment. He replies, "Why then Ile fit you!" (i.e., accommodate you), and assigns the parts in the entertainment so that, in the course of the action, his son's murderers are killed.
5. Shantih. Repeated as here, a formal ending to

an Upanishad. 'The Peace which passeth understanding' is our equivalent to this word [Eliot's note]. The Upanishads are poetic dialogues on Hindu metaphysics, written after the Vedas, the ancient Hindu scriptures, and in part commenting on them. The fact that the benediction is in a language so foreign to Western tradition may indicate that the solution is willed, not achieved.
1. From Joseph Conrad's *Heart of Darkness* (see p. 2304).
2. Every year on Nov. 5, British children build bonfires on which they burn a scarecrow effigy of the traitor Guido [Guy] Fawkes who, in 1605, attempted to blow up the Parliament buildings. For some days before this, they ask people in the streets for pennies with which to buy fireworks.
3. Cf. *The Waste Land*, lines 115 and 195.

II

Eyes I dare not meet in dreams
20   In death's dream kingdom[4]
These do not appear:
There, the eyes are
Sunlight on a broken column
There, is a tree swinging
25   And voices are
In the wind's singing
More distant and more solemn
Than a fading star.

Let me be no nearer
30   In death's dream kingdom
Let me also wear
Such deliberate disguises
Rat's coat, crowskin, crossed staves
In a field[5]
35   Behaving as the wind behaves
No nearer—

Not that final meeting
In the twilight kingdom[6]

III

This is the dead land
40   This is cactus land
Here the stone images[7]
Are raised, here they receive
The supplication of a dead man's hand
Under the twinkle of a fading star.

45   Is it like this
In death's other kingdom
Waking alone
At the hour when we are
Trembling with tenderness
50   Lips that would kiss
Form prayers to broken stone.

IV

The eyes are not here
There are no eyes here
In this valley of dying stars

---

4. At the end of Dante's *Purgatorio* and in *Paradiso* 4, he cannot meet the gaze of Beatrice (see Eliot's 1929 essay, *Dante*).
5. The traditional British scarecrow is made from two sticks tied in the form of a cross (the vertical one stuck in the ground), dressed in cast-off clothes, and sometimes draped with dead vermin.
6. Perhaps a reference to Dante's meeting with Beatrice after he has crossed the river Lethe. There reminded of his sins, he is allowed to proceed to Paradise (*Purgatorio* 30).
7. Cf. *The Waste Land* line 22.

55 In this hollow valley
This broken jaw of our lost kingdoms

In this last of meeting places
We grope together
And avoid speech
60 Gathered on this beach of the tumid river[8]

Sightless, unless
The eyes reappear
As the perpetual star
Multifoliate rose[9]
65 Of death's twilight kingdom
The hope only
Of empty men.

V

Here we go round the prickly pear
Prickly pear prickly pear
70 *Here we go round the prickly pear*
At five o'clock in the morning.[1]

Between the idea
And the reality
Between the motion
75 And the act[2]
Falls the Shadow[3]
            For Thine is the Kingdom[4]

Between the conception
And the creation
80 Between the emotion
And the response
Falls the Shadow
            Life is very long

Between the desire
85 And the spasm
Between the potency
And the existence
Between the essence
And the descent
90 Falls the Shadow
            For Thine is the Kingdom

8. Dante's Acheron, which encircles Hell, and the Congo of Conrad's *Heart of Darkness.*
9. The image of heaven in Dante's *Paradiso* 32.
1. Parodic version of the children's rhyme ending "Here we go round the mulberry bush / On a cold and frosty morning."
2. Cf. Shakespeare's *Julius Caesar* 2.1.63–5: "Between the acting of a dreadful thing / And the first motion, all the interim is / Like a phantasma or a hideous dream."
3. Cf. Ernest Dowson's *Non sum qualis eram bonae sub regno Cynarae*, lines 1–2: "Last night, ah, yesternight, betwixt her lips and mine / There fell thy shadow, Cynara!"
4. Cf. The Lord's Prayer.

For Thine is
Life is
For Thine is the

95   *This is the way the world ends*
     This is the way the world ends
     This is the way the world ends
     Not with a bang but a whimper.

1924–25   1925

Journey of the Magi[1]

'A cold coming we had of it,
Just the worst time of the year
For a journey, and such a long journey:
The ways deep and the weather sharp,
5   The very dead of winter.'[2]
And the camels galled, sore-footed, refractory,
Lying down in the melting snow.
There were times we regretted
The summer palaces on slopes, the terraces,
10   And the silken girls bringing sherbet.
Then the camel men cursing and grumbling
And running away, and wanting their liquor and women,
And the night-fires going out, and the lack of shelters,
And the cities hostile and the towns unfriendly
15   And the villages dirty and charging high prices:
A hard time we had of it.
At the end we preferred to travel all night,
Sleeping in snatches,
With the voices singing in our ears, saying
20   That this was all folly.

     Then at dawn we came down to a temperate valley,
Wet, below the snow line, smelling of vegetation;
With a running stream and a water mill beating the darkness,
And three trees on the low sky.[3]
25   And an old white horse galloped away in the meadow.
Then we came to a tavern with vine-leaves over the lintel,
Six hands at an open door dicing for pieces of silver,[4]
And feet kicking the empty wine-skins.

1. One of the wise men who came from the east to Jerusalem to do homage to the infant Jesus (Matthew 2.1–12) is recalling in old age the meaning of the experience.
2. Adapted from a passage in a Nativity sermon by the 17th-century divine Lancelot Andrewes: "A cold coming they had of it at this time of the year, just the worst time of the year to take a journey, and specially a long journey in. The ways deep, the weather sharp, the days short, the sun farthest off, *in solstitio brumali,* 'the very dead of winter.' "
3. The "three trees" suggest the three crosses, with Christ crucified on the center one; the men "dicing for pieces of silver" (line 27) suggest the soldiers dicing for Christ's garments and Judas's betrayal of him for thirty pieces of silver.
4. "Why, for all of us, out of all that we have heard, seen, felt, in a lifetime, do certain images recur, charged with emotion, rather than others? . . . six ruffians seen through an open window playing cards at night at a small French railway junction where there was a water mill" (Eliot, *The Use of Poetry and the Use of Criticism*).

But there was no information, and so we continued
30   And arrived at evening, not a moment too soon
Finding the place; it was (you may say) satisfactory.

    All this was a long time ago, I remember,
And I would do it again, but set down
This set down
35   This: were we led all that way for
Birth or Death? There was a Birth, certainly,
We had evidence and no doubt. I had seen birth and death,
But had thought they were different; this Birth was
Hard and bitter agony for us, like Death, our death.
40   We returned to our places, these Kingdoms,
But no longer at ease here, in the old dispensation,
With an alien people clutching their gods.
I should be glad of another death.

                                                          1927

Marina[1]

Quis hic locus, quae regio, quae mundi plaga?[2]

    What seas what shores what gray rocks and what islands
What water lapping the bow
And scent of pine and the woodthrush singing through the fog
What images return
5   O my daughter.

    Those who sharpen the tooth of the dog, meaning
Death
Those who glitter with the glory of the hummingbird, meaning
Death
10   Those who sit in the sty of contentment, meaning
Death
Those who suffer the ecstasy of the animals, meaning
Death

    Are become unsubstantial, reduced by a wind,
15   A breath of pine, and the woodsong fog
By this grace dissolved in place

    What is this face, less clear and clearer
The pulse in the arm, less strong and stronger—
Given or lent? more distant than stars and nearer than the eye

1. Pericles' daughter in Shakespeare's *Pericles, Prince of Tyre*: she was born at sea, lost to her father, then as a young woman found by him again.
2. "What place is this, what country, what region of the world?" Spoken by Hercules on regaining sanity after having killed his children in his mad-
ness, in Seneca's *Hercules Furens* (The mad Hercules). This is a situation contrary to the one evoked in the poem. Eliot once wrote to a correspondent that he wished to achieve a "crisscross" between the scenes in the Senecan and the Shakespearean plays.

20   Whispers and small laughter between leaves and hurrying feet
       Under sleep, where all the waters meet.

       Bowsprit cracked with ice and paint cracked with heat.
       I made this, I have forgotten
       And remember.
25   The rigging weak and the canvas rotten
       Between one June and another September.
       Made this unknowing, half conscious, unknown, my own.
       The garboard strake[3] leaks, the seams need caulking.
       This form, this face, this life
30   Living to live in a world of time beyond me; let me
       Resign my life for this life, my speech for that unspoken,
       The awakened, lips parted, the hope, the new ships.

       What seas what shores what granite islands towards my timbers
       And woodthrush calling through the fog
35   My daughter.

                                1930

FROM FOUR QUARTETS

Little Gidding[1]

I

   Midwinter spring is its own season
   Sempiternal° though sodden towards sundown,   *eternal, everlasting*
   Suspended in time, between pole and tropic,
   When the short day is brightest, with frost and fire,
5   The brief sun flames the ice, on pond and ditches,
   In windless cold that is the heart's heat,
   Reflecting in a watery mirror
   A glare that is blindness in the early afternoon.
   And glow more intense than blaze of branch, or brazier,
10 Stirs the dumb spirit: no wind, but pentecostal fire[2]
   In the dark time of the year. Between melting and freezing

3. The planking nearest to the boat's keel—hence its most vital spot.
1. This is the fourth of Eliot's *Four Quartets,* four related poems each divided into five "movements" in a manner reminiscent of the structure of a quartet or a sonata and each dealing with some aspect of the relation of time and eternity, the meaning of history, the achievement of the moment of timeless insight. Although the *Four Quartets* constitute a unified sequence, they were each written separately and can be read as individual poems. "*Little Gidding* can be understood by itself, without reference to the preceding poems, which it yet so beautifully completes" (Helen Gardner). Each of the four is named after a place. Little Gidding is a

village in Huntingdonshire where in 1625 Nicholas Ferrar established an Anglican religious community; it was broken up in 1647, toward the end of the civil war, by the victorious Puritans; the chapel, however, was rebuilt in the 19th century and still exists. Eliot wrote the poem in 1942, when he was taking his turn as a nighttime fire-watcher during the incendiary bombings of London in World War II, and he looks back at the history and meaning of Little Gidding from his own war experience in order to project its present significance.
2. On the Pentecost day after the death and resurrection of Christ, there appeared to His apostles "cloven tongues like as of fire . . . And they were all filled with the Holy Ghost" (Acts 2).

The soul's sap quivers. There is no earth smell
Or smell of living thing. This is the springtime
But not in time's covenant. Now the hedgerow
15 Is blanched for an hour with transitory blossom
Of snow, a bloom more sudden
Than that of summer, neither budding nor fading,
Not in the scheme of generation.
Where is the summer, the unimaginable
Zero summer?

20   If you came this way,
Taking the route you would be likely to take
From the place you would be likely to come from,
If you came this way in may time, you would find the hedges
White again, in May, with voluptuary sweetness.
25 It would be the same at the end of the journey,
If you came at night like a broken king,[3]
If you came by day not knowing what you came for,
It would be the same, when you leave the rough road
And turn behind the pig-sty to the dull façade
30 And the tombstone. And what you thought you came for
Is only a shell, a husk of meaning
From which the purpose breaks only when it is fulfilled
If at all. Either you had no purpose
Or the purpose is beyond the end you figured
35 And is altered in fulfilment. There are other places
Which also are the world's end, some at the sea jaws,
Or over a dark lake, in a desert or a city[4]—
But this is the nearest, in place and time,
Now and in England.

                If you came this way,
40 Taking any route, starting from anywhere,
At any time or at any season,
It would always be the same: you would have to put off
Sense and notion. You are not here to verify,
Instruct yourself, or inform curiosity
45 Or carry report. You are here to kneel
Where prayer has been valid. And prayer is more
Than an order of words, the conscious occupation
Of the praying mind, or the sound of the voice praying.
And what the dead had no speech for, when living,
50 They can tell you, being dead: the communication
Of the dead is tongued with fire beyond the language of the living.
Here, the intersection of the timeless moment
Is England and nowhere. Never and always.

---

3. King Charles I visited Ferrar's community more
than once and is said to have paid his last visit in
secret after his final defeat at the battle of Naseby
in the Civil War.
4. "The 'sea jaws' [Eliot] associated with Iona and
St. Columba and with Lindisfarne and St. Cuth-

bert: the 'dark lake' with the lake of Glendalough
and St. Kevin's hermitage in County Wicklow: the
desert with the hermits of the Thebaid and St.
Antony: the city with Padua and the other St.
Antony" (Gardner, *The Composition of Four Quartets*, p. 163).

II

Ash on an old man's sleeve
55 Is all the ash the burnt roses leave.
Dust in the air suspended
Marks the place where a story ended.[5]
Dust inbreathed was a house—
The wall, the wainscot, and the mouse.
60 The death of hope and despair,
    This is the death of air.[6]

There are flood and drouth
Over the eyes and in the mouth,
Dead water and dead sand
65 Contending for the upper hand.
The parched eviscerate soil
Gapes at the vanity of toil,
Laughs without mirth.
    This is the death of earth.

70 Water and fire succeed
The town, the pasture, and the weed.
Water and fire deride
The sacrifice that we denied.
Water and fire shall rot
75 The marred foundations we forgot,
Of sanctuary and choir.
    This is the death of water and fire.

In the uncertain hour before the morning[7]
    Near the ending of interminable night
80   At the recurrent end of the unending
After the dark dove with the flickering tongue[8]
    Had passed below the horizon of his homing
    While the dead leaves still rattled on like tin
Over the asphalt where no other sound was
85   Between three districts whence the smoke arose
    I met one walking, loitering and hurried
As if blown towards me like the metal leaves
    Before the urban dawn wind unresisting.
    And as I fixed upon the down-turned face
90 That pointed scrutiny with which we challenge
    The first-met stranger in the waning dusk
    I caught the sudden look of some dead master
Whom I had known, forgotten, half recalled

5. Eliot wrote to a friend: "During the Blitz [bomb-ing] the accumulated debris was suspended in the London air for hours after a bombing. Then it would slowly descend and cover one's sleeves and coat with a fine white ash."
6. "The death of air," like that of "earth" and of "water and fire" in the succeeding stanzas, recalls the theory of the creative strife of the four elements propounded by Heraclitus (Greek philosopher of 4th and 5th centuries B.C.E.): "Fire lives in the death of air; water lives in the death of earth; and earth lives in the death of water."
7. The pattern of indentation in the left margin of lines 78–149, their movement and elevated diction, are meant to suggest the *terza rima* of Dante's *Inferno*.
8. The German dive bomber.

Both one and many; in the brown baked features
95   The eyes of a familiar compound ghost[9]
Both intimate and unidentifiable.
    So I assumed a double part, and cried
    And heard another's voice cry: "What! are *you* here?"
Although we were not. I was still the same,
100   Knowing myself yet being someone other—
    And he a face still forming; yet the words sufficed
To compel the recognition they preceded.
    And so, compliant to the common wind,
    Too strange to each other for misunderstanding,
105 In concord at this intersection time
    Of meeting nowhere, no before and after,
    We trod the pavement in a dead patrol.
I said: 'The wonder that I feel is easy,
    Yet ease is cause of wonder. Therefore speak:
110   I may not comprehend, may not remember.'
And he: 'I am not eager to rehearse
    My thought and theory which you have forgotten.
    These things have served their purpose: let them be.
So with your own, and pray they be forgiven
115   By others, as I pray you to forgive
    Both bad and good. Last season's fruit is eaten
And the fullfed beast shall kick the empty pail.
    For last year's words belong to last year's language
    And next year's words await another voice.
120 But, as the passage now presents no hindrance
    To the spirit unappeased and peregrine°   *foreign, wandering*
    Between two worlds become much like each other,
So I find words I never thought to speak
    In streets I never thought I should revisit
125   When I left my body on a distant shore.[1]
Since our concern was speech, and speech impelled us
    To purify the dialect of the tribe[2]
    And urge the mind to aftersight and foresight,
Let me disclose the gifts reserved for age
130   To set a crown upon your lifetime's effort.
    First, the cold friction of expiring sense
Without enchantment, offering no promise
    But bitter tastelessness of shadow fruit
    As body and soul begin to fall asunder.
135 Second, the conscious impotence of rage[3]
    At human folly, and the laceration
    Of laughter at what ceases to amuse.[4]

---

9. This encounter with a ghost "compounded" of W. B. Yeats and his fellow Irishman Jonathan Swift is modeled on Dante's meeting with Brunetto Latini (*Inferno* 15), closing with a direct translation of Dante's cry of horrified recognition: "*Siete voi qui, ser Brunetto?*" Cf. also Shakespeare's Sonnet 86, line 9: "that affable familiar ghost."
1. Yeats died on Jan. 28, 1939, at Roquebrune in the south of France.
2. A rendering of the line "*Donner un sens plus pur*

aux mots de la tribu" in Stéphane Mallarmé's sonnet *Le Tombeau d'Edgar Poe* (The tomb of Edgar Poe).
3. Cf. Yeats's *The Spur*: "You think it horrible that lust and rage / Should dance attention upon my old age."
4. Cf. Yeats's *Swift's Epitaph* (translated from Swift's own Latin): "Savage indignation there / Cannot lacerate his breast."

And last, the rending pain of re-enactment
 Of all that you have done, and been;[5] the shame
140 Of motives late revealed, and the awareness
Of things ill done and done to others' harm
 Which once you took for exercise of virtue.
 Then fools' approval stings, and honour stains.
From wrong to wrong the exasperated spirit
145 Proceeds, unless restored by that refining fire[6]
 Where you must move in measure, like a dancer.'[7]
The day was breaking. In the disfigured street
 He left me, with a kind of valediction,
 And faded on the blowing of the horn.[8]

III

150 There are three conditions which often look alike
Yet differ completely, flourish in the same hedgerow:
Attachment to self and to things and to persons, detachment
From self and from things and from persons; and, growing between
 them, indifference
Which resembles the others as death resembles life,
155 Being between two lives—unflowering, between
The live and the dead nettle.[9] This is the use of memory:
For liberation—not less of love but expanding
Of love beyond desire, and so liberation
From the future as well as the past. Thus, love of a country
160 Begins as attachment to our own field of action
And comes to find that action of little importance
Though never indifferent. History may be servitude,
History may be freedom. See, now they vanish,
The faces and places, with the self which, as it could, loved them,
165 To become renewed, transfigured, in another pattern.

Sin is Behovely, but
All shall be well, and
All manner of thing shall be well.[1]
If I think, again, of this place,
170 And of people, not wholly commendable,
Of no immediate kin or kindness,
But some of peculiar genius,

---

5. Cf. Yeats's *The Man and the Echo*: "All that I have said and done, / Now that I am old and ill, / Turns into a question till / I lie awake night after night / And never get the answer right. / Did that play of mine send out / Certain men the English shot?"
6. Cf. *The Waste Land*, line 428 and n. 8, p. 2626; also the refining fire in Yeats's *Byzantium*, lines 25–32.
7. Cf. Yeats's *Among School Children*, line 64: "How can we know the dancer from the dance?"
8. Cf. *Hamlet* 1.2.157: "It faded on the crowing of the cock." The horn is the all-clear signal after an air raid (the dialogue has taken place between the dropping of the last bomb and the sounding of the all clear). Eliot called the section that ends with

this line "the nearest equivalent to a canto of the *Inferno* or *Purgatorio*" that he could achieve and spoke of his intention to present "a parallel, by means of contrast, between the *Inferno* and the *Purgatorio* . . . and a hallucinated scene after an air raid."
9. Eliot wrote to a friend: "The dead nettle is the family of flowering plants of which the White Archangel is one of the commonest and closely resembles the stinging nettle and is found in its company."
1. A quotation from the 14th-century English mystic Dame Julian of Norwich: "Sin is behovabil [inevitable], but all shall be well and all shall be well and all manner of thing shall be well."

All touched by a common genius,
United in the strife which divided them;
175   If I think of a king at nightfall,[2]
Of three men, and more, on the scaffold
And a few who died forgotten
In other places, here and abroad,
And of one who died blind and quiet[3]
180   Why should we celebrate
These dead men more than the dying?
It is not to ring the bell backward
Nor is it an incantation
To summon the spectre of a Rose.
185   We cannot revive old factions
We cannot restore old policies
Or follow an antique drum.
These men, and those who opposed them
And those whom they opposed
190   Accept the constitution of silence
And are folded in a single party.
Whatever we inherit from the fortunate
We have taken from the defeated
What they had to leave us—a symbol:
195   A symbol perfected in death.
And all shall be well and
All manner of thing shall be well
By the purification of the motive
In the ground of our beseeching.[4]

IV

200   The dove descending breaks the air
With flame of incandescent terror
Of which the tongues declare
The one discharge from sin and error.
The only hope, or else despair
205   Lies in the choice of pyre or pyre—
To be redeemed from fire by fire.

Who then devised the torment? Love.
Love is the unfamiliar Name
Behind the hands that wove
210   The intolerable shirt of flame[5]
Which human power cannot remove.
We only live, only suspire
Consumed by either fire or fire.

2. I.e., Charles I. He died "on the scaffold" in 1649, while his principal advisers, Archbishop Laud and Thomas Wentworth, earl of Strafford, were both executed earlier by the victorious parliamentary forces.
3. I.e., Milton.
4. Dame Julian of Norwich was instructed in a vision that "the ground of our beseeching" is love.
5. Out of love for her husband, Hercules, Deianira gave him the poisoned shirt of Nessus. She had been told that it would increase his love for her, but instead it so corroded his flesh that in his agony he mounted a funeral pyre and burned himself to death.

V

What we call the beginning is often the end
215   And to make an end is to make a beginning.
The end is where we start from. And every phrase
And sentence that is right (where every word is at home,
Taking its place to support the others,
The word neither diffident nor ostentatious,
220   And easy commerce of the old and the new,
The common word exact without vulgarity,
The formal word precise but not pedantic,
The complete consort[6] dancing together)
Every phrase and every sentence is an end and a beginning,
225   Every poem an epitaph. And any action
Is a step to the block, to the fire, down the sea's throat
Or to an illegible stone: and that is where we start.
We die with the dying:
See, they depart, and we go with them.
230   We are born with the dead:
See, they return, and bring us with them.
The moment of the rose and the moment of the yew-tree
Are of equal duration. A people without history
Is not redeemed from time, for history is a pattern
235   Of timeless moments. So, while the light fails
On a winter's afternoon, in a secluded chapel
History is now and England.

With the drawing of this Love and the voice of this Calling[7]

We shall not cease from exploration
240   And the end of all our exploring
Will be to arrive where we started
And know the place for the first time.
Through the unknown, remembered gate
When the last of earth left to discover
245   Is that which was the beginning;
At the source of the longest river
The voice of the hidden waterfall
And the children in the apple tree
Not known, because not looked for
250   But heard, half-heard, in the stillness
Between two waves of the sea.[8]
Quick now, here, now, always—
A condition of complete simplicity
(Costing not less than everything)
255   And all shall be well and
All manner of thing shall be well

6. Company, also harmony of sounds.
7. This line is from the *Cloud of Unknowing*, an anonymous 14th-century mystical work.
8. The voices of the children in the apple tree symbolize the sudden moment of insight. Cf. the conclusion to *Burnt Norton* (the first of the *Four*

Quartets), where the laughter of the children in the garden has a like meaning: "Sudden in a shaft of sunlight / Even while the dust moves / There rises the hidden laughter / Of children in the foliage / Quick now, here, now, always."

When the tongues of flame are in-folded
Into the crowned knot of fire
And the fire and the rose are one.

1942   1942, 1943

Tradition and the Individual Talent[1]

1

In English writing we seldom speak of tradition, though we occasionally apply its name in deploring its absence. We cannot refer to 'the tradition' or to 'a tradition'; at most, we employ the adjective in saying that the poetry of So-and-so is 'traditional' or even 'too traditional.' Seldom, perhaps, does the word appear except in a phrase of censure. If otherwise, it is vaguely approbative, with the implication, as to the work approved, of some pleasing archæological reconstruction. You can hardly make the word agreeable to English ears without this comfortable reference to the reassuring science of archæology.

Certainly the word is not likely to appear in our appreciations of living or dead writers. Every nation, every race, has not only its own creative, but its own critical turn of mind; and is even more oblivious of the shortcomings and limitations of its critical habits than of those of its creative genius. We know, or think we know, from the enormous mass of critical writing that has appeared in the French language the critical method or habit of the French; we only conclude (we are such unconscious people) that the French are 'more critical' than we, and sometimes even plume ourselves a little with the fact, as if the French were the less spontaneous. Perhaps they are; but we might remind ourselves that criticism is as inevitable as breathing, and that we should be none the worse for articulating what passes in our minds when we read a book and feel an emotion about it, for criticizing our own minds in their work of criticism. One of the facts that might come to light in this process is our tendency to insist, when we praise a poet, upon those aspects of his work in which he least resembles anyone else. In these aspects or parts of his work we pretend to find what is individual, what is the peculiar essence of the man. We dwell with satisfaction upon the poet's difference from his predecessors, especially his immediate predecessors; we endeavour to find something that can be isolated in order to be enjoyed. Whereas if we approach a poet without this prejudice we shall often find that not only the best, but the most individual parts of his work may be those in which the dead poets, his ancestors, assert their immortality most vigorously. And I do not mean the impressionable period of adolescence, but the period of full maturity.

Yet if the only form of tradition, of handing down, consisted in following the ways of the immediate generation before us in a blind or timid adherence to its successes, 'tradition' should positively be discouraged. We have seen many such simple currents soon lost in the sand; and novelty is better than repetition. Tradition is a matter of much wider significance. It cannot be inherited, and if you want it you must obtain it by great labour. It involves,

1. First published in the *Egoist* (1919) and later collected in *The Sacred Wood* (1920).

in the first place, the historical sense, which we may call nearly indispensable to any one who would continue to be a poet beyond his twenty-fifth year; and the historical sense involves a perception, not only of the pastness of the past, but of its presence; the historical sense compels a man to write not merely with his own generation in his bones, but with a feeling that the whole of the literature of Europe from Homer and within it the whole of the literature of his own country has a simultaneous existence and composes a simultaneous order. This historical sense, which is a sense of the timeless as well as of the temporal and of the timeless and of the temporal together, is what makes a writer traditional. And it is at the same time what makes a writer most acutely conscious of his place in time, of his own contemporaneity.

No poet, no artist of any art, has his complete meaning alone. His significance, his appreciation is the appreciation of his relation to the dead poets and artists. You cannot value him alone; you must set him, for contrast and comparison, among the dead. I mean this as a principle of æsthetic, not merely historical, criticism. The necessity that he shall conform, that he shall cohere, is not one-sided; what happens when a new work of art is created is something that happens simultaneously to all the works of art which preceded it. The existing monuments form an ideal order among themselves, which is modified by the introduction of the new (the really new) work of art among them. The existing order is complete before the new work arrives; for order to persist after the supervention of novelty, the *whole* existing order must be, if ever so slightly, altered; and so the relations, proportions, values of each work of art toward the whole are readjusted; and this is conformity between the old and the new. Whoever has approved this idea of order, of the form of European, of English literature will not find it preposterous that the past should be altered by the present as much as the present is directed by the past. And the poet who is aware of this will be aware of great difficulties and responsibilities.

In a peculiar sense he will be aware also that he must inevitably be judged by the standards of the past. I say judged, not amputated, by them; not judged to be as good as, or worse or better than, the dead; and certainly not judged by the canons of dead critics. It is a judgment, a comparison, in which two things are measured by each other. To conform merely would be for the new work not really to conform at all; it would not be new, and would therefore not be a work of art. And we do not quite say that the new is more valuable because it fits in; but its fitting in is a test of its value—a test, it is true, which can only be slowly and cautiously applied, for we are none of us infallible judges of conformity. We say: it appears to conform, and is perhaps individual, or it appears individual, and may conform; but we are hardly likely to find that it is one and not the other.

To proceed to a more intelligible exposition of the relation of the poet to the past: he can neither take the past as a lump, an indiscriminate bolus,[2] nor can he form himself wholly on one or two private admirations, nor can he form himself wholly upon one preferred period. The first course is inadmissible, the second is an important experience of youth, and the third is a pleasant and highly desirable supplement. The poet must be very conscious of the main current, which does not at all flow invariably through the most

---

2. A round mass of anything: a large pill.

distinguished reputations. He must be quite aware of the obvious fact that art never improves, but that the material of art is never quite the same. He must be aware that the mind of Europe—the mind of his own country—a mind which he learns in time to be much more important than his own private mind—is a mind which changes, and that this change is a development which abandons nothing *en route,* which does not superannuate either Shakespeare, or Homer, or the rock drawing of the Magdalenian[3] draftsmen. That this development, refinement perhaps, complication certainly, is not, from the point of view of the artist, any improvement. Perhaps not even an improvement from the point of view of the psychologist or not to the extent which we imagine; perhaps only in the end based upon a complication in economics and machinery. But the difference between the present and the past is that the conscious present is an awareness of the past in a way and to an extent which the past's awareness of itself cannot show.

Someone said: 'The dead writers are remote from us because we *know* so much more than they did.' Precisely, and they are that which we know.

I am alive to a usual objection to what is clearly part of my programme for the *métier* of poetry. The objection is that the doctrine requires a ridiculous amount of erudition (pedantry), a claim which can be rejected by appeal to the lives of poets in any pantheon. It will even be affirmed that much learning deadens or perverts poetic sensibility. While, however, we persist in believing that a poet ought to know as much as will not encroach upon his necessary receptivity and necessary laziness, it is not desirable to confine knowledge to whatever can be put into a useful shape for examinations, drawing-rooms, or the still more pretentious modes of publicity. Some can absorb knowledge, the more tardy must sweat for it. Shakespeare acquired more essential history from Plutarch[4] than most men could from the whole British Museum. What is to be insisted upon is that the poet must develop or procure the consciousness of the past and that he should continue to develop this consciousness throughout his career.

What happens is a continual surrender of himself as he is at the moment to something which is more valuable. The progress of an artist is a continual self-sacrifice, a continual extinction of personality.

There remains to define this process of depersonalisation and its relation to the sense of tradition. It is in this depersonalization that art may be said to approach the condition of science. I, therefore, invite you to consider, as a suggestive analogy, the action which takes place when a bit of finely filiated[5] platinum is introduced into a chamber containing oxygen and sulphur dioxide.

II

Honest criticism and sensitive appreciation are directed not upon the poet but upon the poetry. If we attend to the confused cries of the newspaper critics and the susurrus[6] of popular repetition that follows, we shall hear the names of poets in great numbers; if we seek not Blue-book[7] knowledge but

3. The most advanced culture of the European Paleolithic period (from discoveries at La Madeleine, France).
4. Plutarch (1st century C.E.), Greek biographer of famous Greeks and Romans from whose work

Shakespeare drew the plots of his Roman plays.
5. Drawn out like a thread.
6. Murmuring, buzzing (Latin).
7. British official government publication.

the enjoyment of poetry, and ask for a poem, we shall seldom find it. I have tried to point out the importance of the relation of the poem to other poems by other authors, and suggested the conception of poetry as a living whole of all the poetry that has ever been written. The other aspect of this Impersonal theory of poetry is the relation of the poem to its author. And I hinted, by an analogy, that the mind of the mature poet differs from that of the immature one not precisely in any valuation of 'personality,' not being necessarily more interesting, or having 'more to say,' but rather by being a more finely perfected medium in which special, or very varied, feelings are at liberty to enter into new combinations.

The analogy was that of the catalyst.[8] When the two gases previously mentioned are mixed in the presence of a filament of platinum, they form sulphurous acid. This combination takes place only if the platinum is present; nevertheless the newly formed acid contains no trace of platinum, and the platinum itself is apparently unaffected; has remained inert, neutral, and unchanged. The mind of the poet is the shred of platinum. It may partly or exclusively operate upon the experience of the man himself; but, the more perfect the artist, the more completely separate in him will be the man who suffers and the mind which creates; the more perfectly will the mind digest and transmute the passions which are its material.

The experience, you will notice, the elements which enter the presence of the transforming catalyst, are of two kinds: emotions and feelings. The effect of a work of art upon the person who enjoys it is an experience different in kind from any experience not of art. It may be formed out of one emotion, or may be a combination of several; and various feelings, inhering for the writer in particular words or phrases or images, may be added to compose the final result. Or great poetry may be made without the direct use of any emotion whatever: composed out of feelings solely. Canto XV of the *Inferno* (Brunetto Latini)[9] is a working up of the emotion evident in the situation; but the effect, though single as that of any work of art, is obtained by considerable complexity of detail. The last quatrain gives an image, a feeling attaching to an image, which 'came,' which did not develop simply out of what precedes, but which was probably in suspension in the poet's mind until the proper combination arrived for it to add itself to.[1] The poet's mind is in fact a receptacle for seizing and storing up numberless feelings, phrases, images, which remain there until all the particles which can unite to form a new compound are present together.

If you compare several representative passages of the greatest poetry you see how great is the variety of types of combination, and also how completely any semi-ethical criterion of 'sublimity' misses the mark. For it is not the 'greatness,' the intensity, of the emotions, the components, but the intensity of the artistic process, the pressure, so to speak, under which the fusion takes place, that counts. The episode of Paolo and Francesca[2] employs a

8. Substance that triggers a chemical change without itself being affected by the reaction.
9. Dante meets in Hell his old master Brunetto Latini, suffering eternal punishment for unnatural lust yet still loved and admired by Dante, who addresses him with affectionate courtesy (see n. 1, just below).
1. Dante's strange interview with Brunetto is over,

and Brunetto moves off to continue his punishment: "Then he turned round, and seemed like one of those / Who run for the green cloth [in the footrace] at Verona / In the field; and he seemed among them / Not the loser but the winner."
2. Illicit lovers whom Dante meets in the second circle of Hell (*Inferno* 5) and at whose punishment and sorrows he swoons with pity.

definite emotion, but the intensity of the poetry is something quite different from whatever intensity in the supposed experience it may give the impression of. It is no more intense, furthermore, than Canto XXVI,[3] the voyage of Ulysses, which has not the direct dependence upon an emotion. Great variety is possible in the process of transmutation of emotion: the murder of Agamemnon,[4] or the agony of Othello, gives an artistic effect apparently closer to a possible original than the scenes from Dante. In the *Agamemnon,* the artistic emotion approximates to the emotion of an actual spectator; in *Othello* to the emotion of the protagonist himself. But the difference between art and the event is always absolute; the combination which is the murder of Agamemnon is probably as complex as that which is the voyage of Ulysses. In either case there has been a fusion of elements. The ode of Keats contains a number of feelings which have nothing particular to do with the nightingale, but which the nightingale, partly, perhaps, because of its attractive name, and partly because of its reputation, served to bring together.

The point of view which I am struggling to attack is perhaps related to the metaphysical theory of the substantial unity of the soul: for my meaning is, that the poet has, not a 'personality' to express, but a particular medium, which is only a medium and not a personality, in which impressions and experiences combine in peculiar and unexpected ways. Impressions and experiences which are important for the man may take no place in the poetry, and those which become important in the poetry may play quite a negligible part in the man, the personality.

I will quote a passage which is unfamiliar enough to be regarded with fresh attention in the light—or darkness—of these observations:

> And now methinks I could e'en chide myself
> For doating on her beauty, though her death
> Shall be revenged after no common action.
> Does the silkworm expend her yellow labours
> For thee? For thee does she undo herself?
> Are lordships sold to maintain ladyships
> For the poor benefit of a bewildering minute?
> Why does yon fellow falsify highways,
> And put his life between the judge's lips,
> To refine such a thing—keeps horse and men
> To beat their valours for her? . . .[5]

In this passage (as is evident if it is taken in its context) there is a combination of positive and negative emotions: an intensely strong attraction toward beauty and an equally intense fascination by the ugliness which is contrasted with it and which destroys it. This balance of contrasted emotion is in the dramatic situation to which the speech is pertinent, but that situation alone is inadequate to it. This is, so to speak, the structural emotion, provided by the drama. But the whole effect, the dominant tone, is due to the fact that a number of floating feelings, having an affinity to this emotion by no means superficially evident, have combined with it to give us a new art emotion.

It is not in his personal emotions, the emotions provoked by particular

---

3. Of the *Inferno.* Ulysses, suffering in Hell for "false counseling," tells Dante of his final voyage.
4. By his wife, Clytemnestra; the central action of

Aeschylus's play *Agamemnon.*
5. From Cyril Tourneur, *The Revenger's Tragedy* 3.4 (1607).

events in his life, that the poet is in any way remarkable or interesting. His particular emotions may be simple, or crude, or flat. The emotion in his poetry will be a very complex thing, but not with the complexity of the emotions of people who have very complex or unusual emotions in life. One error, in fact, of eccentricity in poetry is to seek for new human emotions to express; and in this search for novelty in the wrong place it discovers the perverse. The business of the poet is not to find new emotions, but to use the ordinary ones and, in working them up into poetry, to express feelings which are not in actual emotions at all. And emotions which he has never experienced will serve his turn as well as those familiar to him. Consequently, we must believe that 'emotion recollected in tranquillity'[6] is an inexact formula. For it is neither emotion, nor recollection, nor, without distortion of meaning, tranquility. It is a concentration, and a new thing resulting from the concentration, of a very great number of experiences which to the practical and active person would not seem to be experiences at all; it is a concentration which does not happen consciously or of deliberation. These experiences are not 'recollected,' and they finally unite in an atmosphere which is 'tranquil' only in that it is a passive attending upon the event. Of course this is not quite the whole story. There is a great deal, in the writing of poetry, which must be conscious and deliberate. In fact, the bad poet is usually unconscious where he ought to be conscious, and conscious where he ought to be unconscious. Both errors tend to make him 'personal.' Poetry is not a turning loose of emotion, but an escape from emotion; it is not the expression of personality, but an escape from personality. But, of course, only those who have personality and emotions know what it means to want to escape from these things.

III

ὁ δὲ νοῦς ἴσως θειότερόν τι καὶ ἀπαθές στιν.[7]

This essay proposes to halt at the frontier of metaphysics or mysticism, and confine itself to such practical conclusions as can be applied by the responsible person interested in poetry. To divert interest from the poet to the poetry is a laudable aim: for it would conduce to a juster estimation of actual poetry, good and bad. There are many people who appreciate the expression of sincere emotion in verse, and there is a smaller number of people who can appreciate technical excellence. But very few know when there is an expression of *significant* emotion, emotion which has its life in the poem and not in the history of the poet. The emotion of art is impersonal. And the poet cannot reach this impersonality without surrendering himself wholly to the work to be done. And he is not likely to know what is to be done unless he lives in what is not merely the present, but the present moment of the past, unless he is conscious, not of what is dead, but of what is already living.

1919, 1920

---

6. Wordsworth's, *Preface to Lyrical Ballads* (2nd ed., 1800). Wordsworth said that poetry "takes its origin from emotion recollected in tranquility."

7. Aristotle's *De Anima* ("On the Soul") 1.4: "The mind is doubtless something more divine and unimpressionable."

KATHERINE MANSFIELD
1888–1923

Kathleen Mansfield Beauchamp was born in Wellington, New Zealand, daughter of a respected businessman who was later knighted. In 1903 the family came to London, where Kathleen and her sisters entered Queen's College, London, the first institution in England founded expressly for the higher education of women. The family returned to New Zealand, leaving the girls in London, but Mr. and Mrs. Beauchamp brought their daughters home in 1906. By this time Kathleen had written a number of poems, sketches, and stories; and after experimenting with different pen names, she eventually adopted that of Katherine Mansfield. She was restless and ambitious and chafed against the narrowness of middle-class life in New Zealand, at that time still very much a new country in the shadow of the British Empire.

In March 1907 her mother gave a garden party in their Wellington house; a fatal street accident to a neighbor living in a poor quarter nearby nearly spoiled the festive atmosphere of the day. (This was to form the basis of her story *The Garden Party,* but Laura's sensibility as portrayed in that story is subtler and finer than anything the author appears to have herself felt at that time. The story, like so much of Mansfield's reworking of her New Zealand experiences in her last years, represents a kind of atonement for her younger self.) In July 1908 she left again for London and never returned to New Zealand. Very much a rebel, she became involved in a number of love affairs and in 1909 suddenly married G. C. Bowden, a teacher of singing and elocution, but left him the same evening. Shortly afterward she became pregnant by another man and went to Germany to await the birth, but she had a miscarriage there. Her experiences in Germany are told in carefully observed sketches full of ironic detail in her first published book, *In a German Pension* (1911).

In 1910 she briefly resumed life with Bowden, who put her in touch with A. R. Orage, editor of the avant garde periodical *The New Age*. There she published a number of her stories and sketches. At the end of 1911 she met the critic John Middleton Murry, editor of *Rhythm*. She became involved with both Murry and *Rhythm* and lived with Murry fairly continuously for the rest of her life, marrying him in 1918 when Bowden finally divorced her. Mansfield experimented in technique and refined her art in an attempt to achieve a kind of short story that by precision of style and imagery and a symbolic patterning of incident would project insights into certain kinds of experience. The death in World War I in October 1915 of her much-loved younger brother sent her imagination back to their childhood days in New Zealand and in doing so gave a fresh charge and significance to her writing. With the publication of *The Garden Party and Other Stories* in February 1922, Mansfield's place as a master of the modern short story was ensured. But she was now gravely ill with tuberculosis and died suddenly in January 1923 at Fontainebleau, France, where she had gone to try to find a cure by adopting the methods of the controversial mystic George Ivanovich Gurdjieff.

Mansfield proceeded through a variety of literary styles, but her best and most characteristic work was produced in the last years of her short life when she was able to combine incident, image, symbol, and structure in a way comparable with, yet interestingly different from, Joyce's method in *Dubliners*. One late story, *Daughters of the Late Colonel*, shows her working characteristically through suggestion rather than explicit development and achieving meaning through the story's meticulously developed atmosphere. The ability to manipulate time is another quality Mansfield shows in some of her best work: she makes particularly effective use of the unobtrusive flashback, where we find ourselves in an earlier phase of the action without quite knowing how we got there although fully aware of its relevance to the total action and atmosphere.

The Garden Party

And after all the weather was ideal. They could not have had a more perfect day for a garden party if they had ordered it. Windless, warm, the sky without a cloud. Only the blue was veiled with a haze of light gold, as it is sometimes in early summer. The gardener had been up since dawn, mowing the lawns and sweeping them, until the grass and the dark flat rosettes where the daisy plants had been seemed to shine. As for the roses, you could not help feeling they understood that roses are the only flowers that impress people at garden parties; the only flowers that everybody is certain of knowing. Hundreds, yes, literally hundreds, had come out in a single night; the green bushes bowed down as though they had been visited by archangels.

Breakfast was not yet over before the men came to put up the marquee.

'Where do you want the marquee put, mother?'

'My dear child, it's no use asking me. I'm determined to leave everything to you children this year. Forget I am your mother. Treat me as an honoured guest.'

But Meg could not possibly go and supervise the men. She had washed her hair before breakfast, and she sat drinking her coffee in a green turban, with a dark wet curl stamped on each cheek. Jose, the butterfly, always came down in a silk petticoat and a kimono jacket.

'You'll have to go, Laura; you're the artistic one.'

Away Laura flew, still holding her piece of bread-and-butter. It's so delicious to have an excuse for eating out of doors, and besides, she loved having to arrange things; she always felt she could do it so much better than anybody else.

Four men in their shirt-sleeves stood grouped together on the garden path. They carried staves covered with rolls of canvas, and they had big tool-bags slung on their backs. They looked impressive. Laura wished now that she had not got the bread-and-butter, but there was nowhere to put it, and she couldn't possibly throw it away. She blushed and tried to look severe and even a little bit short-sighted as she came up to them.

'Good morning,' she said, copying her mother's voice. But that sounded so fearfully affected that she was ashamed, and stammered like a little girl, 'Oh—er—have you come—is it about the marquee?'

'That's right, miss,' said the tallest of the men, a lanky, freckled fellow, and he shifted his tool-bag, knocked back his straw hat and smiled down at her. 'That's about it.'

His smile was so easy, so friendly that Laura recovered. What nice eyes he had, small, but such a dark blue! And now she looked at the others, they were smiling too. 'Cheer up, we won't bite,' their smile seemed to say. How very nice workmen were! And what a beautiful morning! She mustn't mention the morning; she must be business-like. The marquee.

'Well, what about the lily-lawn? Would that do?'

And she pointed to the lily-lawn with the hand that didn't hold the bread-and-butter. They turned, they stared in the direction. A little fat chap thrust out his under-lip, and the tall fellow frowned.

'I don't fancy it,' said he. 'Not conspicuous enough. You see, with a thing like a marquee,' and he turned to Laura in his easy way, 'you want to put it somewhere where it'll give you a bang slap in the eye, if you follow me.'

Laura's upbringing made her wonder for a moment whether it was quite respectful of a workman to talk to her of bangs slap in the eye. But she did quite follow him.

'A corner of the tennis-court,' she suggested. 'But the band's going to be in one corner.'

'H'm, going to have a band, are you?' said another of the workmen. He was pale. He had a haggard look as his dark eyes scanned the tennis-court. What was he thinking?

'Only a very small band,' said Laura gently. Perhaps he wouldn't mind so much if the band was quite small. But the tall fellow interrupted.

'Look here, miss, that's the place. Against those trees. Over there. That'll do fine.'

Against the karakas. Then the karaka-trees would be hidden. And they were so lovely, with their broad, gleaming leaves, and their clusters of yellow fruit. They were like trees you imagined growing on a desert island, proud, solitary, lifting their leaves and fruits to the sun in a kind of silent splendour. Must they be hidden by a marquee?

They must. Already the men had shouldered their staves and were making for the place. Only the tall fellow was left. He bent down, pinched a sprig of lavender, put his thumb and forefinger to his nose and snuffed up the smell. When Laura saw that gesture she forgot all about the karakas in her wonder at him caring for things like that—caring for the smell of lavender. How many men that she knew would have done such a thing? Oh, how extraordinarily nice workmen were, she thought. Why couldn't she have workmen for friends rather than the silly boys she danced with and who came to Sunday night supper? She would get on much better with men like these.

It's all the fault, she decided, as the tall fellow drew something on the back of an envelope, something that was to be looped up or left to hang, of these absurd class distinctions. Well, for her part, she didn't feel them. Not a bit, not an atom . . . And now there came the chock-chock of wooden hammers. Some one whistled, some one sang out, 'Are you right there, matey?' 'Matey!' The friendliness of it, the—the—Just to prove how happy she was, just to show the tall fellow how at home she felt, and how she despised stupid conventions, Laura took a big bite of her bread-and-butter as she stared at the little drawing. She felt just like a work-girl.

'Laura, Laura, where are you? Telephone, Laura!' a voice cried from the house.

'Coming!' Away she skimmed, over the lawn, up the path, up the steps, across the veranda, and into the porch. In the hall her father and Laurie were brushing their hats ready to go to the office.

'I say, Laura,' said Laurie very fast, 'you might just give a squiz at my coat before this afternoon. See if it wants pressing.'

'I will,' said she. Suddenly she couldn't stop herself. She ran at Laurie and gave him a small, quick squeeze. 'Oh, I do love parties, don't you?' gasped Laura.

'Ra-ther,' said Laurie's warm, boyish voice, and he squeezed his sister too, and gave her a gentle push. 'Dash off to the telephone, old girl.'

The telephone. 'Yes, yes; oh yes. Kitty? Good morning, dear. Come to lunch? Do, dear. Delighted of course. It will only be a very scratch meal—just the sandwich crusts and broken meringue-shells and what's left over. Yes, isn't it a perfect morning? Your white? Oh, I certainly should. One moment—hold the line. Mother's calling.' And Laura sat back. 'What, mother? Can't hear.'

Mrs Sheridan's voice floated down the stairs. 'Tell her to wear that sweet hat she had on last Sunday.'

'Mother says you're to wear that sweet hat you had on last Sunday. Good. One o'clock. Bye-bye.'

Laura put back the receiver, flung her arms over her head, took a deep breath, stretched and let them fall. 'Huh,' she sighed, and the moment after the sigh she sat up quickly. She was still, listening. All the doors in the house seemed to be open. The house was alive with soft, quick steps and running voices. The green baize door that led to the kitchen regions swung open and shut with a muffled thud. And now there came a long, chuckling absurd sound. It was the heavy piano being moved on its stiff castors. But the air! If you stopped to notice, was the air always like this? Little faint winds were playing chase in at the tops of the windows, out at the doors. And there were two tiny spots of sun, one on the inkpot, one on a silver photograph frame, playing too. Darling little spots. Especially the one on the inkpot lid. It was quite warm. A warm little silver star. She could have kissed it.

The front door bell pealed, and there sounded the rustle of Sadie's print skirt on the stairs. A man's voice murmured; Sadie answered, careless, 'I'm sure I don't know. Wait. I'll ask Mrs Sheridan.'

'What is it, Sadie?' Laura came into the hall.

'It's the florist, Miss Laura.'

It was, indeed. There, just inside the door, stood a wide, shallow tray full of pots of pink lilies. No other kind. Nothing but lilies—canna lilies, big pink flowers, wide open, radiant, almost frighteningly alive on bright crimson stems.

'O-oh, Sadie!' said Laura, and the sound was like a little moan. She crouched down as if to warm herself at that blaze of lilies; she felt they were in her fingers, on her lips, growing in her breast.

'It's some mistake,' she said faintly. 'Nobody ever ordered so many. Sadie, go and find mother.'

But at that moment Mrs Sheridan joined them.

'It's quite right,' she said calmly. 'Yes, I ordered them. Aren't they lovely?' She pressed Laura's arm. 'I was passing the shop yesterday, and I saw them in the window. And I suddenly thought for once in my life I shall have enough canna lilies. The garden party will be a good excuse.'

'But I thought you said you didn't mean to interfere,' said Laura. Sadie had gone. The florist's man was still outside at his van. She put her arm round her mother's neck and gently, very gently, she bit her mother's ear.

'My darling child, you wouldn't like a logical mother, would you? Don't do that. Here's the man.'

He carried more lilies still, another whole tray.

'Bank them up, just inside the door, on both sides of the porch, please,' said Mrs Sheridan. 'Don't you agree, Laura?'

'Oh, I *do* mother.'

In the drawing-room Meg, Jose and good little Hans had at last succeeded in moving the piano.

'Now, if we put this chesterfield against the wall and move everything out of the room except the chairs, don't you think?'

'Quite.'

'Hans, move these tables into the smoking-room, and bring a sweeper to take these marks off the carpet and—one moment, Hans—' Jose loved giving orders to the servants, and they loved obeying her. She always made them feel they were taking part in some drama. 'Tell mother and Miss Laura to come here at once.'

'Very good, Miss Jose.'

She turned to Meg. 'I want to hear what the piano sounds like, just in case I'm asked to sing this afternoon. Let's try over "This life is Weary."'

Pom! Ta-ta-ta *Tee*-ta! The piano burst out so passionately that Jose's face changed. She clasped her hands. She looked mournfully and enigmatically at her mother and Laura as they came in.

> This Life is *Wee*-ary,
>   A Tear—a Sigh.
> A Love that *Chan*-ges,
>   This Life is *Wee*-ary,
> A Tear—a Sigh.
> A Love that *Chan*-ges,
> And then . . . Good-bye!

But at the word 'Good-bye,' and although the piano sounded more desperate than ever, her face broke into a brilliant, dreadfully unsympathetic smile.

'Aren't I in good voice, mummy?' she beamed.

> This Life is *Wee*-ary,
> Hope comes to Die.
> A Dream—a *Wa*-kening.

But now Sadie interrupted them. 'What is it, Sadie?'

'If you please, m'm, cook says have you got the flags[1] for the sandwiches?'

'The flags for the sandwiches, Sadie?' echoed Mrs Sheridan dreamily. And the children knew by her face that she hadn't got them. 'Let me see.' And she said to Sadie firmly, 'Tell cook I'll let her have them in ten minutes.'

Sadie went.

'Now, Laura,' said her mother quickly. 'Come with me into the smoking-room. I've got the names[2] somewhere on the back of an envelope. You'll have to write them out for me. Meg, go upstairs this minute and take that wet thing off your head. Jose, run and finish dressing this instant. Do you hear me, children, or shall I have to tell your father when he comes home to-night? And—and, Jose, pacify cook if you do go into the kitchen, will you? I'm terrified of her this morning.'

The envelope was found at last behind the dining-room clock, though how it had got there Mrs Sheridan could not imagine.

---

1. Little paper flags stuck in a plate of small triangular sandwiches indicating what is inside the sandwiches on each plate—an English custom adopted by the New Zealand middle class as a sign of gentility.
2. I.e., the names of the sandwich fillings to be written on each flag.

'One of you children must have stolen it out of my bag, because I remember vividly—cream cheese and lemon-curd. Have you done that?'

'Yes.'

'Egg and—' Mrs Sheridan held the envelope away from her. 'It looks like mice. It can't be mice, can it?'

'Olive, pet,' said Laura, looking over her shoulder.

'Yes, of course, olive. What a horrible combination it sounds. Egg and olive.'

They were finished at last, and Laura took them off to the kitchen. She found Jose there pacifying the cook, who did not look at all terrifying.

'I have never seen such exquisite sandwiches,' said Jose's rapturous voice. 'How many kinds did you say there were, cook? Fifteen?'

'Fifteen, Miss Jose.'

'Well, cook, I congratulate you.'

Cook swept up crusts with the long sandwich knife and smiled broadly.

'Godber's has come,' announced Sadie, issuing out of the pantry. She had seen the man pass the window.

That meant the cream puffs had come. Godber's were famous for their cream puffs. Nobody ever thought of making them at home.

'Bring them in and put them on the table, my girl,' ordered cook.

Sadie brought them in and went back to the door. Of course Laura and Jose were far too grown-up to really care about such things. All the same, they couldn't help agreeing that the puffs looked very attractive. Very. Cook began arranging them, shaking off the extra icing sugar.

'Don't they carry one back to all one's parties?' said Laura.

'I suppose they do,' said practical Jose, who never liked to be carried back. 'They look beautifully light and feathery, I must say.'

'Have one each, my dears,' said cook in her comfortable voice. 'Yer ma won't know.'

Oh, impossible. Fancy cream puffs so soon after breakfast. The very idea made one shudder. All the same, two minutes later Jose and Laura were licking their fingers with that absorbed inward look that only comes from whipped cream.

'Let's go into the garden, out by the back way,' suggested Laura. 'I want to see how the men are getting on with the marquee. They're such awfully nice men.'

But the back door was blocked by cook, Sadie, Godber's man and Hans.

Something had happened.

'Tuk-tuk-tuk,' clucked cook like an agitated hen. Sadie had her hand clapped to her cheek as though she had toothache. Hans's face was screwed up in the effort to understand. Only Godber's man seemed to be enjoying himself; it was his story.

'What's the matter? What's happened?'

'There's been a horrible accident,' said cook. 'A man killed.'

'A man killed! Where? How? When?'

But Godber's man wasn't going to have his story snatched from under his very nose.

'Know those little cottages just below here, miss?' Know them? Of course, she knew them. 'Well, there's a young chap living there, name of Scott, a carter. His horse shied at a traction-engine, corner of Hawke Street this morning, and he was thrown out on the back of his head. Killed.'

'Dead!' Laura stared at Godber's man.

'Dead when they picked him up,' said Godber's man with relish. 'They were taking the body home as I come up here.' And he said to the cook, 'He's left a wife and five little ones.'

'Jose, come here.' Laura caught hold of her sister's sleeve and dragged her through the kitchen to the other side of the green baize door. There she paused and leaned against it. 'Jose!' she said, horrified, 'however are we going to stop everything?'

'Stop everything, Laura!' cried Jose in astonishment. 'What do you mean?'

'Stop the garden party, of course.' Why did Jose pretend?

But Jose was still more amazed. 'Stop the garden party? My dear Laura, don't be so absurd. Of course we can't do anything of the kind. Nobody expects us to. Don't be so extravagant.'

'But we can't possibly have a garden party with a man dead just outside the front gate.'

That really was extravagant, for the little cottages were in a lane to themselves at the very bottom of a steep rise that led up to the house. A broad road ran between. True, they were far too near. They were the greatest possible eyesore, and they had no right to be in that neighbourhood at all. They were little mean dwellings painted a chocolate brown. In the garden patches there was nothing but cabbage stalks, sick hens and tomato cans. The very smoke coming out of their chimneys was poverty-stricken. Little rags and shreds of smoke, so unlike the great silvery plumes that uncurled from the Sheridans' chimneys. Washerwomen lived in the lane and sweeps and a cobbler, and a man whose house-front was studded all over with minute bird-cages. Children swarmed. When the Sheridans were little they were forbidden to set foot there because of the revolting language and of what they might catch. But since they were grown up, Laura and Laurie on their prowls sometimes walked through. It was disgusting and sordid. They came out with a shudder. But still one must go everywhere; one must see everything. So through they went.

'And just think of what the band would sound like to that poor woman,' said Laura.

'Oh, Laura!' Jose began to be seriously annoyed. 'If you're going to stop a band playing every time some one has an accident, you'll lead a very strenuous life. I'm every bit as sorry about it as you. I feel just as sympathetic.' Her eyes hardened. She looked at her sister just as she used to when they were little and fighting together. 'You won't bring a drunken workman back to life by being sentimental,' she said softly.

'Drunk! Who said he was drunk?' Laura turned furiously on Jose. She said, just as they had used to say on those occasions, 'I'm going straight up to tell mother.'

'Do, dear,' cooed Jose.

'Mother, can I come into your room?' Laura turned the big glass doorknob.

'Of course, child. Why, what's the matter? What's given you such a colour?' And Mrs Sheridan turned round from her dressing-table. She was trying on a new hat.

'Mother, a man's been killed,' began Laura.

'Not in the garden?' interrupted her mother.

'No, no!'

'Oh, what a fright you gave me!' Mrs Sheridan sighed with relief, and took off the big hat and held it on her knees.

'But listen, mother,' said Laura. Breathless, half-choking, she told the dreadful story. 'Of course, we can't have our party, can we?' she pleaded. 'The band and everybody arriving. They'd hear us, mother; they're nearly neighbours!'

To Laura's astonishment her mother behaved just like Jose; it was harder to bear because she seemed amused. She refused to take Laura seriously.

'But, my dear child, use your common sense. It's only by accident we've heard of it. If some one had died there normally—and I can't understand how they keep alive in those poky little holes—we should still be having our party, shouldn't we?'

Laura had to say 'yes' to that, but she felt it was all wrong. She sat down on her mother's sofa and pinched the cushion frill.

'Mother, isn't it really terribly heartless of us?' she asked.

'Darling!' Mrs Sheridan got up and came over to her, carrying the hat. Before Laura could stop her she had popped it on. 'My child!' said her mother, 'the hat is yours. It's made for you. It's much too young for me. I have never seen you look such a picture. Look at yourself!' And she held up her hand-mirror.

'But, mother,' Laura began again. She couldn't look at herself; she turned aside.

This time Mrs Sheridan lost patience just as Jose had done.

'You are being very absurd, Laura,' she said coldly. 'People like that don't expect sacrifices from us. And it's not very sympathetic to spoil everybody's enjoyment as you're doing now.'

'I don't understand,' said Laura, and she walked quickly out of the room into her own bedroom. There, quite by chance, the first thing she saw was this charming girl in the mirror, in her black hat trimmed with gold daisies, and a long black velvet ribbon. Never had she imagined she could look like that. Is mother right? she thought. And now she hoped her mother was right. Am I being extravagant? Perhaps it was extravagant. Just for a moment she had another glimpse of that poor woman and those little children, and the body being carried into the house. But it all seemed blurred, unreal, like a picture in the newspaper. I'll remember it again after the party's over, she decided. And somehow that seemed quite the best plan . . .

Lunch was over by half past one. By half past two they were all ready for the fray. The green-coated band had arrived and was established in a corner of the tennis-court.

'My dear!' trilled Kitty Maitland, 'aren't they too like frogs for words? You ought to have arranged them round the pond with the conductor in the middle on a leaf.'

Laurie arrived and hailed them on his way to dress. At the sight of him Laura remembered the accident again. She wanted to tell him. If Laurie agreed with the others, then it was bound to be all right. And she followed him into the hall.

'Laurie!'

'Hallo!' He was half-way upstairs, but when he turned round and saw Laura he suddenly puffed out his cheeks and goggled his eyes at her. 'My word, Laura! You do look stunning,' said Laurie. 'What an absolutely topping hat!'

Laura said faintly 'Is it?' and smiled up at Laurie, and didn't tell him after all.

Soon after that people began coming in streams. The band struck up; the hired waiters ran from the house to the marquee. Wherever you looked there were couples strolling, bending to the flowers, greeting, moving on over the lawn. They were like bright birds that had alighted in the Sheridans' garden for this one afternoon, on their way to—where? Ah, what happiness it is to be with people who all are happy, to press hands, press cheeks, smile into eyes.

'Darling Laura, how well you look!'

'What a becoming hat, child!'

'Laura, you look quite Spanish. I've never seen you look so striking.'

And Laura, glowing, answered softly, 'Have you had tea? Won't you have an ice? The passion-fruit ices really are rather special.' She ran to her father and begged him. 'Daddy darling, can't the band have something to drink?'

And the perfect afternoon slowly ripened, slowly faded, slowly its petals closed.

'Never a more delightful garden party . . .' 'The greatest success . . .' 'Quite the most . . .'

Laura helped her mother with the goodbyes. They stood side by side in the porch till it was all over.

'All over, all over, thank heaven,' said Mrs Sheridan. 'Round up the others, Laura. Let's go and have some fresh coffee. I'm exhausted. Yes, it's been very successful. But oh, these parties, these parties! Why will you children insist on giving parties!' And they all of them sat down in the deserted marquee.

'Have a sandwich, daddy dear. I wrote the flag.'

'Thanks.' Mr Sheridan took a bite and the sandwich was gone. He took another. 'I suppose you didn't hear of a beastly accident that happened to-day?' he said.

'My dear,' said Mrs Sheridan, holding up her hand, 'we did. It nearly ruined the party. Laura insisted we should put it off.'

'Oh, mother!' Laura didn't want to be teased about it.

'It was a horrible affair all the same,' said Mr Sheridan. 'The chap was married too. Lived just below in the lane, and leaves a wife and half a dozen kiddies, so they say.'

An awkward little silence fell. Mrs Sheridan fidgeted with her cup. Really, it was very tactless of father . . .

Suddenly she looked up. There on the table were all those sandwiches, cakes, puffs, all un-eaten, all going to be wasted. She had one of her brilliant ideas.

'I know,' she said. 'Let's make up a basket. Let's send that poor creature some of this perfectly good food. At any rate, it will be the greatest treat for the children. Don't you agree? And she's sure to have neighbours calling in and so on. What a point to have it all ready prepared. Laura!' She jumped up. 'Get me the big basket out of the stairs cupboard.'

'But, mother, do you really think it's a good idea?' said Laura.

Again, how curious, she seemed to be different from them all. To take scraps from their party. Would the poor woman really like that?

'Of course! What's the matter with you today? An hour or two ago you were insisting on us being sympathetic, and now—'

Oh well! Laura ran for the basket. It was filled, it was heaped by her mother.

'Take it yourself, darling,' said she. 'Run down just as you are. No, wait, take the arum lilies too. People of that class are so impressed by arum lilies.'

'The stems will ruin her lace frock,' said practical Jose.

So they would. Just in time. 'Only the basket, then. And, Laura!'—her mother followed her out of the marquee—'don't on any account—'

'What mother?'

No, better not put such ideas into the child's head! 'Nothing! Run along.'

It was just growing dusky as Laura shut their garden gates. A big dog ran by like a shadow. The road gleamed white, and down below in the hollow the little cottages were in deep shade. How quiet it seemed after the afternoon. Here she was going down the hill to somewhere where a man lay dead, and she couldn't realize it. Why couldn't she? She stopped a minute. And it seemed to her that kisses, voices, tinkling spoons, laughter, the smell of crushed grass were somehow inside her. She had no room for anything else. How strange! She looked up at the pale sky, and all she thought was, 'Yes, it was the most successful.'

Now the broad road was crossed. The lane began, smoky and dark. Women in shawls and men's tweed caps hurried by. Men hung over the palings; the children played in the doorways. A low hum came from the mean little cottages. In some of them there was a flicker of light, and a shadow, crab-like, moved across the window. Laura bent her head and hurried on. She wished now she had put on a coat. How her frock shone! And the big hat with the velvet streamer—if only it was another hat! Were the people looking at her? They must be. It was a mistake to have come; she knew all along it was a mistake. Should she go back even now?

No, too late. This was the house. It must be. A dark knot of people stood outside. Beside the gate an old, old woman with a crutch sat in a chair, watching. She had her feet on a newspaper. The voices stopped as Laura drew near. The group parted. It was as though she was expected, as though they had known she was coming here.

Laura was terribly nervous. Tossing the velvet ribbon over her shoulder, she said to a woman standing by, 'Is this Mrs Scott's house?' and the woman, smiling queerly, said, 'It is, my lass.'

Oh, to be away from this! She actually said, 'Help me, God,' as she walked up the tiny path and knocked. To be away from those staring eyes, or to be covered up in anything, one of those women's shawls even. I'll just leave the basket and go, she decided. I shan't even wait for it to be emptied.

Then the door opened. A little woman in black showed in the gloom.

Laura said, 'Are you Mrs Scott?' But to her horror the woman answered, 'Walk in please, miss,' and she was shut in the passage.

'No,' said Laura, 'I don't want to come in. I only want to leave this basket. Mother sent—'

The little woman in the gloomy passage seemed not to have heard her. 'Step this way, please, miss,' she said in an oily voice, and Laura followed her.

She found herself in a wretched little low kitchen, lighted by a smoky lamp. There was a woman sitting before the fire.

'Em,' said the little creature who had let her in. 'Em! It's a young lady.' She turned to Laura. She said meaningly, 'I'm her sister, Miss. You'll excuse 'er, won't you?'

'Oh, but of course!' said Laura. 'Please, please don't disturb her. I—I only want to leave—'

But at that moment the woman at the fire turned round. Her face, puffed up, red, with swollen eyes and swollen lips, looked terrible. She seemed as though she couldn't understand why Laura was there. What did it mean? Why was this stranger standing in the kitchen with a basket? What was it all about? And the poor face puckered up again.

'All right, my dear,' said the other. 'I'll thenk the young lady.'

And again she began, 'You'll excuse her, miss, I'm sure,' and her face, swollen too, tried an oily smile.

Laura only wanted to get out, to get away. She was back in the passage. The door opened. She walked straight through into the bedroom where the dead man was lying.

'You'd like a look at 'im, wouldn't you?' said Em's sister, and she brushed past Laura over to the bed. 'Don't be afraid, my lass,'—and now her voice sounded fond and sly, and fondly she drew down the sheet—' 'e looks a picture. There's nothing to show. Come along, my dear.'

Laura came.

There lay a young man, fast asleep—sleeping so soundly, so deeply, that he was far, far away from them both. Oh, so remote, so peaceful. He was dreaming. Never wake him up again. His head was sunk in the pillow, his eyes were closed; they were blind under the closed eyelids. He was given up to his dream. What did garden parties and baskets and lace frocks matter to him? He was far from all those things. He was wonderful, beautiful. While they were laughing and while the band was playing, this marvel had come to the lane. Happy . . . happy . . . All is well, said that sleeping face. This is just as it should be. I am content.

But all the same you had to cry, and she couldn't go out of the room without saying something to him. Laura gave a loud childish sob.

'Forgive my hat,' she said.

And this time she didn't wait for Em's sister. She found her way out of the door, down the path, past all those dark people. At the corner of the lane she met Laurie.

He stepped out of the shadow. 'Is that you, Laura?'

'Yes.'

'Mother was getting anxious. Was it all right?'

'Yes, quite. Oh, Laurie!' She took his arm, she pressed up against him.

'I say, you're not crying, are you?' asked her brother.

Laura shook her head. She was.

Laurie put his arm round her shoulder. 'Don't cry,' he said in his warm, loving voice. 'Was it awful?'

'No,' sobbed Laura. 'It was simply marvellous. But, Laurie—' She stopped, she looked at her brother. 'Isn't life,' she stammered, 'isn't life—' But what life was she couldn't explain. No matter. He quite understood.

'Isn't it, darling?' said Laurie.

1921   1922

SAMUEL BECKETT
1906–1989

Samuel Beckett, born near Dublin in what is now the Republic of Ireland, received a B.A. from Trinity College, Dublin, and, after teaching English at the École Normale Supérieure in Paris for two years, returned there to take his M.A. in 1931. He gave up teaching in 1932 to write, although, having produced an insightful essay on the early stages of James Joyce's *Finnegans Wake* in 1929, he also worked as Joyce's secretary and translator. From the mid-1940s he generally wrote in French and subsequently translated some of his work into an eloquent, Irish-inflected English. His early novels, *Murphy* (1938) and *Watt* (1953), and the trilogy, *Molloy* (1951), *Malone Dies* (1951), and *The Unnameable* (1953), have been hailed as masterpieces and precursors of postmodern fiction; but he is best known for his dramatic work, and in particular for *Waiting for Godot* (1953). He received the Nobel Prize for Literature in 1969.

Not much happens in a Beckett play; there is very little plot, very little incident, and very little characterization. Characters engage in dialogue or dialectical monologues that go nowhere. There is no progression, no development, no resolution. Rambling dialogue and repetitive actions enact the lack of a fixed center, of meaning, of purpose, in the lives depicted. Yet the characters do persist in their habitual, almost ritualistic, activities; they do go on talking, even if only to themselves. So long as there is a stream of discourse, of thought and will, so long as there is a consciousness to question its own meaning and purpose, there is life. In spite of a reiterated theme of nonexistence, the characters go on existing—if minimally. The plays restrict the acting space to a room, to a dustbin, to a mound in which the actor is buried; characters are physically confined or disabled, until *Not I* presents the most minimal embodiment of human consciousness available to theatrical representation: a disembodied mouth.

In *Endgame,* irritable, resentful, spiteful characters talk of leaving, dying, or otherwise ending but simply continue in their peevish, complaining round. Like all of Beckett's work, the play defies definitive interpretation. It draws on vaudeville and other comic traditions but juxtaposes these with the intellectual and the grotesque. Beckett's work shares this tragicomedic quality with Absurdist drama such as Ionesco's *The Bald Soprano* (1958), which, like *Waiting for Godot* and *Endgame,* disrupts the conventions of realist drama. The exaggerated symbolism of Absurdism refuses to provide hierarchies of significance. In *Endgame,* is it significant that Hamm wears a close-fitting cap like that of a judge? Is the gaff symbolic of anything, or merely a piece of flotsam from the wreckage of a life? We do not know; and our attempts to determine or affix significance, constantly thwarted by the playful texts, may represent our need to look for underlying meaning in a universe made up only of surfaces. Like much Absurdist drama, Beckett's plays break and disrupt the conventions of realism to deny the audience the comfortable security of stability and to draw attention to their own fictionality—but also to provide laughs, sometimes at the audience's expense.

Endgame[1]

For Roger Blin

THE CHARACTERS

NAGG
NELL
HAMM
CLOV

Bare interior.
Grey light.
Left and right back, high up, two small windows, curtains drawn.
Front right, a door. Hanging near door, its face to wall, a picture.
Front left, touching each other, covered with an old sheet, two ashbins.
Centre, in an armchair on castors, covered with an old sheet, HAMM.
Motionless by the door, his eyes fixed on HAMM, CLOV. *Very red face.*
Brief tableau.

[CLOV *goes and stands under window left. Stiff, staggering walk. He looks up at window left. He turns and looks at window right. He goes and stands under window right. He looks up at window right. He turns and looks at window left. He goes out, comes back immediately with a small step-ladder, carries it over and sets it down under window left, gets up on it, draws back curtain. He gets down, takes six steps (for example) towards window right, goes back for ladder, carries it over and sets it down under window right, gets up on it, draws back curtain. He gets down, takes three steps towards window left, goes back for ladder, carries it over and sets it down under window left, gets up on it, looks out of window. Brief laugh. He gets down, takes one step towards window right, goes back for ladder, carries it over and sets it down under window right, gets up on it, looks out of window. Brief laugh. He gets down, goes with ladder towards ashbins, halts, turns, carries back ladder and sets it down under window right, goes to ashbins, removes sheet covering them, folds it over his arm. He raises one lid, stoops and looks into bin. Brief laugh. He closes lid. Same with other bin. He goes to* HAMM, *removes sheet covering him, folds it over his arm. In a dressing-gown, a stiff toque[2] on his head, a large blood-stained handkerchief over his face, a whistle hanging from his neck, a rug over his knees, thick socks on his feet,* HAMM *seems to be asleep.* CLOV *looks him over. Brief laugh. He goes to door, halts, turns towards auditorium.*]

CLOV   [*Fixed gaze, tonelessly.*] Finished, it's finished, nearly finished, it must be nearly finished. [*Pause.*] Grain upon grain, one by one, and one day, suddenly, there's a heap, a little heap, the impossible heap. [*Pause.*] I can't be punished any more. [*Pause.*] I'll go now to my kitchen, ten feet by ten feet by ten feet, and wait for him to whistle me. [*Pause.*] Nice dimensions, nice proportions, I'll lean on the table, and look at the wall, and wait for him to whistle me.

---

1. Translated by the author.   2. Small cap with no brim.

[*He remains a moment motionless, then goes out. He comes back imme-diately, goes to window right, takes up the ladder and carries it out. Pause.* HAMM *stirs. He yawns under the handkerchief. He removes the handkerchief from his face. Very red face. Black glasses.*]

HAMM   Me—[*He yawns.*]—to play.[3] [*He holds the handkerchief spread out before him.*] Old Stancher![4] [*He takes off his glasses, wipes his eyes, his face, the glasses, puts them on again, folds the handkerchief and puts it back neatly in the breast-pocket of his dressing-gown. He clears his throat, joins the tips of his fingers.*] Can there be misery—[*He yawns.*]—loftier than mine? No doubt. Formerly. But now? [*Pause.*] My father? [*Pause.*] My mother? [*Pause.*] My . . . dog? [*Pause.*] Oh I am willing to believe they suffer as much as such creatures can suffer. But does that mean their sufferings equal mine? No doubt. [*Pause.*] No, all is a—[*He yawns.*]—bsolute, [*Proudly.*] the bigger a man is the fuller he is. [*Pause. Gloomily.*] And the emptier. [*He sniffs.*] Clov! [*Pause.*] No, alone. [*Pause.*] What dreams! Those forests! [*Pause.*] Enough, it's time it ended, in the shelter too. [*Pause.*] And yet I hesitate, I hesitate to . . . to end. Yes, there it is, it's time it ended and yet I hesitate to—[*He yawns.*]—to end. [*Yawns.*] God, I'm tired, I'd be better off in bed. [*He whistles. Enter* CLOV *immediately. He halts beside the chair.*] You pollute the air! [*Pause.*] Get me ready, I'm going to bed.

CLOV   I've just got you up.

HAMM   And what of it?

CLOV   I can't be getting you up and putting you to bed every five minutes, I have things to do. [*Pause.*]

HAMM   Did you ever see my eyes?

CLOV   No.

HAMM   Did you never have the curiosity, while I was sleeping, to take off my glasses and look at my eyes?

CLOV   Pulling back the lids? [*Pause.*] No.

HAMM   One of these days I'll show them to you. [*Pause.*] It seems they've gone all white. [*Pause.*] What time is it?

CLOV   The same as usual.

HAMM   [*Gesture towards window right.*] Have you looked?

CLOV   Yes.

HAMM   Well?

CLOV   Zero.

HAMM   It'd need to rain.

CLOV   It won't rain. [*Pause.*]

HAMM   Apart from that, how do you feel?

CLOV   I don't complain.

HAMM   You feel normal?

CLOV   [*Irritably.*] I tell you I don't complain.

HAMM   I feel a little queer. [*Pause.*] Clov!

CLOV   Yes.

HAMM   Have you not had enough?

CLOV   Yes! [*Pause.*] Of what?

---

3. Hamm announces that it is his move, as it were in a game of chess, of which the final stage is called the "endgame."

4. Handkerchief that stanches (checks the flow of) blood.

HAMM   Of this . . . this . . . thing.

CLOV   I always had. [*Pause*.] Not you?

HAMM   [*Gloomily*.] Then there's no reason for it to change.

CLOV   It may end. [*Pause*.] All life long the same questions, the same
answers.

HAMM   Get me ready. [CLOV *does not move*.] Go and get the sheet. [CLOV
does not move.] Clov!

CLOV   Yes.

HAMM   I'll give you nothing more to eat.

CLOV   Then we'll die.

HAMM   I'll give you just enough to keep you from dying. You'll be hungry
all the time.

CLOV   Then we won't die. [*Pause*.] I'll go and get the sheet. [*He goes
towards the door*.]

HAMM   No! [CLOV *halts*.] I'll give you one biscuit per day. [*Pause*.] One
and a half. [*Pause*.] Why do you stay with me?

CLOV   Why do you keep me?

HAMM   There's no one else.

CLOV   There's nowhere else. [*Pause*.]

HAMM   You're leaving me all the same.

CLOV   I'm trying.

HAMM   You don't love me.

CLOV   No.

HAMM   You loved me once.

CLOV   Once!

HAMM   I've made you suffer too much. [*Pause*.] Haven't I?

CLOV   It's not that.

HAMM   [*Shocked*.] I haven't made you suffer too much?

CLOV   Yes!

HAMM   [*Relieved*.] Ah you gave me a fright! [*Pause. Coldly*.] Forgive me.
[*Pause. Louder*.] I said, Forgive me.

CLOV   I heard you. [*Pause*.] Have you bled?

HAMM   Less. [*Pause*.] Is it not time for my pain-killer?

CLOV   No. [*Pause*.]

HAMM   How are your eyes?

CLOV   Bad.

HAMM   How are your legs?

CLOV   Bad.

HAMM   But you can move.

CLOV   Yes.

HAMM   [*Violently*.] Then move! [CLOV *goes to back wall, leans against it
with his forehead and hands*.] Where are you?

CLOV   Here.

HAMM   Come back! [CLOV *returns to his place beside the chair*.] Where are
you?

CLOV   Here.

HAMM   Why don't you kill me?

CLOV   I don't know the combination of the cupboard. [*Pause*.]

HAMM   Go and get two bicycle-wheels.

CLOV   There are no more bicycle-wheels.

HAMM   What have you done with your bicycle?

CLOV   I never had a bicycle.

HAMM   The thing is impossible.

CLOV   When there were still bicycles I wept to have one. I crawled at your feet. You told me to go to hell. Now there are none.

HAMM   And your rounds? When you inspected my paupers. Always on foot?

CLOV   Sometimes on horse. [*The lid of one of the bins lifts and the hands of* NAGG *appear, gripping the rim. Then his head emerges. Nightcap. Very white face.* NAGG *yawns, then listens.*] I'll leave you, I have things to do.

HAMM   In your kitchen?

CLOV   Yes.

HAMM   Outside of here it's death. [*Pause.*] All right, be off. [*Exit* CLOV. *Pause.*] We're getting on.

NAGG   Me Pap![5]

HAMM   Accursed progenitor![6]

NAGG   Me pap!

HAMM   The old folks at home! No decency left! Guzzle, guzzle, that's all they think of. [*He whistles. Enter* CLOV. *He halts beside the chair.*] Well! I thought you were leaving me.

CLOV   Oh not just yet, not just yet.

NAGG   Me pap!

HAMM   Give him his pap.

CLOV   There's no more pap.

HAMM   [*To* NAGG.] Do you hear that? There's no more pap. You'll never get any more pap.

NAGG   I want me pap!

HAMM   Give him a biscuit. [*Exit* CLOV.] Accursed fornicator! How are your stumps?

NAGG   Never mind me stumps. [*Enter* CLOV *with biscuit.*]

CLOV   I'm back again, with the biscuit. [*He gives biscuit to* NAGG *who fingers, it, sniffs it.*]

NAGG   [*Plaintively.*] What is it?

CLOV   Spratt's medium.[7]

NAGG   [*As before.*] It's hard! I can't!

HAMM   Bottle him! [CLOV *pushes* NAGG *back into the bin, closes the lid.*]

CLOV   [*Returning to his place beside the chair.*] If age but knew!

HAMM   Sit on him!

CLOV   I can't sit.

HAMM   True. And I can't stand.

CLOV   So it is.

HAMM   Every man his speciality. [*Pause.*] No phone calls? [*Pause.*] Don't we laugh?

CLOV   [*After reflection.*] I don't feel like it.

HAMM   [*After reflection.*] Not I. [*Pause.*] Clov!

CLOV   Yes.

HAMM   Nature has forgotten us.

CLOV   There's no more nature.

5. Mushy food.   7. Brand name of a biscuit (cookie).
6. Parent.

HAMM No more nature! You exaggerate.

CLOV In the vicinity.

HAMM But we breathe, we change! We lose our hair, our teeth! Our bloom! Our ideals!

CLOV Then she hasn't forgotten us.

HAMM But you say there is none.

CLOV [*Sadly.*] No one that ever lived ever thought so crooked as we.

HAMM We do what we can.

CLOV We shouldn't. [*Pause.*]

HAMM You're a bit of all right,[8] aren't you?

CLOV A smithereen.[9] [*Pause.*]

HAMM This is slow work. [*Pause.*] Is it not time for my pain-killer?

CLOV No. [*Pause.*] I'll leave you, I have things to do.

HAMM In your kitchen?

CLOV Yes.

HAMM What, I'd like to know.

CLOV I look at the wall.

HAMM The wall! And what do you see on your wall? Mene, mene?[1] Naked bodies?

CLOV I see my light dying.

HAMM Your light dying! Listen to that! Well, it can die just as well here, *your* light. Take a look at me and then come back and tell me what you think of *your* light. [*Pause.*]

CLOV You shouldn't speak to me like that. [*Pause.*]

HAMM [*Coldly.*] Forgive me. [*Pause. Louder.*] I said, Forgive me.

CLOV I heard you. [*The lid of* NAGG's *bin lifts. His hands appear, gripping the rim. Then his head emerges. In his mouth the biscuit. He listens.*]

HAMM Did your seeds come up?

CLOV No.

HAMM Did you scratch round them to see if they had sprouted?

CLOV They haven't sprouted.

HAMM Perhaps it's still too early.

CLOV If they were going to sprout they would have sprouted. [*Violently.*] They'll never sprout! [*Pause.* NAGG *takes biscuit in his hand.*]

HAMM This is not much fun. [*Pause.*] But that's always the way at the end of the day, isn't it, Clov?

CLOV Always.

HAMM It's the end of the day like any other day, isn't it, Clov?

CLOV Looks like it. [*Pause.*]

HAMM [*Anguished.*] What's happening, what's happening?

CLOV Something is taking its course. [*Pause.*]

HAMM All right, be off. [*He leans back in his chair, remains motionless.* CLOV *does not move, heaves a great groaning sigh.* HAMM *sits up.*] I thought I told you to be off.

CLOV I'm trying. [*He goes to door, halts.*] Ever since I was whelped.[2] [*Exit* CLOV.]

HAMM We're getting on.

---

8. You're pretty good (British slang).
9. A little bit.
1. "Mene mene, tekel, upharsin": words written by a heavenly hand on the wall during the feast of

Balshazzar, king of Babylon. Translated as "Thou art weighed in the balance and found wanting," it foretells his ruin (Daniel 5.25–28).
2. Born (usually applied to puppies: whelps).

[*He leans back in his chair, remains motionless.* NAGG *knocks on the lid of the other bin. Pause. He knocks harder. The lid lifts and the hands of* NELL *appear, gripping the rim. Then her head emerges. Lace cap. Very white face.*]

NELL What is it, my pet? [*Pause.*] Time for love?

NAGG Were you asleep?

NELL Oh no!

NAGG Kiss me.

NELL We can't.

NAGG Try. [*Their heads strain towards each other, fail to meet, fall apart again.*]

NELL Why this farce, day after day? [*Pause.*]

NAGG I've lost me tooth.

NELL When?

NAGG I had it yesterday.

NELL [*Elegiac.*[3]] Ah yesterday! [*They turn painfully towards each other.*]

NAGG Can you see me?

NELL Hardly. And you?

NAGG What?

NELL Can you see me?

NAGG Hardly.

NELL So much the better, so much the better.

NAGG Don't say that. [*Pause.*] Our sight has failed.

NELL Yes. [*Pause. They turn away from each other.*]

NAGG Can you hear me?

NELL Yes. And you?

NAGG Yes. [*Pause.*] Our hearing hasn't failed.

NELL Our what?

NAGG Our hearing.

NELL No. [*Pause.*] Have you anything else to say to me?

NAGG Do you remember—

NELL No.

NAGG When we crashed on our tandem[4] and lost our shanks. [*They laugh heartily.*]

NELL It was in the Ardennes. [*They laugh less heartily.*]

NAGG On the road to Sedan.[5] [*They laugh still less heartily.*] Are you cold?

NELL Yes, perished. And you?

NAGG [*Pause.*] I'm freezing. [*Pause.*] Do you want to go in?

NELL Yes.

NAGG Then go in. [NELL *does not move*] Why don't you go in?

NELL I don't know. [*Pause.*]

NAGG Has he changed your sawdust?

NELL It isn't sawdust. [*Pause. Wearily.*] Can you not be a little accurate, Nagg?

NAGG Your sand then. It's not important.

NELL It is important. [*Pause.*]

3. As though lamenting something lost.
4. A bicycle made for two.
5. Town in northern France where the French Army was defeated in 1870 during the Franco-

Prussian War. Ardennes is a forest in northern France, which was the scene of fierce fighting in both World Wars.

NAGG   It was sawdust once.

NELL   Once!

NAGG   And now it's sand. [*Pause.*] From the shore. [*Pause. Impatiently.*]
Now it's sand he fetches from the shore.

NELL   Now it's sand.

NAGG   Has he changed yours?

NELL   No.

NAGG   Nor mine. [*Pause.*] I won't have it! [*Pause. Holding up the biscuit.*]
Do you want a bit?

NELL   No. [*Pause.*] Of what?

NAGG   Biscuit. I've kept you half. [*He looks at the biscuit. Proudly.*] Three
quarters. For you. Here. [*He proffers the biscuit.*] No? [*Pause.*] Do you
not feel well?

HAMM   [*Wearily.*] Quiet, quiet, you're keeping me awake. [*Pause.*] Talk
softer. [*Pause.*] If I could sleep I might make love. I'd go into the woods.
My eyes would see . . . the sky, the earth. I'd run, run, they wouldn't
catch me. [*Pause.*] Nature! [*Pause.*] There's something dripping in my
head. [*Pause.*] A heart, a heart in my head. [*Pause.*]

NAGG   [*Soft.*] Do you hear him? A heart in his head! [*He chuckles cautiously.*]

NELL   One mustn't laugh at those things, Nagg. Why must you always
laugh at them?

NAGG   Not so loud!

NELL   [*Without lowering her voice.*] Nothing is funnier than unhappiness,
I grant you that. But—

NAGG   [*Shocked.*] Oh!

NELL   Yes, yes, it's the most comical thing in the world. And we laugh, we
laugh, with a will, in the beginning. But it's always the same thing. Yes,
it's like the funny story we have heard too often, we still find it funny,
but we don't laugh any more. [*Pause.*] Have you anything else to say to
me?

NAGG   No.

NELL   Are you quite sure? [*Pause.*] Then I'll leave you.

NAGG   Do you not want your biscuit? [*Pause.*] I'll keep it for you. [*Pause.*]
I thought you were going to leave me.

NELL   I am going to leave you.

NAGG   Could you give me a scratch before you go?

NELL   No. [*Pause.*] Where?

NAGG   In the back.

NELL   No. [*Pause.*] Rub yourself against the rim.

NAGG   It's lower down. In the hollow.

NELL   What hollow?

NAGG   The hollow! [*Pause.*] Could you not? [*Pause.*] Yesterday you
scratched me there.

NELL   [*Elegiac.*] Ah yesterday!

NAGG   Could you not? [*Pause.*] Would you like me to scratch you? [*Pause.*]
Are you crying again?

NELL   I was trying. [*Pause.*]

HAMM   Perhaps it's a little vein. [*Pause.*]

NAGG   What was that he said?

NELL   Perhaps it's a little vein.

NAGG   What does that mean? [*Pause.*] That means nothing. [*Pause.*] Will I tell you the story of the tailor?

NELL   No. [*Pause.*] What for?

NAGG   To cheer you up.

NELL   It's not funny.

NAGG   It always made you laugh. [*Pause.*] The first time I thought you'd die.

NELL   It was on Lake Como.[6] [*Pause.*] One April afternoon. [*Pause.*] Can you believe it?

NAGG   What?

NELL   That we once went out rowing on Lake Como. [*Pause.*] One April afternoon.

NAGG   We had got engaged the day before.

NELL   Engaged!

NAGG   You were in such fits that we capsized. By rights we should have been drowned.

NELL   It was because I felt happy.

NAGG   [*Indignant.*] It was not, it was not, it was my story and nothing else. Happy! Don't you laugh at it still? Every time I tell it. Happy!

NELL   It was deep, deep. And you could see down to the bottom. So white. So clean.

NAGG   Let me tell it again. [*Raconteur's voice.*] An Englishman, needing a pair of striped trousers in a hurry for the New Year festivities, goes to his tailor who takes his measurements. [*Tailor's voice.*] "That's the lot, come back in four days, I'll have it ready." Good. Four days later. [*Tailor's voice.*] "So sorry, come back in a week, I've made a mess of the seat." Good, that's all right, a neat seat can be very ticklish. A week later. [*Tailor's voice.*] "Frightfully sorry, come back in ten days. I've made a hash of the crotch." Good, can't be helped, a snug crotch is always a teaser. Ten days later. [*Tailor's voice.*] "Dreadfully sorry, come back in a fortnight, I've made a balls of the fly." Good, at a pinch, a smart fly is a stiff proposition. [*Pause. Normal voice.*] I never told it worse. [*Pause. Gloomy.*] I tell this story worse and worse. [*Pause. Raconteur's voice.*] Well, to make it short, the bluebells are blowing and he ballockses[7] the buttonholes. [*Customer's voice.*] "God damn you to hell, Sir, no, it's indecent, there are limits! In six days, do you hear me, six days, God made the world. Yes Sir, no less Sir, the WORLD! And you are not bloody well capable of making me a pair of trousers in three months!" [*Tailor's voice, scandalised.*] "But my dear Sir, my dear Sir, look—[*Disdainful gesture, disgustedly.*]—at the world—[*pause*] and look—[*Loving gesture, proudly.*]—at my TROUSERS!"

    [*Pause. He looks at* NELL *who has remained impassive, her eyes unseeing, breaks into a high forced laugh, cuts it short, pokes his head towards* NELL, *launches his laugh again.*]

HAMM   Silence!

    [NAGG *starts, cuts short his laugh.*]

NELL   You could see down to the bottom.

HAMM   [*Exasperated.*] Have you not finished? Will you never finish? [*With

6. Large lake in northern Italy.   7. Botches.

sudden fury.] Will this never finish? [NAGG *disappears into his bin, closes the lid behind him.* NELL *does not move. Frenziedly.*] My kingdom for a nightman![8] [*He whistles. Enter* CLOV.] Clear away this muck! Chuck it in the sea! [CLOV *goes to bins, halts.*]

NELL   So white.

HAMM   What? What's she blathering about? [CLOV *stoops, takes* NELL's *hand, feels her pulse.*]

NELL   [*To* CLOV.] Desert! [CLOV *lets go her hand, pushes her back in the bin, closes the lid.*]

CLOV   [*Returning to his place beside the chair.*] She has no pulse.

HAMM   What was she drivelling about?

CLOV   She told me to go away, into the desert.

HAMM   Damn busybody! Is that all?

CLOV   No.

HAMM   What else?

CLOV   I didn't understand.

HAMM   Have you bottled her?

CLOV   Yes.

HAMM   Are they both bottled?

CLOV   Yes.

HAMM   Screw down the lids. [CLOV *goes towards door.*] Time enough. [CLOV *halts.*] My anger subsides, I'd like to pee.

CLOV   [*With alacrity.*] I'll go and get the catheter. [*He goes towards door.*]

HAMM   Time enough. [CLOV *halts.*] Give me my pain-killer.

CLOV   It's too soon. [*Pause.*] It's too soon on top of your tonic, it wouldn't act.

HAMM   In the morning they brace you up and in the evening they calm you down. Unless it's the other way round. [*Pause.*] That old doctor, he's dead naturally?

CLOV   He wasn't old.

HAMM   But he's dead?

CLOV   Naturally. [*Pause.*] *You* ask *me* that? [*Pause.*]

HAMM   Take me for a little turn. [CLOV *goes behind the chair and pushes it forward.*] Not too fast! [CLOV *pushes chair.*] Right round the world! [CLOV *pushes chair.*] Hug the walls, then back to the centre again. [CLOV *pushes chair.*] I was right in the centre, wasn't I?

CLOV   [*Pushing.*] Yes.

HAMM   We'd need a proper wheel-chair. With big wheels. Bicycle wheels! [*Pause.*] Are you hugging?

CLOV   [*Pushing.*] Yes.

HAMM   [*Groping for wall.*] It's a lie! Why do you lie to me?

CLOV   [*Bearing closer to wall.*] There! There!

HAMM   Stop! [CLOV *stops chair close to back wall.* HAMM *lays his hand against wall.*] Old wall! [*Pause.*] Beyond is the . . . other hell. [*Pause. Violently.*] Closer! Closer! Up against!

CLOV   Take away your hand. [HAMM *withdraws his hand.* CLOV *rams chair against wall.*] There! [HAMM *leans towards wall, applies his ear to it.*]

HAMM   Do you hear? [*He strikes the wall with his knuckles.*] Do you hear?

---

8. A collector of nightsoil (excrement). Cf. Shakespeare's *Richard III* 5.4.7: "A horse! a horse! My kingdom for a horse!"

Hollow bricks! [*He strikes again.*] All that's hollow! [*Pause. He straightens up. Violently.*] That's enough. Back!

CLOV   We haven't done the round.

HAMM   Back to my place! [CLOV *pushes chair back to centre.*] Is that my place?

CLOV   Yes, that's your place.

HAMM   Am I right in the centre?

CLOV   I'll measure it.

HAMM   More or less! More or less!

CLOV   [*Moving chair slightly.*] There!

HAMM   I'm more or less in the centre?

CLOV   I'd say so.

HAMM   You'd say so! Put me right in the centre!

CLOV   I'll go and get the tape.

HAMM   Roughly! Roughly! [CLOV *moves chair slightly.*] Bang in the centre!

CLOV   There! [*Pause.*]

HAMM   I feel a little too far to the left. [CLOV *moves chair slightly.*] Now I feel a little too far to the right. [CLOV *moves chair slightly.*] I feel a little too far forward. [CLOV *moves chair slightly.*] Now I feel a little too far back. [CLOV *moves chair slightly.*] Don't stay there, [*I.e., behind the chair.*] you give me the shivers. [CLOV *returns to his place beside the chair.*]

CLOV   If I could kill him I'd die happy. [*Pause.*]

HAMM   What's the weather like?

CLOV   As usual.

HAMM   Look at the earth.

CLOV   I've looked.

HAMM   With the glass?

CLOV   No need of the glass.

HAMM   Look at it with the glass.

CLOV   I'll go and get the glass. [*Exit* CLOV.]

HAMM   No need of the glass! [*Enter* CLOV *with telescope.*]

CLOV   I'm back again, with the glass. [*He goes to window right, looks up at it.*] I need the steps.

HAMM   Why? Have you shrunk? [*Exit* CLOV *with telescope.*] I don't like that, I don't like that. [*Enter* CLOV *with ladder, but without telescope.*]

CLOV   I'm back again, with the steps. [*He sets down ladder under window right, gets up on it, realises he has not the telescope, gets down.*] I need the glass. [*He goes towards door.*]

HAMM   [*Violently.*] But you have the glass!

CLOV   [*Halting, violently.*] No, I haven't the glass! [*Exit* CLOV.]

HAMM   This is deadly. [*Enter* CLOV *with telescope. He goes towards ladder.*]

CLOV   Things are livening up. [*He gets up on ladder, raises the telescope, lets it fall.*] I did it on purpose. [*He gets down, picks up the telescope, turns it on auditorium.*] I see . . . a multitude . . . in transports . . . of joy.[9] [*Pause.*] That's what I call a magnifier. [*He lowers the telescope, turns towards* HAMM.] Well? Don't we laugh?

9. Cf. Revelation 7.9–10: "After this I beheld, and lo, a great multitude, which . . . cried with a loud voice . . . Salvation."

HAMM   [*After reflection.*] I don't.

CLOV   [*After reflection.*] Nor I. [*He gets up on ladder, turns the telescope on the without.*] Let's see. [*He looks, moving the telescope.*] Zero . . . [*He looks.*] . . . zero . . . [*He looks.*] . . . and zero.

HAMM   Nothing stirs. All is—

CLOV   Zer—

HAMM   [*Violently.*] Wait till you're spoke to! [*Normal voice.*] All is . . . all is . . . all is what? [*Violently.*] All is what?

CLOV   What all is? In a word? Is that what you want to know? Just a moment. [*He turns the telescope on the without, looks, lowers the telescope, turns towards* HAMM.] Corpsed. [*Pause.*] Well? Content?

HAMM   Look at the sea.

CLOV   It's the same.

HAMM   Look at the ocean! [CLOV *gets down, takes a few steps towards window left, goes back for ladder, carries it over and sets it down under window left, gets up on it, turns the telescope on the without, looks at length. He starts, lowers the telescope, examines it, turns it again on the without.*]

CLOV   Never seen anything like that!

HAMM   [*Anxious.*] What? A sail? A fin? Smoke?

CLOV   [*Looking.*] The light is sunk.

HAMM   [*Relieved.*] Pah! We all knew that.

CLOV   [*Looking.*] There was a bit left.

HAMM   The base.

CLOV   [*Looking.*] Yes.

HAMM   And now?

CLOV   [*Looking.*] All gone.

HAMM   No gulls?

CLOV   [*Looking.*] Gulls!

HAMM   And the horizon? Nothing on the horizon?

CLOV   [*Lowering the telescope, turning towards* HAMM, *exasperated.*] What in God's name could there be on the horizon? [*Pause.*]

HAMM   The waves, how are the waves?

CLOV   The waves? [*He turns the telescope on the waves.*] Lead.

HAMM   And the sun?

CLOV   [*Looking.*] Zero.

HAMM   But it should be sinking. Look again.

CLOV   [*Looking.*] Damn the sun.

HAMM   Is it night already then?

CLOV   [*Looking.*] No.

HAMM   Then what is it?

CLOV   [*Looking.*] Grey. [*Lowering the telescope, turning towards* HAMM, *louder.*] Grey! [*Pause. Still louder.*] GRREY! [*Pause. He gets down, approaches* HAMM *from behind, whispers in his ear.*]

HAMM   [*Starting.*] Grey! Did I hear you say grey?

CLOV   Light black. From pole to pole.

HAMM   You exaggerate. [*Pause.*] Don't stay there, you give me the shivers. [CLOV *returns to his place beside the chair.*]

CLOV   Why this farce, day after day?

HAMM   Routine. One never knows. [*Pause.*] Last night I saw inside my breast. There was a big sore.

CLOV   Pah! You saw your heart.

HAMM   No, it was living. [*Pause. Anguished.*] Clov!

CLOV   Yes.

HAMM   What's happening?

CLOV   Something is taking its course. [*Pause.*]

HAMM   Clov!

CLOV   [*Impatiently.*] What is it?

HAMM   We're not beginning to . . . to . . . mean something?

CLOV   Mean something! You and I, mean something! [*Brief laugh.*] Ah that's a good one!

HAMM   I wonder. [*Pause.*] Imagine if a rational being came back to earth, wouldn't he be liable to get ideas into his head if he observed us long enough. [*Voice of rational being.*] Ah, good, now I see what it is, yes, now I understand what they're at! [CLOV *starts, drops the telescope and begins to scratch his belly with both hands. Normal voice.*] And without going so far as that, we ourselves . . . [*With emotion.*] . . . we ourselves . . . at certain moments . . . [*Vehemently.*] To think perhaps it won't all have been for nothing!

CLOV   [*Anguished, scratching himself.*] I have a flea!

HAMM   A flea! Are there still fleas?

CLOV   On me there's one. [*Scratching.*] Unless it's a crablouse.

HAMM   [*Very perturbed.*] But humanity might start from there all over again! Catch him, for the love of God!

CLOV   I'll go and get the powder. [*Exit* CLOV.]

HAMM   A flea! This is awful! What a day! [*Enter* CLOV *with a sprinkling-tin.*]

CLOV   I'm back again, with the insecticide.

HAMM   Let him have it! [CLOV *loosens the top of his trousers, pulls it forward and shakes powder into the aperture. He stoops, looks, waits, starts, frenziedly shakes more powder, stoops, looks, waits.*]

CLOV   The bastard!

HAMM   Did you get him?

CLOV   Looks like it. [*He drops the tin and adjusts his trousers.*] Unless he's laying doggo.

HAMM   Laying! Lying you mean. Unless he's *lying* doggo.

CLOV   Ah? One says lying? One doesn't say laying?

HAMM   Use your head, can't you. If he was laying we'd be bitched.

CLOV   Ah. [*Pause.*] What about that pee?

HAMM   I'm having it.

CLOV   Ah that's the spirit, that's the spirit! [*Pause.*]

HAMM   [*With ardour.*] Let's go from here, the two of us! South! You can make a raft and the currents will carry us away, far away, to other . . . mammals!

CLOV   God forbid!

HAMM   Alone, I'll embark alone! Get working on that raft immediately. Tomorrow I'll be gone for ever.

CLOV   [*Hastening towards door.*] I'll start straight away.

HAMM   Wait! [CLOV *halts.*] Will there be sharks, do you think?

CLOV   Sharks? I don't know. If there are there will be. [*He goes towards door.*]

HAMM Wait! [CLOV *halts.*] Is it not yet time for my pain-killer?

CLOV [*Violently.*] No! [*He goes towards door.*]

HAMM Wait! [CLOV *halts.*] How are your eyes?

CLOV Bad.

HAMM But you can see.

CLOV All I want.

HAMM How are your legs?

CLOV Bad.

HAMM But you can walk.

CLOV I come . . . and go.

HAMM In my house. [*Pause. With prophetic relish.*] One day you'll be blind, like me. You'll be sitting there, a speck in the void, in the dark, for ever, like me. [*Pause.*] One day you'll say to yourself, I'm tired, I'll sit down, and you'll go and sit down. Then you'll say, I'm hungry, I'll get up and get something to eat. But you won't get up. You'll say, I shouldn't have sat down, but since I have I'll sit on a little longer, then I'll get up and get something to eat. But you won't go up and you won't get anything to eat. [*Pause.*] You'll look at the wall a while, then you'll say, I'll close my eyes, perhaps have a little sleep, after that I'll feel better, and you'll close them. And when you open them again there'll be no wall any more. [*Pause.*] Infinite emptiness will be all around you, all the resurrected dead of all the ages wouldn't fill it, and there you'll be like a little bit of grit in the middle of the steppe.[1] [*Pause.*] Yes, one day you'll know what it is, you'll be like me, except that you won't have anyone with you, because you won't have had pity on anyone and because there won't be anyone left to have pity on. [*Pause.*]

CLOV It's not certain. [*Pause.*] And there's one thing you forget.

HAMM Ah?

CLOV I can't sit down.

HAMM [*Impatiently.*] Well you'll lie down then, what the hell! Or you'll come to a standstill, simply stop and stand still, the way you are now. One day you'll say, I'm tired, I'll stop. What does the attitude matter? [*Pause.*]

CLOV So you all want me to leave you.

HAMM Naturally.

CLOV Then I'll leave you.

HAMM You can't leave us.

CLOV Then I won't leave you. [*Pause.*]

HAMM Why don't you finish us? [*Pause.*] I'll tell you the combination of the cupboard if you promise to finish me.

CLOV I couldn't finish you.

HAMM Then you won't finish me. [*Pause.*]

CLOV I'll leave you, I have things to do.

HAMM Do you remember when you came here?

CLOV No. Too small, you told me.

HAMM Do you remember your father?

CLOV [*Wearily.*] Same answer. [*Pause.*] You've asked me these questions millions of times.

---

1. Level grassy plain devoid of forest, especially in southeast Europe and Siberia.

HAMM   I love the old questions. [*With fervour.*] Ah the old questions, the old answers, there's nothing like them! [*Pause.*] It was I was a father to you.

CLOV   Yes. [*He looks at* HAMM *fixedly.*] You were that to me.

HAMM   My house a home for you.

CLOV   Yes. [*He looks about him.*] This was that for me.

HAMM   [*Proudly.*] But for me, [*Gesture towards himself.*] no father. But for Hamm, [*Gesture towards surroundings.*] no home. [*Pause.*]

CLOV   I'll leave you.

HAMM   Did you ever think of one thing?

CLOV   Never.

HAMM   That here we're down in a hole. [*Pause.*] But beyond the hills? Eh? Perhaps it's still green. Eh? [*Pause.*] Flora! Pomona! [*Ecstatically.*] Ceres!² [*Pause.*] Perhaps you won't need to go very far.

CLOV   I can't go very far. [*Pause*] I'll leave you.

HAMM   Is my dog ready?

CLOV   He lacks a leg.

HAMM   Is he silky?

CLOV   He's a kind of Pomeranian.

HAMM   Go and get him.

CLOV   He lacks a leg.

HAMM   Go and get him! [*Exit* CLOV.] We're getting on. [*Enter* CLOV *holding by one of its three legs a black toy dog.*]

CLOV   Your dogs are here. [*He hands the dog to* HAMM *who feels it, fondles it.*]

HAMM   He's white, isn't he?

CLOV   Nearly.

HAMM   What do you mean, nearly? Is he white or isn't he?

CLOV   He isn't. [*Pause.*]

HAMM   You've forgotten the sex.

CLOV   [*Vexed.*] But he isn't finished. The sex goes on at the end. [*Pause.*]

HAMM   You haven't put on his ribbon.

CLOV   [*Angrily.*] But he isn't finished, I tell you! First you finish your dog and then you put on his ribbon! [*Pause.*]

HAMM   Can he stand?

CLOV   I don't know.

HAMM   Try. [*He hands the dog to* CLOV *who places it on the ground.*] Well?

CLOV   Wait! [*He squats down and tries to get the dog to stand on its three legs, fails, lets it go. The dog falls on its side.*]

HAMM   [*Impatiently.*] Well?

CLOV   He's standing.

HAMM   [*Groping for the dog.*] Where? Where is he? [CLOV *holds up the dog in a standing position.*]

CLOV   There. [*He takes* HAMM's *hand and guides it towards the dog's head.*]

HAMM   [*His hand on the dog's head.*] Is he gazing at me?

CLOV   Yes.

HAMM   [*Proudly.*] As if he were asking me to take him for a walk?

---

2. In Roman mythology, respectively, the goddesses of flowers, fruit, and crops.

CLOV   If you like.

HAMM   [*As before.*] Or as if he were begging me for a bone. [*He withdraws his hand.*] Leave him like that, standing there imploring me. [CLOV *straightens up. The dog falls on its side.*]

CLOV   I'll leave you.

HAMM   Have you had your visions?

CLOV   Less.

HAMM   Is Mother Pegg's light on?

CLOV   Light! How could anyone's light be on?

HAMM   Extinguished!

CLOV   Naturally it's extinguished. If it's not on it's extinguished.

HAMM   No, I mean Mother Pegg.

CLOV   But naturally she's extinguished! [*Pause.*] What's the matter with you today?

HAMM   I'm taking my course. [*Pause.*] Is she buried?

CLOV   Buried! Who would have buried her?

HAMM   You.

CLOV   Me! Haven't I enough to do without burying people?

HAMM   But you'll bury me.

CLOV   No I won't bury you. [*Pause.*]

HAMM   She was bonny once, like a flower of the field. [*With reminiscent leer.*] And a great one for the men!

CLOV   We too were bonny—once. It's a rare thing not to have been bonny—once. [*Pause.*]

HAMM   Go and get the gaff.[3] [CLOV *goes to door, halts.*]

CLOV   Do this, do that, and I do it. I never refuse. Why?

HAMM   You're not able to.

CLOV   Soon I won't do it any more.

HAMM   You won't be able to any more. [*Exit* CLOV.] Ah the creatures, the creatures, everything has to be explained to them. [*Enter* CLOV *with gaff.*]

CLOV   Here's your gaff. Stick it up. [*He gives the gaff to* HAMM *who, wielding it like a puntpole,[4] tries to move his chair.*]

HAMM   Did I move?

CLOV   No. [HAMM *throws down the gaff.*]

HAMM   Go and get the oilcan.

CLOV   What for?

HAMM   To oil the castors.

CLOV   I oiled them yesterday.

HAMM   Yesterday! What does that mean? Yesterday!

CLOV   [*Violently.*] That means that bloody awful day, long ago, before this bloody awful day. I use the words you taught me. If they don't mean anything any more, teach me others. Or let me be silent. [*Pause.*]

HAMM   I once knew a madman who thought the end of the world had come. He was a painter—and engraver. I had a great fondness for him. I used to go and see him, in the asylum. I'd take him by the hand and drag him to the window. Look! There! All that rising corn! And there!

---

3. Barbed fishing spear.
4. Long pole, pushed against the bottom of a river to propel a punt (a shallow, flat-bottomed boat).

Look! The sails of the herring fleet! All that loveliness! [*Pause.*] He'd snatch away his hand and go back into his corner. Appalled. All he had seen was ashes. [*Pause.*] He alone had been spared. [*Pause.*] Forgotten. [*Pause.*] It appears the case is . . . was not so . . . so unusual.

CLOV A madman! When was that?

HAMM Oh way back, way back, you weren't in the land of the living.

CLOV God be with the days! [*Pause.* HAMM *raises his toque.*]

HAMM I had a great fondness for him. [*Pause. He puts on his toque again.*] He was a painter—and engraver.

CLOV There are so many terrible things.

HAMM No, no, there are not so many now. [*Pause.*] Clov!

CLOV Yes.

HAMM Do you not think this has gone on long enough?

CLOV Yes! [*Pause.*] What?

HAMM This . . . this . . . thing.

CLOV I've always thought so. [*Pause.*] You not?

HAMM [*Gloomily.*] Then it's a day like any other day.

CLOV As long as it lasts. [*Pause.*] All life long the same inanities.

HAMM I can't leave you.

CLOV I know. And you can't follow me. [*Pause.*]

HAMM If you leave me how shall I know?

CLOV [*Briskly.*] Well you simply whistle me and if I don't come running it means I've left you. [*Pause.*]

HAMM You won't come and kiss me goodbye?

CLOV Oh I shouldn't think so. [*Pause.*]

HAMM But you might be merely dead in your kitchen.

CLOV The result would be the same.

HAMM Yes, but how would I know, if you were merely dead in your kitchen?

CLOV Well . . . sooner or later I'd start to stink.

HAMM You stink already. The whole place stinks of corpses.

CLOV The whole universe.

HAMM [*Angrily.*] To hell with the universe. [*Pause.*] Think of something.

CLOV What?

HAMM An idea, have an idea. [*Angrily.*] A bright idea!

CLOV Ah good. [*He starts pacing to and fro, his eyes fixed on the ground, his hands behind his back. He halts.*] The pains in my legs! It's unbeliev-able! Soon I won't be able to think any more.

HAMM You won't be able to leave me. [CLOV *resumes his pacing.*] What are you doing?

CLOV Having an idea. [*He paces.*] Ah! [*He halts.*]

HAMM What a brain! [*Pause.*] Well?

CLOV Wait! [*He meditates. Not very convinced.*] Yes . . . [*Pause. More convinced.*] Yes! [*He raises his head.*] I have it! I set the alarm. [*Pause.*]

HAMM This is perhaps not one of my bright days, but frankly—

CLOV You whistle me. I don't come. The alarm rings. I'm gone. It doesn't ring. I'm dead. [*Pause.*]

HAMM Is it working? [*Pause. Impatiently.*] The alarm, is it working?

CLOV Why wouldn't it be working?

HAMM Because it's worked too much.

CLOV But it's hardly worked at all.

HAMM [*Angrily.*] Then because it's worked too little!

CLOV I'll go and see. [*Exit* CLOV. *Brief ring of alarm off. Enter* CLOV *with alarm-clock. He holds it against* HAMM's *ear and releases alarm. They listen to it ringing to the end. Pause.*] Fit to wake the dead! Did you hear it?

HAMM Vaguely.

CLOV The end is terrific!

HAMM I prefer the middle. [*Pause.*] Is it not time for my pain-killer?

CLOV No! [*He goes to door, turns.*] I'll leave you.

HAMM It's time for my story. Do you want to listen to my story?

CLOV No.

HAMM Ask my father if he wants to listen to my story. [CLOV *goes to bins, raises the lid of* NAGG's, *stoops, looks into it. Pause. He straightens up.*]

CLOV He's asleep.

HAMM Wake him. [CLOV *stoops, wakes* NAGG *with the alarm. Unintelligible words.* CLOV *straightens up.*]

CLOV He doesn't want to listen to your story.

HAMM I'll give him a bon-bon.[5] [CLOV *stoops. As before.*]

CLOV He wants a sugar-plum.

HAMM He'll get a sugar-plum. [CLOV *stoops. As before.*]

CLOV It's a deal. [*He goes towards door.* NAGG's *hands appear, gripping the rim. Then the head emerges.* CLOV *reaches door, turns.*] Do you believe in the life to come?

HAMM Mine was always that. [*Exit* CLOV.] Got him that time!

NAGG I'm listening.

HAMM Scoundrel! Why did you engender me?

NAGG I didn't know.

HAMM What? What didn't you know?

NAGG That it'd be you. [*Pause.*] You'll give me a sugar-plum?

HAMM After the audition.

NAGG You swear?

HAMM Yes.

NAGG On what?

HAMM My honour. [*Pause. They laugh heartily.*]

NAGG Two.

HAMM One.

NAGG One for me and one for—

HAMM One! Silence! [*Pause.*] Where was I? [*Pause. Gloomily.*] It's finished, we're finished. [*Pause.*] Nearly finished. [*Pause.*] There'll be no more speech. [*Pause.*] Something dripping in my head, ever since the fontanelles.[6] [*Stifled hilarity of* NAGG.] Splash, splash, always on the same spot. [*Pause.*] Perhaps it's a little vein. [*Pause.*] A little artery. [*Pause. More animated.*] Enough of that, it's story time, where was I? [*Pause. Narrative tone.*] The man came crawling towards me, on his belly. Pale, wonderfully pale and thin, he seemed on the point of—[*Pause. Normal tone.*] No, I've done that bit. [*Pause. Narrative tone.*] I calmly filled my pipe—the meerschaum, lit it with . . . let us say a vesta,[7] drew a few

5. Candy (French).
6. Membranous space in infant's skull at the angles of the parietal bones.

7. Vesta is the brand name of a type of match (from Vesta, Roman goddess of the hearth).

puffs. Aah! [*Pause.*] Well, what is it you want? [*Pause.*] It was an extraordinarily bitter day, I remember, zero by the thermometer. But considering it was Christmas Eve there was nothing . . . extra-ordinary about that. Seasonable weather, for once in a way. [*Pause.*] Well, what ill wind blows you my way? He raised his face to me, black with mingled dirt and tears. [*Pause. Normal tone.*] That should do it. [*Narrative tone.*] No, no, don't look at me, don't look at me. He dropped his eyes and mumbled something, apologies I presume. [*Pause.*] I'm a busy man, you know, the final touches, before the festivities, you know what it is. [*Pause. Forcibly.*] Come on now, what is the object of this invasion? [*Pause.*] It was a glorious bright day, I remember, fifty by the heliometer,[8] but already the sun was sinking down into the . . . down among the dead. [*Normal tone.*] Nicely put, that. [*Narrative tone.*] Come on now, come on, present your petition and let me resume my labours. [*Pause. Normal tone.*] There's English for you. Ah well . . . [*Narrative tone.*] It was then he took the plunge. It's my little one, he said. Tsstss, a little one, that's bad. My little boy, he said, as if the sex mattered. Where did he come from? He named the hole. A good half-day, on horse. What are you insinuating? That the place is still inhabited? No no, not a soul, except himself and the child—assuming he existed. Good. I enquired about the situation at Kov,[9] beyond the gulf. Not a sinner. Good. And you expect me to believe you have left your little one back there, all alone, and alive into the bargain? Come now! [*Pause.*] It was a howling wild day, I remember, a hundred by the anemometer.[1] The wind was tearing up the dead pines and sweeping them . . . away. [*Pause. Normal tone.*] A bit feeble, that. [*Narrative tone.*] Come on, man, speak up, what is you want from me, I have to put up my holly. [*Pause.*] Well to make it short it finally transpired that what he wanted from me was . . . bread for his brat? Bread? But I have no bread, it doesn't agree with me. Good. Then perhaps a little corn? [*Pause. Normal tone.*] That should do it. [*Narrative tone.*] Corn, yes, I have corn, it's true, in my granaries. But use your head. I give you some corn, a pound, a pound and a half, you bring it back to your child and you make him—if he's still alive—a nice pot of porridge, [NAGG *reacts.*] a nice pot and a half of porridge, full of nourishment. Good. The colours come back into his little cheeks—perhaps. And then? [*Pause.*] I lost patience. [*Violently.*] Use your head, can't you, use your head, you're on earth, there's no cure for that! [*Pause.*] It was an exceedingly dry day, I remember, zero by the hygrometer. Ideal weather, for my lumbago.[2] [*Pause. Violently.*] But what in God's name do you imagine? That the earth will awake in spring? That the rivers and seas will run with fish again? That there's manna in heaven still for imbeciles like you? [*Pause.*] Gradually I cooled down, sufficiently at least to ask him how long he had taken on the way. Three whole days. Good. In what condition he had left the child. Deep in sleep. [*Forcibly.*] But deep in what sleep, deep in what sleep already? [*Pause.*] Well to make it short I finally offered to take him into my service. He had touched a chord. And then I imagined

---

8. Literally, a sun meter.
9. Conceivably, the town of Kova in southern Siberia (except that it has no gulf); more probably, Hamm's invention.

1. A wind meter.
2. Rheumatic pain in lumbar region of the lower back. "Hygrometer": a moisture meter.

already that I wasn't much longer for this world. [*He laughs. Pause.*] Well? [*Pause.*] Well? Here if you were careful you might die a nice natural death, in peace and comfort. [*Pause.*] Well? [*Pause.*] In the end he asked me would I consent to take in the child as well—if he were still alive. [*Pause.*] It was the moment I was waiting for. [*Pause.*] Would I consent to take in the child . . . [*Pause.*] I can see him still, down on his knees, his hands flat on the ground, glaring at me with his mad eyes, in defiance of my wishes. [*Pause. Normal tone.*] I'll soon have finished with this story. [*Pause.*] Unless I bring in other characters. [*Pause.*] But where would I find them? [*Pause.*] Where would I look for them? [*Pause. He whistles. Enter* CLOV.] Let us pray to God.

NAGG   Me sugar-plum!

CLOV   There's a rat in the kitchen!

HAMM   A rat! Are there still rats?

CLOV   In the kitchen there's one.

HAMM   And you haven't exterminated him?

CLOV   Half. You disturbed us.

HAMM   He can't get away?

CLOV   No.

HAMM   You'll finish him later. Let us pray to God.

CLOV   Again!

NAGG   Me sugar-plum!

HAMM   God first! [*Pause.*] Are you right?

CLOV   [*Resigned.*] Off we go.

HAMM   [*To* NAGG.] And you?

NAGG   [*Clasping his hands, closing his eyes, in a gabble.*] Our Father which art—

HAMM   Silence! In silence! Where are your manners? [*Pause.*] Off we go. [*Attitudes of prayer. Silence. Abandoning his attitude, discouraged.*] Well?

CLOV   [*Abandoning his attitude.*] What a hope! And you?

HAMM   Sweet damn all! [*To* NAGG.] And you?

NAGG   Wait! [*Pause. Abandoning his attitude.*] Nothing doing!

HAMM   The bastard! He doesn't exist!

CLOV   Not yet.

NAGG   Me sugar-plum!

HAMM   There are no more sugar-plums! [*Pause.*]

NAGG   It's natural. After all I'm your father. It's true if it hadn't been me it would have been someone else. But that's no excuse. [*Pause.*] Turkish Delight,[3] for example, which no longer exists, we all know that, there is nothing in the world I love more. And one day I'll ask you for some, in return for a kindness, and you'll promise it to me. One must live with the times. [*Pause.*] Whom did you call when you were a tiny boy, and were frightened, in the dark? Your mother? No. Me. We let you cry. Then we moved you out of earshot, so that we might sleep in peace. [*Pause.*] I was asleep, as happy as a king, and you woke me up to have me listen to you. It wasn't indispensable, you didn't really need to have me listen to you. [*Pause.*] I hope the day will come when you'll really need to have me listen to you, and need to hear my voice, any voice. [*Pause.*] Yes, I

3. A sticky sweet candy (originally from Turkey).

hope I'll live till then, to hear you calling me like when you were a tiny boy, and were frightened, in the dark, and I was your only hope. [*Pause.* NAGG *knocks on lid of* NELL's *bin. Pause.*] Nell! [*Pause. He knocks louder. Pause. Louder.*] Nell! [*Pause.* NAGG *sinks back into his bin, closes the lid behind him. Pause.*]

HAMM   Our revels now are ended.[4] [*He gropes for the dog*] The dog's gone.

CLOV   He's not a real dog, he can't go.

HAMM   [*Groping.*] He's not there.

CLOV   He's lain down.

HAMM   Give him up to me. [CLOV *picks up the dog and gives it to* HAMM. HAMM *holds it in his arms. Pause.* HAMM *throws away the dog.*] Dirty brute! [CLOV *begins to pick up the objects lying on the ground.*] What are you doing?

CLOV   Putting things in order. [*He straightens up. Fervently.*] I'm going to clear everything away! [*He starts picking up again.*]

HAMM   Order!

CLOV   [*Straightening up.*] I love order. It's my dream. A world where all would be silent and still and each thing in its last place, under the last dust. [*He starts picking up again.*]

HAMM   [*Exasperated.*] What in God's name do you think you are doing?

CLOV   [*Straightening up.*] I'm doing my best to create a little order.

HAMM   Drop it! [CLOV *drops the objects he has picked up.*]

CLOV   After all, there or elsewhere. [*He goes towards door.*]

HAMM   [*Irritably.*] What's wrong with your feet?

CLOV   My feet?

HAMM   Tramp! Tramp!

CLOV   I must have put on my boots.

HAMM   Your slippers were hurting you? [*Pause.*]

CLOV   I'll leave you.

HAMM   No!

CLOV   What is there to keep me here?

HAMM   The dialogue. [*Pause.*] I've got on with my story. [*Pause.*] I've got on with it well. [*Pause. Irritably.*] Ask me where I've got to.

CLOV   Oh, by the way, your story?

HAMM   [*Surprised.*] What story?

CLOV   The one you've been telling yourself all your days.

HAMM   Ah you mean my chronicle?

CLOV   That's the one. [*Pause.*]

HAMM   [*Angrily.*] Keep going, can't you, keep going!

CLOV   You've got on with it, I hope.

HAMM   [*Modestly.*] Oh not very far, not very far. [*He sighs.*] There are days like that, one isn't inspired. [*Pause.*] Nothing you can do about it, just wait for it to come. [*Pause.*] No forcing, no forcing, it's fatal. [*Pause.*] I've got on with it a little all the same. [*Pause.*] Technique, you know. [*Pause. Irritably.*] I say I've got on with it a little all the same.

CLOV   [*Admiringly.*] Well I never! In spite of everything you were able to get on with it!

HAMM   [*Modestly.*] Oh not very far, you know, not very far, but nevertheless, better than nothing.

---

4. Words spoken by Prospero in Shakespeare's *The Tempest* 4.1.148.

CLOV   Better than nothing! Is it possible?

HAMM   I'll tell you how it goes. He comes crawling on his belly—

CLOV   Who?

HAMM   What?

CLOV   Who do you mean, he?

HAMM   Who do I mean! Yet another.

CLOV   Ah him! I wasn't sure.

HAMM   Crawling on his belly, whining for bread for his brat. He's offered a job as gardener. Before—[CLOV *bursts out laughing.*] What is there so funny about that?

CLOV   A job as gardener!

HAMM   Is that what tickles you?

CLOV   It must be that.

HAMM   It wouldn't be the bread?

CLOV   Or the brat. [*Pause.*]

HAMM   The whole thing is comical, I grant you that. What about having a good guffaw the two of us together?

CLOV   [*After reflection.*] I couldn't guffaw again today.

HAMM   [*After reflection.*] Nor I. [*Pause.*] I continue then. Before accepting with gratitude he asks if he may have his little boy with him.

CLOV   What age?

HAMM   Oh tiny.

CLOV   He would have climbed the trees.

HAMM   All the little odd jobs.

CLOV   And then he would have grown up.

HAMM   Very likely. [*Pause.*]

CLOV   Keep going, can't you, keep going!

HAMM   That's all. I stopped there. [*Pause.*]

CLOV   Do you see how it goes on.

HAMM   More or less.

CLOV   Will it not soon be the end?

HAMM   I'm afraid it will.

CLOV   Pah! You'll make up another.

HAMM   I don't know. [*Pause.*] I feel rather drained. [*Pause.*] The prolonged creative effort. [*Pause.*] If I could drag myself down to the sea! I'd make a pillow of sand for my head and the tide would come.

CLOV   There's no more tide. [*Pause.*]

HAMM   Go and see is she dead. [CLOV *goes to bins, raises the lid of* NELL's, *stoops, looks into it. Pause.*]

CLOV   Looks like it. [*He closes the lid, straightens up.* HAMM *raises his toque. Pause. He puts it on again.*]

HAMM   [*With his hand to his toque.*] And Nagg? [CLOV *raises lid of* NAGG's *bin, stoops, looks into it. Pause.*]

CLOV   Doesn't look like it. [*He closes the lid, straightens up.*]

HAMM   [*Letting go his toque.*] What's he doing? [CLOV *raises lid of* NAGG's *bin, stoops, looks into it. Pause.*]

CLOV   He's crying. [*He closes lid, straightens up.*]

HAMM   Then he's living. [*Pause.*] Did you ever have an instant of happiness?

CLOV   Not to my knowledge. [*Pause.*]

HAMM   Bring me under the window. [CLOV *goes towards chair.*] I want to feel the light on my face. [CLOV *pushes chair*.] Do you remember, in the beginning, when you took me for a turn? You used to hold the chair too high. At every step you nearly tipped me out. [*With senile quaver*.] Ah great fun, we had, the two of us, great fun. [*Gloomily*.] And then we got into the way of it. [CLOV *stops the chair under window right*.] There already? [*Pause. He tilts back his head*.] Is it light?

CLOV It isn't dark.

HAMM [*Angrily*] I'm asking you is it light.

CLOV Yes. [*Pause*.]

HAMM The curtain isn't closed?

CLOV No.

HAMM What window is it?

CLOV The earth.

HAMM I knew it! [*Angrily*.] But there's no light there! The other! [CLOV *stops the chair under window left*. HAMM *tilts back his head*.] That's what I call light! [*Pause*.] Feels like a ray of sunshine. [*Pause*.] No?

CLOV No.

HAMM It isn't a ray of sunshine I feel on my face?

CLOV No. [*Pause*.]

HAMM Am I very white? [*Pause. Angrily*.] I'm asking you am I very white!

CLOV Not more so than usual. [*Pause*.]

HAMM Open the window.

CLOV What for?

HAMM I want to hear the sea.

CLOV You wouldn't hear it.

HAMM Even if you opened the window?

CLOV No.

HAMM Then it's not worth while opening it?

CLOV No.

HAMM [*Violently*] Then open it! [CLOV *gets up on the ladder, opens the window. Pause*.] Have you opened it?

CLOV Yes. [*Pause*.]

HAMM You swear you've opened it?

CLOV Yes. [*Pause*.]

HAMM Well . . . ! [*Pause*.] It must be very calm. [*Pause. Violently*.] I'm asking you is it very calm!

CLOV Yes.

HAMM It's because there are no more navigators. [*Pause*.] You haven't much conversation all of a sudden. Do you not feel well?

CLOV I'm cold.

HAMM What month are we? [*Pause*.] Close the window, we're going back. [CLOV *closes the window, gets down, pushes the chair back to its place, remains standing behind it, head bowed*.] Don't stay there, you give me the shivers! [CLOV *returns to his place beside the chair*.] Father! [*Pause. Louder*.] Father! [*Pause*.] Go and see did he hear me. [CLOV *goes to* NAGG's *bin, raises the lid, stoops. Unintelligible words*. CLOV *straightens up*.]

CLOV Yes.

HAMM Both times? [CLOV *stoops. As before*.]

CLOV Once only.

HAMM   The first time or the second? [CLOV *stoops. As before.*]

CLOV   He doesn't know.

HAMM   It must have been the second.

CLOV   We'll never know. [*He closes lid.*]

HAMM   Is he still crying?

CLOV   No.

HAMM   The dead go fast. [*Pause.*] What's he doing?

CLOV   Sucking his biscuit.

HAMM   Life goes on. [CLOV *returns to his place beside the chair.*] Give me a rug. I'm freezing.

CLOV   There are no more rugs. [*Pause.*]

HAMM   Kiss me. [*Pause.*] Will you not kiss me?

CLOV   No.

HAMM   On the forehead.

CLOV   I won't kiss you anywhere. [*Pause.*]

HAMM   [*Holding out his hand.*] Give me your hand at least. [*Pause.*] Will you not give me your hand?

CLOV   I won't touch you. [*Pause.*]

HAMM   Give me the dog. [CLOV *looks round for the dog.*] No!

CLOV   Do you not want your dog?

HAMM   No.

CLOV   Then I'll leave you.

HAMM   [*Head bowed, absently.*] That's right. [CLOV *goes to door, turns.*]

CLOV   If I don't kill that rat he'll die.

HAMM   [*As before.*] That's right. [*Exit* CLOV. *Pause.*] Me to play. [*He takes out his handkerchief, unfolds it, holds it spread out before him.*] We're getting on. [*Pause.*] You weep, and weep, for nothing, so as not to laugh, and little by little . . . you begin to grieve. [*He folds the handkerchief, puts it back in his pocket, raises his head.*] All those I might have helped. [*Pause.*] Helped! [*Pause.*] Saved. [*Pause.*] Saved! [*Pause.*] The place was crawling with them! [*Pause. Violently.*] Use your head, can't you, use your head, you're on earth, there's no cure for that! [*Pause.*] Get out of here and love one another! Lick your neighbour as yourself![5] [*Pause. Calmer.*] When it wasn't bread they wanted it was crumpets. [*Pause. Violently.*] Out of my sight and back to your petting parties! [*Pause.*] All that, all that! [*Pause.*] Not even a real dog! [*Calmer.*] The end is in the beginning and yet you go on. [*Pause.*] Perhaps I could go on with my story, end it and begin another. [*Pause.*] Perhaps I could throw myself out on the floor. [*He pushes himself painfully off his seat, falls back again.*] Dig my nails into the cracks and drag myself forward with my fingers. [*Pause.*] It will be the end and there I'll be, wondering what can have brought it on and wondering what can have . . . [*He hesitates.*] . . . why it was so long coming. [*Pause.*] There I'll be, in the old shelter, alone against the silence and . . . [*He hesitates.*] . . . the stillness. If I can hold my peace, and sit quiet, it will be all over with sound, and motion, all over and done with. [*Pause.*] I'll have called my father and I'll have called my . . . [*He hesitates.*] . . . my son. And even twice, or three times, in case they shouldn't have heard me, the first time, or the second. [*Pause.*] I'll

---

5. Parody of Christ's instruction: "Thou shalt love thy neighbor as thyself" (Matthew 19.19).

say to myself, He'll come back. [*Pause.*] And then? [*Pause.*] And then?
[*Pause.*] He couldn't, he has gone too far. [*Pause.*] And then? [*Pause.
Very agitated.*] All kinds of fantasies! That I'm being watched! A rat!
Steps! Breath held and then . . . [*He breathes out.*] Then babble, babble,
words, like the solitary child who turns himself into children, two, three,
so as to be together, and whisper together, in the dark. [*Pause.*] Moment
upon moment, pattering down, like the millet grains of . . . [*He hesitates.*]
. . . that old Greek,[6] and all life long you wait for that to mount up to a
life. [*Pause. He opens his mouth to continue, renounces.*] Ah let's get it
over! [*He whistles. Enter* CLOV *with alarm-clock. He halts beside the
chair.*] What? Neither gone nor dead?

CLOV   In spirit only.
HAMM   Which?
CLOV   Both.
HAMM   Gone from me you'd be dead.
CLOV   And vice versa.
HAMM   Outside of here it's death! [*Pause.*] And the rat?
CLOV   He's got away.
HAMM   He can't go far. [*Pause. Anxious.*] Eh?
CLOV   He doesn't need to go far. [*Pause.*]
HAMM   Is it not time for my pain-killer?
CLOV   Yes.
HAMM   Ah! At last! Give it to me! Quick! [*Pause.*]
CLOV   There's no more pain-killer. [*Pause.*]
HAMM   [*Appalled.*] Good . . . ! [*Pause.*] No more pain-killer!
CLOV   No more pain-killer. You'll never get any more pain-killer. [*Pause.*]
HAMM   But the little round box. It was full!
CLOV   Yes. But now it's empty. [*Pause. CLOV starts to move about the room.
He is looking for a place to put down the alarm-clock.*]
HAMM   [*Soft.*] What'll I do? [*Pause. In a scream.*] What'll I do? [*CLOV sees
the picture, takes it down, stands it on the floor with its face to the wall,
hangs up the alarm-clock in its place.*] What are you doing?
CLOV   Winding up.
HAMM   Look at the earth.
CLOV   Again!
HAMM   Since it's calling to you.
CLOV   Is your throat sore? [*Pause.*] Would you like a lozenge? [*Pause.*] No.
[*Pause.*] Pity. [CLOV *goes, humming, towards window right, halts before
it, looks up at it.*]
HAMM   Don't sing.
CLOV   [*Turning towards* HAMM.] One hasn't the right to sing any more?
HAMM   No.
CLOV   Then how can it end?
HAMM   You want it to end?
CLOV   I want to sing.
HAMM   I can't prevent you. [*Pause. CLOV turns towards window right.*]

6. Zeno of Elea (ca. 450 B.C.E.), a Greek philosopher famous for his paradoxes; e.g., "If a grain of
millet falling makes no sound, how can a bushel of
grains make any sound?" (reported by Aristotle in
his *Physics* 5:250 a.19).

CLOV   What did I do with that steps? [*He looks around for ladder.*] You
    didn't see that steps? [*He sees it.*] Ah, about time. [*He goes towards win-
    dow left.*] Sometimes I wonder if I'm in my right mind. Then it passes
    over and I'm as lucid as before. [*He gets up on ladder, looks out of win-
    dow.*] Christ, she's under water! [*He looks.*] How can that be? [*He pokes
    forward his head, his hand above his eyes.*] It hasn't rained. [*He wipes the
    pane, looks. Pause.*] Ah what a fool I am! I'm on the wrong side! [*He gets
    down, takes a few steps towards window right.*] Under water! [*He goes
    back for ladder.*] What a fool I am! [*He carries ladder towards window
    right.*] Sometimes I wonder if I'm in my right senses. Then it passes off
    and I'm as intelligent as ever. [*He sets down ladder under window right,
    gets up on it, looks out of window. He turns towards* HAMM.] Any particular
    sector you fancy? Or merely the whole thing?
HAMM   Whole thing.
CLOV   The general effect? Just a moment. [*He looks out of window. Pause.*]
HAMM   Clov.
CLOV   [*Absorbed.*] Mmm.
HAMM   Do you know what it is?
CLOV   [*As before.*] Mmm.
HAMM   I was never there. [*Pause.*] Clov!
CLOV   [*Turning towards* HAMM, *exasperated.*] What is it?
HAMM   I was never there.
CLOV   Lucky for you. [*He looks out of window.*]
HAMM   Absent, always. It all happened without me. I don't know what's
    happened. [*Pause.*] Do you know what's happened? [*Pause.*] Clov!
CLOV   [*Turning towards* HAMM, *exasperated.*] Do you want me to look at
    this muckheap, yes or no?
HAMM   Answer me first.
CLOV   What?
HAMM   Do you know what's happened?
CLOV   When? Where?
HAMM   [*Violently.*] When! What's happened? Use your head, can't you!
    What has happened?
CLOV   What for Christ's sake does it matter? [*He looks out of window.*]
HAMM   I don't know. [*Pause.* CLOV *turns towards* HAMM.]
CLOV   [*Harshly.*] When old Mother Pegg asked you for oil for her lamp
    and you told her to get out to hell, you knew what was happening then,
    no? [*Pause.*] You know what she died of, Mother Pegg? Of darkness.
HAMM   [*Feebly.*] I hadn't any.
CLOV   [*As before.*] Yes, you had. [*Pause.*]
HAMM   Have you the glass?
CLOV   No, it's clear enough as it is.
HAMM   Go and get it. [*Pause.* CLOV *casts up his eyes, brandishes his fists.
    He loses balance, clutches on to the ladder. He starts to get down, halts.*]
CLOV   There's one thing I'll never understand. [*He gets down.*] Why I
    always obey you. Can you explain that to me?
HAMM   No. . . . Perhaps it's compassion. [*Pause.*] A kind of great compas-
    sion. [*Pause.*] Oh you won't find it easy, you won't find it easy. [*Pause.
    CLOV begins to move about the room in search of the telescope.*]

CLOV   I'm tired of our goings on, very tired. [*He searches.*] You're not sitting on it? [*He moves the chair, looks at the place where it stood, resumes his search.*]

HAMM   [*Anguished.*] Don't leave me there! [*Angrily* CLOV *restores the chair to its place.*] Am I right in the centre?

CLOV   You'd need a microscope to find this—[*He sees the telescope.*] Ah, about time. [*He picks up the telescope, gets up on the ladder, turns the telescope on the without.*]

HAMM   Give me the dog.

CLOV   [*Looking.*] Quiet!

HAMM   [*Angrily.*] Give me the dog! [CLOV *drops the telescope, clasps his hands to his head. Pause. He gets down precipitately, looks for the dog, sees it, picks it up, hastens towards* HAMM *and strikes him violently on the head with the dog.*]

CLOV   There's your dog for you! [*The dog falls to the ground. Pause.*]

HAMM   He hit me!

CLOV   You drive me mad, I'm mad!

HAMM   If you must hit me, hit me with the axe. [*Pause.*] Or with the gaff, hit me with the gaff. Not with the dog. With the gaff. Or with the axe. [CLOV *picks up the dog and gives it to* HAMM *who takes it in his arms.*]

CLOV   [*Imploringly.*] Let's stop playing!

HAMM   Never! [*Pause.*] Put me in my coffin.

CLOV   There are no more coffins.

HAMM   Then let it end! [CLOV *goes towards ladder.*] With a bang! [CLOV *gets up on ladder, gets down again, looks for telescope, sees it, picks it up, gets up ladder, raises telescope.*] Of darkness! And me? Did anyone ever have pity on me?

CLOV   [*Lowering the telescope, turning towards* HAMM.] What? [*Pause.*] Is it me you're referring to?

HAMM   [*Angrily.*] An aside, ape! Did you never hear an aside before? [*Pause.*] I'm warming up for my last soliloquy.

CLOV   I warn you. I'm going to look at this filth since it's an order. But it's the last time. [*He turns the telescope on the without.*] Let's see. [*He moves the telescope.*] Nothing . . . nothing . . . good . . . good . . . nothing . . . goo—[*He starts, lowers the telescope, examines it, turns it again on the without. Pause.*] Bad luck to it!

HAMM   More complications! [CLOV *gets down.*] Not an underplot, I trust. [CLOV *moves ladder nearer window, gets up on it, turns telescope on the without.*]

CLOV   [*Dismayed.*] Looks like a small boy!

HAMM   [*Sarcastic.*] A small . . . boy!

CLOV   I'll go and see. [*He gets down, drops the telescope, goes towards door, turns.*] I'll take the gaff. [*He looks for the gaff, sees it, picks it up, hastens towards door.*]

HAMM   No! [CLOV *halts.*]

CLOV   No? A potential procreator?

HAMM   If he exists he'll die there or he'll come here. And if he doesn't . . . [*Pause.*]

CLOV   You don't believe me? You think I'm inventing? [*Pause.*]

HAMM It's the end, Clov, we've come to the end. I don't need you any more. [*Pause.*]

CLOV Lucky for you. [*He goes towards door.*]

HAMM Leave me the gaff. [CLOV *gives him the gaff, goes towards door, halts, looks at alarm-clock, takes it down, looks round for a better place to put it, goes to bins, puts it on lid of* NAGG's *bin. Pause.*]

CLOV I'll leave you. [*He goes towards door.*]

HAMM Before you go . . . [CLOV *halts near door.*] . . . say something.

CLOV There is nothing to say.

HAMM A few words . . . to ponder . . . in my heart.

CLOV Your heart!

HAMM Yes. [*Pause. Forcibly.*] Yes! [*Pause.*] With the rest, in the end, the shadows, the murmurs, all the trouble, to end up with. [*Pause.*] Clov. . . . He never spoke to me. Then, in the end, before he went, without my having asked him, he spoke to me. He said . . .

CLOV [*Despairingly.*] Ah . . . !

HAMM Something . . . from your heart.

CLOV My heart!

HAMM A few words . . . from your heart. [*Pause.*]

CLOV [*Fixed gaze, tonelessly, towards auditorium.*] They said to me, That's love, yes, yes, not a doubt, now you see how—

HAMM Articulate!

CLOV [*As before.*] How easy it is. They said to me, That's friendship, yes, yes, no question, you've found it. They said to me, Here's the place, stop, raise your head and look at all that beauty. That order! They said to me. Come now, you're not a brute beast, think upon these things and you'll see how all becomes clear. And simple! They said to me, What skilled attention they get, all these dying of their wounds.

HAMM Enough!

CLOV [*As before.*] I say to myself—sometimes, Clov, you must learn to suffer better than that if you want them to weary of punishing you—one day. I say to myself—sometimes, Clov, you must be there better than that if you want them to let you go—one day. But I feel too old, and too far, to form new habits. Good, it'll never end, I'll never go. [*Pause.*] Then one day, suddenly, it ends, it changes, I don't understand, it dies, or it's me, I don't understand, that either. I ask the words that remain—sleeping, waking, morning, evening. They have nothing to say. [*Pause.*] I open the door of the cell and go. I am so bowed I only see my feet, if I open my eyes, and between my legs a little trail of black dust. I say to myself that the earth is extinguished, though I never saw it lit. [*Pause.*] It's easy going. [*Pause.*] When I fall I'll weep for happiness. [*Pause. He goes towards door.*]

HAMM Clov! [CLOV *halts, without turning.*] Nothing. [CLOV *moves on.*] Clov! [CLOV *halts, without turning.*]

CLOV This is what we call making an exit.

HAMM I'm obliged to you, Clov. For your services.

CLOV [*Turning, sharply.*] Ah pardon, it's I am obliged to you.

HAMM It's we are obliged to each other. [*Pause.* CLOV *goes towards door.*] One thing more. [CLOV *halts.*] A last favour. [*Exit* CLOV.] Cover me with the sheet. [*Long pause.*] No? Good. [*Pause.*] Me to play. [*Pause. Wearily.*] Old endgame lost of old, play and lose and have done with losing. [*Pause. More animated.*] Let me see. [*Pause.*] Ah yes! [*He tries to move the chair, using the gaff as before. Enter* CLOV, *dressed for the road. Panama hat, tweed coat, raincoat over his arm, umbrella, bag. He halts by the door and stands there, impassive and motionless, his eyes fixed on* HAMM, *till the end.* HAMM *gives up.*] Good. [*Pause.*] Discard. [*He throws away the gaff, makes to throw away the dog, thinks better of it.*] Take it easy. [*Pause.*] And now? [*Pause.*] Raise hat. [*He raises his toque.*] Peace to our . . . arses. [*Pause.*] And put on again. [*He puts on his toque.*] Deuce. [*Pause. He takes off his glasses.*] Wipe. [*He takes out his handkerchief and, without unfolding it, wipes his glasses.*] And put on again. [*He puts on his glasses, puts back the handkerchief in his pocket.*] We're coming. A few more squirms like that and I'll call. [*Pause.*] A little poetry. [*Pause.*] You prayed—[*Pause. He corrects himself.*] You CRIED for night; it comes— [*Pause. He corrects himself.*] It FALLS: now cry in darkness. [*He repeats, chanting.*] You cried for night; it falls: now cry in darkness.[7] [*Pause.*] Nicely put, that. [*Pause.*] And now? [*Pause.*] Moments for nothing, now as always, time was never and time is over, reckoning closed and story ended. [*Pause. Narrative tone.*] If he could have his child with him. . . . [*Pause.*] It was the moment I was waiting for. [*Pause.*] You don't want to abandon him? You want him to bloom while you are withering? Be there to solace your last million last moments? [*Pause.*] He doesn't realize, all he knows is hunger, and cold, and death to crown it all. But you! You ought to know what the earth is like, nowadays. Oh I put him before his responsibilities! [*Pause. Normal tone.*] Well, there we are, there I am, that's enough. [*He raises the whistle to his lips, hesitates, drops it. Pause.*] Yes, truly! [*He whistles. Pause. Louder. Pause.*] Good. [*Pause.*] Father! [*Pause. Louder.*] Father! [*Pause.*] Good. [*Pause.*] We're coming. [*Pause.*] And to end up with? [*Pause.*] Discard. [*He throws away the dog. He tears the whistle from his neck.*] With my compliments. [*He throws whistle towards auditorium. Pause. He sniffs. Soft.*] Clov! [*Long pause.*] No? Good. [*He takes out the handkerchief.*] Since that's the way we're playing it . . . [*He unfolds handkerchief.*] . . . let's play it that way . . . [*He unfolds.*] . . . and speak no more about it . . . [*He finishes unfolding.*] . . . speak no more. [*He holds handkerchief spread out before him.*] Old stancher! [*Pause.*] You . . . remain. [*Pause. He covers his face with hand-kerchief, lowers his arms to armrests, remains motionless.*] [*Brief tableau.*]

CURTAIN

1958

7. Parody of a line from Baudelaire's poem *Meditation,* which can be translated as: "You were calling for evening; it falls; it is here."

W. H. AUDEN
1907–1973

Wystan Hugh Auden was born in York and educated at Gresham's School, Holt, Norfolk, and Christ Church, Oxford. After leaving Oxford he taught school from 1930 to 1935 and later worked for a government film unit. His sympathies in the 1930s were with the Left, like those of most intellectuals of his age, and he went to Spain during the Civil War, intending to serve as an ambulance driver on the left-wing Republican side. He found himself to his surprise, however, so disturbed by the sight of the many Roman Catholic churches gutted and looted by the Republicans that he returned to England without fulfilling his ambition. He traveled in Iceland and China before coming to America in 1939; in 1946 he became an American citizen. He taught at a number of American colleges and was Professor of Poetry at Oxford from 1956 to 1960.

Auden was the most active of the group of young English poets who, in the late 1920s and early 1930s, saw themselves bringing new techniques and attitudes to English poetry. Stephen Spender (1909–1995) and Cecil Day Lewis (1904–1972) were at the time the most prominent of the other members of the new school, which soon afterward fell apart, each poet going his own separate way. Like all his generation, Auden learned poetic wit and irony from T. S. Eliot, and he also learned metrical and verbal techniques from Gerard Manley Hopkins and from Wilfred Owen. His English studies at Oxford familiarized him with the rhythms and long alliterative line of Anglo-Saxon poetry as well as with the rapid and rollicking short lines (a sort of inspired doggerel) of the poet John Skelton (ca. 1460–1529); both influenced his own versification. He learned, too, from the songs of the English music hall and, later, from American blues singers.

The Depression that hit America in 1929 hit England soon afterward, and Auden and his contemporaries looked out at an England of industrial stagnation and mass unemployment, seeing not the metaphorical Waste Land of Eliot but a more literal Waste Land of poverty and "depressed areas." His early poetry is much concerned with a diagnosis of the ills of his country. This diagnosis, conducted in a verse that combined deliberate irreverence and sometimes even clowning with a cunning verbal craftsmanship, drew on both Freud and Marx to show England now as a nation of neurotic invalids who must learn to "throw away their rugs" and now as the victim of an antiquated economic system. The liveliness and nervous force of this early poetry of Auden's made a great impression, even though an uncertainty about his audience led him to introduce purely private symbols, intelligible only to a few friends, in some of his poems.

Gradually, Auden learned to clarify his imagery and control his desire to shock, and he produced, in the years around 1940, some poems (such as *Lullaby*) of finely disciplined movement, pellucid clarity, and deep yet unsentimental feeling. At the same time he was developing a more complex view of the world, moving from his earlier diagnosis of modern ills in terms of Freud and Marx to a more religious view of personal responsibility and traditional value without, however, abandoning the ideas and terms he had learned from modern psychology. But he never lost his ear for popular speech or his ability to combine elements from popular art with an extreme technical formality. He was always the experimenter, particularly in ways of bringing together high artifice and a colloquial tone.

For the first part of his career—the English and the early American phase—Auden was very much the poet of his times, first of the Depression and then of the Age of the Refugee. In the poems of this period he preferred to confront modern problems directly rather than to filter them, as Eliot did, through symbolic situations. The poems of the last phase of his career, notably those in *About the House* (1967) and

City without Walls (1970), are increasingly personal in tone and combine an apparent air of offhand informality with remarkable technical skill in versification. Auden grew increasingly hostile to the modern world and skeptical of all remedies offered for modern ills: he took refuge in love and friendship, particularly the love and friendship he shared with Chester Kallmann; emotions grounded in an ever deepening but rarely obtrusive religious feeling. In the last year of his life he returned to England to live in Oxford, feeling the need to be part of a university community as a protection against loneliness. An uneven poet, a poet who in the opinion of some critics never quite fulfilled the enormous promise of his early work, Auden is nevertheless now generally recognized as one of the masters of twentieth-century English poetry, a thoughtful, seriously playful (if one may put it in this paradoxical way) poet whom more than one critic has compared with Dryden in his combination of lively intelligence and immense craftsmanship.

Petition

Sir, no man's enemy, forgiving all
But will his negative inversion, be prodigal:
Send to us power and light, a sovereign touch[1]
Curing the intolerable neural itch,
5   The exhaustion of weaning, the liar's quinsy,°   *tonsillitis*
And the distortions of ingrown virginity.
Prohibit sharply the rehearsed response
And gradually correct the coward's stance;
Cover in time with beams those in retreat
10 That, spotted, they turn though the reverse were great;
Publish each healer that in city lives
Or country houses at the end of drives;
Harrow the house of the dead; look shining at
New styles of architecture, a change of heart.

Oct. 1929   1930

On This Island

Look, stranger, on this island now
The leaping light for your delight discovers,
Stand stable here
And silent be,
5   That through the channels of the ear
May wander like a river
The swaying sound of the sea.

Here at the small field's ending pause
When the chalk wall falls to the foam and its tall ledges
10 Oppose the pluck
And knock of the tide,
And the shingle scrambles after the suck-

1. The king's touch was often regarded as miraculous cure for disease (cf. "sovereign" as an adjective, meaning "supreme, all-dominating").

-ing surf,
And the gull lodges
15 A moment on its sheer side.

Far off like floating seeds the ships
Diverge on urgent voluntary errands,
And the full view
Indeed may enter
20 And move in memory as now these clouds do,
That pass the harbour mirror
And all the summer through the water saunter.

1935   1936

Spain 1937[1]

Yesterday all the past. The language of size
Spreading to China along the trade routes; the diffusion
          Of the counting-frame and the cromlech;[2]
Yesterday the shadow-reckoning in the sunny climates.

5 Yesterday the assessment of insurance by cards,
The divination of water; yesterday the invention
          Of cart-wheels and clocks, the taming of
Horses; yesterday the bustling world of the navigators.

Yesterday the abolition of fairies and giants;
10 The fortress like a motionless eagle eyeing the valley,
          The chapel built in the forest;
Yesterday the carving of angels and of frightening gargoyles;

The trial of heretics among the columns of stone;
Yesterday the theological feuds in the taverns
15   And the miraculous cure at the fountain;
Yesterday the Sabbath of Witches.[3] But to-day the struggle.

Yesterday the installation of dynamos and turbines;
The construction of railways in the colonial desert;
          Yesterday the classic lecture
20 On the origin of Mankind. But to-day the struggle.

Yesterday the belief in the absolute value of Greek;
The fall of the curtain upon the death of a hero;
          Yesterday the prayer to the sunset,
And the adoration of madmen. But to-day the struggle.

1. Written when the Spanish Civil War was raging. The rebellion by General Franco's right-wing
army against the left-wing Spanish government,
which broke out in 1936 and provoked full-scale
civil war, was viewed by British liberal intellectuals
at the time as a testing struggle between fascism
and democracy. The poem first appeared separately in 1937, the proceeds of its sale going to
Medical Aid for Spain. This is Auden's revised version of 1940.
2. Ancient stone circle.
3. Convocation of witches in parody of Christian
service.

25 As the poet whispers, startled among the pines
    Or, where the loose waterfall sings, compact, or upright
                On the crag by the leaning tower:
    "O my vision. O send me the luck of the sailor."

    And the investigator peers through his instruments
30 At the inhuman provinces, the virile bacillus
                Or enormous Jupiter finished:
    "But the lives of my friends. I inquire, I inquire."

    And the poor in their fireless lodgings dropping the sheets
    Of the evening paper: "Our day is our loss. O show us
35   History the operator, the
    Organizer, Time the refreshing river."

    And the nations combine each cry, invoking the life
    That shapes the individual belly and orders
                The private nocturnal terror:
40 "Did you not found once the city state of the sponge,

    "Raise the vast military empires of the shark
    And the tiger, establish the robin's plucky canton?°   district
                Intervene. O descend as a dove or
    A furious papa or a mild engineer: but descend."

45 And the life, if it answers at all, replies from the heart
    And the eyes and the lungs, from the shops and squares of the city:
                "O no, I am not the Mover,
    Not to-day, not to you. To you I'm the

    "Yes-man, the bar-companion, the easily-duped:
50 I am whatever you do; I am your vow to be
                Good, your humorous story;
    I am your business voice; I am your marriage.

    "What's your proposal? To build the Just City? I will.
    I agree. Or is it the suicide pact, the romantic
55   Death? Very well, I accept, for
    I am your choice, your decision: yes, I am Spain."

    Many have heard it on remote peninsulas,
    On sleepy plains, in the aberrant fishermen's islands,
                In the corrupt heart of the city;
60 Have heard and migrated like gulls or the seeds of a flower.

    They clung like burrs to the long expresses that lurch
    Through the unjust lands, through the night, through the alpine tunnel;
                They floated over the oceans;
    They walked the passes: they came to present their lives.

65 On that arid square, that fragment nipped off from hot
    Africa, soldered so crudely to inventive Europe,

On that tableland scored by rivers,
Our fever's menancing shapes are precise and alive.

70 To-morrow, perhaps, the future: the research on fatigue
And the movements of packers; the gradual exploring of all the
Octaves of radiation;
To-morrow the enlarging of consciousness by diet and breathing.

To-morrow the rediscovery of romantic love;
The photographing of ravens; all the fun under
75 Liberty's masterful shadow;
To-morrow the hour of the pageant-master and the musician.

To-morrow for the young the poets exploding like bombs,
The walks by the lake, the winter of perfect communion;
To-morrow the bicycle races
80 Through the suburbs on summer evenings: but to-day the struggle.

To-day the inevitable increase in the chances of death;
The conscious acceptance of guilt in the fact of murder;
To-day the expending of powers
On the flat ephemeral pamphlet and the boring meeting.

85 To-day the makeshift consolations; the shared cigarette;
The cards in the candle-lit barn and the scraping concert,
The masculine jokes; to-day the
Fumbled and unsatisfactory embrace before hurting.

The stars are dead; the animals will not look:
90 We are left alone with our day, and the time is short and
History to the defeated
May say Alas but cannot help or pardon.

1937   1937, 1940

Musée des Beaux Arts[1]

About suffering they were never wrong,
The Old Masters: how well they understood
Its human position; how it takes place
While someone else is eating or opening a window or just walking dully along;
5 How, when the aged are reverently, passionately waiting
For the miraculous birth, there always must be
Children who did not specially want it to happen, skating
On a pond at the edge of the wood:
They never forgot
10 That even the dreadful martyrdom must run its course
Anyhow in a corner, some untidy spot

---

1. Museum of Fine Arts. The reference is to the Museum of Fine Arts in Brussels, which contains Brueghel's *Icarus.*

Where the dogs go on with their doggy life and the torturer's horse
Scratches its innocent behind on a tree.

In Brueghel's *Icarus*,[2] for instance: how everything turns away
15   Quite leisurely from the disaster; the ploughman may
Have heard the splash, the forsaken cry,
But for him it was not an important failure; the sun shone
As it had to on the white legs disappearing into the green
Water; and the expensive delicate ship that must have seen
20   Something amazing, a boy falling out of the sky,
Had somewhere to get to and sailed calmly on.

Dec. 1938   1940

Lullaby

Lay your sleeping head, my love,
Human on my faithless arm;
Time and fevers burn away
Individual beauty from
5   Thoughtful children, and the grave
Proves the child ephemeral:
But in my arms till break of day
Let the living creature lie,
Mortal, guilty, but to me
10   The entirely beautiful.

Soul and body have no bounds:
To lovers as they lie upon
Her tolerant enchanted slope
In their ordinary swoon,
15   Grave the vision Venus sends
Of supernatural sympathy,
Universal love and hope;
While an abstract insight wakes
Among the glaciers and the rocks
20   The hermit's carnal ecstasy.

Certainty, fidelity
On the stroke of midnight pass
Like vibrations of a bell,
And fashionable madmen raise
25   Their pedantic boring cry:
Every farthing[1] of the cost,
All the dreaded cards foretell,
Shall be paid, but from this night

2. Icarus was the son of Daedalus, the cunning craftsman of ancient legend. Together they flew on artificial wings fastened to their shoulders with wax, but Icarus ventured too near the sun, which melted the wax, and so he fell and perished. The painting of the fall of Icarus is by the Flemish painter Pieter Brueghel (ca. 1520–1569): Icarus's legs are disappearing into the sea in one corner of the picture, the rest of which has nothing to do with him.
1. At one time the smallest and least valuable British coin.

Not a whisper, not a thought,
30   Not a kiss nor look be lost.

Beauty, midnight, vision dies:
Let the winds of dawn that blow
Softly round your dreaming head
Such a day of sweetness show
35   Eye and knocking heart may bless,
Find the mortal world enough;
Noons of dryness see you fed
By the involuntary powers,
Nights of insult let you pass
40   Watched by every human love.

Jan. 1937   1940

In Memory of W. B. Yeats

(d. Jan. 1939)

1

He disappeared in the dead of winter:
The brooks were frozen, the airports almost deserted,
And snow disfigured the public statues;
The mercury sank in the mouth of the dying day.
5   What instruments we have agree
The day of his death was a dark cold day.

Far from his illness
The wolves ran on through the evergreen forests,
The peasant river was untempted by the fashionable quays;
10   By mourning tongues
The death of the poet was kept from his poems.

But for him it was his last afternoon as himself,
An afternoon of nurses and rumours;
The provinces of his body revolted,
15   The squares of his mind were empty,
Silence invaded the suburbs,
The current of his feeling failed: he became his admirers.

Now he is scattered among a hundred cities
And wholly given over to unfamiliar affections;
20   To find his happiness in another kind of wood[1]
And be punished under a foreign code of conscience.
The words of a dead man
Are modified in the guts of the living.

1. Cf. Dante's *Inferno* 1.1–3 (translated): "In the middle of the journey of our life I came to myself in a dark wood where the straight way was lost."

But in the importance and noise of to-morrow
25 When the brokers are roaring like beasts on the floor of the
Bourse,° stock exchange
And the poor have the sufferings to which they are fairly accustomed,
And each in the cell of himself is almost convinced of his freedom,
A few thousand will think of this day
As one thinks of a day when one did something slightly unusual.
30 What instruments we have agree
The day of his death was a dark cold day.

2

You were silly like us: your gift survived it all:
The parish of rich women, physical decay,
Yourself. Mad Ireland hurt you into poetry.
35 Now Ireland has her madness and her weather still,
For poetry makes nothing happen: it survives
In the valley of its making where executives
Would never want to tamper, flows on south
From ranches of isolation and the busy griefs,
40 Raw towns that we believe and die in; it survives,
A way of happening, a mouth.

3

Earth, receive an honoured guest:
William Yeats is laid to rest.
Let the Irish vessel lie
45 Emptied of its poetry.[2]

In the nightmare of the dark
All the dogs of Europe bark,
And the living nations wait,
Each sequestered in its hate;

50 Intellectual disgrace
Stares from every human face,
And the seas of pity lie
Locked and frozen in each eye.

Follow, poet, follow right
55 To the bottom of the night,
With your unconstraining voice
Still persuade us to rejoice;

2. Three stanzas that originally followed this were omitted in the 1966 edition of Auden's *Collected Shorter Poems* and thereafter: "Time that is intolerant / Of the brave and innocent, / And indifferent in a week / To a beautiful physique, // Worships language and forgives / Everyone by whom it lives; / Pardons cowardice, conceit, / Lays its honours at their feet. // Time that with this strange excuse / Pardoned Kipling and his views, / And will pardon Paul Claudel, / Pardons him for writing well." Kipling's views were imperialistic. Paul Claudel (1868–1955), French poet, dramatist, and diplomat, was an extreme right-winger in his political ideas. Yeats's own politics were at times antidemocratic and appeared to favor dictatorship.

With the farming of a verse
Make a vineyard of the curse,
60 Sing of human unsuccess
In a rapture of distress;

In the deserts of the heart
Let the healing fountain start,
In the prison of his days
65 Teach the free man how to praise.

Feb. 1939   1940, 1966

Their Lonely Betters

As I listened from a beach-chair in the shade
To all the noises that my garden made,
It seemed to me only proper that words
Should be withheld from vegetables and birds.

5 A robin with no Christian name ran through
The Robin-Anthem which was all it knew,
And rustling flowers for some third party waited
To say which pairs, if any, should get mated.

Not one of them was capable of lying,
10 There was not one which knew that it was dying
Or could have with a rhythm or a rhyme
Assumed responsibility for time.

Let them leave language to their lonely betters
Who count some days and long for certain letters;
15 We, too, make noises when we laugh or weep,
Words are for those with promises to keep.

1950   1951

In Praise of Limestone[1]

If it form the one landscape that we the inconstant ones
    Are consistently homesick for, this is chiefly
Because it dissolves in water. Mark these rounded slopes
    With their surface fragrance of thyme and, beneath,
5 A secret system of caves and conduits; hear the springs
    That spurt out everywhere with a chuckle
Each filling a private pool for its fish and carving
    Its own little ravine whose cliffs entertain
The butterfly and the lizard; examine this region

---

1. The landscape of this poem derives from Auden's native Yorkshire. Cf. his *New Year Letter:* "I see the nature of my kind / As a locality I love / Those limestone moors that stretch from Brough / To Hexham on the Roman Wall / That is my symbol of us all."

10   Of short distances and definite places:
What could be more like Mother or a fitter background
    For her son, for the flirtatious male who lounges
Against a rock in the sunlight, never doubting
That for all his faults he is loved; whose works are but
15   Extensions of his power to charm? From weathered outcrop
    To hill-top temple, from appearing waters to
Conspicuous fountains, from a wild to a formal vineyard,
    Are ingenious but short steps that a child's wish
To receive more attention than his brothers, whether
20   By pleasing or teasing, can easily take.

Watch, then, the band of rivals as they climb up and down
    Their steep stone gennels[2] in twos and threes, at times
Arm in arm, but never, thank God, in step; or engaged
    On the shady side of a square at midday in
25   Voluble discourse, knowing each other too well to think
    There are any important secrets, unable
To conceive a god whose temper-tantrums are moral
    And not to be pacified by a clever line
Or a good lay: for, accustomed to a stone that responds,
30   They have never had to veil their faces in awe
Of a crater whose blazing fury could not be fixed;
    Adjusted to the local needs of valleys
Where everything can be touched or reached by walking,
    Their eyes have never looked into infinite space
35   Through the lattice-work of a nomad's comb;[3] born lucky,
    Their legs have never encountered the fungi
And insects of the jungle, the monstrous forms and lives
    With which we have nothing, we like to hope, in common.
So, when one of them goes to the bad, the way his mind works
40   Remains comprehensible: to become a pimp
Or deal in fake jewelry or ruin a fine tenor voice
    For effects that bring down the house, could happen to all
But the best and the worst of us . . .
                     That is why, I suppose,
    The best and worst never stayed here long but sought
45   Immoderate soils where the beauty was not so external,
    The light less public and the meaning of life
Something more than a mad camp. "Come!" cried the granite wastes,
    "How evasive is your humour, how accidental
Your kindest kiss, how permanent is death." (Saints-to-be
50   Slipped away sighing.) "Come!" purred the clays and gravels.
"On our plains there is room for armies to drill; rivers
    Wait to be tamed and slaves to construct you a tomb
In the grand manner: soft as the earth is mankind and both
    Need to be altered." (Intendant Caesars° rose and   *Roman emperors*
55   Left, slamming the door.) But the really reckless were fetched

2. Long narrow passages between houses (Yorkshire and northern English dialect); here passages between rocks.
3. The context suggests that this might be a popular name for a plant or tree (cf. "traveler's joy" and "traveler's palm"), but Auden is probably using the phrase quite literally to suggest that these people have never led a nomad's (wanderer's) life. The "nomad's comb" might be the fringe of unkempt hair through which the nomad peers at wild landscapes.

By an older colder voice, the oceanic whisper:
"I am the solitude that asks and promises nothing;
   That is how I shall set you free. There is no love;
There are only the various envies, all of them sad."

60   They were right, my dear, all those voices were right
And still are; this land is not the sweet home that it looks,
   Nor its peace the historical calm of a site
Where something was settled once and for all: A backward
   And dilapidated province, connected
65 To the big busy world by a tunnel, with a certain
   Seedy appeal, is that all it is now? Not quite:
It has a worldly duty which in spite of itself
   It does not neglect, but calls into question
All the Great Powers assume; it disturbs our rights. The poet,
70   Admired for his earnest habit of calling
The sun the sun, his mind Puzzle, is made uneasy
   By these marble statues which so obviously doubt
His antimythological myth; and these gamins,°   *urchins*
   Pursuing the scientist down the tiled colonnade
75 With such lively offers, rebuke his concern for Nature's
   Remotest aspects: I, too, am reproached, for what
And how much you know. Not to lose time, not to get caught,
   Not to be left behind, not, please! to resemble
The beasts who repeat themselves, or a thing like water
80   Or stone whose conduct can be predicted, these
Are our Common Prayer, whose greatest comfort is music
   Which can be made anywhere, is invisible,
And does not smell. In so far as we have to look forward
   To death as a fact, no doubt we are right: But if
85 Sins can be forgiven, if bodies rise from the dead,
   These modifications of matter into
Innocent athletes and gesticulating fountains,
   Made solely for pleasure, make a further point:
The blessed will not care what angle they are regarded from,
90   Having nothing to hide. Dear, I know nothing of
Either, but when I try to imagine a faultless love
   Or the life to come, what I hear is the murmur
Of underground streams, what I see is a limestone landscape.

May 1948   1948, 1951

The Shield of Achilles[1]

        She looked over his shoulder
          For vines and olive trees,

1. In books 16 and 17 of Homer's *Iliad*, Achilles, the chief Greek hero in the war against Troy, lends his armor to his friend Patroclus and loses it when Patroclus is killed by the Trojan hero Hector. While Achilles is mourning for his friend, his mother, the goddess Thetis, goes to Mount Olympus to beg Hephaestos, god of fire, to forge new armor for Achilles. The splendid shield that Hephaestos then makes him is described in book 18 of the *Iliad* (lines 478–608). On it he depicts the heavens, the sea, and the earth represented by many scenes such as a city at peace and a city at war.

            Marble well-governed cities
                And ships upon untamed seas,
5   But there on the shining metal
                His hands had put instead
            An artificial wilderness
            And a sky like lead.

no nature

            A plain without a feature, bare and brown,
10   No blade of grass, no sign of neighbourhood,
        Nothing to eat and nowhere to sit down,
                Yet, congregated on its blankness, stood
                An unintelligible multitude,
            A million eyes, a million boots in line,
15   Without expression, waiting for a sign.

            Out of the air a voice without a face
                Proved by statistics that some cause was just
            In tones as dry and level as the place:
                No one was cheered and nothing was discussed;
20   Column by column in a cloud of dust
            They marched away enduring a belief
            Whose logic brought them, somewhere else, to grief.

                She looked over his shoulder
                    For ritual pieties,
25   White flower-garlanded heifers,
                    Libation and sacrifice,[2]
                But there on the shining metal
                    Where the altar should have been,
                She saw by his flickering forge-light
30   Quite another scene.

            Barbed wire enclosed an arbitrary spot
                Where bored officials lounged (one cracked a joke)
            And sentries sweated for the day was hot:
                A crowd of ordinary decent folk
35   Watched from without and neither moved nor spoke
            As three pale figures were led forth and bound
            To three posts driven upright in the ground.

            The mass and majesty of this world, all
                That carries weight and always weighs the same
40   Lay in the hands of others; they were small
                And could not hope for help and no help came:
            What their foes liked to do was done, their shame
            Was all the worst could wish; they lost their pride
            And died as men before their bodies died.

45   She looked over his shoulder
                    For athletes at their games,

---

2. Cf. Keats, *Ode on a Grecian Urn*, lines 31–34: "Who are these coming to the sacrifice? / To what green altar, O mysterious priest, / Lead'st thou that heifer lowing at the skies, / And all her silken flanks with garlands drest?" "Libation": sacrifice of wine or other liquid.

Men and women in a dance
　　Moving their sweet limbs
　　Quick, quick, to music,
50　　But there on the shining shield
His hands had set no dancing-floor
　　But a weed-choked field.

A ragged urchin, aimless and alone,
　　Loitered about that vacancy; a bird
55　Flew up to safety from his well-aimed stone:
　　That girls are raped, that two boys knife a third,
　　Were axioms to him, who'd never heard
Of any world where promises were kept,
Or one could weep because another wept.

60　　　The thin-lipped armourer,
　　　Hephaestos, hobbled away,
　　Thetis of the shining breasts
　　　Cried out in dismay
At what the god had wrought
65　　To please her son, the strong
Iron-hearted man-slaying Achilles
　　Who would not live long.

1952　　　　　　　　　　　　　　　　　　　　　　　　　　　　1955

DYLAN THOMAS
1914–1953

Dylan Thomas was born in Swansea, Wales, and educated at Swansea Grammar School. After working for a time as a newspaper reporter, he was "discovered" as a poet in 1933 through a poetry contest in a popular newspaper. The following year his *Eighteen Poems* caused considerable excitement because of the strange violence of their imagery and their powerfully suggestive obscurity. It looked as though a new kind of strength and romantic picturesqueness had been restored to English poetry after the deliberately muted tones of T. S. Eliot and his followers. Thomas did not, however, turn out to be the founder of a neo-Romantic movement, though some early critics took him to be so. As his poetry became better known, and after he had clarified the somewhat clotted imagery of his early style in his later volumes—*The Map of Love* (1939), *Deaths and Entrances* (1946), *Collected Poems* (1953)—it became clear that he was a master craftsman and not the shouting rhapsodist that some had taken him to be. His images were most carefully ordered in a patterned sequence, and his major theme was the unity of all life, the continuing *process* of life and death and new life that linked the generations to each other. Thomas saw the workings of biology as a magical transformation producing unity out of diversity, and again and again in his poetry he sought a poetic ritual to celebrate this unity ("The force that through the green fuse drives the flower / Drives my green age"). He saw men and women locked in a round of identities—with the beginning of growth also the first movement toward death, the beginning of love leading to procreation, new growth, and so in turn to death again and to life again, and because of this view he comforted himself with the unity of humankind and nature, of past and present, of life and death, and so "refused to mourn the death of a child." In his best poems the closely woven imagery (deriving from the Bible, Welsh folklore and preaching, and Freud) is organized to present aspects of this theme. His more open-worked poems of reminiscence and autobiographical emotion, such as *Poem in October,* communicate more immediately to the reader through their fine lyrical feeling and compelling use of simple natural images.

Thomas was a brilliant talker (when he felt like it), a considerable drinker, a reckless and impulsive man whose short life was packed with emotional ups and downs. He acted the wild bohemian poet as that role had not been played since the 1890s; some thought this behavior wonderful, though others deplored it. He was a brilliant reader of his own and others' poems, and many people who do not normally read poetry were drawn to Thomas's by the magic of his own reading. After his premature death a reaction set in: some critics declared that he had been overrated as a poet because of the sensational role he had played in life. But a balanced view is now possible; it is clear that at his best he was an original poet of great power and beauty.

The Force That Through the Green Fuse Drives the Flower

The force that through the green fuse drives the flower
Drives my green age; that blasts the roots of trees
Is my destroyer.
And I am dumb to tell the crooked rose
5   My youth is bent by the same wintry fever.

The force that drives the water through the rocks
Drives my red blood; that dries the mouthing streams
Turns mine to wax.
And I am dumb to mouth unto my veins
10   How at the mountain spring the same mouth sucks.

The hand that whirls the water in the pool[1]
Stirs the quicksand; that ropes the blowing wind
Hauls my shroud sail.
And I am dumb to tell the hanging man
15   How of my clay is made the hangman's lime.[2]

The lips of time leech to the fountain head;
Love drips and gathers, but the fallen blood
Shall calm her sores.
And I am dumb to tell a weather's wind
20   How time has ticked a heaven round the stars.

And I am dumb to tell the lover's tomb
How at my sheet goes the same crooked worm.

1933

---

1. The hand of the angel who troubles the water of the pool Bethesda, thus rendering it curative, in John 5.1–4.

2. Quicklime was sometimes poured into the graves of victims of the public hangmen to accelerate decomposition.

After the Funeral

(In Memory of Ann Jones)[1]

After the funeral, mule praises, brays,
Windshake of sailshaped ears, muffle-toed tap
Tap happily of one peg in the thick
Grave's foot, blinds down the lids, the teeth in black,
5   The spittled eyes, the salt ponds in the sleeves,
Morning smack of the spade that wakes up sleep,
Shakes a desolate boy who slits his throat
In the dark of the coffin and sheds dry leaves,
That breaks one bone to light with a judgment clout,
10 After the feast of tear-stuffed time and thistles
In a room with a stuffed fox and a stale fern,
I stand, for this memorial's sake, alone
In the snivelling hours with dead, humped Ann
Whose hooded, fountain heart once fell in puddles
15 Round the parched worlds of Wales and drowned each sun
(Though this for her is a monstrous image blindly
Magnified out of praise; her death was a still drop;
She would not have me sinking in the holy
Flood of her heart's fame; she would lie dumb and deep
20 And need no druid[2] of her broken body).
But I, Ann's bard on a raised hearth, call all
The seas to service that her wood-tongued virtue
Babble like a bellbuoy over the hymning heads,
Bow down the walls of the ferned and foxy woods
25 That her love sing and swing through a brown chapel,
Bless her bent spirit with four, crossing birds.
Her flesh was meek as milk, but this skyward statue
With the wild breast and blessed and giant skull
Is carved from her in a room with a wet window
30 In a fiercely mourning house in a crooked year.
I know her scrubbed and sour humble hands
Lie with religion in their cramp, her threadbare
Whisper in a damp word, her wits drilled hollow,
Her fist of a face died clenched on a round pain;
35 And sculptured Ann is seventy years of stone.
These cloud-sopped, marble hands, this monumental
Argument of the hewn voice, gesture and psalm,
Storm me forever over her grave until
The stuffed lung of the fox twitch and cry Love
40 And the strutting fern lay seeds on the black sill.

1938, 1939

---

1. Ann Jones was Thomas's aunt; she lived at a farmhouse called Fern Hill in the Welsh landscape described in *Poem in October* and *Fern Hill*.

2. Priest of the ancient Celtic pagans (ancestors of the modern Welsh).

Poem in October

It was my thirtieth year to heaven
Woke to my hearing from harbour and neighbour wood
And the mussel pooled and the heron
      Priested shore
5   The morning beckon
With water praying and call of seagull and rook
And the knock of sailing boats on the net webbed wall
      Myself to set foot
        That second
10   In the still sleeping town and set forth.

My birthday began with the water-
Birds and the birds of the winged trees flying my name
Above the farms and the white horses
      And I rose
15   In rainy autumn
And walked abroad in a shower of all my days.
High tide and the heron dived when I took the road
      Over the border
        And the gates
20   Of the town closed as the town awoke.

A springful of larks in a rolling
Cloud and the roadside bushes brimming with whistling
Blackbirds and the sun of October
      Summery
25   On the hill's shoulder,
Here were fond climates and sweet singers suddenly
Come in the morning where I wandered and listened
      To the rain wringing
        Wind blow cold
30   In the wood faraway under me.

Pale rain over the dwindling harbour
And over the sea wet church the size of a snail
With its horns through mist and the castle
      Brown as owls
35   But all the gardens
Of spring and summer were blooming in the tall tales
Beyond the border and under the lark full cloud.
      There could I marvel
        My birthday
40   Away but the weather turned around.

It turned away from the blithe country
And down the other air and the blue altered sky
Streamed again a wonder of summer
      With apples
45   Pears and red currants

And I saw in the turning so clearly a child's
Forgotten mornings when he walked with his mother
      Through the parables
        Of sun light
50   And the legends of the green chapels

And the twice told fields of infancy
That his tears burned my cheeks and his heart moved in mine.
    These were the woods the river and sea
      Where a boy
55   In the listening
Summertime of the dead whispered the truth of his joy
To the trees and the stones and the fish in the tide.
      And the mystery
        Sang alive
60   Still in the water and singingbirds.

And there could I marvel my birthday
Away but the weather turned around. And the true
    Joy of the long dead child sang burning
      In the sun.
65   It was my thirtieth
Year to heaven stood there then in the summer noon
Though the town below lay leaved with October blood.
      O may my heart's truth
        Still be sung
70   On this high hill in a year's turning.

                             1945, 1946

Fern Hill[1]

Now as I was young and easy under the apple boughs
About the lilting house and happy as the grass was green,
    The night above the dingle[2] starry,
      Time let me hail and climb
5   Golden in the heydays of his eyes,
And honoured among wagons I was prince of the apple towns
And once below a time I lordly had the trees and leaves
      Trail with daisies and barley
    Down the rivers of the windfall light.

10   And as I was green and carefree, famous among the barns
About the happy yard and singing as the farm was home,
    In the sun that is young once only,
      Time let me play and be
    Golden in the mercy of his means,
15 And green and golden I was huntsman and herdsman, the calves
Sang to my horn, the foxes on the hills barked clear and cold,

1. Name of the Welsh farmhouse, home of Thomas's aunt Ann Jones, where he spent summer holidays as a boy.
2. Deep dell or hollow, usually wooded.

And the sabbath rang slowly
In the pebbles of the holy streams.

All the sun long it was running, it was lovely, the hay
20 Fields high as the house, the tunes from the chimneys, it was air
And playing, lovely and watery
And fire green as grass.
And nightly under the simple stars
As I rode to sleep the owls were bearing the farm away,
25 All the moon long I heard, blessed among stables, the night-jars[3]
Flying with the ricks,° and the horses   *haystacks*
Flashing into the dark.

And then to awake, and the farm, like a wanderer white
With the dew, come back, the cock on his shoulder: it was all
30 Shining, it was Adam and maiden,[4]
The sky gathered again
And the sun grew round that very day.
So it must have been after the birth of the simple light
In the first, spinning place, the spellbound horses walking warm
35 Out of the whinnying green stable
On to the fields of praise.

And honoured among foxes and pheasants by the gay house
Under the new made clouds and happy as the heart was long,
In the sun born over and over,
40 I ran my heedless ways,
My wishes raced through the house high hay
And nothing I cared, at my sky blue trades, that time allows
In all his tuneful turning so few and such morning songs
Before the children green and golden
45 Follow him out of grace,

Nothing I cared, in the lamb white days, that time would take me
Up to the swallow thronged loft by the shadow of my hand,
In the moon that is always rising,
Nor that riding to sleep
50 I should hear him fly with the high fields
And wake to the farm forever fled from the childless land.
Oh as I was young and easy in the mercy of his means,
Time held me green and dying
Though I sang in my chains like the sea.

1946

Do Not Go Gentle into That Good Night

Do not go gentle into that good night,
Old age should burn and rave at close of day;
Rage, rage against the dying of the light.

---

3. Species of bird.   4. Cf. Genesis 1.

Though wise men at their end know dark is right,
5   Because their words had forked no lightning they
Do not go gentle into that good night.

Good men, the last wave by, crying how bright
Their frail deeds might have danced in a green bay,
Rage, rage against the dying of the light.

10   Wild men who caught and sang the sun in flight,
And learn, too late, they grieved it on its way,
Do not go gentle into that good night.

Grave men, near death, who see with blinding sight
Blind eyes could blaze like meteors and be gay,
15   Rage, rage against the dying of the light.

And you, my father, there on the sad height,
Curse, bless, me now with your fierce tears, I pray.
Do not go gentle into that good night.
Rage, rage against the dying of the light.

1951, 1952

PHILIP LARKIN
1922–1985

Philip Larkin was born in Coventry; was educated at its King Henry VIII School and
at St. John's College, Oxford; and was for many years librarian of the Hull University
Library. He wrote the poems of his first book, *The North Ship* (1945), under Yeats's
strong enchantment; but released by his discovery of Hardy's *Collected Poems*, Larkin
found his own voice. Like Hardy, he wrote novels, *Jill* (1946) and *A Girl in Winter*
(1947), and his poems have a novelist's sense of place and skill in the handling of
direct speech. He was the dominant figure in what came to be known as "the Movement," a group of poets that included Kingsley Amis, Donald Davie, and Thom Gunn,
whose work (in the words of Robert Conquest's introduction to his 1956 anthology
New Lines) "is free from both mystical and logical compulsions and—like modern
philosophy—is empirical in its attitude to all that comes."

No other poet presents the welfare-state world of postimperial Britain so vividly,
so unsparingly, and in the last analysis so tenderly. Much has been written of Larkin's
Hardyesque pessimism, his depiction of loneliness, age, and death; however, the many
negatives in his poems imply positives, out of reach of the ironic and self-deprecating
speaker, but available perhaps to others more fortunate, elsewhere. His output was
small; but his four volumes of poetry and his controversial anthology *The Oxford Book
of Twentieth-Century English Verse* (1973) testify to the continuing vitality of a native
English tradition, the tradition of Chaucer, Wordsworth, and Hardy, distinct from
(and, in Larkin's view, opposed to) the imported modernist tradition of Eliot and
Pound.

Church Going

Once I am sure there's nothing going on
I step inside, letting the door thud shut.
Another church: matting, seats, and stone,
And little books; sprawlings of flowers, cut
5   For Sunday, brownish now; some brass and stuff
Up at the holy end; the small neat organ;
And a tense, musty, unignorable silence,
Brewed God knows how long. Hatless, I take off
My cycle-clips in awkward reverence,

10   Move forward, run my hand around the font.
From where I stand, the roof looks almost new—
Cleaned, or restored? Someone would know: I don't.
Mounting the lectern, I peruse a few
Hectoring large-scale verses, and pronounce
15   "Here endeth" much more loudly than I'd meant.
The echoes snigger briefly. Back at the door
I sign the book, donate an Irish sixpence,[1]
Reflect the place was not worth stopping for.

Yet stop I did: in fact I often do,
20   And always end much at a loss like this,
Wondering what to look for; wondering, too,
When churches fall completely out of use
What we shall turn them into, if we shall keep
A few cathedrals chronically on show,
25   Their parchment, plate and pyx[2] in locked cases,
And let the rest rent-free to rain and sheep.
Shall we avoid them as unlucky places?

Or, after dark, will dubious women come
To make their children touch a particular stone;
30   Pick simples° for a cancer; or on some   *medicinal herbs*
Advised night see walking a dead one?
Power of some sort or other will go on
In games, in riddles, seemingly at random;
But superstition, like belief, must die,
35   And what remains when disbelief has gone?
Grass, weedy pavement, brambles, buttress, sky,

A shape less recognisable each week,
A purpose more obscure. I wonder who
Will be the last, the very last, to seek
40   This place for what it was; one of the crew
That tap and jot and know what rood-lofts[3] were?
Some ruin-bibber, randy for antique,

---

1. An Irish sixpence has no value in England.
2. Box in which communion wafers are kept.

3. Galleries on top of carved screens separating the nave of a church from the choir.

Or Christmas-addict, counting on a whiff
Of gown-and-bands and organ-pipes and myrrh?[4]
45   Or will he be my representative,

Bored, uninformed, knowing the ghostly silt
Dispersed, yet tending to this cross of ground
Through suburb scrub because it held unspilt
So long and equably what since is found
50   Only in separation—marriage, and birth,
And death, and thoughts of these—for which was built
This special shell? For, though I've no idea
What this accoutred frowsty barn is worth,
It pleases me to stand in silence here;

55   A serious house on serious earth it is,
In whose blent air all our compulsions meet,
Are recognised, and robed as destinies.
And that much never can be obsolete,
Since someone will forever be surprising
60   A hunger in himself to be more serious,
And gravitating with it to this ground,
Which, he once heard, was proper to grow wise in,
If only that so many dead lie round.

1954   1955

MCMXIV[1]

Those long uneven lines
Standing as patiently
As if they were stretched outside
The Oval or Villa Park,[2]
5   The crowns of hats, the sun
On moustached archaic faces
Grinning as if it were all
An August bank Holiday lark;

And the shut shops, the bleached,
10   Established names on the sunblinds,
The farthings and sovereigns,[3]
And dark-clothed children at play
Called after kings and queens,
The tin advertisements
15   For cocoa and twist,° and the pubs   *tobacco*
Wide open all day;

---

4. Gum resin, from trees of genus *Commiphora*, used in the making of incense; one of three presents given by the Three Wise Men to the infant Jesus. "Gown-and-bands": gown and decorative collar worn by clergymen.
1. 1914, in Roman numerals, as incised on stone memorials to the dead of World War I.
2. London cricket ground and Birmingham football ground.
3. At that time, the least valuable and the most valuable British coins, respectively.

And the countryside not caring:
The place-names all hazed over
With flowering grasses, and fields
20   Shadowing Domesday lines[4]
Under wheat's restless silence;
The differently-dressed servants
With tiny rooms in huge houses,
The dust behind limousines;

25   Never such innocence,
Never before or since,
As changed itself to past
Without a word—the men
Leaving the gardens tidy,
30   The thousands of marriages
Lasting a little while longer:
Never such innocence again.

1960   1964

Talking in Bed

Talking in bed ought to be easiest,
Lying together there goes back so far,
An emblem of two people being honest.

Yet more and more time passes silently.
5   Outside, the wind's incomplete unrest
Builds and disperses clouds about the sky,

And dark towns heap up on the horizon.
None of this cares for us. Nothing shows why
At this unique distance from isolation

10   It becomes still more difficult to find
Words at once true and kind,
Or not untrue and not unkind.

1960   1964

Ambulances

Closed like confessionals,[1] they thread
Loud noons of cities, giving back
None of the glances they absorb.
Light glossy grey, arms on a plaque,

---

4. The still-visible boundaries of medieval farmers' long and narrow plots, ownership of which is recorded in William the Conqueror's *Domesday* *Book* (1085–86).
1. Enclosed stalls in Roman Catholic churches in which priests hear confession.

5   They come to rest at any kerb:
     All streets in time are visited.

     Then children strewn on steps or road,
     Or women coming from the shops
     Past smells of different dinners, see
10   A wild white face that overtops
     Red stretcher-blankets momently
     As it is carried in and stowed,

     And sense the solving emptiness
     That lies just under all we do,
15   And for a second get it whole,
     So permanent and blank and true.
     The fastened doors recede. *Poor soul,*
     They whisper at their own distress;

     For borne away in deadened air
20   May go the sudden shut of loss
     Round something nearly at an end,
     And what cohered in it across
     The years, the unique random blend
     Of families and fashions, there

25   At last begin to loosen. Far
     From the exchange of love to lie
     Unreachable inside a room
     The traffic parts to let go by
     Brings closer what is left to come,
30   And dulls to distance all we are.

1961   1964

High Windows

     When I see a couple of kids
     And guess he's fucking her and she's
     Taking pills or wearing a diaphragm,
     I know this is paradise

5   Everyone old has dreamed of all their lives—
     Bonds and gestures pushed to one side
     Like an outdated combine harvester,
     And everyone young going down the long slide

     To happiness, endlessly. I wonder if
10   Anyone looked at me, forty years back,
     And thought, *That'll be the life;*
     No God any more, or sweating in the dark

     About hell and that, or having to hide
     What you think of the priest. He

15   *And his lot will all go down the long slide*
     Like free bloody birds. And immediately

Rather than words comes the thought of high windows:
The sun-comprehending glass,
And beyond it, the deep blue air, that shows
20   Nothing, and is nowhere, and is endless.

1967   1974

Sad Steps[1]

Groping back to bed after a piss
I part thick curtains, and am startled by
The rapid clouds, the moon's cleanliness.

Four o'clock: wedge-shadowed gardens lie
5   Under a cavernous, a wind-picked sky.
There's something laughable about this,

The way the moon dashes through clouds that blow
Loosely as cannon-smoke to stand apart
(Stone-coloured light sharpening the roofs below)

10   High and preposterous and separate—
     Lozenge of love! Medallion of art!
     O wolves of memory! Immensements! No,

One shivers slightly, looking up there.
The hardness and the brightness and the plain
15   Far-reaching singleness of that wide stare

Is a reminder of the strength and pain
Of being young; that it can't come again,
But is for others undiminished somewhere.

1968   1974

The Explosion

On the day of the explosion
Shadows pointed towards the pithead:°   *mine entrance*
In the sun the slagheap slept.

Down the lane came men in pitboots
5   Coughing oath-edged talk and pipe-smoke,
     Shouldering off the freshened silence.

1. Cf. Sir Philip Sidney's *Astrophil and Stella* 31: "With how sad steps, O Moon, thou climb'st the skies."

One chased after rabbits; lost them;
Came back with a nest of lark's eggs;
Showed them; lodged them in the grasses.

10 So they passed in beards and moleskins,
Fathers, brothers, nicknames, laughter,
Through the tall gates standing open.

At noon, there came a tremor; cows
Stopped chewing for a second; sun,
15 Scarfed as in a heat-haze, dimmed.

The dead go on before us, they
Are sitting in God's house in comfort,
We shall see them face to face—

Plain as lettering in the chapels
20 It was said, and for a second
Wives saw men of the explosion

Larger than in life they managed—
Gold as on a coin, or walking
Somehow from the sun towards them,

25 One showing the eggs unbroken.

1970   1974

Aubade[1]

I work all day, and get half-drunk at night.
Waking at four to soundless dark, I stare.
In time the curtain-edges will grow light.
Till then I see what's really always there:
5 Unresting death, a whole day nearer now,
Making all thought impossible but how
And where and when I shall myself die.
Arid interrogation: yet the dread
Of dying, and being dead,
10 Flashes afresh to hold and horrify.

The mind blanks at the glare. Not in remorse
—The good not done, the love not given, time
Torn off unused—nor wretchedly because
An only life can take so long to climb
15 Clear of its wrong beginnings, and may never;
But at the total emptiness for ever,
The sure extinction that we travel to
And shall be lost in always. Not to be here,

1. Music or poem announcing dawn.

Not to be anywhere,
20   And soon; nothing more terrible, nothing more true.

This is a special way of being afraid
No trick dispels. Religion used to try,
That vast moth-eaten musical brocade
Created to pretend we never die,
25   And specious stuff that says *No rational being*
Can fear a thing it will not feel, not seeing
That this is what we fear—no sight, no sound,
No touch or taste or smell, nothing to think with,
Nothing to love or link with,
30   The anaesthetic from which none come round.

And so it stays just on the edge of vision,
A small unfocused blur, a standing chill
That slows each impulse down to indecision.
Most things may never happen: this one will,
35   And realisation of it rages out
In furnace-fear when we are caught without
People or drink. Courage is no good:
It means not scaring others. Being brave
Lets no one off the grave.
40   Death is no different whined at than withstood.

Slowly light strengthens, and the room takes shape.
It stands plain as a wardrobe, what we know,
Have always known, know that we can't escape,
Yet can't accept. One side will have to go.
45   Meanwhile telephones crouch, getting ready to ring
In locked-up offices, and all the uncaring
Intricate rented world begins to rouse.
The sky is white as clay, with no sun.
Work has to be done.
50   Postmen like doctors go from house to house.

                                                                    1977

NADINE GORDIMER
b. 1923

Perhaps more than the work of any other writer, the novels of Nadine Gordimer have given imaginative and moral shape to the recent history of South Africa. Since the publication of her first book, *The Lying Days* (1953), she has charted the changing patterns of response and resistance to apartheid with her exploration of the place of the European in Africa, her selection of representative themes and governing motifs for novels and short stories, and her accompanying shifts in ideological focus from a liberal to a more radical position. It was in recognition of this achievement, of having borne untiring and lucid narrative witness, that Gordimer was awarded the 1991 Nobel Prize for Literature.

Born in 1923 to Jewish immigrant parents in the South African mining town of Springs, Gordimer began writing early, from the beginning taking as her subject the pathologies and everyday realities of a racially divided society. Her decision to remain in Johannesburg through the years of political repression reflected her commitment to her subject and to her vision of a postapartheid future. In the years since apartheid was dismantled in 1994, Gordimer has continued to live and write in South Africa, and her recent novels, *None to Accompany Me* (1994) and *The House Gun* (1998), retain an uncompromising focus on the inhabitants of a racially fractured culture.

Gordimer's concern—as shown in her incisive and highly acclaimed novels of the 1970s, *The Conservationist* (1974) and *Burger's Daughter* (1979)—is to evoke by way of the personal and the precisely observed particular a broader political and historical totality. It is this that gives her characters, and her novels themselves, their representativeness. As Gordimer has famously said, "politics is character in South Africa." Yet, throughout the long years of political polarization in that country and the banning of three of her own books, Gordimer has distanced herself from polemics and retained a firm humanist belief in what she variously describes as the objectivity and the inwardness of the writer. Narrative for Gordimer helps define and clarify historical experience. Her keen sense of history as formation, and as demanding a continual rewriting, has ensured that her novels can be read as at once contemporary in their reference and symbolic of broader social and historical patterns, as in the paranoia surrounding the case of the buried black body on a white farm in *The Conservationist,* or in the psychosocial portrait of Rosa Burger in *Burger's Daughter.*

Gordimer has drawn criticism both for her apparent lack of attention to feminism in favor of race issues and for the wholeness and unfashionable completeness of her novels—their plottedness, meticulous scene paintings, fully realized characters. However, the searching symbolism and complexity of her narratives generally work against such judgments. As the following short story shows, a prominent feature of her writing is to give a number of different perspectives on a situation, in some cases most poignantly those of apartheid's supporters, and in this way to represent the broader anatomy of a diseased politics. Gordimer's subject, as she emphasizes, is much more than apartheid; it is the human being in history.

The Moment before the Gun Went Off

Marais Van der Vyver shot one of his farm labourers, dead. An accident, there are accidents with guns every day of the week—children playing a fatal game with a father's revolver in the cities where guns are domestic objects, nowadays, hunting mishaps like this one, in the country—but these won't be reported all over the world. Van der Vyver knows his will be. He knows that the story of the Afrikaner farmer—regional Party leader and Commandant of the local security commando—shooting a black man who worked for him will fit exactly *their* version of South Africa, it's made for them. They'll be able to use it in their boycott and divestment campaigns, it'll be another piece of evidence in their truth about the country. The papers at home will quote the story as it has appeared in the overseas press, and in the back-and-forth he and the black man will become those crudely-drawn figures on anti-apartheid banners, units in statistics of white brutality against the blacks quoted at the United Nations—he, whom they will gleefully be able to call "a leading member" of the ruling Party.

People in the farming community understand how he must feel. Bad enough to have killed a man, without helping the Party's, the government's, the country's enemies, as well. They see the truth of that. They know, reading the Sunday papers, that when Van der Vyver is quoted saying he is "terribly shocked," he will "look after the wife and children," none of those Americans and English, and none of those people at home who want to destroy the white man's power will believe him. And how they will sneer when he even says of the farm boy (according to one paper, if you can trust any of those reporters), "He was my friend, I always took him hunting with me." Those city and overseas people don't know it's true: farmers usually have one particular black boy they like to take along with them in the lands; you could call it a kind of friend, yes, friends are not only your own white people, like yourself, you take into your house, pray with in church and work with on the Party committee. But how can those others know that? They don't want to know it. They think all blacks are like the big-mouth agitators in town. And Van der Vyver's face, in the photographs, strangely opened by distress—everyone in the district remembers Marais Van der Vyver as a little boy who would go away and hide himself if he caught you smiling at him, and everyone knows him now as a man who hides any change of expression round his mouth behind a thick, soft moustache, and in his eyes by always looking at some object in hand, leaf of a crop fingered, pen or stone picked up, while concentrating on what he is saying, or while listening to you. It just goes to show what shock can do; when you look at the newspaper photographs you feel like apologising, as if you had stared in on some room where you should not be.

There will be an inquiry; there had better be, to stop the assumption of yet another case of brutality against farm workers, although there's nothing in doubt—an accident, and all the facts fully admitted by Van der Vyver. He made a statement when he arrived at the police station with the dead man in his bakkie.[1] Captain Beetge knows him well, of course; he gave him brandy. He was shaking, this big, calm, clever son of Willem Van der Vyver, who inherited the old man's best farm. The black was stone dead, nothing to be done for him. Beetge will not tell anyone that after the brandy Van der Vyver wept. He sobbed, snot running onto his hands, like a dirty kid. The Captain was ashamed, for him, and walked out to give him a chance to recover himself.

Marais Van der Vyver left his house at three in the afternoon to cull a buck from the family of kudu[2] he protects in the bush areas of his farm. He is interested in wildlife and sees it as the farmers' sacred duty to raise game as well as cattle. As usual, he called at his shed workshop to pick up Lucas, a twenty-year-old farmhand who had shown mechanical aptitude and whom Van der Vyver himself had taught to maintain tractors and other farm machinery. He hooted, and Lucas followed the familiar routine, jumping onto the back of the truck. He liked to travel standing up there, spotting

1. Pickup truck.
2. Large African antelope. The males have long, spirally twisted horns.

game before his employer did. He would lean forward, braced against the cab below him.

Van der Vyver had a rifle and .300 ammunition beside him in the cab. The rifle was one of his father's, because his own was at the gunsmith's in town. Since his father died (Beetge's sergeant wrote "passed on") no one had used the rifle and so when he took it from a cupboard he was sure it was not loaded. His father had never allowed a loaded gun in the house; he himself had been taught since childhood never to ride with a loaded weapon in a vehicle. But this gun was loaded. On a dirt track, Lucas thumped his fist on the cab roof three times to signal: look left. Having seen the white-ripple-marked flank of a kudu, and its fine horns raking through disguising bush, Van der Vyver drove rather fast over a pot-hole. The jolt fired the rifle. Upright, it was pointing straight through the cab roof at the head of Lucas. The bullet pierced the roof and entered Lucas's brain by way of his throat.

That is the statement of what happened. Although a man of such standing in the district, Van der Vyver had to go through the ritual of swearing that it was the truth. It has gone on record, and will be there in the archive of the local police station as long as Van der Vyver lives, and beyond that, through the lives of his children, Magnus, Helena and Karel—unless things in the country get worse, the example of black mobs in the towns spreads to the rural areas and the place is burned down as many urban police stations have been. Because nothing the government can do will appease the agitators and the whites who encourage them. Nothing satisfies them, in the cities: blacks can sit and drink in white hotels, now, the Immorality Act[3] has gone, blacks can sleep with whites. . . . It's not even a crime any more.

Van der Vyver has a high barbed security fence round his farmhouse and garden which his wife, Alida, thinks spoils completely the effect of her artificial stream with its tree-ferns beneath the jacarandas.[4] There is an aerial soaring like a flag-pole in the back yard. All his vehicles, including the truck in which the black man died, have aerials that swing their whips when the driver hits a pot-hole: they are part of the security system the farmers in the district maintain, each farm in touch with every other by radio, twenty-four hours out of twenty-four. It has already happened that infiltrators from over the border have mined remote farm roads, killing white farmers and their families out on their own property for a Sunday picnic. The pot-hole could have set off a land-mine, and Van der Vyver might have died with his farm boy. When neighbours use the communications system to call up and say they are sorry about "that business" with one of Van der Vyver's boys, there goes unsaid: it could have been worse.

It is obvious from the quality and fittings of the coffin that the farmer has provided money for the funeral. And an elaborate funeral means a great deal to blacks; look how they will deprive themselves of the little they have, in their lifetime, keeping up payments to a burial society so they won't go in boxwood to an unmarked grave. The young wife is pregnant (of course) and another little one, wearing red shoes several sizes too large, leans under her jutting belly. He is too young to understand what has happened, what he is witnessing that day, but neither whines nor plays about; he is solemn without

3. South African government act prohibiting sexual relations between whites and other races. 4. Tropical trees with blue flowers.

knowing why. Blacks expose small children to everything, they don't protect them from the sight of fear and pain the way whites do theirs. It is the young wife who rolls her head and cries like a child, sobbing on the breast of this relative and that.

All present work for Van der Vyver or are the families of those who work; and in the weeding and harvest seasons, the women and children work for him, too, carried—wrapped in their blankets, on a truck, singing—at sunrise to the fields. The dead man's mother is a woman who can't be more than in her late thirties (they start bearing children at puberty) but she is heavily mature in a black dress between her own parents, who were already working for old Van der Vyver when Marais, like their daughter, was a child. The parents hold her as if she were a prisoner or a crazy woman to be restrained. But she says nothing, does nothing. She does not look up; she does not look at Van der Vyver, whose gun went off in the truck, she stares at the grave. Nothing will make her look up; there need be no fear that she will look up; at him. His wife, Alida, is beside him. To show the proper respect, as for any white funeral, she is wearing the navy-blue-and-cream hat she wears to church this summer. She is always supportive, although he doesn't seem to notice it; this coldness and reserve—his mother says he didn't mix well as a child—she accepts for herself but regrets that it has prevented him from being nominated, as he should be, to stand as the Party's parliamentary candidate for the district. He does not let her clothing, or that of anyone else gathered closely, make contact with him. He, too, stares at the grave. The dead man's mother and he stare at the grave in communication like that between the black man outside and the white man inside the cab the moment before the gun went off.

The moment before the gun went off was a moment of high excitement shared through the roof of the cab, as the bullet was to pass, between the young black man outside and the white farmer inside the vehicle. There were such moments, without explanation, between them, although often around the farm the farmer would pass the young man without returning a greeting, as if he did not recognize him. When the bullet went off what Van der Vyver saw was the kudu stumble in fright at the report and gallop away. Then he heard the thud behind him, and past the window saw the young man fall out of the vehicle. He was sure he had leapt up and toppled—in fright, like the buck. The farmer was almost laughing with relief, ready to tease, as he opened his door, it did not seem possible that a bullet passing through the roof could have done harm.

The young man did not laugh with him at his own fright. The farmer carried him in his arms, to the truck. He was sure, sure he could not be dead. But the young black man's blood was all over the farmer's clothes, soaking against his flesh as he drove.

How will they ever know, when they file newspaper clippings, evidence, proof, when they look at the photographs and see his face—guilty! guilty! they are right!—how will they know, when the police stations burn with all the evidence of what has happened now, and what the law made a crime in the past. How could they know that *they do not know*. Anything. The young black callously shot through the negligence of the white man was not the farmer's boy; he was his son.

1991

DEREK WALCOTT
b. 1930

Derek Walcott was born on the island of St. Lucia in the British West Indies and educated there at St. Mary's College and at the University of the West Indies in Jamaica. He then moved to Trinidad, where he has worked as a book reviewer, art critic, playwright, and artistic director of a theater workshop. He has also been poet-in-residence at a number of American colleges and universities and is the recipient of a MacArthur Award.

At once flamboyant and disciplined, poems like his wittily titled *A Far Cry from Africa* proclaim his divided roots, as a black poet writing from within both the English literary tradition and the history of a subject people. He has since proved the truth of Yeats's statement that "out of our quarrel with ourselves we make poetry." Isolation is Walcott's theme; and as with Yeats, the writing and producing of plays has increased the emotional and dramatic range of his poetry. The movement of *Another Life* (1973) and *Midsummer* (1984) is freer, more flexible than that of earlier work, but Walcott's language still has the accuracy and energy that proclaim him—more than any of his American contemporaries—the natural heir of his friend Robert Lowell. In 1992, following the publication of his verse epic *Omeros*, which transposes elements of Homeric epic from the Aegean to the Caribbean, Walcott was awarded the Nobel Prize for Literature.

A Far Cry from Africa

A wind is ruffling the tawny pelt
Of Africa. Kikuyu,[1] quick as flies,
Batten upon the bloodstreams of the veldt.[2]
Corpses are scattered through a paradise.
5   Only the worm, colonel of carrion, cries:
"Waste no compassion on these separate dead!"
Statistics justify and scholars seize
The salients of colonial policy.
What is that to the white child hacked in bed?
10   To savages, expendable as Jews?

Threshed out by beaters,[3] the long rushes break
In a white dust of ibises whose cries
Have wheeled since civilization's dawn
From the parched river or beast-teeming plain.
15   The violence of beast on beast is read
As natural law, but upright man
Seeks his divinity by inflicting pain.
Delirious as these worried beasts, his wars
Dance to the tightened carcass of a drum,
20   While he calls courage still that native dread
Of the white peace contracted by the dead.

Again brutish necessity wipes its hands
Upon the napkin of a dirty cause, again

---

1. An east African tribe whose members, as Mau Mau fighters, conducted an eight-year terrorist campaign against British colonial settlers in Kenya.
2. Open country, neither cultivated nor forest (Afrikaans).
3. In big-game hunting, natives are hired to beat the brush, driving birds—such as ibises—and other animals into the open.

A waste of our compassion, as with Spain,[4]
25   The gorilla wrestles with the superman.
I who am poisoned with the blood of both,
Where shall I turn, divided to the vein?
I who have cursed
The drunken officer of British rule, how choose
30   Between this Africa and the English tongue I love?
Betray them both, or give back what they give?
How can I face such slaughter and be cool?
How can I turn from Africa and live?

1962

Nights in the Gardens of Port of Spain[1]

Night, the black summer, simplifies her smells
into a village; she assumes the impenetrable

musk of the negro, grows secret as sweat,
her alleys odorous with shucked oyster shells,

5   coals of gold oranges, braziers of melon.
Commerce and tambourines increase her heat.

Hellfire or the whorehouse: crossing Park Street,
a surf of sailors' faces crests, is gone

with the sea's phosphoresence; the boites-de-nuit[2]
10   tinkle like fireflies in her thick hair.

Blinded by headlamps, deaf to taxi klaxons,
she lifts her face from the cheap, pitch oil flare

towards white stars, like cities, flashing neon,
burning to be the bitch she must become.

15   As daylight breaks the coolie turns his tumbril[3]
of hacked, beheaded coconuts towards home.

1964

The Glory Trumpeter

Old Eddie's face, wrinkled with river lights,
Looked like a Mississippi man's. The eyes,
Derisive and avuncular at once,
Swivelling, fixed me. They'd seen

4. The Spanish Civil War (1936–39).
1. Capital of Trinidad, British West Indies.
2. Nightclubs (French).

3. Open cart used in the French Revolution to carry victims to the guillotine.

5   Too many wakes, too many cathouse nights.
     The bony, idle fingers on the valves
     Of his knee-cradled horn could tear
     Through "Georgia on My Mind" or "Jesus Saves"
     With the same fury of indifference,
10   If what propelled such frenzy was despair.

     Now, as the eyes sealed in the ashen flesh,
     And Eddie, like a deacon at his prayer,
     Rose, tilting the bright horn, I saw a flash
     Of gulls and pigeons from the dunes of coal
15   Near my grandmother's barracks on the wharves,
     I saw the sallow faces of those men
     Who sighed as if they spoke into their graves
     About the Negro in America. That was when
     The Sunday comics sprawled out on her floor,
20   Sent from the States, had a particular odour,
     A smell of money mingled with man's sweat.

     And yet, if Eddie's features held our fate,
     Secure in childhood I did not know then
     A jesus-ragtime or gut-bucket blues
25   To the bowed heads of lean, compliant men
     Back from the States in their funereal serge,
     Black, rusty Homburgs[1] and limp waiters' ties
     With honey accents and lard-coloured eyes
     Was Joshua's ram's horn wailing for the Jews
30   Of patient bitterness or bitter siege.[2]

     Now it was that as Eddie turned his back
     On our young crowd out fêteing, swilling liquor,
     And blew, eyes closed, one foot up, out to sea,
     His horn aimed at those cities of the Gulf,
35   Mobile and Galveston and sweetly meted
     The horn of plenty through a bitter cup,
     In lonely exaltation blaming me
     For all whom race and exile have defeated,
     For my own uncle in America,
40   That living there I never could look up.

                                                    1964

From The Schooner *Flight*

1 Adios,[1] Carenage

In idle August, while the sea soft,
and leaves of brown islands stick to the rim
of this Caribbean, I blow out the light

1. Old-fashioned felt hats. "Funereal serge":
cheap dark suits.
2. At the fall of the city of Jericho (Joshua 6.1–

21).
1. Goodbye (Spanish).

by the dreamless face of Maria Concepcion
5   to ship as a seaman on the schooner *Flight*.
Out in the yard turning grey in the dawn,
I stood like a stone and nothing else move
but the cold sea rippling like galvanize
and the nail holes of stars in the sky roof,
10 till a wind start to interfere with the trees.
I pass me dry neighbour sweeping she yard
as I went downhill, and I nearly said:
"Sweep soft, you witch, 'cause she don't sleep hard,"
but the bitch look through me like I was dead.
15 A route taxi pull up, park-lights still on.
The driver size up my bags with a grin:
"This time, Shabine, like you really gone!"
I ain't answer the ass, I simply pile in
the back seat and watch the sky burn
20 above Laventille pink as the gown
in which the woman I left was sleeping,
and I look in the rearview and see a man
exactly like me, and the man was weeping
for the houses, the streets, the whole fucking island.
25 Christ have mercy on all sleeping things!
From that dog rotting down Wrightson Road
to when I was a dog on these streets;
if loving these islands must be my load,
out of corruption my soul takes wings,
30 But they had started to poison my soul
with their big house, big car, big-time bohbohl,
coolie, nigger, Syrian, and French Creole,
so I leave it for them and their carnival—
I taking a sea-bath, I gone down the road.
35 I know these islands from Monos to Nassau,
a rusty head sailor with sea-green eyes
that they nickname Shabine, the patois for
any red nigger, and I, Shabine, saw
when these slums of empire was paradise.
40 I'm just a red nigger who love the sea,
I had a sound colonial education,
I have Dutch, nigger, and English in me,
and either I'm nobody, or I'm a nation.

But Maria Concepcion was all my thought
45 watching the sea heaving up and down
as the port side of dories, schooners, and yachts
was painted afresh by the strokes of the sun
signing her name with every reflection;
I knew when dark-haired evening put on
50 her bright silk at sunset, and, folding the sea,
sidled under the sheet with her starry laugh,
that there'd be no rest, there'd be no forgetting.
Is like telling mourners round the graveside

about resurrection, they want the dead back,
55 so I smile to myself as the bow rope untied
and the *Flight* swing seaward: "Is no use repeating
that the sea have more fish. I ain't want her
dressed in the sexless light of a seraph,
I want those round brown eyes like a marmoset, and
60 till the day when I can lean back and laugh,
those claws that tickled my back on sweating
Sunday afternoons, like a crab on wet sand."
As I worked, watching the rotting waves come
past the bow that scissor the sea like silk,
65 I swear to you all, by my mother's milk,
by the stars that shall fly from tonight's furnace,
that I loved them, my children, my wife, my home;
I loved them as poets love the poetry
that kills them, as drowned sailors the sea.

70 You ever look up from some lonely beach
and see a far schooner? Well, when I write
this poem, each phrase go be soaked in salt;
I go draw and knot every line as tight
as ropes in this rigging; in simple speech
75 my common language go be the wind,
my pages the sails of the schooner *Flight*.

1979

Midsummer

Certain things here[1] are quietly American—
that chain-link fence dividing the absent roars
of the beach from the empty ball park, its holes
muttering the word umpire instead of empire;
5 the gray, metal light where an early pelican
coasts, with its engine off, over the pink fire
of a sea whose surface is as cold as Maine's.
The light warms up the sides of white, eager Cessnas[2]
parked at the airstrip under the freckling hills
10 of St. Thomas. The sheds, the brown, functional hangar,
are like those of the Occupation in the last war.
The night left a rank smell under the casuarinas,[3]
the villas have fenced-off beaches where the natives walk,
illegal immigrants from unlucky islands
15 who envy the smallest polyp its right to work.
Here the wetback crab and the mollusc are citizens,
and the leaves have green cards. Bulldozers jerk
and gouge out a hill, but we all know that the dust
is industrial and must be suffered. Soon—

---

1. I.e., in Trinidad.
2. Make of small aircraft.

3. Trees with jointed branches.

20   the sea's corrugations are sheets of zinc
soldered by the sun's steady acetylene. This
drizzle that falls now is American rain,
stitching stars in the sand. My own corpuscles
are changing as fast. I fear what the migrant envies:
25   the starry pattern they make—the flag on the post office—
the quality of the dirt, the fealty changing under my foot.

1984

From Omeros

Chapter XXX

1

He yawned and watched the lilac horns of his island
lift the horizon.
        "I know you ain't like to talk,"
the mate said, "but this morning I could use a hand.

Where your mind was whole night?"
               "Africa."
                       "Oh? You walk?"
5   The mate held up his T-shirt, mainly a red hole,
and wriggled it on. He tested the bamboo pole

that trawled the skipping lure from the fast-shearing hull
with the Trade behind them.
               "Mackerel running," he said.
"Africa, right! You get sunstroke, chief. That is all.

10 You best put that damn captain-cap back on your head."
All night he had worked the rods without any sleep,
watching Achille cradled in the bow; he had read

the stars and known how far out they were and how deep
the black troughs were and how long it took them to lift,
15 but he owed it to his captain, who took him on

when he was stale-drunk. He had not noticed the swift.
"You know what we ketch last night? One *mako* size 'ton,' "
using the patois for kingfish, blue albacore.

"Look by your foot."
            The kingfish, steel-blue and silver,
20 lay fresh at his feet, its eye like a globed window
ringing with cold, its rim the circular river

of the current that had carried him back, with the spoon
bait in its jaw, the ton was his deliverer,
now its cold eye in sunlight was blind as the moon.

25 A grey lens clouded the gaze of the albacore
that the mate had gaffed and clubbed. It lay there, gaping,
its blue flakes yielding the oceanic colour

of the steel-cold depth from which it had shot, leaping,
stronger than a stallion's neck tugging its stake,
30 sounding, then bursting its trough, yawning at the lure

of a fishhook moon that was reeled in at daybreak
round the horizon's wrist. Tired of slapping water,
the tail's wedge had drifted into docility.

Achille had slept through the fight. Cradled at the bow
35 like a foetus, like a sea-horse, his memory
dimmed in the sun with the scales of the albacore.

"Look, land!" the mate said. Achille altered the rudder
to keep sideways in the deep troughs without riding
the crests, then he looked up at an old man-o'-war

40 tracing the herring-gulls with that endless gliding
that made it the sea-king.
       "Them stupid gulls does fish
for him every morning. He himself don't catch none,

white slaves for a black king."
        "When?" the mate said. "You wish."
"Look him dropping." Achille pointed. "Look at that son-
45 of-a-bitch stealing his fish for the whole fucking week!"

A herring-gull climbed with silver bent in its beak
and the black magnificent frigate met the gull
halfway with the tribute; the gull dropped the mackerel

but the frigate-bird caught it before it could break
the water and soared.
50   "The black bugger beautiful,
though!" The mate nodded, and Achille felt the phrase lift

his heart as high as the bird whose wings wrote the word
"Afolabe," in the letters of the sea-swift.
"The king going home," he said as he and the mate

55 watched the frigate steer into that immensity
of seraphic space whose cumuli were a gate
dividing for a monarch entering his city.

               1990

SEAMUS HEANEY
b. 1939

Seamus Heaney was born into a Roman Catholic family in the Protestant north of Ireland (or Ulster), and grew up on a farm in County Derry bordered on one side by a stream that marked the frontier with the predominantly Roman Catholic Irish Republic (or Eire) to the south. He won scholarships first to St. Columb's College, a Catholic boarding school, and then to Queen's University in Protestant Belfast. There he became one of a lively group of young poets that included Michael Longley and Derek Mahon, writing with the encouragement of two faculty poets, Laurence Lerner and Philip Hobsbaum. He has been Boylston Professor of Rhetoric and Oratory at Harvard and Professor of Poetry at Oxford.

With *Digging*, placed appropriately as the first poem of his first book, Heaney defined his territory. He dug into his memory, uncovering first his father and then, going deeper, his grandfather. In this and many later poems, his concern has been— like Tony Harrison's—to give a voice to the silent and oppressed. In 1967, his political preoccupations were brought into sharper focus by his reading of *The Bog People* by P. V. Glob, a Danish archaeologist. This opened his eyes—as Jessie L. Weston's *From Ritual to Romance* had opened Eliot's—to deeper levels of mythic and historical congruence. He writes of *The Bog People*:

> It was chiefly concerned with preserved bodies of men and women found in the bogs of Jutland, naked, strangled or with their throats cut, disposed under the peat since early Iron Age times. The author . . . argues convincingly that a number of these, and in particular, the Tollund Man, whose head is now preserved near Aarhus in the museum of Silkeburg, were ritual sacrifices to the Mother Goddess, the goddess of the ground who needed new bridegrooms each winter to bed with her in her sacred place, in the spring. Taken in relation to the tradition of Irish political martyrdom for the cause whose icon is Kathleen Ni Houlihan [mythic figure emblematic of Mother Ireland], this is more than an archaic barbarous rite: it is an archetypal pattern. And the unforgettable photographs of these victims blended in my mind with photographs of atrocities, past and present, in the long rites of Irish political and religious struggles.

Heaney's perception that the Irish "bog is a memory bank," in that it preserves everything thrown into it, produced the powerful bog poems of *North* (1975). By then, feeling constrained by the role of political poet being thrust on him, he had crossed the border to live in the Irish Republic. The troubles of Ireland continue to surface in the poems he has written since, but the richer harmonies of *Field Work* (1979), *Station Island* (1984), *The Haw Lantern* (1987), *Seeing Things* (1991), and *The Spirit Level* (1996) confirm the wisdom of his decision to move south and the truth of Robert Lowell's judgment that Heaney is "the best Irish poet since W. B. Yeats." His *Opened Ground: Poems 1966–1996* ends with "Crediting Poetry," the speech with which he accepted the 1995 Nobel Prize, awarded to him, in the words of the Swedish Academy of Letters, for his "words of lyrical beauty and ethical depth." Heaney is also a noteworthy translator; his verse translation of *Beowulf* appears on pp. 23 to 93 of this volume.

Digging

Between my finger and my thumb
The squat pen rests; snug as a gun.

Under my window, a clean rasping sound
When the spade sinks into gravelly ground:
5 My father, digging. I look down

Till his straining rump among the flowerbeds
Bends low, comes up twenty years away
Stooping in rhythm through potato drills[1]
Where he was digging.

10 The coarse boot nestled on the lug, the shaft
Against the inside knee was levered firmly.
He rooted out tall tops, buried the bright edge deep
To scatter new potatoes that we picked
Loving their cool hardness in our hands.

15 By God, the old man could handle a spade.
Just like his old man.

My grandfather cut more turf[2] in a day
Than any other man on Toner's bog.
Once I carried him milk in a bottle
20 Corked sloppily with paper. He straightened up
To drink it, then fell to right away
Nicking and slicing neatly, heaving sods
Over his shoulder, going down and down
For the good turf. Digging.

25 The cold smell of potato mould, the squelch and slap
Of soggy peat, the curt cuts of an edge
Through living roots awaken in my head.
But I've no spade to follow men like them.

Between my finger and my thumb
30 The squat pen rests.
I'll dig with it.

1966

The Forge

All I know is a door into the dark.
Outside, old axles and iron hoops rusting;
Inside, the hammered anvil's short-pitched ring,
The unpredictable fantail of sparks
5 Or hiss when a new shoe toughens in water.
The anvil must be somewhere in the centre,
Horned as a unicorn, at one end square,
Set there immoveable: an altar

---

1. Small furrows in which seeds are sown.
2. Slabs of peat that, when dried, are a common domestic fuel in Ireland.

Where he expends himself in shape and music.
10   Sometimes, leather-aproned, hairs in his nose,
He leans out on the jamb, recalls a clatter
Of hoofs where traffic is flashing in rows;
Then grunts and goes in, with a slam and flick
To beat real iron out, to work the bellows.

1969

Punishment[1]

I can feel the tug
of the halter at the nape
of her neck, the wind
on her naked front.

5   It blows her nipples
to amber beads,
it shakes the frail rigging
of her ribs.

I can see her drowned
10   body in the bog,
the weighing stone,
the floating rods and boughs.

Under which at first
she was a barked sapling
15   that is dug up
oak-bone, brain-firkin:°   *small cask*

her shaved head
like a stubble of black corn,
her blindfold a soiled bandage,
20   her noose a ring

to store
the memories of love.
Little adultress,
before they punished you

---

1. In 1951 the peat-stained body of a young girl, who lived in the late 1st century C.E., was recovered from a bog in Windeby, Germany. As P. V. Glob describes her in *The Bog People,* she "lay naked in the hole in the peat, a bandage over the eyes and a collar round the neck. The band across the eyes was drawn tight and had cut into the neck and the base of the nose. We may feel sure that it had not been used to close her eyes to this world. There was no mark of strangulation on the neck, so that it had not been used for that purpose." Her hair "had been shaved off with a razor on the left side of the head. . . . When the brain was removed the convolutions and folds of the surface could be clearly seen [Glob reproduces a photograph of her brain]. . . . this girl of only fourteen had had an inadequate winter diet. . . . To keep the young body under, some birch branches and a big stone were laid upon her." According to the Roman historian Tacitus, the Germanic peoples punished adulterous women by shaving off their hair and then scourging them out of the village or killing them. Today, her "betraying sisters" are sometimes shaved, stripped, tarred, and handcuffed by the IRA to the railings of Belfast in punishment for keeping company with British soldiers.

25   you were flaxen-haired,
      undernourished, and your
      tar-black face was beautiful.
      My poor scapegoat,

      I almost love you
30   but would have cast, I know,
      the stones of silence.
      I am the artful voyeur

      of your brain's exposed
      and darkened combs,
35   your muscles' webbing
      and all your numbered bones:

      I who have stood dumb
      when your betraying sisters,
      cauled in tar,
40   wept by the railings,

      who would connive
      in civilized outrage
      yet understand the exact
      and tribal, intimate revenge.

      1975

Casualty

1

      He would drink by himself
      And raise a weathered thumb
      Towards the high shelf,
      Calling another rum
5   And blackcurrant, without
      Having to raise his voice,
      Or order a quick stout°   *strong, dark beer*
      By a lifting of the eyes
      And a discreet dumb-show
10 Of pulling off the top;
      At closing time would go
      In waders and peaked cap
      Into the showery dark,
      A dole-kept[1] breadwinner
15 But a natural for work.
      I loved his whole manner,
      Sure-footed but too sly,
      His deadpan sidling tact,
      His fisherman's quick eye

---

1. I.e., receiving unemployment benefits.

20 And turned observant back.
Incomprehensible
To him, my other life.
Sometimes, on his high stool,
Too busy with his knife
25 At a tobacco plug
And not meeting my eye
In the pause after a slug[2]
He mentioned poetry.
We would be on our own
30 And, always politic
And shy of condescension,
I would manage by some trick
To switch the talk to eels
Or lore of the horse and cart
35 Or the Provisionals.[3]

But my tentative art
His turned back watches too:
He was blown to bits
Out drinking in a curfew
40 Others obeyed, three nights
After they shot dead
The thirteen men in Derry.
PARAS THIRTEEN, the walls said,
BOGSIDE NIL.[4] That Wednesday
45 Everybody held
His breath and trembled.

2

It was a day of cold
Raw silence, wind-blown
Surplice and soutane:[5]
50 Rained-on, flower-laden
Coffin after coffin
Seemed to float from the door
Of the packed cathedral
Like blossoms on slow water.
55 The common funeral
Unrolled its swaddling band,[6]
Lapping, tightening
Till we were braced and bound
Like brothers in a ring.

60 But he would not be held
At home by his own crowd
Whatever threats were phoned,

2. Of liquor.
3. The Provisional Branch of the IRA.
4. This graffito records—in the form of a football match score—that the British Army's Parachute Regiment had killed thirteen people, and the Roman Catholic inhabitants of Londonderry's Bogside district, none.
5. Vestments worn by Roman Catholic priests.
6. Long cloth in which babies were once wrapped to restrain them.

Whatever black flags waved.
I see him as he turned
65 In that bombed offending place,
Remorse fused with terror
In his still knowable face,
His cornered outfaced stare
Blinding in the flash.

70 He had gone miles away
For he drank like a fish
Nightly, naturally
Swimming towards the lure
Of warm lit-up places,
75 The blurred mesh and murmur
Drifting among glasses
In the gregarious smoke.
How culpable was he
That last night when he broke
80 Our tribe's complicity?[7]
"Now you're supposed to be
An educated man,"
I hear him say. "Puzzle me
The right answer to that one."

3

85 I missed his funeral,
Those quiet walkers
And sideways talkers
Shoaling out of his lane
To the respectable
90 Purring of the hearse . . .
They move in equal pace
With the habitual
Slow consolation
Of a dawdling engine,
95 The line lifted, hand
Over fist, cold sunshine
On the water, the land
Banked under fog: that morning
I was taken in his boat,
100 The screw° purling, turning   propellor
Indolent fathoms white,
I tasted freedom with him.
To get out early, haul
Steadily off the bottom,
105 Dispraise the catch, and smile
As you find a rhythm
Working you, slow mile by mile,
Into your proper haunt
Somewhere, well out, beyond . . .

7. The Roman Catholic community's agreement to obey the curfew (of lines 39–40).

110   Dawn-sniffing revenant,[8]
      Plodder through midnight rain,
      Question me again.

                                                          1979

The Skunk

Up, black, striped and damasked like the chasuble[1]
At a funeral mass, the skunk's tail
Paraded the skunk. Night after night
I expected her like a visitor.

5   The refrigerator whinnied into silence.
    My desk light softened beyond the verandah.
    Small oranges loomed in the orange tree.
    I began to be tense as a voyeur.

    After eleven years I was composing
10 Love-letters again, broaching the word "wife"
    Like a stored cask, as if its slender vowel
    Had mutated into the night earth and air

    Of California. The beautiful, useless
    Tang of eucalyptus spelt your absence.
15 The aftermath of a mouthful of wine
    Was like inhaling you off a cold pillow.

    And there she was, the intent and glamorous,
    Ordinary, mysterious skunk,
    Mythologized, demythologized,
20 Snuffing the boards five feet beyond me.

    It all came back to me last night, stirred
    By the sootfall of your things at bedtime,
    Your head-down, tail-up hunt in a bottom drawer
    For the black plunge-line nightdress.

                                                          1979

From Station Island[1]

12

Like a convalescent, I took the hand
stretched down from the jetty, sensed again
an alien comfort as I stepped on ground

8. One returned from the dead.
1. Sleeveless vestment worn by the priest celebrating mass, its color regulated by the feast of the
day.
1. *Station Island* is a sequence of dream encounters with familiar ghosts, set on Station Island on
Lough Derg in Co. Donegal. The island is also
known as St. Patrick's Purgatory because of a tradition that Patrick was the first to establish the
penitential vigil of fasting and praying which still
constitutes the basis of the three-day pilgrimage.
Each unit of the contemporary pilgrim's exercises
is called a 'station,' and a large part of each station
involves walking barefoot and praying round the
'beds,' stone circles which are said to be the
remains of early medieval monastic cells [Heaney's
note]. In this last section of the poem, the familiar
ghost is that of Heaney's countryman James Joyce.

to find the helping hand still gripping mine,
5   fish-cold and bony, but whether to guide
or to be guided I could not be certain

for the tall man in step at my side
seemed blind, though he walked straight as a rush
upon his ash plant,[2] his eyes fixed straight ahead.

10 Then I knew him in the flesh
out there on the tarmac among the cars,
wintered hard and sharp as a blackthorn bush.

His voice eddying with the vowels of all rivers[3]
came back to me, though he did not speak yet,
15 a voice like a prosecutor's or a singer's,

cunning,[4] narcotic, mimic, definite
as a steel nib's downstroke, quick and clean,
and suddenly he hit a litter basket

with his stick, saying, "Your obligation
20 is not discharged by any common rite.
What you must do must be done on your own

so get back in harness. The main thing is to write
for the joy of it. Cultivate a work-lust
that imagines its haven like your hands at night

25 dreaming the sun in the sunspot of a breast.
You are fasted now, light-headed, dangerous.
Take off from here. And don't be so earnest,

let others wear the sackcloth and the ashes.[5]
Let go, let fly, forget.
30 You've listened long enough. Now strike your note."

It was as if I had stepped free into space
alone with nothing that I had not known
already. Raindrops blew in my face

as I came to. "Old father, mother's son,
35 there is a moment in Stephen's diary
for April the thirteenth, a revelation

set among my stars—that one entry
has been a sort of password in my ears,
the collect of a new epiphany,[6]

---

2. Walking stick made of ash. Joyce was almost
blind.
3. The Anna Livia Plurabelle episode of *Finnegans
Wake* (p. 2565) resounds with the names of many
rivers.
4. "The only arms I allow myself to use—silence,
exile, and cunning" (Joyce, *Portrait of the Artist as*

a Young Man).
5. As worn by penitents in biblical times and later.
6. Manifestation of a superhuman being, as of the
infant Jesus to the Magi (Matthew 2). In the Christian calendar, the Feast of the Epiphany is January
6. "Collect": short prayer assigned to a particular
day.

40 the Feast of the Holy Tundish."⁷ "Who cares,"
he jeered, "any more? The English language
belongs to us. You are raking at dead fires,

a waste of time for somebody your age.
That subject people stuff is a cod's° game,   *fool's*
45 infantile, like your peasant pilgrimage.

You lose more of yourself than you redeem
doing the decent thing. Keep at a tangent.
When they make the circle wide, it's time to swim

out on your own and fill the element
50 with signatures on your own frequency,
echo soundings, searches, probes, allurements,

elver-gleams⁸ in the dark of the whole sea."
The shower broke in a cloudburst, the tarmac
fumed and sizzled. As he moved off quickly

55 the downpour loosed its screens round his straight walk.

                                                    1984

The Sharping Stone¹

In an apothecary's° chest of drawers,   *pharmacist's*
Sweet cedar that we'd purchased second hand,
In one of its weighty deep-sliding recesses
I found the sharping stone that was to be
5 Our gift to him. Still in its wrapping paper.
Like a baton of black light I'd failed to pass.

                    •

Airless cinder-depths. But all the same,
The way it lay there, it wakened something too . . .
I thought of us that evening on the logs,
10 Flat on our backs, the pair of us, parallel,
Supported head to heel, arms straight, eyes front,
Listening to the rain drip off the trees
And saying nothing, braced to the damp bark.
What possessed us? The bare, lopped loveliness
15 Of those two winter trunks, the way they seemed
Prepared for launching, at right angles across
A causeway of short fence-posts set like rollers.
Neither of us spoke. The puddles waited.
The workers had gone home, saws fallen silent.
20 And next thing down we lay, babes in the wood,

---

7. See the end of James Joyce's *Portrait of the Artist as a Young Man* [Heaney's note]: "*13 April:* That
tundish [funnel] has been on my mind for a long
time. I looked it up and find it English and good
old blunt English too. Damn the dean of studies
and his funnel! What did he come here for to teach
us his own language or to learn it from us? Damn
him one way or the other!"
8. Gleams as of young eels.
1. Whetstone for sharpening metal blades.

Gazing up at the flood-face of the sky
Until it seemed a flood was carrying us
Out of the forest park, feet first, eyes front,
Out of November, out of middle age,
25 Together, out, across the Sea of Moyle.[2]

•

Sarcophage des époux.[3] In terra cotta.
Etruscan couple shown side by side,
Recumbent on left elbows, husband pointing
With his right arm and watching where he points,
30 Wife in front, her earrings in, her braids
Down to her waist, taking her sexual ease.
He is all eyes, she is all brow and dream,
Her right forearm and hand held out as if
Some bird she sees in her deep inward gaze
35 Might be about to roost there. Domestic
Love, the artist thought, warm tones and property,
The frangibility of terra cotta . . .
Which is how they figured on the colour postcard
(*Louvre, Département des Antiquités*)[4]
40 That we'd sent him once, then found among his things.

•

He loved inspired mistakes: his Spanish grandson's
English transliteration, thanking him
For a boat trip: 'That was a marvellous
Walk on the water, granddad.' And indeed
45 He walked on air himself, never more so
Than when he had been widowed and the youth
In him, the athlete who had wooed her—
Breasting tapes and clearing the high bars—
Grew lightsome once again. Going at eighty
50 On the bendiest roads, going for broke
At every point-to-point[5] and poker-school,
'He commenced his wild career' a second time
And not a bother on him. Smoked like a train
And took the power mower in his stride.
55 Flirted and vaunted. Set fire to his bed.
Fell from a ladder. Learned to microwave.

•

So set the drawer on freshets[6] of thaw water
And place the unused sharping stone inside it:
To be found next summer on a riverbank
60 Where scythes once hung all night in alder trees
And mowers played dawn scherzos[7] on the blades,

---

2. Channel between the northwestern coast of
County Antrim in Ireland and the southwestern
coast of Scotland.
3. Coffin for a married couple.
4. Department of Antiquities, the Louvre
Museum, Paris, in which this Etruscan funerary

statue, known as *The Cerveteri Couple*, is to be
found.
5. Horse race over jumps.
6. Surges of water.
7. Vigorous light and playful musical composition.

Their arms like harpists' arms, one drawing towards,
One sweeping the bright rim of the extreme.

1996

J. M. COETZEE
b. 1940

John Michael Coetzee was born in Cape Town, South Africa, and went to school and university in that city. Earning his Ph.D. at the University of Texas at Austin, he worked in computing for some years before being appointed, first, assistant professor and, subsequently, Butler Professor of English at the State University of New York at Buffalo. In 1984, he returned to South Africa as professor of general literature at the University of Cape Town.

The central concern of Coetzee's fiction—the oppressive nature of colonialism—made its appearance with his first book, *Dusklands* (1974). Since then, he has published six novels, including *In the Heart of the Country* (1977), *Life and Times of Michael K* (1983), and *The Master of Petersburg* (1994), as well as essays and criticism on a number of themes.

Coetzee is at once a passionate political novelist and an intensely literary one, both qualities emerging in his most compelling indictment of colonialism to date, *Waiting for the Barbarians* (1980). This novel takes its title and theme from a well-known poem by the Greek poet Constantine Cavafy (1863–1933), which ends (in Rae Dalven's translation):

> . . . night is here but the barbarians have not come.
> Some people arrived from the frontiers,
> And they said that there are no longer any barbarians.
>
> And now what shall become of us without any barbarians?
> Those people were a kind of solution.

The unspecified empire of Coetzee's novel is said (by its fascist rulers) to be threatened by barbarians who never appear, that threat holding it together against its real enemies, those within. The narrator is poised uneasily between the two. A well-meaning but weak liberal magistrate in charge of a frontier post, he is unable to protect his harmless prisoners from his brutal colleague, Colonel Joll.

From Waiting for the Barbarians

Today, only four days after the departure of the expedition, the first of the Colonel's prisoners arrive. From my window I watch them cross the square between their mounted guards, dusty, exhausted, cringing already from the spectators who crowd about them, the skipping children, the barking dogs. In the shade of the barracks wall the guards dismount; at once the prisoners squat down to rest, save for a little boy who stands on one leg, his arm on his mother's shoulder, staring back curiously at the onlookers. Someone brings a bucket of water and a ladle. They drink thirstily, while the crowd grows and presses in so tight around them that I can no longer see. Impatiently I wait for the guard who now pushes his way through the crowd and crosses the barracks yard.

'How do you explain this?' I shout at him. He bows his head, fumbles at his pockets. 'These are fishing people! How can you bring them back here?'

He holds out a letter. I break the seal and read: 'Please hold these and succeeding detainees incommunicado for my return.' Beneath his signature the seal is repeated, the seal of the Bureau[1] which he has carried with him into the desert and which, if he perished, I would doubtless have to send out a second expedition to recover.

'The man is ridiculous!' I shout. I storm about the room. One should never disparage officers in front of men, fathers in front of children, but towards this man I discover no loyalty in my heart. 'Did no one tell him these are fishing people? It is a waste of time bringing them here! You are supposed to help him track down thieves, bandits, invaders of the Empire! Do these people look like a danger to the Empire?' I fling the letter at the window.

The crowd parts before me till I stand at the centre confronting the dozen pathetic prisoners. They flinch before my anger, the little boy sliding into his mother's arms. I gesture to the guards: 'Clear a way and bring these people into the barracks yard!' They herd the captives along; the barracks gate closes behind us. 'Now explain yourselves,' I say; 'did no one tell him these prisoners are useless to him? Did no one tell him the difference between fishermen with nets and wild nomad horsemen with bows? Did no one tell him they don't even speak the same language?'

One of the soldiers explains. 'When they saw us coming they tried to hide in the reeds. They saw horsemen coming so they tried to hide. So the officer, the Excellency, ordered us to take them in. Because they were hiding.'

I could curse with vexation. A policeman! The reasoning of a policeman! 'Did the Excellency say why he wanted them brought back here? Did he say why he could not ask them his questions out there?'

'None of us could speak their language, sir.'

Of course not! These river people are aboriginal, older even than the nomads. They live in settlements of two or three families along the banks of the river, fishing and trapping for most of the year, paddling to the remote southern shores of the lake in the autumn to catch redworms and dry them, building flimsy reed shelters, groaning with cold through the winter, dressing in skins. Living in fear of everyone, skulking in the reeds, what can they possibly know of a great barbarian enterprise against the Empire?

I send one of the men to the kitchen for food. He comes back with a loaf of yesterday's bread which he offers to the oldest prisoner. The old man accepts the bread reverentially in both hands, sniffs it, breaks it, passes the lumps around. They stuff their mouths with this manna,[2] chewing fast, not raising their eyes. A woman spits masticated bread into her palm and feeds her baby. I motion for more bread. We stand watching them eat as though they are strange animals.

---

1. Government department. "Incommunicado": without allowing them to communicate with any- one.

2. Food from heaven (Exodus 16).

'Let them stay in the yard,' I tell their guards. 'It will be inconvenient for us, but there is nowhere else. If it gets cold tonight I will make another arrangement. See that they are fed. Give them something to do to keep their hands busy. Keep the gate closed. They will not run away but I do not want idlers coming in to stare at them.'

So I check my anger and do as the Colonel instructs: I hold his useless prisoners 'incommunicado' for him. And in a day or two these savages seem to forget they ever had another home. Seduced utterly by the free and plentiful food, above all by the bread, they relax, smile at everyone, move about the barracks yard from one patch of shade to another, doze and wake, grow excited as mealtimes approach. Their habits are frank and filthy. One corner of the yard has become a latrine where men and women squat openly and where a cloud of flies buzzes all day. ('Give them a spade!' I tell the guards; but they do not use it.) The little boy, grown quite fearless, haunts the kitchen, begging sugar from the maids. Aside from bread, sugar and tea are great novelties to them. Every morning they get a small block of pressed tea-leaves which they boil up in a four-gallon pail on a tripod over a fire. They are happy here; indeed unless we chase them away they may stay with us forever, so little does it seem to have taken to lure them out of a state of nature. I spend hours watching them from the upstairs window (other idlers have to watch through the gate). I watch the women picking lice, combing and plaiting each other's long black hair. Some of them have fits of harsh dry coughing. It is striking that there are no children in the group but the baby and the little boy. Did some of them, the nimble, the wakeful, after all succeed in escaping from the soldiers? I hope so. I hope that when we return them to their homes along the river they will have many far-fetched stories to tell their neighbours. I hope that the history of their captivity enters their legends, passed down from grandfather to grandson. But I hope too that memories of the town, with its easy life and its exotic foods, are not strong enough to lure them back. I do not want a race of beggars on my hands.

For a few days the fisherfolk are a diversion, with their strange gabbling, their vast appetites, their animal shamelessness, their volatile tempers. The soldiers lounge in the doorways watching them, making obscene comments about them which they do not understand, laughing; there are always children with their faces pressed to the bars of the gate; and from my window I stare down, invisible behind the glass.

Then, all together, we lose sympathy with them. The filth, the smell, the noise of their quarrelling and coughing become too much. There is an ugly incident when a soldier tries to drag one of their women indoors, perhaps only in play, who knows, and is pelted with stones. A rumour begins to go the rounds that they are diseased, that they will bring an epidemic to the town. Though I make them dig a pit in the corner of the yard and have the nightsoil[3] removed, the kitchen staff refuse them utensils and begin to toss them their food from the doorway as if they were indeed animals. The soldiers lock the door to the barracks hall, the children no longer come to the gate. Someone flings a dead cat over the wall during the night and causes an uproar. Through the long hot days they moon about the empty yard. The baby cries and coughs, cries and coughs till I flee for refuge to the farthest corner of my apartment. I write an angry letter to the Third Bureau, unsleep-

3. Excrement.

ing guardian of the Empire, denouncing the incompetence of one of its agents. 'Why do you not send people with experience of the frontier to investigate frontier unrest?' I write. Wisely I tear up the letter. If I unlock the gate in the dead of night, I wonder, will the fisherfolk sneak away? But I do nothing. Then one day I notice that the baby has stopped crying. When I look from the window it is nowhere to be seen. I send a guard to search and he finds the little corpse under its mother's clothes. She will not yield it up, we have to tear it away from her. After this she squats alone all day with her face covered, refusing to eat. Her people seem to shun her. Have we violated some custom of theirs, I wonder, by taking the child and burying it? I curse Colonel Joll for all the trouble he has brought me, and for the shame too.

Then in the middle of the night he is back. Bugle-calls from the ramparts break into my sleep, the barracks hall erupts in uproar as the soldiers go scrambling for their weapons. My head is confused, I am slow in dressing, by the time I emerge on to the square the column is already passing through the gates, some of the men riding, some leading their mounts. I stand back while the onlookers crowd around, touching and embracing the soldiers, laughing with excitement ('All safe!' someone shouts), until coming up in the middle of the column I see what I have been dreading: the black carriage, then the shuffling group of prisoners roped together neck to neck, shapeless figures in their sheepskin coats under the silver moonlight, then behind them the last of the soldiers leading the carts and pack-horses. As more and more people come running up, some with flaming torches, and the babble mounts, I turn my back on the Colonel's triumph and make my way back to my rooms. This is the point at which I begin to see the disadvantages of living, as I have chosen to do, in the rambling apartment over the storerooms and kitchen intended for the military commandant we have not had for years, rather than in the attractive villa with geraniums in the windows which falls to the lot of the civil magistrate. I would like to be able to stop my ears to the noises coming from the yard below, which has now, it appears, become permanently a prison yard. I feel old and tired, I want to sleep. I sleep whenever I can nowadays and, when I wake up, wake reluctantly. Sleep is no longer a healing bath, a recuperation of vital forces, but an oblivion, a nightly brush with annihilation. Living in the apartment has become bad for me, I think; but not only that. If I lived in the magistrate's villa on the quietest street in town, holding sittings of the court on Mondays and Thursdays, going hunting every morning, occupying my evenings in the classics, closing my ears to the activities of this upstart policeman, if I resolved to ride out the bad times, keeping my own counsel, I might cease to feel like a man who, in the grip of the undertow, gives up the fight, stops swimming, and turns his face towards the open sea and death. But it is the knowledge of how contingent my unease is, how dependent on a baby that wails beneath my window one day and does not wail the next, that brings the worst shame to me, the greatest indifference to annihilation. I know somewhat too much; and from this knowledge, once one has been infected, there seems to be no recovering. I ought never to have taken my lantern to see what was going on in the hut by the granary. On the other hand, there was no way, once I had picked up the lantern, for me to put it down again. The knot loops in upon itself; I cannot find the end.

All the next day the Colonel spends sleeping in his room at the inn, and the staff have to tiptoe about their duties. I try to pay no attention to the new batch of prisoners in the yard. It is a pity that all the doors of the barracks block as well as the stairway leading up to my apartment open on to the yard. I hurry out in the early-morning light, occupy myself all day with municipal rents, dine in the evening with friends. On the way home I meet the young lieutenant who accompanied Colonel Joll into the desert and congratulate him on his safe return. 'But why did you not explain to the Colonel that the fishing people could not possibly help him in his inquiries?' He looks embarrassed. 'I spoke to him,' he tells me, 'but all he said was, "Prisoners are prisoners". I decided it was not my place to argue with him.'

The next day the Colonel begins his interrogations. Once I thought him lazy, little more than a bureaucrat with vicious tastes. Now I see how mistaken I was. In his quest for the truth he is tireless. The questioning starts in the early morning and is still going on when I return after dark. He has enlisted the aid of a hunter who has shot pigs up and down the river all his life and knows a hundred words of the fisherfolk's language. One by one the fisherfolk are taken into the room where the Colonel has established himself, to be asked whether they have seen movements of strange horsemen. Even the child is questioned: 'Have strangers visited your father during the night?' (I guess, of course, at what passes in that room, at the fear, the bewilderment, the abasement.) The prisoners are returned not to the yard but to the main barracks hall: the soldiers have been turned out, quartered on the town. I sit in my rooms with the windows shut, in the stifling warmth of a windless evening, trying to read, straining my ears to hear or not to hear sounds of violence. Finally at midnight the interrogations cease, there is no more banging of doors or tramping of feet, the yard is silent in the moonlight, and I am at liberty to sleep.

* * *

Then, in my office at the courthouse, a visitor is announced. Colonel Joll, wearing his dark eyeshades indoors, enters and sits down opposite me. I offer him tea, surprised at how steady my hand is. He is leaving, he says. Should I try to conceal my joy? He sips his tea, sitting carefully upright, inspecting the room, the shelves upon shelves of papers bundled together and tied with ribbon, the record of decades of humdrum administration, the small bookcase of legal texts, the cluttered desk. He has completed his inquiries for the time being, he says, and is in a hurry to return to the capital and make his report. He has an air of sternly controlled triumph. I nod my understanding. 'Anything that I can do to facilitate your journey . . .' I say. There is a pause. Then into the silence, like a pebble into a pool, I drop my question.

'And your inquiries, Colonel, among the nomad peoples and the aboriginals—have they been as successful as you wished?'

He places his fingers together tip to tip before he answers. I have the feeling that he knows how much his affectations irritate me. 'Yes, Magistrate, I can say that we have had some success. Particularly when you consider that similar investigations are being carried out elsewhere along the frontier in a co-ordinated fashion.'

'That is good. And can you tell us whether we have anything to fear? Can we rest securely at night?'

The corner of his mouth crinkles in a little smile. Then he stands up, bows, turns, and leaves. Early next morning he departs accompanied by his small escort, taking the long east road back to the capital. Throughout a trying period he and I have managed to behave towards each other like civilized people. All my life I have believed in civilized behaviour; on this occasion, however, I cannot deny it, the memory leaves me sick with myself.

My first action is to visit the prisoners. I unlock the barracks hall which has been their jail, my senses already revolting at the sickly smell of sweat and ordure, and throw the doors wide open. 'Get them out of there!' I shout at the half-dressed soldiers who stand about watching me as they eat their porridge. From the gloom inside the prisoners stare apathetically back. 'Go in there and clean up that room!' I shout. 'I want everything cleaned up! Soap and water! I want everything as it was before!' The soldiers hurry to obey; but why is my anger directed at them, they must be asking. Into the daylight emerge the prisoners, blinking, shielding their eyes. One of the women has to be helped. She shakes all the time like an old person, though she is young. There are some too sick to stand up.

I last saw them five days ago (if I can claim ever to have seen them, if I ever did more than pass my gaze over their surface absently, with reluctance). What they have undergone in these five days I do not know. Now herded by their guards they stand in a hopeless little knot in the corner of the yard, nomads and fisherfolk together, sick, famished, damaged, terrified. It would be best if this obscure chapter in the history of the world were terminated at once, if these ugly people were obliterated from the face of the earth and we swore to make a new start, to run an empire in which there would be no more injustice, no more pain. It would cost little to march them out into the desert (having put a meal in them first, perhaps, to make the march possible), to have them dig, with their last strength, a pit large enough for all of them to lie in (or even to dig it for them!), and, leaving them buried there forever and forever, to come back to the walled town full of new intentions, new resolutions. But that will not be my way. The new men of Empire are the ones who believe in fresh starts, new chapters, clean pages; I struggle on with the old story, hoping that before it is finished it will reveal to me why it was that I thought it worth the trouble. Thus it is that, administration of law and order in these parts having today passed back to me, I order that the prisoners be fed, that the doctor be called in to do what he can, that the barracks return to being a barracks, that arrangements be made to restore the prisoners to their former lives as soon as possible, as far as possible.

1980

SALMAN RUSHDIE
b. 1947

The most influential novelist to have come from India is the last fifty years is Ahmed Salman Rushdie, whose dynamic narratives—stories of magic, suffering, and the vitality of human beings in the grip of history—have helped generate the literary renaissance flowering in India today. Born in Bombay two months before the partition of the Indian subcontinent and educated at Cathedral School, Bombay, Rugby School, Warwickshire, and King's College, Cambridge, Rushdie eventually settled in England, working as an actor and as a freelance advertising copywriter (1970–80).

His first novel, *Grimus* (1979), passed unnoticed, but his second, *Midnight's Children* (1981), announced the arrival of a major writer. Taking its title from those who were born—two months later than its author—around midnight on August 15, 1947, when the state of Pakistan was born, *Midnight's Children* is a work of prodigious prodigality, a Dickensian cornucopia as richly fertile in character and incident as the subcontinent that is its setting. The book's triumphant progress across the world culminated in it being adjudged "the Booker of Bookers," the best novel to have won Britain's premier fiction prize in its first twenty-five years. Rushdie has said that "we're all radio-active with history," and the books that have followed *Midnight's Children* have again shown a form of "magic realism"—learned from such Latin American writers as Borges and García Márquez—deployed in the service of a powerful political-historical imagination.

In 1988, Rushdie found himself at the perilous center of a real, rather than a magic-realist, political-historical storm. His novel *The Satanic Verses* was judged by senior religious figures in Iran to have blasphemed the Prophet Mohammad, founder of the Muslim faith, and a *fatwa* (a proclamation calling for his death) was pronounced. He was obliged to go into hiding, and for almost a decade lived under round-the-clock protection from British Secret Service agents, while governments argued for and against the lifting of the *fatwa*, and the author himself became symbolic of the vulnerability of the intellectual in the face of fundamentalism. The *fatwa* was lifted in 1998, allowing Rushdie to reappear in public, but his life remains under constant threat. He is his own best critic and has defended his book in an essay, *In Good Faith* (1990):

> If *The Satanic Verses* is anything, it is a migrant's-eye view of the world. It is written from the very experience of uprooting, disjuncture and metamorphosis (slow or rapid, painful or pleasurable) that is the migrant condition, and from which, I believe, can be derived a metaphor for all humanity.
>
> Standing at the centre of the novel is a group of characters most of whom are British Muslims, or not particularly religious persons of Muslim background, struggling with just the sort of great problems of hybridization and ghettoization, of reconciling the old and the new. Those who oppose the novel most vociferously today are of the opinion that intermingling with a different culture will inevitably weaken and ruin their own. I am of the opposite opinion. *The Satanic Verses* celebrates hybridity, impurity, intermingling, the transformation that comes of new and unexpected combinations of human beings, cultures, ideas, politics, movies, songs. It rejoices in mongrelization and fears the absolutism of the Pure. *Mélange*, hotchpotch, a bit of this and a bit of that is *how newness enters the world*. It is the great possibility that mass migration gives the world, and I have tried to embrace it. *The Satanic Verses* is for change-by-fusion, change-by-conjoining. It is a love-song to our mongrel selves.

An earlier story had invoked the Prophet uncontroversially. *The Prophet's Hair* is at once a moral fable in the tradition of *The Thousand and One Nights* and a magic-realist extravaganza, packed with incident, poetic detail ("water to which the cold of the night had given the cloudy consistency of wild honey"), and humor, all brilliantly interwoven at breakneck speed. Salman Rushdie is the Scheherazade of the twentieth century.

The Prophet's[1] Hair

Early in the year 19—, when Srinagar[2] was under the spell of a winter so fierce it could crack men's bones as if they were glass, a young man upon whose cold-pinked skin there lay, like a frost, the unmistakable sheen of wealth was to be seen entering the most wretched and disreputable part of the city, where the houses of wood and corrugated iron seemed perpetually on the verge of losing their balance, and asking in low, grave tones where he might go to engage the services of a dependably professional burglar. The young man's name was Atta, and the rogues in that part of town directed him gleefully into ever darker and less public alleys, until in a yard wet with the blood of a slaughtered chicken he was set upon by two men whose faces he never saw, robbed of the substantial bank-roll which he had insanely brought on his solitary excursion, and beaten within an inch of his life.

Night fell. His body was carried by anonymous hands to the edge of the lake, whence it was transported by shikara[3] across the water and deposited, torn and bleeding, on the deserted embankment of the canal which led to the gardens of Shalimar. At dawn the next morning a flower-vendor was rowing his boat through water to which the cold of the night had given the cloudy consistency of wild honey when he saw the prone form of young Atta, who was just beginning to stir and moan, and on whose now deathly pale skin the sheen of wealth could still be made out dimly beneath an actual layer of frost.

The flower-vendor moored his craft and by stooping over the mouth of the injured man was able to learn the poor fellow's address, which was mumbled through lips that could scarcely move; whereupon, hoping for a large tip, the hawker rowed Atta home to a large house on the shores of the lake, where a beautiful but inexplicably bruised young woman and her distraught, but equally handsome mother, neither of whom, it was clear from their eyes, had slept a wink from worrying, screamed at the sight of their Atta—who was the elder brother of the beautiful young woman—lying motionless amidst the funereally stunted winter blooms of the hopeful florist.

The flower-vendor was indeed paid off handsomely, not least to ensure his silence, and plays no further part in our story. Atta himself, suffering terribly from exposure as well as a broken skull, entered a coma which caused the city's finest doctors to shrug helplessly. It was therefore all the more remarkable that on the very next evening the most wretched and disreputable part of the city received a second unexpected visitor. This was Huma, the sister of the unfortunate young man, and her question was the same as her brother's, and asked in the same low, grave tones:

'Where may I hire a thief?'

The story of the rich idiot who had come looking for a burglar was already common knowledge in those insalubrious gullies, but this time the young

---

1. The Prophet Mohammed, founder of the Muslim religion, was born in Mecca about 570 and died in 632.
2. Capital of the state of Kashmir.
3. Long swift Kashmiri boat.

woman added: 'I should say that I am carrying no money, nor am I wearing any jewellery items. My father has disowned me and will pay no ransom if I am kidnapped; and a letter has been lodged with the Deputy Commissioner of Police, my uncle, to be opened in the event of my not being safe at home by morning. In that letter he will find full details of my journey here, and he will move Heaven and Earth to punish my assailants.'

Her exceptional beauty, which was visible even through the enormous welts and bruises disfiguring her arms and forehead, coupled with the oddity of her inquiries, had attracted a sizable group of curious onlookers, and because her little speech seemed to them to cover just about everything, no one attempted to injure her in any way, although there were some raucous comments to the effect that it was pretty peculiar for someone who was trying to hire a crook to invoke the protection of a high-up policeman uncle.

She was directed into ever darker and less public alleys until finally in a gully as dark as ink an old woman with eyes which stared so piercingly that Huma instantly understood she was blind motioned her through a doorway from which darkness seemed to be pouring like smoke. Clenching her fists, angrily ordering her heart to behave normally, Huma followed the old woman into the gloom-wrapped house.

The faintest conceivable rivulet of candlelight trickled through the darkness; following this unreliable yellow thread (because she could no longer see the old lady), Huma received a sudden sharp blow to the shins and cried out involuntarily, after which she at once bit her lip, angry at having revealed her mounting terror to whoever or whatever waited before her, shrouded in blackness.

She had, in fact, collided with a low table on which a single candle burned and beyond which a mountainous figure could be made out, sitting cross-legged on the floor. 'Sit, sit,' said a man's calm, deep voice, and her legs, needing no more flowery invitation, buckled beneath her at the terse command. Clutching her left hand in her right, she forced her voice to respond evenly:

'And you, sir, will be the thief I have been requesting?'

Shifting its weight very slightly, the shadow-mountain informed Huma that all criminal activity originating in this zone was well organised and also centrally controlled, so that all requests for what might be termed freelance work had to be channelled through this room.

He demanded comprehensive details of the crime to be committed, including a precise inventory of items to be acquired, also a clear statement of all financial inducements being offered with no gratuities excluded, plus, for filing purposes only, a summary of the motives for the application.

At this, Huma, as though remembering something, stiffened both in body and resolve and replied loudly that her motives were entirely a matter for herself; that she would discuss details with no one but the thief himself; but that the rewards she proposed could only be described as 'lavish'.

'All I am willing to disclose to you, sir, since it appears that I am on the premises of some sort of employment agency, is that in return for such lavish rewards I must have the most desperate criminal at your disposal a man for whom life holds no terrors, not even the fear of God.

'The worst of fellows, I tell you—nothing less will do!'

At this a paraffin storm-lantern was lighted, and Huma saw facing her a grey-haired giant down whose left cheek ran the most sinister of scars, a cicatrice in the shape of the letter *sín* in the Nastaliq[4] script. She was gripped by the insupportably nostalgic notion that the bogeyman of her childhood nursery had risen up to confront her, because her ayah[5] had always forestalled any incipient acts of disobedience by threatening Huma and Atta: 'You don't watch out and I'll send that one to steal you away—that Sheikh[6] Sín, the Thief of Thieves!'

Here, grey-haired but unquestionably scarred, was the notorious criminal himself—and was she out of her mind, were her ears playing tricks, or had he truly just announced that, given the stated circumstances, he himself was the only man for the job?

Struggling hard against the newborn goblins of nostalgia, Huma warned the fearsome volunteer that only a matter of extreme urgency and peril would have brought her unescorted into these ferocious streets.

'Because we can afford no last-minute backings-out,' she continued, 'I am determined to tell you everything, keeping back no secrets whatsoever. If, after hearing me out, you are still prepared to proceed, then we shall do everything in our power to assist you, and to make you rich.'

The old thief shrugged, nodded, spat. Huma began her story.

Six days ago, everything in the household of her father, the wealthy money-lender Hashim, had been as it always was. At breakfast her mother had spooned khichri[7] lovingly on to the moneylender's plate; the conversation had been filled with those expressions of courtesy and solicitude on which the family prided itself.

Hashim was fond of pointing out that while he was not a godly man he set great store by 'living honourably in the world'. In that spacious lakeside residence, all outsiders were greeted with the same formality and respect, even those unfortunates who came to negotiate for small fragments of Hashim's large fortune, and of whom he naturally asked an interest rate of over seventy per cent, partly, as he told his khichri-spooning wife, 'to teach these people the value of money; let them only learn that, and they will be cured of this fever of borrowing borrowing all the time—so you see that if my plans succeed, I shall put myself out of business!'

In their children, Atta and Huma, the moneylender and his wife had successfully sought to inculcate the virtues of thrift, plain dealing and a healthy independence of spirit. On this, too, Hashim was fond of congratulating himself.

Breakfast ended; the family members wished one another a fulfilling day. Within a few hours, however, the glassy contentment of that household, of

---

4. A Persian cursive script, characterized by rounded forms and elongated horizontal strokes.
5. Child's nurse (Anglo-Indian, from Portuguese).
6. Chief (Arabic).
7. Rice and lentils cooked together (Hindi).

that life of porcelain delicacy and alabaster sensibilities, was to be shattered beyond all hope of repair.

The moneylender summoned his personal shikara and was on the point of stepping into it when, attracted by a glint of silver, he noticed a small vial[8] floating between the boat and his private quay. On an impulse, he scooped it out of the glutinous water.

It was a cylinder of tinted glass cased in exquisitely wrought silver, and Hashim saw within its walls a silver pendant bearing a single strand of human hair.

Closing his fist around this unique discovery, he muttered to the boatman that he'd changed his plans, and hurried to his sanctum, where, behind closed doors, he feasted his eyes on his find.

There can be no doubt that Hashim the moneylender knew from the first that he was in possession of the famous relic of the Prophet Muhammad, that revered hair whose theft from its shrine at Hazratbal mosque the previous morning had created an unprecedented hue and cry in the valley.

The thieves—no doubt alarmed by the pandemonium, by the procession through the streets of endless ululating[9] crocodiles of lamentation, by the riots, the political ramifications and by the massive police search which was commanded and carried out by men whose entire careers now hung upon the finding of this lost hair—had evidently panicked and hurled the vial into the gelatine bosom of the lake.

Having found it by a stroke of great good fortune, Hashim's duty as a citizen was clear: the hair must be restored to its shrine, and the state to equanimity and peace.

But the moneylender had a different notion.

All around him in his study was the evidence of his collector's mania. There were enormous glass cases full of impaled butterflies from Gulmarg, three dozen scale models in various metals of the legendary cannon Zamzama,[1] innumerable swords, a Naga spear, ninety-four terracotta camels of the sort sold on railway station platforms, many samovars,[2] and a whole zoology of tiny sandalwood animals, which had originally been carved to serve as children's bathtime toys.

'And after all,' Hashim told himself, 'the Prophet would have disapproved mightily of this relic-worship. He abhorred the idea of being deified! So, by keeping this hair from its distracted devotees, I perform—do I not?—a finer service than I would by returning it! Naturally, I don't want it for its religious value . . . I'm a man of the world, of this world. I see it purely as a secular object of great rarity and blinding beauty. In short, it's the silver vial I desire, more than the hair.

'They say there are American millionaires who purchase stolen art masterpieces and hide them away—they would know how I feel. I must, must have it!'

---

8. Small, cylindrical glass container.
9. Howling.
1. Cf. Rudyard Kipling's *Kim* (p. 1): "The gun Zam-Zammah on her brick platform opposite the old Ajaib-Gher—the Wonder House, as the natives call the Lahore Museum."
2. Apparatus for making tea (Russian for self-boiler).

Every collector must share his treasures with one other human being, and Hashim summoned—and told—his only son Atta, who was deeply perturbed but, having been sworn to secrecy, only spilled the beans when the troubles became too terrible to bear.

The youth excused himself and left his father alone in the crowded solitude of his collections. Hashim was sitting erect in a hard, straight-backed chair, gazing intently at the beautiful vial.

It was well known that the moneylender never ate lunch, so it was not until evening that a servant entered the sanctum[3] to summon his master to the dining-table. He found Hashim as Atta had left him. The same, and not the same—for now the moneylender looked swollen, distended. His eyes bulged even more than they always had, they were red-rimmed, and his knuckles were white.

He seemed to be on the point of bursting! As though, under the influence of the misappropriated relic, he had filled up with some spectral fluid which might at any moment ooze uncontrollably from his every bodily opening.

He had to be helped to the table, and then the explosion did indeed take place.

Seemingly careless of the effect of his words on the carefully constructed and fragile constitution of the family's life, Hashim began to gush, to spume long streams of awful truths. In horrified silence, his children heard their father turn upon his wife, and reveal to her that for many years their marriage had been the worst of his afflictions. 'An end to politeness!' he thundered. 'An end to hypocrisy!'

Next, and in the same spirit, he revealed to his family the existence of a mistress; he informed them also of his regular visits to paid women. He told his wife that, far from being the principal beneficiary of his will, she would receive no more than the eighth portion which was her due under Islamic law. Then he turned upon his children, screaming at Atta for his lack of academic ability—'A dope! I have been cursed with a dope!'—and accusing his daughter of lasciviousness, because she went around the city barefaced, which was unseemly for any good Muslim girl to do. She should, he commanded, enter purdah[4] forthwith.

Hashim left the table without having eaten and fell into the deep sleep of a man who has got many things off his chest, leaving his children stunned, in tears, and the dinner going cold on the sideboard under the gaze of an anticipatory bearer.[5]

At five o'clock the next morning the moneylender forced his family to rise, wash and say their prayers. From then on, he began to pray five times daily for the first time in his life, and his wife and children were obliged to do likewise.

Before breakfast, Huma saw the servants, under her father's direction, constructing a great heap of books in the garden and setting fire to it. The

3. Private room.
4. Area of certain traditional Indian houses in which Hindu or Muslim women live secluded from the sight of men outside their family circle.
5. Servant.

only volume left untouched was the Qur'an,[6] which Hashim wrapped in a silken cloth and placed on a table in the hall. He ordered each member of his family to read passages from this book for at least two hours per day. Visits to the cinema were forbidden. And if Atta invited male friends to the house, Huma was to retire to her room.

By now, the family had entered a state of shock and dismay; but there was worse to come.

That afternoon, a trembling debtor arrived at the house to confess his inability to pay the latest instalment of interest owed, and made the mistake of reminding Hashim, in somewhat blustering fashion, of the Qur'an's strictures against usury. The moneylender flew into a rage and attacked the fellow with one of his large collection of bullwhips.

By mischance, later the same day a second defaulter came to plead for time, and was seen fleeing Hashim's study with a great gash in his arm, because Huma's father had called him a thief of other men's money and had tried to cut off the wretch's right hand with one of the thirty-eight kukri knives[7] hanging on the study walls.

These breaches of the family's unwritten laws of decorum alarmed Atta and Huma, and when, that evening, their mother attempted to calm Hashim down, he struck her on the face with an open hand. Atta leapt to his mother's defence and he, too, was sent flying.

'From now on,' Hashim bellowed, 'there's going to be some discipline around here!'

The moneylender's wife began a fit of hysterics which continued throughout that night and the following day, and which so provoked her husband that he threatened her with divorce, at which she fled to her room, locked the door and subsided into a raga[8] of sniffling. Huma now lost her composure, challenged her father openly, and announced (with that same independence of spirit which he had encouraged in her) that she would wear no cloth over her face; apart from anything else, it was bad for the eyes.

On hearing this, her father disowned her on the spot and gave her one week in which to pack her bags and go.

By the fourth day, the fear in the air of the house had become so thick that it was difficult to walk around. Atta told his shock-numbed sister: 'We are descending to gutter-level—but I know what must be done.'

That afternoon, Hashim left home accompanied by two hired thugs to extract the unpaid dues from his two insolvent clients. Atta went immediately to his father's study. Being the son and heir, he possessed his own key to the moneylender's safe. This he now used, and removing the little vial from its hiding-place, he slipped it into his trouser pocket and re-locked the safe door.

Now he told Huma the secret of what his father had fished out of Lake Dal, and exclaimed: 'Maybe I'm crazy—maybe the awful things that are hap-

6. Muslims' sacred book: collection of the Prophet Muhammad's oral revelations.
7. Curved knives broadening toward the point

(Hindi).
8. Musical improvisation (Sanskrit).

pening have made me cracked—but I am convinced there will be no peace in our house until this hair is out of it.'

His sister at once agreed that the hair must be returned, and Atta set off in a hired shikara to Hazratbal mosque. Only when the boat had delivered him into the throng of the distraught faithful which was swirling around the desecrated shrine did Atta discover that the relic was no longer in his pocket. There was only a hole, which his mother, usually so attentive to household matters, must have overlooked under the stress of recent events.

Atta's initial surge of chagrin was quickly replaced by a feeling of profound relief.

'Suppose', he imagined, 'that I had already announced to the mullahs[9] that the hair was on my person! They would never have believed me now—and this mob would have lynched me! At any rate, it has gone, and that's a load off my mind.' Feeling more contented than he had for days, the young man returned home.

Here he found his sister bruised and weeping in the hall; upstairs, in her bedroom, his mother wailed like a brand-new widow. He begged Huma to tell him what had happened, and when she replied that their father, returning from his brutal business trip, had once again noticed a glint of silver between boat and quay, had once again scooped up the errant relic, and was consequently in a rage to end all rages, having beaten the truth out of her— then Atta buried his face in his hands and sobbed out his opinion, which was that the hair was persecuting them, and had come back to finish the job.

It was Huma's turn to think of a way out of their troubles.

While her arms turned black and blue and great stains spread across her forehead, she hugged her brother and whispered to him that she was determined to get rid of the hair *at all costs*—she repeated this last phrase several times.

'The hair', she then declared, 'was stolen from the mosque; so it can be stolen from this house. But it must be a genuine robbery, carried out by a bona-fide thief, not by one of us who are under the hair's thrall—by a thief so desperate that he fears neither capture nor curses.'

Unfortunately, she added, the theft would be ten times harder to pull off now that their father, knowing that there had already been one attempt on the relic, was certainly on his guard.

'Can you do it?'

Huma, in a room lit by candle and storm-lantern, ended her account with one further question: 'What assurances can you give that the job holds no terrors for you still?'

The criminal, spitting, stated that he was not in the habit of providing references, as a cook might, or a gardener, but he was not alarmed so easily, certainly not by any children's djinni of a curse. Huma had to be content with this boast, and proceeded to describe the details of the proposed burglary.

9. Muslims learned in Islamic theology and sacred law.

'Since my brother's failure to return the hair to the mosque, my father has taken to sleeping with his precious treasure under his pillow. However, he sleeps alone, and very energetically; only enter his room without waking him, and he will certainly have tossed and turned quite enough to make the theft a simple matter. When you have the vial, come to my room,' and here she handed Sheikh Sín a plan of her home, 'and I will hand over all the jewellery owned by my mother and myself. You will find . . . it is worth . . . that is, you will be able to get a fortune for it . . .'

It was evident that her self-control was weakening and that she was on the point of physical collapse.

'Tonight,' she burst out finally. 'You must come tonight!'

No sooner had she left the room than the old criminal's body was convulsed by a fit of coughing: he spat blood into an old vanaspati[1] can. The great Sheikh, the 'Thief of Thieves', had become a sick man, and every day the time drew nearer when some young pretender to his power would stick a dagger in his stomach. A lifelong addiction to gambling had left him almost as poor as he had been when, decades ago, he had started out in this line of work as a mere pickpocket's apprentice; so in the extraordinary commission he had accepted from the moneylender's daughter he saw his opportunity of amassing enough wealth at a stroke to leave the valley for ever, and acquire the luxury of a respectable death which would leave his stomach intact.

As for the Prophet's hair, well, neither he nor his blind wife had ever had much to say for prophets—that was one thing they had in common with the moneylender's thunderstruck clan.

It would not do, however, to reveal the nature of this, his last crime, to his four sons. To his consternation, they had all grown up to be hopelessly devout men, who even spoke of making the pilgrimage to Mecca some day. 'Absurd!' their father would laugh at them. 'Just tell me how you will go?' For, with a parent's absolutist love, he had made sure they were all provided with a lifelong source of high income by crippling them at birth, so that, as they dragged themselves around the city, they earned excellent money in the begging business.

The children, then, could look after themselves.

He and his wife would be off soon with the jewel-boxes of the moneylender's women. It was a timely chance indeed that had brought the beautiful bruised girl into his corner of the town.

That night, the large house on the shore of the lake lay blindly waiting, with silence lapping at its walls. A burglar's night: clouds in the sky and mists on the winter water. Hashim the moneylender was asleep, the only member of his family to whom sleep had come that night. In another room, his son Atta lay deep in the coils of his coma with a blood-clot forming on his brain, watched over by a mother who had let down her long greying hair to show her grief, a mother who placed warm compresses on his head with gestures

---

1. Brand of clarified butter.

redolent of impotence. In a third bedroom Huma waited, fully dressed, amidst the jewel-heavy caskets of her desperation.

At last a bulbul[2] sang softly from the garden below her window and, creeping downstairs, she opened a door to the bird, on whose face there was a scar in the shape of the Nastaliq letter *sín*.

Noiselessly, the bird flew up the stairs behind her. At the head of the staircase they parted, moving in opposite directions along the corridor of their conspiracy without a glance at one another.

Entering the moneylender's room with professional ease, the burglar, Sín, discovered that Huma's predictions had been wholly accurate. Hashim lay sprawled diagonally across his bed, the pillow untenanted by his head, the prize easily accessible. Step by padded step, Sín moved towards the goal.

It was at this point that, in the bedroom next door, young Atta sat bolt upright in his bed, giving his mother a great fright, and without any warning—prompted by goodness knows what pressure of the blood-clot upon his brain—began screaming at the top of his voice:

'Thief! Thief! Thief!'

It seems probable that his poor mind had been dwelling, in these last moments, upon his own father; but it is impossible to be certain, because having uttered these three emphatic words the young man fell back upon his pillow and died.

At once his mother set up a screeching and a wailing and a keening and a howling so earsplittingly intense that they completed the work which Atta's cry had begun—that is, her laments penetrated the walls of her husband's bedroom and brought Hashim wide awake.

Sheikh Sín was just deciding whether to dive beneath the bed or brain the moneylender good and proper when Hashim grabbed the tiger-striped swordstick which always stood propped up in a corner beside his bed, and rushed from the room without so much as noticing the burglar who stood on the opposite side of the bed in the darkness. Sín stooped quickly and removed the vial containing the Prophet's hair from its hiding-place.

Meanwhile Hashim had erupted into the corridor, having unsheathed the sword inside his cane. In his right hand he held the weapon and was waving it about dementedly. His left hand was shaking the stick. A shadow came rushing towards him through the midnight darkness of the passageway and, in his somnolent anger, the moneylender thrust his sword fatally through its heart. Turning up the light, he found that he had murdered his daughter, and under the dire influence of this accident he was so overwhelmed by remorse that he turned the sword upon himself, fell upon it and so extinguished his life. His wife, the sole surviving member of the family, was driven mad by the general carnage and had to be committed to an asylum for the insane by her brother, the city's Deputy Commissioner of Police.

Sheikh Sín had quickly understood that the plan had gone awry.

Abandoning the dream of the jewel-boxes when he was but a few yards

---

2. Asian song thrush.

from its fulfilment, he climbed out of Hashim's window and made his escape during the appalling events described above. Reaching home before dawn, he woke his wife and confessed his failure. It would be necessary, he whispered, for him to vanish for a while. Her blind eyes never opened until he had gone.

The noise in the Hashim household had roused their servants and even managed to awaken the night-watchman, who had been fast asleep as usual on his charpoy by the street-gate. They alerted the police, and the Deputy Commissioner himself was informed. When he heard of Huma's death, the mournful officer opened and read the sealed letter which his niece had given him, and instantly led a large detachment of armed men into the light-repellent gullies of the most wretched and disreputable part of the city.

The tongue of a malicious cat-burglar named Huma's fellow-conspirator; the finger of an ambitious bank-robber pointed at the house in which he lay concealed; and although Sín managed to crawl through a hatch in the attic and attempt a roof-top escape, a bullet from the Deputy Commissioner's own rifle penetrated his stomach and brought him crashing messily to the ground at the feet of Huma's enraged uncle.

From the dead thief's pocket rolled a vial of tinted glass, cased in filigree silver.

The recovery of the Prophet's hair was announced at once on All-India Radio. One month later, the valley's holiest men assembled at the Hazratbal mosque and formally authenticated the relic. It sits to this day in a closely guarded vault by the shores of the loveliest of lakes in the heart of the valley which was once closer than any other place on earth to Paradise.

But before our story can properly be concluded, it is necessary to record that when the four sons of the dead Sheikh awoke on the morning of his death, having unwittingly spent a few minutes under the same roof as the famous hair, they found that a miracle had occurred, that they were all sound of limb and strong of wind, as whole as they might have been if their father had not thought to smash their legs in the first hours of their lives. They were, all four of them, very properly furious, because the miracle had reduced their earning powers by 75 per cent, at the most conservative estimate; so they were ruined men.

Only the Sheikh's widow had some reason for feeling grateful, because although her husband was dead she had regained her sight, so that it was possible for her to spend her last days gazing once more upon the beauties of the valley of Kashmir.

1981

Poems in Process

In all ages, some poets have claimed that their poems were not willed but were inspired, whether by a muse, by divine visitation, or by sudden emergence from the author's subconscious mind. But as the poet Richard Aldington has remarked, "genius is not enough; one must also work." The working manuscripts of the greatest writers show that, however involuntary the origin of a poem, vision was usually followed by laborious revision before the work achieved the seeming inevitability of its final form.

Milton is the first major English author for whom we possess drafts of poems indubitably written in his own hand; the excerpt from his manuscript of *Lycidas* shows the extent to which he worked over and expanded his initial attempt. We have increasing numbers of manuscripts written in the eighteenth century, such as those reproduced below from Pope and Johnson. In the early nineteenth century the working drafts of poets began to be widely preserved, and so remain abundantly available.

The examples from major poets that are transcribed here represent various stages in the composition of a poem, and a variety of procedures by individual poets. In all these examples we look on as poets, no matter how rapidly they achieve a result they are willing to let stand, carry on their inevitably tentative efforts to meet the multiple requirements of meaning, syntax, meter, sound pattern, and the constraints imposed by a chosen stanza. And because these are all very good poets, the seeming conflict between the necessities of significance and form results not in the distortion but in the perfecting of the poetic statement.

Our transcriptions from the poets' drafts attempt to reproduce, as accurately as the change from script to print will allow, the appearance of the original manuscript page. A poet's first attempt at a line or phrase is reproduced in larger type, the emendations in smaller type. The line numbers in the headings that identify an excerpt are those of the final form of the complete poem, as reprinted in this anthology, above. The marginal numbers beside the extract from *The Vanity of Human Wishes* are Johnson's own additions.

SELECTED BIBLIOGRAPHY

Autograph Poetry in the English Language, 2 vols., 1973, compiled by P. J. Croft, reproduces and transcribes one or more pages of manuscript in the poet's own hand, from the 14th century to the present time. Volume 1 includes Blake and Burns; volume 2 includes many of the other poets represented in this volume of *The Norton Anthology of English Literature,* from Wordsworth to Dylan Thomas. Books that discuss the process of composition and revision, with examples from the manuscripts and printed versions of poems, are Charles D. Abbott, ed., *Poets at Work,* 1948; Phyllis Bartlett, *Poems in Process,* 1951; A. F. Scott, *The Poet's Craft,* 1957; George Bornstein, *Poetic Remaking: The Art of Browning, Yeats, and Pound,* 1988. In *Word for Word: A Study of Authors' Alterations,* 1965, Wallace Hildick analyzes the composition of prose fiction as well as poems; a shorter version, *Word for Word: The Rewriting of Fiction,* 1965, discusses the revision of novels by George Eliot, Samuel Butler, Hardy, Lawrence, James, and Woolf. *Byron's "Don Juan,"* ed. T. G. Steffan and W. W. Pratt, 4 vols., 1957, transcribes the manuscript drafts; the Cornell Wordsworth, in process, reproduces, transcribes, and discusses various versions of Wordsworth's poems from the first manuscript drafts to the final publication in his lifetime, and the Cornell Yeats, also in process, does the same for Yeats. For facsimiles and transcripts of Keats's poems, see *John Keats: Poetry Manuscripts at Harvard,* ed. Jack Stillinger, 1990. Jon Stallworthy, *Between the Lines: Yeats's Poetry in the Making,* 1963, reproduces and analyzes the sequential drafts of a number of Yeats's major poems. Valerie Eliot has edited

T. S. Eliot's *The Waste Land: A Facsimile and Transcript of the Original Drafts Including the Annotations of Ezra Pound*, 1971, while Dame Helen Gardner has transcribed and analyzed the manuscript drafts of Eliot's *Four Quartets* in *The Composition of Four Quartets*, 1978.

JOHN MILTON
From Lycidas[1]

[*Lines 1–14*][2]

yet once more O ye laurells and once more

ye myrtl's browne wth Ivie never sere

I come to pluck yor berries harsh and crude

~~before the mellowing yeare~~ and wth forc't fingers rude

~~and crop yor young~~ shatter yor leaves before ye mellowing yeare
bitter constraint, and sad occasion deare

compells me to disturbe yor season due
for ~~young~~ Lycidas is dead, dead ere his prime
young Lycidas and hath not left his peere

who would ^not sing for Lycidas he well knew
himselfe to sing & build the loftie rime
he must not flote upon his watrie beare
unwept, and welter to the parching wind
without the meed of some melodious teare

[*Lines 56–63*]

ay mee I fondly dreame
~~had yee bin there, for~~ what could that have don?
~~what could the golden hayrd Calliope~~
for her inchaunting son ————
~~when shee beheld   (the gods farre sighted bee)~~
~~his goarie scalpe rowle downe the Thracian lee~~

whome universal nature
might lament
~~and heaven and hel deplore~~
~~when his divine head downe~~
the streame was sent
downe the Swift Hebrus to the
Lesbian shore.

[THE THIRD AND FOLLOWING LINES ARE REWRITTEN
ON A SEPARATE PAGE]

✳what could the muse her selfe that Orpheus bore
the muse her selfe for her inchanting son
~~for her inchanting son~~
                                    did
whome universal nature ~~might~~ lament
when by the rout that made the hideous roare
                    gorie
✳goarie his ~~divine~~ visage down the streame was sent
downe the swift Hebrus to ye Lesbian shoare.

1. Transcribed from a manuscript of fifty pages in the library of Trinity College, Cambridge. Among the poems written in Milton's own hand are *Lycidas*, *Comus*, seven sonnets, and several other short poems. The manuscript has been photographically reproduced, with printed transcriptions, by W. Aldis Wright, *Facsimile of the Manuscript of Milton's Minor Poems* (Cambridge, England, 1899).
2. This draft is written on a separate page of the manuscript, which also contains drafts of the passages, "What could the muse her selfe" and "Bring the rathe primrose," transcribed below.

[*Lines 132–53*]

Returne Alpheus the dred voice is past
   that shrunk thy streams, returne Sicilian Muse
   and call the vales and bid them hither cast
   thire bells, and flowrets of a thousand hues
   yee vallies low where the mild wispers use

   of shades, and wanton winds, and goshing brooks   ✳

                                    ✳   ✳ sparely

   on whose fresh lap the swart starre sparely looks   —faintly

✳
   — bring hither all yor quaint enamel'd eyes   ✳   throw
   that on the greene terfe suck the honied showrs

   and purple all the ground wth vernal flowrs
                                ————   Bring the rathe &c.[3]

   to strew the laureat herse where Lycid' lies
   for so to interpose a little ease
         ✳   fraile
   let our sad thoughts dally wth false surmise   ✳ fraile

[LINES 142–50 ARE DRAFTED ON A SEPARATE PAGE, AS FOLLOWS]

   Bring the rathe primrose that unwedded dies
   — collu colouring the pale cheeke of uninjoyd love
   and that sad floure that strove
   to write his owne woes on the vermeil graine

   next adde Narcissus y^t still weeps in vaine

   the woodbine and ye pancie freak't wth jet
   the glowing violet
   the cowslip wan that hangs his pensive head
   and every bud that sorrows liverie weares

                             with
   let Daffadillies fill thire cups teares
   bid Amaranthus all his beautie shed
   to strew the laureat herse &c.

   Bring the rathe primrose that forsaken dies
   the tufted crowtoe and pale Gessamin

                 ye
   the white pinke, and pansie freakt wth jet
   the glowing violet
                the well-attired woodbine
   the muske rose and the garish columbine —

   wth cowslips wan that hang the pensive head
                        weare ✳   weares
   and every flower that sad escutcheon beares imbroidrie beares

   &
 2 let daffadillies fill thire cups wth teares
 1 bid Amaranthus all his beauties shed
   to strew &c.

---

3. I.e., Milton plans to insert here the passage that follows, lines 142–50.

ALEXANDER POPE
From The Rape of the Lock[1]
[1712 Version: Canto 1, Lines 1–24]

WHAT dire Offence from Am'rous Causes springs,
What mighty Quarrels rise from Trivial Things,
I sing—This Verse to C—l, Muse! is due;
This, ev'n *Belinda* may vouchsafe to view:
Slight is the Subject, but not so the Praise,
If she inspire, and He approve my Lays.
Say what strange Motive, Goddess! cou'd compel
A well-bred *Lord* t'assault a gentle *Belle?*
Oh say what stranger Cause, yet unexplor'd,
Cou'd make a gentle *Belle* reject a *Lord?*
And dwells such Rage in *softest Bosoms* then?
And lodge such daring Souls in *Little Men?*
Sol thro' white Curtains did his Beams display,
And op'd those Eyes which brighter shine than they;
Shock just had giv'n himself the rowzing Shake,
And Nymphs prepar'd their *Chocolate* to take;
Thrice the wrought Slipper knock'd against the Ground,
And striking Watches the tenth Hour resound.
Belinda rose, and 'midst attending Dames
Launch'd on the Bosom of the silver *Thames:*
A Train of well-drest Youths around her shone,
And ev'ry Eye was fix'd on her alone;
On her white Breast a sparking *Cross* she wore,
Which *Jews* might kiss, and Infidels adore.

[Revised Version: Canto 1, Lines 1–22]

WHAT dire Offence from am'rous Causes springs,
What mighty Contests rise from trivial Things,
I sing—This Verse to *Caryll*, Muse! is due;
This, ev'n *Belinda* may vouchsafe to view:
Slight is the Subject, but not so the Praise,
If She inspire, and He approve my Lays.
Say what strange Motive, Goddess! cou'd compel
A well-bred *Lord* t'assault a gentle *Belle?*
Oh say what stranger Cause, yet unexplor'd,
Cou'd make a gentle *Belle* reject a *Lord?*

1. The first version of *The Rape of the Lock*, published 1712, consisted of two cantos and a total of 334 lines. Two years later, in 1714, Pope published an enlarged version of five cantos and 794 lines, in which he added the supernatural "machinery" of the Sylphs and Gnomes as well as a number of mock-epic episodes. The excerpts reprinted here show how Pope revised and expanded passages that he retained from the first version of the poem. The revised version includes changes that Pope added in later editions of the enlarged text of 1714.

In Tasks so bold, can Little Men engage,
And in soft Bosoms dwells such mighty Rage?
   Sol thro' white Curtains shot a tim'rous Ray,
And op'd those Eyes that must eclipse the Day;
Now Lapdogs give themselves the rowzing Shake,
And sleepless Lovers, just at Twelve, awake:
Thrice rung the Bell, the Slipper knock'd the Ground,
And the press'd Watch return'd a silver Sound.
Belinda still her downy Pillow prest,
Her Guardian *Sylph* prolong'd the balmy Rest.
'Twas he had summon'd to her silent Bed
The Morning-Dream that hover'd o'er her Head.

[*Revised Version: Canto 2, Lines 1–8*]

Not with more Glories, in th' Etherial Plain,
   The Sun first rises o'er the purpled Main,
   Than issuing forth, the Rival of his Beams
Launch'd on the Bosom of the Silver *Thames*.
Fair Nymphs, and well-drest Youths around her shone,
But ev'ry Eye was fix'd on her alone.
On her white Breast a sparkling *Cross* she wore,
Which *Jews* might kiss, and Infidels adore.

From An Essay on Man[1]

[*From the First Manuscript*]

                        we ourselves
1. Learn ~~then thyself~~, not God presume to scan,
       But
   ~~And~~ know, the Study of Mankind is <u>Man.</u>
Plac'd on this <u>Isthmus</u> of a Middle State,
A Being <u>darkly wise,</u> & <u>rudely</u> <u>great.</u>
With too much <u>knowledge</u> for the <u>Sceptic</u> side,
And too much <u>Weakness</u> for a <u>Stoic's</u> Pride,
He hangs between, uncertain where to rest;
Whether to deem himself a <u>God</u> or <u>Beast;</u>
Whether his <u>Mind</u> or <u>Body</u> to prefer,
Born but to <u>die,</u> & reas'ning but to <u>err;</u>
                        his
Alike in <u>Ignorance,</u> (~~that~~ Reason such)
     ~~Who~~   ~~who thinks~~
Whether he thinks too <u>little</u> or too <u>much</u>:
Chaos of <u>Thought</u> & <u>Passion,</u> all confus'd,
Still by <u>himself</u> abus'd & dis-abus'd:

---

1. Two of Pope's holograph manuscripts of *An Essay on Man* have survived. The earlier one is at the Pierpont Morgan Library in New York. The second one, at the Houghton Library, Harvard, was evidently intended as a fair copy for printing; but Pope, who was an inveterate reviser, intro- duced some last-minute changes. The passage transcribed here from each of these manuscripts is Pope's famed description of man's "middle state" in the great chain of being; in the published ver- sion, it opens Epistle 2, lines 1–18.

Created half to rise, & half to fall;
Great <u>Lord</u> of all things, yet a prey to all;
Sole Judge of Truth, in endless Error hurl'd;
The Glory, Jest, and Riddle of the World.

[*From the Second Manuscript*]²

~~Incipit I~~   Know
~~Incipit III~~   ~~Learn~~ we ourselves, not God presume to scan,
The only Science   Convinc'd,
          ~~But know~~, the Study of Mankind is Man;
(Plac'd on this Isthmus of a Middle State,
A Being darkly wise, and rudely great;
With too much Knowledge for the Sceptic side,
          With
~~And~~ too much Weakness for a Stoic's Pride,
                    in doubt to act or
He hangs between, ~~uncertain where to~~ rest,
                    Part of
Whether To deem himself a ⌄God or Beast;
          In doubt
Whether his Mind, or Body to prefer.
          ~~This born~~   ~~that~~
Born but to die, and reas'ning but to err;
Alike in Ignorance, his Reason such,
          Whether he thinks   or too much.
~~Who thinks~~ too little, ~~or who thinks too much:~~
Chaos of Thought and Passion, all confus'd,
Still by himself abus'd and dis-abus'd:
Created half to rise, and half to fall;
Great Lord of all things, yet a prey to all;
Sole Judge of Truth, in endless error hurl'd;
The Glory, Jest, and Riddle of the World!

2. In this version of the manuscript, Pope inserted some marginal glosses. In the right-hand margin (next to the line beginning "Learn we ourselves . . ."), he wrote, "Of Man, as an Individual," while next to the line beginning "Plac'd on this Isthmus . . . ," he wrote, "His Middle Nature." And in the left-hand margin, a little below the line beginning "With too much knowledge . . . ," he wrote, "His Powers, and Imperfections."

SAMUEL JOHNSON

Johnson told Boswell in 1766 that when composing verses "I have generally had them in my mind, perhaps fifty at a time, walking up and down in my room; and then I have written them down, and often, from laziness, have written only half lines. . . . I remember I wrote a hundred lines of *The Vanity of Human Wishes* in a day." When the first manuscript draft of this poem turned up in the 1940s among Boswell's papers at Malahide Castle, it supported Johnson's account, for it had been written and corrected in haste, with only sparse punctuation; also the second half of each line had been filled out, obviously from memory, at some time after the writing of the first half, in a darker ink. In the transcriptions from this manuscript (which is in the collection of Mary Hyde, Somerville, New Jersey), the half-lines and emendations that Johnson added to his initial draft are printed in boldface type.

The draft was written on the right-hand pages of a small homemade pocket book;

some words in the added half-line, impinging on the right margin of the page, had to be completed above or below the line. The two added lines, "See Nations slowly wise . . . the tardy Bust," were written on the blank left-hand page, at the place where they were to be inserted. The numeration of every tenth line was added by Johnson in the manuscript and incorporates these two additional lines.

Johnson published the poem in 1749 and revised it for a second publication in 1755, when it achieved the final form printed in the selections from Johnson, above. It was in 1755 that Johnson introduced his most famous emendation, when, after his disillusionment with Lord Chesterfield as literary patron, he substituted in line 162 the word "patron" for "garret": "Toil, envy, want, the patron, and the jail."

From The Vanity of Human Wishes

[*Lines 135–64*]

When first the College Rolls receive his nam^e
The young Enthusiast quits his ease for fame

Quick fires his breast
~~Each act betrays~~ the fever of renown
Caught from the strong Contagion of the Gown
On Isis banks he waves, from noise withdrawn
140 In sober state th' imaginary Lawn
O'er Bodley's Dome his future Labours spread
And Bacon's Mansion trembles o'er his head.
Are these thy views, proceed illustrious Youth
And Virtue guard thee to the throne of Trut^h
Yet should thy ~~fate~~ Soul indulge the gen'rous
                                                            Heat
Till Captive Science yields her last Retreat
Should Reason guide thee with her brightest Ray
And pour on misty Doubt resistless day
Should no false kindness lure to loose delight
150 Nor Praise relax, nor difficulty fright
Should tempting Novelty thy cell refrain
                                                            vain
And Sloth's bland opiates shed their fumes in
~~s~~Should Beuty blunt on fops her fatal dart
Nor claim the triumph of a letter'd heart
~~S Nor~~ Should no Disease thy torpid veins invade
Nor Melancholys Spectres haunt thy Shade
                        hope
Yet ~~dream~~ not Life from Grief or Danger free,
Nor think the doom of Man revers'd for thee
Deign   passing   to
~~Turn~~ on the ⌃ world ~~awhile~~ turn thine eyes
160 And pause awhile from Learning to be wise
There mark what ill the Scholar's life assail
                            the
Toil envy Want ~~a~~ Garret and the Jayl
                    Dreams
If ~~Hope~~ yet flatter once again attend
Hear Lydiats life and Galileo's End.

See Nations slowly wise, and meanly just,
To buried merit raise the tardy Bust.

THOMAS GRAY

There are three manuscript versions of the *Elegy* in Gray's handwriting. The one reproduced here in part is the earliest of these, preserved at Eton College, England; Gray entitled it "Stanzas wrote in a Country Church-Yard."

It is evident that Gray originally intended to conclude his poem at the end of the fifth stanza transcribed below. At some later time he bracketed off the last four stanzas, introduced a transitional stanza that incorporated the last two lines of the original conclusion, and then went on to write a new and much enlarged conclusion to the poem, which includes the closing "Epitaph." A comparison with the final version of the *Elegy,* above, will show that the author deleted some of these added stanzas, and also made a number of verbal changes, in his published texts of the poem.

From Elegy Written in a Country Churchyard

[*Lines 69–128*]

The struggleings Pangs of conscious Truth to hide,
To quench the Blushes of ingenuous Shame,
        crown
And at the Shrine of Luxury & Pride
  With   by
~~Burn~~ Incense hallowd in the Muse's Flame.
    kindled at

The thoughtless World to Majesty may bow
Exalt the brave, & idolize Success
But more to Innocence their Safety owe
Than Power & Genius e'er conspired to bless

And thou, who mindful of the unhonour'd Dead
             eir
Dost in these notes thy artless Tale relate
By Night & lonely Contemplation led
To linger in the gloomy Walks of Fate

Hark how the sacred Calm, that broods around
Bids ev'ry fierce tumultuous Passion cease
In still small Accents whisp'ring from the Ground
A grateful Earnest of eternal Peace

No more with Reason & thyself at Strife
Give anxious Cares & endless Wishes room
But thro' the cool sequester'd Vale of Life
Pursue the silent Tenour of thy Doom.

Far from the madding Crowd's ignoble Strife;
Their sober Wishes never knew to stray:
Along the cool sequester'd Vale of Life
          noiseless
They kept the silent Tenour of their Way.

Yet even these Bones from Insult to protect
Some frail Memorial still erected nigh

         With
~~In~~-uncouth Rhime, & shapeless Sculpture deckt
Implores the passing Tribute of a Sigh.

Their Name, their Years, spelt by th' unletter'd Muse
The Place of Fame, & Epitaph supply,
And many a holy Text around she strews
That teach the rustic Moralist to die.

For who to dumb Forgetfulness a Prey
This pleasing anxious Being e'er resign'd;
Left the warm Precincts of the chearful Day,
Nor cast one longing lingring Look behind?

On some fond Breast the parting Soul relies,
Some pious Drops the closing Eye requires:
Even from the Tomb the Voice of Nature cries,
And buried Ashes glow with social Fires
    For Thee, who mindful &c: as above.[1]

If chance that e'er some pensive Spirit more,
By sympathetic Musings here delay'd,
With vain, tho' kind, Enquiry shall explore
Thy once-loved Haunt, this long-deserted Shade.

Haply some hoary-headed Swain shall say,[2]
Oft have we seen him at the Peep of Dawn
With hasty Footsteps brush the Dews away
On the high Brow of yonder hanging Lawn
Him have we seen the Green-wood Side along,
While o'er the Heath we hied, our Labours done,
Oft as the Woodlark piped her farewell Song
With whistful Eyes pursue the setting Sun.
               spreading   nodding
Oft at the Foot of yonder hoary Beech
That wreathes its old fantastic Roots so high
His listless Length at Noontide would he stretch,
And pore upon the Brook that babbles by.
    With Gestures quaint now smileing as in Scorn,
        wayward fancies   ~~loved~~ would he
    Mutt'ring his fond Conceits he ~~wont to~~ rove:
       drooping,
    Now woeful wan, ~~he droop'd,~~ as one forlorn
    Or crazed with Care, or cross'd in hopeless Love.
      One Morn we miss'd him on th' accustom'd Hill,
       Along the   near
      By the Heath-~~side,~~ & at his fav'rite Tree.
      Another came, nor yet beside the Rill,
           by
      Nor up the Lawn, nor at the Wood was he.

---

1. I.e., Gray indicates that the second bracketed stanza, above, is to be inserted here, except that the opening "And thou" is to be altered to "For Thee."

2. At this point in the manuscript Gray ceases to leave a space between the stanzas. The first edition of 1751, at Gray's request, was printed without such spaces. They were, however, inserted in later editions printed during Gray's lifetime.

~~There scatter'd oft, the earliest~~
The next with Dirges meet in sad Array
    by
Slow thro the Church-way Path we saw him born
Approach & read, for thou can'st read the Lay
  Graved carved   yon
Wrote on the Stone beneath that ancient Thorn

                             Year
There scatter'd oft the earliest of y^e ~~Spring~~
              showers of
By Hands unseen are frequent Vi'lets found
  Redbreast
The Robin loves to build & warble there,
And little Footsteps lightly print the Ground.

Here rests his Head upon the Lap of Earth[3]
A Youth to Fortune & to Fame unknown
Fair Science frown'd not on his humble Birth
And Melancholy mark'd him for her own

Large was his Bounty & his Heart sincere;
Heaven did a Recompence as largely send.
He gave to Mis'ry all he had, a Tear.
He gain'd from Heav'n, 'twas all he wish'd, a Friend

No farther seek his Merits to disclose,
    think
Nor seek to draw them from their dread Abode
(His Frailties there in trembling Hope repose)
The Bosom of his Father & his God.

WILLIAM BLAKE
The Tyger[1]

[First Draft]

The Tyger

1   Tyger Tyger burning bright
        In the forests of the night
        What immortal hand or eye
      ~~Dare~~ ~~Could~~ frame thy fearful symmetry

        Burnt in
2   ~~In what~~ distant deeps or skies
   ~~The cruel~~ ~~Burnt the~~ fire of thine eyes
        On what wings dare he aspire
        What the hand dare sieze the fire

3. These last three stanzas (which Gray in the first edition of 1751 labeled "The Epitaph") are written in the right-hand margin, with the page turned crosswise.

1. These drafts have been taken from a notebook used by William Blake, called the Rossetti MS because it was once owned by Dante Gabriel Rossetti, the Victorian poet and painter; David V. Erdman's edition of *The Notebook of William Blake* (1973) contains a photographic facsimile. The stanza and line numbers were written by Blake in the manuscript.

3   And what shoulder & what art
      Could twist the sinews of thy heart
      And when thy heart began to beat
      What dread hand & what dread feet

      ~~Could fetch it from the furnace deep~~
      ~~And in thy horrid ribs dare steep~~
      ~~In the well of sanguine woe~~
      ~~In what clay & what mould~~
      ~~Were thy eyes of fury rolld~~

      ~~Where~~   ~~where~~
4   ~~What~~ the hammer ~~what~~ the chain
      In what furnace was thy brain

                  dread grasp
      What the anvil what the ~~arm~~ arm grasp ~~clasp~~
  Dare ~~Could~~ its deadly terrors ~~clasp grasp~~ clasp

6   Tyger Tyger burning bright
      In the forests of the night
      What immortal hand & eye
           frame
      Dare ~~form~~ thy fearful symmetry

[Trial Stanzas]

      Burnt in distant deeps or skies
      The cruel fire of thine eye
      Could heart descend or wings aspire
      What the hand dare sieze the fire

            dare he ~~smile laugh~~
5 3/ And ~~did he laugh~~ his work to see
         ankle
     ~~What the shoulder what the knee~~
      Dare
   4 ~~Did~~ he who made the lamb make thee
   1 When the stars threw down their spears
   2 And waterd heaven with their tears

[Second Full Draft]

      Tyger Tyger burning bright
      In the forests of the night
      What Immortal hand & eye
      Dare frame thy fearful symmetry

      And what shoulder & what art
      Could twist the sinews of thy heart
      And when thy heart began to beat
      What dread hand & what dread feet

When the stars threw down their spears
And water'd heaven with their tears
Did he smile his work to see
Did he who made the lamb make thee

Tyger Tyger burning bright
In the forests of the night
What immortal hand & eye
Dare frame thy fearful symmetry

[*Final Version, 1794*][2]

The Tyger

Tyger Tyger, burning bright,
In the forests of the night;
What immortal hand or eye,
Could frame thy fearful symmetry?

In what distant deeps or skies
Burnt the fire of thine eyes!
On what wings dare he aspire?
What the hand, dare sieze the fire?

And what shoulder, & what art,
Could twist the sinews of thy heart?
And when thy heart began to beat,
What dread hand? & what dread feet?

What the hammer? what the chain,
In what furnace was thy brain?
What the anvil? what dread grasp,
Dare its deadly terrors clasp?

When the stars threw down their spears
And water'd heaven with their tears:
Did he smile his work to see?
Did he who made the Lamb make thee?

Tyger, Tyger burning bright,
In the forests of the night:
What immortal hand or eye,
Dare frame thy fearful symmetry?

2. As published in *Songs of Experience*.

WILLIAM WORDSWORTH
She dwelt among the untrodden ways

[*Version in a Letter to Coleridge,
December 1798 or January 1799*][1]

My hope was one, from cities far
    Nursed on a lonesome heath:
Her lips were red as roses are,
    Her hair a woodbine wreath.

She lived among the untrodden ways
    Beside the springs of Dove,
A maid whom there were none to praise,
    And very few to love;

A violet by a mossy stone
    Half-hidden from the eye!
Fair as a star when only one
    Is shining in the sky!

And she was graceful as the broom
    That flowers by Carron's side;[2]
But slow distemper checked her bloom,
    And on the Heath she died.

Long time before her head lay low
    Dead to the world was she:
But now she's in her grave, and Oh!
    The difference to me!

[*Final Version, 1800*][3]
Song

She dwelt among th' untrodden ways
    Beside the springs of Dove,
A Maid whom there were none to praise
    And very few to love.

A Violet by a mossy stone
    Half-hidden from the Eye!
—Fair, as a star when only one
    Is shining in the sky!

She *liv'd* unknown, and few could know
    When Lucy ceas'd to be;

---

1. Printed in Ernest de Selincourt's *Early Letters
of William and Dorothy Wordsworth* (1935). By
deleting two stanzas, and making a few verbal
changes, Wordsworth achieved the terse published
form of his great dirge.

2. The Carron is a river in northwestern Scotland.
"Broom" (preceding line) is a shrub with long slender branches and yellow flowers.
3. As published in the second edition of *Lyrical
Ballads.*

But she is in her Grave, and Oh!
The difference to me.

LORD BYRON
From Don Juan[1]

[*First Draft: Canto 3, Stanza 9*]

~~Life is a play and men~~
All tragedies are finished by a death,
All Comedies are ended by a marriage,
~~For Life can go no further.~~
~~These two form the last gasp of Passion's breath~~
~~All further is a blank—I won't disparage~~
~~That holy state—but certainly beneath~~
~~The Sun—of human things~~
~~These two are levellers, and human breath~~
~~So~~ ~~These point the epigram of human breath;~~
~~Or any~~ ~~The future states of both are left to faith,~~
~~Though Life and love I like not to disparage~~
~~The~~ For authors think description might disparage
                              fear
~~Tis strange that poets never try to wreathe~~ [*sic?*]
~~With eith~~ ~~'Tis strange that poets of the Catholic faith~~
~~Neer go beyond—and~~ ~~but seem to dread miscarriage~~
~~So dramas close with death or settlement for life~~
~~veiling~~ ~~Leaving the future states of Love and Life~~
~~The paradise beyond like that of life~~
~~And neer describing either~~
~~To more conjecture of a devil~~ ~~and~~ ~~or wife~~
~~And don't say much of paradise or wife~~
The worlds to come of both—~~&~~ or fall beneath,
~~And all~~ ~~both the worlds would blame them for miscarriage~~
And then both worlds would punish their miscarriage—
~~So leaving both with priest & prayerbook ready~~
So leaving ~~Clerg~~ both a each their Priest and prayerbook ready,
They say no more of death or of the Lady.

[*First Draft: Canto 14, Stanza 95*]

                quote   seldom
Alas! ~~I speak by~~ Experience—~~never~~ yet
~~I had a paramour—and I've had many~~

                              ~~some small~~
~~To whom I did not cause a deep~~ regret—
~~Whom I had not some reason to regret~~
~~For Whom—I did not feel myself~~ a Zany—
Alas! by all experience, seldom yet
(I merely quote what I have heard from many)
Had lovers not some reason to regret
The passion which made Solomon a Zany.
~~I also had a wife—not to forget—~~
I've also seen some wives—not to forget—

---

1. Reproduced from transcripts made of Byron's manuscripts in T. G. Steffan and W. W. Pratt, *Byron's "Don Juan"* (1957). The stanzas were published by Byron in their emended form.

The marriage state—the best or worst of any—
Who ~~was~~ the very ~~paragon~~ of wives,
Yet made the misery of ~~both our~~ lives.

were   paragons

~~many~~
~~several~~
~~of~~ at least two

PERCY BYSSHE SHELLEY

The three stages of this poem labeled "First Draft" are scattered through one of Shelley's notebooks, now in the Huntington Library, San Marino, California; these drafts have been transcribed and analyzed by Bennett Weaver, "Shelley Works Out the Rhythm of *A Lament*," *PMLA* 47 (1932): 570–76. They show Shelley working with fragmentary words and phrases, and simultaneously with a wordless pattern of pulses that marked out the meter of the single lines and the shape of the lyric stanzas. Shelley left this draft unfinished.

Apparently at some later time, Shelley returned to the poem and wrote what is here called the "Second Draft"; from this he then made, on a second page, a revised fair copy that provided the text that Mary Shelley published in 1824, after the poet's death. These two manuscript pages are now in the Bodleian Library, Oxford; the first page is photographically reproduced and discussed by John Carter and John Sparrow, "Shelley, Swinburne, and Housman," *Times Literary Supplement*, November 21, 1968, pp. 1318–19.

O World, O Life, O Time

[*First Draft, Stage 1*]

Ah time, oh night, oh day
~~Ni nal ni na, na ni~~
~~Ni na ni na, ni na~~
Oh life O death, O time
   Time a di
~~Never Time~~
Ah time, a time O-time
  ~~Time!~~

[*First Draft, Stage 2*]

Oh time, oh night oh day
~~O day oh night, alas~~
  ~~O~~ Death time night ~~oh~~
Oh, Time
Oh time o night oh day

[*First Draft, Stage 3*]

Na na, na na ná na
Nă nă na na na—nă nă

Nă nă nă nă nā nā
Na na nă nă nâ ă na

Na na na—nă nă—na na
Na na na na—na na na na na
Na na na na na.
    Na na
Na na na na na
    Na na
Na na na na na ˇ na!

Oh time, oh night, o day
      alas
O day ~~serenest~~, o day
O day alas the day
That thou shouldst sleep when we awake to say

O time time—o death—o day
    for
O day, o death life is far from thee
O thou wert never free
For death is now with thee
~~And life is far from~~
O death, o day for life is far from thee

[*Second Draft*][1]

Out of the day & night   I am
A joy has taken flight   despair
Fresh spring & summer   & winter hoar
Fill my faint heart with grief, but with
                        delight
      No more—o never more!

~~We~~
    O World, o life, o time
~~Will ye~~ On whose last steps I climb
Trembling at those which I have trod[2] before
When will return the glory of yr prime
    No more Oh never more

    Out of the day & night
    A joy has taken flight—
             autumn
~~From~~ Green spring, & ~~summer gra~~[3] & winter hoar

1. Shelley apparently wrote the first stanza of this draft low down on the page, and ran out of space after crowding in the third line of the second stanza; he then, in a lighter ink, wrote a revised form of the whole of the second stanza at the top of the page. In this revision, he left a space after "summer" in line 3, indicating that he planned an insertion that would fill out the four-foot meter of this line, and so make it match the five feet in the corresponding line of the first stanza.
In the upper right-hand corner of this manuscript page Shelley wrote "I am despair"—seemingly to express his bleak mood at the time he wrote the poem.
For this draft and information, and for the transcript of the fair copy that follows, the editors are indebted to Donald H. Reiman.
2. Shelley at first wrote "trod," then overwrote that with "stood." In the following line, Shelley at first wrote "yr," then overwrote "thy."
3. Not clearly legible; it is either "gra" or "gre." A difference in the ink from the rest of the line indicates that Shelley, having left a blank space, later started to fill it in, but thought better of it and crossed out the fragmentary insertion.

[FAIR COPY]

O World   o Life   o Time
On whose last steps I climb
Trembling at that where I had stood before
When will return the glory of yr prime?
    No more, o never more

2

Out of the day & night
A joy has taken flight
Fresh spring & summer   ⁴ & winter hoar
Move my faint heart with grief but with delight
No more, o, never more

JOHN KEATS

From The Eve of St. Agnes¹

[*Stanza 26*]

But soon his heart revives—her prayers said
She lays aside her neck   pearled

        strips her hair of all its ∧ wreathes pearl
Unclasps her bosom jewels
And twist it in one knot upon her head

                                        soon
But soon his heart revives—her praying done,
Of all its wreathed pearl she strips her hair
Unclasps her warmed jewels one by one

        her bursting
Loosens the boddice from her
        her Boddice lace string
        her Boddice and her bosom bar
        her

[HERE KEATS BEGINS A NEW SHEET]

Loosens her fragrant boddice and doth bare
Her

26

Anon
But soon his heart revives—her praying done,
                                        frees:
Of all its wreathe'd pearl her hair she strips
Unclasps her warmed jewels one by one

4. This fair copy of the second draft retains, and even enlarges, the blank space, indicating that Shelley still hasn't made up his mind what to insert after the word "summer." We may speculate, by reference to the fragmentary version of this stanza in the second draft, that he had in mind as possibilities either an adjective, "gray" or "green," or else the noun "autumn." Mary Shelley closed up this space when she published the poem in 1824, with the result that editors, following her version, have until very recently printed this line as though Shelley had intended it to be one metric foot shorter than the corresponding line of stanza 1.

1. Transcribed from what is probably the best known of all manuscripts, that which contains Keats's first draft of all but the first seven stanzas of The Eve of St. Agnes; it is now in the Houghton Library, Harvard University. Keats's published version of the poem, above, contains some further changes in wording.

                                                   by degrees
Loosens her fragrant boddice: ~~and down slips~~
                            ~~to her knees~~
Her sweet attire ~~fails light creeps down by~~

                        creeps rusteling to her knees
                    Mermaid   in sea weed
Half hidden like ~~a Syren of the Sea~~
~~And more melodious~~

                            dreaming
She stands awhile in ^ thought; and sees

                            on
In fancy fair Saint Agnes ~~in~~ her bed
But dares not look behind or all the charm is ~~fl~~ dead

[*Stanza 30*]

     But
~~And still she slept:~~
And still she slept an azure-lidded sleep
    In blanched linen, smooth and lavender'd
While he from frorth the closet brough a heap

                    fruits
Of candied ~~sweets~~ ~~sweets with~~

            apple Quince and plumb and gourd
                                creamed
With jellies soother than the ~~dairy~~ curd

                            tinct
And lucent syrups ~~smooth~~ with ciannamon
~~And sugar'd dates from that oer Euphrates fard~~

                    in Brigantine transferred
Manna and daites in ~~Bragtine transferd~~
                        ~~and manna wild transferd~~
~~And Manna wild and Bragantine~~

                            sugar'd dates transferred
~~In Brigantine from Fez~~
From fez—and spiced danties every one

            glutted
From ~~wealthy~~ Samarchand to cedard lebanon
        silken

To Autumn[2]

Season of Mists and mellow fruitfulness
    Close bosom friend of the naturring sun;
Conspiring with him how to load and bless
    The Vines with fruit that round the thatch eves run
        To bend with apples the moss'd Cottage trees
            And fill all furuits with sweeness to the core

---

2. From an untitled manuscript—apparently
Keats's first draft of the poem—in the Houghton
Library, Harvard University. The many pen-slips
and errors in spelling indicate that Keats wrote rapidly, in a state of creative excitement. Keats made
a few further changes before publishing the poem
in the form included in the selections above.

To swell the gourd, and plump the hazle shells
With a white kernel; to set budding more
And still more later flowers for the bees
Until they think wam days with never cease
For Summer has o'erbrimm'd their clammy cells—

oft amid thy stores?
Who hath not seen thee? ~~for thy haunts are many~~
                                        abroad
Sometimes whoever seeks ~~for thee~~ may find
Thee sitting careless on a granary floorr
Thy hair soft lifted by the winnowing wind

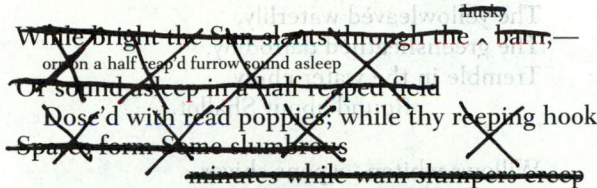

                                    husky
~~While bright the Sun slants through the~~ ∧ ~~barn,—~~
~~or on a half reap'd furrow sound asleep~~
~~Or sound asleep in a half reaped field~~
~~Dose'd with read poppies; while thy reeping hook~~
~~Spares form Some slumbrous~~
~~minutes while wam slumpers creep~~

Or on a half reap'd furrow sound asleep
Dos'd with the fume of poppies, while thy hook
Spares the next swath and all its twined flowers
~~Spares for some slumbrous minutes the next swath;~~
And sometimes like a gleans thost dost keep
Steady thy laden head across the brook;
Or by a Cyder-press with patent look
Thou watchest the last oozing hours by hours

Where are the songs of Sping? Aye where are they?
Think not of them thou hast thy music too—
barred   bloom
While ~~a gold~~ clouds ~~gilds~~ the soft-dying day
And   with
~~And~~ Touching ~~the~~ the stibble plains ∧ rosy hue—
Then in a waiful quire the small gnats mourn
Among the river sallows, ~~on the~~ borne afots
Or sinking as the light wind lives and dies;
And full grown Lambs loud bleat from hilly bourn,
Hedge crickets sing, and now again full soft
The Redbreast whistles from a garden croft:
~~And now flock still~~
And Gather'd Swallows twiter in the Skies—

ALFRED, LORD TENNYSON
From The Lady of Shalott[1]

[Version of 1832]

PART THE FIRST.

On either side the river lie
Long fields of barley and of rye,
That clothe the wold, and meet the sky.
And thro' the field the road runs by
    To manytowered Camelot.
The yellowleavèd waterlily,
The greensheathèd daffodilly,
Tremble in the water chilly,
    Round about Shallot.

Willows whiten, aspens shiver,
The sunbeam-showers break and quiver
In the stream that runneth ever
By the island in the river,
    Flowing down to Camelot.
Four gray walls and four gray towers
Overlook a space of flowers,
And the silent isle imbowers
    The Lady of Shalott.

Underneath the bearded barley,
The reaper, reaping late and early,
Hears her ever chanting cheerly,
Like an angel, singing clearly,
    O'er the stream of Camelot.
Piling the sheaves in furrows airy,
Beneath the moon, the reaper weary
Listening whispers, " 'tis the fairy
    Lady of Shalott."

The little isle is all inrailed
With a rose-fence, and overtrailed
With roses: by the marge unhailed
The shallop flitteth silkensailed,
    Skimming down to Camelot.
A pearlgarland winds her head:
She leaneth on a velvet bed,

---

1. First published in Tennyson's *Poems* of 1832 (dated 1833 on the title page). The volume was severely criticized by some reviewers; partly in response to this criticism, Tennyson radically revised a number of the poems, including *The Lady of Shalott,* before reprinting them in his *Poems* (1842).
    Parts 1 and 4 are reproduced here in the version of 1832. The final form of the poem reprinted in the selections from Tennyson, above, differs from the revised version that Tennyson published in 1842 only in line 157, which in 1842 read: "A corse between the houses high"; Tennyson changed the line to "Dead-pale between the houses high" in 1855.

Full royally apparellèd,
　　　The Lady of Shalott.

　　　　　　*　*　*

PART THE FOURTH.

In the stormy eastwind straining
The pale-yellow woods were waning,
The broad stream in his banks complaining,
Heavily the low sky raining
　　　　　Over towered Camelot:
Outside the isle a shallow boat
Beneath a willow lay afloat,
Below the carven stern she wrote,
　　　THE LADY OF SHALOTT.

A cloudwhite crown of pearl she dight.
All raimented in snowy white
That loosely flew, (her zone in sight,
Clasped with one blinding diamond bright,)
　　　　　Her wide eyes fixed on Camelot,
Though the squally eastwind keenly
Blew, with folded arms serenely
By the water stood the queenly
　　　　　Lady of Shalott.

With a steady, stony glance—
Like some bold seer in a trance,
Beholding all his own mischance,
Mute, with a glassy countenance—
　　　　　She looked down to Camelot.
It was the closing of the day,
She loosed the chain, and down she lay,
The broad stream bore her far away,
　　　　　The Lady of Shalott.

As when to sailors while they roam,
By creeks and outfalls far from home,
Rising and dropping with the foam,
From dying swans wild warblings come,
　　　　　Blown shoreward; so to Camelot
Still as the boathead wound along
The willowy hills and fields among,
They heard her chanting her deathsong,
　　　　　The Lady of Shalott.

A longdrawn carol, mournful, holy,
She chanted loudly, chanted lowly,
Till her eyes were darkened wholly,
And her smooth face sharpened slowly
　　　　　Turned to towered Camelot:
For ere she reached upon the tide

The first house by the waterside,
Singing in her song she died,
   The Lady of Shalott.

Under tower and balcony,
By gardenwall and gallery,
A pale, pale corpse she floated by,
Deadcold, between the houses high.
   Dead into towered Camelot.
Knight and burgher, lord and dame,
To the plankèd wharfage came:
Below the stern they read her name,
   "The Lady of Shalott."

They crossed themselves, their stars they blest,
Knight, ministrel, abbot, squire and guest.
There lay a parchment on her breast,
That puzzled more than all the rest,
   The wellfed wits at Camelot.
"The web was woven curiously
The charm is broken utterly,
Draw near and fear not—this is I,
   The Lady of Shalott."

From Tithonus[2]

[Lines 1–10]

[TRINITY COLLEGE MANUSCRIPT]

Ay me! Ay me! the woods decay & fall
~~The stars blaze out & never rise again~~.
         the
The vapours weep their substance to ground
Man͵ comes & tills the earth & lies beneath
And after many summers dies the ~~rose~~ swan
Me only fatal immortality
Consumes: I wither slowly in thine arms:
Here at the quiet limit of the world
        e yet
A white-haired shade roaming like a dream
The ever-silent spaces of the East
Far-folded mists & gleaming halls of morn.

2. Three manuscript drafts of *Tithonus* are extant. Two are in Tennyson's Notebooks Nos. 20 and 21, at Trinity College, Cambridge; a third one, written 1833, is in the Commonplace Book compiled by Tennyson's friend J. M. Heath, which is in the Fitzwilliam Museum at Cambridge University. According to Tennyson's editor, Christopher Ricks, the Heath version is later than those in the Trinity Manuscripts. The transcriptions here of Tennyson's opening lines are from the first draft (Trinity College manuscript, Notebook 20), and from the Heath manuscript, where the poem is titled "Tithon." These are followed by the final version of *Tithonus* that Tennyson published in 1864. As late as in the edition of 1860, the opening words had remained "Ay me! ay me!" and "field" (line 3) had remained "earth."

[HEATH MANUSCRIPT]

Tithon

Ay me! ay me! the woods decay and fall,
The vapours weep their substance to the ground,
Man comes and tills the earth and lies beneath,
And after many summers dies the rose.
Me only fatal immortality
Consumes: I wither slowly in thine arms,
Here at the quiet limit of the world,
A white-haired shadow roaming like a dream
The ever-silent spaces of the East,
Far-folded mists, and gleaming halls of morn.

[AS PRINTED IN 1864]

Tithonus

The woods decay, the woods decay and fall,
The vapours weep their burthen to the ground,
Man comes and tills the field and lies beneath,
And after many a summer dies the swan.
Me only cruel immortality
Consumes: I wither slowly in thine arms,
Here at the quiet limit of the world,
A white-haired shadow roaming like a dream
The ever-silent spaces of the East,
Far-folded mists, and gleaming halls of morn.

GERARD MANLEY HOPKINS
Thou art indeed just, Lord[1]

*Justus quidem tu es, Domine, si disputem tecum; verumtamen
justa loquar ad te: quare via impiorum prosperatur? etc.*
—Jer. xii 1.

March 17 1889

Lord, if I
Thou art indeed just, ~~were I to~~ contend
        sir,   plead
With thee; but, ~~Lord,~~ so what I ~~speak~~ is just.

Why do sinners' ways prosper? and why must

---

1. From a manuscript in the Bodleian Library, Oxford University; it is a clean copy, made after earlier drafts, which Hopkins goes on to revise further. Differences in the ink show that the emendation "lacèd they are" (line 10) was made during the first writing, but that the other verbal changes were made later. The interlinear markings are Hopkins's metrical indicators; he explains their significance in the "Author's Preface," included in *Poems of Gerard Manley Hopkins* (1970), ed. W. H. Gardner and N. H. MacKenzie.

The epigraph is from the Vulgate translation of Jeremiah 12.1; a literal translation of the Latin is "Thou art indeed just, Lord, [even] if I plead with Thee; nevertheless I will speak what is just to Thee: Why does the way of the wicked prosper? etc."

Disappointment all I endeavour end?
Wert thou my enemy, O thou my friend,
How wouldst thou worse, I wonder, than thou dost
          O the sots and   of
Defeat, thwart me? ~~Ah! sots, revellers~~, thralls to lust
Do in   that
In spare hours ~~do~~ more thrive than I ~~who~~ spend,
     great   See,
Sir, ~~my~~ life on thy cause. ~~Look~~, banks and brakes
Now, leavèd   lacèd they are
~~Leavèd~~ how thick! ~~broidered all~~ again
               look
With fretty chervil, ~~now~~, and fresh winds shakes
Them; birds build—but not I build; no, but strain,
Time's eunuch, and not breed one work that wakes.
     Mine, O   send my
~~Then send~~, thou lord of life, ~~these~~ roots ~~their~~ rain.

WILLIAM BUTLER YEATS

Yeats usually composed very slowly and with painful effort. He tells us in his *Auto-biography* that "five or six lines in two or three laborious hours were a day's work, and I longed for somebody to interrupt me." His manuscripts show the slow evolution of his best poems, which sometimes began with a prose sketch, were then versified, and underwent numerous revisions. In many instances, even after the poems had been published, Yeats continued to revise them, sometimes drastically, in later printings.

The Sorrow of Love[1]

[*Manuscript, 1891*][2]

The quarrel of the sparrows in the eaves,
The full round moon and the star-laden sky,
The song of the ever-singing leaves,
Had hushed away earth's old and weary cry.

And then you came with those red mournful lips,
And with you came the whole of the world's tears,
And all the sorrows of her labouring ships,
And all the burden of her million years.

And now the angry sparrows in the eaves,
The withered moon, the white stars in the sky,

1. Originally composed in Yeats's Pre-Raphaelite mode of the early 1890s, *The Sorrow of Love* was one of his most popular poems. Nonetheless, some thirty years after publication, Yeats rewrote the lyric to give it the greater precision and the collo-

quial vigor of his poetic style in the 1920s.
2. Manuscript version composed in October 1891, as transcribed by Jon Stallworthy, *Between the Lines: Yeats's Poetry in the Making* (Oxford University Press, 1963), pp. 47–48.

The wearisome loud chanting of the leaves,
Are shaken with earth's old and weary cry.

[First Printed Version, 1892][3]

The quarrel of the sparrows in the eaves,
  The full round moon and the star-laden sky,
And the loud song of the ever-singing leaves
  Had hid away earth's old and weary cry.

And then you came with those red mournful lips,
  And with you came the whole of the world's tears,
And all the sorrows of her labouring ships,
  And all burden of her myriad years.

And now the sparrows warring in the eaves,
  The crumbling moon, the white stars in the sky,
And the loud chanting of the unquiet leaves,
  Are shaken with earth's old and weary cry.

[Final Printed Version, 1925][4]

The brawling of a sparrow in the eaves,
The brilliant moon and all the milky sky,
And all that famous harmony of leaves,
Had blotted out man's image and his cry.

A girl arose that had red mournful lips
And seemed the greatness of the world in tears,
Doomed like Odysseus and the labouring ships
And proud as Priam murdered with his peers;

Arose, and on the instant clamorous eaves,
A climbing moon upon an empty sky,
And all that lamentation of the leaves,
Could but compose man's image and his cry.

---

3. From Yeats's *The Countess Kathleen and Various Legends and Lyrics* (1892). In a corrected page proof for this printing, now in the Garvan Collection of the Yale University Library, lines 7–8 originally read: "And all the sorrows of his labouring ships, / And all the burden of his married years." Also, in lines 4 and 12, the adjective was "bitter" instead of "weary." In his *Poems* (1895), Yeats inserted the missing "the" in line 8, and changed "sorrows" (line 7) to "trouble"; "burden" (line 8) to "trouble"; and "crumbling moon" (line 10) to "curd-pale moon."

4. From *Early Poems and Stories* (1925). Yeats wrote in his *Autobiography* (New York, 1938), p.

371, that "in later years" he had "learnt that occasional prosaic words gave the impression of an active man speaking," so that "certain words must be dull and numb. Here and there in correcting my early poems I have introduced such numbness and dullness, turned, for instance, 'the curd-pale moon' into the 'brilliant moon,' that all might seem, as it were, remembered with indifference, except some one vivid image." Yeats, however, did not recall his emendations accurately. He had in 1925 altered "the full round moon" (line 2) to "the brilliant moon," and "the curd-pale moon" (line 10, version of 1895) to "a climbing moon."

Leda and the Swan[5]

[*First Version*]

Annunciation

Now can the swooping Godhead have his will
Yet hovers, though her helpless thighs are pressed
By the webbed toes; and that all powerful bill
Has suddenly bowed her face upon his breast.
How can those terrified vague fingers push
The feathered glory from her loosening thighs?
All the stretched body's laid on that white rush

       strange
And feels the ~~strong~~ heart beating where it lies
A shudder in the loins engenders there
The broken wall, the burning roof and tower
And Agamemnon dead. . . .

                Being so caught up
Did nothing pass before her in the air?
Did she put on his knowledge with his power
Before the indifferent beak could let her drop
              Sept 18 1923

      swooping
The ~~trembl~~ godhead is half hovering still,
     climbs
Yet ~~climbs~~ upon her trembling body pressed
     webbed
By the toes; & ~~through~~ that all powerful bill
       ~~the~~ bowed
Has suddenly ~~bowed~~ her face upon his breast.
How can those terrified vague fingers push
The feathered glory from her loosening thighs
              laid
All the stretched body ~~leans~~ on that white rush
          or
~~Her falling body thrown on the white~~ white rush

Can feel etc
or Her body can but lean on the white rush

But mounts until her trembling thighs are pressed[6]
~~B~~
By the webbed toes; & that all powerful bill
Has suddenly bowed her head on his breast

---

5. From Yeats's manuscript *Journal*, Sections 248 and 250. This *Journal*, including facsimiles and transcriptions of the drafts of *Leda and the Swan*, has been published in W. B. Yeats, *Memoirs*, ed. Denis Donoghue (Macmillan, London, 1972).
    The first version, entitled *Annunciation*, seems to be a clean copy of earlier drafts; Yeats went on to revise it further, especially the opening octave. Neither of the other two complete drafts, each of which Yeats labeled "Final Version," was in fact final. Yeats himself crossed out the first draft. The second, although Yeats published it in 1924, was

subjected to further revision before he published the poem in *The Tower* (1928), in the final form reprinted in the selections from Yeats, above.
    Yeats's handwriting is hasty and very difficult to decipher. The readings of some words, in the manuscripts both of this poem and of *After Long Silence*, below, are uncertain.
6. This passage is written across the blank page opposite the first version; Yeats drew a line indicating that it was to replace the revised lines 2–4, which he had written below the first version.

Final Version

Annunciation

Can hold

The swooping godhead is half hovering still
But mounts, until her trembling thighs are pressed
By the webbed toes, & that all powerful bill
~~Has hung~~ her helpless body
Has suddenly bowed her head upon his breast.
How can those terrified vague fingers push
The feathered glory from her loosening thighs?
~~How~~ now its body leans on
~~With her body laid on the white~~ rush
all the stretched body laid on the white rush
and ~~Can~~ feel the strange heart beating where it lies?
A shudder in the loins engenders there
The broken wall, the burning roof & tower
And Agamemnon dead . . .

Being mastered so
~~Being so caught up~~

So
~~And~~ mastered by the brute blood of the air
~~Being mastered so~~
~~Did nothing pass before her in the air?~~
Did she put on his knowledge with his power
Before the indifferent beak could let her drop.

WBY. Sept 18 1923

swoop
A ~~rush~~ upon great wings & hovering still
~~He sinks until~~
~~He has sunk on her down, & her hair~~
~~The great bird sinks, till~~
The bird descends, & her frail ~~thigh~~ thighs are pressed
By the webbed toes, & that all

that
Now ~~all~~ her body's laid on that white rush[7]
~~All the stretched body laid on~~ that white rush
~~Now that whole~~
Now t~~he body on the white~~ rush
Can fee

Final Version

Leda & the Swan

A rush, a sudden wheel and
~~A swoop upon great wings &~~ hovering still
sinks down   bare frail
stet The bird ~~descends~~ & her ~~frail~~ thighs are pressed
By the ~~toes~~ webbed toes, & that all powerful bill

7. Written on the blank page across from the complete version, with an arrow indicating that it was a revision of the seventh line.

laid
Has ~~driven~~ her helpless face upon his breast.
How can those terrified vague fingers push
The feathered glory from her loosening thighs?

s laid
All the stretched body ~~laid~~ on that white rush
And ~~feel~~ feels the strange heart beating where it lies.
A shudder in the loins engenders there
The broken wall, the burning roof & tower
And Agamemnon dead.
                        Being so caught up
So mastered by the ~~br~~ brute blood of the air
Did she put on his knowledge with his power
Before the indifferent beak could let her drop.

After Long Silence[8]

[Draft 1]

Subject

Your hair is white
My hair is white
Come let us talk of love
What other theme do we know
When we were young
We were in love with one another
~~A O~~ And therefore ignorant

[Draft 2]

Those
s
~~Your~~ other lover being dead & gone

                                        friendly light
                                        hair is white
                ~~on love descent~~   descant
Upon the ~~sole theme~~ supreme theme of art &   song
Wherein there's theme so fitting for the aged.   ;young
We loved each other & were ignorant

[Draft 3]

~~I h~~

Once more I have kissed your hand & it is right—
All other lovers being estranged or dead

8. The drafts of *After Long Silence* are interspersed with other materials on seven pages of a manuscript book, begun in 1928, which includes a number of additional poems that were published in *The Winding Stair and Other Poems* (1933). It begins, like many of Yeats's poems, with a prose sketch, and is labeled simply "Subject." It then passes through a tentative versified stage (Draft 2) in which Yeats sets down four complete lines and a set of possible rhyme words; is subjected to various drafts and revisions; and concludes with the final text that Yeats published in 1933. Yeats did not add the title *After Long Silence* until he wrote out a fair copy for his typist at some time after August 14, 1931.

David R. Clark, "After 'Silence,' The 'Supreme Theme': Eight Lines of Yeats," includes photocopies and transcripts of the drafts of this poem, together with a discussion of its biographical occasion and its interpretation (in *Myth and Reality in Irish Literature*, ed. Joseph Ronsley [Waterloo, Canada, 1977], pp. 149–73).

The heavy curtain drawn—the candlelight
Waging a doubtful battle with the shade

                                 discant,
We call our wisdom up upon our wisdom & descant
Upon the supreme theme of art & song
Decrepitude increases wisdom—young
We loved each other & were ignorant ignor   ignorant

[Draft 4]

Un
The friendly lamplight hidden by its shade
And shutters clapped upon the deepening night—
The candle hidden by its friendly shade
Those curtains drawn upon the deepening night—

The curtains drawn on the unfriendly night—
That we descant & yet again descant
         supreme theme
Upon the supreme theme of art & song— art & song—
Bodily decrepitude is wisdom—young

[Final MS Version]

Speech after long silence; it is right—
                         or
All other lovers being estranged & dead,
                hid
Unfriendly lamp-light hid under its shade,
              upon
The curtain's drawn upon unfriendly night—
That we descant & yet again descant
Upon the supreme theme of art & song,
Bodily decrepitude is wisdom—young
We loved each other & were ignorant

                               Nov
                               Oct 1929

D. H. LAWRENCE
The Piano[1]

Somewhere beneath that piano's superb sleek black
Must hide my mother's piano, little and brown, with
         the back

---

1. Transcribed from a notebook in which Lawrence at first entered various academic assignments while he was a student at the University College of Nottingham, 1906–8, but then used to write drafts of some of his early poems. These were probably composed in the period from 1906 to 1910. The text reproduced here was revised and published with the title *Piano* in Lawrence's *New Poems,* 1918. A comparison of this draft with *Piano,* reprinted above, will show that Lawrence eliminated the first and fourth stanzas (as well as the last two lines of the third stanza); revised the remaining three stanzas, sometimes radically; and

most surprisingly, reversed his original conclusion. As Lawrence himself explained his revisions of some of his early poems, they "had to be altered, where sometimes the hand of commonplace youth had been laid on the mouth of the demon. It is not for technique that these poems are altered: it is to say the real say."

For transcriptions and discussions of this and other poems in Lawrence's early notebook, see Vivian de Sola Pinto, "D.H. Lawrence: Letter-Writer and Craftsman in Verse," in *Renaissance and Modern Studies* 1 (1957): 5–34.

                    stood close to

That ~~was against~~ the wall, and the front's faded silk, both torn
And the keys with little hollows, that my mother's fingers
          had worn.

Softly, in the shadows, a woman is singing to me
Quietly, through the years I have crept back to see
A child sitting under the piano, in the boom of the
        shaking ~~tingling~~ strings
Pressing the little poised feet of the mother who smiles
        as she sings

The full throated woman has chosen a winning, living[2]
        song
And surely the heart that is in me must belong
To the old Sunday evenings, when darkness wandered
        outside
And hymns gleamed on our warm lips, as we watched
        mother's fingers glide

          is
Or is this my sister at home in the old front room
Singing love's first surprised gladness, alone in
        the gloom.
She will start when she sees me, and blushing,
        spread out her hands
To cover my mouth's raillery, till I'm bound in
           heart-spun
        her shame's ~~pleading~~ bands.

A woman is singing me a wild Hungarian
        air
And her arms, and her bosom and the whole
        of her soul is bare
And the great black piano is clamouring as my
      mother's never could clamour
        my mother's [   ]³ tunes are
And the ~~tunes of the past is~~ devoured of this music's
      ravaging glamour.

---

2. A conjectural reading; the word is not clearly
legible.

3. An undecipherable word is crossed out here.

Selected Bibliographies

The Selected Bibliographies consist of a list of Suggested General Readings on English literature, followed by bibliographies for each of the literary periods. For ease of reference, the authors within each period are arranged in alphabetical order.

SUGGESTED GENERAL READINGS

Histories of England and of English Literature

New research and new perspectives have made even the most distinguished of the comprehensive, general histories written in past generations seem outmoded. Innovative research in social, cultural, and political history has made it difficult to write a single, coherent account of England from the Middle Ages to the present, let alone to accommodate in a unified narrative the complex histories of Scotland, Ireland, and Wales. Readers who wish to explore the historical matrix out of which the works of literature collected in this anthology emerged are advised to consult the studies of particular periods listed in the appropriate sections of this bibliography. The multivolume *Oxford History of England* is useful, as are the three-volume *Peoples of the British Isles: A New History*, ed. Stanford Lehmberg, 1992, and the nine-volume *Cambridge Cultural History of Britain*, ed. Boris Ford, 1992. Albert Baugh et al., *A Literary History of England*, rev. 1967, remains a convenient source of factual materials about authors, works, and chronology. Given the cultural centrality of London, readers may find Roy Porter's *London: A Social History*, 1994, valuable. Similar observations may be made about literary history. In the light of such initiatives as women's studies, new historicism, and postcolonialism, the range of authors deemed most significant has expanded in recent years, along with the geographical and conceptual boundaries of literature in English. Attempts to capture in a unified account the great sweep of literature from *Beowulf* to late last night have largely given way to studies of individual genres, carefully delimited time periods, and specific authors. For these more focused accounts, see the listings by period.

Among the large-scale literary surveys, *The Cambridge Guide to Literature in English*, 1993, is useful, as is *The Penguin History of Literature. The Feminist Companion to Literature in English*, ed. Virginia Blain, Isobel Grundy, and Patricia Clements, 1990, is an important resource, and the editorial materials in *The Norton Anthology of*

Literature by Women, 2nd ed., 1996, ed. Sandra M. Gilbert and Susan Gubar, constitute a concise history and set of biographies of women authors since the Middle Ages. *Annals of English Literature, 1475–1950*, rev. 1961, lists important publications year by year, together with the significant literary events for each year. David Daiches, *A Critical History of English Literature*, 2 vols., rev. 1970, provides a running literary appreciation.

Helpful treatments and surveys of English meter, rhyme, and stanza forms are Paul Fussell Jr., *Poetic Meter and Poetic Form*, rev. 1979; Donald Wesling, *The Chances of Rhyme: Device and Modernity*, 1980; Derek Attridge, *The Rhythms of English Poetry*, 1982; Charles O. Hartman, *Free Verse: An Essay in Prosody*, 1983; John Hollander, *Vision and Resonance: Two Senses of Poetic Form*, rev. 1985; and Robert Pinsky, *The Sounds of Poetry: A Brief Guide*, 1998.

On the development of the novel as a form, see Ian Watt, *The Rise of the Novel*, 1957; *The Columbia History of the British Novel*, ed. John Richetti, 1994; and Margaret Doody, *The True Story of the Novel*, 1996. On women novelists and readers, see Nancy Armstrong, *Desire and Domestic Fiction: A Political History of the Novel*, 1987; and Catherine Gallagher, *Nobody's Story: The Vanishing Acts of Women Writers in the Marketplace, 1670–1820*, 1994.

On the history of playhouse design, see Richard Leacroft, *The Development of the English Playhouse: An Illustrated Survey of Theatre Building in England from Medieval to Modern Times*, 1988. For a survey of the plays that have appeared on these and other stages, see Allardyce Nicoll, *British Drama*, rev. 1962, and the eight-volume *Revels History of Drama in English*, gen. eds. Clifford Leech and T. W. Craik, 1975–83.

On some of the key intellectual currents that are at once reflected in and shaped by English literature, Arthur T. Lovejoy's classic studies *The Great Chain of Being*, 1936, and *Essays in the History of Ideas*, 1948, remain valuable, along with such works as Lovejoy and George Boas, *Primitivism and Related Ideas in Antiquity*, 1935; Ernst Kantowicz, *The King's Two Bodies: A Study in Medieval Political Theology*, 1957, new ed. 1997; Richard Popkin, *The History of Skepticism from Erasmus to Descartes*, 1960; M. H. Abrams, *Natural Supernaturalism: Tradition and Revolution in Romantic Literature*, 1971; and Michel Foucault, *Madness and Civilization: A History of Insanity in the Age of Reason*, Eng. trans. 1965, and *The Order of Things: An Archaeology of the Human Sciences*, Eng. trans. 1970.

Reference Works

The single most important tool for the study of literature in English is the *Oxford English Dictionary*, 2nd ed., 1989, also available on CD-ROM. The *OED* is written on historical principles: that is, it attempts not only to describe current word use but also to record the history and development of the language from its origins before the Norman conquest to the present. It thus provides, for familiar as well as archaic and obscure words, the widest possible range of meanings and uses, organized chronologically and illustrated with quotations. Beyond the *OED* there are many other valuable dictionaries, such as *The American Heritage Dictionary*, *The Oxford Dictionary of Etymology*, and an array of reference works from *The Cambridge Encyclopedia of the English Language*, ed. David Crystal, 1995, to guides to specialized vocabularies, slang, regional dialects, and the like.

There is a steady flow of new editions of most major and many minor writers in English, along with a ceaseless outpouring of critical appraisals and scholarship. The *MLA International Bibliography* (also on line) is the best way to keep abreast of the most recent work and to conduct bibliographic searches. *The New Cambridge Bibliography of English Literature* ed. George Watson, 1969–77, updated shorter ed. 1981, is a valuable guide to the huge body of earlier literary criticism and scholarship. *A Guide to English and American Literature*, ed. F. W. Bateson and Harrison Meserole, rev. 1976, is a selected list of editions, as well as scholarly and critical treatments. Further bibliographical aids are described in Arthur G. Kennedy, *A Concise Bibliography for Students of English*, rev. 1972; Richard D. Altick and Andrew Wright, *Selective Bibliography for the Study of English and American Literature* rev. 1979, and James L. Harner, *Literary Research Guide*, rev. 1998.

For compact biographies of English authors, see the multivolume *Dictionary of National Biography*, ed. Leslie Stephen and Sidney Lee, 1885–1900, with supplements that carry the work to 1980; condensed biographies will be found in the *Concise Dictionary of National Biography*, 2 parts (1920, 1988). Handy reference books of authors, works, and various literary terms and allusions are *The Oxford Companion to the Theatre*, Phyllis Hartnoll, rev. 1990; *Princeton Encyclopedia of Poetry and Poetics*, ed. Alex Preminger and others, rev. 1993; and *The Oxford Companion to English Literature*,

ed. Margaret Drabble, rev. 1998. Low-priced handbooks that define and illustrate literary concepts and terms are *The Penguin Dictionary of Literary Terms and Literary Theory*, ed. J. A. Cuddon, 1991; W. F. Thrall and Addison Hibbard, *A Handbook to Literature*, ed. C. Hugh Holman, rev. 1992; *Critical Terms for Literary Study*, ed. Frank Lentricchia and Thomas McLaughlin, rev. 1995; and M. H. Abrams, *A Glossary of Literary Terms*, rev. 1992. On Greek and Roman background, see G. M. Kirkwood, *A Short Guide to Classical Mythology*, 1959; *The Oxford Classical Dictionary*, rev. 1996; and *The Oxford Companion to Classical Literature*, ed. M. C. Howatson and Ian Chilvers, rev. 1993.

Literary Criticism and Theory

Three volumes of the *Cambridge History of Literary Criticism* have been published, 1989–: *Classical Criticism*, ed. George A. Kennedy; *The Eighteenth Century*, ed. H. B. Nisbet and Claude Rawson; and *From Formalism to Poststructuralism*, ed. Raman Selden. See also M. H. Abrams, *The Mirror and the Lamp: Romantic Theory and the Critical Tradition*, 1953; William K. Wimsatt and Cleanth Brooks, *Literary Criticism: A Short History*, 1957; George Watson, *The Literary Critics*, 1962; René Wellek, *A History of Modern Criticism: 1750–1950*, 9 vols., 1955–1993; Frank Lentricchia, *After the New Criticism*, 1980; and *Redrawing the Boundaries: The Transformation of English and American Literary Studies*, ed. Stephen Greenblatt and Giles Gunn, 1992. Raman Selden, Peter Widdowson, and Peter Brooker have written *A Reader's Guide to Contemporary Literary Theory*, 1997.

The following is a selection of books in literary criticism that have been notably influential in shaping modern approaches to English literature and literary forms: Lionel Trilling, *The Liberal Imagination*, 1950; T. S. Eliot, *Selected Essays*, 3rd ed. 1951, and *On Poetry and Poets*, 1957; Erich Auerbach, *Mimesis: The Representation of Reality in Western Literature*, 1953; William Empson, *Seven Types of Ambiguity*, 3rd ed. 1953; William K. Wimsalt, *The Verbal Icon*, 1954; Northrop Frye, *Anatomy of Criticism*, 1957; Wayne C. Booth, *The Rhetoric of Fiction*, 1961, rev. ed. 1983; W. J. Bate, *The Burden of the Past and the English Poet*, 1970; Harold Bloom, *The Anxiety of Influence*, 1973; and Paul de Man, *Allegories of Reading*, 1979.

René Wellek and Austin Warren, *Theory of Literature*, rev. 1970, is a useful introduction to the variety of scholarly and critical approaches to literature up to the time of its publication. Jonathan Culler's *Literary Theory: A Very Short Introduction*, 1997, discusses recurrent issues and debates. Modern feminist literary criticism was fashioned by such works as Particia Meyers Spacks, *The Female Imagination*, 1975; Ellen Moers, *Literary Women*, 1976; Elaine Showalter, *A Literature of Their Own*, 1977; and Sandra Gilbert and Susan Gubar, *The Madwoman in the Attic*, 1979. More recent studies include Jane Gallop, *The Daughter's Seduction: Feminism and Psychoanalysis*, 1982; Gayatri Chakravorty Spivak, *In Other Worlds: Essays in Cultural Politics*, 1987; Sandra Gilbert and Susan Gubar, *No Man's Land: The Place of the Woman Writer in the Twentieth Century*, 2 vols., 1988–89; Barbara Johnson, *A World of Difference*, 1989; Judith Butler, *Gender Trouble*, 1990; and the critical views sampled in Elaine Showalter, *The New Feminist Criticism*, 1985; *Feminist Literary Theory: A Reader*, ed. Mary Eagleton, 2nd ed., 1995; and *Feminisms: An Anthology of Literary Theory and Criticism*, ed. Robyn R. Warhol and Diane Price Herndl, 2nd ed. 1997. Gay and lesbian studies and criticism are represented in *The Lesbian and Gay Studies Reader*, ed. Henry Abelove, Michele Barale, and David Halperin, 1993, and by such books as Eve Sedgwick, *Between Men: English Literature and Male Homosocial Desire*, 1985, and *Epistemology of the Closet*, 1990; Diana Fuss, *Essentially Speaking: Feminism, Nature, and Difference*, 1989; and Gregory Woods, *A History of Gay Literature: The Male Tradition*, 1998. Convenient introductions to structuralist literary criticism include Robert Scholes, *Structuralism in Literature: An Introduction*, 1974, and Jonathan Culler, *Structuralist Poetics*, 1975. The poststructuralist challenges to this approach are discussed in Jonathan Culler, *On Deconstruction*, 1982; Fredric Jameson, *Poststructuralism; or the Cultural Logic of Late Capitalism*, 1991; John McGowan, *Postmodernism and Its Critics*, 1991; and *Beyond Structuralism*, ed. Wendell Harris,

1996. New historicism is represented in Stephen Greenblatt, *Learning to Curse*, 1990, and in the essays collected in *The New Historicism*, ed. Harold Veeser, 1989, and *New Historical Literary Study: Essays on Reproducing Texts, Representing History*, ed. Jeffrey N. Cox and Larry J. Reynolds, 1993. The related social and historical dimension of texts is discussed in Jerome McGann, *Critique of Modern Textual Criticism*, 1983, and D. F. McKenzie, *Bibliography and Sociology of Texts*, 1986. Characteristic of new historicism is an expansion of the field of literary interpretation extended still further in cultural studies; for a broad sampling of the range of interests, see *The Cultural Studies Reader*, ed. Simon During, 1993, and *A Cultural Studies Reader: History, Theory, Practice*, ed. Jessica Munns and Gita Rajan, 1997. This expansion of the field is similarly reflected in postcolonial studies: see *The Post-Colonial Studies Reader*, ed. Bill Ashcroft, Gareth Griffiths, and Helen Tiffin, 1995, and such influential books as Ranajit Guha and Gayatri Chakravorti Spivak, *Selected Subaltern Studies*, 1988; Edward Said, *Culture and Imperialism*, 1993; and Homi Bhabha, *The Location of Culture*, 1994.

Anthologies representing a range of recent approaches include *Modern Criticism and Theory*, ed. David Lodge, 1988, and *Contemporary Literary Criticism*, ed. Robert Con Davis and Ronald Schlieffer, rev. 1998.

THE MIDDLE AGES

Scholarship during this era has been divided into the same three periods as in the General Introduction: Anglo-Saxon England, Anglo-Norman England, and Middle English Literature of the Fourteenth and Fifteenth Centuries. A reference book for the whole era is Joseph Strayer et al., *Dictionary of the Middle Ages*, 1982–.

Anglo-Saxon England

D. Whitelock, *The Beginnings of English Society*, 1952, provides concise historical background for the literature of the period. The most detailed history is F. M. Stenton's authoritative *Anglo-Saxon England*, 3rd ed., 1971. Also highly informative are P. Hunter Blair, *An Introduction to Anglo-Saxon England*, 1956, and *Roman Britain and Early England*, 55 B.C.–A.D. 871, 1963. The classic study of the culture of the primitive Germanic peoples is H. M. Chadwick, *The Heroic Age*, 1912. For those who wish to sample basic historical documents of the period, there is available the translation by G. N. Garmonsway of *The Anglo-Saxon Chronicle*, 1953. *The Age of Bede*, ed. D. H. Farmer, rev. 1983, and *Alfred the Great*, ed. S. Keynes and M. Lapidge, 1983, contain texts documenting two crucial periods of Anglo-Saxon history. Bede's *Ecclesiastical History of the English People* is translated and edited by B. Colgrave and R. A. B.

Mynors, 1969. For studies of Bede, see G. H. Brown, *Bede, the Venerable*, 1987, and J. M. Wallace-Hadrill, *Bede's Ecclesiastical History of the English People: A Historical Commentary*, 1993. A lavishly and finely illustrated introduction to Anglo-Saxon England is *The Anglo-Saxons*, ed. J. Campbell, 1982. C. Fell, *Women in Anglo-Saxon England*, 1984, is pertinent to women's studies. The journal *Anglo-Saxon England* is devoted to all aspects of the history and culture of the period.

All the surviving poetry in Old English is contained in the six volumes edited by G. P. Krapp and E. V. K. Dobbie, *The Anglo-Saxon Poetic Records*, 1931–53, but the absence of glossaries makes this edition difficult for nonspecialists. Excellent texts of the shorter poems translated in this anthology are contained in J. C. Pope, *Seven Old English Poems*, 1966, rev. 1981. The standard text of *Beowulf and the Fight of Finnsburg* is F. Klaeber's 3rd ed., 1950; C. L. Wrenn's edition, *Beowulf, with the Finnsburg Fragment*, rev. W. F. Bolton, 1973, rev. 1988, is very useful; H. D. Chickering Jr. has made a dual-language edition with extensive commentary, and G. B. Jack has prepared *Beowulf: A Student Edition*, 1994. There are individual editions of *The Dream of the Rood* by M. Swanton, 1970; of *The Wanderer* by T. P. Dunning and A. J. Bliss, 1969. *The Wanderer* and *The Wife's Lament* are included in *The*

Old English Elegies: A Critical Edition and Genre Study, ed. A. L. Klinck, 1992. Modern English translations of many of the Old English poems have been published under various titles by R. K. Gordon, C. W. Kennedy, M. Alexander, S. A. J. Bradley, and K. Crossley-Holland. Many translations of *Beowulf* are available. E. T. Donaldson's translation is used in *Beowulf*, A Norton Critical Edition, ed. J. F. Tuso, 1975.

General discussions of Old English literature will be found in Vol. 1 of the *Cambridge History of English Literature*; S. B. Greenfield and D. G. Calder, *New Critical History of Old English Literature*, 1986; C. L. Wrenn, *A Study of Old English Literature*; M. Alexander, *Old English Literature*, 1983; and *The Cambridge Companion to Old English Literature*, ed. M. Godden and M. Lapidge, 1991.

Some useful studies and collections devoted exclusively to Old English poetry are S. B. Greenfield, *The Interpretation of Old English Poems*, 1972; T. A. Shippey, *Old English Verse*, 1972; J. B. Bessinger Jr. and S. J. Kahrl, *Essential Articles for the Study of Old English Poetry*, 1977; D. A. Pearsall, *Old and Middle English Poetry*, 1977; B. C. Raw, *The Art and Background of Old English Poetry*, 1978; *Old English Poetry: Essays on Style*, ed. D. G. Calder, 1979; *The Old English Elegies*, ed. M. Green, 1983; S. B. Greenfield, *Hero and Exile: The Art of Old English Poetry*, 1989; *De Gustibus*, ed. J. M. Foley et al., 1992; *Heroic Poetry in the Anglo-Saxon Period*, ed. H. Damico and J. Leyerle, 1993; *Companion to Old English Poetry*, ed. H. Aertsen and R. H. Bremmer Jr., 1994; and *Old English Shorter Poems: Basic Readings*, ed. K. O'Brien O'Keeffe, 1994.

General collections of essays on Old English literature include *Old English Literature in Context*, ed. J. D. Niles, 1980; *Literature and Learning in Anglo-Saxon England*, ed. M. Lapidge and H. Gneuss, 1985; *Modes of Interpretation in Old English Literature*, ed. P. R. Brown et al., 1986; F. C. Robinson, *The Tomb of Beowulf and Other Essays on Old English*, 1993; and *Studies in English Language and Literature*, ed. M. J. Toswell and E. M. Tyler, 1996.

Some studies of special topics in Old English literature are J. Chance, *Woman as Hero in Old English Literature*, 1986; *New Readings on Women in Old English Literature*, ed. Helen Damico and A. H. Olsen, 1990; A. J. Frantzen, *Desire for Origins: New Language, Old English, and Teaching the Tradition*, 1990; *The Battle of Maldon AD 991*, ed. D. Scragg, 1991; *Class and Gender in Early English Literature*, ed. B. J. Harwood and G. R. Overing, 1994; and *Holy Men, Holy Women: Old English Prose Saints' Lives and Their Contexts*, ed. P. Szarmach, 1996.

Beowulf

Essential backgrounds to the study of the poem are provided by R. W. Chambers, *Beowulf: An Introduction to the Study of the Poem*, 3rd ed., with a supplement by C. L. Wrenn, 1959; and a wide-ranging overview of *Beowulf* scholarship is furnished by *A Beowulf Handbook*, ed. R. E. Bjork and J. D. Niles, 1997. Important critical studies of the poem are found in D. Whitelock, *The Audience of Beowulf*, 1951; A. G. Brodeur, *The Art of Beowulf*, 1959; E. B. Irving Jr., *A Reading of Beowulf*, 1968, *Introduction to Beowulf*, 1969, and *Rereading Beowulf*, 1990; T. A. Shippey, *Beowulf*, 1978; J. D. Niles, *Beowulf: The Poem and Its Tradition*, 1983; G. Clark, *Beowulf*, 1990; J. W. Earl, *Thinking about Beowulf*, 1994; J. M. Hill, *The Cultural World in Beowulf*, 1995; and C. R. Davis, *Beowulf and the Demise of Germanic Legend in England*, 1996.

For anthologies of criticism, see *The Beowulf Poet*, ed. D. K. Fry, 1968; *Beowulf*, A Norton Critical Edition, ed. J. Tuso, 1975; *Interpretations of Beowulf*, ed. R. D. Fulk, 1991; and *Beowulf: Basic Readings*, ed. P. S. Baker, 1995. Special mention should be made of J. R. R. Tolkien's famous lecture, *Beowulf, the Monsters and the Critics*, 1937, reprinted in the anthologies of Fry and Fulk.

Anglo-Norman England

For accounts of the Norman conquest and its historical consequences, see C. Brooke, *From Alfred to Henry III, 871–1272*, 2 vols., 1961; R. A. Brown, *The Normans*, 1984; A. L. Poole, *From Domesday Book to Magna Carta*, 1955; P. Stafford, *A Political and Social History of England in the Tenth and Eleventh Centuries*, 1989; and F. M. Powicke, *The Thirteenth Century, 1216–1307*, 1953. The *Peterborough Chronicle*, a continuation of the *Anglo-Saxon Chronicle* to the year 1154, relates events from the point of view of English monks and can be read in translation in *The Anglo-Saxon Chronicle: a Revised Translation*, ed. by D. Whitelock with D. C. Douglas and S. I. Tucker, 1961, rev. 1965.

Studies of historical writing within the period itself, including the legendary histories of the kings of Britain, are J. S. P. Tatlock, *The Legendary History of Britain*, 1950; R. W. Hanning, *The Vision of History in Early Britain: From Gildas to Geoffrey of Monmouth*, 1966; and M. Otter, *Inventiones: Fiction and Referentiality in Twelfth-Century Historical Writing*.

On **Geoffrey of Monmouth,** in addition to the texts mentioned above, see the translation of his *History of the Kings of Britain* by Lewis Thorpe, 1966; R. W. Leckie Jr., *The Passage of Dominion: Geoffrey of Monmouth and the Periodization of Insular History in the Twelfth Century*, 1981; and M. J. Curley, *Geoffrey of Monmouth*, 1994. The *Brut* of **Layamon** is available in translations by D. G. Bzdyl, 1989; Rosamund Allen, 1992; and in an edition of the Middle English text with facing translation, notes, and commentary by W. R. J. Barron and S. C. Weinberg, 1989. The Arthurian sections of Wace's *Roman de Brut*, translated by Judith Weiss, and of Layamon in Allen's translation are printed together as *The Life of King Arthur*, 1997.

M. D. Legge, *Anglo-Norman Literature and Its*

Background, 1963, is the standard history. The lais of **Marie de France** have been translated by R. H. Hanning and J. Ferrante, 1978, and by G. S. Burgess and K. Busby, 1986. For background and critical interpretations of Marie de France's works, see E. J. Mickel, *Marie de France*, 1974; P. M. Clifford, *Marie de France, Lais*, 1982; and G. S. Burgess, *The Lais of Marie de France*, 1987.

R. M. Wilson's *Early Middle English Literature* focuses primarily on this period. Vol. 1 of the *Oxford History of English Literature*, by J. A. W. Bennett and D. Gray, *Middle English Literature*, 1986, which goes up to 1400 (exclusive of Chaucer), contains excellent discussions of early Middle English texts. Selections of texts from this era with a valuable introduction to the language and annotations are contained in the anthology edited by J. A. W. Bennett and G. V. Smithers, *Early Middle English Verse and Prose*, 2nd ed, 1968.

For discussions of the Arthurian materials in Geoffrey of Monmouth, Wace, Marie de France, and Layamon, see chaps. 4 and 8 to 11 in *Arthurian Literature in the Middle Ages*, ed. R. S. Loomis, 1959.

Middle English Literature of the Fourteenth and Fifteenth Centuries

Histories of the period include G. Holmes, *The Later Middle Ages, 1272–1485*, 1962; M. McKisack, *The Fourteenth Century, 1307–99*, 1959; and E. F. Jacob, *The Fifteenth Century*, 1961. Accounts of life and society during this period are provided by G. G. Coulton in *Chaucer and His England*, 1908, *The Medieval Scene*, 1930, and *Medieval Panorama*, 1938; E. Rickert, *Chaucer's World*, 1948; G. M. Trevelyan, *Chaucer's England and the Early Tudors*, vol. 1 of *The Illustrated English Social History*, 1949; and M. Keen, *English Society in the Later Middle Ages*, 1990. See also the picture books listed under Chaucer. J. Huizinga has written a famous account of the culture and spirit of the late fourteenth to fifteenth centuries, formerly translated as *The Waning of the Middle Ages*, 1924, now available in a fuller text under the more accurate title, *The Autumn of the Middle Ages*, trans. R. J. Payton and U. Mammitzsch, 1996. F. R. H. Du Boulay complements and qualifies Huizinga in *An Age of Ambition*, 1970. Chaps. 6 to 10 in E. Auerbach's *Mimesis: The Representation of Reality in Western Literature*, trans. by W. R. Trask, 1953, although it does not deal with works in this anthology, gives penetrating insights into the reading of medieval texts. C. S. Lewis, *The Discarded Image: An Introduction to Medieval and Renaissance Literature*, 1964, seeks to restore for modern readers the perspective and sensibilities of the earlier age.

For general discussion of late Middle English literature, see the *The Oxford History of English Literature*: J. A. W. Bennett and D. Gray, *Middle English Literature*, 1986, vol. 1, part 2 (up to 1400, exclusive of Chaucer); H. S. Bennett, *Chaucer and the Fifteenth Century*, vol. 2, part 1, 1947, and E. K.

Chambers, *English Literature at the Close of the Middle Ages*, vol. 2, part 2, 1954; also D. A. Pearsall, *Old and Middle English Poetry*, 1977; J. A. Burrow, *Middle English Literature and Its Background*, 1982; and D. S. Brewer, *English Gothic Literature*, 1983.

Critical works devoted to more than one author or genre in the period are G. Kane, *Middle English Literature*, 1951 (chapters on the romances, the religious lyrics, and *Piers Plowman*); J. A. Burrow, *Ricardian Poetry: Chaucer, Gower, Langland, and the Gawain Poet*, 1971; C. Muscatine, *Poetry and Crisis in the Age of Chaucer*, 1972; A. C. Spearing, *Medieval Dream Poetry*, 1976, and *Readings in Medieval Poetry*, 1987; T. Turville-Petre, *The Alliterative Revival*, 1977; *Medieval Literature: Chaucer and the Alliterative Tradition*, vol. 1 of *The New Pelican Guide to English Literature*, ed. Boris Ford, 1982; D. Despres, *Ghostly Sights: Visual Meditation in Late-Medieval Literature*, 1989; S. Justice, *Writing and Rebellion: England in 1381*, 1994; and G. Margherita, *The Romance of Origins: Language and Sexual Difference in Middle English Literature*, 1994. *Middle English Survey: Critical Essays*, ed. E. Vasta, 1965, contains commentary on Langland, *Gawain*, and drama.

For the Middle English language, see Helge Kökeritz, *A Guide to Chaucer's Pronunciation*, 1954; David Burnley, *A Guide to Chaucer's Language*, 1983; and J. A. Burrow and T. Turville-Petre, *A Book of Middle English*, 1996.

The standard bibliography is *A Manual of the Writings in Middle English, 1050–1500*, 6 vols., ed. J. B. Severs, A. E. Hartung, et al., 1967–80, which is based on and supersedes the *Manual* of J. E. Wells, 1916, with nine supplements through 1945.

Geoffrey Chaucer

The standard edition of Chaucer's writing is *The Riverside Chaucer*, 3rd ed., ed. L. D. Benson et al., 1987, based on F. N. Robinson's edition. E. Talbot Donaldson, *Chaucer's Poetry*, 2nd ed., 1975, from which are taken the selections printed here, is helpful to the nonspecialist, as are John H. Fisher, *The Complete Poetry and Prose of Geoffrey Chaucer*, 2nd ed., 1989, and V. A. Kolve and Glending Olson, *The Canterbury Tales: Nine Tales and The "General Prologue,"* Norton Critical Edition, 1989. Vivid presentations of Chaucer in the background of fourteenth-century England are found in D. S. Brewer, *Chaucer and His World*, 1978, which is beautifully illustrated, and *A New Introduction to Chaucer*, 2nd ed., 1998. Pictorial companions to Chaucer's works, especially the *Canterbury Tales*, include R. S. Loomis, *A Mirror of Chaucer's World*, 1965, Maurice Hussey, *Chaucer's World*, 1967, Ian Serraillier, *Chaucer and His World*, 1968, and Roger Hart, *English Life in Chaucer's Day*, 1973.

The raw material for Chaucer's biography is contained in *Chaucer Life-Records*, ed. M. M. Crow and C. C. Olson, 1966. D. R. Howard, *Chaucer: His Life, His Works, His World*, 1987, and D. A. Pearsall, *The Life of Geoffrey Chaucer*, 1992, contain extensive background and interpretation. For succinct accounts of the sources and literary background of Chaucer's works, see R. D. French, *A Chaucer Handbook*, 2nd ed., 1947; reproductions of many of the known sources of the *Canterbury Tales* are contained in *Sources and Analogues of Chaucer's Canterbury Tales*, ed. W. F. Bryan and Germaine Dempster, 1941, 1958. Useful literary materials are collected in R. P. Miller, *Chaucer: Sources and Backgrounds*, 1977. Muriel Bowden, *A Commentary on the General Prologue to the Canterbury Tales*, 1948, provides a wealth of background information on the individual Canterbury pilgrims; see also Jill Mann, *Chaucer and Medieval Estates Satire*, 1973. Various aspects of Chaucer's work are treated by a number of scholars in *Chaucer and Chaucerians*, ed. D. S. Brewer, 1966; *Geoffrey Chaucer (Writers and Their Background)*, ed. D. S. Brewer, 1974; *Companion to Chaucer Studies*, ed. Beryl Rowland, rev. 1979; and *The Cambridge Chaucer Companion*, ed. Piero Boitani and Jill Mann, 1986.

For literary criticism on both *The Canterbury Tales* and other works by Chaucer, the following contain stimulating discussions: G. L. Kittredge, *Chaucer and His Poetry*, 1915; J. L. Lowes, *Geoffrey Chaucer and the Development of His Genius*, 1934; C. Muscatine, *Chaucer and the French Tradition*, 1957; W. C. Curry, *Chaucer and the Medieval Sciences*, rev. 1960; R. O. Payne, *The Key of Remembrance*, 1963; M. Hussey, A. C. Spearing, and J. Winny, *An Introduction to Chaucer*, 1965; E. T. Donaldson, *Speaking of Chaucer*, 1970; T. Ross, *Chaucer's Bawdy*, 1972; D. S. Brewer, *Chaucer*, 3rd ed., 1973; P. Elbow, *Oppositions in Chaucer*, 1975; A. David, *The Strumpet Muse: Art and Morals in Chaucer's Poetry*, 1976; R. Burlin, *Chaucerian Fiction*, 1977; G. Kane, *Chaucer*, 1984; S. Knight, *Geoffrey Chaucer*, 1986; D. Wallace, *Chaucerian Polity: Absolutist Lineages and Associational Forms in England and Italy*, 1997; and R. P. McGerr, *Chaucer's Open Book: Resistance to Closure in Medieval Discourse*, 1998.

Criticism that deals mainly with *The Canterbury Tales* and with earlier commentary on it includes P. Ruggiers, *The Art of The Canterbury Tales*, 1964; D. R. Howard, *The Idea of The Canterbury Tales*, 1976; T. Lawler, *The One and the Many in The Canterbury Tales*, 1980; D. Pearsall, *The Canterbury Tales*, 1985; C. D. Benson, *Chaucer's Drama of Style: Poetic Variety in The Canterbury Tales*, 1986; W. Wetherbee, *Geoffrey Chaucer: The Canterbury Tales*, 1989; H. M. Leicester Jr., *The Disenchanted Self: Representing the Subject in The Canterbury Tales*, 1990; S. Crane, *Gender and Romance in Chaucer's Canterbury Tales*, 1994; and H. Cooper, *The Canterbury Tales*, Oxford Guides to Chaucer, 2nd ed., 1996.

D. W. Robertson's *A Preface to Chaucer*, 1962, is a learned and stimulating introduction to the reading of Chaucer in the light of medieval aesthetic doctrines. V. A. Kolve, *Chaucer and the Imagery of Narrative*, 1984, relates the first five of the *Canterbury Tales* to medieval art. Several recent books stress the importance of oral delivery, performance, and storytelling in the *Canterbury Tales*: Betsy Bowden, *Chaucer Aloud*, 1987; Carl Lindahl, *Earnest Games: Folkloric Patterns in The Canterbury Tales*, 1987; L. M. Koff, *Chaucer and the Art of Storytelling*, 1988; and J. M. Ganim, *Chaucerian Theatricality*, 1990. The following studies relate Chaucer's works to their social and historical background: Paul Strohm, *Social Chaucer*, 1989; Peggy Knapp, *Chaucer and the Social Contest*, 1990; Peter Brown and Andrew Butcher, *The Age of Saturn: Literature and History in The Canterbury Tales*, 1991; and Lee Patterson, *Chaucer and the Subject of History*, 1991. A pioneer feminist study of Chaucer is Carolyn Dinshaw, *Chaucer's Sexual Poetics*, 1989; see also E. T. Hansen, *Chaucer and the Fictions of Gender*, 1992.

The following are collections of critical essays: *Chaucer: Modern Essays in Criticism*, ed. E. C. Wagenknecht, 1959; *Chaucer Criticism: The Canterbury Tales*, ed. R. J. Schoeck and J. Taylor, 1960; *Discussions of The Canterbury Tales*, ed. C. J. Owen, 1961; *Geoffrey Chaucer: A Critical Anthology*, ed. J. A. Burrow, 1969; and *Geoffrey Chaucer Contemporary Studies in Literature*, ed. G. D. Economou, 1975. See also the prefatory remarks on individual works and tales in *The Riverside Chaucer* and the commentary in E. Talbot Donaldson's anthology, cited above.

Perhaps the most reliable glossary is that edited by Norman Davis et al., 1979. The standard bibliographies are E. P. Hammond, *Chaucer: A Bibliographical Manual*, 1908; D. D. Griffith, *Bibliography of Chaucer*, 1955; W. R. Crawford, *1954–63*, 1967; L. Y. Baird, *1964–73*, 1977; and L. Y. Baird-Lange and H. Schnutgen, *1974–85*, 1988. Two very useful annotated bibliographies are by Mark Allen and J. H. Fisher, *The Essential Chaucer*, 1987, and John Leyerle and Anne Quick, *Chaucer: A Bibliographical Introduction*, 1986. *Studies in the Age of Chaucer*, the journal of The New Chaucer Society publishes a current bibliography as well as articles on Chaucer and other medieval literature. See also Caroline Spurgeon, *Five Hundred Years of Chaucer Criticism and Allusion, 1357–1900*, 1925.

Julian of Norwich

The standard Middle English text with a wealth of commentary is *A Book of Showings to the Anchoress Julian of Norwich*, 2 vols., ed. Edmund Colledge and James Walsh, 1978. The editors' translation is published as *Julian of Norwich: Showings*, 1978; another translation of the long text by Clifton Walters is published under the title *Revelations of Divine Love*, 1966. Another edition of the long text, ed. G. R. Crampton, 1994, published for TEAMS (Consortium for the Teaching of the Middle Ages) is designed for students.

General studies of mystical writing in England and on the Continent are W. Riehle, *The Middle English Mystics*, trans. B. Standring, 1981; *An Intro-*

duction to the Medieval Mystics of Europe, ed. P. Szarmach, 1984; A. K. Warren, Anchorites and their Patrons in Medieval England, 1985; F. Beer, Women and Mystical Experience in the Middle Ages, 1992; S. Beckwith, Christ's Body: Identity, Culture, and Society in Late Medieval Writings, 1993; and D. Aers and L. Staley, The Powers of the Holy: Religion, Politics, and Gender in Late Medieval English Culture, 1996. Studies helpful to understanding the mystical thought of Julian of Norwich are B. Pelphrey, Christ Our Mother, 1989, and D. N. Baker, Julian of Norwich's Showing: From Vision to Book, 1994.

Sir Thomas Malory
The Winchester manuscript of Malory's Morte Darthur, with full commentary and valuable discussion, is given in Eugène Vinaver's The Works of Sir Thomas Malory, 3 vols., 2nd ed., 1967; the one-volume edition, 2nd ed., Oxford, 1970, contains the text only. The Caxton version is most readily available in Caxton's Malory, ed. J. W. Spisak, 1983. Vinaver, Malory, 1929, surveys Malory's life and career; see also, P. J. C. Field, The Life and Times of Sir Thomas Malory, 1993. Guides to Malory are B. Dillon, A Malory Handbook, 1978; Terence McCarthy, An Introduction to Malory, rev. ed., 1991; and E. Archibald and A. S. G. Edwards, A Companion to Malory, 1996. A number of critical problems in Malory's work, especially its unity, are discussed in three collections of essays by various scholars: Essays on Malory, ed. J. A. W. Bennett, 1963, Malory's Originality, ed. by R. M. Lumianski, 1964, and Studies in Malory, ed. J. W. Spisak, 1985. Other studies of Malory and the Morte Darthur include Mark Lambert, Malory: Style and Vision in Le Morte Darthur, 1975; L. D. Benson, Malory's Morte Darthur, 1976; and Felicity Riddy, Sir Thomas Malory, 1987.

For reference books and discussions of the development and of the political and social significance of the Arthurian tradition in England, see R. S. Loomis, The Development of Arthurian Romance, 1963; S. Knight, Arthurian Literature and Society, 1983; The Arthurian Handbook, ed. N. J. Lacy and G. Ashe, 2nd ed., 1998; The New Arthurian Encyclopedia, ed. N. J. Lacy, 1991; Approaches to Teaching the Arthurian Tradition, ed. M. Fries and J. Watson, 1992; Culture and the King: the Social Implications of the Arthurian Legend, ed. M. Schichtman and J. Carley, 1994; Arthurian Women: A Casebook, ed. T. Fenster, 1996; and King Arthur: A Casebook, ed. E. D. Kennedy, 1996.

Mystery Plays
E. K. Chambers's classic The Medieval Stage, 1905, remains a mine of information, although its views about the evolution of medieval drama are no longer accepted. A new understanding and appreciation of medieval drama begins with O. B. Har-

dison, Christian Rite and Christian Drama in the Middle Ages, 1965; and for the mysteries, with V. A. Kolve, The Play Called Corpus Christie, 1966. Rosemary Woolf, The English Mystery Plays, 1972, makes detailed comparisons among the extant plays. Individual cycles are studied by Peter Travis in Dramatic Design in the Chester Cycle, 1982, and by Martin Stevens in Four Middle English Mystery Cycles: Textual, Contextual, and Critical Interpretations, 1987. G. M. Gibson fills in the social and religious background in The Theater of Devotion: East Anglian Drama and Society in the Late Middle Ages, 1989. Good selections of Middle English plays are presented by A. C. Cawley, Everyman and Medieval Miracle Plays, 1960; by D. M. Bevington, Medieval Drama, 1975; and by Peter Happé, The English Mystery Plays, 1975. Cawley, The Wakefield Pageants in the Towneley Cycle, 1958, has a discussion of the work of the "Wakefield Master" whose hand is seen in the Second Shepherds' Play. A collection of critical essays has been made by Jerome Taylor and A. H. Nelson in Medieval English Drama, 1972. Approaches to Teaching Medieval Drama, ed. Richard Emmerson, 1990, contains essays by many hands and makes up a nontechnical survey of current opinion. For commentary on Everyman, see the introduction to A. C. Cawley's 1961 edition and Robert Potter's comprehensive The English Morality Play: Origins, History, and Influence of a Dramatic Tradition, 1975.

Sir Gawain and the Green Knight
The standard Middle English edition of the poem is by J. R. R. Tolkien and E. V. Gordon, rev. Norman Davis, 1967. Easier to use are the editions by R. A. Waldron, 1970, rev. for The Poems of the Pearl Manuscript, 1978; and by J. A. Burrow, 1972. For a guide to the poems in the manuscript, see A. Putter, An Introduction to the Gawain-Poet, 1996, and A Companion to the Gawain Poet, ed. D. S. Brewer and J. Gibson, 1997. Discussions of various aspects of the poem appear in Marie Borroff, Sir Gawain and the Green Knight: A Stylistic and Metrical Study, 1962; L. D. Benson, Art and Tradition in Sir Gawain and the Green Knight, 1965; J. A. Burrow, A Reading of Sir Gawain and the Green Knight, 1965; A. C. Spearing, The Gawain Poet: A Critical Study, 1971; And W. Clein, Concepts of Chivalry in Sir Gawain and the Green Knight, 1984.

Collections of essays have been compiled by R. J. Blanch, Sir Gawain and Pearl, 1966, and Text and Matter: New Critical Perspectives of the Pearl-Poet, 1991 D. Fox, Twentieth-Century Interpretations of Sir Gawain and the Green Knight, 1968; and D. R. Howard and C. K. Zacher, Critical Studies of Sir Gawain and the Green Knight, 1968.

THE SIXTEENTH CENTURY

Some important books on society and culture in early modern England are Lawrence Stone, *The Crisis of the Aristocracy, 1558–1641*, 1965, and *The Family, Sex and Marriage in England, 1500–1800*, 1979; Keith Thomas, *Religion and the Decline of Magic*, 1971; J. A. Sharpe, *Early Modern England: A Social History*, 1987; P. G. Emmison, *Elizabethan Life: Disorder*, 1970; David Cressy, *Literacy and the Social Order: Reading and Writing in Tudor and Stuart England*, 1980, and *Birth, Marriage, and Death: Ritual, Religion, and the Life-Cycle in Tudor and Stuart England*, 1997; Keith Wrightson, *English Society, 1580–1680*, 1982; Peter Clark, *The English Alehouse: A Social History, 1200–1830*, 1983; Peter Laslett, *The World We Have Lost, Further Explored*, 1984; Paul Slack, *The Impact of Plague in Tudor and Stuart England*, 1985; Mervyn James, *Society, Politics, and Culture: Studies in Early Modern England*, 1986; Susan Amussen, *An Ordered Society: Gender and Class in Early Modern England*, 1988; Felicity Heal, *Hospitality in Early Modern England*, 1990; Ian Archer, *The Pursuit of Stability: Social Relations in Elizabethan London*, 1991; Illana Ben-Amos, *Adolescence and Youth in Early Modern England*, 1994; Ronald Hutton, *The Rise and Fall of Merry England: The Ritual Year 1400–1700*, 1994; Lena Orlin, *Private Matters and Public Culture in Post-Reformation England*, 1994; and Kim Hall, *Things of Darkness: Economies of Race and Gender in Early Modern England*, 1995.

Useful general studies of the history of the period include J. B. Black, *The Reign of Elizabeth, 1558–1603*, 2nd ed., 1959; G. R. Elton, *England under the Tudors*, 1955, and *Reform and Reformation: England, 1509–1559*, 1977; Conrad Russell, *The Crisis of Parliaments: English History, 1509–1660*, 1971; and John Guy, *Tudor England*, 1988. Political theory in the period is surveyed in Quentin Skinner, *The Foundations of Modern Political Thought*, 2 vols., 1978; and there is an important analysis of the theory of kingship in E. H. Kantorowicz, *The King's Two Bodies*, 1957. Exploration and military history are treated in G. Mattingly, *The Armada*, 1959, and J. A. Williamson, *The Age of Drake*, 4th ed., 1960. For church history and religion, see John Bossy, *The English Catholic Community, 1570–1850*, 1979; Patrick Collinson, *The Religion of Protestants: The Church in English Society, 1559–1625*, 1982, and *The Birthpangs of Protestant England: Religious and Cultural Change in the Sixteenth and Seventeenth Centuries*, 1988; Peter Lake, *Anglicans and Puritans?*, 1988; Debora Shuger, *Habits of Thought in the English Renaissance: Religion, Politics, and the Dominant Culture*, 1990; Eamon Duffy, *The Stripping of the Altars: Traditional Religion in England c. 1400–c. 1580*, 1992; Christopher Haigh, *English Reformations: Religion, Politics, and Society under the Tudors*, 1993; and James Shapiro, *Shakespeare and the Jews*, 1996.

Life at court is described in David Starkey, *The English Court: From the Wars of the Roses to the Civil War*, 1987. Patronage and courtiership, with special reference to literature, are analyzed in David Javitch, *Poetry and Courtliness in Renaissance England*, 1976; *Patronage in the Renaissance*, ed. Guy Fitch Lytle and Stephen Orgel, 1981; and Frank Whigham, *Ambition and Privilege: The Social Tropes of Elizabethan Courtesy Theory*, 1984. On publishing and the book trade, see H. S. Bennett, *English Books and Readers, 1475–1557*, 1952, and *English Books and Readers, 1558–1603*, 1965; Elizabeth L. Eisenstein, *The Printing Press as an Agent of Change*, 2 vols., 1979; and Adrian Johns, *The Nature of the Book: Print and Knowledge in the Making*, 1998.

Several classic studies define the Renaissance in terms of humanism, imitation of the ancients, and individual achievement: Jacob Burckhardt, *The Civilization of the Renaissance*, 1878, rev. 1944; Douglas Bush, *The Renaissance and English Humanism*, 1939; E. M. W. Tillyard, *The Elizabethan World Picture*, 1943; *The Renaissance Philosophy of Man*, ed. Ernst Cassirer et al., 1948; Erwin Panofsky, *Renaissance and Renascences in Western Art*, 2 vols., 1960; and Paul O. Kristeller, *Renaissance Thought*, 2 vols., 1961, 1965. Revisionist analyses by new historicist and cultural materialist critics focus on the interaction of institutions, ideology, and the conditions of cultural production in the social construction of persons and literary texts. Some seminal studies are Stephen Greenblatt, *Renaissance Self-Fashioning*, 1980; *Representing the English Renaissance*, ed. S. Greenblatt, 1988; Richard Helgerson, *Self-Crowned Laureates: Spenser, Jonson, Milton and the Literary System*, 1983, and *Forms of Nationhood: The Elizabethan Writing of England*, 1992; Annabel Patterson, *Censorship and Interpretation: The Conditions of Writing and Reading in Early Modern England*, 1984; Peter Stallybrass and Allon White, *The Politics and Poetics of Transgression*, 1986; and Richard Halpern, *The Poetics of Primitive Accumulation: English Renaissance Culture and the Genealogy of Capital*, 1991. (Others on the theater and on Shakespeare are noted in appropriate sections.)

Science and medicine in this period are discussed in Antonia Mclean, *Humanism and the Rise of Science in Tudor England*, 1972; Roy Porter, *Disease, Medicine and Society in England 1550–1860*, 1987; Thomas Laqueur, *Making Sex: Body and Gender from the Greeks to Freud*, 1990; and Jonathan Sawday, *The Body Emblazoned: Dissection and the Human Body in Renaissance Culture*, 1995. Education is the subject of T. W. Baldwin, *William Shakespere's Small Latine and Lesse Greeke*, 2 vols., 1944, and Kenneth Charlton, *Education in Renaissance England*, 1965. On logic and rhetoric see W. S. Howell, *Logic and Rhetoric in England, 1500–1700*, 1956; Sister Miriam Joseph, *Rhetoric* in Shakespeare's Time, 1962; Frances Yates, The Art of Memory, 1966; and Victoria Kahn, Rhetoric and Skepticism in the Renaissance, 1985.

Some books on Renaissance art and architecture are Marcus Whiffin, An Introduction to Elizabethan and Jacobean Architecture, 1952; J. Buxton, Elizabethan Taste, 1963; Roy Strong, The English Icon: Elizabethan and Jacobean Portraiture, 1969, and The Cult of Elizabeth: Elizabethan Portraiture and Pageantry, 1977; Mark Girouard, Life in the English Country House, 1978; John King, Tudor Royal Iconography: Literature and Art in an Age of Religious Crisis, 1989; Lucy Gent, Picture and Poetry, 1560–1620, 1981; and Norman K. Farmer, Poets and the Visual Arts in Renaissance England, 1984. Renaissance iconology and emblem books often illuminate literary imagery; important studies are Erwin Panofsky, Studies in Iconology, 1939; Rosemary Freeman, English Emblem Books, 1948; Jean Seznec, The Survival of the Pagan Gods, trans. B. F. Sessions, 1963. The attack on religious images is treated by John Phillips, The Reformation of Images: Destruction of Art in England, 1535–1660, 1971; and Ernest B. Gilman, Iconoclasm and Poetry in the English Reformation, 1986.

For Tudor music and musicians in relation to poetry see M. C. Boyd, Elizabethan Music and Music Criticism, 1940; E. H. Fellowes, English Madrigal Verse, rev. 1967; John Stevens, Music and Poetry in the Early Tudor Court, 1961, rpt. 1979; David Price, Patrons and Musicians of the English Renaissance, 1981; and Winifred Meynard, Elizabethan Lyric Poetry and Its Music, 1986. John Hollander studies music as symbol in The Untuning of the Sky: Ideas of Music in English Poetry, 1500–1700, 1961; and Paula Johnson analyzes structural affinities of the two art forms in Form and Transformation in Music and Poetry of the English Renaissance, 1975.

Useful anthologies of Elizabethan literary criticism are G. G. Smith, Elizabethan Critical Essays, 2 vols., 1904, and O. B. Hardison Jr., English Literary Criticism: The Renaissance, 1963. Important studies of Renaissance literary theory and criticism include Rosamond Tuve, Elizabethan and Metaphysical Imagery, 1947; Baxter Hathaway, Marvels and Commonplaces: Renaissance Literary Criticism, 1968; Don C. Allen, Mysteriously Meant: The Rediscovery of Pagan Symbolism and Allegorical Interpretation in the Renaissance, 1970; S. K. Heninger, Touches of Sweet Harmony: Pythagorean Cosmology and Renaissance Poetics, 1974; Margaret W. Ferguson, Trials of Desire: Renaissance Defenses of Poetry, 1983; and Arthur Kinney, Humanist Poetics, 1986.

Some distinguished historical and critical accounts of Renaissance literature include Hallett Smith, Elizabethan Poetry: A Study in Conventions, Meaning, and Expression, 1952, rpt. 1968; C. S. Lewis, English Literature in the Sixteenth Century, Excluding Drama, 1954; Douglas Bush, Mythology and the Renaissance Tradition in English Poetry, rev. 1963; Rosalie Colie, The Resources of Kind: Genre-Theory in the Renaissance, 1973; Thomas M.

Greene, The Light in Troy: Imitation and Discovery in Renaissance Poetry, 1982; Alan Sinfield, Literature in Protestant England, 1560–1660, 1983; and David Norbrook, Poetry and Politics in the English Renaissance, 1984. Important studies of particular Renaissance genres and kinds include J. W. Lever, The Elizabethan Love Sonnet, 1956; Alvin Kernan, The Cankered Muse: Satire of the English Renaissance, 1959; Lily B. Campbell, Divine Poetry and Drama in Sixteenth-Century England, 1959; Angus Fletcher, Allegory: The Theory of a Symbolic Mode, 1964; Douglas L. Peterson, The English Lyric from Wyatt to Donne, 1966; Seventeenth-Century Prose, ed. Stanley Fish, 1971; Patricia Parker, Inescapable Romance, 1979; Anne Ferry, The "Inward" Language: Sonnets of Wyatt, Sidney, Shakespeare, and Donne, 1983; Janel Mueller, The Native Tongue and the Word: Developments in English Prose Style, 1380–1580, 1984; Peter Sacks, The English Elegy: Studies in the Genre from Spenser to Yeats, 1985; Susanne Wofford, The Choice of Achilles: The Ideology of Figure in the Epic, 1992; Arthur Marotti, Manuscript, Print, and the English Renaissance Lyric, 1995; and Paul Alpers, What Is Pastoral?, 1996.

Important studies of stage history, audiences, and the development of dramatic forms include E. K. Chambers, The Elizabethan Stage, 4 vols., 1923; Allardyce Nicoll, British Drama, rev. 1962; Revels History of Drama in English, 8 vols., 1978–83; Muriel D. Bradbrook, A History of Elizabethan Drama, 6 vols., 1935–76; F. T. Bowers, Elizabethan Revenge Tragedy, 1578–1642, 1940; Glynne Wickham, Early English Stages, 1300–1660, 3 vols., 1959–81; Richard Leacroft, The Development of the English Playhouse, 1973; David Bevington, From "Mankind" to Marlowe, 1962; Stephen Orgel, The Illusion of Power: Political Theater in the English Renaissance, 1975, and Impersonations: The Performance of Gender in Shakespeare's England, 1996; Ann Jennalie Cook, The Privileged Playgoers of Shakespeare's London: 1576–1642, 1981; Andrew Gurr, Playgoing in Shakespeare's London, 1987; and Leeds Barroll, Politics, Plague, and Shakespeare's Theater, 1991. Some important studies of drama in relation to contemporary politics and ideology are David Bevington, Tudor Drama and Politics, 1968; Robert Weiman, Shakespeare and the Popular Tradition in the Theater, 1967, rpt. 1987; Jonas Barish, The Antitheatrical Prejudice, 1981; Jonathan Dollimore, Radical Tragedy: Religion, Ideology and Power in the Drama of Shakespeare and his Contemporaries, 1984; Catherine Belsey, The Subject of Tragedy: Identity and Difference in Renaissance Drama, 1985; Jean-Christophe Agnew, Worlds Apart: The Market and the Theatre in Anglo-American Thought, 1550–1750, 1986; Steven Mullaney, The Place of the Stage, 1988; Katharine Maus, Inwardness and Theater in the English Renaissance, 1995; and Louis Montrose, The Purpose of Playing: Shakespeare and the Cultural Politics of the Elizabethan Theatre, 1996.

The many recent studies of the status of women

in early modern England have a distinguished precursor in Alice Clark, *Working Life of Women in the Seventeenth Century*, 1919. On the situation of women in the Renaissance and the achievements of women writers, see Joan Kelly-Gadol, "Did Women Have a Renaissance?" in *Becoming Visible: Women in European History*, ed. R. Bridenthal and C. Koonz, 1977; Ian Maclean, *The Renaissance Notion of Women*, 1980; *Beyond Their Sex: Learned Women of the European Past*, ed. Patricia H. Labalme, 1980; Retha M. Warnicke, *Women of the English Renaissance and Reformation*, 1983; Linda Woodbridge, *Women and the English Renaissance: Literature and the Nature of Womankind, 1540–1640*, 1984; *Rewriting the Renaissance: The Discourses of Sexual Difference in Early Modern Europe*, ed. Margaret Ferguson et al., 1986; Elaine Beilin, *Redeeming Eve: Women Writers of the English Renaissance*, 1987; *The Renaissance Englishwoman in Print: Counterbalancing the Canon*. ed. Anne M. Haselkorn and Betty S. Travitsky, 1990; Constance Jordan, *Renaissance Feminism: Literary Texts and Political Models*, 1990; and Patricia Crawford, *Women and Religion in England, 1500–1720*, 1993. A useful anthology is *The Paradise of Women: Writings by Englishwomen of the Renaissance*, ed. Betty Travitsky, 1981; see also Randall Martin, *Women Writers in Renaissance England*, 1997. On male homosexuality in the period, see Alan Bray, *Homosexuality in Renaissance England*, 1982, and Bruce Smith, *Homosexual Desire in Shakespeare's England*, 1991.

An invaluable tool for the study of early modern literature is the *Oxford English Dictionary*, 2nd ed., 1989, now also on CD-ROM. Also useful are Morris Tilley, *A Dictionary of the Proverbs in England in the Sixteenth and Seventeenth Centuries*, 1950; Richard Jones, *The Triumph of the English Language*, 1953; Richard Lanham, *A Handlist of Rhetorical Terms*, 1968; James Hencke, *Courtesans and Cuckolds: A Glossary of Renaissance Dramatic Bawdy (Exclusive of Shakespeare)*, 1979; Fausto Cercignani, *Shakespeare's Works and Elizabethan Pronunciation*, 1981; Eric Partridge, *Shakespeare's Bawdy*, 3rd ed., 1991; and Charles Barber, *Early Modern English*, rev. ed., 1997.

Michael Drayton

The standard edition is by J. W. Hebel, 5 vols., 1931–41, rpt. 1961; there is a useful selected edition by John Buxton, 1953. The standard biography is B. H. Newdigate, *Michael Drayton and his Circle*, 1941, rpt. 1961. Critical studies include J. A. Berthelot, *Michael Drayton*, 1967; R. F. Hardin, *Michael Drayton and the Passing of Elizabethan England*, 1973; and Jean R. Brink, *Michael Drayton Revisited*, 1990. There are valuable discussions of Drayton in Richard Helgerson, *Forms of Nationhood*, 1992, and Claire McEachern, *The Poetics of English Nationhood, 1590–1612*, 1996.

Queen Elizabeth I

There is no complete edition of Queen Elizabeth's writings. *The Poems of Queen Elizabeth I*, ed.

Leicester Bradner, 1964, prints several of her poems and verse translations. The most inclusive edition of her letters is by G. B. Harrison, 1935; and George P. Rice Jr. prints twenty-one of her speeches in *The Public Speaking of Queen Elizabeth: Selections from her Official Addresses*, 1951, rpt. 1966. Frances Teague surveys Elizabeth's life and writings, and prints a selection of her works, in *Women Writers of the Renaissance and Reformation*, ed. Katharina M. Wilson, 1987; Marc Shell edits and provides an extended commentary on one of her religious translations in *Elizabeth's Glass*, 1993. The standard biography remains J. E. Neale, *Queen Elizabeth I*, 1934, rpt. 1967. Maria Perry has a documentary biography, *The Word of a Prince: The Life of Elizabeth I from Contemporary Documents*, 1990. The queen's significance as political and cultural presence is treated by Frances Yates, *Astraea: The Imperial Theme*, 1975; Marie Axton, *The Queen's Two Bodies: Drama and the Elizabethan Succession*, 1977; Phillippa Berry, *Of Chastity and Power: Elizabethan Literature and the Unmarried Queen*, 1989; and Carole Levin, *"The Heart and Stomach of a King": Elizabeth I and the Politics of Sex and Power*, 1994. Susan Bassnett, *Elizabeth I: A Feminist Perspective*, 1988, approaches the queen's career through her writings; Susan Frye, *Elizabeth I: The Competition for Representation*, 1993, studies Elizabeth's construction of her power within a patriarchal society. *ELR* 23 (1993): 345–54 and 24 (1994): 234–36 survey recent studies of Elizabeth.

The English Bible

Debora Shuger's *The Renaissance Bible: Scholarship, Sacrifice, and Subjectivity*, 1994, is a brilliant analysis of the place of Scripture in a wide range of early modern discourses. Studies of the English Bible include John Coolidge, *The Pauline Renaissance in England: Puritanism and the Bible*, 1970; David Daiches, *The King James Version of the English Bible*, 1968; F. F. Bruce, *History of the Bible in English*, 1978; and A. C. Partridge, *English Biblical Translation*, 1973. William Tyndale's doctrinal treatises were edited by Henry Walter in 1848; there is a modern biography of Tyndale by David Daniell, 1994, and an account of his psychological and literary power in Stephen Greenblatt, *Renaissance Self-Fashioning*, 1980.

The Book of Common Prayer

John Booty edited the 1559 version of the Book of Common Prayer in 1976; Booty also edited *The Godly Kingdom of Tudor England*, 1981, a useful collection of essays on the prayer book, the Book of Homilies, and other Reformation texts.

Mary (Sidney) Herbert, Countess of Pembroke

Margaret P. Hannay et al. edited the *Collected Works*, 2 vols., 1998; there is an important edition of *The Psalms of Sir Philip Sidney and the Countess of Pembroke*, ed J. C. A. Rathmell, 1963. Margaret P. Hannay has written the only literary biography, *Philip's Phoenix*, 1990. Mary Herbert is also one of the three writers treated in Kim Walker, *Women*

Writers of the English Renaissance, 1996. Other important studies are Gary Waller, *Mary Sidney, Countess of Pembroke: A Critical Study of Her Writings and Literary Milieu*, 1979, and Mary Ellen Lamb, *Gender and Authorship in the Sidney Circle*, 1990. Recent studies are surveyed in *ELR* 14 (1984): 426–37 and 24 (1994): 237–38.

Christopher Marlowe

Fredson Bowers has edited the *Complete Works*, 2 vols., 1973, rev. 1981; R. H. Case has a modern-spelling edition, 6 vols., 1930–33, rpt. 1966; of Roma Gill's projected three-volume edition, the first two volumes appeared in 1987. W. W. Greg edited parallel texts of the two versions of *Dr. Faustus* in 1950; the two versions have also been edited by David Bevington and Eric Rasmussen, 1993; and Roma Gill edited the A text (our copy text for *Faustus*) in 1989. Stephen Orgel edited *The Complete Poems and Translations of Christopher Marlowe*, 1971. For Marlowe's biography see John Bakeless, *The Tragicall History of Christopher Marlowe*, 2 vols., 1942, and Charles Nicholl, *The Reckoning: The Murder of Christopher Marlowe*, 1992. Valuable critical studies include Harry Levin, *The Overreacher*, 1952; Douglas Cole, *Suffering and Evil in the Plays of Christopher Marlowe*, 1962; *Two Renaissance Mythmakers: Christopher Marlowe and Ben Jonson*, ed. Alvin B. Kernan, 1977; *Marlowe: The Critical Heritage*, ed. Millar McLure, 1979; Clifford Leech, *Christopher Marlowe: Poet for the Stage*, 1986; Simon Shepherd, *Marlowe and the Politics of Elizabethan Theatre*, 1986; *Christopher Marlowe*, in the series "Modern Critical Views," ed. Harold Bloom, 1986; C. L. Barber, *Creating Elizabethan Tragedy: the Theater of Marlowe and Kyd*, 1988. *Christopher Marlowe's "Doctor Faustus*," in "Modern Critical Interpretations," ed. Harold Bloom, 1988; and *Christopher Marlowe and English Renaissance Culture*, ed. Darryll Grantley and Peter Roberts, 1996. For *Hero and Leander*, Louis L. Martz's facsimile of the first edition, 1972, has an important introduction. On the genre, see William Keach, *Elizabeth Erotic Narratives*, 1977; and Clark Hulse, *Metamorphic Verse: The Elizabethan Minor Epic*, 1981. Recent studies are surveyed in *ELR* 7 (1977): 382–99 and 18 (1988): 329–42.

Thomas Nashe

The standard edition, 5 vols., is by R. W. McKerrow, rev. F. P. Wilson, 1958; there are selected editions by Stanley Wells, 1965, and J. B. Steane, 1972. Charles Nicholl has written *A Cup of News: The Life of Thomas Nashe*, 1984. Useful critical studies include G. R. Hibbard, *Thomas Nashe: A Critical Introduction*, 1962; Jonathan V. Crewe, *Unredeemed Rhetoric: Thomas Nashe and the Scandal of Authorship*, 1982; Stephen S. Hilliard, *The Singularity of Thomas Nashe*, 1986; Lorna Hutson, *Thomas Nashe in Context*, 1989; and Peter Holbrook, *Literature and Degree in Renaissance England: Nashe, Bourgeois Tragedy, Shakespeare*, 1994. *ELR* 25 (1995): 261–64 reviews recent studies.

Sir Walter Ralegh

The collected edition is by William Oldys and Thomas Birch, 8 vols., 1829, rpt. 1965; the standard edition of the poems is by A. M. C. Latham, rev. 1950; a useful edition is *Selected Writings*, ed. Gerard Hammond, 1984. *The Discoverie of the Large, Rich and Bewtiful Empyre of Guiana* has been newly edited, with much contextual and interpretive material, by Neil L. Whitehead, 1997. Biographies include Willard M. Wallace, *Sir Walter Raleigh*, 1959, and Stephen Coote, *A Play of Passion*, 1993. Noteworthy studies include David B. Quinn, *Ralegh and the British Empire*, 1947, rpt. 1962; E. A. Strathmann, *Sir Walter Ralegh, A Study in Elizabethan Skepticism*, 1951; Philip Edwards, *Sir Walter Ralegh*, 1953, rpt. 1976; F. J. Levy in *Tudor Historical Thought*, 1967; Stephen Greenblatt, *Sir Walter Ralegh*, 1973; and Shannon Miller, *Invested with Meaning: The Raleigh Circle in the New World*, 1998. For guides to scholarship, see Jerry L. Mills, *Sir Walter Ralegh: A Reference Guide*, 1986, and Christopher Armitage, *Sir Walter Ralegh, An Annotated Bibliography*, 1987. See also entries under **The Wider World**.

William Shakespeare

Some important editions of the plays are the Variorum (S. B. Hemingway, ed., *1 Henry IV*, 1936, with a supplement by G. B. Evans, 1956); the New Arden (A. R. Humphries, ed., *1 Henry IV*, 1960); and David Bevington, ed., *1 Henry IV*, 1987. Major studies treating *1 Henry IV* are E. M. W. Tillyard, *Shakespeare's History Plays*, 1944; Irving Ribner, *The English History Play in the Age of Shakespeare*, rev. 1965; Robert Ornstein, *A Kingdom for a Stage: The Achievement of Shakespeare's History Plays*, 1972; Phyllis Rackin, *Stages of History: Shakespeare's English Chronicles*, 1990; and Scott McMillin, *Shakespeare in Performance: 1 Henry IV*, 1991.

The objects of obsessive critical attention for centuries, Shakespeare's plays have recently been studied from new historicist, feminist, psychoanalytic, and deconstructive perspectives, among others. The range may be sampled in such collections as *Representing Shakespeare: New Psychoanalytic Essays*, ed. Murray Schwartz and Coppelia Kahn, 1980; *Alternative Shakespeares*, ed. John Drakakis, 1985; *Shakespeare and the Question of Theory*, ed. Patricia Parker and Geoffrey Hartman, 1985; *Shakespeare Reproduced*, ed. Jean Howard and M. O'Connor, 1987; *Political Shakespeare*, ed. Jonathan Dollimore and Alan Sinfield, 1994; and in such books as Lisa Jardine, *Still Harping on Daughters*, 1983; Marjorie Garber, *Shakespeare's Ghost Writers*, 1987; Stephen Greenblatt, *Shakespearean Negotiations*, 1988; Margreta de Grazia, *Shakespeare Verbatim*, 1991; Janet Adelman, *Suffocating Mothers*, 1992; Valerie Traub, *Desire and Anxiety*, 1992; and Harry Berger Jr., *Making Trifles of Terrors*, 1997. Notable performance studies include Marvin Rosenberg, *The Masks of Lear*,

1972; David Bevington, *Action Is Eloquence*, 1984; Michael Goldman, *Acting and Action in Shakespearean Tragedy*, 1985; Peter Donaldson, *Shakespearean Films, Shakespearean Directors*, 1990; and *Shakespeare, the Movie*, ed. Lynda Boose and Richard Burt, 1997.

Hyder Rollins's Variorum edition of the sonnets, 2 vols., 1944, summarizes many commentaries and problems; Stephen Booth's edition, 1977, presents a facsimile of the first edition and a modernized text on facing pages, with elaborate commentary; see, likewise, the Arden Edition (K. Duncan-Jones, ed., 1997) and Helen Vendler, *The Art of Shakespeare's Sonnets*, 1997. Noteworthy criticism of the sonnets and poems includes Stephen Booth, *An Essay on Shakespeare's Sonnets*, 1969; Joel Fineman, *Shakespeare's Perjured Eye: The Invention of Poetic Subjectivity in the Sonnets*, 1986; Heather Dubrow, *Captive Victors: Shakespeare's Narrative Poems and Sonnets*, 1987; Bruce Smith, *Homosexual Desire in Shakespeare's England*, 1991; and Margreta de Grazia, "The Scandal of Shakespeare's Sonnets," in *Shakespeare Survey* 46 (1994): 35–49.

The life and works are treated by E. K. Chambers, *William Shakespeare: A Study of Facts and Problems*, 2 vols., 1930. S. Schoenbaum's important biographical research is recorded in *William Shakespeare: A Documentary Life*, 1975, and *A Compact Documentary Life*, 1977. Some useful aids to scholarship are Geoffrey Bullough, *Narrative and Dramatic Sources of Shakespeare*, 8 vols., 1957–75, and *A New Companion to Shakespeare Studies*, ed. Kenneth Muir and S. Schoenbaum, 1971, rpt. 1976.

Sir Philip Sidney
Oxford editions are standard for everything except the correspondence: the poetry is edited by William A. Ringler Jr., 1962; the *Old Arcadia* by Jean Robertson, 1973; the *New Arcadia* by Victor Skretkowicz, 1987; and the *Miscellaneous Prose* (including the *Defense*) by Katherine Duncan-Jones and Jan Van Dorsten, 1973. Sidney's letters are found in *The Prose Works of Sir Philip Sidney*, 4 vols., ed. Albert Feuillerat, 1912, rpt. 1962, 3: 75–184. There are valuable editions of the *Defense* by Geoffrey Shepherd, 1965, and Van Dorsten, 1966. Maurice Evans edited *The Countess of Pembroke's Arcadia* (the 1593 composite version) in 1977. Useful volumes of selected works are those by David Kalstone, 1970; Duncan-Jones for the Oxford English Authors series, 1989; Catherine Bates (poetry), 1994; and Elizabeth P. Watson, 1997. The earliest biography was by Sidney's friend Fulke Greville, 1652; it is included in Greville's *Prose Works*, ed. John Gouws, 1986. The standard modern biography is Duncan-Jones, *Sir Philip Sidney: Courtier Poet*, 1991. Modern studies of the life and works are John Buxton, *Sir Philip Sidney and the English Renaissance*, 1954, rpt. 1964; James M. Osborn, *Young Philip Sidney*, 1972; and A. C. Hamilton, *Sir Philip Sidney: A Study of His Life and Works*, 1977. Some important critical studies are Walter R. Davis and

Richard Lanham, *Sidney's Arcadia*, 1965; David Kalstone, *Sidney's Poetry: Contexts and Interpretations*, 1965; Neil L. Rudenstine, *Sidney's Poetic Development*, 1967; Andrew Weiner, *Sir Philip Sidney and the Poetics of Protestantism*, 1978; Richard C. McCoy, *Sir Philip Sidney: Rebellion in Arcadia*, 1979; Stephen Greenblatt, "Murdering Peasants: Status, Genre, and the Representation of Rebellion," in *Representations* 1 (1983): 1–29; Joan Rees, *Sir Philip Sidney and "Arcadia,"* 1991; Roland Greene in *Post-Petrarchism*, 1991; and Blair Worden, *The Sound of Virtue: Philip Sidney's "Arcadia" and Elizabethan Politics*, 1996. Dennis Kay edited *Sir Philip Sidney: An Anthology of Modern Criticism*, 1987. *Sidney in Retrospect: Selections from "English Literary Renaissance,"* ed. Arthur F. Kinney, 1988, reprints articles and reviews of recent scholarship from a leading Renaissance journal. Recent studies of *Arcadia* are surveyed in *ELR* 26 (1996): 173–81.

Edmund Spenser
Edwin A. Greenlaw et al. edited a ten-volume Variorum edition, *The Works of Edmund Spenser*, 1932–49. Important editions of *The Faerie Queene* are by A. C. Hamilton, 1977, and Thomas P. Roche Jr., 1978; William A. Oram et al. edited *The Yale Edition of the Shorter Poems of Edmund Spenser*, 1989. The chief biography is *The Life of Edmund Spenser* by Alexander Judson, 1945. Two recent overviews of the life and works are Gary Waller, *Edmund Spenser, A Literary Life*, 1994, and Oram, *Edmund Spenser*, 1997. Important critical studies include C. S. Lewis, *The Allegory of Love*, 1936; Paul J. Alpers, *The Poetry of "The Faerie Queene,"* 1967; Isabel MacCaffrey, *Spenser's Allegory: The Anatomy of Imagination*, 1975; James Nohrnberg, *The Analogy of "The Faerie Queene,"* 1976; Michael O'Connell, *Mirror and Veil: The Historical Dimension of Spenser's "Faerie Queene,"* 1977; Jonathan Goldberg, *Endlesse Worke: Spenser and the Structure of Discourse*, 1981; John Guillory, *Poetic Authority: Spenser, Milton, and Literary History*, 1983; Harry Berger Jr., *Revisionary Play: Studies in the Spenserian Dynamics*, 1988; John N. King, *Spenser's Poetry and the Reformation Tradition*, 1990; Theresa M. Krier, *Gazing on Secret Sights: Spenser, Classical Imitation, and the Decorums of Vision*, 1990; Richard Rambuss, *Spenser's Secret Career*, 1993; Gordon Teskey, *Allegory and Violence*, 1994; Lauren Silberman, *Transforming Desire: Erotic Knowledge in Books III and IV of "The Faerie Queene,"* 1995; and Willy Maley, *Salvaging Spenser: Colonialism, Culture, and Identity*, 1997. Hamilton edited *Essential Articles for the Study of Edmund Spenser*, 1972. A wide range of criticism is reprinted in Hugh Maclean and Anne Lake Prescott's Norton Critical Edition, *Edmund Spenser's Poetry*, rev. 1993. Mihoko Suzuki edited a collection of recent *Critical Essays on Edmund Spenser*, 1996; a parallel collection, issued the same year, is *Edmund Spenser*, ed. Andrew Hadfield. A collection that students may find intriguing is

Approaches to Teaching Spenser's "Faerie Queene," ed. David L. Miller and Alexander Dunlop, 1994. *The Spenser Encyclopedia,* ed. Hamilton et al., 1990, is an invaluable aid. The best guides to recent work are the bibliographies in the encyclopedia and the selected bibliography, with annotations, in Oram's *Edmund Spenser.*

Henry Howard, Earl of Surrey

The complete edition is by F. M. Padelford, 1928, rpt. 1966; Emrys Jones's excellent selected edition, 1964, is widely used. *Tottel's Miscellany* is edited by Hyder E. Rollins, 2 vols., rev. 1965. E. R. Casady's biography, 1938, rpt. 1966, and W. R. Sessions's study of the life and works, 1986, bear the same title, *Henry Howard, Earl of Surrey.* Noteworthy critical studies are Walter R. Davis, "Contexts in Surrey's Poetry," *ELR* 4 (1974): 40–55; the chapters on Surrey in Alastair Fowler, *Conceitful Thought: The Interpretation of English Renaissance Poems,* 1975, and Jonathan Crewe, *Trials of Authorship: Anterior Forms and Poetic Reconstruction from Wyatt to Shakespeare,* 1990, and those on Wyatt and Surrey in Maurice Evans, *English Poetry in the Sixteenth Century,* rev. 1967; Susanne Woods, *Natural Emphasis: English Versification from Chaucer to Dryden,* 1984; A. C. Spearing, *Medieval to Renaissance in English Poetry,* 1985; and Elizabeth Heale, *Wyatt, Surrey and Early Tudor Poetry,* 1998. Scholarship is surveyed in Clyde W. Jentoft, *Sir*

Thomas Wyatt and Henry Howard, Earl of Surrey: A Reference Guide, 1980. Reviews of recent studies are in *ELR* 19 (1989): 389–401 and 28 (1998): 307.

Sir Thomas Wyatt

The most useful edition is by Kenneth Muir and Patricia Thomson, *Collected Poems,* 1969; others are by Richard C. Harrier, 1975; Joost Daalder, 1975; and R. A. Rebholz, 1978. *Tottel's Miscellany* is edited by Hyder E. Rollins, 2 vols., rev. 1965. Letters and life records are included in Muir's biography, 1963; Thomson treats both life and works in *Sir Thomas Wyatt and His Background,* 1964; a more recent, slighter treatment is Stephen M. Foley, *Sir Thomas Wyatt,* 1990. Critical studies include E. M. W. Tillyard, *The Poetry of Sir Thomas Wyatt,* 1929, rpt. 1949; Raymond Southall, *The Courtly Maker,* 1964; Elizabeth W. Pomeroy, *The Elizabethan Miscellanies: Their Development and Conventions,* 1973; Stephen Greenblatt, *Renaissance Self-Fashioning,* 1980; Thomas M. Greene, *The Light in Troy: Imitation and Discovery in Renaissance Poetry,* 1982; and Barbara L. Estrin, *Laura: Uncovering Gender and Genre in Wyatt, Donne, and Marvell,* 1994. Since the sixteenth century, Wyatt and Surrey have often been discussed in tandem: for some modern instances, see **Surrey.** Thomson edited *Wyatt: The Critical Heritage,* 1974. Reviews of recent studies are in *ELR* 19 (1989): 226–46 and 28 (1998): 307–09.

THE EARLY SEVENTEENTH CENTURY

The journal *English Literary Renaissance (ELR)* publishes recent studies of individual sixteenth- and seventeenth-century authors and of some literary topics, on an ongoing basis; they are updated periodically. In its winter issue, annually, the journal *Studies in English Literature* publishes "Recent Studies in the English Renaissance," evaluating the past year's publications. These journals regularly carry important new articles on seventeenth-century topics, as do *English Literary History, Representations, The Seventeenth Century, Seventeenth Century News, Renaissance Studies, John Donne Journal, Milton Studies,* and *Milton Quarterly.*

Politics, Society, and Political Thought

Some general histories of the seventeenth century or some part of it are Christopher Hill, *The Century of Revolution,* 1961; Barry Coward, *The Stuart Age: A History of England, 1603–1714,* 1980; Derek Hirst, *Authority and Conflict: England, 1603–58,* 1986; and Austin Woolrych, *Commonwealth to Protectorate,* 1982. Interpretation of the causes and progress of the English revolution is a contested issue. A series of books by Christopher Hill emphasizes political, social, and ideological conflict: *Puritanism and Revolution,* 1958; *The World Turned Upside Down: Radical Ideas During the English Revolution,* 1972; and *The Experience of Defeat,* 1984.

The "revisionist" view sees this event not as a revolution but as an accidental consequence of politicians' incompetence: it is represented by J. S. Morrill, *Seventeenth-Century Britain, 1603–1714,* 1980; and Conrad Russell, *The Causes of the English Civil War,* 1990, and *Unrevolutionary England, 1603–1642,* 1990. Recent efforts to revise the revisionists include J. P. Sommerville, *Politics and Ideology in England, 1603–1640,* 1986; *Conflict in Early Stuart England: Studies in Religion and Politics, 1603–1642,* ed. Richard Cust and Ann Hughes, 1989, and *Reviving the English Revolution: Reflections and Elaborations on the Work of Christopher Hill,* ed. Geoff Eley and William Hunt, 1988. The complex place of religion, both as doctrine and cultural force, is explored in William Haller, *The Rise of Puritanism,* 1938; Keith Thomas, *Religion and the Decline of Magic: Popular Beliefs in Sixteenth- and Seventeenth-Century England,* 1971; Patrick Collinson, *The Religion of Protestants: The Church in English Society, 1559–1625,* 1982, and *The Birthpangs of Protestant England,* 1986; and David Underdown, *Revel, Riot, and Rebellion: Popular Politics and Culture in England, 1603–1660,* 1985. Suggestive essays on the interrelation of events, religion, and culture are collected in *Culture and Politics in Early Stuart England,* ed. Kevin Sharpe and Peter Lake, 1993.

English society in the seventeenth century was analyzed by the German sociologist Max Weber in a very influential essay, 1904–05, emphasizing the importance of the Protestant doctrine of the calling or vocation for the aspiring capitalist class; that thesis was further developed by R. H. Tawney in *Religion and the Rise of Capitalism*, 1926, but it has been much disputed, notably by H. R. Trevor-Roper. Peter Laslett's book, *The World We Have Lost*, 3rd. ed., 1984, helps in imagining what life was like in a preindustrial society. Studies of early modern society of special interest to students of literature include Lawrence Stone, *The Family, Sex and Marriage in England, 1500–1800*, 1977; Keith Wrightson, *English Society, 1580–1680*, 1982, Susan Amussen, *An Ordered Society: Gender and Class in Early Modern England*, 1988; and Alan Bray, *Homosexuality in Renaissance England*, 1982. Elizabeth Eisenstein, *The Printing Press as an Agent of Change*, 2 vols., 1979, bears directly on the production and transmission of literature. A general study of schools and education in the period is K. Charlton, *Education in Renaissance England*, 1965.

Helpful accounts of political thought in the seventeenth century are found in J. G. A. Pocock's seminal works, *The Ancient Constitution and the Feudal Law*, rev. 1987, and *The Machiavellian Moment: Florentine Political Thought and the Atlantic Republican Tradition*, 1975, as well as in Quentin Skinner, *The Foundations of Modern Political Thought*, 2 vols., 1978, and Richard Tuck, *Philosophy and Government, 1572–1651*, 1993. A useful collection of political treatises in the period has been edited by David Wootton, *Divine Right and Democracy: An Anthology of Political Writing in Stuart England*, 1986. J. H. Burns has edited essays included in *The Cambridge History of Political Thought, 1450–1700*, 1991.

Literature, Culture, and Politics

Several studies focus on the intellectual and cultural milieu of the period as it affects literature. Inherited views of the universe based on hierarchy, order, and analogy, which were still prevalent in poetic imagery, are set forth in E. M. W. Tillyard's concise though oversimplified account, *The Elizabethan World Picture*, 1943. Studies focusing on the challenge of the new science include Rupert Hall, *The Scientific Revolution, 1500–1800*, 1954; William R. Shea, *Galileo's Intellectual Revolution*, 1972; Hans Blumenberg, *The Genesis of the Copernican World*, 1987; and Barbara Shapiro, *Probability and Certainty in Seventeenth-Century England*, 1983. Some sense of the still-powerful influence of the occult—alchemy, magic, hermeticism, and the like—may be gleaned from Wayne Shumaker, *The Occult Sciences in the Renaissance*, 1972. C. A. Patrides and Raymond Waddington have edited a useful collection of essays on various facets of seventeenth-century society and culture, *The Age of Milton: Backgrounds to Seventeenth-Century Literature*, 1980. More focused studies of intellectual currents include Debora Shuger, *Habits*

of Thought in the English Renaissance: Religion, Politics, and the Dominant Culture, 1990; Victoria Kahn, *Machiavellian Rhetoric: From the Counter-Reformation to Milton*, 1994; and John Rogers, *The Matter of Revolution: Science, Poetry, and Politics in the Age of Milton*, 1996. A fine brief account of court culture in the Jacobean and Caroline eras is by Graham Parry, *The Golden Age Restor'd: The Culture of the Stuart Court, 1603–1642*, 1981.

Studies of seventeenth-century literature in relation to political and cultural forces include James Turner, *The Politics of Landscape: Rural Scenery and Society in English Poetry, 1630–1660*, 1979; Annabel Patterson, *Censorship and Interpretation: The Conditions of Writing and Reading in Early Modern England*, 1984; Graham Parry, *Seventeenth Century Poetry: The Social Context*, 1985; Leah Marcus, *The Politics of Mirth: Jonson, Herrick, Milton, Marvell*, 1986; and David Norbrook, *Poetry and Politics in the English Renaissance*, 1984. Several collections of essays treat particular topics and writers in these terms: *The Muses' Common-Weale: Poetry and Politics in the Seventeenth Century*, ed. Claude Summers and Ted-Larry Pebworth, 1988; *The Politics of Discourse: The Literature and History of Seventeenth-Century England*, ed. Kevin Sharpe and Steven Zwicker, 1987; *Patronage, Politics, and Literary Traditions in England, 1558–1658*, ed. Cedric Brown, 1993; and *Religion and Culture in Renaissance England*, ed. C. McEachern and D. Shuger, 1997.

Analyses focusing especially on the Jacobean era are Jonathan Goldberg, *James I and the Politics of Literature: Jonson, Shakespeare, Donne and Their Contemporaries*, 1983; Curtis Perry, *The Making of Jacobean Culture*, 1987; and an important collection of essays edited by Linda Levy Peck, *The Mental World of the Jacobean Court*, 1991. Kevin Sharpe has edited essays pertaining to the Caroline era, *Criticism and Compliment: The Politics of Literature in the England of Charles I*, 1987. Studies treating the literature and culture of the revolutionary era focus on Milton, Marvell, and several royalist poets and prose writers, including Michael Wilding, *Dragon's Teeth: Literature in the English Revolution*, 1987; Nigel Smith, *Literature and Revolution in England, 1640–1660*, 1994, which treats the political uses of various genres; Steven Zwicker, *Lines of Authority: Politics and English Culture, 1649–1689*, 1993; and essays edited by Thomas Healy and Jonathan Sawday, *Literature and the English Civil War*, 1990. Works that attend especially to royalist writers are Raymond Anselment, *Loyalist Resolve: Patient Fortitude in the English Civil War*, 1988; Lois Potter, *Secret Rites and Secret Writing: Royalist Literature, 1641–1660*, 1989; and *Classic and Cavalier: Essays on Jonson and the Sons of Ben*, ed. Claude J. Summers and Ted-Larry Pebworth, 1982. David Norbrook has written an impressive, wide-ranging study of writers who contributed to the emergence of republican thought and culture in England before and during the revolution, *Writing the English Republic: Poetry, Rhetoric and Politics,*

1627–1660, 1999. Joad Raymond has studied the emergence of the newspaper during the revolutionary era in *The Invention of the Newspaper: English Newsbooks 1641–1649*, 1996. Nigel Smith has analyzed the rhetoric and assumptions about language of the revolution's radicals—Quakers, Ranters, Diggers—in *Perfection Proclaimed: Language and Literature in English Radical Religion, 1640–1660*, 1989.

Genre, Style, and Poetics
Valuable perspectives on literary history, the literary institution, and aspects of style in the period are provided in several works. J. E. Spingarn has edited a collection of literary criticism, *Critical Essays of the Seventeenth Century*, reissued, 1957. An illuminating and elegant brief account of the place and uses of genre is supplied by Rosalie Colie in *The Resources of Kind: Genre-Theory in the Renaissance*, 1973. Although the category of Metaphysical poets has generally lost its usefulness, Earl Miner's three volumes provide important surveys of the literature of the era: *The Metaphysical Mode from Donne to Cowley*, 1969; *The Cavalier Mode from Jonson to Cotton*, 1971; and *The Restoration Mode from Milton to Dryden*, 1974. George Parfitt has provided a single-volume survey, *English Poetry of the Seventeenth Century*, 1985. Barbara K. Lewalski, *Protestant Poetics and the Seventeenth-Century Religious Lyric*, 1979, treats the effect of Protestant theology, sermon theory, and devotional practices on poetics and religious poetry, especially Donne, Herbert, Vaughan, and Traherne. Diane McColley has explored the relationship between the poetic language of several major poets and the music of the period in *Poetry and Music in Seventeenth-Century England*, 1997. An important collection of essays that reconsiders canonical poets of period in the light of poststructuralist theory is *Soliciting Interpretation: Literary Theory and Seventeenth-Century Poetry*, ed. Elizabeth D. Harvey and Katharine E. Maus, 1990.

The styles, varieties, and rhetoric of seventeenth-century prose are treated in several important studies: Maurice Croll, in *Style, Rhetoric, and Rhythm: Essays*, ed. J. M. Patrick et al., 1966; Stanley Fish, *Self-Consuming Artifacts: The Experience of Seventeenth-Century Literature*, 1972 (Bacon, Burton, Browne, Milton, Bunyan); Joan Webber, *The Eloquent I: Style and Self in Seventeenth-Century Prose*, 1968; and Roger Pooley, *English Prose of the Seventeenth Century, 1590–1700*, 1992. In *Paradoxia Epidemica*, 1966, Rosalie Colie studied the pervasiveness of paradox in texts of all kinds throughout the century.

Important studies of particular genres in relation to seventeenth-century culture include Rosemary Freeman, *English Emblem Books*, 1948; Paul Delany, *British Autobiography in the Seventeenth Century*, 1969; Ellen Z. Lambert, *Placing Sorrow: A Study of Pastoral Elegy*, 1976; Anthony Low, *Love's Architecture: Devotional Modes in Seventeenth-Century English Poetry*, 1978, and *The Geor-*

gic Revolution, 1985; Paul Salzman, *English Prose Fiction 1558–1700: A Critical History*, 1985; Heather DuBrow, *The Happier Eden: The Politics of Marriage in the Stuart Epithalamium*, 1990; Alastair Fowler, *The Country-House Poem*. 1994; and Amy Boesky, *Founding Fictions: Utopias in Early Modern England*, 1996. Some of the many studies of drama in the Stuart era are Brian Gibbons, *Jacobean City Comedy: A Study of Satiric Plays by Jonson, Marston, and Middleton*, 1968; Margot Heinemann, *Puritanism and Theatre: Thomas Middleton and Opposition Drama Under the Early Stuarts*, 1980; Albert Tricomi, *Anticourt Drama in England, 1603–1642*, 1989; and Richard Strier ed., et al., *The Theatrical City: Culture, Theater, and Politics in London, 1576–1649*, 1995.

Women's Roles and Writing
An important recovery effort is under way in publishing and studying hitherto unknown or little-studied works by early modern women, sometimes highlighting gender issues, sometimes attending to women's self-constructions as patrons and authors, sometimes addressing aesthetic and stylistic matters. Some anthologies of writing by women in (or including) the seventeenth century are *The Paradise of Women*, ed. Betty Travitsky, 1981; *First Feminists: British Women Writers, 1578–1799*, ed. Moira Ferguson, 1985; *Kissing the Rod: An Anthology of Seventeenth-Century Women's Verse*, ed. Germaine Greer et al., 1988; *Women Writers of the Seventeenth Century*, ed. Katharina Wilson and Frank J. Warnke, 1989; and *Her Own Life: Autobiographical Writings by Seventeenth-Century Englishwomen*, ed. Elspeth Graham et al., 1989. An annotated bibliography by Hilda Smith and Susan Cardinale, *Women and the Literature of the Seventeenth Century*, 1900, gives a brief account of all the works by or about women listed in Donald Wing's *Short-Title Catalogue of English books published between 1641 and 1700*. Elaine Hobby in *Virtue of Necessity: English Women's Writing, 1649–88*, 1988, discusses women writers and their several genres, with bibliography. Other important bibliographical resources are Mary Thomas Crane, "Women and the Early Modern Canon: Recent Editions of Works by English Women, 1500–1500," *Renaissance Quarterly* 51 (1998); and recent studies of seventeenth-century women writers by Elizabeth Hageman and Sara Jayne Steen, in *ELR* 14 (1984), 18 (1988), and 24 (1994). Anthologies of texts that illuminate the place of women and women writers in seventeenth-century society are *Half Humankind: Contexts and Texts of the Controversy about Women in England, 1540–1640*, ed. K. Henderson and B. McManus, 1985, and *Daughters, Wives, and Widows: Writings By Men About Women and Marriage in England, 1500–1640*, ed. Joan L. Klein, 1992. Antonia Fraser has written a lively social history of women throughout the century, with many vignettes of particular lives, *The Weaker Vessel*, 1984.

Some important studies and collections of essays

on women, writing, and gender in the period are Linda Woodbridge, *Women and the English Renaissance: Literature and the Nature of Womenkind, 1540–1620,* 1984; *Women in English Society, 1500–1800,* ed. Mary Prior, 1985; *Rewriting the Renaissance: The Discourses of Sexual Difference in Early Modern England,* ed. Margaret Ferguson, Maureen Quilligan, and Nancy Vickers, 1986; and Margaret J. M. Ezell, *The Patriarch's Wife: Literary Evidence and the History of the Family,* 1987. Some of the women writers included in this anthology are treated by Elaine Beilin in *Redeeming Eve: Women Writers of the English Renaissance,* 1987; by Sara Mendelson in *The Mental World of Stuart Women,* 1987; by Tina Krontiris in *Oppositional Voices: Women as Writers and Translators of Literature in the English Renaissance,* 1991; by Barbara K. Lewalski in *Writing Women in Jacobean England,* 1993; and by Louise Schleiner in *Tudor and Stuart Women Writers,* 1994. Phyllis Mack, *Visionary Women: Ecstatic Prophecy in Seventeenth-Century England,* 1992, highlights the emergence of prophecy as a genre for women, especially during the revolution; a complementary study by Bonnelyn Y. Kunze is *Margaret Fell and the Rise of Quakerism,* 1994. Useful collections of essays discussing various women writers are *Ambiguous Realities: Women in the Middle Ages and Renaissance,* ed. Carole Levin and Jeanie Watson, 1987; *The Renaissance Englishwoman in Print: Counterbalancing the Canon,* ed. Anne M. Haselkorn and Travitsky, 1990; Jean Brink, *Privileging Gender in Early Modern England,* 1993; *Women and Literature in Britain, 1500–1700,* ed. Helen Wilcox, 1996; and *Representing Women in Renaissance England,* ed. Claude J. Summers and Ted-Larry Pebworth, 1997.

Margaret Cavendish, Duchess of Newcastle

Kate Lilley has edited *Margaret Cavendish: The Description of a New World Called The Blazing World and Other Writings,* 1992; *The Blazing World* is also included in Paul Salzman's *Anthology of Seventeenth-Century Fiction,* 1991, and he discusses that work in his *English Prose Fiction,* 1985, as does Amy Boesky in *Founding Fictions: Utopias in Early Modern England,* 1996. Two of Cavendish's books have been reprinted in facsimile, *Sociable Letters,* 1969, and *Poems and Fancies,* 1972. There are selections in *Women Writers of the Seventeenth Century,* ed. Katharina Wilson and Frank J. Warnke, and in *Kissing the Rod: An Anthology of Seventeenth-Century Women's Verse* ed. Germaine Greer et al., 1988. Ann Shaver has edited plays by Cavendish in *Convent of Pleasure and Other Plays,* 1999. The best biography is by Kathleen Jones, *A Glorious Fame: The Life of Margaret Cavendish, Duchess of Newcastle, 1623–1673,* 1988. There are substantial scholarly treatments of Cavendish in Hilda Smith, *Reason's Disciples: Seventeenth-Century English Feminists,* 1982; Sara Mendelson, *The Mental World of Stuart Women,* 1987; and Mary Beth Rose, *Women in the Middle Ages and*

Renaissance, 1986. Some useful articles are Catherine Gallagher, "Embracing the Absolute: The Politics of the Female Subject in Seventeenth-Century England," in *Genders* 1 (1988): 24–29, and Eve Keller, "Producing Petty Gods: Margaret Cavendish's Critique of Experimental Science," in *English Literary History* 64 (1997): 447–71.

John Donne

The two-volume edition of Donne's *Poems* edited by H. J. C. Grierson, 1912, is still important, although we now have newer Oxford editions of Donne's several genres: *The Divine Poems,* ed. Helen Gardner, 1952, rev. 1978; *The Elegies and the Songs and Sonnets,* ed. Gardner, 1965; *The Satires, Epigrams, and Verse Letters,* ed. Wesley Milgate, 1967; and *The Epithalamions, Anniversaries, and Epicedes,* ed., Milgate, 1978. George Potter and Evelyn Simpson have edited *The Sermons of John Donne,* 10 vols., 1953–62. Donne's meditations were edited by Anthony Raspa, *John Donne: Devotions upon Emergent Occasions,* 1975. There are several single-volume editions of the English poems, one by C. A. Patrides, 1985, rpt. 1994, and another by A. L. Clements, 1966, rev. 1992. A *Donne Variorum* edition is in progress, 1995–, under the general editorship of Gary Stringer; Vol. 6, *Anniversaries and Epicedes,* and Vol. 8, *Epigrams, Epithalamions, Epitaphs, etc.* have been published. The first biography of Donne was by Izaak Walton, 1640. R. C. Bald's *John Donne: A Life,* 1970, is the standard biography. John Carey, *John Donne: Life, Mind, and Art,* 1981, offers a challenging account of the psychological and social factors influencing Donne's life choices and his poetry. Arthur Marotti, *John Donne: Coterie Poet,* 1986, locates Donne in his social milieu and places his poems in relation to the various audiences they addressed.

T. S. Eliot's essay "The Varieties of Metaphysical Poets," in *Selected Essays, 1917–1932,* 1932, rpt. 1969, was influential in setting terms for analyzing Donne over several decades; Cleanth Brook's reading of "The Canonization" in his *Well Wrought Urn,* 1947, is a classic of the New Criticism. Donne is discussed in many accounts of the period—Earl Miner, *The Metaphysical Mode from Donne to Cowley,* 1969; Barbara K. Lewalski, *Protestant Poetics and the Seventeenth-Century Religious Lyric,* 1979; and Jonathan Goldberg, *James I and the Politics of Literature,* 1983—and has invited several valuable individual studies: Donald Guss, *John Donne: Petrarchist,* 1966; Murray Roston, *The Soul of Wit,* 1974; Lewalski, *Donne's Anniversaries and the Poetry of Praise,* 1973; Stevie Davies, *Reassessing John Donne,* 1986; Terry Sherwood, *Fulfilling the Circle,* 1986; Meg Lota Brown, *Donne and the Politics of Conscience,* 1995. Many significant critical essays are collected in *John Donne: Essays in Celebration,* ed. A. J. Smith, 1972; *John Donne: The Critical Heritage,* ed. Smith, 1975–1996; *John Donne and the Seventeenth-Century Metaphysical Poets,* ed. Harold Bloom, 1986; *The Eagle and the*

Dove: Reassessing John Donne, ed. Claude J. Summers and Ted-Larry Pebworth, 1986; and *Critical Essays on John Donne*, ed. Arthur Marotti, 1994.

George Herbert

The standard edition is *The Works of George Herbert*, ed. F. E. Hutchinson, rev. 1945; C. A. Patrides edited a compact edition of *The English Poems*, 1974. Izaak Walton wrote a contemporary *Life of George Herbert*, 1670; there are modern ones by Amy Charles, *A Life of George Herbert*, 1977, and by Stanley Stewart, *George Herbert*, 1986. Besides the general studies mentioned in the general bibliography for the period, several important critical books on Herbert deal with the interrelation of his religion and his art: Rosemund Tuve, *A Reading of George Herbert*, 1952; Joseph Summers, *George Herbert: His Religion and His Art*, 1954; Stanley Fish, *The Living Temple: George Herbert and Catechizing*, 1978; Diana Benet, *Secretary of Praise: The Poetic Vocation of George Herbert*, 1984; Chana Bloch, *Spelling the Word: George Herbert and the Bible*, 1985; Terry Sherwood, *Herbert's Prayerful Art*, 1989; Richard Strier, *Love Known: Theology and Experience in George Herbert's Poetry*, 1983; and Gene E. Veith, *Reformation Spirituality: The Religion of George Herbert*, 1985. Helen Vendler, in *The Poetry of George Herbert*, 1975, focuses on Herbert's exquisite art. Michael Schoenfeldt, in *Prayer and Power: George Herbert and Renaissance Courtship*, 1991, explores the interdependence of social and religious discourse, to advance a cultural poetics of Herbert's lyrics. There are several essay collections all or partly on Herbert: *"Too Rich to Clothe the Sunne": Essays on George Herbert*, ed. Claude Summers and Ted-Larry Pebworth, 1980; *"Bright Shoots of Everlastingness": The Seventeenth-Century Religious Lyric*, ed. Summers and Pebworth, 1987; and *George Herbert: The Critical Heritage*, ed. C. A. Patrides, 1983. Recent studies are surveyed in *ELR* 18 (1988): 460–75.

Robert Herrick

The standard edition is by L. C. Martin, *Robert Herrick: Poems*, 1965. J. Max Patrick also edited the *Complete Poetry of Robert Herrick* in 1963. There are biographical accounts by Roger Rollin, *Robert Herrick*, 1966, and George W. Scott, *Robert Herrick*, 1974. Important critical studies include Robert Deming, *Ceremony and Art: Robert Herrick's Poetry*, 1974; Leigh DeNeef, *"This Poetic Liturgie:" Robert Herrick's Ceremonial Mode*, 1974; Ann Baynes Coiro, *Robert Herrick's Hesperides and the Epigram Book Tradition*, 1988; as well as essays by Leah Marcus in *The Politics of Mirth*, 1986, and by Aschah Guibbory in *The Muses' Common-Weale: Poetry and Politics in the Seventeenth Century*, ed. Claude Summers and Ted-Larry Pebworth, 1988. A collection of essays edited by Roger Rollin and J. Max Patrick, *Trust to Good Verses: Herrick Tercentenary Essays*, appeared in 1978. Recent studies are surveyed in *ELR* 3 (1973): 462–71.

Ben Jonson

A monumental edition of Jonson's *Works* was edited by C. H. Herford and Percy and Evelyn Simpson, 11 vols., 1925–52. The Yale edition and the paperback series known as the New Mermaids provide good modernized and annotated versions of the major plays (one play to a volume). Robert M. Adams has edited *Ben Jonson's Plays and Masques*, 1979, with critical essays. Stephen Orgel has edited *The Complete Masques*, 1969. Handy editions of the verse are by W. B. Hunter, *The Complete Poetry of Ben Jonson*, 1963, and George Parfitt, *Ben Jonson: The Complete Poems*, 1975. There is an edition of *Timber* by Ralph Walker, 1953. David Riggs has written a fine biography, *Ben Jonson: A Life*, 1989.

Important critical studies include Alexander Leggatt, *Ben Jonson: His Vision and His Art*, 1981; Richard Helgerson, *Self-Crowned Laureates: Spenser, Jonson, Milton and the Literary System*, 1983; Katherine E. Maus, *Ben Jonson and the Roman Frame of Mind*, 1984; Robert N. Watson, *Ben Jonson's Parodic Strategy: Literary Imperialism in the Comedies*, 1987; George Rowe, *Distinguishing Jonson*, 1988; Jonathan Haynes, *The Social Relations of Jonson's Theater*, 1992; and Richard Burt, *Licensed by Authority: Ben Jonson and the Discourses of Censorship*, 1993. Works that deal especially with Jonson's poetry are Sara Van den Berg, *The Action of Ben Jonson's Poetry*, 1987, and Robert C. Evans, *Ben Jonson and the Poetics of Patronage*, 1989. Don E. Wayne, *Penshurst: The Semiotics of Place and the Poetics of History*, 1984, locates Jonson's poem in its social and architectural context; Raymond Williams, *The Country and the City*, 1973, places it within a broad social history of movements affecting agriculture and the land.

Stuart court masques, and Jonson's major contribution to them, are analyzed in two essay collections: *The Court Masque*, ed. David Lindley, 1984, and *The Politics of the Stuart Court Masque*, ed. David Bevington and Peter Holbrook, 1998, and by Orgel in *The Illusion of Power: Political Theater in the English Renaissance*, 1975. The fascinating reproduction of drawings and designs for the masques, published by Orgel and Roy Strong in *Inigo Jones: The Theatre of the Stuart Court*, 2 vols., 1973, gives some sense of what masques looked like in presentation. Collections of critical essays on Jonson include *Classic and Cavalier: Essays on Jonson and the Sons of Ben*, ed. Claude J. Summers and Ted-Larry Pebworth, 1982; *Ben Jonson: A Collection of Critical Essays*, ed. Jonas A. Barish, 1963; and *New Perspectives on Ben Jonson*, ed. James Hirsh, 1997.

Aemilia Lanyer

Susanne Woods has edited *The Poems of Aemelia Lanyer: Salve Deus Rex Judaeorum*, 1993, and has also analyzed her life and works in *Lanyer: A Renaissance Woman Poet*, 1999. The important collection of essays edited by Marshall Grossman, *Aemilia*

Lanyer: Gender, Genre, and the Canon, 1998, includes a valuable annotated bibliography. There are chapters on Lanyer in Elaine Beilin, *Redeeming Eve: Women Writers of the English Renaissance*, 1987; Tina Krontiris, *Oppositional Voices: Women as Writers and Translators of Literature in the English Renaissance*, 1991; Barbara K. Lewalski, *Writing Women in Jacobean England*, 1993; and Louise Schleiner, *Tudor and Stuart Women Writers*, 1994. Other notable essays include Mary Ellen Lamb, "Patronage and Class in Aemilia Lanyer's *Salve Deus Rex Judaeorum*," in *Women, Writing, and the Reproduction of Culture*, ed. Jane Donawerth et al., 1999, and Wendy Wall, "The Body of Christ, Aemilia Lanyer's Passion," in her volume, *The Imprint of Gender: Authorship and Publication in the English Renaissance*, 1993.

Richard Lovelace
C. H. Wilkinson edited the *Poems*, 1930, rpt. 1968. Manfred Weidhorn published a biography, *Richard Lovelace*, 1970; and both the life and works are treated in Cyril Hartmann, *The Cavalier Spirit and Its Influence on the Life and Work of Richard Lovelace (1618–1658)*, 1925. Commentary can be found in Earl Miner, *The Cavalier Mode from Jonson to Cotton, 1971*; in Raymond Anselment, "'Stone Walls' and 'Iron Bars': Richard Lovelace and Seventeenth-Century Prison Literature," in *Renaissance and Reformation* 17 (1993); and in two essay collections edited by Claude J. Summers and Ted-Larry Pebworth: *Classic and Cavalier: Essays on Jonson and the Sons of Ben*, 1982, and *The Wit of Seventeenth-Century Poetry*, 1995. Recent studies are reviewed in *ELR* 7 (1977): 248–52.

Andrew Marvell
The standard edition is *The Poems and Letters of Andrew Marvell*, ed. H. M. Margoliouth, 1927; rev. Pierre Legouis and E. E. Duncan-Jones, 2 vols., 1971. His Restoration prose satires, *The Rehearsal Transpros'd* (2 parts), are edited by D. I. B. Smith, 1971. There are handy editions of Marvell's *Complete Poetry* by George de F. Lord, 1968, rpt. 1984, and Elizabeth Story Donno, 1972. Biographical studies include John Dixon Hunt, *Andrew Marvell: His Life and Writings*, 1978; Patsy Griffin, *The Modest Ambition of Andrew Marvell: A Study of Marvell and His Relation to Lovelace, Fairfax, Cromwell, and Milton*, 1995; and Thomas Wheeler, *Andrew Marvell Revisited*, 1996. Influential studies of his political attitudes and writing in connection with his poetry include John M. Wallace, *Destiny His Choice: The Loyalism of Andrew Marvell*, 1968; Annabel Patterson, *Marvell and the Civic Crown*, 1978; Warren Chernaik, *The Poet's Time: Politics and Religion in the Work of Marvell*, 1983; *The Political Identity of Andrew Marvell*, ed. Conal Condren and A. D. Cousins, 1990; and the important essay by David Norbrook, "Horatian Ode," in *Literature and the English Civil War*, ed. Thomas Healy and Jonathan Sawday, 1990. Important analyses of Marvell's poetic art include Rosalie Colie's elegant and learned study, *'My Ecchoing Song':*

Andrew Marvell's Poetry of Criticism, 1970; Donald Friedman, *Marvell's Pastoral Art*, 1970; Patrick Cullen, *Spenser, Marvell, and Renaissance Pastoral*, 1970; Robert Wilcher, *Andrew Marvell*, 1985; and Christine Rees, *The Judgment of Marvell*, 1989. Donno has edited *Andrew Marvell: The Critical Heritage*, 1978. Important essays dealing with Marvell are included in various tercentenary tributes: *Tercentenary Essays in Honor of Andrew Marvell*, ed. Kenneth Friedenreich, 1977; *Approaches to Marvell*, ed. C. A. Patrides, 1978; and *Andrew Marvell: Essays on the Tercentenary of His Death*, ed. R. L. Brett, 1979. Others are in *Politics of Discourse: The Literature and History of Seventeenth-Century England*, ed. Kevin Sharpe and Steven Zwicker, 1987; in Leah Marcus, *Politics of Mirth: Jonson, Herrick, Milton, Marvell*, 1986; and in Zwicker, *Lines of Authority: Politics and English Culture, 1649–1689*, 1993.

John Milton
The Columbia Milton, *The Works of John Milton*, 18 vols., ed. F. A. Patterson, et al., 1931–40, with its invaluable two-volume index, is the only complete edition of all the poetry and prose, English and Latin. The Yale edition, *Complete Prose Works of John Milton*, 8 vols., ed. Don M. Wolfe et al., 1953–82, supplies excellent historical introductions to all the prose. The single-volume edition, *Complete Poems and Major Prose*, by Merritt Y. Hughes, 1957, is still useful; *The Riverside Milton*, ed. Roy Flannagan, 1998, contains all the poetry and much of the English prose, with updated introductions and bibliography. John Leonard's paperback, *John Milton: The Complete Poems*, 1998, supplies a good text and useful notes; the Longman edition is in two volumes: John Carey, *John Milton: Complete Shorter Poems*, 1972, rev. 1997, and *Paradise Lost*, ed. Alastair Fowler, 1966, rev. 1998. For the prose, C. A. Patrides's paperback edition, *John Milton: Selected Prose*, 1985, offers a judicious selection. Three volumes of the *Variorum Commentary on the Poems of John Milton*, ed. Douglas Bush, et al., 1970–75, have been published, but the volume on *Paradise Lost* is still in process.

The standard biography is William Riley Parker, *Milton: A Biography*, 2 vols., 1968. David Masson's, *The Life of John Milton*, 6 vols. plus index, 1859–91, is still a treasure trove of information about the poet and the period. Christopher Hill's *Milton and the English Revolution*, 1977, has spearheaded an ongoing effort to locate Milton more precisely among his revolutionary contemporaries. Cedric C. Brown's brief biography, *John Milton: A Literary Life*, 1995, offers a useful introduction to the man and his works. Milton is psychoanalyzed by William Kerrigan in *The Sacred Complex: On the Psychogenesis of Paradise Lost*, 1983. The five volumes of J. Milton French's *The Life Records of John Milton*, 1949–58, rpt. 1966, gather much primary material for the life. Gordon Campbell, *A Milton Chronology*, 1997, reexamines, records, and adds to these materials. Aids to the study of Milton include the nine-volume *Milton Encyclopedia*, ed. William Hunter et al., 1978–83, with bibliographies and updates in Vol. 9, and *The Cambridge Companion to Milton*, ed. Dennis Danielson, 1989, rev. 1999.

Valuable critical studies that address all or some considerable part of Milton's career and writing include the following: Kerrigan, *The Prophetic Milton*, 1974; Louis L. Martz, *Milton: Poet of Exile*, 1980; Christopher Kendrick, *Milton: A Study in Ideology and Form*, 1986; Marshall Grossman, *"Authors to Themselves": Milton and the Revelation of History*, 1987; Catherine Belsey, *John Milton: Language, Gender, Power*, 1988; Joan Bennett, *Reviving Liberty: Radical Christian Humanism in Milton's Great Poems*, 1989; Loewenstein, *Milton and the Drama of History*, 1990; John T. Shawcross, *John Milton: The Self and the World*, 1993; Sharon Achinstein, *Milton and the Revolutionary Reader*, 1994; Laura Lunger Knoppers, *Historicizing Milton: Spectacle, Power, and Poetry in Restoration England*, 1994; Lana Cable, *Carnal Rhetoric: Milton's Iconoclasm and the Poetics of Desire*, 1995; John Rumrich, *Milton Unbound: Controversy and Reinterpretation*, 1996; and David Norbrook, *Writing the English Republic: Poetry, Rhetoric, and Politics, 1627–1660*, 1999.

Various approaches to Milton over the centuries can be sampled in two volumes edited by Shawcross, *Milton: The Critical Heritage, 1628–1731*, 1970, and *Milton, 1732–1801: The Critical Heritage*, 1972; in *The Romantics on Milton*, ed. Joseph Wittreich, 1970; and in *Milton: A Collection of Critical Essays*, ed. Louis L. Martz, 1966. Useful essay collections include Mary Nyquist and Margaret Ferguson, *Re-Membering Milton: Essays on the Texts and Traditions*, 1988; *Milton in Italy*, ed. Mario Di Cesare, 1991; *John Milton*, ed. Annabel Patterson, 1992; *Literary Milton: Text, Pretext, Context*, ed. Diana Benet and Michael Lieb, 1994; *Of Poetry and Politics: New Essays on Milton and His World*, ed. Paul G. Stanwood, 1995; *Milton and Republicanism*, ed. David Armitage, Armand Himy, and Quentin Skinner, 1995; *Arenas of Conflict: Milton and the Unfettered Mind*, ed. Kristin McColgan and Charles Durham, 1997; and Stephen B. Dobranski and John P. Rumrich, *Milton and Heresy*, 1998. Milton's views of women and various feminist issues are addressed in several of these collections, and centrally in Diane McColley, *Milton's Eve*, 1983; James Grantham Turner, *One Flesh: Paradisal Marriage and Sexual Relations in the Age of Milton*, 1987; Joseph Wittreich, *Feminist Milton*, 1987; and *Milton and the Idea of Woman*, ed. Julia M. Walker, 1988.

Stella Revard has written an excellent account of Milton's shorter poems, including the Latin poems, *Milton and the Tangles of Neaera's Hair: The Making of the 1645 Poems*, 1997. Rosamond Tuve, *Images and Themes in Five Poems by Milton*, 1957, can still illuminate Milton's most important shorter poems. Brown treats Milton's *Comus* and "Lycidas" in their social and political contexts in *John Milton's Aristocratic Entertainments*, 1985. Patrides has edited a useful collection of essays, *Milton's Lycidas: The Tradition and the Poem*, rev. 1983; and that poem is at the center of Joseph A Wittreich, *Visionary Poetics: Milton's Tradition and His Legacy*, 1980. Milton's prose is discussed in several important books and essays: Arthur Barker, *Milton and the Puritan Dilemma, 1641–1660*, 1942; Thomas A. Kranides, *The Fierce Equation: A Study of Milton's Decorum*, 1964; Joan Webber, *The Eloquent I: Style and Self in Seventeenth-Century Prose*, 1968; Stanley Fish, *Self-Consuming Artifacts*, 1972; Keith W. Staveley, *The Politics of Milton's Prose Style*, 1975; *Achievements of the Left Hand*, ed. Michael Lieb and Shawcross, 1974; Thomas N. Corns, *The Development of Milton's Prose Style*, 1982; and *Politics, Poetics, and Hermeneutics in Milton's Prose*, ed. David Loewenstein and James G. Turner, 1990.

Modern criticism of *Paradise Lost* still engages with issues of interpretation and generic tradition raised in C. S. Lewis, *A Preface to Paradise Lost*, 1942; C. M. Bowra, *From Virgil to Milton*, 1945; and William Empson's provocative attack on the figure of God in the poem, *Milton's God*, rev. 1965. A classic study of Milton's theology in reference to the epic is Maurice Kelley, *This Great Argument: A Study of Milton's De Doctrina Christiana as a Gloss upon Paradise Lost*, 1941; Dennis R. Danielson, *Milton's Good God: A Study in Literary Theodicy*, 1982, revisits that issue. Some important earlier critical books include Joseph Summers, *The Muse's Method: An Introduction to Paradise Lost*, 1962; Christopher Ricks, *Milton's Grand Style*, 1963; Northrop Frye, *The Return to Eden*, 1966; and Fish's very influential reader response criticism, *Surprised by Sin: The Reader in Paradise Lost*, 1967. Collections of critical essays include *Approaches to Paradise Lost*, ed. Patrides, 1968, and *New Essays on Paradise Lost*, ed. Thomas Kranidas, 1969. Concerns in some recent criticism are indicated by the titles: J. M. Evans, *Paradise Lost and the Genesis Tradition*, 1968; Lieb, *The Dialectics of Creation: Patterns of Birth and Regeneration in Paradise Lost*, 1970; John R. Knott, *Milton's Pastoral Vision*, 1971; John Steadman, *Epic and Tragic Structure in Paradise Lost*, 1976; Joan Webber, *Milton and His Epic Tradition*, 1979; Murray Roston, *Milton and the Baroque*, 1980; Maureen Quilligan, *Milton's Spenser: The Politics of Reading*, 1983; Stevie Davies, *Images of Kingship in Paradise Lost*, 1983; Barbara K. Lewalski, *Paradise Lost and the Rhetoric of Literary Forms*, 1985; David Quint, *Epic and Empire: Politics and Generic Form from Virgil to Milton*, 1993; Jason Rosenblatt, *Torah and Law in Paradise Lost*, 1994; and J. Martin Evans, *Milton's Imperial Epic: Paradise Lost and the Discourse of Colonialism*, 1996. Placing Milton's epic in relation to relevant visual traditions is the burden of a beautifully illustrated book by Roland M. Frye, *Milton's Imagery and the Visual Arts: Iconographic Traditions in the Epic Poems*, 1978; and of a broader study by Diane McColley, *A Gust for Paradise: Milton's Eden and the Visual Arts*, 1993.

Milton's brief epic, *Paradise Regained*, is the subject of Lewalski, *Milton's Brief Epic: The Genre, Meaning, and Art of Paradise Regained*, 1966; the poem is treated at some length in Loewenstein, *Milton and the Drama of History*; Knoppers, *Historicizing Milton*; Quint, *Epic and Empire*; Mary Ann Radzinowicz, *Milton's Epics and the Book of Psalms*, 1989; *Calm of Mind*, ed. Joseph Wittreich, 1971; and *The Prison and the Pinnacle*, ed. Balachandra Rajan, 1972, which also contain essays on *Samson Agonistes*. Some important works dealing with Milton's tragedy, *Samson Agonistes*, include William R. Parker, *Milton's Debt to Greek Tragedy in Samson Agonistes*, 1937; Anthony Low, *The Blaze of Noon: A Reading of Samson Agonistes*, 1974; and with reference to competing traditions of interpreting the Samson story, in Wittreich, *Interpreting Samson Agonistes*, 1986. Radzinowicz, *Toward Samson Agonistes: The Growth of Milton's Mind*, 1978, treats themes and concerns in all his writing as leading toward his great tragedy. In 1987 Patrides provided the very useful *Annotated Critical Bibliography of John Milton*.

Katherine Philips

Patrick Thomas has edited *The Collected Works of Katherine Philips: The Matchless Orinda*, 1993. Her translations of Corneille and other French works were edited by Ruth Little, 1991. There are two biographies: Philip W. Souer, *The Matchless Orinda*, 1931, and Patrick Thomas, *Katherine Philips*, 1988. Useful critical studies include Harriette Andreadis, "The Sapphic-Platonics of Katherine Philips, 1632–1664," in *Signs* 15 (1989): 34–60; Elizabeth Hageman, "Katherine Philips: The Matchless Orinda," in *Women Writers of the Renaissance and Reformation*, ed. Katharina M. Wilson, 1987; and Arlene Stiebel, "Subversive Sexuality: Masking the Erotic in Poems by Katherine Philips and Aphra Behn," in *Renaissance Discourses of Desire*, ed. Claude J. Summers and Ted-Larry Pebworth, 1993.

Lady Mary Wroth

Josephine Roberts edited *Poems*, 1983, and also *The First Part of The Countess of Montgomery's Urania*, 1995. Part II of the *Urania* is being published from the manuscript in the Newberry Library. There is a modernized edition of *Poems* edited by R. E. Pritchard, 1996. Wroth's pastoral drama, *Love's Victory*, was edited by Michael Brennan, 1988. There are biographical accounts in Roberts' introductions, and in Kim Walker, *Women Writers of the English Renaissance*, 1996. Critical studies include May Nelson Paulissen, *The Love Sonnets of Lady Mary Wroth: A Critical Introduction*, 1982; Gary Waller, *The Sidney Family Romance: Mary Wroth, William Herbert, and the Early Modern Construction of Gender*, 1993; and Naomi Miller, *Changing the Subject: Mary Wroth and Figurations of Gender in Early Modern England*, 1996. Miller and Waller have also edited a collection of essays, *Reading Mary Wroth: Representing Alternatives in Early Modern England*, 1991. Wroth's works are also treated by Maureen Quilligan in *Unfolded Tales: Essays on Renaissance Romance*, ed. George Logan and Gordon Teskey, 1989; by several hands in *The Renaissance Englishwoman in Print: Counterbalancing the Canon*, ed. Anne M. Haselkorn and Betty Travitsky, 1990; and in Barbara K. Lewalski, *Writing Women in Jacobean England*, 1993. Recent studies are surveyed in *ELR* 18 (1988) and 24 (1994).

THE RESTORATION AND THE EIGHTEENTH CENTURY

In recent decades, historians have placed less emphasis on stories about the ruling classes and their political conflicts and more on the economic and social forces that shape the lives of ordinary people. A good example of this approach is *The Peoples of the British Isles: A New History*, 3 vols., 1992; volume 2, by T. W. Heyck, covers the period from 1688 to 1870. A fuller account is provided by J. R. Jones, *Country and Court: England, 1658–1714*, 1978; W. A. Speck, *Stability and Strife: England, 1714–1760*, 1977; and Ian Christie, *Wars and Revolutions: Britain, 1760–1815*, 1982. Linda Colley, *Britons*, 1992, studies the forging of a new national identity. J. H. Plumb, *England in the Eighteenth Century*, 1950, describes the structure of society, and Roy Porter, *English Society in the Eighteenth Century*, rev. 1990, is a mine of information. John Brewer, *The Pleasures of the Imagination*, 1997, is a wide-ranging history of popular culture. The life and manners of the age are surveyed in *Johnson's England*, 2 vols., ed. A. S. Turberville, 1933; Dorothy Marshall, *English People in the Eighteenth Century*, 1956; and R. B. Schwartz, *Daily Life in Johnson's England*, 1983. *The Birth of a Consumer Society*, 1982, by Neil McKendrick, Brewer, and J. H. Plumb, traces the rise of modern commercialization in the eighteenth century. Useful guides to the historical and cultural contexts of literature include A. R. Humphreys, *The Augustan World*, 1954; Donald Greene, *The Age of Exuberance*, 1970; *The Eighteenth Century*, ed. Pat Rogers, 1978; and James Sambrook, *The Eighteenth Century, 1700–1789*, 2nd ed., 1993.

On the intellectual background of the period, Sir Leslie Stephen, *History of English Thought in the Eighteenth Century*, 2 vols., 1876, remains valuable; so do A. O. Lovejoy, *The Great Chain of Being*, 1942, and *Essays in the History of Ideas*, 1948. Basil Willey, *The Eighteenth Century Background*, 1940, studies ideas about nature, and Keith Thomas, *Man and the Natural World*, 1983, shows the development of a modern sensibility between 1500 and 1800. Gordon Rupp, *Religion in England, 1688–1791*, 1986, is dependable. Volumes 4 to 6 of F. C.

Coplestone, *History of Philosophy*, 1960, deal with the period from Descartes to Kant; Peter Gay, *The Enlightenment: An Interpretation*, 2 vols., 1969, forcefully defends the philosophers of the Age of Reason. Paul Hazard, *The European Mind, 1680–1715*, 1953, and *European Thought in the Eighteenth Century*, 1954, trans. from French by J. L. May, are readable surveys of intellectual movements on the Continent as well as in England. J. W. Johnson, *The Formation of English Neo-Classical Thought*, 1967, and J. M. Levine, *The Battle of the Books: History and Literature in the Augustan Age*, 1991, study the ways that writers came to terms with the past. Burton Feldman and R. D. Richardson, *The Rise of Modern Mythology 1680–1860*, 1972, and Gerald Newman, *The Rise of English Nationalism*, 1987, deal with important new directions of thought. Steven Shapin, *The Scientific Revolution*, 1996, is a brief clear survey. Valuable studies of the influence of scientific ideas include R. F. Jones, *Ancients and Moderns*, 1936; Marjorie Nicolson, *Newton Demands the Muse*, 1946, and *Science and the Imagination*, 1956; and W. P. Jones, *The Rhetoric of Science*, 1966. Myra Reynolds, *The Learned Lady in England, 1650–1760*, 1920, still useful, should be supplemented by Sylvia Myers, *The Bluestocking Circle*, 1990. Sensibility, a set of new ideas and feelings associated especially with women, is the subject of several good books, including Jean Hagstrum, *Sex and Sensibility*, 1970; Janet Todd, *Sensibility: An Introduction*, 1986; John Mullan, *Sentiment and Sociability*, 1988; and G. J. Barker-Benfield, *The Culture of Sensibility*, 1992. Changes in the literary marketplace are illuminated by Pat Rogers, *Grub Street*, 1972; Paula McDowell, *The Women of Grub Street*, 1998; Mark Rose, *Authors and Owners: The Invention of Copyright*, 1993; and Dustin Griffin, *Literary Patronage in England, 1650–1800*, 1996. Martin Price, *To the Palace of Wisdom: Studies in Order and Energy from Dryden to Blake*, 1964; Paul Fussell, *The Rhetorical World of Augustan Humanism*, 1965; W. J. Bate, *The Burden of the Past and the English Poet*, 1970; John Sitter, *Literary Loneliness in Mid-Eighteenth-Century England*, 1982; Howard Weinbrot, *Britannia's Issue: The Rise of British Literature from Dryden to Ossian*, 1993; and Stuart Sherman, *Telling Time: Clocks, Diaries, and English Diurnal Form, 1660–1785*, 1996, are all thoughtful and stimulating studies that relate ideas to literary art.

Good surveys of the literature of the age include George Sherburn, "The Restoration and Eighteenth Century," in *A Literary History of England*, ed. A. C. Baugh, rev. 1967, and *Dryden to Johnson*, ed. Roger Lonsdale, rev. 1987, vol. 4 of the Sphere History of Literature. Far more detailed are three volumes of the *Oxford History of English Literature*: James Sutherland, *English Literature of the Late Seventeenth Century*, 1969; Bonamy Dobrée, *English Literature in the Early Eighteenth Century, 1700–1740*, 1959; and John Butt and Geoffrey Carnall, *English Literature in the Mid-Eighteenth Century*, 1979. On women writers they need to be supple-

mented by Janet Todd, *A Dictionary of British and American Women Writers, 1660–1800*, 1985.

Among books that deal with a single literary mode, James Sutherland, *A Preface to Eighteenth-Century Poetry*, 1948, is a deft introduction, and Eric Rothstein, *Restoration and Eighteenth-Century Poetry, 1660–1780*, 1981, is a fresh, informative survey. Other useful studies include Ian Jack, *Augustan Satire*, 1952; Earl Miner, *The Restoration Mode from Milton to Dryden*, 1974; Rachel Trickett, *The Honest Muse*, 1974; Margaret Doody, *The Daring Muse*, 1985; and Robert Griffin, *Wordsworth's Pope*, 1995. Anne Williams, *Prophetic Strain*, 1984, and Richard Feingold, *Moralized Song*, 1989, both stress the lyricism of eighteenth-century poems. Two anthologies edited by Roger Lonsdale, *The New Oxford Book of Eighteenth Century Verse*, 1984, and *Eighteenth-Century Women Poets*, 1989, have sparked an interest in neglected poems about daily life; Joyce Fullard has edited *Eighteenth-Century Women Poets 1660–1800*, 1990; and David Fairer and Christine Gerrard have edited an annotated anthology, *Eighteenth-Century Poetry*, 1999.

On drama, a good introduction is R. W. Bevis, *English Drama: Restoration and Eighteenth Century, 1660–1789*, 1988. Fuller accounts appear in Allardyce Nicoll, *A History of Restoration Drama 1660–1700*, *A History of Early Eighteenth-Century Drama, 1700–1750*, and *A History of Late Eighteenth-Century Drama, 1750–1800*, rev. 1952; and *The Revels History of Drama in English*, Vol. 5, *1660–1750*, 1976, and Vol. 6, *1750–1880*, 1975. An invaluable store of detailed information is *The London Stage, 1660–1800*, 11 vols., 1960–68, the critical introductions of which have been gathered in five paperback books. Six of the most important plays of the period, together with critical commentary and background material on theaters, staging, and audience, are edited by Scott McMillin in a Norton Critical Edition, *Restoration and Eighteenth-Century Comedy*, 2nd ed., 1997. Two collections, *Restoration Dramatists*, ed. Earl Miner, 1966, and *Restoration Drama*, ed. John Loftis, 1966, provide essays in criticism by various writers; Loftis has also analyzed *Comedy and Society from Congreve to Fielding*, 1959. Walter Graham has surveyed *English Literary Periodicals*, 1930. Letter writing was an important eighteenth-century genre, discussed in *The Familiar Letter in the Eighteenth Century*, ed. Howard Anderson, P. B. Daghlian, and Irvin Ehrenpreis, 1966, and Bruce Redford, *The Converse of the Pen*, 1987. Another important genre, history writing, is examined in Karen O'Brien, *Narratives of Enlightenment*, 1997. D. A. Stauffer, *English Biography before 1700*, 1930, and *The Art of Biography in Eighteenth-Century England*, 2 vols., 1941, are standard surveys; William H. Epstein, *Recognizing Biography*, 1987, is a challenging theoretical study. Bunyan figures prominently in two books on autobiography: John N. Morris, *Versions of the Self*, 1966, and Felicity Nussbaum, *The Autobiographical Subject*, 1989. Patricia Spacks, *Imagining a Self*, 1976, discusses conceptions of personal identity in eighteenth-century autobiographies and novels.

The Cambridge Companion to the Eighteenth-Century Novel, ed. John Richetti, 1996, is a good general survey. E. A. Baker, The History of the English Novel, vols. 3–5, 1930–34, assembles many details. A. D. McKillop, The Early Masters of English Fiction, 1956, and Clive Probyn, English Fiction of the Eighteenth Century, 1700–1789, 1987, offer good introductions to major novelists. Ian Watt, The Rise of the Novel, 1957, an influential study of Defoe, Richardson, and Fielding, set off a long discussion that has been joined by Jane Spencer, The Rise of the Woman Novelist, 1986; Michael McKeon, The Origins of the English Novel, 1987; Nancy Armstrong, Desire and Domestic Fiction, 1987; J. Paul Hunter, Before Novels, 1990; Homer O. Brown, Institutions of the English Novel from Defoe to Scott, 1997; and William B. Warner, Licensing Entertainment, 1998. Interesting studies of special aspects of fiction include Lennard Davis, Factual Fictions, 1983; Terry Castle, Masquerade and Civilization, 1986; John Bender, Imagining the Penitentiary, 1987; Carol Kay, Political Constructions, 1988; and Catherine Gallagher, Nobody's Story, 1994, which has chapters on Oroonoko and Frances Burney.

The most comprehensive account of eighteenth-century criticism is vol. 4 of The Cambridge History of Literary Criticism, ed. H. B. Nisbet and Claude Rawson, 1997. J. E. Spingarn, Critical Essays of the Seventeenth Century, vols. 2 and 3, 1908 (the preface is still useful), and Scott Elledge, Eighteenth-Century Critical Essays, 2 vols., 1961, are valuable collections. R. S. Crane's "Neo-Classical Criticism," in A Dictionary of World Literature, ed. J. T. Shipley, 1943, has not been surpassed. A survey of major critical movements is provided by James Engell, Forming the Critical Mind: Dryden to Coleridge, 1989. René Wellek, A History of Modern Criticism 1750–1950, vol. 1, 1955, and W. K. Wimsatt and Cleanth Brooks, Literary Criticism: A Short History, 1957, review important issues of theory and aesthetics. Raymond Williams, Keywords: A Vocabulary of Culture and Society, 1983, examines the changing meanings of critical terms. A feminist perspective is offered by Marilyn Williamson, Raising Their Voices: British Women Writers, 1650–1750, 1990. The issues explored by Samuel H. Monk's classic study, The Sublime, 1935, have been taken up by many later critics, among them David Morris, The Religious Sublime, 1972, and Steven Knapp, Personification and the Sublime, 1985. The theory of satire has also been a perennial source of interest, most recently in John Sitter, Arguments of Augustan Wit, 1991, and Dustin Griffin, Satire: A Critical Reintroduction, 1994. Though primarily concerned with Romantic theory, M. H. Abrams, The Mirror and the Lamp, 1953, delves deeply into eighteenth-century critical ideas.

The relation of literature to other arts has been the subject of many instructive studies. Jean Hagstrum, The Sister Arts, 1958, compares paintings with poems; John Dixon Hunt, The Figure in the Landscape, 1977, deals with poetry, painting, and gardening; and Richard Wendorf, The Elements of Life, 1990, compares biography with portrait-painting. Lawrence Lipking discusses the first histories of the arts in The Ordering of the Arts in Eighteenth-Century England, 1970; Ronald Paulson, Breaking and Remaking, 1989, explores aesthetic practice from 1700 to 1820; and Murray Roston analyzes Changing Perspectives in Literature and the Visual Arts 1650–1820, 1990. B. Sprague Allen, Tides of English Taste 1619–1800, 2 vols., 1937, on architecture, gardening, and decoration, and Sir Kenneth Clark, The Gothic Revival, 2nd ed., 1950, on architecture, chronicle significant changes in style.

Good collections of criticism have been edited by James L. Clifford, Eighteenth-Century English Literature: Modern Essays in Criticism, 1959, and Leopold Damrosch, Modern Essays on Eighteenth-Century Literature, 1988. Essays that explore new theoretical approaches are collected by Felicity Nussbaum and Laura Brown, The New Eighteenth Century, 1987. Studies in English Literature devotes its summer issue to the Restoration and the eighteenth century and includes an article reviewing important work published in the preceding year. Finally, for elaborate bibliographies and reviews of eighteenth-century studies, the student may consult the bibliography of English literature, 1660–1800, that has appeared annually since 1926 in Philological Quarterly and, since 1976, in yearly volumes, The Eighteenth Century: A Current Bibliography.

Aphra Behn

Janet Todd has edited The Works of Aphra Behn, 7 vols., 1992–96. The Norton Critical Edition of Oroonoko, ed. Joanna Lipking, 1997, includes relevant historical backgrounds and criticism. The paucity of reliable facts about Behn's life prevents any biography from being authoritative, but Maureen Duffy, The Passionate Shepherdess, 1977, is worth reading, and Janet Todd, The Secret Life of Aphra Behn, 1997, is full of interesting speculations and fresh information. Wylie Sypher, Guinea's Captive Kings, 1942, puts Oroonoko in the context of antislavery literature. Mary Ann O'Donnell, Aphra Behn: An Annotated Bibliography, 1986, is a thorough review of primary and secondary sources through 1985.

James Boswell

Modern revaluations of Boswell began with the publication of The Private Papers of James Boswell from Malahide Castle, ed. Geoffrey Scott and Frederick A. Pottle, 18 vols., 1928–34. Pottle described the history of the papers in Pride and Negligence, 1981. A trade edition of Boswell's Journals, 14 vols., 1950–89, has valuable introductions and notes. The Letters, ed. C. B. Tinker, 2 vols., 1924, need to be supplemented by the recovered Correspondence of James Boswell, 1966–97, of which seven volumes have been published. The best edition of the Life of Johnson is L. F. Powell's revision of G. B. Hill's edition, 6 vols., 1934–64. A good one-volume edition by R. W. Chapman and J. D. Fleeman, 1982, is available in paperback.

F. A. Pottle, *James Boswell, The Earlier Years, 1740–1769*, 1966, and Frank Brady, *James Boswell, The Later Years, 1769–1795*, 1984, are the two halves of the standard biography, judicious and well informed. Pottle, *The Literary Career of James Boswell*, 1929, and Mary Hyde, *The Impossible Friendship: Boswell and Mrs. Thrale*, 1972, are both useful. B. H. Bronson, "Boswell's Boswell," in *Johnson and Boswell*, 1944, is a wise and sympathetic study; and J. L. Smith-Dampier, *Who's Who in Boswell?*, 1935, is a helpful guide through the *Life of Johnson*. Greg Clingham has edited a collection of essays, *New Light on Boswell*, 1991.

Frances Burney

The *Diary and Letters* were first edited in a truncated version by Charlotte Barrett, Burney's niece, 7 vols., 1842–46. The original texts of *The Journals and Letters of Fanny Burney (Madame d'Arblay), 1791–1840*, 12 vols., have been superbly edited by Joyce Hemlow et al., 1972–84. Several volumes of *The Early Journals and Letters of Fanny Burney, 1768–1791*, which will eventually fill ten or twelve volumes, have been edited by Lars Troide et al., 1988–94. There is no standard edition of the novels, but Peter Sabor has edited *The Complete Plays of Frances Burney*, 2 vols., 1995. Joyce Hemlow wrote the standard biography, *The History of Fanny Burney*, 1958, and Margaret Doody's critical biography, *Frances Burney: The Life in the Works*, 1988, is lively and thought provoking.

William Collins

The *Works* of Collins, which amount only to one slim volume, have been well edited by Richard Wendorf and Charles Ryskamp, 1979. Lonsdale's edition (see **Gray**) has copious notes. P. L. Carver, *The Life of a Poet*, 1967, is the fullest biography. Wendorf, *William Collins and Eighteenth-Century English Poetry*, 1981, is a fine critical study.

William Cowper

The *Poems*, 3 vols., have been expertly edited by John D. Baird and Charles Ryskamp, 1980–95. James Sambrook's edition of *The Task and Selected Other Poems*, 1994, has useful notes. James King and Ryskamp have edited Cowper's *Letters and Prose Writings*, 5 vols., 1979–86, and one volume of *Selected Letters*, 1989. King, *William Cowper: A Biography*, 1986, is the best full life; Ryskamp's fine *William Cowper of the Inner Temple, Esq.*, 1959, ends in 1768. Useful critical studies include Morris Golden, *In Search of Stability: The Poetry of William Cowper*, 1960; Vincent Newey, *Cowper's Poetry*, 1982; Martin Priestman, *Cowper's Task*, 1983; and the last chapter of Donald Davie, *The Eighteenth-Century Hymn in England*, 1993.

John Dryden

James A. Winn's *John Dryden and His World*, 1987, is the best biography. G. R. Noyes's edition of the *Poetical Works*, 2nd ed., 1950, includes a good bio-

graphical sketch; and Samuel Johnson's *Life of Dryden* is still worth reading. A fine scholarly edition of the *Works*, launched in 1956, under the general editorship first of E. N. Hooker, then H. T. Swedenberg, and lately Alan Roper, has reached twenty volumes. Keith Walker has edited a useful selected *Works*, 1987. The poems have been edited by James Kinsley, 4 vols., 1958, and the essays by W. P. Ker, 2 vols., 1900, and George Watson, 2 vols., 1962. Paul Hammond's new edition of the poems has useful notes; the first two volumes appeared in 1995.

Mark Van Doren, *John Dryden: A Study of His Poetry*, 1920, remains valuable for its fresh critical responses, as do T. S. Eliot's brief studies, *Homage to John Dryden*, 1924, and *John Dryden the Poet, the Dramatist, and the Critic*, 1932. Important modern criticism includes Arthur Hoffman, *John Dryden's Imagery*, 1962; Alan Roper, *Dryden's Poetic Kingdoms*, 1965; and Earl Miner, *Dryden's Poetry*, 1967. David Hopkins, *John Dryden*, 1986, is a good introduction. Steven Zwicker has studied *Politics and Language in Dryden's Poetry*, 1984. The standard work on Dryden's philosophical and religious ideas is Philip Harth, *Contexts of Dryden's Thought*, 1968, and Harth has also analyzed the politics of *Absalom and Achitophel* in *Pen for a Party*, 1993. Robert Hume analyzes *Dryden's Criticism*, 1970; Edward Pechter, *Dryden's Classical Theory of Literature*, 1975; and John C. Aden brings together *The Critical Opinions of John Dryden, A Dictionary*, 1963, under convenient headings. James Winn has edited *Critical Essays on John Dryden*, 1997.

Olaudah Equiano

A facsimile of the first edition of the *Interesting Narrative* was published by Paul Edwards, 2 vols., 1969. Equiano's later revisions of the *Narrative* and other writings have been edited, with useful notes, by Vincent Carretta, 1995. Carretta includes Equiano as well as other eighteenth-century black authors in a good anthology, *Unchained Voices*, 1996. Angelo Costanzo, *Surprizing Narrative: Olaudah Equiano and the Beginnings of Black Autobiography*, 1987; Keith Sandiford, *Measuring the Moment: Strategies of Protest in Eighteenth-Century Afro-English Writing*, 1988; and Peter Fryer, *Staying Power: The History of Black People in Britain*, 1984, place Equiano amid the debates of his time.

Anne Finch, Countess of Winchilsea

Myra Reynolds added a long biographical introduction to her valuable edition of the *Poems*, 1903, which needs to be supplemented by *The Anne Finch Wellesley Manuscript Poems*, ed. Barbara McGovern and Charles Hinnant, 1998. McGovern has written a good critical biography, *Anne Finch and Her Poetry*, 1992. Hinnant, *The Poetry of Anne Finch*, 1994, is an essay in interpretation.

Thomas Gray

The poems of Gray, Collins, and Goldsmith have been edited, with informative notes, by Roger Lonsdale, 1969. The standard edition of Gray's *Works* remains that of Edmund Gosse, 4 vols., rev. 1902–

6; of the *Correspondence*, that of Paget Toynbee and Leonard Whibley, 3 vols., 1935; of the poems, that of H. W. Starr and J. R. Hendrickson, 1966. R. W. Ketton-Cremer, *Thomas Gray*, 1955, is the best biography. Among critical studies, Henry Weinfield, *The Poet without a Name: Gray's Elegy and the Problem of History*, 1991, is thoughtful and searching, and B. Eugene McCarthy, *Thomas Gray: The Progress of a Poet*, 1997, is a good general introduction. *From Sensibility to Romanticism*, ed. F. W. Hilles and Harold Bloom, 1965, includes studies of the *Elegy* by Ian Jack, B. H. Bronson, and Frank Brady.

William Hogarth

The standard, comprehensive critical biography is Ronald Paulson, *Hogarth*, 3 vols., 1991–93. Jenny Uglow, *Hogarth: A Life and a World*, 1997, is perceptive and lively. Paulson has edited *Hogarth's Graphic Works*, 2 vols., 1970, as well as *The Analysis of Beauty*, 1998. The paintings are catalogued by R. B. Beckett, *Hogarth*, 1949, and the drawings by A. P. Oppé, *The Drawings of William Hogarth*, 1948. Sean Shesgreen has edited *Engravings by Hogarth*, 1973, in a generous and inexpensive format. *Hogarth on High Life*, 1970, illuminates *Marriage A-la-Mode* with the famous eighteenth-century commentaries by Georg Christoph Lichtenberg, translated and edited by Arthur Wensinger with W. B. Coley. David Bindman, *Hogarth*, 1981, is a good brief introduction to the art, and Bindman and Scott Wilcox have edited *Among the Whores and Thieves*, 1997, a collection of essays on Hogarth and *The Beggar's Opera*.

Samuel Johnson

Others among Johnson's friends besides Boswell wrote of him: notably, Hester Lynch Thrale Piozzi, whose *Anecdotes* (1786) have been edited, along with William Shaw's *Anecdotes*, by Arthur Sherbo, 1974; Sir John Hawkins, whose *Life* (1787) has been edited and abridged by Bertram H. Davis, 1961; and Frances Burney (Mme D'Arblay), from whose diary C. B. Tinker extracted the Johnsonian passages in *Dr. Johnson and Fanny Burney*, 1911. Pat Rogers, *The Samuel Johnson Encyclopedia*, 1996, is a handy source of information. James L. Clifford, *Young Sam Johnson*, 1955, and *Dictionary Johnson*, 1979, are well-informed studies of the early and middle years that supplement Boswell's rather sketchy account of Johnson's life before their meeting in 1763. There are fine modern biographies by John Wain, 1975, and W. J. Bate, 1977.

The best collected edition of Johnson's *Works* appeared as long ago as 1825. It is being replaced by an excellent scholarly edition, published by Yale, that has been coming out irregularly since 1958. The poems have been edited by D. N. Smith and E. L. McAdam, 2nd ed. rev. by J. D. Fleeman, 1974. G. B. Hill's editions of *Johnsonian Miscellanies*, 2 vols., 1897, and *The Lives of the Poets*, 3 vols., 1905, are still worth consulting for their fine notes. Bruce Redford's edition of the *Letters*, 5 vols., 1992–94, is superb. The *Dictionary* is available on CD-ROM, ed. Anne McDermott, 1996.

Robert DeMaria, *The Life of Samuel Johnson*, 1993, and Lawrence Lipking, *Samuel Johnson: The Life of an Author*, 1998, offer critical overviews of Johnson's literary career. Thomas Woodman, *A Preface to Samuel Johnson*, 1993, and *The Cambridge Companion to Samuel Johnson*, ed. Greg Clingham, 1997, are useful guides. Among critical introductions, W. J. Bate, *The Achievement of Samuel Johnson*, 1955, is inspiring, and Paul Fussell, *Samuel Johnson and the Life of Writing*, 1971, is lively. Good specialized studies include W. K. Wimsatt, *The Prose Style of Samuel Johnson*, 1941; Donald J. Greene, *The Politics of Samuel Johnson*, 2nd ed., 1990; Carey McIntosh, *The Choice of Life: Samuel Johnson and the World of Fiction*, 1973; Robert Folkenflik, *Samuel Johnson, Biographer*, 1978; Nicholas Hudson, *Samuel Johnson and Eighteenth-Century Thought*, 1988; and John Cannon, *Samuel Johnson and the Politics of Hanoverian England*, 1994. Joseph E. Brown collected *The Critical Opinions of Samuel Johnson*, 1926. Jean Hagstrum's fine study of *Samuel Johnson's Literary Criticism*, 1952, has been complemented by Leopold Damrosch, *The Uses of Johnson's Criticism*, 1976, and G. F. Parker, *Johnson's Shakespeare*, 1989. DeMaria, *Johnson's Dictionary and the Language of Learning*, 1986, looks at the range of ideas gathered by Johnson, and Allen Reddick has studied *The Making of Johnson's Dictionary, 1746–1773*, rev. 1996. J. L. Clifford and D. J. Greene's survey and bibliography of critical studies, rev. 1970, was updated through 1985 by Greene and J. A. Vance, 1987.

Lady Mary Wortley Montagu

Isobel Grundy's full-scale biography, *Lady Mary Wortley Montagu: Comet of the Enlightenment*, 1999, adds much information to Robert Halsband's elegant *Life of Lady Mary Wortley Monagu*, 1956. Halsband also edited *The Complete Letters*, 3 vols., 1965–67; *Selected Letters*, 1970; and with Grundy, *Essays and Poems and Simplicity, a Comedy*, 2nd ed., 1993. Grundy has edited the *Romance Writings*, 1996.

Alexander Pope

There is no reliable complete edition of Pope's works. Although defective in many respects, the Victorian edition by Whitwell Elwin and J. W. Courthope, 10 vols., 1871–89, must still be consulted (with caution). The excellent Twickenham Edition of the poems, 11 vols., 1939–67, a cooperative undertaking by several scholars (under John Butt), includes valuable introductory and critical materials and notes. A convenient selection in a single volume, with selected notes, omits the translations of Homer. *The Prose Works* have been edited in 2 vols., by Norman Ault, 1936, and Rosemary Cowler, 1986.

Maynard Mack, *Alexander Pope: A Life*, 1986, is a full and sympathetic biography. George Sherburn, *Early Career of Alexander Pope*, 1934, and Mack, *The Garden and the City*, 1969, on Pope's later career, are valuable studies. David Foxon, *Pope and* the Early Eighteenth-Century Book Trade, 1991, and Brean Hammond, *Professional Imaginative Writing in England, 1670–1740*, 1997, treat Pope's concern with the business of publication. Howard Erskine-Hill has described *The Social Milieu of Alexander Pope*, 1975, and Valerie Rumbold examined *Women's Place in Pope's World*, 1989. Sherburn's edition of the *Correspondence*, 5 vols., 1956, is standard. R. H. Griffith, *Alexander Pope: A Bibliography*, 2 vols., 1962, is a detailed list of Pope's writings.

A good critical introduction to the poems is Geoffrey Tillotson, *On the Poetry of Pope*, 2nd ed., 1950; and Tillotson, *Pope and Human Nature*, 1958, throws light on a difficult subject. David B. Morris, *Alexander Pope: The Genius of Sense*, 1984, offers fine criticism of individual poems. Reuben A. Brower, *Alexander Pope: The Poetry of Allusion*, 1959, is an enlightening study of Pope's lifelong habit of adapting phrases, images, and ideas from earlier poets, especially those of classical antiquity. Much information is gathered up in Robert W. Rogers, *The Major Satires of Alexander Pope*, 1955. Austin Warren, *Alexander Pope as Critic and Humanist*, 1929, is dated but still useful. Aubrey Williams has analyzed *Pope's Dunciad*, 1955, and John Sitter, *The Poetry of Pope's Dunciad*, 1971. Several essays on Pope are included in Maynard Mack, *Collected in Himself*, 1982. Mack has also edited *Essential Articles for the Study of Alexander Pope*, 1964, and with James Winn, *Pope: Recent Essays*, 1980. *The Enduring Legacy*, ed. G. S. Rousseau and Pat Rogers, 1988, collects new essays on Pope, and Brean Hammond has edited *Pope*, 1996, a critical reader.

Jonathan Swift

Irvin Ehrenpreis's standard, comprehensive biography, *Swift: The Man, His Works, and the Age*, consists of three volumes: *Mr. Swift and His Contemporaries*, 1962, *Dr. Swift*, 1967, and *Dean Swift*, 1983. J. A. Downie, *Jonathan Swift, Political*

Writer, 1984, and David Nokes, *Jonathan Swift, A Hypocrite Reversed*, 1985, are good introductions to the life and writings. Louis A. Landa, *Swift and the Church of Ireland*, 1954, is a valuable special study.

The standard edition of the poems is by Sir Harold Williams, 2 vols., 1937, rev., 1958. Pat Rogers's edition of Swift's *Complete Poems*, 1983, is reliable and less expensive. Herbert Davis has edited the prose works in fourteen volumes, 1939–68. Swift's *Correspondence* was edited by Williams, 5 vols., 1963–65. Other distinguished editions include Davis, *The Drapier's Letters*, 1935; Williams, *Journal to Stella*, 2 vols., 1948; A. C. Guthkelch and D. Nichol Smith, *A Tale of a Tub*, 2nd ed., 1958; and Frank H. Ellis, *A Discourse of the Contests and Dissentions between the Nobles and the Commons in Athens and Rome*, 1967. For the Norton Critical Editions series, Robert Greenberg has edited *Gulliver's Travels*, rev. 1971, and with W. B. Piper, *The Writings of Jonathan Swift*, 1973.

Among the abundant critical studies, the student should find especially helpful Ricardo Quintana, *The Mind and Art of Jonathan Swift*, 1936, and *Swift: An Introduction*, 1955. Arthur Case, *Four Essays on Gulliver's Travels*, Herbert Davis, *Jonathan Swift: Essays on his Satire and Other Studies*, 1964; C. J. Rawson, *Gulliver and the Gentle Reader*, 1973; and Robert Phiddian, *Swift's Parodies*, 1995, are all useful. After long neglect, Swift's poems have attracted a wealth of criticism; some of the best has been collected by David Vieth, *Essential Articles for the study of Jonathan Swift's Poetry*, 1984. Three books by Robert C. Elliott, *The Power of Satire*, 1960, *The Shape of Utopia*, 1970, and *The Literary Persona*, 1982, contain interesting chapters on Swift; so do Edward Said, *The World, the Text, and the Critic*, 1983, and Carol Houlihan Flynn, *The Body in Swift and Defoe*, 1990. Two good collections of essays are *Jonathan Swift: A Critical Anthology*, ed. Denis Donoghue, 1971, and *The Character of Swift's Satire*, ed. C. J. Rawson, 1983.

THE ROMANTIC PERIOD

Bibliographies

The most convenient starting points are the surveys by Frank Jordan and others in *The English Romantic Poets, a Review of Research and Criticism*, rev. 1985, on Blake, Wordsworth, Coleridge, Byron, Shelley, and Keats; and Carolyn W. Houtchens and Lawrence H. Houtchens, *The English Romantic Poets and Essayists*, rev. 1966, on Blake, the lesser poets, and the principal essayists. Annual bibliographies of publications about these writers are to be found in *ELH*, 1937–49; *Philological Quarterly*, 1950–64; *English Language Notes*, 1965–79; and *The Romantic Movement: A Selective and Critical Bibliography*, ed. David V. Erdman, 1980–. See also the topical bibliographies in *The Cambridge Companion to British Romanticism*, ed. Stuart Curran, 1993.

Political and Social, and Intellectual Backgrounds

Succinct treatments of the political and social events in this period are the relevant chapters of G. M. Trevelyan, *British History of the Nineteenth Century*, 2nd ed., 1937, and *English Social History*, 1942. More detailed histories are Asa Briggs, *The Making of Modern England: 1783–1867*, 1959; J. Steven Watson, *The Reign of George III, 1760–1815*, 1960; E. P. Thompson, *The Making of the English Working Class*, 1963, and *Customs in Common*, 1991; Marilyn Butler, *Romantics, Rebels, and Reactionaries: English Literature and Its Background, 1760–1830*, 1982; and M. J. Daunton, *Progress and Poverty: An Economic and Social History of Britain, 1700–1850*, 1995. See also Carl Woodring, *Politics in English Romantic Poetry*, 1970;

James Chandler, *England in 1819: The Politics of Literary Culture and the Case of Romantic Historicism*, 1998; and the separate essays in *Romanticism, Race, and Imperial Culture, 1780–1834*, ed. Alan Richardson and Sonia Hofkosh, 1996.

For English literary relations to the French Revolution, see *The Debate on the French Revolution, 1789–1800*, 2nd ed., ed. Alfred Cobban, 1960; Howard Mumford Jones, *Revolution and Romanticism*, 1974; Ronald Paulson, *Representations of Revolution (1789–1820)*, 1983; *Burke, Paine, Godwin, and the Revolution Controversy*, ed. Marilyn Butler, 1984; H. T. Dickinson, *British Radicalism and the French Revolution, 1789–1815*, 1985; Seamus Deane, *The French Revolution and Enlightenment in England, 1789–1832*, 1988; Barton R. Friedman, *Fabricating History: English Writers on the French Revolution*, 1988; Simon Bainbridge, *Napoleon and English Romanticism*, 1995; Kevin Gilmartin, *Print Politics: The Press and Radical Opposition in Early Nineteenth-Century England*, 1996; *The French Revolution and British Culture*, ed. Ceri Crossley and Ian Small, 1989; and *The French Revolution and British Popular Politics*, ed. Mark Philp, 1991.

Illuminating analyses of important intellectual movements will be found in A. O. Lovejoy's *The Great Chain of Being*, 1936, chapters 9 and 10, and *Essays in the History of Ideas*, 1948. Other particularly useful works on intellectual history are Basil Willey, *Nineteenth Century Studies: Coleridge to Matthew Arnold*, 1949; Hoxie Neale Fairchild, *Religious Trends in English Poetry*, of which vol. 3 (1949) deals with 1780–1830; H. W. Piper, *The Active Universe: Pantheism and the Concept of Imagination in the English Romantic Poets*, 1962; and James Engell, *The Creative Imagination: Enlightenment to Romanticism*, 1981. Marilyn Gaull, *English Romanticism: The Human Context*, 1988; and Robert M. Ryan, *The Romantic Reformation: Religious Politics in English Literature, 1789–1824*, 1997. On Romantic literature in its social matrix, see Raymond Williams, *Culture and Society, 1780–1950*, 1960; Jon Klancher, *The Making of English Reading Audiences, 1790–1832*, 1987; Alan Richardson, *Literature, Education, and Romanticism: Reading as Social Practice, 1780–1832*, 1994; and Lee Erickson, *The Economy of Literary Form: English Literature and the Industrialization of Publishing, 1800–1850*, 1996.

Literary History and Criticism

Among the histories of Romantic literature are W. L. Renwick's rather inadequate *English Literature, 1789–1815*, 1963; Ian Jack, *English Literature, 1815–1832*, 1963; and J. R. de J. Jackson, *Poetry of the Romantic Period*, 1980. Mario Praz, *The Romantic Agony*, 2nd ed., 1951, treats Satansim, sadism, vampirism, and others of the more exotic literary interests of the time; G. R. Thompson has edited *The Gothic Imagination: Essays in Dark Romanticism*, 1974; and Peter L. Thorslev Jr.'s *The Byronic Hero: Types and Prototypes*, 1962, discusses the solitary or alienated hero in other writers, as well

as Byron; see also Frank Kermode, *Romantic Image*, 1957, on the concept of the poet at odds with society, from the Romantic period to Yeats. Douglas Bush, *Mythology and the Romantic Tradition in English Poetry*, 1937, is so broad in its range that it constitutes an excellent survey of Romantic poetry in general. Wilson Knight, *The Starlit Dome*, 1941, is an influential early example of the approach to Romantic poets by the analysis of characteristic patterns of imagery. Harold Bloom, *The Visionary Company*, rev. 1971, which relates these poets to the prophetic tradition of Spenser and Milton, includes brief and stimulating commentaries on many of the important poems; Bloom, *The Ringers in the Tower*, 1971, consists of essays on both nineteenth- and twentieth-century "Romantic" writers. David Perkins treats Wordsworth, Shelley, and Keats, in *The Quest for Permanence*, 1959; and Northrop Frye presents an archetypal overview in *A Study of English Romanticism*, 1968. In *Natural Supernaturalism: Tradition and Revolution in Romantic Literature*, 1971, and more recently in *The Correspondent Breeze: Essays on English Romanticism*, 1984, M. H. Abrams deals with persistent themes, concepts, and designs in English and German Romantic literature, and stresses their relation both to the biblical tradition and to the intellectual ambiance of a revolutionary age. Other useful books to be noted are Thomas Weiskel, *The Romantic Sublime: Studies in the Structure and Psychology of Transcendence*, 1976; Anne K. Mellor, *English Romantic Irony*, 1980; Thomas McFarland, *Romanticism and the Forms of Ruin: Wordsworth, Coleridge, and Modalities of Fragmentation*, 1981; Jerome J. McGann, *The Romantic Ideology*, 1983; Charles J. Rzepka, *The Self as Mind: Vision and Identity in Wordsworth, Coleridge, and Keats*, 1986; Clifford Siskin, *The Historicity of Romantic Discourse*, 1988; Peter J. Manning, *Reading Romantics: Texts and Contexts*, 1990; William H. Galperin, *The Return of the Visible in British Romanticism*, 1993; and Jerome McGann, *The Poetics of Sensibility: A Revolution in Literary Style*, 1996. *English Romantic Poets: Modern Essays in Criticism*, ed. M. H. Abrams, 1975, is a collection of representative essays by influential contemporary critics; *Romanticism and Consciousness: Essays in Criticism*, 1970, focuses on some prominent topics in Romantic literature. See also the essays in *Romantic Poetry: Recent Revisionary Criticism*, Kroeber and Gene W. Ruoff, 1993. For critical opinions of the poets during their own lifetime, see Donald H. Reiman, *The Romantics Reviewed: Contemporary Reviews of British Romantic Writers*, 9 vols., 1972.

Following are studies of various forms of Romantic literature. On literary criticism: M. H. Abrams, *The Mirror and the Lamp: Romantic Theory and the Critical Tradition*, 1953; René Wellek, *A History of Modern Criticism: 1750–1950*, vol. 2, *The Romantic Age*, 1955. On poetic genres: Stuart Curran, *Poetic Form and British Romanticism*, 1986, and Susan J. Wolfson, *Formal Charges: The Shaping of Poetry in British Romanticism*, 1997. On the fragment: Marjorie Levinson, *The Romantic Fragment Poem*, 1986. On narrative poetry: Karl Kroeber, *Romantic Narrative Art*, 1960, and Brian Wilkie, *Romantic Poets and Epic Tradition*, 1965. On the novel: Ernest A. Baker, *The History of the English Novel*, vol. 6, 1961; Montague Summers, *The Gothic Quest: A History of the Gothic Novel*, 1938; and Robert Kiely, *The Romantic Novel in England*, 1972. On drama: Allardyce Nicoll, *History of Early Nineteenth-Century Drama, 1800–50*, 2 vols., rev. 1955. On the essay: William F. Bryan and Ronald S. Crane, Introduction, *The English Familiar Essay*, 1916; Marie H. Law, *The English Familiar Essay in the Early Nineteenth Century*, 1934. See also Annette Wheeler Cafarelli, *Prose in the Age of Poets: Romanticism and Biographical Narrative from Johnson to De Quincey*, 1990.

On women writers of the period, see Sandra M. Gilbert and Susan Gubar, *The Madwoman in the Attic: The Woman Writer and the Nineteenth-Century Literary Imagination*, 1979; Mary Poovey, *The Proper Lady and the Woman Writer: Ideology as Style in the Works of Mary Wollstonecraft, Mary Shelley, and Jane Austen*, 1984; Margaret Homans, *Bearing the Word: Language and Female Experience in Nineteenth-Century Women's Writing*, 1986; Marlon B. Ross, *The Contours of Masculine Desire: Romanticism and the Rise of Women's Poetry*, 1989; Gary Kelly, *Women, Writing, and Revolution, 1790–1827*, 1993; Anne K. Mellor, *Romanticism and Gender*, 1993; Judith Pascoe, *Romantic Theatricality: Gender, Poetry, and Spectatorship*, 1997; *Romanticism and Feminism*, ed. Anne K. Mellor, 1988; *Re-Visioning Romanticism: British Women Writers, 1776–1837*, ed. Carol Shiner Wilson and Joel Haefner, 1994; and *Romantic Women Writers: Voices and Countervoices*, ed. Paula R. Feldman and Theresa M. Kelley, 1995.

Anna Letitia Barbauld

The Poems of Anna Letitia Barbauld, ed. William McCarthy and Elizabeth Kraft, 1994, is now the standard edition. For biography, see Betsy Rodgers, *Georgian Chronicle: Mrs. Barbauld and Her Family*, 1958. Among recent critical essays, see Julie Ellison, "The Politics of Fancy in the Age of Sensibility," in *Re-Visioning Romanticism*, ed. Wilson and Haefner, 1994; William Keach, "A Regency Prophecy and the End of Anna Barbauld's Career," *Studies in Romanticism*, 1994; Isobel Armstrong, "The Gush of the Feminine," in *Romantic Women Writers*, ed. Feldman and Kelley, 1995; and William McCarthy, "Repression, Desire, and Gender in Anna Letitia Barbauld's Early Poems," also in Feldman and Kelley.

William Blake

The beautifully printed *The Complete Writings of William Blake*, ed. Geoffrey Keynes, 1957, has been replaced as the scholar's edition by *The Poetry and Prose of William Blake*, ed. David Erdman and Harold Bloom, rev. 1982, which includes painstaking textual notes and brief commentaries on many of the poems. Erdman also prepared a modernized text

of all Blake's verse, with copious explanatory notes by W. H. Stevenson, *The Poems of William Blake* (Longman-Norton Annotated English Poets), 1971. A useful annotated selection of *Blake's Poetry and Designs* has been edited by Mary Lynn Johnson and John E. Grant, 1979. There is a *Life of William Blake* by Mona Wilson, 1927, rev. 1948, and Raymond Lister's *William Blake: An Introduction to the Man and His Work*, 1968; but the first full account, Alexander Gilchrist's *The Life of William Blake*, which appeared in 1863, has been a source book for all later biographers and is available (edited and supplemented by Ruthven Todd) in Everyman's Library, 1945. The most recent biographies are James King's *William Blake: His Life*, 1991, and Peter Ackroyd's *Blake*, 1996. See also *A Concordance to the Writings of William Blake*, ed. David V. Erdman, 1967.

The modern era of the scholarly explication of Blake symbolism was begun by S. Foster Damon's *William Blake: His Philosophy and Symbols*, 1924; the same scholar also published a *Blake Dictionary: The Ideas and Symbols of William Blake*, 1965. Among later books, some of the most useful are Northrop Frye's classic analysis of Blake's moral allegory, *Fearful Symmetry*, 1947; Mark Schorer's study of Blake's characteristic union of political, moral, and religious radicalism, *William Blake: The Politics of Vision*, 1946; David V. Erdman's investigation of the relation of Blake's poetry to the historical events of his time, *Blake: Prophet against Empire*, rev. 1969; Peter Fisher's exposition of Blake's thought, *The Valley of Vision*, 1961; Harold Bloom's commentaries on the individual poems, *Blake's Apocalypse: A Study in Poetic Argument*, 1963; Thomas R. Frosch, *The Awakening of Albion: The Renovation of the Body in the Poetry of William Blake*, 1973; J. A. Wittreich, *Angel of Apocalypse: Blake's Idea of Milton*, 1975; W. J. T. Mitchell, *Blake's Composite Art: A Study of the Illuminated Poetry*, 1978; Leopold Damrosch Jr., *Symbol and Truth in Blake's Myth*, 1980; Robert N. Essick, *William Blake and the Language of Albion*, 1989; Morris Eaves, *The Counter-Arts Conspiracy: Art and Identity in the Age of Blake*, 1992; and E. P. Thompson, *Witness against the Beast: William Blake and the Moral Law*, 1993.

H. M. Margoliouth, *William Blake*, 1951, and Martin K. Nurmi, *William Blake*, 1976, are useful general introductions to the man and his work. Studies emphasizing the shorter poems are Hazard Adams, *William Blake: A Reading of the Shorter Poems*, 1963; Robert F. Gleckner, *The Piper and the Bard*, 1959; E. D. Hirsch Jr., *Innocence and Experience: An Introduction to Blake*, 1964; and Brian Wilkie, *Blake's Thel and Oothoon*, 1990. *Blake's Sublime Allegory*, ed. Stuart Curran and Joseph Anthony Wittreich Jr., 1973, includes essays by various scholars on the major prophecies, *The Four Zoas, Milton*, and *Jerusalem*. On Blake's graphic work see David Bindman, *Blake as an Artist*, 1977; Robert N. Essick, *William Blake, Printmaker*, 1980; Morris Eaves, *William Blake's Theory of Art*, 1982;

and Joseph Vicomi, *Blake and the Idea of the Book*, 1993. There is a large and growing list of books that reproduce (some of them in color) Blake's etched poems, drawings, and engravings; especially useful are *The Illuminated Blake*, ed. David V. Erdman, 1974, of which the subtitle describes the contents: "All of William Blake's Illuminated Works with a Plate-by-Plate Commentary," and Erdman's reproduction, with transcripts and commentary, of *The Notebooks of William Blake*, rev. 1977. The Blake Trust has issued a splendid series of color reproductions of a number of Blake's illuminated works, in expensive limited editions, printed by the Trianon Press.

Robert Burns

The standard references for Burns's poems are the Centenary Edition, ed. W. E. Henley and T. F. Henderson, 4 vols., 1896–97, and *The Poems and Songs of Robert Burns*, ed. James Kinsley, 3 vols., 1968. A good one-volume edition is that by James Kinsley, Oxford Standard Authors. 1969. J. De Lancey Ferguson has given us a reliable edition of *The Letters of Robert Burns*, 2 vols., 1931 (2nd ed., ed. G. Ross Roy, 1985) and a brilliant portrait of Burns, *Pride and Passion*, 1939. The most recent among many biographies are James Mackay, *A Biography of Robert Burns*, 1992; Ian McIntyre, *Dirt and Deity: A Life of Robert Burns*, 1995; and Hugh Douglas, *Robert Burns: The Tinder Heart*, 1996. David Daiches, *Robert Burns*, 1950, provides a critical analysis of the major poems, and Thomas Crawford, *Burns: A Study of the Poems and Songs*, 1960, is a detailed and comprehensive commentary. See also Raymond Bentman, *Robert Burns*, 1987, and *Robert Burns and Cultural Authority*, ed. Robert Crawford, 1997.

George Gordon, Lord Byron

For the poetry, the standard is *Lord Byron: The Complete Poetical Works*, ed. Jerome J. McGann, 7 vols., 1980–93; for the letters, *Byron's Letters and Journals*, ed. Leslie A. Marchand, 12 vols., 1973–82 (with a supplementary volume in 1994); Marchand has also edited the one-volume *Selected Letters and Journals*, 1982. Ernest J. Lovell Jr., *His Very Self and Voice*, 1954, is a compilation of Byron's conversations. The standard biography, a circumstantial and objective narrative, is Marchand, *Byron: A Biography*, 3 vols., 1957; a one-volume condensation by Marchand is *Byron: A Portrait*, 1970. See also Louis Crompton, *Byron and Greek Love: Homophobia in 19th-Century England*, 1985.

Among the many useful books on Byron as poet are Andrew Rutherford, *Byron: A Critical Study*, 1961; Peter L. Thorslev Jr., *The Byronic Hero*, 1962; Jerome J. McGann, *Fiery Dust: Byron's Poetic Development*, 1968; Paul G. Trueblood, *Lord Byron*, rev. 1977; Peter J. Manning, *Byron and His Fictions*, 1978; Frederick L. Beaty, *Byron the Satirist*, 1985; Caroline Franklin, *Byron's Heroines*, 1992; and Jerome Christensen, *Lord Byron's Strength: Romantic Writing and Commercial Society*, 1993. See also *Critical Essays on Lord Byron*, ed. Robert F. Gleckner, 1991, and *Rereading Byron*, ed. Alice Levine and Robert N. Keane, 1993.

The variorum edition of *Don Juan* by Truman Guy Steffan and Willis W. Pratt, 4 vols., 1957, provides an elaborate record of changes that Byron made in his manuscripts; the first volume, by Steffan, is an extended commentary on the poem. Other discussions of Byron's masterpiece include George M. Ridenour, *The Style of "Don Juan,"* 1960; Jerome J. McGann, *"Don Juan" in Context*, 1976; Peter W. Graham, *"Don Juan" and Regency England*, 1990; and Moyra Haslett, *Byron's "Don Juan" and the Don Juan Legend*, 1997.

Samuel Taylor Coleridge

The Complete Works, ed. W. G. T. Shedd, 7 vols., 1853, hitherto the most inclusive collection of Coleridge's works, is being superseded by *The Collected Works* under the general editorship of Kathleen Coburn; thirteen of the projected sixteen volumes have now appeared, beginning in 1969. E. H. Coleridge, *Complete Poetical Works*, 2 vols., 1912 (with a one-volume edition of *Poetical Works* by the same editor in the Oxford Standard Authors series), remains the standard, though it will shortly be replaced by J. C. C. Mays's edition of the poems and plays in volume 16 of the *Collected Works*. The most fully annotated edition of *Biographia Literaria* is that by James Engell and W. Jackson Bate, 2 vols. 1983 (vol. 7 of the *Collected Works*).

Richard Holmes, *Coleridge: Early Visions*, 1989, and *Coleridge: Darker Reflections*, 1998, together constitute the most recent biography, following close upon Rosemary Ashton, *The Life of Samuel Taylor Coleridge: A Critical Biography*, 1987. The definitive edition of Coleridge's *Collected Letters* is edited by E. L. Griggs, 6 vols., 1956–71; see also *Selected Letters*, ed. H. J. Jackson, 1987. The first four volumes of Coleridge's *Notebooks* are available, meticulously edited by Kathleen Coburn and associates, 1957–.

There are good short studies of the life and works by Walter Jackson Bate, *Coleridge*, 1968, and, with emphasis on the philosophical and religious writings, by Basil Willey, *Samuel Taylor Coleridge*, 1972. H. M. Margoliouth has described the most fruitful literary association on record in his *Wordsworth and Coleridge, 1795–1834*, 1953; more sophisticated studies are Paul Magnuson, *Coleridge and Wordsworth: A Lyrical Dialogue*, 1988, and Gene W. Ruoff, *Wordsworth and Coleridge: The Making of the Major Lyrics, 1802–1804*, 1989. The best older critique of Coleridge as poet is Humphry House, *Coleridge*, 1953. More recent studies include Max F. Schulz, *The Poetic Voices of Coleridge*, 1963; George Watson, *Coleridge the Poet*, 1966; Paul Magnuson, *Coleridge's Nightmare Poetry*, 1974; Reeve Parker, *Coleridge's Meditative Art*, 1975; Kelvin Everest, *Coleridge's Secret Ministry*, 1979; M. H. Abrams, *The Correspondent Breeze*, 1984; and Morton D. Paley, *Coleridge's*

Later Poetry, 1996. *The Road to Xanadu*, by J. L. Lowes, 1927, rev. 1930, which investigates the sources and composition of *The Ancient Mariner* and *Kubla Khan*, has achieved the status of a critical classic. Discussion of Coleridge as critic will be found in M. H. Abrams, *The Mirror and the Lamp*, 1953; René Wellek, *A History of Modern Criticism, 1750–1950*, vol. 2, 1955; Richard Harter Fogle, *The Idea of Coleridge's Criticism*, 1962; and J. A. Appleyard, *Coleridge's Philosophy of Literature*, 1965. Norman Fruman, *Coleridge, the Damaged Archangel*, 1971, collects all the charges and evidence concerning Coleridge's "plagiarism." Among the excellent studies of Coleridge's philosophical, theological, and moral interests and achievements are Richard Haven, *Patterns of Consciousness*, 1969; Thomas McFarland's important and wide-ranging study of *Coleridge and the Pantheist Tradition*, 1969; Owen Barfield, *What Coleridge Thought*, 1971; and Lawrence S. Lockridge, *Coleridge the Moralist*, 1977. Recent studies of his political views include Nicholas Roe, *Wordsworth and Coleridge: The Radical Years*, 1988; John Morrow, *Coleridge's Political Thought*, 1990; and Patrick J. Keane, *Coleridge's Submerged Politics*, 1994. On opium, dreaming, and Coleridge's poetry, see Elisabeth Schneider, *Coleridge, Opium and "Kubla Khan,"* 1953; Alethea Hayter, *Opium and the Romantic Imagination*, 1968; M. H. Abrams, *The Milk of Paradise*, rev. 1970; and Jennifer Ford, *Coleridge on Dreaming: Romanticism, Dreams and the Medical Imagination*, 1998. On his developing reputation, see *Coleridge: The Critical Heritage*, ed. J. R. de J. Jackson, 2 vols., 1970, 1991. Modern essays in criticism have been collected by, among others, Kathleen Coburn, *Coleridge*, 1967; John Beer, *Coleridge's Variety*, 1974; Frederick Burwick, *Coleridge's "Biographia Literaria": Text and Meaning*, 1989; and Leonard Orr, *Critical Essays*, 1994.

Felicia Dorothea Hemans
The best complete edition is *The Poetical Works of Felicia Dorothea Hemans*, 1914; a modern selection is in progress under the editorship of Gary Kelly. For criticism, see Peter W. Trinder, *Mrs. Hemans*, 1984; Angela Leighton, *Victorian Women Poets: Writing against the Heart*, 1992; Isobel Armstrong, *Victorian Poetry*, 1993; Tricia Lootens, "Hemans and Home," *PMLA*, 1994; Nanora Sweet, "Hemans and the Post-Napoleonic Moment," in *At the Limits of Romanticism*, ed. Mary A. Favret and Nicola J. Watson, 1994; Susan J. Wolfson, "Felicia Hemans and the Dilemma of Gender," in *Re-Visioning Romanticism*, ed. Wilson and Haefner, 1994; Paula R. Feldman, "Felicia Hemans and the Literary Marketplace," *Keats-Shelley Journal*, 1997.

John Keats
The standard edition of the poetry is Jack Stillinger, *The Poems of John Keats*, 1978. Miriam Allott, *The Poems of John Keats*, 1970, is copiously annotated. Hyder E. Rollins, *The Letters of John Keats*, 2 vols., 1958, provides exact texts based on the manuscripts.

The most frequently cited biographies are Walter Jackson Bate, *John Keats*, 1963; Robert Gittings, *John Keats*, 1968; and Aileen Ward, *John Keats: The Making of a Poet*, rev. 1986. A good shorter life is Douglas Bush, *John Keats*, 1966; Andrew Motion, full-scale *Keats*, 1997, is the most recent.

Among the many critical studies, the following are especially useful: C. D. Thorpe, *The Mind of John Keats*, 1926 (on Keats's thought); M. R. Ridley, *Keats' Craftsmanship*, 1933 (based on the revisions in Keats's manuscripts); Earl Wasserman, *The Finer Tone*, 1953 (a close analysis of the major poems); David Perkins, *The Quest for Permanence*, 1959; Walter Evert, *Aesthetic and Myth in the Poetry of Keats*, 1965; Jack Stillinger, *The Hoodwinking of Madeline and Other Essays on Keats's Poems*, 1971; Stuart Sperry, *Keats the Poet*, 1973; Christopher Ricks's lively and wide-ranging study of *Keats and Embarrassment*, 1974; Robert M. Ryan's analysis of Keats's personal creed, *Keats: The Religious Sense*, 1976; Ronald A. Sharp, *Keats, Skepticism, and the Religion of Beauty*, 1979; Helen Vendler, *The Odes of John Keats*, 1983; Leon Waldoff, *Keats and the Silent Work of Imagination*, 1985; Susan J. Wolfson. *The Questioning Presence: Wordsworth, Keats, and the Interrogative Mode in Romantic Poetry*, 1986; John Barnard, *John Keats*, 1987; Marjorie Levinson, *Keats's Life of Allegory*, 1988; Daniel P. Watkins, *Keats's Poetry and the Poetics of Imagination*, 1989; Nicholas Roe, *John Keats and the Culture of Dissent*, 1997; *The Persistence of Poetry: Bicentennial Essays on Keats*, ed. Robert M. Ryan and Ronald A. Sharp, 1998. For other commentary on the odes, consult Jack Wright Rhodes, *Keats's Major Odes: An Annotated Bibliography of the Criticism*, 1984; and on *The Eve of St. Agnes*, Jack Stillinger's *Reading "The Eve of St. Agnes,"* 1999. For the poet's nineteenth-century reputation, see *Keats: The Critical Heritage*, ed. G. M. Matthews, 1971. Recent collections of essays include *Critical Essays on John Keats*, ed. Hermione de Almeida, 1990, and *Keats and History*, ed. Nicholas Roe, 1995.

Percy Bysshe Shelley
The nearest to a complete collection of Shelley's writings is *The Complete Works*, ed. Roger Ingpen and Walter E. Peck, 10 vols., 1926–30. The most widely used single-volume edition of the poems has been that in the Oxford Standard Authors, ed. Thomas Hutchinson and rev. G. M. Matthews, 1970. *Shelley's Prose* was collected by David Lee Clark in 1954; and *The Letters* were edited by Frederick L. Jones in 2 vols., 1964. Because of the erratic way in which Shelley's poems and essays were published, all the collected editions are faulty; Shelley's writings are now in the process of being revised and reprinted by a number of editors. Neville Rogers's edition of *The Complete Poetical Works*, of which two volumes are in print, 1972–, has been severely criticized by scholars. The best texts are those in *The Lyrics of Shelley*, edited and sensitively interpreted by Judith Chernaik, 1972; and in the large

selection of *Shelley's Poetry and Prose*, A Norton Critical Edition, ed. Donald H. Reiman and Sharon B. Powers, 1977, which also includes a collection of critical essays on Shelley.

The classic life is Newman Ivey White, *Shelley*, 2 vols., 1940, which is also available in a condensed single volume, *Portrait of Shelley*, 1945. Richard Holmes's *Shelley: The Pursuit*, 1974, is not so detailed as White's biography, but provides a vivid sense of Shelley as a human being. Kenneth Neill Cameron, in *The Young Shelley*, 1950, and in the sequel, *Shelley: The Golden Years*, 1974, emphasizes the development of Shelley's radical social and political thinking. C. E. Pulos, *The Deep Truth: A Study of Shelley's Scepticism*, 1954, emphasizes the philosophic skepticism at the center of his idealism.

Shelley's Major Poetry, by Carlos Baker, 1948, provides analyses of the longer poems that stress their ideational content; Carl H. Grabo, in *A Newton among Poets*, 1930, and Desmond King-Hele, in *Shelley: His Thought and Work*, 1960, deal with Shelley's conversion of scientific knowledge into poetic images. *The Imagery of Keats and Shelley*, by Richard H. Fogle, 1949, analyzes the stylistic qualities of Shelley's poetry.

As early as 1900, W. B. Yeats, in "The Philosophy of Shelley's Poetry" (reprinted in *Essays*, 1924), dealt with Shelley as one of the great symbolist poets. More recent treatments of Shelley's symbolic imagery are Peter Butter, *Shelley's Idols of the Cave*, 1954, and Harold Bloom's innovative study, *Shelley's Mythmaking*, 1959, which puts Shelley in the line of visionary poets whose imaginative processes were instinctively mythopoetic. Earl Wasserman's *Shelley: A Critical Reading*, 1971, is a series of close readings of Shelley's most important poems and essays. Other useful critiques are Milton Wilson, *Shelley's Later Poetry*, 1959; R. G. Woodman, *The Apocalyptic Tradition in the Poetry of Shelley*, 1964; Stuart Curran's study of *Shelley's Annus Mirabilis: The Maturing of an Epic Vision*, 1975; Timothy Webb, *Shelley: A Voice Not Understood*, 1977; William Keach, *Shelley's Style*, 1984; Stuart M. Sperry, *Shelley's Major Verse: The Narrative and Dramatic Poetry*, 1988; Stephen C. Behrendt, *Shelley and His Audiences*, 1989; Donald Reiman, *Percy Bysshe Shelley*, rev. 1990, and Susan Wolfson, *Formal Charges*, 1997. Charles Robinson discusses the personal and poetic relations of *Byron and Shelley: The Snake and the Eagle Wreathed in Fight*, 1975. *Shelley*, ed. George M. Ridenour, 1965, is an anthology of modern critical essays.

Mary Wollstonecraft

There is a collected edition, *The Works of Mary Wollstonecraft*, ed. Janet Todd and Marilyn Butler, 7 vols., 1989. Todd has also edited *A Wollstonecraft Anthology*, 1989, and *Mary Wollstonecraft: Political Writings*, 1993. The most important reprints of single works are *A Vindication of the Rights of Men*, facsimile edition by Eleanor Louise Nicholes, 1960; *A Vindication of the Rights of Woman*, in both the annotated edition by Ulrich H. Hardt, 1982, and a

Norton Critical Edition by Carol H. Poston, 1988; *Letters Written during a Short Residence in Sweden, Norway, and Denmark*, ed. Carol H. Poston, 1976; and a reprint in a single volume (ed. Gary Kelly, 1976) of her two novels, the early *Mary, A Fiction*, and *The Wrongs of Woman; or Maria*, which she left unfinished at her death. Ralph Wardle has edited *Collected Letters of Mary Wollstonecraft*, 1979.

Biographers rely for many facts on William Godwin's candid *Memoirs of the Author of "A Vindication of the Rights of Woman,"* 1798. The first modern critical biography is Ralph Wardle's *Mary Wollstonecraft*, 1951; see also Eleanor Flexner, *Mary Wollstonecraft: A Biography*, 1972; Claire Tomlin's *The Life and Death of Mary Wollstonecraft*, 1974; and Emily Sunstein's *A Different Face: The Life of Mary Wollstonecraft*, 1975. Recent studies include Moira Ferguson and Janet Todd, *Mary Wollstonecraft*, 1984; Mary Poovey, *The Proper Lady and the Woman Writer*, 1984; Jennifer Lorch, *Mary Wollstonecraft: The Making of a Radical Feminist*, 1990; Gary Kelly, *Revolutionary Feminism: The Mind and Career of Mary Wollstonecraft*, 1992; and Virginia Sapiro, *A Vindication of Political Virtue: The Political Theory of Mary Wollstonecraft*, 1992.

Dorothy Wordsworth

For the journals, the best editions are *Journals of Dorothy Wordsworth*, ed. Mary Moorman, 1971, and *The Grasmere Journals*, ed. Pamela Woof, 1991. For the poems, consult the appendix of Susan M. Levin's critical study, *Dorothy Wordsworth and Romanticism*, 1987. Dorothy Wordsworth's letters are collected with those of her brother in *The Letters of William and Dorothy Wordsworth*, rev. Chester L. Shaver and others, 8 vols., 1967–93; there is a one-volume selection of her *Letters*, ed. Alan G. Hill, 1985. The 1933 biography by Ernest de Selincourt has been superseded by Robert Gittings and Jo Manton, *Dorothy Wordsworth*, 1985. See also Catherine Macdonald Maclean, *Dorothy Wordsworth, the Early Years*, 1932; Elizabeth Hardwick, *Seduction and Betrayal*, 1974; and Margaret Homans, *Women Writers and Poetic Identity: Dorothy Wordsworth, Emily Brontë, and Emily Dickinson*, 1980.

William Wordsworth

Ernest de Selincourt edited *The Poetical Works* (with Helen Darbishire), 5 vols., 1940–49, and the variorum edition of *The Prelude*, with the texts of 1805 and 1850 on facing pages (rev. Helen Darbishire, 1959). *The Letters of William and Dorothy Wordsworth*, ed. de Selincourt, have been revised by C. L. Shaver, Mary Moorman, and Alan G. Hill, 7 vols., 1967–92. The 1805 and 1850 *Preludes* on facing pages, together with the "Two-Part *Prelude*" of 1799, various manuscript fragments of *The Prelude*, and a selection of recent critical essays on the poem, are available in *The Prelude: 1799, 1805, 1850*. A Norton Critical Edition, ed. Jonathan Wordsworth, M. H. Abrams, and Stephen Gill, 1979. Wordsworth's poems in one volume were edited for The Oxford Authors by Stephen Gill (1984). A series, the Cornell Wordsworth, general ed. Stephen Parrish, begun in 1975 and now close to completion, prints texts of the poems, together with variant readings from the manuscripts (which are reproduced and transcribed) through the final printings in Wordsworth's lifetime. W. J. B. Owen and Jane Worthington Smyser have edited The Prose Works, 3 vols., 1974, and there is a Selected Prose, ed. John O. Hayden, 1988. Owen has also printed from his edition a convenient collection of Wordsworth's Literary Criticism, 1974. Mary Moorman, William Wordsworth, vol. 1, rev. 1968; vol. 2, 1965, has been superseded by Stephen Gill's reliable William Wordsworth: A Life (1984) and by Kenneth B. Johnston's lively and well-researched, if at times speculative, The Hidden Wordsworth (1988), whose emphases are indicated by its subtitle: Poet, Lover, Rebel, Spy. Mark L. Reed's dating of Wordsworth's poems, manuscripts, and the events of his daily life, has reached two volumes, Wordsworth: The Chronology of the Early Years, 1967, and The Chronology of the Middle Years, 1975.

Walter Raleigh, Wordsworth, 1903; Helen Darbishire, The Poet Wordsworth, 1950; and Carl Woodring, Wordsworth, 1965, are useful introductions to Wordsworth's poetry. Paul D. Sheats has written a study of the early poems, The Making of Wordsworth's Poetry, 1785–1798, 1973. Modern interest in Lyrical Ballads is shown in Stephen M. Parrish, The Art of the "Lyrical Ballads," 1973; Mary Jacobus, Tradition and Experiment in Wordsworth's "Lyrical Ballads," 1798, 1976; John E. Jordan, Why the "Lyrical Ballads"? 1976; and Don H. Bialostosky, Making Tales, 1984. Herbert Lindenberger, On Wordsworth's "Prelude," 1963, explores Words-

worth's major achievement; Richard J. Onorato deals with it from a psychoanalytic standpoint in The Character of the Poet: Wordsworth in "The Prelude," 1971; and Mary Jacobus from a feminist standpoint in Romanticism, Writing, and Sexual Difference: Essays on "The Prelude," 1989. Aspects of Wordsworth's thought are explored by James A. W. Heffernan, Wordsworth's Theory of Poetry, 1969, and Geoffrey Durrant, Wordsworth and the Great System, 1970. Prominent critical studies of Wordsworth's poetry are John Jones, The Egotistical Sublime, 1954; David Perkins, Wordsworth and the Poetry of Sincerity, 1964; Geoffrey Hartman's impressive study of Wordsworth's Poetry, 1787–1814, 1964; James H. Averill, Wordsworth and the Poetry of Human Suffering, 1980; Kenneth R. Johnston, Wordsworth and "The Recluse," 1984; Marjorie Levinson, Wordsworth's Great Period Poems, 1986; Susan J. Wolfson, The Questioning Presence: Wordsworth, Keats, and the Interrogative Mode in Romantic Poetry, 1986; David Simpson, Wordsworth's Historical Imagination, 1987; Nicholas Roe, Wordsworth and Coleridge: The Radical Years, 1988; Theresa M. Kelley, Wordsworth's Revisionary Aesthetics, 1988; William H. Galperin, Revision and Authority in Wordsworth, 1989; Alan Liu, Wordsworth, The Sense of History (1989); Peter J. Manning, Reading Romantics, 1990; Judith W. Page, Wordsworth and the Cultivation of Women, 1994. The range and diversity of critical studies are represented in Wordsworth: A Collection of Critical Essays, ed. M. H. Abrams, 1972; The Age of William Wordsworth: Critical Essays on the Romantic Tradition, ed. Kenneth R. Johnston and Gene W. Ruoff, 1987; and Critical Essays on William Wordsworth, ed. George Gilpin, 1990.

THE VICTORIAN AGE

Studies of the Victorian age and its point of view include Richard D. Altick, Victorian People and Ideas: A Companion for the Modern Reader of Victorian Literature, 1973; Patrick Brantlinger, Rule of Darkness: British Literature and Imperialism, 1830–1914, 1988; Asa Briggs, The Age of Improvement, 1962; W. L. Burn, The Age of Equipoise: A Study of the Mid-Victorian Generation, 1964; Jerome Buckley, The Victorian Temper, 1951; David Cannadine, The Decline and Fall of the British Aristocracy, 1990; A. Dwight Culler, The Victorian Mirror of History, 1986; Robin Gilmour, The Victorian Period: The Intellectual and Cultural Context of Victorian Literature, 1830–1890, 1993; Walter E. Houghton, The Victorian Frame of Mind, 1830–1870, 1957; Victorian Britain: An Encyclopedia, ed. Sally Mitchell, 1988; David Newsome, The Victorian World Picture: Perceptions and Introspections in a World of Change, 1997; Mary Poovey, Making a Social Body: British Cultural Formation, 1830–1864, 1995; Richard L. Stein, Victoria's Year: English Literature and Culture, 1837–38, 1988; F. M. L.

Thompson, The Rise of Respectable Society: A Social History of Victorian Britain, 1830–1900, 1988; and G. M. Young, Victorian England: Portrait of an Age, 1936 (republished in 1977 with 215 pages of explanatory notes by George Kitson Clark). Young's essay is a brilliant synthesis, but it can be incomprehensible to readers who are not yet adequately familiar with the history of the age. Such readers should consult David Thomson's England in the Nineteenth Century, 1950, or Derek Beales, From Castlereagh to Gladstone: 1815–1885, 1970.

Studies of special aspects of the age include James Eli Adams, Dandies and Desert Saints: Styles of Victorian Masculinity, 1995; Richard Altick, The English Common Reader, 1957; Asa Briggs, Victorian Things, 1989; Jerome Buckley, The Triumph of Time, 1966; Peter Gay, The Bourgeois Experience: From Victoria to Freud, 2 vols., 1984–86; Mark Girouard, The Return to Camelot, 1981; Bruce Haley, The Healthy Body and Victorian Culture, 1978; Steven Marcus, The Other Victorians: A Study of Sexuality and Pornography in Mid-

Nineteenth-Century England, 1964; Herbert Sussman, Victorians and the Machine, 1968; E. P. Thompson, The Making of the English Working Class, 1963; Frank M. Turner, The Greek Heritage in Victorian Britain, 1981; The Victorian City, ed. H. J. Dyos and Michael Wolff, 2 vols., 1973; Jeffrey Weeks, Sex, Politics and Society: The Regulation of Sexuality Since 1800, 1981; and Michael Wheeler, Death and the Future Life in Victorian Literature and Theology, 1991. For pictures and paintings of the Victorian scene, see Jeremy Maas, Victorian Painters, 1969. Also revealing are the illustrations for Henry Mayhew, London Labour and London Poor, originally published 1851, reprinted 1967, and Gustav Doré, London: A Pilgrimage, originally published 1872 and reprinted 1970. Nature and the Victorian Imagination, ed. U. C. Knoepflmacher and G. B. Tennyson, 1977; Victorian Types, Victorian Shadows: Biblical Typology in Victorian Literature, Art, and Thought, George Landow, 1980; and Victorian Literature and the Victorian Visual Imagination, ed. Carol T. Christ and John O. Jordan, 1995, feature valuable treatments of literature and the visual arts.

Studies of Victorian literature include Isobel Armstrong, Victorian Poetry: Poetry, Poetics, and Politics, 1993; Harold Bloom, The Ringers in the Tower, 1971; William E. Buckler, The Victorian Imagination, 1980; Douglas Bush, Mythology and the Romantic Tradition, 1937; Raymond Chapman, The Sense of the Past in Victorian Literature, 1986; Carol T. Christ, The Finer Optic: The Aesthetic of Particularity in Victorian Poetry, 1975, and Victorian and Modern Poetics, 1984; Peter Allan Dale, The Victorian Critic and the Idea of History, 1977; Oliver Elton, A Survey of English Literature, 1920, vols. 3 and 4; Avrom Fleischman, Figures of Autobiography: The Language of Self in Victorian and Modern England, 1983; Pauline Fletcher, Gardens and Grim Ravines . . . Landscape in Victorian Poetry, 1983; George Ford, Keats and the Victorians, 1944; Hilary Fraser with David Brown, English Prose of the Nineteenth Century, 1997; E. D. H. Johnson, The Alien Vision of Victorian Poetry, 1952; Robert Langbaum, The Poetry of Experience, 1957; John P. McGowan, Representation and Revelation: Victorian Realism from Carlyle to Yeats, 1986; Dorothy Mermin, The Audience in the Poem, 1983; J. Hillis Miller, The Disappearance of God: Five Nineteenth-Century Writers, 1963; John R. Reed, Victorian Conventions, 1975; W. David Shaw, The Lucid Veil: Poetic Truth in the Victorian Age, 1987; René Wellek, A History of Modern Criticism, vol. 4, 1965. Helpful collections of critical essays have been compiled by Robert Preyer in his Victorian Literature: Selected Essays, 1965; Isobel Armstrong, The Major Victorian Poets: Reconsiderations, 1969; and by Michael Timko in Victorian Poetry, Spring 1978. Especially noteworthy is The Art of Victorian Prose, ed. George Levine and William Madden, 1968.

For the status of women in Victorian life and literature, see Nina Auerbach, Woman and the De-

mon, 1982, and Romantic Imprisonment, 1985; Deirdre David, Rule Britannia: Women, Empire, and Victorian Writing, 1996; Sandra Gilbert and Susan Gubar, The Madwoman in the Attic, 1979; Elizabeth Helsinger, Robin Lauterbach Sheets, and William Veeder, The Woman Question, 3 vols., 1980; Margaret Homans, Bearing the Word: Language and Female Experience in Nineteenth-Century Women's Writing, 1986; Elizabeth Langland, Nobody's Angels: Middle Class Women and Domestic Ideology in Victorian Culture, 1995; Angela Leighton, Victorian Women Poets: Writing against the Heart, 1992; Dorothy Mermin, Godiva's Ride: Women of Letters in England, 1830–1880, 1993; Ellen Moers, Literary Women, 1976; Mary Poovey, Uneven Developments: The Ideological Work of Gender in Mid-Victorian England, 1988; Eve Kosofsky Sedgwick, Between Men: English Literature and Male Homosexual Desire. 1985; Elaine Showalter, A Literature of Their Own, 1977; and Martha Vicinus, ed., Suffer and Be Still, 1972, A Widening Sphere, 1977, and Ever Yours, Florence Nightingale, Selected Letters (with Bea Nergaard), 1989.

For classified or annotated lists of other books and articles, see The Victorian Poets: A Guide to Research, ed. F. E. Faverty, rev. 1968; Victorian Fiction: A Guide to Research, ed. Lionel Stevenson, 1964; Victorian Fiction: A Second Guide to Research, ed. George H. Ford, 1978; Victorian Prose: A Guide to Research, ed. David J. DeLaura, 1973; Sharon W. Propas, Victorian Studies: A Research Guide, 1992; and Laurence W. Mazzeno, Victorian Poetry: An Annotated Bibliography, 1995.

For developments in prose fiction during the period, see Lionel Stevenson, The English Novel: A Panorama, 1960, and for introductions to individual novelists, see Victorian Novelists before 1885, ed. Ira Nadel and William Fredeman, Dictionary of Literary Biography, vol. 21, 1983. For special critical issues, see Peter Brooks, Reading for the Plot: Design and Intention in Narrative, 1984; Joseph W. Childers, Novel Possibilities: Fiction and the Formation of Early Victorian Culture, 1995; Catherine Gallagher, The Industrial Reformation of English Fiction: Social Discourse and Narrative Form, 1832–1867, 1985; Peter Garrett, The Victorian Multiplot Novel, 1980; George Levine, The Realistic Imagination, 1981; D. A. Miller, The Novel and the Police, 1988; J. Hillis Miller, The Form of Victorian Fiction, 1968; Robert M. Polhemus, Erotic Faith, 1990; and Donald Stone, The Romantic Impulse in Victorian Fiction, 1980.

Matthew Arnold

The standard edition of Arnold's poetry is the elaborately annotated Poems of Arnold, ed. Miriam Allott, 1979. Cecil Lang is editing The Letters of Matthew Arnold, 1996–. H. F. Lowry has edited The Letters of Arnold to . . . Clough, 1932. R. H. Super has produced an authoritative edition of The Complete Prose Works, 11 vols., 1960–77. For a study of those prose works, see William Robbins's

The Ethical Idealism of Matthew Arnold, 1959, and Joseph Carroll's The Cultural Theory of Matthew Arnold, 1982.

The most satisfactory biography is Park Honan's Matthew Arnold: A Life, 1981, but see also Nicholas Murray, A Life of Matthew Arnold, 1996. Lionel Trilling's excellent Matthew Arnold, 1949, remains a standard critical and biographical study, but see also Dwight Culler's Imaginative Reason, 1966, and G. Robert Stange's The Poet as Humanist, 1967. For two centenary assessments, see Stefan Collini, Arnold, 1988, and David G. Riede, Matthew Arnold and the Betrayal of Language, 1988. Two investigations of Arnold's literary and intellectual background are Leon Gottfried, Matthew Arnold and the Romantics, 1983, and Ruth apRoberts, Arnold and God, 1983. See also Kenneth Allott, Matthew Arnold, 1975, and the selection of essays edited by Harold Bloom, Matthew Arnold, 1987.

Elizabeth Barrett Browning
The standard Complete Works were edited by Charlotte Porter and Helen Clarke, 6 vols., 1900. Margaret Reynolds has edited a Norton Critical Edition of Aurora Leigh, 1996, and Julia Markus had edited Casa Guidi Windows, 1977. Of a projected forty-volume collection, The Brownings' Correspondence, ed. Philip Kelley and Ronald Hudson (1984–), fourteen volumes have been published. The best critical biography is Dorothy Mermin's Elizabeth Barrett Browning: The Origins of a New Poetry, 1989. See also Angela Leighton, Elizabeth Barrett Browning, 1986. Interesting recent discussions of Barrett Browning can be found in Ellen Moers, Literary Women, 1976; Sandra Gilbert and Susan Gubar, The Madwoman in the Attic, 1979; Deirdre David, Intellectual Women and Victorian Patriarchy, 1987; Helen Cooper, Elizabeth Barrett Browning, Woman and Artist, 1988; and Marjorie Stone, Elizabeth Barrett Browning, 1995.

Robert Browning
A standard edition is The Complete Works of Robert Browning, with Variant Readings and Annotations, ed. Roma A. King Jr., et al., 9 vols., 1969–89. Five volumes of a projected seven-volume annotated edition of the poetry only, The Poetical Works of Robert Browning, have appeared, edited by Ian Jack, Margaret Smith, and Robert Inglesfield, 1983–95. John Woolford and Daniel Karlin have also edited The Poems of Browning, 1991, two volumes of which have appeared. A convenient two-volume collection of the poems edited by John Pettigrew and Thomas J. Collins was published in 1981. For the Brownings' correspondence, see entry under **Elizabeth Barrett Browning**. The standard biography is The Book, the Ring, and the Poet, William Irvine and Park Honan, 1974; also see Clyde de L. Ryals, The Life of Robert Browning: A Critical Biography. Gertrude Reese Hudson provides a study of his critical reception in Robert Browning's Literary Life, 1993. W. C. DeVane's A Browning Handbook, rev. 1955, is a compilation of factual data concerning each of Browning's poems: sources, composition, and rep-

utation. Further information is supplied by Norman B. Crowell, A Reader's Guide to Robert Browning, 1972, which also offers simplified summaries of critical discussions for twenty-three monologues.

The critical assessments in G. K. Chesterton's Robert Browning, 1903, are colorfully expressed and often shrewd. Robert Langbaum's The Poetry of Experience relates Browning's monologues to some of the main developments in modern literature. See also Roma A. King Jr., The Bow and the Lyre, 1957; W. O. Raymond, The Infinite Moment, 1965; Donald Hair, Browning's Experiments with Genre; 1972; Ian Jack, Browning's Major Poetry, 1973; Herbert Tucker, Browning's Beginnings, 1980; Loy Martin, Browning's Dramatic Monologues and the Post-Romantic Subject, 1985; and Joseph Bristow, Robert Browning, 1991. Useful collections of essays include The Browning Critics, ed. Boyd Litzinger and K. L. Knickerbocker, 1965; Robert Browning: A Collection of Critical Essays, ed. Philip Drew, 1966; Browning: The Critical Heritage, ed. Boyd Litzinger and Donald Smalley, 1970; Robert Browning, ed. Isobel Armstrong, 1974; Robert Browning: A Collection of Critical Essays, ed. Harold Bloom and Adrienne Munich, 1979; and Critical Essays on Robert Browning, ed. Mary Ellis Gibson, 1992.

Thomas Carlyle
The Works have been edited by H. D. Traill, 30 vols., 1898–1901. Twenty-one volumes of the Collected Letters, projected to extend to thirty volumes, have been published since 1971 (ed. by C. R. Sanders et al.). C. F. Harrold's edition of Sartor Resartus, 1937, is helpful concerning Carlyle's debt to German literature, as is Louis Cazamian's Carlyle, 1932, concerning his religious background. J. A. Froude, Thomas Carlyle, 1882–84, for years the standard biography, has been replaced by Fred Kaplan, Thomas Carlyle, 1983. Recommended as studies of Carlyle's thought are Emery Neff, Carlyle and Mill, 1926; Philip Rosenberg, The Seventh Hero: Thomas Carlyle and the Theory of Radical Activism, 1974; Ruth apRoberts, The Ancient Dialect: Thomas Carlyle and Comparative Religion, 1988; and Chris Vanden Bossche, Carlyle and the Search for Authority, 1991. That he has affinities with twentieth-century "mythmakers" such as D. H. Lawrence is argued by Albert J. LaValley in Carlyle and the Idea of the Modern, 1968. John Holloway's The Victorian Sage, 1953, includes a chapter analyzing Carlyle's rhetoric. George B. Tennyson, Sartor Called Resartus, 1965, is an important critical study. See also George Levine, The Boundaries of Fiction, 1968, on Carlyle, Macaulay, and Newman, and the collection of essays edited by K. J. Fielding and Rodger L. Tarr, Carlyle Past and Present, 1976. Tarr has also compiled Thomas Carlyle: A Descriptive Bibliography, 1990.

Elizabeth Gaskell
The standard edition of Gaskell's fiction is the Knutsford Edition, ed. A. W. Ward, 8 vols, 1906–20; the best modern editions are by Penguin. A modern edition exists of The Letters of Mrs. Gaskell,

ed. J. A. V. Chapple and Arthur Pollard, rev. 1997. Biographies include Winifred Gerin, *Elizabeth Gaskell*, 1980, and Jenny Uglow, *Elizabeth Gaskell: A Habit of Stories*, 1993. For critical studies see W. A. Craik, *Elizabeth Gaskell and the English Provincial Novel*, 1975; Angus Easson, *Elizabeth Gaskell*, 1979; Angus Easson, ed., *Elizabeth Gaskell: The Critical Heritage*, 1991; Hilary M. Schor, *Scheherezade in the Marketplace: Elizabeth Gaskell and the Victorian Novel*, 1992; and Patsy Stoneman, *Elizabeth Gaskell*, 1987.

Gerard Manley Hopkins

Robert Bridges edited the first (posthumous) edition of Hopkins's poems in 1918, which has been the nucleus of all subsequent editions. The most recent is *The Poetical Works of Gerard Manley Hopkins*, ed. Norman H. MacKenzie, 1990. In addition to the poems, Hopkins's letters and parts of his notebooks have been published: *The Letters of Gerard Manley Hopkins to Robert Bridges* and *The Correspondence of G. M. Hopkins and Richard Watson Dixon*, ed. C. C. Abbot, 2 vols., 1935; *Further Letters of Gerard Manley Hopkins*, ed. C. C. Abbott, 1938, rev. 1956; *The Journals and Papers of Gerard Manley Hopkins*, ed. Humphry House and Graham Storey, 1969; and *The Sermons and Devotional Writings of Gerard Manley Hopkins*, ed. Christopher Devlin, 1959. A helpful introduction to these works is Norman H. MacKenzie, *A Reader's Guide to Gerard Manley Hopkins*, 1981.

The two best biographies are Robert Bernard Martin, *Gerard Manley Hopkins: A Very Private Life*, 1991, and Norman White, *Hopkins: A Literary Biography*, 1992. Some useful critical studies are W. H. Gardner, *G. M. Hopkins: A Study of Poetic Idiosyncrasy in Relation to Poetic Tradition*, 2 vols., 1944, 1949; Paul L. Mariani, *A Commentary on the Complete Poems of Gerard Manley Hopkins*, 1970; Alison Sulloway, *Gerard Manley Hopkins and the Victorian Temper*, 1972; Daniel Harris, *Inspirations Unbidden: The "Terrible Sonnets" of Gerard Manley Hopkins*, 1982; Walter J. Ong, *Hopkins, the Self, and God*, 1986; and Virginia Ridley Ellis, *Gerard Manley Hopkins and the Language of Mystery*, 1991. Two good collections of critical essays are *Hopkins*, ed. Geoffrey Hartmann, 1966, and *Hopkins Among the Poets: Studies in Modern Responses to Gerard Manley Hopkins*, ed. Richard F. Giles, 1985.

Christina Rossetti

The standard variorum edition is *The Complete Poems of Christina Rossetti*, ed. R. W. Crump, 3 vols., 1979–90. The first volume of *The Letters of Christina Rossetti*, ed. Anthony H. Harrison, 1997, has been published. See also *Selected Prose of Christina Rossetti*, ed. David A. Kent and P. G. Stanwood, 1998. Two recent biographies are Kathleen Jones, *Learning Not to Be First: The Life of Christina Rossetti*, 1991, and Jan Marsh, *Christina Rossetti: A Writer's Life*, 1995. Virginia Woolf's *Second Common Reader*, 1932, contains an essay on the poet. Dolores Rosenblum's *Christina Rossetti: The Poetry of Endurance*, 1986, and Antony H. Harrison's *Christina Rossetti in Context*, 1988, are good book-length studies of the poetry. David Kent has edited a collection of critical essays, *The Achievement of Christina Rossetti*, 1987.

Bernard Shaw

The first volume of *The Collected Works of Bernard Shaw*, in the Ayot St. Lawrence Edition, 30 vols., appeared in 1930. *Collected Plays with Their Prefaces*, 7 vols., 1975, contains the fully revised texts of all the published plays, together with historical data and miscellaneous Shavian pronouncements on each play. There is a Norton Critical Edition, *Bernard Shaw's Plays*, ed. Warren Sylvester Smith, 1970. Selections of prose include *Bernard Shaw, Selected Prose*, ed. Diarmuid Russell, 1952; *Plays and Players*, ed. A. C. Ward, 1952; *The Nondramatic Literary Criticism of Bernard Shaw*, ed. Stanley Weintraub, 1972; *Shaw on Music*, ed. Eric Bentley, 1972; and *Bernard Shaw on Language*, ed. Abraham Tauber, 1963. The *Collected Letters of Bernard Shaw*, ed. Dan H. Laurence, 1965–, collects his voluminous correspondence.

The standard biography is Michael Holroyd, *Bernard Shaw*, 4 vols, 1988–93. Also of interest is Hesketh Pearson, *George Bernard Shaw: His Life and Personality*, 1963. Other biographical sources are *Shaw: An Autobiography, Selected from His Writings*, 2 vols., ed. Stanley Weintraub, 1969–70, and *Shaw: Interviews and Recollections*, ed. A. M. Gibbs, 1990.

Critical studies include Eric Bentley, *Bernard Shaw: A Reconsideration*, 1947; Charles A. Carpenter, *Bernard Shaw and the Art of Destroying Ideals*, 1969; Louis Crompton, *Shaw the Dramatist*, 1969; *Shaw and Politics*, ed. T. F. Evans, 1991; J. Ellen Gainor, *Shaw's Daughters: Dramatic and Narrative Constructions of Gender*, 1991; Gareth Griffith, *Socialism and Superior Brains: The Political Thought of Bernard Shaw*, 1992; and Sally Peters, *Bernard Shaw: The Ascent of the Superman*, 1996. Two useful collections of essays are *George Bernard Shaw*, ed. Harold Bloom, 1987, and *Critical Essays on George Bernard Shaw*, ed. Elsie B. Adams, 1991.

Alfred, Lord Tennyson

Tennyson's *Works* were edited by his son Hallam, Lord Tennyson, in 9 vols., 1907–8. The *Poems* in one volume were edited by Christopher Ricks in 1969 and extensively revised in three volumes in 1988. Norton Critical Editions of Tennyson's work are *Tennyson's Poetry*, ed. Robert W. Hill, Jr., 1972, and *In Memoriam*, ed. Robert H. Ross, 1974. *In Memoriam* has been edited by Susan Shatto and Marion Shaw, 1982. Three volumes of *The Letters of Alfred, Lord Tennyson*, to 1870, were edited by Cecil Y. Lang and Edgar F. Shannon, 1981–90. Hallam Tennyson's *Alfred, Lord Tennyson: A Memoir*, 2 vols., 1897, is a mine of anecdotes and valuable information. *The Tennyson Archive*, ed. Christopher Ricks and Aidan Day, 23 vols., 1987–89, is a monumental production concerning the manuscripts. The standard biography is Robert Martin, *Tennyson*, 1980. Sir Harold Nicolson, *Ten-*

nyson, 1923, a critical study more than a biography, gives a lively but distorted assessment of Tennyson's achievement. A number of critical studies have successively corrected Nicolson's oversights and have variously demonstrated that Tennyson is one of the finest of poets. These include Jerome H. Buckley, *Tennyson: The Growth of a Poet*, 1961; Christopher Ricks, *Tennyson*, 1972; F. E. L. Priestley, *Language and Structure in Tennyson's Poetry*, 1973; James R. Kincaid, *Tennyson's Major Poems: The Comic and Ironic Patterns*, 1975; W. David Shaw, *Tennyson's Style*, 1976; and, most especially to be recommended, A. Dwight Culler, *The Poetry of Tennyson* 1977. See also Daniel Albright, *Tennyson: The Muses' Tug-of-War*, 1986; Alan Sinfield, *Alfred Tennyson*, 1986; Herbert F. Tucker, *Tennyson and the Doom of Romanticism*, 1988; Donald S. Hair, *Tennyson's Language*, 1991; and Gerhard Joseph, *Tennyson and the Text: The Weaver's Shuttle*, 1992.

Some of the most interesting discussions are in introductory essays to Tennyson's poems by T. S. Eliot, 1936; W. H. Auden, 1944; H. Marshall McLuhan, 1956; Jerome Buckley, 1958; and George MacBeth, 1971. Also useful are A. C. Bradley, *A Commentary on Tennyson's "In Memoriam,"* 1901; E. D. H. Johnson, *The Alien Vision of Victorian Poetry*, 1952; *Critical Essays on the Poetry of Tennyson*, ed. John Kilham, 1960; and Herbert F. Tucker, *Critical Essays on Alfred Lord Tennyson*, 1993. Book-length studies of the *Idylls* have been published by Clyde de L. Ryals, 1967, John R. Reed, 1969, and John D. Rosenberg, 1973. A collection of critical essays on *In Memoriam* was edited by John Dixon Hunt, 1970; and Timothy Peltason has published a study of the poem, *Reading In Memoriam*, 1985.

Oscar Wilde

There is no standard complete edition, but a convenient one-volume collection is *The Complete Works of Oscar Wilde*, 1989. Rupert Hart-Davis has edited the *Letters*, 1962, and its supplement, *More Letters*, 1985. The standard biography is Richard Ellmann, *Oscar Wilde*, 1988. See also the psychoanalytic biography by Melissa Knox, *Oscar Wilde: A Long and Lovely Suicide*, 1994. Earlier biographies include Hesketh Pearson, *The Life of Oscar Wilde: His Life and Wit*, 1946, and H. Montgomery Hyde, *Oscar Wilde: A Biography*, 1975. *Oscar Wilde, a Pictorial Biography*, by Wilde's son, Vyvyan Holland, 1960, has splendid photographs of Wilde and his contemporaries and also provides a concise factual account of his life. The essays by Ian Fletcher and John Stokes in *Anglo-Irish Literature: A Review of Research*, 1976, and *Recent Research on Anglo-Irish Writers*, 1983 (both ed. Richard J. Finneran), provide a full-scale guide to editions of Wilde and studies of his life and work.

Oscar Wilde: A Collection of Critical Essays, ed. Richard Ellmann, 1969, is valuable for its coverage of responses to Wilde by other writers such as Yeats and Shaw. *Oscar Wilde: The Critical Heritage*, ed. Karl Beckson, 1970, is especially helpful with regard to the plays; it covers the period 1881–1927. For an account of the contemporary reception of Wilde, see Regina Gagnier, *Idylls of the Marketplace: Oscar Wilde and the Victorian Public*, 1986. See also Camille Paglia, *Sexual Personae*, 1990; *Critical Essays on Oscar Wilde*, ed. Regina Gagnier, 1991; Ed Cohen, *Talk on the Wilde Side: Toward a Genealogy of Discourse on Male Sexualities*, 1993; Gary Schmidgall, *The Stranger Wilde: Interpreting Oscar*, 1994; Lawrence Damson, *Wilde's Intentions: The Artist in His Criticism*, 1997; *The Cambridge Companion to Oscar Wilde*, ed. Peter Raby, 1997; and Karl Beckson, *The Oscar Wilde Encyclopedia*, 1998. Harold Bloom has edited two anthologies of critical essays: *Oscar Wilde: Modern Critical Views*, 1985, and *Oscar Wilde's The Importance of Being Earnest: Modern Critical Interpretations*, 1988.

THE TWENTIETH CENTURY

Martin Gilbert, *A History of the Twentieth Century*, vol. 1, *1900–33*, 1997, and vol. 2, *1933–51*, 1998, offers a richly informative and readable account of the first half-century; while Peter Conrad, *Modern Times, Modern Places*, 1998, skillfully interweaves the history of the period with its artistic and intellectual movements.

The social and political background is well covered in Paul Fussell, *The Great War and Modern Memory*, 1975, and *Wartime: Understanding and Behaviour in the Second World War*, 1989; Robert Graves and Alan Hodge, *The Long Week-End: A Social History of Great Britain, 1918–1939*, 1940; *The Baldwin Age*, ed. John Raymond, 1960; Julian Symons, *The Thirties*, rev, 1975; Samuel Hynes, *The Auden Generation: Literature and Politics in England in the 1930s*, 1976, and *A War Imagined: The First World War and British Culture*, 1990; Hugh Thomas, *The Spanish Civil War*, 1986; Valentine Cunningham, *British Writers of the Thirties*, 1988; Malcolm Bradbury, *The Social Context of Modern English Literature*, 1971; and *The Twentieth-Century Mind: History, Ideas, and Literature in Britain*, 3 vols., ed. C. B. Cox and A. E. Dyson, 1972, all of which include useful bibliographies.

The following critical works deal with general aspects of modern English literature: Stephen Spender, *The Struggle of the Modern*, 1963; C. K. Stead, *The New Poetic: Yeats to Eliot*, 1964, and *Pound, Yeats, Eliot, and the Modernists*, 1986; M. L. Rosenthal and Sally M. Gall, *The Modern Poetic Sequence: The Genius of Modern Poetry*, 1983; *The Modern Tradition: Backgrounds of Modern Literature*, ed. Richard Ellmann and Charles Feidelson, 1965; Irving Howe, *The Idea of the*

Modern, 1968; Hugh Kenner, *The Pound Era*, 1971; *Modernism 1890–1930*, ed. Malcolm Bradbury and James McFarlane, 1976; Robert Hughes, *The Shock of the New*, 1981; Carol T. Christ, *Victorian and Modern Poetics*, 1984; Sanford Schwartz, *The Matrix of Modernism: Pound, Eliot and Early Twentieth-Century Thought*, 1985; Maud Ellmann, *The Poetics of Impersonality: T. S. Eliot and Ezra Pound*, 1987; Perry Meisel, *The Myth of the Modern: A Study in British Literature and Criticism after 1850*, 1987; James Longenbach, *Stone Cottage: Pound, Yeats, and Modernism*, 1988; John Bayley, *The Short Story: Henry James to Elizabeth Bowen*, 1988; Sandra Gilbert and Susan Gubar, *No Man's Land: The Place of the Woman Writer in the Twentieth Century*, 3 vols., 1988–; George Watson, *British Literature since 1945*, 1991; and Joseph Bristow, *Effeminate England: Homoerotic Writing after 1885*, 1995.

Useful reference books include John L. Somer and Barbara Eck Cooper, *American and British Literature 1945–1975: An Annotated Bibliography of Contemporary Scholarship*, 1980; *An Annotated Critical Bibliography of Modernism*, ed. Alistair Davies, 1982; *Contemporary Dramatists*, 5th ed., ed. K. A. Berney, 1993; *Contemporary Novelists*, 4th ed., ed. D. L. Kirkpatrick and James Vinson, 1986; *Contemporary Poets*, ed. Thomas Riggs, 1996; *The Oxford Companion to Twentieth-Century Poetry*, ed. Ian Hamilton, 1994; and *The Oxford Companion to Irish Literature*, ed. Robert Welch, 1996.

See also entries for **The Rise and Fall of Empire, Voices from World War I,** and **Voices from World War II.**

W. H. Auden

W. H. Auden: Collected Poems, ed. Edward Mendelson, 1976, contains all the poems that the author wished to preserve, in the texts that received his final approval. *The English Auden, Poems, Essays and Dramatic Writings, 1927–1939,* ed. Edward Mendelson, 1977, reprints in their original versions all the poems Auden published in book form during the 1930s, together with some previously unpublished and uncollected poems and a selection of Auden's early prose writings. The definitive collected edition of his works now proceeds, under the editorship of Edward Mendelson, *Plays and Other Dramatic Writings by W. H. Auden, 1928–1938,* 1989; *Libretti, and Other Dramatic Writings 1939–1973,* 1993; and *Prose and Travel Books in Prose and Verse,* Vol. 1, *1926–1938,* 1996. The precanonical poems are available in *Juvenilia 1922–1928,* ed. Katherine Bucknell, 1994. *The Dyer's Hand and Other Essays,* 1968, brings together a selection of his stimulating literary-critical articles, lectures, and reviews. *Forewords and Afterwards,* 1973, is a comparable collection. Auden edited a number of anthologies, including (with Norman Pearson) *Poets of the English Language,* 5 vols., 1950; (with Noah Greenberg and Chester Kallman) *An Elizabethan Songbook,* 1955; and *The Elder*

Edda: A Selection, 1969. The best critical studies are M. K. Spears, *The Poetry of W. H. Auden,* 1963; Justin Replogle, *Auden's Poetry,* 1969; Edward Mendelson, *Early Auden,* 1981; Edward Callan, *Auden: A Carnival of Intellect,* 1983; Stan Smith, *W. H. Auden,* 1985; Lucy McDiarmid, *Auden's Apologies for Poetry,* 1990; and Edward Mendelson, *Later Auden,* 1999. John Fuller, *W. H. Auden: A Commentary,* 1998, provides a commentary on Auden's poetry and drama in chronological order; and Samuel Hynes, *The Auden Generation: Literature and Politics in England in the 1930s,* 1976, is an illuminating study of Auden and his contemporaries in their historical context. The most comprehensive biography is Humphrey Carpenter, *W. H. Auden: A Biography,* 1981, but that by Richard Davenport-Hines, 1995, is a strongly conceived and thematic study. The standard bibliography is by Edward Mendelson and B. C. Bloomfield, 2nd ed., 1972, updated in *Auden Studies,* ed. Katherine Bucknell and Nicholas Jenkins, of which three volumes have so far appeared, 1990, 1994, and 1995.

Samuel Beckett

The standard biography is James Knowlson, *Doomed to Fame: The Life of Samuel Beckett,* 1996, but see also Anthony Cronin, *Samuel Beckett: The Last Modernist,* 1996, and *Conversations with and about Beckett,* ed. Mel Gussow, 1996. On the biographical background to the early work, see John Pilling, *Beckett before Godot,* 1998. Hugh Kenner, *A Reader's Guide to Samuel Beckett,* 1973, and A. Alvarez, *Samuel Beckett,* 1973, are good introductions to his work. On the plays, see Ruby Cohn, *Just Play: Beckett's Theatre,* 1980; Beryl Fletcher and John Fletcher, *A Student's Guide to the Plays of Samuel Beckett,* 1985; and, for the later drama, Rosemary Pountney, *Theatre of Shadows: Samuel Beckett's Drama 1956–1976,* 1998. On the fiction, see Ray Federman, *Journey to Chaos: Samuel Beckett's Early Fiction,* 1965; Rubin Rabinovitz, *Innovation in Samuel Beckett's Fiction,* 1992; and Bob Cochran, *Samuel Beckett: A Study of the Short Fiction,* 1992. On the later work in general, see Steven Connor, *Samuel Beckett: Repetition Theory and Text,* 1986; and Enoch Brater, *Beyond Minimalism: Beckett's Late Style in the Theatre,* 1987, and *The Drama in the Text: Beckett's Late Fiction,* 1994. Among many good general studies are *The Cambridge Companion to Beckett,* ed. John Pilling, 1994; Vivian Mercier, *Beckett / Beckett,* 1977; and Christopher Ricks, *Beckett's Dying Words,* 1993. Also very useful is *Samuel Beckett: The Critical Heritage,* ed. Lawrence Graver and Ray Federman, 1979. There is a Beckett Archive at the University of Reading, and the twice-yearly *Journal of Beckett Studies* began publication in 1976.

J. M. Coetzee

Coetzee's *Dusklands,* 1974, consists of two linked novellas. It was followed by the novels *In the Heart of the Country,* 1977, published as *From the Heart of the Country* in the United States; *Waiting for the*

Barbarians, 1980; *Life and Times of Michael K.*, 1983; *Foe*, 1986; *Age of Iron*, 1990; and *The Master of Petersburg*, 1994. His nonfiction writing includes *Truth in Autobiography*, 1984; *White Writing: On the Culture of Letters in South Africa*, 1988; *Doubling the Point: Essays and Interviews*, 1992, and *Giving Offense: Essays on Censorship*, 1996. Kevin Goddard, John Read and Teresa Dovey, *J. M. Coetzee: A Bibliography*, 1990, is comprehensive of the work to 1990. The most inclusive overview of Coetzee's fiction to date is Dominic Head, *J. M. Coetzee*, 1997, although Dick Penner, *Countries of the Mind: The Fiction of J. M. Coetzee*, 1989, is illuminative of work up to and including *Foe*. Coetzee is examined as a specifically South African writer in David Attwell, *J. M. Coetzee: South Africa and the Politics of Writing*, 1993, and Susan VanZanten Gallagher, *A Story of South Africa: J. M. Coetzee's Fiction in Context*, 1991. More specialized is Claudia Egerer, *Fictions of Inbetweenness*, 1997. An impressive essay dedicated to *Foe* is Derek Attridge, "Oppressive Silence: J. M. Coetzee's *Foe* and the Politics of the Canon" in *Decolonizing Tradition: New Views of Twentieth Century "British" Literary Canon*, ed. Karen R. Lawrence, 1992.

Joseph Conrad

The standard edition of Conrad's works is *The Uniform Edition of the Works of Joseph Conrad*, 22 vols., 1923–38, rpt. 1946–55 as the *Collected Edition of the Works of Joseph Conrad*. Useful critical essays and notes to the novels are provided by the Norton Critical Editions of *Heart of Darkness*, 3rd ed., ed. Robert Kimbrough, 1987; *Lord Jim*, ed. Thomas C. Moser, 1968; and *The Nigger of the "Narcissus*," ed. Robert Kimbrough, 1979. The Modern Library edition of *Nostromo*, 1951, also contains an illuminating introductory essay by Robert Penn Warren. Five volumes of Conrad's letters to 1916 have been published as *The Collected Letters of Joseph Conrad*, ed. Frederick R. Karl and Laurence Davies, 1983–96, and *Letters from Joseph Conrad*, ed. Edward Garnett, 1928, and are supplemented by material in *Joseph Conrad's Letters to R. B. Cunninghame Graham*, ed. C. T. Watts, 1969. Letters concerning as well as by Conrad are collected in *A Portrait in Letters: Correspondence to and about Conrad*, ed. John H. Stape and Owen Knowles, 1996. The most comprehensive biographies are John Batchelor, *The Life of Joseph Conrad: A Critical Biography*, 1993; Frederick Karl, *Joseph Conrad: The Three Lives: A Biography*, 1979; Zdzislaw Najder, *Joseph Conrad: A Chronicle*, 1983, and Cedric Watts, *Joseph Conrad: A Literary Life*, 1989. Memoirs of Conrad include Jessie Conrad, *Joseph Conrad As I Knew Him*, 1926, and *Joseph Conrad and His Circle*, 1935, and Ford Madox Ford, *Joseph Conrad: A Personal Remembrance*, 1989. See also material collected in *Joseph Conrad: Interviews and Recollections*, ed. Martin Ray, 1990. The standard bibliography is *Joseph Conrad: An Annotated Bibliography*, ed. Bruce Teets, 1990.

Robert Hampson, *Joseph Conrad: Betrayal and Identity*, 1992, looks at Conrad's early work, whereas Garry Geddes, *Conrad's Later Novels*, 1980, and Thomas Moser, *Joseph Conrad, Achievement and Decline*, 1957, look at the later work. Studies of the political novels include Eloise Knapp Hay, *The Political Novels of Joseph Conrad*, rev. ed. 1981; Clare Rosenfield, *Paradise of Snakes*, 1967; and Avrom Fleishman, *Conrad's Politics: Community and Anarchy in the Fiction of Joseph Conrad*, 1967. A feminist perspective is offered by Heliéna Krenn, *Conrad's Lingard Trilogy: Empire, Race and Women in the Malay Novels*, 1990, and Ruth Nadelhaft, *Joseph Conrad*, 1991. Conrad is examined through postcolonial theories in Gail Fincham and Myrtle Hooper, *Under Postcolonial Eyes: Joseph Conrad after Empire*, 1996, and Christopher L. GoGwilt, *The Invention of the West: Joseph Conrad and the Double-Mapping of Europe and Empire*, 1995. Also important are John Batchelor, *Lord Jim*, 1988; *Joseph Conrad*, ed. Harold Bloom, 1986; *Joseph Conrad: Critical Assessments*, 4 vols, ed. Keith Carabine, 1992; Peter J. Glassman, *Language and Being: Joseph Conrad and the Literature of Personality*, 1976; Albert J. Guerard, *Conrad the Novelist*, 1958; Jakob Lothe, *Conrad's Narrative Method*, 1989; *Conrad on Film*, ed. Gene M. Moore, 1997; Zdzislaw Najder, *Conrad in Perspective: Essays on Art and Fidelity*, 1997; *Joseph Conrad*, Longman Critical Reader Series, ed. Andrew Michael Roberts, 1998; Edward Said, *Joseph Conrad and the Fiction of Autobiography*, 1966; Daniel R. Schwarz, *Conrad: Almayer's Folly Through Under Western Eyes*, 1980; *Conrad: The Critical Heritage*, ed. Norman Sherry, 1973; *The Cambridge Companion to Joseph Conrad*, ed. J. H. Stape, 1996; Daphna Erdinast Vulcan, *Joseph Conrad and the Modern Temper*, 1991; Ian Watt, *Conrad in the Nineteenth Century*, 1981 (a monumental work, but concerned only with the period before 1900); Cedric Watts, *A Preface to Conrad*, 1982; Anthony Winner, *Culture and Irony: Studies in Joseph Conrad's Major Novels*, 1988, and Mark A. Wollaeger, *Joseph Conrad and the Fictions of Skepticism*, 1990. Important essays on Conrad's work can be found in Dorothy Van Ghent, *The English Novel: Form and Function*, 1953; Warwick Gould, *Modernist Writers and the Marketplace*, 1996; Frederic Jameson, *The Political Unconscious: Narrative as a Socially Symbolic Act*, 1981, and Vincent P. Pecora, *Self and Form in Modern Narrative*, 1989.

T. S. Eliot

The fullest one-volume collections of Eliot's poetry are *Collected Poems, 1909–1963*, 1963, and *The Complete Poems and Plays*, including *Poems Written in Early Youth*, 1969. *The Waste Land: A Facsimile and Transcript of the Original Drafts including the Annotations of Ezra Pound*, ed. Valerie Eliot, 1971, is an indispensable tool for study of *The Waste Land*. See also *Inventions of the March Hare, Poems 1909–17*, ed. Christopher Ricks, 1996. Eliot's most important critical essays are to be found in *The Sacred Wood: Essays on Poetry and Criticism*, 1921; *The Use of Poetry and the Use of Criticism: Studies in the Relation of Criticism to Poetry in England*, 1923; *Notes Towards the Definition of Culture*, 1948; *On Poetry and Poets*, 1957; *To Criticize the Critic and Other Writings*, 1965; and *The Varieties of Metaphysical Poetry*, ed. Ronald Schuchard, 1993. Helen Gardner, *The Composition of* Four Quartets, 1978, describes the growth of the poem from the drafts, and includes new information on its sources.

In the absence of a full-scale biography, one is the more grateful for *Notes on Some Figures behind T. S. Eliot*, Herbert Howarth, 1965; *T. S. Eliot: The Man and His Work*, ed. Allen Tate, 1967; Ronald Bush, *T. S. Eliot: A Study in Character and Style*, 1984; Peter Ackroyd, *T. S. Eliot*, 1984; *The Letters of T. S. Eliot*, Vol. 1: *1898–1922*, ed. Valerie Eliot, 1988; and Lyndall Gordon, *T. S. Eliot: An Imperfect Life*, 1998.

Among the many books on Eliot, F. O. Matthiessen, *The Achievement of T. S. Eliot*, rev. ed. 1947, has the enthusiasm of a pioneer work; Helen Gardner, *The Art of T. S. Eliot*, 1950, is a perceptive critical study of his poetry; B. C. Southam, *A Student's Guide to the Selected Poems of T. S. Eliot*, rev. ed., 1994, and *T. S. Eliot: The Critical Heritage*, 2 vols, ed. Michael Grant, 1982, are useful reference sources for students, and Grover Smith Jr., *T. S. Eliot's Poetry and Plays*, 1956, goes through the poems and plays in an exhaustive manner. More specialized studies include *The Making of T. S. Eliot's Plays*, Martin Browne, 1969; *Eliot in His Time*, ed. A. Walton Litz, 1973; A. D. Moody, *Thomas Stearns Eliot, Poet*, 1979; Grover Smith, *"The Waste Land,"* 1983; Louis Menand, *Discovering Modernism: T. S. Eliot and His Context*, 1987; Robert Crawford, *The Savage and the City in the Work of T. S. Eliot*, 1987; Richard Shusterman, *T. S. Eliot and the Philosophy of Criticism*, 1988; Maud Ellmann, *The Poetics of Impersonality*, 1988; Jeffrey M. Perl, *Scepticism and Modern Enmity: Before and after Eliot*, 1989; Eric Sigg, *The American T. S. Eliot: A Study of the Early Writings*, 1989; Ronald Bush, *T. S. Eliot, The Modernist in History*, 1991; Manju Jain, *T. S. Eliot and American Philosophy: The Harvard Years*, 1992; Gail McDonald, *Learning to Be Modern: Pound, Eliot, and the American University*, 1993; Frank Lentricchia, *Modernist Quartet*, 1994; and Anthony Julius, *T. S. Eliot, Anti-Semitism, and Literary Form*, 1995.

Nadine Gordimer

Gordimer's work includes the novels *The Lying Days*, 1953; *The Late Bourgeois World*, 1966; *A Guest of Honour*, 1971; *A World of Strangers*, 1976; *The Conservationist*, 1976; *Burger's Daughter*, 1979; *July's People*, 1981; *A Sport of Nature*, 1987; *My Son's Story*, 1990; *None to Accompany Me*, 1994; and *The House Gun*, 1998. The short-story collections are *Six Feet of the Country*, 1956; *Some Monday for Sure*, 1976; *A Soldier's Embrace*, 1980;

Something Out There, 1984; and *Jump*, 1991. She has also published two collections of nonfiction essays, *The Essential Gesture: Writing, Politics and Places*, ed. Stephen Clingman, and *Writing and Being*, 1995. Critical accounts of her work include Michael Wade, *Nadine Gordimer*, 1978; Stephen Clingman, *The Novels of Nadine Gordimer: History from the Inside*, 1986; a chapter in Abdul R. JanMohamed, *Manichean Aesthetics: The Politics of Literature in Colonial Africa*, 1983; Judie Newman, *Nadine Gordimer*, 1988; *Critical Essays on Nadine Gordimer*, ed. Rowland Smith, 1990; *The Later Fiction of Nadine Gordimer*, ed. Bruce King, 1993; and Andrew V. Ettin, *Betrayals of the Body Politic: The Literary Commitments of Nadine Gordimer*, 1993.

Thomas Hardy

Hardy published over a dozen volumes of poetry in his lifetime; *The Collected Poems* were issued in one volume in 1932; and *The Complete Poetical Works of Thomas Hardy*, ed. Samuel Hynes, in three volumes in 1982–85. There are several collected editions of Hardy's complete work, notably the Wessex Edition, 21 vols., 1912–14, and the Mellstock Edition, 37 vols., 1919–20. Many of the novels are in paperbound editions; among the most notable are the Norton Critical Editions of *Jude the Obscure*, ed. Norman Page, 1978; *The Mayor of Casterbridge*, ed. James K. Robinson, 1977; *The Return of the Native*, ed. James Gindin, 1969; and *Tess of the D'Urbervilles*, 3rd ed., ed. Scott Elledge, 1990.

The best biographies are Robert Gittings, *Young Thomas Hardy*, 1975, and *Thomas Hardy's Later Years*, 1978; Michael Millgate, *Thomas Hardy: A Biography*, 1982; and Paul Turner, *The Life of Thomas Hardy*, 1998. Michael Millgate and R. Purdy have edited *The Collected Letters of Thomas Hardy*, 7 vols., 1978–88. Millgate has also edited *Selected Letters*, 1990, and Harold Orel has edited *Thomas Hardy's Personal Writings: Prefaces, Literary Opinions, Reminiscences*, 1990.

The Hardy Centennial Number of *The Southern Review*, 1940, was influential in shaping Hardy's critical reputation: the special Hardy issues of *Agenda*, 1970, and *Victorian Poetry*, 1979, are notable. *Hardy: A Collection of Critical Essays*, ed. Albert Guerard, 1963, treats both the prose and the poetry, as do J. Hillis Miller, *Thomas Hardy: Distance and Desire*, 1970; Jean R. Brooks, *Thomas Hardy: The Poetic Structure*, 1971; John Bayley, *An Essay on Hardy*, 1978; *Thomas Hardy After Fifty Years*, ed. Lance St. John Butler, 1977; and *Thomas Hardy: The Writer and His Background*, ed. Norman Page, 1980, which contains a useful bibliography. Ian Gregor, *The Great Web: The Form of Hardy's Major Fiction*, 1974, and *Critical Approaches to the Fiction of Thomas Hardy*, ed. Dale Kramer, 1979, provide good discussions of Hardy's novels. Samuel Hynes, *The Pattern of Hardy's Poetry*, 1956, remains sound and useful; Donald Davie, *Thomas Hardy and British Poetry*, 1973, is worth consulting. Paul Zeitlow, *Moments of Vision: The Poetry of Thomas Hardy*, 1974; Tom Paulin, *Thomas Hardy: The*

Poetry of Perception, 1975; The Poetry of Thomas Hardy, ed. Patricia Clements and Juliet Grindle, 1980; William Earl Buckler, The Poetry of Thomas Hardy: A Study in Art and Ideas, 1983; and Dennis Taylor, Hardy's Metres and Victorian Prosody, 1988, contain good criticism of the poetry; J. O. Bailey, The Poetry of Thomas Hardy, 1970, and F. B. Pinion, A Commentary on the Poems of Thomas Hardy, 1976, are helpful on individual poems.

Seamus Heaney

Open Ground: Poems 1966–1996, 1998, includes selections from Heaney's earlier collections Death of a Naturalist, 1966; Door into the Dark, 1969; Wintering Out, 1972; North, 1975; Field Work, 1979; Sweeney Astray, 1983; Station Island, 1984; The Haw Lantern, 1987; Seeing Things, 1991, and The Spirit Level, 1996. He has published three collections of essays: Preoccupations: Selected Prose, 1968–1978, 1980; The Government of the Tongue, 1988; and The Redress of Poetry: Oxford Lectures, 1995. Heaney's verse translation of Beowulf (2000) is available in volume 1 of The Norton Anthology of English Literature, Seventh Edition. A biography, Michael Parker, Seamus Heaney: The Making of the Poet, was published in 1993. Critical and biographical studies include Blake Morrison, Seamus Heaney, 1982; Neil Corcoran, Seamus Heaney: A Faber Study Guide, 1986; Elmer Andrews, The Poetry of Seamus Heaney: All the Reams of Whisper, 1988; Thomas C. Foster, Seamus Heaney, 1989; H. Hart, Seamus Heaney: Poet of Contrary Progressions, 1992; Bernard O'Donoghue Seamus Heaney, 1994; J. W. Foster, The Achievement of Seamus Heaney, 1995; and Helen Vendler, Seamus Heaney, 1998. Collections of critical essays include Seamus Heaney, ed. Harold Bloom, 1988; Seamus Heaney: A Collection of Critical Essays, ed. Elmer Andrews, 1992; The Art of Seamus Heaney, 3rd ed., ed. Tony Curtis, 1994; and Critical Essays on Seamus Heaney, ed. Robert F. Garratt, 1995. Also indispensable is Michael J. Durkan and Rand Brandes, Seamus Heaney: A Reference Guide, 1996.

James Joyce

The most reliable edition of Ulysses, 1922, is Ulysses: A Critical and Synoptic Edition, 3 vols, ed. Hans Walter Gabler with Wolfhard Steppe and Claus Melchoir, 1984 and rev. ed., 1986. Annotated editions of Dubliners, 1914, and A Portrait of the Artist as a Young Man, 1916, are available in Viking, Penguin, and Oxford World's Classics editions. The Oxford World's Classics edition of Ulysses, ed. Jeri Johnson, 1993, uses the 1922 text and has the most exhaustive notes and supportive critical material. An edition of Stephen Hero, the novel that became the basis for Portrait, was edited by John J. Slocum and Herbert Cahoon, 1955. There is no textually reliable edition of Finnegans Wake, but currently available editions include those of Faber, Minerva, Palladin, and Penguin. The Portable James Joyce, ed. H. Levin, 1968, is useful. For Joyce's critical writing see Critical Writings of James Joyce, ed. Richard Ellmann and Ellsworth Mason, 1959, and for his poems and shorter pieces, James Joyce: Poems and Shorter Writings, ed. Richard Ellmann, A. Walton Litz, and John Whittier Ferguson, 1991. The Letters of James Joyce, 3 vols., has been edited by Stuart Gilbert and Richard Ellmann, 1957–66, and a selection is available, ed. Richard Ellmann, 1975. The standard bibliography of Joyce's work is A Bibliography of James Joyce, ed. John J. Slocum and Herbert Cahoon, 2nd ed., 1971, and Thomas Jackson Rice, James Joyce: A Guide to Research, 1982, is a helpful bibliography of the secondary literature.

The standard biography is Richard Ellmann, James Joyce, 3rd rev. ed., 1983. Also useful are Sylvia Beach, Shakespeare and Company, 1959; Stanislaus Joyce, The Complete Dublin Diary of Stanislaus Joyce, 1971, and My Brother's Keeper: James Joyce's Early Years, ed. Richard Ellmann, 1958; Brenda Maddox, Nora: A Biography of Nora Joyce, 1988; E. H. Mikhail, James Joyce: Interviews and Recollections, 1990; Portraits of the Artist in Exile: Recollections of James Joyce by Europeans, ed. Willard Potts, rpt. 1986; and Arthur Power, Conversations with James Joyce, rpt. 1982.

Good general accounts of Joyce's work can be found in The Cambridge Companion to James Joyce, ed. Derek Attridge, 1990; A Companion to Joyce Studies, ed. Zack Bowen and James F. Carens, 1984; James Joyce: The Critical Heritage, 2 vols., ed. Robert H. Deming, 1970; Richard Ellmann, The Consciousness of Joyce, 1977; Hugh Kenner, Dublin's Joyce, 1955, and Joyce's Voices, 1978; Colin MacCabe, James Joyce and the Revolution of the Word, 1978; James Joyce: New Perspectives, ed. Colin MacCabe, 1982; Vicki Mahaffey, Reauthorizing Joyce, 1988; Patrick Parrinder, James Joyce, 1984; C. H. Peake, James Joyce: The Citizen and the Artist, 1976; and Jean-Michel Rabaté, James Joyce: Authorized Reader, 1991.

More specialized studies include Post-Structuralist Joyce: Essays from the French, ed. Derek Attridge and Daniel Ferrer, 1984; Samuel Beckett et al., Our Exagmination Round His Factification for Incamination of Work in Progress, rpt. 1972; Richard Brown, James Joyce and Sexuality, 1985; Kevin J. H. Dettmar, The Illicit Joyce of Postmodernism: Reading against the Grain, 1996; Patrick McGee, Paperspace: Style as Ideology in Joyce, 1988; Dominic Manganiello, Joyce's Politics, 1980; Margot Norris, Joyce's Web: The Social Unraveling of Modernism, 1992; Fritz Senn, Joyce's Dislocations: Essays on Reading as Translation, 1984; and Robert E. Spoo, James Joyce and the Language of History: Daedalus's Nightmare.

Critical studies of Dubliners and A Portrait of the Artist as a Young Man include Twentieth-Century Interpretations of Dubliners: A Collection of Critical Essays, ed. P. K. Garrett, 1968; James Joyce's Dubliners: Critical Essays, ed. Clive Hart, 1968; and Maud Ellmann, "Disremembering Daedalus: A Portrait of the Artist as a Young Man," in Untying the Text: A Post-Structuralist Reader, ed. Robert Young, 1981.

Among the most helpful of many critical studies of Ulysses are Frank Budgen, James Joyce and the

Making of Ulysses, rpt. 1972; Edna Duffy, *The Subaltern Ulysses*, 1994; Maud Ellmann, "The Ghosts of Ulysses," in *James Joyce: The Artist and the Labyrinth*, ed. Augustine Martin, 1990; Richard Ellmann, *Ulysses on the Liffey*, rev. rpt. 1974; Marilyn French, *The Book as World: James Joyce's Ulysses*, 1976; Don Gifford with Robert J. Seidman, *Ulysses Annotated: Notes for Joyce's Ulysses*, rev. ed. 1988; Stuart Gilbert, *James Joyce's Ulysses: A Study*, rev. ed., 1952; Michael Groden, *Ulysses in Progress*, 1977; *James Joyce's Ulysses: Critical Essays*, ed. Clive Hart and David Hayman, 1974; David Hayman, Ulysses: *The Mechanics of Meaning*, rev. ed. 1982; Hugh Kenner, *Ulysses*, rev. ed. 1987; Karen Lawrence, *The Odyssey of Style in Ulysses*, 1981; James H. Maddox, *Joyce's Ulysses and the Assault upon Character*, 1978; William Schutte, *Joyce and Shakespeare*, 1957; Michael Seidel, *Epic Geography: James Joyce's Ulysses*, 1976; Ulysses: *Fifty Years*, ed. Thomas F. Staley, rpt. 1974; and Weldon Thornton, *Allusions in* Ulysses, 1973. David Pierce, *James Joyce's Ireland*, 1992, provides other useful background material.

Notes and drafts for the novel are examined in Philip Herring, *Joyce's Notes and Early Drafts for* Ulysses: *Selections from the Buffalo Collection*, 1977, and *Joyce's Ulysses Notesheets in the British Museum*, 1972.

The best studies of *Finnegans Wake* include James S. Atherton, *The Books at the Wake: A Study of Literary Allusions in James Joyce's Finnegans Wake*, 2nd ed. 1974; John Bishop, *Joyce's Book of the Dark*: Finnegans Wake, 1986; Kimberly J. Devlin, *Wandering and Return in* Finnegans Wake: *An Integrative Approach to Joyce's Fictions*, 1991; Adaline Glasheen, *A Third Census of* Finnegans Wake: *An Index of the Characters and Their Roles*, 1977; Clive Hart, *Structure and Motif in* Finnegans Wake, 1962, and *A Concordance to Finnegans Wake*, rev. ed. 1974; Thomas C. Hofheinz, *Joyce and the Invention of Irish History:* Finnegans Wake *in Context*, 1995; and Roland McHugh, *Annotations to* Finnegans Wake, 1980.

Philip Larkin

Larkin's *Collected Poems*, ed. Anthony Thwaite, 1988, contains a number of hitherto unpublished poems in addition to the contents of his four collections: *The North Ship*, 1945, rev. 1966; *The Less Deceived*, 1955; *The Whitsun Weddings*, 1964 and *High Windows*, 1974. Thwaite has also edited *Selected Letters of Philip Larkin, 1940–1985*, 1992. Larkin published two early novels: *Jill*, 1946, and *A Girl in Winter*, 1947; a collection of essays on jazz: *All That Jazz: A Record Diary, 1961–68*, 1970; and *Required Writing: Miscellaneous Pieces, 1955–1982*, 1983, containing recollections, interviews, and essays on literature and jazz. He edited *The Oxford Book of Twentieth-Century English Verse*, 1973, and contributed an interview to *Viewpoints: Poets in Conversation with John Haffenden*, 1981. The standard biography is Andrew Motion, *Philip*

Larkin: A Writer's Life, 1993. David Timms, *Philip Larkin*, 1973, was the first full-length study of his poetry. Andrew Tolley, *Larkin at Work*, 1998, offers a useful "study of Larkin's mode of composition as seen in his notebooks," and there are good critical essays in *Phoenix*: Philip Larkin Issue, 11/12 (Autumn and Winter 1973/4); *Larkin at Sixty*, ed. Anthony Thwaite, 1982; and *Philip Larkin*, ed. Stephen Regan, 1998.

D. H. Lawrence

The definitive Cambridge Edition of the Works of Lawrence is now almost complete. The seven volumes of his *Letters*, edited by James Boulton and others, were issued by Cambridge between 1979 and 1993. The best edition of Lawrence's poetry remains the third edition of *The Complete Poems*, ed. V. de Sola Pinto and W. Roberts, 1972. The Penguin paperback texts of the novels and shorter fiction are based on the Cambridge editions, and Oxford World's Classics have also issued useful paperback editions of *The White Peacock, Sons and Lovers, The Rainbow, Women in Love*, and certain other works.

The standard biography is the Cambridge triptych: John Worthen, *D. H. Lawrence: The Early Years 1885–1912*, 1991; Mark Kinkead-Weekes, *D. H. Lawrence: Triumph to Exile 1912–1922*, 1996; and David Ellis, *D. H. Lawrence: Dying Game 1922–1930*, 1998.

Pioneering critical studies include F. R. Leavis, *D. H. Lawrence: Novelist*, 1956; Graham Hough, *The Dark Sun*, 1957; H. M. Daleski, *The Forked Flame*, 1965; George Ford, *Double Measure*, 1965; and Colin Clarke, *River of Dissolution: D. H. Lawrence and English Romanticism*, 1969. Some more recent valuable analyses are *D. H. Lawrence: The Critical Heritage*, ed. R. P. Draper, 1970; Emile Delavenay, *D. H. Lawrence: The Man and His Work: The Formative Years, 1885–1919*, trans. Katharine M. Delavenay, 1972; Sandra Gilbert, *Acts of Attention: The Poems of D. H. Lawrence*, 1972; Frank Kermode, *Lawrence*, 1973; Alastair Niven, *D. H. Lawrence: The Novels*, 1978; John Worthen, *D. H. Lawrence and the Idea of the Novel*, 1979; Paul Delaney, *D. H. Lawrence's Nightmare: The Writer and His Circle in the Years of the Great War*, 1979; Aidan Burns, *Nature and Culture in D. H. Lawrence*, 1980; Graham Holderness, *D. H. Lawrence: History, Ideology and Fiction*, 1982; Hilary Simpson, *D. H. Lawrence and Feminism*, 1982; Sheila Macleod, *Lawrence's Men and Women*, 1985; Cornelia Nixon, *Lawrence's Leadership Politics and the Turn against Women*, 1986; Daniel Schneider, *The Consciousness of D. H. Lawrence: An Intellectual Biography*, 1986; Christopher Heywood, *D. H. Lawrence: New Studies*, 1987; Colin Milton, *Lawrence and Nietzsche: A Study in Influence*, 1987; *D. H. Lawrence: New Studies*, ed. Colin Milton, 1988; M. J. Lockwood, *A Study of the Poems of D. H. Lawrence: Thinking in Poetry*, 1988; *The Challenge of D. H. Lawrence*, ed.

Michael Squires and Keith Cushman, 1990; Tony Pinkney, *D. H. Lawrence* and *D. H. Lawrence and Modernism*, 1990; *Rethinking Lawrence*, ed. Keith Brown, 1990; Michael Black, *D. H. Lawrence: The Early Philosophical Works: A Commentary*, 1991; Barbara Mensch, *D. H. Lawrence and the Authoritarian Personality*, 1991; Charles Ross, *Women in Love: A Novel of Mythic Realism*, 1991; Michael Bell, *D. H. Lawrence: Language and Being*, 1992; *D. H. Lawrence: A Critical Reader*, ed. Peter Widdowson, 1992; Anne Fernihough, *D. H. Lawrence: Aesthetics and Ideology*, 1993; and Robert Montgomery, *The Visionary D. H. Lawrence: Beyond Philosophy and Art*, 1994. An essential reference tool is Paul Poplawski, *D. H. Lawrence: A Reference Companion*, 1996.

Katherine Mansfield

There is a convenient complete one-volume edition of Katherine Mansfield's stories, *The Short Stories of Katherine Mansfield*, 1937. Her *Journal* was edited by Middleton Murry in 1954; *The Critical Writings of Katherine Mansfield*, by Clare Hanson, 1987; *Poems of Katherine Mansfield*, by Vincent O'Sullivan, 1988; *The Collected Letters of Katherine Mansfield*, by Vincent O'Sullivan and Margaret Scott, 1984; and *The Katherine Mansfield Notebooks*, 2 vols., by Scott, 1998. The best biographies are Anthony Alpers, *The Life of Katherine Mansfield*, 2nd ed., 1979, and Claire Tomalin, *Katherine Mansfield: A Secret Life*, 1987.

Critical studies include Marvin Magalener, *The Fiction of Katherine Mansfield*, 1971; Ian A. Gordon, *Undiscovered Country: The New Zealand Stories of Katherine Mansfield*, 1974; Clare Hanson and Andrew Gurr, *Katherine Mansfield*, 1981; C. A. Hankin, *Katherine Mansfield and Her Confessional Stories*, 1983; Kate Fullbrook, *Katherine Mansfield*, 1986; *Critical Essays on Katherine Mansfield*, ed. Rhoda B. Nathan, 1993; and *The Critical Response to Katherine Mansfield*, ed. Jan Pilditch, 1996.

Salman Rushdie

Rushdie's first full-length work of fiction was the magic realist *Grimus: a Novel*, 1975, followed by *Midnight's Children*, 1981; *Shame*, 1983; and *The Satanic Verses*, 1988. He has also written a story for children, *Haroun and the Sea of Stories*, 1990. His nonfiction writing includes *The Jaguar Smile: A Nicaraguan Journey*, 1987, and a collection of essays, *Imaginary Homelands: Essays and Criticism, 1981–1991*, 1991, and he was coeditor, with Elizabeth West, of *The Vintage Book of Indian Writing, 1947–1997*, 1997. More recent publications include *In Good Faith*, 1990; *The Wizard of Oz*, 1992; *East, West*, 1994; *The Moor's Last Sigh*, 1995; and *The Ground Beneath Her Feet*, 1999. Some of the most useful of the abundant critical material on Rushdie's writing includes Linwood Taylor Antrim, *History, Nation, Faith: Salman Rushdie and the Reconstruction of Transcendence*, 1998; Catherine Cundy, *Salman Rushdie*, 1997; Jena Habegger, *Salman Rushdie and the Fictive Nature of Reality*,

1998; James Harrison, *Salman Rushdie*, 1992; Margareta Petersson, *Unending Metamorphoses: Myth, Satire and Religion in Salman Rushdie's Novels*, 1996. Works that focus on the controversy surrounding Rushdie's *Satanic Verses*, and his relationship with Islam, include Lisa Appignanesi, *The Rushdie File*, 1989; Umar Azam, *Rushdie's Satanic Verses: An Islamic Response*, 1990; Daniel Easterman, *New Jerusalems: Reflections on Islam, Fundamentalism and the Rushdie Affair*, 1992; Jorgen S. Nielsen, *The "Rushdie Affair": A Documentation*, 1989; and Malise Ruthven, *A Satanic Affair: Salman Rushdie and the Wrath of Islam*, rev. ed. 1991. The section on Rushdie in Fawzia Afzal-Khan, *Cultural Imperialism and the Indo-English Novel: Genre and Ideology in R. K. Narayan, Anita Desai, Kamala Markandaya, and Salman Rushdie*, 1993, considers him as a postcolonial writer.

Dylan Thomas

The Collected Poems, ed. Walford Davies and Ralph Ward, 1988, is the standard edition of Thomas's poetry. He also wrote the autobiographical prose *Portrait of the Artist as a Young Dog*, 1940; *Adventures in the Skin Trade*, 1955; a radio play, *Under Milk Wood*, 1954, which has proved a great popular success; and *Quite Early One Morning*, 1954, a collection of stories, essays, and minor pieces. Paul Ferris edited *The Collected Letters of Dylan Thomas* in 1985, and *The Notebooks of Dylan Thomas* was edited by Ralph N. Maud in 1967. Maud, *Entrances to Dylan Thomas's Poetry*, 1963; William York Tindall, *A Reader's Guide to Dylan Thomas*, 1962; and William T. Moynahan, *The Craft and Art of Dylan Thomas*, 1966, are good introductions to the workings of the poet's mind. R. B. Kershner, *Dylan Thomas: The Poet and His Critics*, 1976, is an evaluation of criticism with a useful bibliography, and *Critical Essays on Dylan Thomas*, ed. Georg Gaston, 1989, offers more recent critical perspectives. John Ackerman has compiled *A Dylan Thomas Companion*, 1991, and written *Thomas: His Life and Work*, 1996. Constantine Fitzgibbon, *The Life of Dylan Thomas*, 1965, and Paul Ferris, *Dylan Thomas: A Biography*, 1977, are good biographies, Bill Read, *The Days of Dylan Thomas*, 1964, supplements a straightforward narrative with many photographs.

Derek Walcott

Walcott's plays include *Dream on Monkey Mountain*, 1971; *The Joker of Seville*, 1978, and *O Babylon!*, 1978; and *Three Plays: The Last Carnival; Beef, No Chicken; A Branch of the Blue Nile*, 1986. He is better known for his poetry collections: *In a Green Night: Poems 1948–60*, 1960; *The Castaway and Other Poems*, 1965; *The Gulf and Other Poems*, 1969; *Another Life*, 1973; *Sea Grapes*, 1976; *The Fortunate Traveller*, 1981; *Midsummer*, 1984; *The Arkansas Testament*, 1988; *Omeros*, 1991; *The Bounty*, 1997. "The Poet in the Theatre," Derek Walcott's Ronald Duncan Lecture, was published in 1990. The standard bibliography is *Derek Walcott, The Primary Sources: An Annotated Bibliogra-*

phy of His Works, ed. Irma E. Goldstraw, 1984. Critical studies of Walcott's writing include Edward Baugh, *Derek Walcott: Memory and Vision: Another Life*, 1978; Robert D. Hamner, *Critical Perspectives on Derek Walcott*, 1993, and Rei Terada, *Derek Walcott's Poetry: American Mimicry*, 1992. Useful sections on Walcott's work can be found in Tejumola Olaniyan, *Scars of Conquest—Masks of Resistance: The Invention of Cultural Identities in African, African-American, and Caribbean Drama*, 1995, and *Postcolonial Literatures: Achebe, Ngugi, Desai, Walcott*, ed. Michael Parker and Roger Starkey, 1995.

Virginia Woolf

The ten novels, *A Room of One's Own*, and *Three Guineas* are all available in paperback. *The Complete Shorter Fiction* has been edited by Susan Dick, 1985, and *The Essays*, 3 vols., by Andrew McNeillie, 1986–88. Useful selections of her essays edited by Rachel Bowlby, in Penguin paperbacks, are *The Crowded Dance of Modern Life* and *A Woman's Essays*. *The Diary of Virginia Woolf*, 5 vols., ed. Anne Olivier Bell and Andrew McNeillie, 1977–84, and *The Letters of Virginia Woolf*, 6 vols., ed. Nigel Nicolson and Joanne Trautmann, 1975–80, provide commentary on Woolf's life and work. For her early development, see *A Passionate Apprentice: The Early Journals, 1897–1909*, ed. Mitchell A. Leaska, 1990. *Moments of Being*, ed. Jeanne Schulkind, 1976, rev. 1989, contains her autobiographical writings. Her stories are collected in *The Complete Shorter Fiction of Virginia Woolf*, ed. Susan Dick, 1989.

Hermione Lee, *Virginia Woolf*, 1996, offers the fullest and most balanced account of her life and work; Quentin Bell, *Virginia Woolf*, 2 vols., 1972, is still an invaluable firsthand portrait; Phyllis Rose, *Woman of Letters: A Life of Virginia Woolf*, 1978, focuses on her feminism; and Lyndall Gordon, *Virginia Woolf: A Writer's Life*, 1984, shows Woolf's creative use of her own experience. Louise A. DeSalvo, *Virginia Woolf: The Impact of Childhood Sexual Abuse on Her Life and Work*, 1989, offers a revised picture of Woolf's childhood and its effect on her writing. Of interest also are Leonard Woolf's five volumes of autobiography, *Sowing*, 1960; *Growing*, 1961; *Beginning Again*, 1964; *Downhill All the Way*, 1967; *The Journey Not the Arrival Matters*, 1975; and *Letters of Leonard Woolf*, ed. Frederic Spotts, 1989. See also *Bloomsbury Group*, ed. S. P. Rosenbaum, 1975.

Perceptive critical studies include David Daiches, *Virginia Woolf*, rev. 1963; Joan Bennett, *Virginia Woolf: Her Art as a Novelist*, 2nd ed., 1964; H. Lee, *The Novels of Virginia Woolf*, 1977; Avrom Fleishman, *Virginia Woolf: A Critical Reading*, 1975; *New Feminist Essays on Virginia Woolf*, ed. Jane Marcus, 1981; *Virginia Woolf: New Critical Essays*, ed. Patricia Clements and Isobel Grundy, 1983; Alex Zwerdling, *Virginia Woolf and the Real World*, 1986; Rachel Bowlby, *Virginia Woolf: Feminist Destina-*

tions, 1988, rev. 1997; Elizabeth Abel, *Virginia Woolf and the Fictions of Psychoanalysis*, 1989; John Mepham, *Virginia Woolf: A Literary Life*, 1991; Gillian Beer, *Virginia Woolf: The Common Ground*, 1996; Juliet Dusinberre, *Virginia Woolf's Renaissance*, 1997.

William Butler Yeats

In addition to poems and verse plays, Yeats published essays, stories, and autobiographical writings, and produced editions of William Blake (with Edwin Ellis) and of some poems of Spenser. He also edited *The Oxford Book of Modern Verse*, 1936. The major editions of his poems and plays are *The Variorum Edition of the Poems*, ed. Peter Allt and Russell K. Alspach, 1957, corrected 3rd printing, 1966, and *The Variorum Edition of the Plays*, ed. Russell K. Alspach, 1966, corrected 2nd printing, 1966. *Yeats's Poems*, ed. and annotated A. Norman Jeffares with an appendix by Warwick Gould, is the most satisfactory paperback edition. The fullest and most representative selection of the voluminous correspondence is *The Letters of W. B. Yeats*, ed. Allan Wade, 1954. This will be superseded by a multivolume edition, of which the first three volumes have appeared: *The Collected Letters of W. B. Yeats*, ed. John Kelly, 1986–. Yeats's mystical work *A Vision* was first published in 1925; a much-revised edition appeared in 1937. His autobiographical writings are combined in *The Autobiography of W. B. Yeats*, 1938–. Neither the first draft of Yeats's *Autobiography* nor his *Journals* were published until 1972, when Denis Donoghue edited them under the title *Memoirs*. *Mythologies*, 1959, contains the bulk of Yeats's prose fiction; *Essays and Introductions*, 1961, the most important of his critical prose; and *Explorations*, 1962, miscellaneous prose pieces not readily available elsewhere. John P. Frayne has edited *Uncollected Prose by W. B. Yeats*, 2 vols., 1970 and 1975, and William H. O'Donnell, *W. B. Yeats: Prefaces and Introductions*, 1988.

A. N. Jeffares, *W. B. Yeats: A New Biography*, 1989, is the best of the one-volume biographies, but will be superseded by Roy Foster, *W. B. Yeats: A Life*, vol. I of which was published in 1997.

The critical literature on Yeats is more extensive than that on any other twentieth-century poet, and the best guide to this is "W. B. Yeats" in *Anglo-Irish Literature: A Review of Research*, ed. Richard J. Finneran, 1976. Denis Donoghue, *Yeats*, 1971, is the most satisfactory of many short introductory studies, though less substantial than *Yeats: The Man and the Masks*, 1948, and *The Identity of Yeats*, 2nd ed., 1964, both by Richard Ellmann and still the best general accounts of Yeats's work. *The Permanence of Yeats*, ed. James Hall and Martin Steinmann, 1950; *Yeats: A Collection of Critical Essays*, ed. John Unterecker, 1963; *In Excited Reverie*, ed. A. N. Jeffares and K. G. W. Cross, 1965; and *Critical Essays on W. B. Yeats*, ed. Richard Finneran, 1987, are four of several useful collections of critical essays. The most helpful commentaries are A. N. Jeffares,

A New Commentary on the Poems of W. B. Yeats, 1984, and A Commentary on The Collected Plays of W. B. Yeats, 1975. Specialized critical studies of important areas of Yeats's work are Thomas Parkinson, W. B. Yeats, Self Critic: A Study of His Early Verse, 1951, rpt. 1971 with The Later Poetry and a new foreword; Jon Stallworthy, Between the Lines: W. B. Yeats's Poetry in the Making, 1963, corrected 2nd imp., 1965; and Thomas R. Whitaker, Swan and Shadow: Yeats's Dialogue with History, 1964; and Michael J. Sidnell, Yeats's Poetry and Poetics, 1996.

Geographic Nomenclature: England, Great Britain, The United Kingdom

The British Isles refers to the prominent group of islands off the northwest coast of Europe, especially to the two largest, **Great Britain** and **Ireland**. At present these comprise two sovereign states: **The Republic of Ireland**, or **Eire**, and **The United Kingdom of Great Britain and Northern Ireland**—known for short as **The United Kingdom** or **The U.K.** Most of the smaller islands are part of **The U.K.** but a few, like the **Isle of Man** and the tiny **Channel Islands**, are very largely independent. **The U.K.** is often loosely referred to as "**Britain**" or "**Great Britain**" and is sometimes simply called "**England.**" The latter usage, though technically inaccurate and occasionally confusing, is common among Englishmen as well as foreigners, though, for obvious reasons, it is rarely heard among the inhabitants of the other countries of **The U.K.—Scotland, Wales,** and **Northern Ireland** (sometimes called **Ulster**). England is by far the most populous part of the kingdom, as well as the seat of its capital, London.

From the first to the fifth century C.E. most of what is now **England** and **Wales** was a province of the Roman Empire called **Britain** (in Latin, **Britannia**). After the fall of Rome, much of the island was invaded and settled by peoples from northern Germany and Denmark speaking what we now call Old English. They are collectively known as the Anglo-Saxons, and the word **England** is related to the first element of their name. By the time of the Norman Conquest (1066) most of the kingdoms founded by the Anglo-Saxons and subsequent Viking invaders had coalesced into the kingdom of **England**, which, in the latter Middle Ages, conquered and largely absorbed the neighboring Celtic kingdom of **Wales**. In 1603 James VI of **Scotland** inherited the island's other throne as James I of **England**, and for the next hundred years—except for the brief period of Puritan rule—**Scotland** and **England** (with **Wales**) were two kingdoms under a single king. In 1707 the Act of Union welded them together as **The United Kingdom of Great Britain**, which, upon the incorporation of **Ireland** in 1801, became **The United Kingdom of Great Britain and Ireland**. With the division of Ireland and the establishment of **The Irish Free State** after World War I, this name was modified to its present form. In 1949 **The Irish Free State** became **The Republic of Ireland**; and in 1997 **Scotland** voted to restore the separate parliament it had relinquished in 1707, without, however, ceasing to be part of **The United Kingdom**.

The **British Isles** are further divided into counties, which in **Great Britain** are also known as shires. This word, with its vowel shortened in pronunciation, forms the suffix in the names of many counties, such as **Yorkshire, Wiltshire, Somersetshire**.

The Latin names **Britannia (Britain), Caledonia (Scotland),** and **Hibernia (Ireland)** are sometimes used in poetic diction; so too is **Britain**'s ancient Celtic name, **Albion**. Because of its accidental resemblance to *albus* (Latin for "white"), **Albion** is especially associated with the chalk cliffs which seem to gird much of the English coast like defensive walls.

The British Empire took its name from **The British Isles** because it was created not only by the **English** but by the **Irish, Scots,** and **Welsh**, as well as by civilians and servicemen from other constituent countries of the Empire.

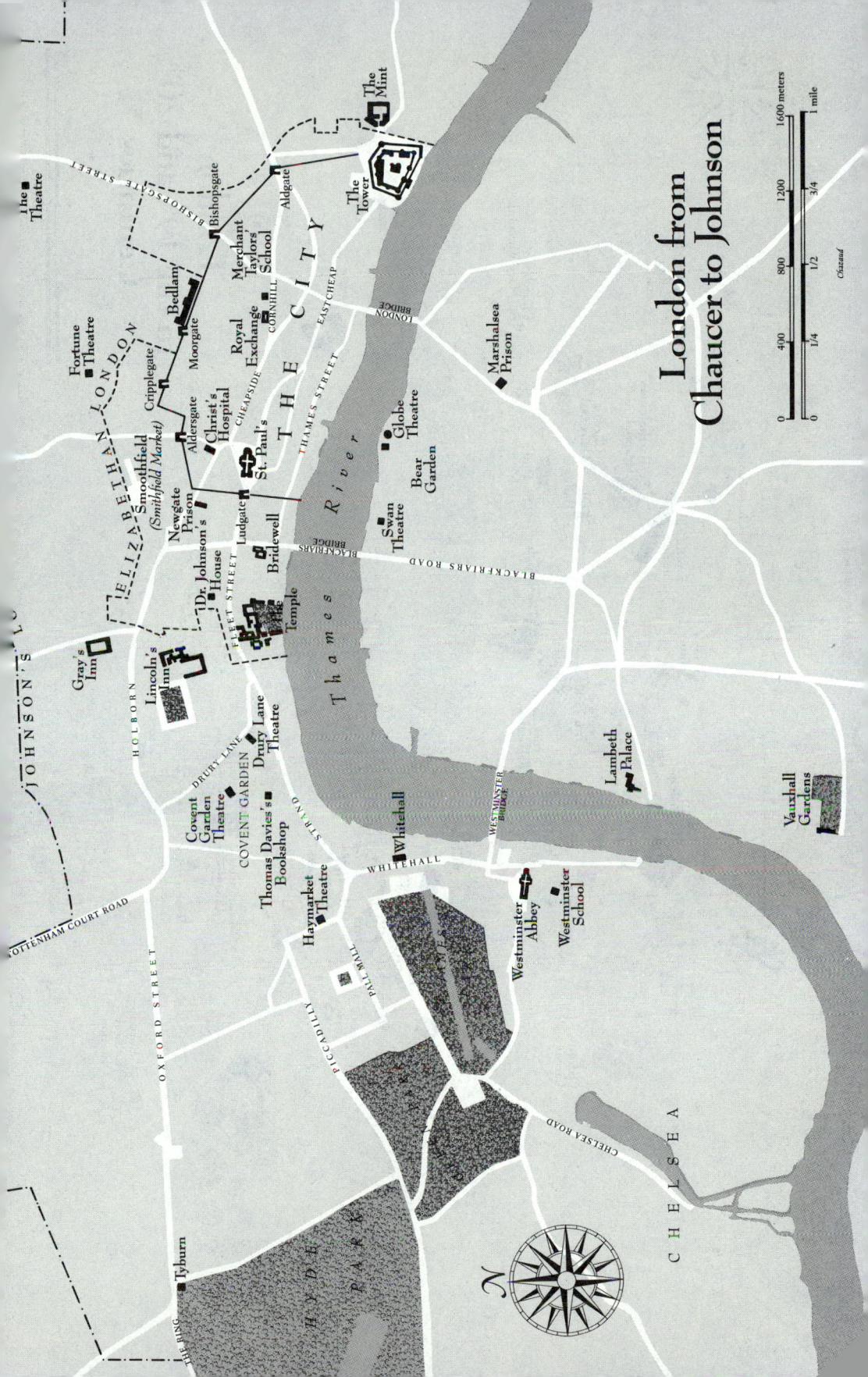

London from Chaucer to Johnson

The Theatre

BISHOPSGATE STREET

Bishopsgate

Merchant Taylors School

Aldgate

The Tower

The Mint

Fortune Theatre

Bedlam

Moorgate

Royal Exchange

CORNHILL

EASTCHEAP

ELIZABETHAN LONDON

Cripplegate

Christ's Hospital

Cheapside

St. Paul's

THAMES STREET

LONDON BRIDGE

THE CITY

Aldersgate

Smoothfield (Smithfield Market)

Newgate Prison

Ludgate

Bridewell

THAMES STREET

Marshalsea Prison

JOHNSON'S LONDON

Gray's Inn

Dr. Johnson's House

FLEET STREET

Temple

Globe Theatre

Bear Garden

HOLBORN

Lincoln's Inn

BLACKFRIARS BRIDGE

Swan Theatre

Thames River

BLACKFRIARS ROAD

Covent Garden Theatre

DRURY LANE

Drury Lane Theatre

COVENT GARDEN

Thomas Davies's Bookshop

STRAND

WESTMINSTER Bridge

Lambeth Palace

TOTTENHAM COURT ROAD

Whitehall

WHITEHALL

Westminster Abbey

Westminster School

Vauxhall Gardens

OXFORD STREET

Haymarket Theatre

PALL MALL

PICCADILLY

CHELSEA ROAD

CHELSEA

Tyburn

THE RING

HYDE PARK

N

London from Chaucer to Johnson

Chatsad

| 0 | 1/4 | 1/2 | 3/4 | 1 mile |

| 0 | 400 | 800 | 1200 | 1600 meters |

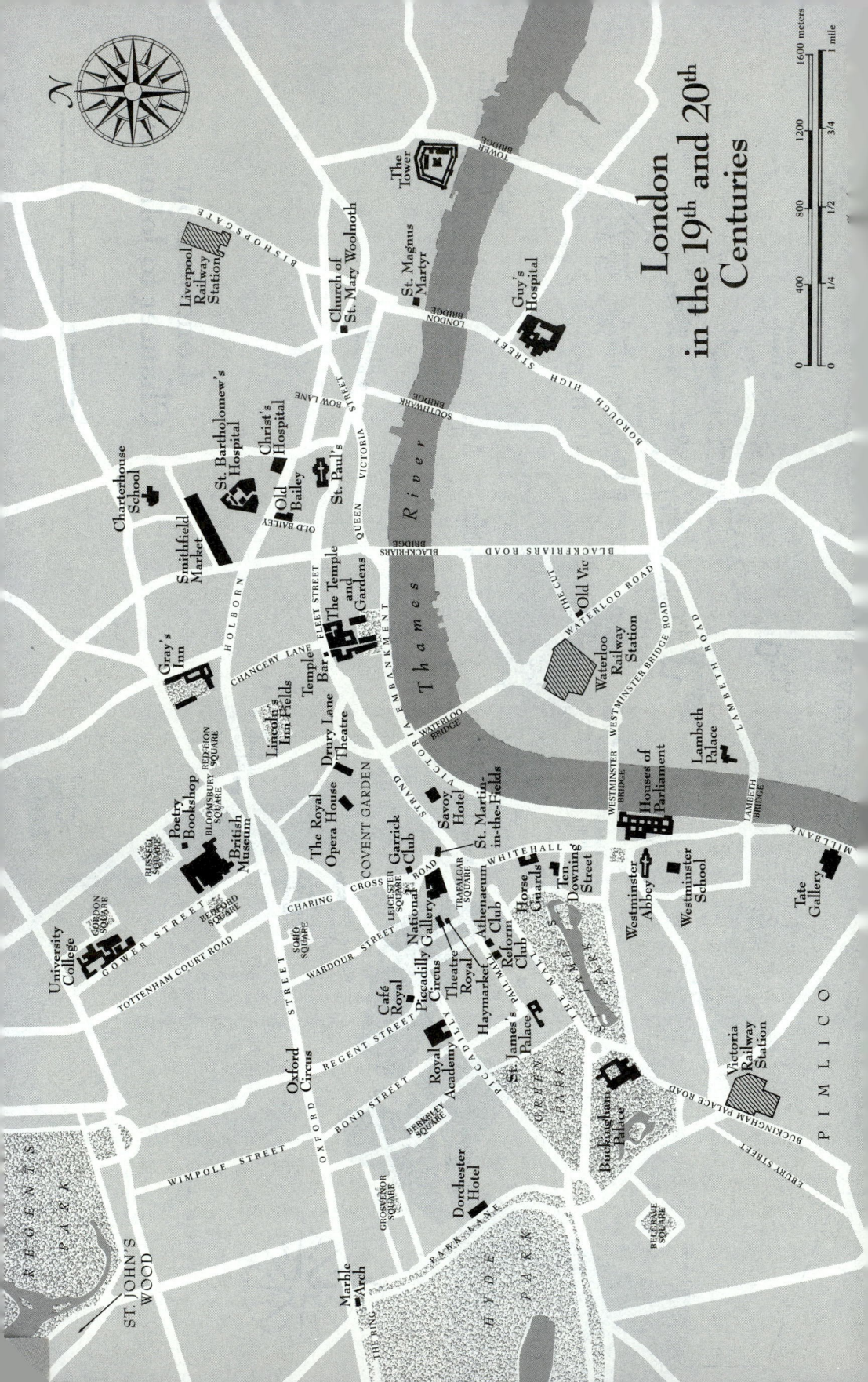

London
in the 19th and 20th Centuries

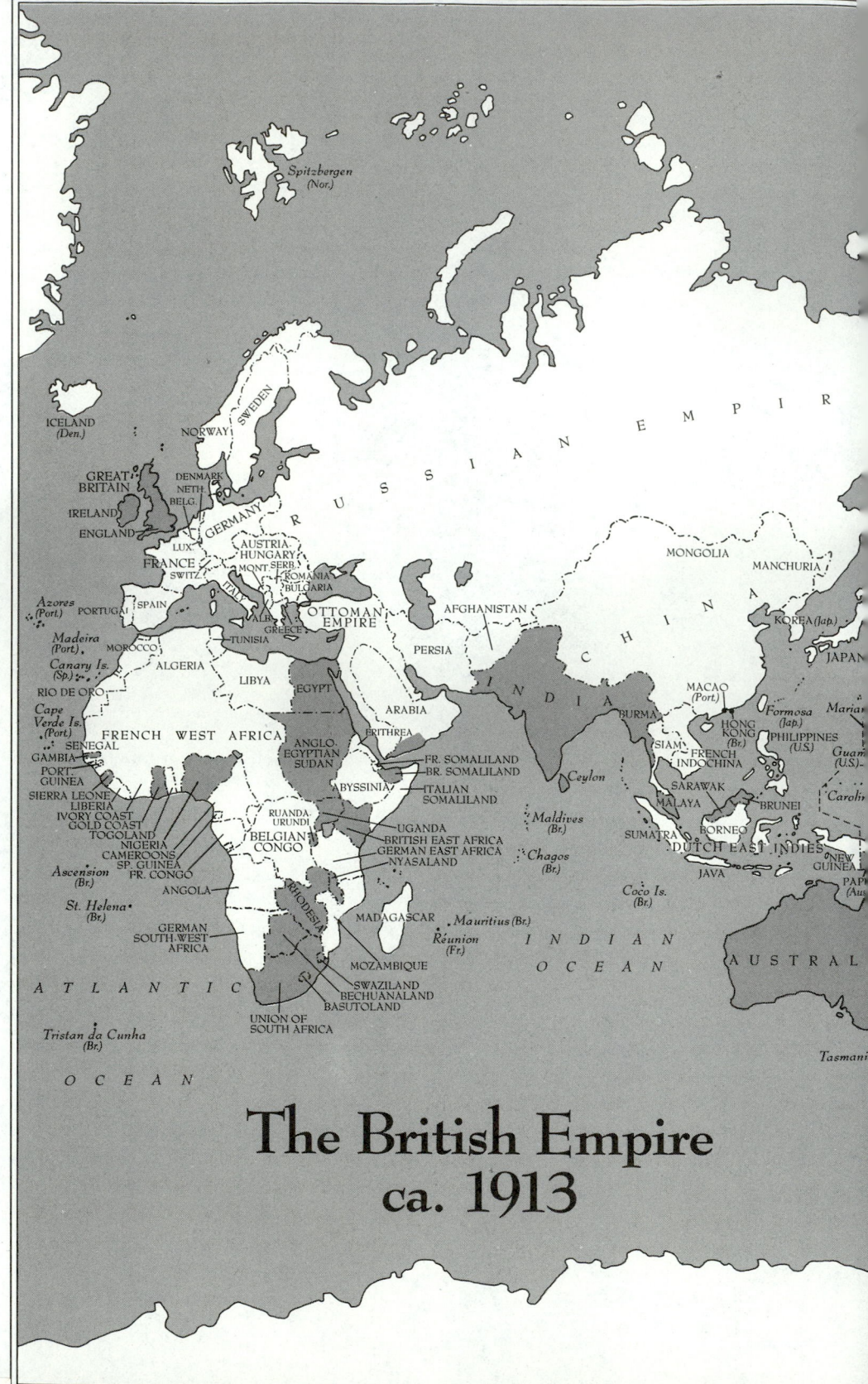

ICELAND
(Den.)

NORWAY

SWEDEN

SPITZBERGEN
(Nor.)

R U S S I A N   E M P I R E

GREAT
BRITAIN

IRELAND

ENGLAND

DENMARK
NETH.
BELG.

GERMANY

FRANCE

LUX.

MONT.

SWITZ.

AUSTRIA-
HUNGARY

SERB.

ROMANIA

BULGARIA

ITALY

ALB.

GREECE

OTTOMAN
EMPIRE

AFGHANISTAN

MONGOLIA

MANCHURIA

Azores
(Port.)

PORTUGAL

SPAIN

Madeira
(Port.)

Canary Is.
(Sp.)

MOROCCO

ALGERIA

TUNISIA

LIBYA

EGYPT

PERSIA

C H I N A

KOREA (Jap.)

JAPAN

RIO DE ORO

Cape
Verde Is.
(Port.)

FRENCH   WEST   AFRICA

ANGLO-
EGYPTIAN
SUDAN

ARABIA

ERITHREA

MACAO
(Port.)

BURMA

Formosa
(Jap.)

Mariai

SENEGAL

GAMBIA

PORT.
GUINEA

SIERRA LEONE

LIBERIA

IVORY COAST

GOLD COAST

TOGOLAND

NIGERIA

CAMEROONS

SP. GUINEA

FR. CONGO

ABYSSINIA

FR. SOMALILAND

BR. SOMALILAND

ITALIAN
SOMALILAND

Ceylon

I N D I A

SIAM

FRENCH
INDOCHINA

HONG
KONG
(Br.)

PHILIPPINES
(U.S.)

Guam
(U.S.)

Caroli

RUANDA-
URUNDI

BELGIAN
CONGO

UGANDA

BRITISH EAST AFRICA

GERMAN EAST AFRICA

NYASALAND

Maldives
(Br.)

Chagos
(Br.)

SUMATRA

MALAYA

SARAWAK

BRUNEI

BORNEO

DUTCH EAST INDIES

JAVA

NEW
GUINEA

PAP
(Au

Ascension
(Br.)

ANGOLA

RHODESIA

St. Helena
(Br.)

GERMAN
SOUTH-WEST
AFRICA

MADAGASCAR

Mauritius (Br.)

Réunion
(Fr.)

Coco Is.
(Br.)

I N D I A N

O C E A N

A U S T R A L

MOZAMBIQUE

SWAZILAND

BECHUANALAND

BASUTOLAND

UNION OF
SOUTH AFRICA

A T L A N T I C

Tristan da Cunha
(Br.)

O C E A N

Tasmania

The British Empire
ca. 1913

British Money

Since 1971, British money has been calculated on the decimal system, with 100 pence to the pound; the pound has fluctuated from a bit more than 2 American dollars to virtual parity—whatever dollars may be worth. Before 1971, the pound consisted of 20 shillings, each containing 12 pence, making 240 pence to the pound. In paper money the change has not been great; 5- and 10-pound notes constitute the mass of bills under both the old and the new systems; nowadays, in addition, 20- and 50-pound notes have been added. But in the smaller coinage the change has been considerable and the simplification remarkable. Most notable is the abolition of the shilling, which goes into retirement now with the mark (worth in its day two-thirds of a pound or 13 shillings 4 pence) and the angel (once 10 shillings but replaced by the 10-shilling note, now in its turn abolished). The guinea, an oddity of the old currency, amounted to a pound and a shilling; though it has not been minted since 1813, a very few quality items or prestige awards (like horse races) may still be quoted in guineas. Colloquially, a pound was (and is) called a quid; a shilling a bob; sixpence a tanner; a penny, half-penny, or farthing, a copper. The common signs were £ for pound, s. for shilling, d. for a penny (from Latin *denarius*). A sum would normally be written £2.19.3, i.e., 2 pounds, 19 shillings, 3 pence. In Joyce's *Ulysses*, that is Leopold Bloom's budget for June 16, 1904. In new currency, it would be about £2.96.

Old	New
1 pound note	1 pound coin (or note in Scotland)
10 shilling (half-pound note)	50 pence
5 shilling (crown)	
	20 pence
2½ shilling (half crown)	
2 shilling (florin)	10 pence
1 shilling	5 pence
6 pence	
2½ pence	1 penny
2 pence	
1 penny	
½ penny	
¼ penny (farthing)	

What the pound was worth at any point in history is ever easy to state. In the first part of the twentieth century, 1 pound equaled about 5 American dollars; but those dollars bought three or four times what they would today. Historians sometimes attempt to calculate the value of the pound in terms of the goods and services it would purchase, but these too vary radically with special circumstances such as wars and poor harvests. Nevertheless, it is clear that money used to be worth much more than it is now. In the early sixteenth century, according to Hugh Latimer, people would say, "Oh, he's a rich man, he's worth £500." Four centuries later, Virginia Woolf argued that £500 a year (along with a room of one's own) was the bare minimum necessary for a woman to be able to write. Whatever Latimer meant by "rich," or Woolf by "necessary," it is clear that the value of the pound had declined drastically over this period, as it has continued to do in the course of the twentieth century. In Britain today, a worker on minimum wage earns more than £500 a month, an income associated with severe poverty.

In the Anglo-Saxon period, the silver penny was the biggest coin in general circulation; 4 of them would buy a sheep. Peasants and craftsmen before the Black Death of the fourteenth century made at most 2 or 3 pence a day—an annual income of £3 or £4; after the onset of the plague, wages nearly doubled, due to the shortage of laborers. Throughout the medieval period, kings and commoners worried less about inflation than about the debasement of the silver currency. In 1124, dozens of mint-masters had their right hands chopped off on Christmas Day for issuing inferior coinage. In the early sixteenth century, under Henry VIII and his son Edward VI, the silver content of coins fell as low as 25 percent. Elizabeth I considered the revaluation of the silver coinage to be one of her greatest achievements as queen. Nevertheless, her reign was marked by sustained inflation of prices, caused in part by the influx of gold and silver from the New World, and in part by the rising population.

In the Elizabethan era, admission to the public theaters cost a penny for those who stood throughout the performance. Playwrights were paid about £6 for each play, so to make a living a writer had to be prolific (or, like Shakespeare, own shares in the theater company). In the same period, 40 pounds a year in independent income (generally rent from lands) was the minimum requirement for a justice of the peace; it marked the threshold of gentry status and was also the sum fixed by King James I at which a man could be forced to accept knighthood (paying a fee to the crown). In 1661, following further inflation, Samuel Pepys calculated his worth at a modest £650 just after he had begun working for the navy; five years later, that good bourgeois was worth more than £6000, and his annual income was about £3000. Of course, he was working for most of this income. Pepys was a rising official and would become a very important one; but he never achieved a title or even knighthood because the smell of commerce had never been washed from his money by possession of land.

Various writers provide examples of the incomes of rich and poor in the eighteenth and nineteenth centuries. Joseph Andrews (in Fielding's novel, published 1742) worked as a footman in the house of Lady Booby for £8 a year; in addition, he got his room, board, and livery, plus the occasional tip. Among the comfortable classes, Mr. Bennet of Jane Austen's *Price and Prejudice* (1813) enjoyed an income of £2000 a year (with a family of five nonearning females to support), while Mr. Darcy had close to £10,000, nearing the level of the aristocracy. In his deepest degradation David Copperfield (of Dickens's 1850 novel) worked in the warehouse of Murdstone & Grinby for 6 or 7 shillings a week (£15 to £18 a year). Mr. Murdstone paid extra for his lodging and laundry, but even so the boy was bitterly impoverished, though he had only himself to feed. When his father died, his mother was thought to be pretty well taken care of with £105 a year, less than £9 per month. Even in 1888, Annie Besant reports workers in Bryant and May's match factory made 4 to 9 shillings a week and paid for their own lodging—this, in the words of Ada Nield Chew, was not a living wage, but "a lingering, dying wage." Far removed from this world is Jack Worthing in Wilde's comedy *The Importance of Being Earnest* (1895), who receives £7000 or £8000 a year from investments and has a country house with about fifteen hundred acres attached to it, though it yields no income worth talking about.

While incomes have risen enormously over the centuries, and the value of the pound declined accordingly, the gap between rich and poor has remained. So too has the gap between the country and the city: London has always been very expensive, and elsewhere a small income goes further. To a large extent, one's position in terms of class and geography determines not only what money can buy but what it means.

We have only to contrast Jack Worthing's vague estimate of his income with the factory workers' exact sense of the value of a shilling. As Woolf acknowledged, having a purse with the power "to breed ten-shilling notes automatically," changes one's view of money and of the world. Perhaps it is because British currency has been so important in shaping people's views of themselves and their society that many Britons are reluctant to let it go. The question of whether the United Kingdom should relinquish the pound and the penny to join the single European currency (the Euro) is a matter of fierce and prolonged debate. For some, the pound, far more than the flag, is an enduring symbol of the nation. Whether or not one holds this view, it can at least be said that over the centuries the pound has undergone as many crises and transformations as the nation itself.

The British Baronage

The English monarchy is in principle hereditary, though at times during the Middle Ages the rules were subject to dispute. In general, authority passes from father to eldest surviving son, from daughters in order of seniority if there is no son, to a brother if there are no children, and in default of direct descendants to collateral lines (cousins, nephews, nieces) in order of closeness. There have been breaks in the order of succession (1066, 1399, 1688), but so far as possible the usurpers have always sought to paper over the break with a legitimate, i.e., a hereditary claim. When a queen succeeds to the throne and takes a husband, he does not become king unless he is in the line of blood succession; rather, he is named prince consort, as Albert was to Victoria. He may father kings, but is not one himself.

The original Saxon nobles were the king's thanes, ealdormen, or earls, who provided the king with military service and counsel in return for booty, gifts, or landed estates. William the Conqueror, arriving from France, where feudalism was fully developed, considerably expanded this group. In addition, as the king distributed the lands of his new kingdom, he also distributed dignities to men who became known collectively as "the baronage." "Baron" in its root meaning signifies simply "man," and barons were the king's men. As the title was common, a distinction was early made between greater and lesser barons, the former gradually assuming loftier and more impressive titles. The first English "duke" was created in 1337; the title of "marquess," or "marquis" (pronounced "markwis"), followed in 1385, and "viscount" ("vyekount") in 1440. Though "earl" is the oldest title of all, it now comes between a marquess and a viscount in order of dignity and precedence, and the old term "baron" now designates a rank just below viscount. "Baronets" were created in 1611 as a means of raising revenue for the crown (the title could be purchased for about £1000); they are marginal nobility and do not sit in the House of Lords.

Kings and queens are addressed as "Your Majesty," princes and princesses as "Your Highness," the other hereditary nobility as "My Lord" or "Your Lordship." Peers receive their titles either by inheritance (like Lord Byron, the sixth baron of that line) or from the monarch (like Alfred Lord Tennyson, created first Baron Tennyson by Victoria). The children, even of a duke, are commoners unless they are specifically granted some other title or inherit their father's title from him. A peerage can be forfeited by act of attainder, as for example when a lord is convicted of treason; and, when forfeited, or lapsed for lack of a successor, can be bestowed on another family. Thus Robert Cecil was made in 1605 first earl of Salisbury in the third creation, the first creation dating from 1149, the second from 1337, the title having been in abeyance since 1539. Titles descend by right of succession and do not depend on tenure of land; thus, a title does not always indicate where a lord dwells or holds power. Indeed, noble titles do not always refer to a real place at all. At Prince Edward's marriage in 1999, the queen created him earl of Wessex, although the old kingdom of Wessex has had no political existence since the Anglo-Saxon period, and the name was all but forgotten until it was resurrected by Thomas Hardy as the setting of his novels. (This is perhaps but one of many ways in which the world of the aristocracy increasingly resembles the realm of literature.)

The king and queen	(These are all of the royal line.)
Prince and princess	
Duke and duchess	(These may or may not be of the royal line, but are
Marquess and marchioness	ordinarily remote from the succession.)
Earl and countess	
Viscount and viscountess	
Baron and baroness	
Baronet and lady	

Scottish peers sat in the parliament of Scotland, as English peers did in the parliament of England, till at the Act of Union (1707) Scots peers were granted sixteen seats in the English House of Lords, to be filled by election. Similarly, Irish peers, when the Irish parliament was abolished in 1801, were granted the right to elect twenty-eight of their number to the House of Lords in Westminster. (Now that the Republic of Ireland is a separate nation, of course, this no longer applies.) The House of Lords still retains some power to influence or delay legislation. But this upper house is now being reformed. All or most of the hereditary peers are to be expelled, while recipients of nonhereditary Life Peerages will remain and vote as before.

Below the peerage the chief title of honor is "knight." Knighthood, which is not hereditary, is generally a reward for services rendered. A knight (Sir John Black) is addressed, using his first name, as "Sir John"; his wife, using the last name, is "Lady Black"—unless she is the daughter of an earl or nobleman of higher rank, in which case she will be "Lady Arabella." The female equivalent of a knight bears the title of "Dame."

Though the word itself comes from the Anglo-Saxon *cniht*, there seems to be some doubt as to whether knighthood amounted to much before the arrival of the Normans. The feudal system required military service as a condition of land tenure, and a man who came to serve his king at the head of an army of tenants required a title of authority and badges of identity—hence the title of knighthood and the coat of arms. During the Crusades, when men were far removed from their land (or had even sold it in order to go on crusade), more elaborate forms of fealty sprang up that soon expanded into orders of knighthood. The Templars, Hospitallers, Knights of the Teutonic Order, Knights of Malta, and Knights of the Golden Fleece were but a few of these companionships; not all of them were available at all times in England.

Gradually, with the rise of centralized government and the decline of feudal tenures, military knighthood became obsolete, and the rank largely honorific; sometimes, as under James I, it degenerated into a scheme of the royal government for making money. For hundreds of years after its establishment in the fourteenth century, the Order of the Garter was the only English order of knighthood, an exclusive courtly companionship. Then, during the late seventeenth, the eighteenth, and the nineteenth centuries, a number of additional orders were created, with names such as the Thistle, Saint Patrick, the Bath, Saint Michael and Saint George, plus a number of special Victorian and Indian orders. They retain the terminology, ceremony, and dignity of knighthood, but the military implications are vestigial.

Although the British Empire now belongs to history, appointments to the Order of the British Empire continue to be conferred for services to that empire at home or abroad. Such honors (commonly referred to as "gongs") are granted by the monarch in her New Year's and Birthday lists, but the decisions are now made by the government in power. In recent years there have been efforts to popularize and democratize the dispensation of honors, with recipients including rock stars and actors. But this does not prevent large sectors of British society from regarding both knighthood and the peerage as largely irrelevant to modern life.

The Royal Lines of England and Great Britain

England

SAXONS AND DANES

Egbert, king of Wessex	802–839
Ethelwulf, son of Egbert	839–858
Ethelbald, second son of Ethelwulf	858–860
Ethelbert, third son of Ethelwulf	860–866
Ethelred I, fourth son of Ethelwulf	866–871
Alfred the Great, fifth son of Ethelwulf	871–899
Edward the Elder, son of Alfred	899–924
Athelstan the Glorious, son of Edward	924–940
Edmund I, third son of Edward	940–946
Edred, fourth son of Edward	946–955
Edwy the Fair, son of Edmund	955–959
Edgar the Peaceful, second son of Edmund	959–975
Edward the Martyr, son of Edgar	975–978 (murdered)
Ethelred II, the Unready, second son of Edgar	978–1016
Edmund II, Ironside, son of Ethelred II	1016–1016
Canute the Dane	1016–1035
Harold I, Harefoot, natural son of Canute	1035–1040
Hardecanute, son of Canute	1040–1042
Edward the Confessor, son of Ethelred II	1042–1066
Harold II, brother-in-law of Edward	1066–1066 (died in battle)

HOUSE OF NORMANDY

William I the Conqueror	1066–1087
William II, Rufus, third son of William I	1087–1100 (shot from ambush)
Henry I, Beauclerc, youngest son of William I	1100–1135

HOUSE OF BLOIS

Stephen, son of Adela, daughter of William I	1135–1154

HOUSE OF PLANTAGENET

Henry II, son of Geoffrey Plantagenet by Matilda, daughter of Henry I	1154–1189
Richard I, Coeur de Lion, son of Henry II	1189–1199
John Lackland, son of Henry II	1199–1216
Henry III, son of John	1216–1272
Edward I, Longshanks, son of Henry III	1272–1307
Edward II, son of Edward I	1307–1327
Edward III of Windsor, son of Edward II	1327–1377
Richard II, grandson of Edward III	1377–1400

HOUSE OF LANCASTER

Henry IV, son of John of Gaunt, son of Edward III	1399–1413
Henry V, Prince Hal, son of Henry IV	1413–1422
Henry VI, son of Henry V	1422–1471 (deposed)

HOUSE OF YORK

Edward IV, great-great-grandson of Edward III	1461–1483
Edward V, son of Edward IV	1483–1483 (murdered)
Richard III, Crookback	1483–1485 (died in battle)

HOUSE OF TUDOR

Henry VII, married daughter of Edward IV	1485–1509
Henry VIII, son of Henry VII	1509–1547
Edward VI, son of Henry VIII	1547–1553
Mary I, "Bloody," daughter of Henry VIII	1553–1558
Elizabeth I, daughter of Henry VIII	1558–1603

HOUSE OF STUART

James I (James VI of Scotland)	1603–1625
Charles I, son of James I	1625–1649 (executed)

COMMONWEALTH & PROTECTORATE

Council of State	1649–1653
Oliver Cromwell, Lord Protector	1653–1658
Richard Cromwell, son of Oliver	1658–1660 (resigned)

HOUSE OF STUART (RESTORED)

Charles II, son of Charles I	1660–1685
James II, second son of Charles I	1685–1688

(INTERREGNUM, 11 DECEMBER 1688 TO 13 FEBRUARY 1689)

William III of Orange, by Mary, daughter of Charles I	1685–1701
and Mary II, daughter of James II	–1694
Anne, second daughter of James II	1702–1714

Great Britain

HOUSE OF HANOVER

George I, son of Elector of Hanover and Sophia, granddaughter of James I	1714–1727
George II, son of George I	1727–1760
George III, grandson of George II	1760–1820
George IV, son of George III	1820–1830
William IV, third son of George III	1830–1837
Victoria, daughter of Edward, fourth son of George III	1837–1901

HOUSE OF SAXE-COBURG AND GOTHA

Edward VII, son of Victoria	1901–1910

HOUSE OF WINDSOR (NAME ADOPTED 17 JULY 1917)

George V, second son of Edward VII	1910–1936
Edward VIII, eldest son of George V	1936–1936 (abdicated)
George VI, second son of George V	1936–1952
Elizabeth II, daughter of George VI	1952–

Religions in England

Religious distinctions and denominations are important in British social history, hence deeply woven into the nation's literature. The numerous (over three hundred) British churches and sects divide along a scale from high to low, depending on the amount of authority they give to the church or the amount of liberty they concede to the individual conscience. At one end of the scale is the Roman Catholic Church, asserting papal infallibility, universal jurisdiction, and the supreme importance of hierarchy as guide and intercessor. For political and social reasons, Catholicism struck deep roots in Ireland but in England was the object of prolonged, bitter hatred on the part of Protestants from the Reformation through the nineteenth century. The Established English (Anglican) Episcopal church has been the official national church since the sixteenth century; it enjoys the support (once direct and exclusive, now indirect and peripheral) of the national government. Its creed is defined by Thirty-Nine Articles, but these are intentionally vague, so there are numerous ways of adhering to the Church of England. Roughly and intermittently, the chief classes of Anglicans have been known as High Church (with its highest portion calling itself Anglo-Catholic); Broad Church, or Latitudinarian (when they get so broad that they admit anyone believing in God, they may be known as Deists, or some may leave the church altogether and be known as Unitarians); and Low Church, whose adherents may stay in the English church and yet come close to shaking hands with Presbyterians or Methodists. These various groups may be arranged, from the High down to the Low Church, in direct relation to the amount of ritual each prefers and in the degree of authority conceded to the upper clergy—and in inverse relation to the importance ascribed to a saving faith directly infused by God into an individual conscience.

All English Protestants who decline to subscribe to the English established church are classed as Dissenters or Nonconformists; for a time in the sixteenth and seventeenth centuries, they were also known as Puritans. (Nowadays, though Puritanism has less distinct theological meaning, it marks a distinct character type; because of his passionate emphasis on individual conscience and moral economy, Bernard Shaw was a prototypical Puritan.) The Presbyterians model their church government on that established by John Calvin in the Swiss city of Geneva. It has no bishops, and therefore is more democratic for the clergy; but it gains energy by associating lay elders with clergymen in matters of social discipline and tends to be strict with the ungodly. From its first reformation the Scottish Kirk was fixed on the Presbyterian model. During the civil wars of the seventeenth century, a great many sects sprang up on the left wing of the Presbyterians, most of them touched by Calvinism but some rebelling against it; a few of these still survive. The Independents became our modern Congregationalists; the Quakers are still Quakers, as Baptists are still Baptists, though multiply divided. But many of the sects flourished and perished within the space of a few years. Among these now vanished groups were the Shakers (though a few groups still exist in America), the Seekers, the Ranters, the Anabaptists, the Muggletonians, the Fifth Monarchy Men, the Family of Love, the Sweet Singers of Israel, and many others, forgotten by all except scholars. During the eighteenth and nineteenth centuries, new sects arose, supplanting old ones; the Methodists, under John and Charles Wesley, became numerous and important, taking root particularly in Wales. (The three "subject" nationalities, Ireland, Scotland, and Wales, thus turned three different ways to avoid the Anglican church.) With the passage of time a small number of Swedenborgians sprang up, followers of the Swedish mystic Emanuel Swedenborg—to be followed by the Plymouth Brethren, Christian Scientists, Jehovah's Witnesses, and countless other nineteenth-century groups. All these sects constantly grow, shrink, split, and occasionally disappear as they succeed or fail in attracting new converts.

Within the various churches and sects, independent of them all but amazingly persistent, there has always survived a stream of esoteric or hermetic thought—a belief in occult powers, and sometimes in magic also, exemplified by the pseudo-sciences of astrology and alchemy but taking many other forms as well. From the mythical Egyptian seer Hermes Trismegistus through Paracelsus, Cornelius Agrippa, Giordano Bruno, Jakob Boehme, the society of Rosicrucians, and a hundred other shadowy figures, the line can be traced to William Blake and William Butler Yeats, who both in their different ways brought hermetic Protestantism close to its ultimate goal, a mystic church of a single consciousness, poised within its mind-elaborated cosmos.

Christianity is not, of course, the only religion present on the British Isles. The few Jews in medieval England were regarded as resident aliens, as were those in other European countries. In 1290 all English Jews who refused baptism were expelled from the kingdom, and officially, there were no Jews living in England between that time and the mid-1650s, when Cromwell encouraged Jewish merchants to settle in London. A considerable number of east European Jews emigrated to England in the first half of the twentieth century (many as refugees), but the country's Jewish population as a whole remains quite small (less than half a million). Hardly any Muslims or Hindus lived in the U.K. before the dissolution of the Empire shortly after World War II. Today both religions have a large and growing representation among ex-colonial immigrants and their children.

Poetic Forms and
Literary Terminology

Systematic literary theory and criticism in English began in the sixteenth century, at a time when the standard education for upper-class students emphasized the study of the classical languages and literatures. As a consequence, the English words that were introduced to describe meter, figures of speech, and literary genres often derive from Latin and Greek roots.

RHYTHM AND METER

Verse is generally distinguished from prose as a more compressed and more regularly rhythmic form of statement. This approximate truth underlines the importance of **meter** in poetry, as the means by which rhythm is measured and described.

In Latin and Greek, meter was established on a **quantitative** basis, by the regular alternation of long and short syllables (that is, syllables classified according to the time taken to pronounce them). Outside of a few experiments (and the songs of Thomas Campion), this system has never proved congenial to Germanic languages such as English, which distinguish, instead, between **stressed** and **unstressed,** or accented and unaccented syllables. Two varieties of accented stress may be distinguished. On the one hand, there is the natural stress pattern of words themselves; *sýllable* is accented on the first syllable, *deplórable* on the second, and so on. Then there is the sort of stress that indicates rhetorical emphasis. If the sentence "You went to Greece?" is given a pronounced accent on the last word, it implies "Greece (of all places)?" If the accent falls on the first word, it implies "you (of all people)?" The meter of poetry—that is, its rhythm—is ordinarily built up out of a regular recurrence of accents, whether established as **word accents** or **rhetorical accents;** once started, it has (like all rhythm) a tendency to persist in the reader's mind.

The unit that is repeated to give steady rhythm to a poem is called a **foot;** in English it usually consists of accented and unaccented syllables in one of five fairly simple patterns:

The **iambic foot** (or **iamb**) consists of an unstressed followed by a stressed syllable, as in *uníte, repeát,* or *insíst.* Most English verse falls naturally into the iambic pattern.

The **trochaic foot** (**trochee**) inverts this order; it is a stressed followed by an unstressed syllable—for example, *únit, réaper,* or *ínstant.*

The **anapestic foot** (**anapest**) consists of two unstressed syllables followed by a stressed syllable, as in *intercéde, disarránged,* or *Cameróon.*

The **dactylic foot** (**dactyl**) consists of a stressed syllable followed by two unstressed syllables, as in *Wáshington, Écuador,* or *ápplejack.*

The **spondaic foot** (**spondee**) consists of two successive stressed syllables, as in *heartbreak, headline,* or *Kashmir.*

In all the examples above, word accent and the quality of the metrical foot coincide exactly. But the metrical foot may well consist of several words, or, on the other hand, one word may well consist of several metrical feet. *Phótolithógraphy* consists of two dactyls in a single word; *dárk and with spóts on it,* though it consists of six words rather than one, is also two dactyls. When we read a piece of poetry with the intention of discovering its underlying metrical pattern, we are said to **scan** it—that is, we go through it line by line, indicating by conventional signs which are the accented and which the unaccented syllables within the feet. We also count the number of feet in each line; a line is, formally, also called a **verse** (from Latin *versus,* which means one "row" of metrical feet). Verse lengths are conventionally described in terms derived from the Greek:

Monometer: one foot (of rare occurrence)
Dimeter: two feet (also rare)
Trimeter: three feet
Tetrameter: four feet
Pentameter: five feet
Hexameter: six feet (six iambic feet make what is called an **Alexandrine**)
Heptameter: seven feet (also rare)

Samuel Johnson wrote a little parody of simpleminded poets which can be scanned this way:

> Ĭ pút m̆y hát ŭpón m̆y héad
> Ănd wálked ĭntó thĕ Stránd
> Ănd thére Ĭ mét ănóthĕr mán
> Whŏse hát wăs ín hĭs hánd.

The poem is iambic in rhythm, alternating tetrameter and trimeter in the length of the verse-lines. The fact that it scans so nicely is, however, no proof that it is good poetry. Quite the contrary. Many of poetry's most subtle effects are achieved by establishing an underlying rhythm and then varying it by means of a whole series of devices, some dramatic and expressive, others designed simply to lend variety and interest to the verse. A well-known sonnet of Shakespeare's (*116*) begins,

> Let me not to the marriage of true minds
> Admit impediments. Love is not love
> Which alters when it alteration finds,
> Or bends with the remover to remove.

It is possible to read the first line of this poem as mechanical iambic pentameter:

Lĕt mé nŏt tó thĕ márrĭăge ŏf trŭe mińds

But of course nobody ever reads it that way, except to make a point; read with normal English accent and some sense of what it is saying, the line would form a pattern something like this:

Lét mĕ nŏt tŏ thĕ márrĭăge ŏf trúe mińds

which is neither pentameter nor in any way iambic. The second line is a little more iambic, but, read expressively also falls short of pentameter:

Ădmít ĭmpédĭmeńts. Lóve ĭs nŏt lóve

Only in the third and fourth lines of the sonnet do we get verses that read as five iambic feet.

The fact is that perfectly regular metrical verse is easy to write and dull to read. Among the devices in common use for varying too regular a pattern are the insertion of a trochaic foot among iambics, especially at the opening of a line, where the soft first syllable of the iambic foot often needs stiffening (see line 1 of the sonnet above); the more or less free addition of extra unaccented syllables; and the use of **caesura,** or strong grammatical pause within a line (conventionally indicated, in scanning, by the sign ‖). The second line of the sonnet above is a good example of caesura:

Admit impediments. ‖ Love is not love

The strength of the caesura, and its placing in the line, may be varied to produce striking variations of effect. More broadly, the whole relation between the poem's sound- and rhythm-patterns and its pattern as a sequence of assertions (phrases, clauses, sentences) may be manipulated by the poet. Sometimes the statements fit neatly within the lines, so that each line ends with a strong mark of punctuation; they are then known as **end-stopped lines.** Sometimes the sense flows over the ends of the lines, creating **run-on lines;** this process is also known, from the French, as **enjambment** (literally, "straddling").

End-stopped lines (Marlowe, *Hero and Leander*, lines 45–48):

> So lovely fair was Hero, Venus' nun,
> As Nature wept, thinking she was undone,
> Because she took more from her than she left
> And of such wondrous beauty her bereft.

Run-on lines (Keats, *Endymion* 1.89–93):

> Full in the middle of this pleasantness
> There stood a marble altar, with a tress
> Of flowers budded newly; and the dew
> Had taken fairy fantasies to strew
> Daisies upon the sacred sward, . . .

Following the example of such poets as Blake, Rimbaud, and Whitman, many twentieth-century poets have undertaken to write what is called **free** verse—that is, verse which has neither a fixed metrical foot nor (consequently) a fixed number of feet in its lines, but which depends for its rhythm on a pattern of cadences, or the rise and fall of the voice in utterance, or the pattern indicated to the reader's eye by the breaks between the verse lines. As in traditional versification, free verse is printed in short lines instead of with the continuity of prose; it differs from such versification, however, by the fact that its stressed syllables are not organized into a regular metric sequence.

SENSE AND SOUND

The words of which poetic lines—whether free or traditional—are composed cause them to have different sounds and produce different effects. Polysyllables, being pronounced fast, often cause a line to move swiftly; monosyllables, especially when heavy and requiring distinct accents, may cause it to move heavily, as in Milton's famous line (*Paradise Lost* 2.621):

> Rocks, caves, lakes, fens, bogs, dens, and shades of death

Poetic assertions are often dramatized and reinforced by means of **alliteration**—that is, the use of several nearby words or stressed syllables beginning with the same consonant. When Shakespeare writes (*Sonnet 64*),

> Ruin hath taught me thus to ruminate
> That Time will come and take my love away,

the alliterative *r*'s and rich internal echoes of the first line contrast with the sharp anxiety and directness of the alliterative *t*'s in the second. When Dryden starts *Absalom and Achitophel* with the couplet,

> In pious times, ere priestcraft did begin,
> Before polygamy was made a sin,

the satiric undercutting is strongly reinforced by the triple alliteration that links "*p*ious" with "*p*riestcraft" and "*p*olygamy."

Assonance, or repetition of the same or similar vowel sounds within a passage (usually in accented syllables), also serves to enrich it, as in two lines from Keats's *Ode on Melancholy*:

> For shade to shade will come too drowsily,
> And drown the wakeful anguish of the soul.

It is clear that the round, hollow tones of "drowsily," repeated in "drown" and darkening to the full *o*-sound of "soul," have much to do with the effect of the passage. A related device is **consonance**, or the repetition of a pattern of consonants with changes in the intervening vowels—for example: *linger, longer, languor; rider, reader, raider, ruder.*

The use of words that seem to reproduce the sounds they designate (known as **onomatopoeia**) has been much attempted, from Virgil's galloping horse—

> *Quadrupedante putrem sonitu quatit ungula campum—*

through Tennyson's account, in *The Princess*, of

> The moan of doves in immemorial elms,
> And murmuring of innumerable bees—

to many poems in the present day.

RHYME AND STANZA

Rhyme consists of a repetition of accented sounds in words, usually those falling at the end of verse lines. If the rhyme sound is the very last syllable of the line (*rebound, sound*), the rhyme is called **masculine**; if the accented syllable is followed by an unaccented syllable (*hounding, bounding*), the rhyme is called **feminine**. Rhymes amounting to three or more syllables, like forced rhymes, generally have a comic effect in English, and have been freely used for this purpose, e.g., by Byron (*intellectual, henpecked-you-all*). Rhymes occurring within a single line are called **internal**; for instance, the Mother Goose rhyme "Mary, Mary, quite contrary," or from Coleridge's *Ancient Mariner* ("We were the first that ever burst / Into that silent sea"). **Eye rhymes** are words used as rhymes that look alike but actually sound different (for example, *alone, done; remove, love*); **off rhymes** (sometimes called **partial, imperfect,** or **slant rhymes**) are occasionally the result of pressing exigencies or lack of skill, but are also, at times, used deliberately by modern poets for special effects. For instance, a poem by Wilfred Owen (*Strange Meeting*) contains such paired words (which Owen called "pararhymes") as *years / yours* or *tigress / progress*.

Blank verse is unrhymed iambic pentameter; until the recent advent of free verse, it was the only unrhymed measure to achieve general popularity in English. Though first used by the earl of Surrey in translating Virgil's *Aeneid*, blank verse was during the sixteenth century employed primarily in plays; *Paradise Lost* was one of the first nondramatic poems in English to use it. But Milton's authority and his success were so great that during the eighteenth and nineteenth centuries blank verse came to be used for a great variety of discursive, descriptive, and philosophical poems—besides remaining the standard metrical form for epics. Thomson's *Seasons*, Cowper's *Task*, Wordsworth's *Prelude*, and Tennyson's *Idylls of the King* were all written in blank verse.

A **stanza** is a recurring unit of a poem, consisting of a number of verses. Certain poems (for example, Dryden's *Alexander's Feast*) have stanzas comprising a variable number of verses, of varying lengths. Others are more regular, and are identified by particular names.

The simplest form of stanza is the **couplet**; it is two lines rhyming together. A single couplet considered in isolation is sometimes called a **distich**; when it expresses a complete thought, ending with a terminal mark of punctuation such as a semicolon or period, it is called a **closed couplet**. The development of very regular end-stopped couplets, their use in so-called heroic tragedies, and their consequent acquisition of the name **heroic couplets** took place for the most part during the mid-seventeenth century. The heroic couplet was the principal form in English neoclassical poems.

Another traditional and challenging form of couplet is the **tetrameter,** or **four-beat couplet.** All rhymed couplets are hard to manage without monotony; and since, in addition, a four-beat line is hard to divide by caesura without splitting it into two tick-tock dimeters, tetrameter couplets have posed a perpetual challenge to poets, and still provide an admirable finger-exercise for aspiring versifiers. An instance of tetrameter couplets managed with marvelous variety, complexity, and expressiveness is Marvell's *To His Coy Mistress*:

> Thou by the Indian Ganges' side
> Shouldst rubies find; I by the tide
> Of Humber would complain. I would
> Love you ten years before the Flood,
> And you should, if you please, refuse
> Till the conversion of the Jews.

English has not done much with rhymes grouped in threes, but has borrowed from Italian the form known as **terza rima,** in which Dante composed his *Divine Comedy*. This form consists of linked groups of three rhymes according to the following pattern: *aba bcb cdc ded*, etc. Shelley's *Ode to the West Wind* is composed in stanzas of *terza rima*, the poem as a whole ending with a couplet.

Quatrains are stanzas of four lines; the lines usually rhyme alternately, *abab*, or in the second and fourth lines, *abcb*. When they alternate tetrameter and trimeter lines, as in Johnson's little poem about men in hats (above), or as in *Sir Patrick Spens*, they are called **ballad stanza.** Dryden's *Annus Mirabilis* and Gray's *Elegy Written in a Country Churchyard* are in **heroic quatrains;** these rhyme alternately *abab*, and employ five-stress iambic verse throughout. Tennyson used for *In Memoriam* a tetrameter quatrain rhymed *abba*, and FitzGerald translated *The Rubáiyát of Omar Khayyám* into a pentameter quatrain rhymed *aaba*; but these forms have not been widely adopted.

Chaucer's *Troilus and Criseide* is the premier example in English of **rhyme royal,** a seven-line iambic pentameter stanza consisting essentially of a quatrain dovetailed onto two couplets, according to the rhyme scheme *ababbcc* (the fourth line serves both as the final line of the quatrain and as the first line of the first couplet). Closely akin to rhyme royal, but differentiated by an extra *a*-rhyme between the two *b*-rhymes, is **ottava rima,** that is, an eight-line stanza rhyming *abababcc*. As its name suggests, ottava rima is of Italian origin; it was first used in English by Wyatt. Its final couplet, being less prepared for than in rhyme royal, and usually set off as a separate verbal unit, is capable of manifesting a witty snap, for which Byron found good use in *Don Juan*.

The longest and most intricate stanza generally used for narrative purposes in English is that devised by Edmund Spenser for *The Faerie Queene*. The **Spenserian stanza** has nine lines rhyming *ababbcbcc*; the first eight lines are pentameter, the last line an Alexandrine. Slow-moving, intricate of pattern, and very demanding in its rhyme scheme (the *b*-sound recurs four times, the *c*-sound three), the Spenserian stanza has nonetheless appealed widely to poets who seek a rich and complicated metrical form. Keats's *Eve of St. Agnes* and Shelley's *Adonais* are brilliantly successful nineteenth-century examples of its use.

The **sonnet,** originally a stanza of Italian origin that has developed into an independent lyric form, is usually defined nowadays as fourteen lines of iambic pentameter. None of the elements in this definition is absolute and in earlier centuries there were sonnets in hexameters (the first of Sidney's *Astrophil and Stella*), and sonnets of as many as twenty lines (Milton's *On the New Forcers of Conscience*). Most, however, approximate the definition. Most Elizabethan sonnets dealt with love; and some poets, like Sidney, Spenser, and Shakespeare, imitated Petrarch in grouping together their sonnets dealing with a particular lady or situation. The term for these gatherings is **sonnet sequences;** the extent to which they tell a sequential story, and the extent to which such stories are autobiographical, vary greatly. Since Elizabethan times, the sonnet has been applied to a wide range of subject matters—religious, political, satiric, moral, and philosophic.

In blank verse or irregularly rhymed verse, where stanzaic divisions do not exist or are indistinct, the poetry sometimes falls into **verse paragraphs,** which are in effect divisions of sense like prose paragraphs. This division can be clearly seen in Milton's *Lycidas* and *Paradise Lost*. An intermediate form, clearly stanzaic but with stanzas of varying patterns of line-length and rhyme, is illustrated by Spenser's *Epithalamion*; in this instance, the division into stanzas is reinforced by a **refrain,** which is simply a line repeated at the end of each stanza. Ballads also customarily have refrains; for example, the refrain of *Lord Randall* is

> mother, make my bed soon,
> For I'm weary wi' hunting, and fain wald lie down.

FIGURATIVE LANGUAGE

The act of bringing words together into rich and vigorous poetic lines is complex and demanding, chiefly because so many variables require control. There is the "thought" of the lines, their verbal texture, their emotional resonance, the developing perspective of the reader—all these to be managed at once. One of the poet's chief resources toward this end is figurative language. Here, as in matters of meter, one may distinguish a great variety of devices, some of which we use in everyday speech without special awareness of their names and natures. When we say someone eats "like a horse" or "like a bird," we are using a **simile,** that is, a comparison marked out by a specific word of likening—"like" or "as." When we omit the word of comparison but imply a likeness—as in the sentence "That hog has guzzled all the champagne"—we are making use of **metaphor.** The **epic simile,** frequent in epic poetry, is an extended simile in which the thing compared is described as an object in its own right, beyond its point of likeness with the main subject. Milton starts to compare Satan to Leviathan, but concludes his simile with the story of a sailor who moored his ship by mistake, one night, to a whale (*Paradise Lost* 1.200–208). Metaphors and similes have been distinguished according to their special effects; they may be, for instance, violent, comic, degrading, decorative, or ennobling.

When we speak of "forty head of cattle" or ask someone to "lend a hand" with a job, we are using **synecdoche**, a figure that substitutes the part for the whole. When we speak of a statement coming "from the White House," or a man much interested in "the turf," (that is, the race-course), we are using **metonymy**, or the substitution of one term for another with which it is closely associated. **Antithesis** is a device for placing opposing ideas in grammatical parallel, as, for example, in the following passage from Alexander Pope's *Rape of the Lock* (5.25–30), where there are more examples of antithesis than there are lines:

> But since, alas! frail beauty must decay,
> Curled or uncurled, since locks will turn to gray;
> Since painted, or not painted, all shall fade,
> And she who scorns a man must die a maid;
> What then remains but well our power to use,
> And keep good humor still whate'er we lose?

Irony is a verbal device that implies an attitude quite different from (and often opposite to) that which is literally expressed. In Pope's *The Rape of the Lock* (4.131–32), after poor Sir Plume has stammered an incoherent request to return the stolen lock of hair, the Baron answers ironically:

> "It grieves me much," replied the Peer again,
> "Who speaks so well should ever speak in vain."

And when Donne "proves," in *The Canonization*, that he and his mistress are going to found a new religion of love, he seems to be inviting us to take a subtly ironic attitude toward religion as well as love.

Because it is easy to see through, **hyperbole**, or willful exaggeration, is a favorite device of irony—which is not to say that it may not be "serious" as well. When she hears that a young man is "dying for love" of her, a sensible young woman does not accept this statement literally, but it may convey a serious meaning to her nonetheless. The **pun**, or play on words (known to the learned, sometimes, as **paronomasia**), may also be serious or comic in intent; witness, for example, the famous series of puns on Donne's name in his *Hymn to God the Father*. **Oxymoron** is a conjunction of two terms that in ordinary use are contraries or incompatible—for instance, Milton's famous description of hell as containing "darkness visible" (*Paradise Lost* 1.63). A **paradox** is a statement that seems absurd but turns out to have rational meaning after all, usually in some unexpected sense; Donne speaks of fear being great courage and high valor (*Satire* 3, line 16), and turns out to mean that fear of God is greater courage than any earthly bravery. A **conceit** is a far-fetched and unusually elaborate comparison. Writing in the fourteenth century, the Italian poet Petrarch popularized a great number of conceits handy for use in love poetry, and readily adapted by his English imitators. Wyatt, for example, is using **Petrarchan conceits** when he compares love to a warrior, or the lover's state to that of a storm-tossed ship; and a hundred other sonneteers developed the themes of the lady's stony heart, incendiary glances, and so forth. On the other hand, the **metaphysical conceit** was a more intellectualized, many-leveled comparison, giving a strong sense of the poet's ingenuity in overcoming obstacles—for instance, Donne's comparison of separated lovers to the legs of a compass (A *Valediction: Forbidding Mourning*) or Herbert's comparison of devotion to a pulley, in the poem of that name.

Personification (or in the term derived from Latin **prosopopoeia**) is the attribution of human qualities to an inanimate object (for example, the Sea) or an abstract concept (Freedom); a special variety of it is called (in a term of John Ruskin's invention) the **pathetic fallacy.** When we speak of leaves "dancing" or a lake "smiling," we attribute human traits to nonhuman objects. Ruskin thought this was false and therefore "morbid"; modern criticism tends to view the practice as artistically and morally neutral. A more formal and abstract variety of personification is **allegory,** in which a narrative (such as *Pilgrim's Progress*) is constructed by representing general concepts (Faithfulness, Sin, Despair) as persons who act out the plot. A **fable** (like Chaucer's *The Nun's Priest's Tale*) represents beasts behaving like humans; a **parable** is a brief story, or simply an observation, with strong moral application; and an **exemplum** is a story told to illustrate a point in a sermon.

A special series of devices, nearly obsolete today, used to be available to poets who could count on readers trained in the classics. These were the devices of **classical allusion**—that is, reference to the mythology (stories about the actions of gods and other supernatural beings) of the Greeks and Romans. In their simplest form, the classic **myths** used to provide a repertoire of agreeable stage properties, and a convenient shorthand for expressing emotional attitudes. Picturesque creatures like centaurs, satyrs, and sphinxes, heroes and heroines like Hector and Helen, and the whole pantheon of Olympic deities could be used to make ready reference to a great many aspects of human nature. One does not have to explain the problems of a man who is "cleaning the Augean stables"; if he is afflicted with an "Achilles' heel," or is assailing "Hydra-headed difficulties," his state is clear. These descriptive phrases, making **allusion** to mythological stories, suggest in a phrase situations that would normally require cumbersome explanations. But because it used to be taken for granted that the classical mythology was the common possession of all educated readers, the classic myths entered into English literature as early as Chaucer. In poets like Spenser and Milton, classical allusion becomes a kind of enormously learned game, in which the poet seeks to make his points as indirectly as possible. For instance, Spenser writes in the *Epithalamion*, lines 328–29:

> Lyke as when Jove with fayre Alcmena lay,
> When he begot the great Tirynthian groome.

The mere mention of Alcmena in the first line suggests, to the informed reader, Hercules, the son of Jupiter (Jove) by Alcmena. Spenser's problem in the second line is to find a way of referring to him that is neither redundant nor heavy-handed. "Tirynthian" reminds the reader of Hercules' long connection with the city of Tiryns, stretching our minds (as it were) across his whole career; and "groome" compresses references to a man-child, a servant, and a bridegroom, all of which apply to different aspects of Hercules' history. Thus, far from simply avoiding redundancy, Spenser has enriched, for the reader who possesses the classical information, the whole texture of his verse, thought, and feeling.

SCHOOLS

Literary scholars and critics often group together in **schools** writers who share stylistic traits or thematic concerns. Whether they considered themselves a group doesn't much matter; although in some cases—for example, the Imagists or the Beat poets—the writers themselves have identified themselves as belonging to a group. None of the **Romantic poets** knew they were being romantic, although Hazlitt, Shelley, and other writers of the time recognized shared features that they called "the spirit of the age." The followers of Spenser are known as **Spenserians;** they knew they admired and to some extent wrote like Spenser, but didn't realize that made them a group. **Cavalier** poets are set decisively apart from **Metaphysical** poets, though pretty surely none of the two-dozen-odd men involved knew that was what they were. And so with the **Gothic novelists,** and the so-called **Graveyard School** of the eighteenth century; these schools are generally grouped, defined, and named by scholars and critics after the event.

Intellectual affinities have led some writers to be classified under the names of the philosophical schools of Greece and Rome. These are chiefly the **Epicureans,** who specify that the aim of life and the source of value is pleasure; the **Stoics,** who emphasize stern virtue and the dignified endurance of what cannot be avoided; and the **Skeptics,** who doubt that anything can be known for certain. These categories are useful as capsule descriptions, but they aren't very tidy, as they are omissive, overlap one another, and cut across other categories. Dryden is an author strongly tinged with skepticism, but many of his poems suggest an unabashed epicureanism. *The Vanity of Human Wishes*, by Samuel Johnson, is the classic poem in English of stoic philosophy, but it also expresses a particularly strong coloring of Christian humanism.

TERMS OF LITERARY ART

The following section defines frequently used literary terms, especially frequently used terms that are closely related or tend to be mistaken for each other.

Allegory, Symbol, Emblem, Type. Allegory is a narrative in which the agents, and sometimes also the setting, are personified concepts or character-types, and the plot represents a doctrine or thesis. John Bunyan's *Pilgrim's Progress*, for example, allegorizes the Christian doctrine of salvation by narrating how the character named Christian, warned by Evangelist, flees the City of Destruction and makes his laborious way to the Celestial City; en route he meets such characters as Faithful and the Giant Despair, and passes through places like the Slough of Despond and Vanity Fair. A literary **symbol** is the representation of an object or event which has a further range of reference beyond itself. Examples of sustainedly symbolic poems are William Blake's *The Sick Rose* and William Butler Yeats's *Sailing to Byzantium*. In the sixteenth and seventeenth centuries, an **emblem** was an enigmatic picture of a physical object, to which was attached a motto and a verse explaining its significance. In present-day usage, an emblem is any object which is widely understood to signify an abstract concept; thus a dove is an emblem of peace, and a cross, of Christianity. In what was once a widespread Christian mode of biblical interpretation, a **type** was a person or event in the Old Testament which was regarded as historically real, but also as "prefiguring" a person or event in the New Testament. Thus Adam was often said to be a type of Christ, and the act of Moses in liberating the children of Israel was said to prefigure Christ in freeing men from Satan.

Baroque and **Mannerist** are terms imported into literary study from the history of art, and applied by analogy. Michelangelo is a **baroque** artist; he holds great masses in powerful dynamic tension, his style is heavily ornamented and restless. In these respects he is sometimes compared to Milton. El Greco is a **mannerist,** whose gaunt and distorted figures often seem to be laboring under great spiritual stress, whose light seems to be focused in spots against a dark background. He has been compared to Donne. Analogies of this sort are occasionally suggestive, but can readily deteriorate into parallels that are forced and nominal rather than substantial.

Bathos. See **Pathos,** the **Sublime,** and **Bathos.**

Burlesque and **Mock Heroic** differ in that the former makes its subject ludicrous by directly cutting it down, the latter by inflating it. In Pope's mock-heroic *Dunciad,* the figure of Dulness (Colley Cibber) is given inappropriately heroic dimensions; in Butler's burlesque *Hudibras,* the knightly hero is characterized by low and vulgar attributes, and persistently engages in inappropriately low behavior. Burlesque contributed to the development of the English novel; and during the nineteenth century, when formal drama tended to be stagy and melodramatic, a vigorous burlesque stage flourished in England, making fun of the classics. See **Imitation** and **Parody.**

Catastrophe and **Catharsis.** The **catastrophe** is the conclusion of a play; the word means "down-turning," and is usually applied only to tragedies, in which a frequent kind of catastrophe is the death of the protagonist. (A term for the precipitating final scene that applies both to tragedy and to comedy is **denouement,** which in French means "unknotting.") **Catharsis** in Greek signifies "purgation" or "purification." In Aristotle's *Poetics,* the special effect of tragedy is the "catharsis" of the "emotions of pity and fear" that have been aroused in the audience by the events of the drama.

Chiasmus and **Zeugma.** **Chiasmus** is an inversion of the word order in two parallel phrases, as in John Denham's *Cooper's Hill*: "Strong without rage, without o'erflowing full." **Zeugma** is the use of a single verb or adjective to control two nouns, as in Pope's *The Rape of the Lock*: "Or stain her honor, or her new brocade."

Classic and **Neoclassic.** See **Gothic, Classic, Neoclassic.**

Convention and **Tradition.** **Conventions** are agreed-upon artistic procedures peculiar to an art form. None of Shakespeare's contemporaries spoke blank verse in everyday life, but characters in his plays do, and the audience accepts it—as the audience at an opera accepts that characters will sing arias to express their feelings. A **tradition** consists of beliefs, attitudes, and ways of representing things that is widely shared by writers over a span of time; it generally includes a number of conventions.

Didactic poetry is designed to teach a branch of knowledge, or to embody in fictional form a moral, religious, or philosophical doctrine. The term is not derogatory. John Milton's *Paradise Lost*, for example, can be called didactic, insofar as it is organized, as Milton claimed in his invocation, to "assert Eternal Providence / And justify the ways of God to men." In the eighteenth century, a number of poets wrote didactic poems called **georgics** (modeled on the Roman Virgil's *Georgics* on rural life and farming), which described such applied arts as making cider or running a sugar plantation.

Dramatic irony and **Dramatic monologue** are quite different literary modes. In **dramatic irony** a stage character says something that has one meaning for him, but quite another for the audience who possesses relevant knowledge that the speaker lacks. The **dramatic monologue** is a form that was perfected by Robert Browning in such poems as *My Last Duchess* and *The Bishop Orders His Tomb*. In it, the poetic speaker unintentionally reveals to the reader his character and temperament by what he says, usually to another person whose presence we infer from the utterance of the speaker.

Eclogue. See **Pastorals.**

Emblem. See **Allegory, Symbol, Emblem, Type.**

Epigram, Epigraph, Epitaph. An **epigram** is a short, witty statement in verse or prose. One of Oscar Wilde's characters remarks, "I can resist everything, except temptation." An **epigraph** is an apposite quotation placed at the beginning of a book or a section of it. An **epitaph** is a brief statement about someone who has died; usually, it is intended to be inscribed on a tombstone.

Eulogy and **Elegy.** The **eulogy** is a work of praise, in prose or poetry, for a person either very distinguished or recently dead. In its usual modern sense, an **elegy** is a formal, and usually long, poetic lament for someone who has died. In an extended sense, the term is also used to designate poems on the transience of earthly things (such as the Old English *The Seafarer*) or poetic meditations on mortality (such as Thomas Gray's *Elegy Written in a Country Churchyard*).

Euphemism and **Euphuism. Euphemism**, or "fine speech," is a verbal device for avoiding an unpleasant concept or expression, as when, instead of saying a person "died," we say he "passed away." Euphues was the hero of a prose romance (published 1579–80) by John Lyly; his adventures are recounted in a mannered style full of puns, alliteration, and antithetical "points." Under the name of **Euphuism** this courtly style enjoyed a brief vogue in the Elizabethan era.

Fancy and **Imagination.** The distinction between these two mental powers was central to the literary theory of S. T. Coleridge. **Fancy** (a word directly derived by contraction from "fantasy") was defined by Coleridge as the power of combining several known properties into new combinations; **imagination**, on the other hand, was the faculty of using such properties to create an integral whole that is entirely new.

Folios, Quartos, etc., are terms used to specify the size of book pages. To make a **folio**, a sheet of paper (14" × 20" or larger) is folded just once (producing thereby four pages); **quartos** are folded twice (producing eight pages). Shakespeare's plays were first printed in quartos (often in several different editions), but when they were collected together, in 1623, they appeared as the First Folio edition.

Genre, Decorum. A **genre** is an established literary form or type, such as stage comedy, the picaresque novel, the epic, the sonnet. Works belonging to a certain genre tend to represent certain characters and events, and to seek a similar effect. **Decorum,** in literary criticism—where it was a central concept from the Renaissance through the eighteenth century—designates the requirement that there should be a propriety, or fitness, in the way that the character, actions, and style are matched to each other in a particular genre. Low characters, actions, and style, for example, were thought appropriate for satire, while epic demanded characters of high estate, engaged in great actions, and speaking in an appropriately high style.

Gothic, Classic, Neoclassic. These terms are used to distinguish prominent tendencies in literature and the other arts. The term **Gothic** originally referred to the Goths, an early Germanic tribe, then came to signify "medieval." In the eighteenth century "Gothic" connoted primitive and irregular work, possessing the qualities of the relatively barbaric North. **Gothic novels** were a very popular type of prose fiction, inaugurated by Horace Walpole's *Castle of Otranto* (1764), usually set in a medieval castle, which aimed to evoke chilling terror from their readers. **Classic** implies lucid, rational, and orderly works, such as are usually attributed to the writers and thinkers in the classic era of the Greeks and Romans. **Neoclassic**—a term often applied to the period in England from 1660 through most of the eighteenth century—implies an ideal of life, art, and thought deliberately modeled on Greek and Roman examples.

Heroic poems, Heroic drama, Heroic couplets. Because they concentrate on the figure of a typical hero (Achilles, Aeneas), epic poems were frequently called **"heroic."** Trying to transfer epic grandeur to the stage, playwrights of the Restoration period wrote what was called **heroic drama,** but usually achieved only grandiosity. The stately iambic pentameter couplets in which they made their characters speak became known as **heroic couplets.**

Humor. See **Wit** and **Humor.**

Humors and **Temperaments** are psychological terms used by Renaissance writers. It was believed that every person's constitution contained four basic humors: the **choleric** (bile), the **sanguine** (blood), the **phlegmatic** (phlegm), and the **melancholy** (black bile). The **temperament,** or mixture, of these four humors was held to determine both a person's physical condition and a person's type of character. When a particular humor predominated, it pushed the character in that direction: choler = anger; sanguine = geniality; phlegm = cold torpor; and melancholy = gloomy self-absorption.

Imagination. See **Fancy** and **Imagination.**

Imitation and **Parody** are forms in which a literary work refers back to a predecessor. In the eighteenth century, an "imitation" was a poem that deliberately echoed an older work, but adapted it to subject matter in the writer's own era, usually with a satirical aim directed against that subject matter; Alexander Pope, for example, wrote a number of satires on contemporary life that he entitled *Imitations of Horace*. A **parody** imitates the characteristic style and other features of a particular literary work—or else of a particular literary type—but in such a way as to satirize that work, by making it either amusing or ridiculous. *Northanger Abbey* (1818) by Jane Austen was a good-humored parody of the popular horror-narratives known as gothic novels. (See **Burlesque** and **Gothic**.)

Irony, Sarcasm. **Irony** and **sarcasm** are both ways of saying one thing but implying something sharply different, often opposite; they differ, however, in the way they go about doing so. **Sarcasm** is a broad and taunting form of using apparent praise in order in fact to denigrate. The patriarch Job is bitterly sarcastic when he replies to his would-be comforters (12.2), "No doubt but ye are the people, and wisdom shall die with you." On the other hand, Jane Austen, in the first sentence of *Pride and Prejudice*, overstates the case just enough to make it drily **ironic** when she writes, "It is a truth universally acknowledged, that a single man in possession of a good fortune, must be in want of a wife." (See **Irony**, in the section "Figurative Language," above.)

Legend. See **Myth** and **Legend**.

Logic. See **Rhetoric** and **Logic**.

Masque. The **Masque**, which flourished during the reigns of Elizabeth I, James I, and Charles I, was an elaborate court entertainment that combined poetic drama, music, song, dance, and splendid costumes and settings. For a discussion of the English masque, see the introduction to Jonson's *Pleasure Reconciled to Virtue*.

Myth and **Legend**. **Myths** are hereditary narratives that purport to account, in supernatural terms, for why the world is as it is, and why people act as they do; they also often provide the rules by which people conduct their lives. Myths often spring up to explain rituals, the original meanings of which have been forgotten. A system of related myths is called a **mythology**—a body of supernatural narratives believed to be true by a particular cultural group. The term "myth" is frequently extended to a set of supernatural narratives that are developed by individual poets such as William Blake and W. B. Yeats. Three great mythologies that have been exploited by poets long after they ceased to be believed are the classical (Greek and Roman), the Celtic, and the Germanic. A **legend** is an old and popularly repeated story, of which the protagonist is not supernatural, but a human being. If a hereditary story concerns supernatural beings who are not gods, and the story is not part of a systematic mythology, it is usually classified as a **folktale**.

Naturalism. See **Realism** and **Naturalism**.

Neo-Classic. See **Gothic, Classic, Neoclassic**.

Novel. See **Romance, Novel**.

Ode. A long lyric poem serious in subject and treatment, written in an elevated style and, usually, in an elaborate stanza. See the discussion of English odes in the headnote to Jonson's *Ode on Cary and Morison*.

Pastoral, Eclogue, and **Pastoral Elegy**. **Pastorals** (from the Latin word for "shepherd") are deliberately conventional poems that project a cultivated poet's nostalgic image of the peace and simplicity of the life of shepherds and other rural folk in an idealized natural setting. The form was established by the Greek poet Theocritus in the third century B.C.E.; it is some-times also called an **eclogue,** which was the title that the Roman poet Virgil gave to his collection of pastorals. The pastorals by Theocritus and later classical poets often included a poem in which a shepherd mourns the death of a fellow shepherd; from these poems developed the highly conventional **pastoral elegy,** a type that includes such great laments as Milton's *Lycidas* and Shelley's *Adonais. Lycidas* is also an example of the extension of the classical pastoral to a Christian range of reference, by way of the use of the term "pastor" (shepherd) for a parish priest or min-ister and the frequent representation of Christ as "the Good Shepherd."

Pathos, the **Sublime,** and **Bathos.** In Greek, **pathos** signified deep feeling, especially suffering; in modern criticism, it is used in a more limited way to signify a scene or passage designed to evoke the feelings of pity or sympathetic sorrow from an audience. An example is the passage in which King Lear is briefly reunited with his daughter Cordelia, beginning

> Pray, do not mock me.
> I am a very foolish fond old man . . .

In the first century the Greek rhetorician Longinus wrote a treatise *On the Sublime,* in which he proposed that sublimity ("loftiness") is the greatest of stylistic qualities in literature; the effect of the sublime on the reader is *elestasis* ("transport"). In 1757 Edmund Burke published a highly influential treatise on *The Sublime and Beautiful,* in which he distin-guished the sublime from the beautiful, not as a stylistic quality, but as the representation of objects that are vast, obscure, and powerful, which evoke from the reader a "delightful horror" that combines pleasure and terror. **Bathos** (Greek for "depth") was used by Pope, in a parodic parallel to Longinus' "sublime," to signify an unintentional descent in literature, when an author, straining to be passionate or elevated, overshoots the mark and falls into the trivial or the ridiculous.

Poetic diction, Poetic license, Poetic justice. Poetic diction denotes a distinctive language used by a poet which is not current in the discourse of the age; an example is the deliberately archaic language of Spenser's *The Faerie Queene.* In modern critical discussion, the term is applied espe-cially to the style of eighteenth-century poets who, according to the reign-ing principle of decorum (see **Decorum**), believed that a poet must adapt the level of his diction to the dignity of the high genres of epic, tragedy, and ode. The results were such phrases as "the finny tribe" for "fish" and "the bleating kind" for "sheep." **Poetic license** designates the freedom of a poet or other literary writer to depart, for special effects, from the norms of common discourse and of literal or historical truth. Examples: the use of archaic words, meter, and rhyme, and the use of other literary conven-tions. (See **Convention.**) **Poetic justice** was coined by Thomas Rymer, in the later seventeenth century, to denote his claim that a narrative or drama should, at the end, distribute rewards and punishments in proportion to the virtues and vices of each character. No important critic since Rymer has adopted this doctrine, except in a highly qualified way.

Quarto. See **Folios, Quartos.**

Realism and **Naturalism** are both terms applied to prose fictions that aim at a faithful representation of actual existence; they differ, however, in the aspects of that existence that they represent and in the manner in which they represent them. The realistic novel attempts to give the effect of representing ordinary life as it commonly occurs. Realistic novelists such as George Eliot in England and William Dean Howells in America present everyday characters experiencing ordinary events, rendered in great detail. **Naturalism,** which the French novelist Émile Zola developed in the 1870s and later, is based on the philosophy that a human being is merely a higher-order animal, whose character and behavior are determined by heredity and environment. Zola, followed by such later naturalistic novelists as the Americans Frank Norris and Theodore Dreiser, typically represents characters who inherit such compulsive instincts as greed and the sexual drive and are shaped by the social and economic forces of family, class, and the milieu into which they are born. Naturalistic novelists also often display an almost medical candor in describing human activities and bodily functions largely unmentioned in earlier fiction.

Rhetoric and **Logic. Rhetoric** was developed by Greek and Roman theorists as the art of using all available means of persuading an audience, either by speech or in writing; it had a great influence on literary criticism in the Renaissance and through the eighteenth century. Rhetorical theorists developed a detailed analysis of figures of speech, largely as effective means to the overall aim of persuasion. In the present century, however, the analysis of such figures has been excerpted from this rhetorical context and made an independent and central concern of language theorists and literary critics. See **Figurative language. Logic** is the study of the principles of reasoning. Logic may be used to persuade an audience, but it does not, like rhetoric, avail itself of all means of persuasion, emotional as well as rational; instead, logic limits itself to a concern with the formal procedures of reasoning from sound premises to valid conclusions.

Romance and **Novel.** Medieval **romances** were verse narratives of adventure, usually about a knightly hero on a quest to gain a lady's favor, who encounters both natural tribulations and supernatural marvels. The term "romance" has since come to be opposed to realism (see **Realism** and **Naturalism**) and is applied to prose fictions that represent characters and events which are more picturesque, fantastic, adventurous, or heroic than one encounters in ordinary life. The **novel,** as distinguished from the prose romance, undertakes to be a more realistic representation of common life and social relationships and tends to avoid the fantastic, the fabulous, and the realm of high derring-do. (See **Realism.**)

Sarcasm. See **Irony, Sarcasm.**

Satire designates literary forms which diminish or derogate a subject by making it ridiculous and by evoking toward it amusement, or scorn, or indignation. In **formal satire,** such as Alexander Pope's *Moral Essays,* the satire is accomplished in a direct, first-person address, either to the audience or to a listener within the work. **Indirect satire** is not a direct address, but is cast in the form of a fictional narrative, as in Swift's *Gulliver's Travels* or Byron's *Don Juan.* For a discussion of the backgrounds of English satire, see the introduction to Donne's *Satire 3.*

Sublime. See **Pathos, the Sublime,** and **Bathos.**

Symbol. See **Allegory, Symbol, Emblem, Type.**

Tradition. See **Convention** and **Tradition.**

Type. See **Allegory, Symbol, Emblem, Type.**

Wit and **Humor,** in their present use, designate elements in a literary work which are designed to amuse or to excite mirth in the reader or audience. **Wit,** through the seventeenth century, had a broad range of meanings, including general intelligence, mental acuity, and ingenuity in literary invention, especially in a brilliant and paradoxical style. From this last application there derived the most common present use of "wit" to denote a kind of verbal expression that is brief, deft, and contrived to produce a shock of comic surprise; a characteristic form of wit, in this sense, is the epigram. (See **Epigram.**) **Humor** goes back to the ancient theory of the four humors and the application of the term "humorous" to a comically eccentric character who has an imbalance of the humors in his or her temperament. (See **Humors** and **Temperament.**) As we now use the word, **humor** is ascribed both to a comic utterance and to the comic appearance or behavior of a literary character. A humorous utterance, unlike a witty utterance, need not be intended to be comic by the speaker, and is not cast in the neat epigrammatic form of a witty saying. In Shakespeare's *Twelfth Night*, for example, Malvolio's utterances, as well as his appearance and behavior, are all found humorous by the audience, but his utterances are never witty and are humorous despite his own very solemn intentions.

Zeugma. See **Chiasmus** and **Zeugma.**

THE UNIVERSE ACCORDING TO PTOLEMY

Ptolemy was a Roman astronomer of Greek descent, born in Egypt during the second century C.E.; after his death, for nearly fifteen hundred years his account of the design of the universe was accepted as standard. During that long period, the basic pattern underwent many detailed modifications and was fitted out with many astrological and pseudoscientific trappings. But in essence Ptolemy's followers agreed in portraying the earth as the center of the universe, with the sun, planets, and fixed stars set in transparent spheres orbiting around it. In this scheme of things, as modified for Christian usage, Hell was usually placed under the earth's surface at the center of the cosmic globe, while Heaven, the abode of the blessed spirits, was in the outermost, uppermost circle, the empyrean. But in 1543 the Polish astronomer Copernicus proposed an alternative hypothesis—that the earth rotates around the sun, not vice versa; and despite theological opposition, observations with the new telescope and careful mathematical calculations insured ultimate acceptance of the new view.

The map of the Ptolemaic universe represented here is a simplified version of a diagram in Peter Apian's *Cosmography* (1584). In such a diagram, the Firmament is the sphere which contained the fixed stars; the Crystalline Sphere, which contained no heavenly bodies, is a late innovation, included to explain certain anomalies in the observed movement of the heavenly bodies; and the Prime Mover is the sphere which, itself put into motion by God, imparts rotation around the earth to all the other spheres.

Milton, writing in mid-seventeenth century, made use of two universes. The Copernican universe, though he alludes to it, was too large, formless, and unfamiliar to serve as the setting for the war between Heaven and Hell in *Paradise Lost*. He therefore adopted as his setting the Ptolemaic cosmos, but placed Heaven well outside this smaller earth-centered universe, Hell far beneath it, and assigned the vast middle space to Chaos.

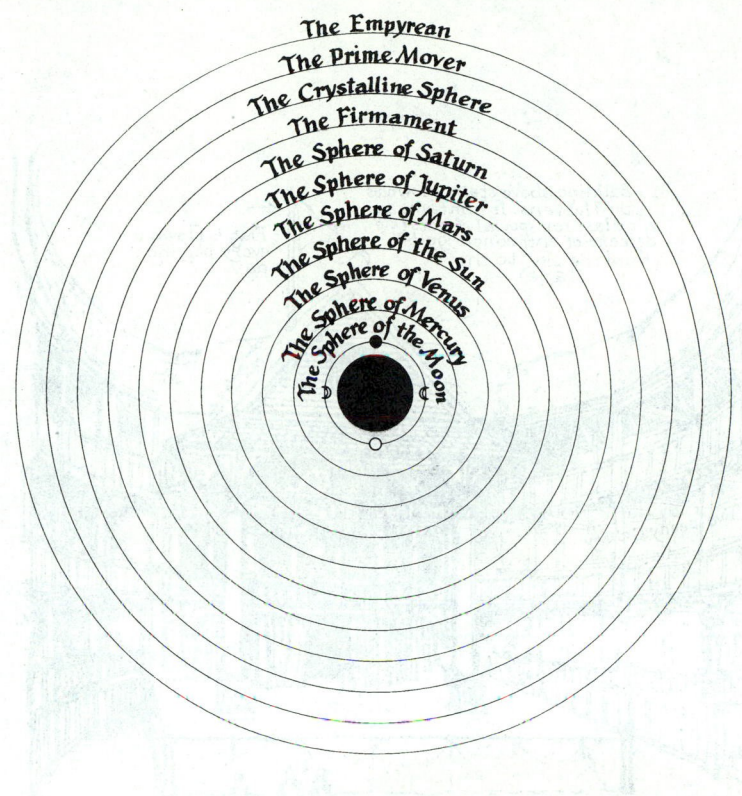

A LONDON PLAYHOUSE OF SHAKESPEARE'S TIME

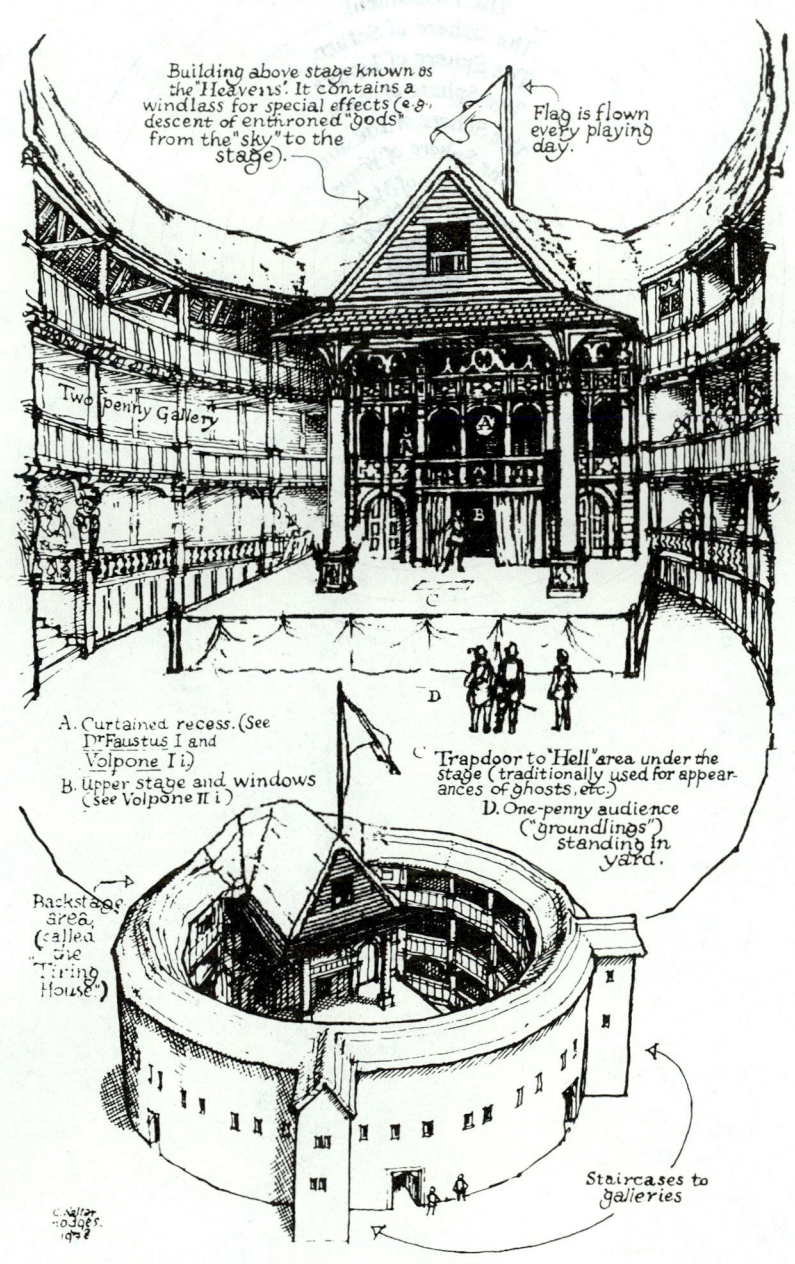

Building above stage known as the "Heavens". It contains a windlass for special effects (e.g. descent of enthroned "gods" from the "sky" to the stage).

Flag is flown every playing day.

Two penny Gallery

A. Curtained recess. (See Dr Faustus I and Volpone I i.)
B. Upper stage and windows (see Volpone II i)

C. Trapdoor to "Hell" area under the stage (traditionally used for appearances of ghosts, etc.)
D. One-penny audience ("groundlings") standing in yard.

Backstage area (called the "Tiring House.")

Staircases to galleries

C. Walter Hodges. 1948

Donald Reiman & Sharon Powers. Copyright © 1977 by Donald H. Reiman and Sharon B. Powers. Reprinted by permission of W. W. Norton & Company, Inc.

Sir Philip Sidney: Selections from THE POEMS OF SIR PHILIP SIDNEY, edited by William A. Ringler, Jr. (1962). Reprinted by permission of Oxford University Press.

Dylan Thomas: *The Force That Through the Green Fuse Drives the Flower*, by Dylan Thomas. Copyright © 1939, 1943 by New Directions Publishing Corp. *After the Funeral* by Dylan Thomas. Copyright © 1938 by New Directions Publishing Corp. *Poem in October* and *Fern Hill* by Dylan Thomas. Copyright © 1945 by The Trustees for the Copyrights of Dylan Thomas, first published in POETRY. *Do Not Go Gentle into That Good Night* by Dylan Thomas. Copyright © 1952 by Dylan Thomas. All from THE POEMS OF DYLAN THOMAS. Reprinted by permission of New Directions Publishing Corp. and David Higham Associates.

Derek Walcott: *A Far Cry from Africa*, XXVII of *Midsummer*, *Nights in the Gardens of Port of Spain*, and *The Glory Trumpeter* all from THE COLLECTED POEMS 1948–1984 by Derek Walcott. Copyright © 1986 by Derek Walcott. XXX from OMEROS by Derek Walcott. Copyright © 1990 by Derek Walcott. All reprinted by permission of Farrar, Straus & Giroux, Inc., and Faber & Faber Ltd. Excerpt of 77 lines of *The Schooner Flight* from THE COLLECTED POEMS 1948–1984 by Derek Walcott. Copyright © 1986 by Derek Walcott. Reprinted by permission of Farrar, Straus & Giroux, Inc.

Mary Wollstonecraft: From A VINDICATION OF THE RIGHTS OF WOMAN: A NORTON CRITICAL EDITION, Second Edition, by Mary Wollstonecraft, edited by Carol H. Poston. Copyright © 1988, 1975 by W. W. Norton & Company, Inc. Reprinted by permission of W. W. Norton & Company, Inc.

Virginia Woolf: *The Mark on the Wall* from A HAUNTED HOUSE AND OTHER SHORT STORIES by Virginia Woolf, copyright 1944 and renewed 1972 by Harcourt, Inc. *Modern Fiction* from THE COMMON READER by Virginia Woolf, copyright 1925 by Harcourt, Inc., and renewed 1953 by Leonard Woolf. *Professions for Women* from THE DEATH OF THE MOTH AND OTHER ESSAYS by Virginia Woolf, copyright 1942 by Harcourt, Inc., and renewed 1970 by Marjorie T. Parsons, Executrix. A ROOM OF ONE'S OWN by Virginia Woolf, copyright © 1929 by Harcourt Brace & Company and renewed 1957 by Leonard Woolf. All reprinted by permission of the publisher and The Society of Authors as the Literary Representative of the Estate of Virginia Woolf. Excerpt from *A Sketch from the Past* in MOMENTS OF BEING by Virginia Woolf, copyright © 1976 by Quentin Bell and Angelica Garnett, reprinted by permission of Harcourt, Inc., and the Hogarth Press on the behalf of the Executors of the Virginia Woolf Estate.

Dorothy Wordsworth: Selections as indicated from THE GRASMERE JOURNALS, edited by Pamela Woof (1991). Reprinted by permission of Oxford University Press. *Grasmere—A Fragment* and *Thoughts on My Sick Bed* from DOROTHY WORDSWORTH AND ROMANTICISM. Reprinted by permission of The Wordsworth Trust, Dove Cottage, Grasmere.

William Wordsworth: Reprinted from William Wordsworth: THE RUINED COTTAGE AND THE PEDLAR. Edited by James A. Butler. Copyright © 1978 by Cornell University. Reprinted from William Wordsworth: THE FOURTEEN-BOOK PRELUDE. Edited by W. J. B. Owen. Copyright © 1985 by Cornell University. Both used by permission of the publisher, Cornell University Press.

Lady Mary Wroth: Poems reprinted with the permission of Louisiana State University Press from THE POEMS OF LADY MARY WROTH, edited, with an introduction and notes, by Josephine A. Roberts. Copyright © 1983.

W. B. Yeats: *The Stolen Child, The Rose of the World, The Lake Isle of Innisfree, The Sorrow of Love, When You Are Old, Who Goes With Fergus?, The Man Who Dreamed of Faeryland, The Secret Rose, The Folly of Being Comforted, Adam's Curse, No Second Troy, The Fascination of What's Difficult, September 1913, To a Shade, A Coat, The Wild Swans at Coole,* and *In Memory of Major Robert Gregory,* all from THE POEMS OF W. B. YEATS: A NEW EDITION, edited by Richard J. Finneran. Reprinted by permission of A. P. Watt on the behalf of Michael B. Yeats. *Easter 1916, The Second Coming,* and *A Prayer for My Daughter,* reprinted with the permission of Simon & Schuster and A. P. Watt on the behalf of Michael B. Yeats from THE POEMS OF W. B. YEATS: A NEW EDITION, edited by Richard J. Finneran. Copyright © 1924 by Macmillan Publishing Company, renewed 1952 by Bertha Georgie Yeats. *Leda and the Swan* reprinted with the permission of Simon & Schuster and A. P. Watt on the behalf of Michael B. Yeats from THE POEMS OF W. B. YEATS: A NEW EDITION, edited by Richard J. Finneran. Copyright © 1928 by Macmillan Publishing Company; copyright renewed © 1956 by Georgie Yeats. *A Dialogue of Self and Soul, For Anne Gregory, Byzantium, Crazy Jane Talks with the Bishop,* and *After Long Silence* reprinted with the permission of Simon & Schuster and A. P. Watt on the behalf of Michael B. Yeats from THE POEMS OF W. B. YEATS: A NEW EDITION, edited by Richard J. Finneran. Copyright © 1933 by Macmillan Publishing Company; copyright renewed © 1961 by Bertha Georgie Yeats. *Lapis Lazuli, Long-Legged Fly, The Circus Animals' Desertion,* and *Under Ben Bulben* reprinted with the permission of Simon & Schuster and A. P. Watt on the behalf of Michael B. Yeats from THE POEMS OF W. B. YEATS: A NEW EDITION, edited by Richard J. Finneran. Copyright 1940 by Georgie Yeats; copyright renewed © 1968 by Bertha Georgie Yeats, Michael Butler Yeats, and Anne Yeats. Excerpts from REVERIES OVER CHILDHOOD AND YOUTH. Reprinted by permission of A. P. Watt on the behalf of Michael B. Yeats. *The Sorrow of Love* (transcription of first printed version) from BETWEEN THE LINES: YEATS'S POETRY IN THE MAKING by Jon Stallworthy (1963). Reprinted by permission of Oxford University Press.

Index